INCLUDES NETTER'S ANATOMY ART

BUCK'S

2019

ICD-10-CM

FOR PHYSICIANS

D1370225

Jackie Grass Koesterman, CPC
JDK Medical Coding EDU, LLC, Lead Technical Collaborator
Coding and Reimbursement Specialist, Grand Forks, North Dakota

ELSEVIER

ELSEVIER

3251 Riverport Lane
St. Louis, Missouri 63043

2019 ICD-10-CM PHYSICIAN EDITION

ISBN: 978-0-323-58273-5

Notice

International Standard Book Number: 978-0-323-58273-5

Content Strategist: Brandi Graham
Senior Content Development Manager: Luke Held
Content Development Specialist: Anna Miller
Publishing Services Manager: Julie Eddy
Project Manager: Abigail Bradberry
Designer: Maggie Reid

Printed in Canada

Last digit is the print number: 9 8 7 6 5 4 3 2 1

 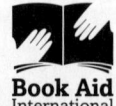

Working together
to grow libraries in
developing countries

www.elsevier.com • www.bookaid.org

DEDICATION

To all the brave medical coders who transitioned the nation into a new coding system. Decades of waiting finally concluded with the implementation of I-10, and you have been the pioneers leading the way.

With greatest appreciations for your efforts!

Carol J. Buck, MS, CPC, CCS-P

CONTENTS

v

GUIDE TO USING THE 2019 ICD-10-CM FOR PHYSICIANS

Medical coding has long been a part of the health care profession. Through the years medical coding systems have become more complex and extensive. Today, medical coding is an intricate and immense process that is present in every health care setting. The increased use of electronic submissions for health care services only increases the need for coders who understand the coding process.

2019 ICD-10-CM for Physicians, Professional Edition was developed to help meet the needs of coding professionals at all levels by offering a comprehensive coding text at a reasonable price.

All material strictly adheres to the latest government versions available at the time of printing. Updates from the *Definitions of Medicare Code Edits* (MCE) will be posted to the companion website (www. codingupdates.com) when available.

Illustrations and Items

The ICD-10-CM Tabular List contains illustrations, pictures, and items to assist you in understanding difficult terminology, diseases/conditions, or coding in a specific category. Items are always printed in ▮▮▮▮▮▮ ink so that the added material is not mistaken for official notations or instructions. ▮▮▮▮▮▮ ink is used for other annotations in the text. Your ideas on what other descriptions or illustrations should be in future editions of this text are always appreciated.

Instructional Notations

Includes Notes

Includes

The word "Includes" appears immediately under certain categories to further define, or give examples of, the content of the category.

Excludes Notes

The ICD-10-CM has two types of excludes notes. Each note has a different definition for use, but they are both similar in that they indicate that codes excluded from each other are independent of each other.

Excludes1

A type 1 Excludes note is a pure excludes. It means "NOT CODED HERE!" An Excludes1 note indicates that the code excluded should never be used at the same time as the code above the Excludes1 note. An Excludes1 is for use when two conditions cannot occur together, such as a congenital form versus an acquired form of the same condition.

Excludes2

A type 2 Excludes note represents "NOT INCLUDED HERE." An Excludes2 note indicates that the condition excluded is not part of the condition it is excluded from but a patient may have both conditions at the same time. When an Excludes2 note appears under a code, it is acceptable to use both the code and the excluded code together.

Code First/Use Additional Code notes (etiology/manifestation paired codes)

Certain conditions have both an underlying etiology and multiple body system manifestations due to the underlying etiology. For such conditions the ICD-10-CM has a coding convention that requires the underlying condition be sequenced first, followed by the manifestation. Wherever such a combination exists, there is a "use additional code" note at the etiology code, and a "code first" note at the manifestation code. These instructional notes indicate the proper sequencing order of the codes, etiology followed by manifestation.

In most cases the manifestation codes will have in the code title, "in diseases classified elsewhere." Codes with this title are a component of the etiology/manifestation convention. The code title indicates that it is a manifestation code. "In diseases classified elsewhere" codes are never permitted to be used as first-listed or principal diagnosis codes. They must be used in conjunction with an underlying condition code, and they must be listed following the underlying condition.

Use additional

The words indicate an instructional note that another code may be needed.

Code first

The words indicate an instructional note that directs the coder to sequence the underlying condition before the manifestation.

Code also

A "code also" note instructs that two codes may be required to fully describe a condition, but the sequencing of the two codes is discretionary, depending on the severity of the conditions and the reason for the encounter.

7th characters and placeholder X

For codes less than 6 characters that require a 7th character a placeholder X should be assigned for all characters less than 6. The 7th character must always be the 7th character of a code.

Annotated

Throughout the manual, revisions, additions, and deleted codes or words are indicated by the following symbols:

⇒   **Revised:** Revisions within the line or code from the previous edition are indicated by the arrow.

▶   **New:** Additions to the previous edition are indicated by the triangle.

deleted   **Deleted:** Deletions from the previous edition are struck through.

ICD-10-CM Tabular List Symbols

●   **Use Additional Character(s):** The red stop sign cautions that the code requires additional character(s) to ensure the greatest specificity.

X   For codes less than 6 characters that require a 7th character, a placeholder X should be assigned for all characters less than 6. The 7th character must always be the 7th character of a code.

OGCR   The *Official Guidelines for Coding and Reporting* symbol includes the placement of a portion of a guideline as that guideline pertains to the code by which it is located. The complete OGCR are located in Part I.

▷   **Manifestation Code:** Describes the manifestation of an underlying disease, not the disease itself, and therefore should not be assigned as a principal diagnosis, according to the *Definitions of Medicare Code Edits* (MCE).

Age conflict: The *Definitions of Medicare Code Edits* (MCE) detects inconsistencies between a patient's age and diagnosis. For example, a 5-year-old patient with benign prostatic hypertrophy or a 78-year-old pregnant female.

The diagnosis is clinically and virtually impossible in a patient of the stated age. Therefore, either the diagnosis or the age is presumed to be incorrect. There are four age categories for diagnoses in the *Definitions of Medicare Code Edits* (MCE):

N   • Newborn. Age of 0 years; a subset of diagnoses intended only for newborns and neonates (e.g., fetal distress, perinatal jaundice).

P   • Pediatric. Age range is 0-17 years inclusive (e.g., Reye's syndrome, routine child health exam).

M   • Maternity. Age range is 12-55 years inclusive (e.g., diabetes in pregnancy, antepartum pulmonary complication).

A   • Adult. Age range is 15-124 years inclusive (e.g., senile delirium, mature cataract).

♀♂   **Sex conflict:** *Definitions of Medicare Code Edits* (MCE) detects inconsistencies between a patient's sex and any diagnosis or procedure on the patient's record. For example, a male patient with cervical cancer (diagnosis) or a female patient with a prostatectomy (procedure). In both instances, the indicated diagnosis or the procedure conflicts with the stated sex of the patient. Therefore, either the patient's diagnosis, procedure, or sex is presumed to be incorrect.

Key words

Highlight identifies key words within similar code descriptions in a particular category.

Coding Clinic Identifies the year, quarter, and page number that presents information about an ICD-10-CM code in the American Hospital Association's *Coding Clinic®* for ICD-10-CM.

Visit codingupdates.com for the full list of 2018 Present on Admission codes.

SYMBOLS AND CONVENTIONS

ICD-10-CM Tabular

Use Additional Character(s): The red stop sign cautions you that the code requires additional character(s) to ensure greatest specificity.

Volume 1, Tabular List

● **K22** Other diseases of esophagus

    Excludes2 esophageal varices (I85.-)

X ● **V00.01** Pedestrian on foot injured in collision with roller-skater

A02.20 Localized salmonella infection, unspecified

Placeholder X: The red X reminds you that for codes less than 6 characters that require a 7th character, a placeholder X should be assigned to all characters less than 6.

Unspecified: These codes are for use when the information in the medical record is insufficient to assign a more specific code. For those categories for which an unspecified code is not provided, the "other specified" code may represent both other and unspecified.

Use additional code: Located at the etiology code and directs you to assign a manifestation code.

A48.3 Toxic shock syndrome

    Use additional code to identify the organism (B95, B96)

Code first indicates the etiology code is to be first-listed before the manifestation code.

B39 Histoplasmosis

    Code first associated AIDS (B20)

Notes define terms or give coding instructions.

E34.0 Carcinoid syndrome

    Note: May be used as an additional code to identify functional activity associated with a carcinoid tumor.

Codes or index entries are for purposes of illustration only and may not be current.

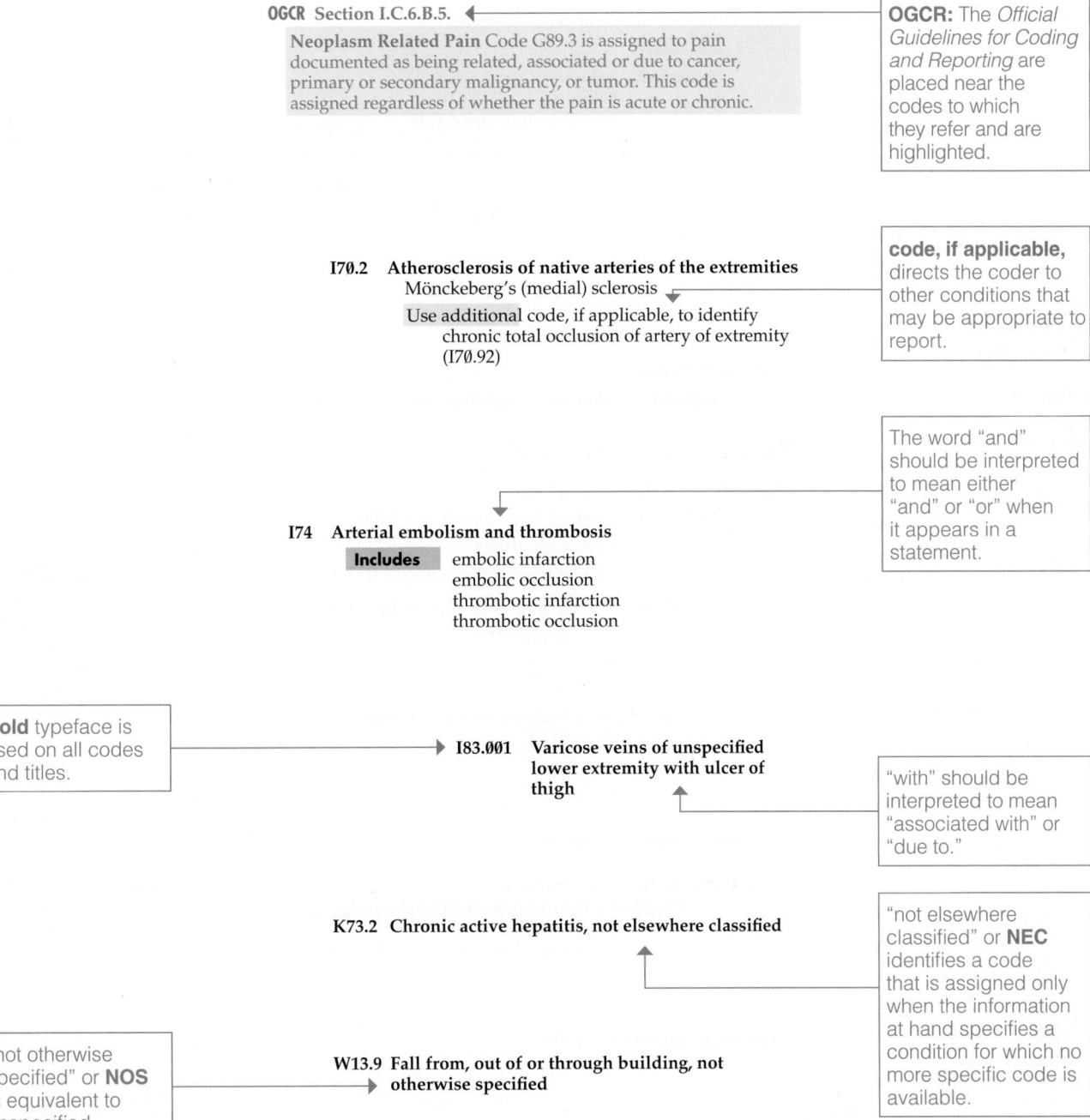

OGCR Section I.C.6.B.5. ←

Neoplasm Related Pain Code G89.3 is assigned to pain documented as being related, associated or due to cancer, primary or secondary malignancy, or tumor. This code is assigned regardless of whether the pain is acute or chronic.

OGCR: The *Official Guidelines for Coding and Reporting* are placed near the codes to which they refer and are highlighted.

I70.2   **Atherosclerosis of native arteries of the extremities**
Mönckeberg's (medial) sclerosis

Use additional code, if applicable, to identify chronic total occlusion of artery of extremity (I70.92)

code, if applicable, directs the coder to other conditions that may be appropriate to report.

The word "and" should be interpreted to mean either "and" or "or" when it appears in a statement.

I74   **Arterial embolism and thrombosis**
Includes   embolic infarction
embolic occlusion
thrombotic infarction
thrombotic occlusion

Bold typeface is used on all codes and titles.

I83.001   **Varicose veins of unspecified lower extremity with ulcer of thigh**

"with" should be interpreted to mean "associated with" or "due to."

K73.2   Chronic active hepatitis, not elsewhere classified

"not elsewhere classified" or **NEC** identifies a code that is assigned only when the information at hand specifies a condition for which no more specific code is available.

"not otherwise specified" or **NOS** is equivalent to unspecified.

W13.9   Fall from, out of or through building, not otherwise specified

Codes or index entries are for purposes of illustration only and may not be current.

Excludes1 means "NOT CODED HERE!" An Excludes1 note indicates that the code excluded should never be assigned at the same time as the code above the Excludes1 note.

M19 Other and unspecified osteoarthritis
- **Excludes1** polyarthritis (M15.-)
- **Excludes2** arthrosis of spine (M47.-)
  hallux rigidus (M20.2)
  osteoarthritis of spine (M47.-)

Excludes2 represents "NOT INCLUDED HERE." An Excludes2 note indicates that the condition excluded is not part of the condition represented by the code, but a patient may have both conditions at the same time and it is acceptable to use both the code and the excluded code together, when appropriate.

Includes: This note appears immediately under a three-character code title to further define, or give examples of, the content.

A06 Amebiasis
- **Includes** infection due to Entamoeba histolytica

E26.01 Conn's syndrome
  Code also adrenal adenoma (D35.0)

Code also instructs that two codes may be required to fully describe a condition, but this note does not provide sequencing direction.

Codes titled "other" or "other specified" are for use when the information in the medical record provides detail for which a specific code does not exist.

E25.8 Other adrenogenital disorders

O00.2 Ovarian pregnancy   M

Maternity DX (Diagnosis) for ages 12-55 according to the *Definitions of Medicare Code Edits* (MCE).

P02.20 Newborn (suspected to be) affected by unspecified morphological and functional abnormalities of placenta   N

Newborn, Age 0, according to the *Definitions of Medicare Code Edits* (MCE).

L21.0 Seborrhea capitis
  Cradle cap   P

Pediatric Age, 0-17, according to the *Definitions of Medicare Code Edits* (MCE).

G30.1 Alzheimer's disease with late onset   A

Adult Age, 15-124, according to the *Definitions of Medicare Code Edits* (MCE).

Females Only according to the *Definitions of Medicare Code Edits* (MCE).

B37.3 Candidiasis of vulva and vagina ♀

C60.1 Malignant neoplasm of glans penis ♂

Males Only according to the *Definitions of Medicare Code Edits* (MCE).

H22 *Disorders of iris and ciliary body in diseases classified elsewhere*

Code first *underlying disease, such as:*
gout (M1A-, M1Ø.-)

Manifestation according to the *Definitions of Medicare Code Edits* (MCE).

Key Term Highlight identifies key words within similar code descriptions in a particular category.

F1Ø.21   Alcohol dependence, in remission

Coding Clinic identifies the year, quarter, and page number that presents information about an ICD-10-PCS code in the American Hospital Association's *Coding Clinic®*.

B96.5   Pseudomonas (aeruginosa) (mallei) (pseudomallei) as the cause of diseases classified elsewhere
Coding Clinic: 2Ø15, Q1, P18

Alphabetic Index

Main terms are in **bold** typeface.

Aberrant (congenital) —*see also* Malposition, congenital
　　adrenal gland Q89.1

Etiology code first followed by the manifestation code in **brackets**. The code in brackets is always to be sequenced second.

Amyloid heart (disease) E85.4 *[I43]*

Amylophagia —*see* Pica

"**see**" indicates another term should be referenced.

Angiofibroma —*see also* Neoplasm, benign, by site

"**see also**" follows a main term and instructs that there is another main term that may also be referenced.

Appendicitis (pneumococcal) (retrocecal) K37
　　with
　　　　perforation NOS K35.32
　　　　peritoneal abscess K35.33

A default code is listed next to the main term and represents that condition most commonly associated with the main term. If a condition is documented in a medical record without any additional information, such as acute or chronic, the default code should be assigned.

Use Additional Character(s):
The red stop sign cautions you that the code requires additional character(s) to ensure greatest specificity.

Abrasion T14.8
　　ankle S90.51-•

Codes or index entries are for purposes of illustration only and may not be current.

CHAPTER 1

CERTAIN INFECTIOUS AND PARASITIC DISEASES (A00-B99)

ARTHROPOD-BORNE VIRAL FEVERS AND VIRAL HEMORRHAGIC FEVERS (A90-A99)

A92   Other mosquito-borne viral fevers

     A92.5   Zika virus disease

New   **Excludes1**   congenital Zika virus disease (P35.4)

MYCOSES (B35-B49)

B39   Histoplasmosis

     Use additional code for any associated manifestations, such as:

Revised   retinitis (H32)

PROTOZOAL DISEASES (B50-B64)

B51   Plasmodium vivax malaria

Revised   **Excludes1**   plasmodium vivax with Plasmodium falciparum (B50.-)

CHAPTER 2

NEOPLASMS (C00-D49)

C43   Malignant melanoma of skin

     C43.1   Malignant melanoma of eyelid, including canthus

         C43.11   Malignant melanoma of right eyelid, including canthus

New   C43.111   Malignant melanoma of right upper eyelid, including canthus

New   C43.112   Malignant melanoma of right lower eyelid, including canthus

         C43.12   Malignant melanoma of left eyelid, including canthus

New   C43.121   Malignant melanoma of left upper eyelid, including canthus

New   C43.122   Malignant melanoma of left lower eyelid, including canthus

C4A   Merkel cell carcinoma

     C4A.1   Merkel cell carcinoma of eyelid, including canthus

         C4A.11   Merkel cell carcinoma of right eyelid, including canthus

New   C4A.111   Merkel cell carcinoma of right upper eyelid, including canthus

New   C4A.112   Merkel cell carcinoma of right lower eyelid, including canthus

         C4A.12   Merkel cell carcinoma of left eyelid, including canthus

New   C4A.121   Merkel cell carcinoma of left upper eyelid, including canthus

New   C4A.122   Merkel cell carcinoma of left lower eyelid, including canthus

C44   Other and unspecified malignant neoplasm of skin

     C44.1   Other and unspecified malignant neoplasm of skin of eyelid, including canthus

         Excludes1   connective tissue of eyelid (C49.0)

         C44.10   Unspecified malignant neoplasm of skin of eyelid, including canthus

             C44.102   Unspecified malignant neoplasm of skin of right eyelid, including canthus

New   C44.1021   Unspecified malignant neoplasm of skin of right upper eyelid, including canthus

New   C44.1022   Unspecified malignant neoplasm of skin of right lower eyelid, including canthus

             C44.109   Unspecified malignant neoplasm of skin of left eyelid, including canthus

New   C44.1091   Unspecified malignant neoplasm of skin of left upper eyelid, including canthus

New   C44.1092   Unspecified malignant neoplasm of skin of left lower eyelid, including canthus

         C44.11   Basal cell carcinoma of skin of eyelid, including canthus

             C44.112   Basal cell carcinoma of skin of right eyelid, including canthus

New   C44.1121   Basal cell carcinoma of skin of right upper eyelid, including canthus

New   C44.1122   Basal cell carcinoma of skin of right lower eyelid, including canthus

             C44.119   Basal cell carcinoma of skin of left eyelid, including canthus

New   C44.1191   Basal cell carcinoma of skin of left upper eyelid, including canthus

New   C44.1192   Basal cell carcinoma of skin of left lower eyelid, including canthus

	C44.12	Squamous cell carcinoma of skin of eyelid, including canthus		
		C44.122	Squamous cell carcinoma of skin of right eyelid, including canthus	
New			C44.1221	Squamous cell carcinoma of skin of right upper eyelid, including canthus
New			C44.1222	Squamous cell carcinoma of skin of right lower eyelid, including canthus
		C44.129	Squamous cell carcinoma of skin of left eyelid, including canthus	
New			C44.1291	Squamous cell carcinoma of skin of left upper eyelid, including canthus
New			C44.1292	Squamous cell carcinoma of skin of left lower eyelid, including canthus
New	C44.13	Sebaceous cell carcinoma of skin of eyelid, including canthus		
New		C44.131	Sebaceous cell carcinoma of skin of unspecified eyelid, including canthus	
New		C44.132	Sebaceous cell carcinoma of skin of right eyelid, including canthus	
New			C44.1321	Sebaceous cell carcinoma of skin of right upper eyelid, including canthus
New			C44.1322	Sebaceous cell carcinoma of skin of right lower eyelid, including canthus
New		C44.139	Sebaceous cell carcinoma of skin of left eyelid, including canthus	
New			C44.1391	Sebaceous cell carcinoma of skin of left upper eyelid, including canthus
New			C44.1392	Sebaceous cell carcinoma of skin of left lower eyelid, including canthus
	C44.19	Other specified malignant neoplasm of skin of eyelid, including canthus		
		C44.192	Other specified malignant neoplasm of skin of right eyelid, including canthus	
New			C44.1921	Other specified malignant neoplasm of skin of right upper eyelid, including canthus
New			C44.1922	Other specified malignant neoplasm of skin of right lower eyelid, including canthus
		C44.199	Other specified malignant neoplasm of skin of left eyelid, including canthus	

New			C44.1991	Other specified malignant neoplasm of skin of left upper eyelid, including canthus
New			C44.1992	Other specified malignant neoplasm of skin of left lower eyelid, including canthus

IN SITU NEOPLASMS (D00-D09)

	D03	Melanoma in situ		
		D03.1	Melanoma in situ of eyelid, including canthus	
			D03.11	Melanoma in situ of right eyelid, including canthus
New				D03.111 Melanoma in situ of right upper eyelid, including canthus
New				D03.112 Melanoma in situ of right lower eyelid, including canthus
			D03.12	Melanoma in situ of left eyelid, including canthus
New				D03.121 Melanoma in situ of left upper eyelid, including canthus
New				D03.122 Melanoma in situ of left lower eyelid, including canthus
	D04	Carcinoma in situ of skin		
		D04.1	Carcinoma in situ of skin of eyelid, including canthus	
			D04.11	Carcinoma in situ of skin of right eyelid, including canthus
New				D04.111 Carcinoma in situ of skin of right upper eyelid, including canthus
New				D04.112 Carcinoma in situ of skin of right lower eyelid, including canthus
			D04.12	Carcinoma in situ of skin of left eyelid, including canthus
New				D04.121 Carcinoma in situ of skin of left upper eyelid, including canthus
New				D04.122 Carcinoma in situ of skin of left lower eyelid, including canthus
	D07	Carcinoma in situ of other and unspecified genital organs		
		D07.2	Carcinoma in situ of vagina	
Revised			Vaginal intraepithelial neoplasia III [VIN III]	

BENIGN NEOPLASMS, EXCEPT BENIGN NEUROENDOCRINE TUMORS (D10-D36)

	D13	Benign neoplasm of other and ill-defined parts of digestive system		
		D13.3	Benign neoplasm of other and unspecified parts of small intestine	
Revised			**Excludes1** benign carcinoid tumors of the small intestine (D3A.01-)	
	D22	Melanocytic nevi		
		D22.1	Melanocytic nevi of eyelid, including canthus	
			D22.11	Melanocytic nevi of right eyelid, including canthus
New				D22.111 Melanocytic nevi of right upper eyelid, including canthus
New				D22.112 Melanocytic nevi of right lower eyelid, including canthus

D22.12 Melanocytic nevi of left eyelid, including canthus

New   D22.121 Melanocytic nevi of left upper eyelid, including canthus

New   D22.122 Melanocytic nevi of left lower eyelid, including canthus

D23 Other benign neoplasms of skin

  D23.1 Other benign neoplasm of skin of eyelid, including canthus

    D23.11 Other benign neoplasm of skin of right eyelid, including canthus

New   D23.111 Other benign neoplasm of skin of right upper eyelid, including canthus

New   D23.112 Other benign neoplasm of skin of right lower eyelid, including canthus

    D23.12 Other benign neoplasm of skin of left eyelid, including canthus

New   D23.121 Other benign neoplasm of skin of left upper eyelid, including canthus

New   D23.122 Other benign neoplasm of skin of left lower eyelid, including canthus

NEOPLASMS OF UNCERTAIN BEHAVIOR, POLYCYTHEMIA VERA AND MYELODYSPLASTIC SYNDROMES (D37-D48)

D47 Other neoplasms of uncertain behavior of lymphoid, hematopoietic and related tissue

  D47.0 Mast cell neoplasms of uncertain behavior

Revised   **Excludes1** congenital cutaneous mastocytosis (Q82.2)

CHAPTER 4

ENDOCRINE, NUTRITIONAL AND METABOLIC DISEASES (E00-E89)

DISORDERS OF OTHER ENDOCRINE GLANDS (E20-E35)

E20 Hypoparathyroidism

Revised   **Excludes1** tetany NOS (R29.0)

E35 Disorders of endocrine glands in diseases classified elsewhere

Revised   Use additional code, if applicable, to identify:

OVERWEIGHT, OBESITY AND OTHER HYPERALIMENTATION (E65-E68)

E67 Other hyperalimentation

Revised   E67.1 Hypercarotenemia

METABOLIC DISORDERS (E70-E88)

E72 Other disorders of amino-acid metabolism

  E72.5 Disorders of glycine metabolism

Revised   E72.53 Primary hyperoxaluria

  E72.8 Other specified disorders of amino-acid metabolism

Deleted   Disorders of beta-amino-acid metabolism
Deleted   Disorders of gamma-glutamyl cycle

New   E72.81 Disorders of gamma aminobutyric acid metabolism

New   4-hydroxybutyric aciduria
New   Disorders of GABA metabolism
New   GABA metabolic defect
New   GABA transaminase deficiency
New   GABA-T deficiency
New   Gamma-hydroxybutyric aciduria
New   SSADHD
New   Succinic semialdehyde dehydrogenase deficiency

New   E72.89 Other specified disorders of amino-acid metabolism
New   Disorders of beta-amino-acid metabolism
New   Disorders of gamma-glutamyl cycle

E75 Disorders of sphingolipid metabolism and other lipid storage disorders

  E75.2 Other sphingolipidosis

New   E75.26 Sulfatase deficiency
New   Multiple sulfatase deficiency (MSD)

    E75.29 Other sphingolipidosis
Deleted   Sulfatase deficiency

E78 Disorders of lipoprotein metabolism and other lipidemias

  E78.2 Mixed hyperlipidemia

Revised   **Excludes1** familial combined hyperlipidemia (E78.49)

  E78.4 Other hyperlipidemia

Deleted   Familial combined hyperlipidemia
New   E78.41 Elevated Lipoprotein(a)
New   Elevated Lp(a)
New   E78.49 Other hyperlipidemia
New   Familial combined hyperlipidemia

E83 Disorders of mineral metabolism

  E83.5 Disorders of calcium metabolism

    E83.59 Other disorders of calcium metabolism
Deleted   Idiopathic hypercalciuria

E88 Other and unspecified metabolic disorders

  E88.0 Disorders of plasma-protein metabolism, not elsewhere classified

New   E88.02 Plasminogen deficiency
New   Dysplasminogenemia
New   Hypoplasminogenemia
New   Type 1 plasminogen deficiency
New   Type 2 plasminogen deficiency
New   Code also, if applicable, ligneous conjunctivitis (H10.51)
New   Use additional code for associated findings, such as:
New   hydrocephalus (G91.4)
New   ligneous conjunctivitis (H10.51)
New   otitis media (H67.-)
New   respiratory disorder related to plasminogen deficiency (J99)

CHAPTER 5

MENTAL, BEHAVIORAL AND NEURODEVELOPMENTAL DISORDERS (F01-F99)

MENTAL AND BEHAVIORAL DISORDERS DUE TO PSYCHOACTIVE SUBSTANCE USE (F10-F19)

F12 Cannabis related disorders

  F12.2 Cannabis dependence

New   F12.23 Cannabis dependence with withdrawal

    F12.28 Cannabis dependence with other cannabis-induced disorder

      F12.288 Cannabis dependence with other cannabis-induced disorder

Deleted   Cannabis withdrawal

  F12.9 Cannabis use, unspecified

New   F12.93 Cannabis use, unspecified with withdrawal

F19   Other psychoactive substance related disorders

     F19.2   Other psychoactive substance dependence

        F19.21   **Other psychoactive substance dependence, in remission**

Revised   Other (or unknown) substance use disorder, severe, in sustained remission

     F19.9   Other psychoactive substance use, unspecified

        F19.98   **Other psychoactive substance use, unspecified with other psychoactive substance-induced disorders**

           F19.988   **Other psychoactive substance use,unspecified with other psychoactive substance-induced disorder**

Revised   Other (or unknown) substance-induced obsessive-compulsive or related disorder, without use disorder

ANXIETY, DISSOCIATIVE, STRESS-RELATED, SOMATOFORM AND OTHER NONPSYCHOTIC MENTAL DISORDERS (F40-F48)

F45   **Somatoform disorders**

Revised   **Excludes2**   factitious disorders (F68.1-, F68.A)

BEHAVIORAL SYNDROMES ASSOCIATED WITH PHYSIOLOGICAL DISTURBANCES AND PHYSICAL FACTORS (F50-F59)

Revised   F53   **Mental and behavioral disorders associated with the puerperium, not elsewhere classified**
Deleted   Postpartum depression

New   F53.0   **Postpartum depression**
New   Postnatal depression, NOS
New   Postpartum depression, NOS

New   F53.1   **Puerperal psychosis**
New   Postpartum psychosis
New   Puerperal psychosis, NOS

DISORDERS OF ADULT PERSONALITY AND BEHAVIOR (F60-F69)

F68   **Other disorders of adult personality and behavior**
Revised   F68.1   **Factitious disorder imposed on self**
Revised   F68.10   **Factitious disorder imposed on self, unspecified**
Revised   F68.11   **Factitious disorder imposed on self with predominantly psychological signs and symptoms**
Revised   F68.12   **Factitious disorder imposed on self with predominantly physical signs and symptoms**
Revised   F68.13   **Factitious disorder imposed on self with combined psychological and physical signs and symptoms**
New   F68.A   **Factitious disorder imposed on another**
New   Factitious disorder by proxy
New   Münchausen's by proxy

CHAPTER 6

DISEASES OF THE NERVOUS SYSTEM (G00-G99)

EXTRAPYRAMIDAL AND MOVEMENT DISORDERS (G20-G26)

G24   **Dystonia**
     G24.0   **Drug induced dystonia**
Revised   Use additional code for adverse effect, if applicable, to identify drug (T36-T50 with fifth or sixth character 5)

NERVE, NERVE ROOT AND PLEXUS DISORDERS (G50-G59)

G51   **Facial nerve disorders**
     G51.3   **Clonic hemifacial spasm**
New   G51.31   **Clonic hemifacial spasm, right**
New   G51.32   **Clonic hemifacial spasm, left**
New   G51.33   **Clonic hemifacial spasm, bilateral**
New   G51.39   **Clonic hemifacial spasm, unspecified**

DISEASES OF MYONEURAL JUNCTION AND MUSCLE (G70-G73)

G71   **Primary disorders of muscles**
     G71.0   **Muscular dystrophy**
New   G71.00   **Muscular dystrophy, unspecified**
New   G71.01   **Duchenne or Becker muscular dystrophy**
New   Autosomal recessive, childhood type, muscular dystrophy resembling Duchenne or Becker muscular dystrophy
New   Benign [Becker] muscular dystrophy
New   Severe [Duchenne] muscular dystrophy
New   G71.02   **Facioscapulohumeral muscular dystrophy**
New   Scapulohumeral muscular dystrophy
New   G71.09   **Other specified muscular dystrophies**
New   Benign scapuloperoneal muscular dystrophy with early contractures [Emery-Dreifuss]
New   Congenital muscular dystrophy NOS
New   Congenital muscular dystrophy with specific morphological abnormalities of the muscle fiber
New   Distal muscular dystrophy
New   Limb-girdle muscular dystrophy
New   Ocular muscular dystrophy
New   Oculopharyngeal muscular dystrophy
New   Scapuloperoneal muscular dystrophy
Deleted   Autosomal recessive, childhood type, muscular dystrophy resembling Duchenne or Becker muscular dystrophy
Deleted   Benign [Becker] muscular dystrophy
Deleted   Benign scapuloperoneal muscular dystrophy with early contractures [Emery-Dreifuss]
Deleted   Congenital muscular dystrophy NOS
Deleted   Congenital muscular dystrophy with specific morphological abnormalities of the muscle fiber
Deleted   Distal muscular dystrophy
Deleted   Facioscapulohumeral muscular dystrophy
Deleted   Limb-girdle muscular dystrophy
Deleted   Ocular muscular dystrophy
Deleted   Oculopharyngeal muscular dystrophy
Deleted   Scapuloperoneal muscular dystrophy
Deleted   Severe [Duchenne] muscular dystrophy

OTHER DISORDERS OF THE NERVOUS SYSTEM (G89-G99)

G89   **Pain, not elsewhere classified**
Revised   **Excludes2**   myalgia (M79.1-)

G91   **Hydrocephalus**
     G91.4   **Hydrocephalus in diseases classified elsewhere**
        Code first underlying condition, such as:
New   plasminogen deficiency (E88.02)

CHAPTER 7

DISEASES OF THE EYE AND ADNEXA (H00-H59)

DISORDERS OF EYELID, LACRIMAL SYSTEM AND ORBIT (H00-H05)

H01 Other inflammation of eyelid
   H01.0 Blepharitis
      H01.00 Unspecified blepharitis
New   H01.00A Unspecified blepharitis right eye, upper and lower eyelids
New   H01.00B Unspecified blepharitis left eye, upper and lower eyelids
      H01.01 Ulcerative blepharitis
New   H01.01A Ulcerative blepharitis right eye, upper and lower eyelids
New   H01.01B Ulcerative blepharitis left eye, upper and lower eyelids
      H01.02 Squamous blepharitis
New   H01.02A Squamous blepharitis right eye, upper and lower eyelids
New   H01.02B Squamous blepharitis left eye, upper and lower eyelids

H02 Other disorders of eyelid
   H02.1 Ectropion of eyelid
New   H02.15 Paralytic ectropion of eyelid
New   H02.151 Paralytic ectropion of right upper eyelid
New   H02.152 Paralytic ectropion of right lower eyelid
New   H02.153 Paralytic ectropion of right eye, unspecified eyelid
New   H02.154 Paralytic ectropion of left upper eyelid
New   H02.155 Paralytic ectropion of left lower eyelid
New   H02.156 Paralytic ectropion of left eye, unspecified eyelid
New   H02.159 Paralytic ectropion of unspecified eye, unspecified eyelid
   H02.2 Lagophthalmos
      H02.20 Unspecified lagophthalmos
New   H02.20A Unspecified lagophthalmos right eye, upper and lower eyelids
New   H02.20B Unspecified lagophthalmos left eye, upper and lower eyelids
New   H02.20C Unspecified lagophthalmos, bilateral, upper and lower eyelids
      H02.21 Cicatricial lagophthalmos
New   H02.21A Cicatricial lagophthalmos right eye, upper and lower eyelids
New   H02.21B Cicatricial lagophthalmos left eye, upper and lower eyelids
New   H02.21C Cicatricial lagophthalmos, bilateral, upper and lower eyelids

      H02.22 Mechanical lagophthalmos
New   H02.22A Mechanical lagophthalmos right eye, upper and lower eyelids [new]
New   H02.22B Mechanical lagophthalmos left eye, upper and lower eyelids
New   H02.22C Mechanical lagophthalmos, bilateral, upper and lower eyelids
      H02.23 Paralytic lagophthalmos
New   H02.23A Paralytic lagophthalmos right eye, upper and lower eyelids
New   H02.23B Paralytic lagophthalmos left eye, upper and lower eyelids
New   H02.23C Paralytic lagophthalmos, bilateral, upper and lower eyelids
   H02.8 Other specified disorders of eyelid
New   H02.88 Meibomian gland dysfunction of eyelid
New   H02.881 Meibomian gland dysfunction right upper eyelid
New   H02.882 Meibomian gland dysfunction right lower eyelid
New   H02.883 Meibomian gland dysfunction of right eye, unspecified eyelid
New   H02.884 Meibomian gland dysfunction left upper eyelid
New   H02.885 Meibomian gland dysfunction left lower eyelid
New   H02.886 Meibomian gland dysfunction of left eye, unspecified eyelid
New   H02.889 Meibomian gland dysfunction of unspecified eye, unspecified eyelid
New   H02.88A Meibomian gland dysfunction right eye, upper and lower eyelids
New   H02.88B Meibomian gland dysfunction left eye, upper and lower eyelids

H04 Disorders of lacrimal system
   H04.2 Epiphora
      H04.20 Unspecified epiphora
Revised   H04.201 Unspecified epiphora, right side
Revised   H04.202 Unspecified epiphora, left side
Revised   H04.203 Unspecified epiphora, bilateral
Revised   H04.209 Unspecified epiphora, unspecified side
      H04.22 Epiphora due to insufficient drainage
Revised   H04.221 Epiphora due to insufficient drainage, right side
Revised   H04.222 Epiphora due to insufficient drainage, left side
Revised   H04.223 Epiphora due to insufficient drainage, bilateral
Revised   H04.229 Epiphora due to insufficient drainage, unspecified side

DISORDERS OF CONJUNCTIVA (H10-H11)

H10 Conjunctivitis
   H10.5 Blepharoconjunctivitis
      H10.51 Ligneous conjunctivitis
New   Code also underlying condition if known, such as:
New   plasminogen deficiency (E88.02)

H10.8   Other conjunctivitis

New   H10.82   Rosacea conjunctivitis
New   *Code first* underlying rosacea dermatitis (L71.-)
New   H10.821   Rosacea conjunctivitis, right eye
New   H10.822   Rosacea conjunctivitis, left eye
New   H10.823   Rosacea conjunctivitis, bilateral
New   H10.829   Rosacea conjunctivitis, unspecified eye

OTHER DISORDERS OF EYE AND ADNEXA (H55-H57)

H57   Other disorders of eye and adnexa
         H57.8   Other specified disorders of eye and adnexa
New   H57.81   Brow ptosis
New   H57.811   Brow ptosis, right
New   H57.812   Brow ptosis, left
New   H57.813   Brow ptosis, bilateral
New   H57.819   Brow ptosis, unspecified
New   H57.89   Other specified disorders of eye and adnexa

CHAPTER 8

DISEASES OF THE EAR AND MASTOID PROCESS (H60-H95)

DISEASES OF MIDDLE EAR AND MASTOID (H65-H75)

H67   Otitis media in diseases classified elsewhere
         Code first underlying disease, such as:
New   plasminogen deficiency (E88.02)

INTRAOPERATIVE AND POSTPROCEDURAL COMPLICATIONS AND DISORDERS OF EAR AND MASTOID PROCESS, NOT ELSEWHERE CLASSIFIED (H95)

H95   Intraoperative and postprocedural complications and disorders of ear and mastoid process, not elsewhere classified
         H95.8   Other intraoperative and postprocedural complications and disorders of the ear and mastoid process, not elsewhere classified
                 H95.88   Other intraoperative complications and disorders of the ear and mastoid process, not elsewhere classified
Revised   Use additional code, if applicable, to further specify disorder

CHAPTER 9

DISEASES OF THE CIRCULATORY SYSTEM (I00-I99)

ISCHEMIC HEART DISEASES (I20-I25)

I22   Subsequent ST elevation (STEMI) and non-ST elevation (NSTEMI) myocardial infarction
         I22.8   Subsequent ST elevation (STEMI) myocardial infarction of other sites
Revised   Subsequent posterior (true) transmural (Q wave) myocardial infarction (acute)

PULMONARY HEART DISEASE AND DISEASES OF PULMONARY CIRCULATION (I26-I28)

I27   Other pulmonary heart diseases
         I27.2   Other secondary pulmonary hypertension
                 I27.29   Other secondary pulmonary hypertension
                         Code also other associated disorders, if known, such as:
Revised   hypertensive chronic kidney disease with end stage renal disease (I12.0, I13.11, I13.2)

OTHER FORMS OF HEART DISEASE (I30-I52)

I44   Atrioventricular and left bundle-branch block
         I44.1   Atrioventricular block, second degree
Revised   Möbitz block, type I and II

CEREBROVASCULAR DISEASES (I60-I69)

         Use additional code to identify presence of:
Revised   hypertension (I10-I16)

I63   Cerebral infarction
         I63.2   Cerebral infarction due to unspecified occlusion or stenosis of precerebral arteries
                 I63.21   Cerebral infarction due to unspecified occlusion or stenosis of vertebral arteries
Revised   I63.219   Cerebral infarction due to unspecified occlusion or stenosis of unspecified vertebral artery
                 I63.23   Cerebral infarction due to unspecified occlusion or stenosis of carotid arteries
Revised   I63.239   Cerebral infarction due to unspecified occlusion or stenosis of unspecified carotid artery
         I63.3   Cerebral infarction due to thrombosis of cerebral arteries
                 I63.33   Cerebral infarction due to thrombosis of posterior cerebral artery
Revised   I63.333   Cerebral infarction due to thrombosis of bilateral posterior cerebral arteries
                 I63.34   Cerebral infarction due to thrombosis of cerebellar artery
Revised   I63.343   Cerebral infarction due to thrombosis of bilateral cerebellar arteries
         I63.8   Other cerebral infarction
New   I63.81   Other cerebral infarction due to occlusion or stenosis of small artery
New   Lacunar infarction
New   I63.89   Other cerebral infarction

I67   Other cerebrovascular diseases
         I67.8   Other specified cerebrovascular diseases
New   I67.85   Hereditary cerebrovascular diseases
New   I67.850   Cerebral autosomal dominant arteriopathy with subcortical infarcts and leukoencephalopathy
New   CADASIL
New   Code also any associated diagnoses, such as:
New   epilepsy (G40.-) stroke (I63.-)
New   vascular dementia (F01.-)
New   I67.858   Other hereditary cerebrovascular disease

DISEASES OF ARTERIES, ARTERIOLES AND CAPILLARIES (I70-I79)

I77   Other disorders of arteries and arterioles
         I77.6   Arteritis, unspecified
                 Excludes1   arteritis or endarteritis:
Revised   giant cell (M31.5, M31.6)

CHAPTER 10

DISEASES OF THE RESPIRATORY SYSTEM (J00-J99)

OTHER DISEASES OF THE RESPIRATORY SYSTEM (J96-J99)

J99   Respiratory disorders in diseases classified elsewhere
Code first underlying disease, such as:
New   plasminogen deficiency (E88.02)

CHAPTER 11

DISEASES OF THE DIGESTIVE SYSTEM (K00-K95)

DISEASES OF APPENDIX (K35-K38)

K35   Acute appendicitis
   K35.2   **Acute appendicitis with generalized peritonitis**
Deleted   Perforated appendix NOS
Deleted   Ruptured appendix NOS
New   K35.20   **Acute appendicitis with generalized peritonitis, without abscess (Acute) appendicitis with generalized peritonitis NOS**
New   K35.21   **Acute appendicitis with generalized peritonitis, with abscess**
   K35.3   **Acute appendicitis with localized peritonitis**
Deleted   Acute appendicitis with or without perforation or rupture with peritonitis NOS
Deleted   Acute appendicitis with or without perforation or rupture with localized peritonitis
Deleted   Acute appendicitis with peritoneal abscess
New   K35.30   **Acute appendicitis with localized peritonitis, without perforation or gangrene**
New   Acute appendicitis with localized peritonitis NOS
New   K35.31   **Acute appendicitis with localized peritonitis and gangrene, without perforation**
New   K35.32   **Acute appendicitis with perforation and localized peritonitis, without abscess**
New   (Acute) appendicitis with perforation NOS
New   Perforated appendix NOS
New   Ruptured appendix (with localized peritonitis) NOS
New   K35.33   **Acute appendicitis with perforation and localized peritonitis, with abscess**
New   (Acute) appendicitis with (peritoneal) abscess NOS
New   Ruptured appendix with localized peritonitis and abscess
   K35.8   **Other and unspecified acute appendicitis**
     K35.89   **Other acute appendicitis**
New   K35.890   **Other acute appendicitis without perforation or gangrene**
New   K35.891   **Other acute appendicitis without perforation, with gangrene**
New   (Acute) appendicitis with gangrene NOS

K37   **Unspecified appendicitis**
Revised   **Excludes1**   -unspecified appendicitis with peritonitis (K35.2-, K35.3)

NONINFECTIVE ENTERITIS AND COLITIS (K50-K52)

K52   **Other and unspecified noninfective gastroenteritis and colitis**
   K52.2   **Allergic and dietetic gastroenteritis and colitis**
     K52.21   **Food protein-induced enterocolitis syndrome**
New   FPIES

OTHER DISEASES OF INTESTINES (K55-K64)

K57   **Diverticular disease of intestine**
New   Code also if applicable peritonitis K65.-

K61   **Abscess of anal and rectal regions**
  Includes   abscess of anal and rectal regions
      cellulitis of anal and rectal regions
   K61.0   **Anal abscess**
Deleted   **Excludes1**   intrasphincteric abscess (K61.4)
New   **Excludes2**   intrasphincteric abscess (K61.4)
   K61.1   **Rectal abscess**
Revised   **Excludes1**   ischiorectal abscess (K61.39)
   K61.3   **Ischiorectal abscess**
Deleted   Abscess of ischiorectal fossa
New   K61.31   **Horseshoe abscess**
New   K61.39   **Other ischiorectal abscess**
New   Abscess of ischiorectal fossa
New   Ischiorectal abscess, NOS
   K61.4   **Intrasphincteric abscess**
New   Intersphincteric abscess
   K61.5   **Supralevator abscess**
New

K63   **Other diseases of intestine**
   K63.0   **Abscess of intestine**
Revised   **Excludes2**   abscess of appendix (K35.3-)
   K63.1   **Perforation of intestine (nontraumatic)**
Revised   **Excludes2**   perforation (nontraumatic) of appendix (K35.2-, K35.3)

DISEASES OF PERITONEUM AND RETROPERITONEUM (K65-K68)

K65   **Peritonitis**
Revised   Use additional code (B95-B97), to identify infectious agent, if known
New   Code also if applicable diverticular disease of intestine (K57.-)
Revised   **Excludes1**   acute appendicitis with generalized peritonitis (K35.2-)
Deleted   diverticulitis of both small and large intestine with peritonitis (K57.4-)
Deleted   diverticulitis of colon with peritonitis (K57.2-)
Deleted   diverticulitis of intestine, NOS, with peritonitis (K57.8-)
Deleted   diverticulitis of small intestine with peritonitis (K57.0-)
Deleted   peritonitis with or following diverticular disease of intestine (K57.-)

K67   **Disorders of peritoneum in infectious diseases classified elsewhere**
Revised   *Code first* underlying disease, such as:

K68   **Disorders of retroperitoneum**
   K68.1   **Retroperitoneal abscess**
     K68.11   **Postprocedural retroperitoneal abscess**
New   **Excludes2**   infection following procedure (T81.4-)

DISEASES OF LIVER (K70-K77)

K74 Fibrosis and cirrhosis of liver
    K74.3 Primary biliary cirrhosis
New   Primary biliary cholangitis
New   **Excludes2** primary schlerosing cholangitis (K83.01)

K75 Other inflammatory liver diseases
    K75.0 Abscess of liver
Revised   **Excludes1** cholangitis without liver abscess (K83.09)

DISORDERS OF GALLBLADDER, BILIARY TRACT AND PANCREAS (K80–K87)

K80 Cholelithiasis
    K80.0 Calculus of gallbladder with acute cholecystitis
New   Use additional code if applicable for associated gangrene of gallbladder (K82.A1), or perforation of gallbladder (K82.A2)
    K80.1 Calculus of gallbladder with other cholecystitis
New   Use additional code if applicable for associated gangrene of gallbladder (K82.A1), or perforation of gallbladder (K82.A2)
    K80.4 Calculus of bile duct with cholecystitis
New   Use additional code if applicable for associated gangrene of gallbladder (K82.A1), or perforation of gallbladder (K82.A2)
    K80.6 Calculus of gallbladder and bile duct with cholecystitis
New   Use additional code if applicable for associated gangrene of gallbladder (K82.A1), or perforation of gallbladder (K82.A2)

K81 Cholecystitis
New   Use additional code if applicable for associated gangrene of gallbladder (K82.A1), or perforation of gallbladder (K82.A2)

K82 Other diseases of gallbladder
    K82.2 Perforation of gallbladder
New   **Excludes1** Perforation of gallbladder in cholecystitis (K82.A2)
New   K82.A Disorders of gallbladder in diseases classified elsewhere
New   *Code first the type of cholecystitis (K81.-), or cholelithiasis with cholecystitis (K80.00-K80.19, K80.40-K80.47, K80.60-K80.67)*
New   K82.A1 Gangrene of gallbladder in cholecystitis
New   K82.A2 Perforation of gallbladder in cholecystitis

K83 Other diseases of biliary tract
    K83.0 Cholangitis
Deleted   Ascending cholangitis
Deleted   Cholangitis NOS
Deleted   Primary cholangitis
Deleted   Recurrent cholangitis
Deleted   Sclerosing cholangitis
Deleted   Secondary cholangitis
Deleted   Stenosing cholangitis
Deleted   Suppurative cholangitis
Deleted   **Excludes1** chronic nonsuppurative destructive cholangitis (K74.3)
New   **Excludes2** chronic nonsuppurative destructive cholangitis (K74.3)
New   primary biliary cholangitis (K74.3)
New   primary biliary cirrhosis (K74.3)
New   K83.01 Primary sclerosing cholangitis

New   K83.09 Other cholangitis
New   Ascending cholangitis
New   Cholangitis NOS
New   Primary cholangitis
New   Recurrent cholangitis
New   Sclerosing cholangitis
New   Secondary cholangitis
New   Stenosing cholangitis
New   Suppurative cholangitis

K87 Disorders of gallbladder, biliary tract and pancreas in diseases classified elsewhere
Revised   **Excludes1** cytomegaloviral pancreatitis (B25.2)

CHAPTER 12

DISEASES OF THE SKIN AND SUBCUTANEOUS TISSUE (L00-L99)

URTICARIA AND ERYTHEMA (L49-L54)

L51 Erythema multiforme
    Use additional code to identify associated manifestations, such as:
Revised   edema of eyelid (H02.84-)

OTHER DISORDERS OF THE SKIN AND SUBCUTANEOUS TISSUE (L80-L99)

L98 Other disorders of skin and subcutaneous tissue, not elsewhere classified
    L98.4 Non-pressure chronic ulcer of skin, not elsewhere classified
        L98.49 Non-pressure chronic ulcer of skin of other sites
            Non-pressure chronic ulcer of skin NOS
Revised   L98.495 Non-pressure chronic ulcer of skin of other sites with muscle involvement without evidence of necrosis
Revised   L98.496 Non-pressure chronic ulcer of skin of other sites with bone involvement without evidence of necrosis
Revised   L98.498 Non-pressure chronic ulcer of skin of other sites with other specified severity

CHAPTER 13

DISEASES OF THE MUSCULOSKELETAL SYSTEM AND CONNECTIVE TISSUE (M00-M99)

This chapter contains the following blocks:

New	M04	Autoinflammatory syndromes
New	M97	Periprosthetic fracture around internal prosthetic joint

DENTOFACIAL ANOMALIES [INCLUDING MALOCCLUSION] AND OTHER DISORDERS OF JAW (M26-M27)

M26 Dentofacial anomalies [including malocclusion]
    M26.2 Anomalies of dental arch relationship
        M26.22 Open occlusal relationship
            M26.220 Open anterior occlusal relationship
Revised   Anterior open bite
            M26.221 Open posterior occlusal relationship
Revised   Posterior open bite

DISORDERS OF MUSCLES (M60-M63)

M62 Other disorders of muscle
Revised   **Excludes1** myalgia (M79.1-)

OTHER SOFT TISSUE DISORDERS (M70-M79)

M79　Other and unspecified soft tissue disorders, not elsewhere classified

　　M79.1　Myalgia

New　　　　M79.10　Myalgia, unspecified site

New　　　　M79.11　Myalgia of mastication muscle

New　　　　M79.12　Myalgia of auxiliary muscles, head and neck

New　　　　M79.18　Myalgia, other site

CHAPTER 14

DISEASES OF THE GENITOURINARY SYSTEM (N00-N99)

OTHER DISEASES OF THE URINARY SYSTEM (N30-N39)

N35　Urethral stricture

　　N35.0　Post-traumatic urethral stricture

　　　　N35.01　Post-traumatic urethral stricture, male

New　　　　　　N35.016　Post-traumatic urethral stricture, male, overlapping sites

　　N35.1　Postinfective urethral stricture, not elsewhere classified

　　　　N35.11　Postinfective urethral stricture, not elsewhere classified, male

New　　　　　　N35.116　Postinfective urethral stricture, not elsewhere classified, male, overlapping sites

　　N35.8　Other urethral stricture

New　　　　N35.81　Other urethral stricture, male

New　　　　　　N35.811　Other urethral stricture, male, meatal

New　　　　　　N35.812　Other urethral bulbous stricture, male

New　　　　　　N35.813　Other membranous urethral stricture, male

New　　　　　　N35.814　Other anterior urethral stricture, male, anterior

New　　　　　　N35.816　Other urethral stricture, male, overlapping sites

New　　　　　　N35.819　Other urethral stricture, male, unspecified site

New　　　　N35.82　Other urethral stricture, female

　　N35.9　Urethral stricture, unspecified

New　　　　N35.91　Urethral stricture, unspecified, male

New　　　　　　N35.911　Unspecified urethral stricture, male, meatal

New　　　　　　N35.912　Unspecified bulbous urethral stricture, male

New　　　　　　N35.913　Unspecified membranous urethral stricture, male

New　　　　　　N35.914　Unspecified anterior urethral stricture, male

New　　　　　　N35.916　Unspecified urethral stricture, male, overlapping sites

New　　　　　　N35.919　Unspecified urethral stricture, male, unspecified site

New　　　　　　　　Pinhole meatus NOS

New　　　　　　　　Urethral stricture NOS

New　　　　N35.92　Unspecified urethral stricture, female

INTRAOPERATIVE AND POSTPROCEDURAL COMPLICATIONS AND DISORDERS OF GENITOURINARY SYSTEM, NOT ELSEWHERE CLASSIFIED (N99)

N99　Intraoperative and postprocedural complications and disorders of genitourinary system, not elsewhere classified

　　N99.1　Postprocedural urethral stricture

　　　　N99.11　Postprocedural urethral stricture, male

New　　　　　　N99.116　Postprocedural urethral stricture, male, overlapping sites

CHAPTER 15

PREGNANCY, CHILDBIRTH AND THE PUERPERIUM (O00-O9A)

Revised　　**Excludes2**　mental and behavioral disorders associated with the puerperium (F53.-)

PREGNANCY WITH ABORTIVE OUTCOME (O00-O08)

O00　Ectopic pregnancy

　　O00.2　Ovarian pregnancy

　　　　O00.21　Ovarian pregnancy with intrauterine pregnancy

Revised　　　　　　O00.212　Left ovarian pregnancy with intrauterine pregnancy

MATERNAL CARE RELATED TO THE FETUS AND AMNIOTIC CAVITY AND POSSIBLE DELIVERY PROBLEMS (O30-O48)

O30　Multiple gestation

　　O30.1　Triplet pregnancy

New　　　　O30.13　Triplet pregnancy, trichorionic/triamniotic

New　　　　　　O30.131　Triplet pregnancy, trichorionic/triamniotic, first trimester

New　　　　　　O30.132　Triplet pregnancy, trichorionic/triamniotic, second trimester

New　　　　　　O30.133　Triplet pregnancy, trichorionic/triamniotic, third trimester

New　　　　　　O30.139　Triplet pregnancy, trichorionic/triamniotic, unspecified trimester

　　O30.2　Quadruplet pregnancy

New　　　　O30.23　Quadruplet pregnancy, quadrachorionic/quadra-amniotic

New　　　　　　O30.231　Quadruplet pregnancy, quadrachorionic/quadra-amniotic, first trimester

New　　　　　　O30.232　Quadruplet pregnancy, quadrachorionic/quadra-amniotic, second trimester

New　　　　　　O30.233　Quadruplet pregnancy, quadrachorionic/quadra-amniotic, third trimester

New　　　　　　O30.239　Quadruplet pregnancy, quadrachorionic/quadra-amniotic, unspecifiedtrimester

　　O30.8　Other specified multiple gestation

New　　　　O30.83　Other specified multiple gestation, number of chorions and amnions are both equalto the number of fetuses

New　　　　　　Pentachorionic, penta-amniotic pregnancy (quintuplets)

New　　　　　　Hexachorionic, hexa-amniotic pregnancy (sextuplets)

New　　　　　　Heptachorionic, hepta-amniotic pregnancy (septuplets)

New　　　　　　O30.831　Other specified multiple gestation, number of chorions and amnions are both equal to the number of fetuses, first trimester

New　　　　　　O30.832　Other specified multiple gestation, number of chorions and amnions are both equal to the number of fetuses, second trimester

New   O30.833   Other specified multiple gestation, number of chorions and amnions are both equal to the number of fetuses, third trimester

New   O30.839   Other specified multiple gestation, number of chorions and amnions areboth equal to the number of fetuses, unspecified trimester

COMPLICATIONS OF LABOR AND DELIVERY (O60-O77)

O75   Other complications of labor and delivery, not elsewhere classified

O75.4   Other complications of obstetric surgery and procedures

Revised   **Excludes2**   infection of obstetrical (surgical) wound (O86.0-)

COMPLICATIONS PREDOMINANTLY RELATED TO THE PUERPERIUM (O85-O92)

Revised   **Excludes2**   mental and behavioral disorders associated with the puerperium (F53.-)

O86   Other puerperal infections

O86.0   Infection of obstetric surgical wound

New   **Excludes1**   complications of procedures, not elsewhere classified (T81.4-)
New   postprocedural fever NOS (R50.82)
New   postprocedural retroperitoneal abscess (K68.11)

New   O86.00   Infection of obstetric surgical wound, unspecified

New   O86.01   Infection of obstetric surgical wound, superficial incisional site
New   Subcutaneous abscess following an obstetrical procedure
New   Stitch abscess following an obstetrical procedure

New   O86.02   Infection of obstetric surgical wound, deep incisional site
New   Intramuscular abscess following an obstetrical procedure
New   Sub-fascial abscess following a procedure

New   O86.03   Infection of obstetric surgical wound, organ and space site
New   Intraabdominal abscess following an obstetrical procedure
New   Subphrenic abscess following an obstetrical procedure

New   O86.04   Sepsis following an obstetrical procedure
New   Use additional code to identify the sepsis

New   O86.09   Infection of obstetric surgical wound, other surgical site

O90   Complications of the puerperium, not elsewhere classified

O90.6   Postpartum mood disturbance

Revised   **Excludes1**   postpartum depression (F53.0)
Revised   puerperal psychosis (F53.1)

OTHER OBSTETRIC CONDITIONS, NOT ELSEWHERE CLASSIFIED (O94-O9A)

O99   Other maternal diseases classifiable elsewhere but complicating pregnancy, childbirth and the puerperium

O99.3   Mental disorders and diseases of the nervous system complicating pregnancy, childbirth and the puerperium

O99.34   Other mental disorders complicating pregnancy, childbirth, and the puerperium

Revised   **Excludes2**   postnatal psychosis (F53.1)
Revised   puerperal psychosis (F53.1)

CHAPTER 16

CERTAIN CONDITIONS ORIGINATING IN THE PERINATAL PERIOD (P00-P96)

NEWBORN AFFECTED BY MATERNAL FACTORS AND BY COMPLICATIONS OF PREGNANCY, LABOR, AND DELIVERY (P00–P04)

P02   Newborn affected by complications of placenta, cord and membranes

P02.7   Newborn affected by chorioamnionitis
Deleted   Newborn affected by amnionitis
Deleted   Newborn affected by membranitis
Deleted   Newborn affected by placentitis

New   P02.70   Newborn affected by fetal inflammatory response syndrome
New   Newborn affected by FIRS

New   P02.78   Newborn affected by other conditions from chorioamnionitis
New   Newborn affected by amnionitis
New   Newborn affected by membranitis
New   Newborn affected by placentitis

P04   Newborn affected by noxious substances transmitted via placenta or breast milk

P04.0   Newborn affected by maternal anesthesia and analgesia in pregnancy, labor and delivery
Revised   Newborn affected by reactions and intoxications from maternal opiates and tranquilizers administered for procedures during pregnancy or labor and delivery

New   **Excludes2**   newborn affected by other maternal medication (P04.1-)

P04.1   Newborn affected by other maternal medication
Deleted   Newborn affected by cancer chemotherapy
Deleted   Newborn affected by cytotoxic drugs
New   *Code first withdrawal symptoms from maternal use of drugs of addiction, if applicable (P96.1)*

Deleted   **Excludes1**   maternal use of drugs of addiction (P04.4-)

New   **Excludes2**   maternal anesthesia and analgesia in pregnancy, labor and delivery (P04.0) maternal use of drugs of addiction (P04.4-)

New   P04.11   Newborn affected by maternal antineoplastic chemotherapy

New   P04.12   Newborn affected by maternal cytotoxic drugs

New   P04.13   Newborn affected by maternal use of anticonvulsants

New   P04.14   Newborn affected by maternal use of opiates

New   P04.15   Newborn affected by maternal use of antidepressants

New   P04.16   Newborn affected by maternal use of amphetamines

New	P04.17	Newborn affected by maternal use of sedative-hypnotics
New	P04.1A	Newborn affected by maternal use of anxiolytics
New	P04.18	Newborn affected by other maternal medication
New	P04.19	Newborn affected by maternal use of unspecified medication
	P04.4	Newborn affected by maternal use of drugs of addiction
New	P04.40	Newborn affected by maternal use of unspecified drugs of addiction
New	P04.42	Newborn affected by maternal use of hallucinogens
New		**Excludes2** newborn affected by other maternal medication (P04.1-)
	P04.8	Newborn affected by other maternal noxious substances
New	P04.81	Newborn affected by maternal use of cannabis
New	P04.89	Newborn affected by other maternal noxious substances

INFECTIONS SPECIFIC TO THE PERINATAL PERIOD (P35-P39)

	P35	Congenital viral diseases
New	P35.4	Congenital Zika virus disease
New		Use additional code to identify manifestations of congenital Zika virus disease

TRANSITORY ENDOCRINE AND METABOLIC DISORDERS SPECIFIC TO NEWBORN (P70-P74)

	P74	Other transitory neonatal electrolyte and metabolic disturbances
	P74.2	Disturbances of sodium balance of newborn
New	P74.21	Hypernatremia of newborn
New	P74.22	Hyponatremia of newborn
	P74.3	Disturbances of potassium balance of newborn
New	P74.31	Hyperkalemia of newborn
New	P74.32	Hypokalemia of newborn
	P74.4	Other transitory electrolyte disturbances of newborn
New	P74.41	Alkalosis of newborn Hyperbicarbonatemia
New	P74.42	Disturbances of chlorine balance of newborn
New	P74.421	Hyperchloremia of newborn Hyperchloremic metabolic acidosis
New		**Excludes2** late metabolic acidosis of the newborn (P77.0)
New	P74.422	Hypochloremia of newborn
New	P74.49	Other transitory electrolyte disturbance of newborn

CONDITIONS INVOLVING THE INTEGUMENT AND TEMPERATURE REGULATION OF NEWBORN (P80-P83)

	P83	Other conditions of integument specific to newborn
	P83.8	Other specified conditions of integument specific to newborn
	P83.81	Umbilical granuloma
Revised		**Excludes2** Granulomatous disorder of the skin and subcutaneous tissue, unspecified (L92.9)

OTHER DISORDERS ORIGINATING IN THE PERINATAL PERIOD (P90-P96)

	P91	Other disturbances of cerebral status of newborn
	P91.8	Other specified disturbances of cerebral status of newborn
	P91.81	Neonatal encephalopathy
	P91.811	*Neonatal encephalopathy in diseases classified elsewhere*
Revised		Code first underlying condition, if known, such as: congenital cirrhosis (of liver) (P78.81)
	P93	Reactions and intoxications due to drugs administered to newborn
Revised		**Excludes1** reactions and intoxications from maternal opiates, tranquilizers and other medication (P04.0-P04.1, P04.4-)

CHAPTER 17

CONGENITAL MALFORMATIONS, DEFORMATIONS AND CHROMOSOMAL ABNORMALITIES (Q00-Q99)

Revised	**Note:** Codes from this chapter are not for use on maternal records

CONGENITAL MALFORMATIONS OF THE NERVOUS SYSTEM (Q00–Q07)

	Q02	Microcephaly
New		Use additional code, if applicable, to identify congenital Zika virus disease

CONGENITAL MALFORMATIONS OF GENITAL ORGANS (Q50-Q56)

	Q51	Congenital malformations of uterus and cervix
	Q51.2	Other doubling of uterus
Revised		Septate uterus
New	Q51.20	Other doubling of uterus, unspecified
New		Septate uterus, unspecified
New	Q51.21	Other complete doubling of uterus
New		Complete septate uterus
New	Q51.22	Other partial doubling of uterus
New		Partial septate uterus
New	Q51.28	Other doubling of uterus, other specified
New		Septate uterus, other specified

CONGENITAL MALFORMATIONS AND DEFORMATIONS OF THE MUSCULOSKELETAL SYSTEM (Q65-Q79)

	Q67	Congenital musculoskeletal deformities of head, face, spine and chest
	Q67.5	Congenital deformity of spine
Revised		**Excludes1** infantile idiopathic scoliosis (M41.0)

CHROMOSOMAL ABNORMALITIES, NOT ELSEWHERE CLASSIFIED (Q90-Q99)

	Q93	Monosomies and deletions from the autosomes, not elsewhere classified
	Q93.5	Other deletions of part of a chromosome
Deleted		Angelman syndrome
New	Q93.51	Angelman syndrome
New	Q93.59	Other deletions of part of a chromosome
	Q93.8	Other deletions from the autosomes
New	Q93.82	Williams syndrome

CHAPTER 18

SYMPTOMS, SIGNS AND ABNORMAL CLINICAL AND LABORATORY FINDINGS, NOT ELSEWHERE CLASSIFIED (R00-R99)

SYMPTOMS AND SIGNS INVOLVING COGNITION, PERCEPTION, EMOTIONAL STATE AND BEHAVIOR (R40-R46)

R40   Somnolence, stupor and coma
    R40.2   Coma
        R40.21   Coma scale, eyes open
            R40.211   Coma scale, eyes open, never
New   Coma scale eye opening score of 1
            R40.212   Coma scale, eyes open, to pain
New   Coma scale eye opening score of 2
            R40.213   Coma scale, eyes open, to sound
New   Coma scale eye opening score of 3
            R40.214   Coma scale, eyes open, spontaneous
New   Coma scale eye opening score of 4
        R40.22   Coma scale, best verbal response
            R40.221   Coma scale, best verbal response, none
New   Coma scale verbal score of 1
            R40.222   Coma scale, best verbal response, incomprehensible words
New   Coma scale verbal score of 2
             R40.223   Coma scale, best verbal response, inappropriate words
New   Coma scale verbal score of 3
            R40.224   Coma scale, best verbal response, confused conversation
New   Coma scale verbal score of 4
            R40.225   Coma scale, best verbal response, oriented
New   Coma scale verbal score of 5
        R40.23   Coma scale, best motor response
            R40.231   Coma scale, best motor response, none
New   Coma scale motor score of 1
            R40.232   Coma scale, best motor response, extension
New   Coma scale motor score of 2
Revised   R40.233   Coma scale, best motor response, abnormal flexion
New   Coma scale motor score of 3
Revised   Abnormal flexure posturing to pain or noxious stimuli (2-5 years of age)
            R40.234   Coma scale, best motor response, flexion withdrawal
New   Coma scale motor score of 4
Revised   Withdraws from pain or noxious stimuli (2-5 years of age)
            R40.235   Coma scale, best motor response, localizes pain
New   Coma scale motor score of 5
            R40.236   Coma scale, best motor response, obeys commands
New   Coma scale motor score of 6

ABNORMAL FINDINGS ON EXAMINATION OF BLOOD, WITHOUT DIAGNOSIS (R70-R79)

R77   Other abnormalities of plasma proteins
Revised   **Excludes1**   disorders of plasma-protein metabolism (E88.0-)

ABNORMAL FINDINGS ON EXAMINATION OF URINE, WITHOUT DIAGNOSIS (R80-R82)

R82   Other and unspecified abnormal findings in urine
    R82.9   Other and unspecified abnormal findings in urine
        R82.99   Other abnormal findings in urine
Deleted   Cells and casts in urine
Deleted   Crystalluria
Deleted   Melanuria
New   R82.991   Hypocitraturia
New   R82.992   Hyperoxaluria
New   **Excludes1**   Primary hyperoxaluria (E72.53)
New   R82.993   Hyperuricoscuria
New   R82.994   Hypercalciuria
New   Idiopathic hypercalciuria
New   R82.998   Other abnormal findings in urine
New   Cells and casts in urine
New   Crystalluria
New   Melanuria

ABNORMAL FINDINGS ON DIAGNOSTIC IMAGING AND IN FUNCTION STUDIES, WITHOUT DIAGNOSIS (R90-R94)

R93   Abnormal findings on diagnostic imaging of other body structures
    R93.6   Abnormal findings on diagnostic imaging of limbs
Revised   **Excludes2**   abnormal finding in skin and subcutaneous tissue (R93.8-)
    R93.8   Abnormal findings on diagnostic imaging of other specified body structures
Deleted   Abnormal finding by radioisotope localization of placenta
Deleted   Abnormal radiological finding in skin and subcutaneous tissue
Deleted   Mediastinal shift
New   R93.81   Abnormal radiologic findings on diagnostic imaging of testis
New   R93.811   Abnormal radiologic findings on diagnostic imaging of right testicle
New   R93.812   Abnormal radiologic findings on diagnostic imaging of left testicle
New   R93.813   Abnormal radiologic findings on diagnostic imaging of testicles, bilateral
New   R93.819   Abnormal radiologic findings on diagnostic imaging of unspecified testicle
New   R93.89   Abnormal findings on diagnostic imaging of other specified body structures
New   Abnormal finding by radioisotope localization of placenta
New   Abnormal radiological finding in skin and subcutaneous tissue
New   Mediastinal shift

CHAPTER 19

INJURY, POISONING AND CERTAIN OTHER CONSEQUENCES OF EXTERNAL CAUSES (S00-T88)

INJURIES TO THE HEAD (S00-S09)

S04   Injury of cranial nerve
    S04.8   Injury of other cranial nerves
        S04.89   Injury of other cranial nerves
Revised   Injury of vagus [10th] nerve

INJURIES TO THE WRIST, HAND AND FINGERS (S60-S69)

S62   Fracture at wrist and hand level
    S62.6   Fracture of other and unspecified finger(s)
        S62.62   Displaced fracture of middle phalanx of finger
Revised   S62.626   Displaced fracture of middle phalanx of right little finger
Revised   S62.627   Displaced fracture of middle phalanx of left little finger
Revised   S62.628   Displaced fracture of middle phalanx of other finger
Revised   Displaced fracture of middle phalanx of specified finger with unspecified laterality
Revised   S62.629   Displaced fracture of middle phalanx of unspecified finger
        S62.65   Nondisplaced fracture of middle phalanx of finger
Revised   S62.654   Nondisplaced fracture of middle phalanx of right ring finger
Revised   S62.655   Nondisplaced fracture of middle phalanx of left ring finger
Revised   S62.656   Nondisplaced fracture of middle phalanx of right little finger
Revised   S62.657   Nondisplaced fracture of middle phalanx of left little finger
Revised   S62.658   Nondisplaced fracture of middle phalanx of other finger
Revised   Nondisplaced fracture of middle phalanx of specified finger with unspecified laterality
Revised   S62.659   Nondisplaced fracture of middle phalanx of unspecified finger

BURNS AND CORROSIONS OF EXTERNAL BODY SURFACE, SPECIFIED BY SITE (T20-T25)

T21   Burn and corrosion of trunk
    T21.0   Burn of unspecified degree of trunk
        T21.01   Burn of unspecified degree of chest wall
Revised   Burn of unspecified degree of breast

POISONING BY, ADVERSE EFFECTS OF AND UNDERDOSING OF DRUGS MEDICAMENTS AND BIOLOGICAL SUBSTANCES (T36-T50)

Code first, for adverse effects, the nature of the adverse effect, such as:
Revised   adverse effect NOS (T88.7)
Revised   blood disorders (D56-D76)
Revised   contact dermatitis (L23-L25)

Revised   T37   Poisoning by, adverse effect of and underdosing of other systemic anti-infectives and antiparasitics

T40   Poisoning by, adverse effect of and underdosing of narcotics and psychodysleptics [hallucinogens]
    T40.8   Poisoning by and adverse effect of lysergide [LSD]
        T40.8X   Poisoning by and adverse effect of lysergide [LSD]
             T40.8X1   Poisoning by lysergide [LSD], accidental (unintentional)
Revised   Poisoning by lysergide [LSD] NOS

T43   Poisoning by, adverse effect of and underdosing of psychotropic drugs, not elsewhere classified
    T43.6   Poisoning by, adverse effect of and underdosing of psychostimulants
New   T43.64   Poisoning by ecstasy
New   Poisoning by MDMA
New   Poisoning by 3,4-methylenedioxymeth-amphetamine
New   T43.641   Poisoning by ecstasy, accidental (unintentional)
New   Poisoning by ecstasy NOS
New   T43.642   Poisoning by ecstasy, intentional self-harm
New   T43.643   Poisoning by ecstasy, assault
New   T43.644   Poisoning by ecstasy, undetermined

OTHER AND UNSPECIFIED EFFECTS OF EXTERNAL CAUSES (T66-T78)

T74   Adult and child abuse, neglect and other maltreatment, confirmed
    T74.3   Psychological abuse, confirmed
New   Bullying and intimidation, confirmed
New   Intimidation through social media, confirmed
New   T74.5   Forced sexual exploitation, confirmed
New   T74.51   Adult forced sexual exploitation, confirmed
New   T74.52   Child sexual exploitation, confirmed
New   T74.6   Forced labor exploitation, confirmed
New   T74.61   Adult forced labor exploitation, confirmed
New   T74.62   Child forced labor exploitation, confirmed

T76   Adult and child abuse, neglect and other maltreatment, suspected
    T76.3   Psychological abuse, suspected
New   Bullying and intimidation, suspected
New   Intimidation through social media, suspected
New   T76.5   Forced sexual exploitation, suspected
New   T76.51   Adult forced sexual exploitation, suspected
New   T76.52   Child sexual exploitation, suspected
New   T76.6   Forced labor exploitation, suspected
New   T76.61   Adult forced labor exploitation, suspected
New   T76.62   Child forced labor exploitation, suspected

COMPLICATIONS OF SURGICAL AND MEDICAL CARE NOT ELSEWHERE CLASSIFIED (T80-T88)

T80   Complications following infusion, transfusion and therapeutic injection
    T80.3   ABO incompatibility reaction due to transfusion of blood or blood products
Revised   **Excludes1**   minor blood group antigens reactions (Duffy) (E) (K) (Kell) (Kidd) (Lewis) (M) (N) (P) (S) (T80.A-)

	T81	**Complications of procedures, not elsewhere classified**	
	T81.4	**Infection following a procedure**	
Deleted		Intra-abdominal abscess following a procedure	
Deleted		Postprocedural infection, not elsewhere classified	
Deleted		Sepsis following a procedure	
Deleted		Stitch abscess following a procedure	
Deleted		Subphrenic abscess following a procedure	
Deleted		Wound abscess following a procedure	
Deleted		**Excludes1** obstetric surgical wound infection (O86.0)	
Deleted		postprocedural fever NOS (R50.82)	
Deleted		postprocedural retroperitoneal abscess (K68.11)	
New		**Excludes2** obstetric surgical wound infection (O86.0-)	
New		postprocedural fever NOS (R50.82)	
New		postprocedural retroperitoneal abscess (K68.11)	

New **T81.40 Infection following a procedure, unspecified**

New **T81.41 Infection following a procedure, superficial incisional surgical site**

New Subcutaneous abscess following a procedure

New Stitch abscess following a procedure

New **T81.42 Infection following a procedure, deep incisional surgical site**

New Intra-muscular abscess following a procedure

New **T81.43 Infection following a procedure, organ and space surgical site**

New Intra-abdominal abscess following a procedure

New Subphrenic abscess following a procedure

New **T81.44 Sepsis following a procedure**

New Use additional code to identify the sepsis

New **T81.49 Infection following a procedure, other surgical site**

T85 Complications of other internal prosthetic devices, implants and grafts

T85.1 Mechanical complication of implanted electronic stimulator of nervous system

T85.11 Breakdown (mechanical) of implanted electronic stimulator of nervous system

T85.113 Breakdown (mechanical) of implanted electronic neurostimulator, generator

Revised Breakdown (mechanical) of implanted electronic neurostimulator generator, brain, peripheral, gastric, spinal

CHAPTER 20

EXTERNAL CAUSES OF MORBIDITY (V00-Y99)

This chapter contains the following blocks:

New | X50 | Overexertion and strenuous or repetitive movements |

TRANSPORT ACCIDENTS (V00-V99)

Note:

Revised (e) A pedestrian is any person involved in an accident who was not at the time of the accident riding in or on a motor vehicle, railway train, streetcar or animal-drawn or other vehicle, or on a pedal cycle or animal. This includes, a person changing a tire, working on a parked car, or a person on foot. It also includes the user of a pedestrian conveyance such as a baby stroller, ice-skates, skis, sled, roller skates, a skateboard, nonmotorized or motorized wheelchair, motorized mobility scooter, or nonmotorized scooter.

Revised (w) A special all-terrain vehicle is a motor vehicle of special design to enable it to negotiate over rough or soft terrain, snow or sand. Examples of special design are high construction, special wheels and tires, tracks, and support on a cushion of air. This includes snow mobiles, all-terrain vehicles (ATV), and dune buggies. It does not include passenger vehicle designated as sport utility vehicles (SUV).

PEDESTRIAN INJURED IN TRANSPORT ACCIDENT (V00-V09)

V00 Pedestrian conveyance accident

V00.1 Rolling-type pedestrian conveyance accident

Revised **Excludes1** accident with baby stroller (V00.82-)

V00.14 Scooter (nonmotorized) accident

Revised **Excludes1** motor scooter accident (V20-V29)

V00.2 Gliding-type pedestrian conveyance accident

V00.21 Ice-skates accident

V00.218 Other ice-skates accident

Revised **Excludes1** ice-skater collision with other land transport vehicle (V01-V09 with 5th character 9)

V00.22 Sled accident

V00.228 Other sled accident

Revised **Excludes1** sled collision with other land transport vehicle (V01-V09 with 5th character 9)

V00.28 Other gliding-type pedestrian conveyance accident

V00.288 Other accident on other gliding-type pedestrian conveyance

Revised **Excludes1** gliding-type pedestrian conveyance collision with other land transport vehicle (V01-V09 with 5th character 9)

V00.3   Flat-bottomed pedestrian conveyance accident

   V00.31   Snowboard accident

      V00.318   Other snowboard accident

Revised   **Excludes1**   snowboarder collision with other land transport vehicle (V01-V09 with 5th character 9)

   V00.32   Snow-ski accident

      V00.328   Other snow-ski accident

Revised   **Excludes1**   snow-skier collision with other land transport vehicle (V01-V09 with 5th character 9)

V00.8   Accident on other pedestrian conveyance

Revised   **V00.82   Accident with baby stroller**

Revised   **V00.821   Fall from baby stroller**

Revised   **V00.822   Baby stroller colliding with stationary object**

Revised   **V00.828   Other accident with baby stroller**

   V00.89   Accident on other pedestrian conveyance

      V00.898   Other accident on other pedestrian conveyance

Revised   **Excludes1**   other pedestrian (conveyance) collision with other land transport vehicle (V01-V09 with 5th character 9)

V01   Pedestrian injured in collision with pedal cycle

   V01.0   Pedestrian injured in collision with pedal cycle in nontraffic accident

      V01.09   Pedestrian with other conveyance injured in collision with pedal cycle in nontraffic accident

Revised   Pedestrian with baby stroller injured in collision with pedal cycle in nontraffic accident

   V01.1   Pedestrian injured in collision with pedal cycle in traffic accident

      V01.19   Pedestrian with other conveyance injured in collision with pedal cycle in traffic accident

Revised   Pedestrian with baby stroller injured in collision with pedal cycle in traffic accident

   V01.9   Pedestrian injured in collision with pedal cycle, unspecified whether traffic or nontraffic accident

      V01.99   Pedestrian with other conveyance injured in collision with pedal cycle, unspecified whether traffic or nontraffic accident

Revised   Pedestrian with baby stroller injured in collision with pedal cycle, unspecified whether traffic or nontraffic accident

V02   Pedestrian injured in collision with two- or three-wheeled motor vehicle

   V02.0   Pedestrian injured in collision with two- or three-wheeled motor vehicle in nontraffic accident

      V02.09   Pedestrian with other conveyance injured in collision with two- or three-wheeled motor vehicle in nontraffic accident

Revised   Pedestrian with baby stroller injured in collision with two- or three-wheeled motor vehicle in nontraffic accident

   V02.1   Pedestrian injured in collision with two- or three-wheeled motor vehicle in traffic accident

      V02.19   Pedestrian with other conveyance injured in collision with two- or three-wheeled motor vehicle in traffic accident

Revised   Pedestrian with baby stroller injured in collision with two- or three-wheeled motor vehicle in traffic accident

   V02.9   Pedestrian injured in collision with two- or three-wheeled motor vehicle, unspecified whether traffic or nontraffic accident

      V02.99   Pedestrian with other conveyance injured in collision with two- or three-wheeled motor vehicle, unspecified whether traffic or nontraffic accident

Revised   Pedestrian with baby stroller injured in collision with two- or three-wheeled motor vehicle, unspecified whether traffic or nontraffic accident

V03   Pedestrian injured in collision with car, pick-up truck or van

   V03.0   Pedestrian injured in collision with car, pick-up truck or van in nontraffic accident

      V03.09   Pedestrian with other conveyance injured in collision with car, pick-up truck or van in nontraffic accident

Revised   Pedestrian with baby stroller injured in collision with car, pick-up truck or van in nontraffic accident

   V03.1   Pedestrian injured in collision with car, pick-up truck or van in traffic accident

      V03.19   Pedestrian with other conveyance injured in collision with car, pick-up truck or van in traffic accident

Revised   Pedestrian with baby stroller injured in collision with car, pick-up truck or van in traffic accident

   V03.9   Pedestrian injured in collision with car, pick-up truck or van, unspecified whether traffic or nontraffic accident

      V03.99   Pedestrian with other conveyance injured in collision with car, pick-up truck or van, unspecified whether traffic or nontraffic accident

Revised   Pedestrian with baby stroller injured in collision with car, pick-up truck or van, unspecified whether traffic or nontraffic accident

V04   Pedestrian injured in collision with heavy transport vehicle or bus

   V04.0   Pedestrian injured in collision with heavy transport vehicle or bus in nontraffic accident

      V04.09   Pedestrian with other conveyance injured in collision with heavy transport vehicle or bus in nontraffic accident

Revised   Pedestrian with baby stroller injured in collision with heavy transport vehicle or bus in nontraffic accident

V04.1   Pedestrian injured in collision with heavy transport vehicle or bus in traffic accident

V04.19   Pedestrian with other conveyance injured in collision with heavy transport vehicle or bus in traffic accident

Revised   Pedestrian with baby stroller injured in collision with heavy transport vehicle or bus in traffic accident

V04.9   Pedestrian injured in collision with heavy transport vehicle or bus, unspecified whether traffic or nontraffic accident

V04.99   Pedestrian with other conveyance injured in collision with heavy transport vehicle or bus, unspecified whether traffic or nontraffic accident

Revised   Pedestrian with baby stroller injured in collision with heavy transport vehicle or bus, unspecified whether traffic or nontraffic accident

V05   Pedestrian injured in collision with railway train or railway vehicle

V05.0   Pedestrian injured in collision with railway train or railway vehicle in nontraffic accident

V05.09   Pedestrian with other conveyance injured in collision with railway train or railway vehicle in nontraffic accident

Revised   Pedestrian with baby stroller injured in collision with railway train or railway vehicle in nontraffic accident

V05.1   Pedestrian injured in collision with railway train or railway vehicle in traffic accident

V05.19   Pedestrian with other conveyance injured in collision with railway train or railway vehicle in traffic accident

Revised   Pedestrian with baby stroller injured in collision with railway train or railway vehicle in traffic accident

V05.9   Pedestrian injured in collision with railway train or railway vehicle, unspecified whether traffic or nontraffic accident

V05.99   Pedestrian with other conveyance injured in collision with railway train or railway vehicle, unspecified whether traffic or nontraffic accident

Revised   Pedestrian with baby stroller injured in collision with railway train or railway vehicle, unspecified whether traffic or nontraffic

V06   Pedestrian injured in collision with other nonmotor vehicle

V06.0   Pedestrian injured in collision with other nonmotor vehicle in nontraffic accident

V06.09   Pedestrian with other conveyance injured in collision with other nonmotor vehicle in nontraffic accident

Revised   Pedestrian with baby stroller injured in collision with other nonmotor vehicle in nontraffic accident

V06.1   Pedestrian injured in collision with other nonmotor vehicle in traffic accident

V06.19   Pedestrian with other conveyance injured in collision with other nonmotor vehicle in traffic accident

Revised   Pedestrian with baby stroller injured in collision with other nonmotor vehicle in nontraffic accident

V06.9   Pedestrian injured in collision with other nonmotor vehicle, unspecified whether traffic or nontraffic accident

V06.99   Pedestrian with other conveyance injured in collision with other nonmotor vehicle, unspecified whether traffic or nontraffic accident

Revised   Pedestrian with baby stroller injured in collision with other nonmotor vehicle, unspecified whether traffic or nontraffic accident

EXPOSURE TO FORCES OF NATURE (X30-X39)

X37   Cataclysmic storm

X37.9   Unspecified cataclysmic storm

Revised   **Excludes1**   collapse of dam or man-made structure causing earth movement (X36.0)

X38   Flood

Revised   **Excludes1**   collapse of dam or man-made structure causing earth movement (X36.0)

Revised   tidal wave caused by storm (X37.42)

X39   Exposure to other forces of nature

X39.0   Exposure to natural radiation

Revised   **Excludes1**   contact with and (suspected) exposure to radon and other naturally occurring radiation (Z77.123)

ASSAULT (X92-Y09)

Y07   Perpetrator of assault, maltreatment and neglect

New   Y07.6   Multiple perpetrators of maltreatment and neglect

MEDICAL DEVICES ASSOCIATED WITH ADVERSE INCIDENTS IN DIAGNOSTIC AND THERAPEUTIC USE (Y70-Y82)

Deleted   **Excludes2**   breakdown or malfunctioning of medical device (after implantation) (during procedure) (ongoing use) (Y70-Y82)

SUPPLEMENTARY FACTORS RELATED TO CAUSES OF MORBIDITY CLASSIFIED ELSEWHERE (Y90-Y99)

Y93   Activity codes

Y93.2   Activities involving ice and snow

Revised   Y93.23   Activity, snow (alpine) (downhill) skiing, snowboarding, sledding, tobogganing and snow tubing

CHAPTER 21

FACTORS INFLUENCING HEALTH STATUS AND CONTACT WITH HEALTH SERVICES (Z00-Z99)

This chapter contains the following blocks:

New | Z19 | Hormone sensitivity malignancy status |

PERSONS ENCOUNTERING HEALTH SERVICES FOR EXAMINATIONS (Z00-Z13)

Z00   **Encounter for general examination without complaint, suspected or reported diagnosis**
    Z00.1   **Encounter for newborn, infant and child health examinations**
        Z00.12   **Encounter for routine child health examination**

Deleted   Encounter for development testing of infant or child
New   Immunizations appropriate for age
New   Routine developmental screening of infant or child
New   Routine vision and hearing testing

Z02   **Encounter for administrative examination**
    Z02.7   **Encounter for issue of medical certificate**
Revised   **Excludes1**   encounter for general medical examination (Z00-Z01, Z02.0-Z02.6, Z02.8-Z02.9)

Z03   **Encounter for medical observation for suspected diseases and conditions ruled out**
Revised   **Excludes1**   encounter for observation and evaluation of newborn for suspected diseases and conditions ruled out (Z05.-)

Z04   **Encounter for examination and observation for other reasons**
    Z04.8   **Encounter for examination and observation for other specified reasons**
New   Z04.81   **Encounter for examination and observation of victim following forced sexual exploitation**
New   Z04.82   **Encounter for examination and observation of victim following forced labor exploitation**
New   Z04.89   **Encounter for examination and observation for other specified reasons**

Z13   **Encounter for screening for other diseases and disorders**
New   Z13.3   **Encounter for screening examination for mental health and behavioral disorders**
New   Z13.30   **Encounter for screening examination for mental health and behavioral disorders, unspecified**
New   Z13.31   **Encounter for screening for depression**
New   Encounter for screening for depression, adult
New   Encounter for screening for depression for child or adolescent
New   Z13.32   **Encounter for screening for maternal depression**
New   Encounter for screening for perinatal depression
New   Z13.39   **Encounter for screening examination for other mental health and behavioral disorders**
New   Encounter for screening for alcoholism
New   Encounter for screening for intellectual disabilities
    Z13.4   **Encounter for screening for certain developmental disorders in childhood**
New   Encounter for development testing of infant or child
Deleted   **Excludes1**   routine development testing of infant or child (Z00.1-)
New   **Excludes2**   encounter for routine child health examination (Z00.12-)
New   Z13.40   **Encounter for screening for unspecified developmental delays**
New   Z13.41   **Encounter for autism screening**

New   Z13.42   **Encounter for screening for global developmental delays (milestones)**
New   Encounter for screening for developmental handicaps in early childhood
New   Z13.49   **Encounter for screening for other developmental delays**

RETAINED FOREIGN BODY FRAGMENTS (Z18)

Z18   **Retained foreign body fragments**
    Z18.2   **Retained plastic fragments**
Revised   Diethylhexylphthalates fragments

PERSONS WITH POTENTIAL HEALTH HAZARDS RELATED TO COMMUNICABLE DISEASES (Z20-Z29)

Z20   **Contact with and (suspected) exposure to communicable diseases**
    Z20.8   **Contact with and (suspected) exposure to other communicable diseases**
        Z20.82   **Contact with and (suspected) exposure to other viral communicable diseases**
New   Z20.821   **Contact with and (suspected) exposure to Zika virus**

Z28   **Immunization not carried out and underimmunization status**
    Z28.8   **Immunization not carried out for other reason**
New   Z28.83   **Immunization not carried out due to unavailability of vaccine**
New   Delay in delivery of vaccine
New   Lack of availability of vaccine
New   Manufacturer delay of vaccine

ENCOUNTERS FOR OTHER SPECIFIC HEALTH CARE (Z40-Z53)

Z40   **Encounter for prophylactic surgery**
    Z40.0   **Encounter for prophylactic surgery for risk factors related to malignant neoplasms**
Revised   Z40.03   **Encounter for prophylactic removal of fallopian tube(s)**

PERSONS WITH POTENTIAL HEALTH HAZARDS RELATED TO SOCIOECONOMIC AND PSYCHOSOCIAL CIRCUMSTANCES (Z55-Z65)

Z62   **Problems related to upbringing**
    Z62.8   **Other specified problems related to upbringing**
        Z62.81   **Personal history of abuse in childhood**
New   Z62.813   **Personal history of forced labor or sexual exploitation in childhood**

BODY MASS INDEX [BMI] (Z68)

Z68   **Body mass index [BMI]**
    Z68.4   **Body mass index (BMI) 40 or greater, adult**
Revised   Z68.43   **Body mass index (BMI) 50-59.9, adult**

PERSONS ENCOUNTERING HEALTH SERVICES IN OTHER CIRCUMSTANCES (Z69-Z76)

Z76   **Persons encountering health services in other circumstances**
    Z76.5   **Malingerer [conscious simulation]**
Revised   **Excludes1**   factitious disorder (F68.1-, F68.A)

PERSONS WITH POTENTIAL HEALTH HAZARDS RELATED TO FAMILY AND PERSONAL HISTORY AND CERTAIN CONDITIONS INFLUENCING HEALTH STATUS (Z77-Z99)

Z77   Other contact with and (suspected) exposures hazardous to health

    Z77.1   Contact with and (suspected) exposure to environmental pollution and hazards in the physical environment

        Z77.12   Contact with and (suspected) exposure to hazards in the physical environment

Revised   Z77.123   Contact with and (suspected) exposure to radon and other naturally occurring radiation

Revised   Z77.2   Contact with and (suspected) exposure to other hazardous substances

Revised   Z77.29   Contact with and (suspected) exposure to other hazardous substances

Z83   Family history of other specific disorders

    Z83.4   Family history of other endocrine, nutritional and metabolic diseases
        Conditions classifiable to E00-E07, E15-E88

New   Z83.43   Family history of other disorder of lipoprotein metabolism and other lipidemias

New   Z83.430   Family history of elevated lipoprotein(a)

New   Family history of elevated Lp(a)

New   Z83.438   Family history of other disorder of lipoprotein metabolism and other lipidemia

New   Family history of familial combined hyperlipidemia

Z91   Personal risk factors, not elsewhere classified

    Z91.4   Personal history of psychological trauma, not elsewhere classified

New   Z91.42   Personal history of forced labor or sexual exploitation

Z95   Presence of cardiac and vascular implants and grafts

    Z95.8   Presence of other cardiac and vascular implants and grafts

        Z95.81   Presence of other cardiac implants and grafts

            Z95.810   Presence of automatic (implantable) cardiac defibrillator

Revised   Presence of automatic (implantable) cardiac defribillator with synchronous cardiac pacemaker

Z99   Dependence on enabling machines and devices, not elsewhere classified

    Z99.3   Dependence on wheelchair
        Wheelchair confinement status

Revised   *Code first cause of dependence, such as:*
        muscular dystrophy (G71.0-)

Introduction

ICD-10-CM Official Guidelines for Coding and Reporting 2019
Narrative changes appear in **bold** text
Items <u>underlined</u> have been moved within the guidelines since the 2018 version
Italics are used to indicate revisions to heading changes

The Centers for Medicare and Medicaid Services (CMS) and the National Center for Health Statistics (NCHS), two departments within the U.S. Federal Government's Department of Health and Human Services (DHHS), provide the following guidelines for coding and reporting using the International Classification of Diseases, 10th Revision, Clinical Modification (ICD-10-CM). These guidelines should be used as a companion document to the official version of the ICD-10-CM as published on the NCHS website. The ICD-10-CM is a morbidity classification published by the United States for classifying diagnoses and reason for visits in all health care settings. The ICD-10-CM is based on the ICD-10, the statistical classification of disease published by the World Health Organization (WHO).

These guidelines have been approved by the four organizations that make up the Cooperating Parties for the ICD-10-CM: the American Hospital Association (AHA), the American Health Information Management Association (AHIMA), CMS, and NCHS.

These guidelines are a set of rules that have been developed to accompany and complement the official conventions and instructions provided within the ICD-10-CM itself. The instructions and conventions of the classification take precedence over guidelines. These guidelines are based on the coding and sequencing instructions in the Tabular List and Alphabetic Index of ICD-10-CM, but provide additional instruction. Adherence to these guidelines when assigning ICD-10-CM diagnosis codes is required under the Health Insurance Portability and Accountability Act (HIPAA). The diagnosis codes (Tabular List and Alphabetic Index)

have been adopted under HIPAA for all health care settings. A joint effort between the health care provider and the coder is essential to achieve complete and accurate documentation, code assignment, and reporting of diagnoses and procedures. These guidelines have been developed to assist both the health care provider and the coder in identifying those diagnoses that are to be reported. The importance of consistent, complete documentation in the medical record cannot be overemphasized. Without such documentation accurate coding cannot be achieved. The entire record should be reviewed to determine the specific reason for the encounter and the conditions treated.

The term "encounter" is used for all settings, including hospital admissions. In the context of these guidelines, the term "provider" is used throughout the guidelines to mean physician or any qualified health care practitioner who is legally accountable for establishing the patient's diagnosis. Only this set of guidelines, approved by the Cooperating Parties, is official.

The guidelines are organized into sections. Section I includes the structure and conventions of the classification and general guidelines that apply to the entire classification, and chapter-specific guidelines that correspond to the chapters as they are arranged in the classification. Section II includes guidelines for selection of principal diagnosis for non-outpatient settings. Section III includes guidelines for reporting additional diagnoses in non-outpatient settings. Section IV is for outpatient coding and reporting. It is necessary to review all sections of the guidelines to fully understand all of the rules and instructions needed to code properly.

ICD-10-CM Official Guidelines for Coding and Reporting

9. Chapter 9: Diseases of the Circulatory System (I00-I99)
   a. Hypertension
   b. Atherosclerotic Coronary Artery Disease and Angina
   c. Intraoperative and Postprocedural Cerebrovascular Accident
   d. Sequelae of Cerebrovascular Disease
   e. Acute myocardial infarction (AMI)
10. Chapter 10: Diseases of the Respiratory System (J00-J99)
    a. Chronic Obstructive Pulmonary Disease [COPD] and Asthma
    b. Acute Respiratory Failure
    c. Influenza due to certain identified influenza viruses
    d. Ventilator associated Pneumonia
11. Chapter 11: Diseases of the Digestive System (K00-K95)
12. Chapter 12: Diseases of the Skin and Subcutaneous Tissue (L00-L99)
    a. Pressure ulcer stage codes
    b. Non-Pressure Chronic Ulcers
13. Chapter 13: Diseases of the Musculoskeletal System and Connective Tissue (M00-M99)
    a. Site and laterality
    b. Acute traumatic versus chronic or recurrent musculoskeletal conditions
    c. Coding of Pathologic Fractures
    d. Osteoporosis
14. Chapter 14: Diseases of Genitourinary System (N00-N99)
    a. Chronic kidney disease
15. Chapter 15: Pregnancy, Childbirth, and the Puerperium (O00-O9A)
    a. General Rules for Obstetric Cases
    b. Selection of OB Principal or First-listed Diagnosis
    c. Pre-existing conditions versus conditions due to the pregnancy
    d. Pre-existing hypertension in pregnancy
    e. Fetal Conditions Affecting the Management of the Mother
    f. HIV Infection in Pregnancy, Childbirth and the Puerperium
    g. Diabetes mellitus in pregnancy
    h. Long term use of insulin and oral hypoglycemics
    i. Gestational (pregnancy induced) diabetes
    j. Sepsis and septic shock complicating abortion, pregnancy, childbirth and the puerperium
    k. Puerperal sepsis
    l. Alcohol, tobacco *and drug* use during pregnancy, childbirth and the puerperium
    m. Poisoning, toxic effects, adverse effects and underdosing in a pregnant patient
    n. Normal Delivery, Code O80
    o. The Peripartum and Postpartum Periods
    p. Code O94, Sequelae of complication of pregnancy, childbirth, and the puerperium
    q. Termination of Pregnancy and Spontaneous abortions
    r. Abuse in a pregnant patient

16. Chapter 16: Certain Conditions Originating in the Perinatal Period (P00-P96)
    a. General Perinatal Rules
    b. Observation and Evaluation of Newborns for Suspected Conditions not Found
    c. Coding Additional Perinatal Diagnoses
    d. Prematurity and Fetal Growth Retardation
    e. Low birth weight and immaturity status
    f. Bacterial Sepsis of Newborn
    g. Stillbirth
17. Chapter 17: Congenital Malformations, Deformations, and Chromosomal Abnormalities (Q00-Q99)
18. Chapter 18: Symptoms, Signs, and Abnormal Clinical and Laboratory Findings, Not Elsewhere Classified (R00-R99)
    a. Use of symptom codes
    b. Use of a symptom code with a definitive diagnosis code
    c. Combination codes that include symptoms
    d. Repeated falls
    e. Coma scale
    f. Functional quadriplegia
    g. SIRS due to Non-Infectious Process
    h. Death NOS
    i. NIHSS Stroke Scale
19. Chapter 19: Injury, Poisoning, and Certain Other Consequences of External Causes (S00-T88)
    a. Application of 7th Characters in Chapter 19
    b. Coding of Injuries
    c. Coding of Traumatic Fractures
    d. Coding of Burns and Corrosions
    e. Adverse Effects, Poisoning, Underdosing and Toxic Effects
    f. Adult and child abuse, neglect and other maltreatment
    g. Complications of care
20. Chapter 20: External Causes of Morbidity (V00-Y99)
    a. General External Cause Coding Guidelines
    b. Place of Occurrence Guideline
    c. Activity Code
    d. Place of Occurrence, Activity, and Status Codes Used with other External Cause Code
    e. If the Reporting Format Limits the Number of External Cause Codes
    f. Multiple External Cause Coding Guidelines
    g. Child and Adult Abuse Guideline
    h. Unknown or Undetermined Intent Guideline
    i. Sequelae (Late Effects) of External Cause Guidelines
    j. Terrorism Guidelines
    k. External cause status
21. Chapter 21: Factors Influencing Health Status and Contact with Health Services (Z00-Z99)
    a. Use of Z codes in any healthcare setting
    b. Z Codes indicate a reason for an encounter
    c. Categories of Z Codes

Section II. Selection of Principal Diagnosis

A. Codes for symptoms, signs, and ill-defined conditions
B. Two or more interrelated conditions, each potentially meeting the definition for principal diagnosis
C. Two or more diagnoses that equally meet the definition for principal diagnosis
D. Two or more comparative or contrasting conditions
E. A symptom(s) followed by contrasting/comparative diagnoses
F. Original treatment plan not carried out
G. Complications of surgery and other medical care
H. Uncertain Diagnosis
I. Admission from Observation Unit
   1. Admission Following Medical Observation
   2. Admission Following Post-Operative Observation
J. Admission from Outpatient Surgery
K. Admissions/Encounters for Rehabilitation

Section III. Reporting Additional Diagnoses

A. Previous conditions
B. Abnormal findings
C. Uncertain Diagnosis

Section IV. Diagnostic Coding and Reporting Guidelines for Outpatient Services

A. Selection of first-listed condition
   1. Outpatient Surgery
   2. Observation Stay
B. Codes from A00.0 through T88.9, Z00-Z99
C. Accurate reporting of ICD-10-CM diagnosis codes
D. Codes that describe symptoms and signs
E. Encounters for circumstances other than a disease or injury
F. Level of Detail in Coding
   1. ICD-10-CM codes with 3, 4, 5, 6, or 7 characters
   2. Use of full number of characters required for a code
G. ICD-10-CM code for the diagnosis, condition, problem, or other reason for encounter/visit
H. Uncertain diagnosis
I. Chronic diseases
J. Code all documented conditions that coexist
K. Patients receiving diagnostic services only
L. Patients receiving therapeutic services only
M. Patients receiving preoperative evaluations only
N. Ambulatory surgery
O. Routine outpatient prenatal visits
P. Encounters for general medical examinations with abnormal findings
Q. Encounters for routine health screenings

Appendix I: Present on Admission Reporting Guidelines

Section I. Conventions, General Coding Guidelines, and Chapter Specific Guidelines

The conventions, general guidelines, and chapter-specific guidelines are applicable to all health care settings unless otherwise indicated. The conventions and instructions of the classification take precedence over guidelines.

A. Conventions for the ICD-10-CM

The conventions for the ICD-10-CM are the general rules for use of the classification independent of the guidelines. These conventions are incorporated within the Alphabetic Index and Tabular List of the ICD-10-CM as instructional notes.

1. **The Alphabetic Index and Tabular List**
The ICD-10-CM is divided into the Alphabetic Index, an alphabetical list of terms and their corresponding code, and the Tabular List, a structured list of codes divided into chapters based on body system or condition. The Alphabetic Index consists of the following parts: the Index of Diseases and Injury, the Index of External Causes of Injury, the Table of Neoplasms, and the Table of Drugs and Chemicals.
See Section I.C2. General guidelines
See Section I.C.19. Adverse effects, poisoning, underdosing and toxic effects

2. **Format and Structure:**
The ICD-10-CM Tabular List contains categories, subcategories and codes. Characters for categories, subcategories and codes may be either a letter or a number. All categories are 3 characters. A 3-character category that has no further subdivision is equivalent to a code. Subcategories are either 4 or 5 characters. Codes may be 3, 4, 5, 6 or 7 characters. That is, each level of subdivision after a category is a subcategory. The final level of subdivision is a code. Codes that have applicable 7th characters are still referred to as codes, not subcategories. A code that has an applicable 7th character is considered invalid without the 7th character.
The ICD-10-CM uses an indented format for ease in reference

3. **Use of codes for reporting purposes**
For reporting purposes only codes are permissible, not categories or subcategories, and any applicable 7th character is required.

4. **Placeholder character**
The ICD-10-CM utilizes a placeholder character "X". The "X" is used as a placeholder at certain codes to allow for future expansion. An example of this is at the poisoning, adverse effect and underdosing codes, categories T36-T50. Where a placeholder exists, the X must be used in order for the code to be considered a valid code.

5. **7th Characters**
Certain ICD-10-CM categories have applicable 7th characters. The applicable 7th character is required for all codes within the category, or as the notes in the Tabular List instruct. The 7th character must always be the 7th character in the data field. If a code that requires a 7th character is not 6 characters, a placeholder X must be used to fill in the empty characters.

6. **Abbreviations**
  a. **Alphabetic Index abbreviations**
    NEC "Not elsewhere classifiable"
      This abbreviation in the Alphabetic Index represents "other specified". When a

specific code is not available for a condition the Alphabetic Index directs the coder to the "other specified" code in the Tabular List.

NOS "Not otherwise specified"
This abbreviation is the equivalent of unspecified.

b. Tabular List abbreviations

NEC "Not elsewhere classifiable"
This abbreviation in the Tabular List represents "other specified". When a specific code is not available for a condition, the Tabular List includes an NEC entry under a code to identify the code as the "other specified" code.

NOS "Not otherwise specified"
This abbreviation is the equivalent of unspecified.

7. Punctuation

[ ] Brackets are used in the Tabular List to enclose synonyms, alternative wording or explanatory phrases. Brackets are used in the Alphabetic Index to identify manifestation codes.

( ) Parentheses are used in both the Alphabetic Index and Tabular List to enclose supplementary words that may be present or absent in the statement of a disease or procedure without affecting the code number to which it is assigned. The terms within the parentheses are referred to as nonessential modifiers. The nonessential modifiers in the Alphabetic Index to Diseases apply to subterms following a main term except when a nonessential modifier and a subentry are mutually exclusive, the subentry takes precedence. For example, in the ICD-10-CM Alphabetic Index under the main term Enteritis, "acute" is a nonessential modifier and "chronic" is a subentry. In this case, the nonessential modifier "acute" does not apply to the subentry "chronic".

: Colons are used in the Tabular List after an incomplete term which needs one or more of the modifiers following the colon to make it assignable to a given category.

8. Use of "and".

See Section I.A.14. Use of the term "And"

9. Other and Unspecified codes

a. "Other" codes

Codes titled "other" or "other specified" are for use when the information in the medical record provides detail for which a specific code does not exist. Alphabetic Index entries with NEC in the line designate "other" codes in the Tabular List. These Alphabetic Index entries represent specific disease entities for which no specific code exists so the term is included within an "other" code.

b. "Unspecified" codes

Codes titled "unspecified" are for use when the information in the medical record is insufficient to assign a more specific code. For those categories for which an unspecified code is not provided, the "other specified" code may represent both other and unspecified.

See Section I.B.18 Use of signs/symptoms/unspecified codes

10. Includes Notes

This note appears immediately under a three-character code title to further define, or give examples of, the content of the category.

11. Inclusion terms

List of terms is included under some codes. These terms are the conditions for which that code is to be used. The terms may be synonyms of the code title, or, in the case of "other specified" codes, the terms are a list of the various conditions assigned to that code. The inclusion terms are not necessarily exhaustive. Additional terms found only in the Alphabetic Index may also be assigned to a code.

12. Excludes Notes

The ICD-10-CM has two types of excludes notes. Each type of note has a different definition for use but they are all similar in that they indicate that codes excluded from each other are independent of each other.

a. Excludes1

A type 1 Excludes note is a pure excludes note. It means "NOT CODED HERE!" An Excludes1 note indicates that the code excluded should never be used at the same time as the code above the Excludes1 note. An Excludes1 is used when two conditions cannot occur together, such as a congenital form versus an acquired form of the same condition.

An exception to the Excludes1 definition is the circumstance when the two conditions are unrelated to each other. If it is not clear whether the two conditions involving an Excludes1 note are related or not, query the provider. For example, code F45.8, Other somatoform disorders, has an Excludes1 note for "sleep related teeth grinding (G47.63)" because "teeth grinding" is an inclusion term under F45.8. Only one of these two codes should be assigned for teeth grinding. However, psychogenic dysmenorrhea is also an inclusion term under F45.8, and a patient could have both this condition and sleep-related teeth grinding. In this case, the two conditions are clearly unrelated to each other, and so it would be appropriate to report F45.8 and G47.63 together.

b. Excludes2

A Type 2 Excludes note represents "Not included here." An excludes2 note indicates that the condition excluded is not part of the condition represented by the code, but a patient may have both conditions at the same time. When an Excludes2 note appears under a code, it is acceptable to use both the code and the excluded code together, when appropriate.

13. **Etiology/manifestation convention ("code first", "use additional code" and "in diseases classified elsewhere" notes)**

    Certain conditions have both an underlying etiology and multiple body system manifestations due to the underlying etiology. For such conditions, the ICD-10-CM has a coding convention that requires the underlying condition be sequenced first, if applicable, followed by the manifestation. Wherever such a combination exists, there is a "use additional code" note at the etiology code, and a "code first" note at the manifestation code. These instructional notes indicate the proper sequencing order of the codes, etiology followed by manifestation.

    In most cases the manifestation codes will have in the code title, "in diseases classified elsewhere." Codes with this title are a component of the etiology/ manifestation convention. The code title indicates that it is a manifestation code. "In diseases classified elsewhere" codes are never permitted to be used as first-listed or principal diagnosis codes. They must be used in conjunction with an underlying condition code and they must be listed following the underlying condition. See category F02, Dementia in other diseases classified elsewhere, for an example of this convention.

    There are manifestation codes that do not have "in diseases classified elsewhere" in the title. For such codes, there is a "use additional code" note at the etiology code and a "code first" note at the manifestation code and the rules for sequencing apply.

    In addition to the notes in the Tabular List, these conditions also have a specific Alphabetic Index entry structure. In the Alphabetic Index both conditions are listed together with the etiology code first followed by the manifestation codes in brackets. The code in brackets is always to be sequenced second.

    An example of the etiology/manifestation convention is dementia in Parkinson's disease. In the Alphabetic Index, code G20 is listed first, followed by code F02.80 or F02.81 in brackets. Code G20 represents the underlying etiology, Parkinson's disease, and must be sequenced first, whereas code F02.80 and F02.81 represent the manifestation of dementia in diseases classified elsewhere, with or without behavioral disturbance.

    "Code first" and "Use additional code" notes are also used as sequencing rules in the classification for certain codes that are not part of an etiology/manifestation combination.

    See Section I.B.7. Multiple coding for a single condition.

14. **"And"**

    The word "and" should be interpreted to mean either "and" or "or" when it appears in a title.

    For example, cases of "tuberculosis of bones", "tuberculosis of joints" and "tuberculosis of bones and joints" are classified to subcategory A18.0, Tuberculosis of bones and joints.

15. **"With"**

    The word "with" or "in" should be interpreted to mean "associated with" or "due to" when it appears in a code title, the Alphabetic Index, **(either under a main term or subterm)** or an instructional note in the Tabular List. The classification presumes a causal relationship between the two conditions linked by these terms in the Alphabetic Index or Tabular List. These conditions should be coded as related even in the absence of provider documentation explicitly linking them, unless the documentation clearly states the conditions are unrelated or when another guideline exists that specifically requires a documented linkage between two conditions (e.g., sepsis guideline for "acute organ dysfunction that is not clearly associated with the sepsis").

    For conditions not specifically linked by these relational terms in the classification or when a guideline requires that a linkage between two conditions be explicitly documented provider documentation must link the conditions in order to code them as related.

    The word "with" in the Alphabetic Index is sequenced immediately following the main term, not in alphabetical order.

16. **"See" and "See Also"**

    The "see" instruction following a main term in the Alphabetic Index indicates that another term should be referenced. It is necessary to go to the main term referenced with the "see" note to locate the correct code.

    A "see also" instruction following a main term in the Alphabetic Index instructs that there is another main term that may also be referenced that may provide additional Alphabetic Index entries that may be useful. It is not necessary to follow the "see also" note when the original main term provides the necessary code.

17. **"Code also" note**

    A "code also" note instructs that two codes may be required to fully describe a condition, but this note does not provide sequencing direction. The sequencing depends on the circumstances of the encounter.

18. **Default codes**

    A code listed next to a main term in the ICD-10-CM Alphabetic Index is referred to as a default code. The default code represents that condition that is most commonly associated with the main term, or is the unspecified code for the condition. If a condition is documented in a medical record (for example, appendicitis) without any additional information, such as acute or chronic, the default code should be assigned.

19. **Code assignment and Clinical Criteria**

    The assignment of a diagnosis code is based on the provider's diagnostic statement that the condition exists. The provider's statement that the patient has a particular condition is sufficient. Code assignment is not based on clinical criteria used by the provider to establish the diagnosis.

B. **General Coding Guidelines**

1. **Locating a code in the ICD-10-CM**

To select a code in the classification that corresponds to a diagnosis or reason for visit documented in a medical record, first locate the term in the Alphabetic Index, and then verify the code in the Tabular List. Read and be guided by instructional notations that appear in both the Alphabetic Index and the Tabular List.

It is essential to use both the Alphabetic Index and Tabular List when locating and assigning a code. The Alphabetic Index does not always provide the full code. Selection of the full code, including laterality and any applicable 7th character can only be done in the Tabular List. A dash (-) at the end of an Alphabetic Index entry indicates that additional characters are required. Even if a dash is not included at the Alphabetic Index entry, it is necessary to refer to the Tabular List to verify that no 7th character is required.

2. **Level of Detail in Coding**

Diagnosis codes are to be used and reported at their highest number of characters available.

ICD-10-CM diagnosis codes are composed of codes with 3, 4, 5, 6, or 7 characters. Codes with three characters are included in ICD-10-CM as the heading of a category of codes that may be further subdivided by the use of fourth and/or fifth characters and/or sixth characters, which provide greater detail.

A three-character code is to be used only if it is not further subdivided. A code is invalid if it has not been coded to the full number of characters required for that code, including the 7th character, if applicable.

3. **Code or codes from A00.0 through T88.9, Z00-Z99.8**

The appropriate code or codes from A00.0 through T88.9, Z00-Z99.8 must be used to identify diagnoses, symptoms, conditions, problems, complaints or other reason(s) for the encounter/visit.

4. **Signs and symptoms**

Codes that describe symptoms and signs, as opposed to diagnoses, are acceptable for reporting purposes when a related definitive diagnosis has not been established (confirmed) by the provider. Chapter 18 of ICD-10-CM, Symptoms, Signs, and Abnormal Clinical and Laboratory Findings, Not Elsewhere Classified (codes R00.0 - R99) contains many, but not all codes for symptoms.

See Section I.B.18 Use of signs/symptoms/ unspecified codes

5. **Conditions that are an integral part of a disease process**

Signs and symptoms that are associated routinely with a disease process should not be assigned as additional codes, unless otherwise instructed by the classification.

6. **Conditions that are not an integral part of a disease process**

Additional signs and symptoms that may not be associated routinely with a disease process should be coded when present.

7. **Multiple coding for a single condition**

In addition to the etiology/manifestation convention that requires two codes to fully describe a single condition that affects multiple body systems, there are other single conditions that also require more than one code. "Use additional code" notes are found in the Tabular List at codes that are not part of an etiology/manifestation pair where a secondary code is useful to fully describe a condition. The sequencing rule is the same as the etiology/manifestation pair, "use additional code" indicates that a secondary code should be added, if known.

For example, for bacterial infections that are not included in Chapter 1, a secondary code from category B95, Streptococcus, Staphylococcus, and Enterococcus, as the cause of diseases classified elsewhere, or B96, Other bacterial agents as the cause of diseases classified elsewhere, may be required to identify the bacterial organism causing the infection. A "use additional code" note will normally be found at the infectious disease code, indicating a need for the organism code to be added as a secondary code.

"Code first" notes are also under certain codes that are not specifically manifestation codes but may be due to an underlying cause. When there is a "code first" note and an underlying condition is present, the underlying condition should be sequenced first, if known.

"Code, if applicable, any causal condition first," notes indicate that this code may be assigned as a principal diagnosis when the causal condition is unknown or not applicable. If a causal condition is known, then the code for that condition should be sequenced as the principal or first-listed diagnosis.

Multiple codes may be needed for sequela, complication codes and obstetric codes to more fully describe a condition. See the specific guidelines for these conditions for further instruction.

8. **Acute and Chronic Conditions**

If the same condition is described as both acute (subacute) and chronic, and separate subentries exist in the Alphabetic Index at the same indentation level, code both and sequence the acute (subacute) code first.

9. **Combination Code**

A combination code is a single code used to classify:

Two diagnoses, or

A diagnosis with an associated secondary process (manifestation)

A diagnosis with an associated complication

Combination codes are identified by referring to subterm entries in the Alphabetic Index and by reading the inclusion and exclusion notes in the Tabular List.

Assign only the combination code when that code fully identifies the diagnostic conditions involved or when the Alphabetic Index so directs. Multiple coding should not be used when the classification provides a combination code that clearly identifies all of the elements documented in the diagnosis. When the combination code lacks necessary specificity in describing the manifestation or complication, an additional code should be used as a secondary code.

10. Sequela (Late Effects)
A sequela is the residual effect (condition produced) after the acute phase of an illness or injury has terminated. There is no time limit on when a sequela code can be used. The residual may be apparent early, such as in cerebral infarction, or it may occur months or years later, such as that due to a previous injury. Examples of sequela include: scar formation resulting from a burn, deviated septum due to a nasal fracture, and infertility due to tubal occlusion from old tuberculosis. Coding of sequela generally requires two codes sequenced in the following order: the condition or nature of the sequela is sequenced first. The sequela code is sequenced second.

An exception to the above guidelines are those instances where the code for the sequela is followed by a manifestation code identified in the Tabular List and title, or the sequela code has been expanded (at the fourth, fifth, or sixth character levels) to include the manifestation(s). The code for the acute phase of an illness or injury that led to the sequela is never used with a code for the late effect.
See Section I.C.9. Sequelae of cerebrovascular disease
See Section I.C.15. Sequelae of complication of pregnancy, childbirth and the puerperium
See Section I.C.19. Application of 7th characters for Chapter 19

11. Impending or Threatened Condition
Code any condition described at the time of discharge as "impending" or "threatened" as follows:
If it did occur, code as confirmed diagnosis.
If it did not occur, reference the Alphabetic Index to determine if the condition has a subentry term for "impending" or "threatened" and also reference main term entries for "Impending" and for "Threatened."
If the subterms are listed, assign the given code.
If the subterms are not listed, code the existing underlying condition(s) and not the condition described as impending or threatened.

12. Reporting Same Diagnosis Code More Than Once
Each unique ICD-10-CM diagnosis code may be reported only once for an encounter. This applies to bilateral conditions when there are no distinct codes identifying laterality or two different conditions classified to the same ICD-10-CM diagnosis code.

13. Laterality
Some ICD-10-CM codes indicate laterality, specifying whether the condition occurs on the left, right or is bilateral. If no bilateral code is provided and the condition is bilateral, assign separate codes for both the left and right side. If the side is not identified in the medical record, assign the code for the unspecified side.

When a patient has a bilateral condition and each side is treated during separate encounters, assign the "bilateral" code (as the condition still exists on both sides), including for the encounter to treat the first side. For the second encounter for treatment after one side has previously been treated and the condition no longer exists on that side, assign the appropriate unilateral code for the side where the condition still exists (e.g., cataract surgery performed on each eye in separate encounters). The bilateral code would not be assigned for the subsequent encounter, as the patient no longer has the condition in the previously-treated site. If the treatment on the first side did not completely resolve the condition, then the bilateral code would still be appropriate.

14. Documentation *by Clinicians Other than the Patient's Provider*
Code assignment is based on the documentation by patient's provider (i.e., physician or other qualified healthcare practitioner legally accountable for establishing the patient's diagnosis). There are a few exceptions, such as codes for the Body Mass Index (BMI), depth of non-pressure chronic ulcers, pressure ulcer stage, coma scale, and NIH stroke scale (NIHSS) codes, code assignment may be based on medical record documentation from clinicians who are not the patient's provider (i.e., physician or other qualified healthcare practitioner legally accountable for establishing the patient's diagnosis), since this information is typically documented by other clinicians involved in the care of the patient (e.g., a dietitian often documents the BMI, a nurse often documents the pressure ulcer stages, and an emergency medical technician often documents the coma scale). However, the associated diagnosis (such as overweight, obesity, acute stroke, or pressure ulcer) must be documented by the patient's provider. If there is conflicting medical record documentation, either from the same clinician or different clinicians, the patient's attending provider should be queried for clarification.

For social determinants of health, such as information found in categories Z55-Z65, Persons with potential health hazards related to socioeconomic and psychosocial circumstances, code assignment may be based on medical record documentation from clinicians involved in the care of the patient who are not the patient's provider since this information represents social information, rather than medical diagnoses.

The BMI, coma scale, and NIHSS codes and categories Z55-Z65 should only be reported as secondary diagnoses.

15. **Syndromes**

    Follow the Alphabetic Index guidance when coding syndromes. In the absence of Alphabetic Index guidance, assign codes for the documented manifestations of the syndrome. Additional codes for manifestations that are not an integral part of the disease process may also be assigned when the condition does not have a unique code.

16. **Documentation of Complications of Care**

    Code assignment is based on the provider's documentation of the relationship between the condition and the care or procedure, unless otherwise instructed by the classification. The guideline extends to any complications of care, regardless of the chapter the code is located in. It is important to note that not all conditions that occur during or following medical care or surgery are classified as complications. There must be a cause-and-effect relationship between the care provided and the condition, and an indication in the documentation that it is a complication. Query the provider for clarification, if the complication is not clearly documented.

17. **Borderline Diagnosis**

    If the provider documents a "borderline" diagnosis at the time of discharge, the diagnosis is coded as confirmed, unless the classification provides a specific entry (e.g., borderline diabetes). If a borderline condition has a specific index entry in ICD-10-CM, it should be coded as such. Since borderline conditions are not uncertain diagnoses, no distinction is made between the care setting (inpatient versus outpatient). Whenever the documentation is unclear regarding a borderline condition, coders are encouraged to query for clarification.

18. **Use of Sign/Symptom/Unspecified Codes**

    Sign/symptom and "unspecified" codes have acceptable, even necessary, uses. While specific diagnosis codes should be reported when they are supported by the available medical record documentation and clinical knowledge of the patient's health condition, there are instances when signs/symptoms or unspecified codes are the best choices for accurately reflecting the healthcare encounter. Each healthcare encounter should be coded to the level of certainty known for that encounter.

    If a definitive diagnosis has not been established by the end of the encounter, it is appropriate to report codes for sign(s) and/or symptom(s) in lieu of a definitive diagnosis. When sufficient clinical information isn't known or available about a particular health condition to assign a more specific code, it is acceptable to report the appropriate "unspecified" code (e.g., a diagnosis of pneumonia has been determined, but not the specific type). Unspecified codes should be reported when they are the codes that most accurately reflect what is known about the patient's condition at the time of that particular

encounter. It would be inappropriate to select a specific code that is not supported by the medical record documentation or conduct medically unnecessary diagnostic testing in order to determine a more specific code.

19. *Coding for Healthcare Encounters in Hurricane Aftermath*

    a. Use of External Cause of Morbidity Codes

    An external cause of morbidity code should be assigned to identify the cause of the injury(ies) incurred as a result of the hurricane. The use of external cause of morbidity codes is supplemental to the application of ICD-10-CM codes. External cause of morbidity codes are never to be recorded as a principal diagnosis (first-listed in non-inpatient settings). The appropriate injury code should be sequenced before any external cause codes. The external cause of morbidity codes capture how the injury or health condition happened (cause), the intent (unintentional or accidental; or intentional, such as suicide or assault), the place where the event occurred, the activity of the patient at the time of the event, and the person's status (e.g., civilian, military). They should not be assigned for encounters to treat hurricane victims' medical conditions when no injury, adverse effect or poisoning is involved. External cause of morbidity codes should be assigned for each encounter for care and treatment of the injury. External cause of morbidity codes may be assigned in all health care settings. For the purpose of capturing complete and accurate ICD-10-CM data in the aftermath of the hurricane, a healthcare setting should be considered as any location where medical care is provided by licensed healthcare professionals.

    b. Sequencing of External Causes of Morbidity Codes

    Codes for cataclysmic events, such as a hurricane, take priority over all other external cause codes except child and adult abuse and terrorism and should be sequenced before other external cause of injury codes. Assign as many external cause of morbidity codes as necessary to fully explain each cause. For example, if an injury occurs as a result of a building collapse during the hurricane, external cause codes for both the hurricane and the building collapse should be assigned, with the external causes code for hurricane being sequenced as the first external cause code. For injuries incurred as a direct result of the hurricane, assign the appropriate code(s) for the injuries, followed by the code X37.0-, Hurricane (with the appropriate 7th character), and any other applicable external cause of injury codes. Code X37.0- also should be assigned when an injury is incurred as a result of flooding caused by a levee breaking related to the hurricane. Code X38.-, Flood (with the appropriate 7th character), should be assigned when an injury is from flooding resulting directly from the storm. Code X36.0.-, Collapse of dam or man-made structure, should not be assigned when the cause of the collapse is due to the hurricane. Use of code X36.0- is limited to collapses of man-made structures due to earth surface movements, not due to storm surges directly from a hurricane.

c. Other External Causes of Morbidity Code Issues

For injuries that are not a direct result of the hurricane, such as an evacuee that has incurred an injury as a result of a motor vehicle accident, assign the appropriate external cause of morbidity code(s) to describe the cause of the injury, but do not assign code X37.0-, Hurricane. If it is not clear whether the injury was a direct result of the hurricane, assume the injury is due to the hurricane and assign code X37.0-, Hurricane, as well as any other applicable external cause of morbidity codes. In addition to code X37.0-, Hurricane, other possible applicable external cause of morbidity codes include:

W54.0-	Bitten by dog
X30-	Exposure to excessive natural heat
X31-	Exposure to excessive natural cold
X38-	Flood

d. Use of Z codes

Z codes (other reasons for healthcare encounters) may be assigned as appropriate to further explain the reasons for presenting for healthcare services, including transfers between healthcare facilities. The ICD-10-CM Official Guidelines for Coding and Reporting identify which codes maybe assigned as principal or first-listed diagnosis only, secondary diagnosis only, or principal/first-listed or secondary (depending on the circumstances). Possible applicable Z codes include:

Z59.0	Homelessness
Z59.1	Inadequate housing
Z59.5	Extreme poverty
Z75.1	Person awaiting admission to adequate facility elsewhere
Z75.3	Unavailability and inaccessibility of health-care facilities
Z75.4	Unavailability and inaccessibility of other helping agencies
Z76.2	Encounter for health supervision and care of other healthy infant and child
Z99.12	Encounter for respirator [ventilator] dependence during power failure

The external cause of morbidity codes and the Z codes listed above are not an all-inclusive list. Other codes may be applicable to the encounter based upon the documentation. Assign as many codes as necessary to fully explain each healthcare encounter. Since patient history information may be very limited, use any available documentation to assign the appropriate external cause of morbidity and Z codes.

C. Chapter-Specific Coding Guidelines

In addition to general coding guidelines, there are guidelines for specific diagnoses and/or conditions in the classification. Unless otherwise indicated, these guidelines apply to all health care settings. Please refer to Section II for guidelines on the selection of principal diagnosis.

1. Chapter 1: Certain Infectious and Parasitic Diseases (A00-B99)

a. Human Immunodeficiency Virus (HIV) Infections

1) Code only confirmed cases

Code only confirmed cases of HIV infection/illness. This is an exception to the hospital inpatient guideline Section II, H.

In this context, "confirmation" does not require documentation of positive serology or culture for HIV; the provider's diagnostic statement that the patient is HIV positive, or has an HIV-related illness is sufficient.

2) Selection and sequencing of HIV codes

(a) **Patient admitted for HIV-related condition**

If a patient is admitted for an HIV-related condition, the principal diagnosis should be B20, Human immunodeficiency virus [HIV] disease followed by additional diagnosis codes for all reported HIV-related conditions.

(b) **Patient with HIV disease admitted for unrelated condition**

If a patient with HIV disease is admitted for an unrelated condition (such as a traumatic injury), the code for the unrelated condition (e.g., the nature of injury code) should be the principal diagnosis. Other diagnoses would be B20 followed by additional diagnosis codes for all reported HIV-related conditions.

(c) **Whether the patient is newly diagnosed**

Whether the patient is newly diagnosed or has had previous admissions/encounters for HIV conditions is irrelevant to the sequencing decision.

(d) **Asymptomatic human immunodeficiency virus**

Z21, Asymptomatic human immunodeficiency virus [HIV] infection status, is to be applied when the patient without any documentation of symptoms is listed as being "HIV positive," "known HIV," "HIV test positive," or similar terminology. Do not use this code if the term "AIDS" is used or if the patient is treated for any HIV-related illness or is described as having any condition(s) resulting from his/her HIV positive status; use B20 in these cases.

(e) **Patients with inconclusive HIV serology**

Patients with inconclusive HIV serology, but no definitive diagnosis or manifestations of the illness, may be assigned code R75, Inconclusive laboratory evidence of human immunodeficiency virus [HIV].

(f) Previously diagnosed HIV-related illness

Patients with any known prior diagnosis of an HIV-related illness should be coded to B20. Once a patient has developed an HIV-related illness, the patient should always be assigned code B20 on every subsequent admission/encounter. Patients previously diagnosed with any HIV illness (B20) should never be assigned to R75 or Z21, Asymptomatic human immunodeficiency virus [HIV] infection status.

(g) HIV Infection in Pregnancy, Childbirth and the Puerperium

During pregnancy, childbirth or the puerperium, a patient admitted (or presenting for a health care encounter) because of an HIV-related illness should receive a principal diagnosis code of O98.7-, Human immunodeficiency [HIV] disease complicating pregnancy, childbirth and the puerperium, followed by B20 and the code(s) for the HIV-related illness(es). Codes from Chapter 15 always take sequencing priority.

Patients with asymptomatic HIV infection status admitted (or presenting for a health care encounter) during pregnancy, childbirth, or the puerperium should receive codes of O98.7- and Z21.

(h) Encounters for testing for HIV

If a patient is being seen to determine his/her HIV status, use code Z11.4, Encounter for screening for human immunodeficiency virus [HIV]. Use additional codes for any associated high risk behavior.

If a patient with signs or symptoms is being seen for HIV testing, code the signs and symptoms. An additional counseling code Z71.7, Human immunodeficiency virus [HIV] counseling, may be used if counseling is provided during the encounter for the test.

When a patient returns to be informed of his/her HIV test results and the test result is negative, use code Z71.7, Human immunodeficiency virus [HIV] counseling.

If the results are positive, see previous guidelines and assign codes as appropriate.

b. Infectious agents as the cause of diseases classified to other chapters

Certain infections are classified in chapters other than Chapter 1 and no organism is identified as part of the infection code. In these instances, it is necessary to use an additional code from Chapter 1 to identify the organism. A code from category B95, Streptococcus, Staphylococcus, and Enterococcus as the cause of diseases classified to other chapters, B96, Other bacterial agents as the cause of diseases classified to other chapters, or B97, Viral agents as the cause of diseases classified to other chapters, is to be used as an additional code to identify the organism. An instructional note will be found at the infection code advising that an additional organism code is required.

c. Infections resistant to antibiotics

Many bacterial infections are resistant to current antibiotics. It is necessary to identify all infections documented as antibiotic resistant. Assign a code from category Z16, Resistance to antimicrobial drugs, following the infection code only if the infection code does not identify drug resistance.

d. Sepsis, Severe Sepsis, and Septic Shock

1) Coding of Sepsis and Severe Sepsis

(a) Sepsis

For a diagnosis of sepsis, assign the appropriate code for the underlying systemic infection. If the type of infection or causal organism is not further specified, assign code A41.9, Sepsis, unspecified organism.

A code from subcategory R65.2, Severe sepsis, should not be assigned unless severe sepsis or an associated acute organ dysfunction is documented.

(i) Negative or inconclusive blood cultures and sepsis
Negative or inconclusive blood cultures do not preclude a diagnosis of sepsis in patients with clinical evidence of the condition, however, the provider should be queried.

(ii) Urosepsis
The term urosepsis is a nonspecific term. It is not to be considered synonymous with sepsis. It has no default code in the Alphabetic Index. Should a provider use this term, he/she must be queried for clarification.

(iii) Sepsis with organ dysfunction
If a patient has sepsis and associated acute organ dysfunction or multiple organ dysfunction (MOD), follow the instructions for coding severe sepsis.

(iv) Acute organ dysfunction that is not clearly associated with the sepsis
If a patient has sepsis and an acute organ dysfunction, but the medical record documentation indicates that the acute organ dysfunction is related to a medical condition other than the sepsis, do not assign a code from subcategory R65.2, Severe sepsis. An acute organ dysfunction must be associated with the sepsis in order to assign the severe sepsis code. If the documentation is not clear as to whether an acute organ dysfunction is related to the sepsis or another medical condition, query the provider.

(b) Severe sepsis

The coding of severe sepsis requires a minimum of 2 codes: first a code for the underlying systemic infection, followed by a code from subcategory

R65.2, Severe sepsis. If the causal organism is not documented, assign code A41.9, Sepsis, unspecified organism, for the infection. Additional code(s) for the associated acute organ dysfunction are also required.

Due to the complex nature of severe sepsis, some cases may require querying the provider prior to assignment of the codes.

2) Septic shock

(a) Septic shock generally refers to circulatory failure associated with severe sepsis, and therefore, it represents a type of acute organ dysfunction.

For all cases of septic shock, the code for the systemic infection should be sequenced first, followed by code R65.21, Severe sepsis with septic shock or code T81.12, Postprocedural septic shock. Any additional codes for the other acute organ dysfunctions should also be assigned. As noted in the sequencing instructions in the Tabular List, the code for septic shock cannot be assigned as a principal diagnosis.

3) Sequencing of severe sepsis

If severe sepsis is present on admission, and meets the definition of principal diagnosis, the underlying systemic infection should be assigned as principal diagnosis followed by the appropriate code from subcategory R65.2 as required by the sequencing rules in the Tabular List. A code from subcategory R65.2 can never be assigned as a principal diagnosis.

When severe sepsis develops during an encounter (it was not present on admission) the underlying systemic infection and the appropriate code from subcategory R65.2 should be assigned as secondary diagnoses.

Severe sepsis may be present on admission but the diagnosis may not be confirmed until sometime after admission. If the documentation is not clear whether severe sepsis was present on admission, the provider should be queried.

4) Sepsis and severe sepsis with a localized infection

If the reason for admission is both sepsis or severe sepsis and a localized infection, such as pneumonia or cellulitis, a code(s) for the underlying systemic infection should be assigned first and the code for the localized infection should be assigned as a secondary diagnosis. If the patient has severe sepsis, a code from subcategory R65.2 should also be assigned as a secondary diagnosis. If the patient is admitted with a localized infection, such as pneumonia, and sepsis/severe sepsis doesn't develop until after admission, the localized infection should be assigned first, followed by the appropriate sepsis/severe sepsis codes.

5) Sepsis due to a postprocedural infection

(a) **Documentation of causal relationship**

As with all postprocedural complications, code assignment is based on the provider's documentation of the relationship between the infection and the procedure.

(b) **Sepsis due to a postprocedural infection** For **infections following a procedure, a code from T81.40, to T81.43**. Infection following a procedure, or **a code from O86.00 to O86.03**, Infection of obstetric surgical wound, **that identifies the site of the infection** should be coded first, **if known. Assign an additional code for sepsis following a procedure (T81.44) or sepsis following an obstetrical procedure (O86.04). Use an additional code to identify the infectious agent.** If the patient has severe sepsis the appropriate code from subcategory R65.2 should also be assigned with the additional code(s) for any acute organ dysfunction.

For infections following infusion, transfusion, therapeutic injection, or immunization, a code from subcategory T80.2, Infections following infusion, transfusion, and therapeutic injection, or code T88.0-, Infection following immunization, should be coded first, followed by the code for the specific infection. If the patient has severe sepsis, the appropriate code from subcategory R65.2 should also be assigned, with the additional codes(s) for any acute organ dysfunction.

(c) **Postprocedural infection and postprocedural septic shock**

If a postprocedural infection has resulted in postprocedural septic shock, **assign the codes indicated above for sepsis due to a postprocedural infection, followed by code T81.12-, Postprocedural septic shock. Do not assign code R65.21, Severe sepsis with septic shock. Additional code(s) should be assigned for any acute organ dysfunction.**

6) Sepsis and severe sepsis associated with a noninfectious process (condition)

In some cases a noninfectious process (condition), such as trauma, may lead to an infection which can result in sepsis or severe sepsis. If sepsis or severe sepsis is documented as associated with a noninfectious condition, such as a burn or serious injury, and this condition meets the definition for principal diagnosis, the code for the noninfectious condition should be sequenced first, followed by the code for the resulting infection. If severe sepsis is present, a code from subcategory R65.2 should also be assigned with any associated organ dysfunction(s) codes. It is not necessary to assign a code from subcategory R65.1, Systemic inflammatory response syndrome (SIRS) of non-infectious origin, for these cases.

If the infection meets the definition of principal diagnosis it should be sequenced before the non-infectious condition. When both the associated non-infectious condition and the infection meet the definition of principal diagnosis either may be assigned as principal diagnosis.

Only one code from category R65, Symptoms and signs specifically associated with systemic

inflammation and infection, should be assigned. Therefore, when a non-infectious condition leads to an infection resulting in severe sepsis, assign the appropriate code from subcategory R65.2, Severe sepsis. Do not additionally assign a code from subcategory R65.1, Systemic inflammatory response syndrome (SIRS) of non-infectious origin.
See Section I.C.18. SIRS due to non-infectious process

7) Sepsis and septic shock complicating abortion, pregnancy, childbirth, and the puerperium
See Section I.C.15. Sepsis and septic shock complicating abortion, pregnancy, childbirth and the puerperium

8) Newborn sepsis
See Section I.C.16. f. Bacterial sepsis of Newborn

e. Methicillin Resistant Staphylococcus aureus (MRSA) Conditions

1) Selection and sequencing of MRSA codes

(a) Combination codes for MRSA infection
When a patient is diagnosed with an infection that is due to methicillin resistant *Staphylococcus aureus* (MRSA), and that infection has a combination code that includes the causal organism (e.g., sepsis, pneumonia) assign the appropriate combination code for the condition (e.g., code A41.02, Sepsis due to Methicillin resistant Staphylococcus aureus or code J15.212, Pneumonia due to Methicillin resistant Staphylococcus aureus). Do not assign code B95.62, Methicillin resistant Staphylococcus aureus infection as the cause of diseases classified elsewhere, as an additional code because the combination code includes the type of infection and the MRSA organism. Do not assign a code from subcategory Z16.11, Resistance to penicillins, as an additional diagnosis.
See Section C.1. for instructions on coding and sequencing of sepsis and severe sepsis.

(b) Other codes for MRSA infection
When there is documentation of a current infection (e.g., wound infection, stitch abscess, urinary tract infection) due to MRSA, and that infection does not have a combination code that includes the causal organism, assign the appropriate code to identify the condition along with code B95.62, Methicillin resistant Staphylococcus aureus infection as the cause of diseases classified elsewhere for the MRSA infection. Do not assign a code from subcategory Z16.11, Resistance to penicillins.

(c) Methicillin susceptible Staphylococcus aureus (MSSA) and MRSA colonization
The condition or state of being colonized or carrying MSSA or MRSA is called colonization or carriage, while an individual person is described as being colonized or being a carrier. Colonization means that MSSA or MSRA is present on or in the body without necessarily causing illness. A positive MRSA colonization test might be documented by the provider as "MRSA screen positive" or "MRSA nasal swab positive".

Assign code Z22.322, Carrier or suspected carrier of Methicillin resistant Staphylococcus

aureus, for patients documented as having MRSA colonization. Assign code Z22.321, Carrier or suspected carrier of Methicillin susceptible Staphylococcus aureus, for patient documented as having MSSA colonization. Colonization is not necessarily indicative of a disease process or as the cause of a specific condition the patient may have unless documented as such by the provider.

(d) MRSA colonization and infection
If a patient is documented as having both MRSA colonization and infection during a hospital admission, code Z22.322, Carrier or suspected carrier of Methicillin resistant Staphylococcus aureus, and a code for the MRSA infection may both be assigned.

f. Zika virus infections

1) Code only confirmed cases
Code only a confirmed diagnosis of Zika virus (A92.5, Zika virus disease) as documented by the provider. This is an exception to the hospital inpatient guideline Section II, H.

In this context, "confirmation" does not require documentation of the type of test performed; the physician's diagnostic statement that the condition is confirmed is sufficient. This code should be assigned regardless of the stated mode of transmission.

If the provider documents "suspected", "possible" or "probable" Zika, do not assign code A92.5. Assign a code(s) explaining the reason for encounter (such as fever, rash, or joint pain) or Z20.821, Contact with and (suspected) exposure to **Zika virus**.

2. Chapter 2: Neoplasms (C00-D49)
General guidelines
Chapter 2 of the ICD-10-CM contains the codes for most benign and all malignant neoplasms. Certain benign neoplasms, such as prostatic adenomas, may be found in the specific body system chapters. To properly code a neoplasm it is necessary to determine from the record if the neoplasm is benign, in-situ, malignant, or of uncertain histologic behavior. If malignant, any secondary (metastatic) sites should also be determined.

Primary malignant neoplasms overlapping site boundaries
> A primary malignant neoplasm that overlaps two or more contiguous (next to each other) sites should be classified to the subcategory/code .8 ("overlapping lesion"), unless the combination is specifically indexed elsewhere. For multiple neoplasms of the same site that are not contiguous such as tumors in different quadrants of the same breast, codes for each site should be assigned.

Malignant neoplasm of ectopic tissue
> Malignant neoplasms of ectopic tissue are to be coded to the site of origin mentioned, e.g., ectopic pancreatic malignant neoplasms involving the stomach are coded to malignant neoplasm of pancreas, unspecified (C25.9).

The neoplasm table in the Alphabetic Index should be referenced first. However, if the histological term is documented, that term should be referenced first, rather than going immediately to the Neoplasm Table, in order to determine which column in the Neoplasm Table is appropriate. For example, if the documentation indicates "adenoma," refer to the term in the Alphabetic Index to review the entries under this term and the instructional note to "see also neoplasm, by site, benign." The table provides the proper code based on the type of neoplasm and the site. It is important to select the proper column in the table that corresponds to the type of neoplasm. The Tabular List should then be referenced to verify that the correct code has been selected from the table and that a more specific site code does not exist.

See Section I.C.21. Factors influencing health status and contact with health services, Status, for information regarding Z15.0, codes for genetic susceptibility to cancer.

a. Treatment directed at the malignancy

If the treatment is directed at the malignancy, designate the malignancy as the principal diagnosis.

The only exception to this guideline is if a patient admission/encounter is solely for the administration of chemotherapy, immunotherapy or external beam radiation therapy, assign the appropriate Z51.— code as the first-listed or principal diagnosis, and the diagnosis or problem for which the service is being performed as a secondary diagnosis.

b. Treatment of secondary site

When a patient is admitted because of a primary neoplasm with metastasis and treatment is directed toward the secondary site only, the secondary neoplasm is designated as the principal diagnosis even though the primary malignancy is still present.

c. Coding and sequencing of complications

Coding and sequencing of complications associated with the malignancies or with the therapy thereof are subject to the following guidelines:

1) Anemia associated with malignancy

When admission/encounter is for management of an anemia associated with the malignancy, and the treatment is only for anemia, the appropriate code for the malignancy is sequenced as the principal or first-listed diagnosis followed by the appropriate code for the anemia (such as code D63.0, Anemia in neoplastic disease).

2) Anemia associated with chemotherapy, immunotherapy and radiation therapy

When the admission/encounter is for management of an anemia associated with an adverse effect of the administration of chemotherapy or immunotherapy and the only treatment is for the anemia, the anemia code is sequenced first followed by the appropriate codes for the neoplasm and the adverse effect (T45.1X5, Adverse effect of antineoplastic and immunosuppressive drugs).

When the admission/encounter is for management of an anemia associated with an adverse effect of radiotherapy, the anemia code should be sequenced first, followed by the appropriate neoplasm code and code Y84.2, Radiological procedure and radiotherapy as the cause of abnormal reaction of the patient, or of later complication, without mention of misadventure at the time of the procedure.

3) Management of dehydration due to the malignancy

When the admission/encounter is for management of dehydration due to the malignancy and only the dehydration is being treated (intravenous rehydration), the dehydration is sequenced first, followed by the code(s) for the malignancy.

4) Treatment of a complication resulting from a surgical procedure

When the admission/encounter is for treatment of a complication resulting from a surgical procedure, designate the complication as the principal or first-listed diagnosis if treatment is directed at resolving the complication.

d. Primary malignancy previously excised

When a primary malignancy has been previously excised or eradicated from its site and there is no further treatment directed to that site and there is no evidence of any existing primary malignancy, **at that site** a code from category Z85, Personal history of malignant neoplasm, should be used to indicate the former site of the malignancy. Any mention of extension, invasion, or metastasis to another site is coded as a secondary malignant neoplasm to that site. The secondary site may be the principal or first-listed with the Z85 code used as a secondary code.

e. Admissions/Encounters involving chemotherapy, immunotherapy and radiation therapy

1) Episode of care involves surgical removal of neoplasm

When an episode of care involves the surgical removal of a neoplasm, primary or secondary site, followed by adjunct chemotherapy or radiation treatment during the same episode of care, the code for the neoplasm should be assigned as principal or first-listed diagnosis.

2) Patient admission/encounter solely for administration of chemotherapy, immunotherapy and radiation therapy

If a patient admission/encounter is solely for the administration of chemotherapy, immunotherapy or external beam radiation therapy assign code Z51.0, Encounter for antineoplastic radiation therapy, or Z51.11, Encounter for antineoplastic chemotherapy, or Z51.12, Encounter for antineoplastic immunotherapy as the first-listed or principal diagnosis. If a patient receives more than one of these therapies during the same admission more than one of these codes may be assigned, in any sequence.

The malignancy for which the therapy is being administered should be assigned as a secondary diagnosis.

If a patient admission/encounter is for the insertion or implantation of radioactive elements (e.g., brachytherapy) the appropriate code for the malignancy is sequenced as the principal or first-listed diagnosis. Code Z51.0 should not be assigned.

3) Patient admitted for radiation therapy, chemotherapy or immunotherapy and develops complications

When a patient is admitted for the purpose of external beam radiotherapy, immunotherapy or chemotherapy and develops complications such as uncontrolled nausea and vomiting or dehydration, the principal or first-listed diagnosis is Z51.0, Encounter for antineoplastic radiation therapy, or Z51.11, Encounter for antineoplastic chemotherapy, or Z51.12, Encounter for antineoplastic immunotherapy followed by any codes for the complications.

When a patient is admitted for the purpose of insertion or implantation of radioactive elements (e.g., brachytherapy) and develops complications such as uncontrolled nausea and vomiting or dehydration, the principal or first-listed diagnosis is the appropriate code for the malignancy followed by any codes for the complications.

f. Admission/encounter to determine extent of malignancy

When the reason for admission/encounter is to determine the extent of the malignancy, or for a procedure such as paracentesis or thoracentesis, the primary malignancy or appropriate metastatic site is designated as the principal or first-listed diagnosis, even though chemotherapy or radiotherapy is administered.

g. Symptoms, signs, and abnormal findings listed in Chapter 18 associated with neoplasms

Symptoms, signs, and ill-defined conditions listed in Chapter 18 characteristic of, or associated with, an existing primary or secondary site malignancy cannot be used to replace the malignancy as principal or first-listed diagnosis, regardless of the number of admissions or encounters for treatment and care of the neoplasm.

See section I.C.21. Factors influencing health status and contact with health services, Encounter for prophylactic organ removal.

h. Admission/encounter for pain control/management

See Section I.C.6. for information on coding admission/encounter for pain control/management.

i. Malignancy in two or more noncontiguous sites

A patient may have more than one malignant tumor in the same organ. These tumors may represent different primaries or metastatic disease, depending on the site. Should the documentation be unclear, the provider should be queried as to the status of each tumor so that the correct codes can be assigned.

j. Disseminated malignant neoplasm, unspecified

Code C80.0, Disseminated malignant neoplasm, unspecified, is for use only in those cases where the patient has advanced metastatic disease and no known primary or secondary sites are specified. It should not be used in place of assigning codes for the primary site and all known secondary sites.

k. Malignant neoplasm without specification of site

Code C80.1, Malignant (primary) neoplasm, unspecified, equates to Cancer, unspecified. This code should only be used when no determination can be made as to the primary site of a malignancy. This code should rarely be used in the inpatient setting.

l. Sequencing of neoplasm codes

1) Encounter for treatment of primary malignancy

If the reason for the encounter is for treatment of a primary malignancy, assign the malignancy as the principal/first-listed diagnosis. The primary site is to be sequenced first, followed by any metastatic sites.

2) Encounter for treatment of secondary malignancy

When an encounter is for a primary malignancy with metastasis and treatment is directed toward the metastatic (secondary) site(s) only, the metastatic site(s) is designated as the principal/first-listed diagnosis. The primary malignancy is coded as an additional code.

3) Malignant neoplasm in a pregnant patient

When a pregnant woman has a malignant neoplasm, a code from subcategory O9A.1-, Malignant neoplasm complicating pregnancy, childbirth, and the puerperium, should be sequenced first, followed by the appropriate code from Chapter 2 to indicate the type of neoplasm.

4) Encounter for complication associated with a neoplasm

When an encounter is for management of a complication associated with a neoplasm, such as dehydration, and the treatment is only for the complication, the complication is coded first, followed by the appropriate code(s) for the neoplasm.

The exception to this guideline is anemia. When the admission/encounter is for management of an anemia associated with the malignancy, and the treatment is only for anemia, the appropriate code for the malignancy is sequenced as the principal or first-listed diagnosis followed by code D63.0, Anemia in neoplastic disease.

5) Complication from surgical procedure for treatment of a neoplasm

When an encounter is for treatment of a complication resulting from a surgical procedure performed for the treatment of the neoplasm, designate the complication as the principal/first-listed diagnosis. See guideline regarding the coding of a current malignancy versus personal history to determine if the code for the neoplasm should also be assigned.

6) Pathologic fracture due to a neoplasm

When an encounter is for a pathological fracture due to a neoplasm, and the focus of treatment is the fracture, a code from subcategory M84.5, Pathological fracture in neoplastic disease, should be sequenced first, followed by the code for the neoplasm.

If the focus of treatment is the neoplasm with an associated pathological fracture, the neoplasm code should be sequenced first, followed by a code from M84.5 for the pathological fracture.

m. Current malignancy versus personal history of malignancy

When a primary malignancy has been excised but further treatment, such as an additional surgery for the malignancy, radiation therapy or chemotherapy is directed to that site, the primary malignancy code should be used until treatment is completed.

When a primary malignancy has been previously excised or eradicated from its site, there is no further treatment (of the malignancy) directed to that site, and there is no evidence of any existing primary malignancy **at that site**, a code from category Z85, Personal history of malignant neoplasm, should be used to indicate the former site of the malignancy.

Subcategories Z85.0 – Z85.7 should only be assigned for the former site of a primary malignancy, not the site of a secondary malignancy. Codes from subcategory Z85.8-, may be assigned for the former site(s) of either a primary or secondary malignancy included in this subcategory.

See Section I.C.21. Factors influencing health status and contact with health services, History (of)

n. Leukemia, Multiple Myeloma, and Malignant Plasma Cell Neoplasms in remission versus personal history

The categories for leukemia, and category C90, Multiple myeloma and malignant plasma cell neoplasms, have codes indicating whether or not the leukemia has achieved remission. There are also codes Z85.6, Personal history of leukemia, and Z85.79, Personal history of other malignant neoplasms of lymphoid, hematopoietic and related tissues. If the documentation is unclear, as to whether the leukemia has achieved remission, the provider should be queried.

See Section I.C.21. Factors influencing health status and contact with health services, History (of)

o. Aftercare following surgery for neoplasm

See Section I.C.21. Factors influencing health status and contact with health services, Aftercare

p. Follow-up care for completed treatment of a malignancy

See Section I.C.21. Factors influencing health status and contact with health services, Follow-up

q. Prophylactic organ removal for prevention of malignancy

See Section I.C. 21, Factors influencing health status and contact with health services, Prophylactic organ removal

r. Malignant neoplasm associated with transplanted organ

A malignant neoplasm of a transplanted organ should be coded as a transplant complication. Assign first the appropriate code from category T86.-, Complications of transplanted organs and tissue, followed by code C80.2, Malignant neoplasm associated with transplanted organ. Use an additional code for the specific malignancy.

3. Chapter 3: Disease of the blood and blood-forming organs and certain disorders involving the immune mechanism (D50-D89)

Reserved for future guideline expansion

4. Chapter 4: Endocrine, Nutritional, and Metabolic Diseases (E00-E89)

a. Diabetes mellitus

The diabetes mellitus codes are combination codes that include the type of diabetes mellitus, the body system affected, and the complications affecting that body system. As many codes within a particular category as are necessary to describe all of the complications of the disease may be used. They should be sequenced based on the reason for a particular encounter. Assign as many codes from categories E08 – E13 as needed to identify all of the associated conditions that the patient has.

1) Type of diabetes

The age of a patient is not the sole determining factor, though most type 1 diabetics develop the condition before reaching puberty. For this reason type 1 diabetes mellitus is also referred to as juvenile diabetes.

2) Type of diabetes mellitus not documented

If the type of diabetes mellitus is not documented in the medical record the default is E11.-, Type 2 diabetes mellitus.

3) Diabetes mellitus and the use of insulin oral hypoglycemics

If the documentation in a medical record does not indicate the type of diabetes but does indicate that the patient uses insulin, code E11, Type 2 diabetes mellitus, should be assigned. An additional code should be assigned from category Z79 to identify the long-term (current) use of insulin or oral hypoglycemic drugs. If the patient is treated with both oral medications and insulin, only the code for long-term (current) use of insulin should be assigned. Code Z79.4 should not be assigned if insulin is given temporarily to bring a type 2 patient's blood sugar under control during an encounter.

4) Diabetes mellitus in pregnancy and gestational diabetes

See Section I.C.15. Diabetes mellitus in pregnancy.
See Section I.C.15. Gestational (pregnancy induced) diabetes

5) Complications due to insulin pump malfunction

(a) Underdose of insulin due to insulin pump failure

An underdose of insulin due to an insulin pump failure should be assigned to a code from subcategory T85.6, Mechanical complication of other specified internal and external prosthetic devices, implants and grafts, that specifies the type of pump malfunction, as the principal or first-listed code, followed by code T38.3X6-, Underdosing of insulin and oral hypoglycemic [antidiabetic] drugs. Additional codes for the type of diabetes mellitus and any associated complications due to the underdosing should also be assigned.

(b) Overdose of insulin due to insulin pump failure

The principal or first-listed code for an encounter due to an insulin pump malfunction resulting in an overdose of insulin, should also be T85.6-, Mechanical complication of other specified internal and external prosthetic devices, implants and grafts, followed by code T38.3X1-, Poisoning by insulin and oral hypoglycemic [antidiabetic] drugs, accidental (unintentional).

6) Secondary diabetes mellitus

Codes under categories E08, Diabetes mellitus due to underlying condition, E09, Drug or chemical induced diabetes mellitus and E13, Other specified diabetes mellitus, identify complications/ manifestations associated with secondary diabetes mellitus. Secondary diabetes is always caused by another condition or event (e.g., cystic fibrosis, malignant neoplasm of pancreas, pancreatectomy, adverse effect of drug, or poisoning).

(a) Secondary diabetes mellitus and the use of insulin or hypoglycemic drugs

For patients with secondary diabetes mellitus who routinely use insulin or oral hypoglycemic drugs, an additional code from category Z79 should be assigned to identify the long-term (current) use of insulin or oral hypoglycemic drugs. If the patient is treated with both oral medications and insulin, only the code for long-term (current) use of insulin should be assigned. Code Z79.4 should not be assigned if insulin is given temporarily to bring a type 2 patient's blood sugar under control during an encounter.

(b) Assigning and sequencing secondary diabetes codes and its causes

The sequencing of the secondary diabetes codes in relationship to codes for the cause of the diabetes is based on the Tabular List instructions for categories E08, E09 and E13.

(i) Secondary diabetes mellitus due to pancreatectomy For postpancreatectomy diabetes mellitus (lack of insulin due to the surgical removal of all or part of the pancreas), assign code E89.1, Postprocedural hypoinsulinemia.

Assign a code from category E13 and a code from subcategory Z90.41-, Acquired absence of pancreas, as additional codes.

(ii) Secondary diabetes due to drugs Secondary diabetes may be caused by an adverse effect of correctly administered medications, poisoning or sequela of poisoning.

See section I.C.19.e for coding of adverse effects and poisoning, and section I.C.20 for external cause code reporting.

5. Chapter 5: Mental, Behavioral and Neurodevelopmental disorders (F01 – F99)

a. Pain disorders related to psychological factors

Assign code F45.41, for pain that is exclusively related to psychological disorders. As indicated by the Excludes 1 note under category G89, a code from category G89 should not be assigned with code F45.41

Code F45.42, Pain disorders with related psychological factors, should be used with a code from category G89, Pain, not elsewhere classified, if there is documentation of a psychological component for a patient with acute or chronic pain.

See Section I.C.6. Pain

b. Mental and behavioral disorders due to psychoactive substance use

1) In Remission

Selection of codes for "in remission" for categories F10-F19, Mental and behavioral disorders due to psychoactive substance use (categories F10-F19 with -.11, -.21) requires the provider's clinical judgment. The appropriate codes for "in remission" are assigned only on the basis of provider documentation (as defined in the Official Guidelines for Coding and Reporting), unless otherwise instructed by the classification.

Mild substance use disorders in early or sustained remission are classified to the appropriate codes for substance abuse in remission, and moderate or severe substance use disorders in early or sustained remission are classified to the appropriate codes for substance dependence in remission.

2) Psychoactive Substance Use, Abuse and Dependence

When the provider documentation refers to use, abuse and dependence of the same substance (e.g., alcohol, opioid, cannabis, etc.), only one code should be assigned to identify the pattern of use based on the following hierarchy:

- If both use and abuse are documented, assign only the code for abuse
- If both abuse and dependence are documented, assign only the code for dependence
- If use, abuse and dependence are all documented, assign only the code for dependence
- If both use and dependence are documented, assign only the code for dependence.

3) Psychoactive Substance Use, *Unspecified*

As with all other **unspecified** diagnoses, the codes for **unspecified** psychoactive substance use disorders (F10.9-, F11.9-, F12.9-, F13.9-, F14.9-, F15.9-, F16.9-, **F18.9-, F19.9-**) should only be assigned based on provider documentation and when they meet the definition of a reportable diagnosis (see Section III, Reporting Additional Diagnoses). These codes are to be used only when the psychoactive substance use is associated with a physical, mental or behavioral disorder, and such a relationship is documented by the provider.

c. Factitious Disorder

Factitious disorder imposed on self or Munchausen's syndrome is a disorder in which a person falsely reports or causes his or her own physical or psychological signs or symptoms. For patients with documented factitious disorder on self or Munchausen's syndrome, assign the appropriate code from subcategory F68.1-, Factitious disorder imposed on self.

Munchausen's syndrome by proxy (MSBP) is a disorder in which a caregiver (perpetrator) falsely reports or causes an illness or injury in another person (victim) under his or her care, such as a child, an elderly adult, or a person who has a disability. The condition is also referred to as "factitious disorder imposed on another" or "factitious disorder by proxy." The perpetrator, not the victim, receives this diagnosis. Assign code F68.A, Factitious disorder imposed on another, to the perpetrator's record. For the victim of a patient suffering from MSBP, assign the appropriate code from categories T74, Adult and child abuse, neglect and other maltreatment, confirmed, or T76, Adult and child abuse, neglect and other maltreatment, suspected.

See Section I.C.19.f. Adult and child abuse, neglect and other maltreatment

6. **Chapter 6: Diseases of the Nervous System (G00-G99)**

a. Dominant/nondominant side

Codes from category G81, Hemiplegia and hemiparesis, and subcategories, G83.1, Monoplegia of lower limb, G83.2, Monoplegia of upper limb, and G83.3, Monoplegia, unspecified, identify whether the dominant or nondominant side is affected. Should the affected side be documented, but not specified as dominant or nondominant, and the classification system does not indicate a default, code selection is as follows:

- For ambidextrous patients, the default should be dominant.
- If the left side is affected, the default is non-dominant.
- If the right side is affected, the default is dominant.

b. Pain - Category G89

1) General coding information

Codes in category G89, Pain, not elsewhere classified, may be used in conjunction with codes from other categories and chapters to provide more detail about acute or chronic pain and neoplasm-related pain, unless otherwise indicated below.

If the pain is not specified as acute or chronic, post-thoracotomy, postprocedural, or neoplasm-related, do not assign codes from category G89.

A code from category G89 should not be assigned if the underlying (definitive) diagnosis is known, unless the reason for the encounter is pain control/management and not management of the underlying condition.

When an admission or encounter is for a procedure aimed at treating the underlying condition (e.g., spinal fusion, kyphoplasty), a code for the underlying condition (e.g., vertebral fracture, spinal stenosis) should be assigned as the principal diagnosis. No code from category G89 should be assigned.

(a) **Category G89 Codes as Principal or First-Listed Diagnosis**

Category G89 codes are acceptable as principal diagnosis or the first-listed code:

- When pain control or pain management is the reason for the admission/encounter (e.g., a patient with displaced intervertebral disc, nerve impingement and severe back pain presents for injection of steroid into the spinal canal). The underlying cause of the pain should be reported as an additional diagnosis, if known.
- When a patient is admitted for the insertion of a neurostimulator for pain control, assign the appropriate pain code as the principal or first-listed diagnosis. When an admission or encounter is for a procedure aimed at treating the underlying condition and a neurostimulator is inserted for pain control during the same admission/encounter, a code for the underlying condition should be assigned as the principal diagnosis and the appropriate pain code should be assigned as a secondary diagnosis.

(b) **Use of Category G89 Codes in Conjunction with Site Specific Pain Codes**

(i) **Assigning Category G89 and Site-Specific Pain Codes**

Codes from category G89 may be used in conjunction with codes that identify the site of pain (including codes from Chapter 18) if the category G89 code provides additional information. For example, if the code describes the site of the pain, but does not fully describe whether the pain is acute or chronic, then both codes should be assigned.

(ii) **Sequencing of Category G89 Codes with Site-Specific Pain Codes**

The sequencing of category G89 codes with site-specific pain codes (including Chapter 18 codes), is dependent on the circumstances of the encounter/admission as follows:

- If the encounter is for pain control or pain management, assign the code from category G89 followed by the code identifying the specific site of pain (e.g., encounter for pain management for acute neck pain from trauma is assigned code G89.11, Acute pain due to trauma, followed by code M54.2, Cervicalgia, to identify the site of pain).
- If the encounter is for any other reason except pain control or pain management, and a related definitive diagnosis has not been established (confirmed) by the provider, assign the code for the specific site of pain first, followed by the appropriate code from category G89.

2) Pain due to devices, implants and grafts
See Section I.C.19. Pain due to medical devices

3) Postoperative Pain
The provider's documentation should be used to guide the coding of postoperative pain, as well as *Section III. Reporting Additional Diagnoses* and *Section IV. Diagnostic Coding and Reporting in the Outpatient Setting.*

The default for post-thoracotomy and other postoperative pain not specified as acute or chronic is the code for the acute form.

Routine or expected postoperative pain immediately after surgery should not be coded.

(a) Postoperative pain not associated with specific postoperative complication
Postoperative pain not associated with a specific postoperative complication is assigned to the appropriate postoperative pain code in category G89.

(b) Postoperative pain associated with specific postoperative complication
Postoperative pain associated with a specific postoperative complication (such as painful wire sutures) is assigned to the appropriate code(s) found in Chapter 19, Injury, poisoning, and certain other consequences of external causes. If appropriate, use additional code(s) from category G89 to identify acute or chronic pain (G89.18 or G89.28).

4) Chronic pain
Chronic pain is classified to subcategory G89.2. There is no time frame defining when pain becomes chronic pain. The provider's documentation should be used to guide use of these codes.

5) Neoplasm Related Pain
Code G89.3 is assigned to pain documented as being related, associated or due to cancer, primary or secondary malignancy, or tumor. This code is assigned regardless of whether the pain is acute or chronic.

This code may be assigned as the principal or first-listed code when the stated reason for the admission/encounter is documented as pain control/pain management. The underlying neoplasm should be reported as an additional diagnosis.

When the reason for the admission/encounter is management of the neoplasm and the pain associated with the neoplasm is also documented, code G89.3 may be assigned as an additional diagnosis. It is not necessary to assign an additional code for the site of the pain.

See Section I.C.2 for instructions on the sequencing of neoplasms for all other stated reasons for the admission/encounter (except for pain control/pain management).

6) Chronic pain syndrome
Central pain syndrome (G89.0) and chronic pain syndrome (G89.4) are different than the term "chronic pain," and therefore codes should only be used when the provider has specifically documented this condition.

See Section I.C.5. Pain disorders related to psychological factors

7. Chapter 7: Diseases of the Eye and Adnexa (H00-H59)

a. Glaucoma

1) Assigning Glaucoma Codes
Assign as many codes from category H40, Glaucoma, as needed to identify the type of glaucoma, the affected eye, and the glaucoma stage.

2) Bilateral glaucoma with same type and stage
When a patient has bilateral glaucoma and both eyes are documented as being the same type and stage, and there is a code for bilateral glaucoma, report only the code for the type of glaucoma, bilateral, with the seventh character for the stage.

When a patient has bilateral glaucoma and both eyes are documented as being the same type and stage, and the classification does not provide a code for bilateral glaucoma (i.e., subcategories H40.10, H40.11 and H40.20) report only one code for the type of glaucoma with the appropriate seventh character for the stage.

3) Bilateral glaucoma stage with different types or stages
When a patient has bilateral glaucoma and each eye is documented as having a different type or stage, and the classification distinguishes laterality, assign the appropriate code for each eye rather than the code for bilateral glaucoma.

When a patient has bilateral glaucoma and each eye is documented as having a different type, and the classification does not distinguish laterality (i.e., subcategories H40.10, H40.11 and H40.20), assign one code for each type of glaucoma with the appropriate seventh character for the stage.

When a patient has bilateral glaucoma and each eye is documented as having the same type, but different stage, and the classification does not distinguish laterality (i.e., subcategories H40.10, H40.11 and H40.20), assign a code for the type of glaucoma for each eye with the seventh character for the specific glaucoma stage documented for each eye.

4) Patient admitted with glaucoma and stage evolves during the admission

If a patient is admitted with glaucoma and the stage progresses during the admission, assign the code for highest stage documented.

5) Indeterminate stage glaucoma

Assignment of the seventh character "4" for "indeterminate stage" should be based on the clinical documentation. The seventh character "4" is used for glaucomas whose stage cannot be clinically determined. This seventh character should not be confused with the seventh character "Ø", unspecified, which should be assigned when there is no documentation regarding the stage of the glaucoma.

b. Blindness

If "blindness" or "low vision" of both eyes is documented but the visual impairment category is not documented, assign code H54.3, Unqualified visual loss, both eyes. If "blindness" or "low vision" in one eye is documented but the visual impairment category is not documented, assign a code from H54.6-, Unqualified visual loss, one eye. If "blindness" or "visual loss" is documented without any information about whether one or both eyes are affected, assign code H54.7, Unspecified visual loss.

8. Chapter 8: Diseases of the Ear and Mastoid Process (H60-H95)

Reserved for future guideline expansion

9. Chapter 9: Diseases of the Circulatory System (I00-I99)

a. Hypertension

The classification presumes a causal relationship between hypertension and heart involvement and between hypertension and kidney involvement, as the two conditions are linked by the term "with" in the Alphabetic Index. These conditions should be coded as related even in the absence of provider documentation explicitly linking them, unless the documentation clearly states the conditions are unrelated.

For hypertension and conditions not specifically linked by relational terms such as "with," "associated with" or "due to" in the classification, provider documentation must link the conditions in order to code them as related.

1) Hypertension with Heart Disease

Hypertension with heart conditions classified to I5Ø.- or **I51.4-I51.7, I51.89, I51.9**, are assigned to, a code from category I11, Hypertensive heart disease. Use additional code(s) from category I5Ø, Heart failure, to identify the type(s) of heart failure in those patients with heart failure.

The same heart conditions (I5Ø.-, **I51.4-I51.7, I51.89, I51.9**) with hypertension are coded separately if the provider has **documented they are unrelated to the hypertension**. Sequence according to the circumstances of the admission/encounter.

2) Hypertensive Chronic Kidney Disease

Assign codes from category I12, Hypertensive chronic kidney disease, when both hypertension and a condition classifiable to category N18, Chronic kidney disease (CKD), are present. CKD should not be coded as hypertensive if the **provider indicates the CKD is not related to the hypertension.**

The appropriate code from category N18 should be used as a secondary code with a code from category I12 to identify the stage of chronic kidney disease.

See Section I.C.14. Chronic kidney disease.

If a patient has hypertensive chronic kidney disease and acute renal failure, an additional code for the acute renal failure is required.

3) Hypertensive Heart and Chronic Kidney Disease

Assign codes from combination category I13, Hypertensive heart and chronic kidney disease, when there is hypertension with both heart and kidney involvement. If heart failure is present, assign an additional code from category I5Ø to identify the type of heart failure.

The appropriate code from category N18, Chronic kidney disease, should be used as a secondary code with a code from category I13 to identify the stage of chronic kidney disease.

See Section I.C.14. Chronic kidney disease.

The codes in category I13, Hypertensive heart and chronic kidney disease, are combination codes that include hypertension, heart disease and chronic kidney disease. The Includes note at I13 specifies that the conditions included at I11 and I12 are included together in I13. If a patient has hypertension, heart disease and chronic kidney disease then a code from I13 should be used, not individual codes for hypertension, heart disease and chronic kidney disease, or codes from I11 or I12.

For patients with both acute renal failure and chronic kidney disease an additional code for acute renal failure is required.

4) Hypertensive Cerebrovascular Disease

For hypertensive cerebrovascular disease, first assign the appropriate code from categories I60-I69, followed by the appropriate hypertension code.

5) Hypertensive Retinopathy

Subcategory H35.Ø, Background retinopathy and retinal vascular changes, should be used with a code from category I10 – I15, Hypertensive disease to include the systemic hypertension. The sequencing is based on the reason for the encounter.

6) Hypertension, Secondary

Secondary hypertension is due to an underlying condition. Two codes are required: one to identify the underlying etiology and one from category I15 to identify the hypertension. Sequencing of codes is determined by the reason for admission/encounter.

7) Hypertension, Transient

Assign code R03.0, Elevated blood pressure reading without diagnosis of hypertension, unless patient has an established diagnosis of hypertension. Assign code O13.-, Gestational [pregnancy-induced] hypertension without significant proteinuria, or O14.-, Pre-eclampsia, for transient hypertension of pregnancy.

8) Hypertension, Controlled
This diagnostic statement usually refers to an existing state of hypertension under control by therapy. Assign the appropriate code from categories I10-I15, Hypertensive diseases.

9) Hypertension, Uncontrolled
Uncontrolled hypertension may refer to untreated hypertension or hypertension not responding to current therapeutic regimen. In either case, assign the appropriate code from categories I10-I15, Hypertensive diseases.

10) Hypertensive Crisis
Assign a code from category I16, Hypertensive crisis, for documented hypertensive urgency, hypertensive emergency or unspecified hypertensive crisis. Code also any identified hypertensive disease (I10-I15). The sequencing is based on the reason for the encounter.

11) Pulmonary Hypertension
Pulmonary hypertension is classified to category I27, Other pulmonary heart diseases. For secondary pulmonary hypertension (I27.1, I27.2-), code also any associated conditions or adverse effects of drugs or toxins. The sequencing is based on the reason for the encounter, **except for adverse effects of drugs.**
See Section I.C.19.e

b. Atherosclerotic Coronary Artery Disease and Angina
ICD-10-CM has combination codes for atherosclerotic heart disease with angina pectoris. The subcategories for these codes are I25.11, Atherosclerotic heart disease of native coronary artery with angina pectoris and I25.7, Atherosclerosis of coronary artery bypass graft(s) and coronary artery of transplanted heart with angina pectoris.

When using one of these combination codes it is not necessary to use an additional code for angina pectoris. A causal relationship can be assumed in a patient with both atherosclerosis and angina pectoris, unless the documentation indicates the angina is due to something other than the atherosclerosis.

If a patient with coronary artery disease is admitted due to an acute myocardial infarction (AMI), the AMI should be sequenced before the coronary artery disease.
See Section I.C.9. Acute myocardial infarction (AMI)

c. Intraoperative and Postprocedural Cerebrovascular Accident
Medical record documentation should clearly specify the cause-and-effect relationship between the medical intervention and the cerebrovascular accident in order to assign a code for intraoperative or postprocedural cerebrovascular accident.

Proper code assignment depends on whether it was an infarction or hemorrhage and whether it occurred intraoperatively or postoperatively. If it was a cerebral hemorrhage, code assignment depends on the type of procedure performed.

d. Sequelae of Cerebrovascular Disease
1) Category I69, Sequelae of Cerebrovascular disease
Category I69 is used to indicate conditions classifiable to categories I60-I67 as the causes of sequela (neurologic deficits), themselves classified elsewhere. These "late effects" include neurologic deficits that persist after initial onset of conditions classifiable to categories I60-I67. The neurologic deficits caused by cerebrovascular disease may be present from the onset or may arise at any time after the onset of the condition classifiable to categories I60-I67.

Codes from category I69, Sequelae of cerebrovascular disease, that specify hemiplegia, hemiparesis and monoplegia identify whether the dominant or nondominant side is affected. Should the affected side be documented, but not specified as dominant or nondominant, and the classification system does not indicate a default, code selection is as follows:
- For ambidextrous patients, the default should be dominant.
- If the left side is affected, the default is non-dominant.
- If the right side is affected, the default is dominant.

2) Codes from category I69 with codes from I60-I67
Codes from category I69 may be assigned on a health care record with codes from I60-I67, if the patient has a current cerebrovascular disease and deficits from an old cerebrovascular disease.

3) Codes from category I69 and Personal history of transient ischemic attack (TIA) and cerebral infarction (Z86.73)
Codes from category I69 should not be assigned if the patient does not have neurologic deficits.
See Section I.C.21. 4. History (of) for use of personal history codes

e. Acute myocardial infarction (AMI)
1) Type 1 ST elevation myocardial infarction (STEMI) and non ST elevation myocardial infarction (NSTEMI)
The ICD-10-CM codes for type 1 acute myocardial infarction (AMI) identify the site, such as anterolateral wall or true posterior wall. Subcategories I21.0-I21.2 and code I21.3 are used for type 1 ST elevation myocardial infarction (STEMI). Code I21.4, Non-ST elevation (NSTEMI) myocardial infarction, is used for type 1 non ST elevation myocardial infarction (NSTEMI) and nontransmural MIs.

If a type 1 NSTEMI evolves to STEMI, assign the STEMI code. If a type 1 STEMI converts to NSTEMI due to thrombolytic therapy, it is still coded as STEMI.

For encounters occurring while the myocardial infarction is equal to, or less than, four weeks old, including transfers to another acute setting or a postacute setting, and the myocardial infarction meets the definition for "other diagnoses" (see Section III, Reporting Additional Diagnoses), codes from category I21 may continue to be reported. For encounters after the 4 week time frame and the patient is still receiving care related to the myocardial infarction, the appropriate aftercare code should be assigned, rather than a code from category I21. For old or healed myocardial infarctions not requiring further care, code I25.2, Old myocardial infarction, may be assigned.

2) Acute myocardial infarction, unspecified
Code I21.9, Acute myocardial infarction, unspecified, is the default for unspecified acute myocardial infarction or unspecified type. If only type 1 STEMI or transmural MI without the site is documented, assign code I21.3, ST elevation (STEMI) myocardial infarction of unspecified site.

3) AMI documented as nontransmural or subendocardial but site provided
If an AMI is documented as nontransmural or subendocardial, but the site is provided, it is still coded as a subendocardial AMI.
See Section I.C.21.3 for information on coding status post administration of tPA in a different facility within the last 24 hours.

4) Subsequent acute myocardial infarction
A code from category I22, Subsequent ST elevation (STEMI) and non ST elevation (NSTEMI) myocardial infarction, is to be used when a patient who has suffered a type 1 or unspecified AMI has a new AMI within the 4 week time frame of the initial AMI. A code from category I22 must be used in conjunction with a code from category I21. The sequencing of the I22 and I21 codes depends on the circumstances of the encounter.

Do not assign code I22 for subsequent myocardial infarctions other than type 1 or unspecified. For subsequent type 2 AMI assign only code I21.A1. For subsequent type 4 or type 5 AMI, assign only code I21.A9.

If a subsequent myocardial infarction of one type occurs within 4 weeks of a myocardial infarction of a different type, assign the appropriate codes from category I21 to identify each type. Do not assign a code from I22. Codes from category I22 should only be assigned if both the initial and subsequent myocardial infarctions are type 1 or unspecified.

5) Other Types of Myocardial Infarction
The ICD-10-CM provides codes for different types of myocardial infarction. Type 1 myocardial infarctions are assigned to codes I21.0-I21.4 **and I21.9**.

Type 2 myocardial infarction, and myocardial infarction due to demand ischemia or secondary to ischemic balance, is assigned to code I21.A1, Myocardial infarction type 2 with a code for the underlying cause. Do not assign code I24.8, Other forms of acute ischemic heart disease for the demand ischemia. Sequencing of type 2 AMI or the underlying cause is dependent on the circumstances of admission. When a type 2 AMI code is described as NSTEMI or STEMI, only assign code I21.A1. Codes I21.01-I21.4 should only be assigned for type 1 AMIs.

Acute myocardial infarctions type 3, 4a, 4b, 4c, and 5 are assigned to code I21.A9, Other myocardial infarction type.

The "Code also" and "Code first" notes should be followed related to complications, and for coding of postprocedural myocardial infarctions during or following cardiac surgery.

10. Chapter 10: Diseases of the Respiratory System (J00-J99)

a. Chronic Obstructive Pulmonary Disease [COPD] and Asthma

1) Acute exacerbation of chronic obstructive bronchitis and asthma
The codes in categories J44 and J45 distinguish between uncomplicated cases and those in acute exacerbation. An acute exacerbation is a worsening or a decompensation of a chronic condition. An acute exacerbation is not equivalent to an infection superimposed on a chronic condition, though an exacerbation may be triggered by an infection.

b. Acute Respiratory Failure

1) Acute respiratory failure as principal diagnosis
A code from subcategory J96.0, Acute respiratory failure, or subcategory J96.2, Acute and chronic respiratory failure, may be assigned as a principal diagnosis when it is the condition established after study to be chiefly responsible for occasioning the admission to the hospital, and the selection is supported by the Alphabetic Index and Tabular List. However, chapter-specific coding guidelines (such as obstetrics, poisoning, HIV, newborn) that provide sequencing direction take precedence.

2) Acute respiratory failure as secondary diagnosis
Respiratory failure may be listed as a secondary diagnosis if it occurs after admission, or if it is present on admission, but does not meet the definition of principal diagnosis.

3) Sequencing of acute respiratory failure and another acute condition
When a patient is admitted with respiratory failure and another acute condition (e.g., myocardial infarction, cerebrovascular accident, aspiration pneumonia), the principal diagnosis will not be the same in every situation. This applies whether the other acute condition is a respiratory or nonrespiratory condition. Selection of the principal diagnosis will be dependent on the circumstances of admission. If both the respiratory failure and the other acute condition are equally responsible for occasioning the admission to the hospital, and there are no chapter-specific sequencing rules, the guideline regarding two or more diagnoses that

equally meet the definition for principal diagnosis *(Section II, C.)* may be applied in these situations.

If the documentation is not clear as to whether acute respiratory failure and another condition are equally responsible for occasioning the admission, query the provider for clarification.

c. Influenza due to certain identified influenza viruses

Code only confirmed cases of influenza due to certain identified influenza viruses (category J09), and due to other identified influenza virus (category J10). This is an exception to the hospital inpatient guideline Section II, H. (Uncertain Diagnosis).

In this context, "confirmation" does not require documentation of positive laboratory testing specific for avian or other novel influenza A or other identified influenza virus. However, coding should be based on the provider's diagnostic statement that the patient has avian influenza, or other novel influenza A, for category J09, or has another particular identified strain of influenza, such as H1N1 or H3N2, but not identified as novel or variant, for category J10.

If the provider records "suspected" or "possible" or "probable" avian influenza, or novel influenza, or other identified influenza, then the appropriate influenza code from category J11, Influenza due to unidentified influenza virus, should be assigned. A code from category J09, Influenza due to certain identified influenza viruses, should not be assigned nor should a code from category J10, Influenza due to other identified influenza virus.

d. Ventilator associated Pneumonia

1) Documentation of Ventilator associated Pneumonia

As with all procedural or postprocedural complications, code assignment is based on the provider's documentation of the relationship between the condition and the procedure.

Code J95.851, Ventilator associated pneumonia, should be assigned only when the provider has documented ventilator associated pneumonia (VAP). An additional code to identify the organism (e.g., Pseudomonas aeruginosa, code B96.5) should also be assigned. Do not assign an additional code from categories J12-J18 to identify the type of pneumonia.

Code J95.851 should not be assigned for cases where the patient has pneumonia and is on a mechanical ventilator and the provider has not specifically stated that the pneumonia is ventilator-associated pneumonia. If the documentation is unclear as to whether the patient has a pneumonia that is a complication attributable to the mechanical ventilator, query the provider.

2) Ventilator associated Pneumonia Develops after Admission

A patient may be admitted with one type of pneumonia (e.g., code J13, Pneumonia due to Streptococcus pneumonia) and subsequently develop VAP. In this instance, the principal diagnosis would be the appropriate code from categories J12-J18 for the pneumonia diagnosed at the time of admission. Code J95.851, Ventilator associated pneumonia, would be assigned as an additional diagnosis when the provider has also documented the presence of ventilator associated pneumonia.

11. **Chapter 11: Diseases of the Digestive System (K00-K95)**
Reserved for future guideline expansion

12. **Chapter 12: Diseases of the Skin and Subcutaneous Tissue (L00-L99)**

a. Pressure ulcer stage codes

1) Pressure ulcer stages

Codes from category L89, Pressure ulcer, identify the site of the pressure ulcer as well as the stage of the ulcer.

The ICD-10-CM classifies pressure ulcer stages based on severity, which is designated by stages 1-4, unspecified stage and unstageable.

Assign as many codes from category L89 as needed to identify all the pressure ulcers the patient has, if applicable.

See Section I.B.14 for pressure ulcer stage documentation by clinicians other than patient's provider

2) Unstageable pressure ulcers

Assignment of the code for unstageable pressure ulcer (L89.--0) should be based on the clinical documentation. These codes are used for pressure ulcers whose stage cannot be clinically determined (e.g., the ulcer is covered by eschar or has been treated with a skin or muscle graft) and pressure ulcers that are documented as deep tissue injury but not documented as due to trauma. This code should not be confused with the codes for unspecified stage (L89.--9). When there is no documentation regarding the stage of the pressure ulcer, assign the appropriate code for unspecified stage (L89.--9).

3) Documented pressure ulcer stage

Assignment of the pressure ulcer stage code should be guided by clinical documentation of the stage or documentation of the terms found in the Alphabetic Index. For clinical terms describing the stage that are not found in the Alphabetic Index, and there is no documentation of the stage, the provider should be queried.

4) Patients admitted with pressure ulcers documented as healed

No code is assigned if the documentation states that the pressure ulcer is completely healed.

5) Patients admitted with pressure ulcers documented as healing

Pressure ulcers described as healing should be assigned the appropriate pressure ulcer stage code based on the documentation in the medical record. If the documentation does not provide information about the stage of the healing pressure ulcer, assign the appropriate code for unspecified stage.

If the documentation is unclear as to whether the patient has a current (new) pressure ulcer or if the patient is being treated for a healing pressure ulcer, query the provider.

For ulcers that were present on admission but healed at the time of discharge, assign the code for the site and stage of the pressure ulcer at the time of admission.

6) Patient admitted with pressure ulcer evolving into another stage during the admission

If a patient is admitted to an inpatient hospital with a pressure ulcer at one stage and it progresses to a higher stage, two separate codes should be assigned: one code for the site and stage of the ulcer on admission and a second code for the same ulcer site and the highest stage reported during the stay.

b. Non-Pressure Chronic Ulcers

1) Patients admitted with non-pressure ulcers documented as healed

No code is assigned if the documentation states that the non-pressure ulcer is completely healed.

2) Patients admitted with non-pressure ulcers documented as healing

Non-pressure ulcers described as healing should be assigned the appropriate non-pressure ulcer code based on the documentation in the medical record. If the documentation does not provide information about the severity of the healing non-pressure ulcer, assign the appropriate code for unspecified severity.

If the documentation is unclear as to whether the patient has a current (new) non-pressure ulcer or if the patient is being treated for a healing non-pressure ulcer, query the provider.

For ulcers that were present on admission but healed at the time of discharge, assign the code for the site and severity of the non-pressure ulcer at the time of admission.

3) Patient admitted with non-pressure ulcer that progresses to another severity level during the admission

If a patient is admitted to an inpatient hospital with a non-pressure ulcer at one severity level and it progresses to a higher severity level, two separate codes should be assigned: one code for the site and severity level of the ulcer on admission and a second code for the same ulcer site and the highest severity level reported during the stay.

See Section I.B.14 for pressure ulcer stage documentation by clinicians other than patient's provider

13. Chapter 13: Diseases of the Musculoskeletal System and Connective Tissue (M00-M99)

a. Site and laterality

Most of the codes within Chapter 13 have site and laterality designations. The site represents the bone, joint or the muscle involved. For some conditions where more than one bone, joint or muscle is usually involved, such as osteoarthritis, there is a "multiple sites" code available. For categories where no multiple site code is provided and more than one bone, joint or muscle is involved, multiple codes should be used to indicate the different sites involved.

1) Bone versus joint

For certain conditions, the bone may be affected at the upper or lower end (e.g., avascular necrosis of bone, M87, Osteoporosis, M80, M81). Though the portion of the bone affected may be at the joint, the site designation will be the bone, not the joint.

b. Acute traumatic versus chronic or recurrent musculoskeletal conditions

Many musculoskeletal conditions are a result of previous injury or trauma to a site, or are recurrent conditions. Bone, joint or muscle conditions that are the result of a healed injury are usually found in Chapter 13. Recurrent bone, joint or muscle conditions are also usually found in Chapter 13. Any current, acute injury should be coded to the appropriate injury code from Chapter 19. Chronic or recurrent conditions should generally be coded with a code from Chapter 13. If it is difficult to determine from the documentation in the record which code is best to describe a condition, query the provider.

c. Coding of Pathologic Fractures

Seventh character A is for use as long as the patient is receiving active treatment for the fracture. While the patient may be seen by a new or different provider over the course of treatment for a pathological fracture, assignment of the 7th character is based on whether the patient is undergoing active treatment and not whether the provider is seeing the patient for the first time.

Seventh character, D is to be used for encounters after the patient has completed active treatment for the fracture and is receiving routine care for the fracture during the healing or recovery phase. The other 7th characters, listed under each subcategory in the Tabular List, are to be used for subsequent encounters for treatment of problems associated with the healing, such as malunions, nonunions, and sequelae.

Care for complications of surgical treatment for fracture repairs during the healing or recovery phase should be coded with the appropriate complication codes.

See Section I.C.19. Coding of traumatic fractures

d. Osteoporosis

Osteoporosis is a systemic condition, meaning that all bones of the musculoskeletal system are affected. Therefore, site is not a component of the codes under category M81, Osteoporosis without current pathological fracture. The site codes under category M80, Osteoporosis with current pathological fracture, identify the site of the fracture, not the osteoporosis.

1) Osteoporosis without pathological fracture

Category M81, Osteoporosis without current pathological fracture, is for use for patients with osteoporosis who do not currently have a pathologic fracture due to the osteoporosis, even if they have had a fracture in the past. For patients with a history of osteoporosis fractures, status code Z87.310, Personal history of (healed) osteoporosis fracture, should follow the code from M81.

2) Osteoporosis with current pathological fracture

Category M80, Osteoporosis with current pathological fracture, is for patients who have a current pathologic fracture at the time of an encounter. The codes under M80 identify the site of the fracture. A code from category M80, not a traumatic fracture code, should be used for any patient with known osteoporosis who suffers a fracture, even if the patient had a minor fall or trauma, if that fall or trauma would not usually break a normal, healthy bone.

14. Chapter 14: Diseases of Genitourinary System (N00-N99)

a. Chronic kidney disease

1) Stages of chronic kidney disease (CKD)

The ICD-10-CM classifies CKD based on severity. The severity of CKD is designated by stages 1-5. Stage 2, code N18.2, equates to mild CKD; stage 3, code N18.3, equates to moderate CKD; and stage 4, code N18.4, equates to severe CKD. Code N18.6, End stage renal disease (ESRD), is assigned when the provider has documented end-stage-renal disease (ESRD).

If both a stage of CKD and ESRD are documented, assign code N18.6 only.

2) Chronic kidney disease and kidney transplant status

Patients who have undergone kidney transplant may still have some form of chronic kidney disease CKD because the kidney transplant may not fully restore kidney function. Therefore, the presence of CKD alone does not constitute a transplant complication. Assign the appropriate N18 code for the patient's stage of CKD and code Z94.0, Kidney transplant status. If a transplant complication such as failure or rejection or other transplant complication is documented, see section I.C.19.g for information on coding complications of a kidney transplant. If the documentation is unclear as to whether the patient has a complication of the transplant, query the provider.

3) Chronic kidney disease with other conditions

Patients with CKD may also suffer from other serious conditions, most commonly diabetes mellitus and hypertension. The sequencing of the CKD code in relationship to codes for other contributing conditions is based on the conventions in the Tabular List.

See I.C.9. Hypertensive chronic kidney disease.
See I.C.19. Chronic kidney disease and kidney transplant complications.

15. Chapter 15: Pregnancy, Childbirth, and the Puerperium (O00-O9A)

a. General Rules for Obstetric Cases

1) Codes from Chapter 15 and sequencing priority

Obstetric cases require codes from Chapter 15, codes in the range O00-O9A, Pregnancy, Childbirth, and the Puerperium. Chapter 15 codes have sequencing priority over codes from other chapters. Additional codes from other chapters may be used in conjunction with Chapter 15 codes to further specify conditions. Should the provider document that the pregnancy is incidental to the encounter, then code Z33.1, Pregnant state, incidental, should be used in place of any Chapter 15 codes. It is the provider's responsibility to state that the condition being treated is not affecting the pregnancy.

2) Chapter 15 codes used only on the maternal record

Chapter 15 codes are to be used only on the maternal record, never on the record of the newborn.

3) Final character for trimester

The majority of codes in Chapter 15 have a final character indicating the trimester of pregnancy. The timeframes for the trimesters are indicated at the beginning of the chapter. If trimester is not a component of a code it is because the condition always occurs in a specific trimester, or the concept of trimester of pregnancy is not applicable. Certain codes have characters for only certain trimesters because the condition does not occur in all trimesters, but it may occur in more than just one.

Assignment of the final character for trimester should be based on the provider's documentation of the trimester (or number of weeks) for the current admission/encounter. This applies to the assignment of trimester for pre-existing conditions as well as those that develop during or are due to the pregnancy. The provider's documentation of the number of weeks may be used to assign the appropriate code identifying the trimester.

Whenever delivery occurs during the current admission, and there is an "in childbirth" option for the obstetric complication being coded, the "in childbirth" code should be assigned.

4) Selection of trimester for inpatient admissions that encompass more than one trimester

In instances when a patient is admitted to a hospital for complications of pregnancy during one trimester and remains in the hospital into a subsequent trimester, the trimester character for the antepartum complication code should be assigned on the basis of the trimester when the complication developed, not the trimester of the discharge. If the condition developed prior to the current admission/encounter or represents a pre-existing condition, the trimester character for the trimester at the time of the admission/encounter should be assigned.

5) Unspecified trimester

Each category that includes codes for trimester has a code for "unspecified trimester." The "unspecified trimester" code should rarely be used, such as when the documentation in the record is insufficient to determine the trimester and it is not possible to obtain clarification.

6) 7th character for Fetus Identification

Where applicable, a 7th character is to be assigned for certain categories (O31, O32, O33.3 - O33.6, O35, O36, O40, O41, O60.1, O60.2, O64, and O69) to identify the fetus for which the complication code applies.

Assign 7th character "0":
- For single gestations
- When the documentation in the record is insufficient to determine the fetus affected and it is not possible to obtain clarification.
- When it is not possible to clinically determine which fetus is affected.

b. Selection of OB Principal or First-listed Diagnosis

1) Routine outpatient prenatal visits

For routine outpatient prenatal visits when no complications are present, a code from category Z34, Encounter for supervision of normal pregnancy, should be used as the first-listed diagnosis. These codes should not be used in conjunction with Chapter 15 codes.

2) Supervision of High-Risk Pregnancy

Codes from category O09, Supervision of high-risk pregnancy, are intended for use only during the prenatal period. For complications during the labor or delivery episode as a result of a high-risk pregnancy, assign the applicable complication codes from Chapter 15. If there are no complications during the labor or delivery episode, assign code O80, Encounter for full-term uncomplicated delivery.

For routine prenatal outpatient visits for patients with high-risk pregnancies, a code from category O09, Supervision of high-risk pregnancy, should be used as the first-listed diagnosis. Secondary Chapter 15 codes may be used in conjunction with these codes if appropriate.

3) Episodes when no delivery occurs

In episodes when no delivery occurs, the principal diagnosis should correspond to the principal complication of the pregnancy which necessitated the encounter. Should more than one complication exist, all of which are treated or monitored, any of the complications codes may be sequenced first.

4) When a delivery occurs

When an obstetric patient is admitted and delivers during that admission, the condition that prompted the admission should be sequenced as the principal diagnosis. If multiple conditions prompted the admission, sequence the one most related to the delivery as the principal diagnosis. A code for any complication of the delivery should be assigned as an additional diagnosis. In cases of cesarean delivery, if the patient was admitted with a condition that resulted in the performance of a cesarean procedure, that condition should be selected as the principal diagnosis. If the reason for the admission was unrelated to the condition resulting in the cesarean delivery, the condition related to the reason for the admission should be selected as the principal diagnosis.

5) Outcome of delivery

A code from category Z37, Outcome of delivery, should be included on every maternal record when a delivery has occurred. These codes are not to be used on subsequent records or on the newborn record.

c. Pre-existing conditions versus conditions due to the pregnancy

Certain categories in Chapter 15 distinguish between conditions of the mother that existed prior to pregnancy (pre-existing) and those that are a direct result of pregnancy. When assigning codes from Chapter 15, it is important to assess if a condition was pre-existing prior to pregnancy or developed during or due to the pregnancy in order to assign the correct code.

Categories that do not distinguish between pre-existing and pregnancy-related conditions may be used for either. It is acceptable to use codes specifically for the puerperium with codes complicating pregnancy and childbirth if a condition arises postpartum during the delivery encounter.

d. Pre-existing hypertension in pregnancy

Category O10, Pre-existing hypertension complicating pregnancy, childbirth and the puerperium, includes codes for hypertensive heart and hypertensive chronic kidney disease. When assigning one of the O10 codes that includes hypertensive heart disease or hypertensive chronic kidney disease, it is necessary to add a secondary code from the appropriate hypertension category to specify the type of heart failure or chronic kidney disease.

See Section I.C.9. Hypertension.

e. Fetal Conditions Affecting the Management of the Mother

1) Codes from categories O35 and O36

Codes from categories O35, Maternal care for known or suspected fetal abnormality and damage, and O36, Maternal care for other fetal problems, are assigned only when the fetal condition is actually responsible for modifying the management of the mother, i.e., by requiring diagnostic studies, additional observation, special care, or termination of pregnancy. The fact that the fetal condition exists does not justify assigning a code from this series to the mother's record.

2) In utero surgery

In cases when surgery is performed on the fetus, a diagnosis code from category O35, Maternal care for known or suspected fetal abnormality and damage, should be assigned identifying the fetal condition. Assign the appropriate procedure code for the procedure performed.

No code from Chapter 16, the perinatal codes, should be used on the mother's record to identify fetal conditions. Surgery performed in utero on a fetus is still to be coded as an obstetric encounter.

f. HIV Infection in Pregnancy, Childbirth and the Puerperium

During pregnancy, childbirth or the puerperium, a patient admitted because of an HIV-related illness should receive a principal diagnosis from subcategory O98.7-, Human immunodeficiency [HIV] disease complicating pregnancy, childbirth and the puerperium, followed by the code(s) for the HIV-related illness(es).

Patients with asymptomatic HIV infection status admitted during pregnancy, childbirth, or the puerperium should receive codes of O98.7- and Z21, Asymptomatic human immunodeficiency virus [HIV] infection status.

g. Diabetes mellitus in pregnancy

Diabetes mellitus is a significant complicating factor in pregnancy. Pregnant women who are diabetic should be assigned a code from category O24, Diabetes mellitus in pregnancy, childbirth, and the puerperium, first, followed by the appropriate diabetes code(s) (E08-E13) from Chapter 4.

h. Long-term use of insulin and oral hypoglycemics

See Section I.C.4.a.3 for information on the long term use of insulin and oral hypoglycemic.

i. Gestational (pregnancy induced) diabetes

Gestational (pregnancy induced) diabetes can occur during the second and third trimester of pregnancy in women who were not diabetic prior to pregnancy. Gestational diabetes can cause complications in the pregnancy similar to those of pre-existing diabetes mellitus. It also puts the woman at greater risk of developing diabetes after the pregnancy. Codes for gestational diabetes are in subcategory O24.4, Gestational diabetes mellitus. No other code from category O24, Diabetes mellitus in pregnancy, childbirth, and the puerperium, should be used with a code from O24.4.

The codes under subcategory O24.4 include diet controlled, insulin controlled, and controlled by oral hypoglycemic drugs. If a patient with gestational diabetes is treated with both diet and insulin, only the code for insulin-controlled is required. If a patient with gestational diabetes is treated with both diet and oral hypoglycemic medications, only the code for "controlled by oral hypoglycemic drugs" is required. Code Z79.4, Long-term (current) use of insulin or code Z79.84, Long-term (current) use of oral hypoglycemic drugs, should not be assigned with codes from subcategory O24.4.

An abnormal glucose tolerance in pregnancy is assigned a code from subcategory O99.81, Abnormal glucose complicating pregnancy, childbirth, and the puerperium.

j. Sepsis and septic shock complicating abortion, pregnancy, childbirth and the puerperium

When assigning a Chapter 15 code for sepsis complicating abortion, pregnancy, childbirth, and the puerperium, a code for the specific type of infection should be assigned as an additional diagnosis. If severe sepsis is present, a code from subcategory R65.2, Severe sepsis, and code(s) for associated organ dysfunction(s) should also be assigned as additional diagnoses.

k. Puerperal sepsis

Code O85, Puerperal sepsis, should be assigned with a secondary code to identify the causal organism (e.g., for a bacterial infection, assign a code from category B95-B96, Bacterial infections in conditions classified elsewhere). A code from category A40, Streptococcal sepsis, or A41, Other sepsis, should not be used for puerperal sepsis. If applicable, use additional codes to identify severe sepsis (R65.2-) and any associated acute organ dysfunction.

l. Alcohol, tobacco *and drug* use during pregnancy, childbirth and the puerperium

1) Alcohol use during pregnancy, childbirth and the puerperium

Codes under subcategory O99.31, Alcohol use complicating pregnancy, childbirth, and the puerperium, should be assigned for any pregnancy case when a mother uses alcohol during the pregnancy or postpartum. A secondary code from category F10, Alcohol related disorders, should also be assigned to identify manifestations of the alcohol use.

2) Tobacco use during pregnancy, childbirth and the puerperium

Codes under subcategory O99.33, Smoking (tobacco) complicating pregnancy, childbirth, and the puerperium, should be assigned for any pregnancy case when a mother uses any type of tobacco product during the pregnancy or postpartum. A secondary code from category F17, Nicotine dependence, should also be assigned to identify the type of nicotine dependence.

3) *Drug use during pregnancy, childbirth and the puerperium*

Codes under subcategory O99.32, Drug use complicating pregnancy, childbirth, and the puerperium, should be assigned for any pregnancy case when a mother uses drugs during the pregnancy or postpartum. This can involve illegal drugs, or inappropriate use or abuse of prescription drugs. Secondary code(s) from categories F11-F16 and F18F19 should also be assigned to identify manifestations of the drug use.

m. Poisoning, toxic effects, adverse effects and underdosing in a pregnant patient

A code from subcategory O9A.2, Injury, poisoning and certain other consequences of external causes complicating pregnancy, childbirth, and the puerperium, should be sequenced first, followed by the appropriate injury, poisoning, toxic effect, adverse effect or underdosing code, and then the additional code(s) that specifies the condition caused by the poisoning, toxic effect, adverse effect or underdosing.

See Section I.C.19. Adverse effects, poisoning, underdosing and toxic effects.

n. Normal Delivery, Code O80

1) Encounter for full term uncomplicated delivery

Code O80 should be assigned when a woman is admitted for a full-term normal delivery and delivers a single, healthy infant without any complications antepartum, during the delivery, or postpartum during the delivery episode. Code O80 is always a principal diagnosis. It is not to be used if any other code from Chapter 15 is needed to describe a current complication of the antenatal, delivery, or perinatal period. Additional codes from other chapters may be used with code O80 if they are not related to or are in any way complicating the pregnancy.

2) Uncomplicated delivery with resolved antepartum complication

Code O80 may be used if the patient had a complication at some point during the pregnancy, but the complication is not present at the time of the admission for delivery.

3) Outcome of delivery for O80

Z37.0, Single live birth, is the only outcome of delivery code appropriate for use with O80.

o. The Peripartum and Postpartum Periods

1) Peripartum and Postpartum periods

The postpartum period begins immediately after delivery and continues for six weeks following delivery. The peripartum period is defined as the last month of pregnancy to five months postpartum.

2) Peripartum and postpartum complication

A postpartum complication is any complication occurring within the six-week period.

3) Pregnancy-related complications after 6 week period

Chapter 15 codes may also be used to describe pregnancy-related complications after the peripartum or postpartum period if the provider documents that a condition is pregnancy related.

4) Admission for routine postpartum care following delivery outside hospital

When the mother delivers outside the hospital prior to admission and is admitted for routine postpartum care and no complications are noted, code Z39.0, Encounter for care and examination of mother immediately after delivery, should be assigned as the principal diagnosis.

5) Pregnancy associated cardiomyopathy

Pregnancy associated cardiomyopathy, code O90.3, is unique in that it may be diagnosed in the third trimester of pregnancy but may continue to progress months after delivery. For this reason, it is referred to as peripartum cardiomyopathy. Code O90.3 is only for use when the cardiomyopathy develops as a result of pregnancy in a woman who did not have pre-existing heart disease.

p. Code O94, Sequelae of complication of pregnancy, childbirth, and the puerperium

1) Code O94

Code O94, Sequelae of complication of pregnancy, childbirth, and the puerperium, is for use in those cases when an initial complication of a pregnancy develops a sequelae requiring care or treatment at a future date.

2) After the initial postpartum period

This code may be used at any time after the initial postpartum period.

3) Sequencing of Code O94

This code, like all sequela codes, is to be sequenced following the code describing the sequelae of the complication.

q. Termination of Pregnancy and Spontaneous abortions

1) Abortion with Liveborn Fetus

When an attempted termination of pregnancy results in a liveborn fetus assign code Z33.2, Encounter for elective termination of pregnancy and a code from category Z37, Outcome of Delivery.

2) Retained Products of Conception following an abortion

Subsequent encounters for retained products of conception following a spontaneous abortion or elective termination of pregnancy, without complications are assigned O03.4, Incomplete spontaneous, abortion without complication or codes O07.4, Failed attempted termination of pregnancy without complication. This advice is appropriate even when the patient was discharged previously with a discharge diagnosis of complete abortion. If the patient has a specific complication associated with the spontaneous abortion or elective termination of pregnancy in addition to retained products of conception, assign the appropriate complication in category O03 or O07 instead of code O03.4 or O07.4

3) Complications leading to abortion

Codes from Chapter 15 may be used as additional codes to identify any documented complications of the pregnancy in conjunction with codes in categories in O04, O07 and O08.

r. Abuse in a pregnant patient

For suspected or confirmed cases of abuse of a pregnant patient, a code(s) from subcategories O9A.3, Physical abuse complicating pregnancy, childbirth, and the puerperium, O9A.4, Sexual abuse complicating pregnancy, childbirth, and the puerperium, and O9A.5, Psychological abuse complicating pregnancy, childbirth, and the puerperium, should be sequenced first, followed by the appropriate codes (if applicable) to identify any associated current injury due to physical abuse, sexual abuse, and the perpetrator of abuse.

See Section I.C.19. Adult and child abuse, neglect and other maltreatment.

16. **Chapter 16: Certain Conditions Originating in the Perinatal Period (P00-P96)**
For coding and reporting purposes the perinatal period is defined as before birth through the 28th day following birth. The following guidelines are provided for reporting purposes

    a. **General Perinatal Rules**

    1) **Use of Chapter 16 Codes**
    Codes in this chapter are never for use on the maternal record. Codes from Chapter 15, the obstetric chapter, are never permitted on the newborn record. Chapter 16 codes may be used throughout the life of the patient if the condition is still present.

    2) **Principal Diagnosis for Birth Record**
    When coding the birth episode in a newborn record, assign a code from category Z38, Liveborn infants according to place of birth and type of delivery, as the principal diagnosis. A code from category Z38 is assigned only once, to a newborn at the time of birth. If a newborn is transferred to another institution, a code from category Z38 should not be used at the receiving hospital.

    A code from category Z38 is used only on the newborn record, not on the mother's record.

    3) **Use of Codes from other Chapters with Codes from Chapter 16**
    Codes from other chapters may be used with codes from Chapter 16 if the codes from the other chapters provide more specific detail. Codes for signs and symptoms may be assigned when a definitive diagnosis has not been established. If the reason for the encounter is a perinatal condition, the code from Chapter 16 should be sequenced first.

    4) **Use of Chapter 16 Codes after the Perinatal Period**
    Should a condition originate in the perinatal period, and continue throughout the life of the patient, the perinatal code should continue to be used regardless of the patient's age.

    5) **Birth process or community acquired conditions**
    If a newborn has a condition that may be either due to the birth process or community acquired and the documentation does not indicate which it is, the default is due to the birth process and the code from Chapter 16 should be used. If the condition is community-acquired, a code from Chapter 16 should not be assigned.

    6) **Code all clinically significant conditions**
    All clinically significant conditions noted on routine newborn examination should be coded. A condition is clinically significant if it requires:
    - clinical evaluation; or
    - therapeutic treatment; or
    - diagnostic procedures; or
    - extended length of hospital stay; or
    - increased nursing care and/or monitoring; or
    - has implications for future health care needs

    Note: The perinatal guidelines listed above are the same as the general coding guidelines for "additional diagnoses", except for the final point regarding implications for future health care needs. Codes should be assigned for conditions that have been specified by the provider as having implications for future health care needs.

    b. **Observation and Evaluation of Newborns for Suspected Conditions not Found**

    1) **Use of Z05 codes**
    Assign a code from category Z05, Observation and evaluation of newborns and infants for suspected conditions ruled out, to identify those instances when a healthy newborn is evaluated for a suspected condition that is determined after study not to be present. Do not use a code from category Z05 when the patient has identified signs or symptoms of a suspected problem; in such cases code the sign or symptom.

    2) **Z05 on Other than the Birth Record**
    A code from category Z05 may also be assigned as a principal or first-listed code for readmissions or encounters when the code from category Z38 code no longer applies. Codes from category Z05 are for use only for healthy newborns and infants for which no condition after study is found to be present.

    3) **Z05 on a birth record**
    A code from category Z05 is to be used as a secondary code after the code from category Z38, Liveborn infants according to place of birth and type of delivery.

    c. **Coding Additional Perinatal Diagnoses**

    1) **Assigning codes for conditions that require treatment**
    Assign codes for conditions that require treatment or further investigation, prolong the length of stay, or require resource utilization.

    2) **Codes for conditions specified as having implications for future health care needs**
    Assign codes for conditions that have been specified by the provider as having implications for future health care needs.

    Note: This guideline should not be used for adult patients.

    d. **Prematurity and Fetal Growth Retardation**
    Providers utilize different criteria in determining prematurity. A code for prematurity should not be assigned unless it is documented. Assignment of codes in categories P05, Disorders of newborn

related to slow fetal growth and fetal malnutrition, and P07, Disorders of newborn related to short gestation and low birth weight, not elsewhere classified, should be based on the recorded birth weight and estimated gestational age.

When both birth weight and gestational age are available, two codes from category P07 should be assigned, with the code for birth weight sequenced before the code for gestational age.

e. Low birth weight and immaturity status

Codes from category P07, Disorders of newborn related to short gestation and low birth weight, not elsewhere classified, are for use for a child or adult who was premature or had a low birth weight as a newborn and this is affecting the patient's current health status.

See Section I.C.21. Factors influencing health status and contact with health services, Status.

f. Bacterial Sepsis of Newborn

Category P36, Bacterial sepsis of newborn, includes congenital sepsis. If a perinate is documented as having sepsis without documentation of congenital or community acquired, the default is congenital and a code from category P36 should be assigned. If the P36 code includes the causal organism, an additional code from category B95, Streptococcus, Staphylococcus, and Enterococcus as the cause of diseases classified elsewhere, or B96, Other bacterial agents as the cause of diseases classified elsewhere, should not be assigned. If the P36 code does not include the causal organism, assign an additional code from category B96. If applicable, use additional codes to identify severe sepsis (R65.2-) and any associated acute organ dysfunction.

g. Stillbirth

Code P95, Stillbirth, is only for use in institutions that maintain separate records for stillbirths. No other code should be used with P95. Code P95 should not be used on the mother's record.

17. Chapter 17: Congenital Malformations, Deformations, and Chromosomal Abnormalities (Q00-Q99)

Assign an appropriate code(s) from categories Q00-Q99, Congenital malformations, deformations, and chromosomal abnormalities when a malformation/deformation or chromosomal abnormality is documented. A malformation/ deformation/or chromosomal abnormality may be the principal/first-listed diagnosis on a record or a secondary diagnosis.

When a malformation/deformation/or chromosomal abnormality does not have a unique code assignment, assign additional code(s) for any manifestations that may be present.

When the code assignment specifically identifies the malformation/deformation/or chromosomal abnormality, manifestations that are an inherent component of the anomaly should not be coded separately. Additional codes should be assigned for manifestations that are not an inherent component.

Codes from Chapter 17 may be used throughout the life of the patient. If a congenital malformation or deformity has been corrected, a personal history code should be used to identify the history of the malformation or deformity. Although present at birth, malformation/deformation/or chromosomal abnormality may not be identified until later in life. Whenever the condition is diagnosed by the physician, it is appropriate to assign a code from codes Q00-Q99.

For the birth admission, the appropriate code from category Z38, Liveborn infants, according to place of birth and type of delivery, should be sequenced as the principal diagnosis, followed by any congenital anomaly codes, Q00-Q99.

18. Chapter 18: Symptoms, Signs, and Abnormal Clinical and Laboratory Findings, Not Elsewhere Classified (R00-R99)

Chapter 18 includes symptoms, signs, abnormal results of clinical or other investigative procedures, and ill-defined conditions regarding which no diagnosis classifiable elsewhere is recorded. Signs and symptoms that point to a specific diagnosis have been assigned to a category in other chapters of the classification.

a. Use of symptom codes

Codes that describe symptoms and signs are acceptable for reporting purposes when a related definitive diagnosis has not been established (confirmed) by the provider.

b. Use of a symptom code with a definitive diagnosis code

Codes for signs and symptoms may be reported in addition to a related definitive diagnosis when the sign or symptom is not routinely associated with that diagnosis, such as the various signs and symptoms associated with complex syndromes. The definitive diagnosis code should be sequenced before the symptom code.

Signs or symptoms that are associated routinely with a disease process should not be assigned as additional codes, unless otherwise instructed by the classification.

c. Combination codes that include symptoms

ICD-10-CM contains a number of combination codes that identify both the definitive diagnosis and common symptoms of that diagnosis. When using one of these combination codes, an additional code should not be assigned for the symptom.

d. Repeated falls

Code R29.6, Repeated falls, is for use for encounters when a patient has recently fallen and the reason for the fall is being investigated.

Code Z91.81, History of falling, is for use when a patient has fallen in the past and is at risk for future falls. When appropriate, both codes R29.6 and Z91.81 may be assigned together.

e. Coma scale

The coma scale codes (R40.2-) can be used in conjunction with traumatic brain injury codes, acute cerebrovascular disease or sequelae of cerebrovascular disease codes. These codes are primarily for use by trauma registries, but they may be used in any setting where this information is collected. The coma scale may also be used to assess the status of the central nervous system for other non-trauma conditions, such as monitoring patients in the intensive care unit regardless of medical condition. The coma scale codes should be sequenced after the diagnosis code(s).

These codes, one from each subcategory, are needed to complete the scale. The 7th character indicates when the scale was recorded. The 7th character should match for all three codes.

At a minimum, report the initial score documented on presentation at your facility. This may be a score from the emergency medicine technician (EMT) or in the emergency department. If desired, a facility may choose to capture multiple coma scale scores.

Assign code R40.24, Glasgow coma scale, total score, when only the total score is documented in the medical record and not the individual score(s).

Do not report codes for individual or total Glasgow coma scale scores for a patient with a medically induced coma or a sedated patient.

See Section I.B.14 for coma scale documentation by clinicians other than patient's provider

f. Functional quadriplegia
GUIDELINE HAS BEEN DELETED EFFECTIVE OCTOBER 1, 2017

g. SIRS due to Non-Infectious Process
The systemic inflammatory response syndrome (SIRS) can develop as a result of certain non-infectious disease processes, such as trauma, malignant neoplasm, or pancreatitis. When SIRS is documented with a noninfectious condition, and no subsequent infection is documented, the code for the underlying condition, such as an injury, should be assigned, followed by code R65.10, Systemic inflammatory response syndrome (SIRS) of non-infectious origin without acute organ dysfunction, or code R65.11, Systemic inflammatory response syndrome (SIRS) of non-infectious origin with acute organ dysfunction. If an associated acute organ dysfunction is documented, the appropriate code(s) for the specific type of organ dysfunction(s) should be assigned in addition to code R65.11. If acute organ dysfunction is documented, but it cannot be determined if the acute organ dysfunction is associated with SIRS or due to another condition (e.g., directly due to the trauma), the provider should be queried.

h. Death NOS
Code R99, Ill-defined and unknown cause of mortality, is only for use in the very limited circumstance when a patient who has already died is brought into an emergency department or other healthcare facility and is pronounced dead upon arrival. It does not represent the discharge disposition of death.

i. NIHSS Stroke Scale
The NIH stroke scale (NIHSS) codes (R29.7- -) can be used in conjunction with acute stroke codes (I63) to identify the patient's neurological status and the severity of the stroke. The stroke scale codes should be sequenced after the acute stroke diagnosis code(s).

At a minimum, report the initial score documented. If desired, a facility may choose to capture multiple stroke scale scores.

See Section I.B.14 for NIHSS stroke scale documentation by clinicians other than patient's provider

19. **Chapter 19: Injury, Poisoning, and Certain Other Consequences of External Causes (S00-T88)**

   a. **Application of 7th Characters in Chapter 19**
   Most categories in Chapter 19 have a 7th character requirement for each applicable code. Most categories in this chapter have three 7th character values (with the exception of fractures): A, initial encounter, D, subsequent encounter and S, sequela. Categories for traumatic fractures have additional 7th character values. While the patient may be seen by a new or different provider over the course of treatment for an injury, assignment of the 7th character is based on whether the patient is undergoing active treatment and not whether the provider is seeing the patient for the first time.

   For complication codes, active treatment refers to treatment for the condition described by the code, even though it may be related to an earlier precipitating problem. For example, code T84.50XA, Infection and inflammatory reaction due to unspecified internal joint prosthesis, initial encounter, is used when active treatment is provided for the infection, even though the condition relates to the prosthetic device, implant or graft that was placed at a previous encounter.

   7th character "A", initial encounter is used for each encounter where the patient is receiving active treatment for the condition.

   7th character "D" subsequent encounter is used for encounters after the patient has completed active treatment of the condition and is receiving routine care for the condition during the healing or recovery phase.

   The aftercare Z codes should not be used for aftercare for conditions such as injuries or poisonings, where 7th characters are provided to identify subsequent care. For example, for aftercare of an injury, assign the acute injury code with the 7th character "D" (subsequent encounter).

   7th character "S", sequela, is for use for complications or conditions that arise as a direct result of a condition, such as scar formation after a burn. The scars are sequelae of the burn. When using 7th character "S", it is necessary to use both the injury code that precipitated the sequela and the code for the sequela itself. The "S" is added only to the injury code, not the sequela code. The 7th character "S" identifies the injury responsible for the sequela. The specific type of sequela (e.g., scar) is sequenced first, followed by the injury code.

   See Section I.B.10. Sequelae, (Late Effects)

b. Coding of Injuries

When coding injuries, assign separate codes for each injury unless a combination code is provided, in which case the combination code is assigned. Codes from category T07, Unspecified multiple injuries should not be assigned in the inpatient setting unless information for a more specific code is not available. Traumatic injury codes (S00-T14.9) are not to be used for normal, healing surgical wounds or to identify complications of surgical wounds.

The code for the most serious injury, as determined by the provider and the focus of treatment, is sequenced first.

1) Superficial injuries

Superficial injuries such as abrasions or contusions are not coded when associated with more severe injuries of the same site.

2) Primary injury with damage to nerves/blood vessels

When a primary injury results in minor damage to peripheral nerves or blood vessels, the primary injury is sequenced first with additional code(s) for injuries to nerves and spinal cord (such as category S04), and/or injury to blood vessels (such as category S15). When the primary injury is to the blood vessels or nerves, that injury should be sequenced first.

c. Coding of Traumatic Fractures

The principles of multiple coding of injuries should be followed in coding fractures. Fractures of specified sites are coded individually by site in accordance with both the provisions within categories S02, S12, S22, S32, S42, S49, S52, S59, S62, S72, S79, S82, S89, S92 and the level of detail furnished by medical record content.

A fracture not indicated as open or closed should be coded to closed. A fracture not indicated whether displaced or not displaced should be coded to displaced.

More specific guidelines are as follows:

1) Initial vs. Subsequent Encounter for Fractures

Traumatic fractures are coded using the appropriate 7th character for initial encounter (A, B, C) for each encounter where the patient is receiving active treatment for the fracture. The appropriate 7th character for initial encounter should also be assigned for a patient who delayed seeking treatment for the fracture or nonunion.

Fractures are coded using the appropriate 7th character for subsequent care for encounters after the patient has completed active treatment of the fracture and is receiving routine care for the fracture during the healing or recovery phase.

Care for complications of surgical treatment for fracture repairs during the healing or recovery phase should be coded with the appropriate complication codes.

Care of complications of fractures, such as malunion and nonunion, should be reported with the appropriate 7th character for subsequent care with nonunion (K, M, N,) or subsequent care with malunion (P, Q, R).

Malunion/nonunion: The appropriate 7th character for initial encounter should also be assigned for a patient who delayed seeking treatment for the fracture or nonunion.

The open fracture designations in the assignment of the 7th character for fractures of the forearm, femur and lower leg, including ankle are based on the Gustilo open fracture classification. When the Gustilo classification type is not specified for an open fracture, the 7th character for open fracture type I or II should be assigned (B, E, H, M, Q).

A code from category M80, not a traumatic fracture code, should be used for any patient with known osteoporosis who suffers a fracture, even if the patient had a minor fall or trauma, if that fall or trauma would not usually break a normal, healthy bone.

See Section I.C.13. Osteoporosis.

The aftercare Z codes should not be used for aftercare for traumatic fractures. For aftercare of a traumatic fracture, assign the acute fracture code with the appropriate 7th character.

2) Multiple fractures sequencing

Multiple fractures are sequenced in accordance with the severity of the fracture.

d. Coding of Burns and Corrosions

The ICD-10-CM makes a distinction between burns and corrosions. The burn codes are for thermal burns, except sunburns, that come from a heat source, such as a fire or hot appliance. The burn codes are also for burns resulting from electricity and radiation. Corrosions are burns due to chemicals. The guidelines are the same for burns and corrosions.

Current burns (T20-T25) are classified by depth, extent and by agent (X code). Burns are classified by depth as first degree (erythema), second degree (blistering), and third degree (full-thickness involvement). Burns of the eye and internal organs (T26-T28) are classified by site, but not by degree.

1) Sequencing of burn and related condition codes

Sequence first the code that reflects the highest degree of burn when more than one burn is present.

a. When the reason for the admission or encounter is for treatment of external multiple burns, sequence first the code that reflects the burn of the highest degree.

b. When a patient has both internal and external burns, the circumstances of admission govern the selection of the principal diagnosis or first-listed diagnosis.

c. When a patient is admitted for burn injuries and other related conditions such as smoke inhalation and/or respiratory failure, the circumstances of admission govern the selection of the principal or first-listed diagnosis.

2) Burns of the same *anatomic* site
Classify burns of the same **anatomic** site **and on the same side** but of different degrees to the subcategory identifying the highest degree recorded in the diagnosis **(e.g., for second and third degree burns of right thigh, assign only code T24.311-).**

3) Non-healing burns
Non-healing burns are coded as acute burns.
Necrosis of burned skin should be coded as a non-healed burn.

4) Infected Burn
For any documented infected burn site, use an additional code for the infection.

5) Assign separate codes for each burn site
When coding burns, assign separate codes for each burn site. Category T30, Burn and corrosion, body region unspecified is extremely vague and should rarely be used.

Codes for burns of "multiple sites" should only be assigned when the medical record documentation does not specify the individual sites.

6) Burns and Corrosions Classified According to Extent of Body Surface Involved
Assign codes from category T31, Burns classified according to extent of body surface involved, or T32, Corrosions classified according to extent of body surface involved, when the site of the burn is not specified or when there is a need for additional data. It is advisable to use category T31 as additional coding when needed to provide data for evaluating burn mortality, such as that needed by burn units. It is also advisable to use category T31 as an additional code for reporting purposes when there is mention of a third-degree burn involving 20 percent or more of the body surface.

Categories T31 and T32 are based on the classic "rule of nines" in estimating body surface involved: head and neck are assigned nine percent, each arm nine percent, each leg 18 percent, the anterior trunk 18 percent, posterior trunk 18 percent, and genitalia one percent. Providers may change these percentage assignments where necessary to accommodate infants and children who have proportionately larger heads than adults, and patients who have large buttocks, thighs, or abdomen that involve burns.

7) Encounters for treatment of sequela of burns
Encounters for the treatment of the late effects of burns or corrosions (i.e., scars or joint contractures) should be coded with a burn or corrosion code with the 7th character "S" for sequela.

8) Sequelae with a late effect code and current burn
When appropriate, both a code for a current burn or corrosion with 7th character "A" or "D" and a burn or corrosion code with 7th character "S" may be assigned on the same record (when both a current burn and sequelae of an old burn exist).

Burns and corrosions do not heal at the same rate and a current healing wound may still exist with sequela of a healed burn or corrosion.
See Section I.B.10. Sequela, (Late Effects)

9) Use of an external cause code with burns and corrosions
An external cause code should be used with burns and corrosions to identify the source and intent of the burn, as well as the place where it occurred.

e. Adverse Effects, Poisoning, Underdosing and Toxic Effects
Codes in categories T36-T65 are combination codes that include the substance that was taken as well as the intent. No additional external cause code is required for poisonings, toxic effects, adverse effects and underdosing codes.

1) Do not code directly from the Table of Drugs
Do not code directly from the Table of Drugs and Chemicals. Always refer back to the Tabular List.

2) Use as many codes as necessary to describe
Use as many codes as necessary to describe completely all drugs, medicinal or biological substances.

3) If the same code would describe the causative agent
If the same code would describe the causative agent for more than one adverse reaction, poisoning, toxic effect or underdosing, assign the code only once.

4) If two or more drugs, medicinal or biological substances
If two or more drugs, medicinal or biological substances are reported, code each individually unless a combination code is listed in the Table of Drugs and Chemicals.

5) The occurrence of drug toxicity is classified in ICD-10-CM as follows:
(a) Adverse Effect
When coding an adverse effect of a drug that has been correctly prescribed and properly administered, assign the appropriate code for the nature of the adverse effect followed by the appropriate code for the adverse effect of the drug (T36-T50). The code for the drug should have a 5th or 6th character "5" (for example T36.0X5-) Examples of the nature of an adverse effect are tachycardia, delirium, gastrointestinal hemorrhaging, vomiting, hypokalemia, hepatitis, renal failure, or respiratory failure.

(b) Poisoning
When coding a poisoning or reaction to the improper use of a medication (e.g., overdose, wrong substance given or taken in error, wrong route of administration), first assign the appropriate code from categories T36-T50. The poisoning codes have an associated intent as their 5th or 6th character (accidental, intentional self-harm, assault and undetermined). If the intent of the poisoning is unknown or unspecified, code

the intent as accidental intent. The undetermined intent is only for use if the documentation in the record specifies that the intent cannot be determined. Use additional code(s) for all manifestations of poisonings.

If there is also a diagnosis of abuse or dependence of the substance, the abuse or dependence is assigned as an additional code.

Examples of poisoning include:

    (i) Error was made in drug prescription Errors made in drug prescription or in the administration of the drug by provider, nurse, patient, or other person.

    (ii) Overdose of a drug intentionally taken If an overdose of a drug was intentionally taken or administered and resulted in drug toxicity, it would be coded as a poisoning.

    (iii) Nonprescribed drug taken with correctly prescribed and properly administered drug.
If a nonprescribed drug or medicinal agent was taken in combination with a correctly prescribed and properly administered drug, any drug toxicity or other reaction resulting from the interaction of the two drugs would be classified as a poisoning.

    (iv) Interaction of drug(s) and alcohol. When a reaction results from the interaction of a drug(s) and alcohol, this would be classified as poisoning.

See Section I.C.4. if poisoning is the result of insulin pump malfunctions.

(c) Underdosing

Underdosing refers to taking less of a medication than is prescribed by a provider or a manufacturer's instruction. **Discontinuing the use of a prescribed medication on the patient's own initiative (not directed by the patient's provider) is also classified as an underdosing.** For underdosing, assign the code from categories T36-T50 (fifth or sixth character "6").

Codes for underdosing should never be assigned as principal or first-listed codes. If a patient has a relapse or exacerbation of the medical condition for which the drug is prescribed because of the reduction in dose, then the medical condition itself should be coded.

Noncompliance (Z91.12-, Z91.13- **and Z91.14-**) or complication of care (Y63.6-Y63.9) codes are to be used with an underdosing code to indicate intent, if known.

(d) Toxic Effects

When a harmful substance is ingested or comes in contact with a person, this is classified as a toxic effect. The toxic effect codes are in categories T51-T65.

Toxic effect codes have an associated intent: accidental, intentional self-harm, assault and undetermined.

f. Adult and child abuse, neglect and other maltreatment

Sequence first the appropriate code from categories T74 (Adult and child abuse, neglect and other maltreatment, confirmed) or T76 (Adult and child abuse, neglect and other maltreatment, suspected) for abuse, neglect and other maltreatment, followed by any accompanying mental health or injury code(s).

If the documentation in the medical record states abuse or neglect it is coded as confirmed (T74.-). It is coded as suspected if it is documented as suspected (T76.-).

For cases of confirmed abuse or neglect an external cause code from the assault section (X92-Y09) should be added to identify the cause of any physical injuries. A perpetrator code (Y07) should be added when the perpetrator of the abuse is known. For suspected cases of abuse or neglect, do not report external cause or perpetrator code.

If a suspected case of abuse, neglect or mistreatment is ruled out during an encounter code Z04.71, Encounter for examination and observation following alleged physical adult abuse, ruled out, or code Z04.72, Encounter for examination and observation following alleged child physical abuse, ruled out, should be used, not a code from T76.

If a suspected case of alleged rape or sexual abuse is ruled out during an encounter code Z04.41, Encounter for examination and observation following alleged adult rape or code Z04.42, Encounter for examination and observation following alleged child rape, should be used, not a code from T76.

If a suspected case of forced sexual exploitation or forced labor exploitation is ruled out during an encounter, code Z04.81, Encounter for examination and observation of victim following forced sexual exploitation, or code Z04.82, Encounter for examination and observation of victim following forced labor exploitation, should be used, not a code from T76.

See Section I.C.15. Abuse in a pregnant patient.

g. Complications of care

1) General guidelines for complications of care

(a) Documentation of complications of care

See Section I.B.16. for information on documentation of complications of care.

2) Pain due to medical devices

Pain associated with devices, implants or grafts left in a surgical site (for example painful hip prosthesis) is assigned to the appropriate code(s) found in Chapter 19, Injury, poisoning, and certain other consequences of external causes. Specific codes for pain due to medical devices are found in the T code section of the ICD-10-CM. Use additional code(s) from category G89 to identify acute or chronic pain due to presence of the device, implant or graft (G89.18 or G89.28).

3) Transplant complications

(a) Transplant complications other than kidney

Codes under category T86, Complications of transplanted organs and tissues, are for use for both complications and rejection of transplanted organs. A transplant complication code is only assigned if the complication affects the function of the transplanted organ. Two codes are required to fully describe a transplant complication: the appropriate code from category T86 and a secondary code that identifies the complication.

Pre-existing conditions or conditions that develop after the transplant are not coded as complications unless they affect the function of the transplanted organs.

See Section I.C.21. for transplant organ removal status
See Section I.C.2. for malignant neoplasm associated with transplanted organ.

(b) Kidney transplant complications

Patients who have undergone kidney transplant may still have some form of chronic kidney disease (CKD) because the kidney transplant may not fully restore kidney function. Code T86.1- should be assigned for documented complications of a kidney transplant, such as transplant failure or rejection or other transplant complication. Code T86.1- should not be assigned for post kidney transplant patients who have chronic kidney (CKD) unless a transplant complication such as transplant failure or rejection is documented. If the documentation is unclear as to whether the patient has a complication of the transplant, query the provider.

Conditions that affect the function of the transplanted kidney, other than CKD, should be assigned a code from subcategory T86.1, Complications of transplanted organ, Kidney, and a secondary code that identifies the complication.

For patients with CKD following a kidney transplant, but who do not have a complication such as failure or rejection, *see Section I.C.14. Chronic kidney disease and kidney transplant status.*

4) Complication codes that include the external cause

As with certain other T codes, some of the complications of care codes have the external cause included in the code. The code includes the nature of the complication as well as the type of procedure that caused the complication. No external cause code indicating the type of procedure is necessary for these codes.

5) Complications of care codes within the body system chapters

Intraoperative and postprocedural complication codes are found within the body system chapters with codes specific to the organs and structures of that body system. These codes should be sequenced first, followed by a code(s) for the specific complication, if applicable.

20. Chapter 20: External Causes of Morbidity (V00-Y99)

The external causes of morbidity codes should never be sequenced as the first-listed or principal diagnosis.

External cause codes are intended to provide data for injury research and evaluation of injury prevention strategies. These codes capture how the injury or health condition happened (cause), the intent (unintentional or accidental; or intentional, such as suicide or assault), the place where the event occurred the activity of the patient at the time of the event, and the person's status (e.g., civilian, military).

There is no national requirement for mandatory ICD-10-CM external cause code reporting. Unless a provider is subject to a state-based external cause code reporting mandate or these codes are required by a particular payer, reporting of ICD-10-CM codes in Chapter 20, External Causes of Morbidity, is not required. In the absence of a mandatory reporting requirement, providers are encouraged to voluntarily report external cause codes, as they provide valuable data for injury research and evaluation of injury prevention strategies.

a. General External Cause Coding Guidelines

1) Used with any code in the range of A00.0-T88.9, Z00-Z99

An external cause code may be used with any code in the range of A00.0-T88.9, Z00-Z99, classification that represents a health condition due to an external cause. Though they are most applicable to injuries, they are also valid for use with such things as infections or diseases due to an external source, and other health conditions, such as a heart attack that occurs during strenuous physical activity.

2) External cause code used for length of treatment

Assign the external cause code, with the appropriate 7th character (initial encounter, subsequent encounter or sequela) for each encounter for which the injury or condition is being treated.

Most categories in Chapter 20 have a 7th character requirement for each applicable code. Most categories in this chapter have three 7th character values: A, initial encounter, D, subsequent encounter and S, sequela. While the patient may be seen by a new or different provider over the course of treatment for an injury or condition, assignment of the 7th character for external cause should match the 7th character of the code assigned for the associated injury or condition for the encounter.

3) Use the full range of external cause codes

Use the full range of external cause codes to completely describe the cause, the intent, the place of occurrence and if applicable, the activity of the patient at the time of the event, and the patient's status, for all injuries, and other health conditions due to an external cause.

4) Assign as many external cause codes as necessary

Assign as many external cause codes as necessary to fully explain each cause. If only one external code can be recorded, assign the code most related to the principal diagnosis.

5) The selection of the appropriate external cause code

The selection of the appropriate external cause code is guided by the Alphabetic Index of External Causes and by Inclusion and Exclusion notes in the Tabular List.

6) External cause code can never be a principal diagnosis

An external cause code can never be a principal (first-listed) diagnosis.

7) Combination external cause codes

Certain of the external cause codes are combination codes that identify sequential events that result in an injury, such as a fall which results in striking against an object. The injury may be due to either event or both. The combination external cause code used should correspond to the sequence of events regardless of which caused the most serious injury.

8) No external cause code needed in certain circumstances

No external cause code from Chapter 20 is needed if the external cause and intent are included in a code from another chapter (e.g., T36.0X1- Poisoning by penicillins, accidental (unintentional)).

b. Place of Occurrence Guideline

Codes from category Y92, Place of occurrence of the external cause, are secondary codes for use after other external cause codes to identify the location of the patient at the time of injury or other condition.

Generally, a place of occurrence code is assigned only once, at the initial encounter for treatment. However, in the rare instance that a new injury occurs during hospitalization, an additional place of occurrence code may be assigned. No 7th characters are used for Y92. Only one code from Y92 should be recorded on a medical record.

Do not use place of occurrence code Y92.9 if the place is not stated or is not applicable.

c. Activity Code

Assign a code from category Y93, Activity code, to describe the activity of the patient at the time the injury or other health condition occurred.

An activity code is used only once, at the initial encounter for treatment. Only one code from Y93 should be recorded on a medical record.

The activity codes are not applicable to poisonings, adverse effects, misadventures or sequela.

Do not assign Y93.9, Unspecified activity, if the activity is not stated.

A code from category Y93 is appropriate for use with external cause and intent codes if identifying the activity provides additional information about the event.

d. Place of Occurrence, Activity, and Status Codes Used with other External Cause Code

When applicable, place of occurrence, activity, and external cause status codes are sequenced after the main external cause code(s). Regardless of the number of external cause codes assigned, there should be only one place of occurrence code, one activity code, and one external cause status code assigned to an encounter.

e. If the Reporting Format Limits the Number of External Cause Codes

If the reporting format limits the number of external cause codes that can be used in reporting clinical data, report the code for the cause/intent most related to the principal diagnosis. If the format permits capture of additional external cause codes, the cause/intent, including medical misadventures, of the additional events should be reported rather than the codes for place, activity, or external status.

f. Multiple External Cause Coding Guidelines

More than one external cause code is required to fully describe the external cause of an illness or injury. The assignment of external cause codes should be sequenced in the following priority:

If two or more events cause separate injuries, an external cause code should be assigned for each cause. The first-listed external cause code will be selected in the following order:

External codes for child and adult abuse take priority over all other external cause codes.
See Section I.C.19., Child and Adult abuse guidelines.

External codes for terrorism events take priority over all other external cause codes except child and adult abuse.

External cause codes for cataclysmic events take priority over all other external cause codes except child and adult abuse and terrorism.

External cause codes for transport accidents take priority over all other external cause codes except cataclysmic events, child and adult abuse and terrorism.

Activity and external cause status codes are assigned following all causal (intent) external cause codes.

The first-listed external cause code should correspond to the cause of the most serious diagnosis due to an assault, accident, or self-harm, following the order of hierarchy listed above.

g. Child and Adult Abuse Guideline

Adult and child abuse, neglect and maltreatment are classified as assault. Any of the assault codes may be used to indicate the external cause of any injury resulting from the confirmed abuse.

For confirmed cases of abuse, neglect and maltreatment, when the perpetrator is known, a code from Y07, Perpetrator of maltreatment and neglect, should accompany any other assault codes.
See Section I.C.19. Adult and child abuse, neglect and other maltreatment

h. Unknown or Undetermined Intent Guideline

If the intent (accident, self-harm, assault) of the cause of an injury or other condition is unknown or unspecified, code the intent as accidental intent. All transport accident categories assume accidental intent.

1) Use of undetermined intent

External cause codes for events of undetermined intent are only for use if the documentation in the record specifies that the intent cannot be determined.

i. Sequelae (Late Effects) of External Cause Guidelines

1) Sequelae external cause codes

Sequela are reported using the external cause code with the 7th character "S" for sequela. These codes should be used with any report of a late effect or sequela resulting from a previous injury.

See Section I.B.1Ø. Sequela (Late Effects)

2) Sequela external cause code with a related current injury

A sequela external cause code should never be used with a related current nature of injury code.

3) Use of sequela external cause codes for subsequent visits

Use a late effect external cause code for subsequent visits when a late effect of the initial injury is being treated. Do not use a late effect external cause code for subsequent visits for follow-up care (e.g., to assess healing, to receive rehabilitative therapy) of the injury when no late effect of the injury has been documented.

j. Terrorism Guidelines

1) Cause of injury identified by the Federal Government (FBI) as terrorism

When the cause of an injury is identified by the Federal Government (FBI) as terrorism, the first-listed external cause code should be a code from category Y38, Terrorism. The definition of terrorism employed by the FBI is found at the inclusion note at the beginning of category Y38. Use additional code for place of occurrence (Y92.-). More than one Y38 code may be assigned if the injury is the result of more than one mechanism of terrorism.

2) Cause of an injury is suspected to be the result of terrorism

When the cause of an injury is suspected to be the result of terrorism a code from category Y38 should not be assigned. Suspected cases should be classified as assault.

3) Code Y38.9, Terrorism, secondary effects

Assign code Y38.9, Terrorism, secondary effects, for conditions occurring subsequent to the terrorist event. This code should not be assigned for conditions that are due to the initial terrorist act.

It is acceptable to assign code Y38.9 with another code from Y38 if there is an injury due to the initial terrorist event and an injury that is a subsequent result of the terrorist event.

k. External cause status

A code from category Y99, External cause status, should be assigned whenever any other external cause code is assigned for an encounter, including an Activity code, except for the events noted below. Assign a code from category Y99, External cause status, to indicate the work status of the person at the time the event occurred. The status code indicates whether the event occurred during military activity, whether a non-military person was at work, whether an individual including a student or volunteer was involved in a non-work activity at the time of the causal event.

A code from Y99, External cause status, should be assigned, when applicable, with other external cause codes, such as transport accidents and falls. The external cause status codes are not applicable to poisonings, adverse effects, misadventures or late effects.

Do not assign a code from category Y99 if no other external cause codes (cause, activity) are applicable for the encounter.

An external cause status code is used only once, at the initial encounter for treatment. Only one code from Y99 should be recorded on a medical record.

Do not assign code Y99.9, Unspecified external cause status, if the status is not stated.

21. Chapter 21: Factors Influencing Health Status and Contact with Health Services (ZØØ-Z99)

Note: The chapter-specific guidelines provide additional information about the use of Z codes for specified encounters.

a. Use of Z codes in any healthcare setting

Z codes are for use in any healthcare setting. Z codes may be used as either a first-listed (principal diagnosis code in the inpatient setting) or secondary code, depending on the circumstances of the encounter. Certain Z codes may only be used as first-listed or principal diagnosis.

b. Z Codes indicate a reason for an encounter

Z codes are not procedure codes. A corresponding procedure code must accompany a Z code to describe any procedure performed.

c. Categories of Z Codes

1) Contact/Exposure

Category Z2Ø indicates contact with, and suspected exposure to, communicable diseases. These codes are for patients who do not show any sign or symptom of a disease but are suspected to have been exposed to it by close personal contact with an infected individual or are in an area where a disease is epidemic.

Category Z77, Other contact with and (suspected) exposures hazardous to health, indicates contact with and suspected exposures hazardous to health.

Contact/exposure codes may be used as a first-listed code to explain an encounter for testing, or, more commonly, as a secondary code to identify a potential risk.

2) Inoculations and vaccinations

Code Z23 is for encounters for inoculations and vaccinations. It indicates that a patient is being seen to receive a prophylactic inoculation against a disease. Procedure codes are required to identify the actual administration of the injection and the type(s) of immunizations given. Code Z23 may be used as a secondary code if the inoculation is given as a routine part of preventive health care, such as a well-baby visit.

3) Status

Status codes indicate that a patient is either a carrier of a disease or has the sequelae or residual of a past disease or condition. This includes such things as the presence of prosthetic or mechanical devices resulting from past treatment. A status code is informative, because the status may affect the course of treatment and its outcome. A status code is distinct from a history code. The history code indicates that the patient no longer has the condition.

A status code should not be used with a diagnosis code from one of the body system chapters, if the diagnosis code includes the information provided by the status code. For example, code Z94.1, Heart transplant status, should not be used with a code from subcategory T86.2, Complications of heart transplant. The status code does not provide additional information. The complication code indicates that the patient is a heart transplant patient.

For encounters for weaning from a mechanical ventilator, assign a code from subcategory J96.1, Chronic respiratory failure, followed by code Z99.11, Dependence on respirator [ventilator] status.

The status Z codes/categories are:

Z14   Genetic carrier
Genetic carrier status indicates that a person carries a gene, associated with a particular disease, which may be passed to offspring who may develop that disease. The person does not have the disease and is not at risk of developing the disease.

Z15   Genetic susceptibility to disease Genetic susceptibility indicates that a person has a gene that increases the risk of that person developing the disease.

Codes from category Z15 should not be used as principal or first-listed codes. If the patient has the condition to which he/she is susceptible, and that condition is the reason for the encounter, the code for the current condition should be sequenced first. If the patient is being seen for follow-up after completed treatment for this condition, and the condition no longer exists, a follow-up code should be sequenced first, followed by the appropriate personal history and genetic susceptibility codes. If the purpose of the encounter is genetic counseling associated with procreative management, code Z31.5, Encounter

for genetic counseling, should be assigned as the first-listed code, followed by a code from category Z15. Additional codes should be assigned for any applicable family or personal history.

Z16   Resistance to antimicrobial drugs
This code indicates that a patient has a condition that is resistant to antimicrobial drug treatment. Sequence the infection code first.

Z17   Estrogen receptor status
Z18   Retained foreign body fragments
Z19   Hormone sensitivity malignancy status
Z21   Asymptomatic HIV infection status This code indicates that a patient has tested positive for HIV but has manifested no signs or symptoms of the disease.

Z22   Carrier of infectious disease Carrier status indicates that a person harbors the specific organisms of a disease without manifest symptoms and is capable of transmitting the infection.

Z28.3   Underimmunization status
Z33.1   Pregnant state, incidental This code is a secondary code only for use when the pregnancy is in no way complicating the reason for visit. Otherwise, a code from the obstetric chapter is required.

Z66   Do not resuscitate
This code may be used when it is documented by the provider that a patient is on do not resuscitate status at any time during the stay.

Z67   Blood type
Z68   Body mass index (BMI)
BMI codes should only be assigned when the associated diagnosis (such as overweight or obesity) meets the definition of a reportable diagnosis (see Section III, Reporting Additional Diagnoses). **Do not assign BMI codes during pregnancy.**

See Section I.B.14 for BMI documentation by clinicians other than the patient's provider.

Z74.01   Bed confinement status
Z76.82   Awaiting organ transplant status
Z78   Other specified health status
Code Z78.1, Physical restraint status, may be used when it is documented by the provider that a patient has been put in restraints during the current encounter. Please note that this code should not be reported when it is documented by the provider that a patient is temporarily restrained during a procedure.

Z79   Long-term (current) drug therapy
Codes from this category indicate a patient's continuous use of a prescribed drug (including such things as aspirin therapy) for the long-term treatment of a condition or for prophylactic use. It is not for use for patients who have addictions to drugs. This subcategory is not for use of medications for detoxification or maintenance programs to prevent withdrawal symptoms in patients with drug dependence (e.g., methadone

maintenance for opiate dependence). Assign the appropriate code for the drug dependence instead.

Assign a code from Z79 if the patient is receiving a medication for an extended period as a prophylactic measure (such as for the prevention of deep vein thrombosis) or as treatment of a chronic condition (such as arthritis) or a disease requiring a lengthy course of treatment (such as cancer). Do not assign a code from category Z79 for medication being administered for a brief period of time to treat an acute illness or injury (such as a course of antibiotics to treat acute bronchitis).

Z88	Allergy status to drugs, medicaments and biological substances Except: Z88.9, Allergy status to unspecified drugs, medicaments and biological substances status
Z89	Acquired absence of limb
Z90	Acquired absence of organs, not elsewhere classified
Z91.0-	Allergy status, other than to drugs and biological substances
Z92.82	Status post administration of tPA (rtPA) in a different facility within the last 24 hours prior to admission to a current facility Assign code Z92.82, Status post administration of tPA (rtPA) in a different facility within the last 24 hours prior to admission to current facility, as a secondary diagnosis when a patient is received by transfer into a facility and documentation indicates they were administered tissue plasminogen activator (tPA) within the last 24 hours prior to admission to the current facility. This guideline applies even if the patient is still receiving the tPA at the time they are received into the current facility. The appropriate code for the condition for which the tPA was administered (such as cerebrovascular disease or myocardial infarction) should be assigned first. Code Z92.82 is only applicable to the receiving facility record and not to the transferring facility record.
Z93	Artificial opening status
Z94	Transplanted organ and tissue status
Z95	Presence of cardiac and vascular implants and grafts
Z96	Presence of other functional implants
Z97	Presence of other devices
Z98	Other postprocedural states

Assign code Z98.85, Transplanted organ removal status, to indicate that a transplanted organ has been previously removed. This code should not be assigned for the encounter in which the transplanted organ is removed. The complication necessitating removal of the transplant organ should be assigned for that encounter.

See Section I.C.19. for information on the coding of organ transplant complications.

Z99	Dependence on enabling machines and devices, not elsewhere classified

Note: Categories Z89-Z90 and Z93-Z99 are for use only if there are no complications or malfunctions of the organ or tissue replaced, the amputation site or the equipment on which the patient is dependent.

4) History (of)

There are two types of history Z codes, personal and family. Personal history codes explain a patient's past medical condition that no longer exists and is not receiving any treatment, but that has the potential for recurrence, and therefore may require continued monitoring.

Family history codes are for use when a patient has a family member(s) who has had a particular disease that causes the patient to be at higher risk of also contracting the disease.

Personal history codes may be used in conjunction with follow-up codes and family history codes may be used in conjunction with screening codes to explain the need for a test or procedure. History codes are also acceptable on any medical record regardless of the reason for visit. A history of an illness, even if no longer present, is important information that may alter the type of treatment ordered.

The history Z code categories are:

Z80	Family history of primary malignant neoplasm
Z81	Family history of mental and behavioral disorders
Z82	Family history of certain disabilities and chronic diseases (leading to disablement)
Z83	Family history of other specific disorders
Z84	Family history of other conditions
Z85	Personal history of malignant neoplasm
Z86	Personal history of certain other diseases
Z87	Personal history of other diseases and conditions
Z91.4-	Personal history of psychological trauma, not elsewhere classified
Z91.5	Personal history of self-harm
Z91.81	History of falling
Z91.82	Personal history of military deployment
Z92	Personal history of medical treatment Except: Z92.0, Personal history of contraception Except: Z92.82, Status post administration of tPA (rtPA) in a different facility within the last 24 hours prior to admission to a current facility

5) Screening

Screening is the testing for disease or disease precursors in seemingly well individuals so that early detection and treatment can be provided for those who test positive for the disease (e.g., screening mammogram).

The testing of a person to rule out or confirm a suspected diagnosis because the patient has some sign or symptom is a diagnostic examination, not a screening. In these cases, the sign or symptom is used to explain the reason for the test.

A screening code may be a first-listed code if the reason for the visit is specifically the screening exam. It may also be used as an additional code if the screening is done during an office visit for other health problems. A screening code is not necessary if the screening is inherent to a routine examination, such as a pap smear done during a routine pelvic examination.

Should a condition be discovered during the screening then the code for the condition may be assigned as an additional diagnosis.

The Z code indicates that a screening exam is planned. A procedure code is required to confirm that the screening was performed.

The screening Z codes/categories:

Z11   Encounter for screening for infectious and parasitic diseases

Z12   Encounter for screening for malignant neoplasms

Z13   Encounter for screening for other diseases and disorders Except: Z13.9, Encounter for screening, unspecified

Z36   Encounter for antenatal screening for mother

6) Observation

There are three observation Z code categories. They are for use in very limited circumstances when a person is being observed for a suspected condition that is ruled out. The observation codes are not for use if an injury or illness or any signs or symptoms related to the suspected condition are present. In such cases the diagnosis/symptom code is used with the corresponding external cause code.

The observation codes are to be used as principal diagnosis only. The only exception to this is when the principal diagnosis is required to be a code from category Z38, Liveborn infants according to place of birth and type of delivery. Then a code from category Z05, Encounter for observation and evaluation of newborn for suspected diseases and conditions ruled out, is sequenced after the Z38 code. Additional codes may be used in addition to the observation code, but only if they are unrelated to the suspected condition being observed.

Codes from subcategory Z03.7 Encounter for suspected maternal and fetal conditions ruled out, may either be used as a first-listed or as an additional code assignment depending on the case. They are for use in very limited circumstances on a maternal record when an encounter is for a suspected maternal or fetal condition that is ruled out during that encounter (for example, a maternal or fetal condition may be suspected due to an abnormal test result). These codes should not be used when the condition is confirmed. In those cases, the confirmed condition should be coded. In addition, these codes are not for use if an illness or any signs or symptoms related to the suspected condition or problem are present. In such cases the diagnosis/symptom code is used.

Additional codes may be used in addition to the code from subcategory Z03.7, but only if they are unrelated to the suspected condition being evaluated.

Codes from subcategory Z03.7 may not be used for encounters for antenatal screening of mother. *See Section I.C.21. Screening.*

For encounters for suspected fetal condition that are inconclusive following testing and evaluation, assign the appropriate code from category O35, O36, O40 or O41.

The observation Z code categories:

Z03   Encounter for medical observation for suspected diseases and conditions ruled out

Z04   Encounter for examination and observation for other reasons Except: Z04.9, Encounter for examination and observation for unspecified reason

Z05   Encounter for observation and evaluation of newborn for suspected diseases and conditions ruled out

7) Aftercare

Aftercare visit codes cover situations when the initial treatment of a disease has been performed and the patient requires continued care during the healing or recovery phase, or for the long-term consequences of the disease. The aftercare Z code should not be used if treatment is directed at a current, acute disease. The diagnosis code is to be used in these cases.

Exceptions to this rule are codes Z51.0, Encounter for antineoplastic radiation therapy, and codes from subcategory Z51.1, Encounter for antineoplastic chemotherapy and immunotherapy. These codes are to be first-listed, followed by the diagnosis code when a patient's encounter is solely to receive radiation therapy, chemotherapy, or immunotherapy for the treatment of a neoplasm. If the reason for the encounter is more than one type of antineoplastic therapy, code Z51.0 and a code from subcategory Z51.1 may be assigned together, in which case one of these codes would be reported as a secondary diagnosis.

The aftercare Z codes should also not be used for aftercare for injuries. For aftercare of an injury, assign the acute injury code with the appropriate 7th character (for subsequent encounter).

The aftercare codes are generally first-listed to explain the specific reason for the encounter. An aftercare code may be used as an additional code when some type of aftercare is provided in addition to the reason for admission and no diagnosis code is applicable. An example of this would be the closure of a colostomy during an encounter for treatment of another condition.

Aftercare codes should be used in conjunction with other aftercare codes or diagnosis codes to provide better detail on the specifics of an aftercare encounter visit, unless otherwise directed by the classification. Should a patient receive multiple types of antineoplastic therapy during the same encounter, code Z51.Ø, Encounter for antineoplastic radiation therapy, and codes from subcategory Z51.1, Encounter for antineoplastic chemotherapy and immunotherapy, may be used together on a record. The sequencing of multiple aftercare codes depends on the circumstances of the encounter.

Certain aftercare Z code categories need a secondary diagnosis code to describe the resolving condition or sequelae. For others, the condition is included in the code title.

Additional Z code aftercare category terms include fitting and adjustment, and attention to artificial openings.

Status Z codes may be used with aftercare Z codes to indicate the nature of the aftercare. For example code Z95.1, Presence of aortocoronary bypass graft, may be used with code Z48.812, Encounter for surgical aftercare following surgery on the circulatory system, to indicate the surgery for which the aftercare is being performed. A status code should not be used when the aftercare code indicates the type of status, such as using Z43.Ø, Encounter for attention to tracheostomy, with Z93.Ø, Tracheostomy status.

The aftercare Z category/codes:

Z42   Encounter for plastic and reconstructive surgery following medical procedure or healed injury

Z43   Encounter for attention to artificial openings

Z44   Encounter for fitting and adjustment of external prosthetic device

Z45   Encounter for adjustment and management of implanted device

Z46   Encounter for fitting and adjustment of other devices

Z47   Orthopedic aftercare

Z48   Encounter for other postprocedural aftercare

Z49   Encounter for care involving renal dialysis

Z51   Encounter for other aftercare and medical care

8) Follow-up

The follow-up codes are used to explain continuing surveillance following completed treatment of a disease, condition, or injury. They imply that the condition has been fully treated and no longer exists. They should not be confused with aftercare codes, or injury codes with a 7th character for subsequent encounter, that explain ongoing care of a healing condition or its sequelae. Follow-up codes may be used in conjunction with history codes to provide the full picture of the healed condition and its treatment. The follow-up code is sequenced first, followed by the history code.

A follow-up code may be used to explain multiple visits. Should a condition be found to have recurred on the follow-up visit, then the diagnosis code for the condition should be assigned in place of the follow-up code.

The follow-up Z code categories:

ZØ8   Encounter for follow-up examination after completed treatment for malignant neoplasm

ZØ9   Encounter for follow-up examination after completed treatment for conditions other than malignant neoplasm

Z39   Encounter for maternal postpartum care and examination

9) Donor

Codes in category Z52, Donors of organs and tissues, are used for living individuals who are donating blood or other body tissue. These codes are only for individuals donating for others, not for self-donations. They are not used to identify cadaveric donations.

1Ø) Counseling

Counseling Z codes are used when a patient or family member receives assistance in the aftermath of an illness or injury, or when support is required in coping with family or social problems.

The counseling Z codes/categories:

Z3Ø.Ø-   Encounter for general counseling and advice on contraception

Z31.5   Encounter for procreative genetic counseling

Z31.6-   Encounter for general counseling and advice on procreation

Z32.2   Encounter for childbirth instruction

Z32.3   Encounter for childcare instruction

Z69   Encounter for mental health services for victim and perpetrator of abuse

Z7Ø   Counseling related to sexual attitude, behavior and orientation

Z71   Persons encountering health services for other counseling and medical advice, not elsewhere classified

Z76.81   Expectant mother prebirth pediatrician visit

11) Encounters for Obstetrical and Reproductive Services

See Section I.C.15. Pregnancy, childbirth, and the puerperium, for further instruction on the use of these codes.

Z codes for pregnancy are for use in those circumstances when none of the problems or complications included in the codes from the Obstetrics chapter exist (a routine prenatal visit or postpartum care). Codes in category Z34, Encounter for supervision of normal pregnancy, are always first listed and are not to be used with any other code from the OB chapter.

Codes in category Z3A, Weeks of gestation, may be assigned to provide additional information about the pregnancy. Category Z3A codes should not be assigned for pregnancies with abortive outcomes (categories OØØ-OØ8), elective termination of pregnancy (code Z33.2), nor for postpartum conditions, as category Z3A is not applicable to these conditions. The date of the admission should be used to determine weeks of gestation for inpatient admissions that encompass more than one gestational week.

The outcome of delivery, category Z37, should be included on all maternal delivery records. It is always a secondary code. Codes in category Z37 should not be used on the newborn record.

Z codes for family planning (contraceptive) or procreative management and counseling should be included on an obstetric record either during the pregnancy or the postpartum stage, if applicable.

Z codes/categories for obstetrical and reproductive services:

Z30	Encounter for contraceptive management
Z31	Encounter for procreative management
Z32.2	Encounter for childbirth instruction
Z32.3	Encounter for childcare instruction
Z33	Pregnant state
Z34	Encounter for supervision of normal pregnancy
Z36	Encounter for antenatal screening of mother
Z3A	Weeks of gestation
Z37	Outcome of delivery
Z39	Encounter for maternal postpartum care and examination
Z76.81	Expectant mother prebirth pediatrician visit

12) Newborns and Infants

See Section I.C.16. Newborn (Perinatal) guidelines, for further instruction on the use of these codes.

Newborn Z codes/categories:

Z76.1	Encounter for health supervision and care of foundling
Z00.1-	Encounter for routine child health examination
Z38	Liveborn infants according to place of birth and type of delivery

13) Routine and administrative examinations

The Z codes allow for the description of encounters for routine examinations, such as, a general check-up, or, examinations for administrative purposes, such as, a pre-employment physical. The codes are not to be used if the examination is for diagnosis of a suspected condition or for treatment purposes. In such cases the diagnosis code is used. During a routine exam, should a diagnosis or condition be discovered, it should be coded as an additional code. Pre-existing and chronic conditions and history codes may also be included as additional codes as long as the examination is for administrative purposes and not focused on any particular condition.

Some of the codes for routine health examinations distinguish between "with" and "without" abnormal findings. Code assignment depends on the information that is known at the time the encounter is being coded. For example, if no abnormal findings were found during the examination, but the encounter is being coded before test results are back, it is acceptable to assign the code for "without abnormal findings." When assigning a code for "with abnormal findings," additional code(s) should be assigned to identify the specific abnormal finding(s).

Pre-operative examination and pre-procedural laboratory examination Z codes are for use only in those situations when a patient is being cleared for a procedure or surgery and no treatment is given.

The Z codes/categories for routine and administrative examinations:

Z00	Encounter for general examination without complaint, suspected or reported diagnosis
Z01	Encounter for other special examination without complaint, suspected or reported diagnosis
Z02	Encounter for administrative examination Except: Z02.9, Encounter for administrative examinations, unspecified
Z32.0-	Encounter for pregnancy test

14) Miscellaneous Z codes

The miscellaneous Z codes capture a number of other health care encounters that do not fall into one of the other categories. Certain of these codes identify the reason for the encounter; others are for use as additional codes that provide useful information on circumstances that may affect a patient's care and treatment.

Prophylactic Organ Removal

For encounters specifically for prophylactic removal of an organ (such as prophylactic removal of breasts due to a genetic susceptibility to cancer or a family history of cancer), the principal or first-listed code should be a code from category Z40, Encounter for prophylactic surgery, followed by the appropriate codes to identify the associated risk factor (such as genetic susceptibility or family history).

If the patient has a malignancy of one site and is having prophylactic removal at another site to prevent either a new primary malignancy or metastatic disease, a code for the malignancy should also be assigned in addition to a code from subcategory Z40.0, Encounter for prophylactic surgery for risk factors related to malignant neoplasms. A Z40.0 code should not be assigned if the patient is having organ removal for treatment of a malignancy, such as the removal of the testes for the treatment of prostate cancer.

Miscellaneous Z codes/categories:

Z28	Immunization not carried out Except: Z28.3, Underimmunization status
Z29	Encounter for other prophylactic measures
Z40	Encounter for prophylactic surgery
Z41	Encounter for procedures for purposes other than remedying health state Except: Z41.9, Encounter for procedure for purposes other than remedying health state, unspecified

GUIDELINES (ICD-10-CM)

Z53   Persons encountering health services for specific procedures and treatment, not carried out

Z55   Problems related to education and literacy

Z56   Problems related to employment and unemployment

Z57   Occupational exposure to risk factors

Z58   Problems related to physical environment

Z59   Problems related to housing and economic circumstances

Z60   Problems related to social environment

Z62   Problems related to upbringing

Z63   Other problems related to primary support group, including family circumstances

Z64   Problems related to certain psychosocial circumstances

Z65   Problems related to other psychosocial circumstances

Z72   Problems related to lifestyle
Note: These codes should be assigned only when the documentation specifies that the patient has an associated problem

Z73   Problems related to life management difficulty

Z74   Problems related to care provider dependency Except: Z74.01, Bed confinement status

Z75   Problems related to medical facilities and other health care

Z76.0   Encounter for issue of repeat prescription

Z76.3   Healthy person accompanying sick person

Z76.4   Other boarder to healthcare facility

Z76.5   Malingerer [conscious simulation]

Z91.1-   Patient's noncompliance with medical treatment and regimen

Z91.83   Wandering in diseases classified elsewhere

Z91.84-   Oral health risk factors

Z91.89   Other specified personal risk factors, not elsewhere classified

See Section I.B.14 for Z55-Z65 Persons with potential health hazards related to socioeconomic and psychosocial circumstances, documentation by clinicians other than the patient's provider

15) Nonspecific Z codes

Certain Z codes are so non-specific, or potentially redundant with other codes in the classification, that there can be little justification for their use in the inpatient setting. Their use in the outpatient setting should be limited to those instances when there is no further documentation to permit more precise coding. Otherwise, any sign or symptom or any other reason for visit that is captured in another code should be used.

Nonspecific Z codes/categories:

Z02.9   Encounter for administrative examinations, unspecified

Z04.9   Encounter for examination and observation for unspecified reason

Z13.9   Encounter for screening, unspecified

Z41.9   Encounter for procedure for purposes other than remedying health state, unspecified

Z52.9   Donor of unspecified organ or tissue

Z86.59   Personal history of other mental and behavioral disorders

Z88.9   Allergy status to unspecified drugs, medicaments and biological substances status

Z92.0   Personal history of contraception

16) Z Codes That May Only be Principal/First-Listed Diagnosis

The following Z codes/categories may only be reported as the principal/first-listed diagnosis, except when there are multiple encounters on the same day and the medical records for the encounters are combined:

Z00   Encounter for general examination without complaint, suspected or reported diagnosis
Except: Z00.6

Z01   Encounter for other special examination without complaint, suspected or reported diagnosis

Z02   Encounter for administrative examination

Z03   Encounter for medical observation for suspected diseases and conditions ruled out

Z04   Encounter for examination and observation for other reasons

Z33.2   Encounter for elective termination of pregnancy

Z31.81   Encounter for male factor infertility in female patient

Z31.83   Encounter for assisted reproductive fertility procedure cycle

Z31.84   Encounter for fertility preservation procedure

Z34   Encounter for supervision of normal pregnancy

Z39   Encounter for maternal postpartum care and examination

Z38   Liveborn infants according to place of birth and type of delivery

Z40   Encounter for prophylactic surgery

Z42   Encounter for plastic and reconstructive surgery following medical procedure or healed injury

Z51.0   Encounter for antineoplastic radiation therapy

Z51.1-   Encounter for antineoplastic chemotherapy and immunotherapy

Z52   Donors of organs and tissues Except: Z52.9, Donor of unspecified organ or tissue

Z76.1   Encounter for health supervision and care of foundling

Z76.2   Encounter for health supervision and care of other healthy infant and child

Z99.12   Encounter for respirator [ventilator] dependence during power failure

Section II. Selection of Principal Diagnosis

The circumstances of inpatient admission always govern the selection of principal diagnosis. The principal diagnosis is defined in the Uniform Hospital Discharge Data Set (UHDDS) as "that condition established after study to be chiefly responsible for occasioning the admission of the patient to the hospital for care."

The UHDDS definitions are used by hospitals to report inpatient data elements in a standardized manner. These data elements and their definitions can be found in the July 31, 1985, Federal Register (Vol. 50, No, 147), pp. 31038-40.

Since that time the application of the UHDDS definitions has been expanded to include all nonoutpatient settings (acute care, short term, long-term care and psychiatric hospitals; home health agencies; rehab facilities; nursing homes, etc). The UHDDS definitions also apply to hospice services (all levels of care).

In determining principal diagnosis, coding conventions in the ICD-10-CM, the Tabular List and Alphabetic Index take precedence over these official coding guidelines.

(See Section I.A., Conventions for the ICD-10-CM)

The importance of consistent, complete documentation in the medical record cannot be overemphasized. Without such documentation the application of all coding guidelines is a difficult, if not impossible, task.

A. Codes for symptoms, signs, and ill-defined conditions

Codes for symptoms, signs, and ill-defined conditions from Chapter 18 are not to be used as principal diagnosis when a related definitive diagnosis has been established.

B. Two or more interrelated conditions, each potentially meeting the definition for principal diagnosis.

When there are two or more interrelated conditions (such as diseases in the same ICD-10-CM chapter or manifestations characteristically associated with a certain disease) potentially meeting the definition of principal diagnosis, either condition may be sequenced first, unless the circumstances of the admission, the therapy provided, the Tabular List, or the Alphabetic Index indicate otherwise.

C. Two or more diagnoses that equally meet the definition for principal diagnosis

In the unusual instance when two or more diagnoses equally meet the criteria for principal diagnosis as determined by the circumstances of admission, diagnostic workup and/or therapy provided, and the Alphabetic Index, Tabular List, or another coding guidelines does not provide sequencing direction, any one of the diagnoses may be sequenced first.

D. Two or more comparative or contrasting conditions.

In those rare instances when two or more contrasting or comparative diagnoses are documented as "either/or" (or similar terminology), they are coded as if the diagnoses were confirmed and the diagnoses are sequenced according to the circumstances of the admission. If no further determination can be made as to which diagnosis should be principal, either diagnosis may be sequenced first.

E. A symptom(s) followed by contrasting/ comparative diagnoses

GUIDELINE HAS BEEN DELETED EFFECTIVE OCTOBER 1, 2014

F. Original treatment plan not carried out

Sequence as the principal diagnosis the condition, which after study occasioned the admission to the hospital, even though treatment may not have been carried out due to unforeseen circumstances.

G. Complications of surgery and other medical care

When the admission is for treatment of a complication resulting from surgery or other medical care, the complication code is sequenced as the principal diagnosis. If the complication is classified to the T80-T88 series and the code lacks the necessary specificity in describing the complication, an additional code for the specific complication should be assigned.

H. Uncertain Diagnosis

If the diagnosis documented at the time of discharge is qualified as "probable", "suspected", "likely", "questionable", "possible", or "still to be ruled out", or other similar terms indicating uncertainty, code the condition as if it existed or was established. The bases for these guidelines are the diagnostic workup, arrangements for further workup or observation, and initial therapeutic approach that correspond most closely with the established diagnosis.

Note: This guideline is applicable only to inpatient admissions to short-term, acute, long-term care and psychiatric hospitals.

I. Admission from Observation Unit

1. Admission Following Medical Observation

When a patient is admitted to an observation unit for a medical condition, which either worsens or does not improve, and is subsequently admitted as an inpatient of the same hospital for this same medical condition, the principal diagnosis would be the medical condition which led to the hospital admission.

2. Admission Following Post-Operative Observation

When a patient is admitted to an observation unit to monitor a condition (or complication) that develops following outpatient surgery, and then is subsequently admitted as an inpatient of the same hospital, hospitals should apply the Uniform Hospital Discharge Data Set (UHDDS) definition of principal diagnosis as "that condition established after study to be chiefly responsible for occasioning the admission of the patient to the hospital for care."

J. Admission from Outpatient Surgery

When a patient receives surgery in the hospital's outpatient surgery department and is subsequently admitted for continuing inpatient care at the same hospital, the following guidelines should be followed in selecting the principal diagnosis for the inpatient admission:

- If the reason for the inpatient admission is a complication, assign the complication as the principal diagnosis.
- If no complication, or other condition, is documented as the reason for the inpatient admission, assign the reason for the outpatient surgery as the principal diagnosis.
- If the reason for the inpatient admission is another condition unrelated to the surgery, assign the unrelated condition as the principal diagnosis.

K. Admissions/Encounters for Rehabilitation

When the purpose for the admission/encounter is rehabilitation, sequence first the code for the condition for which the service is being performed. For example, for an admission/encounter for rehabilitation for right-sided dominant hemiplegia following a cerebrovascular infarction, report code I69.351, Hemiplegia and hemiparesis following cerebral infarction affecting right dominant side, as the first-listed or principal diagnosis.

If the condition for which the rehabilitation service is no longer present, report the appropriate aftercare code as the first-listed or principal diagnosis, unless the rehabilitation service is being provided following an injury. For rehabilitation services following active treatment of an injury, assign the injury code with the appropriate seventh character for subsequent encounter as the first-listed or principal diagnosis. For example, if a patient with severe degenerative osteoarthritis of the hip, underwent hip replacement and the current encounter/admission is for rehabilitation, report code Z47.1, Aftercare following joint replacement surgery, as the first-listed or principal diagnosis. If the patient requires rehabilitation post hip replacement for right intertrochanteric femur fracture, report code S72.141D, Displaced intertrochanteric fracture of right femur, subsequent encounter for closed fracture with routine healing, as the first-listed or principal diagnosis.

See Section I.C.21.c.7, Factors influencing health states and contact with health services, Aftercare.

See Section I.C.19.a for additional information about the use of 7th characters for injury codes.

Section III. Reporting Additional Diagnoses

GENERAL RULES FOR OTHER (ADDITIONAL) DIAGNOSES

For reporting purposes the definition for "other diagnoses" is interpreted as additional conditions that affect patient care in terms of requiring:

    clinical evaluation; or
    therapeutic treatment; or
    diagnostic procedures; or
    extended length of hospital stay; or
    increased nursing care and/or monitoring.

The UHDDS item #11-b defines Other Diagnoses as "all conditions that coexist at the time of admission, that develop subsequently, or that affect the treatment received and/or the length of stay. Diagnoses that relate to an earlier episode which have no bearing on the current hospital stay are to be excluded." UHDDS definitions apply to inpatients in acute care, short-term, long term care and psychiatric hospital setting. The UHDDS definitions are used by acute care short-term hospitals to report inpatient data elements in a standardized manner. These data elements and their definitions can be found in the July 31, 1985, Federal Register (Vol. 50, No, 147), pp. 31038-40.

Since that time the application of the UHDDS definitions has been expanded to include all nonoutpatient settings (acute care, short term, long term care and psychiatric hospitals; home health agencies; rehab facilities; nursing homes, etc). The UHDDS definitions also apply to hospice services (all levels of care).

The following guidelines are to be applied in designating "other diagnoses" when neither the Alphabetic Index nor the Tabular List in ICD-10-CM provide direction. The listing of the diagnoses in the patient record is the responsibility of the attending provider.

A. Previous conditions

If the provider has included a diagnosis in the final diagnostic statement, such as the discharge summary or the face sheet, it should ordinarily be coded. Some providers include in the diagnostic statement resolved conditions or diagnoses and status-post procedures from previous admission that have no bearing on the current stay. Such conditions are not to be reported and are coded only if required by hospital policy.

However, history codes (categories Z80-Z87) may be used as secondary codes if the historical condition or family history has an impact on current care or influences treatment.

B. Abnormal findings

Abnormal findings (laboratory, x-ray, pathologic, and other diagnostic results) are not coded and reported unless the provider indicates their clinical significance. If the findings are outside the normal range and the attending provider has ordered other tests to evaluate the condition or prescribed treatment, it is appropriate to ask the provider whether the abnormal finding should be added.

Please note: This differs from the coding practices in the outpatient setting for coding encounters for diagnostic tests that have been interpreted by a provider.

C. Uncertain Diagnosis

If the diagnosis documented at the time of discharge is qualified as "probable", "suspected", "likely", "questionable", "possible", or "still to be ruled out" or other similar terms indicating uncertainty, code the condition as if it existed or was established. The bases for these guidelines are the diagnostic workup, arrangements for further workup or observation, and initial therapeutic approach that correspond most closely with the established diagnosis.

Note: This guideline is applicable only to inpatient admissions to short-term, acute, long-term care and psychiatric hospitals.

Section IV. Diagnostic Coding and Reporting Guidelines for Outpatient Services

These coding guidelines for outpatient diagnoses have been approved for use by hospitals/ providers in coding and reporting hospital-based outpatient services and provider-based office visits. Guidelines in Section I, Conventions, general coding guidelines and chapter-specific guidelines, should also be applied for outpatient services and office visits.

Information about the use of certain abbreviations, punctuation, symbols, and other conventions used in the ICD-10-CM Tabular List (code numbers and titles), can be found in Section IA of these guidelines, under "Conventions Used in the Tabular List." Section I.B. contains general guidelines that apply to the entire classification. Section I.C. contains chapter-specific guidelines that correspond to the chapters as they are arranged in the classification. Information about the correct sequence to use in finding a code is also described in Section I.

The terms encounter and visit are often used interchangeably in describing outpatient service contacts and, therefore, appear together in these guidelines without distinguishing one from the other.

Though the conventions and general guidelines apply to all settings, coding guidelines for outpatient and provider reporting of diagnoses will vary in a number of instances from those for inpatient diagnoses, recognizing that:

The Uniform Hospital Discharge Data Set (UHDDS) definition of principal diagnosis does not apply to hospital-based outpatient services and provider-based office visits.

Coding guidelines for inconclusive diagnoses (probable, suspected, rule out, etc.) were developed for inpatient reporting and do not apply to outpatients.

A. Selection of first-listed condition

In the outpatient setting, the term first-listed diagnosis is used in lieu of principal diagnosis.

In determining the first-listed diagnosis the coding conventions of ICD-10-CM, as well as the general and disease specific guidelines take precedence over the outpatient guidelines.

Diagnoses often are not established at the time of the initial encounter/visit. It may take two or more visits before the diagnosis is confirmed.

The most critical rule involves beginning the search for the correct code assignment through the Alphabetic Index. Never begin searching initially in the Tabular List as this will lead to coding errors.

1. Outpatient Surgery

When a patient presents for outpatient surgery (same day surgery), code the reason for the surgery as the first-listed diagnosis (reason for the encounter), even if the surgery is not performed due to a contraindication.

2. Observation Stay

When a patient is admitted for observation for a medical condition, assign a code for the medical condition as the first-listed diagnosis.

When a patient presents for outpatient surgery and develops complications requiring admission to observation, code the reason for the surgery as the first reported diagnosis (reason for the encounter), followed by codes for the complications as secondary diagnoses.

B. Codes from A00.0 through T88.9, Z00-Z99

The appropriate code(s) from A00.0 through T88.9, Z00-Z99 must be used to identify diagnoses, symptoms, conditions, problems, complaints, or other reason(s) for the encounter/visit.

C. Accurate reporting of ICD-10-CM diagnosis codes

For accurate reporting of ICD-10-CM diagnosis codes, the documentation should describe the patient's condition, using terminology which includes specific diagnoses as well as symptoms, problems, or reasons for the encounter. There are ICD-10-CM codes to describe all of these.

D. Codes that describe symptoms and signs

Codes that describe symptoms and signs, as opposed to diagnoses, are acceptable for reporting purposes when a diagnosis has not been established (confirmed) by the provider. Chapter 18 of ICD-10-CM, Symptoms, Signs, and Abnormal Clinical and Laboratory Findings Not Elsewhere Classified (codes R00-R99) contains many, but not all codes for symptoms.

E. Encounters for circumstances other than a disease or injury

ICD-10-CM provides codes to deal with encounters for circumstances other than a disease or injury. The Factors Influencing Health Status and Contact with Health Services codes (Z00-Z99) are provided to deal with occasions when circumstances other than a disease or injury are recorded as diagnosis or problems.

See Section I.C.21., Factors influencing health status and contact with health services.

F. Level of Detail in Coding

1. ICD-10-CM codes with 3, 4, 5, 6 or 7 characters

ICD-10-CM is composed of codes with 3, 4, 5, 6 or 7 characters. Codes with three characters are included in ICD-10-CM as the heading of a category of codes that may be further subdivided by the use of fourth, fifth, sixth or seventh characters to provide greater specificity.

2. Use of full number of characters required for a code

A three-character code is to be used only if it is not further subdivided. A code is invalid if it has not been coded to the full number of characters required for that code, including the 7th character, if applicable.

G. ICD-10-CM code for the diagnosis, condition, problem, or other reason for encounter/visit

List first the ICD-10-CM code for the diagnosis, condition, problem, or other reason for encounter/visit shown in the medical record to be chiefly responsible for the services provided. List additional codes that describe any coexisting conditions. In some cases the first-listed diagnosis may be a symptom when a diagnosis has not been established (confirmed) by the physician.

H. Uncertain diagnosis

Do not code diagnoses documented as "probable", "suspected," "questionable," "rule out," or "working diagnosis" or other similar terms indicating uncertainty. Rather, code the condition(s) to the highest degree of certainty for that encounter/visit, such as symptoms, signs, abnormal test results, or other reason for the visit.

Please note: This differs from the coding practices used by short-term, acute care, long-term care and psychiatric hospitals.

I. Chronic diseases

Chronic diseases treated on an ongoing basis may be coded and reported as many times as the patient receives treatment and care for the condition(s)

J. Code all documented conditions that coexist

Code all documented conditions that coexist at the time of the encounter/visit, and require or affect patient care treatment or management. Do not code conditions that were previously treated and no longer exist. However, history codes (categories Z80-Z87) may be used as secondary codes if the historical condition or family history has an impact on current care or influences treatment.

K. Patients receiving diagnostic services only

For patients receiving diagnostic services only during an encounter/visit, sequence first the diagnosis, condition, problem, or other reason for encounter/visit shown in the medical record to be chiefly responsible for the outpatient services provided during the encounter/visit. Codes for other diagnoses (e.g., chronic conditions) may be sequenced as additional diagnoses.

For encounters for routine laboratory/radiology testing in the absence of any signs, symptoms, or associated diagnosis, assign Z01.89, Encounter for other specified special examinations. If routine testing is performed during the same encounter as a test to evaluate a sign, symptom, or diagnosis, it is appropriate to assign both the Z code and the code describing the reason for the non-routine test.

For outpatient encounters for diagnostic tests that have been interpreted by a physician, and the final report is available at the time of coding, code any confirmed or definitive diagnosis(es) documented in the interpretation. Do not code related signs and symptoms as additional diagnoses.

Please note: This differs from the coding practice in the hospital inpatient setting regarding abnormal findings on test results.

L. Patients receiving therapeutic services only

For patients receiving therapeutic services only during an encounter/visit, sequence first the diagnosis, condition, problem, or other reason for encounter/visit shown in the medical record to be chiefly responsible for the outpatient services provided during the encounter/visit. Codes for other diagnoses (e.g., chronic conditions) may be sequenced as additional diagnoses.

The only exception to this rule is that when the primary reason for the admission/encounter is chemotherapy or radiation therapy, the appropriate Z code for the service is listed first, and the diagnosis or problem for which the service is being performed listed second.

M. Patients receiving preoperative evaluations only

For patients receiving preoperative evaluations only, sequence first a code from subcategory Z01.81, Encounter for pre-procedural examinations, to describe the pre-op consultations. Assign a code for the condition to describe the reason for the surgery as an additional diagnosis. Code also any findings related to the pre-op evaluation.

N. Ambulatory surgery

For ambulatory surgery, code the diagnosis for which the surgery was performed. If the postoperative diagnosis is known to be different from the preoperative diagnosis at the time the diagnosis is confirmed, select the postoperative diagnosis for coding, since it is the most definitive.

O. Routine outpatient prenatal visits

See Section I.C.15., Routine outpatient prenatal visits.

P. Encounters for general medical examinations with abnormal findings

The subcategories for encounters for general medical examinations, Z00.0- and encounter for routine child health examination, Z00.12-, provide codes for with and without abnormal findings. Should a general medical examination result in an abnormal finding, the code for general medical examination with abnormal finding should be assigned as the first-listed diagnosis. An examination with abnormal findings refers to a condition/diagnosis that is newly identified or a change in severity of a chronic condition (such as uncontrolled hypertension, or an acute exacerbation of chronic obstructive pulmonary disease) during a routine physical examination. A secondary code for the abnormal finding should also be coded.

Q. Encounters for routine health screenings

See Section I.C.21., Factors influencing health status and contact with health services, Screening

GUIDELINES (ICD-10-CM)

Appendix I
Present on Admission Reporting Guidelines

Introduction

These guidelines are to be used as a supplement to the *ICD-10-CM Official Guidelines for Coding and Reporting* to facilitate the assignment of the Present on Admission (POA) indicator for each diagnosis and external cause of injury code reported on claim forms (UB-04 and 837 Institutional).

These guidelines are not intended to replace any guidelines in the main body of the *ICD-10-CM Official Guidelines for Coding and Reporting*. The POA guidelines are not intended to provide guidance on when a condition should be coded, but rather, how to apply the POA indicator to the final set of diagnosis codes that have been assigned in accordance with Sections I, II, and III of the official coding guidelines. Subsequent to the assignment of the ICD-10-CM codes, the POA indicator should then be assigned to those conditions that have been coded.

As stated in the Introduction to the ICD-10-CM Official Guidelines for Coding and Reporting, a joint effort between the healthcare provider and the coder is essential to achieve complete and accurate documentation, code assignment, and reporting of diagnoses and procedures. The importance of consistent, complete documentation in the medical record cannot be overemphasized. Medical record documentation from any provider involved in the care and treatment of the patient may be used to support the determination of whether a condition was present on admission or not. In the context of the official coding guidelines, the term "provider" means a physician or any qualified healthcare practitioner who is legally accountable for establishing the patient's diagnosis.

These guidelines are not a substitute for the provider's clinical judgment as to the determination of whether a condition was/was not present on admission. The provider should be queried regarding issues related to the linking of signs/symptoms, timing of test results, and the timing of findings.

Please see the CDC website for the detailed list of ICD-10-CM codes that do not require the use of a POA indicator (https://www.cdc.gov/nchs/icd/icd10cm.htm) (https://www.cms.gov/Medicare/Coding/ICD10/2018-ICD-10-CM-and-GEMs.html). The codes and categories on this exempt list are for circumstances regarding the healthcare encounter or factors influencing health status that do not represent a current disease or injury or that describe conditions that are always present on admission.

General Reporting Requirements

All claims involving inpatient admissions to general acute care hospitals or other facilities that are subject to a law or regulation mandating collection of present on admission information.

Present on admission is defined as present at the time the order for inpatient admission occurs—conditions that develop during an outpatient encounter, including emergency department, observation, or outpatient surgery, are considered as present on admission.

POA indicator is assigned to principal and secondary diagnoses (as defined in Section II of the Official Guidelines for Coding and Reporting) and the external cause of injury codes.

Issues related to inconsistent, missing, conflicting or unclear documentation must still be resolved by the provider.

If a condition would not be coded and reported based on UHDDS definitions and current official coding guidelines, then the POA indicator would not be reported.

Reporting Options

Y - Yes

N - No

U - Unknown

W - Clinically undetermined

Unreported/Not used - (Exempt from POA reporting)

Reporting Definitions

Y = present at the time of inpatient admission

N = not present at the time of inpatient admission

U = documentation is insufficient to determine if condition is present on admission

W = provider is unable to clinically determine whether condition was present on admission or not

Timeframe for POA Identification and Documentation

There is no required timeframe as to when a provider (per the definition of "provider" used in these guidelines) must identify or document a condition to be present on admission. In some clinical situations, it may not be possible for a provider to make a definitive diagnosis (or a condition may not be recognized or reported by the patient) for a period of time after admission. In some cases it may be several days before the provider arrives at a definitive diagnosis. This does not mean that the condition was not present on admission. Determination of whether the condition was present on admission or not will be based on the applicable POA guideline as identified in this document, or on the provider's best clinical judgment.

If at the time of code assignment the documentation is unclear as to whether a condition was present on admission or not, it is appropriate to query the provider for clarification.

Assigning the POA Indicator

Condition is on the "Exempt from Reporting" list

Leave the "present on admission" field blank if the condition is on the list of ICD-10-CM codes for which this field is not applicable. This is the only circumstance in which the field may be left blank.

POA Explicitly Documented

Assign Y for any condition the provider explicitly documents as being present on admission.

Assign N for any condition the provider explicitly documents as not present at the time of admission.

Conditions diagnosed prior to inpatient admission

Assign "Y" for conditions that were diagnosed prior to admission (example: hypertension, diabetes mellitus, asthma)

Conditions diagnosed during the admission but clearly present before admission

Assign "Y" for conditions diagnosed during the admission that were clearly present but not diagnosed until after admission occurred.

Diagnoses subsequently confirmed after admission are considered present on admission if at the time of admission they are documented as suspected, possible, rule out, differential diagnosis, or constitute an underlying cause of a symptom that is present at the time of admission.

Condition develops during outpatient encounter prior to inpatient admission

Assign Y for any condition that develops during an outpatient encounter prior to a written order for inpatient admission.

Documentation does not indicate whether condition was present on admission

Assign "U" when the medical record documentation is unclear as to whether the condition was present on admission. "U" should not be routinely assigned and used only in very limited circumstances. Coders are encouraged to query the providers when the documentation is unclear.

Documentation states that it cannot be determined whether the condition was or was not present on admission

Assign "W" when the medical record documentation indicates that it cannot be clinically determined whether or not the condition was present on admission.

Chronic condition with acute exacerbation during the admission

If a single code identifies both the chronic condition and the acute exacerbation, see POA guidelines pertaining to codes that contain multiple clinical concepts.

If a single code only identifies the chronic condition and not the acute exacerbation (e.g., acute exacerbation of chronic leukemia), assign "Y."

Conditions documented as possible, probable, suspected, or rule out at the time of discharge

If the final diagnosis contains a possible, probable, suspected, or rule out diagnosis, and this diagnosis was based on signs, symptoms or clinical findings suspected at the time of inpatient admission, assign "Y."

If the final diagnosis contains a possible, probable, suspected, or rule out diagnosis, and this diagnosis was based on signs, symptoms or clinical findings that were not present on admission, assign "N".

Conditions documented as impending or threatened at the time of discharge

If the final diagnosis contains an impending or threatened diagnosis, and this diagnosis is based on symptoms or clinical findings that were present on admission, assign "Y".

If the final diagnosis contains an impending or threatened diagnosis, and this diagnosis is based on symptoms or clinical findings that were not present on admission, assign "N".

Acute and Chronic Conditions

Assign "Y" for acute conditions that are present at time of admission and N for acute conditions that are not present at time of admission.

Assign "Y" for chronic conditions, even though the condition may not be diagnosed until after admission.

If a single code identifies both an acute and chronic condition, see the POA guidelines for codes that contain multiple clinical concepts.

Codes That Contain Multiple Clinical Concepts

Assign "N" if at least one of the clinical concepts included in the code was not present on admission (e.g., COPD with acute exacerbation and the exacerbation was not present on admission; gastric ulcer that does not start bleeding until after admission; asthma patient develops status asthmaticus after admission).

Assign "Y" if all of the clinical concepts included in the code were present on admission (e.g., duodenal ulcer that perforates prior to admission).

For infection codes that include the causal organism, assign "Y" if the infection (or signs of the infection) were present on admission, even though the culture results may not be known until after admission (e.g., patient is admitted with pneumonia and the provider documents Pseudomonas as the causal organism a few days later).

Same Diagnosis Code for Two or More Conditions

When the same ICD-10-CM diagnosis code applies to two or more conditions during the same encounter (e.g., two separate conditions classified to the same ICD-10-CM diagnosis code):

Assign "Y" if all conditions represented by the single ICD-10-CM code were present on admission (e.g., bilateral unspecified age-related cataracts).

Assign "N" if any of the conditions represented by the single ICD-10-CM code was not present on admission (e.g., traumatic secondary and recurrent hemorrhage and seroma is assigned to a single code T79.2, but only one of the conditions was present on admission).

Obstetrical conditions

Whether or not the patient delivers during the current hospitalization does not affect assignment of the POA indicator. The determining factor for POA assignment is whether the pregnancy complication or obstetrical condition described by the code was present at the time of admission or not.

If the pregnancy complication or obstetrical condition was present on admission (e.g., patient admitted in preterm labor), assign "Y".

If the pregnancy complication or obstetrical condition was not present on admission (e.g., 2nd degree laceration during delivery, postpartum hemorrhage that occurred during current hospitalization, fetal distress develops after admission), assign "N".

If the obstetrical code includes more than one diagnosis and any of the diagnoses identified by the code were not present on admission assign "N".

GUIDELINES (ICD-10-CM)

49

(e.g., Category O11, Pre-existing hypertension with pre-eclampsia)

Perinatal conditions

Newborns are not considered to be admitted until after birth. Therefore, any condition present at birth or that developed in utero is considered present at admission and should be assigned "Y". This includes conditions that occur during delivery (e.g., injury during delivery, meconium aspiration, exposure to streptococcus B in the vaginal canal).

Congenital conditions and anomalies

Assign "Y" for congenital conditions and anomalies except for categories Q00-Q99, Congenital anomalies, which are on the exempt list. Congenital conditions are always considered present on admission.

External cause of injury codes

Assign "Y" for any external cause code representing an external cause of morbidity that occurred prior to inpatient admission (e.g., patient fell out of bed at home, patient fell out of bed in emergency room prior to admission).

Assign "N" for any external cause code representing an external cause of morbidity that occurred during inpatient hospitalization (e.g., patient fell out of hospital bed during hospital stay, patient experienced an adverse reaction to a medication administered after inpatient admission).

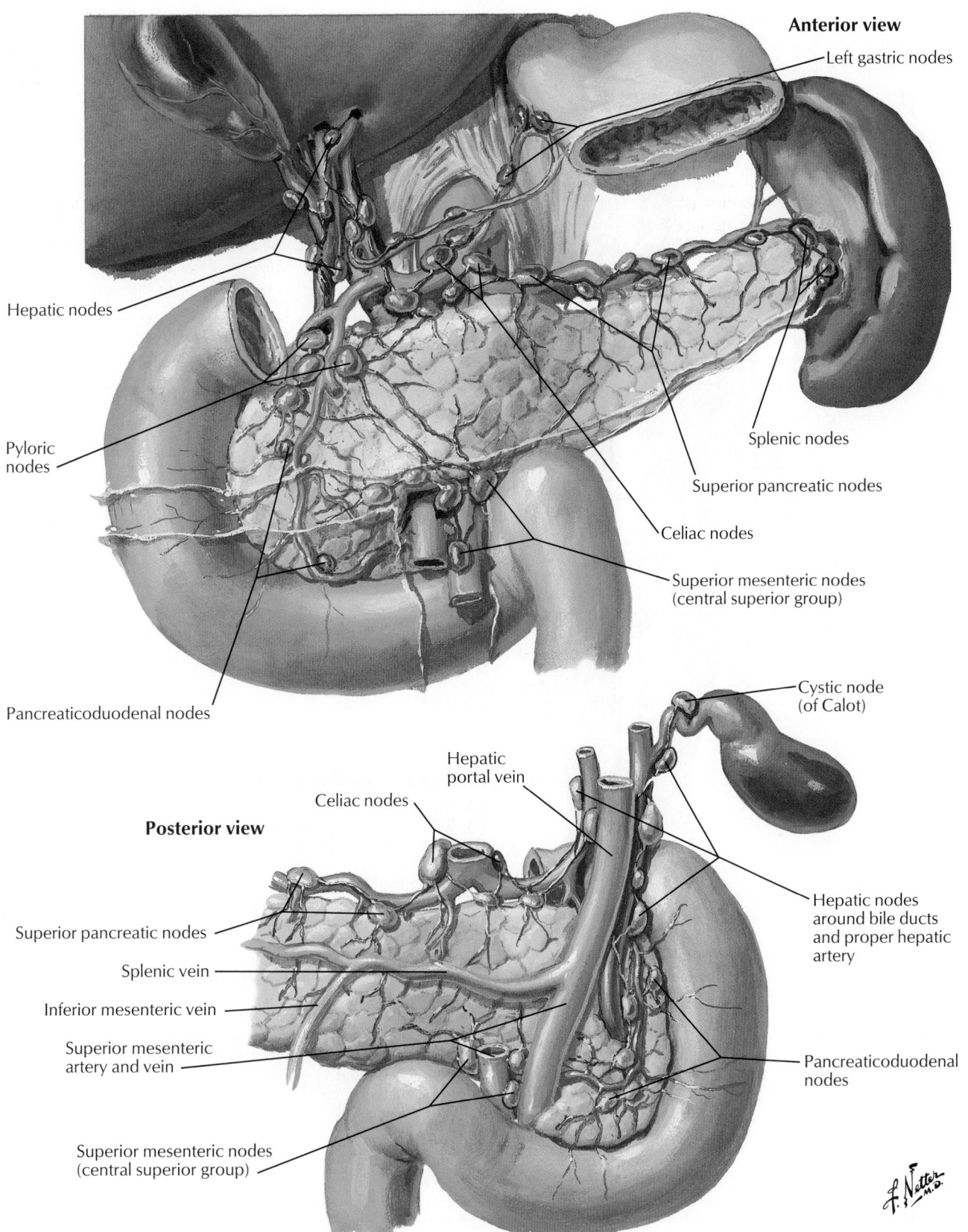

Anterior view

Left gastric nodes

Hepatic nodes

Pyloric nodes

Pancreaticoduodenal nodes

Splenic nodes

Superior pancreatic nodes

Celiac nodes

Superior mesenteric nodes (central superior group)

Cystic node (of Calot)

Posterior view

Hepatic portal vein

Celiac nodes

Hepatic nodes around bile ducts and proper hepatic artery

Superior pancreatic nodes

Splenic vein

Inferior mesenteric vein

Superior mesenteric artery and vein

Pancreaticoduodenal nodes

Superior mesenteric nodes (central superior group)

Plate 315 Lymph Vessels and Nodes of Pancreas. (Netter: Atlas of Human Anatomy, 4 ed, 2006, Saunders.)

Dermatome pattern

Levels of principal dermatomes

C5	Clavicles
C5, 6, 7	Lateral parts of upper limbs
C8; T1	Medial sides of upper limbs
C6	Thumb
C6, 7, 8	Hand
C8	Ring and little fingers
T4	Level of nipples
T10	Level of umbilicus
T12	Inguinal or groin regions
L1, 2, 3, 4	Anterior and inner surfaces of lower limbs
L4, 5; S1	Foot
L4	Medial side of great toe
L5; S1, 2	Outer and posterior sides of lower limbs
S1	Lateral margin of foot and little toe
S2, 3, 4	Perineum

Plate 164 Dermatomes. (Netter: Atlas of Human Anatomy, 4 ed, 2006, Saunders.)

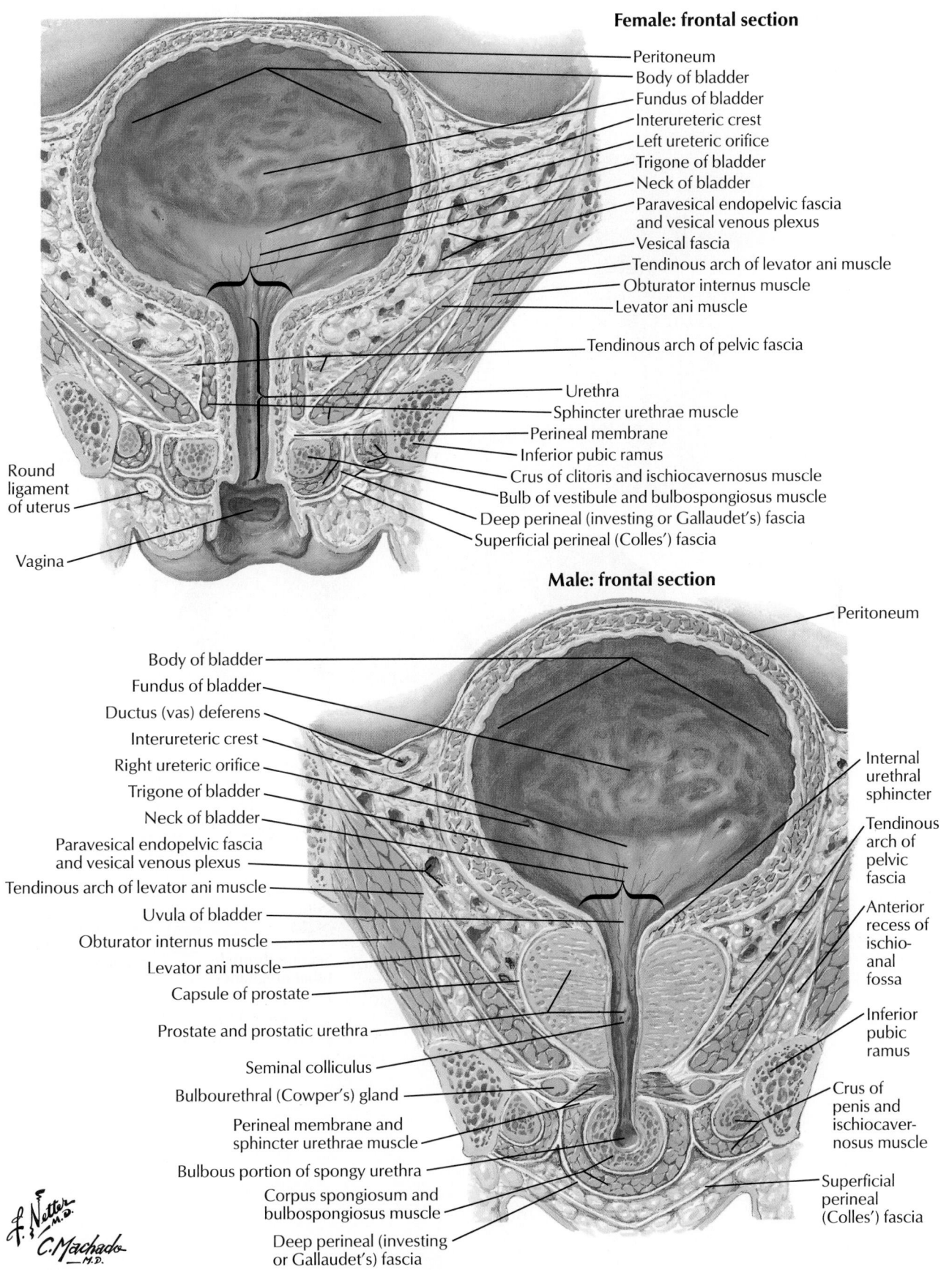

Female: frontal section

Peritoneum
Body of bladder
Fundus of bladder
Interureteric crest
Left ureteric orifice
Trigone of bladder
Neck of bladder
Paravesical endopelvic fascia and vesical venous plexus
Vesical fascia
Tendinous arch of levator ani muscle
Obturator internus muscle
Levator ani muscle
Tendinous arch of pelvic fascia
Urethra
Sphincter urethrae muscle
Perineal membrane
Inferior pubic ramus
Crus of clitoris and ischiocavernosus muscle
Bulb of vestibule and bulbospongiosus muscle
Deep perineal (investing or Gallaudet's) fascia
Superficial perineal (Colles') fascia

Round ligament of uterus

Vagina

Male: frontal section

Body of bladder
Fundus of bladder
Ductus (vas) deferens
Interureteric crest
Right ureteric orifice
Trigone of bladder
Neck of bladder
Paravesical endopelvic fascia and vesical venous plexus
Tendinous arch of levator ani muscle
Uvula of bladder
Obturator internus muscle
Levator ani muscle
Capsule of prostate
Prostate and prostatic urethra
Seminal colliculus
Bulbourethral (Cowper's) gland
Perineal membrane and sphincter urethrae muscle
Bulbous portion of spongy urethra
Corpus spongiosum and bulbospongiosus muscle
Deep perineal (investing or Gallaudet's) fascia

Peritoneum
Internal urethral sphincter
Tendinous arch of pelvic fascia
Anterior recess of ischioanal fossa
Inferior pubic ramus
Crus of penis and ischiocavernosus muscle
Superficial perineal (Colles') fascia

Plate 366   Urinary Bladder: Female and Male. (Netter: Atlas of Human Anatomy, 4 ed, 2006, Saunders.)

Sites of ectopic implantation

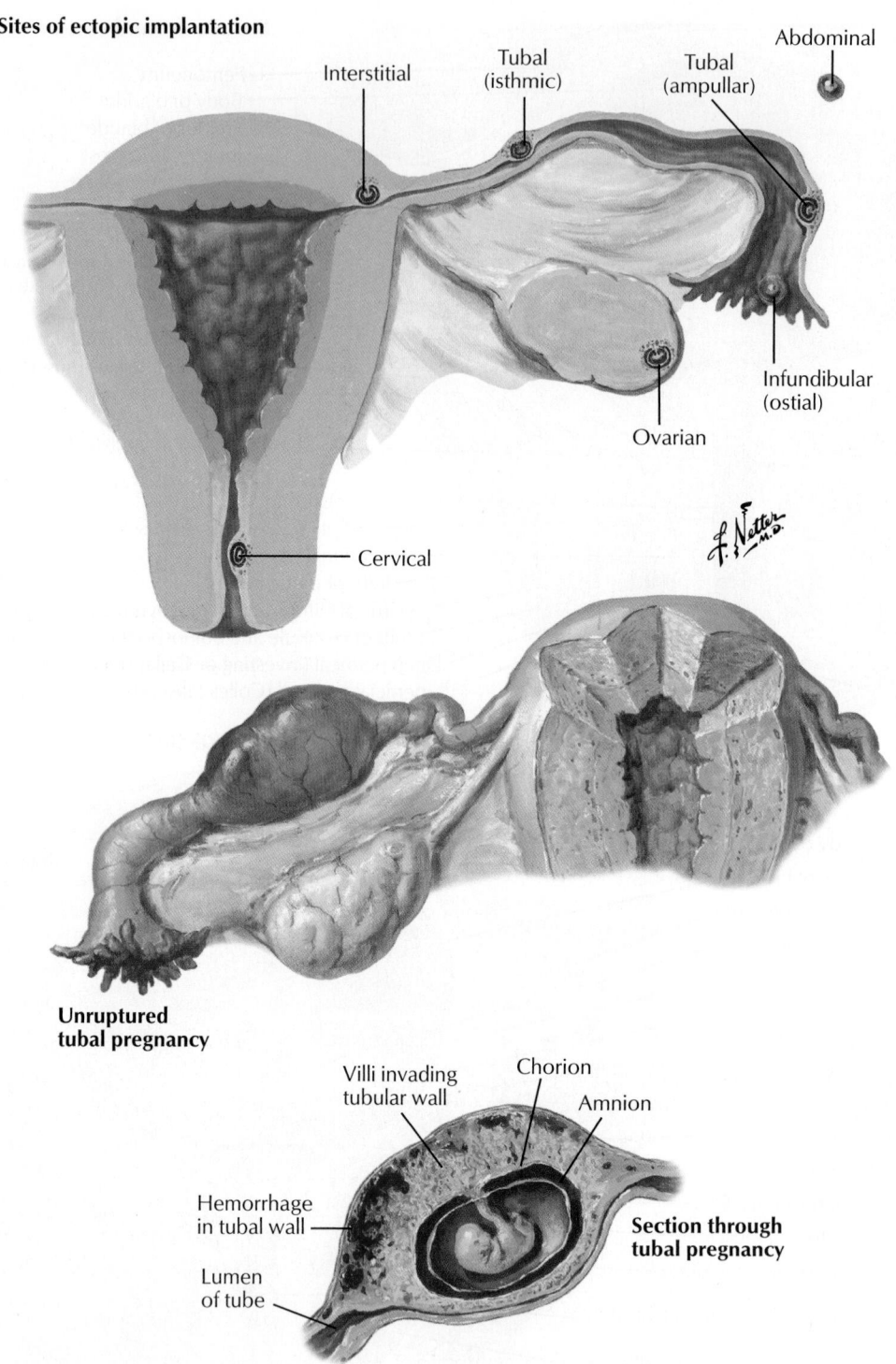

Interstitial

Tubal (isthmic)

Tubal (ampullar)

Abdominal

Infundibular (ostial)

Ovarian

Cervical

Unruptured tubal pregnancy

Villi invading tubular wall

Chorion

Amnion

Hemorrhage in tubal wall

Lumen of tube

Section through tubal pregnancy

Plate 375   Ectopic Pregnancy. (Netter: Atlas of Human Anatomy, 4 ed, 2006, Saunders.)

Skin of penis

Superficial fascia of penis (Colles' fascia)

Deep (Buck's) fascia of penis

Testicular artery

Ductus deferens

Artery to ductus deferens

Genital branch of genitofemoral nerve

Pampiniform (venous) plexus

Epididymis

Appendix of epididymis

Appendix of testis

Testis (covered by visceral layer of tunica vaginalis)

Parietal layer of tunica vaginalis

Superficial inguinal ring

External spermatic fascia

Cremaster muscle and fascia

Septum of scrotum (formed by dartos fascia)

Superficial (dartos) fascia of scrotum

Skin of scrotum

Superficial (dartos) fascia of scrotum

External spermatic fascia

Cremaster muscle and fascia

Internal spermatic fascia

Parietal layer of tunica vaginalis

Epididymis

Testis (covered by visceral layer of tunica vaginalis)

Skin of scrotum

Plate 387 Scrotum and Contents. (Netter: Atlas of Human Anatomy, 4 ed, 2006, Saunders.)

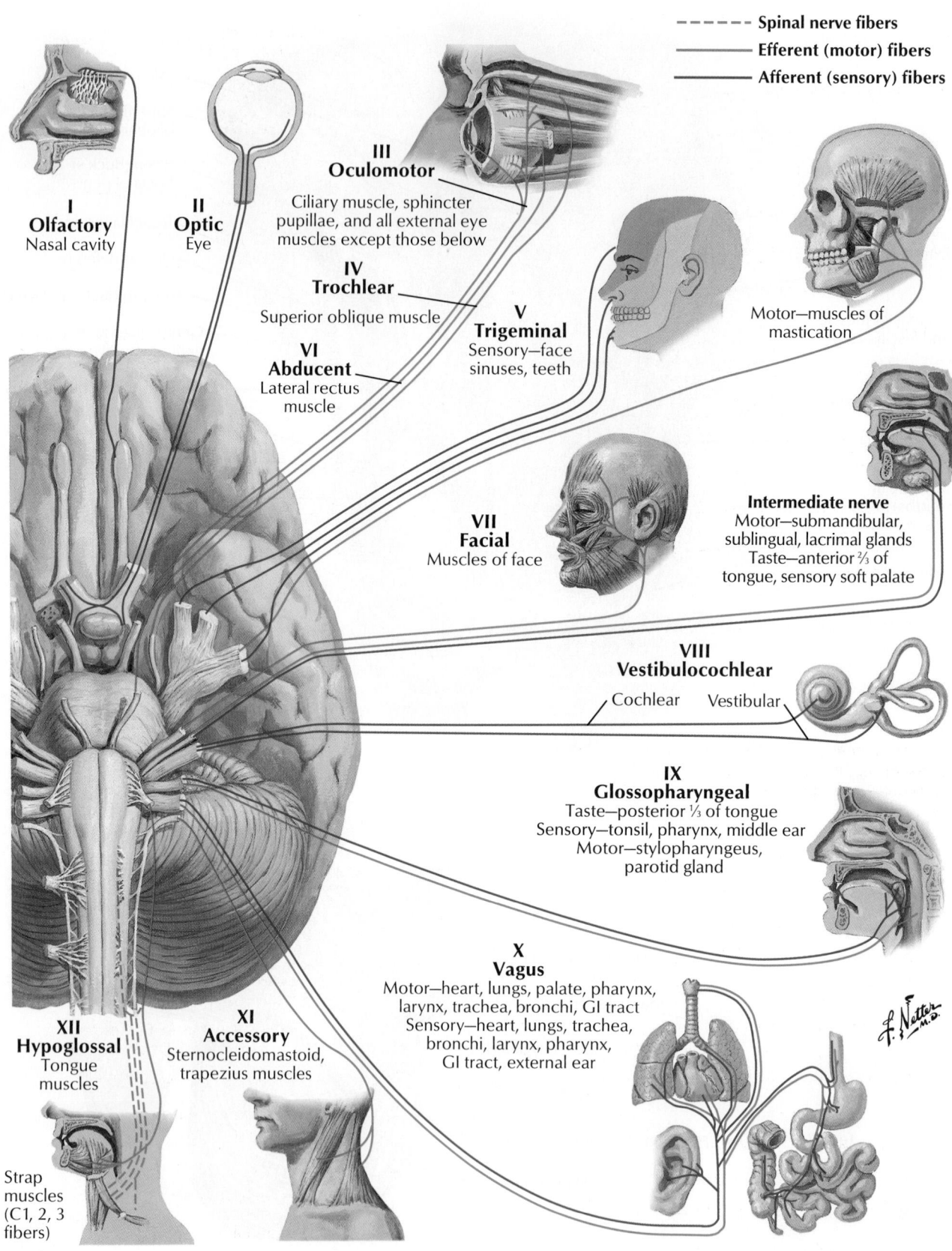

- - - - - - Spinal nerve fibers
———— Efferent (motor) fibers
———— Afferent (sensory) fibers

**I
Olfactory**
Nasal cavity

**II
Optic**
Eye

**III
Oculomotor**
Ciliary muscle, sphincter
pupillae, and all external eye
muscles except those below

**IV
Trochlear**
Superior oblique muscle

**V
Trigeminal**
Sensory—face
sinuses, teeth

**VI
Abducent**
Lateral rectus
muscle

Motor—muscles of
mastication

**VII
Facial**
Muscles of face

Intermediate nerve
Motor—submandibular,
sublingual, lacrimal glands
Taste—anterior ⅔ of
tongue, sensory soft palate

**VIII
Vestibulocochlear**
Cochlear   Vestibular

**IX
Glossopharyngeal**
Taste—posterior ⅓ of tongue
Sensory—tonsil, pharynx, middle ear
Motor—stylopharyngeus,
parotid gland

**X
Vagus**
Motor—heart, lungs, palate, pharynx,
larynx, trachea, bronchi, GI tract
Sensory—heart, lungs, trachea,
bronchi, larynx, pharynx,
GI tract, external ear

**XII
Hypoglossal**
Tongue
muscles

**XI
Accessory**
Sternocleidomastoid,
trapezius muscles

Strap
muscles
(C1, 2, 3
fibers)

Plate 118 Cranial Nerves (Motor and Sensory Distribution): Schema. (Netter: Atlas of Human Anatomy, 4 ed, 2006, Saunders.)

Superior view

Supratrochlear nerve

Medial rectus muscle

Superior oblique muscle

Infratrochlear nerve

Nasociliary nerve

Trochlear nerve (IV)

Common tendinous ring

Ophthalmic nerve (V₁)

Optic nerve (II)

Internal carotid artery
and nerve plexus

Oculomotor nerve (III)

Trochlear nerve (IV)

Abducent nerve (VI)

Tentorium cerebelli

Medial branch
Lateral branch } Supraorbital nerve

Levator palpebrae superioris muscle

Superior rectus muscle

Lacrimal gland

Lacrimal nerve

Lateral rectus muscle

Frontal nerve

Maxillary nerve (V₂)

Meningeal branch
of maxillary nerve

Mandibular nerve (V₃)

Lesser petrosal nerve

Meningeal branch
of mandibular nerve

Greater petrosal nerve

Trigeminal (semilunar) ganglion

Tentorial (meningeal)
branch of ophthalmic nerve

Superior view:
levator palpebrae superioris,
superior rectus, and superior
oblique muscles partially
cut away

Supratrochlear nerve *(cut)*

Supraorbital nerve branches *(cut)*

Infratrochlear nerve

Anterior ethmoidal nerve

Optic nerve (II)

Posterior ethmoidal nerve

Superior branch of
oculomotor nerve (III) *(cut)*

Nasociliary nerve

Internal carotid plexus

Trochlear nerve (IV) *(cut)*

Oculomotor nerve (III)

Abducent nerve (VI)

Long ciliary nerves

Short ciliary nerves

Lacrimal nerve

Ciliary ganglion

Parasympathetic root of ciliary
ganglion (from inferior branch
of oculomotor nerve)

Sympathetic root of ciliary
ganglion (from internal
carotid plexus)

Sensory root of ciliary ganglion
(from nasociliary nerve)

Branches to inferior
and medial rectus muscles

Abducent nerve (VI)

Inferior branch of
oculomotor nerve (III)

Lacrimal nerve

Frontal nerve *(cut)*

Ophthalmic nerve (V₁)

Plate 86 Nerves of Orbit. (Netter: Atlas of Human Anatomy, 4 ed, 2006, Saunders.)

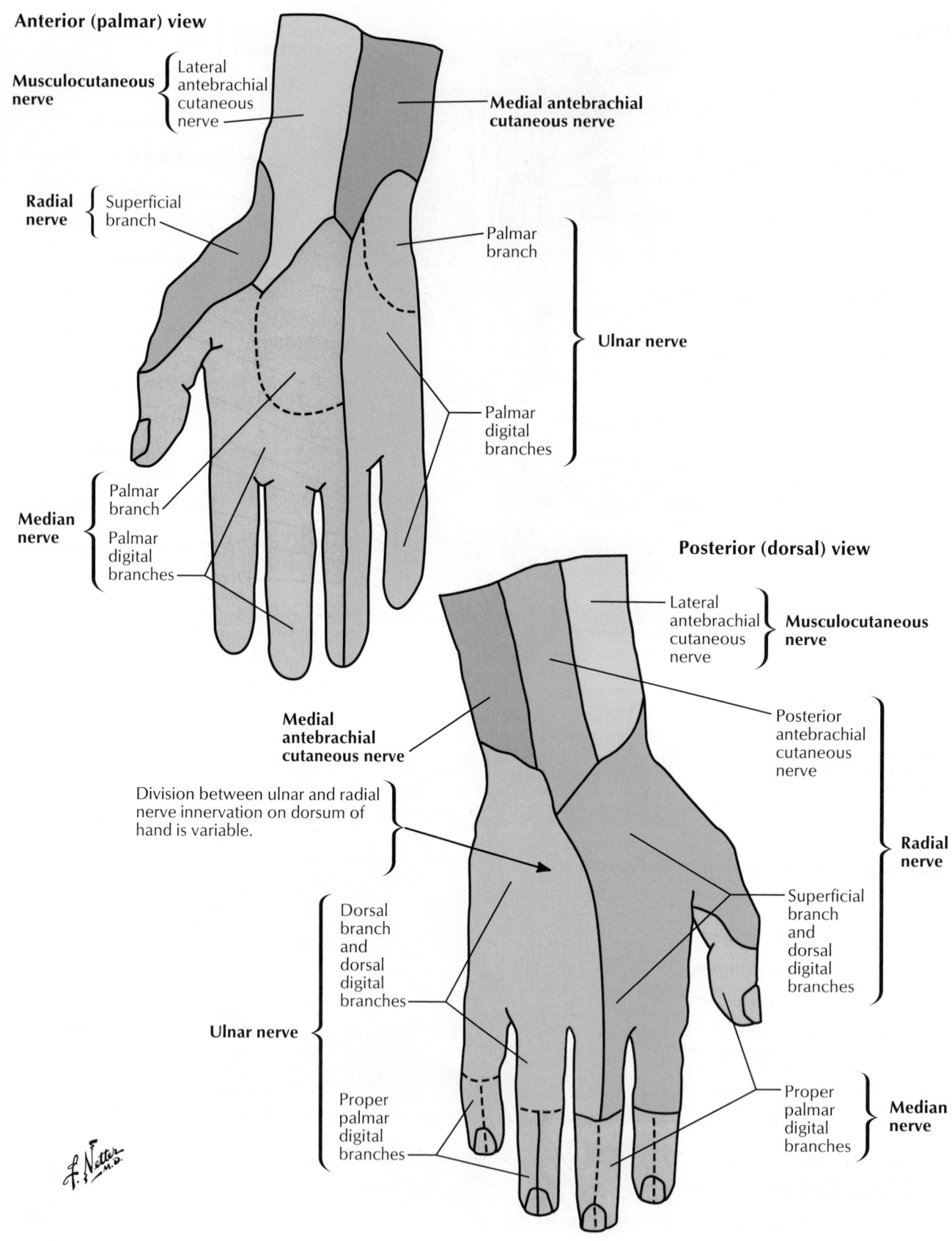

Anterior (palmar) view

Musculocutaneous nerve { Lateral antebrachial cutaneous nerve

Medial antebrachial cutaneous nerve

Radial nerve { Superficial branch

Palmar branch

Ulnar nerve

Palmar digital branches

Median nerve { Palmar branch / Palmar digital branches

Posterior (dorsal) view

Lateral antebrachial cutaneous nerve **Musculocutaneous nerve**

Medial antebrachial cutaneous nerve

Posterior antebrachial cutaneous nerve

Division between ulnar and radial nerve innervation on dorsum of hand is variable.

Radial nerve

Superficial branch and dorsal digital branches

Dorsal branch and dorsal digital branches

Ulnar nerve

Proper palmar digital branches

Proper palmar digital branches **Median nerve**

NETTER'S ANATOMY ILLUSTRATIONS

Plate 472 Cutaneous Innervation of Wrist and Hand. (Netter: Atlas of Human Anatomy, 4 ed, 2006, Saunders.)

Anterior view

Deltoid muscle

Coracobrachialis muscle

Biceps brachii muscle
- Short head (*cut*)
- Long head (*cut*)

Musculocutaneous nerve

Brachialis muscle

Biceps brachii muscle (*cut*) and tendon

Lateral antebrachial cutaneous nerve
(from musculocutaneous nerve)

Radial nerve
- Deep branch
- Superficial branch

Supinator muscle

Brachioradialis muscle

Radial artery

Pronator teres muscle (*partially cut*)

Median nerve

Flexor pollicis longus muscle

Flexor carpi radialis
tendon (*cut*)

Flexor retinaculum
(transverse carpal
ligament)

Superficial branch
of radial nerve

Recurrent (motor)
branch of
median nerve to
thenar muscles

Common palmar
digital branches
of median nerve

Proper palmar
digital branches
of median nerve

Intercostobrachial nerve

Medial brachial
cutaneous nerve

Radial nerve

Ulnar nerve

Medial antebrachial
cutaneous nerve

Median nerve

Brachial artery

Bicipital aponeurosis

Humeral head (*cut*)
Ulnar head
} Pronator teres muscle

Flexor carpi radialis muscle (*cut*)

Humeroulnar head
Radial head
} Flexor digitorum
superficialis muscle (*cut*)

Flexor digitorum profundus muscle

Flexor carpi ulnaris muscle

Ulnar artery and nerve

Dorsal branch of ulnar nerve

Flexor digitorum superficialis tendons (*cut*)

Deep palmar branch of ulnar artery and deep branch of ulnar nerve

Superficial branch of ulnar nerve

Superficial palmar arch (*cut*)

Common palmar digital branch of ulnar nerve

Communicating branch of median nerve with ulnar nerve

Proper palmar digital branches of ulnar nerve

Plate 473 Arteries and Nerves of Upper Limb. (Netter: Atlas of Human Anatomy, 4 ed, 2006, Saunders.)

NETTER'S ANATOMY ILLUSTRATIONS

Lateral cutaneous branch of subcostal nerve

Inguinal ligament (Poupart's)

Superficial circumflex iliac vein

Femoral branches of genitofemoral nerve

Lateral femoral cutaneous nerve

Saphenous opening (fossa ovalis)

Fascia lata

Anterior cutaneous branches of femoral nerve

Patellar nerve plexus

Branches of lateral sural cutaneous nerve (from common fibular [peroneal] nerve)

Deep fascia of leg (crural fascia)

Superficial fibular (peroneal) nerve Medial dorsal cutaneous branch

Intermediate dorsal cutaneous branch

Small saphenous vein and lateral dorsal cutaneous nerve (from sural nerve)

Lateral dorsal digital nerve and vein of 5th toe

Dorsal metatarsal veins

Dorsal digital nerves and veins

Superficial epigastric vein

Ilioinguinal nerve (scrotal branch) (usually passes through superficial inguinal ring)

Genital branch of genitofemoral nerve

Femoral vein

Superficial external pudendal vein

Accessory saphenous vein

Great saphenous vein

Cutaneous branches of obturator nerve

Infrapatellar branch of saphenous nerve

Saphenous nerve (terminal branch of femoral nerve)

Great saphenous vein

Dorsal digital nerves

Dorsal venous arch

Dorsal digital nerve and vein of medial side of great toe

Dorsal digital branch of deep fibular (peroneal) nerve

Plate 544   Superficial Nerves and Veins of Lower Limb: Anterior View. (Netter: Atlas of Human Anatomy, 4 ed, 2006, Saunders.)

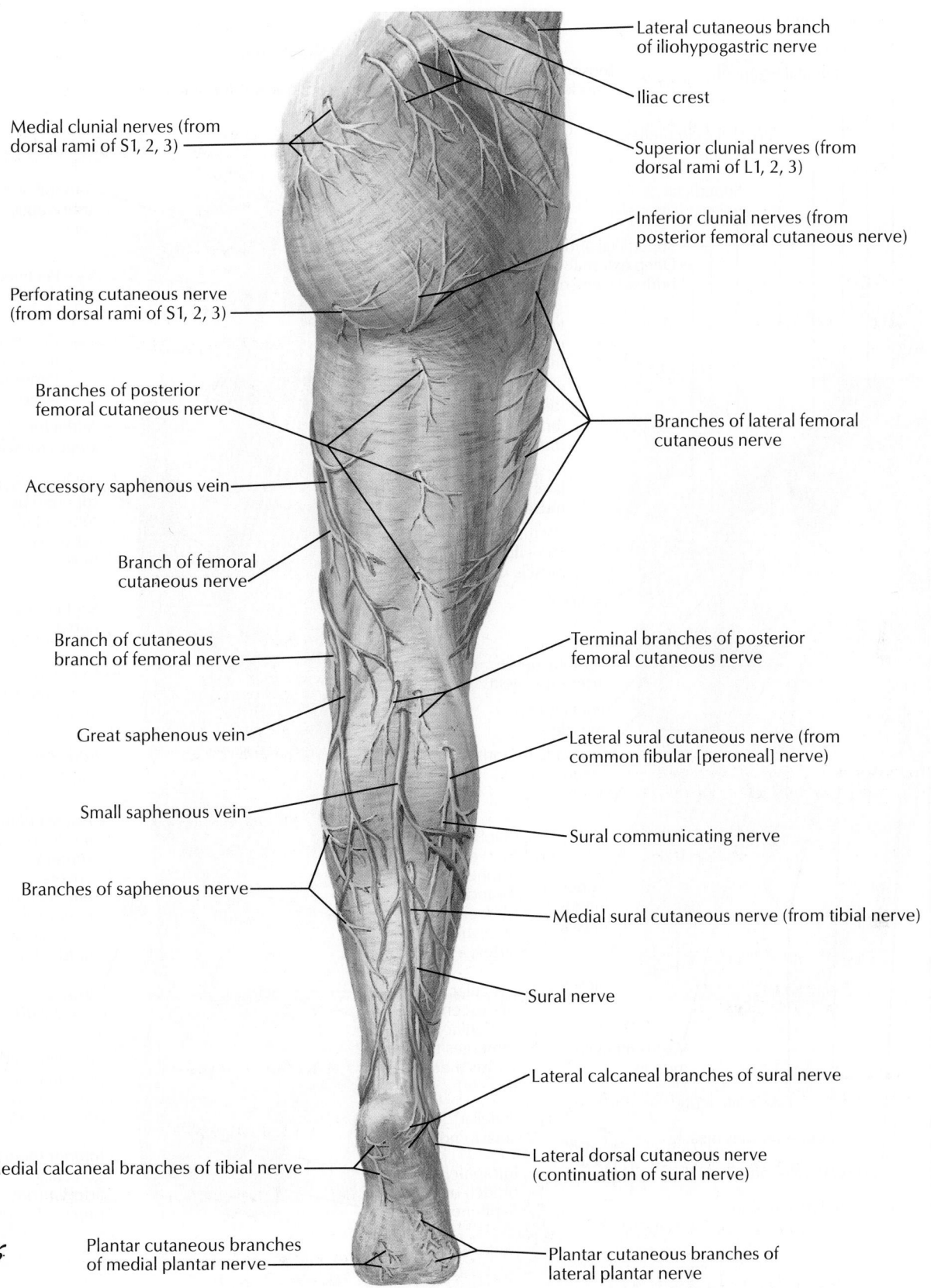

Lateral cutaneous branch
of iliohypogastric nerve

Iliac crest

Medial clunial nerves (from
dorsal rami of S1, 2, 3)

Superior clunial nerves (from
dorsal rami of L1, 2, 3)

Inferior clunial nerves (from
posterior femoral cutaneous nerve)

Perforating cutaneous nerve
(from dorsal rami of S1, 2, 3)

Branches of posterior
femoral cutaneous nerve

Branches of lateral femoral
cutaneous nerve

Accessory saphenous vein

Branch of femoral
cutaneous nerve

Branch of cutaneous
branch of femoral nerve

Terminal branches of posterior
femoral cutaneous nerve

Great saphenous vein

Lateral sural cutaneous nerve (from
common fibular [peroneal] nerve)

Small saphenous vein

Sural communicating nerve

Branches of saphenous nerve

Medial sural cutaneous nerve (from tibial nerve)

Sural nerve

Lateral calcaneal branches of sural nerve

Medial calcaneal branches of tibial nerve

Lateral dorsal cutaneous nerve
(continuation of sural nerve)

Plantar cutaneous branches
of medial plantar nerve

Plantar cutaneous branches of
lateral plantar nerve

Plate 545 Superficial Nerves and Veins of Lower Limb: Posterior View. (Netter: Atlas of Human Anatomy, 4 ed, 2006, Saunders.)

NETTER'S ANATOMY ILLUSTRATIONS

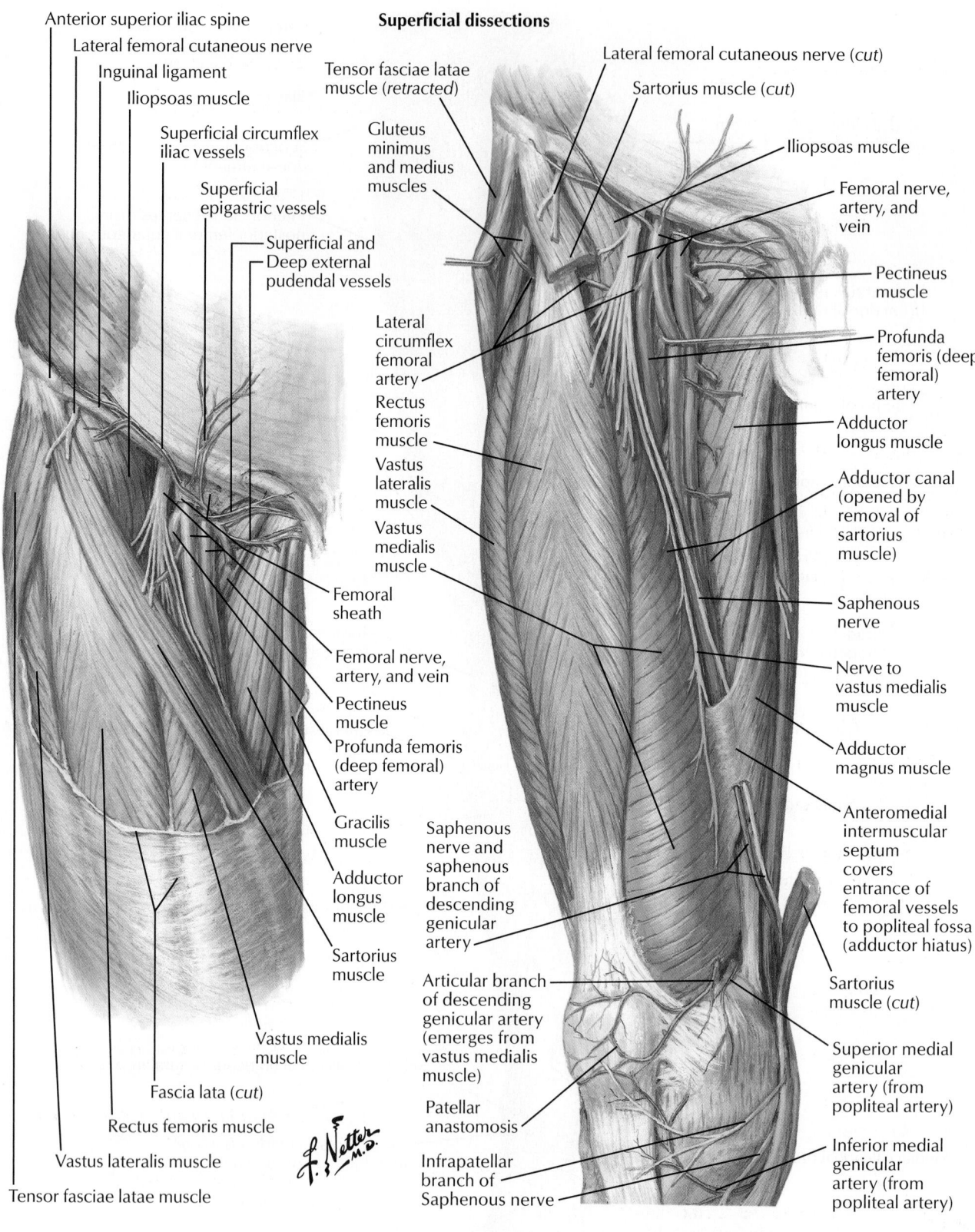

Anterior superior iliac spine

Lateral femoral cutaneous nerve

Inguinal ligament

Iliopsoas muscle

Superficial circumflex iliac vessels

Superficial epigastric vessels

Superficial and Deep external pudendal vessels

Superficial dissections

Tensor fasciae latae muscle (*retracted*)

Gluteus minimus and medius muscles

Lateral circumflex femoral artery

Rectus femoris muscle

Vastus lateralis muscle

Vastus medialis muscle

Femoral sheath

Femoral nerve, artery, and vein

Pectineus muscle

Profunda femoris (deep femoral) artery

Gracilis muscle

Adductor longus muscle

Sartorius muscle

Vastus medialis muscle

Fascia lata (*cut*)

Rectus femoris muscle

Vastus lateralis muscle

Tensor fasciae latae muscle

Lateral femoral cutaneous nerve (*cut*)

Sartorius muscle (*cut*)

Iliopsoas muscle

Femoral nerve, artery, and vein

Pectineus muscle

Profunda femoris (deep femoral) artery

Adductor longus muscle

Adductor canal (opened by removal of sartorius muscle)

Saphenous nerve

Nerve to vastus medialis muscle

Adductor magnus muscle

Anteromedial intermuscular septum covers entrance of femoral vessels to popliteal fossa (adductor hiatus)

Sartorius muscle (*cut*)

Superior medial genicular artery (from popliteal artery)

Inferior medial genicular artery (from popliteal artery)

Saphenous nerve and saphenous branch of descending genicular artery

Articular branch of descending genicular artery (emerges from vastus medialis muscle)

Patellar anastomosis

Infrapatellar branch of Saphenous nerve

f. Netter M.D.

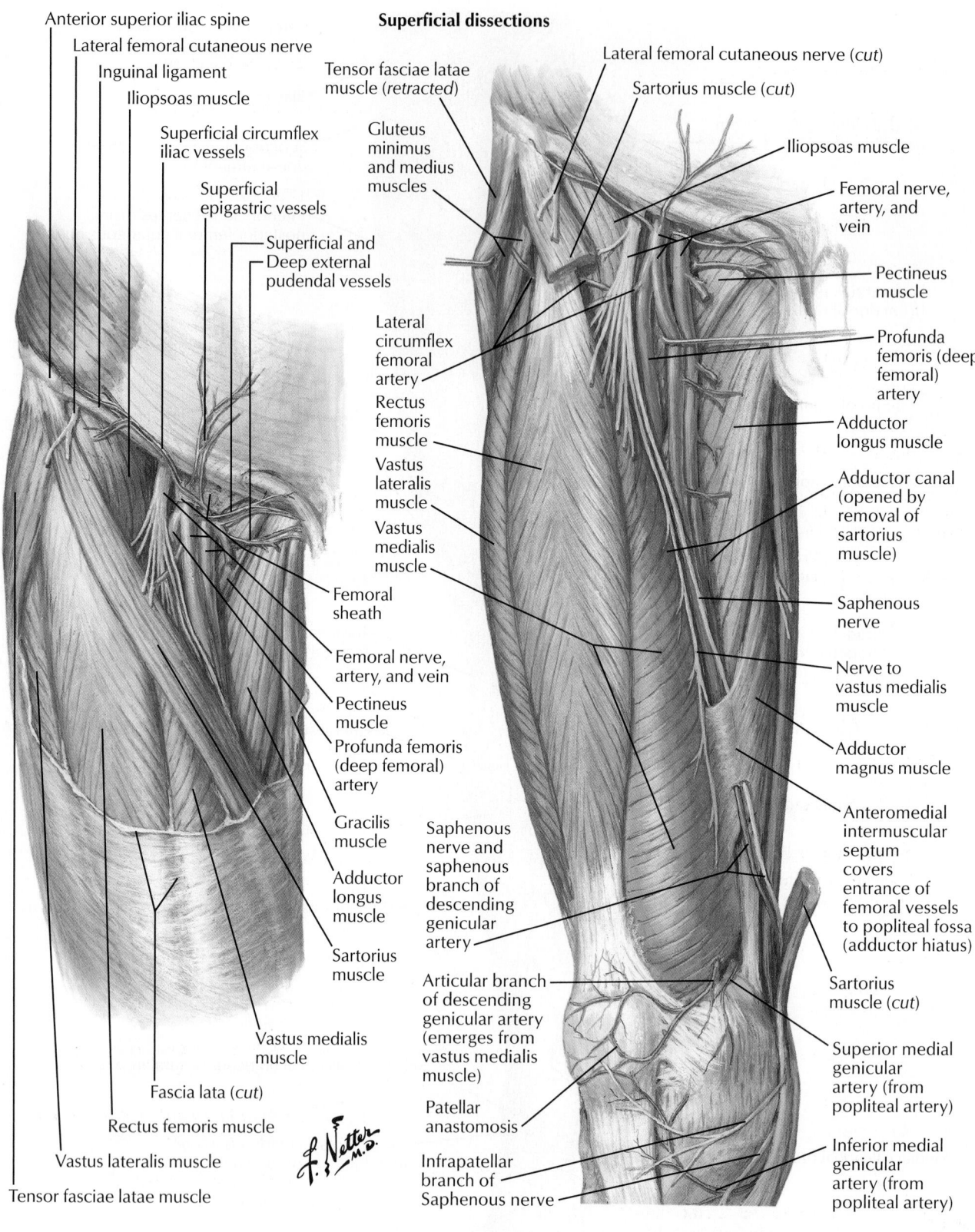

NETTER'S ANATOMY ILLUSTRATIONS

Plate 500   Arteries and Nerves of Thigh: Anterior Views. (Netter: Atlas of Human Anatomy, 4 ed, 2006, Saunders.)

Deep dissection

Deep circumflex iliac artery

Lateral femoral cutaneous nerve

Sartorius muscle (*cut*)

Iliopsoas muscle

Tensor fasciae latae muscle (*retracted*)

Gluteus medius and minimus muscles

Femoral nerve

Rectus femoris muscle (*cut*)

Ascending, transverse and descending branches of Lateral circumflex femoral artery

Medial circumflex femoral artery

Pectineus muscle (*cut*)

Profunda femoris (deep femoral) artery

Perforating branches

Adductor longus muscle (*cut*)

Vastus lateralis muscle

Vastus intermedius muscle

Rectus femoris muscle (*cut*)

Saphenous nerve

Anteromedial intermuscular septum (*opened*)

Vastus medialis muscle

Quadriceps femoris tendon

Patella and patellar anastomosis

Medial patellar retinaculum

Patellar ligament

External iliac artery and vein

Inguinal ligament (Poupart's)

Femoral artery and vein (*cut*)

Pectineus muscle (*cut*)

Obturator canal

Obturator externus muscle

Adductor longus muscle (*cut*)

Anterior branch and Posterior branch of obturator nerve

Quadratus femoris muscle

Adductor brevis muscle

Branches of posterior branch of obturator nerve

Adductor magnus muscle

Gracilis muscle

Cutaneous branch of obturator nerve

Femoral artery and vein (*cut*)

Descending genicular artery
Articular branch
Saphenous branch

Adductor hiatus

Sartorius muscle (*cut*)

Adductor magnus tendon

Adductor tubercle on medial epicondyle of femur

Superior medial genicular artery (from popliteal artery)

Infrapatellar branch of Saphenous nerve

Inferior medial genicular artery (from popliteal artery)

Plate 501   Arteries and Nerves of Thigh: Posterior View. (Netter: Atlas of Human Anatomy, 4 ed, 2006, Saunders.)

Deep dissection

Superior clunial nerves

Gluteus maximus muscle (*cut*)

Medial clunial nerves

Inferior gluteal artery and nerve

Pudendal nerve

Nerve to obturator internus (and superior gemellus)

Posterior femoral cutaneous nerve

Sacrotuberous ligament

Ischial tuberosity

Inferior clunial nerves (*cut*)

Adductor magnus muscle

Gracilis muscle

Sciatic nerve

Muscular branches of sciatic nerve

Semitendinosus muscle (*retracted*)

Semimembranosus muscle

Sciatic nerve

Articular branch

Adductor hiatus

Popliteal vein and artery

Superior medial genicular artery

Medial epicondyle of femur

Tibial nerve

Gastrocnemius muscle (medial head)

Medial sural cutaneous nerve

Small saphenous vein

Iliac crest

Gluteal aponeurosis and gluteus medius muscle (*cut*)

Superior gluteal artery and nerve

Gluteus minimus muscle

Tensor fasciae latae muscle

Piriformis muscle

Gluteus medius muscle (*cut*)

Superior gemellus muscle

Greater trochanter of femur

Obturator internus muscle

Inferior gemellus muscle

Gluteus maximus muscle (*cut*)

Quadratus femoris muscle

Medial circumflex femoral artery

Vastus lateralis muscle and iliotibial tract

Adductor minimus part of adductor magnus muscle

1st perforating artery (from profunda femoris artery)

Adductor magnus muscle

2nd and 3rd perforating arteries (from profunda femoris artery)

4th perforating artery (from profunda femoris artery)

Long head (*retracted*) } Biceps femoris
Short head } muscle

Superior lateral genicular artery

Common fibular (peroneal) nerve

Plantaris muscle

Gastrocnemius muscle (lateral head)

Lateral sural cutaneous nerve

F. Netter M.D.

Plate 502 Arteries and Nerves of Thigh: Posterior View. (Netter: Atlas of Human Anatomy, 4 ed, 2006, Saunders.)

Horizontal section

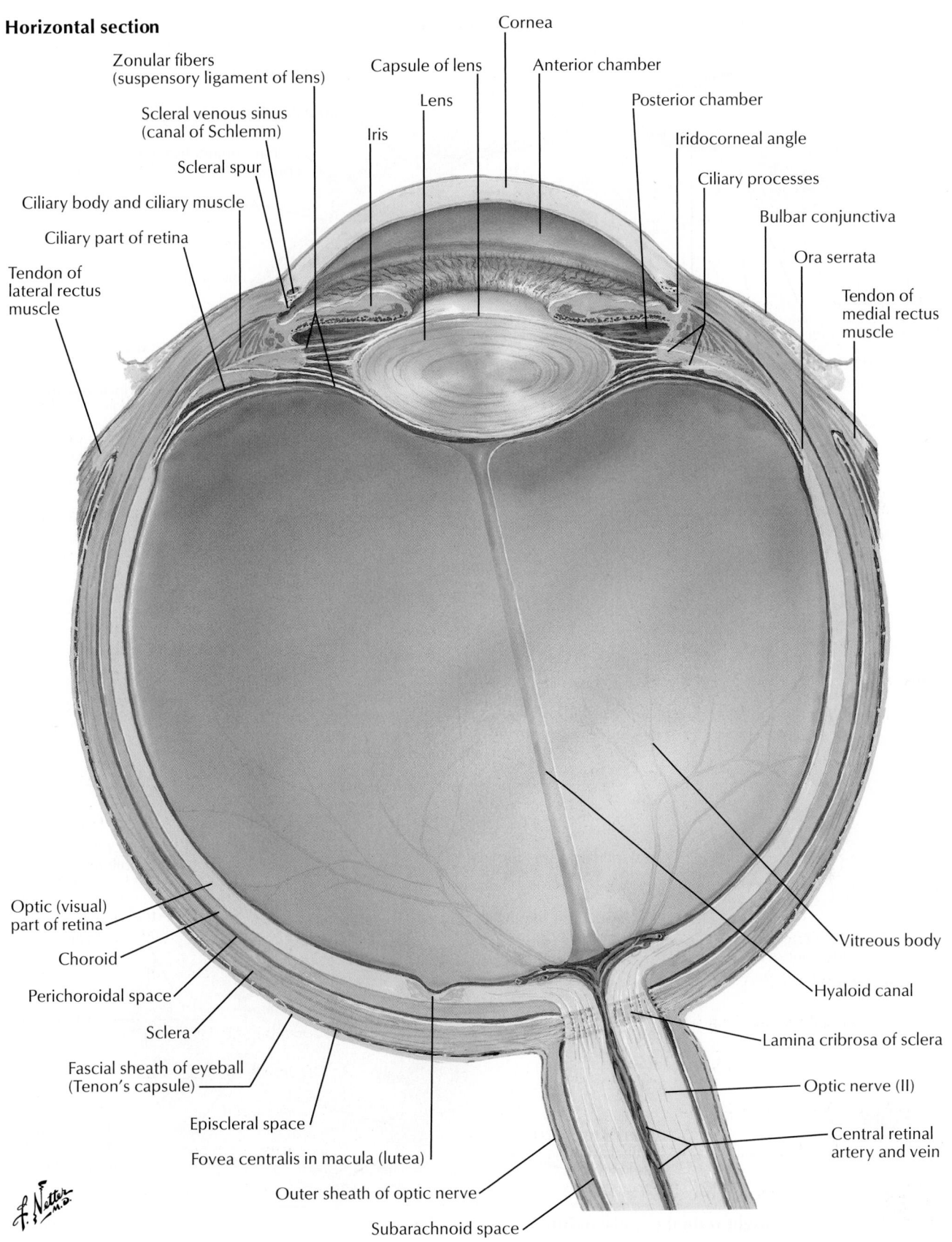

Zonular fibers
(suspensory ligament of lens)

Scleral venous sinus
(canal of Schlemm)

Scleral spur

Ciliary body and ciliary muscle

Ciliary part of retina

Tendon of
lateral rectus
muscle

Iris

Capsule of lens

Lens

Cornea

Anterior chamber

Posterior chamber

Iridocorneal angle

Ciliary processes

Bulbar conjunctiva

Ora serrata

Tendon of
medial rectus
muscle

Optic (visual)
part of retina

Choroid

Perichoroidal space

Sclera

Fascial sheath of eyeball
(Tenon's capsule)

Episcleral space

Fovea centralis in macula (lutea)

Outer sheath of optic nerve

Subarachnoid space

Vitreous body

Hyaloid canal

Lamina cribrosa of sclera

Optic nerve (II)

Central retinal
artery and vein

Plate 87   Eyeball. (Netter: Atlas of Human Anatomy, 4 ed, 2006, Saunders.)

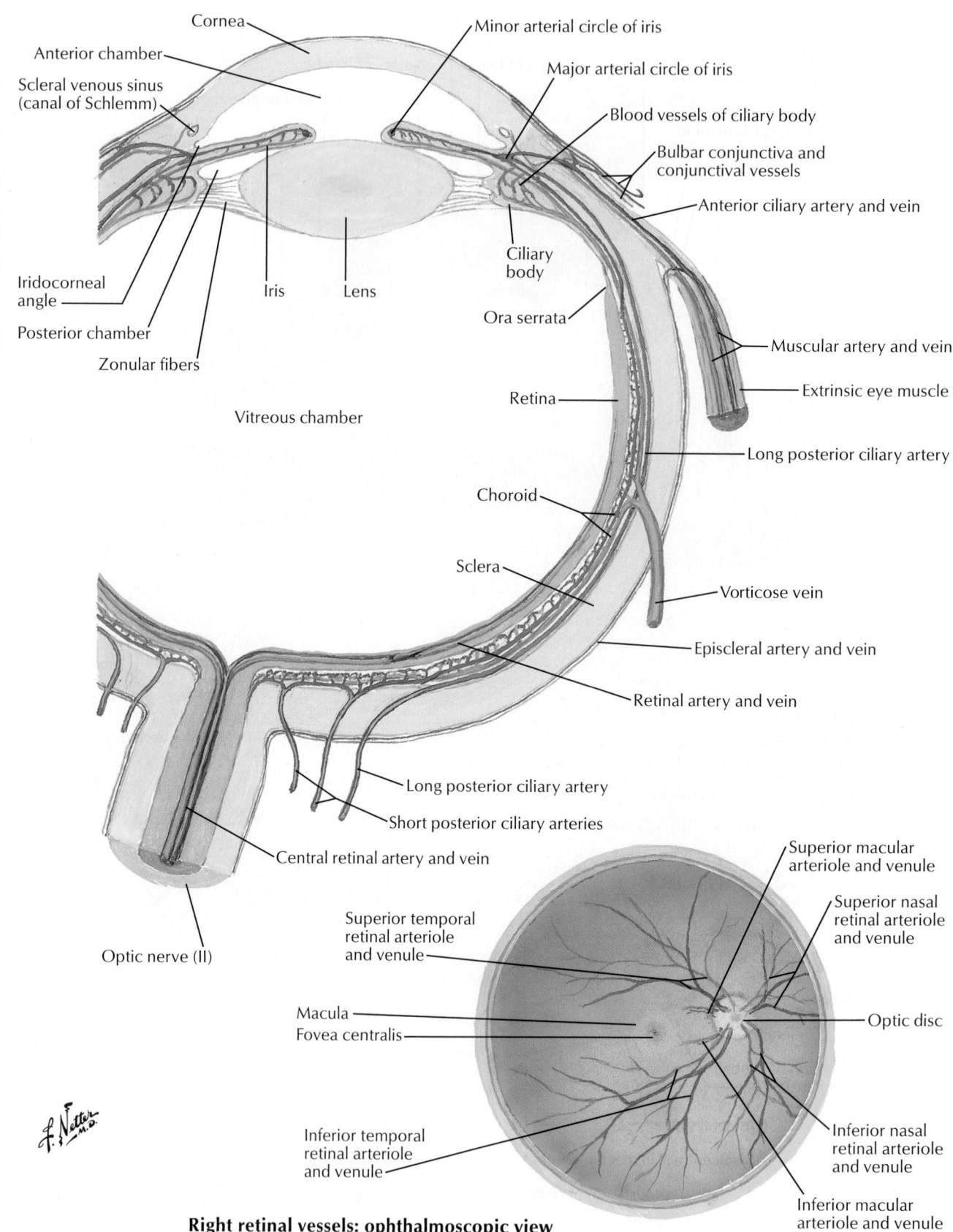

Cornea

Anterior chamber

Scleral venous sinus (canal of Schlemm)

Minor arterial circle of iris

Major arterial circle of iris

Blood vessels of ciliary body

Bulbar conjunctiva and conjunctival vessels

Anterior ciliary artery and vein

Iridocorneal angle

Iris

Lens

Ciliary body

Posterior chamber

Zonular fibers

Ora serrata

Muscular artery and vein

Extrinsic eye muscle

Vitreous chamber

Retina

Long posterior ciliary artery

Choroid

Sclera

Vorticose vein

Episcleral artery and vein

Retinal artery and vein

Long posterior ciliary artery

Short posterior ciliary arteries

Optic nerve (II)

Central retinal artery and vein

Superior temporal retinal arteriole and venule

Superior macular arteriole and venule

Superior nasal retinal arteriole and venule

Macula

Fovea centralis

Optic disc

Inferior temporal retinal arteriole and venule

Inferior nasal retinal arteriole and venule

Inferior macular arteriole and venule

Right retinal vessels: ophthalmoscopic view

Plate 90   Intrinsic Arteries and Veins of Eye. (Netter: Atlas of Human Anatomy, 4 ed, 2006, Saunders.)

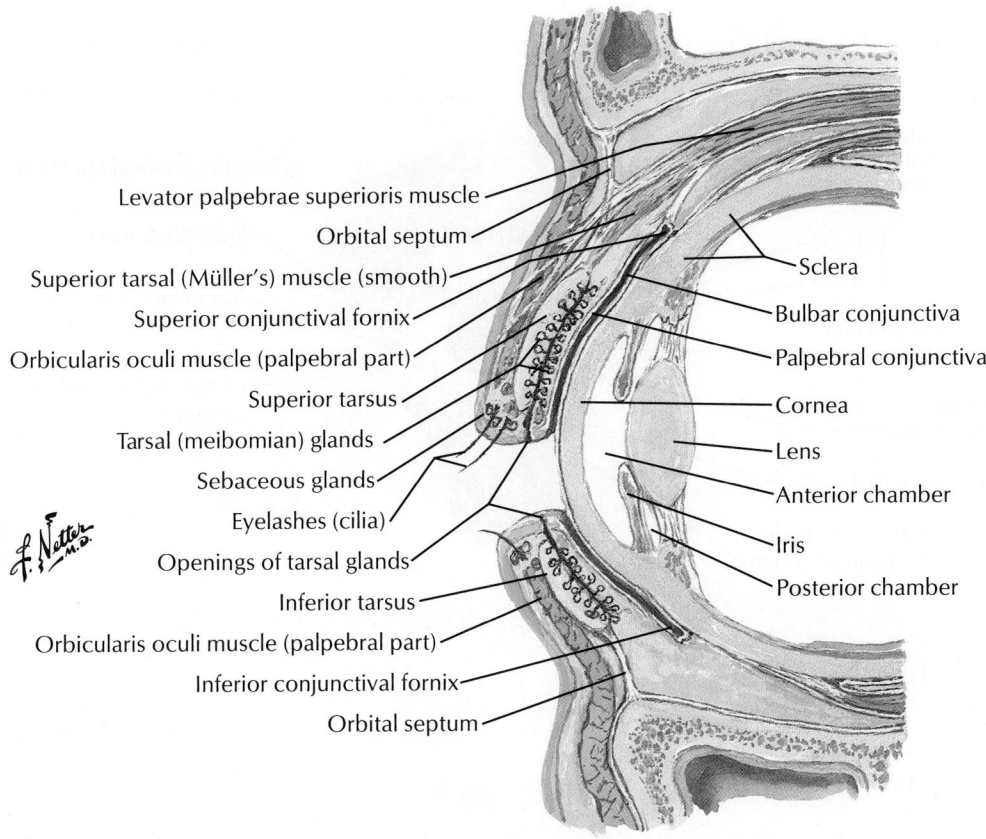

Levator palpebrae superioris muscle
Orbital septum
Superior tarsal (Müller's) muscle (smooth)
Superior conjunctival fornix
Orbicularis oculi muscle (palpebral part)
Superior tarsus
Tarsal (meibomian) glands
Sebaceous glands
Eyelashes (cilia)
Openings of tarsal glands
Inferior tarsus
Orbicularis oculi muscle (palpebral part)
Inferior conjunctival fornix
Orbital septum

Sclera
Bulbar conjunctiva
Palpebral conjunctiva
Cornea
Lens
Anterior chamber
Iris
Posterior chamber

Plate 81, Middle   Eyelids. (Netter: Atlas of Human Anatomy, 4 ed, 2006, Saunders.)

67

NETTER'S ANATOMY ILLUSTRATIONS

Superior palpebral conjunctiva: tarsal (meibomian) glands shining through

Seen through cornea { Pupil / Iris

Corneoscleral junction (corneal limbus)

Bulbar conjunctiva over sclera

Inferior conjunctival fornix

Inferior palpebral conjunctiva: tarsal glands shining through

Superior lacrimal papilla and punctum

Plica semilunaris

Lacrimal caruncle in lacrimal lake (lacus lacrimalis)

Inferior lacrimal papilla and punctum

Plate 81, Upper Eyelid. (Netter: Atlas of Human Anatomy, 4 ed, 2006, Saunders.)

Orbital part of lacrimal gland

Palpebral part of lacrimal gland

Excretory ducts of lacrimal gland

Plica semilunaris

Lacrimal caruncle

Inferior lacrimal papilla and punctum

Superior lacrimal papilla and punctum

Lacrimal canaliculi

Lacrimal sac

Nasolacrimal duct

Opening of nasolacrimal duct

Frontal bone (cut away)

Orbital part of lacrimal gland

Palpebral part of lacrimal gland

Excretory ducts of lacrimal gland

Plica semilunaris and lacrimal lake

Lacrimal caruncle

Inferior lacrimal papilla and punctum

Opening of nasolacrimal duct

Superior lacrimal papilla and punctum

Lacrimal canaliculi

Lacrimal sac

Nasolacrimal duct

Middle nasal concha

Nasal cavity

Inferior nasal concha (cut)

Inferior nasal meatus

Plate 82 Lacrimal Apparatus. (Netter: Atlas of Human Anatomy, 4 ed, 2006, Saunders.)

NETTER'S ANATOMY ILLUSTRATIONS

Frontal section

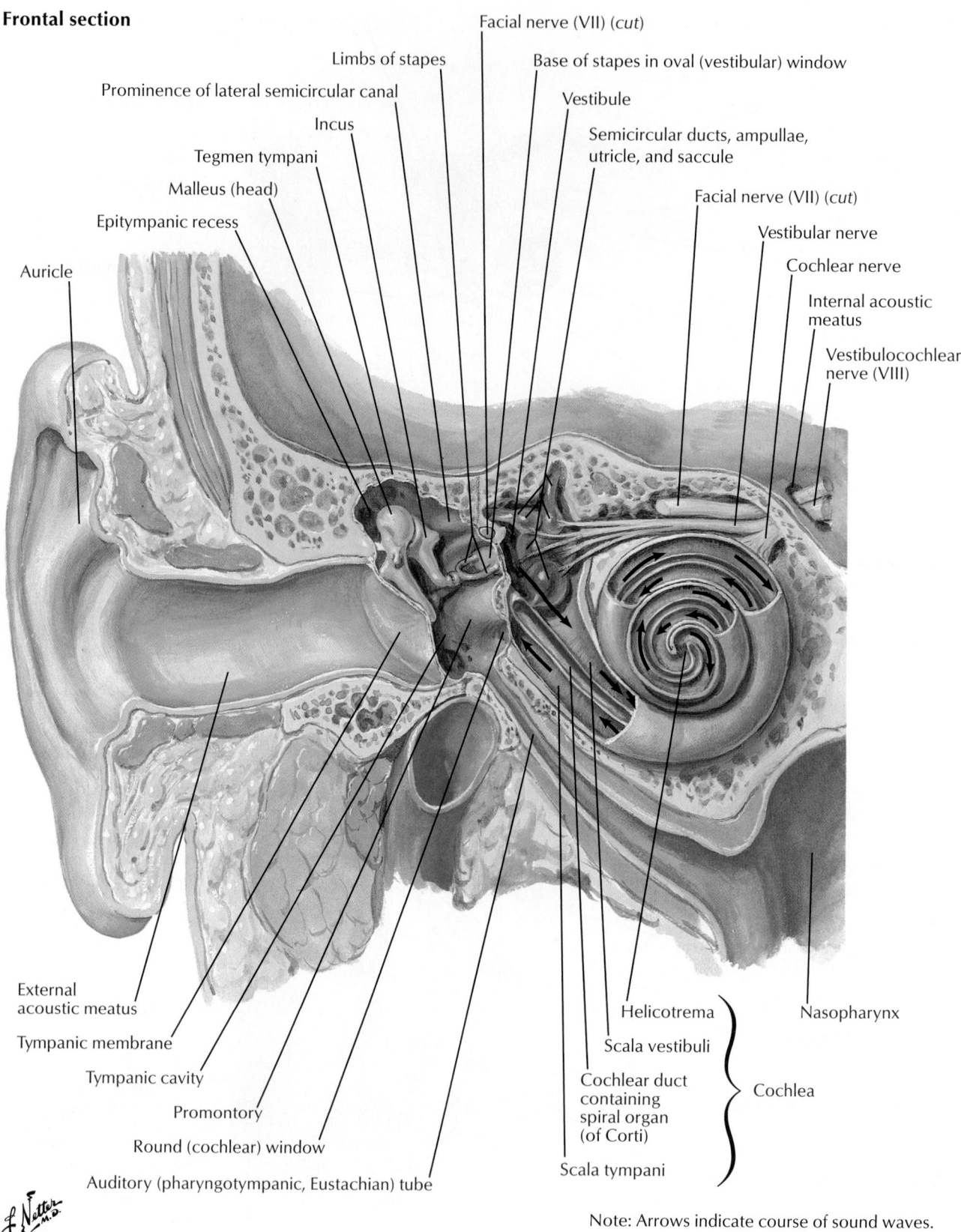

Facial nerve (VII) (*cut*)

Limbs of stapes

Base of stapes in oval (vestibular) window

Prominence of lateral semicircular canal

Vestibule

Incus

Semicircular ducts, ampullae, utricle, and saccule

Tegmen tympani

Malleus (head)

Facial nerve (VII) (*cut*)

Epitympanic recess

Vestibular nerve

Cochlear nerve

Auricle

Internal acoustic meatus

Vestibulocochlear nerve (VIII)

External acoustic meatus

Helicotrema

Nasopharynx

Tympanic membrane

Scala vestibuli

Tympanic cavity

Cochlear duct containing spiral organ (of Corti)

Cochlea

Promontory

Round (cochlear) window

Scala tympani

Auditory (pharyngotympanic, Eustachian) tube

Note: Arrows indicate course of sound waves.

Plate 92 Pathway of Sound Reception. (Netter: Atlas of Human Anatomy, 4 ed, 2006, Saunders.)

Medial wall of tympanic cavity: lateral view

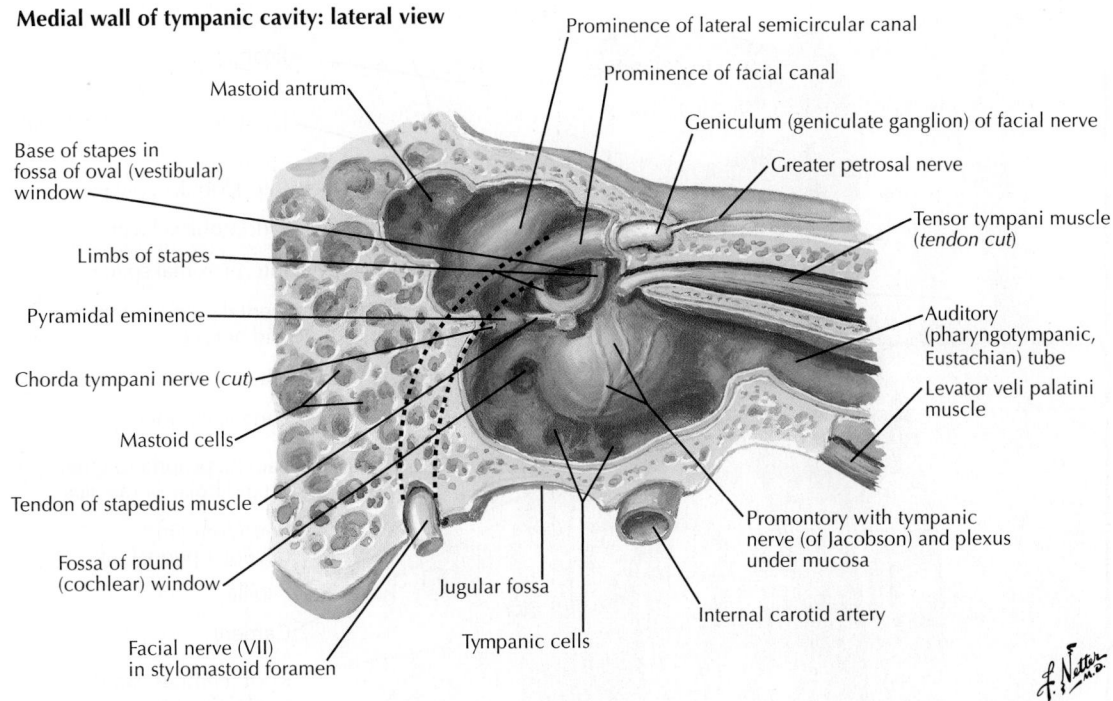

Mastoid antrum

Base of stapes in fossa of oval (vestibular) window

Limbs of stapes

Pyramidal eminence

Chorda tympani nerve (*cut*)

Mastoid cells

Tendon of stapedius muscle

Fossa of round (cochlear) window

Facial nerve (VII) in stylomastoid foramen

Jugular fossa

Tympanic cells

Prominence of lateral semicircular canal

Prominence of facial canal

Geniculum (geniculate ganglion) of facial nerve

Greater petrosal nerve

Tensor tympani muscle (*tendon cut*)

Auditory (pharyngotympanic, Eustachian) tube

Levator veli palatini muscle

Promontory with tympanic nerve (of Jacobson) and plexus under mucosa

Internal carotid artery

Plate 94 Tympanic Cavity. (Netter: Atlas of Human Anatomy, 4 ed, 2006, Saunders.)

Otoscopic view of right tympanic membrane

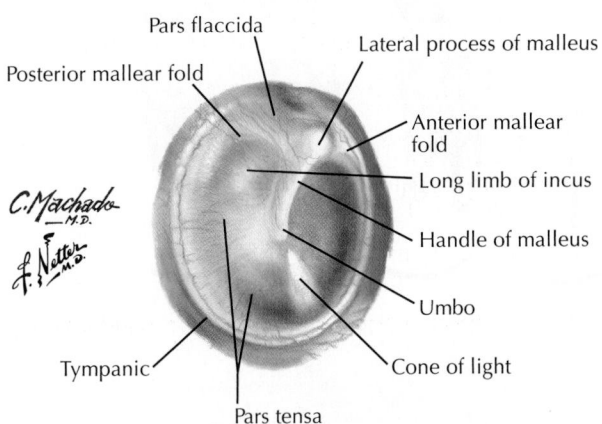

Pars flaccida

Posterior mallear fold

Lateral process of malleus

Anterior mallear fold

Long limb of incus

Handle of malleus

Umbo

Tympanic

Pars tensa

Cone of light

Plate 93 Tympanic Cavity. (Netter: Atlas of Human Anatomy, 4 ed, 2006, Saunders.)

Dissected right bony labyrinth (otic capsule): membranous labyrinth removed

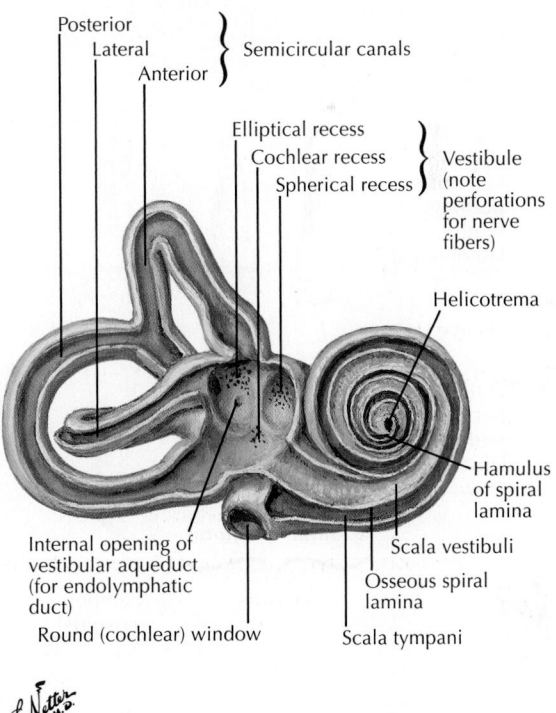

Posterior

Lateral

Anterior

} Semicircular canals

Elliptical recess

Cochlear recess

Spherical recess

} Vestibule (note perforations for nerve fibers)

Helicotrema

Internal opening of vestibular aqueduct (for endolymphatic duct)

Round (cochlear) window

Hamulus of spiral lamina

Scala vestibuli

Osseous spiral lamina

Scala tympani

Plate 95 Bony Membranous Labyrinth. (Netter: Atlas of Human Anatomy, 4 ed, 2006, Saunders.)

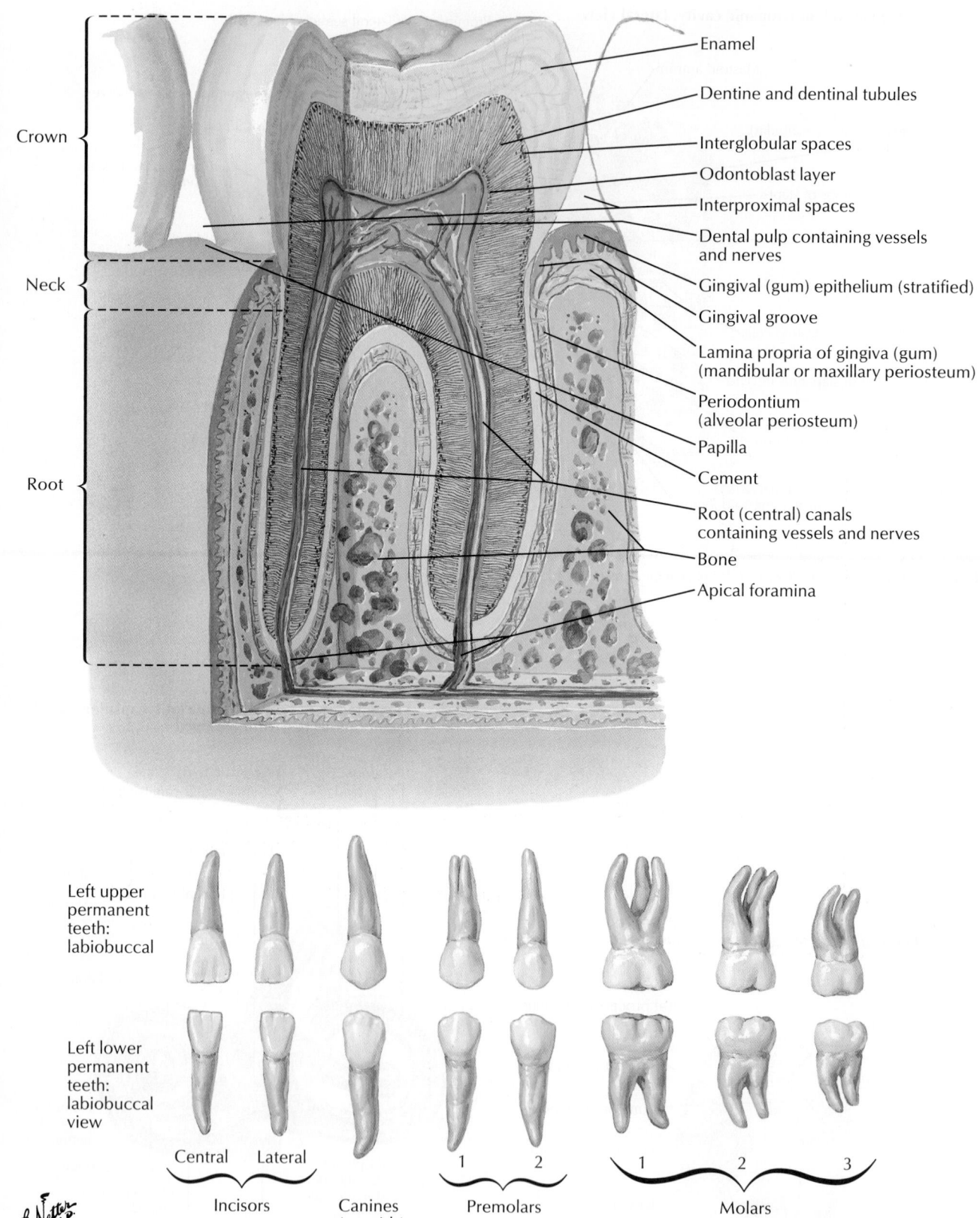

Crown

Neck

Root

Enamel

Dentine and dentinal tubules

Interglobular spaces

Odontoblast layer

Interproximal spaces

Dental pulp containing vessels
and nerves

Gingival (gum) epithelium (stratified)

Gingival groove

Lamina propria of gingiva (gum)
(mandibular or maxillary periosteum)

Periodontium
(alveolar periosteum)

Papilla

Cement

Root (central) canals
containing vessels and nerves

Bone

Apical foramina

Left upper
permanent
teeth:
labiobuccal

Left lower
permanent
teeth:
labiobuccal
view

Central   Lateral

Incisors

Canines
(cuspids)

1   2

Premolars

1   2   3

Molars

Plate 57   Teeth. (Netter: Atlas of Human Anatomy, 4 ed, 2006, Saunders.)

Tongue

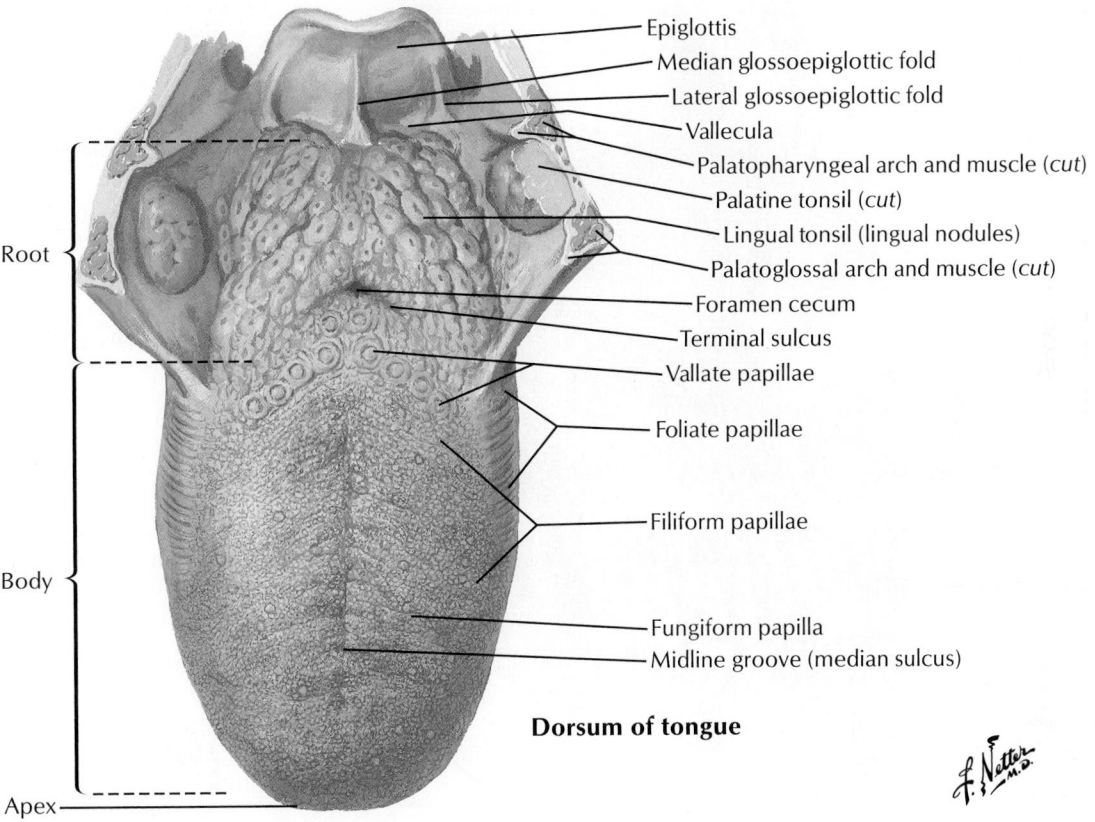

Epiglottis
Median glossoepiglottic fold
Lateral glossoepiglottic fold
Vallecula
Palatopharyngeal arch and muscle (*cut*)
Palatine tonsil (*cut*)
Lingual tonsil (lingual nodules)
Palatoglossal arch and muscle (*cut*)
Foramen cecum
Terminal sulcus
Vallate papillae
Foliate papillae
Filiform papillae
Fungiform papilla
Midline groove (median sulcus)

Root

Body

Apex

Dorsum of tongue

Plate 58   Tongue. (Netter: Atlas of Human Anatomy, 4 ed, 2006, Saunders.)

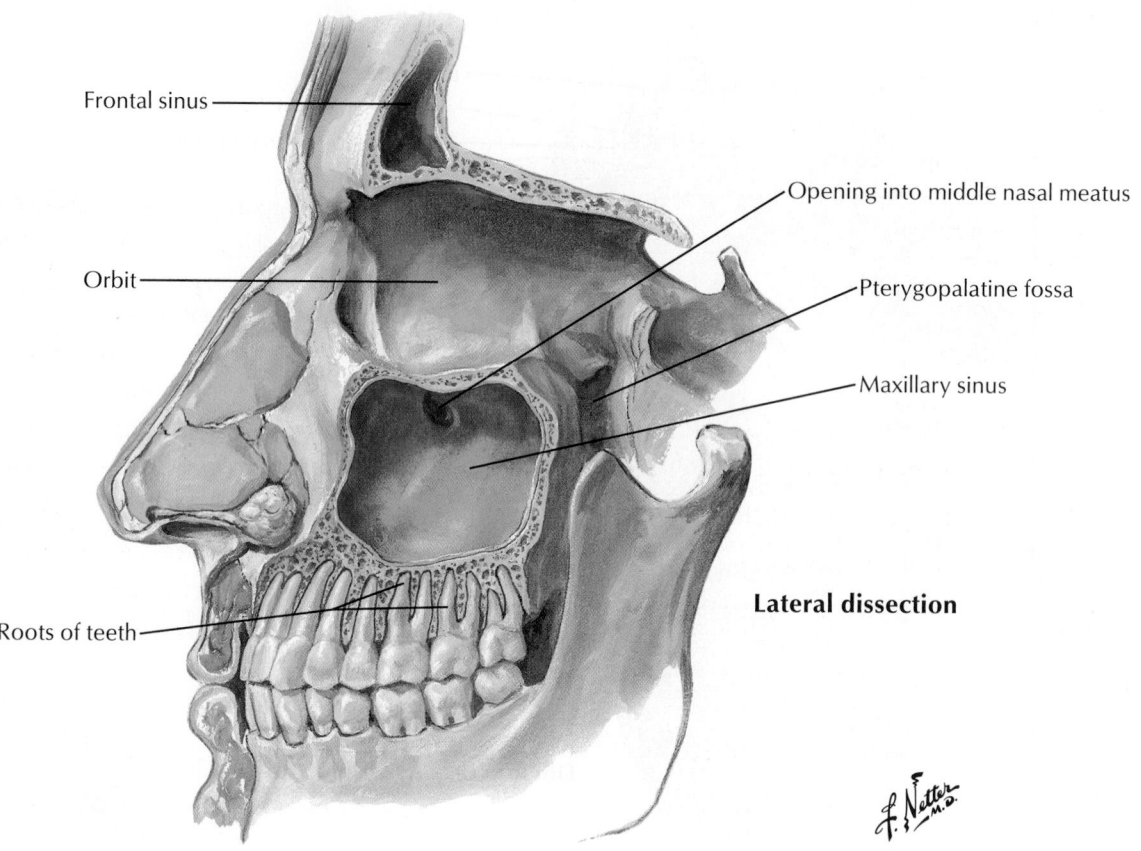

Frontal sinus

Opening into middle nasal meatus

Orbit

Pterygopalatine fossa

Maxillary sinus

Lateral dissection

Roots of teeth

Plate 49   Paranasal Sinuses. (Netter: Atlas of Human Anatomy, 4 ed, 2006, Saunders.)

74

Superficial temporal artery and vein and auriculotemporal nerve

Branches of facial nerve

Transverse facial artery

Accessory parotid gland

Parotid duct

Buccinator muscle (*cut*)

Masseter muscle

Lingual nerve

Submandibular ganglion

Tongue

Frenulum of tongue

Sublingual fold with openings of sublingual ducts

Sublingual caruncle with opening of submandibular duct

Sublingual gland

Submandibular duct

Sublingual artery and vein

Mylohyoid muscle (*cut*)

Digastric muscle (anterior belly)

Submandibular gland

Facial artery and vein

Hyoid bone

Parotid gland

Retromandibular vein (anterior and posterior branches)

Digastric muscle (posterior belly)

Stylohyoid muscle

External jugular vein

Sternocleidomastoid muscle

Common trunk receiving facial, anterior branch of retromandibular, and lingual veins (common facial vein)

Internal jugular vein

External carotid artery

Parotid gland: totally serous

Submandibular gland: mostly serous, partially mucous

Sublingual gland: almost completely mucous

Plate 61   Salivary Glands. (Netter: Atlas of Human Anatomy, 4 ed, 2006, Saunders.)

Coronary Arteries: Arteriographic Views

Right coronary artery: left anterior oblique view

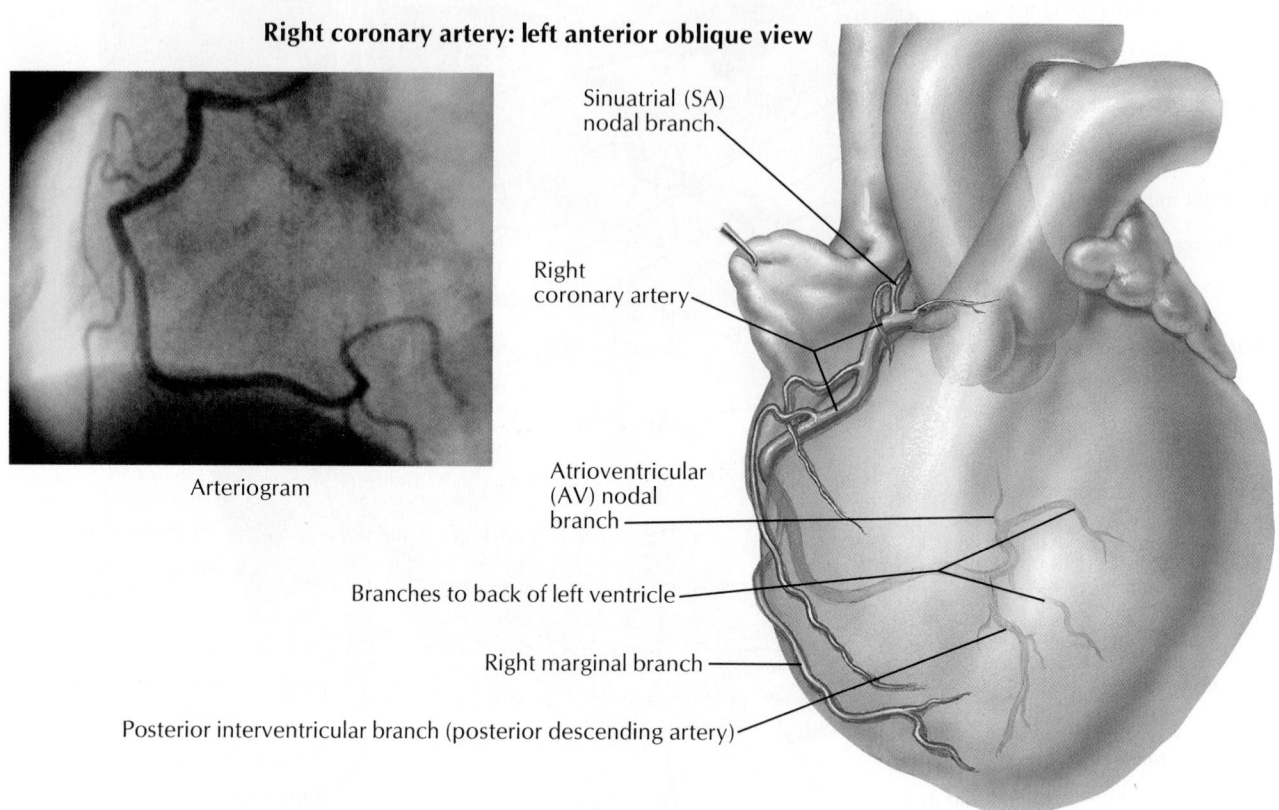

Arteriogram

Sinuatrial (SA) nodal branch

Right coronary artery

Atrioventricular (AV) nodal branch

Branches to back of left ventricle

Right marginal branch

Posterior interventricular branch (posterior descending artery)

Right coronary artery: right anterior oblique view

Sinuatrial (SA) nodal branch

Conus (arteriosus) branch

Right coronary artery

Right marginal branch

Arteriogram

Atrioventricular (AV) nodal branch

Right posterolateral branches (to back of left ventricle)

Posterior interventricular branch (posterior descending artery)

Plate 218   Coronary Arteries: Arteriographic Views. (Netter: Atlas of Human Anatomy, 4 ed, 2006, Saunders.)

76

Left coronary artery: left anterior oblique view

Left coronary artery

Circumflex branch

Arteriogram

Anterior interventricular branch (left anterior descending)

Diagonal branches of anterior interventricular branch

Atrioventricular branch of circumflex branch

Left (obtuse) marginal branch

Posterolateral branches

(Perforating) interventricular septal branches

Left coronary artery: right anterior oblique view

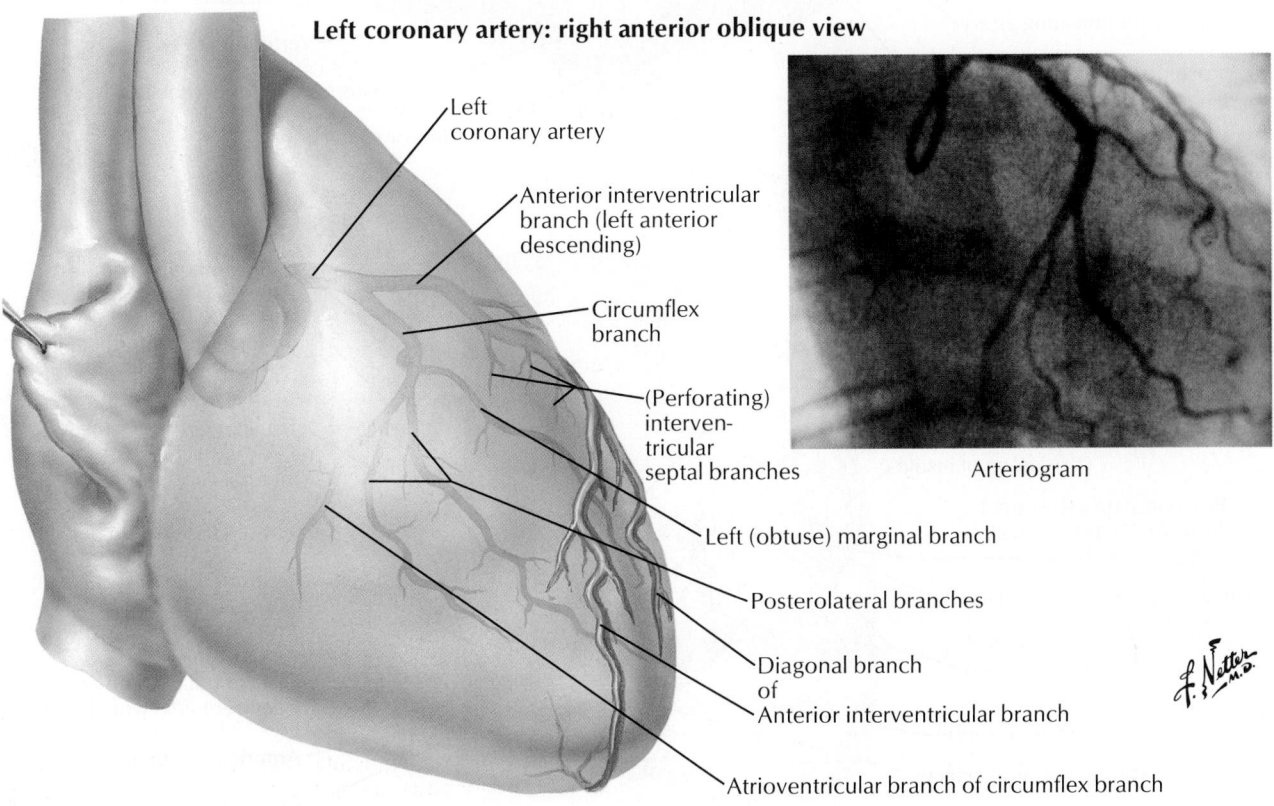

Left coronary artery

Anterior interventricular branch (left anterior descending)

Circumflex branch

(Perforating) interventricular septal branches

Arteriogram

Left (obtuse) marginal branch

Posterolateral branches

Diagonal branch of Anterior interventricular branch

Atrioventricular branch of circumflex branch

Plate 219   Coronary Arteries: Arteriographic Views. (Netter: Atlas of Human Anatomy, 4 ed, 2006, Saunders.)

Corpus callosum

Anterolateral central
(lenticulostriate) arteries

Lateral frontobasal
(orbitofrontal) artery

Prefrontal artery

Precentral (pre-Rolandic)
and central (Rolandic)
sulcal arteries

Anterior parietal
(postcentral sulcal)
artery

Posterior parietal
artery

Branch to
angular gyrus

Temporal branches
(anterior, middle,
and posterior)

Middle cerebral artery
and branches
(deep in lateral cerebral
[Sylvian] sulcus)

Anterior communicating artery

Posterior communicating artery

Anterior inferior cerebellar artery (AICA)

Posterior spinal artery

Paracentral artery

Medial frontal branches

Pericallosal artery

Callosomarginal artery

Polar frontal artery

**Anterior cerebral
arteries**

Medial frontobasal
(orbitofrontal) artery

Distal medial striate
artery (recurrent
artery of Heubner)

Internal carotid
artery

Anterior choroidal
artery

**Posterior cerebral
artery**

Superior cerebellar artery

Basilar and pontine arteries

Labyrinthine (internal
acoustic) artery

Vertebral artery

Posterior inferior cerebellar artery (PICA)

Anterior spinal artery

Corpus striatum
(caudate and lentiform nuclei)

Anterolateral central
(lenticulostriate) arteries

Insula (island of Reil)

Limen of insula

Precentral (pre-Rolandic),
central (Rolandic) sulcal,
and parietal arteries

Lateral cerebral (Sylvian) sulcus

Temporal branches of
middle cerebral artery

Temporal lobe

Middle cerebral artery

Internal carotid artery

Falx cerebri

Callosomarginal arteries
and
Pericallosal arteries
(branches of anterior
cerebral arteries)

Trunk of corpus callosum

Internal capsule

Septum pellucidum

Rostrum of corpus callosum

Anterior cerebral arteries

Distal medial striate artery
(recurrent artery of Heubner)

Anterior communicating artery

Optic chiasm

Plate 141 Arteries of Brain: Frontal View and Section. (Netter: Atlas of Human Anatomy, 4 ed, 2006, Saunders.)

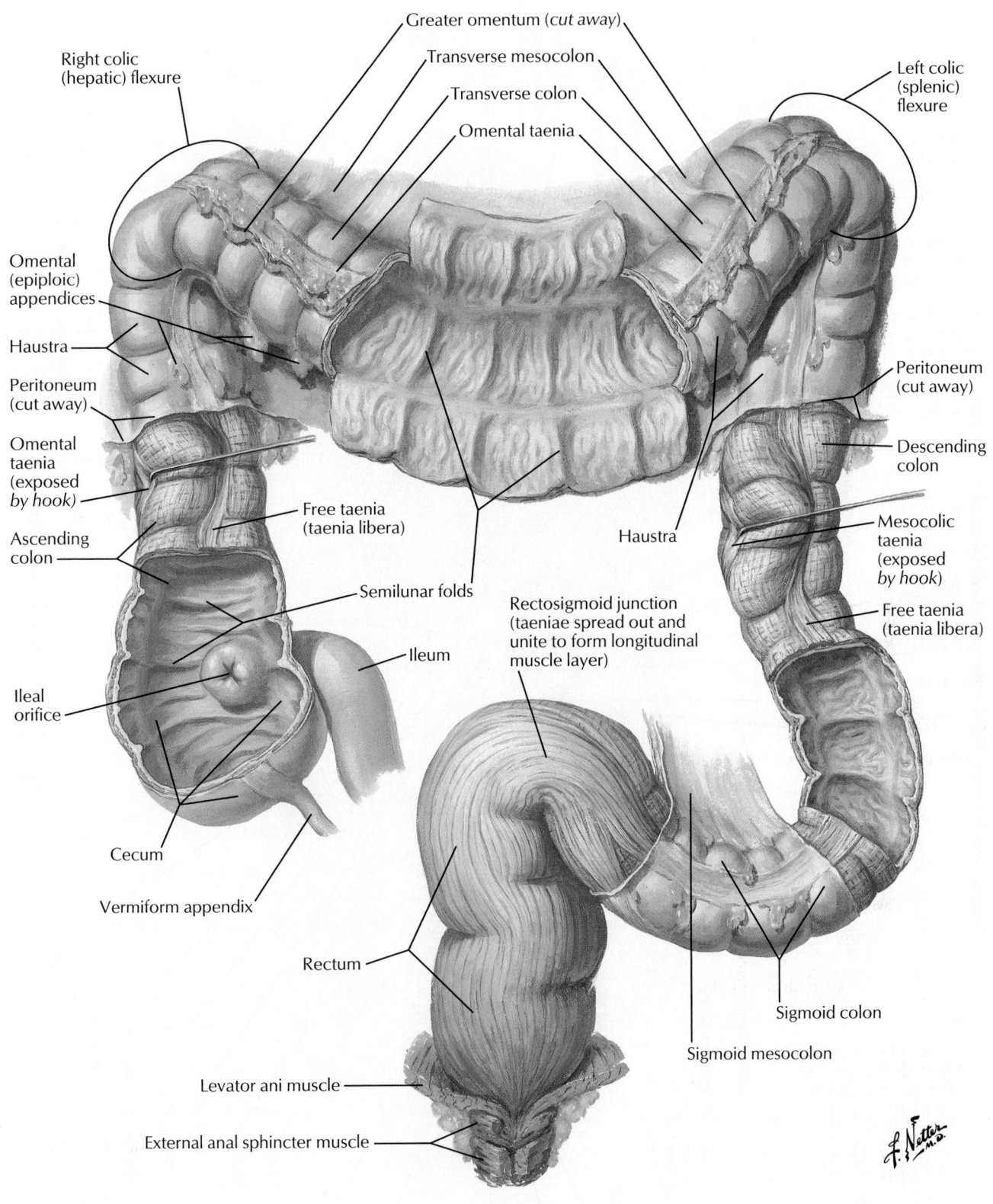

Right colic (hepatic) flexure

Greater omentum (*cut away*)

Transverse mesocolon

Transverse colon

Omental taenia

Left colic (splenic) flexure

Omental (epiploic) appendices

Haustra

Peritoneum (cut away)

Omental taenia (exposed *by hook*)

Ascending colon

Free taenia (taenia libera)

Semilunar folds

Haustra

Peritoneum (cut away)

Descending colon

Mesocolic taenia (exposed *by hook*)

Free taenia (taenia libera)

Ileum

Ileal orifice

Rectosigmoid junction (taeniae spread out and unite to form longitudinal muscle layer)

Cecum

Vermiform appendix

Rectum

Sigmoid colon

Sigmoid mesocolon

Levator ani muscle

External anal sphincter muscle

Plate 284 Mucosa and Musculature of Large Intestine. (Netter: Atlas of Human Anatomy, 4 ed, 2006, Saunders.)

79

NETTER'S ANATOMY ILLUSTRATIONS

Transverse Section: T3–4 Intervertebral Disc, Manubrium

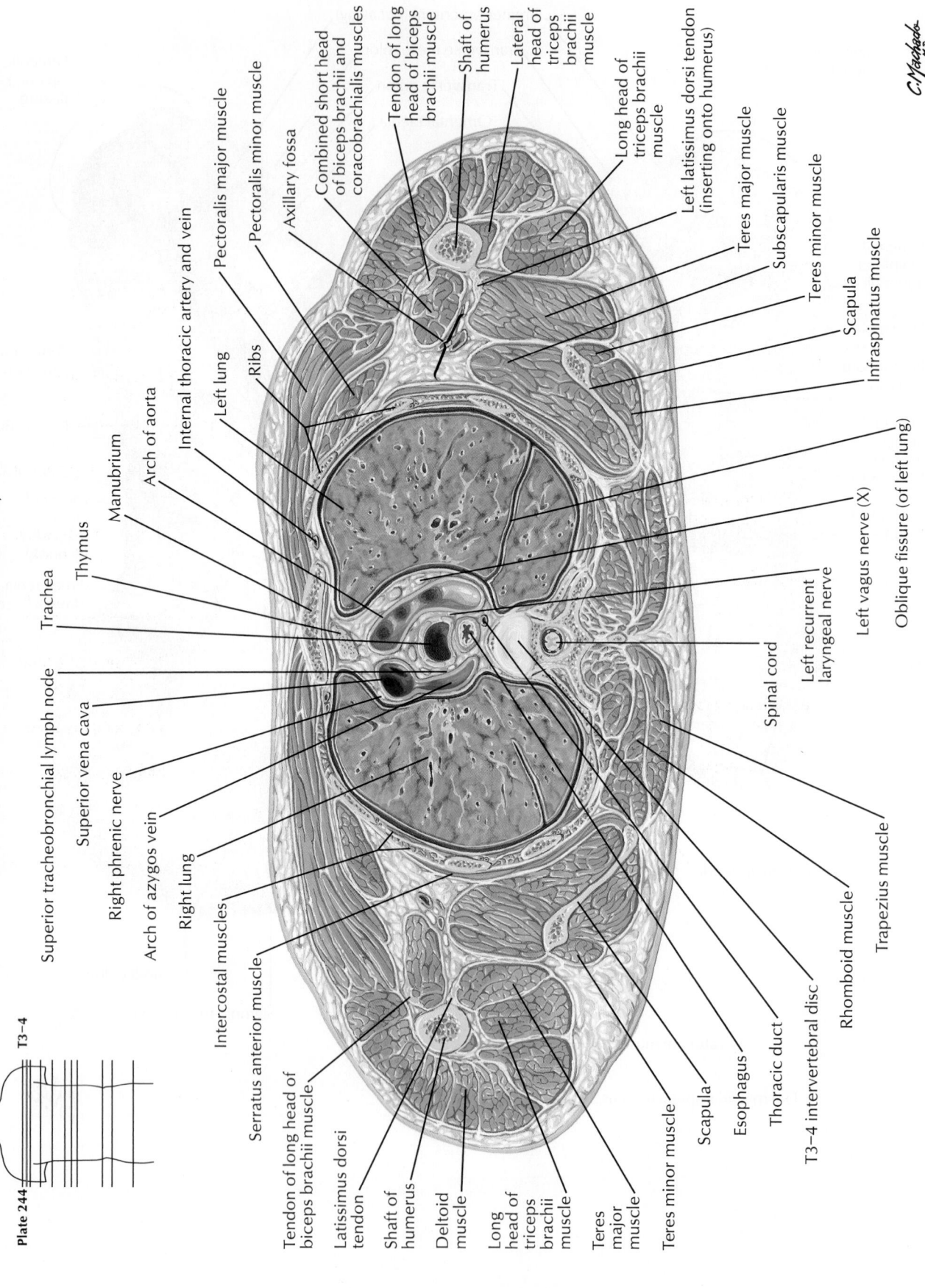

C. Machado
—M.D.

Plate 244

T3–4

Superior tracheobronchial lymph node

Trachea

Thymus

Manubrium

Arch of aorta

Internal thoracic artery and vein

Left lung

Ribs

Pectoralis major muscle

Pectoralis minor muscle

Axillary fossa

Combined short head of biceps brachii and coracobrachialis muscles

Tendon of long head of biceps brachii muscle

Shaft of humerus

Lateral head of triceps brachii muscle

Long head of triceps brachii muscle

Left latissimus dorsi tendon (inserting onto humerus)

Teres major muscle

Subscapularis muscle

Teres minor muscle

Scapula

Infraspinatus muscle

Left vagus nerve (X)

Oblique fissure (of left lung)

Left recurrent laryngeal nerve

Spinal cord

Trapezius muscle

Rhomboid muscle

T3–4 intervertebral disc

Thoracic duct

Esophagus

Scapula

Teres minor muscle

Teres major muscle

Long head of triceps brachii muscle

Deltoid muscle

Shaft of humerus

Latissimus dorsi tendon

Tendon of long head of biceps brachii muscle

Serratus anterior muscle

Intercostal muscles

Right lung

Arch of azygos vein

Right phrenic nerve

Superior vena cava

Plate 244 Cross Section of Thorax at T3-4 Disc Level. (Netter: Atlas of Human Anatomy, 4 ed, 2006, Saunders.)

Right knee in extension: posterior view

Posterior cruciate ligament

Anterior cruciate ligament

Posterior meniscofemoral ligament

Lateral condyle of femur (articular surface)

Popliteus tendon

Fibular collateral ligament

Lateral meniscus

Head of fibula

Adductor tubercle on medial epicondyle of femur

Medial condyle of femur (articular surface)

Medial meniscus

Tibial collateral ligament

Medial condyle of tibia

Plate 509   Knee: Cruciate and Collateral Ligaments. (Netter: Atlas of Human Anatomy, 4 ed, 2006, Saunders.)

Paramedian (sagittal) dissection

Ureter

Uterine (fallopian) tube

Ovary

Ligament of ovary

Round ligament of uterus

Broad ligament (*cut*)

Superior pubic ramus (*cut*)

Inferior pubic ramus (*cut*)

Ischiocavernosus muscle

Body of clitoris

Labia minora

Labium majus

Rectouterine pouch (of Douglas)

Peritoneum (*cut edge*)

Vesicouterine pouch

Rectum

Ureter

Urinary bladder

Vagina

Pelvic diaphragm (levator ani muscle)

Deep transverse perineal muscle (*cut*)

External anal sphincter muscle

Median (sagittal) section

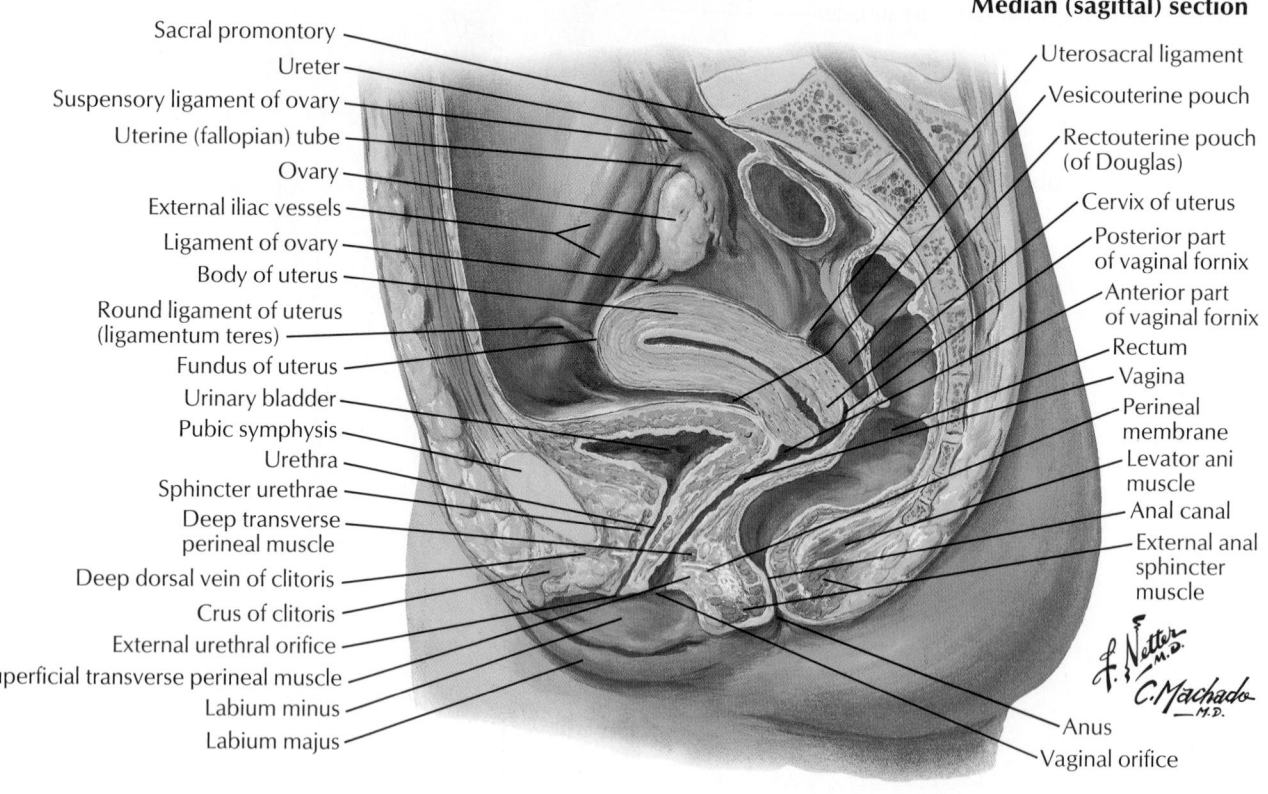

Sacral promontory

Ureter

Suspensory ligament of ovary

Uterine (fallopian) tube

Ovary

External iliac vessels

Ligament of ovary

Body of uterus

Round ligament of uterus (ligamentum teres)

Fundus of uterus

Urinary bladder

Pubic symphysis

Urethra

Sphincter urethrae

Deep transverse perineal muscle

Deep dorsal vein of clitoris

Crus of clitoris

External urethral orifice

Superficial transverse perineal muscle

Labium minus

Labium majus

Uterosacral ligament

Vesicouterine pouch

Rectouterine pouch (of Douglas)

Cervix of uterus

Posterior part of vaginal fornix

Anterior part of vaginal fornix

Rectum

Vagina

Perineal membrane

Levator ani muscle

Anal canal

External anal sphincter muscle

Anus

Vaginal orifice

Plate 360 Pelvic Viscera and Perineum: Female. (Netter: Atlas of Human Anatomy, 4 ed, 2006, Saunders.)

PART II

Alphabetic Index

A

Aarskog's syndrome Q87.1
Abandonment —see Maltreatment
Abasia (-astasia) (hysterical) F44.4
Abderhalden-Kaufmann-Lignac syndrome
(cystinosis) E72.04
Abdomen, abdominal —see also condition
acute R10.0
angina K55.1
muscle deficiency syndrome Q79.4
Abdominalgia —see Pain, abdominal
Abduction contracture, hip or other joint —see
Contraction, joint
Aberrant (congenital) —see also Malposition,
congenital
adrenal gland Q89.1
artery (peripheral) Q27.8
basilar NEC Q28.1
cerebral Q28.3
coronary Q24.5
digestive system Q27.8
eye Q15.8
lower limb Q27.8
precerebral Q28.1
pulmonary Q25.79
renal Q27.2
retina Q14.1
specified site NEC Q27.8
subclavian Q27.8
upper limb Q27.8
vertebral Q28.1
breast Q83.8
endocrine gland NEC Q89.2
hepatic duct Q44.5
pancreas Q45.3
parathyroid gland Q89.2
pituitary gland Q89.2
sebaceous glands, mucous membrane,
mouth, congenital Q38.6
spleen Q89.09
subclavian artery Q27.8
thymus (gland) Q89.2
thyroid gland Q89.2
vein (peripheral) NEC Q27.8
cerebral Q28.3
digestive system Q27.8
lower limb Q27.8
precerebral Q28.1
specified site NEC Q27.8
upper limb Q27.8
Aberration
distantial —see Disturbance, visual
mental F99
Abetalipoproteinemia E78.6
Abiotrophy R68.89
Ablatio, ablation
retinae —see Detachment, retina
Ablepharia, ablepharon Q10.3
Abnormal, abnormality, abnormalities —see
also Anomaly
acid-base balance (mixed) E87.4
albumin R77.0
alphafetoprotein R77.2
alveolar ridge K08.9
anatomical relationship Q89.9
apertures, congenital, diaphragm
Q79.1
auditory perception H93.29-•
diplacusis —see Diplacusis
hyperacusis —see Hyperacusis
recruitment —see Recruitment, auditory
threshold shift —see Shift, auditory
threshold
autosomes Q99.9
fragile site Q95.5
basal metabolic rate R94.8
biosynthesis, testicular androgen
E29.1
bleeding time R79.1

Abnormal, abnormality, abnormalities —
(Continued)
blood level (of)
cobalt R79.0
copper R79.0
iron R79.0
lithium R78.89
magnesium R79.0
mineral NEC R79.0
zinc R79.0
blood pressure
elevated R03.0
low reading (nonspecific) R03.1
blood sugar R73.09
blood-gas level R79.81
bowel sounds R19.15
absent R19.11
hyperactive R19.12
brain scan R94.02
breathing R06.9
caloric test R94.138
cerebrospinal fluid R83.9
cytology R83.6
drug level R83.2
enzyme level R83.0
hormones R83.1
immunology R83.4
microbiology R83.5
nonmedicinal level R83.3
specified type NEC R83.8
chemistry, blood R79.9
C-reactive protein R79.82
drugs —see Findings, abnormal, in blood
gas level R79.81
minerals R79.0
pancytopenia D61.818
PTT R79.1
specified NEC R79.89
toxins —see Findings, abnormal, in
blood
chest sounds (friction) (rales) R09.89
chromosome, chromosomal Q99.9
with more than three X chromosomes,
female Q97.1
analysis result R89.8
bronchial washings R84.8
cerebrospinal fluid R83.8
cervix uteri NEC R87.89
nasal secretions R84.8
nipple discharge R89.8
peritoneal fluid R85.89
pleural fluid R84.8
prostatic secretions R86.8
saliva R85.89
seminal fluid R86.8
sputum R84.8
synovial fluid R89.8
throat scrapings R84.8
vagina R87.89
vulva R87.89
wound secretions R89.8
dicentric replacement Q93.2
ring replacement Q93.2
sex Q99.8
female phenotype Q97.9
specified NEC Q97.8
male phenotype Q98.9
specified NEC Q98.8
structural male Q98.6
specified NEC Q99.8
clinical findings NEC R68.89
coagulation D68.9
newborn, transient P61.6
profile R79.1
time R79.1
communication —see Fistula
conjunctiva, vascular H11.41-•
coronary artery Q24.5
cortisol-binding globulin E27.8
course, eustachian tube Q17.8

Abnormal, abnormality, abnormalities —
(Continued)
creatinine clearance R94.4
cytology
anus R85.619
atypical squamous cells cannot
exclude high grade squamous
intraepithelial lesion (ASC-H)
R85.611
atypical squamous cells of undetermined
significance (ASC-US) R85.610
cytologic evidence of malignancy
R85.614
high grade squamous intraepithelial
lesion (HGSIL) R85.613
human papillomavirus (HPV) DNA test
high risk positive R85.81
low risk postive R85.82
inadequate smear R85.615
low grade squamous intraepithelial
lesion (LGSIL) R85.612
satisfactory anal smear but lacking
transformation zone R85.616
specified NEC R85.618
unsatisfactory smear R85.615
female genital organs —see Abnormal,
Papanicolaou (smear)
dark adaptation curve H53.61
dentofacial NEC —see Anomaly, dentofacial
development, developmental Q89.9
central nervous system Q07.9
diagnostic imaging
abdomen, abdominal region NEC R93.5
biliary tract R93.2
bladder R93.41
breast R92.8
central nervous system NEC R90.89
cerebrovascular NEC R90.89
coronary circulation R93.1
digestive tract NEC R93.3
gastrointestinal (tract) R93.3
➡genitourinary organs R93.89
head R93.0
heart R93.1
➡intrathoracic organ NEC R93.89
kidney R93.42-•
limbs R93.6
liver R93.2
lung (field) R91.8
musculoskeletal system NEC R93.7
renal pelvis R93.41
retroperitoneum R93.5
➡site specified NEC R93.89
➡skin and subcutaneous tissue R93.89
skull R93.0
▶testis R93.81-•
urinary organs specified NEC R93.49
ureter R93.41
direction, teeth, fully erupted M26.30
ear ossicles, acquired NEC H74.39-•
ankylosis —see Ankylosis, ear ossicles
discontinuity —see Discontinuity, ossicles,
ear
partial loss —see Loss, ossicles, ear (partial)
Ebstein Q22.5
echocardiogram R93.1
echoencephalogram R90.81
echogram —see Abnormal, diagnostic
imaging
electrocardiogram [ECG] [EKG] R94.31
electroencephalogram [EEG] R94.01
electrolyte —see Imbalance, electrolyte
electromyogram [EMG] R94.131
electro-oculogram [EOG] R94.110
electrophysiological intracardiac studies
R94.39
electroretinogram [ERG] R94.111
erythrocytes
congenital, with perinatal jaundice D58.9
feces (color) (contents) (mucus) R19.5

Abnormal, abnormality, abnormalities —
   (Continued)
finding —*see* Findings, abnormal, without
      diagnosis
fluid
   amniotic —*see* Abnormal, specimen,
      specified
   cerebrospinal —*see* Abnormal,
      cerebrospinal fluid
   peritoneal —*see* Abnormal, specimen,
      digestive organs
   pleural —*see* Abnormal, specimen,
      respiratory organs
   synovial —*see* Abnormal, specimen,
      specified
   thorax (bronchial washings) (pleural
      fluid) —*see* Abnormal, specimen,
      respiratory organs
   vaginal —*see* Abnormal, specimen, female
      genital organs
form
   teeth K00.2
   uterus —*see* Anomaly, uterus
function studies
   auditory R94.120
   bladder R94.8
   brain R94.09
   cardiovascular R94.30
   ear R94.128
   endocrine NEC R94.7
   eye NEC R94.118
   kidney R94.4
   liver R94.5
   nervous system
      central NEC R94.09
      peripheral NEC R94.138
   pancreas R94.8
   placenta R94.8
   pulmonary R94.2
   special senses NEC R94.128
   spleen R94.8
   thyroid R94.6
   vestibular R94.121
gait —*see* Gait
   hysterical F44.4
gastrin secretion E16.4
globulin R77.1
   cortisol-binding E27.8
   thyroid-binding E07.89
glomerular, minor —*see also* N00-N07 with
      fourth character .0 N05.0
glucagon secretion E16.3
glucose tolerance (test) (non-fasting)
      R73.09
gravitational (G) forces or states (effect of)
      T75.81
hair (color) (shaft) L67.9
   specified NEC L67.8
hard tissue formation in pulp (dental)
      K04.3
head movement R25.0
heart
   rate R00.9
      specified NEC R00.8
   shadow R93.1
   sounds NEC R01.2
hemoglobin (disease) —*see also* Disease,
      hemoglobin D58.2
   trait —*see* Trait, hemoglobin, abnormal
histology NEC R89.7
immunological findings R89.4
   in serum R76.9
      specified NEC R76.8
increase in appetite R63.2
involuntary movement —*see* Abnormal,
      movement, involuntary
jaw closure M26.51
karyotype R89.8
kidney function test R94.4
knee jerk R29.2
leukocyte (cell) (differential) NEC D72.9

Abnormal, abnormality, abnormalities —
   (Continued)
liver function test R94.5
loss of
   height R29.890
   weight R63.4
mammogram NEC R92.8
   calcification (calculus) R92.1
   microcalcification R92.0
Mantoux test R76.11
movement (disorder) —*see also* Disorder,
      movement
   head R25.0
   involuntary R25.9
      fasciculation R25.3
      of head R25.0
      spasm R25.2
      specified type NEC R25.8
      tremor R25.1
myoglobin (Aberdeen) (Annapolis) R89.7
neonatal screening P09
oculomotor study R94.113
palmar creases Q82.8
Papanicolaou (smear)
   anus R85.619
      atypical squamous cells cannot
         exclude high grade squamous
         intraepithelial lesion (ASC-H)
         R85.611
      atypical squamous cells of undetermined
         significance (ASC-US) R85.610
      cytologic evidence of malignancy
         R85.614
      high grade squamous intraepithelial
         lesion (HGSIL) R85.613
      human papillomavirus (HPV)
         DNA test
         high risk positive R85.81
         low risk postive R85.82
      inadequate smear R85.615
      low grade squamous intraepithelial
         lesion (LGSIL) R85.612
      satisfactory anal smear but lacking
         transformation zone R85.616
      specified NEC R85.618
      unsatisfactory smear R85.615
   bronchial washings R84.6
   cerebrospinal fluid R83.6
   cervix R87.619
      atypical squamous cells cannot
         exclude high grade squamous
         intraepithelial lesion (ASC-H)
         R87.611
      atypical squamous cells of undetermined
         significance (ASC-US) R87.610
      cytologic evidence of malignancy
         R87.614
      high grade squamous intraepithelial
         lesion (HGSIL) R87.613
      inadequate smear R87.615
      low grade squamous intraepithelial
         lesion (LGSIL) R87.612
      non-atypical endometrial cells
         R87.618
      satisfactory cervical smear but
         lacking transformation zone
         R87.616
      specified NEC R87.618
      thin preparaton R87.619
      unsatisfactory smear R87.615
   nasal secretions R84.6
   nipple discharge R89.6
   peritoneal fluid R85.69
   pleural fluid R84.6
   prostatic secretions R86.6
   saliva R85.69
   seminal fluid R86.6
   sites NEC R89.6
   sputum R84.6
   synovial fluid R89.6
   throat scrapings R84.6

Abnormal, abnormality, abnormalities —
   (Continued)
Papanicolaou (smear) *(Continued)*
   vagina R87.629
      atypical squamous cells cannot
         exclude high grade squamous
         intraepithelial lesion (ASC-H)
         R87.621
      atypical squamous cells of
         undetermined significance
         (ASC-US) R87.620
      cytologic evidence of malignancy
         R87.624
      high grade squamous intraepithelial
         lesion (HGSIL) R87.623
      inadequate smear R87.625
      low grade squamous intraepithelial
         lesion (LGSIL) R87.622
      specified NEC R87.628
      thin preparation R87.629
      unsatisfactory smear R87.625
   vulva R87.69
   wound secretions R89.6
partial thromboplastin time (PTT) R79.1
pelvis (bony) —*see* Deformity, pelvis
percussion, chest (tympany) R09.89
periods (grossly) —*see* Menstruation
phonocardiogram R94.39
plantar reflex R29.2
plasma
   protein R77.9
      specified NEC R77.8
   viscosity R70.1
pleural (folds) Q34.0
posture R29.3
product of conception O02.9
   specified type NEC O02.89
prothrombin time (PT) R79.1
pulmonary
   artery, congenital Q25.79
   function, newborn P28.89
   test results R94.2
pulsations in neck R00.2
pupillary H21.56-●
   function (reaction) (reflex) —*see* Anomaly,
      pupil, function
radiological examination —*see* Abnormal,
      diagnostic imaging
red blood cell(s) (morphology) (volume)
      R71.8
reflex —*see* Reflex
renal function test R94.4
response to nerve stimulation R94.130
retinal correspondence H53.31
retinal function study R94.111
rhythm, heart —*see also* Arrhythmia
saliva —*see* Abnormal, specimen, digestive
      organs
scan
   kidney R94.4
   liver R93.2
   thyroid R94.6
secretion
   gastrin E16.4
   glucagon E16.3
semen, seminal fluid —*see* Abnormal,
      specimen, male genital organs
serum level (of)
   acid phosphatase R74.8
   alkaline phosphatase R74.8
   amylase R74.8
   enzymes R74.9
      specified NEC R74.8
   lipase R74.8
   triacylglycerol lipase R74.8
shape
   gravid uterus —*see* Anomaly, uterus
sinus venosus Q21.1
size, tooth, teeth K00.2
spacing, tooth, teeth, fully erupted
      M26.30

Abnormal, abnormality, abnormalities —
(Continued)
specimen
digestive organs (peritoneal fluid) (saliva)
R85.9
cytology R85.69
drug level R85.2
enzyme level R85.0
histology R85.7
hormones R85.1
immunology R85.4
microbiology R85.5
nonmedicinal level R85.3
specified type NEC R85.89
female genital organs (secretions) (smears)
R87.9
cytology R87.69
cervix R87.619
human papillomavirus (HPV) DNA
test
high risk positive R87.810
low risk positive R87.820
inadequate (unsatisfactory) smear
R87.615
non-atypical endometrial cells
R87.618
specified NEC R87.618
vagina R87.629
human papillomavirus (HPV) DNA
test
high risk positive R87.811
low risk positive R87.821
inadequate (unsatisfactory) smear
R87.625
vulva R87.69
drug level R87.2
enzyme level R87.0
histological R87.7
hormones R87.1
immunology R87.4
microbiology R87.5
nonmedicinal level R87.3
specified type NEC R87.89
male genital organs (prostatic secretions)
(semen) R86.9
cytology R86.6
drug level R86.2
enzyme level R86.0
histological R86.7
hormones R86.1
immunology R86.4
microbiology R86.5
nonmedicinal level R86.3
specified type NEC R86.8
nipple discharge —see Abnormal,
specimen, specified
respiratory organs (bronchial washings)
(nasal secretions) (pleural fluid)
(sputum) R84.9
cytology R84.6
drug level R84.2
enzyme level R84.0
histology R84.7
hormones R84.1
immunology R84.4
microbiology R84.5
nonmedicinal level R84.3
specified type NEC R84.8
specified organ, system and tissue NOS
R89.9
cytology R89.6
drug level R89.2
enzyme level R89.0
histology R89.7
hormones R89.1
immunology R89.4
microbiology R89.5
nonmedicinal level R89.3
specified type NEC R89.8
synovial fluid —see Abnormal, specimen,
specified

Abnormal, abnormality, abnormalities —
(Continued)
specimen (Continued)
thorax (bronchial washings) (pleural
fluids) —see Abnormal, specimen,
respiratory organs
vagina (secretion) (smear) R87.629
vulva (secretion) (smear) R87.69
wound secretion —see Abnormal,
specimen, specified
spermatozoa —see Abnormal, specimen, male
genital organs
sputum (amount) (color) (odor) R09.3
stool (color) (contents) (mucus) R19.5
bloody K92.1
guaiac positive R19.5
synchondrosis Q78.8
thermography —see also Abnormal,
➠diagnostic imaging R93.89
thyroid-binding globulin E07.89
tooth, teeth (form) (size) K00.2
toxicology (findings) R78.9
transport protein E88.09
tumor marker NEC R97.8
ultrasound results —see Abnormal, diagnostic
imaging
umbilical cord complicating delivery O69.9
urination NEC R39.198
urine (constituents) R82.90
bile R82.2
cytological examination R82.8
drugs R82.5
fat R82.0
glucose R81
heavy metals R82.6
hemoglobin R82.3
histological examination R82.8
ketones R82.4
microbiological examination (culture)
R82.79
myoglobin R82.1
positive culture R82.79
protein —see Proteinuria
➠specified substance NEC R82.998
chromoabnormality NEC R82.91
substances nonmedical R82.6
uterine hemorrhage —see Hemorrhage,
uterus
vectorcardiogram R94.39
visually evoked potential (VEP) R94.112
white blood cells D72.9
specified NEC D72.89
X-ray examination —see Abnormal,
diagnostic imaging
Abnormity (any organ or part) —see Anomaly
Abocclusion M26.29
hemolytic disease (newborn) P55.1
incompatibility reaction ABO —see
Complication(s), transfusion,
incompatibility reaction, ABO
Abolition, language R48.8
Aborter, habitual or recurrent —see Loss (of),
pregnancy, recurrent
Abortion (complete) (spontaneous) O03.9
with
retained products of conception —see
Abortion, incomplete
attempted (elective) (failed) O07.4
complicated by O07.30
afibrinogenemia O07.1
cardiac arrest O07.36
chemical damage of pelvic organ(s)
O07.34
circulatory collapse O07.31
cystitis O07.38
defibrination syndrome O07.1
electrolyte imbalance O07.33
embolism (air) (amniotic fluid) (blood
clot) (fat) (pulmonary) (septic)
(soap) O07.2
endometritis O07.0

Abortion (Continued)
attempted (Continued)
complicated by (Continued)
genital tract and pelvic infection O07.0
hemolysis O07.1
hemorrhage (delayed) (excessive) O07.1
infection
genital tract or pelvic O07.0
urinary tract tract O07.38
intravascular coagulation O07.1
laceration of pelvic organ(s) O07.34
metabolic disorder O07.33
oliguria O07.32
oophoritis O07.0
parametritis O07.0
pelvic peritonitis O07.0
perforation of pelvic organ(s) O07.34
renal failure or shutdown O07.32
salpingitis or salpingo-oophoritis O07.0
sepsis O07.37
shock O07.31
specified condition NEC O07.39
tubular necrosis (renal) O07.32
uremia O07.32
urinary tract infection O07.38
venous complication NEC O07.35
embolism (air) (amniotic fluid) (blood
clot) (fat) (pulmonary) (septic)
(soap) O07.2
complicated (by) (following) O03.80
afibrinogenemia O03.6
cardiac arrest O03.86
chemical damage of pelvic organ(s) O03.84
circulatory collapse O03.81
cystitis O03.88
defibrination syndrome O03.6
electrolyte imbalance O03.83
embolism (air) (amniotic fluid) (blood clot)
(fat) (pulmonary) (septic) (soap) O03.7
endometritis O03.5
genital tract and pelvic infection O03.5
hemolysis O03.6
hemorrhage (delayed) (excessive) O03.6
infection
genital tract or pelvic O03.5
urinary tract O03.88
intravascular coagulation O03.6
laceration of pelvic organ(s) O03.84
metabolic disorder O03.83
oliguria O03.82
oophoritis O03.5
parametritis O03.5
pelvic peritonitis O03.5
perforation of pelvic organ(s) O03.84
renal failure or shutdown O03.82
salpingitis or salpingo-oophoritis
O03.5
sepsis O03.87
shock O03.81
specified condition NEC O03.89
tubular necrosis (renal) O03.82
uremia O03.82
urinary tract infection O03.88
venous complication NEC O03.85
embolism (air) (amniotic fluid) (blood
clot) (fat) (pulmonary) (septic)
(soap) O03.7
failed —see Abortion, attempted
habitual or recurrent N96
with current abortion —see categories
O03-O04
without current pregnancy N96
care in current pregnancy O26.2-●
incomplete (spontaneous) O03.4
complicated (by) (following) O03.30
afibrinogenemia O03.1
cardiac arrest O03.36
chemical damage of pelvic organ(s)
O03.34
circulatory collapse O03.31
cystitis O03.38

▶ New   ➠ Revised   ~~deleted~~ Deleted   ● Use Additional Character(s)

Abortion *(Continued)*
  incomplete *(Continued)*
    complicated *(Continued)*
      defibrination syndrome O03.1
      electrolyte imbalance O03.33
      embolism (air) (amniotic fluid) (blood clot) (fat) (pulmonary) (septic) (soap) O03.2
      endometritis O03.0
      genital tract and pelvic infection O03.0
      hemolysis O03.1
      hemorrhage (delayed) (excessive) O03.1
      infection
        genital tract or pelvic O03.0
        urinary tract O03.38
      intravascular coagulation O03.1
      laceration of pelvic organ(s) O03.34
      metabolic disorder O03.33
      oliguria O03.32
      oophoritis O03.0
      parametritis O03.0
      pelvic peritonitis O03.0
      perforation of pelvic organ(s) O03.34
      renal failure or shutdown O03.32
      salpingitis or salpingo-oophoritis O03.0
      sepsis O03.37
      shock O03.31
      specified condition NEC O03.39
      tubular necrosis (renal) O03.32
      uremia O03.32
      urinary infection O03.38
      venous complication NEC O03.35
        embolism (air) (amniotic fluid) (blood clot) (fat) (pulmonary) (septic) (soap) O03.2
  induced (encounter for) Z33.2
    complicated by O04.80
      afibrinogenemia O04.6
      cardiac arrest O04.86
      chemical damage of pelvic organ(s) O04.84
      circulatory collapse O04.81
      cystitis O04.88
      defibrination syndrome O04.6
      electrolyte imbalance O04.83
      embolism (air) (amniotic fluid) (blood clot) (fat) (pulmonary) (septic) (soap) O04.7
      endometritis O04.5
      genital tract and pelvic infection O04.5
      hemolysis O04.6
      hemorrhage (delayed) (excessive) O04.6
      infection
        genital tract or pelvic O04.5
        urinary tract O04.88
      intravascular coagulation O04.6
      laceration of pelvic organ(s) O04.84
      metabolic disorder O04.83
      oliguria O04.82
      oophoritis O04.5
      parametritis O04.5
      pelvic peritonitis O04.5
      perforation of pelvic organ(s) O04.84
      renal failure or shutdown O04.82
      salpingitis or salpingo-oophoritis O04.5
      sepsis O04.87
      shock O04.81
      specified condition NEC O04.89
      tubular necrosis (renal) O04.82
      uremia O04.82
      urinary tract infection O04.88
      venous complication NEC O04.85
        embolism (air) (amniotic fluid) (blood clot) (fat) (pulmonary) (septic) (soap) O04.7
  missed O02.1
  spontaneous —*see* Abortion (complete) (spontaneous)
  threatened O20.0
  threatened (spontaneous) O20.0

Abortion *(Continued)*
  tubal O00.10-
    with intrauterine pregnancy O00.11-
Abortus fever A23.1
Aboulomania F60.7
Abrami's disease D59.8
Abramov-Fiedler myocarditis (acute isolated myocarditis) I40.1
Abrasion T14.8
  abdomen, abdominal (wall) S30.811
  alveolar process S00.512
  ankle S90.51-●
  antecubital space —*see* Abrasion, elbow
  anus S30.817
  arm (upper) S40.81-●
  auditory canal —*see* Abrasion, ear
  auricle —*see* Abrasion, ear
  axilla —*see* Abrasion, arm
  back, lower S30.810
  breast S20.11-●
  brow S00.81
  buttock S30.810
  calf —*see* Abrasion, leg
  canthus —*see* Abrasion, eyelid
  cheek S00.81
    internal S00.512
  chest wall —*see* Abrasion, thorax
  chin S00.81
  clitoris S30.814
  cornea S05.0-●
  costal region —*see* Abrasion, thorax
  dental K03.1
  digit(s)
    foot —*see* Abrasion, toe
    hand —*see* Abrasion, finger
  ear S00.41-●
  elbow S50.31-●
  epididymis S30.813
  epigastric region S30.811
  epiglottis S10.11
  esophagus (thoracic) S27.818
    cervical S10.11
  eyebrow —*see* Abrasion, eyelid
  eyelid S00.21-●
  face S00.81
  finger(s) S60.41-●
    index S60.41-●
    little S60.41-●
    middle S60.41-●
    ring S60.41-●
  flank S30.811
  foot (except toe(s) alone) S90.81-●
    toe —*see* Abrasion, toe
  forearm S50.81-●
    elbow only —*see* Abrasion, elbow
  forehead S00.81
  genital organs, external
    female S30.816
    male S30.815
  groin S30.811
  gum S00.512
  hand S60.51-●
  head S00.91
    ear —*see* Abrasion, ear
    eyelid —*see* Abrasion, eyelid
    lip S00.511
    nose S00.31
    oral cavity S00.512
    scalp S00.01
    specified site NEC S00.81
  heel —*see* Abrasion, foot
  hip S70.21-●
  inguinal region S30.811
  interscapular region S20.419
  jaw S00.81
  knee S80.21-●
  labium (majus) (minus) S30.814
  larynx S10.11
  leg (lower) S80.81-●
    knee —*see* Abrasion, knee
    upper —*see* Abrasion, thigh

Abrasion *(Continued)*
  lip S00.511
  lower back S30.810
  lumbar region S30.810
  malar region S00.81
  mammary —*see* Abrasion, breast
  mastoid region S00.81
  mouth S00.512
  nail
    finger —*see* Abrasion, finger
    toe —*see* Abrasion, toe
  nape S10.81
  nasal S00.31
  neck S10.91
    specified site NEC S10.81
    throat S10.11
  nose S00.31
  occipital region S00.01
  oral cavity S00.512
  orbital region —*see* Abrasion, eyelid
  palate S00.512
  palm —*see* Abrasion, hand
  parietal region S00.01
  pelvis S30.810
  penis S30.812
  perineum
    female S30.814
    male S30.810
  periocular area —*see* Abrasion, eyelid
  phalanges
    finger —*see* Abrasion, finger
    toe —*see* Abrasion, toe
  pharynx S10.11
  pinna —*see* Abrasion, ear
  popliteal space —*see* Abrasion, knee
  prepuce S30.812
  pubic region S30.810
  pudendum
    female S30.816
    male S30.815
  sacral region S30.810
  scalp S00.01
  scapular region —*see* Abrasion, shoulder
  scrotum S30.813
  shin —*see* Abrasion, leg
  shoulder S40.21-●
  skin NEC T14.8
  sternal region S20.319
  submaxillary region S00.81
  submental region S00.81
  subungual
    finger(s) —*see* Abrasion, finger
    toe(s) —*see* Abrasion, toe
  supraclavicular fossa S10.81
  supraorbital S00.81
  temple S00.81
  temporal region S00.81
  testis S30.813
  thigh S70.31-●
  thorax, thoracic (wall) S20.91
    back S20.41-●
    front S20.31-●
  throat S10.11
  thumb S60.31-●
  toe(s) (lesser) S90.416
    great S90.41-●
  tongue S00.512
  tooth, teeth (dentifrice) (habitual) (hard tissues) (occupational) (ritual) (traditional) K03.1
  trachea S10.11
  tunica vaginalis S30.813
  tympanum, tympanic membrane —*see* Abrasion, ear
  uvula S00.512
  vagina S30.814
  vocal cords S10.11
  vulva S30.814
  wrist S60.81-●
Abrism —*see* Poisoning, food, noxious, plant

Abruptio placentae O45.9-●
  with
    afibrinogenemia O45.01-●
    coagulation defect O45.00-●
      specified NEC O45.09-●
    disseminated intravascular coagulation
      O45.02-●
    hypofibrinogenemia O45.01-●
  specified NEC O45.8-●
Abruption, placenta —see Abruptio placentae
Abscess (connective tissue) (embolic) (fistulous)
    (infective) (metastatic) (multiple)
    (pernicious) (pyogenic) (septic) L02.91
  with
    diverticular disease (intestine) K57.80
      with bleeding K57.81
      large intestine K57.20
        with
          bleeding K57.21
          small intestine K57.40
            with bleeding K57.41
      small intestine K57.00
        with
          bleeding K57.01
          large intestine K57.40
            with bleeding K57.41
    lymphangitis - code by site under
      Abscess
  abdomen, abdominal
    cavity K65.1
    wall L02.211
  abdominopelvic K65.1
  accessory sinus —see Sinusitis
  adrenal (capsule) (gland) E27.8
  alveolar K04.7
    with sinus K04.6
  ambic A06.4
    brain (and liver or lung abscess) A06.6
    genitourinary tract A06.82
    liver (without mention of brain or lung
      abscess) A06.4
    lung (and liver) (without mention of brain
      abscess) A06.5
    specified site NEC A06.89
    spleen A06.89
  anerobic A48.0
  ankle —see Abscess, lower limb
  anorectal K61.2
  antecubital space —see Abscess, upper limb
  antrum (chronic) (Highmore) —see Sinusitis,
    maxillary
  anus K61.0
  apical (tooth) K04.7
    with sinus (alveolar) K04.6
▶appendix K35.33
  areola (acute) (chronic) (nonpuerperal)
    N61.1
    puerperal, postpartum or gestational —see
      Infection, nipple
  arm (any part) —see Abscess, upper limb
  artery (wall) I77.89
  atheromatous I77.2
  auricle, ear —see Abscess, ear, external
  axilla (region) L02.41-●
    lymph gland or node L04.2
  back (any part, except buttock) L02.212
  Bartholin's gland N75.1
    with
      abortion —see Abortion, by type
        complicated by, sepsis
      ectopic or molar pregnancy O08.0
    following ectopic or molar pregnancy O08.0
  Bezold's —see Mastoiditis, acute
  bilharziasis B65.1
  bladder (wall) —see Cystitis, specified type
    NEC
  bone (subperiosteal) —see also Osteomyelitis,
    specified type NEC
    accessory sinus (chronic) —see Sinusitis
    chronic or old —see Osteomyelitis, chronic
    jaw (lower) (upper) M27.2

Abscess (Continued)
  bone (Continued)
    mastoid —see Mastoiditis, acute,
      subperiosteal
    petrous —see Petrositis
    spinal (tuberculous) A18.01
      nontuberculous —see Osteomyelitis,
        vertebra
  bowel K63.0
  brain (any part) (cystic) (otogenic) G06.0
    amebic (with abscess of any other site) A06.6
    gonococcal A54.82
    pheomycotic (chromomycotic) B43.1
    tuberculous A17.81
  breast (acute) (chronic) (nonpuerperal)
    N61.1
    newborn P39.0
    puerperal, postpartum, gestational —see
      Mastitis, obstetric, purulent
  broad ligament N73.2
    acute N73.0
    chronic N73.1
  Brodie's (localized) (chronic) M86.8X-●
  bronchi J98.09
  buccal cavity K12.2
  bulbourethral gland N34.0
  bursa M71.00
    ankle M71.07-●
    elbow M71.02-●
    foot M71.07-●
    hand M71.04-●
    hip M71.05-●
    knee M71.06-●
    multiple sites M71.09
    pharyngeal J39.1
    shoulder M71.01-●
    specified site NEC M71.08
    wrist M71.03-●
  buttock L02.31
  canthus —see Blepharoconjunctivitis
  cartilage —see Disorder, cartilage, specified
    type NEC
▶cecum K35.33
  cerebellum, cerebellar G06.0
    sequelae G09
  cerebral (embolic) G06.0
    sequelae G09
  cervical (meaning neck) L02.11
    lymph gland or node L04.0
  cervix (stump) (uteri) —see Cervicitis
  cheek (external) L02.01
    inner K12.2
  chest J86.9
    with fistula J86.0
    wall L02.213
  chin L02.01
  choroid —see Inflammation, chorioretinal
  circumtonsillar J36
  cold (lung) (tuberculous) —see also
      Tuberculosis, abscess, lung
    articular —see Tuberculosis, joint
  colon (wall) K63.0
  colostomy K94.02
  conjunctiva —see Conjunctivitis, acute
  cornea H16.31-●
  corpus
    cavernosum N48.21
    luteum —see Oophoritis
  Cowper's gland N34.0
  cranium G06.0
  cul-de-sac (Douglas') (posterior) —see
    Peritonitis, pelvic, female
  cutaneous —see Abscess, by site
  dental K04.7
    with sinus (alveolar) K04.6
  dentoalveolar K04.7
    with sinus K04.6
  diaphragm, diaphragmatic K65.1
  Douglas' cul-de-sac or pouch —see
    Peritonitis, pelvic, female
  Dubois A50.59

Abscess (Continued)
  ear (middle) —see also Otitis, media,
      suppurative
    acute —see Otitis, media, suppurative, acute
    external H60.0-●
  entamebic —see Abscess, amebic
  enterostomy K94.12
  epididymis N45.4
  epidural G06.2
    brain G06.0
    spinal cord G06.1
  epiglottis J38.7
  epiploon, epiploic K65.1
  erysipelatous —see Erysipelas
  esophagus K20.8
  ethmoid (bone) (chronic) (sinus) J32.2
  external auditory canal —see Abscess, ear,
    external
  extradural G06.2
    brain G06.0
      sequelae G09
    spinal cord G06.1
  extraperitoneal K68.19
  eye —see Endophthalmitis, purulent
  eyelid H00.03-●
  face (any part, except ear, eye and nose) L02.01
  fallopian tube —see Salpingitis
  fascia M72.8
  fauces J39.1
  fecal K63.0
  femoral (region) —see Abscess, lower limb
  filaria, filarial —see Infestation, filarial
  finger (any) —see also Abscess, hand
    nail —see Cellulitis, finger
  foot L02.61-●
  forehead L02.01
  frontal sinus (chronic) J32.1
  gallbladder K81.0
  genital organ or tract
    female (external) N76.4
    male N49.9
      multiple sites N49.8
      specified NEC N49.8
  gestational mammary O91.11-●
  gestational subareolar O91.11-●
▶gingival —see Peridontitis, ~~aggressive,~~ localized
  gland, glandular (lymph) (acute) —see
    Lymphadenitis, acute
  gluteal (region) L02.31
  gonorrheal —see Gonococcus
  groin L02.214
▶gum —see Peridontitis, ~~aggressive,~~ localized
  hand L02.51-●
  head NEC L02.811
    face (any part, except ear, eye and nose)
      L02.01
  heart —see Carditis
  heel —see Abscess, foot
  helminthic —see Infestation, helminth
  hepatic (cholangitic) (hematogenic)
    (lymphogenic) (pylephlebitic) K75.0
    amebic A06.4
  hip (region) —see Abscess, lower limb
▶horseshoe K61.31
▶ileocecal K35.33
  ileostomy (bud) K94.12
  iliac (region) L02.214
    ▶fossa K35.33
  infraclavicular (fossa) —see Abscess, upper
    limb
  inguinal (region) L02.214
    lymph gland or node L04.1
▶intersphincteric K61.4
  intestine, intestinal NEC K63.0
    rectal K61.1
  intra-abdominal —see also Abscess,
    peritoneum K65.1
  ▶following procedure T81.43
    ▶obstetrical O86.03
  ▶postprocedural T81.49
    retroperitoneal K68.11
  intracranial G06.0

▶ New   ▶ Revised   ~~deleted~~ Deleted   ● Use Additional Character(s)

Abscess *(Continued)*
intramammary —*see* Abscess, breast
▶intramuscular, following procedure T81.44
  ▶obstetrical O86.02
intraorbital —*see* Abscess, orbit
intraperitoneal K65.1
intrasphincteric (anus) K61.4
intraspinal G06.1
intratonsillar J36
➡ischiorectal (fossa) (specified NEC) K61.39
  ~~K61.3~~
jaw (bone) (lower) (upper) M27.2
joint —*see* Arthritis, pyogenic or pyemic
  spine (tuberculous) A18.01
    nontuberculous —*see* Spondylopathy,
      infective
kidney N15.1
  with calculus N20.0
    with hydronephrosis N13.6
  puerperal (postpartum) O86.21
knee —*see also* Abscess, lower limb
  joint M00.9
labium (majus) (minus) N76.4
lacrimal
  caruncle —*see* Inflammation, lacrimal,
    passages, acute
  gland —*see* Dacryoadenitis
  passages (duct) (sac) —*see* Inflammation,
    lacrimal, passages, acute
lacunar N34.0
larynx J38.7
lateral (alveolar) K04.7
  with sinus K04.6
leg (any part) —*see* Abscess, lower limb
lens H27.8
lingual K14.0
  tonsil J36
lip K13.0
Littre's gland N34.0
liver (cholangitic) (hematogenic) (lymphogenic)
  (pylephlebitic) (pyogenic) K75.0
  amebic (due to Entamoeba histolytica)
    (dysenteric) (tropical) A06.4
    with
      brain abscess (and liver or lung
        abscess) A06.6
      lung abscess A06.5
loin (region) L02.211
lower limb L02.41-●
lumbar (tuberculous) A18.01
  nontuberculous L02.212
lung (miliary) (putrid) J85.2
  with pneumonia J85.1
    due to specified organism (*see*
      Pneumonia, in (due to))
  amebic (with liver abscess) A06.5
    with
      brain abscess A06.6
      pneumonia A06.5
lymph, lymphatic, gland or node (acute) —*see
  also* Lymphadenitis, acute
  mesentery I88.0
malar M27.2
mammary gland —*see* Abscess, breast
marginal, anus K61.0
mastoid —*see* Mastoiditis, acute
maxilla, maxillary M27.2
  molar (tooth) K04.7
    with sinus K04.6
  premolar K04.7
  sinus (chronic) J32.0
mediastinum J85.3
meibomian gland —*see* Hordeolum
meninges G06.2
mesentery, mesenteric K65.1
mesosalpinx —*see* Salpingitis
mons pubis L02.215
mouth (floor) K12.2
muscle —*see* Myositis, infective
myocardium I40.0
nabothian (follicle) —*see* Cervicitis
nasal J32.9
nasopharyngeal J39.1

Abscess *(Continued)*
navel L02.216
  newborn P38.9
    with mild hemorrhage P38.1
    without hemorrhage P38.9
neck (region) L02.11
  lymph gland or node L04.0
nephritic —*see* Abscess, kidney
nipple N61.1
  associated with
    lactation —*see* Pregnancy, complicated by
    pregnancy —*see* Pregnancy, complicated
      by
nose (external) (fossa) (septum) J34.0
  sinus (chronic) —*see* Sinusitis
omentum K65.1
➡operative wound T81.49
orbit, orbital —*see* Cellulitis, orbit
otogenic G06.0
ovary, ovarian (corpus luteum) —*see*
  Oophoritis
oviduct —*see* Oophoritis
palate (soft) K12.2
  hard M27.2
palmar (space) —*see* Abscess, hand
pancreas (duct) —*see* Pancreatitis, acute
parafrenal N48.21
parametric, parametrium N73.2
  acute N73.0
  chronic N73.1
paranephric N15.1
parapancreatic —*see* Pancreatitis, acute
parapharyngeal J39.0
pararectal K61.1
parasinus —*see* Sinusitis
parauterine (*see also* Disease, pelvis,
  inflammatory) N73.2
paravaginal —*see* Vaginitis
parietal region (scalp) L02.811
parodontal —*see* Periodontitis, aggressive,
  localized
parotid (duct) (gland) K11.3
  region K12.2
pectoral (region) L02.213
pelvis, pelvic
  female —*see* Disease, pelvis, inflammatory
  male, peritoneal K65.1
penis N48.21
  gonococcal (accessory gland) (periurethral)
    A54.1
perianal K61.0
periapical K04.7
  with sinus (alveolar) K04.6
➡periappendicular K35.33
pericardial I30.1
➡pericecal K35.33
pericemental —*see* Periodontitis, aggressive,
  localized
pericholecystic —*see* Cholecystitis, acute
pericoronal —*see* Periodontitis, aggressive,
  localized
peridental —*see* Periodontitis, aggressive,
  localized
perimetric —*see also* Disease, pelvis,
  inflammatory N73.2
perinephric, perinephritic —*see* Abscess,
  kidney
perineum, perineal (superficial) L02.215
  urethra N34.0
periodontal (parietal) —*see* Periodontitis,
  aggressive, localized
  apical K04.7
periosteum, periosteal —*see also*
  Osteomyelitis, specified type NEC
  with osteomyelitis —*see also* Osteomyelitis,
    specified type NEC
  acute —*see* Osteomyelitis, acute
  chronic —*see* Osteomyelitis, chronic
peripharyngeal J39.0
peripleuritic J86.9
  with fistula J86.0
periprostatic N41.2

Abscess *(Continued)*
perirectal K61.1
perirenal (tissue) —*see* Abscess, kidney
perisinuous (nose) —*see* Sinusitis
peritoneum, peritoneal (perforated)
  (ruptured) K65.1
➡with appendicitis (*see also* Appendicitis)
    K35.33 ~~K35.3~~
  pelvic
    female —*see* Peritonitis, pelvic, female
    male K65.1
➡postoperative T81.49
  puerperal, postpartum, childbirth O85
  tuberculous A18.31
peritonsillar J36
➡perityphlic K35.33
periureteral N28.89
periurethral N34.0
  gonococcal (accessory gland) (periurethral)
    A54.1
periuterine —*see also* Disease, pelvis,
  inflammatory N73.2
perivesical —*see* Cystitis, specified type NEC
petrous bone —*see* Petrositis
phagedenic NOS L02.91
  chancroid A57
pharynx, pharyngeal (lateral) J39.1
pilonidal L05.01
pituitary (gland) E23.6
pleura J86.9
  with fistula J86.0
popliteal —*see* Abscess, lower limb
➡postcecal K35.33
postlaryngeal J38.7
postnasal J34.0
➡postoperative (any site) (*see also* Infection,
  postoperative wound) T81.49 ~~T81.4~~
  retroperitoneal K68.11
postpharyngeal J39.0
posttonsillar J36
post-typhoid A01.09
pouch of Douglas —*see* Peritonitis, pelvic,
  female
premammary —*see* Abscess, breast
prepatellar —*see* Abscess, lower limb
prostate N41.2
  gonococcal (acute) (chronic) A54.22
psoas muscle K68.12
puerperal - code by site under Puerperal,
  abscess
pulmonary —*see* Abscess, lung
pulp, pulpal (dental) K04.01
  irreversible K04.02
  reversible K04.01
rectovaginal septum K63.0
rectovesical —*see* Cystitis, specified type NEC
rectum K61.1
renal —*see* Abscess, kidney
retina —*see* Inflammation, chorioretinal
retrobulbar —*see* Abscess, orbit
retrocecal K65.1
retrolaryngeal J38.7
retromammary —*see* Abscess, breast
retroperitoneal NEC K68.19
  postprocedural K68.11
retropharyngeal J39.0
retrouterine —*see* Peritonitis, pelvic, female
retrovesical —*see* Cystitis, specified type NEC
root, tooth K04.7
  with sinus (alveolar) K04.6
round ligament —*see also* Disease, pelvis,
  inflammatory N73.2
rupture (spontaneous) NOS L02.91
sacrum (tuberculous) A18.01
  nontuberculous M46.28
salivary (duct) (gland) K11.3
scalp (any part) L02.811
scapular —*see* Osteomyelitis, specified type
  NEC
sclera —*see* Scleritis
scrofulous (tuberculous) A18.2
scrotum N49.2

Abscess *(Continued)*
  seminal vesicle N49.0
  septal, dental K04.7
    with sinus (alveolar) K04.6
  serous —*see* Periostitis
  shoulder (region) —*see* Abscess, upper limb
  sigmoid K63.0
  sinus (accessory) (chronic) (nasal) —*see also*
    Sinusitis
    intracranial venous (any) G06.0
  Skene's duct or gland N34.0
  skin —*see* Abscess, by site
  specified site NEC L02.818
  spermatic cord N49.1
  sphenoidal (sinus) (chronic) J32.3
  spinal cord (any part) (staphylococcal) G06.1
    tuberculous A17.81
  spine (column) (tuberculous) A18.01
    epidural G06.1
    nontuberculous —*see* Osteomyelitis,
      vertebra
  spleen D73.3
    amebic A06.89
  stitch T81.41
    ▶following an obstetrical procedure O86.01
  subarachnoid G06.2
    brain G06.0
    spinal cord G06.1
  subareolar —*see* Abscess, breast
  subcecal K35.33
  subcutaneous —*see also* Abscess, by site
    ▶following procedure T81.41
      ▶obstetrical O86.01
    pheomycotic (chromomycotic) B43.2
  subdiaphragmatic K65.1
  subdural G06.2
    brain G06.0
      sequelae G09
    spinal cord G06.1
  ▶sub-fascial, following an obstetrical
    procedure O86.02
  subgaleal L02.811
  subhepatic K65.1
  sublingual K12.2
    gland K11.3
  submammary —*see* Abscess, breast
  submandibular (region) (space) (triangle) K12.2
    gland K11.3
  submaxillary (region) L02.01
    gland K11.3
  submental L02.01
    gland K11.3
  subperiosteal —*see* Osteomyelitis, specified
    type NEC
  subphrenic K65.1
    ▶following an obstetrical procedure O86.03
    postoperative T81.43
  suburethral N34.0
  sudoriparous L75.8
  supraclavicular (fossa) —*see* Abscess, upper
    limb
  ▶supralevator K61.5
  suprapelvic, acute N73.0
  suprarenal (capsule) (gland) E27.8
  sweat gland L74.8
  tear duct —*see* Inflammation, lacrimal,
    passages, acute
  temple L02.01
  temporal region L02.01
  temporosphenoidal G06.0
  tendon (sheath) M65.00
    ankle M65.07-●
    foot M65.07-●
    forearm M65.03-●
    hand M65.04-●
    lower leg M65.06-●
    pelvic region M65.05-●
    shoulder region M65.01-●
    specified site NEC M65.08
    thigh M65.05-●
    upper arm M65.02-●
  testis N45.4
  thigh —*see* Abscess, lower limb

Abscess *(Continued)*
  thorax J86.9
    with fistula J86.0
  throat J39.1
  thumb —*see also* Abscess, hand
    nail —*see* Cellulitis, finger
  thymus (gland) E32.1
  thyroid (gland) E06.0
  toe (any) —*see also* Abscess, foot
    nail —*see* Cellulitis, toe
  tongue (staphylococcal) K14.0
  tonsil(s) (lingual) J36
  tonsillopharyngeal J36
  tooth, teeth (root) K04.7
    with sinus (alveolar) K04.6
    supporting structures NEC —*see*
      Peridontitis, aggressive, localized
  trachea J39.8
  trunk L02.219
    abdominal wall L02.211
    back L02.212
    chest wall L02.213
    groin L02.214
    perineum L02.215
    umbilicus L02.216
  tubal —*see* Salpingitis
  tuberculous —*see* Tuberculosis, abscess
  tubo-ovarian —*see* Salpingo-oophoritis
  tunica vaginalis N49.1
  umbilicus L02.216
  upper
    limb L02.41-●
    respiratory J39.8
  urethral (gland) N34.0
  urinary N34.0
  uterus, uterine (wall) —*see also* Endometritis
    ligament —*see also* Disease, pelvis,
      inflammatory N73.2
    neck —*see* Cervicitis
  uvula K12.2
  vagina (wall) —*see* Vaginitis
  vaginorectal —*see* Vaginitis
  vas deferens N49.1
  vermiform appendix K35.33
  vertebra (column) (tuberculous) A18.01
    nontuberculous —*see* Osteomyelitis,
      vertebra
  vesical —*see* Cystitis, specified type NEC
  vesico-uterine pouch —*see* Peritonitis, pelvic,
    female
  vitreous (humor) —*see* Endophthalmitis,
    purulent
  vocal cord J38.3
  von Bezold's —*see* Mastoiditis, acute
  vulva N76.4
  vulvovaginal gland N75.1
  web space —*see* Abscess, hand
  wound T81.49
  wrist —*see* Abscess, upper limb
Absence (of) (organ or part) (complete or partial)
  adrenal (gland) (congenital) Q89.1
    acquired E89.6
  albumin in blood E88.09
  alimentary tract (congenital) Q45.8
    upper Q40.8
  alveolar process (acquired) —*see* Anomaly,
    alveolar
  ankle (acquired) Z89.44-●
  anus (congenital) Q42.3
    with fistula Q42.2
  aorta (congenital) Q25.41
  appendix, congenital Q42.8
  arm (acquired) Z89.20-●
    above elbow Z89.22-●
      congenital (with hand present) —*see*
        Agenesis, arm, with hand present
        and hand —*see* Agenesis, forearm,
        and hand
    below elbow Z89.21-●
      congenital (with hand present) —*see*
        Agenesis, arm, with hand present
        and hand —*see* Agenesis, forearm,
        and hand

Absence *(Continued)*
  arm *(Continued)*
    congenital —*see* Defect, reduction, upper
      limb
    shoulder (following explantation of
      shoulder joint prosthesis) (joint) (with
      or without presence of antibiotic-
      impregnated cement spacer) Z89.23-●
    congenital (with hand present) —*see*
      Agenesis, arm, with hand present
  artery (congenital) (peripheral) Q27.8
    brain Q28.3
    coronary Q24.5
    pulmonary Q25.79
    specified NEC Q27.8
    umbilical Q27.0
  atrial septum (congenital) Q21.1
  auditory canal (congenital) (external) Q16.1
  auricle (ear), congenital Q16.0
  bile, biliary duct, congenital Q44.5
  bladder (acquired) Z90.6
    congenital Q64.5
  bowel sounds R19.11
  brain Q00.0
    part of Q04.3
  breast(s) (and nipple(s)) (acquired) Z90.1-●
    congenital Q83.8
  broad ligament Q50.6
  bronchus (congenital) Q32.4
  canaliculus lacrimalis, congenital Q10.4
  cerebellum (vermis) Q04.3
  cervix (acquired) (with uterus) Z90.710
    with remaining uterus Z90.712
    congenital Q51.5
  chin, congenital Q18.8
  cilia (congenital) Q10.3
    acquired —*see* Madarosis
  clitoris (congenital) Q52.6
  coccyx, congenital Q76.49
  cold sense R20.8
  congenital
    lumen —*see* Atresia
    organ or site NEC —*see* Agenesis
    septum —*see* Imperfect, closure
  corpus callosum Q04.0
  cricoid cartilage, congenital Q31.8
  diaphragm (with hernia), congenital Q79.1
  digestive organ(s) or tract, congenital Q45.8
    acquired NEC Z90.49
    upper Q40.8
  ductus arteriosus Q28.8
  duodenum (acquired) Z90.49
    congenital Q41.0
  ear, congenital Q16.9
    acquired H93.8-●
    auricle Q16.0
    external Q16.0
    inner Q16.5
    lobe, lobule Q17.8
    middle, except ossicles Q16.4
      ossicles Q16.3
    ossicles Q16.3
  ejaculatory duct (congenital) Q55.4
  endocrine gland (congenital) NEC Q89.2
    acquired E89.89
  epididymis (congenital) Q55.4
    acquired Z90.79
  epiglottis, congenital Q31.8
  esophagus (congenital) Q39.8
    acquired (partial) Z90.49
  eustachian tube (congenital) Q16.2
  extremity (acquired) Z89.9
    congenital Q73.0
    knee (following explantation of knee joint
      prosthesis) (joint) (with or without
      presence of antibiotic-impregnated
      cement spacer) Z89.52-●
    lower (above knee) Z89.619
      below knee Z89.51-●
    upper —*see* Absence, arm
  eye (acquired) Z90.01
    congenital Q11.1
    muscle (congenital) Q10.3

▶ New   ⇒ Revised   ~~deleted~~ Deleted   ● Use Additional Character(s)

Absence (Continued)
  eyeball (acquired) Z90.01
  eyelid (fold) (congenital) Q10.3
    acquired Z90.01
  face, specified part NEC Q18.8
  fallopian tube(s) (acquired) Z90.79
    congenital Q50.6
  family member (causing problem in home)
    NEC —see also Disruption, family Z63.32
  femur, congenital —see Defect, reduction,
    lower limb, longitudinal, femur
  fibrinogen (congenital) D68.2
    acquired D65
  finger(s) (acquired) Z89.02-●
    congenital —see Agenesis, hand
  foot (acquired) Z89.43-●
    congenital —see Agenesis, foot
  forearm (acquired) —see Absence, arm, below
    elbow
  gallbladder (acquired) Z90.49
    congenital Q44.0
  gamma globulin in blood D80.1
    hereditary D80.0
  genital organs
    acquired (female) (male) Z90.79
    female, congenital Q52.8
      external Q52.71
      internal NEC Q52.8
    male, congenital Q55.8
  genitourinary organs, congenital NEC
    female Q52.8
    male Q55.8
  globe (acquired) Z90.01
    congenital Q11.1
  glottis, congenital Q31.8
  hand and wrist (acquired) Z89.11-●
    congenital —see Agenesis, hand
  head, part (acquired) NEC Z90.09
  heat sense R20.8
  hip (following explantation of hip joint
    prosthesis) (joint) (with or without
    presence of antibiotic-impregnated
    cement spacer) Z89.62-●
  hymen (congenital) Q52.4
  ileum (acquired) Z90.49
    congenital Q41.2
  immunoglobulin, isolated NEC D80.3
    IgA D80.2
    IgG D80.3
    IgM D80.4
  incus (acquired) —see Loss, ossicles, ear
    congenital Q16.3
  inner ear, congenital Q16.5
  intestine (acquired) (small) Z90.49
    congenital Q41.9
      specified NEC Q41.8
    large Z90.49
      congenital Q42.9
        specified NEC Q42.8
  iris, congenital Q13.1
  jejunum (acquired) Z90.49
    congenital Q41.1
  joint
    acquired
      hip (following explantation of hip joint
        prosthesis) (with or without
        presence of antibiotic-impregnated
        cement spacer) Z89.62-●
      knee (following explantation of knee
        joint prosthesis) (with or without
        presence of antibiotic-impregnated
        cement spacer) Z89.52-●
      shoulder (following explantation of
        shoulder joint prosthesis) (with or
        without presence of antibiotic-
        impregnated cement spacer)
        Z89.23-●
    congenital NEC Q74.8
  kidney(s) (acquired) Z90.5
    congenital Q60.2
      bilateral Q60.1
      unilateral Q60.0

Absence (Continued)
  knee (following explantation of knee joint
    prosthesis) (joint) (with or without
    presence of antibiotic-impregnated
    cement spacer) Z89.52-●
  labyrinth, membranous Q16.5
  larynx (congenital) Q31.8
    acquired Z90.02
  leg (acquired) (above knee) Z89.61-●
    below knee (acquired) Z89.51-●
    congenital —see Defect, reduction, lower
      limb
  lens (acquired) —see also Aphakia
    congenital Q12.3
    post cataract extraction Z98.4-●
  limb (acquired) —see Absence, extremity
  lip Q38.6
  liver (congenital) Q44.7
  lung (fissure) (lobe) (bilateral) (unilateral)
    (congenital) Q33.3
    acquired (any part) Z90.2
  menstruation —see Amenorrhea
  muscle (congenital) (pectoral) Q79.8
    ocular Q10.3
  neck, part Q18.8
  neutrophil —see Agranulocytosis
  nipple(s) (with breast(s)) (acquired) Z90.1-●
    congenital Q83.2
  nose (congenital) Q30.1
    acquired Z90.09
  organ
    of Corti, congenital Q16.5
    or site, congenital NEC Q89.8
      acquired NEC Z90.89
  osseous meatus (ear) Q16.4
  ovary (acquired)
    bilateral Z90.722
    congenital
      bilateral Q50.02
      unilateral Q50.01
    unilateral Z90.721
  oviduct (acquired)
    bilateral Z90.722
    congenital Q50.6
    unilateral Z90.721
  pancreas (congenital) Q45.0
    acquired Z90.410
      complete Z90.410
      partial Z90.411
      total Z90.410
  parathyroid gland (acquired) E89.2
    congenital Q89.2
  patella, congenital Q74.1
  penis (congenital) Q55.5
    acquired Z90.79
  pericardium (congenital) Q24.8
  pituitary gland (congenital) Q89.2
    acquired E89.3
  prostate (acquired) Z90.79
    congenital Q55.4
  pulmonary valve Q22.0
  punctum lacrimale (congenital) Q10.4
  radius, congenital —see Defect, reduction,
    upper limb, longitudinal, radius
  rectum (congenital) Q42.1
    with fistula Q42.0
    acquired Z90.49
  respiratory organ NOS Q34.9
  rib (acquired) Z90.89
    congenital Q76.6
  sacrum, congenital Q76.49
  salivary gland(s), congenital Q38.4
  scrotum, congenital Q55.29
  seminal vesicles (congenital) Q55.4
    acquired Z90.79
  septum
    atrial (congenital) Q21.1
    between aorta and pulmonary artery Q21.4
    ventricular (congenital) Q20.4
  sex chromosome
    female phenotype Q97.8
    male phenotype Q98.8

Absence (Continued)
  skull bone (congenital) Q75.8
    with
      anencephaly Q00.0
      encephalocele —see Encephalocele
      hydrocephalus Q03.9
        with spina bifida —see Spina
          bifida, by site, with
          hydrocephalus
      microcephaly Q02
  spermatic cord, congenital Q55.4
  spine, congenital Q76.49
  spleen (congenital) Q89.01
    acquired Z90.81
  sternum, congenital Q76.7
  stomach (acquired) (partial) Z90.3
    congenital Q40.2
  superior vena cava, congenital
    Q26.8
  teeth, tooth (congenital) K00.0
    acquired (complete) K08.109
      class I K08.101
      class II K08.102
      class III K08.103
      class IV K08.104
      due to
        caries K08.139
          class I K08.131
          class II K08.132
          class III K08.133
          class IV K08.134
        periodontal disease K08.129
          class I K08.121
          class II K08.122
          class III K08.123
          class IV K08.124
        specified NEC K08.199
          class I K08.191
          class II K08.192
          class III K08.193
          class IV K08.194
        trauma K08.119
          class I K08.111
          class II K08.112
          class III K08.113
          class IV K08.114
    partial K08.409
      class I K08.401
      class II K08.402
      class III K08.403
      class IV K08.404
      due to
        caries K08.439
          class I K08.431
          class II K08.432
          class III K08.433
          class IV K08.434
        periodontal disease K08.429
          class I K08.421
          class II K08.422
          class III K08.423
          class IV K08.424
        specified NEC K08.499
          class I K08.491
          class II K08.492
          class III K08.493
          class IV K08.494
        trauma K08.419
          class I K08.411
          class II K08.412
          class III K08.413
          class IV K08.414
  tendon (congenital) Q79.8
  testis (congenital) Q55.0
    acquired Z90.79
  thumb (acquired) Z89.01-●
    congenital —see Agenesis, hand
  thymus gland Q89.2
  thyroid (gland) (acquired) E89.0
    cartilage, congenital Q31.8
    congenital E03.1

Absence *(Continued)*
  toe(s) (acquired) Z89.42-●
    with foot —*see* Absence, foot and ankle
    congenital —*see* Agenesis, foot
      great Z89.41-●
  tongue, congenital Q38.3
  trachea (cartilage), congenital Q32.1
  transverse aortic arch, congenital Q25.49
  tricuspid valve Q22.4
  umbilical artery, congenital Q27.0
  upper arm and forearm with hand present,
      congenital —*see* Agenesis, arm, with
      hand present
  ureter (congenital) Q62.4
    acquired Z90.6
  urethra, congenital Q64.5
  uterus (acquired) Z90.710
    with cervix Z90.710
    with remaining cervical stump
      Z90.711
    congenital Q51.0
  uvula, congenital Q38.5
  vagina, congenital Q52.0
  vas deferens (congenital) Q55.4
    acquired Z90.79
  vein (peripheral) congenital NEC Q27.8
    cerebral Q28.3
    digestive system Q27.8
    great Q26.8
    lower limb Q27.8
    portal Q26.5
    precerebral Q28.1
    specified site NEC Q27.8
    upper limb Q27.8
  vena cava (inferior) (superior), congenital
      Q26.8
  ventricular septum Q20.4
  vertebra, congenital Q76.49
  vulva, congenital Q52.71
  wrist (acquired) Z89.12-●
Absorbent system disease I87.8
Absorption
  carbohydrate, disturbance K90.49
  chemical —*see* Table of Drugs and Chemicals
    through placenta (newborn) P04.9
      environmental substance P04.6
      nutritional substance P04.5
      obstetric anesthetic or analgesic drug
        P04.0
  drug NEC —*see* Table of Drugs and
      Chemicals
    addictive
    ⇒through placenta (newborn) (*see also*
        Newborn, affected by, maternal,
        use of) P04.40 ~~P04.49~~
      cocaine P04.41
      ▶hallucinogens P04.42
      ▶specified drug NEC P04.49
    medicinal
    ⇒through placenta (newborn) P04.19
  ⇒through placenta (newborn) P04.19
      obstetric anesthetic or analgesic drug
        P04.0
  fat, disturbance K90.49
    pancreatic K90.3
  noxious substance —*see* Table of Drugs and
      Chemicals
  protein, disturbance K90.49
  starch, disturbance K90.49
  toxic substance —*see* Table of Drugs and
      Chemicals
  uremic —*see* Uremia
Abstinence symptoms, syndrome
  alcohol F10.239
    with delirium F10.231
  cocaine F14.23
  neonatal P96.1
  nicotine —*see* Dependence, drug, nicotine,
      with, withdrawal
  opioid F11.93
    with dependence F11.23

Abstinence symptoms, syndrome *(Continued)*
  psychoactive NEC F19.939
    with
      delirium F19.931
      dependence F19.239
        with
          delirium F19.231
          perceptual disturbance F19.232
        uncomplicated F19.230
      perceptual disturbance F19.932
    uncomplicated F19.930
  sedative F13.939
    with
      delirium F13.931
      dependence F13.239
        with
          delirium F13.231
          perceptual disturbance F13.232
        uncomplicated F13.230
      perceptual disturbance F13.932
    uncomplicated F13.930
  stimulant NEC F15.93
    with dependence F15.23
Abulia R68.89
Abulomania F60.7
Abuse
  adult —*see* Maltreatment, adult
    as reason for
      couple seeking advice (including
        offender) Z63.0
  alcohol (non-dependent) F10.10
    with
      anxiety disorder F10.180
      intoxication F10.129
        with delirium F10.121
        uncomplicated F10.120
      mood disorder F10.14
      other specified disorder F10.188
      psychosis F10.159
        delusions F10.150
        hallucinations F10.151
      sexual dysfunction F10.181
      sleep disorder F10.182
      unspecified disorder F10.19
    counseling and surveillance Z71.41
    in remission (early) (sustained) F10.11
  amphetamine (or related substance) —*see*
      Abuse, drug, stimulant NEC
  analgesics (non-prescribed) (over the counter)
      F55.8
  antacids F55.0
  antidepressants —*see* Abuse, drug,
      psychoactive NEC
  anxiolytic —*see* Abuse, drug, sedative
  barbiturates —*see* Abuse, drug, sedative
  caffeine —*see* Abuse, drug, stimulant NEC
  cannabis, cannabinoids —*see* Abuse, drug,
      cannabis
  child —*see* Maltreatment, child
  cocaine —*see* Abuse, drug, cocaine
  drug NEC (non-dependent) F19.10
    with sleep disorder F19.182
    amphetamine type —*see* Abuse, drug,
        stimulant NEC
    analgesics (non-prescribed) (over the
        counter) F55.8
    antacids F55.0
    antidepressants —*see* Abuse, drug,
        psychoactive NEC
    anxiolytics —*see* Abuse, drug, sedative
    barbiturates —*see* Abuse, drug, sedative
    caffeine —*see* Abuse, drug, stimulant NEC
    cannabis F12.10
      with
        anxiety disorder F12.180
        intoxication F12.129
          with
            delirium F12.121
            perceptual disturbance F12.122
          uncomplicated F12.120
        other specified disorder F12.188

Abuse *(Continued)*
  drug NEC *(Continued)*
    cannabis *(Continued)*
      with *(Continued)*
        psychosis F12.159
          delusions F12.150
          hallucinations F12.151
        unspecified disorder F12.19
      in remission (early) (sustained) F12.11
    cocaine F14.10
      with
        anxiety disorder F14.180
        intoxication F14.129
          with
            delirium F14.121
            perceptual disturbance F14.122
          uncomplicated F14.120
        mood disorder F14.14
        other specified disorder F14.188
        psychosis F14.159
          delusions F14.150
          hallucinations F14.151
        sexual dysfunction F14.181
        sleep disorder F14.182
        unspecified disorder F14.19
      in remission (early) (sustained) F14.11
    counseling and surveillance Z71.51
    hallucinogen F16.10
      with
        anxiety disorder F16.180
        flashbacks F16.183
        intoxication F16.129
          with
            delirium F16.121
            perceptual disturbance F16.122
          uncomplicated F16.120
        mood disorder F16.14
        other specified disorder F16.188
        perception disorder, persisting
          F16.183
        psychosis F16.159
          delusions F16.150
          hallucinations F16.151
        unspecified disorder F16.19
      in remission (early) (sustained) F16.11
    hashish —*see* Abuse, drug, cannabis
    herbal or folk remedies F55.1
    hormones F55.3
    hypnotics —*see* Abuse, drug, sedative
    inhalant F18.10
      with
        anxiety disorder F18.180
        dementia, persisting F18.17
        intoxication F18.129
          with delirium F18.121
          uncomplicated F18.120
        mood disorder F18.14
        other specified disorder F18.188
        psychosis F18.159
          delusions F18.150
          hallucinations F18.151
        unspecified disorder F18.19
      in remission (early) (sustained) F18.11
    in remission (early) (sustained) F19.11
    laxatives F55.2
    LSD —*see* Abuse, drug, hallucinogen
    marihuana —*see* Abuse, drug, cannabis
    morphine type (opioids) —*see* Abuse, drug,
        opioid
    opioid F11.10
      with
        intoxication F11.129
          with
            delirium F11.121
            perceptual disturbance F11.122
          uncomplicated F11.120
        mood disorder F11.14
        other specified disorder F11.188
        psychosis F11.159
          delusions F11.150
          hallucinations F11.151

▶ New   ⇒ Revised   ~~deleted~~ Deleted   ● Use Additional Character(s)

Abuse (Continued)
  drug NEC (Continued)
    opioid (Continued)
      with (Continued)
        sexual dysfunction F11.181
        sleep disorder F11.182
        unspecified disorder F11.19
      in remission (early) (sustained) F11.11
    PCP (phencyclidine) (or related substance) —
        see Abuse, drug, hallucinogen
    psychoactive NEC F19.10
      with
        amnestic disorder F19.16
        anxiety disorder F19.180
        dementia F19.17
        intoxication F19.129
          with
            delirium F19.121
            perceptual disturbance F19.122
          uncomplicated F19.120
        mood disorder F19.14
        other specified disorder F19.188
        psychosis F19.159
          delusions F19.150
          hallucinations F19.151
        sexual dysfunction F19.181
        sleep disorder F19.182
        unspecified disorder F19.19
    sedative, hypnotic or anxiolytic F13.10
      with
        anxiety disorder F13.180
        intoxication F13.129
          with delirium F13.121
          uncomplicated F13.120
        mood disorder F13.14
        other specified disorder F13.188
        psychosis F13.159
          delusions F13.150
          hallucinations F13.151
        sexual dysfunction F13.181
        sleep disorder F13.182
        unspecified disorder F13.19
      in remission (early) (sustained) F13.11
    solvent —see Abuse, drug, inhalant
    steroids F55.3
    stimulant NEC F15.10
      with
        anxiety disorder F15.180
        intoxication F15.129
          with
            delirium F15.121
            perceptual disturbance F15.122
          uncomplicated F15.120
        mood disorder F15.14
        other specified disorder F15.188
        psychosis F15.159
          delusions F15.150
          hallucinations F15.151
        sexual dysfunction F15.181
        sleep disorder F15.182
        unspecified disorder F15.19
      in remission (early) (sustained) F15.11
    tranquilizers —see Abuse, drug, sedative
    vitamins F55.4
  hallucinogens —see Abuse, drug, hallucinogen
  hashish —see Abuse, drug, cannabis
  herbal or folk remedies F55.1
  hormones F55.3
  hypnotic —see Abuse, drug, sedative
  inhalant —see Abuse, drug, inhalant
  laxatives F55.2
  LSD —see Abuse, drug, hallucinogen
  marihuana —see Abuse, drug, cannabis
  morphine type (opioids) —see Abuse, drug,
      opioid
  non-psychoactive substance NEC F55.8
    antacids F55.0
    folk remedies F55.1
    herbal remedies F55.1
    hormones F55.3
    laxatives F55.2

Abuse (Continued)
  non-psychoactive substance NEC (Continued)
    steroids F55.3
    vitamins F55.4
  opioids —see Abuse, drug, opioid
  PCP (phencyclidine) (or related substance) —
      see Abuse, drug, hallucinogen
  physical (adult) (child) —see Maltreatment
  psychoactive substance —see Abuse, drug,
      psychoactive NEC
  psychological (adult) (child) —see Maltreatment
  sedative —see Abuse, drug, sedative
  sexual —see Maltreatment
  solvent —see Abuse, drug, inhalant
  steroids F55.3
  vitamins F55.4
Acalculia R48.8
  developmental F81.2
Acanthamebiasis (with) B60.10
  conjunctiva B60.12
  keratoconjunctivitis B60.13
  meningoencephalitis B60.11
  other specified B60.19
Acanthocephaliasis B83.8
Acanthocheilonemiasis B74.4
Acanthocytosis E78.6
Acantholysis L11.9
Acanthosis (acquired) (nigricans) L83
  benign Q82.8
  congenital Q82.8
  seborrheic L82.1
    inflamed L82.0
  tongue K14.3
Acapnia E87.3
Acarbia E87.2
Acardia, acardius Q89.8
Acardiacus amorphus Q89.8
Acardiotrophia I51.4
Acariasis B88.0
  scabies B86
Acarodermatitis (urticarioides) B88.0
Acarophobia F40.218
Acatalasemia, acatalasia E80.3
Acathisia (drug induced) G25.71
Accelerated atrioventricular conduction I45.6
Accentuation of personality traits (type A) Z73.1
Accessory (congenital)
  adrenal gland Q89.1
  anus Q43.4
  appendix Q43.4
  atrioventricular conduction I45.6
  auditory ossicles Q16.3
  auricle (ear) Q17.0
  biliary duct or passage Q44.5
  bladder Q64.79
  blood vessels NEC Q27.9
    coronary Q24.5
  bone NEC Q79.8
  breast tissue, axilla Q83.1
  carpal bones Q74.0
  cecum Q43.4
  chromosome(s) NEC (nonsex) Q92.9
    with complex rearrangements NEC Q92.5
      seen only at prometaphase Q92.8
    13 —see Trisomy, 13
    18 —see Trisomy, 18
    21 —see Trisomy, 21
    partial Q92.9
    sex
      female phenotype Q97.8
  coronary artery Q24.5
  cusp(s), heart valve NEC Q24.8
    pulmonary Q22.3
  cystic duct Q44.5
  digit(s) Q69.9
  ear (auricle) (lobe) Q17.0
  endocrine gland NEC Q89.2
  eye muscle Q10.3
  eyelid Q10.3
  face bone(s) Q75.8
  fallopian tube (fimbria) (ostium) Q50.6

Accessory (Continued)
  finger(s) Q69.0
  foreskin N47.8
  frontonasal process Q75.8
  gallbladder Q44.1
  genital organ(s)
    female Q52.8
      external Q52.79
      internal NEC Q52.8
    male Q55.8
  genitourinary organs NEC Q89.8
    female Q52.8
    male Q55.8
  hallux Q69.2
  heart Q24.8
    valve NEC Q24.8
      pulmonary Q22.3
  hepatic ducts Q44.5
  hymen Q52.4
  intestine (large) (small) Q43.4
  kidney Q63.0
  lacrimal canal Q10.6
  leaflet, heart valve NEC Q24.8
  ligament, broad Q50.6
  liver Q44.7
    duct Q44.5
  lobule (ear) Q17.0
  lung (lobe) Q33.1
  muscle Q79.8
  navicular of carpus Q74.0
  nervous system, part NEC Q07.8
  nipple Q83.3
  nose Q30.8
  organ or site not listed —see Anomaly, by site
  ovary Q50.31
  oviduct Q50.6
  pancreas Q45.3
  parathyroid gland Q89.2
  parotid gland (and duct) Q38.4
  pituitary gland Q89.2
  preauricular appendage Q17.0
  prepuce N47.8
  renal arteries (multiple) Q27.2
  rib Q76.6
    cervical Q76.5
  roots (teeth) K00.2
  salivary gland Q38.4
  sesamoid bones Q74.8
    foot Q74.2
    hand Q74.0
  skin tags Q82.8
  spleen Q89.09
  sternum Q76.7
  submaxillary gland Q38.4
  tarsal bones Q74.2
  teeth, tooth K00.1
  tendon Q79.8
  thumb Q69.1
  thymus gland Q89.2
  thyroid gland Q89.2
  toes Q69.2
  tongue Q38.3
  tooth, teeth K00.1
  tragus Q17.0
  ureter Q62.5
  urethra Q64.79
  urinary organ or tract NEC Q64.8
▶ uterus Q51.28
  vagina Q52.10
  valve, heart NEC Q24.8
    pulmonary Q22.3
  vertebra Q76.49
  vocal cords Q31.8
  vulva Q52.79
Accident
  birth —see Birth, injury
  cardiac —see Infarct, myocardium
  cerebral I63.9
  cerebrovascular (embolic) (ischemic)
      (thrombotic) I63.9
    aborted I63.9

Accident *(Continued)*
  cerebrovascular *(Continued)*
    hemorrhagic —*see* Hemorrhage,
      intracranial, intracerebral
    old (without sequelae) Z86.73
      with sequelae (of) —*see* Sequelae,
        infarction, cerebral
    coronary —*see* Infarct, myocardium
    craniovascular I63.9
    vascular, brain I63.9
Accidental —*see* condition
Accommodation (disorder) —*see also* condition
  hysterical paralysis of F44.89
  insufficiency of H52.4
  paresis —*see* Paresis, of accommodation
  spasm —*see* Spasm, of accommodation
Accouchement —*see* Delivery
Accreta placenta O43.21-●
Accretio cordis (nonrheumatic) I31.0
Accretions, tooth, teeth K03.6
Acculturation difficulty Z60.3
Accumulation secretion, prostate N42.89
Acephalia, acephalism, acephalus, acephaly
    Q00.0
Acephalobrachia monster Q89.8
Acephalochirus monster Q89.8
Acephalogaster Q89.8
Acephalostomus monster Q89.8
Acephalothorax Q89.8
Acerophobia F40.298
Acetonemia R79.89
  in Type 1 diabetes E10.10
    with coma E10.11
Acetonuria R82.4
Achalasia (cardia) (esophagus) K22.0
  congenital Q39.5
  pylorus Q40.0
  sphincteral NEC K59.8
Ache(s) —*see* Pain
Acheilia Q38.6
Achillobursitis —*see* Tendinitis, Achilles
Achillodynia —*see* Tendinitis, Achilles
Achlorhydria, achlorhydric (neurogenic) K31.83
  anemia D50.8
  diarrhea K31.83
  psychogenic F45.8
  secondary to vagotomy K91.1
Achluophobia F40.228
Acholia K82.8
Acholuric jaundice (familial)
    (splenomegalic) —*see also* Spherocytosis
  acquired D59.8
Achondrogenesis Q77.0
Achondroplasia (osteosclerosis congenita) Q77.4
Achroma, cutis L80
Achromat (ism), achromatopsia (acquired)
    (congenital) H53.51
Achromia, congenital —*see* Albinism
Achromia parasitica B36.0
Achylia gastrica K31.89
  psychogenic F45.8
Acid
  burn —*see* Corrosion
  deficiency
    amide nicotinic E52
    ascorbic E54
    folic E53.8
    nicotinic E52
    pantothenic E53.8
  intoxication E87.2
  peptic disease K30
  phosphatase deficiency E83.39
  stomach K30
    psychogenic F45.8
Acidemia E87.2
  argininosuccinic E72.22
  isovaleric E71.110
  metabolic (newborn) P19.9
    first noted before onset of labor P19.0
    first noted during labor P19.1
    noted at birth P19.2

Acidemia *(Continued)*
  methylmalonic E71.120
  pipecolic E72.3
  propionic E71.121
Acidity, gastric (high) K30
  psychogenic F45.8
Acidocytopenia —*see* Agranulocytosis
Acidocytosis D72.1
Acidopenia —*see* Agranulocytosis
Acidosis (lactic) (respiratory) E87.2
  in Type 1 diabetes E10.10
    with coma E10.11
  kidney, tubular N25.89
  lactic E87.2
  metabolic NEC E87.2
  ▶hyperchloremic, of newborn P74.421
    with respiratory acidosis E87.4
    late, of newborn P74.0
  mixed metabolic and respiratory, newborn P84
  newborn P84
  renal (hyperchloremic) (tubular) N25.89
  respiratory E87.2
    complicated by
      metabolic
        acidosis E87.4
        alkalosis E87.4
Aciduria
  ▶4-hydroxybutyric E72.81
  argininosuccinic E72.22
  ▶gamma-hydroxybutyric E72.81
  glutaric (type I) E72.3
    type II E71.313
    type III E71.5-●
  orotic (congenital) (hereditary) (pyrimidine
    deficiency) E79.8
    anemia D53.0
Acladiosis (skin) B36.0
Aclasis, diaphyseal Q78.6
Acleistocardia Q21.1
Aclusion —*see* Anomaly, dentofacial,
    malocclusion
Acne L70.9
  artificialis L70.8
  atrophica L70.2
  cachecticorum (Hebra) L70.8
  conglobata L70.1
  cystic L70.0
  decalvans L66.2
  excoriée (des jeunes filles) L70.5
  frontalis L70.2
  indurata L70.0
  infantile L70.4
  keloid L73.0
  lupoid L70.2
  necrotic, necrotica (miliaris) L70.2
  neonatal L70.4
  nodular L70.0
  occupational L70.8
  picker's L70.5
  pustular L70.0
  rodens L70.2
  rosacea L71.9
  specified NEC L70.8
  tropica L70.3
  varioliformis L70.2
  vulgaris L70.0
Acnitis (primary) A18.4
Acosta's disease T70.29
Acoustic —*see* condition
Acousticophobia F40.298
Acquired —*see also* condition
  immunodeficiency syndrome (AIDS) B20
Acrania Q00.0
Acroangiodermatitis I78.9
Acroasphyxia, chronic I73.89
Acrobystitis N47.7
Acrocephalopolysyndactyly Q87.0
Acrocephalosyndactyly Q87.0
Acrocephaly Q75.0
Acrochondrohyperplasia —*see* Syndrome,
  Marfan's

Acrocyanosis I73.8
  newborn P28.2
    meaning transient blue hands and feet -
      omit code
Acrodermatitis L30.8
  atrophicans (chronica) L90.4
  continua (Hallopeau) L40.2
  enteropathica (hereditary) E83.2
  Hallopeau's L40.2
  infantile papular L44.4
  perstans L40.2
  pustulosa continua L40.2
  recalcitrant pustular L40.2
Acrodynia —*see* Poisoning, mercury
Acromegaly, acromegalia E22.0
Acromelalgia I73.81
Acromicria, acromikria Q79.8
Acronyx L60.0
Acropachy, thyroid —*see* Thyrotoxicosis
Acroparesthesia (simple) (vasomotor) I73.89
Acropathy, thyroid —*see* Thyrotoxicosis
Acrophobia F40.241
Acroposthitis N47.7
Acroscleriasis, acroscleroderma,
  acrosclerosis —*see* Sclerosis, systemic
Acrosphacelus I96
Acrospiroma, eccrine —*see* Neoplasm, skin,
  benign
Acrostealgia —*see* Osteochondropathy
Acrotrophodynia —*see* Immersion
ACTH ectopic syndrome E24.3
Actinic —*see* condition
Actinobacillosis, actinobacillus A28.8
  mallei A24.0
  muris A25.1
Actinomyces israelii (infection) —*see*
  Actinomycosis
Actinomycetoma (foot) B47.1
Actinomycosis, actinomycotic A42.9
  with pneumonia A42.0
  abdominal A42.1
  cervicofacial A42.2
  cutaneous A42.89
  gastrointestinal A42.1
  pulmonary A42.0
  sepsis A42.7
  specified site NEC A42.89
Actinoneuritis G62.82
Action, heart
  disorder I49.9
  irregular I49.9
    psychogenic F45.8
Activated protein C resistance D68.51
Activation
  mast cell (disorder) (syndrome) D89.40
    idiopathic D89.42
    monoclonal D89.41
    secondary D89.43
    specified type NEC D89.49
Active —*see* condition
Acute —*see also* condition
  abdomen R10.0
  gallbladder —*see* Cholecystitis, acute
Acyanotic heart disease (congenital) Q24.9
Acystia Q64.5
Adair-Dighton syndrome (brittle bones and
  blue sclera, deafness) Q78.0
Adamantinoblastoma —*see* Ameloblastoma
Adamantinoma —*see also* Cyst, calcifying
    odontogenic
  long bones C40.90
    lower limb C40.2-●
    upper limb C40.0-●
  malignant C41.1
    jaw (bone) (lower) C41.1
      upper C41.0
  tibial C40.2-●
Adamantoblastoma —*see* Ameloblastoma
Adams-Stokes (-Morgagni) disease or
  syndrome I45.9
Adaption reaction —*see* Disorder, adjustment

▶ New   ⇒ Revised   ~~deleted~~ Deleted   ● Use Additional Character(s)

Addiction —see also Dependence F19.20
  alcohol, alcoholic (ethyl) (methyl) (wood)
    (without remission) F10.20
    with remission F10.21
  drug —see Dependence, drug
  ethyl alcohol (without remission) F10.20
    with remission F10.21
  heroin —see Dependence, drug, opioid
  methyl alcohol (without remission) F10.20
    with remission F10.21
  methylated spirit (without remission) F10.20
    with remission F10.21
  morphine(-like substances) —see
    Dependence, drug, opioid
  nicotine —see Dependence, drug, nicotine
  opium and opioids —see Dependence, drug,
    opioid
  tobacco —see Dependence, drug, nicotine
Addisonian crisis E27.2
Addison's
  anemia (pernicious) D51.0
  disease (bronze) or syndrome E27.1
    tuberculous A18.7
  keloid L94.0
Addison-Biermer anemia (pernicious) D51.0
Addison-Schilder complex E71.528
Additional —see also Accessory
  chromosome(s) Q99.8
    21 —see Trisomy, 21
    sex —see Abnormal, chromosome, sex
Adduction contracture, hip or other joint —see
  Contraction, joint
Adenitis —see also Lymphadenitis
  acute, unspecified site L04.9
  axillary I88.9
    acute L04.2
    chronic or subacute I88.1
  Bartholin's gland N75.8
  bulbourethral gland —see Urethritis
  cervical I88.9
    acute L04.0
    chronic or subacute I88.1
  chancroid (Hemophilus ducreyi) A57
  chronic, unspecified site I88.1
  Cowper's gland —see Urethritis
  due to Pasteurella multocida (P. septica)
    A28.0
  epidemic, acute B27.09
  gangrenous L04.9
  gonorrheal NEC A54.89
  groin I88.9
    acute L04.1
    chronic or subacute I88.1
  infectious (acute) (epidemic) B27.09
  inguinal I88.9
    acute L04.1
    chronic or subacute I88.1
  lymph gland or node, except mesenteric I88.9
    acute —see Lymphadenitis, acute
    chronic or subacute I88.1
  mesenteric (acute) (chronic) (nonspecific)
    (subacute) I88.0
  parotid gland (suppurative) —see Sialoadenitis
  salivary gland (any) (suppurative) —see
    Sialoadenitis
  scrofulous (tuberculous) A18.2
  Skene's duct or gland —see Urethritis
  strumous, tuberculous A18.2
  subacute, unspecified site I88.1
  sublingual gland (suppurative) —see
    Sialoadenitis
  submandibular gland (suppurative) —see
    Sialoadenitis
  submaxillary gland (suppurative) —see
    Sialoadenitis
  tuberculous —see Tuberculosis, lymph gland
  urethral gland —see Urethritis
  Wharton's duct (suppurative) —see
    Sialoadenitis
Adenoacanthoma —see Neoplasm, malignant,
  by site

Adenoameloblastoma —see Cyst, calcifying
  odontogenic
Adenocarcinoid (tumor) —see Neoplasm,
  malignant, by site
Adenocarcinoma —see also Neoplasm,
  malignant, by site
  acidophil
    specified site —see Neoplasm, malignant,
     by site
    unspecified site C75.1
  adrenal cortical C74.0-•
  alveolar —see Neoplasm, lung, malignant
  apocrine
    breast —see Neoplasm, breast, malignant
    in situ
     breast D05.8-•
     specified site NEC —see Neoplasm, skin,
      in situ
     unspecified site D04.9
    specified site NEC —see Neoplasm, skin,
     malignant
    unspecified site C44.99
  basal cell
    specified site —see Neoplasm, skin,
     malignant
    unspecified site C08.9
  basophil
    specified site —see Neoplasm, malignant,
     by site
    unspecified site C75.1
  bile duct type C22.1
    liver C22.1
    specified site NEC —see Neoplasm,
     malignant, by site
    unspecified site C22.1
  bronchiolar —see Neoplasm, lung, malignant
  bronchioloalveolar —see Neoplasm, lung,
    malignant
  ceruminous C44.29-•
  cervix, in situ (see also Carcinoma, cervix
    uteri, in situ) D06.9
  chromophobe
    specified site —see Neoplasm, malignant,
     by site
    unspecified site C75.1
  diffuse type
    specified site —see Neoplasm, malignant,
     by site
    unspecified site C16.9
  duct
    infiltrating
     with Paget's disease —see Neoplasm,
      breast, malignant
     specified site —see Neoplasm,
      malignant, by site
     unspecified site (female) C50.91-•
      male C50.92-•
    specified site —see Neoplasm, malignant,
     by site
    unspecified site
     female C56.9
     male C61
  eosinophil
    specified site —see Neoplasm, malignant,
     by site
    unspecified site C75.1
  follicular
    with papillary C73
    moderately differentiated C73
    specified site —see Neoplasm, malignant,
     by site
    trabecular C73
    unspecified site C73
    well differentiated C73
  Hurthle cell C73
  in
    adenomatous
     polyposis coli C18.9
    infiltrating duct
     with Paget's disease —see Neoplasm,
      breast, malignant

Adenocarcinoma (Continued)
  infiltrating duct (Continued)
    specified site —see Neoplasm, malignant,
     by site
    unspecified site (female) C50.91-•
     male C50.92-•
  inflammatory
    specified site —see Neoplasm, malignant,
     by site
    unspecified site (female) C50.91-•
     male C50.92-•
  intestinal type
    specified site —see Neoplasm, malignant,
     by site
    unspecified site C16.9
  intracystic papillary
  intraductal
    breast D05.1-•
    noninfiltrating
     breast D05.1-•
     papillary
      with invasion
       specified site —see Neoplasm,
        malignant, by site
       unspecified site (female) C50.91-•
        male C50.92-•
      breast D05.1-•
      specified site NEC —see Neoplasm, in
       situ, by site
      unspecified site D05.1-•
     specified site NEC —see Neoplasm, in
      situ, by site
     unspecified site D05.1-•
    papillary
     with invasion
      specified site —see Neoplasm,
       malignant, by site
      unspecified site (female) C50.91-•
       male C50.92-•
     breast D05.1-•
     specified site —see Neoplasm, in situ,
      by site
     unspecified site D05.1-•
    specified site NEC —see Neoplasm, in situ,
     by site
    unspecified site D05.1-•
  islet cell
    with exocrine, mixed
     specified site —see Neoplasm,
      malignant, by site
     unspecified site C25.9
    pancreas C25.4
    specified site NEC —see Neoplasm,
     malignant, by site
    unspecified site C25.4
  lobular
    in situ
     breast D05.0-•
     specified site NEC —see Neoplasm, in
      situ, by site
     unspecified site D05.0-•
    specified site —see Neoplasm, malignant,
     by site
    unspecified site (female) C50.91-•
     male C50.92-•
  mucoid —see also Neoplasm, malignant, by site
    cell
     specified site —see Neoplasm,
      malignant, by site
     unspecified site C75.1
  nonencapsulated sclerosing C73
  papillary
    with follicular C73
    follicular variant C73
    intraductal (noninfiltrating)
     with invasion
      specified site —see Neoplasm,
       malignant, by site
      unspecified site (female) C50.91-•
       male C50.92-•
     breast D05.1-•

Adenocarcinoma *(Continued)*
  papillary *(Continued)*
    intraductal *(Continued)*
      specified site NEC —*see* Neoplasm, in situ, by site
      unspecified site D05.1-●
    serous
      specified site —*see* Neoplasm, malignant, by site
      unspecified site C56.9
  papillocystic
    specified site —*see* Neoplasm, malignant, by site
    unspecified site C56.9
  pseudomucinous
    specified site —*see* Neoplasm, malignant, by site
    unspecified site C56.9
  renal cell C64-●
  sebaceous —*see* Neoplasm, skin, malignant, by site
  serous —*see also* Neoplasm, malignant, by site
    papillary
      specified site —*see* Neoplasm, malignant, by site
      unspecified site C56.9
  sweat gland —*see* Neoplasm, skin, malignant
  water-clear cell C75.0
Adenocarcinoma-in-situ —*see also* Neoplasm, in situ, by site
  breast D05.9-●
Adenofibroma
  clear cell —*see* Neoplasm, benign, by site
  endometrioid D27.9
    borderline malignancy D39.10
    malignant C56-●
  mucinous
    specified site —*see* Neoplasm, benign, by site
    unspecified site D27.9
  papillary
    specified site —*see* Neoplasm, benign, by site
    unspecified site D27.9
  prostate —*see* Enlargement, enlarged, prostate
  serous
    specified site —*see* Neoplasm, benign, by site
    unspecified site D27.9
  specified site —*see* Neoplasm, benign, by site
  unspecified site D27.9
Adenofibrosis
  breast —*see* Fibroadenosis, breast
  endometrioid N80.0
Adenoiditis (chronic) J35.02
  with tonsillitis J35.03
  acute J03.90
    recurrent J03.91
    specified organism NEC J03.80
      recurrent J03.81
    staphylococcal J03.80
      recurrent J03.81
    streptococcal J03.00
      recurrent J03.01
Adenoids —*see* condition
Adenolipoma —*see* Neoplasm, benign, by site
Adenolipomatosis, Launois-Bensaude E88.89
Adenolymphoma
  specified site —*see* Neoplasm, benign, by site
  unspecified site D11.9
Adenoma —*see also* Neoplasm, benign, by site
  acidophil
    specified site —*see* Neoplasm, benign, by site
    unspecified site D35.2
  acidophil-basophil, mixed
    specified site —*see* Neoplasm, benign, by site
    unspecified site D35.2

Adenoma *(Continued)*
  adrenal (cortical) D35.00
    clear cell D35.00
    compact cell D35.00
    glomerulosa cell D35.00
    heavily pigmented variant D35.00
    mixed cell D35.00
  alpha-cell
    pancreas D13.7
    specified site NEC —*see* Neoplasm, benign, by site
    unspecified site D13.7
  alveolar D14.30
  apocrine
    breast D24-●
    specified site NEC —*see* Neoplasm, skin, benign, by site
    unspecified site D23.9
  basal cell D11.9
  basophil
    specified site —*see* Neoplasm, benign, by site
    unspecified site D35.2
  basophil-acidophil, mixed
    specified site —*see* Neoplasm, benign, by site
    unspecified site D35.2
  beta-cell
    pancreas D13.7
    specified site NEC —*see* Neoplasm, benign, by site
    unspecified site D13.7
  bile duct D13.4
    common D13.5
    extrahepatic D13.5
    intrahepatic D13.4
    specified site NEC —*see* Neoplasm, benign, by site
    unspecified site D13.4
  black D35.00
  bronchial D38.1
    cylindroid type —*see* Neoplasm, lung, malignant
  ceruminous D23.2-●
  chief cell D35.1
  chromophobe
    specified site —*see* Neoplasm, benign, by site
    unspecified site D35.2
  colloid
    specified site —*see* Neoplasm, benign, by site
    unspecified site D34
  duct
  eccrine, papillary —*see* Neoplasm, skin, benign
  endocrine, multiple
    single specified site —*see* Neoplasm, uncertain behavior, by site
    two or more specified sites D44-●
    unspecified site D44.9
  endometrioid —*see also* Neoplasm, benign
    borderline malignancy —*see* Neoplasm, uncertain behavior, by site
  eosinophil
    specified site —*see* Neoplasm, malignant, by site
    unspecified site D35.2
  fetal
    specified site —*see* Neoplasm, benign, by site
    unspecified site D34
  follicular
    specified site —*see* Neoplasm, benign, by site
    unspecified site D34
  hepatocellular D13.4
  Hurthle cell D34
  islet cell
    pancreas D13.7
    specified site NEC —*see* Neoplasm, benign, by site
    unspecified site D13.7

Adenoma *(Continued)*
  liver cell D13.4
  macrofollicular
    specified site —*see* Neoplasm, benign, by site
    unspecified site D34
  malignant, malignum —*see* Neoplasm, malignant, by site
  microcystic
    pancreas D13.6
    specified site NEC —*see* Neoplasm, benign, by site
    unspecified site D13.6
  microfollicular
    specified site —*see* Neoplasm, benign, by site
    unspecified site D34
  mucoid cell
    specified site —*see* Neoplasm, benign, by site
    unspecified site D35.2
  multiple endocrine
    single specified site —*see* Neoplasm, uncertain behavior, by site
    two or more specified sites D44-●
    unspecified site D44.9
  nipple D24-●
  papillary —*see also* Neoplasm, benign, by site
    eccrine —*see* Neoplasm, skin, benign, by site
  Pick's tubular
    specified site —*see* Neoplasm, benign, by site
    unspecified site
      female D27.9
      male D29.20
  pleomorphic
    carcinoma in —*see* Neoplasm, salivary gland, malignant
    specified site —*see* Neoplasm, malignant, by site
    unspecified site C08.9
  polypoid —*see also* Neoplasm, benign
    adenocarcinoma in —*see* Neoplasm, malignant, by site
    adenocarcinoma in situ —*see* Neoplasm, in situ, by site
  prostate —*see* Neoplasm, benign, prostate
  rete cell D29.20
  sebaceous —*see* Neoplasm, skin, benign
  Sertoli cell
    specified site —*see* Neoplasm, benign, by site
    unspecified site
      female D27.9
      male D29.20
  skin appendage —*see* Neoplasm, skin, benign
  sudoriferous gland —*see* Neoplasm, skin, benign
  sweat gland —*see* Neoplasm, skin, benign
  testicular
    specified site —*see* Neoplasm, benign, by site
    unspecified site
      female D27.9
      male D29.20
  tubular —*see also* Neoplasm, benign, by site
    adenocarcinoma in —*see* Neoplasm, malignant, by site
    adenocarcinoma in situ —*see* Neoplasm, in situ, by site
    Pick's
      specified site —*see* Neoplasm, benign
      unspecified site
        female D27.9
        male D29.20
  tubulovillous —*see also* Neoplasm, benign, by site
    adenocarcinoma in —*see* Neoplasm, malignant, by site
    adenocarcinoma in situ —*see* Neoplasm, in situ, by site

A

▶ New   ⇒ Revised   ~~deleted~~ Deleted   ● Use Additional Character(s)

Adenoma *(Continued)*
  villous —*see* Neoplasm, uncertain behavior,
    by site
    adenocarcinoma in —*see* Neoplasm,
      malignant, by site
    adenocarcinoma in situ —*see* Neoplasm, in
      situ, by site
  water-clear cell D35.1
Adenomatosis
  endocrine (multiple) E31.20
    single specified site —*see* Neoplasm,
      uncertain behavior, by site
  erosive of nipple D24-•
  pluriendocrine —*see* Adenomatosis,
    endocrine
  pulmonary D38.1
    malignant —*see* Neoplasm, lung,
      malignant
  specified site —*see* Neoplasm, benign, by site
  unspecified site D12.6
Adenomatous
  goiter (nontoxic) E04.9
    with hyperthyroidism —*see* Hyper-
      thyroidism, with, goiter, nodular
    toxic —*see* Hyperthyroidism, with, goiter,
      nodular
Adenomyoma —*see also* Neoplasm, benign, by
  site
  prostate —*see* Enlarged, prostate
Adenomyometritis N80.0
Adenomyosis N80.0
Adenopathy (lymph gland) R59.9
  generalized R59.1
  inguinal R59.0
  localized R59.0
  mediastinal R59.0
  mesentery R59.0
  syphilitic (secondary) A51.49
  tracheobronchial R59.0
    tuberculous A15.4
      primary (progressive) A15.7
  tuberculous —*see also* Tuberculosis, lymph
    gland
    tracheobronchial A15.4
      primary (progressive) A15.7
Adenosalpingitis —*see* Salpingitis
Adenosarcoma —*see* Neoplasm, malignant, by
  site
Adenosclerosis I88.8
Adenosis (sclerosing) breast —*see*
  Fibroadenosis, breast
Adenovirus, as cause of disease classified
  elsewhere B97.0
Adentia (complete) (partial) —*see* Absence,
  teeth
Adherent —*see also* Adhesions
  labia (minora) N90.89
  pericardium (nonrheumatic) I31.0
    rheumatic I09.2
  placenta (with hemorrhage) O72.0
    without hemorrhage O73.0
  prepuce, newborn N47.0
  scar (skin) L90.5
  tendon in scar L90.5
Adhesions, adhesive (postinfective) K66.0
  with intestinal obstruction K56.50
    complete K56.52
    incomplete K56.51
    partial K56.51
  abdominal (wall) —*see* Adhesions, peritoneum
  appendix K38.8
  bile duct (common) (hepatic) K83.8
  bladder (sphincter) N32.89
  bowel —*see* Adhesions, peritoneum
  cardiac I31.0
    rheumatic I09.2
  cecum —*see* Adhesions, peritoneum
  cervicovaginal N88.1
    congenital Q52.8
    postpartal O90.89
      old N88.1

Adhesions, adhesive *(Continued)*
  cervix N88.1
  ciliary body NEC —*see* Adhesions, iris
  clitoris N90.89
  colon —*see* Adhesions, peritoneum
  common duct K83.8
  congenital —*see also* Anomaly, by site
    fingers —*see* Syndactylism, complex, fingers
    omental, anomalous Q43.3
    peritoneal Q43.3
    tongue (to gum or roof of mouth) Q38.3
  conjunctiva (acquired) H11.21-•
    congenital Q15.8
  cystic duct K82.8
  diaphragm —*see* Adhesions, peritoneum
  due to foreign body —*see* Foreign body
  duodenum —*see* Adhesions, peritoneum
  ear
    middle H74.1-•
  epididymis N50.89
  epidural —*see* Adhesions, meninges
  epiglottis J38.7
  eyelid H02.59
  female pelvis N73.6
  gallbladder K82.8
  globe H44.89
  heart I31.0
    rheumatic I09.2
  ileocecal (coil) —*see* Adhesions, peritoneum
  ileum —*see* Adhesions, peritoneum
  intestine —*see also* Adhesions, peritoneum
    with obstruction K56.50
      complete K56.52
      incomplete K56.51
      partial K56.51
  intra-abdominal —*see* Adhesions, peritoneum
  iris H21.50-•
    anterior H21.51-•
    goniosynechiae H21.52-•
    posterior H21.54-•
    to corneal graft T85.898
  joint —*see* Ankylosis
    knee M23.8X
    temporomandibular M26.61-•
  labium (majus) (minus), congenital Q52.5
  liver —*see* Adhesions, peritoneum
  lung J98.4
  mediastinum J98.59
  meninges (cerebral) (spinal) G96.12
    congenital Q07.8
    tuberculous (cerebral) (spinal) A17.0
  mesenteric —*see* Adhesions, peritoneum
  nasal (septum) (to turbinates) J34.89
  ocular muscle —*see* Strabismus, mechanical
  omentum —*see* Adhesions, peritoneum
  ovary N73.6
    congenital (to cecum, kidney or omentum)
      Q50.39
  paraovarian N73.6
  pelvic (peritoneal)
    female N73.6
      postprocedural N99.4
    male —*see* Adhesions, peritoneum
    postpartal (old) N73.6
    tuberculous A18.17
  penis to scrotum (congenital) Q55.8
  periappendiceal —*see also* Adhesions,
    peritoneum
  pericardium (nonrheumatic) I31.0
    focal I31.8
    rheumatic I09.2
    tuberculous A18.84
  pericholecystic K82.8
  perigastric —*see* Adhesions, peritoneum
  periovarian N73.6
  periprostatic N42.89
  perirectal —*see* Adhesions, peritoneum
  perirenal N28.89
  peritoneum, peritoneal (postinfective)
    with obstruction (intestinal) K56.50
      complete K56.52

Adhesions, adhesive *(Continued)*
  peritoneum, peritoneal *(Continued)*
    with obstruction *(Continued)*
      incomplete K56.51
      partial K56.51
    congenital Q43.3
    pelvic, female N73.6
      postprocedural N99.4
    postpartal, pelvic N73.6
    postprocedural K66.0
    to uterus N73.6
  peritubal N73.6
  periureteral N28.89
  periuterine N73.6
  perivesical N32.89
  perivesicular (seminal vesicle) N50.89
  pleura, pleuritic J94.8
    tuberculous NEC A15.6
  pleuropericardial J94.8
  postoperative (gastrointestinal tract) K66.0
    with obstruction —*see also* Obstruction,
      intestine, postoperative K91.30
    due to foreign body accidentally left
      in wound —*see* Foreign body,
      accidentally left during a procedure
    pelvic peritoneal N99.4
    urethra —*see* Stricture, urethra,
      postprocedural
    vagina N99.2
  postpartal, old (vulva or perineum) N90.89
  preputial, prepuce N47.5
  pulmonary J98.4
  pylorus —*see* Adhesions, peritoneum
  sciatic nerve —*see* Lesion, nerve, sciatic
  seminal vesicle N50.89
  shoulder (joint) —*see* Capsulitis, adhesive
  sigmoid flexure —*see* Adhesions, peritoneum
  spermatic cord (acquired) N50.89
    congenital Q55.4
  spinal canal G96.12
  stomach —*see* Adhesions, peritoneum
  subscapular —*see* Capsulitis, adhesive
  temporomandibular M26.61-•
  tendinitis —*see also* Tenosynovitis, specified
    type NEC
    shoulder —*see* Capsulitis, adhesive
  testis N44.8
  tongue, congenital (to gum or roof of mouth)
    Q38.3
    acquired K14.8
  trachea J39.8
  tubo-ovarian N73.6
  tunica vaginalis N44.8
  uterus N73.6
    internal N85.6
    to abdominal wall N73.6
  vagina (chronic) N89.5
    postoperative N99.2
  vitreomacular H43.82-•
  vitreous H43.89
  vulva N90.89
Adiaspiromycosis B48.8
Adie (-Holmes) pupil or syndrome —*see*
  Anomaly, pupil, function, tonic pupil
Adiponecrosis neonatorum P83.88
Adiposis —*see also* Obesity
  cerebralis E23.6
  dolorosa E88.2
Adiposity —*see also* Obesity
  heart —*see* Degeneration, myocardial
  localized E65
Adiposogenital dystrophy E23.6
Adjustment
  disorder —*see* Disorder, adjustment
  implanted device —*see* Encounter (for),
    adjustment (of)
  prosthesis, external —*see* Fitting
  reaction —*see* Disorder, adjustment
Administration of tPA (rtPA) in a different
  facility within the last 24 hours prior to
  admission to current facility Z92.82

Admission (for) —*see also* Encounter (for)
  adjustment (of)
    artificial
      arm Z44.00-●
        complete Z44.01-●
        partial Z44.02-●
      eye Z44.2
      leg Z44.10-●
        complete Z44.11-●
        partial Z44.12-●
    brain neuropacemaker Z46.2
      implanted Z45.42
    breast
      implant Z45.81
      prosthesis (external) Z44.3
    colostomy belt Z46.89
    contact lenses Z46.0
    cystostomy device Z46.6
    dental prosthesis Z46.3
    device NEC
      abdominal Z46.89
      implanted Z45.89
        cardiac Z45.09
          defibrillator (with synchronous
            cardiace pacemaker) Z45.02
          pacemaker (cardiac
            resynchronization therapy
            (CRT-P)) Z45.018
            pulse generator Z45.010
          resynchronization therapy
            defibrillator (CRT-D) Z45.02
        hearing device Z45.328
          bone conduction Z45.320
          cochlear Z45.321
        infusion pump Z45.1
        nervous system Z45.49
          CSF drainage Z45.41
          hearing device —*see* Admission,
            adjustment, device, implanted,
            hearing device
          neuropacemaker Z45.42
          visual substitution Z45.31
        specified NEC Z45.89
        vascular access Z45.2
        visual substitution Z45.31
      nervous system Z46.2
        implanted —*see* Admission,
          adjustment, device, implanted,
          nervous system
      orthodontic Z46.4
      prosthetic Z44.9
        arm —*see* Admission, adjustment,
          artificial, arm
        breast Z44.3
        dental Z46.3
        eye Z44.2
        leg —*see* Admission, adjustment,
          artificial, leg
        specified type NEC Z44.8
      substitution
        auditory Z46.2
          implanted —*see* Admission,
            adjustment, device, implanted,
            hearing device
          nervous system Z46.2
            implanted —*see* Admission,
              adjustment, device, implanted,
              nervous system
          visual Z46.2
            implanted Z45.31
        urinary Z46.6
    hearing aid Z46.1
      implanted —*see* Admission, adjustment,
        device, implanted, hearing device
    ileostomy device Z46.89
    intestinal appliance or device NEC Z46.89
    neuropacemaker (brain) (peripheral nerve)
      (spinal cord) Z46.2
      implanted Z45.42
    orthodontic device Z46.4
    orthopedic (brace) (cast) (device) (shoes)
      Z46.89

Admission (*Continued*)
  adjustment (*Continued*)
    pacemaker (cardiac resynchronization
      therapy (CRT-P))
      cardiac Z45.018
        pulse generator Z45.010
      nervous system Z46.2
        implanted Z45.42
    portacath (port-a-cath) Z45.2
    prosthesis Z44.9
      arm —*see* Admission, adjustment,
        artificial, arm
      breast Z44.3
      dental Z46.3
      eye Z44.2
      leg —*see* Admission, adjustment,
        artificial, leg
      specified NEC Z44.8
    spectacles Z46.0
  aftercare (*see also* Aftercare) Z51.89
    postpartum
      immediately after delivery Z39.0
      routine follow-up Z39.2
    radiation therapy (antineoplastic) Z51.0
  attention to artificial opening (of) Z43.9
    artificial vagina Z43.7
    colostomy Z43.3
    cystostomy Z43.5
    enterostomy Z43.4
    gastrostomy Z43.1
    ileostomy Z43.2
    jejunostomy Z43.4
    nephrostomy Z43.6
    specified site NEC Z43.8
      intestinal tract Z43.4
      urinary tract Z43.6
    tracheostomy Z43.0
    ureterostomy Z43.6
    urethrostomy Z43.6
  breast augmentation or reduction Z41.1
  breast reconstruction following mastectomy
    Z42.1
  change of
    dressing (nonsurgical) Z48.00
    neuropacemaker device (brain) (peripheral
      nerve) (spinal cord) Z46.2
      implanted Z45.42
    surgical dressing Z48.01
  circumcision, ritual or routine (in absence of
    diagnosis) Z41.2
  clinical research investigation (control)
    (normal comparison) (participant) Z00.6
  contraceptive management Z30.9
  cosmetic surgery NEC Z41.1
  counseling (*see also* Counseling)
    dietary Z71.3
    gestational carrier Z31.7
    HIV Z71.7
    human immunodeficiency virus Z71.7
    nonattending third party Z71.0
    procreative management NEC Z31.69
  delivery, full-term, uncomplicated O80
    cesarean, without indication O82
  desensitization to allergens Z51.6
  dietary surveillance and counseling Z71.3
  ear piercing Z41.3
  examination at health care facility (adult) —
    see also Examination Z00.00
    with abnormal findings Z00.01
    clinical research investigation (control)
      (normal comparison) (participant) Z00.6
    dental Z01.20
      with abnormal findings Z01.21
    donor (potential) Z00.5
    ear Z01.10
      with abnormal findings NEC Z01.118
    eye Z01.00
      with abnormal findings Z01.01
    general, specified reason NEC Z00.8
    hearing Z01.10
      with abnormal findings NEC Z01.118
    ▶infant or child (over 28 days old) Z00.129
      ▶with abnormal findings Z00.121

Admission (*Continued*)
  examination at health care facility (*Continued*)
    postpartum checkup Z39.2
    psychiatric (general) Z00.8
      requested by authority Z04.6
    vision Z01.00
      with abnormal findings Z01.01
      ▶infant or child (over 28 days old) Z00.129
        ▶with abnormal findings Z00.121
  fitting (of)
    artificial
      arm —*see* Admission, adjustment,
        artificial, arm
      eye Z44.2
      leg —*see* Admission, adjustment,
        artificial, leg
    brain neuropacemaker Z46.2
      implanted Z45.42
    breast prosthesis (external) Z44.3
    colostomy belt Z46.89
    contact lenses Z46.0
    cystostomy device Z46.6
    dental prosthesis Z46.3
    dentures Z46.3
    device NEC
      abdominal Z46.89
      nervous system Z46.2
        implanted —*see* Admission,
          adjustment, device, implanted,
          nervous system
      orthodontic Z46.4
      prosthetic Z44.9
        breast Z44.3
        dental Z46.3
        eye Z44.2
      substitution
        auditory Z46.2
          implanted —*see* Admission,
            adjustment, device, implanted,
            hearing device
        nervous system Z46.2
          implanted —*see* Admission,
            adjustment, device, implanted,
            nervous system
        visual Z46.2
          implanted Z45.31
    hearing aid Z46.1
    ileostomy device Z46.89
    intestinal appliance or device NEC Z46.89
    neuropacemaker (brain) (peripheral nerve)
      (spinal cord) Z46.2
      implanted Z45.42
    orthodontic device Z46.4
    orthopedic device (brace) (cast) (shoes)
      Z46.89
    prosthesis Z44.9
      arm —*see* Admission, adjustment,
        artificial, arm
      breast Z44.3
      dental Z46.3
      eye Z44.2
      leg —*see* Admission, adjustment,
        artificial, leg
      specified type NEC Z44.8
    spectacles Z46.0
  follow-up examination Z09
  intrauterine device management Z30.431
    initial prescription Z30.014
  mental health evaluation Z00.8
    requested by authority Z04.6
  observation —*see* Observation
  Papanicolaou smear, cervix Z12.4
    for suspected malignant neoplasm Z12.4
  plastic and reconstructive surgery following
    medical procedure or healed injury NEC
    Z42.8
  plastic surgery, cosmetic NEC Z41.1
  postpartum observation
    immediately after delivery Z39.0
    routine follow-up Z39.2
  poststerilization (for restoration) Z31.0
    aftercare Z31.42
  procreative management Z31.9

▶ New   ⇒ Revised   ~~deleted~~ Deleted   ● Use Additional Character(s)

Admission (Continued)
  prophylactic (measure) —see also Encounter,
    prophylactic measures
    organ removal Z40.00
      breast Z40.01
      fallopian tube(s) Z40.03
        with ovary(s) Z40.02
      ovary(s) Z40.02
      specified organ NEC Z40.09
      testes Z40.09
    vaccination Z23
  psychiatric examination (general) Z00.8
    requested by authority Z04.6
  radiation therapy (antineoplastic) Z51.0
  reconstructive surgery following medical
    procedure or healed injury NEC Z42.8
  removal of
    cystostomy catheter Z43.5
    drains Z48.03
    dressing (nonsurgical) Z48.00
    implantable subdermal contraceptive Z30.46
    intrauterine contraceptive device Z30.432
    neuropacemaker (brain) (peripheral nerve)
      (spinal cord) Z46.2
      implanted Z45.42
    staples Z48.02
    surgical dressing Z48.01
    sutures Z48.02
    ureteral stent Z46.6
  respirator [ventilator] use during power
    failure Z99.12
  restoration of organ continuity
    (poststerilization) Z31.0
    aftercare Z31.42
  sensitivity test —see also Test, skin
    allergy NEC Z01.82
    Mantoux Z11.1
  tuboplasty following previous sterilization
    Z31.0
    aftercare Z31.42
  vasoplasty following previous sterilization
    Z31.0
    aftercare Z31.42
  vision examination Z01.00
    with abnormal findings Z01.01
  ▶ infant or child (over 28 days old) Z00.129
    ▶ with abnormal findings Z00.121
  waiting period for admission to other facility
    Z75.1
Adnexitis (suppurative) —see Salpingo-oophoritis
Adolescent X-linked adrenoleukodystrophy
  E71.521
Adrenal (gland) —see condition
Adrenalism, tuberculous A18.7
Adrenalitis, adrenitis E27.8
  autoimmune E27.1
  meningococcal, hemorrhagic A39.1
Adrenarche, premature E27.0
Adrenocortical syndrome —see Cushing's,
  syndrome
Adrenogenital syndrome E25.9
  acquired E25.8
  congenital E25.0
  salt loss E25.0
Adrenogenitalism, congenital E25.0
Adrenoleukodystrophy E71.529
  neonatal E71.511
  X-linked E71.529
    Addison only phenotype E71.528
    Addison-Schilder E71.528
    adolescent E71.521
    adrenomyeloneuropathy E71.522
    childhood cerebral E71.520
    other specified E71.528
Adrenomyeloneuropathy E71.522
Adventitious bursa —see Bursopathy, specified
  type NEC
Adverse effect —see Table of Drugs and
  Chemicals, categories T36-T50, with 6th
  character 5
Advice —see Counseling

Adynamia (episodica) (hereditary) (periodic)
  G72.3
Aeration lung imperfect, newborn —see
  Atelectasis
Aerobullosis T70.3
Aerocele —see Embolism, air
Aerodermectasia
  subcutaneous (traumatic) T79.7
Aerodontalgia T70.29
Aeroembolism T70.3
Aerogenes capsulatus infection A48.0
Aero-otitis media T70.0
Aerophagy, aerophagia (psychogenic) F45.8
Aerophobia F40.228
Aerosinusitis T70.1
Aerotitis T70.0
Affection —see Disease
Afibrinogenemia —see also Defect, coagulation
  D68.8
  acquired D65
  congenital D68.2
  following ectopic or molar pregnancy O08.1
  in abortion —see Abortion, by type,
    complicated by, afibrinogenemia
  puerperal O72.3
African
  sleeping sickness B56.9
  tick fever A68.1
  trypanosomiasis B56.9
    gambian B56.0
    rhodesian B56.1
Aftercare —see also Care Z51.89
  following surgery (for) (on)
    amputation Z47.81
    attention to
      drains Z48.03
      dressings (nonsurgical) Z48.00
        surgical Z48.01
      sutures Z48.02
    circulatory system Z48.812
    delayed (planned) wound closure Z48.1
    digestive system Z48.815
    explanation of joint prosthesis (staged
      procedure)
      hip Z47.32
      knee Z47.33
      shoulder Z47.31
    genitourinary system Z48.816
    joint replacement Z47.1
    neoplasm Z48.3
    nervous system Z48.811
    oral cavity Z48.814
    organ transplant
      bone marrow Z48.290
      heart Z48.21
      heart-lung Z48.280
      kidney Z48.22
      liver Z48.23
      lung Z48.24
      multiple organs NEC Z48.288
      specified NEC Z48.298
    orthopedic NEC Z47.89
    planned wound closure Z48.1
    removal of internal fixation device Z47.2
    respiratory system Z48.813
    scoliosis Z47.82
    sense organs Z48.810
    skin and subcutaneous tissue Z48.817
    specified body system
      circulatory Z48.812
      digestive Z48.815
      genitourinary Z48.816
      nervous Z48.811
      oral cavity Z48.814
      respiratory Z48.813
      sense organs Z48.810
      skin and subcutaneous tissue Z48.817
      teeth Z48.814
    specified NEC Z48.89
    spinal Z47.89
    teeth Z48.814

Aftercare (Continued)
  fracture — code to fracture with seventh
    character D
  involving
    removal of
      drains Z48.03
      dressings (nonsurgical) Z48.00
      staples Z48.02
      surgical dressings Z48.01
      sutures Z48.02
    neuropacemaker (brain) (peripheral nerve)
      (spinal cord) Z46.2
      implanted Z45.42
  orthopedic NEC Z47.89
  postprocedural —see Aftercare, following
    surgery
After-cataract —see Cataract, secondary
Agalactia (primary) O92.3
  elective, secondary or therapeutic O92.5
Agammaglobulinemia (acquired (secondary))
  (nonfamilial) D80.1
  with
    immunoglobulin-bearing B-lymphocytes
      D80.1
    lymphopenia D81.9
  autosomal recessive (Swiss type) D80.0
  Bruton's X-linked D80.0
  common variable (CVAgamma) D80.1
  congenital sex-linked D80.0
  hereditary D80.0
  lymphopenic D81.9
  Swiss type (autosomal recessive) D80.0
  X-linked (with growth hormone deficiency)
    (Bruton) D80.0
Aganglionosis (bowel) (colon) Q43.1
Age (old) —see Senility
Agenesis
  adrenal (gland) Q89.1
  alimentary tract (complete) (partial) NEC Q45.8
    upper Q40.8
  anus, anal (canal) Q42.3
    with fistula Q42.2
  aorta Q25.41
  appendix Q42.8
  arm (complete) Q71.0-•
    with hand present Q71.1-•
  artery (peripheral) Q27.9
    brain Q28.3
    coronary Q24.5
    pulmonary Q25.79
    specified NEC Q27.8
    umbilical Q27.0
  auditory (canal) (external) Q16.1
  auricle (ear) Q16.0
  bile duct or passage Q44.5
  bladder Q64.5
  bone Q79.9
  brain Q00.0
    part of Q04.3
  breast (with nipple present) Q83.8
    with absent nipple Q83.0
  bronchus Q32.4
  canaliculus lacrimalis Q10.4
  carpus —see Agenesis, hand
  cartilage Q79.9
  cecum Q42.8
  cerebellum Q04.3
  cervix Q51.5
  chin Q18.8
  cilia Q10.3
  circulatory system, part NOS Q28.9
  clavicle Q74.0
  clitoris Q52.6
  coccyx Q76.49
  colon Q42.9
    specified NEC Q42.8
  corpus callosum Q04.0
  cricoid cartilage Q31.8
  diaphragm (with hernia) Q79.1
  digestive organ(s) or tract (complete) (partial)
    NEC Q45.8
    upper Q40.8

Agenesis *(Continued)*
ductus arteriosus Q28.8
duodenum Q41.0
ear Q16.9
  auricle Q16.0
  lobe Q17.8
ejaculatory duct Q55.4
endocrine (gland) NEC Q89.2
epiglottis Q31.8
esophagus Q39.8
eustachian tube Q16.2
eye Q11.1
  adnexa Q15.8
eyelid (fold) Q10.3
face
  bones NEC Q75.8
  specified part NEC Q18.8
fallopian tube Q50.6
femur —*see* Defect, reduction, lower limb,
    longitudinal, femur
fibula —*see* Defect, reduction, lower limb,
    longitudinal, fibula
finger (complete) (partial) —*see* Agenesis,
    hand
foot (and toes) (complete) (partial) Q72.3-•
forearm (with hand present) —*see* Agenesis,
    arm, with hand present
  and hand Q71.2-•
gallbladder Q44.0
gastric Q40.2
genitalia, genital (organ(s))
  female Q52.8
    external Q52.71
    internal NEC Q52.8
  male Q55.8
glottis Q31.8
hair Q84.0
hand (and fingers) (complete) (partial) Q71.3-•
heart Q24.8
  valve NEC Q24.8
    pulmonary Q22.0
hepatic Q44.7
humerus —*see* Defect, reduction, upper limb
hymen Q52.4
ileum Q41.2
incus Q16.3
intestine (small) Q41.9
  large Q42.9
    specified NEC Q42.8
iris (dilator fibers) Q13.1
jaw M26.09
jejunum Q41.1
kidney(s) (partial) Q60.2
  bilateral Q60.1
  unilateral Q60.0
labium (majus) (minus) Q52.71
labyrinth, membranous Q16.5
lacrimal apparatus Q10.4
larynx Q31.8
leg (complete) Q72.0-•
  with foot present Q72.1-•
  lower leg (with foot present) —*see*
      Agenesis, leg, with foot present
  and foot Q72.2-•
lens Q12.3
limb (complete) Q73.0
  lower —*see* Agenesis, leg
  upper —*see* Agenesis, arm
lip Q38.0
liver Q44.7
lung (fissure) (lobe) (bilateral) (unilateral)
    Q33.3
mandible, maxilla M26.09
metacarpus —*see* Agenesis, hand
metatarsus —*see* Agenesis, foot
muscle Q79.8
  eyelid Q10.3
  ocular Q15.8
musculoskeletal system NEC Q79.8
nail(s) Q84.3
neck, part Q18.8

Agenesis *(Continued)*
nerve Q07.8
nervous system, part NEC Q07.8
nipple Q83.2
nose Q30.1
nuclear Q07.8
organ
  of Corti Q16.5
  or site not listed —*see* Anomaly, by site
osseous meatus (ear) Q16.1
ovary
  bilateral Q50.02
  unilateral Q50.01
oviduct Q50.6
pancreas Q45.0
parathyroid (gland) Q89.2
parotid gland(s) Q38.4
patella Q74.1
pelvic girdle (complete) (partial) Q74.2
penis Q55.5
pericardium Q24.8
pituitary (gland) Q89.2
prostate Q55.4
punctum lacrimale Q10.4
radioulnar —*see* Defect, reduction, upper limb
radius —*see* Defect, reduction, upper limb,
    longitudinal, radius
rectum Q42.10
  with fistula Q42.0
renal Q60.2
  bilateral Q60.1
  unilateral Q60.0
respiratory organ NEC Q34.8
rib Q76.6
roof of orbit Q75.8
round ligament Q52.8
sacrum Q76.49
salivary gland Q38.4
scapula Q74.0
scrotum Q55.29
seminal vesicles Q55.4
septum
  atrial Q21.1
  between aorta and pulmonary artery Q21.4
  ventricular Q20.4
shoulder girdle (complete) (partial) Q74.0
skull (bone) Q75.8
  with
    anencephaly Q00.0
    encephalocele —*see* Encephalocele
    hydrocephalus Q03.9
      with spina bifida —*see* Spina bifida, by
          site, with hydrocephalus
    microcephaly Q02
spermatic cord Q55.4
spinal cord Q06.0
spine Q76.49
spleen Q89.01
sternum Q76.7
stomach Q40.2
submaxillary gland(s) (congenital) Q38.4
tarsus —*see* Agenesis, foot
tendon Q79.8
testicle Q55.0
thymus (gland) Q89.2
thyroid (gland) E03.1
  cartilage Q31.8
tibia —*see* Defect, reduction, lower limb,
    longitudinal, tibia
tibiofibular —*see* Defect, reduction, lower
    limb, specified type NEC
toe (and foot) (complete) (partial) —*see*
    Agenesis, foot
tongue Q38.3
trachea (cartilage) Q32.1
ulna —*see* Defect, reduction, upper limb,
    longitudinal, ulna
upper limb —*see* Agenesis, arm
ureter Q62.4
urethra Q64.5
urinary tract NEC Q64.8

Agenesis *(Continued)*
uterus Q51.0
uvula Q38.5
vagina Q52.0
vas deferens Q55.4
vein(s) (peripheral) Q27.9
  brain Q28.3
  great NEC Q26.8
  portal Q26.5
vena cava (inferior) (superior) Q26.8
vermis of cerebellum Q04.3
vertebra Q76.49
vulva Q52.71
Ageusia R43.2
Agitated —*see* condition
Agitation R45.1
Aglossia (congenital) Q38.3
Aglossia-adactylia syndrome Q87.0
Aglycogenosis E74.00
Agnosia (body image) (other senses) (tactile)
    R48.1
  developmental F88
  verbal R48.1
    auditory R48.1
      developmental F80.2
    developmental F80.2
  visual (object) R48.3
Agoraphobia F40.00
  with panic disorder F40.01
  without panic disorder F40.02
Agrammatism R48.8
Agranulocytopenia —*see* Agranulocytosis
Agranulocytosis (chronic) (cyclical) (genetic)
    (infantile) (periodic) (pernicious) (*see also*
    Neutropenia) D70.9
  congenital D70.0
  cytoreductive cancer chemotherapy sequela
      D70.1
  drug-induced D70.2
    due to cytoreductive cancer chemotherapy
        D70.1
  due to infection D70.3
  secondary D70.4
    drug-induced D70.2
      due to cytoreductive cancer
          chemotherapy D70.1
Agraphia (absolute) R48.8
  with alexia R48.0
  developmental F81.81
Ague (dumb) —*see* Malaria
Agyria Q04.3
Ahumada-del Castillo syndrome E23.0
Aichomophobia F40.298
AIDS (related complex) B20
Ailment heart —*see* Disease, heart
Ailurophobia F40.218
Ainhum (disease) L94.6
AIN —*see* Neoplasia, intraepithelial, anal
AIPHI (acute idiopathic pulmonary hemorrhage
    in infants (over 28 days old)) R04.81
Air
  anterior mediastinum J98.2
  compressed, disease T70.3
  conditioner lung or pneumonitis J67.7
  embolism (artery) (cerebral) (any site) T79.0
    with ectopic or molar pregnancy O08.2
    due to implanted device NEC —*see*
        Complications, by site and type,
        specified NEC
    following
      abortion —*see* Abortion by type,
          complicated by, embolism
      ectopic or molar pregnancy O08.2
    infusion, therapeutic injection or
        transfusion T80.0
    in pregnancy, childbirth or puerperium —
        see Embolism, obstetric
    traumatic T79.0
  hunger, psychogenic F45.8
  rarefied, effects of —*see* Effect, adverse, high
      altitude
  sickness T75.3

▶ New   ➡ Revised   ~~deleted~~ Deleted   • Use Additional Character(s)

Airplane sickness T75.3
Akathisia (drug-induced) (treatment- induced) G25.71
  neuroleptic induced (acute) G25.71
  tardive G25.71
Akinesia R29.898
Akinetic mutism R41.89
Akureyri's disease G93.3
Alactasia, congenital E73.0
Alagille's syndrome Q44.7
Alastrim B03
Albers-Schönberg syndrome Q78.2
Albert's syndrome —see Tendinitis, Achilles
Albinism, albino E70.30
  with hematologic abnormality E70.339
    Chédiak-Higashi syndrome E70.330
    Hermansky-Pudlak syndrome E70.331
    other specified E70.338
  I E70.320
  II E70.321
  ocular E70.319
    autosomal recessive E70.311
    other specified E70.318
    X-linked E70.310
  oculocutaneous E70.329
    other specified E70.328
    tyrosinase (ty) negative E70.320
    tyrosinase (ty) positive E70.321
  other specified E70.39
Albinismus E70.30
Albright (-McCune)(-Sternberg) syndrome Q78.1
Albuminous —see condition
Albuminuria, albuminuric (acute) (chronic) (subacute) —see also Proteinuria R80.9
  complicating pregnancy —see Proteinuria, gestational
  with
    gestational hypertension —see Pre-eclampsia
    pre-existing hypertension —see Hypertension, complicating pregnancy, pre-existing, with, pre-eclampsia
  gestational —see Proteinuria, gestational
  with
    gestational hypertension —see Pre-eclampsia
    pre-existing hypertension —see Hypertension, complicating pregnancy, pre-existing, with, pre-eclampsia
  orthostatic R80.2
  postural R80.2
  pre-eclamptic —see Pre-eclampsia
  scarlatinal A38.8
Albuminurophobia F40.298
Alcaptonuria E70.29
Alcohol, alcoholic, alcohol-induced
  addiction (without remission) F10.20
    with remission F10.21
  amnestic disorder, persisting F10.96
    with dependence F10.26
  anxiety disorder F10.980
  bipolar and related disorder F10.94
  brain syndrome, chronic F10.97
    with dependence F10.27
  cardiopathy I42.6
  counseling and surveillance Z71.41
    family member Z71.42
  delirium (acute) (tremens) (withdrawal) F10.231
    with intoxication F10.921
    in
      abuse F10.121
      dependence F10.221
  dementia F10.97
    with dependence F10.27
  depressive disorder F10.94
  deterioration F10.97
    with dependence F10.27

Alcohol, alcoholic, alcohol-induced (Continued)
  hallucinosis (acute) F10.951
    in
      abuse F10.151
      dependence F10.251
  insanity F10.959
  intoxication (acute) (without dependence) F10.129
    with
      delirium F10.121
      dependence F10.229
        with delirium F10.221
        uncomplicated F10.220
      uncomplicated F10.120
  jealousy F10.988
  Korsakoff's, Korsakov's, Korsakow's F10.26
  liver K70.9
    acute —see Disease, liver, alcoholic, hepatitis
  major neurocognitive disorder, amnestic-confabulatory type F10.96
  major neurocognitive disorder, nonamnestic-confabulatory type F10.97
  mania (acute) (chronic) F10.959
  mild neurocognitive disorder F10.988
  paranoia, paranoid (type) psychosis F10.950
  pellagra E52
  poisoning, accidental (acute) NEC —see Table of Drugs and Chemicals, alcohol, poisoning
  psychosis —see Psychosis, alcoholic
  psychotic disorder F10.959
  sexual dysfunction F10.981
  sleep disorder F10.982
  withdrawal (without convulsions) F10.239
    with delirium F10.231
Alcoholism (chronic) (without remission) F10.20
  with
    psychosis —see Psychosis, alcoholic
    remission F10.21
  Korsakov's F10.96
    with dependence F10.26
Alder (-Reilly) anomaly or syndrome (leukocyte granulation) D72.0
Aldosteronism E26.9
  familial (type I) E26.02
  glucocorticoid-remediable E26.02
  primary (due to (bilateral) adrenal hyperplasia) E26.09
  primary NEC E26.09
  secondary E26.1
  specified NEC E26.89
Aldosteronoma D44.10
Aldrich(-Wiskott) syndrome (eczema-thrombocytopenia) D82.0
Alektorophobia F40.218
Aleppo boil B55.1
Aleukemic —see condition Aleukia
  congenital D70.0
  hemorrhagica D61.9
    congenital D61.09
  splenica D73.1
Alexia R48.0
  developmental F81.0
  secondary to organic lesion R48.0
Algoneurodystrophy M89.00
  ankle M89.07-●
  foot M89.07-●
  forearm M89.03-●
  hand M89.04-●
  lower leg M89.06-●
  multiple sites M89.0-●
  shoulder M89.01-●
  specified site NEC M89.08
  thigh M89.05-●
  upper arm M89.02-●
Algophobia F40.298
Alienation, mental —see Psychosis
Alkalemia E87.3

Alkalosis E87.3
  metabolic E87.3
    with respiratory acidosis E87.4
 ▶ of newborn P74.41
  respiratory E87.3
Alkaptonuria E70.29
Allen-Masters syndrome N83.8
Allergy, allergic (reaction) (to) T78.40
  air-borne substance NEC (rhinitis) J30.89
  alveolitis (extrinsic) J67.9
    due to
      Aspergillus clavatus J67.4
      Cryptostroma corticale J67.6
      organisms (fungal, thermophilic actinomycete) growing in ventilation (air conditioning) systems J67.7
    specified type NEC J67.8
  anaphylactic reaction or shock T78.2
  angioneurotic edema T78.3
  animal (dander) (epidermal) (hair) (rhinitis) J30.81
  bee sting (anaphylactic shock) —see Toxicity, venom, arthropod, bee
  biological —see Allergy, drug
  colitis —see also Colitis, allergic K52.29
  dander (animal) (rhinitis) J30.81
  dandruff (rhinitis) J30.81
  dental restorative material (existing) K08.55
  dermatitis —see Dermatitis, contact, allergic
  diathesis —see History, allergy
  drug, medicament & biological (any) (external) (internal) T78.40
    correct substance properly administered —see Table of Drugs and Chemicals, by drug, adverse effect
    wrong substance given or taken NEC (by accident) —see Table of Drugs and Chemicals, by drug, poisoning
  due to pollen J30.1
  dust (house) (stock) (rhinitis) J30.89
    with asthma —see Asthma, allergic extrinsic
  eczema —see Dermatitis, contact, allergic
  epidermal (animal) (rhinitis) J30.81
  feathers (rhinitis) J30.89
  food (any) (ingested) NEC T78.1
    anaphylactic shock —see Shock, anaphylactic, due to food
    dermatitis —see Dermatitis, due to, food
    dietary counseling and surveillance Z71.3
    in contact with skin L23.6
    rhinitis J30.5
    status (without reaction) Z91.018
      eggs Z91.012
      milk products Z91.011
      peanuts Z91.010
      seafood Z91.013
      specified NEC Z91.018
  gastrointestinal —see also specific type of allergic reaction
    meaning colitis —see also Colitis, allergic) K52.29
    meaning gastroenteritis —see also Gastroenteritis, allergic) K52.29
    meaning other adverse food reaction not elsewhere classified T78.1
  grain J30.1
  grass (hay fever) (pollen) J30.1
    asthma —see Asthma, allergic extrinsic
  hair (animal) (rhinitis) J30.81
  history (of) —see History, allergy
  horse serum —see Allergy, serum
  inhalant (rhinitis) J30.89
    pollen J30.1
  kapok (rhinitis) J30.89
  medicine —see Allergy, drug
  milk protein —see also Allergy, food Z91.011
    anaphylactic reaction T78.07
    dermatitis L27.2
    enterocolitis syndrome K52.21
    enteropathy K52.22
    gastroenteritis K52.29

Allergy, allergic (Continued)
    milk protein (Continued)
        gastroesophageal reflux —see also Reaction,
            adverse, food) K21.9
            with esophagitis K21.0
        proctocolitis K52.82   ]
    nasal, seasonal due to pollen J30.1
    pneumonia J82
    pollen (any) (hay fever) J30.1
        asthma —see Asthma, allergic extrinsic
    primrose J30.1
    primula J30.1
    proctocolitis K52.82
    purpura D69.0
    ragweed (hay fever) (pollen) J30.1
        asthma —see Asthma, allergic extrinsic
    rose (pollen) J30.1
    seasonal NEC J30.2
    Senecio jacobae (pollen) J30.1
    serum —see also Reaction, serum T80.69
        anaphylactic shock T80.59
    shock (anaphylactic) T78.2
        due to
            administration of blood and blood
                products T80.51
            adverse effect of correct medicinal
                substance properly administered
                T88.6
            immunization T80.52
            serum NEC T80.59
            vaccination T80.52
    specific NEC T78.49
    tree (any) (hay fever) (pollen) J30.1
        asthma —see Asthma, allergic extrinsic
    upper respiratory J30.9
    urticaria L50.0
    vaccine —see Allergy, serum
    wheat —see Allergy, food
Allescheriasis B48.2
Alligator skin disease Q80.9
Allocheiria, allochiria R20.8
Almeida's disease —see
        Paracoccidioidomycosis
Alopecia (hereditaria) (seborrheica)
        L65.9
    androgenic L64.9
        drug-induced L64.0
        specified NEC L64.8
    areata L63.9
        ophiasis L63.2
        specified NEC L63.8
        totalis L63.0
        universalis L63.1
    cicatricial L66.9
        specified NEC L66.8
    circumscripta L63.9
    congenital, congenitalis Q84.0
    due to cytotoxic drugs NEC L65.8
    mucinosa L65.2
    postinfective NEC L65.8
    postpartum L65.0
    premature L64.8
    specific (syphilitic) A51.32
    specified NEC L65.8
    syphilitic (secondary) A51.32
    totalis (capitis) L63.0
    universalis (entire body) L63.1
    X-ray L58.1
Alpers' disease G31.81
Alpine sickness T70.29
Alport syndrome Q87.81
ALTE (apparent life threatening event) in
        newborn and infant R68.13
Alteration (of), Altered
    awareness
        transient R40.4
        unintended under general anesthesia,
            during procedure T88.53
    mental status R41.82
    pattern of family relationships affecting child
        Z62.898

Alteration (of), Altered (Continued)
    sensation
        following
            cerebrovascular disease I69.998
                cerebral infarction I69.398
                intracerebral hemorrhage I69.198
                nontraumatic intracranial hemorrhage
                    NEC I69.298
                specified disease NEC I69.898
                subarachnoid hemorrhage I69.098
Alternating —see condition
Altitude, high (effects) —see Effect, adverse,
        high altitude
Aluminosis (of lung) J63.0
Alveolitis
    allergic (extrinsic) —see Pneumonitis,
        hypersensitivity
    due to
        Aspergillus clavatus J67.4
        Cryptostroma corticale J67.6
    fibrosing (cryptogenic) (idiopathic) J84.112
    jaw M27.3
    sicca dolorosa M27.3
Alveolus, alveolar —see condition
Alymphocytosis D72.810
    thymic (with immunodeficiency) D82.1
Alymphoplasia, thymic D82.1
Alzheimer's disease or sclerosis —see Disease,
        Alzheimer's
Amastia (with nipple present) Q83.8
    with absent nipple Q83.0
Amathophobia F40.228
Amaurosis (acquired) (congenital) —see also
        Blindness
    fugax G45.3
    hysterical F44.6
    Leber's congenital H35.50
    uremic —see Uremia
Amaurotic idiocy (infantile) (juvenile) (late) E75.4
Amaxophobia F40.248
Ambiguous genitalia Q56.4
Amblyopia (congenital) (ex anopsia) (partial)
        (suppression) H53.00-•
    anisometropic —see Amblyopia, refractive
    deprivation H53.01-•
    hysterical F44.6
    nocturnal —see also Blindness, night
        vitamin A deficiency E50.5
    refractive H53.02-•
    strabismic H53.03-•
    suspect H53.04-•
    tobacco H53.8
    toxic NEC H53.8
    uremic —see Uremia
Ameba, amebic (histolytica) —see also Amebiasis
    abscess (liver) A06.4
Amebiasis A06.9
    with abscess —see Abscess, amebic
    acute A06.0
    chronic (intestine) A06.1
        with abscess —see Abscess, amebic
    cutaneous A06.7
    cutis A06.7
    cystitis A06.81
    genitourinary tract NEC A06.82
    hepatic —see Abscess, liver, amebic
    intestine A06.0
    nondysenteric colitis A06.2
    skin A06.7
    specified site NEC A06.89
Ameboma (of intestine) A06.3
Amelia Q73.0
    lower limb —see Agenesis, leg
    upper limb —see Agenesis, arm
Ameloblastoma —see also Cyst, calcifying
        odontogenic
    long bones C40.9-•
        lower limb C40.2-•
        upper limb C40.0-•
    malignant C41.1
        jaw (bone) (lower) C41.1
            upper C41.0
    tibial C40.2-•

Amelogenesis imperfecta K00.5
    nonhereditaria (segmentalis) K00.4
Amenorrhea N91.2
    hyperhormonal E28.8
    primary N91.0
    secondary N91.1
Amentia —see Disability, intellectual
    Meynert's (nonalcoholic) F04
American
    leishmaniasis B55.2
    mountain tick fever A93.2
Ametropia —see Disorder, refraction
AMH (asymptomatic microscopic hematuria)
        R31.21
Amianthosis J61
Amimia R48.8
Amino-acid disorder E72.9
    anemia D53.0
Aminoacidopathy E72.9
Aminoaciduria E72.9
Amnes (t)ic syndrome (post-traumatic) F04
    induced by
        alcohol F10.96
            with dependence F10.26
        psychoactive NEC F19.96
            with
                abuse F19.16
                dependence F19.26
        sedative F13.96
            with dependence F13.26
Amnesia R41.3
    anterograde R41.1
    auditory R48.8
    dissociative F44.0
        with dissociative fugue F44.1
    hysterical F44.0
    postictal in epilepsy —see Epilepsy
    psychogenic F44.0
    retrograde R41.2
    transient global G45.4
Amnion, amniotic —see condition
Amnionitis —see Pregnancy, complicated by
Amok F68.8
Amoral traits F60.89
Amphetamine (or other stimulant) —
        induced
        anxiety disorder F15.980
        bipolar and related disorder F15.94
        delirium F15.921
        depressive disorder F15.94
        obsessive-compulsive and related disorder
            F15.988
        psychotic disorder F15.959
        sexual dysfunction F15.981
        sleep disorder F15.982
        stimulant withdrawal F15.23
Ampulla
    lower esophagus K22.8
    phrenic K22.8
Amputation —see also Absence, by site,
        acquired
    neuroma (postoperative) (traumatic) —see
        Complications, amputation stump,
        neuroma
    stump (surgical)
        abnormal, painful, or with complication
            (late) —see Complications, amputation
            stump
        healed or old NOS Z89.9
    traumatic (complete) (partial)
        arm (upper) (complete) S48.91-•
            at
                elbow S58.01-•
                    partial S58.02-•
                shoulder joint (complete) S48.01-•
                    partial S48.02-•
            between
                elbow and wrist (complete) S58.11-•
                    partial S58.12-•
                shoulder and elbow (complete)
                    S48.11-•
                    partial S48.12-•
            partial S48.92-•

▶ New   ⇒ Revised   ~~deleted~~ Deleted   • Use Additional Character(s)

Amputation (Continued)
  traumatic (Continued)
    breast (complete) S28.21-●
      partial S28.22-●
    clitoris (complete) S38.211
      partial S38.212
    ear (complete) S08.11-●
      partial S08.12-●
    finger (complete) (metacarpophalangeal)
      S68.11-●
      index S68.11-●
      little S68.11-●
      middle S68.11-●
      partial S68.12-●
        index S68.12-●
        little S68.12-●
        middle S68.12-●
        ring S68.12-●
      ring S68.11-●
      thumb —see Amputation, traumatic,
        thumb
      transphalangeal (complete) S68.61-●
        index S68.61-●
        little S68.61-●
        middle S68.61-●
        partial S68.62-●
          index S68.62-●
          little S68.62-●
          middle S68.62-●
          ring S68.62-●
        ring S68.61-●
    foot (complete) S98.91-●
      at ankle level S98.01-●
        partial S98.02-●
      midfoot S98.31-●
        partial S98.32-●
      partial S98.92-●
    forearm (complete) S58.91-●
      at elbow level (complete) S58.01-●
        partial S58.02-●
      between elbow and wrist (complete)
        S58.11-●
        partial S58.12-●
      partial S58.92-●
    genital organ(s) (external)
      female (complete) S38.211
        partial S38.212
      male
        penis (complete) S38.221
          partial S38.222
        scrotum (complete) S38.231
          partial S38.232
        testes (complete) S38.231
          partial S38.232
    hand (complete) (wrist level) S68.41-●
      finger(s) alone —see Amputation,
        traumatic, finger
      partial S68.42-●
      thumb alone —see Amputation,
        traumatic, thumb
      transmetacarpal (complete) S68.71-●
        partial S68.72-●
    head
      ear —see Amputation, traumatic, ear
      nose (partial) S08.812
        complete S08.811
      part S08.89
      scalp S08.0
    hip (and thigh) (complete) S78.91-●
      at hip joint (complete) S78.01-●
        partial S78.02-●
      between hip and knee (complete) S78.11-●
        partial S78.12-●
      partial S78.92-●
    labium (majus) (minus) (complete) S38.21-●
      partial S38.21-●
    leg (lower) S88.91-●
      at knee level S88.01-●
        partial S88.02-●
      between knee and ankle S88.11-●
        partial S88.12-●
      partial S88.92-●

Amputation (Continued)
  traumatic (Continued)
    nose (partial) S08.812
      complete S08.811
    penis (complete) S38.221
      partial S38.222
    scrotum (complete) S38.231
      partial S38.232
    shoulder —see Amputation, traumatic, arm
      at shoulder joint —see Amputation,
        traumatic, arm, at shoulder joint
    testes (complete) S38.231
      partial S38.232
    thigh —see Amputation, traumatic, hip
    thorax, part of S28.1
      breast —see Amputation, traumatic,
        breast
    thumb (complete) (metacarpophalangeal)
      S68.01-●
      partial S68.02-●
      transphalangeal (complete) S68.51-●
        partial S68.52-●
    toe (lesser) S98.13-●
      great S98.11-●
        partial S98.12-●
      more than one S98.21-●
        partial S98.22-●
      partial S98.14-●
    vulva (complete) S38.211
      partial S38.212
Amputee (bilateral) (old) Z89.9
Amsterdam dwarfism Q87.1
Amusia R48.8
  developmental F80.89
Amyelencephalus, amyelencephaly Q00.0
Amyelia Q06.0
Amygdalitis —see Tonsillitis
Amygdalolith J35.8
Amyloid heart (disease) E85.4 [I43]
Amyloidosis (generalized) (primary) E85.9
  with lung involvement E85.4 [J99]
  familial E85.2
  genetic E85.2
  heart E85.4 [I43]
  hemodialysis-associated E85.3
  light chain (AL) E85.81
  liver E85.4 [K77]
  localized E85.4
  neuropathic heredofamilial E85.1
  non-neuropathic heredofamilial E85.0
  organ limited E85.4
  Portuguese E85.1
  pulmonary E85.4 [J99]
  secondary systemic E85.3
  senile systemic (SSA) E85.82
  skin (lichen) (macular) E85.4 [L99]
  specified NEC E85.89
  subglottic E85.4 [J99]
  wild-type transthyretin-related (ATTR)
    E85.82
Amylopectinosis (brancher enzyme deficiency)
  E74.03
Amylophagia —see Pica
Amyoplasia congenita Q79.8
Amyotonia M62.89
  congenita G70.2
Amyotrophia, amyotrophy, amyotrophic G71.8
  congenita Q79.8
  diabetic —see Diabetes, amyotrophy
  lateral sclerosis G12.21
  neuralgic G54.5
  spinal progressive G12.25
Anacidity, gastric K31.83
  psychogenic F45.8
Anaerosis of newborn P28.89
Analbuminemia E88.09
Analgesia —see Anesthesia
Analphalipoproteinemia E78.6
Anaphylactic
  purpura D69.0
  shock or reaction —see Shock, anaphylactic

Anaphylactoid shock or reaction —see Shock,
  anaphylactic
Anaphylactoid syndrome of pregnancy O88.01-●
Anaphylaxis —see Shock, anaphylactic
Anaplasia cervix —see also Dysplasia, cervix
  N87.9
Anaplasmosis, human A77.49
Anarthria R47.1
Anasarca R60.1
  cardiac —see Failure, heart, congestive
  lung J18.2
  newborn P83.2
  nutritional E43
  pulmonary J18.2
  renal N04.9
Anastomosis
  aneurysmal —see Aneurysm
  arteriovenous ruptured brain I60.8
  intestinal K63.89
    complicated NEC K91.89
      involving urinary tract N99.89
  retinal and choroidal vessels (congenital) Q14.8
Anatomical narrow angle H40.03-●
Ancylostoma, ancylostomiasis (braziliense)
  (caninum) (ceylanicum) (duodenale) B76.0
  Necator americanus B76.1
Andersen's disease (glycogen storage) E74.09
Anderson-Fabry disease E75.21
Andes disease T70.29
Andrews' disease (bacterid) L08.89
Androblastoma
  benign
    specified site —see Neoplasm, benign, by
      site
    unspecified site
      female D27.9
      male D29.20
  malignant
    specified site —see Neoplasm, malignant,
      by site
    unspecified site
      female C56.9
      male C62.90
  specified site —see Neoplasm, uncertain
    behavior, by site
  tubular
    with lipid storage
      specified site —see Neoplasm, benign,
        by site
      unspecified site
        female D27.9
        male D29.20
    specified site —see Neoplasm, benign,
      by site
    unspecified site
      female D27.9
      male D29.20
  unspecified site
    female D39.10
    male D40.10
Androgen insensitivity syndrome —see also
  Syndrome, androgen insensitivity E34.50
Androgen resistance syndrome —see also
  Syndrome, androgen insensitivity E34.50
Android pelvis Q74.2
  with disproportion (fetopelvic) O33.3
    causing obstructed labor O65.3
Androphobia F40.290
Anectasis, pulmonary (newborn) —see
  Atelectasis
Anemia (essential) (general) (hemoglobin
  deficiency) (infantile) (primary) (profound)
  D64.9
  with (due to) (in)
    disorder of
      anaerobic glycolysis D55.2
      pentose phosphate pathway D55.1
    koilonychia D50.9
  achlorhydric D50.8
  achrestic D53.1
  Addison (-Biermer) (pernicious) D51.0

Anemia (Continued)
  agranulocytic —see Agranulocytosis
  amino-acid-deficiency D53.0
  aplastic D61.9
    congenital D61.09
    drug-induced D61.1
    due to
      drugs D61.1
      external agents NEC D61.2
      infection D61.2
      radiation D61.2
    idiopathic D61.3
    red cell (pure) D60.9
      chronic D60.0
      congenital D61.01
      specified type NEC D60.8
      transient D60.1
    specified type NEC D61.89
    toxic D61.2
  aregenerative
    congenital D61.09
  asiderotic D50.9
  atypical (primary) D64.9
  Baghdad spring D55.0
  Balantidium coli A07.0
  Biermer's (pernicious) D51.0
  blood loss (chronic) D50.0
    acute D62
  bothriocephalus B70.0 [D63.8]
  brickmaker's B76.9 [D63.8]
  cerebral I67.89
  childhood D58.9
  chlorotic D50.8
  chronic
    blood loss D50.0
    hemolytic D58.9
      idiopathic D59.9
    simple D53.9
  chronica congenita aregenerativa D61.09
  combined system disease NEC D51.0 [G32.0]
    due to dietary vitamin B12 deficiency
      D51.3 [G32.0]
  complicating pregnancy, childbirth
    or puerperium —see Pregnancy,
    complicated by (management affected
    by), anemia
  congenital P61.4
    aplastic D61.09
    due to isoimmunization NOS P55.9
    dyserythropoietic, dyshematopoietic D64.4
    following fetal blood loss P61.3
    Heinz body D58.2
    hereditary hemolytic NOS D58.9
    pernicious D51.0
    spherocytic D58.0
  Cooley's (erythroblastic) D56.1
  cytogenic D51.0
  deficiency D53.9
    2, 3 diphosphoglycurate mutase D55.2
    2, 3 PG D55.2
    6 phosphogluconate dehydrogenase D55.1
    6-PGD D55.1
    amino-acid D53.0
    combined B12 and folate D53.1
    enzyme D55.9
      drug-induced (hemolytic) D59.2
      glucose-6-phosphate dehydrogenase
        (G6PD) D55.0
      glycolytic D55.2
      nucleotide metabolism D55.3
      related to hexose monophosphate
        (HMP) shunt pathway NEC D55.1
      specified type NEC D55.8
    erythrocytic glutathione D55.1
    folate D52.9
      dietary D52.0
      drug-induced D52.1
    folic acid D52.9
      dietary D52.0
      drug-induced D52.1
    G SH D55.1

Anemia (Continued)
  deficiency (Continued)
    G6PD D55.0
    GGS-R D55.1
    glucose-6-phosphate dehydrogenase D55.0
    glutathione reductase D55.1
    glyceraldehyde phosphate dehydrogenase
      D55.2
    hexokinase D55.2
    iron D50.9
      secondary to blood loss (chronic) D50.0
    nutritional D53.9
      with
        poor iron absorption D50.8
        specified deficiency NEC D53.8
    phosphofructo-aldolase D55.2
    phosphoglycerate kinase D55.2
    PK D55.2
    protein D53.0
    pyruvate kinase D55.2
    transcobalamin II D51.2
    triose-phosphate isomerase D55.2
    vitamin B12 NOS D51.9
      dietary D51.3
      due to
        intrinsic factor deficiency D51.0
        selective vitamin B12 malabsorption
          with proteinuria D51.1
      pernicious D51.0
      specified type NEC D51.8
  Diamond-Blackfan (congenital hypoplastic)
    D61.01
  dibothriocephalus B70.0 [D63.8]
  dimorphic D53.1
  diphasic D53.1
  Diphyllobothrium (Dibothriocephalus) B70.0
    [D63.8]
  due to (in) (with)
    antineoplastic chemotherapy D64.81
    blood loss (chronic) D50.0
      acute D62
    chemotherapy, antineoplastic D64.81
    chronic disease classified elsewhere NEC
      D63.8
    chronic kidney disease D63.1
    deficiency
      amino-acid D53.0
      copper D53.8
      folate (folic acid) D52.9
        dietary D52.0
        drug-induced D52.1
      molybdenum D53.8
      protein D53.0
      zinc D53.8
    dietary vitamin B12 deficiency D51.3
    disorder of
      glutathione metabolism D55.1
      nucleotide metabolism D55.3
    drug —see Anemia, by type —see also Table
      of Drugs and Chemicals
    end stage renal disease D63.1
    enzyme disorder D55.9
    fetal blood loss P61.3
    fish tapeworm (D latum) infestation B70.0
      [D63.8]
    hemorrhage (chronic) D50.0
      acute D62
    impaired absorption D50.9
    loss of blood (chronic) D50.0
      acute D62
    myxedema E03.9 [D63.8]
    Necator americanus B76.1 [D63.8]
    prematurity P61.2
    selective vitamin B12 malabsorption with
      proteinuria D51.1
    transcobalamin II deficiency D51.2
  Dyke-Young type (secondary) (symptomatic)
    D59.1
  dyserythropoietic (congenital) D64.4
  dyshematopoietic (congenital) D64.4
  Egyptian B76.9 [D63.8]

Anemia (Continued)
  elliptocytosis —see Elliptocytosis
  enzyme-deficiency, drug-induced D59.2
  epidemic —see also Ancylostomiasis B76.9
    [D63.8]
  erythroblastic
    familial D56.1
    newborn —see also Disease, hemolytic P55.9
    of childhood D56.1
  erythrocytic glutathione deficiency D55.1
  erythropoietin-resistant anemia (EPO
    resistant anemia) D63.1
  Faber's (achlorhydric anemia) D50.9
  factitious (self-induced blood letting) D50.0
  familial erythroblastic D56.1
  Fanconi's (congenital pancytopenia) D61.09
  favism D55.0
  fish tapeworm (D. latum) infestation B70.0
    [D63.8]
  folate (folic acid) deficiency D52.9
  glucose-6-phosphate dehydrogenase (G6PD)
    deficiency D55.0
  glutathione-reductase deficiency D55.1
  goat's milk D52.0
  granulocytic —see Agranulocytosis
  Heinz body, congenital D58.2
  hemolytic D58.9
    acquired D59.9
      with hemoglobinuria NEC D59.6
      autoimmune NEC D59.1
      infectious D59.4
      specified type NEC D59.8
      toxic D59.4
    acute D59.9
      due to enzyme deficiency specified type
        NEC D55.8
    Lederer's D59.1
    autoimmune D59.1
      drug-induced D59.0
    chronic D58.9
      idiopathic D59.9
    cold type (secondary) (symptomatic) D59.1
    congenital (spherocytic) —see Spherocytosis
    due to
      cardiac conditions D59.4
      drugs (nonautoimmune) D59.2
        autoimmune D59.0
      enzyme disorder D55.9
        drug-induced D59.2
      presence of shunt or other internal
        prosthetic device D59.4
    familial D58.9
    hereditary D58.9
      due to enzyme disorder D55.9
        specified type NEC D55.8
      specified type NEC D58.8
    idiopathic (chronic) D59.9
    mechanical D59.4
    microangiopathic D59.4
    nonautoimmune D59.4
      drug-induced D59.2
    nonspherocytic
      congenital or hereditary NEC D55.8
        glucose-6-phosphate dehydrogenase
          deficiency D55.0
        pyruvate kinase deficiency D55.2
        type
          I D55.1
          II D55.2
      type
        I D55.1
        II D55.2
    secondary D59.4
      autoimmune D59.1
    specified (hereditary) type NEC D58.8
    Stransky-Regala type —see also
      Hemoglobinopathy D58.8
    symptomatic D59.4
      autoimmune D59.1
    toxic D59.4
    warm type (secondary) (symptomatic) D59.1

▶ New   ⇨ Revised   ~~deleted~~ Deleted   • Use Additional Character(s)

Anemia *(Continued)*
  hemorrhagic (chronic) D50.0
    acute D62
  Herrick's D57.1
  hexokinase deficiency D55.2
  hookworm B76.9 *[D63.8]*
  hypochromic (idiopathic) (microcytic)
    (normoblastic) D50.9
    due to blood loss (chronic) D50.0
      acute D62
    familial sex-linked D64.0
    pyridoxine-responsive D64.3
    sideroblastic, sex-linked D64.0
  hypoplasia, red blood cells D61.9
    congenital or familial D61.01
  hypoplastic (idiopathic) D61.9
    congenital or familial (of childhood)
      D61.01
  hypoproliferative (refractive) D61.9
  idiopathic D64.9
    aplastic D61.3
    hemolytic, chronic D59.9
  in (due to) (with)
    chronic kidney disease D63.1
    end stage renal disease D63.1
    failure, kidney (renal) D63.1
    neoplastic disease —*see also* Neoplasm
      D63.0
  intertropical —*see also* Ancylostomiasis D63.8
  iron deficiency D50.9
    secondary to blood loss (chronic) D50.0
      acute D62
    specified type NEC D50.8
  Joseph-Diamond-Blackfan (congenital
    hypoplastic) D61.01
  Lederer's (hemolytic) D59.1
  leukoerythroblastic D61.82
  macrocytic D53.9
    nutritional D52.0
    tropical D52.8
  malarial (*see also* Malaria) B54 *[D63.8]*
  malignant (progressive) D51.0
  malnutrition D53.9
  marsh (*see also* Malaria) B54 *[D63.8]*
  Mediterranean (with other
    hemoglobinopathy) D56.9
  megaloblastic D53.1
    combined B12 and folate deficiency
      D53.1
    hereditary D51.1
    nutritional D52.0
    orotic aciduria D53.0
    refractory D53.1
    specified type NEC D53.1
  megalocytic D53.1
  microcytic (hypochromic) D50.9
    due to blood loss (chronic) D50.0
      acute D62
    familial D56.8
  microdrepanocytosis D57.40
  microelliptopoikilocytic (Rietti-Greppi-
    Micheli) D56.9
  miner's B76.9 *[D63.8]*
  myelodysplastic D46.9
  myelofibrosis D75.81
  myelogenous D64.89
  myelopathic D64.89
  myelophthisic D61.82
  myeloproliferative D47.Z9
  newborn P61.4
    due to
      ABO (antibodies, isoimmunization,
        maternal/fetal incompatibility)
        P55.1
      Rh (antibodies, isoimmunization,
        maternal/fetal incompatibility)
        P55.0
    following fetal blood loss P61.3
    posthemorrhagic (fetal) P61.3
  nonspherocytic hemolytic —*see* Anemia,
    hemolytic, nonspherocytic

Anemia *(Continued)*
  normocytic (infectional) D64.9
    due to blood loss (chronic) D50.0
      acute D62
    myelophthisic D61.82
  nutritional (deficiency) D53.9
    with
      poor iron absorption D50.8
      specified deficiency NEC D53.8
    megaloblastic D52.0
  of prematurity P61.2
  orotaciduric (congenital) (hereditary) D53.0
  osteosclerotic D64.89
  ovalocytosis (hereditary) —*see* Elliptocytosis
  paludal —*see also* Malaria B54 *[D63.8]*
  pernicious (congenital) (malignant)
    (progressive) D51.0
  pleochromic D64.89
    of sprue D52.8
  posthemorrhagic (chronic) D50.0
    acute D62
    newborn P61.3
  postoperative (postprocedural)
    due to (acute) blood loss D62
      chronic blood loss D50.0
    specified NEC D64.9
  postpartum O90.81
  pressure D64.89
  progressive D64.9
    malignant D51.0
    pernicious D51.0
  protein-deficiency D53.0
  pseudoleukemica infantum D64.89
  pure red cell D60.9
    congenital D61.01
  pyridoxine-responsive D64.3
  pyruvate kinase deficiency D55.2
  refractory D46.4
    with
      excess of blasts D46.20
        1 (RAEB 1) D46.21
        2 (RAEB 2) D46.22
        in transformation (RAEB T) —*see*
          Leukemia, acute myeloblastic
      hemochromatosis D46.1
      sideroblasts (ring) (RARS) D46.1
    without ring sideroblasts, so stated D46.0
    without sideroblasts without excess of
      blasts D46.0
    megaloblastic D53.1
    sideroblastic D46.1
    sideropenic D50.9
  Rietti-Greppi-Micheli D56.9
  scorbutic D53.2
  secondary to
    blood loss (chronic) D50.0
      acute D62
    hemorrhage (chronic) D50.0
      acute D62
  semiplastic D61.89
  sickle-cell —*see* Disease, sickle-cell
  sideroblastic D64.3
    hereditary D64.0
    hypochromic, sex-linked D64.0
    pyridoxine-responsive NEC D64.3
    refractory D46.1
    secondary (due to)
      disease D64.1
      drugs and toxins D64.2
    specified type NEC D64.3
  sideropenic (refractory) D50.9
    due to blood loss (chronic) D50.0
      acute D62
  simple chronic D53.9
  specified type NEC D64.89
  spherocytic (hereditary) —*see* Spherocytosis
  splenic D64.89
  splenomegalic D64.89
  stomatocytosis D58.8
  syphilitic (acquired) (late) A52.79 *[D63.8]*
  target cell D64.89

Anemia *(Continued)*
  thalassemia D56.9
  thrombocytopenic —*see* Thrombocytopenia
  toxic D61.2
  tropical B76.9 *[D63.8]*
    macrocytic D52.8
  tuberculous A18.89 *[D63.8]*
  vegan D51.3
  vitamin
    B6-responsive D64.3
    B12 deficiency (dietary) pernicious D51.0
  von Jaksch's D64.89
  Witts' (achlorhydric anemia) D50.8
Anemophobia F40.228
Anencephalus, anencephaly Q00.0
Anergasia —*see* Psychosis, organic
Anesthesia, anesthetic R20.0
  complication or reaction NEC —*see also*
    Complications, anesthesia T88.59
    due to
      correct substance properly
        administered —*see* Table of Drugs
        and Chemicals, by drug, adverse
        effect
      overdose or wrong substance given —*see*
        Table of Drugs and Chemicals, by
        drug, poisoning
      unintended awareness under general
        anesthesia during procedure
        T88.53
      personal history of Z92.84
  cornea H18.81-•
  dissociative F44.6
  functional (hysterical) F44.6
  hyperesthetic, thalamic G89.0
  hysterical F44.6
  local skin lesion R20.0
  sexual (psychogenic) F52.1
  shock (due to) T88.2
  skin R20.0
  testicular N50.9
Anetoderma (maculosum) (of) L90.8
  Jadassohn-Pellizzari L90.2
  Schweniger-Buzzi L90.1
Aneurin deficiency E51.9
Aneurysm (anastomotic) (artery) (cirsoid)
  (diffuse) (false) (fusiform) (multiple)
  (saccular) I72.9
  abdominal (aorta) I71.4
    ruptured I71.3
    syphilitic A52.01
  aorta, aortic (nonsyphilitic) I71.9
    abdominal I71.4
      ruptured I71.3
    arch I71.2
      ruptured I71.1
    arteriosclerotic I71.9
      ruptured I71.8
    ascending I71.2
      ruptured I71.1
    congenital Q25.43
    descending I71.9
      abdominal I71.4
        ruptured I71.3
      ruptured I71.8
      thoracic I71.2
        ruptured I71.1
    root Q25.43
    ruptured I71.8
    sinus, congenital Q25.43
    syphilitic A52.01
    thoracic I71.2
      ruptured I71.1
    thoracoabdominal I71.6
      ruptured I71.5
    thorax, thoracic (arch) I71.2
      ruptured I71.1
    transverse I71.2
      ruptured I71.1
    valve (heart) —*see also* Endocarditis, aortic
      I35.8

Aneurysm *(Continued)*
  arteriosclerotic I72.9
    cerebral I67.1
      ruptured —*see* Hemorrhage, intracranial,
        subarachnoid
  arteriovenous (congenital) —*see also*
    Malformation, arteriovenous
    acquired I77.0
      brain I67.1
      coronary I25.41
      pulmonary I28.0
    brain Q28.2
      ruptured I60.8
    peripheral —*see* Malformation,
      arteriovenous, peripheral
    precerebral vessels Q28.0
    specified site NEC —*see also* Malformation,
      arteriovenous
      acquired I77.0
  basal —*see* Aneurysm, brain
  basilar (trunk) I72.5
  berry (congenital) (nonruptured) I67.1
    ruptured I60.7
  brain I67.1
    arteriosclerotic I67.1
      ruptured —*see* Hemorrhage, intracranial,
        subarachnoid
    arteriovenous (congenital) (nonruptured)
      Q28.2
      acquired I67.1
        ruptured I60.8
      ruptured I60.8
    berry (congenital) (nonruptured) I67.1
      ruptured —*see also* Hemorrhage,
        intracranial, subarachnoid I60.7
    congenital Q28.3
      aorta (root) (sinus) Q25.43
      ruptured I60.8
    meninges I67.1
      ruptured I60.8
    miliary (congenital) (nonruptured) I67.1
      ruptured —*see also* Hemorrhage,
        intracranial, subarachnoid I60.7
    mycotic I33.0
      ruptured —*see* Hemorrhage, intracranial,
        subarachnoid
    syphilitic (hemorrhage) A52.05
  cardiac (false) —*see also* Aneurysm, heart
    I25.3
  carotid artery (common) (external) I72.0
    internal (intracranial) I67.1
      extracranial portion I72.0
      ruptured into brain I60.0-●
    syphilitic A52.09
      intracranial A52.05
  cavernous sinus I67.1
    arteriovenous (congenital) (nonruptured)
      Q28.3
      ruptured I60.8
  celiac I72.8
  central nervous system, syphilitic A52.05
  cerebral —*see* Aneurysm, brain
  chest —*see* Aneurysm, thorax
  circle of Willis I67.1
    congenital Q28.3
      ruptured I60.6
    ruptured I60.6
  common iliac artery I72.3
  congenital (peripheral) Q27.8
    aorta (root) (sinus) Q25.43
    brain Q28.3
      ruptured I60.7
    coronary Q24.5
    digestive system Q27.8
    lower limb Q27.8
    pulmonary Q25.79
    retina Q14.1
    specified site NEC Q27.8
    upper limb Q27.8
  conjunctiva —*see* Abnormality, conjunctiva,
    vascular

Aneurysm *(Continued)*
  conus arteriosus —*see* Aneurysm, heart
  coronary (arteriosclerotic) (artery) I25.41
    arteriovenous, congenital Q24.5
    congenital Q24.5
    ruptured —*see* Infarct, myocardium
    syphilitic A52.06
    vein I25.89
  cylindroid (aorta) I71.9
    ruptured I71.8
    syphilitic A52.01
  ductus arteriosus Q25.0
  endocardial, infective (any valve) I33.0
  femoral (artery) (ruptured) I72.4
  gastroduodenal I72.8
  gastroepiploic I72.8
  heart (wall) (chronic or with a stated duration
    of over 4 weeks) I25.3
    valve —*see* Endocarditis
  hepatic I72.8
  iliac (common) (artery) (ruptured) I72.3
  infective I72.9
    endocardial (any valve) I33.0
  innominate (nonsyphilitic) I72.8
    syphilitic A52.09
  interauricular septum —*see* Aneurysm,
    heart
  interventricular septum —*see* Aneurysm,
    heart
  intrathoracic (nonsyphilitic) I71.2
    ruptured I71.1
    syphilitic A52.01
  lower limb I72.4
  lung (pulmonary artery) I28.1
  mediastinal (nonsyphilitic) I72.8
    syphilitic A52.09
  miliary (congenital) I67.1
    ruptured —*see* Hemorrhage, intracerebral,
      subarachnoid, intracranial
  mitral (heart) (valve) I34.8
  mural —*see* Aneurysm, heart
  mycotic I72.9
    endocardial (any valve) I33.0
    ruptured, brain —*see* Hemorrhage,
      intracerebral, subarachnoid
  myocardium —*see* Aneurysm, heart
  neck I72.0
  pancreaticoduodenal I72.8
  patent ductus arteriosus Q25.0
  peripheral NEC I72.8
    congenital Q27.8
      digestive system Q27.8
      lower limb Q27.8
      specified site NEC Q27.8
      upper limb Q27.8
  popliteal (artery) (ruptured) I72.4
  precerebral
    congenital (nonruptured) Q28.1
    specified site, NEC I72.5
  pulmonary I28.1
    arteriovenous Q25.72
      acquired I28.0
    syphilitic A52.09
    valve (heart) —*see* Endocarditis,
      pulmonary
  racemose (peripheral) I72.9
    congenital —*see* Aneurysm,
      congenital
  radial I72.1
  Rasmussen NEC A15.0
  renal (artery) I72.2
  retina —*see also* Disorder, retina,
    microaneurysms
    congenital Q14.1
    diabetic —*see* Diabetes, microaneurysms,
      retinal
  sinus of Valsalva Q25.49
  specified NEC I72.8
  spinal (cord) I72.8
    syphilitic (hemorrhage) A52.09
  splenic I72.8

Aneurysm *(Continued)*
  subclavian (artery) (ruptured) I72.8
    syphilitic A52.09
  superior mesenteric I72.8
  syphilitic (aorta) A52.01
    central nervous system A52.05
    congenital (late) A50.54 *[I79.0]*
    spine, spinal A52.09
  thoracoabdominal (aorta) I71.6
    ruptured I71.5
    syphilitic A52.01
  thorax, thoracic (aorta) (arch) (nonsyphilitic)
    I71.2
    ruptured I71.1
    syphilitic A52.01
  traumatic (complication) (early), specified
    site —*see* Injury, blood vessel
  tricuspid (heart) (valve) I07.8
  ulnar I72.1
  upper limb (ruptured) I72.1
  valve, valvular —*see* Endocarditis
  visceral NEC I72.8
  venous —*see also* Varix I86.8
    congenital Q27.8
      digestive system Q27.8
      lower limb Q27.8
      specified site NEC Q27.8
      upper limb Q27.8
  ventricle —*see* Aneurysm, heart
  vertebral artery I72.6
  visceral NEC I72.8
➧ Angelman syndrome Q93.51
Anger R45.4
Angiectasis, angiectopia I99.8
Angiitis I77.6
  allergic granulomatous M30.1
  hypersensitivity M31.0
  necrotizing M31.9
    specified NEC M31.8
  nervous system, granulomatous I67.7
Angina (attack) (cardiac) (chest) (heart)
  (pectoris) (syndrome) (vasomotor) I20.9
  with
    atherosclerotic heart disease —*see*
      Arteriosclerosis, coronary (artery)
    documented spasm I20.1
  abdominal K55.1
  accelerated —*see* Angina, unstable
  agranulocytic —*see* Agranulocytosis
  angiospastic —*see* Angina, with documented
    spasm
  aphthous B08.5
  crescendo —*see* Angina, unstable
  croupous J05.0
  cruris I73.9
  de novo effort —*see* Angina, unstable
  diphtheritic, membranous A36.0
  equivalent I20.8
  exudative, chronic J37.0
  following acute myocardial infarction
    I23.7
  gangrenous diphtheritic A36.0
  intestinal K55.1
  Ludovici K12.2
  Ludwig's K12.2
  malignant diphtheritic A36.0
  membranous J05.0
    diphtheritic A36.0
    Vincent's A69.1
  mesenteric K55.1
  monocytic —*see* Mononucleosis, infectious
  of effort —*see* Angina, specified NEC
  phlegmonous J36
    diphtheritic A36.0
  post-infarctional I23.7
  pre-infarctional —*see* Angina, unstable
  Prinzmetal —*see* Angina, with documented
    spasm
  progressive —*see* Angina, unstable
  pseudomembranous A69.1
  pultaceous, diphtheritic A36.0

▶ New   ➠ Revised   ~~deleted~~ Deleted   ● Use Additional Character(s)

INDEX TO DISEASES AND INJURIES / Anomaly, anomalous

Angina *(Continued)*
  spasm-induced —*see* Angina, with
      documented spasm
  specified NEC I20.8
  stable I20.8
  stenocardia —*see* Angina, specified NEC
  stridulous, diphtheritic A36.2
  tonsil J36
  trachealis J05.0
  unstable I20.0
  variant —*see* Angina, with documented
      spasm
  Vincent's A69.1
  worsening effort —*see* Angina, unstable
Angioblastoma —*see* Neoplasm, connective
    tissue, uncertain behavior
Angiocholecystitis —*see* Cholecystitis, acute
➡**Angiocholitis** —*see also* Cholecystitis, acute
    K83.09
Angiodysgenesis spinalis G95.19
Angiodysplasia (cecum) (colon) K55.20
  with bleeding K55.21
  duodenum (and stomach) K31.819
    with bleeding K31.811
  stomach (and duodenum) K31.819
    with bleeding K31.811
Angioedema (allergic) (any site) (with urticaria)
    T78.3
  hereditary D84.1
Angioendothelioma —*see* Neoplasm, uncertain
    behavior, by site
  benign D18.00
    intra-abdominal D18.03
    intracranial D18.02
    skin D18.01
    specified site NEC D18.09
  bone —*see* Neoplasm, bone, malignant
  Ewing's —*see* Neoplasm, bone, malignant
Angioendotheliomatosis C85.8-●
Angiofibroma —*see also* Neoplasm, benign, by
    site
  juvenile
    specified site —*see* Neoplasm, benign, by
        site
    unspecified site D10.6
Angiohemophilia (A) (B) D68.0
Angioid streaks (choroid) (macula) (retina)
    H35.33
Angiokeratoma —*see* Neoplasm, skin,
    benign
  corporis diffusum E75.21
Angioleiomyoma —*see* Neoplasm, connective
    tissue, benign
Angiolipoma —*see also* Lipoma
  infiltrating —*see* Lipoma
Angioma —*see also* Hemangioma, by site
  capillary I78.1
  hemorrhagicum hereditaria I78.0
  intra-abdominal D18.03
  intracranial D18.02
  malignant —*see* Neoplasm, connective tissue,
      malignant
  plexiform D18.00
    intra-abdominal D18.03
    intracranial D18.02
    skin D18.01
    specified site NEC D18.09
  senile I78.1
  serpiginosum L81.7
  skin D18.01
  specified site NEC D18.09
  spider I78.1
  stellate I78.1
  venous Q28.3
Angiomatosis Q82.8
  bacillary A79.89
  encephalotrigeminal Q85.8
  hemorrhagic familial I78.0
  hereditary familial I78.0
  liver K76.4
Angiomyolipoma —*see* Lipoma

Angiomyoliposarcoma —*see* Neoplasm,
    connective tissue, malignant
Angiomyoma —*see* Neoplasm, connective
    tissue, benign
Angiomyosarcoma —*see* Neoplasm, connective
    tissue, malignant
Angiomyxoma —*see* Neoplasm, connective
    tissue, uncertain behavior
Angioneurosis F45.8
Angioneurotic edema (allergic) (any site) (with
    urticaria) T78.3
  hereditary D84.1
Angiopathia, angiopathy I99.9
  cerebral I67.9
    amyloid E85.4 *[I68.0]*
  diabetic (peripheral) —*see* Diabetes,
      angiopathy
  peripheral I73.9
    diabetic —*see* Diabetes, angiopathy
    specified type NEC I73.89
  retinae syphilitica A52.05
  retinalis (juvenilis)
    diabetic —*see* Diabetes, retinopathy
    proliferative —*see* Retinopathy,
        proliferative
Angiosarcoma —*see also* Neoplasm, connective
    tissue, malignant
  liver C22.3
Angiosclerosis —*see* Arteriosclerosis
Angiospasm (peripheral) (traumatic) (vessel)
    I73.9
  brachial plexus G54.0
  cerebral G45.9
  cervical plexus G54.2
  nerve
    arm —*see* Mononeuropathy, upper limb
      axillary G54.0
      median —*see* Lesion, nerve, median
      ulnar —*see* Lesion, nerve, ulnar
    axillary G54.0
    leg —*see* Mononeuropathy, lower limb
    median —*see* Lesion, nerve, median
    plantar —*see* Lesion, nerve, plantar
    ulnar —*see* Lesion, nerve, ulnar
Angiospastic disease or edema I73.9
Angiostrongyliasis
  due to
    Parastrongylus
      cantonensis B83.2
      costaricensis B81.3
    intestinal B81.3
Anguillulosis —*see* Strongyloidiasis
Angulation
  cecum —*see* Obstruction, intestine
  coccyx (acquired) —*see also* subcategory
      M43.8
    congenital NEC Q76.49
  femur (acquired) —*see also* Deformity, limb,
      specified type NEC, thigh
    congenital Q74.2
  intestine (large) (small) —*see* Obstruction,
      intestine
  sacrum (acquired) —*see also* subcategory
      M43.8
    congenital NEC Q76.49
  sigmoid (flexure) —*see* Obstruction,
      intestine
  spine —*see* Dorsopathy, deforming,
      specified NEC
  tibia (acquired) —*see also* Deformity, limb,
      specified type NEC, lower leg
    congenital Q74.2
  ureter N13.5
    with infection N13.6
  wrist (acquired) —*see also* Deformity,
      limb, specified type NEC, forearm
    congenital Q74.0
Angulus infectiosus (lips) K13.0
Anhedonia R45.84
  sexual F52.0
Anhidrosis L74.4

Anhydration E86.0
Anhydremia E86.0
Anidrosis L74.4
Aniridia (congenital) Q13.1
Anisakiasis (infection) (infestation) B81.0
Anisakis larvae infestation B81.0
Aniseikonia H52.32
Anisocoria (pupil) H57.02
  congenital Q13.2
Anisocytosis R71.8
Anisometropia (congenital) H52.31
Ankle —*see* condition
Ankyloblepharon (eyelid) (acquired) —*see also*
    Blepharophimosis
  filiforme (adnatum) (congenital) Q10.3
  total Q10.3
Ankyloglossia Q38.1
Ankylosis (fibrous) (osseous) (joint) M24.60
  ankle M24.67-●
  arthrodesis status Z98.1
  cricoarytenoid (cartilage) (joint) (larynx)
      J38.7
  dental K03.5
  ear ossicles H74.31-●
  elbow M24.62-●
  foot M24.67-●
  hand M24.64-●
  hip M24.65-●
  incostapedial joint (infectional) —*see*
      Ankylosis, ear ossicles
  jaw (temporomandibular) M26.61-●
  knee M24.66-●
  lumbosacral (joint) M43.27
  postoperative (status) Z98.1
  produced by surgical fusion, status Z98.1
  sacro-iliac (joint) M43.28
  shoulder M24.61-●
  spine (joint) —*see also* Fusion, spine
    spondylitic —*see* Spondylitis, ankylosing
  surgical Z98.1
  temporomandibular M26.61-●
  tooth, teeth (hard tissues) K03.5
  wrist M24.63-●
Ankylostoma —*see* Ancylostoma
Ankylostomiasis —*see* Ancylostomiasis
Ankylurethria —*see* Stricture, urethra
Annular —*see also* condition
  detachment, cervix N88.8
  organ or site, congenital NEC —*see* Distortion
  pancreas (congenital) Q45.1
Anodontia (complete) (partial) (vera) K00.0
  acquired K08.10
Anomaly, anomalous (congenital) (unspecified
    type) Q89.9
  abdominal wall NEC Q79.59
  acoustic nerve Q07.8
  adrenal (gland) Q89.1
  Alder (-Reilly) (leukocyte granulation)
      D72.0
  alimentary tract Q45.9
    upper Q40.9
  alveolar M26.70
    hyperplasia M26.79
      mandibular M26.72
      maxillary M26.71
    hypoplasia M26.79
      mandibular M26.74
      maxillary M26.73
    ridge (process) M26.79
    specified NEC M26.79
  ankle (joint) Q74.2
  anus Q43.9
  aorta (arch) NEC Q25.40
    coarctation (preductal) (postductal)
        Q25.1
  aortic cusp or valve Q23.9
  appendix Q43.8
  apple peel syndrome Q41.1
  aqueduct of Sylvius Q03.0
    with spina bifida —*see* Spina bifida, with
        hydrocephalus

Anomaly, anomalous *(Continued)*
  arm Q74.0
  arteriovenous NEC
    coronary Q24.5
    gastrointestinal Q27.33
      acquired —*see* Angiodysplasia
  artery (peripheral) Q27.9
    basilar NEC Q28.1
    cerebral Q28.3
    coronary Q24.5
    digestive system Q27.8
    eye Q15.8
    great Q25.9
      specified NEC Q25.8
    lower limb Q27.8
    peripheral Q27.9
      specified NEC Q27.8
    pulmonary NEC Q25.79
    renal Q27.2
    retina Q14.1
    specified site NEC Q27.8
    subclavian Q27.8
      origin Q25.48
    umbilical Q27.0
    upper limb Q27.8
    vertebral NEC Q28.1
  aryteno-epiglottic folds Q31.8
  atrial
    bands or folds Q20.8
    septa Q21.1
  atrioventricular
    excitation I45.6
    septum Q21.0
  auditory canal Q17.8
  auricle
    ear Q17.8
      causing impairment of hearing
        Q16.9
    heart Q20.8
  Axenfeld's Q15.0
  back Q89.9
  band
    atrial Q20.8
    heart Q24.8
    ventricular Q24.8
  Bartholin's duct Q38.4
  biliary duct or passage Q44.5
  bladder Q64.70
    absence Q64.5
    diverticulum Q64.6
    exstrophy Q64.10
      cloacal Q64.12
      extroversion Q64.19
      specified type NEC Q64.19
      supravesical fissure Q64.11
    neck obstruction Q64.31
    specified type NEC Q64.79
  bone Q79.9
    arm Q74.0
    face Q75.9
    leg Q74.2
    pelvic girdle Q74.2
    shoulder girdle Q74.0
    skull Q75.9
      with
        anencephaly Q00.0
        encephalocele —*see* Encephalocele
        hydrocephalus Q03.9
          with spina bifida —*see* Spina bifida,
            by site, with hydrocephalus
        microcephaly Q02
  brain (multiple) Q04.9
    vessel Q28.3
  breast Q83.9
  broad ligament Q50.6
  bronchus Q32.4
  bulbus cordis Q21.9
  bursa Q79.9
  canal of Nuck Q52.4
  canthus Q10.3
  capillary Q27.9

Anomaly, anomalous *(Continued)*
  cardiac Q24.9
    chambers Q20.9
      specified NEC Q20.8
    septal closure Q21.9
      specified NEC Q21.8
    valve NEC Q24.8
      pulmonary Q22.3
  cardiovascular system Q28.8
  carpus Q74.0
  caruncle, lacrimal Q10.6
  cascade stomach Q40.2
  cauda equina Q06.3
  cecum Q43.9
  cerebral Q04.9
    vessels Q28.3
  cervix Q51.9
  Chédiak-Higashi(-Steinbrinck) (congenital
      gigantism of peroxidase granules)
      E70.330
  cheek Q18.9
  chest wall Q67.8
    bones Q76.9
  chin Q18.9
  chordae tendineae Q24.8
  choroid Q14.3
    plexus Q07.8
  chromosomes, chromosomal Q99.9
    D (1) —*see* condition, chromosome 13
    E (3) —*see* condition, chromosome 18
    G —*see* condition, chromosome 21
    sex
      female phenotype Q97.8
      gonadal dysgenesis (pure) Q99.1
      Klinefelter's Q98.4
      male phenotype Q98.9
      Turner's Q96.9
    specified NEC Q99.8
  cilia Q10.3
  circulatory system Q28.9
  clavicle Q74.0
  clitoris Q52.6
  coccyx Q76.49
  colon Q43.9
  common duct Q44.5
  communication
    coronary artery Q24.5
    left ventricle with right atrium Q21.0
  concha (ear) Q17.3
  connection
    portal vein Q26.5
    pulmonary venous Q26.4
      partial Q26.3
      total Q26.2
    renal artery with kidney Q27.2
  cornea (shape) Q13.4
  coronary artery or vein Q24.5
  cranium —*see* Anomaly, skull
  cricoid cartilage Q31.8
  cystic duct Q44.5
  dental
    alveolar —*see* Anomaly, alveolar
    arch relationship M26.20
      specified NEC M26.29
  dentofacial M26.9
    alveolar —*see* Anomaly, alveolar
    dental arch relationship M26.20
      specified NEC M26.29
    functional M26.50
      specified NEC M26.59
    jaw-cranial base relationship M26.10
      asymmetry M26.12
        maxillary M26.11
      specified type NEC M26.19
    jaw size M26.00
      macrogenia M26.05
      mandibular
        hyperplasia M26.03
        hypoplasia M26.04
      maxillary
        hyperplasia M26.01
        hypoplasia M26.02

Anomaly, anomalous *(Continued)*
  dentofacial *(Continued)*
    jaw size *(Continued)*
      microgenia M26.06
      specified type NEC M26.09
    malocclusion M26.4
      dental arch relationship NEC M26.29
      jaw-cranial base relationship —*see*
        Anomaly, dentofacial, jaw-cranial
        base relationship
      jaw size —*see* Anomaly, dentofacial, jaw
        size
    specified type NEC M26.89
    temporomandibular joint M26.60-•
      adhesions M26.61-•
      ankylosis M26.61-•
      arthralgia M26.62-•
      articular disc M26.63-•
      specified type NEC M26.69
    tooth position, fully erupted M26.30
      specified NEC M26.39
  dermatoglyphic Q82.8
  diaphragm (apertures) NEC Q79.1
  digestive organ(s) or tract Q45.9
    lower Q43.9
    upper Q40.9
  distance, interarch (excessive) (inadequate)
    M26.25
  distribution, coronary artery Q24.5
  ductus
    arteriosus Q25.0
    botalli Q25.0
  duodenum Q43.9
  dura (brain) Q04.9
    spinal cord Q06.9
  ear (external) Q17.9
    causing impairment of hearing Q16.9
    inner Q16.5
    middle (causing impairment of hearing)
      Q16.4
    ossicles Q16.3
  Ebstein's (heart) (tricuspid valve) Q22.5
  ectodermal Q82.9
  Eisenmenger's (ventricular septal defect)
    Q21.8
  ejaculatory duct Q55.4
  elbow Q74.0
  endocrine gland NEC Q89.2
  epididymis Q55.4
  epiglottis Q31.8
  esophagus Q39.9
  eustachian tube Q17.8
  eye Q15.9
    anterior segment Q13.9
      specified NEC Q13.89
    posterior segment Q14.9
      specified NEC Q14.8
    ptosis (eyelid) Q10.0
    specified NEC Q15.8
  eyebrow Q18.8
  eyelid Q10.3
    ptosis Q10.0
  face Q18.9
    bone(s) Q75.9
  fallopian tube Q50.6
  fascia Q79.9
  femur NEC Q74.2
  fibula NEC Q74.2
  finger Q74.0
  fixation, intestine Q43.3
  flexion (joint) NOS Q74.9
    hip or thigh Q65.89
  foot NEC Q74.2
    varus (congenital) Q66.3
  foramen
    Botalli Q21.1
    ovale Q21.1
  forearm Q74.0
  forehead Q75.8
  form, teeth K00.2
  fovea centralis Q14.1

▶ New   ⇒ Revised   ~~deleted~~ Deleted   • Use Additional Character(s)

Anomaly, anomalous (Continued)
frontal bone —see Anomaly, skull
gallbladder (position) (shape) (size) Q44.1
Gartner's duct Q52.4
gastrointestinal tract Q45.9
genitalia, genital organ(s) or system
  female Q52.9
    external Q52.70
    internal NOS Q52.9
  male Q55.9
    hydrocele P83.5
    specified NEC Q55.8
genitourinary NEC
  female Q52.9
  male Q55.9
Gerbode Q21.0
glottis Q31.8
granulation or granulocyte, genetic
  (constitutional) (leukocyte) D72.0
gum Q38.6
gyri Q07.9
hair Q84.2
hand Q74.0
hard tissue formation in pulp K04.3
head —see Anomaly, skull
heart Q24.9
  auricle Q20.8
  bands or folds Q24.8
  fibroelastosis cordis I42.4
  obstructive NEC Q22.6
  patent ductus arteriosus (Botalli) Q25.0
  septum Q21.9
    auricular Q21.1
    interatrial Q21.1
    interventricular Q21.0
      with pulmonary stenosis or atresia,
        dextraposition of aorta and
        hypertrophy of right ventricle
        Q21.3
    specified NEC Q21.8
    ventricular Q21.0
      with pulmonary stenosis or atresia,
        dextraposition of aorta and
        hypertrophy of right ventricle
        Q21.3
  tetralogy of Fallot Q21.3
  valve NEC Q24.8
    aortic
      bicuspid valve Q23.1
      insufficiency Q23.1
      stenosis Q23.0
        subaortic Q24.4
    mitral
      insufficiency Q23.3
      stenosis Q23.2
    pulmonary Q22.3
      atresia Q22.0
      insufficiency Q22.2
      stenosis Q22.1
        infundibular Q24.3
        subvalvular Q24.3
    tricuspid
      atresia Q22.4
      stenosis Q22.4
  ventricle Q20.8
heel NEC Q74.2
Hegglin's D72.0
hemianencephaly Q00.0
hemicephaly Q00.0
hemicrania Q00.0
hepatic duct Q44.5
hip NEC Q74.2
hourglass stomach Q40.2
humerus Q74.0
hydatid of Morgagni
  female Q50.5
  male (epididymal) Q55.4
    testicular Q55.29
hymen Q52.4
hypersegmentation of neutrophils, hereditary
  D72.0

Anomaly, anomalous (Continued)
hypophyseal Q89.2
ileocecal (coil) (valve) Q43.9
ileum Q43.9
ilium NEC Q74.2
integument Q84.9
  specified NEC Q84.8
interarch distance (excessive) (inadequate)
  M26.25
intervertebral cartilage or disc Q76.49
intestine (large) (small) Q43.9
  with anomalous adhesions, fixation or
    malrotation Q43.3
iris Q13.2
ischium NEC Q74.2
jaw —see Anomaly, dentofacial
  alveolar —see Anomaly, alveolar
jaw-cranial base relationship —see
    Anomaly, dentofacial, jaw-cranial
    base relationship
jejunum Q43.8
joint Q74.9
  specified NEC Q74.8
Jordan's D72.0
kidney(s) (calyx) (pelvis) Q63.9
  artery Q27.2
  specified NEC Q63.8
Klippel-Feil (brevicollis) Q76.1
knee Q74.1
labium (majus) (minus) Q52.70
labyrinth, membranous Q16.5
lacrimal apparatus or duct Q10.6
larynx, laryngeal (muscle) Q31.9
  web (bed) Q31.0
lens Q12.9
leukocytes, genetic D72.0
  granulation (constitutional) D72.0
lid (fold) Q10.3
ligament Q79.9
  broad Q50.6
  round Q52.8
limb Q74.9
  lower NEC Q74.2
    reduction deformity —see Defect,
      reduction, lower limb
  upper Q74.0
lip Q38.0
liver Q44.7
  duct Q44.5
lower limb NEC Q74.2
lumbosacral (joint) (region) Q76.49
  kyphosis —see Kyphosis, congenital
  lordosis —see Lordosis, congenital
lung (fissure) (lobe) Q33.9
mandible —see Anomaly, dentofacial
maxilla —see Anomaly, dentofacial
May (-Hegglin) D72.0
meatus urinarius NEC Q64.79
meningeal bands or folds Q07.9
  constriction of Q07.8
  spinal Q06.9
meninges Q07.9
  cerebral Q04.8
  spinal Q06.9
meningocele Q05.9
mesentery Q45.9
metacarpus Q74.0
metatarsus NEC Q74.2
middle ear Q16.4
  ossicles Q16.3
mitral (leaflets) (valve) Q23.9
  insufficiency Q23.3
  specified NEC Q23.8
  stenosis Q23.2
mouth Q38.6
Müllerian —see also Anomaly, by site
  uterus NEC Q51.818
multiple NEC Q89.7
muscle Q79.9
  eyelid Q10.3
  musculoskeletal system, except limbs Q79.9

Anomaly, anomalous (Continued)
myocardium Q24.8
nail Q84.6
narrowness, eyelid Q10.3
nasal sinus (wall) Q30.8
neck (any part) Q18.9
nerve Q07.9
  acoustic Q07.8
  optic Q07.8
nervous system (central) Q07.9
nipple Q83.9
nose, nasal (bones) (cartilage) (septum)
  (sinus) Q30.9
  specified NEC Q30.8
ocular muscle Q15.8
omphalomesenteric duct Q43.0
opening, pulmonary veins Q26.4
optic
  disc Q14.2
  nerve Q07.8
opticociliary vessels Q13.2
orbit (eye) Q10.7
organ Q89.9
  of Corti Q16.5
origin
  artery
    innominate Q25.8
    pulmonary Q25.79
    renal Q27.2
    subclavian Q25.48
osseous meatus (ear) Q16.1
ovary Q50.39
oviduct Q50.6
palate (hard) (soft) NEC Q38.5
pancreas or pancreatic duct Q45.3
papillary muscles Q24.8
parathyroid gland Q89.2
paraurethral ducts Q64.79
parotid (gland) Q38.4
patella Q74.1
Pelger-Huët (hereditary hyposegmentation)
  D72.0
pelvic girdle NEC Q74.2
pelvis (bony) NEC Q74.2
  rachitic E64.3
penis (glans) Q55.69
pericardium Q24.8
peripheral vascular system Q27.9
Peter's Q13.4
pharynx Q38.8
pigmentation L81.9
  congenital Q82.8
pituitary (gland) Q89.2
pleural (folds) Q34.0
portal vein Q26.5
  connection Q26.5
position, tooth, teeth, fully erupted M26.30
  specified NEC M26.39
precerebral vessel Q28.1
prepuce Q55.69
prostate Q55.4
pulmonary Q33.9
  artery NEC Q25.79
  valve Q22.3
    atresia Q22.0
    insufficiency Q22.2
    specified type NEC Q22.3
    stenosis Q22.1
      infundibular Q24.3
      subvalvular Q24.3
  venous connection Q26.4
    partial Q26.3
    total Q26.2
pupil Q13.2
  function H57.00
    anisocoria H57.02
    Argyll Robertson pupil H57.01
    miosis H57.03
    mydriasis H57.04
    specified type NEC H57.09
    tonic pupil H57.05-•

Anomaly, anomalous (Continued)
  pylorus Q40.3
  radius Q74.0
  rectum Q43.9
  reduction (extremity) (limb)
    femur (longitudinal) —see Defect,
      reduction, lower limb, longitudinal,
      femur
    fibula (longitudinal) —see Defect,
      reduction, lower limb, longitudinal,
      fibula
    lower limb —see Defect, reduction, lower
      limb
    radius (longitudinal) —see Defect,
      reduction, upper limb, longitudinal,
      radius
    tibia (longitudinal) —see Defect, reduction,
      lower limb, longitudinal, tibia
    ulna (longitudinal) —see Defect, reduction,
      upper limb, longitudinal, ulna
    upper limb —see Defect, reduction, upper
      limb
  refraction —see Disorder, refraction
  renal Q63.9
    artery Q27.2
    pelvis Q63.9
      specified NEC Q63.8
  respiratory system Q34.9
    specified NEC Q34.8
  retina Q14.1
  rib Q76.6
    cervical Q76.5
  Rieger's Q13.81
  rotation —see Malrotation
    hip or thigh Q65.89
  round ligament Q52.8
  sacroiliac (joint) NEC Q74.2
  sacrum NEC Q76.49
    kyphosis —see Kyphosis, congenital
    lordosis —see Lordosis, congenital
  saddle nose, syphilitic A50.57
  salivary duct or gland Q38.4
  scapula Q74.0
  scrotum —see Malformation, testis and
    scrotum
  sebaceous gland Q82.9
  seminal vesicles Q55.4
  sense organs NEC Q07.8
  sex chromosomes NEC —see also Anomaly,
    chromosomes
    female phenotype Q97.8
    male phenotype Q98.9
  shoulder (girdle) (joint) Q74.0
  sigmoid (flexure) Q43.9
  simian crease Q82.8
  sinus of Valsalva Q25.49
  skeleton generalized Q78.9
  skin (appendage) Q82.9
  skull Q75.9
    with
      anencephaly Q00.0
      encephalocele —see Encephalocele
      hydrocephalus Q03.9
        with spina bifida —see Spina bifida, by
          site, with hydrocephalus
      microcephaly Q02
  specified organ or site NEC Q89.8
  spermatic cord Q55.4
  spine, spinal NEC Q76.49
    column NEC Q76.49
      kyphosis —see Kyphosis, congenital
      lordosis —see Lordosis, congenital
    cord Q06.9
    nerve root Q07.8
  spleen Q89.09
    agenesis Q89.01
  stenonian duct Q38.4
  sternum NEC Q76.7
  stomach Q40.3
  submaxillary gland Q38.4
  tarsus NEC Q74.2

Anomaly, anomalous (Continued)
  tendon Q79.9
  testis —see Malformation, testis and
    scrotum
  thigh NEC Q74.2
  thorax (wall) Q67.8
    bony Q76.9
  throat Q38.8
  thumb Q74.0
  thymus gland Q89.2
  thyroid (gland) Q89.2
    cartilage Q31.8
  tibia NEC Q74.2
    saber A50.56
  toe Q74.2
  tongue Q38.3
  tooth, teeth K00.9
    eruption K00.6
    position, fully erupted M26.30
    spacing, fully erupted M26.30
  trachea (cartilage) Q32.1
  tragus Q17.9
  tricuspid (leaflet) (valve) Q22.9
    atresia or stenosis Q22.4
    Ebstein's Q22.5
  Uhl's (hypoplasia of myocardium, right
    ventricle) Q24.8
  ulna Q74.0
  umbilical artery Q27.0
  union
    cricoid cartilage and thyroid cartilage
      Q31.8
    thyroid cartilage and hyoid bone
      Q31.8
    trachea with larynx Q31.8
  upper limb Q74.0
  urachus Q64.4
  ureter Q62.8
    obstructive NEC Q62.39
      cecoureterocele Q62.32
      orthotopic ureterocele Q62.31
  urethra Q64.70
    absence Q64.5
    double Q64.74
    fistula to rectum Q64.73
    obstructive Q64.39
      stricture Q64.32
    prolapse Q64.71
    specified type NEC Q64.79
  urinary tract Q64.9
  uterus Q51.9
    with only one functioning horn Q51.4
  uvula Q38.5
  vagina Q52.4
  valleculae Q31.8
  valve (heart) NEC Q24.8
    coronary sinus Q24.5
    inferior vena cava Q24.8
    pulmonary Q22.3
    sinus coronario Q24.5
    venae cavae inferioris Q24.8
  vas deferens Q55.4
  vascular Q27.9
    brain Q28.3
    ring Q25.45
  vein(s) (peripheral) Q27.9
    brain Q28.3
    cerebral Q28.3
    coronary Q24.5
    developmental Q28.3
    great Q26.9
      specified NEC Q26.8
  vena cava (inferior) (superior) Q26.9
  venous —see Anomaly, vein(s)
  venous return Q26.8
  ventricular
    bands or folds Q24.8
    septa Q21.0
  vertebra Q76.49
    kyphosis —see Kyphosis, congenital
    lordosis —see Lordosis, congenital

Anomaly, anomalous (Continued)
  vesicourethral orifice Q64.79
  vessel(s) Q27.9
    optic papilla Q14.2
    precerebral Q28.1
  vitelline duct Q43.0
  vitreous body or humor Q14.0
  vulva Q52.70
  wrist (joint) Q74.0
Anomia R48.8
Anonychia (congenital) Q84.3
  acquired L60.8
Anophthalmos, anophthalmus (congenital)
    (globe) Q11.1
  acquired Z90.01
Anopia, anopsia H53.46-●
  quadrant H53.46-●
Anorchia, anorchism, anorchidism Q55.0
Anorexia R63.0
  hysterical F44.89
  nervosa F50.00
    atypical F50.9
    binge-eating type F50.2
      with purging F50.02
    restricting type F50.01
Anorgasmy, psychogenic (female)
    F52.31
  male F52.32
Anosmia R43.0
  hysterical F44.6
  postinfectional J39.8
Anosognosia R41.89
Anosteoplasia Q78.9
Anovulatory cycle N97.0
Anoxemia R09.02
  newborn P84
Anoxia (pathological) R09.02
  altitude T70.29
  cerebral G93.1
    complicating
      anesthesia (general) (local) or other
        sedation T88.59
      in labor and delivery O74.3
      in pregnancy O29.21-●
      postpartum, puerperal O89.2
    delivery (cesarean) (instrumental)
      O75.4
    during a procedure G97.81
    newborn P84
    resulting from a procedure G97.82
  due to
    drowning T75.1
    high altitude T70.29
  heart —see Insufficiency, coronary
  intrauterine P84
  myocardial —see Insufficiency, coronary
  newborn P84
  spinal cord G95.11
  systemic (by suffocation) (low content in
    atmosphere) —see Asphyxia,
    traumatic
Anteflexion —see Anteversion
Antenatal
  care (normal pregnancy) Z34.90
  screening (encounter for) of mother —see also
    Encounter, antenatal screening Z36.9
Antepartum —see condition
Anterior —see condition
Antero-occlusion M26.220
Anteversion
  cervix —see Anteversion, uterus
  femur (neck), congenital Q65.89
  uterus, uterine (cervix) (postinfectional)
    (postpartal, old) N85.4
    congenital Q51.818
    in pregnancy or childbirth —see Pregnancy,
      complicated by
Anthophobia F40.228
Anthracosilicosis J60
Anthracosis (lung) (occupational) J60
  lingua K14.3

▶ New   ⇒ Revised   ~~deleted~~ Deleted   ● Use Additional Character(s)

Anthrax A22.9
  with pneumonia A22.1
  cerebral A22.8
  colitis A22.2
  cutaneous A22.0
  gastrointestinal A22.2
  inhalation A22.1
  intestinal A22.2
  meningitis A22.8
  pulmonary A22.1
  respiratory A22.1
  sepsis A22.7
  specified manifestation NEC A22.8
Anthropoid pelvis Q74.2
  with disproportion (fetopelvic) O33.0
Anthropophobia F40.10
  generalized F40.11
Antibodies, maternal (blood group) —see
    Isoimmunization, affecting management of
    pregnancy
  anti-D —see Isoimmunization, affecting
    management of pregnancy, Rh
    newborn P55.0
Antibody
  anticardiolipin R76.0
    with
      hemorrhagic disorder D68.312
      hypercoagulable state D68.61
  antiphosphatidylglycerol R76.0
    with
      hemorrhagic disorder D68.312
      hypercoagulable state D68.61
  antiphosphatidylinositol R76.0
    with
      hemorrhagic disorder D68.312
      hypercoagulable state D68.61
  antiphosphatidylserine R76.0
    with
      hemorrhagic disorder D68.312
      hypercoagulable state D68.61
  antiphospholipid R76.0
    with
      hemorrhagic disorder D68.312
      hypercoagulable state D68.61
Anticardiolipin syndrome D68.61
Anticoagulant, circulating (intrinsic) —see also -
    Disorder, hemorrhagic D68.318
  drug-induced (extrinsic) —see also - Disorder,
    hemorrhagic D68.32
  iatrogenic D68.32
Antidiuretic hormone syndrome E22.2
Antimonial cholera —see Poisoning,
    antimony
Antiphospholipid
  antibody
    with hemorrhagic disorder D68.312
    syndrome D68.61
Antisocial personality F60.2
Antithrombinemia —see Circulating
    anticoagulants
Antithromboplastinemia D68.318
Antithromboplastinogenemia D68.318
Antitoxin complication or reaction —see
    Complications, vaccination
Antlophobia F40.228
Antritis J32.0
  maxilla J32.0
    acute J01.00
      recurrent J01.01
  stomach K29.60
    with bleeding K29.61
Antrum, antral —see condition
Anuria R34
  calculous (impacted) (recurrent) —see also
    Calculus, urinary N20.9
  following
    abortion —see Abortion by type
      complicated by, renal failure
    ectopic or molar pregnancy O08.4
  newborn P96.0
  postprocedural N99.0

Anuria (Continued)
  postrenal N13.8
  traumatic (following crushing) T79.5
Anus, anal —see condition
Anusitis K62.89
Anxiety F41.9
  depression F41.8
  episodic paroxysmal F41.0
  generalized F41.1
  hysteria F41.8
  neurosis F41.1
  panic type F41.0
  reaction F41.1
  separation, abnormal (of childhood) F93.0
  specified NEC F41.8
  state F41.1
Aorta, aortic —see condition
Aortectasia —see Ectasia, aorta
  with aneurysm —see Aneurysm, aorta
Aortitis (nonsyphilitic) (calcific) I77.6
  arteriosclerotic I70.0
  Doehle-Heller A52.02
  luetic A52.02
  rheumatic —see Endocarditis, acute,
    rheumatic
  specific (syphilitic) A52.02
  syphilitic A52.02
    congenital A50.54 [I79.1]
Apathetic thyroid storm —see Thyrotoxicosis
Apathy R45.3
Apeirophobia F40.228
Apepsia K30
  psychogenic F45.8
Aperistalsis, esophagus K22.0
Apertognathia M26.29
Apert's syndrome Q87.0
Aphagia R13.0
  psychogenic F50.9
Aphakia (acquired) (postoperative) H27.0-•
  congenital Q12.3
Aphasia (amnestic) (global) (nominal)
    (semantic) (syntactic) R47.01
  acquired, with epilepsy (Landau-Kleffner
    syndrome) —see Epilepsy, specified
    NEC
  auditory (developmental) F80.2
  developmental (receptive type) F80.2
    expressive type F80.1
    Wernicke's F80.2
  following
    cerebrovascular disease I69.920
      cerebral infarction I69.320
      intracerebral hemorrhage I69.120
      nontraumatic intracranial hemorrhage
        NEC I69.220
      specified disease NEC I69.820
      subarachnoid hemorrhage I69.020
  primary progressive G31.01 [F02.80]
    with behavioral disturbance G31.01
      [F02.81]
  progressive isolated G31.01 [F02.80]
    with behavioral disturbance G31.01
      [F02.81]
  sensory F80.2
  syphilis, tertiary A52.19
  Wernicke's (developmental) F80.2
Aphonia (organic) R49.1
  hysterical F44.4
  psychogenic F44.4
Aphthae, aphthous —see also condition
  Bednar's K12.0
  cachectic K14.0
  epizootic B08.8
  fever B08.8
  oral (recurrent) K12.0
  stomatitis (major) (minor) K12.0
  thrush B37.0
  ulcer (oral) (recurrent) K12.0
    genital organ(s) NEC
      female N76.6
      male N50.89
    larynx J38.7

Apical —see condition
Apiphobia F40.218
Aplasia —see also Agenesis
  abdominal muscle syndrome Q79.4
  alveolar process (acquired) —see Anomaly,
    alveolar
    congenital Q38.6
  aorta (congenital) Q25.41
  axialis extracorticalis (congenita) E75.29
  bone marrow (myeloid) D61.9
    congenital D61.01
  brain Q00.0
    part of Q04.3
  bronchus Q32.4
  cementum K00.4
  cerebellum Q04.3
  cervix (congenital) Q51.5
  congenital pure red cell D61.01
  corpus callosum Q04.0
  cutis congenita Q84.8
  erythrocyte congenital D61.01
  extracortical axial E75.29
  eye Q11.1
  fovea centralis (congenital) Q14.1
  gallbladder, congenital Q44.0
  iris Q13.1
  labyrinth, membranous Q16.5
  limb (congenital) Q73.8
    lower —see Defect, reduction, lower limb
    upper —see Agenesis, arm
  lung, congenital (bilateral) (unilateral) Q33.3
  pancreas Q45.0
  parathyroid-thymic D82.1
  Pelizaeus-Merzbacher E75.29
  penis Q55.5
  prostate Q55.4
  red cell (with thymoma) D60.9
    acquired D60.9
      due to drugs D60.9
    adult D60.9
    chronic D60.0
    congenital D61.01
    constitutional D61.01
    due to drugs D60.9
    hereditary D61.01
    of infants D61.01
    primary D61.01
    pure D61.01
      due to drugs D60.9
    specified type NEC D60.8
    transient D60.1
  round ligament Q52.8
  skin Q84.8
  spermatic cord Q55.4
  spleen Q89.01
  testicle Q55.0
  thymic, with immunodeficiency D82.1
  thyroid (congenital) (with myxedema) E03.1
  uterus Q51.0
  ventral horn cell Q06.1
Apnea, apneic (of) (spells) R06.81
  newborn NEC P28.4
    obstructive P28.4
    sleep (central) (obstructive) (primary) P28.3
  prematurity P28.4
  sleep G47.30
    central (primary) G47.31
      idiopathic G47.31
      in conditions classified elsewhere
        G47.37
    obstructive (adult) (pediatric) G47.33
      hypopnea G47.33
    primary central G47.31
    specified NEC G47.39
Apneumatosis, newborn P28.0
Apocrine metaplasia (breast) —see Dysplasia,
    mammary, specified type NEC
Apophysitis (bone) —see also
    Osteochondropathy
  calcaneus M92.8
  juvenile M92.9

Apoplectiform convulsions (cerebral ischemia) I67.82
Apoplexia, apoplexy, apoplectic
　adrenal A39.1
　heart (auricle) (ventricle) —see Infarct, myocardium
　heat T67.Ø
　hemorrhagic (stroke) —see Hemorrhage, intracranial
　meninges, hemorrhagic —see Hemorrhage, intracranial, subarachnoid
　uremic N18.9 [I68.8]
Appearance
　bizarre R46.1
　specified NEC R46.89
　very low level of personal hygiene R46.Ø
Appendage
　epididymal (organ of Morgagni) Q55.4
　intestine (epiploic) Q43.8
　preauricular Q17.Ø
　testicular (organ of Morgagni) Q55.29
Appendicitis (pneumococcal) (retrocecal) K37
　with
　▶gangrene K35.891
　▶perforation NOS K35.32
　　perforation or rupture K35.2
　⟫peritoneal abscess K35.33
　⟫peritonitis NEC K35.33
　　⟫generalized (with perforation or rupture) K35.2Ø
　　　▶with abscess K35.21
　　⟫localized (with perforation or rupture) K35.3Ø
　　　▶with
　　　　▶gangrene K35.32
　　　　▶perforation K35.32
　　　　　▶and abscess K35.33
　　▶ruptured NOS (with localized peritonitis) K35.32
　acute (catarrhal) (fulminating) (gangrenous) (obstructive) (retrocecal) (suppurative) K35.8Ø
　with
　▶gangrene K35.891
　⟫peritoneal abscess K35.33
　⟫peritonitis NEC K35.33
　　⟫generalized (with perforation or rupture) K35.2Ø
　　　▶with abscess K35.21
　　⟫localized (with perforation or rupture) K35.3Ø
　　　▶with
　　　　▶gangrene K35.32
　　　　▶perforation K35.32
　　　　　▶and abscess K35.33
　⟫specified NEC K35.89Ø
　　▶with gangrene K35.891
　amebic AØ6.89
　chronic (recurrent) K36
　exacerbation —see Appendicitis, acute
　gangrenous —see Appendicitis, acute
　healed (obliterative) K36
　interval K36
　neurogenic K36
　obstructive K36
　recurrent K36
　relapsing K36
　▶ruptured NOS (with localized peritonitis) K35.32
　subacute (adhesive) K36
　subsiding K36
　suppurative —see Appendicitis, acute
　tuberculous A18.32
Appendicopathia oxyurica B8Ø
Appendix, appendicular —see also condition
　epididymis Q55.4
　Morgagni
　　female Q5Ø.5
　　male (epididymal) Q55.4
　　　testicular Q55.29
　testis Q55.29

Appetite
　depraved —see Pica
　excessive R63.2
　lack or loss —see also Anorexia R63.Ø
　　nonorganic origin F5Ø.89
　　psychogenic F5Ø.89
　perverted (hysterical) —see Pica
Apple peel syndrome Q41.1
Apprehension state F41.1
Apprehensiveness, abnormal F41.9
Approximal wear KØ3.Ø
Apraxia (classic) (ideational) (ideokinetic) (ideomotor) (motor) (verbal) R48.2
　following
　　cerebrovascular disease I69.99Ø
　　　cerebral infarction I69.39Ø
　　　intracerebral hemorrhage I69.19Ø
　　　nontraumatic intracranial hemorrhage NEC I69.29Ø
　　　specified disease NEC I69.89Ø
　　　subarachnoid hemorrhage I69.Ø9Ø
　oculomotor, congenital H51.8
Aptyalism K11.7
Apudoma —see Neoplasm, uncertain behavior, by site
Aqueous misdirection H4Ø.83-●
Arabicum elephantiasis —see Infestation, filarial
Arachnitis —see Meningitis
Arachnodactyly —see Syndrome, Marfan's
Arachnoiditis (acute) (adhesive) (basal) (brain) (cerebrospinal) —see Meningitis
Arachnophobia F4Ø.21Ø
Arboencephalitis, Australian A83.4
Arborization block (heart) I45.5
ARC (AIDS-related complex) B2Ø
Arch
　aortic Q25.49
　bovine Q25.49
Arches —see condition
Arcuate uterus Q51.81Ø
Arcuatus uterus Q51.81Ø
Arcus (cornea) senilis —see Degeneration, cornea, senile
Arc-welder's lung J63.4
Areflexia R29.2
Areola —see condition
Argentaffinoma —see also Neoplasm, uncertain behavior, by site
　malignant —see Neoplasm, malignant, by site
　syndrome E34.Ø
Argininemia E72.21
Arginosuccinic aciduria E72.22
Argyll Robertson phenomenon, pupil or syndrome (syphilitic) A52.19
　atypical H57.Ø9
　nonsyphilitic H57.Ø9
Argyria, argyriasis
　conjunctival H11.13-●
　from drug or medicament —see Table of Drugs and Chemicals, by substance
Argyrosis, conjunctival H11.13-●
Arhinencephaly QØ4.1
Ariboflavinosis E53.Ø
Arm —see condition
Arnold-Chiari disease, obstruction or syndrome (type II) QØ7.ØØ
　with
　　hydrocephalus QØ7.Ø2
　　　with spina bifida QØ7.Ø3
　　spina bifida QØ7.Ø1
　　　with hydrocephalus QØ7.Ø3
　type III —see Encephalocele
　type IV QØ4.8
Aromatic amino-acid metabolism disorder E7Ø.9
　specified NEC E7Ø.8
Arousals, confusional G47.51
Arrest, arrested
　cardiac I46.9
　　complicating
　　　abortion —see Abortion, by type, complicated by, cardiac arrest

Arrest, arrested (Continued)
　cardiac (Continued)
　　complicating (Continued)
　　　anesthesia (general) (local) or other sedation —see Table of Drugs and Chemicals, by drug
　　　in labor and delivery O74.2
　　　in pregnancy O29.11-●
　　　postpartum, puerperal O89.1
　　　delivery (cesarean) (instrumental) O75.4
　　due to
　　　cardiac condition I46.2
　　　specified condition NEC I46.8
　　intraoperative I97.71-●
　　newborn P29.81
　　personal history, successfully resuscitated Z86.74
　　postprocedural I97.12-●
　　　obstetric procedure O75.4
　cardiorespiratory —see Arrest, cardiac
　circulatory —see Arrest, cardiac
　deep transverse O64.Ø
　development or growth
　　bone —see Disorder, bone, development or growth
　　child R62.5Ø
　　tracheal rings Q32.1
　epiphyseal
　　complete
　　　femur M89.15-●
　　　humerus M89.12-●
　　　tibia M89.16-●
　　　ulna M89.13-●
　　　forearm M89.13-●
　　　　specified NEC M89.13-●
　　　ulna —see Arrest, epiphyseal, by type, ulna
　　　lower leg M89.16-●
　　　　specified NEC M89.168
　　　tibia —see Arrest, epiphyseal, by type, tibia
　　partial
　　　femur M89.15-●
　　　humerus M89.12-●
　　　tibia M89.16-●
　　　ulna M89.13-●
　　specified NEC M89.18
　granulopoiesis —see Agranulocytosis
　growth plate —see Arrest, epiphyseal
　heart —see Arrest, cardiac
　legal, anxiety concerning Z65.3
　physeal —see Arrest, epiphyseal
　respiratory RØ9.2
　　newborn P28.81
　sinus I45.5
　spermatogenesis (complete) —see Azoospermia
　　incomplete —see Oligospermia
　transverse (deep) O64.Ø
Arrhenoblastoma
　benign
　　specified site —see Neoplasm, benign, by site
　　unspecified site
　　　female D27.9
　　　male D29.2Ø
　malignant
　　specified site —see Neoplasm, malignant, by site
　　unspecified site
　　　female C56.9
　　　male C62.9Ø
　specified site —see Neoplasm, uncertain behavior, by site
　unspecified site
　　female D39.1Ø
　　male D4Ø.1Ø
Arrhythmia (auricle)(cardiac) (juvenile)(nodal) (reflex)(sinus)(supraventricular)(transitory) (ventricle) I49.9
　block I45.9
　extrasystolic I49.49

Arrhythmia *(Continued)*
  newborn
    bradycardia P29.12
    occurring before birth P03.819
      before onset of labor P03.810
      during labor P03.811
    tachycardia P29.11
  psychogenic F45.8
  specified NEC I49.8
  vagal R55
  ventricular re-entry I47.0
Arrillaga-Ayerza syndrome (pulmonary
  sclerosis with pulmonary hypertension)
  I27.0
Arsenical pigmentation L81.8
  from drug or medicament —*see* Table of
    Drugs and Chemicals
Arsenism —*see* Poisoning, arsenic
Arterial —*see* condition
Arteriofibrosis —*see* Arteriosclerosis
Arteriolar sclerosis —*see* Arteriosclerosis
Arteriolith —*see* Arteriosclerosis
Arteriolitis I77.6
  necrotizing, kidney I77.5
  renal —*see* Hypertension, kidney
Arteriolosclerosis —*see* Arteriosclerosis
Arterionephrosclerosis —*see* Hypertension,
  kidney
Arteriopathy I77.9
▶cerebral autosomal dominant, with
    subcortical infarcts and
    leukoencephalopathy
    (CADASIL) I67.850
Arteriosclerosis, arteriosclerotic (diffuse)
  (obliterans) (of) (senile) (with calcification)
  I70.90
  aorta I70.0
  arteries of extremities —*see* Arteriosclerosis,
    extremities
  brain I67.2
  bypass graft
    coronary —*see* Arteriosclerosis, coronary,
      bypass graft
    extremities —*see* Arteriosclerosis,
      extremities, bypass graft
  cardiac —*see* Disease, heart, ischemic,
    atherosclerotic
  cardiopathy —*see* Disease, heart, ischemic,
    atherosclerotic
  cardiorenal —*see* Hypertension, cardiorenal
  cardiovascular —*see* Disease, heart, ischemic,
    atherosclerotic
  carotid —*see also* Occlusion, artery, carotid
    I65.2-●
  central nervous system I67.2
  cerebral I67.2
  cerebrovascular I67.2
  coronary (artery) I25.10
    bypass graft I25.810
      with
        angina pectoris I25.709
          with documented spasm I25.701
          specified type NEC I25.708
          unstable I25.700
        ischemic chest pain I25.709
      autologous artery I25.810
        with
          angina pectoris I25.729
            with documented spasm
              I25.721
            specified type I25.728
            unstable I25.720
          ischemic chest pain I25.729
      autologous vein I25.810
        with
          angina pectoris I25.719
            with documented spasm
              I25.711
            specified type I25.718
            unstable I25.710
          ischemic chest pain I25.719

Arteriosclerosis, arteriosclerotic *(Continued)*
  coronary *(Continued)*
    bypass graft *(Continued)*
      nonautologous biological I25.810
        with
          angina pectoris I25.739
            with documented spasm I25.731
            specified type I25.738
            unstable I25.730
          ischemic chest pain I25.739
      specified type NEC I25.810
        with
          angina pectoris I25.799
            with documented spasm I25.791
            specified type I25.798
            unstable I25.790
          ischemic chest pain I25.799
    due to
      calcified coronary lesion (severely) I25.84
      lipid rich plaque I25.83
    native vessel
      with
        angina pectoris I25.119
          with documented spasm I25.111
          specified type NEC I25.118
          unstable I25.110
        ischemic chest pain I25.119
    transplanted heart I25.811
      bypass graft I25.812
        with
          angina pectoris I25.769
           with documented spasm I25.761
           specified type I25.768
           unstable I25.760
         ischemic chest pain I25.769
      native coronary artery I25.811
        with
          angina pectoris I25.759
           with documented spasm I25.751
           specified type I25.758
           unstable I25.750
         ischemic chest pain I25.759
  extremities (native arteries) I70.209
    bypass graft I70.309
      autologous vein graft I70.409
        leg I70.409
          with
            gangrene (and intermittent
              claudication, rest pain and
              ulcer) I70.469
            intermittent claudication I70.419
            rest pain (and intermittent
              claudication) I70.429
          bilateral I70.403
            with
              gangrene (and intermittent
                claudication, rest pain and
                ulcer) I70.463
             intermittent claudication I70.413
             rest pain (and intermittent
               claudication) I70.423
            specified type NEC I70.493
          left I70.402
            with
              gangrene (and intermittent
                claudication, rest pain and
                ulcer) I70.462
             intermittent claudication
              I70.412
             rest pain (and intermittent
               claudication) I70.422
             ulceration (and intermittent
               claudication and rest
              pain) I70.449
             ankle I70.443
             calf I70.442
             foot site NEC I70.445
             heel I70.444
             lower leg NEC I70.448
             midfoot I70.444
             thigh I70.441
            specified type NEC I70.492

Arteriosclerosis, arteriosclerotic *(Continued)*
  extremities *(Continued)*
    bypass graft *(Continued)*
      autologous vein graft *(Continued)*
        leg *(Continued)*
          right I70.401
            with
             gangrene (and intermittent
              claudication, rest pain and
              ulcer) I70.461
             intermittent claudication I70.411
             rest pain (and intermittent
              claudication) I70.421
             ulceration (and intermittent
              claudication and rest
             pain) I70.439
            ankle I70.433
            calf I70.432
            foot site NEC I70.435
            heel I70.434
            lower leg NEC I70.438
            midfoot I70.434
            thigh I70.431
          specified type NEC I70.491
        specified type NEC I70.499
      specified NEC I70.408
        with
          gangrene (and intermittent
            claudication, rest pain and
            ulcer) I70.468
          intermittent claudication I70.418
          rest pain (and intermittent
            claudication) I70.428
          ulceration (and intermittent
            claudication and rest pain)
            I70.45
          specified type NEC I70.498
      leg I70.309
        with
          gangrene (and intermittent
            claudication, rest pain and
            ulcer) I70.369
          intermittent claudication I70.319
          rest pain (and intermittent
            claudication) I70.329
        bilateral I70.303
          with
           gangrene (and intermittent
            claudication, rest pain and
            ulcer) I70.363
          intermittent claudication I70.313
          rest pain (and intermittent
            claudication) I70.323
          specified type NEC I70.393
        left I70.302
          with
           gangrene (and intermittent
            claudication, rest pain and
            ulcer) I70.362
          intermittent claudication I70.312
          rest pain (and intermittent
            claudication) I70.322
          ulceration (and intermittent
            claudication and rest pain)
            I70.349
          ankle I70.343
          calf I70.342
          foot site NEC I70.345
          heel I70.344
          lower leg NEC I70.348
          midfoot I70.344
          thigh I70.341
        specified type NEC I70.392
        right I70.301
          with
           gangrene (and intermittent
            claudication, rest pain and
            ulcer) I70.361
          intermittent claudication I70.311
          rest pain (and intermittent
            claudication) I70.321

Arteriosclerosis, arteriosclerotic (Continued)
  extremities (Continued)
    bypass graft (Continued)
      nonautologous biological graft
        (Continued)
        leg (Continued)
          with (Continued)
            ulceration (and intermittent
              claudication and rest pain)
              I70.339
              ankle I70.333
              calf I70.332
              foot site NEC I70.335
              heel I70.334
              lower leg NEC I70.338
              midfoot I70.334
              thigh I70.331
            specified type NEC I70.391
          specified type NEC I70.399
      nonautologous biological graft I70.509
        leg I70.509
          with
            gangrene (and intermittent
              claudication, rest pain and
              ulcer) I70.569
            intermittent claudication
              I70.519
            rest pain (and intermittent
              claudication) I70.529
          bilateral I70.503
            with
              gangrene (and intermittent
                claudication, rest pain and
                ulcer) I70.563
              intermittent claudication
                I70.513
              rest pain (and intermittent
                claudication) I70.523
            specified type NEC I70.593
          left I70.502
            with
              gangrene (and intermittent
                claudication, rest pain and
                ulcer) I70.562
              intermittent claudication
                I70.512
              rest pain (and intermittent
                claudication)
                I70.522
              ulceration (and intermittent
                claudication and rest
                pain) I70.549
                ankle I70.543
                calf I70.542
                foot site NEC I70.545
                heel I70.544
                lower leg NEC I70.548
                midfoot I70.544
                thigh I70.541
            specified type NEC I70.592
          right I70.501
            with
              gangrene (and intermittent
                claudication, rest pain and
                ulcer) I70.561
              intermittent claudication
                I70.511
              rest pain (and intermittent
                claudication) I70.521
              ulceration (and intermittent
                claudication and rest
                pain) I70.539
                ankle I70.533
                calf I70.532
                foot site NEC I70.535
                heel I70.534
                lower leg NEC I70.538
                midfoot I70.534
                thigh I70.531
            specified type NEC I70.591
          specified type NEC I70.599

Arteriosclerosis, arteriosclerotic (Continued)
  extremities (Continued)
    bypass graft (Continued)
      nonbiological graft (Continued)
        specified NEC I70.508
          with
            gangrene (and intermittent
              claudication, rest pain and
              ulcer) I70.568
            intermittent claudication I70.518
            rest pain (and intermittent
              claudication) I70.528
            ulceration (and intermittent
              claudication and rest pain)
              I70.55
          specified type NEC I70.598
      nonbiological graft I70.609
        leg I70.609
          with
            gangrene (and intermittent
              claudication, rest pain and
              ulcer) I70.669
            intermittent claudication I70.619
            rest pain (and intermittent
              claudication) I70.629
          bilateral I70.603
            with
              gangrene (and intermittent
                claudication, rest pain and
                ulcer) I70.663
              intermittent claudication
                I70.613
              rest pain (and intermittent
                claudication) I70.623
            specified type NEC I70.693
          left I70.602
            with
              gangrene (and intermittent
                claudication, rest pain and
                ulcer) I70.662
              intermittent claudication
                I70.612
              rest pain (and intermittent
                claudication) I70.622
              ulceration (and intermittent
                claudication and rest
                pain) I70.649
                ankle I70.643
                calf I70.642
                foot site NEC I70.645
                heel I70.644
                lower leg NEC I70.648
                midfoot I70.644
                thigh I70.641
            specified type NEC I70.692
          right I70.601
            with
              gangrene (and intermittent
                claudication, rest pain and
                ulcer) I70.661
              intermittent claudication I70.611
              rest pain (and intermittent
                claudication) I70.621
              ulceration (and intermittent
                claudication and rest
                pain) I70.639
                ankle I70.633
                calf I70.632
                foot site NEC I70.635
                heel I70.634
                lower leg NEC I70.638
                midfoot I70.634
                thigh I70.631
            specified type NEC I70.691
          specified type NEC I70.699
        specified NEC I70.608
          with
            gangrene (and intermittent
              claudication, rest pain and
              ulcer) I70.668
            intermittent claudication I70.618

Arteriosclerosis, arteriosclerotic (Continued)
  extremities (Continued)
    bypass graft (Continued)
      specified graft NEC (Continued)
        leg (Continued)
          with (Continued)
            rest pain (and intermittent
              claudication) I70.628
            ulceration (and intermittent
              claudication and rest pain)
              I70.65
          specified type NEC I70.698
      specified graft NEC I70.709
        leg I70.709
          with
            gangrene (and intermittent
              claudication, rest pain and
              ulcer) I70.769
            intermittent claudication I70.719
            rest pain (and intermittent
              claudication) I70.729
          bilateral I70.703
            with
              gangrene (and intermittent
                claudication, rest pain and
                ulcer) I70.763
              intermittent claudication I70.713
              rest pain (and intermittent
                claudication) I70.723
            specified type NEC I70.793
          left I70.702
            with
              gangrene (and intermittent
                claudication, rest pain and
                ulcer) I70.762
              intermittent claudication I70.712
              rest pain (and intermittent
                claudication) I70.722
              ulceration (and intermittent
                claudication and rest
                pain) I70.749
                ankle I70.743
                calf I70.742
                foot site NEC I70.745
                heel I70.744
                lower leg NEC I70.748
                midfoot I70.744
                thigh I70.741
            specified type NEC I70.792
          right I70.701
            with
              gangrene (and intermittent
                claudication, rest pain and
                ulcer) I70.761
              intermittent claudication
                I70.711
              rest pain (and intermittent
                claudication) I70.721
              ulceration (and intermittent
                claudication and rest
                pain) I70.739
                ankle I70.733
                calf I70.732
                foot site NEC I70.735
                heel I70.734
                lower leg NEC I70.738
                midfoot I70.734
                thigh I70.731
            specified type NEC I70.791
          specified type NEC I70.799
        specified NEC I70.708
          with
            gangrene (and intermittent
              claudication, rest pain and
              ulcer) I70.768
            intermittent claudication I70.718
            rest pain (and intermittent
              claudication) I70.728
            ulceration (and intermittent
              claudication and rest pain)
              I70.75
          specified type NEC I70.798

▶ New　　⇒ Revised　　~~deleted~~ Deleted　　• Use Additional Character(s)

Arteriosclerosis, arteriosclerotic *(Continued)*
extremities *(Continued)*
  bypass graft *(Continued)*
    specified NEC I70.308
      with
        gangrene (and intermittent
          claudication, rest pain and
          ulcer) I70.368
        intermittent claudication I70.318
        rest pain (and intermittent
          claudication) I70.328
        ulceration (and intermittent
          claudication and rest pain)
          I70.35
      specified type NEC I70.398
  leg I70.209
    with
      gangrene (and intermittent claudication,
        rest pain and ulcer) I70.269
      intermittent claudication I70.219
      rest pain (and intermittent
        claudication) I70.229
    bilateral I70.203
      with
        gangrene (and intermittent
          claudication, rest pain and
          ulcer) I70.263
        intermittent claudication I70.213
        rest pain (and intermittent
          claudication) I70.223
      specified type NEC I70.293
    left I70.202
      with
        gangrene (and intermittent
          claudication, rest pain and
          ulcer) I70.262
        intermittent claudication I70.212
        rest pain (and intermittent
          claudication) I70.222
        ulceration (and intermittent
          claudication and rest pain)
          I70.249
          ankle I70.243
          calf I70.242
          foot site NEC I70.245
          heel I70.244
          lower leg NEC I70.248
          midfoot I70.244
          thigh I70.241
      specified type NEC I70.292
    right I70.201
      with
        gangrene (and intermittent
          claudication, rest pain and
          ulcer) I70.261
        intermittent claudication I70.211
        rest pain (and intermittent
          claudication) I70.221
        ulceration (and intermittent
          claudication and rest pain)
          I70.239
          ankle I70.233
          calf I70.232
          foot site NEC I70.235
          heel I70.234
          lower leg NEC I70.238
          midfoot I70.234
          thigh I70.231
      specified type NEC I70.291
    specified type NEC I70.299
  specified site NEC I70.208
    with
      gangrene (and intermittent claudication,
        rest pain and ulcer) I70.268
      intermittent claudication I70.218
      rest pain (and intermittent
        claudication) I70.228
      ulceration (and intermittent
        claudication and rest pain) I70.25
    specified type NEC I70.298
generalized I70.91

Arteriosclerosis, arteriosclerotic *(Continued)*
heart (disease) —*see* Arteriosclerosis,
  coronary (artery)
kidney —*see* Hypertension, kidney
medial —*see* Arteriosclerosis, extremities
mesenteric (artery) K55.1
Mönckeberg's —*see* Arteriosclerosis,
  extremities
myocarditis I51.4
peripheral (of extremities) —*see*
  Arteriosclerosis, extremities
pulmonary (idiopathic) I27.0
renal (arterioles) —*see also* Hypertension,
  kidney
  artery I70.1
retina (vascular) I70.8 [*H35.0-●*]
specified artery NEC I70.8
spinal (cord) G95.19
vertebral (artery) I67.2
Arteriospasm I73.9
Arteriovenous —*see* condition
Arteritis I77.6
allergic M31.0
aorta (nonsyphilitic) I77.6
  syphilitic A52.02
aortic arch M31.4
brachiocephalic M31.4
brain I67.7
  syphilitic A52.04
cerebral I67.7
  in
    diseases classified elsewhere I68.2
    systemic lupus erythematosus M32.19
  listerial A32.89
  syphilitic A52.04
  tuberculous A18.89
coronary (artery) I25.89
  rheumatic I01.8
    chronic I09.89
  syphilitic A52.06
cranial (left) (right), giant cell M31.6
deformans —*see* Arteriosclerosis
giant cell NEC M31.6
  with polymyalgia rheumatica M31.5
necrosing or necrotizing M31.9
  specified NEC M31.8
nodosa M30.0
obliterans —*see* Arteriosclerosis
pulmonary I28.8
rheumatic —*see* Fever, rheumatic
senile —*see* Arteriosclerosis
suppurative I77.2
syphilitic (general) A52.09
  brain A52.04
  coronary A52.06
  spinal A52.09
temporal, giant cell M31.6
young female aortic arch syndrome M31.4
Artery, arterial —*see also* condition
abscess I77.89
single umbilical Q27.0
Arthralgia (allergic) —*see also* Pain, joint
in caisson disease T70.3
temporomandibular M26.62
Arthritis, arthritic (acute) (chronic)
  (nonpyogenic) (subacute) M19.90
allergic —*see* Arthritis, specified form NEC
ankylosing (crippling) (spine) —*see also*
    Spondylitis, ankylosing
  sites other than spine —*see* Arthritis,
    specified form NEC
atrophic —*see* Osteoarthritis
  spine —*see* Spondylitis, ankylosing
back —*see* Spondylopathy, inflammatory
blennorrhagic (gonococcal) A54.42
Charcot's —*see* Arthropathy, neuropathic
  diabetic —*see* Diabetes, arthropathy,
    neuropathic
  syringomyelic G95.0
chylous (filarial) —*see also* category M01 B74.9
climacteric (any site) NEC —*see* Arthritis,
  specified form NEC

Arthritis, arthritic *(Continued)*
crystal (-induced) —*see* Arthritis, in, crystals
deformans —*see* Osteoarthritis
degenerative —*see* Osteoarthritis
due to or associated with
  acromegaly E22.0
  brucellosis —*see* Brucellosis
  caisson disease T70.3
  diabetes —*see* Diabetes, arthropathy
  dracontiasis —*see also* category M01 B72
  enteritis NEC
    regional —*see* Enteritis, regional
  erysipelas —*see also* category M01 A46
  erythema
    epidemic A25.1
    nodosum L52
  filariasis NOS B74.9
  glanders A24.0
  helminthiasis —*see also* category M01 B83.9
  hemophilia D66 [*M36.2*]
  Henoch-(Schönlein) purpura D69.0 [*M36.4*]
  human parvovirus —*see also* category M01
    B97.6
  infectious disease NEC —*see* category M01
  leprosy (*see also* category M01) —*see also*
    Leprosy A30.9
  Lyme disease A69.23
  mycobacteria —*see also* category M01 A31.8
  parasitic disease NEC —*see also* category
    M01 B89
  paratyphoid fever (*see also* category M01)
    —*see also* Fever, paratyphoid A01.4
  rat bite fever —*see also* category M01 A25.1
  regional enteritis —*see* Enteritis, regional
  respiratory disorder NOS J98.9
  serum sickness —*see also* Reaction, serum
    T80.69
  syringomyelia G95.0
  typhoid fever A01.04
epidemic erythema A25.1
febrile —*see* Fever, rheumatic
gonococcal A54.42
gouty (acute) —*see* Gout
in (due to)
  acromegaly —*see also* subcategory
    M14.8-● E22.0
  amyloidosis —*see also* subcategory
    M14.8-● E85.4
  bacterial disease —*see also* subcategory
    M01 A49.9
  Behçet's syndrome M35.2
  caisson disease —*see also* subcategory
    M14.8-● T70.3
  coliform bacilli (Escherichia coli) —*see*
    Arthritis, in, pyogenic organism NEC
  crystals M11.9
    dicalcium phosphate —*see* Arthritis, in,
      crystals, specified type NEC
    hydroxyapatite M11.0-●
    pyrophosphate —*see* Arthritis, in,
      crystals, specified type NEC
    specified type NEC M11.80
      ankle M11.87-●
      elbow M11.82-●
      foot joint M11.87-●
      hand joint M11.84-●
      hip M11.85-●
      knee M11.86-●
      multiple sites M11.8-●
      shoulder M11.81-●
      vertebrae M11.88
      wrist M11.83-●
  dermatoarthritis, lipoid E78.81
  dracontiasis (dracunculiasis) —*see also*
    category M01 B72
  endocrine disorder NEC —*see also*
    subcategory M14.8-● E34.9
  enteritis, infectious NEC —*see also* category
    M01 A09
    specified organism NEC —*see also*
      category M01 A08.8

Arthritis, arthritic *(Continued)*
in *(Continued)*
erythema
multiforme —*see also* subcategory
M14.8-● L51.9
nodosum —*see also* subcategory M14.8-●
L52
gout —*see* Gout
helminthiasis NEC —*see also* category M01
B83.9
hemochromatosis —*see also* subcategory
M14.8-● E83.118
hemoglobinopathy NEC D58.2 *[M36.3]*
hemophilia NEC D66 *[M36.2]*
Hemophilus influenzae M00.8-● *[B96.3]*
Henoch(-Schönlein) purpura D69.0 *[M36.4]*
hyperparathyroidism NEC —*see also*
subcategory M14.8-● E21.3
hypersensitivity reaction NEC T78.49
[M36.4]
hypogammaglobulinemia —*see also*
subcategory M14.8-● D80.1
hypothyroidism NEC —*see also*
subcategory M14.8-● E03.9
infection —*see* Arthritis, pyogenic or pyemic
spine —*see* Spondylopathy, infective
infectious disease NEC —*see also* category M01
leprosy —*see also* category M01 A30.9
leukemia NEC C95.9-● *[M36.1]*
lipoid dermatoarthritis E78.81
Lyme disease A69.23
Mediterranean fever, familial —*see also*
subcategory M14.8-● M04.1
Meningococcus A39.83
metabolic disorder NEC —*see also*
subcategory M14.8-● E88.9
multiple myelomatosis C90.0-● *[M36.1]*
mumps B26.85
mycosis NEC —*see also* category M01 B49
myelomatosis (multiple) C90.0-● *[M36.1]*
neurological disorder NEC G98.0
ochronosis —*see also* subcategory M14.8-●
E70.29
O'nyong-nyong —*see also* category M01
A92.1
parasitic disease NEC —*see also* category
M01 B89
paratyphoid fever —*see also* category M01
A01.4
Pseudomonas —*see* Arthritis, pyogenic,
bacterial NEC
psoriasis L40.50
pyogenic organism NEC —*see* Arthritis,
pyogenic, bacterial NEC
Reiter's disease —*see* Reiter's disease
respiratory disorder NEC —*see also*
subcategory M14.8-● J98.9
reticulosis, malignant —*see also*
subcategory M14.8-● C86.0
rubella B06.82
Salmonella (arizonae) (cholerae-suis)
(enteritidis) (typhimurium) A02.23
sarcoidosis D86.86
specified bacteria NEC —*see* Arthritis,
pyogenic, bacterial NEC
sporotrichosis B42.82
syringomyelia G95.0
thalassemia NEC D56.9 *[M36.3]*
tuberculosis —*see* Tuberculosis, arthritis
typhoid fever A01.04
urethritis, Reiter's —*see* Reiter's disease
viral disease NEC —*see also* category M01
B34.9
infectious or infective —*see also* Arthritis,
pyogenic or pyemic
spine —*see* Spondylopathy, infective
juvenile M08.90
with systemic onset —*see* Still's disease
ankle M08.97-●
elbow M08.92-●
foot joint M08.97-●

Arthritis, arthritic *(Continued)*
juvenile *(Continued)*
hand joint M08.94-●
hip M08.95-●
knee M08.96-●
multiple site M08.99
pauciarticular M08.40
ankle M08.47-●
elbow M08.42-●
foot joint M08.47-●
hand joint M08.44-●
hip M08.45-●
knee M08.46-●
shoulder M08.41-●
vertebrae M08.48
wrist M08.43-●
psoriatic L40.54
rheumatoid —*see* Arthritis, rheumatoid,
juvenile
shoulder M08.91-●
specified type NEC M08.80
ankle M08.87-●
elbow M08.82-●
foot joint M08.87-●
hand joint M08.84-●
hip M08.85-●
knee M08.86-●
multiple site M08.89
shoulder M08.81-●
specified joint NEC M08.88
vertebrae M08.88
wrist M08.83-●
vertebra M08.98
wrist M08.93-●
meaning osteoarthritis —*see* Osteoarthritis
meningococcal A39.83
menopausal (any site) NEC —*see* Arthritis,
specified form NEC
mutilans (psoriatic) L40.52
mycotic NEC —*see also* category M01 B49
neuropathic (Charcot) —*see* Arthropathy,
neuropathic
diabetic —*see* Diabetes, arthropathy,
neuropathic
nonsyphilitic NEC G98.0
syringomyelic G95.0
ochronotic —*see also* subcategory M14.8-●
E70.29
palindromic (any site) —*see* Rheumatism,
palindromic
pneumococcal M00.10
ankle M00.17-●
elbow M00.12-●
foot joint —*see* Arthritis, pneumococcal,
ankle
hand joint M00.14-●
hip M00.15-●
knee M00.16-●
multiple site M00.19
shoulder M00.11-●
vertebra M00.18
wrist M00.13-●
postdysenteric —*see* Arthropathy,
postdysenteric
postmeningococcal A39.84
postrheumatic, chronic —*see* Arthropathy,
postrheumatic, chronic
primary progressive —*see also* Arthritis,
specified form NEC
spine —*see* Spondylitis, ankylosing
psoriatic L40.50
purulent (any site except spine) —*see*
Arthritis, pyogenic or pyemic
spine —*see* Spondylopathy, infective
pyogenic or pyemic (any site except spine)
M00.9
bacterial NEC M00.80
ankle M00.87-●
elbow M00.82-●
foot joint —*see* Arthritis, pyogenic,
bacterial NEC, ankle

Arthritis, arthritic *(Continued)*
pyogenic or pyemic *(Continued)*
bacterial NEC *(Continued)*
hand joint M00.84-●
hip M00.85-●
knee M00.86-●
multiple site M00.89
shoulder M00.81-●
vertebra M00.88
wrist M00.83-●
pneumococcal —*see* Arthritis,
pneumococcal
spine —*see* Spondylopathy, infective
staphylococcal —*see* Arthritis,
staphylococcal
streptococcal —*see* Arthritis, streptococcal
NEC
pneumococcal —*see* Arthritis,
pneumococcal
reactive —*see* Reiter's disease
rheumatic —*see also* Arthritis, rheumatoid
acute or subacute —*see* Fever, rheumatic
rheumatoid M06.9
with
carditis —*see* Rheumatoid, carditis
endocarditis —*see* Rheumatoid, carditis
heart involvement NEC —*see*
Rheumatoid, carditis
lung involvement —*see* Rheumatoid, lung
myocarditis —*see* Rheumatoid, carditis
myopathy —*see* Rheumatoid, myopathy
pericarditis —*see* Rheumatoid, carditis
polyneuropathy —*see* Rheumatoid,
polyneuropathy
rheumatoid factor —*see* Arthritis,
rheumatoid, seropositive
splenoadenomegaly and leukopenia —
see Felty's syndrome
vasculitis —*see* Rheumatoid, vasculitis
visceral involvement NEC —*see*
Rheumatoid, arthritis, with
involvement of organs NEC
juvenile (with or without rheumatoid
factor) M08.00
ankle M08.07-●
elbow M08.02-●
foot joint M08.07-●
hand joint M08.04-●
hip M08.05-●
knee M08.06-●
multiple site M08.09
shoulder M08.01-●
vertebra M08.08
wrist M08.03-●
seronegative M06.00
ankle M06.07-●
elbow M06.02-●
foot joint M06.07-●
hand joint M06.04-●
hip M06.05-●
knee M06.06-●
multiple sites M06.09
shoulder M06.01-●
vertebra M06.08
wrist M06.03-●
seropositive M05.9
without organ involvement M05.70
ankle M05.77-●
elbow M05.72-●
foot joint M05.77-●
hand joint M05.74-●
hip M05.75-●
knee M05.76-●
multiple sites M05.79
shoulder M05.71-●
vertebra —*see* Spondylitis, ankylosing
wrist M05.73-●
specified NEC M05.80
ankle M05.87-●
elbow M05.82-●
foot joint M05.87-●

▶ New   ⇒ Revised   ~~deleted~~ Deleted   ● Use Additional Character(s)

Arthritis, arthritic (Continued)
rheumatoid (Continued)
specified NEC (Continued)
hand joint M05.84-•
hip M05.85-•
knee M05.86-•
multiple sites M05.89
shoulder M05.81-•
vertebra —see Spondylitis, ankylosing
wrist M05.83-•
specified type NEC M06.80
ankle M06.87-•
elbow M06.82-•
foot joint M06.87-•
hand joint M06.84-•
hip M06.85-•
knee M06.86-•
multiple site M06.89
shoulder M06.81-•
vertebra M06.88
wrist M06.83-•
spine —see Spondylitis, ankylosing
rubella B06.82
scorbutic —see also subcategory M14.8-• E54
senile or senescent —see Osteoarthritis
septic (any site except spine) —see Arthritis,
pyogenic or pyemic
spine —see Spondylopathy, infective
serum (nontherapeutic) (therapeutic) —see
Arthropathy, postimmunization
specified form NEC M13.80
ankle M13.87-•
elbow M13.82-•
foot joint M13.87-•
hand joint M13.84-•
hip M13.85-•
knee M13.86-•
multiple site M13.89
shoulder M13.81-•
specified joint NEC M13.88
wrist M13.83-•
spine —see also Spondylopathy, inflammatory
infectious or infective NEC —see
Spondylopathy, infective
Marie-Strümpell —see Spondylitis,
ankylosing
pyogenic —see Spondylopathy, infective
rheumatoid —see Spondylitis, ankylosing
traumatic (old) —see Spondylopathy,
traumatic
tuberculous A18.01
staphylococcal M00.00
ankle M00.07-•
elbow M00.02-•
foot joint —see Arthritis, staphylococcal,
ankle
hand joint M00.04-•
hip M00.05-•
knee M00.06-•
multiple site M00.09
shoulder M00.01-•
vertebra M00.08
wrist M00.03-•
streptococcal NEC M00.20
ankle M00.27-•
elbow M00.22-•
foot joint —see Arthritis, streptococcal, ankle
hand joint M00.24-•
hip M00.25-•
knee M00.26-•
multiple site M00.29
shoulder M00.21-•
vertebra M00.28
wrist M00.23-•
suppurative —see Arthritis, pyogenic or
pyemic
syphilitic (late) A52.16
congenital A50.55 [M12.80]
syphilitica deformans (Charcot) A52.16
temporomandibular M26.69
toxic of menopause (any site) —see Arthritis,
specified form NEC

Arthritis, arthritic (Continued)
transient —see Arthropathy, specified form
NEC
traumatic (chronic) —see Arthropathy,
traumatic
tuberculous A18.02
spine A18.01
uratic —see Gout
urethritica (Reiter's) —see Reiter's disease
vertebral —see Spondylopathy, inflammatory
villous (any site) —see Arthropathy, specified
form NEC
Arthrocele —see Effusion, joint
Arthrodesis status Z98.1
Arthrodynia —see also Pain, joint
Arthrodysplasia Q74.9
Arthrofibrosis, joint —see Ankylosis
Arthrogryposis (congenital) Q68.8
multiplex congenita Q74.3
Arthrokatadysis M24.7
Arthropathy (see also Arthritis) M12.9
Charcot's —see Arthropathy, neuropathic
diabetic —see Diabetes, arthropathy,
neuropathic
syringomyelic G95.0
cricoarytenoid J38.7
crystal(-induced) —see Arthritis, in, crystals
diabetic NEC —see Diabetes, arthropathy
distal interphalangeal, psoriatic L40.51
enteropathic M07.60
ankle M07.67-•
elbow M07.62-•
foot joint M07.67-•
hand joint M07.64-•
hip M07.65-•
knee M07.66-•
multiple site M07.69
shoulder M07.61-•
vertebra M07.68
wrist M07.63-•
following intestinal bypass M02.00
ankle M02.07-•
elbow M02.02-•
foot joint M02.07-•
hand joint M02.04-•
hip M02.05-•
knee M02.06-•
multiple site M02.09
shoulder M02.01-•
vertebra M02.08
wrist M02.03-•
gouty —see also Gout
in (due to)
Lesch-Nyhan syndrome E79.1 [M14.8-•]
sickle-cell disorders D57-• [M14.8-•]
hemophilic NEC D66 [M36.2]
in (due to)
hyperparathyroidism NEC E21.3
[M14.8-•]
metabolic disease NOS E88.9 [M14.8-•]
in (due to)
acromegaly E22.0 [M14.8-•]
amyloidosis E85.4 [M14.8-•]
blood disorder NOS D75.9 [M36.3]
diabetes —see Diabetes, arthropathy
endocrine disease NOS E34.9 [M14.8-•]
erythema
multiforme L51.9 [M14.8-•]
nodosum L52 [M14.8-•]
hemochromatosis E83.118 [M14.8-•]
hemoglobinopathy NEC D58.2 [M36.3]
hemophilia NEC D66 [M36.2]
Henoch-Schönlein purpura D69.0 [M36.4]
hyperthyroidism E05.90 [M14.8-•]
hypothyroidism E03.9 [M14.8-•]
infective endocarditis I33.0 [M12.80]
leukemia NEC C95.9-• [M36.1]
malignant histiocytosis C96.A [M36.1]
metabolic disease NOS E88.9 [M14.8-•]
multiple myeloma C90.0-• [M36.1]
neoplastic disease NOS (see also Neoplasm)
D49.9 [M36.1]

Arthropathy (Continued)
hemochromatosis (Continued)
nutritional deficiency —see also
subcategory M14.8-• E63.9
psoriasis NOS L40.50
sarcoidosis D86.86
syphilis (late) A52.77
congenital A50.55 [M12.80]
thyrotoxicosis —see also subcategory
M14.8-• E05.90
ulcerative colitis K51.90 [M07.60]
viral hepatitis (postinfectious) NEC B19.9
[M12.80]
Whipple's disease —see also subcategory
M14.8-• K90.81
Jaccoud —see Arthropathy, postrheumatic,
chronic
juvenile —see Arthritis, juvenile
psoriatic L40.54
mutilans (psoriatic) L40.52
neuropathic (Charcot) M14.60
ankle M14.67-•
diabetic —see Diabetes, arthropathy,
neuropathic
elbow M14.62-•
foot joint M14.67-•
hand joint M14.64-•
hip M14.65-•
knee M14.66-•
multiple site M14.69
nonsyphilitic NEC G98.0
shoulder M14.61-•
syringomyelic G95.0
vertebra M14.68
wrist M14.63-•
osteopulmonary —see Osteoarthropathy,
hypertrophic, specified NEC
postdysenteric M02.10
ankle M02.17-•
elbow M02.12-•
foot joint M02.17-•
hand joint M02.14-•
hip M02.15-•
knee M02.16-•
multiple site M02.19
shoulder M02.11-•
vertebra M02.18
wrist M02.13-•
postimmunization M02.20
ankle M02.27-•
elbow M02.22-•
foot joint M02.27-•
hand joint M02.24-•
hip M02.25-•
knee M02.26-•
multiple site M02.29
shoulder M02.21-•
vertebra M02.28
wrist M02.23-•
postinfectious NEC B99 [M12.80]
in (due to)
enteritis due to Yersinia enterocolitica
A04.6 [M12.80]
syphilis A52.77
viral hepatitis NEC B19.9
[M12.80]
postrheumatic, chronic (Jaccoud)
M12.00
ankle M12.07-•
elbow M12.02-•
foot joint M12.07-•
hand joint M12.04-•
hip M12.05-•
knee M12.06-•
multiple site M12.09
shoulder M12.01-•
specified joint NEC M12.08
vertebrae M12.08
wrist M12.03-•
psoriatic NEC L40.59
interphalangeal, distal L40.51

Arthropathy *(Continued)*
  reactive M02.9
    in (due to)
      infective endocarditis I33.0 *[M02.9]*
      specified type NEC M02.80
        ankle M02.87-•
        elbow M02.82-•
        foot joint M02.87-•
        hand joint M02.84-•
        hip M02.85-•
        knee M02.86-•
        multiple site M02.89
        shoulder M02.81-•
        vertebra M02.88
        wrist M02.83-•
  specified form NEC M12.80
    ankle M12.87-•
    elbow M12.82-•
    foot joint M12.87-•
    hand joint M12.84-•
    hip M12.85-•
    knee M12.86-•
    multiple site M12.89
    shoulder M12.81-•
    specified joint NEC M12.88
    vertebrae M12.88
    wrist M12.83-•
  syringomyelic G95.0
  tabes dorsalis A52.16
  tabetic A52.16
  transient —*see* Arthropathy, specified form NEC
  traumatic M12.50
    ankle M12.57-•
    elbow M12.52-•
    foot joint M12.57-•
    hand joint M12.54-•
    hip M12.55-•
    knee M12.56-•
    multiple site M12.59
    shoulder M12.51-•
    specified joint NEC M12.58
    vertebrae M12.58
    wrist M12.53-•
Arthropyosis —*see* Arthritis, pyogenic or pyemic
Arthrosis (deformans) (degenerative) (localized) —*see also* Osteoarthritis M19.90
  spine —*see* Spondylosis
Arthus' phenomenon or reaction T78.41
  due to
    drug —*see* Table of Drugs and Chemicals, by drug
Articular —*see* condition
Articulation, reverse (teeth) M26.24
Artificial
  insemination complication —*see* Complications, artificial, fertilization
  opening status (functioning) (without complication) Z93.9
    anus (colostomy) Z93.3
    colostomy Z93.3
    cystostomy Z93.50
      appendico-vesicostomy Z93.52
      cutaneous Z93.51
      specified NEC Z93.59
    enterostomy Z93.4
    gastrostomy Z93.1
    ileostomy Z93.2
    intestinal tract NEC Z93.4
    jejunostomy Z93.4
    nephrostomy Z93.6
    specified site NEC Z93.8
    tracheostomy Z93.0
    ureterostomy Z93.6
    urethrostomy Z93.6
    urinary tract NEC Z93.6
    vagina Z93.8
  vagina status Z93.8
Arytenoid —*see* condition
Asbestosis (occupational) J61

ASC-H (atypical squamous cells cannot exclude high grade squamous intraepithelial lesion on cytologic smear)
  anus R85.611
  cervix R87.611
  vagina R87.621
ASC-US (atypical squamous cells of undetermined significance on cytologic smear)
  anus R85.610
  cervix R87.610
  vagina R87.620
Ascariasis B77.9
  with
    complications NEC B77.89
    intestinal complications B77.0
    pneumonia, pneumonitis B77.81
Ascaridosis, ascaridiasis —*see* Ascariasis
Ascaris (infection) (infestation) (lumbricoides) —*see* Ascariasis
Ascending —*see* condition
Aschoff's bodies —*see* Myocarditis, rheumatic
Ascites (abdominal) R18.8
  cardiac —*see also* Failure, heart, right I50.810
  chylous (nonfilarial) I89.8
    filarial —*see* Infestation, filarial
  due to
    cirrhosis, alcoholic K70.31
    hepatitis
      alcoholic K70.11
      chronic active K71.51
    S. japonicum B65.2
  heart —*see also* Failure, heart, right I50.810
  malignant R18.0
  pseudochylous R18.8
  syphilitic A52.74
  tuberculous A18.31
Aseptic —*see* condition
Asherman's syndrome N85.6
Asialia K11.7
Asiatic cholera —*see* Cholera
Asimultagnosia (simultanagnosia) R48.3
Askin's tumor —*see* Neoplasm, connective tissue, malignant
Asocial personality F60.2
Asomatognosia R41.4
Aspartylglucosaminuria E77.1
Asperger's disease or syndrome F84.5
Aspergilloma —*see* Aspergillosis
Aspergillosis (with pneumonia) B44.9
  bronchopulmonary, allergic B44.81
  disseminated B44.7
  generalized B44.7
  pulmonary NEC B44.1
    allergic B44.81
    invasive B44.0
  specified NEC B44.89
  tonsillar B44.2
Aspergillus (flavus) (fumigatus) (infection) (terreus) —*see* Aspergillosis
Aspermatogenesis —*see* Azoospermia
Aspermia (testis) —*see* Azoospermia
Asphyxia, asphyxiation (by) R09.01
  antenatal P84
  birth P84
  bunny bag —*see* Asphyxia, due to, mechanical threat to breathing, trapped in bed clothes
  crushing S28.0
  drowning T75.1
  gas, fumes, or vapor —*see* Table of Drugs and Chemicals
  inhalation —*see* Inhalation
  intrauterine P84
  local I73.00
    with gangrene I73.01
  mucus —*see also* Foreign body, respiratory tract, causing asphyxia
  newborn P84

Asphyxia, asphyxiation *(Continued)*
  pathological R09.01
  postnatal P84
    mechanical —*see* Asphyxia, due to, mechanical threat to breathing
  prenatal P84
  reticularis R23.1
  strangulation —*see* Asphyxia, due to, mechanical threat to breathing
  submersion T75.1
  traumatic T71.9
    due to
      crushed chest S28.0
      foreign body (in) —*see* Foreign body, respiratory tract, causing asphyxia
      low oxygen content of ambient air T71.20
        due to
          being trapped in
            low oxygen environment T71.29
              in car trunk T71.221
                circumstances undetermined T71.224
                done with intent to harm by another person T71.223
                self T71.222
              in refrigerator T71.231
                circumstances undetermined T71.234
                done with intent to harm by another person T71.233
                self T71.232
          cave-in T71.21
      mechanical threat to breathing (accidental) T71.191
        circumstances undetermined T71.194
        done with intent to harm by another person T71.193
        self T71.192
        hanging T71.161
          circumstances undetermined T71.164
          done with intent to harm by another person T71.163
          self T71.162
        plastic bag T71.121
          circumstances undetermined T71.124
          done with intent to harm by another person T71.123
          self T71.122
        smothering
          in furniture T71.151
            circumstances undetermined T71.154
            done with intent to harm by another person T71.153
            self T71.152
          under
            another person's body T71.141
              circumstances undetermined T71.144
              done with intent to harm T71.143
            pillow T71.111
              circumstances undetermined T71.114
              done with intent to harm by another person T71.113
              self T71.112
        trapped in bed clothes T71.131
          circumstances undetermined T71.134
          done with intent to harm by another person T71.133
          self T71.132
  vomiting, vomitus —*see* Foreign body, respiratory tract, causing asphyxia
Aspiration
  amniotic (clear) fluid (newborn) P24.10
    with
      pneumonia (pneumonitis) P24.11
      respiratory symptoms P24.11

▶ New   ⇒ Revised   ~~deleted~~ Deleted   • Use Additional Character(s)

Aspiration (Continued)
blood
newborn (without respiratory symptoms)
P24.20
with
pneumonia (pneumonitis) P24.21
respiratory symptoms P24.21
specified age NEC —see Foreign body,
respiratory tract
bronchitis J69.0
food or foreign body (with asphyxiation) —
see Asphyxia, food
liquor (amnii) (newborn) P24.10
with
pneumonia (pneumonitis) P24.11
respiratory symptoms P24.11
meconium (newborn) (without respiratory
symptoms) P24.00
with
pneumonitis (pneumonitis) P24.01
respiratory symptoms P24.01
milk (newborn) (without respiratory
symptoms) P24.30
with
pneumonia (pneumonitis) P24.31
respiratory symptoms P24.31
specified age NEC —see Foreign body,
respiratory tract
mucus —see also Foreign body, by site,
causing asphyxia
newborn P24.10
with
pneumonia (pneumonitis) P24.11
respiratory symptoms P24.11
neonatal P24.9
specific NEC (without respiratory
symptoms) P24.80
with
pneumonia (pneumonitis) P24.81
respiratory symptoms P24.81
newborn P24.9
specific NEC (without respiratory
symptoms) P24.80
with
pneumonia (pneumonitis) P24.81
respiratory symptoms P24.81
pneumonia J69.0
pneumonitis J69.0
syndrome of newborn —see Aspiration, by
substance, with pneumonia
vernix caseosa (newborn) P24.80
with
pneumonia (pneumonitis) P24.81
respiratory symptoms P24.81
vomitus —see also Foreign body, respiratory
tract
newborn (without respiratory symptoms)
P24.30
with
pneumonia (pneumonitis) P24.31
respiratory symptoms P24.31
Asplenia (congenital) Q89.01
postsurgical Z90.81
Assam fever B55.0
Assault, sexual —see Maltreatment
Assmann's focus NEC A15.0
Astasia (-abasia) (hysterical) F44.4
Asteatosis cutis L85.3
Astereognosia, astereognosis R48.1
Asterixis R27.8
in liver disease K71.3
Asteroid hyalitis —see Deposit, crystalline
Asthenia, asthenic R53.1
cardiac —see also Failure, heart I50.9
psychogenic F45.8
cardiovascular —see also Failure, heart
I50.9
psychogenic F45.8
heart —see also Failure, heart I50.9
psychogenic F45.8
hysterical F44.4

Asthenia, asthenic (Continued)
myocardial —see also Failure, heart I50.9
psychogenic F45.8
nervous F48.8
neurocirculatory F45.8
neurotic F48.8
psychogenic F48.8
psychoneurotic F48.8
psychophysiologic F48.8
reaction (psychophysiologic) F48.8
senile R54
Asthenopia —see also Discomfort, visual
hysterical F44.6
psychogenic F44.6
Asthenospermia —see Abnormal, specimen,
male genital organs
Asthma, asthmatic (bronchial) (catarrh)
(spasmodic) J45.909
with
chronic obstructive bronchitis J44.9
with
acute lower respiratory infection J44.0
exacerbation (acute) J44.1
chronic obstructive pulmonary disease
J44.9
with
acute lower respiratory infection J44.0
exacerbation (acute) J44.1
exacerbation (acute) J45.901
hay fever —see Asthma, allergic extrinsic
rhinitis, allergic —see Asthma, allergic
extrinsic
status asthmaticus J45.902
allergic extrinsic J45.909
with
exacerbation (acute) J45.901
status asthmaticus J45.902
atopic —see Asthma, allergic extrinsic
cardiac —see Failure, ventricular, left
cardiobronchial I50.1
childhood J45.909
with
exacerbation (acute) J45.901
status asthmaticus J45.902
chronic obstructive J44.9
with
acute lower respiratory infection J44.0
exacerbation (acute) J44.1
collier's J60
cough variant J45.991
detergent J69.8
due to
detergent J69.8
inhalation of fumes J68.3
eosinophilic J82
extrinsic, allergic —see Asthma, allergic
extrinsic
grinder's J62.8
hay —see Asthma, allergic extrinsic
heart I50.1
idiosyncratic —see Asthma, nonallergic
intermittent (mild) J45.20
with
exacerbation (acute) J45.21
status asthmaticus J45.22
intrinsic, nonallergic —see Asthma, nonallergic
Kopp's E32.8
late-onset J45.909
with
exacerbation (acute) J45.901
status asthmaticus J45.902
mild intermittent J45.20
with
exacerbation (acute) J45.21
status asthmaticus J45.22
mild persistent J45.30
with
exacerbation (acute) J45.31
status asthmaticus J45.32
Millar's (laryngismus stridulus) J38.5
miner's J60

Asthma, asthmatic (Continued)
mixed J45.909
with
exacerbation (acute) J45.901
status asthmaticus J45.902
moderate persistent J45.40
with
exacerbation (acute) J45.41
status asthmaticus J45.42
nervous —see Asthma, nonallergic
nonallergic (intrinsic) J45.909
with
exacerbation (acute) J45.901
status asthmaticus J45.902
persistent
mild J45.30
with
exacerbation (acute) J45.31
status asthmaticus J45.32
moderate J45.40
with
exacerbation (acute) J45.41
status asthmaticus J45.42
severe J45.50
with
exacerbation (acute) J45.51
status asthmaticus J45.52
platinum J45.998
pneumoconiotic NEC J64
potter's J62.8
predominantly allergic J45.909
psychogenic F54
pulmonary eosinophilic J82
red cedar J67.8
Rostan's I50.1
sandblaster's J62.8
sequoiosis J67.8
severe persistent J45.50
with
exacerbation (acute) J45.51
status asthmaticus J45.52
specified NEC J45.998
stonemason's J62.8
thymic E32.8
tuberculous —see Tuberculosis, pulmonary
Wichmann's (laryngismus stridulus) J38.5
wood J67.8
Astigmatism (compound) (congenital)
H52.20-●
irregular H52.21-●
regular H52.22-●
Astraphobia F40.220
Astroblastoma
specified site —see Neoplasm, malignant, by
site
unspecified site C71.9
Astrocytoma (cystic)
anaplastic
specified site —see Neoplasm, malignant,
by site
unspecified site C71.9
fibrillary
specified site —see Neoplasm, malignant,
by site
unspecified site C71.9
fibrous
specified site —see Neoplasm, malignant,
by site
unspecified site C71.9
gemistocytic
specified site —see Neoplasm, malignant,
by site
unspecified site C71.9
juvenile
specified site —see Neoplasm, malignant,
by site
unspecified site C71.9
pilocytic
specified site —see Neoplasm, malignant,
by site
unspecified site C71.9

Astrocytoma *(Continued)*
piloid
specified site —*see* Neoplasm, malignant, by site
unspecified site C71.9
protoplasmic
specified site —*see* Neoplasm, malignant, by site
unspecified site C71.9
specified site NEC —*see* Neoplasm, malignant, by site
subependymal D43.2
giant cell
specified site —*see* Neoplasm, uncertain behavior, by site
unspecified site D43.2
specified site —*see* Neoplasm, uncertain behavior, by site
unspecified site D43.2
unspecified site C71.9
Astroglioma
specified site —*see* Neoplasm, malignant, by site
unspecified site C71.9
Asymbolia R48.8
Asymmetry —*see also* Distortion
between native and reconstructed breast N65.1
face Q67.0
jaw (lower) —*see* Anomaly, dentofacial, jaw-cranial base relationship, asymmetry
Asynergia, asynergy R27.8
ventricular I51.89
Asystole (heart) —*see* Arrest, cardiac
At risk
for
dental caries Z91.849
high Z91.843
low Z91.841
moderate Z91.842
falling Z91.81
Ataxia, ataxy, ataxic R27.0
acute R27.8
brain (hereditary) G11.9
cerebellar (hereditary) G11.9
with defective DNA repair G11.3
alcoholic G31.2
early-onset G11.1
in
alcoholism G31.2
myxedema E03.9 *[G13.2]*
neoplastic disease —*see also* Neoplasm D49.9 *[G32.81]*
specified disease NEC G32.81
late-onset (Marie's) G11.2
cerebral (hereditary) G11.9
congenital nonprogressive G11.0
family, familial —*see* Ataxia, hereditary
following
cerebrovascular disease I69.993
cerebral infarction I69.393
intracerebral hemorrhage I69.193
nontraumatic intracranial hemorrhage NEC I69.293
specified disease NEC I69.893
subarachnoid hemorrhage I69.093
Friedreich's (heredofamilial) (cerebellar) (spinal) G11.1
gait R26.0
hysterical F44.4
general R27.8
gluten M35.9 *[G32.81]*
with celiac disease K90.0 *[G32.81]*
hereditary G11.9
with neuropathy G60.2
cerebellar —*see* Ataxia, cerebellar
spastic G11.4
specified NEC G11.8
spinal (Friedreich's) G11.1
heredofamilial —*see* Ataxia, hereditary
Hunt's G11.1
hysterical F44.4

Ataxia, ataxy, ataxic *(Continued)*
locomotor (progressive) (syphilitic) (partial) (spastic) A52.11
diabetic —*see* Diabetes, ataxia
Marie's (cerebellar) (heredofamilial) (late- onset) G11.2
nonorganic origin F44.4
nonprogressive, congenital G11.0
psychogenic F44.4
Roussy-Lévy G60.0
Sanger-Brown's (hereditary) G11.2
spastic hereditary G11.4
spinal
hereditary (Friedreich's) G11.1
progressive (syphilitic) A52.11
spinocerebellar, X-linked recessive G11.1
telangiectasia (Louis-Bar) G11.3
Ataxia-telangiectasia (Louis-Bar) G11.3
Atelectasis (massive) (partial) (pressure) (pulmonary) J98.11
newborn P28.10
due to resorption P28.11
partial P28.19
primary P28.0
secondary P28.19
primary (newborn) P28.0
tuberculous —*see* Tuberculosis, pulmonary
Atelocardia Q24.9
Atelomyelia Q06.1
Atheroembolism
of
extremities
lower I75.02-●
upper I75.01-●
kidney I75.81
specified NEC I75.89
Atheroma, atheromatous —*see also*
Arteriosclerosis I70.90
aorta, aortic I70.0
valve —*see also* Endocarditis, aortic I35.8
aorto-iliac I70.0
artery —*see* Arteriosclerosis
basilar (artery) I67.2
carotid (artery) (common) (internal) I67.2
cerebral (arteries) I67.2
coronary (artery) I25.10
with angina pectoris —*see* Arteriosclerosis, coronary (artery)
degeneration —*see* Arteriosclerosis
heart, cardiac —*see* Disease, heart, ischemic, atherosclerotic
mitral (valve) I34.8
myocardium, myocardial —*see* Disease, heart, ischemic, atherosclerotic
pulmonary valve (heart) —*see also*
Endocarditis, pulmonary I37.8
tricuspid (heart) (valve) I36.8
valve, valvular —*see* Endocarditis
vertebral (artery) I67.2
Atheromatosis —*see* Arteriosclerosis
Atherosclerosis —*see also* Arteriosclerosis
coronary
artery I25.10
with angina pectoris —*see* Arteriosclerosis, coronary (artery), due to
calcified coronary lesion (severely) I25.84
lipid rich plaque I25.83
transplanted heart I25.811
bypass graft I25.812
with angina pectoris —*see* Arteriosclerosis, coronary (artery)
native coronary artery I25.811
with angina pectoris —*see* Arteriosclerosis, coronary (artery)
Athetosis (acquired) R25.8
bilateral (congenital) G80.3
congenital (bilateral) (double) G80.3
double (congenital) G80.3
unilateral R25.8

Athlete's
foot B35.3
heart I51.7
Athrepsia E41
Athyrea (acquired) —*see also* Hypothyroidism
congenital E03.1
Atonia, atony, atonic
bladder (sphincter) (neurogenic) N31.2
capillary I78.8
cecum K59.8
psychogenic F45.8
colon —*see* Atony, intestine
congenital P94.2
esophagus K22.8
intestine K59.8
psychogenic F45.8
stomach K31.89
neurotic or psychogenic F45.8
uterus (during labor) O62.2
with hemorrhage (postpartum) O72.1
postpartum (with hemorrhage) O72.1
without hemorrhage O75.89
Atopy —*see* History, allergy
Atransferrinemia, congenital E88.09
Atresia, atretic
alimentary organ or tract NEC Q45.8
upper Q40.8
ani, anus, anal (canal) Q42.3
with fistula Q42.2
aorta (ring) Q25.29
aortic (orifice) (valve) Q23.0
arch Q25.21
congenital with hypoplasia of ascending aorta and defective development of left ventricle (with mitral stenosis) Q23.4
in hypoplastic left heart syndrome Q23.4
aqueduct of Sylvius Q03.0
with spina bifida —*see* Spina bifida, with hydrocephalus
artery NEC Q27.8
cerebral Q28.3
coronary Q24.5
digestive system Q27.8
eye Q15.8
lower limb Q27.8
pulmonary Q25.5
specified site NEC Q27.8
umbilical Q27.0
upper limb Q27.8
auditory canal (external) Q16.1
bile duct (common) (congenital) (hepatic) Q44.2
acquired —*see* Obstruction, bile duct
bladder (neck) Q64.39
obstruction Q64.31
bronchus Q32.4
cecum Q42.8
cervix (acquired) N88.2
congenital Q51.828
in pregnancy or childbirth —*see* Anomaly, cervix, in pregnancy or childbirth
causing obstructed labor O65.5
choana Q30.0
colon Q42.9
specified NEC Q42.8
common duct Q44.2
cricoid cartilage Q31.8
cystic duct Q44.2
acquired K82.8
with obstruction K82.0
digestive organs NEC Q45.8
duodenum Q41.0
ear canal Q16.1
ejaculatory duct Q55.4
epiglottis Q31.8
esophagus Q39.0
with tracheoesophageal fistula Q39.1
eustachian tube Q17.8
fallopian tube (congenital) Q50.6
acquired N97.1

Atresia, atretic (Continued)
follicular cyst N83.0-●
foramen of
Luschka Q03.1
with spina bifida —see Spina bifida, with hydrocephalus
Magendie Q03.1
with spina bifida —see Spina bifida, with hydrocephalus
gallbladder Q44.1
genital organ
external
female Q52.79
male Q55.8
internal
female Q52.8
male Q55.8
glottis Q31.8
gullet Q39.0
with tracheoesophageal fistula Q39.1
heart valve NEC Q24.8
pulmonary Q22.0
tricuspid Q22.4
hymen Q52.3
acquired (postinfective) N89.6
ileum Q41.2
intestine (small) Q41.9
large Q42.9
specified NEC Q42.8
iris, filtration angle Q15.0
jejunum Q41.1
lacrimal apparatus Q10.4
larynx Q31.8
meatus urinarius Q64.33
mitral valve Q23.2
in hypoplastic left heart syndrome Q23.4
nares (anterior) (posterior) Q30.0
nasopharynx Q34.8
nose, nostril Q30.0
acquired J34.89
organ or site NEC Q89.8
osseous meatus (ear) Q16.1
oviduct (congenital) Q50.6
acquired N97.1
parotid duct Q38.4
acquired K11.8
pulmonary (artery) Q25.5
valve Q22.0
pulmonic Q22.0
pupil Q13.2
rectum Q42.1
with fistula Q42.0
salivary duct Q38.4
acquired K11.8
sublingual duct Q38.4
acquired K11.8
submandibular duct Q38.4
acquired K11.8
submaxillary duct Q38.4
acquired K11.8
thyroid cartilage Q31.8
trachea Q32.1
tricuspid valve Q22.4
ureter Q62.10
pelvic junction Q62.11
vesical orifice Q62.12
ureteropelvic junction Q62.11
ureterovesical orifice Q62.12
urethra (valvular) Q64.39
stricture Q64.32
urinary tract NEC Q64.8
uterus Q51.818
acquired N85.8
vagina (congenital) Q52.4
acquired (postinfectional) (senile) N89.5
vas deferens Q55.3
vascular NEC Q27.8
cerebral Q28.3
digestive system Q27.8

Atresia, atretic (Continued)
vascular NEC (Continued)
lower limb Q27.8
specified site NEC Q27.8
upper limb Q27.8
vein NEC Q27.8
digestive system Q27.8
great Q26.8
lower limb Q27.8
portal Q26.5
pulmonary Q26.4
partial Q26.3
total Q26.2
specified site NEC Q27.8
upper limb Q27.8
vena cava (inferior) (superior) Q26.8
vesicourethral orifice Q64.31
vulva Q52.79
acquired N90.5
Atrichia, atrichosis —see Alopecia
Atrophia —see also Atrophy
cutis senilis L90.8
due to radiation L57.8
gyrata of choroid and retina H31.23
senilis R54
dermatological L90.8
due to radiation (nonionizing) (solar) L57.8
unguium L60.3
congenita Q84.6
Atrophie blanche (en plaque) (de Milian) L95.0
Atrophoderma, atrophodermia (of) L90.9
diffusum (idiopathic) L90.4
maculatum L90.8
et striatum L90.8
due to syphilis A52.79
syphilitic A51.39
neuriticum L90.8
Pasini and Pierini L90.3
pigmentosum Q82.1
reticulatum symmetricum faciei L66.4
senile L90.8
due to radiation (nonionizing) (solar) L57.8
vermiculata (cheeks) L66.4
Atrophy, atrophic (of)
adrenal (capsule) (gland) E27.49
primary (autoimmune) E27.1
alveolar process or ridge (edentulous) K08.20
anal sphincter (disuse) N81.84
appendix K38.8
arteriosclerotic —see Arteriosclerosis
bile duct (common) (hepatic) K83.8
bladder N32.89
neurogenic N31.8
blanche (en plaque) (of Milian) L95.0
bone (senile) NEC —see also Disorder, bone, specified type NEC
due to
tabes dorsalis (neurogenic) A52.11
brain (cortex) (progressive) G31.9
frontotemporal circumscribed G31.01 [F02.80]
with behavioral disturbance G31.01 [F02.81]
senile NEC G31.1
breast N64.2
obstetric —see Disorder, breast, specified type NEC
buccal cavity K13.79
cardiac —see Degeneration, myocardial
cartilage (infectional) (joint) —see Disorder, cartilage, specified NEC
cerebellar —see Atrophy, brain
cerebral —see Atrophy, brain
cervix (mucosa) (senile) (uteri) N88.8
menopausal N95.8
Charcot-Marie-Tooth G60.0
choroid (central) (macular) (myopic) (retina) H31.10-●
diffuse secondary H31.12-●
gyrate H31.23
senile H31.11-●

Atrophy, atrophic (Continued)
ciliary body —see Atrophy, iris
conjunctiva (senile) H11.89
corpus cavernosum N48.89
cortical —see Atrophy, brain
cystic duct K82.8
Déjérine-Thomas G23.8
disuse NEC —see Atrophy, muscle
Duchenne-Aran G12.21
ear H93.8-●
edentulous alveolar ridge K08.20
endometrium (senile) N85.8
cervix N88.8
enteric K63.89
epididymis N50.89
eyeball —see Disorder, globe, degenerated condition, atrophy
eyelid (senile) —see Disorder, eyelid, degenerative
facial (skin) L90.9
fallopian tube (senile) N83.32-●
with ovary N83.33-●
➠ fascioscapulohumeral (Landouzy-Déjérine) G71.02
fatty, thymus (gland) E32.8
gallbladder K82.8
gastric K29.40
with bleeding K29.41
gastrointestinal K63.89
glandular I89.8
globe H44.52-●
gum —see Recession, gingival
hair L67.8
heart (brown) —see Degeneration, myocardial
hemifacial Q67.4
Romberg G51.8
infantile E41
paralysis, acute —see Poliomyelitis, paralytic
intestine K63.89
iris (essential) (progressive) H21.26-●
specified NEC H21.29
kidney (senile) (terminal) —see also Sclerosis, renal N26.1
congenital or infantile Q60.5
bilateral Q60.4
unilateral Q60.3
hydronephrotic —see Hydronephrosis
lacrimal gland (primary) H04.14-●
secondary H04.15-●
➠ Landouzy-Déjérine G71.02
laryngitis, infective J37.0
larynx J38.7
Leber's optic (hereditary) H47.22
lip K13.0
liver (yellow) K72.90
with coma K72.91
acute, subacute K72.00
with coma K72.01
chronic K72.10
with coma K72.11
lung (senile) J98.4
macular (dermatological) L90.8
syphilitic, skin A51.39
striated A52.79
mandible (edentulous) K08.20
minimal K08.21
moderate K08.22
severe K08.23
maxilla K08.20
minimal K08.24
moderate K08.25
severe K08.26
muscle, muscular (diffuse) (general) (idiopathic) (primary) M62.50
ankle M62.57-●
Duchenne-Aran G12.21
foot M62.57-●
forearm M62.53-●
hand M62.54-●
infantile spinal G12.0
lower leg M62.56-●

Atrophy, atrophic (Continued)
  muscle, muscular (Continued)
    multiple sites M62.59
    myelopathic —see Atrophy, muscle, spinal
    myotonic G71.11
    neuritic G58.9
    neuropathic (peroneal) (progressive) G60.0
    pelvic (disuse) N81.84
    peroneal G60.0
    progressive (bulbar) G12.21
      adult G12.1
      infantile (spinal) G12.0
      spinal G12.25
        adult G12.1
        infantile G12.0
    ⇒pseudohypertrophic G71.02
    shoulder region M62.51-●
    specified site NEC M62.58
    spinal G12.9
      adult form G12.1
      Aran-Duchenne G12.21
      childhood form, type II G12.1
      distal G12.1
      hereditary NEC G12.1
      infantile, type I (Werdnig-Hoffmann) G12.0
      juvenile form, type III (Kugelberg-Welander) G12.1
      progressive G12.25
      scapuloperoneal form G12.1
      specified NEC G12.8
    syphilitic A52.78
    thigh M62.55-●
    upper arm M62.52-●
  myocardium —see Degeneration, myocardial
  myometrium (senile) N85.8
    cervix N88.8
  myopathic NEC —see Atrophy, muscle
  myotonia G71.11
  nail L60.3
  nasopharynx J31.1
  nerve —see also Disorder, nerve
    abducens —see Strabismus, paralytic, sixth nerve
    accessory G52.8
    acoustic or auditory —see subcategory H93.3
    cranial G52.9
      eighth (auditory) —see subcategory H93.3
      eleventh (accessory) G52.8
      fifth (trigeminal) G50.8
      first (olfactory) G52.0
      fourth (trochlear) —see Strabismus, paralytic, fourth nerve
      second (optic) H47.20
      sixth (abducens) —see Strabismus, paralytic, sixth nerve
      tenth (pneumogastric) (vagus) G52.2
      third (oculomotor) —see Strabismus, paralytic, third nerve
      twelfth (hypoglossal) G52.3
    hypoglossal G52.3
    oculomotor —see Strabismus, paralytic, third nerve
    olfactory G52.0
    optic (papillomacular bundle)
      syphilitic (late) A52.15
        congenital A50.44
    pneumogastric G52.2
    trigeminal G50.8
    trochlear —see Strabismus, paralytic, fourth nerve
    vagus (pneumogastric) G52.2
  neurogenic, bone, tabetic A52.11
  nutritional E41
  old age R54
  olivopontocerebellar G23.8

Atrophy, atrophic (Continued)
  optic (nerve) H47.20
    glaucomatous H47.23-●
    hereditary H47.22
    primary H47.21-●
    specified type NEC H47.29-●
    syphilitic (late) A52.15
      congenital A50.44
  orbit H05.31-●
  ovary (senile) N83.31-●
    with fallopian tube N83.33-●
  oviduct (senile) —see Atrophy, fallopian tube
  palsy, diffuse (progressive) G12.22
  pancreas (duct) (senile) K86.89
  parotid gland K11.0
  pelvic muscle N81.84
  penis N48.89
  pharynx J39.2
  pluriglandular E31.8
    autoimmune E31.0
  polyarthritis M15.9
  prostate N42.89
  ⇒pseudohypertrophic (muscle) G71.02
  renal —see also Sclerosis, renal N26.1
  retina, retinal (postinfectional) H35.89
  rhinitis J31.0
  salivary gland K11.0
  scar L90.5
  sclerosis, lobar (of brain) G31.09 [F02.80]
    with behavioral disturbance G31.09 [F02.81]
  scrotum N50.89
  seminal vesicle N50.89
  senile R54
    due to radiation (nonionizing) (solar) L57.8
  skin (patches) (spots) L90.9
    degenerative (senile) L90.8
    due to radiation (nonionizing) (solar) L57.8
    senile L90.8
  spermatic cord N50.89
  spinal (acute) (cord) G95.89
    muscular —see Atrophy, muscle, spinal
    paralysis G12.20
      acute —see Poliomyelitis, paralytic
      meaning progressive muscular atrophy G12.21
  spine (column) —see Spondylopathy, specified NEC
  spleen (senile) D73.0
  stomach K29.40
    with bleeding K29.41
  striate (skin) L90.6
    syphilitic A52.79
  subcutaneous L90.9
  sublingual gland K11.0
  submandibular gland K11.0
  submaxillary gland K11.0
  Sudeck's —see Algoneurodystrophy
  suprarenal (capsule) (gland) E27.49
    primary E27.1
  systemic affecting central nervous system in
      myxedema E03.9 [G13.2]
      neoplastic disease —see also Neoplasm D49.9 [G13.1]
      specified disease NEC G13.8
  tarso-orbital fascia, congenital Q10.3
  testis N50.0
  thenar, partial —see Syndrome, carpal tunnel
  thymus (fatty) E32.8
  thyroid (gland) (acquired) E03.4
    with cretinism E03.1
    congenital (with myxedema) E03.1
  tongue (senile) K14.8
    papillae K14.4
  trachea J39.8
  tunica vaginalis N50.89
  turbinate J34.89
  tympanic membrane (nonflaccid) H73.82-●
    flaccid H73.81-●
  upper respiratory tract J39.8

Atrophy, atrophic (Continued)
  uterus, uterine (senile) N85.8
    cervix N88.8
    due to radiation (intended effect) N85.8
      adverse effect or misadventure N99.89
  vagina (senile) N95.2
  vas deferens N50.89
  vascular I99.8
  vertebra (senile) —see Spondylopathy, specified NEC
  vulva (senile) N90.5
  Werdnig-Hoffmann G12.0
  yellow —see Failure, hepatic
Attack, attacks
  with alteration of consciousness (with automatisms) —see Epilepsy, localization-related, symptomatic, with complex partial seizures
  without alteration of consciousness —see Epilepsy, localization-related, symptomatic, with simple partial seizures
  Adams-Stokes I45.9
  akinetic —see Epilepsy, generalized, specified NEC
  angina —see Angina
  atonic —see Epilepsy, generalized, specified NEC
  benign shuddering G25.83
  cataleptic —see Catalepsy
  coronary —see Infarct, myocardium
  cyanotic, newborn P28.2
  drop NEC R55
  epileptic —see Epilepsy
  heart —see infarct, myocardium
  hysterical F44.9
  jacksonian —see Epilepsy, localization-related, symptomatic, with simple partial seizures
  myocardium, myocardial —see Infarct, myocardium
  myoclonic —see Epilepsy, generalized, specified NEC
  panic F41.0
  psychomotor —see Epilepsy, localization-related, symptomatic, with complex partial seizures
  salaam —see Epilepsy, spasms
  schizophreniform, brief F23
  shuddering, benign G25.83
  Stokes-Adams I45.9
  syncope R55
  transient ischemic (TIA) G45.9
    specified NEC G45.8
  unconsciousness R55
    hysterical F44.89
  vasomotor R55
  vasovagal (paroxysmal) (idiopathic) R55
Attention (to)
  artificial
    opening (of) Z43.9
      digestive tract NEC Z43.4
        colon Z43.3
        ilium Z43.2
        stomach Z43.1
      specified NEC Z43.8
      trachea Z43.0
      urinary tract NEC Z43.6
        cystostomy Z43.5
        nephrostomy Z43.6
        ureterostomy Z43.6
        urethrostomy Z43.6
    vagina Z43.7
  colostomy Z43.3
  cystostomy Z43.5
  deficit disorder or syndrome F98.8
    with hyperactivity —see Disorder, attention-deficit hyperactivity
  gastrostomy Z43.1
  ileostomy Z43.2

▶ New ⇒ Revised ~~deleted~~ Deleted ● Use Additional Character(s)

Attention *(Continued)*
  jejunostomy Z43.4
  nephrostomy Z43.6
  surgical dressings Z48.01
  sutures Z48.02
  tracheostomy Z43.0
  ureterostomy Z43.6
  urethrostomy Z43.6
Attrition
  gum —*see* Recession, gingival
  tooth, teeth (excessive) (hard tissues) K03.0
Atypical, atypism —*see also* condition
  cells (on cytolgocial smear) (endocervical)
      (endometrial) (glandular)
    cervix R87.619
    vagina R87.629
  cervical N87.9
  endometrium N85.9
    hyperplasia N85.00
  parenting situation Z62.9
Auditory —*see* condition
Aujeszky's disease B33.8
Aurantiasis, cutis E67.1
Auricle, auricular —*see also* condition
  cervical Q18.2
Auriculotemporal syndrome G50.8
Austin Flint murmur (aortic insufficiency)
    I35.1
Australian
  Q fever A78
  X disease A83.4
Autism, autistic (childhood) (infantile) F84.0
  atypical F84.9
  spectrum disorder F84.0
Autodigestion R68.89
Autoerythrocyte sensitization (syndrome)
    D69.2
Autographism L50.3
Autoimmune
  disease (systemic) M35.9
  inhibitors to clotting factors D68.311
  lymphoproliferative syndrome [ALPS]
      D89.82
  thyroiditis E06.3
Autointoxication R68.89
Automatism G93.89
  with temporal sclerosis G93.81
  epileptic —*see* Epilepsy, localization- related,
      symptomatic, with complex partial
      seizures

Automatism *(Continued)*
  paroxysmal, idiopathic —*see* Epilepsy,
      localization-related, symptomatic, with
      complex partial seizures
Autonomic, autonomous
  bladder (neurogenic) N31.2
  hysteria seizure F44.5
Autosensitivity, erythrocyte D69.2
Autosensitization, cutaneous L30.2
Autosome —*see* condition by chromosome
    involved
Autotopagnosia R48.1
Autotoxemia R68.89
Autumn —*see* condition
Avellis' syndrome G46.8
Aversion
  oral R63.3
    newborn P92.-●
    nonorganic origin F98.2
  sexual F52.1
Aviator's
  disease or sickness —*see* Effect, adverse, high
      altitude
  ear T70.0
Avitaminosis (multiple) —*see also* Deficiency,
    vitamin E56.9
  B E53.9
    with
      beriberi E51.11
      pellagra E52
  B2 E53.0
  B6 E53.1
  B12 E53.8
  D E55.9
    with rickets E55.0
  G E53.0
  K E56.1
  nicotinic acid E52
AVNRT (atrioventricular nodal re-entrant
    tachycardia) I47.1
AVRT (atrioventricular nodal re-entrant
    tachycardia) I47.1
Avulsion (traumatic)
  blood vessel —*see* Injury, blood vessel
  bone —*see* Fracture, by site
  cartilage —*see also* Dislocation, by site
    symphyseal (inner), complicating delivery
        O71.6
  external site other than limb —*see* Wound,
      open, by site

Avulsion *(Continued)*
  eye S05.7-●
  head (intracranial)
    external site NEC S08.89
    scalp S08.0
  internal organ or site —*see* Injury, by site
  joint —*see also* Dislocation, by site
    capsule —*see* Sprain, by site
  kidney S37.06-●
  ligament —*see* Sprain, by site
  limb —*see also* Amputation, traumatic,
      by site
    skin and subcutaneous tissue —*see* Wound,
        open, by site
  muscle —*see* Injury, muscle
  nerve (root) —*see* Injury, nerve
  scalp S08.0
  skin and subcutaneous tissue —*see* Wound,
      open, by site
  spleen S36.032
  symphyseal cartilage (inner), complicating
      delivery O71.6
  tendon —*see* Injury, muscle
  tooth S03.2
Awareness of heart beat R00.2
Axenfeld's
  anomaly or syndrome Q15.0
  degeneration (calcareous) Q13.4
Axilla, axillary —*see also* condition
  breast Q83.1
Axonotmesis —*see* Injury, nerve
Ayerza's disease or syndrome (pulmonary
    artery sclerosis with pulmonary
    hypertension) I27.0
Azoospermia (organic) N46.01
  due to
    drug therapy N46.021
    efferent duct obstruction N46.023
    infection N46.022
    radiation N46.024
    specified cause NEC N46.029
    systemic disease N46.025
Azotemia R79.89
  meaning uremia N19
Aztec ear Q17.3
Azygos
  continuation inferior vena cava Q26.8
  lobe (lung) Q33.1

A

B

Baastrup's disease —see Kissing spine
Babesiosis B60.0
Babington's disease (familial hemorrhagic
 telangiectasia) I78.0
Babinski's syndrome A52.79
Baby
 crying constantly R68.11
 floppy (syndrome) P94.2
Bacillary —see condition
Bacilluria R82.71
Bacillus —see also Infection, bacillus
 abortus infection A23.1
 anthracis infection A22.9
 coli infection —see also Escherichia coli B96.20
 Flexner's A03.1
 mallei infection A24.0
 Shiga's A03.0
 suipestifer infection —see Infection,
  salmonella
Back —see condition
Backache (postural) M54.9
 sacroiliac M53.3
 specified NEC M54.89
Backflow —see Reflux
Backward reading (dyslexia) F81.0
Bacteremia R78.81
 with sepsis —see Sepsis
Bactericholia —see Cholecystitis, acute
Bacterid, bacteride (pustular) L40.3
Bacterium, bacteria, bacterial
 agent NEC, as cause of disease classified
  elsewhere B96.89
 in blood —see Bacteremia
 in urine —see Bacteriuria
Bacteriuria, bacteruria R82.71
 asymptomatic R82.71
Bacteroides
 fragilis, as cause of disease classified
  elsewhere B96.6
Bad
 heart —see Disease, heart
 trip
  due to drug abuse —see Abuse, drug,
   hallucinogen
  due to drug dependence —see Dependence,
   drug, hallucinogen
Baelz's disease (cheilitis glandularis
 apostematosa) K13.0
Baerensprung's disease (eczema marginatum)
 B35.6
Bagasse disease or pneumonitis J67.1
Bagassosis J67.1
Baker's cyst —see Cyst, Baker's
Bakwin-Krida syndrome (metaphyseal
 dysplasia) Q78.5
Balancing side interference M26.56
Balanitis (circinata) (erosiva) (gangrenosa)
 (phagedenic) (vulgaris) N48.1
 amebic A06.82
 candidal B37.42
 due to Haemophilus ducreyi A57
 ➡gonococcal (acute) (chronic) A54.23
 xerotica obliterans N48.0
Balanoposthitis N47.6
 ➡gonococcal (acute) (chronic) A54.23
 ulcerative (specific) A63.8
Balanorrhagia —see Balanitis
Balantidiasis, balantidiosis A07.0
Bald tongue K14.4
Baldness —see also Alopecia
 male-pattern —see Alopecia, androgenic
Balkan grippe A78
Balloon disease —see Effect, adverse, high
 altitude
Balo's disease (concentric sclerosis) G37.5
Bamberger-Marie disease —see
 Osteoarthropathy, hypertrophic, specified
 type NEC
Bancroft's filariasis B74.0

Band(s)
 adhesive —see Adhesions, peritoneum
 anomalous or congenital —see also Anomaly,
  by site
  heart (atrial) (ventricular) Q24.8
  intestine Q43.3
  omentum Q43.3
 cervix N88.1
 constricting, congenital Q79.8
 gallbladder (congenital) Q44.1
 intestinal (adhesive) —see Adhesions,
  peritoneum
 obstructive
  intestine K56.50
   complete K56.52
   incomplete K56.51
   partial K56.51
  peritoneum K56.50
   complete K56.52
   incomplete K56.51
   partial K56.51
 periappendiceal, congenital Q43.3
 peritoneal (adhesive) —see Adhesions,
  peritoneum
 uterus N73.6
  internal N85.6
 vagina N89.5
Bandemia D72.825
Bandl's ring (contraction), complicating
 delivery O62.4
Bangkok hemorrhagic fever A91
Bang's disease (brucella abortus) A23.1
Bankruptcy, anxiety concerning Z59.8
Bannister's disease T78.3
 hereditary D84.1
Banti's disease or syndrome (with cirrhosis)
 (with portal hypertension) K76.6
Bar, median, prostate —see Enlargement,
 enlarged, prostate
Barcoo disease or rot —see Ulcer, skin
Barlow's disease E54
Barodontalgia T70.29
Baron Münchausen syndrome —see Disorder,
 factitious
Barosinusitis T70.1
Barotitis T70.0
Barotrauma T70.29
 odontalgia T70.29
 otitic T70.0
 sinus T70.1
Barraquer (-Simons) disease or syndrome
 (progressive lipodystrophy) E88.1
Barré-Guillain disease or syndrome G61.0
Barré-Liéou syndrome (posterior cervical
 sympathetic) M53.0
Barrel chest M95.4
Barrett's
 disease —see Barrett's, esophagus
 esophagus K22.70
  with dysplasia K22.719
   high grade K22.711
   low grade K22.710
  without dysplasia K22.70
 syndrome —see Barrett's, esophagus
 ulcer K22.10
  with bleeding K22.11
  without bleeding K22.10
Barth syndrome E78.71
Bársony (-Polgár) (-Teschendorf) syndrome
 (corkscrew esophagus) K22.4
Bartholinitis (suppurating) N75.8
 gonococcal (acute) (chronic) (with abscess)
  A54.1
Bartonellosis A44.9
 cutaneous A44.1
 mucocutaneous A44.1
 specified NEC A44.8
 systemic A44.0
Barton's fracture S52.56-●
Bartter's syndrome E26.81
Basal —see condition

Basan's (hidrotic) ectodermal dysplasia Q82.4
Baseball finger —see Dislocation, finger
Basedow's disease (exophthalmic goiter) —see
 Hyperthyroidism, with, goiter
Basic —see condition
Basilar —see condition
Bason's (hidrotic) ectodermal dysplasia Q82.4
Basopenia —see Agranulocytosis
Basophilia D72.824
Basophilism (cortico-adrenal) (Cushing's)
 (pituitary) E24.0
Bassen-Kornzweig disease or syndrome E78.6
Bat ear Q17.5
Bateman's
 disease B08.1
 purpura (senile) D69.2
Bathing cramp T75.1
Bathophobia F40.248
Batten (-Mayou) disease E75.4
 retina E75.4 [H36]
Batten-Steinert syndrome G71.11
Battered —see Maltreatment
Battey Mycobacterium infection A31.0
Battle exhaustion F43.0
Battledore placenta O43.19-●
Baumgarten-Cruveilhier cirrhosis, disease or
 syndrome K74.69
Bauxite fibrosis (of lung) J63.1
Bayle's disease (general paresis) A52.17
Bazin's disease (primary) (tuberculous) A18.4
Beach ear —see Swimmer's, ear
Beaded hair (congenital) Q84.1
Béal conjunctivitis or syndrome B30.2
Beard's disease (neurasthenia) F48.8
Beat(s)
 atrial, premature I49.1
 ectopic I49.49
 elbow —see Bursitis, elbow
 escaped, heart I49.49
 hand —see Bursitis, hand
 knee —see Bursitis, knee
 premature I49.40
  atrial I49.1
  auricular I49.1
  supraventricular I49.1
Beau's
 disease or syndrome —see Degeneration,
  myocardial
 lines (transverse furrows on fingernails) L60.4
Bechterev's syndrome —see Spondylitis,
 ankylosing
Beck's syndrome (anterior spinal artery
 occlusion) I65.8
Becker's
 cardiomyopathy I42.8
 disease
  idiopathic mural endomyocardial disease
   I42.3
  myotonia congenita, recessive form G71.12
 ➡dystrophy G71.01
 pigmented hairy nevus D22.5
Beckwith-Wiedemann syndrome Q87.3
Bed confinement status Z74.01
Bed sore —see Ulcer, pressure, by site
Bedbug bite(s) —see Bite(s), by site, superficial,
 insect
Bedclothes, asphyxiation or suffocation
 by —see Asphyxia, traumatic, due to,
  mechanical, trapped
Bednar's
 aphthae K12.0
 tumor —see Neoplasm, malignant, by site
Bedridden Z74.01
Bedsore —see Ulcer, pressure, by site
Bedwetting —see Enuresis
Bee sting (with allergic or anaphylactic
 shock) —see Toxicity, venom, arthropod,
 bee
Bee drinker's heart (disease) I42.6
Begbie's disease (exophthalmic goiter) —see
 Hyperthyroidism, with, goiter

  ▶ New   ➡ Revised   ~~deleted~~ Deleted   ● Use Additional Character(s)

Behavior
  antisocial
    adult Z72.811
    child or adolescent Z72.810
  disorder, disturbance —*see* Disorder, conduct
  disruptive —*see* Disorder, conduct
  drug seeking Z76.5
  inexplicable R46.2
  marked evasiveness R46.5
  obsessive-compulsive R46.81
  overactivity R46.3
  poor responsiveness R46.4
  self-damaging (life-style) Z72.89
  sleep-incompatible Z72.821
  slowness R46.4
  specified NEC R46.89
  strange (and inexplicable) R46.2
  suspiciousness R46.5
  type A pattern Z73.1
  undue concern or preoccupation with
    stressful events R46.6
  verbosity and circumstantial detail obscuring
    reason for contact R46.7
Behcet's disease or syndrome M35.2
Behr's disease —*see* Degeneration, macula
Beigel's disease or morbus (white piedra)
  B36.2
Bejel A65
Bekhterev's syndrome —*see* Spondylitis,
  ankylosing
Belching —*see* Eructation
Bell's
  mania F30.8
  palsy, paralysis G51.0
    infant or newborn P11.3
▶ spasm G51.3-●
Bence Jones albuminuria or proteinuria NEC
  R80.3
Bends T70.3
Benedikt's paralysis or syndrome G46.3
Benign (*see also* condition)
  prostatic hyperplasia —*see* Hyperplasia,
    prostate
Bennett's fracture (displaced) S62.21-●
Benson's disease —*see* Deposit, crystalline
Bent
  back (hysterical) F44.4
  nose M95.0
    congenital Q67.4
Bereavement (uncomplicated) Z63.4
Bergeron's disease (hysterical chorea) F44.4
Berger's disease —*see* Nephropathy, IgA
Beriberi (dry) E51.11
  heart (disease) E51.12
  polyneuropathy E51.11
  wet E51.12
    involving circulatory system E51.11
Berlin's disease or edema (traumatic) S05.8X-●
Berlock (berloque) dermatitis L56.2
Bernard-Horner syndrome G90.2
Bernard-Soulier disease or thrombopathia
  D69.1
Bernhardt (-Roth) disease —*see*
  Mononeuropathy, lower limb, meralgia
  paresthetica
Bernheim's syndrome —*see* Failure, heart,
  right
Bertielliasis B71.8
Berylliosis (lung) J63.2
Besnier-Boeck (-Schaumann) disease —*see*
  Sarcoidosis
Besnier's
  lupus pernio D86.3
  prurigo L20.0
Bestiality F65.89
Best's disease H35.50
Beta-mercaptolactate-cysteine disulfiduria
  E72.09
Betalipoproteinemia, broad or floating E78.2
Betting and gambling Z72.6
  pathological (compulsive) F63.0

Bezoar T18.9
  intestine T18.3
  stomach T18.2
Bezold's abscess —*see* Mastoiditis, acute
Bianchi's syndrome R48.8
Bicornate or bicornis uterus Q51.3
  in pregnancy or childbirth O34.00
    causing obstructed labor O65.5
Bicuspid aortic valve Q23.1
Biedl-Bardet syndrome Q87.89
Bielschowsky (-Jansky) disease E75.4
Biermer's (pernicious) anemia or disease D51.0
Biett's disease L93.0
Bifid (congenital)
  apex, heart Q24.8
  clitoris Q52.6
  kidney Q63.8
  nose Q30.2
  patella Q74.1
  scrotum Q55.29
  toe NEC Q74.2
  tongue Q38.3
  ureter Q62.8
  uterus Q51.3
  uvula Q35.7
Biforis uterus (suprasimplex) Q51.3
Bifurcation (congenital)
  gallbladder Q44.1
  kidney pelvis Q63.8
  renal pelvis Q63.8
  rib Q76.6
  tongue, congenital Q38.3
  trachea Q32.1
  ureter Q62.8
  urethra Q64.74
  vertebra Q76.49
Big spleen syndrome D73.1
Bigeminal pulse R00.8
Bilateral —*see* condition
Bile
  duct —*see* condition
  pigments in urine R82.2
Bilharziasis —*see also* Schistosomiasis
  chyluria B65.0
  cutaneous B65.3
  galacturia B65.0
  hematochyluria B65.0
  intestinal B65.1
  lipemia B65.9
  lipuria B65.0
  oriental B65.2
  piarhemia B65.9
  pulmonary NOS B65.9 [J99]
    pneumonia B65.9 [J17]
  tropical hematuria B65.0
  vesical B65.0
Biliary —*see* condition
Bilirubin metabolism disorder E80.7
  specified NEC E80.6
Bilirubinemia, familial nonhemolytic E80.4
Bilirubinuria R82.2
Biliuria R82.2
Bilocular stomach K31.2
Binswanger's disease I67.3
Biparta, bipartite
  carpal scaphoid Q74.0
  patella Q74.1
  vagina Q52.10
Bird
  face Q75.8
  fancier's disease or lung J67.2
Birt-Hogg-Dube syndrome Q87.89
Birth
  complications in mother —*see* Delivery,
    complicated
  compression during NOS P15.9
  defect —*see* Anomaly
  immature (less than 37 completed weeks) —
    see Preterm, newborn
    extremely (less than 28 completed
      weeks) —*see* Immaturity, extreme

Birth (*Continued*)
  inattention, at or after —*see* Maltreatment,
    child, neglect
  injury NOS P15.9
    basal ganglia P11.1
    brachial plexus NEC P14.3
    brain (compression) (pressure) P11.2
    central nervous system NOS P11.9
    cerebellum P11.1
    cerebral hemorrhage P10.1
    external genitalia P15.5
    eye P15.3
    face P15.4
    fracture
      bone P13.9
        specified NEC P13.8
      clavicle P13.4
      femur P13.2
      humerus P13.3
      long bone, except femur P13.3
      radius and ulna P13.3
      skull P13.0
      spine P11.5
      tibia and fibula P13.3
    intracranial P11.2
      laceration or hemorrhage P10.9
        specified NEC P10.8
    intraventricular hemorrhage P10.2
    laceration
      brain P10.1
      by scalpel P15.8
      peripheral nerve P14.9
    liver P15.0
    meninges
      brain P11.1
      spinal cord P11.5
    nerve
      brachial plexus P14.3
      cranial NEC (except facial) P11.4
      facial P11.3
      peripheral P14.9
      phrenic (paralysis) P14.2
    paralysis
      facial nerve P11.3
      spinal P11.5
    penis P15.5
    rupture
      spinal cord P11.5
    scalp P12.9
    scalpel wound P15.8
    scrotum P15.5
    skull NEC P13.1
      fracture P13.0
    specified type NEC P15.8
    spinal cord P11.5
    spine P11.5
    spleen P15.1
    sternomastoid (hematoma) P15.2
    subarachnoid hemorrhage P10.3
    subcutaneous fat necrosis P15.6
    subdural hemorrhage P10.0
    tentorial tear P10.4
    testes P15.5
    vulva P15.5
  lack of care, at or after —*see* Maltreatment,
    child, neglect
  neglect, at or after —*see* Maltreatment, child,
    neglect
  palsy or paralysis, newborn, NOS (birth
    injury) P14.9
  premature (infant) —*see* Preterm, newborn
  shock, newborn P96.89
  trauma —*see* Birth, injury
  weight
    4000 grams to 4499 grams P08.1
    4500 grams or more P08.0
    low (2499 grams or less) —*see* Low,
      birthweight
      extremely (999 grams or less) —*see* Low,
        birthweight, extreme
Birthmark Q82.5

Bisalbuminemia E88.09
Biskra's button B55.1
Bite(s) (animal) (human)
  abdomen, abdominal
    wall S31.159
      with penetration into peritoneal cavity
        S31.659
      epigastric region S31.152
        with penetration into peritoneal cavity
          S31.652
      left
        lower quadrant S31.154
          with penetration into peritoneal
            cavity S31.654
        upper quadrant S31.151
          with penetration into peritoneal
            cavity S31.651
      periumbilic region S31.155
        with penetration into peritoneal cavity
          S31.655
      right
        lower quadrant S31.153
          with penetration into peritoneal
            cavity S31.653
        upper quadrant S31.150
          with penetration into peritoneal
            cavity S31.650
      superficial NEC S30.871
        insect S30.861
  alveolar (process) —*see* Bite, oral cavity
  amphibian (venomous) —*see* Venom, bite,
    amphibian
  animal —*see also* Bite, by site
    venomous —*see* Venom
  ankle S91.05-●
    superficial NEC S90.57-●
      insect S90.56-●
  antecubital space —*see* Bite, elbow
  anus S31.835
    superficial NEC S30.877
      insect S30.867
  arm (upper) S41.15-●
    lower —*see* Bite, forearm
    superficial NEC S40.87-●
      insect S40.86-●
  arthropod NEC —*see* Venom, bite, arthropod
  auditory canal (external) (meatus) —
    see Bite, ear
  auricle, ear —*see* Bite, ear
  axilla —*see* Bite, arm
  back —*see also* Bite, thorax, back
    lower S31.050
      with penetration into retroperitoneal
        space S31.051
      superficial NEC S30.870
        insect S30.860
  bedbug —*see* Bite(s), by site, superficial,
    insect
  breast S21.05-●
    superficial NEC S20.17-●
      insect S20.16-●
  brow —*see* Bite, head, specified site NEC
  buttock S31.805
    left S31.825
    right S31.815
    superficial NEC S30.870
      insect S30.860
  calf —*see* Bite, leg
  canaliculus lacrimalis —*see* Bite, eyelid
  canthus, eye —*see* Bite, eyelid
  centipede —*see* Toxicity, venom, arthropod,
    centipede
  cheek (external) S01.45-●
    internal —*see* Bite, oral cavity
    superficial NEC S00.87
      insect S00.86
  chest wall —*see* Bite, thorax
  chigger B88.0
  chin —*see* Bite, head, specified site NEC
  clitoris —*see* Bite, vulva
  costal region —*see* Bite, thorax

Bite *(Continued)*
  digit(s)
    hand —*see* Bite, finger
    toe —*see* Bite, toe
  ear (canal) (external) S01.35-●
    superficial NEC S00.47-●
      insect S00.46-●
  elbow S51.05-●
    superficial NEC S50.37-●
      insect S50.36-●
  epididymis —*see* Bite, testis
  epigastric region —*see* Bite, abdomen
  epiglottis —*see* Bite, neck, specified site
    NEC
  esophagus, cervical S11.25
    superficial NEC S10.17
      insect S10.16
  eyebrow —*see* Bite, eyelid
  eyelid S01.15-●
    superficial NEC S00.27-●
      insect S00.26-●
  face NEC —*see* Bite, head, specified site
    NEC
  finger(s) S61.259
    with
      damage to nail S61.359
    index S61.258
      with
        damage to nail S61.358
      left S61.251
        with
          damage to nail S61.351
      right S61.250
        with
          damage to nail S61.350
      superficial NEC S60.478
        insect S60.46-●
    little S61.25-●
      with
        damage to nail S61.35-●
      superficial NEC S60.47-●
        insect S60.46-●
    middle S61.25-●
      with
        damage to nail S61.35-●
      superficial NEC S60.47-●
        insect S60.46-●
    ring S61.25-●
      with
        damage to nail S61.35-●
      superficial NEC S60.47-●
        insect S60.46-●
    superficial NEC S60.479
      insect S60.469
    thumb —*see* Bite, thumb
  flank —*see* Bite, abdomen, wall
  flea —*see* Bite, by site, superficial,
    insect
  foot (except toe(s) alone) S91.35-●
    superficial NEC S90.87-●
      insect S90.86-●
    toe —*see* Bite, toe
  forearm S51.85-●
    elbow only —*see* Bite, elbow
    superficial NEC S50.87-●
      insect S50.86-●
  forehead —*see* Bite, head, specified site
    NEC
  genital organs, external
    female S31.552
      superficial NEC S30.876
        insect S30.866
      vagina and vulva —*see* Bite, vulva
    male S31.551
      penis —*see* Bite, penis
      scrotum —*see* Bite, scrotum
      superficial NEC S30.875
        insect S30.865
      testes —*see* Bite, testis
  groin —*see* Bite, abdomen, wall
  gum —*see* Bite, oral cavity

Bite *(Continued)*
  hand S61.45-●
    finger —*see* Bite, finger
    superficial NEC S60.57-●
      insect S60.56-●
    thumb —*see* Bite, thumb
  head S01.95
    cheek —*see* Bite, cheek
    ear —*see* Bite, ear
    eyelid —*see* Bite, eyelid
    lip —*see* Bite, lip
    nose —*see* Bite, nose
    oral cavity —*see* Bite, oral cavity
    scalp —*see* Bite, scalp
    specified site NEC S01.85
      superficial NEC S00.87
        insect S00.86
    superficial NEC S00.97
      insect S00.96
    temporomandibular area —*see* Bite, cheek
  heel —*see* Bite, foot
  hip S71.05-●
    superficial NEC S70.27-●
      insect S70.26-●
  hymen S31.45
  hypochondrium —*see* Bite, abdomen, wall
  hypogastric region —*see* Bite, abdomen, wall
  inguinal region —*see* Bite, abdomen, wall
  insect —*see* Bite, by site, superficial, insect
  instep —*see* Bite, foot
  interscapular region —*see* Bite, thorax, back
  jaw —*see* Bite, head, specified site NEC
  knee S81.05-●
    superficial NEC S80.27-●
      insect S80.26-●
  labium (majus) (minus) —*see* Bite, vulva
  lacrimal duct —*see* Bite, eyelid
  larynx S11.015
    superficial NEC S10.17
      insect S10.16
  leg (lower) S81.85-●
    ankle —*see* Bite, ankle
    foot —*see* Bite, foot
    knee —*see* Bite, knee
    superficial NEC S80.87-●
      insect S80.86-●
    toe —*see* Bite, toe
    upper —*see* Bite, thigh
  lip S01.551
    superficial NEC S00.571
      insect S00.561
  lizard (venomous) —*see* Venom, bite, reptile
  loin —*see* Bite, abdomen, wall
  lower back —*see* Bite, back, lower
  lumbar region —*see* Bite, back, lower
  malar region —*see* Bite, head, specified site
    NEC
  mammary —*see* Bite, breast
  marine animals (venomous) —*see* Toxicity,
    venom, marine animal
  mastoid region —*see* Bite, head, specified site
    NEC
  mouth —*see* Bite, oral cavity
  nail
    finger —*see* Bite, finger
    toe —*see* Bite, toe
  nape —*see* Bite, neck, specified site NEC
  nasal (septum) (sinus) —*see* Bite, nose
  nasopharynx —*see* Bite, head, specified site
    NEC
  neck S11.95
    involving
      cervical esophagus —*see* Bite,
        esophagus, cervical
      larynx —*see* Bite, larynx
      pharynx —*see* Bite, pharynx
      thyroid gland S11.15
      trachea —*see* Bite, trachea
    specified site NEC S11.85
      superficial NEC S10.87
        insect S10.86

▶ New   ⇒ Revised   ~~deleted~~ Deleted   ● Use Additional Character(s)

Bite *(Continued)*
  neck *(Continued)*
    superficial NEC S10.97
      insect S10.96
    throat S11.85
      superficial NEC S10.17
        insect S10.16
  nose (septum) (sinus) S01.25
    superficial NEC S00.37
      insect S00.36
  occipital region —*see* Bite, scalp
  oral cavity S01.552
    superficial NEC S00.572
      insect S00.562
  orbital region —*see* Bite, eyelid
  palate —*see* Bite, oral cavity
  palm —*see* Bite, hand
  parietal region —*see* Bite, scalp
  pelvis S31.050
    with penetration into retroperitoneal space S31.051
    superficial NEC S30.870
      insect S30.860
  penis S31.25
    superficial NEC S30.872
      insect S30.862
  perineum
    female —*see* Bite, vulva
    male —*see* Bite, pelvis
  periocular area (with or without lacrimal passages) —*see* Bite, eyelid
  phalanges
    finger —*see* Bite, finger
    toe —*see* Bite, toe
  pharynx S11.25
    superficial NEC S10.17
      insect S10.16
  pinna —*see* Bite, ear
  poisonous —*see* Venom
  popliteal space —*see* Bite, knee
  prepuce —*see* Bite, penis
  pubic region —*see* Bite, abdomen, wall
  rectovaginal septum —*see* Bite, vulva
  red bug B88.0
  reptile NEC —*see also* Venom, bite, reptile
    nonvenomous —*see* Bite, by site
    snake —*see* Venom, bite, snake
  sacral region —*see* Bite, back, lower
  sacroiliac region —*see* Bite, back, lower
  salivary gland —*see* Bite, oral cavity
  scalp S01.05
    superficial NEC S00.07
      insect S00.06
  scapular region —*see* Bite, shoulder
  scrotum S31.35
    superficial NEC S30.873
      insect S30.863
  sea-snake (venomous) —*see* Toxicity, venom, snake, sea snake
  shin —*see* Bite, leg
  shoulder S41.05-●
    superficial NEC S40.27-●
      insect S40.26-●
  snake —*see also* Venom, bite, snake
    nonvenomous —*see* Bite, by site
  spermatic cord —*see* Bite, testis
  spider (venomous) —*see* Toxicity, venom, spider
    nonvenomous —*see* Bite, by site, superficial, insect
  sternal region —*see* Bite, thorax, front
  submaxillary region —*see* Bite, head, specified site NEC
  submental region —*see* Bite, head, specified site NEC
  subungual
    finger(s) —*see* Bite, finger
    toe —*see* Bite, toe
  superficial —*see* Bite, by site, superficial
  supraclavicular fossa S11.85

Bite *(Continued)*
  supraorbital —*see* Bite, head, specified site NEC
  temple, temporal region —*see* Bite, head, specified site NEC
  temporomandibular area —*see* Bite, cheek
  testis S31.35
    superficial NEC S30.873
      insect S30.863
  thigh S71.15-●
    superficial NEC S70.37-●
      insect S70.36-●
  thorax, thoracic (wall) S21.95
    back S21.25-●
      with penetration into thoracic cavity S21.45-●
    breast —*see* Bite, breast
    front S21.15-●
      with penetration into thoracic cavity S21.35-●
    superficial NEC S20.97
      back S20.47-●
      front S20.37-●
      insect S20.96
        back S20.46-●
        front S20.36-●
  throat —*see* Bite, neck, throat
  thumb S61.05-●
    with
      damage to nail S61.15-●
    superficial NEC S60.37-●
      insect S60.36-●
  thyroid S11.15
    superficial NEC S10.87
      insect S10.86
  toe(s) S91.15-●
    with
      damage to nail S91.25-●
    great S91.15-●
      with
        damage to nail S91.25-●
    lesser S91.15-●
      with
        damage to nail S91.25-●
    superficial NEC S90.47-●
      great S90.47-●
      insect S90.46-●
        great S90.46-●
  tongue S01.552
  trachea S11.025
    superficial NEC S10.17
      insect S10.16
  tunica vaginalis —*see* Bite, testis
  tympanum, tympanic membrane —*see* Bite, ear
  umbilical region S31.155
  uvula —*see* Bite, oral cavity
  vagina —*see* Bite, vulva
  venomous —*see* Venom
  vocal cords S11.035
    superficial NEC S10.17
      insect S10.16
  vulva S31.45
    superficial NEC S30.874
      insect S30.864
  wrist S61.55-●
    superficial NEC S60.87-●
      insect S60.86-●
Biting, cheek or lip K13.1
Biventricular failure (heart) I50.82
Björck (-Thorson) syndrome (malignant carcinoid) E34.0
Black
  death A20.9
  eye S00.1-●
  hairy tongue K14.3
  heel (foot) S90.3-●
  lung (disease) J60
  palm (hand) S60.22-●
Blackfan-Diamond anemia or syndrome (congenital hypoplastic anemia) D61.01

Blackhead L70.0
Blackout R55
Bladder —*see* condition
Blast (air) (hydraulic) (immersion) (underwater)
  blindness S05.8X-●
  injury
    abdomen or thorax —*see* Injury, by site
    ear (acoustic nerve trauma) —*see* Injury, nerve, acoustic, specified type NEC
    syndrome NEC T70.8
Blastoma —*see* Neoplasm, malignant, by site
  pulmonary —*see* Neoplasm, lung, malignant
Blastomycosis, blastomycotic B40.9
  Brazilian —*see* Paracoccidioidomycosis
  cutaneous B40.3
  disseminated B40.7
  European —*see* Cryptococcosis
  generalized B40.7
  keloidal B48.0
  North American B40.9
  primary pulmonary B40.0
  pulmonary B40.2
    acute B40.0
    chronic B40.1
  skin B40.3
  South American —*see* Paracoccidioidomycosis
  specified NEC B40.89
Bleb(s) R23.8
  emphysematous (lung) (solitary) J43.9
  endophthalmitis H59.43
  filtering (vitreous), after glaucoma surgery Z98.83
  inflamed (infected), postprocedural H59.40
    stage 1 H59.41
    stage 2 H59.42
    stage 3 H59.43
  lung (ruptured) J43.9
    congenital —*see* Atelectasis
    newborn P25.8
  subpleural (emphysematous) J43.9
Blebitis, postprocedural H59.40
  stage 1 H59.41
  stage 2 H59.42
  stage 3 H59.43
Bleeder (familial) (hereditary) —*see* Hemophilia
Bleeding —*see also* Hemorrhage
  anal K62.5
  anovulatory N97.0
  atonic, following delivery O72.1
  capillary I78.8
    puerperal O72.2
  contact (postcoital) N93.0
  due to uterine subinvolution N85.3
  ear —*see* Otorrhagia
  excessive, associated with menopausal onset N92.4
  familial —*see* Defect, coagulation
  following intercourse N93.0
  gastrointestinal K92.2
  hemorrhoids —*see* Hemorrhoids
  intermenstrual (regular) N92.3
    irregular N92.1
  intraoperative —*see* Complication, intraoperative, hemorrhage
  irregular N92.6
  menopausal N92.4
  newborn, intraventricular —*see* Newborn, affected by, hemorrhage, intraventricular
  nipple N64.59
  nose R04.0
  ovulation N92.3
  postclimacteric N95.0
  postcoital N93.0
  postmenopausal N95.0
  postoperative —*see* Complication, postprocedural, hemorrhage
  preclimacteric N92.4
  pre-pubertal vaginal N93.1
  puberty (excessive, with onset of menstrual periods) N92.2

Bleeding *(Continued)*
  rectum, rectal K62.5
    newborn P54.2
  tendencies —*see* Defect, coagulation
  throat R04.1
  tooth socket (post-extraction) K91.840
  umbilical stump P51.9
  uterus, uterine NEC N93.9
    climacteric N92.4
    dysfunctional or functional N93.8
    menopausal N92.4
    preclimacteric or premenopausal N92.4
    unrelated to menstrual cycle N93.9
  vagina, vaginal (abnormal) N93.9
    dysfunctional or functional N93.8
    newborn P54.6
    pre-pubertal N93.1
  vicarious N94.89
Blennorrhagia, blennorrhagic —*see* Gonorrhea
Blennorrhea (acute) (chronic) —*see also*
    Gonorrhea
  inclusion (neonatal) (newborn) P39.1
  lower genitourinary tract (gonococcal) A54.00
  neonatorum (gonococcal ophthalmia) A54.31
Blepharelosis —*see* Entropion
Blepharitis (angularis) (ciliaris) (eyelid)
    (marginal) (nonulcerative) H01.009
  herpes zoster B02.39
  left H01.006
    lower H01.005
    upper H01.004
    ▶upper and lower H01.00B
  right H01.003
    lower H01.002
    upper H01.001
    ▶upper and lower H01.00A
  squamous H01.029
    left H01.026
      lower H01.025
      upper H01.024
    ▶upper and lower H01.02B
    right H01.023
      lower H01.022
      upper H01.021
    ▶upper and lower H01.02A
  ulcerative H01.019
    left H01.016
      lower H01.015
      upper H01.014
    ▶upper and lower H01.01B
    right H01.013
      lower H01.012
      upper H01.011
    ▶upper and lower H01.01B
Blepharochalasis H02.30
  congenital Q10.0
  left H02.36
    lower H02.35
    upper H02.34
  right H02.33
    lower H02.32
    upper H02.31
Blepharoclonus H02.59
Blepharoconjunctivitis H10.50-●
  angular H10.52-●
  contact H10.53-●
  ligneous H10.51-●
Blepharophimosis (eyelid) H02.529
  congenital Q10.3
  left H02.526
    lower H02.525
    upper H02.524
  right H02.523
    lower H02.522
    upper H02.521
Blepharoptosis H02.40-●
  congenital Q10.0
  mechanical H02.41-●
  myogenic H02.42-●
  neurogenic H02.43-●
  paralytic H02.43-●
Blepharopyorrhea, gonococcal A54.39

Blepharospasm G24.5
  drug induced G24.01
Blighted ovum O02.0
Blind —*see also* Blindness
  bronchus (congenital) Q32.4
  loop syndrome K90.2
    congenital Q43.8
  sac, fallopian tube (congenital) Q50.6
  spot, enlarged —*see* Defect, visual field,
    localized, scotoma, blind spot area
  tract or tube, congenital NEC —*see* Atresia,
    by site
Blindness (acquired) (congenital) (both eyes)
    H54.0X-●
  blast S05.8X-●
  color —*see* Deficiency, color vision
  concussion S05.8X-●
  cortical H47.619
    left brain H47.612
    right brain H47.611
  day H53.11
  due to injury (current episode) S05.9-●
    sequelae — code to injury with seventh
      character S
  eclipse (total) —*see* Retinopathy, solar
  emotional (hysterical) F44.6
  face H53.16
  hysterical F44.6
  legal (both eyes) (USA definition) H54.8
  mind R48.8
  night H53.60
    abnormal dark adaptation curve H53.61
    acquired H53.62
    congenital H53.63
    specified type NEC H53.69
    vitamin A deficiency E50.5
  one eye (other eye normal) H54.40
    left (normal vision on right) H54.42-●
      low vision on right H54.12-●
    low vision, other eye H54.10
    right (normal vision on left) H54.41-●
      low vision on left H54.11-●
  psychic R48.8
  river B73.01
  snow —*see* Photokeratitis
  sun, solar —*see* Retinopathy, solar
  transient —*see* Disturbance, vision, subjective,
    loss, transient
  traumatic (current episode) S05.9-●
  word (developmental) F81.0
    acquired R48.0
    secondary to organic lesion R48.0
Blister (nonthermal)
  abdominal wall S30.821
  alveolar process S00.522
  ankle S90.52-●
  antecubital space —*see* Blister, elbow
  anus S30.827
  arm (upper) S40.82-●
  auditory canal —*see* Blister, ear
  auricle —*see* Blister, ear
  axilla —*see* Blister, arm
  back, lower S30.820
  beetle dermatitis L24.89
  breast S20.12-●
  brow S00.82
  calf —*see* Blister, leg
  canthus —*see* Blister, eyelid
  cheek S00.82
    internal S00.522
  chest wall —*see* Blister, thorax
  chin S00.82
  costal region —*see* Blister, thorax
  digit(s)
    foot —*see* Blister, toe
    hand —*see* Blister, finger
  due to burn —*see* Burn, by site, second degree
  ear S00.42-●
  elbow S50.32-●
  epiglottis S10.12
  esophagus, cervical S10.12
  eyebrow —*see* Blister, eyelid

Blister *(Continued)*
  eyelid S00.22-●
  face S00.82
  fever B00.1
  finger(s) S60.429
    index S60.42-●
    little S60.42-●
    middle S60.42-●
    ring S60.42-●
  foot (except toe(s) alone) S90.82-●
    toe —*see* Blister, toe
  forearm S50.82-●
    elbow only —*see* Blister, elbow
  forehead S00.82
  fracture - omit code
  genital organ
    female S30.826
    male S30.825
  gum S00.522
  hand S60.52-●
  head S00.92
    ear —*see* Blister, ear
    eyelid —*see* Blister, eyelid
    lip S00.521
    nose S00.32
    oral cavity S00.522
    scalp S00.02
    specified site NEC S00.82
  heel —*see* Blister, foot
  hip S70.22-●
  interscapular region S20.429
  jaw S00.82
  knee S80.22-●
  larynx S10.12
  leg (lower) S80.82-●
    knee —*see* Blister, knee
    upper —*see* Blister, thigh
  lip S00.521
  malar region S00.82
  mammary —*see* Blister, breast
  mastoid region S00.82
  mouth S00.522
  multiple, skin, nontraumatic R23.8
  nail
    finger —*see* Blister, finger
    toe —*see* Blister, toe
  nasal S00.32
  neck S10.92
    specified site NEC S10.82
    throat S10.12
  nose S00.32
  occipital region S00.02
  oral cavity S00.522
  orbital region —*see* Blister, eyelid
  palate S00.522
  palm —*see* Blister, hand
  parietal region S00.02
  pelvis S30.820
  penis S30.822
  periocular area —*see* Blister, eyelid
  phalanges
    finger —*see* Blister, finger
    toe —*see* Blister, toe
  pharynx S10.12
  pinna —*see* Blister, ear
  popliteal space —*see* Blister, knee
  scalp S00.02
  scapular region —*see* Blister, shoulder
  scrotum S30.823
  shin —*see* Blister, leg
  shoulder S40.22-●
  sternal region S20.329
  submaxillary region S00.82
  submental region S00.82
  subungual
    finger(s) —*see* Blister, finger
    toe(s) —*see* Blister, toe
  supraclavicular fossa S10.82
  supraorbital S00.82
  temple S00.82
  temporal region S00.82
  testis S30.823

Blister *(Continued)*
thermal —*see* Burn, second degree, by site
thigh S70.32-●
thorax, thoracic (wall) S20.92
back S20.42-●
front S20.32-●
throat S10.12
thumb S60.32-●
toe(s) S90.42-●
great S90.42-●
tongue S00.522
trachea S10.12
tympanum, tympanic membrane —*see* Blister, ear
upper arm —*see* Blister, arm (upper)
uvula S00.522
vagina S30.824
vocal cords S10.12
vulva S30.824
wrist S60.82-●
Bloating R14.0
Bloch-Sulzberger disease or syndrome Q82.3
Block, blocked
alveolocapillary J84.10
arborization (heart) I45.5
arrhythmic I45.9
atrioventricular (incomplete) (partial) I44.30
with atrioventricular dissociation I44.2
complete I44.2
congenital Q24.6
congenital Q24.6
first degree I44.0
second degree (types I and II) I44.1
specified NEC I44.39
third degree I44.2
types I and II I44.1
auriculoventricular —*see* Block, atrioventricular
bifascicular (cardiac) I45.2
bundle-branch (complete) (false) (incomplete) I45.4
bilateral I45.2
left I44.7
with right bundle branch block I45.2
hemiblock I44.60
anterior I44.4
posterior I44.5
incomplete I44.7
with right bundle branch block I45.2
right I45.10
with
left bundle branch block I45.2
left fascicular block I45.2
specified NEC I45.19
Wilson's type I45.19
cardiac I45.9
conduction I45.9
complete I44.2
fascicular (left) I44.60
anterior I44.4
posterior I44.5
right I45.0
specified NEC I44.69
foramen Magendie (acquired) G91.1
congenital Q03.1
with spina bifida —*see* Spina bifida, by site, with hydrocephalus
heart I45.9
bundle branch I45.4
bilateral I45.2
complete (atrioventricular) I44.2
congenital Q24.6
first degree (atrioventricular) I44.0
second degree (atrioventricular) I44.1
specified type NEC I45.5
third degree (atrioventricular) I44.2
hepatic vein I82.0
intraventricular (nonspecific) I45.4
bundle branch
bilateral I45.2
kidney N28.9
postcystoscopic or postprocedural N99.0

Block, blocked *(Continued)*
Mobitz (types I and II) I44.1
myocardial —*see* Block, heart
nodal I45.5
organ or site, congenital NEC —*see* Atresia, by site
portal (vein) I81
second degree (types I and II) I44.1
sinoatrial I45.5
sinoauricular I45.5
third degree I44.2
trifascicular I45.3
tubal N97.1
vein NOS I82.90
Wenckebach (types I and II) I44.1
Blockage —*see* Obstruction
Blocq's disease F44.4
Blood
constituents, abnormal R78.9
disease D75.9
donor —*see* Donor, blood
dyscrasia D75.9
with
abortion —*see* Abortion, by type, complicated by, hemorrhage
ectopic pregnancy O08.1
molar pregnancy O08.1
following ectopic or molar pregnancy O08.1
newborn P61.9
puerperal, postpartum O72.3
flukes NEC —*see* Schistosomiasis
in
feces K92.1
occult R19.5
urine —*see* Hematuria
mole O02.0
occult in feces R19.5
pressure
decreased, due to shock following injury T79.4
examination only Z01.30
fluctuating I99.8
high —*see* Hypertension
borderline R03.0
incidental reading, without diagnosis of hypertension R03.0
low —*see also* Hypotension
incidental reading, without diagnosis of hypotension R03.1
spitting —*see* Hemoptysis
staining cornea —*see* Pigmentation, cornea, stromal
transfusion
reaction or complication —*see* Complications, transfusion
type
A (Rh positive) Z67.10
Rh negative Z67.11
AB (Rh positive) Z67.30
Rh negative Z67.31
B (Rh positive) Z67.20
Rh negative Z67.21
O (Rh positive) Z67.40
Rh negative Z67.41
Rh (positive) Z67.90
negative Z67.91
vessel rupture —*see* Hemorrhage
vomiting —*see* Hematemesis
Blood-forming organs, disease D75.9
Bloodgood's disease —*see* Mastopathy, cystic
Bloom (-Machacek)(-Torre) **syndrome** Q82.8
Blount's disease or osteochondrosis —*see* Osteochondrosis, juvenile, tibia
Blue
baby Q24.9
diaper syndrome E72.09
dome cyst (breast) —*see* Cyst, breast
dot cataract Q12.0
nevus D22.9

Blue *(Continued)*
sclera Q13.5
with fragility of bone and deafness Q78.0
toe syndrome I75.02-●
Blueness —*see* Cyanosis
Blues, postpartal O90.6
baby O90.6
Blurring, visual H53.8
Blushing (abnormal) (excessive) R23.2
BMI —*see* Body, mass index
Boarder, hospital NEC Z76.4
accompanying sick person Z76.3
healthy infant or child Z76.2
foundling Z76.1
Bockhart's impetigo L01.02
Bodechtel-Guttman disease (subacute sclerosing panencephalitis) A81.1
Boder-Sedgwick syndrome (ataxia-telangiectasia) G11.3
Body, bodies
Aschoff's —*see* Myocarditis, rheumatic
asteroid, vitreous —*see* Deposit, crystalline
cytoid (retina) —*see* Occlusion, artery, retina
drusen (degenerative) (macula) (retinal) —*see also* Degeneration, macula, drusen
optic disc —*see* Drusen, optic disc
foreign —*see* Foreign body
loose
joint, except knee —*see* Loose, body, joint
knee M23.4-●
sheath, tendon —*see* Disorder, tendon, specified type NEC
mass index (BMI)
adult
19.9 or less Z68.1
20.0-20.9 Z68.20
21.0-21.9 Z68.21
22.0-22.9 Z68.22
23.0-23.9 Z68.23
24.0-24.9 Z68.24
25.0-25.9 Z68.25
26.0-26.9 Z68.26
27.0-27.9 Z68.27
28.0-28.9 Z68.28
29.0-29.9 Z68.29
30.0-30.9 Z68.30
31.0-31.9 Z68.31
32.0-32.9 Z68.32
33.0-33.9 Z68.33
34.0-34.9 Z68.34
35.0-35.9 Z68.35
36.0-36.9 Z68.36
37.0-37.9 Z68.37
38.0-38.9 Z68.38
39.0-39.9 Z68.39
40.0-44.9 Z68.41
45.0-49.9 Z68.42
50.0-59.9 Z68.43
60.0-69.9 Z68.44
70 and over Z68.45
pediatric
5th percentile to less than 85th percentile for age Z68.52
85th percentile to less than 95th percentile for age Z68.53
greater than or equal to ninety-fifth percentile for age Z68.54
less than fifth percentile for age Z68.51
Mooser's A75.2
rice —*see also* Loose, body, joint
knee M23.4-●
rocking F98.4
Boeck's
disease or sarcoid —*see* Sarcoidosis
lupoid (miliary) D86.3
Boerhaave's syndrome (spontaneous esophageal rupture) K22.3
Boggy
cervix N88.8
uterus N85.8

Boil —*see also* Furuncle, by site
　Aleppo B55.1
　Baghdad B55.1
　Delhi B55.1
　lacrimal
　　gland —*see* Dacryoadenitis
　　passages (duct) (sac) —*see* Inflammation,
　　　lacrimal, passages, acute
　Natal B55.1
　orbit, orbital —*see* Abscess, orbit
　tropical B55.1
Bold hives —*see* Urticaria
Bombé, iris —*see* Membrane, pupillary
Bone —*see* condition
Bonnevie-Ullrich syndrome —*see also* Turner's
　syndrome Q87.1
Bonnier's syndrome —*see* subcategory H81.8
Bonvale dam fever T73.3
Bony block of joint —*see* Ankylosis
BOOP (bronchiolitis obliterans organized
　pneumonia) J84.89
Borderline
　diabetes mellitus R73.03
　hypertension R03.0
　osteopenia M85.8-●
　pelvis, with obstruction during labor O65.1
　personality F60.3
Borna disease A83.9
Bornholm disease B33.0
Boston exanthem A88.0
Botalli, ductus (patent) (persistent) Q25.0
Bothriocephalus latus infestation B70.0
Botulism (foodborne intoxication) A05.1
　infant A48.51
　non-foodborne A48.52
　wound A48.52
Bouba —*see* Yaws
Bouchard's nodes (with arthropathy) M15.2
Bouffée délirante F23
Bouillaud's disease or syndrome (rheumatic
　heart disease) I01.9
Bourneville's disease Q85.1
Boutonniere deformity (finger) —*see*
　Deformity, finger, boutonniere
Bouveret (-Hoffmann) syndrome (paroxysmal
　tachycardia) I47.9
Bovine heart —*see* Hypertrophy, cardiac
Bowel —*see* condition
Bowen's
　dermatosis (precancerous) —*see* Neoplasm,
　　skin, in situ
　disease —*see* Neoplasm, skin, in situ
　epithelioma —*see* Neoplasm, skin, in situ
　type
　　epidermoid carcinoma-in-situ —*see*
　　　Neoplasm, skin, in situ
　　intraepidermal squamous cell carcinoma —
　　　see Neoplasm, skin, in situ
Bowing
　femur —*see also* Deformity, limb, specified
　　type NEC, thigh
　　congenital Q68.3
　fibula —*see also* Deformity, limb, specified
　　type NEC, lower leg
　　congenital Q68.4
　forearm —*see* Deformity, limb, specified type
　　NEC, forearm
　leg(s), long bones, congenital Q68.5
　radius —*see* Deformity, limb, specified type
　　NEC, forearm
　tibia —*see also* Deformity, limb, specified type
　　NEC, lower leg
　　congenital Q68.4
Bowleg(s) (acquired) M21.16-●
　congenital Q68.5
　rachitic E64.3
Boyd's dysentery A03.2
Brachial —*see* condition
Brachycardia R00.1
Brachycephaly Q75.0
Bradley's disease A08.19

Bradyarrhythmia, cardiac I49.8
Bradycardia (sinoatrial) (sinus) (vagal) R00.1
　neonatal P29.12
　reflex G90.09
　tachycardia syndrome I49.5
Bradykinesia R25.8
Bradypnea R06.89
Bradytachycardia I49.5
Brailsford's disease or osteochondrosis —*see*
　Osteochondrosis, juvenile, radius
Brain —*see also* condition
　death G93.82
　syndrome —*see* Syndrome, brain
Branched-chain amino-acid disorder E71.2
Branchial —*see* condition
　cartilage, congenital Q18.2
Branchiogenic remnant (in neck) Q18.0
Brandt's syndrome (acrodermatitis
　enteropathica) E83.2
Brash (water) R12
Bravais-jacksonian epilepsy —*see* Epilepsy,
　localization-related, symptomatic, with
　simple partial seizures
Braxton Hicks contractions —*see* False, labor
Brazilian leishmaniasis B55.2
BRBPR K62.5
Break, retina (without detachment) H33.30-●
　with retinal detachment —*see* Detachment,
　　retina
　horseshoe tear H33.31-●
　multiple H33.33-●
　round hole H33.32-●
Breakdown
　device, graft or implant —*see also*
　　Complications, by site and type,
　　mechanical T85.618
　　arterial graft NEC —*see* Complication,
　　　cardiovascular device, mechanical,
　　　vascular
　　breast (implant) T85.41
　　catheter NEC T85.618
　　　cystostomy T83.010
　　　dialysis (renal) T82.41
　　　　intraperitoneal T85.611
　　　Hopkins T83.018
　　　ileostomy T83.018
　　　infusion NEC T82.514
　　　　cranial T85.610
　　　　epidural T85.610
　　　　intrathecal T85.610
　　　　spinal T85.610
　　　　subarachnoid T85.610
　　　　subdural T85.610
　　　nephrostomy T83.012
　　　urethral indwelling T83.011
　　　urinary NEC T83.018
　　　urostomy T83.018
　　electronic (electrode) (pulse generator)
　　　(stimulator)
　　　bone T84.310
　　　cardiac T82.119
　　　　electrode T82.110
　　　　pulse generator T82.111
　　　　specified type NEC T82.118
　　　nervous system —*see* Complication,
　　　　prosthetic device, mechanical,
　　　　electronic nervous system stimulator
　　　urinary —*see* Complication,
　　　　genitourinary, device, urinary,
　　　　mechanical
　　fixation, internal (orthopedic) NEC —
　　　see Complication, fixation device,
　　　mechanical
　　gastrointestinal —*see* Complications,
　　　prosthetic device, mechanical,
　　　gastrointestinal device
　　genital NEC T83.418
　　　intrauterine contraceptive device T83.31
　　　penile prosthesis (cylinder) (implanted)
　　　　(pump) (resevoir) T83.410
　　　testicular prosthesis T83.411

Breakdown *(Continued)*
　device, graft or implant *(Continued)*
　　heart NEC —*see* Complication,
　　　cardiovascular device, mechanical
　　intrathecal infusion pump T85.615
　　joint prosthesis —*see* Complications..., joint
　　　prosthesis,internal, mechanical, by site
　　nervous system, specified device NEC
　　　T85.615
　　ocular NEC —*see* Complications, prosthetic
　　　device, mechanical, ocular device
　　orthopedic NEC —*see* Complication,
　　　orthopedic, device, mechanical
　　specified NEC T85.618
　　subcutaneous device pocket
　　　nervous system prosthetic device,
　　　　implant, or graft T85.890
　　　other internal prosthetic device, implant,
　　　　or graft T85.898
　　sutures, permanent T85.612
　　　used in bone repair —*see* Complications,
　　　　fixation device, internal
　　　　(orthopedic), mechanical
　　urinary NEC T83.118
　　　graft T83.21
　　　sphincter, implanted T83.111
　　　stent (ileal conduit) (nephroureteral)
　　　　T83.113
　　　　ureteral indwelling T83.112
　　vascular NEC —*see* Complication,
　　　cardiovascular device, mechanical
　　ventricular intracranial shunt T85.01
　nervous F48.8
　perineum O90.1
　respirator J95.850
　　specified NEC J95.859
　ventilator J95.850
　　specified NEC J95.859
Breast —*see also* condition
　buds E30.1
　　in newborn P96.89
　dense R92.2
　nodule —*see also* Lump, breast N63.0
Breath
　foul R19.6
　holder, child R06.89
　holding spell R06.89
　shortness R06.02
Breathing
　labored —*see* Hyperventilation
　mouth R06.5
　　causing malocclusion M26.5
　periodic R06.3
　　high altitude G47.32
Breathlessness R06.81
Breda's disease —*see* Yaws
Breech presentation (mother) O32.1
　causing obstructed labor O64.1
　footling O32.8
　　causing obstructed labor O64.8
　incomplete O32.8
　　causing obstructed labor O64.8
Breisky's disease N90.4
Brennemann's syndrome I88.0
Brenner
　tumor (benign) D27.9
　　borderline malignancy D39.1-●
　　malignant C56
　　proliferating D39.1
Bretonneau's disease or angina A36.0
Breus' mole O02.0
Brevicollis Q76.49
Brickmakers' anemia B76.9 [D63.8]
Bridge, myocardial Q24.5
Bright red blood per rectum (BRBPR) K62.5
Bright's disease —*see also* Nephritis
　arteriosclerotic —*see* Hypertension, kidney
Brill (-Zinsser) disease (recrudescent typhus)
　A75.1
　flea-borne A75.2
　louse-borne A75.1

▶ New　⇒ Revised　~~deleted~~ Deleted　● Use Additional Character(s)

Brill-Symmers' disease C82.90
Brion-Kayser disease —see Fever, parathyroid
Briquet's disorder or syndrome F45.0
Brissaud's
  infantilism or dwarfism E23.0
  motor-verbal tic F95.2
Brittle
  bones disease Q78.0
  nails L60.3
    congenital Q84.6
Broad —see also condition
  beta disease E78.2
  ligament laceration syndrome N83.8
Broad- or floating-betalipoproteinemia E78.2
Brock's syndrome (atelectasis due to enlarged
    lymph nodes) J98.19
Brocq-Duhring disease (dermatitis
    herpetiformis) L13.0
Brodie's abscess or disease M86.8X-•
Broken
  arches —see also Deformity, limb, flat foot
  arm (meaning upper limb) —see Fracture, arm
  back —see Fracture, vertebra
  bone —see Fracture
  implant or internal device —see
    Complications, by site and type,
    mechanical
  leg (meaning lower limb) —see Fracture, leg
  nose S02.2
  tooth, teeth —see Fracture, tooth
Bromhidrosis, bromidrosis L75.0
Bromidism, bromism G92
  chronic (dependence) F13.20
  due to
    correct substance properly administered —
      see Table of Drugs and Chemicals, by
      drug, adverse effect
    overdose or wrong substance given
      or taken —see Table of Drugs and
      Chemicals, by drug, poisoning
Bromidrosiphobia F40.298
Bronchi, bronchial —see condition
Bronchiectasis (cylindrical) (diffuse) (fusiform)
    (localized) (saccular) J47.9
  with
    acute
      bronchitis J47.0
      lower respiratory infection J47.0
    exacerbation (acute) J47.1
  congenital Q33.4
  tuberculous NEC —see Tuberculosis,
    pulmonary
Bronchiolectasis —see Bronchiectasis
Bronchiolitis (acute) (infective) (subacute) J21.9
  with
    bronchospasm or obstruction J21.9
    influenza, flu or grippe —see Influenza,
      with, respiratory manifestations NEC
  chemical (chronic) J68.4
    acute J68.0
  chronic (fibrosing) (obliterative) J44.9
  due to
    external agent —see Bronchitis, acute, due to
    human metapneumovirus J21.1
    respiratory syncytial virus J21.0
    specified organism NEC J21.8
  fibrosa obliterans J44.9
  influenzal —see Influenza, with, respiratory
    manifestations NEC
  obliterans J42
    with organizing pneumonia (BOOP) J84.89
  obliterative (chronic) (subacute) J44.9
    due to chemicals, gases, fumes or vapors
      (inhalation) J68.4
    due to fumes or vapors J68.4
  respiratory, interstitial lung disease J84.115
Bronchitis (diffuse) (fibrinous) (hypostatic)
    (infective) (membranous) J40
  with
    influenza, flu or grippe —see Influenza,
      with, respiratory manifestations NEC

Bronchitis (Continued)
  with (Continued)
    obstruction (airway) (lung) J44.9
    tracheitis (15 years of age and above) J40
      acute or subacute J20.9
      chronic J42
      under 15 years of age J20.9
  acute or subacute (with bronchospasm or
    obstruction) J20.9
    with
      bronchiectasis J47.0
      chronic obstructive pulmonary disease
        J44.0
    chemical (due to gases, fumes or vapors)
      J68.0
    due to
      fumes or vapors J68.0
      Haemophilus influenzae J20.1
      Mycoplasma pneumoniae J20.0
      radiation J70.0
      specified organism NEC J20.8
      Streptococcus J20.2
      virus
        coxsackie J20.3
        echovirus J20.7
        parainfluenzae J20.4
        respiratory syncytial J20.5
        rhinovirus J20.6
    viral NEC J20.8
  allergic (acute) J45.909
    with
      exacerbation (acute) J45.901
      status asthmaticus J45.902
  arachidic T17.528
  aspiration (due to fumes or vapors) J68.0
  asthmatic J45.9
    chronic J44.9
      with
        acute lower respiratory infection J44.0
        exacerbation (acute) J44.1
  capillary —see Pneumonia, broncho
  caseous (tuberculous) A15.5
  Castellani's A69.8
  catarrhal (15 years of age and above) J40
    acute —see Bronchitis, acute
    chronic J41.0
    under 15 years of age J20.9
  chemical (acute) (subacute) J68.0
    chronic J68.4
    due to fumes or vapors J68.0
      chronic J68.4
  chronic J42
    with
      airways obstruction J44.9
      tracheitis (chronic) J42
    asthmatic (obstructive) J44.9
    catarrhal J41.0
    chemical (due to fumes or vapors) J68.4
    due to
      chemicals, gases, fumes or vapors
        (inhalation) J68.4
      radiation J70.1
      tobacco smoking J41.0
    emphysematous J44.9
    mucopurulent J41.1
    non-obstructive J41.0
    obliterans J44.9
    obstructive J44.9
    purulent J41.1
    simple J41.0
  croupous —see Bronchitis, acute
  due to gases, fumes or vapors (chemical)
    J68.0
  emphysematous (obstructive) J44.9
  exudative —see Bronchitis, acute
  fetid J41.1
  grippal —see Influenza, with, respiratory
    manifestations NEC
  in those under 15 years age —see Bronchitis,
    acute
    chronic —see Bronchitis, chronic

Bronchitis (Continued)
  influenzal —see Influenza, with, respiratory
    manifestations NEC
  mixed simple and mucopurulent J41.8
  moulder's J62.8
  mucopurulent (chronic) (recurrent) J41.1
    acute or subacute J20.9
    simple (mixed) J41.8
  obliterans (chronic) J44.9
  obstructive (chronic) (diffuse) J44.9
  pituitous J41.1
  pneumococcal, acute or subacute J20.2
  pseudomembranous, acute or subacute —see
    Bronchitis, acute
  purulent (chronic) (recurrent) J41.1
    acute or subacute —see Bronchitis, acute
  putrid J41.1
  senile (chronic) J42
  simple and mucopurulent (mixed) J41.8
  smokers' J41.0
  spirochetal NEC A69.8
  subacute —see Bronchitis, acute
  suppurative (chronic) J41.1
    acute or subacute —see Bronchitis, acute
  tuberculous A15.5
  under 15 years of age —see Bronchitis, acute
    chronic —see Bronchitis, chronic
  viral NEC, acute or subacute —see also
    Bronchitis, acute J20.8
Bronchoalveolitis J18.0
Bronchoaspergillosis B44.1
Bronchocele meaning goiter E04.0
Broncholithiasis J98.09
  tuberculous NEC A15.5
Bronchomalacia J98.09
  congenital Q32.2
Bronchomycosis NOS B49 [J99]
  candidal B37.1
Bronchopleuropneumonia —see Pneumonia,
    broncho
Bronchopneumonia —see Pneumonia, broncho
Bronchopneumonitis —see Pneumonia,
    broncho
Bronchopulmonary —see condition
Bronchopulmonitis —see Pneumonia, broncho
Bronchorrhagia (see Hemoptysis)
Bronchorrhea J98.09
  acute J20.9
  chronic (infective) (purulent) J42
Bronchospasm (acute) J98.01
  with
    bronchiolitis, acute J21.9
    bronchitis, acute (conditions in J20) —see
      Bronchitis, acute
  due to external agent —see condition,
    respiratory, acute, due to
  exercise induced J45.990
Bronchospirochetosis A69.8
  Castellani A69.8
Bronchostenosis J98.09
Bronchus —see condition
Brontophobia F40.220
Bronze baby syndrome P83.88
Brooke's tumor —see Neoplasm, skin, benign
Brown enamel of teeth (hereditary) K00.5
Brown's sheath syndrome H50.61-•
Brown-Séquard disease, paralysis or
    syndrome G83.81
Bruce sepsis A23.0
Brucellosis (infection) A23.9
  abortus A23.1
  canis A23.3
  dermatitis A23.9
  melitensis A23.0
  mixed A23.8
  sepsis A23.9
    melitensis A23.0
    specified NEC A23.8
  suis A23.2
Bruck-de Lange disease Q87.1
Bruck's disease —see Deformity, limb

BRUE (brief resolved unexplained event) R68.13
Brugsch's syndrome Q82.8
Bruise (skin surface intact) —*see also* Contusion
with
    open wound —*see* Wound, open
  internal organ —*see* Injury, by site
  newborn P54.5
  scalp, due to birth injury, newborn P12.3
  umbilical cord O69.5
Bruit (arterial) R09.89
  cardiac R01.1
Brush burn —*see* Abrasion, by site
Bruton's X-linked agammaglobulinemia D80.0
Bruxism
  psychogenic F45.8
  sleep related G47.63
Bubbly lung syndrome P27.0
Bubo I88.8
  blennorrhagic (gonococcal) A54.89
  chancroidal A57
  climatic A55
  due to Haemophilus ducreyi A57
  gonococcal A54.89
  indolent (nonspecific) I88.8
  inguinal (nonspecific) I88.8
    chancroidal A57
    climatic A55
    due to H. ducreyi A57
    infective I88.8
  scrofulous (tuberculous) A18.2
  soft chancre A57
  suppurating —*see* Lymphadenitis, acute
  syphilitic (primary) A51.0
    congenital A50.07
  tropical A55
  virulent (chancroidal) A57
Bubonic plague A20.0
Bubonocele —*see* Hernia, inguinal
Buccal —*see* condition
Buchanan's disease or osteochondrosis M91.0
Buchem's syndrome (hyperostosis corticalis)
  M85.2
Bucket-handle fracture or tear (semilunar
  cartilage) —*see* Tear, meniscus
Budd-Chiari syndrome (hepatic vein
  thrombosis) I82.0
Budgerigar fancier's disease or lung
  J67.2
Buds
  breast E30.1
    in newborn P96.89
Buerger's disease (thromboangiitis obliterans)
  I73.1
Bulbar —*see* condition
Bulbus cordis (left ventricle) (persistent) Q21.8
Bulimia (nervosa) F50.2
  atypical F50.9
  normal weight F50.9
Bulky
  stools R19.5
  uterus N85.2
Bulla (e) R23.8
  lung (emphysematous) (solitary) J43.9
    newborn P25.8
Bullet wound —*see also* Wound, open
  fracture - code as Fracture, by site
  internal organ —*see* Injury, by site
Bundle
  branch block (complete) (false)
    (incomplete) —*see* Block, bundle-branch
  of His —*see* condition
Bunion M21.61-●
  tailor's M21.62-●
Bunionette M21.62-●
Buphthalmia, buphthalmos (congenital) Q15.0
Burdwan fever B55.0
Bürger-Grütz disease or syndrome E78.3
Buried
  penis (congenital) Q55.64
    acquired N48.83
  roots K08.3

Burke's syndrome K86.89
Burkitt
  cell leukemia C91.0-●
  lymphoma (malignant) C83.7-●
    small noncleaved, diffuse C83.7-●
    spleen C83.77
    undifferentiated C83.7-●
  tumor C83.7-●
  type
    acute lymphoblastic leukemia C91.0-●
    undifferentiated C83.7-●
Burn (electricity) (flame) (hot gas, liquid or hot
  object) (radiation) (steam) (thermal) T30.0
  abdomen, abdominal (muscle) (wall)
    T21.02
    first degree T21.12
    second degree T21.22
    third degree T21.32
  above elbow T22.039
    first degree T22.139
    left T22.032
      first degree T22.132
      second degree T22.232
      third degree T22.332
    right T22.031
      first degree T22.131
      second degree T22.231
      third degree T22.331
    second degree T22.239
    third degree T22.339
  acid (caustic) (external) (internal) —*see*
    Corrosion, by site
  alimentary tract NEC T28.2
    esophagus T28.1
    mouth T28.0
    pharynx T28.0
  alkaline (caustic) (external) (internal) —*see*
    Corrosion, by site
  ankle T25.019
    first degree T25.119
    left T25.012
      first degree T25.112
      second degree T25.212
      third degree T25.312
    multiple with foot —*see* Burn, lower, limb,
      multiple, ankle and foot
    right T25.011
      first degree T25.111
      second degree T25.211
      third degree T25.311
    second degree T25.219
    third degree T25.319
  anus —*see* Burn, buttock
  arm (lower) (upper) —*see* Burn, upper,
    limb
  axilla T22.049
    first degree T22.149
    left T22.042
      first degree T22.142
      second degree T22.242
      third degree T22.342
    right T22.041
      first degree T22.141
      second degree T22.241
      third degree T22.341
    second degree T22.249
    third degree T22.349
  back (lower) T21.04
    first degree T21.14
    second degree T21.24
    third degree T21.34
    upper T21.03
      first degree T21.13
      second degree T21.23
      third degree T21.33
  blisters - code as Burn, second degree, by site
  breast(s) —*see* Burn, chest wall
  buttock(s) T21.05
    first degree T21.15
    second degree T21.25
    third degree T21.35

Burn (*Continued*)
  calf T24.039
    first degree T24.139
    left T24.032
      first degree T24.132
      second degree T24.232
      third degree T24.332
    right T24.031
      first degree T24.131
      second degree T24.231
      third degree T24.331
    second degree T24.239
    third degree T24.339
  canthus (eye) —*see* Burn, eyelid
  caustic acid or alkaline —*see* Corrosion, by
    site
  cervix T28.3
  cheek T20.06
    first degree T20.16
    second degree T20.26
    third degree T20.36
  chemical (acids) (alkalines) (caustics) (external)
    (internal) —*see* Corrosion, by site
  chest wall T21.01
    first degree T21.11
    second degree T21.21
    third degree T21.31
  chin T20.03
    first degree T20.13
    second degree T20.23
    third degree T20.33
  colon T28.2
  conjunctiva (and cornea) —*see* Burn, cornea
  cornea (and conjunctiva) T26.1-●
    chemical —*see* Corrosion, cornea
  corrosion (external) (internal) —*see*
    Corrosion, by site
  deep necrosis of underlying tissue - code as
    Burn, third degree, by site
  dorsum of hand T23.069
    first degree T23.169
    left T23.062
      first degree T23.162
      second degree T23.262
      third degree T23.362
    right T23.061
      first degree T23.161
      second degree T23.261
      third degree T23.361
    second degree T23.269
    third degree T23.369
  due to ingested chemical agent —*see*
    Corrosion, by site
  ear (auricle) (external) (canal) T20.01
    first degree T20.11
    second degree T20.21
    third degree T20.31
  elbow T22.029
    first degree T22.129
    left T22.022
      first degree T22.122
      second degree T22.222
      third degree T22.322
    right T22.021
      first degree T22.121
      second degree T22.221
      third degree T22.321
    second degree T22.229
    third degree T22.329
  epidermal loss - code as Burn, second degree,
    by site
  erythema, erythematous - code as Burn, first
    degree, by site
  esophagus T28.1
  extent (percentage of body surface)
    less than 10 percent T31.0
    10-19 percent T31.10
      with 0-9 percent third degree burns
        T31.10
      with 10-19 percent third degree burns
        T31.11

▶ New   ⇒ Revised   ~~deleted~~ Deleted   ● Use Additional Character(s)

Burn *(Continued)*
  extent *(Continued)*
    20-29 percent T31.20
      with 0-9 percent third degree burns T31.20
      with 10-19 percent third degree burns T31.21
      with 20-29 percent third degree burns T31.22
    30-39 percent T31.30
      with 0-9 percent third degree burns T31.30
      with 10-19 percent third degree burns T31.31
      with 20-29 percent third degree burns T31.32
      with 30-39 percent third degree burns T31.33
    40-49 percent T31.40
      with 0-9 percent third degree burns T31.40
      with 10-19 percent third degree burns T31.41
      with 20-29 percent third degree burns T31.42
      with 30-39 percent third degree burns T31.43
      with 40-49 percent third degree burns T31.44
    50-59 percent T31.50
      with 0-9 percent third degree burns T31.50
      with 10-19 percent third degree burns T31.51
      with 20-29 percent third degree burns T31.52
      with 30-39 percent third degree burns T31.53
      with 40-49 percent third degree burns T31.54
      with 50-59 percent third degree burns T31.55
    60-69 percent T31.60
      with 0-9 percent third degree burns T31.60
      with 10-19 percent third degree burns T31.61
      with 20-29 percent third degree burns T31.62
      with 30-39 percent third degree burns T31.63
      with 40-49 percent third degree burns T31.64
      with 50-59 percent third degree burns T31.65
      with 60-69 percent third degree burns T31.66
    70-79 percent T31.70
      with 0-9 percent third degree burns T31.70
      with 10-19 percent third degree burns T31.71
      with 20-29 percent third degree burns T31.72
      with 30-39 percent third degree burns T31.73
      with 40-49 percent third degree burns T31.74
      with 50-59 percent third degree burns T31.75
      with 60-69 percent third degree burns T31.76
      with 70-79 percent third degree burns T31.77
    80-89 percent T31.80
      with 0-9 percent third degree burns T31.80
      with 10-19 percent third degree burns T31.81
      with 20-29 percent third degree burns T31.82
      with 30-39 percent third degree burns T31.83
      with 40-49 percent third degree burns T31.84

Burn *(Continued)*
  extent *(Continued)*
    80-89 percent T31.80 *(Continued)*
      with 50-59 percent third degree burns T31.85
      with 60-69 percent third degree burns T31.86
      with 70-79 percent third degree burns T31.87
      with 80-89 percent third degree burns T31.88
    90 percent or more T31.90
      with 0-9 percent third degree burns T31.90
      with 10-19 percent third degree burns T31.91
      with 20-29 percent third degree burns T31.92
      with 30-39 percent third degree burns T31.93
      with 40-49 percent third degree burns T31.94
      with 50-59 percent third degree burns T31.95
      with 60-69 percent third degree burns T31.96
      with 70-79 percent third degree burns T31.97
      with 80-89 percent third degree burns T31.98
      with 90 percent or more third degree burns T31.99
  extremity —*see* Burn, limb
  eye(s) and adnexa T26.4-●
    with resulting rupture and destruction of eyeball T26.2-●
    conjunctival sac —*see* Burn, cornea
    cornea —*see* Burn, cornea
    lid —*see* Burn, eyelid
    periocular area —*see* Burn, eyelid
    specified site NEC T26.3-●
  eyeball —*see* Burn, eye
  eyelid(s) T26.0-●
    chemical —*see* Corrosion, eyelid
  face —*see* Burn, head
  finger T23.029
    first degree T23.129
    left T23.022
      first degree T23.122
      second degree T23.222
      third degree T23.322
    multiple sites (without thumb) T23.039
      with thumb T23.049
        first degree T23.149
        left T23.042
          first degree T23.142
          second degree T23.242
          third degree T23.342
        right T23.041
          first degree T23.141
          second degree T23.241
          third degree T23.341
        second degree T23.249
        third degree T23.349
      first degree T23.139
      left T23.032
        first degree T23.132
        second degree T23.232
        third degree T23.332
      right T23.031
        first degree T23.131
        second degree T23.231
        third degree T23.331
      second degree T23.239
      third degree T23.339
    right T23.021
      first degree T23.121
      second degree T23.221
      third degree T23.321
    second degree T23.229
    third degree T23.329
  flank —*see* Burn, abdominal wall

Burn *(Continued)*
  foot T25.029
    first degree T25.129
    left T25.022
      first degree T25.122
      second degree T25.222
      third degree T25.322
    multiple with ankle —*see* Burn, lower, limb, multiple, ankle and foot
    right T25.021
      first degree T25.121
      second degree T25.221
      third degree T25.321
    second degree T25.229
    third degree T25.329
  forearm T22.019
    first degree T22.119
    left T22.012
      first degree T22.112
      second degree T22.212
      third degree T22.312
    right T22.011
      first degree T22.111
      second degree T22.211
      third degree T22.311
    second degree T22.219
    third degree T22.319
  forehead T20.06
    first degree T20.16
    second degree T20.26
    third degree T20.36
  fourth degree - code as Burn, third degree, by site
  friction —*see* Burn, by site
  from swallowing caustic or corrosive substance NEC —*see* Corrosion, by site
  full thickness skin loss - code as Burn, third degree, by site
  gastrointestinal tract NEC T28.2
    from swallowing caustic or corrosive substance T28.7
  genital organs
    external
      female T21.07
        first degree T21.17
        second degree T21.27
        third degree T21.37
      male T21.06
        first degree T21.16
        second degree T21.26
        third degree T21.36
    internal T28.3
      from caustic or corrosive substance T28.8
  groin —*see* Burn, abdominal wall
  hand(s) T23.009
    back —*see* Burn, dorsum of hand
    finger —*see* Burn, finger
    first degree T23.109
    left T23.002
      first degree T23.102
      second degree T23.202
      third degree T23.302
    multiple sites with wrist T23.099
      first degree T23.199
      left T23.092
        first degree T23.192
        second degree T23.292
        third degree T23.392
      right T23.091
        first degree T23.191
        second degree T23.291
        third degree T23.391
      second degree T23.299
      third degree T23.399
    palm —*see* Burn, palm
    right T23.001
      first degree T23.101
      second degree T23.201
      third degree T23.301

▶ New   ⇨ Revised   ~~deleted~~ Deleted   ● Use Additional Character(s)

Burn *(Continued)*
    hand *(Continued)*
        second degree T23.209
        third degree T23.309
        thumb —*see* Burn, thumb
    head (and face) (and neck) T20.00
        cheek —*see* Burn, cheek
        chin —*see* Burn, chin
        ear —*see* Burn, ear
        eye(s) only —*see* Burn, eye
        first degree T20.10
        forehead —*see* Burn, forehead
        lip —*see* Burn, lip
        multiple sites T20.09
            first degree T20.19
            second degree T20.29
            third degree T20.39
        neck —*see* Burn, neck
        nose —*see* Burn, nose
        scalp —*see* Burn, scalp
        second degree T20.20
        third degree T20.30
    hip(s) —*see* Burn, thigh
    inhalation —*see* Burn, respiratory tract
        caustic or corrosive substance (fumes) —*see*
            Corrosion, respiratory tract
    internal organ(s) T28.40
        alimentary tract T28.2
            esophagus T28.1
        eardrum T28.41
        esophagus T28.1
        from caustic or corrosive substance
            (swallowing) NEC —*see* Corrosion,
            by site
        genitourinary T28.3
        mouth T28.0
        pharynx T28.0
        respiratory tract —*see* Burn, respiratory
            tract
        specified organ NEC T28.49
    interscapular region —*see* Burn, back,
        upper
    intestine (large) (small) T28.2
    knee T24.029
        first degree T24.129
        left T24.022
            first degree T24.122
            second degree T24.222
            third degree T24.322
        right T24.021
            first degree T24.121
            second degree T24.221
            third degree T24.321
        second degree T24.229
        third degree T24.329
    labium (majus) (minus) —*see* Burn, genital
        organs, external, female
    lacrimal apparatus, duct, gland or sac —*see*
        Burn, eye, specified site NEC
    larynx T27.0
        with lung T27.1
    leg(s) (lower) (upper) —*see* Burn, lower,
        limb
    lightning —*see* Burn, by site
    limb(s)
        lower (except ankle or foot alone) —*see*
            Burn, lower, limb
        upper —*see* Burn, upper limb
    lip(s) T20.02
        first degree T20.12
        second degree T20.22
        third degree T20.32
    lower
        back —*see* Burn, back
        limb T24.009
            ankle —*see* Burn, ankle
            calf —*see* Burn, calf
            first degree T24.109
            foot —*see* Burn, foot
            hip —*see* Burn, thigh
            knee —*see* Burn, knee

Burn *(Continued)*
    lower *(Continued)*
        limb *(Continued)*
            left T24.002
                first degree T24.102
                second degree T24.202
                third degree T24.302
            multiple sites, except ankle and foot
                T24.099
                ankle and foot T25.099
                    first degree T25.199
                    left T25.092
                        first degree T25.192
                        second degree T25.292
                        third degree T25.392
                    right T25.091
                        first degree T25.191
                        second degree T25.291
                        third degree T25.391
                    second degree T25.299
                    third degree T25.399
                first degree T24.199
                left T24.092
                    first degree T24.192
                    second degree T24.292
                    third degree T24.392
                right T24.091
                    first degree T24.191
                    second degree T24.291
                    third degree T24.391
                second degree T24.299
                third degree T24.399
            right T24.001
                first degree T24.101
                second degree T24.201
                third degree T24.301
            second degree T24.209
            thigh —*see* Burn, thigh
            third degree T24.309
            toe —*see* Burn, toe
    lung (with larynx and trachea) T27.1
    mouth T28.0
    neck T20.07
        first degree T20.17
        second degree T20.27
        third degree T20.37
    nose (septum) T20.04
        first degree T20.14
        second degree T20.24
        third degree T20.34
    ocular adnexa —*see* Burn, eye
    orbit region —*see* Burn, eyelid
    palm T23.059
        first degree T23.159
        left T23.052
            first degree T23.152
            second degree T23.252
            third degree T23.352
        right T23.051
            first degree T23.151
            second degree T23.251
            third degree T23.351
        second degree T23.259
        third degree T23.359
    partial thickness - code as Burn, unspecified
        degree, by site
    pelvis —*see* Burn, trunk
    penis —*see* Burn, genital organs, external,
        male
    perineum
        female —*see* Burn, genital organs, external,
            female
        male —*see* Burn, genital organs, external,
            male
    periocular area —*see* Burn, eyelid
    pharynx T28.0
    rectum T28.2
    respiratory tract T27.3
        larynx —*see* Burn, larynx
        specified part NEC T27.2
        trachea —*see* Burn, trachea

Burn *(Continued)*
    sac, lacrimal —*see* Burn, eye, specified site
        NEC
    scalp T20.05
        first degree T20.15
        second degree T20.25
        third degree T20.35
    scapular region T22.069
        first degree T22.169
        left T22.062
            first degree T22.162
            second degree T22.262
            third degree T22.362
        right T22.061
            first degree T22.161
            second degree T22.261
            third degree T22.361
        second degree T22.269
        third degree T22.369
    sclera —*see* Burn, eye, specified site NEC
    scrotum —*see* Burn, genital organs, external,
        male
    shoulder T22.059
        first degree T22.159
        left T22.052
            first degree T22.152
            second degree T22.252
            third degree T22.352
        right T22.051
            first degree T22.151
            second degree T22.251
            third degree T22.351
        second degree T22.259
        third degree T22.359
    stomach T28.2
    temple —*see* Burn, head
    testis —*see* Burn, genital organs, external, male
    thigh T24.019
        first degree T24.119
        left T24.012
            first degree T24.112
            second degree T24.212
            third degree T24.312
        right T24.011
            first degree T24.111
            second degree T24.211
            third degree T24.311
        second degree T24.219
        third degree T24.319
    thorax (external) —*see* Burn, trunk
    throat (meaning pharynx) T28.0
    thumb(s) T23.019
        first degree T23.119
        left T23.012
            first degree T23.112
            second degree T23.212
            third degree T23.312
        multiple sites with fingers T23.049
            first degree T23.149
            left T23.042
                first degree T23.142
                second degree T23.242
                third degree T23.342
            right T23.041
                first degree T23.141
                second degree T23.241
                third degree T23.341
            second degree T23.249
            third degree T23.349
        right T23.011
            first degree T23.111
            second degree T23.211
            third degree T23.311
        second degree T23.219
        third degree T23.319
    toe T25.039
        first degree T25.139
        left T25.032
            first degree T25.132
            second degree T25.232
            third degree T25.332

▶ New   ⇒ Revised   ~~deleted~~ Deleted   ● Use Additional Character(s)

Burn (Continued)
  toe (Continued)
    right T25.031
      first degree T25.131
      second degree T25.231
      third degree T25.331
    second degree T25.239
    third degree T25.339
  tongue T28.0
  tonsil(s) T28.0
  trachea T27.0
    with lung T27.1
  trunk T21.00
    abdominal wall —see Burn, abdominal
      wall
    anus —see Burn, buttock
    axilla —see Burn, upper limb
    back —see Burn, back
    breast —see Burn, chest wall
    buttock —see Burn, buttock
    chest wall —see Burn, chest wall
    first degree T21.10
    flank —see Burn, abdominal wall
    genital
      female —see Burn, genital organs,
        external, female
      male —see Burn, genital organs, external,
        male
    groin —see Burn, abdominal wall
    interscapular region —see Burn, back,
      upper
    labia —see Burn, genital organs, external,
      female
    lower back —see Burn, back
    penis —see Burn, genital organs, external,
      male
    perineum
      female —see Burn, genital organs,
        external, female
      male —see Burn, genital organs, external,
        male
    scapula region —see Burn, scapular
      region
    scrotum —see Burn, genital organs,
      external, male
    second degree T21.20
    specified site NEC T21.09
      first degree T21.19
      second degree T21.29
      third degree T21.39
    testes —see Burn, genital organs, external,
      male
    third degree T21.30
    upper back —see Burn, back, upper
    vulva —see Burn, genital organs, external,
      female
  unspecified site with extent of body surface
    involved specified
    less than 10 percent T31.0
    10-19 percent (0-9 percent third degree)
      T31.10
      with 10-19 percent third degree
        T31.11
    20-29 percent (0-9 percent third degree)
      T31.20
      with
        10-19 percent third degree T31.21
        20-29 percent third degree T31.22
    30-39 percent (0-9 percent third degree)
      T31.30
      with
        10-19 percent third degree T31.31
        20-29 percent third degree T31.32
        30-39 percent third degree T31.33
    40-49 percent (0-9 percent third degree)
      T31.40
      with
        10-19 percent third degree T31.41
        20-29 percent third degree T31.42
        30-39 percent third degree T31.43
        40-49 percent third degree T31.44

Burn (Continued)
  unspecified site with extent of body surface
    involved specified (Continued)
    50-59 percent (0-9 percent third degree)
      T31.50
      with
        10-19 percent third degree T31.51
        20-29 percent third degree T31.52
        30-39 percent third degree T31.53
        40-49 percent third degree T31.54
        50-59 percent third degree T31.55
    60-69 percent (0-9 percent third degree)
      T31.60
      with
        10-19 percent third degree T31.61
        20-29 percent third degree T31.62
        30-39 percent third degree T31.63
        40-49 percent third degree T31.64
        50-59 percent third degree T31.65
        60-69 percent third degree T31.66
    70-79 percent (0-9 percent third degree)
      T31.70
      with
        10-19 percent third degree T31.71
        20-29 percent third degree T31.72
        30-39 percent third degree T31.73
        40-49 percent third degree T31.74
        50-59 percent third degree T31.75
        60-69 percent third degree T31.76
        70-79 percent third degree T31.77
    80-89 percent (0-9 percent third degree)
      T31.80
      with
        10-19 percent third degree T31.81
        20-29 percent third degree T31.82
        30-39 percent third degree T31.83
        40-49 percent third degree T31.84
        50-59 percent third degree T31.85
        60-69 percent third degree T31.86
        70-79 percent third degree T31.87
        80-89 percent third degree T31.88
    90 percent or more (0-9 percent third
      degree) T31.90
      with
        10-19 percent third degree T31.91
        20-29 percent third degree T31.92
        30-39 percent third degree T31.93
        40-49 percent third degree T31.94
        50-59 percent third degree T31.95
        60-69 percent third degree T31.96
        70-79 percent third degree T31.97
        80-89 percent third degree T31.98
        90-99 percent third degree T31.99
  upper limb T22.00
    above elbow —see Burn, above elbow
    axilla —see Burn, axilla
    elbow —see Burn, elbow
    first degree T22.10
    forearm —see Burn, forearm
    hand —see Burn, hand
    interscapular region —see Burn, back,
      upper
    multiple sites T22.099
      first degree T22.199
      left T22.092
        first degree T22.192
        second degree T22.292
        third degree T22.392
      right T22.091
        first degree T22.191
        second degree T22.291
        third degree T22.391
      second degree T22.299
      third degree T22.399
    scapular region —see Burn, scapular region
    second degree T22.20
    shoulder —see Burn, shoulder
    third degree T22.30
    wrist —see Burn, wrist
  uterus T28.3
  vagina T28.3

Burn (Continued)
  vulva —see Burn, genital organs, external,
    female
  wrist T23.079
    first degree T23.179
    left T23.072
      first degree T23.172
      second degree T23.272
      third degree T23.372
    multiple sites with hand T23.099
      first degree T23.199
      left T23.092
        first degree T23.192
        second degree T23.292
        third degree T23.392
      right T23.091
        first degree T23.191
        second degree T23.291
        third degree T23.391
      second degree T23.299
      third degree T23.399
    right T23.071
      first degree T23.171
      second degree T23.271
      third degree T23.371
    second degree T23.279
    third degree T23.379
Burnett's syndrome E83.52
Burning
  feet syndrome E53.9
  sensation R20.8
  tongue K14.6
Burn-out (state) Z73.0
Burns' disease or osteochondrosis —see
    Osteochondrosis, juvenile, ulna
Bursa —see condition
Bursitis M71.9
  Achilles —see Tendinitis, Achilles
  adhesive —see Bursitis, specified NEC
  ankle —see Enthesopathy, lower limb, ankle,
    specified type NEC
  calcaneal —see Enthesopathy, foot, specified
    type NEC
  collateral ligament, tibial —see Bursitis, tibial
    collateral
  due to use, overuse, pressure —see also
    Disorder, soft tissue, due to use,
    specified type NEC
    specified NEC —see Disorder, soft tissue,
      due to use, specified NEC
  Duplay's M75.0
  elbow NEC M70.3-●
    olecranon M70.2-●
  finger —see Disorder, soft tissue, due to use,
    specified type NEC, hand
  foot —see Enthesopathy, foot, specified type
    NEC
  gonococcal A54.49
  gouty —see Gout
  hand M70.1-●
  hip NEC M70.7-●
    trochanteric M70.6-●
  infective NEC M71.10
    abscess —see Abscess, bursa
    ankle M71.17-●
    elbow M71.12-●
    foot M71.17-●
    hand M71.14-●
    hip M71.15-●
    knee M71.16-●
    multiple sites M71.19
    shoulder M71.11-●
    specified site NEC M71.18
    wrist M71.13-●
  ischial —see Bursitis, hip
  knee NEC M70.5-●
    prepatellar M70.4-●
  occupational NEC —see also Disorder, soft
    tissue, due to, use
  olecranon —see Bursitis, elbow, olecranon
  pharyngeal J39.1

Bursitis *(Continued)*
  popliteal —*see* Bursitis, knee
  prepatellar M70.4-●
  radiohumeral M77.8
  rheumatoid M06.20
    ankle M06.27-●
    elbow M06.22-●
    foot joint M06.27-●
    hand joint M06.24-●
    hip M06.25-●
    knee M06.26-●
    multiple site M06.29
    shoulder M06.21-●
    vertebra M06.28
    wrist M06.23-●
  scapulohumeral —*see* Bursitis, shoulder
  semimembranous muscle (knee) —*see*
      Bursitis, knee
  shoulder M75.5-●
    adhesive —*see* Capsulitis, adhesive
  specified NEC M71.50
    ankle M71.57-●
    due to use, overuse or pressure —*see*
        Disorder, soft tissue, due to, use
    elbow M71.52-●
    foot M71.57-●
    hand M71.54-●

Bursitis *(Continued)*
  specified NEC *(Continued)*
    hip M71.55-●
    knee M71.56-●
    shoulder —*see* Bursitis, shoulder
    specified site NEC M71.58
    tibial collateral M76.4-●
    wrist M71.53-●
  subacromial —*see* Bursitis, shoulder
  subcoracoid —*see* Bursitis, shoulder
  subdeltoid —*see* Bursitis, shoulder
  syphilitic A52.78
  Thornwaldt, Tornwaldt J39.2
  tibial collateral M76.4-●
  toe —*see* Enthesopathy, foot, specified type
      NEC
  trochanteric (area) —*see* Bursitis, hip,
      trochanteric
  wrist —*see* Bursitis, hand
Bursopathy M71.9
  specified type NEC M71.80
    ankle M71.87-●
    elbow M71.82-●
    foot M71.87-●
    hand M71.84-●
    hip M71.85-●
    knee M71.86-●

Bursopathy *(Continued)*
  specified type NEC *(Continued)*
    multiple sites M71.89
    shoulder M71.81-●
    specified site NEC M71.88
    wrist M71.83-●
Burst stitches or sutures (complication of
    surgery) T81.31
  external operation wound T81.31
  internal operation wound T81.32
Buruli ulcer A31.1
Bury's disease L95.1
Buschke's
  disease B45.3
  scleredema —*see* Sclerosis, systemic
Busse-Buschke disease B45.3
Buttock —*see* condition
Button
  Biskra B55.1
  Delhi B55.1
  oriental B55.1
Buttonhole deformity (finger) —*see* Deformity,
    finger, boutonniere
Bwamba fever A92.8
Byssinosis J66.0
Bywaters' syndrome T79.5

▶ New   ⇒ Revised   ~~deleted~~ Deleted   ● Use Additional Character(s)

C

Cachexia R64
cancerous R64
cardiac —*see* Disease, heart
dehydration E86.0
due to malnutrition R64
exophthalmic —*see* Hyperthyroidism
heart —*see* Disease, heart
hypophyseal E23.0
hypopituitary E23.0
lead —*see* Poisoning, lead
malignant R64
marsh —*see* Malaria
nervous F48.8
old age R54
paludal —*see* Malaria
pituitary E23.0
renal N28.9
saturnine —*see* Poisoning, lead
senile R54
Simmonds' E23.0
splenica D73.0
strumipriva E03.4
tuberculous NEC —*see* Tuberculosis
▶CADASIL (cerebral autosomal dominant arteriopathy with subcortical infarcts and leukoencephalopathy) I67.850
Café au lait spots L81.3
Caffeine-induced
anxiety disorder F15.980
sleep disorder F15.982
Caffey's syndrome Q78.8
Caisson disease T70.3
Cake kidney Q63.1
Caked breast (puerperal, postpartum) O92.79
Calabar swelling B74.3
Calcaneal spur —*see* Spur, bone, calcaneal
Calcaneo-apophysitis M92.8
Calcareous —*see* condition
Calcicosis J62.8
Calciferol (vitamin D) deficiency E55.9
with rickets E55.0
Calcification
adrenal (capsule) (gland) E27.49
tuberculous E35 [B90.8]
aorta I70.0
artery (annular) —*see* Arteriosclerosis
auricle (ear) —*see* Disorder, pinna, specified type NEC
basal ganglia G23.8
bladder N32.89
due to Schistosoma hematobium B65.0
brain (cortex) —*see* Calcification, cerebral
bronchus J98.09
bursa M71.40
ankle M71.47-●
elbow M71.42-●
foot M71.47-●
hand M71.44-●
hip M71.45-●
knee M71.46-●
multiple sites M71.49
shoulder M75.3-●
specified site NEC M71.48
wrist M71.43-●
cardiac —*see* Degeneration, myocardial
cerebral (cortex) G93.89
artery I67.2
cervix (uteri) N88.8
choroid plexus G93.89
conjunctiva —*see* Concretion, conjunctiva
corpora cavernosa (penis) N48.89
cortex (brain) —*see* Calcification, cerebral
dental pulp (nodular) K04.2
dentinal papilla K00.4
fallopian tube N83.8
falx cerebri G96.19
gallbladder K82.8
general E83.59
heart —*see also* Degeneration, myocardial
valve —*see* Endocarditis

Calcification (Continued)
idiopathic infantile arterial (IIAC) Q28.8
intervertebral cartilage or disc (postinfective) —*see* Disorder, disc, specified NEC
intracranial —*see* Calcification, cerebral
joint —*see* Disorder, joint, specified type NEC
kidney N28.89
tuberculous N29 [B90.1]
larynx (senile) J38.7
lens —*see* Cataract, specified NEC
lung (active) (postinfectional) J98.4
tuberculous B90.9
lymph gland or node (postinfectional) I89.8
tuberculous —*see also* Tuberculosis, lymph gland B90.8
mammographic R92.1
massive (paraplegic) —*see* Myositis, ossificans, in, quadriplegia
medial —*see* Arteriosclerosis, extremities
meninges (cerebral) (spinal) G96.19
metastatic E83.59
Mönckeberg's —*see* Arteriosclerosis, extremities
muscle M61.9
due to burns —*see* Myositis, ossificans, in, burns
paralytic —*see* Myositis, ossificans, in, quadriplegia
specified type NEC M61.40
ankle M61.47-●
foot M61.47-●
forearm M61.43-●
hand M61.44-●
lower leg M61.46-●
multiple sites M61.49
pelvic region M61.45-●
shoulder region M61.41-●
specified site NEC M61.48
thigh M61.45-●
upper arm M61.42-●
myocardium, myocardial —*see* Degeneration, myocardial
ovary N83.8
pancreas K86.89
penis N48.89
periarticular —*see* Disorder, joint, specified type NEC
pericardium —*see also* Pericarditis I31.1
pineal gland E34.8
pleura J94.8
postinfectional J94.8
tuberculous NEC B90.9
pulpal (dental) (nodular) K04.2
sclera H15.89
spleen D73.89
subcutaneous L94.2
suprarenal (capsule) (gland) E27.49
tendon (sheath) —*see also* Tenosynovitis, specified type NEC
with bursitis, synovitis or tenosynovitis —*see* Tendinitis, calcific
trachea J39.8
ureter N28.89
vitreous —*see* Deposit, crystalline
Calcified —*see* Calcification
Calcinosis (interstitial) (tumoral) (universalis) E83.59
with Raynaud's phenomenon, esophageal dysfunction, sclerodactyly, telangiectasia (CREST syndrome) M34.1
circumscripta (skin) L94.2
cutis L94.2
Calciphylaxis —*see also* Calcification, by site E83.59
Calcium
deposits —*see* Calcification, by site
metabolism disorder E83.50
salts or soaps in vitreous —*see* Deposit, crystalline

⇒Calciuria R82.994
Calculi —*see* Calculus
Calculosis, intrahepatic —*see* Calculus, bile duct
Calculus, calculi, calculous
ampulla of Vater —*see* Calculus, bile duct
anuria (impacted) (recurrent) —*see also* Calculus, urinary N20.9
appendix K38.1
bile duct (common) (hepatic) K80.50
with
calculus of gallbladder —*see* Calculus, gallbladder and bile duct
cholangitis K80.30
with
cholecystitis —*see* Calculus, bile duct, with cholecystitis
obstruction K80.31
acute K80.32
with
chronic cholangitis K80.36
with obstruction K80.37
obstruction K80.33
chronic K80.34
with
acute cholangitis K80.36
with obstruction K80.37
obstruction K80.35
cholecystitis (with cholangitis) K80.40
with obstruction K80.41
acute K80.42
with
chronic cholecystitis K80.46
with obstruction K80.47
obstruction K80.43
chronic K80.44
with
acute cholecystitis K80.46
with obstruction K80.47
obstruction K80.45
obstruction K80.51
biliary —*see also* Calculus, gallbladder
specified NEC K80.80
with obstruction K80.81
bilirubin, multiple —*see* Calculus, gallbladder
bladder (encysted) (impacted) (urinary) (diverticulum) N21.0
bronchus J98.09
calyx (kidney) (renal) —*see* Calculus, kidney
cholesterol (pure) (solitary) —*see* Calculus, gallbladder
common duct (bile) —*see* Calculus, bile duct
conjunctiva —*see* Concretion, conjunctiva
cystic N21.0
duct —*see* Calculus, gallbladder
dental (subgingival) (supragingival) K03.6
diverticulum
bladder N21.0
kidney N20.0
epididymis N50.89
gallbladder K80.20
with
bile duct calculus —*see* Calculus, gallbladder and bile duct
cholecystitis K80.10
with obstruction K80.11
acute K80.00
with
chronic cholecystitis K80.12
with obstruction K80.13
obstruction K80.01
chronic K80.10
with
acute cholecystitis K80.12
with obstruction K80.13
obstruction K80.11
specified NEC K80.18
with obstruction K80.19
obstruction K80.21

Calculus, calculi, calculous (Continued)
- gallbladder and bile duct K80.70
  - with
    - cholecystitis K80.60
      - with obstruction K80.61
      - acute K80.62
        - with
          - chronic cholecystitis K80.66
            - with obstruction K80.67
          - obstruction K80.63
        - chronic K80.64
          - with
            - acute cholecystitis K80.66
              - with obstruction K80.67
            - obstruction K80.65
    - obstruction K80.71
- hepatic (duct) —see Calculus, bile duct
- hepatobiliary K80.80
  - with obstruction K80.81
- ileal conduit N21.8
- intestinal (impaction) (obstruction) K56.49
- kidney (impacted) (multiple) (pelvis) (recurrent) (staghorn) N20.0
  - with calculus, ureter N20.2
  - congenital Q63.8
- lacrimal passages —see Dacryolith
- liver (impacted) —see Calculus, bile duct
- lung J98.4
- mammographic R92.1
- nephritic (impacted) (recurrent) —see Calculus, kidney
- nose J34.89
- pancreas (duct) K86.89
- parotid duct or gland K11.5
- pelvis, encysted —see Calculus, kidney
- prostate N42.0
- pulmonary J98.4
- pyelitis (impacted) (recurrent) N20.0
  - with hydronephrosis N13.2
- pyelonephritis (impacted) (recurrent) —see category N20
  - with hydronephrosis N13.2
- renal (impacted) (recurrent) —see Calculus, kidney
- salivary (duct) (gland) K11.5
- seminal vesicle N50.89
- staghorn —see Calculus, kidney
- Stensen's duct K11.5
- stomach K31.89
- sublingual duct or gland K11.5
  - congenital Q38.4
- submandibular duct, gland or region K11.5
- submaxillary duct, gland or region K11.5
- suburethral N21.8
- tonsil J35.8
- tooth, teeth (subgingival) (supragingival) K03.6
- tunica vaginalis N50.89
- ureter (impacted) (recurrent) N20.1
  - with calculus, kidney N20.2
    - with hydronephrosis N13.2
      - with infection N13.6
- urethra (impacted) N21.1
- urinary (duct) (impacted) (passage) (tract) N20.9
  - with hydronephrosis N13.2
    - with infection N13.6
  - in (due to)
  - lower N21.9
    - specified NEC N21.8
- vagina N89.8
- vesical (impacted) N21.0
- Wharton's duct K11.5
- xanthine E79.8 [N22]

Calicectasis N28.89
Caliectasis N28.89
California
- disease B38.9
- encephalitis A83.5
Caligo cornea —see Opacity, cornea, central
Callositas, callosity (infected) L84

Callus (infected) L84
- bone —see Osteophyte
- excessive, following fracture - code as Sequelae of fracture
CALME (childhood asymmetric labium majus enlargement) N90.61
Calorie deficiency or malnutrition —see also Malnutrition E46
Calvé-Perthes disease —see Legg-Calve-Perthes disease
Calvé's disease —see Osteochondrosis, juvenile, spine
Calvities —see Alopecia, androgenic
Cameroon fever —see Malaria
Camptocormia (hysterical) F44.4
Camurati-Engelmann syndrome Q78.3
Canal —see also condition
- atrioventricular common Q21.2
Canaliculitis (lacrimal) (acute) (subacute) H04.33-●
- Actinomyces A42.89
- chronic H04.42-●
Canavan's disease E75.29
Canceled procedure (surgical) Z53.9
- because of
  - contraindication Z53.09
    - smoking Z53.01
  - left against medical advice (AMA) Z53.21
  - patient's decision Z53.20
    - for reasons of belief or group pressure Z53.1
    - specified reason NEC Z53.29
  - specified reason NEC Z53.8
Cancer —see also Neoplasm, by site, malignant
- bile duct type, liver C22.1
- blood —see Leukemia
- breast —see also Neoplasm, breast, malignant C50.91-●
- hepatocellular C22.0
- lung —see also Neoplasm, lung, malignant C34.90-●
- ovarian —see also Neoplasm, ovary, malignant C56.9-●
- unspecified site (primary) C80.1
Cancer (o)phobia F45.29
Cancerous —see Neoplasm, malignant, by site
Cancrum oris A69.0
Candidiasis, candidal B37.9
- balanitis B37.42
- bronchitis B37.1
- cheilitis B37.83
- congenital P37.5
- cystitis B37.41
- disseminated B37.7
- endocarditis B37.6
- enteritis B37.82
- esophagitis B37.81
- intertrigo B37.2
- lung B37.1
- meningitis B37.5
- mouth B37.0
- nails B37.2
- neonatal P37.5
- onychia B37.2
- oral B37.0
- osteomyelitis B37.89
- otitis externa B37.84
- paronychia B37.2
- perionyxis B37.2
- pneumonia B37.1
- proctitis B37.82
- pulmonary B37.1
- pyelonephritis B37.49
- sepsis B37.7
- skin B37.2
- specified site NEC B37.89
- stomatitis B37.0
- systemic B37.7
- urethritis B37.41
- urogenital site NEC B37.49
- vagina B37.3
- vulva B37.3
- vulvovaginitis B37.3

Candidid L30.2
Candidosis —see Candidiasis
Candiru infection or infestation B88.8
Canities (premature) L67.1
- congenital Q84.2
Canker (mouth) (sore) K12.0
- rash A38.9
Cannabinosis J66.2
Cannabis induced
- anxiety disorder F12.980
- psychotic disorder F12.959
- sleep disorder F12.988
Canton fever A75.9
Cantrell's syndrome Q87.89
Capillariasis (intestinal) B81.1
- hepatic B83.8
Capillary —see condition
Caplan's syndrome —see Rheumatoid, lung
Capsule —see condition
Capsulitis (joint) —see also Enthesopathy
- adhesive (shoulder) M75.0-●
- hepatic K65.8
- labyrinthine —see Otosclerosis, specified NEC
- thyroid E06.9
Caput
- crepitus Q75.8
- medusae I86.8
- succedaneum P12.81
Car sickness T75.3
Carapata (disease) A68.0
Carate —see Pinta
Carbon lung J60
Carbuncle L02.93
- abdominal wall L02.231
- anus K61.0
- auditory canal, external —see Abscess, ear, external
- auricle ear —see Abscess, ear, external
- axilla L02.43-●
- back (any part) L02.232
- breast N61.1
- buttock L02.33
- cheek (external) L02.03
- chest wall L02.233
- chin L02.03
- corpus cavernosum N48.21
- ear (any part) (external) (middle) —see Abscess, ear, external
- external auditory canal —see Abscess, ear, external
- eyelid —see Abscess, eyelid
- face NEC L02.03
- femoral (region) —see Carbuncle, lower limb
- finger —see Carbuncle, hand
- flank L02.231
- foot L02.63-●
- forehead L02.03
- genital —see Abscess, genital
- gluteal (region) L02.33
- groin L02.234
- hand L02.53-●
- head NEC L02.831
- heel —see Carbuncle, foot
- hip —see Carbuncle, lower limb
- kidney —see Abscess, kidney
- knee —see Carbuncle, lower limb
- labium (majus) (minus) N76.4
- lacrimal
  - gland —see Dacryoadenitis
  - passages (duct) (sac) —see Inflammation, lacrimal, passages, acute
- leg —see Carbuncle, lower limb
- lower limb L02.43-●
- malignant A22.0
- navel L02.236
- neck L02.13
- nose (external) (septum) J34.0
- orbit, orbital —see Abscess, orbit
- palmar (space) —see Carbuncle, hand
- partes posteriores L02.33
- pectoral region L02.233
- penis N48.21

▶ New   ⇒ Revised   ~~deleted~~ Deleted   ● Use Additional Character(s)

Carbuncle *(Continued)*
  perineum L02.235
  pinna —*see* Abscess, ear, external
  popliteal —*see* Carbuncle, lower limb
  scalp L02.831
  seminal vesicle N49.0
  shoulder —*see* Carbuncle, upper limb
  specified site NEC L02.838
  temple (region) L02.03
  thumb —*see* Carbuncle, hand
  toe —*see* Carbuncle, foot
  trunk L02.239
    abdominal wall L02.231
    back L02.232
    chest wall L02.233
    groin L02.234
    perineum L02.235
    umbilicus L02.236
  umbilicus L02.236
  upper limb L02.43-●
  urethra N34.0
  vulva N76.4
Carbunculus —*see* Carbuncle
Carcinoid (tumor) —*see* Tumor, carcinoid
Carcinoidosis E34.0
Carcinoma (malignant) —*see also* Neoplasm,
  by site, malignant
  acidophil
    specified site —*see* Neoplasm, malignant,
      by site
    unspecified site C75.1
  acidophil-basophil, mixed
    specified site —*see* Neoplasm, malignant,
      by site
    unspecified site C75.1
  adnexal (skin) —*see* Neoplasm, skin, malignant
  adrenal cortical C74.0-●
  alveolar —*see* Neoplasm, lung, malignant
    cell —*see* Neoplasm, lung, malignant
  ameloblastic C41.1
    upper jaw (bone) C41.0
  apocrine
    breast —*see* Neoplasm, breast, malignant
    specified site NEC —*see* Neoplasm, skin,
      malignant
    unspecified site C44.99
  basal cell (pigmented) (*see also* Neoplasm,
    skin, malignant) C44.91
    fibro-epithelial —*see* Neoplasm, skin,
      malignant
    morphea —*see* Neoplasm, skin, malignant
    multicentric —*see* Neoplasm, skin,
      malignant
  basaloid
  basal-squamous cell, mixed —*see* Neoplasm,
    skin, malignant
  basophil
    specified site —*see* Neoplasm, malignant,
      by site
    unspecified site C75.1
  basophil-acidophil, mixed
    specified site —*see* Neoplasm, malignant,
      by site
    unspecified site C75.1
  basosquamous —*see* Neoplasm, skin, malignant
  bile duct
    with hepatocellular, mixed C22.0
    liver C22.1
    specified site NEC —*see* Neoplasm,
      malignant, by site
    unspecified site C22.1
  branchial or branchiogenic C10.4
  bronchial or bronchogenic —*see* Neoplasm,
    lung, malignant
  bronchiolar —*see* Neoplasm, lung, malignant
  bronchioloalveolar —*see* Neoplasm, lung,
    malignant
  C cell
    specified site —*see* Neoplasm, malignant,
      by site
    unspecified site C73
  ceruminous C44.29-●

Carcinoma *(Continued)*
  cervix uteri
    in situ D06.9
      endocervix D06.0
      exocervix D06.1
      specified site NEC D06.7
  chorionic
    specified site —*see* Neoplasm, malignant,
      by site
    unspecified site
      female C58
      male C62.90
  chromophobe
    specified site —*see* Neoplasm, malignant,
      by site
    unspecified site C75.1
  cloacogenic
    specified site —*see* Neoplasm, malignant,
      by site
    unspecified site C21.2
  diffuse type
    specified site —*see* Neoplasm, malignant,
      by site
    unspecified site C16.9
  duct (cell)
    with Paget's disease —*see* Neoplasm,
      breast, malignant
    infiltrating
      with lobular carcinoma (in situ)
        specified site —*see* Neoplasm,
          malignant, by site
        unspecified site (female) C50.91-●
          male C50.92-●
      specified site —*see* Neoplasm,
        malignant, by site
      unspecified site (female) C50.91-●
        male C50.92-●
  ductal
    with lobular
      specified site —*see* Neoplasm,
        malignant, by site
      unspecified site (female) C50.91-●
        male C50.92-●
  ductular, infiltrating
    specified site —*see* Neoplasm, malignant,
      by site
    unspecified site (female) C50.91-●
      male C50.92-●
  embryonal
    liver C22.7
  endometrioid
    specified site —*see* Neoplasm, malignant,
      by site
    unspecified site
      female C56.9
      male C61
  eosinophil
    specified site —*see* Neoplasm, malignant,
      by site
    unspecified site C75.1
  epidermoid —*see also* Neoplasm, skin
    malignant
    in situ, Bowen's type —*see* Neoplasm, skin,
      in situ
  fibroepithelial, basal cell —*see* Neoplasm,
    skin, malignant
  follicular
    with papillary (mixed) C73
    moderately differentiated C73
    pure follicle C73
    specified site —*see* Neoplasm, malignant,
      by site
    trabecular C73
    unspecified site C73
    well differentiated C73
  generalized, with unspecified primary site
    C80.0
  glycogen-rich —*see* Neoplasm, breast,
    malignant
  granulosa cell C56-●
  hepatic cell C22.0

Carcinoma *(Continued)*
  hepatocellular C22.0
    with bile duct, mixed C22.0
    fibrolamellar C22.0
  hepatocholangiolitic C22.0
  Hurthle cell C73
  in
    adenomatous
      polyposis coli C18.9
    pleomorphic adenoma —*see* Neoplasm,
      salivary glands, malignant
    situ —*see* Carcinoma-in-situ
  infiltrating
    duct
      with lobular
        specified site —*see* Neoplasm,
          malignant, by site
        unspecified site (female) C50.91-●
          male C50.92-●
      with Paget's disease —*see* Neoplasm,
        breast, malignant
      specified site —*see* Neoplasm,
        malignant
      unspecified site (female) C50.91-●
        male C50.92-●
    ductular
      specified site —*see* Neoplasm,
        malignant
      unspecified site (female) C50.91-●
        male C50.92-●
    lobular
      specified site —*see* Neoplasm,
        malignant
      unspecified site (female) C50.91-●
        male C50.92-●
  inflammatory
    specified site —*see* Neoplasm, malignant
    unspecified site (female) C50.91-●
      male C50.92-●
  intestinal type
    specified site —*see* Neoplasm, malignant,
      by site
    unspecified site C16.9
  intracystic
    noninfiltrating —*see* Neoplasm, in situ,
      by site
  intraductal (noninfiltrating)
    with Paget's disease —*see* Neoplasm,
      breast, malignant
    breast D05.1-●
    papillary
      with invasion
        specified site —*see* Neoplasm,
          malignant, by site
        unspecified site (female) C50.91-●
          male C50.92-●
      breast D05.1-●
      specified site NEC —*see* Neoplasm,
        in situ, by site
      unspecified site (female) D05.1-●
    specified site NEC —*see* Neoplasm,
      in situ, by site
    unspecified site (female) D05.1-●
  intraepidermal —*see* Neoplasm, in situ
    squamous cell, Bowen's type —*see*
      Neoplasm, skin, in situ
  intraepithelial —*see* Neoplasm, in situ,
    by site
    squamous cell —*see* Neoplasm, in situ,
      by site
  intraosseous C41.1
    upper jaw (bone) C41.0
  islet cell
    with exocrine, mixed
      specified site —*see* Neoplasm,
        malignant, by site
      unspecified site C25.9
    pancreas C25.4
    specified site NEC —*see* Neoplasm,
      malignant, by site
    unspecified site C25.4

Carcinoma *(Continued)*
 juvenile, breast —*see* Neoplasm, breast,
  malignant
 large cell
  small cell
   specified site —*see* Neoplasm,
    malignant, by site
   unspecified site C34.90
 Leydig cell (testis)
  specified site —*see* Neoplasm, malignant,
   by site
  unspecified site
   female C56.9
   male C62.90
 lipid-rich (female) C50.91-●
  male C50.92-●
 liver cell C22.0
 liver NEC C22.7
 lobular (infiltrating)
  with intraductal
   specified site —*see* Neoplasm,
    malignant, by site
   unspecified site (female) C50.91-●
    male C50.92-●
  noninfiltrating
   breast D05.0-●
   specified site NEC —*see* Neoplasm, in
    situ, by site
   unspecified site D05.0-●
  specified site —*see* Neoplasm, malignant,
   by site
  unspecified site (female) C50.91-●
   male C50.92-●
 medullary
  with
   amyloid stroma
    specified site —*see* Neoplasm,
     malignant, by site
    unspecified site C73
   lymphoid stroma
    specified site —*see* Neoplasm,
     malignant, by site
    unspecified site (female) C50.91-●
     male C50.92-●
 Merkel cell C4A.9
  anal margin C4A.51
  anal skin C4A.51
  canthus C4A.1-●
  ear and external auricular canal C4A.2-●
  external auricular canal C4A.2-●
  eyelid, including canthus C4A.1-●
  face C4A.30
   specified NEC C4A.39
  hip C4A.7-●
  lip C4A.0
  lower limb, including hip C4A.7-●
  neck C4A.4
  nodal presentation C7B.1
  nose C4A.31
  overlapping sites C4A.8
  perianal skin C4A.51
  scalp C4A.4
  secondary C7B.1
  shoulder C4A.6-●
  skin of breast C4A.52
  trunk NEC C4A.59
  upper limb, including shoulder C4A.6-●
  visceral metastatic C7B.1
 metastatic —*see* Neoplasm, secondary
 metatypical —*see* Neoplasm, skin, malignant
 morphea, basal cell —*see* Neoplasm, skin,
  malignant
 mucoid
  cell
   specified site —*see* Neoplasm,
    malignant, by site
   unspecified site C75.1
 neuroendocrine —*see also* Tumor,
   neuroendocrine
  high grade, any site C7A.1
  poorly differentiated, any site C7A.1

Carcinoma *(Continued)*
 nonencapsulated sclerosing C73
 noninfiltrating
  intracystic —*see* Neoplasm, in situ, by site
  intraductal
   breast D05.1-●
   papillary
    breast D05.1-●
    specified site NEC —*see* Neoplasm, in
     situ, by site
    unspecified site D05.1-●
   specified site —*see* Neoplasm, in situ,
    by site
   unspecified site D05.1-●
  lobular
   breast D05.0-●
   specified site NEC —*see* Neoplasm, in
    situ, by site
   unspecified site (female) D05.0-●
 oat cell
  specified site —*see* Neoplasm, malignant,
   by site
  unspecified site C34.90
 odontogenic C41.1
  upper jaw (bone) C41.0
 papillary
  with follicular (mixed) C73
  follicular variant C73
  intraductal (noninfiltrating)
   with invasion
    specified site —*see* Neoplasm,
     malignant, by site
    unspecified site (female) C50.91-●
     male C50.92-●
   breast D05.1-●
   specified site NEC —*see* Neoplasm, in
    situ, by site
   unspecified site D05.1-●
  serous
   specified site —*see* Neoplasm,
    malignant, by site
   surface
    specified site —*see* Neoplasm,
     malignant, by site
    unspecified site C56.9
   unspecified site C56.9
 papillocystic
  specified site —*see* Neoplasm, malignant,
   by site
  unspecified site C56.9
 parafollicular cell
  specified site —*see* Neoplasm, malignant,
   by site
  unspecified site C73
 pilomatrix —*see* Neoplasm, skin, malignant
 pseudomucinous
  specified site —*see* Neoplasm, malignant,
   by site
  unspecified site C56.9
 renal cell C64-●
 Schmincke —*see* Neoplasm, nasopharynx,
  malignant
 Schneiderian
  specified site —*see* Neoplasm, malignant,
   by site
  unspecified site C30.0
 sebaceous —*see* Neoplasm, skin, malignant
 secondary —*see also* Neoplasm, secondary,
   by site
  Merkel cell C7B.1
 secretory, breast —*see* Neoplasm, breast,
  malignant
 serous
  papillary
   specified site —*see* Neoplasm,
    malignant, by site
   unspecified site C56.9
  surface, papillary
   specified site —*see* Neoplasm,
    malignant, by site
   unspecified site C56.9

Carcinoma *(Continued)*
 Sertoli cell
  specified site —*see* Neoplasm, malignant,
   by site
  unspecified site C62.90
   female C56.9
   male C62.90
 skin appendage —*see* Neoplasm, skin,
  malignant
 small cell
  fusiform cell
   specified site —*see* Neoplasm,
    malignant, by site
   unspecified site C34.90
  intermediate cell
   specified site —*see* Neoplasm,
    malignant, by site
   unspecified site C34.90
  large cell
   specified site —*see* Neoplasm,
    malignant, by site
   unspecified site C34.90
 solid
  with amyloid stroma
   specified site —*see* Neoplasm,
    malignant, by site
   unspecified site C73
  microinvasive
   specified site —*see* Neoplasm,
    malignant, by site
   unspecified site C53.9
 sweat gland —*see* Neoplasm, skin,
  malignant
 theca cell C56.-●
 thymic C37
 unspecified site (primary) C80.1
 water-clear cell C75.0
Carcinoma-in-situ —*see also* Neoplasm, in situ,
  by site
 breast NOS D05.9-●
  specified type NEC D05.8-●
 epidermoid —*see also* Neoplasm, in situ, by
   site
  with questionable stromal invasion
   cervix D06.9
   specified site NEC —*see* Neoplasm, in
    situ, by site
   unspecified site D06.9
  Bowen's type —*see* Neoplasm, skin,
   in situ
 intraductal
  breast D05.1-●
  specified site NEC —*see* Neoplasm, in situ,
   by site
  unspecified site D05.1-●
 lobular
  with
   infiltrating duct
    breast (female) C50.91-●
     male C50.92-●
    specified site NEC —*see* Neoplasm,
     malignant
    unspecified site (female) C50.91-●
     male C50.92-●
   intraductal
    breast D05.8-●
    specified site NEC —*see* Neoplasm, in
     situ, by site
    unspecified site (female) D05.8-●
  breast D05.0-●
  specified site NEC —*see* Neoplasm, in situ,
   by site
  unspecified site D05.0-●
 squamous cell —*see also* Neoplasm, in situ,
   by site
  with questionable stromal invasion
   cervix D06.9
   specified site NEC —*see* Neoplasm, in
    situ, by site
   unspecified site D06.9
Carcinomaphobia F45.29

▶ New   ⇒ Revised   ~~deleted~~ Deleted   ● Use Additional Character(s)

Carcinomatosis C80.0
  peritonei C78.6
  unspecified site (primary) (secondary) C80.0
Carcinosarcoma —see Neoplasm, malignant,
    by site
  embryonal —see Neoplasm, malignant, by site
Cardia, cardial —see condition
Cardiac —see also condition
  death, sudden —see Arrest, cardiac
  pacemaker
    in situ Z95.0
    management or adjustment Z45.018
  tamponade I31.4
Cardialgia —see Pain, precordial
Cardiectasis —see Hypertrophy, cardiac
Cardiochalasia K21.9
Cardiomalacia I51.5
Cardiomegalia glycogenica diffusa E74.02 [143]
Cardiomegaly —see also Hypertrophy, cardiac
  congenital Q24.8
  glycogen E74.02 [143]
  idiopathic I51.7
Cardiomyoliposis I51.5
Cardiomyopathy (familial) (idiopathic) I42.9
  alcoholic I42.6
  amyloid E85.4 [143]
    transthyretin-related (ATTR) familial E85.4
  arteriosclerotic —see Disease, heart, ischemic,
    atherosclerotic
  beriberi E51.12
  cobalt-beer I42.6
  congenital I42.4
  congestive I42.0
  constrictive NOS I42.5
  dilated I42.0
  due to
    alcohol I42.6
    beriberi E51.12
    cardiac glycogenosis E74.02 [143]
    drugs I42.7
    external agents NEC I42.7
    Friedreich's ataxia G11.1
    myotonia atrophica G71.11 [143]
    ⇒progressive muscular dystrophy G71.09
        [143]
  glycogen storage E74.02 [143]
  hypertensive —see Hypertension, heart
  hypertrophic (nonobstructive) I42.2
    obstructive I42.1
      congenital Q24.8
  in
    Chagas' disease (chronic) B57.2
      acute B57.0
    sarcoidosis D86.85
  ischemic I25.5
  metabolic E88.9 [143]
    thyrotoxic E05.90 [143]
      with thyroid storm E05.91 [143]
  newborn I42.8
    congenital I42.4
  nutritional E63.9 [143]
    beriberi E51.12
  obscure of Africa I42.8
  peripartum O90.3
  postpartum O90.3
  restrictive NEC I42.5
  rheumatic I09.0
  secondary I42.9
  stress induced I51.81
  takotsubo I51.81
  thyrotoxic E05.90 [143]
    with thyroid storm E05.91 [143]
  toxic NEC I42.7
  transthyretin-related (ATTR) familial amyloid
    E85.4
  tuberculous A18.84
  viral B33.24
Cardionephritis —see Hypertension,
    cardiorenal
Cardionephropathy —see Hypertension,
    cardiorenal

Cardionephrosis —see Hypertension, cardiorenal
Cardiopathia nigra I27.0
Cardiopathy —see also Disease, heart I51.9
  idiopathic I42.9
  mucopolysaccharidosis E76.3 [I52]
Cardiopericarditis —see Pericarditis
Cardiophobia F45.29
Cardiorenal —see condition
Cardiorrhexis —see Infarct, myocardium
Cardiosclerosis —see Disease, heart, ischemic,
    atherosclerotic
Cardiosis —see Disease, heart
Cardiospasm (esophagus) (reflex) (stomach)
    K22.0
  congenital Q39.5
    with megaesophagus Q39.5
Cardiostenosis —see Disease, heart
Cardiosymphysis I31.0
Cardiovascular —see condition
Carditis (acute) (bacterial) (chronic) (subacute)
    I51.89
  meningococcal A39.50
  rheumatic —see Disease, heart, rheumatic
  rheumatoid —see Rheumatoid, carditis
  viral B33.20
Care (of) (for) (following)
  child (routine) Z76.2
  family member (handicapped) (sick)
    creating problem for family Z63.6
    provided away from home for holiday
        relief Z75.5
    unavailable, due to
      absence (person rendering care)
          (sufferer) Z74.2
      inability (any reason) of person
          rendering care Z74.2
  foundling Z76.1
  holiday relief Z75.5
  improper —see Maltreatment
  lack of (at or after birth) (infant) —see
    Maltreatment, child, neglect
  lactating mother Z39.1
  palliative Z51.5
  postpartum
    immediately after delivery Z39.0
    routine follow-up Z39.2
  respite Z75.5
  unavailable, due to
    absence of person rendering care Z74.2
    inability (any reason) of person rendering
        care Z74.2
  well-baby Z76.2
Caries
  bone NEC A18.03
  dental (dentino enamel junction) (early
      childhood) (of dentine) (pre-eruptive)
      (recurrent) (to the pulp) K02.9
    arrested (coronal) (root) K02.3
    chewing surface
      limited to enamel K02.51
      penetrating into dentin K02.52
      penetrating into pulp K02.53
    coronal surface
      chewing surface
        limited to enamel K02.51
        penetrating into dentin K02.52
        penetrating into pulp K02.53
      pit and fissure surface
        limited to enamel K02.51
        penetrating into dentin K02.52
        penetrating into pulp K02.53
      smooth surface
        limited to enamel K02.61
        penetrating into dentin K02.62
        penetrating into pulp K02.63
    pit and fissure surface
      limited to enamel K02.51
      penetrating into dentin K02.52
      penetrating into pulp K02.53
    primary, cervical origin K02.52
    root K02.7

Caries (Continued)
  dental (Continued)
    smooth surface
      limited to enamel K02.61
      penetrating into dentin K02.62
      penetrating into pulp K02.63
  external meatus —see Disorder, ear, external,
    specified type NEC
  hip (tuberculous) A18.02
  initial (tooth)
    chewing surface K02.51
    pit and fissure surface K02.51
    smooth surface K02.61
  knee (tuberculous) A18.02
  labyrinth —see subcategory H83.8
  limb NEC (tuberculous) A18.03
  mastoid process (chronic) —see Mastoiditis,
    chronic
    tuberculous A18.03
  middle ear —see subcategory H74.8
  nose (tuberculous) A18.03
  orbit (tuberculous) A18.03
  ossicles, ear —see Abnormal, ear ossicles
  petrous bone —see Petrositis
  root (dental) (tooth) K02.7
  sacrum (tuberculous) A18.01
  spine, spinal (column) (tuberculous) A18.01
  syphilitic A52.77
    congenital (early) A50.02 [M90.80]
  tooth, teeth —see Caries, dental
  tuberculous A18.03
  vertebra (column) (tuberculous) A18.01
Carious teeth —see Caries, dental
Carneous mole O02.0
Carnitine insufficiency E71.40
⇒Carotenemia (dietary) E67.1
⇒Carotenosis (cutis) (skin) E67.1
Carotid body or sinus syndrome G90.01
Carotidynia G90.01
Carpal tunnel syndrome —see Syndrome,
    carpal tunnel
Carpenter's syndrome Q87.0
Carpopedal spasm —see Tetany
Carr-Barr-Plunkett syndrome Q97.1
Carrier (suspected) of
  amebiasis Z22.1
  bacterial disease NEC Z22.39
    diphtheria Z22.2
    intestinal infectious NEC Z22.1
      typhoid Z22.0
    meningococcal Z22.31
    sexually transmitted Z22.4
    specified NEC Z22.39
    staphylococcal (Methicillin susceptible)
        Z22.321
      Methicillin resistant Z22.322
    streptococcal Z22.338
      group B Z22.330
        complicating pregnancy or delivery
            O99.82-●
    typhoid Z22.0
  cholera Z22.1
  diphtheria Z22.2
  gastrointestinal pathogens NEC Z22.1
  genetic Z14.8
    cystic fibrosis Z14.1
    hemophilia A (asymptomatic) Z14.01
      symptomatic Z14.02
  gestational, pregnant Z33.1
  gonorrhea Z22.4
  HAA (hepatitis Australian-antigen) B18.8
  HB (c)(s)-AG B18.1
  hepatitis (viral) B18.9
    Australia-antigen (HAA) B18.8
    B surface antigen (HBsAg) B18.1
      with acute delta- (super)infection
          B17.0
    C B18.2
    specified NEC B18.8
  human T-cell lymphotropic virus type-1
      (HTLV-1) infection Z22.6

Carrier of *(Continued)*
  infectious organism Z22.9
    specified NEC Z22.8
  meningococci Z22.31
  Salmonella typhosa Z22.0
  serum hepatitis —*see* Carrier, hepatitis
  staphylococci (Methicillin susceptible) Z22.321
    Methicillin resistant Z22.322
  streptococci Z22.338
    group B Z22.330
      complicating pregnancy or delivery
        O99.82-●
  syphilis Z22.4
  typhoid Z22.0
  venereal disease NEC Z22.4
Carrion's disease A44.0
Carter's relapsing fever (Asiatic) A68.1
Cartilage —*see* condition
Caruncle (inflamed)
  conjunctiva (acute) —*see* Conjunctivitis, acute
  labium (majus) (minus) N90.89
  lacrimal —*see* Inflammation, lacrimal,
    passages
  myrtiform N89.8
  urethral (benign) N36.2
Cascade stomach K31.2
Caseation lymphatic gland (tuberculous) A18.2
Cassidy (-Scholte) syndrome (malignant
  carcinoid) E34.0
Castellani's disease A69.8
Castration, traumatic, male S38.231
Casts in urine R82.998
Cat
  cry syndrome Q93.4
  ear Q17.3
  eye syndrome Q92.8
Catabolism, senile R54
Catalepsy (hysterical) F44.2
  schizophrenic F20.2
Cataplexy (idiopathic) —*see* - Narcolepsy
Cataract (cortical) (immature) (incipient) H26.9
  with
    neovascularization —*see* Cataract,
      complicated
  age-related —*see* Cataract, senile
  anterior
    and posterior axial embryonal Q12.0
    pyramidal Q12.0
  associated with
    galactosemia E74.21 *[H28]*
    myotonic disorders G71.19 *[H28]*
  blue Q12.0
  central Q12.0
  cerulean Q12.0
  complicated H26.20
    with
      neovascularization H26.21-●
      ocular disorder H26.22-●
    glaucomatous flecks H26.23-●
  congenital Q12.0
  coraliform Q12.0
  coronary Q12.0
  crystalline Q12.0
  diabetic —*see* Diabetes, cataract
  drug-induced H26.3-●
  due to
    ocular disorder —*see* Cataract, complicated
    radiation H26.8
  electric H26.8
  extraction status Z98.4-●
  glass-blower's H26.8
  heat ray H26.8
  heterochromic —*see* Cataract, complicated
  hypermature —*see* Cataract, senile,
    morgagnian type
  in (due to)
    chronic iridocyclitis —*see* Cataract,
      complicated
    diabetes —*see* Diabetes, cataract
    endocrine disease E34.9 *[H28]*
    eye disease —*see* Cataract, complicated

Cataract *(Continued)*
  in (due to) *(Continued)*
    hypoparathyroidism E20.9 *[H28]*
    malnutrition-dehydration E46 *[H28]*
    metabolic disease E88.9 *[H28]*
    myotonic disorders G71.19 *[H28]*
    nutritional disease E63.9 *[H28]*
  infantile —*see* Cataract, presenile
  irradiational —*see* Cataract, specified NEC
  juvenile —*see* Cataract, presenile
  malnutrition-dehydration E46 *[H28]*
  morgagnian —*see* Cataract, senile,
    morgagnian type
  myotonic G71.19 *[H28]*
  myxedema E03.9 *[H28]*
  nuclear
    embryonal Q12.0
    sclerosis —*see* Cataract, senile, nuclear
  presenile H26.00-●
    combined forms H26.06-●
    cortical H26.01-●
    lamellar —*see* Cataract, presenile, cortical
    nuclear H26.03-●
    specified NEC H26.09
    subcapsular polar (anterior) H26.04-●
      posterior H26.05-●
    zonular —*see* Cataract, presenile, cortical
  secondary H26.40
    Soemmering's ring H26.41-●
    specified NEC H26.49-●
    to eye disease —*see* Cataract, complicated
  senile H25.9
    brunescens —*see* Cataract, senile, nuclear
    combined forms H25.81-●
    coronary —*see* Cataract, senile, incipient
    cortical H25.01-●
    hypermature —*see* Cataract, senile,
      morgagnian type
    incipient (mature) (total) H25.09-●
      cortical —*see* Cataract, senile, cortical
      subcapsular —*see* Cataract, senile,
        subcapsular
    morgagnian type (hypermature) H25.2-●
    nuclear (sclerosis) H25.1-●
    polar subcapsular (anterior) (posterior) —
      see Cataract, senile, incipient
    punctate —*see* Cataract, senile, incipient
    specified NEC H25.89
    subcapsular polar (anterior) H25.03-●
      posterior H25.04-●
  snowflake —*see* Diabetes, cataract
  specified NEC H26.8
  toxic —*see* Cataract, drug-induced
  traumatic H26.10-●
    localized H26.11-●
    partially resolved H26.12-●
    total H26.13-●
  zonular (perinuclear) Q12.0
Cataracta —*see also* Cataract
  brunescens —*see* Cataract, senile, nuclear
  centralis pulverulenta Q12.0
  cerulea Q12.0
  complicata —*see* Cataract, complicated
  congenita Q12.0
  coralliformis Q12.0
  coronaria Q12.0
  diabetica —*see* Diabetes, cataract
  membranacea
    accreta —*see* Cataract, secondary
    congenita Q12.0
  nigra —*see* Cataract, senile, nuclear
  sunflower —*see* Cataract, complicated
Catarrh, catarrhal (acute) (febrile) (infectious)
  (inflammation) (*see also* condition) J00
  bronchial —*see* Bronchitis
  chest —*see* Bronchitis
  chronic J31.0
  due to congenital syphilis A50.03
  enteric —*see* Enteritis
  eustachian H68.009
  fauces —*see* Pharyngitis

Catarrh, catarrhal *(Continued)*
  gastrointestinal —*see* Enteritis
  gingivitis K05.00
    nonplaque induced K05.01
    plaque induced K05.00
  hay —*see* Fever, hay
  intestinal —*see* Enteritis
  larynx, chronic J37.0
  liver B15.9
    with hepatic coma B15.0
  lung —*see* Bronchitis
  middle ear, chronic —*see* Otitis, media,
    nonsuppurative, chronic, serous
  mouth K12.1
  nasal (chronic) —*see* Rhinitis
  nasobronchial J31.1
  nasopharyngeal (chronic) J31.1
    acute J00
  pulmonary —*see* Bronchitis
  spring (eye) (vernal) —*see* Conjunctivitis,
    acute, atopic
  summer (hay) —*see* Fever, hay
  throat J31.2
  tubotympanal —*see also* Otitis, media,
    nonsuppurative
    chronic —*see* Otitis, media,
      nonsuppurative, chronic, serous
Catatonia (schizophrenic) F20.2
Catatonic
  disorder due to known physiologic condition
    F06.1
  schizophrenia F20.2
  stupor R40.1
Cat-scratch —*see also* Abrasion
  disease or fever A28.1
Cauda equina —*see* condition
Cauliflower ear M95.1-●
Causalgia (upper limb) G56.4-●
  lower limb G57.7-●
Cause
  external, general effects T75.89
Caustic burn —*see* Corrosion, by site
Cavare's disease (familial periodic paralysis)
  G72.3
Cave-in, injury
  crushing (severe) —*see* Crush
  suffocation —*see* Asphyxia, traumatic, due to
    low oxygen, due to cave-in
Cavernitis (penis) N48.29
Cavernositis N48.29
Cavernous —*see* condition
Cavitation of lung —*see also* Tuberculosis,
  pulmonary
  nontuberculous J98.4
Cavities, dental —*see* Caries, dental
Cavity
  lung —*see* Cavitation of lung
  optic papilla Q14.2
  pulmonary —*see* Cavitation of lung
Cavovarus foot, congenital Q66.1
Cavus foot (congenital) Q66.7
  acquired —*see* Deformity, limb, foot, specified
    NEC
Cazenave's disease L10.2
Cecitis K52.9
  with perforation, peritonitis, or rupture K65.8
Cecum —*see* condition
Celiac
  artery compression syndrome I77.4
  disease (with steatorrhea) K90.0
  infantilism K90.0
Cell(s), cellular —*see also* condition
  in urine R82.998
Cellulitis (diffuse) (phlegmonous) (septic)
  (suppurative) L03.90
  abdominal wall L03.311
  anaerobic A48.0
  ankle —*see* Cellulitis, lower limb
  anus K61.0
  arm —*see* Cellulitis, upper limb
  auricle (ear) —*see* Cellulitis, ear

▶ New   ➡ Revised   ~~deleted~~ Deleted   ● Use Additional Character(s)

Cellulitis (Continued)
  axilla L03.11-●
  back (any part) L03.312
  breast (acute) (nonpuerperal) (subacute)
      N61.0
    nipple N61.0
  broad ligament
    acute N73.0
  buttock L03.317
  cervical (meaning neck) L03.221
  cervix (uteri) —see Cervicitis
  cheek (external) L03.211
    internal K12.2
  chest wall L03.313
  chronic L03.90
  clostridial A48.0
  corpus cavernosum N48.22
  digit
    finger —see Cellulitis, finger
    toe —see Cellulitis, toe
  Douglas' cul-de-sac or pouch
    acute N73.0
  drainage site (following operation) T81.49
  ear (external) H60.1-●
  eosinophilic (granulomatous) L98.3
  erysipelatous —see Erysipelas
  external auditory canal —see Cellulitis, ear
  eyelid —see Abscess, eyelid
  face NEC L03.211
  finger (intrathecal) (periosteal)
      (subcutaneous) (subcuticular) L03.01-●
  foot —see Cellulitis, lower limb
  gangrenous —see Gangrene
  genital organ NEC
    female (external) N76.4
    male N49.9
      multiple sites N49.8
      specified NEC N49.8
  gluteal (region) L03.317
  gonococcal A54.89
  groin L03.314
  hand —see Cellulitis, upper limb
  head NEC L03.811
    face (any part, except ear, eye and nose)
        L03.211
  heel —see Cellulitis, lower limb
  hip —see Cellulitis, lower limb
  jaw (region) L03.211
  knee —see Cellulitis, lower limb
  labium (majus) (minus) —see Vulvitis
  lacrimal passages —see Inflammation,
      lacrimal, passages
  larynx J38.7
  leg —see Cellulitis, lower limb
  lip K13.0
  lower limb L03.11-●
    toe —see Cellulitis, toe
  mouth (floor) K12.2
  multiple sites, so stated L03.90
  nasopharynx J39.1
  navel L03.316
    newborn P38.9
      with mild hemorrhage P38.1
      without hemorrhage P38.9
  neck (region) L03.221
  nipple (acute) (nonpuerperal) (subacute)
      N61.0
  nose (septum) (external) J34.0
  orbit, orbital H05.01-●
  palate (soft) K12.2
  pectoral (region) L03.313
  pelvis, pelvic (chronic)
    female —see also Disease, pelvis,
        inflammatory N73.2
      acute N73.0
    following ectopic or molar pregnancy
        O08.0
    male K65.0
  penis N48.22
  perineal, perineum L03.315
  periorbital L03.213

Cellulitis (Continued)
  perirectal K61.1
  peritonsillar J36
  periurethral N34.0
  periuterine —see also Disease, pelvis,
      inflammatory N73.2
    acute N73.0
  pharynx J39.1
  preseptal L03.213
  rectum K61.1
  retroperitoneal K68.9
  round ligament
    acute N73.0
  scalp (any part) L03.811
  scrotum N49.2
  seminal vesicle N49.0
  shoulder —see Cellulitis, upper limb
  specified site NEC L03.818
  submandibular (region) (space) (triangle)
      K12.2
    gland K11.3
  submaxillary (region) K12.2
    gland K11.3
  thigh —see Cellulitis, lower limb
  thumb (intrathecal) (periosteal)
      (subcutaneous) (subcuticular) —see
      Cellulitis, finger
  toe (intrathecal) (periosteal) (subcutaneous)
      (subcuticular) L03.03-●
  tonsil J36
  trunk L03.319
    abdominal wall L03.311
    back (any part) L03.312
    buttock L03.317
    chest wall L03.313
    groin L03.314
    perineal, perineum L03.315
    umbilicus L03.316
  tuberculous (primary) A18.4
  umbilicus L03.316
  upper limb L03.11-●
    axilla —see Cellulitis, axilla
    finger —see Cellulitis, finger
    thumb —see Cellulitis, finger
  vaccinal T88.0
  vocal cord J38.3
  vulva —see Vulvitis
  wrist —see Cellulitis, upper limb
Cementoblastoma, benign —see Cyst,
    calcifying odontogenic
Cementoma —see Cyst, calcifying odontogenic
Cementoperiostitis —see Periodontitis
Cementosis K03.4
Central auditory processing disorder H93.25
Central pain syndrome G89.0
Cephalematocele, cephal (o)hematocele
  newborn P52.8
    birth injury P10.8
  traumatic —see Hematoma, brain
Cephalematoma, cephalhematoma (calcified)
  newborn (birth injury) P12.0
  traumatic —see Hematoma, brain
Cephalgia, cephalalgia —see also Headache
  histamine G44.009
    intractable G44.001
    not intractable G44.009
  trigeminal autonomic (TAC) NEC G44.099
    intractable G44.091
    not intractable G44.099
Cephalic —see condition
Cephalitis —see Encephalitis
Cephalocele —see Encephalocele
Cephalomenia N94.89
Cephalopelvic —see condition
Cerclage (with cervical incompetence) in
    pregnancy —see Incompetence, cervix, in
    pregnancy
Cerebellitis —see Encephalitis
Cerebellum, cerebellar —see condition
Cerebral —see condition
Cerebritis —see Encephalitis

Cerebro-hepato-renal syndrome Q87.89
Cerebromalacia —see Softening, brain
  sequelae of cerebrovascular disease I69.398
Cerebroside lipidosis E75.22
Cerebrospasticity (congenital) G80.1
Cerebrospinal —see condition
Cerebrum —see condition
Ceroid-lipofuscinosis, neuronal E75.4
Cerumen (accumulation) (impacted) H61.2-●
Cervical —see also condition
  auricle Q18.2
  dysplasia in pregnancy —see Abnormal,
      cervix, in pregnancy or childbirth
  erosion in pregnancy —see Abnormal, cervix,
      in pregnancy or childbirth
  fibrosis in pregnancy —see Abnormal, cervix,
      in pregnancy or childbirth
  fusion syndrome Q76.1
  rib Q76.5
  shortening (complicating pregnancy)
      O26.87-●
Cervicalgia M54.2
Cervicitis (acute) (chronic) (nonvenereal)
    (senile (atrophic)) (subacute) (with
    ulceration) N72
  with
    abortion —see Abortion, by type
        complicated by genital tract and
        pelvic infection
    ectopic pregnancy O08.0
    molar pregnancy O08.0
  chlamydial A56.09
  gonococcal A54.03
  herpesviral A60.03
  puerperal (postpartum) O86.11
  syphilitic A52.76
  trichomonal A59.09
  tuberculous A18.16
Cervicocolpitis (emphysematosa) (see also
    Cervicitis) N72
Cervix —see condition
Cesarean delivery, previous, affecting
    management of pregnancy O34.219
  classical (vertical) scar O34.212
  low transverse scar O34.211
Céstan (-Chenais) paralysis or syndrome G46.3
Céstan-Raymond syndrome I65.8
Cestode infestation B71.9
  specified type NEC B71.8
Cestodiasis B71.9
Chabert's disease A22.9
Chacaleh E53.8
Chafing L30.4
Chagas' (-Mazza) disease (chronic) B57.2
  with
    cardiovascular involvement NEC B57.2
    digestive system involvement B57.30
      megacolon B57.32
      megaesophagus B57.31
      other specified B57.39
    megacolon B57.32
    megaesophagus B57.31
    myocarditis B57.2
    nervous system involvement B57.40
      meningitis B57.41
      meningoencephalitis B57.42
      other specified B57.49
    specified organ involvement NEC B57.5
  acute (with) B57.1
    cardiovascular NEC B57.0
    myocarditis B57.0
Chagres fever B50.9
Chairridden Z74.09
Chalasia (cardiac sphincter) K21.9
Chalazion H00.19
  left H00.16
    lower H00.15
    upper H00.14
  right H00.13
    lower H00.12
    upper H00.11

Chalcosis —*see also* Disorder, globe,
  degenerative, chalcosis
  cornea —*see* Deposit, cornea
  crystalline lens —*see* Cataract, complicated
  retina H35.89
Chalicosis (pulmonum) J62.8
Chancre (any genital site) (hard) (hunterian)
    (mixed) (primary) (seronegative)
    (seropositive) (syphilitic) A51.0
  congenital A50.07
  conjunctiva NEC A51.2
  Ducrey's A57
  extragenital A51.2
  eyelid A51.2
  lip A51.2
  nipple A51.2
  Nisbet's A57
  of
    carate A67.0
    pinta A67.0
    yaws A66.0
  palate, soft A51.2
  phagedenic A57
  simple A57
  soft A57
    bubo A57
    palate A51.2
  urethra A51.0
  yaws A66.0
Chancroid (anus) (genital) (penis) (perineum)
    (rectum) (urethra) (vulva) A57
Chandler's disease (osteochondritis dissecans,
    hip) —*see* Osteochondritis, dissecans,
    hip
Change(s) (in) (of) —*see also* Removal
  arteriosclerotic —*see* Arteriosclerosis
  bone —*see also* Disorder, bone
    diabetic —*see* Diabetes, bone change
  bowel habit R19.4
  cardiorenal (vascular) —*see* Hypertension,
    cardiorenal
  cardiovascular —*see* Disease, cardiovascular
  circulatory I99.9
  cognitive (mild) (organic) R41.89
  color, tooth, teeth
    during formation K00.8
    posteruptive K03.7
  contraceptive device Z30.433
  corneal membrane H18.30
    Bowman's membrane fold or rupture
      H18.31-●
    Descemet's membrane
      fold H18.32-●
      rupture H18.33-●
  coronary —*see* Disease, heart, ischemic
  degenerative, spine or vertebra —*see*
    Spondylosis
  dental pulp, regressive K04.2
  dressing (nonsurgical) Z48.00
    surgical Z48.01
  heart —*see* Disease, heart
  hip joint —*see* Derangement, joint, hip
  hyperplastic larynx J38.7
  hypertrophic
    nasal sinus J34.89
    turbinate, nasal J34.3
    upper respiratory tract J39.8
  indwelling catheter Z46.6
  inflammatory —*see also* Inflammation
    sacroiliac M46.1
  job, anxiety concerning Z56.1
  joint —*see* Derangement, joint
  life —*see* Menopause
  mental status R41.82
  minimal (glomerular) —*see also* N00-N07
    with fourth character .0 N05.0
  myocardium, myocardial —*see*
    Degeneration, myocardial - of life —*see*
    Menopause
  pacemaker Z45.018
    pulse generator Z45.010

Change *(Continued)*
  personality (enduring) F68.8
    due to (secondary to)
      general medical condition F07.0
      secondary (nonspecific) F60.89
  regressive, dental pulp K04.2
  renal —*see* Disease, renal
  retina H35.9
    myopic —*see also* Myopia, degenerative
      H44.2-●
  sacroiliac joint M53.3
  senile —*see also* condition R54
  sensory R20.8
  skin R23.9
    acute, due to ultraviolet radiation L56.9
      specified NEC L56.8
    chronic, due to nonionizing radiation L57.9
      specified NEC L57.8
    cyanosis R23.0
    flushing R23.2
    pallor R23.1
    petechiae R23.3
    specified change NEC R23.8
    swelling —*see* Mass, localized
    texture R23.4
  trophic
    arm —*see* Mononeuropathy, upper limb
    leg —*see* Mononeuropathy, lower limb
  vascular I99.9
  vasomotor I73.9
  voice R49.9
    psychogenic F44.4
    specified NEC R49.8
Changing sleep-work schedule, affecting sleep
    G47.26
Changuinola fever A93.1
Chapping skin T69.8
Charcot-Marie-Tooth disease, paralysis or
    syndrome G60.0
Charcot's
  arthropathy —*see* Arthropathy, neuropathic
  cirrhosis K74.3
  disease (tabetic arthropathy) A52.16
  joint (disease) (tabetic) A52.16
    diabetic —*see* Diabetes, with, arthropathy
    syringomyelic G95.0
  syndrome (intermittent claudication) I73.9
CHARGE association Q89.8
Charley-horse (quadriceps) M62.831
  traumatic (quadriceps) S76.11-●
Charlouis' disease —*see* Yaws
Cheadle's disease E54
Checking (of)
  cardiac pacemaker (battery) (electrode(s))
    Z45.018
    pulse generator Z45.010
  implantable subdermal contraceptive Z30.46
  intrauterine contraceptive device Z30.431
  wound Z48.0-●
    due to injury - code to Injury, by site, using
      appropriate seventh character for
      subsequent encounter
Check-up —*see* Examination
Chédiak-Higashi (-Steinbrinck) syndrome
    (congenital gigantism of peroxidase
    granules) E70.330
Cheek —*see* condition
Cheese itch B88.0
Cheese-washer's lung J67.8
Cheese-worker's lung J67.8
Cheilitis (acute) (angular) (catarrhal) (chronic)
    (exfoliative) (gangrenous) (glandular)
    (infectional) (suppurative) (ulcerative)
    (vesicular) K13.0
  actinic (due to sun) L56.8
    other than from sun L59.8
  candidal B37.83
Cheilodynia K13.0
Cheiloschisis —*see* Cleft, lip
Cheilosis (angular) K13.0
  with pellagra E52
  due to
    vitamin B2 (riboflavin) deficiency E53.0

Cheiromegaly M79.89
Cheiropompholyx L30.1
Cheloid —*see* Keloid
Chemical burn —*see* Corrosion, by site
Chemodectoma —*see* Paraganglioma,
    nonchromaffin
Chemosis, conjunctiva —*see* Edema,
    conjunctiva
Chemotherapy (session) (for)
  cancer Z51.11
  neoplasm Z51.11
Cherubism M27.8
Chest —*see* condition
Cheyne-Stokes breathing (respiration) R06.3
Chiari's
  disease or syndrome (hepatic vein
    thrombosis) I82.0
  malformation
    type I G93.5
    type II —*see* Spina bifida
  net Q24.8
Chicago disease B40.9
Chickenpox —*see* Varicella
Chiclero ulcer or sore B55.1
Chigger (infestation) B88.0
Chignon (disease) B36.8
  newborn (from vacuum extraction) (birth
    injury) P12.1
Chilaiditi's syndrome (subphrenic
    displacement, colon) Q43.3
Chilblain(s) (lupus) T69.1
Child
  custody dispute Z65.3
Childbirth —*see* Delivery
Childhood
  cerebral X-linked adrenoleukodystrophy
    E71.520
  period of rapid growth Z00.2
Chill(s) R68.83
  with fever R50.9
  without fever R68.83
  congestive in malarial regions B54
Chilomastigiasis A07.8
Chimera 46,XX/46,XY Q99.0
Chin —*see* condition
Chinese dysentery A03.9
Chionophobia F40.228
Chitral fever A93.1
Chlamydia, chlamydial A74.9
  cervicitis A56.09
  conjunctivitis A74.0
  cystitis A56.01
  endometritis A56.11
  epididymitis A56.19
  female
    pelvic inflammatory disease A56.11
    pelviperitonitis A56.11
  orchitis A56.19
  peritonitis A74.81
  pharyngitis A56.4
  proctitis A56.3
  psittaci (infection) A70
  salpingitis A56.11
  sexually-transmitted infection NEC A56.8
  specified NEC A74.89
  urethritis A56.01
  vulvovaginitis A56.02
Chlamydiosis —*see* Chlamydia
Chloasma (skin) (idiopathic) (symptomatic)
    L81.1
  eyelid H02.719
    hyperthyroid E05.90 *[H02.719]*
      with thyroid storm E05.91 *[H02.719]*
    left H02.716
      lower H02.715
      upper H02.714
    right H02.713
      lower H02.712
      upper H02.711
Chloroma C92.3-●
Chlorosis D50.9
  Egyptian B76.9 *[D63.8]*
  miner's B76.9 *[D63.8]*

Chlorotic anemia D50.8
Chocolate cyst (ovary) N80.1
Choked
 disc or disk —see Papilledema
 on food, phlegm, or vomitus NOS —see
   Foreign body, by site
 while vomiting NOS —see Foreign body, by
   site
Chokes (resulting from bends) T70.3
Choking sensation R09.89
Cholangiectasis K83.8
Cholangiocarcinoma
 with hepatocellular carcinoma, combined
   C22.0
 liver C22.1
 specified site NEC —see Neoplasm,
   malignant, by site
 unspecified site C22.1
Cholangiohepatitis K83.8
 due to fluke infestation B66.1
Cholangiohepatoma C22.0
➡Cholangiolitis (acute) (chronic) (extrahepatic)
   (gangrenous) (intrahepatic) K83.09
 paratyphoidal —see Fever, paratyphoid
 typhoidal A01.09
Cholangioma D13.4
 malignant —see Cholangiocarcinoma
➡Cholangitis (ascending) (primary) (recurrent)
   (sclerosing) (secondary) (stenosing)
   (suppurative) K83.09
 with calculus, bile duct —see Calculus, bile
   duct, with cholangitis
 chronic nonsuppurative destructive K74.3
 ▶primary K83.09
  ▶sclerosing K83.01
 ▶sclerosing K83.09
Cholecystectasia K82.8
Cholecystitis K81.9
 with
  calculus, stones in
   bile duct (common) (hepatic) —
     see Calculus, bile duct, with
     cholecystitis
   cystic duct —see Calculus, gallbladder,
     with cholecystitis
   gallbladder —see Calculus, gallbladder,
     with cholecystitis
   choledocholithiasis —see Calculus, bile
     duct, with cholecystitis
   cholelithiasis —see Calculus, gallbladder,
     with cholecystitis
  ▶gangrene of gallbladder K82.A1
  ▶perforation of gallbladder K82.A2
 acute (emphysematous) (gangrenous)
   (suppurative) K81.0
  with
   calculus, stones in
    cystic duct —see Calculus, gallbladder,
      with cholecystitis, acute
    gallbladder —see Calculus, gallbladder,
      with cholecystitis, acute
    choledocholithiasis —see Calculus, bile
      duct, with cholecystitis, acute
    cholelithiasis —see Calculus, gallbladder,
      with cholecystitis, acute
   chronic cholecystitis K81.2
    with gallbladder calculus K80.12
     with obstruction K80.13
 chronic K81.1
  with acute cholecystitis K81.2
   with gallbladder calculus K80.12
    with obstruction K80.13
 emphysematous (acute) —see Cholecystitis,
   acute
 gangrenous —see Cholecystitis, acute
 paratyphoidal, current A01.4
 suppurative —see Cholecystitis, acute
 typhoidal A01.09
Cholecystolithiasis —see Calculus, gallbladder
➡Choledochitis (suppurative) K83.09
Choledocholith —see Calculus, bile duct

Choledocholithiasis (common duct) (hepatic
   duct) —see Calculus, bile duct
 cystic —see Calculus, gallbladder
 typhoidal A01.09
Cholelithiasis (cystic duct) (gallbladder)
   (impacted) (multiple) —see Calculus,
   gallbladder
 bile duct (common) (hepatic) —see Calculus,
   bile duct
 hepatic duct —see Calculus, bile duct
 specified NEC K80.80
  with obstruction K80.81
Cholemia —see also Jaundice
 familial (simple) (congenital) E80.4
 Gilbert's E80.4
Choleperitoneum, choleperitonitis K65.3
Cholera (Asiatic) (epidemic) (malignant) A00.9
 antimonial —see Poisoning, antimony
 classical A00.0
 due to Vibrio cholerae 01 A00.9
  biovar cholerae A00.0
  biovar eltor A00.1
  el tor A00.1
 el tor A00.1
Cholerine —see Cholera
Cholestasis NEC K83.1
 with hepatocyte injury K71.0
 due to total parenteral nutrition (TPN) K76.89
 pure K71.0
Cholesteatoma (ear) (middle) (with reaction)
   H71.9-●
 attic H71.0-●
 external ear (canal) H60.4-●
 mastoid H71.2-●
 postmastoidectomy cavity (recurrent) —see
   Complications, postmastoidectomy,
   recurrent cholesteatoma
 recurrent (postmastoidectomy) —see
   Complications, postmastoidectomy,
   recurrent cholesteatoma
 tympanum H71.1-●
Cholesteatosis, diffuse H71.3-●
Cholesteremia E78.00
Cholesterin in vitreous —see Deposit, crystalline
Cholesterol
 deposit
  retina H35.89
  vitreous —see Deposit, crystalline
 elevated (high) E78.00
  with elevated (high) triglycerides E78.2
  screening for Z13.220
 imbibition of gallbladder K82.4
Cholesterolemia (essential) (pure) E78.00
 familial E78.01
 hereditary E78.01
Cholesterolosis, cholesterosis (gallbladder)
   K82.4
 cerebrotendinous E75.5
Cholocolic fistula K82.3
Choluria R82.2
Chondritis M94.8X9
 aurical H61.03-●
 costal (Tietze's) M94.0
 external ear H61.03-●
 patella, posttraumatic —see Chondromalacia,
   patella
 pinna H61.03-●
 purulent M94.8X-●
 tuberculous NEC A18.02
  intervertebral A18.01
Chondroblastoma —see also Neoplasm, bone,
   benign
 malignant —see Neoplasm, bone, malignant
Chondrocalcinosis M11.20
 ankle M11.27-●
 elbow M11.22-●
 familial M11.10
  ankle M11.17-●
  elbow M11.12-●
  foot joint M11.17-●
  hand joint M11.14-●

Chondrocalcinosis (Continued)
 familial (Continued)
  hip M11.15-●
  knee M11.16-●
  multiple site M11.19
  shoulder M11.11-●
  vertebrae M11.18
  wrist M11.13-●
 foot joint M11.27-●
 hand joint M11.24-●
 hip M11.25-●
 knee M11.26-●
 multiple site M11.29
 shoulder M11.21-●
 specified type NEC M11.20
  ankle M11.27-●
  elbow M11.22-●
  foot joint M11.27-●
  hand joint M11.24-●
  hip M11.25-●
  knee M11.26-●
  multiple site M11.29
  shoulder M11.21-●
  vertebrae M11.28
  wrist M11.23-●
 vertebrae M11.28
 wrist M11.23-●
Chondrodermatitis nodularis helicis or
   anthelicis —see Perichondritis, ear
Chondrodysplasia Q78.9
 with hemangioma Q78.4
 calcificans congenita Q77.3
 fetalis Q77.4
 metaphyseal (Jansen's) (McKusick's)
   (Schmid's) Q78.8
 punctata Q77.3
Chondrodystrophy, chondrodystrophia
   (familial) (fetalis) (hypoplastic) Q78.9
 calcificans congenita Q77.3
 myotonic (congenital) G71.13
 punctata Q77.3
Chondroectodermal dysplasia Q77.6
Chondrogenesis imperfecta Q77.4
Chondrolysis M94.35-●
Chondroma —see also Neoplasm, cartilage,
   benign
 juxtacortical —see Neoplasm, bone, benign
 periosteal —see Neoplasm, bone, benign
Chondromalacia (systemic) M94.20
 acromioclavicular joint M94.21-●
 ankle M94.27-●
 elbow M94.22-●
 foot joint M94.27-●
 glenohumeral joint M94.21-●
 hand joint M94.24-●
 hip M94.25-●
 knee M94.26-●
  patella M22.4-●
 multiple sites M94.29
 patella M22.4-●
 rib M94.28
 sacroiliac joint M94.259
 shoulder M94.21-●
 sternoclavicular joint M94.21-●
 vertebral joint M94.28
 wrist M94.23-●
Chondromatosis —see also Neoplasm, cartilage,
   uncertain behavior
 internal Q78.4
Chondromyxosarcoma —see Neoplasm,
   cartilage, malignant
Chondro-osteodysplasia (Morquio-Brailsford
   type) E76.219
Chondro-osteodystrophy E76.29
Chondro-osteoma —see Neoplasm, bone, benign
Chondropathia tuberosa M94.0
Chondrosarcoma —see Neoplasm, cartilage,
   malignant
 juxtacortical —see Neoplasm, bone, malignant
 mesenchymal —see Neoplasm, connective
   tissue, malignant
 myxoid —see Neoplasm, cartilage, malignant

Chordee (nonvenereal) N48.89
  congenital Q54.4
  gonococcal A54.09
Chorditis (fibrinous) (nodosa) (tuberosa) J38.2
Chordoma —see Neoplasm, vertebral (column), malignant
Chorea (chronic) (gravis) (posthemiplegic) (senile) (spasmodic) G25.5
  with
    heart involvement I02.0
      active or acute (conditions in I01-●) I02.0
      rheumatic I02.9
        with valvular disorder I02.0
      rheumatic heart disease (chronic) (inactive) (quiescent) — code to rheumatic heart condition involved
  drug-induced G25.4
  habit F95.8
  hereditary G10
  Huntington's G10
  hysterical F44.4
  minor I02.9
    with heart involvement I02.0
  progressive G25.5
    hereditary G10
  rheumatic (chronic) I02.9
    with heart involvement I02.0
  Sydenham's I02.9
    with heart involvement —see Chorea, with rheumatic heart disease
  nonrheumatic G25.5
Choreoathetosis (paroxysmal) G25.5
Chorioadenoma (destruens) D39.2
Chorioamnionitis O41.12-●
Chorioangioma D26.7
Choriocarcinoma —see Neoplasm, malignant, by site
  combined with
    embryonal carcinoma —see Neoplasm, malignant, by site
    other germ cell elements —see Neoplasm, malignant, by site
    teratoma —see Neoplasm, malignant, by site
  specified site —see Neoplasm, malignant, by site
  unspecified site
    female C58
    male C62.90
Chorioencephalitis (acute) (lymphocytic) (serous) A87.2
Chorioepithelioma —see Choriocarcinoma
Choriomeningitis (acute) (lymphocytic) (serous) A87.2
Chorionepithelioma —see Choriocarcinoma
Chorioretinitis —see also Inflammation, chorioretinal
  disseminated —see also Inflammation, chorioretinal, disseminated
    in neurosyphilis A52.19
  Egyptian B76.9 [D63.8]
  focal —see also Inflammation, chorioretinal, focal
  histoplasmic B39.9 [H32]
  in (due to)
    histoplasmosis B39.9 [H32]
    syphilis (secondary) A51.43
      late A52.71
    toxoplasmosis (acquired) B58.01
      congenital (active) P37.1 [H32]
    tuberculosis A18.53
  juxtapapillary, juxtapapillaris —see Inflammation, chorioretinal, focal, juxtapapillary
  leprous A30.9 [H32]
  miner's B76.9 [D63.8]
  progressive myopia (degeneration) —see also Myopia, degenerative H44.2-●
  syphilitic (secondary) A51.43
    congenital (early) A50.01 [H32]
      late A50.32
    late A52.71
  tuberculous A18.53

Chorioretinopathy, central serous H35.71-●
Choroid —see condition
Choroideremia H31.21
Choroiditis —see Chorioretinitis
Choroidopathy —see Disorder, choroid
Choroidoretinitis —see Chorioretinitis
Choroidoretinopathy, central serous —see Chorioretinopathy, central serous
Christian-Weber disease M35.6
Christmas disease D67
Chromaffinoma —see also Neoplasm, benign, by site
  malignant —see Neoplasm, malignant, by site
Chromatopsia —see Deficiency, color vision
Chromhidrosis, chromidrosis L75.1
Chromoblastomycosis —see Chromomycosis
Chromoconversion R82.91
Chromomycosis B43.9
  brain abscess B43.1
  cerebral B43.1
  cutaneous B43.0
  skin B43.0
  specified NEC B43.8
  subcutaneous abscess or cyst B43.2
Chromophytosis B36.0
Chromosome —see condition by chromosome involved
  D (1) —see condition, chromosome 13
  E (3) —see condition, chromosome 18
  G —see condition, chromosome 21
Chromotrichomycosis B36.8
Chronic —see condition
  fracture —see Fracture, pathological
Churg-Strauss syndrome M30.1
Chyle cyst, mesentery I89.8
Chylocele (nonfilarial) I89.8
  filarial —see also Infestation, filarial B74.9 [N51]
  tunica vaginalis N50.89
    filarial —see also Infestation, filarial B74.9 [N51]
Chylomicronemia (fasting) (with hyperprebetalipoproteinemia) E78.3
Chylopericardium I31.3
  acute I30.9
Chylothorax (nonfilarial) I89.8
  filarial —see also Infestation, filarial B74.9 [J91.8]
Chylous —see condition
Chyluria (nonfilarial) R82.0
  due to
    bilharziasis B65.0
    Brugia (malayi) B74.1
      timori B74.2
    schistosomiasis (bilharziasis) B65.0
    Wuchereria (bancrofti) B74.0
  filarial —see Infestation, filarial
Cicatricial (deformity) —see Cicatrix
Cicatrix (adherent) (contracted) (painful) (vicious) —see also Scar L90.5
  adenoid (and tonsil) J35.8
  alveolar process M26.79
  anus K62.89
  auricle —see Disorder, pinna, specified type NEC
  bile duct (common) (hepatic) K83.8
  bladder N32.89
  bone —see Disorder, bone, specified type NEC
  brain G93.89
  cervix (postoperative) (postpartal) N88.1
  common duct K83.8
  cornea H17.9
    tuberculous A18.59
  duodenum (bulb), obstructive K31.5
  esophagus K22.2
  eyelid —see Disorder, eyelid function
  hypopharynx J39.2
  lacrimal passages —see Obstruction, lacrimal
  larynx J38.7
  lung J98.4
  middle ear —see subcategory H74.8
  mouth K13.79

Cicatrix (Continued)
  muscle M62.89
    with contracture —see Contraction, muscle NEC
  nasopharynx J39.2
  palate (soft) K13.79
  penis N48.89
  pharynx J39.2
  prostate N42.89
  rectum K62.89
  retina —see Scar, chorioretinal
  semilunar cartilage —see Derangement, meniscus
  seminal vesicle N50.89
  skin L90.5
    infected L08.89
    postinfective L90.5
    tuberculous B90.8
  specified site NEC L90.5
  throat J39.2
  tongue K14.8
  tonsil (and adenoid) J35.8
  trachea J39.8
  tuberculous NEC B90.9
  urethra N36.8
  uterus N85.8
  vagina N89.8
    postoperative N99.2
  vocal cord J38.3
  wrist, constricting (annular) L90.5
CIDP (chronic inflammatory demyelinating polyneuropathy) G61.81
CIN —see Neoplasia, intraepithelial, cervix
CINCA (chronic infantile neurological, cutaneous and articular syndrome) M04.2
Cinchonism —see Deafness, ototoxic
  correct substance properly administered —see Table of Drugs and Chemicals, by drug, adverse effect
  overdose or wrong substance given or taken —see Table of Drugs and Chemicals, by drug, poisoning
Circle of Willis —see condition
Circular —see condition
Circulating anticoagulants —see also - Disorder, hemorrhagic D68.318
  due to drugs —see also - Disorder, hemorrhagic D68.32
  following childbirth O72.3
Circulation
  collateral, any site I99.8
  defective (lower extremity) I99.9
    congenital Q28.9
  embryonic Q28.9
  failure (peripheral) R57.9
    newborn P29.89
  fetal, persistent P29.38
  heart, incomplete Q28.9
Circulatory system —see condition
Circulus senilis (cornea) —see Degeneration, cornea, senile
Circumcision (in absence of medical indication) (ritual) (routine) Z41.2
Circumscribed —see condition
Circumvallate placenta O43.11-●
Cirrhosis, cirrhotic (hepatic) (liver) K74.60
  alcoholic K70.30
    with ascites K70.31
  atrophic —see Cirrhosis, liver
  Baumgarten-Cruveilhier K74.69
  biliary (cholangiolitic) (cholangitic) (hypertrophic) (obstructive) (pericholangiolitic) K74.5
    due to
      Clonorchiasis B66.1
      flukes B66.3
    primary K74.3
    secondary K74.4
  cardiac (of liver) K76.1
  Charcot's K74.3

Cirrhosis, cirrhotic (Continued)
   cholangiolitic, cholangitic, cholostatic
      (primary) K74.3
   congestive K76.1
   Cruveilhier-Baumgarten K74.69
   cryptogenic (liver) K74.69
   due to
      hepatolenticular degeneration E83.01
      Wilson's disease E83.01
      xanthomatosis E78.2
   fatty K76.0
      alcoholic K70.0
   Hanot's (hypertrophic) K74.3
   hepatic —see Cirrhosis, liver
   hypertrophic K74.3
   Indian childhood K74.69
   kidney —see Sclerosis, renal
   Laennec's K70.30
      with ascites K70.31
      alcoholic K70.30
         with ascites K70.31
      nonalcoholic K74.69
   liver K74.60
      alcoholic K70.30
         with ascites K70.31
         fatty K70.0
      congenital P78.81
      syphilitic A52.74
   lung (chronic) J84.10
   macronodular K74.69
      alcoholic K70.30
         with ascites K70.31
   micronodular K74.69
      alcoholic K70.30
         with ascites K70.31
   mixed type K74.69
   monolobular K74.3
   nephritis —see Sclerosis, renal
   nutritional K74.69
      alcoholic K70.30
         with ascites K70.31
   obstructive —see Cirrhosis, biliary
   ovarian N83.8
   pancreas (duct) K86.89
   pigmentary E83.110
   portal K74.69
      alcoholic K70.30
         with ascites K70.31
   postnecrotic K74.69
      alcoholic K70.30
         with ascites K70.31
   pulmonary J84.10
   renal —see Sclerosis, renal
   spleen D73.2
   stasis K76.1
   Todd's K74.3
   unilobar K74.3
   xanthomatous (biliary) K74.5
      due to xanthomatosis (familial) (metabolic)
         (primary) E78.2
Cistern, subarachnoid R93.0
Citrullinemia E72.23
Citrullinuria E72.23
Civatte's disease or poikiloderma L57.3
Clam digger's itch B65.3
Clammy skin R23.1
Clap —see Gonorrhea
Clarke-Hadfield syndrome (pancreatic
   infantilism) K86.89
Clark's paralysis G80.9
Clastothrix L67.8
Claude Bernard-Horner syndrome G90.2
   traumatic —see Injury, nerve, cervical
      sympathetic
Claude's disease or syndrome G46.3
Claudicatio venosa intermittens I87.8
Claudication (intermittent) I73.9
   cerebral (artery) G45.9
   spinal cord (arteriosclerotic) G95.19
      syphilitic A52.09
   venous (axillary) I87.8

Claustrophobia F40.240
Clavus (infected) L84
Clawfoot (congenital) Q66.89
   acquired —see Deformity, limb, clawfoot
Clawhand (acquired) —see also Deformity, limb,
   clawhand
   congenital Q68.1
Clawtoe (congenital) Q66.89
   acquired —see Deformity, toe, specified NEC
Clay eating —see Pica
Cleansing of artificial opening —see Attention
   to, artificial, opening
Cleft (congenital) —see also Imperfect, closure
   alveolar process M26.79
   branchial (persistent) Q18.2
   cyst Q18.0
      fistula Q18.0
      sinus Q18.0
   cricoid cartilage, posterior Q31.8
   foot Q72.7
   hand Q71.6
   lip (unilateral) Q36.9
      with cleft palate Q37.9
         hard Q37.1
            with soft Q37.5
         soft Q37.3
            with hard Q37.5
      bilateral Q36.0
         with cleft palate Q37.8
            hard Q37.0
               with soft Q37.4
            soft Q37.2
               with hard Q37.4
      median Q36.1
   nose Q30.2
   palate Q35.9
      with cleft lip (unilateral) Q37.9
         bilateral Q37.8
      hard Q35.1
         with
            cleft lip (unilateral) Q37.1
               bilateral Q37.0
            soft Q35.5
               with cleft lip (unilateral) Q37.5
                  bilateral Q37.4
      medial Q35.5
      soft Q35.3
         with
            cleft lip (unilateral) Q37.3
               bilateral Q37.2
            hard Q35.5
               with cleft lip (unilateral) Q37.5
                  bilateral Q37.4
   penis Q55.69
   scrotum Q55.29
   thyroid cartilage Q31.8
   uvula Q35.7
Cleidocranial dysostosis Q74.0
Cleptomania F63.2
Clicking hip (newborn) R29.4
Climacteric (female) —see also Menopause
   arthritis (any site) NEC —see Arthritis,
      specified form NEC
   depression (single episode) F32.89
      recurrent episode F33.8
   male (symptoms) (syndrome) NEC N50.89
   melancholia (single episode) F32.89
      recurrent episode F33.8
   paranoid state F22
   polyarthritis NEC —see Arthritis, specified
      form NEC
   symptoms (female) N95.1
Clinical research investigation (clinical trial)
   (control subject) (normal comparison)
   (participant) Z00.6
Clitoris —see condition Cloaca (persistent)
   Q43.7
Clonorchiasis, clonorchis infection (liver)
   B66.1
Clonus R25.8
Closed bite M26.29

Clostridium (C.) perfringens, as cause of
   disease classified elsewhere B96.7
Closure
   congenital, nose Q30.0
   cranial sutures, premature Q75.0
   defective or imperfect NEC —see Imperfect,
      closure
   fistula, delayed —see Fistula
   foramen ovale, imperfect Q21.1
   hymen N89.6
   interauricular septum, defective Q21.1
   interventricular septum, defective Q21.0
   lacrimal duct —see also Stenosis, lacrimal,
      duct
      congenital Q10.5
   nose (congenital) Q30.0
      acquired M95.0
   of artificial opening —see Attention to,
      artificial, opening
   primary angle, without glaucoma damage
      H40.06-●
   vagina N89.5
   valve —see Endocarditis
   vulva N90.5
Clot (blood) —see also Embolism
   artery (obstruction) (occlusion) —see
      Embolism
   bladder N32.89
   brain (intradural or extradural) —see
      Occlusion, artery, cerebral
   circulation I74.9
   heart —see also Infarct, myocardium
      not resulting in infarction I51.3
   vein —see Thrombosis
Clouded state R40.1
   epileptic —see Epilepsy, specified NEC
   paroxysmal —see Epilepsy, specified NEC
Cloudy antrum, antra J32.0
Clouston's (hidrotic) ectodermal dysplasia
   Q82.4
Clubbed nail pachydermoperiostosis M89.40
   [L62]
Clubbing of finger(s) (nails) R68.3
Clubfinger R68.3
   congenital Q68.1
Clubfoot (congenital) Q66.89
   acquired —see Deformity, limb, clubfoot
   equinovarus Q66.0
   paralytic —see Deformity, limb, clubfoot
Clubhand (congenital) (radial) Q71.4-●
   acquired —see Deformity, limb, clubhand
Clubnail R68.3
   congenital Q84.6
Clump, kidney Q63.1
Clumsiness, clumsy child syndrome F82
Cluttering F98.81
Clutton's joints A50.51 [M12.80]
Coagulation, intravascular (diffuse)
   (disseminated) —see also Defibrination
   syndrome
   complicating abortion —see Abortion, by
      type, complicated by, intravascular
      coagulation
   following ectopic or molar pregnancy
      O08.1
Coagulopathy —see also Defect, coagulation
   consumption D65
   intravascular D65
   newborn P60
Coalition
   calcaneo-scaphoid Q66.89
   tarsal Q66.89
Coalminer's
   elbow —see Bursitis, elbow, olecranon
   lung or pneumoconiosis J60
Coalworker's lung or pneumoconiosis
   J60
Coarctation
   aorta (preductal) (postductal) Q25.1
   pulmonary artery Q25.71
Coated tongue K14.3

Coats' disease (exudative retinopathy) —*see*
   Retinopathy, exudative
Cocaine-induced
  anxiety disorder F14.980
  bipolar and related disorder F14.94
  depressive disorder F14.94
  obsessive-compulsive and related disorder
     F14.988
  psychotic disorder F14.959
  sleep disorder F14.982
  sexual dysfunction F14.981
Cocainism —*see* Disorder, cocaine use
Coccidioidomycosis B38.9
  cutaneous B38.3
  disseminated B38.7
  generalized B38.7
  meninges B38.4
  prostate B38.81
  pulmonary B38.2
    acute B38.0
    chronic B38.1
  skin B38.3
  specified NEC B38.89
Coccidioidosis —*see* Coccidioidomycosis
Coccidiosis (intestinal) A07.3
Coccydynia, coccygodynia M53.3
Coccyx —*see* condition
Cochin-China diarrhea K90.1
Cockayne's syndrome Q87.1
Cocked up toe —*see* Deformity, toe, specified
   NEC
Cock's peculiar tumor L72.3
Codman's tumor —*see* Neoplasm, bone, benign
Coenurosis B71.8
Coffee-worker's lung J67.8
Cogan's syndrome H16.32-•
  oculomotor apraxia H51.8
Coitus, painful (female) N94.10
  male N53.12
  psychogenic F52.6
Cold J00
  with influenza, flu, or grippe —*see* Influenza,
     with, respiratory manifestations NEC
  agglutinin disease or hemoglobinuria
     (chronic) D59.1
  bronchial —*see* Bronchitis
  chest —*see* Bronchitis
  common (head) J00
  effects of T69.9
    specified effect NEC T69.8
  excessive, effects of T69.9
    specified effect NEC T69.8
  exhaustion from T69.8
  exposure to T69.9
    specified effect NEC T69.8
  head J00
  injury syndrome (newborn) P80.0
  on lung —*see* Bronchitis
  rose J30.1
  sensitivity, auto-immune D59.1
  symptoms J00
  virus J00
Coldsore B00.1
Colibacillosis A49.8
  as the cause of other disease (*see also*
    Escherichia coli) B96.20
  generalized A41.50
Colic (bilious) (infantile) (intestinal) (recurrent)
   (spasmodic) R10.83
  abdomen R10.83
    psychogenic F45.8
  appendix, appendicular K38.8
  bile duct —*see* Calculus, bile duct
  biliary —*see* Calculus, bile duct
  common duct —*see* Calculus, bile duct
  cystic duct —*see* Calculus, gallbladder
  Devonshire NEC —*see* Poisoning, lead
  gallbladder —*see* Calculus, gallbladder
  gallstone —*see* Calculus, gallbladder
    gallbladder or cystic duct —*see* Calculus,
      gallbladder

Colic (*Continued*)
  hepatic (duct) —*see* Calculus, bile duct
  hysterical F45.8
  kidney N23
  lead NEC —*see* Poisoning, lead
  mucous K58.9
    with diarrhea K58.0
    psychogenic F54
  nephritic N23
  painter's NEC —*see* Poisoning, lead
  pancreas K86.89
  psychogenic F45.8
  renal N23
  saturnine NEC —*see* Poisoning, lead
  ureter N23
  urethral N36.8
    due to calculus N21.1
  uterus NEC N94.89
    menstrual —*see* Dysmenorrhea
  worm NOS B83.9
Colicystitis —*see* Cystitis
Colitis (acute) (catarrhal) (chronic)
   (noninfective) (hemorrhagic) (*see also*
   Enteritis) K52.9
  allergic K52.29
    with
      food protein-induced enterocolitis
        syndrome K52.21
      proctocolitis K52.82
  amebic (acute) —*see also* Amebiasis A06.0
    nondysenteric A06.2
  anthrax A22.2
  bacillary —*see* Infection, Shigella
  balantidial A07.0
  Clostridium difficile
    not specified as recurrent A04.72
    recurrent A04.71
  coccidial A07.3
  collagenous K52.831
  cystica superficialis K52.89
  dietary counseling and surveillance (for) Z71.3
  dietetic —*see also* Colitis, allergic K52.29
  drug-induced K52.1
  due to radiation K52.0
  eosinophilic K52.82
  food hypersensitivity —*see also* Colitis,
    allergic K52.29
  giardial A07.1
  granulomatous —*see* Enteritis, regional, large
    intestine
  infectious —*see* Enteritis, infectious
  indeterminate, so stated K52.3
  ischemic K55.9
    acute (subacute) —*see also* Ischemia,
      intestine, acute K55.039
    chronic K55.1
    due to mesenteric artery insufficiency K55.1
    fulminant (acute) —*see also* Ischemia,
      intestine, acute K55.039
  left sided K51.50
    with
      abscess K51.514
      complication K51.519
        specified NEC K51.518
      fistula K51.513
      obstruction K51.512
      rectal bleeding K51.511
  lymphocytic K52.832
  membranous
    psychogenic F54
  microscopic K52.839
    specified NEC K52.838
  mucous —*see* Syndrome, irritable, bowel
    psychogenic F54
  noninfective K52.9
    specified NEC K52.89
  polyposa —*see* Polyp, colon, inflammatory
  protozoal A07.9
  pseudomembranous
    not specified as recurrent A04.72
    recurrent A04.71

Colitis (*Continued*)
  pseudomucinous —*see* Syndrome, irritable,
    bowel
  regional —*see* Enteritis, regional, large intestine
    infectious A09
  segmental —*see* Enteritis, regional, large
    intestine
  septic —*see* Enteritis, infectious
  spastic K58.9
    with diarrhea K58.0
    psychogenic F54
  staphylococcal A04.8
    foodborne A05.0
  subacute ischemic —*see also* Ischemia,
    intestine, acute K55.039
  thromboulcerative —*see also* Ischemia,
    intestine, acute K55.039
  toxic NEC K52.1
    due to Clostridium difficile
      not specified as recurrent A04.72
      recurrent A04.71
  transmural —*see* Enteritis, regional, large
    intestine
  trichomonal A07.8
  tuberculous (ulcerative) A18.32
  ulcerative (chronic) K51.90
    with
      complication K51.919
        abscess K51.914
        fistula K51.913
        obstruction K51.912
        rectal bleeding K51.911
        specified complication NEC K51.918
    enterocolitis —*see* Enterocolitis, ulcerative
    ileocolitis —*see* Ileocolitis, ulcerative
    mucosal proctocolitis —*see* Proctocolitis,
      mucosal
    proctitis —*see* Proctitis, ulcerative
    pseudopolyposis —*see* Polyp, colon,
      inflammatory
    psychogenic F54
    rectosigmoiditis —*see* Rectosigmoiditis,
      ulcerative
    specified type NEC K51.80
      with
        complication K51.819
          abscess K51.814
          fistula K51.813
          obstruction K51.812
          rectal bleeding K51.811
          specified complication NEC K51.818
Collagenosis, collagen disease (nonvascular)
   (vascular) M35.9
  cardiovascular I42.8
  reactive perforating L87.1
  specified NEC M35.8
Collapse R55
  adrenal E27.2
  cardiorespiratory R57.0
  cardiovascular R57.0
    newborn P29.89
  circulatory (peripheral) R57.9
    during or after labor and delivery O75.1
    following ectopic or molar pregnancy O08.3
    newborn P29.89
  during or
    after labor and delivery O75.1
    resulting from a procedure, not elsewhere
      classified T81.10
  external ear canal —*see* Stenosis, external ear
    canal
  general R55
  heart —*see* Disease, heart
  heat T67.1
  hysterical F44.89
  labyrinth, membranous (congenital) Q16.5
  lung (massive) —*see also* Atelectasis J98.19
    pressure due to anesthesia (general) (local)
      or other sedation T88.2
      during labor and delivery O74.1
      in pregnancy O29.02-•
      postpartum, puerperal O89.09

Collapse *(Continued)*
  myocardial —*see* Disease, heart
  nervous F48.8
  neurocirculatory F45.8
  nose M95.0
  postoperative T81.10
  pulmonary —*see also* Atelectasis J98.19
    newborn —*see* Atelectasis
  trachea J39.8
  tracheobronchial J98.09
  valvular —*see* Endocarditis
  vascular (peripheral) R57.9
    during or after labor and delivery O75.1
    following ectopic or molar pregnancy O08.3
    newborn P29.89
  vertebra M48.50-●
    cervical region M48.52-●
    cervicothoracic region M48.53-●
    in (due to)
      metastasis —*see* Collapse, vertebra, in,
        specified disease NEC
      osteoporosis —*see also* Osteoporosis
        M80.88
        cervical region M80.88
        cervicothoracic region M80.88
        lumbar region M80.88
        lumbosacral region M80.88
        multiple sites M80.88
        occipito-atlanto-axial region M80.88
        sacrococcygeal region M80.88
        thoracic region M80.88
        thoracolumbar region M80.88
      specified disease NEC M48.50-●
        cervical region M48.52-●
        cervicothoracic region M48.53-●
        lumbar region M48.56-●
        lumbosacral region M48.57-●
        occipito-atlanto-axial region M48.51-●
        sacrococcygeal region M48.58-●
        thoracic region M48.54-●
        thoracolumbar region M48.55-●
    lumbar region M48.56-●
    lumbosacral region M48.57-●
    occipito-atlanto-axial region M48.51-●
    sacrococcygeal region M48.58-●
    thoracic region M48.54-●
    thoracolumbar region M48.55-●
Collateral —*see also* condition
  circulation (venous) I87.8
  dilation, veins I87.8
Colles' fracture S52.53-●
Collet (-Sicard) syndrome G52.7
Collier's asthma or lung J60
Collodion baby Q80.2
Colloid nodule (of thyroid) (cystic) E04.1
Coloboma (iris) Q13.0
  eyelid Q10.3
  fundus Q14.8
  lens Q12.2
  optic disc (congenital) Q14.2
    acquired H47.31-●
Coloenteritis —*see* Enteritis
Colon —*see* condition
Colonization
  MRSA (Methicillin resistant Staphylococcus
    aureus) Z22.322
  MSSA (Methicillin susceptible
    Staphylococcus aureus) Z22.321
  status —*see* Carrier (suspected) of
Coloptosis K63.4
Color blindness —*see* Deficiency, color vision
Colostomy
  attention to Z43.3
  fitting or adjustment Z46.89
  malfunctioning K94.03
  status Z93.3
Colpitis (acute) —*see* Vaginitis
Colpocele N81.5
Colpocystitis —*see* Vaginitis
Colpospasm N94.2
Column, spinal, vertebral —*see* condition

Coma R40.20
  with
    motor response (none) R40.231
      abnormal R40.233
      abnormal extensor posturing to pain or
        noxious stimuli (<2 years of age)
        R40.232
      abnormal flexure posturing to pain or
        noxious stimuli (0-5 years of age)
        R40.233
      extension R40.232
      extensor posturing to pain or noxious
        stimuli (2-5 years of age) R40.232
      flexion/decorticate posturing
        (<2 years of age) R40.233
      flexion withdrawal R40.234
      localizes pain (2-5 years of age) R40.235
      normal or spontaneous movement
        (<2 years of age) R40.236
      obeys commands (2-5 years of age)
        R40.236
    ► score of
      ► 1 R40.231
      ► 2 R40.232
      ► 3 R40.233
      ► 4 R40.234
      ► 5 R40.235
      ► 6 R40.236
      withdraws from pain or noxious stimuli
        (0-5 years of age) R40.234
      withdraws to touch (<2 years of age)
        R40.235
    opening of eyes (never) R40.211
      in response to
        pain R40.212
        sound R40.213
    ► score of
      ► 1 R40.211
      ► 2 R40.212
      ► 3 R40.213
      ► 4 R40.214
      spontaneous R40.214
    verbal response (none) R40.221
      confused conversation R40.224
      cooing or babbling or crying
        appropriately (<2 years of age)
        R40.225
      inappropriate crying or screaming
        (<2 years of age) R40.223
      inappropriate words R40.223
      inappropriate words (2-5 years of age)
        R40.224
      incomprehensible sounds (2-5 years of
        age) R40.222
      incomprehensible words R40.222
      irritable cries (<2 years of age) R40.224
      moans/grunts to pain; restless
        (<2 years old) R40.222
      oriented R40.225
    ► score of
      ► 1 R40.221
      ► 2 R40.222
      ► 3 R40.223
      ► 4 R40.224
      ► 5 R40.225
      screaming (2-5 years of age) R40.223
      uses appropriate words (2-5 years of
        age) R40.225
  eclamptic —*see* Eclampsia
  epileptic —*see* Epilepsy
  Glasgow, scale score —*see* Glasgow coma
    scale
  hepatic —*see* Failure, hepatic, by type, with
    coma
  hyperglycemic (diabetic) —*see* Diabetes, by
    type, with hyperosmolarity, with coma
  hyperosmolar (diabetic) —*see* Diabetes, by
    type, with hyperosmolarity, with coma
  hypoglycemic (diabetic) —*see* Diabetes, by
    type, with hypoglycemia, with coma
    nondiabetic E15

Coma *(Continued)*
  in diabetes —*see* Diabetes, coma
  insulin-induced —*see* Coma, hypoglycemic
  ketoacidotic (diabetic) —*see* Diabetes, by
    type, with ketoacidosis, with coma
  myxedematous E03.5
  newborn P91.5
  persistent vegetative state R40.3
  specified NEC, without documented
    Glasgow coma scale score, or with
    partial Glasgow coma scale score
    reported R40.244
Comatose —*see* Coma
Combat fatigue F43.0
Combined —*see* condition
Comedo, comedones (giant) L70.0
Comedocarcinoma —*see also* Neoplasm, breast,
    malignant
  noninfiltrating
    breast D05.8-●
    specified site —*see* Neoplasm, in situ, by site
    unspecified site D05.8-●
Comedomastitis —*see* Ectasia, mammary duct
Comminuted fracture - code as Fracture, closed
Common
  arterial trunk Q20.0
  atrioventricular canal Q21.2
  atrium Q21.1
  cold (head) J00
  truncus (arteriosus) Q20.0
  variable immunodeficiency —*see*
    Immunodeficiency, common variable
  ventricle Q20.4
Commotio, commotion (current)
  brain —*see* Injury, intracranial, concussion
  cerebri —*see* Injury, intracranial, concussion
  retinae S05.8X-●
  spinal cord —*see* Injury, spinal cord, by region
  spinalis —*see* Injury, spinal cord, by region
Communication
  between
    base of aorta and pulmonary artery Q21.4
    left ventricle and right atrium Q20.5
    pericardial sac and pleural sac Q34.8
    pulmonary artery and pulmonary vein,
      congenital Q25.72
  congenital between uterus and digestive or
    urinary tract Q51.7
Compartment syndrome (deep) (posterior)
    (traumatic) T79.A0
  abdomen T79.A3
  lower extremity (hip, buttock, thigh, leg, foot,
    toes) T79.A2
  nontraumatic
    abdomen M79.A3
    lower extremity (hip, buttock, thigh, leg,
      foot, toes) M79.A2-●
    specified site NEC M79.A9
    upper extremity (shoulder, arm, forearm,
      wrist, hand, fingers) M79.A1-●
  specified site NEC T79.A9
  upper extremity (shoulder, arm, forearm,
    wrist, hand, fingers) T79.A1
Compensation
  failure —*see* Disease, heart
  neurosis, psychoneurosis —*see* Disorder,
    factitious
Complaint —*see also* Disease
  bowel, functional K59.9
    psychogenic F45.8
  intestine, functional K59.9
    psychogenic F45.8
  kidney —*see* Disease, renal
  miners' J60
Complete —*see* condition
Complex
  Addison-Schilder E71.528
  cardiorenal —*see* Hypertension, cardiorenal
  Costen's M26.69
  disseminated mycobacterium avium-
    intracellulare (DMAC) A31.2

Complex *(Continued)*
  Eisenmenger's (ventricular septal defect) I27.83
  hypersexual F52.8
  jumped process, spine —*see* Dislocation,
    vertebra
  primary, tuberculous A15.7
  Schilder-Addison E71.528
  subluxation (vertebral) M99.19
    abdomen M99.19
    acromioclavicular M99.17
    cervical region M99.11
    cervicothoracic M99.11
    costochondral M99.18
    costovertebral M99.18
    head region M99.10
    hip M99.15
    lower extremity M99.16
    lumbar region M99.13
    lumbosacral M99.13
    occipitocervical M99.10
    pelvic region M99.15
    pubic M99.15
    rib cage M99.18
    sacral region M99.14
    sacrococcygeal M99.14
    sacroiliac M99.14
    specified NEC M99.19
    sternochondral M99.18
    sternoclavicular M99.17
    thoracic region M99.12
    thoracolumbar M99.12
    upper extremity M99.17
  Taussig-Bing (transposition, aorta and
    overriding pulmonary artery) Q20.1
Complication(s) (from) (of)
  accidental puncture or laceration during
    a procedure (of) —*see* Complications,
    intraoperative (intraprocedural),
    puncture or laceration
  amputation stump (surgical) (late) NEC T87.9
    dehiscence T87.81
    infection or inflammation T87.40
      lower limb T87.4-●
      upper limb T87.4-●
    necrosis T87.50
      lower limb T87.5-●
      upper limb T87.5-●
    neuroma T87.30
      lower limb T87.3-●
      upper limb T87.3-●
    specified type NEC T87.89
  anastomosis (and bypass) —*see also*
    Complications, prosthetic device or
    implant
    intestinal (internal) NEC K91.89
      involving urinary tract N99.89
    urinary tract (involving intestinal tract)
      N99.89
    vascular —*see* Complications,
      cardiovascular device or implant
  anesthesia, anesthetic —*see also* Anesthesia,
    complication T88.59
    brain, postpartum, puerperal O89.2
    cardiac
      in
        labor and delivery O74.2
        pregnancy O29.19-●
      postpartum, puerperal O89.1
    central nervous system
      in
        labor and delivery O74.3
        pregnancy O29.29-●
      postpartum, puerperal O89.2
    difficult or failed intubation T88.4
      in pregnancy O29.6-●
    failed sedation (conscious) (moderate)
      during procedure T88.52
    general, unintended awareness during
      procedure T88.53
    hyperthermia, malignant T88.3
    hypothermia T88.51
    intubation failure T88.4

Complication *(Continued)*
  anesthesia, anesthetic *(Continued)*
    malignant hyperthermia T88.3
    pulmonary
      in
        labor and delivery O74.1
        pregnancy NEC O29.09-●
      postpartum, puerperal O89.09
    shock T88.2
    spinal and epidural
      in
        labor and delivery NEC O74.6
          headache O74.5
        pregnancy NEC O29.5X-●
      postpartum, puerperal NEC O89.5
        headache O89.4
    unintended awareness under general
      anesthesia during procedure T88.53
  anti-reflux device —*see* Complications,
    esophageal anti-reflux device
  aortic (bifurcation) graft —*see* Complications,
    graft, vascular
  aortocoronary (bypass) graft —*see*
    Complications, coronary artery
    (bypass) graft
  aortofemoral (bypass) graft —*see*
    Complications, extremity artery
    (bypass) graft
  arteriovenous
    fistula, surgically created T82.9
      embolism T82.818
      fibrosis T82.828
      hemorrhage T82.838
      infection or inflammation T82.7
      mechanical
        breakdown T82.510
        displacement T82.520
        leakage T82.530
        malposition T82.520
        obstruction T82.590
        perforation T82.590
        protrusion T82.590
      pain T82.848
      specified type NEC T82.898
      stenosis T82.858
      thrombosis T82.868
    shunt, surgically created T82.9
      embolism T82.818
      fibrosis T82.828
      hemorrhage T82.838
      infection or inflammation T82.7
      mechanical
        breakdown T82.511
        displacement T82.521
        leakage T82.531
        malposition T82.521
        obstruction T82.591
        perforation T82.591
        protrusion T82.591
      pain T82.848
      specified type NEC T82.898
      stenosis T82.858
      thrombosis T82.868
  arthroplasty —*see* Complications, joint
    prosthesis
  artificial
    fertilization or insemination N98.9
      attempted introduction (of)
        embryo in embryo transfer N98.3
        ovum following in vitro fertilization
          N98.2
      hyperstimulation of ovaries N98.1
      infection N98.0
      specified NEC N98.8
    heart T82.9
      embolism T82.817
      fibrosis T82.827
      hemorrhage T82.837
      infection or inflammation T82.7
      mechanical
        breakdown T82.512
        displacement T82.522
        leakage T82.532

Complication *(Continued)*
  artificial *(Continued)*
    heart *(Continued)*
      mechanical *(Continued)*
        malposition T82.522
        obstruction T82.592
        perforation T82.592
        protrusion T82.592
      pain T82.847
      specified type NEC T82.897
      stenosis T82.857
      thrombosis T82.867
    opening
      cecostomy —*see* Complications, colostomy
      colostomy —*see* Complications, colostomy
      cystostomy —*see* Complications,
        cystostomy
      enterostomy —*see* Complications,
        enterostomy
      gastrostomy —*see* Complications,
        gastrostomy
      ileostomy —*see* Complications,
        enterostomy
      jejunostomy —*see* Complications,
        enterostomy
      nephrostomy —*see* Complications,
        stoma, urinary tract
      tracheostomy —*see* Complications,
        tracheostomy
      ureterostomy —*see* Complications,
        stoma, urinary tract
      urethrostomy —*see* Complications,
        stoma, urinary tract
  balloon implant or device
    gastrointestinal T85.9
      embolism T85.818
      fibrosis T85.828
      hemorrhage T85.838
      infection and inflammation T85.79
      pain T85.848
      specified type NEC T85.898
      stenosis T85.858
      thrombosis T85.868
    vascular (counterpulsation) T82.9
      embolism T82.818
      fibrosis T82.828
      hemorrhage T82.838
      infection or inflammation T82.7
      mechanical
        breakdown T82.513
        displacement T82.523
        leakage T82.533
        malposition T82.523
        obstruction T82.593
        perforation T82.593
        protrusion T82.593
      pain T82.848
      specified type NEC T82.898
      stenosis T82.858
      thrombosis T82.868
  bariatric procedure
    gastric band procedure K95.09
      infection K95.01
    specified procedure NEC K95.89
      infection K95.81
  bile duct implant (prosthetic) T85.9
    embolism T85.818
    fibrosis T85.828
    hemorrhage T85.838
    infection and inflammation T85.79
    mechanical
      breakdown T85.510
      displacement T85.520
      malfunction T85.510
      malposition T85.520
      obstruction T85.590
      perforation T85.590
      protrusion T85.590
      specified NEC T85.590
    pain T85.848
    specified type NEC T85.898

▶ New   ➡ Revised   ~~deleted~~ Deleted   ● Use Additional Character(s)

Complication (*Continued*)
  bile duct implant (*Continued*)
    stenosis T85.858
    thrombosis T85.868
  bladder device (auxiliary) —*see*
    Complications, genitourinary, device or
    implant, urinary system
  bleeding (postoperative) —*see* Complication,
    postoperative, hemorrhage
    intraoperative —*see* Complication,
      intraoperative, hemorrhage
  blood vessel graft —*see* Complications, graft,
    vascular
  bone
    device NEC T84.9
      embolism T84.81
      fibrosis T84.82
      hemorrhage T84.83
      infection or inflammation T84.7
      mechanical
        breakdown T84.318
        displacement T84.328
        malposition T84.328
        obstruction T84.398
        perforation T84.398
        protrusion T84.398
      pain T84.84
      specified type NEC T84.89
      stenosis T84.85
      thrombosis T84.86
    graft —*see* Complications, graft, bone
    growth stimulator (electrode) —*see*
      Complications, electronic stimulator
      device, bone
    marrow transplant —*see* Complications,
      transplant, bone, marrow
  brain neurostimulator (electrode) —*see*
    Complications, electronic stimulator
    device, brain
  breast implant (prosthetic) T85.9
    capsular contracture T85.44
    embolism T85.818
    fibrosis T85.828
    hemorrhage T85.838
    infection and inflammation T85.79
    mechanical
      breakdown T85.41
      displacement T85.42
      leakage T85.43
      malposition T85.42
      obstruction T85.49
      perforation T85.49
      protrusion T85.49
      specified NEC T85.49
    pain T85.848
    specified type NEC T85.898
    stenosis T85.858
    thrombosis T85.868
  bypass —*see also* Complications, prosthetic
    device or implant
    aortocoronary —*see* Complications,
      coronary artery (bypass) graft
    arterial —*see also* Complications, graft,
      vascular
      extremity —*see* Complications, extremity
        artery (bypass) graft
  cardiac —*see also* Disease, heart
    device, implant or graft T82.9
      embolism T82.817
      fibrosis T82.827
      hemorrhage T82.837
      infection or inflammation T82.7
        valve prosthesis T82.6
      mechanical
        breakdown T82.519
          specified device NEC T82.518
        displacement T82.529
          specified device NEC T82.528
        leakage T82.539
          specified device NEC T82.538
        malposition T82.529
          specified device NEC T82.528

Complication (*Continued*)
  cardiac (*Continued*)
    device, implant or graft (*Continued*)
      mechanical (*Continued*)
        obstruction T82.599
          specified device NEC T82.598
        perforation T82.599
          specified device NEC T82.598
        protrusion T82.599
          specified device NEC T82.598
      pain T82.847
      specified type NEC T82.897
      stenosis T82.857
      thrombosis T82.867
  cardiovascular device, graft or implant T82.9
    aortic graft —*see* Complications, graft,
      vascular
    arteriovenous
      fistula, artificial —*see* Complication,
        arteriovenous, fistula, surgically
        created
      shunt —*see* Complication, arteriovenous,
        shunt, surgically created
    artificial heart —*see* Complication,
      artificial, heart
    balloon (counterpulsation) device —*see*
      Complication, balloon implant,
      vascular
    carotid artery graft —*see* Complications,
      graft, vascular
    coronary bypass graft —*see* Complication,
      coronary artery (bypass) graft
    dialysis catheter (vascular) —*see*
      Complication, catheter, dialysis
    electronic T82.9
      electrode T82.9
        embolism T82.817
        fibrosis T82.827
        hemorrhage T82.837
        infection T82.7
        mechanical
          breakdown T82.110
          displacement T82.120
          leakage T82.190
          obstruction T82.190
          perforation T82.190
          protrusion T82.190
          specified type NEC T82.190
        pain T82.847
        specified NEC T82.897
        stenosis T82.857
        thrombosis T82.867
      embolism T82.817
      fibrosis T82.827
      hemorrhage T82.837
      infection T82.7
      mechanical
        breakdown T82.119
        displacement T82.129
        leakage T82.199
        obstruction T82.199
        perforation T82.199
        protrusion T82.199
        specified type NEC T82.199
      pain T82.847
      pulse generator T82.9
        embolism T82.817
        fibrosis T82.827
        hemorrhage T82.837
        infection T82.7
        mechanical
          breakdown T82.111
          displacement T82.121
          leakage T82.191
          obstruction T82.191
          perforation T82.191
          protrusion T82.191
          specified type NEC T82.191
        pain T82.847
        specified NEC T82.897
        stenosis T82.857
        thrombosis T82.867

Complication (*Continued*)
  cardiovascular device, graft or implant
    (*Continued*)
    electronic (*Continued*)
      specified condition NEC T82.897
      specified device NEC T82.9
        embolism T82.817
        fibrosis T82.827
        hemorrhage T82.837
        infection T82.7
        mechanical
          breakdown T82.118
          displacement T82.128
          leakage T82.198
          obstruction T82.198
          perforation T82.198
          protrusion T82.198
          specified type NEC T82.198
        pain T82.847
        specified NEC T82.897
        stenosis T82.857
        thrombosis T82.867
      stenosis T82.857
      thrombosis T82.867
    extremity artery graft —*see* Complication,
      extremity artery (bypass) graft
    femoral artery graft —*see* Complication,
      extremity artery (bypass) graft
    heart
      transplant —*see* Complication,
        transplant, heart
      valve —*see* Complication, prosthetic
        device, heart valve
        graft —*see* Complication, heart, valve,
          graft
    heart-lung transplant —*see* Complication,
      transplant, heart, with lung
    infection or inflammation T82.7
    umbrella device —*see* Complication,
      umbrella device, vascular
    vascular graft (or anastomosis) —*see*
      Complication, graft, vascular
  carotid artery (bypass) graft —*see*
    Complications, graft, vascular
  catheter (device) NEC —*see also*
    Complications, prosthetic device or
    implant
    cranial infusion
      infection and inflammation T85.735
      mechanical
        breakdown T85.610
        displacement T85.620
        leakage T85.630
        malfunction T85.690
        malposition T85.620
        obstruction T85.690
        perforation T85.690
        protrusion T85.690
        specified NEC T85.690
    cystostomy T83.9
      embolism T83.81
      fibrosis T83.82
      hemorrhage T83.83
      infection and inflammation T83.510
      mechanical
        breakdown T83.010
        displacement T83.020
        leakage T83.030
        malposition T83.020
        obstruction T83.090
        perforation T83.090
        protrusion T83.090
        specified NEC T83.090
      pain T83.84
      specified type NEC T83.89
      stenosis T83.85
      thrombosis T83.86
    dialysis (vascular) T82.9
      embolism T82.818
      fibrosis T82.828
      hemorrhage T82.838

Complication *(Continued)*
  catheter NEC *(Continued)*
    dialysis *(Continued)*
      infection and inflammation T82.7
      intraperitoneal —*see* Complications, catheter, intraperitoneal
      mechanical
        breakdown T82.41
        displacement T82.42
        leakage T82.43
        malposition T82.42
        obstruction T82.49
        perforation T82.49
        protrusion T82.49
      pain T82.848
      specified type NEC T82.898
      stenosis T82.858
      thrombosis T82.868
    epidural infusion T85.9
      embolism T85.810
      fibrosis T85.820
      hemorrhage T85.830
      infection and inflammation T85.735
      mechanical
        breakdown T85.610
        displacement T85.620
        leakage T85.630
        malfunction T85.610
        malposition T85.620
        obstruction T85.690
        perforation T85.690
        protrusion T85.690
        specified NEC T85.690
      pain T85.840
      specified type NEC T85.890
      stenosis T85.850
      thrombosis T85.860
    intraperitoneal dialysis T85.9
      embolism T85.818
      fibrosis T85.828
      hemorrhage T85.838
      infection and inflammation T85.71
      mechanical
        breakdown T85.611
        displacement T85.621
        leakage T85.631
        malfunction T85.611
        malposition T85.621
        obstruction T85.691
        perforation T85.691
        protrusion T85.691
        specified NEC T85.691
      pain T85.848
      specified type NEC T85.898
      stenosis T85.858
      thrombosis T85.868
    intrathecal infusion
      infection and inflammation T85.735
      mechanical
        breakdown T85.610
        displacement T85.620
        leakage T85.630
        malfunction T85.690
        malposition T85.620
        obstruction T85.690
        perforation T85.690
        protrusion T85.690
        specified NEC T85.690
    intravenous infusion T82.9
      embolism T82.818
      fibrosis T82.828
      hemorrhage T82.838
      infection or inflammation T82.7
      mechanical
        breakdown T82.514
        displacement T82.524
        leakage T82.534
        malposition T82.524
        obstruction T82.594
        perforation T82.594
        protrusion T82.594
      pain T82.848

Complication *(Continued)*
  catheter NEC *(Continued)*
    intravenous infusion *(Continued)*
      specified type NEC T82.898
      stenosis T82.858
      thrombosis T82.868
    spinal infusion
      infection and inflammation T85.735
      mechanical
        breakdown T85.610
        displacement T85.620
        leakage T85.630
        malfunction T85.690
        malposition T85.620
        obstruction T85.690
        perforation T85.690
        protrusion T85.690
        specified NEC T85.690
    subarachnoid infusion
      infection and inflammation T85.735
      mechanical
        breakdown T85.610
        displacement T85.620
        leakage T85.630
        malfunction T85.690
        malposition T85.620
        obstruction T85.690
        perforation T85.690
        protrusion T85.690
        specified NEC T85.690
    subdural infusion T85.9
      embolism T85.810
      fibrosis T85.820
      hemorrhage T85.830
      infection and inflammation T85.735
      mechanical
        breakdown T85.610
        displacement T85.620
        leakage T85.630
        malfunction T85.610
        malposition T85.620
        obstruction T85.690
        perforation T85.690
        protrusion T85.690
        specified NEC T85.690
      pain T85.840
      specified type NEC T85.890
      stenosis T85.850
      thrombosis T85.860
    urethral T83.9
      displacement T83.028
      embolism T83.81
      fibrosis T83.82
      hemorrhage T83.83
      indwelling
        breakdown T83.011
        displacement T83.021
        infection and inflammation T83.511
        leakage T83.031
        specified complication NEC T83.091
      infection and inflammation T83.511
      leakage T83.038
      malposition T83.028
      mechanical
        breakdown T83.011
      obstruction (mechanical) T83.091
      pain T83.84
      perforation T83.091
      protrusion T83.091
      specified type NEC T83.091
      stenosis T83.85
      thrombosis T83.86
    urinary NEC
      breakdown T83.018
      displacement T83.028
      infection and inflammation T83.518
      leakage T83.038
      specified complication NEC T83.098
  cecostomy (stoma) —*see* Complications, colostomy

Complication *(Continued)*
  cesarean delivery wound NEC O90.89
    disruption O90.0
    hematoma O90.2
    ➡ infection (following delivery) O86.00
  chemotherapy (antineoplastic) NEC T88.7
  chin implant (prosthetic) —*see* Complication, prosthetic device or implant, specified NEC
  circulatory system I99.8
    intraoperative I97.88
    postprocedural I97.89
      following cardiac surgery —*see also* Infarct, myocardium, associated with revascularization procedure I97.19-●
        postcardiotomy syndrome I97.0
      hypertension I97.3
      lymphedema after mastectomy I97.2
      postcardiotomy syndrome I97.0
      specified NEC I97.89
  colostomy (stoma) K94.00
    hemorrhage K94.01
    infection K94.02
    malfunction K94.03
    mechanical K94.03
    specified complication NEC K94.09
  contraceptive device, intrauterine — *see* Complications, intrauterine, contraceptive device
  cord (umbilical) —*see* Complications, umbilical cord
  corneal graft —*see* Complications, graft, cornea
  coronary artery (bypass) graft T82.9
    atherosclerosis —*see* Arteriosclerosis, coronary (artery)
    embolism T82.818
    fibrosis T82.828
    hemorrhage T82.838
    infection and inflammation T82.7
    mechanical
      breakdown T82.211
      displacement T82.212
      leakage T82.213
      malposition T82.212
      obstruction T82.218
      perforation T82.218
      protrusion T82.218
      specified NEC T82.218
    pain T82.848
    specified type NEC T82.898
    stenosis T82.858
    thrombosis T82.868
  counterpulsation device (balloon), intra-aortic —*see* Complications, balloon implant, vascular
  cystostomy (stoma) N99.518
    catheter —*see* Complications, catheter, cystostomy
    hemorrhage N99.510
    infection N99.511
    malfunction N99.512
    specified type NEC N99.518
  delivery —*see also* Complications, obstetric O75.9
    procedure (instrumental) (manual) (surgical) O75.4
    specified NEC O75.89
  dialysis (peritoneal) (renal) —*see also* Complications, infusion
    catheter (vascular) —*see* Complication, catheter, dialysis
      peritoneal, intraperitoneal —*see* Complications, catheter, intraperitoneal
  dorsal column (spinal) neurostimulator —*see* Complications, electronic stimulator device, spinal cord
  drug NEC T88.7
  ear procedure —*see also* Disorder, ear
    intraoperative H95.88-●
      hematoma —*see* Complications, intraoperative, hematoma (of), ear

Complication (Continued)
ear procedure (Continued)
intraoperative (Continued)
hemorrhage —see Complications,
intraoperative, hemorrhage (of), ear
laceration —see Complications,
intraoperative, puncture or
laceration..., ear
seroma —see Complications,
postprocedural, seroma (of),
mastoid process
specified NEC H95.88-•
postoperative H95.89-•
external ear canal stenosis H95.81-•
hematoma —see Complications,
postprocedural, hemorrhage
(hematoma) (of), ear
hemorrhage —see Complications,
postprocedural, hemorrhage
(hematoma) (of), ear
postmastoidectomy —see Complications,
postmastoidectomy
specified NEC H95.89-•
ectopic pregnancy O08.9
damage to pelvic organs O08.6
embolism O08.2
genital infection O08.0
hemorrhage (delayed) (excessive) O08.1
metabolic disorder O08.5
renal failure O08.4
shock O08.3
specified type NEC O08.0
venous complication NEC O08.7
electronic stimulator device
bladder (urinary) —see Complications,
electronic stimulator device, urinary
bone T84.9
breakdown T84.310
displacement T84.320
embolism T84.81
fibrosis T84.82
hemorrhage T84.83
infection or inflammation T84.7
malfunction T84.310
malposition T84.320
mechanical NEC T84.390
obstruction T84.390
pain T84.84
perforation T84.390
protrusion T84.390
specified type NEC T84.89
stenosis T84.85
thrombosis T84.86
brain T85.9
embolism T85.810
fibrosis T85.820
hemorrhage T85.830
infection and inflammation T85.731
mechanical
breakdown T85.110
displacement T85.120
leakage T85.190
malposition T85.120
obstruction T85.190
perforation T85.190
protrusion T85.190
specified NEC T85.190
pain T85.840
specified type NEC T85.890
stenosis T85.850
thrombosis T85.860
cardiac (defibrillator) (pacemaker) —see
Complications, cardiovascular device
or implant, electronic
generator (brain) (gastric) (peripheral)
(sacral) (spinal)
breakdown T85.113
displacement T85.123
leakage T85.193
malposition T85.123
obstruction T85.193

Complication (Continued)
electronic stimulator device (Continued)
generator (Continued)
perforation T85.193
protrusion T85.193
specified type NEC T85.193
muscle T84.9
breakdown T84.418
displacement T84.428
embolism T84.81
fibrosis T84.82
hemorrhage T84.83
infection or inflammation T84.7
mechanical NEC T84.498
pain T84.84
specified type NEC T84.89
stenosis T84.85
thrombosis T84.86
nervous system T85.9
brain —see Complications, electronic
stimulator device, brain
cranial nerve —see Complications,
electronic stimulator device,
peripheral nerve
embolism T85.810
fibrosis T85.820
gastric nerve —see Complications,
electronic stimulator device,
peripheral nerve
hemorrhage T85.830
infection and inflammation T85.738
mechanical
breakdown T85.118
displacement T85.128
leakage T85.199
malposition T85.128
obstruction T85.199
perforation T85.199
protrusion T85.199
specified NEC T85.199
pain T85.840
peripheral nerve —see Complications,
electronic stimulator device,
peripheral nerve
sacral nerve —see Complications,
electronic stimulator device,
peripheral nerve
specified type NEC T85.890
spinal cord —see Complications, electronic
stimulator device, spinal cord
stenosis T85.850
thrombosis T85.860
vagal nerve —see Complications,
electronic stimulator device,
peripheral nerve
peripheral nerve T85.9
embolism T85.810
fibrosis T85.820
hemorrhage T85.830
infection and inflammation T85.732
mechanical
breakdown T85.111
displacement T85.121
leakage T85.191
malposition T85.121
obstruction T85.191
perforation T85.191
protrusion T85.191
specified NEC T85.191
pain T85.840
specified type NEC T85.890
stenosis T85.850
thrombosis T85.860
spinal cord T85.9
embolism T85.810
fibrosis T85.820
hemorrhage T85.830
infection and inflammation T85.733
mechanical
breakdown T85.112
displacement T85.122

Complication (Continued)
electronic stimulator device (Continued)
spinal cord (Continued)
mechanical (Continued)
leakage T85.192
malposition T85.122
obstruction T85.192
perforation T85.192
protrusion T85.192
specified NEC T85.192
pain T85.840
specified type NEC T85.890
stenosis T85.850
thrombosis T85.860
urinary T83.9
embolism T83.81
fibrosis T83.82
hemorrhage T83.83
infection and inflammation T83.598
mechanical
breakdown T83.110
displacement T83.120
malposition T83.120
perforation T83.190
protrusion T83.190
specified NEC T83.190
pain T83.84
specified type NEC T83.89
stenosis T83.85
thrombosis T83.86
electroshock therapy T88.9
specified NEC T88.8
endocrine E34.9
postprocedural
adrenal hypofunction E89.6
hypoinsulinemia E89.1
hypoparathyroidism E89.2
hypopituitarism E89.3
hypothyroidism E89.0
ovarian failure E89.40
asymptomatic E89.40
symptomatic E89.41
specified NEC E89.89
testicular hypofunction E89.5
endodontic treatment NEC M27.59
enterostomy (stoma) K94.10
hemorrhage K94.11
infection K94.12
malfunction K94.13
mechanical K94.13
specified complication NEC K94.19
episiotomy, disruption O90.1
esophageal anti-reflux device T85.9
embolism T85.818
fibrosis T85.828
hemorrhage T85.838
infection and inflammation T85.79
mechanical
breakdown T85.511
displacement T85.521
malfunction T85.511
malposition T85.521
obstruction T85.591
perforation T85.591
protrusion T85.591
specified NEC T85.591
pain T85.848
specified type NEC T85.898
stenosis T85.858
thrombosis T85.868
esophagostomy K94.30
hemorrhage K94.31
infection K94.32
malfunction K94.33
mechanical K94.33
specified complication NEC K94.39
extracorporeal circulation T80.90
extremity artery (bypass) graft T82.9
arteriosclerosis —see Arteriosclerosis,
extremities, bypass graft
embolism T82.818
fibrosis T82.828

▶ New   ⇒ Revised   ~~deleted~~ Deleted   ● Use Additional Character(s)

Complication (Continued)
  genitourinary (Continued)
    device or implant (Continued)
      genital tract (Continued)
        specified type NEC T83.89
          embolism T83.81
          fibrosis T83.82
          hemorrhage T83.83
          pain T83.84
          specified complication NEC T83.89
          stenosis T83.85
          thrombosis T83.86
        vaginal mesh —see Complications,
          mesh
    urinary system T83.9
      cystostomy catheter —see
        Complication, catheter,
        cystostomy
      electronic stimulator —see
        Complications, electronic
        stimulator device, urinary
      indwelling urethral catheter —see
        Complications, catheter, urethral,
        indwelling
      infection or inflammation T83.598
        indwelling urethral catheter T83.511
      kidney transplant —see Complication,
        transplant, kidney
      organ graft —see Complication, graft,
        urinary organ
      specified type NEC T83.89
        embolism T83.81
        fibrosis T83.82
        hemorrhage T83.83
        mechanical T83.198
          breakdown T83.118
          displacement T83.128
          malfunction T83.118
          malposition T83.128
          obstruction T83.198
          perforation T83.198
          protrusion T83.198
          specified NEC T83.198
        sphincter, implanted T83.191
        stent (ileal conduit) (nephroureteral)
          T83.193
        ureteral indwelling T83.192
        pain T83.84
        specified complication NEC T83.89
        stenosis T83.85
        thrombosis T83.86
      sphincter implant —see Complications,
        implant, urinary sphincter
  postprocedural
    pelvic peritoneal adhesions N99.4
    renal failure N99.0
    specified NEC N99.89
    stoma —see Complications, stoma,
      urinary tract
    urethral stricture —see Stricture, urethra,
      postprocedural
    vaginal
      adhesions N99.2
      vault prolapse N99.3
  graft (bypass) (patch) —see also
    Complications, prosthetic device or
    implant
  aorta —see Complications, graft, vascular
  arterial —see Complication, graft, vascular
  bone T86.839
    failure T86.831
    infection T86.832
    mechanical T84.318
      breakdown T84.318
      displacement T84.328
      protrusion T84.398
      specified type NEC T84.398
    rejection T86.830
    specified type NEC T86.838
  carotid artery —see Complications, graft,
    vascular

Complication (Continued)
  graft (Continued)
    cornea T86.849
      failure T86.841
      infection T86.842
      mechanical T85.398
        breakdown T85.318
        displacement T85.328
        protrusion T85.398
        specified type NEC T85.398
      rejection T86.840
      retroprosthetic membrane T85.398
      specified type NEC T86.848
    femoral artery (bypass) —see Complication,
      extremity artery (bypass) graft
    genital organ or tract —see Complications,
      genitourinary, device or implant,
      genital tract
    muscle T84.9
      breakdown T84.410
      displacement T84.420
      embolism T84.81
      fibrosis T84.82
      hemorrhage T84.83
      infection and inflammation T84.7
      mechanical NEC T84.490
      pain T84.84
      specified type NEC T84.89
      stenosis T84.85
      thrombosis T84.86
    nerve —see Complication, prosthetic device
      or implant, specified NEC
    skin —see Complications, prosthetic device
      or implant, skin graft
    tendon T84.9
      breakdown T84.410
      displacement T84.420
      embolism T84.81
      fibrosis T84.82
      hemorrhage T84.83
      infection and inflammation T84.7
      mechanical NEC T84.490
      pain T84.84
      specified type NEC T84.89
      stenosis T84.85
      thrombosis T84.86
    urinary organ T83.9
      embolism T83.81
      fibrosis T83.82
      hemorrhage T83.83
      infection and inflammation T83.598
        indwelling urethral catheter T83.511
      mechanical
        breakdown T83.21
        displacement T83.22
        erosion T83.24
        exposure T83.25
        leakage T83.23
        malposition T83.22
        obstruction T83.29
        perforation T83.29
        protrusion T83.29
        specified NEC T83.29
      pain T83.84
      specified type NEC T83.89
      stenosis T83.85
      thrombosis T83.86
    vascular T82.9
      embolism T82.818
      femoral artery —see Complication,
        extremity artery (bypass) graft
      fibrosis T82.828
      hemorrhage T82.838
      mechanical
        breakdown T82.319
          aorta (bifurcation) T82.310
          carotid artery T82.311
          specified vessel NEC T82.318
        displacement T82.329
          aorta (bifurcation) T82.320
          carotid artery T82.321
          specified vessel NEC T82.328

Complication (Continued)
  graft (Continued)
    vascular (Continued)
      mechanical (Continued)
        leakage T82.339
          aorta (bifurcation) T82.330
          carotid artery T82.331
          specified vessel NEC T82.338
        malposition T82.329
          aorta (bifurcation) T82.320
          carotid artery T82.321
          specified vessel NEC T82.328
        obstruction T82.399
          aorta (bifurcation) T82.390
          carotid artery T82.391
          specified vessel NEC T82.398
        perforation T82.399
          aorta (bifurcation) T82.390
          carotid artery T82.391
          specified vessel NEC T82.398
        protrusion T82.399
          aorta (bifurcation) T82.390
          carotid artery T82.391
          specified vessel NEC T82.398
      pain T82.848
      specified complication NEC T82.898
      stenosis T82.858
      thrombosis T82.868
  heart I51.9
    assist device
      infection and inflammation T82.7
    following acute myocardial infarction —
      see Complications, following, acute
      myocardial infarction
    postoperative —see Complications,
      circulatory system
    transplant —see Complication, transplant,
      heart
      and lung(s) —see Complications,
        transplant, heart, with lung
    valve
      graft (biological) T82.9
        embolism T82.817
        fibrosis T82.827
        hemorrhage T82.837
        infection and inflammation T82.7
        mechanical T82.228
          breakdown T82.221
          displacement T82.222
          leakage T82.223
          malposition T82.222
          obstruction T82.228
          perforation T82.228
          protrusion T82.228
        pain T82.847
        specified type NEC T82.897
        stenosis T82.857
        thrombosis T82.867
      prosthesis T82.9
        embolism T82.817
        fibrosis T82.827
        hemorrhage T82.837
        infection or inflammation T82.6
        mechanical T82.09
          breakdown T82.01
          displacement T82.02
          leakage T82.03
          malposition T82.02
          obstruction T82.09
          perforation T82.09
          protrusion T82.09
        pain T82.847
        specified type NEC T82.897
          mechanical T82.09
        stenosis T82.857
        thrombosis T82.867
  hematoma
    intraoperative —see Complication,
      intraoperative, hemorrhage
    postprocedural —see Complication,
      postprocedural, hematoma
  hemodialysis —see Complications, dialysis

Complication (Continued)
 hemorrhage
  intraoperative —see Complication,
   intraoperative, hemorrhage
  postprocedural —see Complication,
   postprocedural, hemorrhage
 ileostomy (stoma) —see Complications,
  enterostomy
 immunization (procedure) —see
  Complications, vaccination
 implant —see also Complications, by site and
  type
  urinary sphincter T83.9
   embolism T83.81
   fibrosis T83.82
   hemorrhage T83.83
   infection and inflammation T83.591
   mechanical
    breakdown T83.111
    displacement T83.121
    leakage T83.191
    malposition T83.121
    obstruction T83.191
    perforation T83.191
    protrusion T83.191
    specified NEC T83.191
   pain T83.84
   specified type NEC T83.89
   stenosis T83.85
   thrombosis T83.86
 infusion (procedure) T80.90
  air embolism T80.0
  blood —see Complications, transfusion
  catheter —see Complications, catheter
  infection T80.29
  pump —see Complications, cardiovascular,
   device or implant
  sepsis T80.29
  serum reaction —see also Reaction, serum
   T80.69
   anaphylactic shock —see also Shock,
    anaphylactic T80.59
  specified type NEC T80.89
 inhalation therapy NEC T81.81
 injection (procedure) T80.90
  drug reaction —see Reaction, drug
  infection T80.29
  sepsis T80.29
  serum (prophylactic) (therapeutic) —see
   Complications, vaccination
  specified type NEC T80.89
  vaccine (any) —see Complications,
   vaccination
 inoculation (any) —see Complications,
  vaccination
 insulin pump
  infection and inflammation T85.72
  mechanical
   breakdown T85.614
   displacement T85.624
   leakage T85.633
   malposition T85.624
   obstruction T85.694
   perforation T85.694
   protrusion T85.694
   specified NEC T85.694
 intestinal pouch NEC K91.858
 intraocular lens (prosthetic) T85.9
  embolism T85.818
  fibrosis T85.828
  hemorrhage T85.838
  infection and inflammation T85.79
  mechanical
   breakdown T85.21
   displacement T85.22
   malposition T85.22
   obstruction T85.29
   perforation T85.29
   protrusion T85.29
   specified NEC T85.29
  pain T85.848
  specified type NEC T85.898

Complication (Continued)
 intraocular lens (Continued)
  stenosis T85.858
  thrombosis T85.868
 intraoperative (intraprocedural)
  cardiac arrest —see also Infarct,
   myocardium, associated with
   revascularization procedure
   during cardiac surgery I97.710
   during other surgery I97.711
  cardiac functional disturbance NEC —see
   also Infarct, myocardium, associated
   with revascularization procedure
   during cardiac surgery I97.790
   during other surgery I97.791
  hemorrhage (hematoma) (of)
   circulatory system organ or structure
    during cardiac bypass I97.411
    during cardiac catheterization I97.410
    during other circulatory system
     procedure I97.418
    during other procedure I97.42
   digestive system organ
    during procedure on digestive system
     K91.61
    during procedure on other organ
     K91.62
   ear
    during procedure on ear and mastoid
     process H95.21
    during procedure on other organ
     H95.22
   endocrine system organ or structure
    during procedure on endocrine
     system organ or structure E36.01
    during procedure on other organ
     E36.02
   eye and adnexa
    during ophthalmic procedure H59.11-●
    during other procedure H59.12-●
   genitourinary organ or structure
    during procedure on genitourinary
     organ or structure N99.61
    during procedure on other organ
     N99.62
   mastoid process
    during procedure on ear and mastoid
     process H95.21
    during procedure on other organ
     H95.22
   musculoskeletal structure
    during musculoskeletal surgery
     M96.810
    during non-orthopedic surgery
     M96.811
    during orthopedic surgery M96.810
   nervous system
    during a nervous system procedure
     G97.31
    during other procedure G97.32
   respiratory system
    during other procedure J95.62
    during procedure on respiratory
     system organ or structure
     J95.61
   skin and subcutaneous tissue
    during a dermatologic procedure
     L76.01
    during a procedure on other organ
     L76.02
   spleen
    during a procedure on other organ
     D78.02
    during a procedure on the spleen
     D78.01
  puncture or laceration (accidental)
   (unintentional) (of)
   brain
    during a nervous system procedure
     G97.48
    during other procedure G97.49

Complication (Continued)
 intraoperative (Continued)
  puncture or laceration (Continued)
   circulatory system organ or structure
    during circulatory system procedure
     I97.51
    during other procedure I97.52
   digestive system
    during procedure on digestive system
     K91.71
    during procedure on other organ K91.72
   ear
    during procedure on ear and mastoid
     process H95.31
    during procedure on other organ
     H95.32
   endocrine system organ or structure
    during procedure on endocrine
     system organ or structure E36.11
    during procedure on other organ E36.12
   eye and adnexa
    during ophthalmic procedure H59.21-●
    during other procedure H59.22-●
   genitourinary organ or structure
    during procedure on genitourinary
     organ or structure N99.71
    during procedure on other organ
     N99.72
   mastoid process
    during procedure on ear and mastoid
     process H95.31
    during procedure on other organ
     H95.32
   musculoskeletal structure
    during musculoskeletal surgery
     M96.820
    during non-orthopedic surgery
     M96.821
    during orthopedic surgery M96.820
   nervous system
    during a nervous system procedure
     G97.48
    during other procedure G97.49
   respiratory system
    during other procedure J95.72
    during procedure on respiratory
     system organ or structure J95.71
   skin and subcutaneous tissue
    during a dermatologic procedure
     L76.11
    during a procedure on other organ
     L76.12
   spleen
    during a procedure on other organ
     D78.12
    during a procedure on the spleen
     D78.11
  specified NEC
   circulatory system I97.88
   digestive system K91.81
   ear H95.88
   endocrine system E36.8
   eye and adnexa H59.88
   genitourinary system N99.81
   mastoid process H95.88
   musculoskeletal structure M96.89
   nervous system G97.81
   respiratory system J95.88
   skin and subcutaneous tissue L76.81
   spleen D78.81
 intraperitoneal catheter (dialysis)
  (infusion) —see Complications, catheter,
  intraperitoneal
 intrathecal infusion pump
  infection and inflammation T85.738
  mechanical
   breakdown T85.615
   displacement T85.625
   leakage T85.635
   malfunction T85.695
   malposition T85.625

▶ New   ⇒ Revised   ~~deleted~~ Deleted   ● Use Additional Character(s)

Complication *(Continued)*
 intrathecal infusion pump *(Continued)*
  mechanical *(Continued)*
   obstruction T85.695
   perforation T85.695
   protrusion T85.695
   specified NEC T85.695
 intrauterine
  contraceptive device
   embolism T83.81
   fibrosis T83.82
   hemorrhage T83.83
   infection and inflammation T83.69
   mechanical
    breakdown T83.31
    displacement T83.32
    malposition T83.32
    obstruction T83.39
    perforation T83.39
    protrusion T83.39
    specified NEC T83.39
   pain T83.84
   specified type NEC T83.89
   stenosis T83.85
   thrombosis T83.86
  procedure (fetal), to newborn P96.5
 jejunostomy (stoma) —*see* Complications,
   enterostomy
 joint prosthesis, internal T84.9
  breakage (fracture) T84.01-•
  dislocation T84.02-•
  fracture T84.01-•
  infection or inflammation T84.50
   hip T84.5-•
   knee T84.5-•
   specified joint NEC T84.59
  instability T84.02-•
  malposition —*see* Complications, joint
    prosthesis, mechanical, displacement
  mechanical
   breakage, broken T84.01-•
   dislocation T84.02-•
   fracture T84.01-•
   instability T84.02-•
   leakage —*see* Complications, joint
     prosthesis, mechanical, specified
     NEC
   loosening T84.039
    hip T84.03-•
    knee T84.03-•
    specified joint NEC T84.038
   obstruction —*see* Complications, joint
     prosthesis, mechanical, specified
     NEC
   perforation —*see* Complications, joint
     prosthesis, mechanical, specified
     NEC
    osteolysis T84.059
     hip T84.05-•
     knee T84.05-•
     other specified joint T84.058
   protrusion —*see* Complications, joint
     prosthesis, mechanical, specified
     NEC
   specified complication NEC T84.099
    hip T84.09-•
    knee T84.09-•
    other specified joint T84.098
   subluxation T84.02-•
   wear of articular bearing surface T84.069
    hip T84.06-•
    knee T84.06-•
    other specified joint T84.068
  specified joint NEC T84.89
   embolism T84.81
   fibrosis T84.82
   hemorrhage T84.83
   pain T84.84
   specified complication NEC T84.89
   stenosis T84.85
   thrombosis T84.86
  subluxation T84.02-•

Complication *(Continued)*
 kidney transplant —*see* Complications,
   transplant, kidney
 labor O75.9
  specified NEC O75.89
 liver transplant (immune or nonimmune) —
   see Complications, transplant,
   liver
 lumbar puncture G97.1
  cerebrospinal fluid leak G97.0
  headache or reaction G97.1
 lung transplant —*see* Complications,
   transplant, lung
  and heart —*see* Complications, transplant,
    lung, with heart
 male genital N50.9
  device, implant or graft —*see*
    Complications, genitourinary,
    device or implant, genital tract
  postprocedural or postoperative —*see*
    Complications, genitourinary,
    postprocedural
  specified NEC N99.89
 mastoid (process) procedure
  intraoperative H95.88-•
   hematoma —*see* Complications,
     intraoperative, hemorrhage
     (hematoma) (of), mastoid process
   hemorrhage —*see* Complications,
     intraoperative, hemorrhage
     (hematoma) (of), mastoid process
   laceration —*see* Complications,
     intraoperative, puncture or
     laceration..., mastoid process
   specified NEC H95.88-•
  postmastoidectomy —*see* Complications,
    postmastoidectomy
  postoperative H95.89-•
   external ear canal stenosis H95.81-•
   hematoma —*see* Complications...,
     postprocedural, hematoma (of),
     mastoid process
   hemorrhage —*see* Complications...,
     postprocedural, hemorrhage (of),
     mastoid process
   postmastoidectomy —*see* Complications,
     postmastoidectomy
   seroma —*see* Complications,
     postprocedural, seroma (of),
     mastoid process
   specified NEC H95.89-•
 mastoidectomy cavity —*see* Complications,
   postmastoidectomy
 mechanical —*see* Complications, by site and
   type, mechanical
 medical procedures (see also Complication(s),
   intraoperative) T88.9
 metabolic E88.9
  postoperative E89.89
   specified NEC E89.89
 molar pregnancy NOS O08.9
  damage to pelvic organs O08.6
  embolism O08.2
  genital infection O08.0
  hemorrhage (delayed) (excessive) O08.1
  metabolic disorder O08.5
  renal failure O08.4
  shock O08.3
  specified type NEC O08.0
  venous complication NEC O08.7
 musculoskeletal system —*see also*
   Complication, intraoperative
   (intraprocedural), by site
  device, implant or graft NEC —*see*
    Complications, orthopedic, device or
    implant
  internal fixation (nail) (plate) (rod) —*see*
    Complications, fixation device,
    internal
  joint prosthesis —*see* Complications, joint
    prosthesis

Complication *(Continued)*
 musculoskeletal system *(Continued)*
  postoperative (postprocedural) M96.89
   with osteoporosis —*see* Osteoporosis
   fracture following insertion of device —
     see Fracture, following insertion of
     orthopedic implant, joint prosthesis
     or bone plate
   joint instability after prosthesis removal
     M96.89
   lordosis M96.4
   postlaminectomy syndrome NEC M96.1
    kyphosis M96.2
   pseudarthrosis M96.0
   specified complication NEC M96.89
  post radiation M96.89
   kyphosis M96.3
   scoliosis M96.5
   specified complication NEC M96.89
 nephrostomy (stoma) —*see* Complications,
   stoma, urinary tract, external NEC
 nervous system G98.8
  central G96.9
  device, implant or graft —*see also*
    Complication, prosthetic device or
    implant, specified NEC
   electronic stimulator (electrode(s)) —*see*
     Complications, electronic stimulator
     device
   specified NEC
    infection and inflammation T85.738
    mechanical T85.695
     breakdown T85.615
     displacement T85.625
     leakage T85.635
     malfunction T85.695
     malposition T85.625
     obstruction T85.695
     perforation T85.695
     protrusion T85.695
     specified NEC T85.695
   ventricular shunt —*see* Complications,
     ventricular shunt
  electronic stimulator (electrode(s)) —*see*
    Complications, electronic stimulator
    device
  postprocedural G97.82
   intracranial hypotension G97.2
   specified NEC G97.82
   spinal fluid leak G97.0
 newborn, due to intrauterine (fetal)
   procedure P96.5
 nonabsorbable (permanent) sutures —*see*
   Complication, sutures, permanent
 obstetric O75.9
  procedure (instrumental) (manual)
    (surgical) specified NEC O75.4
  specified NEC O75.89
  surgical wound NEC O90.89
   hematoma O90.2
   ➡ infection O86.00
 ocular lens implant —*see* Complications,
   intraocular lens
 ophthalmologic
  postprocedural bleb —*see* Blebitis
 orbital prosthesis T85.9
  embolism T85.818
  fibrosis T85.828
  hemorrhage T85.838
  infection and inflammation T85.79
  mechanical
   breakdown T85.31-•
   displacement T85.32-•
   malposition T85.32-•
   obstruction T85.39-•
   perforation T85.39-•
   protrusion T85.39-•
   specified NEC T85.39-•
  pain T85.848
  specified type NEC T85.898
  stenosis T85.858
  thrombosis T85.868

Complication *(Continued)*
 organ or tissue transplant (partial) (total) —
  see Complications, transplant
 orthopedic —*see also* Disorder, soft tissue
  device or implant T84.9
   bone
    device or implant —*see* Complication,
     bone, device NEC
    graft —*see* Complication, graft, bone
   breakdown T84.418
   displacement T84.428
   electronic bone stimulator —*see*
    Complications, electronic stimulator
    device, bone
   embolism T84.81
   fibrosis T84.82
   fixation device —*see* Complication,
    fixation device, internal
   hemorrhage T84.83
   infection or inflammation T84.7
   joint prosthesis —*see* Complication, joint
    prosthesis, internal
   malfunction T84.418
   malposition T84.428
   mechanical NEC T84.498
   muscle graft —*see* Complications, graft,
    muscle
   obstruction T84.498
   pain T84.84
   perforation T84.498
   protrusion T84.498
   specified complication NEC T84.89
   stenosis T84.85
   tendon graft —*see* Complications, graft,
    tendon
   thrombosis T84.86
  fracture (following insertion of device) —
   see Fracture, following insertion of
   orthopedic implant, joint prosthesis or
   bone plate
  postprocedural M96.89
   fracture —*see* Fracture, following
    insertion of orthopedic implant,
    joint prosthesis or bone plate
   postlaminectomy syndrome NEC M96.1
    kyphosis M96.3
    lordosis M96.4
   postradiation
    kyphosis M96.2
    scoliosis M96.5
   pseudarthrosis post-fusion M96.0
   specified type NEC M96.89
 pacemaker (cardiac) —*see* Complications,
  cardiovascular device or implant,
  electronic
 pancreas transplant —*see* Complications,
  transplant, pancreas
 penile prosthesis (implant) —*see*
  Complications, prosthetic device, penile
 perfusion NEC T80.90
 perineal repair (obstetrical) NEC O90.89
  disruption O90.1
  hematoma O90.2
  ⇒infection (following delivery) O86.09
 phototherapy T88.9
  specified NEC T88.8
 postmastoidectomy NEC H95.19-●
  cyst, mucosal H95.13-●
  granulation H95.12-●
  inflammation, chronic H95.11-●
  recurrent cholesteatoma H95.0-●
 postoperative —*see* Complications,
  postprocedural
  circulatory —*see* Complications, circulatory
   system
  ear —*see* Complications, ear
  endocrine —*see* Complications,
   endocrine
  eye —*see* Complications, eye
  lumbar puncture G97.1
   cerebrospinal fluid leak G97.0

Complication *(Continued)*
 postoperative *(Continued)*
  nervous system (central) (peripheral) —*see*
   Complications, nervous system
  respiratory system —*see* Complications,
   respiratory system
 postprocedural —*see also* Complications,
  surgical procedure
  cardiac arrest —*see also* Infarct,
   myocardium, associated with
   revascularization procedure
   following cardiac surgery I97.120
   following other surgery I97.121
  cardiac functional disturbance NEC —*see
   also* Infarct, myocardium, associated
   with revascularization procedure
   following cardiac surgery I97.190
   following other surgery I97.191
  cardiac insufficiency
   following cardiac surgery I97.110
   following other surgery I97.111
  chorioretinal scars following retinal
   surgery H59.81-●
  following cataract surgery
   cataract (lens) fragments H59.02-●
   cystoid macular edema H59.03-●
   specified NEC H59.09-●
   vitreous (touch) syndrome H59.01-●
  heart failure
   following cardiac surgery I97.130
   following other surgery I97.131
  hematoma (of)
   circulatory system organ or structure
    following cardiac bypass I97.631
    following cardiac catheterization
     I97.630
    following other circulatory system
     procedure I97.638
    following other procedure I97.621
   digestive system
    following procedure on digestive
     system K91.870
    following procedure on other organ
     K91.871
   ear
    following other procedure H95.52
    following procedure on ear and
     mastoid process H95.51
   endocrine system
    following endocrine system procedure
     E89.820
    following other procedure E89.821
   eye and adnexa
    following ophthalmic procedure
     H59.33-●
    following other procedure H59.34-●
   genitourinary organ or structure
    following procedure on genitourinary
     organ or structure N99.840
    following procedure on other organ
     N99.841
   mastoid process
    following other procedure H95.52
    following procedure on ear and
     mastoid process H95.51
   musculoskeletal structure
    following musculoskeletal surgery
     M96.840
    following non-orthopedic surgery
     M96.841
    following orthopedic surgery M96.840
   nervous system
    following nervous system procedure
     G97.61
    following other procedure G97.62
   respiratory system
    following other procedure J95.861
    following procedure on respiratory
     system organ or structure J95.860
   skin and subcutaneous tissue
    following dermatologic procedure
     L76.31

Complication *(Continued)*
 postprocedural *(Continued)*
  hematoma *(Continued)*
   skin and subcutaneous tissue *(Continued)*
    following procedure on other organ
     L76.32
   spleen
    following procedure on other organ
     D78.32
    following procedure on the spleen
     D78.31
  hemorrhage (of)
   circulatory system organ or structure
    following cardiac bypass I97.611
    following cardiac catheterization
     I97.610
    following other circulatory system
     procedure I97.618
    following other procedure I97.620
   digestive system
    following procedure on digestive
     system K91.840
    following procedure on other organ
     K91.841
   ear
    following other procedure H95.42
    following procedure on ear and
     mastoid process H95.41
   endocrine system
    following endocrine system procedure
     E89.810
    following other procedure E89.811
   eye and adnexa
    following ophthalmic procedure
     H59.31-●
    following other procedure H59.32-●
   genitourinary organ or structure
    following procedure on genitourinary
     organ or structure N99.820
    following procedure on other organ
     N99.821
   mastoid process
    following other procedure H95.42
    following procedure on ear and
     mastoid process H95.41
   musculoskeletal structure
    following musculoskeletal surgery
     M96.830
    following non-orthopedic surgery
     M96.831
    following orthopedic surgery M96.830
   nervous system
    following nervous system procedure
     G97.51
    following other procedure G97.52
   respiratory system
    following other procedure J95.831
    following procedure on respiratory
     system organ or structure J95.830
   skin and subcutaneous tissue
    following dermatologic procedure
     L76.21
    following a procedure on other organ
     L76.22
   spleen
    following procedure on other organ
     D78.22
    following procedure on the spleen
     D78.21
  seroma (of)
   circulatory system organ or structure
    following cardiac bypass I97.641
    following cardiac catheterization
     I97.640
    following other circulatory system
     procedure I97.648
    following other procedure I97.622
   digestive system
    following procedure on digestive
     system K91.872
    following procedure on other organ
     K91.873

▶ New   ⇒ Revised   ~~deleted~~ Deleted   ● Use Additional Character(s)

Complication (Continued)
    postprocedural (Continued)
        seroma (Continued)
            ear
                following other procedure H95.54
                following procedure on ear and
                    mastoid process H95.53
            endocrine system
                following endocrine system procedure
                    E89.822
                following other procedure E89.823
            eye and adnexa
                following ophthalmic procedure
                    H59.35-●
                following other procedure H59.36-●
            genitourinary organ or structure
                following procedure on genitourinary
                    organ or structure N99.842
                following procedure on other organ
                    N99.843
            mastoid process
                following other procedure H95.54
                following procedure on ear and
                    mastoid process H95.53
            musculoskeletal structure
                following musculoskeletal surgery
                    M96.842
                following non-orthopedic surgery
                    M96.843
                following orthopedic surgery M96.842
            nervous system
                following nervous system procedure
                    G97.63
                following other procedure G97.64
            respiratory system
                following other procedure J95.863
                following procedure on respiratory
                    system organ or structure J95.862
            skin and subcutaneous tissue
                following dermatologic procedure
                    L76.33
                following procedure on other organ
                    L76.34
            spleen
                following procedure on other organ
                    D78.34
                following procedure on the spleen
                    D78.33
        specified NEC
            circulatory system I97.89
            digestive K91.89
            ear H95.89
            endocrine E89.89
            eye and adnexa H59.89
            genitourinary N99.89
            mastoid process H95.89
            metabolic E89.89
            musculoskeletal structure M96.89
            nervous system G97.82
            respiratory system J95.89
            skin and subcutaneous tissue L76.82
            spleen D78.89
    pregnancy NEC —see Pregnancy,
        complicated by
    prosthetic device or implant T85.9
        bile duct —see Complications, bile duct
            implant
        breast —see Complications, breast
            implant
        bulking agent
            ureteral
                erosion T83.714
                exposure T83.724
            urethral
                erosion T83.713
                exposure T83.723
        cardiac and vascular NEC —see
            Complications, cardiovascular device
            or implant
        corneal transplant —see Complications,
            graft, cornea

Complication (Continued)
    prosthetic device or implant (Continued)
        electronic nervous system stimulator —see
            Complications, electronic stimulator
            device
        epidural infusion catheter —see
            Complications, catheter, epidural
        esophageal anti-reflux device —see
            Complications, esophageal anti-reflux
            device
        genital organ or tract —see Complications,
            genitourinary, device or implant,
            genital tract
            specified NEC T83.79
        heart valve —see Complications, heart,
            valve, prosthesis
        infection or inflammation T85.79
            intestine transplant T86.892
            liver transplant T86.43
            lung transplant T86.812
            pancreas transplant T86.892
            skin graft T86.822
        intraocular lens —see Complications,
            intraocular lens
        intraperitoneal (dialysis) catheter —
            see Complications, catheter,
            intraperitoneal
        joint —see Complications, joint prosthesis,
            internal
        mechanical NEC T85.698
            dialysis catheter (vascular) —see also
                Complication, catheter, dialysis,
                mechanical
                peritoneal —see Complication, catheter,
                    intraperitoneal, mechanical
            gastrointestinal device T85.598
            ocular device T85.398
            subdural (infusion) catheter T85.690
            suture, permanent T85.692
                that for bone repair —see
                    Complications, fixation device,
                    internal (orthopedic), mechanical
            ventricular shunt
                breakdown T85.01
                displacement T85.02
                leakage T85.03
                malposition T85.02
                obstruction T85.09
                perforation T85.09
                protrusion T85.09
                specified NEC T85.09
        mesh
            erosion (to surrounding organ or tissue)
                T83.718
                urethral (into pelvic floor muscles)
                    T83.712
                vaginal (into pelvic floor muscles)
                    T83.711
            exposure (into surrounding organ or
                tissue) T83.728
                urethral (through urethral wall)
                    T83.722
                vaginal (into vagina) (through vaginal
                    wall) T83.721
        orbital —see Complications, orbital
            prosthesis
        penile T83.9
            embolism T83.81
            fibrosis T83.82
            hemorrhage T83.83
            infection and inflammation T83.61
            mechanical
                breakdown T83.410
                displacement T83.420
                leakage T83.490
                malposition T83.420
                obstruction T83.490
                perforation T83.490
                protrusion T83.490
                specified NEC T83.490
            pain T83.84

Complication (Continued)
    prosthetic device or implant (Continued)
        penile (Continued)
            specified type NEC T83.89
            stenosis T83.85
            thrombosis T83.86
        prosthetic materials NEC
            erosion (to surrounding organ or tissue)
                T83.718
            exposure (into surrounding organ or
                tissue) T83.728
        skin graft T86.829
            artificial skin or decellularized
                allodermis
                embolism T85.818
                fibrosis T85.828
                hemorrhage T85.838
                infection and inflammation T85.79
                mechanical
                    breakdown T85.613
                    displacement T85.623
                    malfunction T85.613
                    malposition T85.623
                    obstruction T85.693
                    perforation T85.693
                    protrusion T85.693
                    specified NEC T85.693
                pain T85.848
                specified type NEC T85.898
                stenosis T85.858
                thrombosis T85.868
            failure T86.821
            infection T86.822
            rejection T86.820
            specified NEC T86.828
        sling
            urethral (female) (male)
                erosion T83.712
                exposure T83.722
        specified NEC T85.9
            embolism T85.818
            fibrosis T85.828
            hemorrhage T85.838
            infection and inflammation T85.79
            mechanical
                breakdown T85.618
                displacement T85.628
                leakage T85.638
                malfunction T85.618
                malposition T85.628
                obstruction T85.698
                perforation T85.698
                protrusion T85.698
                specified NEC T85.698
            pain T85.848
            specified type NEC T85.898
            stenosis T85.858
            thrombosis T85.868
        subdural infusion catheter —see
            Complications, catheter, subdural
        sutures —see Complications, sutures
        urinary organ or tract NEC —see
            Complications, genitourinary, device
            or implant, urinary system
        vascular —see Complications,
            cardiovascular device or implant
        ventricular shunt —see Complications,
            ventricular shunt (device)
    puerperium —see Puerperal
    puncture, spinal G97.1
        cerebrospinal fluid leak G97.0
        headache or reaction G97.1
    pyelogram N99.89
    radiation
        kyphosis M96.2
        scoliosis M96.5
    reattached
        extremity (infection) (rejection)
            lower T87.1X-●
            upper T87.0X-●
        specified body part NEC T87.2

Complication *(Continued)*
  reconstructed breast
    asymmetry between native and
      reconstructed breast N65.1
    deformity N65.0
    disproportion between native and
      reconstructed breast N65.1
    excess tissue N65.0
    misshappen N65.0
  reimplant NEC —*see also* Complications,
    prosthetic device or implant
    limb (infection) (rejection) —*see*
      Complications, reattached,
      extremity
    organ (partial) (total) —*see* Complications,
      transplant
    prosthetic device NEC —*see* Complications,
      prosthetic device
  renal N28.9
    allograft —*see* Complications, transplant,
      kidney
    dialysis —*see* Complications, dialysis
  respirator
    mechancial J95.850
      specified NEC J95.859
  respiratory system J98.9
    device, implant or graft —*see*
      Complication, prosthetic device or
      implant, specified NEC
    lung transplant —*see* Complications,
      prosthetic device or implant, lung
      transplant
    postoperative J95.89
      air leak J95.812
      Mendelson's syndrome (chemical
        pneumonitis) J95.4
      pneumothorax J95.811
      pulmonary insufficiency (acute) (after
        nonthoracic surgery) J95.2
        chronic J95.3
        following thoracic surgery J95.1
      respiratory failure (acute) J95.821
        acute and chronic J95.822
      specified NEC J95.89
      subglottic stenosis J95.5
      tracheostomy complication —*see*
        Complications, tracheostomy
    therapy T81.89
  sedation during labor and delivery O74.9
    cardiac O74.2
    central nervous system O74.3
    pulmonary NEC O74.1
  shunt —*see also* Complications, prosthetic
    device or implant
    arteriovenous —*see* Complications,
      arteriovenous, shunt
    ventricular (communicating) —*see*
      Complications, ventricular shunt
  skin
    graft T86.829
      failure T86.821
      infection T86.822
      rejection T86.820
      specified type NEC T86.828
  spinal
    anesthesia —*see* Complications, anesthesia,
      spinal
    catheter (epidural) (subdural) —*see*
      Complications, catheter
    puncture or tap G97.1
      cerebrospinal fluid leak G97.0
      headache or reaction G97.1
  stent
    bile duct —*see* Complications, bile duct
      prosthesis
    ureteral indwelling
      breakdown T83.112
      displacement T83.122
      leakage T83.192
      malposition T83.122

Complication *(Continued)*
  stent *(Continued)*
    ureteral indwelling *(Continued)*
      obstruction T83.192
      perforation T83.192
      protrusion T83.192
      specified NEC T83.192
    urinary (ileal conduit) (nephroureteral)
      T83.193
      embolism T83.81
      fibrosis T83.82
      hemorrhage T83.83
      infection and inflammation T83.593
      mechanical
        breakdown T83.113
        displacement T83.123
        leakage T83.193
        malposition T83.123
        obstruction T83.193
        perforation T83.193
        protrusion T83.193
        specified NEC T83.193
      pain T83.84
      specified type NEC T83.89
      stenosis T83.85
      thrombosis T83.86
    vascular
      end stent stenosis —*see* Restenosis,
        stent
      in stent stenosis —*see* Restenosis, stent
  stoma
    digestive tract
      colostomy —*see* Complications,
        colostomy
      enterostomy —*see* Complications,
        enterostomy
      esophagostomy —*see* Complications,
        esophagostomy
      gastrostomy —*see* Complications,
        gastrostomy
    urinary tract N99.528
      continent N99.538
        hemorrhage N99.530
        herniation N99.533
        infection N99.531
        malfunction N99.532
        specified type NEC N99.538
        stenosis N99.534
      cystostomy —*see* Complications,
        cystostomy
      external NOS N99.528
      hemorrhage N99.520
      herniation N99.523
      incontinent N99.528
        hemorrhage N99.520
        herniation N99.523
        infection N99.521
        malfunction N99.522
        specified type NEC N99.528
        stenosis N99.524
      infection N99.521
      malfunction N99.522
      specified type NEC N99.528
      stenosis N99.524
  stomach banding —*see* Complication(s),
    bariatric procedure
  stomach stapling —*see* Complication(s),
    bariatric procedure
  surgical material, nonabsorbable —*see*
    Complication, suture, permanent
  surgical procedure (on) T81.9
    amputation stump (late) —*see*
      Complications, amputation stump
    cardiac —*see* Complications, circulatory
      system
    cholesteatoma, recurrent —*see*
      Complications, postmastoidectomy,
      recurrent cholesteatoma
    circulatory (early) —*see* Complications,
      circulatory system

Complication *(Continued)*
  surgical procedure *(Continued)*
    digestive system —*see* Complications,
      gastrointestinal
    dumping syndrome (postgastrectomy)
      K91.1
    ear —*see* Complications, ear
    elephantiasis or lymphedema I97.89
      postmastectomy I97.2
    emphysema (surgical) T81.82
    endocrine —*see* Complications, endocrine
    eye —*see* Complications, eye
    fistula (persistent postoperative) T81.83
    foreign body inadvertently left in wound
      (sponge) (suture) (swab) —*see* Foreign
      body, accidentally left during a
      procedure
    gastrointestinal —*see* Complications,
      gastrointestinal
    genitourinary NEC N99.89
    hematoma
      intraoperative —*see* Complication,
        intraoperative, hemorrhage
      postprocedural —*see* Complication,
        postprocedural, hematoma
    hemorrhage
      intraoperative —*see* Complication,
        intraoperative, hemorrhage
      postprocedural —*see* Complication,
        postprocedural, hemorrhage
    hepatic failure K91.82
    hyperglycemia (postpancreatectomy) E89.1
    hypoinsulinemia (postpancreatectomy)
      E89.1
    hypoparathyroidism
      (postparathyroidectomy) E89.2
    hypopituitarism (posthypophysectomy)
      E89.3
    hypothyroidism (post-thyroidectomy)
      E89.0
    intestinal obstruction —*see also*
      Obstruction, intestine, postoperative
      K91.30
    intracranial hypotension following
      ventricular shunting
      (ventriculostomy) G97.2
    lymphedema I97.89
      postmastectomy I97.2
    malabsorption (postsurgical) NEC K91.2
      osteoporosis —*see* Osteoporosis,
        postsurgical malabsorption
    mastoidectomy cavity NEC —*see*
      Complications, postmastoidectomy
    metabolic E89.89
      specified NEC E89.89
    musculoskeletal —*see* Complications,
      musculoskeletal system
    nervous system (central) (peripheral) —*see*
      Complications, nervous system
    ovarian failure E89.40
      asymptomatic E89.40
      symptomatic E89.41
    peripheral vascular —*see* Complications,
      surgical procedure, vascular
    postcardiotomy syndrome I97.0
    postcholecystectomy syndrome K91.5
    postcommissurotomy syndrome I97.0
    postgastrectomy dumping syndrome K91.1
    postlaminectomy syndrome NEC M96.1
      kyphosis M96.3
    postmastectomy lymphedema syndrome
      I97.2
    postmastoidectomy cholesteatoma —*see*
      Complications, postmastoidectomy,
      recurrent cholesteatoma
    postvagotomy syndrome K91.1
    postvalvulotomy syndrome I97.0
    pulmonary insufficiency (acute) J95.2
      chronic J95.3
      following thoracic surgery J95.1

▶ New   ⇒ Revised   ~~deleted~~ Deleted   ● Use Additional Character(s)

Complication *(Continued)*
  vascular I99.9
    device or implant T82.9
      embolism T82.818
      fibrosis T82.828
      hemorrhage T82.838
      infection or inflammation T82.7
      mechanical
        breakdown T82.519
          specified device NEC T82.518
        displacement T82.529
          specified device NEC T82.528
        leakage T82.539
          specified device NEC T82.538
        malposition T82.529
          specified device NEC T82.528
        obstruction T82.599
          specified device NEC T82.598
        perforation T82.599
          specified device NEC T82.598
        protrusion T82.599
          specified device NEC T82.598
      pain T82.848
      specified type NEC T82.898
      stenosis T82.858
      thrombosis T82.868
    dialysis catheter —*see* Complication,
        catheter, dialysis
    following infusion, therapeutic injection or
        transfusion T80.1
    graft T82.9
      embolism T82.818
      fibrosis T82.828
      hemorrhage T82.838
      mechanical
        breakdown T82.319
          aorta (bifurcation) T82.310
          carotid artery T82.311
          specified vessel NEC T82.318
        displacement T82.329
          aorta (bifurcation) T82.320
          carotid artery T82.321
          specified vessel NEC T82.328
        leakage T82.339
          aorta (bifurcation) T82.330
          carotid artery T82.331
          specified vessel NEC T82.338
        malposition T82.329
          aorta (bifurcation) T82.320
          carotid artery T82.321
          specified vessel NEC T82.328
        obstruction T82.399
          aorta (bifurcation) T82.390
          carotid artery T82.391
          specified vessel NEC T82.398
        perforation T82.399
          aorta (bifurcation) T82.390
          carotid artery T82.391
          specified vessel NEC T82.398
        protrusion T82.399
          aorta (bifurcation) T82.390
          carotid artery T82.391
          specified vessel NEC T82.398
      pain T82.848
      specified complication NEC T82.898
      stenosis T82.858
      thrombosis T82.868
    postoperative —*see* Complications,
        postoperative, circulatory
    vena cava device (filter) (sieve) (umbrella) —
        see Complications, umbrella device,
        vascular
    ventilation therapy NEC T81.81
    ventilator
      mechanical J95.850
        specified NEC J95.859
    ventricular (communicating) shunt (device)
        T85.9
      embolism T85.810
      fibrosis T85.820
      hemorrhage T85.830

Complication *(Continued)*
  ventricular shunt *(Continued)*
    infection and inflammation T85.730
    mechanical
      breakdown T85.01
      displacement T85.02
      leakage T85.03
      malposition T85.02
      obstruction T85.09
      perforation T85.09
      protrusion T85.09
      specified NEC T85.09
    pain T85.840
    specified type NEC T85.890
    stenosis T85.850
    thrombosis T85.860
  wire suture, permanent (implanted) —*see*
      Complications, suture, permanent
Compressed air disease T70.3
Compression
  with injury - code by Nature of injury
  artery I77.1
    celiac, syndrome I77.4
  brachial plexus G54.0
  brain (stem) G93.5
    due to
      contusion (diffuse) —*see* Injury,
          intracranial, diffuse
        focal —*see* Injury, intracranial, focal
      injury NEC —*see* Injury, intracranial,
          diffuse
      traumatic —*see* Injury, intracranial, diffuse
  bronchus J98.09
  cauda equina G83.4
  celiac (artery) (axis) I77.4
  cerebral —*see* Compression, brain
  cervical plexus G54.2
  cord
    spinal —*see* Compression, spinal
    umbilical —*see* Compression, umbilical
        cord
  cranial nerve G52.9
    eighth —*see* subcategory H93.3
    eleventh G52.8
    fifth G50.8
    first G52.0
    fourth —*see* Strabismus, paralytic, fourth
        nerve
    ninth G52.1
    second —*see* Disorder, nerve, optic
    seventh G51.8
    sixth —*see* Strabismus, paralytic, sixth
        nerve
    tenth G52.2
    third —*see* Strabismus, paralytic, third
        nerve
    twelfth G52.3
  diver's squeeze T70.3
  during birth (newborn) P15.9
  esophagus K22.2
  eustachian tube —*see* Obstruction, eustachian
      tube, cartilaginous
  facies Q67.1
  fracture
    nontraumatic NOS —*see* Collapse, vertebra
    pathological —*see* Fracture, pathological
    traumatic —*see* Fracture, traumatic
  heart —*see* Disease, heart
  intestine —*see* Obstruction, intestine
  laryngeal nerve, recurrent G52.2
    with paralysis of vocal cords and larynx
        J38.00
      bilateral J38.02
      unilateral J38.01
  lumbosacral plexus G54.1
  lung J98.4
  lymphatic vessel I89.0
  medulla —*see* Compression, brain
  nerve —*see also* Disorder, nerve G58.9
    arm NEC —*see* Mononeuropathy, upper
        limb

Compression *(Continued)*
  nerve *(Continued)*
    axillary G54.0
    cranial —*see* Compression, cranial nerve
    leg NEC —*see* Mononeuropathy, lower
        limb
    median (in carpal tunnel) —*see* Syndrome,
        carpal tunnel
    optic —*see* Disorder, nerve, optic
    plantar —*see* Lesion, nerve, plantar
    posterior tibial (in tarsal tunnel) —*see*
        Syndrome, tarsal tunnel
    root or plexus NOS (in) G54.9
      intervertebral disc disorder NEC —
          see Disorder, disc, with,
          radiculopathy
        with myelopathy —*see* Disorder, disc,
            with, myelopathy
      neoplastic disease —*see also* Neoplasm
          D49.9 [G55]
      spondylosis —*see* Spondylosis, with
          radiculopathy
    sciatic (acute) —*see* Lesion, nerve, sciatic
    sympathetic G90.8
    traumatic —*see* Injury, nerve
    ulnar —*see* Lesion, nerve, ulnar
    upper extremity NEC —*see*
        Mononeuropathy, upper limb
  spinal (cord) G95.20
    by displacement of intervertebral disc
        NEC —*see also* Disorder, disc, with,
        myelopathy
    nerve root NOS G54.9
      due to displacement of intervertebral
          disc NEC —*see* Disorder, disc, with,
          radiculopathy
        with myelopathy —*see* Disorder, disc,
            with, myelopathy
    specified NEC G95.29
    spondylogenic (cervical) (lumbar,
        lumbosacral) (thoracic) —*see*
        Spondylosis, with myelopathy NEC
    anterior —*see* Syndrome, anterior, spinal
        artery, compression
    traumatic —*see* Injury, spinal cord, by
        region
  subcostal nerve (syndrome) —*see*
      Mononeuropathy, upper limb, specified
      NEC
  sympathetic nerve NEC G90.8
  syndrome T79.5
  trachea J39.8
  ulnar nerve (by scar tissue) —*see* Lesion,
      nerve, ulnar
  umbilical cord
    complicating delivery O69.2
      cord around neck O69.1
      prolapse O69.0
      specified NEC O69.2
  ureter N13.5
  vein I87.1
  vena cava (inferior) (superior) I87.1
Compulsion, compulsive
  gambling F63.0
  neurosis F42.8
  personality F60.5
  states F42.8
  swearing F42.8
    in Gilles de la Tourette's syndrome F95.2
  tics and spasms F95.9
Concato's disease (pericardial polyserositis)
    A19.9
  nontubercular I31.1
  pleural —*see* Pleurisy, with effusion
Concavity chest wall M95.4
➡Concealed penis Q55.64
Concern (normal) about sick person in family
    Z63.6
Concrescence (teeth) K00.2
Concretio cordis I31.1
  rheumatic I09.2

▶ New ➡ Revised ~~deleted~~ Deleted ● Use Additional Character(s)

Concretion —*see also* Calculus
  appendicular K38.1
  canaliculus —*see* Dacryolith
  clitoris N90.89
  conjunctiva H11.12-●
  eyelid —*see* Disorder, eyelid, specified type
    NEC
  lacrimal passages —*see* Dacryolith
  prepuce (male) N47.8
  salivary gland (any) K11.5
  seminal vesicle N50.89
  tonsil J35.8
Concussion (brain) (cerebral) (current)
  S06.0X9
  with
    loss of consciousness of 30 minutes or less
      S06.0X1
    loss of consciousness of unspecified
      duration S06.0X9
  blast (air) (hydraulic) (immersion)
    (underwater)
    abdomen or thorax —*see* Injury, blast, by
      site
    ear with acoustic nerve injury —*see* Injury,
      nerve, acoustic, specified type NEC
  cauda equina S34.3
  conus medullaris S34.02
  ocular S05.8X-●
  spinal (cord)
    cervical S14.0
    lumbar S34.01
    sacral S34.02
    thoracic S24.0
  syndrome F07.81
  Without loss of consciousness S06.0X0
Condition —*see* Disease
Conditions arising in the perinatal period —
  see Newborn, affected by
Conduct disorder —*see* Disorder, conduct
Condyloma A63.0
  acuminatum A63.0
  gonorrheal A54.09
  latum A51.31
  syphilitic A51.31
    congenital A50.07
  venereal, syphilitic A51.31
Conflagration —*see also* Burn
  asphyxia (by inhalation of gases, fumes or
    vapors) —*see also* Table of Drugs and
    Chemicals T59.9-●
Conflict (with) —*see also* Discord
  family Z73.9
  marital Z63.0
    involving divorce or estrangement Z63.5
  parent-child Z62.820
    parent-adopted child Z62.821
    parent-biological child Z62.820
    parent-foster child Z62.822
  social role NEC Z73.5
Confluent —*see* condition
Confusion, confused R41.0
  epileptic F05
  mental state (psychogenic) F44.89
  psychogenic F44.89
  reactive (from emotional stress, psychological
    trauma) F44.89
Confusional arousals G47.51
Congelation T69.9
Congenital —*see also* condition
  aortic septum Q25.49
  intrinsic factor deficiency D51.0
  malformation —*see* Anomaly
Congestion, congestive
  bladder N32.89
  bowel K63.89
  brain G93.89
  breast N64.59
  bronchial J98.09
  catarrhal J31.0
  chest R09.89
  chill, malarial —*see* Malaria

Congestion, congestive *(Continued)*
  circulatory NEC I99.8
  duodenum K31.89
  eye —*see* Hyperemia, conjunctiva
  facial, due to birth injury P15.4
  general R68.89
  glottis J37.0
  heart —*see* Failure, heart, congestive
  hepatic K76.1
  hypostatic (lung) —*see* Edema, lung
  intestine K63.89
  kidney N28.89
  labyrinth —*see* subcategory H83.8
  larynx J37.0
  liver K76.1
  lung R09.89
    active or acute —*see* Pneumonia
  malaria, malarial —*see* Malaria
  nasal R09.81
  nose R09.81
  orbit, orbital —*see also* Exophthalmos
    inflammatory (chronic) —*see* Inflammation,
      orbit
  ovary N83.8
  pancreas K86.89
  pelvic, female N94.89
  pleural J94.8
  prostate (active) N42.1
  pulmonary —*see* Congestion, lung
  renal N28.89
  retina H35.81
  seminal vesicle N50.1
  spinal cord G95.19
  spleen (chronic) D73.2
  stomach K31.89
  trachea —*see* Tracheitis
  urethra N36.8
  uterus N85.8
    with subinvolution N85.3
  venous (passive) I87.8
  viscera R68.89
Congestive —*see* Congestion
Conical
  cervix (hypertrophic elongation) N88.4
  cornea —*see* Keratoconus
  teeth K00.2
Conjoined twins Q89.4
Conjugal maladjustment Z63.0
  involving divorce or estrangement Z63.5
Conjunctiva —*see* condition
Conjunctivitis (staphylococcal) (streptococcal)
  NOS H10.9
  Acanthamoeba B60.12
  acute H10.3-●
    atopic H10.1-●
    chemical —*see also* Corrosion, cornea
      H10.21-●
    mucopurulent H10.02-●
      follicular H10.01-●
    pseudomembranous H10.22-●
    serous except viral H10.23-●
      viral —*see* Conjunctivitis, viral
    toxic H10.21-●
  adenoviral (acute) (follicular) B30.1
  allergic (acute) —*see* Conjunctivitis, acute,
    atopic
    chronic H10.45
      vernal H10.44
  anaphylactic —*see* Conjunctivitis, acute,
    atopic
  Apollo B30.3
  atopic (acute) —*see* Conjunctivitis, acute,
    atopic
  Béal's B30.2
  blennorrhagic (gonococcal) (neonatorum)
    A54.31
  chemical (acute) —*see also* Corrosion, cornea
    H10.21-●
  chlamydial A74.0
    due to trachoma A71.1
    neonatal P39.1

Conjunctivitis *(Continued)*
  chronic (nodosa) (petrificans) (phlyctenular)
    H10.40-●
    allergic H10.45
      vernal H10.44
    follicular H10.43-●
    giant papillary H10.41-●
    simple H10.42-●
    vernal H10.44
  coxsackievirus 24 B30.3
  diphtheritic A36.86
  due to
    dust —*see* Conjunctivitis, acute, atopic
    filariasis B74.9
    mucocutaneous leishmaniasis B55.2
  enterovirus type 70 (hemorrhagic) B30.3
  epidemic (viral) B30.9
    hemorrhagic B30.3
  gonococcal (neonatorum) A54.31
  granular (trachomatous) A71.1
    sequelae (late effect) B94.0
  hemorrhagic (acute) (epidemic) B30.3
  herpes zoster B02.31
  in (due to)
    Acanthamoeba B60.12
    adenovirus (acute) (follicular) B30.1
    Chlamydia A74.0
    coxsackievirus 24 B30.3
    diphtheria A36.86
    enterovirus type 70 (hemorrhagic) B30.3
    filariasis B74.9
    gonococci A54.31
    herpes (simplex) virus B00.53
      zoster B02.31
    infectious disease NEC B99
    meningococci A39.89
    mucocutaneous leishmaniasis B55.2
   ➧ rosacea H10.82-●
    syphilis (late) A52.71
    zoster B02.31
  inclusion A74.0
  infantile P39.1
    gonococcal A54.31
  Koch-Weeks' —*see* Conjunctivitis, acute,
    mucopurulent
  light —*see* Conjunctivitis, acute, atopic
  ligneous —*see* Blepharoconjunctivitis,
    ligneous
  meningococcal A39.89
  mucopurulent —*see* Conjunctivitis, acute,
    mucopurulent
  neonatal P39.1
    gonococcal A54.31
  Newcastle B30.8
  of Béal B30.2
  parasitic
    filariasis B74.9
    mucocutaneous leishmaniasis B55.2
  Parinaud's H10.89
  petrificans H10.89
  ➧ rosacea H10.82-●
  specified NEC H10.89
  swimming-pool B30.1
  trachomatous A71.1
    acute A71.0
    sequelae (late effect) B94.0
  traumatic NEC H10.89
  tuberculous A18.59
  tularemic A21.1
  tularensis A21.1
  viral B30.9
    due to
      adenovirus B30.1
      enterovirus B30.3
      specified NEC B30.8
Conjunctivochalasis H11.82-●
Connective tissue —*see* condition
Conn's syndrome E26.01
Conradi (-Hunermann) disease Q77.3
Consanguinity Z84.3
  counseling Z71.89

Conscious simulation (of illness) Z76.5
Consecutive —*see* condition
Consolidation lung (base) —*see* Pneumonia, lobar
Constipation (atonic) (neurogenic) (simple) (spastic) K59.00
  chronic K59.09
    idiopathic K59.04
  drug-induced K59.03
  functional K59.04
  outlet dysfunction K59.02
  psychogenic F45.8
  slow transit K59.01
  specified NEC K59.09
Constitutional —*see also* condition
  substandard F60.7
Constitutionally substandard F60.7
Constriction —*see also* Stricture
  auditory canal —*see* Stenosis, external ear canal
  bronchial J98.09
  duodenum K31.5
  esophagus K22.2
  external
    abdomen, abdominal (wall) S30.841
    alveolar process S00.542
    ankle S90.54-●
    antecubital space —*see* Constriction, external, forearm
    arm (upper) S40.84-●
    auricle —*see* Constriction, external, ear
    axilla —*see* Constriction, external, arm
    back, lower S30.840
    breast S20.14-●
    brow S00.84
    buttock S30.840
    calf —*see* Constriction, external, leg
    canthus —*see* Constriction, external, eyelid
    cheek S00.84
      internal S00.542
    chest wall —*see* Constriction, external, thorax
    chin S00.84
    clitoris S30.844
    costal region —*see* Constriction, external, thorax
    digit(s)
      foot —*see* Constriction, external, toe
      hand —*see* Constriction, external, finger
    ear S00.44-●
    elbow S50.34-●
    epididymis S30.843
    epigastric region S30.841
    esophagus, cervical S10.14
    eyebrow —*see* Constriction, external, eyelid
    eyelid S00.24-●
    face S00.84
    finger(s) S60.44-●
      index S60.44-●
      little S60.44-●
      middle S60.44-●
      ring S60.44-●
    flank S30.841
    foot (except toe(s) alone) S90.84-●
      toe —*see* Constriction, external, toe
    forearm S50.84-●
      elbow only —*see* Constriction, external, elbow
    forehead S00.84
    genital organs, external
      female S30.846
      male S30.845
    groin S30.841
    gum S00.542
    hand S60.54-●
    head S00.94
      ear —*see* Constriction, external, ear
      eyelid —*see* Constriction, external, eyelid
      lip S00.541
      nose S00.34
      oral cavity S00.542

Constriction *(Continued)*
  external *(Continued)*
    head *(Continued)*
      scalp S00.04
      specified site NEC S00.84
    heel —*see* Constriction, external, foot
    hip S70.24-●
    inguinal region S30.841
    interscapular region S20.449
    jaw S00.84
    knee S80.24-●
    labium (majus) (minus) S30.844
    larynx S10.14
    leg (lower) S80.84-●
      knee —*see* Constriction, external, knee
      upper —*see* Constriction, external, thigh
    lip S00.541
    lower back S30.840
    lumbar region S30.840
    malar region S00.84
    mammary —*see* Constriction, external, breast
    mastoid region S00.84
    mouth S00.542
    nail
      finger —*see* Constriction, external, finger
      toe —*see* Constriction, external, toe
    nasal S00.34
    neck S10.94
      specified site NEC S10.84
      throat S10.14
    nose S00.34
    occipital region S00.04
    oral cavity S00.542
    orbital region —*see* Constriction, external, eyelid
    palate S00.542
    palm —*see* Constriction, external, hand
    parietal region S00.04
    pelvis S30.840
    penis S30.842
    perineum
      female S30.844
      male S30.840
    periocular area —*see* Constriction, external, eyelid
    phalanges
      finger —*see* Constriction, external, finger
      toe —*see* Constriction, external, toe
    pharynx S10.14
    pinna —*see* Constriction, external, ear
    popliteal space —*see* Constriction, external, knee
    prepuce S30.842
    pubic region S30.840
    pudendum
      female S30.846
      male S30.845
    sacral region S30.840
    scalp S00.04
    scapular region —*see* Constriction, external, shoulder
    scrotum S30.843
    shin —*see* Constriction, external, leg
    shoulder S40.24-●
    sternal region S20.349
    submaxillary region S00.84
    submental region S00.84
    subungual
      finger(s) —*see* Constriction, external, finger
      toe(s) —*see* Constriction, external, toe
    supraclavicular fossa S10.84
    supraorbital S00.84
    temple S00.84
    temporal region S00.84
    testis S30.843
    thigh S70.34-●
    thorax, thoracic (wall) S20.94
      back S20.44-●
      front S20.34-●

Constriction *(Continued)*
  external *(Continued)*
    throat S10.14
    thumb S60.34-●
    toe(s) (lesser) S90.44-●
      great S90.44-●
    tongue S00.542
    trachea S10.14
    tunica vaginalis S30.843
    uvula S00.542
    vagina S30.844
    vulva S30.844
    wrist S60.84-●
  gallbladder —*see* Obstruction, gallbladder
  intestine —*see* Obstruction, intestine
  larynx J38.6
    congenital Q31.8
      specified NEC Q31.8
      subglottic Q31.1
  organ or site, congenital NEC —*see* Atresia, by site
  prepuce (acquired) (congenital) N47.1
  pylorus (adult hypertrophic) K31.1
    congenital or infantile Q40.0
    newborn Q40.0
  ring dystocia (uterus) O62.4
  spastic —*see also* Spasm
    ureter N13.5
  ureter N13.5
    with infection N13.6
  urethra —*see* Stricture, urethra
  visual field (peripheral) (functional) —*see* Defect, visual field
Constrictive —*see* condition
Consultation
  without complaint or sickness Z71.9
    feared complaint unfounded Z71.1
    specified reason NEC Z71.89
  medical —*see* Counseling, medical
  religious Z71.81
  specified reason NEC Z71.89
  spiritual Z71.81
Consumption —*see* Tuberculosis
Contact (with) —*see also* Exposure (to)
  acariasis Z20.7
  AIDS virus Z20.6
  air pollution Z77.110
  algae and algae toxins Z77.121
  algae bloom Z77.121
  anthrax Z20.810
  aromatic (hazardous) compounds NEC Z77.028
  aromatic amines Z77.020
  aromatic dyes NOS Z77.028
  arsenic Z77.010
  asbestos Z77.090
  bacterial disease NEC Z20.818
  benzene Z77.021
  blue-green algae bloom Z77.121
  body fluids (potentially hazardous) Z77.21
  brown tide Z77.121
  chemicals (chiefly nonmedicinal) (hazardous) NEC Z77.098
  cholera Z20.09
  chromium compounds Z77.018
  communicable disease Z20.9
    bacterial NEC Z20.818
    specified NEC Z20.89
    viral NEC Z20.828
  ▶ Zika virus Z20.821
  cyanobacteria bloom Z77.121
  dyes Z77.098
  Escherichia coli (E. coli) Z20.01
  fiberglass —*see* Table of Drugs and Chemicals, fiberglass
  German measles Z20.4
  gonorrhea Z20.2
  hazardous metals NEC Z77.018
  hazardous substances NEC Z77.29
  hazards in the physical environment NEC Z77.128
  hazards to health NEC Z77.9

▶ New   ⇒ Revised   ~~deleted~~ Deleted   ● Use Additional Character(s)

Contact (Continued)
HIV Z20.6
HTLV-III/LAV Z20.6
human immunodeficiency virus (HIV) Z20.6
infection Z20.9
　specified NEC Z20.89
infestation (parasitic) NEC Z20.7
intestinal infectious disease NEC Z20.09
　Escherichia coli (E. coli) Z20.01
lead Z77.011
meningococcus Z20.811
mold (toxic) Z77.120
nickel dust Z77.018
noise Z77.122
parasitic disease Z20.7
pediculosis Z20.7
pfiesteria piscicida Z77.121
poliomyelitis Z20.89
pollution
　air Z77.110
　environmental NEC Z77.118
　soil Z77.112
　water Z77.111
polycyclic aromatic hydrocarbons Z77.028
rabies Z20.3
radiation, naturally occurring NEC Z77.123
radon Z77.123
red tide (Florida) Z77.121
rubella Z20.4
sexually-transmitted disease Z20.2
smallpox (laboratory) Z20.89
syphilis Z20.2
tuberculosis Z20.1
uranium Z77.012
varicella Z20.820
venereal disease Z20.2
viral disease NEC Z20.828
viral hepatitis Z20.5
water pollution Z77.111
▶ Zika virus Z20.821
Contamination, food —see Intoxication,
　foodborne
Contraception, contraceptive
advice Z30.09
counseling Z30.09
device (intrauterine) (in situ) Z97.5
　causing menorrhagia T83.83
　checking Z30.431
　complications —see Complications,
　　intrauterine, contraceptive device
　in place Z97.5
　initial prescription Z30.014
　reinsertion Z30.433
　removal Z30.432
　replacement Z30.433
emergency (postcoital) Z30.012
initial prescription Z30.019
　　barrier Z30.018
　　diaphragm Z30.018
　injectable Z30.013
　intrauterine device Z30.014
　pills Z30.011
　postcoital (emergency) Z30.012
　specified type NEC Z30.018
　subdermal implantable Z30.017
　transdermal patch hormonal Z30.016
　vaginal ring hormonal Z30.015
maintenance Z30.40
　barrier Z30.49
　diaphragm Z30.49
　examination Z30.8
　injectable Z30.42
　intrauterine device Z30.431
　pills Z30.41
　specified type NEC Z30.49
　subdermal implantable Z30.46
　transdermal patch hormonal Z30.45
　vaginal ring hormonal Z30.44
management Z30.9
　specified NEC Z30.8
postcoital (emergency) Z30.012
prescription Z30.019
　repeat Z30.40

Contraception, contraceptive (Continued)
sterilization Z30.2
surveillance (drug) —see Contraception,
　maintenance
Contraction(s), contracture, contracted
Achilles tendon —see also Short, tendon,
　Achilles
　congenital Q66.89
amputation stump (surgical) (flexion) (late)
　next proximal joint T87.89
anus K59.8
bile duct (common) (hepatic) K83.8
bladder N32.89
　neck or sphincter N32.0
bowel, cecum, colon or intestine, any part —
　see Obstruction, intestine
Braxton Hicks —see False, labor
breast implant, capsular T85.44
bronchial J98.09
burn (old) —see Cicatrix
cervix —see Stricture, cervix
cicatricial —see Cicatrix
conjunctiva, trachomatous, active A71.1
　sequelae (late effect) B94.0
Dupuytren's M72.0
eyelid —see Disorder, eyelid function
fascia (lata) (postural) M72.8
　Dupuytren's M72.0
　palmar M72.0
　plantar M72.2
finger NEC —see also Deformity, finger
　congenital Q68.1
　joint —see Contraction, joint, hand
flaccid —see Contraction, paralytic
gallbladder K82.0
heart valve —see Endocarditis
hip —see Contraction, joint, hip
hourglass
　bladder N32.89
　　congenital Q64.79
　gallbladder K82.0
　　congenital Q44.1
　stomach K31.89
　　congenital Q40.2
　　psychogenic F45.8
　uterus (complicating delivery) O62.4
hysterical F44.4
internal os —see Stricture, cervix
joint (abduction) (acquired) (adduction)
　(flexion) (rotation) M24.50
　ankle M24.57-●
　congenital NEC Q68.8
　　hip Q65.89
　elbow M24.52-●
　foot joint M24.57-●
　hand joint M24.54-●
　hip M24.55-●
　　congenital Q65.89
　hysterical F44.4
　knee M24.56-●
　shoulder M24.51-●
　wrist M24.53-●
kidney (granular) (secondary) N26.9
　congenital Q63.8
　hydronephritic —see Hydronephrosis
　　Page N26.2
　pyelonephritic —see Pyelitis, chronic
　　tuberculous A18.11
ligament —see also Disorder, ligament
　congenital Q79.8
muscle (postinfective) (postural) NEC M62.40
　with contracture of joint —see Contraction,
　　joint
　ankle M62.47-●
　congenital Q79.8
　　sternocleidomastoid Q68.0
　extraocular —see Strabismus
　eye (extrinsic) —see Strabismus
　foot M62.47-●
　forearm M62.43-●
　hand M62.44-●

Contraction, contracture, contracted
　(Continued)
muscle (Continued)
　hysterical F44.4
　ischemic (Volkmann's) T79.6
　lower leg M62.46-●
　multiple sites M62.49
　pelvic region M62.45-●
　posttraumatic —see Strabismus, paralytic
　psychogenic F45.8
　　conversion reaction F44.4
　shoulder region M62.41-●
　specified site NEC M62.48
　thigh M62.45-●
　upper arm M62.42-●
neck —see Torticollis
ocular muscle —see Strabismus
organ or site, congenital NEC —see Atresia,
　by site
outlet (pelvis) —see Contraction, pelvis
palmar fascia M72.0
paralytic
　joint —see Contraction, joint
　muscle —see also Contraction, muscle NEC
　　ocular —see Strabismus, paralytic
pelvis (acquired) (general) M95.5
　with disproportion (fetopelvic) O33.1
　　causing obstructed labor O65.1
　　inlet O33.2
　　mid-cavity O33.3
　　outlet O33.3
plantar fascia M72.2
premature
　atrium I49.1
　auriculoventricular I49.49
　heart I49.49
　junctional I49.2
　supraventricular I49.1
　ventricular I49.3
prostate N42.89
pylorus NEC —see also Pylorospasm
　psychogenic F45.8
rectum, rectal (sphincter) K59.8
ring (Bandl's) (complicating delivery) O62.4
scar —see Cicatrix
spine —see Dorsopathy, deforming
sternocleidomastoid (muscle), congenital
　Q68.0
stomach K31.89
　hourglass K31.89
　　congenital Q40.2
　　psychogenic F45.8
　psychogenic F45.8
tendon (sheath) M62.40
　with contracture of joint —see Contraction,
　　joint
　Achilles —see Short, tendon, Achilles
　ankle M62.47-●
　　Achilles —see Short, tendon, Achilles
　foot M62.47-●
　forearm M62.43-●
　hand M62.44-●
　lower leg M62.46-●
　multiple sites M62.49
　neck M62.48
　pelvic region M62.45-●
　shoulder region M62.41-●
　specified site NEC M62.48
　thigh M62.45-●
　thorax M62.48
　trunk M62.48
　upper arm M62.42-●
toe —see Deformity, toe, specified NEC
ureterovesical orifice (postinfectional) N13.5
　with infection N13.6
urethra —see also Stricture, urethra
　orifice N32.0
uterus N85.8
　abnormal NEC O62.9
　clonic (complicating delivery) O62.4
　dyscoordinate (complicating delivery) O62.4

Contraction, contracture, contracted
(Continued)
uterus (Continued)
hourglass (complicating delivery) O62.4
hypertonic O62.4
hypotonic NEC O62.2
inadequate
primary O62.0
secondary O62.1
incoordinate (complicating delivery) O62.4
poor O62.2
tetanic (complicating delivery) O62.4
vagina (outlet) N89.5
vesical N32.89
neck or urethral orifice N32.0
visual field —see Defect, visual field, generalized
Volkmann's (ischemic) T79.6
Contusion (skin surface intact) T14.8
abdomen, abdominal (muscle) (wall) S30.1
adnexa, eye NEC S05.8X-●
adrenal gland S37.812
alveolar process S00.532
ankle S90.0-●
antecubital space —see Contusion, forearm
anus S30.3
arm (upper) S40.02-●
lower (with elbow) —see Contusion, forearm
auditory canal —see Contusion, ear
auricle —see Contusion, ear
axilla —see Contusion, arm, upper
back —see also Contusion, thorax, back
lower S30.0
bile duct S36.13
bladder S37.22
bone NEC T14.8
brain (diffuse) —see Injury, intracranial, diffuse
focal —see Injury, intracranial, focal
brainstem S06.38-●
breast S20.0-●
broad ligament S37.892
brow S00.83
buttock S30.0
canthus, eye S00.1-●
cauda equina S34.3
cerebellar, traumatic S06.37-●
cerebral S06.33-●
left side S06.32-●
right side S06.31-●
cheek S00.83
internal S00.532
chest (wall) —see Contusion, thorax
chin S00.83
clitoris S30.23
colon —see Injury, intestine, large, contusion
common bile duct S36.13
conjunctiva S05.1-●
with foreign body (in conjunctival sac) —see Foreign body, conjunctival sac
conus medullaris (spine) S34.139
cornea —see Contusion, eyeball
with foreign body —see Foreign body, cornea
corpus cavernosum S30.21
cortex (brain) (cerebral) —see Injury, intracranial, diffuse
focal —see Injury, intracranial, focal
costal region —see Contusion, thorax
cystic duct S36.13
diaphragm S27.802
duodenum S36.420
ear S00.43-●
elbow S50.0-●
with forearm —see Contusion, forearm
epididymis S30.22
epigastric region S30.1
epiglottis S10.0
esophagus (thoracic) S27.812
cervical S10.0
eyeball S05.1-●

Contusion (Continued)
eyebrow S00.1-●
eyelid (and periocular area) S00.1-●
face NEC S00.83
fallopian tube S37.529
bilateral S37.522
unilateral S37.521
femoral triangle S30.1
finger(s) S60.00
with damage to nail (matrix) S60.10
index S60.02-●
with damage to nail S60.12-●
little S60.05-●
with damage to nail S60.15-●
middle S60.03-●
with damage to nail S60.13-●
ring S60.04-●
with damage to nail S60.14-●
thumb —see Contusion, thumb
flank S30.1
foot (except toe(s) alone) S90.3-●
toe —see Contusion, toe
forearm S50.1-●
elbow only —see Contusion, elbow
forehead S00.83
gallbladder S36.122
genital organs, external
female S30.202
male S30.201
globe (eye) —see Contusion, eyeball
groin S30.1
gum S00.532
hand S60.22-●
finger(s) —see Contusion, finger
wrist —see Contusion, wrist
head S00.93
ear —see Contusion, ear
eyelid —see Contusion, eyelid
lip S00.531
nose S00.33
oral cavity S00.532
scalp S00.03
specified part NEC S00.83
heart —see also Injury, heart S26.91
heel —see Contusion, foot
hepatic duct S36.13
hip S70.0-●
ileum S36.428
iliac region S30.1
inguinal region S30.1
interscapular region S20.229
intra-abdominal organ S36.92
colon —see Injury, intestine, large, contusion
liver S36.112
pancreas —see Contusion, pancreas
rectum S36.62
small intestine —see Injury, intestine, small, contusion
specified organ NEC S36.892
spleen —see Contusion, spleen
stomach S36.32
iris (eye) —see Contusion, eyeball
jaw S00.83
jejunum S36.428
kidney S37.01-●
major (greater than 2 cm) S37.02-●
minor (less than 2 cm) S37.01-●
knee S80.0-●
labium (majus) (minus) S30.23
lacrimal apparatus, gland or sac S05.8X-●
larynx S10.0
leg (lower) S80.1-●
knee —see Contusion, knee
lens —see Contusion, eyeball
lip S00.531
liver S36.112
lower back S30.0
lumbar region S30.0
lung S27.329
bilateral S27.322
unilateral S27.321

Contusion (Continued)
malar region S00.83
mastoid region S00.83
membrane, brain —see Injury, intracranial, diffuse
focal —see Injury, intracranial, focal
mesentery S36.892
mesosalpinx S37.892
mouth S00.532
muscle —see Contusion, by site
nail
finger —see Contusion, finger, with damage to nail
toe —see Contusion, toe, with damage to nail
nasal S00.33
neck S10.93
specified site NEC S10.83
throat S10.0
nerve —see Injury, nerve
newborn P54.5
nose S00.33
occipital
lobe (brain) —see Injury, intracranial, diffuse
focal —see Injury, intracranial, focal
region (scalp) S00.03
orbit (region) (tissues) S05.1-●
ovary S37.429
bilateral S37.422
unilateral S37.421
palate S00.532
pancreas S36.229
body S36.221
head S36.220
tail S36.222
parietal
lobe (brain) —see Injury, intracranial, diffuse
focal —see Injury, intracranial, focal
region (scalp) S00.03
pelvic organ S37.92
adrenal gland S37.812
bladder S37.22
fallopian tube —see Contusion, fallopian tube
kidney —see Contusion, kidney
ovary —see Contusion, ovary
prostate S37.822
specified organ NEC S37.892
ureter S37.12
urethra S37.32
uterus S37.62
pelvis S30.0
penis S30.21
perineum
female S30.23
male S30.0
periocular area S00.1-●
peritoneum S36.81
periurethral tissue —see Contusion, urethra
pharynx S10.0
pinna —see Contusion, ear
popliteal space —see Contusion, knee
prepuce S30.21
prostate S37.822
pubic region S30.1
pudendum
female S30.202
male S30.201
quadriceps femoris —see Contusion, thigh
rectum S36.62
retroperitoneum S36.892
round ligament S37.892
sacral region S30.0
scalp S00.03
due to birth injury P12.3
scapular region —see Contusion, shoulder
sclera —see Contusion, eyeball

Contusion *(Continued)*
scrotum S30.22
seminal vesicle S37.892
shoulder S40.01-●
skin NEC T14.8
small intestine —*see* Injury, intestine, small, contusion
spermatic cord S30.22
spinal cord —*see* Injury, spinal cord, by region
    cauda equina S34.3
    conus medullaris S34.139
spleen S36.029
  major S36.021
  minor S36.020
sternal region S20.219
stomach S36.32
subconjunctival S05.1-●
subcutaneous NEC T14.8
submaxillary region S00.83
submental region S00.83
subperiosteal NEC T14.8
subungual
  finger —*see* Contusion, finger, with damage to nail
  toe —*see* Contusion, toe, with damage to nail
supraclavicular fossa S10.83
supraorbital S00.83
suprarenal gland S37.812
temple (region) S00.83
temporal
  lobe (brain) —*see* Injury, intracranial, diffuse
  focal —*see* Injury, intracranial, focal
  region S00.83
testis S30.22
thigh S70.1-●
thorax (wall) S20.20
  back S20.22-●
  front S20.21-●
throat S10.0
thumb S60.01-●
  with damage to nail S60.11-●
toe(s) (lesser) S90.12-●
  with damage to nail S90.22-●
  great S90.11-●
    with damage to nail S90.21-●
tongue S00.532
trachea (cervical) S10.0
  thoracic S27.52
tunica vaginalis S30.22
tympanum, tympanic membrane —*see* Contusion, ear
ureter S37.12
urethra S37.32
urinary organ NEC S37.892
uterus S37.62
uvula S00.532
vagina S30.23
vas deferens S37.892
vesical S37.22
vocal cord(s) S10.0
vulva S30.23
wrist S60.21-●
Conus (congenital) (any type) Q14.8
cornea —*see* Keratoconus
medullaris syndrome G95.81
Conversion hysteria, neurosis or reaction F44.9
Converter, tuberculosis (test reaction) R76.11
Conviction (legal), anxiety concerning Z65.0
with imprisonment Z65.1
Convulsions (idiopathic) —*see also* Seizure(s) R56.9
apoplectiform (cerebral ischemia) I67.82
dissociative F44.5
epileptic —*see* Epilepsy
epileptiform, epileptoid —*see* Seizure, epileptiform

Convulsions *(Continued)*
ether (anesthetic) —*see* Table of Drugs and Chemicals, by drug
febrile R56.00
  with status epilepticus G40.901
  complex R56.01
    with status epilepticus G40.901
  simple R56.00
hysterical F44.5
infantile P90
  epilepsy —*see* Epilepsy
jacksonian —*see* Epilepsy, localization-related, symptomatic, with simple partial seizures
myoclonic G25.3
newborn P90
obstetrical (nephritic) (uremic) —*see* Eclampsia
paretic A52.17
post traumatic R56.1
psychomotor —*see* Epilepsy, localization-related, symptomatic, with complex partial seizures
recurrent R56.9
reflex R25.8
scarlatinal A38.8
tetanus, tetanic —*see* Tetanus
thymic E32.8
Convulsive —*see also* Convulsions
Cooley's anemia D56.1
Coolie itch B76.9
Cooper's
disease —*see* Mastopathy, cystic
hernia —*see* Hernia, abdomen, specified site NEC
Copra itch B88.0
Coprophagy F50.89
Coprophobia F40.298
Coproporphyria, hereditary E80.29
Cor
biloculare Q20.8
bovis, bovinum —*see* Hypertrophy, cardiac
pulmonale (chronic) I27.81
  acute I26.09
triatriatum, triatrium Q24.2
triloculare Q20.8
  biatrium Q20.4
  biventriculare Q21.1
Corbus' disease (gangrenous balanitis) N48.1
Cord —*see also* condition
around neck
  complicating delivery O69.81
  with compression O69.1
bladder G95.89
  tabetic A52.19
Cordis ectopia Q24.8
Corditis (spermatic) N49.1
Corectopia Q13.2
Cori's disease (glycogen storage) E74.03
Corkhandler's disease or lung J67.3
Corkscrew esophagus K22.4
Corkworker's disease or lung J67.3
Corn (infected) L84
Cornea —*see also* condition
donor Z52.5
plana Q13.4
Cornelia de Lange syndrome Q87.1
Cornu cutaneum L85.8
Cornual gestation or pregnancy O00.80
with intrauterine pregnancy O00.81
Coronary (artery) —*see* condition
Coronavirus, as cause of disease classified elsewhere B97.29
SARS-associated B97.21
Corpora —*see also* condition
amylacea, prostate N42.89
cavernosa —*see* condition
Corpulence —*see* Obesity
Corpus —*see* condition
Corrected transposition Q20.5

Corrosion (injury) (acid) (caustic) (chemical) (lime) (external) (internal) T30.4
abdomen, abdominal (muscle) (wall) T21.42
  first degree T21.52
  second degree T21.62
  third degree T21.72
above elbow T22.439
  first degree T22.539
  left T22.432
    first degree T22.532
    second degree T22.632
    third degree T22.732
  right T22.431
    first degree T22.531
    second degree T22.631
    third degree T22.731
  second degree T22.639
  third degree T22.739
alimentary tract NEC T28.7
ankle T25.419
  first degree T25.519
  left T25.412
    first degree T25.512
    second degree T25.612
    third degree T25.712
  multiple with foot —*see* Corrosion, lower, limb, multiple, ankle and foot
  right T25.411
    first degree T25.511
    second degree T25.611
    third degree T25.711
  second degree T25.619
  third degree T25.719
anus —*see* Corrosion, buttock
arm(s) (meaning upper limb(s)) —*see* Corrosion, upper limb
axilla T22.449
  first degree T22.549
  left T22.442
    first degree T22.542
    second degree T22.642
    third degree T22.742
  right T22.441
    first degree T22.541
    second degree T22.641
    third degree T22.741
  second degree T22.649
  third degree T22.749
back (lower) T21.44
  first degree T21.54
  second degree T21.64
  third degree T21.74
  upper T21.43
    first degree T21.53
    second degree T21.63
    third degree T21.73
blisters - code as Corrosion, second degree, by site
breast(s) —*see* Corrosion, chest wall
buttock(s) T21.45
  first degree T21.55
  second degree T21.65
  third degree T21.75
calf T24.439
  first degree T24.539
  left T24.432
    first degree T24.532
    second degree T24.632
    third degree T24.732
  right T24.431
    first degree T24.531
    second degree T24.631
    third degree T24.731
  second degree T24.639
  third degree T24.739
canthus (eye) —*see* Corrosion, eyelid
cervix T28.8
cheek T20.46
  first degree T20.56
  second degree T20.66
  third degree T20.76

Corrosion *(Continued)*
  chest wall T21.41
    first degree T21.51
    second degree T21.61
    third degree T21.71
  chin T20.43
    first degree T20.53
    second degree T20.63
    third degree T20.73
  colon T28.7
  conjunctiva (and cornea) —*see* Corrosion, cornea
  cornea (and conjunctiva) T26.6-•
  deep necrosis of underlying tissue - code as Corrosion, third degree, by site
  dorsum of hand T23.469
    first degree T23.569
    left T23.462
      first degree T23.562
      second degree T23.662
      third degree T23.762
    right T23.461
      first degree T23.561
      second degree T23.661
      third degree T23.761
    second degree T23.669
    third degree T23.769
  ear (auricle) (external) (canal) T20.41
    drum T28.91
    first degree T20.51
    second degree T20.61
    third degree T20.71
  elbow T22.429
    first degree T22.529
    left T22.422
      first degree T22.522
      second degree T22.622
      third degree T22.722
    right T22.421
      first degree T22.521
      second degree T22.621
      third degree T22.721
    second degree T22.629
    third degree T22.729
  entire body —*see* Corrosion, multiple body regions
  epidermal loss - code as Corrosion, second degree, by site
  epiglottis T27.4
  erythema, erythematous - code as Corrosion, first degree, by site
  esophagus T28.6
  extent (percentage of body surface)
    less than 10 percent T32.0
    10-19 percent (0-9 percent third degree) T32.10
      with 10-19 percent third degree T32.11
    20-29 percent (0-9 percent third degree) T32.20
      with
        10-19 percent third degree T32.21
        20-29 percent third degree T32.22
    30-39 percent (0-9 percent third degree) T32.30
      with
        10-19 percent third degree T32.31
        20-29 percent third degree T32.32
        30-39 percent third degree T32.33
    40-49 percent (0-9 percent third degree) T32.40
      with
        10-19 percent third degree T32.41
        20-29 percent third degree T32.42
        30-39 percent third degree T32.43
        40-49 percent third degree T32.44
    50-59 percent (0-9 percent third degree) T32.50
      with
        10-19 percent third degree T32.51
        20-29 percent third degree T32.52

Corrosion *(Continued)*
  extent *(Continued)*
    50-59 percent *(Continued)*
      with *(Continued)*
        30-39 percent third degree T32.53
        40-49 percent third degree T32.54
        50-59 percent third degree T32.55
    60-69 percent (0-9 percent third degree) T32.60
      with
        10-19 percent third degree T32.61
        20-29 percent third degree T32.62
        30-39 percent third degree T32.63
        40-49 percent third degree T32.64
        50-59 percent third degree T32.65
        60-69 percent third degree T32.66
    70-79 percent (0-9 percent third degree) T32.70
      with
        10-19 percent third degree T32.71
        20-29 percent third degree T32.72
        30-39 percent third degree T32.73
        40-49 percent third degree T32.74
        50-59 percent third degree T32.75
        60-69 percent third degree T32.76
        70-79 percent third degree T32.77
    80-89 percent (0-9 percent third degree) T32.80
      with
        10-19 percent third degree T32.81
        20-29 percent third degree T32.82
        30-39 percent third degree T32.83
        40-49 percent third degree T32.84
        50-59 percent third degree T32.85
        60-69 percent third degree T32.86
        70-79 percent third degree T32.87
        80-89 percent third degree T32.88
    90 percent or more (0-9 percent third degree) T32.90
      with
        10-19 percent third degree T32.91
        20-29 percent third degree T32.92
        30-39 percent third degree T32.93
        40-49 percent third degree T32.94
        50-59 percent third degree T32.95
        60-69 percent third degree T32.96
        70-79 percent third degree T32.97
        80-89 percent third degree T32.98
        90-99 percent third degree T32.99
  extremity —*see* Corrosion, limb
  eye(s) and adnexa T26.9-•
    with resulting rupture and destruction of eyeball T26.7-•
    conjunctival sac —*see* Corrosion, cornea
    cornea —*see* Corrosion, cornea
    lid —*see* Corrosion, eyelid
    periocular area —*see* Corrosion eyelid
    specified site NEC T26.8-•
  eyeball —*see* Corrosion, eye
  eyelid(s) T26.5-•
  face —*see* Corrosion, head
  finger T23.429
    first degree T23.529
    left T23.422
      first degree T23.522
      second degree T23.622
      third degree T23.722
    multiple sites (without thumb) T23.439
      with thumb T23.449
        first degree T23.549
        left T23.442
          first degree T23.542
          second degree T23.642
          third degree T23.742
        right T23.441
          first degree T23.541
          second degree T23.641
          third degree T23.741
      second degree T23.649
      third degree T23.749

Corrosion *(Continued)*
  finger *(Continued)*
    multiple sites *(Continued)*
      first degree T23.539
      left T23.432
        first degree T23.532
        second degree T23.632
        third degree T23.732
      right T23.431
        first degree T23.531
        second degree T23.631
        third degree T23.731
      second degree T23.639
      third degree T23.739
    right T23.421
      first degree T23.521
      second degree T23.621
      third degree T23.721
    second degree T23.629
    third degree T23.729
  flank —*see* Corrosion, abdomen
  foot T25.429
    first degree T25.529
    left T25.422
      first degree T25.522
      second degree T25.622
      third degree T25.722
    multiple with ankle —*see* Corrosion, lower, limb, multiple, ankle and foot
    right T25.421
      first degree T25.521
      second degree T25.621
      third degree T25.721
    second degree T25.629
    third degree T25.729
  forearm T22.419
    first degree T22.519
    left T22.412
      first degree T22.512
      second degree T22.612
      third degree T22.712
    right T22.411
      first degree T22.511
      second degree T22.611
      third degree T22.711
    second degree T22.619
    third degree T22.719
  forehead T20.46
    first degree T20.56
    second degree T20.66
    third degree T20.76
  fourth degree - code as Corrosion, third degree, by site
  full thickness skin loss - code as Corrosion, third degree, by site
  gastrointestinal tract NEC T28.7
  genital organs
    external
      female T21.47
        first degree T21.57
        second degree T21.67
        third degree T21.77
      male T21.46
        first degree T21.56
        second degree T21.66
        third degree T21.76
    internal T28.8
  groin —*see* Corrosion, abdominal wall
  hand(s) T23.409
    back —*see* Corrosion, dorsum of hand
    finger —*see* Corrosion, finger
    first degree T23.509
    left T23.402
      first degree T23.502
      second degree T23.602
      third degree T23.702
    multiple sites with wrist T23.499
      first degree T23.599
      left T23.492
        first degree T23.592
        second degree T23.692
        third degree T23.792

▶ New   ⇒ Revised   ~~deleted~~ Deleted   • Use Additional Character(s)

Corrosion *(Continued)*
  hand(s) *(Continued)*
    multiple sites *(Continued)*
      right T23.491
        first degree T23.591
        second degree T23.691
        third degree T23.791
      second degree T23.699
      third degree T23.799
    palm —*see* Corrosion, palm
    right T23.401
      first degree T23.501
      second degree T23.601
      third degree T23.701
    second degree T23.609
    third degree T23.709
    thumb —*see* Corrosion, thumb
  head (and face) (and neck) T20.40
    cheek —*see* Corrosion, cheek
    chin —*see* Corrosion, chin
    ear —*see* Corrosion, ear
    eye(s) only —*see* Corrosion, eye
    first degree T20.50
    forehead —*see* Corrosion, forehead
    lip —*see* Corrosion, lip
    multiple sites T20.49
      first degree T20.59
      second degree T20.69
      third degree T20.79
    neck —*see* Corrosion, neck
    nose —*see* Corrosion, nose
    scalp —*see* Corrosion, scalp
    second degree T20.60
    third degree T20.70
  hip(s) —*see* Corrosion, lower, limb
  inhalation —*see* Corrosion, respiratory
    tract
  internal organ(s) *(see also* Corrosion, by site)
    T28.90
    alimentary tract T28.7
      esophagus T28.6
    esophagus T28.6
    genitourinary T28.8
    mouth T28.5
    pharynx T28.5
    specified organ NEC T28.99
  interscapular region —*see* Corrosion, back,
    upper
  intestine (large) (small) T28.7
  knee T24.429
    first degree T24.529
    left T24.422
      first degree T24.522
      second degree T24.622
      third degree T24.722
    right T24.421
      first degree T24.521
      second degree T24.621
      third degree T24.721
    second degree T24.629
    third degree T24.729
  labium (majus) (minus) —*see* Corrosion,
    genital organs, external, female
  lacrimal apparatus, duct, gland or sac —*see*
    Corrosion, eye, specified site NEC
  larynx T27.4
    with lung T27.5
  leg(s) (meaning lower limb(s)) —*see*
    Corrosion, lower limb
  limb(s)
    lower —*see* Corrosion, lower, limb
    upper —*see* Corrosion, upper limb
  lip(s) T20.42
    first degree T20.52
    second degree T20.62
    third degree T20.72
  lower
    back —*see* Corrosion, back
    limb T24.409
      ankle —*see* Corrosion, ankle
      calf —*see* Corrosion, calf

Corrosion *(Continued)*
  lower *(Continued)*
    limb *(Continued)*
      first degree T24.509
      foot —*see* Corrosion, foot
      hip —*see* Corrosion, thigh
      knee —*see* Corrosion, knee
      left T24.402
        first degree T24.502
        second degree T24.602
        third degree T24.702
      multiple sites, except ankle and foot
        T24.499
        ankle and foot T25.499
          first degree T25.599
          left T25.492
            first degree T25.592
            second degree T25.692
            third degree T25.792
          right T25.491
            first degree T25.591
            second degree T25.691
            third degree T25.791
          second degree T25.699
          third degree T25.799
        first degree T24.599
        left T24.492
          first degree T24.592
          second degree T24.692
          third degree T24.792
        right T24.491
          first degree T24.591
          second degree T24.691
          third degree T24.791
        second degree T24.699
        third degree T24.799
      right T24.401
        first degree T24.501
        second degree T24.601
        third degree T24.701
      second degree T24.609
      thigh —*see* Corrosion, thigh
      third degree T24.709
  lung (with larynx and trachea)
    T27.5
  mouth T28.5
  neck T20.47
    first degree T20.57
    second degree T20.67
    third degree T20.77
  nose (septum) T20.44
    first degree T20.54
    second degree T20.64
    third degree T20.74
  ocular adnexa —*see* Corrosion, eye
  orbit region —*see* Corrosion, eyelid
  palm T23.459
    first degree T23.559
    left T23.452
      first degree T23.552
      second degree T23.652
      third degree T23.752
    right T23.451
      first degree T23.551
      second degree T23.651
      third degree T23.751
    second degree T23.659
    third degree T23.759
  partial thickness - code as Corrosion,
    unspecified degree, by site
  pelvis —*see* Corrosion, trunk
  penis —*see* Corrosion, genital organs,
    external, male
  perineum
    female —*see* Corrosion, genital organs,
      external, female
    male —*see* Corrosion, genital organs,
      external, male
  periocular area —*see* Corrosion, eyelid
  pharynx T28.5
  rectum T28.7

Corrosion *(Continued)*
  respiratory tract T27.7
    larynx —*see* Corrosion, larynx
    specified part NEC T27.6
    trachea —*see* Corrosion, larynx
  sac, lacrimal —*see* Corrosion, eye,
    specified site NEC
  scalp T20.45
    first degree T20.55
    second degree T20.65
    third degree T20.75
  scapular region T22.469
    first degree T22.569
    left T22.462
      first degree T22.562
      second degree T22.662
      third degree T22.762
    right T22.461
      first degree T22.561
      second degree T22.661
      third degree T22.761
    second degree T22.669
    third degree T22.769
  sclera —*see* Corrosion, eye, specified site
    NEC
  scrotum —*see* Corrosion, genital organs,
    external, male
  shoulder T22.459
    first degree T22.559
    left T22.452
      first degree T22.552
      second degree T22.652
      third degree T22.752
    right T22.451
      first degree T22.551
      second degree T22.651
      third degree T22.751
    second degree T22.659
    third degree T22.759
  stomach T28.7
  temple —*see* Corrosion, head
  testis —*see* Corrosion, genital organs,
    external, male
  thigh T24.419
    first degree T24.519
    left T24.412
      first degree T24.512
      second degree T24.612
      third degree T24.712
    right T24.411
      first degree T24.511
      second degree T24.611
      third degree T24.711
    second degree T24.619
    third degree T24.719
  thorax (external) —*see* Corrosion, trunk
  throat (meaning pharynx) T28.5
  thumb(s) T23.419
    first degree T23.519
    left T23.412
      first degree T23.512
      second degree T23.612
      third degree T23.712
    multiple sites with fingers T23.449
      first degree T23.549
      left T23.442
        first degree T23.542
        second degree T23.642
        third degree T23.742
      right T23.441
        first degree T23.541
        second degree T23.641
        third degree T23.741
      second degree T23.649
      third degree T23.749
    right T23.411
      first degree T23.511
      second degree T23.611
      third degree T23.711
    second degree T23.619
    third degree T23.719

Corrosion (*Continued*)
toe T25.439
  first degree T25.539
  left T25.432
    first degree T25.532
    second degree T25.632
    third degree T25.732
  right T25.431
    first degree T25.531
    second degree T25.631
    third degree T25.731
  second degree T25.639
  third degree T25.739
tongue T28.5
tonsil(s) T28.5
total body —*see* Corrosion, multiple body
    regions
trachea T27.4
  with lung T27.5
trunk T21.40
  abdominal wall —*see* Corrosion,
      abdominal wall
  anus —*see* Corrosion, buttock
  axilla —*see* Corrosion, upper limb
  back —*see* Corrosion, back
  breast —*see* Corrosion, chest wall
  buttock —*see* Corrosion, buttock
  chest wall —*see* Corrosion, chest wall
  first degree T21.50
  flank —*see* Corrosion, abdominal wall
  genital
    female —*see* Corrosion, genital organs,
        external, female
    male —*see* Corrosion, genital organs,
        external, male
  groin —*see* Corrosion, abdominal wall
  interscapular region —*see* Corrosion, back,
      upper
  labia —*see* Corrosion, genital organs,
      external, female
  lower back —*see* Corrosion, back
  penis —*see* Corrosion, genital organs,
      external, male
  perineum
    female —*see* Corrosion, genital organs,
        external, female
    male —*see* Corrosion, genital organs,
        external, male
  scapular region —*see* Corrosion, upper
      limb
  scrotum —*see* Corrosion, genital organs,
      external, male
  second degree T21.60
  shoulder —*see* Corrosion, upper limb
  specified site NEC T21.49
    first degree T21.59
    second degree T21.69
    third degree T21.79
  testes —*see* Corrosion, genital organs,
      external, male
  third degree T21.70
  upper back —*see* Corrosion, back, upper
  vagina T28.8
  vulva —*see* Corrosion, genital organs,
      external, female
unspecified site with extent of body surface
    involved specified
  less than 10 percent T32.0
  10-19 percent (0-9 percent third degree)
      T32.10
    with 10-19 percent third degree T32.11
  20-29 percent (0-9 percent third degree)
      T32.20
    with
      10-19 percent third degree T32.21
      20-29 percent third degree T32.22
  30-39 percent (0-9 percent third degree)
      T32.30
    with
      10-19 percent third degree T32.31
      20-29 percent third degree T32.32
      30-39 percent third degree T32.33

Corrosion (*Continued*)
unspecified site with extent of body surface
    involved specified (*Continued*)
  40-49 percent (0-9 percent third degree)
      T32.40
    with
      10-19 percent third degree T32.41
      20-29 percent third degree T32.42
      30-39 percent third degree T32.43
      40-49 percent third degree T32.44
  50-59 percent (0-9 percent third degree)
      T32.50
    with
      10-19 percent third degree T32.51
      20-29 percent third degree T32.52
      30-39 percent third degree T32.53
      40-49 percent third degree T32.54
      50-59 percent third degree T32.55
  60-69 percent (0-9 percent third degree)
      T32.60
    with
      10-19 percent third degree T32.61
      20-29 percent third degree T32.62
      30-39 percent third degree T32.63
      40-49 percent third degree T32.64
      50-59 percent third degree T32.65
      60-69 percent third degree T32.66
  70-79 percent (0-9 percent third degree)
      T32.70
    with
      10-19 percent third degree T32.71
      20-29 percent third degree T32.72
      30-39 percent third degree T32.73
      40-49 percent third degree T32.74
      50-59 percent third degree T32.75
      60-69 percent third degree T32.76
      70-79 percent third degree T32.77
  80-89 percent (0-9 percent third degree)
      T32.80
    with
      10-19 percent third degree T32.81
      20-29 percent third degree T32.82
      30-39 percent third degree T32.83
      40-49 percent third degree T32.84
      50-59 percent third degree T32.85
      60-69 percent third degree T32.86
      70-79 percent third degree T32.87
      80-89 percent third degree T32.88
  90 percent or more (0-9 percent third
      degree) T32.90
    with
      10-19 percent third degree T32.91
      20-29 percent third degree T32.92
      30-39 percent third degree T32.93
      40-49 percent third degree T32.94
      50-59 percent third degree T32.95
      60-69 percent third degree T32.96
      70-79 percent third degree T32.97
      80-89 percent third degree T32.98
      90-99 percent third degree T32.99
upper limb (axilla) (scapular region) T22.40
  above elbow —*see* Corrosion, above elbow
  axilla —*see* Corrosion, axilla
  elbow —*see* Corrosion, elbow
  first degree T22.50
  forearm —*see* Corrosion, forearm
  hand —*see* Corrosion, hand
  interscapular region —*see* Corrosion, back,
      upper
  multiple sites T22.499
    first degree T22.599
    left T22.492
      first degree T22.592
      second degree T22.692
      third degree T22.792
    right T22.491
      first degree T22.591
      second degree T22.691
      third degree T22.791
    second degree T22.699
    third degree T22.799

Corrosion (*Continued*)
upper limb (axilla) (scapular region)
    (*Continued*)
  scapular region —*see* Corrosion, scapular
      region
  second degree T22.60
  shoulder —*see* Corrosion, shoulder
  third degree T22.70
  wrist —*see* Corrosion, hand
uterus T28.8
vagina T28.8
vulva —*see* Corrosion, genital organs,
    external, female
wrist T23.479
  first degree T23.579
  left T23.472
    first degree T23.572
    second degree T23.672
    third degree T23.772
  multiple sites with hand T23.499
    first degree T23.599
    left T23.492
      first degree T23.592
      second degree T23.692
      third degree T23.792
    right T23.491
      first degree T23.591
      second degree T23.691
      third degree T23.791
    second degree T23.699
    third degree T23.799
  right T23.471
    first degree T23.571
    second degree T23.671
    third degree T23.771
  second degree T23.679
  third degree T23.779
Corrosive burn —*see* Corrosion
Corsican fever —*see* Malaria
Cortical —*see* condition
Cortico-adrenal —*see* condition
Coryza (acute) J00
  with grippe or influenza —*see* Influenza,
      with, respiratory manifestations
      NEC
  syphilitic
    congenital (chronic) A50.05
Costen's syndrome or complex M26.69
Costiveness —*see* Constipation
Costochondritis M94.0
Cot death R99
Cotard's syndrome F22
Cotia virus B08.8
Cotton wool spots (retinal) H35.81
Cotungo's disease —*see* Sciatica
Cough (affected) (chronic) (epidemic) (nervous)
    R05
  with hemorrhage —*see* Hemoptysis
  bronchial R05
    with grippe or influenza —*see* Influenza,
        with, respiratory manifestations
        NEC
  functional F45.8
  hysterical F45.8
  laryngeal, spasmodic R05
  psychogenic F45.8
  smokers' J41.0
  tea taster's B49
Counseling (for) Z71.9
  abuse NEC
    perpetrator Z69.82
    victim Z69.81
  alcohol abuser Z71.41
    family Z71.42
  child abuse
    nonparental
      perpetrator Z69.021
      victim Z69.020
    parental
      perpetrator Z69.011
      victim Z69.010

▶ New   ⇒ Revised   ~~deleted~~ Deleted   ● Use Additional Character(s)

Counseling (Continued)
consanguinity Z71.89
contraceptive Z30.09
dietary Z71.3
drug abuser Z71.51
family member Z71.52
exercise Z71.82
family Z71.89
fertility preservation (prior to cancer therapy)
(prior to removal of gonads) Z31.62
for non-attending third party Z71.0
related to sexual behavior or orientation
Z70.2
genetic
nonprocreative Z71.83
procreative NEC Z31.5
gestational carrier Z31.7
health (advice) (education) (instruction) —see
Counseling, medical
human immunodeficiency virus (HIV)
Z71.7
impotence Z70.1
insulin pump use Z46.81
medical (for) Z71.9
boarding school resident Z59.3
consanguinity Z71.89
feared complaint and no disease found Z71.1
human immunodeficiency virus (HIV) Z71.7
institutional resident Z59.3
on behalf of another Z71.0
related to sexual behavior or orientation
Z70.2
person living alone Z60.2
specified reason NEC Z71.89
natural family planning
procreative Z31.61
to avoid pregnancy Z30.02
perpetrator (of)
abuse NEC Z69.82
child abuse
non-parental Z69.021
parental Z69.011
rape NEC Z69.82
spousal abuse Z69.12
procreative NEC Z31.69
fertility preservation (prior to cancer
therapy) (prior to removal of
gonads) Z31.62
using natural family planning Z31.61
promiscuity Z70.1
rape victim Z69.81
religious Z71.81
sex, sexual (related to) Z70.9
attitude(s) Z70.0
behavior or orientation Z70.1
combined concerns Z70.3
non-responsiveness Z70.1
on behalf of third party Z70.2
specified reason NEC Z70.8
specified reason NEC Z71.89
spiritual Z71.81
spousal abuse (perpetrator) Z69.12
victim Z69.11
substance abuse Z71.89
alcohol Z71.41
drug Z71.51
tobacco Z71.6
tobacco use Z71.6
use (of)
insulin pump Z46.81
victim (of)
abuse Z69.81
child abuse
by parent Z69.010
non-parental Z69.020
rape NEC Z69.81
Coupled rhythm R00.8
Couvelaire syndrome or uterus (complicating
delivery) O45.8X-●
Cowperitis —see Urethritis
Cowper's gland —see condition

Cowpox B08.010
due to vaccination T88.1
Coxa
magna M91.4-●
plana M91.2-●
valga (acquired) —see also Deformity, limb,
specified type NEC, thigh
congenital Q65.81
sequelae (late effect) of rickets E64.3
vara (acquired) —see also Deformity, limb,
specified type NEC, thigh
congenital Q65.82
sequelae (late effect) of rickets E64.3
Coxalgia, coxalgic (nontuberculous) —see also
Pain, joint, hip
tuberculous A18.02
Coxitis —see Monoarthritis, hip
Coxsackie (virus) (infection) B34.1
as cause of disease classified elsewhere B97.11
carditis B33.20
central nervous system NEC A88.8
endocarditis B33.21
enteritis A08.39
meningitis (aseptic) A87.0
myocarditis B33.22
pericarditis B33.23
pharyngitis B08.5
pleurodynia B33.0
specific disease NEC B33.8
Crabs, meaning pubic lice B85.3
Crack baby P04.41
Cracked nipple N64.0
associated with
lactation O92.13
pregnancy O92.11-●
puerperium O92.12
Cracked tooth K03.81
Cradle cap L21.0
Craft neurosis F48.8
Cramp(s) R25.2
abdominal —see Pain, abdominal
bathing T75.1
colic R10.83
psychogenic F45.8
due to immersion T75.1
fireman T67.2
heat T67.2
immersion T75.1
intestinal —see Pain, abdominal
psychogenic F45.8
leg, sleep related G47.62
limb (lower) (upper) NEC R25.2
sleep related G47.62
linotypist's F48.8
organic G25.89
muscle (limb) (general) R25.2
due to immersion T75.1
psychogenic F45.8
occupational (hand) F48.8
organic G25.89
salt-depletion E87.1
sleep related, leg G47.62
stoker's T67.2
swimmer's T75.1
telegrapher's F48.8
organic G25.89
typist's F48.8
organic G25.89
uterus N94.89
menstrual —see Dysmenorrhea
writer's F48.8
organic G25.89
Cranial —see condition
Craniocleidodysostosis Q74.0
Craniofenestria (skull) Q75.8
Craniolacunia (skull) Q75.8
Craniopagus Q89.4
Craniopathy, metabolic M85.2
Craniopharyngeal —see condition
Craniopharyngioma D44.4
Craniorachischisis (totalis) Q00.1

Cranioschisis Q75.8
Craniostenosis Q75.0
Craniosynostosis Q75.0
Craniotabes (cause unknown) M83.8
neonatal P96.3
rachitic E64.3
syphilitic A50.56
Cranium —see condition
Craw-craw —see Onchocerciasis
Creaking joint —see Derangement, joint,
specified type NEC
Creeping
eruption B76.9
palsy or paralysis G12.22
Crenated tongue K14.8
Creotoxism A05.9
Crepitus
caput Q75.8
joint —see Derangement, joint, specified type
NEC
Crescent or conus choroid, congenital Q14.3
CREST syndrome M34.1
Cretin, cretinism (congenital) (endemic)
(nongoitrous) (sporadic) E00.9
pelvis
with disproportion (fetopelvic) O33.0
causing obstructed labor O65.0
type
hypothyroid E00.1
mixed E00.2
myxedematous E00.1
neurological E00.0
Creutzfeldt-Jakob disease or syndrome (with
dementia) A81.00
familial A81.09
iatrogenic A81.09
specified NEC A81.09
sporadic A81.09
variant (vCJD) A81.01
Crib death R99
Cribriform hymen Q52.3
Cri-du-chat syndrome Q93.4
Crigler-Najjar disease or syndrome E80.5
Crime, victim of Z65.4
Crimean hemorrhagic fever A98.0
Criminalism F60.2
Crisis
abdomen R10.0
acute reaction F43.0
addisonian E27.2
adrenal (cortical) E27.2
celiac K90.0
Dietl's N13.8
emotional —see also Disorder, adjustment
acute reaction to stress F43.0
specific to childhood and adolescence F93.8
glaucomatocyclitic —see Glaucoma,
secondary, inflammation
heart —see Failure, heart
nitritoid I95.2
correct substance properly administered —
see Table of Drugs and Chemicals, by
drug, adverse effect
overdose or wrong substance given
or taken —see Table of Drugs and
Chemicals, by drug, poisoning
oculogyric H51.8
psychogenic F45.8
Pel's (tabetic) A52.11
psychosexual identity F64.2
renal N28.0
sickle-cell D57.00
with
acute chest syndrome D57.01
splenic sequestration D57.02
state (acute reaction) F43.0
tabetic A52.11
thyroid —see Thyrotoxicosis with thyroid
storm
thyrotoxic —see Thyrotoxicosis with thyroid
storm

Crocq's disease (acrocyanosis) I73.89
Crohn's disease —see Enteritis, regional
Crooked septum, nasal J34.2
Cross syndrome E70.328
Crossbite (anterior) (posterior) M26.24
Cross-eye —see Strabismus, convergent
    concomitant
Croup, croupous (catarrhal) (infectious)
    (inflammatory) (nondiphtheritic) J05.0
  bronchial J20.9
  diphtheritic A36.2
  false J38.5
  spasmodic J38.5
    diphtheritic A36.2
  stridulous J38.5
    diphtheritic A36.2
Crouzon's disease Q75.1
Crowding, tooth, teeth, fully erupted M26.31
CRST syndrome M34.1
Cruchet's disease A85.8
Cruelty in children —see also Disorder, conduct
Crural ulcer —see Ulcer, lower limb
Crush, crushed, crushing T14.8
  abdomen S38.1
  ankle S97.0-●
  arm (upper) (and shoulder) S47.-●
  axilla —see Crush, arm
  back, lower S38.1
  buttock S38.1
  cheek S07.0
  chest S28.0
  cranium S07.1
  ear S07.0
  elbow S57.0-●
  extremity
    lower
      ankle —see Crush, ankle
      below knee —see Crush, leg
      foot —see Crush, foot
      hip —see Crush, hip
      knee —see Crush, knee
      thigh —see Crush, thigh
      toe —see Crush, toe
    upper
      below elbow S67.9-●
      elbow —see Crush, elbow
      finger —see Crush, finger
      forearm —see Crush, forearm
      hand —see Crush, hand
      thumb —see Crush, thumb
      upper arm —see Crush, arm
      wrist —see Crush, wrist
  face S07.0
  finger(s) S67.1-●
    with hand (and wrist) —see Crush, hand,
        specified site NEC
    index S67.19-●
    little S67.19-●
    middle S67.19-●
    ring S67.19-●
    thumb —see Crush, thumb
  foot S97.8-●
    toe —see Crush, toe
  forearm S57.8-●
  genitalia, external
    female S38.002
      vagina S38.03
      vulva S38.03
    male S38.001
      penis S38.01
      scrotum S38.02
      testis S38.02
  hand (except fingers alone) S67.2-●
    with wrist S67.4-●
  head S07.9
    specified NEC S07.8
  heel —see Crush, foot
  hip S77.0-●
    with thigh S77.2-●
  internal organ (abdomen, chest, or pelvis)
      NEC T14.8

Crush, crushed, crushing (Continued)
  knee S87.0-●
  labium (majus) (minus) S38.03
  larynx S17.0
  leg (lower) S87.8-●
    knee —see Crush, knee
  lip S07.0
  lower
    back S38.1
    leg —see Crush, leg
  neck S17.9
  nerve —see Injury, nerve
  nose S07.0
  pelvis S38.1
  penis S38.01
  scalp S07.8
  scapular region —see Crush, arm
  scrotum S38.02
  severe, unspecified site T14.8
  shoulder (and upper arm) —see Crush, arm
  skull S07.1
  syndrome (complication of trauma) T79.5
  testis S38.02
  thigh S77.1-●
    with hip S77.2-●
  throat S17.8
  thumb S67.0-●
    with hand (and wrist) —see Crush, hand,
        specified site NEC
  toe(s) S97.10-●
    great S97.11-●
    lesser S97.12-●
  trachea S17.0
  vagina S38.03
  vulva S38.03
  wrist S67.3-●
    with hand S67.4-●
Crusta lactea L21.0
Crusts R23.4
Crutch paralysis —see Injury, brachial plexus
Cruveilhier-Baumgarten cirrhosis, disease or
    syndrome K74.69
Cruveilhier's atrophy or disease G12.8
Crying (constant) (continuous) (excessive)
  child, adolescent, or adult R45.83
  infant (baby) (newborn) R68.11
Cryofibrinogenemia D89.2
Cryoglobulinemia (essential) (idiopathic)
    (mixed) (primary) (purpura) (secondary)
    (vasculitis) D89.1
  with lung involvement D89.1 [J99]
Cryptitis (anal) (rectal) K62.89
Cryptococcosis, cryptococcus (infection)
    (neoformans) B45.9
  bone B45.3
  cerebral B45.1
  cutaneous B45.2
  disseminated B45.7
  generalized B45.7
  meningitis B45.1
  meningocerebralis B45.1
  osseous B45.3
  pulmonary B45.0
  skin B45.2
  specified NEC B45.8
Cryptopapillitis (anus) K62.89
Cryptophthalmos Q11.2
  syndrome Q87.0
Cryptorchid, cryptorchism, cryptorchidism
    Q53.9
  bilateral Q53.20
    abdominal Q53.211
    perineal Q53.22
  unilateral Q53.10
    abdominal Q53.111
    perineal Q53.12
Cryptosporidiosis A07.2
  hepatobiliary B88.8
  respiratory B88.8
Cryptostromosis J67.6
Crystalluria R82.998

Cubitus
  congenital Q68.8
  valgus (acquired) M21.0-●
    congenital Q68.8
    sequelae (late effect) of rickets E64.3
  varus (acquired) M21.1-●
    congenital Q68.8
    sequelae (late effect) of rickets E64.3
Cultural deprivation or shock Z60.3
Curling esophagus K22.4
Curling's ulcer —see Ulcer, peptic, acute
Curschmann (-Batten) (-Steinert) disease or
    syndrome G71.11
Curse, Ondine's —see Apnea, sleep
Curvature
  organ or site, congenital NEC —see Distortion
  penis (lateral) Q55.61
  Pott's (spinal) A18.01
  radius, idiopathic, progressive (congenital)
    Q74.0
  spine (acquired) (angular) (idiopathic)
    (incorrect) (postural) —see Dorsopathy,
    deforming
    congenital Q67.5
    due to or associated with
      Charcot-Marie-Tooth disease —see also
        subcategory M49.8 G60.0
      osteitis
        deformans M88.88
        fibrosa cystica —see also subcategory
          M49.8 E21.0
      tuberculosis (Pott's curvature) A18.01
    sequelae (late effect) of rickets E64.3
    tuberculous A18.01
Cushingoid due to steroid therapy E24.2
  correct substance properly administered —see
    Table of Drugs and Chemicals, by drug,
    adverse effect
  overdose or wrong substance given
    or taken —see Table of Drugs and
    Chemicals, by drug, poisoning
Cushing's
  syndrome or disease E24.9
    drug-induced E24.2
    iatrogenic E24.2
    pituitary-dependent E24.0
    specified NEC E24.8
  ulcer —see Ulcer, peptic, acute
Cusp, Carabelli - omit code
Cut (external) —see also Laceration
  muscle —see Injury, muscle
Cutaneous —see also condition
  hemorrhage R23.3
  larva migrans B76.9
Cutis —see also condition
  hyperelastica Q82.8
    acquired L57.4
  laxa (hyperelastica) —see Dermatolysis
  marmorata R23.8
  osteosis L94.2
  pendula —see Dermatolysis
  rhomboidalis nuchae L57.2
  verticis gyrata Q82.8
    acquired L91.8
Cyanosis R23.0
  due to
    patent foramen botalli Q21.1
    persistent foramen ovale Q21.1
  enterogenous D74.8
  paroxysmal digital —see Raynaud's disease
    with gangrene I73.01
  retina, retinal H35.89
Cyanotic heart disease I24.9
  congenital Q24.9
Cycle
  anovulatory N97.0
  menstrual, irregular N92.6
Cyclencephaly Q04.9
Cyclical vomiting (see also Vomiting, cyclical)
    G43.A0
  psychogenic F50.89

Cyclitis —see also Iridocyclitis H20.9
  chronic —see Iridocyclitis, chronic
  Fuchs' heterochromic H20.81-●
  granulomatous —see Iridocyclitis, chronic
  lens-induced —see Iridocyclitis,
    lens-induced
  posterior H30.2-●
Cycloid personality F34.0
Cyclophoria H50.54
Cyclopia, cyclops Q87.0
Cyclopism Q87.0
Cyclosporiasis A07.4
Cyclothymia F34.0
Cyclothymic personality F34.0
Cyclotropia H50.41-●
Cylindroma —see also Neoplasm, malignant,
  by site
  eccrine dermal —see Neoplasm, skin,
    benign
  skin —see Neoplasm, skin, benign
Cylindruria R82.998
Cynanche
  diphtheritic A36.2
  tonsillaris J36
Cynophobia F40.218
Cynorexia R63.2
Cyphosis —see Kyphosis
Cyprus fever —see Brucellosis
Cyst (colloid) (mucous) (simple) (retention)
  adenoid (infected) J35.8
  adrenal gland E27.8
    congenital Q89.1
  air, lung J98.4
  allantoic Q64.4
  alveolar process (jaw bone) M27.40
  amnion, amniotic O41.8X-●
  aneurysmal M27.49
  anterior
    chamber (eye) —see Cyst, iris
    nasopalatine K09.1
  antrum J34.1
  anus K62.89
  apical (tooth) (periodontal) K04.8
  appendix K38.8
  arachnoid, brain (acquired) G93.0
    congenital Q04.6
  arytenoid J38.7
  Baker's M71.2-●
    ruptured M66.0
    tuberculous A18.02
  Bartholin's gland N75.0
  bile duct (common) (hepatic) K83.5
  bladder (multiple) (trigone) N32.89
  blue dome (breast) —see Cyst, breast
  bone (local) NEC M85.60
    aneurysmal M85.50
      ankle M85.57-●
      foot M85.57-●
      forearm M85.53-●
      hand M85.54-●
      jaw M27.49
      lower leg M85.56-●
      multiple site M85.59
      neck M85.58
      rib M85.58
      shoulder M85.51-●
      skull M85.58
      specified site NEC M85.58
      thigh M85.55-●
      toe M85.57-●
      upper arm M85.52-●
      vertebra M85.58
    solitary M85.40
      ankle M85.47-●
      fibula M85.46-●
      foot M85.47-●
      hand M85.44-●
      humerus M85.42-●
      jaw M27.49
      neck M85.48
      pelvis M85.45-●

Cyst (Continued)
  bone NEC (Continued)
    solitary (Continued)
      radius M85.43-●
      rib M85.48
      shoulder M85.41-●
      skull M85.48
      specified site NEC M85.48
      tibia M85.46-●
      toe M85.47-●
      ulna M85.43-●
      vertebra M85.48
    specified type NEC M85.60
      ankle M85.67-●
      foot M85.67-●
      forearm M85.63-●
      hand M85.64-●
      jaw M27.40
        developmental (nonodontogenic) K09.1
          odontogenic K09.0
        latent M27.0
      lower leg M85.66-●
      multiple site M85.69
      neck M85.68
      rib M85.68
      shoulder M85.61-●
      skull M85.68
      specified site NEC M85.68
      thigh M85.65-●
      toe M85.67-●
      upper arm M85.62-●
      vertebra M85.68
  brain (acquired) G93.0
    congenital Q04.6
    hydatid B67.99 [G94]
    third ventricle (colloid), congenital
      Q04.6
  branchial (cleft) Q18.0
  branchiogenic Q18.0
  breast (benign) (blue dome) (pedunculated)
    (solitary) N60.0-●
    involution —see Dysplasia, mammary,
      specified type NEC
    sebaceous —see Dysplasia, mammary,
      specified type NEC
  broad ligament (benign) N83.8
  bronchogenic (mediastinal) (sequestration)
    J98.4
    congenital Q33.0
  buccal K09.8
  bulbourethral gland N36.8
  bursa, bursal NEC M71.30
    with rupture —see Rupture, synovium
    ankle M71.37-●
    elbow M71.32-●
    foot M71.37-●
    hand M71.34-●
    hip M71.35-●
    multiple sites M71.39
    pharyngeal J39.2
    popliteal space —see Cyst, Baker's
    shoulder M71.31-●
    specified site NEC M71.38
    wrist M71.33-●
  calcifying odontogenic D16.5
    upper jaw (bone) (maxilla) D16.4
  canal of Nuck (female) N94.89
    congenital Q52.4
  canthus —see Cyst, conjunctiva
  carcinomatous —see Neoplasm, malignant,
    by site
  cauda equina G95.89
  cavum septi pellucidi —see Cyst, brain
  celomic (pericardium) Q24.8
  cerebellopontine (angle) —see Cyst, brain
  cerebellum —see Cyst, brain
  cerebral —see Cyst, brain
  cervical lateral Q18.0
  cervix NEC N88.8
    embryonic Q51.6
    nabothian N88.8

Cyst (Continued)
  chiasmal optic NEC —see Disorder, optic,
    chiasm
  chocolate (ovary) N80.1
  choledochus, congenital Q44.4
  chorion O41.8X-●
  choroid plexus G93.0
  ciliary body —see Cyst, iris
  clitoris N90.7
  colon K63.89
  common (bile) duct K83.5
  congenital NEC Q89.8
    adrenal gland Q89.1
    epiglottis Q31.8
    esophagus Q39.8
    fallopian tube Q50.4
    kidney Q61.00
      more than one (multiple) Q61.02
        specified as polycystic Q61.3
          adult type Q61.2
          infantile type NEC Q61.19
            collecting duct dilation Q61.11
      solitary Q61.01
    larynx Q31.8
    liver Q44.6
    lung Q33.0
    mediastinum Q34.1
    ovary Q50.1
    oviduct Q50.4
    periurethral (tissue) Q64.79
    prepuce Q55.69
    salivary gland (any) Q38.4
    sublingual Q38.6
    submaxillary gland Q38.6
    thymus (gland) Q89.2
    tongue Q38.3
    ureterovesical orifice Q62.8
    vulva Q52.79
  conjunctiva H11.44-●
  cornea H18.89-●
  corpora quadrigemina G93.0
  corpus
    albicans N83.29-●
    luteum (hemorrhagic) (ruptured) N83.1-●
  Cowper's gland (benign) (infected) N36.8
  cranial meninges G93.0
  craniobuccal pouch E23.6
  craniopharyngeal pouch E23.6
  cystic duct K82.8
  Cysticercus —see Cysticercosis
  Dandy-Walker Q03.1
    with spina bifida —see Spina bifida
  dental (root) K04.8
    developmental K09.0
    eruption K09.0
    primordial K09.0
  dentigerous (mandible) (maxilla) K09.0
  dermoid —see Neoplasm, benign, by site
    with malignant transformation C56.-●
    implantation
      external area or site (skin) NEC L72.0
      iris —see Cyst, iris, implantation
      vagina N89.8
      vulva N90.7
    mouth K09.8
    oral soft tissue K09.8
    sacrococcygeal —see Cyst, pilonidal
  developmental K09.1
    odontogenic K09.0
    oral region (nonodontogenic) K09.1
    ovary, ovarian Q50.1
  dura (cerebral) G93.0
    spinal G96.19
  ear (external) Q18.1
  echinococcal —see Echinococcus
  embryonic
    cervix uteri Q51.6
    fallopian tube Q50.4
    vagina Q52.4
  endometrium, endometrial (uterus) N85.8
    ectopic —see Endometriosis

Cyst (Continued)
enterogenous Q43.8
epidermal, epidermoid (inclusion) (see also Cyst, skin) L72.0
 mouth K09.8
 oral soft tissue K09.8
epididymis N50.3
epiglottis J38.7
epiphysis cerebri E34.8
epithelial (inclusion) L72.0
epoophoron Q50.5
eruption K09.0
esophagus K22.8
ethmoid sinus J34.1
external female genital organs NEC N90.7
eye NEC H57.89
 congenital Q15.8
eyelid (sebaceous) H02.829
 infected —see Hordeolum
 left H02.826
  lower H02.825
  upper H02.824
 right H02.823
  lower H02.822
  upper H02.821
fallopian tube N83.8
 congenital Q50.4
fimbrial (twisted) Q50.4
fissural (oral region) K09.1
follicle (graafian) (hemorrhagic) N83.0-●
 nabothian N88.8
follicular (atretic) (hemorrhagic) (ovarian) N83.0-●
 dentigerous K09.0
 odontogenic K09.0
 skin L72.9
  specified NEC L72.8
frontal sinus J34.1
gallbladder K82.8
ganglion —see Ganglion
Gartner's duct Q52.4
gingiva K09.0
gland of Moll —see Cyst, eyelid
globulomaxillary K09.1
graafian follicle (hemorrhagic) N83.0-●
granulosal lutein (hemorrhagic) N83.1-●
hemangiomatous D18.00
 intra-abdominal D18.03
 intracranial D18.02
 skin D18.01
 specified site NEC D18.09
hemorrhagic M27.49
hydatid —see also Echinococcus B67.90
 brain B67.99 [G94]
 liver —see also Cyst, liver, hydatid B67.8
 lung NEC B67.99 [J99]
 Morgagni
  female Q50.5
  male (epididymal) Q55.4
   testicular Q55.29
 specified site NEC B67.99
hymen N89.8
 embryonic Q52.4
hypophysis, hypophyseal (duct) (recurrent) E23.6
 cerebri E23.6
implantation (dermoid)
 external area or site (skin) NEC L72.0
 iris —see Cyst, iris, implantation
 vagina N89.8
 vulva N90.7
incisive canal K09.1
inclusion (epidermal) (epithelial) (epidermoid) (squamous) L72.0
 not of skin - code under Cyst, by site
intestine (large) (small) K63.89
intracranial —see Cyst, brain
intraligamentous —see also Disorder, ligament
 knee —see Derangement, knee

Cyst (Continued)
intrasellar E23.6
iris H21.309
 exudative H21.31-●
 idiopathic H21.30-●
 implantation H21.32-●
 parasitic H21.33-●
 pars plana (primary) H21.34-●
  exudative H21.35-●
jaw (bone) M27.40
 aneurysmal M27.49
 developmental (odontogenic) K09.0
 fissural K09.1
 hemorrhagic M27.49
 traumatic M27.49
joint NEC —see Disorder, joint, specified type NEC
kidney (acquired) N28.1
 calyceal —see Hydronephrosis
 congenital Q61.00
 more than one (multiple) Q61.02
  specified as polycystic Q61.3
   adult type (autosomal dominant) Q61.2
   infantile type (autosomal recessive) NEC Q61.19
    collecting duct dilation Q61.11
 pyelogenic —see Hydronephrosis
 simple N28.1
 solitary (single) Q61.01
  acquired N28.1
labium (majus) (minus) N90.7
 sebaceous N90.7
lacrimal —see also Disorder, lacrimal system, specified NEC
 gland H04.13-●
 passages or sac —see Disorder, lacrimal system, specified NEC
larynx J38.7
lateral periodontal K09.0
lens H27.8
 congenital Q12.8
lip (gland) K13.0
liver (idiopathic) (simple) K76.89
 congenital Q44.6
 hydatid B67.8
  granulosus B67.0
  multilocularis B67.5
lung J98.4
 congenital Q33.0
 giant bullous J43.9
lutein N83.1-●
lymphangiomatous D18.1
lymphoepithelial, oral soft tissue K09.8
macula —see Degeneration, macula, hole
malignant —see Neoplasm, malignant, by site
mammary gland —see Cyst, breast
mandible M27.40
 dentigerous K09.0
 radicular K04.8
maxilla M27.40
 dentigerous K09.0
 radicular K04.8
medial, face and neck Q18.8
median
 anterior maxillary K09.1
 palatal K09.1
mediastinum, congenital Q34.1
meibomian (gland) —see Chalazion
 infected —see Hordeolum
membrane, brain G93.0
meninges (cerebral) G93.0
 spinal G96.19
meniscus, knee —see Derangement, knee, meniscus, cystic
mesentery, mesenteric K66.8
 chyle I89.8
mesonephric duct
 female Q50.5
 male Q55.4
milk N64.89

Cyst (Continued)
Morgagni (hydatid)
 female Q50.5
 male (epididymal) Q55.4
  testicular Q55.29
mouth K09.8
Müllerian duct Q50.4
 appendix testis Q55.29
 cervix Q51.6
 fallopian tube Q50.4
 female Q50.4
 male Q55.29
 prostatic utricle Q55.4
 vagina (embryonal) Q52.4
multilocular (ovary) D39.10
 benign —see Neoplasm, benign, by site
myometrium N85.8
nabothian (follicle) (ruptured) N88.8
nasoalveolar K09.1
nasolabial K09.1
nasopalatine (anterior) (duct) K09.1
nasopharynx J39.2
neoplastic —see Neoplasm, uncertain behavior, by site
 benign —see Neoplasm, benign, by site
nervous system NEC G96.8
neuroenteric (congenital) Q06.8
nipple —see Cyst, breast
nose (turbinates) J34.1
 sinus J34.1
odontogenic, developmental K09.0
omentum (lesser) K66.8
 congenital Q45.8
ora serrata —see Cyst, retina, ora serrata
oral
 region K09.9
  developmental (nonodontogenic) K09.1
  specified NEC K09.8
 soft tissue K09.9
  specified NEC K09.8
orbit H05.81-●
ovary, ovarian (twisted) N83.20-●
 adherent N83.20-●
 chocolate N80.1
 corpus
  albicans N83.29-●
  luteum (hemorrhagic) N83.1-●
 dermoid D27.9
 developmental Q50.1
 due to failure of involution NEC N83.20-●
 endometrial N80.1
 follicular (graafian) (hemorrhagic) N83.0-●
 hemorrhagic N83.20-●
 in pregnancy or childbirth O34.8-●
  with obstructed labor O65.5
 multilocular D39.10
 pseudomucinous D27.9
 retention N83.29-●
 serous N83.20-●
 specified NEC N83.29-●
 theca lutein (hemorrhagic) N83.1-●
 tuberculous A18.18
oviduct N83.8
palate (median) (fissural) K09.1
palatine papilla (jaw) K09.1
pancreas, pancreatic (hemorrhagic) (true) K86.2
 congenital Q45.2
 false K86.3
paralabral
 hip M24.85-●
 shoulder S43.43-●
paramesonephric duct Q50.4
 female Q50.4
 male Q55.29
paranephric N28.1
paraphysis, cerebri, congenital Q04.6
parasitic B89
parathyroid (gland) E21.4
paratubal N83.8
paraurethral duct N36.8
paroophoron Q50.5

Cyst (Continued)
parotid gland K11.6
parovarian Q50.5
pelvis, female N94.89
in pregnancy or childbirth O34.8-•
causing obstructed labor O65.5
penis (sebaceous) N48.89
periapical K04.8
pericardial (congenital) Q24.8
acquired (secondary) I31.8
pericoronal K09.0
periodontal K04.8
lateral K09.0
peripelvic (lymphatic) N28.1
peritoneum K66.8
chylous I89.8
periventricular, acquired, newborn P91.1
pharynx (wall) J39.2
pilar L72.11
pilonidal (infected) (rectum) L05.91
with abscess L05.01
malignant C44.59-•
pituitary (duct) (gland) E23.6
placenta O43.19-•
pleura J94.8
popliteal —see Cyst, Baker's
porencephalic Q04.6
acquired G93.0
postanal (infected) —see Cyst, pilonidal
postmastoidectomy cavity (mucosal) —see
Complications, postmastoidectomy, cyst
preauricular Q18.1
prepuce N47.4
congenital Q55.69
primordial (jaw) K09.0
prostate N42.83
pseudomucinous (ovary) D27.9
pupillary, miotic H21.27-•
radicular (residual) K04.8
radiculodental K04.8
ranular K11.8
Rathke's pouch E23.6
rectum (epithelium) (mucous) K62.89
renal —see Cyst, kidney
residual (radicular) K04.8
retention (ovary) N83.29-•
salivary gland K11.6
retina H33.19-•
ora serrata H33.11-•
parasitic H33.12-•
retroperitoneal K68.9
sacrococcygeal (dermoid) —see Cyst,
pilonidal
salivary gland or duct (mucous extravasation
or retention) K11.6
Sampson's N80.1
sclera H15.89
scrotum L72.9
sebaceous L72.3
sebaceous (duct) (gland) L72.3
breast —see Dysplasia, mammary, specified
type NEC
eyelid —see Cyst, eyelid
genital organ NEC
female N94.89
male N50.89
scrotum L72.3
semilunar cartilage (knee) (multiple) —see
Derangement, knee, meniscus, cystic
seminal vesicle N50.89
serous (ovary) N83.20-•
sinus (accessory) (nasal) J34.1
Skene's gland N36.8
skin L72.9
breast —see Dysplasia, mammary, specified
type NEC
epidermal, epidermoid L72.0
epithelial L72.0
eyelid —see Cyst, eyelid
genital organ NEC
female N90.7
male N50.89

Cyst (Continued)
skin (Continued)
inclusion L72.0
scrotum L72.9
sebaceous L72.3
sweat gland or duct L74.8
solitary
bone —see Cyst, bone, solitary
jaw M27.40
kidney N28.1
spermatic cord N50.89
sphenoid sinus J34.1
spinal meninges G96.19
spleen NEC D73.4
congenital Q89.09
hydatid —see also Echinococcus B67.99 [D77]
Stafne's M27.0
subarachnoid intrasellar R93.0
subcutaneous, pheomycotic (chromomycotic)
B43.2
subdural (cerebral) G93.0
spinal cord G96.19
sublingual gland K11.6
submandibular gland K11.6
submaxillary gland K11.6
suburethral N36.8
suprarenal gland E27.8
suprasellar —see Cyst, brain
sweat gland or duct L74.8
synovial —see also Cyst, bursa
ruptured —see Rupture, synovium
tarsal —see Chalazion
tendon (sheath) —see Disorder, tendon,
specified type NEC
testis N44.2
tunica albuginea N44.1
theca lutein (ovary) N83.1-•
Thornwaldt's J39.2
thymus (gland) E32.8
thyroglossal duct (infected) (persistent)
Q89.2
thyroid (gland) E04.1
thyrolingual duct (infected) (persistent)
Q89.2
tongue K14.8
tonsil J35.8
tooth —see Cyst, dental
Tornwaldt's J39.2
trichilemmal (proliferating) L72.12
trichodermal L72.12
tubal (fallopian) N83.8
inflammatory —see Salpingitis, chronic
tubo-ovarian N83.8
inflammatory N70.13
tunica
albuginea testis N44.1
vaginalis N50.89
turbinate (nose) J34.1
Tyson's gland N48.89
urachus, congenital Q64.4
ureter N28.89
ureterovesical orifice N28.89
urethra, urethral (gland) N36.8
uterine ligament N83.8
uterus (body) (corpus) (recurrent)
N85.8
embryonic Q51.818
cervix Q51.6
vagina, vaginal (implantation) (inclusion)
(squamous cell) (wall) N89.8
embryonic Q52.4
vallecula, vallecular (epiglottis) J38.7
vesical (orifice) N32.89
vitreous body H43.89
vulva (implantation) (inclusion) N90.7
congenital Q52.79
sebaceous gland N90.7
vulvovaginal gland N90.7
wolffian
female Q50.5
male Q55.4

Cystadenocarcinoma —see Neoplasm,
malignant, by site
bile duct C22.1
endometrioid —see Neoplasm, malignant,
by site
specified site —see Neoplasm, malignant,
by site
unspecified site
female C56.9
male C61
mucinous
papillary
specified site —see Neoplasm,
malignant, by site
unspecified site C56.9
specified site —see Neoplasm, malignant,
by site
unspecified site C56.9
papillary
mucinous
specified site —see Neoplasm,
malignant, by site
unspecified site C56.9
pseudomucinous
specified site —see Neoplasm,
malignant, by site
unspecified site C56.9
serous
specified site —see Neoplasm,
malignant, by site
unspecified site C56.9
specified site —see Neoplasm, malignant,
by site
unspecified site C56.9
pseudomucinous
papillary
specified site —see Neoplasm,
malignant, by site
unspecified site C56.9
specified site —see Neoplasm, malignant,
by site
unspecified site C56.9
serous
papillary
specified site —see Neoplasm,
malignant, by site
unspecified site C56.9
specified site —see Neoplasm, malignant,
by site
unspecified site C56.9
Cystadenofibroma
clear cell —see Neoplasm, benign, by site
endometrioid D27.9
borderline malignancy D39.1-•
malignant C56.-•
mucinous
specified site —see Neoplasm, benign, by site
unspecified site D27.9
serous
specified site —see Neoplasm, benign, by site
unspecified site D27.9
specified site —see Neoplasm, benign, by site
unspecified site D27.9
Cystadenoma —see also Neoplasm, benign, by
site
bile duct D13.4
endometrioid —see Neoplasm, benign, by site
borderline malignancy —see Neoplasm,
uncertain behavior, by site
malignant —see Neoplasm, malignant, by site
mucinous
borderline malignancy
ovary C56.-•
specified site NEC —see Neoplasm,
uncertain behavior, by site
unspecified site C56.9
papillary
borderline malignancy
ovary C56.-•
specified site NEC —see Neoplasm,
uncertain behavior, by site
unspecified site C56.9

Cystadenoma (Continued)
    mucinous (Continued)
        papillary (Continued)
            specified site —see Neoplasm, benign,
                by site
            unspecified site D27.9
        specified site —see Neoplasm, benign, by site
        unspecified site D27.9
    papillary
        borderline malignancy
            ovary C56.-●
            specified site NEC —see Neoplasm,
                uncertain behavior, by site
            unspecified site C56.9
        lymphomatosum
            specified site —see Neoplasm, benign,
                by site
            unspecified site D11.9
        mucinous
            borderline malignancy
                ovary C56.-●
                specified site NEC —see Neoplasm,
                    uncertain behavior, by site
                unspecified site C56.9
            specified site —see Neoplasm, benign,
                by site
            unspecified site D27.9
        pseudomucinous
            borderline malignancy
                ovary C56.-●
                specified site NEC —see Neoplasm,
                    uncertain behavior, by site
                unspecified site C56.9
            specified site —see Neoplasm, benign,
                by site
            unspecified site D27.9
        serous
            borderline malignancy
                ovary C56.-●
                specified site NEC —see Neoplasm,
                    uncertain behavior, by site
                unspecified site C56.9
            specified site —see Neoplasm, benign,
                by site
            unspecified site D27.9
        specified site —see Neoplasm, benign, by site
        unspecified site D27.9
    pseudomucinous
        borderline malignancy
            ovary C56.-●
            specified site NEC —see Neoplasm,
                uncertain behavior, by site
            unspecified site C56.9
        papillary
            borderline malignancy
                ovary C56.-●
                specified site NEC —see Neoplasm,
                    uncertain behavior, by site
                unspecified site C56.9
            specified site —see Neoplasm, benign,
                by site
            unspecified site D27.9
        specified site —see Neoplasm, benign, by site
        unspecified site D27.9
    serous
        borderline malignancy
            ovary C56.-●
            specified site NEC —see Neoplasm,
                uncertain behavior, by site
            unspecified site C56.9
        papillary
            borderline malignancy
                ovary C56.-●
                specified site NEC —see Neoplasm,
                    uncertain behavior, by site
                unspecified site C56.9
            specified site —see Neoplasm, benign,
                by site
            unspecified site D27.9
        specified site —see Neoplasm, benign, by site
        unspecified site D27.9

Cystathionine synthase deficiency E72.11
Cystathioninemia E72.19
Cystathioninuria E72.19
Cystic —see also condition
    breast (chronic) —see Mastopathy, cystic
    corpora lutea (hemorrhagic) N83.1-●
    duct —see condition
    eyeball (congenital) Q11.0
    fibrosis —see Fibrosis, cystic
    kidney (congenital) Q61.9
        adult type Q61.2
        infantile type NEC Q61.19
            collecting duct dilatation Q61.11
        medullary Q61.5
    liver, congenital Q44.6
    lung disease J98.4
        congenital Q33.0
    mastitis, chronic —see Mastopathy, cystic
    medullary, kidney Q61.5
    meniscus —see Derangement, knee,
        meniscus, cystic
    ovary N83.20-●
Cysticercosis, cysticerciasis B69.9
    with
        epileptiform fits B69.0
        myositis B69.81
    brain B69.0
    central nervous system B69.0
    cerebral B69.0
    ocular B69.1
    specified NEC B69.89
Cysticercus cellulose infestation —see
    Cysticercosis
Cystinosis (malignant) E72.04
Cystinuria E72.01
Cystitis (exudative) (hemorrhagic) (septic)
    (suppurative) N30.90
    with
        fibrosis —see Cystitis, chronic, interstitial
        hematuria N30.91
        leukoplakia —see Cystitis, chronic,
            interstitial
        malakoplakia —see Cystitis, chronic,
            interstitial
        metaplasia —see Cystitis, chronic, interstitial
        prostatitis N41.3
    acute N30.00
        with hematuria N30.01
        of trigone N30.30
            with hematuria N30.31
    allergic —see Cystitis, specified type NEC
    amebic A06.81
    bilharzial B65.9 [N33]
    blennorrhagic (gonococcal) A54.01
    bullous —see Cystitis, specified type NEC
    calculous N21.0
    chlamydial A56.01
    chronic N30.20
        with hematuria N30.21
        interstitial N30.10
            with hematuria N30.11
        of trigone N30.30
            with hematuria N30.31
        specified NEC N30.20
            with hematuria N30.21
    cystic (a) —see Cystitis, specified type NEC
    diphtheritic A36.85
    echinococcal
        granulosus B67.39
        multilocularis B67.69
    emphysematous —see Cystitis, specified type
        NEC
    encysted —see Cystitis, specified type NEC
    eosinophilic —see Cystitis, specified type
        NEC
    follicular —see Cystitis, of trigone
    gangrenous —see Cystitis, specified type
        NEC
    glandularis —see Cystitis, specified type
        NEC

Cystitis (Continued)
    gonococcal A54.01
    incrusted —see Cystitis, specified type
        NEC
    interstitial (chronic) —see Cystitis, chronic,
        interstitial
    irradiation N30.40
        with hematuria N30.41
    irritation —see Cystitis, specified type
        NEC
    malignant —see Cystitis, specified type
        NEC
    of trigone N30.30
        with hematuria N30.31
    panmural —see Cystitis, chronic, interstitial
    polyposa —see Cystitis, specified type NEC
    prostatic N41.3
    puerperal (postpartum) O86.22
    radiation —see Cystitis, irradiation
    specified type NEC N30.80
        with hematuria N30.81
    subacute —see Cystitis, chronic
    submucous —see Cystitis, chronic, interstitial
    syphilitic (late) A52.76
    trichomonal A59.03
    tuberculous A18.12
    ulcerative —see Cystitis, chronic, interstitial
Cystocele (-urethrocele)
    female N81.10
        with prolapse of uterus —see Prolapse,
            uterus
        lateral N81.12
        midline N81.11
        paravaginal N81.12
    in pregnancy or childbirth O34.8-●
        causing obstructed labor O65.5
    male N32.89
Cystolithiasis N21.0
Cystoma —see also Neoplasm, benign, by site
    endometrial, ovary N80.1
    mucinous
        specified site —see Neoplasm, benign, by site
        unspecified site D27.9
    serous
        specified site —see Neoplasm, benign, by site
        unspecified site D27.9
    simple (ovary) N83.29-●
Cystoplegia N31.2
Cystoptosis N32.89
Cystopyelitis —see Pyelonephritis
Cystorrhagia N32.89
Cystosarcoma phyllodes D48.6-●
    benign D24-●
    malignant —see Neoplasm, breast, malignant
Cystostomy
    attention to Z43.5
    complication —see Complications, cystostomy
    status Z93.50
        appendico-vesicostomy Z93.52
        cutaneous Z93.51
        specified NEC Z93.59
Cystourethritis —see Urethritis
Cystourethrocele —see also Cystocele
    female N81.10
        with uterine prolapse —see Prolapse,
            uterus
        lateral N81.12
        midline N81.11
        paravaginal N81.12
    male N32.89
Cytomegalic inclusion disease
    congenital P35.1
Cytomegalovirus infection B25.9
Cytomycosis (reticuloendothelial) B39.4
Cytopenia D75.9
    refractory
        with multilineage dysplasia D46.A
            and ring sideroblasts (RCMD RS) D46.B
Czerny's disease (periodic hydrarthrosis of the
    knee) —see Effusion, joint, knee

► New   ⇒ Revised   ~~deleted~~ Deleted   ● Use Additional Character(s)

D

Daae (-Finsen) disease (epidemic pleurodynia) B33.0
Dabney's grip B33.0
Da Costa's syndrome F45.8
Dacryoadenitis, dacryadenitis H04.00-●
  acute H04.01-●
  chronic H04.02-●
Dacryocystitis H04.30-●
  acute H04.32-●
  chronic H04.41-●
  neonatal P39.1
  phlegmonous H04.31-●
  syphilitic A52.71
    congenital (early) A50.01
  trachomatous, active A71.1
    sequelae (late effect) B94.0
Dacryocystoblenorrhea —see Inflammation, lacrimal, passages, chronic
Dacryocystocele —see Disorder, lacrimal system, changes
Dacryolith, dacryolithiasis H04.51-●
Dacryoma —see Disorder, lacrimal system, changes
Dacryopericystitis —see Dacryocystitis
Dacryops H04.11-●
Dacryostenosis —see also Stenosis, lacrimal
  congenital Q10.5
Dactylitis
  bone —see Osteomyelitis
  sickle-cell D57.00
    Hb C D57.219
    Hb SS D57.00
    specified NEC D57.819
  skin L08.9
  syphilitic A52.77
  tuberculous A18.03
Dactylolysis spontanea (ainhum) L94.6
Dactylosymphysis Q70.9
  fingers —see Syndactylism, complex, fingers
  toes —see Syndactylism, complex, toes
Damage
  arteriosclerotic —see Arteriosclerosis
  brain (nontraumatic) G93.9
    anoxic, hypoxic G93.1
      resulting from a procedure G97.82
    child NEC G80.9
    due to birth injury P11.2
  cardiorenal (vascular) —see Hypertension, cardiorenal
  cerebral NEC —see Damage, brain
  coccyx, complicating delivery O71.6
  coronary —see Disease, heart, ischemic
  eye, birth injury P15.3
  liver (nontraumatic) K76.9
    alcoholic K70.9
    due to drugs —see Disease, liver, toxic
    toxic —see Disease, liver, toxic
  medication T88.7
  pelvic
    joint or ligament, during delivery O71.6
    organ NEC
      during delivery O71.5
      following ectopic or molar pregnancy O08.6
  renal —see Disease, renal
  subendocardium, subendocardial —see Degeneration, myocardial
  vascular I99.9
Dana-Putnam syndrome (subacute combined sclerosis with pernicious anemia) —see Degeneration, combined
Danbolt (-Cross) syndrome (acrodermatitis enteropathica) E83.2
Dandruff L21.0
Dandy-Walker syndrome Q03.1
  with spina bifida —see Spina bifida
Danlos' syndrome Q79.6

Darier (-White) disease (congenital) Q82.8
  meaning erythema annulare centrifugum L53.1
Darier-Roussy sarcoid D86.3
Darling's disease or histoplasmosis B39.4
Darwin's tubercle Q17.8
Dawson's (inclusion body) encephalitis A81.1
De Beurmann (-Gougerot) disease B42.1
De la Tourette's syndrome F95.2
De Lange's syndrome Q87.1
De Morgan's spots (senile angiomas) I78.1
De Quervain's
  disease (tendon sheath) M65.4
  syndrome E34.51
  thyroiditis (subacute granulomatous thyroiditis) E06.1
De Toni-Fanconi (-Debré) syndrome E72.09
  with cystinosis E72.04
Dead
  fetus, retained (mother) O36.4
    early pregnancy O02.1
  labyrinth —see subcategory H83.2
  ovum, retained O02.0
Deaf nonspeaking NEC H91.3
Deafmutism (acquired) (congenital) NEC H91.3
  hysterical F44.6
  syphilitic, congenital —see also subcategory H94.8 A50.09
Deafness (acquired) (complete) (hereditary) (partial) H91.9-●
  with blue sclera and fragility of bone Q78.0
  auditory fatigue —see Deafness, specified type NEC
  aviation T70.0
    nerve injury —see Injury, nerve, acoustic, specified type NEC
  boilermaker's —see subcategory H83.3
  central —see Deafness, sensorineural
  conductive H90.2
    and sensorineural
      mixed H90.8
        bilateral H90.6
      bilateral H90.0
      unilateral H90.1-●
        with restricted hearing on the contralateral side H90.A-●
  congenital H90.5
    with blue sclera and fragility of bone Q78.0
  due to toxic agents —see Deafness, ototoxic
  emotional (hysterical) F44.6
  functional (hysterical) F44.6
  high frequency H91.9-●
  hysterical F44.6
  low frequency H91.9-●
  mental R48.8
  mixed conductive and sensorineural H90.8
    bilateral H90.6
    unilateral H90.7-●
  nerve —see Deafness, sensorineural
  neural —see Deafness, sensorineural
  noise-induced —see also subcategory H83.3
    nerve injury —see Injury, nerve, acoustic, specified type NEC
  nonspeaking H91.3
  ototoxic —see subcategory H91.0
  perceptive —see Deafness, sensorineural
  psychogenic (hysterical) F44.6
  sensorineural H90.5
    and conductive
      mixed H90.8
        bilateral H90.6
      bilateral H90.3
      unilateral H90.4-●
        with restricted hearing on the contralateral side H90.A-●
  sensory —see Deafness, sensorineural
  specified type NEC —see subcategory H91.8
  sudden (idiopathic) H91.2-●

Deafness (Continued)
  syphilitic A52.15
  transient ischemic H93.01-●
  traumatic —see Injury, nerve, acoustic, specified type NEC
  word (developmental) H93.25
Death (cause unknown) (of) (unexplained) (unspecified cause) R99
  brain G93.82
  cardiac (sudden) (with successful resuscitation) — code to underlying disease
    family history of Z82.41
    personal history of Z86.74
  family member (assumed) Z63.4
Debility (chronic) (general) (nervous) R53.81
  congenital or neonatal NOS P96.9
  nervous R53.81
  old age R54
  senile R54
Débove's disease (splenomegaly) R16.1
Decalcification
  bone —see Osteoporosis
  teeth K03.89
Decapsulation, kidney N28.89
Decay
  dental —see Caries, dental
  senile R54
  tooth, teeth —see Caries, dental
Deciduitis (acute)
  following ectopic or molar pregnancy O08.0
Decline (general) —see Debility
  cognitive, age-associated R41.81
Decompensation
  cardiac (acute) (chronic) —see Disease, heart
  cardiovascular —see Disease, cardiovascular
  heart —see Disease, heart
  hepatic —see Failure, hepatic
  myocardial (acute) (chronic) —see Disease, heart
  respiratory J98.8
Decompression sickness T70.3
Decrease (d)
  absolute neutrophile count —see Neutropenia
  blood
    platelets —see Thrombocytopenia
    pressure R03.1
      due to shock following injury T79.4
        operation T81.19
  estrogen E28.39
    postablative E89.40
      asymptomatic E89.40
      symptomatic E89.41
  fragility of erythrocytes D58.8
  function
    lipase (pancreatic) K90.3
    ovary in hypopituitarism E23.0
    parenchyma of pancreas K86.89
    pituitary (gland) (anterior) (lobe) E23.0
      posterior (lobe) E23.0
  functional activity R68.89
  glucose R73.09
  hematocrit R71.0
  hemoglobin R71.0
  leukocytes D72.819
    specified NEC D72.818
  libido R68.82
  lymphocytes D72.810
  platelets D69.6
  respiration, due to shock following injury T79.4
  sexual desire R68.82
  tear secretion NEC —see Syndrome, dry eye
  tolerance
    fat K90.49
    glucose R73.09
    pancreatic K90.3
    salt and water E87.8
  vision NEC H54.7
  white blood cell count D72.819
    specified NEC D72.818

Decubitus (ulcer) —see Ulcer, pressure, by site
  cervix N86
Deepening acetabulum —see Derangement,
  joint, specified type NEC, hip
Defect, defective Q89.9
  3-beta-hydroxysteroid dehydrogenase E25.0
  11-hydroxylase E25.0
  21-hydroxylase E25.0
  abdominal wall, congenital Q79.59
  antibody immunodeficiency D80.9
  aorticopulmonary septum Q21.4
  atrial septal (ostium secundum type) Q21.1
    following acute myocardial infarction
      (current complication) I23.1
    ostium primum type Q21.2
  atrioventricular
    canal Q21.2
    septum Q21.2
  auricular septal Q21.1
  bilirubin excretion NEC E80.6
  biosynthesis, androgen (testicular) E29.1
  bulbar septum Q21.0
  catalase E80.3
  cell membrane receptor complex (CR3) D71
  circulation I99.9
    congenital Q28.9
    newborn Q28.9
  coagulation (factor) —see also Deficiency,
    factor D68.9
    with
      ectopic pregnancy O08.1
      molar pregnancy O08.1
    acquired D68.4
    antepartum with hemorrhage —see
      Hemorrhage, antepartum, with
      coagulation defect
    due to
      liver disease D68.4
      vitamin K deficiency D68.4
    hereditary NEC D68.2
    intrapartum O67.0
    newborn, transient P61.6
    postpartum O99.13
      with hemorrhage O72.3
    specified type NEC D68.8
  complement system D84.1
  conduction (heart) I45.9
    bone —see Deafness, conductive
  congenital, organ or site not listed —see
    Anomaly, by site
  coronary sinus Q21.1
  cushion, endocardial Q21.2
  degradation, glycoprotein E77.1
  dental bridge, crown, fillings —see Defect,
    dental restoration
  dental restoration K08.50
    specified NEC K08.59
  dentin (hereditary) K00.5
  Descemet's membrane, congenital Q13.89
  developmental —see also Anomaly
    cauda equina Q06.3
  diaphragm
    with elevation, eventration or hernia —see
      Hernia, diaphragm
    congenital Q79.1
      with hernia Q79.0
      gross (with hernia) Q79.0
  ectodermal, congenital Q82.9
  Eisenmenger's Q21.8
  enzyme
    catalase E80.3
    peroxidase E80.3
  esophagus, congenital Q39.9
  extensor retinaculum M62.89
  fibrin polymerization D68.2
  filling
    bladder R93.41
    kidney R93.42-•
    renal pelvis R93.41
    stomach R93.3
    ureter R93.41
    urinary organs, specified NEC R93.49

Defect, defective (Continued)
▶GABA (gamma aminobutyric acid) metabolic
  E72.81
  Gerbode Q21.0
  glycoprotein degradation E77.1
  Hageman (factor) D68.2
  hearing —see Deafness
  high grade F70
  interatrial septal Q21.1
  interauricular septal Q21.1
  interventricular septal Q21.0
    with dextroposition of aorta, pulmonary
      stenosis and hypertrophy of right
      ventricle Q21.3
    in tetralogy of Fallot Q21.3
  learning (specific) —see Disorder, learning
  lymphocyte function antigen-1 (LFA-1) D84.0
  lysosomal enzyme, post-translational
    modification E77.0
  major osseous M89.70
    ankle M89.77-•
    carpus M89.74-•
    clavicle M89.71-•
    femur M89.75-•
    fibula M89.76-•
    fingers M89.74-•
    foot M89.77-•
    forearm M89.73-•
    hand M89.74-•
    humerus M89.72-•
    lower leg M89.76-•
    metacarpus M89.74-•
    metatarsus M89.77-•
    multiple sites M89.79
    pelvic region M89.75-•
    pelvis M89.75-•
    radius M89.73-•
    scapula M89.71-•
    shoulder region M89.71-•
    specified NEC M89.78
    tarsus M89.77-•
    thigh M89.75-•
    tibia M89.76-•
    toes M89.77-•
    ulna M89.73-•
  mental —see Disability, intellectual
  modification, lysosomal enzymes, post-
    translational E77.0
  obstructive, congenital
    renal pelvis Q62.39
    ureter Q62.39
      atresia —see Atresia, ureter
      cecoureterocele Q62.32
      megaureter Q62.2
      orthotopic ureterocele Q62.31
  osseous, major M89.70
    ankle M89.77-•
    carpus M89.74-•
    clavicle M89.71-•
    femur M89.75-•
    fibula M89.76-•
    fingers M89.74-•
    foot M89.77-•
    forearm M89.73-•
    hand M89.74-•
    humerus M89.72-•
    lower leg M89.76-•
    metacarpus M89.74-•
    metatarsus M89.77-•
    multiple sites M89.9
    pelvic region M89.75-•
    pelvis M89.75-•
    radius M89.73-•
    scapula M89.71-•
    shoulder region M89.71-•
    specified NEC M89.78
    tarsus M89.77-•
    thigh M89.75-•
    tibia M89.76-•
    toes M89.77-•
    ulna M89.73-•

Defect, defective (Continued)
  osteochondral NEC —see also Deformity
    M95.8-•
  ostium
    primum Q21.2
    secundum Q21.1
  peroxidase E80.3
  placental blood supply —see Insufficiency,
    placental
  platelets, qualitative D69.1
    constitutional D68.0
  postural NEC, spine —see Dorsopathy,
    deforming
  reduction
    limb Q73.8
      lower Q72.9-•
        absence —see Agenesis, leg
          foot —see Agenesis, foot
        longitudinal
          femur Q72.4-•
          fibula Q72.6-•
          tibia Q72.5-•
        specified type NEC Q72.89-•
        split foot Q72.7-•
      specified type NEC Q73.8
      upper Q71.9-•
        absence —see Agenesis, arm
          forearm —see Agenesis, forearm
          hand —see Agenesis, hand
        lobster-claw hand Q71.6-•
        longitudinal
          radius Q71.4-•
          ulna Q71.5-•
        specified type NEC Q71.89-•
  renal pelvis Q63.8
    obstructive Q62.39
  respiratory system, congenital Q34.9
  restoration, dental K08.50
    specified NEC K08.59
  retinal nerve bundle fibers H35.89
  septal (heart) NOS Q21.9
    acquired (atrial) (auricular) (ventricular)
      (old) I51.0
    atrial Q21.1
      concurrent with acute myocardial
        infarction —see Infarct, myocardium
      following acute myocardial infarction
        (current complication) I23.1
      ventricular —see also Defect, ventricular
        septal Q21.0
  sinus venosus Q21.1
  speech R47.9
    developmental F80.9
    specified NEC R47.89
  Taussig-Bing (aortic transposition and
    overriding pulmonary artery) Q20.1
  teeth, wedge K03.1
  vascular (local) I99.9
    congenital Q27.9
  ventricular septal Q21.0
    concurrent with acute myocardial
      infarction —see Infarct, myocardium
    following acute myocardial infarction
      (current complication) I23.2
    in tetralogy of Fallot Q21.3
  vision NEC H54.7
  visual field H53.40
    bilateral
      heteronymous H53.47
      homonymous H53.46-•
    generalized contraction H53.48-•
    localized
      arcuate H53.43-•
      scotoma (central area) H53.41-•
        blind spot area H53.42-•
      sector H53.43-•
      specified type NEC H53.45-•
  voice R49.9
    specified NEC R49.8
  wedge, tooth, teeth (abrasion) K03.1
Deferentitis N49.1
  gonorrheal (acute) (chronic) A54.23

▶ New   ⇒ Revised   ~~deleted~~ Deleted   • Use Additional Character(s)

Defibrination (syndrome) D65
  antepartum —see Hemorrhage, antepartum,
      with coagulation defect, disseminated
      intravascular coagulation
  following ectopic or molar pregnancy O08.1
  intrapartum O67.0
  newborn P60
  postpartum O72.3
Deficiency, deficient
  3-beta hydroxysteroid dehydrogenase E25.0
  11-hydroxylase E25.0
  21-hydroxylase E25.0
  5-alpha reductase (with male
      pseudohermaphroditism) E29.1
  abdominal muscle syndrome Q79.4
  AC globulin (congenital) (hereditary) D68.2
    acquired D68.4
  accelerator globulin (Ac G) (blood) D68.2
  acid phosphatase E83.39
  activating factor (blood) D68.2
  adenosine deaminase (ADA) D81.3
  aldolase (hereditary) E74.19
  alpha-1-antitrypsin E88.01
  amino-acids E72.9
  anemia —see Anemia
  aneurin E51.9
  antibody with
    hyperimmunoglobulinemia D80.6
    near-normal immunoglobins D80.6
  antidiuretic hormone E23.2
  anti-hemophilic
    factor (A) D66
      B D67
      C D68.1
    globulin (AHG) NEC D66
  antithrombin (antithrombin III) D68.59
  ascorbic acid E54
  attention (disorder) (syndrome) F98.8
    with hyperactivity —see Disorder,
        attention-deficit hyperactivity
  autoprothrombin
    I D68.2
    II D67
    C D68.2
  beta-glucuronidase E76.29
  biotin E53.8
  biotin-dependent carboxylase D81.819
  biotinidase D81.810
  brancher enzyme (amylopectinosis) E74.03
  C1 esterase inhibitor (C1-INH) D84.1
  calciferol E55.9
    with
      adult osteomalacia M83.8
      rickets —see Rickets
  calcium (dietary) E58
  calorie, severe E43
    with marasmus E41
      and kwashiorkor E42
  cardiac —see Insufficiency, myocardial
  carnitine E71.40
    due to
      hemodialysis E71.43
      inborn errors of metabolism E71.42
      Valproic acid therapy E71.43
    iatrogenic E71.43
    muscle palmityltransferase E71.314
    primary E71.41
    secondary E71.448
  carotene E50.9
  central nervous system G96.8
  ceruloplasmin (Wilson) E83.01
  choline E53.8
  Christmas factor D67
  chromium E61.4
  clotting (blood) —see also Deficiency,
      coagulation factor D68.9
  clotting factor NEC (hereditary) —see also
      Deficiency, factor D68.2
  coagulation NOS D68.9
    with
      ectopic pregnancy O08.1
      molar pregnancy O08.1

Deficiency, deficient (Continued)
  coagulation NOS (Continued)
    acquired (any) D68.4
    antepartum hemorrhage —see
        Hemorrhage, antepartum, with
        coagulation defect
    clotting factor NEC —see also Deficiency,
        factor D68.2
    due to
      hyperprothrombinemia D68.4
      liver disease D68.4
      vitamin K deficiency D68.4
    newborn, transient P61.6
    postpartum O72.3
    specified NEC D68.8
  cognitive F09
  color vision H53.50
    achromatopsia H53.51
    acquired H53.52
    deuteranomaly H53.53
    protanomaly H53.54
    specified type NEC H53.59
    tritanomaly H53.55
  combined glucocorticoid and
      mineralocorticoid E27.49
  contact factor D68.2
  copper (nutritional) E61.0
  corticoadrenal E27.40
    primary E27.1
  craniofacial axis Q75.0
  cyanocobalamin E53.8
  debrancher enzyme (limit dextrinosis) E74.03
  dehydrogenase
    long chain/very long chain acyl CoA
        E71.310
    medium chain acyl CoA E71.311
    short chain acyl CoA E71.312
  diet E63.9
  dihydropyrimidine dehydrogenase (DPD)
      E88.89
  disaccharidase E73.9
  edema —see Malnutrition, severe
  endocrine E34.9
  energy-supply —see Malnutrition
  enzymes, circulating NEC E88.09
  ergosterol E55.9
    with
      adult osteomalacia M83.8
      rickets —see Rickets
  essential fatty acid (EFA) E63.0
  factor —see also Deficiency, coagulation
    Hageman D68.2
    I (congenital) (hereditary) D68.2
    II (congenital) (hereditary) D68.2
    IX (congenital) (functional) (hereditary)
        (with functional defect) D67
    multiple (congenital) D68.8
      acquired D68.4
    V (congenital) (hereditary) D68.2
    VII (congenital) (hereditary) D68.2
    VIII (congenital) (functional) (hereditary)
        (with functional defect) D66
      with vascular defect D68.0
    X (congenital) (hereditary) D68.2
    XI (congenital) (hereditary) D68.1
    XII (congenital) (hereditary) D68.2
    XIII (congenital) (hereditary) D68.2
  femoral, proximal focal (congenital) —
      see Defect, reduction, lower limb,
      longitudinal, femur
  fibrin-stabilizing factor (congenital)
      (hereditary) D68.2
    acquired D68.4
  fibrinase D68.2
  fibrinogen (congenital) (hereditary) D68.2
    acquired D65
  folate E53.8
  folic acid E53.8
  foreskin N47.3
  fructokinase E74.11
  fructose 1,6-diphosphatase E74.19

Deficiency, deficient (Continued)
  fructose-1-phosphate aldolase E74.19
  ▶GABA (gamma aminobutyric acid)
      transaminase E72.81
  ▶GABA-T (gamma aminobutyric acid
      transaminase) E72.81
  galactokinase E74.29
  galactose-1-phosphate uridyl transferase
      E74.29
  gammaglobulin in blood D80.1
    hereditary D80.0
  glass factor D68.2
  glucocorticoid E27.49
    mineralocorticoid E27.49
  glucose-6-phosphatase E74.01
  glucose-6-phosphate dehydrogenase anemia
      D55.0
  glucuronyl transferase E80.5
  glycogen synthetase E74.09
  gonadotropin (isolated) E23.0
  growth hormone (idiopathic) (isolated) E23.0
  Hageman factor D68.2
  hemoglobin D64.9
  hepatophosphorylase E74.09
  homogentisate 1,2-dioxygenase E70.29
  hormone
    anterior pituitary (partial) NEC E23.0
      growth E23.0
    growth (isolated) E23.0
    pituitary E23.0
    testicular E29.1
  hypoxanthine-(guanine)-
      phosphoribosyltransferase (HG-PRT)
      (total HG-PRT) E79.1
  immunity D84.9
    cell-mediated D84.8
      with thrombocytopenia and eczema D82.0
    combined D81.9
    humoral D80.9
    IgA (secretory) D80.2
    IgG D80.3
    IgM D80.4
  immuno —see Immunodeficiency
  immunoglobulin, selective
    A (IgA) D80.2
    G (IgG) (subclasses) D80.3
    M (IgM) D80.4
  inositol (B complex) E53.8
  intrinsic
    factor (congenital) D51.0
    sphincter N36.42
      with urethral hypermobility N36.43
  iodine E61.8
    congenital syndrome —see Syndrome,
        iodine-deficiency, congenital
  iron E61.1
    anemia D50.9
  kalium E87.6
  kappa-light chain D80.8
  labile factor (congenital) (hereditary) D68.2
    acquired D68.4
  lacrimal fluid (acquired) —see also Syndrome,
      dry eye
    congenital Q10.6
  lactase
    congenital E73.0
    secondary E73.1
  Laki-Lorand factor D68.2
  lecithin cholesterol acyltransferase E78.6
  lipocaic K86.89
  lipoprotein (familial) (high density) E78.6
  liver phosphorylase E74.09
  lysosomal alpha-1, 4 glucosidase E74.02
  magnesium E61.2
  major histocompatibility complex
    class I D81.6
    class II D81.7
  manganese E61.3
  menadione (vitamin K) E56.1
    newborn P53
  mental (familial) (hereditary) —see Disability,
      intellectual

Deficiency, deficient (Continued)
  methylenetetrahydrofolate reductase
      (MTHFR) E72.12
  mevalonate kinase M04.1
  mineral NEC E61.8
  mineralocorticoid E27.49
      with glucocorticoid E27.49
  molybdenum (nutritional) E61.5
  moral F60.2
  multiple nutrient elements E61.7
▶ multiple sulfatase (MSD) E75.26
  muscle
      carnitine (palmityltransferase) E71.314
      phosphofructokinase E74.09
  myoadenylate deaminase E79.2
  myocardial —see Insufficiency, myocardial
  myophosphorylase E74.04
  NADH diaphorase or reductase (congenital)
      D74.0
  NADH-methemoglobin reductase
      (congenital) D74.0
  natrium E87.1
  niacin (amide) (-tryptophan) E52
  nicotinamide E52
  nicotinic acid E52
  number of teeth —see Anodontia
  nutrient element E61.9
      multiple E61.7
      specified NEC E61.8
  nutrition, nutritional E63.9
      sequelae —see Sequelae, nutritional
          deficiency
      specified NEC E63.8
  of interleukin 1 receptor antagonist [DIRA]
      M04.8
  ornithine transcarbamylase E72.4
  ovarian E28.39
  oxygen —see Anoxia
  pantothenic acid E53.8
  parathyroid (gland) E20.9
  perineum (female) N81.89
  phenylalanine hydroxylase E70.1
  phosphoenolpyruvate carboxykinase E74.4
  phosphofructokinase E74.19
  phosphomannomutase E74.8
  phosphomannose isomerase E74.8
  phosphomannosyl mutase E74.8
  phosphorylase kinase, liver E74.09
  pituitary hormone (isolated) E23.0
  plasma thromboplastin
      antecedent (PTA) D68.1
      component (PTC) D67
▶ plasminogen (type 1) (type 2) E88.02
  platelet NEC D69.1
      constitutional D68.0
  polyglandular E31.8
      autoimmune E31.0
  potassium (K) E87.6
  prepuce N47.3
  proaccelerin (congenital) (hereditary) D68.2
      acquired D68.4
  proconvertin factor (congenital) (hereditary)
      D68.2
      acquired D68.4
  protein —see also Malnutrition E46
      anemia D53.0
      C D68.59
      S D68.59
  prothrombin (congenital) (hereditary) D68.2
      acquired D68.4
  Prower factor D68.2
  pseudocholinesterase E88.09
  PTA (plasma thromboplastin antecedent) D68.1
  PTC (plasma thromboplastin component) D67
  purine nucleoside phosphorylase (PNP) D81.5
  pyracin (alpha) (beta) E53.1
  pyridoxal E53.1
  pyridoxamine E53.1
  pyridoxine (derivatives) E53.1
  pyruvate
      carboxylase E74.4
      dehydrogenase E74.4

Deficiency, deficient (Continued)
  riboflavin (vitamin B2) E53.0
  salt E87.1
  secretion
      ovary E28.39
      salivary gland (any) K11.7
      urine R34
  selenium (dietary) E59
  serum antitrypsin, familial E88.01
  short stature homeobox gene (SHOX)
      with
          dyschondrosteosis Q78.8
          short stature (idiopathic) E34.3
          Turner's syndrome Q96.9
  sodium (Na) E87.1
  SPCA (factor VII) D68.2
  sphincter, intrinsic N36.42
      with urethral hypermobility N36.43
  stable factor (congenital) (hereditary) D68.2
      acquired D68.4
  Stuart-Prower (factor X) D68.2
▶ succinic semialdehyde dehydrogenase E72.81
  sucrase E74.39
⇉ sulfatase E75.26
  sulfite oxidase E72.19
  thiamin, thiaminic (chloride) E51.9
      beriberi (dry) E51.11
          wet E51.12
  thrombokinase D68.2
      newborn P53
  thyroid (gland) —see Hypothyroidism
  tocopherol E56.0
  tooth bud K00.0
  transcobalamine II (anemia) D51.2
  vanadium E61.6
  vascular I99.9
  vasopressin E23.2
  vertical ridge K06.8
  viosterol —see Deficiency, calciferol
  vitamin (multiple) NOS E56.9
      A E50.9
          with
              Bitot's spot (corneal) E50.1
              follicular keratosis E50.8
              keratomalacia E50.4
              manifestations NEC E50.8
              night blindness E50.5
              scar of cornea, xerophthalmic E50.6
              xeroderma E50.8
              xerophthalmia E50.7
              xerosis
                  conjunctival E50.0
                      and Bitot's spot E50.1
                  cornea E50.2
                      and ulceration E50.3
          sequelae E64.1
      B (complex) NOS E53.9
          with
              beriberi (dry) E51.11
                  wet E51.12
              pellagra E52
      B1 NOS E51.9
          beriberi (dry) E51.11
              with circulatory system
                  manifestations E51.11
              wet E51.12
      B12 E53.8
      B2 (riboflavin) E53.0
      B6 E53.1
      C E54
          sequelae E64.2
      D E55.9
          with
              adult osteomalacia M83.8
              rickets —see Rickets
          25-hydroxylase E83.32
      E E56.0
      folic acid E53.8
      G E53.0
      group B E53.9
          specified NEC E53.8

Deficiency, deficient (Continued)
  vitamin (Continued)
      H (biotin) E53.8
      K E56.1
          of newborn P53
      nicotinic E52
      P E56.8
      PP (pellagra-preventing) E52
      specified NEC E56.8
      thiamin E51.9
          beriberi —see Beriberi
  zinc, dietary E60
Deficit —see also Deficiency
  attention and concentration R41.840
      following
          cerebral infarction I69.310
          cerebrovascular disease I69.910
              specified disease NEC I69.810
          nontraumatic
              intracerebral hemorrhage I69.110
              specified intracranial hemorrhage
                  NEC I69.210
              subarachnoid hemorrhage I69.010
      disorder —see Attention, deficit
  cognitive
      communication R41.841
      emotional
          following
              cerebral infarction I69.315
              cerebrovascular disease I69.915
                  specified disease NEC I69.815
              nontraumatic
                  intracerebral hemorrhage I69.115
                  specified intracranial hemorrhage
                      NEC I69.215
                  subarachnoid hemorrhage I69.015
      following
          cerebral infarction I69.319
          cerebrovascular disease I69.919
              specified disease NEC I69.819
          nontraumatic
              intracerebral hemorrhage I69.119
              specified intracranial hemorrhage
                  NEC I69.219
              subarachnoid hemorrhage I69.019
      social
          following
              cerebral infarction I69.315
              cerebrovascular disease I69.915
                  specified disease NEC I69.815
              nontraumatic
                  intracerebral hemorrhage I69.115
                  specified intracranial hemorrhage
                      NEC I69.215
                  subarachnoid hemorrhage I69.015
  cognitive NEC R41.89
      following
          cerebral infarction I69.318
          cerebrovascular disease I69.918
              specified disease NEC I69.818
          nontraumatic
              intracerebral hemorrhage I69.118
              specified intracranial hemorrhage
                  NEC I69.218
              subarachnoid hemorrhage I69.018
  concentration R41.840
  executive function R41.844
      following
          cerebral infarction I69.314
          cerebrovascular disease I69.914
              specified disease NEC I69.814
          nontraumatic
              intracerebral hemorrhage I69.114
              specified intracranial hemorrhage
                  NEC I69.214
              subarachnoid hemorrhage I69.014
  frontal lobe R41.844
      following
          cerebral infarction I69.314
          cerebrovascular disease I69.914
              specified disease NEC I69.814

Deficit *(Continued)*
frontal lobe *(Continued)*
following *(Continued)*
nontraumatic
intracerebral hemorrhage I69.114
specified intracranial hemorrhage NEC I69.214
subarachnoid hemorrhage I69.014
memory
following
cerebral infarction I69.311
cerebrovascular disease I69.911
specified disease NEC I69.811
nontraumatic
intracerebral hemorrhage I69.111
specified intracranial hemorrhage NEC I69.211
subarachnoid hemorrhage I69.011
neurologic NEC R29.818
ischemic
reversible (RIND) I63.9
prolonged (PRIND) I63.9
oxygen R09.02
prolonged reversible ischemic neurologic (PRIND) I63.9
psychomotor R41.843
following
cerebral infarction I69.313
cerebrovascular disease I69.913
specified disease NEC I69.813
nontraumatic
intracerebral hemorrhage I69.113
specified intracranial hemorrhage NEC I69.213
subarachnoid hemorrhage I69.013
visuospatial R41.842
following
cerebral infarction I69.312
cerebrovascular disease I69.912
specified disease NEC I69.812
nontraumatic
intracerebral hemorrhage I69.112
specified intracranial hemorrhage NEC I69.212
subarachnoid hemorrhage I69.012
Deflection
radius —*see* Deformity, limb, specified type NEC, forearm
septum (acquired) (nasal) (nose) J34.2
spine —*see* Curvature, spine
turbinate (nose) J34.2
Defluvium
capillorum —*see* Alopecia
ciliorum —*see* Madarosis
unguium L60.8
Deformity Q89.9
abdomen, congenital Q89.9
abdominal wall
acquired M95.8
congenital Q79.59
acquired (unspecified site) M95.9
adrenal gland Q89.1
alimentary tract, congenital Q45.9
upper Q40.9
ankle (joint) (acquired) —*see also* Deformity, limb, lower leg
abduction —*see* Contraction, joint, ankle
congenital Q68.8
contraction —*see* Contraction, joint, ankle
specified type NEC —*see* Deformity, limb, foot, specified NEC
anus (acquired) K62.89
congenital Q43.9
aorta (arch) (congenital) Q25.40
acquired I77.89
aortic
arch, acquired I77.89
cusp or valve (congenital) Q23.8
acquired —*see also* Endocarditis, aortic I35.8

Deformity *(Continued)*
arm (acquired) (upper) —*see also* Deformity, limb, upper arm
congenital Q68.8
forearm —*see* Deformity, limb, forearm
artery (congenital) (peripheral) NOS Q27.9
acquired I77.89
coronary (acquired) I25.9
congenital Q24.5
umbilical Q27.0
atrial septal Q21.1
auditory canal (external) (congenital) —*see also* Malformation, ear, external
acquired —*see* Disorder, ear, external, specified type NEC
auricle
ear (congenital) —*see also* Malformation, ear, external
acquired —*see* Disorder, pinna, deformity
back —*see* Dorsopathy, deforming
bile duct (common) (congenital) (hepatic) Q44.5
acquired K83.8
biliary duct or passage (congenital) Q44.5
acquired K83.8
bladder (neck) (trigone) (sphincter) (acquired) N32.89
congenital Q64.79
bone (acquired) NOS M95.9
congenital Q79.9
turbinate M95.0
brain (congenital) Q04.9
acquired G93.89
reduction Q04.3
breast (acquired) N64.89
congenital Q83.9
reconstructed N65.0
bronchus (congenital) Q32.4
acquired NEC J98.09
bursa, congenital Q79.9
canaliculi (lacrimalis) (acquired) —*see also* Disorder, lacrimal system, changes
congenital Q10.6
canthus, acquired —*see* Disorder, eyelid, specified type NEC
capillary (acquired) I78.8
cardiovascular system, congenital Q28.9
caruncle, lacrimal (acquired) —*see also* Disorder, lacrimal system, changes
congenital Q10.6
cascade, stomach K31.2
cecum (congenital) Q43.9
acquired K63.89
cerebral, acquired G93.89
congenital Q04.9
cervix (uterus) (acquired) NEC N88.8
congenital Q51.9
cheek (acquired) M95.2
congenital Q18.9
chest (acquired) (wall) M95.4
congenital Q67.8
sequelae (late effect) of rickets E64.3
chin (acquired) M95.2
congenital Q18.9
choroid (congenital) Q14.3
acquired H31.8
plexus Q07.8
acquired G96.19
cicatricial —*see* Cicatrix
cilia, acquired —*see* Disorder, eyelid, specified type NEC
clavicle (acquired) M95.8
congenital Q68.8
clitoris (congenital) Q52.6
acquired N90.89
clubfoot —*see* Clubfoot
coccyx (acquired) —*see* subcategory M43.8
colon (congenital) Q43.9
acquired K63.89

Deformity *(Continued)*
concha (ear), congenital —*see also* Malformation, ear, external
acquired —*see* Disorder, pinna, deformity
cornea (acquired) H18.70
congenital Q13.4
descemetocele —*see* Descemetocele
ectasia —*see* Ectasia, cornea
specified NEC H18.79-●
staphyloma —*see* Staphyloma, cornea
coronary artery (acquired) I25.9
congenital Q24.5
cranium (acquired) —*see* Deformity, skull
cricoid cartilage (congenital) Q31.8
acquired J38.7
cystic duct (congenital) Q44.5
acquired K82.8
Dandy-Walker Q03.1
with spina bifida —*see* Spina bifida
diaphragm (congenital) Q79.1
acquired J98.6
digestive organ NOS Q45.9
ductus arteriosus Q25.0
duodenal bulb K31.89
duodenum (congenital) Q43.9
acquired K31.89
dura —*see* Deformity, meninges
ear (acquired) —*see also* Disorder, pinna, deformity
congenital (external) Q17.9
internal Q16.5
middle Q16.4
ossicles Q16.3
ossicles Q16.3
ectodermal (congenital) NEC Q84.9
ejaculatory duct (congenital) Q55.4
acquired N50.89
elbow (joint) (acquired) —*see also* Deformity, limb, upper arm
congenital Q68.8
contraction —*see* Contraction, joint, elbow
endocrine gland NEC Q89.2
epididymis (congenital) Q55.4
acquired N50.89
epiglottis (congenital) Q31.8
acquired J38.7
esophagus (congenital) Q39.9
acquired K22.8
eustachian tube (congenital) NEC Q17.8
eye, congenital Q15.9
eyebrow (congenital) Q18.8
eyelid (acquired) —*see also* Disorder, eyelid, specified type NEC
congenital Q10.3
face (acquired) M95.2
congenital Q18.9
fallopian tube, acquired N83.8
femur (acquired) —*see* Deformity, limb, specified type NEC, thigh
fetal
with fetopelvic disproportion O33.7
causing obstructed labor O66.3
finger (acquired) M20.00-●
boutonniere M20.02-●
congenital Q68.1
flexion contracture —*see* Contraction, joint, hand
mallet finger M20.01-●
specified NEC M20.09-●
swan-neck M20.03-●
flexion (joint) (acquired) —*see also* Deformity, limb, flexion M21.20
congenital NOS Q74.9
hip Q65.89
foot (acquired) —*see also* Deformity, limb, lower leg
cavovarus (congenital) Q66.1
congenital NOS Q66.9
specified type NEC Q66.89

▶ New   ⟹ Revised   ~~deleted~~ Deleted   ● Use Additional Character(s)

Deformity (Continued)
  foot (Continued)
    specified type NEC —see Deformity, limb,
      foot, specified NEC
    valgus (congenital) Q66.6
      acquired —see Deformity, valgus, ankle
    varus (congenital) NEC Q66.3
      acquired —see Deformity, varus, ankle
  forearm (acquired) —see also Deformity, limb,
    forearm
    congenital Q68.8
  forehead (acquired) M95.2
    congenital Q75.8
  frontal bone (acquired) M95.2
    congenital Q75.8
  gallbladder (congenital) Q44.1
    acquired K82.8
  gastrointestinal tract (congenital) NOS
    Q45.9
    acquired K63.89
  genitalia, genital organ(s) or system NEC
    female (congenital) Q52.9
      acquired N94.89
      external Q52.70
    male (congenital) Q55.9
      acquired N50.89
  globe (eye) (congenital) Q15.8
    acquired H44.89
  gum, acquired NEC K06.8
  hand (acquired) —see Deformity, limb,
    hand
    congenital Q68.1
  head (acquired) M95.2
    congenital Q75.8
  heart (congenital) Q24.9
    septum Q21.9
      auricular Q21.1
      ventricular Q21.0
    valve (congenital) NEC Q24.8
      acquired —see Endocarditis
  heel (acquired) —see Deformity, foot
  hepatic duct (congenital) Q44.5
    acquired K83.8
  hip (joint) (acquired) —see also Deformity,
    limb, thigh
    congenital Q65.9
    due to (previous) juvenile
      osteochondrosis —see Coxa, plana
    flexion —see Contraction, joint, hip
  hourglass —see Contraction, hourglass
  humerus (acquired) M21.82-●
    congenital Q74.0
  hypophyseal (congenital) Q89.2
  ileocecal (coil) (valve) (acquired) K63.89
    congenital Q43.9
  ileum (congenital) Q43.9
    acquired K63.89
  ilium (acquired) M95.5
    congenital Q74.2
  integument (congenital) Q84.9
  intervertebral cartilage or disc (acquired) —
    see Disorder, disc, specified NEC
  intestine (large) (small) (congenital) NOS
    Q43.9
    acquired K63.89
  intrinsic minus or plus (hand) —see
    Deformity, limb, specified type NEC,
    forearm
  iris (acquired) H21.89
    congenital Q13.2
  ischium (acquired) M95.5
    congenital Q74.2
  jaw (acquired) (congenital) M26.9
  joint (acquired) NEC M21.90
    congenital Q68.8
    elbow M21.92-●
    hand M21.94-●
    hip M21.95-●
    knee M21.96-●
    shoulder M21.92-●
    wrist M21.93-●

Deformity (Continued)
  kidney(s) (calyx) (pelvis) (congenital) Q63.9
    acquired N28.89
    artery (congenital) Q27.2
      acquired I77.89
  Klippel-Feil (brevicollis) Q76.1
  knee (acquired) NEC —see also Deformity,
    limb, lower leg
    congenital Q68.2
  labium (majus) (minus) (congenital) Q52.79
    acquired N90.89
  lacrimal passages or duct (congenital) NEC
    Q10.6
    acquired —see Disorder, lacrimal system,
      changes
  larynx (muscle) (congenital) Q31.8
    acquired J38.7
    web (glottic) Q31.0
  leg (upper) (acquired) NEC —see also
    Deformity, limb, thigh
    congenital Q68.8
    lower leg —see Deformity, limb, lower leg
  lens (acquired) H27.8
    congenital Q12.9
  lid (fold) (acquired) —see also Disorder,
    eyelid, specified type NEC
    congenital Q10.3
  ligament (acquired) —see Disorder, ligament
    congenital Q79.9
  limb (acquired) M21.90
    clawfoot M21.53-●
    clawhand M21.51-●
    clubfoot M21.54-●
    clubhand M21.52-●
    congenital, except reduction deformity
      Q74.9
    flat foot M21.4-●
    flexion M21.20
      ankle M21.27-●
      elbow M21.22-●
      finger M21.24-●
      hip M21.25-●
      knee M21.26-●
      shoulder M21.21-●
      toe M21.27-●
      wrist M21.23-●
    foot
      claw —see Deformity, limb, clawfoot
      club —see Deformity, limb, clubfoot
      drop M21.37-●
      flat —see Deformity, limb, flat foot
      specified NEC M21.6X-●
    forearm M21.93-●
    hand M21.94-●
    lower leg M21.96-●
    specified type NEC M21.80
      forearm M21.83-●
      lower leg M21.86-●
      thigh M21.85-●
      upper arm M21.82-●
    thigh M21.95-●
    unequal length M21.70
      short site is
        femur M21.75-●
        fibula M21.76-●
        humerus M21.72-●
        radius M21.73-●
        tibia M21.76-●
        ulna M21.73-●
      upper arm M21.92-●
    valgus —see Deformity, valgus
    varus —see Deformity, varus
    wrist drop M21.33-●
  lip (acquired) NEC K13.0
    congenital Q38.0
  liver (congenital) Q44.7
    acquired K76.89
  lumbosacral (congenital) (joint) (region) Q76.49
    acquired subcategory M43.8
    kyphosis —see Kyphosis, congenital
    lordosis —see Lordosis, congenital

Deformity (Continued)
  lung (congenital) Q33.9
    acquired J98.4
  lymphatic system, congenital Q89.9
  Madelung's (radius) Q74.0
  mandible (acquired) (congenital) M26.9
  maxilla (acquired) (congenital) M26.9
  meninges or membrane (congenital) Q07.9
    cerebral Q04.8
      acquired G96.19
    spinal cord (congenital) G96.19
      acquired G96.19
  metacarpus (acquired) —see Deformity, limb,
    forearm
    congenital Q74.0
  metatarsus (acquired) —see Deformity,
    foot
    congenital Q66.9
  middle ear (congenital) Q16.4
    ossicles Q16.3
  mitral (leaflets) (valve) I05.8
    parachute Q23.2
    stenosis, congenital Q23.2
  mouth (acquired) K13.79
    congenital Q38.6
  multiple, congenital NEC Q89.7
  muscle (acquired) M62.89
    congenital Q79.9
      sternocleidomastoid Q68.0
  musculoskeletal system (acquired) M95.9
    congenital Q79.9
    specified NEC M95.8
  nail (acquired) L60.8
    congenital Q84.6
  nasal —see Deformity, nose
  neck (acquired) M95.3
    congenital Q18.9
      sternocleidomastoid Q68.0
  nervous system (congenital) Q07.9
  nipple (congenital) Q83.9
    acquired N64.89
  nose (acquired) (cartilage) M95.0
    bone (turbinate) M95.0
    congenital Q30.9
      bent or squashed Q67.4
    saddle M95.0
      syphilitic A50.57
    septum (acquired) J34.2
      congenital Q30.8
    sinus (wall) (congenital) Q30.8
      acquired M95.0
    syphilitic (congenital) A50.57
      late A52.73
  ocular muscle (congenital) Q10.3
    acquired —see Strabismus, mechanical
  opticociliary vessels (congenital) Q13.2
  orbit (eye) (acquired) H05.30
    atrophy —see Atrophy, orbit
    congenital Q10.7
    due to
      bone disease NEC H05.32-●
      trauma or surgery H05.33-●
    enlargement —see Enlargement, orbit
    exostosis —see Exostosis, orbit
  organ of Corti (congenital) Q16.5
  ovary (congenital) Q50.39
    acquired N83.8
  oviduct, acquired N83.8
  palate (congenital) Q38.5
    acquired K27.8
    cleft (congenital) —see Cleft, palate
  pancreas (congenital) Q45.3
    acquired K86.89
  parathyroid (gland) Q89.2
  parotid (gland) (congenital) Q38.4
    acquired K11.8
  patella (acquired) —see Disorder, patella,
    specified NEC
  pelvis, pelvic (acquired) (bony) M95.5
    with disproportion (fetopelvic) O33.0
      causing obstructed labor O65.0

▶ New ⇒ Revised ~~deleted~~ Deleted ● Use Additional Character(s)

Deformity (Continued)

pelvis, pelvic (Continued)
congenital Q74.2
rachitic sequelae (late effect) E64.3
penis (glans) (congenital) Q55.69
acquired N48.89
pericardium (congenital) Q24.8
acquired —see Pericarditis
pharynx (congenital) Q38.8
acquired J39.2
pinna, acquired —see also Disorder, pinna, deformity
congenital Q17.9
pituitary (congenital) Q89.2
posture —see Dorsopathy, deforming
prepuce (congenital) Q55.69
acquired N47.8
prostate (congenital) Q55.4
acquired N42.89
pupil (congenital) Q13.2
acquired —see Abnormality, pupillary
pylorus (congenital) Q40.3
acquired K31.89
rachitic (acquired), old or healed E64.3
radius (acquired) —see also Deformity, limb, forearm
congenital Q68.8
rectum (congenital) Q43.9
acquired K62.89
reduction (extremity) (limb), congenital (see also condition and site) Q73.8
brain Q04.3
lower —see Defect, reduction, lower limb
upper —see Defect, reduction, upper limb
renal —see Deformity, kidney
respiratory system (congenital) Q34.9
rib (acquired) M95.4
congenital Q76.6
cervical Q76.5
rotation (joint) (acquired) —see Deformity, limb, specified site NEC
congenital Q74.9
hip —see Deformity, limb, specified type NEC, thigh
congenital Q65.89
sacroiliac joint (congenital) Q74.2
acquired —see subcategory M43.8
sacrum (acquired) —see subcategory M43.8
saddle
back —see Lordosis
nose M95.0
syphilitic A50.57
salivary gland or duct (congenital) Q38.4
acquired K11.8
scapula (acquired) M95.8
congenital Q68.8
scrotum (congenital) —see also Malformation, testis and scrotum
acquired N50.89
seminal vesicles (congenital) Q55.4
acquired N50.89
septum, nasal (acquired) J34.2
shoulder (joint) (acquired) —see Deformity, limb, upper arm
congenital Q74.0
contraction —see Contraction, joint, shoulder
sigmoid (flexure) (congenital) Q43.9
acquired K63.89
skin (congenital) Q82.9
skull (acquired) M95.2
congenital Q75.8
with
anencephaly Q00.0
encephalocele —see Encephalocele
hydrocephalus Q03.9
with spina bifida —see Spina bifida, by site, with hydrocephalus
microcephaly Q02

Deformity (Continued)

soft parts, organs or tissues (of pelvis)
in pregnancy or childbirth NEC O34.8-•
causing obstructed labor O65.5
spermatic cord (congenital) Q55.4
acquired N50.89
torsion —see Torsion, spermatic cord
spinal —see Dorsopathy, deforming
column (acquired) —see Dorsopathy, deforming
congenital Q67.5
cord (congenital) Q06.9
acquired G95.89
nerve root (congenital) Q07.9
spine (acquired) —see also Dorsopathy, deforming
congenital Q67.5
rachitic E64.3
specified NEC —see Dorsopathy, deforming, specified NEC
spleen
acquired D73.89
congenital Q89.09
Sprengel's (congenital) Q74.0
sternocleidomastoid (muscle), congenital Q68.0
sternum (acquired) M95.4
congenital NEC Q76.7
stomach (congenital) Q40.3
acquired K31.89
submandibular gland (congenital) Q38.4
submaxillary gland (congenital) Q38.4
acquired K11.8
talipes —see Talipes
testis (congenital) —see also Malformation, testis and scrotum
acquired N44.8
torsion —see Torsion, testis
thigh (acquired) —see also Deformity, limb, thigh
congenital NEC Q68.8
thorax (acquired) (wall) M95.4
congenital Q67.8
sequelae of rickets E64.3
thumb (acquired) —see also Deformity, finger
congenital NEC Q68.1
thymus (tissue) (congenital) Q89.2
thyroid (gland) (congenital) Q89.2
cartilage Q31.8
acquired J38.7
tibia (acquired) —see also Deformity, limb, specified type NEC, lower leg
congenital NEC Q68.8
saber (syphilitic) A50.56
toe (acquired) M20.6-•
congenital Q66.9
hallux rigidus M20.2-•
hallux valgus M20.1-•
hallux varus M20.3-•
hammer toe M20.4-•
specified NEC M20.5X-•
tongue (congenital) Q38.3
acquired K14.8
tooth, teeth K00.2
trachea (rings) (congenital) Q32.1
acquired J39.8
transverse aortic arch (congenital) Q25.49
tricuspid (leaflets) (valve) I07.8
atresia or stenosis Q22.4
Ebstein's Q22.5
trunk (acquired) M95.8
congenital Q89.9
ulna (acquired) —see also Deformity, limb, forearm
congenital NEC Q68.8
urachus, congenital Q64.4
ureter (opening) (congenital) Q62.8
acquired N28.89
urethra (congenital) Q64.79
acquired N36.8

Deformity (Continued)

urinary tract (congenital) Q64.9
urachus Q64.4
uterus (congenital) Q51.9
acquired N85.8
uvula (congenital) Q38.5
vagina (acquired) N89.8
congenital Q52.4
valgus NEC M21.00
ankle M21.07-•
elbow M21.02-•
hip M21.05-•
knee M21.06-•
valve, valvular (congenital) (heart) Q24.8
acquired —see Endocarditis
varus NEC M21.10
ankle M21.17-•
elbow M21.12-•
hip M21.15
knee M21.16-•
tibia —see Osteochondrosis, juvenile, tibia
vas deferens (congenital) Q55.4
acquired N50.89
vein (congenital) Q27.9
great Q26.9
vertebra —see Dorsopathy, deforming
vertical talus (congenital) Q66.80
left foot Q66.82
right foot Q66.81
vesicourethral orifice (acquired) N32.89
congenital NEC Q64.79
vessels of optic papilla (congenital) Q14.2
visual field (contraction) —see Defect, visual field
vitreous body, acquired H43.89
vulva (congenital) Q52.79
acquired N90.89
wrist (joint) (acquired) —see also Deformity, limb, forearm
congenital Q68.8
contraction —see Contraction, joint, wrist

Degeneration, degenerative

adrenal (capsule) (fatty) (gland) (hyaline) (infectional) E27.8
amyloid —see also Amyloidosis E85.9
anterior cornua, spinal cord G12.29
anterior labral S43.49-•
aorta, aortic I70.0
fatty I77.89
aortic valve (heart) —see Endocarditis, aortic
arteriovascular —see Arteriosclerosis
artery, arterial (atheromatous) (calcareous) —see also Arteriosclerosis
cerebral, amyloid E85.4 [I68.0]
medial —see Arteriosclerosis, extremities
articular cartilage NEC —see Derangement, joint, articular cartilage, by site
atheromatous —see Arteriosclerosis
basal nuclei or ganglia G23.9
specified NEC G23.8
bone NEC —see Disorder, bone, specified type NEC
brachial plexus G54.0
brain (cortical) (progressive) G31.9
alcoholic G31.2
arteriosclerotic I67.2
childhood G31.9
specified NEC G31.89
cystic G31.89
congenital Q04.6
in
alcoholism G31.2
beriberi E51.2
cerebrovascular disease I67.9
congenital hydrocephalus Q03.9
with spina bifida —see also Spina bifida
Fabry-Anderson disease E75.21
Gaucher's disease E75.22
Hunter's syndrome E76.1

Degeneration, degenerative *(Continued)*
  brain *(Continued)*
    in *(Continued)*
      lipidosis
        cerebral E75.4
        generalized E75.6
      mucopolysaccharidosis —*see*
        Mucopolysaccharidosis
      myxedema E03.9 *[G32.89]*
      neoplastic disease —*see also* Neoplasm
        D49.6 *[G32.89]*
      Niemann-Pick disease E75.249 *[G32.89]*
      sphingolipidosis E75.3 *[G32.89]*
      vitamin B12 deficiency E53.8 *[G32.89]*
    senile NEC G31.1
  breast N64.89
  Bruch's membrane —*see* Degeneration,
    choroid
  capillaries (fatty) I78.8
    amyloid E85.89 *[I79.8]*
  cardiac —*see also* Degeneration, myocardial
    valve, valvular —*see* Endocarditis
  cardiorenal —*see* Hypertension, cardiorenal
  cardiovascular —*see also* Disease,
    cardiovascular
    renal —*see* Hypertension, cardiorenal
  cerebellar NOS G31.9
    alcoholic G31.2
    primary (hereditary) (sporadic) G11.9
  cerebral —*see* Degeneration, brain
  cerebrovascular I67.9
    due to hypertension I67.4
  cervical plexus G54.2
  cervix N88.8
    due to radiation (intended effect) N88.8
      adverse effect or misadventure N99.89
  chamber angle H21.21-●
  changes, spine or vertebra —*see* Spondylosis
  chorioretinal —*see also* Degeneration, choroid
    hereditary H31.20
  choroid (colloid) (drusen) H31.10-●
    atrophy —*see* Atrophy, choroidal
    hereditary —*see* Dystrophy, choroidal,
      hereditary
  ciliary body H21.22-●
  cochlear —*see* subcategory H83.8
  combined (spinal cord) (subacute) E53.8
    [G32.0]
    with anemia (pernicious) D51.0 *[G32.0]*
      due to dietary vitamin B12 deficiency
        D51.3 *[G32.0]*
    in (due to)
      vitamin B12 deficiency E53.8 *[G32.0]*
        anemia D51.9 *[G32.0]*
  conjunctiva H11.10
    concretions —*see* Concretion, conjunctiva
    deposits —*see* Deposit, conjunctiva
    pigmentations —*see* Pigmentation,
      conjunctiva
    pinguecula —*see* Pinguecula
    xerosis —*see* Xerosis, conjunctiva
  cornea H18.40
    calcerous H18.43
      band keratopathy H18.42-●
    familial, hereditary —*see* Dystrophy, cornea
    hyaline (of old scars) H18.49
    keratomalacia —*see* Keratomalacia
    nodular H18.45-●
    peripheral H18.46-●
    senile H18.41-●
    specified type NEC H18.49
  cortical (cerebellar) (parenchymatous)
    G31.89
    alcoholic G31.2
    diffuse, due to arteriopathy I67.2
  corticobasal G31.85
  cutis L98.8
    amyloid E85.4 *[L99]*
  dental pulp K04.2
  disc disease —*see* Degeneration,
    intervertebral disc NEC

Degeneration, degenerative *(Continued)*
  dorsolateral (spinal cord) —*see* Degeneration,
    combined
  extrapyramidal G25.9
  eye, macular —*see also* Degeneration, macula
    congenital or hereditary —*see* Dystrophy,
      retina
  facet joints —*see* Spondylosis
  fatty
    liver NEC K76.0
      alcoholic K70.0
  grey matter (brain) (Alpers') G31.81
  heart —*see also* Degeneration, myocardial
    amyloid E85.4 *[I43]*
    atheromatous —*see* Disease, heart,
      ischemic, atherosclerotic
    ischemic —*see* Disease, heart, ischemic
  hepatolenticular (Wilson's) E83.01
  hepatorenal K76.7
  hyaline (diffuse) (generalized)
    localized —*see* Degeneration, by site
  infrapatellar fat pad M79.4
  intervertebral disc NOS
    with
      myelopathy —*see* Disorder, disc, with,
        myelopathy
      radiculitis or radiculopathy —*see*
        Disorder, disc, with, radiculopathy
    cervical, cervicothoracic —*see* Disorder,
      disc, cervical, degeneration
      with
        myelopathy —*see* Disorder, disc,
          cervical, with myelopathy
        neuritis, radiculitis or
          radiculopathy —*see* Disorder,
          disc, cervical, with neuritis
    lumbar region M51.36
      with
        myelopathy M51.06
        neuritis, radiculitis, radiculopathy or
          sciatica M51.16
    lumbosacral region M51.37
      with
        neuritis, radiculitis, radiculopathy or
          sciatica M51.17
    sacrococcygeal region M53.3
    thoracic region M51.34
      with
        myelopathy M51.04
        neuritis, radiculitis, radiculopathy
          M51.14
    thoracolumbar region M51.35
      with
        myelopathy M51.05
        neuritis, radiculitis, radiculopathy
          M51.15
  intestine, amyloid E85.4
  iris (pigmentary) H21.23-●
  ischemic —*see* Ischemia
  joint disease —*see* Osteoarthritis
  kidney N28.89
    amyloid E85.4 *[N29]*
    cystic, congenital Q61.9
    fatty N28.89
    polycystic Q61.3
      adult type (autosomal dominant)
        Q61.2
      infantile type (autosomal recessive) NEC
        Q61.19
        collecting duct dilatation Q61.11
  Kuhnt-Junius —*see also* Degeneration, macula
    H35.32-●
  lens —*see* Cataract
  lenticular (familial) (progressive) (Wilson's)
    (with cirrhosis of liver) E83.01
  liver (diffuse) NEC K76.89
    amyloid E85.4 *[K77]*
    cystic K76.89
      congenital Q44.6
    fatty NEC K76.0
      alcoholic K70.0

Degeneration, degenerative *(Continued)*
  liver *(Continued)*
    hypertrophic K76.89
    parenchymatous, acute or subacute
      K72.00
      with coma K72.01
    pigmentary K76.89
    toxic (acute) K71.9
  lung J98.4
  lymph gland I89.8
    hyaline I89.8
  macula, macular (acquired) (age-related)
    (senile) H35.30
    angioid streaks H35.33
    atrophic age-related H35.31-●
    congenital or hereditary —*see* Dystrophy,
      retina
    cystoid H35.35-●
    drusen H35.36-●
    dry age-related H35.31-●
    exudative H35.32-●
    hole H35.34-●
    nonexudative H35.31-●
    puckering H35.37-●
    toxic H35.38-●
    wet age-related H35.32-●
  membranous labyrinth, congenital (causing
    impairment of hearing) Q16.5
  meniscus —*see* Derangement, meniscus
  mitral —*see* Insufficiency, mitral
  Mönckeberg's —*see* Arteriosclerosis,
    extremities
  motor centers, senile G31.1
  multi-system G90.3
  mural —*see* Degeneration, myocardial
  muscle (fatty) (fibrous) (hyaline)
    (progressive) M62.89
    heart —*see* Degeneration, myocardial
  myelin, central nervous system G37.9
  myocardial, myocardium (fatty) (hyaline)
    (senile) I51.5
    with rheumatic fever (conditions in I00)
      I09.0
      active, acute or subacute I01.2
        with chorea I02.0
      inactive or quiescent (with chorea) I09.0
    hypertensive —*see* Hypertension, heart
    rheumatic —*see* Degeneration, myocardial,
      with rheumatic fever
    syphilitic A52.06
  nasal sinus (mucosa) J32.9
    frontal J32.1
    maxillary J32.0
  nerve —*see* Disorder, nerve
  nervous system G31.9
    alcoholic G31.2
    amyloid E85.4 *[G99.8]*
    autonomic G90.9
    fatty G31.89
    specified NEC G31.89
  nipple N64.89
  olivopontocerebellar (hereditary) (familial)
    G23.8
  osseous labyrinth —*see* subcategory H83.8
  ovary N83.8
    cystic N83.20-●
    microcystic N83.20-●
  pallidal pigmentary (progressive) G23.0
  pancreas K86.89
    tuberculous A18.83
  penis N48.89
  pigmentary (diffuse) (general)
    localized —*see* Degeneration, by site
    pallidal (progressive) G23.0
  pineal gland E34.8
  pituitary (gland) E23.6
  popliteal fat pad M79.4
  posterolateral (spinal cord) —*see*
    Degeneration, combined
  pulmonary valve (heart) I37.8
  pulp (tooth) K04.2

▶ New   ⇒ Revised   ~~deleted~~ Deleted   ● Use Additional Character(s)

Degeneration, degenerative (Continued)
  pupillary margin H21.24-●
  renal —see Degeneration, kidney
  retina H35.9
    hereditary (cerebroretinal) (congenital)
      (juvenile) (macula) (peripheral)
      (pigmentary) —see Dystrophy, retina
    Kuhnt-Junius —see also Degeneration,
      macula H35.32-●
    macula (cystic) (exudative) (hole)
      (nonexudative) (pseudohole) (senile)
      (toxic) —see Degeneration, macula
    peripheral H35.40
      lattice H35.41-●
      microcystoid H35.42-●
      paving stone H35.43-●
      secondary
        pigmentary H35.45-●
        vitreoretinal H35.46-●
      senile reticular H35.44-●
    pigmentary (primary) —see also Dystrophy,
      retina
    secondary —see Degeneration, retina,
      peripheral, secondary
    posterior pole —see Degeneration, macula
  saccule, congenital (causing impairment of
    hearing) Q16.5
  senile R54
    brain G31.1
    cardiac, heart or myocardium —see
      Degeneration, myocardial
    motor centers G31.1
    vascular —see Arteriosclerosis
  sinus (cystic) —see also Sinusitis
    polypoid J33.1
  skin L98.8
    amyloid E85.4 [L99]
    colloid L98.8
  spinal (cord) G31.89
    amyloid E85.4 [G32.89]
    combined (subacute) —see Degeneration,
      combined
    dorsolateral —see Degeneration, combined
    familial NEC G31.89
    fatty G31.89
    funicular —see Degeneration, combined
    posterolateral —see Degeneration,
      combined
    subacute combined —see Degeneration,
      combined
    tuberculous A17.81
  spleen D73.0
    amyloid E85.4 [D77]
  stomach K31.89
  striatonigral G23.2
  suprarenal (capsule) (gland) E27.8
  synovial membrane (pulpy) —see Disorder,
    synovium, specified type NEC
  tapetoretinal —see Dystrophy, retina
  thymus (gland) E32.8
    fatty E32.8
  thyroid (gland) E07.89
  tricuspid (heart) (valve) I07.9
  tuberculous NEC —see Tuberculosis
  turbinate J34.89
  uterus (cystic) N85.8
  vascular (senile) —see Arteriosclerosis
    hypertensive —see Hypertension
  vitreoretinal, secondary —see Degeneration,
    retina, peripheral, secondary, vitreoretinal
  vitreous (body) H43.81-●
  Wallerian —see Disorder, nerve
  Wilson's hepatolenticular E83.01
Deglutition
  paralysis R13.0
    hysterical F44.4
  pneumonia J69.0
Degos' disease I77.89
Dehiscence (of)
  amputation stump T87.81
  cesarean wound O90.0

Dehiscence (Continued)
  closure of
    cornea T81.31
    craniotomy T81.32
    fascia (muscular) (superficial) T81.32
    internal organ or tissue T81.32
    laceration (external) (internal) T81.33
    ligament T81.32
    mucosa T81.31
    muscle or muscle flap T81.32
    ribs or rib cage T81.32
    skin and subcutaneous tissue (full-
      thickness) (superficial) T81.31
    skull T81.32
    sternum (sternotomy) T81.32
    tendon T81.32
    traumatic laceration (external) (internal)
      T81.33
  episiotomy O90.1
  operation wound NEC T81.31
    external operation wound (superficial)
      T81.31
    internal operation wound (deep)
      T81.32
  perineal wound (postpartum) O90.1
  traumatic injury wound repair T81.33
  wound T81.30
    traumatic repair T81.33
Dehydration E86.0
  newborn P74.1
Déjérine-Roussy syndrome G93.89
Déjérine-Sottas disease or neuropathy
  (hypertrophic) G60.0
Déjérine-Thomas atrophy G23.8
Delay, delayed
  any plane in pelvis
    complicating delivery O66.9
  birth or delivery NOS O63.9
  closure, ductus arteriosus (Botalli) P29.38
  coagulation —see Defect, coagulation
  conduction (cardiac) (ventricular) I45.9
  delivery, second twin, triplet, etc O63.2
  development R62.50
    global F88
    intellectual (specific) F81.9
    language F80.9
      due to hearing loss F80.4
    learning F81.9
    pervasive F84.9
    physiological R62.50
      specified stage NEC R62.0
    reading F81.0
    sexual E30.0
    speech F80.9
      due to hearing loss F80.4
    spelling F81.81
  ejaculation F52.32
  gastric emptying K30
  menarche E30.0
  menstruation (cause unknown) N91.0
  milestone R62.0
  passage of meconium (newborn)
    P76.0
  primary respiration P28.9
  puberty (constitutional) E30.0
  separation of umbilical cord P96.82
  sexual maturation, female E30.0
  sleep phase syndrome G47.21
  union, fracture —see Fracture, by site
  vaccination Z28.9
Deletion(s)
  autosome Q93.9
    identified by fluorescence in situ
      hybridization (FISH) Q93.89
    identified by in situ hybridization (ISH)
      Q93.89
  chromosome
    with complex rearrangements NEC
      Q93.7
  ⇒part of NEC Q93.59
    seen only at prometaphase Q93.89

Deletion (Continued)
  chromosome (Continued)
    short arm
      4 Q93.3
      5p Q93.4
      22q11.2 Q93.81
      specified NEC Q93.89
    long arm chromosome 18 or 21 Q93.89
      with complex rearrangements NEC
        Q93.7
    microdeletions NEC Q93.88
Delhi boil or button B55.1
Delinquency (juvenile) (neurotic) F91.8
  group Z72.810
Delinquent immunization status Z28.3
Delirium, delirious (acute or subacute) (not
    alcohol or drug-induced) (with dementia)
    R41.0
  alcoholic (acute) (tremens) (withdrawal)
    F10.921
    with intoxication F10.921
      in
        abuse F10.121
        dependence F10.221
  due to (secondary to)
    alcohol
      intoxication F10.921
        in
          abuse F10.121
          dependence F10.221
      withdrawal F10.231
    amphetamine intoxication F15.921
      in
        abuse F15.121
        dependence F15.221
    anxiolytic
      intoxication F13.921
        in
          abuse F13.121
          dependence F13.221
      withdrawal F13.231
    cannabis intoxication (acute) F12.921
      in
        abuse F12.121
        dependence F12.221
    cocaine intoxication (acute) F14.921
      in
        abuse F14.121
        dependence F14.221
    general medical condition F05
    hallucinogen intoxication F16.921
      in
        abuse F16.121
        dependence F16.221
    hypnotic
      intoxication F13.921
        in
          abuse F13.121
          dependence F13.221
      withdrawal F13.231
    inhalant intoxication (acute) F18.921
      in
        abuse F18.121
        dependence F18.221
    multiple etiologies F05
    opioid intoxication (acute) F11.921
      in
        abuse F11.121
        dependence F11.221
    other (or unknown) substance
      F19.921
    phencyclidine intoxication (acute)
      F16.921
      in
        abuse F16.121
        dependence F16.221
    psychoactive substance NEC intoxication
      (acute) F19.921
      in
        abuse F19.121
        dependence F19.221

Delirium, delirious *(Continued)*
  due to *(Continued)*
    sedative
      intoxication F13.921
        in
          abuse F13.121
          dependence F13.221
        withdrawal F13.231
      unknown etiology F05
    exhaustion F43.0
    hysterical F44.89
    postprocedural (postoperative) F05
    puerperal F05
    thyroid —*see* Thyrotoxicosis with thyroid
      storm
    traumatic —*see* Injury, intracranial
    tremens (alcohol-induced) F10.231
      sedative-induced F13.231
Delivery (childbirth) (labor)
  arrested active phase O62.1
  cesarean (for)
    without indication O82
    abnormal
      pelvis (bony) (deformity) (major) NEC
        with disproportion (fetopelvic)
          O33.0
        with obstructed labor O65.0
      presentation or position O32.9
    abruptio placentae —*see also* Abruptio
      placentae 045.9-●
    acromion presentation O32.2
    atony, uterus O62.2
    breech presentation O32.1
      incomplete O32.8
    brow presentation O32.3
    cephalopelvic disproportion O33.9
    cerclage O34.3-●
    chin presentation O32.3
    cicatrix of cervix O34.4-●
    contracted pelvis (general)
      inlet O33.2
      outlet O33.3
    cord presentation or prolapse O69.0
    cystocele O34.8-●
    deformity (acquired) (congenital)
      pelvic organs or tissues NEC O34.8-●
      pelvis (bony) NEC O33.0
    disproportion NOS O33.9
    eclampsia —*see* Eclampsia
    face presentation O32.3
    failed
      forceps O66.5
      induction of labor O61.9
        instrumental O61.1
        mechanical O61.1
        medical O61.0
        specified NEC O61.8
        surgical O61.1
      trial of labor NOS O66.40
        following previous cesarean delivery
          O66.41
      vacuum extraction O66.5
      ventouse O66.5
    fetal-maternal hemorrhage O43.01-●
    hemorrhage (intrapartum) O67.9
      with coagulation defect O67.0
      specified cause NEC O67.8
    high head at term O32.4
    hydrocephalic fetus O33.6
    incarceration of uterus O34.51-●
    incoordinate uterine action O62.4
    increased size, fetus O33.5
    inertia, uterus O62.2
      primary O62.0
      secondary O62.1
    lateroversion, uterus O34.59-●
    mal lie O32.9
    malposition
      fetus O32.9
      pelvic organs or tissues NEC O34.8-●
      uterus NEC O34.59-●

Delivery *(Continued)*
  cesarean *(Continued)*
    malpresentation NOS O32.9
    oblique presentation O32.2
    occurring after 37 completed weeks of
      gestation but before 39 completed
      weeks gestation due to (spontaneous)
      onset of labor O75.82
    oversize fetus O33.5
    pelvic tumor NEC O34.8-●
    placenta previa O44.0-●
      complete O44.0-●
        with hemorrhage O44.1-●
    placental insufficiency O36.51-●
    planned, occurring after 37 completed
      weeks of gestation but before 39
      completed weeks gestation due to
      (spontaneous) onset of labor O75.82
    polyp, cervix O34.4-●
      causing obstructed labor O65.5
    poor dilatation, cervix O62.0
    pre-eclampsia O14.94
      mild O14.04
      moderate O14.04
      severe O14.14
        with hemolysis, elevated liver
          enzymes and low platelet count
          (HELLP) O14.24
    previous
      cesarean delivery O34.219
        classical (vertical) scar O34.212
        low transverse scar O34.211
      surgery (to)
        cervix O34.4-●
        gynecological NEC O34.8-●
        rectum O34.7-●
        uterus O34.29
        vagina O34.6-●
    prolapse
      arm or hand O32.2
      uterus O34.52-●
    prolonged labor NOS O63.9
    rectocele O34.8-●
    retroversion
      uterus O34.53-●
    rigid
      cervix O34.4-●
      pelvic floor O34.8-●
      perineum O34.7-●
      vagina O34.6-●
      vulva O34.7-●
    sacculation, pregnant uterus O34.59-●
    scar(s)
      cervix O34.4-●
      cesarean delivery O34.219
        classical (vertical) O34.212
        low transverse O34.211
      transmural uterine O34.29
      uterus O34.29
    Shirodkar suture in situ O34.3-●
    shoulder presentation O32.2
    stenosis or stricture, cervix O34.4-●
    streptococcus group B (GBS) carrier state
      O99.824
    transmural uterine scar O34.29
    transverse presentation or lie O32.2
    tumor, pelvic organs or tissues NEC
      O34.8-●
      cervix O34.4-●
    umbilical cord presentation or prolapse
      O69.0
  completely normal case O80
  complicated O75.9
    by
      abnormal, abnormality (of)
        forces of labor O62.9
          specified type NEC O62.8
        glucose O99.814
        uterine contractions NOS O62.9
      abruptio placentae —*see also* Abruptio
        placentae O45.9-●

Delivery *(Continued)*
  complicated *(Continued)*
    by *(Continued)*
      abuse
        physical O9A.32
        psychological O9A.52
        sexual O9A.42
      adherent placenta O72.0
        without hemorrhage O73.0
      alcohol use O99.314
      anemia (pre-existing) O99.02
      anesthetic death O74.8
      annular detachment of cervix O71.3
      atony, uterus O62.2
      attempted vacuum extraction and
        forceps O66.5
      Bandl's ring O62.4
      bariatric surgery status O99.844
      biliary tract disorder O26.62
      bleeding —*see* Delivery, complicated by,
        hemorrhage
      blood disorder NEC O99.12
      cervical dystocia (hypotonic) O62.2
        primary O62.0
        secondary O62.1
      circulatory system disorder O99.42
      compression of cord (umbilical) NEC
        O69.2
      condition NEC O99.89
      contraction, contracted ring O62.4
      cord (umbilical)
        around neck
          with compression O69.1
          without compression O69.81
        bruising O69.5
        complication O69.9
          specified NEC O69.89
        compression NEC O69.2
        entanglement O69.2
          without compression O69.82
        hematoma O69.5
        presentation O69.0
        prolapse O69.0
        short O69.3
        thrombosis (vessels) O69.5
        vascular lesion O69.5
      Couvelaire uterus O45.8X-●
      damage to (injury to) NEC
        perineum O71.82
        periurethral tissue O71.82
        vulva O71.82
      delay following rupture of membranes
        (spontaneous) —*see* Pregnancy,
        complicated by, premature rupture
        of membranes
      depressed fetal heart tones O76
      diabetes O24.92
        gestational O24.429
          diet controlled O24.420
          insulin controlled O24.424
          oral drug controlled (antidiabetic)
            (hypoglycemic) O24.425
        pre-existing O24.32
          specified NEC O24.82
          type 1 O24.02
          type 2 O24.12
      diastasis recti (abdominis) O71.89
      dilatation
        bladder O66.8
        cervix incomplete, poor or slow O62.0
      disease NEC O99.89
      disruptio uteri —*see* Delivery,
        complicated by, rupture, uterus
      drug use O99.324
      dysfunction, uterus NOS O62.9
        hypertonic O62.4
        hypotonic O62.2
          primary O62.0
          secondary O62.1
        incoordinate O62.4
      eclampsia O15.1

▶ New   ⇒ Revised   ~~deleted~~ Deleted   ● Use Additional Character(s)

Delivery *(Continued)*
    complicated *(Continued)*
        by *(Continued)*
            embolism (pulmonary) —*see* Embolism,
                obstetric
            endocrine, nutritional or metabolic
                disease NEC O99.284
            failed
                attempted vaginal birth after
                    previous cesarean delivery
                    O66.41
                induction of labor O61.9
                    instrumental O61.1
                    mechanical O61.1
                    medical O61.0
                    specified NEC O61.8
                    surgical O61.1
                trial of labor O66.40
            female genital mutilation O65.5
            fetal
                abnormal acid-base balance O68
                acidemia O68
                acidosis O68
                alkalosis O68
                death, early O02.1
                deformity O66.3
                heart rate or rhythm (abnormal) (non-
                    reassuring) O76
                hypoxia O77.8
                stress O77.9
                    due to drug administration O77.1
                    electrocardiographic evidence of
                        O77.8
                    specified NEC O77.8
                    ultrasound evidence of O77.8
            fever during labor O75.2
            gastric banding status O99.844
            gastric bypass status O99.844
            gastrointestinal disease NEC O99.62
            gestational
                diabetes O24.429
                    diet controlled O24.420
                    insulin (and diet) controlled
                        O24.424
                    oral drug controlled (antidiabetic)
                        (hypoglycemic) O24.425
                edema O12.04
                    with proteinuria O12.24
                proteinuria O12.14
            gonorrhea O98.22
            hematoma O71.7
                ischial spine O71.7
                pelvic O71.7
                vagina O71.7
                vulva or perineum O71.7
            hemorrhage (uterine) O67.9
                associated with
                    afibrinogenemia O67.0
                    coagulation defect O67.0
                    hyperfibrinolysis O67.0
                    hypofibrinogenemia O67.0
                due to
                    low implantation of placenta
                        O44.5-•
                    low-lying placenta O44.5-•
                    placenta previa O44.1-•
                        marginal O44.3-•
                        partial O44.3-•
                    premature separation of placenta
                        (normally implanted) *(see also*
                        Abruptio placentae) O45.9-•
                    retained placenta O72.0
                    uterine leiomyoma O67.8
                placenta NEC O67.8
                postpartum NEC (atonic) (immediate)
                    O72.1
                    with retained or trapped placenta
                        O72.0
                    delayed O72.2
                    secondary O72.2
                    third stage O72.0

Delivery *(Continued)*
    complicated *(Continued)*
        by *(Continued)*
            hourglass contraction, uterus O62.4
            hypertension, hypertensive (pre-
                existing) —*see* Hypertension,
                complicated by, childbirth (labor)
            hypotension O26.5-•
            incomplete dilatation (cervix) O62.0
            incoordinate uterus contractions O62.4
            inertia, uterus O62.2
                during latent phase of labor O62.0
                primary O62.0
                secondary O62.1
            infection (maternal) O98.92
                carrier state NEC O99.834
                gonorrhea O98.22
                human immunodeficiency virus (HIV)
                    O98.72
                sexually transmitted NEC O98.32
                specified NEC O98.82
                syphilis O98.12
                tuberculosis O98.02
                viral hepatitis O98.42
                viral NEC O98.52
            injury (to mother) *(see also* Delivery,
                complicated, by, damage to)
                O71.9
                nonobstetric O9A.22
                    caused by abuse —*see* Delivery,
                        complicated by, abuse
            intrauterine fetal death, early O02.1
            inversion, uterus O71.2
            laceration (perineal) O70.9
                anus (sphincter) O70.4
                    with third degree laceration —*see*
                        also Delivery, complicated, by,
                        laceration, perineum, third
                        degree O70.20
                        with mucosa O70.3
                    without third degree laceration
                        O70.4
                bladder (urinary) O71.5
                bowel O71.5
                cervix (uteri) O71.3
                fourchette O70.0
                hymen O70.0
                labia O70.0
                pelvic
                    floor O70.1
                    organ NEC O71.5
                perineum, perineal O70.9
                    first degree O70.0
                    fourth degree O70.3
                    muscles O70.1
                    second degree O70.1
                    skin O70.0
                    slight O70.0
                    third degree O70.20
                        with
                            both external anal sphincter
                                (EAS) and internal anal
                                sphincter (IAS) torn (IIIc)
                                O70.23
                            less than 50% of external anal
                                sphincter (EAS) thickness
                                torn (IIIa) O70.21
                            more than 50% external anal
                                sphincter (EAS) thickness
                                torn (IIIb) O70.22
                        IIIa O70.21
                        IIIb O70.22
                        IIIc O70.23
                peritoneum (pelvic) O71.5
                rectovaginal (septum) (without
                    perineal laceration) O71.4
                    with perineum —*see also* Delivery,
                        complicated, by, laceration,
                        perineum, third degree
                        O70.20
                        with anal or rectal mucosa O70.3

Delivery *(Continued)*
    complicated *(Continued)*
        by *(Continued)*
            laceration *(Continued)*
                specified NEC O71.89
                sphincter ani —*see* Delivery,
                    complicated, by, laceration, anus
                    (sphincter)
                urethra O71.5
                uterus O71.81
                    before labor O71.81
                vagina, vaginal (deep) (high)
                    (without perineal laceration)
                    O71.4
                    with perineum O70.0
                    muscles, with perineum O70.1
                vulva O70.0
            liver disorder O26.62
            malignancy O9A.12
            malnutrition O25.2
            malposition, malpresentation
                without obstruction O32.9 —*see*
                    also Delivery, complicated by,
                    obstruction
                breech O32.1
                compound O32.6
                face (brow) (chin) O32.3
                footling O38.8
                high head O32.4
                oblique O32.2
                specified NEC O32.8
                transverse O32.2
                unstable lie O32.0
            placenta O44.0-•
                with hemorrhage O44.1-•
            uterus or cervix O65.5
            meconium in amniotic fluid O77.0
            mental disorder NEC O99.344
            metrorrhexis —*see* Delivery, complicated
                by, rupture, uterus
            nervous system disorder O99.354
            obesity (pre-existing) O99.214
            obesity surgery status O99.844
            obstetric trauma O71.9
                specified NEC O71.89
            obstructed labor
                due to
                    breech (complete) (frank)
                        presentation O64.1
                        incomplete O64.8
                    brow presenation O64.3
                    buttock presentation O64.1
                    chin presentation O64.2
                    compound presentation O64.5
                    contracted pelvis O65.1
                    deep transverse arrest O64.0
                    deformed pelvis O65.0
                    dystocia (fetal) O66.9
                        due to
                            conjoined twins O66.3
                            fetal
                                abnormality NEC O66.3
                                ascites O66.3
                                hydrops O66.3
                                meningomyelocele O66.3
                                sacral teratoma O66.3
                                tumor O66.3
                            hydrocephalic fetus O66.3
                            shoulder O66.0
                    face presentation O64.2
                    fetopelvic disproportion O65.4
                    footling presentation O64.8
                    impacted shoulders O66.0
                    incomplete rotation of fetal head
                        O64.0
                    large fetus O66.2
                    locked twins O66.1
                    malposition O64.9
                        specified NEC O64.8
                    malpresentation O64.9
                        specified NEC O64.8

Delivery (Continued)
  complicated (Continued)
    by (Continued)
      obstructed labor (Continued)
        due to (Continued)
          multiple fetuses NEC O66.6
          pelvic
            abnormality (maternal) O65.9
              organ O65.5
              specified NEC O65.8
            contraction
              inlet O65.2
              mid-cavity O65.3
              outlet O65.3
            persistent (position)
              occipitoiliac O64.0
              occipitoposterior O64.0
              occipitosacral O64.0
              occipitotransverse O64.0
            prolapsed arm O64.4
            shoulder presentation O64.4
          specified NEC O66.8
      pathological retraction ring, uterus O62.4
      penetration, pregnant uterus by instrument O71.1
      perforation —see Delivery, complicated by, laceration
      placenta, placental
        ablatio —see also Abruptio placentae O45.9-●
        abnormality O43.9-●
          specified NEC O43.89-●
        abruptio —see also Abruptio placentae O45.9-●
        accreta O43.21-●
        adherent (with hemorrhage) O72.0
          without hemorrhage O73.0
        detachment (premature) —see also Abruptio placentae O45.9-●
        disorder O43.9-●
          specified NEC O43.89-●
        hemorrhage NEC O67.8
        increta O43.22-●
        low (implantation) (lying) O44.4-●
          with hemorrhage O44.5-●
        malformation O43.10-●
        malposition O44.0-●
          without hemorrhage O44.1-●
        percreta O43.23-●
        previa (central) (complete) (lateral) (total) O44.0-●
          with hemorrhage O44.1-●
            marginal O44.2-●
              with hemorrhage O44.3-●
            partial O44.2-●
              with hemorrhage O44.3-●
        retained (with hemorrhage) O72.0
          without hemorrhage O73.0
        separation (premature) O45.9-●
          specified NEC O45.8X-●
        vicious insertion O44.1-●
      precipitate labor O62.3
      premature rupture, membranes (see also Pregnancy, complicated by, premature rupture of membranes) O42.90
      prolapse
        arm or hand O32.2
        cord (umbilical) O69.0
        foot or leg O32.8
        uterus O34.52-●
      prolonged labor O63.9
        first stage O63.0
        second stage O63.1
      protozoal disease (maternal) O98.62
      respiratory disease NEC O99.52
      retained membranes or portions of placenta O72.2
        without hemorrhage O73.1
      retarded birth O63.9

Delivery (Continued)
  complicated (Continued)
    by (Continued)
      retention of secundines (with hemorrhage) O72.0
        without hemorrhage O73.0
        partial O72.2
          without hemorrhage O73.1
      rupture
        bladder (urinary) O71.5
        cervix O71.3
        pelvic organ NEC O71.5
        urethra O71.5
        uterus (during or after labor) O71.1
          before labor O71.0-●
      separation, pubic bone (symphysis pubis) O71.6
      shock O75.1
      shoulder presentation O64.4
      skin disorder NEC O99.72
      spasm, cervix O62.4
      stenosis or stricture, cervix O65.5
      streptococcus group B (GBS) carrier state O99.824
      subluxation of symphysis (pubis) O26.72
      syphilis (maternal) O98.12
      tear —see Delivery, complicated by, laceration
      tetanic uterus O62.4
      trauma (obstetrical) —see also Delivery, complicated, by, damage to O71.9
        non-obstetric O9A.22
        periurethral O71.82
        specified NEC O71.89
      tuberculosis (maternal) O98.02
      tumor, pelvic organs or tissues NEC O65.5
      umbilical cord around neck
        with compression O69.1
        without compression O69.81
      uterine inertia O62.2
        during latent phase of labor O62.0
        primary O62.0
        secondary O62.1
      vasa previa O69.4
      velamentous insertion of cord O43.12-●
    specified complication NEC O75.89
  delayed NOS O63.9
    following rupture of membranes artificial O75.5
    second twin, triplet, etc. O63.2
  forceps, low following failed vacuum extraction O66.5
  missed (at or near term) O36.4
  normal O80
  obstructed —see Delivery, complicated by, obstructed labor
  precipitate O62.3
  preterm —see also Pregnancy, complicated by, preterm labor O60.10
  spontaneous O80
  term pregnancy NOS O80
  uncomplicated O80
  vaginal, following previous cesarean delivery O34.219
    classical (vertical) scar O34.212
    low transverse scar O34.211
Delusions (paranoid) —see Disorder, delusional
Dementia (degenerative (primary)) (old age) (persisting) F03.90
  with
    aggressive behavior F03.91
    behavioral disturbance F03.91
    combative behavior F03.91
    Lewy bodies G31.83 [F02.80]
      with behavioral disturbance G31.83 [F02.81]
    Parkinson's disease G20 [F02.80]
      with behavioral disturbance G20 [F02.81]

Dementia (Continued)
  with (Continued)
    Parkinsonism G31.83 [F02.80]
      with behavioral disturbance G31.83 [F02.81]
    violent behavior F03.91
  alcoholic F10.97
    with dependence F10.27
  Alzheimer's type —see Disease, Alzheimer's
  arteriosclerotic —see Dementia, vascular
  atypical, Alzheimer's type —see Disease, Alzheimer's, specified NEC
  congenital —see Disability, intellectual
  frontal (lobe) G31.09 [F02.80]
    with behavioral disturbance G31.09 [F02.81]
  frontotemporal G31.09 [F02.80]
    with behavioral disturbance G31.09 [F02.81]
    specified NEC G31.09 [F02.80]
      with behavioral disturbance G31.09 [F02.81]
  in (due to)
    alcohol F10.97
      with dependence F10.27
    Alzheimer's disease —see Disease, Alzheimer's
    arteriosclerotic brain disease —see Dementia, vascular
    cerebral lipidoses E75.-● [F02.80]
      with behavioral disturbance E75.-● [F02.81]
    Creutzfeldt-Jakob disease —see also Creutzfeldt-Jakob disease or syndrome (with dementia) A81.00
    epilepsy G40.-● [F02.80]
      with behavioral disturbance G40.-● [F02.81]
    hepatolenticular degeneration E83.01 [F02.80]
      with behavioral disturbance E83.01 [F02.81]
    human immunodeficiency virus (HIV) disease B20 [F02.80]
      with behavioral disturbance B20 [F02.81]
    Huntington's disease or chorea G10 [F02.80]
      with behavioral disturbance G10 [F02.81]
    hypercalcemia E83.52 [F02.80]
      with behavioral disturbance E83.52 [F02.81]
    hypothyroidism, acquired E03.9 [F02.80]
      with behavioral disturbance E03.9 [F02.81]
      due to iodine deficiency E01.8 [F02.80]
        with behavioral disturbance E01.8 [F02.81]
    inhalants F18.97
      with dependence F18.27
    multiple
      etiologies F03
      sclerosis G35 [F02.80]
        with behavioral disturbance G35 [F02.81]
    neurosyphilis A52.17 [F02.80]
      with behavioral disturbance A52.17 [F02.81]
      juvenile A50.49 [F02.80]
        with behavioral disturbance A50.49 [F02.81]
    niacin deficiency E52 [F02.80]
      with behavioral disturbance E52 [F02.81]
    paralysis agitans G20 [F02.80]
      with behavioral disturbance G20 [F02.81]
    Parkinson's disease G20 [F02.80]
    pellagra E52 [F02.80]
      with behavioral disturbance E52 [F02.81]
    Pick's G31.01 [F02.80]
      with behavioral disturbance G31.01 [F02.81]
    polyarteritis nodosa M30.0 [F02.80]
      with behavioral disturbance M30.0 [F02.81]

▶ New   ⇒ Revised   ~~deleted~~ Deleted   ● Use Additional Character(s)

Dementia (Continued)
  in (Continued)
    psychoactive drug F19.97
      with dependence F19.27
      inhalants F18.97
        with dependence F18.27
      sedatives, hypnotics or anxiolytics
        F13.97
        with dependence F13.27
      sedatives, hypnotics or anxiolytics F13.97
        with dependence F13.27
      systemic lupus erythematosus
        M32.- ● [F02.80]
        with behavioral disturbance
          M32.- ● [F02.81]
      trypanosomiasis
        African B56.9 [F02.80]
        with behavioral disturbance B56.9
          [F02.81]
      unknown etiology F03
      vitamin B12 deficiency E53.8 [F02.80]
        with behavioral disturbance E53.8
          [F02.81]
      volatile solvents F18.97
        with dependence F18.27
  infantile, infantilis F84.3
  Lewy body G31.83 [F02.80]
    with behavioral disturbance G31.83
      [F02.81]
  multi-infarct —see Dementia, vascular
  paralytica, paralytic (syphilitic) A52.17
    [F02.80]
    with behavioral disturbance A52.17
      [F02.81]
    juvenilis A50.45
  paretic A52.17
  praecox —see Schizophrenia
  presenile F03
    Alzheimer's type —see Disease,
      Alzheimer's, early onset
  primary degenerative F03
  progressive, syphilitic A52.17
  senile F03
    with acute confusional state F05
    Alzheimer's type —see Disease,
      Alzheimer's, late onset
    depressed or paranoid type F03
  vascular (acute onset) (mixed) (multi-infarct)
    (subcortical) F01.50
    with behavioral disturbance F01.51
Demineralization, bone —see Osteoporosis
Demodex folliculorum (infestation) B88.0
Demophobia F40.248
Demoralization R45.3
Demyelination, demyelinization
  central nervous system G37.9
    specified NEC G37.8
  corpus callosum (central) G37.1
  disseminated, acute G36.9
    specified NEC G36.8
  global G35
  in optic neuritis G36.0
Dengue (classical) (fever) A90
  hemorrhagic A91
  sandfly A93.1
Dennie-Marfan syphilitic syndrome
  A50.45
Dens evaginatus, in dente or invaginatus
  K00.2
Dense breasts R92.2
Density
  increased, bone (disseminated) (generalized)
    (spotted) —see Disorder, bone, density
    and structure, specified type NEC
  lung (nodular) J98.4
Dental —see also condition
  examination Z01.20
    with abnormal findings Z01.21
  restoration
    aesthetically inadequate or displeasing
      K08.56

Dental (Continued)
  restoration (Continued)
    defective K08.50
      specified NEC K08.59
    failure of marginal integrity K08.51
    failure of periodontal anatomical integrity
      K08.54
Dentia praecox K00.6
Denticles (pulp) K04.2
Dentigerous cyst K09.0
Dentin
  irregular (in pulp) K04.3
  opalescent K00.5
  secondary (in pulp) K04.3
  sensitive K03.89
Dentinogenesis imperfecta K00.5
Dentinoma —see Cyst, calcifying odontogenic
Dentition (syndrome) K00.7
  delayed K00.6
  difficult K00.7
  precocious K00.6
  premature K00.6
  retarded K00.6
Dependence (on) (syndrome) F19.20
  with remission F19.21
  alcohol (ethyl) (methyl) (without remission)
    F10.20
    with
      amnestic disorder, persisting F10.26
      anxiety disorder F10.280
      dementia, persisting F10.27
      intoxication F10.229
        with delirium F10.221
        uncomplicated F10.220
      mood disorder F10.24
      psychotic disorder F10.259
        with
          delusions F10.250
          hallucinations F10.251
      remission F10.21
      sexual dysfunction F10.281
      sleep disorder F10.282
      specified disorder NEC F10.288
      withdrawal F10.239
        with
          delirium F10.231
          perceptual disturbance F10.232
        uncomplicated F10.230
    counseling and surveillance Z71.41
  amobarbital —see Dependence, drug,
    sedative
  amphetamine(s) (type) —see Dependence,
    drug, stimulant NEC
  amytal (sodium) —see Dependence, drug,
    sedative
  analgesic NEC F55.8
  anesthetic (agent) (gas) (general) (local)
    NEC —see Dependence, drug,
    psychoactive NEC
  anxiolytic NEC —see Dependence, drug,
    sedative
  barbital(s) —see Dependence, drug, sedative
  barbiturate(s) (compounds) (drugs
    classifiable to T42) —see Dependence,
    drug, sedative
  benzedrine —see Dependence, drug,
    stimulant NEC
  bhang —see Dependence, drug, cannabis
  bromide(s) NEC —see Dependence, drug,
    sedative
  caffeine —see Dependence, drug, stimulant
    NEC
  cannabis (sativa) (indica) (resin) (derivatives)
    (type) —see Dependence, drug, cannabis
  chloral (betaine) (hydrate) —see Dependence,
    drug, sedative
  chlordiazepoxide —see Dependence, drug,
    sedative
  coca (leaf) (derivatives) —see Dependence,
    drug, cocaine
  cocaine —see Dependence, drug, cocaine

Dependence (Continued)
  codeine —see Dependence, drug, opioid
  combinations of drugs F19.20
  dagga —see Dependence, drug, cannabis
  demerol —see Dependence, drug, opioid
  dexamphetamine —see Dependence, drug,
    stimulant NEC
  dexedrine —see Dependence, drug, stimulant
    NEC
  dextromethorphan —see Dependence, drug,
    opioid
  dextromoramide —see Dependence, drug,
    opioid
  dextro-nor-pseudo-ephedrine —see
    Dependence, drug, stimulant NEC
  dextrorphan —see Dependence, drug, opioid
  diazepam —see Dependence, drug, sedative
  dilaudid —see Dependence, drug, opioid
  D-lysergic acid diethylamide —see
    Dependence, drug, hallucinogen
  drug NEC F19.20
    with sleep disorder F19.282
    cannabis F12.20
      with
        anxiety disorder F12.280
        intoxication F12.229
          with
            delirium F12.221
            perceptual disturbance F12.222
          uncomplicated F12.220
        other specified disorder F12.288
        psychosis F12.259
          delusions F12.250
          hallucinations F12.251
        unspecified disorder F12.29
      ▶ withdrawal F12.23
      in remission F12.21
    cocaine F14.20
      with
        anxiety disorder F14.280
        intoxication F14.229
          with
            delirium F14.221
            perceptual disturbance F14.222
          uncomplicated F14.220
        mood disorder F14.24
        other specified disorder F14.288
        psychosis F14.259
          delusions F14.250
          hallucinations F14.251
        sexual dysfunction F14.281
        sleep disorder F14.282
        unspecified disorder F14.29
        withdrawal F14.23
      in remission F14.21
      withdrawal symptoms in newborn P96.1
    counseling and surveillance Z71.51
    hallucinogen F16.20
      with
        anxiety disorder F16.280
        flashbacks F16.283
        intoxication F16.229
          with delirium F16.221
          uncomplicated F16.220
        mood disorder F16.24
        other specified disorder F16.288
        perception disorder, persisting F16.283
        psychosis F16.259
          delusions F16.250
          hallucinations F16.251
        unspecified disorder F16.29
      in remission F16.21
    in remission F19.21
    inhalant F18.20
      with
        anxiety disorder F18.280
        dementia, persisting F18.27
        intoxication F18.229
          with delirium F18.221
          uncomplicated F18.220
        mood disorder F18.24

Dependence *(Continued)*
 drug NEC *(Continued)*
  inhalant *(Continued)*
   with *(Continued)*
    other specified disorder F18.288
    psychosis F18.259
     delusions F18.250
     hallucinations F18.251
    unspecified disorder F18.29
   in remission F18.21
  nicotine F17.200
   with disorder F17.209
    in remission F17.201
    specified disorder NEC F17.208
    withdrawal F17.203
   chewing tobacco F17.220
    with disorder F17.229
     in remission F17.221
     specified disorder NEC F17.228
     withdrawal F17.223
   cigarettes F17.210
    with disorder F17.219
     in remission F17.211
     specified disorder NEC F17.218
     withdrawal F17.213
   specified product NEC F17.290
    with disorder F17.299
     remission F17.291
     specified disorder NEC F17.298
     withdrawal F17.293
  opioid F11.20
   with
    intoxication F11.229
     with
      delirium F11.221
      perceptual disturbance F11.222
     uncomplicated F11.220
    mood disorder F11.24
    other specified disorder F11.288
    psychosis F11.259
     delusions F11.250
     hallucinations F11.251
    sexual dysfunction F11.281
    sleep disorder F11.282
    unspecified disorder F11.29
    withdrawal F11.23
   in remission F11.21
  psychoactive NEC F19.20
   with
    amnestic disorder F19.26
    anxiety disorder F19.280
    dementia F19.27
    intoxication F19.229
     with
      delirium F19.221
      perceptual disturbance F19.222
     uncomplicated F19.220
    mood disorder F19.24
    other specified disorder F19.288
    psychosis F19.259
     delusions F19.250
     hallucinations F19.251
    sexual dysfunction F19.281
    sleep disorder F19.282
    unspecified disorder F19.29
    withdrawal F19.239
     with
      delirium F19.231
      perceptual disturbance
       F19.232
     uncomplicated F19.230
  sedative, hypnotic or anxiolytic F13.20
   with
    amnestic disorder F13.26
    anxiety disorder F13.280
    dementia, persisting F13.27
    intoxication F13.229
     with delirium F13.221
     uncomplicated F13.220
    mood disorder F13.24
    other specified disorder F13.288

Dependence *(Continued)*
 drug NEC *(Continued)*
  sedative, hypnotic or anxiolytic *(Continued)*
   with *(Continued)*
    psychosis F13.259
     delusions F13.250
     hallucinations F13.251
    sexual dysfunction F13.281
    sleep disorder F13.282
    unspecified disorder F13.29
    withdrawal F13.239
     with
      delirium F13.231
      perceptual disturbance F13.232
     uncomplicated F13.230
   in remission F13.21
  stimulant NEC F15.20
   with
    anxiety disorder F15.280
    intoxication F15.229
     with
      delirium F15.221
      perceptual disturbance F15.222
     uncomplicated F15.220
    mood disorder F15.24
    other specified disorder F15.288
    psychosis F15.259
     delusions F15.250
     hallucinations F15.251
    sexual dysfunction F15.281
    sleep disorder F15.282
    unspecified disorder F15.29
    withdrawal F15.23
   in remission F15.21
 ethyl
  alcohol (without remission) F10.20
   with remission F10.21
  bromide —*see* Dependence, drug,
   sedative
  carbamate F19.20
  chloride F19.20
  morphine —*see* Dependence, drug, opioid
 ganja —*see* Dependence, drug, cannabis
 glue (airplane) (sniffing) —*see* Dependence,
  drug, inhalant
 glutethimide —*see* Dependence, drug,
  sedative
 hallucinogenics —*see* Dependence, drug,
  hallucinogen
 hashish —*see* Dependence, drug, cannabis
 hemp —*see* Dependence, drug, cannabis
 heroin (salt) (any) —*see* Dependence, drug,
  opioid
 hypnotic NEC —*see* Dependence, drug,
  sedative
 Indian hemp —*see* Dependence, drug,
  cannabis
 inhalants —*see* Dependence, drug, inhalant
 khat —*see* Dependence, drug, stimulant NEC
 laudanum —*see* Dependence, drug, opioid
 LSD (-25) (derivatives) —*see* Dependence,
  drug, hallucinogen
 luminal —*see* Dependence, drug, sedative
 lysergic acid —*see* Dependence, drug,
  hallucinogen
 maconha —*see* Dependence, drug, cannabis
 marihuana —*see* Dependence, drug, cannabis
 meprobamate —*see* Dependence, drug,
  sedative
 mescaline —*see* Dependence, drug,
  hallucinogen
 methadone —*see* Dependence, drug, opioid
 methamphetamine(s) —*see* Dependence,
  drug, stimulant NEC
 methaqualone —*see* Dependence, drug,
  sedative
 methyl
  alcohol (without remission) F10.20
   with remission F10.21
  bromide —*see* Dependence, drug, sedative
  morphine —*see* Dependence, drug, opioid

Dependence *(Continued)*
 methyl *(Continued)*
  phenidate —*see* Dependence, drug,
   stimulant NEC
  sulfonal —*see* Dependence, drug, sedative
 morphine (sulfate) (sulfite) (type) —*see*
  Dependence, drug, opioid
 narcotic (drug) NEC —*see* Dependence, drug,
  opioid
 nembutal —*see* Dependence, drug, sedative
 neraval —*see* Dependence, drug, sedative
 neravan —*see* Dependence, drug, sedative
 neurobarb —*see* Dependence, drug, sedative
 nicotine —*see* Dependence, drug, nicotine
 nitrous oxide F19.20
 nonbarbiturate sedatives and tranquilizers
  with similar effect —*see* Dependence,
  drug, sedative
 on
  artificial heart (fully implantable)
   (mechanical) Z95.812
  aspirator Z99.0
  care provider (because of) Z74.9
   impaired mobility Z74.09
   need for
    assistance with personal care Z74.1
    continuous supervision Z74.3
   no other household member able to
    render care Z74.2
   specified reason NEC Z74.8
  machine Z99.89
   enabling NEC Z99.89
   specified type NEC Z99.89
  renal dialysis (hemodialysis) (peritoneal)
   Z99.2
  respirator Z99.11
  ventilator Z99.11
  wheelchair Z99.3
 opiate —*see* Dependence, drug, opioid
 opioids —*see* Dependence, drug, opioid
 opium (alkaloids) (derivatives) (tincture) —
  see Dependence, drug, opioid
 oxygen (long-term) (supplemental) Z99.81
 paraldehyde —*see* Dependence, drug,
  sedative
 paregoric —*see* Dependence, drug, opioid
 PCP (phencyclidine) (or related substance) —
  see Dependence, drug, hallucinogen
 pentobarbital —*see* Dependence, drug,
  sedative
 pentobarbitone (sodium) —*see* Dependence,
  drug, sedative
 pentothal —*see* Dependence, drug, sedative
 peyote —*see* Dependence, drug, hallucinogen
 phencyclidine (PCP) (or related substance) —
  see Dependence, drug, hallucinogen
 phenmetrazine —*see* Dependence, drug,
  stimulant NEC
 phenobarbital —*see* Dependence, drug,
  sedative
 polysubstance F19.20
 psilocibin, psilocin, psilocyn, psilocyline —*see*
  Dependence, drug, hallucinogen
 psychostimulant NEC —*see* Dependence,
  drug, stimulant NEC
 secobarbital —*see* Dependence, drug, sedative
 seconal —*see* Dependence, drug, sedative
 sedative NEC —*see* Dependence, drug,
  sedative
 specified drug NEC —*see* Dependence, drug
 stimulant NEC —*see* Dependence, drug,
  stimulant NEC
 substance NEC —*see* Dependence, drug
 supplemental oxygen Z99.81
 tobacco —*see* Dependence, drug, nicotine
  counseling and surveillance Z71.6
 tranquilizer NEC —*see* Dependence, drug,
  sedative
 vitamin B6 E53.1
 volatile solvents —*see* Dependence, drug,
  inhalant

▶ New   ⟹ Revised   ~~deleted~~ Deleted   ● Use Additional Character(s)

Dependency
  care-provider Z74.9
  passive F60.7
  reactions (persistent) F60.7
Depersonalization (in neurotic state) (neurotic)
    (syndrome) F48.1
Depletion
  extracellular fluid E86.9
  plasma E86.1
  potassium E87.6
    nephropathy N25.89
  salt or sodium E87.1
    causing heat exhaustion or prostration T67.4
    nephropathy N28.9
  volume NOS E86.9
Deployment (current) (military) status Z56.82
  in theater or in support of military war,
        peacekeeping and humanitarian
        operations Z56.82
  personal history of Z91.82
    military war, peacekeeping and
        humanitarian deployment (current or
        past conflict) Z91.82
    returned from Z91.82
Depolarization, premature I49.40
  atrial I49.1
  junctional I49.2
  specified NEC I49.49
  ventricular I49.3
Deposit
  bone in Boeck's sarcoid D86.89
  calcareous, calcium —see Calcification
  cholesterol
    retina H35.89
    vitreous (body) (humor) —see Deposit,
        crystalline
  conjunctiva H11.11-●
  cornea H18.00-●
    argentous H18.02-●
    due to metabolic disorder H18.03-●
    Kayser-Fleischer ring H18.04-●
    pigmentation —see Pigmentation, cornea
  crystalline, vitreous (body) (humor) H43.2-●
  hemosiderin in old scars of cornea —see
        Pigmentation, cornea, stromal
  metallic in lens —see Cataract, specified NEC
  skin R23.8
  tooth, teeth (betel) (black) (green) (materia
        alba) (orange) (tobacco) K03.6
  urate, kidney —see Calculus, kidney
Depraved appetite —see Pica
Depressed
  HDL cholesterol E78.6
Depression (acute) (mental) F32.9
  agitated (single episode) F32.2
  anaclitic —see Disorder, adjustment
  anxiety F41.8
    persistent F34.1
  arches —see also Deformity, limb, flat foot
  atypical (single episode) F32.89
    recurrent episode F33.8
  basal metabolic rate R94.8
  bone marrow D75.89
  central nervous system R09.2
  cerebral R29.818
    newborn P91.4
  cerebrovascular I67.9
  chest wall M95.4
  climacteric (single episode) F32.89
    recurrent episode F33.8
  endogenous (without psychotic symptoms)
        F33.2
    with psychotic symptoms F33.3
  functional activity R68.89
  hysterical F44.89
  involutional (single episode) F32.89
    recurrent episode F33.8
  major F32.9
    with psychotic symptoms F32.3
    recurrent —see Disorder, depressive,
        recurrent

Depression (Continued)
  manic-depressive —see Disorder, depressive,
        recurrent
  masked (single episode) F32.89
  medullary G93.89
  menopausal (single episode) F32.89
    recurrent episode F33.8
  metatarsus —see Depression, arches
  monopolar F33.9
  nervous F34.1
  neurotic F34.1
  nose M95.0
  postnatal (NOS) F53.0
  postpartum (NOS) F53.0
  post-psychotic of schizophrenia F32.89
  post-schizophrenic F32.89
  psychogenic (reactive) (single episode) F32.9
  psychoneurotic F34.1
  psychotic (single episode) F32.3
    recurrent F33.3
  reactive (psychogenic) (single episode) F32.9
    psychotic (single episode) F32.3
  recurrent —see Disorder, depressive,
        recurrent
  respiratory center G93.89
  seasonal —see Disorder, depressive, recurrent
  senile F03
  severe, single episode F32.2
  situational F43.21
  skull Q67.4
  specified NEC (single episode) F32.89
  sternum M95.4
  visual field —see Defect, visual field
  vital (recurrent) (without psychotic
        symptoms) F33.2
    with psychotic symptoms F33.3
    single episode F32.2
Deprivation
  cultural Z60.3
  effects NOS T73.9
    specified NEC T73.8
  emotional NEC Z65.8
    affecting infant or child —see
        Maltreatment, child, psychological
  food T73.0
  protein —see Malnutrition
  sleep Z72.820
  social Z60.4
    affecting infant or child —see
        Maltreatment, child, psychological
  specified NEC T73.8
  vitamins —see Deficiency, vitamin
  water T73.1
Derangement
  ankle (internal) —see Derangement, joint,
        ankle
  cartilage (articular) NEC —see Derangement,
        joint, articular cartilage, by site
    recurrent —see Dislocation, recurrent
  cruciate ligament, anterior, current injury —
        see Sprain, knee, cruciate, anterior
  elbow (internal) —see Derangement, joint,
        elbow
  hip (joint) (internal) (old) —see Derangement,
        joint, hip
  joint (internal) M24.9
    ankylosis —see Ankylosis
    articular cartilage M24.10
      ankle M24.17-●
      elbow M24.12-●
      foot M24.17-●
      hand M24.14-●
      hip M24.15-●
      knee NEC M23.9-●
      loose body —see Loose, body
      shoulder M24.11-●
      wrist M24.13-●
    contracture —see Contraction, joint
    current injury —see also Dislocation
      knee, meniscus or cartilage —see Tear,
        meniscus

Derangement (Continued)
  joint (Continued)
    dislocation
      pathological —see Dislocation,
        pathological
      recurrent —see Dislocation, recurrent
    knee —see Derangement, knee
    ligament —see Disorder, ligament
    loose body —see Loose, body
    recurrent —see Dislocation, recurrent
    specified type NEC M24.80
      ankle M24.87-●
      elbow M24.82-●
      foot joint M24.87-●
      hand joint M24.84-●
      hip M24.85-●
      shoulder M24.81-●
      wrist M24.83-●
    temporomandibular M26.69
  knee (recurrent) M23.9-●
    ligament disruption, spontaneous
        M23.60-●
      anterior cruciate M23.61-●
      capsular M23.67-●
      instability, chronic M23.5-●
      lateral collateral M23.64-●
      medial collateral M23.63-●
      posterior cruciate M23.62-●
    loose body M23.4-●
    meniscus M23.30-●
      cystic M23.00-●
        lateral M23.002
          anterior horn M23.04-●
          posterior horn M23.05-●
          specified NEC M23.06-●
        medial M23.005
          anterior horn M23.01-●
          posterior horn M23.02-●
          specified NEC M23.03-●
      degenerate —see Derangement, knee,
        meniscus, specified NEC
      detached —see Derangement, knee,
        meniscus, specified NEC
      due to old tear or injury M23.20-●
        lateral M23.20-●
          anterior horn M23.24-●
          posterior horn M23.25-●
          specified NEC M23.26-●
        medial M23.20-●
          anterior horn M23.21-●
          posterior horn M23.22-●
          specified NEC M23.23-●
      retained —see Derangement, knee,
        meniscus, specified NEC
      specified NEC M23.30-●
        lateral M23.30-●
          anterior horn M23.34-●
          posterior horn M23.35-●
          specified NEC M23.36-●
        medial M23.30-●
          anterior horn M23.31-●
          posterior horn M23.32-●
          specified NEC M23.33-●
    old M23.8X-●
    specified NEC —see subcategory M23.8
  low back NEC —see Dorsopathy, specified
        NEC
  meniscus —see Derangement, knee,
        meniscus
  mental —see Psychosis
  patella, specified NEC —see Disorder,
        patella, derangement NEC
  semilunar cartilage (knee) —see
        Derangement, knee, meniscus,
        specified NEC
  shoulder (internal) —see Derangement,
        joint, shoulder
Dercum's disease E88.2
Derealization (neurotic) F48.1
Dermal —see condition
Dermaphytid —see Dermatophytosis

Dermatitis (eczematous) L30.9
  ab igne L59.0
  acarine B88.0
  actinic (due to sun) L57.8
    other than from sun L59.8
  allergic —see Dermatitis, contact, allergic
  ambustionis, due to burn or scald —see Burn
  amebic A06.7
  ammonia L22
  arsenical (ingested) L27.8
  artefacta L98.1
    psychogenic F54
  atopic L20.9
    psychogenic F54
    specified NEC L20.89
  autoimmune progesterone L30.8
  berlock, berloque L56.2
  blastomycotic B40.3
  blister beetle L24.89
  bullous, bullosa L13.9
    mucosynechial, atrophic L12.1
    seasonal L30.8
    specified NEC L13.8
  calorica L59.0
    due to burn or scald —see Burn
  caterpillar L24.89
  cercarial B65.3
  combustionis L59.0
    due to burn or scald —see Burn
  congelationis T69.1
  contact (occupational) L25.9
    allergic L23.9
      due to
        adhesives L23.1
        cement L23.5
        chemical products NEC L23.5
        chromium L23.0
        cosmetics L23.2
        dander (cat) (dog) L23.81
        drugs in contact with skin L23.3
        dyes L23.4
        food in contact with skin L23.6
        hair (cat) (dog) L23.81
        insecticide L23.5
        metals L23.0
        nickel L23.0
        plants, non-food L23.7
        plastic L23.5
        rubber L23.5
        specified agent NEC L23.89
    due to
      cement L25.3
      chemical products NEC L25.3
      cosmetics L25.0
      dander (cat) (dog) L23.81
      drugs in contact with skin L25.1
      dyes L25.2
      food in contact with skin L25.4
      hair (cat) (dog) L23.81
      plants, non-food L25.5
      specified agent NEC L25.8
    irritant L24.9
      due to
        cement L24.5
        chemical products NEC L24.5
        cosmetics L24.3
        detergents L24.0
        drugs in contact with skin L24.4
        food in contact with skin L24.6
        oils and greases L24.1
        plants, non-food L24.7
        solvents L24.2
        specified agent NEC L24.89
  contusiformis L52
  diabetic —see E08-E13 with .620
  diaper L22
  diphtheritica A36.3
  dry skin L85.3
  due to
    acetone (contact) (irritant) L24.2
    acids (contact) (irritant) L24.5

Dermatitis (Continued)
  due to (Continued)
    adhesive(s) (allergic) (contact) (plaster)
      L23.1
      irritant L24.5
    alcohol (irritant) (skin contact) (substances
      in category T51) L24.2
      taken internally L27.8
    alkalis (contact) (irritant) L24.5
    arsenic (ingested) L27.8
    carbon disulfide (contact) (irritant) L24.2
    caustics (contact) (irritant) L24.5
    cement (contact) L25.3
    cereal (ingested) L27.2
    chemical(s) NEC L25.3
      taken internally L27.8
    chlorocompounds L24.2
    chromium (contact) (irritant) L24.81
    coffee (ingested) L27.2
    cold weather L30.8
    cosmetics (contact) L25.0
      allergic L23.2
      irritant L24.3
    cyclohexanes L24.2
    dander (cat) (dog) L23.81
    Demodex species B88.0
    Dermanyssus gallinae B88.0
    detergents (contact) (irritant) L24.0
    dichromate L24.81
    drugs and medicaments (generalized)
      (internal use) L27.0
      external —see Dermatitis, due to, drugs,
        in contact with skin
      in contact with skin L25.1
        allergic L23.3
        irritant L24.4
      localized skin eruption L27.1
      specified substance —see Table of Drugs
        and Chemicals
    dyes (contact) L25.2
      allergic L23.4
      irritant L24.89
    epidermophytosis —see Dermatophytosis
    esters L24.2
    external irritant NEC L24.9
    fish (ingested) L27.2
    flour (ingested) L27.2
    food (ingested) L27.2
      in contact with skin L25.4
    fruit (ingested) L27.2
    furs (allergic) (contact) L23.81
    glues —see Dermatitis, due to, adhesives
    glycols L24.2
    greases NEC (contact) (irritant) L24.1
    hair (cat) (dog) L23.81
    hot
      objects and materials —see Burn
      weather or places L59.0
    hydrocarbons L24.2
    infrared rays L59.8
    ingestion, ingested substance L27.9
      chemical NEC L27.8
      drugs and medicaments —see
        Dermatitis, due to, drugs
      food L27.2
      specified NEC L27.8
    insecticide in contact with skin L24.5
    internal agent L27.9
      drugs and medicaments (generalized) —
        see Dermatitis, due to, drugs
      food L27.2
    irradiation —see Dermatitis, due to,
      radioactive substance
    ketones L24.2
    lacquer tree (allergic) (contact) L23.7
    light (sun) NEC L57.8
      acute L56.8
      other L59.8
    Liponyssoides sanguineus B88.0
    low temperature L30.8
    meat (ingested) L27.2

Dermatitis (Continued)
  due to (Continued)
    metals, metal salts (contact) (irritant)
      L24.81
    milk (ingested) L27.2
    nickel (contact) (irritant) L24.81
    nylon (contact) (irritant) L24.5
    oils NEC (contact) (irritant) L24.1
    paint solvent (contact) (irritant) L24.2
    petroleum products (contact) (irritant)
      (substances in T52) L24.2
    plants NEC (contact) L25.5
      allergic L23.7
      irritant L24.7
    plasters (adhesive) (any) (allergic) (contact)
      L23.1
      irritant L24.5
    plastic (contact) L25.3
    preservatives (contact) —see Dermatitis,
      due to, chemical, in contact with
      skin
    primrose (allergic) (contact) L23.7
    primula (allergic) (contact) L23.7
    radiation L59.8
      nonionizing (chronic exposure) L57.8
      sun NEC L57.8
        acute L56.8
    radioactive substance L58.9
      acute L58.0
      chronic L58.1
    radium L58.9
      acute L58.0
      chronic L58.1
    ragweed (allergic) (contact) L23.7
    Rhus (allergic) (contact) (diversiloba)
      (radicans) (toxicodendron) (venenata)
      (verniciflua) L23.7
    rubber (contact) L24.5
    Senecio jacobaea (allergic) (contact)
      L23.7
    solvents (contact) (irritant) (substances in
      categories T52) L24.2
    specified agent NEC (contact) L25.8
      allergic L23.89
      irritant L24.89
    sunshine NEC L57.8
      acute L56.8
    tetrachlorethylene (contact) (irritant)
      L24.2
    toluene (contact) (irritant) L24.2
    turpentine (contact) L24.2
    ultraviolet rays (sun NEC) (chronic
      exposure) L57.8
      acute L56.8
    vaccine or vaccination L27.0
      specified substance —see Table of Drugs
        and Chemicals
    varicose veins —see Varix, leg, with,
      inflammation
    X-rays L58.9
      acute L58.0
      chronic L58.1
  dyshydrotic L30.1
  dysmenorrheica N94.6
  escharotica —see Burn
  exfoliative, exfoliativa (generalized) L26
    neonatorum L00
  eyelid —see also Dermatosis, eyelid
    allergic H01.119
      left H01.116
        lower H01.115
        upper H01.114
      right H01.113
        lower H01.112
        upper H01.111
    contact —see Dermatitis, eyelid,
      allergic
    due to
      Demodex species B88.0
      herpes (zoster) B02.39
        simplex B00.59

▶ New   ⇒ Revised   ~~deleted~~ Deleted   ● Use Additional Character(s)

Dermatitis *(Continued)*
  eyelid *(Continued)*
    eczematous H01.139
      left H01.136
        lower H01.135
        upper H01.134
      right H01.133
        lower H01.132
        upper H01.131
  facta, factitia, factitial L98.1
    psychogenic F54
  flexural NEC L20.82
  friction L30.4
  fungus B36.9
    specified type NEC B36.8
  gangrenosa, gangrenous infantum L08.0
  harvest mite B88.0
  heat L59.0
  herpesviral, vesicular (ear) (lip) B00.1
  herpetiformis (bullous) (erythematous)
      (pustular) (vesicular) L13.0
    juvenile L12.2
    senile L12.0
  hiemalis L30.8
  hypostatic, hypostatica —*see* Varix, leg, with,
      inflammation
  infectious eczematoid L30.3
  infective L30.3
  irritant —*see* Dermatitis, contact, irritant
  Jacquet's (diaper dermatitis) L22
  Leptus B88.0
  lichenified NEC L28.0
  medicamentosa (generalized) (internal
      use) —*see* Dermatitis, due to drugs
  mite B88.0
  multiformis L13.0
    juvenile L12.2
  napkin L22
  neurotica L13.0
  nummular L30.0
  papillaris capillitii L73.0
  pellagrous E52
  perioral L71.0
  photocontact L56.2
  polymorpha dolorosa L13.0
  pruriginosa L13.0
  pruritic NEC L30.8
  psychogenic F54
  purulent L08.0
  pustular
    contagious B08.02
    subcorneal L13.1
  pyococcal L08.0
  pyogenica L08.0
  repens L40.2
  Ritter's (exfoliativa) L00
  Schamberg's L81.7
  schistosome B65.3
  seasonal bullous L30.8
  seborrheic L21.9
    infantile L21.1
    specified NEC L21.8
  sensitization NOS L23.9
  septic L08.0
  solare L57.8
  specified NEC L30.8
  stasis I87.2
    with
      varicose ulcer —*see* Varix, leg, with ulcer,
          with inflammation
      varicose veins —*see* Varix, leg, with,
          inflammation
    due to postthrombotic syndrome —*see*
        Syndrome, postthrombotic
  suppurative L08.0
  traumatic NEC L30.4
  trophoneurotica L13.0
  ultraviolet (sun) (chronic exposure) L57.8
    acute L56.8
  varicose —*see* Varix, leg, with, inflammation
  vegetans L10.1

Dermatitis *(Continued)*
  verrucosa B43.0
  vesicular, herpesviral B00.1
Dermatoarthritis, lipoid E78.81
Dermatochalasis, eyelid H02.839
  left H02.836
    lower H02.835
    upper H02.834
  right H02.833
    lower H02.832
    upper H02.831
Dermatofibroma (lenticulare) —*see* Neoplasm,
    skin, benign
  protuberans —*see* Neoplasm, skin, uncertain
      behavior
Dermatofibrosarcoma (pigmented)
    (protuberans) —*see* Neoplasm, skin,
    malignant
Dermatographia L50.3
Dermatolysis (exfoliativa) (congenital) Q82.8
  acquired L57.4
  eyelids —*see* Blepharochalasis
  palpebrarum —*see* Blepharochalasis
  senile L57.4
Dermatomegaly NEC Q82.8
Dermatomucosomyositis M33.10
  with
    myopathy M33.12
    respiratory involvement M33.11
    specified organ involvement NEC M33.19
Dermatomycosis B36.9
  furfuracea B36.0
  specified type NEC B36.8
Dermatomyositis (acute) (chronic) —*see also*
    Dermatopolymyositis
  adult —*see also* Dermatomyositis, specified
      NEC M33.10
  in (due to) neoplastic disease —*see also*
      Neoplasm D49.9 *[M36.0]*
  juvenile M33.00
    with
      myopathy M33.02
      respiratory involvement M33.01
      specified organ involvement NEC
          M33.09
    without myopathy M33.03
  specified NEC M33.10
    with
      myopathy M33.12
      respiratory involvement M33.11
      specified organ involvement NEC M33.19
    without myopathy M33.13
Dermatoneuritis of children —*see* Poisoning,
    mercury
Dermatophilosis A48.8
Dermatophytid L30.2
Dermatophytide —*see* Dermatophytosis
Dermatophytosis (epidermophyton) (infection)
    (Microsporum) (tinea) (Trichophyton)
    B35.9
  beard B35.0
  body B35.4
  capitis B35.0
  corporis B35.4
  deep-seated B35.8
  disseminated B35.8
  foot B35.3
  granulomatous B35.8
  groin B35.6
  hand B35.2
  nail B35.1
  perianal (area) B35.6
  scalp B35.0
  specified NEC B35.8
Dermatopolymyositis M33.90
  with
    myopathy M33.92
    respiratory involvement M33.91
    specified organ involvement NEC M33.99
  in neoplastic disease (*see also* Neoplasm)
      D49.9 *[M36.0]*

Dermatopolymyositis *(Continued)*
  juvenile M33.00
    with
      myopathy M33.02
      respiratory involvement M33.01
      specified organ involvement NEC M33.09
  specified NEC M33.10
    myopathy M33.12
    respiratory involvement M33.11
    specified organ involvement NEC M33.19
  without myopathy M33.93
Dermatopolyneuritis —*see* Poisoning, mercury
Dermatorrhexis Q79.6
  acquired L57.4
Dermatosclerosis —*see also* Scleroderma
  localized L94.0
Dermatosis L98.9
  Andrews' L08.89
  Bowen's —*see* Neoplasm, skin, in situ
  bullous L13.9
    specified NEC L13.8
  exfoliativa L26
  eyelid (noninfectious)
    dermatitis —*see* Dermatitis, eyelid
    discoid lupus erythematosus —*see* Lupus,
        erythematosus, eyelid
    xeroderma —*see* Xeroderma, acquired,
        eyelid
  factitial L98.1
  febrile neutrophilic L98.2
  gonococcal A54.89
  herpetiformis L13.0
    juvenile L12.2
  linear IgA L13.8
  menstrual NEC L98.8
  neutrophilic, febrile L98.2
  occupational —*see* Dermatitis, contact
  papulosa nigra L82.1
  pigmentary L81.9
    progressive L81.7
    Schamberg's L81.7
  psychogenic F54
  purpuric, pigmented L81.7
  pustular, subcorneal L13.1
  transient acantholytic L11.1
Dermographia, dermographism L50.3
Dermoid (cyst) —*see also* Neoplasm, benign,
    by site
  with malignant transformation C56-●
  due to radiation (nonionizing) L57.8
Dermopathy
  infiltrative with thyrotoxicosis —*see*
      Thyrotoxicosis
  nephrogenic fibrosing L90.8
Dermophytosis —*see* Dermatophytosis
Descemetocele H18.73-●
Descemet's membrane —*see* condition
Descending —*see* condition
Descensus uteri —*see* Prolapse, uterus
Desert
  rheumatism B38.0
  sore —*see* Ulcer, skin
Desertion (newborn) —*see* Maltreatment
Desmoid (extra-abdominal) (tumor) —*see*
    Neoplasm, connective tissue, uncertain
    behavior
  abdominal D48.1
Despondency F32.9
Desquamation, skin R23.4
Destruction, destructive —*see also* Damage
  articular facet —*see also* Derangement, joint,
      specified type NEC
    knee M23.8X-●
    vertebra —*see* Spondylosis
  bone —*see also* Disorder, bone, specified type
      NEC
    syphilitic A52.77
  joint —*see also* Derangement, joint, specified
      type NEC
    sacroiliac M53.3
  rectal sphincter K62.89

Destruction, destructive *(Continued)*
  septum (nasal) J34.89
  tuberculous NEC —*see* Tuberculosis
  tympanum, tympanic membrane
      (nontraumatic) —*see* Disorder, tympanic
      membrane, specified NEC
  vertebral disc —*see* Degeneration,
      intervertebral disc
Destructiveness —*see also* Disorder, conduct
  adjustment reaction —*see* Disorder,
      adjustment
Desultory labor O62.2
Detachment
  cartilage —*see* Sprain
  cervix, annular N88.8
      complicating delivery O71.3
  choroid (old) (postinfectional) (simple)
      (spontaneous) H31.40-●
      hemorrhagic H31.41-●
      serous H31.42-●
  ligament —*see* Sprain
  meniscus (knee) —*see also* Derangement,
      knee, meniscus, specified NEC
      current injury —*see* Tear, meniscus
      due to old tear or injury —*see*
          Derangement, knee, meniscus, due to
          old tear
  retina (without retinal break) (serous)
      H33.2-●
      with retinal:
          break H33.00-●
              giant H33.03-●
              multiple H33.02-●
              single H33.01-●
          dialysis H33.04-●
      pigment epithelium —*see* Degeneration,
          retina, separation of layers, pigment
          epithelium detachment
      rhegmatogenous —*see* Detachment, retina,
          with retinal, break
      specified NEC H33.8
      total H33.05-●
      traction H33.4-●
  vitreous (body) H43.81
Detergent asthma J69.8
Deterioration
  epileptic F06.8
  general physical R53.81
  heart, cardiac —*see* Degeneration,
      myocardial
  mental —*see* Psychosis
  myocardial, myocardium —*see* Degeneration,
      myocardial
  senile (simple) R54
Deuteranomaly (anomalous trichromat) H53.53
Deuteranopia (complete) (incomplete) H53.53
Development
  abnormal, bone Q79.9
  arrested R62.50
      bone —*see* Arrest, development or growth,
          bone
      child R62.50
      due to malnutrition E45
  defective, congenital —*see also* Anomaly, by
      site
      cauda equina Q06.3
      left ventricle Q24.8
          in hypoplastic left heart syndrome Q23.4
      valve Q24.8
          pulmonary Q22.3
  delayed *(see also* Delay, development) R62.50
      arithmetical skills F81.2
      language (skills) (expressive) F80.1
      learning skill F81.9
      mixed skills F88
      motor coordination F82
      reading F81.0
      specified learning skill NEC F81.89
      speech F80.9
      spelling F81.81
      written expression F81.81

Development *(Continued)*
  imperfect, congenital —*see also* Anomaly, by
      site
      heart Q24.9
      lungs Q33.6
  incomplete
      bronchial tree Q32.4
      organ or site not listed —*see* Hypoplasia,
          by site
      respiratory system Q34.9
  sexual, precocious NEC E30.1
  tardy, mental *(see also* Disability, intellectual)
      F79
Developmental —*see* condition
  testing, infant or child —*see* Examination,
      child
Devergie's disease (pityriasis rubra pilaris)
      L44.0
Deviation (in)
  conjugate palsy (eye) (spastic) H51.0
  esophagus (acquired) K22.8
  eye, skew H51.8
  midline (jaw) (teeth) (dental arch) M26.29
      specified site NEC —*see* Malposition
  nasal septum J34.2
      congenital Q67.4
  opening and closing of the mandible M26.53
  organ or site, congenital NEC —*see*
      Malposition, congenital
  septum (nasal) (acquired) J34.2
      congenital Q67.4
  sexual F65.9
      bestiality F65.89
      erotomania F52.8
      exhibitionism F65.2
      fetishism, fetishistic F65.0
          transvestism F65.1
      frotteurism F65.81
      masochism F65.51
      multiple F65.89
      necrophilia F65.89
      nymphomania F52.8
      pederosis F65.4
      pedophilia F65.4
      sadism, sadomasochism F65.52
      satyriasis F52.8
      specified type NEC F65.89
      transvestism F64.1
      voyeurism F65.3
  teeth, midline M26.29
  trachea J39.8
  ureter, congenital Q62.61
Device
  cerebral ventricle (communicating) in situ
      Z98.2
  contraceptive —*see* Contraceptive, device
  drainage, cerebrospinal fluid, in situ Z98.2
Devic's disease G36.0
Devil's
  grip B33.0
  pinches (purpura simplex) D69.2
Devitalized tooth K04.99
Devonshire colic —*see* Poisoning, lead
Dextraposition, aorta Q20.3
  in tetralogy of Fallot Q21.3
Dextrinosis, limit (debrancher enzyme
      deficiency) E74.03
Dextrocardia (true) Q24.0
  with
      complete transposition of viscera Q89.3
      situs inversus Q89.3
Dextrotransposition, aorta Q20.3
d-glycericacidemia E72.59
Dhat syndrome F48.8
Dhobi itch B35.6
Di George's syndrome D82.1
Di Guglielmo's disease C94.0-●
Diabetes, diabetic (mellitus) (sugar) E11.9
  with
      amyotrophy E11.44
      arthropathy NEC E11.618

Diabetes, diabetic *(Continued)*
  with *(Continued)*
      autonomic (poly)neuropathy E11.43
      cataract E11.36
      Charcot's joints E11.610
      chronic kidney disease E11.22
      circulatory complication NEC E11.59
      complication E11.8
          specified NEC E11.69
      dermatitis E11.620
      foot ulcer E11.621
      gangrene E11.52
      gastroparalysis E11.43
      gastroparesis E11.43
      glomerulonephrosis, intracapillary E11.21
      glomerulosclerosis, intercapillary E11.21
      hyperglycemia E11.65
      hyperosmolarity E11.00
          with coma E11.01
      hypoglycemia E11.649
          with coma E11.641
      ketoacidosis E11.10
          with coma E11.11
      kidney complications NEC E11.29
      Kimmelstiel-Wilson disease E11.21
      loss of protective sensation (LOPS) —*see*
          Diabetes, by type, with neuropathy
      mononeuropathy E11.41
      myasthenia E11.44
      necrobiosis lipoidica E11.620
      nephropathy E11.21
      neuralgia E11.42
      neurologic complication NEC E11.49
      neuropathic arthropathy E11.610
      neuropathy E11.40
      ophthalmic complication NEC E11.39
      oral complication NEC E11.638
      osteomyelitis E11.69
      periodontal disease E11.630
      peripheral angiopathy E11.51
          with gangrene E11.52
      polyneuropathy E11.42
      renal complication NEC E11.29
      renal tubular degeneration E11.29
      retinopathy E11.319
          with macular edema E11.311
              resolved following treatment
                  E11.37
          nonproliferative E11.329
              with macular edema E11.321
              mild E11.329
                  with macular edema E11.321
              moderate E11.339
                  with macular edema E11.331
              severe E11.349
                  with macular edema E11.341
          proliferative E11.359
              with
                  combined traction retinal
                      detachment and
                      rhegmatogenous retinal
                      detachment E11.354
                  macular edema E11.351
                  stable proliferative diabetic
                      retinopathy E11.355
                  traction retinal detachment
                      involving the macula E11.352
                  traction retinal detachment not
                      involving the macula E11.353
      skin complication NEC E11.628
      skin ulcer NEC E11.622
  brittle —*see* Diabetes, type 1
  bronzed E83.110
  complicating pregnancy —*see* Pregnancy,
      complicated by, diabetes
  dietary counseling and surveillance Z71.3
  due to
      autoimmune process —*see* Diabetes, type 1
      immune mediated pancreatic islet
          beta-cell destruction —*see* Diabetes,
              type 1

▶ New   ➡ Revised   ~~deleted~~ Deleted   ● Use Additional Character(s)

Diabetes, diabetic (Continued)
  due to drug or chemical E09.9
    with
      amyotrophy E09.44
      arthropathy NEC E09.618
      autonomic (poly)neuropathy E09.43
      cataract E09.36
      Charcot's joints E09.610
      chronic kidney disease E09.22
      circulatory complication NEC E09.59
      complication E09.8
        specified NEC E09.69
      dermatitis E09.620
      foot ulcer E09.621
      gangrene E09.52
      gastroparalysis E09.43
      gastroparesis E09.43
      glomerulonephrosis, intracapillary
        E09.21
      glomerulosclerosis, intercapillary E09.21
      hyperglycemia E09.65
      hyperosmolarity E09.00
        with coma E09.01
      hypoglycemia E09.649
        with coma E09.641
      ketoacidosis E09.10
        with coma E09.11
      kidney complications NEC E09.29
      Kimmelsteil-Wilson disease E09.21
      mononeuropathy E09.41
      myasthenia E09.44
      necrobiosis lipoidica E09.620
      nephropathy E09.21
      neuralgia E09.42
      neurologic complication NEC E09.49
      neuropathic arthropathy E09.610
      neuropathy E09.40
      ophthalmic complication NEC E09.39
      oral complication NEC E09.638
      periodontal disease E09.630
      peripheral angiopathy E09.51
        with gangrene E09.52
      polyneuropathy E09.42
      renal complication NEC E09.29
      renal tubular degeneration E09.29
      retinopathy E09.319
        with macular edema E09.311
          resolved following treatment
            E09.37
        nonproliferative E09.329
          with macular edema E09.321
          mild E09.329
            with macular edema E09.321
          moderate E09.339
            with macular edema E09.331
          severe E09.349
            with macular edema E09.341
        proliferative E09.359
          with
            combined traction retinal
              detachment and
              rhegmatogenous retinal
              detachment E09.354
            macular edema E09.351
            stable proliferative diabetic
              retinopathy E09.355
            traction retinal detachment
              involving the macula
              E09.352
            traction retinal detachment not
              involving the macula
              E09.353
      skin complication NEC E09.628
      skin ulcer NEC E09.622
  due to underlying condition E08.9
    with
      amyotrophy E08.44
      arthropathy NEC E08.618
      autonomic (poly)neuropathy E08.43
      cataract E08.36
      Charcot's joints E08.610

Diabetes, diabetic (Continued)
  due to underlying condition (Continued)
    with (Continued)
      chronic kidney disease E08.22
      circulatory complication NEC E08.59
      complication E08.8
        specified NEC E08.69
      dermatitis E08.620
      foot ulcer E08.621
      gangrene E08.52
      gastroparalysis E08.43
      gastroparesis E08.43
      glomerulonephrosis, intracapillary
        E08.21
      glomerulosclerosis, intercapillary E08.21
      hyperglycemia E08.69
      hyperosmolarity E08.00
        with coma E08.01
      hypoglycemia E08.649
        with coma E08.641
      ketoacidosis E08.10
        with coma E08.11
      kidney complications NEC E08.29
      Kimmelsteil-WIlson disease E08.21
      mononeuropathy E08.41
      myasthenia E08.44
      necrobiosis lipoidica E08.620
      nephropathy E08.21
      neuralgia E08.42
      neurologic complication NEC E08.49
      neuropathic arthropathy E08.610
      neuropathy E08.40
      ophthalmic complication NEC
        E08.39
      oral complication NEC E08.638
      periodontal disease E08.630
      peripheral angiopathy E08.51
        with gangrene E08.52
      polyneuropathy E08.42
      renal complication NEC E08.29
      renal tubular degeneration E08.29
      retinopathy E08.319
        with macular edema E08.311
          resolved following treatment E08.37

        nonproliferative E08.329
          with macular edema E08.321
          mild E08.329
            with macular edema E08.321
          moderate E08.339
            with macular edema E08.331
          severe E08.349
            with macular edema E08.341
        proliferative E08.359
          with
            combined traction retinal
              detachment and
              rhegmatogenous retinal
              detachment E08.354
            macular edema E08.351
            stable proliferative diabetic
              retinopathy E08.355
            traction retinal detachment
              involving the macula
              E08.352
            traction retinal detachment not
              involving the macula
              E08.353
      skin complication NEC E08.628
      skin ulcer NEC E08.622
  gestational (in pregnancy) O24.419
    affecting newborn P70.0
    diet-controlled O24.410
    in childbirth O24.429
      diet-controlled O24.420
      insulin (and diet) controlled O24.424
      oral drug controlled (antidiabetic)
        (hypoglycemic) O24.425
    insulin (and diet) controlled O24.414
    oral drug controlled (antidiabetic)
      (hypoglycemic) O24.415

Diabetes, diabetic (Continued)
  gestational (in pregnancy) (Continued)
    puerperal O24.439
      diet-controlled O24.430
      insulin (and diet) controlled O24.434
      oral drug controlled (antidiabetic)
        (hypoglycemic) O24.435
  hepatogenous E13.9
  idiopathic —see Diabetes, type 1
  inadequately controlled — code to Diabetes,
    by type, with hyperglycemia
  insipidus E23.2
    nephrogenic N25.1
    pituitary E23.2
    vasopressin resistant N25.1
  insulin dependent — code to type of diabetes
  juvenile-onset —see Diabetes, type 1
  ketosis-prone —see Diabetes, type 1
  latent R73.03
  neonatal (transient) P70.2
  non-insulin dependent — code to type of
    diabetes
  out of control — code to Diabetes, by type,
    with hyperglycemia
  phosphate E83.39
  poorly controlled — code to Diabetes, by
    type, with hyperglycemia
  postpancreatectomy —see Diabetes, specified
    type NEC
  postprocedural —see Diabetes, specified type
    NEC
  secondary diabetes mellitus NEC —see
    Diabetes, specified type NEC
  specified type NEC E13.9
    with
      amyotrophy E13.44
      arthropathy NEC E13.618
      autonomic (poly)neuropathy E13.43
      cataract E13.36
      Charcot's joints E13.610
      chronic kidney disease E13.22
      circulatory complication NEC E13.59
      complication E13.8
        specified NEC E13.69
      dermatitis E13.620
      foot ulcer E13.621
      gangrene E13.52
      gastroparalysis E13.43
      gastroparesis E13.43
      glomerulonephrosis, intracapillary
        E13.21
      glomerulosclerosis, intercapillary E13.21
      hyperglycemia E13.65
      hyperosmolarity E13.00
        with coma E13.01
      hypoglycemia E13.649
        with coma E13.641
      ketoacidosis E13.10
        with coma E13.11
      kidney complications NEC E13.29
      Kimmelsteil-Wilson disease E13.21
      mononeuropathy E13.41
      myasthenia E13.44
      necrobiosis lipoidica E13.620
      nephropathy E13.21
      neuralgia E13.42
      neurologic complication NEC E13.49
      neuropathic arthropathy E13.610
      neuropathy E13.40
      ophthalmic complication NEC E13.39
      oral complication NEC E13.638
      periodontal disease E13.630
      peripheral angiopathy E13.51
        with gangrene E13.52
      polyneuropathy E13.42
      renal complication NEC E13.29
      renal tubular degeneration E13.29
      retinopathy E13.319
        with macular edema E13.311
          resolved following treatment
            E13.37

Diabetes, diabetic *(Continued)*
  specified type NEC *(Continued)*
    with *(Continued)*
      retinopathy *(Continued)*
        nonproliferative E13.329
          with macular edema E13.321
          mild E13.329
            with macular edema E13.321
          moderate E13.339
            with macular edema E13.331
          severe E13.349
            with macular edema E13.341
        proliferative E13.359
          with
            combined traction retinal
              detachment and
              rhegmatogenous retinal
              detachment E13.354
            macular edema E13.351
            stable proliferative diabetic
              retinopathy E13.355
            traction retinal detachment
              involving the macula
              E13.352
            traction retinal detachment not
              involving the macula
              E13.353
      skin complication NEC E13.628
      skin ulcer NEC E13.622
  steroid-induced —*see* Diabetes, due to, drug
    or chemical
  type 1 E10.9
    with
      amyotrophy E10.44
      arthropathy NEC E10.618
      autonomic (poly)neuropathy E10.43
      cataract E10.36
      Charcot's joints E10.610
      chronic kidney disease E10.22
      circulatory complication NEC E10.59
      complication E10.8
        specified NEC E10.69
      dermatitis E10.620
      foot ulcer E10.621
      gangrene E10.52
      gastroparalysis E10.43
      gastroparesis E10.43
      glomerulonephrosis, intracapillary E10.21
      glomerulosclerosis, intercapillary E10.21
      hyperglycemia E10.65
      hypoglycemia E10.649
        with coma E10.641
      ketoacidosis E10.10
        with coma E10.11
      kidney complications NEC E10.29
      Kimmelstiel-Wilson disease E10.21
      mononeuropathy E10.41
      myasthenia E10.44
      necrobiosis lipoidica E10.620
      nephropathy E10.21
      neuralgia E10.42
      neurologic complication NEC E10.49
      neuropathic arthropathy E10.610
      neuropathy E10.40
      ophthalmic complication NEC E10.39
      oral complication NEC E10.638
      osteomyelitis E10.69
      periodontal disease E10.630
      peripheral angiopathy E10.51
        with gangrene E10.52
      polyneuropathy E10.42
      renal complication NEC E10.29
      renal tubular degeneration E10.29
      retinopathy E10.319
        with macular edema E10.311
          resolved following treatment E10.37
        nonproliferative E10.329
          with macular edema E10.321
          mild E10.329
            with macular edema E10.321
          moderate E10.339
            with macular edema E10.331

Diabetes, diabetic *(Continued)*
  type 1 *(Continued)*
    with *(Continued)*
      retinopathy *(Continued)*
        nonproliferative *(Continued)*
          severe E10.349
            with macular edema E10.341
        proliferative E10.359
          with
            combined traction retinal
              detachment and
              rhegmatogenous retinal
              detachment E13.354
            macular edema E13.351
            stable proliferative diabetic
              retinopathy E13.355
            traction retinal detachment
              involving the macula E13.352
            traction retinal detachment not
              involving the macula E13.353
      skin complication NEC E10.628
      skin ulcer NEC E10.622
  type 2 E11.9
    with
      amyotrophy E11.44
      arthropathy NEC E11.618
      autonomic (poly)neuropathy E11.43
      cataract E11.36
      Charcot's joints E11.610
      chronic kidney disease E11.22
      circulatory complication NEC E11.59
      complication E11.8
        specified NEC E11.69
      dermatitis E11.620
      foot ulcer E11.621
      gangrene E11.52
      gastroparalysis E11.43
      gastroparesis E11.43
      glomerulonephrosis, intracapillary E11.21
      glomerulosclerosis, intercapillary E11.21
      hyperglycemia E11.65
      hyperosmolarity E11.00
        with coma E11.01
      hypoglycemia E11.649
        with coma E11.641
      ketoacidosis E11.10
        with coma E11.11
      kidney complications NEC E11.29
      Kimmelstiel-Wilson disease E11.21
      mononeuropathy E11.41
      myasthenia E11.44
      necrobiosis lipoidica E11.620
      nephropathy E11.21
      neuralgia E11.42
      neurologic complication NEC E11.49
      neuropathic arthropathy E11.610
      neuropathy E11.40
      ophthalmic complication NEC E11.39
      oral complication NEC E11.638
      osteomyelitis E11.69
      periodontal disease E11.630
      peripheral angiopathy E11.51
        with gangrene E11.52
      polyneuropathy E11.42
      renal complication NEC E11.29
      renal tubular degeneration E11.29
      retinopathy E11.319
        with macular edema E11.311
          resolved following treatment E11.37
        nonproliferative E11.329
          with macular edema E11.321
          mild E11.329
            with macular edema E11.321
          moderate E11.339
            with macular edema E11.331
          severe E11.349
            with macular edema E11.341
        proliferative E11.359
          with
            combined traction retinal
              detachment and
              rhegmatogenous retinal
              detachment E11.354

Diabetes, diabetic *(Continued)*
  type 2 *(Continued)*
    with *(Continued)*
      retinopathy *(Continued)*
        proliferative *(Continued)*
          with *(Continued)*
            macular edema E11.351
            stable proliferative diabetic
              retinopathy E11.355
            traction retinal detachment
              involving the macula E11.352
            traction retinal detachment not
              involving the macula E11.353
      skin complication NEC E11.628
      skin ulcer NEC E11.622
  uncontrolled
    meaning
      hyperglycemia —*see* Diabetes, by type,
        with, hyperglycemia
      hypoglycemia —*see* Diabetes, by type,
        with, hypoglycemia
Diacyclothrombopathia D69.1
Diagnosis deferred R69
Dialysis (intermittent) (treatment)
  noncompliance (with) Z91.15
  renal (hemodialysis) (peritoneal), status Z99.2
  retina, retinal —*see* Detachment, retina, with
    retinal, dialysis
Diamond-Blackfan anemia (congenital
  hypoplastic) D61.01
Diamond-Gardener syndrome
  (autoerythrocyte sensitization) D69.2
Diaper rash L22
Diaphoresis (excessive) R61
Diaphragm —*see* condition
Diaphragmalgia R07.1
Diaphragmatitis, diaphragmitis J98.6
Diaphysial aclasis Q78.6
Diaphysitis —*see* Osteomyelitis, specified type
  NEC
Diarrhea, diarrheal (disease) (infantile)
  (inflammatory) R19.7
  achlorhydric K31.83
  allergic K52.29
    due to
      colitis —*see* Colitis, allergic
      enteritis —*see* Enteritis, allergic
  amebic —*see also* Amebiasis A06.0
    with abscess —*see* Abscess, amebic
    acute A06.0
    chronic A06.1
    nondysenteric A06.2
  bacillary —*see* Dysentery, bacillary
  balantidial A07.0
  cachectic NEC K52.89
  Chilomastix A07.8
  choleriformis A00.1
  chronic (noninfectious) K52.9
  coccidial A07.3
  Cochin-China K90.1
    strongyloidiasis B78.0
  Dientamoeba A07.8
  dietetic —*see also* Diarrhea, allergic K52.29
  drug-induced K52.1
  due to
    bacteria A04.9
      specified NEC A04.8
    Campylobacter A04.5
    Capillaria philippinensis B81.1
    Clostridium difficile
      not specified as recurrent A04.72
      recurrent A04.71
    Clostridium perfringens (C) (F) A04.8
    Cryptosporidium A07.2
    drugs K52.1
    Escherichia coli A04.4
      enteroaggregative A04.4
      enterohemorrhagic A04.3
      enteroinvasive A04.2
      enteropathogenic A04.0
      enterotoxigenic A04.1
      specified NEC A04.4

▶ New   ⮕ Revised   ~~deleted~~ Deleted   ● Use Additional Character(s)

Diarrhea, diarrheal *(Continued)*
  due to *(Continued)*
    food hypersensitivity —*see also* Diarrhea,
      allergic K52.29
    Necator americanus B76.1
    S. japonicum B65.2
    specified organism NEC A08.8
      bacterial A04.8
      viral A08.39
    Staphylococcus A04.8
    Trichuris trichiuria B79
    virus —*see* Enteritis, viral
    Yersinia enterocolitica A04.6
  dysenteric A09
  endemic A09
  epidemic A09
  flagellate A07.9
  Flexner's (ulcerative) A03.1
  functional K59.1
    following gastrointestinal surgery
      K91.89
    psychogenic F45.8
  Giardia lamblia A07.1
  giardial A07.1
  hill K90.1
  infectious A09
  malarial —*see* Malaria
  mite B88.0
  mycotic NEC B49
  neonatal (noninfectious) P78.3
  nervous F45.8
  neurogenic K59.1
  noninfectious K52.9
  postgastrectomy K91.1
  postvagotomy K91.1
  protozoal A07.9
    specified NEC A07.8
  psychogenic F45.8
  specified
    bacterium NEC A04.8
    virus NEC A08.39
  strongyloidiasis B78.0
  toxic K52.1
  trichomonal A07.8
  tropical K90.1
  tuberculous A18.32
  viral —*see* Enteritis, viral
Diastasis
  cranial bones M84.88
    congenital NEC Q75.8
  joint (traumatic) —*see* Dislocation
  muscle M62.00
    ankle M62.07-●
    congenital Q79.8
    foot M62.07-●
    forearm M62.03-●
    hand M62.04-●
    lower leg M62.06-●
    pelvic region M62.05-●
    shoulder region M62.01-●
    specified site NEC M62.08
    thigh M62.05-●
    upper arm M62.02-●
  recti (abdomen)
    complicating delivery O71.89
    congenital Q79.59
Diastema, tooth, teeth, fully erupted
  M26.32
Diastematomyelia Q06.2
Diataxia, cerebral G80.4
Diathesis
  allergic —*see* History, allergy
  bleeding (familial) D69.9
  cystine (familial) E72.00
  gouty —*see* Gout
  hemorrhagic (familial) D69.9
    newborn NEC P53
  spasmophilic R29.0
Diaz's disease or osteochondrosis (juvenile)
  (talus) —*see* Osteochondrosis, juvenile,
    tarsus

Dibothriocephalus, dibothriocephaliasis
  (latus) (infection) (infestation) B70.0
  larval B70.1
Dicephalus, dicephaly Q89.4
Dichotomy, teeth K00.2
Dichromat, dichromatopsia (congenital) —*see*
  Deficiency, color vision
Dichuchwa A65
Dicroceliasis B66.2
Didelphia, didelphys —*see* Double uterus
Didymytis N45.1
  with orchitis N45.3
Dietary
  inadequacy or deficiency E63.9
  surveillance and counseling Z71.3
Dietl's crisis N13.8
Dieulafoy lesion (hemorrhagic)
  duodenum K31.82
  esophagus K22.8
  intestine (colon) K63.81
  stomach K31.82
Difficult, difficulty (in)
  acculturation Z60.3
  feeding R63.3
    newborn P92.9
      breast P92.5
      specified NEC P92.8
    nonorganic (infant or child) F98.29
  intubation, in anesthesia T88.4
  mechanical, gastroduodenal stoma K91.89
    causing obstruction —*see also* Obstruction,
      intestine, postoperative K91.30
  micturition
    need to immediately re-void R39.191
    position dependent R39.192
    specified NEC R39.198
  reading (developmental) F81.0
    secondary to emotional disorders F93.9
  spelling (specific) F81.81
    with reading disorder F81.89
    due to inadequate teaching Z55.8
  swallowing —*see* Dysphagia
  walking R26.2
  work
    conditions NEC Z56.5
    schedule Z56.3
Diffuse —*see* condition
DiGeorge's syndrome (thymic hypoplasia)
  D82.1
Digestive —*see* condition
Dihydropyrimidine dehydrogenase disease
  (DPD) E88.89
Diktyoma —*see* Neoplasm, malignant, by site
Dilaceration, tooth K00.4
Dilatation
  anus K59.8
    venule —*see* Hemorrhoids
  aorta (focal) (general) —*see* Ectasia, aorta
    with aneurysm —*see* Aneurysm, aorta
    congenital Q25.44
  artery —*see* Aneurysm
  bladder (sphincter) N32.89
    congenital Q64.79
  blood vessel I99.8
  bronchial J47.9
    with
      exacerbation (acute) J47.1
      lower respiratory infection J47.0
  calyx (due to obstruction) —*see*
    Hydronephrosis
  capillaries I78.8
  cardiac (acute) (chronic) —*see also*
    Hypertrophy, cardiac
    congenital Q24.8
      valve NEC Q24.8
        pulmonary Q22.3
    valve —*see* Endocarditis
  cavum septi pellucidi Q06.8
  cervix (uteri) —*see also* Incompetency, cervix
    incomplete, poor, slow complicating
      delivery O62.0

Dilatation *(Continued)*
  colon K59.39
    congenital Q43.1
    psychogenic F45.8
    toxic K59.31
  common duct (acquired) K83.8
    congenital Q44.5
  cystic duct (acquired) K82.8
    congenital Q44.5
  duct, mammary —*see* Ectasia, mammary duct
  duodenum K59.8
  esophagus K22.8
    congenital Q39.5
    due to achalasia K22.0
  eustachian tube, congenital Q17.8
  gallbladder K82.8
  gastric —*see* Dilatation, stomach
  heart (acute) (chronic) —*see also* Hypertrophy,
    cardiac
    congenital Q24.8
    valve —*see* Endocarditis
  ileum K59.8
    psychogenic F45.8
  jejunum K59.8
    psychogenic F45.8
  kidney (calyx) (collecting structures) (cystic)
    (parenchyma) (pelvis) (idiopathic)
    N28.89
  lacrimal passages or duct —*see* Disorder,
    lacrimal system, changes
  lymphatic vessel I89.0
  mammary duct —*see* Ectasia, mammary
    duct
  Meckel's diverticulum (congenital) Q43.0
    malignant —*see* Table of Neoplasms, small
      intestine, malignant
  myocardium (acute) (chronic) —*see*
    Hypertrophy, cardiac organ or site,
    congenital NEC —*see* Distortion
  pancreatic duct K86.89
  pericardium —*see* Pericarditis
  pharynx J39.2
  prostate N42.89
  pulmonary
    artery (idiopathic) I28.8
    valve, congenital Q22.3
  pupil H57.04
  rectum K59.39
  saccule, congenital Q16.5
  salivary gland (duct) K11.8
  sphincter ani K62.89
  stomach K31.89
    acute K31.0
    psychogenic F45.8
  submaxillary duct K11.8
  trachea, congenital Q32.1
  ureter (idiopathic) N28.82
    congenital Q62.2
    due to obstruction N13.4
  urethra (acquired) N36.8
  vasomotor I73.9
  vein I86.8
  ventricular, ventricle (acute) (chronic) —*see*
    also Hypertrophy, cardiac
    cerebral, congenital Q04.8
  venule NEC I86.8
  vesical orifice N32.89
Dilated, dilation —*see* Dilatation
Diminished, diminution
  hearing (acuity) —*see* Deafness
  sense or sensation (cold) (heat) (tactile)
    (vibratory) R20.8
  vision NEC H54.7
  vital capacity R94.2
Diminuta taenia B71.0
Dimitri-Sturge-Weber disease Q85.8
Dimple
  congenital sacral Q82.6
  parasacral Q82.6
  pilonidal or postanal —*see* Cyst,
    pilonidal

Dioctophyme renalis (infection) (infestation)
B83.8
Dipetalonemiasis B74.4
Diphallus Q55.69
Diphtheria, diphtheritic (gangrenous)
(hemorrhagic) A36.9
carrier (suspected) Z22.2
cutaneous A36.3
faucial A36.0
infection of wound A36.3
laryngeal A36.2
myocarditis A36.81
nasal, anterior A36.89
nasopharyngeal A36.1
neurological complication A36.89
pharyngeal A36.0
specified site NEC A36.89
tonsillar A36.0
Diphyllobothriasis (intestine) B70.0
larval B70.1
Diplacusis H93.22-●
Diplegia (upper limbs) G83.0
congenital (cerebral) G80.8
facial G51.0
lower limbs G82.20
spastic G80.1
Diplococcus, diplococcal —see condition
Diplopia H53.2
Dipsomania F10.20
with
psychosis —see Psychosis, alcoholic
remission F10.21
Dipylidiasis B71.1
DIRA (deficiency of interleukin 1 receptor
antagonist) M04.8
Direction, teeth, abnormal, fully erupted
M26.30
Dirofilariasis B74.8
Dirt-eating child F98.3
Disability, disabilities
heart —see Disease, heart
intellectual F79
with
autistic features F84.9
mild (I.Q. 50-69) F70
moderate (I.Q. 35-49) F71
profound (I.Q. under 20) F73
severe (I.Q. 20-34) F72
specified level NEC F78
knowledge acquisition F81.9
learning F81.9
limiting activities Z73.6
spelling, specific F81.81
Disappearance of family member Z63.4
Disarticulation —see Amputation
meaning traumatic amputation —see
Amputation, traumatic
Discharge (from)
abnormal finding in —see Abnormal,
specimen
breast (female) (male) N64.52
diencephalic autonomic idiopathic —see
Epilepsy, specified NEC
ear —see also Otorrhea
blood —see Otorrhagia
excessive urine R35.8
nipple N64.52
penile R36.9
postnasal R09.82
prison, anxiety concerning Z65.2
urethral R36.9
without blood R36.0
hematospermia R36.1
vaginal N89.8
Discitis, diskitis M46.40
cervical region M46.42
cervicothoracic region M46.43
lumbar region M46.46
lumbosacral region M46.47
multiple sites M46.49
occipito-atlanto-axial region M46.41

Discitis, diskitis (Continued)
pyogenic —see Infection, intervertebral
disc, pyogenic
sacrococcygeal region M46.48
thoracic region M46.44
thoracolumbar region M46.45
Discoid
meniscus (congenital) Q68.6
semilunar cartilage (congenital) —see
Derangement, knee, meniscus,
specified NEC
Discoloration
nails L60.8
teeth (posteruptive) K03.7
during formation K00.8
Discomfort
chest R07.89
visual H53.14-●
Discontinuity, ossicles, ear H74.2-●
Discord (with)
boss Z56.4
classmates Z55.4
counselor Z64.4
employer Z56.4
family Z63.8
fellow employees Z56.4
in-laws Z63.1
landlord Z59.2
lodgers Z59.2
neighbors Z59.2
probation officer Z64.4
social worker Z64.4
teachers Z55.4
workmates Z56.4
Discordant connection
atrioventricular (congenital)
Q20.5
ventriculoarterial Q20.3
Discrepancy
centric occlusion maximum intercuspation
M26.55
leg length (acquired) —see Deformity, limb,
unequal length
congenital —see Defect, reduction, lower
limb
uterine size date O26.84-●
Discrimination
ethnic Z60.5
political Z60.5
racial Z60.5
religious Z60.5
sex Z60.5
Disease, diseased —see also Syndrome
absorbent system I87.8
acid-peptic K30
Acosta's T70.29
Adams-Stokes (-Morgagni) (syncope with
heart block) I45.9
Addison's anemia (pernicious) D51.0
adenoids (and tonsils) J35.9
adrenal (capsule) (cortex) (gland) (medullary)
E27.9
hyperfunction E27.0
specified NEC E27.8
ainhum L94.6
airway
obstructive, chronic J44.9
due to
cotton dust J66.0
specific organic dusts NEC J66.8
reactive —see Asthma
akamushi (scrub typhus) A75.3
Albers-Schönberg (marble bones)
Q78.2
Albert's —see Tendinitis, Achilles
alimentary canal K63.9
alligator-skin Q80.9
acquired L85.0
alpha heavy chain C88.3
alpine T70.29
altitude T70.20

Disease, diseased (Continued)
alveolar ridge
edentulous K06.9
specified NEC K06.8
alveoli, teeth K08.9
Alzheimer's G30.9 [F02.80]
with behavioral disturbance G30.9 [F02.81]
early onset G30.0 [F02.80]
with behavioral disturbance G30.0
[F02.81]
late onset G30.1 [F02.80]
with behavioral disturbance G30.1
[F02.81]
specified NEC G30.8 [F02.80]
with behavioral disturbance G30.8
[F02.81]
amyloid —see Amyloidosis
Andersen's (glycogenosis IV) E74.09
Andes T70.29
Andrews' (bacterid) L08.89
angiospastic I73.9
cerebral G45.9
vein I87.8
anterior
chamber H21.9
horn cell G12.29
antiglomerular basement membrane
(anti-GBM) antibody M31.0
tubulo-interstitial nephritis N12
antral —see Sinusitis, maxillary
anus K62.9
specified NEC K62.89
aorta (nonsyphilitic) I77.9
syphilitic NEC A52.02
aortic (heart) (valve) I35.9
rheumatic I06.9
Apollo B30.3
aponeuroses —see Enthesopathy
appendix K38.9
specified NEC K38.8
aqueous (chamber) H21.9
Arnold-Chiari —see Arnold-Chiari disease
arterial I77.9
occlusive —see Occlusion, by site
due to stricture or stenosis I77.1
arteriocardiorenal —see Hypertension,
cardiorenal
arteriolar (generalized) (obliterative) I77.9
arteriorenal —see Hypertension, kidney
arteriosclerotic —see also Arteriosclerosis
cardiovascular —see Disease, heart,
ischemic, atherosclerotic
coronary (artery) —see Disease, heart,
ischemic, atherosclerotic
heart —see Disease, heart, ischemic,
atherosclerotic
artery I77.9
cerebral I67.9
coronary I25.10
with angina pectoris —see Arteriosclerosis,
coronary (artery),
arthropod-borne NOS (viral) A94
specified type NEC A93.8
atticoantral, chronic H66.20
left H66.22
with right H66.23
right H66.21
with left H66.23
auditory canal —see Disorder, ear, external
auricle, ear NEC —see Disorder, pinna
Australian X A83.4
autoimmune (systemic) NOS M35.9
hemolytic (cold type) (warm type) D59.1
drug-induced D59.0
thyroid E06.3
▶autoinflammatory M04.9
▶NOD2-associated M04.8
▶specified type NEC M04.8
aviator's —see Effect, adverse, high altitude
Ayerza's (pulmonary artery sclerosis with
pulmonary hypertension) I27.0

▶ New ⟹ Revised deleted Deleted ● Use Additional Character(s)

Disease, diseased (Continued)
 Babington's (familial hemorrhagic
   telangiectasia) I78.0
 bacterial A49.9
  specified NEC A48.8
  zoonotic A28.9
   specified type NEC A28.8
 Baelz's (cheilitis glandularis apostematosa)
   K13.0
 bagasse J67.1
 balloon —see Effect, adverse, high altitude
 Bang's (brucella abortus) A23.1
 Bannister's T78.3
 barometer makers' —see Poisoning, mercury
 Barraquer (-Simons') (progressive
   lipodystrophy) E88.1
 Barrett's —see Barrett's, esophagus
 Bartholin's gland N75.9
 basal ganglia G25.9
  degenerative G23.9
   specified NEC G23.8
  specified NEC G25.89
 Basedow's (exophthalmic goiter) —see
   Hyperthyroidism, with, goiter (diffuse)
 Bateman's B08.1
 Batten-Steinert G71.11
 Battey A31.0
 Beard's (neurasthenia) F48.8
 Becker
  idiopathic mural endomyocardial I42.3
  myotonia congenita G71.12
 Begbie's (exophthalmic goiter) —see
   Hyperthyroidism, with, goiter (diffuse)
 behavioral, organic F07.9
 Beigel's (white piedra) B36.2
 Benson's —see Deposit, crystalline
 Bernard-Soulier (thrombopathy) D69.1
 Bernhardt (-Roth) —see Mononeuropathy,
   lower limb, meralgia paresthetica
 Biermer's (pernicious anemia) D51.0
 bile duct (common) (hepatic) K83.9
  with calculus, stones —see Calculus, bile
   duct
  specified NEC K83.8
 biliary (tract) K83.9
  specified NEC K83.8
 Billroth's —see Spina bifida
 bird fancier's J67.2
 black lung J60
 bladder N32.9
  in (due to)
   schistosomiasis (bilharziasis) B65.0 [N33]
  specified NEC N32.89
 bleeder's D66
 blood D75.9
  forming organs D75.9
  vessel I99.9
 Bloodgood's —see Mastopathy, cystic
 Bodechtel-Guttmann (subacute sclerosing
   panencephalitis) A81.1
 bone —see also Disorder, bone
  aluminum M83.4
  fibrocystic NEC
   jaw M27.49
 bone-marrow D75.9
 Borna A83.9
 Bornholm (epidemic pleurodynia) B33.0
 Bouchard's (myopathic dilatation of the
   stomach) K31.0
 Bouillaud's (rheumatic heart disease) I01.9
 Bourneville (-Brissaud) (tuberous sclerosis)
   Q85.1
 Bouveret (-Hoffmann) (paroxysmal
   tachycardia) I47.9
 bowel K63.9
  functional K59.9
   psychogenic F45.8
 brain G93.9
  arterial, artery I67.9
  arteriosclerotic I67.2
  congenital Q04.9

Disease, diseased (Continued)
 brain (Continued)
  degenerative —see Degeneration, brain
  inflammatory —see Encephalitis
  organic G93.9
   arteriosclerotic I67.2
  parasitic NEC B71.9 [G94]
  senile NEC G31.1
  specified NEC G93.89
 breast (see also Disorder, breast) N64.9
  cystic (chronic) —see Mastopathy, cystic
  fibrocystic —see Mastopathy, cystic
  Paget's
   female, unspecified side C50.91-●
   male, unspecified side C50.92-●
  specified NEC N64.89
 Breda's —see Yaws
 Bretonneau's (diphtheritic malignant angina)
   A36.0
 Bright's —see Nephritis
  arteriosclerotic —see Hypertension, kidney
 Brill's (recrudescent typhus) A75.1
 Brill-Zinsser (recrudescent typhus) A75.1
 Brion-Kayser —see Fever, paratyphoid
 broad
  beta E78.2
  ligament (noninflammatory) N83.9
   inflammatory —see Disease, pelvis,
    inflammatory
   specified NEC N83.8
 Brocq-Duhring (dermatitis herpetiformis)
   L13.0
 Brocq's
  meaning
   dermatitis herpetiformis L13.0
   prurigo L28.2
 bronchopulmonary J98.4
 bronchus NEC J98.09
 bronze Addison's E27.1
  tuberculous A18.7
 budgerigar fancier's J67.2
 Buerger's (thromboangiitis obliterans)
   I73.1
 bullous L13.9
  chronic of childhood L12.2
  specified NEC L13.8
 Bürger-Grütz (essential familial
   hyperlipemia) E78.3
 bursa —see Bursopathy
 caisson T70.3
 California —see Coccidioidomycosis
 capillaries I78.9
  specified NEC I78.8
 Carapata A68.0
 cardiac —see Disease, heart
 cardiopulmonary, chronic I27.9
 cardiorenal (hepatic) (hypertensive)
   (vascular) —see Hypertension,
   cardiorenal
 cardiovascular (atherosclerotic) I25.10
  with angina pectoris —see Arteriosclerosis,
   coronary (artery),
  congenital Q28.9
  hypertensive —see Hypertension, heart
  newborn P29.9
   specified NEC P29.89
  renal (hypertensive) —see Hypertension,
   cardiorenal
  syphilitic (asymptomatic) A52.00
 cartilage —see Disorder, cartilage
 Castellani's A69.8
 Castleman (unicentric) (multicentric)
   D47.Z2
  HHV-8-associated —see also Herpesvirus,
   human, 8 D47.Z2
 cat-scratch A28.1
 Cavare's (familial periodic paralysis) G72.3
 cecum K63.9
 celiac (adult) (infantile) (with steatorrhea)
   K90.0
 cellular tissue L98.9

Disease, diseased (Continued)
 central core G71.2
 cerebellar, cerebellum —see Disease, brain
 cerebral —see also Disease, brain
  degenerative —see Degeneration, brain
 cerebrospinal G96.9
 cerebrovascular I67.9
  acute I67.89
   embolic I63.4-●
   thrombotic I63.3-●
  arteriosclerotic I67.2
  ▶hereditary NEC I67.858
  specified NEC I67.89
 cervix (uteri) (noninflammatory) N88.9
  inflammatory —see Cervicitis
  specified NEC N88.8
 Chabert's A22.9
 Chandler's (osteochondritis dissecans, hip) —
   see Osteochondritis, dissecans, hip
 Charlouis —see Yaws
 Chédiak-Steinbrinck (-Higashi) (congenital
   gigantism of peroxidase granules) E70.330
 chest J98.9
 Chiari's (hepatic vein thrombosis) I82.0
 Chicago B40.9
 Chignon B36.8
 chigo, chigoe B88.1
 childhood granulomatous D71
 Chinese liver fluke B66.1
 chlamydial A74.9
  specified NEC A74.89
 cholecystic K82.9
 choroid H31.9
  specified NEC H31.8
 Christmas D67
 chronic bullous of childhood L12.2
 chylomicron retention E78.3
 ciliary body H21.9
  specified NEC H21.89
 circulatory (system) NEC I99.8
  newborn P29.9
  syphilitic A52.00
   congenital A50.54
 coagulation factor deficiency (congenital) —
   see Defect, coagulation
 coccidioidal —see Coccidioidomycosis
 cold
  agglutinin or hemoglobinuria D59.1
   paroxysmal D59.6
  hemagglutinin (chronic) D59.1
 collagen NOS (nonvascular) (vascular) M35.9
  specified NEC M35.8
 colon K63.9
  functional K59.9
   congenital Q43.2
  ischemic —see also Ischemia, intestine,
   acute K55.039
 colonic inflammatory bowel, unclassified
   (IBDU) K52.3
 combined system —see Degeneration,
   combined
 compressed air T70.3
 Concato's (pericardial polyserositis) A19.9
  nontubercular I31.1
  pleural —see Pleurisy, with effusion
 conjunctiva H11.9
  chlamydial A74.9
  specified NEC H11.89
  viral B30.9
   specified NEC B30.8
 connective tissue, systemic (diffuse) M35.9
  in (due to)
   hypogammaglobulinemia D80.1 [M36.8]
   ochronosis E70.29 [M36.8]
  specified NEC M35.8
 Conor and Bruch's (boutonneuse fever) A77.1
 Cooper's —see Mastopathy, cystic
 Cori's (glycogenosis III) E74.03
 corkhandler's or corkworker's J67.3
 cornea H18.9
  specified NEC H18.89-●

Disease, diseased (Continued)
  coronary (artery) —see Disease, heart,
      ischemic, atherosclerotic
    congenital Q24.5
    ostial, syphilitic (aortic) (mitral)
        (pulmonary) A52.03
  corpus cavernosum N48.9
    specified NEC N48.89
  Cotugno's —see Sciatica
  coxsackie (virus) NEC B34.1
  cranial nerve NOS G52.9
  Creutzfeldt-Jakob —see Creutzfeldt-Jakob
      disease or syndrome
  Crocq's (acrocyanosis) I73.89
  Crohn's —see Enteritis, regional
  Curschmann G71.11
  cystic
    breast (chronic) —see Mastopathy, cystic
    kidney, congenital Q61.9
    liver, congenital Q44.6
    lung J98.4
      congenital Q33.0
  cytomegalic inclusion (generalized) B25.9
    with pneumonia B25.0
    congenital P35.1
  cytomegaloviral B25.9
    specified NEC B25.8
  Czerny's (periodic hydrarthrosis of the
      knee) —see Effusion, joint, knee
  Daae (-Finsen) (epidemic pleurodynia) B33.0
  Darling's —see Histoplasmosis capsulati
  Débove's (splenomegaly) R16.1
  deer fly —see Tularemia
  Degos' I77.8
  demyelinating, demyelinizating (nervous
      system) G37.9
    multiple sclerosis G35
    specified NEC G37.8
  dense deposit —see also N00-N07 with fourth
      character .6 N05.6
  deposition, hydroxyapatite —see Disease,
      hydroxyapatite deposition
  de Quervain's (tendon sheath) M65.4
    thyroid (subacute granulomatous
        thyroiditis) E06.1
  Devergie's (pityriasis rubra pilaris) L44.0
  Devic's G36.0
  diaphorase deficiency D74.0
  diaphragm J98.6
  diarrheal, infectious NEC A09
  digestive system K92.9
    specified NEC K92.89
  disc, degenerative —see Degeneration,
      intervertebral disc
  discogenic —see also Displacement,
      intervertebral disc NEC
    with myelopathy —see Disorder, disc, with,
        myelopathy
  diverticular —see Diverticula
  Dubois (thymus) A50.59 [E35]
➡ Duchenne-Griesinger G71.01
  Duchenne's
➡   muscular dystrophy G71.01
➡   pseudohypertrophy, muscles G71.01
  ductless glands E34.9
  Duhring's (dermatitis herpetiformis) L13.0
  duodenum K31.9
    specified NEC K31.89
  Dupré's (meningism) R29.1
  Dupuytren's (muscle contracture) M72.0
  Durand-Nicholas-Favre (climatic bubo) A55
  Duroziez's (congenital mitral stenosis) Q23.2
  ear —see Disorder, ear
  Eberth's —see Fever, typhoid
  Ebola (virus) A98.4
  Ebstein's heart Q22.5
  Echinococcus —see Echinococcus
  echovirus NEC B34.1
  Eddowes' (brittle bones and blue sclera) Q78.0
  edentulous (alveolar) ridge K06.9
    specified NEC K06.8

Disease, diseased (Continued)
  Edsall's T67.2
  Eichstedt's (pityriasis versicolor) B36.0
  Eisenmenger's (irreversible) I27.83
  Ellis-van Creveld (chondroectodermal
      dysplasia) Q77.6
  end stage renal (ESRD) N18.6
    due to hypertension I12.0
  endocrine glands or system NEC E34.9
  endomyocardial (eosinophilic) I42.3
  English (rickets) E55.0
  enteroviral, enterovirus NEC B34.1
    central nervous system NEC A88.8
  epidemic B99.9
    specified NEC B99.8
  epididymis N50.9
➡ Erb (-Landouzy) G71.02
  Erdheim-Chester (ECD) E88.89
  esophagus K22.9
    functional K22.4
    psychogenic F45.8
    specified NEC K22.8
  Eulenburg's (congenital paramyotonia) G71.19
  eustachian tube —see Disorder, eustachian tube
  external
    auditory canal —see Disorder, ear, external
    ear —see Disorder, ear, external
  extrapyramidal G25.9
    specified NEC G25.89
  eye H57.9
    anterior chamber H21.9
➡   inflammatory NEC H57.89
    muscle (external) —see Strabismus
➡   specified NEC H57.89
    syphilitic —see Oculopathy, syphilitic
  eyeball H44.9
    specified NEC H44.89
  eyelid —see Disorder, eyelid
    specified NEC —see Disorder, eyelid,
        specified type NEC
  eyeworm of Africa B74.3
  facial nerve (seventh) G51.9
    newborn (birth injury) P11.3
  Fahr (of brain) G23.8
  Fahr Volhard (of kidney) I12.-•
  fallopian tube (noninflammatory) N83.9
    inflammatory —see Salpingo-oophoritis
    specified NEC N83.8
  familial periodic paralysis G72.3
  Fanconi's (congenital pancytopenia) D61.09
  fascia NEC —see also Disorder, muscle
    inflammatory —see Myositis
    specified NEC M62.89
  Fauchard's (periodontitis) —see Periodontitis
  Favre-Durand-Nicolas (climatic bubo) A55
  Fede's K14.0
  Feer's —see Poisoning, mercury
  female pelvic inflammatory —see also Disease,
      pelvis, inflammatory N73.9
    syphilitic (secondary) A51.42
    tuberculous A18.17
  Fernels' (aortic aneurysm) I71.9
  fibrocaseous of lung —see Tuberculosis,
      pulmonary
  fibrocystic —see Fibrocystic disease
  Fiedler's (leptospiral jaundice) A27.0
  fifth B08.3
  file-cutter's —see Poisoning, lead
  fish-skin Q80.9
    acquired L85.0
  Flajani (-Basedow) (exophthalmic goiter) —
      see Hyperthyroidism, with, goiter
      (diffuse)
  flax-dresser's J66.1
  fluke —see Infestation, fluke
  foot and mouth B08.8
  foot process N04.9
  Forbes' (glycogenosis III) E74.03
  Fordyce-Fox (apocrine miliaria) L75.2
  Fordyce's (ectopic sebaceous glands) (mouth)
      Q38.6

Disease, diseased (Continued)
  Forestier's (rhizomelic pseudopolyarthritis)
      M35.3
    meaning ankylosing hyperostosis —see
        Hyperostosis, ankylosing
  Fothergill's
    neuralgia —see Neuralgia, trigeminal
    scarlatina anginosa A38.9
  Fournier (gangrene) N49.3
    female N76.89
  fourth B08.8
  Fox (-Fordyce) (apocrine miliaria) L75.2
  Francis' —see Tularemia
  Franklin C88.2
  Frei's (climatic bubo) A55
  Friedreich's
    combined systemic or ataxia G11.1
    myoclonia G25.3
  frontal sinus —see Sinusitis, frontal
  fungus NEC B49
  Gaisböck's (polycythemia hypertonica) D75.1
  gallbladder K82.9
    calculus —see Calculus, gallbladder
    cholecystitis —see Cholecystitis
    cholesterolosis K82.4
    fistula —see Fistula, gallbladder
    hydrops K82.1
    obstruction —see Obstruction, gallbladder
    perforation K82.2
    specified NEC K82.8
  gamma heavy chain C88.2
  Gamna's (siderotic splenomegaly) D73.2
  Gamstorp's (adynamia episodica hereditaria)
      G72.3
  Gandy-Nanta (siderotic splenomegaly) D73.2
  ganister J62.8
  gastric —see Disease, stomach
  gastroesophageal reflux (GERD) K21.9
    with esophagitis K21.0
  gastrointestinal (tract) K92.9
    amyloid E85.4
    functional K59.9
      psychogenic F45.8
    specified NEC K92.89
  Gee (-Herter) (-Heubner) (-Thaysen)
      (nontropical sprue) K90.0
  genital organs
    female N94.9
    male N50.9
  Gerhardt's (erythromelalgia) I73.81
  Gibert's (pityriasis rosea) L42
  Gierke's (glycogenosis I) E74.01
  Gilles de la Tourette's (motor-verbal tic) F95.2
  gingiva K06.9
    plaque induced K05.00
    specified NEC K06.8
  gland (lymph) I89.9
  Glanzmann's (hereditary hemorrhagic
      thrombasthenia) D69.1
  glass-blower's (cataract) —see Cataract,
      specified NEC
    salivary gland hypertrophy K11.1
  Glisson's —see Rickets
  globe H44.9
    specified NEC H44.89
  glomerular —see also Glomerulonephritis
    with edema —see Nephrosis
    acute —see Nephritis, acute
    chronic —see Nephritis, chronic
    minimal change N05.0
    rapidly progressive N01.9
  glycogen storage E74.00
    Andersen's E74.09
    Cori's E74.03
    Forbes' E74.03
    generalized E74.00
    glucose-6-phosphatase deficiency E74.01
    heart E74.02 [I43]
    hepatorenal E74.09
    Hers' E74.09
    liver and kidney E74.09

▶ New   ➡ Revised   deleted Deleted   • Use Additional Character(s)

Disease, diseased *(Continued)*
  glycogen storage *(Continued)*
    McArdle's E74.04
    muscle phosphofructokinase E74.09
    myocardium E74.02 *[I43]*
    Pompe's E74.02
    Tauri's E74.09
    type Ø E74.09
    type I E74.01
    type II E74.02
    type III E74.03
    type IV E74.09
    type V E74.04
    type VI-XI E74.09
    Von Gierke's E74.01
  Goldstein's (familial hemorrhagic
    telangiectasia) I78.0
  gonococcal NOS A54.9
  graft-versus-host (GVH) D89.813
    acute D89.810
    acute on chronic D89.812
    chronic D89.811
  grainhandler's J67.8
  granulomatous (childhood) (chronic) D71
  Graves' (exophthalmic goiter) —*see*
    Hyperthyroidism, with, goiter
    (diffuse)
  Griesinger's —*see* Ancylostomiasis
  Grisel's M43.6
  Gruby's (tinea tonsurans) B35.0
  Guillain-Barré G61.0
  Guinon's (motor-verbal tic) F95.2
  gum K06.9
  gynecological N94.9
  H (Hartnup's) E72.02
  Haff —*see* Poisoning, mercury
  Hageman (congenital factor XII deficiency)
    D68.2
  hair (color) (shaft) L67.9
    follicles L73.9
      specified NEC L73.8
  Hamman's (spontaneous mediastinal
    emphysema) J98.2
  hand, foot and mouth B08.4
  Hansen's —*see* Leprosy
  Hantavirus, with pulmonary manifestations
    B33.4
    with renal manifestations A98.5
  Harada's H30.81-•
  Hartnup (pellagra-cerebellar ataxia-renal
    aminoaciduria) E72.02
  Hart's (pellagra-cerebellar ataxia-renal
    aminoaciduria) E72.02
  Hashimoto's (struma lymphomatosa) E06.3
  Hb —*see* Disease, hemoglobin
  heart (organic) I51.9
    with
      pulmonary edema (acute) —*see also*
        Failure, ventricular, left I50.1
      rheumatic fever (conditions in I00)
        active I01.9
          with chorea I02.0
          specified NEC I01.8
        inactive or quiescent (with chorea)
          I09.9
          specified NEC I09.89
    amyloid E85.4 *[I43]*
    aortic (valve) I35.9
    arteriosclerotic or sclerotic (senile) —
      see Disease, heart, ischemic,
      atherosclerotic
    artery, arterial —*see* Disease, heart,
      ischemic, atherosclerotic
    beer drinkers' I42.6
    beriberi (wet) E51.12
    black I27.0
    congenital Q24.9
      cyanotic Q24.9
      specified NEC Q24.8
    coronary —*see* Disease, heart, ischemic
    cryptogenic I51.9

Disease, diseased *(Continued)*
  heart *(Continued)*
    fibroid —*see* Myocarditis
    functional I51.89
      psychogenic F45.8
    glycogen storage E74.02 *[I43]*
    gonococcal A54.83
    hypertensive —*see* Hypertension, heart
    hyperthyroid —*see also* Hyperthyroidism
      E05.90 *[I43]*
      with thyroid storm E05.91 *[I43]*
    ischemic (chronic or with a stated duration
      of over 4 weeks) I25.9
      atherosclerotic (of) I25.10
        with angina pectoris —*see*
          Arteriosclerosis, coronary (artery)
        coronary artery bypass graft —*see*
          Arteriosclerosis, coronary
          (artery),
      cardiomyopathy I25.5
      diagnosed on ECG or other special
        investigation, but currently
        presenting no symptoms I25.6
      silent I25.6
      specified form NEC I25.89
    kyphoscoliotic I27.1
    meningococcal A39.50
      endocarditis A39.51
      myocarditis A39.52
      pericarditis A39.53
    mitral I05.9
      specified NEC I05.8
    muscular —*see* Degeneration, myocardial
    psychogenic (functional) F45.8
    pulmonary (chronic) I27.9
      in schistosomiasis B65.9 *[I52]*
      specified NEC I27.89
    rheumatic (chronic) (inactive) (old)
      (quiescent) (with chorea) I09.9
      active or acute I01.9
        with chorea (acute) (rheumatic)
          (Sydenham's) I02.0
      specified NEC I09.89
    senile —*see* Myocarditis
    syphilitic A52.06
      aortic A52.03
        aneurysm A52.01
      congenital A50.54 *[I52]*
    thyrotoxic —*see also* Thyrotoxicosis E05.90
      [I43]
      with thyroid storm E05.91 *[I43]*
    valve, valvular (obstructive)
      (regurgitant) —*see also* Endocarditis
      congenital NEC Q24.8
        pulmonary Q22.3
    vascular —*see* Disease, cardiovascular
  heavy chain NEC C88.2
    alpha C88.3
    gamma C88.2
    mu C88.2
  Hebra's
    pityriasis
      maculata et circinata L42
      rubra pilaris L44.0
    prurigo L28.2
  hematopoietic organs D75.9
  hemoglobin or Hb
    abnormal (mixed) NEC D58.2
      with thalassemia D56.9
    AS genotype D57.3
    Bart's D56.0
    C (Hb-C) D58.2
      with other abnormal hemoglobin NEC
        D58.2
      elliptocytosis D58.1
      Hb-S D57.2-•
      sickle-cell D57.2-•
      thalassemia D56.8
    Constant Spring D58.2
    D (Hb-D) D58.2
    E (Hb-E) D58.2

Disease, diseased *(Continued)*
  hemoglobin or Hb *(Continued)*
    E-beta thalassemia D56.5
    elliptocytosis D58.1
    H (Hb-H) (thalassemia) D56.0
      with other abnormal hemoglobin NEC
        D56.9
      Constant Spring D56.0
    I thalassemia D56.9
    M D74.0
    S or SS D57.1
    SC D57.2-•
    SD D57.8-•
    SE D57.8-•
    spherocytosis D58.0
    unstable, hemolytic D58.2
  hemolytic (newborn) P55.9
    autoimmune (cold type) (warm type) D59.1
    drug-induced D59.0
    due to or with
      incompatibility
        ABO (blood group) P55.1
        ➡blood (group) (Duffy) (K) (Kell)
          (Kidd) (Lewis) (M) (S) NEC P55.8
        Rh (blood group) (factor) P55.0
        Rh negative mother P55.0
    specified type NEC P55.8
    unstable hemoglobin D58.2
  hemorrhagic D69.9
    newborn P53
  Henoch (-Schönlein) (purpura nervosa) D69.0
  hepatic —*see* Disease, liver
  hepatobiliary K83.9
    toxic K71.9
  hepatolenticular E83.01
  heredodegenerative NEC
    spinal cord G95.89
  herpesviral, disseminated B00.7
  Hers' (glycogenosis VI) E74.09
  Herter (-Gee) (-Heubner) (nontropical sprue)
    K90.0
  Heubner-Herter (nontropical sprue) K90.0
  high fetal gene or hemoglobin thalassemia
    D56.9
  Hildenbrand's —*see* Typhus
  hip (joint) M25.9
    congenital Q65.89
    suppurative M00.9
    tuberculous A18.02
  His (-Werner) (trench fever) A79.0
  Hodgson's I71.2
    ruptured I71.1
  Holla —*see* Spherocytosis
  hookworm B76.9
    specified NEC B76.8
  host-versus-graft D89.813
    acute D89.810
    acute on chronic D89.812
    chronic D89.811
  human immunodeficiency virus (HIV) B20
  Huntington's G10
    with dementia G10 *[F02.80]*
  Hutchinson's (cheiropompholyx) —*see*
    Hutchinson's disease
  hyaline (diffuse) (generalized)
    membrane (lung) (newborn) P22.0
    adult J80
  hydatid —*see* Echinococcus
  hydroxyapatite deposition M11.00
    ankle M11.07-•
    elbow M11.02-•
    foot joint M11.07-•
    hand joint M11.04-•
    hip M11.05-•
    knee M11.06-•
    multiple site M11.09
    shoulder M11.01-•
    vertebra M11.08
    wrist M11.03-•
  hyperkinetic —*see* Hyperkinesia
  hypertensive —*see* Hypertension

Disease, diseased (Continued)
 hypophysis E23.7
 Iceland G93.3
 I-cell E77.0
 immune D89.9
 immunoproliferative (malignant) C88.9
  small intestinal C88.3
  specified NEC C88.8
 inclusion B25.9
  salivary gland B25.9
 infectious, infective B99.9
  congenital P37.9
   specified NEC P37.8
   viral P35.9
    specified type NEC P35.8
  specified NEC B99.8
 inflammatory
  penis N48.29
   abscess N48.21
   cellulitis N48.22
  prepuce N47.7
   balanoposthitis N47.6
  tubo-ovarian —see Salpingo-oophoritis
 intervertebral disc —see also Disorder, disc
  with myelopathy —see Disorder, disc, with,
    myelopathy
  cervical, cervicothoracic —see Disorder,
    disc, cervical
   with
    myelopathy —see Disorder, disc,
     cervical, with myelopathy
    neuritis, radiculitis or
     radiculopathy —see Disorder,
     disc, cervical, with neuritis
    specified NEC —see Disorder, disc,
     cervical, specified type NEC
  lumbar (with)
   myelopathy M51.06
   neuritis, radiculitis, radiculopathy or
     sciatica M51.16
   specified NEC M51.86
  lumbosacral (with)
   neuritis, radiculitis, radiculopathy or
     sciatica M51.17
   specified NEC M51.87
  specified NEC —see Disorder, disc,
    specified NEC
  thoracic (with)
   myelopathy M51.04
   neuritis, radiculitis or radiculopathy
     M51.14
   specified NEC M51.84
  thoracolumbar (with)
   myelopathy M51.05
   neuritis, radiculitis or radiculopathy
     M51.15
   specified NEC M51.85
 intestine K63.9
  functional K59.9
   psychogenic F45.8
   specified NEC K59.8
  organic K63.9
  protozoal A07.9
  specified NEC K63.89
 iris H21.9
  specified NEC H21.89
 iron metabolism or storage E83.10
 island (scrub typhus) A75.3
 itai-itai —see Poisoning, cadmium
 Jakob-Creutzfeldt —see Creutzfeldt-Jakob
   disease or syndrome
 jaw M27.9
  fibrocystic M27.49
  specified NEC M27.8
 jigger B88.1
 joint —see also Disorder, joint
  Charcot's —see Arthropathy, neuropathic
    (Charcot)
  degenerative —see Osteoarthritis
   multiple M15.9
   spine —see Spondylosis

Disease, diseased (Continued)
 joint (Continued)
  hypertrophic —see Osteoarthritis
  sacroiliac M53.3
  specified NEC —see Disorder, joint,
    specified type NEC
  spine NEC —see Dorsopathy
  suppurative —see Arthritis, pyogenic or
    pyemic
 Jourdain's (acute gingivitis) K05.00
  nonplaque induced K05.01
  plaque induced K05.00
 Kaschin-Beck (endemic polyarthritis)
   M12.10
  ankle M12.17-•
  elbow M12.12-•
  foot joint M12.17-•
  hand joint M12.14-•
  hip M12.15-•
  knee M12.16-•
  multiple site M12.19
  shoulder M12.11-•
  vertebra M12.18
  wrist M12.13-•
 Katayama B65.2
 Kedani (scrub typhus) A75.3
 Keshan E59
 kidney (functional) (pelvis) N28.9
  chronic N18.9
   hypertensive —see Hypertension, kidney
   stage 1 N18.1
   stage 2 (mild) N18.2
   stage 3 (moderate) N18.3
   stage 4 (severe) N18.4
   stage 5 N18.5
  complicating pregnancy —see Pregnancy,
    complicated by, renal disease
  cystic (congenital) Q61.9
  diabetic —see E08-E13 with .22
  fibrocystic (congenital) Q61.8
  hypertensive —see Hypertension, kidney
  in (due to)
   schistosomiasis (bilharziasis) B65.9 [N29]
  multicystic Q61.4
  polycystic Q61.3
   adult type Q61.2
   childhood type NEC Q61.19
    collecting duct dilatation Q61.11
 Kimmelstiel (-Wilson) (intercapillary polycystic
   (congenital) glomerulosclerosis) —see
   E08-E13 with .21
 Kimura D21.9
  specified site (see Neoplasm, connective
    tissue benign)
 Kinnier Wilson's (hepatolenticular
   degeneration) E83.01
 kissing —see Mononucleosis, infectious
 Klebs' —see also Glomerulonephritis N05.-•
 Klippel-Feil (brevicollis) Q76.1
 Köhler-Pellegrini-Stieda (calcification, knee
   joint) —see Bursitis, tibial collateral
 Kok Q89.8
 König's (osteochondritis dissecans) —see
   Osteochondritis, dissecans
 Korsakoff's (nonalcoholic) F04
  alcoholic F10.96
   with dependence F10.26
 Kostmann's (infantile genetic
   agranulocytosis) D70.0
 kuru A81.81
 Kyasanur Forest A98.2
 labyrinth, ear —see Disorder, ear, inner
 lacrimal system —see Disorder, lacrimal
   system
 Lafora's —see Epilepsy, generalized,
   idiopathic
 Lancereaux-Mathieu (leptospiral jaundice)
   A27.0
 Landry's G61.0
 Larrey-Weil (leptospiral jaundice) A27.0
 larynx J38.7

Disease, diseased (Continued)
 legionnaires' A48.1
  nonpneumonic A48.2
 Lenegre's I44.2
 lens H27.9
  specified NEC H27.8
 Lev's (acquired complete heart block) I44.2
 Lewy body (dementia) G31.83 [F02.80]
  with behavioral disturbance G31.83 [F02.81]
 Lichtheim's (subacute combined sclerosis
   with pernicious anemia) D51.0
 Lightwood's (renal tubular acidosis) N25.89
 Lignac's (cystinosis) E72.04
 lip K13.0
 lipid-storage E75.6
  specified NEC E75.5
 Lipschütz's N76.6
 liver (chronic) (organic) K76.9
  alcoholic (chronic) K70.9
   acute —see Disease, liver, alcoholic,
     hepatitis
   cirrhosis K70.30
    with ascites K70.31
   failure K70.40
    with coma K70.41
   fatty liver K70.0
   fibrosis K70.2
   hepatitis K70.10
    with ascites K70.11
   sclerosis K70.2
  cystic, congenital Q44.6
  drug-induced (idiosyncratic) (toxic)
    (predictable) (unpredictable) —see
    Disease, liver, toxic
  end stage K72.90
   due to hepatitis —see Hepatitis
  fatty, nonalcoholic (NAFLD) K76.0
   alcoholic K70.0
  fibrocystic (congenital) Q44.6
  fluke
   Chinese B66.1
   oriental B66.1
   sheep B66.3
  gestational alloimmune (GALD) P78.84
  glycogen storage E74.09 [K77]
  in (due to)
   schistosomiasis (bilharziasis) B65.9 [K77]
  inflammatory K75.9
   alcoholic K70.1
   specified NEC K75.89
  polycystic (congenital) Q44.6
  toxic K71.9
   with
    cholestasis K71.0
    cirrhosis (liver) K71.7
    fibrosis (liver) K71.7
    focal nodular hyperplasia K71.8
    hepatic granuloma K71.8
    hepatic necrosis K71.10
     with coma K71.11
    hepatitis NEC K71.6
     acute K71.2
     chronic
      active K71.50
       with ascites K71.51
      lobular K71.4
      persistent K71.3
     lupoid K71.50
      with ascites K71.51
    peliosis hepatis K71.8
    veno-occlusive disease (VOD) of liver
      K71.8
  veno-occlusive K76.5
 Lobo's (keloid blastomycosis) B48.0
 Lobstein's (brittle bones and blue sclera) Q78.0
 Ludwig's (submaxillary cellulitis) K12.2
 lumbosacral region M53.87
 lung J98.4
  black J60
  congenital Q33.9
  cystic J98.4
   congenital Q33.0

▶ New   ➡ Revised   ~~deleted~~ Deleted   • Use Additional Character(s)

Disease, diseased (Continued)

lung (Continued)
  fibroid (chronic) —see Fibrosis, lung
  fluke B66.4
    oriental B66.4
  in
    amyloidosis E85.4 [I99]
    sarcoidosis D86.0
    Sjögren's syndrome M35.02
    systemic
      lupus erythematosus M32.13
      sclerosis M34.81
  interstitial J84.9
    of childhood, specified NEC J84.848
    respiratory bronchiolitis J84.115
    specified NEC J84.89
  obstructive (chronic) J44.9
    with
      acute
        bronchitis J44.0
          exacerbation NEC J44.1
          lower respiratory infection J44.0
      alveolitis, allergic J67.9
      asthma J44.9
      bronchiectasis J47.9
        with
          exacerbation (acute) J47.1
          lower respiratory infection J47.0
      bronchitis J44.9
        with
          exacerbation (acute) J44.1
          lower respiratory infection J44.0
      emphysema J43.9
      hypersensitivity pneumonitis J67.9
    decompensated J44.1
      with
        exacerbation (acute) J44.1
  polycystic J98.4
    congenital Q33.0
  rheumatoid (diffuse) (interstitial) —see
    Rheumatoid, lung
Lutembacher's (atrial septal defect with
  mitral stenosis) Q21.1
Lyme A69.20
lymphatic (gland) (system) (channel) (vessel)
  I89.9
lymphoproliferative D47.9
  specified NEC D47.Z9
  T-gamma D47.Z9
  X-linked D82.3
Magitot's M27.2
malarial —see Malaria
malignant —see also Neoplasm, malignant,
  by site
Manson's B65.1
maple bark J67.6
maple-syrup-urine E71.0
Marburg (virus) A98.3
Marion's (bladder neck obstruction) N32.0
Marsh's (exophthalmic goiter) —see
  Hyperthyroidism, with, goiter (diffuse)
mastoid (process) —see Disorder, ear, middle
Mathieu's (leptospiral jaundice) A27.0
Maxcy's A75.2
McArdle (-Schmid-Pearson) (glycogenosis
  V) E74.04
mediastinum J98.59
medullary center (idiopathic) (respiratory)
  G93.89
Meige's (chronic hereditary edema) Q82.0
meningococcal —see Infection, meningococcal
mental F99
  organic F09
mesenchymal M35.9
mesenteric embolic —see also Ischemia,
  intestine, acute K55.039
metabolic, metabolism E88.9
  bilirubin E80.7
metal-polisher's J62.8
metastatic —see also Neoplasm, secondary, by
  site C79.9

Disease, diseased (Continued)

microvascular — code to condition
microvillus
  atrophy Q43.8
  inclusion (MVD) Q43.8
middle ear —see Disorder, ear, middle
Mikulicz' (dryness of mouth, absent or
  decreased lacrimation) K11.8
Milroy's (chronic hereditary edema) Q82.0
Minamata —see Poisoning, mercury
minicore G71.2
Minor's G95.19
Minot's (hemorrhagic disease, newborn) P53
Minot-von Willebrand-Jürgens
  (angiohemophilia) D68.0
Mitchell's (erythromelalgia) I73.81
mitral (valve) I05.9
  nonrheumatic I34.9
mixed connective tissue M35.1
moldy hay J67.0
Monge's T70.29
Morgagni-Adams-Stokes (syncope with heart
  block) I45.9
Morgagni's (syndrome) (hyperostosis
  frontalis interna) M85.2
Morton's (with metatarsalgia) —see Lesion,
  nerve, plantar
Morvan's G60.8
motor neuron (bulbar) (mixed type) (spinal)
  G12.20
  amyotrophic lateral sclerosis G12.21
  familial G12.24
  progressive bulbar palsy G12.22
  specified NEC G12.29
moyamoya I67.5
mu heavy chain disease C88.2
multicore G71.2
muscle —see also Disorder, muscle
  inflammatory —see Myositis
  ocular (external) —see Strabismus
musculoskeletal system, soft tissue —see also
  Disorder, soft tissue
  specified NEC —see Disorder, soft tissue,
    specified type NEC
mushroom workers' J67.5
mycotic B49
myelodysplastic, not classified C94.6
myeloproliferative, not classified C94.6
  chronic D47.1
myocardium, myocardial —see also
  Degeneration, myocardial I51.5
  primary (idiopathic) I42.9
myoneural G70.9
Naegeli's D69.1
nails L60.9
  specified NEC L60.8
Nairobi (sheep virus) A93.8
nasal J34.9
nemaline body G71.2
nerve —see Disorder, nerve
nervous system G98.8
  autonomic G90.9
  central G96.9
    specified NEC G96.8
  congenital Q07.9
  parasympathetic G90.9
  specified NEC G98.8
  sympathetic G90.9
  vegetative G90.9
neuromuscular system G70.9
Newcastle B30.8
Nicolas (-Durand)-Favre (climatic bubo) A55
nipple N64.9
  Paget's C50.01-●
    female C50.01-●
    male C50.02-●
Nishimoto (-Takeuchi) I67.5
nonarthropod-borne NOS (viral) B34.9
  enterovirus NEC B34.1
nonautoimmune hemolytic D59.4
  drug-induced D59.2

Disease, diseased (Continued)

Nonne-Milroy-Meige (chronic hereditary
  edema) Q82.0
nose J34.9
nucleus pulposus —see Disorder, disc
nutritional E63.9
oast-house-urine E72.19
ocular
  herpesviral B00.50
  zoster B02.30
obliterative vascular I77.1
Ohara's —see Tularemia
Opitz's (congestive splenomegaly)
  D73.2
Oppenheim-Urbach (necrobiosis lipoidica
  diabeticorum) —see E08-E13 with .620
optic nerve NEC —see Disorder, nerve, optic
  orbit —see Disorder, orbit
Oriental liver fluke B66.1
Oriental lung fluke B66.4
Ormond's N13.5
Oropouche virus A93.0
Osler-Rendu (familial hemorrhagic
  telangiectasia) I78.0
osteofibrocystic E21.0
Otto's M24.7
outer ear —see Disorder, ear, external
ovary (noninflammatory) N83.9
  cystic N83.20-●
  inflammatory —see Salpingo-oophoritis
  polycystic E28.2
  specified NEC N83.8
Owren's (congenital) —see Defect,
  coagulation
pancreas K86.9
  cystic K86.2
  fibrocystic E84.9
  specified NEC K86.89
panvalvular I08.9
  specified NEC I08.8
parametrium (noninflammatory) N83.9
parasitic B89
  cerebral NEC B71.9 [G94]
  intestinal NOS B82.9
  mouth B37.0
  skin NOS B88.9
  specified type —see Infestation
  tongue B37.0
parathyroid (gland) E21.5
  specified NEC E21.4
Parkinson's G20
parodontal K05.6
Parrot's (syphilitic osteochondritis) A50.02
Parry's (exophthalmic goiter) —see
  Hyperthyroidism, with, goiter (diffuse)
Parson's (exophthalmic goiter) —see
  Hyperthyroidism, with, goiter (diffuse)
Paxton's (white piedra) B36.2
pearl-worker's —see Osteomyelitis, specified
  type NEC
Pellegrini-Stieda (calcification, knee joint) —
  see Bursitis, tibial collateral
pelvis, pelvic
  female NOS N94.9
    specified NEC N94.89
  gonococcal (acute) (chronic) A54.24
  inflammatory (female) N73.9
    acute N73.0
      chlamydial A56.11
    chronic N73.1
    specified NEC N73.8
    syphilitic (secondary) A51.42
      late A52.76
    tuberculous A18.17
  organ, female N94.9
  peritoneum, female NEC N94.89
penis N48.9
  inflammatory N48.29
    abscess N48.21
    cellulitis N48.22
  specified NEC N48.89

Disease, diseased *(Continued)*
  periapical tissues NOS K04.90
  periodontal K05.6
    specified NEC K05.5
  periosteum —*see* Disorder, bone, specified
      type NEC
  peripheral
    arterial I73.9
    autonomic nervous system G90.9
    nerves —*see* Polyneuropathy
    vascular NOS I73.9
  peritoneum K66.9
    pelvic, female NEC N94.89
    specified NEC K66.8
  persistent mucosal (middle ear) H66.20
    left H66.22
      with right H66.23
    right H66.21
      with left H66.23
  Petit's —*see* Hernia, abdomen, specified site
      NEC
  pharynx J39.2
    specified NEC J39.2
  Phocas' —*see* Mastopathy, cystic
  photochromogenic (acid-fast bacilli)
      (pulmonary) A31.0
    nonpulmonary A31.9
  Pick's G31.01 *[F02.80]*
    with behavioral disturbance G31.01
        [F02.81]
    brain G31.01 *[F02.80]*
      with behavioral disturbance G31.01
          [F02.81]
    of pericardium (pericardial pseudocirrhosis
        of liver) I31.1
  pigeon fancier's J67.2
  pineal gland E34.8
  pink —*see* Poisoning, mercury
  Pinkus' (lichen nitidus) L44.1
  pinworm B80
  Piry virus A93.8
  pituitary (gland) E23.7
  pituitary-snuff-taker's J67.8
  pleura (cavity) J94.9
    specified NEC J94.8
  pneumatic drill (hammer) T75.21
  Pollitzer's (hidradenitis suppurativa)
      L73.2
  polycystic
    kidney or renal Q61.3
      adult type Q61.2
      childhood type NEC Q61.19
        collecting duct dilatation Q61.11
    liver or hepatic Q44.6
    lung or pulmonary J98.4
      congenital Q33.0
    ovary, ovaries E28.2
    spleen Q89.09
  polyethylene T84.05-•
  Pompe's (glycogenosis II) E74.02
  Posadas-Wernicke B38.9
  Potain's (pulmonary edema) —*see* Edema,
      lung
  prepuce N47.8
    inflammatory N47.7
      balanoposthitis N47.6
  Pringle's (tuberous sclerosis) Q85.1
  prion, central nervous system A81.9
    specified NEC A81.89
  prostate N42.9
    specified NEC N42.89
  protozoal B64
    acanthamebiasis —*see* Acanthamebiasis
    African trypanosomiasis —*see* African
        trypanosomiasis
    babesiosis B60.0
    Chagas disease —*see* Chagas disease
    intestine, intestinal A07.9
    leishmaniasis —*see* Leishmaniasis
    malaria —*see* Malaria
    naegleriasis B60.2

Disease, diseased *(Continued)*
  protozoal *(Continued)*
    pneumocystosis B59
    specified organism NEC B60.8
    toxoplasmosis —*see* Toxoplasmosis
  pseudo-Hurler's E77.0
  psychiatric F99
  psychotic —*see* Psychosis
  Puente's (simple glandular cheilitis) K13.0
  puerperal —*see also* Puerperal O90.89
  pulmonary —*see also* Disease, lung
    artery I28.9
    chronic obstructive J44.9
      with
        acute bronchitis J44.0
        exacerbation (acute) J44.1
        lower respiratory infection (acute)
            J44.0
      decompensated J44.1
        with
          exacerbation (acute) J44.1
    heart I27.9
      specified NEC I27.89
    hypertensive (vascular) —*see also*
        Hypertension, pulmonary I27.20
      primary (idiopathic) I27.0
    valve I37.9
      rheumatic I09.89
  pulp (dental) NOS K04.90
  pulseless M31.4
  Putnam's (subacute combined sclerosis with
      pernicious anemia) D51.0
  Pyle (-Cohn) (metaphyseal dysplasia) Q78.5
  ragpicker's or ragsorter's A22.1
  Raynaud's —*see* Raynaud's disease
  reactive airway —*see* Asthma
  Reclus' (cystic) —*see* Mastopathy, cystic
  rectum K62.9
    specified NEC K62.89
  Refsum's (heredopathia atactica
      polyneuritiformis) G60.1
  renal (functional) (pelvis) —*see also* Disease,
      kidney N28.9
    with
      edema —*see* Nephrosis
      glomerular lesion —*see*
          Glomerulonephritis
        with edema —*see* Nephrosis
      interstitial nephritis N12
    acute N28.9
    chronic —*see also* Disease, kidney, chronic
        N18.9
    cystic, congenital Q61.9
    diabetic —*see* E08-E13 with .22
    end-stage (failure) N18.6
      due to hypertension I12.0
    fibrocystic (congenital) Q61.8
    hypertensive —*see* Hypertension,
        kidney
    lupus M32.14
    phosphate-losing (tubular) N25.0
    polycystic (congenital) Q61.3
      adult type Q61.2
      childhood type NEC Q61.19
        collecting duct dilatation Q61.11
    rapidly progressive N01.9
    subacute N01.9
  Rendu-Osler-Weber (familial hemorrhagic
      telangiectasia) I78.0
  renovascular (arteriosclerotic) —*see*
      Hypertension, kidney
  respiratory (tract) J98.9
    acute or subacute NOS J06.9
      due to
        chemicals, gases, fumes or vapors
            (inhalation) J68.3
        external agent J70.9
          specified NEC J70.8
        radiation J70.0
        smoke inhalation J70.5
      noninfectious J39.8

Disease, diseased *(Continued)*
  respiratory *(Continued)*
    chronic NOS J98.9
      due to
        chemicals, gases, fumes or vapors
            J68.4
        external agent J70.9
          specified NEC J70.8
        radiation J70.1
      newborn P27.9
        specified NEC P27.8
    due to
      chemicals, gases, fumes or vapors J68.9
        acute or subacute NEC J68.3
        chronic J68.4
      external agent J70.9
        specified NEC J70.8
    newborn P28.9
      specified type NEC P28.89
    upper J39.9
      acute or subacute J06.9
      noninfectious NEC J39.8
      specified NEC J39.8
      streptococcal J06.9
  retina, retinal H35.9
    Batten's or Batten-Mayou E75.4 *[H36]*
    specified NEC H35.89
  rheumatoid —*see* Arthritis, rheumatoid
  rickettsial NOS A79.9
    specified type NEC A79.89
  Riga (-Fede) (cachectic aphthae) K14.0
  Riggs' (compound periodontitis) —*see*
      Periodontitis
  Ritter's L00
  Rivalta's (cervicofacial actinomycosis)
      A42.2
  Robles' (onchocerciasis) B73.01
  Roger's (congenital interventricular septal
      defect) Q21.0
  Rosenthal's (factor XI deficiency) D68.1
  Ross River B33.1
  Rossbach's (hyperchlorhydria) K30
  Rotes Quérol —*see* Hyperostosis, ankylosing
  Roth (-Bernhardt) —*see* Mononeuropathy,
      lower limb, meralgia paresthetica
  Runeberg's (progressive pernicious anemia)
      D51.0
  sacroiliac NEC M53.3
  salivary gland or duct K11.9
    inclusion B25.9
    specified NEC K11.8
    virus B25.9
  sandworm B76.9
  Schimmelbusch's —*see* Mastopathy, cystic
  Schmorl's —*see* Schmorl's disease or nodes
  Schönlein (-Henoch) (purpura rheumatica)
      D69.0
  Schottmüller's —*see* Fever, paratyphoid
  Schultz's (agranulocytosis) —*see*
      Agranulocytosis
  Schwalbe-Ziehen-Oppenheim G24.1
  Schwartz-Jampel G71.13
  sclera H15.9
    specified NEC H15.89
  scrofulous (tuberculous) A18.2
  scrotum N50.9
  sebaceous glands L73.9
  semilunar cartilage, cystic —*see also*
      Derangement, knee, meniscus, cystic
  seminal vesicle N50.9
  serum NEC —*see also* Reaction, serum T80.69
  sexually transmitted A64
    anogenital
      herpesviral infection —*see* Herpes,
          anogenital
      warts A63.0
    chancroid A57
    chlamydial infection —*see* Chlamydia
    gonorrhea —*see* Gonorrhea
    granuloma inguinale A58
    specified organism NEC A63.8

► New   ⇒ Revised   ~~deleted~~ Deleted   • Use Additional Character(s)

Disease, diseased *(Continued)*
  sexually transmitted *(Continued)*
    syphilis —*see* Syphilis
    trichomoniasis —*see* Trichomoniasis
  Sézary C84.1-●
  shimamushi (scrub typhus) A75.3
  shipyard B30.0
  sickle-cell D57.1
    with crisis (vasoocclusive pain) D57.00
      with
        acute chest syndrome D57.01
        splenic sequestration D57.02
    elliptocytosis D57.8-●
    Hb-C D57.20
      with crisis (vasoocclusive pain) D57.219
        with
          acute chest syndrome D57.211
          splenic sequestration D57.212
      without crisis D57.20
    Hb-SD D57.80
      with crisis D57.819
        with
          acute chest syndrome D57.811
          splenic sequestration D57.812
    Hb-SE D57.80
      with crisis D57.819
        with
          acute chest syndrome D57.811
          splenic sequestration D57.812
    specified NEC D57.80
      with crisis D57.819
        with
          acute chest syndrome D57.811
          splenic sequestration D57.812
    spherocytosis D57.80
      with crisis D57.819
        with
          acute chest syndrome D57.811
          splenic sequestration D57.812
    thalassemia D57.40
      with crisis (vasoocclusive pain) D57.419
        with
          acute chest syndrome D57.411
          splenic sequestration D57.412
      without crisis D57.40
  silo-filler's J68.8
    bronchitis J68.0
    pneumonitis J68.0
    pulmonary edema J68.1
  simian B B00.4
  Simons' (progressive lipodystrophy) E88.1
  sin nombre virus B33.4
  sinus —*see* Sinusitis
  Sirkari's B55.0
  sixth B08.20
    due to human herpesvirus 6 B08.21
    due to human herpesvirus 7 B08.22
  skin L98.9
    due to metabolic disorder NEC E88.9
      [L99]
    specified NEC L98.8
  slim (HIV) B20
  small vessel I73.9
  Sneddon-Wilkinson (subcorneal pustular
    dermatosis) L13.1
  South African creeping B88.0
  spinal (cord) G95.9
    congenital Q06.9
    specified NEC G95.89
  spine —*see also* Spondylopathy
    joint —*see* Dorsopathy
    tuberculous A18.01
  spinocerebellar (hereditary) G11.9
    specified NEC G11.8
  spleen D73.9
    amyloid E85.4 *[D77]*
    organic D73.9
    polycystic Q89.09
    postinfectional D73.89
  sponge-diver's —*see* Toxicity, venom, marine
    animal, sea anemone

Disease, diseased *(Continued)*
  Startle Q89.8
  Steinert's G71.11
  Sticker's (erythema infectiosum) B08.3
  Stieda's (calcification, knee joint) —*see*
    Bursitis, tibial collateral
  Stokes' (exophthalmic goiter) —*see*
    Hyperthyroidism, with, goiter (diffuse)
  Stokes-Adams (syncope with heart block)
    I45.9
  stomach K31.9
    functional, psychogenic F45.8
    specified NEC K31.89
  stonemason's J62.8
  storage
    glycogen —*see* Disease, glycogen storage
    mucopolysaccharide —*see*
      Mucopolysaccharidosis
  striatopallidal system NEC G25.89
  Stuart-Prower (congenital factor X deficiency)
    D68.2
  Stuart's (congenital factor X deficiency) D68.2
  subcutaneous tissue —*see* Disease, skin
  supporting structures of teeth K08.9
    specified NEC K08.89
  suprarenal (capsule) (gland) E27.9
    hyperfunction E27.0
    specified NEC E27.8
  sweat glands L74.9
    specified NEC L74.8
  Sweeley-Klionsky E75.21
  Swift (-Feer) —*see* Poisoning, mercury
  swimming-pool granuloma A31.1
  Sylvest's (epidemic pleurodynia) B33.0
  sympathetic nervous system G90.9
  synovium —*see* Disorder, synovium
  syphilitic —*see* Syphilis
  systemic tissue mast cell C96.20
  tanapox (virus) B08.71
  Tangier E78.6
  Tarral-Besnier (pityriasis rubra pilaris) L44.0
  Tauri's E74.09
  tear duct —*see* Disorder, lacrimal system
  tendon, tendinous —*see also* Disorder, tendon
    nodular —*see* Trigger finger
  terminal vessel I73.9
  testis N50.9
  thalassemia Hb-S —*see* Disease, sickle-cell,
    thalassemia
  Thaysen-Gee (nontropical sprue) K90.0
  Thomsen G71.12
  throat J39.2
    septic J02.0
  thromboembolic —*see* Embolism
  thymus (gland) E32.9
    specified NEC E32.8
  thyroid (gland) E07.9
    heart —*see also* Hyperthyroidism E05.90
      [I43]
      with thyroid storm E05.91 *[I43]*
    specified NEC E07.8
  Tietze's M94.0
  tongue K14.9
    specified NEC K14.89
  tonsils, tonsillar (and adenoids) J35.9
  tooth, teeth K08.9
    hard tissues K03.9
      specified NEC K03.89
    pulp NEC K04.99
    specified NEC K08.89
  Tourette's F95.2
  trachea NEC J39.8
  tricuspid I07.9
    nonrheumatic I36.9
  triglyceride-storage E75.5
  trophoblastic —*see* Mole, hydatidiform
  tsutsugamushi A75.3
  tube (fallopian) (noninflammatory) N83.9
    inflammatory —*see* Salpingitis
    specified NEC N83.8
  tuberculous NEC —*see* Tuberculosis

Disease, diseased *(Continued)*
  tubo-ovarian (noninflammatory) N83.9
    inflammatory —*see* Salpingo-oophoritis
    specified NEC N83.8
  tubotympanic, chronic —*see* Otitis, media,
    suppurative, chronic, tubotympanic
  tubulo-interstitial N15.9
    specified NEC N15.8
  tympanum —*see* Disorder, tympanic
    membrane
  Uhl's Q24.8
  Underwood's (sclerema neonatorum) P83.0
  Unverricht (-Lundborg) —*see* Epilepsy,
    generalized, idiopathic
  Urbach-Oppenheim (necrobiosis lipoidica
    diabeticorum) —*see* E08-E13 with .620
  ureter N28.9
    in (due to)
      schistosomiasis (bilharziasis) B65.0 *[N29]*
  urethra N36.9
    specified NEC N36.8
  urinary (tract) N39.9
    bladder N32.9
      specified NEC N32.89
    specified NEC N39.8
  uterus (noninflammatory) N85.9
    infective —*see* Endometritis
    inflammatory —*see* Endometritis
    specified NEC N85.8
  uveal tract (anterior) H21.9
    posterior H31.9
  vagabond's B85.1
  vagina, vaginal (noninflammatory) N89.9
    inflammatory NEC N76.89
    specified NEC N89.8
  valve, valvular I38
    multiple I08.9
      specified NEC I08.8
  van Creveld-von Gierke (glycogenosis I)
    E74.01
  vas deferens N50.9
  vascular I99.9
    arteriosclerotic —*see* Arteriosclerosis
    ciliary body NEC —*see* Disorder, iris,
      vascular
    hypertensive —*see* Hypertension
    iris NEC —*see* Disorder, iris, vascular
    obliterative I77.1
      peripheral I73.9
    occlusive I99.8
    peripheral (occlusive) I73.9
      in diabetes mellitus —*see* E08-E13 with .51
  vasomotor I73.9
  vasospastic I73.9
  vein I87.9
  venereal —*see also* Disease, sexually
    transmitted A64
    chlamydial NEC A56.8
      anus A56.3
      genitourinary NOS A56.2
      pharynx A56.4
      rectum A56.3
    fifth A55
    sixth A55
    specified nature or type NEC A63.8
  vertebra, vertebral —*see also* Spondylopathy
    disc —*see* Disorder, disc
  vibration —*see* Vibration, adverse effects
  viral, virus —*see also* Disease, by type of virus
    B34.9
    arbovirus NOS A94
    arthropod-borne NOS A94
    congenital P35.9
      specified NEC P35.8
    Hanta (with renal manifestations)
      (Dobrava) (Puumala) (Seoul) A98.5
      with pulmonary manifestations (Andes)
        (Bayou) (Bermejo) (Black Creek
        Canal) (Choclo) (Juquitiba) (Laguna
        negra) (Lechiguanas) (New York)
        (Oran) (Sin nombre) B33.4

Disease, diseased *(Continued)*
  viral, virus *(Continued)*
    Hantaan (Korean hemorrhagic fever) A98.5
    human immunodeficiency (HIV) B20
    Kunjin A83.4
    nonarthropod-borne NOS B34.9
    Powassan A84.8
    Rocio (encephalitis) A83.6
    Sin nombre (Hantavirus) (cardio)-
        pulmonary syndrome B33.4
    Tahyna B33.8
    vesicular stomatitis A93.8
  vitreous H43.9
    specified NEC H43.89
  vocal cord J38.3
  Volkmann's, acquired T79.6
  von Eulenburg's (congenital paramyotonia)
      G71.19
  von Gierke's (glycogenosis I) E74.01
  von Graefe's —*see* Strabismus, paralytic,
      ophthalmoplegia, progressive
  von Willebrand (-Jürgens) (angiohemophilia)
      D68.0
  Vrolik's (osteogenesis imperfecta) Q78.0
  vulva (noninflammatory) N90.9
    inflammatory NEC N76.89
    specified NEC N90.89
  Wallgren's (obstruction of splenic vein with
      collateral circulation) I87.8
  Wassilieff's (leptospiral jaundice) A27.0
  wasting NEC R64
    due to malnutrition E41
  Waterhouse-Friderichsen A39.1
  Wegner's (syphilitic osteochondritis) A50.02
  Weil's (leptospiral jaundice of lung) A27.0
  Weir Mitchell's (erythromelalgia) I73.81
  Werdnig-Hoffmann G12.0
  Wermer's E31.21
  Werner-His (trench fever) A79.0
  Werner-Schultz (neutropenic splenomegaly)
      D73.81
  Wernicke-Posadas B38.9
  whipworm B79
  white blood cells D72.9
    specified NEC D72.89
  white matter R90.82
  white-spot, meaning lichen sclerosus et
      atrophicus L90.0
    penis N48.0
    vulva N90.4
  Wilkie's K55.1
  Wilkinson-Sneddon (subcorneal pustular
      dermatosis) L13.1
  Willis' —*see* Diabetes
  Wilson's (hepatolenticular degeneration) E83.01
  woolsorter's A22.1
  yaba monkey tumor B08.72
  yaba pox (virus) B08.72
  Zika virus A92.5
  zoonotic, bacterial A28.9
  ▶congenital P35.4
    specified type NEC A28.8
Disfigurement (due to scar) L90.5
Disgerminoma —*see* Dysgerminoma
DISH (diffuse idiopathic skeletal
    hyperostosis) —*see* Hyperostosis,
    ankylosing
Disinsertion, retina —*see* Detachment, retina
Dislocatable hip, congenital Q65.6
Dislocation (articular)
  with fracture —*see* Fracture
  acromioclavicular (joint) S43.10-●
    with displacement
      100%-200% S43.12-●
      more than 200% S43.13-●
    inferior S43.14-●
    posterior S43.15-●
  ankle S93.0-●
  astragalus —*see* Dislocation, ankle
  atlantoaxial S13.121
  atlantooccipital S13.111

Dislocation *(Continued)*
  atloidooccipital S13.111
  breast bone S23.29
  capsule, joint code by site under Dislocation
  carpal (bone) —*see* Dislocation, wrist
  carpometacarpal (joint) NEC S63.05-●
    thumb S63.04-●
  cartilage (joint) - code by site under
      Dislocation
  cervical spine (vertebra) —*see* Dislocation,
      vertebra, cervical
  chronic —*see* Dislocation, recurrent
  clavicle —*see* Dislocation, acromioclavicular
      joint
  coccyx S33.2
  congenital NEC Q68.8
  coracoid —*see* Dislocation, shoulder
  costal cartilage S23.29
  costochondral S23.29
  cricoarytenoid articulation S13.29
  cricothyroid articulation S13.29
  dorsal vertebra —*see* Dislocation, vertebra,
      thoracic
  ear ossicle —*see* Discontinuity, ossicles, ear
  elbow S53.10-●
    congenital Q68.8
    pathological —*see* Dislocation, pathological
        NEC, elbow
    radial head alone —*see* Dislocation, radial
        head
    recurrent —*see* Dislocation, recurrent,
        elbow
    traumatic S53.10-●
      anterior S53.11-●
      lateral S53.14-●
      medial S53.13-●
      posterior S53.12-●
      specified type NEC S53.19-●
  eye, nontraumatic —*see* Luxation, globe
  eyeball, nontraumatic —*see* Luxation, globe
  femur
    distal end —*see* Dislocation, knee
    proximal end —*see* Dislocation, hip
  fibula
    distal end —*see* Dislocation, ankle
    proximal end —*see* Dislocation, knee
  finger S63.25-●
    index S63.25-●
    interphalangeal S63.27-●
      distal S63.29-●
        index S63.29-●
        little S63.29-●
        middle S63.29-●
        ring S63.29-●
      index S63.27-●
      little S63.27-●
      middle S63.27-●
      proximal S63.28-●
        index S63.28-●
        little S63.28-●
        middle S63.28-●
        ring S63.28-●
      ring S63.27-●
    little S63.25-●
    metacarpophalangeal S63.26-●
      index S63.26-●
      little S63.26-●
      middle S63.26-●
      ring S63.26-●
    middle S63.25-●
    recurrent —*see* Dislocation, recurrent,
        finger
    ring S63.25-●
    thumb —*see* Dislocation, thumb
  foot S93.30-●
    recurrent —*see* Dislocation, recurrent,
        foot
    specified site NEC S93.33-●
    tarsal joint S93.31-●
    tarsometatarsal joint S93.32-●
    toe —*see* Dislocation, toe

Dislocation *(Continued)*
  fracture —*see* Fracture
  glenohumeral (joint) —*see* Dislocation,
      shoulder
  glenoid —*see* Dislocation, shoulder
  habitual —*see* Dislocation, recurrent
  hip S73.00-●
    anterior S73.03-●
      obturator S73.02-●
    central S73.04-●
    congenital (total) Q65.2
      bilateral Q65.1
      partial Q65.5
        bilateral Q65.4
        unilateral Q65.3-●
      unilateral Q65.0-●
    developmental M24.85-●
    pathological —*see* Dislocation, pathological
        NEC, hip
    posterior S73.01-●
    recurrent —*see* Dislocation, recurrent,
        hip
  humerus, proximal end —*see* Dislocation,
      shoulder
  incomplete —*see* Subluxation, by site
  incus —*see* Discontinuity, ossicles, ear
  infracoracoid —*see* Dislocation, shoulder
  innominate (pubic junction) (sacral junction)
      S33.39
    acetabulum —*see* Dislocation, hip
  interphalangeal (joint(s))
    finger S63.279
      distal S63.29-●
        index S63.29-●
        little S63.29-●
        middle S63.29-●
        ring S63.29-●
      index S63.27-●
      little S63.27-●
      middle S63.27-●
      proximal S63.28-●
        index S63.28-●
        little S63.28-●
        middle S63.28-●
        ring S63.28-●
      ring S63.27-●
    foot or toe —*see* Dislocation, toe
    thumb S63.12-●
      ~~distal joint S63.14~~
      ~~proximal joint S63.13~~
  jaw (cartilage) (meniscus) S03.0-●
  joint prosthesis —*see* Complications, joint
      prosthesis, mechanical, displacement,
      by site
  knee S83.106
    cap —*see* Dislocation, patella
    congenital Q68.2
    old M23.8X-●
    patella —*see* Dislocation, patella
    pathological —*see* Dislocation, pathological
        NEC, knee
    proximal tibia
      anteriorly S83.11-●
      laterally S83.14-●
      medially S83.13-●
      posteriorly S83.12-●
    recurrent —*see also* Derangement, knee,
        specified NEC
    specified type NEC S83.19-●
  lacrimal gland H04.16-●
  lens (complete) H27.10-●
    anterior H27.12-●
    congenital Q12.1
    ocular implant —*see* Complications,
        intraocular lens
    partial H27.11-●
    posterior H27.13-●
    traumatic S05.8X-●
  ligament code by site under Dislocation
  lumbar (vertebra) —*see* Dislocation, vertebra,
      lumbar

▶ New   ⇒ Revised   ~~deleted~~ Deleted   ● Use Additional Character(s)

Dislocation *(Continued)*
  lumbosacral (vertebra) —*see also* Dislocation, vertebra, lumbar
    congenital Q76.49
  mandible S03.0-●
  meniscus (knee) —*see* Tear, meniscus
    other sites code by site under Dislocation
  metacarpal (bone)
    distal end —*see* Dislocation, finger
    proximal end S63.06-●
  metacarpophalangeal (joint)
    finger S63.26-●
      index S63.26-●
      little S63.26-●
      middle S63.26-●
      ring S63.26-●
      thumb S63.11-●
  metatarsal (bone) —*see* Dislocation, foot
  metatarsophalangeal (joint(s)) —*see* Dislocation, toe
  midcarpal (joint) S63.03-●
  midtarsal (joint) —*see* Dislocation, foot
  neck S13.20
    specified site NEC S13.29
    vertebra —*see* Dislocation, vertebra, cervical
  nose (septal cartilage) S03.1
  occipitoatloid S13.111
  old —*see* Derangement, joint, specified type NEC
  ossicles, ear —*see* Discontinuity, ossicles, ear
  partial —*see* Subluxation, by site
  patella S83.006
    congenital Q74.1
    lateral S83.01-●
    recurrent (nontraumatic) M22.0-●
      incomplete M22.1-●
    specified type NEC S83.09-●
  pathological NEC M24.30
    ankle M24.37-●
    elbow M24.32-●
    foot joint M24.37-●
    hand joint M24.34-●
    hip M24.35-●
    knee M24.36-●
    lumbosacral joint —*see* subcategory M53.2
    pelvic region —*see* Dislocation, pathological, hip
    sacroiliac —*see* subcategory M53.2
    shoulder M24.31-●
    wrist M24.33-●
  pelvis NEC S33.30
    specified NEC S33.39
  phalanx
    finger or hand —*see* Dislocation, finger
    foot or toe —*see* Dislocation, toe
  prosthesis, internal —*see* Complications, prosthetic device, by site, mechanical
  radial head S53.006
    anterior S53.01-●
    posterior S53.02-●
    specified type NEC S53.09-●
  radiocarpal (joint) S63.02-●
  radiohumeral (joint) —*see* Dislocation, radial head
  radioulnar (joint)
    distal S63.01-●
    proximal —*see* Dislocation, elbow
  radius
    distal end —*see* Dislocation, wrist
    proximal end —*see* Dislocation, radial head
  recurrent M24.40
    ankle M24.47-●
    elbow M24.42-●
    finger M24.44-●
    foot joint M24.47-●
    hand joint M24.44-●
    hip M24.45-●
    knee M24.46-●
      patella —*see* Dislocation, patella, recurrent

Dislocation *(Continued)*
  recurrent *(Continued)*
    patella —*see* Dislocation, patella, recurrent
    sacroiliac —*see* subcategory M53.2
    shoulder M24.41-●
    toe M24.47-●
    vertebra —*see also* subcategory M43.5
      atlantoaxial M43.4
        with myelopathy M43.3
    wrist M24.43-●
  rib (cartilage) S23.29
  sacrococcygeal S33.2
  sacroiliac (joint) (ligament) S33.2
    congenital Q74.2
    recurrent —*see* subcategory M53.2
  sacrum S33.2
  scaphoid (bone) (hand) (wrist) —*see* Dislocation, wrist
    foot —*see* Dislocation, foot
  scapula —*see* Dislocation, shoulder, girdle, scapula
  semilunar cartilage, knee —*see* Tear, meniscus
  septal cartilage (nose) S03.1
  septum (nasal) (old) J34.2
  sesamoid bone code by site under Dislocation
  shoulder (blade) (ligament) (joint) (traumatic) S43.006
    acromioclavicular —*see* Dislocation, acromioclavicular
    chronic —*see* Dislocation, recurrent, shoulder
    congenital Q68.8
    girdle S43.30-●
      scapula S43.31-●
      specified site NEC S43.39-●
    humerus S43.00-●
      anterior S43.01-●
      inferior S43.03-●
      posterior S43.02-●
    pathological —*see* Dislocation, pathological NEC, shoulder
    recurrent —*see* Dislocation, recurrent, shoulder
    specified type NEC S43.08-●
  spine
    cervical —*see* Dislocation, vertebra, cervical
    congenital Q76.49
    due to birth trauma P11.5
    lumbar —*see* Dislocation, vertebra, lumbar
    thoracic —*see* Dislocation, vertebra, thoracic
  spontaneous —*see* Dislocation, pathological
  sternoclavicular (joint) S43.206
    anterior S43.21-●
    posterior S43.22-●
  sternum S23.29
  subglenoid —*see* Dislocation, shoulder
  symphysis pubis S33.4
  talus —*see* Dislocation, ankle
  tarsal (bone(s)) (joint(s)) —*see* Dislocation, foot
  tarsometatarsal (joint(s)) —*see* Dislocation, foot
  temporomandibular (joint) S03.0-●
  thigh, proximal end —*see* Dislocation, hip
  thorax S23.20
    specified site NEC S23.29
    vertebra —*see* Dislocation, vertebra
  thumb S63.10-●
    interphalangeal joint —*see* Dislocation, interphalangeal (joint), thumb
    metacarpophalangeal joint —*see* Dislocation, metacarpophalangeal (joint), thumb
  thyroid cartilage S13.29
  tibia
    distal end —*see* Dislocation, ankle
    proximal end —*see* Dislocation, knee
  tibiofibular (joint)
    distal —*see* Dislocation, ankle
    superior —*see* Dislocation, knee

Dislocation *(Continued)*
  toe(s) S93.106
    great S93.10-●
      interphalangeal joint S93.11-●
      metatarsophalangeal joint S93.12-●
    interphalangeal joint S93.119
    lesser S93.106
      interphalangeal joint S93.11-●
      metatarsophalangeal joint S93.12-●
    metatarsophalangeal joint S93.12-●
  tooth S03.2
  trachea S23.29
  ulna
    distal end S63.07-●
    proximal end —*see* Dislocation, elbow
  ulnohumeral (joint) —*see* Dislocation, elbow
  vertebra (articular process) (body) (traumatic)
    cervical S13.101
      atlantoaxial joint S13.121
      atlantooccipital joint S13.111
      atloidooccipital joint S13.111
      joint between
        C0 and C1 S13.111
        C1 and C2 S13.121
        C2 and C3 S13.131
        C3 and C4 S13.141
        C4 and C5 S13.151
        C5 and C6 S13.161
        C6 and C7 S13.171
        C7 and T1 S13.181
      occipitoatloid joint S13.111
    congenital Q76.49
    lumbar S33.101
      joint between
        L1 and L2 S33.111
        L2 and L3 S33.121
        L3 and L4 S33.131
        L4 and L5 S33.141
    nontraumatic —*see* Displacement, intervertebral disc
    partial —*see* Subluxation, by site
    recurrent NEC —*see* subcategory M43.5
    thoracic S23.101
      joint between
        T1 and T2 S23.111
        T2 and T3 S23.121
        T3 and T4 S23.123
        T4 and T5 S23.131
        T5 and T6 S23.133
        T6 and T7 S23.141
        T7 and T8 S23.143
        T8 and T9 S23.151
        T9 and T10 S23.153
        T10 and T11 S23.161
        T11 and T12 S23.163
        T12 and L1 S23.171
  wrist (carpal bone) S63.006
    carpometacarpal joint —*see* Dislocation, carpometacarpal (joint)
    distal radioulnar joint —*see* Dislocation, radioulnar (joint), distal
    metacarpal bone, proximal —*see* Dislocation, metacarpal (bone), proximal end
    midcarpal —*see* Dislocation, midcarpal (joint)
    radiocarpal joint —*see* Dislocation, radiocarpal (joint)
    recurrent —*see* Dislocation, recurrent, wrist
    specified site NEC S63.09-●
    ulna —*see* Dislocation, ulna, distal end
  xiphoid cartilage S23.29
Disorder (of) —*see also* Disease
  acantholytic L11.9
    specified NEC L11.8
  acute
    psychotic —*see* Psychosis, acute
    stress F43.0

Disorder (Continued)
adjustment (grief) F43.20
  with
    anxiety F43.22
      with depressed mood F43.23
    conduct disturbance F43.24
      with emotional disturbance F43.25
    depressed mood F43.21
      with anxiety F43.23
    other specified symptom F43.29
adrenal (capsule) (gland) (medullary) E27.9
  specified NEC E27.8
adrenogenital E25.9
  drug-induced E25.8
  iatrogenic E25.8
  idiopathic E25.8
adult personality (and behavior) F69
  specified NEC F68.8
affective (mood) —see Disorder, mood
aggressive, unsocialized F91.1
alcohol-related F10.99
  with
    amnestic disorder, persisting F10.96
    anxiety disorder F10.980
    dementia, persisting F10.97
    intoxication F10.929
      with delirium F10.921
      uncomplicated F10.920
    mood disorder F10.94
    other specified F10.988
    psychotic disorder F10.959
      with
        delusions F10.950
        hallucinations F10.951
    sexual dysfunction F10.981
    sleep disorder F10.982
alcohol use
  mild F10.10
    with
      alcohol-induced
        anxiety disorder F10.180
        bipolar and related disorder
          F10.14
        depressive disorder F10.14
        psychotic disorder F10.159
        sexual dysfunction F10.181
        sleep disorder F10.182
      alcohol intoxication F10.129
        delirium F10.121
    in remission (early) (sustained) F10.11
  moderate or severe F10.20
    with
      alcohol-induced
        anxiety disorder F10.280
        bipolar and related disorder F10.24
        depressive disorder F10.24
        major neurocognitive disorder,
          amnestic-confabulatory type
          F10.26
        major neurocognitive disorder,
          nonamnestic-confabulatory
          type F10.27
        mild neurocognitive disorder
          F10.288
        psychotic disorder F10.259
        sexual dysfunction F10.281
        sleep disorder F10.282
      alcohol intoxication F10.229
        delirium F10.221
    in remission (early) (sustained) F10.21
allergic —see Allergy
alveolar NEC J84.09
amino-acid
  cystathioninuria E72.19
  cystinosis E72.04
  cystinuria E72.01
  glycinuria E72.09
  homocystinuria E72.11
  metabolism —see Disturbance,
    metabolism, amino-acid
  ➟ specified NEC E72.89
  neonatal, transitory P74.8

Disorder (Continued)
amino-acid (Continued)
  renal transport NEC E72.09
  transport NEC E72.09
amnesic, amnestic
  alcohol-induced F10.96
    with dependence F10.26
  due to (secondary to) general medical
    condition F04
  psychoactive NEC-induced F19.96
    with
      abuse F19.16
      dependence F19.26
  sedative, hypnotic or anxiolytic-●
    induced F13.96
    with dependence F13.26
amphetamine-type substance use
  mild F15.10
    in remission (early) (sustained) F15.11
  moderate F15.20
    in remission (early) (sustained) F15.21
  severe F15.20
    in remission (early) (sustained) F15.21
amphetamine (or other stimulant) use
  mild
    with
      amphetamine (or other stimulant)
        -induced
        anxiety disorder F15.180
        bipolar and related disorder
          F15.14
        depressive disorder F15.14
        obsessive-compulsive and related
          disorder F15.188
        psychotic disorder F15.159
        sexual dysfunction F15.181
      amphetamine, cocaine, or other
        stimulant intoxication
        with perceptual disturbances
          F15.122
        without perceptual disturbances
          F15.129
      intoxication delirium F15.121
  moderate or severe
    with
      amphetamine (or other stimulant)
        -induced
        anxiety disorder F15.280
        obsessive-compulsive and related
          disorder F15.288
        sexual dysfunction F15.281
        bipolar and related disorder
          F15.24
        depressive disorder F15.24
        psychotic disorder F15.259
      amphetamine, cocaine, or other
        stimulant intoxication
        with perceptual disturbances
          F15.222
        without perceptual disturbances
          F15.229
      intoxication delirium F15.221
anaerobic glycolysis with anemia D55.2
anxiety F41.9
  due to (secondary to)
    alcohol F10.980
      in
        abuse F10.180
        dependence F10.280
    amphetamine F15.980
      in
        abuse F15.180
        dependence F15.280
    anxiolytic F13.980
      in
        abuse F13.180
        dependence F13.280
    caffeine F15.980
      in
        abuse F15.180
        dependence F15.280

Disorder (Continued)
anxiety (Continued)
  due to (Continued)
    cannabis F12.980
      in
        abuse F12.180
        dependence F12.280
    cocaine F14.980
      in
        abuse F14.180
        dependence F14.180
    general medical condition F06.4
    hallucinogen F16.980
      in
        abuse F16.180
        dependence F16.280
    hypnotic F13.980
      in
        abuse F13.180
        dependence F13.280
    inhalant F18.980
      in
        abuse F18.180
        dependence F18.280
    phencyclidine F16.980
      in
        abuse F16.180
        dependence F16.280
    psychoactive substance NEC F19.980
      in
        abuse F19.180
        dependence F19.280
    sedative F13.980
      in
        abuse F13.180
        dependence F13.280
    volatile solvents F18.980
      in
        abuse F18.180
        dependence F18.280
  generalized F41.1
  illness F45.21
  mixed
    with depression (mild) F41.8
    specified NEC F41.3
  organic F06.4
  phobic F40.9
    of childhood F40.8
  specified NEC F41.8
aortic valve —see Endocarditis, aortic
aromatic amino-acid metabolism E70.9
  specified NEC E70.8
arteriole NEC I77.89
artery NEC I77.89
articulation —see Disorder, joint
attachment (childhood)
  disinhibited F94.2
  reactive F94.1
attention-deficit hyperactivity (adolescent)
  (adult) (child) F98.8
  combined
    presentation F90.2
    type F90.2
  hyperactive
    impulsive presentation F90.1
    type F90.1
  inattentive
    presentation F90.0
    type F90.0
  specified type NEC F90.8
attention-deficit without hyperactivity
  (adolescent) (adult) (child) F90.0
auditory processing (central) H93.25
autism spectrum F84.0
autistic F84.0
autoimmune D89.89
autonomic nervous system G90.9
  specified NEC G90.8
avoidant
  child or adolescent F40.10
  restrictive food intake F50.82

Disorder *(Continued)*
 balance
  acid-base E87.8
   mixed E87.4
  electrolyte E87.8
  fluid NEC E87.8
 behavioral (disruptive) —*see* Disorder,
   conduct
 beta-amino-acid metabolism E72.89
 bile acid and cholesterol metabolism E78.70
  Barth syndrome E78.71
  other specified E78.79
  Smith-Lemli-Opitz syndrome E78.72
 bilirubin excretion E80.6
 binge eating F50.81
 binocular
  movement H51.9
   convergence
    excess H51.12
    insufficiency H51.11
   internuclear ophthalmoplegia —*see*
     Ophthalmoplegia, internuclear
   palsy of conjugate gaze H51.0
   specified type NEC H51.8
  vision NEC —*see* Disorder, vision, binocular
 bipolar (I) (type 1) F31.9
  and related due to a known physiological
    condition
   with
    manic features F06.33
    manic- or hypomanic-like episodes
      F06.33
    mixed features F06.34
  current (or most recent) episode
   depressed F31.9
    with psychotic features F31.5
    without psychotic features F31.30
     mild F31.31
     moderate F31.32
     severe (without psychotic features)
       F31.4
      with psychotic features F31.5
   hypomanic F31.0
   manic F31.9
    with psychotic features F31.2
    without psychotic features F31.10
     mild F31.11
     moderate F31.12
     severe (without psychotic features)
       F31.13
      with psychotic features F31.2
   mixed F31.60
    mild F31.61
    moderate F31.62
    severe (without psychotic features)
      F31.63
     with psychotic features F31.64
    severe depression (without psychotic
      features) F31.4
     with psychotic features F31.5
  II (type 2) F31.81
  in remission (currently) F31.70
   in full remission
    most recent episode
     depressed F31.76
     hypomanic F31.72
     manic F31.74
     mixed F31.78
   in partial remission
    most recent episode
     depressed F31.75
     hypomanic F31.71
     manic F31.73
     mixed F31.77
  organic F06.30
  single manic episode F30.9
   mild F30.11
   moderate F30.12
   hhsevere (without psychotic symptoms)
     F30.13
    with psychotic symptoms F30.2
  specified NEC F31.89

Disorder *(Continued)*
 bladder N32.9
  functional NEC N31.9
  in schistosomiasis B65.0 *[N33]*
  specified NEC N32.89
 bleeding D68.9
 blood D75.9
  in congenital early syphilis A50.09
    [D77]
 body dysmorphic F45.22
 bone M89.9
  continuity M84.9
   specified type NEC M84.80
    ankle M84.87-•
    fibula M84.86-•
    foot M84.87-•
    hand M84.84-•
    humerus M84.82-•
    neck M84.88
    pelvis M84.859
    radius M84.83-•
    rib M84.88
    shoulder M84.81-•
    skull M84.88
    thigh M84.85-•
    tibia M84.86-•
    ulna M84.83-•
    vertebra M84.88
  density and structure M85.9
   cyst —*see also* Cyst, bone, specified type
     NEC
    aneurysmal —*see* Cyst, bone,
      aneurysmal
    solitary —*see* Cyst, bone, solitary
   diffuse idiopathic skeletal
     hyperostosis —*see* Hyperostosis,
     ankylosing
   fibrous dysplasia (monostotic) —*see*
     Dysplasia, fibrous, bone
   fluorosis —*see* Fluorosis, skeletal
   hyperostosis of skull M85.2
   osteitis condensans —*see* Osteitis,
     condensans
   specified type NEC M85.8-•
    ankle M85.87-•
    foot M85.87-•
    forearm M85.83-•
    hand M85.84-•
    lower leg M85.86-•
    multiple sites M85.89
    neck M85.88
    rib M85.88
    shoulder M85.81-•
    skull M85.88
    thigh M85.85-•
    upper arm M85.82-•
    vertebra M85.88
  development and growth NEC M89.20
   carpus M89.24-•
   clavicle M89.21-•
   femur M89.25-•
   fibula M89.26-•
   finger M89.24-•
   humerus M89.22-•
   ilium M89.259
   ischium M89.259
   metacarpus M89.24-•
   metatarsus M89.27-•
   multiple sites M89.29
   neck M89.28
   radius M89.23-•
   rib M89.28
   scapula M89.21-•
   skull M89.28
   tarsus M89.27-•
   tibia M89.26-•
   toe M89.27-•
   ulna M89.23-•
   vertebra M89.28
  specified type NEC M89.8X-•
 brachial plexus G54.0

Disorder *(Continued)*
 branched-chain amino-acid metabolism E71.2
  specified NEC E71.19
 breast N64.9
  agalactia —*see* Agalactia
  associated with
   lactation O92.70
    specified NEC O92.79
   pregnancy O92.20
    specified NEC O92.29
   puerperium O92.20
    specified NEC O92.29
  cracked nipple —*see* Cracked nipple
  galactorrhea —*see* Galactorrhea
  hypogalactia O92.4
  lactation disorder NEC O92.79
  mastitis —*see* Mastitis
  nipple infection —*see* Infection, nipple
  retracted nipple —*see* Retraction, nipple
  specified type NEC N64.89
 Briquet's F45.0
 bullous, in diseases classified elsewhere L14
 caffeine use
  mild
   with
    caffeine-induced
     anxiety disorder F15.180
     sleep disorder F15.182
  moderate or severe
   with
    caffeine-induced
     anxiety disorder F15.280
     sleep disorder F15.282
 cannabis use
  mild F12.10
   with
    cannabis-induced
     anxiety disorder F12.180
     psychotic disorder F12.159
     sleep disorder F12.188
    cannabis intoxication delirium F12.121
     with perceptual disturbances
       F12.122
     without perceptual disturbances
       F12.129
   in remission (early) (sustained) F12.11
  moderate or severe F12.20
   with
    cannabis-induced
     anxiety disorder F12.280
     psychotic disorder F12.259
     sleep disorder F12.288
    cannabis intoxication
     with perceptual disturbances
       F12.222
     without perceptual disturbances
       F12.229
    delirium F12.221
   in remission (early) (sustained) F12.21
 carbohydrate
  absorption, intestinal NEC E74.39
  metabolism (congenital) E74.9
   specified NEC E74.8
 cardiac, functional I51.89
 carnitine metabolism E71.40
 cartilage M94.9
  articular NEC —*see* Derangement, joint,
    articular cartilage
  chondrocalcinosis —*see*
    Chondrocalcinosis
  specified type NEC M94.8X-•
   articular —*see* Derangement, joint,
     articular cartilage
   multiple sites M94.8X0
 catatonia (due to known physiological
   condition) (with another mental
   disorder) F06.1
 catatonic
  due to (secondary to) known physiological
    condition F06.1
  organic F06.1

Disorder (Continued)
 central auditory processing H93.25
 cervical
  region NEC M53.82
  root (nerve) NEC G54.2
 character NOS F60.9
 childhood disintegrative NEC F84.3
 cholesterol and bile acid metabolism E78.70
  Barth syndrome E78.71
  other specified E78.79
  Smith-Lemli-Opitz syndrome E78.72
 choroid H31.9
  atrophy —see Atrophy, choroid
  degeneration —see Degeneration, choroid
  detachment —see Detachment, choroid
  dystrophy —see Dystrophy, choroid
  hemorrhage —see Hemorrhage, choroid
  rupture —see Rupture, choroid
  scar —see Scar, chorioretinal
  solar retinopathy —see Retinopathy, solar
  specified type NEC H31.8
 ciliary body —see Disorder, iris
  degeneration —see Degeneration, ciliary
   body
 coagulation (factor) (see also Defect,
   coagulation) D68.9
  newborn, transient P61.6
 cocaine use
  mild F14.10
   with
    amphetamine, cocaine, or other
     stimulant intoxication
     with perceptual disturbances
      F14.122
     without perceptual disturbances
      F14.129
    cocaine-induced
     anxiety disorder F14.180
     bipolar and related disorder F14.14
     depressive disorder F14.14
     obsessive-compulsive and related
      disorder F14.188
     psychotic disorder F14.159
     sexual dysfunction F14.181
     sleep disorder F14.182
    cocaine intoxication delirium F14.121
   in remission (early) (sustained) F14.11
  moderate or severe F14.20
   with
    amphetamine, cocaine, or other
     stimulant intoxication
     with perceptual disturbances
      F14.222
     without perceptual disturbances
      F14.229
    cocaine-induced
     anxiety disorder F14.280
     bipolar and related disorder
      F14.24
     depressive disorder F14.24
     obsessive-compulsive and related
      disorder F14.288
     psychotic disorder F14.259
     sexual dysfunction F14.281
     sleep disorder F14.282
    cocaine intoxication delirium F14.221
   in remission (early) (sustained) F14.21
 coccyx NEC M53.3
 cognitive F09
  due to (secondary to) general medical
   condition F09
  persisting R41.89
   due to
    alcohol F10.97
     with dependence F10.27
    anxiolytics F13.97
     with dependence F13.27
    hypnotics F13.97
     with dependence F13.27
    sedatives F13.97
     with dependence F13.27

Disorder (Continued)
 cognitive (Continued)
  persisting (Continued)
   due to (Continued)
    specified substance NEC
     F19.97
     with
      abuse F19.17
      dependence F19.27
 communication F80.9
  social pragmatic F80.82
 conduct (childhood) F91.9
  adjustment reaction —see Disorder,
   adjustment
  adolescent onset type F91.2
  childhood onset type F91.1
  compulsive F63.9
  confined to family context F91.0
  depressive F91.8
  group type F91.2
  hyperkinetic —see Disorder, attention-
   deficit hyperactivity
  oppositional defiance F91.3
  socialized F91.2
  solitary aggressive type F91.1
  specified NEC F91.8
  unsocialized (aggressive) F91.1
 conduction, heart I45.9
 congenital glycosylation (CDG) E74.8
 conjunctiva H11.9
  infection —see Conjunctivitis
 connective tissue, localized L94.9
  specified NEC L94.8
 conversion (functional neurological symptom
   disorder)
  with
   abnormal movement F44.4
   anesthesia or sensory loss F44.6
   attacks or seizures F44.5
   mixed symptoms F44.7
   special sensory symptoms F44.6
   speech symptoms F44.4
   swallowing symptoms F44.4
   weakness or paralysis F44.4
 convulsive (secondary) —see Convulsions
 cornea H18.9
  deformity —see Deformity, cornea
  degeneration —see Degeneration, cornea
  deposits —see Deposit, cornea
  due to contact lens H18.82-●
   specified as edema —see Edema, cornea
  edema —see Edema, cornea
  keratitis —see Keratitis
  keratoconjunctivitis —see
    Keratoconjunctivitis
  membrane change —see Change, corneal
    membrane
  neovascularization —see
    Neovascularization, cornea
  scar —see Opacity, cornea
  specified type NEC H18.89-●
  ulcer —see Ulcer, cornea
 corpus cavernosum N48.9
 cranial nerve —see Disorder, nerve, cranial
 cyclothymic F34.0
 defiant oppositional F91.3
 delusional (persistent) (systematized) F22
  induced F24
 depersonalization F48.1
 depressive F32.9
  due to known physiological condition
   with
    depressive features F06.31
    major depressive-like episode F06.32
    mixed features F06.34
  major F32.9
   with psychotic symptoms F32.3
   in remission (full) F32.5
    partial F32.4
   recurrent F33.9
    with psychotic features F33.3

Disorder (Continued)
 depressive (Continued)
  major (Continued)
   single episode F32.9
    mild F32.0
    moderate F32.1
    severe (without psychotic symptoms)
     F32.2
     with psychotic symptoms
      F32.3
   organic F06.31
   persistent F34.1
   recurrent F33.9
    current episode
     mild F33.0
     moderate F33.1
     severe (without psychotic symptoms)
      F33.2
      with psychotic symptoms F33.3
    in remission F33.40
     full F33.42
     partial F33.41
    specified NEC F33.8
   single episode —see Episode,
     depressive
   specified NEC F32.89
  developmental F89
   arithmetical skills F81.2
   coordination (motor) F82
   expressive writing F81.81
   language F80.9
    expressive F80.1
    mixed receptive and expressive
     F80.2
    receptive type F80.2
    specified NEC F80.89
   learning F81.9
    arithmetical F81.2
    reading F81.0
   mixed F88
   motor coordination or function F82
   pervasive F84.9
    specified NEC F84.8
   phonological F80.0
   reading F81.0
   scholastic skills —see also Disorder,
     learning
    mixed F81.89
    specified NEC F88
   speech F80.9
    articulation F80.0
    specified NEC F80.89
   written expression F81.81
  diaphragm J98.6
  digestive (system) K92.9
   newborn P78.9
    specified NEC P78.89
   postprocedural —see Complication,
     gastrointestinal
   psychogenic F45.8
  disc (intervertebral) M51.9
   with
    myelopathy
     cervical region M50.00
     cervicothoracic region M50.03
     high cervical region M50.01
     lumbar region M51.06
     mid-cervical region M50.020
     sacrococcygeal region M53.3
     thoracic region M51.04
     thoracolumbar region M51.05
    radiculopathy
     cervical region M50.10
     cervicothoracic region M50.13
     high cervical region M50.11
     lumbar region M51.16
     lumbosacral region M51.17
     mid-cervical region M50.120
     sacrococcygeal region M53.3
     thoracic region M51.14
     thoracolumbar region M51.15

Disorder *(Continued)*
disc (intervertebral) *(Continued)*
  cervical M50.90
    with
      myelopathy M50.00
        C2-C3 M50.01
        C3-C4 M50.01
        C4-C5 M50.021
        C5-C6 M50.022
        C6-C7 M50.023
        C7-T1 M50.03
        cervicothoracic region M50.03
        high cervical region M50.01
        mid-cervical region M50.020
      neuritis, radiculitis or radiculopathy M50.10
        C2-C3 M50.11
        C3-C4 M50.11
        C4-C5 M50.121
        C5-C6 M50.122
        C6-C7 M50.123
        C7-T1 M50.13
        cervicothoracic region M50.13
        high cervical region M50.11
        mid-cervical region M50.120
    C2-C3 M50.91
    C3-C4 M50.91
    C4-C5 M50.921
    C5-C6 M50.922
    C6-C7 M50.923
    C7-T1 M50.93
    cervicothoracic region M50.93
    degeneration M50.30
      C2-C3 M50.31
      C3-C4 M50.31
      C4-C5 M50.321
      C5-C6 M50.322
      C6-C7 M50.323
      C7-T1 M50.33
      cervicothoracic region M50.33
      high cervical region M50.31
      mid-cervical region M50.320
    displacement M50.20
      C2-C3 M50.21
      C3-C4 M50.21
      C4-C5 M50.221
      C5-C6 M50.222
      C6-C7 M50.223
      C7-T1 M50.23
      cervicothoracic region M50.23
      high cervical region M50.21
      mid-cervical region M50.220
    high cervical region M50.91
    mid-cervical region M50.920
    specified type NEC M50.80
      C2-C3 M50.81
      C3-C4 M50.81
      C4-C5 M50.821
      C5-C6 M50.822
      C6-C7 M50.823
      C7-T1 M50.83
      cervicothoracic region M50.83
      high cervical region M50.81
      mid-cervical region M50.820
  specified NEC
    lumbar region M51.86
    lumbosacral region M51.87
    sacrococcygeal region M53.3
    thoracic region M51.84
    thoracolumbar region M51.85
disinhibited attachment (childhood) F94.2
disintegrative, childhood NEC F84.3
disruptive F91.9
  mood dysregulation F34.81
  specified NEC F91.8
disruptive behavior —*see* Disorder, conduct
dissocial personality F60.2
dissociative F44.9
  affecting
    motor function F44.4
      and sensation F44.7

Disorder *(Continued)*
dissociative *(Continued)*
  affecting *(Continued)*
    sensation F44.6
      and motor function F44.7
  brief reactive F43.0
  due to (secondary to) general medical condition F06.8
  mixed F44.7
  organic F06.8
  other specified NEC F44.89
double heterozygous sickling —*see* Disease, sickle-cell
dream anxiety F51.5
drug induced hemorrhagic D68.32
drug related F19.99
  abuse —*see* Abuse, drug
  dependence —*see* Dependence, drug
dysmorphic body F45.22
dysthymic F34.1
ear H93.9-●
  bleeding —*see* Otorrhagia
  deafness —*see* Deafness
  degenerative H93.09-●
  discharge —*see* Otorrhea
  external H61.9-●
    auditory canal stenosis —*see* Stenosis, external ear canal
    exostosis —*see* Exostosis, external ear canal
    impacted cerumen —*see* Impaction, cerumen
    otitis —*see* Otitis, externa
    perichondritis —*see* Perichondritis, ear
    pinna —*see* Disorder, pinna
    specified type NEC H61.89-●
      in diseases classified elsewhere H62.8X-●
  inner H83.9-●
    vestibular dysfunction —*see* Disorder, vestibular function
  middle H74.9-●
    adhesive H74.1-●
    ossicle —*see* Abnormal, ear ossicles
    polyp —*see* Polyp, ear (middle)
    specified NEC, in diseases classified elsewhere H75.8-●
  postprocedural —*see* Complications, ear, procedure
  specified NEC, in diseases classified elsewhere H94.8-●
eating (adult) (psychogenic) F50.9
  anorexia —*see* Anorexia
  binge F50.81
  bulimia F50.2
  child F98.29
    pica F98.3
    rumination disorder F98.21
  pica F50.89
    childhood F98.3
electrolyte (balance) NEC E87.8
  with
    abortion —*see* Abortion by type complicated by specified condition NEC
    ectopic pregnancy O08.5
    molar pregnancy O08.5
    acidosis (metabolic) (respiratory) E87.2
    alkalosis (metabolic) (respiratory) E87.3
elimination, transepidermal L87.9
  specified NEC L87.8
emotional (persistent) F34.9
  of childhood F93.9
    specified NEC F93.8
endocrine E34.9
  postprocedural E89.89
    specified NEC E89.89
erectile (male) (organic) —*see also* Dysfunction, sexual, male, erectile N52.9
  nonorganic F52.21
erythematous —*see* Erythema

Disorder *(Continued)*
esophagus K22.9
  functional K22.4
  psychogenic F45.8
eustachian tube H69.9-●
  infection —*see* Salpingitis, eustachian
  obstruction —*see* Obstruction, eustachian tube
  patulous —*see* Patulous, eustachian tube
  specified NEC H69.8-●
exhibitionistic F65.2
extrapyramidal G25.9
  in diseases classified elsewhere —*see* category G26
  specified type NEC G25.89
eye H57.9
  postprocedural —*see* Complication, postprocedural, eye
eyelid H02.9
  cyst —*see* Cyst, eyelid
  degenerative H02.70
    chloasma —*see* Chloasma, eyelid
    madarosis —*see* Madarosis
    specified type NEC H02.79
    vitiligo —*see* Vitiligo, eyelid
    xanthelasma —*see* Xanthelasma
  dermatochalasis —*see* Dermato-chalasis
  edema —*see* Edema, eyelid
  elephantiasis —*see* Elephantiasis, eyelid
  foreign body, retained —*see* Foreign body, retained, eyelid
  function H02.59
    abnormal innervation syndrome —*see* Syndrome, abnormal innervation
    blepharochalasis —*see* Blepharochalasis
    blepharoclonus —*see* Blepharoclonus
    blepharophimosis —*see* Blepharophimosis
    blepharoptosis —*see* Blepharoptosis
    lagophthalmos —*see* Lagophthalmos
    lid retraction —*see* Retraction, lid
    hypertrichosis —*see* Hypertrichosis, eyelid
    specified type NEC H02.89
  vascular H02.879
    left H02.876
      lower H02.875
      upper H02.874
    right H02.873
      lower H02.872
      upper H02.871
▥factitious
  ▶by proxy F68.A
  ▶imposed on another F68.A
  ▶imposed on self F68.10
    ▶with predominantly
      ▶psychological symptoms F68.11
        ▶with physical symptoms F68.13
      ▶physical symptoms F68.12
        ▶with psychological symptoms F68.13
  with predominantly
    physical symptoms F68.12
      with psychological symptoms F68.13
    psychological symptoms F68.11
      with physical symptoms F68.13
factor, coagulation —*see* Defect, coagulation
fatty acid
  metabolism E71.30
    specified NEC E71.39
  oxidation
    LCAD E71.310
    MCAD E71.311
    SCAD E71.312
    specified deficiency NEC E71.318
feeding (infant or child) —*see also* Disorder, eating R63.3-●
  or eating disorder F50.9
  specified NEC F50.9
feigned (with obvious motivation) Z76.5
  without obvious motivation —*see* Disorder, factitious

Disorder *(Continued)*
  female
    hypoactive sexual desire F52.0
    orgasmic F52.31
    sexual interest/arousal F52.22
  fetishistic F65.0
  fibroblastic M72.9
    specified NEC M72.8
  fluency
    adult onset F98.5
    childhood onset F80.81
    following
      cerebral infarction I69.323
      cerebrovascular disease I69.923
        specified disease NEC I69.823
      intracerebral hemorrhage I69.123
      nontraumatic intracranial hemorrhage
        NEC I69.223
      subarachnoid hemorrhage I69.023
    in conditions classified elsewhere R47.82
  fluid balance E87.8
  follicular (skin) L73.9
    specified NEC L73.8
  frotteuristic F65.81
  fructose metabolism E74.10
    essential fructosuria E74.11
    fructokinase deficiency E74.11
    fructose-1, 6-diphosphatase deficiency
      E74.19
    hereditary fructose intolerance E74.12
    other specified E74.19
  functional polymorphonuclear neutrophils
    D71
  gallbladder, biliary tract and pancreas in
    diseases classified elsewhere K87
  gambling F63.0
▶ gamma aminobutyric acid (GABA)
    metabolism E72.81
⇒ gamma-glutamyl cycle E72.89
  gastric (functional) K31.9
    motility K30
    psychogenic F45.8
    secretion K30
  gastrointestinal (functional) NOS K92.9
    newborn P78.9
    psychogenic F45.8
  gender-identity or -role F64.9
    childhood F64.2
    effect on relationship F66
    of adolescence or adulthood F64.0
      nontranssexual F64.8
    specified NEC F64.8
    uncertainty F66
  genito-pelvic pain penetration F52.6
  genitourinary system
    female N94.9
    male N50.9
    psychogenic F45.8
  globe H44.9
    degenerated condition H44.50
      absolute glaucoma H44.51-●
      atrophy H44.52-●
      leucocoria H44.53-●
    degenerative H44.30
      chalcosis H44.31-●
      myopia —*see also* Myopia, degenerative
        H44.2-●
      siderosis H44.32-●
      specified type NEC H44.39-●
    endophthalmitis —*see* Endophthalmitis
    foreign body, retained —*see* Foreign body,
      intraocular, old, retained
    hemophthalmos —*see* Hemophthalmos
    hypotony H44.40
      due to
        ocular fistula H44.42-●
        specified disorder NEC H44.43-●
      flat anterior chamber H44.41-●
      primary H44.44-●
    luxation —*see* Luxation, globe
    specified type NEC H44.89

Disorder *(Continued)*
  glomerular (in) N05.9
    amyloidosis E85.4 *[N08]*
    cryoglobulinemia D89.1 *[N08]*
    disseminated intravascular coagulation
      D65 *[N08]*
    Fabry's disease E75.21 *[N08]*
    familial lecithin cholesterol acyltransferase
      deficiency E78.6 *[N08]*
    Goodpasture's syndrome M31.0
    hemolytic-uremic syndrome D59.3
    Henoch (-Schönlein) purpura D69.0 *[N08]*
    malariae malaria B52.0
    microscopic polyangiitis M31.7 *[N08]*
    multiple myeloma C90.0-● *[N08]*
    mumps B26.83
    schistosomiasis B65.9 *[N08]*
    sepsis NEC A41.-● *[N08]*
      streptococcal A40.-● *[N08]*
    sickle-cell disorders D57.-● *[N08]*
    strongyloidiasis B78.9 *[N08]*
    subacute bacterial endocarditis I33.0 *[N08]*
    syphilis A52.75
    systemic lupus erythematosus M32.14
    thrombotic thrombocytopenic purpura
      M31.1 *[N08]*
    Waldenström macroglobulinemia C88.0
      [N08]
    Wegener's granulomatosis M31.31
  gluconeogenesis E74.4
  glucosaminoglycan metabolism —
    see Disorder, metabolism,
    glucosaminoglycan
  glycine metabolism E72.50
    d-glycericacidemia E72.59
    hyperhydroxyprolinemia E72.59
▶   hyperoxaluria R82.992
    ▶ primary E72.53
    hyperprolinemia E72.59
    non-ketotic hyperglycinemia E72.51
    oxalosis E72.53
    oxaluria E72.53
    sarcosinemia E72.59
    trimethylaminuria E72.52
  glycoprotein metabolism E77.9
    specified NEC E77.8
  habit (and impulse) F63.9
    involving sexual behavior NEC F65.9
    specified NEC F63.89
  hallucinogen use
    mild F16.10
      with
        hallucinogen-induced
          anxiety disorder F16.180
          bipolar and related disorder F16.14
          depressive disorder F16.14
          psychotic disorder F16.159
        hallucinogen intoxication delirium
          F16.121
        other hallucinogen intoxication
          F16.129
      in remission (early) (sustained) F16.11
    moderate or severe F16.20
      with
        hallucinogen-induced
          anxiety disorder F16.280
          bipolar and related disorder
            F16.24
          depressive disorder F16.24
          psychotic disorder F16.259
        hallucinogen intoxication delirium
          F16.221
        other hallucinogen intoxication
          F16.229
      in remission (early) (sustained)
        F16.21
  heart action I49.9
  hematological D75.9
    newborn (transient) P61.9
    specified NEC P61.8
  hematopoietic organs D75.9

Disorder *(Continued)*
  hemorrhagic NEC D69.9
    drug-induced D68.32
    due to
      extrinsic circulating anticoagulants
        D68.32
      increase in
        anti-IIa D68.32
        anti-Xa D68.32
      intrinsic
        circulating anticoagulants D68.318
        increase in
          antithrombin D68.318
          anti-VIIIa D68.318
          anti-IXa D68.318
          anti-XIa D68.318
    following childbirth O72.3
  hemostasis —*see* Defect, coagulation
  histidine metabolism E70.40
    histidinemia E70.41
    other specified E70.49
  hoarding F42.3
  hyperkinetic —*see* Disorder, attention-deficit
    hyperactivity
  hyperleucine-isoleucinemia E71.19
  hypervalinemia E71.19
  hypoactive sexual desire F52.0
  hypochondriacal F45.20
    body dysmorphic F45.22
    neurosis F45.21
    other specified F45.29
  identity
    dissociative F44.81
    illness anxiety F45.21
    of childhood F93.8
  immune mechanism (immunity) D89.9
    specified type NEC D89.89
  impaired renal tubular function N25.9
    specified NEC N25.89
  impulse (control) F63.9
  inflammatory
    pelvic, in diseases classified elsewhere —
      see category N74
    penis N48.29
      abscess N48.21
      cellulitis N48.22
  inhalant use
    mild F18.10
      with
        inhalant-induced
          anxiety disorder F18.180
          depressive disorder F18.14
          major neurocognitive disorder
            F18.17
          mild neurocognitive disorder
            F18.188
          psychotic disorder F18.159
        inhalant intoxication F18.129
        inhalant intoxication delirium F18.121
      in remission (early) (sustained) F18.11
    moderate or severe F18.20
      with
        inhalant-induced
          anxiety disorder F18.280
          depressive disorder F18.24
          major neurocognitive disorder
            F18.27
          mild neurocognitive disorder
            F18.288
          psychotic disorder F18.259
        inhalant intoxication F18.229
        inhalant intoxication delirium F18.221
      in remission (early) (sustained) F18.21
  integument, newborn P83.9
    specified NEC P83.88
  intermittent explosive F63.81
  internal secretion pancreas —*see* Increased,
    secretion, pancreas, endocrine
  intestine, intestinal
    carbohydrate absorption NEC E74.39
      postoperative K91.2

▶ New   ⇒ Revised   ~~deleted~~ Deleted   ● Use Additional Character(s)

Disorder *(Continued)*
  intestine, intestinal *(Continued)*
    functional NEC K59.9
      postoperative K91.89
    psychogenic F45.8
    vascular K55.9
      chronic K55.1
      specified NEC K55.8
  intraoperative (intraprocedural) —*see* Complications, intraoperative
  involuntary emotional expression (IEED) F48.2
  iris H21.9
    adhesions —*see* Adhesions, iris
    atrophy —*see* Atrophy, iris
    chamber angle recession —*see* Recession, chamber angle
    cyst —*see* Cyst, iris
    degeneration —*see* Degeneration, iris
    in diseases classified elsewhere H22
    iridodialysis —*see* Iridodialysis
    iridoschisis —*see* Iridoschisis
    miotic pupillary cyst —*see* Cyst, pupillary
    pupillary
      abnormality —*see* Abnormality, pupillary
      membrane —*see* Membrane, pupillary
    specified type NEC H21.89
    vascular NEC H21.1X-●
  iron metabolism E83.10
    specified NEC E83.19
  isovaleric acidemia E71.110
  jaw, developmental M27.0
    temporomandibular —*see also* Anomaly, dentofacial, temporomandibular joint M26.60-●
  joint M25.9
    derangement —*see* Derangement, joint
    effusion —*see* Effusion, joint
    fistula —*see* Fistula, joint
    hemarthrosis —*see* Hemarthrosis
    instability —*see* Instability, joint
    osteophyte —*see* Osteophyte
    pain —*see* Pain, joint
    psychogenic F45.8
    specified type NEC M25.80
      ankle M25.87-●
      elbow M25.82-●
      foot joint M25.87-●
      hand joint M25.84-●
      hip M25.85-●
      knee M25.86-●
      shoulder M25.81-●
      wrist M25.83-●
    stiffness —*see* Stiffness, joint
  ketone metabolism E71.32
  kidney N28.9
    functional (tubular) N25.9
    in
      schistosomiasis B65.9 [N29]
    tubular function N25.9
    specified NEC N25.89
  lacrimal system H04.9
    changes H04.69
      fistula —*see* Fistula, lacrimal
    gland H04.19
      atrophy —*see* Atrophy, lacrimal gland
      cyst —*see* Cyst, lacrimal, gland
      dacryops —*see* Dacryops
      dislocation —*see* Dislocation, lacrimal gland
      dry eye syndrome —*see* Syndrome, dry eye
      infection —*see* Dacryoadenitis
      granuloma —*see* Granuloma, lacrimal
      inflammation —*see* Inflammation, lacrimal
    obstruction —*see* Obstruction, lacrimal
    specified NEC H04.89
  lactation NEC O92.79
  language (developmental) F80.9
    expressive F80.1
    mixed receptive and expressive F80.2
    receptive F80.2

Disorder *(Continued)*
  late luteal phase dysphoric N94.89
  learning (specific) F81.9
    acalculia R48.8
    alexia R48.0
    mathematics F81.2
    reading F81.0
    specified
      with impairment in
        mathematics F81.2
        reading F81.0
        written expression F81.81
    specified NEC F81.89
    spelling F81.81
    written expression F81.81
  lens H27.9
    aphakia —*see* Aphakia
    cataract —*see* Cataract
    dislocation —*see* Dislocation, lens
    specified type NEC H27.8
  ligament M24.20
    ankle M24.27-●
    attachment, spine —*see* Enthesopathy, spinal
    elbow M24.22-●
    foot joint M24.27-●
    hand joint M24.24-●
    hip M24.25-●
    knee —*see* Derangement, knee, specified NEC
    shoulder M24.21-●
    vertebra M24.28
    wrist M24.23-●
  ligamentous attachments —*see also* Enthesopathy
    spine —*see* Enthesopathy, spinal
  lipid
    metabolism, congenital E78.9
    storage E75.6
      specified NEC E75.5
  lipoprotein
    deficiency (familial) E78.6
    metabolism E78.9
      specified NEC E78.89
  liver K76.9
    malarial B54 [K77]
  low back —*see also* Dorsopathy, specified NEC
  lumbosacral
    plexus G54.1
    root (nerve) NEC G54.4
  lung, interstitial, drug-induced J70.4
    acute J70.2
    chronic J70.3
  lymphoproliferative, post-transplant (PTLD) D47.Z1
  lysine and hydroxylysine metabolism E72.3
  major neurocognitive —*see* Dementia, in (due to)
  male
    erectile (organic) —*see also* Dysfunction, sexual, male, erectile N52.9
      nonorganic F52.21
    hypoactive sexual desire F52.0
    orgasmic F52.32
  manic F30.9
    organic F06.33
  mast cell activation —*see* Activation, mast cell
  mastoid —*see also* Disorder, ear, middle
    postprocedural —*see* Complications, ear, procedure
  meniscus —*see* Derangement, knee, meniscus
  menopausal N95.9
    specified NEC N95.8
  menstrual N92.6
    psychogenic F45.8
    specified NEC N92.5
  mental (or behavioral) (nonpsychotic) F99
    due to (secondary to)
      amphetamine
        due to drug abuse —*see* Abuse, drug, stimulant

Disorder *(Continued)*
  mental *(Continued)*
    due to (secondary to) *(Continued)*
      amphetamine *(Continued)*
        due to drug dependence —*see* Dependence, drug, stimulant
      brain disease, damage and dysfunction F09
      caffeine use
        due to drug abuse —*see* Abuse, drug, stimulant
        due to drug dependence —*see* Dependence, drug, stimulant
      cannabis use
        due to drug abuse —*see* Abuse, drug, cannabis
        due to drug dependence —*see* Dependence, drug, cannabis
      general medical condition F09
      sedative or hypnotic use
        due to drug abuse —*see* Abuse, drug, sedative
        due to drug dependence —*see* Dependence, drug, sedative
      tobacco (nicotine) use —*see* Dependence, drug, nicotine
    following organic brain damage F07.9
      frontal lobe syndrome F07.0
      personality change F07.0
      postconcussional syndrome F07.81
      specified NEC F07.89
    infancy, childhood or adolescence F98.9
    neurotic —*see* Neurosis
    organic or symptomatic F09
    presenile, psychotic F03
    problem NEC
    psychoneurotic —*see* Neurosis
    psychotic —*see* Psychosis
    puerperal F53.0
    senile, psychotic NEC F03
  metabolic, amino acid, transitory, newborn P74.8
  metabolism NOS E88.9
    amino-acid E72.9
      aromatic E70.9
        albinism —*see* Albinism
        histidine E70.40
          histidinemia E70.41
          other specified E70.49
        hyperphenylalaninemia E70.1
          classical phenylketonuria E70.0
        other specified E70.8
        tryptophan E70.5
        tyrosine E70.20
          hypertyrosinemia E70.21
          other specified E70.29
      branched chain E71.2
        3-methylglutaconic aciduria E71.111
        hyperleucine-isoleucinemia E71.19
        hypervalinemia E71.19
        isovaleric acidemia E71.110
        maple syrup urine disease E71.0
        methylmalonic acidemia E71.120
        organic aciduria NEC E71.118
        other specified E71.19
        proprionate NEC E71.128
        proprionic acidemia E71.121
      glycine E72.50
        d-glycericacidemia E72.59
        hyperhydroxyprolinemia E72.59
        hyperoxaluria R82.992
          primary E72.53
        hyperprolinemia E72.59
        non-ketotic hyperglycinemia E72.51
        other specified E72.59
        sarcosinemia E72.59
        trimethylaminuria E72.52
      hydroxylysine E72.3
      lysine E72.3
      ornithine E72.4

Disorder *(Continued)*
  metabolism *(Continued)*
    amino-acid *(Continued)*
      ▸ other specified E72.89
        ▸ beta-amino acid E72.89
        ▸ gamma-glutamyl cycle E72.89
      ▸ straight-chain E72.89
        sulfur-bearing E72.10
          homocystinuria E72.11
          methylenetetrahydrofolate reductase
            deficiency E72.12
          other specified E72.19
    bile acid and cholesterol metabolism E78.70
    bilirubin E80.7
      specified NEC E80.6
    calcium E83.50
      hypercalcemia E83.52
      hypocalcemia E83.51
      other specified E83.59
    carbohydrate E74.9
      specified NEC E74.8
    cholesterol and bile acid metabolism
      E78.70
    congenital E88.9
    copper E83.00
      specified type NEC E83.09
      Wilson's disease E83.01
    cystinuria E72.01
    fructose E74.10
    galactose E74.20
    glucosaminoglycan E76.9
      mucopolysaccharidosis —*see*
        Mucopolysaccharidosis
      specified NEC E76.8
    ▸ glutamine E72.89
    glycine E72.50
    glycogen storage (hepatorenal) E74.09
    glycoprotein E77.9
      specified NEC E77.8
    glycosaminoglycan E76.9
      specified NEC E76.8
    in labor and delivery O75.89
    iron E83.10
    isoleucine E71.19
    leucine E71.19
    lipoid E78.9
    lipoprotein E78.9
      specified NEC E78.89
    magnesium E83.40
      hypermagnesemia E83.41
      hypomagnesemia E83.42
      other specified E83.49
    mineral E83.9
      specified NEC E83.89
    mitochondrial E88.40
      MELAS syndrome E88.41
      MERRF syndrome (myoclonic epilepsy
        associated with ragged-red fibers)
        E88.42
      other specified E88.49
    ornithine E72.4
    phosphatases E83.30
    phosphorus E83.30
      acid phosphatase deficiency E83.39
      hypophosphatasia E83.39
      hypophosphatemia E83.39
        familial E83.31
      other specified E83.39
      pseudovitamin D deficiency E83.32
    plasma protein NEC E88.09
    porphyrin —*see* Porphyria
    postprocedural E89.89
      specified NEC E89.89
    purine E79.9
      specified NEC E79.8
    pyrimidine E79.9
      specified NEC E79.8
    pyruvate E74.4
    ▸ serine E72.89
    sodium E87.8
    specified NEC E88.89

Disorder *(Continued)*
  metabolism *(Continued)*
    ▸ threonine E72.89
    valine E71.19
    zinc E83.2
  methylmalonic acidemia E71.120
  micturition NEC —*see also* Difficulty,
    micturition R39.198
    feeling of incomplete emptying
      R39.14
    hesitancy R39.11
    poor stream R39.12
    psychogenic F45.8
    split stream R39.13
    straining R39.16
    urgency R39.15
  mild neurocognitive G31.84
  mitochondrial metabolism E88.40
  mitral (valve) —*see* Endocarditis, mitral
  mixed
    anxiety and depressive F41.8
    of scholastic skills (developmental)
      F81.89
    receptive expressive language F80.2
  mood F39
    bipolar —*see* Disorder, bipolar
    depressive —*see* Disorder, depressive
    due to (secondary to)
      alcohol F10.94
      amphetamine F15.94
        in
          abuse F15.14
          dependence F15.24
      anxiolytic F13.94
        in
          abuse F13.14
          dependence F13.24
      cocaine F14.94
        in
          abuse F14.14
          dependence F14.24
      general medical condition F06.30
      hallucinogen F16.94
        in
          abuse F16.14
          dependence F16.24
      hypnotic F13.94
        in
          abuse F13.14
          dependence F13.24
      inhalant F18.94
        in
          abuse F18.14
          dependence F18.24
      opioid F11.94
        in
          abuse F11.14
          dependence F11.24
      phencyclidine (PCP) F16.94
        in
          abuse F16.14
          dependence F16.24
      physiological condition F06.30
        with
          depressive features F06.31
          major depressive-like episode
            F06.32
          manic features F06.33
          mixed features F06.34
      psychoactive substance NEC F19.94
        in
          abuse F19.14
          dependence F19.24
      sedative F13.94
        in
          abuse F13.14
          dependence F13.24
      volatile solvents F18.94
        in
          abuse F18.14
          dependence F18.24

Disorder *(Continued)*
  mood *(Continued)*
    manic episode F30.9
      with psychotic symptoms F30.2
      without psychotic symptoms F30.10
        mild F30.11
        moderate F30.12
        severe F30.13
      in remission (full) F30.4
        partial F30.3
      specified type NEC F30.8
    organic F06.30
      right hemisphere F07.89
    persistent F34.9
      cyclothymia F34.0
      dysthymia F34.1
      specified type NEC F34.89
    recurrent F39
    right hemisphere organic F07.89
  movement G25.9
    drug-induced G25.70
      akathisia G25.71
      specified NEC G25.79
    hysterical F44.4
    in diseases classified elsewhere —*see*
      category G26
    periodic limb G47.61
      sleep related G47.61
    sleep related NEC G47.69
    specified NEC G25.89
    stereotyped F98.4
    treatment-induced G25.9
  multiple personality F44.81
  muscle M62.9
    attachment, spine —*see* Enthesopathy, spinal
    in trichinellosis —*see* Trichinellosis, with
      muscle disorder
    psychogenic F45.8
    specified type NEC M62.89
    tone, newborn P94.9
      specified NEC P94.8
  muscular
    attachments —*see also* Enthesopathy
      spine —*see* Enthesopathy, spinal
    urethra N36.44
  musculoskeletal system, soft tissue —*see*
    Disorder, soft tissue
    postprocedural M96.89
    psychogenic F45.8
  myoneural G70.9
    due to lead G70.1
    specified NEC G70.89
    toxic G70.1
  myotonic NEC G71.19
  nail, in diseases classified elsewhere L62
  neck region NEC —*see* Dorsopathy, specified
    NEC
  neonatal onset multisystemic inflammatory
    (NOMID) M04.2
  nerve G58.9
    abducent NEC —*see* Strabismus, paralytic,
      sixth nerve
    accessory G52.8
    acoustic —*see* subcategory H93.3
    auditory —*see* subcategory H93.3
    auriculotemporal G50.8
    axillary G54.0
    cerebral —*see* Disorder, nerve, cranial
    cranial G52.9
      eighth —*see* subcategory H93.3
      eleventh G52.8
      fifth G50.9
      first G52.0
      fourth NEC —*see* Strabismus, paralytic,
        fourth nerve
      multiple G52.7
      ninth G52.1
      second NEC —*see* Disorder, nerve, optic
      seventh NEC G51.8
      sixth NEC —*see* Strabismus, paralytic,
        sixth nerve

Disorder *(Continued)*
nerve *(Continued)*
cranial *(Continued)*
specified NEC G52.8
tenth G52.2
third NEC —*see* Strabismus, paralytic,
third nerve
twelfth G52.3
entrapment —*see* Neuropathy, entrapment
facial G51.9
specified NEC G51.8
femoral —*see* Lesion, nerve, femoral
glossopharyngeal NEC G52.1
hypoglossal G52.3
intercostal G58.0
lateral
cutaneous of thigh —*see*
Mononeuropathy, lower limb,
meralgia paresthetica
popliteal —*see* Lesion, nerve, popliteal
lower limb —*see* Mononeuropathy, lower
limb
medial popliteal —*see* Lesion, nerve,
popliteal, medial
median NEC —*see* Lesion, nerve, median
multiple G58.7
oculomotor NEC —*see* Strabismus,
paralytic, third nerve
olfactory G52.0
optic NEC H47.09-•
hemorrhage into sheath —*see*
Hemorrhage, optic nerve
ischemic H47.01-•
peroneal —*see* Lesion, nerve, popliteal
phrenic G58.8
plantar —*see* Lesion, nerve, plantar
pneumogastric G52.2
posterior tibial —*see* Syndrome, tarsal
tunnel
radial —*see* Lesion, nerve, radial
recurrent laryngeal G52.2
root G54.9
cervical G54.2
lumbosacral G54.1
specified NEC G54.8
thoracic G54.3
sciatic NEC —*see* Lesion, nerve, sciatic
specified NEC G58.8
lower limb —*see* Mononeuropathy,
lower limb, specified NEC
upper limb —*see* Mononeuropathy,
upper limb, specified NEC
sympathetic G90.9
tibial —*see* Lesion, nerve, popliteal, medial
trigeminal G50.9
specified NEC G50.8
trochlear NEC —*see* Strabismus, paralytic,
fourth nerve
ulnar —*see* Lesion, nerve, ulnar
upper limb —*see* Mononeuropathy, upper
limb
vagus G52.2
nervous system G98.8
autonomic (peripheral) G90.9
specified NEC G90.8
central G96.9
specified NEC G96.8
parasympathetic G90.9
specified NEC G98.8
sympathetic G90.9
vegetative G90.9
neurocognitive R41.9
major
with
aggressive behavior F01.51
combative behavior F01.51
violent behavior F01.51
due to vascular disease, with behavioral
disturbance F01.51
in (due to) (other diseases classified
elsewhere) —*see also* Dementia, in
(due to) F02.80

Disorder *(Continued)*
neurocognitive *(Continued)*
major *(Continued)*
in *(Continued)*
with
aggressive behavior F02.81
combative behavior F02.81
violent behavior F02.81
without behavioral disturbance F01.50
mild G31.84
neurodevelopmental F89
specified NEC F88
neurohypophysis NEC E23.3
neurological NEC R29.818
neuromuscular G70.9
hereditary NEC G71.9
specified NEC G70.89
toxic G70.1
neurotic F48.9
specified NEC F48.8
neutrophil, polymorphonuclear D71
nicotine use —*see* Dependence, drug, nicotine
nightmare F51.5
non-rapid eye movement sleep arousal
sleep terror type F51.4
sleepwalking type F51.3
nose J34.9
specified NEC J34.89
obsessive-compulsive F42.9
and related disorder due to a known
physiological condition F06.8
odontogenesis NOS K00.9
opioid use
with
opioid-induced psychotic disorder F11.959
with
delusions F11.950
hallucinations F11.951
due to drug abuse —*see* Abuse, drug,
opioid
due to drug dependence —*see* Dependence,
drug, opioid
mild F11.10
with
opioid-induced
anxiety disorder F11.188
depressive disorder F11.14
sexual dysfunction F11.181
opioid intoxication
with perceptual disturbances F11.122
delirium F11.121
without perceptual disturbances
F11.129
in remission (early) (sustained) F11.11
moderate or severe F11.20
with
opioid-induced
anxiety disorder F11.288
anxiety disorder F11.988
depressive disorder F11.24
depressive disorder F11.94
sexual dysfunction F11.281
sexual dysfunction F11.981
opioid intoxication
with perceptual disturbances F11.222
delirium F11.221
without perceptual disturbances
F11.229
in remission (early) (sustained) F11.21
oppositional defiant F91.3
optic
chiasm H47.49
due to
inflammatory disorder H47.41
neoplasm H47.42
vascular disorder H47.43
disc H47.39-•
coloboma —*see* Coloboma, optic disc
drusen —*see* Drusen, optic disc
pseudopapilledema —*see*
Pseudopapilledema

Disorder *(Continued)*
optic *(Continued)*
radiations —*see* Disorder, visual, pathway
tracts —*see* Disorder, visual, pathway
orbit H05.9
cyst —*see* Cyst, orbit
deformity —*see* Deformity, orbit
edema —*see* Edema, orbit
enophthalmos —*see* Enophthalmos
exophthalmos —*see* Exophthalmos
hemorrhage —*see* Hemorrhage, orbit
inflammation —*see* Inflammation, orbit
myopathy —*see* Myopathy, extraocular
muscles
retained foreign body —*see* Foreign body,
orbit, old
specified type NEC H05.89
organic
anxiety F06.4
catatonic F06.1
delusional F06.2
dissociative F06.8
emotionally labile (asthenic) F06.8
mood (affective) F06.30
schizophrenia-like F06.2
orgasmic (female) F52.31
male F52.32
ornithine metabolism E72.4
overanxious F41.1
of childhood F93.8
pain
with related psychological factors F45.42
exclusively related to psychological factors
F45.41
genito-pelvic penetration disorder F52.6
pancreatic internal secretion E16.9
specified NEC E16.8
panic F41.0
with agoraphobia F40.01
papulosquamous L44.9
in diseases classified elsewhere L45
specified NEC L44.8
paranoid F22
induced F24
shared F24
paraphilic F65.9
specified NEC F65.89
parathyroid (gland) E21.5
specified NEC E21.4
parietoalveolar NEC J84.09
paroxysmal, mixed R56.9
patella M22.9-•
chondromalacia —*see* Chondromalacia,
patella
derangement NEC M22.3X-•
recurrent
dislocation —*see* Dislocation, patella,
recurrent
subluxation —*see* Dislocation, patella,
recurrent, incomplete
specified NEC M22.8X-•
patellofemoral M22.2X-•
pedophilic F65.4
pentose phosphate pathway with anemia
D55.1
perception, due to hallucinogens F16.983
in
abuse F16.183
dependence F16.283
peripheral nervous system NEC G64
peroxisomal E71.50
biogenesis
neonatal adrenoleukodystrophy E71.511
specified disorder NEC E71.518
Zellweger syndrome E71.510
rhizomelic chondrodysplasia punctata
E71.540
specified form NEC E71.548
group 1 E71.518
group 2 E71.53
group 3 E71.542

▶ New   ⟹ Revised   ~~deleted~~ Deleted   • Use Additional Character(s)

Disorder (Continued)
  retina (Continued)
    neovascularization —see
      Neovascularization, retina
    retinopathy —see Retinopathy
    separation of layers H35.70
      central serous chorioretinopathy H35.71-●
      pigment epithelium detachment (serous)
        H35.72-●
        hemorrhagic H35.73-●
    specified type NEC H35.89
    telangiectasis —see Telangiectasis, retina
    vasculitis —see Vasculitis, retina
  retroperitoneal K68.9
  right hemisphere organic affective F07.89
  rumination (infant or child) F98.21
  sacrum, sacrococcygeal NEC M53.3
  schizoaffective F25.9
    bipolar type F25.0
    depressive type F25.1
    manic type F25.0
    mixed type F25.0
    specified NEC F25.8
  schizoid of childhood F84.5
  schizophrenia spectrum and other psychotic
    disorder F29
    specified NEC F28
  schizophreniform F20.81
    brief F23
  schizotypal (personality) F21
  secretion, thyrocalcitonin E07.0
  sedative, hypnotic, or anxiolytic use
    mild F13.10
      with
        sedative, hypnotic, or
          anxiolytic-induced
        anxiety disorder F13.180
        bipolar and related disorder F13.14
        depressive disorder F13.14
        psychotic disorder F13.159
        sexual dysfunction F13.181
        sedative, hypnotic, or anxiolytic
          intoxication F13.129
        sedative, hypnotic, or anxiolytic
          intoxication delirium F13.121
      in remission (early) (sustained) F13.11
    moderate or severe F13.20
      with
        sedative, hypnotic, or
          anxiolytic-induced
        anxiety disorder F13.280
        bipolar and related disorder F13.24
        depressive disorder F13.24
        major neurocognitive disorder F13.27
        mild neurocognitive disorder F13.288
        psychotic disorder F13.259
        sexual dysfunction F13.281
        sedative, hypnotic, or anxiolytic
          intoxication F13.229
         sedative, hypnotic, or anxiolytic
          intoxication delirium F13.221
      in remission (early) (sustained) F13.21
  seizure —see also Epilepsy G40.909
    intractable G40.919
      with status epilepticus G40.911
  semantic pragmatic F80.89
    with autism F84.0
  sense of smell R43.1
    psychogenic F45.8
  separation anxiety, of childhood F93.0
  sexual
    arousal, female F52.22
    aversion F52.1
    function, psychogenic F52.9
    interest/arousal, female F52.22
    masochism F65.51
    maturation F66
    nonorganic F52.9
    preference —see also Deviation, sexual F65.9
      fetishistic transvestism F65.1
    relationship F66
    sadism F65.52

Disorder (Continued)
  shyness, of childhood and adolescence F40.10
  sibling rivalry F93.8
  sickle-cell (sickling) (homozygous) —see
    Disease, sickle-cell
    heterozygous D57.3
    specified type NEC D57.8-●
    trait D57.3
  sinus (nasal) J34.9
    specified NEC J34.89
  skin L98.9
    atrophic L90.9
      specified NEC L90.8
    granulomatous L92.9
      specified NEC L92.8
    hypertrophic L91.9
      specified NEC L91.8
    infiltrative NEC L98.6
    newborn P83.9
      specified NEC P83.88
    picking F42.4
    psychogenic (allergic) (eczematous) F54
  sleep G47.9
    breathing-related —see Apnea, sleep
    circadian rhythm G47.20
      advance sleep phase type G47.22
      delayed sleep phase type G47.21
      due to
        alcohol
          abuse F10.182
          dependence F10.282
          use F10.982
        amphetamines
          abuse F15.182
          dependence F15.282
          use F15.982
        caffeine
          abuse F15.182
          dependence F15.282
          use F15.982
        cocaine
          abuse F14.182
          dependence F14.282
          use F14.982
        drug NEC
          abuse F19.182
          dependence F19.282
          use F19.982
        opioid
          abuse F11.182
          dependence F11.282
          use F11.982
        psychoactive substance NEC
          abuse F19.182
          dependence F19.282
          use F19.982
        sedative, hypnotic, or anxiolytic
          abuse F13.182
          dependence F13.282
          use F13.982
        stimulant NEC
          abuse F15.182
          dependence F15.282
          use F15.982
      free running type G47.24
      in conditions classified elsewhere
        G47.27
      irregular sleep wake type G47.23
      jet lag type G47.25
      non-24-hour sleep-wake type G47.24
      shift work type G47.26
      specified NEC G47.29
    due to
      alcohol
        abuse F10.182
        dependence F10.282
        use F10.982
      amphetamine
        abuse F15.182
        dependence F15.282
        use F15.982

Disorder (Continued)
  sleep (Continued)
    due to (Continued)
      anxiolytic
        abuse F13.182
        dependence F13.282
        use F13.982
      caffeine
        abuse F15.182
        dependence F15.282
        use F15.982
      cocaine
        abuse F14.182
        dependence F14.282
        use F14.982
      drug NEC
        abuse F19.182
        dependence F19.282
        use F19.982
      hypnotic
        abuse F13.182
        dependence F13.282
        use F13.982
      opioid
        abuse F11.182
        dependence F11.282
        use F11.982
      psychoactive substance NEC
        abuse F19.182
        dependence F19.282
        use F19.982
      sedative
        abuse F13.182
        dependence F13.282
        use F13.982
      stimulant NEC
        abuse F15.182
        dependence F15.282
        use F15.982
    emotional F51.9
    excessive somnolence —see Hypersomnia
    hypersomnia type —see Hypersomnia
    initiating or maintaining —see Insomnia
    nightmares F51.5
    nonorganic F51.9
      specified NEC F51.8
    parasomnia type G47.50
    specified NEC G47.8
    terrors F51.4
    walking F51.3
  sleep-wake pattern or schedule —see also
    Disorder, sleep, circadian rhythm
    G47.9
    specified NEC G47.8
  social
    anxiety (of childhood) F40.10
      generalized F40.11
    functioning in childhood F94.9
      specified NEC F94.8
    pragmatic F80.82
  soft tissue M79.9
    ankle M79.9
    due to use, overuse and pressure M70.90
      ankle M70.97-●
      bursitis —see Bursitis
      foot M70.97-●
      forearm M70.93-●
      hand M70.94-●
      lower leg M70.96-●
      multiple sites M70.99
      pelvic region M70.95-●
      shoulder region M70.91-●
      specified site NEC M70.98
      specified type NEC M70.80
        ankle M70.87-●
        foot M70.87-●
        forearm M70.83-●
        hand M70.84-●
        lower leg M70.86-●
        multiple sites M70.89
        pelvic region M70.85-●

Disorder *(Continued)*
  soft tissue *(Continued)*
    due to use, overuse and pressure
        (Continued)
      specified type NEC *(Continued)*
        shoulder region M70.81-•
        specified site NEC M70.88
        thigh M70.85-•
        upper arm M70.82-•
      thigh M70.95-•
      upper arm M70.92-•
    foot M79.9
    forearm M79.9
    hand M79.9
    lower leg M79.9
    multiple sites M79.9
    occupational —see Disorder, soft tissue,
        due to use, overuse and pressure
    pelvic region M79.9
    shoulder region M79.9
    specified type NEC M79.89
    thigh M79.9
    upper arm M79.9
  somatic symptom F45.1
  somatization F45.0
  somatoform F45.9
    pain (persistent) F45.41
    somatization (multiple) (long-lasting) F45.0
    specified NEC F45.8
    undifferentiated F45.1
  somnolence, excessive —see Hypersomnia
  specific
    arithmetical F81.2
    developmental, of motor F82
    reading F81.0
    speech and language F80.9
    spelling F81.81
    written expression F81.81
  speech R47.9
    articulation (functional) (specific) F80.0
    developmental F80.9
    specified NEC R47.89
  speech-sound F80.0
  spelling (specific) F81.81
  spine —see also Dorsopathy
    ligamentous or muscular attachments,
        peripheral —see Enthesopathy, spinal
    specified NEC —see Dorsopathy, specified
        NEC
  stereotyped, habit or movement F98.4
  stimulant use (other) (unspecified)
    mild F15.10
      in remission (early) (sustained) F15.11
    moderate or severe F15.20
      in remission (early) (sustained) F15.21
  stomach (functional) —see Disorder, gastric
  stress F43.9
    acute F43.0
    post-traumatic F43.10
      acute F43.11
      chronic F43.12
  substance use (other) (unknown)
    mild F19.10
      with substance-induced
        anxiety disorder F19.180
        bipolar and related disorder F19.14
        depressive disorder F19.14
        major neurocognitive disorder F19.17
        mild neurocognitive disorder F19.188
        obsessive-compulsive and related
            disorder F19.188
        sexual dysfunction F19.181
      substance intoxication F19.129
      substance intoxication delirium F19.121
    moderate or severe F19.20
      with substance-induced
        anxiety disorder F19.280
        bipolar and related disorder F19.24
        depressive disorder F19.24
        major neurocognitive disorder F19.27
        mild neurocognitive disorder F19.288

Disorder *(Continued)*
  substance use (other) (unknown) *(Continued)*
    moderate or severe *(Continued)*
      with substance-induced anxiety
          disorder*(Continued)*
        obsessive-compulsive and related
            disorder F19.288
        sexual dysfunction F19.281
      in remission (early) (sustained) F19.21
      substance intoxication F19.229
      substance intoxication delirium F19.221
  sulfur-bearing amino-acid metabolism E72.10
  sweat gland (eccrine) L74.9
    apocrine L75.9
      specified NEC L75.8
    specified NEC L74.8
  synovium M67.90
    acromioclavicular M67.91-•
    ankle M67.97-•
    elbow M67.92-•
    foot M67.97-•
    forearm M67.93-•
    hand M67.94-•
    hip M67.95-•
    knee M67.96-•
    multiple sites M67.99
    rupture —see Rupture, synovium
    shoulder M67.91-•
    specified type NEC M67.80
      acromioclavicular M67.81-•
      ankle M67.87-•
      elbow M67.82-•
      foot M67.87-•
      hand M67.84-•
      hip M67.85-•
      knee M67.86-•
      multiple sites M67.89
      wrist M67.83-•
    synovitis —see Synovitis
    upper arm M67.92-•
    wrist M67.93-•
  temperature regulation, newborn P81.9
    specified NEC P81.8
  temporomandibular joint M26.60-•
  tendon M67.90
    acromioclavicular M67.91-•
    ankle M67.97-•
    contracture —see Contracture, tendon
    elbow M67.92-•
    foot M67.97-•
    forearm M67.93-•
    hand M67.94-•
    hip M67.95-•
    knee M67.96-•
    multiple sites M67.99
    rupture —see Rupture, tendon
    shoulder M67.91-•
    specified type NEC M67.80
      acromioclavicular M67.81-•
      ankle M67.87-•
      elbow M67.82-•
      foot M67.87-•
      hand M67.84-•
      hip M67.85-•
      knee M67.86-•
      multiple sites M67.89
      trunk M67.88
      wrist M67.83-•
    synovitis —see Synovitis
    tendinitis —see Tendinitis
    tenosynovitis —see Tenosynovitis
    trunk M67.98
    upper arm M67.92-•
    wrist M67.93-•
  thoracic root (nerve) NEC G54.3
  thyrocalcitonin hypersecretion E07.0
  thyroid (gland) E07.9
    function NEC, neonatal, transitory P72.2
    iodine-deficiency related E01.8
    specified NEC E07.89
  tic —see Tic

Disorder *(Continued)*
  tobacco use
    chewing tobacco (mild) (moderate) (severe)
      in remission (early) (sustained) F17.221
    cigarettes (mild) (moderate) (severe)
      in remission (early) (sustained) F17.211
    mild Z72.0
      in remission (early) (sustained) F17.201
    moderate F17.200
      in remission (early) (sustained) F17.201
    severe F17.200
      in remission (early) (sustained) F17.201
    specified product NEC (mild) (moderate)
        (severe)
      in remission (early) (sustained) F17.291
  tooth K08.9
    development K00.9
      specified NEC K00.8
    eruption K00.6
  Tourette's F95.2
  trance and possession F44.89
  transvestic F65.1
  trauma and stressor-related F43.9
    other specified F43.8
  tricuspid (valve) —see Endocarditis, tricuspid
  tryptophan metabolism E70.5
  tubular, phosphate-losing N25.0
  tubulo-interstitial (in)
    brucellosis A23.9 *[N16]*
    cystinosis E72.04
    diphtheria A36.84
    glycogen storage disease E74.00 *[N16]*
    leukemia NEC C95.9-• *[N16]*
    lymphoma NEC C85.9-• *[N16]*
    mixed cryoglobulinemia D89.1 *[N16]*
    multiple myeloma C90.0-• *[N16]*
    Salmonella infection A02.25
    sarcoidosis D86.84
    sepsis A41.9 *[N16]*
      streptococcal A40.9 *[N16]*
    systemic lupus erythematosus M32.15
    toxoplasmosis B58.83
    transplant rejection T86.91 *[N16]*
    Wilson's disease E83.01 *[N16]*
  tubulo-renal function, impaired N25.9
    specified NEC N25.89
  tympanic membrane H73.9-•
    atrophy —see Atrophy, tympanic membrane
    infection —see Myringitis
    perforation —see Perforation, tympanum
    specified NEC H73.89-•
  unsocialized aggressive F91.1
  urea cycle metabolism E72.20
    argininemia E72.21
    arginosuccinic aciduria E72.22
    citrullinemia E72.23
    ornithine transcarbamylase deficiency E72.4
    other specified E72.29
  ureter (in) N28.9
    schistosomiasis B65.0 *[N29]*
    tuberculosis A18.11
  urethra N36.9
    specified NEC N36.8
  urinary system N39.9
    specified NEC N39.8
  valve, heart
    aortic —see Endocarditis, aortic
    mitral —see Endocarditis, mitral
    pulmonary —see Endocarditis, pulmonary
    rheumatic
      aortic —see Endocarditis, aortic,
          rheumatic
      mitral —see Endocarditis, mitral
      pulmonary —see Endocarditis,
          pulmonary, rheumatic
      tricuspid —see Endocarditis, tricuspid
    tricuspid —see Endocarditis, tricuspid
  vestibular function H81.9-•
    specified NEC —see subcategory H81.8
      in diseases classified elsewhere H82.-•
  vertigo —see Vertigo

▶ New   ⇒ Revised   ~~deleted~~ Deleted   • Use Additional Character(s)

Disorder (Continued)
vision, binocular H53.30
abnormal retinal correspondence H53.31
diplopia H53.2
fusion with defective stereopsis H53.32
simultaneous perception H53.33
suppression H53.34
visual
cortex
blindness H47.619
left brain H47.612
right brain H47.611
due to
inflammatory disorder H47.629
left brain H47.622
right brain H47.621
neoplasm H47.639
left brain H47.632
right brain H47.631
vascular disorder H47.649
left brain H47.642
right brain H47.641
pathway H47.9
due to
inflammatory disorder H47.51-•
neoplasm H47.52-•
vascular disorder H47.53-•
optic chiasm —see Disorder, optic, chiasm
vitreous body H43.9
crystalline deposits —see Deposit,
crystalline
degeneration —see Degeneration, vitreous
hemorrhage —see Hemorrhage, vitreous
opacities —see Opacity, vitreous
prolapse —see Prolapse, vitreous
specified type NEC H43.89
voice R49.9
specified type NEC R49.8
volatile solvent use
due to drug abuse —see Abuse, drug,
inhalant
due to drug dependence —see Dependence,
drug, inhalant
voyeuristic F65.3
white blood cells D72.9
specified NEC D72.89
withdrawing, child or adolescent
F40.10
Disorientation R41.0
Displacement, displaced
acquired traumatic of bone, cartilage, joint,
tendon NEC —see Dislocation
adrenal gland (congenital) Q89.1
appendix, retrocecal (congenital) Q43.8
auricle (congenital) Q17.4
bladder (acquired) N32.89
congenital Q64.19
brachial plexus (congenital) Q07.8
brain stem, caudal (congenital) Q04.8
canaliculus (lacrimalis), congenital Q10.6
cardia through esophageal hiatus (congenital)
Q40.1
cerebellum, caudal (congenital) Q04.8
cervix —see Malposition, uterus
colon (congenital) Q43.3
device, implant or graft —see also
Complications, by site and type,
mechanical T85.628
arterial graft NEC —see Complication,
cardiovascular device, mechanical,
vascular
breast (implant) T85.42
catheter NEC T85.628
dialysis (renal) T82.42
intraperitoneal T85.621
infusion NEC T82.524
spinal (epidural) (subdural) T85.620
urinary
cystostomy T83.020
Hopkins T83.028
ileostomy T83.028

Displacement, displaced (Continued)
device, implant or graft (Continued)
catheter NEC (Continued)
urinary (Continued)
indwelling T83.021
nephrostomy T83.022
specified NEC T83.028
urostomy T83.028
electronic (electrode) (pulse generator)
(stimulator) —see Complication,
electronic stimulator
fixation, internal (orthopedic) NEC —
see Complication, fixation device,
mechanical
gastrointestinal —see Complications,
prosthetic device, mechanical,
gastrointestinal device
genital NEC T83.428
intrauterine contraceptive device (string)
T83.32
penile prosthesis (cylinder) (implanted)
(pump) (resevoir) T83.420
testicular prosthesis T83.421
heart NEC —see Complication,
cardiovascular device, mechanical
joint prosthesis —see Complications, joint
prosthesis, mechanical
ocular —see Complications, prosthetic
device, mechanical, ocular device
orthopedic NEC —see Complication,
orthopedic, device or graft,
mechanical
specified NEC T85.628
urinary NEC T83.128
graft T83.22
sphincter, implanted T83.121
stent (ileal conduit) (nephroureteral)
T83.123
ureteral indwelling T83.122
vascular NEC —see Complication,
cardiovascular device, mechanical
ventricular intracranial shunt T85.02
electronic stimulator
bone T84.320
cardiac —see Complications, cardiac
device, electronic
nervous system —see Complication,
prosthetic device, mechanical,
electronic nervous system
stimulator
urinary —see Complications, electronic
stimulator, urinary
esophageal mucosa into cardia of stomach,
congenital Q39.8
esophagus (acquired) K22.8
congenital Q39.8
eyeball (acquired) (lateral) (old) —see
Displacement, globe
congenital Q15.8
current —see Avulsion, eye
fallopian tube (acquired) N83.4-•
congenital Q50.6
opening (congenital) Q50.6
gallbladder (congenital) Q44.1
gastric mucosa (congenital) Q40.2
globe (acquired) (old) (lateral) H05.21-•
current —see Avulsion, eye
heart (congenital) Q24.8
acquired I51.89
hymen (upward) (congenital) Q52.4
intervertebral disc NEC
with myelopathy —see Disorder, disc, with,
myelopathy
cervical, cervicothoracic (with)
M50.20
myelopathy —see Disorder, disc,
cervical, with myelopathy
neuritis, radiculitis or radiculopathy —
see Disorder, disc, cervical, with
neuritis
due to trauma —see Dislocation, vertebra

Displacement, displaced (Continued)
intervertebral disc NEC (Continued)
lumbar region M51.26
with
neuritis, radiculitis, radiculopathy or
sciatica M51.16
lumbosacral region M51.27
with
myelopathy M51.07
neuritis, radiculitis, radiculopathy or
sciatica M51.17
sacrococcygeal region M53.3
thoracic region M51.24
with
myelopathy M51.04
neuritis, radiculitis, radiculopathy
M51.14
thoracolumbar region M51.25
with
myelopathy M51.05
neuritis, radiculitis, radiculopathy
M51.15
intrauterine device (string) T83.32
kidney (acquired) N28.83
congenital Q63.2
lachrymal, lacrimal apparatus or duct
(congenital) Q10.6
lens, congenital Q12.1
macula (congenital) Q14.1
Meckel's diverticulum Q43.0
malignant —see Table of Neoplasms, small
intestine, malignant
nail (congenital) Q84.6
acquired L60.8
opening of Wharton's duct in mouth Q38.4
organ or site, congenital NEC —see
Malposition, congenital
ovary (acquired) N83.4-•
congenital Q50.39
free in peritoneal cavity (congenital)
Q50.39
into hernial sac N83.4-•
oviduct (acquired) N83.4-•
congenital Q50.6
parathyroid (gland) E21.4
parotid gland (congenital) Q38.4
punctum lacrimale (congenital) Q10.6
sacro-iliac (joint) (congenital) Q74.2
current injury S33.2
old —see subcategory M53.2
salivary gland (any) (congenital) Q38.4
spleen (congenital) Q89.09
stomach, congenital Q40.2
sublingual duct Q38.4
tongue (downward) (congenital) Q38.3
tooth, teeth, fully erupted M26.30
horizontal M26.33
vertical M26.34
trachea (congenital) Q32.1
ureter or ureteric opening or orifice
(congenital) Q62.62
uterine opening of oviducts or fallopian tubes
Q50.6
uterus, uterine —see Malposition, uterus
ventricular septum Q21.0
with rudimentary ventricle Q20.4
Disproportion
between native and reconstructed breast N65.1
fiber-type G71.2
Disruptio uteri —see Rupture, uterus
Disruption (of)
ciliary body NEC H21.89
closure of
cornea T81.31
craniotomy T81.32
fascia (muscular) (superficial) T81.32
internal organ or tissue T81.32
laceration (external) (internal) T81.33
ligament T81.32
mucosa T81.31
muscle or muscle flap T81.32

Disruption (Continued)
  closure of (Continued)
    ribs or rib cage T81.32
    skin and subcutaneous tissue (full-
        thickness) (superficial) T81.31
    skull T81.32
    sternum (sternotomy) T81.32
    tendon T81.32
    traumatic laceration (external) (internal)
        T81.33
  family Z63.8
    due to
      absence of family member due to
          military deployment Z63.31
      absence of family member NEC Z63.32
      alcoholism and drug addiction in family
          Z63.72
      bereavement Z63.4
      death (assumed) or disappearance of
          family member Z63.4
      divorce or separation Z63.5
      drug addiction in family Z63.72
      return of family member from military
          deployment (current or past
          conflict) Z63.71
      stressful life events NEC Z63.79
  iris NEC H21.89
  ligament(s) —see also Sprain
    knee
      current injury —see Dislocation, knee
      old (chronic) —see Derangement, knee,
          ligament, instability, chronic
      spontaneous NEC —see Derangement,
          knee, disruption ligament
  ossicular chain —see Discontinuity, ossicles,
      ear
  pelvic ring (stable) S32.810
    unstable S32.811
  traumatic injury wound repair T81.33
  wound T81.30
    episiotomy O90.1
    operation T81.31
      cesarean O90.0
      external operation wound (superficial)
          T81.31
      internal operation wound (deep) T81.32
    perineal (obstetric) O90.1
  traumatic injury repair T81.33
Dissatisfaction with
  employment Z56.9
  school environment Z55.4
Dissecting —see condition
Dissection
  aorta I71.00
    abdominal I71.02
    thoracic I71.01
    thoracoabdominal I71.03
  artery I77.70
    basilar (trunk) I77.75
    carotid I77.71
    cerebral (nonruptured) I67.0
      ruptured —see Hemorrhage, intracranial,
          subarachnoid
    coronary I25.42
    extremity
      lower I77.77
      upper I77.76
    iliac I77.72
    precerebral
      congenital (nonruptured) Q28.1
      specified site NEC I77.75
    renal I77.73
    specified NEC I77.79
    vertebral I77.74
  precerebral artery, congenital (nonruptured)
      Q28.1
    Heartland A93.8
  traumatic —see Wound, open, by site
  vascular I99.8
  wound —see Wound, open
Disseminated —see condition

Dissociation
  auriculoventricular or atrioventricular (AV)
      (any degree) (isorhythmic) I45.89
    with heart block I44.2
  interference I45.89
Dissociative reaction, state F44.9
Dissolution, vertebra —see Osteoporosis
Distension, distention
  abdomen R14.0
  bladder N32.89
  cecum K63.89
  colon K63.89
  gallbladder K82.8
  intestine K63.89
  kidney N28.89
  liver K76.89
  seminal vesicle N50.89
  stomach K31.89
    acute K31.0
    psychogenic F45.8
  ureter —see Dilatation, ureter
  uterus N85.8
Distoma hepaticum infestation B66.3
Distomiasis B66.9
  bile passages B66.3
  hemic B65.9
  hepatic B66.3
    due to Clonorchis sinensis B66.1
  intestinal B66.5
  liver B66.3
    due to Clonorchis sinensis B66.1
  lung B66.4
  pulmonary B66.4
Distomolar (fourth molar) K00.1
Disto-occlusion (Division I) (Division II)
    M26.212
Distortion(s) (congenital)
  adrenal (gland) Q89.1
  arm NEC Q68.8
  bile duct or passage Q44.5
  bladder Q64.79
  brain Q04.9
  cervix (uteri) Q51.9
  chest (wall) Q67.8
    bones Q76.8
  clavicle Q74.0
  clitoris Q52.6
  coccyx Q76.49
  common duct Q44.5
  coronary Q24.5
  cystic duct Q44.5
  ear (auricle) (external) Q17.3
    inner Q16.5
    middle Q16.4
      ossicles Q16.3
  endocrine NEC Q89.2
  eustachian tube Q17.8
  eye (adnexa) Q15.8
  face bone(s) NEC Q75.8
  fallopian tube Q50.6
  femur NEC Q68.8
  fibula NEC Q68.8
  finger(s) Q68.1
  foot Q66.9
  genitalia, genital organ(s)
    female Q52.8
      external Q52.79
      internal NEC Q52.8
  gyri Q04.8
  hand bone(s) Q68.1
  heart (auricle) (ventricle) Q24.8
    valve (cusp) Q24.8
  hepatic duct Q44.5
  humerus NEC Q68.8
  hymen Q52.4
  intrafamilial communications Z63.8
  jaw NEC M26.89
  labium (majus) (minus) Q52.79
  leg NEC Q68.8
  lens Q12.8
  liver Q44.7

Distortion (Continued)
  lumbar spine Q76.49
    with disproportion O33.8
      causing obstructed labor O65.0
  lumbosacral (joint) (region) Q76.49
    kyphosis —see Kyphosis, congenital
    lordosis —see Lordosis, congenital
  nerve Q07.8
  nose Q30.8
  organ
    of Corti Q16.5
    or site not listed —see Anomaly, by site
      ossicles, ear Q16.3
  oviduct Q50.6
  pancreas Q45.3
  parathyroid (gland) Q89.2
  pituitary (gland) Q89.2
  radius NEC Q68.8
  sacroiliac joint Q74.2
  sacrum Q76.49
  scapula Q74.0
  shoulder girdle Q74.0
  skull bone(s) NEC Q75.8
    with
      anencephalus Q00.0
      encephalocele —see Encephalocele
      hydrocephalus Q03.9
        with spina bifida —see Spina bifida,
          with hydrocephalus
      microcephaly Q02
  spinal cord Q06.8
  spine Q76.49
    kyphosis —see Kyphosis, congenital
    lordosis —see Lordosis, congenital
  spleen Q89.09
  sternum NEC Q76.7
  thorax (wall) Q67.8
    bony Q76.8
  thymus (gland) Q89.2
  thyroid (gland) Q89.2
  tibia NEC Q68.8
  toe(s) Q66.9
  tongue Q38.3
  trachea (cartilage) Q32.1
  ulna NEC Q68.8
  ureter Q62.8
  urethra Q64.79
    causing obstruction Q64.39
  uterus Q51.9
  vagina Q52.4
  vertebra Q76.49
    kyphosis —see Kyphosis, congenital
    lordosis —see Lordosis, congenital
  visual —see also Disturbance, vision
    shape and size H53.15
  vulva Q52.79
  wrist (bones) (joint) Q68.8
Distress
  abdomen —see Pain, abdominal
  acute respiratory R06.03
    syndrome (adult) (child) J80
  epigastric R10.13
  fetal P84
    complicating pregnancy —see Stress, fetal
  gastrointestinal (functional) K30
    psychogenic F45.8
  intestinal (functional) NOS K59.9
    psychogenic F45.8
  maternal, during labor and delivery O75.0
  relationship, with spouse or intimate partner
      Z63.0
  respiratory (adult) (child) R06.03
    newborn P22.9
      specified NEC P22.8
    orthopnea R06.01
    psychogenic F45.8
    shortness of breath R06.02
    specified type NEC R06.09
Distribution vessel, atypical Q27.9
  coronary artery Q24.5
  precerebral Q28.1

Districhiasis L68.8
Disturbance(s) —see also Disease
absorption K90.9
    calcium E58
    carbohydrate K90.49
    fat K90.49
        pancreatic K90.3
    protein K90.49
    starch K90.49
    vitamin —see Deficiency, vitamin
acid-base equilibrium E87.8
    mixed E87.4
activity and attention (with hyperkinesis) —
    see Disorder, attention-deficit
    hyperactivity
amino acid transport E72.00
assimilation, food K90.9
auditory nerve, except deafness —see
    subcategory H93.3
behavior —see Disorder, conduct
blood clotting (mechanism) —see also Defect,
    coagulation D68.9
cerebral
    nerve —see Disorder, nerve, cranial
    status, newborn P91.9
        specified NEC P91.88
circulatory I99.9
conduct —see also Disorder, conduct F91.9
    adjustment reaction —see Disorder,
        adjustment
    compulsive F63.9
    disruptive F91.9
    hyperkinetic —see Disorder, attention-
        deficit hyperactivity
    socialized F91.2
    specified NEC F91.8
    unsocialized F91.1
coordination R27.8
cranial nerve —see Disorder, nerve, cranial
deep sensibility —see Disturbance, sensation
digestive K30
    psychogenic F45.8
electrolyte —see also Imbalance, electrolyte
⇢newborn, transitory P74.49
    hyperammonemia P74.6
    ▶hyperchloremia P74.421
    ▶hyperchloremic metabolic acidosis
        P74.421
    ▶hypochloremia P74.422
    ⇢potassium balance
        ▶hyperkalemia P74.31
        ▶hypokalemia P74.32
    ⇢sodium balance
        ▶hypernatremia P74.21
        ▶hyponatremia P74.22
    ⇢specified type NEC P74.49
emotions specific to childhood and
    adolescence F93.9
    with
        anxiety and fearfulness NEC F93.8
        elective mutism F94.0
        oppositional disorder F91.3
        sensitivity (withdrawal) F40.10
        shyness F40.10
        social withdrawal F40.10
    involving relationship problems F93.8
    mixed F93.8
    specified NEC F93.8
endocrine (gland) E34.9
    neonatal, transitory P72.9
        specified NEC P72.8
equilibrium R42
fructose metabolism E74.10
gait —see Gait
    hysterical F44.4
    psychogenic F44.4
gastrointestinal (functional) K30
    psychogenic F45.8
habit, child F98.9
hearing, except deafness and tinnitus —see
    Abnormal, auditory perception

Disturbance (Continued)
heart, functional (conditions in I44-I50)
    due to presence of (cardiac) prosthesis
        I97.19-•
    postoperative I97.89
        cardiac surgery —see also Infarct,
            myocardium, associated with
            revascularization procedure I97.19-•
hormones E34.9
innervation uterus (parasympathetic)
    (sympathetic) N85.8
keratinization NEC
    gingiva K05.10
        nonplaque induced K05.11
        plaque induced K05.10
    lip K13.0
    oral (mucosa) (soft tissue) K13.29
    tongue K13.29
learning (specific) —see Disorder, learning
memory —see Amnesia
    mild, following organic brain damage F06.8
mental F99
    associated with diseases classified
        elsewhere F54
metabolism E88.9
    with
        abortion —see Abortion, by type with
            other specified complication
        ectopic pregnancy O08.5
        molar pregnancy O08.5
    amino-acid E72.9
        aromatic E70.9
        branched-chain E71.2
        ⇢straight-chain E72.89
        sulfur-bearing E72.10
    ammonia E72.20
    arginine E72.21
    arginosuccinic acid E72.22
    carbohydrate E74.9
    cholesterol E78.9
    citrulline E72.23
    cystathionine E72.19
    general E88.9
    ⇢glutamine E72.89
    histidine E70.40
    homocystine E72.19
    hydroxylysine E72.3
    in labor or delivery O75.89
    iron E83.10
    lipoid E78.9
    lysine E72.3
    methionine E72.19
    neonatal, transitory P74.9
        calcium and magnesium P71.9
            specified type NEC P71.8
        carbohydrate metabolism P70.9
            specified type NEC P70.8
        specified NEC P74.8
    ornithine E72.4
    phosphate E83.39
    sodium NEC E87.8
    ⇢threonine E72.89
    tryptophan E70.5
    tyrosine E70.20
    urea cycle E72.20
motor R29.2
nervous, functional R45.0
neuromuscular mechanism (eye), due to
    syphilis A52.15
nutritional E63.9
    nail L60.3
ocular motion H51.9
    psychogenic F45.8
oculogyric H51.8
    psychogenic F45.8
oculomotor H51.9
    psychogenic F45.8
olfactory nerve R43.1
optic nerve NEC —see Disorder, nerve, optic
oral epithelium, including tongue NEC
    K13.29

Disturbance (Continued)
perceptual due to
    alcohol withdrawal F10.232
    amphetamine intoxication F15.922
        in
            abuse F15.122
            dependence F15.222
    anxiolytic withdrawal F13.232
    cannabis intoxication (acute) F12.922
        in
            abuse F12.122
            dependence F12.222
    cocaine intoxication (acute) F14.922
        in
            abuse F14.122
            dependence F14.222
    hypnotic withdrawal F13.232
    opioid intoxication (acute) F11.922
        in
            abuse F11.122
            dependence F11.222
    phencyclidine intoxication (acute)
        F16.122
    sedative withdrawal F13.232
personality (pattern) (trait) —see also
    Disorder, personality F60.9
    following organic brain damage
        F07.9
polyglandular E31.9
    specified NEC E31.8
⇢potassium balance, newborn
    ▶hyperkalemia P74.31
    ▶hypokalemia P74.32
psychogenic F45.9
psychomotor F44.4
psychophysical visual H53.16
pupillary —see Anomaly, pupil, function
reflex R29.2
rhythm, heart I49.9
salivary secretion K11.7
sensation (cold) (heat) (localization) (tactile
    discrimination) (texture) (vibratory)
    NEC R20.9
    hysterical F44.6
    skin R20.9
        anesthesia R20.0
        hyperesthesia R20.3
        hypoesthesia R20.1
        paresthesia R20.2
        specified type NEC R20.8
    smell R43.9
        and taste (mixed) R43.8
        anosmia R43.0
        parosmia R43.1
        specified NEC R43.8
    taste R43.9
        and smell (mixed) R43.8
        parageusia R43.2
        specified NEC R43.8
sensory —see Disturbance, sensation
situational (transient) —see also Disorder,
    adjustment
    acute F43.0
sleep G47.9
    nonorganic origin F51.9
smell —see Disturbance, sensation, smell
sociopathic F60.2
⇢sodium balance, newborn
    ▶hypernatremia P74.21
    ▶hyponatremia P74.22
speech R47.9
    developmental F80.9
    specified NEC R47.89
stomach (functional) K31.9
sympathetic (nerve) G90.9
taste —see Disturbance, sensation, taste
temperature
    regulation, newborn P81.9
        specified NEC P81.8
    sense R20.8
        hysterical F44.6

Disturbance *(Continued)*
  tooth
    eruption K00.6
    formation K00.4
    structure, hereditary NEC K00.5
  touch —*see* Disturbance, sensation
  vascular I99.9
    arteriosclerotic —*see* Arteriosclerosis
  vasomotor I73.9
  vasospastic I73.9
  vision, visual H53.9
    following
      cerebral infarction I69.398
      cerebrovascular disease I69.998
        specified NEC I69.898
      intracerebral hemorrhage I69.198
      nontraumatic intracranial hemorrhage
        NEC I69.298
      specified disease NEC I69.898
      subarachnoid hemorrhage I69.098
    psychophysical H53.16
    specified NEC H53.8
    subjective H53.10
      day blindness H53.11
      discomfort H53.14-•
      distortions of shape and size H53.15
      loss
        sudden H53.13-•
        transient H53.12-•
      specified type NEC H53.19
  voice R49.9
    psychogenic F44.4
    specified NEC R49.8
Diuresis R35.8
Diver's palsy, paralysis or squeeze T70.3
Diverticulitis (acute) K57.92
  bladder —*see* Cystitis
  ileum —*see* Diverticulitis, intestine, small
  intestine K57.92
    with
      abscess, perforation or peritonitis
        K57.80
        with bleeding K57.81
      bleeding K57.93
    congenital Q43.8
    large K57.32
      with
        abscess, perforation or peritonitis
          K57.20
          with bleeding K57.21
        bleeding K57.33
        small intestine K57.52
          with
            abscess, perforation or peritonitis
              K57.40
              with bleeding K57.41
            bleeding K57.53
    small K57.12
      with
        abscess, perforation or peritonitis
          K57.00
          with bleeding K57.01
        bleeding K57.13
        large intestine K57.52
          with
            abscess, perforation or peritonitis
              K57.40
              with bleeding K57.41
            bleeding K57.53
Diverticulosis K57.90
  with bleeding K57.91
  large intestine K57.30
    with
      bleeding K57.31
      small intestine K57.50
        with bleeding K57.51
  small intestine K57.10
    with
      bleeding K57.11
      large intestine K57.50
        with bleeding K57.51

Diverticulum, diverticula (multiple) K57.90
  appendix (noninflammatory) K38.2
  bladder (sphincter) N32.3
    congenital Q64.6
  bronchus (congenital) Q32.4
    acquired J98.09
  calyx, calyceal (kidney) N28.89
  cardia (stomach) K31.4
  cecum —*see* Diverticulosis, intestine, large
    congenital Q43.8
  colon —*see* Diverticulosis, intestine, large
    congenital Q43.8
  duodenum —*see* Diverticulosis, intestine,
    small
    congenital Q43.8
  epiphrenic (esophagus) K22.5
  esophagus (congenital) Q39.6
    acquired (epiphrenic) (pulsion) (traction)
      K22.5
  eustachian tube —*see* Disorder, eustachian
    tube, specified NEC
  fallopian tube N83.8
  gastric K31.4
  heart (congenital) Q24.8
  ileum —*see* Diverticulosis, intestine, small
  jejunum —*see* Diverticulosis, intestine, small
  kidney (pelvis) (calyces) N28.89
    with calculus —*see* Calculus, kidney
  Meckel's (displaced) (hypertrophic) Q43.0
    malignant —*see* Table of Neoplasms, small
      intestine, malignant
  midthoracic K22.5
  organ or site, congenital NEC —*see* Distortion
  pericardium (congenital) (cyst) Q24.8
    acquired I31.8
  pharyngoesophageal (congenital) Q39.6
    acquired K22.5
  pharynx (congenital) Q38.7
  rectosigmoid —*see* Diverticulosis, intestine,
    large
    congenital Q43.8
  rectum —*see* Diverticulosis, intestine, large
  Rokitansky's K22.5
  seminal vesicle N50.89
  sigmoid —*see* Diverticulosis, intestine, large
    congenital Q43.8
  stomach (acquired) K31.4
    congenital Q40.2
  trachea (acquired) J39.8
  ureter (acquired) N28.89
    congenital Q62.8
  ureterovesical orifice N28.89
  urethra (acquired) N36.1
    congenital Q64.79
  ventricle, left (congenital) Q24.8
  vesical N32.3
    congenital Q64.6
  Zenker's (esophagus) K22.5
Division
  cervix uteri (acquired) N88.8
  glans penis Q55.69
  labia minora (congenital) Q52.79
  ligament (partial or complete) (current) —*see*
    also Sprain
    with open wound —*see* Wound, open
  muscle (partial or complete) (current) —*see*
    also Injury, muscle
    with open wound —*see* Wound, open
  nerve (traumatic) —*see* Injury, nerve
  spinal cord —*see* Injury, spinal cord,
    by region
  vein I87.8
Divorce, causing family disruption Z63.5
Dix-Hallpike neurolabyrinthitis —*see*
  Neuronitis, vestibular
Dizziness R42
  hysterical F44.89
  psychogenic F45.8
DMAC (disseminated mycobacterium avium-
  intracellulare complex) A31.2
DNR (do not resuscitate) Z66

Doan-Wiseman syndrome (primary splenic
  neutropenia) —*see* Agranulocytosis
Doehle-Heller aortitis A52.02
Dog bite —*see* Bite
Dohle body panmyelopathic syndrome D72.0
Dolichocephaly Q67.2
Dolichocolon Q43.8
Dolichostenomelia —*see* Syndrome, Marfan's
Donohue's syndrome E34.8
Donor (organ or tissue) Z52.9
  blood (whole) Z52.000
    autologous Z52.010
    specified component (lymphocytes)
      (platelets) NEC Z52.008
      autologous Z52.018
      specified donor NEC Z52.098
    specified donor NEC Z52.090
    stem cells Z52.001
      autologous Z52.011
      specified donor NEC Z52.091
  bone Z52.20
    autologous Z52.21
    marrow Z52.3
    specified type NEC Z52.29
  cornea Z52.5
  egg (Oocyte) Z52.819
    age 35 and over Z52.812
      anonymous recipient Z52.812
      designated recipient Z52.813
    under age 35 Z52.810
      anonymous recipient Z52.810
      designated recipient Z52.811
  kidney Z52.4
  liver Z52.6
  lung Z52.89
  lymphocyte —*see* Donor, blood, specified
    components NEC
  Oocyte —*see* Donor, egg
  platelets Z52.008
  potential, examination of Z00.5
  semen Z52.89
  skin Z52.10
    autologous Z52.11
    specified type NEC Z52.19
  specified organ or tissue NEC Z52.89
  sperm Z52.89
Donovanosis A58
Dorsalgia M54.9
  psychogenic F45.41
  specified NEC M54.89
Dorsopathy M53.9
  deforming M43.9
    specified NEC —*see* subcategory M43.8
  specified NEC M53.80
    cervical region M53.82
    cervicothoracic region M53.83
    lumbar region M53.86
    lumbosacral region M53.87
    occipito-atlanto-axial region M53.81
    sacrococcygeal region M53.88
    thoracic region M53.84
    thoracolumbar region M53.85
Double
  albumin E88.09
  aortic arch Q25.45
  auditory canal Q17.8
  auricle (heart) Q20.8
  bladder Q64.79
  cervix Q51.820
    with doubling of uterus (and vagina)
      Q51.10
      with obstruction Q51.11
  inlet ventricle Q20.4
  kidney with double pelvis (renal) Q63.0
  meatus urinarius Q64.75
  monster Q89.4
  outlet
    left ventricle Q20.2
    right ventricle Q20.1
  pelvis (renal) with double ureter Q62.5
  tongue Q38.3

▶ New   ⇒ Revised   ~~deleted~~ Deleted   • Use Additional Character(s)

Double *(Continued)*
  ureter (one or both sides) Q62.5
    with double pelvis (renal) Q62.5
  urethra Q64.74
  urinary meatus Q64.75
  uterus Q51.2∅
    with
      doubling of cervix (and vagina) Q51.1∅
        with obstruction Q51.11
    complete Q51.21
      in pregnancy or childbirth O34.59-•
        causing obstructed labor O65.5
    partial Q51.22
    specified NEC Q51.28
    vagina Q52.1∅
      with doubling of uterus (and cervix)
        Q51.1∅
        with obstruction Q51.11
    vision H53.2
    vulva Q52.79
Douglas' pouch, cul-de-sac —*see* condition
Down syndrome Q90.9
  meiotic nondisjunction Q90.∅
  mitotic nondisjunction Q90.1
  mosaicism Q90.1
  translocation Q90.2
DPD (dihydropyrimidine dehydrogenase
    deficiency) E88.89
Dracontiasis B72
Dracunculiasis, dracunculosis B72
Dream state, hysterical F44.89
Drepanocytic anemia —*see* Disease, sickle-cell
Dresbach's syndrome (elliptocytosis) D58.1
Dreschlera (hawaiiensis) (infection) B43.8
Dressler's syndrome I24.1
Drift, ulnar —*see* Deformity, limb, specified
    type NEC, forearm
Drinking (alcohol)
  excessive, to excess NEC (without
    dependence) F10.10
    habitual (continual) (without remission)
      F10.20
        with remission F10.21
Drip, postnasal (chronic) R09.82
  due to
    allergic rhinitis —*see* Rhinitis, allergic
    common cold J00
    gastroesophageal reflux —*see* Reflux,
      gastroesophageal
    nasopharyngitis —*see* Nasopharyngitis
    other known condition — code to
      condition
    sinusitis —*see* Sinusitis
Droop
  facial R29.810
    cerebrovascular disease I69.992
      cerebral infarction I69.392
      intracerebral hemorrhage I69.192
      nontraumatic intracranial hemorrhage
        NEC I69.292
      specified disease NEC I69.892
      subarachnoid hemorrhage I69.092
Drop (in)
  attack NEC R55
  finger —*see* Deformity, finger
  foot —*see* Deformity, limb, foot, drop
  hematocrit (precipitous) R71.∅
  hemoglobin R71.∅
  toe —*see* Deformity, toe, specified NEC
  wrist —*see* Deformity, limb, wrist drop
Dropped heart beats I45.9
Dropsy, dropsical —*see also* Hydrops
  abdomen R18.8
  brain —*see* Hydrocephalus
  cardiac, heart —*see* Failure, heart, congestive
  gangrenous —*see* Gangrene
  heart —*see* Failure, heart, congestive
  kidney —*see* Nephrosis
  lung —*see* Edema, lung
  newborn due to isoimmunization P56.∅
  pericardium —*see* Pericarditis

Drowned, drowning (near) T75.1
Drowsiness R40.∅
Drug
  abuse counseling and surveillance Z71.51
  addiction —*see* Dependence
  dependence —*see* Dependence
  habit —*see* Dependence
  harmful use —*see* Abuse, drug
  induced fever R50.2
  overdose —*see* Table of Drugs and Chemicals,
    by drug, poisoning
  poisoning —*see* Table of Drugs and
    Chemicals, by drug, poisoning
  resistant organism infection —*see also*
    Resistant, organism, to, drug Z16.30
  therapy
    long term (current) (prophylactic) —*see*
      Therapy, drug long-term (current)
      (prophylactic)
    short term - omit code
  wrong substance given or taken in error —*see*
    Table of Drugs and Chemicals, by drug,
    poisoning
Drunkenness (without dependence) F10.129
  acute in alcoholism F10.229
  chronic (without remission) F10.20
    with remission F10.21
  pathological (without dependence) F10.129
    with dependence F10.229
  sleep F51.9
Drusen
  macula (degenerative) (retina) —*see*
    Degeneration, macula, drusen
  optic disc H47.32-•
Dry, dryness —*see also* condition
  larynx J38.7
  mouth R68.2
    due to dehydration E86.∅
  nose J34.89
  socket (teeth) M27.3
  throat J39.2
DSAP L56.5
Duane's syndrome H50.81-•
Dubin-Johnson disease or syndrome E80.6
Dubois' disease (thymus gland) A50.59 *[E35]*
Dubowitz' syndrome Q87.1
Duchenne-Aran muscular atrophy G12.21
Duchenne-Griesinger disease G71.01
Duchenne's
  disease or syndrome
    motor neuron disease G12.22
    muscular dystrophy G71.01
  locomotor ataxia (syphilitic) A52.11
  paralysis
    birth injury P14.∅
    due to or associated with
      motor neuron disease G12.22
      muscular dystrophy G71.01
Ducrey's chancre A57
Duct, ductus —*see* condition
Duhring's disease (dermatitis herpetiformis)
  L13.∅
Dullness, cardiac (decreased) (increased) R01.2
Dumb ague —*see* Malaria
Dumbness —*see* Aphasia
Dumdum fever B55.∅
Dumping syndrome (postgastrectomy) K91.1
Duodenitis (nonspecific) (peptic) K29.80
  with bleeding K29.81
Duodenocholangitis —*see* Cholangitis
Duodenum, duodenal —*see* condition
Duplay's bursitis or periarthritis —*see*
  Tendinitis, calcific, shoulder
Duplication, duplex —*see also* Accessory
  alimentary tract Q45.8
  anus Q43.4
  appendix (and cecum) Q43.4
  biliary duct (any) Q44.5
  bladder Q64.79
  cecum (and appendix) Q43.4
  cervix Q51.82∅

Duplication, duplex *(Continued)*
  chromosome NEC
    with complex rearrangements NEC Q92.5
    seen only at prometaphase Q92.8
  cystic duct Q44.5
  digestive organs Q45.8
  esophagus Q39.8
  frontonasal process Q75.8
  intestine (large) (small) Q43.4
  kidney Q63.∅
  liver Q44.7
  pancreas Q45.3
  penis Q55.69
  respiratory organs NEC Q34.8
  salivary duct Q38.4
  spinal cord (incomplete) Q06.2
  stomach Q40.2
Dupré's disease (meningism) R29.1
Dupuytren's contraction or disease M72.∅
Durand-Nicolas-Favre disease A55
Durotomy (inadvertent) (incidental) G97.41
Duroziez's disease (congenital mitral stenosis)
  Q23.2
Dutton's relapsing fever (West African) A68.1
Dwarfism E34.3
  achondroplastic Q77.4
  congenital E34.3
  constitutional E34.3
  hypochondroplastic Q77.4
  hypophyseal E23.∅
  infantile E34.3
  Laron-type E34.3
  Lorain (-Levi) type E23.∅
  metatropic Q77.8
  nephrotic-glycosuric (with
    hypophosphatemic rickets) E72.09
  nutritional E45
  pancreatic K86.89
  pituitary E23.∅
  renal N25.∅
  thanatophoric Q77.1
Dyke-Young anemia (secondary)
  (symptomatic) D59.1
Dysacusis —*see* Abnormal, auditory
  perception
Dysadrenocortism E27.9
  hyperfunction E27.∅
Dysarthria R47.1
  following
    cerebral infarction I69.322
    cerebrovascular disease I69.922
      specified disease NEC I69.822
    intracerebral hemorrhage I69.122
    nontraumatic intracranial hemorrhage
      NEC I69.222
    subarachnoid hemorrhage I69.022
Dysautonomia (familial) G90.1
Dysbarism T70.3
Dysbasia R26.2
  angiosclerotica intermittens I73.9
  hysterical F44.4
  lordotica (progressiva) G24.1
  nonorganic origin F44.4
  psychogenic F44.4
Dysbetalipoproteinemia (familial) E78.2
Dyscalculia R48.8
  developmental F81.2
Dyschezia K59.00
Dyschondroplasia (with hemangiomata) Q78.4
Dyschromia (skin) L81.9
Dyscollagenosis M35.9
Dyscranio-pygo-phalangy Q87.∅
Dyscrasia
  blood (with) D75.9
    antepartum hemorrhage —*see* Hemorrhage,
      antepartum, with coagulation defect
    intrapartum hemorrhage O67.∅
    newborn P61.9
      specified type NEC P61.8
    puerperal, postpartum O72.3
  polyglandular, pluriglandular E31.9

Dysendocrinism E34.9

Dysentery, dysenteric (catarrhal) (diarrhea) (epidemic) (hemorrhagic) (infectious) (sporadic) (tropical) A09
  abscess, liver A06.4
  amebic —see also Amebiasis A06.0
    with abscess —see Abscess, amebic
    acute A06.0
    chronic A06.1
  arthritis —see also category M01 A09
    bacillary —see also category M01 A03.9
  bacillary A03.9
    arthritis —see also category M01 A03.9
    Boyd A03.2
    Flexner A03.1
    Schmitz (-Stutzer) A03.0
    Shiga (-Kruse) A03.0
    Shigella A03.9
      boydii A03.2
      dysenteriae A03.0
      flexneri A03.1
      group A A03.0
      group B A03.1
      group C A03.2
      group D A03.3
      sonnei A03.3
      specified type NEC A03.8
    Sonne A03.3
    specified type NEC A03.8
  balantidial A07.0
  Balantidium coli A07.0
  Boyd's A03.2
  candidal B37.82
  Chilomastix A07.8
  Chinese A03.9
  coccidial A07.3
  Dientamoeba (fragilis) A07.8
  Embadomonas A07.8
  Entamoeba, entamebic —see Dysentery, amebic
  Flexner-Boyd A03.2
  Flexner's A03.1
  Giardia lamblia A07.1
  Hiss-Russell A03.1
  Lamblia A07.1
  leishmanial B55.0
  malarial —see Malaria
  metazoal B82.0
  monilial B37.82
  protozoal A07.9
  Salmonella A02.0
  schistosomal B65.1
  Schmitz (-Stutzer) A03.0
  Shiga (-Kruse) A03.0
  Shigella NOS —see Dysentery, bacillary
  Sonne A03.3
  strongyloidiasis B78.0
  trichomonal A07.8
  viral —see also Enteritis, viral A08.4

Dysequilibrium R42

Dysesthesia R20.8
  hysterical F44.6

Dysfibrinogenemia (congenital) D68.2

Dysfunction
  adrenal E27.9
    hyperfunction E27.0
  autonomic
    due to alcohol G31.2
    somatoform F45.8
  bladder N31.9
    neurogenic NOS —see Dysfunction, bladder, neuromuscular
    neuromuscular NOS N31.9
      atonic (motor) (sensory) N31.2
      autonomous N31.2
      flaccid N31.2
      nonreflex N31.2
      reflex N31.1
      specified NEC N31.8
      uninhibited N31.0
  bleeding, uterus N93.8

Dysfunction (Continued)
  cerebral G93.89
  colon K59.9
    psychogenic F45.8
  colostomy K94.03
  cystic duct K82.8
  cystostomy (stoma) —see Complications, cystostomy
  ejaculatory N53.19
    anejaculatory orgasm N53.13
    painful N53.12
    premature F52.4
    retarded N53.11
  endocrine NOS E34.9
  endometrium N85.8
  enterostomy K94.13
  erectile —see Dysfunction, sexual, male, erectile
  gallbladder K82.8
  gastrostomy (stoma) K94.23
  gland, glandular NOS E34.9
  ▶meibomian, of eyelid -see Dysfunction, meibomian gland
  heart I51.89
  hemoglobin D75.89
  hepatic K76.89
  hypophysis E23.7
  hypothalamic NEC E23.3
  ileostomy (stoma) K94.13
  jejunostomy (stoma) K94.13
  kidney —see Disease, renal
  labyrinthine —see subcategory H83.2
  left ventricular, following sudden emotional stress I51.81
  liver K76.89
  male —see Dysfunction, sexual, male
  ▶meibomian gland, of eyelid H02.889
    ▶left H02.886
      ▶lower H02.885
      ▶upper H02.884
      ▶upper and lower eyelids H02.88B
    ▶right H02.883
      ▶lower H02.882
      ▶upper H02.881
      ▶upper and lower eyelids H02.88A
  orgasmic (female) F52.31
    male F52.32
  ovary E28.9
    specified NEC E28.8
  papillary muscle I51.89
  parathyroid E21.4
  physiological NEC R68.89
    psychogenic F59
  pineal gland E34.8
  pituitary (gland) E23.3
  platelets D69.1
  polyglandular E31.9
    specified NEC E31.8
  psychophysiologic F59
  psychosexual F52.9
    with
      dyspareunia F52.6
      premature ejaculation F52.4
      vaginismus F52.5
  pylorus K31.9
  rectum K59.9
    psychogenic F45.8
  reflex (sympathetic) —see Syndrome, pain, complex regional I
  segmental —see Dysfunction, somatic
  senile R54
  sexual (due to) R37
    alcohol F10.981
    amphetamine F15.981
      in
        abuse F15.181
        dependence F15.281
    anxiolytic F13.981
      in
        abuse F13.181
        dependence F13.281

Dysfunction (Continued)
  sexual (Continued)
    cocaine F14.981
      in
        abuse F14.181
        dependence F14.281
    excessive sexual drive F52.8
    failure of genital response (male) F52.21
      female F52.22
    female N94.9
      aversion F52.1
      dyspareunia N94.10
        psychogenic F52.6
      frigidity F52.22
      nymphomania F52.8
      orgasmic F52.31
      psychogenic F52.9
        aversion F52.1
        dyspareunia F52.6
        frigidity F52.22
        nymphomania F52.8
        orgasmic F52.31
        vaginismus F52.5
      vaginismus N94.2
        psychogenic F52.5
    hypnotic F13.981
      in
        abuse F13.181
        dependence F13.281
    inhibited orgasm (female) F52.31
      male F52.32
    lack
      of sexual enjoyment F52.1
      or loss of sexual desire F52.0
    male N53.9
      anejaculatory orgasm N53.13
      ejaculatory N53.19
        painful N53.12
        premature F52.4
        retarded N53.11
      erectile N52.9
        drug induced N52.2
        due to
          disease classified elsewhere N52.1
          drug N52.2
        postoperative (postprocedural) N52.39
          following
            cryotherapy N52.37
            interstitial seed therapy N52.36
            prostate ablative therapy N52.37
            prostatectomy N52.34
              radical N52.31
            radiation therapy N52.35
            radical cystectomy N52.32
            ultrasound ablative therapy N52.37
            urethral surgery N52.33
        psychogenic F52.21
        specified cause NEC N52.8
        vasculogenic
          arterial insufficiency N52.01
            with corporo-venous occlusive N52.03
          corporo-venous occlusive N52.02
            with arterial insufficiency N52.03
      impotence —see Dysfunction, sexual, male, erectile
      psychogenic F52.9
        aversion F52.1
        erectile F52.21
        orgasmic F52.32
        premature ejaculation F52.4
        satyriasis F52.8
        specified type NEC F52.8
      specified type NEC N53.8
    nonorganic F52.9
      specified NEC F52.8
    opioid F11.981
      in
        abuse F11.181
        dependence F11.281

▶ New   ⇒ Revised   deleted Deleted   ● Use Additional Character(s)

Dysfunction *(Continued)*
  sexual *(Continued)*
    orgasmic dysfunction (female) F52.31
      male F52.32
    premature ejaculation F52.4
    psychoactive substances NEC F19.981
      in
        abuse F19.181
        dependence F19.281
    psychogenic F52.9
    sedative F13.981
      in
        abuse F13.181
        dependence F13.281
    sexual aversion F52.1
    vaginismus (nonorganic) (psychogenic)
      F52.5
  sinoatrial node I49.5
  somatic M99.09
    abdomen M99.09
    acromioclavicular M99.07
    cervical region M99.01
    cervicothoracic M99.01
    costochondral M99.08
    costovertebral M99.08
    head region M99.00
    hip M99.05
    lower extremity M99.06
    lumbar region M99.03
    lumbosacral M99.03
    occipitocervical M99.00
    pelvic region M99.05
    pubic M99.05
    rib cage M99.08
    sacral region M99.04
    sacrococcygeal M99.04
    sacroiliac M99.04
    specified NEC M99.09
    sternochondral M99.08
    sternoclavicular M99.07
    thoracic region M99.02
    thoracolumbar M99.02
    upper extremity M99.07
  somatoform autonomic F45.8
  stomach K31.89
    psychogenic F45.8
  suprarenal E27.9
    hyperfunction E27.0
  symbolic R48.9
    specified type NEC R48.8
  temporomandibular (joint) M26.69
    joint-pain syndrome M26.62-●
  testicular (endocrine) E29.9
    specified NEC E29.8
  thymus E32.9
  thyroid E07.9
  ureterostomy (stoma) —*see* Complications,
    stoma, urinary tract
  urethrostomy (stoma) —*see* Complications,
    stoma, urinary tract
  uterus, complicating delivery O62.9
    hypertonic O62.4
    hypotonic O62.2
      primary O62.0
      secondary O62.1
  ventricular I51.9
    with congestive heart failure —*see also*
      Failure, heart I50.9
    left, reversible, following sudden
      emotional stress I51.81
Dysgenesis
  gonadal (due to chromosomal anomaly) Q96.9
    pure Q99.1
  renal Q60.5
    bilateral Q60.4
    unilateral Q60.3
  reticular D72.0
  tidal platelet D69.3
Dysgerminoma
  specified site —*see* Neoplasm, malignant,
    by site

Dysgerminoma *(Continued)*
  unspecified site
    female C56.9
    male C62.90
Dysgeusia R43.2
Dysgraphia R27.8
Dyshidrosis, dysidrosis L30.1
Dyskaryotic cervical smear R87.619
Dyskeratosis L85.8
  cervix —*see* Dysplasia, cervix
  congenital Q82.8
  uterus NEC N85.8
Dyskinesia G24.9
  biliary (cystic duct or gallbladder)
    K82.8
  drug induced
    orofacial G24.01
  esophagus K22.4
  hysterical F44.4
  intestinal K59.8
  nonorganic origin F44.4
  orofacial (idiopathic) G24.4
    drug induced G24.01
  psychogenic F44.4
  subacute, drug induced G24.01
  tardive G24.01
    neuroleptic induced G24.01
  trachea J39.8
  tracheobronchial J98.09
Dyslalia (developmental) F80.0
Dyslexia R48.0
  developmental F81.0
Dyslipidemia E78.5
  depressed HDL cholesterol E78.6
  elevated fasting triglycerides E78.1
Dysmaturity —*see also* Light for dates
  pulmonary (newborn) (Wilson-Mikity)
    P27.0
Dysmenorrhea (essential) (exfoliative)
  N94.6
  congestive (syndrome) N94.6
  primary N94.4
  psychogenic F45.8
  secondary N94.5
Dysmetabolic syndrome X E88.81
Dysmetria R27.8
Dysmorphism (due to)
  alcohol Q86.0
  exogenous cause NEC Q86.8
  hydantoin Q86.1
  warfarin Q86.2
Dysmorphophobia (nondelusional) F45.22
  delusional F22
Dysnomia R47.01
Dysorexia R63.0
  psychogenic F50.89
Dysostosis
  cleidocranial, cleidocranialis Q74.0
  craniofacial Q75.1
  Fairbank's (idiopathic familial generalized
    osteophytosis) Q78.9
  mandibulofacial (incomplete) Q75.4
  multiplex E76.01
  oculomandibular Q75.5
Dyspareunia (female) N94.10
  deep N94.12
  male N53.12
  nonorganic F52.6
  psychogenic F52.6
  secondary N94.19
  specified NEC N94.19
  superficial (introital) N94.11
Dyspepsia R10.13
  atonic K30
  functional (allergic) (congenital)
    (gastrointestinal) (occupational)
    (reflex) K30
  intestinal K59.8
  nervous F45.8
  neurotic F45.8
  psychogenic F45.8

Dysphagia R13.10
  cervical R13.19
  following
    cerebral infarction I69.391
    cerebrovascular disease I69.991
      specified NEC I69.891
    intracerebral hemorrhage I69.191
    nontraumatic intracranial hemorrhage
      NEC I69.291
    specified disease NEC I69.891
    subarachnoid hemorrhage I69.091
  functional (hysterical) F45.8
  hysterical F45.8
  nervous (hysterical) F45.8
  neurogenic R13.19
  oral phase R13.11
  oropharyngeal phase R13.12
  pharyngeal phase R13.13
  pharyngoesophageal phase R13.14
  psychogenic F45.8
  sideropenic D50.1
  spastica K22.4
  specified NEC R13.19
Dysphagocytosis, congenital D71
Dysphasia R47.02
  developmental
    expressive type F80.1
    receptive type F80.2
  following
    cerebrovascular disease I69.921
      cerebral infarction I69.321
      intracerebral hemorrhage I69.121
    nontraumatic intracranial hemorrhage NEC
      I69.221
      specified disease NEC I69.821
      subarachnoid hemorrhage I69.021
Dysphonia R49.0
  functional F44.4
  hysterical F44.4
  psychogenic F44.4
  spastica J38.3
Dysphoria
  gender F64.9
    in
      adolescence and adulthood F64.0
      children F64.2
    specified NEC F64.8
    postpartal O90.6
Dyspituitarism E23.3
Dysplasia —*see also* Anomaly
  acetabular, congenital Q65.89
  alveolar capillary, with vein misalignment
    J84.843
  anus (histologically confirmed) (mild)
    (moderate) K62.82
    severe D01.3
  arrhythmogenic right ventricular I42.8
  arterial, fibromuscular I77.3
  asphyxiating thoracic (congenital) Q77.2
  brain Q07.9
  bronchopulmonary, perinatal P27.1
  cervix (uteri) N87.9
    mild N87.0
    moderate N87.1
    severe D06.9
  chondroectodermal Q77.6
  colon D12.6
  craniometaphyseal Q78.58
  dentinal K00.5
  diaphyseal, progressive Q78.3
  dystrophic Q77.5
  ectodermal (anhidrotic) (congenital)
    (hereditary) Q82.4
    hidrotic Q82.8
  epithelial, uterine cervix —*see* Dysplasia,
    cervix
  eye (congenital) Q11.2
  fibrous
    bone NEC (monostotic) M85.00
      ankle M85.07-●
      foot M85.07-●

Dysplasia *(Continued)*
  fibrous *(Continued)*
    bone NEC *(Continued)*
      forearm M85.03-●
      hand M85.04-●
      lower leg M85.06-●
      multiple site M85.09
      neck M85.08
      rib M85.08
      shoulder M85.01-●
      skull M85.08
      specified site NEC M85.08
      thigh M85.05-●
      toe M85.07-●
      upper arm M85.02-●
      vertebra M85.08
    diaphyseal, progressive Q78.3
    jaw M27.8
    polyostotic Q78.1
  florid osseous —*see also* Cyst, calcifying odontogenic
  high grade, focal D12.6
  hip, congenital Q65.89
  joint, congenital Q74.8
  kidney Q61.4
    multicystic Q61.4
  leg Q74.2
  lung, congenital (not associated with short gestation) Q33.6
  mammary (gland) (benign) N60.9-●
    cyst (solitary) —*see* Cyst, breast
    cystic —*see* Mastopathy, cystic
    duct ectasia —*see* Ectasia, mammary duct
    fibroadenosis —*see* Fibroadenosis, breast
    fibrosclerosis —*see* Fibrosclerosis, breast
    specified type NEC N60.8-●
  metaphyseal Q78.5
  muscle Q79.8
  oculodentodigital Q87.0
  periapical (cemental) (cemento-osseous) —*see* Cyst, calcifying odontogenic
  periosteum —*see* Disorder, bone, specified type NEC
  polyostotic fibrous Q78.1
  prostate —*see also* Neoplasia, intraepithelial, prostate N42.30
    severe D07.5
    specified NEC N42.39
  renal Q61.4
    multicystic Q61.4
  retinal, congenital Q14.1
  right ventricular, arrhythmogenic I42.8
  septo-optic Q04.4
  skin L98.8
  spinal cord Q06.1
  spondyloepiphyseal Q77.7
  thymic, with immunodeficiency D82.1
  vagina N89.3
    mild N89.0
    moderate N89.1
    severe NEC D07.2
  vulva N90.3
    mild N90.0
    moderate N90.1
    severe NEC D07.1
Dysplasminogenemia E88.02
Dyspnea (nocturnal) (paroxysmal) R06.00
  asthmatic (bronchial) J45.909
    with
      bronchitis J45.909
        with
          exacerbation (acute) J45.901
          status asthmaticus J45.902
        chronic J44.9
      exacerbation (acute) J45.901
      status asthmaticus J45.902
    cardiac —*see* Failure, ventricular, left
  cardiac —*see* Failure, ventricular, left
  functional F45.8
  hyperventilation R06.4
  hysterical F45.8

Dyspnea *(Continued)*
  newborn P28.89
  psychogenic F45.8
  shortness of breath R06.02
  specified type NEC R06.09
Dyspraxia R27.8
  developmental (syndrome) F82
Dysproteinemia E88.09
Dysreflexia, autonomic G90.4
Dysrhythmia
  cardiac I49.9
    newborn
      bradycardia P29.12
      occurring before birth P03.819
        before onset of labor P03.810
        during labor P03.811
      tachycardia P29.11
    postoperative I97.89
  cerebral or cortical —*see* Epilepsy
Dyssomnia —*see* Disorder, sleep
Dyssynergia
  biliary K83.8
  bladder sphincter N36.44
  cerebellaris myoclonica (Hunt's ataxia) G11.1
Dysthymia F34.1
Dysthyroidism E07.9
Dystocia O66.9
  affecting newborn P03.1
  cervical (hypotonic) O62.2
    affecting newborn P03.6
    primary O62.0
    secondary O62.1
  contraction ring O62.4
  fetal O66.9
    abnormality NEC O66.3
    conjoined twins O66.3
    oversize O66.2
  maternal O66.9
  positional O64.9
  shoulder (girdle) O66.0
    causing obstructed labor O66.0
  uterine NEC O62.4
Dystonia G24.9
  cervical G24.3
  deformans progressiva G24.1
  drug induced NEC G24.09
    acute G24.02
    specified NEC G24.09
  familial G24.1
  idiopathic G24.1
    familial G24.1
    nonfamilial G24.2
    orofacial G24.4
  lenticularis G24.8
  musculorum deformans G24.1
  neuroleptic induced (acute) G24.02
  orofacial (idiopathic) G24.4
  oromandibular G24.4
    due to drug G24.01
  specified NEC G24.8
  torsion (familial) (idiopathic) G24.1
    acquired G24.8
    genetic G24.1
    symptomatic (nonfamilial) G24.2
Dystonic movements R25.8
Dystrophy, dystrophia
  adiposogenital E23.6
  autosomal recessive, childhood type, muscular dystrophy resembling Duchenne or Becker G71.01
  Becker's type G71.01
  cervical sympathetic G90.2
  choroid (hereditary) H31.20
    central areolar H31.22
    choroideremia H31.21
    gyrate atrophy H31.23
    specified type NEC H31.29
  cornea (hereditary) H18.50
    endothelial H18.51
    epithelial H18.52

Dystrophy, dystrophia *(Continued)*
  cornea *(Continued)*
    granular H18.53
    lattice H18.54
    macular H18.55
    specified type NEC H18.59
  Duchenne's type G71.01
  due to malnutrition E45
  Erb's G71.02
  Fuchs' H18.51
  Gower's muscular G71.01
  hair L67.8
  infantile neuraxonal G31.89
  Landouzy-Déjérine G71.02
  Leyden-Möbius G71.09
  muscular G71.00
    autosomal recessive, childhood type, muscular dystrophy resembling Duchenne or Becker G71.01
    benign (Becker type) G71.01
      scapuloperoneal with early contractures [Emery-Dreifuss] G71.09
    congenital (hereditary) (progressive) (with specific morphological abnormalities of the muscle fiber) G71.09
      myotonic G71.11
    distal G71.09
    Duchenne type G71.01
    Emery-Dreifuss G71.09
    Erb type G71.02
    facioscapulohumeral G71.02
    Gower's G71.01
    hereditary (progressive) G71.09
    Landouzy-Déjérine type G71.02
    limb-girdle G71.09
      myotonic G71.11
    progressive (hereditary) G71.09
      Charcot-Marie (-Tooth) type G60.0
    pseudohypertrophic (infantile) G71.01
    scapulohumeral G71.02
    scapuloperoneal G71.09
    severe (Duchenne type) G71.01
    specified type NEC G71.09
  myocardium, myocardial —*see* Degeneration, myocardial
  nail L60.3
    congenital Q84.6
  nutritional E45
  ocular G71.09
  oculocerebrorenal E72.03
  oculopharyngeal G71.09
  ovarian N83.8
  polyglandular E31.8
  reflex (neuromuscular) (sympathetic) — *see* Syndrome, pain, complex regional I
  retinal (hereditary) H35.50
    in
      lipid storage disorders E75.6 [H36]
      systemic lipidoses E75.6 [H36]
    involving
      pigment epithelium H35.54
      sensory area H35.53
    pigmentary H35.52
    vitreoretinal H35.51
  Salzmann's nodular —*see* Degeneration, cornea, nodular
  scapuloperoneal G71.09
  skin NEC L98.8
  sympathetic (reflex) —*see* Syndrome, pain, complex regional I
    cervical G90.2
  tapetoretinal H35.54
  thoracic, asphyxiating Q77.2
  unguium L60.3
    congenital Q84.6
  vitreoretinal H35.51
  vulva N90.4
  yellow (liver) —*see* Failure, hepatic
Dysuria R30.0
  psychogenic F45.8

▶ New   ⇒ Revised   ~~deleted~~ Deleted   ● Use Additional Character(s)

E

Eales' disease H35.06-●
Ear —see also condition
  piercing Z41.3
  tropical NEC B36.9 *[H62.40]*
    in
      aspergillosis B44.89
      candidiasis B37.84
      moniliasis B37.84
  wax (impacted) H61.20
    left H61.22
      with right H61.23
    right H61.21
      with left H61.23
Earache —see subcategory H92.0
Early satiety R68.81
Eaton-Lambert syndrome—see Syndrome,
    Lambert-Eaton
Eberth's disease (typhoid fever) A01.00
Ebola virus disease A98.4
Ebstein's anomaly or syndrome (heart) Q22.5
Eccentro-osteochondrodysplasia E76.29
Ecchondroma —see Neoplasm, bone, benign
Ecchondrosis D48.0
Ecchymosis R58
  conjunctiva —see Hemorrhage, conjunctiva
  eye (traumatic) —see Contusion, eyeball
  eyelid (traumatic) —see Contusion, eyelid
  newborn P54.5
  spontaneous R23.3
  traumatic —see Contusion
Echinococciasis —see Echinococcus
Echinococcosis —see Echinococcus
Echinococcus (infection) B67.90
  granulosus B67.4
    bone B67.2
    liver B67.0
    lung B67.1
    multiple sites B67.32
    specified site NEC B67.39
    thyroid B67.31
  liver NOS B67.8
    granulosus B67.0
    multilocularis B67.5
  lung NEC B67.99
    granulosus B67.1
    multilocularis B67.69
  multilocularis B67.7
    liver B67.5
    multiple sites B67.61
    specified site NEC B67.69
  specified site NEC B67.99
    granulosus B67.39
    multilocularis B67.69
  thyroid NEC B67.99
    granulosus B67.31
    multilocularis B67.69 *[E35]*
Echinorhynchiasis B83.8
Echinostomiasis B66.8
Echolalia R48.8
Echovirus, as cause of disease classified
    elsewhere B97.12
Eclampsia, eclamptic (coma) (convulsions)
    (delirium) (with hypertension) NEC O15.9
  complicating
    labor and delivery O15.1
    postpartum O15.2
    pregnancy O15.0-●
    puerperium O15.2
Economic circumstances affecting care Z59.9
Economo's disease A85.8
Ectasia, ectasis
  annuloaortic I35.8
  aorta I77.819
    with aneurysm —see Aneurysm, aorta
      abdominal I77.811
      thoracic I77.810
      thoracoabdominal I77.812
  breast —see Ectasia, mammary duct
  capillary I78.8
  cornea H18.71-●

Ectasia, ectasis *(Continued)*
  gastric antral vascular (GAVE) K31.819
    with hemorrhage K31.811
    without hemorrhage K31.819
  mammary duct N60.4-●
  salivary gland (duct) K11.8
  sclera —see Sclerectasia
Ecthyma L08.0
  contagiosum B08.02
  gangrenosum L08.0
  infectiosum B08.02
Ectocardia Q24.8
Ectodermal dysplasia (anhidrotic) Q82.4
Ectodermosis erosiva pluriorificialis
    L51.1
Ectopic, ectopia (congenital)
  abdominal viscera Q45.8
    due to defect in anterior abdominal wall
        Q79.59
  ACTH syndrome E24.3
  adrenal gland Q89.1
  anus Q43.5
  atrial beats I49.1
  beats I49.49
    atrial I49.1
    ventricular I49.3
  bladder Q64.10
  bone and cartilage in lung Q33.5
  brain Q04.8
  breast tissue Q83.8
  cardiac Q24.8
  cerebral Q04.8
  cordis Q24.8
  endometrium —see Endometriosis
  gastric mucosa Q40.2
  gestation —see Pregnancy, by site
  heart Q24.8
  hormone secretion NEC E34.2
  kidney (crossed) (pelvis) Q63.2
  lens, lentis Q12.1
  mole —see Pregnancy, by site
  organ or site NEC —see Malposition,
      congenital
  pancreas Q45.3
  pregnancy —see Pregnancy, ectopic
  pupil —see Abnormality, pupillary
  renal Q63.2
  sebaceous glands of mouth Q38.6
  spleen Q89.09
  testis Q53.00
    bilateral Q53.02
    unilateral Q53.01
  thyroid Q89.2
  tissue in lung Q33.5
  ureter Q62.63
  ventricular beats I49.3
  vesicae Q64.10
Ectromelia Q73.8
  lower limb —see Defect, reduction, limb,
      lower, specified type NEC
  upper limb —see Defect, reduction, limb,
      upper, specified type NEC
Ectropion H02.109
  cervix N86
    with cervicitis N72
  congenital Q10.1
▶ eyelid H02.109
    cicatricial H02.119
      left H02.116
        lower H02.115
        upper H02.114
      right H02.113
        lower H02.112
        upper H02.111
    congenital Q10.1
    left H02.106
      lower H02.105
      upper H02.104
    mechanical H02.129
      left H02.126
        lower H02.125
        upper H02.124

Ectropion *(Continued)*
  eyelid *(Continued)*
    mechanical *(Continued)*
      right H02.123
        lower H02.122
        upper H02.121
  ▶ paralytic H02.159
    ▶ left H02.156
      ▶ lower H02.155
      ▶ upper H02.154
    ▶ right H02.153
      ▶ lower H02.152
      ▶ upper H02.151
    right H02.103
      lower H02.102
      upper H02.101
    senile H02.139
      left H02.136
        lower H02.135
        upper H02.134
      right H02.133
        lower H02.132
        upper H02.131
    spastic H02.149
      left H02.146
        lower H02.145
        upper H02.144
      right H02.143
        lower H02.142
        upper H02.141
  iris H21.89
  lip (acquired) K13.0
    congenital Q38.0
  urethra N36.8
  uvea H21.89
Eczema (acute) (chronic) (erythematous)
    (fissum) (rubrum) (squamous) (see also
    Dermatitis) L30.9
  contact —see Dermatitis, contact
  dyshydrotic L30.1
  external ear —see Otitis, externa, acute,
      eczematoid
  flexural L20.82
  herpeticum B00.0
  hypertrophicum L28.0
  hypostatic —see Varix, leg, with,
      inflammation
  impetiginous L01.1
  infantile (due to any substance) L20.83
    intertriginous L21.1
    seborrheic L21.1
  intertriginous NEC L30.4
    infantile L21.1
  intrinsic (allergic) L20.84
  lichenified NEC L28.0
  marginatum (hebrae) B35.6
  pustular L30.3
  stasis I87.2
    with varicose veins —see Varix, leg, with,
        inflammation
  vaccination, vaccinatum T88.1
  varicose —see Varix, leg, with, inflammation
Eczematid L30.2
Eddowes (-Spurway) syndrome Q78.0
Edema, edematous (infectious) (pitting)
    (toxic) R60.9
  with nephritis —see Nephrosis
  allergic T78.3
  amputation stump (surgical) (sequelae
      (late effect)) T87.89
  angioneurotic (allergic) (any site) (with
      urticaria) T78.3
    hereditary D84.1
  angiospastic I73.9
  Berlin's (traumatic) S05.8X-●
  brain (cytotoxic) (vasogenic) G93.6
    due to birth injury P11.0
    newborn (anoxia or hypoxia) P52.4
      birth injury P11.0
    traumatic —see Injury, intracranial,
        cerebral edema
  cardiac —see Failure, heart, congestive

Edema, edematous (Continued)
- cardiovascular —see Failure, heart, congestive
- cerebral —see Edema, brain
- cerebrospinal —see Edema, brain
- cervix (uteri) (acute) N88.8
  - puerperal, postpartum O90.89
- chronic hereditary Q82.0
- circumscribed, acute T78.3
  - hereditary D84.1
- conjunctiva H11.42-●
- cornea H18.2-●
  - idiopathic H18.22-●
  - secondary H18.23-●
    - due to contact lens H18.21-●
- due to
  - lymphatic obstruction I89.0
  - salt retention E87.0
- epiglottis —see Edema, glottis
- essential, acute T78.3
  - hereditary D84.1
- extremities, lower —see Edema, legs
- eyelid NEC H02.849
  - left H02.846
    - lower H02.845
    - upper H02.844
  - right H02.843
    - lower H02.842
    - upper H02.841
- familial, hereditary Q82.0
- famine —see Malnutrition, severe
- generalized R60.1
- glottis, glottic, glottidis (obstructive) (passive) J38.4
  - allergic T78.3
    - hereditary D84.1
- heart —see Failure, heart, congestive
- heat T67.7
- hereditary Q82.0
- inanition —see Malnutrition, severe
- intracranial G93.6
- iris H21.89
- joint —see Effusion, joint
- larynx —see Edema, glottis
- legs R60.0
  - due to venous obstruction I87.1
  - hereditary Q82.0
- localized R60.0
  - due to venous obstruction I87.1
- lower limbs —see Edema, legs
- lung J81.1
  - with heart condition or failure —see Failure, ventricular, left
  - acute J81.0
  - chemical (acute) J68.1
    - chronic J68.1
  - chronic J81.1
    - due to
      - chemicals, gases, fumes or vapors (inhalation) J68.1
      - external agent J70.9
        - specified NEC J70.8
      - radiation J70.1
  - due to
    - chemicals, fumes or vapors (inhalation) J68.1
    - external agent J70.9
      - specified NEC J70.8
    - high altitude T70.29
    - near drowning T75.1
    - radiation J70.0
  - meaning failure, left ventricle I50.1
- lymphatic I89.0
  - due to mastectomy I97.2
- macula H35.81
  - cystoid, following cataract surgery —see Complications, postprocedural, following cataract surgery
  - diabetic —see Diabetes, by type, with, retinopathy, with macular edema
- malignant —see Gangrene, gas
- Milroy's Q82.0

Edema, edematous (Continued)
- nasopharynx J39.2
- newborn P83.30
  - hydrops fetalis —see Hydrops, fetalis
  - specified NEC P83.39
- nutritional —see also Malnutrition, severe
  - with dyspigmentation, skin and hair E40
- optic disc or nerve —see Papilledema
- orbit H05.22-●
- pancreas K86.89
- papilla, optic —see Papilledema
- penis N48.89
- periodic T78.3
  - hereditary D84.1
- pharynx J39.2
- pulmonary —see Edema, lung
- Quincke's T78.3
  - hereditary D84.1
- renal —see Nephrosis
- retina H35.81
  - diabetic —see Diabetes, by type, with, retinopathy, with macular edema
- salt E87.0
- scrotum N50.89
- seminal vesicle N50.89
- spermatic cord N50.89
- spinal (cord) (vascular) (nontraumatic) G95.19
- starvation —see Malnutrition, severe
- stasis —see Hypertension, venous, (chronic)
- subglottic —see Edema, glottis
- supraglottic —see Edema, glottis
- testis N44.8
- tunica vaginalis N50.89
- vas deferens N50.89
- vulva (acute) N90.89

Edentulism —see Absence, teeth, acquired
Edsall's disease T67.2
Educational handicap Z55.9
- specified NEC Z55.8
Edward's syndrome —see Trisomy, 18
Effect, adverse
- abnormal gravitational (G) forces or states T75.81
- abuse —see Maltreatment
- air pressure T70.9
  - specified NEC T70.8
- altitude (high) —see Effect, adverse, high altitude
- anesthesia —see also Anesthesia T88.59
  - in labor and delivery O74.9
  - local, toxic
    - in labor and delivery O74.4-●
    - in pregnancy NEC O29.3-●
    - postpartum, puerperal O89.3
  - postpartum, puerperal O89.9
  - specified NEC T88.59
    - in labor and delivery O74.8
    - postpartum, puerperal O89.8
  - spinal and epidural T88.59
    - headache T88.59
      - in labor and delivery O74.5
      - postpartum, puerperal O89.4
    - specified NEC
      - in labor and delivery O74.6
      - postpartum, puerperal O89.5
- antitoxin —see Complications, vaccination
- atmospheric pressure T70.9
  - due to explosion T70.8
  - high T70.3
  - low —see Effect, adverse, high altitude
  - specified effect NEC T70.8
- biological, correct substance properly administered —see Effect, adverse, drug
- blood (derivatives) (serum) (transfusion) — see Complications, transfusion
- chemical substance —see Table of Drugs and Chemicals
- cold (temperature) (weather) T69.9
  - chilblains T69.1
  - frostbite —see Frostbite
  - specified effect NEC T69.8

Effect, adverse (Continued)
- drugs and medicaments T88.7
  - specified drug —see Table of Drugs and Chemicals, by drug, adverse effect
  - specified effect — code to condition
- electric current, electricity (shock) T75.4
  - burn —see Burn
- exertion (excessive) T73.3
- exposure —see Exposure
- external cause NEC T75.89
- foodstuffs T78.1
  - allergic reaction —see Allergy, food
    - causing anaphylaxis —see Shock, anaphylactic, due to food
  - noxious —see Poisoning, food, noxious
- gases, fumes, or vapors T59.9-●
  - specified agent —see Table of Drugs and Chemicals
- glue (airplane) sniffing
  - due to drug abuse —see Abuse, drug, inhalant
  - due to drug dependence —see Dependence, drug, inhalant
- heat —see Heat
- high altitude NEC T70.29
  - anoxia T70.29
  - on
    - ears T70.0
    - sinuses T70.1
  - polycythemia D75.1
- high pressure fluids T70.4
- hot weather —see Heat
- hunger T73.0
- immersion, foot —see Immersion
- immunization —see Complications, vaccination
- immunological agents —see Complications, vaccination
- infrared (radiation) (rays) NOS T66
  - dermatitis or eczema L59.8
- infusion —see Complications, infusion
- lack of care of infants —see Maltreatment, child
- lightning —see Lightning
- medical care T88.9
  - specified NEC T88.8
- medicinal substance, correct, properly administered —see Effect, adverse, drug
- motion T75.3
- noise, on inner ear —see subcategory H83.3
- overheated places —see Heat
- psychosocial, of work environment Z56.5
- radiation (diagnostic) (infrared) (natural source) (therapeutic) (ultraviolet) (X-ray) NOS T66
  - dermatitis or eczema —see Dermatitis, due to, radiation
  - fibrosis of lung J70.1
  - pneumonitis J70.0
  - pulmonary manifestations
    - acute J70.0
    - chronic J70.1
  - skin L59.9
- radioactive substance NOS
  - dermatitis or eczema —see Radiodermatitis
- reduced temperature T69.9
  - immersion foot or hand —see Immersion
  - specified effect NEC T69.8
- serum NEC (see also Reaction, serum) T80.69
- specified NEC T78.8
  - external cause NEC T75.89
- strangulation —see Asphyxia, traumatic
- submersion T75.1
- thirst T73.1
- toxic —see Toxicity
- transfusion —see Complications, transfusion
- ultraviolet (radiation) (rays) NOS T66
  - burn —see Burn
  - dermatitis or eczema —see Dermatitis, due to, ultraviolet rays
    - acute L56.8

▶ New ⇒ Revised ~~deleted~~ Deleted ● Use Additional Character(s)

Effect, adverse *(Continued)*
vaccine (any) —*see* Complications, vaccination
vibration —*see* Vibration, adverse effects
water pressure NEC T70.9
specified NEC T70.8
weightlessness T75.82
whole blood —*see* Complications, transfusion
work environment Z56.5
Effect(s) (of) (from) —*see* Effect, adverse NEC
Effects, late —*see* Sequelae
Effluvium
anagen L65.1
telogen L65.0
Effort syndrome (psychogenic) F45.8
Effusion
amniotic fluid —*see* Pregnancy, complicated
by, prematue rupture of membranes
brain (serous) G93.6
bronchial —*see* Bronchitis
cerebral G93.6
cerebrospinal —*see also* Meningitis
vessel G93.6
chest —*see* Effusion, pleura
chylous, chyliform (pleura) J94.0
intracranial G93.6
joint M25.40
ankle M25.47-●
elbow M25.42-●
foot joint M25.47-●
hand joint M25.44-●
hip M25.45-●
knee M25.46-●
shoulder M25.41-●
specified joint NEC M25.48
wrist M25.43-●
malignant pleural J91.0
meninges —*see* Meningitis
pericardium, pericardial (noninflammatory)
I31.3
acute —*see* Pericarditis, acute
peritoneal (chronic) R18.8
pleura, pleurisy, pleuritic, pleuropericardial
J90
chylous, chyliform J94.0
due to systemic lupus erythematosis
M32.13
in conditions classified elsewhere J91.8
influenzal —*see* Influenza, with, respiratory
manifestations NEC
malignant J91.0
newborn P28.89
tuberculous NEC A15.6
primary (progressive) A15.7
spinal —*see* Meningitis
thorax, thoracic —*see* Effusion, pleura
Egg shell nails L60.3
congenital Q84.6
Egyptian splenomegaly B65.1
Ehlers-Danlos syndrome Q79.6
Ehrlichiosis A77.40
due to
E. chafeensis A77.41
E. sennetsu A79.81
specified organism NEC A77.49
Eichstedt's disease B36.0
Eisenmenger's
complex or syndrome I27.83
defect Q21.8
Ejaculation
delayed F52.32
painful N53.12
premature F52.4
retarded N53.11
retrograde N53.14
semen, painful N53.12
psychogenic F52.6
Ekbom's syndrome (restless legs) G25.81
Ekman's syndrome (brittle bones and blue
sclera) Q78.0
Elastic skin Q82.8
acquired L57.4

Elastofibroma —*see* Neoplasm, connective
tissue, benign
Elastoma (juvenile) Q82.8
Miescher's L87.2
Elastomyofibrosis I42.4
Elastosis
actinic, solar L57.8
atrophicans (senile) L57.4
perforans serpiginosa L87.2
senilis L57.4
Elbow —*see* condition
Electric current, electricity, effects (concussion)
(fatal) (nonfatal) (shock) T75.4
burn —*see* Burn
Electric feet syndrome E53.8
Electrocution T75.4
from electroshock gun (taser) T75.4
Electrolyte imbalance E87.8
with
abortion —*see* Abortion by type,
complicated by, electrolyte imbalance
ectopic pregnancy O08.5
molar pregnancy O08.5
Elephantiasis (nonfilarial) I89.0
arabicum —*see* Infestation, filarial
bancroftian B74.0
congenital (any site) (hereditary) Q82.0
due to
Brugia (malayi) B74.1
timori B74.2
mastectomy I97.2
Wuchereria (bancrofti) B74.0
eyelid H02.859
left H02.856
lower H02.855
upper H02.854
right H02.853
lower H02.852
upper H02.851
filarial, filariensis —*see* Infestation, filarial
glandular I89.0
graecorum A30.9
lymphangiectatic I89.0
lymphatic vessel I89.0
due to mastectomy I97.2
scrotum (nonfilarial) I89.0
streptococcal I89.0
surgical I97.89
postmastectomy I97.2
telangiectodes I89.0
vulva (nonfilarial) N90.89
Elevated, elevation
antibody titer R76.0
basal metabolic rate R94.8
blood pressure —*see also* Hypertension
reading (incidental) (isolated) (nonspecific),
no diagnosis of hypertension R03.0
blood sugar R73.9
body temperature (of unknown origin) R50.9
C-reactive protein (CRP) R79.82
cancer antigen 125 [CA 125] R97.1
carcinoembryonic antigen [CEA] R97.0
cholesterol E78.00
with high triglycerides E78.2
conjugate, eye H51.0
diaphragm, congenital Q79.1
erythrocyte sedimentation rate R70.0
fasting glucose R73.01
fasting triglycerides E78.1
finding on laboratory examination —*see*
Findings, abnormal, inconclusive,
without diagnosis, by type of exam
GFR (glomerular filtration rate) —*see*
Findings, abnormal, inconclusive,
without diagnosis, by type of exam
glucose tolerance (oral) R73.02
immunoglobulin level R76.8
indoleacetic acid R82.5
lactic acid dehydrogenase (LDH) level R74.0
leukocytes D72.829
➠lipoprotein a (Lp(a)) level E78.41

Elevated, elevation *(Continued)*
liver function
study R94.5
test R79.89
alkaline phosphatase R74.8
aminotransferase R74.0
bilirubin R17
hepatic enzyme R74.8
lactate dehydrogenase R74.0
▶(Lp(a)) (lipoprotein(a)) E78.41
lymphocytes D72.820
prostate specific antigen [PSA] R97.20
Rh titer —*see* Complication(s), transfusion,
incompatibility reaction, Rh (factor)
scapula, congenital Q74.0
sedimentation rate R70.0
SGOT R74.0
SGPT R74.0
transaminase level R74.0
triglycerides E78.1
with high cholesterol E78.2
tumor associated antigens [TAA] NEC R97.8
tumor specific antigens [TSA] NEC R97.8
urine level of
17-ketosteroids R82.5
catecholamine R82.5
indoleacetic acid R82.5
steroids R82.5
vanillylmandelic acid (VMA) R82.5
venous pressure I87.8
white blood cell count D72.829
specified NEC D72.828
Elliptocytosis (congenital) (hereditary) D58.1
Hb C (disease) D58.1
hemoglobin disease D58.1
sickle-cell (disease) D57.8-●
trait D57.3
Ellison-Zollinger syndrome E16.4
Ellis-van Creveld syndrome
(chondroectodermal dysplasia) Q77.6
Elongated, elongation (congenital) —*see also*
Distortion
bone Q79.9
cervix (uteri) Q51.828
acquired N88.4
hypertrophic N88.4
colon Q43.8
common bile duct Q44.5
cystic duct Q44.5
frenulum, penis Q55.69
labia minora (acquired) N90.69
ligamentum patellae Q74.1
petiolus (epiglottidis) Q31.8
tooth, teeth K00.2
uvula Q38.6
Eltor cholera A00.1
Emaciation (due to malnutrition) E41
Embadomoniasis A07.8
Embedded tooth, teeth K01.0
root only K08.3
Embolic —*see* condition
Embolism (multiple) (paradoxical) I74.9
air (any site) (traumatic) T79.0
following
abortion —*see* Abortion by type
complicated by embolism
ectopic pregnancy O08.2
infusion, therapeutic injection or
transfusion T80.0
molar pregnancy O08.2
procedure NEC
artery T81.719
mesenteric T81.710
renal T81.711
specified NEC T81.718
vein T81.72
in pregnancy, childbirth or puerperium —
see Embolism, obstetric
amniotic fluid (pulmonary) —*see also*
Embolism, obstetric
following
abortion —*see* Abortion by type
complicated by embolism

Embolism *(Continued)*
  amniotic fluid *(Continued)*
    following *(Continued)*
      ectopic pregnancy O08.2
      molar pregnancy O08.2
  aorta, aortic I74.10
    abdominal I74.09
      saddle I74.01
    bifurcation I74.09
    saddle I74.01
    thoracic I74.11
  artery I74.9
    auditory, internal I65.8
    basilar —*see* Occlusion, artery, basilar
    carotid (common) (internal) —*see*
      Occlusion, artery, carotid
    cerebellar (anterior inferior) (posterior
      inferior) (superior) I66.3
    cerebral —*see* Occlusion, artery, cerebral
    choroidal (anterior) I65.8
    communicating posterior I65.8
    coronary —*see also* Infarct, myocardium
      not resulting in infarction I24.0
    extremity I74.4
      lower I74.3
      upper I74.2
    hypophyseal I65.8
    iliac I74.5
    limb I74.4
      lower I74.3
      upper I74.2
    mesenteric (with gangrene) —*see also*
      Ischemia, intestine, acute K55.09
    ophthalmic —*see* Occlusion, artery, retina
    peripheral I74.4
    pontine I65.8
    precerebral —*see* Occlusion, artery,
      precerebral
    pulmonary —*see* Embolism, pulmonary
    renal N28.0
    retinal —*see* Occlusion, artery, retina
    septic I76
    specified NEC I74.8
    vertebral —*see* Occlusion, artery, vertebral
  basilar (artery) I65.1
  blood clot
    following
      abortion —*see* Abortion by type
        complicated by embolism
      ectopic or molar pregnancy O08.2
    in pregnancy, childbirth or puerperium —
      see Embolism, obstetric
  brain —*see also* Occlusion, artery, cerebral
    following
      abortion —*see* Abortion by type
        complicated by embolism
      ectopic or molar pregnancy O08.2
    puerperal, postpartum, childbirth —*see*
      Embolism, obstetric
  capillary I78.8
  cardiac —*see also* Infarct, myocardium
    not resulting in infarction I51.3
  carotid (artery) (common) (internal) —*see*
    Occlusion, artery, carotid
  cavernous sinus (venous) —*see* Embolism,
    intracranial venous sinus
  cerebral —*see* Occlusion, artery, cerebral
  cholesterol —*see* Atheroembolism
  coronary (artery or vein) (systemic) —*see*
    Occlusion, coronary
  due to device, implant or graft —*see also*
    Complications, by site and type,
    specified NEC
    arterial graft NEC T82.818
    breast (implant) T85.818
    catheter NEC T85.818
      dialysis (renal) T82.818
        intraperitoneal T85.818
      infusion NEC T82.818
        spinal (epidural) (subdural) T85.810
      urinary (indwelling) T83.81

Embolism *(Continued)*
  due to device, implant or graft *(Continued)*
    electronic (electrode) (pulse generator)
      (stimulator)
      bone T84.81
      cardiac T82.817
      nervous system (brain) (peripheral
        nerve) (spinal) T85.810
      urinary T83.81
    fixation, internal (orthopedic) NEC T84.81
    gastrointestinal (bile duct) (esophagus)
      T85.818
    genital NEC T83.81
    heart (graft) (valve) T82.817
    joint prosthesis T84.81
    ocular (corneal graft) (orbital implant)
      T85.818
    orthopedic (bone graft) NEC T86.838
    specified NEC T85.818
    urinary (graft) NEC T83.81
    vascular NEC T82.818
    ventricular intracranial shunt T85.810
  extremities
    lower —*see* Embolism, vein, lower
      extremity
      arterial I74.3
    upper I74.2
  eye H34.9
  fat (cerebral) (pulmonary) (systemic) T79.1
    complicating delivery —*see* Embolism,
      obstetric
    following
      abortion —*see* Abortion by type
        complicated by embolism
      ectopic or molar pregnancy O08.2
  following
    abortion —*see* Abortion by type
      complicated by embolism
    ectopic or molar pregnancy O08.2
    infusion, therapeutic injection or
      transfusion
      air T80.0
  heart (fatty) —*see also* Infarct, myocardium
    not resulting in infarction I51.3
  hepatic (vein) I82.0
  in pregnancy, childbirth or puerperium —*see*
    Embolism, obstetric
  intestine (artery) (vein) (with gangrene) —*see*
    also Ischemia, intestine, acute K55.039
  intracranial —*see also* Occlusion, artery,
    cerebral
    venous sinus (any) G08
      nonpyogenic I67.6
  intraspinal venous sinuses or veins G08
    nonpyogenic G95.19
  kidney (artery) N28.0
  lateral sinus (venous) —*see* Embolism,
    intracranial, venous sinus
  leg —*see* Embolism, vein, lower extremity
    arterial I74.3
  longitudinal sinus (venous) —*see* Embolism,
    intracranial, venous sinus
  lung (massive) —*see* Embolism, pulmonary
  meninges I66.8
  mesenteric (artery) (vein) (with gangrene) —
    see also Ischemia, intestine, acute
    K55.059
  obstetric (in) (pulmonary)
    childbirth O88.22
      air O88.02
      amniotic fluid O88.12
      blood clot O88.22
      fat O88.82
      pyemic O88.32
      septic O88.32
      specified type NEC O88.82
    pregnancy O88.21-•
      air O88.01-•
      amniotic fluid O88.11-•
      blood clot O88.21-•
      fat O88.81-•

Embolism *(Continued)*
  obstetric *(Continued)*
    pregnancy *(Continued)*
      pyemic O88.31-•
      septic O88.31-•
      specified type NEC O88.81-•
    puerperal O88.23
      air O88.03
      amniotic fluid O88.13
      blood clot O88.23
      fat O88.83
      pyemic O88.33
      septic O88.33
      specified type NEC O88.83
  ophthalmic —*see* Occlusion, artery, retina
  penis N48.81
  peripheral artery NOS I74.4
  pituitary E23.6
  popliteal (artery) I74.3
  portal (vein) I81
  postoperative, postprocedural
    artery T81.719
      mesenteric T81.710
      renal T81.711
      specified NEC T81.718
    vein T81.72
  precerebral artery —*see* Occlusion, artery,
    precerebral
  puerperal —*see* Embolism, obstetric
  pulmonary (acute) (artery) (vein) I26.99
    with acute cor pulmonale I26.09
    chronic I27.82
    following
      abortion —*see* Abortion by type
        complicated by embolism
      ectopic or molar pregnancy O08.2
    healed or old Z86.711
    in pregnancy, childbirth or puerperium —
      see Embolism, obstetric
    personal history of Z86.711
    saddle I26.92
      with acute cor pulmonale I26.02
    septic I26.90
      with acute cor pulmonale I26.01
  pyemic (multiple) I76
    following
      abortion —*see* Abortion by type
        complicated by embolism
      ectopic or molar pregnancy O08.2
    Hemophilus influenzae A41.3
    pneumococcal A40.3
      with pneumonia J13
    puerperal, postpartum, childbirth (any
      organism) —*see* Embolism, obstetric
    specified organism NEC A41.89
    staphylococcal A41.2
    streptococcal A40.9
  renal (artery) N28.0
    vein I82.3
  retina, retinal —*see* Occlusion, artery,
    retina
  saddle
    abdominal aorta I74.01
    pulmonary artery I26.92
      with acute cor pulmonale I26.02
  septic (arterial) I76
    complicating abortion —*see* Abortion, by
      type, complicated by, embolism
  sinus —*see* Embolism, intracranial, venous
    sinus
  soap complicating abortion —*see* Abortion,
    by type, complicated by, embolism
  spinal cord G95.19
    pyogenic origin G06.1
  spleen, splenic (artery) I74.8
  upper extremity I74.2
  vein (acute) I82.90
    antecubital I82.61-•
      chronic I82.71-•
    axillary I82.A1-•
      chronic I82.A2-•

▶ New   ⇒ Revised   ~~deleted~~ Deleted   • Use Additional Character(s)

Embolism *(Continued)*
  vein *(Continued)*
    basilic I82.61-•
      chronic I82.71-•
    brachial I82.62-•
      chronic I82.72-•
    brachiocephalic (innominate) I82.290
      chronic I82.291
    cephalic I82.61-•
      chronic I82.71-•
    chronic I82.91
    deep (DVT) I82.40-•
      calf I82.4Z-•
        chronic I82.5Z-•
      lower leg I82.4Z-•
        chronic I82.5Z-•
      thigh I82.4Y-•
        chronic I82.5Y-•
      upper leg I82.4Y
        chronic I82.5y--•
    femoral I82.41-•
      chronic I82.51-•
    iliac (iliofemoral) I82.42-•
      chronic I82.52-•
    innominate I82.290
      chronic I82.291
    internal jugular I82.C1-•
      chronic I82.C2-•
    lower extremity
      deep I82.40-•
        chronic I82.50-•
        specified NEC I82.49-•
          chronic NEC I82.59-•
      distal
        deep I82.4Z-•
      proximal
        deep I82.4Y-•
          chronic I82.5Y-•
      superficial I82.81-•
    popliteal I82.43-•
      chronic I82.53-•
    radial I82.62-•
      chronic I82.72-•
    renal I82.3
    saphenous (greater) (lesser) I82.81-•
    specified NEC I82.890
      chronic NEC I82.891
    subclavian I82.B1-•
      chronic I82.B2-•
    thoracic NEC I82.290
      chronic I82.291
    tibial I82.44-•
      chronic I82.54-•
    ulnar I82.62-•
      chronic I82.72-•
    upper extremity I82.60-•
      chronic I82.70-•
      deep I82.62-•
        chronic I82.72-•
      superficial I82.61-•
        chronic I82.71-•
  vena cava
    inferior (acute) I82.220
      chronic I82.221
    superior (acute) I82.210
      chronic I82.211
  venous sinus G08
  vessels of brain —*see* Occlusion, artery,
    cerebral
Embolus —*see* Embolism
Embryoma —*see also* Neoplasm, uncertain
  behavior, by site
  benign —*see* Neoplasm, benign, by site
  kidney C64.-•
  liver C22.0
  malignant —*see also* Neoplasm, malignant,
    by site
    kidney C64.-•
    liver C22.0
    testis C62.9-•
      descended (scrotal) C62.1-•
      undescended C62.0-•

Embryoma *(Continued)*
  testis C62.9-•
    descended (scrotal) C62.1-•
    undescended C62.0-•
Embryonic
  circulation Q28.9
  heart Q28.9
  vas deferens Q55.4
Embryopathia NOS Q89.9
Embryotoxon Q13.4
Emesis —*see* Vomiting
Emotional lability R45.86
Emotionality, pathological F60.3
Emotogenic disease —*see* Disorder,
  psychogenic
Emphysema (atrophic) (bullous) (chronic)
  (interlobular) (lung) (obstructive)
  (pulmonary) (senile) (vesicular)
  J43.9
  cellular tissue (traumatic) T79.7
    surgical T81.82
  centrilobular J43.2
  compensatory J98.3
  congenital (interstitial) P25.0
  conjunctiva H11.89
  connective tissue (traumatic) T79.7
    surgical T81.82
  due to chemicals, gases, fumes or vapors
    J68.4
  eyelid(s) —*see* Disorder, eyelid, specified type
    NEC
    surgical T81.82
    traumatic T79.7
  interstitial J98.2
    congenital P25.0
    perinatal period P25.0
  laminated tissue T79.7
    surgical T81.82
  mediastinal J98.2
    newborn P25.2
  orbit, orbital —*see* Disorder, orbit, specified
    type NEC
  panacinar J43.1
  panlobular J43.1
  specified NEC J43.8
  subcutaneous (traumatic) T79.7
    nontraumatic J98.2
    postprocedural T81.82
    surgical T81.82
  surgical T81.82
  thymus (gland) (congenital) E32.8
  traumatic (subcutaneous) T79.7
  unilateral J43.0
Empty nest syndrome Z60.0
Empyema (acute) (chest) (double) (pleura)
  (supradiaphragmatic) (thorax) J86.9
  with fistula J86.0
  accessory sinus (chronic) —*see* Sinusitis
  antrum (chronic) —*see* Sinusitis, maxillary
  brain (any part) —*see* Abscess, brain
  ethmoidal (chronic) (sinus) —*see* Sinusitis,
    ethmoidal
  extradural —*see* Abscess, extradural
  frontal (chronic) (sinus) —*see* Sinusitis,
    frontal
  gallbladder K81.0
  mastoid (process) (acute) —*see* Mastoiditis,
    acute
  maxilla, maxillary M27.2
    sinus (chronic) —*see* Sinusitis,
      maxillary
  nasal sinus (chronic) —*see* Sinusitis
  sinus (accessory) (chronic) (nasal) —*see*
    Sinusitis
  sphenoidal (sinus) (chronic) —*see* Sinusitis,
    sphenoidal
  subarachnoid —*see* Abscess, extradural
  subdural —*see* Abscess, subdural
  tuberculous A15.6
  ureter —*see* Ureteritis
  ventricular —*see* Abscess, brain

En coup de sabre lesion L94.1
Enamel pearls K00.2
Enameloma K00.2
Enanthema, viral B09
Encephalitis (chronic) (hemorrhagic)
  (idiopathic) (nonepidemic) (spurious)
  (subacute) G04.90
  acute —*see also* Encephalitis, viral A86
    disseminated G04.00
      infectious G04.01
      noninfectious G04.81
      postimmunization (postvaccination)
        G04.02
      postinfectious G04.01
    inclusion body A85.8
    necrotizing hemorrhagic G04.30
      postimmunization G04.32
      postinfectious G04.31
      specified NEC G04.39
  arboviral, arbovirus NEC A85.2
  arthropod-borne NEC (viral) A85.2
  Australian A83.4
  California (virus) A83.5
  Central European (tick-borne) A84.1
  Czechoslovakian A84.1
  Dawson's (inclusion body) A81.1
  diffuse sclerosing A81.1
  disseminated, acute G04.00
  due to
    cat scratch disease A28.1
    human immunodeficiency virus (HIV)
      disease B20 *[G05.3]*
    malaria —*see* Malaria
    rickettsiosis —*see* Rickettsiosis
    smallpox inoculation G04.02
    typhus —*see* Typhus
  Eastern equine A83.2
  endemic (viral) A86
  epidemic NEC (viral) A86
  equine (acute) (infectious) (viral) A83.9
    Eastern A83.2
    Venezuelan A92.2
    Western A83.1
  Far Eastern (tick-borne) A84.0
  following vaccination or other immunization
    procedure G04.02
  herpes zoster B02.0
  herpesviral B00.4
    due to herpesvirus 6 B10.01
    due to herpesvirus 7 B10.09
    specified NEC B10.09
  Ilheus (virus) A83.8
  in (due to)
    actinomycosis A42.82
    adenovirus A85.1
    African trypanosomiasis B56.9 *[G05.3]*
    Chagas' disease (chronic) B57.42
    cytomegalovirus B25.8
    enterovirus A85.0
    herpes (simplex) virus B00.4
      due to herpesvirus 6 B10.01
      due to herpesvirus 7 B10.09
      specified NEC B10.09
    infectious disease NEC B99 *[G05.3]*
    influenza —*see* Influenza, with,
      encephalopathy
    listeriosis A32.12
    measles B05.0
    mumps B26.2
    naegleriasis B60.2
    parasitic disease NEC B89 *[G05.3]*
    poliovirus A80.9 *[G05.3]*
    rubella B06.01
    syphilis
      congenital A50.42
      late A52.14
    systemic lupus erythematosus M32.19
    toxoplasmosis (acquired) B58.2
      congenital P37.1
    tuberculosis A17.82
    zoster B02.0

Encephalitis *(Continued)*
inclusion body A81.1
infectious (acute) (virus) NEC A86
Japanese (B type) A83.0
La Crosse A83.5
lead —*see* Poisoning, lead
lethargica (acute) (infectious) A85.8
louping ill A84.8
lupus erythematosus, systemic M32.19
lymphatica A87.2
Mengo A85.8
meningococcal A39.81
Murray Valley A83.4
otitic NEC H66.40 *[G05.3]*
parasitic NOS B71.9
periaxial G37.0
periaxialis (concentrica) (diffuse) G37.5
postchickenpox B01.11
postexanthematous NEC B09
postimmunization G04.02
postinfectious NEC G04.01
postmeasles B05.0
postvaccinal G04.02
postvaricella B01.11
postviral NEC A86
Powassan A84.8
Rasmussen G04.81
Rio Bravo A85.8
Russian
autumnal A83.0
spring-summer (taiga) A84.0
saturnine —*see* Poisoning, lead
specified NEC G04.81
St. Louis A83.3
subacute sclerosing A81.1
summer A83.0
suppurative G04.81
tick-borne A84.9
Torula, torular (cryptococcal) B45.1
toxic NEC G92
trichinosis B75 *[G05.3]*
type
B A83.0
C A83.3
van Bogaert's A81.1
Venezuelan equine A92.2
Vienna A85.8
viral, virus A86
arthropod-borne NEC A85.2
mosquito-borne A83.9
Australian X disease A83.4
California virus A83.5
Eastern equine A83.2
Japanese (B type) A83.0
Murray Valley A83.4
specified NEC A83.8
St. Louis A83.3
type B A83.0
type C A83.3
Western equine A83.1
tick-borne A84.9
biundulant A84.1
central European A84.1
Czechoslovakian A84.1
diphasic meningoencephalitis A84.1
Far Eastern A84.0
Russian spring-summer (taiga)
A84.0
specified NEC A84.8
specified type NEC A85.8
Western equine A83.1
Encephalocele Q01.9
frontal Q01.0
nasofrontal Q01.1
occipital Q01.2
specified NEC Q01.8
Encephalocystocele —*see* Encephalocele
Encephaloduroarteriomyosynangiosis
(EDAMS) I67.5
Encephalomalacia (brain) (cerebellar)
(cerebral) —*see* Softening, brain

Encephalomeningitis —*see*
Meningoencephalitis
Encephalomeningocele —*see* Encephalocele
Encephalomeningomyelitis —*see*
Meningoencephalitis
Encephalomyelitis —*see also* Encephalitis
G04.90
acute disseminated G04.00
infectious G04.01
noninfectious G04.81
postimmunization G04.02
postinfectious G04.01
acute necrotizing hemorrhagic G04.30
postimmunization G04.32
postinfectious G04.31
specified NEC G04.39
benign myalgic G93.3
equine A83.9
Eastern A83.2
Venezuelan A92.2
Western A83.1
in diseases classified elsewhere G05.3
myalgic, benign G93.3
postchickenpox B01.11
postinfectious NEC G04.01
postmeasles B05.0
postvaccinal G04.02
postvaricella B01.11
rubella B06.01
specified NEC G04.81
Venezuelan equine A92.2
Encephalomyelocele —*see* Encephalocele
Encephalomyelomeningitis —*see*
Meningoencephalitis
Encephalomyelopathy G96.9
Encephalomyeloradiculitis (acute) G61.0
Encephalomyeloradiculoneuritis (acute)
(Guillain-Barré) G61.0
Encephalomyeloradiculopathy G96.9
Encephalopathia hyperbilirubinemica,
newborn P57.9
due to isoimmunization (conditions in P55)
P57.0
Encephalopathy (acute) G93.40
acute necrotizing hemorrhagic G04.30
postimmunization G04.32
postinfectious G04.31
specified NEC G04.39
alcoholic G31.2
anoxic —*see* Damage, brain, anoxic
arteriosclerotic I67.2
centrolobar progressive (Schilder) G37.0
congenital Q07.9
degenerative, in specified disease NEC
G32.89
due to
drugs (*see also* Table of Drugs and
Chemicals) G92
demyelinating callosal G37.1
hepatic —*see* Failure, hepatic
hyperbilirubinemic, newborn P57.9
due to isoimmunization (conditions in P55)
P57.0
hypertensive I67.4
hypoglycemic E16.2
hypoxic —*see* Damage, brain, anoxic
hypoxic ischemic P91.60
mild P91.61
moderate P91.62
severe P91.63
in (due to) (with)
birth injury P11.1
hyperinsulinism E16.1 *[G94]*
influenza —*see* Influenza, with,
encephalopathy
lack of vitamin (*see also* Deficiency, vitamin)
E56.9 *[G32.89]*
neoplastic disease (*see also* Neoplasm)
D49.9 *[G13.1]*
serum (*see also* Reaction, serum) T80.69
syphilis A52.17

Encephalopathy *(Continued)*
in *(Continued)*
trauma (postconcussional) F07.81
current injury —*see* Injury, intracranial
vaccination G04.02
lead —*see* Poisoning, lead
metabolic G93.41
drug induced G92
toxic G92
myoclonic, early, symptomatic —*see* Epilepsy,
generalized, specified NEC
necrotizing, subacute (Leigh) G31.82
neonatal P91.819
in diseases classified elsewhere P91.811
pellagrous E52 *[G32.89]*
portosystemic —*see* Failure, hepatic
postcontusional F07.81
current injury —*see* Injury, intracranial,
diffuse
posthypoglycemic (coma) E16.1 *[G94]*
postradiation G93.89
saturnine —*see* Poisoning, lead
septic G93.41
specified NEC G93.49
spongioform, subacute (viral) A81.09
toxic G92
metabolic G92
traumatic (postconcussional) F07.81
current injury —*see* Injury, intracranial
vitamin B deficiency NEC E53.9 *[G32.89]*
vitamin B1 E51.2
Wernicke's E51.2
Encephalorrhagia —*see* Hemorrhage,
intracranial, intracerebral
Encephalosis, posttraumatic F07.81
Enchondroma —*see also* Neoplasm, bone,
benign
Enchondromatosis (cartilaginous) (multiple)
Q78.4
Encopresis R15.9
functional F98.1
nonorganic origin F98.1
psychogenic F98.1
Encounter (with health service) (for) Z76.89
adjustment and management (of)
breast implant Z45.81
implanted device NEC Z45.89
myringotomy device (stent) (tube) Z45.82
administrative purpose only Z02.9
examination for
adoption Z02.82
armed forces Z02.3
disability determination Z02.71
driving license Z02.4
employment Z02.1
insurance Z02.6
medical certificate NEC Z02.79
paternity testing Z02.81
residential institution admission Z02.2
school admission Z02.0
sports Z02.5
specified reason NEC Z02.89
aftercare —*see* Aftercare
antenatal screening Z36.9
cervical length Z36.86
chromosomal anomalies Z36.0
congenital cardiac abnormalities Z36.83
elevated maternal serum alphafetoprotein
level Z36.1
fetal growth retardation Z36.4
fetal lung maturity Z36.84
fetal macrosomia Z36.88
hydrops fetalis Z36.81
intrauterine growth restriction (IUGR)/
small-for-dates Z36.4
isoimmunization Z36.5
large-for-dates Z36.88
malformations Z36.3
non-visualized anatomy on a previous scan
Z36.2
nuchal translucency Z36.82

▶ New ⇒ Revised ~~deleted~~ Deleted ● Use Additional Character(s)

Encounter *(Continued)*
  antenatal screening *(Continued)*
    raised alphafetoprotein level Z36.1
    risk of pre-term labor Z36.86
    specified type NEC Z36.89
    specified follow-up NEC Z36.2
    specified genetic defects NEC Z36.8A
    Streptococcus B Z36.85
    suspected anomaly Z36.3
    uncertain dates Z36.87
  assisted reproductive fertility procedure cycle Z31.83
  blood typing Z01.83
    Rh typing Z01.83
  breast augmentation or reduction Z41.1
  breast implant exchange (different material) (different size) Z45.81
  breast reconstruction following mastectomy Z42.1
  check-up —*see* Examination
  chemotherapy for neoplasm Z51.11
  colonoscopy, screening Z12.11
  counseling —*see* Counseling
  delivery, full-term, uncomplicated O80
    cesarean, without indication O82
  desensitization to allergens Z51.6
  ear piercing Z41.3
  examination —*see* Examination
  expectant parent(s) (adoptive) pre-birth pediatrician visit Z76.81
  fertility preservation procedure (prior to cancer therapy) (prior to removal of gonads) Z31.84
  fitting (of) —*see* Fitting (and adjustment) (of)
  genetic
    counseling
      nonprocreative Z71.83
      procreative Z31.5
    testing —*see* Test, genetic
  hearing conservation and treatment Z01.12
  immunotherapy for neoplasm Z51.12
  in vitro fertilization cycle Z31.83
  instruction (in)
    child care (postpartal) (prenatal) Z32.3
    childbirth Z32.2
    natural family planning
      procreative Z31.61
      to avoid pregnancy Z30.02
  insulin pump titration Z46.81
  joint prosthesis insertion following prior explantation of joint prosthesis (staged procedure)
    hip Z47.32
    knee Z47.33
    shoulder Z47.31
  laboratory (as part of a general medical examination) Z00.00
    with abnormal findings Z00.01
  mental health services (for)
    abuse NEC
      perpetrator Z69.82
      victim Z69.81
    child abuse
      nonparental
        perpetrator Z69.021
        victim Z69.020
      parental
        perpetrator Z69.011
        victim Z69.010
    child neglect
      nonparental
        perpetrator Z69.021
        victim Z69.020
      parental
        perpetrator Z69.011
        victim Z69.010
    child psychological abuse
      nonparental
        perpetrator Z69.021
        victim Z69.020

Encounter *(Continued)*
  mental health services *(Continued)*
    child psychological abuse *(Continued)*
      parental
        perpetrator Z69.011
        victim Z69.010
    child sexual abuse
      nonparental
        perpetrator Z69.021
        victim Z69.020
      parental
        perpetrator Z69.011
        victim Z69.010
    non-spousal adult abuse (perpetrator) (victim) Z69.81
    spousal or partner
      abuse
        perpetrator Z69.12
        victim Z69.11
      neglect
        perpetrator Z69.12
        victim Z69.11
      psychological abuse
        perpetrator Z69.12
        victim Z69.11
      violence
        perpetrator (physical) (sexual) Z69.12
        victim (physical) Z69.11
          sexual Z69.81
  observation (for) (ruled out)
    exposure to (suspected)
      anthrax Z03.810
      biological agent NEC Z03.818
  pediatrician visit, by expectant parent(s) (adoptive) Z76.81
  placental sample (taken vaginally) —*see also* Encounter, antenatal screening Z36.9
  plastic and reconstructive surgery following medical procedure or healed injury NEC Z42.8
  pregnancy
    supervision of —*see* Pregnancy, supervision of
    test Z32.00
      result negative Z32.02
      result positive Z32.01
  procreative management and counseling for gestational carrier Z31.7
  prophylactic measures Z29.9
    antivenin Z29.12
    fluoride administration Z29.3
    immunotherapy for respiratory syncytial virus (RSV) Z29.11
    rabies immune globin Z29.14
    Rho (D) immune globulin Z29.13
    specified NEC Z29.8
  radiation therapy (antineoplastic) Z51.0
  radiological (as part of a general medical examination) Z00.00
    with abnormal findings Z00.01
  reconstructive surgery following medical procedure or healed injury NEC Z42.8
  removal (of) —*see also* Removal
    artificial
      arm Z44.00-●
        complete Z44.01-●
        partial Z44.02-●
      eye Z44.2-●
      leg Z44.10-●
        complete Z44.11-●
        partial Z44.12-●
    breast implant Z45.81
      tissue expander (without synchronous insertion of permanent implant) Z45.81
    device Z46.9
      specified NEC Z46.89
    external
      fixation device — code to fracture with seventh character D

Encounter *(Continued)*
  removal *(Continued)*
    external *(Continued)*
      prosthesis, prosthetic device Z44.9
        breast Z44.3-●
        specified NEC Z44.8
    implanted device NEC Z45.89
    insulin pump Z46.81
    internal fixation device Z47.2
    myringotomy device (stent) (tube) Z45.82
    nervous system device NEC Z46.2
      brain neuropacemaker Z46.2
      visual substitution device Z46.2
        implanted Z45.31
    non-vascular catheter Z46.82
    orthodontic device Z46.4
    stent
      ureteral Z46.6
    urinary device Z46.6
  repeat cervical smear to confirm findings of recent normal smear following initial abnormal smear Z01.42
  respirator [ventilator] use during power failure (Z99.12)
  Rh typing Z01.83
  screening —*see* Screening
  specified NEC Z76.89
  sterilization Z30.2
  suspected condition, ruled out
    amniotic cavity and membrane Z03.71
    cervical shortening Z03.75
    fetal anomaly Z03.73
    fetal growth Z03.74
    maternal and fetal conditions NEC Z03.79
    oligohydramnios Z03.71
    placental problem Z03.72
    polyhydramnios Z03.71
  suspected exposure (to), ruled out
    anthrax Z03.810
    biological agents NEC Z03.818
  termination of pregnancy, elective Z33.2
  testing —*see* Test
  therapeutic drug level monitoring Z51.81
  titration, insulin pump Z46.81
  to determine fetal viability of pregnancy O36.80
  training
    insulin pump Z46.81
  X-ray of chest (as part of a general medical examination Z00.00)
    with abnormal findings Z00.01
Encystment —*see* Cyst
Endarteritis (bacterial, subacute) (infective) I77.6
  brain I67.7
  cerebral or cerebrospinal I67.7
  deformans —*see* Arteriosclerosis
  embolic —*see* Embolism
  obliterans —*see also* Arteriosclerosis
    pulmonary I28.8
  pulmonary I28.8
  retina —*see* Vasculitis, retina
  senile —*see* Arteriosclerosis
  syphilitic A52.09
    brain or cerebral A52.04
    congenital A50.54 [*I79.8*]
  tuberculous A18.89
Endemic —*see* condition
Endocarditis (chronic) (marantic) (nonbacterial) (thrombotic) (valvular) I38
  with rheumatic fever (conditions in I00)
    active —*see* Endocarditis, acute, rheumatic
    inactive or quiescent (with chorea) I09.1
  acute or subacute I33.9
    infective I33.0
    rheumatic (aortic) (mitral) (pulmonary) (tricuspid) I01.1
      with chorea (acute) (rheumatic) (Sydenham's) I02.0

Endocarditis *(Continued)*
  aortic (heart) (nonrheumatic) (valve) I35.8
    with
      mitral disease I08.0
        with tricuspid (valve) disease I08.3
        active or acute I01.1
          with chorea (acute) (rheumatic)
            (Sydenham's) I02.0
        rheumatic fever (conditions in I00)
          active —*see* Endocarditis, acute,
            rheumatic
          inactive or quiescent (with chorea)
            I06.9
        tricuspid (valve) disease I08.2
          with mitral (valve) disease I08.3
    acute or subacute I33.9
    arteriosclerotic I35.8
    rheumatic I06.9
      with mitral disease I08.0
        with tricuspid (valve) disease I08.3
        active or acute I01.1
          with chorea (acute) (rheumatic)
            (Sydenham's) I02.0
      active or acute I01.1
        with chorea (acute) (rheumatic)
          (Sydenham's) I02.0
      specified NEC I06.8
    specified cause NEC I35.8
    syphilitic A52.03
  arteriosclerotic I38
  atypical verrucous (Libman-Sacks) M32.11
  bacterial (acute) (any valve) (subacute) I33.0
  candidal B37.6
  congenital Q24.8
  constrictive I33.0
  Coxiella burnetii A78 *[I39]*
  Coxsackie B33.21
  due to
    prosthetic cardiac valve T82.6
    Q fever A78 *[I39]*
    Serratia marcescens I33.0
    typhoid (fever) A01.02
  gonococcal A54.83
  infectious or infective (acute) (any valve)
    (subacute) I33.0
  lenta (acute) (any valve) (subacute) I33.0
  Libman-Sacks M32.11
  listerial A32.82
  Löffler's I42.3
  malignant (acute) (any valve) (subacute) I33.0
  meningococcal A39.51
  mitral (chronic) (double) (fibroid) (heart)
    (inactive) (valve) (with chorea) I05.9
    with
      aortic (valve) disease I08.0
        with tricuspid (valve) disease I08.3
        active or acute I01.1
          with chorea (acute) (rheumatic)
            (Sydenham's) I02.0
        rheumatic fever (conditions in I00)
          active —*see* Endocarditis, acute,
            rheumatic
          inactive or quiescent (with chorea)
            I05.9
      tricuspid (valve) disease I08.1
        with aortic (valve) disease I08.3
    active or acute I01.1
      with chorea (acute) (rheumatic)
        (Sydenham's) I02.0
    bacterial I33.0
    arteriosclerotic I34.8
    nonrheumatic I34.8
      acute or subacute I33.9
    specified NEC I05.8
  monilial B37.6
  multiple valves I08.9
    specified disorders I08.8
  mycotic (acute) (any valve) (subacute) I33.0
  pneumococcal (acute) (any valve) (subacute)
    I33.0
  pulmonary (chronic) (heart) (valve) I37.8

Endocarditis *(Continued)*
  pulmonary *(Continued)*
    with rheumatic fever (conditions in I00)
      active —*see* Endocarditis, acute,
        rheumatic
      inactive or quiescent (with chorea) I09.89
        with aortic, mitral or tricuspid disease
          I08.8
    acute or subacute I33.9
      rheumatic I01.1
        with chorea (acute) (rheumatic)
          (Sydenham's) I02.0
    arteriosclerotic I37.8
    congenital Q22.2
    rheumatic (chronic) (inactive) (with chorea)
      I09.89
      active or acute I01.1
        with chorea (acute) (rheumatic)
          (Sydenham's) I02.0
    syphilitic A52.03
  purulent (acute) (any valve) (subacute) I33.0
  Q fever A78 *[I39]*
  rheumatic (chronic) (inactive) (with chorea)
    I09.1
    active or acute (aortic) (mitral)
      (pulmonary) (tricuspid) I01.1
      with chorea (acute) (rheumatic)
        (Sydenham's) I02.0
  rheumatoid —*see* Rheumatoid, carditis
  septic (acute) (any valve) (subacute) I33.0
  streptococcal (acute) (any valve) (subacute)
    I33.0
  subacute —*see* Endocarditis, acute
  suppurative (acute) (any valve) (subacute)
    I33.0
  syphilitic A52.03
  toxic I33.9
  tricuspid (chronic) (heart) (inactive)
    (rheumatic) (valve) (with chorea) I07.9
    with
      aortic (valve) disease I08.2
        mitral (valve) disease I08.3
      mitral (valve) disease I08.1
        aortic (valve) disease I08.3
      rheumatic fever (conditions in I00)
        active —*see* Endocarditis, acute,
          rheumatic
        inactive or quiescent (with chorea)
          I07.8
    active or acute I01.1
      with chorea (acute) (rheumatic)
        (Sydenham's) I02.0
    arteriosclerotic I36.8
    nonrheumatic I36.8
      acute or subacute I33.9
    specified cause, except rheumatic I36.8
  tuberculous —*see* Tuberculosis, endocarditis
  typhoid A01.02
  ulcerative (acute) (any valve) (subacute) I33.0
  vegetative (acute) (any valve) (subacute) I33.0
  verrucous (atypical) (nonbacterial)
    (nonrheumatic) M32.11
Endocardium, endocardial —*see also* condition
  cushion defect Q21.2
Endocervicitis —*see also* Cervicitis
  due to intrauterine (contraceptive) device
    T83.69
  hyperplastic N72
Endocrine —*see* condition
Endocrinopathy, pluriglandular E31.9
Endodontic
  overfill M27.52
  underfill M27.53
Endodontitis K04.01
  irreversible K04.02
  reversible K04.01
Endomastoiditis —*see* Mastoiditis
Endometrioma N80.9
Endometriosis N80.9
  appendix N80.5
  bladder N80.8

Endometriosis *(Continued)*
  bowel N80.5
  broad ligament N80.3
  cervix N80.0
  colon N80.5
  cul-de-sac (Douglas') N80.3
  exocervix N80.0
  fallopian tube N80.2
  female genital organ NEC N80.8
  gallbladder N80.8
  in scar of skin N80.6
  internal N80.0
  intestine N80.5
  lung N80.8
  myometrium N80.0
  ovary N80.1
  parametrium N80.3
  pelvic peritoneum N80.3
  peritoneal (pelvic) N80.3
  rectovaginal septum N80.4
  rectum N80.5
  round ligament N80.3
  skin (scar) N80.6
  specified site NEC N80.8
  stromal D39.0
  thorax N80.8
  umbilicus N80.8
  uterus (internal) N80.0
  vagina N80.4
  vulva N80.8
Endometritis (decidual) (nonspecific) (purulent)
    (senile (atrophic) (suppurative) N71.9
  with ectopic pregnancy O08.0
  acute N71.0
  blenorrhagic (gonococcal) (acute) (chronic)
    A54.24
  cervix, cervical (with erosion or ectropion) —
    see also Cervicitis
    hyperplastic N72
  chlamydial A56.11
  chronic N71.1
  following
    abortion —*see* Abortion by type
      complicated by genital infection
    ectopic or molar pregnancy O08.0
  gonococcal, gonorrheal (acute) (chronic) A54.24
  hyperplastic —*see also* Hyperplasia,
      endometrial N85.00-•
    cervix N72
  puerperal, postpartum, childbirth O86.12
  subacute N71.0
  tuberculous A18.17
Endometrium —*see* condition
Endomyocardiopathy, South African I42.3
Endomyocarditis —*see* Endocarditis
Endomyofibrosis I42.3
Endomyometritis —*see* Endometritis
Endopericarditis —*see* Endocarditis
Endoperineuritis —*see* Disorder, nerve
Endophlebitis —*see* Phlebitis
Endophthalmia —*see* Endophthalmitis,
    purulent
Endophthalmitis (acute) (infective) (metastatic)
    (subacute) H44.009
  bleb associated H59.4 —*see also* Bleb,
      inflamed (infected), postprocedural
  gonorrheal A54.39
  in (due to)
    cysticercosis B69.1
    onchocerciasis B73.01
    toxocariasis B83.0
  panuveitis —*see* Panuveitis
  parasitic H44.12-•
  purulent H44.00-•
    panophthalmitis —*see* Panophthalmitis
    vitreous abscess H44.02-•
  specified NEC H44.19
  sympathetic —*see* Uveitis, sympathetic
Endosalpingioma D28.2
Endosalpingiosis N94.89
Endosteitis —*see* Osteomyelitis

▶ New   ⟾ Revised   ~~deleted~~ Deleted   • Use Additional Character(s)

Endothelioma, bone —*see* Neoplasm, bone, malignant
Endotheliosis (hemorrhagic infectional) D69.8
Endotoxemia — code to condition
Endotrachelitis —*see* Cervicitis
Engelmann (-Camurati) syndrome Q78.3
English disease —*see* Rickets
Engman's disease L30.3
Engorgement
   breast N64.59
      newborn P83.4
      puerperal, postpartum O92.79
   lung (passive) —*see* Edema, lung
   pulmonary (passive) —*see* Edema, lung
   stomach K31.89
   venous, retina —*see* Occlusion, retina, vein, engorgement
Enlargement, enlarged —*see also* Hypertrophy
   adenoids J35.2
      with tonsils J35.3
   alveolar ridge K08.89
      congenital —*see* Anomaly, alveolar
   apertures of diaphragm (congenital) Q79.1
   gingival K06.1
   heart, cardiac —*see* Hypertrophy, cardiac
   labium majus, childhood asymmetric (CALME) N90.61
   lacrimal gland, chronic H04.03-•
   liver —*see* Hypertrophy, liver
   lymph gland or node R59.9
      generalized R59.1
      localized R59.0
   orbit H05.34-•
   organ or site, congenital NEC —*see* Anomaly, by site
   parathyroid (gland) E21.0
   pituitary fossa R93.0
   prostate N40.0
      with lower urinary tract symptoms (LUTS) N40.1
      without lower urinary tract symptoms (LUTS) N40.0
   sella turcica R93.0
   spleen —*see* Splenomegaly
   thymus (gland) (congenital) E32.0
   thyroid (gland) —*see* Goiter
   tongue K14.8
   tonsils J35.1
      with adenoids J35.3
   uterus N85.2
   vestibular aqueduct Q16.5
Enophthalmos H05.40-•
   due to
      orbital tissue atrophy H05.41-•
      trauma or surgery H05.42-•
Enostosis M27.8
Entamebic, entamebiasis —*see* Amebiasis
Entanglement
   umbilical cord(s) O69.82
      with compression O69.2
      around neck (with compression) O69.81
         with compression O69.1
         without compression O69.81
      of twins in monoamniotic sac O69.2
      without compression O69.82
Enteralgia —*see* Pain, abdominal
Enteric —*see* condition
Enteritis (acute) (diarrheal) (hemorrhagic) (noninfective) K52.9
   adenovirus A08.2
   aertrycke infection A02.0
   allergic K52.29
      with
         eosinophilic gastritis or gastroenteritis K52.81
         food protein-induced enterocolitis syndrome K52.21
         food protein-induced enteropathy K52.22
      ▶FPIES K52.21

Enteritis *(Continued)*
   amebic (acute) A06.0
      with abscess —*see* Abscess, amebic
      chronic A06.1
         with abscess —*see* Abscess, amebic
         nondysenteric A06.2
      nondysenteric A06.2
   astrovirus A08.32
   bacillary NOS A03.9
   bacterial A04.9
      specified NEC A04.8
   calicivirus A08.31
   candidal B37.82
   Chilomastix A07.8
   choleriformis A00.1
   chronic (noninfectious) K52.9
      ulcerative —*see* Colitis, ulcerative
   cicatrizing (chronic) —*see* Enteritis, regional, small intestine
   Clostridium
      botulinum (food poisoning) A05.1
      difficile
         not specified as recurrent A04.72
         recurrent A04.71
   coccidial A07.3
   coxsackie virus A08.39
   dietetic —*see also* Enteritis, allergic K52.29
   drug-induced K52.1
   due to
      astrovirus A08.32
      calicivirus A08.31
      coxsackie virus A08.39
      drugs K52.1
      echovirus A08.39
      enterovirus NEC A08.39
      food hypersensitivity —*see also* Enteritis, allergic K52.29
      infectious organism (bacterial) (viral) —*see* Enteritis, infectious
      torovirus A08.39
      Yersinia enterocolitica A04.6
   echovirus A08.39
   eltor A00.1
   enterovirus NEC A08.39
   eosinophilic K52.81
   epidemic (infectious) A09
   fulminant —*see also* Ischemia, intestine, acute K55.019
   gangrenous —*see* Enteritis, infectious
   giardial A07.1
   infectious NOS A09
      due to
         adenovirus A08.2
         Aerobacter aerogenes A04.8
         Arizona (bacillus) A02.0
         bacteria NOS A04.9
            specified NEC A04.8
         Campylobacter A04.5
         Clostridium difficile
            not specified as recurrent A04.72
            recurrent A04.71
         Clostridium perfringens A04.8
         Enterobacter aerogenes A04.8
         enterovirus A08.39
         Escherichia coli A04.4
            enteroaggregative A04.4
            enterohemorrhagic A04.3
            enteroinvasive A04.2
            enteropathogenic A04.0
            enterotoxigenic A04.1
            specified NEC A04.4
         specified
            bacteria NEC A04.8
            virus NEC A08.39
         Staphylococcus A04.8
         virus NEC A08.4
            specified type NEC A08.39
         Yersinia enterocolitica A04.6
      specified organism NEC A08.8
   influenzal —*see* Influenza, with, digestive manifestations

Enteritis *(Continued)*
   ischemic K55.9
      acute —*see also* Ischemia, intestine, acute K55.019
      chronic K55.1
   microsporidial A07.8
   mucomembranous, myxomembranous —*see* Syndrome, irritable bowel
   mucous —*see* Syndrome, irritable bowel
   necroticans A05.2
   necrotizing of newborn —*see* Enterocolitis, necrotizing, in newborn
   neurogenic —*see* Syndrome, irritable bowel
   newborn necrotizing —*see* Enterocolitis, necrotizing, in newborn
   noninfectious K52.9
   norovirus A08.11
   parasitic NEC B82.9
   paratyphoid (fever) —*see* Fever, paratyphoid
   protozoal A07.9
      specified NEC A07.8
   radiation K52.0
   regional (of) K50.90
      with
         complication K50.919
            abscess K50.914
            fistula K50.913
            intestinal obstruction K50.912
            rectal bleeding K50.911
            specified complication NEC K50.918
      colon —*see* Enteritis, regional, large intestine
      duodenum —*see* Enteritis, regional, small intestine
      ileum —*see* Enteritis, regional, small intestine
      jejunum —*see* Enteritis, regional, small intestine
      large bowel —*see* Enteritis, regional, large intestine
      large intestine (colon) (rectum) K50.10
         with
            complication K50.119
               abscess K50.114
               fistula K50.113
               intestinal obstruction K50.112
               rectal bleeding K50.111
               small intestine (duodenum) (ileum) (jejunum) involvement K50.80
                  with
                     complication K50.819
                        abscess K50.814
                        fistula K50.813
                        intestinal obstruction K50.812
                        rectal bleeding K50.811
                        specified complication NEC K50.818
               specified complication NEC K50.118
      rectum —*see* Enteritis, regional, large intestine
      small intestine (duodenum) (ileum) (jejunum) K50.00
         with
            complication K50.019
               abscess K50.014
               fistula K50.013
               intestinal obstruction K50.012
               large intestine (colon) (rectum) involvement K50.80
                  with
                     complication K50.819
                        abscess K50.814
                        fistula K50.813
                        intestinal obstruction K50.812
                        rectal bleeding K50.811
                        specified complication NEC K50.818
               rectal bleeding K50.011
               specified complication NEC K50.018
   rotaviral A08.0

Enteritis *(Continued)*
　Salmonella, salmonellosis (arizonae)
　　(cholerae-suis) (enteritidis)
　　(typhimurium) A02.0
　segmental —see Enteritis, regional
　septic A09
　Shigella —see Infection, Shigella
　small round structured NEC A08.19
　spasmodic, spastic —see Syndrome, irritable
　　bowel
　staphylococcal A04.8
　　due to food A05.0
　torovirus A08.39
　toxic NEC K52.1
　　due to Clostridium difficile
　　　not specified as recurrent A04.72
　　　recurrent A04.71
　trichomonal A07.8
　tuberculous A18.32
　typhosa A01.00
　ulcerative (chronic) —see Colitis, ulcerative
　viral A08.4
　　adenovirus A08.2
　　enterovirus A08.39
　　Rotavirus A08.0
　　small round structured NEC A08.19
　　specified NEC A08.39
　　virus specified NEC A08.39
Enterobiasis B80
Enterobius vermicularis (infection) (infestation)
　B80
Enterocele —see also Hernia, abdomen
　pelvic, pelvis (acquired) (congenital) N81.5
　vagina, vaginal (acquired) (congenital)
　　NEC N81.5
Enterocolitis —see also Enteritis K52.9
　due to Clostridium difficile
　　not specified as recurrent A04.72
　　recurrent A04.71
　fulminant ischemic —see also Ischemia,
　　intestine, acute K55.059
　granulomatous —see Enteritis, regional
　hemorrhagic (acute) —see also Ischemia,
　　intestine, acute K55.059
　　chronic K55.1
　infectious NEC A09
　ischemic K55.9
　necrotizing K55.30
　　with
　　　perforation K55.33
　　　pneumatosis K55.32
　　　and perforation K55.33
　　due to Clostridium difficile
　　　not specified as recurrent A04.72
　　　recurrent A04.71
　　in non-newborn K55.30
　　　stage 1 (without pneumatosis, without
　　　　perforation) K55.31
　　　stage 2 (with pneumatosis, without
　　　　perforation) K55.32
　　　stage 3 (with pneumatosis, with
　　　　perforation) K55.33
　　in newborn P77.9
　　　stage 1 (without pneumatosis, without
　　　　perforation) P77.1
　　　stage 2 (with pneumatosis, without
　　　　perforation) P77.2
　　　stage 3 (with pneumatosis, with
　　　　perforation) P77.3
　　without pneumatosis or perforation K55.31
　noninfectious K52.9
　　newborn —see Enterocolitis, necrotizing, in
　　　newborn
　pseudomembranous (newborn)
　　not specified as recurrent A04.72
　　recurrent A04.71
　radiation K52.0
　　newborn —see Enterocolitis, necrotizing, in
　　　newborn
　ulcerative (chronic) —see Pancolitis,
　　ulcerative (chronic)

Enterogastritis —see Enteritis
Enteropathy K63.9
　celiac-gluten-sensitive K90.0
　　non-celiac K90.41
　food protein-induced enterocolitis (FPIES)
　　K52.22
　hemorrhagic, terminal —see also Ischemia,
　　intestine, acute K55.059
　protein-losing K90.49
Enteroperitonitis —see Peritonitis
Enteroptosis K63.4
Enterorrhagia K92.2
Enterospasm —see also Syndrome, irritable,
　bowel
　psychogenic F45.8
Enterostenosis —see also Obstruction, intestine,
　specified NEC K56.699
Enterostomy
　complication —see Complication,
　　enterostomy
　status Z93.4
Enterovirus, as cause of disease classified
　elsewhere B97.10
　coxsackievirus B97.11
　echovirus B97.12
　other specified B97.19
Enthesopathy (peripheral) M77.9
　Achilles tendinitis —see Tendinitis, Achilles
　ankle and tarsus M77.9
　　specified type NEC —see Enthesopathy,
　　　foot, specified type NEC
　anterior tibial syndrome M76.81-●
　calcaneal spur —see Spur, bone, calcaneal
　elbow region M77.8
　　lateral epicondylitis —see Epicondylitis,
　　　lateral
　　medial epicondylitis —see Epicondylitis,
　　　medial
　foot NEC M77.9
　　metatarsalgia —see Metatarsalgia
　　specified type NEC M77.5-●
　forearm M77.9
　gluteal tendinitis —see Tendinitis, gluteal
　hand M77.9
　hip —see Enthesopathy, lower limb, specified
　　type NEC
　iliac crest spur —see Spur, bone, iliac crest
　iliotibial band syndrome —see Syndrome,
　　iliotibial band
　knee —see Enthesopathy, lower limb, lower
　　leg, specified type NEC
　lateral epicondylitis —see Epicondylitis,
　　lateral
　lower limb (excluding foot) M76.9
　　Achilles tendinitis —see Tendinitis, Achilles
　　anterior tibial syndrome M76.81-●
　　gluteal tendinitis —see Tendinitis, gluteal
　　iliac crest spur —see Spur, bone, iliac crest
　　iliotibial band syndrome —see Syndrome,
　　　iliotibial band
　　patellar tendinitis —see Tendinitis, patellar
　　pelvic region —see Enthesopathy, lower
　　　limb, specified type NEC
　　peroneal tendinitis —see Tendinitis,
　　　peroneal
　　posterior tibial syndrome M76.82-●
　　psoas tendinitis —see Tendinitis, psoas
　　shoulder M77.9
　　specified type NEC M76.89-●
　　tibial collateral bursitis —see Bursitis, tibial
　　　collateral
　medial epicondylitis —see Epicondylitis,
　　medial
　multiple sites M77.9
　patellar tendinitis —see Tendinitis, patellar
　pelvis M77.9
　periarthritis of wrist —see Periarthritis,
　　wrist
　peroneal tendinitis —see Tendinitis, peroneal
　posterior tibial syndrome M76.82-●
　psoas tendinitis —see Tendinitis, psoas

Enthesopathy *(Continued)*
　shoulder region —see Lesion, shoulder
　specified site NEC M77.9
　specified type NEC M77.8
　spinal M46.00
　　cervical region M46.02
　　cervicothoracic region M46.03
　　lumbar region M46.06
　　lumbosacral region M46.07
　　multiple sites M46.09
　　occipito-atlanto-axial region M46.01
　　sacrococcygeal region M46.08
　　thoracic region M46.04
　　thoracolumbar region M46.05
　tibial collateral bursitis —see Bursitis, tibial
　　collateral
　upper arm M77.9
　wrist and carpus NEC M77.8
　　calcaneal spur —see Spur, bone, calcaneal
　　periarthritis of wrist —see Periarthritis,
　　　wrist
Entomophobia F40.218
Entomophthoromycosis B46.8
Entrance, air into vein —see Embolism, air
Entrapment, nerve —see Neuropathy,
　entrapment
Entropion (eyelid) (paralytic) H02.009
　cicatricial H02.019
　　left H02.016
　　　lower H02.015
　　　upper H02.014
　　right H02.013
　　　lower H02.012
　　　upper H02.011
　congenital Q10.2
　left H02.006
　　lower H02.005
　　upper H02.004
　mechanical H02.029
　　left H02.026
　　　lower H02.025
　　　upper H02.024
　　right H02.023
　　　lower H02.022
　　　upper H02.021
　right H02.003
　　lower H02.002
　　upper H02.001
　senile H02.039
　　left H02.036
　　　lower H02.035
　　　upper H02.034
　　right H02.033
　　　lower H02.032
　　　upper H02.031
　spastic H02.049
　　left H02.046
　　　lower H02.045
　　　upper H02.044
　　right H02.043
　　　lower H02.042
　　　upper H02.041
Enucleated eye (traumatic, current) S05.7-●
Enuresis R32
　functional F98.0
　habit disturbance F98.0
　nocturnal N39.44
　　psychogenic F98.0
　nonorganic origin F98.0
　psychogenic F98.0
Eosinopenia —see Agranulocytosis
Eosinophilia (allergic) (hereditary) (idiopathic)
　(secondary) D72.1
　with
　　angiolymphoid hyperplasia (ALHE)
　　　D18.01
　infiltrative J82
　Löffler's J82
　peritoneal —see Peritonitis, eosinophilic
　pulmonary NEC J82
　tropical (pulmonary) J82

Epilepsy, epileptic, epilepsia *(Continued)*
- spasms G40.822
  - intractable G40.824
    - with status epilepticus G40.823
    - without status epilepticus G40.824
  - not intractable G40.822
    - with status epilepticus G40.821
    - without status epilepticus G40.822
- specified NEC G40.802
  - intractable G40.804
    - with status epilepticus G40.803
    - without status epilepticus G40.804
  - not intractable G40.802
    - with status epilepticus G40.801
    - without status epilepticus G40.802
- syndromes
  - generalized
    - idiopathic G40.309
      - intractable G40.319
        - with status epilepticus G40.311
        - without status epilepticus G40.319
      - not intractable G40.309
        - with status epilepticus G40.301
        - without status epilepticus G40.309
    - specified NEC G40.409
      - intractable G40.419
        - with status epilepticus G40.411
        - without status epilepticus G40.419
      - not intractable G40.409
        - with status epilepticus G40.401
        - without status epilepticus G40.409
  - localization-related (focal) (partial)
    - idiopathic G40.009
      - with seizures of localized onset G40.009
      - intractable G40.019
        - with status epilepticus G40.011
        - without status epilepticus G40.019
      - not intractable G40.009
        - with status epilepticus G40.001
        - without status epilepticus G40.009
    - symptomatic
      - with complex partial seizures G40.209
        - intractable G40.219
          - with status epilepticus G40.211
          - without status epilepticus G40.219
        - not intractable G40.209
          - with status epilepticus G40.201
          - without status epilepticus G40.209
      - with simple partial seizures G40.109
        - intractable G40.119
          - with status epilepticus G40.111
          - without status epilepticus G40.119
        - not intractable G40.109
          - with status epilepticus G40.101
          - without status epilepticus G40.109
    - specified NEC G40.802
      - intractable G40.804
        - with status epilepticus G40.803
        - without status epilepticus G40.804
      - not intractable G40.802
        - with status epilepticus G40.801
        - without status epilepticus G40.802
- tonic (-clonic) —*see* Epilepsy, generalized, specified NEC
- twilight F05
- uncinate (gyrus) —*see* Epilepsy, localization-related, symptomatic, with complex partial seizures
- Unverricht (-Lundborg) (familial myoclonic) — *see* Epilepsy, generalized, idiopathic
- visceral —*see* Epilepsy, specified NEC
- visual —*see* Epilepsy, specified NEC
Epiloia Q85.1
Epimenorrhea N92.0
Epipharyngitis —*see* Nasopharyngitis
Epiphora H04.20-•
- due to
  - excess lacrimation H04.21-•
  - insufficient drainage H04.22-•

Epiphyseal arrest —*see* Arrest, epiphyseal
Epiphyseolysis, epiphysiolysis —*see* Osteochondropathy
Epiphysitis —*see also* Osteochondropathy
- juvenile M92.9
- syphilitic (congenital) A50.02
Epiplocele —*see* Hernia, abdomen
Epiploitis —*see* Peritonitis
Epiplosarcomphalocele —*see* Hernia, umbilicus
Episcleritis (suppurative) H15.10-•
- in (due to)
  - syphilis A52.71
  - tuberculosis A18.51
- nodular H15.12-•
- periodica fugax H15.11-•
  - angioneurotic —*see* Edema, angioneurotic
- syphilitic (late) A52.71
- tuberculous A18.51
Episode
- affective, mixed F39
- depersonalization (in neurotic state) F48.1
- depressive F32.9
  - major F32.9
    - mild F32.0
    - moderate F32.1
    - severe (without psychotic symptoms) F32.2
      - with psychotic symptoms F32.3
  - recurrent F33.9
    - brief F33.8
  - specified NEC F32.89
- hypomanic F30.8
- manic F30.9
  - with
    - psychotic symptoms F30.2
    - remission (full) F30.4
      - partial F30.3
  - without psychotic symptoms F30.10
    - mild F30.11
    - moderate F30.12
    - severe (without psychotic symptoms) F30.13
      - with psychotic symptoms F30.2
  - other specified F30.8
  - recurrent F31.89
- psychotic F23
  - organic F06.8
- schizophrenic (acute) NEC, brief F23
Epispadias (female) (male) Q64.0
Episplenitis D73.89
Epistaxis (multiple) R04.0
- hereditary I78.0
- vicarious menstruation N94.89
Epithelioma (malignant) —*see also* Neoplasm, malignant, by site
- adenoides cysticum —*see* Neoplasm, skin, benign
- basal cell —*see* Neoplasm, skin, malignant
- benign —*see* Neoplasm, benign, by site
- Bowen's —*see* Neoplasm, skin, in situ
- calcifying, of Malherbe —*see* Neoplasm, skin, benign
- external site —*see* Neoplasm, skin, malignant
- intraepidermal, Jadassohn —*see* Neoplasm, skin, benign
- squamous cell —*see* Neoplasm, malignant, by site
Epitheliomatosis pigmented Q82.1
Epitheliopathy, multifocal placoid pigment H30.14-•
Epithelium, epithelial —*see* condition
Epituberculosis (with atelectasis) (allergic) A15.7
Eponychia Q84.6
Epstein's
- nephrosis or syndrome —*see* Nephrosis
- pearl K09.8
Epulis (gingiva) (fibrous) (giant cell) K06.8
Equinia A24.0
Equinovarus (congenital) (talipes) Q66.0
- acquired —*see* Deformity, limb, clubfoot

Equivalent
- convulsive (abdominal) —*see* Epilepsy, specified NEC
- epileptic (psychic) —*see* Epilepsy, localization-related, symptomatic, with complex partial seizures
Erb (-Duchenne) **paralysis** (birth injury) (newborn) P14.0
Erb's
- ⟹disease G71.02
- palsy, paralysis (brachial) (birth) (newborn) P14.0
  - spinal (spastic) syphilitic A52.17
- ⟹pseudohypertrophic muscular dystrophy G71.02
Erb-Goldflam disease or syndrome G70.00
- with exacerbation (acute) G70.01
- in crisis G70.01
Erdheim's syndrome (acromegalic macrospondylitis) E22.0
Erection, painful (persistent) —*see* Priapism
Ergosterol deficiency (vitamin D) E55.9
- with
  - adult osteomalacia M83.8
  - rickets —*see* Rickets
Ergotism —*see also* Poisoning, food, noxious, plant
- from ergot used as drug (migraine therapy) —*see* Table of Drugs and Chemicals
Erosio interdigitalis blastomycetica B37.2
Erosion
- artery I77.2
  - without rupture I77.89
- bone —*see* Disorder, bone, density and structure, specified NEC
- bronchus J98.09
- cartilage (joint) —*see* Disorder, cartilage, specified type NEC
- cervix (uteri) (acquired) (chronic) (congenital) N86
  - with cervicitis N72
- cornea (nontraumatic) —*see* Ulcer, cornea
  - recurrent H18.83-•
  - traumatic —*see* Abrasion, cornea
- dental (idiopathic) (occupational) (due to diet, drugs or vomiting) K03.2
- duodenum, postpyloric —*see* Ulcer, duodenum
- esophagus K22.10
  - with bleeding K22.11
- gastric —*see* Ulcer, stomach
- gastrojejunal —*see* Ulcer, gastrojejunal
- implanted mesh —*see* Complications, mesh
- intestine K63.3
- lymphatic vessel I89.8
- pylorus, pyloric (ulcer) —*see* Ulcer, stomach
- spine, aneurysmal A52.09
- stomach —*see* Ulcer, stomach
- subcutaneous device pocket
  - nervous system prosthetic device, implant, or graft T85.890
  - other internal prosthetic device, implant, or graft T85.898
- teeth (idiopathic) (occupational) (due to diet, drugs or vomiting) K03.2
- urethra N36.8
- uterus N85.8
Erotomania F52.8
Error
- metabolism, inborn —*see* Disorder, metabolism
- refractive —*see* Disorder, refraction
Eructation R14.2
- nervous or psychogenic F45.8
Eruption
- creeping B76.9
- drug (generalized) (taken internally) L27.0
  - fixed L27.1
  - in contact with skin —*see* Dermatitis, due to drugs
  - localized L27.1

▶ New   ⟹ Revised   ~~deleted~~ Deleted   • Use Additional Character(s)

Evidence *(Continued)*
  cytologic *(Continued)*
    of malignancy on cervical smear R87.614
    of malignancy on vaginal smear R87.624
Evisceration
  birth injury P15.8
  traumatic NEC
    eye —*see* Enucleated eye
Evulsion —*see* Avulsion
Ewing's sarcoma or tumor —*see* Neoplasm,
    bone, malignant
Examination (for) (following) (general) (of)
    (routine) Z00.00
  with abnormal findings Z00.01
  abuse, physical (alleged), ruled out
    adult Z04.71
    child Z04.72
  adolescent (development state) Z00.3
  alleged rape or sexual assault (victim), ruled
    out
    adult Z04.41
    child Z04.42
  allergy Z01.82
  annual (adult) (periodic) (physical) Z00.00
    with abnormal findings Z00.01
    gynecological Z01.419
      with abnormal findings Z01.411
  antibody response Z01.84
  blood —*see* Examination, laboratory
  blood pressure Z01.30
    with abnormal findings Z01.31
  cancer staging —*see* Neoplasm, malignant,
    by site
  cervical Papanicolaou smear Z12.4
    as part of routine gynecological
      examination Z01.419
      with abnormal findings Z01.411
  child (over 28 days old) Z00.129
    with abnormal findings Z00.121
    under 28 days old —*see* Newborn,
      examination
  clinical research control or normal
    comparison (control) (participant) Z00.6
  contraceptive (drug) maintenance (routine)
    Z30.8
    device (intrauterine) Z30.431
  dental Z01.20
    with abnormal findings Z01.21
  developmental —*see* Examination, child
  donor (potential) Z00.5
  ear Z01.10
    with abnormal findings NEC Z01.118
  eye Z01.00
    with abnormal findings Z01.01
  following
    accident NEC Z04.3
      transport Z04.1
      work Z04.2
    assault, alleged, ruled out
      adult Z04.71
      child Z04.72
    motor vehicle accident Z04.1
    treatment (for) Z09
      combined NEC Z09
        fracture Z09
        malignant neoplasm Z08
      malignant neoplasm Z08
      mental disorder Z09
      specified condition NEC Z09
  follow-up (routine) (following) Z09
    chemotherapy NEC Z09
      malignant neoplasm Z08
    fracture Z09
    malignant neoplasm Z08
    postpartum Z39.2
    psychotherapy Z09
    radiotherapy NEC Z09
      malignant neoplasm Z08
    surgery NEC Z09
      malignant neoplasm Z08
  ▶forced sexual exploitation Z04.81

Examination *(Continued)*
  ▶forced labor exploitation Z04.82
  gynecological Z01.419
    with abnormal findings Z01.411
    for contraceptive maintenance Z30.8
  health —*see* Examination, medical
  hearing Z01.10
    with abnormal findings NEC Z01.118
  ▶infant or child (over 28 days old) Z00.129
    ▶with abnormal findings Z00.121
    following failed hearing screening Z01.110
  immunity status testing Z01.84
  laboratory (as part of a general medical
    examination) Z00.00
    with abnormal findings Z00.01
    preprocedural Z01.812
  lactating mother Z39.1
  medical (adult) (for) (of) Z00.00
    with abnormal findings Z00.01
    administrative purpose only Z02.9
      specified NEC Z02.89
    admission to
      armed forces Z02.3
      old age home Z02.2
      prison Z02.89
      residential institution Z02.2
      school Z02.0
        following illness or medical treatment
        Z02.0
      summer camp Z02.89
    adoption Z02.82
    blood alcohol or drug level Z02.83
    camp (summer) Z02.89
    clinical research, normal subject (control)
      (participant) Z00.6
    control subject in clinical research (normal
      comparison) (participant) Z00.6
    donor (potential) Z00.5
    driving license Z02.4
    general (adult) Z00.00
      with abnormal findings Z00.01
    immigration Z02.89
    insurance purposes Z02.6
    marriage Z02.89
  ⇒medicolegal reasons NEC Z04.89
    naturalization Z02.89
    participation in sport Z02.5
    paternity testing Z02.81
    population survey Z00.8
    pre-employment Z02.1
    pre-operative —*see* Examination,
      pre-procedural
    pre-procedural
      cardiovascular Z01.810
      respiratory Z01.811
      specified NEC Z01.818
    preschool children
      for admission to school Z02.0
    prisoners
      for entrance into prison Z02.89
    recruitment for armed forces Z02.3
    specified NEC Z00.8
    sport competition Z02.5
  ⇒medicolegal reason NEC Z04.89
  ▶forced sexual exploitation Z04.81
  ▶forced labor exploitation Z04.82
  newborn —*see* Newborn, examination
  pelvic (annual) (periodic) Z01.419
    with abnormal findings Z01.411
  period of rapid growth in childhood Z00.2
  periodic (adult) (annual) (routine) Z00.00
    with abnormal findings Z00.01
  physical (adult) —*see also* Examination,
    medical Z00.00
    sports Z02.5
  postpartum
    immediately after delivery Z39.0
    routine follow-up Z39.2
  pre-chemotherapy (antineoplastic) Z01.818
  prenatal (normal pregnancy) —*see also*
    Pregnancy, normal Z34.9-●

Examination *(Continued)*
  pre-procedural (pre-operative)
    cardiovascular Z01.810
    laboratory Z01.812
    respiratory Z01.811
    specified NEC Z01.818
  prior to chemotherapy (antineoplastic)
    Z01.818
  psychiatric NEC Z00.8
    follow-up not needing further care Z09
    requested by authority Z04.6
  radiological (as part of a general medical
    examination) Z00.00
    with abnormal findings Z00.01
  repeat cervical smear to confirm findings of
    recent normal smear following initial
    abnormal smear Z01.42
  skin (hypersensitivity) Z01.82
  special —*see also* Examination, by type Z01.89
    specified type NEC Z01.89
  ⇒specified type or reason NEC Z04.89
  teeth Z01.20
    with abnormal findings Z01.21
  urine —*see* Examination, laboratory
  vision Z01.00
    with abnormal findings Z01.01
    ▶infant or child (over 28 days old) Z00.129
      ▶with abnormal findings Z00.121
Exanthem, exanthema —*see also* Rash
  with enteroviral vesicular stomatitis B08.4
  Boston A88.0
  epidemic with meningitis A88.0 *[G02]*
  subitum B08.20
    due to human herpesvirus 6 B08.21
    due to human herpesvirus 7 B08.22
  viral, virus B09
    specified type NEC B08.8
Excess, excessive, excessively
  alcohol level in blood R78.0
  androgen (ovarian) E28.1
  attrition, tooth, teeth K03.0
  carotene, carotin (dietary) E67.1
  cold, effects of T69.9
    specified effect NEC T69.8
  convergence H51.12
  crying
    in child, adolescent, or adult R45.83
    in infant R68.11
  development, breast N62
  divergence H51.8
  drinking (alcohol) NEC (without
    dependence) F10.10
    habitual (continual) (without remission)
      F10.20
  eating R63.2
  estrogen E28.0
  fat —*see also* Obesity
    in heart —*see* Degeneration, myocardial
    localized E65
  foreskin N47.8
  gas R14.0
  glucagon E16.3
  heat —*see* Heat
  intermaxillary vertical dimension of fully
    erupted teeth M26.37
  interocclusal distance of fully erupted teeth
    M26.37
  kalium E87.5
  large
    colon K59.39
      congenital Q43.8
    infant P08.0
    organ or site, congenital NEC —*see*
      Anomaly, by site
  long
    organ or site, congenital NEC —*see*
      Anomaly, by site
  menstruation (with regular cycle) N92.0
    with irregular cycle N92.1
  napping Z72.821
  natrium E87.0

▶ New   ⇒ Revised   ~~deleted~~ Deleted   ● Use Additional Character(s)

Excess, excessive, excessively (Continued)
  number of teeth K00.1
  nutrient (dietary) NEC R63.2
  potassium (K) E87.5
  salivation K11.7
  secretion —see also Hypersecretion
    milk O92.6
    sputum R09.3
    sweat R61
  sexual drive F52.8
  short
    organ or site, congenital NEC —see
      Anomaly, by site
    umbilical cord in labor or delivery O69.3
  skin L98.7
    and subcutaneous tissue L98.7
    eyelid (acquired) —see Blepharochalasis
      congenital Q10.3
  sodium (Na) E87.0
  spacing of fully erupted teeth M26.32
  sputum R09.3
  sweating R61
  thirst R63.1
    due to deprivation of water T73.1
  tuberosity of jaw M26.07
  vitamin
    A (dietary) E67.0
      administered as drug (prolonged
        intake) —see Table of Drugs and
        Chemicals, vitamins, adverse
        effect
      overdose or wrong substance given
        or taken —see Table of Drugs and
        Chemicals, vitamins, poisoning
    D (dietary) E67.3
      administered as drug (prolonged
        intake) —see Table of Drugs and
        Chemicals, vitamins, adverse
        effect
      overdose or wrong substance given
        or taken —see Table of Drugs and
        Chemicals, vitamins, poisoning
  weight
    gain R63.5
    loss R63.4
Excitability, abnormal, under minor stress
    (personality disorder) F60.3
Excitation
  anomalous atrioventricular I45.6
  psychogenic F30.8
  reactive (from emotional stress, psychological
    trauma) F30.8
Excitement
  hypomanic F30.8
  manic F30.9
  mental, reactive (from emotional stress,
    psychological trauma) F30.8
  state, reactive (from emotional stress,
    psychological trauma) F30.8
Excoriation (traumatic) —see also Abrasion
  neurotic L98.1
  skin picking disorder F42.4
Exfoliation
  due to erythematous conditions according to
    extent of body surface involved L49.0
    10-19 percent of body surface L49.1
    20-29 percent of body surface L49.2
    30-39 percent of body surface L49.3
    40-49 percent of body surface L49.4
    50-59 percent of body surface L49.5
    60-69 percent of body surface L49.6
    70-79 percent of body surface L49.7
    80-89 percent of body surface L49.8
    90-99 percent of body surface L49.9
    less than 10 percent of body surface L49.0
  teeth, due to systemic causes K08.0
Exfoliative —see condition
Exhaustion, exhaustive (physical NEC) R53.83
  battle F43.0
  cardiac —see Failure, heart
  delirium F43.0

Exhaustion, exhaustive (Continued)
  due to
    cold T69.8
    excessive exertion T73.3
    exposure T73.2
    neurasthenia F48.8
  heart —see Failure, heart
  heat —see also Heat, exhaustion T67.5
    due to
      salt depletion T67.4
      water depletion T67.3
  maternal, complicating delivery O75.81
  mental F48.8
  myocardium, myocardial —see Failure, heart
  nervous F48.8
  old age R54
  psychogenic F48.8
  psychosis F43.0
  senile R54
  vital NEC Z73.0
Exhibitionism F65.2
Exocervicitis —see Cervicitis
Exomphalos Q79.2
  meaning hernia —see Hernia, umbilicus
Exophoria H50.52
  convergence, insufficiency H51.11
  divergence, excess H51.8
Exophthalmos H05.2-•
  congenital Q15.8
  constant NEC H05.24-•
  displacement, globe —see Displacement,
    globe
  due to thyrotoxicosis (hyperthyroidism) —see
    Hyperthyroidism, with, goiter (diffuse)
  dysthyroid —see Hyperthyroidism, with,
    goiter (diffuse)
  goiter —see Hyperthyroidism, with, goiter
    (diffuse)
  intermittent NEC H05.25-•
  malignant —see Hyperthyroidism, with,
    goiter (diffuse)
  orbital
    edema —see Edema, orbit
    hemorrhage —see Hemorrhage, orbit
  pulsating NEC H05.26-•
  thyrotoxic, thyrotropic —see
    Hyperthyroidism, with, goiter (diffuse)
Exostosis —see also Disorder, bone
  cartilaginous —see Neoplasm, bone, benign
  congenital (multiple) Q78.6
  external ear canal H61.81-•
  gonococcal A54.49
  jaw (bone) M27.8
  multiple, congenital Q78.6
  orbit H05.35-•
  osteocartilaginous —see Neoplasm, bone,
    benign
  syphilitic A52.77
Exotropia —see Strabismus, divergent
    concomitant
Explanation of
  investigation finding Z71.2
  medication Z71.89
Exposure (to) —see also Contact, with T75.89
  acariasis Z20.7
  AIDS virus Z20.6
  air pollution Z77.110
  algae and algae toxins Z77.121
  algae bloom Z77.121
  anthrax Z20.810
  aromatic amines Z77.020
  aromatic (hazardous) compounds NEC
    Z77.028
  aromatic dyes NOS Z77.028
  arsenic Z77.010
  asbestos Z77.090
  bacterial disease NEC Z20.818
  benzene Z77.021
  blue-green algae bloom Z77.121
  body fluids (potentially hazardous) Z77.21
  brown tide Z77.121

Exposure (Continued)
  chemicals (chiefly nonmedicinal) (hazardous)
    NEC Z77.098
  cholera Z20.09
  chromium compounds Z77.018
  cold, effects of T69.9
    specified effect NEC T69.8
  communicable disease Z20.9
    bacterial NEC Z20.818
    specified NEC Z20.89
    viral NEC Z20.828
    ▶ Zika virus Z20.821
  cyanobacteria bloom Z77.121
  disaster Z65.5
  discrimination Z60.5
  dyes Z77.098
  effects of T73.9
  environmental tobacco smoke (acute)
    (chronic) Z77.22
  Escherichia coli (E. coli) Z20.01
  exhaustion due to T73.2
  fiberglass —see Table of Drugs and
    Chemicals, fiberglass
  German measles Z20.4
  gonorrhea Z20.2
  hazardous metals NEC Z77.018
  hazardous substances NEC Z77.29
  hazards in the physical environment NEC
    Z77.128
  hazards to health NEC Z77.9
  human immunodeficiency virus (HIV) Z20.6
  human T-lymphotropic virus type-1 (HTLV-1)
    Z20.89
  implanted
    mesh —see Complications, mesh
    prosthetic materials NEC —see
      Complications, prosthetic materials
      NEC
  infestation (parasitic) NEC Z20.7
  intestinal infectious disease NEC Z20.09
    Escherichia coli (E. coli) Z20.01
  lead Z77.011
  meningococcus Z20.811
  mold (toxic) Z77.120
  nickel dust Z77.018
  noise Z77.122
  occupational
    air contaminants NEC Z57.39
    dust Z57.2
    environmental tobacco smoke Z57.31
    extreme temperature Z57.6
    noise Z57.0
    radiation Z57.1
    risk factors Z57.9
      specified NEC Z57.8
    toxic agents (gases) (liquids) (solids)
      (vapors) in agriculture Z57.4
    toxic agents (gases) (liquids) (solids)
      (vapors) in industry NEC Z57.5
    vibration Z57.7
  parasitic disease NEC Z20.7
  pediculosis Z20.7
  persecution Z60.5
  pfiesteria piscicida Z77.121
  poliomyelitis Z20.89
  pollution
    air Z77.110
    environmental NEC Z77.118
    soil Z77.112
    water Z77.111
  polycyclic aromatic hydrocarbons
    Z77.028
  prenatal (drugs) (toxic chemicals) —see
    Newborn, affected by, noxious
    substances transmitted via placenta or
    breast milk
  rabies Z20.3
  radiation, naturally occurring NEC Z77.123
  radon Z77.123
  red tide (Florida) Z77.121
  rubella Z20.4

Exposure *(Continued)*
  second hand tobacco smoke (acute) (chronic)
      Z77.22
    in the perinatal period P96.81
  sexually-transmitted disease Z20.2
  smallpox (laboratory) Z20.89
  syphilis Z20.2
  terrorism Z65.4
  torture Z65.4
  tuberculosis Z20.1
  uranium Z77.012
  varicella Z20.820
  venereal disease Z20.2
  viral disease NEC Z20.828
  war Z65.5
  water pollution Z77.111
  ▶Zika virus Z20.821
Exsanguination —*see* Hemorrhage
Exstrophy
  abdominal contents Q45.8
  bladder Q64.10
    cloacal Q64.12
    specified type NEC Q64.19
    supravesical fissure Q64.11

Extensive —*see* condition
Extra —*see also* Accessory
  marker chromosomes (normal individual)
      Q92.61
    in abnormal individual Q92.62
  rib Q76.6
    cervical Q76.5
Extrasystoles (supraventricular) I49.49
  atrial I49.1
  auricular I49.1
  junctional I49.2
  ventricular I49.3
Extrauterine gestation or pregnancy —*see*
    Pregnancy, by site
Extravasation
  blood R58
  chyle into mesentery I89.8
  pelvicalyceal N13.8
  pyelosinus N13.8
  urine (from ureter) R39.0
  vesicant agent
    antineoplastic chemotherapy T80.810
    other agent NEC T80.818

Extremity —*see* condition, limb
Extrophy —*see* Exstrophy
Extroversion
  bladder Q64.19
  uterus N81.4
    complicating delivery O71.2
    postpartal (old) N81.4
Extruded tooth (teeth) M26.34
Extrusion
  breast implant (prosthetic) T85.42
  eye implant (globe) (ball) T85.328
  intervertebral disc —*see* Displacement,
      intervertebral disc
  ocular lens implant (prosthetic) —*see*
      Complications, intraocular lens
  vitreous —*see* Prolapse, vitreous
Exudate
  pleural —*see* Effusion, pleura
  retina H35.89
Exudative —*see* condition
Eye, eyeball, eyelid —*see* condition
Eyestrain —*see* Disturbance, vision, subjective
Eyeworm disease of Africa B74.3

▶ New   ⟹ Revised   ~~deleted~~ Deleted   ● Use Additional Character(s)

F

Faber's syndrome (achlorhydric anemia) D50.9
Fabry (-Anderson) disease E75.21
Faciocephalalgia, autonomic —see also
    Neuropathy, peripheral, autonomic G90.09
Factor(s)
  psychic, associated with diseases classified
    elsewhere F54
  psychological
    affecting physical conditions F54
    or behavioral
      affecting general medical condition F54
      associated with disorders or diseases
        classified elsewhere F54
Fahr disease (of brain) G23.8
Fahr Volhard disease (of kidney) I12.-•
Failure, failed
  abortion —see Abortion, attempted
  aortic (valve) I35.8
    rheumatic I06.8
  attempted abortion —see Abortion, attempted
  biventricular I50.82
    due to left heart failure I50.814
  bone marrow —see Anemia, aplastic
  cardiac —see Failure, heart
  cardiorenal (chronic) —see also Failure, renal,
    and Failure, heart I50.9
    hypertensive I13.2
  cardiorespiratory (see also Failure, heart)
    R09.2
  cardiovascular (chronic) —see Failure, heart
  cerebrovascular I67.9
  cervical dilatation in labor O62.0
  circulation, circulatory (peripheral) R57.9
    newborn P29.89
  compensation —see Disease, heart
  compliance with medical treatment or
    regimen —see Noncompliance
  congestive —see Failure, heart, congestive
  dental implant (endosseous) M27.69
    due to
      failure of dental prosthesis M27.63
      lack of attached gingiva M27.62
      occlusal trauma (poor prosthetic design)
        M27.62
      parafunctional habits M27.62
      periodontal infection (peri-implantitis)
        M27.62
      poor oral hygiene M27.62
    osseointegration M27.61
      due to
        complications of systemic disease
          M27.61
        poor bone quality M27.61
      iatrogenic M27.61
    post-osseointegration
      biological M27.62
      due to complications of systemic disease
        M27.62
      iatrogenic M27.62
      mechanical M27.63
    pre-integration M27.61
    pre-osseointegration M27.61
    specified NEC M27.69
  descent of head (at term) of pregnancy
    (mother) O32.4
  endosseous dental implant —see Failure,
    dental implant
  engagement of head (term of pregnancy)
    (mother) O32.4
  erection (penile) —see also Dysfunction,
    sexual, male, erectile N52.9
    nonorganic F52.21
  examination(s), anxiety concerning Z55.2
  expansion terminal respiratory units
    (newborn) (primary) P28.0
  forceps NOS (with subsequent cesarean
    delivery) O66.5

Failure, failed (Continued)
  gain weight (child over 28 days old) R62.51
    adult R62.7
    newborn P92.6
  genital response (male) F52.21
    female F52.22
  heart (acute) (senile) (sudden) I50.9
    with
      acute pulmonary edema —see Failure,
        ventricular, left
      decompensation —see also Failure, heart,
        by type as diastolic or systolic,
        acute and chronic I50.9
      dilatation —see Disease, heart
      normal ejection fraction —see Failure,
        heart, diastolic
      preserved ejection fraction —see Failure,
        heart, diastolic
      reduced ejection fraction —see Failure,
        heart, systolic
    arteriosclerotic I70.90
    biventricular I50.82
      due to left heart failure I50.814
    combined left-right sided I50.82
      due to left heart failure I50.814
    compensated —see also Failure, heart, by
      type as diastolic or systolic, chronic
      I50.9
    complicating
      anesthesia (general) (local) or other
        sedation
        in labor and delivery O74.2
        in pregnancy O29.12-•
        postpartum, puerperal O89.1
      delivery (cesarean) (instrumental) O75.4
    congestive I50.9
      with rheumatic fever (conditions in I00)
        active I01.8
        inactive or quiescent (with chorea)
          I09.81
      newborn P29.0
      rheumatic (chronic) (inactive) (with
        chorea) I09.81
        active or acute I01.8
          with chorea I02.0
    decompensated —see also Failure, heart, by
      type as diastolic or systolic, acute and
      chronic I50.9
    degenerative —see Degeneration,
      myocardial
    diastolic (congestive) (left ventricular)
      I50.30
      acute (congestive) I50.31
        and (on) chronic (congestive) I50.33
      chronic (congestive) I50.32
        and (on) acute (congestive) I50.33
      combined with systolic (congestive)
        I50.40
        acute (congestive) I50.41
          and (on) chronic (congestive) I50.43
        chronic (congestive) I50.42
          and (on) acute (congestive) I50.43
    due to presence of cardiac prosthesis I97.13-•
    end stage —see also Failure, heart, by type
      as diastolic or systolic, chronic I50.84
    following cardiac surgery I97.13-•
    high output NOS I50.83
    hypertensive —see Hypertension, heart
    left (ventricular) —see also Failure,
      ventricular, left
      combined diastolic and systolic —see
        Failure, heart, diastolic, combined
        with systolic
      diastolic —see Failure, heart, diastolic
      systolic —see Failure, heart, systolic
    low output (syndrome) NOS I50.9
    newborn P29.0
    organic —see Disease, heart
    peripartum O90.3

Failure, failed (Continued)
  heart (Continued)
    postprocedural I97.13-•
    rheumatic (chronic) (inactive) I09.9
    right (isolated) (ventricular) I50.810
      acute I50.811
        and (on) chronic I50.813
      chronic I50.812
        and acute I50.813
      secondary to left heart failure I50.814
    specified NEC I50.89

> Note: heart failure stages A, B, C, and
> D are based on the American College of
> Cardiology and American Heart Association
> stages of heart failure, which complement
> and should not be confused with the New
> York Heart Association Classification of
> Heart Failure, into Class I, Class II, Class III,
> and Class IV

    stage A Z91.89
    stage B (see also Failure, heart, by type as
      diastolic or systolic) I50.9
    stage C (see also Failure, heart, by type as
      diastolic or systolic) I50.9
    stage D (see also Failure, heart, by type as
      diastolic or systolic, chronic) I50.84
    systolic (congestive) (left ventricular)
      I50.20
      acute (congestive) I50.21
        and (on) chronic (congestive) I50.23
      chronic (congestive) I50.22
        and (on) acute (congestive) I50.23
      combined with diastolic (congestive)
        I50.40
        acute (congestive) I50.41
          and (on) chronic (congestive) I50.43
        chronic (congestive) I50.42
          and (on) acute (congestive) I50.43
    thyrotoxic (see also Thyrotoxicosis) E05.90
      [I43]
      with
        high output (see also Thyrotoxicosis)
          I50.83
        thyroid storm E05.91 [I43]
          high output (see also
            Thyrotoxicosis) I50.83
    valvular —see Endocarditis
  hepatic K72.90
    with coma K72.91
    acute or subacute K72.00
      with coma K72.01
      due to drugs K71.10
        with coma K71.11
    alcoholic (acute) (chronic) (subacute)
      K70.40
      with coma K70.41
    chronic K72.10
      with coma K72.11
      due to drugs (acute) (subacute) (chronic)
        K71.10
        with coma K71.11
    due to drugs (acute) (subacute) (chronic)
      K71.10
      with coma K71.11
    postprocedural K91.82
  hepatorenal K76.7
  induction (of labor) O61.9
    abortion —see Abortion, attempted
    by
      oxytocic drugs O61.0
      prostaglandins O61.0
    instrumental O61.1
    mechanical O61.1
    medical O61.0
    specified NEC O61.8
    surgical O61.1

Failure, failed (Continued)
  intubation during anesthesia T88.4
    in pregnancy O29.6-•
    labor and delivery O74.7
    postpartum, puerperal O89.6
  involution, thymus (gland) E32.0
  kidney —see also Disease, kidney, chronic N19
    acute —see also Failure, renal, acute
      N17.9-•
    diabetic —see E08-E13 with .22
  lactation (complete) O92.3
    partial O92.4
  Leydig's cell, adult E29.1
  liver —see Failure, hepatic
  menstruation at puberty N91.0
  mitral I05.8
  myocardial, myocardium —see also Failure,
    heart I50.9
    chronic —see also Failure, heart, congestive
      I50.9
    congestive —see also Failure, heart,
      congestive I50.9
  orgasm (female) (psychogenic) F52.31
    male F52.32
  ovarian (primary) E28.39
    iatrogenic E89.40
      asymptomatic E89.40
      symptomatic E89.41
    postprocedural (postablative)
      (postirradiation) (postsurgical) E89.40
      asymptomatic E89.40
      symptomatic E89.41
  ovulation causing infertility N97.0
  polyglandular, autoimmune E31.0
  prosthetic joint implant —see Complications,
    joint prosthesis, mechanical, breakdown,
    by site
  renal N19
    with
      tubular necrosis (acute) N17.0
    acute N17.9
      with
        cortical necrosis N17.1
        medullary necrosis N17.2
        tubular necrosis N17.0
      specified NEC N17.8
    chronic N18.9
      hypertensive —see Hypertension, kidney
    congenital P96.0
    end stage (chronic) N18.6
      due to hypertension I12.0
    following
      abortion —see Abortion by type
        complicated by specified
          condition NEC
      crushing T79.5
      ectopic or molar pregnancy O08.4
      labor and delivery (acute) O90.4
    hypertensive —see Hypertension, kidney
    postprocedural N99.0
  respiration, respiratory J96.9
    with
      hypercapnia J96.92
      hypercarbia J96.02
      hypoxia J96.91
    acute J96.00
      with
        hypercapnia J96.02
        hypercarbia J96.02
        hypoxia J96.01
      acute and (on) chronic J96.20
        with
          hypercapnia J96.22
          hypercarbia J96.22
          hypoxia J96.21
      center G93.89
      chronic J96.10
        with
          hypercapnia J96.12
          hypercarbia J96.12
          hypoxia J96.11

Failure, failed (Continued)
  respiration, respiratory (Continued)
    newborn P28.5
    postprocedural (acute) J95.821
      acute and chronic J95.822
  rotation
    cecum Q43.3
    colon Q43.3
    intestine Q43.3
    kidney Q63.2
  sedation (conscious) (moderate) during
    procedure T88.52
    history of Z92.83
  segmentation —see also Fusion
    fingers —see Syndactylism, complex,
      fingers
    vertebra Q76.49
      with scoliosis Q76.3
  seminiferous tubule, adult E29.1
  senile (general) R54
  sexual arousal (male) F52.21
    female F52.22
  testicular endocrine function E29.1
  to thrive (child over 28 days old) R62.51
    adult R62.7
    newborn P92.6
  transplant T86.92
    bone T86.831
      marrow T86.02
    cornea T86.841
    heart T86.22
      with lung(s) T86.32
    intestine T86.851
    kidney T86.12
    liver T86.42
    lung(s) T86.811
      with heart T86.32
    pancreas T86.891
    skin (allograft) (autograft) T86.821
    specified organ or tissue NEC T86.891
    stem cell (peripheral blood) (umbilical
      cord) T86.5
  trial of labor (with subsequent cesarean
    delivery) O66.40
    following previous cesarean delivery
      O66.41
  tubal ligation N99.89
  urinary —see Disease, kidney, chronic
  vacuum extraction NOS (with subsequent
    cesarean delivery) O66.5
  vasectomy N99.89
  ventouse NOS (with subsequent cesarean
    delivery) O66.5
  ventricular —see also Failure, heart I50.9
    left —see also Failure, heart, left I50.1
      with rheumatic fever (conditions
        in I00)
        active I01.8
          with chorea I02.0
        inactive or quiescent (with chorea)
          I09.81
      rheumatic (chronic) (inactive) (with
        chorea) I09.81
        active or acute I01.8
          with chorea I02.0
    right —see Failure, heart, right
  vital centers, newborn P91.88
Fainting (fit) R55
Fallen arches —see Deformity, limb, flat foot
Falling, falls (repeated) R29.6
  any organ or part —see Prolapse
Fallopian
  insufflation Z31.41
  tube —see condition
Fallot's
  pentalogy Q21.8
  tetrad or tetralogy Q21.3
  triad or trilogy Q22.3
False —see also condition
  croup J38.5
  joint —see Nonunion, fracture

False (Continued)
  labor (pains) O47.9
    at or after 37 completed weeks of gestation
      O47.1
    before 37 completed weeks of gestation
      O47.0-•
  passage, urethra (prostatic) N36.5
  pregnancy F45.8
Family, familial —see also condition
  disruption Z63.8
    involving divorce or separation
      Z63.5
  Li-Fraumeni (syndrome) Z15.01
  planning advice Z30.09
  problem Z63.9
    specified NEC Z63.8
  retinoblastoma C69.2-•
Famine (effects of) T73.0
  edema —see Malnutrition, severe
Fanconi (-de Toni)(-Debré) syndrome
    E72.09
  with cystinosis E72.04
Fanconi's anemia (congenital pancytopenia)
    D61.09
Farber's disease or syndrome E75.29
Farcy A24.0
Farmer's
  lung J67.0
  skin L57.8
Farsightedness —see Hypermetropia
Fascia —see condition
Fasciculation R25.3
Fasciitis M72.9
  diffuse (eosinophilic) M35.4
  infective M72.8
    necrotizing M72.6
  necrotizing M72.6
  nodular M72.4
  perirenal (with ureteral obstruction)
    N13.5
    with infection N13.6
  plantar M72.2
  specified NEC M72.8
  traumatic (old) M72.8
    current - code by site under Sprain
Fascioliasis B66.3
Fasciolopsis, fasciolopsiasis (intestinal)
    B66.5
➡ Fascioscapulohumeral myopathy G71.02
Fast pulse R00.0
Fat
  embolism —see Embolism, fat
  excessive —see also Obesity
    in heart —see Degeneration, myocardial
  in stool R19.5
  localized (pad) E65
    heart —see Degeneration, myocardial
    knee M79.4
    retropatellar M79.4
  necrosis
    breast N64.1
    mesentery K65.4
    omentum K65.4
  pad E65
    knee M79.4
Fatigue R53.83
  auditory deafness —see Deafness
  chronic R53.82
  combat F43.0
  general R53.83
    psychogenic F48.8
  heat (transient) T67.6
  muscle M62.89
  myocardium —see Failure, heart
  neoplasm-related R53.0
  nervous, neurosis F48.8
  operational F48.8
  psychogenic (general) F48.8
  senile R54
  voice R49.8
Fatness —see Obesity

Fatty —*see also* condition
  apron E65
  degeneration —*see* Degeneration, fatty
  heart (enlarged) —*see* Degeneration,
    myocardial
  liver NEC K76.0
    alcoholic K70.0
    nonalcoholic K76.0
  necrosis —*see* Degeneration, fatty
Fauces —*see* condition
Fauchard's disease (periodontitis) —*see*
    Periodontitis
Faucitis J02.9
Favism (anemia) D55.0
Favus —*see* Dermatophytosis
Fazio-Londe disease or syndrome
    G12.1
Fear complex or reaction F40.9
Fear of —*see* Phobia
Feared complaint unfounded Z71.1
Febris, febrile —*see also* Fever
  flava —*see also* Fever, yellow A95.9
  melitensis A23.0
  pestis —*see* Plague
  recurrens —*see* Fever, relapsing
  rubra A38.9
Fecal
  incontinence R15.9
  smearing R15.1
  soiling R15.1
  urgency R15.2
Fecalith (impaction) K56.41
  appendix K38.1
  congenital P76.8
Fede's disease K14.0
Feeble rapid pulse due to shock following
    injury T79.4
Feeble-minded F70
Feeding
  difficulties R63.3
  problem R63.3
    newborn P92.9
      specified NEC P92.8
    nonorganic (adult) —*see* Disorder,
      eating
Feeling (of)
  foreign body in throat R09.89
Feer's disease —*see* Poisoning, mercury
Feet —*see* condition
Feigned illness Z76.5
Feil-Klippel syndrome (brevicollis) Q76.1
Feinmesser's (hidrotic) ectodermal dysplasia
    Q82.4
Felinophobia F40.218
Felon —*see also* Cellulitis, digit
  with lymphangitis —*see* Lymphangitis,
    acute, digit
Felty's syndrome M05.00
  ankle M05.07-●
  elbow M05.02-●
  foot joint M05.07-●
  hand joint M05.04-●
  hip M05.05-●
  knee M05.06-●
  multiple site M05.09
  shoulder M05.01-●
  vertebra —*see* Spondylitis, ankylosing
  wrist M05.03-●
Female genital cutting status —*see*
    Female genital mutilation status
    (FGM)
Female genital mutilation status (FGM)
    N90.810
  specified NEC N90.818
  type I (clitorectomy status) N90.811
  type II (clitorectomy with excision
    of labia minora status)
    N90.812
  type III (infibulation status)
    N90.813
  type IV N90.818

Femur, femoral —*see* condition
Fenestration, fenestrated —*see also* Imperfect,
    closure
  aortico-pulmonary Q21.4
  cusps, heart valve NEC Q24.8
    pulmonary Q22.3
  pulmonic cusps Q22.3
Fernell's disease (aortic aneurysm) I71.9
Fertile eunuch syndrome E23.0
Fetid
  breath R19.6
  sweat L75.0
Fetishism F65.0
  transvestic F65.1
Fetus, fetal —*see also* condition
  alcohol syndrome (dysmorphic) Q86.0
  compressus O31.0-●
  hydantoin syndrome Q86.1
  lung tissue P28.0
  papyraceous O31.0-●
Fever (inanition) (of unknown origin)
    (persistent) (with chills) (with rigor) R50.9
  abortus A23.1
  Aden (dengue) A90
  African tick-borne A68.1
  American
    mountain (tick) A93.2
    spotted A77.0
  aphthous B08.8
  arbovirus, arboviral A94
    hemorrhagic A94
    specified NEC A93.8
  Argentinian hemorrhagic A96.0
  Assam B55.0
  Australian Q A78
  Bangkok hemorrhagic A91
  Barmah forest A92.8
  Bartonella A44.0
  bilious, hemoglobinuric B50.8
  blackwater B50.8
  blister B00.1
  Bolivian hemorrhagic A96.1
  Bonvale dam T73.3
  boutonneuse A77.1
  brain —*see* Encephalitis
  Brazilian purpuric A48.4
  breakbone A90
  Bullis A77.0
  Bunyamwera A92.8
  Burdwan B55.0
  Bwamba A92.8
  Cameroon —*see* Malaria
  Canton A75.9
  catarrhal (acute) J00
    chronic J31.0
  cat-scratch A28.1
  Central Asian hemorrhagic A98.0
  cerebral —*see* Encephalitis
  cerebrospinal meningococcal A39.0
  Chagres B50.9
  Chandipura A92.8
  Changuinola A93.1
  Charcot's (biliary) (hepatic) (intermittent) —
    see Calculus, bile duct
  Chikungunya (viral) (hemorrhagic) A92.0
  Chitral A93.1
  Colombo —*see* Fever, paratyphoid
  Colorado tick (virus) A93.2
  congestive (remittent) —*see* Malaria
  Congo virus A98.0
  continued malarial B50.9
  Corsican —*see* Malaria
  Crimean-Congo hemorrhagic A98.0
  Cyprus —*see* Brucellosis
  dandy A90
  deer fly —*see* Tularemia
  dengue (virus) A90
    hemorrhagic A91
    sandfly A93.1
  desert B38.0
  drug induced R50.2

Fever (*Continued*)
  due to
    conditions classified elsewhere
      R50.81
    heat T67.0
  enteric A01.00
  enteroviral exanthematous (Boston
      exanthem) A88.0
  ephemeral (of unknown origin) R50.9
  epidemic hemorrhagic A98.5
  erysipelatous —*see* Erysipelas
  estivo-autumnal (malarial) B50.9
  famine A75.0
  five day A79.0
  following delivery O86.4
  Fort Bragg A27.89
  gastroenteric A01.00
  gastromalarial —*see* Malaria
  Gibraltar —*see* Brucellosis
  glandular —*see* Mononucleosis, infectious
  Guama (viral) A92.8
  Haverhill A25.1
  hay (allergic) J30.1
    with asthma (bronchial) J45.909
      with
        exacerbation (acute) J45.901
        status asthmaticus J45.902
    due to
      allergen other than pollen J30.89
      pollen, any plant or tree J30.1
  heat (effects) T67.0
  hematuric, bilious B50.8
  hemoglobinuric (malarial) (bilious) B50.8
  hemorrhagic (arthropod-borne) NOS A94
    with renal syndrome A98.5
    arenaviral A96.9
      specified NEC A96.8
    Argentinian A96.0
    Bangkok A91
    Bolivian A96.1
    Central Asian A98.0
    Chikungunya A92.0
    Crimean-Congo A98.0
    dengue (virus) A91
    epidemic A98.5
    Junin (virus) A96.0
    Korean A98.5
    Kyasanur forest A98.2
    Machupo (virus) A96.1
    mite-borne A93.8
    mosquito-borne A92.8
    Omsk A98.1
    Philippine A91
    Russian A98.5
    Singapore A91
    Southeast Asia A91
    Thailand A91
    tick-borne NEC A93.8
    viral A99
      specified NEC A98.8
  hepatic —*see* Cholecystitis
  herpetic —*see* Herpes
  icterohemorrhagic A27.0
  Indiana A93.8
  infective B99.9
    specified NEC B99.8
  intermittent (bilious) —*see also* Malaria
    of unknown origin R50.9
    pernicious B50.9
  iodide R50.2
  Japanese river A75.3
  jungle —*see also* Malaria
    yellow A95.0
  Junin (virus) hemorrhagic A96.0
  Katayama B65.2
  kedani A75.3
  Kenya (tick) A77.1
  Kew Garden A79.1
  Korean hemorrhagic A98.5
  Lassa A96.2
  Lone Star A77.0

Fever *(Continued)*
  Machupo (virus) hemorrhagic A96.1
  malaria, malarial —*see* Malaria
  Malta A23.9
  Marseilles A77.1
  marsh —*see* Malaria
  Mayaro (viral) A92.8
  Mediterranean —*see also* Brucellosis A23.9
    familial M04.1
    tick A77.1
  meningeal —*see* Meningitis
  Meuse A79.0
  Mexican A75.2
  mianeh A68.1
  miasmatic —*see* Malaria
  mosquito-borne (viral) A92.9
    hemorrhagic A92.8
  mountain —*see also* Brucellosis
    meaning Rocky Mountain spotted fever
      A77.0
    tick (American) (Colorado) (viral) A93.2
  Mucambo (viral) A92.8
  mud A27.9
  Neapolitan —*see* Brucellosis
  neutropenic D70.9
  newborn P81.9
    environmental P81.0
  Nine-Mile A78
  non-exanthematous tick A93.2
  North Asian tick-borne A77.2
  Omsk hemorrhagic A98.1
  O'nyong-nyong (viral) A92.1
  Oropouche (viral) A93.0
  Oroya A44.0
  paludal —*see* Malaria
  Panama (malarial) B50.9
  Pappataci A93.1
  paratyphoid A01.4
    A A01.1
    B A01.2
    C A01.3
  parrot A70
  periodic (Mediterranean) M04.1
  persistent (of unknown origin) R50.9
  petechial A39.0
  pharyngoconjunctival B30.2
  Philippine hemorrhagic A91
  phlebotomus A93.1
  Piry (virus) A93.8
  Pixuna (viral) A92.8
  Plasmodium ovale B53.0
  polioviral (nonparalytic) A80.4
  Pontiac A48.2
  postimmunization R50.83
  postoperative R50.82
  ➡ due to infection T81.40
  posttransfusion R50.84
  postvaccinian R50.83
  presenting with conditions classified
    elsewhere R50.81
  pretibial A27.89
  puerperal O86.4
  Q A78
  quadrilateral A78
  quartan (malaria) B52.9
  Queensland (coastal) (tick) A77.3
  quintan A79.0
  rabbit —*see* Tularemia
  rat-bite A25.9
    due to
      Spirillum A25.0
      Streptobacillus moniliformis A25.1
  recurrent —*see* Fever, relapsing
  relapsing (Borrelia) A68.9
    Carter's (Asiatic) A68.1
    Dutton's (West African) A68.1
    Koch's A68.9
    louse-borne A68.0
    Novy's
      louse-borne A68.0
      tick-borne A68.1

Fever *(Continued)*
  relapsing (Borrelia) *(Continued)*
    Obermeyer's (European) A68.0
    tick-borne A68.1
  remittent (bilious) (congestive) (gastric) —*see*
    Malaria
  rheumatic (active) (acute) (chronic) (subacute)
    I00
    with central nervous system involvement
      I02.9
    active with heart involvement —*see*
      category I01
    inactive or quiescent with
      cardiac hypertrophy I09.89
      carditis I09.9
      endocarditis I09.1
        aortic (valve) I06.9
          with mitral (valve) disease I08.0
        mitral (valve) I05.9
          with aortic (valve) disease I08.0
        pulmonary (valve) I09.89
        tricuspid (valve) I07.8
      heart disease NEC I09.89
      ➡ heart failure (congestive) (conditions in
        category I50.) I09.81
      left ventricular failure (conditions in
        I50.- I50.4-) I09.81
      myocarditis, myocardial degeneration
        (conditions in I51.4) I09.0
      pancarditis I09.9
      pericarditis I09.2
  Rift Valley (viral) A92.4
  Rocky Mountain spotted A77.0
  rose J30.1
  Ross River B33.1
  Russian hemorrhagic A98.5
  San Joaquin (Valley) B38.0
  sandfly A93.1
  Sao Paulo A77.0
  scarlet A38.9
  seven day (leptospirosis) (autumnal)
    (Japanese) A27.89
    dengue A90
  shin-bone A79.0
  Singapore hemorrhagic A91
  solar A90
  Songo A98.5
  sore B00.1
  South African tick-bite A68.1
  Southeast Asia hemorrhagic A91
  spinal —*see* Meningitis
  spirillary A25.0
  splenic —*see* Anthrax
  spotted A77.9
    American A77.0
    Brazilian A77.0
    cerebrospinal meningitis A39.0
    Colombian A77.0
    due to Rickettsia
      australis A77.3
      conorii A77.1
      rickettsii A77.0
      sibirica A77.2
      specified type NEC A77.8
    Ehrlichiosis A77.40
      due to
        E. chafeensis A77.41
        specified organism NEC A77.49
    Rocky Mountain A77.0
  steroid R50.2
  streptobacillary A25.1
  subtertian B50.9
  Sumatran mite A75.3
  sun A90
  swamp A27.9
  swine A02.8
  sylvatic, yellow A95.0
  Tahyna B33.8
  tertian —*see* Malaria, tertian
  Thailand hemorrhagic A91
  thermic T67.0

Fever *(Continued)*
  three-day A93.1
  tick
    American mountain A93.2
    Colorado A93.2
    Kemerovo A93.8
    Mediterranean A77.1
    mountain A93.2
    nonexanthematous A93.2
    Quaranfil A93.8
  tick-bite NEC A93.8
  tick-borne (hemorrhagic) NEC A93.8
  trench A79.0
  tsutsugamushi A75.3
  typhogastric A01.00
  typhoid (abortive) (hemorrhagic)
    (intermittent) (malignant) A01.00
    complicated by
      arthritis A01.04
      heart involvement A01.02
      meningitis A01.01
      osteomyelitis A01.05
      pneumonia A01.03
      specified NEC A01.09
  typhomalarial —*see* Malaria
  typhus —*see* Typhus (fever)
  undulant —*see* Brucellosis
  unknown origin R50.9
  uveoparotid D86.89
  valley B38.0
  Venezuelan equine A92.2
  vesicular stomatitis A93.8
  viral hemorrhagic —*see* Fever, hemorrhagic,
    by type of virus
  Volhynian A79.0
  Wesselsbron (viral) A92.8
  West
    African B50.8
    Nile (viral) A92.30
      with
        complications NEC A92.39
        cranial nerve disorders A92.32
        encephalitis A92.31
        encephalomyelitis A92.31
        neurologic manifestation NEC
          A92.32
        optic neuritis A92.32
        polyradiculitis A92.32
  Whitmore's —*see* Melioidosis
  Wolhynian A79.0
  worm B83.9
  yellow A95.9
    jungle A95.0
    sylvatic A95.0
    urban A95.1
  Zika virus A92.5
Fibrillation
  atrial or auricular (established) I48.91
    chronic I48.2
    paroxysmal I48.0
    permanent I48.2
    persistent I48.1
  cardiac I49.8
  heart I49.8
  muscular M62.89
  ventricular I49.01
Fibrin
  ball or bodies, pleural (sac) J94.1
  chamber, anterior (eye) (gelatinous
    exudate) —*see* Iridocyclitis, acute
Fibrinogenolysis —*see* Fibrinolysis
Fibrinogenopenia D68.8
  acquired D65
  congenital D68.2
Fibrinolysis (hemorrhagic) (acquired) D65
  antepartum hemorrhage —*see* Hemorrhage,
    antepartum, with coagulation defect
  following
    abortion —*see* Abortion by type
      complicated by hemorrhage
    ectopic or molar pregnancy O08.1

  ▶ New   ➡ Revised   ~~deleted~~ Deleted   ● Use Additional Character(s)

Fibrinolysis *(Continued)*
intrapartum O67.0
newborn, transient P60
postpartum O72.3
Fibrinopenia (hereditary) D68.2
acquired D68.4
Fibrinopurulent —*see* condition
Fibrinous —*see* condition
Fibroadenoma
cellular intracanalicular D24-●
giant D24-●
intracanalicular
cellular D24-●
giant D24-●
specified site —*see* Neoplasm, benign, by site
unspecified site D24-●
juvenile D24-●
pericanalicular
specified site —*see* Neoplasm, benign, by site
unspecified site D24-●
phyllodes D24-●
prostate D29.1
specified site NEC —*see* Neoplasm, benign, by site
unspecified site D24-●
Fibroadenosis, breast (chronic) (cystic) (diffuse) (periodic) (segmental) N60.2-●
Fibroangioma —*see also* Neoplasm, benign, by site
juvenile
specified site —*see* Neoplasm, benign, by site
unspecified site D10.6
Fibrochondrosarcoma —*see* Neoplasm, cartilage, malignant
Fibrocystic
disease —*see also* Fibrosis, cystic
breast —*see* Mastopathy, cystic
jaw M27.49
kidney (congenital) Q61.8
liver Q44.6
pancreas E84.9
kidney (congenital) Q61.8
Fibrodysplasia ossificans progressiva —*see* Myositis, ossificans, progressiva
Fibroelastosis (cordis) (endocardial) (endomyocardial) I42.4
Fibroid (tumor) —*see also* Neoplasm, connective tissue, benign
disease, lung (chronic) —*see* Fibrosis, lung
heart (disease) —*see* Myocarditis
in pregnancy or childbirth O34.1-●
causing obstructed labor O65.5
induration, lung (chronic) —*see* Fibrosis, lung
lung —*see* Fibrosis, lung
pneumonia (chronic) —*see* Fibrosis, lung
uterus —*see also* Leiomyoma, uterus D25.9
Fibrolipoma —*see* Lipoma
Fibroliposarcoma —*see* Neoplasm, connective tissue, malignant
Fibroma —*see also* Neoplasm, connective tissue, benign
ameloblastic —*see* Cyst, calcifying odontogenic
bone (nonossifying) —*see* Disorder, bone, specified type NEC
ossifying —*see* Neoplasm, bone, benign
cementifying —*see* Neoplasm, bone, benign
chondromyxoid —*see* Neoplasm, bone, benign
desmoplastic —*see* Neoplasm, connective tissue, uncertain behavior
durum —*see* Neoplasm, connective tissue, benign
fascial —*see* Neoplasm, connective tissue, benign
invasive —*see* Neoplasm, connective tissue, uncertain behavior
molle —*see* Lipoma

Fibroma *(Continued)*
myxoid —*see* Neoplasm, connective tissue, benign
nasopharynx, nasopharyngeal (juvenile) D10.6
nonosteogenic (nonossifying) —*see* Dysplasia, fibrous
odontogenic (central) —*see* Cyst, calcifying odontogenic
ossifying —*see* Neoplasm, bone, benign
periosteal —*see* Neoplasm, bone, benign
soft —*see* Lipoma
Fibromatosis M72.9
abdominal —*see* Neoplasm, connective tissue, uncertain behavior
aggressive —*see* Neoplasm, connective tissue, uncertain behavior
congenital generalized —*see* Neoplasm, connective tissue, uncertain behavior
Dupuytren's M72.0
gingival K06.1
palmar (fascial) M72.0
plantar (fascial) M72.2
pseudosarcomatous (proliferative) (subcutaneous) M72.4
retroperitoneal D48.3
specified NEC M72.8
Fibromyalgia M79.7
Fibromyoma —*see also* Neoplasm, connective tissue, benign
uterus (corpus) —*see also* Leiomyoma, uterus
in pregnancy or childbirth —*see* Fibroid, in pregnancy or childbirth
causing obstructed labor O65.5
Fibromyositis M79.7
Fibromyxolipoma D17.9
Fibromyxoma —*see* Neoplasm, connective tissue, benign
Fibromyxosarcoma —*see* Neoplasm, connective tissue, malignant
Fibro-odontoma, ameloblastic —*see* Cyst, calcifying odontogenic
Fibro-osteoma —*see* Neoplasm, bone, benign
Fibroplasia, retrolental H35.17
Fibropurulent —*see* condition
Fibrosarcoma —*see also* Neoplasm, connective tissue, malignant
ameloblastic C41.1
upper jaw (bone) C41.0
congenital —*see* Neoplasm, connective tissue, malignant
fascial —*see* Neoplasm, connective tissue, malignant
infantile —*see* Neoplasm, connective tissue, malignant
odontogenic C41.1
upper jaw (bone) C41.0
periosteal —*see* Neoplasm, bone, malignant
Fibrosclerosis
breast N60.3-●
multifocal M35.5
penis (corpora cavernosa) N48.6
Fibrosis, fibrotic
adrenal (gland) E27.8
amnion O41.8X-●
anal papillae K62.89
arteriocapillary —*see* Arteriosclerosis
bladder N32.89
interstitial —*see* Cystitis, chronic, interstitial
localized submucosal —*see* Cystitis, chronic, interstitial
panmural —*see* Cystitis, chronic, interstitial
breast —*see* Fibrosclerosis, breast
capillary —*see also* Arteriosclerosis I70.90
lung (chronic) —*see* Fibrosis, lung
cardiac —*see* Myocarditis
cervix N88.8
chorion O41.8X-●
corpus cavernosum (sclerosing) N48.6
cystic (of pancreas) E84.9

Fibrosis, fibrotic *(Continued)*
cystic *(Continued)*
with
distal intestinal obstruction syndrome E84.19
fecal impaction E84.19
intestinal manifestations NEC E84.19
pulmonary manifestations E84.0
specified manifestations NEC E84.8
due to device, implant or graft —*see also* Complications, by site and type, specified NEC T85.828
arterial graft NEC T82.828
breast (implant) T85.828
catheter NEC T85.828
dialysis (renal) T82.828
intraperitoneal T85.828
infusion NEC T82.828
spinal (epidural) (subdural) T85.820
urinary (indwelling) T83.82
electronic (electrode) (pulse generator) (stimulator)
bone T84.82
cardiac T82.827
nervous system (brain) (peripheral nerve) (spinal) T85.820
urinary T83.82
fixation, internal (orthopedic) NEC T84.82
gastrointestinal (bile duct) (esophagus) T85.828
genital NEC T83.82
heart NEC T82.827
joint prosthesis T84.82
ocular (corneal graft) (orbital implant) NEC T85.828
orthopedic NEC T84.82
specified NEC T85.828
urinary NEC T83.82
vascular NEC T82.828
ventricular intracranial shunt T85.820
ejaculatory duct N50.89
endocardium —*see* Endocarditis
endomyocardial (tropical) I42.3
epididymis N50.89
eye muscle —*see* Strabismus, mechanical
heart —*see* Myocarditis
hepatic —*see* Fibrosis, liver
hepatolienal (portal hypertension) K76.6
hepatosplenic (portal hypertension) K76.6
infrapatellar fat pad M79.4
intrascrotal N50.89
kidney N26.9
liver K74.0
with sclerosis K74.2
alcoholic K70.2
lung (atrophic) (chronic) (confluent) (massive) (perialveolar) (peribronchial) J84.10
with
anthracosilicosis J60
anthracosis J60
asbestosis J61
bagassosis J67.1
bauxite J63.1
berylliosis J63.2
byssinosis J66.0
calcicosis J62.8
chalicosis J62.8
dust reticulation J64
farmer's lung J67.0
ganister disease J62.8
graphite J63.3
pneumoconiosis NOS J64
siderosis J63.4
silicosis J62.8
capillary J84.10
congenital P27.8
diffuse (idiopathic) J84.10
chemicals, gases, fumes or vapors (inhalation) J68.4

Fibrosis, fibrotic *(Continued)*
  lung *(Continued)*
    diffuse *(Continued)*
      interstitial J84.10
        acute J84.114
      talc J62.0
    following radiation J70.1
    idiopathic J84.112
    postinflammatory J84.10
    silicotic J62.8
    tuberculous —*see* Tuberculosis, pulmonary
  lymphatic gland I89.8
  median bar —*see* Hyperplasia, prostate
  mediastinum (idiopathic) J98.59
  meninges G96.19
  myocardium, myocardial —*see* Myocarditis
  ovary N83.8
  oviduct N83.8
  pancreas K86.89
  penis NEC N48.6
  pericardium I31.0
  perineum, in pregnancy or childbirth O34.7-●
    causing obstructed labor O65.5
  pleura J94.1
  popliteal fat pad M79.4
  prostate (chronic) —*see* Hyperplasia, prostate
  pulmonary —*see also* Fibrosis, lung J84.10
    congenital P27.8
    idiopathic J84.112
  rectal sphincter K62.89
  retroperitoneal, idiopathic (with ureteral obstruction) N13.5
    with infection N13.6
  sclerosing mesenteric (idiopathic) K65.4
  scrotum N50.89
  seminal vesicle N50.89
  senile R54
  skin L90.5
  spermatic cord N50.89
  spleen D73.89
    in schistosomiasis (bilharziasis) B65.9
      [D77]
  subepidermal nodular —*see* Neoplasm, skin, benign
  submucous (oral) (tongue) K13.5
  testis N44.8
    chronic, due to syphilis A52.76
  thymus (gland) E32.8
  tongue, submucous K13.5
  tunica vaginalis N50.89
  uterus (non-neoplastic) N85.8
  vagina N89.8
  valve, heart —*see* Endocarditis
  vas deferens N50.89
  vein I87.8
Fibrositis (periarticular) M79.7
  nodular, chronic (Jaccoud's) (rheumatoid) — *see* Arthropathy, postrheumatic, chronic
Fibrothorax J94.1
Fibrotic —*see* Fibrosis
Fibrous —*see* condition
Fibroxanthoma —*see also* Neoplasm, connective tissue, benign
  atypical —*see* Neoplasm, connective tissue, uncertain behavior
  malignant —*see* Neoplasm, connective tissue, malignant
Fibroxanthosarcoma —*see* Neoplasm, connective tissue, malignant
Fiedler's
  disease (icterohemorrhagic leptospirosis) A27.0
  myocarditis (acute) I40.1
Fifth disease B08.3
  venereal A55
Filaria, filarial, filariasis —*see* Infestation, filarial
Filatov's disease —*see* Mononucleosis, infectious
File-cutter's disease —*see* Poisoning, lead

Filling defect
  biliary tract R93.2
  bladder R93.41
  duodenum R93.3
  gallbladder R93.2
  gastrointestinal tract R93.3
  intestine R93.3
  kidney R93.42-●
  stomach R93.3
  ureter R93.41
  urinary organs, specified NEC R93.49
Fimbrial cyst Q50.4
Financial problem affecting care NOS Z59.9
  bankruptcy Z59.8
  foreclosure on loan Z59.8
Findings, abnormal, inconclusive, without diagnosis —*see also* Abnormal
  17-ketosteroids, elevated R82.5
  acetonuria R82.4
  alcohol in blood R78.0
  anisocytosis R71.8
  antenatal screening of mother O28.9
    biochemical O28.1
    chromosomal O28.5
    cytological O28.2
    genetic O28.5
    hematological O28.0
    radiological O28.4
    specified NEC O28.8
    ultrasonic O28.3
  antibody titer, elevated R76.0
  anticardiolipin antibody R76.0
  antiphosphatidylglycerol antibody R76.0
  antiphosphatidylinositol antibody R76.0
  antiphosphatidylserine antibody R76.0
  antiphospholipid antibody R76.0
  bacteriuria R82.71
  bicarbonate E87.8
  bile in urine R82.2
  blood sugar R73.09
    high R73.9
    low (transient) E16.2
  body fluid or substance, specified NEC R88.8
  casts, urine R82.998
  catecholamines R82.5
  cells, urine R82.998
  chloride E87.8
  cholesterol E78.9
    high E78.00
      with high triglycerides E78.2
  chyluria R82.0
  cloudy
    dialysis effluent R88.0
    urine R82.90
  creatinine clearance R94.4
  crystals, urine R82.998
  culture
    blood R78.81
    positive —*see* Positive, culture
  echocardiogram R93.1
  electrolyte level, urinary R82.998
  function study NEC R94.8
    bladder R94.8
    endocrine NEC R94.7
      thyroid R94.6
    kidney R94.4
    liver R94.5
    pancreas R94.8
    placenta R94.8
    pulmonary R94.2
    spleen R94.8
  gallbladder, nonvisualization R93.2
  glucose (tolerance test) (non-fasting) R73.09
  glycosuria R81
  heart
    shadow R93.1
    sounds R01.2
  hematinuria R82.3
  hematocrit drop (precipitous) R71.0
  hemoglobinuria R82.3

Findings, abnormal, inconclusive, without diagnosis *(Continued)*
  human papillomavirus (HPV) DNA test positive
    cervix
      high risk R87.810
      low risk R87.820
    vagina
      high risk R87.811
      low risk R87.821
  in blood (of substance not normally found in blood) R78.9
    addictive drug NEC R78.4
    alcohol (excessive level) R78.0
    cocaine R78.2
    hallucinogen R78.3
    heavy metals (abnormal level) R78.79
    lead R78.71
    lithium (abnormal level) R78.89
    opiate drug R78.1
    psychotropic drug R78.5
    specified substance NEC R78.89
    steroid agent R78.6
  indoleacetic acid, elevated R82.5
  ketonuria R82.4
  lactic acid dehydrogenase (LDH) R74.0
  liver function test R79.89
  mammogram NEC R92.8
    calcification (calculus) R92.1
    inconclusive result (due to dense breasts) R92.2
    microcalcification R92.0
  mediastinal shift R93.89
  melanin, urine R82.998
  myoglobinuria R82.1
  neonatal screening P09
  nonvisualization of gallbladder R93.2
  odor of urine NOS R82.90
  Papanicolaou cervix R87.619
    non-atypical endometrial cells R87.618
  pneumoencephalogram R93.0
  poikilocytosis R71.8
  potassium (deficiency) E87.6
    excess E87.5
  PPD R76.11
  radiologic (X-ray) R93.89
    abdomen R93.5
    biliary tract R93.2
    breast R92.8
    gastrointestinal tract R93.3
    genitourinary organs R93.89
    head R93.0
    inconclusive due to excess body fat of patient R93.9
    intrathoracic organs NEC R93.1
    placenta R93.89
    retroperitoneum R93.5
    skin R93.89
    skull R93.0
    subcutaneous tissue R93.89
    testis R93.81-●
  red blood cell (count) (morphology) (sickling) (volume) R71.8
  scan NEC R94.8
    bladder R94.8
    bone R94.8
    kidney R94.4
    liver R93.2
    lung R94.2
    pancreas R94.8
    placental R94.8
    spleen R94.8
    thyroid R94.6
  sedimentation rate, elevated R70.0
  SGOT R74.0
  SGPT R74.0
  sodium (deficiency) E87.1
    excess E87.0
  specified body fluid NEC R88.8
  stress test R94.39
  thyroid (function) (metabolic rate) (scan) (uptake) R94.6

▶ New   ⇒ Revised   ~~deleted~~ Deleted   ● Use Additional Character(s)

Findings, abnormal, inconclusive, without
    diagnosis (Continued)
  transaminase (level) R74.0
  triglycerides E78.9
    high E78.1
      with high cholesterol E78.2
  tuberculin skin test (without active
    tuberculosis) R76.11
  urine R82.90
    acetone R82.4
    bacteria R82.71
    bile R82.2
    ⇒casts or cells R82.998
    chyle R82.0
    culture positive R82.79
    glucose R81
    hemoglobin R82.3
    ketone R82.4
    sugar R81
  vanillylmandelic acid (VMA), elevated
    R82.5
  vectorcardiogram (VCG) R94.39
  ventriculogram R93.0
  white blood cell (count) (differential)
    (morphology) D72.9
  xerography R92.8
Finger —see condition
Fire, Saint Anthony's —see Erysipelas
Fire-setting
  pathological (compulsive) F63.1
Fish hook stomach K31.89
Fishmeal-worker's lung J67.8
Fissure, fissured
  anus, anal K60.2
    acute K60.0
    chronic K60.1
    congenital Q43.8
  ear, lobule, congenital Q17.8
  epiglottis (congenital) Q31.8
  larynx J38.7
    congenital Q31.8
  lip K13.0
    congenital —see Cleft, lip
  nipple N64.0
    associated with
      lactation O92.13
      pregnancy O92.11-●
      puerperium O92.12
  nose Q30.2
  palate (congenital) —see Cleft, palate
  skin R23.4
  spine (congenital) —see also Spina bifida
    with hydrocephalus —see Spina bifida, by
      site, with hydrocephalus
  tongue (acquired) K14.5
    congenital Q38.3
Fistula (cutaneous) L98.8
  abdomen (wall) K63.2
    bladder N32.2
    intestine NEC K63.2
    ureter N28.89
    uterus N82.5
  abdominorectal K63.2
  abdominosigmoidal K63.2
  abdominothoracic J86.0
  abdominouterine N82.5
    congenital Q51.7
  abdominovesical N32.2
  accessory sinuses —see Sinusitis
  actinomycotic —see Actinomycosis
  alveolar antrum —see Sinusitis, maxillary
  alveolar process K04.6
  anorectal K60.5
  antrobuccal —see Sinusitis, maxillary
  antrum —see Sinusitis, maxillary
  anus, anal (recurrent) (infectional) K60.3
    congenital Q43.6
      with absence, atresia and stenosis Q42.2
    tuberculous A18.32
  aorta-duodenal I77.2
  appendix, appendicular K38.3

Fistula (Continued)
  arteriovenous (acquired) (nonruptured) I77.0
    brain I67.1
      congenital Q28.2
        ruptured I60.8
      ruptured I60.8
    cerebral —see Fistula, arteriovenous, brain
    congenital (peripheral) —see also
      Malformation, arteriovenous
      brain Q28.2
        ruptured I60.8
      coronary Q24.5
      pulmonary Q25.72
    coronary I25.41
      congenital Q24.5
    pulmonary I28.0
      congenital Q25.72
    surgically created (for dialysis) Z99.2
      complication —see Complication,
        arteriovenous, fistula, surgically
        created
    traumatic —see Injury, blood vessel
  artery I77.2
  aural (mastoid) —see Mastoiditis, chronic
  auricle —see also Disorder, pinna, specified
    type NEC
    congenital Q18.1
  Bartholin's gland N82.8
  bile duct (common) (hepatic) K83.3
    with calculus, stones —see Calculus, bile
      duct
  biliary (tract) —see Fistula, bile duct
  bladder (sphincter) NEC —see also Fistula,
    vesico- N32.2
    into seminal vesicle N32.2
  bone —see also Disorder, bone, specified type
    NEC
    with osteomyelitis, chronic —see
      Osteomyelitis, chronic, with draining
      sinus
  brain G93.89
    arteriovenous (acquired) I67.1
      congenital Q28.2
  branchial (cleft) Q18.0
  branchiogenous Q18.0
  breast N61.0
    puerperal, postpartum or gestational, due
      to mastitis (purulent) —see Mastitis,
      obstetric, purulent
  bronchial J86.0
  bronchocutaneous, bronchomediastinal,
    bronchopleural,
    bronchopleuromediastinal (infective)
    J86.0
    tuberculous NEC A15.5
  bronchoesophageal J86.0
    congenital Q39.2
      with atresia of esophagus Q39.1
  bronchovisceral J86.0
  buccal cavity (infective) K12.2
  cecosigmoidal K63.2
  cecum K63.2
  cerebrospinal (fluid) G96.0
  cervical, lateral Q18.1
  cervicoaural Q18.1
  cervicosigmoidal N82.4
  cervicovesical N82.1
  cervix N82.8
  chest (wall) J86.0
  cholecystenteric —see Fistula, gallbladder
  cholecystocolic —see Fistula, gallbladder
  cholecystocolonic —see Fistula, gallbladder
  cholecystoduodenal —see Fistula, gallbladder
  cholecystogastric —see Fistula, gallbladder
  cholecystointestinal —see Fistula, gallbladder
  choledochoduodenal —see Fistula, bile duct
  cholocolic K82.3
  coccyx —see Sinus, pilonidal
  colon K63.2
  colostomy K94.09
  common duct —see Fistula, bile duct

Fistula (Continued)
  congenital, site not listed —see Anomaly, by
    site
  coronary, arteriovenous I25.41
    congenital Q24.5
  costal region J86.0
  cul-de-sac, Douglas' N82.8
  cystic duct —see also Fistula, gallbladder
    congenital Q44.5
  dental K04.6
  diaphragm J86.0
  duodenum K31.6
  ear (external) (canal) —see Disorder, ear,
    external, specified type NEC
  enterocolic K63.2
  enterocutaneous K63.2
  enterouterine N82.4
    congenital Q51.7
  enterovaginal N82.4
    congenital Q52.2
    large intestine N82.3
    small intestine N82.2
  enterovesical N32.1
  epididymis N50.89
    tuberculous A18.15
  esophagobronchial J86.0
    congenital Q39.2
      with atresia of esophagus Q39.1
  esophagocutaneous K22.8
  esophagopleural-cutaneous J86.0
  esophagotracheal J86.0
    congenital Q39.2
      with atresia of esophagus Q39.1
  esophagus K22.8
    congenital Q39.2
      with atresia of esophagus Q39.1
  ethmoid —see Sinusitis, ethmoidal
  eyeball (cornea) (sclera) —see Disorder, globe,
    hypotony
  eyelid H01.8
  fallopian tube, external N82.5
  fecal K63.2
    congenital Q43.6
  from periapical abscess K04.6
  frontal sinus —see Sinusitis, frontal
  gallbladder K82.3
    with calculus, cholelithiasis, stones —see
      Calculus, gallbladder
  gastric K31.6
  gastrocolic K31.6
    congenital Q40.2
    tuberculous A18.32
  gastroenterocolic K31.6
  gastroesophageal K31.6
  gastrojejunal K31.6
  gastrojejunocolic K31.6
  genital tract (female) N82.9
    specified NEC N82.8
    to intestine NEC N82.4
    to skin N82.5
  hepatic artery-portal vein, congenital Q26.6
  hepatopleural J86.0
  hepatopulmonary J86.0
  ileorectal or ileosigmoidal K63.2
  ileovaginal N82.2
  ileovesical N32.1
  ileum K63.2
  in ano K60.3
    tuberculous A18.32
  inner ear (labyrinth) —see subcategory
    H83.1
  intestine NEC K63.2
  intestinocolonic (abdominal) K63.2
  intestinoureteral N28.89
  intestinouterine N82.4
  intestinovaginal N82.4
    large intestine N82.3
    small intestine N82.2
  intestinovesical N32.1
  ⇒ischiorectal (fossa) K61.39
  jejunum K63.2

Fistula (Continued)
- joint M25.10
  - ankle M25.17-●
  - elbow M25.12-●
  - foot joint M25.17-●
  - hand joint M25.14-●
  - hip M25.15-●
  - knee M25.16-●
  - shoulder M25.11-●
  - specified joint NEC M25.18
  - tuberculous —see Tuberculosis, joint
  - vertebrae M25.18
  - wrist M25.13-●
- kidney N28.89
- labium (majus) (minus) N82.8
- labyrinth —see subcategory H83.1
- lacrimal (gland) (sac) H04.61-●
- lacrimonasal duct —see Fistula, lacrimal
- laryngotracheal, congenital Q34.8
- larynx J38.7
- lip K13.0
  - congenital Q38.0
- lumbar, tuberculous A18.01
- lung J86.0
- lymphatic I89.8
- mammary (gland) N61.0
- mastoid (process) (region) —see Mastoiditis, chronic
- maxillary J32.0
- medial, face and neck Q18.8
- mediastinal J86.0
- mediastinobronchial J86.0
- mediastinocutaneous J86.0
- middle ear —see subcategory H74.8
- mouth K12.2
- nasal J34.89
  - sinus —see Sinusitis
- nasopharynx J39.2
- nipple N64.0
- nose J34.89
- oral (cutaneous) K12.2
  - maxillary J32.0
  - nasal (with cleft palate) —see Cleft, palate
- orbit, orbital —see Disorder, orbit, specified type NEC
- oroantral J32.8
- oviduct, external N82.5
- palate (hard) M27.8
- pancreatic K86.89
- pancreaticoduodenal K86.89
- parotid (gland) K11.4
  - region K12.2
- penis N48.89
- perianal K60.3
- pericardium (pleura) (sac) —see Pericarditis
- pericecal K63.2
- perineorectal K60.4 perineosigmoidal K63.2
- perineosigmoidal K63.2
- perineum, perineal (with urethral involvement) NEC N36.0
  - tuberculous A18.13
  - ureter N28.89
- perirectal K60.4
  - tuberculous A18.32
- peritoneum K65.9
- pharyngoesophageal J39.2
- pharynx J39.2
  - branchial cleft (congenital) Q18.0
- pilonidal (infected) (rectum) —see Sinus, pilonidal
- pleura, pleural, pleurocutaneous, pleuroperitoneal J86.0
  - tuberculous NEC A15.6
- pleuropericardial I31.8
- portal vein-hepatic artery, congenital Q26.6
- postauricular H70.81-●
- postoperative, persistent T81.83
  - specified site —see Fistula, by site
- preauricular (congenital) Q18.1
- prostate N42.89

Fistula (Continued)
- pulmonary J86.0
  - arteriovenous I28.0
    - congenital Q25.72
  - tuberculous —see Tuberculosis, pulmonary
- pulmonoperitoneal J86.0
- rectolabial N82.4
- rectosigmoid (intercommunicating) K63.2
- rectoureteral N28.89
- rectourethral N36.0
  - congenital Q64.73
- rectouterine N82.4
  - congenital Q51.7
- rectovaginal N82.3
  - congenital Q52.2
  - tuberculous A18.18
- rectovesical N32.1
  - congenital Q64.79
- rectovesicovaginal N82.3
- rectovulval N82.4
  - congenital Q52.79
- rectum (to skin) K60.4
  - congenital Q43.6
    - with absence, atresia and stenosis Q42.0
  - tuberculous A18.32
- renal N28.89
- retroauricular —see Fistula, postauricular
- salivary duct or gland (any) K11.4
  - congenital Q38.4
- scrotum (urinary) N50.89
  - tuberculous A18.15
- semicircular canals —see subcategory H83.1
- sigmoid K63.2
  - to bladder N32.1
- sinus —see Sinusitis
- skin L98.8
  - to genital tract (female) N82.5
- splenocolic D73.89
- stercoral K63.2
- stomach K31.6
- sublingual gland K11.4
- submandibular gland K11.4
- submaxillary (gland) K11.4
  - region K12.2
- thoracic J86.0
  - duct I89.8
- thoracoabdominal J86.0
- thoracogastric J86.0
- thoracointestinal J86.0
- thorax J86.0
- thyroglossal duct Q89.2
- thyroid E07.89
- trachea, congenital (external) (internal) Q32.1
- tracheoesophageal J86.0
  - congenital Q39.2
    - with atresia of esophagus Q39.1
  - following tracheostomy J95.04
- traumatic arteriovenous —see Injury, blood vessel, by site
- tuberculous - code by site under Tuberculosis
- typhoid A01.09
- umbilicourinary Q64.8
- urachus, congenital Q64.4
- ureter (persistent) N28.89
- ureteroabdominal N28.89
- ureterorectal N28.89
- ureterosigmoido-abdominal N28.89
- ureterovaginal N82.1
- ureterovesical N32.2
- urethra N36.0
  - congenital Q64.79
  - tuberculous A18.13
- urethroperineal N36.0
- urethroperineovesical N32.2
- urethrorectal N36.0
  - congenital Q64.73
- urethroscrotal N50.89
- urethrovaginal N82.1
- urethrovesical N32.2
- urinary (tract) (persistent) (recurrent) N36.0

Fistula (Continued)
- uteroabdominal N82.5
  - congenital Q51.7
- uteroenteric, uterointestinal N82.4
  - congenital Q51.7
- uterorectal N82.4
  - congenital Q51.7
- uteroureteric N82.1
- uterourethral Q51.7
- uterovaginal N82.8
- uterovesical N82.1
  - congenital Q51.7
- uterus N82.8
- vagina (postpartal) (wall) N82.8
- vaginocutaneous (postpartal) N82.5
- vaginointestinal NEC N82.4
  - large intestine N82.3
  - small intestine N82.2
- vaginoperineal N82.5
- vasocutaneous, congenital Q55.7
- vesical NEC N32.2
- vesicoabdominal N32.2
- vesicocervicovaginal N82.1
- vesicocolic N32.1
- vesicocutaneous N32.2
- vesicoenteric N32.1
- vesicointestinal N32.1
- vesicometrorectal N82.4
- vesicoperineal N32.2
- vesicorectal N32.1
  - congenital Q64.79
- vesicosigmoidal N32.1
- vesicosigmoidovaginal N82.3
- vesicoureteral N32.2
- vesicoureterovaginal N82.1
- vesicourethral N32.2
- vesicourethrorectal N32.1
- vesicouterine N82.1
  - congenital Q51.7
- vesicovaginal N82.0
- vulvorectal N82.4
  - congenital Q52.79
Fit R56.9
- epileptic —see Epilepsy
- fainting R55
- hysterical F44.5
- newborn P90
Fitting (and adjustment) (of)
- artificial
  - arm —see Admission, adjustment, artificial, arm
  - breast Z44.3
  - eye Z44.2
  - leg —see Admission, adjustment, artificial, leg
- automatic implantable cardiac defibrillator (with synchronous cardiac pacemaker) Z45.02
- brain neuropacemaker Z46.2
  - implanted Z45.42
- cardiac defibrillator —see Fitting (and adjustment) (of), automatic implantable cardiac defibrillator
- catheter, non-vascular Z46.82
- colostomy belt Z46.89
- contact lenses Z46.0
- CRT-D (resynchronization therapy defibrillator) Z45.02
- CRT-P (cardiac resynchronization therapy pacemaker) Z45.018
  - pulse generator Z45.010
- cystostomy device Z46.6
- defibrillator, cardiac —see Fitting (and adjustment) (of), automatic implantable cardiac defibrillator
- dentures Z46.3
- device NOS Z46.9
  - abdominal Z46.89
  - gastrointestinal NEC Z46.59
  - implanted NEC Z45.89
  - nervous system Z46.2
    - implanted —see Admission, adjustment, device, implanted, nervous system

▶ New   ⇒ Revised   ~~deleted~~ Deleted   ● Use Additional Character(s)

Folliculitis (Continued)
  decalvans L66.2
  deep —see Furuncle, by site
  gonococcal (acute) (chronic) A54.01
  keloid, keloidalis L73.0
  pustular L01.02
  ulerythematosa reticulata L66.4
Folliculome lipidique
  specified site —see Neoplasm, benign, by site
  unspecified site
    female D27.9
    male D29.20
Følling's disease E70.0
Follow-up —see Examination, follow-up
Fong's syndrome (hereditary osteo-
    onychodysplasia) Q87.2
Food
  allergy L27.2
  asphyxia (from aspiration or inhalation) —see
      Foreign body, by site
  choked on —see Foreign body, by site
  deprivation T73.0
    specified kind of food NEC E63.8
  intoxication —see Poisoning, food
  lack of T73.0
  poisoning —see Poisoning, food
  rejection NEC —see Disorder, eating
  strangulation or suffocation —see Foreign
      body, by site
  toxemia —see Poisoning, food
Foot —see condition
Foramen ovale (nonclosure) (patent)
    (persistent) Q21.1
Forbes' glycogen storage disease E74.03
Fordyce-Fox disease L75.2
Fordyce's disease (mouth) Q38.6
Forearm —see condition
Foreign body
  with
    laceration —see Laceration, by site, with
        foreign body
    puncture wound —see Puncture, by site,
        with foreign body
  accidentally left following a procedure
      T81.509
    aspiration T81.506
      resulting in
        adhesions T81.516
        obstruction T81.526
        perforation T81.536
        specified complication NEC T81.596
    cardiac catheterization T81.505
      resulting in
        acute reaction T81.60
          aseptic peritonitis T81.61
          specified NEC T81.69
        adhesions T81.515
        obstruction T81.525
        perforation T81.535
        specified complication NEC T81.595
    causing
      acute reaction T81.60
        aseptic peritonitis T81.61
        specified complication NEC T81.69
      adhesions T81.519
      aseptic peritonitis T81.61
      obstruction T81.529
      perforation T81.539
      specified complication NEC T81.599
    endoscopy T81.504
      resulting in
        adhesions T81.514
        obstruction T81.524
        perforation T81.534
        specified complication NEC T81.594
    immunization T81.503
      resulting in
        adhesions T81.513
        obstruction T81.523
        perforation T81.533
        specified complication NEC T81.593

Foreign body (Continued)
  accidentally left following a procedure
      (Continued)
    infusion T81.501
      resulting in
        adhesions T81.511
        obstruction T81.521
        perforation T81.531
        specified complication NEC T81.591
    injection T81.503
      resulting in
        adhesions T81.513
        obstruction T81.523
        perforation T81.533
        specified complication NEC T81.593
    kidney dialysis T81.502
      resulting in
        adhesions T81.512
        obstruction T81.522
        perforation T81.532
        specified complication NEC T81.592
    packing removal T81.507
      resulting in
        acute reaction T81.60
          aseptic peritonitis T81.61
          specified NEC T81.69
        adhesions T81.517
        obstruction T81.527
        perforation T81.537
        specified complication NEC T81.597
    puncture T81.506
      resulting in
        adhesions T81.516
        obstruction T81.526
        perforation T81.536
        specified complication NEC T81.596
    specified procedure NEC T81.508
      resulting in
        acute reaction T81.60
          aseptic peritonitis T81.61
          specified NEC T81.69
        adhesions T81.518
        obstruction T81.528
        perforation T81.538
        specified complication NEC
            T81.598
    surgical operation T81.500
      resulting in
        acute reaction T81.60
          aseptic peritonitis T81.61
          specified NEC T81.69
        adhesions T81.510
        obstruction T81.520
        perforation T81.530
        specified complication NEC T81.590
    transfusion T81.501
      resulting in
        adhesions T81.511
        obstruction T81.521
        perforation T81.531
        specified complication NEC T81.591
  alimentary tract T18.9
    anus T18.5
    colon T18.4
    esophagus —see Foreign body, esophagus
    mouth T18.0
    multiple sites T18.8
    rectosigmoid (junction) T18.5
    rectum T18.5
    small intestine T18.3
    specified site NEC T18.8
    stomach T18.2
  anterior chamber (eye) S05.5-●
  auditory canal —see Foreign body, entering
      through orifice, ear
  bronchus T17.508
    causing
      asphyxiation T17.500
        food (bone) (seed) T17.520
        gastric contents (vomitus) T17.510
        specified type NEC T17.590

Foreign body (Continued)
  bronchus (Continued)
    causing (Continued)
      injury NEC T17.508
        food (bone) (seed) T17.528
        gastric contents (vomitus) T17.518
        specified type NEC T17.598
  canthus —see Foreign body, conjunctival sac
  ciliary body (eye) S05.5-●
  conjunctival sac T15.1-●
  cornea T15.0-●
  entering through orifice
    accessory sinus T17.0
    alimentary canal T18.9
      multiple parts T18.8
      specified part NEC T18.8
    alveolar process T18.0
    antrum (Highmore's) T17.0
    anus T18.5
    appendix T18.4
    auditory canal —see Foreign body, entering
        through orifice, ear
    auricle —see Foreign body, entering
        through orifice, ear
    bladder T19.1
    bronchioles —see Foreign body, respiratory
        tract, specified site NEC
    bronchus (main) —see Foreign body,
        bronchus
    buccal cavity T18.0
    canthus (inner) —see Foreign body,
        conjunctival sac
    cecum T18.4
    cervix (canal) (uteri) T19.3
    colon T18.4
    conjunctival sac —see Foreign body,
        conjunctival sac
    cornea —see Foreign body, cornea
    digestive organ or tract NOS T18.9
      multiple parts T18.8
      specified part NEC T18.8
    duodenum T18.3
    ear (external) T16.-●
    esophagus —see Foreign body, esophagus
    eye (external) NOS T15.9-●
      conjunctival sac —see Foreign body,
          conjunctival sac
      cornea —see Foreign body, cornea
      specified part NEC T15.8-●
    eyeball —see also Foreign body, entering
        through orifice, eye, specified part
        NEC
      with penetrating wound —see Puncture,
          eyeball
    eyelid —see also Foreign body, conjunctival
        sac
      with
        laceration —see Laceration, eyelid,
            with foreign body
        puncture —see Puncture, eyelid, with
            foreign body
        superficial injury —see Foreign body,
            superficial, eyelid
    gastrointestinal tract T18.9
      multiple parts T18.8
      specified part NEC T18.8
    genitourinary tract T19.9
      multiple parts T19.8
      specified part NEC T19.8
    globe —see Foreign body, entering through
        orifice, eyeball
    gum T18.0
    Highmore's antrum T17.0
    hypopharynx —see Foreign body, pharynx
    ileum T18.3
    intestine (small) T18.3
      large T18.4
    lacrimal apparatus (punctum) —see
        Foreign body, entering through orifice,
        eye, specified part NEC
    large intestine T18.4

Foreign body *(Continued)*
  superficial, without open wound *(Continued)*
    calf —*see* Foreign body, superficial, leg
    canthus —*see* Foreign body, superficial,
        eyelid
    cheek S00.85
      internal S00.552
    chest wall —*see* Foreign body, superficial,
        thorax
    chin S00.85
    clitoris S30.854
    costal region —*see* Foreign body,
        superficial, thorax
    digit(s)
      foot —*see* Foreign body, superficial, toe
      hand —*see* Foreign body, superficial,
          finger
    ear S00.45-●
    elbow S50.35-●
    epididymis S30.853
    epigastric region S30.851
    epiglottis S10.15
    esophagus, cervical S10.15
    eyebrow —*see* Foreign body, superficial,
        eyelid
    eyelid S00.25-●
    face S00.85
    finger(s) S60.459
      index S60.45-●
      little S60.45-●
      middle S60.45-●
      ring S60.45-●
    flank S30.851
    foot (except toe(s) alone) S90.85-●
      toe —*see* Foreign body, superficial, toe
    forearm S50.85-●
      elbow only —*see* Foreign body,
          superficial, elbow
    forehead S00.85
    genital organs, external
      female S30.856
      male S30.855
    groin S30.851
    gum S00.552
    hand S60.55-●
    head S00.95
      ear —*see* Foreign body, superficial, ear
      eyelid —*see* Foreign body, superficial,
          eyelid
      lip S00.551
      nose S00.35
      oral cavity S00.552
      scalp S00.05
      specified site NEC S00.85
    heel —*see* Foreign body, superficial, foot
    hip S70.25-●
    inguinal region S30.851
    interscapular region S20.459
    jaw S00.85
    knee S80.25-●
    labium (majus) (minus) S30.854
    larynx S10.15
    leg (lower) S80.85-●
      knee —*see* Foreign body, superficial,
          knee
      upper —*see* Foreign body, superficial,
          thigh
    lip S00.551
    lower back S30.850
    lumbar region S30.850
    malar region S00.85
    mammary —*see* Foreign body, superficial,
        breast
    mastoid region S00.85
    mouth S00.552
    nail
      finger —*see* Foreign body, superficial,
          finger
      toe —*see* Foreign body, superficial, toe
    nape S10.85
    nasal S00.35

Foreign body *(Continued)*
  superficial, without open wound *(Continued)*
    neck S10.95
      specified site NEC S10.85
      throat S10.15
    nose S00.35
    occipital region S00.05
    oral cavity S00.552
    orbital region —*see* Foreign body,
        superficial, eyelid
    palate S00.552
    palm —*see* Foreign body, superficial, hand
    parietal region S00.05
    pelvis S30.850
    penis S30.852
    perineum
      female S30.854
      male S30.850
    periocular area —*see* Foreign body,
        superficial, eyelid
    phalanges
      finger —*see* Foreign body, superficial,
          finger
      toe —*see* Foreign body, superficial, toe
    pharynx S10.15
    pinna —*see* Foreign body, superficial, ear
    popliteal space —*see* Foreign body,
        superficial, knee
    prepuce S30.852
    pubic region S30.850
    pudendum
      female S30.856
      male S30.855
    sacral region S30.850
    scalp S00.05
    scapular region —*see* Foreign body,
        superficial, shoulder
    scrotum S30.853
    shin —*see* Foreign body, superficial, leg
    shoulder S40.25-●
    sternal region S20.359
    submaxillary region S00.85
    submental region S00.85
    subungual
      finger(s) —*see* Foreign body, superficial,
          finger
      toe(s) —*see* Foreign body, superficial, toe
    supraclavicular fossa S10.85
    supraorbital S00.85
    temple S00.85
    temporal region S00.85
    testis S30.853
    thigh S70.35-●
    thorax, thoracic (wall) S20.95
      back S20.45-●
      front S20.35-●
    throat S10.15
    thumb S60.35-●
    toe(s) (lesser) S90.456
      great S90.45-●
    tongue S00.552
    trachea S10.15
    tunica vaginalis S30.853
    tympanum, tympanic membrane —*see*
        Foreign body, superficial, ear
    uvula S00.552
    vagina S30.854
    vocal cords S10.15
    vulva S30.854
    wrist S60.85-●
  swallowed T18.9
  trachea T17.408
    causing
      asphyxiation T17.400
        food (bone) (seed) T17.420
        gastric contents (vomitus) T17.410
        specified type NEC T17.490
      injury NEC T17.408
        food (bone) (seed) T17.428
        gastric contents (vomitus) T17.418
        specified type NEC T17.498

Foreign body *(Continued)*
  type of fragment —*see* Retained, foreign body
      fragments (type of)
  vitreous (humor) S05.5-●
Forestier's disease (rhizomelic
    pseudopolyarthritis) M35.3-●
  meaning ankylosing hyperostosis —*see*
      Hyperostosis, ankylosing
Formation
  hyalin in cornea —*see* Degeneration, cornea
  sequestrum in bone (due to infection) —*see*
      Osteomyelitis, chronic
  valve
    colon, congenital Q43.8
    ureter (congenital) Q62.39
Formication R20.2
Fort Bragg fever A27.89
Fossa —*see also* condition
  pyriform —*see* condition
Foster-Kennedy syndrome H47.14-●
Fothergill's
  disease (trigeminal neuralgia) —*see also*
      Neuralgia, trigeminal
  scarlatina anginosa A38.9
Foul breath R19.6
Foundling Z76.1
Fournier disease or gangrene N49.3
  female N76.89
Fourth
  cranial nerve —*see* condition
  molar K00.1
Foville's (peduncular) disease or syndrome G46.3
Fox (-Fordyce) disease (apocrine miliaria) L75.2
▶FPIES (food protein-induced enteropathy
    syndrome) K52.21
Fracture, burst —*see* Fracture, traumatic, by site
Fracture, chronic —*see* Fracture, pathological,
    by site
Fracture, insufficiency —*see* Fracture,
    pathological, by site
Fracture, nontraumatic, NEC
  atypical
    femur M84.750-●
      complete
        oblique M84.759
          left side M84.758
          right side M84.757
        transverse M84.756
          left side M84.755
          right side M84.754
      incomplete M84.753
        left side M84.752
        right side M84.751
Fracture, pathological (pathologic) —*see also*
    Fracture, traumatic M84.40
  ankle M84.47-●
  carpus M84.44-●
  clavicle M84.41-●
  compression (not due to trauma) —*see also*
      Collapse, vertebra M48.50-●
  dental implant M27.63
  dental restorative material K08.539
    with loss of material K08.531
    without loss of material K08.530
  due to
    neoplastic disease NEC —*see also*
        Neoplasm M84.50
      ankle M84.57-●
      carpus M84.54-●
      clavicle M84.51-●
      femur M84.55-●
      fibula M84.56-●
      finger M84.54-●
      hip M84.559
      humerus M84.52-●
      ilium M84.550
      ischium M84.550
      metacarpus M84.54-●
      metatarsus M84.57-●
      neck M84.58
      pelvis M84.550
      radius M84.53-●

▶ New   ⇒ Revised   ~~deleted~~ Deleted   ● Use Additional Character(s)

Fracture, traumatic *(Continued)*
  due to
    birth injury —*see* Birth, injury, fracture
    osteoporosis —*see* Osteoporosis, with
      fracture
  Dupuytren's —*see* Fracture, ankle, lateral
    malleolus
  elbow S42.40-●
  ethmoid (bone) (sinus) —*see* Fracture, skull,
    base
  face bone S02.92
  fatigue —*see also* Fracture, stress
    vertebra M48.40
      cervical region M48.42
      cervicothoracic region M48.43
      lumbar region M48.46
      lumbosacral region M48.47
      occipito-atlanto-axial region M48.41
      sacrococcygeal region M48.48
      thoracic region M48.44
      thoracolumbar region M48.45
  femur, femoral S72.9-●
    basicervical (basal) S72.0
    birth injury P13.2
    capital epiphyseal S79.01-●
    condyles, epicondyles —*see* Fracture,
      femur, lower end
    distal end —*see* Fracture, femur, lower end
    epiphysis
      head —*see* Fracture, femur, upper end,
        epiphysis
      lower —*see* Fracture, femur, lower end,
        epiphysis
      upper —*see* Fracture, femur, upper end,
        epiphysis
    following insertion of implant, prosthesis
      or plate M96.66-●
    head —*see* Fracture, femur, upper end,
      head
    intertrochanteric —*see* Fracture, femur,
      trochanteric
    intratrochanteric —*see* Fracture, femur,
      trochanteric
    lower end S72.40-●
      condyle (displaced) S72.41-●
        lateral (displaced) S72.42-●
          nondisplaced S72.42-●
        medial (displaced) S72.43-●
          nondisplaced S72.43-●
        nondisplaced S72.41-●
      epiphysis (displaced) S72.44-●
        nondisplaced S72.44-●
      physeal S79.10-●
        Salter-Harris
          Type I S79.11-●
          Type II S79.12-●
          Type III S79.13-●
          Type IV S79.14-●
        specified NEC S79.19-●
      specified NEC S72.49-●
      supracondylar (displaced) S72.45-●
        with intracondylar extension
          (displaced) S72.46-●
          nondisplaced S72.46-●
        nondisplaced S72.45-●
      torus S72.47-●
    neck —*see* Fracture, femur, upper end, neck
    pertrochanteric —*see* Fracture, femur,
      trochanteric
    shaft (lower third) (middle third) (upper
      third) S72.30-●
      comminuted (displaced) S72.35-●
        nondisplaced S72.35-●
      oblique (displaced) S72.33-●
        nondisplaced S72.33-●
      segmental (displaced) S72.36-●
        nondisplaced S72.36-●
      specified NEC S72.39-●
      spiral (displaced) S72.34-●
        nondisplaced S72.34-●
      transverse (displaced) S72.32-●
        nondisplaced S72.32-●

Fracture, traumatic *(Continued)*
  femur, femoral *(Continued)*
    specified site NEC —*see* subcategory S72.8
    subcapital (displaced) S72.01-●
    subtrochanteric (region) (section)
      (displaced) S72.2-●
      nondisplaced S72.2-●
    transcervical —*see* Fracture, femur, upper
      end, neck
    transtrochanteric —*see* Fracture, femur,
      trochanteric
    trochanteric S72.10-●
      apophyseal (displaced) S72.13-●
        nondisplaced S72.13-●
      greater trochanter (displaced) S72.11-●
        nondisplaced S72.11-●
      intertrochanteric (displaced) S72.14-●
        nondisplaced S72.14-●
      lesser trochanter (displaced) S72.12-●
        nondisplaced S72.12-●
    upper end S72.00-●
      apophyseal (displaced) S72.13-●
        nondisplaced S72.13-●
      cervicotrochanteric —*see* Fracture,
        femur, upper end, neck, base
      epiphysis (displaced) S72.02-●
        nondisplaced S72.02-●
      head S72.05-●
        articular (displaced) S72.06-●
          nondisplaced S72.06-●
        specified NEC S72.09-●
      intertrochanteric (displaced) S72.14-●
        nondisplaced S72.14-●
      intracapsular S72.01-●
      midcervical (displaced) S72.03-●
        nondisplaced S72.03-●
      neck S72.00-●
        base (displaced) S72.04-●
          nondisplaced S72.04-●
        specified NEC S72.09-●
      pertrochanteric —*see* Fracture, femur,
        upper end, trochanteric
      physeal S79.00-●
        Salter-Harris type I S79.01-●
        specified NEC S79.09-●
      subcapital (displaced) S72.01-●
      subtrochanteric (displaced) S72.2-●
        nondisplaced S72.2-●
      transcervical —*see* Fracture, femur,
        upper end, midcervical
      trochanteric S72.10-●
        greater (displaced) S72.11-●
          nondisplaced S72.11-●
        lesser (displaced) S72.12-●
          nondisplaced S72.12-●
  fibula (shaft) (styloid) S82.40-●
    comminuted (displaced) S82.45-●
      nondisplaced S82.45-●
    following insertion of implant, prosthesis
      or plate M96.67-●
    involving ankle or malleolus —*see*
      Fracture, fibula, lateral malleolus
    lateral malleolus (displaced) S82.6-●
      nondisplaced S82.6-●
    lower end
      physeal S89.30-●
        Salter-Harris
          Type I S89.31-●
          Type II S89.32-●
        specified NEC S89.39-●
      specified NEC S82.83-●
      torus S82.82-●
    oblique (displaced) S82.43-●
      nondisplaced S82.43-●
    segmental (displaced) S82.46-●
      nondisplaced S82.46-●
    specified NEC S82.49-●
    spiral (displaced) S82.44-●
      nondisplaced S82.44-●
    transverse (displaced) S82.42-●
      nondisplaced S82.42-●

Fracture, traumatic *(Continued)*
  fibula (shaft) (styloid) *(Continued)*
    upper end
      physeal S89.20-●
        Salter-Harris
          Type I S89.21-●
          Type II S89.22-●
        specified NEC S89.29-●
      specified NEC S82.83-●
      torus S82.81-●
  finger (except thumb) S62.60-●
    distal phalanx (displaced) S62.63-●
      nondisplaced S62.66-●
    index S62.60-●
      distal phalanx (displaced) S62.63-●
        nondisplaced S62.66-●
    ➣ middle phalanx (displaced) S62.62-●
        nondisplaced S62.65-●
      proximal phalanx (displaced) S62.61-●
        nondisplaced S62.64-●
    little S62.60-●
      distal phalanx (displaced) S62.63-●
        nondisplaced S62.66-●
    ➣ middle phalanx (displaced) S62.62-●
        nondisplaced S62.65-●
      proximal phalanx (displaced) S62.61-●
        nondisplaced S62.64-●
    ➣ middle phalanx (displaced) S62.62-●
      nondisplaced S62.65-●
    middle S62.60-●
      distal phalanx (displaced) S62.63-●
        nondisplaced S62.66-●
    ➣ middle phalanx (displaced) S62.62-●
        nondisplaced S62.65-●
      proximal phalanx (displaced) S62.61-●
        nondisplaced S62.64-●
    proximal phalanx (displaced) S62.61-●
      nondisplaced S62.64-●
    ring S62.60-●
      distal phalanx (displaced) S62.63-●
        nondisplaced S62.66-●
    ➣ middle phalanx (displaced) S62.62-●
        nondisplaced S62.65-●
      proximal phalanx (displaced) S62.61-●
        nondisplaced S62.64-●
    thumb —*see* Fracture, thumb
  following insertion (intraoperative)
    (postoperative) of orthopedic implant,
    joint prosthesis or bone plate M96.69
    femur M96.66-●
    fibula M96.67-●
    humerus M96.62-●
    pelvis M96.65
    radius M96.63-●
    specified bone NEC M96.69
    tibia M96.67-●
    ulna M96.63-●
  foot S92.90-●
    astragalus —*see* Fracture, tarsal, talus
    calcaneus —*see* Fracture, tarsal, calcaneus
    cuboid —*see* Fracture, tarsal, cuboid
    cuneiform —*see* Fracture, tarsal, cuneiform
    metatarsal —*see* Fracture, metatarsal
    navicular —*see* Fracture, tarsal, navicular
    sesamoid S92.81-●
    specified NEC S92.81-●
    talus —*see* Fracture, tarsal, talus
    tarsal —*see* Fracture, tarsal
    toe —*see* Fracture, toe
  forearm S52.9-●
    radius —*see* Fracture, radius
    ulna —*see* Fracture, ulna
  fossa (anterior) (middle) (posterior) S02.19
  frontal (bone) (skull) S02.0
    sinus S02.19
  glenoid (cavity) (scapula) —*see* Fracture,
    scapula, glenoid cavity
  greenstick —*see* Fracture, by site
  hallux —*see* Fracture, toe, great
  hand S62.9-●
    carpal —*see* Fracture, carpal bone

▶ New   ➡ Revised   ~~deleted~~ Deleted   ● Use Additional Character(s)

Fracture, traumatic *(Continued)*
  metastatic —*see* Fracture, pathological,
      due to, neoplastic disease —*see also*
      Neoplasm
  metatarsal bone S92.30-●
    fifth (displaced) S92.35-●
      nondisplaced S92.35-●
    first (displaced) S92.31-●
      nondisplaced S92.31-●
    fourth (displaced) S92.34-●
      nondisplaced S92.34-●
    physeal S99.10-●
      Salter-Harris
        Type I S99.11-●
        Type II S99.12-●
        Type III S99.13-●
        Type IV S99.14-●
      specified NEC S99.19-●
    second (displaced) S92.32-●
      nondisplaced S92.32-●
    third (displaced) S92.33-●
      nondisplaced S92.33-●
  Monteggia's —*see* Monteggia's
      fracture
  multiple
    hand (and wrist) NEC —*see* Fracture, by
        site
    ribs —*see* Fracture, rib, multiple
  nasal (bone(s)) S02.2
  navicular (scaphoid) (foot) —*see also* Fracture,
      tarsal, navicular
    hand —*see* Fracture, carpal, navicular
  neck S12.9
    cervical vertebra S12.9
      fifth (displaced) S12.400
        nondisplaced S12.401
        specified type NEC (displaced)
            S12.490
          nondisplaced S12.491
      first (displaced) S12.000
        burst (stable) S12.01
          unstable S12.02
        lateral mass (displaced) S12.040
          nondisplaced S12.041
        nondisplaced S12.001
        posterior arch (displaced) S12.030
          nondisplaced S12.031
        specified type NEC (displaced)
            S12.090
          nondisplaced S12.091
      fourth (displaced) S12.300
        nondisplaced S12.301
        specified type NEC (displaced)
            S12.390
          nondisplaced S12.391
      second (displaced) S12.100
        dens (anterior) (displaced) (type II)
            S12.110
          nondisplaced S12.112
          posterior S12.111
        specified type NEC (displaced)
            S12.120
          nondisplaced S12.121
        nondisplaced S12.101
        specified type NEC (displaced)
            S12.190
          nondisplaced S12.191
      seventh (displaced) S12.600
        nondisplaced S12.601
        specified type NEC (displaced) S12.690
          nondisplaced S12.691
      sixth (displaced) S12.500
        nondisplaced S12.501
        specified type NEC (displaced)
            S12.590
          nondisplaced S12.591
      third (displaced) S12.200
        nondisplaced S12.201
        specified type NEC (displaced)
            S12.290
          nondisplaced S12.291

Fracture, traumatic *(Continued)*
  neck *(Continued)*
    hyoid bone S12.8
    larynx S12.8
    specified site NEC S12.8
    thyroid cartilage S12.8
    trachea S12.8
  neoplastic NEC —*see* Fracture, pathological,
      due to, neoplastic disease
  neural arch —*see* Fracture, vertebra
  newborn —*see* Birth, injury, fracture
  nontraumatic —*see* Fracture, pathological
  nonunion —*see* Nonunion, fracture
  nose, nasal (bone) (septum) S02.2
  occiput —*see* Fracture, skull, base, occiput
  odontoid process —*see* Fracture, neck,
      cervical vertebra, second
  olecranon (process) (ulna) —*see* Fracture,
      ulna, upper end, olecranon process
  orbit, orbital (bone) (region) S02.8-●
    floor (blow-out) S02.3-●
    roof S02.19
  os
    calcis —*see* Fracture, tarsal, calcaneus
    magnum —*see* Fracture, carpal, capitate
    pubis —*see* Fracture, pubis
  palate S02.8-●
  parietal bone (skull) S02.0
  patella S82.00-●
    comminuted (displaced) S82.04-●
      nondisplaced S82.04-●
    longitudinal (displaced) S82.02-●
      nondisplaced S82.02-●
    osteochondral (displaced) S82.01-●
      nondisplaced S82.01-●
    specified NEC S82.09-●
    transverse (displaced) S82.03-●
      nondisplaced S82.03-●
  pedicle (of vertebral arch) —*see* Fracture,
      vertebra
  pelvis, pelvic (bone) S32.9
    acetabulum —*see* Fracture, acetabulum
    circle —*see* Disruption, pelvic ring
    following insertion of implant, prosthesis
        or plate M96.65
    ilium —*see* Fracture, ilium
    ischium —*see* Fracture, ischium
    multiple
      with disruption of pelvic ring (circle) —
          see Disruption, pelvic ring
      without disruption of pelvic ring (circle)
          S32.82
    pubis —*see* Fracture, pubis
    sacrum —*see* Fracture, sacrum
    specified site NEC S32.89
  periprosthetic, around internal prosthetic
      joint M97.9
    ankle M97.2-●
    elbow M97.4-●
    finger M97.8
    hip M97.0-●
    knee M97.1-●
    shoulder M97.3-●
    specified joint NEC M97.8
    spine M97.8
    toe M97.8
    wrist M97.8
  phalanx
    foot —*see* Fracture, toe
    hand —*see* Fracture, finger
  pisiform —*see* Fracture, carpal, pisiform
  pond —*see* Fracture, skull
  prosthetic device, internal —*see*
      Complications, prosthetic device, by site,
      mechanical
  pubis S32.50-●
    with disruption of pelvic ring —*see*
        Disruption, pelvic ring
    specified site NEC S32.59-●
    superior rim S32.59-●

Fracture, traumatic *(Continued)*
  radius S52.9-●
    distal end —*see* Fracture, radius,
        lower end
    following insertion of implant, prosthesis
        or plate M96.63-●
    head —*see* Fracture, radius, upper end,
        head
    lower end S52.50-●
      Barton's —*see* Barton's fracture
      Colles' —*see* Colles' fracture
      extraarticular NEC S52.55-●
      intraarticular NEC S52.57-●
      physeal S59.20-●
        Salter-Harris
          Type I S59.21-●
          Type II S59.22-●
          Type III S59.23-●
          Type IV S59.24-●
        specified NEC S59.29-●
      Smith's —*see* Smith's fracture
      specified NEC S52.59-●
      styloid process (displaced) S52.51-●
        nondisplaced S52.51-●
      torus S52.52-●
    neck —*see* Fracture, radius, upper end
    proximal end —*see* Fracture, radius, upper
        end
    shaft S52.30-●
      bent bone S52.38-●
      comminuted (displaced) S52.35-●
        nondisplaced S52.35-●
      Galeazzi's —*see* Galeazzi's fracture
      greenstick S52.31-●
      oblique (displaced) S52.33-●
        nondisplaced S52.33-●
      segmental (displaced) S52.36-●
        nondisplaced S52.36-●
      specified NEC S52.39-●
      spiral (displaced) S52.34-●
        nondisplaced S52.34-●
      transverse (displaced) S52.32-●
        nondisplaced S52.32-●
    upper end S52.10-●
      head (displaced) S52.12-●
        nondisplaced S52.12-●
      neck (displaced) S52.13-●
        nondisplaced S52.13-●
      physeal S59.10-●
        Salter-Harris
          Type I S59.11-●
          Type II S59.12-●
          Type III S59.13-●
          Type IV S59.14-●
        specified NEC S59.19-●
      specified NEC S52.18-●
      torus S52.11-●
  ramus
    inferior or superior, pubis —*see* Fracture,
        pubis
    mandible —*see* Fracture, mandible
  restorative material (dental) K08.539
    with loss of material K08.531
    without loss of material K08.530
  rib S22.3-●
    with flail chest —*see* Flail, chest
    multiple S22.4-●
      with flail chest —*see* Flail, chest
  root, tooth —*see* Fracture, tooth
  sacrum S32.10
    specified NEC S32.19
    Type
      1 S32.14
      2 S32.15
      3 S32.16
      4 S32.17
    Zone
      I S32.119
        displaced (minimally) S32.111
          severely S32.112
        nondisplaced S32.110

▶ New   ⇒ Revised   ~~deleted~~ Deleted   ● Use Additional Character(s)

▶ New   ⇒ Revised   ~~deleted~~ Deleted   • Use Additional Character(s)

Fracture, traumatic *(Continued)*
 tibia *(Continued)*
  condyles —*see* Fracture, tibia, upper end
  distal end —*see* Fracture, tibia, lower end
  epiphysis
   lower —*see* Fracture, tibia, lower end
   upper —*see* Fracture, tibia, upper end
  following insertion of implant, prosthesis
    or plate M96.67-●
  head (involving knee joint) —*see* Fracture,
    tibia, upper end
  intercondyloid eminence —*see* Fracture,
    tibia, upper end
  involving ankle or malleolus —*see*
    Fracture, ankle, medial malleolus
  lower end S82.30-●
   physeal S89.10-●
    Salter-Harris
     Type I S89.11-●
     Type II S89.12-●
     Type III S89.13-●
     Type IV S89.14-●
     specified NEC S89.19-●
   pilon (displaced) S82.87-●
    nondisplaced S82.87-●
   specified NEC S82.39-●
   torus S82.31-●
  malleolus —*see* Fracture, ankle, medial
    malleolus
  oblique (displaced) S82.23-●
   nondisplaced S82.23-●
  pilon —*see* Fracture, tibia, lower end, pilon
  proximal end —*see* Fracture, tibia, upper
    end
  segmental (displaced) S82.26-●
   nondisplaced S82.26-●
  specified NEC S82.29-●
  spine —*see* Fracture, tibia, upper end, spine
  spiral (displaced) S82.24-●
   nondisplaced S82.24-●
  transverse (displaced) S82.22-●
   nondisplaced S82.22-●
  tuberosity —*see* Fracture, tibia, upper end,
    tuberosity
  upper end S82.10-●
   bicondylar (displaced) S82.14-●
    nondisplaced S82.14-●
   lateral condyle (displaced) S82.12-●
    nondisplaced S82.12-●
   medial condyle (displaced) S82.13-●
    nondisplaced S82.13-●
   physeal S89.00-●
    Salter-Harris
     Type I S89.01-●
     Type II S89.02-●
     Type III S89.03-●
     Type IV S89.04-●
     specified NEC S89.09-●
   plateau —*see* Fracture, tibia, upper end,
     bicondylar
   specified NEC S82.19-●
   spine (displaced) S82.11-●
    nondisplaced S82.11-●
   torus S82.16-●
   tuberosity (displaced) S82.15-●
    nondisplaced S82.15-●
 toe S92.91-●
  great (displaced) S92.40-●
   distal phalanx (displaced) S92.42-●
    nondisplaced S92.42-●
   nondisplaced S92.40-●
   proximal phalanx (displaced)
     S92.41-●
    nondisplaced S92.41-●
   specified NEC S92.49-●
  lesser (displaced) S92.50-●
   distal phalanx (displaced) S92.53-●
    nondisplaced S92.53-●
   medial phalanx (displaced) S92.52-●
    nondisplaced S92.52-●
   nondisplaced S92.50-●

Fracture, traumatic *(Continued)*
 toe *(Continued)*
  lesser *(Continued)*
   proximal phalanx (displaced) S92.51-●
    nondisplaced S92.51-●
   specified NEC S92.59-●
  physeal
   phalanx S99.20-●
    Salter-Harris
     Type I S99.21-●
     Type II S99.22-●
     Type III S99.23-●
     Type IV S99.24-●
     specified NEC S99.29-●
 tooth (root) S02.5
 trachea (cartilage) S12.8
 transverse process —*see* Fracture, vertebra
 trapezium or trapezoid bone —*see* Fracture,
   carpal
 trimalleolar —*see* Fracture, ankle, trimalleolar
 triquetrum (cuneiform of carpus) —*see*
   Fracture, carpal, triquetrum
 trochanter —*see* Fracture, femur, trochanteric
 tuberosity (external) —*see* Fracture,
   traumatic, by site
 ulna (shaft) S52.20-●
  bent bone S52.28-●
  coronoid process —*see* Fracture, ulna,
    upper end, coronoid process
  distal end —*see* Fracture, ulna, lower end
  following insertion of implant, prosthesis
    or plate M96.63-●
  head S52.60-●
  lower end S52.60-●
   physeal S59.00-●
    Salter-Harris
     Type I S59.01-●
     Type II S59.02-●
     Type III S59.03-●
     Type IV S59.04-●
     specified NEC S59.09-●
   specified NEC S52.69-●
   styloid process (displaced) S52.61-●
    nondisplaced S52.61-●
   torus S52.62-●
  proximal end —*see* Fracture, ulna, upper
    end
  shaft S52.20-●
   comminuted (displaced) S52.25-●
    nondisplaced S52.25-●
   greenstick S52.21-●
   Monteggia's —*see* Monteggia's fracture
   oblique (displaced) S52.23-●
    nondisplaced S52.23-●
   segmental (displaced) S52.26-●
    nondisplaced S52.26-●
   specified NEC S52.29-●
   spiral (displaced) S52.24-●
    nondisplaced S52.24-●
   transverse (displaced) S52.22-●
    nondisplaced S52.22-●
  upper end S52.00-●
   coronoid process (displaced) S52.04-●
    nondisplaced S52.04-●
   olecranon process (displaced) S52.02-●
    with intraarticular extension S52.03-●
    nondisplaced S52.02-●
     with intraarticular extension S52.03-●
   specified NEC S52.09-●
   torus S52.01-●
 unciform —*see* Fracture, carpal, hamate
 vault of skull S02.0
 vertebra, vertebral (arch) (body) (column)
   (neural arch) (pedicle) (spinous process)
   (transverse process)
  atlas —*see* Fracture, neck, cervical vertebra,
    first
  axis —*see* Fracture, neck, cervical vertebra,
    second
  cervical (teardrop) S12.9
   axis —*see* Fracture, neck, cervical
     vertebra, second

Fracture, traumatic *(Continued)*
 vertebra, vertebral *(Continued)*
  cervical *(Continued)*
   first (atlas) —*see* Fracture, neck, cervical
     vertebra, first
   second (axis) —*see* Fracture, neck,
     cervical vertebra, second
  chronic M84.48
  coccyx S32.2
  dorsal —*see* Fracture, thorax, vertebra
  lumbar S32.009
   burst (stable) S32.001
    unstable S32.002
   fifth S32.059
    burst (stable) S32.051
     unstable S32.052
    specified type NEC S32.058
    wedge compression S32.050
   first S32.019
    burst (stable) S32.011
     unstable S32.012
    specified type NEC S32.018
    wedge compression S32.010
   fourth S32.049
    burst (stable) S32.041
     unstable S32.042
    specified type NEC S32.048
    wedge compression S32.040
   second S32.029
    burst (stable) S32.021
     unstable S32.022
    specified type NEC S32.028
    wedge compression S32.020
   specified type NEC S32.008
   third S32.039
    burst (stable) S32.031
     unstable S32.032
    specified type NEC S32.038
    wedge compression S32.030
   wedge compression S32.000
  metastatic —*see* Collapse, vertebra, in,
    specified disease NEC —*see also*
    Neoplasm
  newborn (birth injury) P11.5
  sacrum S32.10
   specified NEC S32.19
   Type
    1 S32.14
    2 S32.15
    3 S32.16
    4 S32.17
   Zone
    I S32.119
     displaced (minimally) S32.111
      severely S32.112
     nondisplaced S32.110
    II S32.129
     displaced (minimally) S32.121
      severely S32.122
     nondisplaced S32.120
    III S32.139
     displaced (minimally) S32.131
      severely S32.132
     nondisplaced S32.130
  thoracic —*see* Fracture, thorax, vertebra
 vertex S02.0
 vomer (bone) S02.2
 wrist S62.10-●
  carpal —*see* Fracture, carpal bone
  navicular (scaphoid) (hand) —*see* Fracture,
    carpal, navicular
 xiphisternum, xiphoid (process) S22.24
 zygoma S02.442
  left side S02.40F
  right side S02.40E
Fragile, fragility
 autosomal site Q95.5
 bone, congenital (with blue sclera) Q78.0
 capillary (hereditary) D69.8
 hair L67.8
 nails L60.3
 non-sex chromosome site Q95.5
 X chromosome Q99.2

▶ New   ⇒ Revised   ~~deleted~~ Deleted   ● Use Additional Character(s)

Fragilitas
crinium L67.8
ossium (with blue sclerae) (hereditary) Q78.0
unguium L60.3
congenital Q84.6
Fragments, cataract (lens), following cataract
surgery H59.02-●
retained foreign body —see Retained, foreign
body fragments (type of)
Frailty (frail) R54
mental R41.81
Frambesia, frambesial (tropica) —see also Yaws
initial lesion or ulcer A66.0
primary A66.0
Frambeside
gummatous A66.4
of early yaws A66.2
Frambesioma A66.1
Franceschetti-Klein (-Wildervanck) disease or
syndrome Q75.4
Francis' disease —see Tularemia
Franklin disease C88.2
Frank's essential thrombocytopenia D69.3
Fraser's syndrome Q87.0
Freckle(s) L81.2
malignant melanoma in —see Melanoma
melanotic (Hutchinson's) —see Melanoma,
in situ
retinal D49.81
Frederickson's hyperlipoproteinemia, type
I and V E78.3
IIA E78.00
IIB and III E78.2
IV E78.1
Freeman Sheldon syndrome Q87.0
Freezing —see also Effect, adverse, cold T69.9
Freiberg's disease (infraction of metatarsal head
or osteochondrosis) —see Osteochondrosis,
juvenile, metatarsus
Frei's disease A55
Fremitus, friction, cardiac R01.2
Frenum, frenulum
external os Q51.828
tongue (shortening) (congenital) Q38.1
Frequency micturition (nocturnal) R35.0
psychogenic F45.8
Frey's syndrome
auriculotemporal G50.8
hyperhidrosis L74.52
Friction
burn —see Burn, by site
fremitus, cardiac R01.2
precordial R01.2
sounds, chest R09.89
Friderichsen-Waterhouse syndrome or disease
A39.1
Friedländer's B (bacillus) NEC —see also
condition A49.8
Friedreich's
ataxia G11.1
combined systemic disease G11.1
facial hemihypertrophy Q67.4
sclerosis (cerebellum) (spinal cord) G11.1
Frigidity F52.22
Fröhlich's syndrome E23.6
Frontal —see also condition
lobe syndrome F07.0
Frostbite (superficial) T33.90
with
partial thickness skin loss —see Frostbite
(superficial), by site
tissue necrosis T34.90
abdominal wall T33.3
with tissue necrosis T34.3
ankle T33.81-●
with tissue necrosis T34.81-●
arm T33.4-●
with tissue necrosis T34.4-●
finger(s) —see Frostbite, finger
hand —see Frostbite, hand
wrist —see Frostbite, wrist

Frostbite (Continued)
ear T33.01-●
with tissue necrosis T34.01-●
face T33.09
with tissue necrosis T34.09
finger T33.53-●
with tissue necrosis T34.53-●
foot T33.82-●
with tissue necrosis T34.82-●
hand T33.52-●
with tissue necrosis T34.52-●
head T33.09
with tissue necrosis T34.09
ear —see Frostbite, ear
nose —see Frostbite, nose
hip (and thigh) T33.6-●
with tissue necrosis T34.6-●
knee T33.7-●
with tissue necrosis T34.7-●
leg T33.9-●
with tissue necrosis T34.9-●
ankle —see Frostbite, ankle
foot —see Frostbite, foot
knee —see Frostbite, knee
lower T33.7-●
with tissue necrosis T34.7-●
thigh —see Frostbite, hip
toe —see Frostbite, toe
limb
lower T33.99
with tissue necrosis T34.99
upper —see Frostbite, arm
neck T33.1
with tissue necrosis T34.1
nose T33.02
with tissue necrosis T34.02
pelvis T33.3
with tissue necrosis T34.3
specified site NEC T33.99
with tissue necrosis T34.99
thigh —see Frostbite, hip
thorax T33.2
with tissue necrosis T34.2
toes T33.83-●
with tissue necrosis T34.83-●
trunk T33.99
with tissue necrosis T34.99
wrist T33.51-●
with tissue necrosis T34.51-●
Frotteurism F65.81
Frozen —see also Effect, adverse, cold T69.9
pelvis (female) N94.89
male K66.8
shoulder —see Capsulitis, adhesive
Fructokinase deficiency E74.11
Fructose 1,6 diphosphatase deficiency E74.19
Fructosemia (benign) (essential) E74.12
Fructosuria (benign) (essential) E74.11
Fuchs'
black spot (myopic) —see also Myopia,
degenerative H44.2-●
dystrophy (corneal endothelium) H18.51
heterochromic cyclitis —see Cyclitis, Fuchs'
heterochromic
Fucosidosis E77.1
Fugue R68.89
dissociative F44.1
hysterical (dissociative) F44.1
postictal in epilepsy —see Epilepsy
reaction to exceptional stress (transient)
F43.0
Fulminant, fulminating —see condition
Functional —see also condition
bleeding (uterus) N93.8
Functioning, intellectual, borderline R41.83
Fundus —see condition
Fungemia NOS B49
Fungus, fungous
cerebral G93.89
disease NOS B49
infection —see Infection, fungus

Funiculitis (acute) (chronic) (endemic)
N49.1
gonococcal (acute) (chronic) A54.23
tuberculous A18.15
Funnel
breast (acquired) M95.4
congenital Q67.6
sequelae (late effect) of rickets E64.3
chest (acquired) M95.4
congenital Q67.6
sequelae (late effect) of rickets E64.3
pelvis (acquired) M95.5
with disproportion (fetopelvic) O33.3
causing obstructed labor O65.3
congenital Q74.2
FUO (fever of unknown origin) R50.9
Furfur L21.0
microsporon B36.0
Furrier's lung J67.8
Furrowed K14.5
nail(s) (transverse) L60.4
congenital Q84.6
tongue K14.5
congenital Q38.3
Furuncle L02.92
abdominal wall L02.221
ankle —see Furuncle, lower limb
antecubital space —see Furuncle, upper
limb
anus K61.0
arm —see Furuncle, upper limb
auditory canal, external —see Abscess, ear,
external
auricle (ear) —see Abscess, ear, external
axilla (region) L02.42-●
back (any part) L02.222
breast N61.1
buttock L02.32
cheek (external) L02.02
chest wall L02.223
chin L02.02
corpus cavernosum N48.21
ear, external —see Abscess, ear, external
external auditory canal —see Abscess, ear,
external
eyelid —see Abscess, eyelid
face L02.02
femoral (region) —see Furuncle, lower
limb
finger —see Furuncle, hand
flank L02.221
foot L02.62-●
forehead L02.02
gluteal (region) L02.32
groin L02.224
hand L02.52-●
head L02.821
face L02.02
hip —see Furuncle, lower limb
kidney —see Abscess, kidney
knee —see Furuncle, lower limb
labium (majus) (minus) N76.4
lacrimal
gland —see Dacryoadenitis
passages (duct) (sac) —see Inflammation,
lacrimal, passages, acute
leg (any part) —see Furuncle, lower limb
lower limb L02.42-●
malignant A22.0
mouth K12.2
navel L02.226
neck L02.12
nose J34.0
orbit, orbital —see Abscess, orbit
palmar (space) —see Furuncle, hand
partes posteriores L02.32
pectoral region L02.223
penis N48.21
perineum L02.225
pinna —see Abscess, ear, external
popliteal —see Furuncle, lower limb

Furuncle (Continued)
  prepatellar —see Furuncle, lower limb
  scalp L02.821
  seminal vesicle N49.0
  shoulder —see Furuncle, upper limb
  specified site NEC L02.828
  submandibular K12.2
  temple (region) L02.02
  thumb —see Furuncle, hand
  toe —see Furuncle, foot
  trunk L02.229
    abdominal wall L02.221
    back L02.222
    chest wall L02.223
    groin L02.224
    perineum L02.225
    umbilicus L02.226
  umbilicus L02.226
  upper limb L02.42-●
  vulva N76.4
Furunculosis —see Furuncle
Fused —see Fusion, fused
Fusion, fused (congenital)
  astragaloscaphoid Q74.2
  atria Q21.1
  auditory canal Q16.1
  auricles, heart Q21.1
  binocular with defective stereopsis H53.32
  bone Q79.8
  cervical spine M43.22

Fusion, fused (Continued)
  choanal Q30.0
  commissure, mitral valve Q23.2
  cusps, heart valve NEC Q24.8
    mitral Q23.2
    pulmonary Q22.1
    tricuspid Q22.4
  ear ossicles Q16.3
  fingers Q70.0-●
  hymen Q52.3
  joint (acquired) —see also Ankylosis
    congenital Q74.8
  kidneys (incomplete) Q63.1
  labium (majus) (minus) Q52.5
  larynx and trachea Q34.8
  limb, congenital Q74.8
    lower Q74.2
    upper Q74.0
  lobes, lung Q33.8
  lumbosacral (acquired) M43.27
    arthrodesis status Z98.1
    congenital Q76.49
    postprocedural status Z98.1
  nares, nose, nasal, nostril(s) Q30.0
  organ or site not listed —see Anomaly,
    by site
  ossicles Q79.9
    auditory Q16.3
  pulmonic cusps Q22.1
  ribs Q76.6

Fusion, fused (Continued)
  sacroiliac (joint) (acquired) M43.28
    arthrodesis status Z98.1
    congenital Q74.2
    postprocedural status Z98.1
  spine (acquired) NEC M43.20
    arthrodesis status Z98.1
    cervical region M43.22
    cervicothoracic region M43.23
    congenital Q76.49
    lumbar M43.26
    lumbosacral region M43.27
    occipito-atlanto-axial region M43.21
    postoperative status Z98.1
    sacrococcygeal region M43.28
    thoracic region M43.24
    thoracolumbar region M43.25
  sublingual duct with submaxillary duct at
    opening in mouth Q38.4
  testes Q55.1
  toes Q70.2
  tooth, teeth K00.2
  trachea and esophagus Q39.8
  twins Q89.4
  vagina Q52.4
  ventricles, heart Q21.0
  vertebra (arch) —see Fusion, spine
  vulva Q52.5
Fusospirillosis (mouth) (tongue) (tonsil) A69.1
Fussy baby R68.12

▶ New　⇒ Revised　deleted Deleted　● Use Additional Character(s)

G

Gain in weight (abnormal) (excessive) —*see also* Weight, gain
Gaisböck's disease (polycythemia hypertonica) D75.1
Gait abnormality R26.9
 ataxic R26.0
 falling R29.6
 hysterical (ataxic) (staggering) F44.4
 paralytic R26.1
 spastic R26.1
 specified type NEC R26.89
 staggering R26.0
 unsteadiness R26.81
 walking difficulty NEC R26.2
Galactocele (breast) N64.89
 puerperal, postpartum O92.79
Galactokinase deficiency E74.29
Galactophoritis N61.0
 gestational, puerperal, postpartum O91.2-●
Galactorrhea O92.6
 not associated with childbirth N64.3
Galactosemia (classic) (congenital) E74.21
Galactosuria E74.29
Galacturia R82.0
 schistosomiasis (bilharziasis) B65.0
GALD (gestational alloimmune liver disease) P78.84
Galeazzi's fracture S52.37-●
Galen's vein —*see* condition
Galeophobia F40.218
Gall duct —*see* condition
Gallbladder —*see also* condition
 acute K81.0
Gallop rhythm R00.8
Gallstone (colic) (cystic duct) (gallbladder) (impacted) (multiple) —*see also* Calculus, gallbladder
 with
  cholecystitis —*see* Calculus, gallbladder, with cholecystitis
 bile duct (common) (hepatic) —*see* Calculus, bile duct
 causing intestinal obstruction K56.3
 specified NEC K80.80
  with obstruction K80.81
Gambling Z72.6
 pathological (compulsive) F63.0
Gammopathy (of undetermined significance [MGUS]) D47.2
 associated with lymphoplasmacytic dyscrasia D47.2
 monoclonal D47.2
 polyclonal D89.0
Gamna's disease (siderotic splenomegaly) D73.1
Gamophobia F40.298
Gampsodactylia (congenital) Q66.7
Gamstorp's disease (adynamia episodica hereditaria) G72.3
Gandy-Nanta disease (siderotic splenomegaly) D73.1
Gang
 membership offenses Z72.810
Gangliocytoma D36.10
Ganglioglioma —*see* Neoplasm, uncertain behavior, by site
Ganglion (compound) (diffuse) (joint) (tendon (sheath)) M67.40
 ankle M67.47-●
 foot M67.47-●
 forearm M67.43-●
 hand M67.44-●
 lower leg M67.46-●
 multiple sites M67.49
 of yaws (early) (late) A66.6
 pelvic region M67.45-●
 periosteal —*see* Periostitis
 shoulder region M67.41-●
 specified site NEC M67.48
 thigh region M67.45-●

Ganglion (Continued)
 tuberculous A18.09
 upper arm M67.42-●
 wrist M67.43-●
Ganglioneuroblastoma —*see* Neoplasm, nerve, malignant
Ganglioneuroma D36.10
 malignant —*see* Neoplasm, nerve, malignant
Ganglioneuromatosis D36.10
Ganglionitis
 fifth nerve —*see* Neuralgia, trigeminal
 gasserian (postherpetic) (postzoster) B02.21
 geniculate G51.1
  newborn (birth injury) P11.3
  postherpetic, postzoster B02.21
 herpes zoster B02.21
 postherpetic geniculate B02.21
Gangliosidosis E75.10
 GM1 E75.19
 GM2 E75.00
  other specified E75.09
  Sandhoff disease E75.01
  Tay-Sachs disease E75.02
 GM3 E75.19
 mucolipidosis IV E75.11
Gangosa A66.5
Gangrene, gangrenous (connective tissue) (dropsical) (dry) (moist) (skin) (ulcer) —*see also* Necrosis I96
 with diabetes (mellitus) —*see* Diabetes, gangrene
 abdomen (wall) I96
 alveolar M27.3
 appendix K35.80
  with
   ~~perforation or rupture K35.2~~
   ~~peritoneal abscess K35.3~~
   ⇒peritonitis, localized (*see also* Appendicitis) K35.31
    ~~generalized (with perforation or rupture) K35.2~~
    ~~localized (with perforation or rupture) K35.3~~
 arteriosclerotic (general) (senile) —*see* Arteriosclerosis, extremities, with, gangrene
 auricle I96
 Bacillus welchii A48.0
 bladder (infectious) —*see* Cystitis, specified type NEC
 bowel, cecum, or colon —*see* Gangrene, intestine
 Clostridium perfringens or welchii A48.0
 cornea H18.89-●
 corpora cavernosa N48.29
  noninfective N48.89
 cutaneous, spreading I96
 decubital —*see* Ulcer, pressure, by site
 diabetic (any site) —*see* Diabetes, gangrene
 emphysematous —*see* Gangrene, gas
 epidemic —*see* Poisoning, food, noxious, plant
 epididymis (infectional) N45.1
 erysipelas —*see* Erysipelas
 extremity (lower) (upper) I96
 Fournier N49.3
  female N76.89
 fusospirochetal A69.0
 gallbladder —*see* Cholecystitis, acute
 gas (bacillus) A48.0
  following
   abortion —*see* Abortion by type complicated by infection
   ectopic or molar pregnancy O08.0
 glossitis K14.0
 hernia —*see* Hernia, by site, with gangrene
 intestine, intestinal (hemorrhagic) (massive) —*see also* Infarct, intestine K55.069
  with
   mesenteric embolism —*see also* Infarct, intestine K55.069
   obstruction —*see* Obstruction, intestine

Gangrene, gangrenous (Continued)
 laryngitis J04.0
 limb (lower) (upper) I96
 lung J85.0
  spirochetal A69.8
 lymphangitis I89.1
 Meleney's (synergistic) —*see* Ulcer, skin
 mesentery —*see also* Infarct, intestine K55.069
  with
   embolism —*see also* Infarct, intestine K55.069
   intestinal obstruction —*see* Obstruction, intestine
 mouth A69.0
 ovary —*see* Oophoritis
 pancreas —*see* Pancreatitis, acute
 penis N48.29
  noninfective N48.89
 perineum I96
 pharynx —*see also* Pharyngitis
  Vincent's A69.1
 presenile I73.1
 progressive synergistic —*see* Ulcer, skin
 pulmonary J85.0
 pulpal (dental) K04.1
 quinsy J36
 Raynaud's (symmetric gangrene) I73.01
 retropharyngeal J39.2
 scrotum N49.3
  noninfective N50.89
 senile (atherosclerotic) —*see* Arteriosclerosis, extremities, with, gangrene
 spermatic cord N49.1
  noninfective N50.89
 spine I96
 spirochetal NEC A69.8
 spreading cutaneous I96
 stomatitis A69.0
 symmetrical I73.01
 testis (infectional) N45.2
  noninfective N44.8
 throat —*see also* Pharyngitis
  diphtheritic A36.0
  Vincent's A69.1
 thyroid (gland) E07.89
 tooth (pulp) K04.1
 tuberculous NEC —*see* Tuberculosis
 tunica vaginalis N49.1
  noninfective N50.89
 umbilicus I96
 uterus —*see* Endometritis
 uvulitis K12.2
 vas deferens N49.1
  noninfective N50.89
 vulva N76.89
Ganister disease J62.8
Ganser's syndrome (hysterical) F44.89
Gardner-Diamond syndrome (autoerythrocyte sensitization) D69.2
Gargoylism E76.01
Garré's disease, osteitis (sclerosing), osteomyelitis —*see* Osteomyelitis, specified type NEC
Garrod's pad, knuckle M72.1
Gartner's duct
 cyst Q52.4
 persistent Q50.6
Gas R14.3
 asphyxiation, inhalation, poisoning, suffocation NEC —*see* Table of Drugs and Chemicals
 excessive R14.0
 gangrene A48.0
  following
   abortion —*see* Abortion by type complicated by infection
   ectopic or molar pregnancy O08.0
 on stomach R14.0
 pains R14.1
Gastralgia —*see also* Pain, abdominal
Gastrectasis K31.0
 psychogenic F45.8

Gastric —*see* condition
Gastrinoma
  malignant
    pancreas C25.4
    specified site NEC —*see* Neoplasm,
      malignant, by site
    unspecified site C25.4
  specified site —*see* Neoplasm, uncertain
    behavior
  unspecified site D37.9
Gastritis (simple) K29.70
  with bleeding K29.71
  acute (erosive) K29.00
    with bleeding K29.01
  alcoholic K29.20
    with bleeding K29.21
  allergic K29.60
    with bleeding K29.61
  atrophic (chronic) K29.40
    with bleeding K29.41
  chronic (antral) (fundal) K29.50
    with bleeding K29.51
    atrophic K29.40
      with bleeding K29.41
    superficial K29.30
      with bleeding K29.31
  dietary counseling and surveillance Z71.3
  due to diet deficiency E63.9
  eosinophilic K52.81
  giant hypertrophic K29.60
    with bleeding K29.61
  granulomatous K29.60
    with bleeding K29.61
  hypertrophic (mucosa) K29.60
    with bleeding K29.61
  nervous F54
  spastic K29.60
    with bleeding K29.61
  specified NEC K29.60
    with bleeding K29.61
  superficial chronic K29.30
    with bleeding K29.31
  tuberculous A18.83
  viral NEC A08.4
Gastrocarcinoma —*see* Neoplasm, malignant,
    stomach
Gastrocolic —*see* condition
Gastrodisciasis, gastrodiscoidiasis B66.8
Gastroduodenitis K29.90
  with bleeding K29.91
  virus, viral A08.4
    specified type NEC A08.39
Gastrodynia —*see* Pain, abdominal
Gastroenteritis (acute) (chronic) (noninfectious)
    (*see also* Enteritis) K52.9
  allergic K52.29
  with
    eosinophilic gastritis or gastroenteritis
      K52.81
    food protein-induced enterocolitis
      syndrome K52.21
    food protein-induced enteropathy K52.22
  dietetic —*see also* Gastroenteritis, allergic
    K52.29
  drug-induced K52.1
  due to
    Cryptosporidium A07.2
    drugs K52.1
    food poisoning —*see* Intoxication,
      foodborne
    radiation K52.0
  eosinophilic K52.81
  epidemic (infectious) A09
  food hypersensitivity —*see also*
      Gastroenteritis, allergic K52.29
  infectious —*see* Enteritis, infectious
  influenzal —*see* Influenza, with
      gastroenteritis
  noninfectious K52.9
    specified NEC K52.89
  rotaviral A08.0

Gastroenteritis (*Continued*)
  Salmonella A02.0
  toxic K52.1
  viral NEC A08.4
    acute infectious A08.39
      type Norwalk A08.11
    infantile (acute) A08.39
    Norwalk agent A08.11
    rotaviral A08.0
    severe of infants A08.39
    specified type NEC A08.39
Gastroenteropathy —*see also* Gastroenteritis
    K52.9
  acute, due to Norovirus A08.11
  acute, due to Norwalk agent A08.11
  infectious A09
Gastroenteroptosis K63.4
Gastroesophageal laceration-hemorrhage
    syndrome K22.6
Gastrointestinal —*see* condition
Gastrojejunal —*see* condition
Gastrojejunitis —*see also* Enteritis K52.9
Gastrojejunocolic —*see* condition
Gastroliths K31.89
Gastromalacia K31.89
Gastroparalysis K31.84
  diabetic —*see* Diabetes, gastroparalysis
Gastroparesis K31.84
  diabetic —*see* Diabetes, by type, with
      gastroparesis
Gastropathy K31.9
  congestive portal K31.89
  erythematous K29.70
  exudative K90.89
  portal hypertensive K31.89
Gastroptosis K31.89
Gastrorrhagia K92.2
  psychogenic F45.8
Gastroschisis (congenital) Q79.3
Gastrospasm (neurogenic) (reflex) K31.89
  neurotic F45.8
  psychogenic F45.8
Gastrostaxis —*see* Gastritis, with bleeding
Gastrostenosis K31.89
Gastrostomy
  attention to Z43.1
  status Z93.1
Gastrosuccorrhea (continuous) (intermittent)
    K31.89
  neurotic F45.8
  psychogenic F45.8
Gatophobia F40.218
Gaucher's disease or splenomegaly (adult)
    (infantile) E75.22
Gee (-Herter)(-Thaysen) disease (nontropical
    sprue) K90.0
Gélineau's syndrome G47.419
  with cataplexy G47.411
Gemination, tooth, teeth K00.2
Gemistocytoma
  specified site —*see* Neoplasm, malignant, by
    site
  unspecified site C71.9
General, generalized —*see* condition
Genetic
  carrier (status)
    cystic fibrosis Z14.1
    hemophilia A (asymptomatic) Z14.01
      symptomatic Z14.02
    specified NEC Z14.8
  susceptibility to disease NEC Z15.89
    malignant neoplasm Z15.09
      breast Z15.01
      endometrium Z15.04
      ovary Z15.02
      prostate Z15.03
      specified NEC Z15.09
    multiple endocrine neoplasia Z15.81
Genital —*see* condition
Genito-anorectal syndrome A55
Genitourinary system —*see* condition

Genu
  congenital Q74.1
  extrorsum (acquired) —*see also* Deformity,
      varus, knee
    congenital Q74.1
    sequelae (late effect) of rickets E64.3
  introrsum (acquired) —*see also* Deformity,
      valgus, knee
    congenital Q74.1
    sequelae (late effect) of rickets E64.3
  rachitic (old) E64.3
  recurvatum (acquired) —*see also* Deformity,
      limb, specified type NEC, lower leg
    congenital Q68.2
    sequelae (late effect) of rickets E64.3
  valgum (acquired) (knock-knee) M21.06-●
    congenital Q74.1
    sequelae (late effect) of rickets E64.3
  varum (acquired) (bowleg) M21.16-●
    congenital Q74.1
    sequelae (late effect) of rickets E64.3
Geographic tongue K14.1
Geophagia —*see* Pica
Geotrichosis B48.3
  stomatitis B48.3
Gephyrophobia F40.242
Gerbode defect Q21.0
GERD (gastroesophageal reflux disease) K21.9
Gerhardt's
  disease (erythromelalgia) I73.81
  syndrome (vocal cord paralysis)
      J38.00
    bilateral J38.02
    unilateral J38.01
German measles —*see also* Rubella
  exposure to Z20.4
Germinoblastoma (diffuse) C85.9-●
  follicular C82.9-●
Germinoma —*see* Neoplasm, malignant, by site
Gerontoxon —*see* Degeneration, cornea, senile
Gerstmann-Sträussler-Scheinker syndrome
    (GSS) A81.82
Gerstmann's syndrome R48.8
  developmental F81.2
Gestation (period) —*see also* Pregnancy
  ectopic —*see* Pregnancy, by site
  multiple O30.9-●
    greater than quadruplets —*see* Pregnancy,
      multiple (gestation), specified NEC
    specified NEC —*see* Pregnancy, multiple
      (gestation), specified NEC
Gestational
  mammary abscess O91.11-●
  purulent mastitis O91.11-●
  subareolar abscess O91.11-●
Ghon tubercle, primary infection A15.7
Ghost
  teeth K00.4
  vessels (cornea) H16.41-●
Ghoul hand A66.3
Gianotti-Crosti disease L44.4
Giant
  cell
    epulis K06.8
    peripheral granuloma K06.8
  esophagus, congenital Q39.5
  kidney, congenital Q63.3
  urticaria T78.3
    hereditary D84.1
Giardiasis A07.1
Gibert's disease or pityriasis L42
Giddiness R42
  hysterical F44.89
  psychogenic F45.8
Gierke's disease (glycogenosis I) E74.01
Gigantism (cerebral) (hypophyseal) (pituitary)
    E22.0
  constitutional E34.4
Gilbert's disease or syndrome E80.4
Gilchrist's disease B40.9
Gilford-Hutchinson disease E34.8

▶ New   ➠ Revised   ~~deleted~~ Deleted   ● Use Additional Character(s)

Gilles de la Tourette's disease or syndrome
(motor-verbal tic) F95.2
Gingivitis K05.10
acute (catarrhal) K05.00
necrotizing A69.1
nonplaque induced K05.01
plaque induced K05.00
chronic (desquamative) (hyperplastic)
(simple marginal) (pregnancy
associated) (ulcerative) K05.10
nonplaque induced K05.11
plaque induced K05.10
expulsiva —see Periodontitis
necrotizing ulcerative (acute) A69.1
pellagrous E52
acute necrotizing A69.1
Vincent's A69.1
Gingivoglossitis K14.0
Gingivopericementitis —see Periodontitis
Gingivosis —see Gingivitis, chronic
Gingivostomatitis K05.10
herpesviral B00.2
necrotizing ulcerative (acute) A69.1
Gland, glandular —see condition
Glanders A24.0
Glanzmann (-Naegeli) disease or
thrombasthenia D69.1
Glasgow coma scale
total score
3-8 R40.243
9-12 R40.242
13-15 R40.241
Glass-blower's disease (cataract) —see
Cataract, specified NEC
Glaucoma H40.9
with
increased episcleral venous pressure
H40.81-●
pseudoexfoliation of lens —see Glaucoma,
open angle, primary, capsular
absolute H44.51-●
angle-closure (primary) H40.20-●
acute (attack) (crisis) H40.21-●
chronic H40.22-●
intermittent H40.23-●
residual stage H40.24-●
borderline H40.00-●
capsular (with pseudoexfoliation of lens) —
see Glaucoma, open angle, primary,
capsular
childhood Q15.0
closed angle —see Glaucoma, angle-closure
congenital Q15.0
corticosteroid-induced —see Glaucoma,
secondary, drugs
hypersecretion H40.82-●
in (due to)
amyloidosis E85.4 [H42]
aniridia Q13.1 [H42]
concussion of globe —see Glaucoma,
secondary, trauma
dislocation of lens —see Glaucoma,
secondary
disorder of lens NEC —see Glaucoma,
secondary
drugs —see Glaucoma, secondary, drugs
endocrine disease NOS E34.9 [H42]
eye
inflammation —see Glaucoma,
secondary, inflammation
trauma —see Glaucoma, secondary,
trauma
hypermature cataract —see Glaucoma,
secondary
iridocyclitis —see Glaucoma, secondary,
inflammation
lens disorder —see Glaucoma, secondary,
Lowe's syndrome E72.03 [H42]
metabolic disease NOS E88.9 [H42]
ocular disorders NEC —see Glaucoma,
secondary

Glaucoma (Continued)
in (due to) (Continued)
onchocerciasis B73.02
pupillary block —see Glaucoma, secondary
retinal vein occlusion —see Glaucoma,
secondary
Rieger's anomaly Q13.81 [H42]
rubeosis of iris —see Glaucoma, secondary
tumor of globe —see Glaucoma, secondary
infantile Q15.0
low tension —see Glaucoma, open angle,
primary, low-tension
malignant H40.83-●
narrow angle —see Glaucoma, angle-closure
newborn Q15.0
noncongestive (chronic) —see Glaucoma,
open angle
nonobstructive —see Glaucoma, open angle
obstructive —see also Glaucoma,
angle-closure
due to lens changes —see Glaucoma,
secondary
open angle H40.10-●
primary H40.11-●
capsular (with pseudoexfoliation of lens)
H40.14-●
low-tension H40.12-●
pigmentary H40.13-●
residual stage H40.15-●
phacolytic —see Glaucoma, secondary
pigmentary —see Glaucoma, open angle,
primary, pigmentary
postinfectious —see Glaucoma, secondary,
inflammation
secondary (to) H40.5-●
drugs H40.6-●
inflammation H40.4-●
trauma H40.3-●
simple (chronic) H40.11-●
simplex H40.11-●
specified type NEC H40.89
suspect H40.00-●
syphilitic A52.71
traumatic —see also Glaucoma, secondary,
trauma
newborn (birth injury) P15.3
tuberculous A18.59
Glaucomatous flecks (subcapsular) —see
Cataract, complicated
Glazed tongue K14.4
Gleet (gonococcal) A54.01
Glénard's disease K63.4
Glioblastoma (multiforme)
with sarcomatous component
specified site —see Neoplasm, malignant,
by site
unspecified site C71.9
giant cell
specified site —see Neoplasm, malignant,
by site
unspecified site C71.9
specified site —see Neoplasm, malignant, by
site
unspecified site C71.9
Glioma (malignant)
astrocytic
specified site —see Neoplasm, malignant,
by site
unspecified site C71.9
mixed
specified site —see Neoplasm, malignant,
by site
unspecified site C71.9
nose Q30.8
specified site NEC —see Neoplasm,
malignant, by site
subependymal D43.2
specified site —see Neoplasm, uncertain
behavior, by site
unspecified site D43.2
unspecified site C71.9

Gliomatosis cerebri C71.0
Glioneuroma —see Neoplasm, uncertain
behavior, by site
Gliosarcoma
specified site —see Neoplasm, malignant, by
site
unspecified site C71.9
Gliosis (cerebral) G93.89
spinal G95.89
Glisson's disease —see Rickets
Globinuria R82.3
Globus (hystericus) F45.8
Glomangioma D18.00
intra-abdominal D18.03
intracranial D18.02
skin D18.01
specified site NEC D18.09
Glomangiomyoma D18.00
intra-abdominal D18.03
intracranial D18.02
skin D18.01
specified site NEC D18.09
Glomangiosarcoma —see Neoplasm, connective
tissue, malignant
Glomerular
disease in syphilis A52.75
nephritis —see Glomerulonephritis
Glomerulitis —see Glomerulonephritis
Glomerulonephritis —see also Nephritis N05.9
with
edema —see Nephrosis
minimal change N05.0
minor glomerular abnormality N05.0
acute N00.9
chronic N03.9
crescentic (diffuse) NEC —see also N00-N07
with fourth character .7 N05.7
dense deposit —see also N00-N07 with fourth
character .6 N05.6
diffuse
crescentic —see also N00-N07 with fourth
character .7 N05.7
endocapillary proliferative —see also
N00N07 with fourth character .4
N05.4
membranous —see also N00-N07 with
fourth character .2 N05.2
mesangial proliferative —see also N00-N07
with fourth character .3 N05.3
mesangiocapillary —see also N00-N07 with
fourth character .5 N05.5
sclerosing N18.9
endocapillary proliferative (diffuse) NEC —
see also N00-N07 with fourth character
.4 N05.4
extracapillary NEC —see also N00-N07 with
fourth character .7 N05.7
focal (and segmental) —see also N00-N07 with
fourth character .1 N05.1
hypocomplementemic —
see Glomerulonephritis,
membranoproliferative
IgA —see Nephropathy, IgA
immune complex (circulating) NEC
N05.8
in (due to)
amyloidosis E85.4 [N08]
bilharziasis B65.9 [N08]
cryoglobulinemia D89.1 [N08]
defibrination syndrome D65 [N08]
diabetes mellitus —see Diabetes,
glomerulosclerosis
disseminated intravascular coagulation
D65 [N08]
Fabry (-Anderson) disease E75.21 [N08]
Goodpasture's syndrome M31.0
hemolytic-uremic syndrome D59.3
Henoch (-Schönlein) purpura D69.0
[N08]
lecithin cholesterol acyltransferase
deficiency E78.6 [N08]

Glomerulonephritis (Continued)
  in (Continued)
    microscopic polyangiitis M31.7 [N08]
    multiple myeloma C90.0-● [N08]
    Plasmodium malariae B52.0
    schistosomiasis B65.9 [N08]
    sepsis A41.9-● [N08]
      streptococcal A40-● [N08]
    sickle-cell disorders D57.-● [N08]
    strongyloidiasis B78.9 [N08]
    subacute bacterial endocarditis I33.0
      [N08]
    syphilis (late) congenital A50.59 [N08]
    systemic lupus erythematosus M32.14
    thrombotic thrombocytopenic purpura
      M31.1 [N08]
    typhoid fever A01.09
    Waldenström macroglobulinemia C88.0
      [N08]
    Wegener's granulomatosis M31.31
  latent or quiescent N03.9
  lobular, lobulonodular —
    see Glomerulonephritis,
    membranoproliferative
  membranoproliferative (diffuse) (type 1
    or 3) —see also N00-N07 with fourth
    character .5 N05.5
    dense deposit (type 2) NEC —see also
      N00-N07 with fourth character .6
      N05.6
  membranous (diffuse) NEC —see also
    N00-N07 with fourth character .2 N05.2
  mesangial
    IgA/IgG —see Nephropathy, IgA
    proliferative (diffuse) NEC —see also
      N00-N07 with fourth character .3
      N05.3
  mesangiocapillary (diffuse) NEC —see also
    N00-N07 with fourth character .5 N05.5
  necrotic, necrotizing NEC —see also N00-N07
    with fourth character .8 N05.8
  nodular —see Glomerulonephritis,
    membranoproliferative
  poststreptococcal NEC N05.9
    acute N00.9
    chronic N03.9
    rapidly progressive N01.9
  proliferative NEC —see also N00-N07 with
    fourth character .8 N05.8
    diffuse (lupus) M32.14
  rapidly progressive N01.9
  sclerosing, diffuse N18.9
  specified pathology NEC —see also N00-N07
    with fourth character .8 N05.8
  subacute N01.9
Glomerulopathy —see Glomerulonephritis
Glomerulosclerosis —see also Sclerosis, renal
  intercapillary (nodular) (with diabetes) —see
    Diabetes, glomerulosclerosis
  intracapillary —see Diabetes,
    glomerulosclerosis
Glossagra K14.6
Glossalgia K14.6
Glossitis (chronic superficial) (gangrenous)
  (Moeller's) K14.0
  areata exfoliativa K14.1
  atrophic K14.4
  benign migratory K14.1
  cortical superficial, sclerotic K14.0
  Hunter's D51.0
  interstitial, sclerous K14.0
  median rhomboid K14.2
  pellagrous E52
  superficial, chronic K14.0
Glossocele K14.8
Glossodynia K14.6
  exfoliativa K14.4
Glossoncus K14.8
Glossopathy K14.9
Glossophytia K14.3
Glossoplegia K14.8

Glossoptosis K14.8
Glossopyrosis K14.6
Glossotrichia K14.3
Glossy skin L90.8
Glottis —see condition
Glottitis —see also Laryngitis J04.0
Glucagonoma
  pancreas
    benign D13.7
    malignant C25.4
    uncertain behavior D37.8
  specified site NEC
    benign —see Neoplasm, benign, by site
    malignant —see Neoplasm, malignant, by
      site
    uncertain behavior —see Neoplasm,
      uncertain behavior, by site
  unspecified site
    benign D13.7
    malignant C25.4
    uncertain behavior D37.8
Glucoglycinuria E72.51
Glucose-galactose malabsorption E74.39
Glue
  ear —see Otitis, media, nonsuppurative,
    chronic, mucoid
  sniffing (airplane) —see Abuse, drug,
    inhalant
    dependence —see Dependence, drug,
      inhalant
Glutaric aciduria E72.3
Glycinemia E72.51
Glycinuria (renal) (with ketosis) E72.09
Glycogen
  infiltration —see Disease, glycogen storage
  storage disease —see Disease, glycogen
    storage
Glycogenosis (diffuse) (generalized) —see also
  Disease, glycogen storage
  cardiac E74.02 [I43]
  diabetic, secondary —see Diabetes,
    glycogenosis, secondary
  pulmonary interstitial J84.842
Glycopenia E16.2
Glycosuria R81
  renal E74.8
Gnathostoma spinigerum (infection)
  (infestation), gnathostomiasis (wandering
  swelling) B83.1
Goiter (plunging) (substernal) E04.9
  with
    hyperthyroidism (recurrent) —see
      Hyperthyroidism, with, goiter
    thyrotoxicosis —see Hyperthyroidism,
      with, goiter
  adenomatous —see Goiter, nodular
  cancerous C73
  congenital (nontoxic) E03.0
    diffuse E03.0
    parenchymatous E03.0
    transitory, with normal functioning
      P72.0
  cystic E04.2
    due to iodine-deficiency E01.1
  due to
    enzyme defect in synthesis of thyroid
      hormone E07.1
    iodine-deficiency (endemic) E01.2
  dyshormonogenetic (familial) E07.1
  endemic (iodine-deficiency) E01.2
    diffuse E01.0
    multinodular E01.1
  exophthalmic —see Hyperthyroidism, with,
    goiter
  iodine-deficiency (endemic) E01.2
    diffuse E01.0
    multinodular E01.1
    nodular E01.1
  lingual Q89.2
  lymphadenoid E06.3
  malignant C73

Goiter (Continued)
  multinodular (cystic) (nontoxic) E04.2
    toxic or with hyperthyroidism E05.20
      with thyroid storm E05.21
  neonatal NEC P72.0
  nodular (nontoxic) (due to) E04.9
    with
      hyperthyroidism E05.20
        with thyroid storm E05.21
      thyrotoxicosis E05.20
        with thyroid storm E05.21
    endemic E01.1
    iodine-deficiency E01.1
    sporadic E04.9
    toxic E05.20
      with thyroid storm E05.21
  nontoxic E04.9
    diffuse (colloid) E04.0
    multinodular E04.2
    simple E04.0
    specified NEC E04.8
    uninodular E04.1
  simple E04.0
  toxic —see Hyperthyroidism, with, goiter
  uninodular (nontoxic) E04.1
    toxic or with hyperthyroidism E05.10
      with thyroid storm E05.11
Goiter-deafness syndrome E07.1
Goldberg syndrome Q89.8
Goldberg-Maxwell syndrome E34.51
Goldblatt's hypertension or kidney I70.1
Goldenhar (-Gorlin) syndrome Q87.0
Goldflam-Erb disease or syndrome G70.00
  with exacerbation (acute) G70.01
  in crisis G70.01
Goldscheider's disease Q81.8
Goldstein's disease (familial hemorrhagic
  telangiectasia) I78.0
Golfer's elbow —see Epicondylitis, medial
Gonadoblastoma
  specified site —see Neoplasm, uncertain
    behavior, by site
  unspecified site
    female D39.10
    male D40.10
Gonecystitis —see Vesiculitis
Gongylonemiasis B83.8
Goniosynechiae —see Adhesions, iris,
  goniosynechiae
Gonococcemia A54.86
Gonococcus, gonococcal (disease) (infection)
  —see also condition A54.9
  anus A54.6
  bursa, bursitis A54.49
  conjunctiva, conjunctivitis (neonatorum)
    A54.31
  endocardium A54.83
  eye A54.30
    conjunctivitis A54.31
    iridocyclitis A54.32
    keratitis A54.33
    newborn A54.31
    other specified A54.39
  fallopian tubes (acute) (chronic) A54.24
  genitourinary (organ) (system) (tract) (acute)
    lower A54.00
      with abscess (accessory gland)
        (periurethral) A54.1
    upper —see also condition A54.29
  heart A54.83
  iridocyclitis A54.32
  joint A54.42
  lymphatic (gland) (node) A54.89
  meninges, meningitis A54.81
  musculoskeletal A54.40
    arthritis A54.42
    osteomyelitis A54.43
    other specified A54.49
    spondylopathy A54.41
  pelviperitonitis A54.24
  pelvis (acute) (chronic) A54.24

▶ New   ➡ Revised   ~~deleted~~ Deleted   ● Use Additional Character(s)

Granuloma (Continued)
  colon K63.89
  conjunctiva H11.22-●
  dental K04.5
  ear, middle —see Cholesteatoma
  eosinophilic C96.6
    bone C96.6
    lung C96.6
    oral mucosa K13.4
    skin L92.2
  eyelid H01.8
  facial (e) L92.2
  foreign body (in soft tissue) NEC M60.20
    ankle M60.27-●
    foot M60.27-●
    forearm M60.23-●
    hand M60.24-●
    in operation wound —see Foreign body,
      accidentally left during a procedure
    lower leg M60.26-●
    pelvic region M60.25-●
    shoulder region M60.21-●
    skin L92.3
    specified site NEC M60.28
    subcutaneous tissue L92.3
    thigh M60.25-●
    upper arm M60.22-●
  gangraenescens M31.2
  genito-inguinale A58
  giant cell (central) (reparative) (jaw) M27.1
    gingiva (peripheral) K06.8
  gland (lymph) I88.8
  hepatic NEC K75.3
    in (due to)
      berylliosis J63.2 [K77]
      sarcoidosis D86.89
  Hodgkin C81.9
  ileum K63.89
  infectious B99.9
    specified NEC B99.8
  inguinale (Donovan) (venereal) A58
  intestine NEC K63.89
  intracranial (any site) G06.0
  intraspinal (any part) G06.1
  iridocyclitis —see Iridocyclitis, chronic
  jaw (bone) (central) M27.1
    reparative giant cell M27.1
  kidney —see also Infection, kidney N15.8
  lacrimal H04.81-●
  larynx J38.7
  lethal midline (faciale (e)) M31.2
  liver NEC —see Granuloma, hepatic
  lung (infectious) —see also Fibrosis, lung
    coccidioidal B38.1
    eosinophilic C96.6
  Majocchi's B35.8
  malignant (facial (e)) M31.2
  mandible (central) M27.1
  midline (lethal) M31.2
  monilial (cutaneous) B37.2
  nasal sinus —see Sinusitis
  operation wound T81.89
    foreign body —see Foreign body,
      accidentally left during a procedure
    stitch T81.89
    talc —see Foreign body, accidentally left
      during a procedure
  oral mucosa K13.4
  orbit, orbital H05.11-●
  paracoccidioidal B41.8
  penis, venereal A58
  periapical K04.5
  peritoneum K66.8
    due to ova of helminths NOS —see also
      Helminthiasis B83.9 [K67]
  postmastoidectomy cavity —see
    Complications, postmastoidectomy,
      recurrent cholesteatoma
  prostate N42.89
  pudendi (ulcerating) A58
  pulp, internal (tooth) K03.3

Granuloma (Continued)
  pyogenic, pyogenicum (of) (skin) L98.0
    gingiva K06.8
    maxillary alveolar ridge K04.5
    oral mucosa K13.4
  rectum K62.89
  reticulohistiocytic D76.3
  rubrum nasi L74.8
  Schistosoma —see Schistosomiasis
  septic (skin) L98.0
  silica (skin) L92.3
  sinus (accessory) (infective) (nasal) —see
    Sinusitis
  skin L92.9
    from residual foreign body L92.3
    pyogenicum L98.0
  spine
    syphilitic (epidural) A52.19
    tuberculous A18.01
  stitch (postoperative) T81.89
  suppurative (skin) L98.0
  swimming pool A31.1
  talc —see also Granuloma, foreign body
    in operation wound —see Foreign body,
      accidentally left during a procedure
  telangiectaticum (skin) L98.0
  tracheostomy J95.09
  trichophyticum B35.8
  tropicum A66.4
  umbilical P83.81
  umbilicus P83.81
  urethra N36.8
  uveitis —see Iridocyclitis, chronic
  vagina A58
  venereum A58
  vocal cord J38.3
Granulomatosis L92.9
  lymphoid C83.8-●
  miliary (listerial) A32.89
  necrotizing, respiratory M31.30
  progressive septic D71
  specified NEC L92.8
  Wegener's M31.30
    with renal involvement M31.31
Granulomatous tissue (abnormal) (excessive)
  L92.9
Granulosis rubra nasi L74.8
Graphite fibrosis (of lung) J63.3
Graphospasm F48.8
  organic G25.89
Grating scapula M89.8X1
Gravel (urinary) —see Calculus, urinary
Graves' disease —see Hyperthyroidism, with,
  goiter
Gravis —see condition
Grawitz tumor C64.-●
Gray syndrome (newborn) P93.0
Grayness, hair (premature) L67.1
  congenital Q84.2
Green sickness D50.8
Greenfield's disease
  meaning
    concentric sclerosis (encephalitis periaxialis
      concentrica) G37.5
    metachromatic leukodystrophy E75.25
Greenstick fracture - code as Fracture, by site
Grey syndrome (newborn) P93.0
Grief F43.21
  prolonged F43.29
  reaction —see also Disorder, adjustment F43.20
Griesinger's disease B76.9
Grinder's lung or pneumoconiosis J62.8
Grinding, teeth
  psychogenic F45.8
  sleep related G47.63
Grip
  Dabney's B33.0
  devil's B33.0
Grippe, grippal —see also Influenza
  Balkan A78
  summer, of Italy A93.1
Grisel's disease M43.6

Groin —see condition
Grooved tongue K14.5
Ground itch B76.9
Grover's disease or syndrome L11.1
Growing pains, children R29.898
Growth (fungoid) (neoplastic) (new) —see also
    Neoplasm
  adenoid (vegetative) J35.8
  benign —see Neoplasm, benign, by site
  malignant —see Neoplasm, malignant, by site
  rapid, childhood Z00.2
  secondary —see Neoplasm, secondary, by site
Gruby's disease B35.0
Gubler-Millard paralysis or syndrome G46.3
Guerin-Stern syndrome Q74.3
Guidance, insufficient anterior (occlusal) M26.54
Guillain-Barré disease or syndrome G61.0
  sequelae G65.0
Guinea worms (infection) (infestation) B72
Guinon's disease (motor-verbal tic) F95.2
Gull's disease E03.4
Gum —see condition
Gumboil K04.7
  with sinus K04.6
Gumma (syphilitic) A52.79
  artery A52.09
    cerebral A52.04
  bone A52.77
    of yaws (late) A66.6
  brain A52.19
  cauda equina A52.19
  central nervous system A52.3
  ciliary body A52.71
  congenital A50.59
  eyelid A52.71
  heart A52.06
  intracranial A52.19
  iris A52.71
  kidney A52.75
  larynx A52.73
  leptomeninges A52.19
  liver A52.74
  meninges A52.19
  myocardium A52.06
  nasopharynx A52.73
  neurosyphilitic A52.3
  nose A52.73
  orbit A52.71
  palate (soft) A52.79
  penis A52.76
  pericardium A52.06
  pharynx A52.73
  pituitary A52.79
  scrofulous (tuberculous) A18.4
  skin A52.79
  specified site NEC A52.79
  spinal cord A52.19
  tongue A52.79
  tonsil A52.73
  trachea A52.73
  tuberculous A18.4
  ulcerative due to yaws A66.4
  ureter A52.75
  yaws A66.4
    bone A66.6
Gunn's syndrome Q07.8
Gunshot wound —see also Wound, open
  fracture - code as Fracture, by site
  internal organs —see Injury, by site
Gynandrism Q56.0
Gynandroblastoma
  specified site —see Neoplasm, uncertain
    behavior, by site
  unspecified site
    female D39.10
    male D40.10
Gynecological examination (periodic) (routine)
  Z01.419
  with abnormal findings Z01.411
Gynecomastia N62
Gynephobia F40.291
Gyrate scalp Q82.8

▶ New   ⇒ Revised   ~~deleted~~ Deleted   ● Use Additional Character(s)

H

H (Hartnup's) disease E72.02
Haas' disease or osteochondrosis (juvenile)
    (head of humerus) —see Osteochondrosis,
    juvenile, humerus
Habit, habituation
  bad sleep Z72.821
  chorea F95.8
  disturbance, child F98.9
  drug —see Dependence, drug
  irregular sleep Z72.821
  laxative F55.2
  spasm —see Tic
  tic —see Tic
Haemophilus (H.) influenzae, as cause of
    disease classified elsewhere B96.3
Haff disease —see Poisoning, mercury
Hageman's factor defect, deficiency or disease
    D68.2
Haglund's disease or osteochondrosis
    (juvenile) (os tibiale externum) —see
    Osteochondrosis, juvenile, tarsus
Hailey-Hailey disease Q82.8
Hair —see also condition
  plucking F63.3
    in stereotyped movement disorder F98.4
  tourniquet syndrome —see also Constriction,
    external, by site
    finger S60.44-●
    penis S30.842
    thumb S60.34-●
    toe S90.44-●
Hairball in stomach T18.2
Hair-pulling, pathological (compulsive) F63.3
Hairy black tongue K14.3
Half vertebra Q76.49
Halitosis R19.6
Hallerman-Streiff syndrome Q87.0
Hallervorden-Spatz disease G23.0
Hallopeau's acrodermatitis or disease L40.2
Hallucination R44.3
  auditory R44.0
  gustatory R44.2
  olfactory R44.2
  specified NEC R44.2
  tactile R44.2
  visual R44.1
Hallucinosis (chronic) F28
  alcoholic (acute) F10.951
    in
      abuse F10.151
      dependence F10.251
  drug-induced F19.951
    cannabis F12.951
    cocaine F14.951
    hallucinogen F16.151
    in
      abuse F19.151
        cannabis F12.151
        cocaine F14.151
        hallucinogen F16.151
        inhalant F18.151
        opioid F11.151
        sedative, anxiolytic or hypnotic
          F13.151
        stimulant NEC F15.151
      dependence F19.251
        cannabis F12.251
        cocaine F14.251
        hallucinogen F16.251
        inhalant F18.251
        opioid F11.251
        sedative, anxiolytic or hypnotic
          F13.251
        stimulant NEC F15.251
    inhalant F18.951
    opioid F11.951
    sedative, anxiolytic or hypnotic F13.951
    stimulant NEC F15.951
  organic F06.0

Hallux
  deformity (acquired) NEC M20.5X-●
  limitus M20.5X-●
  malleus (acquired) NEC M20.3-●
  rigidus (acquired) M20.2-●
    congenital Q74.2
    sequelae (late effect) of rickets E64.3
  valgus (acquired) M20.1-●
    congenital Q66.6
  varus (acquired) M20.3-●
    congenital Q66.3
Halo, visual H53.19
Hamartoma, hamartoblastoma Q85.9
  epithelial (gingival), odontogenic, central
    or peripheral —see Cyst, calcifying
    odontogenic
Hamartosis Q85.9
Hamman-Rich syndrome J84.114
Hammer toe (acquired) NEC —see also
    Deformity, toe, hammer toe
  congenital Q66.89
  sequelae (late effect) of rickets E64.3
Hand —see condition
Hand-foot syndrome L27.1
Handicap, handicapped
  educational Z55.9
    specified NEC Z55.8
Hand-Schüller-Christian disease or syndrome
    C96.5
Hanging (asphyxia) (strangulation)
    (suffocation) —see Asphyxia, traumatic,
    due to mechanical threat
Hangnail —see also Cellulitis, digit
  with lymphangitis —see Lymphangitis, acute,
    digit
Hangover (alcohol) F10.129
Hanhart's syndrome Q87.0
Hanot-Chauffard (-Troisier) syndrome E83.19
Hanot's cirrhosis or disease K74.3
Hansen's disease —see Leprosy
Hantaan virus disease (Korean hemorrhagic
    fever) A98.5
Hantavirus disease (with renal manifestations)
    (Dobrava) (Puumala) (Seoul) A98.5
  with pulmonary manifestations (Andes)
    (Bayou) (Bermejo) (Black Creek Canal)
    (Choclo) (Juquitiba) (Laguna negra)
    (Lechiguanas) (New York) (Oran) (Sin
    nombre) B33.4
⇒ Happy puppet syndrome Q93.59
Harada's disease or syndrome H30.81-●
Hardening
  artery —see Arteriosclerosis
  brain G93.89
Harelip (complete) (incomplete) —see Cleft, lip
Harlequin (newborn) Q80.4
Harley's disease D59.6
Harmful use (of)
  alcohol F10.10
  anxiolytics —see Abuse, drug, sedative
  cannabinoids —see Abuse, drug, cannabis
  cocaine —see Abuse, drug, cocaine
  drug —see Abuse, drug
  hallucinogens —see Abuse, drug,
    hallucinogen
  hypnotics —see Abuse, drug, sedative -
    opioids —see Abuse, drug, opioid
  PCP (phencyclidine) —see Abuse, drug,
    hallucinogen
  sedatives —see Abuse, drug, sedative
  stimulants NEC —see Abuse, drug, stimulant
Harris' lines —see Arrest, epiphyseal
Hartnup's disease E72.02
Harvester's lung J67.0
Harvesting ovum for in vitro fertilization
    Z31.83
Hashimoto's disease or thyroiditis E06.3
Hashitoxicosis (transient) E06.3
Hassal-Henle bodies or warts (cornea) H18.49
Haut mal —see Epilepsy, generalized, specified
    NEC

Haverhill fever A25.1
Hay fever —see also Fever, hay J30.1
Hayem-Widal syndrome D59.8
Haygarth's nodes M15.8
Haymaker's lung J67.0
Hb (abnormal)
  Bart's disease D56.0
  disease —see Disease, hemoglobin
  trait —see Trait
Head —see condition
Headache R51
  allergic NEC G44.89
  associated with sexual activity
    G44.82
  chronic daily R51
  cluster G44.009
    chronic G44.029
      intractable G44.021
      not intractable G44.029
    episodic G44.019
      intractable G44.011
      not intractable G44.019
    intractable G44.001
    not intractable G44.009
  cough (primary) G44.83
  daily chronic R51
  drug-induced NEC G44.40
    intractable G44.41
    not intractable G44.40
  exertional (primary) G44.84
  histamine G44.009
    intractable G44.001
    not intractable G44.009
  hypnic G44.81
  lumbar puncture G97.1
  medication overuse G44.40
    intractable G44.41
    not intractable G44.40
  menstrual —see Migraine, menstrual
  migraine (type) —see also Migraine
    G43.909
  nasal septum R51
  neuralgiform, short lasting unilateral, with
    conjunctival injection and tearing
    (SUNCT) G44.059
    intractable G44.051
    not intractable G44.059
  new daily persistent (NDPH) G44.52
  orgasmic G44.82
  periodic syndromes in adults and children
    G43.C0
    with refractory migraine G43.C1
    intractable G43.C1
    not intractable G43.C0
    without refractory migraine G43.C0
  postspinal puncture G97.1
  post-traumatic G44.309
    acute G44.319
      intractable G44.311
      not intractable G44.319
    chronic G44.329
      intractable G44.321
      not intractable G44.329
    intractable G44.301
    not intractable G44.309
  pre-menstrual —see Migraine, menstrual
  preorgasmic G44.82
  primary
    cough G44.83
    exertional G44.84
    stabbing G44.85
    thunderclap G44.53
  rebound G44.40
    intractable G44.41
    not intractable G44.40
  short lasting unilateral neuralgiform, with
    conjunctival injection and tearing
    (SUNCT) G44.059
    intractable G44.051
    not intractable G44.059
  specified syndrome NEC G44.89

Headache *(Continued)*
　spinal and epidural anesthesia - induced
　　　T88.59
　　in labor and delivery O74.5
　　in pregnancy O29.4-●
　　postpartum, puerperal O89.4
　spinal fluid loss (from puncture) G97.1
　stabbing (primary) G44.85
　tension (-type) G44.209
　　chronic G44.229
　　　intractable G44.221
　　　not intractable G44.229
　　episodic G44.219
　　　intractable G44.211
　　　not intractable G44.219
　　intractable G44.201
　　not intractable G44.209
　thunderclap (primary) G44.53
　vascular NEC G44.1
Healthy
　infant
　　accompanying sick mother Z76.3
　　receiving care Z76.2
　person accompanying sick person Z76.3
Hearing examination Z01.10
　with abnormal findings NEC Z01.118
▶infant or child (over 28 days old) Z00.129
　　▶with abnormal findings Z00.121
　following failed hearing screening Z01.110
　for hearing conservation and treatment Z01.12
Heart —*see* condition
Heart beat
　abnormality R00.9
　　specified NEC R00.8
　awareness R00.2
　rapid R00.0
　slow R00.1
Heartburn R12
　psychogenic F45.8
Heartland virus disease A93.8
Heat (effects) T67.9
　apoplexy T67.0
　burn —*see also* Burn L55.9
　collapse T67.1
　cramps T67.2
　dermatitis or eczema L59.0
　edema T67.7
　erythema - code by site under Burn, first degree
　excessive T67.9
　　specified effect NEC T67.8
　exhaustion T67.5
　　anhydrotic T67.3
　　due to
　　　salt (and water) depletion T67.4
　　　water depletion T67.3
　　　　with salt depletion T67.4
　fatigue (transient) T67.6
　fever T67.0
　hyperpyrexia T67.0
　prickly L74.0
　prostration —*see* Heat, exhaustion
　pyrexia T67.0
　rash L74.0
　specified effect NEC T67.8
　stroke T67.0
　sunburn —*see* Sunburn
　syncope T67.1
Heavy-for-dates NEC (infant) (4000g to 4499g)
　　P08.1
　exceptionally (4500g or more) P08.0
Hebephrenia, hebephrenic (schizophrenia) F20.1
Heberden's disease or nodes (with
　　arthropathy) M15.1
Hebra's
　pityriasis L26
　prurigo L28.2
Heel —*see* condition
Heerfordt's disease D86.89
Hegglin's anomaly or syndrome D72.0
Heilmeyer-Schoner disease D45
Heine-Medin disease A80.9

Heinz body anemia, congenital D58.2
Heliophobia F40.228
Heller's disease or syndrome F84.3
HELLP syndrome (hemolysis, elevated liver
　　enzymes and low platelet count) O14.2-●
　complicating
　　childbirth O14.24
　　puerperium O14.25
Helminthiasis —*see also* Infestation, helminth
　Ancylostoma B76.0
　intestinal B82.0
　　mixed types (types classifiable to more
　　　than one of the titles B65.0-B81.3 and
　　　B81.8) B81.4
　　specified type NEC B81.8
　mixed types (intestinal) (types classifiable to
　　more than one of the titles B65.0-B81.3
　　and B81.8) B81.4
　Necator (americanus) B76.1
　specified type NEC B83.8
Heloma L84
Hemangioblastoma —*see* Neoplasm,
　　connective tissue, uncertain behavior
　malignant —*see* Neoplasm, connective tissue,
　　malignant
Hemangioendothelioma —*see also* Neoplasm,
　　uncertain behavior, by site
　benign D18.00
　　intra-abdominal D18.03
　　intracranial D18.02
　　skin D18.01
　　specified site NEC D18.09
　bone (diffuse) —*see* Neoplasm, bone,
　　malignant
　epithelioid —*see also* Neoplasm, uncertain
　　behavior, by site
　　malignant —*see* Neoplasm, malignant, by
　　　site
　malignant —*see* Neoplasm, connective tissue,
　　malignant
Hemangiofibroma —*see* Neoplasm, benign,
　　by site
Hemangiolipoma —*see* Lipoma
Hemangioma D18.00
　arteriovenous D18.00
　　intra-abdominal D18.03
　　intracranial D18.02
　　skin D18.01
　　specified site NEC D18.09
　capillary D18.00
　　intra-abdominal D18.03
　　intracranial D18.02
　　skin D18.01
　　specified site NEC D18.09
　cavernous D18.00
　　intra-abdominal D18.03
　　intracranial D18.02
　　skin D18.01
　　specified site NEC D18.09
　epithelioid D18.00
　　intra-abdominal D18.03
　　intracranial D18.02
　　skin D18.01
　　specified site NEC D18.09
　histiocytoid D18.00
　　intra-abdominal D18.03
　　intracranial D18.02
　　skin D18.01
　　specified site NEC D18.09
　infantile D18.00
　　intra-abdominal D18.03
　　intracranial D18.02
　　skin D18.01
　　specified site NEC D18.09
　intra-abdominal D18.03
　intracranial D18.02
　intramuscular D18.00
　　intra-abdominal D18.03
　　intracranial D18.02
　　skin D18.01
　　specified site NEC D18.09

Hemangioma *(Continued)*
　intrathoracic structures D18.09
　juvenile D18.00
　malignant —*see* Neoplasm, connective tissue,
　　malignant
　plexiform D18.00
　　intra-abdominal D18.03
　　intracranial D18.02
　　skin D18.01
　　specified site NEC D18.09
　racemose D18.00
　　intra-abdominal D18.03
　　intracranial D18.02
　　skin D18.01
　　specified site NEC D18.09
　sclerosing —*see* Neoplasm, skin, benign
　simplex D18.00
　　intra-abdominal D18.03
　　intracranial D18.02
　　skin D18.01
　　specified site NEC D18.09
　skin D18.01
　specified site NEC D18.09
　venous D18.00
　　intra-abdominal D18.03
　　intracranial D18.02
　　skin D18.01
　　specified site NEC D18.09
　verrucous keratotic D18.00
　　intra-abdominal D18.03
　　intracranial D18.02
　　skin D18.01
　　specified site NEC D18.09
Hemangiomatosis (systemic) I78.8
　involving single site —*see* Hemangioma
Hemangiopericytoma —*see also* Neoplasm,
　　connective tissue, uncertain behavior
　benign —*see* Neoplasm, connective tissue,
　　benign
　malignant —*see* Neoplasm, connective tissue,
　　malignant
Hemangiosarcoma —*see* Neoplasm, connective
　　tissue, malignant
Hemarthrosis (nontraumatic) M25.00
　ankle M25.07-●
　elbow M25.02-●
　foot joint M25.07-●
　hand joint M25.04-●
　hip M25.05-●
　in hemophilic arthropathy —*see* Arthropathy,
　　hemophilic
　knee M25.06-●
　shoulder M25.01-●
　specified joint NEC M25.08
　traumatic —*see* Sprain, by site
　vertebrae M25.08
　wrist M25.03-●
Hematemesis K92.0
　with ulcer - code by site under Ulcer, with
　　hemorrhage K27.4
　newborn, neonatal P54.0
　　due to swallowed maternal blood
　　　P78.2
Hematidrosis L74.8
Hematinuria —*see also* Hemoglobinuria
　malarial B50.8
Hematobilia K83.8
Hematocele
　female NEC N94.89
　　with ectopic pregnancy O00.90
　　　with intrauterine pregnancy O00.91
　　ovary N83.8
　male N50.1
Hematochezia —*see also* Melena K92.1
Hematochyluria —*see also* Infestation, filarial
　schistosomiasis (bilharziasis) B65.0
Hematocolpos (with hematometra or
　　hematosalpinx) N89.7
Hematocornea —*see* Pigmentation, cornea,
　　stromal
Hematogenous —*see* condition

▶ New　　⇒ Revised　　~~deleted~~ Deleted　　● Use Additional Character(s)

Hematoma (traumatic) (skin surface intact) — *see also* Contusion
with
  injury of internal organs — *see* Injury, by site
  open wound — *see* Wound, open
amputation stump (surgical) (late) T87.89
aorta, dissecting I71.00
  abdominal I71.02
  thoracic I71.01
  thoracoabdominal I71.03
aortic intramural — *see* Dissection, aorta
arterial (complicating trauma) — *see* Injury, blood vessel, by site
auricle — *see* Contusion, ear
  nontraumatic — *see* Disorder, pinna, hematoma
birth injury NEC P15.8
brain (traumatic)
with
  cerebral laceration or contusion (diffuse) — *see* Injury, intracranial, diffuse
  focal — *see* Injury, intracranial, focal
cerebellar, traumatic S06.37-●
intracerebral, traumatic — *see* Injury, intracranial, intracerebral hemorrhage
newborn NEC P52.4
  birth injury P10.1
nontraumatic — *see* Hemorrhage, intracranial
subarachnoid, arachnoid, traumatic — *see* Injury, intracranial, subarachnoid hemorrhage
subdural, traumatic — *see* Injury, intracranial, subdural hemorrhage
breast (nontraumatic) N64.89
broad ligament (nontraumatic) N83.7
  traumatic S37.892
cerebellar, traumatic S06.37-●
cerebral — *see* Hematoma, brain
cerebrum S06.36-●
  left S06.35-●
  right S06.34-●
cesarean delivery wound O90.2
complicating delivery (perineal) (pelvic) (vagina) (vulva) O71.7
corpus cavernosum (nontraumatic) N48.89
epididymis (nontraumatic) N50.1
epidural (traumatic) — *see* Injury, intracranial, epidural hemorrhage
  spinal — *see* Injury, spinal cord, by region
episiotomy O90.2
face, birth injury P15.4
genital organ NEC (nontraumatic)
  female (nonobstetric) N94.89
    traumatic S30.202
  male N50.1
    traumatic S30.201
internal organs — *see* Injury, by site
intracerebral, traumatic — *see* Injury, intracranial, intracerebral hemorrhage
intraoperative — *see* Complications, intraoperative, hemorrhage
labia (nontraumatic) (nonobstetric) N90.8
liver (subcapsular) (nontraumatic) K76.89
  birth injury P15.0
mediastinum — *see* Injury, intrathoracic
mesosalpinx (nontraumatic) N83.7
  traumatic S37.898
muscle - code by site under Contusion
nontraumatic
  muscle M79.81
  soft tissue M79.81
obstetrical surgical wound O90.2
orbit, orbital (nontraumatic) — *see also* Hemorrhage, orbit
  traumatic — *see* Contusion, orbit
pelvis (female) (nontraumatic) (nonobstetric) N94.89
  obstetric O71.7
  traumatic — *see* Injury, by site

Hematoma (*Continued*)
penis (nontraumatic) N48.89
  birth injury P15.5
perianal (nontraumatic) K64.5
perineal S30.23
  complicating delivery O71.7
perirenal — *see* Injury, kidney
pinna — *see* Contusion, ear
  nontraumatic — *see* Disorder, pinna, hematoma
placenta O43.89-●
postoperative (postprocedural) — *see* Complication, postprocedural, hematoma
retroperitoneal (nontraumatic) K66.1
  traumatic S36.892
scrotum, superficial S30.22
  birth injury P15.5
seminal vesicle (nontraumatic) N50.1
  traumatic S37.892
spermatic cord (traumatic) S37.892
  nontraumatic N50.1
spinal (cord) (meninges) — *see also* Injury, spinal cord, by region
  newborn (birth injury) P11.5
spleen D73.5
  intraoperative — *see* Complications, intraoperative, hemorrhage, spleen
  postprocedural (postoperative) — *see* Complications, postprocedural, hemorrhage, spleen
sternocleidomastoid, birth injury P15.2
sternomastoid, birth injury P15.2
subarachnoid (traumatic) — *see* Injury, intracranial, subarachnoid hemorrhage
  newborn (nontraumatic) P52.5
    due to birth injury P10.3
  nontraumatic — *see* Hemorrhage, intracranial, subarachnoid
subdural (traumatic) — *see* Injury, intracranial, subdural hemorrhage
  newborn (localized) P52.8
    birth injury P10.0
  nontraumatic — *see* Hemorrhage, intracranial, subdural
superficial, newborn P54.5
testis (nontraumatic) N50.1
  birth injury P15.5
tunica vaginalis (nontraumatic) N50.1
umbilical cord, complicating delivery O69.5
uterine ligament (broad) (nontraumatic) N83.7
  traumatic S37.892
vagina (ruptured) (nontraumatic) N89.8
  complicating delivery O71.7
vas deferens (nontraumatic) N50.1
  traumatic S37.892
vitreous — *see* Hemorrhage, vitreous
vulva (nontraumatic) (nonobstetric) N90.89
  complicating delivery O71.7
  newborn (birth injury) P15.5
Hematometra N85.7
  with hematocolpos N89.7
Hematomyelia (central) G95.19
  newborn (birth injury) P11.5
  traumatic T14.8
Hematomyelitis G04.90
Hematoperitoneum — *see* Hemoperitoneum
Hematophobia F40.230
Hematopneumothorax (*see* Hemothorax)
Hematopoiesis, cyclic D70.4
Hematoporphyria — *see* Porphyria
Hematorachis, hematorrhachis G95.19
  newborn (birth injury) P11.5
Hematosalpinx N83.6
with
  hematocolpos N89.7
  hematometra N85.7
    with hematocolpos N89.7
  infectional — *see* Salpingitis
Hematospermia R36.1

Hematothorax (*see* Hemothorax)
Hematuria R31.9
  benign (familial) (of childhood) — *see also* Hematuria, idiopathic
    essential microscopic R31.1
  due to sulphonamide, sulfonamide — *see* Table of Drugs and Chemicals, by drug
  endemic — *see also* Schistosomiasis B65.0
  gross R31.0
  idiopathic N02.9
  with glomerular lesion
    crescentic (diffuse) glomerulonephritis N02.7
    dense deposit disease N02.6
    endocapillary proliferative glomerulonephritis N02.4
    focal and segmental hyalinosis or sclerosis N02.1
    membranoproliferative (diffuse) N02.5
    membranous (diffuse) N02.2
    mesangial proliferative (diffuse) N02.3
    mesangiocapillary (diffuse) N02.5
    minor abnormality N02.0
    proliferative NEC N02.8
    specified pathology NEC N02.8
  intermittent — *see* Hematuria, idiopathic
  malarial B50.8
  microscopic NEC (with symptoms) R31.29
    asymptomatic R31.21
    benign essential R31.1
  paroxysmal — *see also* Hematuria, idiopathic
    nocturnal D59.5
  persistent — *see* Hematuria, idiopathic
  recurrent — *see* Hematuria, idiopathic
  tropical — *see also* Schistosomiasis B65.0
  tuberculous A18.13
Hemeralopia (day blindness) H53.11
  vitamin A deficiency E50.5
Hemi-akinesia R41.4
Hemianalgesia R20.0
Hemianencephaly Q00.0
Hemianesthesia R20.0
Hemianopia, hemianopsia (heteronymous) H53.47
  homonymous H53.46-●
  syphilitic A52.71
Hemiathetosis R25.8
Hemiatrophy R68.89
  cerebellar G31.9
  face, facial, progressive (Romberg) G51.8
  tongue K14.8
Hemiballism (us) G25.5
Hemicardia Q24.8
Hemicephalus, hemicephaly Q00.0
Hemichorea G25.5
Hemicolitis, left — *see* Colitis, left sided
Hemicrania
  congenital malformation Q00.0
  continua G44.51
  meaning migraine — *see also* Migraine G43.909
  paroxysmal G44.039
    chronic G44.049
      intractable G44.041
      not intractable G44.049
    episodic G44.039
      intractable G44.031
      not intractable G44.039
    intractable G44.031
    not intractable G44.039
Hemidystrophy — *see* Hemiatrophy
Hemiectromelia Q73.8
Hemihypalgesia R20.8
Hemihypesthesia R20.1
Hemi-inattention R41.4
Hemimelia Q73.8
  lower limb — *see* Defect, reduction, lower limb, specified type NEC
  upper limb — *see* Defect, reduction, upper limb, specified type NEC
Hemiparalysis — *see* Hemiplegia
Hemiparesis — *see* Hemiplegia

Hemiparesthesia R20.2
Hemiparkinsonism G20
Hemiplegia G81.9-●
   alternans facialis G83.89
   ascending NEC G81.90
      spinal G95.89
   congenital (cerebral) G80.8
      spastic G80.2
   embolic (current episode) I63.4-●
   flaccid G81.0-●
   following
      cerebrovascular disease I69.959
         cerebral infarction I69.35-●
         intracerebral hemorrhage I69.15-●
         nontraumatic intracranial hemorrhage
            NEC I69.25-●
         specified disease NEC I69.85-●
         stroke NOS I69.35-●
         subarachnoid hemorrhage I69.05-●
   hysterical F44.4
   newborn NEC P91.88
      birth injury P11.9
   spastic G81.1-●
      congenital G80.2
   thrombotic (current episode) I63.3-●
Hemisection, spinal cord —*see* Injury, spinal
   cord, by region
Hemispasm (facial) R25.2
Hemisporosis B48.8
Hemitremor R25.1
Hemivertebra Q76.49
   failure of segmentation with scoliosis Q76.3
   fusion with scoliosis Q76.3
Hemochromatosis E83.119
   with refractory anemia D46.1
   due to repeated red blood cell transfusion
      E83.111
   hereditary (primary) E83.110
   neonatal P78.84
   primary E83.110
   specified NEC E83.118
Hemoglobin —*see also* condition
   abnormal (disease) —*see* Disease, hemoglobin
   AS genotype D57.3
   Constant Spring D58.2
   E-beta thalassemia D56.5
   fetal, hereditary persistence (HPFH) D56.4
   H Constant Spring D56.0
   low NOS D64.9
   S (Hb S), heterozygous D57.3
Hemoglobinemia D59.9
   due to blood transfusion T80.89
   paroxysmal D59.6
      nocturnal D59.5
Hemoglobinopathy (mixed) D58.2
   with thalassemia D56.8
   sickle-cell D57.1
      with thalassemia D57.40
         with crisis (vasoocclusive pain) D57.419
            with
               acute chest syndrome D57.411
               splenic sequestration D57.412
         without crisis D57.40
Hemoglobinuria R82.3
   with anemia, hemolytic, acquired (chronic)
      NEC D59.6
   cold (agglutinin) (paroxysmal) (with
      Raynaud's syndrome) D59.6
   due to exertion or hemolysis NEC D59.6
   intermittent D59.6
   malarial B50.8
   march D59.6
   nocturnal (paroxysmal) D59.5
   paroxysmal (cold) D59.6
      nocturnal D59.5
Hemolymphangioma D18.1
Hemolysis
   intravascular
      with
         abortion —*see* Abortion, by type,
            complicated by, hemorrhage
         ectopic or molar pregnancy O08.1

Hemolysis *(Continued)*
   intravascular *(Continued)*
      with *(Continued)*
         hemorrhage
            antepartum —*see* Hemorrhage,
               antepartum, with coagulation
               defect
            intrapartum —*see also* Hemorrhage,
               complicating, delivery O67.0
   postpartum O72.3
   neonatal (excessive) P58.9
      specified NEC P58.8
Hemolytic —*see* condition
Hemopericardium I31.2
   following acute myocardial infarction
      (current complication) I23.0
   newborn P54.8
   traumatic —*see* Injury, heart, with
      hemopericardium
Hemoperitoneum K66.1
   infectional K65.9
   traumatic S36.899
      with open wound —*see* Wound, open, with
         penetration into peritoneal cavity
Hemophilia (classical) (familial) (hereditary)
   D66
   A D66
   B D67
   C D68.1
   acquired D68.311
   autoimmune D68.311
   calcipriva —*see also* Defect, coagulation D68.4
   nonfamilial —*see also* Defect, coagulation
      D68.4
   secondary D68.311
   vascular D68.0
Hemophthalmos H44.81-●
Hemopneumothorax —*see also* Hemothorax
   traumatic S27.2
Hemoptysis R04.2
   newborn P26.9
   tuberculous —*see* Tuberculosis, pulmonary
Hemorrhage, hemorrhagic (concealed) R58
   abdomen R58
   accidental antepartum —*see* Hemorrhage,
      antepartum
   acute idiopathic pulmonary, in infants
      R04.81
   adenoid J35.8
   adrenal (capsule) (gland) E27.49
      medulla E27.8
      newborn P54.4
   after delivery —*see* Hemorrhage, postpartum
   alveolar
      lung, newborn P26.8
      process K08.89
   alveolus K08.89
   amputation stump (surgical) T87.89
   anemia (chronic) D50.0
      acute D62
   antepartum (with) O46.90
      with coagulation defect O46.00-●
         afibrinogenemia O46.01-●
         disseminated intravascular coagulation
            O46.02-●
         hypofibrinogenemia O46.01-●
         specified defect NEC O46.09-●
      before 20 weeks gestation O20.9
         specified type NEC O20.8
         threatened abortion O20.0
      due to
         abruptio placenta —*see also* Abruptio
            placentae O45.9-●
         leiomyoma, uterus —*see* Hemorrhage,
            antepartum, specified cause NEC
         placenta previa O44.1-●
      specified cause NEC —*see* subcategory
         O46.8X-●
   anus (sphincter) K62.5
   apoplexy (stroke) —*see* Hemorrhage,
      intracranial, intracerebral

Hemorrhage, hemorrhagic *(Continued)*
   arachnoid —*see* Hemorrhage, intracranial,
      subarachnoid
   artery R58
      brain —*see* Hemorrhage, intracranial,
         intracerebral
   basilar (ganglion) I61.0
   bladder N32.89
   bowel K92.2
      newborn P54.3
   brain (miliary) (nontraumatic) —*see*
      Hemorrhage, intracranial, intracerebral
      due to
         birth injury P10.1
         syphilis A52.05
      epidural or extradural (traumatic) —
         see Injury, intracranial, epidural
         hemorrhage
      newborn P52.4
         birth injury P10.1
      subarachnoid —*see* Hemorrhage,
         intracranial, subarachnoid
      subdural —*see* Hemorrhage, intracranial,
         subdural
   brainstem (nontraumatic) I61.3
      traumatic S06.38-●
   breast N64.59
   bronchial tube —*see* Hemorrhage, lung
   bronchopulmonary —*see* Hemorrhage, lung
   bronchus —*see* Hemorrhage, lung
   bulbar I61.5
   capillary I78.8
      primary D69.8
   cecum K92.2
   cerebellar, cerebellum (nontraumatic) I61.4
      newborn P52.6
      traumatic S06.37-●
   cerebral, cerebrum —*see also* Hemorrhage,
      intracranial, intracerebral
      lobe I61.1
      newborn (anoxic) P52.4
         birth injury P10.1
   cerebromeningeal I61.8
   cerebrospinal —*see* Hemorrhage, intracranial,
      intracerebral
   cervix (uteri) (stump) NEC N88.8
   chamber, anterior (eye) —*see* Hyphema
   childbirth —*see* Hemorrhage, complicating,
      delivery
   choroid H31.30-●
      expulsive H31.31-●
   ciliary body —*see* Hyphema
   cochlea —*see* subcategory H83.8
   colon K92.2
   complicating
      abortion —*see* Abortion, by type,
         complicated by, hemorrhage
      delivery O67.9
         associated with coagulation defect
            (afibrinogenemia) (DIC)
            (hyperfibrinolysis) O67.0
         specified cause NEC O67.8
      surgical procedure —*see* Hemorrhage,
         intraoperative
   conjunctiva H11.3-●
      newborn P54.8
   cord, newborn (stump) P51.9
   corpus luteum (ruptured) cyst N83.1-●
   cortical (brain) I61.1
   cranial —*see* Hemorrhage, intracranial
   cutaneous R23.3
      due to autosensitivity, erythrocyte D69.2
      newborn P54.5
   delayed
      following ectopic or molar pregnancy
         O08.1
      postpartum O72.2
   diathesis (familial) D69.9
   disease D69.9
      newborn P53
      specified type NEC D69.8

▶ New   ⇒ Revised   ~~deleted~~ Deleted   ● Use Additional Character(s)

Hemorrhage, hemorrhagic *(Continued)*
  due to or associated with
    afibrinogenemia or other coagulation defect
      (conditions in categories D65-D69)
      antepartum —*see* Hemorrhage,
        antepartum, with coagulation
        defect
      intrapartum O67.0
    dental implant M27.61
    device, implant or graft —*see also*
      Complications, by site and type,
      specified NEC T85.838
      arterial graft NEC T82.838
      breast T85.838
      catheter NEC T85.838
        dialysis (renal) T82.838
          intraperitoneal T85.838
        infusion NEC T82.838
          spinal (epidural) (subdural)
            T85.830
        urinary (indwelling) T83.83
      electronic (electrode) (pulse generator)
        (stimulator)
        bone T84.83
        cardiac T82.837
        nervous system (brain) (peripheral
          nerve) (spinal) T85.830
        urinary T83.83
      fixation, internal (orthopedic) NEC T84.83
      gastrointestinal (bile duct) (esophagus)
        T85.838
      genital NEC T83.83
      heart NEC T82.837
      joint prosthesis T84.83
      ocular (corneal graft) (orbital implant)
        NEC T85.838
      orthopedic NEC T84.83
        bone graft T86.838
      specified NEC T85.838
      urinary NEC T83.83
      vascular NEC T82.838
      ventricular intracranial shunt T85.838
  duodenum, duodenal K92.2
    ulcer —*see* Ulcer, duodenum, with
      hemorrhage
  dura mater —*see* Hemorrhage, intracranial,
    subdural
  endotracheal —*see* Hemorrhage, lung
  epicranial subaponeurotic (massive), birth
    injury P12.2
  epidural (traumatic) —*see also* Injury,
    intracranial, epidural hemorrhage
    nontraumatic I62.1
  esophagus K22.8
    varix I85.01
      secondary I85.11
  excessive, following ectopic gestation
    (subsequent episode) O08.1
  extradural (traumatic) —*see* Injury,
    intracranial, epidural hemorrhage
    birth injury P10.8
    newborn (anoxic) (nontraumatic) P52.8
    nontraumatic I62.1
➡ eye NEC H57.89
    fundus —*see* Hemorrhage, retina
    lid —*see* Disorder, eyelid, specified type
      NEC
  fallopian tube N83.6
  fibrinogenolysis —*see* Fibrinolysis
  fibrinolytic (acquired) —*see* Fibrinolysis
  from
    ear (nontraumatic) —*see* Otorrhagia
    tracheostomy stoma J95.01
  fundus, eye —*see* Hemorrhage, retina
  funis —*see* Hemorrhage, umbilicus, cord
  gastric —*see* Hemorrhage, stomach
  gastroenteric K92.2
    newborn P54.3
  gastrointestinal (tract) K92.2
    newborn P54.3
  genital organ, male N50.1

Hemorrhage, hemorrhagic *(Continued)*
  genitourinary (tract) NOS R31.9
  gingiva K06.8
  globe (eye) —*see* Hemophthalmos
  graafian follicle cyst (ruptured) N83.0-●
  gum K06.8
  heart I51.89
  hypopharyngeal (throat) R04.1
  intermenstrual (regular) N92.3
    irregular N92.1
  internal (organs) NEC R58
    capsule I61.0
    ear —*see* subcategory H83.8
    newborn P54.8
  intestine K92.2
    newborn P54.3
  intra-abdominal R58
  intra-alveolar (lung), newborn P26.8
  intracerebral (nontraumatic) —*see*
    Hemorrhage, intracranial,
    intracerebral
  intracranial (nontraumatic) I62.9
    birth injury P10.9
    epidural, nontraumatic I62.1
    extradural, nontraumatic I62.1
    intracerebral (nontraumatic) (in) I61.9
      brain stem I61.3
      cerebellum I61.4
      hemisphere I61.2
        cortical (superficial) I61.1
        subcortical (deep) I61.0
      intraoperative
        during a nervous system procedure
          G97.31
        during other procedure G97.32
      intraventricular I61.5
      multiple localized I61.6
      newborn P52.4
        birth injury P10.1
      postprocedural
        following a nervous system procedure
          G97.51
        following other procedure
          G97.52
      specified NEC I61.8
      superficial I61.1
      traumatic (diffuse) —*see* Injury,
        intracranial, diffuse
        focal —*see* Injury, intracranial, focal
    newborn P52.9
      specified NEC P52.8
    subarachnoid (nontraumatic) (from) I60.9
      intracranial (cerebral) artery I60.7
        anterior communicating I60.2
        basilar I60.4
        carotid siphon and bifurcation
          I60.0-●
        communicating I60.7
          anterior I60.2
          posterior I60.3-●
        middle cerebral I60.1-●
        posterior communicating I60.3-●
        specified artery NEC I60.6
        vertebral I60.5-●
      newborn P52.5
        birth injury P10.3
      specified NEC I60.8
      traumatic S06.6X-●
    subdural (nontraumatic) I62.00
      acute I62.01
      birth injury P10.0
      chronic I62.03
      newborn (anoxic) (hypoxic) P52.8
        birth injury P10.0
      spinal G95.19
      subacute I62.02
      traumatic —*see* Injury, intracranial,
        subdural hemorrhage
    traumatic —*see* Injury, intracranial, focal
      brain injury
  intramedullary NEC G95.19

Hemorrhage, hemorrhagic *(Continued)*
  intraocular —*see* Hemophthalmos
  intraoperative, intraprocedural —*see*
    Complication, hemorrhage (hematoma),
    intraoperative (intraprocedural), by site
  intrapartum —*see* Hemorrhage, complicating,
    delivery
  intrapelvic
    female N94.89
    male K66.1
  intraperitoneal K66.1
  intrapontine I61.3
  intraprocedural —*see* Complication,
    hemorrhage (hematoma), intraoperative
    (intraprocedural), by site
  intrauterine N85.7
    complicating delivery —*see also* Hemorrhage,
      complicating, delivery O67.9
    postpartum —*see* Hemorrhage, postpartum
  intraventricular I61.5
    newborn (nontraumatic) —*see also* Newborn,
      affected by, hemorrhage P52.3
      due to birth injury P10.2
      grade
        1 P52.0
        2 P52.1
        3 P52.21
        4 P52.22
  intravesical N32.89
  iris (postinfectional) (postinflammatory)
    (toxic) —*see* Hyphema
  joint (nontraumatic) —*see* Hemarthrosis
  kidney N28.89
  knee (joint) (nontraumatic) —*see*
    Hemarthrosis, knee
  labyrinth —*see* subcategory H83.8
  lenticular striate artery I61.0
  ligature, vessel —*see* Hemorrhage,
    postoperative
  liver K76.89
  lung R04.89
    newborn P26.9
      massive P26.1
      specified NEC P26.8
    tuberculous —*see* Tuberculosis, pulmonary
  massive umbilical, newborn P51.0
  mediastinum —*see* Hemorrhage, lung
  medulla I61.3
  membrane (brain) I60.8
    spinal cord —*see* Hemorrhage, spinal cord
  meninges, meningeal (brain) (middle) I60.8
    spinal cord —*see* Hemorrhage, spinal cord
  mesentery K66.1
  metritis —*see* Endometritis
  mouth K13.79
  mucous membrane NEC R58
    newborn P54.8
  muscle M62.89
  nail (subungual) L60.8
  nasal turbinate R04.0
    newborn P54.8
  navel, newborn P51.9
  newborn P54.9
    specified NEC P54.8
  nipple N64.59
  nose R04.0
    newborn P54.8
  omentum K66.1
  optic nerve (sheath) H47.02-●
  orbit, orbital H05.23-●
  ovary NEC N83.8
  oviduct N83.6
  pancreas K86.89
  parathyroid (gland) (spontaneous) E21.4
  parturition —*see* Hemorrhage, complicating,
    delivery
  penis N48.89
  pericardium, pericarditis I31.2
  peritoneum, peritoneal K66.1
  peritonsillar tissue J35.8
    due to infection J36

▶ New   ➡ Revised   ~~deleted~~ Deleted   • Use Additional Character(s)

Hepatitis (Continued)
- history of
  - B Z86.19
  - C Z86.19
- homologous serum —see Hepatitis, viral, type B
- in (due to)
  - mumps B26.81
  - toxoplasmosis (acquired) B58.1
    - congenital (active) P37.1 [K77]
- infectious, infective B15.9
  - acute (subacute) B17.9
  - chronic B18.9
- inoculation —see Hepatitis, viral, type B
- interstitial (chronic) K74.69
- lupoid NEC K75.2
- malignant NEC (with hepatic failure) K72.90
  - with coma K72.91
- neonatal giant cell P59.29
- neonatal (idiopathic) (toxic) P59.29
- newborn P59.29
- postimmunization —see Hepatitis, viral, type B
- post-transfusion —see Hepatitis, viral, type B
- reactive, nonspecific K75.2
- serum —see Hepatitis, viral, type B
- specified type NEC
  - with hepatic failure —see Failure, hepatic
- syphilitic (late) A52.74
  - congenital (early) A50.08 [K77]
    - late A50.59 [K77]
  - secondary A51.45
- toxic —see also Disease, liver, toxic K71.6
- tuberculous A18.83
- viral, virus B19.9
  - with hepatic coma B19.0
  - acute B17.9
  - chronic B18.9
    - specified NEC B18.8
    - type
      - B B18.1
        - with delta-agent B18.0
      - C B18.2
  - congenital P35.3
  - coxsackie B33.8 [K77]
  - cytomegalic inclusion B25.1
  - in remission, any type — code to Hepatitis, chronic, by type
  - non-A, non-B B17.8
  - specified type NEC (with or without coma) B17.8
  - type
    - A B15.9
      - with hepatic coma B15.0
    - B B19.10
      - with hepatic coma B19.11
      - acute B16.9
        - with
          - delta-agent (coinfection) (without hepatic coma) B16.1
            - with hepatic coma B16.0
          - hepatic coma (without delta-agent coinfection) B16.2
      - chronic B18.1
        - with delta-agent B18.0
    - C B19.20
      - with hepatic coma B19.21
      - acute B17.10
        - with hepatic coma B17.11
      - chronic B18.2
    - E B17.2
    - non-A, non-B B17.8
- **Hepatization lung** (acute) —see Pneumonia, lobar
- **Hepatoblastoma** C22.2
- **Hepatocarcinoma** C22.0
- **Hepatocholangiocarcinoma** C22.0
- **Hepatocholangioma, benign** D13.4
- **Hepatocholangitis** K75.89
- **Hepatolenticular degeneration** E83.01

Hepatoma (malignant) C22.0
- benign D13.4
- embryonal C22.0
Hepatomegaly —see also Hypertrophy, liver
- with splenomegaly R16.2
- congenital Q44.7
- in mononucleosis
  - gammaherpesviral B27.09
  - infectious specified NEC B27.89
Hepatoptosis K76.89
Hepatorenal syndrome following labor and delivery O90.4
Hepatosis K76.89
Hepatosplenomegaly R16.2
- hyperlipemic (Bürger-Grütz type) E78.3 [K77]
Hereditary —see condition
Heredodegeneration, macular —see Dystrophy, retina
Heredopathia atactica polyneuritiformis G60.1
Heredosyphilis —see Syphilis, congenital
Herlitz' syndrome Q81.1
Hermansky-Pudlak syndrome E70.331
Hermaphrodite, hermaphroditism (true) Q56.0
- 46,XX with streak gonads Q99.1
- 46,XX/46,XY Q99.0
- 46,XY with streak gonads Q99.1
- chimera 46,XX/46,XY Q99.0
Hernia, hernial (acquired) (recurrent) K46.9
- with
  - gangrene —see Hernia, by site, with, gangrene
  - incarceration —see Hernia, by site, with, obstruction
  - irreducible —see Hernia, by site, with, obstruction
  - obstruction —see Hernia, by site, with, obstruction
  - strangulation —see Hernia, by site, with, obstruction
- abdomen, abdominal K46.9
  - with
    - gangrene (and obstruction) K46.1
    - obstruction K46.0
  - femoral —see Hernia, femoral
  - incisional —see Hernia, incisional
  - inguinal —see Hernia, inguinal
  - specified site NEC K45.8
    - with
      - gangrene (and obstruction) K45.1
      - obstruction K45.0
  - umbilical —see Hernia, umbilical
  - wall —see Hernia, ventral
- appendix —see Hernia, abdomen
- bladder (mucosa) (sphincter)
  - congenital (female) (male) Q79.51
  - female —see Cystocele
  - male N32.89
- brain, congenital —see Encephalocele
- cartilage, vertebra —see Displacement, intervertebral disc
- cerebral, congenital —see also Encephalocele endaural Q01.8
- ciliary body (traumatic) S05.2-●
- colon —see Hernia, abdomen
- Cooper's —see Hernia, abdomen, specified site NEC
- crural —see Hernia, femoral
- diaphragm, diaphragmatic K44.9
  - with
    - gangrene (and obstruction) K44.1
    - obstruction K44.0
  - congenital Q79.0
- direct (inguinal) —see Hernia, inguinal
- diverticulum, intestine —see Hernia, abdomen
- double (inguinal) —see Hernia, inguinal, bilateral
- due to adhesions (with obstruction) K56.50
- epigastric —see also Hernia, ventral K43.9
- esophageal hiatus —see Hernia, hiatal

Hernia, hernial (Continued)
- external (inguinal) —see Hernia, inguinal
- fallopian tube N83.4-●
- fascia M62.89
- femoral K41.90
  - with
    - gangrene (and obstruction) K41.40
      - not specified as recurrent K41.40
      - recurrent K41.41
    - obstruction K41.30
      - not specified as recurrent K41.30
      - recurrent K41.31
  - bilateral K41.20
    - with
      - gangrene (and obstruction) K41.10
        - not specified as recurrent K41.10
        - recurrent K41.11
      - obstruction K41.00
        - not specified as recurrent K41.00
        - recurrent K41.01
    - not specified as recurrent K41.20
    - recurrent K41.21
  - not specified as recurrent K41.90
  - recurrent K41.91
  - unilateral K41.90
    - with
      - gangrene (and obstruction) K41.40
        - not specified as recurrent K41.40
        - recurrent K41.41
      - obstruction K41.30
        - not specified as recurrent K41.30
        - recurrent K41.31
    - not specified as recurrent K41.90
    - recurrent K41.91
- foramen magnum G93.5
  - congenital Q01.8
- funicular (umbilical) —see also Hernia, umbilicus
- spermatic (cord) —see Hernia, inguinal
- gastrointestinal tract —see Hernia, abdomen
- Hesselbach's —see Hernia, femoral, specified site NEC
- hiatal (esophageal) (sliding) K44.9
  - with
    - gangrene (and obstruction) K44.1
    - obstruction K44.0
  - congenital Q40.1
- hypogastric —see Hernia, ventral
- incarcerated —see also Hernia, by site, with obstruction
  - with gangrene —see Hernia, by site, with gangrene
- incisional K43.92
  - with
    - gangrene (and obstruction) K43.1
    - obstruction K43.0
- indirect (inguinal) —see Hernia, inguinal
- inguinal (direct) (external) (funicular) (indirect) (internal) (oblique) (scrotal) (sliding) K40.90
  - with
    - gangrene (and obstruction) K40.40
      - not specified as recurrent K40.40
      - recurrent K40.41
    - obstruction K40.30
      - not specified as recurrent K40.30
      - recurrent K40.31
  - bilateral K40.20
    - with
      - gangrene (and obstruction) K40.10
        - not specified as recurrent K40.10
        - recurrent K40.11
      - obstruction K40.00
        - not specified as recurrent K40.00
        - recurrent K40.01
    - not specified as recurrent K40.20
    - recurrent K40.21
  - not specified as recurrent K40.90
  - recurrent K40.91

Hernia, hernial *(Continued)*
  inguinal *(Continued)*
    unilateral K40.90
      with
        gangrene (and obstruction) K40.40
          not specified as recurrent K40.40
          recurrent K40.41
        obstruction K40.30
          not specified as recurrent K40.30
          recurrent K40.31
      not specified as recurrent K40.90
      recurrent K40.91
  internal —*see also* Hernia, abdomen
    inguinal —*see* Hernia, inguinal
  interstitial —*see* Hernia, abdomen
  intervertebral cartilage or disc —*see*
    Displacement, intervertebral disc
  intestine, intestinal —*see* Hernia, by site
  intra-abdominal —*see* Hernia, abdomen
  iris (traumatic) S05.2-●
  irreducible —*see also* Hernia, by site, with
    obstruction
    with gangrene —*see* Hernia, by site, with
      gangrene
  ischiatic —*see* Hernia, abdomen, specified
    site NEC
  ischiorectal —*see* Hernia, abdomen, specified
    site NEC
  lens (traumatic) S05.2-●
  linea (alba) (semilunaris) —*see* Hernia,
    ventral
  Littre's —*see* Hernia, abdomen
  lumbar —*see* Hernia, abdomen, specified site
    NEC
  lung (subcutaneous) J98.4
  mediastinum J98.59
  mesenteric (internal) —*see* Hernia, abdomen
  midline —*see* Hernia, ventral
  muscle (sheath) M62.89
  nucleus pulposus —*see* Displacement,
    intervertebral disc
  oblique (inguinal) —*see* Hernia, inguinal
  obstructive —*see also* Hernia, by site, with
    obstruction
    with gangrene —*see* Hernia, by site, with
      gangrene
  obturator —*see* Hernia, abdomen, specified
    site NEC
  omental —*see* Hernia, abdomen
  ovary N83.4-●
  oviduct N83.4-●
  paraesophageal —*see also* Hernia, diaphragm
    congenital Q40.1
  parastomal K43.5
    with
      gangrene (and obstruction) K43.4
      obstruction K43.3
  paraumbilical —*see* Hernia, umbilicus
  perineal —*see* Hernia, abdomen, specified
    site NEC
  Petit's —*see* Hernia, abdomen, specified site
    NEC
  postoperative —*see* Hernia, incisional
  pregnant uterus —*see* Abnormal, uterus in
    pregnancy or childbirth
  prevesical N32.89
  properitoneal —*see* Hernia, abdomen,
    specified site NEC
  pudendal —*see* Hernia, abdomen, specified
    site NEC
  rectovaginal N81.6
  retroperitoneal —*see* Hernia, abdomen,
    specified site NEC
  Richter's —*see* Hernia, abdomen, with
    obstruction
  Rieux's, Riex's —*see* Hernia, abdomen,
    specified site NEC
  sac condition (adhesion) (dropsy)
    (inflammation) (laceration)
    (suppuration) - code by site under
    Hernia

Hernia, hernial *(Continued)*
  sciatic —*see* Hernia, abdomen, specified site
    NEC
  scrotum, scrotal —*see* Hernia, inguinal
  sliding (inguinal) —*see also* Hernia,
    inguinal
    hiatus —*see* Hernia, hiatal
  spigelian —*see* Hernia, ventral
  spinal —*see* Spina bifida
  strangulated —*see also* Hernia, by site, with
    obstruction
    with gangrene —*see* Hernia, by site, with
      gangrene
  subxiphoid —*see* Hernia, ventral
  supra-umbilicus —*see* Hernia, ventral
  tendon —*see* Disorder, tendon, specified type
    NEC
  Treitz's (fossa) —*see* Hernia, abdomen,
    specified site NEC
  tunica vaginalis Q55.29
  umbilicus, umbilical K42.9
    with
      gangrene (and obstruction) K42.1
      obstruction K42.0
  ureter N28.89
  urethra, congenital Q64.79
  urinary meatus, congenital Q64.79
  uterus N81.4
    pregnant —*see* Abnormal, uterus in
      pregnancy or childbirth
  vaginal (anterior) (wall) —*see* Cystocele
  Velpeau's —*see* Hernia, femoral
  ventral K43.9
    with
      gangrene (and obstruction) K43.7
      obstruction K43.6
    incisional K43.2
      with
        gangrene (and obstruction) K43.1
        obstruction K43.0
      recurrent —*see* Hernia, incisional
    specified NEC K43.9
      with
        gangrene (and obstruction) K43.7
        obstruction K43.6
  vesical
    congenital (female) (male) Q79.51
    female —*see* Cystocele
    male N32.89
  vitreous (into wound) S05.2-●
    into anterior chamber —*see* Prolapse,
      vitreous
Herniation —*see also* Hernia
  brain (stem) G93.5
  cerebral G93.5
  mediastinum J98.59
  nucleus pulposus —*see* Displacement,
    intervertebral disc
Herpangina B08.5
Herpes, herpesvirus, herpetic B00.9
  anogenital A60.9
    perianal skin A60.1
    rectum A60.1
    urogenital tract A60.00
      cervix A60.03
      male genital organ NEC A60.02
      penis A60.01
      specified site NEC A60.09
      vagina A60.04
      vulva A60.04
  blepharitis (zoster) B02.39
    simplex B00.59
  circinatus B35.4
    bullosus L12.0
  conjunctivitis (simplex) B00.53
    zoster B02.31
  cornea B02.33
  encephalitis B00.4
    due to herpesvirus 6 B10.01
    due to herpesvirus 7 B10.09
    specified NEC B10.09

Herpes, herpesvirus, herpetic *(Continued)*
  eye (zoster) B02.30
    simplex B00.50
  eyelid (zoster) B02.39
    simplex B00.59
  facialis B00.1
  febrilis B00.1
  geniculate ganglionitis B02.21
  genital, genitalis A60.00
    female A60.09
    male A60.02
  gestational, gestationis O26.4-●
  gingivostomatitis B00.2
  human B00.9
    1 —*see* Herpes, simplex
    2 —*see* Herpes, simplex
    3 —*see* Varicella
    4 —*see* Mononucleosis, Epstein-Barr (virus)
    5 —*see* Disease, cytomegalic inclusion
      (generalized)
    6
      encephalitis B10.01
      specified NEC B10.81
    7
      encephalitis B10.09
      specified NEC B10.82
    8 B10.89
  infection NEC B10.89
    Kaposi's sarcoma associated B10.89
  iridocyclitis (simplex) B00.51
    zoster B02.32
  iris (vesicular erythema multiforme) L51.9
  iritis (simplex) B00.51
  Kaposi's sarcoma associated B10.89
  keratitis (simplex) (dendritic) (disciform)
    (interstitial) B00.52
    zoster (interstitial) B02.33
  keratoconjunctivitis (simplex) B00.52
    zoster B02.33
  labialis B00.1
  lip B00.1
  meningitis (simplex) B00.3
    zoster B02.1
  ophthalmicus (zoster) NEC B02.30
    simplex B00.50
  penis A60.01
  perianal skin A60.1
  pharyngitis, pharyngotonsillitis B00.2
  rectum A60.1
  scrotum A60.02
  sepsis B00.7
  simplex B00.9
    complicated NEC B00.89
    congenital P35.2
    conjunctivitis B00.53
    external ear B00.1
    eyelid B00.59
    hepatitis B00.81
    keratitis (interstitial) B00.52
    myelitis B00.82
    specified complication NEC B00.89
    visceral B00.89
  stomatitis B00.2
  tonsurans B35.0
  visceral B00.89
  vulva A60.04
  whitlow B00.89
  zoster —*see also* condition B02.9
    auricularis B02.21
    complicated NEC B02.8
    conjunctivitis B02.31
    disseminated B02.7
    encephalitis B02.0
    eye(lid) B02.39
    geniculate ganglionitis B02.21
    keratitis (interstitial) B02.33
    meningitis B02.1
    myelitis B02.24
    neuritis, neuralgia B02.29
    ophthalmicus NEC B02.30
    oticus B02.21

▶ New   ⇒ Revised   ~~deleted~~ Deleted   ● Use Additional Character(s)

Herpes, herpesvirus, herpetic *(Continued)*
zoster *(Continued)*
polyneuropathy B02.23
specified complication NEC B02.8
trigeminal neuralgia B02.22
Herpesvirus (human) —*see* Herpes
Herpetophobia F40.218
Herrick's anemia —*see* Disease, sickle-cell
Hers' disease E74.09
Herter-Gee syndrome K90.0
Herxheimer's reaction R68.89
Hesitancy
of micturition R39.11
urinary R39.11
Hesselbach's hernia —*see* Hernia, femoral,
specified site NEC
Heterochromia (congenital) Q13.2
cataract —*see* Cataract, complicated
cyclitis (Fuchs) —*see* Cyclitis, Fuchs'
heterochromic
hair L67.1
iritis —*see* Cyclitis, Fuchs' heterochromic
retained metallic foreign body
(nonmagnetic) —*see* Foreign body,
intraocular, old, retained
magnetic —*see* Foreign body, intraocular,
old, retained, magnetic
uveitis —*see* Cyclitis, Fuchs' heterochromic
Heterophoria —*see* Strabismus, heterophoria
Heterophyes, heterophyiasis (small intestine)
B66.8
Heterotopia, heterotopic —*see also* Malposition,
congenital
cerebralis Q04.8
Heterotropia —*see* Strabismus
Heubner-Herter disease K90.0
Hexadactylism Q69.9
HGSIL (cytology finding) (high grade
squamous intraepithelial lesion on
cytologic smear) (Pap smear finding)
anus R85.613
cervix R87.613
biopsy (histology) finding — *see* Neoplasia,
intraepithelial, cervix, grade II or
grade III
vagina R87.623
biopsy (histology) finding — *see* Neoplasia,
intraepithelial, vagina, grade II or
grade III
Hibernoma —*see* Lipoma
Hiccup, hiccough R06.6
epidemic B33.0
psychogenic F45.8
Hidden penis (congenital) Q55.64
acquired N48.83
Hidradenitis (axillaris) (suppurative) L73.2
Hidradenoma (nodular) —*see also* Neoplasm,
skin, benign
clear cell —*see* Neoplasm, skin, benign
papillary —*see* Neoplasm, skin, benign
Hidrocystoma —*see* Neoplasm, skin, benign
High
altitude effects T70.20
anoxia T70.29
on
ears T70.0
sinuses T70.1
polycythemia D75.1
arch
foot Q66.7
palate, congenital Q38.5
arterial tension —*see* Hypertension
basal metabolic rate R94.8
blood pressure —*see also* Hypertension
borderline R03.0
reading (incidental) (isolated)
(nonspecific), without diagnosis of
hypertension R03.0
cholesterol E78.00
with high triglycerides E78.2
diaphragm (congenital) Q79.1

High *(Continued)*
expressed emotional level within family Z63.8
head at term O32.4
palate, congenital Q38.5
risk
infant NEC Z76.2
sexual behavior (heterosexual) Z72.51
bisexual Z72.53
homosexual Z72.52
scrotal testis, testes
bilateral Q53.23
unilateral Q53.13
temperature (of unknown origin) R50.9
thoracic rib Q76.6
triglycerides E78.1
with high cholesterol E78.2
Hildenbrand's disease A75.0
Hilum —*see* condition
Hip —*see* condition
Hippel's disease Q85.8
Hippophobia F40.218
Hippus H57.09
Hirschsprung's disease or megacolon Q43.1
Hirsutism, hirsuties L68.0
Hirudiniasis
external B88.3
internal B83.4
Hiss-Russell dysentery A03.1
Histidinemia, histidinuria E70.41
Histiocytoma —*see also* Neoplasm, skin, benign
fibrous —*see also* Neoplasm, skin, benign
atypical —*see* Neoplasm, connective tissue,
uncertain behavior
malignant —*see* Neoplasm, connective
tissue, malignant
Histiocytosis D76.3
acute differentiated progressive C96.0
Langerhans' cell NEC C96.6
multifocal X
multisystemic (disseminated) C96.0
unisystemic C96.5
pulmonary, adult (adult PLCH) J84.82
unifocal (X) C96.6
lipid, lipoid D76.3
essential E75.29
malignant C96.A
mononuclear phagocytes NEC D76.1
Langerhans' cells C96.6
non-Langerhans cell D76.3
polyostotic sclerosing D76.3
sinus, with massive lymphadenopathy D76.3
syndrome NEC D76.3
X NEC C96.6
acute (progressive) C96.0
chronic C96.6
multifocal C96.5
multisystemic C96.0
unifocal C96.6
Histoplasmosis B39.9
with pneumonia NEC B39.2
African B39.5
American —*see* Histoplasmosis, capsulati
capsulati B39.4
disseminated B39.3
generalized B39.3
pulmonary B39.2
acute B39.0
chronic B39.1
Darling's B39.4
duboisii B39.5
lung NEC B39.2
History
family (of) —*see also* History, personal (of)
alcohol abuse Z81.1
allergy NEC Z84.89
anemia Z83.2
arthritis Z82.61
asthma Z82.5
blindness Z82.1
cardiac death (sudden) Z82.41
carrier of genetic disease Z84.81
chromosomal anomaly Z82.79

History *(Continued)*
family *(Continued)*
chronic
disabling disease NEC Z82.8
lower respiratory disease Z82.5
colonic polyps Z83.71
congenital malformations and
deformations Z82.79
polycystic kidney Z82.71
consanguinity Z84.3
deafness Z82.2
diabetes mellitus Z83.3
disability NEC Z82.8
disease or disorder (of)
allergic NEC Z84.89
behavioral NEC Z81.8
blood and blood-forming organs Z83.2
cardiovascular NEC Z82.49
chronic disabling NEC Z82.8
digestive Z83.79
ear NEC Z83.52
▶ elevated lipoprotein(a) (Lp(a)) Z83.430
endocrine NEC Z83.49
eye NEC Z83.518
glaucoma Z83.511
familial hypercholesterolemia Z83.42
genitourinary NEC Z84.2
glaucoma Z83.511
hematological Z83.2
immune mechanism Z83.2
infectious NEC Z83.1
ischemic heart Z82.49
kidney Z84.1
▶ lipoprotein metabolism Z83.438
mental NEC Z81.8
metabolic Z83.49
musculoskeletal NEC Z82.69
neurological NEC Z82.0
nutritional Z83.49
parasitic NEC Z83.1
psychiatric NEC Z81.8
respiratory NEC Z83.6
skin and subcutaneous tissue NEC Z84.0
specified NEC Z84.89
drug abuse NEC Z81.3
▶ elevated lipoprotein(a) (Lp(a)) Z83.430
epilepsy Z82.0
familial hypercholesterolemia Z83.42
genetic disease carrier Z84.81
glaucoma Z83.511
hearing loss Z82.2
human immunodeficiency virus (HIV)
infection Z83.0
Huntington's chorea Z82.0
▶ hyperlipidemia, familial combined
Z83.438
intellectual disability Z81.0
leukemia Z80.6
▶ lipidemia NEC Z83.438
malignant neoplasm (of) NOS Z80.9
bladder Z80.52
breast Z80.3
bronchus Z80.1
digestive organ Z80.0
gastrointestinal tract Z80.0
genital organ Z80.49
ovary Z80.41
prostate Z80.42
specified organ NEC Z80.49
testis Z80.43
hematopoietic NEC Z80.7
intrathoracic organ NEC Z80.2
kidney Z80.51
lung Z80.1
lymphatic NEC Z80.7
ovary Z80.41
prostate Z80.42
respiratory organ NEC Z80.2
specified site NEC Z80.8
testis Z80.43
trachea Z80.1

History *(Continued)*
 family *(Continued)*
  malignant neoplasm *(Continued)*
   urinary organ or tract Z80.59
    bladder Z80.52
    kidney Z80.51
  mental
   disorder NEC Z81.8
  multiple endocrine neoplasia (MEN)
    syndrome Z83.41
  osteoporosis Z82.62
  polycystic kidney Z82.71
  polyps (colon) Z83.71
  psychiatric disorder Z81.8
  psychoactive substance abuse NEC Z81.3
  respiratory condition NEC Z83.6
   asthma and other lower respiratory
     conditions Z82.5
  self-harmful behavior Z81.8
  SIDS (sudden infant death syndrome)
    Z84.82
  skin condition Z84.0
  specified condition NEC Z84.89
  stroke (cerebrovascular) Z82.3
  substance abuse NEC Z81.4
   alcohol Z81.1
   drug NEC Z81.3
   psychoactive NEC Z81.3
   tobacco Z81.2
  sudden
   cardiac death Z82.41
   infant death syndrome (SIDS) Z84.82
  tobacco abuse Z81.2
  violence, violent behavior Z81.8
  visual loss Z82.1
 personal (of) —*see also* History, family (of)
  abuse
   adult Z91.419
   ▶forced labor or sexual exploitation
     Z91.42
    physical and sexual Z91.410
    psychological Z91.411
   childhood Z62.819
   ▶forced labor or sexual exploitation in
     childhood Z62.813
    physical Z62.810
    psychological Z62.811
    sexual Z62.810
  alcohol dependence F10.21
  allergy (to) Z88.9
   analgesic agent NEC Z88.6
   anesthetic Z88.4
   antibiotic agent NEC Z88.1
   anti-infective agent NEC Z88.3
   contrast media Z91.041
   drugs, medicaments and biological
     substances Z88.9
    specified NEC Z88.8
   food Z91.018
    additives Z91.02
    eggs Z91.012
    milk products Z91.011
    peanuts Z91.010
    seafood Z91.013
    specified food NEC Z91.018
   insect Z91.038
    bee Z91.030
   latex Z91.040
   medicinal agents Z88.9
    specified NEC Z88.8
   narcotic agent NEC Z88.5
   nonmedicinal agents Z91.048
   penicillin Z88.0
   serum Z88.7
   specified NEC Z91.09
   sulfonamides Z88.2
   vaccine Z88.7
  anaphylactic shock Z87.892
  anaphylaxis Z87.892
  behavioral disorders Z86.59
  benign carcinoid tumor Z86.012

History *(Continued)*
 personal *(Continued)*
  benign neoplasm Z86.018
   brain Z86.011
   carcinoid Z86.012
   colonic polyps Z86.010
  brain injury (traumatic) Z87.820
  breast implant removal Z98.86
  calculi, renal Z87.442
  cancer —*see* History, personal (of),
    malignant neoplasm (of)
  cardiac arrest (death), successfully
    resuscitated Z86.74
  cerebral infarction without residual deficit
    Z86.73
  cervical dysplasia Z87.410
  chemotherapy for neoplastic condition
    Z92.21
  childhood abuse —*see* History, personal
    (of), abuse
  cleft lip (corrected) Z87.730
  cleft palate (corrected) Z87.730
  collapsed vertebra (healed) Z87.311
   due to osteoporosis Z87.310
  combat and operational stress reaction
    Z86.51
  congenital malformation (corrected)
    Z87.798
   circulatory system (corrected) Z87.74
   digestive system (corrected) NEC Z87.738
   ear (corrected) Z87.721
   eye (corrected) Z87.720
   face and neck (corrected) Z87.790
   genitourinary system (corrected) NEC
     Z87.718
   heart (corrected) Z87.74
   integument (corrected) Z87.76
   limb(s) (corrected) Z87.76
   musculoskeletal system (corrected)
     Z87.76
   neck (corrected) Z87.790
   nervous system (corrected) NEC Z87.728
   respiratory system (corrected) Z87.75
   sense organs (corrected) NEC Z87.728
   specified NEC Z87.798
  contraception Z92.0
  deployment (military) Z91.82
  diabetic foot ulcer Z86.31
  disease or disorder (of) Z87.898
   blood and blood-forming organs Z86.2
   circulatory system Z86.79
    specified condition NEC Z86.79
   connective tissue NEC Z87.39
   digestive system Z87.19
    colonic polyp Z86.010
    peptic ulcer disease Z87.11
    specified condition NEC Z87.19
   ear Z86.69
   endocrine Z86.39
    diabetic foot ulcer Z86.31
    gestational diabetes Z86.32
    specified type NEC Z86.39
   eye Z86.69
   genital (track) system NEC
    female Z87.42
    male Z87.438
   hematological Z86.2
   Hodgkin Z85.71
   immune mechanism Z86.2
   infectious Z86.19
    malaria Z86.13
    Methicillin resistant Staphylococcus
      aureus (MRSA) Z86.14
    poliomyelitis Z86.12
    specified NEC Z86.19
    tuberculosis Z86.11
   mental NEC Z86.59
   metabolic Z86.39
    diabetic foot ulcer Z86.31
    gestational diabetes Z86.32
    specified type NEC Z86.39

History *(Continued)*
 personal *(Continued)*
  disease or disorder (of) *(Continued)*
   musculoskeletal NEC Z87.39
   nervous system Z86.69
   nutritional Z86.39
   parasitic Z86.19
   respiratory system NEC Z87.09
   sense organs Z86.69
   skin Z87.2
   specified site or type NEC Z87.898
   subcutaneous tissue Z87.2
   trophoblastic Z87.59
   urinary system NEC Z87.448
  drug dependence —*see* Dependence, drug,
    by type, in remission
  drug therapy
   antineoplastic chemotherapy Z92.21
   estrogen Z92.23
   immunosupression Z92.25
   inhaled steroids Z92.240
   monoclonal drug Z92.22
   specified NEC Z92.29
   steroid Z92.241
   systemic steroids Z92.241
  dysplasia
   cervical (mild) (moderate) Z87.410
    severe (grade III) Z86.001
   prostatic Z87.430
   vaginal Z87.411
   vulvar (mild) (moderate) Z87.412
    severe (grade III) Z86.008
  embolism (venous) Z86.718
   pulmonary Z86.711
  encephalitis Z86.61
  estrogen therapy Z92.23
  extracorporeal membrane oxygenation
    (ECMO) Z92.81
  failed conscious sedation Z92.83
  failed moderate sedation Z92.83
  fall, falling Z91.81
  ▶forced labor or sexual exploitation Z91.42
   ▶in childhood Z62.813
  fracture (healed)
   fatigue Z87.312
   fragility Z87.310
   osteoporosis Z87.310
   pathological NEC Z87.311
   stress Z87.312
   traumatic Z87.81
  gestational diabetes Z86.32
  hepatitis
   B Z86.19
   C Z86.19
  Hodgkin disease Z85.71
  hyperthermia, malignant Z88.4
  hypospadias (corrected) Z87.710
  hysterectomy Z90.710
  immunosupression therapy Z92.25
  in situ neoplasm
   breast Z86.000
   cervix uteri Z86.001
   specified NEC Z86.008
  infection NEC Z86.19
   central nervous system Z86.61
   Methicillin resistant Staphylococcus
     aureus (MRSA) Z86.14
   urinary (tract) Z87.41
  injury NEC Z87.828
  in utero procedure during pregnancy
    Z98.870
  in utero procedure while a fetus Z98.871
  irradiation Z92.3
  kidney stones Z87.442
  leukemia Z85.6
  lymphoma (non-Hodgkin) Z85.72
  malignant melanoma (skin) Z85.820
  malignant neoplasm (of) Z85.9
   accessory sinuses Z85.22
   anus NEC Z85.048
    carcinoid Z85.040

▶ New   ⇒ Revised   ~~deleted~~ Deleted   ● Use Additional Character(s)

History *(Continued)*
  personal *(Continued)*
    malignant neoplasm *(Continued)*
      bladder Z85.51
      bone Z85.830
      brain Z85.841
      breast Z85.3
      bronchus NEC Z85.118
        carcinoid Z85.110
      carcinoid —*see* History, personal (of),
        malignant neoplasm, by site,
        carcinioid
      cervix Z85.41
      colon NEC Z85.038
        carcinoid Z85.030
      digestive organ Z85.00
        specified NEC Z85.09
      endocrine gland NEC Z85.858
      epididymis Z85.48
      esophagus Z85.01
      eye Z85.840
      gastrointestinal tract —*see* History,
        malignant neoplasm, digestive
        organ
      genital organ
        female Z85.40
          specified NEC Z85.44
        male Z85.45
          specified NEC Z85.49
      hematopoietic NEC Z85.79
      intrathoracic organ Z85.20-●
      kidney NEC Z85.528
        carcinoid Z85.520
      large intestine NEC Z85.038
        carcinoid Z85.030
      larynx Z85.21
      liver Z85.05
      lung NEC Z85.118
        carcinoid Z85.110
      mediastinum Z85.29
      Merkel cell Z85.821
      middle ear Z85.22
      nasal cavities Z85.22
      nervous system NEC Z85.848
      oral cavity Z85.819
        specified site NEC Z85.818
      ovary Z85.43
      pancreas Z85.07
      pelvis Z85.53
      pharynx Z85.819
        specified site NEC Z85.818
      pleura Z85.29
      prostate Z85.46
      rectosigmoid junction NEC Z85.048
        carcinoid Z85.040
      rectum NEC Z85.048
        carcinoid Z85.040
      respiratory organ Z85.20
      sinuses, accessory Z85.22
      skin NEC Z85.828
        melanoma Z85.820
        Merkel cell Z85.821
      small intestine NEC Z85.068
        carcinoid Z85.060
      soft tissue Z85.831
      specified site NEC Z85.89
      stomach NEC Z85.028
        carcinoid Z85.020
      testis Z85.47
      thymus NEC Z85.238
        carcinoid Z85.230
      thyroid Z85.850
      tongue Z85.810
      trachea Z85.12
      ureter Z85.54
      urinary organ or tract Z85.50
        specified NEC Z85.59
      uterus Z85.42
    maltreatment Z91.89
    medical treatment NEC Z92.89
    melanoma (malignant) (skin) Z85.820

History *(Continued)*
  personal *(Continued)*
    meningitis Z86.61
    mental disorder Z86.59
    Merkel cell carcinoma (skin) Z85.821
    Methicillin resistant Staphylococcus aureus
      (MRSA) Z86.14
    military deployment Z91.82
    military war, peacekeeping and
      humanitarian deployment (current or
      past conflict) Z91.82
    myocardial infarction (old) I25.2
    neglect (in)
      adult Z91.412
      childhood Z62.812
    neoplasm
      benign Z86.018
        brain Z86.011
        colon polyp Z86.010
      in situ
        breast Z86.000
        cervix uteri Z86.001
        specified NEC Z86.008
      malignant —*see* History of, malignant
        neoplasm
      uncertain behavior Z86.03
    nephrotic syndrome Z87.441
    nicotine dependence Z87.891
    noncompliance with medical treatment or
      regimen —*see* Noncompliance
    nutritional deficiency Z86.39
    obstetric complications Z87.59
      childbirth Z87.59
      pregnancy Z87.59
      pre-term labor Z87.51
      puerperium Z87.59
    osteoporosis fractures Z87.31
    parasuicide (attempt) Z91.5
    physical trauma NEC Z87.828
      self-harm or suicide attempt Z91.5
    pneumonia (recurrent) Z87.01
    poisoning NEC Z91.89
      self-harm or suicide attempt Z91.5
    poor personal hygiene Z91.89
    preterm labor Z87.51
    procedure during pregnancy Z98.870
    procedure while a fetus Z98.871
    prolonged reversible ischemic neurologic
      deficit (PRINO) Z86.73
    prostatic dysplasia Z87.430
    psychiatric disorder NEC Z87.89
    psychological
      abuse
        adult Z91.411
        child Z62.811
      trauma, specified NEC Z91.49
    radiation therapy Z92.3
    removal
      implant
        breast Z98.86
    renal calculi Z87.442
    respiratory condition NEC Z87.09
    retained foreign body fully removed Z87.821
    risk factors NEC Z91.89
    self-harm Z91.5
    self-poisoning attempt Z91.5
    sex reassignment Z87.890
    sleep-wake cycle problem Z72.821
    specified NEC Z87.898
    steroid therapy (systemic) Z92.241
      inhaled Z92.240
    stroke without residual deficits Z86.73
    substance abuse NEC F10-F19
    sudden cardiac arrest Z86.74
    sudden cardiac death successfully
      resuscitated Z86.74
    suicide attempt Z91.5
    surgery NEC Z98.890
      with uterine scar Z98.891
      sex reassignment Z87.890
      transplant —*see* Transplant

History *(Continued)*
  personal *(Continued)*
    thrombophlebitis Z86.72
    thrombosis (venous) Z86.718
      pulmonary Z86.711
    tobacco dependence Z87.891
    transient ischemic attack (TIA) without
      residual deficits Z86.73
    trauma (physical) NEC Z87.828
      psychological NEC Z91.49
      self-harm Z91.5
    traumatic brain injury Z87.820
    unhealthy sleep-wake cycle Z72.821
    unintended awareness under general
      anesthesia Z92.84
    urinary (recurrent) (tract) infection(s) Z87.440
    urinary calculi Z87.42
    uterine scar from previous surgery Z98.891
    vaginal dysplasia Z87.411
    venous thrombosis or embolism Z86.718
      pulmonary Z86.711
    vulvar dysplasia Z87.412
His-Werner disease A79.0
HIV —*see also* Human, immunodeficiency virus
  B20
  laboratory evidence (nonconclusive) R75
  nonconclusive test (in infants) R75
  positive, seropositive Z21
Hives (bold) —*see* Urticaria
Hoarseness R49.0
Hobo Z59.0
Hodgkin disease —*see* Lymphoma, Hodgkin
Hodgson's disease I71.2
  ruptured I71.1
Hoffa-Kastert disease E88.89
Hoffa's disease E88.89
Hoffmann-Bouveret syndrome I47.9
Hoffmann's syndrome E03.9 *[G73.7]*
Hole (round)
  macula H35.34-●
  retina (without detachment) —*see* Break,
    retina, round hole
    with detachment —*see* Detachment, retina,
      with retinal, break
Holiday relief care Z75.5
Hollenhorst's plaque —*see* Occlusion, artery,
  retina
Hollow foot (congenital) Q66.7
  acquired —*see* Deformity, limb, foot, specified
    NEC
Holoprosencephaly Q04.2
Holt-Oram syndrome Q87.2
Homelessness Z59.0
Homesickness —*see* Disorder, adjustment
Homocystinemia, homocystinuria E72.11
Homogentisate 1,2-dioxygenase deficiency
  E70.29
Homologous serum hepatitis (prophylactic)
  (therapeutic) —*see* Hepatitis, viral, type B
Honeycomb lung J98.4
  congenital Q33.0
Hooded
  clitoris Q52.6
  penis Q55.69
Hookworm (anemia) (disease) (infection)
  (infestation) B76.9
  specified NEC B76.8
Hordeolum (eyelid) (externum) (recurrent)
  H00.019
  internum H00.029
    left H00.026
      lower H00.025
      upper H00.024
    right H00.023
      lower H00.022
      upper H00.021
  left H00.016
    lower H00.015
    upper H00.014
  right H00.013
    lower H00.012
    upper H00.011

Horn
  cutaneous L85.8
  nail L60.2
    congenital Q84.6
Horner (-Claude Bernard) syndrome G90.2
  traumatic —see Injury, nerve, cervical
    sympathetic
Horseshoe kidney (congenital) Q63.1
Horton's headache or neuralgia G44.099
  intractable G44.091
  not intractable G44.099
Hospital hopper syndrome —see Disorder,
    factitious
Hospitalism in children —see Disorder,
    adjustment
Hostility R45.5
  towards child Z62.3
Hot flashes
  menopausal N95.1
Hourglass (contracture) —see also Contraction,
    hourglass
  stomach K31.89
    congenital Q40.2
    stricture K31.2
Household, housing circumstance affecting
    care Z59.9
  specified NEC Z59.8
Housemaid's knee —see Bursitis, prepatellar
Hudson (-Stähli) line (cornea) —see
    Pigmentation, cornea, anterior
Human
  bite (open wound) —see also Bite
    intact skin surface —see Bite, superficial
  herpesvirus —see Herpes
  immunodeficiency virus (HIV) disease
      (infection) B20
    asymptomatic status Z21
    contact Z20.6
    counseling Z71.7
    dementia B20 [F02.80]
      with behavioral disturbance B20 [F02.81]
    exposure to Z20.6
    laboratory evidence R75
    type-2 (HIV 2) as cause of disease classified
      elsewhere B97.35
  papillomavirus (HPV)
    DNA test positive
      high risk
        cervix R87.810
        vagina R87.811
      low risk
        cervix R87.820
        vagina R87.821
    screening for Z11.51
  T-cell lymphotropic virus
    type-1 (HTLV-I) infection B33.3
      as cause of disease classified elsewhere
        B97.33
      carrier Z22.6
    type-2 (HTLV-II) as cause of disease
      classified elsewhere B97.34
Humidifier lung or pneumonitis J67.7
Humiliation (experience) in childhood Z62.898
Humpback (acquired) —see Kyphosis
Hunchback (acquired) —see Kyphosis
Hunger T73.0
  air, psychogenic F45.8
Hungry bone syndrome E83.81
Hunner's ulcer —see Cystitis, chronic,
    interstitial
Hunter's
  glossitis D51.0
  syndrome E76.1
Huntington's disease or chorea G10
  with dementia G10 [F02.80]
    with behavioral disturbance G10 [F02.81]
Hunt's
  disease or syndrome (herpetic geniculate
      ganglionitis) B02.21
    dyssynergia cerebellaris myoclonica G11.1
  neuralgia B02.21

Hurler (-Scheie) disease or syndrome E76.02
Hurst's disease G36.1
Hurthle cell
  adenocarcinoma C73
  adenoma D34
  carcinoma C73
  tumor D34
Hutchinson-Boeck disease or syndrome —see
    Sarcoidosis
Hutchinson-Gilford disease or syndrome E34.8
Hutchinson's
  disease, meaning
    angioma serpiginosum L81.7
    pompholyx (cheiropompholyx) L30.1
    prurigo estivalis L56.4
    summer eruption or summer prurigo L56.4
  melanotic freckle —see Melanoma, in situ
    malignant melanoma in —see Melanoma
  teeth or incisors (congenital syphilis) A50.52
  triad (congenital syphilis) A50.53
Hyalin plaque, sclera, senile H15.89
Hyaline membrane (disease) (lung)
    (pulmonary) (newborn) P22.0
Hyalinosis
  cutis (et mucosae) E78.89
  focal and segmental (glomerular) —see also
    N00-N07 with fourth character .1 N05.1
Hyalitis, hyalosis, asteroid —see also Deposit,
    crystalline
  syphilitic (late) A52.71
Hydatid
  cyst or tumor —see Echinococcus
  mole —see Hydatidiform mole
  Morgagni
    female Q50.5
    male (epididymal) Q55.4
      testicular Q55.29
Hydatidiform mole (benign) (complicating
    pregnancy) (delivered) (undelivered) O01.9
  classical O01.0
  complete O01.0
  incomplete O01.1
  invasive D39.2
  malignant D39.2
  partial O01.1
Hydatidosis —see Echinococcus
Hydradenitis (axillaris) (suppurative) L73.2
Hydradenoma —see Hidradenoma
Hydramnios O40.-●
Hydrancephaly, hydranencephaly Q04.3
  with spina bifida —see Spina bifida, with
    hydrocephalus
Hydrargyrism NEC —see Poisoning, mercury
Hydrarthrosis —see also Effusion, joint
  gonococcal A54.42
  intermittent M12.40
    ankle M12.47-●
    elbow M12.42-●
    foot joint M12.47-●
    hand joint M12.44-●
    hip M12.45-●
    knee M12.46-●
    multiple site M12.49
    shoulder M12.41-●
    specified joint NEC M12.48
    wrist M12.43-●
  of yaws (early) (late) —see also subcategory
    M14.8-● A66.6
  syphilitic (late) A52.77
    congenital A50.55 [M12.80]
Hydremia D64.89
Hydrencephalocele (congenital) —see
    Encephalocele
Hydrencephalomeningocele (congenital) —see
    Encephalocele
Hydroa R23.8
  aestivale L56.4
  vacciniforme L56.4
Hydroadenitis (axillaris) (suppurative)
    L73.2
Hydrocalycosis —see Hydronephrosis

Hydrocele (spermatic cord) (testis) (tunica
    vaginalis) N43.3
  canal of Nuck N94.89
  communicating N43.2
    congenital P83.5
  congenital P83.5
  encysted N43.0
  female NEC N94.89
  infected N43.1
  newborn P83.5
  round ligament N94.89
  specified NEC N43.2
  spinalis —see Spina bifida
  vulva N90.89
Hydrocephalus (acquired) (external) (internal)
    (malignant) (recurrent) G91.9
  aqueduct Sylvius stricture Q03.0
  causing disproportion O33.6
    with obstructed labor O66.3
  communicating G91.0
  congenital (external) (internal) Q03.9
    with spina bifida Q05.4
      cervical Q05.0
      dorsal Q05.1
      lumbar Q05.2
      lumbosacral Q05.2
      sacral Q05.3
      thoracic Q05.1
      thoracolumbar Q05.1
    specified NEC Q03.8
  due to toxoplasmosis (congenital) P37.1
  foramen Magendie block (acquired) G91.1
    congenital —see also Hydrocephalus,
      congenital Q03.1
  in (due to)
    infectious disease NEC B89 [G91.4]
    neoplastic disease NEC (see also Neoplasm)
      G91.4
    parasitic disease B89 [G91.4]
  newborn Q03.9
    with spina bifida —see Spina bifida, with
      hydrocephalus
  noncommunicating G91.1
  normal pressure G91.2
    secondary G91.0
  obstructive G91.1
  otitic G93.2
  post-traumatic NEC G91.3
  secondary G91.4
    post-traumatic G91.3
  specified NEC G91.8
  syphilitic, congenital A50.49
Hydrocolpos (congenital) N89.8
Hydrocystoma —see Neoplasm, skin, benign
Hydroencephalocele (congenital) —see
    Encephalocele
Hydroencephalomeningocele (congenital) —
    see Encephalocele
Hydrohematopneumothorax —see Hemothorax
Hydromeningitis —see Meningitis
Hydromeningocele (spinal) —see also Spina
    bifida
  cranial —see Encephalocele
Hydrometra N85.8
Hydrometrocolpos N89.8
Hydromicrocephaly Q02
Hydromphalos (since birth) Q45.8
Hydromyelia Q06.4
Hydromyelocele —see Spina bifida
Hydronephrosis (atrophic) (early)
    (functionless) (intermittent) (primary)
    (secondary) NEC N13.30
  with
    infection N13.6
    obstruction (by) (of)
      renal calculus N13.2
        with infection N13.6
      ureteral NEC N13.1
        with infection N13.6
        calculus N13.2
          with infection N13.6

▶ New   ⇒ Revised   ~~deleted~~ Deleted   ● Use Additional Character(s)

Hyperfructosemia E74.19
Hyperfunction
  adrenal cortex, not associated with Cushing's
      syndrome E27.0
    medulla E27.5
      adrenomedullary E27.5
    virilism E25.9
      congenital E25.0
  ovarian E28.8
  pancreas K86.89
  parathyroid (gland) E21.3
  pituitary (gland) (anterior) E22.9
    specified NEC E22.8
  polyglandular E31.1
  testicular E29.0
Hypergammaglobulinemia D89.2
  polyclonal D89.0
  Waldenström D89.0
Hypergastrinemia E16.4
Hyperglobulinemia R77.1
Hyperglycemia, hyperglycemic (transient)
    R73.9
  coma —see Diabetes, by type, with coma
  postpancreatectomy E89.1
Hyperglyceridemia (endogenous) (essential)
    (familial) (hereditary) (pure) E78.1
  mixed E78.3
Hyperglycinemia (non-ketotic) E72.51
Hypergonadism
  ovarian E28.8
  testicular (primary) (infantile) E29.0
Hyperheparinemia D68.32
Hyperhidrosis, hyperidrosis R61
  focal
    primary L74.519
      axilla L74.510
      face L74.511
      palms L74.512
      soles L74.513
    secondary L74.52
  generalized R61
  localized
    primary L74.519
      axilla L74.510
      face L74.511
      palms L74.512
      soles L74.513
    secondary L74.52
  psychogenic F45.8
  secondary R61
    focal L74.52
Hyperhistidinemia E70.41
Hyperhomocysteinemia E72.11
Hyperhydroxyprolinemia E72.59
Hyperinsulinism (functional) E16.1
  with
    coma (hypoglycemic) E15
    encephalopathy E16.1 [G94]
  ectopic E16.1
  therapeutic misadventure (from
      administration of insulin) —see
      subcategory T38.3
Hyperkalemia E87.5
Hyperkeratosis —see also Keratosis L85.9
  cervix N88.0
  due to yaws (early) (late) (palmar or plantar)
      A66.3
  follicularis Q82.8
    penetrans (in cutem) L87.0
  palmoplantaris climacterica L85.1
  pinta A67.1
  senile (with pruritus) L57.0
  universalis congenita Q80.8
  vocal cord J38.3
  vulva N90.4
Hyperkinesia, hyperkinetic (disease) (reaction)
    (syndrome) (childhood) (adolescence) —
    see also Disorder, attention-deficit
    hyperactivity
  heart I51.89
Hyperleucine-isoleucinemia E71.19

Hyperlipemia, hyperlipidemia E78.5
  combined E78.2
  familial E78.49
  group
    A E78.00
    B E78.1
    C E78.2
    D E78.3
  mixed E78.2
  specified NEC E78.49
Hyperlipidosis E75.6
  hereditary NEC E75.5
Hyperlipoproteinemia E78.5
  Fredrickson's type
    I E78.3
    IIa E78.00
    IIb E78.2
    III E78.2
    IV E78.1
    V E78.3
  low-density-lipoprotein-type (LDL) E78.00
  very-low-density-lipoprotein-type (VLDL)
      E78.1
Hyperlucent lung, unilateral J43.0
Hyperlysinemia E72.3
Hypermagnesemia E83.41
  neonatal P71.8
Hypermenorrhea N92.0
Hypermethioninemia E72.19
Hypermetropia (congenital) H52.0-●
Hypermobility, hypermotility
  cecum —see Syndrome, irritable bowel
  coccyx —see subcategory M53.2
  colon —see Syndrome, irritable bowel
    psychogenic F45.8
  ileum K58.9
  intestine —see also Syndrome, irritable bowel
      K58.9
    psychogenic F45.8
  meniscus (knee) —see Derangement, knee,
      meniscus
  scapula —see Instability, joint, shoulder
  stomach K31.89
    psychogenic F45.8
  syndrome M35.7
  urethra N36.41
    with intrinsic sphincter deficiency
        N36.43
Hypernasality R49.21
Hypernatremia E87.0
Hypernephroma C64.-●
Hyperopia —see Hypermetropia
Hyperorexia nervosa F50.2
Hyperornithinemia E72.4
Hyperosmia R43.1
Hyperosmolality E87.0
Hyperostosis (monomelic) —see also Disorder,
    bone, density and structure, specified
    NEC
  ankylosing (spine) M48.10
    cervical region M48.12
    cervicothoracic region M48.13
    lumbar region M48.16
    lumbosacral region M48.17
    multiple sites M48.19
    occipito-atlanto-axial region M48.11
    sacrococcygeal region M48.18
    thoracic region M48.14
    thoracolumbar region M48.15
  cortical (skull) M85.2
    infantile M89.8X-●
  frontal, internal of skull M85.2
  interna frontalis M85.2
  skeletal, diffuse idiopathic —see
      Hyperostosis, ankylosing
  skull M85.2
    congenital Q75.8
  vertebral, ankylosing —see Hyperostosis,
      ankylosing
Hyperovarism E28.8
Hyperoxaluria (primary) R82.992

Hyperparathyroidism E21.3
  primary E21.0
  secondary (renal) N25.81
    non-renal E21.1
  specified NEC E21.2
  tertiary E21.2
Hyperpathia R20.8
Hyperperistalsis R19.2
  psychogenic F45.8
Hyperpermeability, capillary I78.8
Hyperphagia R63.2
Hyperphenylalaninemia NEC E70.1
Hyperphoria (alternating) H50.53
Hyperphosphatemia E83.39
Hyperpiesis, hyperpiesia —see Hypertension
Hyperpigmentation —see also Pigmentation
  melanin NEC L81.4
  postinflammatory L81.0
Hyperpinealism E34.8
Hyperpituitarism E22.9
Hyperplasia, hyperplastic
  adenoids J35.2
  adrenal (capsule) (cortex) (gland) E27.8
    with
      sexual precocity (male) E25.9
        congenital E25.0
      virilism, adrenal E25.9
        congenital E25.0
      virilization (female) E25.9
        congenital E25.0
    congenital E25.0
    salt-losing E25.0
  adrenomedullary E27.5
  angiolymphoid, eosinophilia (ALHE) D18.01
  appendix (lymphoid) K38.0
  artery, fibromuscular I77.3
  bone —see also Hypertrophy, bone
    marrow D75.89
  breast —see also Hypertrophy, breast
    ductal (atypical) N60.9-●
  C-cell, thyroid E07.0
  cementation (tooth) (teeth) K03.4
  cervical gland R59.0
  cervix (uteri) (basal cell) (endometrium)
      (polypoid) —see also Dysplasia, cervix
    congenital Q51.828
  clitoris, congenital Q52.6
  denture K06.2
  endocervicitis N72
  endometrium, endometrial (adenomatous)
      (benign) (cystic) (glandular) (glandular-
      cystic) (polypoid) N85.00
    with atypia N85.02
    cervix —see Dysplasia, cervix
    complex (without atypia) N85.01
    simple (without atypia) N85.01
  epithelial L85.9
    focal, oral, including tongue K13.29
    nipple N62
    skin L85.9
    tongue K13.29
    vaginal wall N89.3
  erythroid D75.89
  fibromuscular of artery (carotid) (renal)
      I77.3
  genital
    female NEC N94.89
    male N50.89
  gingiva K06.1
  glandularis cystica uteri (interstitialis) —see
      also Hyperplasia, endometrial N85.00-●
  gum K06.1
  hymen, congenital Q52.4
  irritative, edentulous (alveolar) K06.2
  jaw M26.09
    alveolar M26.79
      lower M26.03
        alveolar M26.72
      upper M26.01
        alveolar M26.71
  kidney (congenital) Q63.3

▶ New   ⇒ Revised   ~~deleted~~ Deleted   ● Use Additional Character(s)

Hyperplasia, hyperplastic *(Continued)*
labia N90.69
   epithelial N90.3
liver (congenital) Q44.7
   nodular, focal K76.89
lymph gland or node R59.9
mandible, mandibular M26.03
   alveolar M26.72
   unilateral condylar M27.8
maxilla, maxillary M26.01
   alveolar M26.71
myometrium, myometrial N85.2
neuroendocrine cell, of infancy J84.841
nose
   lymphoid J34.89
   polypoid J33.9
oral mucosa (irritative) K13.6
organ or site, congenital NEC —*see* Anomaly,
      by site
ovary N83.8
palate, papillary (irritative) K13.6
pancreatic islet cells E16.9
   alpha E16.8
      with excess
         gastrin E16.4
         glucagon E16.3
   beta E16.1
parathyroid (gland) E21.0
pharynx (lymphoid) J39.2
prostate (adenofibromatous) (nodular) N40.0
   with lower urinary tract symptoms (LUTS)
      N40.1
   without lower urinary tract symptoms
      (LUTS) N40.0
renal artery I77.89
reticulo-endothelial (cell) D75.89
salivary gland (any) K11.1
Schimmelbusch's —*see* Mastopathy, cystic
suprarenal capsule (gland) E27.8
thymus (gland) (persistent) E32.0
thyroid (gland) —*see* Goiter
tonsils (faucial) (infective) (lingual)
      (lymphoid) J35.1
   with adenoids J35.3
unilateral condylar M27.8
uterus, uterine N85.2
   endometrium (glandular) —*see also*
      Hyperplasia, endometrial N85.00-•
vulva N90.69
   epithelial N90.3
Hyperpnea —*see* Hyperventilation
Hyperpotassemia E87.5
Hyperprebetalipoproteinemia (familial) E78.1
Hyperprolactinemia E22.1
Hyperprolinemia (type I) (type II) E72.59
Hyperproteinemia E88.09
Hyperprothrombinemia, causing coagulation
   factor deficiency D68.4
Hyperpyrexia R50.9
heat (effects) T67.0
malignant, due to anesthetic T88.3
rheumatic —*see* Fever, rheumatic
unknown origin R50.9
Hyper-reflexia R29.2
Hypersalivation K11.7
Hypersecretion
ACTH (not associated with Cushing's
      syndrome) E27.0
   pituitary E24.0
adrenaline E27.5
adrenomedullary E27.5
androgen (testicular) E29.0
   ovarian (drug-induced) (iatrogenic) E28.1
calcitonin E07.0
catecholamine E27.5
corticoadrenal E24.9
cortisol E24.9
epinephrine E27.5
estrogen E28.0
gastric K31.89
   psychogenic F45.8

Hypersecretion *(Continued)*
gastrin E16.4
glucagon E16.3
hormone(s)
   ACTH (not associated with Cushing's
         syndrome) E27.0
      pituitary E24.0
   antidiuretic E22.2
   growth E22.0
   intestinal NEC E34.1
   ovarian androgen E28.1
   pituitary E22.9
   testicular E29.0
   thyroid stimulating E05.80
      with thyroid storm E05.81
insulin —*see* Hyperinsulinism
lacrimal glands —*see* Epiphora
medulloadrenal E27.5
milk O92.6
ovarian androgens E28.1
salivary gland (any) K11.7
thyrocalcitonin E07.0
upper respiratory J39.8
Hypersegmentation, leukocytic, hereditary D72.0
Hypersensitive, hypersensitiveness,
      hypersensitivity —*see also* Allergy
carotid sinus G90.01
colon —*see* Irritable, colon
drug T88.7
gastrointestinal K52.29
   immediate K52.29
   psychogenic F45.8
labyrinth —*see* subcategory H83.2
pain R20.8
pneumonitis —*see* Pneumonitis, allergic
reaction T78.40
   upper respiratory tract NEC J39.3
Hypersomnia (organic) G47.10
due to
   alcohol
      abuse F10.182
      dependence F10.282
      use F10.982
   amphetamines
      abuse F15.182
      dependence F15.282
      use F15.982
   caffeine
      abuse F15.182
      dependence F15.282
      use F15.982
   cocaine
      abuse F14.182
      dependence F14.282
      use F14.982
   drug NEC
      abuse F19.182
      dependence F19.282
      use F19.982
   medical condition G47.14
   mental disorder F51.13
   opioid
      abuse F11.182
      dependence F11.282
      use F11.982
   psychoactive substance NEC
      abuse F19.182
      dependence F19.282
      use F19.982
   sedative, hypnotic, or anxiolytic
      abuse F13.182
      dependence F13.282
      use F13.982
   stimulant NEC
      abuse F15.182
      dependence F15.282
      use F15.982
idiopathic G47.11
   with long sleep time G47.11
   without long sleep time G47.12
menstrual related G47.13

Hypersomnia *(Continued)*
nonorganic origin F51.11
   specified NEC F51.19
not due to a substance or known
      physiological condition F51.11
   specified NEC F51.19
primary F51.11
recurrent G47.13
specified NEC G47.19
Hypersplenia, hypersplenism D73.1
Hyperstimulation, ovaries (associated with
   induced ovulation) N98.1
Hypersusceptibility —*see* Allergy
Hypertelorism (ocular) (orbital) Q75.2
Hypertension, hypertensive (accelerated)
      (benign) (essential) (idiopathic)
      (malignant) (systemic) I10
with
   heart failure (congestive) I11.0
   heart involvement (conditions in I50.-,
      I51.4-I51.9 due to hypertension) —*see*
      Hypertension, heart
   kidney involvement —*see* Hypertension,
      kidney
benign, intracranial G93.2
borderline R03.0
cardiorenal (disease) I13.10
   with heart failure I13.0
      with stage 1 through stage 4 chronic
         kidney disease I13.0
      with stage 5 or end stage renal disease
         I13.2
   without heart failure I13.10
      with stage 1 through stage 4 chronic
         kidney disease I13.10
      with stage 5 or end stage renal disease
         I13.11
cardiovascular
   disease (arteriosclerotic) (sclerotic) —*see*
      Hypertension, heart
   renal (disease) —*see* Hypertension,
      cardiorenal
chronic venous —*see* Hypertension, venous
   (chronic)
complicating
   childbirth (labor) O16.4
      pre-existing O10.92
         with
            heart disease O10.12
               with renal disease O10.32
            pre-eclampsia O11.4
            renal disease O10.22
               with heart disease O10.32
         essential O10.02
         secondary O10.42
   pregnancy O16.-•
      with edema —*see also* Pre-eclampsia
         O14.9-•
      gestational (pregnancy induced) O13.-•
         (without proteinuria) O13.-•
         with proteinuria O14.9-•
            mild pre-eclampsia O14.0-•
            moderate pre-eclampsia O14.0-•
            severe pre-eclampsia O14.1-•
               with hemolysis, elevated liver
                  enzymes and low platelet
                  count (HELLP) O14.2-•
      pre-existing O10.91-•
         with
            heart disease O10.11-•
               with renal disease O10.31-•
            pre-eclampsia —*see* category O11
            renal disease O10.21-•
               with heart disease O10.31-•
         essential O10.01-•
         secondary O10.41-•
      transient O13.-•
   puerperium pre-existing O16.5
      pre-existing
         with
            heart disease O10.13
               with renal disease O10.33

Hypertension, hypertensive *(Continued)*
  complicating *(Continued)*
    puerperium pre-existing *(Continued)*
      pre-existing *(Continued)*
        with *(Continued)*
          pre-eclampsia O11.5
          renal disease O10.23
            with heart disease O10.33
          essential O10.03
        pregnancy-induced O13.9
        secondary O10.43
  crisis I16.9
  due to
    endocrine disorders I15.2
    pheochromocytoma I15.2
    renal disorders NEC I15.1
      arterial I15.0
    renovascular disorders I15.0
    specified disease NEC I15.8
  emergency I16.1
  encephalopathy I67.4
  gestational (without significant proteinuria)
      (pregnancy-induced) (transient) O13.-●
    with significant proteinuria —*see*
        Pre-eclampsia
    complicating
      delivery O13.4
      puerperium O13.5
  Goldblatt's I70.1
  heart (disease) (conditions in I51.4-I51.9 due
      to hypertension) I11.9
    with
      heart failure (congestive) I11.0
      kidney disease (chronic) —*see*
          Hypertension, cardiorenal
  intracranial (benign) G93.2
  kidney I12.9
    with
      heart disease —*see* Hypertension,
          cardiorenal
      stage 1 through stage 4 chronic kidney
          disease I12.9
      stage 5 chronic kidney disease (CKD) or
          end stage renal disease (ESRD)
          I12.0
  lesser circulation I27.0
  maternal O16.-●
  newborn P29.2
    pulmonary (persistent) P29.30
  ocular H40.05-●
  pancreatic duct — code to underlying
      condition
    with chronic pancreatitis K86.1
  portal (due to chronic liver disease)
      (idiopathic) K76.6
    gastropathy K31.89
    in (due to) schistosomiasis (bilharziasis)
        B65.9 [K77]
  postoperative I97.3
  psychogenic F45.8
  pulmonary NEC I27.20
    with
      cor pulmonale (chronic) I27.29
        acute I26.09
      right heart ventricular strain/failure
          I27.29
        acute I26.09
      right to left shunt related to congenital
          heart disease I27.83
      unclear multifactorial mechanisms
          I27.29
    arterial (associated) (drug-induced)
        (toxin-induced) I27.21
    chronic thromboembolic I27.24
    due to
      hematologic disorders I27.29
      left heart disease I27.22
      lung diseases and hypoxia I27.23
      metabolic disorders I27.29
      specified systemic disorders NEC
          I27.29

Hypertension, hypertensive *(Continued)*
  pulmonary *(Continued)*
    group 1 (associated) (drug-induced) (toxin-
        induced) I27.21
    group 2 I27.22
    group 3 I27.23
    group 4 I27.24
    group 5 I27.29
    of newborn (persistent) P29.30
    secondary
      arterial I27.21
      specified NEC I27.29
    primary (idiopathic) I27.0
  renal —*see* Hypertension, kidney
  renovascular I15.0
  secondary NEC I15.9
    due to
      endocrine disorders I15.2
      pheochromocytoma I15.2
      renal disorders NEC I15.1
        arterial I15.0
      renovascular disorders I15.0
    specified NEC I15.8
  ~~transient, of pregnancy O13.-~~
  ▶transient R03.0
    ▶of pregnancy O13.●
  urgency I16.0
  venous (chronic)
    due to
      deep vein thrombosis —*see* Syndrome,
          postthrombotic
    idiopathic I87.309
      with
        inflammation I87.32-●
          with ulcer I87.33-●
        specified complication NEC I87.39-●
        ulcer I87.31-●
          with inflammation I87.33-●
      asymptomatic I87.30-●
Hypertensive urgency —*see* Hypertension
Hyperthecosis ovary E28.8
Hyperthermia (of unknown origin) —*see also*
    Hyperpyrexia
  malignant, due to anesthesia T88.3
  newborn P81.9
    environmental P81.0
Hyperthyroid (recurrent) —*see* Hyperthyroidism
Hyperthyroidism (latent) (pre-adult)
    (recurrent) E05.90
  with
    goiter (diffuse) E05.00
      with thyroid storm E05.01
      nodular (multinodular) E05.20
        with thyroid storm E05.21
        uninodular E05.10
          with thyroid storm E05.11
    storm E05.91
  due to ectopic thyroid tissue E05.30
    with thyroid storm E05.31
  neonatal, transitory P72.1
  specified NEC E05.80
    with thyroid storm E05.81
Hypertony, hypertonia, hypertonicity
  bladder N31.8
  congenital P94.1
  stomach K31.89
    psychogenic F45.8
  uterus, uterine (contractions) (complicating
      delivery) O62.4
Hypertrichosis L68.9
  congenital Q84.2
  eyelid H02.869
    left H02.866
      lower H02.865
      upper H02.864
    right H02.863
      lower H02.862
      upper H02.861
  lanuginosa Q84.2
    acquired L68.1
  localized L68.2
  specified NEC L68.8

Hypertriglyceridemia, essential E78.1
Hypertrophy, hypertrophic
  adenofibromatous, prostate —*see*
      Enlargement, enlarged, prostate
  adenoids (infective) J35.2
    with tonsils J35.3
  adrenal cortex E27.8
  alveolar process or ridge —*see* Anomaly,
      alveolar
  anal papillae K62.89
  artery I77.89
    congenital NEC Q27.8
      digestive system Q27.8
      lower limb Q27.8
      specified site NEC Q27.8
      upper limb Q27.8
  auricular —*see* Hypertrophy, cardiac
  Bartholin's gland N75.8
  bile duct (common) (hepatic) K83.8
  bladder (sphincter) (trigone) N32.89
  bone M89.30
    carpus M89.34-●
    clavicle M89.31-●
    femur M89.35-●
    fibula M89.36-●
    finger M89.34-●
    humerus M89.32-●
    ilium M89.359
    ischium M89.359
    metacarpus M89.34-●
    metatarsus M89.37-●
    multiple sites M89.39
    neck M89.38
    radius M89.33-●
    rib M89.38
    scapula M89.31-●
    skull M89.38
    tarsus M89.37-●
    tibia M89.36-●
    toe M89.37-●
    ulna M89.33-●
    vertebra M89.38
  brain G93.89
  breast N62
    cystic —*see* Mastopathy, cystic
    newborn P83.4
    pubertal, massive N62
    puerperal, postpartum —*see* Disorder,
        breast, specified type NEC
    senile (parenchymatous) N62
  cardiac (chronic) (idiopathic) I51.7
    with rheumatic fever (conditions in I00)
        active I01.8
        inactive or quiescent (with chorea) I09.89
    congenital NEC Q24.8
    fatty —*see* Degeneration, myocardial
    hypertensive —*see* Hypertension, heart
    rheumatic (with chorea) I09.89
      active or acute I01.8
        with chorea I02.0
    valve —*see* Endocarditis
  cartilage —*see* Disorder, cartilage, specified
      type NEC
  cecum —*see* Megacolon
  cervix (uteri) N88.8
    congenital Q51.828
    elongation N88.4
  clitoris (cirrhotic) N90.89
    congenital Q52.6
  colon —*see also* Megacolon
    congenital Q43.2
  conjunctiva, lymphoid H11.89
  corpora cavernosa N48.89
  cystic duct K82.8
  duodenum K31.89
  endometrium (glandular) —*see also*
      Hyperplasia, endometrial N85.00-●
    cervix N88.8
  epididymis N50.89
  esophageal hiatus (congenital) Q79.1
    with hernia —*see* Hernia, hiatal

▶ New   ⇒ Revised   ~~deleted~~ Deleted   ● Use Additional Character(s)

Hypertrophy, hypertrophic *(Continued)*
  eyelid —*see* Disorder, eyelid, specified type
      NEC
  fat pad E65
    knee (infrapatellar) (popliteal) (prepatellar)
        (retropatellar) M79.4
  foot (congenital) Q74.2
  frenulum, frenum (tongue) K14.8
    lip K13.0
  gallbladder K82.8
  gastric mucosa K29.60
    with bleeding K29.61
  gland, glandular R59.9
    generalized R59.1
    localized R59.0
  gum (mucous membrane) K06.1
  heart (idiopathic) —*see also* Hypertrophy,
      cardiac
    valve —*see also* Endocarditis I38
  hemifacial Q67.4
  hepatic —*see* Hypertrophy, liver
  hiatus (esophageal) Q79.1
  hilus gland R59.0
  hymen, congenital Q52.4
  ileum K63.89
  intestine NEC K63.89
  jejunum K63.89
  kidney (compensatory) N28.81
    congenital Q63.3
  labium (majus) (minus) N90.60
  ligament —*see* Disorder, ligament
  lingual tonsil (infective) J35.1
    with adenoids J35.3
  lip K13.0
    congenital Q18.6
  liver R16.0
    acute K76.89
    cirrhotic —*see* Cirrhosis, liver
    congenital Q44.7
    fatty —*see* Fatty, liver
  lymph, lymphatic gland R59.9
    generalized R59.1
    localized R59.0
    tuberculous —*see* Tuberculosis, lymph
        gland
  mammary gland —*see* Hypertrophy, breast
  Meckel's diverticulum (congenital) Q43.0
    malignant —*see* Table of Neoplasms,
        small intestine, malignant
  median bar —*see* Hyperplasia, prostate
  meibomian gland —*see* Chalazion
  meniscus, knee, congenital Q74.1
  metatarsal head —*see* Hypertrophy, bone,
      metatarsus
  metatarsus —*see* Hypertrophy, bone,
      metatarsus
  mucous membrane
    alveolar ridge K06.2
    gum K06.1
    nose (turbinate) J34.3
  muscle M62.89
  muscular coat, artery I77.89
  myocardium —*see also* Hypertrophy, cardiac
    idiopathic I42.2
  myometrium N85.2
  nail L60.2
    congenital Q84.5
  nasal J34.89
    alae J34.89
    bone J34.89
    cartilage J34.89
    mucous membrane (septum) J34.3
    sinus J34.89
    turbinate J34.3
  nasopharynx, lymphoid (infectional) (tissue)
      (wall) J35.2
  nipple N62
  organ or site, congenital NEC —*see* Anomaly,
      by site - ovary N83.8
  palate (hard) M27.8
    soft K13.79

Hypertrophy, hypertrophic *(Continued)*
  pancreas, congenital Q45.3
  parathyroid (gland) E21.0
  parotid gland K11.1
  penis N48.89
  pharyngeal tonsil J35.2
  pharynx J39.2
    lymphoid (infectional) (tissue) (wall) J35.2
  pituitary (anterior) (fossa) (gland) E23.6
  prepuce (congenital) N47.8
    female N90.89
  prostate —*see* Enlargement, enlarged, prostate
    congenital Q55.4
▶ pseudomuscular G71.09
  pylorus (adult) (muscle) (sphincter) K31.1
    congenital or infantile Q40.0
  rectal, rectum (sphincter) K62.89
  rhinitis (turbinate) J31.0
  salivary gland (any) K11.1
    congenital Q38.4
  scaphoid (tarsal) —*see* Hypertrophy, bone,
      tarsus
  scar L91.0
  scrotum N50.89
  seminal vesicle N50.89
  sigmoid —*see* Megacolon
  skin L91.9
    specified NEC L91.8
  spermatic cord N50.89
  spleen —*see* Splenomegaly
  spondylitis —*see* Spondylosis
  stomach K31.89
  sublingual gland K11.1
  submandibular gland K11.1
  suprarenal cortex (gland) E27.8
  synovial NEC M67.20
    acromioclavicular M67.21-●
    ankle M67.27-●
    elbow M67.22-●
    foot M67.27-●
    hand M67.24-●
    hip M67.25-●
    knee M67.26-●
    multiple sites M67.29
    specified site NEC M67.28
    wrist M67.23-●
  tendon —*see* Disorder, tendon, specified type
      NEC
  testis N44.8
    congenital Q55.29
  thymic, thymus (gland) (congenital) E32.0
  thyroid (gland) —*see* Goiter
  toe (congenital) Q74.2
    acquired —*see also* Deformity, toe, specified
        NEC
  tongue K14.8
    congenital Q38.2
    papillae (foliate) K14.3
  tonsils (faucial) (infective) (lingual)
      (lymphoid) J35.1
    with adenoids J35.3
  tunica vaginalis N50.89
  ureter N28.89
  urethra N36.8
  uterus N85.2
    neck (with elongation) N88.4
    puerperal O90.89
  uvula K13.79
  vagina N89.8
  vas deferens N50.89
  vein I87.8
  ventricle, ventricular (heart) —*see also*
      Hypertrophy, cardiac
    congenital Q24.8
    in tetralogy of Fallot Q21.3
  verumontanum N36.8
  vocal cord J38.3
  vulva N90.60
    stasis (nonfilarial) N90.69
Hypertropia H50.2-●
Hypertyrosinemia E70.21

Hyperuricemia (asymptomatic) E79.0
▶ Hyperuricoscuria R82.993
Hypervalinemia E71.19
Hyperventilation (tetany) R06.4
  hysterical F45.8
  psychogenic F45.8
  syndrome F45.8
Hypervitaminosis (dietary) NEC E67.8
  A E67.0
    administered as drug (prolonged intake) —
        see Table of Drugs and Chemicals,
        vitamins, adverse effect
    overdose or wrong substance given
        or taken —*see* Table of Drugs and
        Chemicals, vitamins, poisoning
  B6 E67.2
  D E67.3
    administered as drug (prolonged intake) —
        see Table of Drugs and Chemicals,
        vitamins, adverse effect
    overdose or wrong substance given
        or taken —*see* Table of Drugs and
        Chemicals, vitamins, poisoning
  K E67.8
    administered as drug (prolonged intake) —
        see Table of Drugs and Chemicals,
        vitamins, adverse effect
    overdose or wrong substance given
        or taken —*see* Table of Drugs and
        Chemicals, vitamins, poisoning
Hypervolemia E87.70
  specified NEC E87.79
Hypesthesia R20.1
  cornea —*see* Anesthesia, cornea
Hyphema H21.0-●
  traumatic S05.1-●
Hypoacidity, gastric K31.89
  psychogenic F45.8
Hypoadrenalism, hypoadrenia E27.40
  primary E27.1
  tuberculous A18.7
Hypoadrenocorticism E27.40
  pituitary E23.0
  primary E27.1
Hypoalbuminemia E88.09
Hypoaldosteronism E27.40
Hypoalphalipoproteinemia E78.6
Hypobarism T70.29
Hypobaropathy T70.29
Hypobetalipoproteinemia (familial) E78.6
Hypocalcemia E83.51
  dietary E58
  neonatal P71.1
    due to cow's milk P71.0
  phosphate-loading (newborn) P71.1
Hypochloremia E87.8
Hypochlorhydria K31.89
  neurotic F45.8
  psychogenic F45.8
Hypochondria, hypochondriac,
    hypochondriasis (reaction) F45.21
  sleep F51.03
Hypochondrogenesis Q77.0
Hypochondroplasia Q77.4
Hypochromasia, blood cells D50.8
Hypodontia —*see* Anodontia
▶ Hypocitraturia R82.991
Hypoeosinophilia D72.89
Hypoesthesia R20.1
Hypofibrinogenemia D68.8
  acquired D65
  congenital (hereditary) D68.2
Hypofunction
  adrenocortical E27.40
    drug-induced E27.3
    postprocedural E89.6
    primary E27.1
  adrenomedullary, postprocedural E89.6
  cerebral R29.818
  corticoadrenal NEC E27.40
  intestinal K59.8

Hypofunction *(Continued)*
  labyrinth —*see* subcategory H83.2
  ovary E28.39
  pituitary (gland) (anterior) E23.0
  testicular E29.1
    postprocedural (postsurgical)
      (postirradiation) (iatrogenic)
      E89.5
Hypogalactia O92.4
Hypogammaglobulinemia —*see also*
    Agammaglobulinemia D80.1
  hereditary D80.0
  nonfamilial D80.1
  transient, of infancy D80.7
Hypogenitalism (congenital) —*see*
    Hypogonadism
Hypoglossia Q38.3
Hypoglycemia (spontaneous) E16.2
  coma E15
    diabetic —*see* Diabetes, by type, with
      hypoglycemia, with coma
  diabetic —*see* Diabetes, hypoglycemia
  dietary counseling and surveillance Z71.3
  drug-induced E16.0
    with coma (nondiabetic) E15
  due to insulin E16.0
    with coma (nondiabetic) E15
    therapeutic misadventure —*see*
      subcategory T38.3
  functional, nonhyperinsulinemic E16.1
  iatrogenic E16.0
    with coma (nondiabetic) E15
  in infant of diabetic mother P70.1
    gestational diabetes P70.0
  infantile E16.1
  leucine-induced E71.19
  neonatal (transitory) P70.4
    iatrogenic P70.3
  reactive (not drug-induced) E16.1
  transitory neonatal P70.4
Hypogonadism
  female E28.39
  hypogonadotropic E23.0
  male E29.1
  ovarian (primary) E28.39
  pituitary E23.0
  testicular (primary) E29.1
Hypohidrosis, hypoidrosis L74.4
Hypoinsulinemia, postprocedural E89.1
Hypokalemia E87.6
Hypoleukocytosis —*see* Agranulocytosis
Hypolipoproteinemia (alpha) (beta) E78.6
Hypomagnesemia E83.42
  neonatal P71.2
Hypomania, hypomanic reaction F30.8
Hypomenorrhea —*see* Oligomenorrhea
Hypometabolism R63.8
Hypomotility
  gastrointestinal (tract) K31.89
    psychogenic F45.8
  intestine K59.8
    psychogenic F45.8
  stomach K31.89
    psychogenic F45.8
Hyponasality R49.22
Hyponatremia E87.1
Hypo-osmolality E87.1
Hypo-ovarianism, hypo-ovarism E28.39
Hypoparathyroidism E20.9
  familial E20.8
  idiopathic E20.0
  neonatal, transitory P71.4
  postprocedural E89.2
  specified NEC E20.8
Hypoperfusion (in)
  newborn P96.89
Hypopharyngitis —*see* Laryngopharyngitis
Hypophoria H50.53
Hypophosphatemia, hypophosphatasia
    (acquired) (congenital) (renal) E83.39
  familial E83.31

Hypophyseal, hypophysis —*see also* condition
  dwarfism E23.0
  gigantism E22.0
Hypopiesis —*see* Hypotension
Hypopinealism E34.8
Hypopituitarism (juvenile) E23.0
  drug-induced E23.1
  due to
    hypophysectomy E89.3
    radiotherapy E89.3
  iatrogenic NEC E23.1
  postirradiation E89.3
  postpartum O99.285
  postprocedural E89.3
Hypoplasia, hypoplastic
  adrenal (gland), congenital Q89.1
  alimentary tract, congenital Q45.8
    upper Q40.8
  anus, anal (canal) Q42.3
    with fistula Q42.2
  aorta, aortic Q25.42
    ascending, in hypoplastic left heart
      syndrome Q23.4
    valve Q23.1
      in hypoplastic left heart syndrome
        Q23.4
  areola, congenital Q83.8
  arm (congenital) —*see* Defect, reduction,
    upper limb
  artery (peripheral) Q27.8
    brain (congenital) Q28.3
    coronary Q24.5
    digestive system Q27.8
    lower limb Q27.8
    pulmonary Q25.79
      functional, unilateral J43.0
    retinal (congenital) Q14.1
    specified site NEC Q27.8
    umbilical Q27.0
    upper limb Q27.8
  auditory canal Q17.8
    causing impairment of hearing Q16.9
  biliary duct or passage Q44.5
  bone NOS Q79.9
    face Q75.8
    marrow D61.9
      megakaryocytic D69.49
    skull —*see* Hypoplasia, skull
  brain Q02
    gyri Q04.3
    part of Q04.3
  breast (areola) N64.82
  bronchus Q32.4
  cardiac Q24.8
  carpus —*see* Defect, reduction, upper limb,
    specified type NEC
  cartilage hair Q78.8
  cecum Q42.8
  cementum K00.4
  cephalic Q02
  cerebellum Q04.3
  cervix (uteri), congenital Q51.821
  clavicle (congenital) Q74.0
  coccyx Q76.49
  colon Q42.9
    specified NEC Q42.8
  corpus callosum Q04.0
  cricoid cartilage Q31.2
  digestive organ(s) or tract NEC Q45.8
    upper (congenital) Q40.8
  ear (auricle) (lobe) Q17.2
    middle Q16.4
  enamel of teeth (neonatal) (postnatal)
    (prenatal) K00.4
  endocrine (gland) NEC Q89.2
  endometrium N85.8
  epididymis (congenital) Q55.4
  epiglottis Q31.2
  erythroid, congenital D61.01
  esophagus (congenital) Q39.8
  eustachian tube Q17.8

Hypoplasia, hypoplastic *(Continued)*
  eye Q11.2
  eyelid (congenital) Q10.3
  face Q18.8
    bone(s) Q75.8
  femur (congenital) —*see* Defect,
    reduction, lower limb, specified
    type NEC
  fibula (congenital) —*see* Defect, reduction,
    lower limb, specified type NEC
  finger (congenital) —*see* Defect, reduction,
    upper limb, specified type NEC
  focal dermal Q82.8
  foot —*see* Defect, reduction, lower limb,
    specified type NEC
  gallbladder Q44.0
  genitalia, genital organ(s)
    female, congenital Q52.8
      external Q52.79
      internal NEC Q52.8
    in adiposogenital dystrophy E23.6
  glottis Q31.2
  hair Q84.2
  hand (congenital) —*see* Defect, reduction,
    upper limb, specified type NEC
  heart Q24.8
  humerus (congenital) —*see* Defect,
    reduction, upper limb, specified
    type NEC
  intestine (small) Q41.9
    large Q42.9
      specified NEC Q42.8
  jaw M26.09
    alveolar M26.79
    lower M26.04
      alveolar M26.74
    upper M26.02
      alveolar M26.73
  kidney(s) Q60.5
    bilateral Q60.4
    unilateral Q60.3
  labium (majus) (minus), congenital Q52.79
  larynx Q31.2
  left heart syndrome Q23.4
  leg (congenital) —*see* Defect, reduction, lower
    limb
  limb Q73.8
    lower (congenital) —*see* Defect, reduction,
      lower limb
    upper (congenital) —*see* Defect, reduction,
      upper limb
  liver Q44.7
  lung (lobe) (not associated with short
    gestation) Q33.6
    associated with immaturity, low birth
      weight, prematurity, or short gestation
      P28.0
  mammary (areola), congenital Q83.8
  mandible, mandibular M26.04
    alveolar M26.74
    unilateral condylar M27.8
  maxillary M26.02
    alveolar M26.73
  medullary D61.9
  megakaryocytic D69.49
  metacarpus —*see* Defect, reduction, upper
    limb, specified type NEC
  metatarsus —*see* Defect, reduction, lower
    limb, specified type NEC
  muscle Q79.8
  nail(s) Q84.6
  nose, nasal Q30.1
  optic nerve H47.03-●
  osseous meatus (ear) Q17.8
  ovary, congenital Q50.39
  pancreas Q45.0
  parathyroid (gland) Q89.2
  parotid gland Q38.4
  patella Q74.1
  pelvis, pelvic girdle Q74.2
  penis (congenital) Q55.62

▶ New   ⇒ Revised   ~~deleted~~ Deleted   ● Use Additional Character(s)

Hypoplasia, hypoplastic *(Continued)*
  peripheral vascular system Q27.8
    digestive system Q27.8
    lower limb Q27.8
    specified site NEC Q27.8
    upper limb Q27.8
  pituitary (gland) (congenital) Q89.2
  pulmonary (not associated with short
      gestation) Q33.6
    artery, functional J43.0
    associated with short gestation P28.0
  radioulnar —*see* Defect, reduction, upper
      limb, specified type NEC
  radius —*see* Defect, reduction, upper limb
  rectum Q42.1
    with fistula Q42.0
  respiratory system NEC Q34.8
  rib Q76.6
  right heart syndrome Q22.6
  sacrum Q76.49
  scapula Q74.0
  scrotum Q55.1
  shoulder girdle Q74.0
  skin Q82.8
  skull (bone) Q75.8
    with
      anencephaly Q00.0
      encephalocele —*see* Encephalocele
      hydrocephalus Q03.9
        with spina bifida —*see* Spina bifida, by
            site, with hydrocephalus
      microcephaly Q02
  spinal (cord) (ventral horn cell)
      Q06.1
  spine Q76.49
  sternum Q76.7
  tarsus —*see* Defect, reduction, lower limb,
      specified type NEC
  testis Q55.1
  thymic, with immunodeficiency D82.1
  thymus (gland) Q89.2
    with immunodeficiency D82.1
  thyroid (gland) E03.1
    cartilage Q31.2
  tibiofibular (congenital) —*see* Defect,
      reduction, lower limb, specified type
      NEC
  toe —*see* Defect, reduction, lower limb,
      specified type NEC
  tongue Q38.3
  Turner's K00.4
  ulna (congenital) —*see* Defect, reduction,
      upper limb
  umbilical artery Q27.0
  unilateral condylar M27.8
  ureter Q62.8
  uterus, congenital Q51.811
  vagina Q52.4
  vascular NEC peripheral Q27.8
    brain Q28.3
    digestive system Q27.8
    lower limb Q27.8
    specified site NEC Q27.8
    upper limb Q27.8
  vein(s) (peripheral) Q27.8
    brain Q28.3
    digestive system Q27.8
    great Q26.8
    lower limb Q27.8
    specified site NEC Q27.8
    upper limb Q27.8

Hypoplasia, hypoplastic *(Continued)*
  vena cava (inferior) (superior) Q26.8
  vertebra Q76.49
  vulva, congenital Q52.79
  zonule (ciliary) Q12.8
▶Hypoplasminogenemia E88.02
Hypopnea, obstructive sleep apnea G47.33
Hypopotassemia E87.6
Hypoproconvertinemia, congenital
    (hereditary) D68.2
Hypoproteinemia E77.8
Hypoprothrombinemia (congenital)
    (hereditary) (idiopathic) D68.2
  acquired D68.4
  newborn, transient P61.6
Hypoptyalism K11.7
Hypopyon (eye) (anterior chamber) —*see*
    Iridocyclitis, acute, hypopyon
Hypopyrexia R68.0
Hyporeflexia R29.2
Hyposecretion
  ACTH E23.0
  antidiuretic hormone E23.2
  ovary E28.39
  salivary gland (any) K11.7
  vasopressin E23.2
Hyposegmentation, leukocytic, hereditary
    D72.0
Hyposiderinemia D50.9
Hypospadias Q54.9
  balanic Q54.0
  coronal Q54.0
  glandular Q54.0
  penile Q54.1
  penoscrotal Q54.2
  perineal Q54.3
  specified NEC Q54.8
Hypospermatogenesis —*see* Oligospermia
Hyposplenism D73.0
Hypostasis pulmonary, passive —*see* Edema,
    lung
Hypostatic —*see* condition
Hyposthenuria N28.89
Hypotension (arterial) (constitutional)
    I95.9
  chronic I95.89
  drug-induced I95.2
  due to (of) hemodialysis I95.3
  iatrogenic I95.89
  idiopathic (permanent) I95.0
  intracranial, following ventricular shunting
      (ventriculostomy) G97.2
  intra-dialytic I95.3
  maternal, syndrome (following labor and
      delivery) O26.5-●
  neurogenic, orthostatic G90.3
  orthostatic (chronic) I95.1
    due to drugs I95.2
    neurogenic G90.3
  postoperative I95.81
  postural I95.1
  specified NEC I95.89
Hypothermia (accidental) T68
  due to anesthesia, anesthetic T88.51
  low environmental temperature T68
  neonatal P80.9
    environmental (mild) NEC P80.8
    mild P80.8
    severe (chronic) (cold injury syndrome)
        P80.0
    specified NEC P80.8

Hypothermia *(Continued)*
  not associated with low environmental
      temperature R68.0
Hypothyroidism (acquired) E03.9
  autoimmune —*see* Thyroiditis, autoimmune
  congenital (without goiter) E03.1
    with goiter (diffuse) E03.0
  due to
    exogenous substance NEC E03.2
    iodine-deficiency, acquired E01.8
      subclinical E02
    irradiation therapy E89.0
    medicament NEC E03.2
    P-aminosalicylic acid (PAS) E03.2
    phenylbutazone E03.2
    resorcinol E03.2
    sulfonamide E03.2
    surgery E89.0
    thiourea group drugs E03.2
  iatrogenic NEC E03.2
  iodine-deficiency (acquired) E01.8
    congenital —*see* Syndrome, iodine-
        deficiency, congenital
    subclinical E02
  neonatal, transitory P72.2
  postinfectious E03.3
  postirradiation E89.0
  postprocedural E89.0
  postsurgical E89.0
  specified NEC E03.8
  subclinical, iodine-deficiency related
      E02
Hypotonia, hypotonicity, hypotony
  bladder N31.2
  congenital (benign) P94.2
  eye —*see* Disorder, globe, hypotony
Hypotrichosis —*see* Alopecia
Hypotropia H50.2-●
Hypoventilation R06.89
  congenital central alveolar G47.35
  sleep related
    idiopathic nonobstructive alveolar
        G47.34
    in conditions classified elsewhere
        G47.36
Hypovitaminosis —*see* Deficiency, vitamin
Hypovolemia E86.1
  surgical shock T81.19
  traumatic (shock) T79.4
Hypoxemia R09.02
  newborn P84
  sleep related, in conditions classified
      elsewhere G47.36
Hypoxia —*see also* Anoxia R09.02
  cerebral, during a procedure NEC G97.81
    postprocedural NEC G97.82
  intrauterine P84
  myocardial —*see* Insufficiency, coronary
  newborn P84
  sleep-related G47.34
Hypsarhythmia —*see* Epilepsy, generalized,
    specified NEC
Hysteralgia, pregnant uterus O26.89-●
Hysteria, hysterical (conversion) (dissociative
    state) F44.9
  anxiety F41.8
  convulsions F44.5
  psychosis, acute F44.9
Hysteroepilepsy F44.5

I

IBDU (colonic inflammatory bowel disseasae unclassified) K52.3
Ichthyoparasitism due to Vandellia cirrhosa B88.8
Ichthyosis (congenital) Q80.9
  acquired L85.0
  fetalis Q80.4
  hystrix Q80.8
  lamellar Q80.2
  lingual K13.29
  palmaris and plantaris Q82.8
  simplex Q80.0
  vera Q80.8
  vulgaris Q80.0
  X-linked Q80.1
Ichthyotoxism —see Poisoning, fish
  bacterial —see Intoxication, foodborne
Icteroanemia, hemolytic (acquired) D59.9
  congenital —see Spherocytosis
Icterus —see also Jaundice
  conjunctiva R17
  gravis, newborn P55.0
  hematogenous (acquired) D59.9
  hemolytic (acquired) D59.9
    congenital —see Spherocytosis
  hemorrhagic (acute) (leptospiral) (spirochetal) A27.0
    newborn P53
  infectious B15.9
    with hepatic coma B15.0
    leptospiral A27.0
    spirochetal A27.0
  neonatorum —see Jaundice, newborn
  newborn P59.9
  spirochetal A27.0
Ictus solaris, solis T67.0
Ideation
  homicidal R45.850
  suicidal R45.851
Identity disorder (child) F64.9
  gender role F64.2
  psychosexual F64.2
Idioglossia F80.0
Idiopathic —see condition
Idiot, idiocy (congenital) F73
  amaurotic (Bielschowsky(-Jansky)) (family) (infantile (late)) (juvenile (late)) (Vogt-Spielmeyer) E75.4
  microcephalic Q02
Id reaction (due to bacteria) L30.2
IgE asthma J45.909
IIAC (idiopathic infantile arterial calcification) Q28.8
Ileitis (chronic) (noninfectious) —see also Enteritis K52.9
  backwash —see Pancolitis, ulcerative (chronic)
  infectious A09
  regional (ulcerative) —see Enteritis, regional, small intestine
  segmental —see Enteritis, regional
  terminal (ulcerative) —see Enteritis, regional, small intestine
Ileocolitis —see also Enteritis K52.9
  infectious A09
  regional —see Enteritis, regional
  ulcerative K51.0-●
Ileostomy
  attention to Z43.2
  malfunctioning K94.13
  status Z93.2
    with complication —see Complications, enterostomy
Ileotyphus —see Typhoid
Ileum —see condition
Ileus (bowel) (colon) (inhibitory) (intestine) K56.7
  adynamic K56.0
  due to gallstone (in intestine) K56.3
  duodenal (chronic) K31.5

Ileus (Continued)
  gallstone K56.3
  mechanical NEC —see also Obstruction, intestine, specified K56.699
  meconium P76.0
    in cystic fibrosis E84.11
    meaning meconium plug (without cystic fibrosis) P76.0
  myxedema K59.8
  neurogenic K56.0
    Hirschsprung's disease or megacolon Q43.1
  newborn
    due to meconium P76.0
      in cystic fibrosis E84.11
      meaning meconium plug (without cystic fibrosis) P76.0
    transitory P76.1
  obstructive —see also Obstruction, intestine, specified K56.699
  paralytic K56.0
  postoperative K91.89
Iliac —see condition
Iliotibial band syndrome M76.3-●
Illiteracy Z55.0
Illness —see also Disease R69
  manic-depressive —see Disorder, bipolar
Imbalance R26.89
  autonomic G90.8
  constituents of food intake E63.1
  electrolyte E87.8
    with
      abortion —see Abortion by type, complicated by, electrolyte imbalance
      molar pregnancy O08.5
    due to hyperemesis gravidarum O21.1
    following ectopic or molar pregnancy O08.5
    neonatal, transitory NEC P74.49
      potassium
        hyperkalemia P74.31
        hypokalemia P74.32
      sodium
        hypernatremia P74.21
        hyponatremia P74.22
  endocrine E34.9
  eye muscle NOS H50.9
  hormone E34.9
  hysterical F44.4
  labyrinth —see subcategory H83.2
  posture R29.3
  protein-energy —see Malnutrition
  sympathetic G90.8
Imbecile, imbecility (I.Q. 35-49) F71
Imbedding, intrauterine device T83.39
Imbibition, cholesterol (gallbladder) K82.4
Imbrication, teeth, fully erupted M26.30
Imerslund (-Gräsbeck) syndrome D51.1
Immature —see also Immaturity
  birth (less than 37 completed weeks) —see Preterm, newborn
    extremely (less than 28 completed weeks) —see Immaturity, extreme
  personality F60.89
Immaturity (less than 37 completed weeks) — see also Preterm, newborn
  extreme of newborn (less than 28 completed weeks of gestation) (less than 196 completed days of gestation) (unspecified weeks of gestation) P07.20
    gestational age
      23 completed weeks (23 weeks, 0 days through 23 weeks, 6 days) P07.22
      24 completed weeks (24 weeks, 0 days through 24 weeks, 6 days) P07.23
      25 completed weeks (25 weeks, 0 days through 25 weeks, 6 days) P07.24
      26 completed weeks (26 weeks, 0 days through 26 weeks, 6 days) P07.25
      27 completed weeks (27 weeks, 0 days through 27 weeks, 6 days) P07.26
      less than 23 completed weeks P07.21

Immaturity (Continued)
  fetus or infant light-for-dates —see Light-for-dates
  lung, newborn P28.0
  organ or site NEC —see Hypoplasia
  pulmonary, newborn P28.0
  reaction F60.89
  sexual (female) (male), after puberty E30.0
Immersion T75.1
  foot T69.02-●
  hand T69.01-●
Immobile, immobility
  complete, due to severe physical disability or frailty R53.2
  intestine K59.8
  syndrome (paraplegic) M62.3
Immune reconstitution (inflammatory) syndrome [IRIS] D89.3
Immunization —see also Vaccination
  ABO —see Incompatibility, ABO
    in newborn P55.1
▶appropriate for age
  ▶child (over 28 days old) Z00.129
    ▶with abnormal findings Z00.121
  complication —see Complications, vaccination
  encounter for Z23
  not done (not carried out) Z28.9
    because (of)
      acute illness of patient Z28.01
      allergy to vaccine (or component) Z28.04
      caregiver refusal Z28.82
      chronic illness of patient Z28.02
      contraindication NEC Z28.09
      ▶delay in delivery of vaccine Z28.83
      group pressure Z28.1
      guardian refusal Z28.82
      immune compromised state of patient Z28.03
      ▶lack of availability of vaccine Z28.83
      ▶manufacturer delay of vaccine Z28.83
      parent refusal Z28.82
      patient's belief Z28.1
      patient had disease being vaccinated against Z28.81
      patient refusal Z28.21
      religious beliefs of patient Z28.1
      specified reason NEC Z28.89
        of patient Z28.29
      ▶unavailability of vaccine Z28.83
      unspecified patient reason Z28.20
  Rh factor
    affecting management of pregnancy NEC O36.09-●
      anti-D antibody O36.01-●
    from transfusion —see Complication(s), transfusion, incompatibility reaction, Rh (factor)
Immunocytoma C83.0-●
Immunodeficiency D84.9
  with
    adenosine-deaminase deficiency D81.3
    antibody defects D80.9
      specified type NEC D80.8
    hyperimmunoglobulinemia D80.6
    increased immunoglobulin M (IgM) D80.5
    major defect D82.9
      specified type NEC D82.8
    partial albinism D82.8
    short-limbed stature D82.2
    thrombocytopenia and eczema D82.0
  antibody with
    hyperimmunoglobulinemia D80.6
    near-normal immunoglobulins D80.6
  autosomal recessive, Swiss type D80.0
  combined D81.9
    biotin-dependent carboxylase D81.819
      biotinidase D81.810
      holocarboxylase synthetase D81.818
      specified type NEC D81.818

▶ New   ➡ Revised   deleted Deleted   ● Use Additional Character(s)

Immunodeficiency (Continued)
  combined (Continued)
    severe (SCID) D81.9
      with
        low or normal B-cell numbers D81.2
        low T- and B-cell numbers D81.1
        reticular dysgenesis D81.0
    specified type NEC D81.89
  common variable D83.9
    with
      abnormalities of B-cell numbers and
        function D83.0
      autoantibodies to B- or T-cells D83.2
      immunoregulatory T-cell disorders D83.1
    specified type NEC D83.8
  following hereditary defective response to
    Epstein-Barr virus (EBV) D82.3
  selective, immunoglobulin
    A (IgA) D80.2
    G (IgG) (subclasses) D80.3
    M (IgM) D80.4
  severe combined (SCID) D81.9
  specified type NEC D84.8
  X-linked, with increased IgM D80.5
Immunotherapy (encounter for)
  antineoplastic Z51.12
Impaction, impacted
  bowel, colon, rectum —see also Impaction,
    fecal K56.49
    by gallstone K56.3
  calculus —see Calculus
  cerumen (ear) (external) H61.2-•
  cuspid —see Impaction, tooth
  dental (same or adjacent tooth) K01.1
  fecal, feces K56.41
  fracture —see Fracture, by site
  gallbladder —see Calculus, gallbladder
  gallstone(s) —see Calculus, gallbladder
    bile duct (common) (hepatic) —see
      Calculus, bile duct
    cystic duct —see Calculus, gallbladder
    in intestine, with obstruction (any part) K56.3
  intestine (calculous) NEC —see also
    Impaction, fecal K56.49
    gallstone, with ileus K56.3
  intrauterine device (IUD) T83.39
  molar —see Impaction, tooth
  shoulder, causing obstructed labor O66.0
  tooth, teeth K01.1
  turbinate J34.89
Impaired, impairment (function)
  auditory discrimination —see Abnormal,
    auditory perception
  cognitive, mild, so stated G31.84
  dual sensory Z73.82
  fasting glucose R73.01
  glucose tolerance (oral) R73.02
  hearing —see Deafness
  heart —see Disease, heart
  kidney N28.9
    disorder resulting from N25.9
      specified NEC N25.89
  liver K72.90
    with coma K72.91
  mastication K08.89
  mild cognitive, so stated G31.84
  mobility
    ear ossicles —see Ankylosis, ear ossicles
    requiring care provider Z74.09
  myocardium, myocardial —see Insufficiency,
    myocardial
  rectal sphincter R19.8
  renal (acute) (chronic) N28.9
    disorder resulting from N25.9
      specified NEC N25.89
  vision NEC H54.7
    both eyes H54.3
Impediment, speech R47.9
  psychogenic (childhood) F98.8
  slurring R47.81
  specified NEC R47.89

Impending
  coronary syndrome I20.0
  delirium tremens F10.239
  myocardial infarction I20.0
Imperception auditory (acquired) —see also
  Deafness
  congenital H93.25
Imperfect
  aeration, lung (newborn) NEC —see
    Atelectasis
  closure (congenital)
    alimentary tract NEC Q45.8
      lower Q43.8
      upper Q40.8
    atrioventricular ostium Q21.2
    atrium (secundum) Q21.1
    branchial cleft NOS Q18.2
      cyst Q18.0
      fistula Q18.0
      sinus Q18.0
    choroid Q14.3
    cricoid cartilage Q31.8
    cusps, heart valve NEC Q24.8
      pulmonary Q22.3
    ductus
      arteriosus Q25.0
      Botalli Q25.0
    ear drum (causing impairment of hearing)
      Q16.4
    esophagus with communication to
      bronchus or trachea Q39.1
    eyelid Q10.3
    foramen
      botalli Q21.1
      ovale Q21.1
    genitalia, genital organ(s) or system
      female Q52.8
        external Q52.79
        internal NEC Q52.8
      male Q55.8
    glottis Q31.8
    interatrial ostium or septum
      Q21.1
    interauricular ostium or septum
      Q21.1
    interventricular ostium or septum
      Q21.0
    larynx Q31.8
    lip —see Cleft, lip
    nasal septum Q30.3
    nose Q30.2
    omphalomesenteric duct Q43.0
    optic nerve entry Q14.2
    organ or site not listed —see Anomaly,
      by site
    ostium
      interatrial Q21.1
      interauricular Q21.1
      interventricular Q21.0
    palate —see Cleft, palate
    preauricular sinus Q18.1
    retina Q14.1
    roof of orbit Q75.8
    sclera Q13.5
    septum
      aorticopulmonary Q21.4
      atrial (secundum) Q21.1
      between aorta and pulmonary artery
        Q21.4
      heart Q21.9
      interatrial (secundum) Q21.1
      interauricular (secundum) Q21.1
      interventricular Q21.0
        in tetralogy of Fallot Q21.3
      nasal Q30.3
      ventricular Q21.0
        with pulmonary stenosis or atresia,
          dextraposition of aorta, and
          hypertrophy of right ventricle
          Q21.3
        in tetralogy of Fallot Q21.3

Imperfect (Continued)
  closure (Continued)
    skull Q75.0
      with
        anencephaly Q00.0
        encephalocele —see Encephalocele
        hydrocephalus Q03.9
          with spina bifida —see Spina bifida,
            by site, with hydrocephalus
        microcephaly Q02
    spine (with meningocele) —see Spina
      bifida
    trachea Q32.1
    tympanic membrane (causing impairment
      of hearing) Q16.4
    uterus Q51.818
    vitelline duct Q43.0
  erection —see Dysfunction, sexual, male,
    erectile
  fusion —see Imperfect, closure
  inflation, lung (newborn) —see Atelectasis
  posture R29.3
  rotation, intestine Q43.3
  septum, ventricular Q21.0
Imperfectly descended testis —see
  Cryptorchid
Imperforate (congenital) —see also Atresia
  anus Q42.3
    with fistula Q42.2
  cervix (uteri) Q51.828
  esophagus Q39.0
    with tracheoesophageal fistula Q39.1
  hymen Q52.3
  jejunum Q41.1
  pharynx Q38.8
  rectum Q42.1
    with fistula Q42.0
  urethra Q64.39
  vagina Q52.4
Impervious (congenital) —see also Atresia
  anus Q42.3
    with fistula Q42.2
  bile duct Q44.2
  esophagus Q39.0
    with tracheoesophageal fistula Q39.1
  intestine (small) Q41.9
    large Q42.9
      specified NEC Q42.8
  rectum Q42.1
    with fistula Q42.0
  ureter —see Atresia, ureter
  urethra Q64.39
Impetiginization of dermatoses L01.1
Impetigo (any organism) (any site) (circinate)
    (contagiosa) (simplex) (vulgaris)
    L01.00
  Bockhart's L01.02
  bullous, bullosa L01.03
  external ear L01.00 [H62.40]
  follicularis L01.02
  furfuracea L30.5
  herpetiformis L40.1
    nonobstetrical L40.1
  neonatorum L01.03
  nonbullous L01.01
  specified type NEC L01.09
  ulcerative L01.09
Impingement (on teeth)
  soft tissue
    anterior M26.81
    posterior M26.82
Implant, endometrial N80.9
Implantation
  anomalous —see Anomaly, by site
    ureter Q62.63
  cyst
    external area or site (skin) NEC L72.0
    iris —see Cyst, iris, implantation
    vagina N89.8
    vulva N90.7
  dermoid (cyst) —see Implantation, cyst

Impotence (sexual) N52.9
 counseling Z70.1
 organic origin —see also Dysfunction, sexual,
  male, erectile N52.9
 psychogenic F52.21
Impression, basilar Q75.8
Imprisonment, anxiety concerning Z65.1
Improper care (child) (newborn) —see
  Maltreatment
Improperly tied umbilical cord (causing
  hemorrhage) P51.8
Impulsiveness (impulsive) R45.87
Inability to swallow —see Aphagia
Inaccessible, inaccessibility
 health care NEC Z75.3
  due to
   waiting period Z75.2
    for admission to facility elsewhere
     Z75.1
 other helping agencies Z75.4
Inactive —see condition
Inadequate, inadequacy
 aesthetics of dental restoration K08.56
 biologic, constitutional, functional, or social
  F60.7
 development
  child R62.50
  genitalia
   after puberty NEC E30.0
   congenital
    female Q52.8
     external Q52.79
     internal Q52.8
    male Q55.8
  lungs Q33.6
   associated with short gestation P28.0
  organ or site not listed —see Anomaly, by
   site
 diet (causing nutritional deficiency) E63.9
 eating habits Z72.4
 environment, household Z59.1
 family support Z63.8
 food (supply) NEC Z59.4
  hunger effects T73.0
 functional F60.7
 household care, due to
  family member
   handicapped or ill Z74.2
   on vacation Z75.5
   temporarily away from home Z74.2
  technical defects in home Z59.1
  temporary absence from home of person
   rendering care Z74.2
 housing (heating) (space) Z59.1
 income (financial) Z59.6
 intrafamilial communication Z63.8
 material resources Z59.9
 mental —see Disability, intellectual
 parental supervision or control of child
  Z62.0
 personality F60.7
 pulmonary
  function R06.89
   newborn P28.5
  ventilation, newborn P28.5
 sample of cytologic smear
  anus R85.615
  cervix R87.615
  vagina R87.625
 social F60.7
  insurance Z59.7
  skills NEC Z73.4
 supervision of child by parent Z62.0
 teaching affecting education Z55.8
 welfare support Z59.7
Inanition R64
 with edema —see Malnutrition, severe
 due to
  deprivation of food T73.0
  malnutrition —see Malnutrition
 fever R50.9

Inappropriate
 change in quantitative human chorionic
  gonadotropin (hCG) in early pregnancy
  O02.81
 diet or eating habits Z72.4
 level of quantitative human chorionic
  gonadotropin (hCG) for gestational age
  in early pregnancy O02.81
 secretion
  antidiuretic hormone (ADH) (excessive)
   E22.2
  deficiency E23.2
  pituitary (posterior) E22.2
Inattention at or after birth —see Neglect
Incarceration, incarcerated
 enterocele K46.0
  gangrenous K46.1
 epiplocele K46.0
  gangrenous K46.1
 exomphalos K42.0
  gangrenous K42.1
 hernia —see also Hernia, by site, with
  obstruction
  with gangrene —see Hernia, by site, with
   gangrene
 iris, in wound —see Injury, eye, laceration,
  with prolapse
 lens, in wound —see Injury, eye, laceration,
  with prolapse
 omphalocele K42.0
 prison, anxiety concerning Z65.1
 rupture —see Hernia, by site
 sarcoepiplocele K46.0
  gangrenous K46.1
 sarcoepiplomphalocele K42.0
  with gangrene K42.1
 uterus N85.8
  gravid O34.51-●
   causing obstructed labor O65.5
Incised wound
 external —see Laceration
 internal organs —see Injury, by site
Incision, incisional
 hernia K43.2
  with
   gangrene (and obstruction) K43.1
   obstruction K43.0
  surgical, complication —see Complications,
   surgical procedure
 traumatic
  external —see Laceration
  internal organs —see Injury, by site
Inclusion
 azurophilic leukocytic D72.0
 blennorrhea (neonatal) (newborn) P39.1
 gallbladder in liver (congenital) Q44.1
Incompatibility
 ABO
  affecting management of pregnancy
   O36.11-●
   anti-A sensitization O36.11-●
   anti-B sensitization O36.19-●
   specified NEC O36.19-●
  infusion or transfusion reaction —see
   Complication(s), transfusion,
   incompatibility reaction, ABO
  newborn P55.1
 ⇒blood (group) (Duffy) (K) (Kell) (Kidd)
  (Lewis) (M) (S) NEC
  affecting management of pregnancy
   O36.11-●
   anti-A sensitization O36.11-●
   anti-B sensitization O36.19-●
  infusion or transfusion reaction
   T80.89
  newborn P55.8
 divorce or estrangement Z63.5
 Rh (blood group) (factor) Z31.82
  affecting management of pregnancy NEC
   O36.09-●
   anti-D antibody O36.01-●

Incompatibility (Continued)
 Rh (Continued)
  infusion or transfusion reaction —see
   Complication(s), transfusion,
   incompatibility reaction, Rh (factor)
  newborn P55.0
 rhesus —see Incompatibility, Rh
Incompetency, incompetent, incompetence
 annular
  aortic (valve) —see Insufficiency, aortic
  mitral (valve) I34.0
  pulmonary valve (heart) I37.1
 aortic (valve) —see Insufficiency, aortic
 cardiac valve —see Endocarditis
 cervix, cervical (os) N88.3
  in pregnancy O34.3-●
 chronotropic I45.89
  with
   autonomic dysfunction G90.8
   ischemic heart disease I25.89
   left ventricular dysfunction I51.89
   sinus node dysfunction I49.8
 esophagogastric (junction) (sphincter) K22.0
 mitral (valve) —see Insufficiency, mitral
 pelvic fundus N81.89
 pubocervical tissue N81.82
 pulmonary valve (heart) I37.1
  congenital Q22.3
 rectovaginal tissue N81.83
 tricuspid (annular) (valve) —see Insufficiency,
  tricuspid
 valvular —see Endocarditis
  congenital Q24.8
 vein, venous (saphenous) (varicose) —see
  Varix, leg
Incomplete —see also condition
 bladder, emptying R33.9
 defecation R15.0
 expansion lungs (newborn) NEC —see
  Atelectasis
 rotation, intestine Q43.3
Inconclusive
 diagnostic imaging due to excess body fat of
  patient R93.9
 findings on diagnostic imaging of breast NEC
  R92.8
 mammogram (due to dense breasts) R92.2
Incontinence R32
 anal sphincter R15.9
 coital N39.491
 feces R15.9
  nonorganic origin F98.1
 insensible (urinary) N39.42
 overflow N39.490
 postural (urinary) N39.492
 psychogenic F45.8
 rectal R15.9
 reflex N39.498
 stress (female) (male) N39.3
  and urge N39.46
 urethral sphincter R32
 urge N39.41
  and stress (female) (male) N39.46
 urine (urinary) R32
  continuous N39.45
  due to cognitive impairment, or severe
   physical disability or immobility
   R39.81
  functional R39.81
  insensible N39.42
  mixed (stress and urge) N39.46
  nocturnal N39.44
  nonorganic origin F98.0
  overflow N39.490
  post dribbling N39.43
  postural N39.492
  reflex N39.498
  specified NEC N39.498
  stress (female) (male) N39.3
   and urge N39.46
  total N39.498

▶ New   ⇒ Revised   ~~deleted~~ Deleted   ● Use Additional Character(s)

Infarct, infarction (Continued)
  myocardium, myocardial (Continued)
    past (diagnosed on ECG or other
      investigation, but currently presenting
      no symptoms) I25.2
    postprocedural —see also Infarct,
      myocardium, associated with
      revascularization procedure
      following cardiac surgery —see also
        Infarct, myocardium, type 4 or
        type 5 I97.19Ø
      following other surgery I97.191
    Q wave —see also Infarct, myocardium, by
      site I21.3
    secondary to
      demand ischemia I21.A1
      ischemic imbalance I21.A1
    ST elevation (STEMI) I21.3
      anterior (anteroapical) (anterolateral)
        (anteroseptal) (Q wave) (wall) I21.Ø9
        subsequent I22.Ø
      inferior (diaphragmatic) (inferolateral)
        (inferoposterior) (wall) NEC I21.19
        subsequent I22.1
      inferoposterior transmural (Q wave)
        I21.11
      involving
        coronary artery of anterior wall NEC
          I21.Ø9
        coronary artery of inferior wall NEC
          I21.19
        diagonal coronary artery I21.Ø2
        left anterior descending coronary
          artery I21.Ø2
        left circumflex coronary artery I21.21
        left main coronary artery I21.Ø1
        oblique marginal coronary artery
          I21.21
        right coronary artery I21.11
      lateral (apical-lateral) (basal-lateral)
        (high) I21.29
        subsequent I22.8
      posterior (posterobasal) (posterolateral)
        (posteroseptal) (true) I21.29
        subsequent I22.8
      septal I21.29
        subsequent I22.8
      specified NEC I21.29
        subsequent I22.8
    subsequent I22.9
    subsequent (recurrent) (reinfarction) I22.9
      anterior (anteroapical) (anterolateral)
        (anteroseptal) (wall) I22.Ø
      diaphragmatic (wall) I22.1
      inferior (diaphragmatic) (inferolateral)
        (inferoposterior) (wall) I22.1
      lateral (apical-lateral) (basal-lateral)
        (high) I22.8
      non-ST elevation (NSTEMI) I22.2
      posterior (posterobasal) (posterolateral)
        (posteroseptal) (true) I22.8
      septal I22.8
      specified NEC I22.8
      ST elevation I22.9
        anterior (anteroapical) (anterolateral)
          (anteroseptal) (wall) I22.Ø
        inferior (diaphragmatic) (inferolateral)
          (inferoposterior) (wall) I22.1
        specified NEC I22.8
      subendocardial I22.2
      transmural I22.9
        anterior (anteroapical) (anterolateral)
          (anteroseptal) (wall) I22.Ø
        diaphragmatic (wall) I22.1
        inferior (diaphragmatic) (inferolateral)
          (inferoposterior) (wall) I22.1
        lateral (apical-lateral) (basal-lateral)
          (high) I22.8
        posterior (posterobasal) (posterolateral)
          (posteroseptal) (true) I22.8
        specified NEC I22.8

Infarct, infarction (Continued)
  myocardium, myocardial (Continued)
    subsequent (Continued)
      type 1 —see also Infarction, myocardial,
        subsequent, by site, or by ST
        elevation or non-ST elevation I22.9
      type 2 I21.A1
      type 3 I21.A9
      type 4 I21.A9
      type 5 I21.A9
    syphilitic A52.Ø6
    transmural I21.9
      anterior (anteroapical) (anterolateral)
        (anteroseptal) (Q wave) (wall) NEC
        I21.Ø9
      inferior (diaphragmatic) (inferolateral)
        (inferoposterior) (Q wave) (wall)
        NEC I21.19
      inferoposterior (Q wave) I21.11
      lateral (apical-lateral) (basal-lateral)
        (high) NEC I21.29
      posterior (posterobasal) (posterolateral)
        (posteroseptal) (true) NEC I21.29
      septal NEC I21.29
      specified NEC I21.29
      type 1 —see also Infarction, myocardial,
        by site, or by ST elevation or non-ST
        elevation I21.9
      type 2 I21.A1
      type 3 I21.A9
      type 4 (a) (b) (c) I21.A9
      type 5 I21.A9
    nontransmural I21.4
  omentum —see also Infarct, intestine K55.Ø69
  ovary N83.8
  pancreas K86.89
  papillary muscle —see Infarct, myocardium
  parathyroid gland E21.4
  pituitary (gland) E23.6
  placenta O43.81-●
  prostate N42.89
  pulmonary (artery) (vein) (hemorrhagic) —
    see Embolism, pulmonary
  renal (embolic) (thrombotic) N28.Ø
  retina, retinal (artery) —see Occlusion, artery,
    retina
  spinal (cord) (acute) (embolic) (nonembolic)
    G95.11
  spleen D73.5
    embolic or thrombotic I74.8
  subendocardial (acute) (nontransmural) I21.4
  suprarenal (capsule) (gland) E27.49
  testis N50.1
  thrombotic —see also Thrombosis
    artery, arterial —see Embolism
  thyroid (gland) E07.89
  ventricle (heart) —see Infarct, myocardium
Infecting —see condition
Infection, infected, infective (opportunistic) B99.9
  with
    drug resistant organism —see Resistance
      (to), drug —see also specific organism
    lymphangitis —see Lymphangitis
    organ dysfunction (acute) R65.2Ø
      with septic shock R65.21
  abscess (skin) - code by site under Abscess
  Absidia —see Mucormycosis
  Acanthamoeba —see Acanthamebiasis
  Acanthocheilonema (perstans) (streptocerca)
    B74.4
  accessory sinus (chronic) —see Sinusitis
  achorion —see Dermatophytosis
  Acremonium falciforme B47.Ø
  acromioclavicular MØØ.9
  Actinobacillus (actinomycetem-comitans)
    A28.8
    mallei A24.Ø
    muris A25.1
  Actinomadura B47.1
  Actinomyces (israelii) —see also
    Actinomycosis A42.9

Infection, infected, infective (Continued)
  Actinomycetales —see Actinomycosis
  actinomycotic NOS —see Actinomycosis
  adenoid (and tonsil) JØ3.9Ø
    chronic J35.Ø2
  adenovirus NEC
    as cause of disease classified elsewhere
      B97.Ø
    unspecified nature or site B34.Ø
  aerogenes capsulatus A48.Ø
  aertrycke —see Infection, salmonella
  alimentary canal NOS —see Enteritis,
    infectious
  Allescheria boydii B48.2
  Alternaria B48.8
  alveolus, alveolar (process) KØ4.7
  Ameba, amebic (histolytica) —see Amebiasis
  amniotic fluid, sac or cavity O41.1Ø-●
    chorioamnionitis O41.12-●
    placentitis O41.14-●
  amputation stump (surgical) —see
    Complication, amputation stump,
    infection
  Ancylostoma (duodenalis) B76.Ø
  Anisakiasis, Anisakis larvae B81.Ø
  anthrax —see Anthrax
  antrum (chronic) —see Sinusitis, maxillary
  anus, anal (papillae) (sphincter) K62.89
  arbovirus (arbor virus) A94
    specified type NEC A93.8
  artificial insemination N98.Ø
  Ascaris lumbricoides —see Ascariasis
  Ascomycetes B47.Ø
  Aspergillus (flavus) (fumigatus) (terreus) —
    see Aspergillosis
  atypical
    acid-fast (bacilli) —see Mycobacterium,
      atypical
    mycobacteria —see Mycobacterium, atypical
    virus A81.9
      specified type NEC A81.89
  auditory meatus (external) —see Otitis,
    externa, infective
  auricle (ear) —see Otitis, externa, infective
  axillary gland (lymph) LØ4.2
  Bacillus A49.9
    abortus A23.1
    anthracis —see Anthrax
    Ducrey's (any location) A57
    Flexner's AØ3.1
    Friedländer's NEC A49.8
    gas (gangrene) A48.Ø
    mallei A24.Ø
    melitensis A23.Ø
    paratyphoid, paratyphosus AØ1.4
      A AØ1.1
      B AØ1.2
      C AØ1.3
    Shiga (-Kruse) AØ3.Ø
    suipestifer —see Infection, salmonella
    swimming pool A31.1
    typhosa AØ1.ØØ
    welchii —see Gangrene, gas
  bacterial NOS A49.9
    as cause of disease classified elsewhere
      B96.89
      Bacteroides fragilis [B. fragilis] B96.6
      Clostridium perfringens [C. perfringens]
        B96.7
      Enterobacter sakazakii B96.89
      Enterococcus B95.2
      Escherichia coli [E. coli] (see also
        Escherichia coli) B96.2Ø
      Helicobacter pylori [H.pylori] B96.81
      Hemophilus influenzae [H. influenzae]
        B96.3
      Klebsiella pneumoniae [K. pneumoniae]
        B96.1
      Mycoplasma pneumoniae [M.
        pneumoniae] B96.Ø
      Proteus (mirabilis) (morganii) B96.4

▶ New   ⇒ Revised   ~~deleted~~ Deleted   ● Use Additional Character(s)

Infection, infected, infective *(Continued)*
  bacterial NOS *(Continued)*
    as cause of disease classified elsewhere
      (Continued)
      Pseudomonas (aeruginosa) (mallei)
        (pseudomallei) B96.5
      Staphylococcus B95.8
        aureus (methicillin susceptible)
          (MSSA) B95.61
          methicillin resistant (MRSA) B95.62
        specified NEC B95.7
      Streptococcus B95.5
        group A B95.0
        group B B95.1
        pneumoniae B95.3
        specified NEC B95.4
      Vibrio vulnificus B96.82
    specified NEC A48.8
  Bacterium
    paratyphosum A01.4
      A A01.1
      B A01.2
      C A01.3
    typhosum A01.00
  Bacteroides NEC A49.8
    fragilis, as cause of disease classified
      elsewhere B96.6
  Balantidium coli A07.0
  Bartholin's gland N75.8
  Basidiobolus B46.8
  bile duct (common) (hepatic) —*see*
    Cholangitis
  bladder —*see* Cystitis
  Blastomyces, blastomycotic —*see also*
    Blastomycosis
    brasiliensis —*see* Paracoccidioidomycosis
    dermatitidis —*see* Blastomycosis
    European —*see* Cryptococcosis
    Loboi B48.0
    North American B40.9
    South American —*see*
      Paracoccidioidomycosis
  bleb, postprocedure —*see* Blebitis
  bone —*see* Osteomyelitis
  Bordetella —*see* Whooping cough
  Borrelia bergdorfi A69.20
  brain —*see also* Encephalitis G04.90
    membranes —*see* Meningitis
    septic G06.0
    meninges —*see* Meningitis, bacterial
  branchial cyst Q18.0
  breast —*see* Mastitis
  bronchus —*see* Bronchitis
  Brucella A23.9
    abortus A23.1
    canis A23.3
    melitensis A23.0
    mixed A23.8
    specified NEC A23.8
    suis A23.2
  Brugia (malayi) B74.1
    timori B74.2
  bursa —*see* Bursitis, infective
  buttocks (skin) L08.9
  Campylobacter, intestinal A04.5
    as cause of disease classified elsewhere
      B96.81
  Candida (albicans) (tropicalis) —*see*
    Candidiasis
  candiru B88.8
  Capillaria (intestinal) B81.1
    hepatica B83.8
    philippinensis B81.1
  cartilage —*see* Disorder, cartilage, specified
    type NEC
  catheter-related bloodstream (CRBSI) T80.211
  cat liver fluke B66.0
  cellulitis - code by site under Cellulitis
  central line-associated T80.219
    bloodstream (CLABSI) T80.211
    specified NEC T80.218

Infection, infected, infective *(Continued)*
  Cephalosporium falciforme B47.0
  cerebrospinal —*see* Meningitis
  cervical gland (lymph) L04.0
  cervix —*see* Cervicitis
▶ cesarean delivery wound (puerperal) O86.00
  cestodes —*see* Infestation, cestodes
  chest J22
  Chilomastix (intestinal) A07.8
  Chlamydia, chlamydial A74.9
    anus A56.3
    genitourinary tract A56.2
      lower A56.00
        specified NEC A56.19
    lymphogranuloma A55
    pharynx A56.4
    psittaci A70
    rectum A56.3
    sexually transmitted NEC A56.8
  cholera —*see* Cholera
  Cladosporium
    bantianum (brain abscess) B43.1
    carrionii B43.0
    castellanii B36.1
    trichoides (brain abscess) B43.1
    werneckii B36.1
  Clonorchis (sinensis) (liver) B66.1
  Clostridium NEC
    bifermentans A48.0
    botulinum (food poisoning) A05.1
      infant A48.51
      wound A48.52
    difficile
      as cause of disease classified elsewhere
        B96.89
      foodborne (disease)
        not specified as recurrent A04.72
        recurrent A04.71
      gas gangrene A48.0
      necrotizing enterocolitis
        not specified as recurrent A04.72
        recurrent A04.71
      sepsis A41.4
    gas-forming NEC A48.0
    histolyticum A48.0
    novyi, causing gas gangrene A48.0
    oedematiens A48.0
    perfringens
      as cause of disease classified elsewhere
        B96.7
      due to food A05.2
      foodborne (disease) A05.2
      gas gangrene A48.0
      sepsis A41.4
    septicum, causing gas gangrene A48.0
    sordellii, causing gas gangrene A48.0
    welchii
      as cause of disease classified elsewhere
        B96.7
      foodborne (disease) A05.2
      gas gangrene A48.0
      necrotizing enteritis A05.2
      sepsis A41.4
  Coccidioides (immitis) —*see*
    Coccidioidomycosis
  colon —*see* Enteritis, infectious
  colostomy K94.02
  common duct —*see* Cholangitis
  congenital P39.9
    Candida (albicans) P37.5
    cytomegalovirus P35.1
    hepatitis, viral P35.3
    herpes simplex P35.2
    infectious or parasitic disease P37.9
      specified NEC P37.8
    listeriosis (disseminated) P37.2
    malaria NEC P37.4
      falciparum P37.3
    Plasmodium falciparum P37.3
    poliomyelitis P35.8
    rubella P35.0

Infection, infected, infective *(Continued)*
  congenital *(Continued)*
    skin P39.4
    toxoplasmosis (acute) (subacute) (chronic)
      P37.1
    tuberculosis P37.0
    urinary (tract) P39.3
    vaccinia P35.8
    virus P35.9
      specified type NEC P35.8
  Conidiobolus B46.8
  coronavirus NEC B34.2
    as cause of disease classified elsewhere
      B97.29
    severe acute respiratory syndrome (SARS
      associated) B97.21
  corpus luteum —*see* Salpingo-oophoritis
  Corynebacterium diphtheriae —*see* Diphtheria
  cotia virus B08.8
  Coxiella burnetii A78
  coxsackie —*see* Coxsackie
  Cryptococcus neoformans —*see*
    Cryptococcosis
  Cryptosporidium A07.2
  Cunninghamella —*see* Mucormycosis
  cyst —*see* Cyst
  cystic duct —*see also* Cholecystitis K81.9
  Cysticercus cellulosae —*see* Cysticercosis
  cytomegalovirus, cytomegaloviral B25.9
    congenital P35.1
    maternal, maternal care for (suspected)
      damage to fetus O35.3
    mononucleosis B27.10
      with
        complication NEC B27.19
        meningitis B27.12
        polyneuropathy B27.11
  delta-agent (acute), in hepatitis B carrier B17.0
  dental (pulpal origin) K04.7
  Deuteromycetes B47.0
  Dicrocoelium dendriticum B66.2
  Dipetalonema (perstans) (streptocerca) B74.4
  diphtherial —*see* Diphtheria
  Diphyllobothrium (adult) (latum) (pacificum)
    B70.0
    larval B70.1
  Diplogonoporus (grandis) B71.8
  Dipylidium caninum B67.4
  Dirofilaria B74.8
  Dracunculus medinensis B72
  Drechslera (hawaiiensis) B43.8
  Ducrey Haemophilus (any location) A57
  due to or resulting from
    artificial insemination N98.0
    central venous catheter T80.219
      bloodstream T80.211
      exit or insertion site T80.212
      localized T80.212
      port or reservoir T80.212
      specified NEC T80.218
      tunnel T80.212
    device, implant or graft —*see also*
      Complications, by site and type,
      infection or inflammation T85.79
      arterial graft NEC T82.7
      breast (implant) T85.79
      catheter NEC T85.79
        dialysis (renal) T82.7
          intraperitoneal T85.71
        infusion NEC T82.7
          cranial T85.735
          intrathecal T85.735
          spinal (epidural) (subdural) T85.735
          subarachnoid T85.735
        urinary T83.518
          cystostomy T83.510
          Hopkins T83.518
          ileostomy T83.518
          nephrostomy T83.512
          specified NEC T83.518
          urethral indwelling T83.511
          urostomy T83.518

Infection, infected, infective *(Continued)*
 due to or resulting from *(Continued)*
  device, implant or graft *(Continued)*
   electronic (electrode) (pulse generator)
     (stimulator)
    bone T84.7
    cardiac T82.7
    nervous system T85.738
     brain T85.731
     cranial nerve T85.732
     gastric nerve T85.732
     generator pocket T85.734
     neurostimulator generator T85.734
     peripheral nerve T85.732
     sacral nerve T85.732
     spinal cord T85.733
     vagal nerve T85.732
    urinary T83.590
   fixation, internal (orthopedic) NEC —
     see Complication, fixation device,
     infection
   gastrointestinal (bile duct) (esophagus)
     T85.79
    neurostimulator electrode (lead)
      T85.732
   genital NEC T83.69
   heart NEC T82.7
    valve (prosthesis) T82.6
    graft T82.7
   joint prosthesis —*see* Complication, joint
     prosthesis, infection
   ocular (corneal graft) (orbital implant)
     NEC T85.79
   orthopedic NEC T84.7
   penile (cylinder) (pump) (resevoir) T83.61
   specified NEC T85.79
   testicular T83.62
   urinary NEC T83.598
    ileal conduit stent T83.593
    implanted neurostimulation T83.590
    implanted sphincter T83.591
    indwelling ureteral stent T83.592
    nephroureteral stent T83.593
    specified stent NEC T83.593
   vascular NEC T82.7
   ventricular intracranial (communicating)
     shunt T85.730
  Hickman catheter T80.219
   bloodstream T80.211
   localized T80.212
   specified NEC T80.218
  immunization or vaccination T88.0
  infusion, injection or transfusion NEC
    T80.29
   acute T80.22
  injury NEC - code by site under Wound,
    open
  peripherally inserted central catheter
    (PICC) T80.219
   bloodstream T80.211
   localized T80.212
   specified NEC T80.218
  portacath (port-a-cath) T80.219
   bloodstream T80.211
   localized T80.212
   specified NEC T80.218
  pulmonary artery catheter —*see* Infection,
    due to or resulting from, central
    venous catheter
 ⇒surgery T81.40
  Swan Ganz catheter —*see* Infection, due
    to or resulting from, central venous
    catheter
  triple lumen catheter T80.219
   bloodstream T80.211
   localized T80.212
   specified NEC T80.218
  umbilical venous catheter T80.219
   bloodstream T80.211
   localized T80.212
   specified NEC T80.218

Infection, infected, infective *(Continued)*
 during labor NEC O75.3
 ear (middle) —*see also* Otitis media
  external —*see* Otitis, externa, infective
  inner —*see* subcategory H83.0
 Eberthella typhosa A01.00
 Echinococcus —*see* Echinococcus
 echovirus
  as cause of disease classified elsewhere
    B97.12
  unspecified nature or site B34.1
 endocardium I33.0
 endocervix —*see* Cervicitis
 Entamoeba —*see* Amebiasis
 enteric —*see* Enteritis, infectious
 Enterobacter sakazakii B96.89
 Enterobius vermicularis B80
 enterostomy K94.12
 enterovirus B34.1
  as cause of disease classified elsewhere
    B97.10
   coxsackievirus B97.11
   echovirus B97.12
   specified NEC B97.19
 Entomophthora B46.8
 Epidermophyton —*see* Dermatophytosis
 epididymis —*see* Epididymitis
⇒episiotomy (puerperal) O86.09
 Erysipelothrix (insidiosa) (rhusiopathiae) —
   see Erysipeloid
 erythema infectiosum B08.3
 Escherichia (E.) coli NEC A49.8
  as cause of disease classified elsewhere —
    see also Escherichia coli B96.20
   congenital P39.8
    sepsis P36.4
   generalized A41.51
   intestinal —*see* Enteritis, infectious, due to,
     Escherichia coli
 ethmoidal (chronic) (sinus) —*see* Sinusitis,
   ethmoidal
 eustachian tube (ear) —*see* Salpingitis,
   eustachian
 external auditory canal (meatus) NEC —*see*
   Otitis, externa, infective
 eye (purulent) —*see* Endophthalmitis, purulent
 eyelid —*see* Inflammation, eyelid
 fallopian tube —*see* Salpingo-oophoritis
 Fasciola (gigantica) (hepatica) (indica) B66.3
 Fasciolopsis (buski) B66.5
 filarial —*see* Infestation, filarial
 finger (skin) L08.9
  nail L03.01-●
   fungus B35.1
 fish tapeworm B70.0
  larval B70.1
 flagellate, intestinal A07.9
 fluke —*see* Infestation, fluke
 focal
  teeth (pulpal origin) K04.7
  tonsils J35.01
 Fonsecaea (compactum) (pedrosoi) B43.0
 food —*see* Intoxication, foodborne
 foot (skin) L08.9
  dermatophytic fungus B35.3
 Francisella tularensis —*see* Tularemia
 frontal (sinus) (chronic) —*see* Sinusitis, frontal
 fungus NOS B49
  beard B35.0
  dermatophytic —*see* Dermatophytosis
  foot B35.3
  groin B35.6
  hand B35.2
  nail B35.1
  pathogenic to compromised host only B48.8
  perianal (area) B35.6
  scalp B35.0
  skin B36.9
   foot B35.3
   hand B35.2
   toenails B35.1

Infection, infected, infective *(Continued)*
 Fusarium B48.8
 gallbladder —*see* Cholecystitis
 gas bacillus —*see* Gangrene, gas
 gastrointestinal —*see* Enteritis, infectious
 generalized NEC —*see* Sepsis
 generator pocket, implanted electronic
   neurostimulator T85.734
 genital organ or tract
  female —*see* Disease, pelvis, inflammatory
  male N49.9
   multiple sites N49.8
   specified NEC N49.8
 Ghon tubercle, primary A15.7
 Giardia lamblia A07.1
 gingiva (chronic) K05.10
  acute K05.00
   nonplaque induced K05.01
   plaque induced K05.00
  nonplaque induced K05.11
  plaque induced K05.10
 glanders A24.0
 glenosporopsis B48.0
 Gnathostoma (spinigerum) B83.1
 Gongylonema B83.8
 gonococcal —*see* Gonococcus
 gram-negative bacilli NOS A49.9
 guinea worm B72
 gum (chronic) K05.10
  acute K05.00
   nonplaque induced K05.01
   plaque induced K05.00
  nonplaque induced K05.11
  plaque induced K05.10
 Haemophilus —*see* Infection, Hemophilus
 heart —*see* Carditis
 Helicobacter pylori A04.8
  as cause of disease classified elsewhere
    B96.81
 helminths B83.9
  intestinal B82.0
   mixed (types classifiable to more than
     one of the titles B65.0-B81.3 and
     B81.8) B81.4
   specified type NEC B81.8
  specified type NEC B83.8
 Hemophilus
  aegyptius, systemic A48.4
  ducrey (any location) A57
  generalized A41.3
  influenzae NEC A49.2
   as cause of disease classified elsewhere
     B96.3
 herpes (simplex) —*see also* Herpes
  congenital P35.2
  disseminated B00.7
  zoster B02.9
 herpesvirus, herpesviral —*see* Herpes
 Heterophyes (heterophyes) B66.8
 hip (joint) NEC M00.9
  due to internal joint prosthesis
   left T84.52
   right T84.51
  skin NEC L08.9
 Histoplasma —*see* Histoplasmosis
  American B39.4
  capsulatum B39.4
 hookworm B76.9
 human
  papilloma virus A63.0
  T-cell lymphotropic virus type-1 (HTLV-1)
    B33.3
 hydrocele N43.0
 Hymenolepis B71.0
 hypopharynx —*see* Pharyngitis
 inguinal (lymph) glands L04.1
  due to soft chancre A57
 intervertebral disc, pyogenic M46.30
  cervical region M46.32
  cervicothoracic region M46.33
  lumbar region M46.36

Infection, infected, infective *(Continued)*
  intervertebral disc, pyogenic *(Continued)*
    lumbosacral region M46.37
    multiple sites M46.39
    occipito-atlanto-axial region M46.31
    sacrococcygeal region M46.38
    thoracic region M46.34
    thoracolumbar region M46.35
  intestine, intestinal —*see* Enteritis, infectious
    specified NEC A08.8
  intra-amniotic affecting newborn NEC P39.2
  Isospora belli or hominis A07.3
  Japanese B encephalitis A83.0
  jaw (bone) (lower) (upper) M27.2
  joint NEC M00.9
    due to internal joint prosthesis T84.50
  kidney (cortex) (hematogenous) N15.9
    with calculus N20.0
      with hydronephrosis N13.6
    following ectopic gestation O08.83
    pelvis and ureter (cystic) N28.85
    puerperal (postpartum) O86.21
    specified NEC N15.8
  Klebsiella (K.) pneumoniae NEC A49.8
    as cause of disease classified elsewhere
      B96.1
  knee (joint) NEC M00.9
    due to internal joint prosthesis
      left T84.54
      right T84.53
    joint M00.9
    skin L08.9
  Koch's —*see* Tuberculosis
  labia (majora) (minora) (acute) —*see* Vulvitis
  lacrimal
    gland —*see* Dacryoadenitis
    passages (duct) (sac) —*see* Inflammation,
      lacrimal, passages
  lancet fluke B66.2
  larynx NEC J38.7
  leg (skin) NOS L08.9
  Legionella pneumophila A48.1
    nonpneumonic A48.2
  Leishmania —*see also* Leishmaniasis
    aethiopica B55.1
    braziliensis B55.2
    chagasi B55.0
    donovani B55.0
    infantum B55.0
    major B55.1
    mexicana B55.1
    tropica B55.1
  lentivirus, as cause of disease classified
    elsewhere B97.31
  Leptosphaeria senegalensis B47.0
  Leptospira interrogans A27.9
    autumnalis A27.89
    canicola A27.89
    hebdomadis A27.89
    icterohaemorrhagiae A27.0
    pomona A27.89
    specified type NEC A27.89
  leptospirochetal NEC —*see* Leptospirosis
  Listeria monocytogenes —*see also* Listeriosis
    congenital P37.2
  Loa loa B74.3
    with conjunctival infestation B74.3
    eyelid B74.3
  Loboa loboi B48.0
  local, skin (staphylococcal) (streptococcal)
    L08.9
    abscess - code by site under Abscess
    cellulitis - code by site under Cellulitis
    specified NEC L08.89
    ulcer —*see* Ulcer, skin
  Loefflerella mallei A24.0
  lung —*see also* Pneumonia J18.9
    atypical Mycobacterium A31.0
    spirochetal A69.8
    tuberculous —*see* Tuberculosis, pulmonary
    virus —*see* Pneumonia, viral

Infection, infected, infective *(Continued)*
  lymph gland —*see also* Lymphadenitis, acute
    mesenteric I88.0
  lymphoid tissue, base of tongue or posterior
    pharynx, NEC (chronic) J35.03
  Madurella (grisea) (mycetomii) B47.0
  major
    following ectopic or molar pregnancy
      O08.0
    puerperal, postpartum, childbirth O85
  Malassezia furfur B36.0
  Malleomyces
    mallei A24.0
    pseudomallei (whitmori) —*see* Melioidosis
  mammary gland N61.0
  Mansonella (ozzardi) (perstans) (streptocerca)
    B74.4
  mastoid —*see* Mastoiditis
  maxilla, maxillary M27.2
    sinus (chronic) —*see* Sinusitis, maxillary
  mediastinum J98.51
  Medina (worm) B72
  meibomian cyst or gland —*see* Hordeolum
  meninges —*see* Meningitis, bacterial
  meningococcal —*see also* condition A39.9
    adrenals A39.1
    brain A39.81
    cerebrospinal A39.0
    conjunctiva A39.89
    endocardium A39.51
    heart A39.50
      endocardium A39.51
      myocardium A39.52
      pericardium A39.53
    joint A39.83
    meninges A39.0
    meningococcemia A39.4
      acute A39.2
      chronic A39.3
    myocardium A39.52
    pericardium A39.53
    retrobulbar neuritis A39.82
    specified site NEC A39.89
  mesenteric lymph nodes or glands NEC I88.0
  Metagonimus B66.8
  metatarsophalangeal M00.9
  methicillin
    resistant Staphylococcus aureus (MRSA)
      A49.02
    susceptible Staphylococcus aureus (MSSA)
      A49.01
  Microsporum, microsporic —*see*
    Dermatophytosis
  mixed flora (bacterial) NEC A49.8
  Monilia —*see* Candidiasis
  Monosporium apiospermum B48.2
  mouth, parasitic B37.0
  Mucor —*see* Mucormycosis
  muscle NEC —*see* Myositis, infective
  mycelium NOS B49
  mycetoma B47.9
    actinomycotic NEC B47.1
    mycotic NEC B47.0
  Mycobacterium, mycobacterial —*see*
    Mycobacterium
  Mycoplasma NEC A49.3
    pneumoniae, as cause of disease classified
      elsewhere B96.0
  mycotic NOS B49
    pathogenic to compromised host only
      B48.8
    skin NOS B36.9
  myocardium NEC I40.0
  nail (chronic)
    with lymphangitis —*see* Lymphangitis,
      acute, digit
    finger L03.01-●
      fungus B35.1
    ingrowing L60.0
    toe L03.03-●
      fungus B35.1

Infection, infected, infective *(Continued)*
  nasal sinus (chronic) —*see* Sinusitis
  nasopharynx —*see* Nasopharyngitis
  navel L08.82
  Necator americanus B76.1
  Neisseria —*see* Gonococcus
  Neotestudina rosatii B47.0
  newborn P39.9
    intra-amniotic NEC P39.2
    skin P39.4
    specified type NEC P39.8
  nipple N61.0
    associated with
      lactation O91.03
      pregnancy O91.01-●
      puerperium O91.02
  Nocardia —*see* Nocardiosis
  ▶obstetrical surgical wound (puerperal) O86.00
    ▶incisional site
      ▶deep O86.02
      ▶superficial O86.01
    ▶organ and space site O86.03
    ▶surgical site specified NEC O86.09
  Oesophagostomum (apiostomum) B81.8
  Oestrus ovis —*see* Myiasis
  Oidium albicans B37.9
  Onchocerca (volvulus) —*see* Onchocerciasis -
    oncovirus, as cause of disease classified
      elsewhere B97.32
  ▶operation wound T81.49
  Opisthorchis (felineus) (viverrini) B66.0
  orbit, orbital —*see* Inflammation, orbit
  orthopoxvirus NEC B08.09
  ovary —*see* Salpingo-oophoritis
  Oxyuris vermicularis B80
  pancreas (acute) —*see* Pancreatitis, acute
    abscess —*see* Pancreatitis, acute
    specified NEC —*see also* Pancreatitis, acute
      K85.80
  papillomavirus, as cause of disease classified
    elsewhere B97.7
  papovavirus NEC B34.4
  Paracoccidioides brasiliensis —*see*
    Paracoccidioidomycosis
  Paragonimus (westermani) B66.4
  parainfluenza virus B34.8
  parameningococcus NOS A39.9
  parapoxvirus B08.60
    specified NEC B08.69
  parasitic B89
  Parastrongylus
    cantonensis B83.2
    costaricensis B81.3
  paratyphoid A01.4
    Type A A01.1
    Type B A01.2
    Type C A01.3
  paraurethral ducts N34.2
  parotid gland —*see* Sialoadenitis
  parvovirus NEC B34.3
    as cause of disease classified elsewhere
      B97.6
  Pasteurella NEC A28.0
    multocida A28.0
    pestis —*see* Plague
    pseudotuberculosis A28.0
    septica (cat bite) (dog bite) A28.0
    tularensis —*see* Tularemia
  pelvic, female —*see* Disease, pelvis,
    inflammatory
  Penicillium (marneffei) B48.4
  penis (glans) (retention) NEC N48.29
  periapical K04.5
  peridental, periodontal K05.20
    generalized —*see* Peridontitis, aggressive,
      generalized
    localized —*see* Peridontitis, aggressive,
      localized
  perinatal period P39.9
    specified type NEC P39.8
  ▶perineal repair (puerperal) O86.09

Infection, infected, infective *(Continued)*
  periorbital —*see* Inflammation, orbit
  perirectal K62.89
  perirenal —*see* Infection, kidney
  peritoneal —*see* Peritonitis
  periureteral N28.89
  Petriellidium boydii B48.2
  pharynx —*see also* Pharyngitis
    coxsackievirus B08.5
    posterior, lymphoid (chronic) J35.03
  Phialophora
    gougerotii (subcutaneous abscess or cyst)
      B43.2
    jeanselmei (subcutaneous abscess or cyst)
      B43.2
    verrucosa (skin) B43.0
  Piedraia hortae B36.3
  pinta A67.9
    intermediate A67.1
    late A67.2
    mixed A67.3
    primary A67.0
  pinworm B80
  pityrosporum furfur B36.0
  pleuro-pneumonia-like organism (PPLO)
      NEC A49.3
    as cause of disease classified elsewhere
      B96.0
  pneumococcus, pneumococcal NEC A49.1
    as cause of disease classified elsewhere B95.3
    generalized (purulent) A40.3
      with pneumonia J13
  Pneumocystis carinii (pneumonia) B59
  Pneumocystis jiroveci (pneumonia) B59
  port or reservoir T80.212
▸ postoperative T81.40
▸ postoperative wound T81.49
▸ postprocedural T81.40
  ▸ surgical site
    ▸ deep incisional T81.42
    ▸ organ and space T81.43
    ▸ specified NEC T81.49
    ▸ superficial incisional T81.41
  postvaccinal T88.0
  prepuce NEC N47.7
    with penile inflammation N47.6
  prion —*see* Disease, prion, central nervous
      system
  prostate (capsule) —*see* Prostatitis
  Proteus (mirabilis) (morganii) (vulgaris) NEC
      A49.8
    as cause of disease classified elsewhere
      B96.4
  protozoal NEC B64
    intestinal A07.9
      specified NEC A07.8
    specified NEC B60.8
  Pseudoallescheria boydii B48.2
  Pseudomonas NEC A49.8
    as cause of disease classified elsewhere
      B96.5
    mallei A24.0
    pneumonia J15.1
    pseudomallei —*see* Melioidosis
  puerperal O86.4
    genitourinary tract NEC O86.89
    major or generalized O85
    minor O86.4
    specified NEC O86.89
  pulmonary —*see* Infection, lung
  purulent —*see* Abscess
  Pyrenochaeta romeroi B47.0
  Q fever A78
  rectum (sphincter) K62.89
  renal —*see also* Infection, kidney
    pelvis and ureter (cystic) N28.85
  reovirus, as cause of disease classified
      elsewhere B97.5
  respiratory (tract) NEC J98.8
    acute J22
    chronic J98.8

Infection, infected, infective *(Continued)*
  respiratory (tract) NEC *(Continued)*
    influenzal (upper) (acute) —*see* Influenza,
        with, respiratory manifestations
        NEC
    lower (acute) J22
      chronic —*see* Bronchitis, chronic
    rhinovirus J00
    syncytial virus, as cause of disease
        classified elsewhere B97.4
    upper (acute) NOS J06.9
      chronic J39.8
      streptococcal J06.9
      viral NOS J06.9
  resulting from
    presence of internal prosthesis, implant,
        graft —*see* Complications, by site and
        type, infection
  retortamoniasis A07.8
  retroperitoneal NEC K68.9
  retrovirus B33.3
    as cause of disease classified elsewhere
        B97.30
    human
      immunodeficiency, type 2 (HIV 2)
          B97.35
      T-cell lymphotropic
        type I (HTLV-I) B97.33
        type II (HTLV-II) B97.34
    lentivirus B97.31
    oncovirus B97.32
    specified NEC B97.39
  Rhinosporidium (seeberi) B48.1
  rhinovirus
    as cause of disease classified elsewhere
        B97.89
    unspecified nature or site B34.8
  Rhizopus —*see* Mucormycosis
  rickettsial NOS A79.9
  roundworm (large) NEC B82.0
    Ascariasis —*see also* Ascariasis B77.9
  rubella —*see* Rubella
  Saccharomyces —*see* Candidiasis
  salivary duct or gland (any) —*see*
      Sialoadenitis
  Salmonella (aertrycke) (arizonae)
      (callinarum) (cholerae-suis)
      (enteritidis) (suipestifer) (typhimurium)
      A02.9
    with
      (gastro) enteritis A02.0
      sepsis A02.1
      specified manifestation NEC A02.8
    due to food (poisoning) A02.9
    hirschfeldii A01.3
    localized A02.20
      arthritis A02.23
      meningitis A02.21
      osteomyelitis A02.24
      pneumonia A02.22
      pyelonephritis A02.25
      specified NEC A02.29
    paratyphi A01.4
      A A01.1
      B A01.2
      C A01.3
    schottmuelleri A01.2
    typhi, typhosa —*see* Typhoid
  Sarcocystis A07.8
  scabies B86
  Schistosoma —*see* Infestation,
      Schistosoma
  scrotum (acute) NEC N49.2
  seminal vesicle —*see* Vesiculitis
  septic
    localized, skin —*see* Abscess
  sheep liver fluke B66.3
  Shigella A03.9
    boydii A03.2
    dysenteriae A03.0
    flexneri A03.1

Infection, infected, infective *(Continued)*
  Shigella *(Continued)*
    group
      A A03.0
      B A03.1
      C A03.2
      D A03.3
    Schmitz (-Stutzer) A03.0
    schmitzii A03.0
    shigae A03.0
    sonnei A03.3
    specified NEC A03.8
  shoulder (joint) NEC M00.9
    due to internal joint prosthesis T84.59
    skin NEC L08.9
  sinus (accessory) (chronic) (nasal) —*see also*
      Sinusitis
    pilonidal —*see* Sinus, pilonidal
    skin NEC L08.89
  Skene's duct or gland —*see* Urethritis
  skin (local) (staphylococcal) (streptococcal)
      L08.9
    abscess - code by site under Abscess
    cellulitis - code by site under Cellulitis
    due to fungus B36.9
      specified type NEC B36.8
    mycotic B36.9
      specified type NEC B36.8
    newborn P39.4
    ulcer —*see* Ulcer, skin
  slow virus A81.9
    specified NEC A81.89
  Sparganum (mansoni) (proliferum) (baxteri)
      B70.1
  specific —*see also* Syphilis
    to perinatal period —*see* Infection,
        congenital
  specified NEC B99.8
  spermatic cord NEC N49.1
  sphenoidal (sinus) —*see* Sinusitis, sphenoidal
  spinal cord NOS —*see also* Myelitis G04.91
    abscess G06.1
    meninges —*see* Meningitis
    streptococcal G04.89
  Spirillum A25.0
  spirochetal NOS A69.9
    lung A69.8
    specified NEC A69.8
  Spirometra larvae B70.1
  spleen D73.89
  Sporotrichum, Sporothrix (schenckii) —*see*
      Sporotrichosis
  staphylococcal, unspecified site
    aureus (methicillin susceptible) (MSSA)
        A49.01
      methicillin resistant (MRSA) A49.02
    as cause of disease classified elsewhere
        B95.8
      aureus (methicillin susceptible) (MSSA)
          B95.61
        methicillin resistant (MRSA)
            B95.62
      specified NEC B95.7
    food poisoning A05.0
    generalized (purulent) A41.2
    pneumonia —*see* Pneumonia,
        staphylococcal
  Stellantchasmus falcatus B66.8
  streptobacillus moniliformis A25.1
  streptococcal NEC A49.1
    as cause of disease classified elsewhere
        B95.5
    B genitourinary complicating
      childbirth O98.82
        pregnancy O98.81-●
      puerperium O98.83
    congenital
      sepsis P36.10
        group B P36.0
        specified NEC P36.19
    generalized (purulent) A40.9

▸ New   ⇒ Revised   ~~deleted~~ Deleted   ● Use Additional Character(s)

Infection, infected, infective (Continued)
Streptomyces B47.1
Strongyloides (stercoralis) —see
   Strongyloidiasis
stump (amputation) (surgical) —see
   Complication, amputation stump,
   infection
subcutaneous tissue, local L08.9
suipestifer —see Infection, salmonella
swimming pool bacillus A31.1
Taenia —see Infestation, Taenia
Taeniarhynchus saginatus B68.1
tapeworm —see Infestation, tapeworm
tendon (sheath) —see Tenosynovitis, infective
   NEC
Ternidens diminutus B81.8
testis —see Orchitis
threadworm B80
throat —see Pharyngitis
thyroglossal duct K14.8
toe (skin) L08.9
   cellulitis L03.03-•
      fungus B35.1
   nail L03.03-•
      fungus B35.1
tongue NEC K14.0
   parasitic B37.0
tonsil (and adenoid) (faucial) (lingual)
   (pharyngeal) —see Tonsillitis
tooth, teeth K04.7
   irreversible K04.02
   periapical K04.7
   peridental, periodontal K05.20
      generalized —see Peridontitis,
         aggressive, generalized
      localized —see Peridontitis, aggressive,
         localized
   pulp K04.01
      irreversible K04.02
      reversible K04.01
TORCH —see Infection, congenital
   without active infection P00.2
Torula histolytica —see Cryptococcosis
Toxocara (canis) (cati) (felis) B83.0
Toxoplasma gondii —see Toxoplasma
trachea, chronic J42
trematode NEC —see Infestation, fluke
trench fever A79.0
Treponema pallidum —see Syphilis
Trichinella (spiralis) B75
Trichomonas A59.9
   cervix A59.09
   intestine A07.8
   prostate A59.02
   specified site NEC A59.8
   urethra A59.03
   urogenitalis A59.00
   vagina A59.01
   vulva A59.01
Trichophyton, trichophytic —see
   Dermatophytosis
Trichosporon (beigelii) cutaneum B36.2
Trichostrongylus B81.2
Trichuris (trichiura) B79
Trombicula (irritans) B88.0
Trypanosoma
   brucei
      gambiense B56.0
      rhodesiense B56.1
   cruzi —see Chagas' disease
tubal —see Salpingo-oophoritis
tuberculous NEC —see Tuberculosis
tubo-ovarian —see Salpingo-oophoritis
tunica vaginalis N49.1
tunnel T80.212
tympanic membrane NEC —see Myringitis
typhoid (abortive) (ambulant) (bacillus) —see
   Typhoid
typhus A75.9
   flea-borne A75.2
   mite-borne A75.3

Infection, infected, infective (Continued)
typhus (Continued)
   recrudescent A75.1
   tick-borne A77.9
      African A77.1
      North Asian A77.2
umbilicus L08.82
ureter N28.86
urethra —see Urethritis
urinary (tract) N39.0
   bladder —see Cystitis
   complicating
      pregnancy O23.4-•
         specified type NEC O23.3-•
   kidney —see Infection, kidney
   newborn P39.3
   puerperal (postpartum) O86.20
   tuberculous A18.13
   urethra —see Urethritis
uterus, uterine —see Endometritis
vaccination T88.0
vaccinia not from vaccination B08.011
vagina (acute) —see Vaginitis
varicella B01.9
varicose veins —see Varix
vas deferens NEC N49.1
vesical —see Cystitis
Vibrio
   cholerae A00.0
      El Tor A00.1
   parahaemolyticus (food poisoning)
      A05.3
   vulnificus
      as cause of disease classified elsewhere
         B96.82
      foodborne intoxication A05.5
Vincent's (gum) (mouth) (tonsil)
   A69.1
virus, viral NOS B34.9
   adenovirus
      as cause of disease classified elsewhere
         B97.0
      unspecified nature or site B34.0
   arborvirus, arbovirus arthropod-borne
      A94
   as cause of disease classified elsewhere
      B97.89
   adenovirus B97.0
   coronavirus B97.29
      SARS-associated B97.21
   coxsackievirus B97.11
   echovirus B97.12
   enterovirus B97.10
      coxsackievirus B97.11
      echovirus B97.12
      specified NEC B97.19
   human
      immunodeficiency, type 2 (HIV 2)
         B97.35
      metapneumovirus B97.81
      T-cell lymphotropic,
         type I (HTLV-I) B97.33
         type II (HTLV-II) B97.34
   papillomavirus B97.7
   parvovirus B97.6
   reovirus B97.5
   respiratory syncytial B97.4
   retrovirus B97.30
      human
         immunodeficiency, type 2 (HIV 2)
            B97.35
         T-cell lymphotropic,
            type I (HTLV-I) B97.33
            type II (HTLV-II) B97.34
      lentivirus B97.31
      oncovirus B97.32
      specified NEC B97.39
   specified NEC B97.89
   central nervous system A89
      atypical A81.9
         specified NEC A81.89

Infection, infected, infective (Continued)
virus, viral NOS (Continued)
   central nervous system (Continued)
      enterovirus NEC A88.8
         meningitis A87.0
      slow virus A81.9
         specified NEC A81.89
      specified NEC A88.8
   chest J98.8
   cotia B08.8
   coxsackie —see also Infection, coxsackie B34.1
      as cause of disease classified elsewhere
         B97.11
   ECHO
      as cause of disease classified elsewhere
         B97.12
      unspecified nature or site B34.1
   encephalitis, tick-borne A84.9
   enterovirus, as cause of disease classified
      elsewhere B97.10
   coxsackievirus B97.11
   echovirus B97.12
   specified NEC B97.19
   exanthem NOS B09
   human metapneumovirus as cause of
      disease classified elsewhere B97.81
   human papilloma as cause of disease
      classified elsewhere B97.7
   intestine —see Enteritis, viral
   respiratory syncytial
      as cause of disease classified elsewhere
         B97.4
      bronchopneumonia J12.1
      common cold syndrome J00
      nasopharyngitis (acute) J00
   rhinovirus
      as cause of disease classified elsewhere
         B97.89
      unspecified nature or site B34.8
   slow A81.9
      specified NEC A81.89
   specified type NEC B33.8
      as cause of disease classified elsewhere
         B97.89
      unspecified nature or site B34.8
   unspecified nature or site B34.9
   West Nile —see Virus, West Nile
   vulva (acute) —see Vulvitis
   West Nile —see Virus, West Nile
   whipworm B79
   worms B83.9
      specified type NEC B83.8
   Wuchereria (bancrofti) B74.0
      malayi B74.1
      yatapoxvirus B08.70
         specified NEC B08.79
   yeast (see also Candidiasis) B37.9
   yellow fever —see Fever, yellow
   Yersinia
      enterocolitica (intestinal) A04.6
      pestis —see Plague
      pseudotuberculosis A28.2
   Zeis' gland —see Hordeolum
   Zika virus A92.5
   ►congenital P35.4
   zoonotic bacterial NOS A28.9
   Zopfia senegalensis B47.0
Infective, infectious —see condition
Infertility
   female N97.9
      age-related N97.8
      associated with
         anovulation N97.0
         cervical (mucus) disease or anomaly
            N88.3
         congenital anomaly
            cervix N88.3
            fallopian tube N97.1
            uterus N97.2
            vagina N97.8
         dysmucorrhea N88.3

Infertility (Continued)
  female (Continued)
    associated with (Continued)
      fallopian tube disease or anomaly N97.1
      pituitary-hypothalamic origin E23.0
      specified origin NEC N97.8
      Stein-Leventhal syndrome E28.2
      uterine disease or anomaly N97.2
      vaginal disease or anomaly N97.8
    due to
      cervical anomaly N88.3
      fallopian tube anomaly N97.1
      ovarian failure E28.39
      Stein-Leventhal syndrome E28.2
      uterine anomaly N97.2
      vaginal anomaly N97.8
    nonimplantation N97.2
    origin
      cervical N88.3
      tubal (block) (occlusion) (stenosis) N97.1
      uterine N97.2
      vaginal N97.8
  male N46.9
    azoospermia N46.01
      extratesticular cause N46.029
        drug therapy N46.021
        efferent duct obstruction N46.023
        infection N46.022
        radiation N46.024
        specified cause NEC N46.029
        systemic disease N46.025
    oligospermia N46.11
      extratesticular cause N46.129
        drug therapy N46.121
        efferent duct obstruction N46.123
        infection N46.122
        radiation N46.124
        specified cause NEC N46.129
        systemic disease N46.125
    specified type NEC N46.8

Infestation B88.9
  Acanthocheilonema (perstans) (streptocerca) B74.4
  Acariasis B88.0
    demodex folliculorum B88.0
    sarcoptes scabiei B86
    trombiculae B88.0
  Agamofilaria streptocerca B74.4
  Ancylostoma, ankylostoma (braziliense) (caninum) (ceylanicum) (duodenale) B76.0
    americanum B76.1
    new world B76.1
  Anisakis larvae, anisakiasis B81.0
  arthropod NEC B88.2
  Ascaris lumbricoides —see Ascariasis
  Balantidium coli A07.0
  beef tapeworm B68.1
  Bothriocephalus (latus) B70.0
    larval B70.1
  broad tapeworm B70.0
    larval B70.1
  Brugia (malayi) B74.1
    timori B74.2
  candiru B88.8
  Capillaria
    hepatica B83.8
    philippinensis B81.1
  cat liver fluke B66.0
  cestodes B71.9
    diphyllobothrium —see Infestation, diphyllobothrium
    dipylidiasis B71.1
    hymenolepiasis B71.0
    specified type NEC B71.8
  chigger B88.0
  chigo, chigoe B88.1
  Clonorchis (sinensis) (liver) B66.1
  coccidial A07.3
  crab-lice B85.3
  Cysticercus cellulosae —see Cysticercosis

Infestation (Continued)
  Demodex (folliculorum) B88.0
  Dermanyssus gallinae B88.0
  Dermatobia (hominis) —see Myiasis
  Dibothriocephalus (latus) B70.0
    larval B70.1
  Dicrocoelium dendriticum B66.2
  Diphyllobothrium (adult) (latum) (intestinal) (pacificum) B70.0
    larval B70.1
  Diplogonoporus (grandis) B71.8
  Dipylidium caninum B67.4
  Distoma hepaticum B66.3
  dog tapeworm B67.4
  Dracunculus medinensis B72
  dragon worm B72
  dwarf tapeworm B71.0
  Echinococcus —see Echinococcus
  Echinostomum ilocanum B66.8
  Entamoeba (histolytica) —see Infection, Ameba
  Enterobius vermicularis B80
  eyelid
    in (due to)
      leishmaniasis B55.1
      loiasis B74.3
      onchocerciasis B73.09
      phthiriasis B85.3
    parasitic NOS B89
  eyeworm B74.3
  Fasciola (gigantica) (hepatica) (indica) B66.3
  Fasciolopsis (buski) (intestine) B66.5
  filarial B74.9
    bancroftian B74.0
    conjunctiva B74.9
    due to
      Acanthocheilonema (perstans) (streptocerca) B74.4
      Brugia (malayi) B74.1
        timori B74.2
      Dracunculus medinensis B72
      guinea worm B72
      loa loa B74.3
      Mansonella (ozzardi) (perstans) (streptocerca) B74.4
      Onchocerca volvulus B73.00
        eye B73.00
        eyelid B73.09
      Wuchereria (bancrofti) B74.0
    Malayan B74.1
    ozzardi B74.4
    specified type NEC B74.8
  fish tapeworm B70.0
    larval B70.1
  fluke B66.9
    blood NOS —see Schistosomiasis
    cat liver B66.0
    intestinal B66.5
    lancet B66.2
    liver (sheep) B66.3
      cat B66.0
      Chinese B66.1
      due to clonorchiasis B66.1
      oriental B66.1
    lung (oriental) B66.4
    sheep liver B66.3
    specified type NEC B66.8
  fly larvae —see Myiasis
  Gasterophilus (intestinalis) —see Myiasis
  Gastrodiscoides hominis B66.8
  Giardia lamblia A07.1
  Gnathostoma (spinigerum) B83.1
  Gongylonema B83.8
  guinea worm B72
  helminth B83.9
    angiostrongyliasis B83.2
      intestinal B81.3
    gnathostomiasis B83.1
    hirudiniasis, internal B83.4

Infestation (Continued)
  helminth (Continued)
    intestinal B82.0
      angiostrongyliasis B81.3
      anisakiasis B81.0
      ascariasis —see Ascariasis
      capillariasis B81.1
      cysticercosis —see Cysticercosis
      diphyllobothriasis —see Infestation, diphyllobothriasis
      dracunculiasis B72
      echinococcus —see Echinococcosis
      enterobiasis B80
      filariasis —see Infestation, filarial
      fluke —see Infestation, fluke
      hookworm —see Infestation, hookworm
      mixed (types classifiable to more than one of the titles B65.0-B81.3 and B81.8) B81.4
      onchocerciasis —see Onchocerciasis
      schistosomiasis —see Infestation, schistosoma
      specified
        cestode NEC —see Infestation, cestode
        type NEC B81.8
      strongyloidiasis —see Strongyloidiasis
      taenia —see Infestation, taenia
      trichinellosis B75
      trichostrongyliasis B81.2
      trichuriasis B79
    specified type NEC B83.8
    syngamiasis B83.3
    visceral larva migrans B83.0
  Heterophyes (heterophyes) B66.8
  hookworm B76.9
    ancylostomiasis B76.0
    necatoriasis B76.1
    specified type NEC B76.8
  Hymenolepis (diminuta) (nana) B71.0
  intestinal NEC B82.9
  leeches (aquatic) (land) —see Hirudiniasis
  Leishmania —see Leishmaniasis
  lice, louse —see Infestation, Pediculus
  Linguatula B88.8
  Liponyssoides sanguineus B88.0
  Loa loa B74.3
    conjunctival B74.3
    eyelid B74.3
  louse —see Infestation, Pediculus
  maggots —see Myiasis
  Mansonella (ozzardi) (perstans) (streptocerca) B74.4
  Medina (worm) B72
  Metagonimus (yokogawai) B66.8
  microfilaria streptocerca —see Onchocerciasis
    eye B73.00
    eyelid B73.09
  mites B88.9
    scabic B86
  Monilia (albicans) —see Candidiasis
  mouth B37.0
  Necator americanus B76.1
  nematode NEC (intestinal) B82.0
    Ancylostoma B76.0
    conjunctiva NEC B83.9
    Enterobius vermicularis B80
    Gnathostoma spinigerum B83.1
    physaloptera B80
    specified NEC B81.8
    trichostrongylus B81.2
    trichuris (trichuria) B79
  Oesophagostomum (apiostomum) B81.8
  Oestrus ovis —see also Myiasis B87.9
  Onchocerca (volvulus) —see Onchocerciasis
  Opisthorchis (felineus) (viverrini) B66.0
  orbit, parasitic NOS B89
  Oxyuris vermicularis B80
  Paragonimus (westermani) B66.4

▶ New   ⇒ Revised   ~~deleted~~ Deleted   ● Use Additional Character(s)

Infestation *(Continued)*
parasite, parasitic B89
 eyelid B89
 intestinal NOS B82.9
 mouth B37.0
 skin B88.9
 tongue B37.0
Parastrongylus
 cantonensis B83.2
 costaricensis B81.3
Pediculus B85.2
 body B85.1
 capitis (humanus) (any site) B85.0
 corporis (humanus) (any site) B85.1
 head B85.0
 mixed (classifiable to more than one of the
  titles B85.0-B85.3) B85.4
 pubis (any site) B85.3
Pentastoma B88.8
Phthirus (pubis) (any site) B85.3
 with any infestation classifiable to
  B85.0-B85.2 B85.4
pinworm B80
pork tapeworm (adult) B68.0
protozoal NEC B64
 intestinal A07.9
  specified NEC A07.8
 specified NEC B60.8
pubic, louse B85.3
rat tapeworm B71.0
red bug B88.0
roundworm (large) NEC B82.0
 Ascariasis —*see also* Ascariasis B77.9
sandflea B88.1
Sarcoptes scabiei B86
scabies B86
Schistosoma B65.9
 bovis B65.8
 cercariae B65.3
 haematobium B65.0
 intercalatum B65.8
 japonicum B65.2
 mansoni B65.1
 mattheei B65.8
 mekongi B65.8
 specified type NEC B65.8
 spindale B65.8
screw worms —*see* Myiasis
skin NOS B88.9
Sparganum (mansoni) (proliferum) (baxteri)
  B70.1
 larval B70.1
specified type NEC B88.8
Spirometra larvae B70.1
Stellantchasmus falcatus B66.8
Strongyloides stercoralis —*see*
  Strongyloidiasis
Taenia B68.9
 diminuta B71.0
 echinococcus —*see* Echinococcus
 mediocanellata B68.1
 nana B71.0
 saginata B68.1
 solium (intestinal form) B68.0
  larval form —*see* Cysticercosis
Taeniarhynchus saginatus B68.1
tapeworm B71.9
 beef B68.1
 broad B70.0
  larval B70.1
 dog B67.4
 dwarf B71.0
 fish B70.0
  larval B70.1
 pork B68.0
 rat B71.0
Ternidens diminutus B81.8
Tetranychus molestissimus B88.0
threadworm B80
tongue B37.0
Toxocara (canis) (cati) (felis) B83.0

Infestation *(Continued)*
trematode(s) NEC —*see* Infestation, fluke
Trichinella (spiralis) B75
Trichocephalus B79
Trichomonas —*see* Trichomoniasis
Trichostrongylus B81.2
Trichuris (trichiura) B79
Trombicula (irritans) B88.0
Tunga penetrans B88.1
Uncinaria americana B76.1
Vandellia cirrhosa B88.8
whipworm B79
worms B83.9
 intestinal B82.0
Wuchereria (bancrofti) B74.0
Infiltrate, infiltration
amyloid (generalized) (localized) —*see*
  Amyloidosis
calcareous NEC R89.7
 localized —*see* Degeneration, by site
calcium salt R89.7
cardiac
 fatty —*see* Degeneration, myocardial
 glycogenic E74.02 *[I43]*
corneal —*see* Edema, cornea
eyelid —*see* Inflammation, eyelid
glycogen, glycogenic —*see* Disease, glycogen
  storage
heart, cardiac
 fatty —*see* Degeneration, myocardial
 glycogenic E74.02 *[I43]*
inflammatory in vitreous H43.89
kidney N28.89
leukemic —*see* Leukemia
liver K76.89
 fatty —*see* Fatty, liver NEC
 glycogen —*see also* Disease, glycogen
  storage E74.03 *[K77]*
lung R91.8
 eosinophilic J82
lymphatic —*see also* Leukemia, lymphatic
  C91.9-●
 gland I88.9
muscle, fatty M62.89
myocardium, myocardial
 fatty —*see* Degeneration, myocardial
 glycogenic E74.02 *[I43]*
on chest x-ray R91.8
pulmonary R91.8
 with eosinophilia J82
skin (lymphocytic) L98.6
thymus (gland) (fatty) E32.8
urine R39.0
vesicant agent
 antineoplastic chemotherapy T80.810
 other agent NEC T80.818
vitreous body H43.89
Infirmity R68.89
senile R54
Inflammation, inflamed, inflammatory (with
  exudation)
abducent (nerve) —*see* Strabismus, paralytic,
  sixth nerve
accessory sinus (chronic) —*see* Sinusitis
adrenal (gland) E27.8
alveoli, teeth M27.3
 scorbutic E54
anal canal, anus K62.89
antrum (chronic) —*see* Sinusitis, maxillary
appendix —*see* Appendicitis
arachnoid —*see* Meningitis
areola N61.0
 puerperal, postpartum or gestational —*see*
  Infection, nipple
areolar tissue NOS L08.9
artery —*see* Arteritis
auditory meatus (external) —*see* Otitis,
  externa
Bartholin's gland N75.8
bile duct (common) (hepatic) or passage —*see*
  Cholangitis

Inflammation, inflamed, inflammatory
  (Continued)
bladder —*see* Cystitis
bone —*see* Osteomyelitis
brain —*see also* Encephalitis
 membrane —*see* Meningitis
breast N61.0
 puerperal, postpartum, gestational —*see*
  Mastitis, obstetric
broad ligament —*see* Disease, pelvis,
  inflammatory
bronchi —*see* Bronchitis
catarrhal J00
cecum —*see* Appendicitis
cerebral —*see also* Encephalitis
 membrane —*see* Meningitis
cerebrospinal
 meningococcal A39.0
cervix (uteri) —*see* Cervicitis
chest J98.8
chorioretinal H30.9-●
 cyclitis —*see* Cyclitis
 disseminated H30.10-●
  generalized H30.13-●
  peripheral H30.12-●
  posterior pole H30.11-●
 epitheliopathy —*see* Epitheliopathy
 focal H30.00-●
  juxtapapillary H30.01-●
  macular H30.04-●
  paramacular —*see* Inflammation,
   chorioretinal, focal, macular
  peripheral H30.03-●
  posterior pole H30.02-●
 specified type NEC H30.89-●
choroid —*see* Inflammation, chorioretinal
chronic, postmastoidectomy cavity —*see*
  Complications, postmastoidectomy,
  inflammation
colon —*see* Enteritis
connective tissue (diffuse) NEC —*see*
  Disorder, soft tissue, specified type NEC
cornea —*see* Keratitis
corpora cavernosa N48.29
cranial nerve —*see* Disorder, nerve, cranial
Douglas' cul-de-sac or pouch (chronic) N73.0
due to device, implant or graft —*see also*
  Complications, by site and type,
  infection or inflammation
 arterial graft T82.7
 breast (implant) T85.79
 catheter T85.79
  dialysis (renal) T82.7
   intraperitoneal T85.71
  infusion T82.7
   cranial T85.735
   intrathecal T85.735
   spinal (epidural) (subdural) T85.735
   subarachnoid T85.735
  urinary T83.518
   cystostomy T83.510
   Hopkins T83.518
   ileostomy T83.518
   nephrostomy T83.512
   specified NEC T83.518
   urethral indwelling T83.511
   urostomy T83.518
 electronic (electrode) (pulse generator)
  (stimulator)
  bone T84.7
  cardiac T82.7
  nervous system T85.738
   brain T85.731
   cranial nerve T85.732
   gastric nerve T85.732
   neurostimulator generator T85.734
   peripheral nerve T85.732
   sacral nerve T85.732
   spinal cord T85.733
   vagal nerve T85.732
  urinary T83.590

Inflammation, inflamed, inflammatory
  (Continued)
  due to device, implant or graft *(Continued)*
    fixation, internal (orthopedic) NEC —
        see Complication, fixation device,
        infection
    gastrointestinal (bile duct) (esophagus)
        T85.79
      neurostimulator electrode (lead) T85.732
    genital NEC T83.69
    heart NEC T82.7
      valve (prosthesis) T82.6
        graft T82.7
    joint prosthesis —*see* Complication, joint
        prosthesis, infection
    ocular (corneal graft) (orbital implant)
        NEC T85.79
    orthopedic NEC T84.7
    penile (cylinder) (pump) (resevoir) T83.61
    specified NEC T85.79
    testicular T83.62
    urinary NEC T83.598
      ileal conduit stent T83.593
      implanted neurostimulation T83.590
      implanted sphincter T83.591
      indwelling ureteral stent T83.592
      nephroureteral stent T83.593
      specified stent NEC T83.593
    vascular NEC T82.7
    ventricular intracranial (communicating)
        shunt T85.730
  duodenum K29.80
    with bleeding K29.81
  dura mater —*see* Meningitis
  ear (middle) —*see also* Otitis, media
    external —*see* Otitis, externa
    inner —*see* subcategory H83.0
  epididymis —*see* Epididymitis
  esophagus K20.9
  ethmoidal (sinus) (chronic) —*see* Sinusitis,
      ethmoidal
  eustachian tube (catarrhal) —*see* Salpingitis,
      eustachian
  eyelid H01.9
    abscess —*see* Abscess, eyelid
    blepharitis —*see* Blepharitis
    chalazion —*see* Chalazion
    dermatosis (noninfectious) —*see*
        Dermatosis, eyelid
    hordeolum —*see* Hordeolum
    specified NEC H01.8
  fallopian tube —*see* Salpingo-oophoritis
  fascia —*see* Myositis
  follicular, pharynx J31.2
  frontal (sinus) (chronic) —*see* Sinusitis, frontal
  gallbladder —*see* Cholecystitis
  gastric —*see* Gastritis
  gastrointestinal —*see* Enteritis
  genital organ (internal) (diffuse)
    female —*see* Disease, pelvis, inflammatory
    male N49.9
      multiple sites N49.8
      specified NEC N49.8
  gland (lymph) —*see* Lymphadenitis
  glottis —*see* Laryngitis
  granular, pharynx J31.2
  gum K05.10
    nonplaque induced K05.11
    plaque induced K05.10
  heart —*see* Carditis
  hepatic duct —*see* Cholangitis
  ileoanal (internal) pouch K91.850
  ileum —*see also* Enteritis
    regional or terminal —*see* Enteritis, regional
  intestinal pouch K91.850
  intestine (any part) —*see* Enteritis
  jaw (acute) (bone) (chronic) (lower)
      (suppurative) (upper) M27.2
  joint NEC —*see* Arthritis
    sacroiliac M46.1
  kidney —*see* Nephritis

Inflammation, inflamed, inflammatory
  (Continued)
  knee (joint) M13.169
    tuberculous A18.02
  labium (majus) (minus) —*see* Vulvitis
  lacrimal
    gland —*see* Dacryoadenitis
    passages (duct) (sac) —*see also* Dacryocystitis
      canaliculitis —*see* Canaliculitis, lacrimal
  larynx —*see* Laryngitis
  leg NOS L08.9
  lip K13.0
  liver (capsule) —*see also* Hepatitis
    chronic K73.9
    suppurative K75.0
  lung —*see also* Pneumonia
    chronic J98.4
  lymphatic vessel —*see* Lymphangitis
  lymph gland or node —*see* Lymphadenitis
  maxilla, maxillary M27.2
    sinus (chronic) —*see* Sinusitis, maxillary
  membranes of brain or spinal cord —*see*
      Meningitis
  meninges —*see* Meningitis
  mouth K12.1
  muscle —*see* Myositis
  myocardium —*see* Myocarditis
  nasal sinus (chronic) —*see* Sinusitis
  nasopharynx —*see* Nasopharyngitis
  navel L08.82
  nerve NEC —*see* Neuralgia
  nipple N61.0
    puerperal, postpartum or gestational —*see*
        Infection, nipple
  nose —*see* Rhinitis
  oculomotor (nerve) —*see* Strabismus,
      paralytic, third nerve
  optic nerve —*see* Neuritis, optic
  orbit (chronic) H05.10
    acute H05.00
      abscess —*see* Abscess, orbit
      cellulitis —*see* Cellulitis, orbit
      osteomyelitis —*see* Osteomyelitis, orbit
      periostitis —*see* Periostitis, orbital
      tenonitis —*see* Tenonitis, eye
    granuloma —*see* Granuloma, orbit
    myositis —*see* Myositis, orbital
  ovary —*see* Salpingo-oophoritis
  oviduct —*see* Salpingo-oophoritis
  pancreas (acute) —*see* Pancreatitis
  parametrium N73.0
  parotid region L08.9
  pelvis, female —*see* Disease, pelvis,
      inflammatory
  penis (corpora cavernosa) N48.29
  perianal K62.89
  pericardium —*see* Pericarditis
  perineum (female) (male) L08.9
  perirectal K62.89
  peritoneum —*see* Peritonitis
  periuterine —*see* Disease, pelvis, inflammatory
  perivesical —*see* Cystitis
  petrous bone (acute) (chronic) —*see* Petrositis
  pharynx (acute) —*see* Pharyngitis
  pia mater —*see* Meningitis
  pleura —*see* Pleurisy
  polyp, colon —*see also* Polyp, colon,
      inflammatory K51.40
  prostate —*see also* Prostatitis
    specified type NEC N41.8
  rectosigmoid —*see* Rectosigmoiditis
  rectum —*see also* Proctitis K62.89
  respiratory, upper —*see also* Infection,
      respiratory, upper J06.9
    acute, due to radiation J70.0
    chronic, due to external agent —*see*
        condition, respiratory, chronic, due to
    due to
      chemicals, gases, fumes or vapors
          (inhalation) J68.2
      radiation J70.1

Inflammation, inflamed, inflammatory
  (Continued)
  retina —*see* Chorioretinitis
  retrocecal —*see* Appendicitis
  retroperitoneal —*see* Peritonitis
  salivary duct or gland (any) (suppurative) —
      see Sialoadenitis
  scorbutic, alveoli, teeth E54
  scrotum N49.2
  seminal vesicle —*see* Vesiculitis
  sigmoid —*see* Enteritis
  sinus —*see* Sinusitis
  Skene's duct or gland —*see* Urethritis
  skin L08.9
  spermatic cord N49.1
  sphenoidal (sinus) —*see* Sinusitis, sphenoidal
  spinal
    cord —*see* Encephalitis
    membrane —*see* Meningitis
    nerve —*see* Disorder, nerve
  spine —*see* Spondylopathy, inflammatory
  spleen (capsule) D73.89
  stomach —*see* Gastritis
  subcutaneous tissue L08.9
  suprarenal (gland) E27.8
  synovial —*see* Tenosynovitis
  tendon (sheath) NEC —*see* Tenosynovitis
  testis —*see* Orchitis
  throat (acute) —*see* Pharyngitis
  thymus (gland) E32.8
  thyroid (gland) —*see* Thyroiditis
  tongue K14.0
  tonsil —*see* Tonsillitis
  trachea —*see* Tracheitis
  trochlear (nerve) —*see* Strabismus, paralytic,
      fourth nerve
  tubal —*see* Salpingo-oophoritis
  tuberculous NEC —*see* Tuberculosis
  tubo-ovarian —*see* Salpingo-oophoritis
  tunica vaginalis N49.1
  tympanic membrane —*see* Tympanitis
  umbilicus, umbilical L08.82
  uterine ligament —*see* Disease, pelvis,
      inflammatory
  uterus (catarrhal) —*see* Endometritis
  uveal tract (anterior) NOS —*see also*
      Iridocyclitis
    posterior —*see* Chorioretinitis
  vagina —*see* Vaginitis
  vas deferens N49.1
  vein —*see also* Phlebitis
    intracranial or intraspinal (septic) G08
    thrombotic I80.9
      leg —*see* Phlebitis, leg
      lower extremity —*see* Phlebitis, leg
  vocal cord J38.3
  vulva —*see* Vulvitis
  Wharton's duct (suppurative) —*see*
      Sialoadenitis
Inflation, lung, imperfect (newborn) —*see*
    Atelectasis
Influenza (bronchial) (epidemic) (respiratory
    (upper)) (unidentified influenza virus) J11.1
  with
    digestive manifestations J11.2
    encephalopathy J11.81
    enteritis J11.2
    gastroenteritis J11.2
    gastrointestinal manifestations J11.2
    laryngitis J11.1
    myocarditis J11.82
    otitis media J11.83
    pharyngitis J11.1
    pneumonia J11.00
      specified type J11.08
    respiratory manifestations NEC J11.1
    specified manifestation NEC J11.89
  A/H5N1 —*see also* Influenza, due to,
      identified novel influenza A virus J09.X2
  avian —*see also* Influenza, due to, identified
      novel influenza A virus J09.X2

Influenza (Continued)
  bird —see also Influenza, due to, identified
    novel influenza A virus J09.X2
  novel (2009) H1N1 influenza —see also
    Influenza, due to, identified influenza
    virus NEC J10.1
  novel influenza A/H1N1 —see also Influenza,
    due to, identified influenza virus NEC
    J10.1
  due to
    avian (see also Influenza, due to, identified
      novel influenza A virus) J09.X2
    identified influenza virus NEC J10.1
      with
        digestive manifestations J10.2
        encephalopathy J10.81
        enteritis J10.2
        gastroenteritis J10.2
        gastrointestinal manifestations J10.2
        laryngitis J10.1
        myocarditis J10.82
        otitis media J10.83
        pharyngitis J10.1
        pneumonia (unspecified type) J10.00
          with same identified influenza virus
            J10.01
          specified type NEC J10.08
        respiratory manifestations NEC J10.1
        specified manifestation NEC J10.89
    identified novel influenza A virus J09.X2
      with
        digestive manifestations J09.X3
        encephalopathy J09.X9
        enteritis J09.X3
        gastroenteritis J09.X3
        gastrointestinal manifestations J09.X3
        laryngitis J09.X2
        myocarditis J09.X9
        otitis media J09.X9
        pharyngitis J09.X2
        pneumonia J09.X1
        respiratory manifestations NEC J09.X2
        specified manifestation NEC J09.X9
        upper respiratory symptoms J09.X2
    of other animal origin, not bird or swine (see
      also Influenza, due to, identified novel
      influenza A virus) J09.X2
    swine (viruses that normally cause infections
      in pigs) —see also Influenza, due to,
      identified novel influenza A virus J09.X2
Influenza-like disease —see Influenza
Influenzal —see Influenza
Infraction, Freiberg's (metatarsal head) —see
    Osteochondrosis, juvenile, metatarsus
Infraeruption of tooth (teeth) M26.34
Infusion complication, misadventure, or
    reaction —see Complications, infusion
Ingestion
  chemical —see Table of Drugs and Chemicals,
    by substance, poisoning
  drug or medicament
    correct substance properly administered —
      see Table of Drugs and Chemicals, by
      drug, adverse effect
    overdose or wrong substance given
      or taken —see Table of Drugs and
      Chemicals, by drug, poisoning
  foreign body —see Foreign body, alimentary
    tract
  tularemia A21.3
Ingrowing
  hair (beard) L73.1
  nail (finger) (toe) L60.0
Inguinal —see also condition
  testicle Q53.9
    bilateral Q53.212
    unilateral Q53.112
Inhalant-induced
  anxiety disorder F18.980
  depressive disorder F18.94
  major neurocognitive disorder F18.97

Inhalant-induced (Continued)
  mild neurocognitive disorder F18.988
  psychotic disorder F18.959
Inhalation
  anthrax A22.1
  flame T27.3
  food or foreign body —see Foreign body, by
    site
  gases, fumes, or vapors NEC T59.9-●
    specified agent —see Table of Drugs and
      Chemicals, by substance
  liquid or vomitus —see Asphyxia
  meconium (newborn) P24.00
    with
      with respiratory symptoms P24.01
      pneumonia (pneumonitis) P24.01
  mucus —see Asphyxia, mucus
  oil or gasoline (causing suffocation) —see
    Foreign body, by site
  smoke J70.5
    due to chemicals, gases, fumes and vapors
      J68.9
  steam —see Toxicity, vapors
  stomach contents or secretions —see Foreign
    body, by site
    due to anesthesia (general) (local) or other
      sedation T88.59
      in labor and delivery O74.0
      in pregnancy O29.01-●
      postpartum, puerperal O89.01
Inhibition, orgasm
  female F52.31
  male F52.32
Inhibitor, systemic lupus erythematosus
  (presence of) D68.62
Iniencephalus, iniencephaly Q00.2
Injection, traumatic jet (air) (industrial) (water)
  (paint or dye) T70.4
Injury —see also specified injury type T14.90
  abdomen, abdominal S39.91
    blood vessel —see Injury, blood vessel,
      abdomen
    cavity —see Injury, intra-abdominal
    contusion S30.1
    internal —see Injury, intra-abdominal
    intra-abdominal organ —see Injury,
      intra-abdominal
    nerve —see Injury, nerve, abdomen
    open —see Wound, open, abdomen
    specified NEC S39.81
    superficial —see Injury, superficial,
      abdomen
  Achilles tendon S86.00-●
    laceration S86.02-●
    specified type NEC S86.09-●
    strain S86.01-●
  acoustic, resulting in deafness —see Injury,
    nerve, acoustic
  adrenal (gland) S37.819
    contusion S37.812
    laceration S37.813
    specified type NEC S37.818
  alveolar (process) S09.93
  ankle S99.91-●
    contusion —see Contusion, ankle
    dislocation —see Dislocation, ankle
    fracture —see Fracture, ankle
    nerve —see Injury, nerve, ankle
    open —see Wound, open, ankle
    specified type NEC S99.91-●
    sprain —see Sprain, ankle
    superficial —see Injury, superficial,
      ankle
  anterior chamber, eye —see Injury, eye,
    specified site NEC
  anus —see Injury, abdomen
  aorta (thoracic) S25.00
    abdominal S35.00
      laceration (minor) (superficial) S35.01
        major S35.02
      specified type NEC S35.09

Injury (Continued)
  aorta (thoracic) (Continued)
    laceration (minor) (superficial) S25.01
      major S25.02
    specified type NEC S25.09
  arm (upper) S49.9-●
    blood vessel —see Injury, blood vessel, arm
    contusion —see Contusion, arm, upper
    fracture —see Fracture, humerus
    lower —see Injury, forearm
    muscle —see Injury, muscle, shoulder
    nerve —see Injury, nerve, arm
    open —see Wound, open, arm
    specified type NEC S49.8-●
    superficial —see Injury, superficial, arm
  artery (complicating trauma) —see also Injury,
    blood vessel, by site
    cerebral or meningeal —see Injury,
      intracranial
  auditory canal (external) (meatus) S09.91
  auricle, auris, ear S09.91
  axilla —see Injury, shoulder
  back —see Injury, back, lower
  bile duct S36.13
  birth —see also Birth, injury P15.9
  bladder (sphincter) S37.20
    at delivery O71.5
    contusion S37.22
    laceration S37.23
    obstetrical trauma O71.5
    specified type NEC S37.29
  blast (air) (hydraulic) (immersion)
    (underwater) NEC T14.8
    acoustic nerve trauma —see Injury, nerve,
      acoustic
    bladder —see Injury, bladder
    brain —see Concussion
    colon —see Injury, intestine, large, blast
      injury
    ear (primary) S09.31-●
      secondary S09.39-●
    generalized T70.8
    lung —see Injury, intrathoracic, lung, blast
      injury
    multiple body organs T70.8
    peritoneum S36.81
    rectum S36.61
    retroperitoneum S36.898
    small intestine S36.419
      duodenum S36.410
      specified site NEC S36.418
    specified
      intra-abdominal organ NEC S36.898
      pelvic organ NEC S37.899
  blood vessel NEC T14.8
    abdomen S35.9-●
      aorta —see Injury, aorta, abdominal
      celiac artery —see Injury, blood vessel,
        celiac artery
      iliac vessel —see Injury, blood vessel, iliac
      laceration S35.91
      mesenteric vessel —see Injury, mesenteric
      portal vein —see Injury, blood vessel,
        portal vein
      renal vessel —see Injury, blood vessel,
        renal
      specified vessel NEC S35.8X-●
      splenic vessel —see Injury, blood vessel,
        splenic
      vena cava —see Injury, vena cava, inferior
    ankle —see Injury, blood vessel, foot
    aorta (abdominal) (thoracic) —see Injury,
      aorta
    arm (upper) NEC S45.90-●
      forearm —see Injury, blood vessel, forearm
      laceration S45.91-●
      specified
        site NEC S45.80-●
          laceration S45.81-●
          specified type NEC S45.89-●
        type NEC S45.99-●

Injury *(Continued)*
blood vessel NEC *(Continued)*
precerebral —*see* Injury, blood vessel, neck
pulmonary (artery) (vein) —*see* Injury,
blood vessel, thoracic, pulmonary
radial artery (forearm level) S55.10-●
hand and wrist (level) S65.10-●
laceration S65.11-●
specified type NEC S65.19-●
laceration S55.11-●
specified type NEC S55.19-●
renal
artery S35.40-●
laceration S35.41-●
specified NEC S35.49-●
vein S35.40-●
laceration S35.41-●
specified NEC S35.49-●
saphenous vein (greater) (lower leg
level) —*see* Injury, blood vessel,
greater saphenous
hip and thigh level —*see* Injury, blood
vessel, greater saphenous, hip level
lesser —*see* Injury, blood vessel, lesser
saphenous
shoulder
specified NEC —*see* Injury, blood vessel,
arm, specified site NEC
superficial vein —*see* Injury, blood
vessel, arm, superficial vein
specified NEC T14.8
splenic
artery —*see* Injury, blood vessel, celiac
artery, branch
vein S35.329
laceration S35.321
specified NEC S35.328
subclavian —*see* Injury, blood vessel,
thoracic, innominate
thigh —*see* Injury, blood vessel, hip
thoracic S25.90
aorta S25.00
laceration (minor) (superficial) S25.01
major S25.02
specified type NEC S25.09
azygos vein —*see* Injury, blood vessel,
thoracic, specified, site NEC
innominate
artery S25.10-●
laceration (minor) (superficial)
S25.11-●
major S25.12-●
specified type NEC S25.19-●
vein S25.30-●
laceration (minor) (superficial)
S25.31-●
major S25.32-●
specified type NEC S25.39-●
intercostal S25.50-●
laceration S25.51-●
specified type NEC S25.59-●
laceration S25.91
mammary vessel —*see* Injury, blood
vessel, thoracic, specified, site NEC
pulmonary S25.40-●
laceration (minor) (superficial)
S25.41-●
major S25.42-●
specified type NEC S25.49-●
specified
site NEC S25.80-●
laceration S25.81-●
specified type NEC S25.89-●
type NEC S25.99
subclavian —*see* Injury, blood vessel,
thoracic, innominate
vena cava (superior) S25.20
laceration (minor) (superficial)
S25.21
major S25.22
specified type NEC S25.29

Injury *(Continued)*
blood vessel NEC *(Continued)*
thumb S65.40-●
laceration S65.41-●
specified type NEC S65.49-●
tibial artery S85.10-●
anterior S85.13-●
laceration S85.14-●
specified injury NEC S85.15-●
laceration S85.11-●
posterior S85.16-●
laceration S85.17-●
specified injury NEC S85.18-●
specified injury NEC S85.12-●
ulnar artery (forearm level) S55.00-●
hand and wrist (level) S65.00-●
laceration S65.01-●
specified type NEC S65.09-●
laceration S55.01-●
specified type NEC S55.09-●
upper arm (level) —*see* Injury, blood vessel,
arm
superficial vein —*see* Injury, blood
vessel, arm, superficial vein
uterine S35.5-●
artery S35.53-●
vein S35.53-●
vena cava —*see* Injury, vena cava
vertebral artery S15.10-●
laceration (minor) (superficial) S15.11-●
major S15.12-●
specified type NEC S15.19-●
wrist (level) —*see* Injury, blood vessel, hand
brachial plexus S14.3
newborn P14.3
brain (traumatic) S06.9-●
diffuse (axonal) S06.2X-●
focal S06.30-●
brainstem S06.38-●
breast NOS S29.9
broad ligament —*see* Injury, pelvic organ,
specified site NEC
bronchus, bronchi —*see* Injury, intrathoracic,
bronchus
brow S09.90
buttock S39.92
canthus, eye S05.90
cardiac plexus —*see* Injury, nerve, thorax,
sympathetic
cauda equina S34.3
cavernous sinus —*see* Injury, intracranial
cecum —*see* Injury, colon
celiac ganglion or plexus —*see* Injury, nerve,
lumbosacral, sympathetic
cerebellum —*see* Injury, intracranial
cerebral —*see* Injury, intracranial
cervix (uteri) —*see* Injury, uterus
cheek (wall) S09.93
chest —*see* Injury, thorax
childbirth (newborn) —*see also* Birth, injury
maternal NEC O71.9
chin S09.93
choroid (eye) —*see* Injury, eye, specified site
NEC
clitoris S39.94
coccyx —*see also* Injury, back, lower
complicating delivery O71.6
colon —*see* Injury, intestine, large
common bile duct —*see* Injury, liver
conjunctiva (superficial) —*see* Injury, eye,
conjunctiva
conus medullaris —*see* Injury, spinal, sacral
cord
spermatic (pelvic region) S37.898
scrotal region S39.848
spinal —*see* Injury, spinal cord, by region
cornea —*see* Injury, eye, specified site NEC
abrasion —*see* Injury, eye, cornea,
abrasion
cortex (cerebral) —*see also* Injury, intracranial
visual —*see* Injury, nerve, optic

Injury *(Continued)*
costal region NEC S29.9
costochondral NEC S29.9
cranial
cavity —*see* Injury, intracranial
nerve —*see* Injury, nerve, cranial
crushing —*see* Crush
cutaneous sensory nerve
cystic duct —*see* Injury, liver
deep tissue —*see* Contusion, by site
meaning pressure ulcer —*see* Ulcer,
pressure, unstageable, by site
delivery (newborn) P15.9
maternal NEC O71.9
Descemet's membrane —*see* Injury, eyeball,
penetrating
diaphragm —*see* Injury, intrathoracic,
diaphragm
duodenum —*see* Injury, intestine, small,
duodenum
ear (auricle) (external) (canal) S09.91
abrasion —*see* Abrasion, ear
bite —*see* Bite, ear
blister —*see* Blister, ear
bruise —*see* Contusion, ear
contusion —*see* Contusion, ear
external constriction —*see* Constriction,
external, ear
hematoma —*see* Hematoma, ear
inner —*see* Injury, ear, middle
laceration —*see* Laceration, ear
middle S09.30-●
blast —*see* Injury, blast, ear
specified NEC S09.39-●
puncture —*see* Puncture, ear
superficial —*see* Injury, superficial, ear
eighth cranial nerve (acoustic or auditory) —
see Injury, nerve, acoustic
elbow S59.90-●
contusion —*see* Contusion, elbow
dislocation —*see* Dislocation, elbow
fracture —*see* Fracture, ulna, upper
end
open —*see* Wound, open, elbow
specified NEC S59.80-●
sprain —*see* Sprain, elbow
superficial —*see* Injury, superficial,
elbow
eleventh cranial nerve (accessory) —*see*
Injury, nerve, accessory
epididymis S39.94
epigastric region S39.91
epiglottis NEC S19.89
esophageal plexus —*see* Injury, nerve, thorax,
sympathetic
esophagus (thoracic part) —*see also* Injury,
intrathoracic, esophagus
cervical NEC S19.85
eustachian tube S09.30-●
eye S05.9-●
avulsion S05.7-●
ball —*see* Injury, eyeball
conjunctiva S05.0-●
cornea
abrasion S05.0-●
laceration S05.3-●
with prolapse S05.2-●
lacrimal apparatus S05.8X-●
orbit penetration S05.4-●
specified site NEC S05.8X-●
eyeball S05.8X-●
contusion S05.1-●
penetrating S05.6-●
with
foreign body S05.5-●
prolapse or loss of intraocular tissue
S05.2-●
without prolapse or loss of intraocular
tissue S05.3-●
specified type NEC S05.8-●
eyebrow S09.93

Injury *(Continued)*
  eyelid S09.93
    abrasion —*see* Abrasion, eyelid
    contusion —*see* Contusion, eyelid
    open —*see* Wound, open, eyelid
  face S09.93
  fallopian tube S37.509
    bilateral S37.502
      blast injury S37.512
      contusion S37.522
      laceration S37.532
      specified type NEC S37.592
    blast injury (primary) S37.519
      bilateral S37.512
        secondary —*see* Injury, fallopian tube,
          specified type NEC
        unilateral S37.511
    contusion S37.529
      bilateral S37.522
      unilateral S37.521
    laceration S37.539
      bilateral S37.532
      unilateral S37.531
    specified type NEC S37.599
      bilateral S37.592
      unilateral S37.591
    unilateral S37.501
      blast injury S37.511
      contusion S37.521
      laceration S37.531
      specified type NEC S37.591
  fascia —*see* Injury, muscle
  fifth cranial nerve (trigeminal) —*see* Injury,
    nerve, trigeminal
  finger (nail) S69.9-•
    blood vessel —*see* Injury, blood vessel,
      finger
    contusion —*see* Contusion, finger
    dislocation —*see* Dislocation, finger
    fracture —*see* Fracture, finger
    muscle —*see* Injury, muscle, finger
    nerve —*see* Injury, nerve, digital, finger
    open —*see* Wound, open, finger
    specified NEC S69.8-•
    sprain —*see* Sprain, finger
    superficial —*see* Injury, superficial, finger
  first cranial nerve (olfactory) —*see* Injury,
    nerve, olfactory
  flank —*see* Injury, abdomen
  foot S99.92-•
    blood vessel —*see* Injury, blood vessel, foot
    contusion —*see* Contusion, foot
    dislocation —*see* Dislocation, foot
    fracture —*see* Fracture, foot
    muscle —*see* Injury, muscle, foot
    open —*see* Wound, open, foot
    specified type NEC S99.82-•
    sprain —*see* Sprain, foot
    superficial —*see* Injury, superficial, foot
  forceps NOS P15.9
  forearm S59.91-•
    blood vessel —*see* Injury, blood vessel,
      forearm
    contusion —*see* Contusion, forearm
    fracture —*see* Fracture, forearm
    muscle —*see* Injury, muscle, forearm
    nerve —*see* Injury, nerve, forearm
    open —*see* Wound, open, forearm
    specified NEC S59.81-•
    superficial —*see* Injury, superficial, forearm
  forehead S09.90
  fourth cranial nerve (trochlear) —*see* Injury,
    nerve, trochlear
  gallbladder S36.129
    contusion S36.122
    laceration S36.123
    specified NEC S36.128
  ganglion
    celiac, coeliac —*see* Injury, nerve,
      lumbosacral, sympathetic
    gasserian —*see* Injury, nerve, trigeminal

Injury *(Continued)*
  ganglion *(Continued)*
    stellate —*see* Injury, nerve, thorax,
      sympathetic
    thoracic sympathetic —*see* Injury, nerve,
      thorax, sympathetic
  gasserian ganglion —*see* Injury, nerve,
    trigeminal
  gastric artery —*see* Injury, blood vessel, celiac
    artery, branch
  gastroduodenal artery —*see* Injury, blood
    vessel, celiac artery, branch
  gastrointestinal tract —*see* Injury,
    intra-abdominal
    with open wound into abdominal cavity —
      see Wound, open, with penetration
      into peritoneal cavity
    colon —*see* Injury, intestine, large
    rectum —*see* Injury, intestine, large, rectum
      with open wound into abdominal cavity
        S36.61
    small intestine —*see* Injury, intestine, small
    specified site NEC —*see* Injury, intra-
      abdominal, specified, site NEC
    stomach —*see* Injury, stomach
  genital organ(s)
    external S39.94
      specified NEC S39.848
    internal S37.90
      fallopian tube —*see* Injury, fallopian tube
      ovary —*see* Injury, ovary
      prostate —*see* Injury, prostate
      seminal vesicle —*see* Injury, pelvis,
        organ, specified site NEC
      uterus —*see* Injury, uterus
      vas deferens —*see* Injury, pelvis, organ,
        specified site NEC
    obstetrical trauma O71.9
  gland
    lacrimal laceration —*see* Injury, eye,
      specified site NEC
    salivary S09.93
    thyroid NEC S19.84
  globe (eye) S05.90
    specified NEC S05.8X-•
  groin —*see* Injury, abdomen
  gum S09.90
  hand S69.9-•
    blood vessel —*see* Injury, blood vessel,
      hand
    contusion —*see* Contusion, hand
    fracture —*see* Fracture, hand
    muscle —*see* Injury, muscle, hand
    nerve —*see* Injury, nerve, hand
    open —*see* Wound, open, hand
    specified NEC S69.8-•
    sprain —*see* Sprain, hand
    superficial —*see* Injury, superficial, hand
  head S09.90
    with loss of consciousness S06.9-•
    specified NEC S09.8-•
  heart S26.90
    with hemopericardium S26.00
      contusion S26.01
      laceration (mild) S26.020
        major S26.022
        moderate S26.021
      specified type NEC S26.09
    without hemopericardium S26.10
      contusion S26.11
      laceration S26.12
      specified type NEC S26.19
    contusion S26.91
    laceration S26.92
    specified type NEC S26.99
  heel —*see* Injury, foot
  hepatic
    artery —*see* Injury, blood vessel, celiac
      artery, branch
    duct —*see* Injury, liver
    vein —*see* Injury, vena cava, inferior

Injury *(Continued)*
  hip S79.91-•
    blood vessel —*see* Injury, blood vessel,
      hip
    contusion —*see* Contusion, hip
    dislocation —*see* Dislocation, hip
    fracture —*see* Fracture, femur, neck
    muscle —*see* Injury, muscle, hip
    nerve —*see* Injury, nerve, hip
    open —*see* Wound, open, hip
    specified NEC S79.81-•
    sprain —*see* Sprain, hip
    superficial —*see* Injury, superficial, hip
  hymen S39.94
  hypogastric
    blood vessel —*see* Injury, blood vessel,
      iliac
    plexus —*see* Injury, nerve, lumbosacral,
      sympathetic
  ileum —*see* Injury, intestine, small
  iliac region S39.91
  instrumental (during surgery) —*see*
    Laceration, accidental complicating
    surgery
    birth injury —*see* Birth, injury
    nonsurgical —*see* Injury, by site
  obstetrical O71.9
    bladder O71.5
    cervix O71.3
    high vaginal O71.4
    perineal NOS O70.9
    urethra O71.5
    uterus O71.5
      with rupture or perforation O71.1
  internal T14.8
    aorta —*see* Injury, aorta
    bladder (sphincter) —*see* Injury, bladder
      with
        ectopic or molar pregnancy O08.6
        following ectopic or molar pregnancy
          O08.6
        obstetrical trauma O71.5
    bronchus, bronchi —*see* Injury,
      intrathoracic, bronchus
    cecum —*see* Injury, intestine, large
    cervix (uteri) —*see also* Injury, uterus
      with ectopic or molar pregnancy
        O08.6
      following ectopic or molar pregnancy
        O08.6
      obstetrical trauma O71.3
    chest —*see* Injury, intrathoracic
    gastrointestinal tract —*see* Injury,
      intra-abdominal
    heart —*see* Injury, heart
    intestine NEC —*see* Injury, intestine
    intrauterine —*see* Injury, uterus
    mesentery —*see* Injury, intra-abdominal,
      specified, site NEC
    pelvis, pelvic (organ) S37.90
      following ectopic or molar pregnancy
        (subsequent episode) O08.6
      obstetrical trauma NEC O71.5
        rupture or perforation O71.1
      specified NEC S39.83
    rectum —*see* Injury, intestine, large,
      rectum
    stomach —*see* Injury, stomach
    ureter —*see* Injury, ureter
    urethra (sphincter) following ectopic or
      molar pregnancy O08.6
    uterus —*see* Injury, uterus
  interscapular area —*see* Injury, thorax
  intestine
    large S36.509
      ascending (right) S36.500
        blast injury (primary) S36.510
          secondary S36.590
        contusion S36.520
        laceration S36.530
        specified type NEC S36.590

▶ New   ⇒ Revised   ~~deleted~~ Deleted   • Use Additional Character(s)

Injury *(Continued)*
  intestine *(Continued)*
    large *(Continued)*
      blast injury (primary) S36.519
        ascending (right) S36.510
        descending (left) S36.512
        rectum S36.61
        sigmoid S36.513
        specified site NEC S36.518
        transverse S36.511
      contusion S36.529
        ascending (right) S36.520
        descending (left) S36.522
        rectum S36.62
        sigmoid S36.523
        specified site NEC S36.528
        transverse S36.521
      descending (left) S36.502
        blast injury (primary) S36.512
          secondary S36.592
        contusion S36.522
        laceration S36.532
        specified type NEC S36.592
      laceration S36.539
        ascending (right) S36.530
        descending (left) S36.532
        rectum S36.63
        sigmoid S36.533
        specified site NEC S36.538
        transverse S36.531
      rectum S36.60
        blast injury (primary) S36.61
          secondary S36.69
        contusion S36.62
        laceration S36.63
        specified type NEC S36.69
      sigmoid S36.503
        blast injury (primary) S36.513
          secondary S36.593
        contusion S36.523
        laceration S36.533
        specified type NEC S36.593
      specified
        site NEC S36.508
          blast injury (primary) S36.518
            secondary S36.598
          contusion S36.528
          laceration S36.538
          specified type NEC S36.598
        type NEC S36.599
          ascending (right) S36.590
          descending (left) S36.592
          rectum S36.69
          sigmoid S36.593
          specified site NEC S36.598
          transverse S36.591
      transverse S36.501
        blast injury (primary) S36.511
          secondary S36.591
        contusion S36.521
        laceration S36.531
        specified type NEC S36.591
    small S36.409
      blast injury (primary) S36.419
        duodenum S36.410
        secondary S36.499
          duodenum S36.490
          specified site NEC S36.498
        specified site NEC S36.418
      contusion S36.429
        duodenum S36.420
        specified site NEC S36.428
      duodenum S36.400
        blast injury (primary) S36.410
          secondary S36.490
        contusion S36.420
        laceration S36.430
        specified NEC S36.490
      laceration S36.439
        duodenum S36.430
        specified site NEC S36.438

Injury *(Continued)*
  intestine *(Continued)*
    small *(Continued)*
      specified
        site NEC S36.408
        type NEC S36.499
          duodenum S36.490
          specified site NEC S36.498
  intra-abdominal S36.90
    adrenal gland —*see* Injury, adrenal gland
    bladder —*see* Injury, bladder
    colon —*see* Injury, intestine, large
    contusion S36.92
    fallopian tube —*see* Injury, fallopian tube
    gallbladder —*see* Injury, gallbladder
    intestine —*see* Injury, intestine
    kidney —*see* Injury, kidney
    laceration S36.93
    liver —*see* Injury, liver
    ovary —*see* Injury, ovary
    pancreas —*see* Injury, pancreas
    pelvic NOS S37.90
    peritoneum —*see* Injury, intra-abdominal, specified, site NEC
    prostate —*see* Injury, prostate
    rectum —*see* Injury, intestine, large, rectum
    retroperitoneum —*see* Injury, intra-abdominal, specified, site NEC
    seminal vesicle —*see* Injury, pelvis, organ, specified site NEC
    small intestine —*see* Injury, intestine, small
    specified
      pelvic S37.90
        specified
          site NEC S37.899
            specified type NEC S37.898
            type NEC S37.99
      site NEC S36.899
        contusion S36.892
        laceration S36.893
        specified type NEC S36.898
      type NEC S36.99
    spleen —*see* Injury, spleen
    stomach —*see* Injury, stomach
    ureter —*see* Injury, ureter
    urethra —*see* Injury, urethra
    uterus —*see* Injury, uterus
    vas deferens —*see* Injury, pelvis, organ, specified site NEC
  intracranial (traumatic) S06.9-●
    cerebellar hemorrhage, traumatic —*see* Injury, intracranial, focal
    cerebral edema, traumatic S06.1X-●
      diffuse S06.1X-●
      focal S06.1X-●
    diffuse (axonal) S06.2X-●
    epidural hemorrhage (traumatic) S06.4X-●
    focal brain injury S06.30-●
      contusion —*see* Contusion, cerebral
      laceration —*see* Laceration, cerebral
    intracerebral hemorrhage, traumatic S06.36-●
      left side S06.35-●
      right side S06.34-●
    subarachnoid hemorrhage, traumatic S06.6X-●
    subdural hemorrhage, traumatic S06.5X-●
  intraocular —*see* Injury, eyeball, penetrating
  intrathoracic S27.9
    bronchus S27.409
      bilateral S27.402
      blast injury (primary) S27.419
        bilateral S27.412
        secondary —*see* Injury, intrathoracic, bronchus, specified type NEC
        unilateral S27.411
      contusion S27.429
        bilateral S27.422
        unilateral S27.421
      laceration S27.439
        bilateral S27.432
        unilateral S27.431

Injury *(Continued)*
  intrathoracic *(Continued)*
    bronchus *(Continued)*
      specified type NEC S27.499
        bilateral S27.492
        unilateral S27.491
      unilateral S27.401
    diaphragm S27.809
      contusion S27.802
      laceration S27.803
      specified type NEC S27.808
    esophagus (thoracic) S27.819
      contusion S27.812
      laceration S27.813
      specified type NEC S27.818
    heart —*see* Injury, heart
    hemopneumothorax S27.2
    hemothorax S27.1
    lung S27.309
      aspiration J69.0
      bilateral S27.302
      blast injury (primary) S27.319
        bilateral S27.312
        secondary —*see* Injury, intrathoracic, lung, specified type NEC
        unilateral S27.311
      contusion S27.329
        bilateral S27.322
        unilateral S27.321
      laceration S27.339
        bilateral S27.332
        unilateral S27.331
      specified type NEC S27.399
        bilateral S27.392
        unilateral S27.391
      unilateral S27.301
    pleura S27.60
      laceration S27.63
      specified type NEC S27.69
    pneumothorax S27.0
    specified organ NEC S27.899
      contusion S27.892
      laceration S27.893
      specified type NEC S27.898
    thoracic duct —*see* Injury, intrathoracic, specified organ NEC
    thymus gland —*see* Injury, intrathoracic, specified organ NEC
    trachea, thoracic S27.50
      blast (primary) S27.51
      contusion S27.52
      laceration S27.53
      specified type NEC S27.59
  iris —*see* Injury, eye, specified site NEC
    penetrating —*see* Injury, eyeball, penetrating
  jaw S09.93
  jejunum —*see* Injury, intestine, small
  joint NOS T14.8
    old or residual —*see* Disorder, joint, specified type NEC
  kidney S37.00-●
    acute (nontraumatic) N17.9
    contusion —*see* Contusion, kidney
    laceration —*see* Laceration, kidney
    specified NEC S37.09-●
  knee S89.9-●
    contusion —*see* Contusion, knee
    dislocation —*see* Dislocation, knee
    meniscus (lateral) (medial) —*see* Sprain, knee, specified site NEC
      old injury or tear —*see* Derangement, knee, meniscus, due to old injury
    open —*see* Wound, open, knee
    specified NEC S89.8-●
    sprain —*see* Sprain, knee
    superficial —*see* Injury, superficial, knee
  labium (majus) (minus) S39.94
  labyrinth, ear S09.30-●
  lacrimal apparatus, duct, gland, or sac —*see* Injury, eye, specified site NEC

Injury *(Continued)*
- larynx NEC S19.81
- leg (lower) S89.9-●
  - blood vessel —*see* Injury, blood vessel, leg
  - contusion —*see* Contusion, leg
  - fracture —*see* Fracture, leg
  - muscle —*see* Injury, muscle, leg
  - nerve —*see* Injury, nerve, leg
  - open —*see* Wound, open, leg
  - specified NEC S89.8-●
  - superficial —*see* Injury, superficial, leg
- lens, eye —*see* Injury, eye, specified site NEC
  - penetrating —*see* Injury, eyeball,
    - penetrating
- limb NEC T14.8
- lip S09.93
- liver S36.119
  - contusion S36.112
  - laceration S36.113
    - major (stellate) S36.116
    - minor S36.114
    - moderate S36.115
  - specified NEC S36.118
- lower back S39.92
  - specified NEC S39.82
- lumbar, lumbosacral (region) S39.92
  - plexus —*see* Injury, lumbosacral plexus
- lumbosacral plexus S34.4
- lung —*see also* Injury, intrathoracic, lung
  - aspiration J69.0
  - transfusion-related (TRALI) J95.84
- lymphatic thoracic duct —*see* Injury,
  - intrathoracic, specified organ NEC
- malar region S09.93
- mastoid region S09.90
- maxilla S09.93
- mediastinum —*see* Injury, intrathoracic,
  - specified organ NEC
- membrane, brain —*see* Injury, intracranial
- meningeal artery —*see* Injury, intracranial,
  - subdural hemorrhage
- meninges (cerebral) —*see* Injury, intracranial
- mesenteric
  - artery
    - branch S35.299
      - laceration (minor) (superficial) S35.291
        - major S35.292
      - specified NEC S35.298
    - inferior S35.239
      - laceration (minor) (superficial) S35.231
        - major S35.232
      - specified NEC S35.238
    - superior S35.229
      - laceration (minor) (superficial) S35.221
        - major S35.222
      - specified NEC S35.228
    - plexus (inferior) (superior) —*see* Injury,
      - nerve, lumbosacral, sympathetic
  - vein
    - inferior S35.349
      - laceration S35.341
      - specified NEC S35.348
    - superior S35.339
      - laceration S35.331
      - specified NEC S35.338
- mesentery —*see* Injury, intra-abdominal,
  - specified site NEC
- mesosalpinx —*see* Injury, pelvic organ,
  - specified site NEC
- middle ear S09.30-●
- midthoracic region NOS S29.9
- mouth S09.93
- multiple NOS T07
- muscle (and fascia) (and tendon)
  - abdomen S39.001
    - laceration S39.021
    - specified type NEC S39.091
    - strain S39.011
  - abductor
    - thumb, forearm level —*see* Injury,
      - muscle, thumb, abductor

Injury *(Continued)*
- muscle *(Continued)*
  - adductor
    - thigh S76.20-●
      - laceration S76.22-●
      - specified type NEC S76.29-●
      - strain S76.21-●
    - ankle —*see* Injury, muscle, foot
    - anterior muscle group, at leg level (lower)
      - S86.20-●
      - laceration S86.22-●
      - specified type NEC S86.29-●
      - strain S86.21-●
    - arm (upper) —*see* Injury, muscle,
      - shoulder
    - biceps (parts NEC) S46.20-●
      - laceration S46.22-●
      - long head S46.10-●
        - laceration S46.12-●
        - specified type NEC S46.19-●
        - strain S46.11-●
      - specified type NEC S46.29-●
      - strain S46.21-●
  - extensor
    - finger(s) (other than thumb) —*see* Injury,
      - muscle, finger by site, extensor
    - forearm level, specified NEC —*see*
      - Injury, muscle, forearm, extensor
    - thumb —*see* Injury, muscle, thumb,
      - extensor
    - toe (large) (ankle level) (foot level) —*see*
      - Injury, muscle, toe, extensor
  - finger
    - extensor (forearm level) S56.40-●
      - hand level S66.309
        - laceration S66.329
        - specified type NEC S66.399
        - strain S66.319
      - laceration S56.429
      - specified type NEC S56.499
      - strain S56.419
    - flexor (forearm level) S56.10-●
      - hand level S66.109
        - laceration S66.129
        - specified type NEC S66.199
        - strain S66.119
      - laceration S56.129
      - specified type NEC S56.199
      - strain S56.119
    - index
      - extensor (forearm level)
        - hand level S66.308
          - laceration S66.32-●
          - specified type NEC S66.39-●
          - strain S66.31-●
        - specified type NEC S56.492-●
      - flexor (forearm level)
        - hand level S66.108
          - laceration S66.12-●
          - specified type NEC
            - S66.19-●
          - strain S66.11-●
        - specified type NEC S56.19-●
        - strain S56.11-●
      - intrinsic S66.50-●
        - laceration S66.52-●
        - specified type NEC S66.59-●
        - strain S66.51-●
    - intrinsic S66.509
      - laceration S66.529
      - specified type NEC S66.599
      - strain S66.519
    - little
      - extensor (forearm level)
        - hand level S66.30-●
          - laceration S66.32-●
          - specified type NEC S66.39-●
          - strain S66.31-●
        - laceration S56.42-●
        - specified type NEC S56.49-●
        - strain S56.41-●

Injury *(Continued)*
- muscle *(Continued)*
  - finger *(Continued)*
    - little *(Continued)*
      - flexor (forearm level)
        - hand level S66.10-●
          - laceration S66.12-●
          - specified type NEC S66.19-●
          - strain S66.11-●
        - laceration S56.12-●
        - specified type NEC S56.19-●
        - strain S56.11-●
      - intrinsic S66.50-●
        - laceration S66.52-●
        - specified type NEC S66.59-●
        - strain S66.51-●
    - middle
      - extensor (forearm level)
        - hand level S66.30-●
          - laceration S66.32-●
          - specified type NEC
            - S66.39-●
          - strain S66.31-●
        - laceration S56.42-●
        - specified type NEC
          - S56.49-●
        - strain S56.41-●
      - flexor (forearm level)
        - hand level S66.10-●
          - laceration S66.12-●
          - specified type NEC
            - S66.19-●
          - strain S66.11-●
        - laceration S56.12-●
        - specified type NEC S56.19-●
        - strain S56.11-●
      - intrinsic S66.50-●
        - laceration S66.52-●
        - specified type NEC S66.59-●
        - strain S66.51-●
    - ring
      - extensor (forearm level)
        - hand level S66.30-●
          - laceration S66.32-●
          - specified type NEC S66.39-●
          - strain S66.31-●
        - laceration S56.42-●
        - specified type NEC S56.49-●
        - strain S56.41-●
      - flexor (forearm level)
        - hand level S66.10-●
          - laceration S66.12-●
          - specified type NEC S66.19-●
          - strain S66.11-●
        - laceration S56.12-●
        - specified type NEC S56.19-●
        - strain S56.11-●
      - intrinsic S66.50-●
        - laceration S66.52-●
        - specified type NEC S66.59-●
        - strain S66.51-●
  - flexor
    - finger(s) (other than thumb) —*see* Injury,
      - muscle, finger
    - forearm level, specified NEC —
      - *see* Injury, muscle, forearm,
      - flexor
    - thumb —*see* Injury, muscle, thumb,
      - flexor
    - toe (long) (ankle level) (foot level) —*see*
      - Injury, muscle, toe, flexor
  - foot S96.90-●
    - intrinsic S96.20-●
      - laceration S96.22-●
      - specified type NEC S96.29-●
      - strain S96.21-●
    - laceration S96.92-●
    - long extensor, toe —*see* Injury, muscle,
      - toe, extensor
    - long flexor, toe —*see* Injury, muscle, toe,
      - flexor

▶ New　　⇒ Revised　　~~deleted~~ Deleted　　● Use Additional Character(s)

Injury (Continued)
  muscle (Continued)
    foot (Continued)
      specified
        site NEC S96.80-●
          laceration S96.82-●
          specified type NEC S96.89-●
          strain S96.81-●
        type NEC S96.99-●
      strain S96.91-●
    forearm (level) S56.90-●
      extensor S56.50-●
        laceration S56.52-●
        specified type NEC S56.59-●
        strain S56.51-●
      flexor S56.20-●
        laceration S56.22-●
        specified type NEC S56.29-●
        strain S56.21-●
      laceration S56.92-●
      specified S56.99-●
        site NEC S56.80-●
          laceration S56.82-●
          strain S56.81-●
        type NEC S56.89-●
      strain S56.91-●
    hand (level) S66.90-●
      laceration S66.92-●
      specified
        site NEC S66.80-●
          laceration S66.82-●
          specified type NEC S66.89-●
          strain S66.81-●
        type NEC S66.99-●
      strain S66.91-●
    head S09.10
      laceration S09.12
      specified type NEC S09.19
      strain S09.11
    hip NEC S76.00-●
      laceration S76.02-●
      specified type NEC S76.09-●
      strain S76.01-●
    intrinsic
      ankle and foot level —see Injury, muscle, foot, intrinsic
      finger (other than thumb) —see Injury, muscle, finger by site, intrinsic
      foot (level) —see Injury, muscle, foot, intrinsic
      thumb —see Injury, muscle, thumb, intrinsic
    leg (level) (lower) S86.90-●
      Achilles tendon —see Injury, Achilles tendon
      anterior muscle group —see Injury, muscle, anterior muscle group
      laceration S86.92-●
      peroneal muscle group —see Injury, muscle, peroneal muscle group
      posterior muscle group —see Injury, muscle, posterior muscle group, leg level
      specified
        site NEC S86.80-●
          laceration S86.82-●
          specified type NEC S86.89-●
          strain S86.81-●
        type NEC S86.99-●
      strain S86.91-●
    long
      extensor toe, at ankle and foot level —see Injury, muscle, toe, extensor
      flexor, toe, at ankle and foot level —see Injury, muscle, toe, flexor
      head, biceps —see Injury, muscle, biceps, long head
    lower back S39.002
      laceration S39.022
      specified type NEC S39.092
      strain S39.012

Injury (Continued)
  muscle (Continued)
    neck (level) S16.9
      laceration S16.2
      specified type NEC S16.8
      strain S16.1
    pelvis S39.003
      laceration S39.023
      specified type NEC S39.093
      strain S39.013
    peroneal muscle group, at leg level (lower) S86.30-●
      laceration S86.32-●
      specified type NEC S86.39-●
      strain S86.31-●
    posterior muscle (group)
      leg level (lower) S86.10-●
        laceration S86.12-●
        specified type NEC S86.19-●
        strain S86.11-●
      thigh level S76.30-●
        laceration S76.32-●
        specified type NEC S76.39-●
        strain S76.31-●
    quadriceps (thigh) S76.10-●
      laceration S76.12-●
      specified type NEC S76.19-●
      strain S76.11-●
    shoulder S46.90-●
      laceration S46.92-●
      rotator cuff —see Injury, rotator cuff
      specified site NEC S46.80-●
        laceration S46.82-●
        specified type NEC S46.89-●
        strain S46.81-●
      specified type NEC S46.99-●
      strain S46.91-●
    thigh NEC (level) S76.90-●
      adductor —see Injury, muscle, adductor, thigh
      laceration S76.92-●
      posterior muscle (group) —see Injury, muscle, posterior muscle, thigh level
      quadriceps —see Injury, muscle, quadriceps
      specified
        site NEC S76.80-●
          laceration S76.82-●
          specified type NEC S76.89-●
          strain S76.81-●
        type NEC S76.99-●
      strain S76.91-●
    thorax (level) S29.009
      back wall S29.002
      front wall S29.001
      laceration S29.029
        back wall S29.022
        front wall S29.021
      specified type NEC S29.099
        back wall S29.092
        front wall S29.091
      strain S29.019
        back wall S29.012
        front wall S29.011
    thumb
      abductor (forearm level) S56.30-●
        laceration S56.32-●
        specified type NEC S56.39-●
        strain S56.31-●
      extensor (forearm level) S56.30-●
        hand level S66.20-●
          laceration S66.22-●
          specified type NEC S66.29-●
          strain S66.21-●
        laceration S56.32-●
        specified type NEC S56.39-●
        strain S56.31-●
      flexor (forearm level) S56.00-●
        hand level S66.00-●
          laceration S66.02-●
          specified type NEC S66.09-●
          strain S66.01-●

Injury (Continued)
  muscle (Continued)
    thumb (Continued)
      flexor (Continued)
        laceration S56.02-●
        specified type NEC S56.09-●
        strain S56.01-●
        wrist level —see Injury, muscle, thumb, flexor, hand level
      intrinsic S66.40-●
        laceration S66.42-●
        specified type NEC S66.49-●
        strain S66.41-●
    toe —see also Injury, muscle, foot
      extensor, long S96.10-●
        laceration S96.12-●
        specified type NEC S96.19-●
        strain S96.11-●
      flexor, long S96.00-●
        laceration S96.02-●
        specified type NEC S96.09-●
        strain S96.01-●
    triceps S46.30-●
      laceration S46.32-●
      specified type NEC S46.39-●
      strain S46.31-●
    wrist (and hand) level —see Injury, muscle, hand
  musculocutaneous nerve —see Injury, nerve, musculocutaneous
  myocardium —see Injury, heart
  nape —see Injury, neck
  nasal (septum) (sinus) S09.92
  nasopharynx S09.92
  neck S19.9
    specified NEC S19.80
      specified site NEC S19.89
  nerve NEC T14.8
    abdomen S34.9
      peripheral S34.6
      specified site NEC S34.8
    abducens S04.4-●
      contusion S04.4-●
      laceration S04.4-●
      specified type NEC S04.4-●
    abducent —see Injury, nerve, abducens
    accessory S04.7-●
      contusion S04.7-●
      laceration S04.7-●
      specified type NEC S04.7-●
    acoustic S04.6-●
      contusion S04.6-●
      laceration S04.6-●
      specified type NEC S04.6-●
    ankle S94.9-●
      cutaneous sensory S94.3-●
      specified site NEC —see subcategory S94.8
    anterior crural, femoral —see Injury, nerve, femoral
    arm (upper) S44.9-●
      axillary —see Injury, nerve, axillary
      cutaneous —see Injury, nerve, cutaneous, arm
      median —see Injury, nerve, median, upper arm
      musculocutaneous —see Injury, nerve, musculocutaneous
      radial —see Injury, nerve, radial, upper arm
      specified site NEC —see subcategory S44.8
      ulnar —see Injury, nerve, ulnar, arm
    auditory —see Injury, nerve, acoustic
    axillary S44.3-●
    brachial plexus —see Injury, brachial plexus
    cervical sympathetic S14.5

Injury *(Continued)*
  nerve NEC *(Continued)*
    cranial S04.9
      contusion S04.9
      eighth (acoustic or auditory) —*see* Injury,
        nerve, acoustic
      eleventh (accessory) —*see* Injury,
        nerve, accessory
      fifth (trigeminal) —*see* Injury, nerve,
        trigeminal
      first (olfactory) —*see* Injury, nerve,
        olfactory
      fourth (trochlear) —*see* Injury, nerve,
        trochlear
      laceration S04.9
      ninth (glossopharyngeal) —*see* Injury,
        nerve, glossopharyngeal
      second (optic) —*see* Injury, nerve,
        optic
      seventh (facial) —*see* Injury, nerve,
        facial
      sixth (abducent) —*see* Injury, nerve,
        abducens
      specified
        nerve NEC S04.89-●
          contusion S04.89-●
          laceration S04.89-●
          specified type NEC S04.89-●
        type NEC S04.9
      tenth (pneumogastric or vagus) —*see*
        Injury, nerve, vagus
      third (oculomotor) —*see* Injury, nerve,
        oculomotor
      twelfth (hypoglossal) —*see* Injury, nerve,
        hypoglossal
    cutaneous sensory
      ankle (level) S94.3-●
      arm (upper) (level) S44.5-●
      foot (level) —*see* Injury, nerve, cutaneous
        sensory, ankle
      forearm (level) S54.3-●
      hip (level) S74.2-●
      leg (lower level) S84.2-●
      shoulder (level) —*see* Injury, nerve,
        cutaneous sensory, arm
      thigh (level) —*see* Injury, nerve,
        cutaneous sensory, hip
    deep peroneal —*see* Injury, nerve, peroneal,
      foot
    digital
      finger S64.4-●
        index S64.49-●
        little S64.49-●
        middle S64.49-●
        ring S64.49-●
        thumb S64.3-●
      toe —*see* Injury, nerve, ankle, specified
        site NEC
    eighth cranial (acoustic or auditory) —*see*
      Injury, nerve, acoustic
    eleventh cranial (accessory) —*see* Injury,
      nerve, accessory
    facial S04.5-●
      contusion S04.5-●
      laceration S04.5-●
      newborn P11.3
      specified type NEC S04.5-●
    femoral (hip level) (thigh level) S74.1-●
    fifth cranial (trigeminal) —*see* Injury, nerve,
      trigeminal
    finger (digital) —*see* Injury, nerve, digital,
      finger
    first cranial (olfactory) —*see* Injury, nerve,
      olfactory
    foot S94.9-●
      cutaneous sensory S94.3-●
      deep peroneal S94.2-●
      lateral plantar S94.0-●
      medial plantar S94.1-●
      specified site NEC —*see* subcategory
        S94.8

Injury *(Continued)*
  nerve NEC *(Continued)*
    forearm (level) S54.9-●
      cutaneous sensory —*see* Injury, nerve,
        cutaneous sensory, forearm
      median —*see* Injury, nerve, median
      radial —*see* Injury, nerve, radial
      specified site NEC —*see* subcategory
        S54.8
      ulnar —*see* Injury, nerve, ulnar
    fourth cranial (trochlear) —*see* Injury,
      nerve, trochlear
    glossopharyngeal S04.89-●
      specified type NEC S04.89-●
    hand S64.9-●
      median —*see* Injury, nerve, median,
        hand
      radial —*see* Injury, nerve, radial, hand
      specified NEC —*see* subcategory S64.8
      ulnar —*see* Injury, nerve, ulnar, hand
    hip (level) S74.9-●
      cutaneous sensory —*see* Injury, nerve,
        cutaneous sensory, hip
      femoral —*see* Injury, nerve, femoral
      sciatic —*see* Injury, nerve, sciatic
      specified site NEC —*see* subcategory
        S74.8
    hypoglossal S04.89-●
      specified type NEC S04.89-●
    lateral plantar S94.0-●
    leg (lower) S84.9-●
      cutaneous sensory —*see* Injury, nerve,
        cutaneous sensory, leg
      peroneal —*see* Injury, nerve, peroneal
      specified site NEC —*see* subcategory S84.8
      tibial —*see* Injury, nerve, tibial
      upper —*see* Injury, nerve, thigh
    lower
      back —*see* Injury, nerve, abdomen,
        specified site NEC
        peripheral —*see* Injury, nerve,
          abdomen, peripheral
      limb —*see* Injury, nerve, leg
    lumbar plexus —*see* Injury, nerve,
      lumbosacral, sympathetic
    lumbar spinal —*see* Injury, nerve, spinal,
      lumbar
    lumbosacral
      plexus —*see* Injury, nerve, lumbosacral,
        sympathetic
      sympathetic S34.5
    medial plantar S94.1-●
    median (forearm level) S54.1-●
      hand (level) S64.1-●
      upper arm (level) S44.1-●
      wrist (level) —*see* Injury, nerve, median,
        hand
    musculocutaneous S44.4-●
    musculospiral (upper arm level) —*see*
      Injury, nerve, radial, upper arm
    neck S14.9
      peripheral S14.4
      specified site NEC S14.8
      sympathetic S14.5
    ninth cranial (glossopharyngeal) —*see*
      Injury, nerve, glossopharyngeal
    oculomotor S04.1-●
      contusion S04.1-●
      laceration S04.1-●
      specified type NEC S04.1-●
    olfactory S04.81-●
      specified type NEC S04.81-●
    optic S04.01-●
      contusion S04.01-●
      laceration S04.01-●
      specified type NEC S04.01-●
    pelvic girdle —*see* Injury, nerve, hip
    pelvis —*see* Injury, nerve, abdomen,
      specified site NEC
    peripheral —*see* Injury, nerve, abdomen,
      peripheral

Injury *(Continued)*
  nerve NEC *(Continued)*
    peripheral NEC T14.8
      abdomen —*see* Injury, nerve, abdomen,
        peripheral
      lower back —*see* Injury, nerve, abdomen,
        peripheral
      neck —*see* Injury, nerve, neck, peripheral
      pelvis —*see* Injury, nerve, abdomen,
        peripheral
      specified NEC T14.8
    peroneal (lower leg level) S84.1-●
      foot S94.2-●
    plexus
      brachial —*see* Injury, brachial plexus
      celiac, coeliac —*see* Injury, nerve,
        lumbosacral, sympathetic
      mesenteric, inferior —*see* Injury, nerve,
        lumbosacral, sympathetic
      sacral —*see* Injury, lumbosacral plexus
      spinal
        brachial —*see* Injury, brachial
          plexus
        lumbosacral —*see* Injury, lumbosacral
          plexus
    pneumogastric —*see* Injury, nerve, vagus
    radial (forearm level) S54.2-●
      hand (level) S64.2-●
      upper arm (level) S44.2-●
      wrist (level) —*see* Injury, nerve, radial,
        hand
    root —*see* Injury, nerve, spinal, root
    sacral plexus —*see* Injury, lumbosacral
      plexus
    sacral spinal —*see* Injury, nerve, spinal,
      sacral
    sciatic (hip level) (thigh level) S74.0-●
    second cranial (optic) —*see* Injury, nerve,
      optic
    seventh cranial (facial) —*see* Injury, nerve,
      facial
    shoulder —*see* Injury, nerve, arm
    sixth cranial (abducent) —*see* Injury, nerve,
      abducens
    spinal
      plexus —*see* Injury, nerve, plexus, spinal
      root
        cervical S14.2
        dorsal S24.2
        lumbar S34.21
        sacral S34.22
        thoracic —*see* Injury, nerve, spinal,
          root, dorsal
    splanchnic —*see* Injury, nerve, lumbosacral,
      sympathetic
    sympathetic NEC —*see* Injury, nerve,
      lumbosacral, sympathetic
      cervical —*see* Injury, nerve, cervical
        sympathetic
    tenth cranial (pneumogastric or vagus) —
      see Injury, nerve, vagus
    thigh (level) —*see* Injury, nerve, hip
      cutaneous sensory —*see* Injury, nerve,
        cutaneous sensory, hip
      femoral —*see* Injury, nerve, femoral
      sciatic —*see* Injury, nerve, sciatic
      specified NEC —*see* Injury, nerve, hip
    third cranial (oculomotor) —*see* Injury,
      nerve, oculomotor
    thorax S24.9
      peripheral S24.3
      specified site NEC S24.8
      sympathetic S24.4
    thumb, digital —*see* Injury, nerve, digital,
      thumb
    tibial (lower leg level) (posterior) S84.0-●
    toe —*see* Injury, nerve, ankle
    trigeminal S04.3-●
      contusion S04.3-●
      laceration S04.3-●
      specified type NEC S04.3-●

Injury *(Continued)*
  nerve NEC *(Continued)*
    trochlear S04.2-●
      contusion S04.2-●
      laceration S04.2-●
      specified type NEC S04.2-●
    twelfth cranial (hypoglossal) —*see* Injury,
        nerve, hypoglossal
    ulnar (forearm level) S54.0-●
      arm (upper) (level) S44.0-●
      hand (level) S64.0-●
      wrist (level) —*see* Injury, nerve, ulnar,
          hand
    vagus S04.89-●
      specified type NEC S04.89-●
    wrist (level) —*see* Injury, nerve, hand
    ninth cranial nerve (glossopharyngeal) —*see*
        Injury, nerve, glossopharyngeal
  nose (septum) S09.92
  obstetrical O71.9
    specified NEC O71.89
  occipital (region) (scalp) S09.90
    lobe —*see* Injury, intracranial
  optic chiasm S04.02
  optic radiation S04.03-●
  optic tract and pathways S04.03-●
  orbit, orbital (region) —*see* Injury,
      eye
    penetrating (with foreign body) —*see*
        Injury, eye, orbit, penetrating
    specified NEC —*see* Injury, eye, specified
        site NEC
  ovary, ovarian S37.409
    bilateral S37.402
      contusion S37.422
      laceration S37.432
      specified type NEC S37.492
    blood vessel —*see* Injury, blood vessel,
        ovarian
    contusion S37.429
      bilateral S37.422
      unilateral S37.421
    laceration S37.439
      bilateral S37.432
      unilateral S37.431
    specified type NEC S37.499
      bilateral S37.492
      unilateral S37.491
    unilateral S37.401
      contusion S37.421
      laceration S37.431
      specified type NEC S37.491
  palate (hard) (soft) S09.93
  pancreas S36.209
    body S36.201
      contusion S36.221
      laceration S36.231
        major S36.261
        minor S36.241
        moderate S36.251
      specified type NEC S36.291
    contusion S36.229
    head S36.200
      contusion S36.220
      laceration S36.230
        major S36.260
        minor S36.240
        moderate S36.250
      specified type NEC S36.290
    laceration S36.239
      major S36.269
      minor S36.249
      moderate S36.259
    specified type NEC S36.299
    tail S36.202
      contusion S36.222
      laceration S36.232
        major S36.262
        minor S36.242
        moderate S36.252
      specified type NEC S36.292

Injury *(Continued)*
  parietal (region) (scalp) S09.90
    lobe —*see* Injury, intracranial
  patellar ligament (tendon) S76.10-●
    laceration S76.12-●
    specified NEC S76.19-●
    strain S76.11-●
  pelvis, pelvic (floor) S39.93
    complicating delivery O70.1
    joint or ligament, complicating delivery
        O71.6
    organ S37.90
      with ectopic or molar pregnancy
          O08.6
      complication of abortion —*see* Abortion
      contusion S37.92
      following ectopic or molar pregnancy
          O08.6
      laceration S37.93
      obstetrical trauma NEC O71.5
      specified
        site NEC S37.899
          contusion S37.892
          laceration S37.893
          specified type NEC S37.898
        type NEC S37.99
    specified NEC S39.83
  penis S39.94
  perineum S39.94
  peritoneum S36.81
    laceration S36.893
  periurethral tissue —*see* Injury, urethra
    complicating delivery O71.82
  phalanges
    foot —*see* Injury, foot
    hand —*see* Injury, hand
  pharynx NEC S19.85
  pleura —*see* Injury, intrathoracic, pleura
  plexus
    brachial —*see* Injury, brachial plexus
    cardiac —*see* Injury, nerve, thorax,
        sympathetic
    celiac, coeliac —*see* Injury, nerve,
        lumbosacral, sympathetic
    esophageal —*see* Injury, nerve, thorax,
        sympathetic
    hypogastric —*see* Injury, nerve,
        lumbosacral, sympathetic
    lumbar, lumbosacral —*see* Injury,
        lumbosacral plexus
    mesenteric —*see* Injury, nerve, lumbosacral,
        sympathetic
    pulmonary —*see* Injury, nerve, thorax,
        sympathetic
  postcardiac surgery (syndrome) I97.0
  prepuce S39.94
  prostate S37.829
    contusion S37.822
    laceration S37.823
    specified type NEC S37.828
  pubic region S39.94
  pudendum S39.94
  pulmonary plexus —*see* Injury, nerve, thorax,
      sympathetic
  rectovaginal septum NEC S39.83
  rectum —*see* Injury, intestine, large, rectum
  retina —*see* Injury, eye, specified site NEC
    penetrating —*see* Injury, eyeball,
        penetrating
  retroperitoneal —*see* Injury, intra-abdominal,
      specified site NEC
  rotator cuff (muscle(s)) (tendon(s))
      S46.00-●
    laceration S46.02-●
    specified type NEC S46.09-●
    strain S46.01-●
  round ligament —*see* Injury, pelvic organ,
      specified site NEC
  sacral plexus —*see* Injury, lumbosacral
      plexus
  salivary duct or gland S09.93

Injury *(Continued)*
  scalp S09.90
    newborn (birth injury) P12.9
      due to monitoring (electrode) (sampling
          incision) P12.4
      specified NEC P12.89
        caput succedaneum P12.81
  scapular region —*see* Injury, shoulder
  sclera —*see* Injury, eye, specified site NEC
    penetrating —*see* Injury, eyeball,
        penetrating
  scrotum S39.94
  second cranial nerve (optic) —*see* Injury,
      nerve, optic
  seminal vesicle —*see* Injury, pelvic organ,
      specified site NEC
  seventh cranial nerve (facial) —*see* Injury,
      nerve, facial
  shoulder S49.9-●
    blood vessel —*see* Injury, blood vessel,
        arm
    contusion —*see* Contusion, shoulder
    dislocation —*see* Dislocation, shoulder
    fracture —*see* Fracture, shoulder
    muscle —*see* Injury, muscle, shoulder
    nerve —*see* Injury, nerve, shoulder
    open —*see* Wound, open, shoulder
    specified type NEC S49.8-●
    sprain —*see* Sprain, shoulder girdle
    superficial —*see* Injury, superficial,
        shoulder
  sinus
    cavernous —*see* Injury, intracranial
    nasal S09.92
  sixth cranial nerve (abducent) —*see* Injury,
      nerve, abducens
  skeleton, birth injury P13.9
    specified part NEC P13.8
  skin NEC T14.8
    surface intact —*see* Injury, superficial
  skull NEC S09.90
  specified NEC T14.8
  spermatic cord (pelvic region) S37.898
    scrotal region S39.848
  spinal (cord)
    cervical (neck) S14.109
      anterior cord syndrome S14.139
        C1 level S14.131
        C2 level S14.132
        C3 level S14.133
        C4 level S14.134
        C5 level S14.135
        C6 level S14.136
        C7 level S14.137
        C8 level S14.138
      Brown-Séquard syndrome S14.149
        C1 level S14.141
        C2 level S14.142
        C3 level S14.143
        C4 level S14.144
        C5 level S14.145
        C6 level S14.146
        C7 level S14.147
        C8 level S14.148
      C1 level S14.101
      C2 level S14.102
      C3 level S14.103
      C4 level S14.104
      C5 level S14.105
      C6 level S14.106
      C7 level S14.107
      C8 level S14.108
      central cord syndrome S14.129
        C1 level S14.121
        C2 level S14.122
        C3 level S14.123
        C4 level S14.124
        C5 level S14.125
        C6 level S14.126
        C7 level S14.127
        C8 level S14.128

Injury *(Continued)*
  spinal *(Continued)*
    cervical *(Continued)*
      complete lesion S14.119
        C1 level S14.111
        C2 level S14.112
        C3 level S14.113
        C4 level S14.114
        C5 level S14.115
        C6 level S14.116
        C7 level S14.117
        C8 level S14.118
      concussion S14.0
      edema S14.0
      incomplete lesion specified NEC S14.159
        C1 level S14.151
        C2 level S14.152
        C3 level S14.153
        C4 level S14.154
        C5 level S14.155
        C6 level S14.156
        C7 level S14.157
        C8 level S14.158
      posterior cord syndrome S14.159
        C1 level S14.151
        C2 level S14.152
        C3 level S14.153
        C4 level S14.154
        C5 level S14.155
        C6 level S14.156
        C7 level S14.157
        C8 level S14.158
    dorsal —*see* Injury, spinal, thoracic
    lumbar S34.109
      complete lesion S34.119
        L1 level S34.111
        L2 level S34.112
        L3 level S34.113
        L4 level S34.114
        L5 level S34.115
      concussion S34.01
      edema S34.01
      incomplete lesion S34.129
        L1 level S34.121
        L2 level S34.122
        L3 level S34.123
        L4 level S34.124
        L5 level S34.125
      L1 level S34.101
      L2 level S34.102
      L3 level S34.103
      L4 level S34.104
      L5 level S34.105
    nerve root NEC
      cervical —*see* Injury, nerve, spinal, root,
        cervical
      dorsal —*see* Injury, nerve, spinal, root,
        dorsal
      lumbar S34.21
      sacral S34.22
      thoracic —*see* Injury, nerve, spinal, root,
        dorsal
    plexus
      brachial —*see* Injury, brachial plexus
      lumbosacral —*see* Injury, lumbosacral
        plexus
    sacral S34.139
      complete lesion S34.131
      incomplete lesion S34.132
    thoracic S24.109
      anterior cord syndrome S24.139
        T1 level S24.131
        T2-T6 level S24.132
        T7-T10 level S24.133
        T11-T12 level S24.134
      Brown-Séquard syndrome
        S24.149
        T1 level S24.141
        T2-T6 level S24.142
        T7-T10 level S24.143
        T11-T12 level S24.144

Injury *(Continued)*
  spinal *(Continued)*
    thoracic *(Continued)*
      complete lesion S24.119
        T1 level S24.111
        T2-T6 level S24.112
        T7-T10 level S24.113
        T11-T12 level S24.114
      concussion S24.0
      edema S24.0
      incomplete lesion specified NEC S24.159
        T1 level S24.151
        T2-T6 level S24.152
        T7-T10 level S24.153
        T11-T12 level S24.154
      posterior cord syndrome S24.159
        T1 level S24.151
        T2-T6 level S24.152
        T7-T10 level S24.153
        T11-T12 level S24.154
      T1 level S24.101
      T2-T6 level S24.102
      T7-T10 level S24.103
      T11-T12 level S24.104
  splanchnic nerve —*see* Injury, nerve,
    lumbosacral, sympathetic
  spleen S36.00
    contusion S36.029
      major S36.021
      minor S36.020
    laceration S36.039
      major (massive) (stellate) S36.032
      moderate S36.031
      superficial (capsular) (minor) S36.030
    specified type NEC S36.09
  splenic artery —*see* Injury, blood vessel, celiac
    artery, branch
  stellate ganglion —*see* Injury, nerve, thorax,
    sympathetic
  sternal region S29.9
  stomach S36.30
    contusion S36.32
    laceration S36.33
    specified type NEC S36.39
  subconjunctival —*see* Injury, eye, conjunctiva
  subcutaneous NEC T14.8
  submaxillary region S09.93
  submental region S09.93
  subungual
    fingers —*see* Injury, hand
    toes —*see* Injury, foot
  superficial NEC T14.8
    abdomen, abdominal (wall) S30.92
      abrasion S30.811
      bite S30.871
        insect S30.861
      contusion S30.1
      external constriction S30.841
      foreign body S30.851
    abrasion —*see* Abrasion, by site
    adnexa, eye NEC —*see* Injury, eye,
      specified site NEC
    alveolar process —*see* Injury, superficial,
      oral cavity
    ankle S90.91-•
      abrasion —*see* Abrasion, ankle
      bite —*see* Bite, ankle
      blister —*see* Blister, ankle
      contusion —*see* Contusion, ankle
      external constriction —*see* Constriction,
        external, ankle
      foreign body —*see* Foreign body,
        superficial, ankle
    anus S30.98
    arm (upper) S40.92-•
      abrasion —*see* Abrasion, arm
      bite —*see* Bite, superficial, arm
      blister —*see* Blister, arm (upper)
      contusion —*see* Contusion, arm
      external constriction —*see* Constriction,
        external, arm

Injury *(Continued)*
  superficial NEC *(Continued)*
    arm *(Continued)*
      foreign body —*see* Foreign body,
        superficial, arm
    auditory canal (external) (meatus) —*see*
      Injury, superficial, ear
    auricle —*see* Injury, superficial, ear
    axilla —*see* Injury, superficial, arm
    back —*see also* Injury, superficial, thorax,
      back
      lower S30.91
        abrasion S30.810
        contusion S30.0
        external constriction S30.840
        superficial
          bite NEC S30.870
            insect S30.860
          foreign body S30.850
    bite NEC —*see* Bite, superficial NEC, by
      site
    blister —*see* Blister, by site
    breast S20.10-•
      abrasion —*see* Abrasion, breast
      bite —*see* Bite, superficial, breast
      contusion —*see* Contusion, breast
      external constriction —*see* Constriction,
        external, breast
      foreign body —*see* Foreign body,
        superficial, breast
    brow —*see* Injury, superficial, head,
      specified NEC
    buttock S30.91
    calf —*see* Injury, superficial, leg
    canthus, eye —*see* Injury, superficial,
      periocular area
    cheek (external) —*see* Injury, superficial,
      head, specified NEC
      internal —*see* Injury, superficial, oral
        cavity
    chest wall —*see* Injury, superficial, thorax
    chin —*see* Injury, superficial, head NEC
    clitoris S30.95
    conjunctiva —*see* Injury, eye, conjunctiva
      with foreign body (in conjunctival
        sac) —*see* Foreign body,
        conjunctival sac
    contusion —*see* Contusion, by site
    costal region —*see* Injury, superficial,
      thorax
    digit(s)
      hand —*see* Injury, superficial, finger
    ear (auricle) (canal) (external) S00.40-•
      abrasion —*see* Abrasion, ear
      bite —*see* Bite, superficial, ear
      contusion —*see* Contusion, ear
      external constriction —*see* Constriction,
        external, ear
      foreign body —*see* Foreign body,
        superficial, ear
    elbow S50.90-•
      abrasion —*see* Abrasion, elbow
      bite —*see* Bite, superficial, elbow
      blister —*see* Blister, elbow
      contusion —*see* Contusion, elbow
      external constriction —*see* Constriction,
        external, elbow
      foreign body —*see* Foreign body,
        superficial, elbow
    epididymis S30.94
    epigastric region S30.92
    epiglottis —*see* Injury, superficial, throat
    esophagus
      cervical —*see* Injury, superficial, throat
    external constriction —*see* Constriction,
      external, by site
    extremity NEC T14.8
    eyeball NEC —*see* Injury, eye, specified
      site NEC
    eyebrow —*see* Injury, superficial,
      periocular area

Injury *(Continued)*
 superficial NEC *(Continued)*
  eyelid S00.20-•
   abrasion —*see* Abrasion, eyelid
   bite —*see* Bite, superficial, eyelid
   contusion —*see* Contusion, eyelid
   external constriction —*see* Constriction, external, eyelid
   foreign body —*see* Foreign body, superficial, eyelid
  face NEC —*see* Injury, superficial, head, specified NEC
  finger(s) S60.949
   abrasion —*see* Abrasion, finger
   bite —*see* Bite, superficial, finger
   blister —*see* Blister, finger
   contusion —*see* Contusion, finger
   external constriction —*see* Constriction, external, finger
   foreign body —*see* Foreign body, superficial, finger
   index S60.94-•
   insect bite —*see* Bite, by site, superficial, insect
   little S60.94-•
   middle S60.94-•
   ring S60.94-•
  flank S30.92
  foot S90.92-•
   abrasion —*see* Abrasion, foot
   bite —*see* Bite, foot
   blister —*see* Blister, foot
   contusion —*see* Contusion, foot
   external constriction —*see* Constriction, external, foot
   foreign body —*see* Foreign body, superficial, foot
  forearm S50.91-•
   abrasion —*see* Abrasion, forearm
   bite —*see* Bite, forearm, superficial
   blister —*see* Blister, forearm
   contusion —*see* Contusion, forearm
   elbow only —*see* Injury, superficial, elbow
   external constriction —*see* Constriction, external, forearm
   foreign body —*see* Foreign body, superficial, forearm
  forehead —*see* Injury, superficial, head NEC
  foreign body —*see* Foreign body, superficial
  genital organs, external
   female S30.97
   male S30.96
  globe (eye) —*see* Injury, eye, specified site NEC
  groin S30.92
  gum —*see* Injury, superficial, oral cavity
  hand S60.92-•
   abrasion —*see* Abrasion, hand
   bite —*see* Bite, superficial, hand
   contusion —*see* Contusion, hand
   external constriction —*see* Constriction, external, hand
   foreign body —*see* Foreign body, superficial, hand
  head S00.90
   ear —*see* Injury, superficial, ear
   eyelid —*see* Injury, superficial, eyelid
   nose S00.30
   oral cavity S00.502
   scalp S00.00
   specified site NEC S00.80
  heel —*see* Injury, superficial, foot
  hip S70.91-•
   abrasion —*see* Abrasion, hip
   bite —*see* Bite, superficial, hip
   blister —*see* Blister, hip
   contusion —*see* Contusion, hip

Injury *(Continued)*
 superficial NEC *(Continued)*
  hip *(Continued)*
   external constriction —*see* Constriction, external, hip
   foreign body —*see* Foreign body, superficial, hip
  iliac region —*see* Injury, superficial, abdomen
  inguinal region —*see* Injury, superficial, abdomen
  insect bite —*see* Bite, by site, superficial, insect
  interscapular region —*see* Injury, superficial, thorax, back
  jaw —*see* Injury, superficial, head, specified NEC
  knee S80.91-•
   abrasion —*see* Abrasion, knee
   bite —*see* Bite, superficial, knee
   blister —*see* Blister, knee
   contusion —*see* Contusion, knee
   external constriction —*see* Constriction, external, knee
   foreign body —*see* Foreign body, superficial, knee
  labium (majus) (minus) S30.95
  lacrimal (apparatus) (gland) (sac) —*see* Injury, eye, specified site NEC
  larynx —*see* Injury, superficial, throat
  leg (lower) S80.92-•
   abrasion —*see* Abrasion, leg
   bite —*see* Bite, superficial, leg
   contusion —*see* Contusion, leg
   external constriction —*see* Constriction, external, leg
   foreign body —*see* Foreign body, superficial, leg
   knee —*see* Injury, superficial, knee
  limb NEC T14.8
  lip S00.501
  lower back S30.91
  lumbar region S30.91
  malar region —*see* Injury, superficial, head, specified NEC
  mammary —*see* Injury, superficial, breast
  mastoid region —*see* Injury, superficial, head, specified NEC
  mouth —*see* Injury, superficial, oral cavity
  muscle NEC T14.8
  nail NEC T14.8
   finger —*see* Injury, superficial, finger
   toe —*see* Injury, superficial, toe
  nasal (septum) —*see* Injury, superficial, nose
  neck S10.90
   specified site NEC S10.80
  nose (septum) S00.30
  occipital region —*see* Injury, superficial, scalp
  oral cavity S00.502
  orbital region —*see* Injury, superficial, periocular area
  palate —*see* Injury, superficial, oral cavity
  palm —*see* Injury, superficial, hand
  parietal region —*see* Injury, superficial, scalp
  pelvis S30.91
   girdle —*see* Injury, superficial, hip
  penis S30.93
  perineum
   female S30.95
   male S30.91
  periocular area S00.20-•
   abrasion —*see* Abrasion, eyelid
   bite —*see* Bite, superficial, eyelid
   contusion —*see* Contusion, eyelid
   external constriction —*see* Constriction, external, eyelid
   foreign body —*see* Foreign body, superficial, eyelid

Injury *(Continued)*
 superficial NEC *(Continued)*
  phalanges
   finger —*see* Injury, superficial, finger
   toe —*see* Injury, superficial, toe
  pharynx —*see* Injury, superficial, throat
  pinna —*see* Injury, superficial, ear
  popliteal space —*see* Injury, superficial, knee
  prepuce S30.93
  pubic region S30.91
  pudendum
   female S30.97
   male S30.96
  sacral region S30.91
  scalp S00.00
  scapular region —*see* Injury, superficial, shoulder
  sclera —*see* Injury, eye, specified site NEC
  scrotum S30.94
  shin —*see* Injury, superficial, leg
  shoulder S40.91-•
   abrasion —*see* Abrasion, shoulder
   bite —*see* Bite, superficial, shoulder
   blister —*see* Blister, shoulder
   contusion —*see* Contusion, shoulder
   external constriction —*see* Constriction, external, shoulder
   foreign body —*see* Foreign body, superficial, shoulder
  skin NEC T14.8
  sternal region —*see* Injury, superficial, thorax, front
  subconjunctival —*see* Injury, eye, specified site NEC
  subcutaneous NEC T14.8
  submaxillary region —*see* Injury, superficial, head, specified NEC
  submental region —*see* Injury, superficial, head, specified NEC
  subungual
   finger(s) —*see* Injury, superficial, finger
   toe(s) —*see* Injury, superficial, toe
  supraclavicular fossa —*see* Injury, superficial, neck
  supraorbital —*see* Injury, superficial, head, specified NEC
  temple —*see* Injury, superficial, head, specified NEC
  temporal region —*see* Injury, superficial, head, specified NEC
  testis S30.94
  thigh S70.92-•
   abrasion —*see* Abrasion, thigh
   bite —*see* Bite, superficial, thigh
   blister —*see* Blister, thigh
   contusion —*see* Contusion, thigh
   external constriction —*see* Constriction, external, thigh
   foreign body —*see* Foreign body, superficial, thigh
  thorax, thoracic (wall) S20.90
   abrasion —*see* Abrasion, thorax
   back S20.40-•
   bite —*see* Bite, thorax, superficial
   blister —*see* Blister, thorax
   contusion —*see* Contusion, thorax
   external constriction —*see* Constriction, external, thorax
   foreign body —*see* Foreign body, superficial, thorax
   front S20.30-•
  throat S10.10
   abrasion S10.11
   bite S10.17
    insect S10.16
   blister S10.12
   contusion S10.0
   external constriction S10.14
   foreign body S10.15

Injury (Continued)
  superficial NEC (Continued)
    thumb S60.93-●
      abrasion —see Abrasion, thumb
      bite —see Bite, superficial, thumb
      blister —see Blister, thumb
      contusion —see Contusion, thumb
      external constriction —see Constriction,
        external, thumb
      foreign body —see Foreign body,
        superficial, thumb
      insect bite —see Bite, by site, superficial,
        insect
      specified type NEC S60.39-●
    toe(s) S90.93-●
      abrasion —see Abrasion, toe
      bite —see Bite, toe
      blister —see Blister, toe
      contusion —see Contusion, toe
      external constriction —see Constriction,
        external, toe
      foreign body —see Foreign body,
        superficial, toe
      great S90.93-●
    tongue —see Injury, superficial, oral cavity
    tooth, teeth —see Injury, superficial, oral
      cavity
    trachea S10.10
    tunica vaginalis S30.94
    tympanum, tympanic membrane —see
      Injury, superficial, ear
    uvula —see Injury, superficial, oral cavity
    vagina S30.95
    vocal cords —see Injury, superficial, throat
    vulva S30.95
    wrist S60.91-●
  supraclavicular region —see Injury, neck
  supraorbital S09.93
  suprarenal gland (multiple) —see Injury,
    adrenal
  surgical complication (external or internal
    site) —see Laceration, accidental
    complicating surgery
  temple S09.90
  temporal region S09.90
  tendon —see also Injury, muscle, by site
    abdomen —see Injury, muscle, abdomen
    Achilles —see Injury, Achilles tendon
    lower back —see Injury, muscle, lower
      back
    pelvic organs —see Injury, muscle, pelvis
  tenth cranial nerve (pneumogastric or
    vagus) —see Injury, nerve, vagus
  testis S39.94
  thigh S79.92-●
    blood vessel —see Injury, blood vessel,
      hip
    contusion —see Contusion, thigh
    fracture —see Fracture, femur
    muscle —see Injury, muscle, thigh
    nerve —see Injury, nerve, thigh
    open —see Wound, open, thigh
    specified NEC S79.82-●
    superficial —see Injury, superficial, thigh
  third cranial nerve (oculomotor) —see Injury,
    nerve, oculomotor
  thorax, thoracic S29.9
    blood vessel —see Injury, blood vessel,
      thorax
    cavity —see Injury, intrathoracic
    dislocation —see Dislocation, thorax
    external (wall) S29.9
      contusion —see Contusion, thorax
      nerve —see Injury, nerve, thorax
      open —see Wound, open, thorax
      specified NEC S29.8
      sprain —see Sprain, thorax
      superficial —see Injury, superficial,
        thorax
    fracture —see Fracture, thorax
    internal —see Injury, intrathoracic

Injury (Continued)
  thorax, thoracic (Continued)
    intrathoracic organ —see Injury, intrathoracic
    sympathetic ganglion —see Injury, nerve,
      thorax, sympathetic
  throat —see also Injury, neck S19.9
  thumb S69.9-●
    blood vessel —see Injury, blood vessel,
      thumb
    contusion —see Contusion, thumb
    dislocation —see Dislocation, thumb
    fracture —see Fracture, thumb
    muscle —see Injury, muscle, thumb
    nerve —see Injury, nerve, digital, thumb
    open —see Wound, open, thumb
    specified NEC S69.8-●
    sprain —see Sprain, thumb
    superficial —see Injury, superficial, thumb
  thymus (gland) —see Injury, intrathoracic,
    specified organ NEC
  thyroid (gland) NEC S19.84
  toe S99.92-●
    contusion —see Contusion, toe
    dislocation —see Dislocation, toe
    fracture —see Fracture, toe
    muscle —see Injury, muscle, toe
    open —see Wound, open, toe
    specified type NEC S99.82-●
    sprain —see Sprain, toe
    superficial —see Injury, superficial, toe
  tongue S09.93
  tonsil S09.93
  tooth S09.93
  trachea (cervical) NEC S19.82
    thoracic —see Injury, intrathoracic, trachea,
      thoracic
  transfusion-related acute lung (TRALI) J95.84
  tunica vaginalis S39.94
  twelfth cranial nerve (hypoglossal) —see
    Injury, nerve, hypoglossal
  ureter S37.10
    contusion S37.12
    laceration S37.13
    specified type NEC S37.19
  urethra (sphincter) S37.30
    at delivery O71.5
    contusion S37.32
    laceration S37.33
    specified type NEC S37.38
  urinary organ S37.899
    contusion S37.92
    laceration S37.93
    specified
      site NEC S37.899
        contusion S37.892
        laceration S37.893
        specified type NEC S37.898
      type NEC S37.99
  uterus, uterine S37.60
    with ectopic or molar pregnancy O08.6
    blood vessel —see Injury, blood vessel, iliac
    contusion S37.62
    laceration S37.63
      cervix at delivery O71.3
    rupture associated with obstetrics —see
      Rupture, uterus
    specified type NEC S37.69
  uvula S09.93
  vagina S39.93
    abrasion S30.814
    bite S31.45
      insect S30.864
      superficial NEC S30.874
    contusion S30.23
    crush S38.03
    during delivery —see Laceration, vagina,
      during delivery
    external constriction S30.844
    insect bite S30.864
    laceration S31.41
      with foreign body S31.42

Injury (Continued)
  vagina (Continued)
    open wound S31.40
    puncture S31.43
      with foreign body S31.44
    superficial S30.95
      foreign body S30.854
  vas deferens —see Injury, pelvic organ,
    specified site NEC
  vascular NEC T14.8
  vein —see Injury, blood vessel
  vena cava (superior) S25.20
    inferior S35.10
      laceration (minor) (superficial) S35.11
        major S35.12
      specified type NEC S35.19
    laceration (minor) (superficial) S25.21
      major S25.22
    specified type NEC S25.29
  vesical (sphincter) —see Injury, bladder
  visual cortex S04.04-●
  vitreous (humor) S05.90
    specified NEC S05.8X-●
  vocal cord NEC S19.83
  vulva S39.94
    abrasion S30.814
    bite S31.45
      insect S30.864
      superficial NEC S30.874
    contusion S30.23
    crush S38.03
    during delivery —see Laceration,
      perineum, female, during delivery
    external constriction S30.844
    insect bite S30.864
    laceration S31.41
      with foreign body S31.42
    open wound S31.40
    puncture S31.43
      with foreign body S31.44
    superficial S30.95
      foreign body S30.854
  whiplash (cervical spine) S13.4
  wrist S69.9-●
    blood vessel —see Injury, blood vessel,
      hand
    contusion —see Contusion, wrist
    dislocation —see Dislocation, wrist
    fracture —see Fracture, wrist
    muscle —see Injury, muscle, hand
    nerve —see Injury, nerve, hand
    open —see Wound, open, wrist
    specified NEC S69.8-●
    sprain —see Sprain, wrist
    superficial —see Injury, superficial, wrist
Inoculation —see also Vaccination
  complication or reaction —see Complications,
    vaccination
Insanity, insane —see also Psychosis
  adolescent —see Schizophrenia
  confusional F28
    acute or subacute F05
  delusional F22
  senile F03
Insect
  bite —see Bite, by site, superficial, insect
  venomous, poisoning NEC (by) —see Venom,
    arthropod
Insensitivity
  adrenocorticotropin hormone (ACTH)
    E27.49
  androgen E34.50
    complete E34.51
    partial E34.52
Insertion
  cord (umbilical) lateral or velamentous
    O43.12-●
  intrauterine contraceptive device (encounter
    for) —see Intrauterine contraceptive
    device
Insolation (sunstroke) T67.0

▶ New   ⇒ Revised   ~~deleted~~ Deleted   ● Use Additional Character(s)

Insomnia (organic) G47.00
  without objective findings F51.02
  adjustment F51.02
  adjustment disorder F51.02
  behavioral, of childhood Z73.819
    combined type Z73.812
    limit setting type Z73.811
    sleep-onset association type Z73.810
  childhood Z73.819
  chronic F51.04
    somatized tension F51.04
  conditioned F51.04
  due to
    alcohol
      abuse F10.182
      dependence F10.282
      use F10.982
    amphetamines
      abuse F15.182
      dependence F15.282
      use F15.982
    anxiety disorder F51.05
    caffeine
      abuse F15.182
      dependence F15.282
      use F15.982
    cocaine
      abuse F14.182
      dependence F14.282
      use F14.982
    depression F51.05
    drug NEC
      abuse F19.182
      dependence F19.282
      use F19.982
    medical condition G47.01
    mental disorder NEC F51.05
    opioid
      abuse F11.182
      dependence F11.282
      use F11.982
    psychoactive substance NEC
      abuse F19.182
      dependence F19.282
      use F19.982
    sedative, hypnotic, or anxiolytic
      abuse F13.182
      dependence F13.282
      use F13.982
    stimulant NEC
      abuse F15.182
      dependence F15.282
      use F15.982
  fatal familial (FFI) A81.83
  idiopathic F51.01
  learned F51.3
  nonorganic origin F51.01
  not due to a substance or known
      physiological condition F51.01
    specified NEC F51.09
  paradoxical F51.03
  primary F51.01
  psychiatric F51.05
  psychophysiologic F51.04
  related to psychopathology F51.05
  short-term F51.02
  specified NEC G47.09
  stress-related F51.02
  transient F51.02
Inspiration
  food or foreign body —see Foreign body, by
      site
  mucus —see Asphyxia, mucus
Inspissated bile syndrome (newborn) P59.1
Instability
  emotional (excessive) F60.3
  joint (post-traumatic) M25.30
    ankle M25.37-•
    due to old ligament injury —see Disorder,
        ligament
    elbow M25.32-•

Instability (Continued)
  joint (Continued)
    flail —see Flail, joint
    foot M25.37-•
    hand M25.34-•
    hip M25.35-•
    knee M25.36-•
    lumbosacral —see subcategory M53.2
    prosthesis —see Complications, joint
        prosthesis, mechanical, displacement,
        by site
    sacroiliac —see subcategory M53.2
    secondary to
      old ligament injury —see Disorder,
          ligament
      removal of joint prosthesis M96.89
    shoulder (region) M25.31-•
    spine —see subcategory M53.2
    wrist M25.33-•
  knee (chronic) M23.5-•
  lumbosacral —see subcategory M53.2
  nervous F48.8
  personality (emotional) F60.3
  spine —see Instability, joint, spine
  vasomotor R55
Institutional syndrome (childhood)
    F94.2
Institutionalization, affecting child
    Z62.22
  disinhibited attachment F94.2
Insufficiency, insufficient
  accommodation, old age H52.4
  adrenal (gland) E27.40
    primary E27.1
  adrenocortical E27.40
    drug-induced E27.3
    iatrogenic E27.3
    primary E27.1
  anatomic crown height K08.89
  anterior (occlusal) guidance M26.54
  anus K62.89
  aortic (valve) I35.1
    with
      mitral (valve) disease I08.0
        with tricuspid (valve) disease I08.3
      stenosis I35.2
      tricuspid (valve) disease I08.2
        with mitral (valve) disease I08.3
    congenital Q23.1
    rheumatic I06.1
      with
        mitral (valve) disease I08.0
          with tricuspid (valve) disease I08.3
        stenosis I06.2
          with mitral (valve) disease I08.0
            with tricuspid (valve) disease
                I08.3
        tricuspid (valve) disease I08.2
          with mitral (valve) disease I08.3
    specified cause NEC I35.1
    syphilitic A52.03
  arterial I77.1
    basilar G45.0
    carotid (hemispheric) G45.1
    cerebral I67.81
    coronary (acute or subacute) I24.8
    mesenteric K55.1
    peripheral I73.9
    precerebral (multiple) (bilateral) G45.2
    vertebral G45.0
  arteriovenous I99.8
  biliary K83.8
  cardiac —see also Insufficiency, myocardial
    due to presence of (cardiac) prosthesis
        I97.11-•
    postprocedural I97.11-•
  cardiorenal, hypertensive I13.2
  cardiovascular —see Disease, cardiovascular
  cerebrovascular (acute) I67.81
    with transient focal neurological signs and
        symptoms G45.8

Insufficiency, insufficient (Continued)
  circulatory NEC I99.8
    newborn P29.89
  clinical crown length K08.89
  convergence H51.11
  coronary (acute or subacute) I24.8
    chronic or with a stated duration of over 4
        weeks I25.89
  corticoadrenal E27.40
    primary E27.1
  dietary E63.9
  divergence H51.8
  food T73.0
  gastroesophageal K22.8
  gonadal
    ovary E28.39
    testis E29.1
  heart —see also Insufficiency, myocardial
    newborn P29.89
    valve —see Endocarditis
  hepatic —see Failure, hepatic
  idiopathic autonomic G90.09
  interocclusal distance of fully erupted teeth
      (ridge) M26.36
  kidney N28.9
    acute N28.9
    chronic N18.9
  lacrimal (secretion) H04.12-•
    passages —see Stenosis, lacrimal
  liver —see Failure, hepatic
  lung —see Insufficiency, pulmonary
  mental (congenital) —see Disability,
      intellectual
  mesenteric K55.1
  mitral (valve) I34.0
    with
      aortic valve disease I08.0
        with tricuspid (valve) disease I08.3
      obstruction or stenosis I05.2
        with aortic valve disease I08.0
      tricuspid (valve) disease I08.1
        with aortic (valve) disease I08.3
    congenital Q23.3
    rheumatic I05.1
      with
        aortic valve disease I08.0
          with tricuspid (valve) disease I08.3
        obstruction or stenosis I05.2
          with aortic valve disease I08.0
            with tricuspid (valve) disease
                I08.3
        tricuspid (valve) disease I08.1
          with aortic (valve) disease I08.3
      active or acute I01.1
        with chorea, rheumatic (Sydenham's)
            I02.0
    specified cause, except rheumatic I34.0
  muscle —see also Disease, muscle
    heart —see Insufficiency, myocardial
  ocular NEC H50.9
  myocardial, myocardium (with
      arteriosclerosis) —see also Failure, heart
      I50.9
    with
      rheumatic fever (conditions in I00) I09.0
        active, acute or subacute I01.2
          with chorea I02.0
        inactive or quiescent (with chorea)
            I09.0
    congenital Q24.8
    hypertensive —see Hypertension, heart
    newborn P29.0
    rheumatic I09.0
      active, acute, or subacute I01.2
    syphilitic A52.06
  nourishment T73.0
  pancreatic K86.89
    exocrine K86.81
  parathyroid (gland) E20.9
  peripheral vascular (arterial) I73.9
  pituitary E23.0

Insufficiency, insufficient (Continued)
placental (mother) O36.51-•
platelets D69.6
prenatal care affecting management of
pregnancy O09.3-•
progressive pluriglandular E31.0
pulmonary J98.4
acute, following surgery (nonthoracic) J95.2
thoracic J95.1
chronic, following surgery J95.3
following
shock J98.4
trauma J98.4
newborn P28.5
valve I37.1
with stenosis I37.2
congenital Q22.2
rheumatic I09.89
with aortic, mitral or tricuspid (valve)
disease I08.8
pyloric K31.89
renal (acute) N28.9
chronic N18.9
respiratory R06.89
newborn P28.5
rotation —see Malrotation
sleep syndrome F51.12
social insurance Z59.7
suprarenal E27.40
primary E27.1
tarso-orbital fascia, congenital Q10.3
testis E29.1
thyroid (gland) (acquired) E03.9
congenital E03.1
tricuspid (valve) (rheumatic) I07.1
with
aortic (valve) disease I08.2
with mitral (valve) disease I08.3
mitral (valve) disease I08.1
with aortic (valve) disease I08.3
obstruction or stenosis I07.2
with aortic (valve) disease I08.2
with mitral (valve) disease I08.3
congenital Q22.8
nonrheumatic I36.1
with stenosis I36.2
urethral sphincter R32
valve, valvular (heart) I38
aortic —see Insufficiency, aortic (valve)
mitral —see Insufficiency, mitral (valve)
pulmonary —see Insufficiency, pulmonary,
valve
tricuspid —see Insufficiency, tricuspid
(valve)
congenital Q24.8
vascular I99.8
intestine K55.9
acute —see also Ischemia, intestine, acute
K55.059
mesenteric K55.1
peripheral I73.9
renal —see Hypertension, kidney
velopharyngeal
acquired K13.79
congenital Q38.8
venous (chronic) (peripheral) I87.2
ventricular —see Insufficiency, myocardial
welfare support Z59.7
Insufflation, fallopian Z31.41
Insular —see condition
Insulinoma
pancreas
benign D13.7
malignant C25.4
uncertain behavior D37.8
specified site
benign —see Neoplasm, by site, benign
malignant —see Neoplasm, by site,
malignant
uncertain behavior —see Neoplasm, by site,
uncertain behavior

Insulinoma (Continued)
unspecified site
benign D13.7
malignant C25.4
uncertain behavior D37.8
Insuloma —see Insulinoma
Interference
balancing side M26.56
non-working side M26.56
Intermenstrual —see condition
Intermittent —see condition
Internal —see condition
Interrogation
cardiac defibrillator (automatic) (implantable)
Z45.02
cardiac pacemaker Z45.018
cardiac (event) (loop) recorder Z45.09
infusion pump (implanted) (intrathecal) Z45.1
neurostimulator Z46.2
Interruption
aortic arch Q25.21
phase-shift, sleep cycle —see Disorder, sleep,
circadian rhythm
sleep phase-shift, or 24 hour sleep-wake
cycle —see Disorder, sleep, circadian
rhythm
Interstitial —see condition
Intertrigo L30.4
labialis K13.0
Intervertebral disc —see condition
Intestine, intestinal —see condition
Intolerance
carbohydrate K90.49
disaccharide, hereditary E73.0
fat NEC K90.49
pancreatic K90.3
food K90.49
dietary counseling and surveillance Z71.3
fructose E74.10
hereditary E74.12
glucose(-galactose) E74.39
gluten K90.01
lactose E73.9
specified NEC E73.8
lysine E72.3
milk NEC K90.49
lactose E73.9
protein K90.49
starch NEC K90.49
sucrose (-isomaltose) E74.31
Intoxicated NEC (without dependence) —see
Alcohol, intoxication
Intoxication
acid E87.2
alcoholic (acute) (without dependence) —see
Alcohol, intoxication
alimentary canal K52.1
amphetamine (without dependence) —
see Abuse, drug, stimulant, with
intoxication
with dependence —see Dependence, drug,
stimulant, with intoxication
anxiolytic (acute) (without dependence) —see
Abuse, drug, sedative, with intoxication
with dependence —see Dependence, drug,
sedative, with intoxication
caffeine F15.929
with dependence —see Dependence, drug,
stimulant, with intoxication
cannabinoids (acute) (without
dependence) —see Use, cannabis, with
intoxication
with
abuse —see Abuse, drug, cannabis, with
intoxication
dependence —see Dependence, drug,
cannabis, with intoxication
chemical —see Table of Drugs and Chemicals
via placenta or breast milk —see -
Absorption, chemical, through
placenta

Intoxication (Continued)
cocaine (acute) (without dependence) —see
Abuse, drug, cocaine, with intoxication
with dependence —see Dependence, drug,
cocaine, with intoxication
drug
acute (without dependence) —see Abuse,
drug, by type with intoxication
with dependence —see Dependence,
drug, by type with intoxication
addictive
via placenta or breast milk —see
Absorption, drug, addictive,
through placenta
newborn P93.8
gray baby syndrome P93.0
overdose or wrong substance given
or taken —see Table of Drugs and
Chemicals, by drug, poisoning
enteric K52.1
foodborne A05.9
bacterial A05.9
classical (Clostridium botulinum) A05.1
due to
Bacillus cereus A05.4
bacterium A05.9
specified NEC A05.8
Clostridium
botulinum A05.1
perfringens A05.2
welchii A05.2
Salmonella A02.9
with
(gastro) enteritis A02.0
localized infection(s) A02.20
arthritis A02.23
meningitis A02.21
osteomyelitis A02.24
pneumonia A02.22
pyelonephritis A02.25
specified NEC A02.29
sepsis A02.1
specified manifestation NEC A02.8
Staphylococcus A05.0
Vibrio
parahaemolyticus A05.3
vulnificus A05.5
enterotoxin, staphylococcal A05.0
noxious —see Poisoning, food, noxious
gastrointestinal K52.1
hallucinogenic (without dependence) —
see Abuse, drug, hallucinogen, with
intoxication
with dependence —see Dependence, drug,
hallucinogen, with intoxication
hypnotic (acute) (without dependence) —see
Abuse, drug, sedative, with intoxication
with dependence —see Dependence, drug,
sedative, with intoxication
inhalant (acute) (without dependence) —see
Abuse, drug, inhalant, with intoxication
with dependence —see Dependence, drug,
inhalant, with intoxication
meaning
inebriation —see category F10
poisoning —see Table of Drugs and
Chemicals
methyl alcohol (acute) (without
dependence) —see Alcohol, intoxication
opioid (acute) (without dependence) —see
Abuse, drug, opioid, with intoxication
with dependence —see Dependence, drug,
opioid, with intoxication
pathologic NEC (without dependence) —see
Alcohol, intoxication
phencyclidine (without dependence) —see
Abuse, drug, hallucinogen, with
intoxication
with dependence —see Dependence, drug,
hallucinogen, with intoxication
potassium (K) E87.5

▶ New   ⇒ Revised   ~~deleted~~ Deleted   • Use Additional Character(s)

Intoxication *(Continued)*
  psychoactive substance NEC (without
    dependence) —*see* Abuse, drug,
    psychoactive NEC, with intoxication
    with dependence —*see* Dependence,
     drug, psychoactive NEC, with
     intoxication
  sedative (acute) (without dependence) —
    see Abuse, drug, sedative, with
    intoxication
    with dependence —*see* Dependence, drug,
     sedative, with intoxication
  serum —*see also* Reaction, serum T80.69
  uremic —*see* Uremia
  volatile solvents (acute) (without
    dependence) —*see* Abuse, drug,
    inhalant, with intoxication
    with dependence —*see* Dependence, drug,
     inhalant, with intoxication
  water E87.79
Intraabdominal testis, testes
  bilateral Q53.211
  unilateral Q53.111
Intracranial —*see* condition
Intrahepatic gallbladder Q44.1
Intraligamentous —*see* condition
Intrathoracic —*see also* condition
  kidney Q63.2
Intrauterine contraceptive device
  checking Z30.431
  in situ Z97.5
  insertion Z30.430
    immediately following removal Z30.433
  management Z30.431
  reinsertion Z30.433
  removal Z30.432
  replacement Z30.433
  retention in pregnancy O26.3-●
Intraventricular —*see* condition
Intrinsic deformity —*see* Deformity
Intubation, difficult or failed T88.4
Intumescence, lens (eye) (cataract) —*see*
  Cataract
Intussusception (bowel) (colon) (enteric)
  (ileocecal) (ileocolic) (intestine) (rectum)
  K56.1
  appendix K38.8
  congenital Q43.8
  ureter (with obstruction) N13.5
Invagination (bowel, colon, intestine or rectum)
  K56.1
Inversion
  albumin-globulin (A-G) ratio E88.09
  bladder N32.89
  cecum —*see* Intussusception
  cervix N88.8
  chromosome in normal individual Q95.1
  circadian rhythm —*see* Disorder, sleep,
    circadian rhythm
  nipple N64.59
    congenital Q83.8
    gestational —*see* Retraction, nipple
    puerperal, postpartum —*see* Retraction,
     nipple
  nyctohemeral rhythm —*see* Disorder, sleep,
    circadian rhythm
  optic papilla Q14.2
  organ or site, congenital NEC —*see* Anomaly,
    by site
  sleep rhythm —*see* Disorder, sleep, circadian
    rhythm
  testis (congenital) Q55.29
  uterus (chronic) (postinfectional) (postpartal,
    old) N85.5
    postpartum O71.2
  vagina (posthysterectomy) N99.3
  ventricular Q20.5
Investigation —*see also* Examination Z04.9
  clinical research subject (control) (normal
    comparison) (participant) Z00.6
Involuntary movement, abnormal R25.9

Involution, involutional —*see also* condition
  breast, cystic —*see* Dysplasia, mammary,
    specified type NEC
  depression (single episode) F32.89
    recurrent episode F33.9
  melancholia (single episode) F32.89
    recurrent episode F33.8
  ovary, senile —*see* Atrophy, ovary
  thymus failure E32.8
I.Q.
  under 20 F73
  20-34 F72
  35-49 F71
  50-69 F70
IRDS (type I) P22.0
  type II P22.1
Irideremia Q13.1
Iridis rubeosis —*see* Disorder, iris, vascular
Iridochoroiditis (panuveitis) —*see* Panuveitis
Iridocyclitis H20.9-●
  acute H20.0-●
    hypopyon H20.05-●
    primary H20.01-●
    recurrent H20.02-●
    secondary (noninfectious) H20.04-●
     infectious H20.03-●
  chronic H20.1-●
  due to allergy —*see* Iridocyclitis, acute,
    secondary
  endogenous —*see* Iridocyclitis, acute, primary
  Fuchs' —*see* Cyclitis, Fuchs' heterochromic
  gonococcal A54.32
  granulomatous —*see* Iridocyclitis, chronic
  herpes, herpetic (simplex) B00.51
    zoster B02.32
  hypopyon —*see* Iridocyclitis, acute,
    hypopyon
  in (due to)
    ankylosing spondylitis M45.9
    gonococcal infection A54.32
    herpes (simplex) virus B00.51
     zoster B02.32
    infectious disease NOS B99
    parasitic disease NOS B89 *[H22]*
    sarcoidosis D86.83
    syphilis A51.43
    tuberculosis A18.54
    zoster B02.32
  lens-induced H20.2-●
  nongranulomatous —*see* Iridocyclitis, acute
  recurrent —*see* Iridocyclitis, acute, recurrent
  rheumatic —*see* Iridocyclitis, chronic
  subacute —*see* Iridocyclitis, acute
  sympathetic —*see* Uveitis, sympathetic
  syphilitic (secondary) A51.43
  tuberculous (chronic) A18.54
  Vogt-Koyanagi H20.82-●
Iridocyclochoroiditis (panuveitis) —*see*
  Panuveitis
Iridodialysis H21.53-●
Iridodonesis H21.89
Iridoplegia (complete) (partial) (reflex) H57.09
Iridoschisis H21.25-●
Iris —*see also* condition
  bombé —*see* Membrane, pupillary
Iritis —*see also* Iridocyclitis
  chronic —*see* Iridocyclitis, chronic
  diabetic —*see* E08-E13 with .39
  due to
    herpes simplex B00.51
    leprosy A30.9 *[H22]*
  gonococcal A54.32
  gouty —*see also* Gout, by type M10.9 *[H22]*
  granulomatous —*see* Iridocyclitis, chronic
  lens induced —*see* Iridocyclitis, lens-induced
  papulosa (syphilitic) A52.71
  rheumatic —*see* Iridocyclitis, chronic
  syphilitic (secondary) A51.43
    congenital (early) A50.01
    late A52.71
  tuberculous A18.54

Iron —*see* condition
Iron-miner's lung J63.4
Irradiated enamel (tooth, teeth) K03.89
Irradiation effects, adverse T66
Irreducible, irreducibility —*see* condition
Irregular, irregularity
  action, heart I49.9
  alveolar process K08.89
  bleeding N92.6
  breathing R06.89
  contour of cornea (acquired) —*see* Deformity,
    cornea
    congenital Q13.4
  contour, reconstructed breast N65.0
  dentin (in pulp) K04.3
  eye movements H55.89
    nystagmus —*see* Nystagmus
    saccadic H55.81
  labor O62.2
  menstruation (cause unknown) N92.6
  periods N92.6
  prostate N42.9
  pupil —*see* Abnormality, pupillary
  reconstructed breast N65.0
  respiratory R06.89
  septum (nasal) J34.2
  shape, organ or site, congenital NEC —*see*
    Distortion
  sleep-wake pattern (rhythm) G47.23
Irritable, irritability R45.4
  bladder N32.89
  bowel (syndrome) K58.9
    with
     constipation K58.1
     diarrhea K58.0
    mixed K58.2
    psychogenic F45.8
    specified NEC K58.8
  bronchial —*see* Bronchitis
  cerebral, in newborn P91.3
  colon —*see also* Irritable, bowel K58.9
    with diarrhea K58.0
    psychogenic F45.8
  duodenum K59.8
  heart (psychogenic) F45.8
  hip —*see* Derangement, joint, specified type
    NEC, hip
  ileum K59.8
  infant R68.12
  jejunum K59.8
  rectum K59.8
  stomach K31.89
    psychogenic F45.8
  sympathetic G90.8
  urethra N36.8
Irritation
  anus K62.89
  axillary nerve G54.0
  bladder N32.89
  brachial plexus G54.0
  bronchial —*see* Bronchitis
  cervical plexus G54.2
  cervix —*see* Cervicitis
  choroid, sympathetic —*see* Endophthalmitis
  cranial nerve —*see* Disorder, nerve, cranial
  gastric K31.89
    psychogenic F45.8
  globe, sympathetic —*see* Uveitis,
    sympathetic
  labyrinth —*see* subcategory H83.2
  lumbosacral plexus G54.1
  meninges (traumatic) —*see* Injury, intracranial
    nontraumatic —*see* Meningismus
  nerve —*see* Disorder, nerve
  nervous R45.0
  penis N48.89
  perineum NEC L29.3
  peripheral autonomic nervous system
    G90.8
  peritoneum —*see* Peritonitis
  pharynx J39.2

Irritation *(Continued)*
 plantar nerve —*see* Lesion, nerve, plantar
 spinal (cord) (traumatic) —*see also* Injury,
   spinal cord, by region
  nerve G58.9
   root NEC —*see* Radiculopathy
  nontraumatic —*see* Myelopathy
 stomach K31.89
  psychogenic F45.8
 sympathetic nerve NEC G90.8
 ulnar nerve —*see* Lesion, nerve, ulnar
 vagina N89.8
Ischemia, ischemic I99.8
 bowel (transient)
  acute —*see also* Ischemia, intestine, acute
    K55.059
  chronic K55.1
  due to mesenteric artery insufficiency
    K55.1
 brain —*see* Ischemia, cerebral
 cardiac (*see* Disease, heart, ischemic)
 cardiomyopathy I25.5
 cerebral (chronic) (generalized) I67.82
  arteriosclerotic I67.2
  intermittent G45.9
  newborn P91.0
  recurrent focal G45.8
  transient G45.9
 colon chronic (due to mesenteric artery
   insufficiency) K55.1
 coronary —*see* Disease, heart, ischemic
 demand (coronary) —*see also* Angina I24.8
  with myocardial infarction I21.A1
  resulting in myocardial infarction I21.A1
 heart (chronic or with a stated duration of
   over 4 weeks) I25.9
  acute or with a stated duration of 4 weeks
    or less I24.9
  subacute I24.9
 infarction, muscle —*see* Infarct, muscle
 intestine (large) (small) (transient) K55.9
  acute K55.059
   diffuse K55.052
   focal K55.051
   large K55.039
    diffuse K55.032
    focal K55.031
   small K55.019
    diffuse K55.012
    focal K55.011
  chronic K55.1
  due to mesenteric artery insufficiency
    K55.1
 kidney N28.0
 mesenteric, acute —*see also* Ischemia,
   intestine, acute K55.059

Ischemia, ischemic *(Continued)*
 muscle, traumatic T79.6
 myocardium, myocardial (chronic or with a
   stated duration of over 4 weeks) I25.9
  acute, without myocardial infarction
    I51.3
  silent (asymptomatic) I25.6
  transient of newborn P29.4
 renal N28.0
 retina, retinal —*see* Occlusion, artery, retina
 small bowel
  acute K55.019
   diffuse K55.012
   focal K55.011
  chronic K55.1
  due to mesenteric artery insufficiency
    K55.1
 spinal cord G95.11
 subendocardial —*see* Insufficiency,
   coronary
 supply (coronary) —*see also* Angina I25.9
  due to vasospasm I20.1
Ischial spine —*see* condition
Ischialgia —*see* Sciatica
Ischiopagus Q89.4
Ischium, ischial —*see* condition
Ischuria R34
Iselin's disease or osteochondrosis —*see*
   Osteochondrosis, juvenile, metatarsus
Islands of
 parotid tissue in
  lymph nodes Q38.6
  neck structures Q38.6
 submaxillary glands in
  fascia Q38.6
  lymph nodes Q38.6
  neck muscles Q38.6
Islet cell tumor, pancreas D13.7
Isoimmunization NEC —*see also*
  Incompatibility
  affecting management of pregnancy (ABO)
   (with hydrops fetalis) O36.11-•
   anti-A sensitization O36.11-•
   anti-B sensitization O36.19-•
   anti-c sensitization O36.09-•
   anti-C sensitization O36.09-•
   anti-e sensitization O36.09-•
   anti-E sensitization O36.09-•
   Rh NEC O36.09-•
    anti-D antibody O36.01-•
   specified NEC O36.19-•
  newborn P55.9
   with
    hydrops fetalis P56.0
    kernicterus P57.0
   ABO (blood groups) P55.1

Isoimmunization NEC *(Continued)*
 newborn *(Continued)*
  Rhesus (Rh) factor P55.0
  specified type NEC P55.8
Isolation, isolated
 dwelling Z59.8
 family Z63.79
 social Z60.4
Isoleucinosis E71.19
Isomerism atrial appendages (with asplenia or
   polysplenia) Q20.6
Isosporiasis, isosporosis A07.3
Isovaleric acidemia E71.110
Issue of
 medical certificate Z02.79
  for disability determination Z02.71
 repeat prescription (appliance) (glasses)
   (medicinal substance, medicament,
   medicine) Z76.0
  contraception —*see* Contraception
Itch, itching —*see also* Pruritus
 baker's L23.6
 barber's B35.0
 bricklayer's L24.5
 cheese B88.0
 clam digger's B65.3
 coolie B76.9
 copra B88.0
 dew B76.9
 dhobi B35.6
 filarial —*see* Infestation, filarial
 grain B88.0
 grocer's B88.0
 ground B76.9
 harvest B88.0
 jock B35.6
 Malabar B35.5
  beard B35.0
  foot B35.3
  scalp B35.0
 meaning scabies B86
 Norwegian B86
 perianal L29.0
 poultrymen's B88.0
 sarcoptic B86
 scabies B86
 scrub B88.0
 straw B88.0
 swimmer's B65.3
 water B76.9
 winter L29.8
Ivemark's syndrome (asplenia with congenital
   heart disease) Q89.01
Ivory bones Q78.2
Ixodiasis NEC B88.8

J

Jaccoud's syndrome —*see* Arthropathy,
 postrheumatic, chronic
Jackson's
 membrane Q43.3
 paralysis or syndrome G83.89
 veil Q43.3
Jacquet's dermatitis (diaper dermatitis) L22
Jadassohn-Pellizari's disease or anetoderma
 L90.2
Jadassohn's
 blue nevus —*see* Nevus
 intraepidermal epithelioma —*see* Neoplasm,
  skin, benign
Jaffe-Lichtenstein (-Uehlinger) syndrome —*see*
 Dysplasia, fibrous, bone NEC
Jakob-Creutzfeldt disease or syndrome —*see*
 Creutzfeldt-Jakob disease or syndrome
Jaksch-Luzet disease D64.89
Jamaican
 neuropathy G92
 paraplegic tropical ataxic-spastic syndrome
  G92
Janet's disease F48.8
Janiceps Q89.4
Jansky-Bielschowsky amaurotic idiocy
 E75.4
Japanese
 B-type encephalitis A83.0
 river fever A75.3
Jaundice (yellow) R17
 acholuric (familial) (splenomegalic) —*see also*
  Spherocytosis
  acquired D59.8
 breast-milk (inhibitor) P59.3
 catarrhal (acute) B15.9
  with hepatic coma B15.0
 cholestatic (benign) R17
 due to or associated with
  delayed conjugation P59.8
   associated with (due to) preterm
    delivery P59.0
  preterm delivery P59.0
 epidemic (catarrhal) B15.9
  with hepatic coma B15.0
  leptospiral A27.0
  spirochetal A27.0
 familial nonhemolytic (congenital) (Gilbert)
  E80.4
  Crigler-Najjar E80.5
 febrile (acute) B15.9
  with hepatic coma B15.0
  leptospiral A27.0
  spirochetal A27.0
 hematogenous D59.9
 hemolytic (acquired) D59.9
  congenital —*see* Spherocytosis

Jaundice *(Continued)*
 hemorrhagic (acute) (leptospiral)
  (spirochetal) A27.0
 infectious (acute) (subacute) B15.9
  with hepatic coma B15.0
  leptospiral A27.0
  spirochetal A27.0
 leptospiral (hemorrhagic) A27.0
 malignant (without coma) K72.90
  with coma K72.91
 neonatal —*see* Jaundice, newborn
 newborn P59.9
  due to or associated with
   ABO
    antibodies P55.1
    incompatibility, maternal/fetal
     P55.1
    isoimmunization P55.1
   absence or deficiency of enzyme
    system for bilirubin conjugation
    (congenital) P59.8
   bleeding P58.1
   breast milk inhibitors to conjugation
    P59.3
    associated with preterm delivery
     P59.0
   bruising P58.0
   Crigler-Najjar syndrome E80.5
   delayed conjugation P59.8
    associated with preterm delivery
     P59.0
   drugs or toxins
    given to newborn P58.42
    transmitted from mother P58.41
   excessive hemolysis P58.9
    due to
     bleeding P58.1
     bruising P58.0
     drugs or toxins
      given to newborn P58.42
      transmitted from mother P58.41
     infection P58.2
     polycythemia P58.3
     swallowed maternal blood P58.5
    specified type NEC P58.8
   galactosemia E74.21
   Gilbert syndrome E80.4
   hemolytic disease P55.9
    ABO isoimmunization P55.1
    Rh isoimmunization P55.0
    specified NEC P55.8
   hepatocellular damage P59.20
    specified NEC P59.29
   hereditary hemolytic anemia P58.8
   hypothyroidism, congenital E03.1
   incompatibility, maternal/fetal NOS
    P55.9
   infection P58.2

Jaundice *(Continued)*
 newborn *(Continued)*
  due to or associated with *(Continued)*
   inspissated bile syndrome P59.1
   isoimmunization NOS P55.9
   mucoviscidosis E84.9
   polycythemia P58.3
   preterm delivery P59.0
   Rh
    antibodies P55.0
    incompatibility, maternal/fetal P55.0
    isoimmunization P55.0
   specified cause NEC P59.8
   swallowed maternal blood P58.5
   spherocytosis (congenital) D58.0
  nonhemolytic congenital familial (Gilbert)
   E80.4
  nuclear, newborn —*see also* Kernicterus of
   newborn P57.9
  obstructive —*see also* Obstruction, bile duct
   K83.1
  post-immunization —*see* Hepatitis, viral,
   type, B
  post-transfusion —*see* Hepatitis, viral, type, B
  regurgitation —*see also* Obstruction, bile duct
   K83.1
  serum (homologous) (prophylactic)
   (therapeutic) —*see* Hepatitis, viral,
   type, B
  spirochetal (hemorrhagic) A27.0
  symptomatic R17
   newborn P59.9
Jaw —*see* condition
Jaw-winking phenomenon or syndrome Q07.8
Jealousy
 alcoholic F10.988
 childhood F93.8
 sibling F93.8
Jejunitis —*see* Enteritis
Jejunostomy status Z93.4
Jejunum, jejunal —*see* condition
Jensen's disease —*see* Inflammation,
 chorioretinal, focal, juxtapapillary
Jerks, myoclonic G25.3
Jervell-Lange-Nielsen syndrome I45.81
Jeune's disease Q77.2
Jigger disease B88.1
Job's syndrome (chronic granulomatous
 disease) D71
Joint —*see also* condition
 mice —*see* Loose, body, joint
  knee M23.4-●
Jordan's anomaly or syndrome D72.0
Joseph-Diamond-Blackfan anemia (congenital
 hypoplastic) D61.01
Jungle yellow fever A95.0
Jüngling's disease —*see* Sarcoidosis
Juvenile —*see* condition

K

Kahler's disease C90.0-●
Kakke E51.11
Kala-azar B55.0
Kallmann's syndrome E23.0
Kanner's syndrome (autism) —see Psychosis, childhood
Kaposi's
  dermatosis (xeroderma pigmentosum) Q82.1
  lichen ruber L44.0
    acuminatus L44.0
  sarcoma
    colon C46.4
    connective tissue C46.1
    gastrointestinal organ C46.4
    lung C46.5-●
    lymph node (multiple) C46.3
    palate (hard) (soft) C46.2
    rectum C46.4
    skin (multiple sites) C46.0
    specified site NEC C46.7
    stomach C46.4
    unspecified site C46.9
  varicelliform eruption B00.0
    vaccinia T88.1
Kartagener's syndrome or triad (sinusitis, bronchiectasis, situs inversus) Q89.3
Karyotype
  with abnormality except iso (Xq) Q96.2
  45,X Q96.0
  46,X
    iso (Xq) Q96.1
  46,XX Q98.3
    with streak gonads Q50.32
    hermaphrodite (true) Q99.1
    male Q98.3
  46,XY
    with streak gonads Q56.1
    female Q97.3
    hermaphrodite (true) Q99.1
  47,XXX Q97.0
  47,XXY Q98.0
  47,XYY Q98.5
Kaschin-Beck disease —see Disease, Kaschin-Beck
Katayama's disease or fever B65.2
Kawasaki's syndrome M30.3
Kayser-Fleischer ring (cornea) (pseudosclerosis) H18.04-●
Kaznelson's syndrome (congenital hypoplastic anemia) D61.01
Kearns-Sayre syndrome H49.81-●
Kedani fever A75.3
Kelis L91.0
Kelly (-Patterson) syndrome (sideropenic dysphagia) D50.1
Keloid, cheloid L91.0
  acne L73.0
  Addison's L94.0
  cornea —see Opacity, cornea
  Hawkin's L91.0
  scar L91.0
Keloma L91.0
Kenya fever A77.1
Keratectasia —see also Ectasia, cornea
  congenital Q13.4
Keratinization of alveolar ridge mucosa
  excessive K13.23
  minimal K13.22
Keratinized residual ridge mucosa
  excessive K13.23
  minimal K13.22
Keratitis (nodular) (nonulcerative) (simple) (zonular) H16.9
  with ulceration (central) (marginal) (perforated) (ring) —see Ulcer, cornea
  actinic —see Photokeratitis
  arborescens (herpes simplex) B00.52
  areolar H16.11-●
  bullosa H16.8

Keratitis (Continued)
  deep H16.309
    specified type NEC H16.399
  dendritic (a) (herpes simplex) B00.52
  disciform (is) (herpes simplex) B00.52
    varicella B01.81
  filamentary H16.12-●
  gonococcal (congenital or prenatal) A54.33
  herpes, herpetic (simplex) B00.52
    zoster B02.33
  in (due to)
    acanthamebiasis B60.13
    adenovirus B30.0
    exanthema —see also Exanthem B09
    herpes (simplex) virus B00.52
    measles B05.81
    syphilis A50.31
    tuberculosis A18.52
    zoster B02.33
  interstitial (nonsyphilitic) H16.30-●
    diffuse H16.32-●
    herpes, herpetic (simplex) B00.52
      zoster B02.33
    sclerosing H16.33-●
    specified type NEC H16.39-●
    syphilitic (congenital) (late) A50.31
    tuberculous A18.52
  macular H16.11-●
  nummular H16.11-●
  oyster shuckers' H16.8
  parenchymatous —see Keratitis, interstitial
  petrificans H16.8
  postmeasles B05.81
  punctata
    leprosa A30.9 [H16.14-●]
    syphilitic (profunda) A50.31
  punctate H16.14-●
  purulent H16.8
  rosacea L71.8
  sclerosing H16.33-●
  specified type NEC H16.8
  stellate H16.11-●
  striate H16.11-●
  superficial H16.10-●
    with conjunctivitis —see Keratoconjunctivitis
    due to light —see Photokeratitis
  suppurative H16.8
  syphilitic (congenital) (prenatal) A50.31
  trachomatous A71.1
    sequelae B94.0
  tuberculous A18.52
  vesicular H16.8
  xerotic —see also Keratomalacia H16.8
    vitamin A deficiency E50.4
Keratoacanthoma L85.8
Keratocele —see Descemetocele
Keratoconjunctivitis H16.20-●
  Acanthamoeba B60.13
  adenoviral B30.0
  epidemic B30.0
  exposure H16.21-●
  herpes, herpetic (simplex) B00.52
    zoster B02.33
  in exanthema —see also Exanthem B09
  infectious B30.0
  lagophthalmic —see Keratoconjunctivitis, specified type NEC
  neurotrophic H16.23-●
  phlyctenular H16.25-●
  postmeasles B05.81
  shipyard B30.0
  sicca (Sjogren's) M35.0-●
    not Sjogren's H16.22-●
  specified type NEC H16.29-●
  tuberculous (phlyctenular) A18.52
  vernal H16.26-●
Keratoconus H18.60-●
  congenital Q13.4
  stable H18.61-●
  unstable H18.62-●

Keratocyst (dental) (odontogenic) —see Cyst, calcifying odontogenic
Keratoderma, keratodermia (congenital) (palmaris et plantaris) (symmetrical) Q82.8
  acquired L85.1
    in diseases classified elsewhere L86
  climactericum L85.1
  gonococcal A54.89
  gonorrheal A54.89
  punctata L85.2
  Reiter's —see Reiter's disease
Keratodermatocele —see Descemetocele
Keratoglobus H18.79
  congenital Q15.8
    with glaucoma Q15.0
Keratohemia —see Pigmentation, cornea, stromal
Keratoiritis —see also Iridocyclitis
  syphilitic A50.39
  tuberculous A18.54
Keratoma L57.0
  palmaris and plantaris hereditarium Q82.8
  senile L57.0
Keratomalacia H18.44-●
  vitamin A deficiency E50.4
Keratomegaly Q13.4
Keratomycosis B49
  nigrans, nigricans (palmaris) B36.1
Keratopathy H18.9
  band H18.42-●
  bullous H18.1-●
  bullous (aphakic), following cataract surgery H59.01-●
Keratoscleritis, tuberculous A18.52
Keratosis L57.0
  actinic L57.0
  arsenical L85.8
  congenital, specified NEC Q80.8
  female genital NEC N94.89
  follicularis Q82.8
    acquired L11.0
    congenita Q82.8
    et parafollicularis in cutem penetrans L87.0
    spinulosa (decalvans) Q82.8
    vitamin A deficiency E50.8
  gonococcal A54.89
  male genital (external) N50.89
  nigricans L83
  obturans, external ear (canal) —see Cholesteatoma, external ear
  palmaris et plantaris (inherited) (symmetrical) Q82.8
    acquired L85.1
  penile N48.89
  pharynx J39.2
  pilaris, acquired L85.8
  punctata (palmaris et plantaris) L85.2
  scrotal N50.89
  seborrheic L82.1
    inflamed L82.0
  senile L57.0
  solar L57.0
  tonsillaris J35.8
  vagina N89.4
  vegetans Q82.8
  vitamin A deficiency E50.8
  vocal cord J38.3
Kerato-uveitis —see Iridocyclitis
Kerion (celsi) B35.0
Kernicterus of newborn (not due to isoimmunization) P57.9
  due to isoimmunization (conditions in P55.0-P55.9) P57.0
  specified type NEC P57.8
Kerunoparalysis T75.09
Keshan disease E59
Ketoacidosis E87.2
  diabetic —see Diabetes, by type, with ketoacidosis
Ketonuria R82.4

▶ New   ⇥ Revised   ~~deleted~~ Deleted   ● Use Additional Character(s)

Ketosis NEC E88.89
  diabetic —*see* Diabetes, by type, with
    ketoacidosis
Kew Garden fever A79.1
Kidney —*see* condition
Kienböck's disease —*see also* Osteochondrosis,
    juvenile, hand, carpal lunate
  adult M93.1
Kimmelstiel (-Wilson) disease —*see* Diabetes,
    Kimmelstiel (-Wilson) disease
Kimura disease D21.9
  specified site (*see* Neoplasm, connective
    tissue benign)
Kink, kinking
  artery I77.1
  hair (acquired) L67.8
  ileum or intestine —*see* Obstruction,
    intestine
  Lane's —*see* Obstruction, intestine
  organ or site, congenital NEC —*see* Anomaly,
    by site
  ureter (pelvic junction) N13.5
    with
      hydronephrosis N13.1
        with infection N13.6
      pyelonephritis (chronic) N11.1
    congenital Q62.39
  vein(s) I87.8
    caval I87.1
    peripheral I87.1
Kinnier Wilson's disease (hepatolenticular
    degeneration) E83.01
Kissing spine M48.20
  cervical region M48.22
  cervicothoracic region M48.23
  lumbar region M48.26
  lumbosacral region M48.27
  occipito-atlanto-axial region M48.21
  thoracic region M48.24
  thoracolumbar region M48.25
Klatskin's tumor C24.0
Klauder's disease A26.8
Klebs' disease —*see also* Glomerulonephritis
    N05.-●
Klebsiella (K.) pneumoniae, as cause of
    disease classified elsewhere B96.1
Klein (e)-Levin syndrome G47.13
Kleptomania F63.2
Klinefelter's syndrome Q98.4
  karyotype 47,XXY Q98.0
  male with more than two X chromosomes
    Q98.1
Klippel-Feil deficiency, disease, or syndrome
    (brevicollis) Q76.1
Klippel's disease I67.2
Klippel-Trenaunay (-Weber) syndrome
    Q87.2
Klumpke (-Déjerine) palsy, paralysis (birth)
    (newborn) P14.1
Knee —*see* condition
Knock knee (acquired) M21.06-●
  congenital Q74.1

Knot(s)
  intestinal, syndrome (volvulus) K56.2
  surfer S89.8-●
  umbilical cord (true) O69.2
Knotting (of)
  hair L67.8
  intestine K56.2
Knuckle pad (Garrod's) M72.1
Koch's
  infection —*see* Tuberculosis
  relapsing fever A68.9
Koch-Weeks' conjunctivitis —*see*
    Conjunctivitis, acute, mucopurulent
Köebner's syndrome Q81.8
Köenig's disease (osteochondritis dissecans) —
    see Osteochondritis, dissecans
Köhler-Pellegrini-Steida disease or syndrome
    (calcification, knee joint) —*see* Bursitis,
    tibial collateral
Köhler's disease
  patellar —*see* Osteochondrosis, juvenile,
    patella
  tarsal navicular —*see* Osteochondrosis,
    juvenile, tarsus
Koilonychia L60.3
  congenital Q84.6
Kojevnikov's, epilepsy —*see* Kozhevnikof's
    epilepsy
Koplik's spots B05.9
Kopp's asthma E32.8
Korsakoff's (Wernicke) disease, psychosis or
    syndrome (alcoholic) F10.96
  with dependence F10.26
  drug-induced
    due to drug abuse —*see* Abuse, drug, by
      type, with amnestic disorder
    due to drug dependence —*see* Dependence,
      drug, by type, with amnestic disorder
  nonalcoholic F04
Korsakov's disease, psychosis or syndrome —
    see Korsakoff's disease
Korsakow's disease, psychosis or syndrome —
    see Korsakoff's disease
Kostmann's disease or syndrome (infantile
    genetic agranulocytosis) —*see*
    Agranulocytosis
Kozhevnikof's epilepsy G40.109
  intractable G40.119
    with status epilepticus G40.111
    without status epilepticus G40.119
  not intractable G40.109
    with status epilepticus G40.101
    without status epilepticus G40.109
Krabbe's
  disease E75.23
  syndrome, congenital muscle hypoplasia
    Q79.8
Kraepelin-Morel disease —*see* Schizophrenia
Kraft-Weber-Dimitri disease Q85.8
Kraurosis
  ani K62.89
  penis N48.0

Kraurosis (*Continued*)
  vagina N89.8
  vulva N90.4
Kreotoxism A05.9
Krukenberg's
  spindle —*see* Pigmentation, cornea, posterior
  tumor C79.6-●
Kufs' disease E75.4
Kugelberg-Welander disease G12.1
Kuhnt-Junius degeneration —*see also*
    Degeneration, macula H35.32-●
Kümmell's disease or spondylitis —*see*
    Spondylopathy, traumatic
Kupffer cell sarcoma C22.3
Kuru A81.81
Kussmaul's
  disease M30.0
  respiration E87.2
    in diabetic acidosis —*see* Diabetes, by type,
      with ketoacidosis
Kwashiorkor E40
  marasmic, marasmus type E42
Kyasanur Forest disease A98.2
Kyphoscoliosis, kyphoscoliotic (acquired) —
    see also Scoliosis M41.9
  congenital Q67.5
  heart (disease) I27.1
  sequelae of rickets E64.3
  tuberculous A18.01
Kyphosis, kyphotic (acquired) M40.209
  cervical region M40.202
  cervicothoracic region M40.203
  congenital Q76.419
    cervical region Q76.412
    cervicothoracic region Q76.413
    occipito-atlanto-axial region Q76.411
    thoracic region Q76.414
    thoracolumbar region Q76.415
  Morquio-Brailsford type (spinal) —*see also*
    subcategory M49.8 E76.219
  postlaminectomy M96.3
  postradiation therapy M96.2
  postural (adolescent) M40.00
    cervicothoracic region M40.03
    thoracic region M40.04
    thoracolumbar region M40.05
  secondary NEC M40.10
    cervical region M40.12
    cervicothoracic region M40.13
    thoracic region M40.14
    thoracolumbar region M40.15
  sequelae of rickets E64.3
  specified type NEC M40.299
    cervical region M40.292
    cervicothoracic region M40.293
    thoracic region M40.294
    thoracolumbar region M40.295
  syphilitic, congenital A50.56
  thoracic region M40.204
  thoracolumbar region M40.205
  tuberculous A18.01
Kyrle disease L87.0

L

Labia, labium —*see* condition
Labile
  blood pressure R09.89
  vasomotor system I73.9
Labioglossal paralysis G12.29
Labium leporinum —*see* Cleft, lip
Labor —*see* Delivery
Labored breathing —*see* Hyperventilation
Labyrinthitis (circumscribed) (destructive)
  (diffuse) (inner ear) (latent) (purulent)
  (suppurative) (*see also* subcategory)
  H83.0
  syphilitic A52.79
Laceration
  with abortion —*see* Abortion, by type,
    complicated by laceration of pelvic
    organs
  abdomen, abdominal
    wall S31.119
      with
        foreign body S31.129
        penetration into peritoneal cavity
          S31.619
          with foreign body S31.629
      epigastric region S31.112
        with
          foreign body S31.122
          penetration into peritoneal cavity
            S31.612
            with foreign body S31.622
      left
        lower quadrant S31.114
          with
            foreign body S31.124
            penetration into peritoneal cavity
              S31.614
              with foreign body S31.624
        upper quadrant S31.111
          with
            foreign body S31.121
            penetration into peritoneal cavity
              S31.611
              with foreign body S31.621
      periumbilic region S31.115
        with
          foreign body S31.125
          penetration into peritoneal cavity
            S31.615
            with foreign body S31.625
      right
        lower quadrant S31.113
          with
            foreign body S31.123
            penetration into peritoneal cavity
              S31.613
              with foreign body S31.623
        upper quadrant S31.110
          with
            foreign body S31.120
           penetration into peritoneal cavity
              S31.610
              with foreign body S31.620
  accidental, complicating surgery —*see*
    Complications, surgical, accidental
    puncture or laceration
  Achilles tendon S86.02-●
  adrenal gland S37.813
  alveolar (process) —*see* Laceration, oral cavity
  ankle S91.01-●
    with
      foreign body S91.02-●
  antecubital space —*see* Laceration, elbow
  anus (sphincter) S31.831
    with
      ectopic or molar pregnancy O08.6
      foreign body S31.832
    complicating delivery —*see* Delivery,
      complicated, by, laceration, anus
      (sphincter)

Laceration (*Continued*)
  anus (*Continued*)
    following ectopic or molar pregnancy
      O08.6
    nontraumatic, nonpuerperal —*see* Fissure,
      anus
  arm (upper) S41.11-●
    with foreign body S41.12-●
    lower —*see* Laceration, forearm
  auditory canal (external) (meatus) —*see*
    Laceration, ear
  auricle, ear —*see* Laceration, ear
  axilla —*see* Laceration, arm
  back —*see also* Laceration, thorax, back
    lower S31.010
      with
        foreign body S31.020
          with penetration into
            retroperitoneal space S31.021
        penetration into retroperitoneal space
          S31.011
  bile duct S36.13
  bladder S37.23
    with ectopic or molar pregnancy O08.6
    following ectopic or molar pregnancy
      O08.6
    obstetrical trauma O71.5
  blood vessel —*see* Injury, blood vessel
  bowel —*see also* Laceration, intestine
    with ectopic or molar pregnancy O08.6
    complicating abortion —*see* Abortion,
      by type, complicated by, specified
      condition NEC
    following ectopic or molar pregnancy
      O08.6
    obstetrical trauma O71.5
  brain (any part) (cortex) (diffuse)
    (membrane) —*see also* Injury,
    intracranial, diffuse
    during birth P10.8
      with hemorrhage P10.1
    focal —*see* Injury, intracranial, focal brain
      injury
  brainstem S06.38-●
  breast S21.01-●
    with foreign body S21.02-●
  broad ligament S37.893
    with ectopic or molar pregnancy O08.6
    following ectopic or molar pregnancy
      O08.6
    laceration syndrome N83.8
    obstetrical trauma O71.6
    syndrome (laceration) N83.8
  buttock S31.801
    with foreign body S31.802
    left S31.821
      with foreign body S31.822
    right S31.811
      with foreign body S31.812
  calf —*see* Laceration, leg
  canaliculus lacrimalis —*see* Laceration,
    eyelid
  canthus, eye —*see* Laceration, eyelid
  capsule, joint —*see* Sprain
  causing eversion of cervix uteri (old) N86
  central (perineal), complicating delivery
    O70.9
  cerebellum, traumatic S06.37-●
  cerebral S06.33-●
    during birth P10.8
      with hemorrhage P10.1
    left side S06.32-●
    right side S06.31-●
  cervix (uteri)
    with ectopic or molar pregnancy O08.6
    following ectopic or molar pregnancy
      O08.6
    nonpuerperal, nontraumatic N88.1
    obstetrical trauma (current) O71.3
    old (postpartal) N88.1
    traumatic S37.63

Laceration (*Continued*)
  cheek (external) S01.41-●
    with foreign body S01.42-●
    internal —*see* Laceration, oral cavity
  chest wall —*see* Laceration, thorax
  chin —*see* Laceration, head, specified site
    NEC
  chordae tendinae NEC I51.1
    concurrent with acute myocardial
      infarction —*see* Infarct, myocardium
    following acute myocardial infarction
      (current complication) I23.4
  clitoris —*see* Laceration, vulva
  colon —*see* Laceration, intestine, large,
    colon
  common bile duct S36.13
  cortex (cerebral) —*see* Injury, intracranial,
    diffuse
  costal region —*see* Laceration, thorax
  cystic duct S36.13
  diaphragm S27.803
  digit(s)
    foot —*see* Laceration, toe
    hand —*see* Laceration, finger
  duodenum S36.430
  ear (canal) (external) S01.31-●
    with foreign body S01.32-●
    drum S09.2-●
  elbow S51.01-●
    with
      foreign body S51.02-●
  epididymis —*see* Laceration, testis
  epigastric region —*see* Laceration, abdomen,
    wall, epigastric region
  esophagus K22.8
    traumatic
      cervical S11.21
        with foreign body S11.22
      thoracic S27.813
  eye (ball) S05.3-●
    with prolapse or loss of intraocular tissue
      S05.2-●
    penetrating S05.6-●
  eyebrow —*see* Laceration, eyelid
  eyelid S01.11-●
    with foreign body S01.12-●
  face NEC —*see* Laceration, head, specified
    site NEC
  fallopian tube S37.539
    bilateral S37.532
    unilateral S37.531
  finger(s) S61.219
    with
      damage to nail S61.319
        with
          foreign body S61.329
      foreign body S61.229
    index S61.218
      with
        damage to nail S61.318
          with
            foreign body S61.328
        foreign body S61.228
      left S61.211
        with
          damage to nail S61.311
            with
              foreign body S61.321
          foreign body S61.221
      right S61.210
        with
          damage to nail S61.310
            with
              foreign body S61.320
          foreign body S61.220
    little S61.218
      with
        damage to nail S61.318
          with
            foreign body S61.328
        foreign body S61.228

▶ New   ⇒ Revised   ~~deleted~~ Deleted   ● Use Additional Character(s)

Laceration (Continued)
  finger (Continued)
    little (Continued)
      left S61.217
        with
          damage to nail S61.317
            with
              foreign body S61.327
          foreign body S61.227
      right S61.216
        with
          damage to nail S61.316
            with
              foreign body S61.326
          foreign body S61.226
    middle S61.218
      with
        damage to nail S61.318
          with
            foreign body S61.328
        foreign body S61.228
      left S61.213
        with
          damage to nail S61.313
            with
              foreign body S61.323
          foreign body S61.223
      right S61.212
        with
          damage to nail S61.312
            with
              foreign body S61.322
          foreign body S61.222
    ring S61.218
      with
        damage to nail S61.318
          with
            foreign body S61.328
        foreign body S61.228
      left S61.215
        with
          damage to nail S61.315
            with
              foreign body S61.325
          foreign body S61.225
      right S61.214
        with
          damage to nail S61.314
            with
              foreign body S61.324
          foreign body S61.224
  flank S31.119
    with foreign body S31.129
  foot (except toe(s) alone) S91.319
    with foreign body S91.329
    left S91.312
      with foreign body S91.322
    right S91.311
      with foreign body S91.321
    toe —see Laceration, toe
  forearm S51.819
    with
      foreign body S51.829
    elbow only —see Laceration,
      elbow
    left S51.812
      with
        foreign body S51.822
    right S51.811
      with
        foreign body S51.821
  forehead S01.81
    with foreign body S01.82
  fourchette O70.0
    with ectopic or molar pregnancy
      O08.6
    complicating delivery O70.0
    following ectopic or molar pregnancy
      O08.6
  gallbladder S36.123

Laceration (Continued)
  genital organs, external
    female S31.512
      with foreign body S31.522
      vagina —see Laceration, vagina
      vulva —see Laceration, vulva
    male S31.511
      with foreign body S31.521
      penis —see Laceration, penis
      scrotum —see Laceration, scrotum
      testis —see Laceration, testis
  groin —see Laceration, abdomen, wall
  gum —see Laceration, oral cavity
  hand S61.419
    with
      foreign body S61.429
    finger —see Laceration, finger
    left S61.412
      with
        foreign body S61.422
    right S61.411
      with
        foreign body S61.421
    thumb —see Laceration, thumb
  head S01.91
    with foreign body S01.92
    cheek —see Laceration, cheek
    ear —see Laceration, ear
    eyelid —see Laceration, eyelid
    lip —see Laceration, lip
    nose —see Laceration, nose
    oral cavity —see Laceration, oral
      cavity
    scalp S01.01
      with foreign body S01.02
    specified site NEC S01.81
      with foreign body S01.82
    temporomandibular area —see Laceration,
      cheek
  heart —see Injury, heart, laceration
  heel —see Laceration, foot
  hepatic duct S36.13
  hip S71.019
    with foreign body S71.029
    left S71.012
      with foreign body S71.022
    right S71.011
      with foreign body S71.021
  hymen —see Laceration, vagina
  hypochondrium —see Laceration, abdomen,
    wall
  hypogastric region —see Laceration,
    abdomen, wall
  ileum S36.438
  inguinal region —see Laceration, abdomen,
    wall
  instep —see Laceration, foot
  internal organ —see Injury, by site
  interscapular region —see Laceration, thorax,
    back
  intestine
    large
      colon S36.539
        ascending S36.530
        descending S36.532
        sigmoid S36.533
        specified site NEC S36.538
      rectum S36.63
        transverse S36.531
    small S36.439
      duodenum S36.430
      specified site NEC S36.438
  intra-abdominal organ S36.93
    intestine —see Laceration, intestine
    liver —see Laceration, liver
    pancreas —see Laceration, pancreas
    peritoneum S36.81
    specified site NEC S36.893
    spleen —see Laceration, spleen
    stomach —see Laceration, stomach

Laceration (Continued)
  intracranial NEC —see also Injury,
    intracranial, diffuse
    birth injury P10.9
  jaw —see Laceration, head, specified site NEC
  jejunum S36.438
  joint capsule —see Sprain, by site
  kidney S37.03-●
    major (greater than 3 cm) (massive)
      (stellate) S37.06-●
    minor (less than 1 cm) S37.04-●
    moderate (1 to 3 cm) S37.05-●
    multiple S37.06-●
  knee S81.01-●
    with foreign body S81.02-●
  labium (majus) (minus) —see Laceration,
    vulva
  lacrimal duct —see Laceration, eyelid
  large intestine —see Laceration, intestine,
    large
  larynx S11.011
    with foreign body S11.012
  leg (lower) S81.819
    with foreign body S81.829
    foot —see Laceration, foot
    knee —see Laceration, knee
    left S81.812
      with foreign body S81.822
    right S81.811
      with foreign body S81.821
    upper —see Laceration, thigh
  ligament —see Sprain
  lip S01.511
    with foreign body S01.521
  liver S36.113
    major (stellate) S36.116
    minor S36.114
    moderate S36.115
  loin —see Laceration, abdomen, wall
  lower back —see Laceration, back, lower
  lumbar region —see Laceration, back, lower
  lung S27.339
    bilateral S27.332
    unilateral S27.331
  malar region —see Laceration, head, specified
    site NEC
  mammary —see Laceration, breast
  mastoid region —see Laceration, head,
    specified site NEC
  meninges —see Injury, intracranial, diffuse
  meniscus —see Tear, meniscus
  mesentery S36.893
  mesosalpinx S37.893
  mouth —see Laceration, oral cavity
  muscle —see Injury, muscle, by site,
    laceration
  nail
    finger —see Laceration, finger, with
      damage to nail
    toe —see Laceration, toe, with damage to nail
  nasal (septum) (sinus) —see Laceration, nose
  nasopharynx —see Laceration, head, specified
    site NEC
  neck S11.91
    with foreign body S11.92
    involving
      cervical esophagus S11.21
        with foreign body S11.22
      larynx —see Laceration, larynx
      pharynx —see Laceration, pharynx
      thyroid gland —see Laceration, thyroid
        gland
      trachea —see Laceration, trachea
    specified site NEC S11.81
      with foreign body S11.82
  nerve —see Injury, nerve
  nose (septum) (sinus) S01.21
    with foreign body S01.22
  ocular NOS S05.3-●
    adnexa NOS S01.11-●

Laceration (Continued)
    oral cavity S01.512
        with foreign body S01.522
    orbit (eye) —see Wound, open, ocular, orbit
    ovary S37.439
        bilateral S37.432
        unilateral S37.431
    palate —see Laceration, oral cavity
    palm —see Laceration, hand
    pancreas S36.239
        body S36.231
            major S36.261
            minor S36.241
            moderate S36.251
        head S36.230
            major S36.260
            minor S36.240
            moderate S36.250
        major S36.269
        minor S36.249
        moderate S36.259
        tail S36.232
            major S36.262
            minor S36.242
            moderate S36.252
    pelvic S31.010
        with
            foreign body S31.020
                penetration into retroperitoneal cavity
                    S31.021
            penetration into retroperitoneal cavity
                S31.011
        floor —see also Laceration, back, lower
            with ectopic or molar pregnancy O08.6
            complicating delivery O70.1
            following ectopic or molar pregnancy
                O08.6
            old (postpartal) N81.89
        organ S37.93
            with ectopic or molar pregnancy
                O08.6
            adrenal gland S37.813
            bladder S37.23
            fallopian tube —see Laceration, fallopian
                tube
            following ectopic or molar pregnancy
                O08.6
            kidney —see Laceration, kidney
            obstetrical trauma O71.5
            ovary —see Laceration, ovary
            prostate S37.823
            specified site NEC S37.893
            ureter S37.13
            urethra S37.33
            uterus S37.63
    penis S31.21
        with foreign body S31.22
    perineum
        female S31.41
            with
                ectopic or molar pregnancy O08.6
                foreign body S31.42
            during delivery O70.9
                first degree O70.0
                fourth degree O70.3
                second degree O70.1
                third degree —see also Delivery,
                    complicated, by, laceration,
                    perineum, third degree
                    O70.20
            old (postpartal) N81.89
            postpartal N81.89
            secondary (postpartal) O90.1
        male S31.119
            with foreign body S31.129
    periocular area (with or without lacrimal
        passages) —see Laceration, eyelid
    peritoneum S36.893
    periumbilic region —see Laceration,
        abdomen, wall, periumbilic

Laceration (Continued)
    periurethral tissue —see Laceration, urethra
    phalanges
        finger —see Laceration, finger
        toe —see Laceration, toe
    pharynx S11.21
        with foreign body S11.22
    pinna —see Laceration, ear
    popliteal space —see Laceration, knee
    prepuce —see Laceration, penis
    prostate S37.823
    pubic region S31.119
        with foreign body S31.129
    pudendum —see Laceration, genital organs,
        external
    rectovaginal septum —see Laceration, vagina
    rectum S36.63
    retroperitoneum S36.893
    round ligament S37.893
    sacral region —see Laceration, back, lower
    sacroiliac region —see Laceration, back, lower
    salivary gland —see Laceration, oral cavity
    scalp S01.01
        with foreign body S01.02
    scapular region —see Laceration, shoulder
    scrotum S31.31
        with foreign body S31.32
    seminal vesicle S37.893
    shin —see Laceration, leg
    shoulder S41.019
        with foreign body S41.029
        left S41.012
            with foreign body S41.022
        right S41.011
            with foreign body S41.021
    small intestine —see Laceration, intestine,
        small
    spermatic cord —see Laceration, testis
    spinal cord (meninges) —see also Injury,
        spinal cord, by region
        due to injury at birth P11.5
        newborn (birth injury) P11.5
    spleen S36.039
        major (massive) (stellate) S36.032
        moderate S36.031
        superficial (minor) S36.030
    sternal region —see Laceration, thorax, front
    stomach S36.33
    submaxillary region —see Laceration, head,
        specified site NEC
    submental region —see Laceration, head,
        specified site NEC
    subungual
        finger(s) —see Laceration, finger, with
            damage to nail
        toe(s) —see Laceration, toe, with damage
            to nail
    suprarenal gland —see Laceration, adrenal
        gland
    temple, temporal region —see Laceration,
        head, specified site NEC
    temporomandibular area —see Laceration,
        cheek
    tendon —see Injury, muscle, by site,
        laceration
        Achilles S86.02-•
    tentorium cerebelli —see Injury, intracranial,
        diffuse
    testis S31.31
        with foreign body S31.32
    thigh S71.11-•
        with foreign body S71.12-•
    thorax, thoracic (wall) S21.91
        with foreign body S21.92
            back S21.22-•
                with penetration into thoracic cavity
                    S21.42-•
            front S21.12-•
                with penetration into thoracic cavity
                    S21.32-•

Laceration (Continued)
    thorax, thoracic (Continued)
        back S21.21-•
            with
                foreign body S21.22-•
                    with penetration into thoracic
                        cavity S21.42-•
                penetration into thoracic cavity
                    S21.41-•
        breast —see Laceration, breast
        front S21.11-•
            with
                foreign body S21.12-•
                    with penetration into thoracic
                        cavity S21.32-•
                penetration into thoracic cavity
                    S21.31-•
    thumb S61.019
        with
            damage to nail S61.119
                with
                    foreign body S61.129
            foreign body S61.029
        left S61.012
            with
                damage to nail S61.112
                    with
                        foreign body S61.122
                foreign body S61.022
        right S61.011
            with
                damage to nail S61.111
                    with
                        foreign body S61.121
                foreign body S61.021
    thyroid gland S11.11
        with foreign body S11.12
    toe(s) S91.119
        with
            damage to nail S91.219
                with
                    foreign body S91.229
            foreign body S91.129
        great S91.113
            with
                damage to nail S91.213
                    with
                        foreign body S91.223
                foreign body S91.123
            left S91.112
                with
                    damage to nail S91.212
                        with
                            foreign body S91.222
                    foreign body S91.122
            right S91.111
                with
                    damage to nail S91.211
                        with
                            foreign body S91.221
                    foreign body S91.121
        lesser S91.116
            with
                damage to nail S91.216
                    with
                        foreign body S91.226
                foreign body S91.126
            left S91.115
                with
                    damage to nail S91.215
                        with
                            foreign body S91.225
                    foreign body S91.125
            right S91.114
                with
                    damage to nail S91.214
                        with
                            foreign body S91.224
                    foreign body S91.124
    tongue —see Laceration, oral cavity

▶ New   ⇒ Revised   ~~deleted~~ Deleted   • Use Additional Character(s)

Laceration *(Continued)*
 trachea S11.021
  with foreign body S11.022
 tunica vaginalis —*see* Laceration, testis
 tympanum, tympanic membrane —*see*
   Laceration, ear, drum
 umbilical region S31.115
  with foreign body S31.125
 ureter S37.13
 urethra S37.33
  with or following ectopic or molar
    pregnancy O08.6
  obstetrical trauma O71.5
 urinary organ NEC S37.893
 uterus S37.63
  with ectopic or molar pregnancy O08.6
  following ectopic or molar pregnancy O08.6
  nonpuerperal, nontraumatic N85.8
  obstetrical trauma NEC O71.81
  old (postpartal) N85.8
 uvula —*see* Laceration, oral cavity
 vagina S31.41
  with
   ectopic or molar pregnancy O08.6
   foreign body S31.42
  during delivery O71.4
   with perineal laceration —*see* Laceration,
     perineum, female, during delivery
  following ectopic or molar pregnancy
    O08.6
  nonpuerperal, nontraumatic N89.8
  old (postpartal) N89.8
 vas deferens S37.893
 vesical —*see* Laceration, bladder
 vocal cords S11.031
  with foreign body S11.032
 vulva S31.41
  with
   ectopic or molar pregnancy O08.6
   foreign body S31.42
  complicating delivery O70.0
  following ectopic or molar pregnancy
    O08.6
  nonpuerperal, nontraumatic N90.89
  old (postpartal) N90.89
 wrist S61.519
  with
   foreign body S61.529
  left S61.512
   with
    foreign body S61.522
  right S61.511
   with
    foreign body S61.521
Lack of
 achievement in school Z55.3
 adequate
  food Z59.4
  intermaxillary vertical dimension of fully
    erupted teeth M26.36
  sleep Z72.820
 appetite (*see* Anorexia) R63.0
 awareness R41.9
 care
  in home Z74.2
  of infant (at or after birth) T76.02
   confirmed T74.02
 cognitive functions R41.9
 coordination R27.9
  ataxia R27.0
  specified type NEC R27.8
 development (physiological) R62.50
  failure to thrive (child over 28 days old)
    R62.51
   adult R62.7
   newborn P92.6
  short stature R62.52
  specified type NEC R62.59
 energy R53.83
 financial resources Z59.6

Lack of *(Continued)*
 food T73.0
 growth R62.52
 heating Z59.1
 housing (permanent) (temporary) Z59.0
  adequate Z59.1
 learning experiences in childhood Z62.898
 leisure time (affecting life-style) Z73.2
 material resources Z59.9
 memory —*see also* Amnesia
  mild, following organic brain damage
    F06.8
 ovulation N97.0
 parental supervision or control of child
   Z62.0
 person able to render necessary care
   Z74.2
 physical exercise Z72.3
 play experience in childhood Z62.898
 posterior occlusal support M26.57
 relaxation (affecting life-style) Z73.2
 sexual
  desire F52.0
  enjoyment F52.1
 shelter Z59.0
 sleep (adequate) Z72.820
 supervision of child by parent Z62.0
 support, posterior occlusal M26.57
 water T73.1
Lacrimal —*see* condition
Lacrimation, abnormal —*see* Epiphora
Lacrimonasal duct —*see* condition
Lactation, lactating (breast) (puerperal,
   postpartum)
 associated
  cracked nipple O92.13
  retracted nipple O92.03
 defective O92.4
 disorder NEC O92.79
 excessive O92.6
 failed (complete) O92.3
  partial O92.4
 mastitis NEC —*see* Mastitis, obstetric
 mother (care and/or examination) Z39.1
 nonpuerperal N64.3
Lacticemia, excessive E87.2
Lacunar skull Q75.8
Laennec's cirrhosis K70.30
 with ascites K70.31
 nonalcoholic K74.69
Lafora's disease —*see* Epilepsy, generalized,
   idiopathic
Lag, lid (nervous) —*see* Retraction, lid
Lagophthalmos (eyelid) (nervous) H02.209
►bilateral, upper and lower eyelids H02.20C
 cicatricial H02.219
  ►bilateral, upper and lower eyelids H02.21C
   left H02.216
    lower H02.215
    upper H02.214
   ►upper and lower eyelids H02.21B
   right H02.213
    lower H02.212
    upper H02.211
   ►upper and lower eyelids H02.21A
 keratoconjunctivitis —*see* Keratoconjunctivitis
 left H02.206
  lower H02.205
  upper H02.204
 ►upper and lower eyelids H02.20B
 mechanical H02.229
  ►bilateral, upper and lower eyelids H02.22C
   left H02.226
    lower H02.225
    upper H02.224
   ►upper and lower eyelids H02.22B
   right H02.223
    lower H02.222
    upper H02.221
   ►upper and lower eyelids H02.22A

Lagophthalmos *(Continued)*
 paralytic H02.239
  ►bilateral, upper and lower eyelids H02.23C
   left H02.236
    lower H02.235
    upper H02.234
   ►upper and lower eyelids H02.23B
   right H02.233
    lower H02.232
    upper H02.231
   ►upper and lower eyelids H02.23A
 right H02.203
  lower H02.202
  upper H02.201
 ►upper and lower eyelids H02.20A
Laki-Lorand factor deficiency —*see* Defect,
   coagulation, specified type NEC
Lalling F80.0
Lambert-Eaton syndrome —*see* Syndrome,
   Lambert-Eaton
Lambliasis, lambliosis A07.1
Landau-Kleffner syndrome —*see* Epilepsy,
   specified NEC
➡Landouzy-Déjérine dystrophy or
   facioscapulohumeral atrophy G71.02
Landouzy's disease (icterohemorrhagic
   leptospirosis) A27.0
Landry-Guillain-Barré, syndrome or paralysis
   G61.0
Landry's disease or paralysis G61.0
Lane's
 band Q43.3
 kink —*see* Obstruction, intestine
 syndrome K90.2
Langdon Down's syndrome —*see* Trisomy, 21
Lapsed immunization schedule status Z28.3
Large
 baby (regardless of gestational age) (4000g to
   4499g) P08.1
 ear, congenital Q17.1
 physiological cup Q14.2
 stature R68.89
Large-for-dates NEC (infant) (4000g to 4499g)
   P08.1
 affecting management of pregnancy O36.6-●
 exceptionally (4500g or more) P08.0
Larsen-Johansson disease
   orosteochondrosis —*see* Osteochondrosis,
   juvenile, patella
Larsen's syndrome (flattened facies and
   multiple congenital dislocations) Q74.8
Larva migrans
 cutaneous B76.9
  Ancylostoma B76.0
 visceral B83.0
Laryngeal —*see* condition
Laryngismus (stridulus) J38.5
 congenital P28.89
 diphtheritic A36.2
Laryngitis (acute) (edematous) (fibrinous)
   (infective) (infiltrative) (malignant)
   (membranous) (phlegmonous)
   (pneumococcal) (pseudomembranous)
   (septic) (subglottic) (suppurative)
   (ulcerative) J04.0
 with
  influenza, flu, or grippe —*see* Influenza,
    with, laryngitis
  tracheitis (acute) —*see* Laryngotracheitis
 atrophic J37.0
 catarrhal J37.0
 chronic J37.0
  with tracheitis (chronic) J37.1
 diphtheritic A36.2
 due to external agent —*see* Inflammation,
    respiratory, upper, due to
 Hemophilus influenzae J04.0
 H. influenzae J04.0
 hypertrophic J37.0
 influenzal —*see* Influenza, with, respiratory
    manifestations NEC

Laryngitis *(Continued)*
  obstructive J05.0
  sicca J37.0
  spasmodic J05.0
    acute J04.0
  streptococcal J04.0
  stridulous J05.0
  syphilitic (late) A52.73
    congenital A50.59 *[J99]*
      early A50.03 *[J99]*
  tuberculous A15.5
  Vincent's A69.1
Laryngocele (congenital) (ventricular) Q31.3
Laryngofissure J38.7
  congenital Q31.8
Laryngomalacia (congenital) Q31.5
Laryngopharyngitis (acute) J06.0
  chronic J37.0
  due to external agent —*see* Inflammation,
    respiratory, upper, due to
Laryngoplegia J38.00
  bilateral J38.02
  unilateral J38.01
Laryngoptosis J38.7
Laryngospasm J38.5
Laryngostenosis J38.6
Laryngotracheitis (acute) (Infectional)
    (infective) (viral) J04.2
  atrophic J37.1
  catarrhal J37.1
  chronic J37.1
  diphtheritic A36.2
  due to external agent —*see* Inflammation,
    respiratory, upper, due to
  Hemophilus influenzae J04.2
  hypertrophic J37.1
  influenzal —*see* Influenza, with, respiratory
    manifestations NEC
  pachydermic J38.7
  sicca J37.1
  spasmodic J38.5
    acute J05.0
  streptococcal J04.2
  stridulous J38.5
  syphilitic (late) A52.73
    congenital A50.59 *[J99]*
      early A50.03 *[J99]*
  tuberculous A15.5
  Vincent's A69.1
Laryngotracheobronchitis —*see* Bronchitis
Larynx, laryngeal —*see* condition
Lassa fever A96.2
Lassitude —*see* Weakness
Late
  talker R62.0
  walker R62.0
Late effect(s) —*see* Sequelae
Latent —*see* condition
Laterocession —*see* Lateroversion
Lateroflexion —*see* Lateroversion
Lateroversion
  cervix —*see* Lateroversion, uterus
  uterus, uterine (cervix) (postinfectional)
      (postpartal, old) N85.4
    congenital Q51.818
    in pregnancy or childbirth O34.59-●
Lathyrism —*see* Poisoning, food, noxious,
    plant
Launois' syndrome (pituitary gigantism) E22.0
Launois-Bensaude adenolipomatosis E88.89
Laurence-Moon (-Bardet)-Biedl syndrome
    Q87.89
Lax, laxity —*see also* Relaxation
  ligament (ous) —*see also* Disorder, ligament
    familial M35.7
    knee —*see* Derangement, knee
  skin (acquired) L57.4
    congenital Q82.8
Laxative habit F55.2
Lazy leukocyte syndrome D70.8
Lead miner's lung J63.6

Leak, leakage
  air NEC J93.82
    postprocedural J95.812
  amniotic fluid —*see* Rupture, membranes,
    premature
  blood (microscopic), fetal, into maternal
    circulation affecting management
    of pregnancy —*see* Pregnancy,
    complicated by
  cerebrospinal fluid G96.0
    from spinal (lumbar) puncture G97.0
  device, implant or graft —*see also*
    Complications, by site and type,
    mechanical
    arterial graft NEC —*see* Complication,
      cardiovascular device, mechanical,
      vascular
    breast (implant) T85.43
    catheter NEC T85.638
      dialysis (renal) T82.43
        intraperitoneal T85.631
      infusion NEC T82.534
        spinal (epidural) (subdural) T85.630
      urinary T83.038
        cystostomy T83.030
        Hopkins T83.038
        ileostomy T83.038
        indwelling T83.031
        nephrostomy T83.032
        specified NEC T83.038
        urostomy T83.038
    gastrointestinal —*see* Complications,
      prosthetic device, mechanical,
      gastrointestinal device
    genital NEC T83.498
      penile prosthesis (cylinder) (implanted)
        (pump) (resevoir) T83.490
      testicular prosthesis T83.491
    heart NEC —*see* Complication,
      cardiovascular device, mechanical
    joint prosthesis —*see* Complications, joint
      prosthesis, mechanical, specified NEC,
      by site
    ocular NEC —*see* Complications, prosthetic
      device, mechanical, ocular device
    orthopedic NEC —*see* Complication,
      orthopedic, device, mechanical
    persistent air J93.82
    specified NEC T85.638
    urinary NEC —*see also* Complication,
      genitourinary, device, urinary,
      mechanical
      graft T83.23
    vascular NEC —*see* Complication,
      cardiovascular device, mechanical
    ventricular intracranial shunt T85.03
  urine —*see* Incontinence
Leaky heart —*see* Endocarditis
Learning defect (specific) F81.9
Leather bottle stomach C16.9
Leber's
  congenital amaurosis H35.50
  optic atrophy (hereditary) H47.22
Lederer's anemia D59.1
Leeches (external) —*see* Hirudiniasis
Leg —*see* condition
Legg (-Calvé)-Perthes disease, syndrome or
    osteochondrosis M91.1-●
Legionellosis A48.1
  nonpneumonic A48.2
Legionnaires'
  disease A48.1
    nonpneumonic A48.2
  pneumonia A48.1
Leigh's disease G31.82
Leiner's disease L21.1
Leiofibromyoma —*see* Leiomyoma
Leiomyoblastoma —*see* Neoplasm, connective
    tissue, benign
Leiomyofibroma —*see also* Neoplasm,
    connective tissue, benign
  uterus (cervix) (corpus) D25.9

Leiomyoma —*see also* Neoplasm, connective
    tissue, benign
  bizarre —*see* Neoplasm, connective tissue,
    benign
  cellular —*see* Neoplasm, connective tissue,
    benign
  epithelioid —*see* Neoplasm, connective
    tissue, benign
  uterus (cervix) (corpus) D25.9
    intramural D25.1
    submucous D25.0
    subserosal D25.2
  vascular —*see* Neoplasm, connective tissue,
    benign
Leiomyoma, leiomyomatosis (intravascular) —
    see Neoplasm, connective tissue, uncertain
    behavior
Leiomyosarcoma —*see also* Neoplasm,
    connective tissue, malignant
  epithelioid —*see* Neoplasm, connective
    tissue, malignant
  myxoid —*see* Neoplasm, connective tissue,
    malignant
Leishmaniasis B55.9
  American (mucocutaneous) B55.2
    cutaneous B55.1
  Asian Desert B55.1
  Brazilian B55.2
  cutaneous (any type) B55.1
  dermal —*see also* Leishmaniasis, cutaneous
    post-kala-azar B55.0
  eyelid B55.1
  infantile B55.0
  Mediterranean B55.0
  mucocutaneous (American) (New World)
    B55.2
  naso-oral B55.2
  nasopharyngeal B55.2
  old world B55.1
  tegumentaria diffusa B55.1
  visceral B55.0
Leishmanoid, dermal —*see also* Leishmaniasis,
    cutaneous
  post-kala-azar B55.0
Lenegre's disease I44.2
Lengthening, leg —*see* Deformity, limb,
    unequal length
Lennert's lymphoma —*see* Lymphoma,
    Lennert's
Lennox-Gastaut syndrome G40.812
  intractable G40.814
    with status epilepticus G40.813
    without status epilepticus G40.814
  not intractable G40.812
    with status epilepticus G40.811
    without status epilepticus G40.812
Lens —*see* condition
Lenticonus (anterior) (posterior) (congenital)
    Q12.8
Lenticular degeneration, progressive E83.01
Lentiglobus (posterior) (congenital) Q12.8
Lentigo (congenital) L81.4
  maligna —*see also* Melanoma, in situ
    melanoma —*see* Melanoma
Lentivirus, as cause of disease classified
    elsewhere B97.31
Leontiasis
  ossium M85.2
  syphilitic (late) A52.78
    congenital A50.59
Lepothrix A48.8
Lepra —*see* Leprosy
Leprechaunism E34.8
Leprosy A30.-●
  with muscle disorder A30.9 *[M63.80]*
    ankle A30.9 *[M63.87-●]*
    foot A30.9 *[M63.87-●]*
    forearm A30.9 *[M63.83-●]*
    hand A30.9 *[M63.84-●]*
    lower leg A30.9 *[M63.86-●]*
    multiple sites A30.9 *[M63.89]*

Leprosy (Continued)
  with muscle disorder (Continued)
    pelvic region A30.9 [M63.85-•]
    shoulder region A30.9 [M63.81-•]
    specified site NEC A30.9 [M63.88]
    thigh A30.9 [M63.85-•]
    upper arm A30.9 [M63.82-•]
  anesthetic A30.9
  BB A30.3
  BL A30.4
  borderline (infiltrated) (neuritic) A30.3
    lepromatous A30.4
    tuberculoid A30.2
  BT A30.2
  dimorphous (infiltrated) (neuritic) A30.3
  I A30.0
  indeterminate (macular) (neuritic) A30.0
  lepromatous (diffuse) (infiltrated) (macular)
      (neuritic) (nodular) A30.5
  LL A30.5
  macular (early) (neuritic) (simple) A30.9
  maculoanesthetic A30.9
  mixed A30.3
  neural A30.9
  nodular A30.5
  primary neuritic A30.3
  specified type NEC A30.8
  TT A30.1
  tuberculoid (major) (minor) A30.1
Leptocytosis, hereditary D56.9
Leptomeningitis (chronic) (circumscribed)
    (hemorrhagic) (nonsuppurative) —see
    Meningitis
Leptomeningopathy G96.19
Leptospiral —see condition
Leptospirochetal —see condition
Leptospirosis A27.9
  canicola A27.89
  due to Leptospira interrogans serovar
      icterohaemorrhagiae A27.0
  icterohemorrhagica A27.0
  pomona A27.89
  Weil's disease A27.0
Leptus dermatitis B88.0
Leriche's syndrome (aortic bifurcation
    occlusion) I74.09
Leri's pleonosteosis Q78.8
Leri-Weill syndrome Q77.8
Lermoyez' syndrome —see Vertigo, peripheral
    NEC
Lesch-Nyhan syndrome E79.1
Leser-Trélat disease L82.1
  inflamed L82.0
Lesion(s) (nontraumatic)
  abducens nerve —see Strabismus, paralytic,
      sixth nerve
  alveolar process K08.9
  angiocentric immunoproliferative D47.Z9
  anorectal K62.9
  aortic (valve) I35.9
  auditory nerve —see subcategory H93.3
  basal ganglion G25.9
  bile duct —see Disease, bile duct
  biomechanical M99.9
    specified type NEC M99.89
      abdomen M99.89
      acromioclavicular M99.87
      cervical region M99.81
      cervicothoracic M99.81
      costochondral M99.88
      costovertebral M99.88
      head region M99.80
      hip M99.85
      lower extremity M99.86
      lumbar region M99.83
      lumbosacral M99.83
      occipitocervical M99.80
      pelvic region M99.85
      pubic M99.85
      rib cage M99.88
      sacral region M99.84

Lesion (Continued)
  biomechanical (Continued)
    specified type NEC (Continued)
      sacrococcygeal M99.84
      sacroiliac M99.84
      specified NEC M99.89
      sternochondral M99.88
      sternoclavicular M99.87
      thoracic region M99.82
      thoracolumbar M99.82
      upper extremity M99.87
  bladder N32.9
  bone —see Disorder, bone
  brachial plexus G54.0
  brain G93.9
    congenital Q04.9
    vascular I67.9
      degenerative I67.9
      hypertensive I67.4
  buccal cavity K13.79
  calcified —see Calcification
  canthus —see Disorder, eyelid
  carate —see Pinta, lesions
  cardia K31.9
  cardiac —see also Disease, heart I51.9
    congenital Q24.9
    valvular —see Endocarditis
  cauda equina G83.4
  cecum K63.9
  cerebral —see Lesion, brain
  cerebrovascular I67.9
    degenerative I67.9
    hypertensive I67.4
  cervical (nerve) root NEC G54.2
  chiasmal —see Disorder, optic, chiasm
  chorda tympani G51.8
  coin, lung R91.1
  colon K63.9
  combined periodontic - endodontic K05.5
  congenital —see Anomaly, by site
  conjunctiva H11.9
  conus medullaris —see Injury, conus
      medullaris
  coronary artery —see Ischemia, heart
  cranial nerve G52.9
    eighth —see Disorder, ear
    eleventh G52.9
    fifth G50.9
    first G52.0
    fourth —see Strabismus, paralytic, fourth
        nerve
    seventh G51.9
    sixth —see Strabismus, paralytic, sixth nerve
    tenth G52.2
    twelfth G52.3
  cystic —see Cyst
  degenerative —see Degeneration
  duodenum K31.9
  edentulous (alveolar) ridge, associated with
      trauma, due to traumatic occlusion K06.2
  en coup de sabre L94.1
  eyelid —see Disorder, eyelid
  gasserian ganglion G50.8
  gastric K31.9
  gastroduodenal K31.9
  gastrointestinal K63.9
  gingiva, associated with trauma K06.2
  glomerular
    focal and segmental —see also N00-N07
        with fourth character .1 N05.1
    minimal change —see also N00-N07 with
        fourth character .0 N05.0
  heart (organic) —see Disease, heart
  hyperchromic, due to pinta (carate) A67.1
  hyperkeratotic —see Hyperkeratosis
  hypothalamic E23.7
  ileocecal K63.9
  ileum K63.9
  iliohypogastric nerve G57.8-•
  inflammatory —see Inflammation
  intestine K63.9

Lesion (Continued)
  intracerebral —see Lesion, brain
  intrachiasmal (optic) —see Disorder, optic,
      chiasm
  intracranial, space-occupying R90.0
  joint —see Disorder, joint
    sacroiliac (old) M53.3
  keratotic —see Keratosis
  kidney —see Disease, renal
  laryngeal nerve (recurrent) G52.2
  lip K13.0
  liver K76.9
  lumbosacral
    plexus G54.1
    root (nerve) NEC G54.4
  lung (coin) R91.1
  maxillary sinus J32.0
  mitral I05.9
  Morel-Lavallée —see Hematoma,
      by site
  motor cortex NEC G93.89
  mouth K13.79
  nerve G58.9
    femoral G57.2-•
    median G56.1-•
      carpal tunnel syndrome —see Syndrome,
          carpal tunnel
    plantar G57.6-•
    popliteal (lateral) G57.3-•
      medial G57.4-•
    radial G56.3-•
    sciatic G57.0-•
    spinal —see Injury, nerve, spinal
    ulnar G56.2-•
  nervous system, congenital Q07.9
  nonallopathic —see Lesion, biomechanical
  nose (internal) J34.89
  obstructive —see Obstruction
  obturator nerve G57.8-•
  oral mucosa K13.70
  organ or site NEC —see Disease, by site
  osteolytic —see Osteolysis
  peptic K27.9
  periodontal, due to traumatic occlusion K05.5
  pharynx J39.2
  pigment, pigmented (skin) L81.9
  pinta —see Pinta, lesions
  polypoid —see Polyp
  prechiasmal (optic) —see Disorder, optic,
      chiasm
  primary —see also Syphilis, primary A51.0
    carate A67.0
    pinta A67.0
    yaws A66.0
  pulmonary J98.4
    valve I37.9
  pylorus K31.9
  rectosigmoid K63.9
  retina, retinal H35.9
  sacroiliac (joint) (old) M53.3
  salivary gland K11.9
    benign lymphoepithelial K11.8
  saphenous nerve G57.8-•
  sciatic nerve G57.0-•
  secondary —see Syphilis, secondary
  shoulder (region) M75.9-•
    specified NEC M75.8-•
  sigmoid K63.9
  sinus (accessory) (nasal) J34.89
  skin L98.9
    suppurative L08.0
  SLAP S43.43-•
  spinal cord G95.9
    congenital Q06.9
  spleen D73.89
  stomach K31.9
  superior glenoid labrum S43.43-•
  syphilitic —see Syphilis
  tertiary —see Syphilis, tertiary
  thoracic root (nerve) NEC G54.3
  tonsillar fossa J35.9

Lesion *(Continued)*
  tooth, teeth K08.9
    white spot
      chewing surface K02.51
      pit and fissure surface K02.51
      smooth surface K02.61
  traumatic —*see* specific type of injury by site
  tricuspid (valve) I07.9
    nonrheumatic I36.9
  trigeminal nerve G50.9
  ulcerated or ulcerative —*see* Ulcer, skin
  uterus N85.9
▶ vagina N89.8
▶ vulva N90.89
  vagus nerve G52.2
  valvular —*see* Endocarditis
  vascular I99.9
    affecting central nervous system I67.9
    following trauma NEC T14.8
    umbilical cord, complicating delivery
      O69.5
  warty —*see* Verruca
  white spot (tooth)
    chewing surface K02.51
    pit and fissure surface K02.51
    smooth surface K02.61
Lethargic —*see* condition
Lethargy R53.83
Letterer-Siwe's disease C96.0
Leukemia, leukemic C95.9-•
  acute basophilic C94.8-•
  acute bilineal C95.0-•
  acute erythroid C94.0-•
  acute lymphoblastic C91.0-•
  acute megakaryoblastic C94.2-•
  acute megakaryocytic C94.2-•
  acute mixed lineage C95.0-•
  acute monoblastic (monoblastic/monocytic)
    C93.0-•
  acute monocytic (monoblastic/monocytic)
    C93.0-•
  acute myeloblastic (minimal differentiation)
    (with maturation) C92.0-•
➡ acute myeloid, NOS C92.0-•
    with
      11q23-abnormality C92.6-•
      dysplasia of remaining hematopoesis
        and/or myelodysplastic disease in
        its history C92.A-•
      multilineage dysplasia C92.A-•
      variation of MLL-gene C92.6-•
    M6 (a)(b) C94.0-•
    M7 C94.2-•
  acute myelomonocytic C92.5-•
  acute promyelocytic C92.4-•
  adult T-cell (HTLV-1-associated) (acute
    variant) (chronic variant)
    (lymphomatoid variant) (smouldering
    variant) C91.5-•
  aggressive NK-cell C94.8-•
  AML (1/ETO) (M0) (M1) (M2) (without a
    FAB classification) C92.0-•
  AML M3 C92.4-•
  AML M4 (Eo with inv(16) or t(16;16)) C92.5-•
  AML M5 C93.0-•
  AML M5a C93.0-•
  AML M5b C93.0-•
  AML Me with t (15;17) and variants C92.4-•
  atypical chronic myeloid, BCR/ABL-negative
    C92.2-•
  biphenotypic acute C95.0-•
  blast cell C95.0-•
  Burkitt-type, mature B-cell C91.A-•
  chronic lymphocytic, of B-cell type C91.1-•
  chronic monocytic C93.1-•
  chronic myelogenous (Philadelphia
    chromosome (Ph1) positive) (t(9;22))
    (q34;q11) (with crisis of blast cells)
    C92.1-•
  chronic myeloid, BCR/ABL-positive C92.1-•
    atypical, BCR/ABL-negative C92.2-•

Leukemia, leukemic *(Continued)*
  chronic myelomonocytic C93.1-•
  chronic neutrophilic D47.1
  CMML (-1) (-2) (with eosinophilia) C93.1-•
  granulocytic —*see also* Category C92 C92.9-•
  hairy-cell C91.4-•
  juvenile myelomonocytic C93.3-•
  lymphoid C91.9-•
    specified NEC C91.Z-•
  mast cell C94.3-•
  mature B-cell, Burkitt-type C91.A-•
  monocytic (subacute) C93.9-•
    specified NEC C93.Z-•
  myelogenous —*see also* Category
    C92 C92.9-•
  myeloid C92.9-•
    specified NEC C92.Z-•
  plasma cell C90.1-•
  plasmacytic C90.1-•
  prolymphocytic
    of B-cell type C91.3-•
    of T-cell type C91.6-•
  specified NEC C94.8-•
  stem cell, of unclear lineage C95.0-•
  subacute lymphocytic C91.9-•
  T-cell large granular lymphocytic C91.Z-•
  unspecified cell type C95.9-•
    acute C95.0-•
    chronic C95.1-•
Leukemoid reaction —*see also* Reaction,
  leukemoid D72.823-•
Leukoaraiosis (hypertensive) I67.81
Leukoariosis —*see* Leukoaraiosis
Leukocoria —*see* Disorder, globe, degenerated
  condition, leucocoria
Leukocytopenia D72.819
Leukocytosis D72.829
  eosinophilic D72.1
Leukoderma, leukodermia NEC L81.5
  syphilitic A51.39
    late A52.79
Leukodystrophy E75.29
Leukoedema, oral epithelium K13.29
Leukoencephalitis G04.81
  acute (subacute) hemorrhagic G36.1
    postimmunization or postvaccinal
      G04.02
  postinfectious G04.01
  subacute sclerosing A81.1
  van Bogaert's (sclerosing) A81.1
Leukoencephalopathy —*see also*
  Encephalopathy G93.49
  Binswanger's I67.3
  heroin vapor G92
  metachromatic E75.25
  multifocal (progressive) A81.2
  postimmunization and postvaccinal
    G04.02
  progressive multifocal A81.2
  reversible, posterior G93.6
  van Bogaert's (sclerosing) A81.1
  vascular, progressive I67.3
Leukoerythroblastosis D75.9
Leukokeratosis —*see also* Leukoplakia
  mouth K13.21
  nicotina palati K13.24
  oral mucosa K13.21
  tongue K13.21
  vocal cord J38.3
Leukokraurosis vulva (e) N90.4
Leukoma (cornea) —*see also* Opacity, cornea
  adherent H17.0-•
  interfering with central vision —*see* Opacity,
    cornea, central
Leukomalacia, cerebral, newborn P91.2
  periventricular P91.2
Leukomelanopathy, hereditary D72.0
Leukonychia (punctata) (striata) L60.8
  congenital Q84.4
Leukopathia unguium L60.8
  congenital Q84.4

Leukopenia D72.819
  basophilic D72.818
  chemotherapy (cancer) induced D70.1
  congenital D70.0
  cyclic D70.0
  drug induced NEC D70.2
    due to cytoreductive cancer chemotherapy
      D70.1
  eosinophilic D72.818
  familial D70.0
  infantile genetic D70.0
  malignant D70.9
  periodic D70.0
  transitory neonatal P61.5
Leukopenic —*see* condition
Leukoplakia
  anus K62.89
  bladder (postinfectional) N32.89
  buccal K13.21
  cervix (uteri) N88.0
  esophagus K22.8
  gingiva K13.21
  hairy (oral mucosa) (tongue) K13.3
  kidney (pelvis) N28.89
  larynx J38.7
  lip K13.21
  mouth K13.21
  oral epithelium, including tongue (mucosa)
    K13.21
  palate K13.21
  pelvis (kidney) N28.89
  penis (infectional) N48.0
  rectum K62.89
  syphilitic (late) A52.79
  tongue K13.21
  ureter (postinfectional) N28.89
  urethra (postinfectional) N36.8
  uterus N85.8
  vagina N89.4
  vocal cord J38.3
  vulva N90.4
Leukorrhea N89.8
  due to Trichomonas (vaginalis)
    A59.00
  trichomonal A59.00
Leukosarcoma C85.9
Levocardia (isolated) Q24.1
  with situs inversus Q89.3
Levotransposition Q20.5
Lev's disease or syndrome (acquired complete
  heart block) I44.2
Levulosuria —*see* Fructosuria
Levurid L30.2
Lewy body (ies) (dementia) (disease)
  G31.83
➡ Leyden-Moebius dystrophy G71.09
Leydig cell
  carcinoma
    specified site —*see* Neoplasm, malignant,
      by site
    unspecified site
      female C56.9-•
      male C62.9-•
  tumor
    benign
      specified site —*see* Neoplasm, benign,
        by site
      unspecified site
        female D27.-•
        male D29.2-•
    malignant
      specified site —*see* Neoplasm,
        malignant, by site
      unspecified site
        female C56.-•
        male C62.9-•
    specified site —*see* Neoplasm, uncertain
      behavior, by site
    unspecified site
      female D39.1-•
      male D40.1-•

▶ New   ➡ Revised   ~~deleted~~ Deleted   • Use Additional Character(s)

Leydig-Sertoli cell tumor
  specified site —see Neoplasm, benign, by site
  unspecified site
    female D27.-•
    male D29.2-•
LGSIL (Low grade squamous intraepithelial lesion on cytologic smear of)
  anus R85.612
  cervix R87.612
  vagina R87.622
Liar, pathologic F60.2
Libido
  decreased R68.82
Libman-Sacks disease M32.11
Lice (infestation) B85.2
  body (Pediculus corporis) B85.1
  crab B85.3
  head (Pediculus capitis) B85.0
  mixed (classifiable to more than one of the titles B85.0-B85.3) B85.4
  pubic (Phthirus pubis) B85.3
Lichen L28.0
  albus L90.0
    penis N48.0
    vulva N90.4
  amyloidosis E85.4 [L99]
  atrophicus L90.0
    penis N48.0
    vulva N90.4
  congenital Q82.8
  myxedematosus L98.5
  nitidus L44.1
  pilaris Q82.8
    acquired L85.8
  planopilaris L66.1
  planus (chronicus) L43.9
    annularis L43.8
    bullous L43.1
    follicular L66.1
    hypertrophic L43.0
    moniliformis L44.3
    of Wilson L43.9
    specified NEC L43.8
    subacute (active) L43.3
    tropicus L43.3
  ruber
    acuminatus L44.0
    moniliformis L44.3
    planus L43.9
  sclerosus (et atrophicus) L90.0
    penis N48.0
    vulva N90.4
  scrofulosus (primary) (tuberculous) A18.4
  simplex (chronicus) (circumscriptus) L28.0
  striatus L44.2
  urticatus L28.2
Lichenification L28.0
Lichenoides tuberculosis (primary) A18.4
Lichtheim's disease or syndrome —see Degeneration, combined
Lien migrans D73.89
Ligament —see condition
Light
  for gestational age —see Light for dates
  headedness R42
Light-for-dates (infant) P05.00
  with weight of
    499 grams or less P05.01
    500-749 grams P05.02
    750-999 grams P05.03
    1000-1249 grams P05.04
    1250-1499 grams P05.05
    1500-1749 grams P05.06
    1750-1999 grams P05.07
    2000-2499 grams P05.08
    2500 grams and over P05.09
  affecting management of pregnancy O36.59-•
  and small-for-dates —see Small for dates
  specified NEC P05.09

Lightning (effects) (stroke) (struck by) T75.00
  burn —see Burn
  foot E53.8
  shock T75.01
  specified effect NEC T75.09
Lightwood-Albright syndrome N25.89
Lightwood's disease or syndrome (renal tubular acidosis) N25.89
Lignac (-de Toni) (-Fanconi) (-Debré) disease or syndrome E72.09
  with cystinosis E72.04
Ligneous thyroiditis E06.5
Likoff's syndrome I20.8
Limb —see condition
Limbic epilepsy personality syndrome F07.0
Limitation, limited
  activities due to disability Z73.6
  cardiac reserve —see Disease, heart
  eye muscle duction, traumatic —see Strabismus, mechanical
  mandibular range of motion M26.52
Lindau (-von Hippel) disease Q85.8
Line(s)
  Beau's L60.4
  Harris' —see Arrest, epiphyseal
  Hudson's (cornea) —see Pigmentation, cornea, anterior
  Stähli's (cornea) —see Pigmentation, cornea, anterior
Linea corneae senilis —see Change, cornea, senile
Lingua
  geographica K14.1
  nigra (villosa) K14.3
  plicata K14.5
  tylosis K13.29
Lingual —see condition
Linguatulosis B88.8
Linitis (gastric) plastica C16.9
Lip —see condition
Lipedema —see Edema
Lipemia —see also Hyperlipidemia
  retina, retinalis E78.3
Lipidosis E75.6
  cerebral (infantile) (juvenile) (late) E75.4
  cerebroretinal E75.4
  cerebroside E75.22
  cholesterol (cerebral) E75.5
  glycolipid E75.21
  hepatosplenomegalic E78.3
  sphingomyelin —see Niemann-Pick disease or syndrome
  sulfatide E75.29
Lipoadenoma —see Neoplasm, benign, by site
Lipoblastoma —see Lipoma
Lipoblastomatosis —see Lipoma
Lipochondrodystrophy E76.01
Lipochrome histiocytosis (familial) D71
Lipodermatosclerosis —see Varix, leg, with, inflammation
  ulcerated —see Varix, leg, with, ulcer, with inflammation by site
Lipodystrophia progressiva E88.1
Lipodystrophy (progressive) E88.1
  insulin E88.1
  intestinal K90.81
  mesenteric K65.4
Lipofibroma —see Lipoma
Lipofuscinosis, neuronal (with ceroidosis) E75.4
Lipogranuloma, sclerosing L92.8
Lipogranulomatosis E78.89
Lipoid —see also condition
  histiocytosis D76.3
    essential E75.29
  nephrosis N04.9
  proteinosis of Urbach E78.89
Lipoidemia —see Hyperlipidemia
Lipoidosis —see Lipidosis

Lipoma D17.9
  fetal D17.9
  fat cell D17.9
  infiltrating D17.9
  intramuscular D17.9
  pleomorphic D17.9
  site classification
    arms (skin) (subcutaneous) D17.2-•
    connective tissue D17.30
      intra-abdominal D17.5
      intrathoracic D17.4
      peritoneum D17.79
      retroperitoneum D17.79
      specified site NEC D17.39
      spermatic cord D17.6
    face (skin) (subcutaneous) D17.0
    genitourinary organ NEC D17.72
    head (skin) (subcutaneous) D17.0
    intra-abdominal D17.5
    intrathoracic D17.4
    kidney D17.71
    legs (skin) (subcutaneous) D17.2-•
    neck (skin) (subcutaneous) D17.0
    peritoneum D17.79
    retroperitoneum D17.79
    skin D17.30
      specified site NEC D17.39
    specified site NEC D17.79
    spermatic cord D17.6
    subcutaneous D17.30
      specified site NEC D17.39
    trunk (skin) (subcutaneous) D17.1
    unspecified D17.9
  spindle cell D17.9
Lipomatosis E88.2
  dolorosa (Dercum) E88.2
  fetal —see Lipoma
  Launois-Bensaude E88.89
Lipomyoma —see Lipoma
Lipomyxoma —see Lipoma
Lipomyxosarcoma —see Neoplasm, connective tissue, malignant
Lipoprotein metabolism disorder E78.9
Lipoproteinemia E78.5
  broad-beta E78.2
  floating-beta E78.2
  hyper-pre-beta E78.1
Liposarcoma —see also Neoplasm, connective tissue, malignant
  dedifferentiated —see Neoplasm, connective tissue, malignant
  differentiated type —see Neoplasm, connective tissue, malignant
  embryonal —see Neoplasm, connective tissue, malignant
  mixed type —see Neoplasm, connective tissue, malignant
  myxoid —see Neoplasm, connective tissue, malignant
  pleomorphic —see Neoplasm, connective tissue, malignant
  round cell —see Neoplasm, connective tissue, malignant
  well differentiated type —see Neoplasm, connective tissue, malignant
Liposynovitis prepatellaris E88.89
Lipping, cervix N86
Lipschütz disease or ulcer N76.6
Lipuria R82.0
  schistosomiasis (bilharziasis) B65.0
Lisping F80.0
Lissauer's paralysis A52.17
Lissencephalia, lissencephaly Q04.3
Listeriosis, listerellosis A32.9
  congenital (disseminated) P37.2
  cutaneous A32.0
  neonatal, newborn (disseminated) P37.2
  oculoglandular A32.81
  specified NEC A32.89
Lithemia E79.0
Lithiasis —see Calculus

▶ New   ⇒ Revised   deleted Deleted   • Use Additional Character(s)

Lithosis J62.8

➡ Lithuria R82.998

Litigation, anxiety concerning Z65.3

Little leaguer's elbow —see Epicondylitis, medial

Little's disease G80.9

Littre's

  gland —see condition

  hernia —see Hernia, abdomen

Littritis —see Urethritis

Livedo (annularis) (racemosa) (reticularis) R23.1

Liver —see condition

Living alone (problems with) Z60.2

  with handicapped person Z74.2

Lloyd's syndrome —see Adenomatosis, endocrine

Loa loa, loaiasis, loasis B74.3

Lobar —see condition

Lobomycosis B48.0

Lobo's disease B48.0

Lobotomy syndrome F07.0

Lobstein (-Ekman) disease or syndrome Q78.0

Lobster-claw hand Q71.6-●

Lobulation (congenital) —see also Anomaly, by site

  kidney, Q63.1

  liver, abnormal Q44.7

  spleen Q89.09

Lobule, lobular —see condition

Local, localized —see condition

Locked twins causing obstructed labor O66.1

Locked-in state G83.5

Locking

  joint —see Derangement, joint, specified type NEC

    knee —see Derangement, knee

Lockjaw —see Tetanus

Löffler's

  endocarditis I42.3

  eosinophilia J82

  pneumonia J82

  syndrome (eosinophilic pneumonitis) J82

Loiasis (with conjunctival infestation) (eyelid) B74.3

Lone Star fever A77.0

Long

  labor O63.9

    first stage O63.0

    second stage O63.1

  QT syndrome I45.81

Long-term (current) (prophylactic) drug therapy (use of)

  agents affecting estrogen receptors and estrogen levels NEC Z79.818

  anastrozole (Arimidex) Z79.811

  antibiotics Z79.2

    short-term use - omit code

  anticoagulants Z79.01

  anti-inflammatory, non-steroidal (NSAID) Z79.1

  antiplatelet Z79.02

  antithrombotics Z79.02

  aromatase inhibitors Z79.811

  aspirin Z79.82

  birth control pill or patch Z79.3

  bisphosphonates Z79.83

  contraceptive, oral Z79.3

  drug, specified NEC Z79.899

  estrogen receptor downregulators Z79.818

  Evista Z79.810

  exemestane (Aromasin) Z79.811

  Fareston Z79.810

  fulvestrant (Faslodex) Z79.818

  gonadotropin-releasing hormone (GnRH) agonist Z79.818

  goserelin acetate (Zoladex) Z79.818

  hormone replacement Z79.890

  insulin Z79.4

  letrozole (Femara) Z79.811

Long-term (Continued)

  leuprolide acetate (leuprorelin) (Lupron) Z79.818

  megestrol acetate (Megace) Z79.818

  methadone for pain management Z79.891

  Nolvadex Z79.810

  non-steroidal anti-inflammatories (NSAID) Z79.1

  opiate analgesic Z79.891

  oral

    antidiabetic Z79.84

    contraceptive Z79.3

    hypoglycemic Z79.84

  raloxifene (Evista) Z79.810

  selective estrogen receptor modulators (SERMs) Z79.810

  steroids

    inhaled Z79.51

    systemic Z79.52

  tamoxifen (Nolvadex) Z79.810

  toremifene (Fareston) Z79.810

Longitudinal stripes or grooves, nails L60.8

  congenital Q84.6

Loop

  intestine —see Volvulus

  vascular on papilla (optic) Q14.2

Loose —see also condition

  body

    joint M24.00

      ankle M24.07-●

      elbow M24.02-●

      hand M24.04-●

      hip M24.05-●

      knee M23.4-●

      shoulder (region) M24.01-●

      specified site NEC M24.08

      toe M24.07-●

      vertebra M24.08

      wrist M24.03-●

    knee M23.4-●

    sheath, tendon —see Disorder, tendon, specified type NEC

  cartilage —see Loose, body, joint

  skin and subcutaneous tissue (following bariatric surgery weight loss) (following dietary weight loss) L98.7

  tooth, teeth K08.89

Loosening

  aseptic

    joint prosthesis —see Complications, joint prosthesis, mechanical, loosening, by site

    epiphysis —see Osteochondropathy

  mechanical

    joint prosthesis —see Complications, joint prosthesis, mechanical, loosening, by site

Looser-Milkman (-Debray) syndrome M83.8

Lop ear (deformity) Q17.3

Lorain (-Levi) short stature syndrome E23.0

Lordosis M40.50

  acquired —see Lordosis, specified type NEC

  congenital Q76.429

    lumbar region Q76.426

    lumbosacral region Q76.427

    sacral region Q76.428

    sacrococcygeal region Q76.428

    thoracolumbar region Q76.425

  lumbar region M40.56

  lumbosacral region M40.57

  postsurgical M96.4

  postural —see Lordosis, specified type NEC

  rachitic (late effect) (sequelae) E64.3

  sequelae of rickets E64.3

  specified type NEC M40.40

    lumbar region M40.46

    lumbosacral region M40.47

    thoracolumbar region M40.45

  thoracolumbar region M40.55

  tuberculous A18.01

Loss (of)

  appetite (see Anorexia) R63.0

    hysterical F50.89

    nonorganic origin F50.89

    psychogenic F50.89

  blood —see Hemorrhage

  bone —see Loss, substance of, bone

  consciousness, transient R55

    traumatic —see Injury, intracranial

  control, sphincter, rectum R15.9

    nonorganic origin F98.1

  elasticity, skin R23.4

  family (member) in childhood Z62.898

  fluid (acute) E86.9

  function of labyrinth —see subcategory H83.2

  hair, nonscarring —see Alopecia

  hearing —see also Deafness

    central NOS H90.5

    conductive H90.2

      bilateral H90.0

      unilateral

        with

          restricted hearing on the contralateral side H90.A1-●

          unrestricted hearing on the contralateral side H90.1-●

    mixed conductive and sensorineural hearing loss H90.8

      bilateral H90.6

      unilateral

        with

          restricted hearing on the contralateral side H90.A3-●

          unrestricted hearing on the contralateral side H90.7-●

    neural NOS H90.5

    perceptive NOS H90.5

    sensorineural NOS H90.5

      bilateral H90.3

      unilateral

        with

          restricted hearing on the contralateral side H90.A2-●

          unrestricted hearing on the contralateral side H90.4-●

    sensory NOS H90.5

  height R29.890

  limb or member, traumatic, current —see Amputation, traumatic

  love relationship in childhood Z62.898

  memory —see also Amnesia

    mild, following organic brain damage F06.8

  mind —see Psychosis

  occlusal vertical dimension of fully erupted teeth M26.37

  organ or part —see also Absence, by site, acquired

  ossicles, ear (partial) H74.32-●

  parent in childhood Z63.4

  pregnancy, recurrent N96

    without current pregnancy N96

    care in current pregnancy O26.2-●

  recurrent pregnancy —see Loss, pregnancy, recurrent

  self-esteem, in childhood Z62.898

  sense of

    smell —see Disturbance, sensation, smell

    taste —see Disturbance, sensation, taste

    touch R20.8

  sensory R44.9

    dissociative F44.6

  sexual desire F52.0

  sight (acquired) (complete) (congenital) —see Blindness

  substance of

    bone —see Disorder, bone, density and structure, specified NEC

      horizontal alveolar K06.3

    cartilage —see Disorder, cartilage, specified type NEC

      auricle (ear) —see Disorder, pinna, specified type NEC

    vitreous (humor) H15.89

▶ New ⇒ Revised ~~deleted~~ Deleted ● Use Additional Character(s)

Loss (Continued)
tooth, teeth —see Absence, teeth, acquired
vision, visual H54.7
  both eyes H54.3
  one eye H54.60
    left (normal vision on right) H54.62
    right (normal vision on left) H54.61
  specified as blindness —see Blindness
  subjective
    sudden H53.13-●
    transient H53.12-●
  vitreous —see Prolapse, vitreous
  voice —see Aphonia
  weight (abnormal) (cause unknown) R63.4
Louis-Bar syndrome (ataxia-telangiectasia) G11.3
Louping ill (encephalitis) A84.8
Louse, lousiness —see Lice
Low
achiever, school Z55.3
back syndrome M54.5
basal metabolic rate R94.8
birthweight (2499 grams or less) P07.10
  with weight of
    1000-1249 grams P07.14
    1250-1499 grams P07.15
    1500-1749 grams P07.16
    1750-1999 grams P07.17
    2000-2499 grams P07.18
  extreme (999 grams or less) P07.00
    with weight of
      499 grams or less P07.01
      500-749 grams P07.02
      750-999 grams P07.03
  for gestational age —see Light for dates
blood pressure —see also Hypotension
  reading (incidental) (isolated) (nonspecific) R03.1
cardiac reserve —see Disease, heart
function —see also Hypofunction
  kidney N28.9
hematocrit D64.9
hemoglobin D64.9
income Z59.6
level of literacy Z55.0
lying
  kidney N28.89
  organ or site, congenital —see Malposition, congenital
output syndrome (cardiac) —see Failure, heart
platelets (blood) —see Thrombocytopenia
reserve, kidney N28.89
salt syndrome E87.1
self esteem R45.81
set ears Q17.4
vision H54.2X-
  one eye (other eye normal) H54.50
    left (normal vision on right) H54.52A-
    other eye blind —see Blindness
    right (normal vision on left) H54.511-
Low-density-lipoprotein-type (LDL) hyperlipoproteinemia E78.00
Lowe's syndrome E72.03
Lown-Ganong-Levine syndrome I45.6
LSD reaction (acute) (without dependence) F16.90
  with dependence F16.20
L-shaped kidney Q63.8
Ludwig's angina or disease K12.2
Lues (venerea), luetic —see Syphilis
Luetscher's syndrome (dehydration) E86.0
Lumbago, lumbalgia M54.5
  with sciatica M54.4-●
    due to intervertebral disc disorder M51.17
  due to displacement, intervertebral disc M51.27
    with sciatica M51.17
Lumbar —see condition
Lumbarization, vertebra, congenital Q76.49
Lumbermen's itch B88.0

Lump —see also Mass
breast N63.0
  axillary tail
    left N63.32
    right N63.31
  left
    lower inner quadrant N63.24
    lower outer quadrant N63.23
    unspecified quadrant N63.20
    upper inner quadrant N63.22
    upper outer quadrant N63.21
  right
    lower inner quadrant N63.14
    lower outer quadrant N63.13
    unspecified quadrant N63.10
    upper inner quadrant N63.12
    upper outer quadrant N63.11
  subareolar
    left N63.42
    right N63.41
Lunacy —see Psychosis
Lung —see condition
Lupoid (miliary) of Boeck D86.3
Lupus
anticoagulant D68.62
  with
    hemorrhagic disorder D68.312
    hypercoagulable state D68.62
  finding without diagnosis R76.0
discoid (local) L93.0
erythematosus (discoid) (local) L93.0
  disseminated —see Lupus, erythematosus, systemic
  eyelid H01.129
    left H01.126
      lower H01.125
      upper H01.124
    right H01.123
      lower H01.122
      upper H01.121
  profundus L93.2
  specified NEC L93.2
  subacute cutaneous L93.1
  systemic M32.9
    with organ or system involvement M32.10
      endocarditis M32.11
      lung M32.13
      pericarditis M32.12
      renal (glomerular) M32.14
        tubulo-interstitial M32.15
      specified organ or system NEC M32.19
    drug-induced M32.0
    inhibitor (presence of) D68.62
      with
        hemorrhagic disorder D68.312
        hypercoagulable state D68.62
      finding without diagnosis R76.0
    specified NEC M32.8
exedens A18.4
hydralazine M32.0
  correct substance properly administered — see Table of Drugs and Chemicals, by drug, adverse effect
  overdose or wrong substance given or taken —see Table of Drugs and Chemicals, by drug, poisoning
nephritis (chronic) M32.14
nontuberculous, not disseminated L93.0
panniculitis L93.2
pernio (Besnier) D86.3
systemic —see Lupus, erythematosus, systemic
tuberculous A18.4
  eyelid A18.4
vulgaris A18.4
  eyelid A18.4
Luteinoma D27.-●
Lutembacher's disease or syndrome (atrial septal defect with mitral stenosis) Q21.1
Luteoma D27.-●

Lutz (-Splendore-de Almeida) disease —see Paracoccidioidomycosis
Luxation —see also Dislocation
eyeball (nontraumatic) —see Luxation, globe
  birth injury P15.3
globe, nontraumatic H44.82-●
lacrimal gland —see Dislocation, lacrimal gland
lens (old) (partial) (spontaneous)
  congenital Q12.1
  syphilitic A50.39
Lycanthropy F22
Lyell's syndrome L51.2
due to drug L51.2
  correct substance properly administered — see Table of Drugs and Chemicals, by drug, adverse effect
  overdose or wrong substance given or taken —see Table of Drugs and Chemicals, by drug, poisoning
Lyme disease A69.20
Lymph
gland or node —see condition
scrotum —see Infestation, filarial
Lymphadenitis I88.9
with ectopic or molar pregnancy O08.0
acute L04.9
  axilla L04.2
  face L04.0
  head L04.0
  hip L04.3
  limb
    lower L04.3
    upper L04.2
  neck L04.0
  shoulder L04.2
  specified site NEC L04.8
  trunk L04.1
anthracosis (occupational) J60
any site, except mesenteric I88.9
  chronic I88.1
  subacute I88.1
breast
  gestational —see Mastitis, obstetric
  puerperal, postpartum (nonpurulent) O91.22
chancroidal (congenital) A57
chronic I88.1
  mesenteric I88.0
due to
  Brugia (malayi) B74.1
    timori B74.2
  chlamydial lymphogranuloma A55
  diphtheria (toxin) A36.89
  lymphogranuloma venereum A55
  Wuchereria bancrofti B74.0
following ectopic or molar pregnancy O08.0
gonorrheal A54.89
infective —see Lymphadenitis, acute
mesenteric (acute) (chronic) (nonspecific) (subacute) I88.0
  due to Salmonella typhi A01.09
  tuberculous A18.39
mycobacterial A31.8
purulent —see Lymphadenitis, acute
pyogenic —see Lymphadenitis, acute
regional, nonbacterial I88.8
septic —see Lymphadenitis, acute
subacute, unspecified site I88.1
suppurative —see Lymphadenitis, acute
syphilitic (early) (secondary) A51.49
  late A52.79
tuberculous —see Tuberculosis, lymph gland
venereal (chlamydial) A55
Lymphadenoid goiter E06.3
Lymphadenopathy (generalized) R59.1
angioimmunoblastic, with dysproteinemia (AILD) C86.5
due to toxoplasmosis (acquired) B58.89
  congenital (acute) (subacute) (chronic) P37.1
localized R59.0
syphilitic (early) (secondary) A51.49

Lymphadenosis R59.1
Lymphangiectasis I89.0
  conjunctiva H11.89
  postinfectional I89.0
  scrotum I89.0
Lymphangiectatic elephantiasis, nonfilarial
      I89.0
Lymphangioendothelioma D18.1
  malignant —see Neoplasm, connective tissue,
      malignant
Lymphangioleiomyomatosis J84.81
Lymphangioma D18.1
  capillary D18.1
  cavernous D18.1
  cystic D18.1
  malignant —see Neoplasm, connective tissue,
      malignant
Lymphangiomyoma D18.1
Lymphangiomyomatosis J84.81
Lymphangiosarcoma —see Neoplasm,
      connective tissue, malignant
Lymphangitis I89.1
  with
    abscess - code by site under Abscess
    cellulitis - code by site under Cellulitis
    ectopic or molar pregnancy O08.0
  acute L03.91
    abdominal wall L03.321
    ankle —see Lymphangitis, acute, lower
      limb
    arm —see Lymphangitis, acute, upper limb
    auricle (ear) —see Lymphangitis, acute, ear
    axilla L03.12-●
    back (any part) L03.322
    buttock L03.327
    cervical (meaning neck) L03.222
    cheek (external) L03.212
    chest wall L03.323
    digit
      finger —see Lymphangitis, acute, finger
      toe —see Lymphangitis, acute, toe
    ear (external) H60.1-●
    external auditory canal —see
        Lymphangitis, acute, ear
    eyelid —see Abscess, eyelid
    face NEC L03.212
    finger (intrathecal) (periosteal)
        (subcutaneous) (subcuticular)
        L03.02-●
    foot —see Lymphangitis, acute, lower
      limb
    gluteal (region) L03.327
    groin L03.324
    hand —see Lymphangitis, acute, upper
      limb
    head NEC L03.891
      face (any part, except ear, eye and nose)
          L03.212
    heel —see Lymphangitis, acute, lower limb
    hip —see Lymphangitis, acute, lower limb
    jaw (region) L03.212
    knee —see Lymphangitis, acute, lower limb
    leg —see Lymphangitis, acute, lower limb
    lower limb L03.12-●
      toe —see Lymphangitis, acute, toe
    navel L03.326
    neck (region) L03.222
    orbit, orbital —see Cellulitis, orbit
    pectoral (region) L03.323
    perineal, perineum L03.325
    scalp (any part) L03.891
    shoulder —see Lymphangitis, acute, upper
      limb
    specified site NEC L03.898
    thigh —see Lymphangitis, acute, lower
      limb
    thumb (intrathecal) (periosteal)
        (subcutaneous) (subcuticular) —see
        Lymphangitis, acute, finger
    toe (intrathecal) (periosteal) (subcutaneous)
        (subcuticular) L03.04-●

Lymphangitis (Continued)
  acute (Continued)
    trunk L03.329
      abdominal wall L03.321
      back (any part) L03.322
      buttock L03.327
      chest wall L03.323
      groin L03.324
      perineal, perineum L03.325
      umbilicus L03.326
    umbilicus L03.326
    upper limb L03.12-●
      axilla —see Lymphangitis, acute, axilla
      finger —see Lymphangitis, acute, finger
      thumb —see Lymphangitis, acute, finger
      wrist —see Lymphangitis, acute, upper
          limb
  breast
    gestational —see Mastitis, obstetric
  chancroidal A57
  chronic (any site) I89.1
  due to
    Brugia (malayi) B74.1
      timori B74.2
    Wuchereria bancrofti B74.0
  following ectopic or molar pregnancy
      O08.89
  penis
    acute N48.29
    gonococcal (acute) (chronic) A54.09
  puerperal, postpartum, childbirth O86.89
  strumous, tuberculous A18.2
  subacute (any site) I89.1
  tuberculous —see Tuberculosis, lymph gland
Lymphatic (vessel) —see condition
Lymphatism E32.8
Lymphectasia I89.0
Lymphedema (acquired) —see also Elephantiasis
  congenital Q82.0
  hereditary (chronic) (idiopathic) Q82.0
  postmastectomy I97.2
  praecox I89.0
  secondary I89.0
  surgical NEC I97.89
    postmastectomy (syndrome) I97.2
Lymphoblastic —see condition
Lymphoblastoma (diffuse) —see Lymphoma,
      lymphoblastic (diffuse)
  giant follicular —see Lymphoma,
      lymphoblastic (diffuse)
  macrofollicular —see Lymphoma,
      lymphoblastic (diffuse)
Lymphocele I89.8
Lymphocytic
  chorioencephalitis (acute) (serous) A87.2
  choriomeningitis (acute) (serous) A87.2
  meningoencephalitis A87.2
Lymphocytoma, benign cutis L98.8
Lymphocytopenia D72.810
Lymphocytosis (symptomatic) D72.820
  infectious (acute) B33.8
Lymphoepithelioma —see Neoplasm,
      malignant, by site
Lymphogranuloma (malignant) —see also
      Lymphoma, Hodgkin
  chlamydial A55
  inguinale A55
  venereum (any site) (chlamydial) (with
      stricture of rectum) A55
Lymphogranulomatosis (malignant) —see also
      Lymphoma, Hodgkin
  benign (Boeck's sarcoid) (Schaumann's)
      D86.1
Lymphohistiocytosis, hemophagocytic
      (familial) D76.1
Lymphoid —see condition
Lymphoma (of) (malignant) C85.90
  adult T-cell (HTLV-1-associated) (acute
      variant) (chronic variant)
      (lymphomatoid variant) (smouldering
      variant) C91.5-●

Lymphoma (Continued)
  anaplastic large cell
    ALK-negative C84.7-●
    ALK-positive C84.6-●
    CD30-positive C84.6-●
    primary cutaneous C86.6
  angioimmunoblastic T-cell C86.5
  BALT C88.4
  B-cell C85.1-●
  B-precursor C83.5-●
  blastic NK-cell C86.4
  blastic plasmacytoid dendritic cell neoplasm
      (BPDCN) C86.4
  bronchial-associated lymphoid tissue
      [BALT-lymphoma] C88.4
  Burkitt (atypical) C83.7-●
  Burkitt-like C83.7-●
  centrocytic C83.1-●
  cutaneous follicle center C82.6-●
  cutaneous T-cell C84.A-●
  diffuse follicle center C82.5-●
  diffuse large cell C83.3-●
    anaplastic C83.3-●
    B-cell C83.3-●
    CD30-positive C83.3-●
    centroblastic C83.3-●
    immunoblastic C83.3-●
    plasmablastic C83.3-●
    subtype not specified C83.3-●
    T-cell rich C83.3-●
  enteropathy-type (associated) (intestinal)
      T-cell C86.2
  extranodal marginal zone B-cell
      lymphoma of mucosa-associated
      lymphoid tissue [MALT-lymphoma]
      C88.4
  extranodal NK/T-cell, nasal type C86.0
  follicular C82.9-●
    grade
      I C82.0-●
      II C82.1-●
      III C82.2-●
      IIIa C82.3-●
      IIIb C82.4-●
    specified NEC C82.8-●
  hepatosplenic T-cell (alpha-beta) (gamma-
      delta) C86.1
  histiocytic C85.9-●
    true C96.A
  Hodgkin C81.9
    lymphocyte-rich (classical) C81.4-●
    lymphocyte depleted (classical)
        C81.3-●
    mixed cellularity (classical) C81.2-●
    nodular sclerosis (classical) C81.1-●
    specified NEC (classical) C81.7-●
    lymphocyte-rich classical C81.4-●
    lymphocyte depleted classical C81.3-●
    mixed cellularity classical C81.2-●
    nodular
      lymphocyte predominant C81.0-●
      sclerosis (classical) C81.1-●
  intravascular large B-cell C83.8-●
  Lennert's C84.4-●
  lymphoblastic (diffuse) C83.5-●
  lymphoblastic B-cell C83.5-●
  lymphoblastic T-cell C83.5-●
  lymphoepithelioid C84.4-●
  lymphoplasmacytic C83.0-●
    with IgM-production C88.0
  MALT C88.4
  mantle cell C83.1-●
  mature T-cell NEC C84.4-●
  mature T/NK-cell C84.9-●
    specified NEC C84.Z-●
  mediastinal (thymic) large B-cell
      C85.2-●
  Mediterranean C88.3
  mucosa-associated lymphoid tissue
      [MALT-lymphoma] C88.4
  NK/T cell C84.9-●

Lymphoma *(Continued)*
  nodal marginal zone C83.0-●
  non-follicular (diffuse) C83.9-●
    specified NEC C83.8-●
  non-Hodgkin —*see also* Lymphoma, by type
    C85.9-●
    specified NEC C85.8-●
  non-leukemic variant of B-CLL C83.0-●
  peripheral T-cell, not classified C84.4-●
  primary cutaneous
    anaplastic large cell C86.6
    CD30-positive large T-cell C86.6
  primary effusion B-cell C83.8-●

Lymphoma *(Continued)*
  SALT C88.4
  skin-associated lymphoid tissue
    [SALT-lymphoma] C88.4
  small cell B-cell C83.0-●
  splenic marginal zone C83.0-●
  subcutaneous panniculitis-like T-cell
    C86.3
  T-precursor C83.5-●
  true histiocytic C96.A
Lymphomatosis —*see* Lymphoma
Lymphopathia venereum, veneris A55
Lymphopenia D72.810

Lymphoplasmacytic leukemia —*see* Leukemia,
  chronic lymphocytic, B-cell type
Lymphoproliferation, X-linked disease D82.3
Lymphoreticulosis, benign (of inoculation)
  A28.1
Lymphorrhea I89.8
Lymphosarcoma (diffuse) —*see also* Lymphoma
  C85.9-●
Lymphostasis I89.8
Lypemania —*see* Melancholia
Lysine and hydroxylysine metabolism
  disorder E72.3
Lyssa —*see* Rabies

M

Macacus ear Q17.3
Maceration, wet feet, tropical (syndrome)
  T69.02-●
MacLeod's syndrome J43.0
Macrocephalia, macrocephaly Q75.3
Macrocheilia, macrochilia (congenital)Q18.6
Macrocolon —see also Megacolon Q43.1
Macrocornea Q15.8
  with glaucoma Q15.0
Macrocytic —see condition
Macrocytosis D75.89
Macrodactylia, macrodactylism (fingers)
    (thumbs) Q74.0
  toes Q74.2
Macrodontia K00.2
Macrogenia M26.05
Macrogenitosomia (adrenal) (male) (praecox)
    E25.9
  congenital E25.0
Macroglobulinemia (idiopathic) (primary)
    C88.0
  monoclonal (essential) D47.2
  Waldenström C88.0
Macroglossia (congenital) Q38.2
  acquired K14.8
Macrognathia, macrognathism (congenital)
    (mandibular) (maxillary) M26.09
Macrogyria (congenital) Q04.8
Macrohydrocephalus —see Hydrocephalus
Macromastia —see Hypertrophy, breast
Macrophthalmos Q11.3
  in congenital glaucoma Q15.0
Macropsia H53.15
Macrosigmoid K59.39
  congenital Q43.2
Macrospondylitis, acromegalic E22.0
Macrostomia (congenital) Q18.4
Macrotia (external ear) (congenital) Q17.1
Macula
  cornea, corneal —see Opacity, cornea
  degeneration (atrophic) (exudative)
      (senile) —see also Degeneration, macula
    hereditary —see Dystrophy, retina
Maculae ceruleae —B85.1
Maculopathy, toxic —see Degeneration, macula,
    toxic
Madarosis (eyelid) H02.729
  left H02.726
    lower H02.725
    upper H02.724
  right H02.723
    lower H02.722
    upper H02.721
Madelung's
  deformity (radius) Q74.0
  disease
    radial deformity Q74.0
    symmetrical lipomas, neck E88.89
Madness —see Psychosis
Madura
  foot B47.9
    actinomycotic B47.1
    mycotic B47.0
Maduromycosis B47.0
Maffucci's syndrome Q78.4
Magnesium metabolism disorder —see
    Disorder, metabolism, magnesium
Main en griffe (acquired) —see also Deformity,
    limb, clawhand
  congenital Q74.0
Maintenance (encounter for)
  antineoplastic chemotherapy Z51.11
  antineoplastic radiation therapy Z51.0
  methadone F11.20
Majocchi's
  disease L81.7
  granuloma B35.8
Major —see condition
Malabar itch (any site) B35.5

Malabsorption K90.9
  calcium K90.89
  carbohydrate K90.49
  disaccharide E73.9
  fat K90.49
  galactose E74.20
  glucose(-galactose) E74.39
  intestinal K90.9
    specified NEC K90.89
  isomaltose E74.31
  lactose E73.9
  methionine E72.19
  monosaccharide E74.39
  postgastrectomy K91.2
  postsurgical K91.2
  protein K90.49
  starch K90.49
  sucrose E74.39
  syndrome K90.9
    postsurgical K91.2
Malacia, bone (adult) M83.9
  juvenile —see Rickets
Malacoplakia
  bladder N32.89
  pelvis (kidney) N28.89
  ureter N28.89
  urethra N36.8
Malacosteon, juvenile —see Rickets
Maladaptation —see Maladjustment
Maladie de Roger Q21.0
Maladjustment
  conjugal Z63.0
    involving divorce or estrangement Z63.5
  educational Z55.4
  family Z63.9
  marital Z63.0
    involving divorce or estrangement Z63.5
  occupational NEC Z56.89
  simple, adult —see Disorder, adjustment
  situational —see Disorder, adjustment
  social Z60.9
    due to
      acculturation difficulty Z60.3
      discrimination and persecution
          (perceived) Z60.5
      exclusion and isolation Z60.4
      life-cycle (phase of life) transition Z60.0
      rejection Z60.4
      specified reason NEC Z60.8
Malaise R53.81
Malakoplakia —see Malacoplakia
Malaria, malarial (fever) B54
  with
    blackwater fever B50.8
      hemoglobinuric (bilious) B50.8
    hemoglobinuria B50.8
  accidentally induced (therapeutically) - code
      by type under Malaria
  algid B50.9
  cerebral B50.0 [G94]
  clinically diagnosed (without parasitological
      confirmation) B54
  congenital NEC P37.4
    falciparum P37.3
  congestion, congestive B54
  continued (fever) B50.9
  estivo-autumnal B50.9
  falciparum B50.9
    with complications NEC B50.8
      cerebral B50.0 [G94]
    severe B50.8
  hemorrhagic B54
  malariae B52.9
    with
      complications NEC B52.8
      glomerular disorder B52.0
  malignant (tertian) —see Malaria, falciparum
  mixed infections — code to first listed type
      in B50-B53
  ovale B53.0
  parasitologically confirmed NEC B53.8

Malaria, malarial (Continued)
  pernicious, acute —see Malaria, falciparum
  Plasmodium (P.)
    falciparum NEC —see Malaria, falciparum
    malariae NEC B52.9
      with Plasmodium
        falciparum (and or vivax) —see
            Malaria, falciparum
        vivax —see also Malaria, vivax
            and falciparum —see Malaria,
            falciparum
    ovale B53.0
      with Plasmodium malariae —see also
          Malaria, malariae
        and vivax —see also Malaria, vivax
            and falciparum —see Malaria,
            falciparum
    simian B53.1
      with Plasmodium malariae —see also
          Malaria, malariae
        and vivax —see also Malaria, vivax
            and falciparum —see Malaria,
            falciparum
    vivax NEC B51.9
      with Plasmodium falciparum —see
          Malaria, falciparum
  quartan —see Malaria, malariae
  quotidian —see Malaria, falciparum
  recurrent B54
  remittent B54
  specified type NEC (parasitologically
      confirmed) B53.8
  spleen B54
  subtertian (fever) —see Malaria, falciparum
  tertian (benign) —see also Malaria, vivax
    malignant B50.9
  tropical B50.9
  typhoid B54
  vivax B51.9
    with
      complications NEC B51.8
      ruptured spleen B51.0
Malassez's disease (cystic) N50.89
Malassimilation K90.9
Mal de los pintos —see Pinta
Mal de mer T75.3
Maldescent, testis Q53.9
  bilateral Q53.20
    abdominal Q53.211
    perineal Q53.22
  unilateral Q53.10
    abdominal Q53.111
    perineal Q53.12
Maldevelopment —see also Anomaly
  brain Q07.9
  colon Q43.9
  hip Q74.2
    congenital dislocation Q65.2
      bilateral Q65.1
      unilateral Q65.0-●
  mastoid process Q75.8
  middle ear Q16.4
    except ossicles Q16.4
    ossicles Q16.3
  ossicles Q16.3
  spine Q76.49
  toe Q74.2
Male type pelvis Q74.2
  with disproportion (fetopelvic) O33.3
    causing obstructed labor O65.3
Malformation (congenital) —see also Anomaly
  adrenal gland Q89.1
  affecting multiple systems with skeletal
      changes NEC Q87.5
  alimentary tract Q45.9
    specified type NEC Q45.8
    upper Q40.9
      specified type NEC Q40.8
  aorta Q25.40
    absence Q25.41
    aneurysm, congenital Q25.43

Malformation *(Continued)*
  aorta *(Continued)*
    aplasia Q25.41
    atresia Q25.29
      aortic arch Q25.21
    coarctation (preductal) (postductal) Q25.1
    dilatation, congenital Q25.44
    hypoplasia Q25.42
    patent ductus arteriosus Q25.0
    specified type NEC Q25.49
    stenosis Q25.1
      supravalvular Q25.3
  aortic valve Q23.9
    specified NEC Q23.8
  arteriovenous, aneurysmatic (congenital) Q27.30
    brain Q28.2
    cerebral Q28.2
    peripheral Q27.30
      digestive system Q27.33
      lower limb Q27.32
      other specified site Q27.39
      renal vessel Q27.34
      upper limb Q27.31
    precerebral vessels (nonruptured) Q28.0
  auricle
    ear (congenital) Q17.3
      acquired H61.119
        left H61.112
          with right H61.113
        right H61.111
          with left H61.113
  bile duct Q44.5
  bladder Q64.79
    aplasia Q64.5
    diverticulum Q64.6
    exstrophy —*see* Exstrophy, bladder
    neck obstruction Q64.31
  bone Q79.9
    face Q75.9
      specified type NEC Q75.8
    skull Q75.9
      specified type NEC Q75.8
  brain (multiple) Q04.9
    arteriovenous Q28.2
    specified type NEC Q04.8
  branchial cleft Q18.2
  breast Q83.9
    specified type NEC Q83.8
  broad ligament Q50.6
  bronchus Q32.4
  bursa Q79.9
  cardiac
    chambers Q20.9
      specified type NEC Q20.8
    septum Q21.9
      specified type NEC Q21.8
  cerebral Q04.9
    vessels Q28.3
  cervix uteri Q51.9
    specified type NEC Q51.828
  Chiari
    Type I G93.5
    Type II Q07.01
  choroid (congenital) Q14.3
    plexus Q07.8
  circulatory system Q28.9
  cochlea Q16.5
  cornea Q13.4
  coronary vessels Q24.5
  corpus callosum (congenital) Q04.0
  diaphragm Q79.1
  digestive system NEC, specified type NEC Q45.8
  dura Q07.9
    brain Q04.9
    spinal Q06.9
  ear Q17.9
    causing impairment of hearing Q16.9

Malformation *(Continued)*
  ear *(Continued)*
    external Q17.9
      accessory auricle Q17.0
      causing impairment of hearing Q16.9
        absence of
          auditory canal Q16.1
          auricle Q16.0
      macrotia Q17.1
      microtia Q17.2
      misplacement Q17.4
      misshapen NEC Q17.3
      prominence Q17.5
      specified type NEC Q17.8
    inner Q16.5
    middle Q16.4
      absence of eustachian tube Q16.2
      ossicles (fusion) Q16.3
    ossicles Q16.3
    specified type NEC Q17.8
  epididymis Q55.4
  esophagus Q39.9
    specified type NEC Q39.8
  eye Q15.9
    lid Q10.3
    specified NEC Q15.8
  fallopian tube Q50.6
  genital organ —*see* Anomaly, genitalia
  great
    artery Q25.9
      aorta —*see* Malformation, aorta
      pulmonary artery —*see* Malformation, pulmonary, artery
      specified type NEC Q25.8
    vein Q26.9
      anomalous
        portal venous connection Q26.5
        pulmonary venous connection Q26.4
          partial Q26.3
          total Q26.2
      persistent left superior vena cava Q26.1
      portal vein-hepatic artery fistula Q26.6
      specified type NEC Q26.8
      vena cava stenosis, congenital Q26.0
  gum Q38.6
  hair Q84.2
  heart Q24.9
    specified type NEC Q24.8
  integument Q84.9
    specified type NEC Q84.8
  internal ear Q16.5
  intestine Q43.9
    specified type NEC Q43.8
  iris Q13.2
  joint Q74.9
    ankle Q74.2
    lumbosacral Q76.49
    sacroiliac Q74.2
    specified type NEC Q74.8
  kidney Q63.9
    accessory Q63.0
    giant Q63.3
    horseshoe Q63.1
    hydronephrosis Q62.0
    malposition Q63.2
    specified type NEC Q63.8
  lacrimal apparatus Q10.6
  lingual Q38.3
  lip Q38.0
  liver Q44.7
  lung Q33.9
  meninges or membrane (congenital) Q07.9
    cerebral Q04.8
    spinal (cord) Q06.9
  middle ear Q16.4
    ossicles Q16.3
  mitral valve Q23.9
    specified NEC Q23.8
  Mondini's (congenital) (malformation, cochlea) Q16.5

Malformation *(Continued)*
  mouth (congenital) Q38.6
  multiple types NEC Q89.7
  musculoskeletal system Q79.9
  myocardium Q24.8
  nail Q84.6
  nervous system (central) Q07.9
  nose Q30.9
    specified type NEC Q30.8
  optic disc Q14.2
  orbit Q10.7
  ovary Q50.39
  palate Q38.5
  parathyroid gland Q89.2
  pelvic organs or tissues NEC
    in pregnancy or childbirth O34.8- •
      causing obstructed labor O65.5
  penis Q55.69
    aplasia Q55.5
    curvature (lateral) Q55.61
    hypoplasia Q55.62
  pericardium Q24.8
  peripheral vascular system Q27.9
    specified type NEC Q27.8
  pharynx Q38.8
  precerebral vessels Q28.1
  prostate Q55.4
  pulmonary
    arteriovenous Q25.72
    artery Q25.9
      atresia Q25.5
      specified type NEC Q25.79
      stenosis Q25.6
    valve Q22.3
  renal artery Q27.2
  respiratory system Q34.9
  retina Q14.1
  scrotum —*see* Malformation, testis and scrotum
  seminal vesicles Q55.4
  sense organs NEC Q07.9
  skin Q82.9
  specified NEC Q89.8
  spinal
    cord Q06.9
    nerve root Q07.8
  spine Q76.49
    kyphosis —*see* Kyphosis, congenital
    lordosis —*see* Lordosis, congenital
  spleen Q89.09
  stomach Q40.3
    specified type NEC Q40.2
  teeth, tooth K00.9
  tendon Q79.9
  testis and scrotum Q55.20
    aplasia Q55.0
    hypoplasia Q55.1
    polyorchism Q55.21
    retractile testis Q55.22
    scrotal transposition Q55.23
    specified NEC Q55.29
  thorax, bony Q76.9
  throat Q38.8
  thyroid gland Q89.2
  tongue (congenital) Q38.3
    hypertrophy Q38.2
    tie Q38.1
  trachea Q32.1
  tricuspid valve Q22.9
    specified type NEC Q22.8
  umbilical cord NEC (complicating delivery) O69.89
  umbilicus Q89.9
  ureter Q62.8
    agenesis Q62.4
    duplication Q62.5
    malposition —*see* Malposition, congenital, ureter
    obstructive defect —*see* Defect, obstructive, ureter
    vesico-uretero-renal reflux Q62.7

Malformation *(Continued)*
  urethra Q64.79
    aplasia Q64.5
    duplication Q64.74
    posterior valves Q64.2
    prolapse Q64.71
    stricture Q64.32
  urinary system Q64.9
  uterus Q51.9
    specified type NEC Q51.818
  vagina Q52.4
  vascular system, peripheral Q27.9
  vas deferens Q55.4
    atresia Q55.3
  venous —*see* Anomaly, vein(s)
  vulva Q52.70
Malfunction —*see also* Dysfunction
  cardiac electronic device T82.119
    electrode T82.110
    pulse generator T82.111
    specified type NEC T82.118
  catheter device NEC T85.618
    cystostomy T83.010
    dialysis (renal) (vascular) T82.41
      intraperitoneal T85.611
    infusion NEC T82.514
      cranial T85.610
      epidural T85.610
      intrathecal T85.610
      spinal T85.610
      subarachnoid T85.610
      subdural T85.610
    urinary —*see also* Breakdown, device,
        catheter T83.018
  colostomy K94.03
    valve K94.03
  cystostomy (stoma) N99.512
    catheter T83.010
  enteric stoma K94.13
  enterostomy K94.13
  esophagostomy K94.33
  gastroenteric K31.89
  gastrostomy K94.23
  ileostomy K94.13
    valve K94.13
  intrathecal infusion pump T85.615
  jejunostomy K94.13
  nervous system device, implant or graft,
      specified NEC T85.615
  pacemaker —*see* Malfunction, cardiac
      electronic device
  prosthetic device, internal —*see*
      Complications, prosthetic device, by site,
      mechanical
  tracheostomy J95.03
  urinary device NEC —*see* Complication,
      genitourinary, device, urinary,
      mechanical
  valve
    colostomy K94.03
    heart T82.09
    ileostomy K94.13
  vascular graft or shunt NEC —*see*
      Complication, cardiovascular device,
      mechanical, vascular
  ventricular (communicating shunt) T85.01
Malherbe's tumor —*see* Neoplasm, skin,
    benign
Malibu disease L98.8-●
Malignancy —*see also* Neoplasm, malignant,
    by site
  unspecified site (primary) C80.1
Malignant —*see* condition
Malingerer, malingering Z76.5
Mallet finger (acquired) —*see* Deformity, finger,
    mallet finger
  congenital Q74.0
  sequelae of rickets E64.3
Malleus A24.0
Mallory's bodies R89.7
Mallory-Weiss syndrome K22.6

Malnutrition E46
  degree
    first E44.1
    mild (protein) E44.1
    moderate (protein) E44.0
    second E44.0
    severe (protein-energy) E43
      intermediate form E42
        with
          kwashiorkor (and marasmus) E42
          marasmus E41
    third E43
  following gastrointestinal surgery K91.2
  intrauterine
    light-for-dates —*see* Light for dates
    small-for-dates —*see* Small for dates
  lack of care, or neglect (child) (infant) T76.02
    confirmed T74.02
  malignant E40
  protein E46
    calorie E46
      mild E44.1
      moderate E44.0
      severe E43
        intermediate form E42
          with
            kwashiorkor (and marasmus)
                E42
            marasmus E41
    energy E46
      mild E44.1
      moderate E44.0
      severe E43
        intermediate form E42
          with
            kwashiorkor (and marasmus)
                E42
            marasmus E41
  severe (protein-energy) E43
    with
      kwashiorkor (and marasmus) E42
      marasmus E41
Malocclusion (teeth) M26.4
  Angle's M26.219
    class I M26.211
    class II M26.212
    class III M26.213
  due to
    abnormal swallowing M26.59
    mouth breathing M26.59
    tongue, lip or finger habits M26.59
  temporomandibular (joint) M26.69
Malposition
  cervix —*see* Malposition, uterus
  congenital
    adrenal (gland) Q89.1
    alimentary tract Q45.8
      lower Q43.8
      upper Q40.8
    aorta Q25.49
    appendix Q43.8
    arterial trunk Q20.0
    artery (peripheral) Q27.8
      coronary Q24.5
      digestive system Q27.8
      lower limb Q27.8
      pulmonary Q25.79
      specified site NEC Q27.8
      upper limb Q27.8
    auditory canal Q17.8
      causing impairment of hearing Q16.9
    auricle (ear) Q17.4
      causing impairment of hearing Q16.9
    cervical Q18.2
    biliary duct or passage Q44.5
    bladder (mucosa) —*see* Exstrophy,
        bladder
    brachial plexus Q07.8
    brain tissue Q04.8
    breast Q83.8
    bronchus Q32.4

Malposition *(Continued)*
  congenital *(Continued)*
    cecum Q43.8
    clavicle Q74.0
    colon Q43.8
    digestive organ or tract NEC Q45.8
      lower Q43.8
      upper Q40.8
    ear (auricle) (external) Q17.4
      ossicles Q16.3
    endocrine (gland) NEC Q89.2
    epiglottis Q31.8
    eustachian tube Q17.8
    eye Q15.8
    facial features Q18.8
    fallopian tube Q50.6
    finger(s) Q68.1
      supernumerary Q69.0
    foot Q66.9
    gallbladder Q44.1
    gastrointestinal tract Q45.8
    genitalia, genital organ(s) or tract
      female Q52.8
        external Q52.79
        internal NEC Q52.8
      male Q55.8
    glottis Q31.8
    hand Q68.1
    heart Q24.8
      dextrocardia Q24.0
        with complete transposition of viscera
            Q89.3
    hepatic duct Q44.5
    hip (joint) Q65.89
    intestine (large) (small) Q43.8
      with anomalous adhesions, fixation or
          malrotation Q43.3
    joint NEC Q68.8
    kidney Q63.2
    larynx Q31.8
    limb Q68.8
      lower Q68.8
      upper Q68.8
    liver Q44.7
    lung (lobe) Q33.8
    nail(s) Q84.6
    nerve Q07.8
    nervous system NEC Q07.8
    nose, nasal (septum) Q30.8
    organ or site not listed —*see* Anomaly,
        by site
    ovary Q50.39
    pancreas Q45.3
    parathyroid (gland) Q89.2
    patella Q74.1
    peripheral vascular system Q27.8
    pituitary (gland) Q89.2
    respiratory organ or system NEC
        Q34.8
    rib (cage) Q76.6
      supernumerary in cervical region
          Q76.5
    scapula Q74.0
    shoulder Q74.0
    spinal cord Q06.8
    spleen Q89.09
    sternum NEC Q76.7
    stomach Q40.2
    symphysis pubis Q74.2
    thymus (gland) Q89.2
    thyroid (gland) (tissue) Q89.2
      cartilage Q31.8
    toe(s) Q66.9
      supernumerary Q69.2
    tongue Q38.3
    trachea Q32.1
    ureter Q62.60
      deviation Q62.61
      displacement Q62.62
      ectopia Q62.63
      specified type NEC Q62.69

▶ New   ⇒ Revised   ~~deleted~~ Deleted   ● Use Additional Character(s)

Malposition *(Continued)*
congenital *(Continued)*
uterus Q51.818
vein(s) (peripheral) Q27.8
great Q26.8
vena cava (inferior) (superior) Q26.8
device, implant or graft —*see also*
Complications, by site and type,
mechanical T85.628
arterial graft NEC —*see* Complication,
cardiovascular device, mechanical,
vascular
breast (implant) T85.42
catheter NEC T85.628
cystostomy T83.020
dialysis (renal) T82.42
intraperitoneal T85.621
infusion NEC T82.524
spinal (epidural) (subdural) T85.620
urinary —*see also* Displacement, device,
catheter, urinary T83.028
electronic (electrode) (pulse generator)
(stimulator)
bone T84.320
cardiac T82.129
electrode T82.120
pulse generator T82.121
specified type NEC T82.128
nervous system —*see* Complication,
prosthetic device, mechanical,
electronic nervous system
stimulator
urinary —*see* Complication,
genitourinary, device, urinary,
mechanical
fixation, internal (orthopedic) NEC —
see Complication, fixation device,
mechanical
gastrointestinal —*see* Complications,
prosthetic device, mechanical,
gastrointestinal device
genital NEC T83.428
intrauterine contraceptive device (string)
T83.32
penile prosthesis (cylinder) (implanted)
(pump) (resevoir) T83.420
testicular prosthesis T83.421
heart NEC —*see* Complication,
cardiovascular device, mechanical
joint prosthesis —*see* Complication, joint
prosthesis, mechanical
ocular NEC —*see* Complications,
prosthetic device, mechanical,
ocular device
orthopedic NEC —*see* Complication,
orthopedic, device, mechanical
specified NEC T85.628
urinary NEC —*see also* Complication,
genitourinary, device, urinary,
mechanical
graft T83.22
vascular NEC —*see* Complication,
cardiovascular device, mechanical
ventricular intracranial shunt T85.02
fetus —*see* Pregnancy, complicated by
(management affected by), presentation,
fetal
gallbladder K82.8
gastrointestinal tract, congenital Q45.8
heart, congenital NEC Q24.8
joint prosthesis —*see* Complications, joint
prosthesis, mechanical, displacement,
by site
stomach K31.89
congenital Q40.2
tooth, teeth, fully erupted M26.30
uterus (acute) (acquired) (adherent)
(asymptomatic) (postinfectional)
(postpartal, old) N85.4
anteflexion or anteversion N85.4
congenital Q51.818

Malposition *(Continued)*
uterus *(Continued)*
flexion N85.4
lateral —*see* Lateroversion, uterus
inversion N85.5
lateral (flexion) (version) —*see*
Lateroversion, uterus
in pregnancy or childbirth —*see*
subcategory O34.5
retroflexion or retroversion —*see*
Retroversion, uterus
Malposture R29.3
Malrotation
cecum Q43.3
colon Q43.3
intestine Q43.3
kidney Q63.2
Malta fever —*see* Brucellosis
Maltreatment
adult
abandonment
confirmed T74.01
suspected T76.01
►bullying
►confirmed T74.31
►suspected T76.31
confirmed T74.91
history of Z91.419
►intimidation (through social media)
►confirmed T74.31
►suspected T76.31
neglect
confirmed T74.01
suspected T76.01
physical abuse
confirmed T74.11
suspected T76.11
psychological abuse
confirmed T74.31
history of Z91.411
suspected T76.31
sexual abuse
confirmed T74.21
suspected T76.21
suspected T76.91
child
abandonment
confirmed T74.02
suspected T76.02
►bullying
►confirmed T74.32
►suspected T76.32
confirmed T74.92
history of —*see* History, personal (of),
abuse
►intimidation (through social media)
►confirmed T74.32
►suspected T76.32
neglect
confirmed T74.02
history of —*see* History, personal (of),
abuse
suspected T76.02
physical abuse
confirmed T74.12
history of —*see* History, personal (of),
abuse
suspected T76.12
psychological abuse
confirmed T74.32
history of —*see* History, personal (of),
abuse
suspected T76.32
sexual abuse
confirmed T74.22
history of —*see* History, personal (of),
abuse
suspected T76.22
suspected T76.92
personal history of Z91.89
Maltworker's lung J67.4

Malunion, fracture —*see* Fracture, by site
Mammillitis N61.0
puerperal, postpartum O91.02
Mammitis —*see* Mastitis
Mammogram (examination) Z12.39
routine Z12.31
Mammoplasia N62
Management (of)
bone conduction hearing device (implanted)
Z45.320
cardiac pacemaker NEC Z45.018
cerebrospinal fluid drainage device Z45.41
cochlear device (implanted) Z45.321
contraceptive Z30.9
specified NEC Z30.8
implanted device Z45.9
specified NEC Z45.89
infusion pump Z45.1
procreative Z31.9
male factor infertility in female Z31.81
specified NEC Z31.89
prosthesis (external) —*see also* Fitting
Z44.9
implanted Z45.9
specified NEC Z45.89
renal dialysis catheter Z49.01
vascular access device Z45.2
Mangled —*see* specified injury by site
Mania (monopolar) —*see also* Disorder, mood,
manic episode
with psychotic symptoms F30.2
without psychotic symptoms F30.10
mild F30.11
moderate F30.12
severe F30.13
Bell's F30.8
chronic (recurrent) F31.89
hysterical F44.89
puerperal F30.8
recurrent F31.89
Manic depression F31.9
Manic-depressive insanity, psychosis, or
syndrome —*see* Disorder, bipolar
Mannosidosis E77.1
Mansonelliasis, mansonellosis B74.4
Manson's
disease B65.1
schistosomiasis B65.1
Manual —*see* condition
Maple-bark-stripper's lung (disease) J67.6
Maple-syrup-urine disease E71.0
Marable's syndrome (celiac artery
compression) I77.4
Marasmus E41
due to malnutrition E41
intestinal E41
nutritional E41
senile R54
tuberculous NEC —*see* Tuberculosis
Marble
bones Q78.2
skin R23.8
Marburg virus disease A98.3
March
fracture —*see* Fracture, traumatic, stress, by
site
hemoglobinuria D59.6
Marchesani (-Weill) syndrome Q87.0
Marchiafava (-Bignami) syndrome or disease
G37.1
Marchiafava-Micheli syndrome D59.5
Marcus Gunn's syndrome Q07.8
Marfan's syndrome —*see* Syndrome, Marfan's
Marie-Bamberger disease —*see*
Osteoarthropathy, hypertrophic, specified
NEC
Marie-Charcot-Tooth neuropathic muscular
atrophy G60.0
Marie's
cerebellar ataxia (late-onset) G11.2
disease or syndrome (acromegaly) E22.0

Marie-Strümpell arthritis, disease or
   spondylitis —see Spondylitis, ankylosing
Marion's disease (bladder neck obstruction)
   N32.0
Marital conflict Z63.0
Mark
   port wine Q82.5
   raspberry Q82.5
   strawberry Q82.5
   stretch L90.6
   tattoo L81.8
Marker heterochromatin —see Extra, marker
   chromosomes
Maroteaux-Lamy syndrome (mild) (severe)
   E76.29
Marrow (bone)
   arrest D61.9
   poor function D75.89
Marseilles fever A77.1
Marsh fever —see Malaria
Marshall's (hidrotic) ectodermal dysplasia
   Q82.4
Marsh's disease (exophthalmic goiter)
   E05.00
   with storm E05.01
Masculinization (female) with adrenal
   hyperplasia E25.9
   congenital E25.0
Masculinovoblastoma D27.-●
Masochism (sexual) F65.51
Mason's lung J62.8
Mass
   abdominal R19.00
      epigastric R19.06
      generalized R19.07
      left lower quadrant R19.04
      left upper quadrant R19.02
      periumbilic R19.05
      right lower quadrant R19.03
      right upper quadrant R19.01
      specified site NEC R19.09
   breast —see also Lump, breast N63.0
   chest R22.2
   cystic —see Cyst
   ear H93.8-●
   head R22.0
   intra-abdominal (diffuse) (generalized) —see
      Mass, abdominal
   kidney N28.89
   liver R16.0
   localized (skin) R22.9
      chest R22.2
      head R22.0
      limb
         lower R22.4-●
         upper R22.3-●
      neck R22.1
      trunk R22.2
   lung R91.8
   malignant —see Neoplasm, malignant,
      by site
   neck R22.1
   pelvic (diffuse) (generalized) —see Mass,
      abdominal
   specified organ NEC —see Disease, by site
   splenic R16.1
   substernal thyroid —see Goiter
   superficial (localized) R22.9
   umbilical (diffuse) (generalized) R19.09
Massive —see condition
Mast cell
   disease, systemic tissue D47.02
   leukemia C94.3-●
   neoplasm
      malignant C96.20
         specified type NEC C96.29
      of uncertain behavior NEC D47.09
   sarcoma C96.22
   tumor D47.09
Mastalgia N64.4
Masters-Allen syndrome N83.8

Mastitis (acute) (diffuse) (nonpuerperal)
   (subacute) N61.0
   with abscess N61.1
   chronic (cystic) —see Mastopathy, cystic
   cystic (Schimmelbusch's type) —see
      Mastopathy, cystic
   fibrocystic —see Mastopathy, cystic
   infective N61.0
      newborn P39.0
   interstitial, gestational or puerperal —see
      Mastitis, obstetric
   neonatal (noninfective) P83.4
      infective P39.0
   obstetric (interstitial) (nonpurulent)
      associated with
         lactation O91.23
         pregnancy O91.21-●
         puerperium O91.22
      purulent
         associated with
            lactation O91.13
            pregnancy O91.11-●
            puerperium O91.12
   periductal —see Ectasia, mammary duct
   phlegmonous —see Mastopathy, cystic
   plasma cell —see Ectasia, mammary duct
   without abscess N61.0
Mastocytoma (extracutaneous) D47.09
   malignant C96.29
   solitary D47.01
Mastocytosis D47.09
   aggressive systemic C96.21
   cutaneous (diffuse) (maculopapular) D47.01
      congenital Q82.2
      of neonatal onset Q82.2
      of newborn onset Q82.2
   indolent systemic D47.02
   isolated bone marrow D47.02
   malignant C96.29
   systemic (indolent) (smoldering)
      with an associated hematological
         non-mast cell lineage disease
         (SM-AHNMD) D47.02
Mastodynia N64.4
Mastoid —see condition
Mastoidalgia —see subcategory H92.0
Mastoiditis (coalescent) (hemorrhagic)
   (suppurative) H70.9-●
   acute, subacute H70.00-●
      complicated NEC H70.09-●
      subperiosteal H70.01-●
   chronic (necrotic) (recurrent) H70.1-●
   in (due to)
      infectious disease NEC B99 [H75.0-●]
      parasitic disease NEC B89 [H75.0-●]
      tuberculosis A18.03
   petrositis —see Petrositis
   postauricular fistula —see Fistula,
      postauricular
   specified NEC H70.89-●
   tuberculous A18.03
Mastopathy, mastopathia N64.9
   chronica cystica —see Mastopathy, cystic
   cystic (chronic) (diffuse) N60.1
      with epithelial proliferation N60.3-●
   diffuse cystic —see Mastopathy, cystic
   estrogenic, oestrogenica N64.89
   ovarian origin N64.89
Mastoplasia, mastoplastia N62
Masturbation (excessive) F98.8
Maternal care (for) —see Pregnancy
   (complicated by) (management affected by)
Matheiu's disease (leptospiral jaundice) A27.0
Mauclaire's disease or osteochondrosis —
   see Osteochondrosis, juvenile, hand,
   metacarpal
Maxcy's disease A75.2
Maxilla, maxillary —see condition
May (-Hegglin) anomaly or syndrome D72.0
McArdle (-Schmid)(-Pearson) disease
   (glycogen storage) E74.04

McCune-Albright syndrome Q78.1
McQuarrie's syndrome (idiopathic familial
   hypoglycemia) E16.2
Meadow's syndrome Q86.1
Measles (black) (hemorrhagic) (suppressed)
   B05.9
   with
      complications NEC B05.89
      encephalitis B05.0
      intestinal complications B05.4
      keratitis (keratoconjunctivitis) B05.81
      meningitis B05.1
      otitis media B05.3
      pneumonia B05.2
   French —see Rubella
   German —see Rubella
   Liberty —see Rubella
Meatitis, urethral —see Urethritis
Meatus, meatal —see condition
Meat-wrappers' asthma J68.9
Meckel-Gruber syndrome Q61.9
Meckel's diverticulitis, diverticulum
   (displaced) (hypertrophic) Q43.0
Meconium
   ileus, newborn P76.0
      in cystic fibrosis E84.11
      meaning meconium plug (without cystic
         fibrosis) P76.0
   obstruction, newborn P76.0
      due to fecaliths P76.0
      in mucoviscidosis E84.11
   peritonitis P78.0
   plug syndrome (newborn) NEC P76.0
Median —see also condition
   arcuate ligament syndrome I77.4
   bar (prostate) (vesical orifice) —see
      Hyperplasia, prostate
   rhomboid glossitis K14.2
▶Mediastinal shift R93.89
Mediastinitis (acute) (chronic) J98.51
   syphilitic A52.73
   tuberculous A15.8
Mediastinopericarditis —see also Pericarditis
   acute I30.9
   adhesive I31.0
   chronic I31.8
   rheumatic I09.2
Mediastinum, mediastinal —see condition
Medicine poisoning —see Table of Drugs and
   Chemicals, by drug, poisoning
Mediterranean
   fever —see Brucellosis
      familial M04.1
      tick A77.1
   kala-azar B55.0
   leishmaniasis B55.0
   tick fever A77.1
Medulla —see condition
Medullary cystic kidney Q61.5
Medullated fibers
   optic (nerve) Q14.8
   retina Q14.1
Medulloblastoma
   desmoplastic C71.6
   specified site —see Neoplasm, malignant, by
      site
   unspecified site C71.6
Medulloepithelioma —see also Neoplasm,
   malignant, by site
   teratoid —see Neoplasm, malignant, by site
Medullomyoblastoma
   specified site —see Neoplasm, malignant, by
      site
   unspecified site C71.6
Meekeren-Ehlers-Danlos syndrome Q79.6
Megacolon (acquired) (functional) (not
   Hirschsprung's disease) (in) K59.39
   Chagas' disease B57.32
   congenital, congenitum (aganglionic)
      Q43.1
   Hirschsprung's (disease) Q43.1

▶ New   ⇒ Revised   ~~deleted~~ Deleted   ● Use Additional Character(s)

Megacolon (Continued)
   toxic NEC K59.31
      due to Clostridium difficile
         not specified as recurrent A04.72
         recurrent A04.71
Megaesophagus (functional) K22.0
   congenital Q39.5
   in (due to) Chagas' disease B57.31
Megalencephaly Q04.5
Megalerythema (epidemic) B08.3
Megaloappendix Q43.8
Megalocephalus, megalocephaly NEC Q75.3
Megalocornea Q15.8
   with glaucoma Q15.0
Megalocytic anemia D53.1
Megalodactylia (fingers) (thumbs) (congenital)
   Q74.0
   toes Q74.2
Megaloduodenum Q43.8
Megaloesophagus (functional) K22.0
   congenital Q39.5
Megalogastria (acquired) K31.89
   congenital Q40.2
Megalophthalmos Q11.3
Megalopsia H53.15
Megalosplenia —see Splenomegaly
Megaloureter N28.82
   congenital Q62.2
Megarectum K62.89
Megasigmoid K59.39
   congenital Q43.2
Megaureter N28.82
   congenital Q62.2
Megavitamin-B6 syndrome E67.2
Megrim —see Migraine
Meibomian
   cyst, infected —see Hordeolum
   gland —see condition
   sty, stye —see Hordeolum
Meibomitis —see Hordeolum
Meige-Milroy disease (chronic hereditary
   edema) Q82.0
Meige's syndrome Q82.0
Melalgia, nutritional E53.8
Melancholia F32.9
   climacteric (single episode) F32.89
      recurrent episode F33.8
   hypochondriac F45.29
   intermittent (single episode) F32.89
      recurrent episode F33.8
   involutional (single episode) F32.89
      recurrent episode F33.8
   menopausal (single episode) F32.89
      recurrent episode F33.8
   puerperal F32.89
   reactive (emotional stress or trauma) F32.3
   recurrent F33.9
   senile F03
   stuporous (single episode) F32.89
      recurrent episode F33.8
Melanemia R79.89
Melanoameloblastoma —see Neoplasm, bone,
   benign
Melanoblastoma —see Melanoma
Melanocarcinoma —see Melanoma
Melanocytoma, eyeball D31.9-●
Melanocytosis, neurocutaneous Q82.8
Melanoderma, melanodermia L81.4
Melanodontia, infantile K03.89
Melanodontoclasia K03.89
Melanoepithelioma —see Melanoma
Melanoma (malignant) C43.9
   acral lentiginous, malignant —see Melanoma,
      skin, by site
   amelanotic —see Melanoma, skin, by site
   balloon cell —see Melanoma, skin, by site
   benign —see Nevus
   desmoplastic, malignant —see Melanoma,
      skin, by site
   epithelioid cell —see Melanoma, skin, by site
      with spindle cell, mixed —see Melanoma,
        skin, by site

Melanoma (Continued)
   in
      giant pigmented nevus —see Melanoma,
        skin, by site
      Hutchinson's melanotic freckle —see
        Melanoma, skin, by site
      junctional nevus —see Melanoma, skin,
        by site
      precancerous melanosis —see Melanoma,
        skin, by site
   in situ D03.9
      abdominal wall D03.59
      ala nasi D03.39
      ankle D03.7-●
      anus, anal (margin) (skin) D03.51
      arm D03.6-●
      auditory canal D03.2-●
      auricle (ear) D03.2-●
      auricular canal (external) D03.2-●
      axilla, axillary fold D03.59
      back D03.59
      breast D03.52
      brow D03.39
      buttock D03.59
      canthus (eye) D03.1-●
      cheek (external) D03.39
      chest wall D03.59
      chin D03.39
      choroid D03.8
      conjunctiva D03.8
      ear (external) D03.2-●
      external meatus (ear) D03.2-●
      eye D03.8
      eyebrow D03.39
      eyelid (lower) (upper) D03.1-●
      face D03.30
         specified NEC D03.39
      female genital organ (external) NEC D03.8
      finger D03.6-●
      flank D03.59
      foot D03.7-●
      forearm D03.6-●
      forehead D03.39
      foreskin D03.8
      gluteal region D03.59
      groin D03.59
      hand D03.6-●
      heel D03.7-●
      helix D03.2-●
      hip D03.7-●
      interscapular region D03.59
      iris D03.8
      jaw D03.39
      knee D03.7-●
      labium (majus) (minus) D03.8
      lacrimal gland D03.8
      leg D03.7-●
      lip (lower) (upper) D03.0
      lower limb NEC D03.7-●
      male genital organ (external) NEC D03.8
      nail D03.9
         finger D03.6-●
         toe D03.7-●
      neck D03.4
      nose (external) D03.39
      orbit D03.8
      penis D03.8
      perianal skin D03.51
      perineum D03.51
      pinna D03.2-●
      popliteal fossa or space D03.7-●
      prepuce D03.8
      pudendum D03.8
      retina D03.8
      retrobulbar D03.8
      scalp D03.4
      scrotum D03.8
      shoulder D03.6-●
      specified site NEC D03.8
      submammary fold D03.52
      temple D03.39

Melanoma (Continued)
   in situ (Continued)
      thigh D03.7-●
      toe D03.7-●
      trunk NEC D03.59
      umbilicus D03.59
      upper limb NEC D03.6-●
      vulva D03.8
   juvenile —see Nevus
   malignant, of soft parts except skin —see
      Neoplasm, connective tissue, malignant
   metastatic
      breast C79.81
      genital organ C79.82
      specified site NEC C79.89
   neurotropic, malignant —see Melanoma, skin,
      by site
   nodular —see Melanoma, skin, by site
   regressing, malignant —see Melanoma, skin,
      by site
   skin C43.9
      abdominal wall C43.59
      ala nasi C43.31
      ankle C43.7-●
      anus, anal (skin) C43.51
      arm C43.6-●
      auditory canal (external) C43.2-●
      auricle (ear) C43.2-●
      auricular canal (external) C43.2-●
      axilla, axillary fold C43.59
      back C43.59
      breast (female) (male) C43.52
      brow C43.39
      buttock C43.59
      canthus (eye) C43.1-●
      cheek (external) C43.39
      chest wall C43.59
      chin C43.39
      ear (external) C43.2-●
      elbow C43.6-●
      external meatus (ear) C43.2-●
      eyebrow C43.39
      eyelid (lower) (upper) C43.1-●
      face C43.30
         specified NEC C43.39
      female genital organ (external) NEC C51.9
      finger C43.6-●
      flank C43.59
      foot C43.7-●
      forearm C43.6-●
      forehead C43.39
      foreskin C60.0
      glabella C43.39
      gluteal region C43.59
      groin C43.59
      hand C43.6-●
      heel C43.7-●
      helix C43.2-●
      hip C43.7-●
      interscapular region C43.59
      jaw (external) C43.39
      knee C43.7-●
      labium C51.9
         majus C51.0
         minus C51.1
      leg C43.7-●
      lip (lower) (upper) C43.0
      lower limb NEC C43.7-●
      male genital organ (external) NEC C63.9
      nail
         finger C43.6-●
         toe C43.7-●
      nasolabial groove C43.39
      nates C43.59
      neck C43.4
      nose (external) C43.31
      overlapping site C43.8
      palpebra C43.1-●
      penis C60.9
      perianal skin C43.51
      perineum C43.51

Merzbacher-Pelizaeus disease E75.29
Mesaortitis —see Aortitis
Mesarteritis —see Arteritis
Mesencephalitis —see Encephalitis
Mesenchymoma —see also Neoplasm,
    connective tissue, uncertain behavior
  benign —see Neoplasm, connective tissue,
    benign
  malignant —see Neoplasm, connective tissue,
    malignant
Mesenteritis
  retractile K65.4
  sclerosing K65.4
Mesentery, mesenteric —see condition
Mesiodens, mesiodentes K00.1
Mesio-occlusion M26.213
Mesocolon —see condition
Mesonephroma (malignant) —see Neoplasm,
    malignant, by site
  benign —see Neoplasm, benign, by site
Mesophlebitis —see Phlebitis
Mesostromal dysgenesis Q13.89
Mesothelioma (malignant) C45.9
  benign
    mesentery D19.1
    mesocolon D19.1
    omentum D19.1
    peritoneum D19.1
    pleura D19.0
    specified site NEC D19.7
    unspecified site D19.9
  biphasic C45.9
    benign
      mesentery D19.1
      mesocolon D19.1
      omentum D19.1
      peritoneum D19.1
      pleura D19.0
      specified site NEC D19.7
      unspecified site D19.9
  cystic D48.4
  epithelioid C45.9
    benign
      mesentery D19.1
      mesocolon D19.1
      omentum D19.1
      peritoneum D19.1
      pleura D19.0
      specified site NEC D19.7
      unspecified site D19.9
  fibrous C45.9
    benign
      mesentery D19.1
      mesocolon D19.1
      omentum D19.1
      peritoneum D19.1
      pleura D19.0
      specified site NEC D19.7
      unspecified site D19.9
  site classification
    liver C45.7
    lung C45.7
    mediastinum C45.7
    mesentery C45.1
    mesocolon C45.1
    omentum C45.1
    pericardium C45.2
    peritoneum C45.1
    pleura C45.0
      parietal C45.0
    retroperitoneum C45.7
    specified site NEC C45.7
    unspecified C45.9
Metabolic syndrome E88.81
Metagonimiasis B66.8
Metagonimus infestation (intestine)
    B66.8
Metal
  pigmentation L81.8
  polisher's disease J62.8
Metamorphopsia H53.15

Metaplasia
  apocrine (breast) —see Dysplasia, mammary,
    specified type NEC
  cervix (squamous) —see Dysplasia, cervix
  endometrium (squamous) (uterus) N85.8
  esophagus K22.7-●
  kidney (pelvis) (squamous) N28.89
  myelogenous D73.1
  myeloid (agnogenic) (megakaryocytic) D73.1
  spleen D73.1
  squamous cell, bladder N32.89
Metastasis, metastatic
  abscess —see Abscess
  calcification E83.59
  cancer
    from specified site —see Neoplasm,
      malignant, by site
    to specified site —see Neoplasm, secondary,
      by site
  deposits (in) —see Neoplasm, secondary, by
    site
  disease (see also Neoplasm, secondary, by site)
    C79.9
  spread (to) —see Neoplasm, secondary, by site
Metastrongyliasis B83.8
Metatarsalgia M77.4-●
  anterior G57.6-●
  Morton's G57.6-●
Metatarsus, metatarsal —see also condition
  adductus, congenital Q66.22
  valgus (abductus), congenital Q66.6
  varus (congenital) Q66.22
    primus Q66.21
Methadone use —see Use, opioid
Methemoglobinemia D74.9
  acquired (with sulfhemoglobinemia) D74.8
  congenital D74.0
  enzymatic (congenital) D74.0
  Hb M disease D74.0
  hereditary D74.0
  toxic D74.8
Methemoglobinuria —see Hemoglobinuria
Methioninemia E72.19
Methylmalonic acidemia E71.120
Metritis (catarrhal) (hemorrhagic) (septic)
    (suppurative) —see also Endometritis
  cervical —see Cervicitis
Metropathia hemorrhagica N93.8
Metroperitonitis —see Peritonitis, pelvic,
    female
Metrorrhagia N92.1
  climacteric N92.4
  menopausal N92.4
  postpartum NEC (atonic) (following delivery
    of placenta) O72.1
    delayed or secondary O72.2
  preclimacteric or premenopausal N92.4
  psychogenic F45.8
Metrorrhexis —see Rupture, uterus
Metrosalpingitis N70.91
Metrostaxis N93.8
Metrovaginitis —see Endometritis
Meyer-Schwickerath and Weyers syndrome
    Q87.0
Meynert's amentia (nonalcoholic) F04
  alcoholic F10.96
    with dependence F10.26
Mibelli's disease (porokeratosis) Q82.8
Mice, joint —see Loose, body, joint
  knee M23.4
Micrencephalon, micrencephaly Q02
Microalbuminuria R80.9
Microaneurysm, retinal —see also Disorder,
    retina, microaneurysms
  diabetic —see E08-E13 with .31
Microangiopathy (peripheral) I73.9
  thrombotic M31.1
Microcalcifications, breast R92.0
Microcephalus, microcephalic, microcephaly
    Q02
  due to toxoplasmosis (congenital) P37.1

Microcheilia Q18.7
Microcolon (congenital) Q43.8
Microcornea (congenital) Q13.4
Microcytic —see condition D57.40
Microdeletions NEC Q93.88
Microdontia K00.2
Microdrepanocytosis D57.40
  with crisis (vasoocclusive pain) D57.419
    with
      acute chest syndrome D57.411
      splenic sequestration D57.412
Microembolism
  atherothrombotic —see Atheroembolism
  retinal —see Occlusion, artery, retina
Microencephalon Q02
Microfilaria streptocerca infestation —see
    Onchocerciasis
Microgastria (congenital) Q40.2
Microgenia M26.06
Microgenitalia, congenital
  female Q52.8
  male Q55.8
Microglioma —see Lymphoma, non-Hodgkin,
    specified NEC
Microglossia (congenital) Q38.3
Micrognathia, micrognathism (congenital)
    (mandibular) (maxillary) M26.09
Microgyria (congenital) Q04.3
Microinfarct of heart —see Insufficiency,
    coronary
Microlentia (congenital) Q12.8
Microlithiasis, alveolar, pulmonary
    J84.02
Micromastia N64.82
Micromyelia (congenital) Q06.8
Micropenis Q55.62
Microphakia (congenital) Q12.8
Microphthalmos, microphthalmia (congenital)
    Q11.2
  due to toxoplasmosis P37.1
Micropsia H53.15
Microscopic polyangiitis (polyarteritis)
    M31.7
Microsporidiosis B60.8
  intestinal A07.8
Microsporon furfur infestation B36.0
Microsporosis —see also Dermatophytosis
  nigra B36.1
Microstomia (congenital) Q18.5
Microtia (congenital) (external ear) Q17.2
Microtropia H50.40
Microvillus inclusion disease (MVD) (MVID)
    Q43.8
Micturition
  disorder NEC —see also Difficulty, micturition
    R39.198
  psychogenic F45.8
  frequency R35.0
    psychogenic F45.8
  hesitancy R39.11
  incomplete emptying R39.14
  nocturnal R35.1
  painful R30.9
    dysuria R30.0
    psychogenic F45.8
    tenesmus R30.1
  poor stream R39.12
  position dependent R39.192
  split stream R39.13
  straining R39.16
  urgency R39.15
Mid plane —see condition
Middle
  ear —see condition
  lobe (right) syndrome J98.19
Miescher's elastoma L87.2
Mietens' syndrome Q87.2
Migraine (idiopathic) G43.909
  with refractory migraine G43.919
    with status migrainosus G43.911
    without status migrainosus G43.919

Migraine *(Continued)*
with aura (acute-onset) (prolonged) (typical)
  (without headache) G43.109
  with refractory migraine G43.119
    with status migrainosus G43.111
    without status migrainosus G43.119
  intractable G43.119
    with status migrainosus G43.111
    without status migrainosus G43.119
  not intractable G43.109
    with status migrainosus G43.101
    without status migrainosus G43.109
  persistent G43.509
    with cerebral infarction G43.609
      with refractory migraine G43.619
        with status migrainosus G43.611
        without status migrainosus G43.619
      intractable G43.619
        with status migrainosus G43.611
        without status migrainosus G43.619
      not intractable G43.609
        with status migrainosus G43.601
        without status migrainosus G43.609
      without refractory migraine G43.609
        with status migrainosus G43.601
        without status migrainosus G43.609
    without cerebral infarction G43.509
      with refractory migraine G43.519
        with status migrainosus G43.511
        without status migrainosus G43.519
      intractable G43.519
        with status migrainosus G43.511
        without status migrainosus G43.519
      not intractable G43.509
        with status migrainosus G43.501
        without status migrainosus G43.509
      without refractory migraine G43.509
        with status migrainosus G43.501
        without status migrainosus G43.509
  without mention of refractory migraine
    G43.109
    with status migrainosus G43.101
    without status migrainosus G43.109
abdominal G43.D0
  with refractory migraine G43.D1
  intractable G43.D1
  not intractable G43.D0
  without refractory migraine G43.D0
basilar —*see* Migraine, with aura
classical —*see* Migraine, with aura
common —*see* Migraine, without aura
complicated G43.109
equivalents —*see* Migraine, with aura
familiar —*see* Migraine, hemiplegic
hemiplegic G43.409
  with refractory migraine G43.419
    with status migrainosus G43.411
    without status migrainosus G43.419
  intractable G43.419
    with status migrainosus G43.411
    without status migrainosus G43.419
  not intractable G43.409
    with status migrainosus G43.401
    without status migrainosus G43.409
  without refractory migraine G43.409
    with status migrainosus G43.401
    without status migrainosus G43.409
intractable G43.919
  with status migrainosus G43.911
  without status migrainosus G43.919
menstrual G43.829
  with refractory migraine G43.839
    with status migrainosus G43.831
    without status migrainosus G43.839
  intractable G43.839
    with status migrainosus G43.831
    without status migrainosus G43.839
  not intractable G43.829
    with status migrainosus G43.821
    without status migrainosus G43.829
  without refractory migraine G43.829
    with status migrainosus G43.821
    without status migrainosus G43.829

Migraine *(Continued)*
menstrually related —*see* Migraine,
  menstrual
not intractable G43.909
  with status migrainosus G43.901
  without status migrainosus G43.919
ophthalmoplegic G43.B0
  with refractory migraine G43.B1
  intractable G43.B1
  not intractable G43.B0
    without refractory migraine
      G43.B0
persistent aura (with, without) cerebral
  infarction —*see* Migraine, with aura,
  persistent
preceded or accompanied by transient focal
  neurological phenomena —*see* Migraine,
  with aura
pre-menstrual —*see* Migraine, menstrual
pure menstrual —*see* Migraine, menstrual
retinal —*see* Migraine, with aura
specified NEC G43.809
  intractable G43.819
    with status migrainosus G43.811
    without status migrainosus G43.819
  not intractable G43.809
    with status migrainosus G43.801
    without status migrainosus G43.809
sporadic —*see* Migraine, hemiplegic
transformed —*see* Migraine, without aura,
  chronic
triggered seizures —*see* Migraine, with aura
without aura G43.009
  with refractory migraine G43.019
    with status migrainosus G43.011
    without status migrainosus G43.019
  chronic G43.709
    with refractory migraine G43.719
      with status migrainosus G43.711
      without status migrainosus G43.719
    intractable
      with status migrainosus G43.711
      without status migrainosus G43.719
    not intractable
      with status migrainosus G43.701
      without status migrainosus G43.709
    without refractory migraine G43.709
      with status migrainosus G43.701
      without status migrainosus
        G43.709
  intractable
    with status migrainosus G43.011
    without status migrainosus G43.019
  not intractable
    with status migrainosus G43.001
    without status migrainosus G43.009
  without mention of refractory migraine
    G43.009
    with status migrainosus G43.001
    without status migrainosus G43.009
  without refractory migraine G43.909
    with status migrainosus G43.901
    without status migrainosus G43.919
Migrant, social Z59.0
Migration, anxiety concerning Z60.3
Migratory, migrating —*see also* condition
  person Z59.0
  testis Q55.29
Mikity-Wilson disease or syndrome
  P27.0
Mikulicz' disease or syndrome K11.8
Miliaria L74.3
  alba L74.1
  apocrine L75.2
  crystallina L74.1
  profunda L74.2
  rubra L74.0
  tropicalis L74.2
Miliary —*see* condition
Milium L72.0
  colloid L57.8

Milk
  crust L21.0
  excessive secretion O92.6
  poisoning —*see* Poisoning, food, noxious
  retention O92.79
  sickness —*see* Poisoning, food, noxious
  spots I31.0
Milk-alkali disease or syndrome E83.52
Milk-leg (deep vessels) (nonpuerperal) —*see*
  Embolism, vein, lower extremity
  complicating pregnancy O22.3- •
  puerperal, postpartum, childbirth O87.1
Milkman's disease or syndrome M83.8
Milky urine —*see* Chyluria
Millard-Gubler (-Foville) **paralysis or**
  syndrome G46.3
Millar's asthma J38.5
Miller-Fisher syndrome G61.0
Mills' disease —*see* Hemiplegia
Millstone maker's pneumoconiosis J62.8
Milroy's disease (chronic hereditary edema)
  Q82.0
Minamata disease T56.1- •
Miners' asthma or lung J60
Minkowski-Chauffard syndrome —*see*
  Spherocytosis
Minor —*see* condition
Minor's disease (hematomyelia) G95.19
Minot's disease (hemorrhagic disease),
  newborn P53
Minot-von Willebrand-Jurgens disease or
  syndrome (angiohemophilia) D68.0
Minus (and plus) hand (intrinsic) —*see*
  Deformity, limb, specified type NEC,
  forearm
Miosis (pupil) H57.03
Mirizzi's syndrome (hepatic duct stenosis) K83.1
Mirror writing F81.0
Misadventure (of) (prophylactic) (therapeutic) —
  see also Complications T88.9
  administration of insulin (by accident) —*see*
    subcategory T38.3
  infusion —*see* Complications, infusion
  local applications (of fomentations, plasters,
    etc.) T88.9
    burn or scald —*see* Burn
    specified NEC T88.8
  medical care (early) (late) T88.9
    adverse effect of drugs or chemicals —*see*
      Table of Drugs and Chemicals
  medical care (early) (late)
    burn or scald —*see* Burn
    specified NEC T88.8
  specified NEC T88.8
  surgical procedure (early) (late) —*see*
    Complications, surgical procedure
  transfusion —*see* Complications, transfusion
  vaccination or other immunological
    procedure —*see* Complications,
    vaccination
Miscarriage O03.9
Misdirection, aqueous H40.83- •
Misperception, sleep state F51.02
Misplaced, misplacement
  ear Q17.4
  kidney (acquired) N28.89
    congenital Q63.2
  organ or site, congenital NEC —*see*
    Malposition, congenital
Missed
  abortion O02.1
  delivery O36.4
Missing —*see also* Absence
  string of intrauterine contraceptive device
    T83.32
Misuse of drugs F19.99
Mitchell's disease (erythromelalgia) I73.81
Mite(s) (infestation) B88.9
  diarrhea B88.0
  grain (itch) B88.0
  hair follicle (itch) B88.0
  in sputum B88.0

▶ New   ⇛ Revised   ~~deleted~~ Deleted   • Use Additional Character(s)

Mitral —see condition
Mittelschmerz N94.0
Mixed —see condition
MMN (multifocal motor neuropathy) G61.82
MNGIE (Mitochondrial Neurogastrointestinal
  Encephalopathy) syndrome E88.49
Mobile, mobility
  cecum Q43.3
  excessive —see Hypermobility
  gallbladder, congenital Q44.1
  kidney N28.89
  organ or site, congenital NEC —see
    Malposition, congenital
Mobitz heart block (atrioventricular) I44.1
Moebius, Möbius
  disease (ophthalmoplegic migraine) —see
    Migraine, ophthalmoplegic
  syndrome Q87.0
    congenital oculofacial paralysis (with other
      anomalies) Q87.0
    ophthalmoplegic migraine —see Migraine,
      ophthalmoplegic
Moeller's glossitis K14.0
Mohr's syndrome (Types I and II) Q87.0
Mola destruens D39.2
Molar pregnancy O02.0
Molarization of premolars K00.2
Molding, head (during birth) - omit code
Mole (pigmented) —see also Nevus
  blood O02.0
  Breus' O02.0
  cancerous —see Melanoma
  carneous O02.0
  destructive D39.2
  fleshy O02.0
  hydatid, hydatidiform (benign) (complicating
    pregnancy) (delivered) (undelivered)
    O01.9
    classical O01.0
    complete O01.0
    incomplete O01.1
    invasive D39.2
    malignant D39.2
    partial O01.1
  intrauterine O02.0
  invasive (hydatidiform) D39.2
  malignant
    meaning
      malignant hydatidiform mole D39.2
      melanoma —see Melanoma
  nonhydatidiform O02.0
  nonpigmented —see Nevus
  pregnancy NEC O02.0
  skin —see Nevus
  tubal O00.10-
    with intrauterine pregnancy O00.11-
  vesicular —see Mole, hydatidiform
Molimen, molimina (menstrual) N94.3
Molluscum contagiosum (epitheliale) B08.1
Mönckeberg's arteriosclerosis, disease, or
  sclerosis —see Arteriosclerosis, extremities
Mondini's malformation (cochlea) Q16.5
Mondor's disease I80.8
Monge's disease T70.29
Monilethrix (congenital) Q84.1
Moniliasis —see also Candidiasis B37.9
  neonatal P37.5
Monitoring (encounter for)
  therapeutic drug level Z51.81
Monkey malaria B53.1
Monkeypox B04
Monoarthritis M13.10
  ankle M13.17-●
  elbow M13.12-●
  foot joint M13.17-●
  hand joint M13.14-●
  hip M13.15-●
  knee M13.16-●
  shoulder M13.11-●
  wrist M13.13-●
Monoblastic —see condition

Monochromat (ism), monochromatopsia
  (acquired) (congenital) H53.51
Monocytic —see condition
Monocytopenia D72.818
Monocytosis (symptomatic) D72.821
Monomania —see Psychosis
Mononeuritis G58.9
  cranial nerve —see Disorder, nerve, cranial
  femoral nerve G57.2-●
  lateral
    cutaneous nerve of thigh G57.1-●
    popliteal nerve G57.3-●
  lower limb G57.9-●
    specified nerve NEC G57.8-●
  medial popliteal nerve G57.4-●
  median nerve G56.1-●
  multiplex G58.7
  plantar nerve G57.6-●
  posterior tibial nerve G57.5-●
  radial nerve G56.3-●
  sciatic nerve G57.0-●
  specified NEC G58.8
  tibial nerve G57.4-●
  ulnar nerve G56.2-●
  upper limb G56.9-●
    specified nerve NEC G56.8-●
  vestibular —see subcategory H93.3
Mononeuropathy G58.9
  carpal tunnel syndrome —see Syndrome,
    carpal tunnel
  diabetic NEC —see E08-E13 with .41
  femoral nerve —see Lesion, nerve, femoral
  ilioinguinal nerve G57.8-●
  in diseases classified elsewhere —see category
    G59
  intercostal G58.0
  lower limb G57.9-●
    causalgia —see Causalgia, lower limb
    femoral nerve —see Lesion, nerve,
      femoral
    meralgia paresthetica G57.1-●
    plantar nerve —see Lesion, nerve, plantar
    popliteal nerve —see Lesion, nerve, popliteal
    sciatic nerve —see Lesion, nerve, sciatic
    specified NEC G57.8-●
    tarsal tunnel syndrome —see Syndrome,
      tarsal tunnel
  median nerve —see Lesion, nerve, median
  multiplex G58.7
  obturator nerve G57.8-●
  popliteal nerve —see Lesion, nerve, popliteal
  radial nerve —see Lesion, nerve, radial
  saphenous nerve G57.8-●
  specified NEC G58.8
  tarsal tunnel syndrome —see Syndrome,
    tarsal tunnel
  tuberculous A17.83
  ulnar nerve —see Lesion, nerve, ulnar
  upper limb G56.9-●
    carpal tunnel syndrome —see Syndrome,
      carpal tunnel
    causalgia —see Causalgia
    median nerve —see Lesion, nerve, median
    radial nerve —see Lesion, nerve, radial
    specified site NEC G56.8-●
    ulnar nerve —see Lesion, nerve, ulnar
Mononucleosis, infectious B27.90
  with
    complication NEC B27.99
    meningitis B27.92
    polyneuropathy B27.91
  cytomegaloviral B27.10
    with
      complication NEC B27.19
      meningitis B27.12
      polyneuropathy B27.11
  Epstein-Barr (virus) B27.00
    with
      complication NEC B27.09
      meningitis B27.02
      polyneuropathy B27.01

Mononucleosis, infectious (Continued)
  gammaherpesviral B27.00
    with
      complication NEC B27.09
      meningitis B27.02
      polyneuropathy B27.01
  specified NEC B27.80
    with
      complication NEC B27.89
      meningitis B27.82
      polyneuropathy B27.81
Monoplegia G83.3-●
  congenital (cerebral) G80.8
    spastic G80.1
  embolic (current episode) I63.4-●
  following
    cerebrovascular disease
      cerebral infarction
        lower limb I69.34-●
        upper limb I69.33-●
      intracerebral hemorrhage
        lower limb I69.14-●
        upper limb I69.13-●
      lower limb I69.94-●
      nontraumatic intracranial hemorrhage
        NEC
        lower limb I69.24-●
        upper limb I69.23-●
      specified disease NEC
        lower limb I69.84-●
        upper limb I69.83-●
      stroke NOS
        lower limb I69.34-●
        upper limb I69.33-●
      subarachnoid hemorrhage
        lower limb I69.04-●
        upper limb I69.03-●
      upper limb I69.93-●
  hysterical (transient) F44.4
  lower limb G83.1-●
  psychogenic (conversion reaction) F44.4
  thrombotic (current episode) I63.3-●
  transient R29.818
  upper limb G83.2-●
Monorchism, monorchidism Q55.0
Monosomy —see also Deletion, chromosome
  Q93.9
  specified NEC Q93.89
  whole chromosome
    meiotic nondisjunction Q93.0
    mitotic nondisjunction Q93.1
    mosaicism Q93.1
  X Q96.9
Monster, monstrosity (single) Q89.7
  acephalic Q00.0
  twin Q89.4
Monteggia's fracture (-dislocation) S52.27-●
Mooren's ulcer (cornea) —see Ulcer, cornea,
  Mooren's
Moore's syndrome —see Epilepsy, specified
  NEC
Mooser-Neill reaction A75.2
Mooser's bodies A75.2
Morbidity not stated or unknown R69
Morbilli —see Measles
Morbus —see also Disease
  angelicus, anglorum E55.0
  Beigel B36.2
  caducus —see Epilepsy
  celiacus K90.0
  comitialis —see Epilepsy
  cordis —see also Disease, heart I51.9
    valvulorum —see Endocarditis
  coxae senilis M16.9
    tuberculous A18.02
  hemorrhagicus neonatorum P53
  maculosus neonatorum P54.5
Morel (-Stewart)(-Morgagni) syndrome
  M85.2
Morel-Kraepelin disease —see Schizophrenia
Morel-Moore syndrome M85.2

M

Morgagni's
  cyst, organ, hydatid, or appendage
    female Q50.5
    male (epididymal) Q55.4
      testicular Q55.29
  syndrome M85.2
Morgagni-Stewart-Morel syndrome M85.2
Morgagni-Stokes-Adams syndrome I45.9
Morgagni-Turner (-Albright) syndrome Q96.9
Moria F07.0
Moron (I.Q. 50-69) F70
Morphea L94.0
Morphinism (without remission) F11.20
  with remission F11.21
Morphinomania (without remission) F11.20
  with remission F11.21
Morquio (-Ullrich)(-Brailsford) disease or
  syndrome —see Mucopolysaccharidosis
Mortification (dry) (moist) —see Gangrene
Morton's metatarsalgia (neuralgia)(neuroma)
  (syndrome) G57.6
Morvan's disease or syndrome G60.8
Mosaicism, mosaic (autosomal) (chromosomal)
  45,X/46,XX Q96.3
  45,X/other cell lines NEC with abnormal sex
    chromosome Q96.4
  sex chromosome
    female Q97.8
    lines with various numbers of
      X chromosomes Q97.2
    male Q98.7
  XY Q96.3
Moschowitz' disease M31.1
Mother yaw A66.0
Motion sickness (from travel, any vehicle)
  (from roundabouts or swings) T75.3
Mottled, mottling, teeth (enamel) (endemic)
  (nonendemic) K00.3
Mounier-Kuhn syndrome Q32.4
  with bronchiectasis J47.9
    exacerbation (acute) J47.1
    lower respiratory infection J47.0
  acquired J98.09
    with bronchiectasis J47.9
      with
        exacerbation (acute) J47.1
        lower respiratory infection J47.0
Mountain
  sickness T70.29
    with polycythemia , acquired (acute) D75.1
  tick fever A93.2
Mouse, joint —see Loose, body, joint
  knee M23.4-•
Mouth —see condition
Movable
  coccyx —see subcategory M53.2
  kidney N28.89
    congenital Q63.8
  spleen D73.89
Movements, dystonic R25.8
Moyamoya disease I67.5
MRSA (Methicillin resistant Staphylococcus
    aureus)
  infection A49.02
    as the cause of diseases classified
      elsewhere B95.62
  sepsis A41.02
▶MSD (multiple sulfatase deficiency) E75.26
MSSA (Methicillin susceptible Staphylococcus
    aureus)
  infection A49.01
    as the cause of diseases classified
      elsewhere B95.61
  sepsis A41.01
Mucha-Habermann disease L41.0
Mucinosis (cutaneous) (focal) (papular)
  (reticular erythematous) (skin) L98.5
  oral K13.79
Mucocele
  appendix K38.8
  buccal cavity K13.79

Mucocele (Continued)
  gallbladder K82.1
  lacrimal sac, chronic H04.43-•
  nasal sinus J34.1
  nose J34.1
  salivary gland (any) K11.6
  sinus (accessory) (nasal) J34.1
  turbinate (bone) (middle) (nasal) J34.1
  uterus N85.8
Mucolipidosis
  I E77.1
  II, III E77.0
  IV E75.11
Mucopolysaccharidosis E76.3
  beta-gluduronidase deficiency E76.29
  cardiopathy E76.3 [I52]
  Hunter's syndrome E76.1
  Hurler's syndrome E76.01
  Hurler-Scheie syndrome E76.02
  Maroteaux-Lamy syndrome E76.29
  Morquio syndrome E76.219
    A E76.210
    B E76.211
    classic E76.210
  Sanfilippo syndrome E76.22
  Scheie's syndrome E76.03
  specified NEC E76.29
  type
    I
      Hurler's syndrome E76.01
      Hurler-Scheie syndrome E76.02
      Scheie's syndrome E76.03
    II E76.1
    III E76.22
    IV E76.219
    IVA E76.210
    IVB E76.211
    VI E76.29
    VII E76.29
Mucormycosis B46.5
  cutaneous B46.3
  disseminated B46.4
  gastrointestinal B46.2
  generalized B46.4
  pulmonary B46.0
  rhinocerebral B46.1
  skin B46.3
  subcutaneous B46.3
Mucositis (ulcerative) K12.30
  due to drugs NEC K12.32
  gastrointestinal K92.81
  mouth (oral) (oropharyngeal) K12.30
    due to antineoplastic therapy K12.31
    due to drugs NEC K12.32
    due to radiation K12.33
    specified NEC K12.39
    viral K12.39
  nasal J34.81
  oral cavity —see Mucositis, mouth
  oral soft tissues —see Mucositis, mouth
  vagina and vulva N76.81
Mucositis necroticans agranulocytica —see
    Agranulocytosis
Mucous —see also condition
  patches (syphilitic) A51.39
    congenital A50.07
Mucoviscidosis E84.9
  with meconium obstruction E84.11
Mucus
  asphyxia or suffocation —see Asphyxia,
    mucus
  in stool R19.5
  plug —see Asphyxia, mucus
Muguet B37.0
Mulberry molars (congenital syphilis)
  A50.52
Müllerian mixed tumor
  specified site —see Neoplasm, malignant, by
    site
  unspecified site C54.9
Multicystic kidney (development) Q61.4

Multiparity (grand) Z64.1
  affecting management of pregnancy, labor
    and delivery (supervision only) O09.4-•
  requiring contraceptive management —see
    Contraception
Multipartita placenta O43.19-•
Multiple, multiplex —see also condition
  digits (congenital) Q69.9
  endocrine neoplasia —see Neoplasia,
    endocrine, multiple [MEN]
  personality F44.81
Mumps B26.9
  arthritis B26.85
  complication NEC B26.89
  encephalitis B26.2
  hepatitis B26.81
  meningitis (aseptic) B26.1
  meningoencephalitis B26.2
  myocarditis B26.82
  oophoritis B26.89
  orchitis B26.0
  pancreatitis B26.3
  polyneuropathy B26.84
Mumu —see also Infestation, filarial B74.9 [N51]
Münchhausen's syndrome —see Disorder,
  factitious
Münchmeyer's syndrome —see Myositis,
  ossificans, progressiva
Mural —see condition
Murmur (cardiac) (heart) (organic) R01.1
  abdominal R19.15
  aortic (valve) —see Endocarditis, aortic
  benign R01.0
  diastolic —see Endocarditis
  Flint I35.1
  functional R01.0
  Graham Steell I37.1
  innocent R01.0
  mitral (valve) —see Insufficiency, mitral
  nonorganic R01.0
  presystolic, mitral —see Insufficiency, mitral
  pulmonic (valve) I37.8
  systolic R01.1
  tricuspid (valve) I07.9
  valvular —see Endocarditis
Murri's disease (intermittent hemoglobinuria)
  D59.6
Muscle, muscular —see also condition
  carnitine (palmityltransferase) deficiency
    E71.314
Musculoneuralgia —see Neuralgia
Mushroom-workers' (pickers') disease or lung
  J67.5
Mushrooming hip —see Derangement, joint,
  specified NEC, hip
Mutation(s)
  factor V Leiden D68.51
  surfactant, of lung J84.83
  prothrombin gene D68.52
Mutism —see also Aphasia
  deaf (acquired) (congenital) NEC H91.3
  elective (adjustment reaction) (childhood)
    F94.0
  hysterical F44.4
  selective (childhood) F94.0
MVD (microvillus inclusion disease) Q43.8
MVID (microvillus inclusion disease) Q43.8
➡Myalgia M79.10
▶auxiliary muscles, head and neck M79.12
  epidemic (cervical) B33.0
▶mastication muscle M79.11
▶site specified NEC M79.18
  traumatic NEC T14.8
Myasthenia G70.9
  congenital G70.2
  cordis —see Failure, heart
  developmental G70.2
  gravis G70.00
    with exacerbation (acute) G70.01
    in crisis G70.01
    neonatal, transient P94.0

Myasthenia *(Continued)*
 gravis *(Continued)*
  pseudoparalytica G70.00
   with exacerbation (acute) G70.01
   in crisis G70.01
 stomach, psychogenic F45.8
 syndrome
  in
   diabetes mellitus —*see* E08-E13 with .44
   neoplastic disease —*see also* Neoplasm
     D49.9 *[G73.3]*
   pernicious anemia D51.0 *[G73.3]*
   thyrotoxicosis E05.90 *[G73.3]*
    with thyroid storm E05.91 *[G73.3]*
Myasthenic M62.81
Mycelium infection B49
Mycetismus —*see* Poisoning, food, noxious,
  mushroom
Mycetoma B47.9
 actinomycotic B47.1
 bone (mycotic) B47.9 *[M90.80]*
 eumycotic B47.0
 foot B47.9
  actinomycotic B47.1
  mycotic B47.0
 madurae NEC B47.9
  mycotic B47.0
 maduromycotic B47.0
 mycotic B47.0
 nocardial B47.1
Mycobacteriosis —*see* Mycobacterium
Mycobacterium, mycobacterial (infection)
  A31.9
 anonymous A31.9
 atypical A31.9
  cutaneous A31.1
  pulmonary A31.0
   tuberculous —*see* Tuberculosis,
     pulmonary
  specified site NEC A31.8
 avium (intracellulare complex) A31.0
 balnei A31.1
 Battey A31.0
 chelonei A31.8
 cutaneous A31.1
 extrapulmonary systemic A31.8
 fortuitum A31.8
 intracellulare (Battey bacillus) A31.0
 kakaferifu A31.8
 kansasii (yellow bacillus) A31.0
 kasongo A31.8
 leprae —*see also* Leprosy A30.9
 luciflavum A31.1
 marinum (M. balnei) A31.1
 nonspecific —*see* Mycobacterium, atypical
 pulmonary (atypical) A31.0
  tuberculous —*see* Tuberculosis, pulmonary
 scrofulaceum A31.8
 simiae A31.8
 systemic, extrapulmonary A31.8
 szulgai A31.8
 terrae A31.8
 triviale A31.8
 tuberculosis (human, bovine) —*see*
   Tuberculosis
 ulcerans A31.1
 xenopi A31.8
Mycoplasma (M.) pneumoniae, as cause of
  disease classified elsewhere B96.0
Mycosis, mycotic B49
 cutaneous NEC B36.9
 ear B36.9
  in
   aspergillosis B44.89
   candidiasis B37.84
   moniliasis B37.84
 fungoides (extranodal) (solid organ) C84.0-•
 mouth B37.0
 nails B35.1
 opportunistic B48.8
 skin NEC B36.9

Mycosis, mycotic *(Continued)*
 specified NEC B48.8
 stomatitis B37.0
 vagina, vaginitis (candidal) B37.3
Mydriasis (pupil) H57.04
Myelatelia Q06.1
Myelinolysis, pontine, central G37.2
Myelitis (acute) (ascending) (childhood)
   (chronic) (descending) (diffuse)
   (disseminated) (idiopathic) (pressure)
   (progressive) (spinal cord) (subacute) —*see
   also* Encephalitis G04.91
 herpes simplex B00.82
 herpes zoster B02.24
 in diseases classified elsewhere
   G05.4
 necrotizing, subacute G37.4
 optic neuritis in G36.0
 postchickenpox B01.12
 postherpetic B02.24
 postimmunization G04.02
 postinfectious NEC G04.89
 postvaccinal G04.02
 specified NEC G04.89
 syphilitic (transverse) A52.14
 toxic G92
 transverse (in demyelinating diseases of
   central nervous system) G37.3
 tuberculous A17.82
 varicella B01.12
Myeloblastic —*see* condition
Myeloblastoma
 granular cell —*see also* Neoplasm, connective
   tissue
  malignant —*see* Neoplasm, connective
    tissue, malignant
  tongue D10.1
Myelocele —*see* Spina bifida
Myelocystocele —*see* Spina bifida
Myelocytic —*see* condition
Myelodysplasia D46.9
 specified NEC D46.Z
 spinal cord (congenital) Q06.1
Myelodysplastic syndrome D46.9
 with
  5q deletion D46.C
  isolated del (5q) chromosomal abnormality
    C46.C
 specified NEC D46.Z
Myeloencephalitis —*see* Encephalitis
Myelofibrosis D75.81
 with myeloid metaplasia D47.4
 acute C94.4-•
 idiopathic (chronic) D47.4
 primary D47.1
 secondary D75.81
  in myeloproliferative disease
    D47.4
Myelogenous —*see* condition
Myeloid —*see* condition
Myelokathexis D70.9
Myeloleukodystrophy E75.29
Myelolipoma —*see* Lipoma
Myeloma (multiple) C90.0-•
 monostotic C90.3
  plasma cell C90.0-•
 plasma cell C90.0-•
 solitary —*see also* Plasmacytoma, solitary
   C90.3-•
Myelomalacia G95.89
Myelomatosis C90.0-•
Myelomeningitis —*see* Meningoencephalitis
Myelomeningocele (spinal cord) —*see* Spina
  bifida
Myelo-osteo-musculodysplasia hereditaria
  Q79.8
Myelopathic
 anemia D64.89
 muscle atrophy —*see* Atrophy, muscle,
   spinal
 pain syndrome G89.0

Myelopathy (spinal cord) G95.9
 drug-induced G95.89
 in (due to)
  degeneration or displacement,
    intervertebral disc NEC —*see*
     Disorder, disc, with, myelopathy
  infection —*see* Encephalitis
  intervertebral disc disorder —*see also*
     Disorder, disc, with, myelopathy
  mercury —*see* subcategory T56.1
  neoplastic disease —*see also* Neoplasm
    D49.9 *[G99.2]*
  pernicious anemia D51.0 *[G99.2]*
  spondylosis —*see* Spondylosis, with
    myelopathy NEC
 necrotic (subacute) (vascular) G95.19
 radiation-induced G95.89
 spondylogenic NEC —*see* Spondylosis, with
   myelopathy NEC
 toxic G95.89
 transverse, acute G37.3
 vascular G95.19
 vitamin B12 E53.8 *[G32.0]*
Myelophthisis D61.82
Myeloradiculitis G04.91
Myeloradiculodysplasia (spinal) Q06.1
Myelosarcoma C92.3-•
Myelosclerosis D75.89
 with myeloid metaplasia D47.4
 disseminated, of nervous system G35
 megakaryocytic D47.4
  with myeloid metaplasia D47.4
Myelosis
 acute C92.0-•
 aleukemic C92.9-•
 chronic D47.1
 erythremic (acute) C94.0-•
 megakaryocytic C94.2-•
 nonleukemic D72.828
 subacute C92.9-•
Myiasis (cavernous) B87.9
 aural B87.4
 creeping B87.0
 cutaneous B87.0
 dermal B87.0
 ear (external) (middle) B87.4
 eye B87.2
 genitourinary B87.81
 intestinal B87.82
 laryngeal B87.3
 nasopharyngeal B87.3
 ocular B87.2
 orbit B87.2
 skin B87.0
 specified site NEC B87.89
 traumatic B87.1
 wound B87.1
Myoadenoma, prostate —*see* Hyperplasia,
  prostate
Myoblastoma
 granular cell —*see also* Neoplasm, connective
   tissue, benign
  malignant —*see* Neoplasm, connective
    tissue, malignant
 tongue D10.1
Myocardial —*see* condition
Myocardiopathy (congestive) (constrictive)
   (familial) (hypertrophic nonobstructive)
   (idiopathic) (infiltrative) (obstructive)
   (primary) (restrictive) (sporadic) —*see also*
   Cardiomyopathy I42.9
 alcoholic I42.6
 cobalt-beer I42.6
 glycogen storage E74.02 *[I43]*
 hypertrophic obstructive I42.1
 in (due to)
  beriberi E51.12
  cardiac glycogenosis E74.02 *[I43]*
  Friedreich's ataxia G11.1 *[I43]*
  myotonia atrophica G71.11 *[I43]*
  ⟹ progressive muscular dystrophy G71.03
    [I43]

Myocardiopathy *(Continued)*
  obscure (African) I42.8
  secondary I42.9
  thyrotoxic E05.90 *[I43]*
    with storm E05.91 *[I43]*
  toxic NEC I42.7
Myocarditis (with arteriosclerosis) (chronic)
    (fibroid) (interstitial) (old) (progressive)
    (senile) I51.4
  with
    rheumatic fever (conditions in I00) I09.0
      active —*see* Myocarditis, acute,
        rheumatic
      inactive or quiescent (with chorea) I09.0
  active I40.9
    rheumatic I01.2
      with chorea (acute) (rheumatic)
        (Sydenham's) I02.0
  acute or subacute (interstitial) I40.9
    due to
      streptococcus (beta-hemolytic) I01.2
    idiopathic I40.1
    rheumatic I01.2
      with chorea (acute) (rheumatic)
        (Sydenham's) I02.0
    specified NEC I40.8
  aseptic of newborn B33.22
  bacterial (acute) I40.0
  Coxsackie (virus) B33.22
  diphtheritic A36.81
  eosinophilic I40.1
  epidemic of newborn (Coxsackie) B33.22
  Fiedler's (acute) (isolated) I40.1
  giant cell (acute) (subacute) I40.1
  gonococcal A54.83
  granulomatous (idiopathic) (isolated)
    (nonspecific) I40.1
  hypertensive —*see* Hypertension, heart
  idiopathic (granulomatous) I40.1
  in (due to)
    diphtheria A36.81
    epidemic louse-borne typhus A75.0 *[I41]*
    Lyme disease A69.29
    sarcoidosis D86.85
    scarlet fever A38.1
    toxoplasmosis (acquired) B58.81
    typhoid A01.02
    typhus NEC A75.9 *[I41]*
  infective I40.0
  influenzal —*see* Influenza, with, myocarditis
  isolated (acute) I40.1
  meningococcal A39.52
  mumps B26.82
  nonrheumatic, active I40.9
  parenchymatous I40.9
  pneumococcal I40.0
  rheumatic (chronic) (inactive) (with chorea)
    I09.0
    active or acute I01.2
      with chorea (acute) (rheumatic)
        (Sydenham's) I02.0
  rheumatoid —*see* Rheumatoid, carditis
  septic I40.0
  staphylococcal I40.0
  suppurative I40.0
  syphilitic (chronic) A52.06
  toxic I40.8
    rheumatic —*see* Myocarditis, acute,
      rheumatic
  tuberculous A18.84
  typhoid A01.02
  valvular —*see* Endocarditis
  virus, viral I40.0
    of newborn (Coxsackie) B33.22
Myocardium, myocardial —*see* condition
Myocardosis —*see* Cardiomyopathy
Myoclonus, myoclonic, myoclonia (familial)
    (essential) (multifocal) (simplex) G25.3
  drug-induced G25.3
  epilepsy —*see also* Epilepsy, generalized,
    specified NEC G40.4-●
  familial (progressive) G25.3

Myoclonus, myoclonic, myoclonia *(Continued)*
  epileptica G40.409
    with status epilepticus G40.401
  ⇒facial G51.3-●
  familial progressive G25.3
  Friedreich's G25.3
  jerks G25.3
  massive G25.3
  palatal G25.3
  pharyngeal G25.3
Myocytolysis I51.5
Myodiastasis —*see* Diastasis, muscle
Myoendocarditis —*see* Endocarditis
Myoepithelioma —*see* Neoplasm, benign, by
  site
Myofasciitis (acute) —*see* Myositis
Myofibroma —*see also* Neoplasm, connective
    tissue, benign
  uterus (cervix) (corpus) —*see* Leiomyoma
Myofibromatosis D48.1
  infantile Q89.8
Myofibrosis M62.89
  heart —*see* Myocarditis
  scapulohumeral —*see* Lesion, shoulder,
    specified NEC
Myofibrositis M79.7
  scapulohumeral —*see* Lesion, shoulder,
    specified NEC
Myoglobulinuria, myoglobinuria (primary)
  R82.1
Myokymia, facial G51.4
Myolipoma —*see* Lipoma
Myoma —*see also* Neoplasm, connective tissue,
    benign
  malignant —*see* Neoplasm, connective tissue,
    malignant
  prostate D29.1
  uterus (cervix) (corpus) —*see* Leiomyoma
Myomalacia M62.89
Myometritis —*see* Endometritis
Myometrium —*see* condition
Myonecrosis, clostridial A48.0
Myopathy G72.9
  acute
    necrotizing G72.81
      quadriplegic G72.81
  alcoholic G72.1
  benign congenital G71.2
  central core G71.2
  centronuclear G71.2
  congenital (benign) G71.2
  critical illness G72.81
  ⇒distal G71.09
  drug-induced G72.0
  endocrine NEC E34.9 *[G73.7]*
  extraocular muscles H05.82-●
  ⇒facioscapulohumeral G71.02
  hereditary G71.9
    specified NEC G71.8
  immune NEC G72.49
  in (due to)
    Addison's disease E27.1 *[G73.7]*
    alcohol G72.1
    amyloidosis E85.0 *[G73.7]*
    cretinism E00.9 *[G73.7]*
    Cushing's syndrome E24.9 *[G73.7]*
    drugs G72.0
    endocrine disease NEC E34.9 *[G73.7]*
    giant cell arteritis M31.6 *[G73.7]*
    glycogen storage disease E74.00 *[G73.7]*
    hyperadrenocorticism E24.9 *[G73.7]*
    hyperparathyroidism NEC E21.3 *[G73.7]*
    hypoparathyroidism E20.9 *[G73.7]*
    hypopituitarism E23.0 *[G73.7]*
    hypothyroidism E03.9 *[G73.7]*
    infectious disease NEC B99 *[G73.7]*
    lipid storage disease E75.6 *[G73.7]*
    metabolic disease NEC E88.9 *[G73.7]*
    myxedema E03.9 *[G73.7]*
    parasitic disease NEC B89 *[G73.7]*
    polyarteritis nodosa M30.0 *[G73.7]*

Myopathy *(Continued)*
  in (due to) *(Continued)*
    rheumatoid arthritis —*see* Rheumatoid,
      myopathy
    sarcoidosis D86.87
    scleroderma M34.82
    sicca syndrome M35.03
    Sjögren's syndrome M35.03
    systemic lupus erythematosus M32.19
    thyrotoxicosis (hyperthyroidism) E05.90
      [G73.7]
      with thyroid storm E05.91 *[G73.7]*
    toxic agent NEC G72.2
  inflammatory NEC G72.49
  intensive care (ICU) G72.81
  ⇒limb-girdle G71.09
  mitochondrial NEC G71.3
  myotubular G71.2
  mytonic, proximal (PROMM) G71.11
  nemaline G71.2
  ⇒ocular G71.09
  ⇒oculopharyngeal G71.09
  of critical illness G72.81
  primary G71.9
    specified NEC G71.8
  progressive NEC G72.89
  proximal myotonic (PROMM) G71.11
  rod G71.2
  ⇒scapulohumeral G71.02
  specified NEC G72.89
  toxic G72.2
Myopericarditis —*see also* Pericarditis
  chronic rheumatic I09.2
Myopia (axial) (congenital) H52.1-●
  degenerative (malignant) H44.20
    with
      choroidal neovascularization H44.2A-●
      foveoschisis H44.2D-●
      macular hole H44.2B-●
      retinal detachment H44.2C-●
      specified maculopathy NEC H44.2E-●
    bilateral H44.23
    left eye H44.22
    right eye H44.21
  malignant —*see also* Myopia, degenerative
    H44.2-●
  pernicious —*see also* Myopia, degenerative
    H44.2-●
  progressive high (degenerative) —*see also*
    Myopia, degenerative H44.2-●
Myosarcoma —*see* Neoplasm, connective tissue,
  malignant
Myosis (pupil) H57.03
  stromal (endolymphatic) D39.0
Myositis M60.9
  clostridial A48.0
  due to posture —*see* Myositis, specified type
    NEC
  epidemic B33.0
  fibrosa or fibrous (chronic), Volkmann's
    T79.6
  foreign body granuloma —*see* Granuloma,
    foreign body
  in (due to)
    bilharziasis B65.9 *[M63.8-●]*
    cysticercosis B69.81
    leprosy A30.9 *[M63.8-●]*
    mycosis B49 *[M63.8-●]*
    sarcoidosis D86.87
    schistosomiasis B65.9 *[M63.8-●]*
    syphilis
      late A52.78
      secondary A51.49
    toxoplasmosis (acquired) B58.82
    trichinellosis B75 *[M63.8-●]*
    tuberculosis A18.09
  inclusion body [IBM] G72.41
  infective M60.009
    arm M60.002
      left M60.001
      right M60.000

Myositis *(Continued)*
  infective *(Continued)*
    leg M60.005
      left M60.004
      right M60.003
    lower limb M60.005
      ankle M60.07-●
      foot M60.07-●
      lower leg M60.06-●
      thigh M60.05-●
      toe M60.07-●
    multiple sites M60.09
    specified site NEC M60.08
    upper limb M60.002
      finger M60.04-●
      forearm M60.03-●
      hand M60.04-●
      shoulder region M60.01-●
      upper arm M60.02-●
  interstitial M60.10
    ankle M60.17-●
    foot M60.17-●
    forearm M60.13-●
    hand M60.14-●
    lower leg M60.16-●
    multiple sites M60.19
    shoulder region M60.11-●
    specified site NEC M60.18
    thigh M60.15-●
    upper arm M60.12-●
  mycotic B49 [*M63.8-●*]
  ossificans or ossifying (circumscripta) —*see also* Ossification, muscle, specified NEC
    in (due to)
      burns M61.30
        ankle M61.37-●
        foot M61.37-●
        forearm M61.33-●
        hand M61.34-●
        lower leg M61.36-●
        multiple sites M61.39
        pelvic region M61.35-●
        shoulder region M61.31-●
        specified site NEC M61.38
        thigh M61.35-●
        upper arm M61.32-●
      quadriplegia or paraplegia M61.20
        ankle M61.27-●
        foot M61.27-●
        forearm M61.23-●
        hand M61.24-●
        lower leg M61.26-●
        multiple sites M61.29
        pelvic region M61.25-●

Myositis *(Continued)*
  ossificans or ossifying *(Continued)*
    in (due to) *(Continued)*
      quadriplegia or paraplegia *(Continued)*
        shoulder region M61.21-●
        specified site NEC M61.28
        thigh M61.25-●
        upper arm M61.22-●
    progressiva M61.10
      ankle M61.17-●
      finger M61.14-●
      foot M61.17-●
      forearm M61.13-●
      hand M61.14-●
      lower leg M61.16-●
      multiple sites M61.19
      pelvic region M61.15-●
      shoulder region M61.11-●
      specified site NEC M61.18
      thigh M61.15-●
      toe M61.17-●
      upper arm M61.12-●
    traumatica M61.00
      ankle M61.07-●
      foot M61.07-●
      forearm M61.03-●
      hand M61.04-●
      lower leg M61.06-●
      multiple sites M61.09
      pelvic region M61.05-●
      shoulder region M61.01-●
      specified site NEC M61.08
      thigh M61.05-●
      upper arm M61.02-●
  purulent —*see* Myositis, infective
  specified type NEC M60.80
    ankle M60.87-●
    foot M60.87-●
    forearm M60.83-●
    hand M60.84-●
    lower leg M60.86-●
    multiple sites M60.89
    pelvic region M60.85-●
    shoulder region M60.81-●
    specified site NEC M60.88
    thigh M60.85-●
    upper arm M60.82-●
  suppurative —*see* Myositis, infective
  traumatic (old) —*see* Myositis, specified type NEC
Myospasia impulsiva F95.2
Myotonia (acquisita) (intermittens) M62.89
  atrophica G71.11
  chondrodystrophic G71.13

Myotonia *(Continued)*
  congenita (acetazolamide responsive) (dominant) (recessive) G71.12
  drug-induced G71.14
  dystrophica G71.11
  fluctuans G71.19
  levior G71.12
  permanens G71.19
  symptomatic G71.19
Myotonic pupil —*see* Anomaly, pupil, function, tonic pupil
Myriapodiasis B88.2
Myringitis H73.2-●
  with otitis media —*see* Otitis, media
  acute H73.00-●
    bullous H73.01-●
    specified NEC H73.09-●
  bullous —*see* Myringitis, acute, bullous
  chronic H73.1-●
Mysophobia F40.228
Mytilotoxism —*see* Poisoning, fish
Myxadenitis labialis K13.0
Myxedema (adult) (idiocy) (infantile) (juvenile) —*see also* Hypothyroidism E03.9
  circumscribed E05.90
    with storm E05.91
  coma E03.5
  congenital E00.1
  cutis L98.5
  localized (pretibial) E05.90
    with storm E05.91
  papular L98.5
Myxochondrosarcoma —*see* Neoplasm, cartilage, malignant
Myxofibroma —*see* Neoplasm, connective tissue, benign
  odontogenic —*see* Cyst, calcifying odontogenic
Myxofibrosarcoma —*see* Neoplasm, connective tissue, malignant
Myxolipoma D17.9
Myxoliposarcoma —*see* Neoplasm, connective tissue, malignant
Myxoma —*see also* Neoplasm, connective tissue, benign
  nerve sheath —*see* Neoplasm, nerve, benign
  odontogenic —*see* Cyst, calcifying odontogenic
Myxosarcoma —*see* Neoplasm, connective tissue, malignant

M

► New   ⇒ Revised   ~~deleted~~ Deleted   ● Use Additional Character(s)

N

Naegeli's
   disease Q82.8
   leukemia, monocytic C93.1-●
Naegleriasis (with meningoencephalitis)
      B60.2
Naffziger's syndrome G54.0
Naga sore —see Ulcer, skin
Nägele's pelvis M95.5
   with disproportion (fetopelvic) O33.0
      causing obstructed labor O65.0
Nail —see also condition
   biting F98.8
   patella syndrome Q87.2
Nanism, nanosomia —see Dwarfism
Nanophyetiasis B66.8
Nanukayami A27.89
Napkin rash L22
Narcolepsy G47.419
   with cataplexy G47.411
   in conditions classified elsewhere
      G47.429
      with cataplexy G47.421
Narcosis R06.89
Narcotism —see Dependence
NARP (Neuropathy, Ataxia and Retinitis
      pigmentosa) syndrome E88.49
Narrow
   anterior chamber angle H40.03-●
   gingival width (of periodontal soft tissue)
      K05.5
   pelvis —see Contraction, pelvis
Narrowing —see also Stenosis
   artery I77.1
      auditory, internal I65.8
      basilar —see Occlusion, artery, basilar
      carotid —see Occlusion, artery, carotid
      cerebellar —see Occlusion, artery, cerebellar
      cerebral —see Occlusion artery, cerebral
      choroidal —see Occlusion, artery, cerebral,
         specified NEC
      communicating posterior —see Occlusion,
         artery, cerebral, specified NEC
      coronary —see also Disease, heart, ischemic,
         atherosclerotic
         congenital Q24.5
            syphilitic A50.54 [I52]
         due to syphilis NEC A52.06
      hypophyseal —see Occlusion, artery,
         cerebral, specified NEC
      pontine —see Occlusion, artery, cerebral,
         specified NEC
      precerebral —see Occlusion, artery,
         precerebral
      vertebral —see Occlusion, artery, vertebral
   auditory canal (external) —see Stenosis,
      external ear canal
   eustachian tube —see Obstruction, eustachian
      tube
   eyelid —see Disorder, eyelid function
   larynx J38.6
   mesenteric artery —see also Ischemia,
      intestine, acute K55.059
   palate M26.89
   palpebral fissure —see Disorder, eyelid
      function
   ureter N13.5
      with infection N13.6
   urethra —see Stricture, urethra
Narrowness, abnormal, eyelid Q10.3
Nasal —see condition
Nasolachrymal, nasolacrimal —see condition
Nasopharyngeal —see also condition
   pituitary gland Q89.2
   torticollis M43.6
Nasopharyngitis (acute) (infective)
      (streptococcal) (subacute) J00
   chronic (suppurative) (ulcerative) J31.1
Nasopharynx, nasopharyngeal —see condition
Natal tooth, teeth K00.6

Nausea (without vomiting) R11.0
   with vomiting R11.2
   gravidarum —see Hyperemesis, gravidarum
   marina T75.3
   navalis T75.3
Navel —see condition
Neapolitan fever —see Brucellosis
Near drowning T75.1
Nearsightedness —see Myopia
Near-syncope R55
Nebula, cornea —see Opacity, cornea
Necator americanus infestation B76.1
Necatoriasis B76.1
Neck —see condition
Necrobiosis R68.89
   lipoidica NEC L92.1
      with diabetes —see E08-E13 with .620
Necrolysis, toxic epidermal L51.2
   due to drug
      correct substance properly administered —
         see Table of Drugs and Chemicals, by
         drug, adverse effect
      overdose or wrong substance given
         or taken —see Table of Drugs and
         Chemicals, by drug, poisoning
Necrophilia F65.89
Necrosis, necrotic (ischemic) —see also
      Gangrene
   adrenal (capsule) (gland) E27.49
   amputation stump (surgical) (late) T87.50
      arm T87.5-●
      leg T87.5-●
   antrum J32.0
   aorta (hyaline) —see also Aneurysm, aorta
      cystic medial —see Dissection, aorta
   artery I77.5
   bladder (aseptic) (sphincter) N32.89
   bone —see also Osteonecrosis M87.9
      aseptic or avascular —see Osteonecrosis
         idiopathic M87.00
      ethmoid J32.2
      jaw M27.2
      tuberculous —see Tuberculosis, bone
   brain I67.89
   breast (aseptic) (fat) (segmental) N64.1
   bronchus J98.09
   central nervous system NEC I67.89
   cerebellar I67.89
   cerebral I67.89
   colon —see also Infarct, intestine K55.049
   cornea H18.89-●
   cortical (acute) (renal) N17.1
   cystic medial (aorta) —see Dissection, aorta
   dental pulp K04.1
   esophagus K22.8
   ethmoid (bone) J32.2
   eyelid —see Disorder, eyelid, degenerative
   fat, fatty (generalized) —see also Disorder, soft
         tissue, specified type NEC
      abdominal wall K65.4
      breast (aseptic) (segmental) N64.1
      localized —see Degeneration, by site, fatty
      mesentery K65.4
      omentum K65.4
      pancreas K86.89
      peritoneum K65.4
      skin (subcutaneous), newborn P83.0
      subcutaneous, due to birth injury P15.6
   gallbladder —see Cholecystitis, acute
   heart —see Infarct, myocardium
   hip, aseptic or avascular —see Osteonecrosis,
         by type, femur
   intestine (acute) (hemorrhagic) (massive) —
         see also Infarct, intestine K55.069
   jaw M27.2
   kidney (bilateral) N28.0
      acute N17.9
      cortical (acute) (bilateral) N17.1
         with ectopic or molar pregnancy O08.4
      medullary (bilateral) (in acute renal failure)
         (papillary) N17.2

Necrosis, necrotic (Continued)
   kidney (Continued)
      papillary (bilateral) (in acute renal
         failure) N17.2
      tubular N17.0
         with ectopic or molar pregnancy
            O08.4
         complicating
            abortion —see Abortion, by type,
               complicated by, tubular necrosis
            ectopic or molar pregnancy O08.4
            pregnancy —see Pregnancy,
               complicated by, diseases of,
               specified type or system NEC
         following ectopic or molar pregnancy
            O08.4
         traumatic T79.5
   larynx J38.7
   liver (with hepatic failure) (cell) —see Failure,
      hepatic
      hemorrhagic, central K76.2
   lung J85.0
   lymphatic gland —see Lymphadenitis, acute
   mammary gland (fat) (segmental) N64.1
   mastoid (chronic) —see Mastoiditis, chronic
   medullary (acute) (renal) N17.2
   mesentery —see also Infarct, intestine
         K55.069
      fat K65.4
   mitral valve —see Insufficiency, mitral
   myocardium, myocardial —see Infarct,
      myocardium
   nose J34.0
   omentum (with mesenteric infarction) —see
         also Infarct, intestine K55.069
      fat K65.4
   orbit, orbital —see Osteomyelitis, orbit
   ossicles, ear —see Abnormal, ear ossicles
   ovary N70.92
   pancreas (aseptic) (duct) (fat) K86.89
      acute (infective) —see Pancreatitis, acute
      infective —see Pancreatitis, acute
   papillary (acute) (renal) N17.2
   perineum N90.89
   peritoneum (with mesenteric infarction) —see
         also Infarct, intestine K55.069
      fat K65.4
   pharynx J02.9
      in granulocytopenia —see Neutropenia
         Vincent's A69.1
   phosphorus —see subcategory T54.2
   pituitary (gland) E23.0
      postpartum O99.285
      Sheehan O99.285
   pressure —see Ulcer, pressure, by site
   pulmonary J85.0
   pulp (dental) K04.1
   radiation —see Necrosis, by site
   radium —see Necrosis, by site
   renal —see Necrosis, kidney
   sclera H15.89
   scrotum N50.89
   skin or subcutaneous tissue NEC I96
   spine, spinal (column) —see also
         Osteonecrosis, by type, vertebra
      cord G95.19
   spleen D73.5
   stomach K31.89
   stomatitis (ulcerative) A69.0
   subcutaneous fat, newborn P83.88
   subendocardial (acute) I21.4
      chronic I25.89
   suprarenal (capsule) (gland) E27.49
   testis N50.89
   thymus (gland) E32.8
   tonsil J35.8
   trachea J39.8
   tuberculous NEC —see Tuberculosis
   tubular (acute) (anoxic) (renal) (toxic)
         N17.0
      postprocedural N99.0

Necrosis, necrotic *(Continued)*
  vagina N89.8
  vertebra —*see also* Osteonecrosis, by type,
      vertebra
    tuberculous A18.01
  vulva N90.89
  X-ray —*see* Necrosis, by site
Necrospermia —*see* Infertility, male
Need (for)
  care provider because of (of)
    assistance with personal care Z74.1
    continuous supervision required Z74.3
    impaired mobility Z74.09
    no other household member able to render
        care Z74.2
    specified reason NEC Z74.8
  immunization —*see* Vaccination
  vaccination —*see* Vaccination
Neglect
  adult
    confirmed T74.01
    history of Z91.412
    suspected T76.01
  child (childhood)
    confirmed T74.02
    history of Z62.812
    suspected T76.02
  emotional, in childhood Z62.898
  hemispatial R41.4
  left-sided R41.4
  sensory R41.4
  visuospatial R41.4
Neisserian infection NEC —*see* Gonococcus
Nelaton's syndrome G60.8
Nelson's syndrome E24.1
Nematodiasis (intestinal) B82.0
  Ancylostoma B76.0
Neonatal —*see also* Newborn
  acne L70.4
  bradycardia P29.12
  screening, abnormal findings on P09
  tachycardia P29.11
  tooth, teeth K00.6
Neonatorum —*see* condition
Neoplasia
  endocrine, multiple (MEN) E31.20
    type I E31.21
    type IIA E31.22
    type IIB E31.23
  intraepithelial (histologically confirmed)
    anal (AIN) (histologically confirmed)
        K62.82
      grade I K62.82
      grade II K62.82
      severe D01.3
    cervical glandular (histologically
        confirmed) D06.9
    cervix (uteri) (CIN) (histologically
        confirmed) N87.9
      glandular D06.9
      grade I N87.0
      grade II N87.1
      grade III (severe dysplasia) —*see also*
          Carcinoma, cervix uteri, in situ
          D06.9
    prostate (histologically confirmed) (PIN)
        N42.31
      grade I N42.31
      grade II N42.31
      grade III (severe dysplasia) D07.5
    vagina (histologically confirmed) (VAIN)
        N89.3
      grade I N89.0
      grade II N89.1
      grade III (severe dysplasia) D07.2
    vulva (histologically confirmed) (VIN)
        N90.3
      grade I N90.0
      grade II N90.1
      grade III (severe dysplasia)
          D07.1

Neoplasm, neoplastic —*see also* Table of
    Neoplasms
  lipomatous, benign —*see* Lipoma
  malignant mast cell C96.20
    specified type NEC C96.29
  mast cell, of uncertain behavior NEC D47.09
Neovascularization
  ciliary body —*see* Disorder, iris, vascular
  cornea H16.40-●
    deep H16.44-●
    ghost vessels —*see* Ghost, vessels
    localized H16.43-●
    pannus —*see* Pannus
  iris —*see* Disorder, iris, vascular
  retina H35.05-●
Nephralgia N23
Nephritis, nephritic (albuminuric) (azotemic)
    (congenital) (disseminated) (epithelial)
    (familial) (focal) (granulomatous)
    (hemorrhagic) (infantile) (nonsuppurative,
    excretory) (uremic) N05.9
  with
    dense deposit disease N05.6
    diffuse
      crescentic glomerulonephritis N05.7
      endocapillary proliferative
          glomerulonephritis N05.4
      membranous glomerulonephritis N05.2
      mesangial proliferative
          glomerulonephritis N05.3
      mesangiocapillary glomerulonephritis
          N05.5
    edema —*see* Nephrosis
    focal and segmental glomerular lesions
        N05.1
    foot process disease N04.9
    glomerular lesion
      diffuse sclerosing N05.8
      hypocomplementemic —*see* Nephritis,
          membranoproliferative
      IgA —*see* Nephropathy, IgA
      lobular, lobulonodular —*see* Nephritis,
          membranoproliferative
      nodular —*see* Nephritis,
          membranoproliferative
    lesion of
      glomerulonephritis, proliferative N05.8
      renal necrosis N05.9
    minor glomerular abnormality N05.0
    specified morphological changes NEC
        N05.8
  acute N00.9
    with
      dense deposit disease N00.6
      diffuse
        crescentic glomerulonephritis
            N00.7
        endocapillary proliferative
            glomerulonephritis N00.4
        membranous glomerulonephritis
            N00.2
        mesangial proliferative
            glomerulonephritis N00.3
        mesangiocapillary glomerulonephritis
            N00.5
      focal and segmental glomerular lesions
          N00.1
      minor glomerular abnormality N00.0
      specified morphological changes NEC
          N00.8
  amyloid E85.4 *[N08]*
  antiglomerular basement membrane (anti-
      GBM) antibody NEC
    in Goodpasture's syndrome M31.0
  antitubular basement membrane (tubulo-
      interstitial) NEC N12
    toxic —*see* Nephropathy, toxic
  arteriolar —*see* Hypertension, kidney
  arteriosclerotic —*see* Hypertension, kidney
  ascending —*see* Nephritis, tubulo-interstitial
  atrophic N03.9

Nephritis, nephritic *(Continued)*
  Balkan (endemic) N15.0
  calculous, calculus —*see* Calculus,
      kidney
  cardiac —*see* Hypertension, kidney
  cardiovascular —*see* Hypertension,
      kidney
  chronic N03.9
    with
      dense deposit disease N03.6
      diffuse
        crescentic glomerulonephritis
            N03.7
        endocapillary proliferative
            glomerulonephritis N03.4
        membranous glomerulonephritis
            N03.2
        mesangial proliferative
            glomerulonephritis N03.3
        mesangiocapillary glomerulonephritis
            N03.5
      focal and segmental glomerular lesions
          N03.1
      minor glomerular abnormality
          N03.0
      specified morphological changes
          NEC N03.8
  arteriosclerotic —*see* Hypertension,
      kidney
  cirrhotic N26.9
  complicating pregnancy O26.83-●
  croupous N00.9
  degenerative —*see* Nephrosis
  diffuse sclerosing N05.8
  due to
    diabetes mellitus —*see* E08-E13 with .21
    subacute bacterial endocarditis I33.0
    systemic lupus erythematosus (chronic)
        M32.14
    typhoid fever A01.09
  gonococcal (acute) (chronic) A54.21
  hypocomplementemic —*see* Nephritis,
      membranoproliferative
  IgA —*see* Nephropathy, IgA
  immune complex (circulating) NEC N05.8
  infective —*see* Nephritis, tubulo-interstitial
  interstitial —*see* Nephritis, tubulo-interstitial
  lead N14.3
  membranoproliferative (diffuse) (type 1
      or 3) —*see also* N00-N07 with fourth
      character .5 N05.5
    type 2 —*see also* N00-N07 with fourth
        character .6 N05.6
  minimal change N05.0
  necrotic, necrotizing NEC —*see also*
      N00-N07 with fourth character .8
      N05.8
  nephrotic —*see* Nephrosis
  nodular —*see* Nephritis,
      membranoproliferative
  polycystic Q61.3
    adult type Q61.2
    autosomal
      dominant Q61.2
      recessive NEC Q61.19
    childhood type NEC Q61.19
    infantile type NEC Q61.19
  poststreptococcal N05.9
    acute N00.9
    chronic N03.9
    rapidly progressive N01.9
  proliferative NEC —*see also* N00-N07 with
      fourth character .8 N05.8
  purulent —*see* Nephritis, tubulo-interstitial
  rapidly progressive N01.9
    with
      dense deposit disease N01.6
      diffuse
        crescentic glomerulonephritis N01.7
        endocapillary proliferative
            glomerulonephritis N01.4

▶ New   ⇒ Revised   ~~deleted~~ Deleted   ● Use Additional Character(s)

Nephritis, nephritic *(Continued)*
  rapidly progressive *(Continued)*
    with *(Continued)*
      diffuse *(Continued)*
        membranous glomerulonephritis N01.2
        mesangial proliferative glomerulonephritis N01.3
        mesangiocapillary glomerulonephritis N01.5
        focal and segmental glomerular lesions N01.1
        minor glomerular abnormality N01.0
        specified morphological changes NEC N01.8
  salt losing or wasting NEC N28.89
  saturnine N14.3
  sclerosing, diffuse N05.8
  septic —*see* Nephritis, tubulo-interstitial
  specified pathology NEC —*see also* N00-N07
    with fourth character .8 N05.8
  subacute N01.9
  suppurative —*see* Nephritis, tubulo-interstitial
  syphilitic (late) A52.75
    congenital A50.59 *[N08]*
    early (secondary) A51.44
  toxic —*see* Nephropathy, toxic
  tubal, tubular —*see* Nephritis, tubulo-interstitial
  tuberculous A18.11
  tubulo-interstitial (in) N12
    acute (infectious) N10
    chronic (infectious) N11.9
      nonobstructive N11.8
        reflux-associated N11.0
      obstructive N11.1
      specified NEC N11.8
    due to
      brucellosis A23.9 *[N16]*
      cryoglobulinemia D89.1 *[N16]*
      glycogen storage disease E74.00 *[N16]*
    Sjögren's syndrome M35.04
  vascular —*see* Hypertension, kidney
  war N00.9
Nephroblastoma (epithelial) (mesenchymal) C64-●
Nephrocalcinosis E83.59 *[N29]*
Nephrocystitis, pustular —*see* Nephritis, tubulo-interstitial
Nephrolithiasis (congenital) (pelvis) (recurrent) —*see also* Calculus, kidney
Nephroma C64-●
  mesoblastic D41.0-●
Nephronephritis —*see* Nephrosis
Nephronophthisis Q61.5
Nephropathia epidemica A98.5
Nephropathy —*see also* Nephritis N28.9
  with
    edema —*see* Nephrosis
    glomerular lesion —*see* Glomerulonephritis
  amyloid, hereditary E85.0
  analgesic N14.0
    with medullary necrosis, acute N17.2
  Balkan (endemic) N15.0
  chemical —*see* Nephropathy, toxic
  diabetic —*see* E08-E13 with .21
  drug-induced N14.2
    specified NEC N14.1
  focal and segmental hyalinosis or sclerosis N02.1
  heavy metal-induced N14.3
  hereditary NEC N07.9
    with
      dense deposit disease N07.6
      diffuse
        crescentic glomerulonephritis N07.7
        endocapillary proliferative glomerulonephritis N07.4

Nephropathy *(Continued)*
  hereditary NEC *(Continued)*
    with *(Continued)*
      diffuse *(Continued)*
        membranous glomerulonephritis N07.2
        mesangial proliferative glomerulonephritis N07.3
        mesangiocapillary glomerulonephritis N07.5
        focal and segmental glomerular lesions N07.1
        minor glomerular abnormality N07.0
        specified morphological changes NEC N07.8
  hypercalcemic N25.89
  hypertensive —*see* Hypertension, kidney
  hypokalemic (vacuolar) N25.89
  IgA N02.8
    with glomerular lesion N02.9
      focal and segmental hyalinosis or sclerosis N02.1
      membranoproliferative (diffuse) N02.5
      membranous (diffuse) N02.2
      mesangial proliferative (diffuse) N02.3
      mesangiocapillary (diffuse) N02.5
      proliferative NEC N02.8
      specified pathology NEC N02.8
  lead N14.3
  membranoproliferative (diffuse) N02.5
  membranous (diffuse) N02.2
  mesangial (IgA/IgG) —*see* Nephropathy, IgA
    proliferative (diffuse) N02.3
  mesangiocapillary (diffuse) N02.5
  obstructive N13.8
  phenacetin N17.2
  phosphate-losing N25.0
  potassium depletion N25.89
  pregnancy-related O26.83-●
  proliferative NEC (*see also* N00-N07 with fourth character .8) N05.8
  protein-losing N25.89
  saturnine N14.3
  sickle-cell D57.-● *[N08]*
  toxic NEC N14.4
    due to
      drugs N14.2
        analgesic N14.0
        specified NEC N14.1
      heavy metals N14.3
  vasomotor N17.0
  water-losing N25.89
Nephroptosis N28.83
Nephropyosis —*see* Abscess, kidney
Nephrorrhagia N28.89
Nephrosclerosis (arteriolar) (arteriosclerotic) (chronic) (hyaline) —*see also* Hypertension, kidney
  hyperplastic —*see* Hypertension, kidney
  senile N26.9
Nephrosis, nephrotic (Epstein's) (syndrome) (congenital) N04.9
  with
    foot process disease N04.9
    glomerular lesion N04.1
    hypocomplementemic N04.5
  acute N04.9
  anoxic —*see* Nephrosis, tubular
  chemical —*see* Nephrosis, tubular
  cholemic K76.7
  diabetic —*see* E08-E13 with .21
  Finnish type (congenital) Q89.8
  hemoglobin N10
  hemoglobinuric —*see* Nephrosis, tubular
  in
    amyloidosis E85.4 *[N08]*
    diabetes mellitus —*see* E08-E13 with .21
    epidemic hemorrhagic fever A98.5
    malaria (malariae) B52.0
  ischemic —*see* Nephrosis, tubular
  lipoid N04.9

Nephrosis, nephrotic *(Continued)*
  lower nephron —*see* Nephrosis, tubular
  malarial (malariae) B52.0
  minimal change N04.0
  myoglobin N10
  necrotizing —*see* Nephrosis, tubular
  osmotic (sucrose) N25.89
  radiation N04.9
  syphilitic (late) A52.75
  toxic —*see* Nephrosis, tubular
  tubular (acute) N17.0
    postprocedural N99.0
    radiation N04.9
Nephrosonephritis, hemorrhagic (endemic) A98.5
Nephrostomy
  attention to Z43.6
  status Z93.6
Nerve —*see also* condition
  injury —*see* Injury, nerve, by body site
Nerves R45.0
Nervous —*see also* condition R45.0
  heart F45.8
  stomach F45.8
  tension R45.0
Nervousness R45.0
Nesidioblastoma
  pancreas D13.7
  specified site NEC —*see* Neoplasm, benign, by site
  unspecified site D13.7
Nettleship's syndrome —*see* Urticaria pigmentosa
Neumann's disease or syndrome L10.1
Neuralgia, neuralgic (acute) M79.2
  accessory (nerve) G52.8
  acoustic (nerve) —*see* subcategory H93.3
  auditory (nerve) —*see* subcategory H93.3
  ciliary G44.009
    intractable G44.001
    not intractable G44.009
  cranial
    nerve —*see also* Disorder, nerve, cranial
      fifth or trigeminal —*see* Neuralgia, trigeminal
    postherpetic, postzoster B02.29
  ear —*see* subcategory H92.0
  facialis vera G51.1
  Fothergill's —*see* Neuralgia, trigeminal
  glossopharyngeal (nerve) G52.1
  Horton's G44.099
    intractable G44.091
    not intractable G44.099
  Hunt's B02.21
  hypoglossal (nerve) G52.3
  infraorbital —*see* Neuralgia, trigeminal
  malarial —*see* Malaria
  migrainous G44.009
    intractable G44.001
    not intractable G44.009
  Morton's G57.6-●
  nerve, cranial —*see* Disorder, nerve, cranial
  nose G52.0
  occipital M54.81
  olfactory G52.0
  penis N48.9
  perineum R10.2
  postherpetic NEC B02.29
    trigeminal B02.22
  pubic region R10.2
  scrotum R10.2
  Sluder's G44.89
  specified nerve NEC G58.8
  spermatic cord R10.2
  sphenopalatine (ganglion) G90.09
  trifacial —*see* Neuralgia, trigeminal
  trigeminal G50.0
    postherpetic, postzoster B02.22
  vagus (nerve) G52.2
  writer's F48.8
    organic G25.89

Neurapraxia —*see* Injury, nerve
Neurasthenia F48.8
  cardiac F45.8
  gastric F45.8
  heart F45.8
Neurilemmoma —*see also* Neoplasm, nerve, benign
  acoustic (nerve) D33.3
  malignant —*see also* Neoplasm, nerve, malignant
    acoustic (nerve) C72.4
Neurilemmosarcoma —*see* Neoplasm, nerve, malignant
Neurinoma —*see* Neoplasm, nerve, benign
Neurinomatosis —*see* Neoplasm, nerve, uncertain behavior
Neuritis (rheumatoid) M79.2
  abducens (nerve) —*see* Strabismus, paralytic, sixth nerve
  accessory (nerve) G52.8
  acoustic (nerve) —*see also* subcategory H93.3
    in (due to)
      infectious disease NEC B99 [H94.0-●]
      parasitic disease NEC B89 [H94.0-●]
    syphilitic A52.15
  alcoholic G62.1
    with psychosis —*see* Psychosis, alcoholic
  amyloid, any site E85.4 [G63]
  auditory (nerve) —*see* subcategory H93.3
  brachial —*see* Radiculopathy
    due to displacement, intervertebral disc —*see* Disorder, disc, cervical, with neuritis
  cranial nerve
    due to Lyme disease A69.22
    eighth or acoustic or auditory —*see* subcategory H93.3
    eleventh or accessory G52.8
    fifth or trigeminal G51.0
    first or olfactory G52.0
    fourth or trochlear —*see* Strabismus, paralytic, fourth nerve
    second or optic —*see* Neuritis, optic
    seventh or facial G51.8
      newborn (birth injury) P11.3
    sixth or abducent —*see* Strabismus, paralytic, sixth nerve
    tenth or vagus G52.2
    third or oculomotor —*see* Strabismus, paralytic, third nerve
    twelfth or hypoglossal G52.3
  Déjérine-Sottas G60.0
  diabetic (mononeuropathy) —*see* E08-E13 with .41
    polyneuropathy —*see* E08-E13 with .42
  due to
    beriberi E51.11
    displacement, prolapse or rupture, intervertebral disc —*see* Disorder, disc, with, radiculopathy
    herniation, nucleus pulposus M51.9 [G55]
  endemic E51.11
  facial G51.8
    newborn (birth injury) P11.3
  general —*see* Polyneuropathy
  geniculate ganglion G51.1
    due to herpes (zoster) B02.21
  gouty —*see also* Gout, by type M10.9 [G63]
  hypoglossal (nerve) G52.3
  ilioinguinal (nerve) G57.9-●
  infectious (multiple) NEC G61.0
  interstitial hypertrophic progressive G60.0
  lumbar M54.16
  lumbosacral M54.17
  multiple —*see also* Polyneuropathy
    endemic E51.11
    infective, acute G61.0
  multiplex endemica E51.11
  nerve root —*see* Radiculopathy
  oculomotor (nerve) —*see* Strabismus, paralytic, third nerve

Neuritis (Continued)
  olfactory nerve G52.0
  optic (nerve) (hereditary) (sympathetic) H46.9
    with demyelination G36.0
    in myelitis G36.0
    nutritional H46.2
    papillitis —*see* Papillitis, optic
    retrobulbar H46.1-●
    specified type NEC H46.8
    toxic H46.3
  peripheral (nerve) G62.9
    multiple —*see* Polyneuropathy
    single —*see* Mononeuritis
  pneumogastric (nerve) G52.2
  postherpetic, postzoster B02.29
  progressive hypertrophic interstitial G60.0
  retrobulbar —*see also* Neuritis, optic, retrobulbar
    in (due to)
      late syphilis A52.15
      meningococcal infection A39.82
    meningococcal A39.82
    syphilitic A52.15
  sciatic (nerve) —*see also* Sciatica
    due to displacement of intervertebral disc —*see* Disorder, disc, with, radiculopathy
  serum —*see also* Reaction, serum T80.69
  shoulder-girdle G54.5
  specified nerve NEC G58.8
  spinal (nerve) root —*see* Radiculopathy
  syphilitic A52.15
  thenar (median) G56.1-●
  thoracic M54.14
  toxic NEC G62.2
  trochlear (nerve) —*see* Strabismus, paralytic, fourth nerve
  vagus (nerve) G52.2
Neuroastrocytoma —*see* Neoplasm, uncertain behavior, by site
Neuroavitaminosis E56.9 [G99.8]
Neuroblastoma
  olfactory C30.0
  specified site —*see* Neoplasm, malignant, by site
  unspecified site C74.90
Neurochorioretinitis —*see* Chorioretinitis
Neurocirculatory asthenia F45.8
Neurocysticercosis B69.0
Neurocytoma —*see* Neoplasm, benign, by site
Neurodermatitis (circumscribed) (circumscripta) (local) L28.0
  atopic L20.81
  diffuse (Brocq) L20.81
  disseminated L20.81
Neuroencephalomyelopathy, optic G36.0
Neuroepithelioma —*see also* Neoplasm, malignant, by site
  olfactory C30.0
Neurofibroma —*see also* Neoplasm, nerve, benign
  melanotic —*see* Neoplasm, nerve, benign
  multiple —*see* Neurofibromatosis
  plexiform —*see* Neoplasm, nerve, benign
Neurofibromatosis (multiple) (nonmalignant) Q85.00
  acoustic Q85.02
  malignant —*see* Neoplasm, nerve, malignant
  specified NEC Q85.09
  type 1 (von Recklinghausen) Q85.01
  type 2 Q85.02
Neurofibrosarcoma —*see* Neoplasm, nerve, malignant
Neurogenic —*see also* condition
  bladder (*see also* Dysfunction, bladder, neuromuscular) N31.9
    cauda equina syndrome G83.4
  bowel NEC K59.2
  heart F45.8
Neuroglioma —*see* Neoplasm, uncertain behavior, by site

Neurolabyrinthitis (of Dix and Hallpike) —*see* Neuronitis, vestibular
Neurolathyrism —*see* Poisoning, food, noxious, plant
Neuroleprosy A30.9
Neuroma —*see also* Neoplasm, nerve, benign
  acoustic (nerve) D33.3
  amputation (stump) (traumatic) (surgical complication) (late) T87.3-●
    arm T87.3-●
    leg T87.3-●
  digital (toe) G57.6-●
  interdigital G58.8
    lower limb toe G57.8-●
    upper limb G56.8-●
  intermetatarsal G57.8-●
  Morton's G57.6-●
  nonneoplastic
    arm G56.9-●
    leg G57.9-●
    lower extremity G57.9-●
    upper extremity G56.9-●
  optic (nerve) D33.3
  plantar G57.6-●
  plexiform —*see* Neoplasm, nerve, benign
  surgical (nonneoplastic)
    arm G56.9-●
    leg G57.9-●
    lower extremity G57.9-●
    upper extremity G56.9-●
Neuromyalgia —*see* Neuralgia
Neuromyasthenia (epidemic) (postinfectious) G93.3
Neuromyelitis G36.9
  ascending G61.0
  optica G36.0
Neuromyopathy G70.9
  paraneoplastic D49.9 [G13.0]
Neuromyotonia (Isaacs) G71.19
Neuronevus —*see* Nevus
Neuronitis G58.9
  ascending (acute) G57.2-●
  vestibular H81.2-●
Neuroparalytic —*see* condition
Neuropathy, neuropathic G62.9
  acute motor G62.81
  alcoholic G62.1
    with psychosis —*see* Psychosis, alcoholic
  arm G56.9-●
  autonomic, peripheral —*see* Neuropathy, peripheral, autonomic
  axillary G56.9-●
  bladder N31.9
    atonic (motor) (sensory) N31.2
    autonomous N31.2
    flaccid N31.2
    nonreflex N31.2
    reflex N31.1
    uninhibited N31.0
  brachial plexus G54.0
  cervical plexus G54.2
  chronic
    progressive segmentally demyelinating G62.89
    relapsing demyelinating G62.89
  Déjérine-Sottas G60.0
  diabetic —*see* E08-E13 with .40
    mononeuropathy —*see* E08-E13 with .41
    polyneuropathy —*see* E08-E13 with .42
  entrapment G58.9
    iliohypogastric nerve G57.8-●
    ilioinguinal nerve G57.8-●
    lateral cutaneous nerve of thigh G57.1-●
    median nerve G56.0-●
    obturator nerve G57.8-●
    peroneal nerve G57.3-●
    posterior tibial nerve G57.5-●
    saphenous nerve G57.8-●
    ulnar nerve G56.2-●

Neuropathy, neuropathic (Continued)
  facial nerve G51.9
  hereditary G60.9
    motor and sensory (types I-IV) G60.0
    sensory G60.8
    specified NEC G60.8
  hypertrophic G60.0
    Charcot-Marie-Tooth G60.0
    Déjérine-Sottas G60.0
    interstitial progressive G60.0
    of infancy G60.0
    Refsum G60.1
  idiopathic G60.9
    progressive G60.3
    specified NEC G60.8
  in association with hereditary ataxia G60.2
  intercostal G58.0
  ischemic —see Disorder, nerve
  Jamaica (ginger) G62.2
  leg NEC G57.9-●
  lower extremity G57.9-●
  lumbar plexus G54.1
  median nerve G56.1-●
  motor and sensory —see also Polyneuropathy
    hereditary (types I-IV) G60.0
  multifocal motor (MMN) G61.82
  multiple (acute) (chronic) —see
    Polyneuropathy
  optic (nerve) —see also Neuritis, optic
    ischemic H47.01-●
  paraneoplastic (sensorial) (Denny Brown)
    D49.9 [G13.0]
  peripheral (nerve) —see also Polyneuropathy
    G62.9
    autonomic G90.9
      idiopathic G90.09
      in (due to)
        amyloidosis E85.4 [G99.0]
        diabetes mellitus —see E08-E13 with
          .43
        endocrine disease NEC E34.9 [G99.0]
        gout M10.00 [G99.0]
        hyperthyroidism E05.90 [G99.0]
          with thyroid storm E05.91 [G99.0]
        metabolic disease NEC E88.9 [G99.0]
    idiopathic G60.9
      progressive G60.3
      in (due to)
        antitetanus serum G62.0
        arsenic G62.2
        drugs NEC G62.0
        lead G62.2
        organophosphate compounds G62.2
        toxic agent NEC G62.2
    plantar nerves G57.6-●
  progressive
    hypertrophic interstitial G60.0
    inflammatory G62.81
  radicular NEC —see Radiculopathy
  sacral plexus G54.1
  sciatic G57.0-●
  serum G61.1
  toxic NEC G62.2
  trigeminal sensory G50.8
  ulnar nerve G56.2-●
  uremic N18.9 [G63]
  vitamin B12 E53.8 [G63]
    with anemia (pernicious) D51.0 [G63]
      due to dietary deficiency D51.3 [G63]
Neurophthisis —see also Disorder, nerve
  peripheral, diabetic —see E08-E13 with .42
Neuroretinitis —see Chorioretinitis
Neuroretinopathy, hereditary optic H47.22
Neurosarcoma —see Neoplasm, nerve, malignant
Neurosclerosis —see Disorder, nerve
Neurosis, neurotic F48.9
  anankastic F42.8
  anxiety (state) F41.1
    panic type F41.0
  asthenic F48.8
  bladder F45.8

Neurosis, neurotic (Continued)
  cardiac (reflex) F45.8
  cardiovascular F45.8
  character F60.9
  colon F45.8
  compensation F68.10
  compulsive, compulsion F42.8
  conversion F44.9
  craft F48.8
  cutaneous F45.8
  depersonalization F48.1
  depressive (reaction) (type) F34.1
  environmental F48.8
  excoriation L98.1
  fatigue F48.8
  functional —see Disorder, somatoform
  gastric F45.8
  gastrointestinal F45.8
  heart F45.8
  hypochondriacal F45.21
  hysterical F44.9
  incoordination F45.8
    larynx F45.8
    vocal cord F45.8
  intestine F45.8
  larynx (sensory) F45.8
    hysterical F44.4
  mixed NEC F48.8
  musculoskeletal F45.8
  obsessional F42.8
  obsessive-compulsive F42.8
  occupational F48.8
  ocular NEC F45.8
  organ —see Disorder, somatoform
  pharynx F45.8
  phobic F40.9
  posttraumatic (situational) F43.10
    acute F43.11
    chronic F43.12
  psychasthenic (type) F48.8
  railroad F48.8
  rectum F45.8
  respiratory F45.8
  rumination F45.8
  sexual F65.9
  situational F48.8
  social F40.10
    generalized F40.11
  specified type NEC F48.8
  state F48.9
    with depersonalization episode F48.1
  stomach F45.8
  traumatic F43.10
    acute F43.11
    chronic F43.12
  vasomotor F45.8
  visceral F45.8
  war F48.8
Neurospongioblastosis diffusa Q85.1
Neurosyphilis (arrested) (early) (gumma) (late)
    (latent) (recurrent) (relapse) A52.3
  with ataxia (cerebellar) (locomotor) (spastic)
    (spinal) A52.19
  aneurysm (cerebral) A52.05
  arachnoid (adhesive) A52.13
  arteritis (any artery) (cerebral) A52.04
  asymptomatic A52.2
  congenital A50.40
  dura (mater) A52.13
  general paresis A52.17
  hemorrhagic A52.05
  juvenile (asymptomatic) (meningeal)
    A50.40
  leptomeninges (aseptic) A52.13
  meningeal, meninges (adhesive) A52.13
  meningitis A52.13
  meningovascular (diffuse) A52.13
  optic atrophy A52.15
  parenchymatous (degenerative) A52.19
  paresis, paretic A52.17
    juvenile A50.45

Neurosyphilis (Continued)
  remission in (sustained) A52.3
  serological (without symptoms) A52.2
  specified nature or site NEC A52.19
  tabes, tabetic (dorsalis) A52.11
    juvenile A50.45
  taboparesis A52.17
    juvenile A50.45
  thrombosis (cerebral) A52.05
  vascular (cerebral) NEC A52.05
Neurothekeoma —see Neoplasm, nerve, benign
Neurotic —see Neurosis
Neurotoxemia —see Toxemia
Neuroclusion M26.211
Neutropenia, neutropenic (chronic) (genetic)
    (idiopathic) (immune) (infantile)
    (malignant) (pernicious) (splenic) D70.9
  congenital (primary) D70.0
  cyclic D70.4
  cytoreductive cancer chemotherapy sequela
    D70.1
  drug-induced D70.2
    due to cytoreductive cancer chemotherapy
      D70.1
  due to infection D70.3
  fever D70.9
  neonatal, transitory (isoimmune) (maternal
    transfer) P61.5
  periodic D70.4
  secondary (cyclic) (periodic) (splenic) D70.4
    drug-induced D70.2
      due to cytoreductive cancer
        chemotherapy D70.1
  toxic D70.8
Neutrophilia, hereditary giant D72.0
Nevocarcinoma —see Melanoma
Nevus D22.9
  achromic —see Neoplasm, skin, benign
  amelanotic —see Neoplasm, skin, benign
  angiomatous D18.00
    intra-abdominal D18.03
    intracranial D18.02
    skin D18.01
    specified site NEC D18.09
  araneus I78.1
  balloon cell —see Neoplasm, skin, benign
  bathing trunk D48.5
  blue —see Neoplasm, skin, benign
    cellular —see Neoplasm, skin, benign
    giant —see Neoplasm, skin, benign
    Jadassohn's —see Neoplasm, skin, benign
    malignant —see Melanoma
  capillary D18.00
    intra-abdominal D18.03
    intracranial D18.02
    skin D18.01
    specified site NEC D18.09
  cavernous D18.00
    intra-abdominal D18.03
    intracranial D18.02
    skin D18.01
    specified site NEC D18.09
  cellular —see Neoplasm, skin, benign
    blue —see Neoplasm, skin, benign
  choroid D31.3-●
  comedonicus Q82.5
  conjunctiva D31.0-●
  dermal —see Neoplasm, skin, benign
    with epidermal nevus —see Neoplasm,
      skin, benign
  dysplastic —see Neoplasm, skin, benign
  eye D31.9-●
  flammeus Q82.5
  hemangiomatous D18.00
    intra-abdominal D18.03
    intracranial D18.02
    skin D18.01
    specified site NEC D18.09
  iris D31.4-●
  lacrimal gland D31.5-●
  lymphatic D18.1

N

Nevus (Continued)
  magnocellular
    specified site —see Neoplasm, benign, by
      site
    unspecified site D31.40
  malignant —see Melanoma
  meaning hemangioma D18.00
    intra-abdominal D18.03
    intracranial D18.02
    skin D18.01
    specified site NEC D18.09
  mouth (mucosa) D10.30
    specified site NEC D10.39
    white sponge Q38.6
  multiplex Q85.1
  non-neoplastic I78.1
  oral mucosa D10.30
    specified site NEC D10.39
    white sponge Q38.6
  orbit D31.6-●
  pigmented
    giant —see also Neoplasm, skin, uncertain
      behavior D48.5
      malignant melanoma in —see Melanoma
  portwine Q82.5
  retina D31.2-●
  retrobulbar D31.6-●
  sanguineous Q82.5
  senile I78.1
  skin D22.9
    abdominal wall D22.5
    ala nasi D22.39
    ankle D22.7-●
    anus, anal D22.5
    arm D22.6-●
    auditory canal (external) D22.2-●
    auricle (ear) D22.2-●
    auricular canal (external) D22.2-●
    axilla, axillary fold D22.5
    back D22.5
    breast D22.5
    brow D22.39
    buttock D22.5
    canthus (eye) D22.1-●
    cheek (external) D22.39
    chest wall D22.5
    chin D22.39
    ear (external) D22.2-●
    external meatus (ear) D22.2-●
    eyebrow D22.39
    eyelid (lower) (upper) D22.1-●
    face D22.30
      specified NEC D22.39
    female genital organ (external) NEC D28.0
    finger D22.6-●
    flank D22.5
    foot D22.7-●
    forearm D22.6-●
    forehead D22.39
    foreskin D29.0
    genital organ (external) NEC
      female D28.0
      male D29.9
    gluteal region D22.5
    groin D22.5
    hand D22.6-●
    heel D22.7-●
    helix D22.2-●
    hip D22.7-●
    interscapular region D22.5
    jaw D22.39
    knee D22.7-●
    labium (majus) (minus) D28.0
    leg D22.7-●
    lip (lower) (upper) D22.0
    lower limb D22.7-●
    male genital organ (external) D29.9
    nail D22.9
      finger D22.6-●
      toe D22.7-●
    nasolabial groove D22.39
    nates D22.5

Nevus (Continued)
  skin (Continued)
    neck D22.4
    nose (external) D22.39
    palpebra D22.1-●
    penis D29.0
    perianal skin D22.5
    perineum D22.5
    pinna D22.2-●
    popliteal fossa or space D22.7-●
    prepuce D29.0
    pudendum D28.0
    scalp D22.4
    scrotum D29.4
    shoulder D22.6-●
    submammary fold D22.5
    temple D22.39
    thigh D22.7-●
    toe D22.7-●
    trunk NEC D22.5
    umbilicus D22.5
    upper limb D22.6-●
    vulva D28.0
  specified site NEC —see Neoplasm, benign,
    by site
  spider I78.1
  stellar I78.1
  strawberry Q82.5
  Sutton's benign D22.9
  unius lateris Q82.5
  Unna's Q82.5
  vascular Q82.5
  verrucous Q82.5
Newborn (infant) (liveborn) (singleton) Z38.2
  abstinence syndrome P96.1
  acne L70.4
  affected by
    abnormalities of membranes P02.9
      specified NEC P02.8
    abruptio placenta P02.1
    amino-acid metabolic disorder, transitory
      P74.8
    amniocentesis (while in utero) P00.6
    ⇒amnionitis P02.78
    apparent life threatening event (ALTE)
      R68.13
    bleeding (into)
      cerebral cortex P52.22
      germinal matrix P52.0
      ventricles P52.1
    breech delivery P03.0
    cardiac arrest P29.81
    cardiomyopathy I42.8
      congenital I42.4
    cerebral ischemia P91.0
    Cesarean delivery P03.4
    ⇒chemotherapy agents P04.11
    ⇒chorioamnionitis P02.78
    cocaine (crack) P04.41
    complications of labor and delivery P03.9
      specified NEC P03.89
    compression of umbilical cord NEC P02.5
    contracted pelvis P03.1
    delivery P03.9
      Cesarean P03.4
      forceps P03.2
      vacuum extractor P03.3
    ▶drugs of addiction P04.40
      ▶cocaine P04.41
      ▶hallucinogens P04.42
      ▶specified drug NEC P04.49
    entanglement (knot) in umbilical cord P02.5
    environmental chemicals P04.6
    fetal (intrauterine)
      growth retardation P05.9
      ▶inflammatory response syndrome (FIRS)
        P02.70
      malnutrition not light or small for
        gestational age P05.2
    ▶FIRS (fetal inflammatory response
      syndrome) P02.70

Newborn (Continued)
  affected by (Continued)
    forceps delivery P03.2
    heart rate abnormalities
      bradycardia P29.12
      intrauterine P03.819
        before onset of labor P03.810
        during labor P03.811
      tachycardia P29.11
    hemorrhage (antepartum) P02.1
      cerebellar (nontraumatic) P52.6
      intracerebral (nontraumatic) P52.4
      intracranial (nontraumatic) P52.9
        specified NEC P52.8
      intraventricular (nontraumatic) P52.3
        grade 1 P52.0
        grade 2 P52.1
        grade 3 P52.21
        grade 4 P52.22
      posterior fossa (nontraumatic) P52.6
      subarachnoid (nontraumatic) P52.5
      subependymal P52.0
        with intracerebral extension P52.22
        with intraventricular extension P52.1
          with enlargment of ventricles
            P52.21
          without intraventricular extension
            P52.0
    hypoxic ischemic encephalopathy [HIE]
      P91.60
      mild P91.61
      moderate P91.62
      severe P91.63
    induction of labor P03.89
    intestinal perforation P78.0
    intrauterine (fetal) blood loss P50.9
      due to (from)
        cut end of co-twin cord P50.5
        hemorrhage into
          co-twin P50.3
          maternal circulation P50.4
        placenta P50.2
        ruptured cord blood P50.1
        vasa previa P50.0
      specified NEC P50.8
    intrauterine (fetal) hemorrhage P50.9
    intrauterine (in utero) procedure P96.5
    malpresentation (malposition) NEC P03.1
    maternal (complication of) (use of)
      alcohol P04.3
      ▶amphetamines P04.16
      analgesia (maternal) P04.0
      anesthesia (maternal) P04.0
      ▶anticonvulsants P04.13
      ▶antidepressants P04.15
      ▶antineoplastic chemotherapy P04.11
      ▶anxiolytics P04.1A
      blood loss P02.1
      ▶cannabis P04.81
      circulatory disease P00.3
      condition P00.9
        specified NEC P00.89
      ▶cytotoxic drugs P04.12
      delivery P03.9
        Cesarean P03.4
        forceps P03.2
        vacuum extractor P03.3
      diabetes mellitus (pre-existing) P70.1
      disorder P00.9
        specified NEC P00.89
      drugs (addictive) (illegal) NEC P04.49
      ectopic pregnancy P01.4
      gestational diabetes P70.0
      hemorrhage P02.1
      hypertensive disorder P00.0
      incompetent cervix P01.0
      infectious disease P00.2
      injury P00.5
      labor and delivery P03.9
      malpresentation before labor P01.7
      maternal death P01.6

▶ New   ⇒ Revised   ~~deleted~~ Deleted   ● Use Additional Character(s)

Newborn *(Continued)*
  affected by *(Continued)*
    maternal *(Continued)*
      medical procedure P00.7
      medication P04.19
        specified type NEC P04.18
      multiple pregnancy P01.5
      nutritional disorder P00.4
      oligohydramnios P01.2
      opiates P04.14
        administered for procedures during pregnancy or labor and delivery P04.0
      parasitic disease P00.2
      periodontal disease P00.81
      placenta previa P02.0
      polyhydramnios P01.3
      precipitate delivery P03.5
      pregnancy P01.9
        specified P01.8
      premature rupture of membranes P01.1
      renal disease P00.1
      respiratory disease P00.3
      sedative-hypnotics P04.17
      surgical procedure P00.6
      tranquilizers administered for procedures during pregnancy or labor and delivery P04.0
      urinary tract disease P00.1
      uterine contraction (abnormal) P03.6
    meconium peritonitis P78.0
    medication (legal) (maternal use) (prescribed) P04.19
    membrane abnormalities P02.9
      specified NEC P02.8
    membranitis P02.78
    methamphetamine(s) P04.49
    mixed metabolic and respiratory acidosis P84
    neonatal abstinence syndrome P96.1
    noxious substances transmitted via placenta or breast milk P04.9
      cannabis P04.81
      specified NEC P04.89
    nutritional supplements P04.5
    placenta previa P02.0
    placental
      abnormality (functional) (morphological) P02.20
        specified NEC P02.29
      dysfunction P02.29
      infarction P02.29
      insufficiency P02.29
      separation NEC P02.1
      transfusion syndromes P02.3
    placentitis P02.78
    precipitate delivery P03.5
    prolapsed cord P02.4
    respiratory arrest P28.81
    slow intrauterine growth P05.9
    tobacco P04.2
    twin to twin transplacental transfusion P02.3
    umbilical cord (tightly) around neck P02.5
    umbilical cord condition P02.60
      short cord P02.69
      specified NEC P02.69
    uterine contractions (abnormal) P03.6
    vasa previa P02.69
      from intrauterine blood loss P50.0
  apnea P28.4
    obstructive P28.4
    primary P28.3
    sleep (central) (obstructive) (primary) P28.3
  born in hospital Z38.00
    by cesarean Z38.01
  born outside hospital Z38.1
  breast buds P96.89
  breast engorgement P83.4
  check-up —*see* Newborn, examination
  convulsion P90
  dehydration P74.1

Newborn *(Continued)*
  examination
    8 to 28 days old Z00.111
    under 8 days old Z00.110
  fever P81.9
    environmentally-induced P81.0
  hyperbilirubinemia P59.9
    of prematurity P59.0
  hypernatremia P74.21
  hyponatremia P74.22
  infection P39.9
    candidal P37.5
    specified NEC P39.8
    urinary tract P39.3
  jaundice P59.9
    due to
      breast milk inhibitor P59.3
      hepatocellular damage P59.20
        specified NEC P59.29
      preterm delivery P59.0
    of prematurity P59.0
    specified NEC P59.8
  late metabolic acidosis P74.0
  mastitis P39.0
    infective P39.0
    noninfective P83.4
  multiple born NEC Z38.8
    born in hospital Z38.68
      by cesarean Z38.69
    born outside hospital Z38.7
  omphalitis P38.9
    with mild hemorrhage P38.1
    without hemorrhage P38.9
  post-term P08.21
  prolonged gestation (over 42 completed weeks) P08.22
  quadruplet Z38.8
    born in hospital Z38.63
      by cesarean Z38.64
    born outside hospital Z38.7
  quintuplet Z38.8
    born in hospital Z38.65
      by cesarean Z38.66
    born outside hospital Z38.7
  seizure P90
  sepsis (congenital) P36.9
    due to
      anaerobes NEC P36.5
      Escherichia coli P36.4
      Staphylococcus P36.30
        aureus P36.2
        specified NEC P36.39
      Streptococcus P36.10
        group B P36.0
        specified NEC P36.19
      specified NEC P36.8
  triplet Z38.8
    born in hospital Z38.61
      by cesarean Z38.62
    born outside hospital Z38.7
  twin Z38.5
    born in hospital Z38.30
      by cesarean Z38.31
    born outside hospital Z38.4
  vomiting P92.09
    bilious P92.01
  weight check Z00.111
Newcastle conjunctivitis or disease B30.8
Nezelof's syndrome (pure alymphocytosis) D81.4
Niacin (amide) deficiency E52
Nicolas (-Durand)-Favre disease A55
Nicotine —*see* Tobacco
Nicotinic acid deficiency E52
Niemann-Pick disease or syndrome E75.249
  specified NEC E75.248
  type
    A E75.240
    B E75.241
    C E75.242
    D E75.243

Night
  blindness —*see* Blindness, night
  sweats R61
  terrors (child) F51.4
Nightmares (REM sleep type) F51.5
NIHSS (National Institutes of Health Stroke Scale) score R29.7-•
Nipple —*see* condition
Nisbet's chancre A57
Nishimoto (-Takeuchi) disease I67.5
Nitritoid crisis or reaction —*see* Crisis, nitritoid
Nitrosohemoglobinemia D74.8
Njovera A65
Nocardiosis, nocardiasis A43.9
  cutaneous A43.1
  lung A43.0
  pneumonia A43.0
  pulmonary A43.0
  specified site NEC A43.8
Nocturia R35.1
  psychogenic F45.8
Nocturnal —*see* condition
Nodal rhythm I49.8
Node(s) —*see also* Nodule
  Bouchard's (with arthropathy) M15.2
  Haygarth's M15.8
  Heberden's (with arthropathy) M15.1
  larynx J38.7
  lymph —*see* condition
  milker's B08.03
  Osler's I33.0
  Schmorl's —*see* Schmorl's disease
  singer's J38.2
  teacher's J38.2
  tuberculous —*see* Tuberculosis, lymph gland
  vocal cord J38.2
Nodule(s), nodular
  actinomycotic —*see* Actinomycosis
  breast NEC —*see also* Lump, breast N63.0
  colloid (cystic), thyroid E04.1
  cutaneous —*see* Swelling, localized
  endometrial (stromal) D26.1
  Haygarth's M15.8
  inflammatory —*see* Inflammation
  juxta-articular
    syphilitic A52.77
    yaws A66.7
  larynx J38.7
  lung, solitary (subsegmental branch of the bronchial tree) R91.1
    multiple R91.8
  milker's B08.03
  prostate N40.2
    with lower urinary tract symptoms (LUTS) N40.3
    without lower urinary tract symptoms (LUTS) N40.2
  pulmonary, solitary (subsegmental branch of the bronchial tree) R91.1
  retrocardiac R09.89
  rheumatoid M06.30
    ankle M06.37-•
    elbow M06.32-•
    foot joint M06.37-•
    hand joint M06.34-•
    hip M06.35-•
    knee M06.36-•
    multiple site M06.39
    shoulder M06.31-•
    vertebra M06.38
    wrist M06.33-•
  scrotum (inflammatory) N49.2
  singer's J38.2
  solitary, lung (subsegmental branch of the bronchial tree) R91.1
    multiple R91.8
  subcutaneous —*see* Swelling, localized
  teacher's J38.2

Nodule(s), nodular *(Continued)*
 thyroid (cold) (gland) (nontoxic) E04.1
  with thyrotoxicosis E05.20
   with thyroid storm E05.21
  toxic or with hyperthyroidism E05.20
   with thyroid storm E05.21
 vocal cord J38.2
Noma (gangrenous) (hospital) (infective)
  A69.0
 auricle I96
 mouth A69.0
 pudendi N76.89
 vulvae N76.89
Nomad, nomadism Z59.0
NOMID (neonatal onset multisystemic
  inflammatory disorder) M04.2
Nonadherence to medical treatment Z91.19
Nonautoimmune hemolytic anemia D59.4
 drug-induced D59.2
Nonclosure —*see also* Imperfect, closure
 ductus arteriosus (Botallo's) Q25.0
 foramen
  botalli Q21.1
  ovale Q21.1
Noncompliance Z91.19
 with
  dialysis Z91.15
  dietary regimen Z91.11
  medical treatment Z91.19
  medication regimen NEC Z91.14
   underdosing —*see also* Table of Drugs
    and Chemicals, categories T36-T50,
    with final character 6 Z91.14
   intentional NEC Z91.128
    due to financial hardship of patient
     Z91.120
   unintentional NEC Z91.138
    due to patient's age related debility
     Z91.130
  renal dialysis Z91.15
Nondescent (congenital) —*see also* Malposition,
  congenital
 cecum Q43.3
 colon Q43.3
 testicle Q53.9
  bilateral Q53.20
   abdominal Q53.211
   perineal Q53.22
  unilateral Q53.10
   abdominal Q53.111
   perineal Q53.12
Nondevelopment
 brain Q02
  part of Q04.3

Nondevelopment *(Continued)*
 heart Q24.8
 organ or site, congenital NEC —*see*
  Hypoplasia
Nonengagement
 head NEC O32.4
  in labor, causing obstructed labor
   O64.8
Nonexanthematous tick fever A93.2
Nonexpansion, lung (newborn) P28.0
Nonfunctioning
 cystic duct —*see also* Disease, gallbladder
  K82.8
 gallbladder —*see also* Disease, gallbladder
  K82.8
 kidney N28.9
 labyrinth —*see* subcategory H83.2
Non-Hodgkin lymphoma NEC —*see*
  Lymphoma, non-Hodgkin
Nonimplantation, ovum N97.2
Noninsufflation, fallopian tube N97.1
Non-ketotic hyperglycinemia E72.51
Nonne-Milroy syndrome Q82.0
Nonovulation N97.0
Non-palpable testicle(s)
  bilateral R39.84
  unilateral R39.83
Nonpatent fallopian tube N97.1
Nonpneumatization, lung NEC P28.0
Nonrotation —*see* Malrotation
Nonsecretion, urine —*see* Anuria
Nonunion
 fracture —*see* Fracture, by site
 joint, following fusion or arthrodesis
  M96.0
 organ or site, congenital NEC —*see*
  Imperfect, closure
 symphysis pubis, congenital Q74.2
Nonvisualization, gallbladder R93.2
Nonvital, nonvitalized tooth K04.99
Non-working side interference
  M26.56
Noonan's syndrome Q87.1
Normocytic anemia (infectional) due to
   blood loss (chronic) D50.0
 acute D62
Norrie's disease (congenital) Q15.8
North American blastomycosis B40.9
Norwegian itch B86
Nose, nasal —*see* condition
Nosebleed R04.0
Nose-picking F98.8
Nosomania F45.21
Nosophobia F45.22

Nostalgia F43.20
Notch of iris Q13.2
Notching nose, congenital (tip)
  Q30.2
Nothnagel's
 syndrome —*see* Strabismus, paralytic, third
  nerve
 vasomotor acroparesthesia I73.89
Novy's relapsing fever A68.9
 louse-borne A68.0
 tick-borne A68.1
Noxious
 foodstuffs, poisoning by —*see* Poisoning,
  food, noxious, plant
 substances transmitted through placenta or
  breast milk P04.9
Nucleus pulposus —*see* condition
Numbness R20.0
Nuns' knee —*see* Bursitis, prepatellar
Nursemaid's elbow S53.03-●
Nutcracker esophagus K22.4
Nutmeg liver K76.1
Nutrient element deficiency E61.9
 specified NEC E61.8
Nutrition deficient or insufficient —*see also*
   Malnutrition E46
 due to
  insufficient food T73.0
  lack of
   care (child) T76.02
    adult T76.01
   food T73.0
Nutritional stunting E45
Nyctalopia (night blindness) —*see* Blindness,
   night
Nycturia R35.1
 psychogenic F45.8
Nymphomania F52.8
Nystagmus H55.00
 benign paroxysmal —*see* Vertigo, benign
   paroxysmal
 central positional H81.4-●
 congenital H55.01
 dissociated H55.04
 latent H55.02
 miners' H55.09
 positional
  benign paroxysmal H81.4-●
  central H81.4-●
 specified form NEC H55.09
 visual deprivation H55.03

▶ New ⇒ Revised ~~deleted~~ Deleted ● Use Additional Character(s)

O

Obermeyer's relapsing fever (European)
A68.0
Obesity E66.9
 with alveolar hypoventilation E66.2
 adrenal E27.8
 complicating
  childbirth O99.214
  pregnancy O99.21-●
  puerperium O99.215
 constitutional E66.8
 dietary counseling and surveillance Z71.3
 drug-induced E66.1
 due to
  drug E66.1
  excess calories E66.09
   morbid E66.01
   severe E66.01
 endocrine E66.8
 endogenous E66.8
 exogenous E66.09
 familial E66.8
 glandular E66.8
 hypothyroid —see Hypothyroidism
 hypoventilation syndrome (OHS)
  E66.2
 morbid E66.01
  with
   alveolar hypoventilation E66.2
   obesity hypoventilation syndrome
    (OHS) E66.2
  due to excess calories E66.01
 nutritional E66.09
 pituitary E23.6
 severe E66.01
 specified type NEC E66.8
Oblique —see condition
Obliteration
 appendix (lumen) K38.8
 artery I77.1
 bile duct (noncalculous) K83.1
 common duct (noncalculous) K83.1
 cystic duct —see Obstruction, gallbladder
 disease, arteriolar I77.1
 endometrium N85.8
 eye, anterior chamber —see Disorder, globe,
  hypotony
 fallopian tube N97.1
 lymphatic vessel I89.0
  due to mastectomy I97.2
 organ or site, congenital NEC —see Atresia,
  by site
 ureter N13.5
  with infection N13.6
 urethra —see Stricture, urethra
 vein I87.8
 vestibule (oral) K08.89
Observation (following) (for) (without need for
 further medical care) Z04.9
 accident NEC Z04.3
  at work Z04.2
  transport Z04.1
 adverse effect of drug Z03.6
 alleged rape or sexual assault (victim),
  ruled out
  adult Z04.41
  child Z04.42
 ⟹criminal assault Z04.89
 development state
  adolescent Z00.3
  period of rapid growth in childhood Z00.2
  puberty Z00.3
 disease, specified NEC Z03.89
 following work accident Z04.2
 ▶forced sexual exploitation Z04.81
 ▶forced labor exploitation Z04.82
 growth and development state —see
  Observation, development state
 injuries (accidental) NEC —see also
  Observation, accident

Observation (Continued)
 newborn (for)
  suspected condition, related to exposure
   from the mother or birth process —
   see Newborn, affected by,
   maternal
   ruled out Z05.9
    cardiac Z05.0
    connective tissue Z05.73
    gastrointestinal Z05.5
    genetic Z05.41
    genitourinary Z05.6
    immunologic Z05.43
    infectious Z05.1
    metabolic Z05.42
    musculoskeletal Z05.72
    neurological Z05.2
    respiratory Z05.3
    skin and subcutaneous tissue
     Z05.71
    specified condition NEC
     Z05.8
 postpartum
  immediately after delivery Z39.0
  routine follow-up Z39.2
 pregnancy (normal) (without complication)
  Z34.9-●
  high risk O09.9-●
 suicide attempt, alleged NEC Z03.89
  self-poisoning Z03.6
 suspected, ruled out —see also Suspected
  condition, ruled out
  abuse, physical
   adult Z04.71
   child Z04.72
  accident at work Z04.2
  adult battering victim Z04.71
  child battering victim Z04.72
  condition NEC Z03.89
   newborn —see also Observation,
    newborn (for), suspected condition,
    ruled out Z05.9
  drug poisoning or adverse effect
   Z03.6
  exposure (to)
   anthrax Z03.810
   biological agent NEC Z03.818
  ⟹inflicted injury NEC Z04.89
  suicide attempt, alleged Z03.89
   self-poisoning Z03.6
  toxic effects from ingested substance (drug)
   (poison) Z03.6
 toxic effects from ingested substance (drug)
  (poison) Z03.6
Obsession, obsessional state F42.8
 mixed thoughts and acts F42.2
Obsessive-compulsive neurosis or reaction
 F42.8
Obstetric embolism, septic —see Embolism,
 obstetric, septic
Obstetrical trauma (complicating delivery)
 O71.9
 with or following ectopic or molar pregnancy
  O08.6
 specified type NEC O71.89
Obstipation —see Constipation
Obstruction, obstructed, obstructive
 airway J98.8
  with
   allergic alveolitis J67.9
   asthma J45.909
    with
     exacerbation (acute) J45.901
     status asthmaticus J45.902
   bronchiectasis J47.9
    with
     exacerbation (acute) J47.1
     lower respiratory infection
      J47.0
   bronchitis (chronic) J44.9
   emphysema J43.9

Obstruction, obstructed, obstructive
 (Continued)
 airway (Continued)
  chronic J44.9
   with
    allergic alveolitis —see Pneumonitis,
     hypersensitivity
    bronchiectasis J47.9
     with
      exacerbation (acute) J47.1
      lower respiratory infection J47.0
  due to
   foreign body —see Foreign body, by site,
    causing asphyxia
   inhalation of fumes or vapors J68.9
   laryngospasm J38.5
 ampulla of Vater K83.1
 aortic (heart) (valve) —see Stenosis, aortic
 aortoiliac I74.09
 aqueduct of Sylvius G91.1
  congenital Q03.0
   with spina bifida —see Spina bifida, by
    site, with hydrocephalus
 Arnold-Chiari —see Arnold-Chiari disease
 artery (see also Atherosclerosis, artery) I70.9
  basilar (complete) (partial) —see Occlusion,
   artery, basilar
  carotid (complete) (partial) —see Occlusion,
   artery, carotid
  cerebellar —see Occlusion, artery, cerebellar
  cerebral (anterior) (middle) (posterior) —
   see Occlusion, artery, cerebral
  precerebral —see Occlusion, artery,
   precerebral
  renal N28.0
  retinal NEC —see Occlusion, artery, retina
  stent —see Restenosis, stent
  vertebral (complete) (partial) —see
   Occlusion, artery, vertebral
 band (intestinal) —see also Obstruction,
  intestine, specified NEC K56.699
 bile duct or passage (common) (hepatic)
  (noncalculous) K83.1
  with calculus K80.51
  congenital (causing jaundice) Q44.3
 biliary (duct) (tract) K83.1
  gallbladder K82.0
 bladder-neck (acquired) N32.0
  congenital Q64.31
  due to hyperplasia (hypertrophy) of
   prostate —see Hyperplasia, prostate
 bowel —see Obstruction, intestine
 bronchus J98.09
 canal, ear —see Stenosis, external ear canal
 cardia K22.2
 caval veins (inferior) (superior) I87.1
 cecum —see Obstruction, intestine
 circulatory I99.8
 colon —see Obstruction, intestine
 common duct (noncalculous) K83.1
 coronary (artery) —see Occlusion, coronary
 cystic duct —see also Obstruction, gallbladder
  with calculus K80.21
 device, implant or graft —see also
  Complications, by site and type,
  mechanical T85.698
  arterial graft NEC —see Complication,
   cardiovascular device, mechanical,
   vascular
  catheter NEC T85.628
   cystostomy T83.090
   dialysis (renal) T82.49
    intraperitoneal T85.691
   Hopkins T83.098
   ileostomy T83.098
   infusion NEC T82.594
    spinal (epidural) (subdural) T85.690
   nephrostomy T83.092
   urethral indwelling T83.091
   urinary T83.098
   urostomy T83.098

Obstruction, obstructed, obstructive
(Continued)
  device, implant or graft (Continued)
    due to infection T85.79
    gastrointestinal —see Complications,
        prosthetic device, mechanical,
        gastrointestinal device
    genital NEC T83.498
      intrauterine contraceptive device T83.39
      penile prosthesis (cylinder) (implanted)
          (pump) (resevoir) T83.490
      testicular prosthesis T83.491
    heart NEC —see Complication,
        cardiovascular device, mechanical
    joint prosthesis —see Complications, joint
        prosthesis, mechanical, specified NEC,
        by site
    orthopedic NEC —see Complication,
        orthopedic, device, mechanical
    specified NEC T85.628
    urinary NEC —see also Complication,
        genitourinary, device, urinary,
        mechanical
      graft T83.29
    vascular NEC —see Complication,
        cardiovascular device, mechanical
    ventricular intracranial shunt T85.09
  due to foreign body accidentally left in
      operative wound T81.529
  duodenum K31.5
  ejaculatory duct N50.89
  esophagus K22.2
  eustachian tube (complete) (partial) H68.10-●
    cartilagenous (extrinsic) H68.13-●
      intrinsic H68.12-●
    osseous H68.11-●
  fallopian tube (bilateral) N97.1
  fecal K56.41
    with hernia —see Hernia, by site, with
        obstruction
  foramen of Monro (congenital) Q03.8
    with spina bifida —see Spina bifida,
        by site, with hydrocephalus
  foreign body —see Foreign body
  gallbladder K82.0
    with calculus, stones K80.21
    congenital Q44.1
  gastric outlet K31.1
  gastrointestinal —see Obstruction, intestine
  hepatic K76.89
    duct (noncalculous) K83.1
  hepatobiliary K83.1
  ileum —see Obstruction, intestine
  iliofemoral (artery) I74.5
  intestine K56.609
    complete K56.601
    incomplete K56.600
    partial K56.600
    with
      adhesions (intestinal) (peritoneal) K56.50
        complete K56.52
        incomplete K56.51
        partial K56.51
    adynamic K56.0
    by gallstone K56.3
    congenital (small) Q41.9
      large Q42.9
        specified part NEC Q42.8
    neurogenic K56.0
      Hirschsprung's disease or megacolon
          Q43.1
    newborn P76.9
      due to
        fecaliths P76.8
        inspissated milk P76.2
        meconium (plug) P76.0
          in mucoviscidosis E84.11
      specified NEC P76.8
    postoperative K91.30
      complete K91.32
      incomplete K91.31
      partial K91.31

Obstruction, obstructed, obstructive
(Continued)
  intestine (Continued)
    reflex K56.0
    specified NEC K56.699
      complete K56.691
      incomplete K56.690
      partial K56.690
    volvulus K56.2
  intracardiac ball valve prosthesis T82.09
  jejunum —see Obstruction, intestine
  joint prosthesis —see Complications, joint
      prosthesis, mechanical, specified NEC,
      by site
  kidney (calices) N28.89
  labor —see Delivery
  lacrimal (passages) (duct)
    by
      dacryolith —see Dacryolith
      stenosis —see Stenosis, lacrimal
    congenital Q10.5
    neonatal H04.53-●
  lacrimonasal duct —see Obstruction, lacrimal
  lacteal, with steatorrhea K90.2
  laryngitis —see Laryngitis
  larynx NEC J38.6
    congenital Q31.8
  lung J98.4
    disease, chronic J44.9
  lymphatic I89.0
  meconium (plug)
    newborn P76.0
      due to fecaliths P76.0
      in mucoviscidosis E84.11
  mitral —see Stenosis, mitral
  nasal J34.89
  nasolacrimal duct —see also Obstruction,
      lacrimal
    congenital Q10.5
  nasopharynx J39.2
  nose J34.89
  organ or site, congenital NEC —see Atresia,
      by site
  pancreatic duct K86.89
  parotid duct or gland K11.8
  pelviureteral junction N13.5
    with hydronephrosis N13.0
    congenital Q62.39
  pharynx J39.2
  portal (circulation) (vein) I81
  prostate —see also Hyperplasia, prostate
    valve (urinary) N32.0
  pulmonary valve (heart) I37.0
  pyelonephritis (chronic) N11.1
  pylorus
    adult K31.1
    congenital or infantile Q40.0
  rectosigmoid —see Obstruction,
      intestine
  rectum K62.4
  renal N28.89
    outflow N13.8
    pelvis, congenital Q62.39
  respiratory J98.8
    chronic J44.9
  retinal (vessels) H34.9
  salivary duct (any) K11.8
    with calculus K11.5
  sigmoid —see Obstruction, intestine
  sinus (accessory) (nasal) J34.89
  Stensen's duct K11.8
  stomach NEC K31.89
    acute K31.0
    congenital Q40.2
    due to pylorospasm K31.3
  submandibular duct K11.8
  submaxillary gland K11.8
    with calculus K11.5
  thoracic duct I89.0
  thrombotic —see Thrombosis
  trachea J39.8

Obstruction, obstructed, obstructive
(Continued)
  tracheostomy airway J95.03
  tricuspid (valve) —see Stenosis, tricuspid
  upper respiratory, congenital Q34.8
  ureter (functional) (pelvic junction) NEC N13.5
    with
      hydronephrosis N13.1
        with infection N13.6
      pyelonephritis (chronic) N11.1
    congenital Q62.39
    due to calculus —see Calculus, ureter
  urethra NEC N36.8
    congenital Q64.39
  urinary (moderate) N13.9
    due to hyperplasia (hypertrophy) of
        prostate —see Hyperplasia, prostate
    organ or tract (lower) N13.9
    prostatic valve N32.0
    specified NEC N13.8
  uropathy N13.9
  uterus N85.8
  vagina N89.5
  valvular —see Endocarditis
  vein, venous I87.1
    caval (inferior) (superior) I87.1
      thrombotic —see Thrombosis
    vena cava (inferior) (superior) I87.1
  vesical NEC N32.0
  vesicourethral orifice N32.0
    congenital Q64.31
  vessel NEC I99.8
  stent —see Restenosis, stent
Obturator —see condition
Occlusal wear, teeth K03.0
Occlusio pupillae —see Membrane, pupillary
Occlusion, occluded
  anus K62.4
    congenital Q42.3
      with fistula Q42.2
  aortoiliac (chronic) I74.09
  aqueduct of Sylvius G91.1
    congenital Q03.0
      with spina bifida —see Spina bifida, by
          site, with hydrocephalus
  artery —see also Atherosclerosis, artery I70.9
    auditory, internal I65.8
    basilar I65.1
      with
        infarction I63.22
          due to
            embolism I63.12
            thrombosis I63.02
    brain or cerebral I66.9
      with infarction (due to) I63.5-●
        embolism I63.4-●
        thrombosis I63.3-●
    carotid I65.2-●
      with
        infarction I63.23-●
          due to
            embolism I63.13-●
            thrombosis I63.03-●
    cerebellar (anterior inferior) (posterior
        inferior) (superior) I66.3
      with infarction I63.54-●
        due to
          embolism I63.44-●
          thrombosis I63.34-●
    cerebral I66.9
      with infarction I63.50
        due to
          embolism I63.40
            specified NEC I63.49
          thrombosis I63.30
            specified NEC I63.39
      anterior I66.1-●
        with infarction I63.52-●
          due to
            embolism I63.42-●
            thrombosis I63.32-●

Occlusion, occluded (Continued)
  artery (Continued)
    cerebral (Continued)
      middle I66.0-●
        with infarction I63.51-●
          due to
            embolism I63.41-●
            thrombosis I63.31-●
      posterior I66.2-●
        with infarction I63.53-●
          due to
            embolism I63.43-●
            thrombosis I63.33-●
      specified NEC I66.8
        with infarction I63.59
          due to
            embolism I63.4-●
            thrombosis I63.3-●
    choroidal (anterior) —see Occlusion,
        artery, cerebral, specified NEC
    communicating posterior —see Occlusion,
        artery, precerebral, specified NEC
    complete
      coronary I25.82
      extremities I70.92
    coronary (acute) (thrombotic) (without
        myocardial infarction) I24.0
      with myocardial infarction —see
          Infarction, myocardium
      chronic total I25.82
      complete I25.82
      healed or old I25.2
      total (chronic) I25.82
    hypophyseal —see Occlusion, artery,
        precerebral, specified NEC
    iliac I74.5
    lower extremities due to stenosis or
        stricture I77.1
    mesenteric (embolic) (thrombotic) —see also
        Infarct, intestine K55.069
    perforating —see Occlusion, artery,
        cerebral, specified NEC
    peripheral I77.9
      thrombotic or embolic I74.4
    pontine —see Occlusion, artery, precerebral,
        specified NEC
    precerebral I65.9
      with infarction I63.20
        due to
          embolism I63.10
            specified NEC I63.19
          thrombosis I63.00
            specified NEC I63.09
        specified NEC I63.29
      basilar —see Occlusion, artery, basilar
      carotid —see Occlusion, artery, carotid
      puerperal O88.23
      specified NEC I65.8
        with infarction I63.29
          due to
            embolism I63.19
            thrombosis I63.09
      vertebral —see Occlusion, artery,
          vertebral
    renal N28.0
    retinal
      branch H34.23-●
      central H34.1-●
      partial H34.21-●
      transient H34.0-●
    spinal —see Occlusion, artery, precerebral,
        vertebral
    total (chronic)
      coronary I25.82
      extremities I70.92
    vertebral I65.0-●
      with
        infarction I63.21-●
          due to
            embolism I63.11-●
            thrombosis I63.01-●

Occlusion, occluded (Continued)
  basilar artery —see Occlusion, artery, basilar
  bile duct (common) (hepatic) (noncalculous)
      K83.1
  bowel —see Obstruction, intestine
  carotid (artery) (common) (internal) —see
      Occlusion, artery, carotid
  centric (of teeth) M26.59
    maximum intercuspation discrepancy
        M26.55
  cerebellar (artery) —see Occlusion, artery,
      cerebellar
  cerebral (artery) —see Occlusion, artery,
      cerebral
  cerebrovascular —see also Occlusion, artery,
      cerebral
    with infarction I63.5-●
  cervical canal —see Stricture, cervix
  cervix (uteri) —see Stricture, cervix
  choanal Q30.0
  choroidal (artery) —see Occlusion, artery,
      precerebral, specified NEC
  colon —see Obstruction, intestine
  communicating posterior artery —see
      Occlusion, artery, precerebral, specified
      NEC
  coronary (artery) (vein) (thrombotic) —see
      also Infarct, myocardium
    chronic total I25.82
    healed or old I25.2
    not resulting in infarction I24.0
    total (chronic) I25.82
  cystic duct —see Obstruction, gallbladder
  embolic —see Embolism
  fallopian tube N97.1
    congenital Q50.6
  gallbladder —see also Obstruction,
      gallbladder
    congenital (causing jaundice) Q44.1
  gingiva, traumatic K06.2
  hymen N89.6
    congenital Q52.3
  hypophyseal (artery) —see Occlusion, artery,
      precerebral, specified NEC
  iliac artery I74.5
  intestine —see Obstruction, intestine
  lacrimal passages —see Obstruction, lacrimal
  lung J98.4
  lymph or lymphatic channel I89.0
  mammary duct N64.89
  mesenteric artery (embolic) (thrombotic) —
      see also Infarct, intestine K55.069
  nose J34.89
    congenital Q30.0
  organ or site, congenital NEC —see Atresia,
      by site
  oviduct N97.1
    congenital Q50.6
  peripheral arteries
    due to stricture or stenosis I77.1
    upper extremity I74.2
  pontine (artery) —see Occlusion, artery,
      precerebral, specified NEC
  posterior lingual, of mandibular teeth M26.29
  precerebral artery —see Occlusion, artery,
      precerebral
  punctum lacrimale —see Obstruction,
      lacrimal
  pupil —see Membrane, pupillary
  pylorus, adult —see also Stricture, pylorus
      K31.1
  renal artery N28.0
  retina, retinal
    artery —see Occlusion, artery, retinal
    vein (central) H34.81-●
      engorgement H34.82-●
      tributary H34.83-●
    vessels H34.9
  spinal artery —see Occlusion, artery,
      precerebral, vertebral
  teeth (mandibular) (posterior lingual) M26.29

Occlusion, occluded (Continued)
  thoracic duct I89.0
  thrombotic —see Thrombosis, artery
  traumatic
    edentulous (alveolar) ridge K06.2
    gingiva K06.2
    periodontal K05.5
  tubal N97.1
  ureter (complete) (partial) N13.5
    congenital Q62.10
  ureteropelvic junction N13.5
    congenital Q62.11
  ureterovesical orifice N13.5
    congenital Q62.12
  urethra —see Stricture, urethra
  uterus N85.8
  vagina N89.5
  vascular NEC I99.8
  vein —see Thrombosis
    retinal —see Occlusion, retinal, vein
  vena cava (inferior) (superior) —see
      Embolism, vena cava
  ventricle (brain) NEC G91.1
  vertebral (artery) —see Occlusion, artery,
      vertebral
  vessel (blood) I99.8
  vulva N90.5
Occult
  blood in feces (stools) R19.5
Occupational
  problems NEC Z56.89
Ochlophobia —see Agoraphobia
Ochronosis (endogenous) E70.29
Ocular muscle —see condition
Oculogyric crisis or disturbance H51.8
  psychogenic F45.8
Oculomotor syndrome H51.9
Oculopathy
  syphilitic NEC A52.71
    congenital
      early A50.01
      late A50.30
    early (secondary) A51.43
    late A52.71
Oddi's sphincter spasm K83.4
Odontalgia K08.89
Odontoameloblastoma —see Cyst, calcifying
    odontogenic
Odontoclasia K03.89
Odontodysplasia, regional K00.4
Odontogenesis imperfecta K00.5
Odontoma (ameloblastic) (complex)
    (compound) (fibroameloblastic) —see Cyst,
    calcifying odontogenic
Odontomyelitis (closed) (open) K04.01
  irreversible K04.02
  reversible K04.01
Odontorrhagia K08.89
Odontosarcoma, ameloblastic C41.1
  upper jaw (bone) C41.0
Oestriasis —see Myiasis
Oguchi's disease H53.63
Ohara's disease —see Tularemia
OHS (obesity hypoventilation syndrome) E66.2

Oidiomycosis —see Candidiasis
Oidium albicans infection —see Candidiasis
Old (previous) myocardial infarction
    I25.2
Old age (without mention of debility) R54-●
  dementia F03
Olfactory —see condition
Oligemia —see Anemia
Oligoastrocytoma
  specified site —see Neoplasm, malignant,
      by site
  unspecified site C71.9
Oligocythemia D64.9
Oligodendroblastoma
  specified site —see Neoplasm, malignant
  unspecified site C71.9

Oligodendroglioma
    anaplastic type
        specified site —*see* Neoplasm, malignant,
            by site
        unspecified site C71.9
    specified site —*see* Neoplasm, malignant,
        by site
    unspecified site C71.9
Oligodontia —*see* Anodontia
Oligoencephalon Q02
Oligohidrosis L74.4
Oligohydramnios O41.0-●
Oligohydrosis L74.4
Oligomenorrhea N91.5
    primary N91.3
    secondary N91.4
Oligophrenia —*see also* Disability, intellectual
    phenylpyruvic E70.0
Oligospermia N46.11
    due to
        drug therapy N46.121
        efferent duct obstruction N46.123
        infection N46.122
        radiation N46.124
        specified cause NEC N46.129
        systemic disease N46.125
Oligotrichia —*see* Alopecia
Oliguria R34
    with, complicating or following ectopic or
        molar pregnancy O08.4
    postprocedural N99.0
Ollier's disease Q78.4
Omenotocele —*see* Hernia, abdomen, specified
    site NEC
Omentitis —*see* Peritonitis
Omentum, omental —*see* condition
Omphalitis (congenital) (newborn) P38.9
    with mild hemorrhage P38.1
    without hemorrhage P38.9
    not of newborn L08.82
    tetanus A33
Omphalocele Q79.2
Omphalomesenteric duct, persistent Q43.0
Omphalorrhagia, newborn P51.9
Omsk hemorrhagic fever A98.1
Onanism (excessive) F98.8
Onchocerciasis, onchocercosis B73.1
    with
        eye disease B73.00
            endophthalmitis B73.01
            eyelid B73.09
            glaucoma B73.02
            specified NEC B73.09
        eye NEC B73.00
        eyelid B73.09
Oncocytoma —*see* Neoplasm, benign, by site
Oncovirus, as cause of disease classified
    elsewhere B97.32
Ondine's curse —*see* Apnea, sleep
Oneirophrenia F23
Onychauxis L60.2
    congenital Q84.5
Onychia —*see also* Cellulitis, digit
    with lymphangitis —*see* Lymphangitis, acute,
        digit
    candidal B37.2
    dermatophytic B35.1
Onychitis —*see also* Cellulitis, digit
    with lymphangitis —*see* Lymphangitis, acute,
        digit
Onychocryptosis L60.0
Onychodystrophy L60.3
    congenital Q84.6
Onychogryphosis, onychogryposis L60.2
Onycholysis L60.1
Onychomadesis L60.8
Onychomalacia L60.3
Onychomycosis (finger) (toe) B35.1
Onycho-osteodysplasia Q87.2
Onychophagia F98.8
Onychophosis L60.8

Onychoptosis L60.8
Onychorrhexis L60.3
    congenital Q84.6
Onychoschizia L60.3
Onyxis (finger) (toe) L60.0
Onyxitis —*see also* Cellulitis, digit
    with lymphangitis —*see* Lymphangitis, acute,
        digit
Oophoritis (cystic) (infectional) (interstitial)
    N70.92
    with salpingitis N70.93
    acute N70.02
        with salpingitis N70.03
    chronic N70.12
        with salpingitis N70.13
    complicating abortion —*see* Abortion, by
        type, complicated by, oophoritis
Oophorocele N83.4-●
Opacity, opacities
    cornea H17.-●
        central H17.1-●
        congenital Q13.3
        degenerative —*see* Degeneration, cornea
        hereditary —*see* Dystrophy, cornea
        inflammatory —*see* Keratitis
        minor H17.81-●
        peripheral H17.82-●
        sequelae of trachoma (healed) B94.0
        specified NEC H17.89
    enamel (teeth) (fluoride) (nonfluoride) K00.3
    lens —*see* Cataract
    snowball —*see* Deposit, crystalline
    vitreous (humor) NEC H43.39-●
        congenital Q14.0
        membranes and strands H43.31-●
Opalescent dentin (hereditary) K00.5
Open, opening
    abnormal, organ or site, congenital —*see*
        Imperfect, closure
    angle with
        borderline
            findings
                high risk H40.02-●
                low risk H40.01-●
            intraocular pressure H40.00-●
        cupping of discs H40.01-●
        glaucoma (primary) —*see* Glaucoma, open
            angle
    bite
        anterior M26.220
        posterior M26.221
    false —*see* Imperfect, closure
    margin on tooth restoration K08.51
    restoration margins of tooth K08.51
    wound —*see* Wound, open
Operational fatigue F48.8
Operative —*see* condition
Operculitis —*see* Periodontitis
Operculum —*see* Break, retina
Ophiasis L63.2
Ophthalmia —*see also* Conjunctivitis H10.9
    actinic rays —*see* Photokeratitis
    allergic (acute) —*see* Conjunctivitis, acute,
        atopic
    blennorrhagic (gonococcal) (neonatorum)
        A54.31
    diphtheritic A36.86
    Egyptian A71.1
    electrica —*see* Photokeratitis
    gonococcal (neonatorum) A54.31
    metastatic —*see* Endophthalmitis, purulent
    migraine —*see* Migraine, ophthalmoplegic
    neonatorum, newborn P39.1
        gonococcal A54.31
    nodosa H16.24-●
    purulent —*see* Conjunctivitis, acute,
        mucopurulent
    spring —*see* Conjunctivitis, acute, atopic
    sympathetic —*see* Uveitis, sympathetic
Ophthalmitis —*see* Ophthalmia
Ophthalmocele (congenital) Q15.8

Ophthalmoneuromyelitis G36.0
Ophthalmoplegia —*see also* Strabismus,
    paralytic
    anterior internuclear —*see* Ophthalmoplegia,
        internuclear
    ataxia-areflexia G61.0
    diabetic —*see* E08-E13 with .39
    exophthalmic E05.00
        with thyroid storm E05.01
    external H49.88-●
        progressive H49.4-●
            with pigmentary retinopathy —*see*
                Kearns-Sayre syndrome
        total H49.3-●
    internal (complete) (total) H52.51-●
    internuclear H51.2-●
    migraine —*see* Migraine, ophthalmoplegic
    Parinaud's H49.88-●
    progressive external —*see* Ophthalmoplegia,
        external, progressive
    supranuclear, progressive G23.1
    total (external) —*see* Ophthalmoplegia,
        external, total
Opioid(s)
    abuse —*see* Abuse, drug, opioids
    dependence —*see* Dependence, drug, opioids
    induced, without use disorder
        anxiety disorder F11.988
        delirium F11.921
        depressive disorder F11.94
        sexual dysfunction F11.981
        sleep disorder F11.982
Opisthognathism M26.09
Opisthorchiasis (felineus) (viverrini) B66.0
Opitz' disease D73.2
Opiumism —*see* Dependence, drug, opioid
Oppenheim's disease G70.2
Oppenheim-Urbach disease (necrobiosis
    lipoidica diabeticorum) —*see* E08-E13 with
    .620
Optic nerve —*see* condition
Orbit —*see* condition
Orchioblastoma C62.9-●
Orchitis (gangrenous) (nonspecific) (septic)
    (suppurative) N45.2
    blennorrhagic (gonococcal) (acute) (chronic)
        A54.23
    chlamydial A56.19
    filarial —*see also* Infestation, filarial B74.9
        [N51]
    gonococcal (acute) (chronic) A54.23
    mumps B26.0
    syphilitic A52.76
    tuberculous A18.15
Orf (virus disease) B08.02
Organic —*see also* condition
    brain syndrome F09
    heart —*see* Disease, heart
    mental disorder F09
    psychosis F09
Orgasm
    anejaculatory N53.13
Oriental
    bilharziasis B65.2
    schistosomiasis B65.2
Orifice —*see* condition
Origin of both great vessels from right
    ventricle Q20.1
Ormond's disease (with ureteral obstruction)
    N13.5
    with infection N13.6
Ornithine metabolism disorder E72.4
Ornithinemia (Type I) (Type II) E72.4
Ornithosis A70
Orotaciduria, oroticaciduria (congenital)
    (hereditary) (pyrimidine deficiency) E79.8
    anemia D53.0
Orthodontics
    adjustment Z46.4
    fitting Z46.4
Orthopnea R06.01

▶ New ⇒ Revised ~~deleted~~ Deleted ● Use Additional Character(s)

Orthopoxvirus B08.09
  specified NEC B08.09
Os, uterus —see condition
Osgood-Schlatter disease or
    osteochondrosis —see Osteochondrosis,
    juvenile, tibia
Osler (-Weber)-Rendu disease I78.0
Osler's nodes I33.0
Osmidrosis L75.0
Osseous —see condition
Ossification
  artery —see Arteriosclerosis
  auricle (ear) —see Disorder, pinna, specified
    type NEC
  bronchial J98.09
  cardiac —see Degeneration, myocardial
  cartilage (senile) —see Disorder, cartilage,
    specified type NEC
  coronary (artery) —see Disease, heart,
    ischemic, atherosclerotic
  diaphragm J98.6
  ear, middle —see Otosclerosis
  falx cerebri G96.19
  fontanel, premature Q75.0
  heart —see also Degeneration, myocardial
    valve —see Endocarditis
  larynx J38.7
  ligament —see Disorder, tendon, specified
    type NEC
    posterior longitudinal —see
      Spondylopathy, specified NEC
  meninges (cerebral) (spinal) G96.19
  multiple, eccentric centers —see Disorder,
    bone, development or growth
  muscle —see also Calcification, muscle
    due to burns —see Myositis, ossificans, in,
      burns
    paralytic —see Myositis, ossificans, in,
      quadriplegia
    progressive —see Myositis, ossificans,
      progressiva
    specified NEC M61.50
      ankle M61.57-●
      foot M61.57-●
      forearm M61.53-●
      hand M61.54-●
      lower leg M61.56-●
      multiple sites M61.59
      pelvic region M61.55-●
      shoulder region M61.51-●
      specified site NEC M61.58
      thigh M61.55-●
      upper arm M61.52-●
    traumatic —see Myositis, ossificans,
      traumatica
  myocardium, myocardial —see Degeneration,
    myocardial
  penis N48.89
  periarticular —see Disorder, joint, specified
    type NEC
  pinna —see Disorder, pinna, specified type
    NEC
  rider's bone —see Ossification, muscle,
    specified NEC
  sclera H15.89
  subperiosteal, post-traumatic M89.8X-●
  tendon —see Disorder, tendon, specified
    type NEC
  trachea J39.8
  tympanic membrane —see Disorder,
    tympanic membrane, specified NEC
  vitreous (humor) —see Deposit, crystalline
Osteitis —see also Osteomyelitis
  alveolar M27.3
  condensans M85.30
    ankle M85.37-●
    foot M85.37-●
    forearm M85.33-●
    hand M85.34-●
    lower leg M85.36-●
    multiple site M85.39

Osteitis (Continued)
  condensans (Continued)
    neck M85.38
    rib M85.38
    shoulder M85.31-●
    skull M85.38
    specified site NEC M85.38
    thigh M85.35-●
    toe M85.37-●
    upper arm M85.32-●
    vertebra M85.38
  deformans M88.9
    in (due to)
      malignant neoplasm of bone
        C41.9 [M90.60]
      neoplastic disease —see also Neoplasm
        D49.9 [M90.60]
        carpus D49.9 [M90.64-●]
        clavicle D49.9 [M90.61-●]
        femur D49.9 [M90.65-●]
        fibula D49.9 [M90.66-●]
        finger D49.9 [M90.64-●]
        humerus D49.9 [M90.62-●]
        ilium D49.9 [M90.65-●]
        ischium D49.9 [M90.65-●]
        metacarpus D49.9 [M90.64-●]
        metatarsus D49.9 [M90.67-●]
        multiple sites D49.9 [M90.69]
        neck D49.9 [M90.68]
        radius D49.9 [M90.63-●]
        rib D49.9 [M90.68]
        scapula D49.9 [M90.61-●]
        skull D49.9 [M90.68]
        tarsus D49.9 [M90.67-●]
        tibia D49.9 [M90.66-●]
        toe D49.9 [M90.67-●]
        ulna D49.9 [M90.63-●]
        vertebra D49.9 [M90.68]
    skull M88.0
    specified NEC —see Paget's disease, bone,
      by site
    vertebra M88.1
  due to yaws A66.6
  fibrosa NEC —see Cyst, bone, by site
    circumscripta —see Dysplasia, fibrous,
      bone NEC
    cystica (generalisata) E21.0
    disseminata Q78.1
    osteoplastica E21.0
  fragilitans Q78.0
  Garr's (sclerosing) —see Osteomyelitis,
    specified type NEC
  jaw (acute) (chronic) (lower) (suppurative)
    (upper) M27.2
  parathyroid E21.0
  petrous bone (acute) (chronic) —see Petrositis
  sclerotic, nonsuppurative —see Osteomyelitis,
    specified type NEC
  tuberculosa A18.09
    cystica D86.89
    multiplex cystoides D86.89
Osteoarthritis M19.90
  ankle M19.07-●
  elbow M19.02-●
  foot joint M19.07-●
  generalized M15.9
    erosive M15.4
    primary M15.0
    specified NEC M15.8
  hand joint M19.04-●
    first carpometacarpal joint M18.9-●
  hip M16.1-●
    bilateral M16.0
    due to hip dysplasia (unilateral)
      M16.3-●
    bilateral M16.2
  interphalangeal
    distal (Heberden) M15.1
    proximal (Bouchard) M15.2
  knee M17.1-●
    bilateral M17.0

Osteoarthritis (Continued)
  post-traumatic NEC M19.92
    ankle M19.17-●
    elbow M19.12-●
    foot joint M19.17-●
    hand joint M19.14-●
      first carpometacarpal joint M18.3-●
        bilateral M18.2
    hip M16.5-●
      bilateral M16.4
    knee M17.3-●
      bilateral M17.2
    shoulder M19.11-●
    wrist M19.13-●
  primary M19.91
    ankle M19.07-●
    elbow M19.02-●
    foot joint M19.07-●
    hand joint M19.04-●
      first carpometacarpal joint M18.1-●
        bilateral M18.0
    hip M16.1-●
      bilateral M16.0
    knee M17.1-●
      bilateral M17.0
    shoulder M19.01-●
    spine —see Spondylosis
    wrist M19.03-●
  secondary M19.93
    ankle M19.27-●
    elbow M19.22-●
    foot joint M19.27-●
    hand joint M19.24-●
      first carpometacarpal joint M18.5-●
        bilateral M18.4
    hip M16.7
      bilateral M16.6
    knee M17.5
      bilateral M17.4
    multiple M15.3
    shoulder M19.21-●
    spine —see Spondylosis
    wrist M19.23-●
  shoulder M19.01-●
  spine —see Spondylosis
  wrist M19.03-●
Osteoarthropathy (hypertrophic) M19.90
  ankle —see Osteoarthritis, primary, ankle
  elbow —see Osteoarthritis, primary, elbow
  foot joint —see Osteoarthritis, primary, foot
  hand joint —see Osteoarthritis, primary, hand
    joint
  knee joint —see Osteoarthritis, primary, knee
  multiple site —see Osteoarthritis, primary,
    multiple joint
  pulmonary —see also Osteoarthropathy,
    specified type NEC
    hypertrophic —see Osteoarthropathy,
      hypertrophic, specified type NEC
  secondary —see Osteoarthropathy, specified
    type NEC
  secondary hypertrophic —see
    Osteoarthropathy, specified type NEC
  shoulder —see Osteoarthritis, primary,
    shoulder
  specified joint NEC —see Osteoarthritis,
    primary, specified joint NEC
  specified type NEC M89.40
    carpus M89.44-●
    clavicle M89.41-●
    femur M89.45-●
    fibula M89.46-●
    finger M89.44-●
    humerus M89.42-●
    ilium M89.459
    ischium M89.459
    metacarpus M89.44-●
    metatarsus M89.47-●
    multiple sites M89.49
    neck M89.48
    radius M89.43-●

Osteoarthropathy *(Continued)*
  specified type NEC *(Continued)*
    rib M89.48
    scapula M89.41-●
    skull M89.48
    tarsus M89.47-●
    tibia M89.46-●
    toe M89.47-●
    ulna M89.43-●
    vertebra M89.48
  spine —*see* Spondylosis
  wrist —*see* Osteoarthritis, primary, wrist
Osteoarthrosis (degenerative) (hypertrophic)
    (joint) —*see also* Osteoarthritis
  deformans alkaptonurica E70.29 *[M36.8]*
  erosive M15.4
  generalized M15.9
    primary M15.0
  polyarticular M15.9
  spine —*see* Spondylosis
Osteoblastoma —*see* Neoplasm, bone, benign
  aggressive —*see* Neoplasm, bone, uncertain
    behavior
Osteochondroarthrosis deformans
    endemica —*see* Disease, Kaschin-Beck
Osteochondritis —*see also* Osteochondropathy,
    by site
  Brailsford's —*see* Osteochondrosis, juvenile,
    radius
  dissecans M93.20
    ankle M93.27-●
    elbow M93.22-●
    foot M93.27-●
    hand M93.24-●
    hip M93.25-●
    knee M93.26-●
    multiple sites M93.29
    shoulder joint M93.21-●
    specified site NEC M93.28
    wrist M93.23-●
  juvenile M92.9
    patellar —*see* Osteochondrosis, juvenile,
      patella
  syphilitic (congenital) (early) A50.02
      [M90.80]
    ankle A50.02 *[M90.87-●]*
    elbow A50.02 *[M90.82-●]*
    foot A50.02 *[M90.87-●]*
    forearm A50.02 *[M90.83-●]*
    hand A50.02 *[M90.84-●]*
    hip A50.02 *[M90.85-●]*
    knee A50.02 *[M90.86●-]*
    multiple sites A50.02 *[M90.89]*
    shoulder joint A50.02 *[M90.81-●]*
    specified site NEC A50.02 *[M90.88]*
Osteochondrodysplasia Q78.9
  with defects of growth of tubular bones and
    spine Q77.9
    specified NEC Q77.8
  specified NEC Q78.8
Osteochondrodystrophy E78.9
Osteochondrolysis —*see* Osteochondritis,
    dissecans
Osteochondroma —*see* Neoplasm, bone, benign
Osteochondromatosis D48.0
  syndrome Q78.4
Osteochondromyxosarcoma —*see* Neoplasm,
    bone, malignant
Osteochondropathy M93.90
  ankle M93.97-●
  elbow M93.92-●
  foot M93.97-●
  hand M93.94-●
  hip M93.95-●
  Kienböck's disease of adults M93.1
  knee M93.96-●
  multiple joints M93.99
  osteochondritis dissecans —*see*
    Osteochondritis, dissecans
  osteochondrosis —*see* Osteochondrosis
  shoulder region M93.91-●

Osteochondropathy *(Continued)*
  slipped upper femoral epiphysis —*see*
    Slipped, epiphysis, upper femoral
  specified joint NEC M93.98
  specified type NEC M93.80
    ankle M93.87-●
    elbow M93.82-●
    foot M93.87-●
    hand M93.84-●
    hip M93.85-●
    knee M93.86-●
    multiple joints M93.89
    shoulder region M93.81-●
    specified joint NEC M93.88
    wrist M93.83-●
  syphilitic, congenital
    early A50.02 *[M90.80]*
    late A50.56 *[M90.80]*
  wrist M93.93-●
Osteochondrosarcoma —*see* Neoplasm, bone,
    malignant
Osteochondrosis —*see also* Osteochondropathy,
    by site
  acetabulum (juvenile) M91.0
  adult —*see* Osteochondropathy, specified
    type NEC, by site
  astragalus (juvenile) —*see* Osteochondrosis,
    juvenile, tarsus
  Blount's —*see* Osteochondrosis, juvenile, tibia
  Buchanan's M91.0
  Burns' —*see* Osteochondrosis, juvenile, ulna
  calcaneus (juvenile) —*see* Osteochondrosis,
    juvenile, tarsus
  capitular epiphysis (femur) (juvenile) —*see*
    Legg-Calvé-Perthes disease
  carpal (juvenile) (lunate) (scaphoid) —*see*
    Osteochondrosis, juvenile, hand, carpal
    lunate
    adult M93.1
  coxae juvenilis —*see* Legg-Calvé-Perthes
    disease
  deformans juvenilis, coxae —*see* Legg-Calvé-
    Perthes disease
  Diaz's —*see* Osteochondrosis, juvenile, tarsus
  dissecans (knee) (shoulder) —*see*
    Osteochondritis, dissecans
  femoral capital epiphysis (juvenile) —*see*
    Legg-Calvé-Perthes disease
  femur (head), juvenile —*see* Legg-Calvé-
    Perthes disease
  fibula (juvenile) —*see* Osteochondrosis,
    juvenile, fibula
  foot NEC (juvenile) M92.8
  Freiberg's —*see* Osteochondrosis, juvenile,
    metatarsus
  Haas' (juvenile) —*see* Osteochondrosis,
    juvenile, humerus
  Haglund's —*see* Osteochondrosis, juvenile,
    tarsus
  hip (juvenile) —*see* Legg-Calvé-Perthes disease
  humerus (capitulum) (head) (juvenile) —*see*
    Osteochondrosis, juvenile, humerus
  ilium, iliac crest (juvenile) M91.0
  ischiopubic synchondrosis M91.0
  Iselin's —*see* Osteochondrosis, juvenile,
    metatarsus
  juvenile, juvenilis M92.9
    after congenital dislocation of hip
      reduction —*see* Osteochondrosis,
      juvenile, hip, specified NEC
    arm —*see* Osteochondrosis, juvenile, upper
      limb NEC
    capitular epiphysis (femur) —*see* Legg-
      Calvé-Perthes disease
    clavicle, sternal epiphysis —*see*
      Osteochondrosis, juvenile, upper limb
      NEC
    coxae —*see* Legg-Calvé-Perthes disease
    deformans M92.9
    fibula M92.5-●
    foot NEC M92.8

Osteochondrosis *(Continued)*
  juvenile, juvenilis *(Continued)*
    hand M92.20-●
      carpal lunate M92.21-●
      metacarpal head M92.22-●
      specified site NEC M92.29-●
    head of femur —*see* Legg-Calvé-Perthes
      disease
    hip and pelvis M91.9-●
      coxa plana —*see* Coxa, plana
      femoral head —*see* Legg-Calvé-Perthes
        disease
      pelvis M91.0
      pseudocoxalgia —*see* Pseudocoxalgia
      specified NEC M91.8-●
    humerus M92.0-●
    limb
      lower NEC M92.8
      upper NEC —*see* Osteochondrosis,
        juvenile, upper limb NEC
    medial cuneiform bone —*see*
      Osteochondrosis, juvenile, tarsus
    metatarsus M92.7-●
    patella M92.4-●
    radius M92.1-●
    specified site NEC M92.8
    spine M42.00
      cervical region M42.02
      cervicothoracic region M42.03
      lumbar region M42.06
      lumbosacral region M42.07
      multiple sites M42.09
      occipito-atlanto-axial region M42.01
      sacrococcygeal region M42.08
      thoracic region M42.04
      thoracolumbar region M42.05
    tarsus M92.6-●
    tibia M92.5-●
    ulna M92.1-●
    upper limb NEC M92.3-●
    vertebra (body) (epiphyseal plates)
        (Calvé's) (Scheuermann's) —*see*
        Osteochondrosis, juvenile, spine
  Kienböck's —*see* Osteochondrosis, juvenile,
    hand, carpal lunate
    adult M93.1
  Köhler's
    patellar —*see* Osteochondrosis, juvenile,
      patella
    tarsal navicular —*see* Osteochondrosis,
      juvenile, tarsus
  Legg-Perthes (-Calvé's) (-Waldenström) —*see*
    Legg-Calvé-Perthes disease
  limb
    lower NEC (juvenile) M92.8
    upper NEC (juvenile) —*see*
      Osteochondrosis, juvenile, upper limb
      NEC
  lunate bone (carpal) (juvenile) —*see also*
    Osteochondrosis, juvenile, hand, carpal
    lunate
    adult M93.1
  Mauclaire's —*see* Osteochondrosis, juvenile,
    hand, metacarpal
  metacarpal (head) (juvenile) —*see*
    Osteochondrosis, juvenile, hand,
    metacarpal
  metatarsus (fifth) (head) (juvenile)
      (second) —*see* Osteochondrosis, juvenile,
      metatarsus
  navicular (juvenile) —*see* Osteochondrosis,
    juvenile, tarsus
  os
    calcis (juvenile) —*see* Osteochondrosis,
      juvenile, tarsus
    tibiale externum (juvenile) —*see*
      Osteochondrosis, juvenile, tarsus
  Osgood-Schlatter —*see* Osteochondrosis,
    juvenile, tibia
  Panner's —*see* Osteochondrosis, juvenile,
    humerus

▶ New   ⇒ Revised   ~~deleted~~ Deleted   ● Use Additional Character(s)

Osteochondrosis (Continued)
  patellar center (juvenile) (primary)
    (secondary) —see Osteochondrosis,
    juvenile, patella
  pelvis (juvenile) M91.0
  Pierson's M91.0
  radius (head) (juvenile) —see
    Osteochondrosis, juvenile, radius
  Scheuermann's —see Osteochondrosis,
    juvenile, spine
  Sever's —see Osteochondrosis, juvenile,
    tarsus
  Sinding-Larsen —see Osteochondrosis,
    juvenile, patella
  spine M42.9
    adult M42.10
      cervical region M42.12
      cervicothoracic region M42.13
      lumbar region M42.16
      lumbosacral region M42.17
      multiple sites M42.19
      occipito-atlanto-axial region M42.11
      sacrococcygeal region M42.18
      thoracic region M42.14
      thoracolumbar region M42.15
    juvenile —see Osteochondrosis, juvenile,
      spine
  symphysis pubis (juvenile) M91.0
  syphilitic (congenital) A50.02
  talus (juvenile) —see Osteochondrosis,
    juvenile, tarsus
  tarsus (navicular) (juvenile) —see
    Osteochondrosis, juvenile, tarsus
  tibia (proximal) (tubercle) (juvenile) —see
    Osteochondrosis, juvenile, tibia
  tuberculous —see Tuberculosis, bone
  ulna (lower) (juvenile) —see Osteochondrosis,
    juvenile, ulna
  van Neck's M91.0
  vertebral —see Osteochondrosis,
    spine
Osteoclastoma D48.0
  malignant —see Neoplasm, bone,
    malignant
Osteodynia —see Disorder, bone,
  specified type NEC
Osteodystrophy Q78.9
  azotemic N25.0
  congenital Q78.9
  parathyroid, secondary E21.1
  renal N25.0
Osteofibroma —see Neoplasm, bone,
  benign
Osteofibrosarcoma —see Neoplasm,
  bone, malignant
Osteogenesis imperfecta Q78.0
Osteogenic —see condition
Osteolysis M89.50
  carpus M89.54-●
  clavicle M89.51-●
  femur M89.55-●
  fibula M89.56-●
  finger M89.54-●
  humerus M89.52-●
  ilium M89.559
  ischium M89.559
  joint prosthesis (periprosthetic) —see
    Complications, joint prosthesis,
    mechanical, periprosthetic, osteolysis,
    by site
  metacarpus M89.54-●
  metatarsus M89.57-●
  multiple sites M89.59
  neck M89.58
  periprosthetic —see Complications, joint
    prosthesis, mechanical, periprosthetic,
    osteolysis, by site
  radius M89.53-●
  rib M89.58
  scapula M89.51-●
  skull M89.58

Osteolysis (Continued)
  tarsus M89.57-●
  tibia M89.56-●
  toe M89.57-●
  ulna M89.53-●
  vertebra M89.58
Osteoma —see also Neoplasm, bone, benign
  osteoid —see also Neoplasm, bone, benign
    giant —see Neoplasm, bone, benign
Osteomalacia M83.9
  adult M83.9
    drug-induced NEC M83.5
    due to
      malabsorption (postsurgical) M83.2
      malnutrition M83.3
    specified NEC M83.8
  aluminium-induced M83.4
  infantile —see Rickets
  juvenile —see Rickets
  oncogenic E83.89
  pelvis M83.8
  puerperal M83.0
  senile M83.1
  vitamin-D-resistant in adults E83.31
    [M90.8-●]
    carpus E83.31 [M90.84-●]
    clavicle E83.31 [M90.81-●]
    femur E83.31 [M90.85-●]
    fibula E83.31 [M90.86-●]
    finger E83.31 [M90.84-●]
    humerus E83.31 [M90.82-●]
    ilium E83.31 [M90.859]
    ischium E83.31 [M90.859]
    metacarpus E83.31 [M90.84-●]
    metatarsus E83.31 [M90.87-●]
    multiple sites E83.31 [M90.89]
    neck E83.31 [M90.88]
    radius E83.31 [M90.83-●]
    rib E83.31 [M90.88]
    scapula E83.31 [M90.819]
    skull E83.31 [M90.88]
    tarsus E83.31 [M90.879]
    tibia E83.31 [M90.869]
    toe E83.31 [M90.879]
    ulna E83.31 [M90.839]
    vertebra E83.31 [M90.88]
Osteomyelitis (general) (infective)
  (localized) (neonatal) (purulent)
  (septic) (staphylococcal) (streptococcal)
  (suppurative) (with periostitis) M86.9
  acute M86.10
    carpus M86.14-●
    clavicle M86.11-●
    femur M86.15-●
    fibula M86.16-●
    finger M86.14-●
    hematogenous M86.00
      carpus M86.04-●
      clavicle M86.01-●
      femur M86.05-●
      fibula M86.06-●
      finger M86.04-●
      humerus M86.02-●
      ilium M86.059
      ischium M86.059
      mandible M27.2
      metacarpus M86.04-●
      metatarsus M86.07-●
      multiple sites M86.09
      neck M86.08
      orbit H05.02-●
      petrous bone —see Petrositis
      radius M86.03-●
      rib M86.08
      scapula M86.01-●
      skull M86.08
      tarsus M86.07-●
      tibia M86.06-●
      toe M86.07-●
      ulna M86.03-●
      vertebra —see Osteomyelitis, vertebra

Osteomyelitis (Continued)
  acute (Continued)
    humerus M86.12-●
    ilium M86.159
    ischium M86.159
    mandible M27.2
    metacarpus M86.14-●
    metatarsus M86.17-●
    multiple sites M86.19
    neck M86.18
    orbit H05.02-●
    petrous bone —see Petrositis
    radius M86.13-●
    rib M86.18
    scapula M86.11-●
    skull M86.18
    tarsus M86.17-●
    tibia M86.16-●
    toe M86.17-●
    ulna M86.13-●
    vertebra —see Osteomyelitis, vertebra
  chronic (or old) M86.60
    with draining sinus M86.40
      carpus M86.44-●
      clavicle M86.41-●
      femur M86.45-●
      fibula M86.46-●
      finger M86.44-●
      humerus M86.42-●
      ilium M86.459
      ischium M86.459
      mandible M27.2
      metacarpus M86.44-●
      metatarsus M86.47-●
      multiple sites M86.49
      neck M86.48
      orbit H05.02-●
      petrous bone —see Petrositis
      radius M86.43-●
      rib M86.48
      scapula M86.41-●
      skull M86.48
      tarsus M86.47-●
      tibia M86.46-●
      toe M86.47-●
      ulna M86.43-●
      vertebra —see Osteomyelitis,
        vertebra
    carpus M86.64-●
    clavicle M86.61-●
    femur M86.65-●
    fibula M86.66-●
    finger M86.64-●
    hematogenous NEC M86.50
      carpus M86.54-●
      clavicle M86.51-●
      femur M86.55-●
      fibula M86.56-●
      finger M86.54-●
      humerus M86.52-●
      ilium M86.559
      ischium M86.559
      mandible M27.2
      metacarpus M86.54-●
      metatarsus M86.57-●
      multifocal M86.30
        carpus M86.34-●
        clavicle M86.31-●
        femur M86.35-●
        fibula M86.36-●
        finger M86.34-●
        humerus M86.32-●
        ilium M86.359
        ischium M86.359
        metacarpus M86.34-●
        metatarsus M86.37-●
        multiple sites M86.39
        neck M86.38
        radius M86.33-●
        rib M86.38
        scapula M86.31-●

Osteomyelitis *(Continued)*
  chronic *(Continued)*
    hematogenous NEC *(Continued)*
      multifocal *(Continued)*
        skull M86.38
        tarsus M86.37-●
        tibia M86.36-●
        toe M86.37-●
        ulna M86.33-●
        vertebra —*see* Osteomyelitis, vertebra
      multiple sites M86.59
      neck M86.58
      orbit H05.02-●
      petrous bone —*see* Petrositis
      radius M86.53-●
      rib M86.58
      scapula M86.51-●
      skull M86.58
      tarsus M86.57-●
      tibia M86.56-●
      toe M86.57-●
      ulna M86.53-●
      vertebra —*see* Osteomyelitis, vertebra
    humerus M86.62-●
    ilium M86.659
    ischium M86.659
    mandible M27.2
    metacarpus M86.64-●
    metatarsus M86.67-●
    multifocal —*see* Osteomyelitis, chronic,
      hematogenous, multifocal
    multiple sites M86.69
    neck M86.68
    orbit H05.02-●
    petrous bone —*see* Petrositis
    radius M86.63-●
    rib M86.68
    scapula M86.61-●
    skull M86.68
    tarsus M86.67-●
    tibia M86.66-●
    toe M86.67-●
    ulna M86.63-●
    vertebra —*see* Osteomyelitis, vertebra
  echinococcal B67.2
  Garr's —*see* Osteomyelitis, specified type
    NEC
  in diabetes mellitus —*see* E08-E13 with .69
  jaw (acute) (chronic) (lower) (neonatal)
    (suppurative) (upper) M27.2
  nonsuppurating —*see* Osteomyelitis,
    specified type NEC
  orbit H05.02-●
  petrous bone —*see* Petrositis
  Salmonella (arizonae) (cholerae-suis)
    (enteritidis) (typhimurium) A02.24
  sclerosing, nonsuppurative —*see*
    Osteomyelitis, specified type NEC
  specified type NEC —*see also* subcategory
    M86.8X-●
    mandible M27.2
    orbit H05.02-●
    petrous bone —*see* Petrositis
    vertebra —*see* Osteomyelitis, vertebra
  subacute M86.20
    carpus M86.24-●
    clavicle M86.21-●
    femur M86.25-●
    fibula M86.26-●
    finger M86.24-●
    humerus M86.22-●
    mandible M27.2
    metacarpus M86.24-●
    metatarsus M86.27-●
    multiple sites M86.29
    neck M86.28
    orbit H05.02-●
    petrous bone —*see* Petrositis
    radius M86.23-●
    rib M86.28
    scapula M86.21-●

Osteomyelitis *(Continued)*
  subacute *(Continued)*
    skull M86.28
    tarsus M86.27-●
    tibia M86.26-●
    toe M86.27-●
    ulna M86.23-●
    vertebra —*see* Osteomyelitis, vertebra
  syphilitic A52.77
    congenital (early) A50.02 [M90.80]
  tuberculous —*see* Tuberculosis, bone
  typhoid A01.05
  vertebra M46.20
    cervical region M46.22
    cervicothoracic region M46.23
    lumbar region M46.26
    lumbosacral region M46.27
    occipito-atlanto-axial region
      M46.21
    sacrococcygeal region M46.28
    thoracic region M46.24
    thoracolumbar region M46.25
Osteomyelofibrosis D47.4
Osteomyelosclerosis D75.89
Osteonecrosis M87.9
  due to
    drugs —*see* Osteonecrosis, secondary, due
      to, drugs
    trauma —*see* Osteonecrosis, secondary, due
      to, trauma
  idiopathic aseptic M87.00
    ankle M87.07-●
    carpus M87.03-●
    clavicle M87.01-●
    femur M87.05-●
    fibula M87.06-●
    finger M87.04-●
    humerus M87.02-●
    ilium M87.050
    ischium M87.050
    metacarpus M87.04-●
    metatarsus M87.07-●
    multiple sites M87.09
    neck M87.08
    pelvis M87.050
    radius M87.03-●
    rib M87.08
    scapula M87.01-●
    skull M87.08
    tarsus M87.07-●
    tibia M87.06-●
    toe M87.07-●
    ulna M87.03-●
    vertebra M87.08
  secondary NEC M87.30
    carpus M87.33-●
    clavicle M87.31-●
    due to
      drugs M87.10
        carpus M87.13-●
        clavicle M87.11-●
        femur M87.15-●
        fibula M87.16-●
        finger M87.14-●
        humerus M87.12-●
        ilium M87.159
        ischium M87.159
        jaw M87.180
        metacarpus M87.14-●
        metatarsus M87.17-●
        multiple sites M87.19
        neck M87.18
        radius M87.13-●
        rib M87.18
        scapula M87.11-●
        skull M87.18
        tarsus M87.17-●
        tibia M87.16-●
        toe M87.17-●
        ulna M87.13-●
        vertebra M87.18

Osteonecrosis *(Continued)*
  secondary NEC *(Continued)*
    due to *(Continued)*
      hemoglobinopathy NEC D58.2
        [M90.50]
        carpus D58.2 [M90.54-●]
        clavicle D58.2 [M90.51-●]
        femur D58.2 [M90.55-●]
        fibula D58.2 [M90.56-●]
        finger D58.2 [M90.54-●]
        humerus D58.2 [M90.52-●]
        ilium D58.2 [M90.55-●]
        ischium D58.2 [M90.55-●]
        metacarpus D58.2 [M90.54-●]
        metatarsus D58.2 [M90.57-●]
        multiple sites D58.2 [M90.58]
        neck D58.2 [M90.58]
        radius D58.2 [M90.53-●]
        rib D58.2 [M90.58]
        scapula D58.2 [M90.51-●]
        skull D58.2 [M90.58]
        tarsus D58.2 [M90.57-●]
        tibia D58.2 [M90.56-●]
        toe D58.2 [M90.57-●]
        ulna D58.2 [M90.53-●]
        vertebra D58.2 [M90.58]
      trauma (previous) M87.20
        carpus M87.23-●
        clavicle M87.21-●
        femur M87.25-●
        fibula M87.26-●
        finger M87.24-●
        humerus M87.22-●
        ilium M87.25-●
        ischium M87.25-●
        metacarpus M87.24-●
        metatarsus M87.27-●
        multiple sites M87.29
        neck M87.28
        radius M87.23-●
        rib M87.28
        scapula M87.21-●
        skull M87.28
        tarsus M87.27-●
        tibia M87.26-●
        toe M87.27-●
        ulna M87.23-●
        vertebra M87.28
    femur M87.35-●
    fibula M87.36-●
    finger M87.34-●
    humerus M87.32
    ilium M87.350
    in
      caisson disease T70.3 [M90.50]
        carpus T70.3 [M90.54-●]
        clavicle T70.3 [M90.51-●]
        femur T70.3 [M90.55-●]
        fibula T70.3 [M90.56-●]
        finger T70.3 [M90.54-●]
        humerus T70.3 [M90.52-●]
        ilium T70.3 [M90.55-●]
        ischium T70.3 [M90.55-●]
        metacarpus T70.3 [M90.54-●]
        metatarsus T70.3 [M90.57-●]
        multiple sites T70.3 [M90.59]
        neck T70.3 [M90.58]
        radius T70.3 [M90.53-●]
        rib T70.3 [M90.58]
        scapula T70.3 [M90.51-●]
        skull T70.3 [M90.58]
        tarsus T70.3 [M90.57-●]
        tibia T70.3 [M90.56-●]
        toe T70.3 [M90.57-●]
        ulna T70.3 [M90.53-●]
        vertebra T70.3 [M90.58]
    ischium M87.350
    metacarpus M87.34-●
    metatarsus M87.37-●
    multiple site M87.39
    neck M87.38

► New   ⇒ Revised   ~~deleted~~ Deleted   ● Use Additional Character(s)

Otitis *(Continued)*
  externa *(Continued)*
    mycotic NEC B36.9 *[H62.40]*
      in
        aspergillosis B44.89
        candidiasis B37.84
        moniliasis B37.84
    necrotizing —*see* Otitis, externa,
      malignant
    Pseudomonas aeruginosa —*see* Otitis,
      externa, malignant
    reactive —*see* Otitis, externa, acute,
      reactive
    specified NEC —*see* subcategory H60.8
    tropical NEC B36.9 *[H62.40]*
      in
        aspergillosis B44.89
        candidiasis B37.84
        moniliasis B37.84
  insidiosa —*see* Otosclerosis
  interna —*see* subcategory H83.0
  media (hemorrhagic) (staphylococcal)
    (streptococcal) H66.9-●
    with effusion (nonpurulent) —*see* Otitis,
      media, nonsuppurative
    acute, subacute H66.90
      allergic —*see* Otitis, media,
        nonsuppurative, acute, allergic
      exudative —*see* Otitis, media,
        suppurative, acute
      mucoid —*see* Otitis, media,
        nonsuppurative, acute
      necrotizing —*see also* Otitis, media,
        suppurative, acute
        in
          measles B05.3
          scarlet fever A38.0
      nonsuppurative NEC —*see* Otitis, media,
        nonsuppurative, acute
      purulent —*see* Otitis, media,
        suppurative, acute
      sanguinous —*see* Otitis, media,
        nonsuppurative, acute
      secretory —*see* Otitis, media,
        nonsuppurative, acute, serous
      seromucinous —*see* Otitis, media,
        nonsuppurative, acute
      serous —*see* Otitis, media,
        nonsuppurative, acute, serous
      suppurative —*see* Otitis, media,
        suppurative, acute
    allergic —*see* Otitis, media, nonsuppurative
    catarrhal —*see* Otitis, media,
      nonsuppurative
    chronic H66.90
      with effusion (nonpurulent) —*see* Otitis,
        media, nonsuppurative, chronic
      allergic —*see* Otitis, media,
        nonsuppurative, chronic, allergic
      benign suppurative —*see* Otitis, media,
        suppurative, chronic, tubotympanic
      catarrhal —*see* Otitis, media,
        nonsuppurative, chronic, serous
      exudative —*see* Otitis, media,
        suppurative, chronic
      mucinous —*see* Otitis, media,
        nonsuppurative, chronic, mucoid
      mucoid —*see* Otitis, media,
        nonsuppurative, chronic, mucoid
      nonsuppurative NEC —*see* Otitis, media,
        nonsuppurative, chronic
      purulent —*see* Otitis, media,
        suppurative, chronic
      secretory —*see* Otitis, media,
        nonsuppurative, chronic, mucoid
      seromucinous —*see* Otitis, media,
        nonsuppurative, chronic
      serous —*see* Otitis, media,
        nonsuppurative, chronic, serous
      suppurative —*see* Otitis, media,
        suppurative, chronic

Otitis *(Continued)*
  media *(Continued)*
    chronic *(Continued)*
      transudative —*see* Otitis, media,
        nonsuppurative, chronic, mucoid
      exudative —*see* Otitis, media,
        nonsuppurative
    in (due to) (with)
      influenza —*see* Influenza, with, otitis
        media
      measles B05.3
      scarlet fever A38.0
      tuberculosis A18.6
      viral disease NEC B34.-● *[H67.-●]*
    mucoid —*see* Otitis, media, nonsuppurative
    nonsuppurative H65.9-●
      acute or subacute NEC H65.19-●
        allergic H65.11-●
          recurrent H65.11-●
        recurrent H65.19-●
        secretory —*see* Otitis, media,
          nonsuppurative, serous
        serous H65.0-●
          recurrent H65.0-●
      chronic H65.49-●
        allergic H65.41-●
        mucoid H65.3-●
        serous H65.2-●
      postmeasles B05.3
      purulent —*see* Otitis, media, suppurative
      secretory —*see* Otitis, media,
        nonsuppurative
      seromucinous —*see* Otitis, media,
        nonsuppurative
      serous —*see* Otitis, media, nonsuppurative
    suppurative H66.4-●
      acute H66.00-●
        with rupture of ear drum H66.01-●
        recurrent H66.00-●
          with rupture of ear drum H66.01-●
      chronic —*see also* subcategory H66.3
        atticoantral H66.2-●
        benign —*see* Otitis, media,
          suppurative, chronic,
          tubotympanic
        tubotympanic H66.1-●
      transudative —*see* Otitis, media,
        nonsuppurative
      tuberculous A18.6
Otocephaly Q18.2
Otolith syndrome —*see* subcategory H81.8
Otomycosis (diffuse) NEC B36.9 *[H62.40]*
  in
    aspergillosis B44.89
    candidiasis B37.84
    moniliasis B37.84
Otoporosis —*see* Otosclerosis
Otorrhagia (nontraumatic) H92.2-●
  traumatic - code by Type of injury
Otorrhea H92.1-●
  cerebrospinal G96.0
Otosclerosis (general) H80.9-●
  cochlear (endosteal) H80.2-●
  involving
    otic capsule —*see* Otosclerosis, cochlear
    oval window
      nonobliterative H80.0-●
      obliterative H80.1-●
    round window —*see* Otosclerosis, cochlear
  nonobliterative —*see* Otosclerosis, involving,
    oval window, nonobliterative
  obliterative —*see* Otosclerosis, involving, oval
    window, obliterative
  specified NEC H80.8-●
Otospongiosis —*see* Otosclerosis
Otto's disease or pelvis M24.7
Outcome of delivery Z37.9
  multiple births Z37.9
    all liveborn Z37.50
      quadruplets Z37.52
      quintuplets Z37.53

Outcome of delivery *(Continued)*
  multiple births *(Continued)*
    all liveborn *(Continued)*
      sextuplets Z37.54
      specified number NEC Z37.59
      triplets Z37.51
    all stillborn Z37.7
    some liveborn Z37.60
      quadruplets Z37.62
      quintuplets Z37.63
      sextuplets Z37.64
      specified number NEC Z37.69
      triplets Z37.61
  single NEC Z37.9
    liveborn Z37.0
    stillborn Z37.1
  twins NEC Z37.9
    both liveborn Z37.2
    both stillborn Z37.4
    one liveborn, one stillborn Z37.3
Outlet —*see* condition
Ovalocytosis (congenital) (hereditary) —*see*
  Elliptocytosis
Ovarian —*see* Condition
Ovariocele N83.4-●
Ovaritis (cystic) —*see* Oophoritis
Ovary, ovarian —*see also* condition
  resistant syndrome E28.39
  vein syndrome N13.8
Overactive —*see also* Hyperfunction
  adrenal cortex NEC E27.0
  bladder N32.81
  hypothalamus E23.3
  thyroid —*see* Hyperthyroidism
Overactivity R46.3
  child —*see* Disorder, attention-deficit
    hyperactivity
Overbite (deep) (excessive) (horizontal)
  (vertical) M26.29
Overbreathing —*see* Hyperventilation
Overconscientious personality F60.5
Overdevelopment —*see* Hypertrophy
Overdistension —*see* Distension
Overdose, overdosage (drug) —*see* Table of
  Drugs and Chemicals, by drug, poisoning
Overeating R63.2
  nonorganic origin F50.89
  psychogenic F50.89
Overexertion (effects) (exhaustion) T73.3
Overexposure (effects) T73.9
  exhaustion T73.2
Overfeeding —*see* Overeating
  newborn P92.4
Overfill, endodontic M27.52
Overgrowth, bone —*see* Hypertrophy, bone
Overhanging of dental restorative material
  (unrepairable) K08.52
Overheated (places) (effects) —*see* Heat
Overjet (excessive horizontal) M26.23
Overlaid, overlying (suffocation) —*see* Asphyxia,
  traumatic, due to mechanical threat
Overlap, excessive horizontal (teeth) M26.23
Overlapping toe (acquired) —*see also*
  Deformity, toe, specified NEC
  congenital (fifth toe) Q66.89
Overload
  circulatory, due to transfusion (blood) (blood
    components) (TACO) E87.71
  fluid E87.70
    due to transfusion (blood) (blood
      components) E87.71
    specified NEC E87.79
  iron, due to repeated red blood cell
    transfusions E83.111
  potassium (K) E87.5
  sodium (Na) E87.0
Overnutrition —*see* Hyperalimentation
Overproduction —*see also* Hypersecretion
  ACTH E27.0
  catecholamine E27.5
  growth hormone E22.0

Overprotection, child by parent Z62.1
Overriding
  aorta Q25.49
  finger (acquired) —*see* Deformity, finger
    congenital Q68.1
  toe (acquired) —*see also* Deformity, toe,
    specified NEC
    congenital Q66.89
Overstrained R53.83
  heart —*see* Hypertrophy, cardiac

Overuse, muscle NEC
  M70.8-●
Overweight E66.3
Overworked R53.83
Oviduct —*see* condition
Ovotestis Q56.0
Ovulation (cycle)
  failure or lack of N97.0
  pain N94.0
Ovum —*see* condition

Owren's disease or syndrome (parahemophilia)
  D68.2
Ox heart —*see* Hypertrophy, cardiac
Oxalosis E72.53
Oxaluria E72.53
Oxycephaly, oxycephalic Q75.0
  syphilitic, congenital A50.02
Oxyuriasis B80
Oxyuris vermicularis (infestation) B80
Ozena J31.0

P

Pachyderma, pachydermia L85.9
  larynx (verrucosa) J38.7
Pachydermatocele (congenital) Q82.8
Pachydermoperiostosis —see also
    Osteoarthropathy, hypertrophic, specified
    type NEC
  clubbed nail M89.40 [L62]
Pachygyria Q04.3
Pachymeningitis (adhesive) (basal) (brain)
    (cervical) (chronic) (circumscribed)
    (external) (fibrous) (hemorrhagic)
    (hypertrophic) (internal) (purulent) (spinal)
    (suppurative) —see Meningitis
Pachyonychia (congenital) Q84.5
Pacinian tumor —see Neoplasm, skin, benign
Pad, knuckle or Garrod's M72.1
Paget-Schroetter syndrome I82.890
Paget's disease
  with infiltrating duct carcinoma —see
      Neoplasm, breast, malignant
  bone M88.9
    carpus M88.84-●
    clavicle M88.81-●
    femur M88.85-●
    fibula M88.86-●
    finger M88.84-●
    humerus M88.82-●
    ilium M88.85-●
    in neoplastic disease —see Osteitis,
        deformans, in neoplastic disease
    ischium M88.85-●
    metacarpus M88.84-●
    metatarsus M88.87-●
    multiple sites M88.89
    neck M88.88
    radius M88.83-●
    rib M88.88
    scapula M88.81-●
    skull M88.0
    tarsus M88.87-●
    tibia M88.86-●
    toe M88.87-●
    ulna M88.83-●
    vertebra M88.88
  breast (female) C50.01-●
    male C50.02-●
  extramammary —see also Neoplasm, skin,
      malignant
    anus C21.0
      margin C44.590
      skin C44.590
  intraductal carcinoma —see Neoplasm,
      breast, malignant
  malignant —see Neoplasm, skin, malignant
    breast (female) C50.01-●
      male C50.02-●
    unspecified site (female) C50.01-●
      male C50.02-●
  mammary —see Paget's disease, breast
  nipple —see Paget's disease, breast
  osteitis deformans —see Paget's disease, bone
Pain(s) —see also Painful R52
  abdominal R10.9
    colic R10.83
    generalized R10.84
      with acute abdomen R10.0
    lower R10.30
      left quadrant R10.32
      pelvic or perineal R10.2
      periumbilical R10.33
      right quadrant R10.31
    rebound —see Tenderness, abdominal,
        rebound
    severe with abdominal rigidity R10.0
    tenderness —see Tenderness, abdominal
    upper R10.10
      epigastric R10.13
      left quadrant R10.12
      right quadrant R10.11

Pain (Continued)
  acute R52
    due to trauma G89.11
    neoplasm related G89.3
    postprocedural NEC G89.18
    post-thoracotomy G89.12
    specified by site — code to Pain, by site
  adnexa (uteri) R10.2
  anginoid —see Pain, precordial
  anus K62.89
  arm —see Pain, limb, upper
  axillary (axilla) M79.62-●
  back (postural) M54.9
  bladder R39.89
    associated with micturition —see
        Micturition, painful
    chronic R39.82
  bone —see Disorder, bone, specified type
      NEC
  breast N64.4
  broad ligament R10.2
  cancer associated (acute) (chronic) G89.3
  cecum —see Pain, abdominal
  cervicobrachial M53.1
  chest (central) R07.9
    anterior wall R07.89
    atypical R07.89
    ischemic I20.9
    musculoskeletal R07.89
    non-cardiac R07.89
    on breathing R07.1
    pleurodynia R07.81
    precordial R07.2
    wall (anterior) R07.89
  chronic G89.29
    associated with significant psychosocial
        dysfunction G89.4
    due to trauma G89.21
    neoplasm related G89.3
    postoperative NEC G89.28
    postprocedural NEC G89.28
    post-thoracotomy G89.22
    specified NEC G89.29
  coccyx M53.3
  colon —see Pain, abdominal
  coronary —see Angina
  costochondral R07.1
  diaphragm R07.1
  due to cancer G89.3
  due to device, implant or graft —see also
      Complications, by site and type,
      specified NEC T85.848
    arterial graft NEC T82.848
    breast (implant) T85.848
    catheter NEC T85.848
      dialysis (renal) T82.848
        intraperitoneal T85.848
      infusion NEC T82.848
        spinal (epidural) (subdural) T85.840
      urinary (indwelling) T83.84
    electronic (electrode) (pulse generator)
        (stimulator)
      bone T84.84
      cardiac T82.847
      nervous system (brain) (peripheral
          nerve) (spinal) T85.840
      urinary T83.84
    fixation, internal (orthopedic) NEC T84.84
    gastrointestinal (bile duct) (esophagus)
        T85.848
    genital NEC T83.84
    heart NEC T82.847
    infusion NEC T85.848
    joint prosthesis T84.84
    ocular (corneal graft) (orbital implant)
        NEC T85.848
    orthopedic NEC T84.84
    specified NEC T85.848
    urinary NEC T83.84
    vascular NEC T82.848
    ventricular intracranial shunt T85.840

Pain (Continued)
  due to malignancy (primary) (secondary)
      G89.3
  ear —see subcategory H92.0
  epigastric, epigastrium R10.13
  eye —see Pain, ocular
  face, facial R51
    atypical G50.1
  female genital organs NEC N94.89
  finger —see Pain, limb, upper
  flank —see Pain, abdominal
  foot —see Pain, limb, lower
  gallbladder K82.9
  gas (intestinal) R14.1
  gastric —see Pain, abdominal
  generalized NOS R52
  genital organ
    female N94.89
    male N50.89
  groin —see Pain, abdominal, lower
  hand —see Pain, limb, upper
  head —see Headache
  heart —see Pain, precordial
  infra-orbital —see Neuralgia, trigeminal
  intercostal R07.82
  intermenstrual N94.0
  jaw R68.84
  joint M25.50
    ankle M25.57-●
    elbow M25.52-●
    finger M25.54-●
    foot M25.57-●
    hand M25.54-●
    hip M25.55-●
    knee M25.56-●
    shoulder M25.51-●
    toe M25.57-●
    wrist M25.53-●
  kidney N23
  laryngeal R07.0
  leg —see Pain, limb, lower
  limb M79.609
    lower M79.60-●
      foot M79.67-●
      lower leg M79.66-●
      thigh M79.65-●
      toe M79.67-●
    upper M79.60-●
      axilla M79.62-●
      finger M79.64-●
      forearm M79.63-●
      hand M79.64-●
      upper arm M79.62-●
  loin M54.5
  low back M54.5
  lumbar region M54.5
  mandibular R68.84
  mastoid —see subcategory H92.0
  maxilla R68.84
  menstrual —see also Dysmenorrhea N94.6
  metacarpophalangeal (joint) —see Pain, joint,
      hand
  metatarsophalangeal (joint) —see Pain, joint,
      foot
  mouth K13.79
  muscle —see Myalgia
  musculoskeletal —see also Pain, by site M79.18
  myofascial M79.18
  nasal J34.89
  nasopharynx J39.2
  neck NEC M54.2
  nerve NEC —see Neuralgia
  neuromuscular —see Neuralgia
  nose J34.89
  ocular H57.1-●
  ophthalmic —see Pain, ocular
  orbital region —see Pain, ocular
  ovary N94.89
  over heart —see Pain, precordial
  ovulation N94.0
  pelvic (female) R10.2

► New   ⇒ Revised   ~~deleted~~ Deleted   ● Use Additional Character(s)

Pain *(Continued)*
  penis N48.89
  pericardial —*see* Pain, precordial
  perineal, perineum R10.2
  pharynx J39.2
  pleura, pleural, pleuritic R07.81
  postoperative NOS G89.18
  postprocedural NOS G89.18
  post-thoracotomy G89.12
  precordial (region) R07.2
  premenstrual N94.3
  psychogenic (persistent) (any site) F45.41
  radicular (spinal) —*see* Radiculopathy
  rectum K62.89
  respiration R07.1
  retrosternal R07.2
  rheumatoid, muscular —*see* Myalgia
  rib R07.81
  root (spinal) —*see* Radiculopathy
  round ligament (stretch) R10.2
  sacroiliac M53.3
  sciatic —*see* Sciatica
  scrotum N50.82
  seminal vesicle N50.89
  shoulder M25.51-●
  spermatic cord N50.89
  spinal root —*see* Radiculopathy
  spine M54.9
    cervical M54.2
    low back M54.5
      with sciatica M54.4-●
    thoracic M54.6
  stomach —*see* Pain, abdominal
  substernal R07.2
  temporomandibular (joint) M26.62-●
  testis N50.81-●
  thoracic spine M54.6
    with radicular and visceral pain
      M54.14
  throat R07.0
  tibia —*see* Pain, limb, lower
  toe —*see* Pain, limb, lower
  tongue K14.6
  tooth K08.89
  trigeminal —*see* Neuralgia, trigeminal
  tumor associated G89.3
  ureter N23
  urinary (organ) (system) N23
  uterus NEC N94.89
  vagina R10.2
  vertebrogenic (syndrome) M54.89
  vesical R39.89
    associated with micturition —*see*
      Micturition, painful
  vulva R10.2
Painful —*see also* Pain
  coitus
    female N94.10
    male N53.12
    psychogenic F52.6
  ejaculation (semen) N53.12
    psychogenic F52.6
  erection —*see* Priapism
  feet syndrome E53.8
  joint replacement (hip) (knee) T84.84
  menstruation —*see* Dysmenorrhea
    psychogenic F45.8
  micturition —*see* Micturition, painful
  respiration R07.1
  scar NEC L90.5
  wire sutures T81.89
Painter's colic —*see* subcategory T56.0
Palate —*see* condition
Palatoplegia K13.79
Palatoschisis —*see* Cleft, palate
Palilalia R48.8
Palliative care Z51.5
Pallor R23.1
  optic disc, temporal —*see* Atrophy, optic
Palmar —*see also* condition
  fascia —*see* condition

Palpable
  cecum K63.89
  kidney N28.89
  ovary N83.8
  prostate N42.9
  spleen —*see* Splenomegaly
Palpitations (heart) R00.2
  psychogenic F45.8
Palsy —*see also* Paralysis G83.9
  atrophic diffuse (progressive) G12.22
  Bell's —*see also* Palsy, facial
    newborn P11.3
  brachial plexus NEC G54.0
    newborn (birth injury) P14.3
  brain —*see* Palsy, cerebral
  bulbar (progressive) (chronic) G12.22
    of childhood (Fazio-Londe) G12.1
    pseudo NEC G12.29
    supranuclear (progressive) G23.1
  cerebral (congenital) G80.9
    ataxic G80.4
    athetoid G80.3
    choreathetoid G80.3
    diplegic G80.8
      spastic G80.1
    dyskinetic G80.3
      athetoid G80.3
      choreathetoid G80.3
      distonic G80.3
    dystonic G80.3
    hemiplegic G80.8
      spastic G80.2
    mixed G80.8
    monoplegic G80.8
      spastic G80.1
    paraplegic G80.8
      spastic G80.1
    quadriplegic G80.8
      spastic G80.0
    spastic G80.1
      diplegic G80.1
      hemiplegic G80.2
      monoplegic G80.1
      quadriplegic G80.0
      specified NEC G80.1
      tetrapelgic G80.0
    specified NEC G80.8
    syphilitic A52.12
      congenital A50.49
    tetraplegic G80.8
      spastic G80.0
  cranial nerve —*see also* Disorder, nerve,
    cranial
    multiple G52.7
      in
        infectious disease B99 *[G53]*
        neoplastic disease —*see also* Neoplasm
          D49.9 *[G53]*
        parasitic disease B89 *[G53]*
        sarcoidosis D86.82
  creeping G12.22
  diver's T70.3
  Erb's P14.0
  facial G51.0
    newborn (birth injury) P11.3
  glossopharyngeal G52.1
  Klumpke (-Déjérine) P14.1
  lead —*see* subcategory T56.0
  median nerve (tardy) G56.1-●
  nerve G58.9
    specified NEC G58.8
  peroneal nerve (acute) (tardy) G57.3-●
  progressive supranuclear G23.1
  pseudobulbar NEC G12.29
  radial nerve (acute) G56.3-●
  seventh nerve —*see also* Palsy, facial
    newborn P11.3
  shaking —*see* Parkinsonism
  spastic (cerebral) (spinal) G80.1
  ulnar nerve (tardy) G56.2-●
  wasting G12.29

Paludism —*see* Malaria
Panangiitis M30.0
Panaris, panaritium —*see also* Cellulitis, digit
  with lymphangitis —*see* Lymphangitis, acute,
    digit
Panarteritis nodosa M30.0
  brain or cerebral I67.7
Pancake heart R93.1
  with cor pulmonale (chronic) I27.81
Pancarditis (acute) (chronic) I51.89
  rheumatic I09.89
    active or acute I01.8
Pancoast's syndrome or tumor C34.1-●
Pancolitis, ulcerative (chronic) K51.00
  with
    abscess K51.014
    complication K51.019
    fistula K51.013
    obstruction K51.012
    rectal bleeding K51.011
    specified complication NEC K51.018
Pancreas, pancreatic —*see* condition
Pancreatitis (annular) (apoplectic) (calcareous)
    (edematous) (hemorrhagic) (malignant)
    (recurrent) (subacute) (suppurative) K85.90

  with necrosis (uninfected) K85.91
    infected K85.92
  acute (without necrosis or infection)
      K85.90
    with necrosis (uninfected) K85.91
      infected K85.92
    alcohol induced (without necrosis or
        infection) K85.20
      with necrosis (uninfected) K85.21
        infected K85.22
    biliary (without necrosis or infection)
        K85.10
      with necrosis (uninfected) K85.11
        infected K85.12
    drug induced (without necrosis or
        infection) K85.30
      with necrosis (uninfected) K85.31
        infected K85.32
    gallstone (without necrosis or infection)
        K85.10
      with necrosis (uninfected) K85.11
        infected K85.12
    idiopathic (without necrosis or infection)
        K85.00
      with necrosis (uninfected) K85.01
        infected K85.02
    specified NEC (without necrosis or
        infection) K85.80
      with necrosis (uninfected)
          K85.81
        infected K85.82
  chronic (infectious) K86.1
    alcohol-induced K86.0
    recurrent K86.1
    relapsing K86.1
  cystic (chronic) K86.1
  cytomegaloviral B25.2
  fibrous (chronic) K86.1
  gallstone (without necrosis or infection)
      K85.10
    with necrosis (uninfected)
        K85.11
      infected K85.12
  gangrenous —*see* Pancreatitis, acute
  interstitial (chronic) K86.1
    acute —*see also* Pancreatitis, acute
        K85.80
  mumps B26.3
  recurrent (chronic) K86.1
  relapsing, chronic K86.1
  syphilitic A52.74
Pancreatoblastoma —*see* Neoplasm, pancreas,
    malignant
Pancreolithiasis K86.89
Pancytolysis D75.89

▶ New   ⇒ Revised   ~~deleted~~ Deleted   ● Use Additional Character(s)

Pancytopenia (acquired) D61.818
  with
    malformations D61.09
    myelodysplastic syndrome —see
      Syndrome, myelodysplastic
  antineoplastic chemotherapy induced
    D61.810
  congenital D61.09
  drug-induced NEC D61.811
PANDAS (pediatric autoimmune
  neuropsychiatric disorders associated with
  streptococcal infections syndrome) D89.89
Panencephalitis, subacute, sclerosing
  A81.1
Panhematopenia D61.9
  congenital D61.09
  constitutional D61.09
  splenic, primary D73.1
Panhemocytopenia D61.9
  congenital D61.09
  constitutional D61.09
Panhypogonadism E29.1
Panhypopituitarism E23.0
  prepubertal E23.0
Panic (attack) (state) F41.0
  reaction to exceptional stress (transient) F43.0
Panmyelopathy, familial, constitutional D61.09
Panmyelophthisis D61.82
  congenital D61.09
Panmyelosis (acute) (with myelofibrosis)
  C94.4-•
Panner's disease —see Osteochondrosis,
  juvenile, humerus
Panneuritis endemica E51.11
Panniculitis (nodular) (nonsuppurative) M79.3
  back M54.00
    cervical region M54.02
    cervicothoracic region M54.03
    lumbar region M54.06
    lumbosacral region M54.07
    multiple sites M54.09
    occipito-atlanto-axial region M54.01
    sacrococcygeal region M54.08
    thoracic region M54.04
    thoracolumbar region M54.05
  lupus L93.2
  mesenteric K65.4
  neck M54.02
    cervicothoracic region M54.03
    occipito-atlanto-axial region M54.01
  relapsing M35.6
Panniculus adiposus (abdominal) E65
Pannus (allergic) (cornea) (degenerativus)
  (keratic) H16.42-•
  abdominal (symptomatic) E65
  trachomatosus, trachomatous (active) A71.1
Panophthalmitis H44.01-•
Pansinusitis (chronic) (hyperplastic)
  (nonpurulent) (purulent) J32.4
  acute J01.40
    recurrent J01.41
  tuberculous A15.8
Panuveitis (sympathetic) H44.11-•
Panvalvular disease I08.9
  specified NEC I08.8
PAPA (pyogenic arthritis, pyoderma
  gangrenosum, and acne syndrome) M04.8
Papanicolaou smear, cervix Z12.4
  as part of routine gynecological examination
    Z01.419
    with abnormal findings Z01.411
  for suspected neoplasm Z12.4
  nonspecific abnormal finding R87.619
  routine Z01.419
    with abnormal findings Z01.411
Papilledema (choked disc) H47.10
  associated with
    decreased ocular pressure H47.12
    increased intracranial pressure H47.11
    retinal disorder H47.13
  Foster-Kennedy syndrome H47.14-•

Papillitis H46.00
  anus K62.89
  chronic lingual K14.4
  necrotizing, kidney N17.2
  optic H46.0-•
  rectum K62.89
  renal, necrotizing N17.2
  tongue K14.0
Papilloma —see also Neoplasm, benign,
  by site
  acuminatum (female) (male) (anogenital)
    A63.0
  basal cell L82.1
    inflamed L82.0
  benign pinta (primary) A67.0
  bladder (urinary) (transitional cell) D41.4
  choroid plexus (lateral ventricle) (third
    ventricle) D33.0
    anaplastic C71.5
    fourth ventricle D33.1
    malignant C71.5
  renal pelvis (transitional cell) D41.1-•
    benign D30.1-•
  Schneiderian
    specified site —see Neoplasm, benign, by
      site
    unspecified site D14.0
  serous surface
    borderline malignancy
      specified site —see Neoplasm, uncertain
        behavior, by site
      unspecified site D39.10
    specified site —see Neoplasm, benign, by
      site
    unspecified site D27.9
  transitional (cell)
    bladder (urinary) D41.4
    inverted type —see Neoplasm, uncertain
      behavior, by site
    renal pelvis D41.1-•
    ureter D41.2-•
  ureter (transitional cell) D41.2-•
    benign D30.2-•
  urothelial —see Neoplasm, uncertain
    behavior, by site
  villous —see Neoplasm, uncertain behavior,
    by site
    adenocarcinoma in —see Neoplasm,
      malignant, by site
    in situ —see Neoplasm, in situ
  yaws, plantar or palmar A66.1
Papillomata, multiple, of yaws A66.1
Papillomatosis —see also Neoplasm, benign,
  by site
  confluent and reticulated L83
  cystic, breast —see Mastopathy, cystic
  ductal, breast —see Mastopathy, cystic
  intraductal (diffuse) —see Neoplasm, benign,
    by site
  subareolar duct D24-•
Papillomavirus, as cause of disease classified
  elsewhere B97.7
Papillon-Léage and Psaume syndrome
  Q87.0
Papule(s) R23.8
  carate (primary) A67.0
  fibrous, of nose D22.39
  Gottron's L94.4
  pinta (primary) A67.0
Papulosis
  lymphomatoid C86.6
  malignant I77.89
Papyraceous fetus O31.0-•
Para-albuminemia E88.09
Paracephalus Q89.7
Parachute mitral valve Q23.2
Paracoccidioidomycosis B41.9
  disseminated B41.7
  generalized B41.7
  mucocutaneous-lymphangitic B41.8
  pulmonary B41.0

Paracoccidioidomycosis (Continued)
  specified NEC B41.8
  visceral B41.8
Paradentosis K05.4
Paraffinoma T88.8
Paraganglioma D44.7
  adrenal D35.0-•
    malignant C74.1-•
  aortic body D44.7
    malignant C75.5
  carotid body D44.6
    malignant C75.4
  chromaffin —see also Neoplasm, benign, by
    site
    malignant —see Neoplasm, malignant, by
      site
  extra-adrenal D44.7
    malignant C75.5
      specified site —see Neoplasm,
        malignant, by site
      unspecified site C75.5
    specified site —see Neoplasm, uncertain
      behavior, by site
    unspecified site D44.7
  gangliocytic D13.2
    specified site —see Neoplasm, benign, by
      site
    unspecified site D13.2
  glomus jugulare D44.7
    malignant C75.5
  jugular D44.7
  malignant C75.5
    specified site —see Neoplasm, malignant,
      by site
    unspecified site C75.5
  nonchromaffin D44.7
    malignant C75.5
      specified site —see Neoplasm,
        malignant, by site
      unspecified site C75.5
    specified site —see Neoplasm, uncertain
      behavior, by site
    unspecified site D44.7
  parasympathetic D44.7
    specified site —see Neoplasm, uncertain
      behavior, by site
    unspecified site D44.7
  specified site —see Neoplasm, uncertain
    behavior, by site
  sympathetic D44.7
    specified site —see Neoplasm, uncertain
      behavior, by site
    unspecified site D44.7
  unspecified site D44.7
Parageusia R43.2
  psychogenic F45.8
Paragonimiasis B66.4
Paragranuloma, Hodgkin —see Lymphoma,
  Hodgkin, specified NEC
Parahemophilia —see also Defect, coagulation
  D68.2
Parakeratosis R23.4
  variegata L41.0
Paralysis, paralytic (complete) (incomplete)
  G83.9
  with
    syphilis A52.17
  abducens, abducent (nerve) —see Strabismus,
    paralytic, sixth nerve
  abductor, lower extremity G57.9-•
  accessory nerve G52.8
  accommodation —see also Paresis, of
    accommodation
    hysterical F44.89
  acoustic nerve (except Deafness) —see
    subcategory H93.3
  agitans —see also Parkinsonism G20
    arteriosclerotic G21.4
  alternating (oculomotor) G83.89
  amyotrophic G12.21

Paralysis, paralytic *(Continued)*
ankle G57.9-●
anus (sphincter) K62.89
arm —*see* Monoplegia, upper limb
ascending (spinal), acute G61.0
association G12.29
asthenic bulbar G70.00
  with exacerbation (acute) G70.01
  in crisis G70.01
ataxic (hereditary) G11.9
  general (syphilitic) A52.17
atrophic G58.9
  infantile, acute —*see* Poliomyelitis, paralytic
  progressive G12.22
  spinal (acute) —*see* Poliomyelitis, paralytic
axillary G54.0
Babinski-Nageotte's G83.89
Bell's G51.0
  newborn P11.3
Benedikt's G46.3
birth injury P14.9
  spinal cord P11.5
bladder (neurogenic) (sphincter) N31.2
bowel, colon or intestine K56.0
brachial plexus G54.0
  birth injury P14.3
  newborn (birth injury) P14.3
brain G83.9
  diplegia G83.0
  triplegia G83.89
bronchial J98.09
Brown-Séquard G83.81
bulbar (chronic) (progressive) G12.22
  infantile —*see* Poliomyelitis, paralytic
  poliomyelitic —*see* Poliomyelitis, paralytic
  pseudo G12.29
bulbospinal G70.00
  with exacerbation (acute) G70.01
  in crisis G70.01
cardiac —*see also* Failure, heart I50.9
cerebrocerebellar, diplegic G80.1
cervical
  plexus G54.2
  sympathetic G90.09
Céstan-Chenais G46.3
Charcot-Marie-Tooth type G60.0
Clark's G80.9
colon K56.0
compressed air T70.3
compression
  arm G56.9-●
  leg G57.9-●
  lower extremity G57.9-●
  upper extremity G56.9-●
congenital (cerebral) —*see* Palsy, cerebral
conjugate movement (gaze) (of eye) H51.0
  cortical (nuclear) (supranuclear) H51.0
cordis —*see* Failure, heart
cranial or cerebral nerve G52.9
creeping G12.22
crossed leg G83.89
crutch —*see* Injury, brachial plexus
deglutition R13.0
  hysterical F44.4
dementia A52.17
descending (spinal) NEC G12.29
diaphragm (flaccid) J98.6
  due to accidental dissection of phrenic nerve during procedure —*see* Puncture, accidental complicating surgery
digestive organs NEC K59.8
diplegic —*see* Diplegia
divergence (nuclear) H51.8
diver's T70.3
Duchenne's
  birth injury P14.0
  due to or associated with
    motor neuron disease G12.22
➠   muscular dystrophy G71.01

Paralysis, paralytic *(Continued)*
due to intracranial or spinal birth injury —*see* Palsy, cerebral
embolic (current episode) I63.4-●
Erb (-Duchenne) (birth) (newborn) P14.0
Erb's syphilitic spastic spinal A52.17
esophagus K22.8
eye muscle (extrinsic) H49.9
  intrinsic —*see also* Paresis, of accommodation
facial (nerve) G51.0
  birth injury P11.3
  congenital P11.3
  following operation NEC —*see* Puncture, accidental complicating surgery
  newborn (birth injury) P11.3
familial (recurrent) (periodic) G72.3
  spastic G11.4
fauces J39.2
finger G56.9-●
gait R26.1
gastric nerve (nondiabetic) G52.2
gaze, conjugate H51.0
general (progressive) (syphilitic) A52.17
  juvenile A50.45
glottis J38.00
  bilateral J38.02
  unilateral J38.01
gluteal G54.1
Gubler (-Millard) G46.3
hand —*see* Monoplegia, upper limb
heart —*see* Arrest, cardiac
hemiplegic —*see* Hemiplegia
hyperkalemic periodic (familial) G72.3
hypoglossal (nerve) G52.3
hypokalemic periodic G72.3
hysterical F44.4
ileus K56.0
infantile —*see also* Poliomyelitis, paralytic A80.30
  bulbar —*see* Poliomyelitis, paralytic
  cerebral —*see* Palsy, cerebral
  spastic —*see* Palsy, cerebral, spastic
infective —*see* Poliomyelitis, paralytic
inferior nuclear G83.9
internuclear —*see* Ophthalmoplegia, internuclear
intestine K56.0
iris H57.09
  due to diphtheria (toxin) A36.89
ischemic, Volkmann's (complicating trauma) T79.6
Jackson's G83.89
jake —*see* Poisoning, food, noxious, plant
Jamaica ginger (jake) G62.2
juvenile general A50.45
Klumpke (-Déjérine) (birth) (newborn) P14.1
labioglossal (laryngeal) (pharyngeal) G12.29
Landry's G61.0
laryngeal nerve (recurrent) (superior) (unilateral) J38.00
  bilateral J38.02
  unilateral J38.01
larynx J38.00
  bilateral J38.02
  due to diphtheria (toxin) A36.2
  unilateral J38.01
lateral G12.23
lead —*see* subcategory T56.0
left side —*see* Hemiplegia
leg G83.1-●
  both —*see* Paraplegia
  crossed G83.89
  hysterical F44.4
  psychogenic F44.4
  transient or transitory R29.818
    traumatic NEC —*see* Injury, nerve, leg
levator palpebrae superioris —*see* Blepharoptosis, paralytic
limb —*see* Monoplegia
lip K13.0

Paralysis, paralytic *(Continued)*
Lissauer's A52.17
lower limb —*see* Monoplegia, lower limb
  both —*see* Paraplegia
lung J98.4
median nerve G56.1-●
medullary (tegmental) G83.89
mesencephalic NEC G83.89
  tegmental G83.89
middle alternating G83.89
Millard-Gubler-Foville G46.3
monoplegic —*see* Monoplegia
motor G83.9
muscle, muscular NEC G72.89
  due to nerve lesion G58.9
  eye (extrinsic) H49.9
    intrinsic —*see* Paresis, of accommodation
    oblique —*see* Strabismus, paralytic, fourth nerve
  iris sphincter H21.9
  ischemic (Volkmann's) (complicating trauma) T79.6
  progressive G12.21
➠ pseudohypertrophic G71.02
musculocutaneous nerve G56.9-●
musculospiral G56.9-●
nerve —*see also* Disorder, nerve
  abducent —*see* Strabismus, paralytic, sixth nerve
  accessory G52.8
  auditory (except Deafness) —*see* subcategory H93.3
  birth injury P14.9
  cranial or cerebral G52.9
  facial G51.0
    birth injury P11.3
    congenital P11.3
    newborn (birth injury) P11.3
  fourth or trochlear —*see* Strabismus, paralytic, fourth nerve
  newborn (birth injury) P14.9
  oculomotor —*see* Strabismus, paralytic, third nerve
  phrenic (birth injury) P14.2
  radial G56.3-●
  seventh or facial G51.0
    newborn (birth injury) P11.3
  sixth or abducent —*see* Strabismus, paralytic, sixth nerve
  syphilitic A52.15
  third or oculomotor —*see* Strabismus, paralytic, third nerve
  trigeminal G50.9
  trochlear —*see* Strabismus, paralytic, fourth nerve
  ulnar G56.2-●
normokalemic periodic G72.3
ocular H49.9
  alternating G83.89
oculofacial, congenital (Moebius) Q87.0
oculomotor (external bilateral) (nerve) —*see* Strabismus, paralytic, third nerve
palate (soft) K13.79
paratrigeminal G50.9
periodic (familial) (hyperkalemic) (hypokalemic) (myotonic) (normokalemic) (potassium sensitive) (secondary) G72.3
peripheral autonomic nervous system —*see* Neuropathy, peripheral, autonomic
peroneal (nerve) G57.3-●
pharynx J39.2
phrenic nerve G56.8-●
plantar nerve(s) G57.6-●
pneumogastric nerve G52.2
poliomyelitis (current) —*see* Poliomyelitis, paralytic
popliteal nerve G57.3-●
postepileptic transitory G83.84

Paralysis, paralytic (Continued)
  progressive (atrophic) (bulbar) (spinal)
      G12.22
    general A52.17
    infantile acute —see Poliomyelitis, paralytic
    supranuclear G23.1
  pseudobulbar G12.29
  pseudohypertrophic (muscle) G71.09
  psychogenic F44.4
  quadriceps G57.9-●
  quadriplegic —see Tetraplegia
  radial nerve G56.3-●
  rectus muscle (eye) H49.9
  recurrent isolated sleep G47.53
  respiratory (muscle) (system) (tract) R06.81
    center NEC G93.89
    congenital P28.89
    newborn P28.89
  right side —see Hemiplegia
  saturnine —see subcategory T56.0
  sciatic nerve G57.0-●
  senile G83.9
  shaking —see Parkinsonism
  shoulder G56.9-●
  sleep, recurrent isolated G47.53
  spastic G83.9
    cerebral —see Palsy, cerebral, spastic
    congenital (cerebral) —see Palsy, cerebral,
        spastic
    familial G11.4
    hereditary G11.4
    quadriplegic G80.0
    syphilitic (spinal) A52.17
  sphincter, bladder —see Paralysis, bladder
  spinal (cord) G83.9
    accessory nerve G52.8
    acute —see Poliomyelitis, paralytic
    ascending acute G61.0
    atrophic (acute) —see also Poliomyelitis,
        paralytic
      spastic, syphilitic A52.17
    congenital NEC —see Palsy, cerebral
    hereditary G95.89
    infantile —see Poliomyelitis, paralytic
    progressive G12.21
    sequelae NEC G83.89
  sternomastoid G52.8
  stomach K31.84
    diabetic —see Diabetes, by type, with
        gastroparesis
    nerve G52.2
      diabetic —see Diabetes, by type, with
          gastroparesis
  stroke —see Infarct, brain
  subcapsularis G56.8-●
  supranuclear (progressive) G23.1
  sympathetic G90.8
    cervical G90.09
    nervous system —see Neuropathy,
        peripheral, autonomic
  syndrome G83.9
    specified NEC G83.89
  syphilitic spastic spinal (Erb's) A52.17
  thigh G57.9-●
  throat J39.2
    diphtheritic A36.0
    muscle J39.2
  thrombotic (current episode) I63.3-●
  thumb G56.9-●
  tick —see Toxicity, venom, arthropod,
      specified NEC
  Todd's (postepileptic transitory paralysis)
      G83.84
  toe G57.6-●
  tongue K14.8
  transient R29.5
    arm or leg NEC R29.818
    traumatic NEC —see Injury, nerve
  trapezius G52.8
  traumatic, transient NEC —see Injury,
      nerve

Paralysis, paralytic (Continued)
  trembling —see Parkinsonism
  triceps brachii G56.9-●
  trigeminal nerve G50.9
  trochlear (nerve) —see Strabismus, paralytic,
      fourth nerve
  ulnar nerve G56.2-●
  upper limb —see Monoplegia, upper limb
  uremic N18.9 [G99.8]
  uveoparotitic D86.89
  uvula K13.79
    postdiphtheritic A36.0
  vagus nerve G52.2
  vasomotor NEC G90.8
  velum palati K13.79
  vesical —see Paralysis, bladder
  vestibular nerve (except Vertigo) —see
      subcategory H93.3
  vocal cords J38.00
    bilateral J38.02
    unilateral J38.01
  Volkmann's (complicating trauma)
      T79.6
  wasting G12.29
  Weber's G46.3
  wrist C56.9-●
Paramedial urethrovesical orifice
    Q64.79
Paramenia N92.6
Parametritis —see also Disease, pelvis,
    inflammatory N73.2
  acute N73.0
  complicating abortion —see Abortion, by
      type, complicated by, parametritis
Parametrium, parametric —see condition
Paramnesia —see Amnesia
Paramolar K00.1
Paramyloidosis E85.89
Paramyoclonus multiplex G25.3
Paramyotonia (congenita) G71.19
Parangi —see Yaws
Paranoia (querulans) F22
  senile F03
Paranoid
  dementia (senile) F03
    praecox —see Schizophrenia
  personality F60.0
  psychosis (climacteric) (involutional)
      (menopausal) F22
    psychogenic (acute) F23
    senile F03
  reaction (acute) F23
    chronic F22
  schizophrenia F20.0
  state (climacteric) (involutional)
      (menopausal) (simple) F22
    senile F03
  tendencies F60.0
  traits F60.0
  trends F60.0
  type, psychopathic personality F60.0
Paraparesis —see Paraplegia
Paraphasia R47.02
Paraphilia F65.9
Paraphimosis (congenital) N47.2
  chancroidal A57
Paraphrenia, paraphrenic (late) F22
  schizophrenia F20.0
Paraplegia (lower) G82.20
  ataxic —see Degeneration, combined, spinal
      cord
  complete G82.21
  congenital (cerebral) G80.8
    spastic G80.1
  familial spastic G11.4
  functional (hysterical) F44.4
  hereditary, spastic G11.4
  hysterical F44.4
  incomplete G82.22
  Pott's A18.01
  psychogenic F44.4

Paraplegia (Continued)
  spastic
    Erb's spinal, syphilitic A52.17
      hereditary G11.4
      tropical G04.1
    syphilitic (spastic) A52.17
  ▶traumatic
    ▶current injury - code to injury with seventh
        character A
      ▶sequela of previous injury - code to
          injury with seventh character S
    tropical spastic G04.1
Parapoxvirus B08.60
  specified NEC B08.69
Paraproteinemia D89.2
  benign (familial) D89.2
  monoclonal D47.2
  secondary to malignant disease D47.2
Parapsoriasis L41.9
  en plaques L41.4
  guttata L41.1
  large plaque L41.4
  retiform, retiformis L41.5
  small plaque L41.3
  specified NEC L41.8
  varioliformis (acuta) L41.0
Parasitic —see also condition
  disease NEC B89
  stomatitis B37.0
  sycosis (beard) (scalp) B35.0
  twin Q89.4
Parasitism B89
  intestinal B82.9
  skin B88.9
  specified —see Infestation
Parasitophobia F40.218
Parasomnia G47.50
  due to
    alcohol
      abuse F10.182
      dependence F10.282
      use F10.982
    amphetamines
      abuse F15.182
      dependence F15.282
      use F15.982
    caffeine
      abuse F15.182
      dependence F15.282
      use F15.982
    cocaine
      abuse F14.182
      dependence F14.282
      use F14.982
    drug NEC
      abuse F19.182
      dependence F19.282
      use F19.982
    opioid
      abuse F11.182
      dependence F11.282
      use F11.982
    psychoactive substance NEC
      abuse F19.182
      dependence F19.282
      use F19.982
    sedative, hypnotic, or anxiolytic
      abuse F13.182
      dependence F13.282
      use F13.982
    stimulant NEC
      abuse F15.182
      dependence F15.282
      use F15.982
  in conditions classified elsewhere
      G47.54
  nonorganic origin F51.8
  organic G47.50
  specified NEC G47.59
Paraspadias Q54.9
Paraspasmus facialis G51.8

▶ New   ⇒ Revised   ~~deleted~~ Deleted   ● Use Additional Character(s)

Parasuicide (attempt)
  history of (personal) Z91.5
    in family Z81.8
Parathyroid gland —see condition
Parathyroid tetany E20.9
Paratrachoma A74.0
Paratyphilitis —see Appendicitis
Paratyphoid (fever) —see Fever, paratyphoid
Paratyphus —see Fever, paratyphoid
Paraurethral duct Q64.79
  nonorganic origin F51.5
Paraurethritis —see also Urethritis
  gonococcal (acute) (chronic) (with abscess) A54.1
Paravaccinia NEC B08.04
Paravaginitis —see Vaginitis
Parencephalitis —see also Encephalitis
  sequelae G09
Parent-child conflict —see Conflict, parent-child
  estrangement NEC Z62.890
Paresis —see also Paralysis
  accommodation —see Paresis, of accommodation
  Bernhardt's G57.1-●
  bladder (sphincter) —see also Paralysis, bladder
    tabetic A52.17
  bowel, colon or intestine K56.0
  extrinsic muscle, eye H49.9
  general (progressive) (syphilitic) A52.17
    juvenile A50.45
  heart —see Failure, heart
  insane (syphilitic) A52.17
  juvenile (general) A50.45
  of accommodation H52.52-●
  peripheral progressive (idiopathic) G60.3
▶pseudohypertrophic G71.09
  senile G83.9
  syphilitic (general) A52.17
    congenital A50.45
  vesical NEC N31.2
Paresthesia —see also Disturbance, sensation, skin R20.2
  Bernhardt G57.1-●
Paretic —see condition
Parinaud's
  conjunctivitis H10.89
  oculoglandular syndrome H10.89
  ophthalmoplegia H49.88
Parkinsonism (idiopathic) (primary) G20
  with neurogenic orthostatic hypotension (symptomatic) G90.3
  arteriosclerotic G21.4
  dementia G31.83 [F02.80]
    with behavioral disturbance G31.83 [F02.81]
  due to
    drugs NEC G21.19
      neuroleptic G21.11
    medication-induced NEC G21.19
  neuroleptic induced G21.11
  postencephalitic G21.3
  secondary G21.9
    due to
      arteriosclerosis G21.4
      drugs NEC G21.19
        neuroleptic G21.11
      encephalitis G21.3
      external agents NEC G21.2
      syphilis A52.19
    specified NEC G21.8
  syphilitic A52.19
  treatment-induced NEC G21.19
  vascular G21.4
Parkinson's disease, syndrome or tremor —see Parkinsonism
Parodontitis —see Periodontitis
Parodontosis K05.4
Paronychia —see also Cellulitis, digit
  with lymphangitis —see Lymphangitis, acute, digit
  candidal (chronic) B37.2
  tuberculous (primary) A18.4

Parorexia (psychogenic) F50.89
Parosmia R43.1
  psychogenic F45.8
Parotid gland —see condition
Parotitis, parotiditis (allergic) (nonspecific toxic) (purulent) (septic) (suppurative) —see also Sialoadenitis
  epidemic —see Mumps
  infectious —see Mumps
  postoperative K91.89
  surgical K91.89
Parrot fever A70
Parrot's disease (early congenital syphilitic pseudoparalysis) A50.02
Parry-Romberg syndrome G51.8
Parry's disease or syndrome E05.00
  with thyroid storm E05.01
Pars planitis —see Cyclitis
Parsonage (-Aldren)-Turner syndrome G54.5
Parson's disease (exophthalmic goiter) E05.00
  with thyroid storm E05.01
Particolored infant Q82.8
Parturition —see Delivery
Parulis K04.7
  with sinus K04.6
Parvovirus, as cause of disease classified elsewhere B97.6
Pasini and Pierini's atrophoderma L90.3
Passage
  false, urethra N36.5
  meconium (newborn) during delivery P03.82
  of sounds or bougies —see Attention to, artificial, opening
Passive —see condition
  smoking Z77.22
Pasteurella septica A28.0
Pasteurellosis —see Infection, Pasteurella
PAT (paroxysmal atrial tachycardia) I47.1
Patau's syndrome —see Trisomy, 13
Patches
  mucous (syphilitic) A51.39
    congenital A50.07
  smokers' (mouth) K13.24
Patellar —see condition
Patent —see also Imperfect, closure
  canal of Nuck Q52.4
  cervix N88.3
  ductus arteriosus or Botallo's Q25.0
  foramen
    botalli Q21.1
    ovale Q21.1
  interauricular septum Q21.1
  interventricular septum Q21.0
  omphalomesenteric duct Q43.0
  os (uteri) —see Patent, cervix
  ostium secundum Q21.1
  urachus Q64.4
  vitelline duct Q43.0
Paterson (-Brown)(-Kelly) syndrome or web D50.1
Pathologic, pathological —see also condition
  asphyxia R09.01
  fire-setting F63.1
  gambling F63.0
  ovum O02.0
  resorption, tooth K03.3
  stealing F63.2
Pathology (of) —see Disease
  periradicular, associated with previous endodontic treatment NEC M27.59
Pattern, sleep-wake, irregular G47.23
Patulous —see also Imperfect, closure (congenital)
  alimentary tract Q45.8
    lower Q43.8
    upper Q40.8
  eustachian tube H69.0-●
Pause, sinoatrial I49.5
Paxton's disease B36.2
Pearl(s)
  enamel K00.2
  Epstein's K09.8

Pearl-worker's disease —see Osteomyelitis, specified type NEC
Pectenosis K62.4
Pectoral —see condition
Pectus
  carinatum (congenital) Q67.7
    acquired M95.4
    rachitic sequelae (late effect) E64.3
  excavatum (congenital) Q67.6
    acquired M95.4
    rachitic sequelae (late effect) E64.3
  recurvatum (congenital) Q67.6
Pedatrophia E41
Pederosis F65.4
Pediculosis (infestation) B85.2
  capitis (head-louse) (any site) B85.0
  corporis (body-louse) (any site) B85.1
  eyelid B85.0
  mixed (classifiable to more than one of the titles B85.0-B85.3) B85.4
  pubis (pubic louse) (any site) B85.3
  vestimenti B85.1
  vulvae B85.3
Pediculus (infestation) —see Pediculosis
Pedophilia F65.4
Peg-shaped teeth K00.2
Pelade —see Alopecia, areata
Pelger-Huët anomaly or syndrome D72.0
Peliosis (rheumatica) D69.0
  hepatis K76.4
    with toxic liver disease K71.8
Pelizaeus-Merzbacher disease E75.29
Pellagra (alcoholic) (with polyneuropathy) E52
Pellagra-cerebellar-ataxia-renal aminoaciduria syndrome E72.02
Pellegrini (-Stieda) disease or syndrome —see Bursitis, tibial collateral
Pellizzi's syndrome E34.8
Pel's crisis A52.11
Pelvic —see also condition
  examination (periodic) (routine) Z01.419
    with abnormal findings Z01.411
  kidney, congenital Q63.2
Pelviolithiasis —see Calculus, kidney
Pelviperitonitis —see also Peritonitis, pelvic
  gonococcal A54.24
  puerperal O85
Pelvis —see condition or type
Pemphigoid L12.9
  benign, mucous membrane L12.1
  bullous L12.0
  cicatricial L12.1
  juvenile L12.2
  ocular L12.1
  specified NEC L12.8
Pemphigus L10.9
  benign familial (chronic) Q82.8
  Brazilian L10.3
  circinatus L13.0
  conjunctiva L12.1
  drug-induced L10.5
  erythematosus L10.4
  foliaceous L10.2
  gangrenous —see Gangrene
  neonatorum L01.03
  ocular L12.1
  paraneoplastic L10.81
  specified NEC L10.89
  syphilitic (congenital) A50.06
  vegetans L10.1
  vulgaris L10.0
  wildfire L10.3
Pendred's syndrome E07.1
Pendulous
  abdomen, in pregnancy —see Pregnancy, complicated by, abnormal, pelvic organs or tissues NEC
  breast N64.89
Penetrating wound —see also Puncture
  with internal injury —see Injury, by site
  eyeball —see Puncture, eyeball

Perforation, perforated *(Continued)*
  tympanum, tympanic *(Continued)*
    total H72.82-●
    traumatic, current episode S09.2-●
  typhoid, gastrointestinal —*see* Typhoid
  ulcer —*see* Ulcer, by site, with perforation
  ureter N28.89
    traumatic S37.19
  urethra N36.8
    with ectopic or molar pregnancy O08.6
    following ectopic or molar pregnancy O08.6
    obstetrical trauma O71.5
    traumatic S37.39
      at delivery O71.5
  uterus
    with ectopic or molar pregnancy O08.6
    by intrauterine contraceptive device T83.39
    following ectopic or molar pregnancy
      O08.6
    obstetrical trauma O71.1
    traumatic S37.69
      obstetric O71.1
  uvula K13.79
    syphilitic A52.79
  vagina
    obstetrical trauma O71.4
    other trauma - *see* Puncture, vagina
Periadenitis mucosa necrotica recurrens K12.0
Periappendicitis (acute) —*see* Appendicitis
Periarteritis nodosa (disseminated) (infectious)
  (necrotizing) M30.0
Periarthritis (joint) —*see also* Enthesopathy
  Duplay's M75.0-●
  gonococcal A54.42
  humeroscapularis —*see* Capsulitis, adhesive
  scapulohumeral —*see* Capsulitis, adhesive
  shoulder —*see* Capsulitis, adhesive
  wrist M77.2-●
Periarthrosis (angioneural) —*see* Enthesopathy
Pericapsulitis, adhesive (shoulder) —*see*
  Capsulitis, adhesive
Pericarditis (with decompensation) (with
  effusion) I31.9
  with rheumatic fever (conditions in I00)
    active —*see* Pericarditis, rheumatic
    inactive or quiescent I09.2
  acute (hemorrhagic) (nonrheumatic) (Sicca)
    I30.9
    with chorea (acute) (rheumatic)
      (Sydenham's) I02.0
    benign I30.8
    nonspecific I30.0
    rheumatic I01.0
      with chorea (acute) (Sydenham's) I02.0
  adhesive or adherent (chronic) (external)
    (internal) I31.0
    acute —*see* Pericarditis, acute
    rheumatic I09.2
  bacterial (acute) (subacute) (with serous or
    seropurulent effusion) I30.1
  calcareous I31.1
  cholesterol (chronic) I31.8
    acute I30.9
  chronic (nonrheumatic) I31.9
    rheumatic I09.2
  constrictive (chronic) I31.1
  coxsackie B33.23
  fibrinocaseous (tuberculous) A18.84
  fibrinopurulent I30.1
  fibrinous I30.8
  fibrous I31.0
  gonococcal A54.83
  idiopathic I30.0
  in systemic lupus erythematosus M32.12
  infective I30.1
  meningococcal A39.53
  neoplastic (chronic) I31.8
    acute I30.9
  obliterans, obliterating I31.0
  plastic I31.0
  pneumococcal I30.1

Pericarditis *(Continued)*
  postinfarction I24.1
  purulent I30.1
  rheumatic (active) (acute) (with effusion)
    (with pneumonia) I01.0
    with chorea (acute) (rheumatic)
      (Sydenham's) I02.0
    chronic or inactive (with chorea) I09.2
  rheumatoid —*see* Rheumatoid, carditis
  septic I30.1
  serofibrinous I30.8
  staphylococcal I30.1
  streptococcal I30.1
  suppurative I30.1
  syphilitic A52.06
  tuberculous A18.84
  uremic N18.9 *[I32]*
  viral I30.1
Pericardium, pericardial —*see* condition
Pericellulitis —*see* Cellulitis
Pericementitis (chronic) (suppurative) —*see also*
  Periodontitis
  acute K05.20
    generalized —*see* Peridontitis, aggressive,
      generalized
    localized —*see* Peridontitis, aggressive,
      localized
Perichondritis
  auricle —*see* Perichondritis, ear
  bronchus J98.09
  ear (external) H61.00-●
    acute H61.01-●
    chronic H61.02-●
  external auditory canal —*see* Perichondritis,
    ear
  larynx J38.7
    syphilitic A52.73
    typhoid A01.09
  nose J34.89
  pinna —*see* Perichondritis, ear
  trachea J39.8
Periclasia K05.4
Pericoronitis —*see* Periodontitis
Pericystitis N30.90
  with hematuria N30.91
Peridiverticulitis (intestine) K57.92
  cecum —*see* Diverticulitis, intestine, large
  colon —*see* Diverticulitis, intestine, large
  duodenum —*see* Diverticulitis, intestine,
    small
  intestine —*see* Diverticulitis, intestine
  jejunum —*see* Diverticulitis, intestine, small
  rectosigmoid —*see* Diverticulitis, intestine,
    large
  rectum —*see* Diverticulitis, intestine, large
  sigmoid —*see* Diverticulitis, intestine, large
Periendocarditis —*see* Endocarditis
Periepididymitis N45.1
Perifolliculitis L01.02
  abscedens, caput, scalp L66.3
  capitis, abscedens (et suffodiens) L66.3
  superficial pustular L01.02
Perihepatitis K65.8
Perilabyrinthitis (acute) —*see* subcategory H83.0
Perimeningitis —*see* Meningitis
Perimetritis —*see* Endometritis
Perimetrosalpingitis —*see* Salpingo-oophoritis
Perineocele N81.81
Perinephric, perinephritic —*see* condition
Perinephritis —*see also* Infection, kidney
  purulent —*see* Abscess, kidney
Perineum, perineal —*see* condition
Perineuritis NEC —*see* Neuralgia
Periodic —*see* condition
Periodontitis (chronic) (complex) (compound)
  (local) (simplex) K05.30
  acute K05.20
    generalized K05.229
      moderate K05.222
      severe K05.223
      slight K05.221

Periodontitis *(Continued)*
  acute *(Continued)*
    localized K05.219
      moderate K05.212
      severe K05.213
      slight K05.211
  apical K04.5
    acute (pulpal origin) K04.4
  generalized K05.329
    moderate K05.322
    severe K05.323
    slight K05.321
  localized K05.319
    moderate K05.312
    severe K05.313
    slight K05.311
Periodontoclasia K05.4
Periodontosis (juvenile) K05.4
Periods —*see also* Menstruation
  heavy N92.0
  irregular N92.6
  shortened intervals (irregular) N92.1
Perionychia —*see also* Cellulitis, digit
  with lymphangitis —*see* Lymphangitis, acute,
    digit
Perioophoritis —*see* Salpingo-oophoritis
Periorchitis N45.2
Periosteum, periosteal —*see* condition
Periostitis (albuminosa) (circumscribed)
  (diffuse) (infective) (monomelic) —*see also*
    Osteomyelitis
  alveolar M27.3
  alveolodental M27.3
  dental M27.3
  gonorrheal A54.43
  jaw (lower) (upper) M27.2
  orbit H05.03-●
  syphilitic A52.77
    congenital (early) A50.02 *[M90.80]*
    secondary A51.46
  tuberculous —*see* Tuberculosis, bone
  yaws (hypertrophic) (early) (late) A66.6
    [M90.80]
Periostosis (hyperplastic) —*see also* Disorder,
  bone, specified type NEC
  with osteomyelitis —*see* Osteomyelitis,
    specified type NEC
Peripartum
  cardiomyopathy O90.3
Periphlebitis —*see* Phlebitis
Periproctitis K62.89
Periprostatitis —*see* Prostatitis
Perirectal —*see* condition
Perirenal —*see* condition
Perisalpingitis —*see* Salpingo-oophoritis
Perisplenitis (infectional) D73.89
Peristalsis, visible or reversed R19.2
Peritendinitis —*see* Enthesopathy
Peritoneum, peritoneal —*see* condition
Peritonitis (adhesive) (bacterial) (fibrinous)
  (hemorrhagic) (idiopathic) (localized)
  (perforative) (primary) (with adhesions)
  (with effusion) K65.9
  with or following
    abscess K65.1
    ⯈ appendicitis
      ⯈ with perforation or rupture K35.32
      ⯈ generalized (*see also* Appendicitis) K35.20
      ⯈ localized (*see also* Appendicitis) K35.30
    diverticular disease (intestine) K57.80
      with bleeding K57.81
      ectopic or molar pregnancy O08.0
      large intestine K57.20
        with
          bleeding K57.21
          small intestine K57.40
            with bleeding K57.41
      small intestine K57.00
        with
          bleeding K57.01
          large intestine K57.40
            with bleeding K57.41

Peritonitis *(Continued)*
  acute (generalized) K65.0
  aseptic T81.61
  bile, biliary K65.3
  chemical T81.61
  chlamydial A74.81
  chronic proliferative K65.8
  complicating abortion —*see* Abortion, by
      type, complicated by, pelvic peritonitis
  congenital P78.1
  diaphragmatic K65.0
  diffuse K65.0
  diphtheritic A36.89
  disseminated K65.0
  due to
    bile K65.3
    foreign
      body or object accidentally left during
          a procedure (instrument) (sponge)
          (swab) T81.599
      substance accidentally left during a
          procedure (chemical) (powder)
          (talc) T81.61
    talc T81.61
    urine K65.8
  eosinophilic K65.8
    acute K65.0
  fibrocaseous (tuberculous) A18.31
  fibropurulent K65.0
  following ectopic or molar pregnancy
      O08.0
  general (ized) K65.0
  gonococcal A54.85
  meconium (newborn) P78.0
  neonatal P78.1
    meconium P78.0
  pancreatic K65.0
  paroxysmal, familial E85.0
    benign E85.0
  pelvic
    female N73.5
      acute N73.3
      chronic N73.4
        with adhesions N73.6
    male K65.0
  periodic, familial E85.0
  proliferative, chronic K65.8
  puerperal, postpartum, childbirth O85
  purulent K65.0
  septic K65.0
  specified NEC K65.8
  spontaneous bacterial K65.2
  subdiaphragmatic K65.0
  subphrenic K65.0
  suppurative K65.0
  syphilitic A52.74
    congenital (early) A50.08 *[K67]*
  talc T81.61
  tuberculous A18.31
  urine K65.8
Peritonsillar —*see* condition
Peritonsillitis J36
Perityphlitis K37
Periureteritis N28.89
Periurethral —*see* condition
Periurethritis (gangrenous) —*see* Urethritis
Periuterine —*see* condition
Perivaginitis —*see* Vaginitis
Perivasculitis, retinal H35.06-●
Perivasitis (chronic) N49.1
Perivesiculitis (seminal) —*see* Vesiculitis
Perlèche NEC K13.0
  due to
    candidiasis B37.83
    moniliasis B37.83
    riboflavin deficiency E53.0
    vitamin B2 (riboflavin) deficiency E53.0
Pernicious —*see* condition
Pernio, perniosis T69.1
Perpetrator (of abuse) —*see* Index to External
    Causes of Injury, Perpetrator

Persecution
  delusion F22
  social Z60.5
Perseveration (tonic) R48.8
Persistence, persistent (congenital)
  anal membrane Q42.3
    with fistula Q42.2
  arteria stapedia Q16.3
  atrioventricular canal Q21.2
  branchial cleft NOS Q18.2
    cyst Q18.0
    fistula Q18.0
    sinus Q18.0
  bulbus cordis in left ventricle Q21.8
  canal of Cloquet Q14.0
  capsule (opaque) Q12.8
  cilioretinal artery or vein Q14.8
  cloaca Q43.7
  communication —*see* Fistula, congenital
  convolutions
    aortic arch Q25.46
    fallopian tube Q50.6
    oviduct Q50.6
    uterine tube Q50.6
  double aortic arch Q25.45
  ductus arteriosus (Botalli) Q25.0
  fetal
    circulation P29.38
    form of cervix (uteri) Q51.828
    hemoglobin, hereditary (HPFH) D56.4
  foramen
    Botalli Q21.1
    ovale Q21.1
  Gartner's duct Q52.4
  hemoglobin, fetal (hereditary) (HPFH)
      D56.4
  hyaloid
    artery (generally incomplete) Q14.0
    system Q14.8
  hymen, in pregnancy or childbirth —*see*
      Pregnancy, complicated by, abnormal,
      vulva
  lanugo Q84.2
  left
    posterior cardinal vein Q26.8
    root with right arch of aorta Q25.49
    superior vena cava Q26.1
  Meckel's diverticulum Q43.0
    malignant —*see* Table of Neoplasms, small
        intestine, malignant
  mucosal disease (middle ear) —*see*
      Otitis, media, suppurative, chronic,
      tubotympanic
  nail(s), anomalous Q84.6
  omphalomesenteric duct Q43.0
  organ or site not listed —*see* Anomaly, by site
  ostium
    atrioventriculare commune Q21.2
    primum Q21.2
    secundum Q21.1
  ovarian rests in fallopian tube Q50.6
  pancreatic tissue in intestinal tract Q43.8
  primary (deciduous)
    teeth K00.6
    vitreous hyperplasia Q14.0
  pupillary membrane Q13.89
  rhesus (Rh)titer —*see* Complication(s),
      transfusion, incompatibility reaction, Rh
      (factor)
  right aortic arch Q25.47
  sinus
    urogenitalis
      female Q52.8
      male Q55.8
    venosus with imperfect incorporation in
        right auricle Q26.8
  thymus (gland) (hyperplasia) E32.0
  thyroglossal duct Q89.2
  thyrolingual duct Q89.2
  truncus arteriosus or communis Q20.0
  tunica vasculosa lentis Q12.2

Persistence, persistent *(Continued)*
  umbilical sinus Q64.4
  urachus Q64.4
  vitelline duct Q43.0
Person (with)
  admitted for clinical research, as a
      control subject (normal comparison)
      (participant) Z00.6
  awaiting admission to adequate facility
      elsewhere Z75.1
  concern (normal) about sick person in family
      Z63.6
  consulting on behalf of another Z71.0
  feigning illness Z76.5
  living (in)
    without
      adequate housing (heating) (space) Z59.1
      housing (permanent) (temporary) Z59.0
      person able to render necessary care
          Z74.2
      shelter Z59.0
    alone Z60.2
    boarding school Z59.3
    residential institution Z59.3
  on waiting list Z75.1
  sick or handicapped in family Z63.6
Personality (disorder) F60.9
  accentuation of traits (type A pattern) Z73.1
  affective F34.0
  aggressive F60.3
  amoral F60.2
  anacastic, anankastic F60.5
  antisocial F60.2
  anxious F60.6
  asocial F60.2
  asthenic F60.7
  avoidant F60.6
  borderline F60.3
  change due to organic condition (enduring)
      F07.0
  compulsive F60.5
  cycloid F34.0
  cyclothymic F34.0
  dependent F60.7
  depressive F34.1
  dissocial F60.2
  dual F44.81
  eccentric F60.89
  emotionally unstable F60.3
  expansive paranoid F60.0
  explosive F60.3
  fanatic F60.0
  haltlose type F60.89
  histrionic F60.4
  hyperthymic F34.0
  hypothymic F34.1
  hysterical F60.4
  immature F60.89
  inadequate F60.7
  labile (emotional) F60.3
  mixed (nonspecific) F60.89
  morally defective F60.2
  multiple F44.81
  narcissistic F60.81
  obsessional F60.5
  obsessive (-compulsive) F60.5
  organic F07.0
  overconscientious F60.5
  paranoid F60.0
  passive (-dependent) F60.7
  passive-aggressive F60.89
  pathologic F60.9
  pattern defect or disturbance F60.9
  pseudopsychopathic (organic) F07.0
  pseudoretarded (organic) F07.0
  psychoinfantile F60.4
  psychoneurotic NEC F60.89
  psychopathic F60.2
  querulant F60.0
  sadistic F60.89
  schizoid F60.1

► New   ⇒ Revised   ~~deleted~~ Deleted   ● Use Additional Character(s)

Personality (Continued)
  self-defeating F60.7
  sensitive paranoid F60.0
  sociopathic (amoral) (antisocial) (asocial)
      (dissocial) F60.2
  specified NEC F60.89
  type A Z73.1
  unstable (emotional) F60.3
Perthes' disease —see Legg-Calvé-Perthes
    disease
Pertussis (see also Whooping cough) A37.90
Perversion, perverted
  appetite F50.89
    psychogenic F50.89
  function
    pituitary gland E23.2
      posterior lobe E22.2
  sense of smell and taste R43.8
    psychogenic F45.8
  sexual —see Deviation, sexual
Pervious, congenital —see also Imperfect, closure
  ductus arteriosus Q25.0
Pes (congenital) —see also Talipes
  acquired —see also Deformity, limb, foot,
      specified NEC
    planus —see Deformity, limb, flat foot
  adductus Q66.89
  cavus Q66.7
  deformity NEC, acquired —see Deformity,
      limb, foot, specified NEC
  planus (acquired) (any degree) —see also
      Deformity, limb, flat foot
    rachitic sequelae (late effect) E64.3
  valgus Q66.6
Pest, pestis —see Plague
Petechia, petechiae R23.3
  newborn P54.5
Petechial typhus A75.9
Peter's anomaly Q13.4
Petit mal seizure —see Epilepsy, generalized,
    specified NEC
Petit's hernia —see Hernia, abdomen, specified
    site NEC
Petrellidosis B48.2
Petrositis H70.20-●
  acute H70.21-●
  chronic H70.22-●
Peutz-Jeghers disease or syndrome Q85.8
Peyronie's disease N48.6
PFAPA (periodic fever, aphthous stomatitis,
    pharyngitis, and adenopathy syndrome)
    M04.8
Pfeiffer's disease —see Mononucleosis,
    infectious
Phagedena (dry) (moist) (sloughing) —see also
    Gangrene
  geometric L88
  penis N48.29
  tropical —see Ulcer, skin
  vulva N76.6
Phagedenic —see condition
Phakoma H35.89
Phakomatosis —see also specific eponymous
    syndromes Q85.9
  Bourneville's Q85.1
  specified NEC Q85.8
Phantom limb syndrome (without pain) G54.7
  with pain G54.6
Pharyngeal pouch syndrome D82.1
Pharyngitis (acute) (catarrhal) (gangrenous)
    (infective) (malignant) (membranous)
    (phlegmonous) (pseudomembranous)
    (simple) (subacute) (suppurative)
    (ulcerative) (viral) J02.9
  with influenza, flu, or grippe —see Influenza,
      with, pharyngitis
  aphthous B08.5
  atrophic J31.2
  chlamydial A56.4
  chronic (atrophic) (granular) (hypertrophic)
      J31.2

Pharyngitis (Continued)
  coxsackievirus B08.5
  diphtheritic A36.0
  enteroviral vesicular B08.5
  follicular (chronic) J31.2
  fusospirochetal A69.1
  gonococcal A54.5
  granular (chronic) J31.2
  herpesviral B00.2
  hypertrophic J31.2
  infectional, chronic J31.2
  influenzal —see Influenza, with, respiratory
      manifestations NEC
  lymphonodular, acute (enteroviral) B08.8
  pneumococcal J02.8
  purulent J02.9
  putrid J02.9
  septic J02.0
  sicca J31.2
  specified organism NEC J02.8
  staphylococcal J02.8
  streptococcal J02.0
  syphilitic, congenital (early) A50.03
  tuberculous A15.8
  vesicular, enteroviral B08.5
  viral NEC J02.8
Pharyngoconjunctivitis, viral B30.2
Pharyngolaryngitis (acute) J06.0
  chronic J37.0
Pharyngoplegia J39.2
Pharyngotonsillitis, herpesviral B00.2
Pharyngotracheitis, chronic J42
Pharynx, pharyngeal —see condition
Phencyclidine-induced
  anxiety disorder F16.980
  bipolar and related disorder F16.94
  depressive disorder F16.94
  psychotic disorder F16.959
Phenomenon
  Arthus' —see Arthus' phenomenon
  jaw-winking Q07.8
  lupus erythematosus (LE) cell M32.9
  Raynaud's (secondary) I73.00
    with gangrene I73.01
  vasomotor R55
  vasospastic I73.9
  vasovagal R55
  Wenckebach's I44.1
Phenylketonuria E70.1
  classical E70.0
  maternal E70.1
Pheochromoblastoma
  specified site —see Neoplasm, malignant, by
      site
  unspecified site C74.10
Pheochromocytoma
  malignant
    specified site —see Neoplasm, malignant,
        by site
    unspecified site C74.10
  specified site —see Neoplasm, benign, by site
  unspecified site D35.00
Pheohyphomycosis —see Chromomycosis
Pheomycosis —see Chromomycosis
Phimosis (congenital) (due to infection) N47.1
  chancroidal A57
Phlebectasia —see also Varix
  congenital Q27.4
Phlebitis (infective) (pyemic) (septic)
    (suppurative) I80.9
  antepartum —see Thrombophlebitis,
      antepartum
  blue —see Phlebitis, leg, deep
  breast, superficial I80.8
  cavernous (venous) sinus —see Phlebitis,
      intracranial (venous) sinus
  cerebral (venous) sinus —see Phlebitis,
      intracranial (venous) sinus
  chest wall, superficial I80.8
  cranial (venous) sinus —see Phlebitis,
      intracranial (venous) sinus

Phlebitis (Continued)
  deep (vessels) —see Phlebitis, leg, deep
  due to implanted device —see Complications,
      by site and type, specified NEC
  during or resulting from a procedure
      T81.72
  femoral vein (superficial) I80.1-●
  femoropopliteal vein I80.0-●
  gestational —see Phlebopathy, gestational
  hepatic veins I80.8
  iliofemoral —see Phlebitis, femoral vein
  intracranial (venous) sinus (any) G08
    nonpyogenic I67.6
  intraspinal venous sinuses and veins G08
    nonpyogenic G95.19
  lateral (venous) sinus —see Phlebitis,
      intracranial (venous) sinus
  leg I80.3
    antepartum —see Thrombophlebitis,
        antepartum
    deep (vessels) NEC I80.20-●
      iliac I80.21-●
      popliteal vein I80.22-●
      specified vessel NEC I80.29-●
      tibial vein I80.23-●
    femoral vein (superficial) I80.1-●
    superficial (vessels) I80.0-●
  longitudinal sinus —see Phlebitis, intracranial
      (venous) sinus
  lower limb —see Phlebitis, leg
  migrans, migrating (superficial) I82.1
  pelvic
    with ectopic or molar pregnancy O08.0
    following ectopic or molar pregnancy
        O08.0
    puerperal, postpartum O87.1
  popliteal vein —see Phlebitis, leg, deep,
      popliteal
  portal (vein) K75.1
  postoperative T81.72
  pregnancy —see Thrombophlebitis,
      antepartum
  puerperal, postpartum, childbirth O87.0
    deep O87.1
    pelvic O87.1
    superficial O87.0
  retina —see Vasculitis, retina
  saphenous (accessory) (great) (long)
      (small) —see Phlebitis, leg, superficial
  sinus (meninges) —see Phlebitis, intracranial
      (venous) sinus
  specified site NEC I80.8
  syphilitic A52.09
  tibial vein —see Phlebitis, leg, deep, tibial
  ulcerative I80.9
    leg —see Phlebitis, leg
  umbilicus I80.8
  uterus (septic) —see Endometritis
  varicose (leg) (lower limb) —see Varix, leg,
      with, inflammation
Phlebofibrosis I87.8
Phleboliths I87.8
Phlebopathy
  gestational O22.9-●
  puerperal O87.9
Phlebosclerosis I87.8
Phlebothrombosis —see also Thrombosis
  antepartum —see Thrombophlebitis,
      antepartum
  pregnancy —see Thrombophlebitis,
      antepartum
  puerperal —see Thrombophlebitis,
      puerperal
Phlebotomus fever A93.1
Phlegmasia
  alba dolens O87.1
    nonpuerperal —see Phlebitis, femoral
        vein
  cerulea dolens —see Phlebitis, leg, deep
Phlegmon —see Abscess
Phlegmonous —see condition

P

Phlyctenulosis (allergic) (keratoconjunctivitis) (nontuberculous) —see also Keratoconjunctivitis
  cornea —see Keratoconjunctivitis
  tuberculous A18.52
Phobia, phobic F40.9
  animal F40.218
    spiders F40.210
  examination F40.298
  reaction F40.9
  simple F40.298
  social F40.10
    generalized F40.11
  specific (isolated) F40.298
    animal F40.218
      spiders F40.210
    blood F40.230
    injection F40.231
    injury F40.233
    men F40.290
    natural environment F40.228
      thunderstorms F40.220
    situational F40.248
      bridges F40.242
      closed in spaces F40.240
      flying F40.243
      heights F40.241
    specified focus NEC F40.298
    transfusion F40.231
    women F40.291
  specified NEC F40.8
    medical care NEC F40.232
  state F40.9
Phocas' disease —see Mastopathy, cystic
Phocomelia Q73.1
  lower limb —see Agenesis, leg, with foot present
  upper limb —see Agenesis, arm, with hand present
Phoria H50.50
Phosphate-losing tubular disorder N25.0
Phosphatemia E83.39
Phosphaturia E83.39
Photodermatitis (sun) L56.8
  chronic L57.8
  due to drug L56.8
  light other than sun L59.8
Photokeratitis H16.13-●
Photophobia H53.14-●
Photophthalmia —see Photokeratitis
Photopsia H53.19
Photoretinitis —see Retinopathy, solar
Photosensitivity, photosensitization (sun) skin L56.8
  light other than sun L59.8
Phrenitis —see Encephalitis
Phrynoderma (vitamin A deficiency) E50.8
Phthiriasis (pubis) B85.3
  with any infestation classifiable to B85.0-B85.2 B85.4
Phthirus infestation —see Phthiriasis
Phthisis —see also Tuberculosis
  bulbi (infectional) —see Disorder, globe, degenerated condition, atrophy
  eyeball (due to infection) —see Disorder, globe, degenerated condition, atrophy
Phycomycosis —see Zygomycosis
Physalopteriasis B81.8
Physical restraint status Z78.1
Phytobezoar T18.9
  intestine T18.3
  stomach T18.2
Pian —see Yaws
Pianoma A66.1
Pica F50.89
  in adults F50.89
  infant or child F98.3
Picking, nose F98.8
Pick-Niemann disease —see Niemann-Pick disease or syndrome

Pick's
  cerebral atrophy G31.01 [F02.80]
    with behavioral disturbance G31.01 [F02.81]
  disease or syndrome (brain) G31.01 [F02.80]
    with behavioral disturbance G31.01 [F02.81]
    brain G31.01 [F02.80]
      with behavioral disturbance G31.01 [F02.81]
    pericardium (pericardial pseudocirrhosis of liver) I31.1
  syndrome
    brain G31.01 [F02.80]
      with behavioral disturbance G31.01 [F02.81]
    of heart (pericardial pseudocirrhosis of liver) I31.1
Pickwickian syndrome E66.2
Piebaldism E70.39
Piedra (beard) (scalp) B36.8
  black B36.3
  white B36.2
Pierre Robin deformity or syndrome Q87.0
Pierson's disease or osteochondrosis M91.0
Pig-bel A05.2
Pigeon
  breast or chest (acquired) M95.4
    congenital Q67.7
      rachitic sequelae (late effect) E64.3
  breeder's disease or lung J67.2
  fancier's disease or lung J67.2
  toe —see Deformity, toe, specified NEC
Pigmentation (abnormal) (anomaly) L81.9
  conjunctiva H11.13-●
  cornea (anterior) H18.01-●
    posterior H18.05-●
    stromal H18.06-●
  diminished melanin formation NEC L81.6
  iron L81.8
  lids, congenital Q82.8
  limbus corneae —see Pigmentation, cornea
  metals L81.8
  optic papilla, congenital Q14.2
  retina, congenital (grouped) (nevoid) Q14.1
  scrotum, congenital Q82.8
  tattoo L81.8
Piles —see also Hemorrhoids K64.9
Pili
  annulati or torti (congenital) Q84.1
  incarnati L73.1
Pill roller hand (intrinsic) —see Parkinsonism
Pilomatrixoma —see Neoplasm, skin, benign
  malignant —see Neoplasm, skin, malignant
Pilonidal —see condition
Pimple R23.8
PIN —see Neoplasia, intraepithelial, prostate
Pinched nerve —see Neuropathy, entrapment
Pindborg tumor —see Cyst, calcifying odontogenic
Pineal body or gland —see condition
Pinealoblastoma C75.3
Pinealoma D44.5
  malignant C75.3
Pineoblastoma C75.3
Pineocytoma D44.5
Pinguecula H11.15-●
Pingueculitis H10.81-●
➡ Pinhole meatus —see also Stricture, urethra N35.919
Pink
  disease —see subcategory T56.1
  eye —see Conjunctivitis, acute, mucopurulent
Pinkus' disease (lichen nitidus) L44.1
Pinpoint
  meatus —see Stricture, urethra
  os (uteri) —see Stricture, cervix
Pins and needles R20.2
Pinta A67.9
  cardiovascular lesions A67.2
  chancre (primary) A67.0

Pinta (Continued)
  erythematous plaques A67.1
  hyperchromic lesions A67.1
  hyperkeratosis A67.1
  lesions A67.9
    cardiovascular A67.2
    hyperchromic A67.1
    intermediate A67.1
    late A67.2
    mixed A67.3
    primary A67.0
    skin (achromic) (cicatricial) (dyschromic) A67.2
      hyperchromic A67.1
      mixed (achromic and hyperchromic) A67.3
  papule (primary) A67.0
  skin lesions (achromic) (cicatricial) (dyschromic) A67.2
    hyperchromic A67.1
    mixed (achromic and hyperchromic) A67.3
  vitiligo A67.2
Pintids A67.1
Pinworm (disease) (infection) (infestation) B80
Piroplasmosis B60.0
Pistol wound —see Gunshot wound
Pitchers' elbow —see Derangement, joint, specified type NEC, elbow
Pithecoid pelvis Q74.2
  with disproportion (fetopelvic) O33.0
    causing obstructed labor O65.0
Pithiatism F48.8
Pitted —see Pitting
Pitting —see also Edema R60.9
  lip R60.0
  nail L60.8
  teeth K00.4
Pituitary gland —see condition
Pituitary-snuff-taker's disease J67.8
Pityriasis (capitis) L21.0
  alba L30.5
  circinata (et maculata) L42
  furfuracea L21.0
  Hebra's L26
  lichenoides L41.0
    chronica L41.1
    et varioliformis (acuta) L41.0
  maculata (et circinata) L30.5
  nigra B36.1
  pilaris, Hebra's L44.0
  rosea L42
  rotunda L44.8
  rubra (Hebra) pilaris L44.0
  simplex L30.5
  specified type NEC L30.5
  streptogenes L30.5
  versicolor (scrotal) B36.0
Placenta, placental —see Pregnancy, complicated by (care of) (management affected by), specified condition
Placentitis O41.14-●
Plagiocephaly Q67.3
Plague A20.9
  abortive A20.8
  ambulatory A20.8
  asymptomatic A20.8
  bubonic A20.0
  cellulocutaneous A20.1
  cutaneobubonic A20.1
  lymphatic gland A20.0
  meningitis A20.3
  pharyngeal A20.8
  pneumonic (primary) (secondary) A20.2
  pulmonary, pulmonic A20.2
  septicemic A20.7
  tonsillar A20.8
    septicemic A20.7
Planning, family
  contraception Z30.9
  procreation Z31.69

Pneumonia *(Continued)*
  Butyrivibrio (fibriosolvens) J15.8
  Candida B37.1
  caseous —*see* Tuberculosis, pulmonary
  catarrhal —*see* Pneumonia, broncho
  chlamydial J16.0
    congenital P23.1
  cholesterol J84.89
  cirrhotic (chronic) —*see* Fibrosis, lung
  Clostridium (haemolyticum) (novyi) J15.8
  confluent —*see* Pneumonia, broncho
  congenital (infective) P23.9
    due to
      bacterium NEC P23.6
      Chlamydia P23.1
      Escherichia coli P23.4
      Haemophilus influenzae P23.6
      infective organism NEC P23.8
      Klebsiella pneumoniae P23.6
      Mycoplasma P23.6
      Pseudomonas P23.5
      Staphylococcus P23.2
      Streptococcus (except group B) P23.6
        group B P23.3
      viral agent P23.0
    specified NEC P23.8
  croupous —*see* Pneumonia, lobar
  cryptogenic organizing J84.116
  cytomegalic inclusion B25.0
  cytomegaloviral B25.0
  deglutition —*see* Pneumonia, aspiration
  desquamative interstitial J84.117
  diffuse —*see* Pneumonia, broncho
  diplococcal, diplococcus (broncho-) (lobar) J13
  disseminated (focal) —*see* Pneumonia, broncho
  Eaton's agent J15.7
  embolic, embolism —*see* Embolism, pulmonary
  Enterobacter J15.6
  eosinophilic J82
  Escherichia coli (E. coli) J15.5
  Eubacterium J15.8
  fibrinous —*see* Pneumonia, lobar
  fibroid, fibrous (chronic) —*see* Fibrosis, lung
  Friedländer's bacillus J15.0
  Fusobacterium (nucleatum) J15.8
  gangrenous J85.0
  giant cell (measles) B05.2
  gonococcal A54.84
  gram-negative bacteria NEC J15.6
    anaerobic J15.8
  Hemophilus influenzae (broncho) (lobar) J14
  human metapneumovirus J12.3
  hypostatic (broncho) (lobar) J18.2
  in (due to)
    actinomycosis A42.0
    adenovirus J12.0
    anthrax A22.1
    ascariasis B77.81
    aspergillosis B44.9
    Bacillus anthracis A22.1
    Bacterium anitratum J15.6
    candidiasis B37.1
    chickenpox B01.2
    Chlamydia J16.0
      neonatal P23.1
    coccidioidomycosis B38.2
      acute B38.0
      chronic B38.1
    cytomegalovirus disease B25.0
    Diplococcus (pneumoniae) J13
    Eaton's agent J15.7
    Enterobacter J15.6
    Escherichia coli (E. coli) J15.5
    Friedländer's bacillus J15.0
    fumes and vapors (chemical) (inhalation) J68.0
    gonorrhea A54.84
    Hemophilus influenzae (H. influenzae) J14

Pneumonia *(Continued)*
  in *(Continued)*
    Herellea J15.6
    histoplasmosis B39.2
      acute B39.0
      chronic B39.1
    human metapneumovirus J12.3
    Klebsiella (pneumoniae) J15.0
    measles B05.2
    Mycoplasma (pneumoniae) J15.7
    nocardiosis, nocardiasis A43.0
    ornithosis A70
    parainfluenza virus J12.2
    pleuro-pneumonia-like-organism (PPLO) J15.7
    pneumococcus J13
    pneumocystosis (Pneumocystis carinii) (Pneumocystis jiroveci) B59
    Proteus J15.6
    Pseudomonas NEC J15.1
      pseudomallei A24.1
    psittacosis A70
    Q fever A78
    respiratory syncytial virus J12.1
    rheumatic fever I00 *[J17]*
    rubella B06.81
    Salmonella (infection) A02.22
      typhi A01.03
    schistosomiasis B65.9 *[J17]*
    Serratia marcescens J15.6
    specified
      bacterium NEC J15.8
      organism NEC J16.8
    spirochetal NEC A69.8
    Staphylococcus J15.20
      aureus (methicillin susceptible) (MSSA) J15.211
        methicillin resistant (MRSA) J15.212
      specified NEC J15.29
    Streptococcus J15.4
      group B J15.3
      pneumoniae J13
      specified NEC J15.4
    toxoplasmosis B58.3
    tularemia A21.2
    typhoid (fever) A01.03
    varicella B01.2
    virus —*see* Pneumonia, viral
    whooping cough A37.91
      due to
        Bordetella parapertussis A37.11
        Bordetella pertussis A37.01
        specified NEC A37.81
    Yersinia pestis A20.2
  inhalation of food or vomit —*see* Pneumonia, aspiration
  interstitial J84.9
    chronic J84.111
    desquamative J84.117
    due to
      collagen vascular disease J84.17
      known underlying cause J84.17
    idiopathic NOS J84.111
    in disease classified elsewhere J84.17
    lymphocytic (due to collagen vascular disease) (in diseases classified elsewhere) J84.17
    lymphoid J84.2
    non-specific J84.89
      due to
        collagen vascular disease J84.17
        known underlying cause J84.17
      idiopathic J84.113
      in diseases classified elsewhere J84.17
    plasma cell B59
    pseudomonas J15.1
    usual J84.112
      due to collagen vascular disease J84.17
      idiopathic J84.112
      in diseases classified elsewhere J84.17

Pneumonia *(Continued)*
  Klebsiella (pneumoniae) J15.0
  lipid, lipoid (exogenous) J69.1
    endogenous J84.89
  lobar (disseminated) (double) (interstitial) J18.1
    bacterial J15.9
      specified NEC J15.8
    chronic —*see* Fibrosis, lung
    Escherichia coli (E. coli) J15.5
    Friedländer's bacillus J15.0
    Hemophilus influenzae J14
    hypostatic J18.2
    Klebsiella (pneumoniae) J15.0
    pneumococcal J13
    Proteus J15.6
    Pseudomonas J15.1
    specified organism NEC J16.8
    staphylococcal —*see* Pneumonia, staphylococcal
    streptococcal NEC J15.4
    Streptococcus pneumoniae J13
    viral, virus —*see* Pneumonia, viral
  lobular —*see* Pneumonia, broncho
  Löffler's J82
  lymphoid interstitial J84.2
  massive —*see* Pneumonia, lobar
  meconium P24.01
  MRSA (Methicillin resistant Staphylococcus aureus) J15.212
  MSSA (methicillin susceptible Staphylococcus aureus) J15.211
  multilobar —*see* Pneumonia, by type
  Mycoplasma (pneumoniae) J15.7
  necrotic J85.0
  neonatal P23.9
    aspiration —*see* Aspiration, by substance, with pneumonia
  nitrogen dioxide J68.0
  organizing J84.89
    due to
      collagen vascular disease J84.17
      known underlying cause J84.17
    in diseases classified elsewhere J84.17
  orthostatic J18.2
  parainfluenza virus J12.2
  parenchymatous —*see* Fibrosis, lung
  passive J18.2
  patchy —*see* Pneumonia, broncho
  Peptococcus J15.8
  Peptostreptococcus J15.8
  plasma cell (of infants) B59
  pleurolobar —*see* Pneumonia, lobar
  pleuro-pneumonia-like organism (PPLO) J15.7
  pneumococcal (broncho) (lobar) J13
  Pneumocystis (carinii) (jiroveci) B59
  postinfectional NEC B99 *[J17]*
  postmeasles B05.2
  Proteus J15.6
  Pseudomonas J15.1
  psittacosis A70
  radiation J70.0
  respiratory syncytial virus J12.1
  resulting from a procedure J95.89
  rheumatic I00 *[J17]*
  Salmonella (arizonae) (cholerae-suis) (enteritidis) (typhimurium) A02.22
    typhi A01.03
    typhoid fever A01.03
  SARS-associated coronavirus J12.81
  segmented, segmental —*see* Pneumonia, broncho-•
  Serratia marcescens J15.6
  specified NEC J18.8
    bacterium NEC J15.8
    organism NEC J16.8
    virus NEC J12.89
  spirochetal NEC A69.8

▶ New   ➠ Revised   ~~deleted~~ Deleted   ● Use Additional Character(s)

Pneumonia (Continued)
staphylococcal (broncho) (lobar) J15.20
   aureus (methicillin susceptible) (MSSA)
      J15.211
         methicillin resistant (MRSA) J15.212
      specified NEC J15.29
static, stasis J18.2
streptococcal NEC (broncho) (lobar) J15.4
   group
      A J15.4
      B J15.3
      specified NEC J15.4
Streptococcus pneumoniae J13
syphilitic, congenital (early) A50.04
traumatic (complication) (early) (secondary)
   T79.8
tuberculous (any) —see Tuberculosis,
   pulmonary
tularemic A21.2
varicella B01.2
Veillonella J15.8
ventilator associated J95.851
viral, virus (broncho) (interstitial) (lobar) J12.9
   adenoviral J12.0
   congenital P23.0
   human metapneumovirus J12.3
   parainfluenza J12.2
   respiratory syncytial J12.1
   SARS-associated coronavirus J12.81
   specified NEC J12.89
white (congenital) A50.04
Pneumonic —see condition
Pneumonitis (acute) (primary) —see also
   Pneumonia
air-conditioner J67.7
allergic (due to) J67.9
   organic dust NEC J67.8
   red cedar dust J67.8
   sequoiosis J67.8
   wood dust J67.8
aspiration J69.0
   due to
      anesthesia J95.4
         during
            labor and delivery O74.0
            pregnancy O29.01-●
            puerperium O89.01
      fumes or gases J68.0
   obstetric O74.0
chemical (due to gases, fumes or vapors)
   (inhalation) J68.0
   due to anesthesia J95.4
cholesterol J84.89
chronic —see Fibrosis, lung
congenital rubella P35.0
crack (cocaine) J68.0
due to
   beryllium J68.0
   cadmium J68.0
   crack (cocaine) J68.0
   detergent J69.8
   fluorocarbon-polymer J68.0
   food, vomit (aspiration) J69.0
   fumes or vapors J68.0
   gases, fumes or vapors (inhalation) J68.0
   inhalation
      blood J69.8
      essences J69.1
      food (regurgitated), milk, vomit
         J69.0
      oils, essences J69.1
      saliva J69.0
      solids, liquids NEC J69.8
   manganese J68.0
   nitrogen dioxide J68.0
   oils, essences J69.1
   solids, liquids NEC J69.8
   toxoplasmosis (acquired) B58.3
      congenital P37.1
   vanadium J68.0
   ventilator J95.851

Pneumonitis (Continued)
eosinophilic J82
hypersensitivity J67.9
   air conditioner lung J67.7
   bagassosis J67.1
   bird fancier's lung J67.2
   farmer's lung J67.0
   maltworker's lung J67.4
   maple bark-stripper's lung J67.6
   mushroom worker's lung J67.5
   specified organic dust NEC J67.8
   suberosis J67.3
interstitial (chronic) J84.89
   acute J84.114
   lymphoid J84.2
   non-specific J84.89
      idiopathic J84.113
lymphoid, interstitial J84.2
meconium P24.01
postanesthetic J95.4
   correct substance properly administered —
      see Table of Drugs and Chemcials, by
      drug, adverse effect
   in labor and delivery O74.0
   in pregnancy O29.01-●
   obstetric O74.0
   overdose or wrong substance given or taken
      (by accident) —see Table of Drugs and
      Chemicals, by drug, poisoning
   postpartum, puerperal O89.01
postoperative J95.4
   obstetric O74.0
radiation J70.0
rubella, congenital P35.0
ventilation (air-conditioning) J67.7
ventilator associated J95.851
wood-dust J67.8
Pneumonoconiosis —see Pneumoconiosis
Pneumoparotid K11.8
Pneumopathy NEC J98.4
alveolar J84.09
due to organic dust NEC J66.8
parietoalveolar J84.09
Pneumopericarditis —see also Pericarditis
acute I30.9
Pneumopericardium —see also Pericarditis
congenital P25.3
newborn P25.3
traumatic (post) —see Injury, heart
Pneumophagia (psychogenic) F45.8
Pneumopleurisy, pneumopleuritis —see also
   Pneumonia J18.8
Pneumopyopericardium I30.1
Pneumopyothorax —see Pyopneumothorax
with fistula J86.0
Pneumorrhagia —see also Hemorrhage, lung
tuberculous —see Tuberculosis, pulmonary
Pneumothorax NOS J93.9
acute J93.83
chronic J93.81
congenital P25.1
perinatal period P25.1
postprocedural J95.811
specified NEC J93.83
spontaneous NOS J93.83
   newborn P25.1
   primary J93.11
   secondary J93.12
   tension J93.0
tense valvular, infectional J93.0
tension (spontaneous) J93.0
traumatic S27.0
   with hemothorax S27.2
tuberculous —see Tuberculosis, pulmonary
Podagra —see also Gout M10.9
Podencephalus Q01.9
Poikilocytosis R71.8
Poikiloderma L81.6
Civatte's L57.3
congenital Q82.8
vasculare atrophicans L94.5

Poikilodermatomyositis M33.10
with
   myopathy M33.12
   respiratory involvement M33.11
   specified organ involvement NEC M33.19
Pointed ear (congenital) Q17.3
Poison ivy, oak, sumac or other plant
   dermatitis (allergic) (contact) L23.7
Poisoning (acute) —see also Table of Drugs and
   Chemicals
algae and toxins T65.82-●
Bacillus B (aertrycke) (cholerae (suis))
   (paratyphosus) (suipestifer) A02.9
   botulinus A05.1
bacterial toxins A05.9
berries, noxious —see Poisoning, food,
   noxious, berries
botulism A05.1
ciguatera fish T61.0-●
Clostridium botulinum A05.1
death-cap (Amanita phalloides) (Amanita
   verna) —see Poisoning, food, noxious,
   mushrooms
drug —see Table of Drugs and Chemicals, by
   drug, poisoning
epidemic, fish (noxious) —see Poisoning,
   seafood
   bacterial A05.9
fava bean D55.0
fish (noxious) T61.9-●
   bacterial —see Intoxication, foodborne, by
      agent
   ciguatera fish —see Poisoning, ciguatera
      fish
   scombroid fish —see Poisoning, scombroid
      fish
   specified type NEC T61.77-●
food (acute) (diseased) (infected) (noxious)
   NEC T62.9-●
   bacterial —see Intoxication, foodborne, by
      agent
   due to
      Bacillus (aertrycke) (choleraesuis)
         (paratyphosus) (suipestifer) A02.9
         botulinus A05.1
      Clostridium (perfringens) (Welchii)
         A05.2
      salmonella (aertrycke) (callinarum)
         (choleraesuis) (enteritidis)
         (paratyphi) (suipestifer) A02.9
         with
            gastroenteritis A02.0
            sepsis A02.1
      staphylococcus A05.0
      Vibrio
         parahaemolyticus A05.3
         vulnificus A05.5
   noxious or naturally toxic T62.9-●
      berries —see subcategory T62.1-●
      fish —see Poisoning, seafood
      mushrooms —see subcategory T62.0X-●
      plants NEC —see subcategory T62.2X-●
      seafood —see Poisoning, seafood
      specified NEC —see subcategory
         T62.8X-●
ichthyotoxism —see Poisoning, seafood
kreotoxism, food A05.9
latex T65.81-●
lead T56.0-●
mushroom —see Poisoning, food, noxious,
   mushroom
mussels —see also Poisoning, shellfish
   bacterial —see Intoxication, foodborne, by
      agent
nicotine (tobacco) T65.2-●
noxious foodstuffs —see Poisoning, food,
   noxious
plants, noxious —see Poisoning, food,
   noxious, plants NEC
ptomaine —see Poisoning, food
radiation J70.0

Poisoning (Continued)
  Salmonella (arizonae) (cholerae-suis)
      (enteritidis) (typhimurium) A02.9
  scombroid fish T61.1-●
  seafood (noxious) T61.9-●
    bacterial —see Intoxication, foodborne, by
        agent
    fish —see Poisoning, fish
    shellfish —see Poisoning, shellfish
    specified NEC —see subcategory T61.8X-●
  shellfish (amnesic) (azaspiracid) (diarrheic)
      (neurotoxic) (noxious) (paralytic)
      T61.78-●
    bacterial —see Intoxication, foodborne, by
        agent
    ciguatera mollusk —see Poisoning,
        ciguatera fish
  specified substance NEC T65.891
  Staphylococcus, food A05.0
  tobacco (nicotine) T65.2-●
  water E87.79
Poker spine —see Spondylitis, ankylosing
Poland syndrome Q79.8
Polioencephalitis (acute) (bulbar) A80.9
  inferior G12.22
  influenzal —see Influenza, with,
      encephalopathy
  superior hemorrhagic (acute) (Wernicke's)
      E51.2
  Wernicke's E51.2
Polioencephalomyelitis (acute) (anterior) A80.9
  with beriberi E51.2
Polioencephalopathy, superior hemorrhagic
      E51.2
  with
    beriberi E51.11
    pellagra E52
Poliomeningoencephalitis —see
      Meningoencephalitis
Poliomyelitis (acute) (anterior) (epidemic)
      A80.9
  with paralysis (bulbar) —see Poliomyelitis,
      paralytic
  abortive A80.4
  ascending (progressive) —see Poliomyelitis,
      paralytic
  bulbar (paralytic) —see Poliomyelitis,
      paralytic
  congenital P35.8
  nonepidemic A80.9
  nonparalytic A80.4
  paralytic A80.30
    specified NEC A80.39
    vaccine-associated A80.0
    wild virus
      imported A80.1
      indigenous A80.2
  spinal, acute A80.9
Poliosis (eyebrow) (eyelashes) L67.1
  circumscripta, acquired L67.1
Pollakiuria R35.0
  psychogenic F45.8
Pollinosis J30.1
Pollitzer's disease L73.2
Polyadenitis —see also Lymphadenitis
  malignant A20.0
Polyalgia M79.89
Polyangiitis M30.0
  microscopic M31.7
  overlap syndrome M30.8
Polyarteritis
  microscopic M31.7
  nodosa M30.0
    with lung involvement M30.1
    juvenile M30.2
    related condition NEC M30.8
Polyarthralgia —see Pain, joint
Polyarthritis, polyarthropathy —see also
      Arthritis M13.0
  due to or associated with other specified
      conditions —see Arthritis

Polyarthritis, polyarthropathy (Continued)
  epidemic (Australian) (with exanthema)
      B33.1
  infective —see Arthritis, pyogenic or
      pyemic
  inflammatory M06.4
  juvenile (chronic) (seronegative)
      M08.3
  migratory —see Fever, rheumatic
  rheumatic, acute —see Fever, rheumatic
Polyarthrosis M15.9
  post-traumatic M15.3
  primary M15.0
  specified NEC M15.8
Polycarential syndrome of infancy E40
Polychondritis (atrophic) (chronic) —see also
      Disorder, cartilage, specified type
      NEC
  relapsing M94.1
Polycoria Q13.2
Polycystic (disease)
  degeneration, kidney Q61.3
    autosomal dominant (adult type) Q61.2
    autosomal recessive (infantile type) NEC
        Q61.19
  kidney Q61.3
    autosomal
      dominant Q61.2
      recessive NEC Q61.19
    autosomal dominant (adult type) Q61.2
    autosomal recessive (childhood type) NEC
        Q61.19
    infantile type NEC Q61.19
  liver Q44.6
  lung J98.4
    congenital Q33.0
  ovary, ovaries E28.2
  spleen Q89.09
Polycythemia (secondary) D75.1
  acquired D75.1
  benign (familial) D75.0
  due to
    donor twin P61.1
    erythropoietin D75.1
    fall in plasma volume D75.1
    high altitude D75.1
    maternal-fetal transfusion P61.1
    stress D75.1
  emotional D75.1
  erythropoietin D75.1
  familial (benign) D75.0
  Gaisböck's (hypertonica) D75.1
  high altitude D75.1
  hypertonica D75.1
  hypoxemic D75.1
  neonatorum P61.1
  nephrogenous D75.1
  relative D75.1
  secondary D75.1
  spurious D75.1
  stress D75.1
  vera D45
Polycytosis cryptogenica D75.1
Polydactylism, polydactyly Q69.9
  toes Q69.2
Polydipsia R63.1
Polydystrophy, pseudo-Hurler E77.0
Polyembryoma —see Neoplasm, malignant,
      by site
Polyglandular
  deficiency E31.0
  dyscrasia E31.9
  dysfunction E31.9
  syndrome E31.8
Polyhydramnios O40.-●
Polymastia Q83.1
Polymenorrhea N92.0
Polymyalgia M35.3
  arteritica, giant cell M31.5
  rheumatica M35.3
    with giant cell arteritis M31.5

Polymyositis (acute) (chronic) (hemorrhagic)
      M33.20
  with
    myopathy M33.22
    respiratory involvement M33.21
    skin involvement —see
        Dermatopolymyositis
    specified organ involvement NEC M33.29
  ossificans (generalisata) (progressiva) —see
      Myositis, ossificans, progressiva
Polyneuritis, polyneuritic —see also
      Polyneuropathy
  acute (post-)infective G61.0
  alcoholic G62.1
  cranialis G52.7
  demyelinating, chronic inflammatory (CIDP)
      G61.81
  diabetic —see Diabetes, polyneuropathy
  diphtheritic A36.83
  due to lack of vitamin NEC E56.9 [G63]
  endemic E51.11
  erythredema —see subcategory T56.1
  febrile, acute G61.0
  hereditary ataxic G60.1
  idiopathic, acute G61.0
  infective (acute) G61.0
  inflammatory, chronic demyelinating (CIDP)
      G61.81
  nutritional E63.9 [G63]
  postinfective (acute) G61.0
  specified NEC G62.89
Polyneuropathy (peripheral) G62.9
  alcoholic G62.1
  amyloid (Portuguese) E85.1 [G63]
    transthyretin-related (ATTR) familial E85.1
  arsenical G62.2
  critical illness G62.81
  demyelinating, chronic inflammatory (CIDP)
      G61.81
  diabetic —see Diabetes, polyneuropathy
  drug-induced G62.0
  hereditary G60.9
    specified NEC G60.8
  idiopathic G60.9
    progressive G60.3
  in (due to)
    alcohol G62.1
      sequelae G65.2
    amyloidosis, familial (Portuguese) E85.1
        [G63]
    antitetanus serum G61.1
    arsenic G62.2
      sequelae G65.2
    avitaminosis NEC E56.9 [G63]
    beriberi E51.11
    collagen vascular disease NEC M35.9 [G63]
    deficiency (of)
      B (-complex) vitamins E53.9 [G63]
      vitamin B6 E53.1 [G63]
    diabetes —see Diabetes, polyneuropathy
    diphtheria A36.83
    drug or medicament G62.0
      correct substance properly
          administered —see Table of Drugs
          and Chemicals, by drug, adverse
          effect
      overdose or wrong substance given
          or taken —see Table of Drugs and
          Chemicals, by drug, poisoning
    endocrine disease NEC E34.9 [G63]
    herpes zoster B02.23
    hypoglycemia E16.2 [G63]
    infectious
      disease NEC B99 [G63]
      mononucleosis B27.91
    lack of vitamin NEC E56.9 [G63]
    lead G62.2
      sequelae G65.2
    leprosy A30.9 [G63]
    Lyme disease A69.22
    metabolic disease NEC E88.9 [G63]

▶ New   ⇒ Revised   ~~deleted~~ Deleted   ● Use Additional Character(s)

Polyneuropathy *(Continued)*
  in *(Continued)*
    microscopic polyangiitis M31.7 *[G63]*
    mumps B26.84
    neoplastic disease —*see also* Neoplasm
      D49.9 *[G63]*
    nutritional deficiency NEC E63.9 *[G63]*
    organophosphate compounds G62.2
      sequelae G65.2
    parasitic disease NEC B89 *[G63]*
    pellagra E52 *[G63]*
    polyarteritis nodosa M30.0
    porphyria E80.20 *[G63]*
    radiation G62.82
    rheumatoid arthritis —*see* Rheumatoid,
      polyneuropathy
    sarcoidosis D86.89
    serum G61.1
    syphilis (late) A52.15
      congenital A50.43
    systemic
      connective tissue disorder M35.9 *[G63]*
      lupus erythematosus M32.19
    toxic agent NEC G62.2
      sequelae G65.2
    transthyretin-related (ATTR) familial
      amyloid E85.1
    triorthocresyl phosphate G62.2
      sequelae G65.2
    tuberculosis A17.89
    uremia N18.9 *[G63]*
    vitamin B12 deficiency E53.8 *[G63]*
      with anemia (pernicious) D51.0
        [G63]
        due to dietary deficiency D51.3
          [G63]
    zoster B02.23
  inflammatory G61.9
    chronic demyelinating (CIDP) G61.81
    sequelae G65.1
    specified NEC G61.89
  lead G62.2
    sequelae G65.2
  nutritional NEC E63.9 *[G63]*
  postherpetic (zoster) B02.23
  progressive G60.3
  radiation-induced G62.82
  sensory (hereditary) (idiopathic) G60.8
  specified NEC G62.89
  syphilitic (late) A52.15
    congenital A50.43
Polyopia H53.8
Polyorchism, polyorchidism Q55.21
Polyosteoarthritis —*see also* Osteoarthritis,
  generalized M15.9-•
  post-traumatic M15.3
  specified NEC M15.8
Polyostotic fibrous dysplasia Q78.1
Polyotia Q17.0
Polyp, polypus
  accessory sinus J33.8
  adenocarcinoma in —*see* Neoplasm,
    malignant, by site
  adenocarcinoma in situ in —*see* Neoplasm, in
    situ, by site
  adenoid tissue J33.0
  adenomatous —*see also* Neoplasm, benign,
    by site
    adenocarcinoma in —*see* Neoplasm,
      malignant, by site
    adenocarcinoma in situ in —*see* Neoplasm,
      in situ, by site
    carcinoma in —*see* Neoplasm, malignant,
      by site
    carcinoma in situ in —*see* Neoplasm, in
      situ, by site
    multiple —*see* Neoplasm, benign
      adenocarcinoma in —*see* Neoplasm,
        malignant, by site
      adenocarcinoma in situ in —*see*
        Neoplasm, in situ, by site

Polyp, polypus *(Continued)*
  antrum J33.8
  anus, anal (canal) K62.0
  Bartholin's gland N84.3
  bladder D41.4
  carcinoma in —*see* Neoplasm, malignant, by
    site
  carcinoma in situ in —*see* Neoplasm, in situ,
    by site
  cecum D12.0
  cervix (uteri) N84.1
    in pregnancy or childbirth —*see* Pregnancy,
      complicated by, abnormal, cervix
    mucous N84.1
    nonneoplastic N84.1
  choanal J33.0
  cholesterol K82.4
  clitoris N84.3
  colon K63.5
    adenomatous D12.6
    ascending D12.2
    cecum D12.0
    descending D12.4
    inflammatory K51.40
      with
        abscess K51.414
        complication K51.419
          specified NEC K51.418
        fistula K51.413
        intestinal obstruction K51.412
        rectal bleeding K51.411
    sigmoid D12.5
    transverse D12.3
  corpus uteri N84.0
  dental K04.01
    irreversible K04.02
    reversible K04.01
  duodenum K31.7
  ear (middle) H74.4-•
  endometrium N84.0
  ethmoidal (sinus) J33.8
  fallopian tube N84.8
  female genital tract N84.9
    specified NEC N84.8
  frontal (sinus) J33.8
  gallbladder K82.4
  gingiva, gum K06.8
  labia, labium (majus) (minus) N84.3
  larynx (mucous) J38.1
    adenomatous D14.1
  malignant —*see* Neoplasm, malignant, by site
  maxillary (sinus) J33.8
  middle ear —*see* Polyp, ear (middle)
  myometrium N84.0
  nares
    anterior J33.9
    posterior J33.0
  nasal (mucous) J33.9
    cavity J33.0
    septum J33.0
  nasopharyngeal J33.0
  nose (mucous) J33.9
  oviduct N84.8
  pharynx J39.2
  placenta O90.89
  prostate —*see* Enlargement, enlarged,
    prostate
  pudenda, pudendum N84.3
  pulpal (dental) K04.01
    irreversible K04.02
    reversible K04.01
  rectum (nonadenomatous) K62.1
    adenomatous —*see* Polyp, adenomatous
  septum (nasal) J33.0
  sinus (accessory) (ethmoidal) (frontal)
    (maxillary) (sphenoidal) J33.8
  sphenoidal (sinus) J33.8
  stomach K31.7
    adenomatous D13.1
  tube, fallopian N84.8
  turbinate, mucous membrane J33.8

Polyp, polypus *(Continued)*
  umbilical, newborn P83.6
  ureter N28.89
  urethra N36.2
  uterus (body) (corpus) (mucous) N84.0
    cervix N84.1
    in pregnancy or childbirth —*see* Pregnancy,
      complicated by, tumor, uterus
  vagina N84.2
  vocal cord (mucous) J38.1
  vulva N84.3
Polyphagia R63.2
Polyploidy Q92.7
Polypoid —*see* condition
Polyposis —*see also* Polyp
  coli (adenomatous) D12.6
    adenocarcinoma in C18.9
    adenocarcinoma in situ in —*see* Neoplasm,
      in situ, by site
    carcinoma in C18.9
  colon (adenomatous) D12.6
  familial D12.6
    adenocarcinoma in situ in —*see* Neoplasm,
      in situ, by site
  intestinal (adenomatous) D12.6
  malignant lymphomatous C83.1
  multiple, adenomatous —*see also* Neoplasm,
    benign D36.9
Polyradiculitis —*see* Polyneuropathy
Polyradiculoneuropathy (acute) (postinfective)
  (segmentally demyelinating) G61.0
Polyserositis
  due to pericarditis I31.1
  pericardial I31.1
  periodic, familial E85.0
  tuberculous A19.9
    acute A19.1
    chronic A19.8
Polysplenia syndrome Q89.09
Polysyndactyly —*see also* Syndactylism,
  syndactyly Q70.4
Polytrichia L68.3
Polyunguia Q84.6
Polyuria R35.8
  nocturnal R35.1
  psychogenic F45.8
Pompe's disease (glycogen storage) E74.02
Pompholyx L30.1
Poncet's disease (tuberculous rheumatism)
  A18.09
Pond fracture —*see* Fracture, skull
Ponos B55.0
Pons, pontine —*see* condition
Poor
  aesthetic of existing restoration of tooth
    K08.56
  contractions, labor O62.2
  gingival margin to tooth restoration K08.51
  personal hygiene R46.0
  prenatal care, affecting management of
    pregnancy —*see* Pregnancy, complicated
    by, insufficient, prenatal care
  sucking reflex (newborn) R29.2
  urinary stream R39.12
  vision NEC H54.7
Poradenitis, nostras inguinalis or venerea A55
Porencephaly (congenital) (developmental)
  (true) Q04.6
  acquired G93.0
  nondevelopmental G93.0
  traumatic (post) F07.89
Porocephaliasis B88.8
Porokeratosis Q82.8
Poroma, eccrine —*see* Neoplasm, skin, benign
Porphyria (South African) E80.20
  acquired E80.20
  acute intermittent (hepatic) (Swedish) E80.21

Porphyria *(Continued)*
  cutanea tarda (hereditary) (symptomatic) E80.1
  due to drugs E80.20
    correct substance properly administered —
      see Table of Drugs and Chemicals, by
      drug, adverse effect
    overdose or wrong substance given
      or taken —*see* Table of Drugs and
      Chemicals, by drug, poisoning
  erythropoietic (congenital) (hereditary) E80.0
  hepatocutaneous type E80.1
  secondary E80.20
  toxic NEC E80.20
  variegata E80.20
Porphyrinuria —*see* Porphyria
Porphyruria —*see* Porphyria
Portal —*see* condition
Port wine nevus, mark, or stain Q82.5
Posadas-Wernicke disease B38.9
Positive
  culture (nonspecific)
    blood R78.81
    bronchial washings R84.5
    cerebrospinal fluid R83.5
    cervix uteri R87.5
    nasal secretions R84.5
    nipple discharge R89.5
    nose R84.5
      staphylococcus (Methicillin susceptible)
        Z22.321
        Methicillin resistant Z22.322
    peritoneal fluid R85.5
    pleural fluid R84.5
    prostatic secretions R86.5
    saliva R85.5
    seminal fluid R86.5
    sputum R84.5
    synovial fluid R89.5
    throat scrapings R84.5
    urine R82.79
    vagina R87.5
    vulva R87.5
    wound secretions R89.5
  PPD (skin test) R76.11
  serology for syphilis A53.0
    with signs or symptoms - code as Syphilis,
      by site and stage
    false R76.8
  skin test, tuberculin (without active
    tuberculosis) R76.11
  test, human immunodeficiency virus (HIV)
    R75
  VDRL A53.0
    with signs or symptoms - code by site and
      stage under Syphilis A53.9
  Wassermann reaction A53.0
Postcardiotomy syndrome I97.0
Postcaval ureter Q62.62
Postcholecystectomy syndrome K91.5
Postclimacteric bleeding N95.0
Postcommissurotomy syndrome I97.0
Postconcussional syndrome F07.81
Postcontusional syndrome F07.81
Postcricoid region —*see* condition
Post-dates (40-42 weeks) (pregnancy) (mother)
  O48.0
  more than 42 weeks gestation O48.1
Postencephalitic syndrome F07.89
Posterior —*see* condition
Posterolateral sclerosis (spinal cord) —*see*
  Degeneration, combined
Postexanthematous —*see* condition
Postfebrile —*see* condition
Postgastrectomy dumping syndrome K91.1
Posthemiplegic chorea —*see* Monoplegia
Posthemorrhagic anemia (chronic) D50.0
  acute D62
  newborn P61.3
Postherpetic neuralgia (zoster) B02.29
  trigeminal B02.22
Posthitis N47.7

Postimmunization complication or reaction —
  see Complications, vaccination
Postinfectious —*see* condition
Postlaminectomy syndrome NEC M96.1
Postleukotomy syndrome F07.0
Postmastectomy lymphedema (syndrome) I97.2
Postmaturity, postmature (over 42 weeks)
  maternal (over 42 weeks gestation) O48.1
  newborn P08.22
Postmeasles complication NEC —*see also*
  condition B05.89
Postmenopausal
  endometrium (atrophic) N95.8
    suppurative —*see also* Endometritis N71.9
  osteoporosis —*see* Osteoporosis,
    postmenopausal
Postnasal drip R09.82
  due to
    allergic rhinitis —*see* Rhinitis, allergic
    common cold J00
    gastroesophageal reflux —*see* Reflux,
      gastroesophageal
    nasopharyngitis —*see* Nasopharyngitis
    other know condition — code to condition
    sinusitis —*see* Sinusitis
Postnatal —*see* condition
Postoperative (postprocedural) —*see*
  Complication, postoperative
  pneumothorax, therapeutic Z98.3
  state NEC Z98.890
Postpancreatectomy hyperglycemia E89.1
Postpartum —*see* Puerperal
Postphlebitic syndrome —*see* Syndrome,
  postthrombotic
Postpolio (myelitic) syndrome G14
Postpoliomyelitic —*see also* condition
  osteopathy —*see* Osteopathy, after
    poliomyelitis
Postprocedural —*see also* Postoperative
  hypoinsulinemia E89.1
Postschizophrenic depression F32.89
Postsurgery status —*see also* Status (post)
  pneumothorax, therapeutic Z98.3
Post-term (40-42 weeks) (pregnancy) (mother)
  O48.0
  infant P08.21
  more than 42 weeks gestation (mother) O48.1
Post-traumatic brain syndrome, nonpsychotic
  F07.81
Post-typhoid abscess A01.09
Postures, hysterical F44.2
Postvaccinal reaction or complication —*see*
  Complications, vaccination
Postvalvulotomy syndrome I97.0
Potain's
  disease (pulmonary edema) —*see* Edema, lung
  syndrome (gastrectasis with dyspepsia) K31.0
Potter's
  asthma J62.8
  facies Q60.6
  lung J62.8
  syndrome (with renal agenesis) Q60.6
Pott's
  curvature (spinal) A18.01
  disease or paraplegia A18.01
  spinal curvature A18.01
  tumor, puffy —*see* Osteomyelitis, specified
    type NEC
Pouch
  bronchus Q32.4
  Douglas' —*see* condition
  esophagus, esophageal, congenital Q39.6
    acquired K22.5
  gastric K31.4
  Hartmann's K82.8
  pharynx, pharyngeal (congenital) Q38.7
Pouchitis K91.850
Poultrymen's itch B88.0
Poverty NEC Z59.6
  extreme Z59.5
Poxvirus NEC B08.8

Prader-Willi syndrome Q87.1
Preauricular appendage or tag Q17.0
Prebetalipoproteinemia (acquired) (essential)
  (familial) (hereditary) (primary)
  (secondary) E78.1
  with chylomicronemia E78.3
Precipitate labor or delivery O62.3
Preclimacteric bleeding (menorrhagia) N92.4
Precocious
  adrenarche E30.1
  menarche E30.1
  menstruation E30.1
  pubarche E30.1
  puberty E30.1
    central E22.8
  sexual development NEC E30.1
  thelarche E30.8
Precocity, sexual (constitutional) (cryptogenic)
  (female) (idiopathic) (male) E30.1
  with adrenal hyperplasia E25.9
    congenital E25.0
Precordial pain R07.2
Predeciduous teeth K00.2
Prediabetes, prediabetic R73.03
  complicating
    pregnancy —*see* Pregnancy, complicated
      by, diseases of, specified type or
      system NEC
    puerperium O99.89
Predislocation status of hip at birth Q65.6
Pre-eclampsia O14.9-●
  with pre-existing hypertension —*see*
    Hypertension, complicating pregnancy,
    pre-existing, with, pre-eclampsia
  complicating
    childbirth O14.94
    puerperium O14.95
  mild O14.0-●
    complicating
      childbirth O14.04
      puerperium O14.05
  moderate O14.0-●
    complicating
      childbirth O14.04
      puerperium O14.05
  severe O14.1-●
    with hemolysis, elevated liver enzymes
      and low platelet count (HELLP)
      O14.2-●
      complicating
        childbirth O14.24
        puerperium O14.25
    complicating
      childbirth O14.14
      puerperium O14.15
Pre-eruptive color change, teeth, tooth
  K00.8
Pre-excitation atrioventricular conduction
  I45.6
Preglaucoma H40.00-●
Pregnancy (single) (uterine) —*see also* Delivery
  and Puerperal

Note: The Tabular must be reviewed for
assignment of the appropriate character
indicating the trimester of the pregnancy

Note: The Tabular must be reviewed for
assignment of appropriate seventh character
for multiple gestation codes in Chapter 15

  abdominal (ectopic) O00.00
    with intrauterine pregnancy O00.01
    with viable fetus O36.7-●
  ampullar O00.10-●
    with intrauterine pregnancy O00.11-●
  biochemical O02.81
  broad ligament O00.80
    with intrauterine pregnancy O00.81
  cervical O00.80
    with intrauterine pregnancy O00.81

▶ New   ➡ Revised   ~~deleted~~ Deleted   ● Use Additional Character(s)

Pregnancy (Continued)
  chemical O02.81
  complicated NOS O26.9-●
  complicated by (care of) (management affected by)
    abnormal, abnormality
      cervix O34.4-●
        causing obstructed labor O65.5
      cord (umbilical) O69.9
      fetal heart rate or rhythm O36.83-●
      findings on antenatal screening of mother O28.9
        biochemical O28.1
        chromosomal O28.5
        cytological O28.2
        genetic O28.5
        hematological O28.0
        radiological O28.4
        specified NEC O28.8
        ultrasonic O28.3
      glucose (tolerance) NEC O99.810
      pelvic organs O34.9-●
        specified NEC O34.8-●
          causing obstructed labor O65.5
      pelvis (bony) (major) NEC O33.0
      perineum O34.7-●
      position
        placenta O44.0-●
          with hemorrhage O44.1-●
        uterus O34.59-●
      uterus O34.59-●
        causing obstructed labor O65.5
        congenital O34.0-●
      vagina O34.6-●
        causing obstructed labor O65.5
      vulva O34.7-●
        causing obstructed labor O65.5
    abruptio placentae —see Abruptio placentae
    abscess or cellulitis
      bladder O23.1-●
      breast O91.11-●
      genital organ or tract O23.9-●
    abuse
      physical O9A.31-●
      psychological O9A.51-●
      sexual O9A.41-●
    adverse effect anesthesia O29.9-●
      aspiration pneumonitis O29.01-●
      cardiac arrest O29.11-●
      cardiac complication NEC O29.19-●
      cardiac failure O29.12-●
      central nervous system complication NEC O29.29-●
      cerebral anoxia O29.21-●
      failed or difficult intubation O29.6-●
      inhalation of stomach contents or secretions NOS O29.01-●
      local, toxic reaction O29.3X
      Mendelson's syndrome O29.01-●
      pressure collapse of lung O29.02-●
      pulmonary complications NEC O29.09-●
      specified NEC O29.8X
      spinal and epidural type NEC O29.5X
        induced headache O29.4-●
    albuminuria —see also Proteinuria, gestational O12.1-●
    alcohol use O99.31-●
    amnionitis O41.12-●
    anaphylactoid syndrome of pregnancy O88.01-●
    anemia (conditions in D50-D64) (pre-existing) O99.01-●
      complicating the puerperium O99.03
    antepartum hemorrhage O46.9-●
      with coagulation defect —see Hemorrhage, antepartum, with coagulation defect
      specified NEC O46.8X-●
    appendicitis O99.61-●
    atrophy (yellow) (acute) liver (subacute) O26.61-●

Pregnancy (Continued)
  complicated by (Continued)
    bariatric surgery status O99.84-●
    bicornis or bicornuate uterus O34.0-●
    biliary tract problems O26.61-●
    breech presentation O32.1
    cardiovascular diseases (conditions in I00-I09, I20-I52, I70-I99) O99.41-●
    cerebrovascular disorders (conditions in I60-I69) O99.41-●
    cervical shortening O26.87-●
    cervicitis O23.51-●
    chloasma (gravidarum) O26.89-●
    cholecystitis O99.61-●
    cholestasis (intrahepatic) O26.61-●
    chorioamnionitis O41.12-●
    circulatory system disorder (conditions in I00-I09, I20-I99, O99.41-●)
    compound presentation O32.6
    conjoined twins O30.02-●
    connective system disorders (conditions in M00-M99) O99.89
    contracted pelvis (general) O33.1
      inlet O33.2
      outlet O33.3
    convulsions (eclamptic) (uremic) —see also Eclampsia O15.9-●
    cracked nipple O92.11-●
    cystitis O23.1-●
    cystocele O34.8-●
    death of fetus (near term) O36.4
      early pregnancy O02.1
      of one fetus or more in multiple gestation O31.2-●
    deciduitis O41.14-●
    decreased fetal movement O36.81-●
    dental problems O99.61-●
    diabetes (mellitus) O24.91-●
      gestational (pregnancy induced) —see Diabetes, gestational
      pre-existing O24.31-●
        specified NEC O24.81-●
        type 1 O24.01-●
        type 2 O24.11-●
    digestive system disorders (conditions in K00-K93) O99.61-●
    diseases of —see Pregnancy, complicated by, specified body system disease
      biliary tract O26.61-●
      blood NEC (conditions in D65-D77) O99.11-●
      liver O26.61-●
      specified NEC O99.89
    disorders of —see Pregnancy, complicated by, specified body system disorder
      amniotic fluid and membranes O41.9-●
        specified NEC O41.8X-●
      biliary tract O26.61-●
      ear and mastoid process (conditions in H60-H95) O99.89
      eye and adnexa (conditions in H00-H59) O99.89
      liver O26.61-●
      skin (conditions in L00-L99) O99.71-●
      specified NEC O99.89
    displacement, uterus NEC O34.59-●
      causing obstructed labor O65.5
    disproportion (due to) O33.9
      fetal (ascites) (hydrops) (meningomyelocele) (sacral teratoma) (tumor) deformities NEC O33.7
      generally contracted pelvis O33.1
      hydrocephalic fetus O33.6
      inlet contraction of pelvis O33.2
      mixed maternal and fetal origin O33.4
      specified NEC O33.8
    double uterus O34.0-●
      causing obstructed labor O65.5
    drug use (conditions in F11-F19) O99.32-●

Pregnancy (Continued)
  complicated by (Continued)
    eclampsia, eclamptic (coma) (convulsions) (delirium) (nephritis) (uremia) (see also Eclampsia) O15-●
    ectopic pregnancy —see Pregnancy, ectopic
    edema O12.0-●
      with
        gestational hypertension, mild —see also Pre-eclampsia O14.0-●
        proteinuria O12.2-●
    effusion, amniotic fluid —see Pregnancy, complicated by, premature rupture of membranes
    elderly
      multigravida O09.52-●
      primigravida O09.51-●
    embolism —see also Embolism, obstetric, pregnancy O88.-●
    endocrine diseases NEC O99.28-●
    endometritis O86.12
    excessive weight gain O26.0-●
    exhaustion O26.81-●
      during labor and delivery O75.81
    face presentation O32.3
    failed induction of labor O61.9
    failed or difficult intubation for anesthesia O29.6-●
      instrumental O61.1
      mechanical O61.1
      medical O61.0
      specified NEC O61.8
      surgical O61.1
    false labor (pains) O47.9
      at or after 37 completed weeks of pregnancy O47.1
      before 37 completed weeks of pregnancy O47.0-●
    fatigue O26.81-●
      during labor and delivery O75.81
    fatty metamorphosis of liver O26.61-●
    female genital mutilation O34.8-● [N90.81-●]
    fetal (maternal care for)
      abnormality or damage O35.9
        acid-base balance O68
        specified type NEC O35.8
      acidemia O68
      acidosis O68
      alkalosis O68
      anemia and thrombocytopenia O36.82-●
      anencephaly O35.0
      chromosomal abnormality (conditions in Q90-Q99) O35.1
      conjoined twins O30.02-●
      damage from
        amniocentesis O35.7
        biopsy procedures O35.7
        drug addiction O35.5
        hematological investigation O35.7
        intrauterine contraceptive device O35.7
        maternal
          alcohol addiction O35.4
          cytomegalovirus infection O35.3
          disease NEC O35.8
          drug addiction O35.5
          listeriosis O35.8
          rubella O35.3
          toxoplasmosis O35.8
          viral infection O35.3
        medical procedure NEC O35.7
        radiation O35.6
      death (near term) O36.4
        early pregnancy O02.1
      decreased movement O36.81-●
      disproportion due to deformity (fetal) O33.7
      excessive growth (large for dates) O36.6-●
      growth retardation O36.59-●
        light for dates O36.59-●
        small for dates O36.59-●

Pregnancy (Continued)
  complicated by (Continued)
    fetal (Continued)
      heart rate irregularity (bradycardia)
        (decelerations) (tachycardia) O76
      hereditary disease O35.2
      hydrocephalus O35.0
      intrauterine death O36.4
      poor growth O36.59-●
        light for dates O36.59-●
        small for dates O36.59-●
      problem O36.9-●
        specified NEC O36.89-●
      reduction (elective) O31.3-●
      selective termination O31.3-●
      spina bifida O35.0
      thrombocytopenia O36.82-●
    fibroid (tumor) (uterus) O34.1-●
    fissure of nipple O92.11-●
    gallstones O99.61-●
    gastric banding status O99.84-●
    gastric bypass status O99.84-●
    genital herpes (asymptomatic) (history of)
      (inactive) O98.3-●
    genital tract infection O23.9-●
    glomerular diseases (conditions in
      N00-N07) O26.83-●
      with hypertension, pre-existing —see
        Hypertension, complicating,
        pregnancy, pre-existing, with, renal
        disease
    gonorrhea O98.21-●
    grand multiparity O09.4
    habitual aborter —see Pregnancy,
      complicated by, recurrent pregnancy
      loss
    HELLP syndrome (hemolysis, elevated
      liver enzymes and low platelet count)
      O14.2-●
    hemorrhage
      antepartum —see Hemorrhage,
        antepartum
      before 20 completed weeks gestation
        O20.9
        specified NEC O20.8
      due to premature separation, placenta —
        see also Abruptio placentae O45.9-●
      early O20.9
        specified NEC O20.8
      threatened abortion O20.0
    hemorrhoids O22.4-●
    hepatitis (viral) O98.41-●
    herniation of uterus O34.59-●
    high
      head at term O32.4
      risk —see Supervision (of) (for), high-risk
    history of in utero procedure during
      previous pregnancy O09.82-●
    HIV O98.71-●
    human immunodeficiency virus (HIV)
      disease O98.71-●
    hydatidiform mole —see also Mole,
      hydatidiform O01.9-●
    hydramnios O40.-●
    hydrocephalic fetus (disproportion) O33.6
    hydrops
      amnii O40.-●
      fetalis O36.2-●
        associated with isoimmunization —see
        also Pregnancy, complicated by,
        isoimmunization O36.11-●
    hydrorrhea O42.90
    hyperemesis (gravidarum) (mild) —see also
      Hyperemesis, gravidarum O21.0-●
    hypertension —see Hypertension,
      complicating pregnancy
    hypertensive
      heart and renal disease, pre-existing —
        see Hypertension, complicating,
        pregnancy, pre-existing, with, heart
        disease, with renal disease

Pregnancy (Continued)
  complicated by (Continued)
    hypertensive (Continued)
      heart disease, pre-existing —see
        Hypertension, complicating,
        pregnancy, pre-existing, with, heart
        disease
      renal disease, pre-existing —see
        Hypertension, complicating,
        pregnancy, pre-existing, with, renal
        disease
    hypotension O26.5-●
    immune disorders NEC (conditions in
      D80-D89) O99.11-●
    incarceration, uterus O34.51-●
    incompetent cervix O34.3-●
    inconclusive fetal viability O36.80
    infection(s) O98.91-●
      amniotic fluid or sac O41.10-●
      bladder O23.1-●
      carrier state NEC O99.830
        streptococcus B O99.820
      genital organ or tract O23.9-●
        specified NEC O23.59-●
      genitourinary tract O23.9-●
      gonorrhea O98.21-●
      hepatitis (viral) O98.41-●
      HIV O98.71-●
      human immunodeficiency virus (HIV)
        O98.71-●
      kidney O23.0-●
      nipple O91.01-●
      parasitic disease O98.91-●
        specified NEC O98.81-●
      protozoal disease O98.61-●
      sexually transmitted NEC O98.31-●
      specified type NEC O98.81-●
      syphilis O98.11-●
      tuberculosis O98.01-●
      urethra O23.2-●
      urinary (tract) O23.4-●
        specified NEC O23.3-●
      viral disease O98.51-●
    injury or poisoning (conditions in S00-T88)
      O9A.21-●
    due to abuse
      physical O9A.31-●
      psychological O9A.51-●
      sexual O9A.41-●
    insufficient
      prenatal care O09.3-●
      weight gain O26.1-●
    insulin resistance O26.89
    intrauterine fetal death (near term) O36.4
      early pregnancy O02.1
      multiple gestation (one fetus or more)
        O31.2-●
    isoimmunization O36.11-●
      anti-A sensitization O36.11-●
      anti-B sensitization O36.19-●
      Rh O36.09-●
        anti-D antibody O36.01-●
      specified NEC O36.19-●
    laceration of uterus NEC O71.81
    malformation
      placenta, placental (vessel) O43.10-●
        specified NEC O43.19-●
      uterus (congenital) O34.0-●
    malnutrition (conditions in E40-E46)
      O25.1-●
    maternal hypotension syndrome O26.5-●
    mental disorders (conditions in F01-F09,
      F20-F99) O99.34-●
      alcohol use O99.31-●
      drug use O99.32-●
      smoking O99.33-●
    mentum presentation O32.3
    metabolic disorders O99.28-●
    missed
      abortion O02.1
      delivery O36.4

Pregnancy (Continued)
  complicated by (Continued)
    multiple gestations O30.9-●
      conjoined twins O30.02-●
      quadruplet —see Pregnancy, quadruplet
      specified complication NEC O31.8X-●
      specified number of multiples NEC —see
        Pregnancy, multiple (gestation),
        specified NEC
      triplet —see Pregnancy, triplet
      twin —see Pregnancy, twin
    musculoskeletal condition (conditions is
      M00-M99) O99.89
    necrosis, liver (conditions in K72)
      O26.61-●
    neoplasm
      benign
        cervix O34.4-●
        corpus uteri O34.1-●
        uterus O34.1-●
      malignant O9A.11-●
    nephropathy NEC O26.83-●
    nervous system condition (conditions in
      G00-G99) O99.35-●
    nutritional diseases NEC O99.28-●
    obesity (pre-existing) O99.21-●
    obesity surgery status O99.84-●
    oblique lie or presentation O32.2
    older mother —see Pregnancy, complicated
      by, elderly
    oligohydramnios O41.0-●
      with premature rupture of
        membranes —see also Pregnancy,
        complicated by, premature rupture
        of membranes O42-●
    onset (spontaneous) of labor after 37
      completed weeks of gestation but
      before 39 completed weeks gestation,
      with delivery by (planned) cesarean
      section O75.82
    oophoritis O23.52-●
    overdose, drug —see also Table of Drugs
      and Chemicals, by drug, poisoning
      O9A.21-●
    oversize fetus O33.5
    papyraceous fetus O31.0-●
    pelvic inflammatory disease O99.89
    periodontal disease O99.61-●
    peripheral neuritis O26.82-●
    peritoneal (pelvic) adhesions O99.89
    phlebitis O22.9-●
    phlebopathy O22.9-●
    phlebothrombosis (superficial) O22.2-●
      deep O22.3-●
    placenta accreta O43.21-●
    placenta increta O43.22-●
    placenta percreta O43.23-●
    placenta previa O44.0-●
      complete O44.0-●
        with hemorrhage O44.1-●
      marginal O44.2-●
        with hemorrhage O44.3-●
      partial O44.2-●
        with hemorrhage O44.3-●
    placental disorder O43.9-●
      specified NEC O43.89-●
    placental dysfunction O43.89-●
    placental infarction O43.81-●
    placental insufficiency O36.51-●
    placental transfusion syndromes
      fetomaternal O43.01-●
      fetus to fetus O43.02-●
      maternofetal O43.01-●
    placentitis O41.14-●
    pneumonia O99.51-●
    poisoning —see also Table of Drugs and
      Chemicals O9A.21-●
    polyhydramnios O40-●
    polymorphic eruption of pregnancy
      O26.86
    poor obstetric history NEC O09.29-●

▶ New   ⇒ Revised   ~~deleted~~ Deleted   ● Use Additional Character(s)

Pregnancy *(Continued)*
  complicated by *(Continued)*
    postmaturity (post-term) (40 to 42 weeks)
      O48.0
      more than 42 completed weeks gestation
        (prolonged) O48.1
    pre-eclampsia O14.9-●
      mild O14.0-●
      moderate O14.0-●
      severe O14.1-●
        with hemolysis, elevated liver
          enzymes and low platelet count
          (HELLP) O14.2-●
    premature labor —*see* Pregnancy,
      complicated by, preterm labor
    premature rupture of membranes O42.90
      full-term, unspecified as to length of
        time between rupture and onset of
        labor O42.92
      with onset of labor
        within 24 hours O42.00
          at or after 37 weeks gestation,
            onset of labor within
            24 hours of rupture
            O42.02
          pre-term (before 37 completed
            weeks of gestation)
            O42.01-●
        after 24 hours O42.10
          at or after 37 weeks gestation,
            onset of labor more than
            24 hours following rupture
            O42.12
          pre-term (before 37 completed
            weeks of gestation)
            O42.11-●
      at or after 37 weeks gestation,
        unspecified as to length of time
        between rupture and onset of labor
        O42.92
      pre-term (before 37 completed weeks of
        gestation) O42.91-●
    premature separation of placenta —*see also*
      Abruptio placentae O45.9-●
    presentation, fetal —*see* Delivery,
      complicated by, malposition
    preterm delivery O60.10
    preterm labor
      with delivery O60.10
        preterm O60.10
        term O60.20
      second trimester
        with preterm delivery
          second trimester O60.12
          third trimester O60.13
        with term delivery O60.22
        without delivery O60.02
      third trimester
        with term delivery O60.23
        with third trimester preterm delivery
          O60.14
        without delivery O60.03
      without delivery O60.00
        second trimester O60.02
        third trimester O60.03
    previous history of —*see* Pregnancy,
      supervision of, high-risk
    prolapse, uterus O34.52-●
    proteinuria (gestational) —*see also*
      Proteinuria, gestational O12.1-●
      with edema O12.2-●
    pruritic urticarial papules and plaques of
      pregnancy (PUPPP) O26.86
    pruritus (neurogenic) O26.89-●
    ➡ psychosis or psychoneurosis (puerperal)
      F53.1
    ptyalism O26.89-●
    PUPPP (pruritic urticarial papules and
      plaques of pregnancy) O26.86
    pyelitis O23.0-●
    recurrent pregnancy loss O26.2-●

Pregnancy *(Continued)*
  complicated by *(Continued)*
    renal disease or failure NEC O26.83-●
      with secondary hypertension, pre-
        existing —*see* Hypertension,
        complicating, pregnancy, pre-
        existing, secondary
      hypertensive, pre-existing —*see*
        Hypertension, complicating,
        pregnancy, pre-existing, with, renal
        disease
    respiratory condition (conditions in
      J00-J99) O99.51-●
    retained, retention
      dead ovum O02.0
      intrauterine contraceptive device
        O26.3-●
    retroversion, uterus O34.53-●
    Rh immunization, incompatibility or
      sensitization NEC O36.09-●
      anti-D antibody O36.01-●
    rupture
      amnion (premature) —*see also*
        Pregnancy, complicated by,
        premature rupture of membranes
        O42-●
      membranes (premature) —*see also*
        Pregnancy, complicated by,
        premature rupture of membranes
        O42-●
      uterus (during labor) O71.1
        before onset of labor O71.0-●
    salivation (excessive) O26.89-●
    salpingitis O23.52-●
    salpingo-oophoritis O23.52-●
    sepsis (conditions in A40, A41) O98.81-●
    size date discrepancy (uterine) O26.84-●
    skin condition (conditions in L00-L99)
      O99.71-●
    smoking (tobacco) O99.33-●
    social problem O09.7-●
    specified condition NEC O26.89-●
    spotting O26.85-●
    streptococcus group B (GBS) carrier state
      O99.820
    subluxation of symphysis (pubis) O26.71-●
    syphilis (conditions in A50-A53) O98.11-●
    threatened
      abortion O20.0
      labor O47.9
        at or after 37 completed weeks of
          gestation O47.1
        before 37 completed weeks of
          gestation O47.0-●
    thrombophlebitis (superficial) O22.2-●
    thrombosis O22.9-●
      cerebral venous O22.5-●
      cerebrovenous sinus O22.5-●
      deep O22.3-●
    tobacco use disorder (smoking) O99.33-●
    torsion of uterus O34.59-●
    toxemia O14.9-●
    transverse lie or presentation O32.2
    tuberculosis (conditions in A15-A19)
      O98.01-●
    tumor (benign)
      cervix O34.4-●
      malignant O9A.11-●
      uterus O34.1-●
    unstable lie O32.0
    upper respiratory infection O99.51-●
    urethritis O23.2-●
    uterine size date discrepancy O26.84-●
    vaginitis or vulvitis O23.59-●
    varicose veins (lower extremities) O22.0-●
      genitals O22.1-●
      legs O22.0-●
      perineal O22.1-●
      vaginal or vulval O22.1-●
    venereal disease NEC (conditions in A63.8)
      O98.31-●

Pregnancy *(Continued)*
  complicated by *(Continued)*
    venous disorders O22.9-●
      specified NEC O22.8X-●
    very young mother —*see* Pregnancy,
      complicated by, young mother
    viral diseases (conditions in A80-B09,
      B25-B34) O98.51-●
    vomiting O21.9
      due to diseases classified elsewhere O21.8
      hyperemesis gravidarum (mild) —*see*
        also Hyperemesis, gravidarum
        O21.0-●
      late (occurring after 20 weeks of
        gestation) O21.2
    young mother
      multigravida O09.62-●
      primigravida O09.61-●
  concealed O09.3-●
  continuing following
    elective fetal reduction of one or more fetus
      O31.3-●
    intrauterine death of one or more fetus
      O31.2-●
    spontaneous abortion of one or more fetus
      O31.1-●
  cornual O00.80
    with intrauterine pregnancy O00.81
  ectopic (ruptured) O00.90
    with intrauterine pregnancy O00.91
    abdominal O00.00
      with
        intrauterine pregnancy O00.01
        viable fetus O36.7-●
    cervical O00.80
      with intrauterine pregnancy O00.81
    complicated (by) O08.9
      afibrinogenemia O08.1
      cardiac arrest O08.81
      chemical damage of pelvic organ(s)
        O08.6
      circulatory collapse O08.3
      defibrination syndrome O08.1
      electrolyte imbalance O08.5
      embolism (amniotic fluid) (blood clot)
        (pulmonary) (septic) O08.2
      endometritis O08.0
      genital tract and pelvic infection O08.0
      hemorrhage (delayed) (excessive) O08.1
      infection
        genital tract or pelvic O08.0
        kidney 008.83
        urinary tract O08.83
      intravascular coagulation O08.1
      laceration of pelvic organ(s)
        O08.6
      metabolic disorder O08.5
      oliguria O08.4
      oophoritis O08.0
      parametritis O08.0
      pelvic peritonitis O08.0
      perforation of pelvic organ(s)
        O08.6
      renal failure or shutdown O08.4
      salpingitis or salpingo-oophoritis
        O08.0
      sepsis O08.82
      shock O08.83
        septic O08.82
      specified condition NEC O08.89
      tubular necrosis (renal) O08.4
      uremia O08.4
      urinary infection O08.83
      venous complication NEC O08.7
        embolism O08.2
    cornual O00.80
      with intrauterine pregnancy
        O00.81
    intraligamentous O00.80
      with intrauterine pregnancy
        O00.81

Pregnancy *(Continued)*
  ectopic *(Continued)*
    mural O00.80
      with intrauterine pregnancy O00.81
    ovarian O00.20-●
      with intrauterine pregnancy O00.21-●
    specified site NEC O00.80
      with intrauterine pregnancy O00.81
    tubal (ruptured) O00.10-●
      with intrauterine pregnancy O00.11-●
  examination (normal) Z34.9-●
    first Z34.0-●
    high-risk *—see* Pregnancy, supervision of,
      high-risk
    specified Z34.8-●
  extrauterine *—see* Pregnancy, ectopic
  fallopian O00.10-●
    with intrauterine pregnancy O00.11-●
  false F45.8
  gestational carrier Z33.3
  ▶heptachorionic, hepta-amniotic (septuplets)
    O30.83-●
  ▶hexachorionic, hexa-amniotic (sextuplets)
    O30.83-●
  hidden O09.3-●
  high-risk *—see* Pregnancy, supervision of,
    high-risk
  incidental finding Z33.1
  interstitial O00.80
    with intrauterine pregnancy O00.81
  intraligamentous O00.80
    with intrauterine pregnancy O00.81
  intramural O00.80
    with intrauterine pregnancy O00.81
  intraperitoneal O00.00
    with intrauterine pregnancy O00.01
  isthmian O00.10-●
    with intrauterine pregnancy O00.11-●
  mesometric (mural) O00.80
    with intrauterine pregnancy O00.81
  molar NEC O02.0
    complicated (by) O08.9
      afibrinogenemia O08.1
      cardiac arrest O08.81
      chemical damage of pelvic organ(s) O08.6
      circulatory collapse O08.3
      defibrination syndrome O08.1
      electrolyte imbalance O08.5
      embolism (amniotic fluid) (blood clot)
        (pulmonary) (septic) O08.2
      endometritis O08.0
      genital tract and pelvic infection O08.0
      hemorrhage (delayed) (excessive) O08.1
      infection
        genital tract or pelvic O08.0
        kidney O08.83
        urinary tract O08.83
      intravascular coagulation O08.1
      laceration of pelvic organ(s) O08.6
      metabolic disorder O08.5
      oliguria O08.4
      oophoritis O08.0
      parametritis O08.0
      pelvic peritonitis O08.0
      perforation of pelvic organ(s) O08.6
      renal failure or shutdown O08.4
      salpingitis or salpingo-oophoritis O08.0
      sepsis O08.82
      shock O08.3
        septic O08.82
      specified condition NEC O08.89
      tubular necrosis (renal) O08.4
      uremia O08.4
      urinary infection O08.83
      venous complication NEC O08.7
        embolism O08.2
  hydatidiform *—see also* Mole, hydatidiform
    O01.9-●
  multiple (gestation) O30.9-●
    greater than quadruplets *—see* Pregnancy,
      multiple (gestation), specified NEC

Pregnancy *(Continued)*
  multiple (gestation) *(Continued)*
    specified NEC O30.80-●
      with
        two or more monoamniotic fetuses
          O30.82-●
        two or more monochorionic fetuses
          O30.81-●
      ▶number of chorions and amnions are
        both equal to the number of fetuses
        O30.83-●
      two or more monoamniotic fetuses
        O30.82-●
      two or more monochorionic fetuses
        O30.81-●
      unable to determine number of placenta
        and number of amniotic sacs
        O30.89-●
      unspecified number of placenta and
        unspecified number of amniotic
        sacs O30.80-●
  mural O00.80
    with intrauterine pregnancy O00.81
  normal (supervision of) Z34.9-●
    first Z34.0-●
    high-risk *—see* Pregnancy, supervision of,
      high-risk
    specified Z34.8-●
  ovarian O00.20-●
    with intrauterine pregnancy O00.21-●
  ▶pentachorionic, penta-amniotic (quintuplets)
    O30.83-●
  postmature (40 to 42 weeks) O48.0
    more than 42 weeks gestation O48.1
  post-term (40 to 42 weeks) O48.0
  prenatal care only Z34.9-●
    first Z34.0-●
    high-risk *—see* Pregnancy, supervision of,
      high-risk
    specified Z34.8-●
  prolonged (more than 42 weeks gestation)
    O48.1
  quadruplet O30.20-●
    with
      two or more monoamniotic fetuses
        O30.22-●
      two or more monochorionic fetuses
        O30.21-●
    ▶quadrachorionic/quadra-amniotic O30.23-●
    two or more monoamniotic fetuses O30.22-●
    two or more monochorionic fetuses
      O30.21-●
    unable to determine number of placenta
      and number of amniotic sacs O30.29-●
    unspecified number of placenta and
      unspecified number of amniotic sacs
      O30.20-●
  quintuplet *—see* Pregnancy, multiple
    (gestation), specified NEC
  sextuplet *—see* Pregnancy, multiple
    (gestation), specified NEC
  supervision of
    concealed pregnancy O09.3-●
    elderly mother
      multigravida O09.52-●
      primigravida O09.51-●
    hidden pregnancy O09.3-●
    high-risk O09.9-●
      due to (history of)
        ectopic pregnancy O09.1-●
        elderly *—see* Pregnancy, supervision,
          elderly mother
        grand multiparity O09.4
        infertility O09.0-●
        insufficient prenatal care O09.3-●
        in utero procedure during previous
          pregnancy O09.82-●
        in vitro fertilization O09.81-●
        molar pregnancy O09.A-●
        multiple previous pregnancies O09.4-●
        older mother *—see* Pregnancy,
          supervision of, elderly mother

Pregnancy *(Continued)*
  supervision of *(Continued)*
    high-risk *(Continued)*
      due to *(Continued)*
        poor reproductive or obstetric history
          NEC O09.29-●
        pre-term labor O09.21-●
        previous
          neonatal death O09.29-●
        social problems O09.7-●
        specified NEC O09.89-●
        very young mother *—see* Pregnancy,
          supervision, young mother
      resulting from in vitro fertilization
        O09.81-●
    normal Z34.9-●
      first Z34.0-●
      specified NEC Z34.8-●
    young mother
      multigravida O09.62-●
      primigravida O09.61-●
  triplet O30.10-●
    with
      two or more monoamniotic fetuses
        O30.12-●
      two or more monochorionic fetuses
        O30.11-●
    ▶trichorionic/triamniotic O30.13-●
    two or more monoamniotic fetuses O30.12-●
    two or more monochorionic fetuses O30.11-●
    unable to determine number of placenta
      and number of amniotic sacs O30.19-●
    unspecified number of placenta and
      unspecified number of amniotic sacs
      O30.10-●
  tubal (with abortion) (with rupture) O00.10-●
    with intrauterine pregnancy O00.11-●
  twin O30.00-●
    conjoined O30.02-●
    dichorionic/diamniotic (two placenta, two
      amniotic sacs) O30.04-●
    monochorionic/diamniotic (one placenta,
      two amniotic sacs) O30.03-●
    monochorionic/monoamniotic (one
      placenta, one amniotic sac) O30.01-●
    unable to determine number of placenta
      and number of amniotic sacs O30.09-●
    unspecified number of placenta and
      unspecified number of amniotic sacs
      O30.00-●
  unwanted Z64.0
  weeks of gestation
    8 weeks Z3A.08
    9 weeks Z3A.09
    10 weeks Z3A.10
    11 weeks Z3A.11
    12 weeks Z3A.12
    13 weeks Z3A.13
    14 weeks Z3A.14
    15 weeks Z3A.15
    16 weeks Z3A.16
    17 weeks Z3A.17
    18 weeks Z3A.18
    19 weeks Z3A.19
    20 weeks Z3A.20
    21 weeks Z3A.21
    22 weeks Z3A.22
    23 weeks Z3A.23
    24 weeks Z3A.24
    25 weeks Z3A.25
    26 weeks Z3A.26
    27 weeks Z3A.27
    28 weeks Z3A.28
    29 weeks Z3A.29
    30 weeks Z3A.30
    31 weeks Z3A.31
    32 weeks Z3A.32
    33 weeks Z3A.33
    34 weeks Z3A.34
    35 weeks Z3A.35
    36 weeks Z3A.36

▶ New   ⟹ Revised   ~~deleted~~ Deleted   ● Use Additional Character(s)

Pregnancy (Continued)
  weeks of gestation (Continued)
    37 weeks Z3A.37
    38 weeks Z3A.38
    39 weeks Z3A.39
    40 weeks Z3A.40
    41 weeks Z3A.41
    42 weeks Z3A.42
    greater than 42 weeks Z3A.49
    less than 8 weeks Z3A.01
    not specified Z3A.00
Preiser's disease —see Osteonecrosis,
    secondary, due to, trauma, metacarpus
Pre-kwashiorkor —see Malnutrition, severe
Preleukemia (syndrome) D46.9
Preluxation, hip, congenital Q65.6
Premature —see also condition
  adrenarche E27.0
  aging E34.8
  beats I49.40
    atrial I49.1
    auricular I49.1
    supraventricular I49.1
  birth NEC —see Preterm, newborn
  closure, foramen ovale Q21.8
  contraction
    atrial I49.1
    atrioventricular I49.49
    auricular I49.1
    auriculoventricular I49.2
    heart (extrasystole) I49.49
    junctional I49.2
    ventricular I49.3
  delivery —see also Pregnancy, complicated by,
      preterm labor O60.10
  ejaculation F52.4
  infant NEC —see Preterm, newborn
    light-for-dates —see Light for dates
  labor —see Pregnancy, complicated by,
      preterm labor
  lungs P28.0
  menopause E28.319
    asymptomatic E28.319
    symptomatic E28.310
  newborn
    extreme (less than 28 completed weeks) —
        see Immaturity, extreme
    less than 37 completed weeks —see
        Preterm, newborn
  puberty E30.1
  rupture membranes or amnion —see
      Pregnancy, complicated by, premature
      rupture of membranes
  senility E34.8
  thelarche E30.8
  ventricular systole I49.3
Prematurity NEC (less than 37 completed
    weeks) —see Preterm, newborn
  extreme (less than 28 completed weeks) —see
      Immaturity, extreme
Premenstrual
  dysphoric disorder (PMDD) F32.81
  tension (syndrome) N94.3
Premolarization, cuspids K00.2
Prenatal
  care, normal pregnancy —see Pregnancy,
      normal
  screening of mother —see also Encounter,
      antenatal Z36.9
  teeth K00.6
Preparatory care for subsequent treatment NEC
  for dialysis Z49.01
    peritoneal Z49.02
Prepartum —see condition
Preponderance, left or right ventricular I51.7
Prepuce —see condition
PRES (posterior reversible encephalopathy
    syndrome) I67.83
Presbycardia R54
Presbycusis, presbyacusia H91.1-•
Presbyesophagus K22.8

Presbyophrenia F03
Presbyopia H52.4
Prescription of contraceptives (initial) Z30.019
  barrier Z30.018
  diaphragm Z30.018
  emergency (postcoital) Z30.012
  implantable subdermal Z30.017
  injectable Z30.013
  intrauterine contraceptive device Z30.014
  pills Z30.011
  postcoital (emergency) Z30.012
  repeat Z30.40
    barrier Z30.49
    diaphragm Z30.49
    implantable subdermal Z30.46
    injectable Z30.42
    pills Z30.41
    specified type NEC Z30.49
    transdermal patch hormonal Z30.45
    vaginal ring hormonal Z30.44
  specified type NEC Z30.018
    transdermal patch hormonal Z30.016
    vaginal ring hormonal Z30.015
Presence (of)
  ankle-joint implant (functional) (prosthesis)
      Z96.66-•
  aortocoronary (bypass) graft Z95.1
  arterial-venous shunt (dialysis) Z99.2
  artificial
    eye (globe) Z97.0
    heart (fully implantable) (mechanical)
        Z95.812
      valve Z95.2
    larynx Z96.3
    lens (intraocular) Z96.1
    limb (complete) (partial) Z97.1-•
      arm Z97.1-•
        bilateral Z97.15
      leg Z97.1-•
        bilateral Z97.16
  audiological implant (functional) Z96.29
  bladder implant (functional) Z96.0
  bone
    conduction hearing device Z96.29
    implant (functional) NEC Z96.7
    joint (prosthesis) —see Presence, joint
        implant
  cardiac
    defibrillator (functional) (with synchronous
        cardiac pacemaker) Z95.810
    implant or graft Z95.9
      specified type NEC Z95.818
    pacemaker Z95.0
    resynchronization therapy
      defibrillator Z95.810
      pacemaker Z95.0
  cerebrospinal fluid drainage device Z98.2
  cochlear implant (functional) Z96.21
  contact lens (es) Z97.3
  coronary artery graft or prosthesis Z95.5
  CRT-D (cardiac resynchronization therapy
      defibrillator) Z95.810
  CRT-P (cardiac resynchronization therapy
      pacemaker) Z95.0
  cardioverter-defibrillator (ICD) Z95.810
  CSF shunt Z98.2
  dental prosthesis device Z97.2
  dentures Z97.2
  device (external) NEC Z97.8
    cardiac NEC Z95.818
    heart assist Z95.811
    implanted (functional) Z96.9
      specified NEC Z96.89
    prosthetic Z97.8
  ear implant Z96.20
    cochlear implant Z96.21
    myringotomy tube Z96.22
    specified type NEC Z96.29
  elbow-joint implant (functional) (prosthesis)
      Z96.62-•
  endocrine implant (functional) NEC Z96.49

Presence (Continued)
  eustachian tube stent or device (functional)
      Z96.29
  external hearing-aid or device Z97.4
  finger-joint implant (functional) (prosthetic)
      Z96.69-•
  functional implant Z96.9
    specified NEC Z96.89
  graft
    cardiac NEC Z95.818
    vascular NEC Z95.828
  hearing-aid or device (external) Z97.4
    implant (bone) (cochlear) (functional) Z96.21
  heart assist device Z95.811
  heart valve implant (functional) Z95.2
    prosthetic Z95.2
    specified type NEC Z95.4
    xenogenic Z95.3
  hip-joint implant (functional) (prosthesis)
      Z96.64-•
  ICD (cardioverter-defibrillator) Z95.810
  implanted device (artificial) (functional)
      (prosthetic) Z96.9
    automatic cardiac defibrillator (with
        synchronous cardiac pacemaker)
        Z95.810
    cardiac pacemaker Z95.0
    cochlear Z96.21
    dental Z96.5
    heart Z95.812
    heart valve Z95.2
      prosthetic Z95.2
      specified NEC Z95.4
      xenogenic Z95.3
    insulin pump Z96.41
    intraocular lens Z96.1
    joint Z96.60
      ankle Z96.66-•
      elbow Z96.62-•
      finger Z96.69-•
      hip Z96.64-•
      knee Z96.65-•
      shoulder Z96.61-•
      specified NEC Z96.698
      wrist Z96.63-•
    larynx Z96.3
    myringotomy tube Z96.22
    otological Z96.20
      cochlear Z96.21
      eustachian stent Z96.29
      myringotomy Z96.22
      specified NEC Z96.29
      stapes Z96.29
    skin Z96.81
    skull plate Z96.7
    specified NEC Z96.89
    urogenital Z96.0
  insulin pump (functional) Z96.41
  intestinal bypass or anastomosis Z98.0
  intraocular lens (functional) Z96.1
  intrauterine contraceptive device (IUD) Z97.5
  intravascular implant (functional) (prosthetic)
      NEC Z95.9
    coronary artery Z95.5
    defibrillator (with synchronous cardiac
        pacemaker) Z95.810
    peripheral vessel (with angioplasty) Z95.820
  joint implant (prosthetic) (any) Z96.60
    ankle —see Presence, ankle joint implant
    elbow —see Presence, elbow joint implant
    finger —see Presence, finger joint implant
    hip —see Presence, hip joint implant
    knee —see Presence, knee joint implant
    shoulder —see Presence, shoulder joint
        implant
    specified joint NEC Z96.698
    wrist —see Presence, wrist joint implant
  knee-joint implant (functional) (prosthesis)
      Z96.65-•
  laryngeal implant (functional) Z96.3
  mandibular implant (dental) Z96.5

Presence *(Continued)*
  myringotomy tube(s) Z96.22
  orthopedic-joint implant (prosthetic) (any) —
    see Presence, joint implant
  otological implant (functional) Z96.29
  shoulder-joint implant (functional)
    (prosthesis) Z96.61-●
  skull-plate implant Z96.7
  spectacles Z97.3
  stapes implant (functional) Z96.29
  systemic lupus erythematosus [SLE] inhibitor
    D68.62
  tendon implant (functional) (graft) Z96.7
  tooth root(s) implant Z96.5
  ureteral stent Z96.0
  urethral stent Z96.0
  urogenital implant (functional) Z96.0
  vascular implant or device Z95.9
    access port device Z95.828
    specified type NEC Z95.828
  wrist-joint implant (functional) (prosthesis)
    Z96.63-●
Presenile —*see also* condition
  dementia F03
  premature aging E34.8
Presentation, fetal —*see* Delivery, complicated
  by, malposition
Prespondylolisthesis (congenital) Q76.2
Pressure
  area, skin —*see* Ulcer, pressure, by site
  brachial plexus G54.0
  brain G93.5
    injury at birth NEC P11.1
  cerebral —*see* Pressure, brain
  chest R07.89
  cone, tentorial G93.5
  hyposystolic —*see also* Hypotension
    incidental reading, without diagnosis of
      hypotension R03.1
  increased
    intracranial (benign) G93.2
      injury at birth P11.0
    intraocular H40.05-●
  lumbosacral plexus G54.1
  mediastinum J98.59
  necrosis (chronic) —*see* Ulcer, pressure,
    by site
  parental, inappropriate (excessive) Z62.6
  sore (chronic) —*see* Ulcer, pressure, by site
  spinal cord G95.20
  ulcer (chronic) —*see* Ulcer, pressure, by site
  venous, increased I87.8
Pre-syncope R55
Preterm
  delivery (*see also* Pregnancy, complicated by,
    preterm labor) O60.10
  labor —*see* Pregnancy, complicated by,
    preterm labor
  newborn (infant) P07.30
    gestational age
      28 completed weeks (28 weeks, 0 days
        through 28 weeks, 6 days) P07.31
      29 completed weeks (29 weeks, 0 days
        through 29 weeks, 6 days) P07.32
      30 completed weeks (30 weeks, 0 days
        through 30 weeks, 6 days) P07.33
      31 completed weeks (31 weeks, 0 days
        through 31 weeks, 6 days) P07.34
      32 completed weeks (32 weeks, 0 days
        through 32 weeks, 6 days) P07.35
      33 completed weeks (33 weeks, 0 days
        through 33 weeks, 6 days) P07.36
      34 completed weeks (34 weeks, 0 days
        through 34 weeks, 6 days) P07.37
      35 completed weeks (35 weeks, 0 days
        through 35 weeks, 6 days) P07.38
      36 completed weeks (36 weeks, 0 days
        through 36 weeks, 6 days) P07.39
Previa
  placenta (total) (without hemorrhage)
    O44.0-●

Previa *(Continued)*
  placenta *(Continued)*
    with hemorrhage O44.1-●
    complete O44.0-●
      with hemorrhage O44.1-●
    low —*see also* Delivery, complicated, by,
      placenta, low O44.4-●
      with hemorrhage O44.5-●
    marginal O44.2-●
      with hemorrhage O44.3-●
    partial O44.2-●
      with hemorrhage O44.3-●
  vasa O69.4
Priapism N48.30
  due to
    disease classified elsewhere N48.32
    drug N48.33
    specified cause NEC N48.39
    trauma N48.31
Prickling sensation (skin) R20.2
Prickly heat L74.0
Primary —*see* condition
Primigravida
  elderly, affecting management of pregnancy,
    labor and delivery (supervision only) —
    see Pregnancy, complicated by, elderly,
    primigravida
  older, affecting management of pregnancy,
    labor and delivery (supervision only) —
    see Pregnancy, complicated by, elderly,
    primigravida
  very young, affecting management of
    pregnancy, labor and delivery (supervision
    only) —*see* Pregnancy, complicated by,
    young mother, primigravida
Primipara
  elderly, affecting management of pregnancy,
    labor and delivery (supervision only) —
    see Pregnancy, complicated by, elderly,
    primigravida
  older, affecting management of pregnancy,
    labor and delivery (supervision only) —
    see Pregnancy, complicated by, elderly,
    primigravida
  very young, affecting management
    of pregnancy, labor and delivery
    (supervision only) —*see* Pregnancy,
    complicated by, young mother,
    primigravida
Primus varus (bilateral) Q66.2
PRIND (Prolonged reversible ischemic
  neurologic deficit) I63.9
Pringle's disease (tuberous sclerosis) Q85.1
Prinzmetal angina I20.1
Prizefighter ear —*see* Cauliflower ear
Problem (with) (related to)
  academic Z55.8
  acculturation Z60.3
  adjustment (to)
    change of job Z56.1
    life-cycle transition Z60.0
    pension Z60.0
    retirement Z60.0
  adopted child Z62.821
  alcoholism in family Z63.72
  atypical parenting situation Z62.9
  bankruptcy Z59.8
  behavioral (adult) F69
    drug seeking Z76.5
  birth of sibling affecting child Z62.898
  care (of)
    provider dependency Z74.9
      specified NEC Z74.8
    sick or handicapped person in family or
      household Z63.6
  child
    abuse (affecting the child) —*see*
      Maltreatment, child
    custody or support proceedings Z65.3
    in care of non-parental family member
      Z62.21

Problem *(Continued)*
  child *(Continued)*
    in foster care Z62.21
    in welfare custody Z62.21
    living in orphanage or group home Z62.22
  child-rearing Z62.9
    specified NEC Z62.898
  communication (developmental) F80.9
  conflict or discord (with)
    boss Z56.4
    classmates Z55.4
    counselor Z64.4
    employer Z56.4
    family Z63.9
      specified NEC Z63.8
    probation officer Z64.4
    social worker Z64.4
    teachers Z55.4
    workmates Z56.4
  conviction in legal proceedings Z65.0
    with imprisonment Z65.1
  counselor Z64.4
  creditors Z59.8
  digestive K92.9
  drug addict in family Z63.72
  ear —*see* Disorder, ear
  economic Z59.9
    affecting care Z59.9
    specified NEC Z59.8
  education Z55.9
    specified NEC Z55.8
  employment Z56.9
    change of job Z56.1
    discord Z56.4
    environment Z56.5
    sexual harassment Z56.81
    specified NEC Z56.89
    stress NEC Z56.6
    stressful schedule Z56.3
    threat of job loss Z56.2
    unemployment Z56.0
  enuresis, child F98.0
  eye H57.9
  failed examinations (school) Z55.2
  falling Z91.81
  family —*see also* Disruption, family Z63.9-●
    specified NEC Z63.8
  feeding (elderly) (infant) R63.3
    newborn P92.9
      breast P92.5
      overfeeding P92.4
      slow P92.2
      specified NEC P92.8
      underfeeding P92.3
    nonorganic F50.89
  finance Z59.9
    specified NEC Z59.8
  foreclosure on loan Z59.8
  foster child Z62.822
  frightening experience(s) in childhood
    Z62.898
  genital NEC
    female N94.9
    male N50.9
  health care Z75.9
    specified NEC Z75.8
  hearing —*see* Deafness
  homelessness Z59.0
  housing Z59.9
    inadequate Z59.1
    isolated Z59.8
    specified NEC Z59.8
  identity (of childhood) F93.8
  illegitimate pregnancy (unwanted) Z64.0
  illiteracy Z55.0
  impaired mobility Z74.09
  imprisonment or incarceration Z65.1
  inadequate teaching affecting education
    Z55.8
  inappropriate (excessive) parental pressure
    Z62.6

▶ New   ⇨ Revised   ~~deleted~~ Deleted   ● Use Additional Character(s)

Problem (Continued)
  influencing health status NEC Z78.9
  in-law Z63.1
  institutionalization, affecting child
      Z62.22
  intrafamilial communication Z63.8
  jealousy, child F93.8
  landlord Z59.2
  language (developmental) F80.9
  learning (developmental) F81.9
  legal Z65.3
    conviction without imprisonment
        Z65.0
    imprisonment Z65.1
    release from prison Z65.2
  life-management Z73.9
    specified NEC Z73.89
  life-style Z72.9
    gambling Z72.6
    high-risk sexual behavior (heterosexual)
        Z72.51
      bisexual Z72.53
      homosexual Z72.52
    inappropriate eating habits Z72.4
    self-damaging behavior NEC Z72.89
    specified NEC Z72.89
    tobacco use Z72.0
  literacy Z55.9
    low level Z55.0
    specified NEC Z55.8
  living alone Z60.2
  lodgers Z59.2
  loss of love relationship in childhood
      Z62.898
  marital Z63.0
    involving
      divorce Z63.5
      estrangement Z63.5
      gender identity F66
  mastication K08.89
  medical
    care, within family Z63.6
    facilities Z75.9
      specified NEC Z75.8
  mental F48.9
  multiparity Z64.1
  negative life events in childhood Z62.9
    altered pattern of family relationships
        Z62.898
    frightening experience Z62.898
    loss of
      love relationship Z62.898
      self-esteem Z62.898
    physical abuse (alleged) —see
        Maltreatment, child
    removal from home Z62.29
    specified event NEC Z62.898
  neighbor Z59.2
  neurological NEC R29.818
  new step-parent affecting child Z62.898
  none (feared complaint unfounded) Z71.1
  occupational NEC Z56.89
  parent-child —see Conflict, parent-child
  personal hygiene Z91.89
  personality F69
  phase-of-life transition, adjustment Z60.0
  presence of sick or disabled person
        in family or household Z63.79
      needing care Z63.6
  primary support group (family) Z63.9
    specified NEC Z63.8
  probation officer Z64.4
  psychiatric F99
  psychosexual (development) F66
  psychosocial Z65.9
    religious or spiritual Z65.8
    specified NEC Z65.8
  relationship Z63.9
    childhood F93.8
  release from prison Z65.2
    religious or spiritual Z65.8

Problem (Continued)
  removal from home affecting child
      Z62.29
  seeking and accepting known hazardous and
      harmful
    behavioral or psychological interventions
        Z65.8
    chemical, nutritional or physical
        interventions Z65.8
  sexual function (nonorganic) F52.9
  sight H54.7
  sleep disorder, child F51.9
  smell —see Disturbance, sensation, smell
  social
    environment Z60.9
      specified NEC Z60.8
    exclusion and rejection Z60.4
    worker Z64.4
  speech R47.9
    developmental F80.9
    specified NEC R47.89
  swallowing —see Dysphagia
  taste —see Disturbance, sensation, taste
  tic, child F95.0
  underachievement in school Z55.3
  unemployment Z56.0
    threatened Z56.2
  unwanted pregnancy Z64.0
  upbringing Z62.9
    specified NEC Z62.898
  urinary N39.9
  voice production R47.89
  work schedule (stressful) Z56.3
Procedure (surgical)
  converted
    arthroscopic to open Z53.33
    laparoscopic to open Z53.31
    specified procedure NEC to open
        Z53.39
    thoracoscopic to open Z53.32
  for purpose other than remedying health
      state Z41.9
    specified NEC Z41.8
  not done Z53.9
    because of
      administrative reasons Z53.8
      contraindication Z53.09
        smoking Z53.01
      patient's decision Z53.20
        for reasons of belief or group pressure
            Z53.1
        left against medical advice (AMA)
            Z53.21
      specified reason NEC Z53.29
    specified reason NEC Z53.8
Procidentia (uteri) N81.3
Proctalgia K62.89
  fugax K59.4
  spasmodic K59.4
Proctitis K62.89
  amebic (acute) A06.0
  chlamydial A56.3
  gonococcal A54.6
  granulomatous —see Enteritis, regional, large
      intestine
  herpetic A60.1
  radiation K62.7
  tuberculous A18.32
  ulcerative (chronic) K51.20
    with
      complication K51.219
        abscess K51.214
        fistula K51.213
        obstruction K51.212
        rectal bleeding K51.211
        specified NEC K51.218
Proctocele
  female (without uterine prolapse) N81.6
    with uterine prolapse N81.2
      complete N81.3
  male K62.3

Proctocolitis
  food-induced eosinophilic K52.82
  food protein-induced K52.82
  milk protein-induced K52.82
  mucosal —see Rectosigmoiditis, ulcerative
Proctoptosis K62.3
Proctorrhagia K62.5
Proctosigmoiditis K63.89
  ulcerative (chronic) —see Rectosigmoiditis,
      ulcerative
Proctospasm K59.4
  psychogenic F45.8
Profichet's disease —see Disorder, soft tissue,
    specified type NEC
Progeria E34.8
Prognathism (mandibular) (maxillary) M26.19
Progonoma (melanotic) —see Neoplasm,
    benign, by site
Progressive —see condition
Prolactinoma
  specified site —see Neoplasm, benign,
      by site
  unspecified site D35.2
Prolapse, prolapsed
  anus, anal (canal) (sphincter) K62.2
  arm or hand O32.2
    causing obstructed labor O64.4
  bladder (mucosa) (sphincter) (acquired)
    congenital Q79.4
    female —see Cystocele
    male N32.89
  breast implant (prosthetic) T85.49
  cecostomy K94.09
  cecum K63.4
  cervix, cervical (hypertrophied) N81.2
    anterior lip, obstructing labor O65.5
    congenital Q51.828
    postpartal, old N81.2
    stump N81.85
  ciliary body (traumatic) —see Laceration,
      eye(ball), with prolapse or loss of
      interocular tissue
  colon (pedunculated) K63.4
  colostomy K94.09
  disc (intervertebral) —see Displacement,
      intervertebral disc
  eye implant (orbital) T85.398
    lens (ocular) —see Complications,
        intraocular lens
  fallopian tube N83.4-•
  gastric (mucosa) K31.89
  genital, female N81.9
    specified NEC N81.89
  globe, nontraumatic —see Luxation, globe
  ileostomy bud K94.19
  intervertebral disc —see Displacement,
      intervertebral disc
  intestine (small) K63.4
  iris (traumatic) —see Laceration, eye(ball),
      with prolapse or loss of interocular
      tissue
    nontraumatic H21.89
  kidney N28.83
    congenital Q63.2
  laryngeal muscles or ventricle J38.7
  liver K76.89
  meatus urinarius N36.8
  mitral (valve) I34.1
  ocular lens implant —see Complications,
      intraocular lens
  organ or site, congenital NEC —see
      Malposition, congenital
  ovary N83.4-•
  pelvic floor, female N81.89
  perineum, female N81.89
  rectum (mucosa) (sphincter) K62.3
    due to trichuris trichuria B79
  spleen D73.89
  stomach K31.89
  umbilical cord
    complicating delivery O69.0

Prolapse, prolapsed *(Continued)*
  urachus, congenital Q64.4
  ureter N28.89
    with obstruction N13.5
      with infection N13.6
  ureterovesical orifice N28.89
  urethra (acquired) (infected) (mucosa)
      N36.8
    congenital Q64.71
  urinary meatus N36.8
    congenital Q64.72
  uterovaginal N81.4
    complete N81.3
    incomplete N81.2
  uterus (with prolapse of vagina) N81.4
    complete N81.3
    congenital Q51.818
    first degree N81.2
    in pregnancy or childbirth —*see*
        Pregnancy, complicated by,
        abnormal, uterus
    incomplete N81.2
    postpartal (old) N81.4
    second degree N81.2
    third degree N81.3
  uveal (traumatic) —*see* Laceration, eye(ball),
      with prolapse or loss of interocular
      tissue
  vagina (anterior) (wall) —*see* Cystocele
    with prolapse of uterus N81.4
      complete N81.3
      incomplete N81.2
    posterior wall N81.6
    posthysterectomy N99.3
  vitreous (humor) H43.0-•
    in wound —*see* Laceration, eye(ball), with
        prolapse or loss of interocular tissue
  womb —*see* Prolapse, uterus
Prolapsus, female N81.9
  specified NEC N81.89
Proliferation(s)
  primary cutaneous CD30-positive large T-cell
      C86.6
  prostate, atypical small acinar N42.32
Proliferative —*see* condition
Prolonged, prolongation (of)
  bleeding (time) (idiopathic) R79.1
  coagulation (time) R79.1
  gestation (over 42 completed weeks)
    mother O48.1
    newborn P08.22
  interval I44.0
  labor O63.9
    first stage O63.0
    second stage O63.1
  partial thromboplastin time (PTT) R79.1
  pregnancy (more than 42 weeks gestation)
      O48.1
  prothrombin time R79.1
  QT interval I45.81
  uterine contractions in labor O62.4
Prominence, prominent
  with disproportion (fetopelvic) O33.0
    causing obstructed labor O65.0
  auricle (congenital) (ear) Q17.5
  ischial spine or sacral promontory
  nose (congenital) acquired M95.0
Promiscuity —*see* High, risk, sexual behavior
Pronation
  ankle —*see* Deformity, limb, foot, specified
      NEC
  foot —*see also* Deformity, limb, foot, specified
      NEC
    congenital Q74.2
Prophylactic
  administration of
    antibiotics, long-term Z79.2
      short-term use - omit code
    drug —*see also* Long-term (current) drug
        therapy (use of) Z79.899-•
  medication Z79.899

Prophylactic *(Continued)*
  organ removal (for neoplasia management)
      Z40.00
    breast Z40.01
    fallopian tube(s) Z40.03
      with ovary(s) Z40.02
    ovary(s) Z40.02
    specified site NEC Z40.09
  surgery Z40.9
    for risk factors related to malignant
        neoplasm —*see* Prophylactic, organ
        removal
    specified NEC Z40.8
  vaccination Z23
Propionic acidemia E71.121
Proptosis (ocular) —*see also* Exophthalmos
  thyroid —*see* Hyperthyroidism, with goiter
Prosecution, anxiety concerning Z65.3
Prosopagnosia R48.3
Prostadynia N42.81
Prostate, prostatic —*see* condition
Prostatism —*see* Hyperplasia, prostate
Prostatitis (congestive) (suppurative) (with
      cystitis) N41.9
  acute N41.0
  cavitary N41.8
  chronic N41.1
  diverticular N41.8
  due to Trichomonas (vaginalis) A59.02
  fibrous N41.1
  gonococcal (acute) (chronic) A54.22
  granulomatous N41.4
  hypertrophic N41.1
  subacute N41.1
  trichomonal A59.02
  tuberculous A18.14
Prostatocystitis N41.3
Prostatorrhea N42.89
Prostatosis N42.82
Prostration R53.83
  heat —*see also* Heat, exhaustion
    anhydrotic T67.3
    due to
      salt (and water) depletion T67.4
      water depletion T67.3
  nervous F48.8
  senile R54
Protanomaly (anomalous trichromat) H53.54
Protanopia (complete) (incomplete) H53.54
Protection (against) (from) —*see* Prophylactic
Protein
  deficiency NEC —*see* Malnutrition
  malnutrition —*see* Malnutrition
  sickness —*see also* Reaction, serum T80.69
Proteinemia R77.9
Proteinosis
  alveolar (pulmonary) J84.01
  lipid or lipoid (of Urbach) E78.89
Proteinuria R80.9
  Bence Jones R80.3
  complicating pregnancy —*see* Proteinuria,
      gestational
  gestational
    complicating
      childbirth O12.14
      pregnancy O12.1-•
        with edema O12.2-•
    puerperium O12.15
  idiopathic R80.0
  isolated R80.0
    with glomerular lesion N06.9
      dense deposit disease N06.6
      diffuse
        crescentic glomerulonephritis N06.7
        endocapillary proliferative
            glomerulonephritis N06.4
        mesangiocapillary glomerulonephritis
            N06.5
      focal and segmental hyalinosis or
          sclerosis N06.1
      membranous (diffuse) N06.2

Proteinuria *(Continued)*
  isolated *(Continued)*
    with glomerular lesion *(Continued)*
      mesangial proliferative (diffuse)
          N06.3
      minimal change N06.0
      specified pathology NEC N06.8
  orthostatic R80.2
    with glomerular lesion —*see* Proteinuria,
        isolated, with glomerular lesion
  persistent R80.1
    with glomerular lesion —*see* Proteinuria,
        isolated, with glomerular lesion
  postural R80.2
    with glomerular lesion —*see* Proteinuria,
        isolated, with glomerular lesion
  pre-eclamptic —*see* Pre-eclampsia
  puerperal O12.15
  specified type NEC R80.8
Proteolysis, pathologic D65
Proteus (mirabilis) (morganii), as cause of
    disease classified elsewhere B96.4
Prothrombin gene mutation D68.52
Protoporphyria, erythropoietic E80.0
Protozoal —*see also* condition
  disease B64
  specified NEC B60.8
Protrusion, protrusio
  acetabuli M24.7
  acetabulum (into pelvis) M24.7
  device, implant or graft —*see also*
      Complications, by site and type,
      mechanical T85.698
    arterial graft NEC —*see* Complication,
        cardiovascular device, mechanical,
        vascular
    breast (implant) T85.49
    catheter NEC T85.698
      cystostomy T83.090
      dialysis (renal) T82.49
        intraperitoneal T85.691
      infusion NEC T82.594
        spinal (epidural) (subdural)
            T85.690
      urinary —*see also* Complications,
          catheter, urinary T83.098
    electronic (electrode) (pulse generator)
        (stimulator)
      bone T84.390
      nervous system —*see* Complication,
          prosthetic device, mechanical,
          electronic nervous system
          stimulator
    fixation, internal (orthopedic) NEC —
        see Complication, fixation device,
        mechanical
    gastrointestinal —*see* Complications,
        prosthetic device, mechanical,
        gastrointestinal device
    genital NEC T83.498
      intrauterine contraceptive device
          T83.39
      penile prosthesis (cylinder) (implanted)
          (pump) (resevoir) T83.490
      testicular prosthesis T83.491
    heart NEC —*see* Complication,
        cardiovascular device, mechanical
    joint prosthesis —*see* Complications, joint
        prosthesis, mechanical, specified NEC,
        by site
    ocular NEC —*see* Complications, prosthetic
        device, mechanical, ocular device
    orthopedic NEC —*see* Complication,
        orthopedic, device, mechanical
    specified NEC T85.628
    urinary NEC —*see also* Complication,
        genitourinary, device, urinary,
        mechanical
      graft T83.29
    vascular NEC —*see* Complication,
        cardiovascular device, mechanical

Protrusion, protrusio (Continued)
  device, implant or graft (Continued)
    ventricular intracranial shunt T85.09
  intervertebral disc —see Displacement,
    intervertebral disc
  joint prosthesis —see Complications, joint
    prosthesis, mechanical, specified NEC,
    by site
  nucleus pulposus —see Displacement,
    intervertebral disc
Prune belly (syndrome) Q79.4
Prurigo (ferox) (gravis) (Hebrae) (Hebra's)
    (mitis) (simplex) L28.2
  Besnier's L20.0
  estivalis L56.4
  nodularis L28.1
  psychogenic F45.8
Pruritus, pruritic (essential) L29.9
  ani, anus L29.0
    psychogenic F45.8
  anogenital L29.3
    psychogenic F45.8
  due to onchocerca volvulus B73.1
  gravidarum —see Pregnancy, complicated by,
    specified pregnancy-related condition
    NEC
  hiemalis L29.8
  neurogenic (any site) F45.8
  perianal L29.0
  psychogenic (any site) F45.8
  scroti, scrotum L29.1
    psychogenic F45.8
  senile, senilis L29.8
  specified NEC L29.8
    psychogenic F45.8
  Trichomonas A59.9
  vulva, vulvae L29.2
    psychogenic F45.8
Pseudarthrosis, pseudoarthrosis (bone) —see
    Nonunion, fracture
  clavicle, congenital Q74.0
  joint, following fusion or arthrodesis M96.0
Pseudoaneurysm —see Aneurysm
Pseudoangina (pectoris) —see Angina
Pseudoangioma I81
Pseudoarteriosus Q28.8
Pseudoarthrosis —see Pseudarthrosis
Pseudobulbar affect (PBA) F48.2
Pseudochromhidrosis L67.8
Pseudocirrhosis, liver, pericardial I31.1
Pseudocowpox B08.03
Pseudocoxalgia M91.3-●
Pseudocroup J38.5
Pseudo-Cushing's syndrome, alcohol-induced
    E24.4
Pseudocyesis F45.8
Pseudocyst
  lung J98.4
  pancreas K86.3
  retina —see Cyst, retina
Pseudoelephantiasis neuroarthritica Q82.0
Pseudoexfoliation, capsule (lens) —see
    Cataract, specified NEC
Pseudofolliculitis barbae L73.1
Pseudoglioma H44.89
Pseudohemophilia (Bernuth's) (hereditary)
    (type B) D68.0
  Type A D69.8
  vascular D69.8
Pseudohermaphroditism Q56.3
  adrenal E25.8
  female Q56.2
    with adrenocortical disorder E25.8
    without adrenocortical disorder
      Q56.2
    adrenal (congenital) E25.0
    unspecified E25.9
  male Q56.1
    with
      adrenocortical disorder E25.8
      androgen resistance E34.51

Pseudohermaphroditism (Continued)
  male (Continued)
    with (Continued)
      cleft scrotum Q56.1
      feminizing testis E34.51
      5-alpha-reductase deficiency E29.1
    without gonadal disorder Q56.1
    adrenal E25.8
    unspecified E25.9
Pseudo-Hurler's polydystrophy E77.0
Pseudohydrocephalus G93.2
➡ Pseudohypertrophic muscular dystrophy
    (Erb's) G71.02
➡ Pseudohypertrophy, muscle G71.09
Pseudohypoparathyroidism E20.1
Pseudoinsomnia F51.03
Pseudoleukemia, infantile D64.89
Pseudomembranous —see condition
Pseudomeningocele (cerebral) (infective) (post-
    traumatic) G96.19
  postprocedural (spinal) G97.82
Pseudomenses (newborn) P54.6
Pseudomenstruation (newborn) P54.6
Pseudomonas
  aeruginosa, as cause of disease classified
    elsewhere B96.5
  mallei infection A24.0
    as cause of disease classified elsewhere
      B96.5
  pseudomallei, as cause of disease classified
    elsewhere B96.5
Pseudomyotonia G71.19
Pseudomyxoma peritonei C78.6
Pseudoneuritis, optic (nerve) (disc) (papilla),
    congenital Q14.2
Pseudo-obstruction intestine (acute) (chronic)
    (idiopathic) (intermittent secondary)
    (primary) K59.8
Pseudopapilledema H47.33-●
  congenital Q14.2
Pseudoparalysis
  arm or leg R29.818
  atonic, congenital P94.2
Pseudopelade L66.0
Pseudophakia Z96.1
Pseudopolyarthritis, rhizomelic M35.3
Pseudopolycythemia D75.1
Pseudopseudohypoparathyroidism E20.1
Pseudopterygium H11.81-●
Pseudoptosis (eyelid) —see Blepharochalasis
Pseudopuberty, precocious
  female heterosexual E25.8
  male isosexual E25.8
Pseudorickets (renal) N25.0
Pseudorubella B08.20
Pseudosclerema, newborn P83.88
Pseudosclerosis (brain)
  Jakob's —see Creutzfeldt-Jakob disease or
    syndrome
  of Westphal (Strüümpell) E83.01
  spastic —see Creutzfeldt-Jakob disease or
    syndrome
Pseudotetanus —see Convulsions
Pseudotetany R29.0
  hysterical F44.5
Pseudotruncus arteriosus Q25.49
Pseudotuberculosis A28.2
  enterocolitis A04.8
  pasteurella (infection) A28.0
Pseudotumor
  cerebri G93.2
  orbital H05.11-●
Pseudoxanthoma elasticum Q82.8
Psilosis (sprue) (tropical) K90.1
  nontropical K90.0
Psittacosis A70
Psoitis M60.88
Psoriasis L40.9
  arthropathic L40.50
    arthritis mutilans L40.52
    distal interphalangeal L40.51

Psoriasis (Continued)
  arthropathic (Continued)
    juvenile L40.54
    other specified L40.59
    spondylitis L40.53
  buccal K13.29
  flexural L40.8
  guttate L40.4
  mouth K13.29
  nummular L40.0
  plaque L40.0
  psychogenic F54
  pustular (generalized) L40.1
    palmaris et plantaris L40.3
  specified NEC L40.8
  vulgaris L40.0
Psychasthenia F48.8
Psychiatric disorder or problem F99
Psychogenic —see also condition
  factors associated with physical conditions
    F54
Psychological and behavioral factors affecting
    medical condition F59
Psychoneurosis, psychoneurotic —see also
    Neurosis
  anxiety (state) F41.1
  depersonalization F48.1
  hypochondriacal F45.21
  hysteria F44.9
  neurasthenic F48.8
  personality NEC F60.89
Psychopathy, psychopathic
  affectionless F94.2
  autistic F84.5
  constitution, post-traumatic F07.81
  personality —see Disorder, personality
  sexual —see Deviation, sexual
  state F60.2
Psychosexual identity disorder of childhood
    F64.2
Psychosis, psychotic F29
  acute (transient) F23
    hysterical F44.9
  affective —see Disorder, mood
  alcoholic F10.959
    with
      abuse F10.159
      anxiety disorder F10.980
        with
          abuse F10.180
          dependence F10.280
      delirium tremens F10.231
      delusions F10.950
        with
          abuse F10.150
          dependence F10.250
      dementia F10.97
        with dependence F10.27
      dependence F10.259
      hallucinosis F10.951
        with
          abuse F10.151
          dependence F10.251
      mood disorder F10.94
        with
          abuse F10.14
          dependence F10.24
      paranoia F10.950
        with
          abuse F10.150
          dependence F10.250
      persisting amnesia F10.96
        with dependence F10.26
    amnestic confabulatory F10.96
      with dependence F10.26
    delirium tremens F10.231
    Korsakoff's, Korsakov's, Korsakow's F10.26
    paranoid type F10.950
      with
        abuse F10.150
        dependence F10.250

Psychosis, psychotic (Continued)
  anergastic —see Psychosis, organic
  arteriosclerotic (simple type) (uncomplicated)
      F01.50
    with behavioral disturbance F01.51
  childhood F84.0
    atypical F84.8
  climacteric —see Psychosis, involutional
  confusional F29
    acute or subacute F05
    reactive F23
  cycloid F23
  depressive —see Disorder, depressive
  disintegrative (childhood) F84.3
  drug-induced —see F11-F19 with .x59
    paranoid and hallucinatory states —see
        F11-F19 with .x50 or .x51
  due to or associated with
    addiction, drug —see F11-F19 with .X59
    dependence
      alcohol F10.259
      drug —see F11-F19 with .x59
    epilepsy F06.8
    Huntington's chorea F06.8
    ischemia, cerebrovascular (generalized)
        F06.8
    multiple sclerosis F06.8
    physical disease F06.8
    presenile dementia F03
    senile dementia F03
    vascular disease (arteriosclerotic) (cerebral)
        F01.50
      with behavioral disturbance F01.51
  epileptic F06.8
  episode F23
    due to or associated with physical
        condition F06.8
  exhaustive F43.0
  hallucinatory, chronic F28
  hypomanic F30.8
  hysterical (acute) F44.9
  induced F24
  infantile F84.0
    atypical F84.8
  infective (acute) (subacute) F05
  involutional F28
    depressive —see Disorder, depressive
    melancholic —see Disorder, depressive
    paranoid (state) F22
  Korsakoff's, Korsakov's, Korsakow's
      (nonalcoholic) F04
    alcoholic F10.96
      in dependence F10.26
    induced by other psychoactive
        substance —see categories F11-F19
        with .x5x
  mania, manic (single episode) F30.2
    recurrent type F31.89
  manic-depressive —see Disorder, bipolar
  menopausal —see Psychosis, involutional
  mixed schizophrenic and affective F25.8
  multi-infarct (cerebrovascular) F01.50
    with behavioral disturbance F01.51
  nonorganic F29
    specified NEC F28
  organic F09
    due to or associated with
      arteriosclerosis (cerebral) —see
          Psychosis, arteriosclerotic
      cerebrovascular disease,
          arteriosclerotic —see Psychosis,
          arteriosclerotic
      childbirth —see Psychosis, puerperal
      Creutzfeldt-Jakob disease or
          syndrome —see Creutzfeldt-Jakob
          disease or syndrome
      dependence, alcohol F10.259
      disease
        alcoholic liver F10.259
        brain, arteriosclerotic —see Psychosis,
            arteriosclerotic

Psychosis, psychotic (Continued)
  organic (Continued)
    due to or associated with (Continued)
      disease (Continued)
        cerebrovascular F01.50
          with behavioral disturbance F01.51
        Creutzfeldt-Jakob —see Creutzfeldt-
            Jakob disease or syndrome
        endocrine or metabolic F06.8
          acute or subacute F05
        liver, alcoholic F10.259
      epilepsy transient (acute) F05
      infection
        brain (intracranial) F06.8
          acute or subacute F05
      intoxication
        alcoholic (acute) F10.259
        drug F19 with .X59 F11-
        ▶drug F11-F19 with .x59
      ischemia, cerebrovascular (generalized) —
          see Psychosis, arteriosclerotic
      puerperium —see Psychosis, puerperal
      trauma, brain (birth) (from electric
          current) (surgical) F06.8
        acute or subacute F05
    infective F06.8
      acute or subacute F05
    post-traumatic F06.8
      acute or subacute F05
  paranoiac F22
  paranoid (climacteric) (involutional)
      (menopausal) F22
    psychogenic (acute) F23
    schizophrenic F20.0
    senile F03
  ⇒postpartum F53.1
  presbyophrenic (type) F03
  presenile F03
  psychogenic (paranoid) F23
    depressive F32.3
  ⇒puerperal F53.1
    specified type —see Psychosis, by type
  reactive (brief) (transient) (emotional stress)
      (psychological trauma) F23
    depressive F32.3
      recurrent F33.3
    excitative type F30.8
  schizoaffective F25.9
    depressive type F25.1
    manic type F25.0
  schizophrenia, schizophrenic —see
      Schizophrenia
  schizophrenia-like, in epilepsy F06.2
  schizophreniform F20.81
    affective type F25.9
    brief F23
    confusional type F23
    mixed type F25.0
  senile NEC F03
    depressed or paranoid type F03
    simple deterioration F03
    specified type — code to condition
  shared F24
  situational (reactive) F23
  symbiotic (childhood) F84.3
  symptomatic F09
Psychosomatic —see Disorder,
    psychosomatic
Psychosyndrome, organic F07.9
Psychotic episode due to or associated with
    physical condition F06.8
Pterygium (eye) H11.00-●
  amyloid H11.01-●
  central H11.02-●
  colli Q18.3
  double H11.03-●
  peripheral
    progressive H11.05-●
    stationary H11.04-●
  recurrent H11.06-●
Ptilosis (eyelid) —see Madarosis

Ptomaine (poisoning) —see Poisoning, food
Ptosis —see also Blepharoptosis
  adiposa (false) —see Blepharoptosis
  breast N64.81
  ▶brow H57.81-●
  cecum K63.4
  colon K63.4
  congenital (eyelid) Q10.0
    specified site NEC —see Anomaly, by site
  ▶eyebrow H57.81-●
  eyelid —see Blepharoptosis
    congenital Q10.0
  gastric K31.89
  intestine K63.4
  kidney N28.83
  liver K76.89
  renal N28.83
  splanchnic K63.4
  spleen D73.89
  stomach K31.89
  viscera K63.4
PTP D69.51
Ptyalism (periodic) K11.7
  hysterical F45.8
  pregnancy —see Pregnancy, complicated by,
      specified pregnancy-related condition
      NEC
  psychogenic F45.8
Ptyalolithiasis K11.5
Pubarche, precocious E30.1
Pubertas praecox E30.1
Puberty (development state) Z00.3
  bleeding (excessive) N92.2
  delayed E30.0
  precocious (constitutional) (cryptogenic)
      (idiopathic) E30.1
    central E22.8
    due to
      ovarian hyperfunction E28.1
        estrogen E28.0
      testicular hyperfunction E29.0
  premature E30.1
    due to
      adrenal cortical hyperfunction E25.8
      pineal tumor E34.8
      pituitary (anterior) hyperfunction E22.8
Puckering, macula —see Degeneration, macula,
    puckering
Pudenda, pudendum —see condition
Puente's disease (simple glandular cheilitis)
    K13.0
Puerperal, puerperium (complicated by,
    complications)
  abnormal glucose (tolerance test) O99.815
  abscess
    areola O91.02
      associated with lactation O91.03
    Bartholin's gland O86.19
    breast O91.12
      associated with lactation O91.13
    cervix (uteri) O86.11
    genital organ NEC O86.19
    kidney O86.21
    mammary O91.12
      associated with lactation O91.13
    nipple O91.02
      associated with lactation O91.03
    peritoneum O85
    subareolar O91.12
      associated with lactation O91.13
    urinary tract —see Puerperal, infection,
        urinary
    uterus O86.12
    vagina (wall) O86.13
    vaginorectal O86.13
    vulvovaginal gland O86.13
  adnexitis O86.19
  afibrinogenemia, or other coagulation defect
      O72.3
  albuminuria (acute) (subacute) —see
      Proteinuria, gestational

▶ New   ⇒ Revised   ~~deleted~~ Deleted   ● Use Additional Character(s)

Puerperal, puerperium (Continued)
alcohol use O99.315
anemia O90.81
    pre-existing (pre-pregnancy) O99.03
anesthetic death O89.8
apoplexy O99.43
bariatric surgery status O99.845
blood disorder NEC O99.13
blood dyscrasia O72.3
cardiomyopathy O90.3
cerebrovascular disorder (conditions in
    I60-I69) O99.43
cervicitis O86.11
circulatory system disorder O99.43
coagulopathy (any) O99.13
    with hemorrhage O72.3
complications O90.9
    specified NEC O90.89
convulsions —see Eclampsia
cystitis O86.22
cystopyelitis O86.29
delirium NEC F05
diabetes O24.93
    gestational —see Puerperal, gestational
        diabetes
    pre-existing O24.33
        specified NEC O24.83
        type 1 O24.03
        type 2 O24.13
digestive system disorder O99.63
disease O90.9
    breast NEC O92.29
    cerebrovascular (acute) O99.43
    nonobstetric NEC O99.89
    tubo-ovarian O86.19
    Valsuani's O99.03
disorder O90.9
    biliary tract O26.63
    lactation O92.70
    liver O26.63
    nonobstetric NEC O99.89
disruption
    cesarean wound O90.0
    episiotomy wound O90.1
    perineal laceration wound O90.1
drug use O99.325
eclampsia (with pre-existing hypertension)
    O15.2
embolism (pulmonary) (blood clot) —see
    Embolism, obstetric, puerperal
endocrine, nutritional or metabolic disease
    NEC O99.285
endophlebitis —see Puerperal, phlebitis
endotrachelitis O86.11
failure
    lactation (complete) O92.3
        partial O92.4
    renal, acute O90.4
fever (of unknown origin) O86.4
    septic O85
fissure, nipple O92.12
    associated with lactation O92.13
fistula
    breast (due to mastitis) O91.12
        associated with lactation O91.13
    nipple O91.02
        associated with lactation O91.03
galactophoritis O91.22
    associated with lactation O91.23
galactorrhea O92.6
gastric banding status O99.845
gastric bypass status O99.845
gastrointestinal disease NEC O99.63
gestational
    diabetes O24.439
        diet controlled O24.430
        insulin (and diet) controlled O24.434
        oral drug controlled (antidiabetic)
            (hypoglycemic) O24.435
    edema O12.05
        with proteinuria O12.25
    proteinuria O12.15

Puerperal, puerperium (Continued)
gonorrhea O98.23
hematoma, subdural O99.43
hemiplegia, cerebral O99.355-•
    due to cerebrovascular disorder
        O99.43
hemorrhage O72.1
    brain O99.43
    bulbar O99.43
    cerebellar O99.43
    cerebral O99.43
    cortical O99.43
    delayed or secondary O72.2
    extradural O99.43
    internal capsule O99.43
    intracranial O99.43
    intrapontine O99.43
    meningeal O99.43
    pontine O99.43
    retained placenta O72.0
    subarachnoid O99.43
    subcortical O99.43
    subdural O99.43
    third stage O72.0
    uterine, delayed O72.2
    ventricular O99.43
hemorrhoids O87.2
hepatorenal syndrome O90.4
hypertension —see Hypertension,
    complicating, puerperium
hypertrophy, breast O92.29
induration breast (fibrous) O92.29
infection O86.4
    cervix O86.11
    generalized O85
    genital tract NEC O86.19
    obstetric surgical wound O86.09
    kidney (bacillus coli) O86.21
    maternal O98.93
        carrier state NEC O99.835
        gonorrhea O98.23
        human immunodeficiency virus (HIV)
            O98.73
        protozoal O98.63
        sexually transmitted NEC O98.33
        specified NEC O98.83
        streptococcus group B (GBS) carrier state
            O99.825
        syphilis O98.13
        tuberculosis O98.03
        viral hepatitis O98.43
        viral NEC O98.53
    nipple O91.02
        associated with lactation O91.03
    peritoneum O85
    renal O86.21
    specified NEC O86.89
    urinary (asymptomatic) (tract) NEC
        O86.20
        bladder O86.22
        kidney O86.21
        specified site NEC O86.29
        urethra O86.22
    vagina O86.13
    vein —see Puerperal, phlebitis
ischemia, cerebral O99.43
lymphangitis O86.89
    breast O91.22
        associated with lactation
            O91.23
malignancy O9A.13
malnutrition O25.3
mammillitis O91.02
    associated with lactation O91.03
mammitis O91.22
    associated with lactation O91.23
mania F30.8
mastitis O91.22
    associated with lactation O91.23
    purulent O91.12
        associated with lactation O91.13

Puerperal, puerperium (Continued)
melancholia —see Disorder, depressive
mental disorder NEC O99.345
metroperitonitis O85
metrorrhagia —see Hemorrhage,
    postpartum
metrosalpingitis O86.19
metrovaginitis O86.13
milk leg O87.1
monoplegia, cerebral O99.43
mood disturbance O90.6
necrosis, liver (acute) (subacute)
    (conditions in subcategory K72.0)
    O26.63
    with renal failure O90.4
nervous system disorder O99.355
neuritis O90.89
obesity (pre-existing prior to pregnancy)
    O99.215
obesity surgery status O99.845
occlusion, precerebral artery O99.43
paralysis
    bladder (sphincter) O90.89
    cerebral O99.43
paralytic stroke O99.43
parametritis O85
paravaginitis O86.13
pelviperitonitis O85
perimetritis O86.12
perimetrosalpingitis O86.19
perinephritis O86.21
periphlebitis —see Puerperal phlebitis
peritoneal infection O85
peritonitis (pelvic) O85
perivaginitis O86.13
phlebitis O87.0
    deep O87.1
    pelvic O87.1
    superficial O87.0
phlebothrombosis, deep O87.1
phlegmasia alba dolens O87.1
placental polyp O90.89
pneumonia, embolic —see Embolism,
    obstetric, puerperal
pre-eclampsia —see Pre-eclampsia
psychosis F53.1
pyelitis O86.21
pyelocystitis O86.29
pyelonephritis O86.21
pyelonephrosis O86.21
pyemia O85
pyocystitis O86.29
pyohemia O85
pyometra O86.12
pyonephritis O86.21
pyosalpingitis O86.19
pyrexia (of unknown origin) O86.4
renal
    disease NEC O90.89
    failure O90.4
respiratory disease NEC O99.53
retention
    decidua —see Retention, decidua
    placenta O72.0
    secundines —see Retention,
        secundines
retracted nipple O92.02
salpingo-ovaritis O86.19
salpingoperitonitis O85
secondary perineal tear O90.1
sepsis O85
sepsis (pelvic) O85
septic thrombophlebitis O86.81
skin disorder NEC O99.73
specified condition NEC O99.89
stroke O99.43
subinvolution (uterus) O90.89
subluxation of symphysis (pubis)
    O26.73
suppuration —see Puerperal, abscess
tetanus A34

Puerperal, puerperium *(Continued)*
  thelitis O91.02
    associated with lactation O91.03
  thrombocytopenia O72.3
  thrombophlebitis (superficial) O87.0
    deep O87.1
    pelvic O87.1
    septic O86.81
  thrombosis (venous) —*see* Thrombosis,
      puerperal
  thyroiditis O90.5
  toxemia (eclamptic) (pre-eclamptic)
      (with convulsions) O15.2
  trauma, non-obstetric O9A.23
    caused by abuse (physical) (suspected)
        O9A.33
      confirmed O9A.33
      psychological (suspected)
          O9A.53
        confirmed O9A.53
      sexual (suspected) O9A.43
        confirmed O9A.43
  uremia (due to renal failure)
      O90.4
  urethritis O86.22
  vaginitis O86.13
  varicose veins (legs) O87.4
    vulva or perineum O87.8
  venous O87.9
  vulvitis O86.19
  vulvovaginitis O86.13
  white leg O87.1
Puerperium —*see* Puerperal
Pulmolithiasis J98.4
Pulmonary —*see* condition
Pulpitis (acute) (anachoretic) (chronic)
    (hyperplastic) (putrescent) (suppurative)
    (ulcerative) K04.01
  irreversible K04.02
  reversible K04.01
Pulpless tooth K04.99
Pulse
  alternating R00.8
  bigeminal R00.8
  fast R00.0
  feeble, rapid due to shock following injury
      T79.4
  rapid R00.0
  weak R09.89
Pulsus alternans or trigeminus R00.8
Punch drunk F07.81
Punctum lacrimale occlusion —*see* Obstruction,
    lacrimal
Puncture
  abdomen, abdominal
    wall S31.139
      with
        foreign body S31.149
        penetration into peritoneal cavity
            S31.639
          with foreign body S31.649
      epigastric region S31.132
        with
          foreign body S31.142
          penetration into peritoneal cavity
              S31.632
            with foreign body S31.642
      left
        lower quadrant S31.134
          with
            foreign body S31.144
            penetration into peritoneal cavity
                S31.634
              with foreign body S31.644
        upper quadrant S31.131
          with
            foreign body S31.141
            penetration into peritoneal cavity
                S31.631
              with foreign body S31.641

Puncture *(Continued)*
  abdomen, abdominal *(Continued)*
    wall *(Continued)*
      periumbilic region S31.135
        with
          foreign body S31.145
          penetration into peritoneal cavity
              S31.635
            with foreign body S31.645
      right
        lower quadrant S31.133
          with
            foreign body S31.143
            penetration into peritoneal cavity
                S31.633
              with foreign body S31.643
        upper quadrant S31.130
          with
            foreign body S31.140
            penetration into peritoneal cavity
                S31.630
              with foreign body S31.640
  accidental, complicating surgery —*see*
      Complication, accidental puncture or
      laceration
  alveolar (process) —*see* Puncture, oral cavity
  ankle S91.039
    with
      foreign body S91.049
    left S91.032
      with
        foreign body S91.042
    right S91.031
      with
        foreign body S91.041
  anus S31.833
    with foreign body S31.834
  arm (upper) S41.139
    with foreign body S41.149
    left S41.132
      with foreign body S41.142
    lower —*see* Puncture, forearm
    right S41.131
      with foreign body S41.141
  auditory canal (external) (meatus) —*see*
      Puncture, ear
  auricle, ear —*see* Puncture, ear
  axilla —*see* Puncture, arm
  back —*see also* Puncture, thorax, back
    lower S31.030
      with
        foreign body S31.040
          with penetration into
              retroperitoneal space S31.041
        penetration into retroperitoneal space
            S31.031
  bladder (traumatic) S37.29
    nontraumatic N32.89
  breast S21.039
    with foreign body S21.049
    left S21.032
      with foreign body S21.042
    right S21.031
      with foreign body S21.041
  buttock S31.803
    with foreign body S31.804
    left S31.823
      with foreign body S31.824
    right S31.813
      with foreign body S31.814
  by
    device, implant or graft —*see*
        Complications, by site and type,
        mechanical
    foreign body left accidentally in operative
        wound T81.539
    instrument (any) during a procedure,
        accidental —*see* Puncture, accidental
        complicating surgery
  calf —*see* Puncture, leg
  canaliculus lacrimalis —*see* Puncture, eyelid

Puncture *(Continued)*
  canthus, eye —*see* Puncture, eyelid
  cervical esophagus S11.23
    with foreign body S11.24
  cheek (external) S01.439
    with foreign body S01.449
    internal —*see* Puncture, oral cavity
    left S01.432
      with foreign body S01.442
    right S01.431
      with foreign body S01.441
  chest wall —*see* Puncture, thorax
  chin —*see* Puncture, head, specified site NEC
  clitoris —*see* Puncture, vulva
  costal region —*see* Puncture, thorax
  digit(s)
    foot —*see* Puncture, toe
    hand —*see* Puncture, finger
  ear (canal) (external) S01.339
    with foreign body S01.349
    drum S09.2-●
    left S01.332
      with foreign body S01.342
    right S01.331
      with foreign body S01.341
  elbow S51.039
    with
      foreign body S51.049
    left S51.032
      with
        foreign body S51.042
    right S51.031
      with
        foreign body S51.041
  epididymis —*see* Puncture, testis
  epigastric region —*see* Puncture, abdomen,
      wall, epigastric
  epiglottis S11.83
    with foreign body S11.84
  esophagus
    cervical S11.23
      with foreign body S11.24
    thoracic S27.818
  eyeball S05.6-●
    with foreign body S05.5-●
  eyebrow —*see* Puncture, eyelid
  eyelid S01.13-●
    with foreign body S01.14-●
    left S01.132
      with foreign body S01.142
    right S01.131
      with foreign body S01.141
  face NEC —*see* Puncture, head, specified site
      NEC
  finger(s) S61.239
    with
      damage to nail S61.339
        with
          foreign body S61.349
      foreign body S61.249
    index S61.238
      with
        damage to nail S61.338
          with
            foreign body S61.348
        foreign body S61.248
      left S61.231
        with
          damage to nail S61.331
            with
              foreign body S61.341
          foreign body S61.241
      right S61.230
        with
          damage to nail S61.330
            with
              foreign body S61.340
          foreign body S61.240
    little S61.238
      with
        damage to nail S61.338

▶ New　　⇒ Revised　　~~deleted~~ Deleted　　● Use Additional Character(s)

Puncture *(Continued)*
  finger *(Continued)*
    with *(Continued)*
      with *(Continued)*
        damage to nail *(Continued)*
          with
            foreign body S61.348
          foreign body S61.248
      left S61.237
        with
          damage to nail S61.337
            with
              foreign body S61.347
          foreign body S61.247
      right S61.236
        with
          damage to nail S61.336
            with
              foreign body S61.346
          foreign body S61.246
    middle S61.238
      with
        damage to nail S61.338
          with
            foreign body S61.348
        foreign body S61.248
      left S61.233
        with
          damage to nail S61.333
            with
              foreign body S61.343
          foreign body S61.243
      right S61.232
        with
          damage to nail S61.332
            with
              foreign body S61.342
          foreign body S61.242
    ring S61.238
      with
        damage to nail S61.338
          with
            foreign body S61.348
        foreign body S61.248
      left S61.235
        with
          damage to nail S61.335
            with
              foreign body S61.345
          foreign body S61.245
      right S61.234
        with
          damage to nail S61.334
            with
              foreign body S61.344
          foreign body S61.244
  flank S31.139
    with foreign body S31.149
  foot (except toe(s) alone) S91.339
    with foreign body S91.349
    left S91.332
      with foreign body S91.342
    right S91.331
      with foreign body S91.341
    toe —*see* Puncture, toe
  forearm S51.839
    with
      foreign body S51.849
    elbow only —*see* Puncture, elbow
    left S51.832
      with
        foreign body S51.842
    right S51.831
      with
        foreign body S51.841
  forehead —*see* Puncture, head, specified site NEC
  genital organs, external
    female S31.532
      with foreign body S31.542
      vagina —*see* Puncture, vagina
      vulva —*see* Puncture, vulva

Puncture *(Continued)*
  genital organs, external *(Continued)*
    male S31.531
      with foreign body S31.541
      penis —*see* Puncture, penis
      scrotum —*see* Puncture, scrotum
      testis —*see* Puncture, testis
  groin —*see* Puncture, abdomen, wall
  gum —*see* Puncture, oral cavity
  hand S61.439
    with
      foreign body S61.449
    finger —*see* Puncture, finger
    left S61.432
      with
        foreign body S61.442
    right S61.431
      with
        foreign body S61.441
    thumb —*see* Puncture, thumb
  head S01.93
    with foreign body S01.94
    cheek —*see* Puncture, cheek
    ear —*see* Puncture, ear
    eyelid —*see* Puncture, eyelid
    lip —*see* Puncture, oral cavity
    nose —*see* Puncture, nose
    oral cavity —*see* Puncture, oral cavity
    scalp S01.03
      with foreign body S01.04
    specified site NEC S01.83
      with foreign body S01.84
    temporomandibular area —*see* Puncture, cheek
  heart S26.99
    with hemopericardium S26.09
    without hemopericardium S26.19
  heel —*see* Puncture, foot
  hip S71.039
    with foreign body S71.049
    left S71.032
      with foreign body S71.042
    right S71.031
      with foreign body S71.041
  hymen —*see* Puncture, vagina
  hypochondrium —*see* Puncture, abdomen, wall
  hypogastric region —*see* Puncture, abdomen, wall
  inguinal region —*see* Puncture, abdomen, wall
  instep —*see* Puncture, foot
  internal organs —*see* Injury, by site
  interscapular region —*see* Puncture, thorax, back
  intestine
    large
      colon S36.599
        ascending S36.590
        descending S36.592
        sigmoid S36.593
        specified site NEC S36.598
        transverse S36.591
      rectum S36.69
    small S36.499
      duodenum S36.490
      specified site NEC S36.498
  intra-abdominal organ S36.99
    gallbladder S36.128
    intestine —*see* Puncture, intestine
    liver S36.118
    pancreas —*see* Puncture, pancreas
    peritoneum S36.81
    specified site NEC S36.898
    spleen S36.09
    stomach S36.39
  jaw —*see* Puncture, head, specified site NEC
  knee S81.039
    with foreign body S81.049
    left S81.032
      with foreign body S81.042

Puncture *(Continued)*
  knee *(Continued)*
    right S81.031
      with foreign body S81.041
  labium (majus) (minus) —*see* Puncture, vulva
  lacrimal duct —*see* Puncture, eyelid
  larynx S11.013
    with foreign body S11.014
  leg (lower) S81.839
    with foreign body S81.849
    foot —*see* Puncture, foot
    knee —*see* Puncture, knee
    left S81.832
      with foreign body S81.842
    right S81.831
      with foreign body S81.841
    upper —*see* Puncture, thigh
  lip S01.531
    with foreign body S01.541
  loin —*see* Puncture, abdomen, wall
  lower back —*see* Puncture, back, lower
  lumbar region —*see* Puncture, back, lower
  malar region —*see* Puncture, head, specified site NEC
  mammary —*see* Puncture, breast
  mastoid region —*see* Puncture, head, specified site NEC
  mouth —*see* Puncture, oral cavity
  nail
    finger —*see* Puncture, finger, with damage to nail
    toe —*see* Puncture, toe, with damage to nail
  nasal (septum) (sinus) —*see* Puncture, nose
  nasopharynx —*see* Puncture, head, specified site NEC
  neck S11.93
    with foreign body S11.94
    involving
      cervical esophagus —*see* Puncture, cervical esophagus
      larynx —*see* Puncture, larynx
      pharynx —*see* Puncture, pharynx
      thyroid gland —*see* Puncture, thyroid gland
      trachea —*see* Puncture, trachea
    specified site NEC S11.83
      with foreign body S11.84
  nose (septum) (sinus) S01.23
    with foreign body S01.24
  ocular —*see* Puncture, eyeball - oral cavity S01.532
    with foreign body S01.542
  orbit S05.4-●
  palate —*see* Puncture, oral cavity
  palm —*see* Puncture, hand
  pancreas S36.299
    body S36.291
    head S36.290
    tail S36.292
  pelvis —*see* Puncture, back, lower
  penis S31.23
    with foreign body S31.24
  perineum
    female S31.43
      with foreign body S31.44
    male S31.139
      with foreign body S31.149
  periocular area (with or without lacrimal passages) —*see* Puncture, eyelid
  phalanges
    finger —*see* Puncture, finger
    toe —*see* Puncture, toe
  pharynx S11.23
    with foreign body S11.24
  pinna —*see* Puncture, ear
  popliteal space —*see* Puncture, knee
  prepuce —*see* Puncture, penis
  pubic region S31.139
    with foreign body S31.149

Puncture *(Continued)*
  pudendum —*see* Puncture, genital organs, external
  rectovaginal septum —*see* Puncture, vagina
  sacral region —*see* Puncture, back, lower
  sacroiliac region —*see* Puncture, back, lower
  salivary gland —*see* Puncture, oral cavity
  scalp S01.03
    with foreign body S01.04
  scapular region —*see* Puncture, shoulder
  scrotum S31.33
    with foreign body S31.34
  shin —*see* Puncture, leg
  shoulder S41.039
    with foreign body S41.049
    left S41.032
      with foreign body S41.042
    right S41.031
      with foreign body S41.041
  spermatic cord —*see* Puncture, testis
  sternal region —*see* Puncture, thorax, front
  submaxillary region —*see* Puncture, head, specified site NEC
  submental region —*see* Puncture, head, specified site NEC
  subungual
    finger(s) —*see* Puncture, finger, with damage to nail
    toe —*see* Puncture, toe, with damage to nail
  supraclavicular fossa —*see* Puncture, neck, specified site NEC
  temple, temporal region —*see* Puncture, head, specified site NEC
  temporomandibular area —*see* Puncture, cheek
  testis S31.33
    with foreign body S31.34
  thigh S71.139
    with foreign body S71.149
    left S71.132
      with foreign body S71.142
    right S71.131
      with foreign body S71.141
  thorax, thoracic (wall) S21.93
    with foreign body S21.94
    back S21.23-•
      with
        foreign body S21.24-•
          with penetration S21.44
        penetration S21.43
    breast —*see* Puncture, breast
    front S21.13-•
      with
        foreign body S21.14-•
          with penetration S21.34
        penetration S21.33
  throat —*see* Puncture, neck
  thumb S61.039
    with
      damage to nail S61.139
        with
          foreign body S61.149
      foreign body S61.049
    left S61.032
      with
        damage to nail S61.132
          with
            foreign body S61.142
        foreign body S61.042
    right S61.031
      with
        damage to nail S61.131
          with
            foreign body S61.141
        foreign body S61.041

Puncture *(Continued)*
  thyroid gland S11.13
    with foreign body S11.14
  toe(s) S91.139
    with
      damage to nail S91.239
        with
          foreign body S91.249
      foreign body S91.149
    great S91.133
      with
        damage to nail S91.233
          with
            foreign body S91.243
        foreign body S91.143
      left S91.132
        with
          damage to nail S91.232
            with
              foreign body S91.242
          foreign body S91.142
      right S91.131
        with
          damage to nail S91.231
            with
              foreign body S91.241
          foreign body S91.141
    lesser S91.136
      with
        damage to nail S91.236
          with
            foreign body S91.246
        foreign body S91.146
      left S91.135
        with
          damage to nail S91.235
            with
              foreign body S91.245
          foreign body S91.145
      right S91.134
        with
          damage to nail S91.234
            with
              foreign body S91.244
          foreign body S91.144
  tongue —*see* Puncture, oral cavity
  trachea S11.023
    with foreign body S11.024
  tunica vaginalis —*see* Puncture, testis
  tympanum, tympanic membrane S09.2-•
  umbilical region S31.135
    with foreign body S31.145
  uvula —*see* Puncture, oral cavity
  vagina S31.43
    with foreign body S31.44
  vocal cords S11.033
    with foreign body S11.034
  vulva S31.43
    with foreign body S31.44
  wrist S61.539
    with
      foreign body S61.549
    left S61.532
      with
        foreign body S61.542
    right S61.531
      with
        foreign body S61.541
PUO (pyrexia of unknown origin) R50.9
Pupillary membrane (persistent) Q13.89
Pupillotonia —*see* Anomaly, pupil, function, tonic pupil
Purpura D69.2
  abdominal D69.0
  allergic D69.0
  anaphylactoid D69.0
  annularis telangiectodes L81.7
  arthritic D69.0
  autoerythrocyte sensitization D69.2
  autoimmune D69.0

Purpura *(Continued)*
  bacterial D69.0
  Bateman's (senile) D69.2
  capillary fragility (hereditary) (idiopathic) D69.8
  cryoglobulinemic D89.1
  Devil's pinches D69.2
  fibrinolytic —*see* Fibrinolysis
  fulminans, fulminous D65
  gangrenous D65
  hemorrhagic, hemorrhagica D69.3
    not due to thrombocytopenia D69.0
  Henoch (-Schönlein) (allergic) D69.0
  hypergammaglobulinemic (benign) (Waldenström's) D89.0
  idiopathic (thrombocytopenic) D69.3
    nonthrombocytopenic D69.0
  immune thrombocytopenic D69.3
  infectious D69.0
  malignant D69.0
  neonatorum P54.5
  nervosa D69.0
  newborn P54.5
  nonthrombocytopenic D69.2
    hemorrhagic D69.0
    idiopathic D69.0
  nonthrombopenic D69.2
  peliosis rheumatica D69.0
  posttransfusion (post-transfusion) (from (fresh) whole blood or blood products) D69.51
  primary D69.49
  red cell membrane sensitivity D69.2
  rheumatica D69.0
  Schönlein (-Henoch) (allergic) D69.0
  scorbutic E54 *[D77]*
  senile D69.2
  simplex D69.2
  symptomatica D69.0
  telangiectasia annularis L81.7
  thrombocytopenic D69.49
    congenital D69.42
    hemorrhagic D69.3
    hereditary D69.42
    idiopathic D69.3
    immune D69.3
    neonatal, transitory P61.0
    thrombotic M31.1
  thrombohemolytic —*see* Fibrinolysis
  thrombolytic —*see* Fibrinolysis
  thrombopenic D69.49
  thrombotic, thrombocytopenic M31.1
  toxic D69.0
  vascular D69.0
  visceral symptoms D69.0
Purpuric spots R23.3
Purulent —*see* condition
Pus
  in
    stool R19.5
    urine N39.0
  tube (rupture) —*see* Salpingo-oophoritis
Pustular rash L08.0
Pustule (nonmalignant) L08.9
  malignant A22.0
Pustulosis palmaris et plantaris L40.3
Putnam (-Dana) disease or syndrome —*see* Degeneration, combined
Putrescent pulp (dental) K04.1
Pyarthritis, pyarthrosis —*see* Arthritis, pyogenic or pyemic
  tuberculous —*see* Tuberculosis, joint
Pyelectasis —*see* Hydronephrosis
Pyelitis (congenital) (uremic) —*see also* Pyelonephritis
  with
    calculus —*see* category N20
      with hydronephrosis N13.2
    contracted kidney N11.9

▶ New   ⇒ Revised   ~~deleted~~ Deleted   • Use Additional Character(s)

Pyelitis *(Continued)*
  acute N10
  chronic N11.9
    with calculus —*see* category N20
      with hydronephrosis N13.2
  cystica N28.84
  puerperal (postpartum) O86.21
  tuberculous A18.11
Pyelocystitis —*see* Pyelonephritis
Pyelonephritis —*see also* Nephritis,
    tubulo-interstitial
  with
    calculus —*see* category N20
      with hydronephrosis N13.2
    contracted kidney N11.9
  acute N10
  calculus —*see* category N20
    with hydronephrosis N13.2
  chronic N11.9
    with calculus —*see* category N20
      with hydronephrosis N13.2
    associated with ureteral obstruction or
        stricture N11.1
    nonobstructive N11.8
      with reflux (vesicoureteral) N11.0
    obstructive N11.1
    specified NEC N11.8
  in (due to)
    brucellosis A23.9 *[N16]*
    cryoglobulinemia (mixed) D89.1 *[N16]*
    cystinosis E72.04
    diphtheria A36.84
    glycogen storage disease E74.09 *[N16]*
    leukemia NEC C95.9-● *[N16]*
    lymphoma NEC C85.90 *[N16]*
    multiple myeloma C90.0-● *[N16]*
    obstruction N11.1
    Salmonella infection A02.25
    sarcoidosis D86.84
    sepsis A41.9 *[N16]*
    Sjögren's disease M35.04
    toxoplasmosis B58.83
    transplant rejection T86.91 *[N16]*
    Wilson's disease E83.01 *[N16]*
  nonobstructive N12
    with reflux (vesicoureteral) N11.0
    chronic N11.8
  syphilitic A52.75

Pyelonephrosis (obstructive) N11.1
  chronic N11.9
Pyelophlebitis I80.8
Pyeloureteritis cystica N28.85
Pyemia, pyemic (fever) (infection) (purulent) —
    see also Sepsis
  joint —*see* Arthritis, pyogenic or pyemic
  liver K75.1
  pneumococcal A40.3
  portal K75.1
  postvaccinal T88.0
  puerperal, postpartum, childbirth O85
  specified organism NEC A41.89
  tuberculous —*see* Tuberculosis, miliary
Pygopagus Q89.4
Pyknoepilepsy (idiopathic) —*see* Pyknolepsy
Pyknolepsy G40.A09
  intractable G40.A19
    with status epilepticus G40.A11
    without status epilepticus G40.A19
  not intractable G40.A09
    with status epilepticus G40.A01
    without status epilepticus G40.A09
Pylephlebitis K75.1
Pyle's syndrome Q78.5
Pylethrombophlebitis K75.1
Pylethrombosis K75.1
Pyloritis K29.90
  with bleeding K29.91
Pylorospasm (reflex) NEC K31.3
  congenital or infantile Q40.0
  neurotic F45.8
  newborn Q40.0
  psychogenic F45.8
Pylorus, pyloric —*see* condition
Pyoarthrosis —*see* Arthritis, pyogenic or
    pyemic
Pyocele
  mastoid —*see* Mastoiditis, acute
  sinus (accessory) —*see* Sinusitis
  turbinate (bone) J32.9
  urethra —*see also* Urethritis N34.0
Pyocolpos —*see* Vaginitis
Pyocystitis N30.80
  with hematuria N30.81
Pyoderma, pyodermia L08.0
  gangrenosum L88
  newborn P39.4

Pyoderma, pyodermia *(Continued)*
  phagedenic L88
  vegetans L08.81
Pyodermatitis L08.0
  vegetans L08.81
Pyogenic —*see* condition
Pyohydronephrosis N13.6
Pyometra, pyometrium, pyometritis —*see*
    Endometritis
Pyomyositis (tropical) —*see* Myositis,
    infective
Pyonephritis N12
Pyonephrosis N13.6
  tuberculous A18.11
Pyo-oophoritis —*see* Salpingo-oophoritis
Pyo-ovarium —*see* Salpingo-oophoritis
Pyopericarditis, pyopericardium
    I30.1
Pyophlebitis —*see* Phlebitis
Pyopneumopericardium I30.1
Pyopneumothorax (infective) J86.9
  with fistula J86.0
  tuberculous NEC A15.6
Pyosalpinx, pyosalpingitis —*see also*
    Salpingo-oophoritis
Pyothorax J86.9
  with fistula J86.0
  tuberculous NEC A15.6
Pyoureter N28.89
  tuberculous A18.11
Pyramidopallidonigral syndrome
    G20
Pyrexia (of unknown origin) R50.9
  atmospheric T67.0
  during labor NEC O75.2
  heat T67.0
  newborn P81.9
    environmentally-induced P81.0
  persistent R50.9
  puerperal O86.4
Pyroglobulinemia NEC E88.09
Pyromania F63.1
Pyrosis R12
Pyuria (bacterial) N39.0

Q

Q fever A78
  with pneumonia A78
Quadricuspid aortic valve Q23.8
Quadrilateral fever A78
Quadriparesis —*see* Quadriplegia
  meaning muscle weakness M62.81
Quadriplegia G82.50-●
  complete
    C1-C4 level G82.51
    C5-C7 level G82.53
  congenital (cerebral) (spinal) G80.8
    spastic G80.0

Quadriplegia *(Continued)*
  embolic (current episode) I63.4-●
  functional R53.2
  incomplete
    C1-C4 level G82.52
    C5-C7 level G82.54
  thrombotic (current episode) I63.3-●
  traumatic — code to injury with seventh
    character S
    current episode —*see* Injury, spinal (cord),
      cervical
Quadruplet, pregnancy —*see* Pregnancy,
  quadruplet
Quarrelsomeness F60.3

Queensland fever A77.3
Quervain's disease M65.4
  thyroid E06.1
Queyrat's erythroplasia D07.4
  penis D07.4
  specified site —*see* Neoplasm, skin,
    in situ
  unspecified site D07.4
Quincke's disease or edema T78.3
  hereditary D84.1
Quinsy (gangrenous) J36
Quintan fever A79.0
Quintuplet, pregnancy —*see* Pregnancy,
  quintuplet

▶ New   ➡ Revised   ~~deleted~~ Deleted   ● Use Additional Character(s)

R

Rabbit fever —see Tularemia
Rabies A82.9
  contact Z20.3
  exposure to Z20.3
  inoculation reaction —see Complications, vaccination
  sylvatic A82.0
  urban A82.1
Rachischisis —see Spina bifida
Rachitic —see also condition
  deformities of spine (late effect) (sequelae) E64.3
  pelvis (late effect) (sequelae) E64.3
    with disproportion (fetopelvic) O33.0
      causing obstructed labor O65.0
Rachitis, rachitism (acute) (tarda) —see also Rickets
  renalis N25.0
  sequelae E64.3
Radial nerve —see condition
Radiation
  burn —see Burn
  effects NOS T66
  sickness NOS T66
  therapy, encounter for Z51.0
Radiculitis (pressure) (vertebrogenic) —see Radiculopathy
Radiculomyelitis —see also Encephalitis
  toxic, due to
    Clostridium tetani A35
    Corynebacterium diphtheriae A36.82
Radiculopathy M54.10
  cervical region M54.12
  cervicothoracic region M54.13
  due to
    disc disorder
      C3 M50.11
      C4 M50.11
      C5 M50.121
      C6 M50.122
      C7 M50.123
      C8 M50.13
    displacement of intervertebral disc —see Disorder, disc, with, radiculopathy
  leg M54.1-●
  lumbar region M54.16
  lumbosacral region M54.17
  occipito-atlanto-axial region M54.11
  postherpetic B02.29
  sacrococcygeal region M54.18
  syphilitic A52.11
  thoracic region (with visceral pain) M54.14
  thoracolumbar region M54.15
Radiodermal burns (acute, chronic, or occupational) —see Burn
Radiodermatitis L58.9
  acute L58.0
  chronic L58.1
Radiotherapy session Z51.0
RAEB (refractory anemia with excess blasts) D46.2-●
Rage, meaning rabies —see Rabies
Ragpicker's disease A22.1
Ragsorter's disease A22.1
Raillietiniasis B71.8
Railroad neurosis F48.8
Railway spine F48.8
Raised —see also Elevated
  antibody titer R76.0
Rake teeth, tooth M26.39
Rales R09.89
Ramifying renal pelvis Q63.8
Ramsay-Hunt disease or syndrome —see also Hunt's disease B02.21
  meaning dyssynergia cerebellaris myoclonica G11.1
Ranula K11.6
  congenital Q38.4

Rape
  adult
    confirmed T74.21
    suspected T76.21
  alleged, observation or examination, ruled out
    adult Z04.41
    child Z04.42
  child
    confirmed T74.22
    suspected T76.22
Rapid
  feeble pulse, due to shock, following injury T79.4
  heart (beat) R00.0
    psychogenic F45.8
  second stage (delivery) O62.3
▶time-zone change syndrome G47.25
Rarefaction, bone —see Disorder, bone, density and structure, specified NEC
Rash (toxic) R21
  canker A38.9
  diaper L22
  drug (internal use) L27.0
    contact —see also Dermatitis, due to, drugs, external L25.1
  following immunization T88.1
  food —see Dermatitis, due to, food
  heat L74.0
  napkin (psoriasiform) L22
  nettle —see Urticaria
  pustular L08.0
  rose R21
    epidemic B06.9
  scarlet A38.9
  serum —see also Reaction, serum T80.69
  wandering tongue K14.1
Rasmussen aneurysm —see Tuberculosis, pulmonary
Rasmussen encephalitis G04.81
Rat-bite fever A25.9
  due to Streptobacillus moniliformis A25.1
  spirochetal (morsus muris) A25.0
Rathke's pouch tumor D44.3
Raymond (-Céstan) syndrome I65.8
Raynaud's disease, phenomenon or syndrome (secondary) I73.00
  with gangrene (symmetric) I73.01
RDS (newborn) (type I) P22.0
  type II P22.1
Reaction —see also Disorder
  adaptation —see Disorder, adjustment
  adjustment (anxiety) (conduct disorder) (depressiveness) (distress) —see Disorder, adjustment
    with
      mutism, elective (child) (adolescent) F94.0
  adverse
    food (any) (ingested) NEC T78.1
      anaphylactic —see Shock, anaphylactic, due to food
  anaphylactoid —see Shock, anaphylactic
  affective —see Disorder, mood
  allergic —see Allergy
  anaphylactic —see Shock, anaphylactic
  anesthesia —see Anesthesia, complication
  antitoxin (prophylactic) (therapeutic) —see Complications, vaccination
  anxiety F41.1
  Arthus —see Arthus' phenomenon
  asthenic F48.8
  combat and operational stress F43.0
  compulsive F42.8
  conversion F44.9
  crisis, acute F43.0
  deoxyribonuclease (DNA) (DNase) hypersensitivity D69.2
  depressive (single episode) F32.9
    affective (single episode) F31.4
      recurrent episode F33.9
    neurotic F34.1
    psychoneurotic F34.1

Reaction (Continued)
  depressive (Continued)
    psychotic F32.3
    recurrent —see Disorder, depressive, recurrent
  dissociative F44.9
  drug NEC T88.7
    addictive —see Dependence, drug
      transmitted via placenta or breast milk —see Absorption, drug, addictive, through placenta
    allergic —see Allergy, drug
    lichenoid L43.2
    newborn P93.8
      gray baby syndrome P93.0
    overdose or poisoning (by accident) —see Table of Drugs and Chemicals, by drug, poisoning
    photoallergic L56.1
    phototoxic L56.0
    withdrawal —see Dependence, by drug, with, withdrawal
      infant of dependent mother P96.1
      newborn P96.1
    wrong substance given or taken (by accident) —see Table of Drugs and Chemicals, by drug, poisoning
  fear F40.9
    child (abnormal) F93.8
  febrile nonhemolytic transfusion (FNHTR) R50.84
  fluid loss, cerebrospinal G97.1
  foreign
    body NEC —see Granuloma, foreign body
      in operative wound (inadvertently left) —see Foreign body, accidentally left during a procedure
    substance accidentally left during a procedure (chemical) (powder) (talc) T81.60
      aseptic peritonitis T81.61
      body or object (instrument) (sponge) (swab) —see Foreign body, accidentally left during a procedure
      specified reaction NEC T81.69
  grief —see Disorder, adjustment
  Herxheimer's R68.89
  hyperkinetic —see Hyperkinesia
  hypochondriacal F45.20
  hypoglycemic, due to insulin E16.0
    with coma (diabetic) —see Diabetes, coma
      nondiabetic E15
    therapeutic misadventure —see subcategory T38.3
  hypomanic F30.8
  hysterical F44.9
  immunization —see Complications, vaccination
  incompatibility
    ABO blood group (infusion) (transfusion) —see Complication(s), transfusion, incompatibility reaction, ABO
      delayed serologic T80.39
    ▶minor blood group (Duffy) (E) (K) (Kell) (Kidd) (Lewis) (M) (N) (P) (S) T80.89
    Rh (factor) (infusion) (transfusion) —see Complication(s), transfusion, incompatibility reaction, Rh (factor)
  inflammatory —see Infection
  infusion —see Complications, infusion
  inoculation (immune serum) —see Complications, vaccination
  insulin T38.3-●
  involutional psychotic —see Disorder, depressive
  leukemoid D72.823
    basophilic D72.823
    lymphocytic D72.823
    monocytic D72.823
    myelocytic D72.823
    neutrophilic D72.823

Reaction (Continued)
  LSD (acute)
    due to drug abuse —see Abuse, drug,
      hallucinogen
    due to drug dependence —see Dependence,
      drug, hallucinogen
  lumbar puncture G97.1
  manic-depressive —see Disorder, bipolar
  neurasthenic F48.8
  neurogenic —see Neurosis
  neurotic F48.9
  neurotic-depressive F34.1
  nitritoid —see Crisis, nitritoid - obsessive-
    compulsive F42
  nonspecific
    to
      cell mediated immunity measurement
        of gamma interferon antigen
        response without active
        tuberculosis R76.12
      QuantiFERON-TB test (QFT) without
        active tuberculosis R76.12
      tuberculin test —see also Reaction,
        tuberculin skin test R76.11
  obsessive-compulsive F42.8
  organic, acute or subacute —see Delirium
  paranoid (acute) F23
    chronic F22
    senile F03
  passive dependency F60.7
  phobic F40.9
  post-traumatic stress, uncomplicated
    Z73.3
  psychogenic F99
  psychoneurotic —see also Neurosis
    compulsive F42.8
    depersonalization F48.1
    depressive F34.1
    hypochondriacal F45.20
    neurasthenic F48.8
    obsessive F42.8
  psychophysiologic —see Disorder,
    somatoform
  psychosomatic —see Disorder, somatoform
  psychotic —see Psychosis
  scarlet fever toxin —see Complications,
    vaccination
  schizophrenic F23
    acute (brief) (undifferentiated) F23
    latent F21
    undifferentiated (acute) (brief) F23
  serological for syphilis —see Serology for
    syphilis
  serum T80.69
    anaphylactic (immediate) —see also Shock,
      anaphylactic T80.59
    specified reaction NEC
      due to
        administration of blood and blood
          products T80.61
        immunization T80.62
        serum specified NEC T80.69
        vaccination T80.62
  situational —see Disorder, adjustment
  somatization —see Disorder, somatoform
  spinal puncture G97.1
  stress (severe) F43.9
    acute (agitation) ("daze") (disorientation)
      (disturbance of consciousness) (flight
      reaction) (fugue) F43.0
    specified NEC F43.8
  surgical procedure —see Complications,
    surgical procedure
  tetanus antitoxin —see Complications,
    vaccination
  toxic, to local anesthesia T81.59
    in labor and delivery O74.4
    in pregnancy O29.3X-●
    postpartum, puerperal O89.3
  toxin-antitoxin —see Complications,
    vaccination

Reaction (Continued)
  transfusion (blood) (bone marrow)
    (lymphocytes) (allergic) —see
    Complications, transfusion
  tuberculin skin test, abnormal R76.11
  vaccination (any) —see Complications,
    vaccination
  withdrawing, child or adolescent F93.8
Reactive airway disease —see Asthma
Reactive depression —see Reaction, depressive
Rearrangement
  chromosomal
    balanced (in) Q95.9
      abnormal individual (autosomal) Q95.2
        non-sex (autosomal) chromosomes
          Q95.2
        sex/non-sex chromosomes Q95.3
      specified NEC Q95.8
Recalcitrant patient —see Noncompliance
Recanalization, thrombus —see Thrombosis
Recession, receding
  chamber angle (eye) H21.55-●
  chin M26.09
  gingival (postinfective) (postoperative)
    generalized K06.020
      minimal K06.021
      moderate K06.022
      severe K06.023
    localized K06.010
      minimal K06.011
      moderate K06.012
      severe K06.013
Recklinghausen's disease Q85.01
  bones E21.0
Reclus' disease (cystic) —see Mastopathy, cystic
Recrudescent typhus (fever) A75.1
Recruitment, auditory H93.21-●
Rectalgia K62.89
Rectitis K62.89
Rectocele
  female (without uterine prolapse) N81.6
    with uterine prolapse N81.4
    incomplete N81.2
  in pregnancy —see Pregnancy, complicated
    by, abnormal, pelvic organs or tissues
    NEC
  male K62.3
Rectosigmoid junction —see condition
Rectosigmoiditis K63.89
  ulcerative (chronic) K51.30
    with
      complication K51.319
        abscess K51.314
        fistula K51.313
        obstruction K51.312
        rectal bleeding K51.311
        specified NEC K51.318
Rectourethral —see condition
Rectovaginal —see condition
Rectovesical —see condition
Rectum, rectal —see condition
Recurrent —see condition
  pregnancy loss —see Loss (of), pregnancy,
    recurrent
Red bugs B88.0
Red-cedar lung or pneumonitis J67.8
Red tide —see also Table of Drugs and
  Chemicals T65.82-●
Reduced
  mobility Z74.09
  ventilatory or vital capacity R94.2
Redundant, redundancy
  anus (congenital) Q43.8
  clitoris N90.89
  colon (congenital) Q43.8
  foreskin (congenital) N47.8
  intestine (congenital) Q43.8

Redundant, redundancy (Continued)
  labia N90.69
  organ or site, congenital NEC —see Accessory
  panniculus (abdominal) E65
  prepuce (congenital) N47.8
  pylorus K31.89
  rectum (congenital) Q43.8
  scrotum N50.89
  sigmoid (congenital) Q43.8
  skin L98.7
    and subcutaneous tissue L98.7
      of face L57.4
      eyelids —see Blepharochalasis
  stomach K31.89
Reduplication —see Duplication
Reflex R29.2
  hyperactive gag J39.2
  pupillary, abnormal —see Anomaly, pupil,
    function
  vasoconstriction I73.9
  vasovagal R55
Reflux K21.9
  acid K21.9
  esophageal K21.9
    with esophagitis K21.0
    newborn P78.83
  gastroesophageal K21.9
    with esophagitis K21.0
  mitral —see Insufficiency, mitral
  ureteral —see Reflux, vesicoureteral
  vesicoureteral (with scarring) N13.70
    with
      nephropathy N13.729
        with hydroureter N13.739
          bilateral N13.732
          unilateral N13.731
        without hydroureter N13.729
          bilateral N13.722
          unilateral N13.721
      bilateral N13.722
      unilateral N13.721
      pyelonephritis (chronic) N11.0
    without nephropathy N13.71
    congenital Q62.7
Reforming, artificial openings —see Attention
  to, artificial, opening
Refractive error —see Disorder, refraction
Refsum's disease or syndrome G60.1
Refusal of
  food, psychogenic F50.89
  treatment (because of) Z53.20
    left against medical advice (AMA) Z53.21
    patient's decision NEC Z53.29
    reasons of belief or group pressure Z53.1
Regional —see condition
Regurgitation R11.10
  aortic (valve) —see Insufficiency, aortic
  food —see also Vomiting
    with reswallowing —see Rumination
    newborn P92.1
  gastric contents —see Vomiting
  heart —see Endocarditis
  mitral (valve) —see Insufficiency, mitral
    congenital Q23.3
  myocardial —see Endocarditis
  pulmonary (valve) (heart) I37.1
    congenital Q22.2
    syphilitic A52.03
  tricuspid —see Insufficiency, tricuspid
  valve, valvular —see Endocarditis
    congenital Q24.8
  vesicoureteral —see Reflux, vesicoureteral
Reichmann's disease or syndrome K31.89
Reifenstein syndrome E34.52
Reinsertion
  implantable subdermal contraceptive Z30.46
  intrauterine contraceptive device Z30.433
Reiter's disease, syndrome, or urethritis
  M02.30
  ankle M02.37-●
  elbow M02.32-●

▶ New   ⇥ Revised   ~~deleted~~ Deleted   ● Use Additional Character(s)

Reiter's disease, syndrome, or urethritis *(Continued)*
  foot joint M02.37-●
  hand joint M02.34-●
  hip M02.35-●
  knee M02.36-●
  multiple site M02.39
  shoulder M02.31-●
  vertebra M02.38
  wrist M02.33-●
Rejection
  food, psychogenic F50.89
  transplant T86.91
    bone T86.830
      marrow T86.01
    cornea T86.840
    heart T86.21
      with lung(s) T86.31
    intestine T86.850
    kidney T86.11
    liver T86.41
    lung(s) T86.810
      with heart T86.31
    organ (immune or nonimmune cause) T86.91
    pancreas T86.890
    skin (allograft) (autograft) T86.820
    specified NEC T86.890
    stem cell (peripheral blood) (umbilical cord) T86.5
Relapsing fever A68.9
  Carter's (Asiatic) A68.1
  Dutton's (West African) A68.1
  Koch's A68.9
  louse-borne (epidemic) A68.0
  Novy's (American) A68.1
  Obermeyers's (European) A68.0
  Spirillum A68.9
  tick-borne (endemic) A68.1
Relationship
  occlusal
    open anterior M26.220
    open posterior M26.221
Relaxation
  anus (sphincter) K62.89
    psychogenic F45.8
  arch (foot) —*see also* Deformity, limb, flat foot
  back ligaments —*see* Instability, joint, spine
  bladder (sphincter) N31.2
  cardioesophageal K21.9
  cervix —*see* Incompetency, cervix
  diaphragm J98.6
  joint (capsule) (ligament) (paralytic) —*see* Flail, joint
    congenital NEC Q74.8
  lumbosacral (joint) —*see* subcategory M53.2
  pelvic floor N81.89
  perineum N81.89
  posture R29.3
  rectum (sphincter) K62.89
  sacroiliac (joint) —*see* subcategory M53.2
  scrotum N50.89
  urethra (sphincter) N36.44
  vesical N31.2
Release from prison, anxiety concerning Z65.2
Remains
  canal of Cloquet Q14.0
  capsule (opaque) Q14.8
Remittent fever (malarial) B54
Remnant
  canal of Cloquet Q14.0
  capsule (opaque) Q14.8
  cervix, cervical stump (acquired) (postoperative) N88.8
  cystic duct, postcholecystectomy K91.5
  fingernail L60.8
    congenital Q84.6
  meniscus, knee —*see* Derangement, knee, meniscus, specified NEC
  thyroglossal duct Q89.2
  tonsil J35.8
    infected (chronic) J35.01
  urachus Q64.4

Removal (from) (of)
  artificial
    arm Z44.00-●
      complete Z44.01-●
      partial Z44.02-●
    eye Z44.2-●
    leg Z44.10-●
      complete Z44.11-●
      partial Z44.12-●
  breast implant Z45.81
  cardiac pulse generator (battery) (end-of-life) Z45.010
  catheter (urinary) (indwelling) Z46.6
    from artificial opening —*see* Attention to, artificial, opening
    non-vascular Z46.82
    vascular NEC Z45.2
  device Z46.9
    contraceptive Z30.432
      implantable subdermal Z30.46
    implanted NEC Z45.89
    specified NEC Z46.89
  drains Z48.03
  dressing (nonsurgical) Z48.00
    surgical Z48.01
  external
    fixation device — code to fracture with seventh character D
    prosthesis, prosthetic device Z44.9
      breast Z44.3-●
      specified NEC Z44.8
  home in childhood (to foster home or institution) Z62.29
  ileostomy Z43.2
  insulin pump Z46.81
  myringotomy device (stent) (tube) Z45.82
  nervous system device NEC Z46.2
    brain neuropacemaker Z46.2
    visual substitution device Z46.2
      implanted Z45.31
  non-vascular catheter Z46.82
  organ, prophylactic (for neoplasia management) —*see* Prophylactic, organ removal
  orthodontic device Z46.4
  staples Z48.02
  stent
    ureteral Z46.6
  suture Z48.02
  urinary device Z46.6
  vascular access device or catheter Z45.2
Ren
  arcuatus Q63.1
  mobile, mobilis N28.89
    congenital Q63.8
  unguliformis Q63.1
Renal —*see* condition
Rendu-Osler-Weber disease or syndrome I78.0
Reninoma D41.0-●
Renon-Delille syndrome E23.3
Reovirus, as cause of disease classified elsewhere B97.5
Repeated falls NEC R29.6
Replaced chromosome by dicentric ring Q93.2
Replacement by artificial or mechanical device or prosthesis of
  bladder Z96.0
  blood vessel NEC Z95.828
  bone NEC Z96.7
  cochlea Z96.21
  coronary artery Z95.5
  eustachian tube Z96.29
  eye globe Z97.0
  heart Z95.812
    valve Z95.2
      prosthetic Z95.2
      specified NEC Z95.4
      xenogenic Z95.3
  intestine Z96.89
  joint Z96.60
    hip —*see* Presence, hip joint implant
    knee —*see* Presence, knee joint implant
    specified site NEC Z96.698

Replacement by artificial or mechanical device or prosthesis of *(Continued)*
  larynx Z96.3
  lens Z96.1
  limb(s) —*see* Presence, artificial, limb
  mandible NEC (for tooth root implant(s)) Z96.5
  organ NEC Z96.89
  peripheral vessel NEC Z95.828
  stapes Z96.29
  teeth Z97.2
  tendon Z96.7
  tissue NEC Z96.89
  tooth root(s) Z96.5
  vessel NEC Z95.828
    coronary (artery) Z95.5
➡ **Request for expert evidence** Z04.89
Reserve, decreased or low
  cardiac —*see* Disease, heart
  kidney N28.89
Residual —*see also* condition
  ovary syndrome N99.83
  state, schizophrenic F20.5
  urine R39.198
Resistance, resistant (to)
  activated protein C D68.51
  complicating pregnancy O26.89
  insulin E88.81
  organism(s)
    to
      drug Z16.30
        aminoglycosides Z16.29
        amoxicillin Z16.11
        ampicillin Z16.11
        antibiotic(s) Z16.20
          multiple Z16.24
          specified NEC Z16.29
        antifungal Z16.32
        antimicrobial (single) Z16.30
          multiple Z16.35
          specified NEC Z16.39
        antimycobacterial (single) Z16.341
          multiple Z16.342
        antiparasitic Z16.31
        antiviral Z16.33
        beta lactam antibiotics Z16.10
          specified NEC Z16.19
        cephalosporins Z16.19
        extended beta lactamase (ESBL) Z16.12
        fluoroquinolones Z16.23
        macrolides Z16.29
        methicillin —*see* MRSA
        multiple drugs (MDRO)
          antibiotics Z16.24
          antimicrobial Z16.35
          antimycobacterials Z16.342
        penicillins Z16.11
        quinine (and related compounds) Z16.31
        quinolones Z16.23
        sulfonamides Z16.29
        tetracyclines Z16.29
        tuberculostatics (single) Z16.341
          multiple Z16.342
        vancomycin Z16.21
          related antibiotics Z16.22
  thyroid hormone E07.89
Resorption
  dental (roots) K03.3
    alveoli M26.79
  teeth (external) (internal) (pathological) (roots) K03.3
Respiration
  Cheyne-Stokes R06.3
  decreased due to shock, following injury T79.4
  disorder of, psychogenic F45.8
  insufficient, or poor R06.89
    newborn P28.5
  painful R07.1
  sighing, psychogenic F45.8

Respiratory —see also condition
  distress syndrome (newborn) (type I)
      P22.0
    type II P22.1
  syncytial virus, as cause of disease classified
      elsewhere B97.4
Respite care Z75.5
Response (drug)
  photoallergic L56.1
  phototoxic L56.0
Restenosis
  stent
    vascular
      end stent
        adjacent to stent —see
            Arteriosclerosis
        within the stent
          coronary T82.855
          peripheral T82.856
      in stent
        coronary vessel T82.855
        peripheral vessel T82.856
Restless legs (syndrome) G25.81
Restlessness R45.1
Restoration (of)
  dental
    aesthetically inadequate or displeasing
        K08.56
    defective K08.50
      specified NEC K08.59
    failure of marginal integrity K08.51
    failure of periodontal anatomical intergrity
        K08.54
    organ continuity from previous sterilization
        (tuboplasty) (vasoplasty) Z31.0
      aftercare Z31.42
    tooth (existing)
      contours biologically incompatible with
          oral health K08.54
      open margins K08.51
      overhanging K08.52
      poor aesthetic K08.56
      poor gingival margins K08.51
    unsatisfactory, of tooth K08.50
      specified NEC K08.59
Restorative material (dental)
  allergy to K08.55
  fractured K08.539
    with loss of material K08.531
    without loss of material K08.530
  unrepairable overhanging of K08.52
Restriction of housing space Z59.1
Rests, ovarian, in fallopian tube Q50.6
Restzustand (schizophrenic) F20.5
Retained —see also Retention
  cholelithiasis following cholecystectomy
      K91.86
  foreign body fragments (type of) Z18.9
    acrylics Z18.2
    animal quill(s) or spines Z18.31
    cement Z18.83
    concrete Z18.83
    crystalline Z18.83
    depleted isotope Z18.09
    depleted uranium Z18.01
➡diethylhexyl phthalates Z18.2
    glass Z18.81
    isocyanate Z18.2
    magnetic metal Z18.11
    metal Z18.10
    nonmagnetic metal Z18.12
    nontherapeutic radioactive Z18.09
    organic NEC Z18.39
    plastic Z18.2
    quill(s) (animal) Z18.31
    radioactive (nontherapeutic) NEC Z18.09
    specified NEC Z18.89
    spine(s) (animal) Z18.31
    stone Z18.83
    tooth (teeth) Z18.32
    wood Z18.33

Retained (Continued)
  fragments (type of) Z18.9
    acrylics Z18.2
    animal quill(s) or spines Z18.31
    cement Z18.83
    concrete Z18.83
    crystalline Z18.83
    depleted isotope Z18.09
    depleted uranium Z18.01
➡diethylhexyl phthalates Z18.2
    glass Z18.81
    isocyanate Z18.2
    magnetic metal Z18.11
    metal Z18.10
    nonmagnectic metal Z18.12
    nontherapeutic radioactive Z18.09
    organic NEC Z18.39
    plastic Z18.2
    quill(s) (animal) Z18.31
    radioactive (nontherapeutic) NEC Z18.09
    specified NEC Z18.89
    spine(s) (animal) Z18.31
    stone Z18.83
    tooth (teeth) Z18.32
    wood Z18.33
  gallstones, following cholecystectomy K91.86
Retardation
  development, developmental, specific —see
      Disorder, developmental
  endochondral bone growth —see Disorder,
      bone, development or growth
  growth R62.50
    due to malnutrition E45
  mental —see Disability, intellectual
  motor function, specific F82
  physical (child) R62.52
    due to malnutrition E45
  reading (specific) F81.0
  spelling (specific) (without reading disorder)
      F81.81
Retching —see Vomiting
Retention —see also Retained
  bladder —see Retention, urine
  carbon dioxide E87.2
  cholelithiasis following cholecystectomy K91.86
  cyst —see Cyst
  dead
    fetus (at or near term) (mother) O36.4
      early fetal death O02.1
    ovum O02.0
  decidua (fragments) (following delivery)
      (with hemorrhage) O72.2
    without hemorrhage O73.1
  deciduous tooth K00.6
  dental root K08.3
  fecal —see Constipation
  fetus
    dead O36.4
    early O02.1
  fluid R60.9
  foreign body —see also Foreign body, retained
    current trauma - code as Foreign body, by
        site or type
  gallstones, following cholecystectomy K91.86
  gastric K31.89
  intrauterine contraceptive device, in
      pregnancy —see Pregnancy, complicated
      by, retention, intrauterine device
  membranes (complicating delivery) (with
      hemorrhage) O72.2
    with abortion —see Abortion, by type
    without hemorrhage O73.1
  meniscus —see Derangement, meniscus
  menses N94.89
  milk (puerperal, postpartum) O92.79
  nitrogen, extrarenal R39.2
  ovary syndrome N99.83
  placenta (total) (with hemorrhage) O72.0
    without hemorrhage O73.0
    portions or fragments (with hemorrhage)
        O72.2
      without hemorrhage O73.1

Retention (Continued)
  products of conception
    early pregnancy (dead fetus) O02.1
    following
      delivery (with hemorrhage) O72.2
        without hemorrhage O73.1
    secundines (following delivery) (with
        hemorrhage) O72.0
      without hemorrhage O73.0
    complicating puerperium (delayed
        hemorrhage) O72.2
    partial O72.2
      without hemorrhage O73.1
  smegma, clitoris N90.89
  urine R33.9
    drug-induced R33.0
    due to hyperplasia (hypertrophy) of
        prostate —see Hyperplasia, prostate
    organic R33.8
      drug-induced R33.0
    psychogenic F45.8
    specified NEC R33.8
  water (in tissues) —see Edema
Reticular erythematous mucinosis L98.5
Reticulation, dust —see Pneumoconiosis
Reticulocytosis R70.1
Reticuloendotheliosis
  acute infantile C96.0
  leukemic C91.4-●
  nonlipid C96.0
Reticulohistiocytoma (giant-cell) D76.3
Reticuloid, actinic L57.1
Reticulosis (skin)
  acute of infancy C96.0
  hemophagocytic, familial D76.1
  histiocytic medullary C96.A
  lipomelanotic I89.8
  malignant (midline) C86.0
  polymorphic C86.0
  Sézary —see Sézary disease
Retina, retinal —see also condition
  dark area D49.81
Retinitis —see also Inflammation,
    chorioretinal
  albuminurica N18.9 [H32]
  diabetic —see Diabetes, retinitis
  disciformis —see Degeneration, macula
  focal —see Inflammation, chorioretinal, focal
  gravidarum —see Pregnancy, complicated by,
      specified pregnancy-related condition
      NEC
  juxtapapillaris —see Inflammation,
      chorioretinal, focal, juxtapapillary
  luetic —see Retinitis, syphilitic
  pigmentosa H35.52
  proliferans —see Disorder, globe,
      degenerative, specified type NEC
  proliferating —see Disorder, globe,
      degenerative, specified type NEC
  renal N18.9 [H32]
  syphilitic (early) (secondary) A51.43
    central, recurrent A52.71
    congenital (early) A50.01 [H32]
    late A52.71
  tuberculous A18.53
Retinoblastoma C69.2-●
  differentiated C69.2-●
  undifferentiated C69.2-●
Retinochoroiditis —see also Inflammation,
    chorioretinal
  disseminated —see Inflammation,
      chorioretinal, disseminated
    syphilitic A52.71
  focal —see Inflammation, chorioretinal
  juxtapapillaris —see Inflammation,
      chorioretinal, focal, juxtapapillary
Retinopathy (background) H35.00
  arteriosclerotic I70.8 [H35.0-●]
  atherosclerotic I70.8 [H35.0-●]
  central serous —see Chorioretinopathy,
      central serous

▶ New   ➡ Revised   ~~deleted~~ Deleted   ● Use Additional Character(s)

Rheumatoid (Continued)
  vasculitis (Continued)
    shoulder M05.21-●
    vertebra —see Spondylitis, ankylosing
    wrist M05.23-●
Rhinitis (atrophic) (catarrhal) (chronic)
    (croupous) (fibrinous) (granulomatous)
    (hyperplastic) (hypertrophic)
    (membranous) (obstructive) (purulent)
    (suppurative) (ulcerative) J31.0
  with
    sore throat —see Nasopharyngitis
  acute J00
  allergic J30.9
    with asthma J45.909
      with
        exacerbation (acute) J45.901
        status asthmaticus J45.902
    due to
      food J30.5
      pollen J30.1
    nonseasonal J30.89
    perennial J30.89
    seasonal NEC J30.2
    specified NEC J30.89
  infective J00
  pneumococcal J00
  syphilitic A52.73
    congenital A50.05 [J99]
  tuberculous A15.8
  vasomotor J30.0
Rhinoantritis (chronic) —see Sinusitis,
    maxillary
Rhinodacryolith —see Dacryolith
Rhinolith (nasal sinus) J34.89
Rhinomegaly J34.89
Rhinopharyngitis (acute) (subacute) —see also
    Nasopharyngitis
  chronic J31.1
  destructive ulcerating A66.5
  mutilans A66.5
Rhinophyma L71.1
Rhinorrhea J34.89
  cerebrospinal (fluid) G96.0
  paroxysmal —see Rhinitis, allergic
  spasmodic —see Rhinitis, allergic
Rhinosalpingitis —see Salpingitis, eustachian
Rhinoscleroma A48.8
Rhinosporidiosis B48.1
Rhinovirus infection NEC B34.8
Rhizomelic chondrodysplasia punctata E71.540
Rhythm
  atrioventricular nodal I49.8
  disorder I49.9
    coronary sinus I49.8
    ectopic I49.8
    nodal I49.8
  escape I49.9
  heart, abnormal I49.9
  idioventricular I44.2
  nodal I49.8
  sleep, inversion G47.2-●
    nonorganic origin —see Disorder, sleep,
      circadian rhythm, psychogenic
Rhytidosis facialis L98.8
Rib —see also condition
  cervical Q76.5
Riboflavin deficiency E53.0
Rice bodies —see also Loose, body, joint
  knee M23.4-●
Richter syndrome —see Leukemia, chronic
    lymphocytic, B-cell type
Richter's hernia —see Hernia, abdomen, with
    obstruction
Ricinism —see Poisoning, food, noxious, plant
Rickets (active) (acute) (adolescent) (chest wall)
    (congenital) (current) (infantile) (intestinal)
    E55.0
  adult —see Osteomalacia
  celiac K90.0
  hypophosphatemic with nephrotic-glycosuric
    dwarfism E72.09
  inactive E64.3

Rickets (Continued)
  kidney N25.0
  renal N25.0
  sequelae, any E64.3
  vitamin-D-resistant E83.31 [M90.80]
Rickettsial disease A79.9
  specified type NEC A79.89
Rickettsialpox (Rickettsia akari) A79.1
Rickettsiosis A79.9
  due to
    Ehrlichia sennetsu A79.81
    Rickettsia akari (rickettsialpox) A79.1
  specified type NEC A79.89
  tick-borne A77.9
  vesicular A79.1
Rider's bone —see Ossification, muscle,
    specified NEC
Ridge, alveolus —see also condition
  flabby K06.8
Ridged ear, congenital Q17.3
Riedel's
  lobe, liver Q44.7
  struma, thyroiditis or disease E06.5
Rieger's anomaly or syndrome Q13.81
Riehl's melanosis L81.4
Rietti-Greppi-Micheli anemia D56.9
Rieux's hernia —see Hernia, abdomen, specified
    site NEC
Riga (-Fede) disease K14.0
Riggs' disease —see Periodontitis
Right aortic arch Q25.47
Right middle lobe syndrome J98.11
Rigid, rigidity —see also condition
  abdominal R19.30
    with severe abdominal pain R10.0
    epigastric R19.36
    generalized R19.37
    left lower quadrant R19.34
    left upper quadrant R19.32
    periumbilic R19.35
    right lower quadrant R19.33
    right upper quadrant R19.31
  articular, multiple, congenital Q68.8
  cervix (uteri) in pregnancy —see Pregnancy,
    complicated by, abnormal, cervix
  hymen (acquired) (congenital) N89.6
  nuchal R29.1
  pelvic floor in pregnancy —see Pregnancy,
    complicated by, abnormal, pelvic organs
    or tissues NEC
  perineum or vulva in pregnancy —see
    Pregnancy, complicated by, abnormal,
    vulva
  spine —see Dorsopathy, specified NEC
  vagina in pregnancy —see Pregnancy,
    complicated by, abnormal, vagina
Rigors R68.89
  with fever R50.9
Riley-Day syndrome G90.1
RIND (reversible ischemic neurologic deficit)
    I63.9
Ring(s)
  aorta (vascular) Q25.45
  Bandl's O62.4
  contraction, complicating delivery O62.4
  esophageal, lower (muscular) K22.2
  Fleischer's (cornea) H18.04-●
  hymenal, tight (acquired) (congenital) N89.6
  Kayser-Fleischer (cornea) H18.04-●
  retraction, uterus, pathological O62.4
  Schatzki's (esophagus) (lower) K22.2
    congenital Q39.3
  Soemmerring's —see Cataract, secondary
  vascular (congenital) Q25.8
    aorta Q25.45
Ringed hair (congenital) Q84.1
Ringworm B35.9
  beard B35.0
  black dot B35.0
  body B35.4
  Burmese B35.5
  corporeal B35.4
  foot B35.3

Ringworm (Continued)
  groin B35.6
  hand B35.2
  honeycomb B35.0
  nails B35.1
  perianal (area) B35.6
  scalp B35.0
  specified NEC B35.8
  Tokelau B35.5
Rise, venous pressure I87.8
Rising, PSA following treatment for malignant
    neoplasm of prostate R97.21
Risk
  for
    dental caries Z91.849
      high Z91.843
      low Z91.841
      moderate Z91.842
  suicidal
    meaning personal history of attempted
      suicide Z91.5
    meaning suicidal ideation —see Ideation,
      suicidal
Ritter's disease L00
Rivalry, sibling Z62.891
Rivalta's disease A42.2
River blindness B73.01
Robert's pelvis Q74.2
  with disproportion (fetopelvic) O33.0
    causing obstructed labor O65.0
Robin (-Pierre) syndrome Q87.0
Robinow-Silvermann-Smith syndrome Q87.1
Robinson's (hidrotic) ectodermal dysplasia or
    syndrome Q82.4
Robles' disease B73.01
Rocky Mountain (spotted) fever A77.0
Roetheln —see Rubella
Roger's disease Q21.0
Rokitansky-Aschoff sinuses (gallbladder) K82.8
Rolando's fracture (displaced) S62.22-●
  nondisplaced S62.22-●
Romano-Ward (prolonged QT interval)
    syndrome I45.81
Romberg's disease or syndrome G51.8
Roof, mouth —see condition
Rosacea L71.9
  acne L71.9
  keratitis L71.8
  specified NEC L71.8
Rosary, rachitic E55.0
Rose
  cold J30.1
  fever J30.1
  rash R21
    epidemic B06.9
Rosenbach's erysipeloid A26.0
Rosenthal's disease or syndrome D68.1
Roseola B09
  infantum B08.20
    due to human herpesvirus 6 B08.21
    due to human herpesvirus 7 B08.22
Ross River disease or fever B33.1
Rossbach's disease K31.89
  psychogenic F45.8
Rostan's asthma (cardiac) —see Failure,
    ventricular, left
Rotation
  anomalous, incomplete or insufficient,
    intestine Q43.3
  cecum (congenital) Q43.3
  colon (congenital) Q43.3
  spine, incomplete or insufficient —see
    Dorsopathy, deforming, specified NEC
  tooth, teeth, fully erupted M26.35
  vertebra, incomplete or insufficient —see
    Dorsopathy, deforming, specified NEC
Rotes Quérol disease or syndrome —see
    Hyperostosis, ankylosing
Roth (-Bernhardt) disease or syndrome —see
    Meralgia paraesthetica
Rothmund (-Thomson) syndrome Q82.8

▶ New   ⇒ Revised   ~~deleted~~ Deleted   ● Use Additional Character(s)

Rotor's disease or syndrome E80.6
Round
  back (with wedging of vertebrae) —*see*
      Kyphosis
    sequelae (late effect) of rickets E64.3
  worms (large) (infestation) NEC B82.0
    Ascariasis —*see also* Ascariasis B77.9
Roussy-Lévy syndrome G60.0
Rubella (German measles) B06.9
  complication NEC B06.09
    neurological B06.00
  congenital P35.0
  contact Z20.4
  exposure to Z20.4
  maternal
    care for (suspected) damage to fetus O35.3
    manifest rubella in infant P35.0
    suspected damage to fetus affecting
        management of pregnancy O35.3
  specified complications NEC B06.89
Rubeola (meaning measles) —*see* Measles
  meaning rubella —*see* Rubella
Rubeosis, iris —*see* Disorder, iris, vascular
Rubinstein-Taybi syndrome Q87.2
Rudimentary (congenital) —*see also* Agenesis
  arm —*see* Defect, reduction, upper limb
  bone Q79.9
  cervix uteri Q51.828
  eye Q11.2
  lobule of ear Q17.3
  patella Q74.1
  respiratory organs in thoracopagus Q89.4
  tracheal bronchus Q32.4
  uterus Q51.818
    in male Q56.1
  vagina Q52.0
Ruled out condition —*see* Observation, suspected
Rumination R11.10
  with nausea R11.2
  disorder of infancy F98.21
  neurotic F42.8
  newborn P92.1
  obsessional F42.8
  psychogenic F42.8
Runeberg's disease D51.0
Runny nose R09.89
Rupia (syphilitic) A51.39
  congenital A50.06
  tertiary A52.79
Rupture, ruptured
  abscess (spontaneous) - code by site under
      Abscess
  aneurysm —*see* Aneurysm
  anus (sphincter) —*see* Laceration, anus
  aorta, aortic I71.8
    abdominal I71.3
    arch I71.1
    ascending I71.1
    descending I71.8
      abdominal I71.3
      thoracic I71.1
    syphilitic A52.01
    thoracoabdominal I71.5
    thorax, thoracic I71.1
    transverse I71.1
    traumatic —*see* Injury, aorta, laceration,
        major
  valve or cusp —*see also* Endocarditis, aortic
      I35.8
⇒appendix (with peritonitis) (*see also*
      Appendicitis) K35.32
⇒with localized peritonitis (*see also*
      Appendicitis) K35.32
  arteriovenous fistula, brain I60.8
  artery I77.2
    brain —*see* Hemorrhage, intracranial,
        intracerebral
    coronary —*see* Infarct, myocardium
    heart —*see* Infarct, myocardium
    pulmonary I28.8
    traumatic (complication) —*see* Injury,
        blood vessel

Rupture, ruptured (*Continued*)
  bile duct (common) (hepatic) K83.2
    cystic K82.2
  bladder (sphincter) (nontraumatic)
      (spontaneous) N32.89
    following ectopic or molar pregnancy O08.6
    obstetrical trauma O71.5
    traumatic S37.29
  blood vessel —*see also* Hemorrhage
    brain —*see* Hemorrhage, intracranial,
        intracerebral
    heart —*see* Infarct, myocardium
    traumatic (complication) —*see* Injury,
        blood vessel, laceration, major, by site
  bone —*see* Fracture
  bowel (nontraumatic) K63.1
  brain
    aneurysm (congenital) —*see also*
        Hemorrhage, intracranial,
        subarachnoid
      syphilitic A52.05
    hemorrhagic —*see* Hemorrhage,
        intracranial, intracerebral
  capillaries I78.8
  cardiac (auricle) (ventricle) (wall) I23.3
    with hemopericardium I23.0
    infectional I40.9
    traumatic —*see* Injury, heart
  cartilage (articular) (current) —*see also* Sprain
    knee S83.3-●
    semilunar —*see* Tear, meniscus
  cecum (with peritonitis) K65.0
  ⇒with peritoneal abscess K35.33
    traumatic S36.598
  celiac artery, traumatic —*see* Injury, blood
      vessel, celiac artery, laceration, major
  cerebral aneurysm (congenital) (*see*
      Hemorrhage, intracranial, subarachnoid)
  cervix (uteri)
    with ectopic or molar pregnancy O08.6
    following ectopic or molar pregnancy O08.6
    obstetrical trauma O71.3
    traumatic S37.69
  chordae tendineae NEC I51.1
    concurrent with acute myocardial
        infarction —*see* Infarct, myocardium
    following acute myocardial infarction
        (current complication) I23.4
  choroid (direct) (indirect) (traumatic) H31.32-●
  circle of Willis I60.6
  colon (nontraumatic) K63.1
    traumatic —*see* Injury, intestine, large
  cornea (traumatic) —*see* Injury, eye, laceration
  coronary (artery) (thrombotic) —*see* Infarct,
      myocardium
  corpus luteum (infected) (ovary) N83.1-●
  cyst —*see* Cyst
  cystic duct K82.2
  Descemet's membrane —*see* Change, corneal
      membrane, Descemet's, rupture
    traumatic —*see* Injury, eye, laceration
  diaphragm, traumatic —*see* Injury,
      intrathoracic, diaphragm
  disc —*see* Rupture, intervertebral disc
  diverticulum (intestine) K57.80
    with bleeding K57.81
    bladder N32.3
    large intestine K57.20
      with
        bleeding K57.21
        small intestine K57.40
          with bleeding K57.41
    small intestine K57.00
      with
        bleeding K57.01
        large intestine K57.40
          with bleeding K57.41
  duodenal stump K31.89
  ear drum (nontraumatic) —*see also*
      Perforation, tympanum
    traumatic S09.2-●
      due to blast injury —*see* Injury, blast, ear
  esophagus K22.3

Rupture, ruptured (*Continued*)
  eye (without prolapse or loss of intraocular
      tissue) —*see* Injury, eye, laceration
  fallopian tube NEC (nonobstetric)
      (nontraumatic) N83.8
    due to pregnancy O00.10-●
      with intrauterine pregnancy O00.11-●
  fontanel P13.1
  gallbladder K82.2
    traumatic S36.128
  gastric —*see also* Rupture, stomach
    vessel K92.2
  globe (eye) (traumatic) —*see* Injury, eye,
      laceration
  graafian follicle (hematoma) N83.0-●
  heart —*see* Rupture, cardiac
  hymen (nontraumatic) (nonintentional) N89.8
  internal organ, traumatic —*see* Injury, by site
  intervertebral disc —*see* Displacement,
      intervertebral disc
    traumatic —*see* Rupture, traumatic,
        intervertebral disc
  intestine NEC (nontraumatic) K63.1
    traumatic —*see* Injury, intestine
  iris —*see also* Abnormality, pupillary
    traumatic —*see* Injury, eye, laceration
  joint capsule, traumatic —*see* Sprain
  kidney (traumatic) S37.06-●
    birth injury P15.8
    nontraumatic N28.89
  lacrimal duct (traumatic) —*see* Injury, eye,
      specified site NEC
  lens (cataract) (traumatic) —*see* Cataract,
      traumatic
  ligament, traumatic —*see* Rupture, traumatic,
      ligament, by site
  liver S36.116
    birth injury P15.0
  lymphatic vessel I89.8
  marginal sinus (placental) (with
      hemorrhage) —*see* Hemorrhage,
      antepartum, specified cause NEC
  membrana tympani (nontraumatic) —*see*
      Perforation, tympanum
  membranes (spontaneous)
    artificial
      delayed delivery following O75.5
    delayed delivery following —*see*
        Pregnancy, complicated by, premature
        rupture of membranes
  meningeal artery I60.8
  meniscus (knee) —*see also* Tear, meniscus
    old —*see* Derangement, meniscus
    site other than knee - code as Sprain
  mesenteric artery, traumatic —*see* Injury,
      mesenteric, artery, laceration, major
  mesentery (nontraumatic) K66.8
    traumatic —*see* Injury, intra-abdominal,
        specified, site NEC
  mitral (valve) I34.8
  muscle (traumatic) —*see also* Strain
    diastasis —*see* Diastasis, muscle
    nontraumatic M62.10
      ankle M62.17-●
      foot M62.17-●
      forearm M62.13-●
      hand M62.14-●
      lower leg M62.16-●
      pelvic region M62.15-●
      shoulder region M62.11-●
      specified site NEC M62.18
      thigh M62.15-●
      upper arm M62.12-●
    traumatic —*see* Strain, by site
  musculotendinous junction NEC,
      nontraumatic —*see* Rupture, tendon,
      spontaneous
  mycotic aneurysm causing cerebral
      hemorrhage —*see* Hemorrhage,
      intracranial, subarachnoid
  myocardium, myocardial —*see* Rupture,
      cardiac
    traumatic —*see* Injury, heart

Rupture, ruptured *(Continued)*
 nontraumatic, meaning hernia —*see* Hernia
 obstructed —*see* Hernia, by site, obstructed
 operation wound —*see* Disruption, wound,
   operation
 ovary, ovarian N83.8
  corpus luteum cyst N83.1-●
  follicle (graafian) N83.0-●
 oviduct (nonobstetric) (nontraumatic) N83.8
  due to pregnancy O00.10-●
   with intrauterine pregnancy O00.11-●
 pancreas (nontraumatic) K86.89
  traumatic S36.299
 papillary muscle NEC I51.2
  following acute myocardial infarction
    (current complication) I23.5
 pelvic
  floor, complicating delivery O70.1
  organ NEC, obstetrical trauma O71.5
 perineum (nonobstetric) (nontraumatic)
    N90.89
  complicating delivery —*see* Delivery,
    complicated, by, laceration, anus
    (sphincter)
 postoperative wound —*see* Disruption,
   wound, operation
 prostate (traumatic) S37.828
 pulmonary
  artery I28.8
  valve (heart) I37.8
  vein I28.8
  vessel I28.8
 pus tube —*see* Salpingitis
 pyosalpinx —*see* Salpingitis
 rectum (nontraumatic) K63.1
  traumatic S36.69
 retina, retinal (traumatic) (without
   detachment) —*see also* Break, retina
  with detachment —*see* Detachment, retina,
    with retinal, break
 rotator cuff (nontraumatic) M75.10-●
  complete M75.12-●
  incomplete M75.11-●
 sclera —*see* Injury, eye, laceration
 sigmoid (nontraumatic) K63.1
  traumatic S36.593
 spinal cord —*see also* Injury, spinal cord, by
   region
  due to injury at birth P11.5
  newborn (birth injury) P11.5
 spleen (traumatic) S36.09
  birth injury P15.1
  congenital (birth injury) P15.1
  due to P. vivax malaria B51.0
  nontraumatic D73.5
  spontaneous D73.5
 splenic vein R58
  traumatic —*see* Injury, blood vessel,
    splenic vein
 stomach (nontraumatic) (spontaneous) K31.89
  traumatic S36.39
 supraspinatus (complete) (incomplete)
   (nontraumatic) —*see* Tear, rotator cuff
 symphysis pubis
  obstetric O71.6
  traumatic S33.4
 synovium (cyst) M66.10
  ankle M66.17-●
  elbow M66.12-●
  finger M66.14-●
  foot M66.17-●
  forearm M66.13-●
  hand M66.14-●
  pelvic region M66.15-●
  shoulder region M66.11-●
  specified site NEC M66.18
  thigh M66.15-●
  toe M66.17-●
  upper arm M66.12-●
  wrist M66.13-●
 tendon (traumatic) —*see* Strain
  nontraumatic (spontaneous) M66.9
   ankle M66.87-●

Rupture, ruptured *(Continued)*
 tendon *(Continued)*
  nontraumatic *(Continued)*
   extensor M66.20
    ankle M66.27-●
    foot M66.27-●
    forearm M66.23-●
    hand M66.24-●
    lower leg M66.26-●
    multiple sites M66.29
    pelvic region M66.25-●
    shoulder region M66.21-●
    specified site NEC M66.28
    thigh M66.25-●
    upper arm M66.22-●
   flexor M66.30
    ankle M66.37-●
    foot M66.37-●
    forearm M66.33-●
    hand M66.34-●
    lower leg M66.36-●
    multiple sites M66.39
    pelvic region M66.35-●
    shoulder region M66.31-●
    specified site NEC M66.38
    thigh M66.35-●
    upper arm M66.32-●
   foot M66.87-●
   forearm M66.83-●
   hand M66.84-●
   lower leg M66.86-●
   multiple sites M66.89
   pelvic region M66.85-●
   shoulder region M66.81-●
   specified
    site NEC M66.88
    tendon M66.80
   thigh M66.85-●
   upper arm M66.82-●
 thoracic duct I89.8
 tonsil J35.8
 traumatic
  aorta —*see* Injury, aorta, laceration, major
  diaphragm —*see* Injury, intrathoracic,
    diaphragm
  external site —*see* Wound, open, by site
  eye —*see* Injury, eye, laceration
  internal organ —*see* Injury, by site
  intervertebral disc
   cervical S13.0
   lumbar S33.0
   thoracic S23.0
  kidney S37.06-●
  ligament —*see also* Sprain
   ankle —*see* Sprain, ankle
   carpus —*see* Rupture, traumatic,
     ligament, wrist
   collateral (hand) —*see* Rupture,
     traumatic, ligament, finger, collateral
   finger (metacarpophalangeal)
     (interphalangeal) S63.40-●
    collateral S63.41-●
     index S63.41-●
     little S63.41-●
     middle S63.41-●
     ring S63.41-●
    index S63.40-●
    little S63.40-●
    middle S63.40-●
    palmar S63.42-●
     index S63.42-●
     little S63.42-●
     middle S63.42-●
     ring S63.42-●
    ring S63.40-●
    specified site NEC S63.499
     index S63.49-●
     little S63.49-●
     middle S63.49-●
     ring S63.49-●
    volar plate S63.43-●
     index S63.43-●
     little S63.43-●

Rupture, ruptured *(Continued)*
 traumatic *(Continued)*
  ligament *(Continued)*
   finger *(Continued)*
    volar plate *(Continued)*
     middle S63.43-●
     ring S63.43-●
   foot —*see* Sprain, foot
   radial collateral S53.2-●
   radiocarpal —*see* Rupture, traumatic,
     ligament, wrist, radiocarpal
   ulnar collateral S53.3-●
   ulnocarpal —*see* Rupture, traumatic,
     ligament, wrist, ulnocarpal
   wrist S63.30-●
    collateral S63.31-●
    radiocarpal S63.32-●
    specified site NEC S63.39-●
    ulnocarpal (palmar) S63.33-●
  liver S36.116
  membrana tympani —*see* Rupture, ear
    drum, traumatic
  muscle or tendon —*see* Strain
  myocardium —*see* Injury, heart
  pancreas S36.299
  rectum S36.69
  sigmoid S36.593
  spleen S36.09
  stomach S36.39
  symphysis pubis S33.4
  tympanum, tympanic (membrane) —*see*
    Rupture, ear drum, traumatic
  ureter S37.19
  uterus S37.69
  vagina —*see* Injury, vagina
  vena cava —*see* Injury, vena cava,
    laceration, major
 tricuspid (heart) (valve) I07.8
 tube, tubal (nonobstetric) (nontraumatic)
    N83.8
  abscess —*see* Salpingitis
  due to pregnancy O00.10-●
   with intrauterine pregnancy O00.11-●
 tympanum, tympanic (membrane)
   (nontraumatic) —*see also* Perforation,
   tympanic membrane H72.9-●
  traumatic —*see* Rupture, ear drum, traumatic
 umbilical cord, complicating delivery O69.89
 ureter (traumatic) S37.19
  nontraumatic N28.89
 urethra (nontraumatic) N36.8
  with ectopic or molar pregnancy O08.6
  following ectopic or molar pregnancy
    O08.6
  obstetrical trauma O71.5
  traumatic S37.39
 uterosacral ligament (nonobstetric)
   (nontraumatic) N83.8
 uterus (traumatic) S37.69
  before labor O71.0-●
  during or after labor O71.1
  nonpuerperal, nontraumatic N85.8
  pregnant (during labor) O71.1
   before labor O71.0-●
 vagina —*see* Injury, vagina
 valve, valvular (heart) —*see* Endocarditis
 varicose vein —*see* Varix
 varix —*see* Varix
 vena cava R58
  traumatic —*see* Injury, vena cava,
    laceration, major
 vesical (urinary) N32.89
 vessel (blood) R58
  pulmonary I28.8
  traumatic —*see* Injury, blood vessel
 viscus R19.8
 vulva complicating delivery O70.0
Russell-Silver syndrome Q87.1
Russian spring-summer type encephalitis A84.0
Rust's disease (tuberculous cervical spondylitis)
  A18.01
Ruvalcaba-Myhre-Smith syndrome E71.440
Rytand-Lipsitch syndrome I44.2

▶ New   ⇒ Revised   ~~deleted~~ Deleted   ● Use Additional Character(s)

S

Saber, sabre shin or tibia (syphilitic) A50.56 [M90.8-●]
Sac lacrimal —see condition
Saccharomyces infection B37.9
Saccharopinuria E72.3
Saccular —see condition
Sacculation
　aorta (nonsyphilitic) —see Aneurysm, aorta
　bladder N32.3
　intralaryngeal (congenital) (ventricular) Q31.3
　larynx (congenital) (ventricular) Q31.3
　organ or site, congenital —see Distortion
　pregnant uterus —see Pregnancy, complicated by, abnormal, uterus
　ureter N28.89
　urethra N36.1
　vesical N32.3
Sachs' amaurotic familial idiocy or disease E75.02
Sachs-Tay disease E75.02
Sacks-Libman disease M32.11
Sacralgia M53.3
Sacralization Q76.49
Sacrodynia M53.3
Sacroiliac joint —see condition
Sacroiliitis NEC M46.1
Sacrum —see condition
Saddle
　back —see Lordosis
　embolus
　　abdominal aorta I74.01
　　pulmonary artery I26.92
　　　with acute cor pulmonale I26.02
　injury — code to condition
　nose M95.0
　　due to syphilis A50.57
Sadism (sexual) F65.52
Sadness, postpartal O90.6
Sadomasochism F65.50
Saemisch's ulcer (cornea) —see Ulcer, cornea, central
Sagging
　skin and subcutaneous tissue (following bariatric surgery weight loss) (following dietary weight loss) L98.7
Sahib disease B55.0
Sailors' skin L57.8
Saint
　Anthony's fire —see Erysipelas
　triad —see Hernia, diaphragm
　Vitus' dance —see Chorea, Sydenham's
Salaam
　attack(s) —see Epilepsy, spasms
　tic R25.8
Salicylism
　abuse F55.8
　overdose or wrong substance given —see Table of Drugs and Chemicals, by drug, poisoning
Salivary duct or gland —see condition
Salivation, excessive K11.7
Salmonella —see Infection, Salmonella
Salmonellosis A02.0
Salpingitis (catarrhal) (fallopian tube) (nodular) (pseudofollicular) (purulent) (septic) N70.91
　with oophoritis N70.93
　acute N70.01
　　with oophoritis N70.03
　chlamydial A56.11
　chronic N70.11
　　with oophoritis N70.13
　complicating abortion —see Abortion, by type, complicated by, salpingitis
　ear —see Salpingitis, eustachian
　eustachian (tube) H68.00-●
　　acute H68.01-●
　　chronic H68.02-●

Salpingitis (Continued)
　follicularis N70.11
　　with oophoritis N70.13
　gonococcal (acute) (chronic) A54.24
　interstitial, chronic N70.11
　　with oophoritis N70.13
　isthmica nodosa N70.11
　　with oophoritis N70.13
　specific (gonococcal) (acute) (chronic) A54.24
　tuberculous (acute) (chronic) A18.17
　venereal (gonococcal) (acute) (chronic) A54.24
Salpingocele N83.4-●
Salpingo-oophoritis (catarrhal) (purulent) (ruptured) (septic) (suppurative) N70.93
　acute N70.03
　　with ectopic or molar pregnancy O08.0
　　following ectopic or molar pregnancy O08.0
　　gonococcal A54.24
　chronic N70.13
　following ectopic or molar pregnancy O08.0
　gonococcal (acute) (chronic) A54.24
　puerperal O86.19
　specific (gonococcal) (acute) (chronic) A54.24
　subacute N70.03
　tuberculous (acute) (chronic) A18.17
　venereal (gonococcal) (acute) (chronic) A54.24
Salpingo-ovaritis —see Salpingo-oophoritis
Salpingoperitonitis —see Salpingo-oophoritis
Salzmann's nodular dystrophy —see Degeneration, cornea, nodular
Sampson's cyst or tumor N80.1
San Joaquin (Valley) fever B38.0
Sandblaster's asthma, lung or pneumoconiosis J62.8
Sander's disease (paranoia) F22
Sandfly fever A93.1
Sandhoff's disease E75.01
Sanfilippo (Type B) (Type C) (Type D) syndrome E76.22
Sanger-Brown ataxia G11.2
Sao Paulo fever or typhus A77.0
Saponification, mesenteric K65.8
Sarcocele (benign)
　syphilitic A52.76
　　congenital A50.59
Sarcocystosis A07.8
Sarcoepiplocele —see Hernia
Sarcoepiplomphalocele Q79.2
Sarcoid —see also Sarcoidosis
　arthropathy D86.86
　Boeck's D86.9
　Darier-Roussy D86.3
　iridocyclitis D86.83
　meningitis D86.81
　myocarditis D86.85
　myositis D86.87
　pyelonephritis D86.84
　Spiegler-Fendt L08.89
Sarcoidosis D86.9
　with
　　cranial nerve palsies D86.82
　　hepatic granuloma D86.89
　　polyarthritis D86.86
　　tubulo-interstitial nephropathy D86.84
　combined sites NEC D86.89
　lung D86.0
　　and lymph nodes D86.2
　lymph nodes D86.1
　　and lung D86.2
　meninges D86.81
　skin D86.3
　specified type NEC D86.89
Sarcoma (of) —see also Neoplasm, connective tissue, malignant
　alveolar soft part —see Neoplasm, connective tissue, malignant
　ameloblastic C41.1
　　upper jaw (bone) C41.0
　botryoid —see Neoplasm, connective tissue, malignant

Sarcoma (Continued)
　botryoides —see Neoplasm, connective tissue, malignant
　cerebellar C71.6
　　circumscribed (arachnoidal) C71.6
　circumscribed (arachnoidal) cerebellar C71.6
　clear cell —see also Neoplasm, connective tissue, malignant
　　kidney C64.-●
　dendritic cells (accessory cells) C96.4
　embryonal —see Neoplasm, connective tissue, malignant
　endometrial (stromal) C54.1
　　isthmus C54.0
　epithelioid (cell) —see Neoplasm, connective tissue, malignant
　Ewing's —see Neoplasm, bone, malignant
　follicular dendritic cell C96.4
　germinoblastic (diffuse) —see Lymphoma, diffuse, large cell
　　follicular —see Lymphoma, follicular, specified NEC
　giant cell (except of bone) —see also Neoplasm, connective tissue, malignant
　　bone —see Neoplasm, bone, malignant
　glomoid —see Neoplasm, connective tissue, malignant
　granulocytic C92.3-●
　hemangioendothelial —see Neoplasm, connective tissue, malignant
　hemorrhagic, multiple —see Sarcoma, Kaposi's
　histiocytic C96.A
　Hodgkin —see Lymphoma, Hodgkin
　immunoblastic (diffuse) —see Lymphoma, diffuse large cell
　interdigitating dendritic cell C96.4
　Kaposi's
　　colon C46.4
　　connective tissue C46.1
　　gastrointestinal organ C46.4
　　lung C46.5-●
　　lymph node(s) C46.3
　　palate (hard) (soft) C46.2
　　rectum C46.4
　　skin C46.0
　　specified site NEC C46.7
　　stomach C46.4
　　unspecified site C46.9
　Kupffer cell C22.3
　Langerhans cell C96.4
　leptomeningeal —see Neoplasm, meninges, malignant
　liver NEC C22.4
　lymphangioendothelial —see Neoplasm, connective tissue, malignant
　lymphoblastic —see Lymphoma, lymphoblastic (diffuse)
　lymphocytic —see Lymphoma, small cell B-cell
　mast cell C96.22
　melanotic —see Melanoma
　meningeal —see Neoplasm, meninges, malignant
　meningothelial —see Neoplasm, meninges, malignant
　mesenchymal —see also Neoplasm, connective tissue, malignant
　mixed —see Neoplasm, connective tissue, malignant
　mesothelial —see Mesothelioma
　monstrocellular
　　specified site —see Neoplasm, malignant, by site
　　unspecified site C71.9
　myeloid C92.3-●
　neurogenic —see Neoplasm, nerve, malignant
　odontogenic C41.1
　　upper jaw (bone) C41.0

Sarcoma *(Continued)*
  osteoblastic —*see* Neoplasm, bone, malignant
  osteogenic —*see also* Neoplasm, bone, malignant
    juxtacortical —*see* Neoplasm, bone, malignant
    periosteal —*see* Neoplasm, bone, malignant
  periosteal —*see also* Neoplasm, bone, malignant
    osteogenic —*see* Neoplasm, bone, malignant
  pleomorphic cell —*see* Neoplasm, connective tissue, malignant
  reticulum cell (diffuse) —*see* Lymphoma, diffuse large cell
    nodular —*see* Lymphoma, follicular
    pleomorphic cell type —*see* Lymphoma, diffuse large cell
  rhabdoid —*see* Neoplasm, malignant, by site
  round cell —*see* Neoplasm, connective tissue, malignant
  small cell —*see* Neoplasm, connective tissue, malignant
  soft tissue —*see* Neoplasm, connective tissue, malignant
  spindle cell —*see* Neoplasm, connective tissue, malignant
  stromal (endometrial) C54.1
    isthmus C54.0
  synovial —*see also* Neoplasm, connective tissue, malignant
    biphasic —*see* Neoplasm, connective tissue, malignant
    epithelioid cell —*see* Neoplasm, connective tissue, malignant
    spindle cell —*see* Neoplasm, connective tissue, malignant
Sarcomatosis
  meningeal —*see* Neoplasm, meninges, malignant
  specified site NEC —*see* Neoplasm, connective tissue, malignant
  unspecified site C80.1
Sarcopenia (age-related) M62.84
Sarcosinemia E72.59
Sarcosporidiosis (intestinal) A07.8
Satiety, early R68.81
Saturnine —*see* condition
Saturnism
  overdose or wrong substance given or taken —*see* Table of Drugs and Chemicals, by drug, poisoning
Satyriasis F52.8
Sauriasis —*see* Ichthyosis
SBE (subacute bacterial endocarditis) I33.0
Scabies (any site) B86
Scabs R23.4
Scaglietti-Dagnini syndrome E22.0
Scald —*see* Burn
Scalenus anticus (anterior) **syndrome** G54.0
Scales R23.4
Scaling, skin R23.4
Scalp —*see* condition
Scapegoating affecting child Z62.3
Scaphocephaly Q75.0
Scapulalgia M89.8X1
➡ **Scapulohumeral myopathy** G71.02
Scar, scarring —*see also* Cicatrix L90.5
  adherent L90.5
  atrophic L90.5
  cervix
    in pregnancy or childbirth —*see* Pregnancy, complicated by, abnormal cervix
  cheloid L91.0
  chorioretinal H31.00-●
    posterior pole macula H31.01-●
    postsurgical H59.81-●
    solar retinopathy H31.02-●
    specified type NEC H31.09-●

Scar, scarring *(Continued)*
  choroid —*see* Scar, chorioretinal
  conjunctiva H11.24-●
  cornea H17.9
    xerophthalmic —*see also* Opacity, cornea
      vitamin A deficiency E50.6
  duodenum, obstructive K31.5
  hypertrophic L91.0
  keloid L91.0
  labia N90.89
  lung (base) J98.4
  macula —*see* Scar, chorioretinal, posterior pole
  muscle M62.89
  myocardium, myocardial I25.2
  painful L90.5
  posterior pole (eye) —*see* Scar, chorioretinal, posterior pole
  retina —*see* Scar, chorioretinal
  trachea J39.8
  transmural uterine, in pregnancy O34.29
  uterus N85.8
    in pregnancy O34.29
  vagina N89.8
    postoperative N99.2
  vulva N90.89
Scarabiasis B88.2
Scarlatina (anginosa) (maligna) A38.9
  myocarditis (acute) A38.1
    old —*see* Myocarditis
  otitis media A38.0
  ulcerosa A38.8
Scarlet fever (albuminuria) (angina) A38.9
Schamberg's disease (progressive pigmentary dermatosis) L81.7
Schatzki's ring (acquired) (esophagus) (lower) K22.2
  congenital Q39.3
Schaufenster krankheit I20.8
Schaumann's
  benign lymphogranulomatosis D86.1
  disease or syndrome —*see* Sarcoidosis
Scheie's syndrome E76.03
Schenck's disease B42.1
Scheuermann's disease or osteochondrosis — *see* Osteochondrosis, juvenile, spine
Schilder (-Flatau) **disease** G37.0
Schilling-type monocytic leukemia C93.0-●
Schimmelbusch's disease, cystic mastitis, or hyperplasia —*see* Mastopathy, cystic
Schistosoma infestation —*see* Infestation, Schistosoma
Schistosomiasis B65.9
  with muscle disorder B65.9 *[M63.80]*
    ankle B65.9 *[M63.87-●]*
    foot B65.9 *[M63.87-●]*
    forearm B65.9 *[M63.83-●]*
    hand B65.9 *[M63.84-●]*
    lower leg B65.9 *[M63.86-●]*
    multiple sites B65.9 *[M63.89]*
    pelvic region B65.9 *[M63.85-●]*
    shoulder region B65.9 *[M63.81-●]*
    specified site NEC B65.9 *[M63.88]*
    thigh B65.9 *[M63.85-●]*
    upper arm B65.9 *[M63.82-●]*
  Asiatic B65.2
  bladder B65.0
  chestermani B65.8
  colon B65.1
  cutaneous B65.3
  due to
    S. haematobium B65.0
    S. japonicum B65.2
    S. mansoni B65.1
    S. mattheii B65.8
  Eastern B65.2
  genitourinary tract B65.0
  intestinal B65.1
  lung NEC B65.9 *[J99]*
    pneumonia B65.9 *[J17]*
  Manson's (intestinal) B65.1

Schistosomiasis *(Continued)*
  oriental B65.2
  pulmonary NEC B65.9 *[J99]*
    pneumonia B65.9
  Schistosoma
    haematobium B65.0
    japonicum B65.2
    mansoni B65.1
  specified type NEC B65.8
  urinary B65.0
  vesical B65.0
Schizencephaly Q04.6
Schizoaffective psychosis F25.9
Schizodontia K00.2
Schizoid personality F60.1
Schizophrenia, schizophrenic F20.9
  acute (brief) (undifferentiated) F23
  atypical (form) F20.3
  borderline F21
  catalepsy F20.2
  catatonic (type) (excited) (withdrawn) F20.2
  cenesthopathic, cenesthesiopathic F20.89
  childhood type F84.5
  chronic undifferentiated F20.5
  cyclic F25.0
  disorganized (type) F20.1
  flexibilitas cerea F20.2
  hebephrenic (type) F20.1
  incipient F21
  latent F21
  negative type F20.5
  paranoid (type) F20.0
  paraphrenic F20.0
  post-psychotic depression F32.89
  prepsychotic F21
  prodromal F21
  pseudoneurotic F21
  pseudopsychopathic F21
  reaction F23
  residual (state) (type) F20.5
  restzustand F20.5
  schizoaffective (type) —*see* Psychosis, schizoaffective
  simple (type) F20.89
  simplex F20.89
  specified type NEC F20.89
  spectrum and other psychotic disorder F29
    specified NEC F28
  stupor F20.2
  syndrome of childhood F84.5
  undifferentiated (type) F20.3
    chronic F20.5
Schizothymia (persistent) F60.1
Schlatter-Osgood disease or osteochondrosis —*see* Osteochondrosis, juvenile, tibia
Schlatter's tibia —*see* Osteochondrosis, juvenile, tibia
Schmidt's syndrome (polyglandular, autoimmune) E31.0
Schmincke's carcinoma or tumor —*see* Neoplasm, nasopharynx, malignant
Schmitz (-Stutzer) **dysentery** A03.0
Schmorl's disease or nodes
  lumbar region M51.46
  lumbosacral region M51.47
  sacrococcygeal region M53.3
  thoracic region M51.44
  thoracolumbar region M51.45
Schneiderian
  papilloma —*see* Neoplasm, nasopharynx, benign
    specified site —*see* Neoplasm, benign, by site
    unspecified site D14.0
  specified site —*see* Neoplasm, malignant, by site
  unspecified site C30.0
Scholte's syndrome (malignant carcinoid) E34.0
Scholz (-Bielchowsky-Henneberg) **disease or syndrome** E75.25
Schönlein (-Henoch) **disease or purpura** (primary) (rheumatic) D69.0

▶ New   ➡ Revised   ~~deleted~~ Deleted   ● Use Additional Character(s)

Schottmuller's disease A01.4
Schroeder's syndrome (endocrine
  hypertensive) E27.0
Schüller-Christian disease or syndrome C96.5
Schultze's type acroparesthesia, simple I73.89
Schultz's disease or syndrome —see
  Agranulocytosis
Schwalbe-Ziehen-Oppenheim disease G24.1
Schwannoma —see also Neoplasm, nerve,
  benign
  malignant —see also Neoplasm, nerve,
    malignant
    with rhabdomyoblastic differentiation —
      see Neoplasm, nerve, malignant
  melanocytic —see Neoplasm, nerve, benign
  pigmented —see Neoplasm, nerve, benign
Schwannomatosis Q85.03
Schwartz (-Jampel) syndrome G71.13
Schwartz-Bartter syndrome E22.2
Schweniger-Buzzi anetoderma L90.1
Sciatic —see condition
Sciatica (infective)
  with lumbago M54.4-●
    due to intervertebral disc disorder —see
      Disorder, disc, with, radiculopathy
  due to displacement of intervertebral disc
    (with lumbago) —see Disorder, disc,
    with, radiculopathy
  wallet M54.3-●
Scimitar syndrome Q26.8
Sclera —see condition
Sclerectasia H15.84-●
Scleredema
  adultorum —see Sclerosis, systemic
  Buschke's —see Sclerosis, systemic
  newborn P83.0
Sclerema (adiposum) (edematosum)
    (neonatorum) (newborn) P83.0
  adultorum —see Sclerosis, systemic
Scleriasis —see Scleroderma
Scleritis H15.00-●
  with corneal involvement H15.04-●
  anterior H15.01-●
  brawny H15.02-●
  in (due to) zoster B02.34
  posterior H15.03-●
  specified type NEC H15.09-●
  syphilitic A52.71
  tuberculous (nodular) A18.51
Sclerochoroiditis H31.8
Scleroconjunctivitis —see Scleritis
Sclerocystic ovary syndrome E28.2
Sclerodactyly, sclerodactylia L94.3
Scleroderma, sclerodermia (acrosclerotic)
    (diffuse) (generalized) (progressive)
    (pulmonary) —see also Sclerosis, systemic
    M34.9-●
  circumscribed L94.0
  linear L94.1
  localized L94.0
  newborn P83.88
  systemic M34.9
Sclerokeratitis H16.8
  tuberculous A18.52
Scleroma nasi A48.8
Scleromalacia (perforans) H15.05-●
Scleromyxedema L98.5
Sclérose en plaques G35
Sclerosis, sclerotic
  adrenal (gland) E27.8
  Alzheimer's —see Disease, Alzheimer's
  amyotrophic (lateral) G12.21
  aorta, aortic I70.0
    valve —see Endocarditis, aortic
  artery, arterial, arteriolar, arteriovascular —
    see Arteriosclerosis
  ascending multiple G35
  brain (generalized) (lobular) G37.9
    artery, arterial I67.2
    diffuse G37.0
    disseminated G35

Sclerosis, sclerotic (Continued)
  brain (Continued)
    insular G35
    Krabbe's E75.23
    miliary G35
    multiple G35
    presenile (Alzheimer's) —see Disease,
      Alzheimer's, early onset
    senile (arteriosclerotic) I67.2
    stem, multiple G35
    tuberous Q85.1
  bulbar, multiple G35
  bundle of His I44.39
  cardiac —see Disease, heart, ischemic,
    atherosclerotic
  cardiorenal —see Hypertension, cardiorenal
  cardiovascular —see also Disease,
    cardiovascular
    renal —see Hypertension, cardiorenal
  cerebellar —see Sclerosis, brain
  cerebral —see Sclerosis, brain
  cerebrospinal (disseminated) (multiple) G35
  cerebrovascular I67.2
  choroid —see Degeneration, choroid
  combined (spinal cord) —see also
    Degeneration, combined
    multiple G35
  concentric (Balo) G37.5
  cornea —see Opacity, cornea
  coronary (artery) I25.10
    with angina pectoris —see Arteriosclerosis,
      coronary (artery),
  corpus cavernosum
    female N90.89
    male N48.6
  diffuse (brain) (spinal cord) G37.0
  disseminated G35
  dorsal G35
  dorsolateral (spinal cord) —see Degeneration,
    combined
  endometrium N85.5
  extrapyramidal G25.9
  eye, nuclear (senile) —see Cataract, senile,
    nuclear
  focal and segmental (glomerular) —see also
    N00-N07 with fourth character .1 N05.1
  Friedreich's (spinal cord) G11.1
  funicular (spermatic cord) N50.89
  general (vascular) —see Arteriosclerosis
  gland (lymphatic) I89.8
  hepatic K74.1
    alcoholic K70.2
  hereditary
    cerebellar G11.9
    spinal (Friedreich's ataxia) G11.1
  hippocampal G93.81
  insular G35
  kidney —see Sclerosis, renal
  larynx J38.7
  lateral (amyotrophic) (descending) (spinal)
    G12.21
    primary G12.23
  lens, senile nuclear —see Cataract, senile,
    nuclear
  liver K74.1
    with fibrosis K74.2
      alcoholic K70.2
    alcoholic K70.2
    cardiac K76.1
  lung —see Fibrosis, lung
  mastoid —see Mastoiditis, chronic
  mesial temporal G93.81
  mitral I05.8
  Mönckeberg's (medial) —see Arteriosclerosis,
    extremities
  multiple (brain stem) (cerebral) (generalized)
    (spinal cord) G35
  myocardium, myocardial —see Disease, heart,
    ischemic, atherosclerotic
  nuclear (senile), eye —see Cataract, senile,
    nuclear

Sclerosis, sclerotic (Continued)
  ovary N83.8
  pancreas K86.89
  penis N48.6
  peripheral arteries —see Arteriosclerosis,
    extremities
  plaques G35
  pluriglandular E31.8
  polyglandular E31.8
  posterolateral (spinal cord) —see
    Degeneration, combined
  presenile (Alzheimer's) —see Disease,
    Alzheimer's, early onset
  primary, lateral G12.23
  progressive, systemic M34.0
  pulmonary —see Fibrosis, lung
    artery I27.0
    valve (heart) —see Endocarditis,
      pulmonary
  renal N26.9
    with
      cystine storage disease E72.09
      hypertensive heart disease (conditions in
        I11) —see Hypertension, cardiorenal
    arteriolar (hyaline) (hyperplastic) —see
      Hypertension, kidney
  retina (senile) (vascular) H35.00
  senile (vascular) —see Arteriosclerosis
  spinal (cord) (progressive) G95.89
    ascending G61.0
    combined —see also Degeneration,
      combined
      multiple G35
      syphilitic A52.11
    disseminated G35
    dorsolateral —see Degeneration,
      combined
    hereditary (Friedreich's) (mixed form)
      G11.1
    lateral (amyotrophic) G12.23
    multiple G35
    posterior (syphilitic) A52.11
  stomach K31.89
  subendocardial, congenital I42.4
  systemic M34.9
    with
      lung involvement M34.81
      myopathy M34.82
      polyneuropathy M34.83
    drug-induced M34.2
    due to chemicals NEC M34.2
    progressive M34.0
    specified NEC M34.89
  temporal (mesial) G93.81
  tricuspid (heart) (valve) I07.8
  tuberous (brain) Q85.1
  tympanic membrane —see Disorder,
    tympanic membrane, specified NEC
  valve, valvular (heart) —see Endocarditis
  vascular —see Arteriosclerosis
  vein I87.8
Scoliosis (acquired) (postural) M41.9
  adolescent (idiopathic) —see Scoliosis,
    idiopathic, adolescent
  congenital Q67.5
    due to bony malformation Q76.3
    failure of segmentation (hemivertebra)
      Q76.3
    hemivertebra fusion Q76.3
    postural Q67.5
  idiopathic M41.20
    adolescent M41.129
      cervical region M41.122
      cervicothoracic region M41.123
      lumbar region M41.126
      lumbosacral region M41.127
      thoracic region M41.124
      thoracolumbar region
        M41.125
    cervical region M41.22
    cervicothoracic region M41.23

Scoliosis *(Continued)*
  idiopathic *(Continued)*
    infantile M41.00
      cervical region M41.02
      cervicothoracic region M41.03
      lumbar region M41.06
      lumbosacral region M41.07
      sacrococcygeal region M41.08
      thoracic region M41.04
      thoracolumbar region M41.05
    juvenile M41.119
      cervical region M41.112
      cervicothoracic region M41.113
      lumbar region M41.116
      lumbosacral region M41.117
      thoracic region M41.114
      thoracolumbar region M41.115
    lumbar region M41.26
    lumbosacral region M41.27
    thoracic region M41.24
    thoracolumbar region M41.25
  infantile —*see* Scoliosis, idiopathic,
    infantile
  neuromuscular M41.40
    cervical region M41.42
    cervicothoracic region M41.43
    lumbar region M41.46
    lumbosacral region M41.47
    occipito-atlanto-axial region M41.41
    thoracic region M41.44
    thoracolumbar region M41.45
  paralytic —*see* Scoliosis, neuromuscular
  postradiation therapy M96.5
  rachitic (late effect or sequelae) E64.3
    [M49.80]
    cervical region E64.3 *[M49.82]*
    cervicothoracic region E64.3 *[M49.83]*
    lumbar region E64.3 *[M49.86]*
    lumbosacral region E64.3 *[M49.87]*
    multiple sites E64.3 *[M49.89]*
    occipito-atlanto-axial region E64.3
      [M49.81]
    sacrococcygeal region E64.3 *[M49.88]*
    thoracic region E64.3 *[M49.84]*
    thoracolumbar region E64.3 *[M49.85]*
  sciatic M54.4-•
  secondary (to) NEC M41.50
    cerebral palsy, Friedreich's ataxia,
      poliomyelitis, neuromuscular
      disorders —*see* Scoliosis,
      neuromuscular
    cervical region M41.52
    cervicothoracic region M41.53
    lumbar region M41.56
    lumbosacral region M41.57
    thoracic region M41.54
    thoracolumbar region M41.55
  specified form NEC M41.80
    cervical region M41.82
    cervicothoracic region M41.83
    lumbar region M41.86
    lumbosacral region M41.87
    thoracic region M41.84
    thoracolumbar region M41.85
  thoracogenic M41.30
    thoracic region M41.34
    thoracolumbar region M41.35
  tuberculous A18.01
Scoliotic pelvis
  with disproportion (fetopelvic) O33.0
    causing obstructed labor O65.0
Scorbutus, scorbutic —*see also* Scurvy
  anemia D53.2
Score, NIHSS (National Institutes of Health
  Stroke Scale) R29.7-•
Scotoma (arcuate) (Bjerrum) (central) (ring) —
  see also Defect, visual field, localized,
  scotoma
  scintillating H53.19
Scratch —*see* Abrasion
Scratchy throat R09.89

Screening (for) Z13.9
  alcoholism Z13.33
  anemia Z13.0
  anomaly, congenital Z13.89
  antenatal, of mother —*see also* Encounter,
    antenatal Z36.9
  arterial hypertension Z13.6
  arthropod-borne viral disease NEC Z11.59
  autism Z13.41
  bacteriuria, asymptomatic Z13.89
    specified NEC Z13.39
  behavioral disorder Z13.30
  brain injury, traumatic Z13.850
  bronchitis, chronic Z13.83
  brucellosis Z11.2
  cardiovascular disorder Z13.6
  cataract Z13.5
  chlamydial diseases Z11.8
  cholera Z11.0
  chromosomal abnormalities (nonprocreative)
    NEC Z13.79
  colonoscopy Z12.11
  congenital
    dislocation of hip Z13.89
    eye disorder Z13.5
    malformation or deformation Z13.89
  contamination NEC Z13.88
  cystic fibrosis Z13.228
  dengue fever Z11.59
  dental disorder Z13.84
  depression (adult) (adolescent) (child) Z13.31
    maternal Z13.32
    perinatal Z13.32
  developmental
    delays Z13.40
      global (milestones) Z13.42
      specified NEC Z13.49
    handicap Z13.42
      in early childhood Z13.42
  ~~developmental handicap Z13.42~~
    ~~in early childhood Z13.42~~
    ~~infant Z13.41~~
  diabetes mellitus Z13.1
  diphtheria Z11.2
  disability, intellectual Z13.39
    ~~infant Z13.41~~
  disease or disorder Z13.9
    bacterial NEC Z11.2
      intestinal infectious Z11.0
      respiratory tuberculosis Z11.1
    behavioral Z13.30
      specified NEC Z13.39
    developmental delays Z13.40
      global (milestones) Z13.42
      specified NEC Z13.49
    mental health and behavioral Z13.30
      specified NEC Z13.39
    blood or blood-forming organ Z13.0
    cardiovascular Z13.6
    Chagas' Z11.6
    chlamydial Z11.8
    dental Z13.89
    ~~developmental Z13.42~~
      ~~in child Z13.42~~
      ~~infant Z13.41~~
    digestive tract NEC Z13.818
      lower GI Z13.811
      upper GI Z13.810
    ear Z13.5
    endocrine Z13.29
    eye Z13.5
    genitourinary Z13.89
    heart Z13.6
    human immunodeficiency virus (HIV)
      infection Z11.4
    immunity Z13.0
    infection
      intestinal Z11.0
        specified NEC Z11.6
    infectious Z11.9
    ~~mental Z13.89~~

Screening *(Continued)*
  disease or disorder *(Continued)*
    metabolic Z13.228
    neurological Z13.89
    nutritional Z13.21
      metabolic Z13.228
        lipoid disorders Z13.220
    protozoal Z11.6
      intestinal Z11.0
    respiratory Z13.83
    rheumatic Z13.828
    rickettsial Z11.8
    sexually-transmitted NEC Z11.3
      human immunodeficiency virus (HIV)
        Z11.4
    sickle-cell (trait) Z13.0
    skin Z13.89
    specified NEC Z13.89
    spirochetal Z11.8
    thyroid Z13.29
    vascular Z13.6
    venereal Z11.3
    viral NEC Z11.59
      human immunodeficiency virus (HIV)
        Z11.4
      intestinal Z11.0
  elevated titer Z13.89
  emphysema Z13.83
  encephalitis, viral (mosquito- or tick-borne)
    Z11.59
  exposure to contaminants (toxic) Z13.88
  fever
    dengue Z11.59
    hemorrhagic Z11.59
    yellow Z11.59
  filariasis Z11.6
  galactosemia Z13.228
  gastrointestinal condition Z13.818
  genetic (nonprocreative)- for procreative
    management —*see* Testing, genetic, for
    procreative management
    disease carrier status (nonprocreative)
      Z13.71
    specified NEC (nonprocreative) Z13.79
  genitourinary condition Z13.89
  glaucoma Z13.5
  gonorrhea Z11.3
  gout Z13.89
  helminthiasis (intestinal) Z11.6
  hematopoietic malignancy Z12.89
  hemoglobinopathies NEC Z13.0
  hemorrhagic fever Z11.59
  Hodgkin disease Z12.89
  human immunodeficiency virus (HIV) Z11.4
  human papillomavirus Z11.51
  hypertension Z13.6
  infant or child (over 28 days old) Z00.129
    with abnormal findings Z00.121
  immunity disorders Z13.0
  infection
    mycotic Z11.8
    parasitic Z11.8
  ingestion of radioactive substance Z13.88
  intellectual disability Z13.39
    ~~infant Z13.41~~
  intestinal
    helminthiasis Z11.6
    infectious disease Z11.0
  leishmaniasis Z11.6
  leprosy Z11.2
  leptospirosis Z11.8
  leukemia Z12.89
  lymphoma Z12.89
  malaria Z11.6
  malnutrition Z13.29
    metabolic Z13.228
    nutritional Z13.21
  measles Z11.59
  mental health disorder Z13.30
    specified NEC Z13.39
  ~~mental disorder Z13.89~~

▶ New   ⇒ Revised   ~~deleted~~ Deleted   • Use Additional Character(s)

Screening *(Continued)*
  metabolic errors, inborn Z13.228
  multiphasic Z13.89
  musculoskeletal disorder Z13.828
    osteoporosis Z13.820
  mycoses Z11.8
  myocardial infarction (acute) Z13.6
  neoplasm (malignant) (of) Z12.9
    bladder Z12.6
    blood Z12.89
    breast Z12.39
      routine mammogram Z12.31
    cervix Z12.4
    colon Z12.11
    genitourinary organs NEC Z12.79
      bladder Z12.6
      cervix Z12.4
      ovary Z12.73
      prostate Z12.5
      testis Z12.71
      vagina Z12.72
    hematopoietic system Z12.89
    intestinal tract Z12.10
      colon Z12.11
      rectum Z12.12
      small intestine Z12.13
    lung Z12.2
    lymph (glands) Z12.89
    nervous system Z12.82
    oral cavity Z12.81
    prostate Z12.5
    rectum Z12.12
    respiratory organs Z12.2
    skin Z12.83
    small intestine Z12.13
    specified site NEC Z12.89
    stomach Z12.0
  nephropathy Z13.89
  nervous system disorders NEC Z13.858
  neurological condition Z13.89
  osteoporosis Z13.820
  parasitic infestation Z11.9
    specified NEC Z11.8
  phenylketonuria Z13.228
  plague Z11.2
  poisoning (chemical) (heavy metal) Z13.88
  poliomyelitis Z11.59
  postnatal, chromosomal abnormalities Z13.89
  prenatal, of mother —*see also* Encounter,
      antenatal Z36.9
  protozoal disease Z11.6
    intestinal Z11.0
  pulmonary tuberculosis Z11.1
  radiation exposure Z13.88
  respiratory condition Z13.83
  respiratory tuberculosis Z11.1
  rheumatoid arthritis Z13.828
  rubella Z11.59
  schistosomiasis Z11.6
  sexually-transmitted disease NEC Z11.3
    human immunodeficiency virus (HIV) Z11.4
  sickle-cell disease or trait Z13.0
  skin condition Z13.89
  sleeping sickness Z11.6
  special Z13.9
    specified NEC Z13.89
  syphilis Z11.3
  tetanus Z11.2
  trachoma Z11.8
  traumatic brain injury Z13.850
  trypanosomiasis Z11.6
  tuberculosis, respiratory Z11.1
  venereal disease Z11.3
  viral encephalitis (mosquito- or tick-borne)
      Z11.59
  whooping cough Z11.2
  worms, intestinal Z11.6
  yaws Z11.8
  yellow fever Z11.59
Scrofula, scrofulosis (tuberculosis of cervical
    lymph glands) A18.2

Scrofulide (primary) (tuberculous) A18.4
Scrofuloderma, scrofulodermia (any site)
    (primary) A18.4
Scrofulosus lichen (primary) (tuberculous) A18.4
Scrofulous —*see* condition
Scrotal tongue K14.5
Scrotum —*see* condition
Scurvy, scorbutic E54
  anemia D53.2
  gum E54
  infantile E54
  rickets E55.0 [M90.80]
Sealpox B08.62
Seasickness T75.3
Seatworm (infection) (infestation) B80
Sebaceous —*see also* condition
  cyst —*see* Cyst, sebaceous
Seborrhea, seborrheic L21.9
  capillitii R23.8
  capitis L21.0
  dermatitis L21.9
    infantile L21.1
  eczema L21.9
    infantile L21.1
  sicca L21.0
Seckel's syndrome Q87.1
Seclusion, pupil —*see* Membrane, pupillary
Second hand tobacco smoke exposure (acute)
    (chronic) Z77.22
  in the perinatal period P96.81
Secondary
  dentin (in pulp) K04.3
  neoplasm, secondaries —*see* Table of
      Neoplasms, secondary
Secretion
  antidiuretic hormone, inappropriate E22.2
  catecholamine, by pheochromocytoma E27.5
  hormone
    antidiuretic, inappropriate (syndrome) E22.2
    by
      carcinoid tumor E34.0
      pheochromocytoma E27.5
    ectopic NEC E34.2
  urinary
    excessive R35.8
    suppression R34
Section
  nerve, traumatic —*see* Injury, nerve
Sedative, hypnotic, or anxiolytic-induced
  anxiety disorder F13.980
  bipolar and related disorder F13.94
  delirium F13.921
  depressive disorder F13.94
  major neurocognitive disorder F13.97
  mild neurocognitive disorder F13.988
  psychotic disorder F13.959
  sexual dysfunction F13.981
  sleep disorder F13.982
Segmentation, incomplete (congenital) —*see
    also* Fusion
  bone NEC Q78.8
  lumbosacral (joint) (vertebra) Q76.49
Seitelberger's syndrome (infantile neuraxonal
    dystrophy) G31.89
Seizure(s) —*see also* Convulsions R56.9
  akinetic —*see* Epilepsy, generalized, specified
      NEC
  atonic —*see* Epilepsy, generalized, specified
      NEC
  autonomic (hysterical) F44.5
  convulsive —*see* Convulsions
  cortical (focal) (motor) —*see* Epilepsy,
      localization-related, symptomatic, with
      simple partial seizures
  disorder —*see also* Epilepsy G40.909
  due to stroke —*see* Sequelae (of), disease,
      cerebrovascular, by type, specified NEC
  epileptic —*see* Epilepsy
  febrile (simple) R56.00
    with status epilepticus G40.901
    complex (atypical) (complicated) R56.01
      with status epilepticus G40.901

Seizure *(Continued)*
  grand mal G40.409
    intractable G40.419
      with status epilepticus G40.411
      without status epilepticus G40.419
    not intractable G40.409
      with status epilepticus G40.401
      without status epilepticus G40.409
  heart —*see* Disease, heart
  hysterical F44.5
  intractable G40.919
    with status epilepticus G40.911
  Jacksonian (focal) (motor type) (sensory
      type) —*see* Epilepsy, localization-related,
      symptomatic, with simple partial
      seizures
  newborn P90
  nonspecific epileptic
    atonic —*see* Epilepsy, generalized, specified
        NEC
    clonic —*see* Epilepsy, generalized, specified
        NEC
    myoclonic —*see* Epilepsy, generalized,
        specified NEC
    tonic —*see* Epilepsy, generalized, specified
        NEC
    tonic-clonic —*see* Epilepsy, generalized,
        specified NEC
  partial, developing into secondarily
      generalized seizures
    complex —*see* Epilepsy, localization-
        related, symptomatic, with complex
        partial seizures
    simple —*see* Epilepsy, localization-related,
        symptomatic, with simple partial
        seizures
  petit mal G40.409
    intractable G40.419
      with status epilepticus G40.411
      without status epilepticus G40.419
    not intractable G40.409
      with status epilepticus G40.401
      without status epilepticus G40.409
  post traumatic R56.1
  recurrent G40.909
  specified NEC G40.89
  uncinate —*see* Epilepsy, localization-related,
      symptomatic, with complex partial
      seizures
Selenium deficiency, dietary E59
Self-damaging behavior (life-style) Z72.89
Self-harm (attempted)
  history (personal) Z91.5
    in family Z81.8
Self-mutilation (attempted)
  history (personal) Z91.5
    in family Z81.8
Self-poisoning
  history (personal) Z91.5
    in family Z81.8
  observation following (alleged) attempt Z03.6
Semicoma R40.1
Seminal vesiculitis N49.0
Seminoma C62.9-●
  specified site —*see* Neoplasm, malignant, by
      site
Senear-Usher disease or syndrome L10.4
Senectus R54
Senescence (without mention of psychosis) R54
Senile, senility —*see also* condition R41.81
  with
    acute confusional state F05
    mental changes NOS F03
    psychosis NEC —*see* Psychosis, senile
  asthenia R54
  cervix (atrophic) N88.8
  debility R54
  endometrium (atrophic) N85.8
  fallopian tube (atrophic) —*see* Atrophy,
      fallopian tube
  heart (failure) R54

Senile, senility (Continued)
  ovary (atrophic) —see Atrophy, ovary
  premature E34.8
  vagina, vaginitis (atrophic) N95.2
  wart L82.1
Sensation
  burning (skin) R20.8
    tongue K14.6
  loss of R20.8
  prickling (skin) R20.2
  tingling (skin) R20.2
Sense loss
  smell —see Disturbance, sensation, smell
  taste —see Disturbance, sensation, taste
  touch R20.8
Sensibility disturbance (cortical) (deep)
      (vibratory) R20.9
Sensitive, sensitivity —see also Allergy
  carotid sinus G90.01
  child (excessive) F93.8
  cold, autoimmune D59.1
  dentin K03.89
  gluten (non-celiac) K90.41
  latex Z91.040
  methemoglobin D74.8
  tuberculin, without clinical or radiological
      symptoms R76.11
  visual
    glare H53.71
    impaired contrast H53.72
Sensitiver Beziehungswahn F22
Sensitization, auto-erythrocytic D69.2
Separation
  anxiety, abnormal (of childhood) F93.0
  apophysis, traumatic - code as Fracture, by site
  choroid —see Detachment, choroid
  epiphysis, epiphyseal
    nontraumatic —see also Osteochondropathy,
        specified type NEC
      upper femoral —see Slipped, epiphysis,
          upper femoral
    traumatic - code as Fracture, by site
  fracture —see Fracture
  infundibulum cardiac from right ventricle by
      a partition Q24.3
  joint (traumatic) (current) - code by site under
      Dislocation
  pubic bone, obstetrical trauma O71.6
  retina, retinal —see Detachment, retina
  symphysis pubis, obstetrical trauma O71.6
  tracheal ring, incomplete, congenital Q32.1
Sepsis (generalized) (unspecified organism)
      A41.9
  with
    organ dysfunction (acute) (multiple) R65.20
      with septic shock R65.21
  actinomycotic A42.7
  adrenal hemorrhage syndrome
      (meningococcal) A39.1
  anaerobic A41.4
  Bacillus anthracis A22.7
  Brucella —see also Brucellosis A23.9
  candidal B37.7
  cryptogenic A41.9
  due to device, implant or graft T85.79
    arterial graft NEC T82.7
    breast (implant) T85.79
    catheter NEC T85.79
      dialysis (renal) T82.7
        intraperitoneal T85.71
      infusion NEC T82.7
        spinal (cranial) (epidural) (intrathecal)
            (spinal) (subarachnoid)
            (subdural) T85.735
      urethral indwelling T83.511
      urinary T83.518
    ectopic or molar pregnancy O08.82
    electronic (electrode) (pulse generator)
        (stimulator)
      bone T84.7
      cardiac T82.7

Sepsis (Continued)
  due to device, implant or graft (Continued)
    electronic (Continued)
      nervous system T85.738
        brain T85.731
        neurostimulator generator T85.734
        peripheral nerve T85.732
        spinal cord T85.733
      urinary T83.590
    fixation, internal (orthopedic) —see
        Complication, fixation device,
        infection
    gastrointestinal (bile duct) (esophagus)
        T85.79
    neurostimulator electrode (lead) T85.732
    genital T83.69
    heart NEC T82.7
      valve (prosthesis) T82.6
        graft T82.7
    joint prosthesis —see Complication, joint
        prosthesis, infection
    ocular (corneal graft) (orbital implant)
        T85.79
    orthopedic NEC T84.7
      fixation device, internal —see
          Complication, fixation device,
          infection
    specified NEC T85.79
    vascular T82.7
    ventricular intracranial (communicating)
        shunt T85.730
  during labor O75.3
  Enterococcus A41.81
  Erysipelothrix (rhusiopathiae) (erysipeloid)
      A26.7
  Escherichia coli (E. coli) A41.5
  extraintestinal yersiniosis A28.2
  following
    abortion (subsequent episode) O08.0
      current episode —see Abortion
    ectopic or molar pregnancy O08.82
    immunization T88.0
    infusion, therapeutic injection or
        transfusion NEC T80.29
  ▶obstetrical procedure O86.04
  gangrenous A41.9
  gonococcal A54.86
  Gram-negative (organism) A41.5
    anaerobic A41.4
  Haemophilus influenzae A41.3
  herpesviral B00.7
  intra-abdominal K65.1
  intraocular —see Endophthalmitis, purulent
  Listeria monocytogenes A32.7
  localized — code to specific localized
      infection
  ▶in operation wound T81.49
    skin —see Abscess
  malleus A24.0
  melioidosis A24.1
  meningeal —see Meningitis
  meningococcal A39.4
    acute A39.2
    chronic A39.3
  MSSA (Methicillin susceptible
      Staphylococcus aureus) A41.01
  newborn P36.9
    due to
      anaerobes NEC P36.5
      Escherichia coli P36.4
      Staphylococcus P36.30
        aureus P36.2
        specified NEC P36.39
      Streptococcus P36.10
        group B P36.0
        specified NEC P36.19
    specified NEC P36.8
  Pasteurella multocida A28.0
  pelvic, puerperal, postpartum, childbirth O85
  pneumococcal A40.3
  ▶postprocedural T81.44

Sepsis (Continued)
  puerperal, postpartum, childbirth (pelvic) O85
  Salmonella (arizonae) (cholerae-suis)
      (enteritidis) (typhimurium) A02.1
  severe R65.20
    with septic shock R65.21
  Shigella (see also Dysentery, bacillary) A03.9
  skin, localized —see Abscess
  specified organism NEC A41.89
  Staphylococcus, staphylococcal A41.2
    aureus (methicillin susceptible) (MSSA)
        A41.01
      methicillin resistant (MRSA) A41.02
    coagulase-negative A41.1
    specified NEC A41.1
  Streptococcus, streptococcal A40.9
    agalactiae A40.1
    group
      A A40.0
      B A40.1
      D A41.81
    neonatal P36.10
      group B P36.0
      specified NEC P36.19
    pneumoniae A40.3
    pyogenes A40.0
    specified NEC A40.8
  tracheostomy stoma J95.02
  tularemic A21.7
  umbilical, umbilical cord (newborn) —see
      Sepsis, newborn
  Yersinia pestis A20.7
Septate —see Septum
Septic —see condition
  arm —see Cellulitis, upper limb
    with lymphangitis —see Lymphangitis,
        acute, upper limb
  embolus —see Embolism
  finger —see Cellulitis, digit
    with lymphangitis —see Lymphangitis,
        acute, digit
  foot —see Cellulitis, lower limb
    with lymphangitis —see Lymphangitis,
        acute, lower limb
  gallbladder (acute) K81.0
  hand —see Cellulitis, upper limb
    with lymphangitis —see Lymphangitis,
        acute, upper limb
  joint —see Arthritis, pyogenic or pyemic
  leg —see Cellulitis, lower limb
    with lymphangitis —see Lymphangitis,
        acute, lower limb
  nail —see also Cellulitis, digit
    with lymphangitis —see Lymphangitis,
        acute, digit
  sore —see also Abscess
    throat J02.0
      streptococcal J02.0
  spleen (acute) D73.89
  teeth, tooth (pulpal origin) K04.4
  throat —see Pharyngitis
  thrombus —see Thrombosis
  toe —see Cellulitis, digit
    with lymphangitis —see Lymphangitis,
        acute, digit
  tonsils, chronic J35.01
    with adenoiditis J35.03
  uterus —see Endometritis
Septicemia A41.9
  meaning sepsis —see Sepsis
Septum, septate (congenital) —see also
    Anomaly, by site
  anal Q42.3
    with fistula Q42.2
  aqueduct of Sylvius Q03.0
    with spina bifida —see Spina bifida, by site,
        with hydrocephalus
  ▶uterus (complete) (partial) Q51.20
    ▶complete Q51.21
    ▶partial Q51.22
    ▶specified NEC Q51.28

S

▶ New   ⇒ Revised   ~~deleted~~ Deleted   • Use Additional Character(s)

Septum, septate (Continued)
  vagina Q52.10
    in pregnancy —see Pregnancy, complicated
      by, abnormal vagina
      causing obstructed labor O65.5
    longitudinal Q52.129
      microperforate
        left side Q52.124
        right side Q52.123
      nonobstruction Q52.120
      obstructing Q52.129
        left side Q52.122
        right side Q52.121
    transverse Q52.11
Sequelae (of) —see also condition
  abscess, intracranial or intraspinal (conditions
    in G06) G09
  amputation — code to injury with seventh
    character S
  burn and corrosion — code to injury with
    seventh character S
  calcium deficiency E64.8
  cerebrovascular disease —see Sequelae,
    disease, cerebrovascular
  childbirth O94
  contusion — code to injury with seventh
    character S
  corrosion —see Sequelae, burn and corrosion
  crushing injury — code to injury with
    seventh character S
  disease
    cerebrovascular I69.90
      alteration of sensation I69.998
      aphasia I69.920
      apraxia I69.990
      ataxia I69.993
      cognitive deficits I69.91
      disturbance of vision I69.998
      dysarthria I69.922
      dysphagia I69.991
      dysphasia I69.921
      facial droop I69.992
      facial weakness I69.992
      fluency disorder I69.923
      hemiplegia I69.95-●
      hemorrhage
        intracerebral —see Sequelae,
          hemorrhage, intracerebral
        intracranial, nontraumatic NEC —
          see Sequelae, hemorrhage,
          intracranial, nontraumatic
        subarachnoid —see Sequelae,
          hemorrhage, subarachnoid
      language deficit I69.928
      monoplegia
        lower limb I69.94-●
        upper limb I69.93-●
      paralytic syndrome I69.96-●
      specified effect NEC I69.998
      specified type NEC I69.80
        alteration of sensation I69.898
        aphasia I69.820
        apraxia I69.890
        ataxia I69.893
        cognitive deficits I69.81
        disturbance of vision I69.898
        dysarthria I69.822
        dysphagia I69.891
        dysphasia I69.821
        facial droop I69.892
        facial weakness I69.892
        fluency disorder I69.823
        hemiplegia I69.85-●
        language deficit I69.828
        monoplegia
          lower limb I69.84-●
          upper limb I69.83-●
        paralytic syndrome I69.86-●
        specified effect NEC I69.898
      speech deficit I69.928
        speech deficit I69.828
      stroke NOS —see Sequelae, stroke NOS

Sequelae (Continued)
  dislocation — code to injury with seventh
    character S
  encephalitis or encephalomyelitis (conditions
    in G04) G09
    in infectious disease NEC B94.8
    viral B94.1
  external cause — code to injury with seventh
    character S
  foreign body entering natural orifice — code
    to injury with seventh character S
  fracture — code to injury with seventh
    character S
  frostbite — code to injury with seventh
    character S
  Hansen's disease B92
  hemorrhage
    intracerebral I69.10
      alteration of sensation I69.198
      aphasia I69.120
      apraxia I69.190
      ataxia I69.193
      cognitive deficits I69.11
      disturbance of vision I69.198
      dysarthria I69.122
      dysphagia I69.191
      dysphasia I69.121
      facial droop I69.192
      facial weakness I69.192
      fluency disorder I69.123
      hemiplegia I69.15-●
      language deficit NEC I69.128
      monoplegia
        lower limb I69.14-●
        upper limb I69.13-●
      paralytic syndrome I69.16-●
      specified effect NEC I69.198
      speech deficit NEC I69.128
    intracranial, nontraumatic NEC I69.20
      alteration of sensation I69.298
      aphasia I69.220
      apraxia I69.290
      ataxia I69.293
      cognitive deficits I69.21
      disturbance of vision I69.298
      dysarthria I69.222
      dysphagia I69.291
      dysphasia I69.221
      facial droop I69.292
      facial weakness I69.292
      fluency disorder I69.223
      hemiplegia I69.25-●
      language deficit NEC I69.228
      monoplegia
        lower limb I69.24-●
        upper limb I69.23-●
      paralytic syndrome I69.26-●
      specified effect NEC I69.298
      speech deficit NEC I69.228
    subarachnoid I69.00
      alteration of sensation I69.098
      aphasia I69.020
      apraxia I69.090
      ataxia I69.093
      cognitive deficits —see subcategory
        I69.01-●
      disturbance of vision I69.098
      dysarthria I69.022
      dysphagia I69.091
      dysphasia I69.021
      facial droop I69.092
      facial weakness I69.092
      fluency disorder I69.023
      hemiplegia I69.05-●
      language deficit NEC I69.028
      monoplegia
        lower limb I69.04-●
        upper limb I69.03-●
      paralytic syndrome I69.06-●
      specified effect NEC I69.098
      speech deficit NEC I69.028

Sequelae (Continued)
  hepatitis, viral B94.2
  hyperalimentation E68
  infarction
    cerebral I69.30
      alteration of sensation I69.398
      aphasia I69.320
      apraxia I69.390
      ataxia I69.393
      cognitive deficits I69.31
      disturbance of vision I69.398
      dysarthria I69.322
      dysphagia I69.391
      dysphasia I69.321
      facial droop I69.392
      facial weakness I69.392
      fluency disorder I69.323
      hemiplegia I69.35-●
      language deficit NEC I69.328
      monoplegia
        lower limb I69.34-●
        upper limb I69.33-●
      paralytic syndrome I69.36-●
      specified effect NEC I69.398
      speech deficit NEC I69.328
  infection, pyogenic, intracranial or intraspinal
    G09
  infectious disease B94.9
    specified NEC B94.8
  injury — code to injury with seventh
    character S
  leprosy B92
  meningitis
    bacterial (conditions in G00) G09
    other or unspecified cause (conditions in
      G03) G09
  muscle (and tendon) injury — code to injury
    with seventh character S
  myelitis —see Sequelae, encephalitis
  niacin deficiency E64.8
  nutritional deficiency E64.9
    specified NEC E64.8
  obstetrical condition O94
  parasitic disease B94.9
  phlebitis or thrombophlebitis of intracranial
    or intraspinal venous sinuses and veins
    (conditions in G08) G09
  poisoning — code to poisoning with seventh
    character S
    nonmedicinal substance —see Sequelae,
      toxic effect, nonmedicinal substance
  poliomyelitis (acute) B91
  pregnancy O94
  protein-energy malnutrition E64.0
  puerperium O94
  rickets E64.3
  selenium deficiency E64.8
  sprain and strain — code to injury with
    seventh character S
  stroke NOS I69.30
    alteration in sensation I69.398
    aphasia I69.320
    apraxia I69.390
    ataxia I69.393
    cognitive deficits I69.31
    disturbance of vision I69.398
    dysarthria I69.322
    dysphagia I69.391
    dysphasia I69.321
    facial droop I69.392
    facial weakness I69.392
    hemiplegia I69.35-●
    language deficit NEC I69.328
    monoplegia
      lower limb I69.34-●
      upper limb I69.33-●
    paralytic syndrome I69.36-●
    specified effect NEC I69.398
    speech deficit NEC I69.328
  tendon and muscle injury — code to injury
    with seventh character S

Sequelae *(Continued)*
thiamine deficiency E64.8
trachoma B94.0
tuberculosis B90.9
bones and joints B90.2
central nervous system B90.0
genitourinary B90.1
pulmonary (respiratory) B90.9
specified organs NEC B90.8
viral
encephalitis B94.1
hepatitis B94.2
vitamin deficiency NEC E64.8
A E64.1
B E64.8
C E64.2
wound, open — code to injury with seventh
character S
Sequestration *—see also* Sequestrum
disk *—see* Displacement, intervertebral
disk
lung, congenital Q33.2
Sequestrum
bone *—see* Osteomyelitis, chronic
dental M27.2
jaw bone M27.2
orbit *—see* Osteomyelitis, orbit
sinus (accessory) (nasal) *—see* Sinusitis
Sequoiosis lung or pneumonitis J67.8
Serology for syphilis
doubtful
with signs or symptoms - code by site and
stage under Syphilis
follow-up of latent syphilis *—see* Syphilis,
latent
negative, with signs or symptoms — code by
site and stage under Syphilis
positive A53.0
with signs or symptoms - code by site and
stage under Syphilis
reactivated A53.0
Seroma *—see also* Hematoma
postprocedural *—see* Complication,
postprocedural, seroma
traumatic, secondary and recurrent
T79.2
Seropurulent *—see* condition
Serositis, multiple K65.8
pericardial I31.1
peritoneal K65.8
Serous *—see* condition
Sertoli cell
adenoma
specified site *—see* Neoplasm, benign, by
site
unspecified site
female D27.9
male D29.20
carcinoma
specified site *—see* Neoplasm, malignant,
by site
unspecified site (male) C62.9-●
female C56.9
tumor
with lipid storage
specified site *—see* Neoplasm, benign,
by site
unspecified site
female D27.9
male D29.20
specified site *—see* Neoplasm, benign, by
site
unspecified site
female D27.9
male D29.20
Sertoli-Leydig cell tumor *—see* Neoplasm,
benign, by site
specified site *—see* Neoplasm, benign, by site
unspecified site
female D27.9
male D29.20

Serum
allergy, allergic reaction *—see also* Reaction,
serum T80.69
shock *—see also* Shock, anaphylactic T80.59
arthritis *—see also* Reaction, serum T80.69
complication or reaction NEC *—see also*
Reaction, serum T80.69
disease NEC *—see also* Reaction, serum T80.69
hepatitis *—see also* Hepatitis, viral, type B
carrier (suspected) of B18.1
intoxication *—see also* Reaction, serum T80.69
neuritis *—see also* Reaction, serum T80.69
neuropathy G61.1
poisoning NEC *—see also* Reaction, serum
T80.69
rash NEC *—see also* Reaction, serum T80.69
reaction NEC *—see also* Reaction, serum
T80.69
sickness NEC *—see also* Reaction, serum
T80.69
urticaria *—see also* Reaction, serum T80.69
Sesamoiditis M25.8-●
Sever's disease or osteochondrosis *—see*
Osteochondrosis, juvenile, tarsus
Severe sepsis R65.20
with septic shock R65.21
Sex
chromosome mosaics Q97.8
lines with various numbers of
X chromosomes Q97.2
education Z70.8
reassignment surgery status Z87.890
Sextuplet pregnancy *—see* Pregnancy,
sextuplet
Sexual
function, disorder of (psychogenic) F52.9
immaturity (female) (male) E30.0
impotence (psychogenic) organic origin
NEC *—see* Dysfunction, sexual, male
precocity (constitutional) (cryptogenic)
(female) (idiopathic) (male) E30.1
Sexuality, pathologic *—see* Deviation, sexual
Sézary disease C84.1-●
Shadow, lung R91.8
Shaking palsy or paralysis *—see* Parkinsonism
Shallowness, acetabulum *—see* Derangement,
joint, specified type NEC, hip
Shaver's disease J63.1
Sheath (tendon) *—see* condition
Sheathing, retinal vessels H35.01-●
Shedding
nail L60.8
premature, primary (deciduous) teeth
K00.6
Sheehan's disease or syndrome E23.0
Shelf, rectal K62.89
Shell teeth K00.5
Shellshock (current) F43.0
lasting state *—see* Disorder, post-traumatic
stress
Shield kidney Q63.1
Shift
auditory threshold (temporary) H93.24-●
mediastinal R93.89
Shifting sleep-work schedule (affecting sleep)
G47.26
Shiga (-Kruse) dysentery A03.0
Shiga's bacillus A03.0
Shigella (dysentery) *—see* Dysentery,
bacillary
Shigellosis A03.9
Group A A03.0
Group B A03.1
Group C A03.2
Group D A03.3
Shin splints S86.89
Shingles *—see* Herpes, zoster
Shipyard disease or eye B30.0
Shirodkar suture, in pregnancy *—see*
Pregnancy, complicated by, incompetent
cervix

Shock R57.9
with ectopic or molar pregnancy O08.3
adrenal (cortical) (Addisonian) E27.2
adverse food reaction (anaphylactic) *—see*
Shock, anaphylactic, due to food
allergic *—see* Shock, anaphylactic
anaphylactic T78.2
chemical *—see* Table of Drugs and
Chemicals
due to drug or medicinal substance
correct substance properly administered
T88.6
overdose or wrong substance given or
taken (by accident) *—see* Table of
Drugs and Chemicals, by drug,
poisoning
due to food (nonpoisonous) T78.00
additives T78.06
dairy products T78.07
eggs T78.08
fish T78.03
shellfish T78.02
fruit T78.04
milk T78.07
nuts T78.05
multiple types T78.05
peanuts T78.01
peanuts T78.01
seeds T78.05
specified type NEC T78.09
vegetable T78.04
following sting(s) *—see* Venom
immunization T80.52
serum T80.59
blood and blood products T80.51
immunization T80.52
specified NEC T80.59
vaccination T80.52
anaphylactoid *—see* Shock, anaphylactic
anesthetic
correct substance properly administered
T88.2
overdose or wrong substance given
or taken *—see* Table of Drugs and
Chemicals, by drug, poisoning
specified anesthetic *—see* Table of
Drugs and Chemicals, by drug,
poisoning
cardiogenic R57.0
chemical substance *—see* Table of Drugs and
Chemicals
complicating ectopic or molar pregnancy O08.3
culture *—see* Disorder, adjustment
drug
due to correct substance properly
administered T88.6
overdose or wrong substance given or
taken (by accident) *—see* Table of
Drugs and Chemicals, by drug,
poisoning
during or after labor and delivery O75.1
electric T75.4
(taser) T75.4
endotoxic R65.21
postprocedural (resulting from a procedure,
not elsewhere classified) T81.12
following
ectopic or molar pregnancy O08.3
injury (immediate) (delayed) T79.4
labor and delivery O75.1
food (anaphylactic) *—see* Shock, anaphylactic,
due to food
from electroshock gun (taser) T75.4
gram-negative R65.21
postprocedural (resulting from a procedure,
not elsewhere classified) T81.12
hematologic R57.8
hemorrhagic R57.8
surgery (intraoperative) (postoperative)
T81.19
trauma T79.4

Shock *(Continued)*
hypovolemic R57.1
  surgical T81.19
  traumatic T79.4
insulin E15
  therapeutic misadventure —*see*
    subcategory T38.3
kidney N17.0
  traumatic (following crushing) T79.5
lightning T75.01
liver K72.00
lung J80
obstetric O75.1
  with ectopic or molar pregnancy O08.3
  following ectopic or molar pregnancy O08.3
pleural (surgical) T81.19
  due to trauma T79.4
postprocedural (postoperative) T81.10
  with ectopic or molar pregnancy O08.3
  cardiogenic T81.11
  endotoxic T81.12
  following ectopic or molar pregnancy O08.3
  gram-negative T81.12
  hypovolemic T81.19
  septic T81.12
  specified type NEC T81.19
psychic F43.0
septic (due to severe sepsis) R65.21
specified NEC R57.8
surgical T81.10
taser gun (taser) T75.4
therapeutic misadventure NEC T81.10
thyroxin
  overdose or wrong substance given
    or taken —*see* Table of Drugs and
    Chemicals, by drug, poisoning
toxic, syndrome A48.3
transfusion —*see* Complications, transfusion
traumatic (immediate) (delayed) T79.4
Shoemaker's chest M95.4
Short, shortening, shortness
arm (acquired) —*see also* Deformity, limb,
  unequal length
  congenital Q71.81-●
  forearm —*see* Deformity, limb, unequal
    length
bowel syndrome K91.2
breath R06.02
cervical (complicating pregnancy) O26.87-●
  non-gravid uterus N88.3
common bile duct, congenital Q44.5
cord (umbilical), complicating delivery O69.3
cystic duct, congenital Q44.5
esophagus (congenital) Q39.8
femur (acquired) —*see* Deformity, limb,
  unequal length, femur
  congenital —*see* Defect, reduction, lower
    limb, longitudinal, femur
frenum, frenulum, linguae (congenital) Q38.1
hip (acquired) —*see also* Deformity, limb,
  unequal length
  congenital Q65.89
leg (acquired) —*see also* Deformity, limb,
  unequal length
  congenital Q72.81-●
  lower leg —*see also* Deformity, limb,
    unequal length
limbed stature, with immunodeficiency D82.2
lower limb (acquired) —*see also* Deformity,
  limb, unequal length
  congenital Q72.81-●
organ or site, congenital NEC —*see* Distortion
palate, congenital Q38.5
radius (acquired) —*see also* Deformity, limb,
  unequal length
  congenital —*see* Defect, reduction, upper
    limb, longitudinal, radius
rib syndrome Q77.2
stature (child) (hereditary) (idiopathic) NEC
  R62.52
  constitutional E34.3
  due to endocrine disorder E34.3
  Laron-type E34.3

Short, shortening, shortness *(Continued)*
tendon —*see also* Contraction, tendon
  with contracture of joint —*see* Contraction,
    joint
  Achilles (acquired) M67.0-●
    congenital Q66.89
  congenital Q79.8
thigh (acquired) —*see also* Deformity, limb,
  unequal length, femur
  congenital —*see* Defect, reduction, lower
    limb, longitudinal, femur
tibialis anterior (tendon) —*see* Contraction,
  tendon
umbilical cord
  complicating delivery O69.3
upper limb, congenital —*see* Defect,
  reduction, upper limb, specified type
  NEC
urethra N36.8
uvula, congenital Q38.5
vagina (congenital) Q52.4
Shortsightedness —*see* Myopia
Shoshin (acute fulminating beriberi) E51.11
Shoulder —*see* condition
Shovel-shaped incisors K00.2
Shower, thromboembolic —*see* Embolism
Shunt
arterial-venous (dialysis) Z99.2
arteriovenous, pulmonary (acquired) I28.0
  congenital Q25.72
cerebral ventricle (communicating) in situ
  Z98.2
surgical, prosthetic, with complications —*see*
  Complications, cardiovascular, device or
  implant Shutdown, renal N28.9
Shutdown, renal N28.9
Shy-Drager syndrome G90.3
Sialadenitis, sialadenosis (any gland) (chronic)
  (periodic) (suppurative) —*see* Sialoadenitis
Sialectasia K11.8
Sialidosis E77.1
Sialitis, silitis (any gland) (chronic)
  (suppurative) —*see* Sialoadenitis
Sialoadenitis (any gland) (periodic)
  (suppurative) K11.20
  acute K11.21
    recurrent K11.22
  chronic K11.23
Sialoadenopathy K11.9
Sialoangitis —*see* Sialoadenitis
Sialodochitis (fibrinosa) —*see* Sialoadenitis
Sialodocholithiasis K11.5
Sialolithiasis K11.5
Sialometaplasia, necrotizing K11.8
Sialorrhea —*see also* Ptyalism
  periodic —*see* Sialoadenitis
Sialosis K11.7
Siamese twin Q89.4
Sibling rivalry Z62.891
Sicard's syndrome G52.7
Sicca syndrome M35.00
  with
    keratoconjunctivitis M35.01
    lung involvement M35.02
    myopathy M35.03
    renal tubulo-interstitial disorders M35.04
    specified organ involvement NEC M35.09
Sick R69
  or handicapped person in family Z63.79
    needing care at home Z63.6
  sinus (syndrome) I49.5
Sick-euthyroid syndrome E07.81
Sickle-cell
anemia —*see* Disease, sickle-cell
trait D57.3
Sicklemia —*see also* Disease, sickle-cell
trait D57.3
Sickness
air (travel) T75.3
airplane T75.3
alpine T70.29

Sickness *(Continued)*
altitude T70.20
Andes T70.29
aviator's T70.29
balloon T70.29
car T75.3
compressed air T70.3
decompression T70.3
green D50.8
milk —*see* Poisoning, food, noxious
motion T75.3
mountain T70.29
  acute D75.1
protein —*see also* Reaction, serum T80.69
radiation T66
roundabout (motion) T75.3
sea T75.3
serum NEC —*see also* Reaction, serum T80.69
sleeping (African) B56.9
  by Trypanosoma B56.9
    brucei
      gambiense B56.0
      rhodesiense B56.1
  East African B56.1
  Gambian B56.0
  Rhodesian B56.1
  West African B56.0
swing (motion) T75.3
train (railway) (travel) T75.3
travel (any vehicle) T75.3
Sideropenia —*see* Anemia, iron deficiency
Siderosilicosis J62.8
Siderosis (lung) J63.4
eye (globe) —*see* Disorder, globe,
  degenerative, siderosis
Siemens' syndrome (ectodermal dysplasia) Q82.8
Sighing R06.89
psychogenic F45.8
Sigmoid —*see also* condition
flexure —*see* condition
kidney Q63.1
Sigmoiditis —*see also* Enteritis K52.9
infectious A09
noninfectious K52.9
Silfversköld's syndrome Q78.9
Silicosiderosis J62.8
Silicosis, silicotic (simple) (complicated) J62.8
with tuberculosis J65
Silicotuberculosis J65
Silo-fillers' disease J68.8
bronchitis J68.0
pneumonitis J68.0
pulmonary edema J68.1
Silver's syndrome Q87.1
Simian malaria B53.1
Simmonds' cachexia or disease E23.0
Simons' disease or syndrome (progressive
  lipodystrophy) E88.1
Simple, simplex —*see* condition
Simulation, conscious (of illness) Z76.5
Simultanagnosia (asimultagnosia) R48.3
Sin Nombre virus disease (Hantavirus)
  (cardio)-pulmonary syndrome) B33.4
Sinding-Larsen disease or osteochondrosis —
  see Osteochondrosis, juvenile, patella
Singapore hemorrhagic fever A91
Singer's node or nodule J38.2
Single
atrium Q21.2
coronary artery Q24.5
umbilical artery Q27.0
ventricle Q20.4
Singultus R06.6
epidemicus B33.0
Sinus —*see also* Fistula
abdominal K63.89
arrest I45.5
arrhythmia I49.8
bradycardia R00.1
branchial cleft (internal) (external) Q18.0
coccygeal —*see* Sinus, pilonidal

Sinus *(Continued)*
  dental K04.6
  dermal (congenital) Q06.8
    with abscess Q06.8
      coccygeal, pilonidal —*see* Sinus,
        coccygeal
  infected, skin NEC L08.89
  marginal, ruptured or bleeding —*see*
    Hemorrhage, antepartum, specified
    cause NEC
  medial, face and neck Q18.8
  pause I45.5
  pericranii Q01.9
  pilonidal (infected) (rectum) L05.92
    with abscess L05.02
  preauricular Q18.1
  rectovaginal N82.3
  Rokitansky-Aschoff (gallbladder) K82.8
  sacrococcygeal (dermoid) (infected) —*see*
    Sinus, pilonidal
  tachycardia R00.0
    paroxysmal I47.1
  tarsi syndrome M25.57-●
  testis N50.89
  tract (postinfective) —*see* Fistula
  urachus Q64.4
Sinusitis (accessory) (chronic) (hyperplastic)
  (nasal) (nonpurulent) (purulent) J32.9
  acute J01.90
    ethmoidal J01.20
      recurrent J01.21
    frontal J01.10
      recurrent J01.11
    involving more than one sinus, other than
      pansinusitis J01.80
      recurrent J01.81
    maxillary J01.00
      recurrent J01.01
    pansinusitis J01.40
      recurrent J01.41
    recurrent J01.91
    specified NEC J01.80
      recurrent J01.81
    sphenoidal J01.30
      recurrent J01.31
  allergic —*see* Rhinitis, allergic
  due to high altitude T70.1
  ethmoidal J32.2
    acute J01.20
      recurrent J01.21
  frontal J32.1
    acute J01.10
      recurrent J01.11
  influenzal —*see* Influenza, with, respiratory
    manifestations NEC
  involving more than one sinus but not
    pansinusitis J32.8
    acute J01.80
      recurrent J01.81
  maxillary J32.0
    acute J01.00
      recurrent J01.01
  sphenoidal J32.3
    acute J01.30
      recurrent J01.31
  tuberculous, any sinus A15.8
Sinusitis-bronchiectasis-situs inversus
  (syndrome) (triad) Q89.3
Sipple's syndrome E31.22
Sirenomelia (syndrome) Q87.2
Siriasis T67.0
Sirkari's disease B55.0
Siti A65
Situation, psychiatric F99
Situational
  disturbance (transient) —*see* Disorder,
    adjustment
    acute F43.0
  maladjustment —*see* Disorder, adjustment
  reaction —*see* Disorder, adjustment
    acute F43.0

Situs inversus or transversus (abdominalis)
  (thoracis) Q89.3
Sixth disease B08.20
  due to human herpesvirus 6 B08.21
  due to human herpesvirus 7 B08.22
Sjögren-Larsson syndrome Q87.1
Sjögren's syndrome or disease —*see* Sicca
  syndrome
Skeletal —*see* condition
Skene's gland —*see* condition
Skenitis —*see* Urethritis
Skerljevo A65
Skevas-Zerfus disease —*see* Toxicity, venom,
  marine animal, sea anemone
Skin —*see also* condition
  clammy R23.1
  donor —*see* Donor, skin
  hidebound M35.9
Slate-dressers' or slate-miners' lung J62.8
Sleep
  apnea —*see* Apnea, sleep
  deprivation Z72.820
  disorder or disturbance G47.9
    child F51.9
    nonorganic origin F51.9
    specified NEC G47.8
  disturbance G47.9
    nonorganic origin F51.9
  drunkenness F51.9
  rhythm inversion G47.2-●
  terrors F51.4
  walking F51.3
    hysterical F44.89
Sleep hygiene
  abuse Z72.821
  inadequate Z72.821
  poor Z72.821
Sleeping sickness —*see* Sickness, sleeping
Sleeplessness —*see* Insomnia
  menopausal N95.11
Sleep-wake schedule disorder G47.20
Slim disease (in HIV infection) B20
Slipped, slipping
  epiphysis (traumatic) —*see also*
    Osteochondropathy, specified type
    NEC
    capital femoral (traumatic)
      acute (on chronic) S79.01-●
    current traumatic - code as Fracture, by site
    upper femoral (nontraumatic) M93.00-●
      acute M93.01-●
        on chronic M93.03-●
      chronic M93.02-●
  intervertebral disc —*see* Displacement,
    intervertebral disc
  ligature, umbilical P51.8
  patella —*see* Disorder, patella, derangement
    NEC
  rib M89.8X8
  sacroiliac joint —*see* subcategory M53.2
  tendon —*see* Disorder, tendon
  ulnar nerve, nontraumatic —*see* Lesion,
    nerve, ulnar
  vertebra NEC —*see* Spondylolisthesis
Slocumb's syndrome E27.0
Sloughing (multiple) (phagedena) (skin) —*see*
  also Gangrene
  abscess —*see* Abscess
  appendix K38.8
  fascia —*see* Disorder, soft tissue, specified
    type NEC
  scrotum N50.89
  tendon —*see* Disorder, tendon
  transplanted organ —*see* Rejection, transplant
  ulcer —*see* Ulcer, skin
Slow
  feeding, newborn P92.2
  flow syndrome, coronary I20.8
  heart(beat) R00.1
Slowing, urinary stream R39.198
Sluder's neuralgia (syndrome) G44.89

Slurred, slurring speech R47.81
Small (ness)
  for gestational age —*see* Small for dates
  introitus, vagina N89.6
  kidney (unknown cause) N27.9
    bilateral N27.1
    unilateral N27.0
  ovary (congenital) Q50.39
  pelvis
    with disproportion (fetopelvic) O33.1
      causing obstructed labor O65.1
  uterus N85.8
  white kidney N03.9
Small-and-light-for-dates —*see* Small for
  dates
Small-for-dates (infant) P05.10
  with weight of
    499 grams or less P05.11
    500-749 grams P05.12
    750-999 grams P05.13
    1000-1249 grams P05.14
    1250-1499 grams P05.15
    1500-1749 grams P05.16
    1750-1999 grams P05.17
    2000-2499 grams P05.18
    2500 grams and over P05.19
  specified NEC P05.19
Smallpox B03
Smearing, fecal R15.1
Smith-Lemli-Opitz syndrome E78.72
Smith's fracture S52.54-●
Smoker —*see* Dependence, drug, nicotine
Smoker's
  bronchitis J41.0
  cough J41.0
  palate K13.24
  throat J31.2
  tongue K13.24
Smoking
  passive Z77.22
Smothering spells R06.81
Snaggle teeth, tooth M26.39
Snapping
  finger —*see* Trigger finger
  hip —*see* Derangement, joint, specified type
    NEC, hip
    involving the iliotibial band M76.3-●
  knee —*see* Derangement, knee
    involving the iliotibial band M76.3-●
Sneddon-Wilkinson disease or syndrome (subcorneal pustular dermatosis) L13.1
Sneezing (intractable) R06.7
Sniffing
  cocaine
    abuse —*see* Abuse, drug, cocaine
    dependence —*see* Dependence, drug,
      cocaine
  gasoline
    abuse —*see* Abuse, drug, inhalant
    dependence —*see* Dependence, drug,
      inhalant
  glue (airplane)
    abuse —*see* Abuse, drug, inhalant
    drug dependence —*see* Dependence, drug,
      inhalant
Sniffles
  newborn P28.89
Snoring R06.83
Snow blindness —*see* Photokeratitis
Snuffles (non-syphilitic) R06.5
  newborn P28.89
  syphilitic (infant) A50.05 [J99]
Social
  exclusion Z60.4
    due to discrimination or persecution
      (perceived) Z60.5
  migrant Z59.0
    acculturation difficulty Z60.3
  rejection Z60.4
    due to discrimination or persecution
      Z60.5

Social *(Continued)*
  role conflict NEC Z73.5
  skills inadequacy NEC Z73.4
  transplantation Z60.3
Sodoku A25.Ø
Soemmerring's ring —*see* Cataract, secondary
Soft —*see also* condition
  nails L60.3
Softening
  bone —*see* Osteomalacia
  brain (necrotic) (progressive) G93.89
    congenital Q04.8
    embolic I63.4-•
    hemorrhagic —*see* Hemorrhage,
        intracranial, intracerebral
    occlusive I63.5-•
    thrombotic I63.3-•
  cartilage M94.2-•
    patella M22.4-•
  cerebellar —*see* Softening, brain
  cerebral —*see* Softening, brain
  cerebrospinal —*see* Softening, brain
  myocardial, heart —*see* Degeneration,
      myocardial
  spinal cord G95.89
  stomach K31.89
Soldier's
  heart F45.8
  patches I31.Ø
Solitary
  cyst, kidney N28.1
  kidney, congenital Q60.Ø
Solvent abuse —*see* Abuse, drug, inhalant
  dependence —*see* Dependence, drug,
      inhalant
Somatization reaction, somatic reaction —*see*
    Disorder, somatoform
Somnambulism F51.3
  hysterical F44.89
Somnolence R40.Ø
  nonorganic origin F51.11
Sonne dysentery A03.3
Soor B37.Ø
Sore
  bed —*see* Ulcer, pressure, by site
  chiclero B55.1
  Delhi B55.1
  desert —*see* Ulcer, skin
  eye H57.1-•
  Lahore B55.1
  mouth K13.79
    canker K12.Ø
  muscle M79.1Ø
  Naga —*see* Ulcer, skin
  of skin —*see* Ulcer, skin - oriental B55.1
  pressure —*see* Ulcer, pressure, by site
  skin L98.9
  soft A57
  throat (acute) —*see also* Pharyngitis
    with influenza, flu, or grippe —*see*
        Influenza, with, respiratory
        manifestations NEC
    chronic J31.2
    coxsackie (virus) B08.5
    diphtheritic A36.Ø
    herpesviral B00.2
    influenzal —*see* Influenza, with, respiratory
        manifestations NEC
    septic J02.Ø
    streptococcal (ulcerative) J02.Ø
    viral NEC J02.8
      coxsackie B08.5
    tropical —*see* Ulcer, skin
    veldt —*see* Ulcer, skin
Soto's syndrome (cerebral gigantism) Q87.3
South African cardiomyopathy syndrome I42.8
Southeast Asian hemorrhagic fever A91
Spacing
  abnormal, tooth, teeth, fully erupted M26.3Ø
  excessive, tooth, fully erupted M26.32
Spade-like hand (congenital) Q68.1

Spading nail L60.8
  congenital Q84.6
Spanish collar N47.1
Sparganosis B70.1
Spasm(s), spastic, spasticity —*see also* condition
    R25.2
  accommodation —*see* Spasm, of
      accommodation
  ampulla of Vater K83.4
  anus, ani (sphincter) (reflex) K59.4
    psychogenic F45.8
  artery I73.9
    cerebral G45.9
  Bell's G51.3-•
  bladder (sphincter, external or internal) N32.89
    psychogenic F45.8
  bronchus, bronchiole J98.01
  cardia K22.Ø
  cardiac I20.1
  carpopedal —*see* Tetany
  cerebral (arteries) (vascular) G45.9
  cervix, complicating delivery O62.4
  ciliary body (of accommodation) —*see* Spasm,
      of accommodation
  colon —*see also* Irritable, bowel K58.9
    with diarrhea K58.Ø
    psychogenic F45.8
  common duct K83.8
  compulsive —*see* Tic
  conjugate H51.8
  coronary (artery) I20.1
  diaphragm (reflex) R06.6
    epidemic B33.Ø
    psychogenic F45.8
  duodenum K59.8
  epidemic diaphragmatic (transient) B33.Ø
  esophagus (diffuse) K22.4
    psychogenic F45.8
  facial G51.3-•
  fallopian tube N83.8
  gastrointestinal (tract) K31.89
    psychogenic F45.8
  glottis J38.5
    hysterical F44.4
    psychogenic F45.8
      conversion reaction F44.4
    reflex through recurrent laryngeal nerve
        J38.5
  habit —*see* Tic
  heart I20.1
  hemifacial (clonic) G51.3-•
  hourglass —*see* Contraction, hourglass
  hysterical F44.4
  infantile —*see* Epilepsy, spasms
  inferior oblique, eye H51.8
  intestinal —*see also* Syndrome, irritable bowel
      K58.9
    psychogenic F45.8
  larynx, laryngeal J38.5
    hysterical F44.4
    psychogenic F45.8
      conversion reaction F44.4
  levator palpebrae superioris —*see* Disorder,
      eyelid function
  muscle NEC M62.838
    back M62.830
  nerve, trigeminal G51.Ø
  nervous F45.8
  nodding F98.4
  occupational F48.8
  oculogyric H51.8
    psychogenic F45.8
  of accommodation H52.53-•
  ophthalmic artery —*see* Occlusion, artery,
      retina
  perineal, female N94.89
  peroneo-extensor —*see also* Deformity, limb,
      flat foot
  pharynx (reflex) J39.2
    hysterical F45.8
    psychogenic F45.8

Spasm(s), spastic, spasticity *(Continued)*
  psychogenic F45.8
  pylorus NEC K31.3
    adult hypertrophic K31.89
    congenital or infantile Q40.Ø
    psychogenic F45.8
  rectum (sphincter) K59.4
    psychogenic F45.8
  retinal (artery) —*see* Occlusion, artery, retina
  sigmoid —*see also* Syndrome, irritable bowel
      K58.9
    psychogenic F45.8
  sphincter of Oddi K83.4
  stomach K31.89
    neurotic F45.8
  throat J39.2
    hysterical F45.8
    psychogenic F45.8
  tic F95.9
    chronic F95.1
    transient of childhood F95.Ø
  tongue K14.8
  torsion (progressive) G24.1
  trigeminal nerve —*see* Neuralgia, trigeminal
  ureter N13.5
  urethra (sphincter) N35.919
  uterus N85.8
    complicating labor O62.4
  vagina N94.2
    psychogenic F52.5
  vascular I73.9
  vasomotor I73.9
  vein NEC I87.8
  viscera —*see* Pain, abdominal
Spasmodic —*see* condition
Spasmophilia —*see* Tetany
Spasmus nutans F98.4
Spastic, spasticity —*see also* Spasm
  child (cerebral) (congenital) (paralysis) G80.1
Speaker's throat R49.8
Specific, specified —*see* condition
Speech
  defect, disorder, disturbance, impediment
      R47.9
    psychogenic, in childhood and adolescence
        F98.8
    slurring R47.81
    specified NEC R47.89
Spencer's disease A08.19
Spens' syndrome (syncope with heart block)
    I45.9
Sperm counts (fertility testing) Z31.41
  postvasectomy Z30.8
    reversal Z31.42
Spermatic cord —*see* condition
Spermatocele N43.40
  congenital Q55.4
  multiple N43.42
  single N43.41
Spermatocystitis N49.Ø
Spermatocytoma C62.9-•
  specified site —*see* Neoplasm, malignant, by
      site
Spermatorrhea N50.89
Sphacelus —*see* Gangrene
Sphenoidal —*see* condition
Sphenoiditis (chronic) —*see* Sinusitis,
    sphenoidal
Sphenopalatine ganglion neuralgia G90.09
Sphericity, increased, lens (congenital)
    Q12.4
Spherocytosis (congenital) (familial)
    (hereditary) D58.Ø
  hemoglobin disease D58.Ø
  sickle-cell (disease) D57.8-•
Spherophakia Q12.4
Sphincter —*see* condition
Sphincteritis, sphincter of Oddi —*see*
    Cholangitis
Sphingolipidosis E75.3
  specified NEC E75.29

Sphingomyelinosis E75.3
Spicule tooth K00.2
Spider
  bite —*see* Toxicity, venom, spider
  fingers —*see* Syndrome, Marfan's
  nevus I78.1
  toes —*see* Syndrome, Marfan's
  vascular I78.1
Spiegler-Fendt
  benign lymphocytoma L98.8
  sarcoid L08.89
Spielmeyer-Vogt disease E75.4
Spina bifida (aperta) Q05.9
  with hydrocephalus NEC Q05.4
  cervical Q05.5
    with hydrocephalus Q05.0
  dorsal Q05.6
    with hydrocephalus Q05.1
  lumbar Q05.7
    with hydrocephalus Q05.2
  lumbosacral Q05.7
    with hydrocephalus Q05.2
  occulta Q76.0
  sacral Q05.8
    with hydrocephalus Q05.3
  thoracic Q05.6
    with hydrocephalus Q05.1
  thoracolumbar Q05.6
    with hydrocephalus Q05.1
Spindle, Krukenberg's —*see* Pigmentation,
    cornea, posterior
Spine, spinal —*see* condition
Spiradenoma (eccrine) —*see* Neoplasm, skin,
    benign
Spirillosis A25.0
Spirillum
  minus A25.0
  obermeieri infection A68.0
Spirochetal —*see* condition
Spirochetosis A69.9
  arthritic, arthritica A69.9
  bronchopulmonary A69.8
  icterohemorrhagic A27.0
  lung A69.8
Spirometrosis B70.1
Spitting blood —*see* Hemoptysis
Splanchnoptosis K63.4
Spleen, splenic —*see* condition
Splenectasis —*see* Splenomegaly
Splenitis (interstitial) (malignant) (nonspecific)
    D73.89
  malarial —*see also* Malaria B54 [D77]
  tuberculous A18.85
Splenocele D73.89
Splenomegaly, splenomegalia (Bengal)
    (cryptogenic) (idiopathic) (tropical) R16.1
  with hepatomegaly R16.2
  cirrhotic D73.2
  congenital Q89.09
  congestive, chronic D73.2
  Egyptian B65.1
  Gaucher's E75.22
  malarial —*see also* Malaria B54 [D77]
  neutropenic D73.81
  Niemann-Pick —*see* Niemann-Pick disease or
    syndrome
  siderotic D73.2
  syphilitic A52.79
    congenital (early) A50.08 [D77]
Splenopathy D73.9
Splenoptosis D73.89
Splenosis D73.89
Splinter —*see* Foreign body, superficial, by site
Split, splitting
  foot Q72.7-•
  hand Q71.6
  heart sounds R01.2
  lip, congenital —*see* Cleft, lip
  nails L60.3
  urinary stream R39.13
Spondylarthrosis —*see* Spondylosis

Spondylitis (chronic) —*see also* Spondylopathy,
    inflammatory
  ankylopoietica —*see* Spondylitis, ankylosing
  ankylosing (chronic) M45.9
    with lung involvement M45.9 [J99]
    cervical region M45.2
    cervicothoracic region M45.3
    juvenile M08.1
    lumbar region M45.6
    lumbosacral region M45.7
    multiple sites M45.0
    occipito-atlanto-axial region M45.1
    sacrococcygeal region M45.8
    thoracic region M45.4
    thoracolumbar region M45.5
  atrophic (ligamentous) —*see* Spondylitis,
    ankylosing
  deformans (chronic) —*see* Spondylosis
  gonococcal A54.41
  gouty —*see also* Gout, by type, vertebrae
    M10.08
  in (due to)
    brucellosis A23.9 [M49.80]
      cervical region A23.9 [M49.82]
      cervicothoracic region A23.9 [M49.83]
      lumbar region A23.9 [M49.86]
      lumbosacral region A23.9 [M49.87]
      multiple sites A23.9 [M49.89]
      occipito-atlanto-axial region A23.9
        [M49.81]
      sacrococcygeal region A23.9 [M49.88]
      thoracic region A23.9 [M49.84]
      thoracolumbar region A23.9 [M49.85]
    enterobacteria —*see also* subcategory M49.8
      A04.9
    tuberculosis A18.01
  infectious NEC —*see* Spondylopathy,
    infective
  juvenile ankylosing (chronic) M08.1
  Kümmell's —*see* Spondylopathy, traumatic
  Marie-Strümpell —*see* Spondylitis,
    ankylosing
  muscularis —*see* Spondylopathy, specified
    NEC
  psoriatic L40.53
  rheumatoid —*see* Spondylitis, ankylosing
  rhizomelica —*see* Spondylitis, ankylosing
  sacroiliac NEC M46.1
  senescent, senile —*see* Spondylosis
  traumatic (chronic) or post-traumatic —*see*
    Spondylopathy, traumatic
  tuberculous A18.01
  typhosa A01.05
Spondylolisthesis (acquired) (degenerative)
    M43.10
  with disproportion (fetopelvic) O33.0
    causing obstructed labor O65.0
  cervical region M43.12
  cervicothoracic region M43.13
  congenital Q76.2
  lumbar region M43.16
  lumbosacral region M43.17
  multiple sites M43.19
  occipito-atlanto-axial region M43.11
  sacrococcygeal region M43.18
  thoracic region M43.14
  thoracolumbar region M43.15
  traumatic (old) M43.10
    acute
      fifth cervical (displaced) S12.430
        nondisplaced S12.431
        specified type NEC (displaced)
          S12.450
          nondisplaced S12.451
        type III S12.44
      fourth cervical (displaced) S12.330
        nondisplaced S12.331
        specified type NEC (displaced)
          S12.350
          nondisplaced S12.351
        type III S12.34

Spondylolisthesis (Continued)
  traumatic (Continued)
    acute (Continued)
      second cervical (displaced) S12.130
        nondisplaced S12.131
        specified type NEC (displaced)
          S12.150
          nondisplaced S12.151
        type III S12.14
      seventh cervical (displaced) S12.630
        nondisplaced S12.631
        specified type NEC (displaced)
          S12.650
          nondisplaced S12.651
        type III S12.64
      sixth cervical (displaced) S12.530
        nondisplaced S12.531
        specified type NEC (displaced)
          S12.550
          nondisplaced S12.551
        type III S12.54
      third cervical (displaced) S12.230
        nondisplaced S12.231
        specified type NEC (displaced)
          S12.250
          nondisplaced S12.251
        type III S12.24
Spondylolysis (acquired) M43.00
  cervical region M43.02
  cervicothoracic region M43.03
  congenital Q76.2
  lumbar region M43.06
  lumbosacral region M43.07
    with disproportion (fetopelvic) O33.0
      causing obstructed labor O65.8
  multiple sites M43.09
  occipito-atlanto-axial region M43.01
  sacrococcygeal region M43.08
  thoracic region M43.04
  thoracolumbar region M43.05
Spondylopathy M48.9
  infective NEC M46.50
    cervical region M46.52
    cervicothoracic region M46.53
    lumbar region M46.56
    lumbosacral region M46.57
    multiple sites M46.59
    occipito-atlanto-axial region M46.51
    sacrococcygeal region M46.58
    thoracic region M46.54
    thoracolumbar region M46.55
  inflammatory M46.90
    cervical region M46.92
    cervicothoracic region M46.93
    lumbar region M46.96
    lumbosacral region M46.97
    multiple sites M46.99
    occipito-atlanto-axial region M46.91
    sacrococcygeal region M46.98
    specified type NEC M46.80
      cervical region M46.82
      cervicothoracic region M46.83
      lumbar region M46.86
      lumbosacral region M46.87
      multiple sites M46.89
      occipito-atlanto-axial region M46.81
      sacrococcygeal region M46.88
      thoracic region M46.84
      thoracolumbar region M46.85
    thoracic region M46.94
    thoracolumbar region M46.95
  neuropathic, in
    syringomyelia and syringobulbia G95.0
    tabes dorsalis A52.11
  specified NEC —*see* subcategory M48.8
  traumatic M48.30
    cervical region M48.32
    cervicothoracic region M48.33
    lumbar region M48.36
    lumbosacral region M48.37
    occipito-atlanto-axial region M48.31

▶ New   ⇒ Revised   ~~deleted~~ Deleted   • Use Additional Character(s)

Spondylopathy (Continued)
traumatic (Continued)
sacrococcygeal region M48.38
thoracic region M48.34
thoracolumbar region M48.35
Spondylosis M47.9
with
disproportion (fetopelvic) O33.0
causing obstructed labor O65.0
myelopathy NEC M47.10
cervical region M47.12
cervicothoracic region M47.13
lumbar region M47.16
occipito-atlanto-axial region M47.11
thoracic region M47.14
thoracolumbar region M47.15
radiculopathy M47.20
cervical region M47.22
cervicothoracic region M47.23
lumbar region M47.26
lumbosacral region M47.27
occipito-atlanto-axial region M47.21
sacrococcygeal region M47.28
thoracic region M47.24
thoracolumbar region M47.25
without myelopathy or radiculopathy M47.819
cervical region M47.812
cervicothoracic region M47.813
lumbar region M47.816
lumbosacral region M47.817
occipito-atlanto-axial region M47.811
sacrococcygeal region M47.818
thoracic region M47.814
thoracolumbar region M47.815
specified NEC M47.899
cervical region M47.892
cervicothoracic region M47.893
lumbar region M47.896
lumbosacral region M47.897
occipito-atlanto-axial region M47.891
sacrococcygeal region M47.898
thoracic region M47.894
thoracolumbar region M47.895
traumatic —see Spondylopathy, traumatic
Sponge
inadvertently left in operation wound —see Foreign body, accidentally left during a procedure
kidney (medullary) Q61.5
Sponge-diver's disease —see Toxicity, venom, marine animal, sea anemone
Spongioblastoma (any type) —see Neoplasm, malignant, by site
specified site —see Neoplasm, malignant, by site
unspecified site C71.9
Spongioneuroblastoma —see Neoplasm, malignant, by site
Spontaneous —see also condition
fracture (cause unknown) —see Fracture, pathological
Spoon nail L60.3
congenital Q84.6
Sporadic —see condition
Sporothrix schenckii infection —see Sporotrichosis
Sporotrichosis B42.9
arthritis B42.82
disseminated B42.7
generalized B42.7
lymphocutaneous (fixed) (progressive) B42.1
pulmonary B42.0
specified NEC B42.89
Spots, spotting (in) (of)
Bitot's —see also Pigmentation, conjunctiva
in the young child E50.1
vitamin A deficiency E50.1

Spots, spotting (Continued)
café, au lait L81.3
Cayenne pepper I78.1
cotton wool, retina —see Occlusion, artery, retina
de Morgan's (senile angiomas) I78.1
Fuchs' black (myopic) —see also Myopia, degenerative H44.2-●
intermenstrual (regular) N92.0
irregular N92.1
Koplik's B05.9
liver L81.4
pregnancy O26.85-●
purpuric R23.3
ruby I78.1
Spotted fever —see Fever, spotted N92.3
Sprain (joint) (ligament)
acromioclavicular joint or ligament S43.5-●
ankle S93.40-●
calcaneofibular ligament S93.41-●
deltoid ligament S93.42-●
internal collateral ligament —see Sprain, ankle, specified ligament NEC
specified ligament NEC S93.49-●
talofibular ligament —see Sprain, ankle, specified ligament NEC
tibiofibular ligament S93.43-●
anterior longitudinal, cervical S13.4
atlas, atlanto-axial, atlanto-occipital S13.4
breast bone —see Sprain, sternum
calcaneofibular —see Sprain, ankle
carpal —see Sprain, wrist
carpometacarpal —see Sprain, hand, specified site NEC
cartilage
costal S23.41
semilunar (knee) —see Sprain, knee, specified site NEC
with current tear —see Tear, meniscus
thyroid region S13.5
xiphoid —see Sprain, sternum
cervical, cervicodorsal, cervicothoracic S13.4
chondrosternal S23.421
coracoclavicular S43.8-●
coracohumeral S43.41-●
coronary, knee —see Sprain, knee, specified site NEC
costal cartilage S23.41
cricoarytenoid articulation or ligament S13.5
cricothyroid articulation S13.5
cruciate, knee —see Sprain, knee, cruciate
deltoid, ankle —see Sprain, ankle
dorsal (spine) S23.3
elbow S53.40-●
radial collateral ligament S53.43-●
radiohumeral S53.41-●
rupture
radial collateral ligament —see Rupture, traumatic, ligament, radial collateral
ulnar collateral ligament —see Rupture, traumatic, ligament, ulnar collateral
specified type NEC S53.49-●
ulnar collateral ligament S53.44-●
ulnohumeral S53.42-●
femur, head —see Sprain, hip
fibular collateral, knee —see Sprain, knee, collateral
fibulocalcaneal —see Sprain, ankle
finger(s) S63.61-●
index S63.61-●
interphalangeal (joint) S63.63-●
index S63.63-●
little S63.63-●
middle S63.63-●
ring S63.63-●
little S63.61-●
metacarpophalangeal (joint) S63.65-●
middle S63.61-●
ring S63.61-●

Sprain (Continued)
finger(s) (Continued)
specified site NEC S63.69-●
index S63.69-●
little S63.69-●
middle S63.69-●
ring S63.69-●
foot S93.60-●
specified ligament NEC S93.69-●
tarsal ligament S93.61-●
tarsometatarsal ligament S93.62-●
toe —see Sprain, toe
hand S63.9-●
finger —see Sprain, finger
specified site NEC —see subcategory S63.8
thumb —see Sprain, thumb
head S03.9
hip S73.10-●
iliofemoral ligament S73.11-●
ischiocapsular (ligament) S73.12-●
specified NEC S73.19-●
iliofemoral —see Sprain, hip
innominate
acetabulum —see Sprain, hip
sacral junction S33.6
internal
collateral, ankle —see Sprain, ankle
semilunar cartilage —see Sprain, knee, specified site NEC
interphalangeal
finger —see Sprain, finger, interphalangeal (joint)
toe —see Sprain, toe, interphalangeal joint
ischiocapsular —see Sprain, hip
ischiofemoral —see Sprain, hip
jaw (articular disc) (cartilage) (meniscus) S03.4-●
old M26.69
knee S83.9-●
collateral ligament S83.40-●
lateral (fibular) S83.42-●
medial (tibial) S83.41-●
cruciate ligament S83.50-●
anterior S83.51-●
posterior S83.52-●
lateral (fibular) collateral ligament S83.42-●
medial (tibial) collateral ligament S83.41-●
patellar ligament S76.11-●
specified site NEC S83.8X-●
superior tibiofibular joint (ligament) S83.6-●
lateral collateral, knee —see Sprain, knee, collateral
lumbar (spine) S33.5
lumbosacral S33.9
mandible (articular disc) S03.4-●
old M26.69
medial collateral, knee —see Sprain, knee, collateral
meniscus
jaw S03.4-●
old M26.69
knee —see Sprain, knee, specified site NEC
with current tear —see Tear, meniscus
old —see Derangement, knee, meniscus, due to old tear
mandible S03.4-●
old M26.69
metacarpal (distal) (proximal) —see Sprain, hand, specified site NEC
metacarpophalangeal —see Sprain, finger, metacarpophalangeal (joint)
metatarsophalangeal —see Sprain, toe, metatarsophalangeal joint
midcarpal —see Sprain, hand, specified site NEC
midtarsal —see Sprain, foot, specified site NEC
neck S13.9
anterior longitudinal cervical ligament S13.4
atlanto-axial joint S13.4

Sprain *(Continued)*
  neck *(Continued)*
    atlanto-occipital joint S13.4
    cervical spine S13.4
    cricoarytenoid ligament S13.5
    cricothyroid ligament S13.5
    specified site NEC S13.8
    thyroid region (cartilage) S13.5
  nose S03.8
  orbicular, hip —*see* Sprain, hip
  patella —*see* Sprain, knee, specified site NEC
  patellar ligament S76.11-•
  pelvis NEC S33.8
  phalanx
    finger —*see* Sprain, finger
    toe —*see* Sprain, toe
  pubofemoral —*see* Sprain, hip
  radiocarpal —*see* Sprain, wrist
  radiohumeral —*see* Sprain, elbow
  radius, collateral —*see* Rupture, traumatic, ligament, radial collateral
  rib (cage) S23.41
  rotator cuff (capsule) S43.42-•
  sacroiliac (region)
    chronic or old —*see* subcategory M53.2
    joint S33.6
  scaphoid (hand) —*see* Sprain, hand, specified site NEC
  scapula (r) —*see* Sprain, shoulder girdle, specified site NEC
  semilunar cartilage (knee) —*see* Sprain, knee, specified site NEC
    with current tear —*see* Tear, meniscus
      old —*see* Derangement, knee, meniscus, due to old tear
  shoulder joint S43.40-•
    acromioclavicular joint (ligament) —*see* Sprain, acromioclavicular joint
    blade —*see* Sprain, shoulder, girdle, specified site NEC
    coracoclavicular joint (ligament) —*see* Sprain, coracoclavicular joint
    coracohumeral ligament —*see* Sprain, coracohumeral joint
    girdle S43.9-•
      specified site NEC S43.8-•
    rotator cuff —*see* Sprain, rotator cuff
    specified site NEC S43.49-•
    sternoclavicular joint (ligament) —*see* Sprain, sternoclavicular joint
  spine
    cervical S13.4
    lumbar S33.5
    thoracic S23.3
  sternoclavicular joint S43.6-•
  sternum S23.429
    chondrosternal joint S23.421
    specified site NEC S23.428
    sternoclavicular (joint) (ligament) S23.420
  symphysis
    jaw S03.4-•
      old M26.69
    mandibular S03.4-•
      old M26.69
  talofibular —*see* Sprain, ankle
  tarsal —*see* Sprain, foot, specified site NEC
  tarsometatarsal —*see* Sprain, foot, specified site NEC
  temporomandibular S03.4-•
    old M26.69
  thorax S23.9
    ribs S23.41
    specified site NEC S23.8
    spine S23.3
    sternum —*see* Sprain, sternum
  thumb S63.60-•
    interphalangeal (joint) S63.62-•
    metacarpophalangeal (joint) S63.64-•
    specified site NEC S63.68-•
  thyroid cartilage or region S13.5

Sprain *(Continued)*
  tibia (proximal end) —*see* Sprain, knee, specified site NEC
  tibial collateral, knee —*see* Sprain, knee, collateral
  tibiofibular
    distal —*see* Sprain, ankle
    superior —*see* Sprain, knee, specified site NEC
  toe(s) S93.50-•
    great S93.50-•
    interphalangeal joint S93.51-•
      great S93.51-•
      lesser S93.51-•
    lesser S93.50-•
    metatarsophalangeal joint S93.52-•
      great S93.52-•
      lesser S93.52-•
  ulna, collateral —*see* Rupture, traumatic, ligament, ulnar collateral
  ulnohumeral —*see* Sprain, elbow
  wrist S63.50-•
    carpal S63.51-•
    radiocarpal S63.52-•
    specified site NEC S63.59-•
  xiphoid cartilage —*see* Sprain, sternum
Sprengel's deformity (congenital) Q74.0
Sprue (tropical) K90.1
  celiac K90.0
  idiopathic K90.49
  meaning thrush B37.0
  nontropical K90.0
Spur, bone —*see also* Enthesopathy
  calcaneal M77.3-•
  iliac crest M76.2-•
  nose (septum) J34.89
Spurway's syndrome Q78.0
Sputum
  abnormal (amount) (color) (odor) (purulent) R09.3
  blood-stained R04.2
  excessive (cause unknown) R09.3
Squamous —*see also* condition
  epithelium in
    cervical canal (congenital) Q51.828
    uterine mucosa (congenital) Q51.818
Squashed nose M95.0
  congenital Q67.4
Squeeze, diver's T70.3
Squint —*see also* Strabismus
  accommodative —*see* Strabismus, convergent concomitant
►SSADHD (succinic semialdehyde dehydrogenase deficiency) E72.81
St. Hubert's disease A82.9
Stab —*see also* Laceration
  internal organs —*see* Injury, by site
Stafne's cyst or cavity M27.0
Staggering gait R26.0
  hysterical F44.4
Staghorn calculus —*see* Calculus, kidney
Stähli's line (cornea) (pigment) —*see* Pigmentation, cornea, anterior
Stain, staining
  meconium (newborn) P96.83
  port wine Q82.5
  tooth, teeth (hard tissues) (extrinsic) K03.6
    due to
      accretions K03.6
      deposits (betel) (black) (green) (materia alba) (orange) (soft) (tobacco) K03.6
      metals (copper) (silver) K03.7
      nicotine K03.6
      pulpal bleeding K03.7
      tobacco K03.6
    intrinsic K00.8
Stammering —*see also* Disorder, fluency F80.81
Standstill
  auricular I45.5
  cardiac —*see* Arrest, cardiac
  sinoatrial I45.5
  ventricular —*see* Arrest, cardiac

Stannosis J63.5
Stanton's disease —*see* Melioidosis
Staphylitis (acute) (catarrhal) (chronic) (gangrenous) (membranous) (suppurative) (ulcerative) K12.2
Staphylococcal scalded skin syndrome L00
Staphylococcemia A41.2
Staphylococcus, staphylococcal —*see also* condition
  as cause of disease classified elsewhere B95.8
    aureus (methicillin susceptible) (MSSA) B95.61
      methicillin resistant (MRSA) B95.62
    specified NEC, as cause of disease classified elsewhere B95.7
Staphyloma (sclera)
  cornea H18.72-•
  equatorial H15.81-•
  localized (anterior) H15.82-•
  posticum H15.83-•
  ring H15.85-•
Stargardt's disease —*see* Dystrophy, retina
Starvation (inanition) (due to lack of food) T73.0
  edema —*see* Malnutrition, severe
Stasis
  bile (noncalculous) K83.1
  bronchus J98.09
    with infection —*see* Bronchitis
  cardiac —*see* Failure, heart, congestive
  cecum K59.8
  colon K59.8
  dermatitis I87.2
    with
      varicose ulcer —*see* Varix, leg, with ulcer, with inflammation
      varicose veins —*see* Varix, leg, with, inflammation
    due to postthrombotic syndrome —*see* Syndrome, postthrombotic
  duodenal K31.5
  eczema —*see* Varix, leg, with, inflammation
  edema —*see* Hypertension, venous (chronic), idiopathic
  foot T69.0-•
  ileocecal coil K59.8
  ileum K59.8
  intestinal K59.8
  jejunum K59.8
  kidney N19
  liver (cirrhotic) K76.1
  lymphatic I89.8
  pneumonia J18.2
  pulmonary —*see* Edema, lung
  rectal K59.8
  renal N19
    tubular N17.0
  ulcer —*see* Varix, leg, with, ulcer
    without varicose veins I87.2
  urine —*see* Retention, urine
  venous I87.8
State (of)
  affective and paranoid, mixed, organic psychotic F06.8
  agitated R45.1
    acute reaction to stress F43.0
  anxiety (neurotic) F41.1
  apprehension F41.1
  burn-out Z73.0
  climacteric, female Z78.0
    symptomatic N95.1
  compulsive F42.8
    mixed with obsessional thoughts F42.2
  confusional (psychogenic) F44.89
    acute —*see also* Delirium
      with
        arteriosclerotic dementia F01.50
          with behavioral disturbance F01.51
        senility or dementia F05
        alcoholic F10.231

▶ New   ⇒ Revised   ~~deleted~~ Deleted   • Use Additional Character(s)

State *(Continued)*
  confusional (psychogenic) *(Continued)*
    epileptic F05
    reactive (from emotional stress,
      psychological trauma) F44.89
    subacute —*see* Delirium
  convulsive —*see* Convulsions
  crisis F43.0
  depressive F32.9
    neurotic F34.1
  dissociative F44.9
  emotional shock (stress) R45.7
  hypercoagulation —*see* Hypercoagulable
  locked-in G83.5
  menopausal Z78.0
    symptomatic N95.1
  neurotic F48.9
    with depersonalization F48.1
  obsessional F42.8
  oneiroid (schizophrenia-like) F23
  organic
    hallucinatory (nonalcoholic) F06.0
    paranoid (-hallucinatory) F06.2
  panic F41.0
  paranoid F22
    climacteric F22
    involutional F22
    menopausal F22
    organic F06.2
    senile F03
    simple F22
  persistent vegetative R40.3
  phobic F40.9
  postleukotomy F07.0
  pregnant
    gestational carrier Z33.3
    incidental Z33.1
  psychogenic, twilight F44.89
  psychopathic (constitutional) F60.2
  psychotic, organic —*see also* Psychosis,
    organic
    mixed paranoid and affective F06.8
    senile or presenile F03
    transient NEC F06.8
      with
        depression F06.31
        hallucinations F06.0
  residual schizophrenic F20.5
  restlessness R45.1
  stress (emotional) R45.7
  tension (mental) F48.9
    specified NEC F48.8
  transient organic psychotic NEC F06.8
    depressive type F06.31
    hallucinatory type F06.0
  twilight
    epileptic F05
    psychogenic F44.89
  vegetative, persistent R40.3
  vital exhaustion Z73.0
  withdrawal —*see* Withdrawal, state
Status (post) —*see also* Presence (of)
  absence, epileptic —*see* Epilepsy, by type,
    with status epilepticus
  administration of tPA (rtPA) in a different
    facility within the last 24 hours prior to
    admission to the current facility
    Z92.82
  adrenalectomy (unilateral) (bilateral)
    E89.6
  anastomosis Z98.0
  anginosus I20.9
  angioplasty (peripheral) Z98.62
    with implant Z95.820
    coronary artery Z98.61
      with implant Z95.5
  aortocoronary bypass Z95.1
  arthrodesis Z98.1
  artificial opening (of) Z93.9
    gastrointestinal tract Z93.4
    specified NEC Z93.8

Status *(Continued)*
  artificial opening (of) *(Continued)*
    urinary tract Z93.6
    vagina Z93.8
  asthmaticus —*see* Asthma, by type, with
    status asthmaticus
  awaiting organ transplant Z76.82
  bariatric surgery Z98.84
  bed confinement Z74.01
  bleb, filtering (vitreous), after glaucoma
    surgery Z98.83
  breast implant Z98.82
    removal Z98.86
  cataract extraction Z98.4-●
  cholecystectomy Z90.49
  clitorectomy N90.811
    with excision of labia minora N90.812
  colectomy (complete) (partial) Z90.49
  colonization —*see* Carrier (suspected) of
  colostomy Z93.3
  convulsivus idiopathicus —*see* Epilepsy, by
    type, with status epilepticus
  coronary artery angioplasty —*see* Status,
    angioplasty, coronary artery
  coronary artery bypass graft Z95.1
  cystectomy (urinary bladder) Z90.6
  cystostomy Z93.50
    appendico-vesicostomy Z93.52
    cutaneous Z93.51
    specified NEC Z93.59
  delinquent immunization Z28.3
  dental Z98.818
    crown Z98.811
    fillings Z98.811
    restoration Z98.811
    sealant Z98.810
    specified NEC Z98.818
  deployment (current) (military) Z56.82
  dialysis (hemodialysis) (peritoneal) Z99.2
  do not resuscitate (DNR) Z66
  donor —*see* Donor
  embedded fragments —*see* Retained, foreign
    body fragments (type of)
  embedded splinter —*see* Retained, foreign
    body fragments (type of)
  enterostomy Z93.4
  epileptic, epilepticus —*see also* Epilepsy, by
    type, with status epilepticus G40.901
  estrogen receptor
    negative Z17.1
    positive Z17.0
  female genital cutting —*see* Female genital
    mutilation status
  female genital mutilation —*see* Female genital
    mutilation status
  filtering (vitreous) bleb after glaucoma
    surgery Z98.83
  gastrectomy (complete) (partial) Z90.3
  gastric banding Z98.84
  gastric bypass for obesity Z98.84
  gastrostomy Z93.1
  human immunodeficiency virus (HIV)
    infection, asymptomatic Z21
  hysterectomy (complete) (total) Z90.710
    partial (with remaining cervial stump)
      Z90.711
  ileostomy Z93.2
  implant
    breast Z98.82
  infibulation N90.813
  intestinal bypass Z98.0
  jejunostomy Z93.4
  lapsed immunization schedule Z28.3
  laryngectomy Z90.02
  lymphaticus E32.8
  malignancy
    castrate resistant prostate Z19.2
    hormone resistant Z19.2
    hormone sensitive Z19.1
  marmoratus G80.3
  mastectomy (unilateral) (bilateral)
    Z90.1-●

Status *(Continued)*
  military deployment status (current) Z56.82
    in theater or in support of military war,
      peacekeeping and humanitarian
      operations Z56.82
  nephrectomy (unilateral) (bilateral) Z90.5
  nephrostomy Z93.6
  obesity surgery Z98.84
  oophorectomy
    bilateral Z90.722
    unilateral Z90.721
  organ replacement
    by artificial or mechanical device or
      prosthesis of
      artery Z95.828
      bladder Z96.0
      blood vessel Z95.828
      breast Z97.8
      eye globe Z97.0
      heart Z95.812
        valve Z95.2
      intestine Z97.8
      joint Z96.60
        hip —*see* Presence, hip joint implant
        knee —*see* Presence, knee joint
          implant
        specified site NEC Z96.698
      kidney Z97.8
      larynx Z96.3
      lens Z96.1
      limbs —*see* Presence, artificial, limb
      liver Z97.8
      lung Z97.8
      pancreas Z97.8
    by organ transplant (heterologous)
      (homologous) —*see* Transplant
  pacemaker
    brain Z96.89
    cardiac Z95.0
    specified NEC Z96.89
  pancreatectomy Z90.410
    complete Z90.410
    partial Z90.411
    total Z90.410
  pneumonectomy (complete) (partial) Z90.2
  pneumothorax, therapeutic Z98.3
  postcommotio cerebri F07.81
  postoperative (postprocedural) NEC
    Z98.890
    breast implant Z98.82
    dental Z98.818
      crown Z98.811
      fillings Z98.811
      restoration Z98.811
      sealant Z98.810
      specified NEC Z98.818
    pneumothorax, therapeutic Z98.3
    uterine scar Z98.891
  postpartum (routine follow-up) Z39.2
    care immediately after delivery Z39.0
  postsurgical (postprocedural) NEC
    Z98.890
    pneumothorax, therapeutic Z98.3
  pregnancy, incidental Z33.1
  prosthesis coronary angioplasty Z95.5
  pseudophakia Z96.1
  renal dialysis (hemodialysis) (peritoneal)
    Z99.2
  retained foreign body —*see* Retained, foreign
    body fragments (type of)
  reversed jejunal transposition (for bypass
    Z98.0
  salpingo-oophorectomy
    bilateral Z90.722
    unilateral Z90.721
  sex reassignment surgery status Z87.890
  shunt
    arteriovenous (for dialysis) Z99.2
    cerebrospinal fluid Z98.2
    ventricular (communicating) (for
      drainage) Z98.2

Status *(Continued)*
 splenectomy Z90.81
 thymicolymphaticus E32.8
 thymicus E32.8
 thymolymphaticus E32.8
 thyroidectomy (hypothyroidism) E89.0
 tooth (teeth) extraction —*see also* Absence,
  teeth, acquired K08.409
 tPA (rtPA) administration in a different
  facility within the last 24 hours prior to
  admission to current facility Z92.82
 tracheostomy Z93.0
 transplant —*see* Transplant
  organ removed Z98.85
 tubal ligation Z98.51
 underimmunization Z28.3
 ureterostomy Z93.6
 urethrostomy Z93.6
 vagina, artificial Z93.8
 vasectomy Z98.52
 wheelchair confinement Z99.3
Stealing
 child problem F91.8
  in company with others Z72.810
 pathological (compulsive) F63.2
Steam burn —*see* Burn
Steatocystoma multiplex L72.2
Steatohepatitis (nonalcoholic) (NASH)
  K75.81
Steatoma L72.3
 eyelid (cystic) —*see* Dermatosis, eyelid
 infected —*see* Hordeolum
Steatorrhea (chronic) K90.9
 with lacteal obstruction K90.2
 idiopathic (adult) (infantile) K90.9
 pancreatic K90.3
 primary K90.0
 tropical K90.1
Steatosis E88.89
 heart —*see* Degeneration, myocardial
 kidney N28.89
 liver NEC K76.0
Steele-Richardson-Olszewski disease or
  syndrome G23.1
Steinbrocker's syndrome G90.8
Steinert's disease G71.11
Stein-Leventhal syndrome E28.2
Stein's syndrome E28.2
STEMI —*see also* Infarct, myocardium, ST
  elevation I21.3
Stenocardia I20.8
Stenocephaly Q75.8
Stenosis, stenotic (cicatricial) —*see also*
  Stricture
 ampulla of Vater K83.1
 anus, anal (canal) (sphincter) K62.4
  and rectum K62.4
  congenital Q42.3
   with fistula Q42.2
 aorta (ascending) (supraventricular)
  (congenital) Q25.1
  arteriosclerotic I70.0
  calcified I70.0
  supravalvular Q25.3
 aortic (valve) I35.0
  with insufficiency I35.2
  congenital Q23.0
  rheumatic I06.0
   with
    incompetency, insufficiency or
     regurgitation I06.2
     with mitral (valve) disease I08.0
      with tricuspid (valve) disease
       I08.3
    mitral (valve) disease I08.0
     with tricuspid (valve) disease
      I08.3
    tricuspid (valve) disease I08.2
     with mitral (valve) disease I08.3
  specified cause NEC I35.0
  syphilitic A52.03

Stenosis, stenotic *(Continued)*
 aqueduct of Sylvius (congenital) Q03.0
  with spina bifida —*see* Spina bifida,
   by site, with hydrocephalus
  acquired G91.1
 artery NEC —*see also* Arteriosclerosis
  I77.1
  celiac I77.4
  cerebral —*see* Occlusion, artery, cerebral
  extremities —*see* Arteriosclerosis,
   extremities
  precerebral —*see* Occlusion, artery,
   precerebral
  pulmonary (congenital) Q25.6
   acquired I28.8
  renal I70.1
  stent
   coronary T82.855
   peripheral T82.856
 bile duct (common) (hepatic) K83.1
  congenital Q44.3
 bladder-neck (acquired) N32.0
  congenital Q64.31
 brain G93.89
 bronchus J98.09
  congenital Q32.3
  syphilitic A52.72
 cardia (stomach) K22.2
  congenital Q39.3
 cardiovascular —*see* Disease, cardiovascular
 caudal M48.08
 cervix, cervical (canal) N88.2
  congenital Q51.828
  in pregnancy or childbirth —*see* Pregnancy,
   complicated by, abnormal cervix
 colon —*see also* Obstruction, intestine
  congenital Q42.9
  specified NEC Q42.8
 colostomy K94.03
 common (bile) duct K83.1
  congenital Q44.3
 coronary (artery) —*see* Disease, heart,
   ischemic, atherosclerotic
 cystic duct —*see* Obstruction, gallbladder
 due to presence of device, implant or
   graft —*see also* Complications, by site
   and type, specified NEC T85.858
  arterial graft NEC T82.858
  breast (implant) T85.858
  catheter T85.858
   dialysis (renal) T82.858
    intraperitoneal T85.858
   infusion NEC T82.858
    spinal (epidural) (subdural)
     T85.850
   urinary (indwelling) T83.85
  fixation, internal (orthopedic) NEC
   T84.85
  gastrointestinal (bile duct) (esophagus)
   T85.858
  genital NEC T83.85
  heart NEC T82.857
  joint prosthesis T84.85
  ocular (corneal graft) (orbital implant)
   NEC T85.858
  orthopedic NEC T84.85
  specified NEC T85.858
  urinary NEC T83.85
  vascular NEC T82.858
  ventricular intracranial shunt T85.850
 duodenum K31.5
  congenital Q41.0
 ejaculatory duct NEC N50.89
 endocervical os —*see* Stenosis, cervix
 enterostomy K94.13
 esophagus K22.2
  congenital Q39.3
  syphilitic A52.79
   congenital A50.59 *[K23]*
 eustachian tube —*see* Obstruction, eustachian
  tube

Stenosis, stenotic *(Continued)*
 external ear canal (acquired) H61.30-•
  congenital Q16.1
  due to
   inflammation H61.32-•
   trauma H61.31-•
  postprocedural H95.81-•
  specified cause NEC H61.39-•
 gallbladder —*see* Obstruction, gallbladder
 glottis J38.6
 heart valve (congenital) Q24.8
  aortic Q23.0
  mitral Q23.2
  pulmonary Q22.1
  tricuspid Q22.4
 hepatic duct K83.1
 hymen N89.6
 hypertrophic subaortic (idiopathic) I42.1
 ileum —*see also* Obstruction, intestine,
   specified NEC K56.699
  congenital Q41.2
 infundibulum cardia Q24.3
 intervertebral foramina —*see also* Lesion,
   biomechanical, specified NEC
  connective tissue M99.79
   abdomen M99.79
   cervical region M99.71
   cervicothoracic M99.71
   head region M99.70
   lumbar region M99.73
   lumbosacral M99.73
   occipitocervical M99.70
   sacral region M99.74
   sacrococcygeal M99.74
   sacroiliac M99.74
   specified NEC M99.79
   thoracic region M99.72
   thoracolumbar M99.72
  disc M99.79
   abdomen M99.79
   cervical region M99.71
   cervicothoracic M99.71
   head region M99.70
   lower extremity M99.76
   lumbar region M99.73
   lumbosacral M99.73
   occipitocervical M99.70
   pelvic M99.75
   rib cage M99.78
   sacral region M99.74
   sacrococcygeal M99.74
   sacroiliac M99.74
   specified NEC M99.79
   thoracic region M99.72
   thoracolumbar M99.72
   upper extremity M99.77
  osseous M99.69
   abdomen M99.69
   cervical region M99.61
   cervicothoracic M99.61
   head region M99.60
   lower extremity M99.66
   lumbar region M99.63
   lumbosacral M99.63
   occipitocervical M99.60
   pelvic M99.65
   rib cage M99.68
   sacral region M99.64
   sacrococcygeal M99.64
   sacroiliac M99.64
   specified NEC M99.69
   thoracic region M99.62
   thoracolumbar M99.62
   upper extremity M99.67
  subluxation —*see* Stenosis, intervertebral
   foramina, osseous
 intestine —*see also* Obstruction, intestine
  congenital (small) Q41.9
   large Q42.9
    specified NEC Q42.8
   specified NEC Q41.8

▶ New   ➡ Revised   ~~deleted~~ Deleted   • Use Additional Character(s)

▶ New   ⇒ Revised   ~~deleted~~ Deleted   ● Use Additional Character(s)

Strangulation, strangulated *(Continued)*
intestine (large) (small) K56.2
  with hernia —*see also* Hernia, by site, with
    obstruction
    with gangrene —*see* Hernia, by site, with
      gangrene
mesentery K56.2
mucus —*see* Asphyxia, mucus
omentum K56.2
organ or site, congenital NEC —*see* Atresia,
  by site
ovary —*see* Torsion, ovary
penis N48.89
  foreign body T19.4
rupture —*see* Hernia, by site, with obstruction
stomach due to hernia —*see also* Hernia, by
  site, with obstruction
  with gangrene —*see* Hernia, by site, with
    gangrene
vesicourethral orifice N32.0
Strangury R30.0
Straw itch B88.0
Strawberry
gallbladder K82.4
mark Q82.5
tongue (red) (white) K14.3
Streak(s)
macula, angioid H35.33
ovarian Q50.32
Strephosymbolia F81.0
secondary to organic lesion R48.8
Streptobacillary fever A25.1
Streptobacillosis A25.1
Streptobacillus moniliformis A25.1
Streptococcus, streptococcal —*see also*
  condition
as cause of disease classified elsewhere B95.5
group
  A, as cause of disease classified elsewhere
    B95.0
  B, as cause of disease classified elsewhere
    B95.1
  D, as cause of disease classified elsewhere
    B95.2
pneumoniae, as cause of disease classified
  elsewhere B95.3
specified NEC, as cause of disease classified
  elsewhere B95.4
Streptomycosis B47.1
Streptotrichosis A48.8
Stress F43.9
family —*see* Disruption, family
fetal P84
  complicating pregnancy O77.9
    due to drug administration O77.1
mental NEC Z73.3
  work-related Z56.6
physical NEC Z73.3
  work-related Z56.6
polycythemia D75.1
reaction —*see also* Reaction, stress F43.9
work schedule Z56.3
Stretching, nerve —*see* Injury, nerve
Striae albicantes, atrophicae or distensae
  (cutis) L90.6
Stricture —*see also* Stenosis
ampulla of Vater K83.1
anus (sphincter) K62.4
  congenital Q42.3
    with fistula Q42.2
  infantile Q42.3
    with fistula Q42.2
aorta (ascending) (congenital) Q25.1
  arteriosclerotic I70.0
  calcified I70.0
  supravalvular, congenital Q25.3
aortic (valve) —*see* Stenosis, aortic
aqueduct of Sylvius (congenital) Q03.0
  with spina bifida —*see* Spina bifida, by site,
    with hydrocephalus
  acquired G91.1

Stricture *(Continued)*
artery I77.1
  basilar —*see* Occlusion, artery, basilar
  carotid —*see* Occlusion, artery, carotid
  celiac I77.4
  congenital (peripheral) Q27.8
    cerebral Q28.3
    coronary Q24.5
    digestive system Q27.8
    lower limb Q27.8
    retinal Q14.1
    specified site NEC Q27.8
    umbilical Q27.0
    upper limb Q27.8
  coronary —*see* Disease, heart, ischemic,
    atherosclerotic
    congenital Q24.5
  precerebral —*see* Occlusion, artery,
    precerebral
  pulmonary (congenital) Q25.6
    acquired I28.8
  renal I70.1
  vertebral —*see* Occlusion, artery, vertebral
auditory canal (external) (congenital)
  acquired —*see* Stenosis, external ear canal
bile duct (common) (hepatic) K83.1
  congenital Q44.3
  postoperative K91.89
bladder N32.89
  neck N32.0
bowel —*see* Obstruction, intestine
brain G93.89
bronchus J98.09
  congenital Q32.3
  syphilitic A52.72
cardia (stomach) K22.2
  congenital Q39.3
cardiac —*see also* Disease, heart
  orifice (stomach) K22.2
cecum —*see* Obstruction, intestine
cervix, cervical (canal) N88.2
  congenital Q51.828
  in pregnancy —*see* Pregnancy, complicated
    by, abnormal cervix
    causing obstructed labor O65.5
colon —*see also* Obstruction, intestine
  congenital Q42.9
    specified NEC Q42.8
colostomy K94.03
common (bile) duct K83.1
coronary (artery) —*see* Disease, heart,
  ischemic, atherosclerotic
cystic duct —*see* Obstruction, gallbladder
digestive organs NEC, congenital Q45.8
duodenum K31.5
  congenital Q41.0
ear canal (external) (congenital) Q16.1
  acquired —*see* Stricture, auditory canal,
    acquired
ejaculatory duct N50.89
enterostomy K94.13
esophagus K22.2
  congenital Q39.3
  syphilitic A52.79
    congenital A50.59 *[K23]*
eustachian tube —*see also* Obstruction,
  eustachian tube
  congenital Q17.8
fallopian tube N97.1
  gonococcal A54.24
  tuberculous A18.17
gallbladder —*see* Obstruction, gallbladder
glottis J38.6
heart —*see also* Disease, heart
  valve (*see also* Endocarditis) I38
    aortic Q23.0
    mitral Q23.2
    pulmonary Q22.1
    tricuspid Q22.4
hepatic duct K83.1
hourglass, of stomach K31.2

Stricture *(Continued)*
hymen N89.6
hypopharynx J39.2
ileum —*see also* Obstruction, intestine,
  specified NEC K56.699
  congenital Q41.2
intestine —*see also* Obstruction, intestine
  congenital (small) Q41.9
    large Q42.9
      specified NEC Q42.8
    specified NEC Q41.8
  ischemic K55.1
jejunum —*see also* Obstruction, intestine,
  specified NEC K56.699
  congenital Q41.1
lacrimal passages —*see also* Stenosis, lacrimal
  congenital Q10.5
larynx J38.6
  congenital NEC Q31.8
    subglottic Q31.1
  syphilitic A52.73
    congenital A50.59 *[J99]*
meatus
  ear (congenital) Q16.1
    acquired —*see* Stricture, auditory canal,
      acquired
    osseous (ear) (congenital) Q16.1
      acquired —*see* Stricture, auditory canal,
        acquired
  urinarius —*see also* Stricture, urethra
    congenital Q64.33
mitral (valve) —*see* Stenosis, mitral
myocardium, myocardial I51.5
  hypertrophic subaortic (idiopathic) I42.1
nares (anterior) (posterior) J34.89
  congenital Q30.0
nasal duct —*see also* Stenosis, lacrimal, duct
  congenital Q10.5
nasolacrimal duct —*see also* Stenosis, lacrimal,
  duct
  congenital Q10.5
nasopharynx J39.2
  syphilitic A52.73
nose J34.89
  congenital Q30.0
nostril (anterior) (posterior) J34.89
  congenital Q30.0
  syphilitic A52.73
    congenital A50.59 *[J99]*
organ or site, congenital NEC —*see* Atresia,
  by site
os uteri —*see* Stricture, cervix
osseous meatus (ear) (congenital) Q16.1
  acquired —*see* Stricture, auditory canal,
    acquired
oviduct —*see* Stricture, fallopian tube
pelviureteric junction (congenital) Q62.11
  acquired, with hydronephrosis N13.0
penis, by foreign body T19.4
pharynx J39.2
prostate N42.89
pulmonary, pulmonic
  artery (congenital) Q25.6
    acquired I28.8
    noncongenital I28.8
  infundibulum (congenital) Q24.3
  valve I37.0
    congenital Q22.1
  vein, acquired I28.8
  vessel NEC I28.8
punctum lacrimale —*see also* Stenosis,
  lacrimal, punctum
  congenital Q10.5
pylorus (hypertrophic) K31.1
  adult K31.1
  congenital Q40.0
  infantile Q40.0
rectosigmoid —*see also* Obstruction, intestine,
  specified NEC K56.699
rectum (sphincter) K62.4
  congenital Q42.1
    with fistula Q42.0

Stricture (Continued)
  rectum (Continued)
    due to
      chlamydial lymphogranuloma A55
      irradiation K91.89
      lymphogranuloma venereum A55
    gonococcal A54.6
    inflammatory (chlamydial) A55
    syphilitic A52.74
    tuberculous A18.32
  renal artery I70.1
    congenital Q27.1
  salivary duct or gland (any) K11.8
  sigmoid (flexure) —see Obstruction, intestine
  spermatic cord N50.89
  stoma (following) (of)
    colostomy K94.03
    enterostomy K94.13
    gastrostomy K94.23
    ileostomy K94.13
    tracheostomy J95.03
  stomach K31.89
    congenital Q40.2
    hourglass K31.2
  subaortic Q24.4
    hypertrophic (acquired) (idiopathic) I42.1
  subglottic J38.6
  syphilitic NEC A52.79
  trachea J39.8
    congenital Q32.1
    syphilitic A52.73
    tuberculous NEC A15.5
  tracheostomy J95.03
  tricuspid (valve) —see Stenosis, tricuspid
  tunica vaginalis N50.89
  ureter (postoperative) N13.5
    with
      hydronephrosis N13.1
        with infection N13.6
      pyelonephritis (chronic) N11.1
    congenital —see Atresia, ureter
    tuberculous A18.11
  ureteropelvic junction (congenital) Q62.11
    acquired, with hydronephrosis N13.0
  ureterovesical orifice N13.5
    with infection N13.6
⇒ urethra (organic) (spasmodic) (see also
      Stricture, urethra, male N35.919)
    associated with schistosomiasis B65.0 [N37]
    congenital Q64.39
      valvular (posterior) Q64.2
    due to
      infection —see Stricture, urethra,
        postinfective
      trauma —see Stricture, urethra,
        post-traumatic
  ▶ female N35.92
    gonococcal, gonorrheal A54.01
    infective NEC —see Stricture, urethra,
      postinfective
    late effect (sequelae) of injury —see
      Stricture, urethra, post-traumatic
  ▶ male N35.919
    ▶ anterior urethra N35.914
    ▶ bulbous urethra N35.912
    ▶ meatal N35.911
    ▶ membranous urethra N35.913
    ▶ overlapping sites N35.916
    postcatheterization —see Stricture, urethra,
      postprocedural
    postinfective NEC
      female N35.12
      male N35.119
        anterior urethra N35.114
        bulbous urethra N35.112
        meatal N35.111
        membranous urethra N35.113
      ▶ overlapping sites N35.116
    postobstetric N35.021
    postoperative —see Stricture, urethra,
      postprocedural

Stricture (Continued)
  urethra (organic) (spasmodic) (Continued)
    postprocedural
      female N99.12
      male N99.114
        anterior bulbous urethra N99.113
        bulbous urethra N99.111
        fossa navicularis N99.115
        meatal N99.110
        membranous urethra N99.112
      ▶ overlapping sites N35.116
    post-traumatic
      female N35.028
        due to childbirth N35.021
      male N35.014
        anterior urethra N35.013
        bulbous urethra N35.011
        meatal N35.010
        membranous urethra N35.012
      ▶ overlapping sites N35.016
    sequela (late effect) of
      childbirth N35.021
      injury —see Stricture, urethra,
        post-traumatic
  ⇒ specified cause NEC
    ▶ female N35.82
    ▶ male N35.819
      ▶ anterior urethra N35.814
      ▶ bulbous urethra N35.812
      ▶ meatal N35.811
      ▶ membranous urethra N35.813
      ▶ overlapping sites N35.816
    syphilitic A52.76
    traumatic —see Stricture, urethra,
      post-traumatic
    valvular (posterior), congenital Q64.2
  urinary meatus —see Stricture, urethra
  uterus, uterine (synechiae) N85.6
    os (external) (internal) —see Stricture, cervix
  vagina (outlet) —see Stenosis, vagina
  valve (cardiac) (heart) —see also Endocarditis
    congenital
      aortic Q23.0
      mitral Q23.2
      pulmonary Q22.1
      tricuspid Q22.4
  vas deferens N50.89
    congenital Q55.4
  vein I87.1
  vena cava (inferior) (superior) NEC I87.1
    congenital Q26.0
  vesicourethral orifice N32.0
    congenital Q64.31
  vulva (acquired) N90.5
Stridor R06.1
  congenital (larynx) P28.89
Stridulous —see condition
Stroke (apoplectic) (brain) (embolic) (ischemic)
    (paralytic) (thrombotic) I63.9
  cryptogenic —see also infarction, cerebral I63.9
  epileptic —see Epilepsy
  heat T67.0
  in evolution I63.9
  intraoperative
    during cardiac surgery I97.810
    during other surgery I97.811
  lightning —see Lightning
  meaning
    cerebral hemorrhage — code to
      Hemorrhage, intracranial
    cerebral infarction — code to Infarction,
      cerebral
  postprocedural
    following cardiac surgery I97.820
    following other surgery I97.821
  unspecified (NOS) I63.9
Stromatosis, endometrial D39.0
Strongyloidiasis, strongyloidosis B78.9
  cutaneous B78.1
  disseminated B78.7
  intestinal B78.0

Strophulus pruriginosus L28.2
Struck by lightning —see Lightning
Struma —see also Goiter
  Hashimoto E06.3
  lymphomatosa E06.3
  nodosa (simplex) E04.9
    endemic E01.2
      multinodular E01.1
    multinodular E04.2
      iodine-deficiency related E01.1
    toxic or with hyperthyroidism E05.20
      with thyroid storm E05.21
      multinodular E05.20
        with thyroid storm E05.21
      uninodular E05.10
        with thyroid storm E05.11
    toxicosa E05.20
      with thyroid storm E05.21
      multinodular E05.20
        with thyroid storm E05.21
      uninodular E05.10
        with thyroid storm E05.11
    uninodular E04.1
  ovarii D27.-●
  Riedel's E06.5
Strumipriva cachexia E03.4
Strümpell-Marie spine —see Spondylitis,
    ankylosing
Strümpell-Westphal pseudosclerosis E83.01
Stuart deficiency disease (factor X) D68.2
Stuart-Prower factor deficiency (factor X) D68.2
Student's elbow —see Bursitis, elbow, olecranon
Stump —see Amputation
Stunting, nutritional E45
Stupor (catatonic) R40.1
  depressive (single episode) F32.89
    recurrent episode F33.8
  dissociative F44.2
  manic F30.2
  manic-depressive F31.89
  psychogenic (anergic) F44.2
  reaction to exceptional stress (transient)
    F43.0
Sturge (-Weber) (-Dimitri) (-Kalischer) disease
    or syndrome Q85.8
Stuttering F80.81
  adult onset F98.5
  childhood onset F80.81
  following cerebrovascular disease —
    see Disorder, fluency, following
    cerebrovascular disease
  in conditions classified elsewhere R47.82
Sty, stye (external) (internal) (meibomian)
    (zeisian) —see Hordeolum
Subacidity, gastric K31.89
  psychogenic F45.8
Subacute —see condition
Subarachnoid —see condition
Subcortical —see condition
Subcostal syndrome, nerve compression —see
    Mononeuropathy, upper limb, specified
    site NEC
Subcutaneous, subcuticular —see condition
Subdural —see condition
Subendocardium —see condition
Subependymoma
  specified site —see Neoplasm, uncertain
    behavior, by site
  unspecified site D43.2
Suberosis J67.3
Subglossitis —see Glossitis
Subhemophilia D66
Subinvolution
  breast (postlactational) (postpuerperal)
    N64.89
  puerperal O90.89
  uterus (chronic) (nonpuerperal) N85.3
    puerperal O90.89
Sublingual —see condition
Sublinguitis —see Sialoadenitis
Subluxatable hip Q65.6

Subluxation —see also Dislocation
 acromioclavicular S43.11-•
 ankle S93.0-•
 atlantoaxial, recurrent M43.4
  with myelopathy M43.3
 carpometacarpal (joint) NEC S63.05-•
  thumb S63.04-•
 complex, vertebral —see Complex,
  subluxation
 congenital —see also Malposition, congenital
  hip —see Dislocation, hip, congenital,
   partial
  joint (excluding hip)
   lower limb Q68.8
   shoulder Q68.8
   upper limb Q68.8
 elbow (traumatic) S53.10-•
  anterior S53.11-•
  lateral S53.14-•
  medial S53.13-•
  posterior S53.12-•
  specified type NEC S53.19-•
 finger S63.20-•
  index S63.20-•
  interphalangeal S63.22-•
   distal S63.24-•
    index S63.24-•
    little S63.24-•
    middle S63.24-•
    ring S63.24-•
   index S63.22-•
   little S63.22-•
   middle S63.22-•
   proximal S63.23-•
    index S63.23-•
    little S63.23-•
    middle S63.23-•
    ring S63.23-•
   ring S63.22-•
  little S63.20-•
  metacarpophalangeal S63.21-•
   index S63.21-•
   little S63.21-•
   middle S63.21-•
   ring S63.21-•
  middle S63.20-•
  ring S63.20-•
 foot S93.30-•
  specified site NEC S93.33-•
  tarsal joint S93.31-•
  tarsometatarsal joint S93.32-•
  toe —see Subluxation, toe
 hip S73.00-•
  anterior S73.03-•
   obturator S73.02-•
  central S73.04-•
  posterior S73.01-•
 interphalangeal (joint)
  finger S63.22-•
   distal joint S63.24-•
    index S63.24-•
    little S63.24-•
    middle S63.24-•
    ring S63.24-•
   index S63.22-•
   little S63.22-•
   middle S63.22-•
   proximal joint S63.23-•
    index S63.23-•
    little S63.23-•
    middle S63.23-•
    ring S63.23-•
   ring S63.22-•
  thumb S63.12-•
   distal joint S63.14-
   proximal joint S63.13-
  toe S93.13-•
   great S93.13-•
   lesser S93.13-•
 joint prosthesis —see Complications, joint
  prosthesis, mechanical, displacement,
  by site

Subluxation (Continued)
 knee S83.10-•
  cap —see Subluxation, patella
  patella —see Subluxation, patella
  proximal tibia
   anteriorly S83.11-•
   laterally S83.14-•
   medially S83.13-•
   posteriorly S83.12-•
  specified type NEC S83.19-•
 lens —see Dislocation, lens, partial
 ligament, traumatic —see Sprain,
  by site
 metacarpal (bone)
  proximal end S63.06-•
 metacarpophalangeal (joint)
  finger S63.21-•
   index S63.21-•
   little S63.21-•
   middle S63.21-•
   ring S63.21-•
  thumb S63.11-•
 metatarsophalangeal joint S93.14-•
  great toe S93.14-•
  lesser toe S93.14-•
 midcarpal (joint) S63.03-•
 patella S83.00-•
  lateral S83.01-•
  recurrent (nontraumatic) —see
   Dislocation, patella, recurrent,
   incomplete
  specified type NEC S83.09-•
 pathological —see Dislocation, pathological
 radial head S53.00-•
  anterior S53.01-•
  nursemaid's elbow S53.03-•
  posterior S53.02-•
  specified type NEC S53.09-•
 radiocarpal (joint) S63.02-•
 radioulnar (joint)
  distal S63.01-•
  proximal —see Subluxation, elbow
 shoulder
  congenital Q68.8
  girdle S43.30-•
   scapula S43.31-•
   specified site NEC S43.39-•
  traumatic S43.00-•
   anterior S43.01-•
   inferior S43.03-•
   posterior S43.02-•
   specified type NEC S43.08-•
 sternoclavicular (joint) S43.20-•
  anterior S43.21-•
  posterior S43.22-•
 symphysis (pubis)
 thumb S63.103
  interphalangeal joint —see Subluxation,
   interphalangeal (joint), thumb
  metacarpophalangeal joint —see
   Subluxation, metacarpophalangeal
   (joint), thumb
 toe(s) S93.10-•
  great S93.10-•
   interphalangeal joint S93.13-•
   metatarsophalangeal joint S93.14-•
  interphalangeal joint S93.13-•
  lesser S93.10-•
   interphalangeal joint S93.13-•
   metatarsophalangeal joint S93.14-•
  metatarsophalangeal joint S93.149
 ulnohumeral joint —see Subluxation,
  elbow
 vertebral
  recurrent NEC —see subcategory
   M43.5
  traumatic
   cervical S13.100
    atlantoaxial joint S13.120
    atlantooccipital joint S13.110
    atloidooccipital joint S13.110

Subluxation (Continued)
 vertebral (Continued)
  traumatic (Continued)
   cervical (Continued)
    joint between
     C0 and C1 S13.110
     C1 and C2 S13.120
     C2 and C3 S13.130
     C3 and C4 S13.140
     C4 and C5 S13.150
     C5 and C6 S13.160
     C6 and C7 S13.170
     C7 and T1 S13.180
    occipitoatloid joint S13.110
   lumbar S33.100
    joint between
     L1 and L2 S33.110
     L2 and L3 S33.120
     L3 and L4 S33.130
     L4 and L5 S33.140
   thoracic S23.100
    joint between
     T1 and T2 S23.110
     T2 and T3 S23.120
     T3 and T4 S23.122
     T4 and T5 S23.130
     T5 and T6 S23.132
     T6 and T7 S23.140
     T7 and T8 S23.142
     T8 and T9 S23.150
     T9 and T10 S23.152
     T10 and T11 S23.160
     T11 and T12 S23.162
     T12 and L1 S23.170
 ulna
  distal end S63.07-•
  proximal end —see Subluxation, elbow
 wrist (carpal bone) S63.00-•
  carpometacarpal joint —see Subluxation,
   carpometacarpal (joint)
  distal radioulnar joint —see Subluxation,
   radioulnar (joint), distal
  metacarpal bone, proximal —see Subluxation,
   metacarpal (bone), proximal end
  midcarpal —see Subluxation, midcarpal
   (joint)
  radiocarpal joint —see Subluxation,
   radiocarpal (joint)
  recurrent —see Dislocation, recurrent, wrist
  specified site NEC S63.09-•
  ulna —see Subluxation, ulna, distal end
Submaxillary —see condition
Submersion (fatal) (nonfatal) T75.1
Submucous —see condition
Subnormal, subnormality
 accommodation (old age) H52.4
 mental —see Disability, intellectual
 temperature (accidental) T68
Subphrenic —see condition
Subscapular nerve —see condition
Subseptus uterus Q51.28
Subsiding appendicitis K36
Substance (other psychoactive) -induced
 anxiety disorder F19.980
 bipolar and related disorder F19.94
 delirium F19.921
 depressive disorder F19.94
 major neurocognitive disorder F19.97
 mild neurocognitive disorder F19.988
 obsessive-compulsive and related disorder
  F19.988
 psychotic disorder F19.959
 sexual dysfunction F19.981
 sleep disorder F19.982
Substernal thyroid E04.9
 congenital Q89.2
Substitution disorder F44.9
Subtentorial —see condition
Subthyroidism (acquired) —see also
 Hypothyroidism
 congenital E03.1

Succenturiate placenta O43.19-●
Sucking thumb, child (excessive) F98.8
Sudamen, sudamina L74.1
Sudanese kala-azar B55.0
Sudden
  hearing loss —see Deafness, sudden
  heart failure —see Failure, heart
Sudeck's atrophy, disease, or syndrome —see
    Algoneurodystrophy
Suffocation —see Asphyxia, traumatic
Sugar
  blood
    high (transient) R73.9
    low (transient) E16.2
  in urine R81
Suicide, suicidal (attempted) T14.91
  by poisoning —see Table of Drugs and
      Chemicals
  history of (personal) Z91.5
    in family Z81.8
  ideation —see Ideation, suicidal
  risk
    meaning personal history of attempted
        suicide Z91.5
    meaning suicidal ideation —see Ideation,
        suicidal
  tendencies
    meaning personal history of attempted
        suicide Z91.5
    meaning suicidal ideation —see Ideation,
        suicidal
  trauma —see nature of injury by site
Suipestifer infection —see Infection, salmonella
Sulfhemoglobinemia, sulphemoglobinemia
    (acquired) (with methemoglobinemia)
    D74.8
Sumatran mite fever A75.3
Summer —see condition
Sunburn L55.9
  due to
    tanning bed (acute) L56.8
      chronic L57.8
    ultraviolet radiation (acute) L56.8
      chronic L57.8
  first degree L55.0
  second degree L55.1
  third degree L55.2
SUNCT (short lasting unilateral neuralgiform
    headache with conjunctival injection and
    tearing) G44.059
  intractable G44.051
  not intractable G44.059
Sundowning F05
Sunken acetabulum —see Derangement, joint,
    specified type NEC, hip
Sunstroke T67.0
Superfecundation —see Pregnancy, multiple
Superfetation —see Pregnancy, multiple
Superinvolution (uterus) N85.8
Supernumerary (congenital)
  aortic cusps Q23.8
  auditory ossicles Q16.3
  bone Q79.8
  breast Q83.1
  carpal bones Q74.0
  cusps, heart valve NEC Q24.8
    aortic Q23.8
    mitral Q23.2
    pulmonary Q22.3
  digit(s) Q69.9
  ear (lobule) Q17.0
  fallopian tube Q50.6
  finger Q69.0
  hymen Q52.4
  kidney Q63.0
  lacrimonasal duct Q10.6
  lobule (ear) Q17.0
  mitral cusps Q23.2
  muscle Q79.8
  nipple(s) Q83.3
  organ or site not listed —see Accessory

Supernumerary (Continued)
  ossicles, auditory Q16.3
  ovary Q50.31
  oviduct Q50.6
  pulmonary, pulmonic cusps Q22.3
  rib Q76.6
    cervical or first (syndrome) Q76.5
  roots (of teeth) K00.2
  spleen Q89.09
  tarsal bones Q74.2
  teeth K00.1
  testis Q55.29
  thumb Q69.1
  toe Q69.2
  ▶uterus Q51.28
  vagina Q52.1
  vertebra Q76.49
Supervision (of)
  contraceptive —see Prescription,
      contraceptives
  dietary (for) Z71.3
    allergy (food) Z71.3
    colitis Z71.3
    diabetes mellitus Z71.3
    food allergy or intolerance Z71.3
    gastritis Z71.3
    hypercholesterolemia Z71.3
    hypoglycemia Z71.3
    intolerance (food) Z71.3
    obesity Z71.3
    specified NEC Z71.3
  healthy infant or child Z76.2
    foundling Z76.1
  high-risk pregnancy —see Pregnancy,
      complicated by, high, risk
  lactation Z39.1
  pregnancy —see Pregnancy, supervision of
Supplemental teeth K00.1
Suppression
  binocular vision H53.34
  lactation O92.5
  menstruation N94.89
  ovarian secretion E28.39
  renal N28.9
  urine, urinary secretion R34
Suppuration, suppurative —see also condition
  accessory sinus (chronic) —see Sinusitis
  adrenal gland
  antrum (chronic) —see Sinusitis, maxillary
  bladder —see Cystitis
  brain G06.0
    sequelae G09
  breast N61.1
    puerperal, postpartum or gestational —see
        Mastitis, obstetric, purulent
  dental periosteum M27.3
  ear (middle) —see also Otitis, media
    external NEC —see Otitis, externa,
        infective
    internal —see subcategory H83.0
  ethmoidal (chronic) (sinus) —see Sinusitis,
      ethmoidal
  fallopian tube —see Salpingo-oophoritis
  frontal (chronic) (sinus) —see Sinusitis, frontal
  gallbladder (acute) K81.0
  gum K05.20
    generalized —see Peridontitis, aggressive,
        generalized
    localized —see Peridontitis, aggressive,
        localized
  intracranial G06.0
  joint —see Arthritis, pyogenic or pyemic
  labyrinthine —see subcategory H83.0
  lung —see Abscess, lung
  mammary gland N61.1
    puerperal, postpartum O91.12
      associated with lactation O91.13
  maxilla, maxillary M27.2
    sinus (chronic) —see Sinusitis, maxillary
  muscle —see Myositis, infective
  nasal sinus (chronic) —see Sinusitis

Suppuration, suppurative (Continued)
  pancreas, acute —see also Pancreatitis, acute
      K85.80
  parotid gland —see Sialoadenitis
  pelvis, pelvic
    female —see Disease, pelvis, inflammatory
    male K65.0
  pericranial —see Osteomyelitis
  salivary duct or gland (any) —see
      Sialoadenitis
  sinus (accessory) (chronic) (nasal) —see
      Sinusitis
  sphenoidal sinus (chronic) —see Sinusitis,
      sphenoidal
  thymus (gland) E32.1
  thyroid (gland) E06.0
  tonsil —see Tonsillitis
  uterus —see Endometritis
Supraeruption of tooth (teeth) M26.34
Supraglottitis J04.30
  with obstruction J04.31
Suprarenal (gland) —see condition
Suprascapular nerve —see condition
Suprasellar —see condition
Surfer's knots or nodules S89.8-●
Surgical
  emphysema T81.82
  procedures, complication or misadventure —
      see Complications, surgical procedures
  shock T81.10
Surveillance (of) (for) —see also Observation
  alcohol abuse Z71.41
  contraceptive —see Prescription, contraceptives
  dietary Z71.3
  drug abuse Z71.51
Susceptibility to disease, genetic Z15.89
  malignant neoplasm Z15.09
    breast Z15.01
    endometrium Z15.04
    ovary Z15.02
    prostate Z15.03
    specified NEC Z15.09
  multiple endocrine neoplasia Z15.81
Suspected condition, ruled out —see also
      Observation, suspected
  amniotic cavity and membrane Z03.71
  cervical shortening Z03.75
  fetal anomaly Z03.73
  fetal growth Z03.74
  maternal and fetal conditions NEC Z03.79
  newborn —see also Observation, newborn,
      suspected condition ruled out Z05.9
  oligohydramnios Z03.71
  placental problem Z03.72
  polyhydramnios Z03.71
Suspended uterus
  in pregnancy or childbirth —see Pregnancy,
      complicated by, abnormal uterus
Sutton's nevus D22.9
Suture
  burst (in operation wound) T81.31
    external operation wound T81.31
    internal operation wound T81.32
  inadvertently left in operation wound —see
      Foreign body, accidentally left during a
      procedure
  removal Z48.02
Swab inadvertently left in operation wound —
    see Foreign body, accidentally left during a
    procedure
Swallowed, swallowing
  difficulty —see Dysphagia
  foreign body —see Foreign body, alimentary
      tract
Swan-neck deformity (finger) —see Deformity,
    finger, swan-neck
Swearing, compulsive F42.8
  in Gilles de la Tourette's syndrome F95.2
Sweat, sweats
  fetid L75.0
  night R61

▶ New   ⇒ Revised   ~~deleted~~ Deleted   ● Use Additional Character(s)

Sweating, excessive R61
Sweeley-Klionsky disease E75.21
Sweet's disease or dermatosis L98.2
Swelling (of) R60.9
  abdomen, abdominal (not referable to any
      particular organ) —see Mass,
      abdominal
  ankle —see Effusion, joint, ankle
  arm M79.89
    forearm M79.89
  breast —see also Lump, breast N63.0
  Calabar B74.3
  cervical gland R59.0
  chest, localized R22.2
  ear H93.8-•
  extremity (lower) (upper) —see Disorder, soft
    tissue, specified type NEC
  finger M79.89
  foot M79.89
  glands R59.9
    generalized R59.1
    localized R59.0
  hand M79.89
  head (localized) R22.0
  inflammatory —see Inflammation
  intra-abdominal —see Mass, abdominal
  joint —see Effusion, joint
  leg M79.89
    lower M79.89
  limb —see Disorder, soft tissue, specified type
    NEC
  localized (skin) R22.9
    chest R22.2
    head R22.0
    limb
      lower —see Mass, localized, limb, lower
      upper —see Mass, localized, limb, upper
    neck R22.1
    trunk R22.2
  neck (localized) R22.1
  pelvic —see Mass, abdominal
  scrotum N50.89
  splenic —see Splenomegaly
  testis N50.89
  toe M79.89
  umbilical R19.09
  wandering, due to Gnathostoma
    (spinigerum) B83.1
  white —see Tuberculosis, arthritis
Swift (-Feer) disease
  overdose or wrong substance given
    or taken —see Table of Drugs and
    Chemicals, by drug, poisoning
Swimmer's
  cramp T75.1
  ear H60.33-•
  itch B65.3
Swimming in the head R42
Swollen —see Swelling
Swyer syndrome Q99.1
Sycosis L73.8
  barbae (not parasitic) L73.8
  contagiosa (mycotic) B35.0
  lupoides L73.8
  mycotic B35.0
  parasitic B35.0
  vulgaris L73.8
Sydenham's chorea —see Chorea, Sydenham's
Sylvatic yellow fever A95.0
Sylvest's disease B33.0
Symblepharon H11.23-•
  congenital Q10.3
Symond's syndrome G93.2
Sympathetic —see condition
Sympatheticotonia G90.8
Sympathicoblastoma
  specified site —see Neoplasm, malignant, by
    site
  unspecified site C74.90
Sympathogonioma —see Sympathicoblastoma
Symphalangy (fingers) (toes) Q70.9

Symptoms NEC R68.89
  breast NEC N64.59
  cold J00
  development NEC R63.8
  factitious, self-induced —see Disorder,
    factitious
  genital organs, female R10.2
  involving
    abdomen NEC R19.8
    appearance NEC R46.89
    awareness R41.9
      altered mental status R41.82
      amnesia —see Amnesia
      borderline intellectual functioning
        R41.83
      coma —see Coma
      disorientation R41.0
      neurologic neglect syndrome R41.4
      senile cognitive decline R41.81
      specified symptom NEC R41.89
    behavior NEC R46.89
    cardiovascular system NEC R09.89
    chest NEC R09.89
    circulatory system NEC R09.89
    cognitive functions R41.9
      altered mental status R41.82
      amnesia —see Amnesia
      borderline intellectual functioning
        R41.83
      coma —see Coma
      disorientation R41.0
      neurologic neglect syndrome
        R41.4
      senile cognitive decline R41.81
      specified symptom NEC R41.89
    development NEC R62.50
    digestive system NEC R19.8
    emotional state NEC R45.89
      emotional lability R45.86
    food and fluid intake R63.8
    general perceptions and sensations
      R44.9
      specified NEC R44.8
    musculoskeletal system R29.91
      specified NEC R29.898
    nervous system R29.90
      specified NEC R29.818
    pelvis NEC R19.8
    respiratory system NEC R09.89
    skin and integument R23.9
    urinary system R39.9
  menopausal N95.1
  metabolism NEC R63.8
  neurotic F48.8
  of infancy R68.19
  pelvis NEC, female R10.2
  skin and integument NEC R23.9
  subcutaneous tissue NEC R23.9
  viral cold J00
Sympus Q74.2
Syncephalus Q89.4
Synchondrosis
  abnormal (congenital) Q78.8
  ischiopubic M91.0
Synchysis (scintillans) (senile) (vitreous body)
  H43.89
Syncope (near) (pre-) R55
  anginosa I20.8
  bradycardia R00.1
  cardiac R55
  carotid sinus G90.01
  due to spinal (lumbar) puncture G97.1
  heart R55
  heat T67.1
  laryngeal R05
  psychogenic F48.8
  tussive R05
  vasoconstriction R55
  vasodepressor R55
  vasomotor R55
  vasovagal R55

Syndactylism, syndactyly Q70.9
  complex (with synostosis)
    fingers Q70.0-•
    toes Q70.2-•
  simple (without synostosis)
    fingers Q70.1-•
    toes Q70.3-•
Syndrome —see also Disease
  5q minus NOS D46.C
  48,XXXX Q97.1
  49,XXXXX Q97.1
  abdominal
    acute R10.0
    muscle deficiency Q79.4
  abnormal innervation H02.519
    left H02.516
      lower H02.515
      upper H02.514
    right H02.513
      lower H02.512
      upper H02.511
  abstinence, neonatal P96.1
  acid pulmonary aspiration, obstetric O74.0
  acquired immunodeficiency —see Human,
    immunodeficiency virus (HIV) disease
  acute abdominal R10.0
  acute respiratory distress (adult) (child) J80
    idiopathic J84.114
  Adair-Dighton Q78.0
  Adams-Stokes (-Morgagni) I45.9
  adiposogenital E23.6
  adrenal
    hemorrhage (meningococcal) A39.1
    meningococcic A39.1
  adrenocortical —see Cushing's, syndrome
  adrenogenital E25.9
    congenital, associated with enzyme
      deficiency E25.0
  afferent loop NEC K91.89
  Alagille's Q44.7
  alcohol withdrawal (without convulsions) —
    see Dependence, alcohol, with,
    withdrawal
  Alder's D72.0
  Aldrich (-Wiskott) D82.0
  alien hand R41.4
  Alport Q87.81
  alveolar hypoventilation E66.2
  alveolocapillary block J84.10
  amnesic, amnestic (confabulatory) (due to) —
    see Disorder, amnesic
  amyostatic (Wilson's disease) E83.01
  androgen insensitivity E34.50
    complete E34.51
    partial E34.52
  androgen resistance (see also Syndrome,
    androgen insensitivity) E34.50
  ➡ Angelman Q93.51
  anginal —see Angina
  ankyloglossia superior Q38.1
  anterior
    chest wall R07.89
    cord G83.82
    spinal artery G95.19
      compression M47.019
        cervical region M47.012
        cervicothoracic region M47.013
        lumbar region M47.016
        occipito-atlanto-axial region M47.011
        thoracic region M47.014
        thoracolumbar region M47.015
    tibial M76.81-•
  antibody deficiency D80.9
    agammaglobulinemic D80.1
      hereditary D80.0
    congenital D80.0
    hypogammaglobulinemic D80.1
      hereditary D80.0
  anticardiolipin (-antibody) D68.61
  antidepressant discontinuation T43.205
  antiphospholipid (-antibody) D68.61

Syndrome *(Continued)*

aortic
  arch M31.4
  bifurcation I74.09
aortomesenteric duodenum occlusion K31.5
apical ballooning (transient left ventricular)
  I51.81
arcuate ligament I77.4
argentaffin, argintaffinoma E34.0
Arnold-Chiari —*see* Arnold-Chiari disease
Arrillaga-Ayerza I27.0
arterial tortuosity Q87.82
arteriovenous steal T82.898-●
Asherman's N85.6
aspiration, of newborn —*see* Aspiration, by
  substance, with pneumonia
  meconium P24.01
ataxia-telangiectasia G11.3
auriculotemporal G50.8
autoerythrocyte sensitization (Gardner-
  Diamond) D69.2
autoimmune lymphoproliferative [ALPS]
  D89.82
autoimmune polyglandular E31.0
autoinflammatory M04.9
  specified type NEC M04.8
autosomal —*see* Abnormal, autosomes
Avellis' G46.8
Ayerza (-Arrillaga) I27.0
Babinski-Nageotte G83.89
Bakwin-Krida Q78.5
bare lymphocyte D81.6
Barré-Guillain G61.0
Barré-Liéou M53.0
Barrett's —*see* Barrett's, esophagus
Barsony-Polgar K22.4
Barsony-Teschendorf K22.4
Barth E78.71
Bartter's E26.81
basal cell nevus Q87.89
Basedow's E05.00
  with thyroid storm E05.01
basilar artery G45.0
Batten-Steinert G71.11
battered
  baby or child —*see* Maltreatment, child,
    physical abuse
  spouse —*see* Maltreatment, adult, physical
    abuse
Beals Q87.40
Beau's I51.5
Beck's I65.8
Benedikt's G46.3
Béquez César (-Steinbrinck-Chédiak-Higashi)
  D70.330
Bernhardt-Roth —*see* Meralgia paresthetica
Bernheim's —*see* Failure, heart, right
big spleen D73.1
bilateral polycystic ovarian E28.2
Bing-Horton's —*see* Horton's headache
Birt-Hogg-Dube syndrome Q87.89
Björck (-Thorsen) E34.0
black
  lung J60
  widow spider bite —*see* Toxicity, venom,
    spider, black widow
Blackfan-Diamond D61.01
Blau M04.8
blind loop K90.2
  congenital Q43.8
  postsurgical K91.2
blue sclera Q78.0
blue toe I75.02-●
Boder-Sedgewick G11.3
Boerhaave's K22.3
Borjeson Forssman Lehmann Q89.8
Bouillaud's I01.9
Bourneville (-Pringle) Q85.1
Bouveret (-Hoffman) I47.9
brachial plexus G54.0
bradycardia-tachycardia I49.5

Syndrome *(Continued)*

brain (nonpsychotic) F09
  with psychosis, psychotic reaction F09
  acute or subacute —*see* Delirium
  congenital —*see* Disability, intellectual
  organic F09
    post-traumatic (nonpsychotic) F07.81
      psychotic F09
  personality change F07.0
  postcontusional F07.81
  post-traumatic, nonpsychotic F07.81
  psycho-organic F09
  psychotic F06.8
brain stem stroke G46.3
Brandt's (acrodermatitis enteropathica) E83.2
broad ligament laceration N83.8
Brock's J98.11
bronze baby P83.88
Brown-Sequard G83.81
Brugada I49.8
bubbly lung P27.0
Buchem's M85.2
Budd-Chiari I82.0
bulbar (progressive) G12.22
Bürger-Grütz E78.3
Burke's K86.89
Burnett's (milk-alkali) E83.52
burning feet E53.9
Bywaters' T79.5
Call-Fleming I67.841
carbohydrate-deficient glycoprotein (CDGS)
  E77.8
carcinogenic thrombophlebitis I82.1
carcinoid E34.0
cardiac asthma I50.1
cardiacos negros I27.0
cardiofaciocutaneous Q87.89
cardiopulmonary-obesity E66.2
cardiorenal —*see* Hypertension, cardiorenal
cardiorespiratory distress (idiopathic),
  newborn P22.0
cardiovascular renal —*see* Hypertension,
  cardiorenal
carotid
  artery (hemispheric) (internal) G45.1
  body G90.01
  sinus G90.01
carpal tunnel G56.0-●
Cassidy (-Scholte) E34.0
cat-cry Q93.4
cat eye Q92.8
cauda equina G83.4
causalgia —*see* Causalgia
celiac K90.0
  artery compression I77.4
  axis I77.4
central pain G89.0
cerebellar
  hereditary G11.9
  stroke G46.4
cerebellomedullary malformation —*see* Spina
  bifida
cerebral
  artery
    anterior G46.1
    middle G46.0
    posterior G46.2
  gigantism E22.0
cervical (root) M53.1
  disc —*see* Disorder, disc, cervical, with
    neuritis
  fusion Q76.1
  posterior, sympathicus M53.0
  rib Q76.5
  sympathetic paralysis G90.2
cervicobrachial (diffuse) M53.1
cervicocranial M53.0
cervicodorsal outlet G54.2
cervicothoracic outlet G54.0
Céstan (-Raymond) I65.8
Charcot's (angina cruris) (intermittent
  claudication) I73.9

Syndrome *(Continued)*

Charcot-Weiss-Baker G90.09
CHARGE Q89.8
Chédiak-Higashi (-Steinbrinck) E70.330
chest wall R07.1
Chiari's (hepatic vein thrombosis) I82.0
Chilaiditi's Q43.3
child maltreatment —*see* Maltreatment, child
chondrocostal junction M94.0
chondroectodermal dysplasia Q77.6
chromosome 4 short arm deletion Q93.3
chromosome 5 short arm deletion Q93.4
chronic
  infantile neurological, cutaneous and
    articular (CINCA) M04.2
  pain G89.4
    personality F68.8
Clarke-Hadfield K86.89
Clerambault's automatism G93.89
Clouston's (hidrotic ectodermal dysplasia)
  Q82.4
clumsiness, clumsy child F82
cluster headache G44.009
  intractable G44.001
  not intractable G44.009
Coffin-Lowry Q89.8
cold injury (newborn) P80.0
combined immunity deficiency D81.9
compartment (deep) (posterior) (traumatic)
  T79.A0
  abdomen T79.A3
  lower extremity (hip, buttock, thigh, leg,
    foot, toes) T79.A2
  nontraumatic
    abdomen M79.A3
    lower extremity (hip, buttock, thigh, leg,
      foot, toes) M79.A2-●
    specified site NEC M79.A9
    upper extremity (shoulder, arm, forearm,
      wrist, hand, fingers) M79.A1-●
  postprocedural —*see* Syndrome
    compartment, nontraumatic
  specified site NEC T79.A9
  upper extremity (shoulder, arm, forearm,
    wrist, hand, fingers) T79.A1
complex regional pain —*see* Syndrome, pain,
  complex regional
compression T79.5
  anterior spinal —*see* Syndrome, anterior,
    spinal artery, compression
  cauda equina G83.4
  celiac artery I77.4
  vertebral artery M47.029
    cervical region M47.022
    occipito-atlanto-axial region M47.021
concussion F07.81
congenital
  affecting multiple systems NEC Q87.89
  central alveolar hypoventilation G47.35
  facial diplegia Q87.0
  muscular hypertrophy-cerebral Q87.89
  oculo-auriculovertebral Q87.0
  oculofacial diplegia (Moebius) Q87.0
  rubella (manifest) P35.0
congestion-fibrosis (pelvic), female N94.89
congestive dysmenorrhea N94.6
Conn's E26.01
connective tissue M35.9
  overlap NEC M35.1
conus medullaris G95.81
cord
  anterior G83.82
  posterior G83.83
coronary
  acute NEC I24.9
  insufficiency or intermediate I20.0
  slow flow I20.8
Costen's (complex) M26.69
costochondral junction M94.0
costoclavicular G54.0
costovertebral E22.0

▶ New   ⇒ Revised   ~~deleted~~ Deleted   ● Use Additional Character(s)

Syndrome *(Continued)*
  Cowden Q85.8
  craniovertebral M53.0
  Creutzfeldt-Jakob —*see* Creutzfeldt-Jakob
    disease or syndrome
  cri-du-chat Q93.4
  crib death R99
  cricopharyngeal —*see* Dysphagia
  croup J05.0
  CRPS I —*see* Syndrome, pain, complex
    regional I
  crush T79.5
  cubital tunnel —*see* Lesion, nerve, ulnar
  Curschmann (-Batten) (-Steinert) G71.11
  Cushing's E24.9
    alcohol-induced E24.4
    drug-induced E24.2
    due to
      alcohol
        drugs E24.2
        ectopic ACTH E24.3
        overproduction of pituitary ACTH
          E24.0
      overdose or wrong substance given
        or taken —*see* Table of Drugs and
        Chemicals, by drug, poisoning
    pituitary-dependent E24.0
    specified type NEC E24.8
  cryopyrin-associated periodic M04.2
  cryptophthalmos Q87.0
  cystic duct stump K91.5
  Dana-Putnam D51.0
  Danbolt (-Cross) (acrodermatitis
    enteropathica) E83.2
  Dandy-Walker Q03.1
    with spina bifida Q07.01
  Danlos' Q79.6
  defibrination —*see also* Fibrinolysis
    with
      antepartum hemorrhage —*see*
        Hemorrhage, antepartum, with
        coagulation defect
      intrapartum hemorrhage —*see*
        Hemorrhage, complicating,
        delivery
    newborn P60
    postpartum O72.3
  Degos' I77.8
  Déjérine-Roussy G89.0
  delayed sleep phase G47.21
  demyelinating G37.9
  dependence —*see* F10-F19 with fourth
    character .2
  depersonalization (-derealization) F48.1
  De Quervain E34.51
  de Toni-Fanconi (-Debré) E72.09
    with cystinosis E72.04
  diabetes mellitus-hypertension-nephrosis —
    see Diabetes, nephrosis
  diabetes mellitus in newborn infant P70.2
  diabetes-nephrosis —*see* Diabetes, nephrosis
  diabetic amyotrophy —*see* Diabetes,
    amyotrophy
  dialysis associated steal T82.898-●
  Diamond-Blackfan D61.01
  Diamond-Gardener D69.2
  DIC (diffuse or disseminated intravascular
    coagulopathy) D65
  di George's D82.1
  Dighton's Q78.0
  disequilibrium E87.8
  Döhle body-panmyelopathic D72.0
  dorsolateral medullary G46.4
  double athetosis G80.3
  Down (*see also* Down syndrome) Q90.9
  Dresbach's (elliptocytosis) D58.1
  Dressler's (postmyocardial infarction) I24.1
    postcardiotomy I97.0
  drug withdrawal, infant of dependent mother
    P96.1
  dry eye H04.12-●

Syndrome *(Continued)*
  due to abnormality
    chromosomal Q99.9
      sex
        female phenotype Q97.9
        male phenotype Q98.9
        specified NEC Q99.8
  dumping (postgastrectomy) K91.1
    nonsurgical K31.89
  Dupré's (meningism) R29.1
  dysmetabolic X E88.81
  dyspraxia, developmental F82
  Eagle-Barrett Q79.4
  Eaton-Lambert —*see* Syndrome,
    Lambert-Eaton
  Ebstein's Q22.5
  ectopic ACTH E24.3
  eczema-thrombocytopenia D82.0
  Eddowes' Q78.0
  effort (psychogenic) F45.8
  Ehlers-Danlos Q79.6
  Eisenmenger's I27.83
  Ekman's Q78.0
  electric feet E53.8
  Ellis-van Creveld Q77.6
  empty nest Z60.0
  endocrine-hypertensive E27.0
  entrapment —*see* Neuropathy,
    entrapment
  eosinophilia-myalgia M35.8
  epileptic —*see also* Epilepsy, by type
    absence G40.A09
      intractable G40.A19
        with status epilepticus G40.A11
        without status epilepticus G40.A19
      not intractable G40.A09
        with status epilepticus G40.A01
        without status epilepticus G40.A09
  Erdheim-Chester (ECD) E88.89
  Erdheim's E22.0
  erythrocyte fragmentation D59.4
  Evans D69.41
  exhaustion F48.8
  extrapyramidal G25.9
    specified NEC G25.89
  eye retraction —*see* Strabismus
  eyelid-malar-mandible Q87.0
  Faber's D50.9
  facial pain, paroxysmal G50.0
  Fallot's Q21.3
  familial cold autoinflammatory M04.2
  familial eczema-thrombocytopenia (Wiskott-
    Aldrich) D82.0
  Fanconi (-de Toni) (-Debré) E72.09
    with cystinosis E72.04
  Fanconi's (anemia) (congenital pancytopenia)
    D61.09
  fatigue
    chronic R53.82
    psychogenic F48.8
  faulty bowel habit K59.39
  Feil-Klippel (brevicollis) Q76.1
  Felty's —*see* Felty's syndrome
  fertile eunuch E23.0
  fetal
    alcohol (dysmorphic) Q86.0
    hydantoin Q86.1
  Fiedler's I40.1
  first arch Q87.0
  ⇒fish odor E72.89
  Fisher's G61.0
  Fitzhugh-Curtis
    due to
      Chlamydia trachomatis A74.81
      Neisseria gonorrhorea (gonococcal
        peritonitis) A54.85
  Fitz's —*see also* Pancreatitis, acute
    K85.80
  Flajani (-Basedow) E05.00
    with thyroid storm E05.01
  flatback —*see* Flatback syndrome

Syndrome *(Continued)*
  floppy
    baby P94.2
    iris (intraoeprative) (IFIS) H21.81
    mitral valve I34.1
  flush E34.0
  Foix-Alajouanine G95.19
  Fong's Q87.2
  ⇒food protein-induced enterocolitis (FPIES)
    K52.21
  foramen magnum G93.5
  Foster-Kennedy H47.14-●
  Foville's (peduncular) G46.3
  fragile X Q99.2
  Franceschetti Q75.4
  Frey's
    auriculotemporal G50.8
    hyperhidrosis L74.52
  Friderichsen-Waterhouse A39.1
  Froin's G95.89
  frontal lobe F07.0
  Fukuhara E88.49
  functional
    bowel K59.9
    prepubertal castrate E29.1
  Gaisböck's D75.1
  ganglion (basal ganglia brain) G25.9
    geniculi G51.1
  Gardner-Diamond D69.2
  gastroesophageal
    junction K22.0
    laceration-hemorrhage K22.6
  gastrojejunal loop obstruction K91.89
  Gee-Herter-Heubner K90.0
  Gelineau's G47.419
    with cataplexy G47.411
  genito-anorectal A55
  Gerstmann-Sträussler-Scheinker (GSS) A81.82
  Gianotti-Crosti L44.4
  giant platelet (Bernard-Soulier) D69.1
  Gilles de la Tourette's F95.2
  goiter-deafness E07.1
  Goldberg Q89.8
  Goldberg-Maxwell E34.51
  Good's D83.8
  Gopalan' (burning feet) E53.8
  Gorlin's Q87.89
  Gougerot-Blum L81.7
  Gouley's I31.1
  Gower's R55
  gray or grey (newborn) P93.0
    platelet D69.1
  Gubler-Millard G46.3
  Guillain-Barré (-Strohl) G61.0
  gustatory sweating G50.8
  Hadfield-Clarke K86.89
  hair tourniquet —*see* Constriction, external,
    by site
  Hamman's J98.19
  hand-foot L27.1
  hand-shoulder G90.8
  hantavirus (cardio)-pulmonary (HPS) (HCPS)
    B33.4
  ⇒happy puppet Q93.51
  Harada's H30.81-●
  Hayem-Faber D50.9
  headache NEC G44.89
    complicated NEC G44.59
  Heberden's I20.8
  Hedinger's E34.0
  Hegglin's D72.0
  HELLP (hemolysis, elevated liver enzymes
    and low platelet count) O14.2-●
    complicating
      childbirth O14.24
        puerperium O14.25
  hemolytic-uremic D59.3
  hemophagocytic, infection-associated D76.2
  Henoch-Schönlein D69.0
  hepatic flexure K59.8
  hepatopulmonary K76.81

Syndrome *(Continued)*
hepatorenal K76.7
  following delivery O90.4
  postoperative or postprocedural K91.83
  postpartum, puerperal O90.4
hepatourologic K76.7
Herter (-Gee) (nontropical sprue) K90.0
Heubner-Herter K90.0
Heyd's K76.7
Hilger's G90.09
histamine-like (fish poisoning) —*see*
      Poisoning, fish
histiocytic D76.3
histiocytosis NEC D76.3
HIV infection, acute B20
Hoffmann-Werdnig G12.0
Hollander-Simons E88.1
Hoppe-Goldflam G70.00
  with exacerbation (acute) G70.01
  in crisis G70.01
Horner's G90.2
hungry bone E83.81
hunterian glossitis D51.0
Hutchinson's triad A50.53
hyperabduction G54.0
hyperammonemia-hyperornithinemia-
      homocitrullinemia E72.4
hypereosinophilic (idiopathic) D72.1
hyperimmunoglobulin D M04.1
hyperimmunoglobulin E (IgE) D82.4
hyperkalemic E87.5
hyperkinetic —*see* Hyperkinesia
hypermobility M35.7
hypernatremia E87.0
hyperosmolarity E87.0
hyperperfusion G97.82
hypersplenic D73.1
hypertransfusion, newborn P61.1
hyperventilation F45.8
hyperviscosity (of serum)
  polycythemic D75.1
  sclerothymic D58.8
hypoglycemic (familial) (neonatal) E16.2
hypokalemic E87.6
hyponatremic E87.1
hypopituitarism E23.0
hypoplastic left-heart Q23.4
hypopotassemia E87.6
hyposmolality E87.1
hypotension, maternal O26.5- •
hypothenar hammer I73.89
hypoventilation, obesity (OHS) E66.2
ICF (intravascular coagulation-fibrinolysis)
      D65
idiopathic
  cardiorespiratory distress, newborn P22.0
  nephrotic (infantile) N04.9
iliotibial band M76.3- •
immobility, immobilization (paraplegic)
      M62.3
immune reconstitution D89.3
immune reconstitution inflammatory [IRIS]
      D89.3
immunity deficiency, combined D81.9
immunodeficiency
  acquired —*see* Human, immunodeficiency
      virus (HIV) disease
  combined D81.9
impending coronary I20.0
impingement, shoulder M75.4- •
inappropriate secretion of antidiuretic
      hormone E22.2
infant
  gestational diabetes P70.0
  of diabetic mother P70.1
infantilism (pituitary) E23.0
inferior vena cava I87.1
inspissated bile (newborn) P59.1
institutional (childhood) F94.2
insufficient sleep F51.12
intermediate coronary (artery) I20.0

Syndrome *(Continued)*
interspinous ligament —*see* Spondylopathy,
      specified NEC
intestinal
  carcinoid E34.0
  knot K56.2
intravascular coagulation-fibrinolysis (ICF)
      D65
iodine-deficiency, congenital E00.9
  type
    mixed E00.2
    myxedematous E00.1
    neurological E00.0
IRDS (idiopathic respiratory distress,
      newborn) P22.0
irritable
  bowel K58.9
    with
      constipation K58.1
      diarrhea K58.0
    mixed K58.2
    psychogenic F45.8
    specified NEC K58.8
  heart (psychogenic) F45.8
  weakness F48.8
ischemic
  bowel (transient) K55.9
    chronic K55.1
    due to mesenteric artery insufficiency
        K55.1
  steal T82.898
IVC (intravascular coagulopathy) D65
Ivemark's Q89.01
Jaccoud's —*see* Arthropathy, postrheumatic,
      chronic
Jackson's G83.89
Jakob-Creutzfeldt —*see* Creutzfeldt-Jakob
      disease or syndrome
jaw-winking Q07.8
Jervell-Lange-Nielsen I45.81
jet lag G47.25
Job's D71
Joseph-Diamond-Blackfan D61.01
jugular foramen G52.7
Kabuki Q89.8
Kanner's (autism) F84.0
Kartagener's Q89.3
Kelly's D50.1
Kimmelstiel-Wilson —*see* Diabetes, specified
      type, with Kimmelstiel-Wilson disease
Klein (e)-Levine G47.13
Klippel-Feil (brevicollis) Q76.1
Köhler-Pellegrini-Steida —*see* Bursitis, tibial
      collateral
König's K59.8
Korsakoff (-Wernicke) (nonalcoholic) F04
  alcoholic F10.26
Kostmann's D70.0
Krabbe's congenital muscle hypoplasia Q79.8
labyrinthine —*see* subcategory H83.2
lacunar NEC G46.7
Lambert-Eaton G70.80
  in
    neoplastic disease G73.1
    specified disease NEC G70.81
Landau-Kleffner —*see* Epilepsy, specified NEC
Larsen's Q74.8
lateral
  cutaneous nerve of thigh G57.1- •
  medullary G46.4
Launois' E22.0
lazy
  leukocyte D70.8
  posture M62.3
Lemiere I80.8
Lennox-Gastaut G40.812
  intractable G40.814
    with status epilepticus G40.813
    without status epilepticus G40.814
  not intractable G40.812
    with status epilepticus G40.811
    without status epilepticus G40.812

Syndrome *(Continued)*
lenticular, progressive E83.01
Leopold-Levi's E05.90
Lev's I44.2
Li-Fraumeni Z15.01
Lichtheim's D51.0
Lightwood's N25.89
Lignac (de Toni) (-Fanconi) (-Debré) E72.09
  with cystinosis E72.04
Likoff's I20.8
limbic epilepsy personality F07.0
liver-kidney K76.7
lobotomy F07.0
Loffler's J82
long arm 18 or 21 deletion Q93.89
long QT I45.81
Louis-Barré G11.3
low
  atmospheric pressure T70.29
  back M54.5
  output (cardiac) I50.9
lower radicular, newborn (birth injury) P14.8
Luetscher's (dehydration) E86.0
Lupus anticoagulant D68.62
Lutembacher's Q21.1
macrophage activation D76.1
  due to infection D76.2
magnesium-deficiency R29.0
Majeed M04.8
Mal de Debarquement R42
malabsorption K90.9
  postsurgical K91.2
malformation, congenital, due to
  alcohol Q86.0
  exogenous cause NEC Q86.8
  hydantoin Q86.1
  warfarin Q86.2
malignant
  carcinoid E34.0
  neuroleptic G21.0
Mallory-Weiss K22.6
mandibulofacial dysostosis Q75.4
manic-depressive —*see* Disorder, bipolar
maple-syrup-urine E71.0
Marable's I77.4
Marfan's Q87.40
  with
    cardiovascular manifestations Q87.418
      aortic dilation Q87.410
    ocular manifestations Q87.42
    skeletal manifestations Q87.43
Marie's (acromegaly) E22.0
mast cell activation —*see* Activation, mast
      cell
maternal hypotension —*see* Syndrome,
      hypotension, maternal
May (-Hegglin) D72.0
McArdle (-Schmidt) (-Pearson) E74.04
McQuarrie's E16.2
meconium plug (newborn) P76.0
median arcuate ligament I77.4
Meekeren-Ehlers-Danlos Q79.6
megavitamin-B6 E67.2
Meige G24.4
MELAS E88.41
Mendelson's O74.0
MERRF (myoclonic epilepsy associated with
      ragged-red fibers) E88.42
mesenteric
  artery (superior) K55.1
  vascular insufficiency K55.1
metabolic E88.81
metastatic carcinoid E34.0
micrognathia-glossoptosis Q87.0
midbrain NEC G93.89
middle lobe (lung) J98.19
middle radicular G54.0
migraine —*see also* Migraine G43.909- •
Mikulicz' K11.8
milk-alkali E83.52
Millard-Gubler G46.3

▶ New   ⇒ Revised   ~~deleted~~ Deleted   • Use Additional Character(s)

Syndrome *(Continued)*
  Miller-Dieker Q93.88
  Miller-Fisher G61.0
  Minkowski-Chauffard D58.0
  Mirizzi's K83.1
  MNGIE (Mitochondrial Neurogastrointestinal Encephalopathy) E88.49
  Möbius, ophthalmoplegic migraine —*see* Migraine, ophthalmoplegic
  monofixation H50.42
  Morel-Moore M85.2
  Morel-Morgagni M85.2
  Morgagni (-Morel) (-Stewart) M85.2
  Morgagni-Adams-Stokes I45.9
  Mounier-Kuhn Q32.4
    with bronchiectasis J47.9
      with
        exacerbation (acute) J47.1
        lower respiratory infection J47.0
    acquired J98.09
      with bronchiectasis J47.9
        with
          exacerbation (acute) J47.1
          lower respiratory infection J47.0
  Muckle-Wells M04.2
  mucocutaneous lymph node (acute febrile) (MCLS) M30.3
  multiple endocrine neoplasia (MEN) —*see* Neoplasia, endocrine, multiple (MEN}
  multiple operations —*see* Disorder, factitious
  myasthenic G70.9
    in
      diabetes mellitus —*see* Diabetes, amyotrophy
      endocrine disease NEC E34.9 *[G73.3]*
      neoplastic disease —*see also* Neoplasm D49.9 *[G73.3]*
      thyrotoxicosis (hyperthyroidism) E05.90 *[G73.3]*
        with thyroid storm E05.91 *[G73.3]*
  myelodysplastic D46.9
    with
      5q deletion D46.C
      isolated del (5q) chromosomal abnormality D46.C
    lesions, low grade D46.20
    specified NEC D46.Z
  myelopathic pain G89.0
  myeloproliferative (chronic) D47.1
  myofascial pain M79.18
  Naffziger's G54.0
  nail patella Q87.2
  NARP (Neuropathy, Ataxia and Retinitis pigmentosa) E88.49
  neonatal abstinence P96.1
  nephritic —*see also* Nephritis
    with edema —*see* Nephrosis
    acute N00.9
    chronic N03.9
    rapidly progressive N01.9
  nephrotic (congenital) —*see also* Nephrosis N04.9
    with
      dense deposit disease N04.6
      diffuse
        crescentic glomerulonephritis N04.7
        endocapillary proliferative glomerulonephritis N04.4
        membranous glomerulonephritis N04.2
        mesangial proliferative glomerulonephritis N04.3
        mesangiocapillary glomerulonephritis N04.5
      focal and segmental glomerular lesions N04.1
      minor glomerular abnormality N04.0
      specified morphological changes NEC N04.8
    diabetic —*see* Diabetes, nephrosis

Syndrome *(Continued)*
  neurologic neglect R41.4
  Nezelof's D81.4
  Nonne-Milroy-Meige Q82.0
  Nothnagel's vasomotor acroparesthesia I73.89
  obesity hypoventilation (OHS) E66.2
  oculomotor H51.9
  ophthalmoplegia-cerebellar ataxia —*see* Strabismus, paralytic, third nerve
  oral allergy T78.1
  oral-facial-digital Q87.0
  organic
    affective F06.30
    amnesic (not alcohol- or drug-induced) F04
    brain F09
    depressive F06.31
    hallucinosis F06.0
    personality F07.0
  Ormond's N13.5
  oro-facial-digital Q87.0
  os trigonum Q68.8
  Osler-Weber-Rendu I78.0
  osteoporosis-osteomalacia M83.8
  Osterreicher-Turner Q87.2
  otolith —*see* subcategory H81.8
  oto-palatal-digital Q87.0
  outlet (thoracic) G54.0
  ovary
    polycystic E28.2
    resistant E28.39
    sclerocystic E28.2
  Owren's D68.2
  Paget-Schroetter I82.890
  pain —*see also* Pain
    complex regional I G90.50
      lower limb G90.52-●
      specified site NEC G90.59
      upper limb G90.51-●
    complex regional II —*see* Causalgia
  painful
    bruising D69.2
    feet E53.8
    prostate N42.81
  paralysis agitans —*see* Parkinsonism
  paralytic G83.9
    specified NEC G83.89
  Parinaud's H51.0
  parkinsonian —*see* Parkinsonism
  Parkinson's —*see* Parkinsonism
  paroxysmal facial pain G50.0
  Parry's E05.00
    with thyroid storm E05.01
  Parsonage (-Aldren)-Turner G54.5
  patella clunk M25.86-●
  Paterson (-Brown) (-Kelly) D50.1
  pectoral girdle I77.89
  pectoralis minor I77.89
  pediatric autoimmune neuropsychiatric disorders associated with streptococcal infections (PANDAS) D89.89
  Pelger-Huet D72.0
  pellagra-cerebellar ataxia-renal aminoaciduria E72.02
  pellagroid E52
  Pellegrini-Stieda —*see* Bursitis, tibial collateral
  pelvic congestion-fibrosis, female N94.89
  penta X Q97.1
  peptic ulcer —*see* Ulcer, peptic
  perabduction I77.89
  periodic fever M04.1
  periodic fever, aphthous stomatitis, pharyngitis, and adenopathy [PFAPA] M04.8
  periodic headache, in adults and children — *see* Headache, periodic syndromes in adults and children
  periurethral fibrosis N13.5
  phantom limb (without pain) G54.7
    with pain G54.6
  pharyngeal pouch D82.1
  Pick's —*see* Disease, Pick's
  Pickwickian E66.2

Syndrome *(Continued)*
  PIE (pulmonary infiltration with eosinophilia) J82
  pigmentary pallidal degeneration (progressive) G23.0
  pineal E34.8
  pituitary E22.0
  placental transfusion —*see* Pregnancy, complicated by, placental transfusion syndromes
  plantar fascia M72.2
  plateau iris (post-iridectomy) (postprocedural) H21.82
  Plummer-Vinson D50.1
  pluricarential of infancy E40
  plurideficiency E40
  pluriglandular (compensatory) E31.8
    autoimmune E31.0
  pneumatic hammer T75.21
  polyangiitis overlap M30.8
  polycarential of infancy E40
  polyglandular E31.8
    autoimmune E31.0
  polysplenia Q89.09
  pontine NEC G93.89
  popliteal
    artery entrapment I77.89
    web Q87.89
  postcardiac injury
    postcardiotomy I97.0
    postmyocardial infarction I24.1
  postcardiotomy I97.0
  post chemoembolization — code to associated conditions
  postcholecystectomy K91.5
  postcommissurotomy I97.0
  postconcussional F07.81
  postcontusional F07.81
  postencephalitic F07.89
  posterior
    cervical sympathetic M53.0
    cord G83.83
    fossa compression G93.5
    reversible encephalopathy (PRES) I67.83
  postgastrectomy (dumping) K91.1
  postgastric surgery K91.1
  postinfarction I24.1
  postlaminectomy NEC M96.1
  postleukotomy F07.0
  postmastectomy lymphedema I97.2
  postmyocardial infarction I24.1
  postoperative NEC T81.9
    blind loop K90.2
  postpartum panhypopituitary (Sheehan) E23.0
  postpolio (myelitic) G14
  postthrombotic I87.009
    with
      inflammation I87.02-●
        with ulcer I87.03-●
      specified complication NEC I87.09-●
      ulcer I87.01-●
        with inflammation I87.03-●
    asymptomatic I87.00-●
  postvagotomy K91.1
  postvalvulotomy I97.0
  postviral NEC G93.3
    fatigue G93.3
  Potain's K31.0
  potassium intoxication E87.5
  precerebral artery (multiple) (bilateral) G45.2
  preinfarction I20.0
  preleukemic D46.9
  premature senility E34.8
  premenstrual dysphoric F32.89
  premenstrual tension N94.3
  Prinzmetal-Massumi R07.1
  prune belly Q79.4
  pseudocarpal tunnel (sublimis) —*see* Syndrome, carpal tunnel

Syndrome *(Continued)*
  pseudoparalytica G70.00
    with exacerbation (acute) G70.01
    in crisis G70.01
  pseudo-Turner's Q87.1
  psycho-organic (nonpsychotic severity) F07.9
    acute or subacute F05
    depressive type F06.31
    hallucinatory type F06.0
    nonpsychotic severity F07.0
    specified NEC F07.89
  pulmonary
    arteriosclerosis I27.0
    dysmaturity (Wilson-Mikity) P27.0
    hypoperfusion (idiopathic) P22.0
    renal (hemorrhagic) (Goodpasture's) M31.0
  pure
    motor lacunar G46.5
    sensory lacunar G46.6
  Putnam-Dana D51.0
  pyogenic arthritis, pyoderma gangrenosum, and acne [PAPA] M04.8
  pyramidopallidonigral G20
  pyriformis —*see* Lesion, nerve, sciatic
  QT interval prolongation I45.81
  radicular NEC —*see* Radiculopathy
    upper limbs, newborn (birth injury) P14.3
  rapid time-zone change G47.25
  Rasmussen G04.81
  Raymond (-Céstan) I65.8
  Raynaud's I73.00
    with gangrene I73.01
  RDS (respiratory distress syndrome, newborn) P22.0
  reactive airways dysfunction J68.3
  Refsum's G60.1
  Reifenstein E34.52
  renal glomerulohyalinosis-diabetic —*see* Diabetes, nephrosis
  Rendu-Osler-Weber I78.0
  residual ovary N99.83
  resistant ovary E28.39
  respiratory
    distress
      acute J80
        adult J80
        child J80
        idiopathic J84.114
        newborn (idiopathic) (type I) P22.0
          type II P22.1
  restless legs G25.81
  retinoblastoma (familial) C69.2
  retroperitoneal fibrosis N13.5
  retroviral seroconversion (acute) Z21
  Reye's G93.7
  Richter —*see* Leukemia, chronic lymphocytic, B-cell type
  Ridley's I50.1
  right
    heart, hypoplastic Q22.6
    ventricular obstruction —*see* Failure, heart, congestive
  Romano-Ward (prolonged QT interval) I45.81
  rotator cuff, shoulder —*see also* Tear, rotator cuff M75.10-●
  Rotes Quérol —*see* Hyperostosis, ankylosing
  Roth —*see* Meralgia paresthetica
  rubella (congenital) P35.0
  Ruvalcaba-Myhre-Smith E71.440
  Rytand-Lipsitch I44.2
  salt
    depletion E87.1
      due to heat NEC T67.8
        causing heat exhaustion or prostration T67.4
    low E87.1
  salt-losing N28.89
  Scaglietti-Dagnini E22.0
  scalenus anticus (anterior) G54.0
  scapulocostal —*see* Mononeuropathy, upper limb, specified site NEC

Syndrome *(Continued)*
  scapuloperoneal G71.09
  schizophrenic, of childhood NEC F84.5
  Schnitzler D47.2
  Scholte's E34.0
  Schroeder's E27.0
  Schüller-Christian C96.5
  Schwachman's —*see* Syndrome, Shwachman's
  Schwartz (-Jampel) G71.13
  Schwartz-Bartter E22.2
  scimitar Q26.8
  sclerocystic ovary E28.2
  Seitelberger's G31.89
  septicemic adrenal hemorrhage A39.1
  seroconversion, retroviral (acute) Z21
  serous meningitis G93.2
  severe acute respiratory (SARS) J12.81
  shaken infant T74.4
  shock (traumatic) T79.4
    kidney N17.0
      following crush injury T79.5
    toxic A48.3
  shock-lung J80
  Shone's — code to specific anomalies
  short
    bowel K91.2
    rib Q77.2
  shoulder-hand —*see* Algoneurodystrophy
  Shwachman's D70.4
  sicca —*see* Sicca syndrome
  sick
    cell E87.1
    sinus I49.5
  sick-euthyroid E07.81
  sideropenic D50.1
  Siemens' ectodermal dysplasia Q82.4
  Silfversköld's Q78.9
  Simons' E88.1
  sinus tarsi M25.57-●
  sinusitis-bronchiectasis-situs inversus Q89.3
  Sipple's E31.22
  sirenomelia Q87.2
  Slocumb's E27.0
  slow flow, coronary I20.8
  Sluder's G44.89
  Smith-Magenis Q93.88
  Sneddon-Wilkinson L13.1
  Sotos' Q87.3
  South African cardiomyopathy I42.8
  spasmodic
    upward movement, eyes H51.8
    winking F95.8
  Spen's I45.9
  splenic
    agenesis Q89.01
    flexure K59.8
    neutropenia D73.81
  Spurway's Q78.0
  staphylococcal scalded skin L00
  steal
    arteriovenous T82.898-●
    ischemic T82.898-●
    subclavian G45.8
  Stein-Leventhal E28.2
  Stein's E28.2
  Stevens-Johnson syndrome L51.1
    toxic epidermal necrolysis overlap L51.3
  Stewart-Morel M85.2
  Stickler Q89.8
  stiff baby Q89.8
  stiff man G25.82
  Still-Felty —*see* Felty's syndrome
  Stokes (-Adams) I45.9
  stone heart I50.1
  straight back, congenital Q76.49
  subclavian steal G45.8
  subcoracoid-pectoralis minor G54.0
  subcostal nerve compression I77.89
  subphrenic interposition Q43.3

Syndrome *(Continued)*
  superior
    cerebellar artery I63.89
      mesenteric artery K55.1
      semi-circular canal dehiscence H83.8X-●
    vena cava I87.1
  supine hypotensive (maternal) —*see* Syndrome, hypotension, maternal
  suprarenal cortical E27.0
  supraspinatus —*see also* Tear, rotator cuff M75.10-●
  Susac G93.49
  swallowed blood P78.2
  sweat retention L74.0
  Swyer Q99.1
  Symond's G93.2
  sympathetic
    cervical paralysis G90.2
    pelvic, female N94.89
  systemic inflammatory response (SIRS), of non-infectious origin (without organ dysfunction) R65.10
    with acute organ dysfunction R65.11
  tachycardia-bradycardia I49.5
  takotsubo I51.81
  TAR (thrombocytopenia with absent radius) Q87.2
  tarsal tunnel G57.5-●
  teething K00.7
  tegmental G93.89
  telangiectasic-pigmentation-cataract Q82.8
  temporal pyramidal apex —*see* Otitis, media, suppurative, acute
  temporomandibular joint-pain-dysfunction M26.62-●
  Terry's —*see also* Myopia, degenerative H44.2-●
  testicular feminization —*see also* Syndrome, androgen insensitivity E34.51
  thalamic pain (hyperesthetic) G89.0
  thoracic outlet (compression) G54.0
  Thorson-Björck E34.0
  thrombocytopenia with absent radius (TAR) Q87.2
  thyroid-adrenocortical insufficiency E31.0
  tibial
    anterior M76.81-●
    posterior M76.82-●
  Tietze's M94.0
  time-zone (rapid) G47.25
  Toni-Fanconi E72.09
    with cystinosis E72.04
  Touraine's Q79.8
  tourniquet —*see* Constriction, external, by site
  toxic shock A48.3
  transient left ventricular apical ballooning I51.81
  traumatic vasospastic T75.22
  Treacher Collins Q75.4
  triple X, female Q97.0
  trisomy Q92.9
    13 Q91.7
      meiotic nondisjunction Q91.4
      mitotic nondisjunction Q91.5
      mosaicism Q91.5
      translocation Q91.6
    18 Q91.3
      meiotic nondisjunction Q91.0
      mitotic nondisjunction Q91.1
      mosaicism Q91.1
      translocation Q91.2
    20 (q)(p) Q92.8
    21 Q90.9
      meiotic nondisjunction Q90.0
      mitotic nondisjunction Q90.1
      mosaicism Q90.1
      translocation Q90.2
    22 Q92.8
  tropical wet feet T69.0-●
  Trousseau's I82.1

▶ New   ⇒ Revised   ~~deleted~~ Deleted   ● Use Additional Character(s)

Syndrome *(Continued)*
    tumor lysis (following antineoplastic chemotherapy) (spontaneous) NEC E88.3
    tumor necrosis factor receptor associated periodic (TRAPS) M04.1
    Twiddler's (due to)
        automatic implantable defibrillator T82.198
        cardiac pacemaker T82.198
    Unverricht (-Lundborg) —*see* Epilepsy, generalized, idiopathic
    upward gaze H51.8
    uremia, chronic —*see also* Disease, kidney, chronic N18.9
    urethral N34.3
    urethro-oculo-articular —*see* Reiter's disease
    urohepatic K76.7
    vago-hypoglossal G52.7
    van Buchem's M85.2
    van der Hoeve's Q78.0
    vascular NEC in cerebrovascular disease G46.8
    vasoconstriction, reversible cerebrovascular I67.841
    vasomotor I73.9
    vasospastic (traumatic) T75.22
    vasovagal R55
    VATER Q87.2
    velo-cardio-facial Q93.81
    vena cava (inferior) (superior) (obstruction) I87.1
    vertebral
        artery G45.0
            compression —*see* Syndrome, anterior, spinal artery, compression
        steal G45.0
    vertebro-basilar artery G45.0
    vertebrogenic (pain) M54.89
    vertiginous —*see* Disorder, vestibular function
    Vinson-Plummer D50.1
    virus B34.9
    visceral larva migrans B83.0
    visual disorientation H53.8
    vitamin B6 deficiency E53.1
    vitreal corneal H59.01-●
    vitreous (touch) H59.01-●
    Vogt-Koyanagi H20.82-●
    Volkmann's T79.6
    von Schroetter's I82.890
    von Willebrand (-Jürgen) D68.0
    Waldenström-Kjellberg D50.1
    Wallenberg's G46.3
    water retention E87.79
    Waterhouse (-Friderichsen) A39.1
    Weber-Gubler G46.3
    Weber-Leyden G46.3
    Weber's G46.3
    Wegener's M31.30
        with
            kidney involvement M31.31
            lung involvement M31.30
                with kidney involvement M31.31
    Weingarten's (tropical eosinophilia) J82
    Weiss-Baker G90.09
    Werdnig-Hoffman G12.0
    Werner's E31.21
    Werner's E34.8
    Wernicke-Korsakoff (nonalcoholic) F04
        alcoholic F10.26
    West's —*see* Epilepsy, spasms
    Westphal-Strümpell E83.01
    wet
        feet (maceration) (tropical) T69.0-●
        lung, newborn P22.1
    whiplash S13.4
    whistling face Q87.0
    Wilkie's K55.1
    Wilkinson-Sneddon L13.1
    Willebrand (-Jürgens) D68.0

Syndrome *(Continued)*
    ▶Williams Q93.82
    Wilson's (hepatolenticular degeneration) E83.01
    Wiskott-Aldrich D82.0
    withdrawal —*see* Withdrawal, state
        drug
            infant of dependent mother P96.1
            therapeutic use, newborn P96.2
    Woakes' (ethmoiditis) J33.1
    Wright's (hyperabduction) G54.0
    X I20.9
    XXXX Q97.1
    XXXXX Q97.1
    XXXXY Q98.1
    XXY Q98.0
    ▶Yao M04.8
    yellow nail L60.5
    Zahorsky's B08.5
    Zellweger syndrome E71.510
    Zellweger-like syndrome E71.541
Synechia (anterior) (iris) (posterior) (pupil) —*see also* Adhesions, iris
    intra-uterine (traumatic) N85.6
Synesthesia R20.8
Syngamiasis, syngamosis B83.3
Synodontia K00.2
Synorchidism, synorchism Q55.1
Synostosis (congenital) Q78.8
    astragalo-scaphoid Q74.2
    radioulnar Q74.0
Synovial sarcoma —*see* Neoplasm, connective tissue, malignant
Synovioma (malignant) —*see also* Neoplasm, connective tissue, malignant
    benign —*see* Neoplasm, connective tissue, benign
Synoviosarcoma —*see* Neoplasm, connective tissue, malignant
Synovitis —*see also* Tenosynovitis M65.9
    crepitant
        hand M70.0-●
        wrist M70.03-●
    gonococcal A54.49
    gouty —*see* Gout
    in (due to)
        crystals M65.8-●
        gonorrhea A54.49
        syphilis (late) A52.78
        use, overuse, pressure —*see* Disorder, soft tissue, due to use
    infective NEC —*see* Tenosynovitis, infective NEC
    specified NEC —*see* Tenosynovitis, specified type NEC
    syphilitic A52.78
        congenital (early) A50.02
    toxic —*see* Synovitis, transient
    transient M67.3-●
        ankle M67.37-●
        elbow M67.32-●
        foot joint M67.37-●
        hand joint M67.34-●
        hip M67.35-●
        knee M67.36-●
        multiple site M67.39
        pelvic region M67.35-●
        shoulder M67.31-●
        specified joint NEC M67.38
        wrist M67.33-●
    traumatic, current —*see* Sprain
    tuberculous —*see* Tuberculosis, synovitis
    villonodular (pigmented) M12.2-●
        ankle M12.27-●
        elbow M12.22-●
        foot joint M12.27-●
        hand joint M12.24-●
        hip M12.25-●
        knee M12.26-●
        multiple site M12.29
        pelvic region M12.25-●
        shoulder M12.21-●
        specified joint NEC M12.28

Synovitis *(Continued)*
    villonodular (pigmented) *(Continued)*
        vertebrae M12.28
        wrist M12.23-●
Syphilid A51.39
    congenital A50.06
    newborn A50.06
    tubercular (late) A52.79
Syphilis, syphilitic (acquired) A53.9
    abdomen (late) A52.79
    acoustic nerve A52.15
    adenopathy (secondary) A51.49
    adrenal (gland) (with cortical hypofunction) A52.79
    age under 2 years NOS —*see also* Syphilis, congenital, early
        acquired A51.9
    alopecia (secondary) A51.32
    anemia (late) A52.79 [D63.8]
    aneurysm (aorta) (ruptured) A52.01
        central nervous system A52.05
        congenital A50.54 [I79.0]
    anus (late) A52.74
        primary A51.1
        secondary A51.39
    aorta (arch) (abdominal) (thoracic) A52.02
        aneurysm A52.01
    aortic (insufficiency) (regurgitation) (stenosis) A52.03
        aneurysm A52.01
    arachnoid (adhesive) (cerebral) (spinal) A52.13
    asymptomatic —*see* Syphilis, latent
    ataxia (locomotor) A52.11
    atrophoderma maculatum A51.39
    auricular fibrillation A52.06
    bladder (late) A52.76
    bone A52.77
        secondary A51.46
    brain A52.17
    breast (late) A52.79
    bronchus (late) A52.72
    bubo (primary) A51.0
    bulbar palsy A52.19
    bursa (late) A52.78
    cardiac decompensation A52.06
    cardiovascular A52.00
    central nervous system (late) (recurrent) (relapse) (tertiary) A52.3
        with
            ataxia A52.11
            general paralysis A52.17
                juvenile A50.45
            paresis (general) A52.17
                juvenile A50.45
            tabes (dorsalis) A52.11
                juvenile A50.45
            taboparesis A52.17
                juvenile A50.45
        aneurysm A52.05
        congenital A50.40
        juvenile A50.40
        remission in (sustained) A52.3
        serology doubtful, negative, or positive A52.3
        specified nature or site NEC A52.19
        vascular A52.05
    cerebral A52.17
        meningovascular A52.13
        nerves (multiple palsies) A52.15
        sclerosis A52.17
        thrombosis A52.05
    cerebrospinal (tabetic type) A52.12
    cerebrovascular A52.05
    cervix (late) A52.76
    chancre (multiple) A51.0
        extragenital A51.2
        Rollet's A51.0
    Charcot's joint A52.16
    chorioretinitis A51.43
        congenital A50.01
        late A52.71
        prenatal A50.01

S

Syphilis, syphilitic *(Continued)*
  choroiditis —*see* Syphilitic chorioretinitis
  choroidoretinitis —*see* Syphilitic
      chorioretinitis
  ciliary body (secondary) A51.43
    late A52.71
  colon (late) A52.74
  combined spinal sclerosis A52.11
  condyloma (latum) A51.31
  congenital A50.9
    with
      paresis (general) A50.45
      tabes (dorsalis) A50.45
      taboparesis A50.45
    chorioretinitis, choroiditis A50.01 [H32]
    early, or less than 2 years after birth NEC
        A50.2
      with manifestations —*see* Syphilis,
          congenital, early, symptomatic
      latent (without manifestations) A50.1
        negative spinal fluid test A50.1
        serology positive A50.1
      symptomatic A50.09
        cutaneous A50.06
        mucocutaneous A50.07
        oculopathy A50.01
        osteochondropathy A50.02
        pharyngitis A50.03
        pneumonia A50.04
        rhinitis A50.05
        visceral A50.08
    interstitial keratitis A50.31
    juvenile neurosyphilis A50.45
    late, or 2 years or more after birth NEC
        A50.7
      chorioretinitis, choroiditis A50.32
      interstitial keratitis A50.31
      juvenile neurosyphilis A50.45
      latent (without manifestations) A50.6
        negative spinal fluid test A50.6
        serology positive A50.6
      symptomatic or with manifestations
          NEC A50.59
        arthropathy A50.55
        cardiovascular A50.54
        Clutton's joints A50.51
        Hutchinson's teeth A50.52
        Hutchinson's triad A50.53
        osteochondropathy A50.56
        saddle nose A50.57
  conjugal A53.9
    tabes A52.11
  conjunctiva (late) A52.71
  contact Z20.2
  cord bladder A52.19
  cornea, late A52.71
  coronary (artery) (sclerosis) A52.06
  coryza, congenital A50.05
  cranial nerve A52.15
    multiple palsies A52.15
  cutaneous —*see* Syphilis, skin
  dacryocystitis (late) A52.71
  degeneration, spinal cord A52.12
  dementia paralytica A52.17
    juvenilis A50.45
  destruction of bone A52.77
  dilatation, aorta A52.01
  due to blood transfusion A53.9
  dura mater A52.13
  ear A52.79
    inner A52.79
      nerve (eighth) A52.15
      neurorecurrence A52.15
  early A51.9
    cardiovascular A52.00
    central nervous system A52.3
    latent (without manifestations) (less than 2
        years after infection) A51.5
      negative spinal fluid test A51.5
      serological relapse after treatment A51.5
      serology positive A51.5

Syphilis, syphilitic *(Continued)*
  early *(Continued)*
    relapse (treated, untreated) A51.9
    skin A51.39
    symptomatic A51.9
      extragenital chancre A51.2
      primary, except extragenital chancre
          A51.0
      secondary —*see also* Syphilis, secondary
          A51.39
        relapse (treated, untreated) A51.49
      ulcer A51.39
  eighth nerve (neuritis) A52.15
  endemic A65
  endocarditis A52.03
    aortic A52.03
    pulmonary A52.03
  epididymis (late) A52.76
  epiglottis (late) A52.73
  epiphysitis (congenital) (early) A50.02
  episcleritis (late) A52.71
  esophagus A52.79
  eustachian tube A52.73
  exposure to Z20.2
  eye A52.71
  eyelid (late) (with gumma) A52.71
  fallopian tube (late) A52.76
  fracture A52.77
  gallbladder (late) A52.74
  gastric (polyposis) (late) A52.74
  general A53.9
    paralysis A52.17
      juvenile A50.45
  genital (primary) A51.0
  glaucoma A52.71
  gumma NEC A52.79
    cardiovascular system A52.00
    central nervous system A52.3
    congenital A50.59
  heart (block) (decompensation) (disease)
      (failure) A52.06 [I52]
    valve NEC A52.03
  hemianesthesia A52.19
  hemianopsia A52.71
  hemiparesis A52.17
  hemiplegia A52.17
  hepatic artery A52.09
  hepatis A52.74
  hepatomegaly, congenital A50.08
  hereditaria tarda —*see* Syphilis, congenital,
      late
  hereditary —*see* Syphilis, congenital
  Hutchinson's teeth A50.52
  hyalitis A52.71
  inactive —*see* Syphilis, latent
  infantum —*see* Syphilis, congenital
  inherited —*see* Syphilis, congenital
  internal ear A52.79
  intestine (late) A52.74
  iris, iritis (secondary) A51.43
    late A52.71
  joint (late) A52.77
  keratitis (congenital) (interstitial) (late) A50.31
  kidney (late) A52.75
  lacrimal passages (late) A52.71
  larynx (late) A52.73
  late A52.9
    cardiovascular A52.00
    central nervous system A52.3
    kidney A52.75
    latent or 2 years or more after infection
        (without manifestations) A52.8
      negative spinal fluid test A52.8
      serology positive A52.8
    paresis A52.17
    specified site NEC A52.79
    symptomatic or with manifestations A52.79
    tabes A52.11
  latent A53.0
    with signs or symptoms - code by site and
        stage under Syphilis

Syphilis, syphilitic *(Continued)*
  latent *(Continued)*
    central nervous system A52.2
    date of infection unspecified A53.0
    early, or less than 2 years after infection
        A51.5
    follow-up of latent syphilis A53.0
      date of infection unspecified A53.0
      late, or 2 years or more after infection
          A52.8
    late, or 2 years or more after infection
        A52.8
    positive serology (only finding) A53.0
      date of infection unspecified A53.0
      early, or less than 2 years after infection
          A51.5
      late, or 2 years or more after infection
          A52.8
  lens (late) A52.71
  leukoderma A51.39
    late A52.79
  lienitis A52.79
  lip A51.39
    chancre (primary) A51.2
    late A52.79
  Lissauer's paralysis A52.17
  liver A52.74
  locomotor ataxia A52.11
  lung A52.72
  lymph gland (early) (secondary) A51.49
    late A52.79
  lymphadenitis (secondary) A51.49
  macular atrophy of skin A51.39
    striated A52.79
  mediastinum (late) A52.73
  meninges (adhesive) (brain) (spinal cord)
      A52.13
  meningitis A52.13
    acute (secondary) A51.41
    congenital A50.41
  meningoencephalitis A52.14
  meningovascular A52.13
    congenital A50.41
  mesarteritis A52.09
    brain A52.04
  middle ear A52.77
  mitral stenosis A52.03
  monoplegia A52.17
  mouth (secondary) A51.39
    late A52.79
  mucocutaneous (secondary) A51.39
    late A52.79
  mucous
    membrane (secondary) A51.39
      late A52.79
    patches A51.39
      congenital A50.07
  mulberry molars A50.52
  muscle A52.78
  myocardium A52.06
  nasal sinus (late) A52.73
  neonatorum —*see* Syphilis, congenital
  nephrotic syndrome (secondary)
      A51.44
  nerve palsy (any cranial nerve) A52.15
    multiple A52.15
  nervous system, central A52.3
  neuritis A52.15
    acoustic A52.15
  neurorecidive of retina A52.19
  neuroretinitis A52.19
  newborn —*see* Syphilis, congenital
  nodular superficial (late) A52.79
  nonvenereal A65
  nose (late) A52.73
    saddle back deformity A50.57
  occlusive arterial disease A52.09
  oculopathy A52.71
  ophthalmic (late) A52.71
  optic nerve (atrophy) (neuritis) (papilla)
      A52.15

▶ New   ⇒ Revised   ~~deleted~~ Deleted   • Use Additional Character(s)

Syphilis, syphilitic (Continued)
orbit (late) A52.71
organic A53.9
osseous (late) A52.77
osteochondritis (congenital) (early) A50.02
 [M90.80]
osteoporosis A52.77
ovary (late) A52.76
oviduct (late) A52.76
palate (late) A52.79
pancreas (late) A52.74
paralysis A52.17
 general A52.17
 juvenile A50.45
paresis (general) A52.17
 juvenile A50.45
paresthesia A52.19
Parkinson's disease or syndrome A52.19
paroxysmal tachycardia A52.06
pemphigus (congenital) A50.06
penis (chancre) A51.0
 late A52.76
pericardium A52.06
perichondritis, larynx (late) A52.73
periosteum (late) A52.77
 congenital (early) A50.02 [M90.80]
 early (secondary) A51.46
peripheral nerve A52.79
petrous bone (late) A52.77
pharynx (late) A52.73
 secondary A51.39
pituitary (gland) A52.79
pleura (late) A52.73
pneumonia, white A50.04
pontine lesion A52.17
portal vein A52.09
primary A51.0
 anal A51.1
 and secondary —see Syphilis, secondary
 central nervous system A52.3
 extragenital chancre NEC A51.2
 fingers A51.2
 genital A51.0
 lip A51.2
 specified site NEC A51.2
 tonsils A51.2
prostate (late) A52.76
ptosis (eyelid) A52.71
pulmonary (late) A52.72
 artery A52.09
pyelonephritis (late) A52.75
recently acquired, symptomatic A51.9
rectum (late) A52.74
respiratory tract (late) A52.73
retina, late A52.71
retrobulbar neuritis A52.15
salpingitis A52.76
sclera (late) A52.71
sclerosis
 cerebral A52.17
 coronary A52.06
 multiple A52.11
scotoma (central) A52.71
scrotum (late) A52.76

Syphilis, syphilitic (Continued)
secondary (and primary) A51.49
 adenopathy A51.49
 anus A51.39
 bone A51.46
 chorioretinitis, choroiditis A51.43
 hepatitis A51.45
 liver A51.45
 lymphadenitis A51.49
 meningitis (acute) A51.41
 mouth A51.39
 mucous membranes A51.39
 periosteum, periostitis A51.46
 pharynx A51.39
 relapse (treated, untreated) A51.49
 skin A51.39
 specified form NEC A51.49
 tonsil A51.39
 ulcer A51.39
 viscera NEC A51.49
 vulva A51.39
seminal vesicle (late) A52.76
seronegative with signs or symptoms - code
 by site and stage under Syphilis
seropositive
 with signs or symptoms - code by site and
 stage under Syphilis
 follow-up of latent syphilis —see Syphilis,
 latent
 only finding —see Syphilis, latent
seventh nerve (paralysis) A52.15
sinus, sinusitis (late) A52.73
skeletal system A52.77
skin (with ulceration) (early) (secondary)
 A51.39
 late or tertiary A52.79
small intestine A52.74
spastic spinal paralysis A52.17
spermatic cord (late) A52.76
spinal (cord) A52.12
spleen A52.79
splenomegaly A52.79
spondylitis A52.77
staphyloma A52.71
stigmata (congenital) A50.59
stomach A52.74
synovium A52.78
tabes dorsalis (late) A52.11
 juvenile A50.45
tabetic type A52.11
 juvenile A50.45
taboparesis A52.17
 juvenile A50.45
tachycardia A52.06
tendon (late) A52.78
tertiary A52.9
 with symptoms NEC A52.79
 cardiovascular A52.00
 central nervous system A52.3
 multiple NEC A52.79
 specified site NEC A52.79
testis A52.76
thorax A52.73
throat A52.73

Syphilis, syphilitic (Continued)
thymus (gland) (late) A52.79
thyroid (late) A52.79
tongue (late) A52.79
tonsil (lingual) (late) A52.73
 primary A51.2
 secondary A51.39
trachea (late) A52.73
tunica vaginalis (late) A52.76
ulcer (any site) (early) (secondary)
 A51.39
 late A52.79
 perforating A52.79
 foot A52.11
urethra (late) A52.76
urogenital (late) A52.76
uterus (late) A52.76
uveal tract (secondary) A51.43
 late A52.71
uveitis (secondary) A51.43
 late A52.71
uvula (late) (perforated) A52.79
vagina A51.0
 late A52.76
valvulitis NEC A52.03
vascular A52.00
 brain (cerebral) A52.05
ventriculi A52.74
vesicae urinariae (late) A52.76
viscera (abdominal) (late) A52.74
 secondary A51.49
vitreous (opacities) (late) A52.71
 hemorrhage A52.71
vulva A51.0
 late A52.76
 secondary A51.39
Syphiloma A52.79
 cardiovascular system A52.00
 central nervous system A52.3
 circulatory system A52.00
 congenital A50.59
Syphilophobia F45.29
Syringadenoma —see also Neoplasm, skin,
 benign
 papillary —see Neoplasm, skin, benign
Syringobulbia G95.0
Syringocystadenoma —see Neoplasm, skin,
 benign
 papillary —see Neoplasm, skin, benign
Syringoma —see also Neoplasm, skin, benign
 chondroid —see Neoplasm, skin, benign
Syringomyelia G95.0
Syringomyelitis —see Encephalitis
Syringomyelocele —see Spina bifida
Syringopontia G95.0
System, systemic —see also condition
 disease, combined —see Degeneration,
 combined
 inflammatory response syndrome (SIRS) of
 non-infectious origin (without organ
 dysfunction) R65.10
 with acute organ dysfunction R65.11
 lupus erythematosus M32.9
 inhibitor present D68.62

T

Tabacism, tabacosis, tabagism —see also
    Poisoning, tobacco
    meaning dependence (without remission)
      F17.200
      with
        disorder F17.299
          in remission F17.211
          specified disorder NEC F17.298
        withdrawal F17.203
Tabardillo A75.9
    flea-borne A75.2
    louse-borne A75.0
Tabes, tabetic A52.10
    with
      central nervous system syphilis A52.10
      Charcot's joint A52.16
      cord bladder A52.19
      crisis, viscera (any) A52.19
      paralysis, general A52.17
      paresis (general) A52.17
      perforating ulcer (foot) A52.19
    arthropathy (Charcot) A52.16
    bladder A52.19
    bone A52.11
    cerebrospinal A52.12
    congenital A50.45
    conjugal A52.10
    dorsalis A52.11
      juvenile A50.49
    juvenile A50.49
    latent A52.19
    mesenterica A18.39
    paralysis, insane, general A52.17
    spasmodic A52.17
    syphilis (cerebrospinal) A52.12
Taboparalysis A52.17
Taboparesis (remission) A52.17
    juvenile A50.45
TAC (trigeminal autonomic cephalgia) NEC
    G44.099
    intractable G44.091
    not intractable G44.099
Tache noir S60.22-•
Tachyalimentation K91.2
Tachyarrhythmia, tachyrhythmia —see
    Tachycardia
Tachycardia R00.0
    atrial (paroxysmal) I47.1
    auricular I47.1
    AV nodal re-entry (re-entrant) I47.1
    junctional (paroxysmal) I47.1
    newborn P29.11
    nodal (paroxysmal) I47.1
    non-paroxysmal AV nodal I45.89
    paroxysmal (sustained) (nonsustained)
      I47.9
      with sinus bradycardia I49.5
      atrial (PAT) I47.1
      atrioventricular (AV) (re-entrant) I47.1
        psychogenic F54
      junctional I47.1
        ectopic I47.1
      nodal I47.1
      psychogenic (atrial) (supraventricular)
        (ventricular) F54
      supraventricular (sustained) I47.1
        psychogenic F54
      ventricular I47.2
        psychogenic F54
    psychogenic F45.8
    sick sinus I49.5
    sinoauricular NOS R00.0
      paroxysmal I47.1
    sinus [sinusal] NOS R00.0
      paroxysmal I47.1
    supraventricular I47.1
    ventricular (paroxysmal) (sustained) I47.2
      psychogenic F54
Tachygastria K31.89

Tachypnea R06.82
    hysterical F45.8
    newborn (idiopathic) (transitory) P22.1
    psychogenic F45.8
    transitory, of newborn P22.1
TACO (transfusion associated circulatory
    overload) E87.71
Taenia (infection) (infestation) B68.9
    diminuta B71.0
    echinococcal infestation B67.90
    mediocanellata B68.1
    nana B71.0
    saginata B68.1
    solium (intestinal form) B68.0
      larval form —see Cysticercosis
Taeniasis (intestine) —see Taenia
Tag (hypertrophied skin) (infected) L91.8
    adenoid J35.8
    anus K64.4
    hemorrhoidal K64.4
    hymen N89.8
    perineal N90.89
    preauricular Q17.0
    sentinel K64.4
    skin L91.8
      accessory (congenital) Q82.8
      anus K64.4
      congenital Q82.8
      preauricular Q17.0
    tonsil J35.8
    urethra, urethral N36.8
    vulva N90.89
Tahyna fever B33.8
Takahara's disease E80.3
Takayasu's disease or syndrome M31.4
Talcosis (pulmonary) J62.0
Talipes (congenital) Q66.89
    acquired, planus —see Deformity, limb, flat
      foot
    asymmetric Q66.89
    calcaneovalgus Q66.4
    calcaneovarus Q66.1
    calcaneus Q66.89
    cavus Q66.7
    equinovalgus Q66.6
    equinovarus Q66.0
    equinus Q66.89
    percavus Q66.7
    planovalgus Q66.6
    planus (acquired) (any degree) —see also
      Deformity, limb, flat foot
      congenital Q66.5-•
      due to rickets (sequelae) E64.3
    valgus Q66.6
    varus Q66.3
Tall stature, constitutional E34.4
Talma's disease M62.89
Talon noir S90.3-•
    hand S60.22-•
    heel S90.3-•
    toe S90.1-•
Tamponade, heart I31.4
Tanapox (virus disease) B08.71
Tangier disease E78.6
Tantrum, child problem F91.8
Tapeworm (infection) (infestation) —see
    Infestation, tapeworm
Tapia's syndrome G52.7
TAR (thrombocytopenia with absent radius)
    syndrome Q87.2
Tarral-Besnier disease L44.0
Tarsal tunnel syndrome —see Syndrome, tarsal
    tunnel
Tarsalgia —see Pain, limb, lower
Tarsitis (eyelid) H01.8
    syphilitic A52.71
    tuberculous A18.4
Tartar (teeth) (dental calculus) K03.6
Tattoo (mark) L81.8
Tauri's disease E74.09
Taurodontism K00.2

Taussig-Bing syndrome Q20.1
Taybi's syndrome Q87.2
Tay-Sachs amaurotic familial idiocy or disease
    E75.02
TBI (traumatic brain injury) S06.9
Teacher's node or nodule J38.2
Tear, torn (traumatic) —see also Laceration
    with abortion —see Abortion
    annular fibrosis M51.35
    anus, anal (sphincter) S31.831
      complicating delivery
        with third degree perineal laceration —
          see also Delivery, complicated, by,
          laceration, perineum, third degree
          O70.20
          with mucosa O70.3
        without third degree perineal laceration
          O70.4
      nontraumatic (healed) (old) K62.81
    articular cartilage, old —see Derangement,
      joint, articular cartilage, by site
    bladder
      with ectopic or molar pregnancy O08.6
      following ectopic or molar pregnancy
        O08.6
      obstetrical O71.5
      traumatic —see Injury, bladder
    bowel
      with ectopic or molar pregnancy O08.6
      following ectopic or molar pregnancy
        O08.6
      obstetrical trauma O71.5
    broad ligament
      with ectopic or molar pregnancy O08.6
      following ectopic or molar pregnancy O08.6
      obstetrical trauma O71.6
    bucket handle (knee) (meniscus) —see Tear,
      meniscus
    capsule, joint —see Sprain
    cartilage —see also Sprain
      articular, old —see Derangement, joint,
        articular cartilage, by site
    cervix
      with ectopic or molar pregnancy O08.6
      following ectopic or molar pregnancy
        O08.6
      obstetrical trauma (current) O71.3
      old N88.1
      traumatic —see Injury, uterus
    dural G97.41
      nontraumatic G96.11
    internal organ —see Injury, by site
    knee cartilage
      articular (current) S83.3-•
      old —see Derangement, knee, meniscus,
        due to old tear
    ligament —see Sprain
    meniscus (knee) (current injury) S83.209
      bucket-handle S83.20-•
      lateral
        bucket-handle S83.25-•
        complex S83.27-•
        peripheral S83.26-•
        specified type NEC S83.28-•
      medial
        bucket-handle S83.21-•
        complex S83.23-•
        peripheral S83.22-•
        specified type NEC S83.24-•
      old —see Derangement, knee, meniscus,
        due to old tear
      site other than knee - code as Sprain
      specified type NEC S83.20-•
    muscle —see Strain
    pelvic
      floor, complicating delivery O70.1
      organ NEC, obstetrical trauma O71.5
        with ectopic or molar pregnancy O08.6
        following ectopic or molar pregnancy
          O08.6
    perineal, secondary O90.1

▶ New   ⇒ Revised   ~~deleted~~ Deleted   • Use Additional Character(s)

Tear, torn *(Continued)*
  periurethral tissue, obstetrical trauma O71.82
    with ectopic or molar pregnancy O08.6
    following ectopic or molar pregnancy O08.6
  rectovaginal septum —*see* Laceration, vagina
  retina, retinal (without detachment) (horseshoe) —*see also* Break, retina, horseshoe
    with detachment —*see* Detachment, retina, with retinal, break
  rotator cuff (nontraumatic) M75.10-●
    complete M75.12-●
    incomplete M75.11-●
    traumatic S46.01-●
      capsule S43.42-●
  semilunar cartilage, knee —*see* Tear, meniscus
  supraspinatus (complete) (incomplete) (nontraumatic) —*see also* Tear, rotator cuff M75.10-●
  tendon —*see* Strain
  tentorial, at birth P10.4
  umbilical cord
    complicating delivery O69.89
  urethra
    with ectopic or molar pregnancy O08.6
    following ectopic or molar pregnancy O08.6
    obstetrical trauma O71.5
  uterus —*see* Injury, uterus
  vagina —*see* Laceration, vagina
  vessel, from catheter —*see* Puncture, accidental complicating surgery
  vulva, complicating delivery O70.0
Tear-stone —*see* Dacryolith
Teeth —*see also* condition
  grinding
    psychogenic F45.8
    sleep related G47.63
Teething (syndrome) K00.7
Telangiectasia, telangiectasis (verrucous) I78.1
  ataxic (cerebellar) (Louis-Bar) G11.3
  familial I78.0
  hemorrhagic, hereditary (congenital) (senile) I78.0
  hereditary, hemorrhagic (congenital) (senile) I78.0
  juxtafoveal H35.07-●
  macular H35.07-●
  macularis eruptiva perstans D47.01
  parafoveal H35.07-●
  retinal (idiopathic) (juxtafoveal) (macular) (parafoveal) H35.07-●
  spider I78.1
Telephone scatologia F65.89
Telescoped bowel or intestine K56.1
  congenital Q43.8
Temperature
  body, high (of unknown origin) R50.9
  cold, trauma from T69.9
    newborn P80.0
    specified effect NEC T69.8
Temple —*see* condition
Temporal —*see* condition
Temporomandibular joint pain-dysfunction syndrome M26.62-●
Temporosphenoidal —*see* condition
Tendency
  bleeding —*see* Defect, coagulation
  suicide
    meaning personal history of attempted suicide Z91.5
    meaning suicidal ideation —*see* Ideation, suicidal
  to fall R29.6
Tenderness, abdominal R10.819
  epigastric R10.816
  generalized R10.817
  left lower quadrant R10.814
  left upper quadrant R10.812
  periumbilic R10.815

Tenderness, abdominal *(Continued)*
  rebound R10.829
    epigastric R10.826
    generalized R10.827
    left lower quadrant R10.824
    left upper quadrant R10.822
    periumbilic R10.825
    right lower quadrant R10.823
    right upper quadrant R10.821
  right lower quadrant R10.813
  right upper quadrant R10.811
Tendinitis, tendonitis —*see also* Enthesopathy
  Achilles M76.6-●
  adhesive —*see* Tenosynovitis, specified type NEC
    shoulder —*see* Capsulitis, adhesive
  bicipital M75.2-●
  calcific M65.2-●
    ankle M65.27-●
    foot M65.27-●
    forearm M65.23-●
    hand M65.24-●
    lower leg M65.26-●
    multiple sites M65.29
    pelvic region M65.25-●
    shoulder M75.3-●
    specified site NEC M65.28
    thigh M65.25-●
    upper arm M65.22-●
  due to use, overuse, pressure —*see also* Disorder, soft tissue, due to use
    specified NEC —*see* Disorder, soft tissue, due to use, specified NEC
  gluteal M76.0-●
  patellar M76.5-●
  peroneal M76.7-●
  psoas M76.1-●
  tibial (posterior) M76.82-●
    anterior M76.81-●
  trochanteric —*see* Bursitis, hip, trochanteric
Tendon —*see* condition
Tendosynovitis —*see* Tenosynovitis
Tenesmus (rectal) R19.8
  vesical R30.1
Tennis elbow —*see* Epicondylitis, lateral
Tenonitis —*see also* Tenosynovitis
  eye (capsule) H05.04-●
Tenontosynovitis —*see* Tenosynovitis
Tenontothecitis —*see* Tenosynovitis
Tenophyte —*see* Disorder, synovium, specified type NEC
Tenosynovitis —*see also* Synovitis M65.9
  adhesive —*see* Tenosynovitis, specified type NEC
    shoulder —*see* Capsulitis, adhesive
  bicipital (calcifying) —*see* Tendinitis, bicipital
  gonococcal A54.49
  in (due to)
    crystals M65.8-●
    gonorrhea A54.49
    syphilis (late) A52.78
    use, overuse, pressure —*see also* Disorder, soft tissue, due to use
      specified NEC —*see* Disorder, soft tissue, due to use, specified NEC
  infective NEC M65.1-●
    ankle M65.17-●
    foot M65.17-●
    forearm M65.13-●
    hand M65.14-●
    lower leg M65.16-●
    multiple sites M65.19
    pelvic region M65.15-●
    shoulder region M65.11-●
    specified site NEC M65.18
    thigh M65.15-●
    upper arm M65.12-●
  radial styloid M65.4
  shoulder region M65.81-●
    adhesive —*see* Capsulitis, adhesive

Tenosynovitis *(Continued)*
  specified type NEC M65.88-●
    ankle M65.87-●
    foot M65.87-●
    forearm M65.83-●
    hand M65.84-●
    lower leg M65.86-●
    multiple sites M65.89
    pelvic region M65.85-●
    shoulder region M65.81-●
    specified site NEC M65.88
    thigh M65.85-●
    upper arm M65.82-●
  tuberculous —*see* Tuberculosis, tenosynovitis
Tenovaginitis —*see* Tenosynovitis
Tension
  arterial, high —*see also* Hypertension
    without diagnosis of hypertension R03.0
  headache G44.209
    intractable G44.201
    not intractable G44.209
  nervous R45.0
  pneumothorax J93.0
  premenstrual N94.3
  state (mental) F48.9
Tentorium —*see* condition
Teratencephalus Q89.8
Teratism Q89.7
Teratoblastoma (malignant) —*see* Neoplasm, malignant, by site
Teratocarcinoma —*see also* Neoplasm, malignant, by site
  liver C22.7
Teratoma (solid) —*see also* Neoplasm, uncertain behavior, by site
  with embryonal carcinoma, mixed —*see* Neoplasm, malignant, by site
  with malignant transformation —*see* Neoplasm, malignant, by site
  adult (cystic) —*see* Neoplasm, benign, by site
  benign —*see* Neoplasm, benign, by site
  combined with choriocarcinoma —*see* Neoplasm, malignant, by site
  cystic (adult) —*see* Neoplasm, benign, by site
  differentiated —*see* Neoplasm, benign, by site
  embryonal —*see also* Neoplasm, malignant, by site
    liver C22.7
  immature —*see* Neoplasm, malignant, by site
  liver C22.7
    adult, benign, cystic, differentiated type or mature D13.4
  malignant —*see also* Neoplasm, malignant, by site
    anaplastic —*see* Neoplasm, malignant, by site
    intermediate —*see* Neoplasm, malignant, by site
    specified site —*see* Neoplasm, malignant, by site
    unspecified site C62.90
    undifferentiated —*see* Neoplasm, malignant, by site
  mature —*see* Neoplasm, uncertain behavior, by site
    malignant —*see* Neoplasm, by site, malignant, by site
  ovary D27.-●
    embryonal, immature or malignant C56-●
  solid —*see* Neoplasm, uncertain behavior, by site
  testis C62.9-●
    adult, benign, cystic, differentiated type or mature D29.2-●
    scrotal C62.1-●
    undescended C62.0-●
Termination
  anomalous —*see also* Malposition, congenital
    right pulmonary vein Q26.3
  pregnancy, elective Z33.2

Ternidens diminutus infestation B81.8
Ternidensiasis B81.8
Terror(s) night (child) F51.4
Terrorism, victim of Z65.4
Terry's syndrome —see also Myopia,
    degenerative H44.2-•
Tertiary —see condition
Test, tests, testing (for)
    adequacy (for dialysis)
      hemodialysis Z49.31
      peritoneal Z49.32
    blood pressure Z01.30
      abnormal reading —see Blood, pressure
    blood typing Z01.83
      Rh typing Z01.83
    blood-alcohol Z04.89
      positive —see Findings, abnormal, in blood
    blood-drug Z04.89
      positive —see Findings, abnormal, in blood
    cardiac pulse generator (battery) Z45.010
    fertility Z31.41
    genetic
      disease carrier status for procreative
        management
        female Z31.430
        male Z31.440
      male partner of patient with recurrent
        pregnancy loss Z31.441
      procreative management NEC
        female Z31.438
        male Z31.448
    hearing Z01.10
      with abnormal findings NEC Z01.118
      infant or child (over 28 days old) Z00.129
        with abnormal findings Z00.121
    HIV (human immunodeficiency virus)
      nonconclusive (in infants) R75
      positive Z21
      seropositive Z21
    immunity status Z01.84
    intelligence NEC Z01.89
    laboratory (as part of a general medical
      examination) Z00.00
      with abnormal finding Z00.01
      for medicolegal reason NEC Z04.89
    male partner of patient with recurrent
      pregnancy loss Z31.441
    Mantoux (for tuberculosis) Z11.1
      abnormal result R76.11
    pregnancy, positive first pregnancy —see
      Pregnancy, normal, first
    procreative Z31.49
      fertility Z31.41
    skin, diagnostic
      allergy Z01.82
        special screening examination —see
          Screening, by name of disease
      Mantoux Z11.1
      tuberculin Z11.1
    specified NEC Z01.89
    tuberculin Z11.1
      abnormal result R76.11
    vision Z01.00
      with abnormal findings Z01.01
      infant or child (over 28 days old) Z00.129
        with abnormal findings Z00.121
    Wassermann Z11.3
      positive —see Serology for syphilis, positive
Testicle, testicular, testis —see also condition
    feminization syndrome —see also Syndrome,
      androgen insensitivity E34.51
    migrans Q55.29
Tetanus, tetanic (cephalic) (convulsions) A35
    with
      abortion A34
      ectopic or molar pregnancy O08.0
    following ectopic or molar pregnancy O08.0
    inoculation reaction (due to serum) —see
      Complications, vaccination
    neonatorum A33
    obstetrical A34
    puerperal, postpartum, childbirth A34

Tetany (due to) R29.0
    alkalosis E87.3
    associated with rickets E55.0
    convulsions R29.0
      hysterical F44.5
    functional (hysterical) F44.5
    hyperkinetic R29.0
      hysterical F44.5
    hyperpnea R06.4
      hysterical F44.5
      psychogenic F45.8
    hyperventilation —see also Hyperventilation
      R06.4
      hysterical F44.5
    neonatal (without calcium or magnesium
      deficiency) P71.3
    parathyroid (gland) E20.9
    parathyroprival E89.2
    post- (para)thyroidectomy E89.2
    postoperative E89.2
    pseudotetany R29.0
    psychogenic (conversion reaction) F44.5
Tetralogy of Fallot Q21.3
Tetraplegia (chronic) —see also Quadriplegia
    G82.50-•
Thailand hemorrhagic fever A91
Thalassanemia —see Thalassemia
Thalassemia (anemia) (disease) D56.9
    with other hemoglobinopathy D56.8
    alpha (major) (severe) (triple gene defect)
      D56.0
      minor D56.3
      silent carrier D56.3
      trait D56.3
    beta (severe) D56.1
      homozygous D56.1
      major D56.1
      minor D56.3
      trait D56.3
    delta-beta (homozygous) D56.2
      minor D56.3
      trait D56.3
    dominant D56.8
    hemoglobin
      C D56.8
      E-beta D56.5
    intermedia D56.1
    major D56.1
    minor D56.3
    mixed D56.8
    sickle-cell —see Disease, sickle-cell,
      thalassemia
    specified type NEC D56.8
    trait D56.3
    variants D56.8
Thanatophoric dwarfism or short stature Q77.1
Thaysen-Gee disease (nontropical sprue) K90.0
Thaysen's disease K90.0
Thecoma D27-•
    luteinized D27-•
    malignant C56-•
Thelarche, premature E30.8
Thelaziasis B83.8
Thelitis N61.0
    puerperal, postpartum or gestational —see
      Infection, nipple
Therapeutic —see condition
Therapy
    drug, long-term (current) (prophylactic)
      agents affecting estrogen receptors and
        estrogen levels NEC Z79.818
      anastrozole (Arimidex) Z79.811
      antibiotics Z79.2
        short-term use - omit code
      anticoagulants Z79.01
      anti-inflammatory Z79.1
      antiplatelet Z79.02
      antithrombotics Z79.02
      aromatase inhibitors Z79.811
      aspirin Z79.82
      birth control pill or patch Z79.3

Therapy (Continued)
    drug, long-term (Continued)
      bisphosphonates Z79.83
      contraceptive, oral Z79.3
      drug, specified NEC Z79.899
      estrogen receptor downregulators
        Z79.818
      Evista Z79.810
      exemestane (Aromasin) Z79.811
      Fareston Z79.810
      fulvestrant (Faslodex) Z79.818
      gonadotropin-releasing hormone (GnRH)
        agonist Z79.818
      goserelin acetate (Zoladex) Z79.818
      hormone replacement Z79.890
      insulin Z79.4
      letrozole (Femara) Z79.811
      leuprolide acetate (leuprorelin) (Lupron)
        Z79.818
      megestrol acetate (Megace) Z79.818
      methadone
        for pain management Z79.891
        maintenance therapy F11.20
      Nolvadex Z79.810
      opiate analgesic Z79.891
      oral contraceptive Z79.3
      raloxifene (Evista) Z79.810
      selective estrogen receptor modulators
        (SERMs) Z79.810
      short term - omit code
      steroids
        inhaled Z79.51
        systemic Z79.52
      tamoxifen (Nolvadex) Z79.810
      toremifene (Fareston) Z79.810
Thermic —see condition
Thermography (abnormal) —see also Abnormal,
    diagnostic imaging R93.89
    breast R92.8
Thermoplegia T67.0
Thesaurismosis, glycogen —see Disease,
    glycogen storage
Thiamin deficiency E51.9
    specified NEC E51.8
Thiaminic deficiency with beriberi E51.11
Thibierge-Weissenbach syndrome —see
    Sclerosis, systemic
Thickening
    bone —see Hypertrophy, bone
    breast N64.59
    endometrium R93.89
    epidermal L85.9
      specified NEC L85.8
    hymen N89.6
    larynx J38.7
    nail L60.2
      congenital Q84.5
    periosteal —see Hypertrophy, bone
    pleura J92.9
      with asbestos J92.0
    skin R23.4
    subepiglottic J38.7
    tongue K14.8
    valve, heart —see Endocarditis
Thigh —see condition
Thinning vertebra —see Spondylopathy,
    specified NEC
Thirst, excessive R63.1
    due to deprivation of water T73.1
Thomsen disease G71.12
Thoracic —see also condition
    kidney Q63.2
    outlet syndrome G54.0
Thoracogastroschisis (congenital)
    Q79.8
Thoracopagus Q89.4
Thorax —see condition
Thorn's syndrome N28.89
Thorson-Björck syndrome E34.0
Threadworm (infection) (infestation)
    B80

▶ New   ⇒ Revised   ~~deleted~~ Deleted   • Use Additional Character(s)

Threatened
abortion O20.0
with subsequent abortion O03.9
job loss, anxiety concerning Z56.2
labor (without delivery) O47.9
at or after 37 completed weeks of gestation
O47.1
before 37 completed weeks of gestation
O47.0-•
loss of job, anxiety concerning Z56.2
miscarriage O20.0
unemployment, anxiety concerning Z56.2
Three-day fever A93.1
Threshers' lung J67.0
Thrix annulata (congenital) Q84.1
Throat —see condition
Thrombasthenia (Glanzmann) (hemorrhagic)
(hereditary) D69.1
Thromboangiitis I73.1
obliterans (general) I73.1
cerebral I67.89
vessels
brain I67.89
spinal cord I67.89
Thromboarteritis —see Arteritis
Thromboasthenia (Glanzmann) (hemorrhagic)
(hereditary) D69.1
Thrombocytasthenia (Glanzmann) D69.1
Thrombocythemia (essential) (hemorrhagic)
(idiopathic) (primary) D47.3
Thrombocytopathy (dystrophic) (granulopenic)
D69.1
Thrombocytopenia, thrombocytopenic
D69.6
with absent radius (TAR) Q87.2
congenital D69.42
dilutional D69.59
due to
drugs D69.59
extracorporeal circulation of blood
D69.59
(massive)blood transfusion D69.59
platelet alloimmunization D69.59
essential D69.3
heparin induced (HIT) D75.82
hereditary D69.42
idiopathic D69.3
neonatal, transitory P61.0
due to
exchange transfusion P61.0
idiopathic maternal thrombocytopenia
P61.0
isoimmunization P61.0
primary NEC D69.49
idiopathic D69.3
puerperal, postpartum O72.3
secondary D69.59
transient neonatal P61.0
Thrombocytosis, essential D47.3
primary D47.3
Thromboembolism —see Embolism
Thrombopathy (Bernard-Soulier) D69.1
constitutional D68.0
Willebrand-Jurgens D68.0
Thrombopenia —see Thrombocytopenia
Thrombophilia D68.59
primary NEC D68.59
secondary NEC D68.69
specified NEC D68.69
Thrombophlebitis I80.9
antepartum O22.2-•
deep O22.3-•
superficial O22.2-•
cavernous (venous) sinus G08
complicating pregnancy O22.5-•
nonpyogenic I67.6
cerebral (sinus) (vein) G08
nonpyogenic I67.6
sequelae G09
due to implanted device —see Complications,
by site and type, specified NEC

Thrombophlebitis (Continued)
during or resulting from a procedure NEC
T81.72
femoral vein (superficial) I80.1-•
femoropopliteal vein I80.0-•
hepatic (vein) I80.8
idiopathic, recurrent I82.1
iliofemoral I80.1-•
intracranial venous sinus (any) G08
nonpyogenic I67.6
sequelae G09
intraspinal venous sinuses and veins G08
nonpyogenic G95.19
lateral (venous) sinus G08
nonpyogenic I67.6
leg I80.3
superficial I80.0-•
longitudinal (venous) sinus G08
nonpyogenic I67.6
lower extremity I80.299
migrans, migrating I82.1
pelvic
with ectopic or molar pregnancy
O08.0
following ectopic or molar pregnancy
O08.0
puerperal O87.1
popliteal vein —see Phlebitis, leg, deep,
popliteal
portal (vein) K75.1
postoperative T81.72
pregnancy —see Thrombophlebitis,
antepartum
puerperal, postpartum, childbirth O87.0
deep O87.1
pelvic O87.1
septic O86.81
superficial O87.0
saphenous (greater) (lesser) I80.0-•
sinus (intracranial) G08
nonpyogenic I67.6
specified site NEC I80.8
tibial vein I80.23-•
Thrombosis, thrombotic (bland) (multiple)
(progressive) (silent) (vessel) I82.90
anal K64.5
antepartum —see Thrombophlebitis,
antepartum
aorta, aortic I74.10
abdominal I74.09
saddle I74.01
bifurcation I74.09
saddle I74.01
specified site NEC I74.19
terminal I74.09
thoracic I74.11
valve —see Endocarditis, aortic
apoplexy I63.3-•
artery, arteries (postinfectional) I74.9
auditory, internal —see Occlusion, artery,
precerebral, specified NEC
basilar —see Occlusion, artery, basilar
carotid (common) (internal) —see
Occlusion, artery, carotid
cerebellar (anterior inferior) (posterior
inferior) (superior) —see Occlusion,
artery, cerebellar
cerebral —see Occlusion, artery, cerebral
choroidal (anterior) —see Occlusion, artery,
precerebral, specified NEC
communicating, posterior —see Occlusion,
artery, precerebral, specified NEC
coronary —see also Infarct, myocardium
not resulting in infarction I24.0
hepatic I74.8
hypophyseal —see Occlusion, artery,
precerebral, specified NEC
iliac I74.5
limb I74.4
lower I74.3
upper I74.2

Thrombosis, thrombotic (Continued)
artery, arteries (Continued)
meningeal, anterior or posterior —see
Occlusion, artery, cerebral, specified
NEC
mesenteric (with gangrene) —see also
Infarct, intestine K55.069
ophthalmic —see Occlusion, artery, retina
pontine —see Occlusion, artery, precerebral,
specified NEC
precerebral —see Occlusion, artery,
precerebral
pulmonary (iatrogenic) —see Embolism,
pulmonary
renal N28.0
retinal —see Occlusion, artery, retina
spinal, anterior or posterior G95.11
traumatic NEC T14.8
vertebral —see Occlusion, artery, vertebral
atrium, auricular —see also Infarct, myocardium
following acute myocardial infarction
(current complication) I23.6
not resulting in infarction I51.3
old I51.3
basilar (artery) —see Occlusion, artery, basilar
brain (artery) (stem) —see also Occlusion,
artery, cerebral
due to syphilis A52.05
puerperal O99.43
sinus —see Thrombosis, intracranial
venous sinus
capillary I78.8
cardiac —see also Infarct, myocardium
not resulting in infarction I51.3
valve —see Endocarditis
old I51.3
carotid (artery) (common) (internal) —see
Occlusion, artery, carotid
cavernous (venous) sinus —see Thrombosis,
intracranial venous sinus
cerebellar artery (anterior inferior) (posterior
inferior) (superior) I66.3
cerebral (artery) —see Occlusion, artery,
cerebral
cerebrovenous sinus —see also Thrombosis,
intracranial venous sinus
puerperium O87.3
chronic I82.91
coronary (artery) (vein) —see also Infarct,
myocardium
not resulting in infarction I24.0
corpus cavernosum N48.89
cortical I66.9
deep —see Embolism, vein, lower extremity
due to device, implant or graft —see also
Complications, by site and type,
specified NEC T85.868
arterial graft NEC T82.868
breast (implant) T85.868
catheter NEC T85.868
dialysis (renal) T82.868
intraperitoneal T85.868
infusion NEC T82.868
spinal (epidural) (subdural) T85.860
urinary (indwelling) T83.86
electronic (electrode) (pulse generator)
(stimulator)
bone T84.86
cardiac T82.867
nervous system (brain) (peripheral
nerve) (spinal) T85.860
urinary T83.86
fixation, internal (orthopedic) NEC T84.86
gastrointestinal (bile duct) (esophagus)
T85.868
genital NEC T83.86
heart T82.867
joint prosthesis T84.86
ocular (corneal graft) (orbital implant)
NEC T85.868
orthopedic NEC T84.86

Thrombosis, thrombotic *(Continued)*
  due to device, implant or graft *(Continued)*
    specified NEC T85.868
    urinary NEC T83.86
    vascular NEC T82.868
    ventricular intracranial shunt T85.860
  during the puerperium —*see* Thrombosis, puerperal
  endocardial —*see also* Infarct, myocardium
    not resulting in infarction I51.3
  eye —*see* Occlusion, retina
  genital organ
    female NEC N94.89
      pregnancy —*see* Thrombophlebitis, antepartum
    male N50.1
  gestational —*see* Phlebopathy, gestational
  heart (chamber) —*see also* Infarct, myocardium
    not resulting in infarction I51.3
    old I51.3
  hepatic (vein) I82.0
    artery I74.8
  history (of) Z86.718
  intestine (with gangrene) —*see also* Infarct, intestine K55.069
  intracardiac NEC (apical) (atrial) (auricular) (ventricular) (old) I51.3
  intracranial (arterial) I66.9
    venous sinus (any) G08
      nonpyogenic origin I67.6
      puerperium O87.3
  intramural —*see also* Infarct, myocardium
    not resulting in infarction I51.3
    old I51.3
  intraspinal venous sinuses and veins G08
    nonpyogenic G95.19
  kidney (artery) N28.0
  lateral (venous) sinus —*see* Thrombosis, intracranial venous sinus
  leg —*see* Thrombosis, vein, lower extremity
    arterial I74.3
  liver (venous) I82.0
    artery I74.8
    portal vein I81
  longitudinal (venous) sinus —*see* Thrombosis, intracranial venous sinus
  lower limb —*see* Thrombosis, vein, lower extremity
  lung (iatrogenic) (postoperative) —*see* Embolism, pulmonary
  meninges (brain) (arterial) I66.8
  mesenteric (artery) (with gangrene) —*see also* Infarct, intestine K55.069
    vein (inferior) (superior) I81
  mitral I34.8
  mural —*see also* Infarct, myocardium
    due to syphilis A52.06
    not resulting in infarction I51.3
    old I51.3
  omentum (with gangrene) —*see also* Infarct, intestine K55.069
  ophthalmic —*see* Occlusion, retina
  pampiniform plexus (male) N50.1
  parietal —*see also* Infarct, myocardium
    not resulting in infarction I24.0
  penis, superficial vein N48.81
  perianal venous K64.5
  peripheral arteries I74.4
    upper I74.2
  personal history (of) Z86.718
  portal I81
    due to syphilis A52.09
  precerebral artery —*see* Occlusion, artery, precerebral
  puerperal, postpartum O87.0
    brain (artery) O99.43
      venous (sinus) O87.3
    cardiac O99.43
    cerebral (artery) O99.43
      venous (sinus) O87.3
    superficial O87.0

Thrombosis, thrombotic *(Continued)*
  pulmonary (artery) (iatrogenic) (postoperative) (vein) —*see* Embolism, pulmonary
  renal (artery) N28.0
    vein I82.3
  resulting from presence of device, implant or graft —*see* Complications, by site and type, specified NEC
  retina, retinal —*see* Occlusion, retina
  scrotum N50.1
  seminal vesicle N50.1
  sigmoid (venous) sinus —*see* Thrombosis, intracranial venous sinus
  sinus, intracranial (any) —*see* Thrombosis, intracranial venous sinus
  specified site NEC I82.890
    chronic I82.891
  spermatic cord N50.1
  spinal cord (arterial) G95.11
    due to syphilis A52.09
    pyogenic origin G06.1
  spleen, splenic D73.5
    artery I74.8
  testis N50.1
  traumatic NEC T14.8
  tricuspid I07.8
  tumor —*see* Neoplasm, by site
  tunica vaginalis N50.1
  umbilical cord (vessels), complicating delivery O69.5
  vas deferens N50.1
  vein (acute) I82.90
    antecubital I82.61-●
      chronic I82.71-●
    axillary I82.A1-●
      chronic I82.A2-●
    basilic I82.61-●
      chronic I82.71-●
    brachial I82.62-●
      chronic I82.72-●
    brachiocephalic (innominate) I82.290
      chronic I82.291
    cerebral, nonpyogenic I67.6
    cephalic I82.61-●
      chronic I82.71-●
    chronic I82.91
    deep (DVT) I82.40-●
      calf I82.4Z-●
        chronic I82.5Z-●
      lower leg I82.4Z-●
        chronic I82.5Z-●
      thigh I82.4Y-●
        chronic I82.5Y-●
      upper leg I82.4Y
        chronic I82.5y-●
    femoral I82.41-●
      chronic I82.51-●
    iliac (iliofemoral) I82.42-●
      chronic I82.52-●
    innominate I82.290
      chronic I82.291
    internal jugular I82.C1-●
      chronic I82.C2-●
    lower extremity
      deep I82.40-●
        chronic I82.50-●
        specified NEC I82.49-●
          chronic NEC I82.59-●
      distal
        deep I82.4Z-●
      proximal
        deep I82.4Y-●
          chronic I82.5Y-●
      superficial I82.81-●
    perianal K64.5
    popliteal I82.43-●
      chronic I82.53-●
    radial I82.62-●
      chronic I82.72-●
    renal I82.3

Thrombosis, thrombotic *(Continued)*
  vein *(Continued)*
    saphenous (greater) (lesser) I82.81-●
    specified NEC I82.890
      chronic NEC I82.891
    subclavian I82.B1-●
      chronic I82.B2-●
    thoracic NEC I82.290
      chronic I82.291
    tibial I82.44-●
      chronic I82.54-●
    ulnar I82.62-●
      chronic I82.72-●
    upper extremity I82.60-●
      chronic I82.70-●
      deep I82.62-●
        chronic I82.72-●
      superficial I82.61-●
        chronic I82.71-●
  vena cava
    inferior I82.220
      chronic I82.221
    superior I82.210
      chronic I82.211
  venous, perianal K64.5
  ventricle —*see also* Infarct, myocardium
    following acute myocardial infarction (current complication) I23.6
    not resulting in infarction I24.0
    old I51.3
Thrombus —*see* Thrombosis
Thrush —*see also* Candidiasis
  newborn P37.5
  oral B37.0
  vaginal B37.3
Thumb —*see also* condition
  sucking (child problem) F98.8
Thymitis E32.8
Thymoma (benign) D15.0
  malignant C37
Thymus, thymic (gland) —*see* condition
Thyrocele —*see* Goiter
Thyroglossal —*see also* condition
  cyst Q89.2
  duct, persistent Q89.2
Thyroid (gland) (body) —*see also* condition
  hormone resistance E07.89
  lingual Q89.2
  nodule (cystic) (nontoxic) (single) E04.1
Thyroiditis E06.9
  acute (nonsuppurative) (pyogenic) (suppurative) E06.0
  autoimmune E06.3
  chronic (nonspecific) (sclerosing) E06.5
    with thyrotoxicosis, transient E06.2
    fibrous E06.5
    lymphadenoid E06.3
    lymphocytic E06.3
    lymphoid E06.3
  de Quervain's E06.1
  drug-induced E06.4
  fibrous (chronic) E06.5
  giant-cell (follicular) E06.1
  granulomatous (de Quervain) (subacute) E06.1
  Hashimoto's (struma lymphomatosa) E06.3
  iatrogenic E06.4
  ligneous E06.5
  lymphocytic (chronic) E06.3
  lymphoid E06.3
  lymphomatous E06.3
  nonsuppurative E06.1
  postpartum, puerperal O90.5
  pseudotuberculous E06.1
  pyogenic E06.0
  radiation E06.4
  Riedel's E06.5
  subacute (granulomatous) E06.1
  suppurative E06.0
  tuberculous A18.81
  viral E06.1
  woody E06.5

▶ New   ⇒ Revised   ~~deleted~~ Deleted   ● Use Additional Character(s)

Thyrolingual duct, persistent Q89.2
Thyromegaly E01.0
Thyrotoxic
  crisis —see Thyrotoxicosis
  heart disease or failure —see also
      Thyrotoxicosis E05.90 [I43]
    with thyroid storm E05.91 [I43]
  storm —see Thyrotoxicosis
Thyrotoxicosis (recurrent) E05.90
  with
    goiter (diffuse) E05.00
      with thyroid storm E05.01
      adenomatous uninodular E05.10
        with thyroid storm E05.11
      multinodular E05.20
        with thyroid storm E05.21
      nodular E05.20
        with thyroid storm E05.21
      uninodular E05.10
        with thyroid storm E05.11
    infiltrative
      dermopathy E05.00
        with thyroid storm E05.01
      ophthalmopathy E05.00
        with thyroid storm E05.01
    single thyroid nodule E05.10
      with thyroid storm E05.11
    thyroid storm E05.91
  due to
    ectopic thyroid nodule or tissue E05.30
      with thyroid storm E05.31
    ingestion of (excessive) thyroid material
      E05.40
      with thyroid storm E05.41
    overproduction of thyroid-stimulating
      hormone E05.80
      with thyroid storm E05.81
    specified cause NEC E05.80
      with thyroid storm E05.81
  factitia E05.40
    with thyroid storm E05.41
  heart —see also Failure, heart, high-output
    E05.90 [I43]
    with thyroid storm —see also Failure, heart,
      high-output E05.91 [I43]
    failure —see also Failure, heart, high-output
      E05.90 [I43]
  neonatal (transient) P72.1
  transient with chronic thyroiditis E06.2
Tibia vara —see Osteochondrosis, juvenile, tibia
Tic (disorder) F95.9
  breathing F95.8
  child problem F95.0
  compulsive F95.1
  de la Tourette F95.2
  degenerative (generalized) (localized) G25.69
    facial G25.69
  disorder
    chronic
      motor F95.1
      vocal F95.1
    combined vocal and multiple motor F95.2
    transient F95.0
  douloureux G50.0
    atypical G50.1
    postherpetic, postzoster B02.22
  drug-induced G25.61
  eyelid F95.8
  habit F95.9
    chronic F95.1
    transient of childhood F95.0
  lid, transient of childhood F95.0
  motor-verbal F95.2
  occupational F48.8
  orbicularis F95.8
    transient of childhood F95.0
  organic origin G25.69
  postchoreic G25.69
  provisional F95.0
  psychogenic, compulsive F95.1
  salaam R25.8

Tic (Continued)
  spasm (motor or vocal) F95.9
    chronic F95.1
    transient of childhood F95.0
  specified NEC F95.8
Tick-borne —see condition
Tietze's disease or syndrome M94.0
Tight, tightness
  anus K62.89
  chest R07.89
  fascia (lata) M62.89
  foreskin (congenital) N47.1
  hymen, hymenal ring N89.6
  introitus (acquired) (congenital) N89.6
  rectal sphincter K62.89
  tendon —see Short, tendon
  urethral sphincter N35.919
Tilting vertebra —see Dorsopathy, deforming,
    specified NEC
Timidity, child F93.8
Tin-miner's lung J63.5
Tinea (intersecta) (tarsi) B35.9
  amiantacea L44.8
  asbestina B35.0
  barbae B35.0
  beard B35.0
  black dot B35.0
  blanca B36.2
  capitis B35.0
  corporis B35.4
  cruris B35.6
  flava B36.0
  foot B35.3
  furfuracea B36.0
  imbricata (Tokelau) B35.5
  kerion B35.0
  manuum B35.2
  microsporic —see Dermatophytosis
  nigra B36.1
  nodosa —see Piedra
  pedis B35.3
  scalp B35.0
  specified NEC B35.8
  sycosis B35.0
  tonsurans B35.0
  trichophytic —see Dermatophytosis
  unguium B35.1
  versicolor B36.0
Tingling sensation (skin) R20.2
Tinnitus NOS H93.1-•
  audible H93.1-•
  aurium H93.1-•
  pulsatile H93.A-•
  subjective H93.1-•
Tipped tooth (teeth) M26.33
Tipping
  pelvis M95.5
    with disproportion (fetopelvic) O33.0
      causing obstructed labor O65.0
  tooth (teeth), fully erupted M26.33
Tiredness R53.83
Tissue —see condition
Tobacco (nicotine)
  abuse —see Tobacco, use
  dependence —see Dependence, drug, nicotine
  harmful use Z72.0
  heart —see Tobacco, toxic effect
  maternal use, affecting newborn P04.2
  toxic effect —see Table of Drugs and
    Chemicals, by substance, poisoning
    chewing tobacco —see Table of Drugs
      and Chemicals, by substance, poisoning
    cigarettes —see Table of Drugs and
      Chemicals, by substance, poisoning
  use Z72.0
    complicating
      childbirth O99.334
      pregnancy O99.33-•
      puerperium O99.335
    counseling and surveillance Z71.6
    history Z87.891

Tobacco (Continued)
  withdrawal state —see also Dependence,
    drug, nicotine F17.203
Tocopherol deficiency E56.0
Todd's
  cirrhosis K74.3
  paralysis (postepileptic) (transitory) G83.84
Toe —see condition
Toilet, artificial opening —see Attention to,
    artificial, opening
Tokelau (ringworm) B35.5
Tollwut —see Rabies
Tommaselli's disease R31.9
  correct substance properly administered —see
    Table of Drugs and Chemicals, by drug,
    adverse effect
  overdose or wrong substance given
    or taken —see Table of Drugs and
    Chemicals, by drug, poisoning
Tongue —see also condition
  tie Q38.1
Tonic pupil —see Anomaly, pupil, function,
    tonic pupil
Toni-Fanconi syndrome (cystinosis) E72.09
  with cystinosis E72.04
Tonsil —see condition
Tonsillitis (acute) (catarrhal) (croupous)
    (follicular) (gangrenous) (infective)
    (lacunar) (lingual) (malignant)
    (membranous) (parenchymatous)
    (phlegmonous) (pseudomembranous)
    (purulent) (septic) (subacute) (suppurative)
    (toxic) (ulcerative) (vesicular) (viral) J03.90
  chronic J35.01
    with adenoiditis J35.03
  diphtheritic A36.0
  hypertrophic J35.01
    with adenoiditis J35.03
  recurrent J03.91
  specified organism NEC J03.80
    recurrent J03.81
  staphylococcal J03.80
    recurrent J03.81
  streptococcal J03.00
    recurrent J03.01
  tuberculous A15.8
  Vincent's A69.1
Tooth, teeth —see condition
Toothache K08.89
Topagnosis R20.8
Tophi —see Gout, chronic
TORCH infection —see Infection, congenital
  without active infection P00.2
Torn —see Tear
Tornwaldt's cyst or disease J39.2
Torsion
  accessory tube —see Torsion, fallopian tube
  adnexa (female) —see Torsion, fallopian tube
  aorta, acquired I77.1
  appendix epididymis N44.04
  appendix testis N44.03
  bile duct (common) (hepatic) K83.8
    congenital Q44.5
  bowel, colon or intestine K56.2
  cervix —see Malposition, uterus
  cystic duct K82.8
  dystonia —see Dystonia, torsion
  epididymis (appendix) N44.04
  fallopian tube N83.52-•
    with ovary N83.53
  gallbladder K82.8
    congenital Q44.1
  hydatid of Morgagni
    female N83.52-•
    male N44.03
  kidney (pedicle) (leading to infarction) N28.0
  Meckel's diverticulum (congenital) Q43.0
    malignant —see Table of Neoplasms, small
      intestine, malignant
  mesentery K56.2
  omentum K56.2

Torsion (Continued)
  organ or site, congenital NEC —see Anomaly,
    by site
  ovary (pedicle) N83.51-●
    with fallopian tube N83.53
    congenital Q50.2
  oviduct —see Torsion, fallopian tube
  penis (acquired) N48.82
    congenital Q55.63
  spasm —see Dystonia, torsion
  spermatic cord N44.02
    extravaginal N44.01
    intravaginal N44.02
  spleen D73.5
  testis, testicle N44.00
    appendix N44.03
  tibia —see Deformity, limb, specified type
    NEC, lower leg
  uterus —see Malposition, uterus
Torticollis (intermittent) (spastic) M43.6
  congenital (sternomastoid) Q68.0
  due to birth injury P15.8
  hysterical F44.4
  ocular R29.891
  psychogenic F45.8
    conversion reaction F44.4
  rheumatic M43.6
  rheumatoid M06.88
  spasmodic G24.3
  traumatic, current S13.4
Tortipelvis G24.1
Tortuous
  aortic arch Q25.46
  artery I77.1
  organ or site, congenital NEC —see Distortion
  retinal vessel, congenital Q14.1
  ureter N13.8
  urethra N36.8
  vein —see Varix
Torture, victim of Z65.4
Torula, torular (histolytica) (infection) —see
  Cryptococcosis
Torulosis —see Cryptococcosis
Torus (mandibularis) (palatinus) M27.0
  fracture —see Fracture, by site, torus
Touraine's syndrome Q79.8
Tourette's syndrome F95.2
Tourniquet syndrome —see Constriction,
  external, by site
Tower skull Q75.0
  with exophthalmos Q87.0
Toxemia R68.89
  bacterial —see Sepsis
  burn —see Burn
  eclamptic (with pre-existing hypertension) —
    see Eclampsia
  erysipelatous —see Erysipelas
  fatigue R68.89
  food —see Poisoning, food
  gastrointestinal K52.1
  intestinal K52.1
  kidney —see Uremia
  malarial —see Malaria
  myocardial —see Myocarditis, toxic
  of pregnancy —see Pre-eclampsia
  pre-eclamptic —see Pre-eclampsia
  small intestine K52.1
  staphylococcal, due to food A05.0
  stasis R68.89
  uremic —see Uremia
  urinary —see Uremia
Toxemica cerebropathia psychica
  (nonalcoholic) F04
  alcoholic —see Alcohol, amnestic disorder
Toxic (poisoning) —see also condition T65.91
  effect —see Table of Drugs and Chemicals, by
    substance, poisoning
  shock syndrome A48.3
  thyroid (gland) —see Thyrotoxicosis
Toxicemia —see Toxemia
Toxicity —see Table of Drugs and Chemicals, by
  substance, poisoning

Toxic (Continued)
  fava bean D55.0
  food, noxious —see Poisoning, food
  from drug or nonmedicinal substance —see
    Table of Drugs and Chemicals, by drug
Toxicosis —see also Toxemia
  capillary, hemorrhagic D69.0
Toxinfection, gastrointestinal K52.1
Toxocariasis B83.0
Toxoplasma, toxoplasmosis (acquired) B58.9
  with
    hepatitis B58.1
    meningoencephalitis B58.2
    ocular involvement B58.00
    other organ involvement B58.89
    pneumonia, pneumonitis B58.3
  congenital (acute) (subacute) (chronic) P37.1
  maternal, manifest toxoplasmosis in infant
    (acute) (subacute) (chronic) P37.1
tPA (rtPA) administation in a different facility
    within the last 24 hours prior to admission
    to current facility Z92.82
Trabeculation, bladder N32.89
Trachea —see condition
Tracheitis (catarrhal) (infantile) (membranous)
    (plastic) (septal) (suppurative) (viral) J04.10
  with
    bronchitis (15 years of age and above) J40
      acute or subacute —see Bronchitis, acute
      chronic J42
      tuberculous NEC A15.5
      under 15 years of age J20.9
    laryngitis (acute) J04.2
      chronic J37.1
      tuberculous NEC A15.5
  acute J04.10
    with obstruction J04.11
  chronic J42
    with
      bronchitis (chronic) J42
      laryngitis (chronic) J37.1
  diphtheritic (membranous) A36.89
  due to external agent —see Inflammation,
    respiratory, upper, due to
  syphilitic A52.73
  tuberculous A15.5
Trachelitis (nonvenereal) —see Cervicitis
Tracheobronchial —see condition
Tracheobronchitis (15 years of age and
    above) —see also Bronchitis
  due to
    Bordetella bronchiseptica A37.80
      with pneumonia A37.81
    Francisella tularensis A21.8
Tracheobronchomegaly Q32.4
  with bronchiectasis J47.9
    with
      exacerbation (acute) J47.1
      lower respiratory infection J47.0
  acquired J98.09
    with bronchiectasis J47.9
      with
        exacerbation (acute) J47.1
        lower respiratory infection J47.0
Tracheobronchopneumonitis —see Pneumonia,
  broncho-●
Tracheocele (external) (internal) J39.8
  congenital Q32.1
Tracheomalacia J39.8
  congenital Q32.0
Tracheopharyngitis (acute) J06.9
  chronic J42
  due to external agent —see Inflammation,
    respiratory, upper, due to
Tracheostenosis J39.8
Tracheostomy
  complication —see Complication,
    tracheostomy
  status Z93.0
    attention to Z43.0
    malfunctioning J95.03

Trachoma, trachomatous A71.9
  active (stage) A71.1
  contraction of conjunctiva A71.1
  dubium A71.0
  healed or sequelae B94.0
  initial (stage) A71.0
  pannus A71.1
  Türck's J37.0
Traction, vitreomacular H43.82-●
Train sickness T75.3
Trait(s)
  Hb-S D57.3
  hemoglobin
    abnormal NEC D58.2
      with thalassemia D56.3
    C —see Disease, hemoglobin C
    S (Hb-S) D57.3
  Lepore D56.3
  personality, accentuated Z73.1
  sickle-cell D57.3
    with elliptocytosis or spherocytosis D57.3
  type A personality Z73.1
Tramp Z59.0
Trance R41.89
  hysterical F44.89
Transaminasemia R74.0
Transection
  abdomen (partial) S38.3
  aorta (incomplete) —see also Injury, aorta
    complete —see Injury, aorta, laceration,
      major
  carotid artery (incomplete) —see also Injury,
    blood vessel, carotid, laceration
    complete —see Injury, blood vessel, carotid,
      laceration, major
  celiac artery (incomplete) S35.211
    branch (incomplete) S35.291
      complete S35.292
    complete S35.212
  innominate
    artery (incomplete) —see also Injury, blood
      vessel, thoracic, innominate, artery,
      laceration
      complete —see Injury, blood vessel,
        thoracic, innominate, artery,
        laceration, major
    vein (incomplete) —see also Injury, blood
      vessel, thoracic, innominate, vein,
      laceration
      complete —see Injury, blood vessel,
        thoracic, innominate, vein,
        laceration, major
  jugular vein (external) (incomplete) —see
    also Injury, blood vessel, jugular vein,
    laceration
    complete —see Injury, blood vessel, jugular
      vein, laceration, major
    internal (incomplete) —see also Injury,
      blood vessel, jugular vein, internal,
      laceration
      complete —see Injury, blood vessel,
        jugular vein, internal, laceration,
        major
  mesenteric artery (incomplete) —see also
    Injury, mesenteric, artery, laceration
    complete —see Injury, mesenteric artery,
      laceration, major
  pulmonary vessel (incomplete) —see also
    Injury, blood vessel, thoracic, pulmonary,
    laceration
    complete —see Injury, blood vessel,
      thoracic, pulmonary, laceration, major
  subclavian —see Transection, innominate
  vena cava (incomplete) —see also Injury, vena
    cava
    complete —see Injury, vena cava,
      laceration, major
  vertebral artery (incomplete) —see also Injury,
    blood vessel, vertebral, laceration
    complete —see Injury, blood vessel,
      vertebral, laceration, major

▶ New   ⇒ Revised   ~~deleted~~ Deleted   ● Use Additional Character(s)

Transfusion
associated (red blood cell) hemochromatosis
E83.111
blood
ABO incompatible —see Complication(s),
transfusion, incompatibility reaction,
ABO
➧minor blood group (Duffy) (E) (K) (Kell)
(Kidd) (Lewis) (M) (N) (P) (S)
T80.89
reaction or complication —see
Complications, transfusion
fetomaternal (mother) —see Pregnancy,
complicated by, placenta, transfusion
syndrome
maternofetal (mother) —see Pregnancy,
complicated by, placenta, transfusion
syndrome
placental (syndrome) (mother) —see
Pregnancy, complicated by, placenta,
transfusion syndrome
reaction (adverse) —see Complications,
transfusion
related acute lung injury (TRALI) J95.84
twin-to-twin —see Pregnancy, complicated
by, placenta, transfusion syndrome, fetus
to fetus
Transient (meaning homeless) —see also
condition Z59.0
Translocation
balanced autosomal Q95.9
in normal individual Q95.0
chromosomes NEC Q99.8
balanced and insertion in normal
individual Q95.0
Down's syndrome Q90.2
trisomy
13 Q91.6
18 Q91.2
21 Q90.2
Translucency, iris —see Degeneration, iris
Transmission of chemical substances through
the placenta —see Absorption, chemical,
through placenta
Transparency, lung, unilateral J43.0
Transplant (ed) (status) Z94.9
awaiting organ Z76.82
bone Z94.6
marrow Z94.81
candidate Z76.82
complication —see Complication, transplant
cornea Z94.7
heart Z94.1
and lung(s) Z94.3
valve Z95.2
prosthetic Z95.2
specified NEC Z95.4
xenogenic Z95.3
intestine Z94.82
kidney Z94.0
liver Z94.4
lung(s) Z94.2
and heart Z94.3
organ (failure) (infection) (rejection)Z94.9
removal status Z98.85
pancreas Z94.83
skin Z94.5
social Z60.3
specified organ or tissue NEC Z94.89
stem cells Z94.84
tissue Z94.9
Transplants, ovarian, endometrial N80.1
Transposed —see Transposition
Transposition (congenital) —see also
Malposition, congenital
abdominal viscera Q89.3
aorta (dextra) Q20.3
appendix Q43.8
colon Q43.8
corrected Q20.5
great vessels (complete) (partial) Q20.3

Transposition (Continued)
heart Q24.0
with complete transposition of viscera
Q89.3
intestine (large) (small) Q43.8
reversed jejunal (for bypass) (status) Z98.0
scrotum Q55.23
stomach Q40.2
with general transposition of viscera
Q89.3
tooth, teeth, fully erupted M26.30
vessels, great (complete) (partial) Q20.3
viscera (abdominal) (thoracic) Q89.3
Transsexualism F64.0
Transverse —see also condition
arrest (deep), in labor O64.0
lie (mother) O32.2
causing obstructed labor O64.8
Transvestism, transvestitism (dual-role)
F64.1
fetishistic F65.1
Trapped placenta (with hemorrhage) O72.0
without hemorrhage O73.0
TRAPS (tumor necrosis factor receptor
associated periodic syndrome) M04.1
Trauma, traumatism —see also Injury
acoustic —see subcategory H83.3
birth —see Birth, injury
complicating ectopic or molar pregnancy
O08.6
during delivery O71.9
following ectopic or molar pregnancy O08.6
obstetric O71.9
specified NEC O71.89
occlusal
primary K08.81
secondary K08.82
Traumatic —see also condition
brain injury S06.9
Treacher Collins syndrome Q75.4
Treitz's hernia —see Hernia, abdomen, specified
site NEC
Trematode infestation —see Infestation, fluke
Trematodiasis —see Infestation, fluke
Trembling paralysis —see Parkinsonism
Tremor(s) R25.1
drug induced G25.1
essential (benign) G25.0
familial G25.0
hereditary G25.0
hysterical F44.4
intention G25.2
medication induced postural G25.1
mercurial —see subcategory T56.1
Parkinson's —see Parkinsonism
psychogenic (conversion reaction) F44.4
senilis R54
specified type NEC G25.2
Trench
fever A79.0
foot —see Immersion, foot
mouth A69.1
Treponema pallidum infection —see Syphilis
Treponematosis
due to
T. pallidum —see Syphilis
T. pertenue —see Yaws
Triad
Hutchinson's (congenital syphilis) A50.53
Kartagener's Q89.3
Saint's —see Hernia, diaphragm
Trichiasis (eyelid) H02.059
with entropion —see Entropion
left H02.056
lower H02.055
upper H02.054
right H02.053
lower H02.052
upper H02.051
Trichinella spiralis (infection) (infestation)
B75

Trichinellosis, trichiniasis, trichinelliasis,
trichinosis B75
with muscle disorder B75 [M63.80]
ankle B75 [M63.87-●]
foot B75 [M63.87-●]
forearm B75 [M63.83-●]
hand B75 [M63.84-●]
lower leg B75 [M63.86-●]
multiple sites B75 [M63.89]
pelvic region B75 [M63.85-●]
shoulder region B75 [M63.81-●]
specified site NEC B75 [M63.88]
thigh B75 [M63.85-●]
upper arm B75 [M63.82-●]
Trichobezoar T18.9
intestine T18.3
stomach T18.2
Trichocephaliasis, trichocephalosis B79
Trichocephalus infestation B79
Trichoclasis L67.8
Trichoepithelioma —see also Neoplasm, skin,
benign
malignant —see Neoplasm, skin, malignant
Trichofolliculoma —see Neoplasm, skin,
benign
Tricholemmoma —see Neoplasm, skin,
benign
Trichomoniasis A59.9
bladder A59.03
cervix A59.09
intestinal A07.8
prostate A59.02
seminal vesicles A59.09
specified site NEC A59.8
urethra A59.03
urogenitalis A59.00
vagina A59.01
vulva A59.01
Trichomycosis
axillaris A48.8
nodosa, nodularis B36.8
Trichonodosis L67.8
Trichophytid, trichophyton infection —see
Dermatophytosis
Trichophytobezoar T18.9
intestine T18.3
stomach T18.2
Trichophytosis —see Dermatophytosis
Trichoptilosis L67.8
Trichorrhexis (nodosa) (invaginata) L67.0
Trichosis axillaris A48.8
Trichosporosis nodosa B36.2
Trichostasis spinulosa (congenital) Q84.1
Trichostrongyliasis, trichostrongylosis (small
intestine) B81.2
Trichostrongylus infection B81.2
Trichotillomania F63.3
Trichromat, trichromatopsia, anomalous
(congenital) H53.55
Trichuriasis B79
Trichuris trichiura (infection) (infestation) (any
site) B79
Tricuspid (valve) —see condition
Trifid —see also Accessory
kidney (pelvis) Q63.8
tongue Q38.3
Trigeminal neuralgia —see Neuralgia,
trigeminal
Trigeminy R00.8
Trigger finger (acquired) M65.30
congenital Q74.0
index finger M65.32-●
little finger M65.35-●
middle finger M65.33-●
ring finger M65.34-●
thumb M65.31-●
Trigonitis (bladder) (chronic)
(pseudomembranous) N30.30
with hematuria N30.31
Trigonocephaly Q75.0
Trilocular heart —see Cor triloculare

Trimethylaminuria E72.52
Tripartite placenta O43.19-●
Triphalangeal thumb Q74.0
Triple —see also Accessory
    kidneys Q63.0
    uteri Q51.818
    X, female Q97.0
Triplegia G83.89
    congenital G80.8
Triplet (newborn) —see also Newborn, triplet
    complicating pregnancy —see Pregnancy,
        triplet
Triplication —see Accessory
Triploidy Q92.7
Trismus R25.2
    neonatorum A33
    newborn A33
Trisomy (syndrome) Q92.9
    13 (partial) Q91.7
        meiotic nondisjunction Q91.4
        mitotic nondisjunction Q91.5
        mosaicism Q91.5
        translocation Q91.6
    18 (partial) Q91.3
        meiotic nondisjunction Q91.0
        mitotic nondisjunction Q91.1
        mosaicism Q91.1
        translocation Q91.2
    20 Q92.8
    21 (partial) Q90.9
        meiotic nondisjunction Q90.0
        mitotic nondisjunction Q90.1
        mosaicism Q90.1
        translocation Q90.2
    22 Q92.8
    autosomes Q92.9
    chromosome specified NEC Q92.8
        partial Q92.2
            due to unbalanced translocation Q92.5
        specified NEC Q92.8
        whole (nonsex chromosome)
            meiotic nondisjunction Q92.0
            mitotic nondisjunction Q92.1
            mosaicism Q92.1
    due to
        dicentrics —see Extra, marker
            chromosomes
        extra rings —see Extra, marker
            chromosomes
        isochromosomes —see Extra, marker
            chromosomes
    specified NEC Q92.8
    whole chromosome Q92.9
        meiotic nondisjunction Q92.0
        mitotic nondisjunction Q92.1
        mosaicism Q92.1
        partial Q92.9
        specified NEC Q92.8
Tritanomaly, tritanopia H53.55
Trombiculosis, trombiculiasis, trombidiosis
    B88.0
Trophedema (congenital) (hereditary) Q82.0
Trophoblastic disease —see also Mole,
    hydatidiform O01.9
Tropholymphedema Q82.0
Trophoneurosis NEC G96.8
    disseminated M34.9
Tropical —see condition
Trouble —see also Disease
    heart —see Disease, heart
    kidney —see Disease, renal
    nervous R45.0
    sinus —see Sinusitis
Trousseau's syndrome (thrombophlebitis
    migrans) I82.1
Truancy, childhood
    from school Z72.810
Truncus
    arteriosus (persistent) Q20.0
    communis Q20.0
Trunk —see condition

Trypanosomiasis
    African B56.9
        by Trypanosoma brucei
            gambiense B56.0
            rhodesiense B56.1
        American —see Chagas' disease
        Brazilian —see Chagas' disease
        by Trypanosoma
            brucei gambiense B56.0
            brucei rhodesiense B56.1
            cruzi —see Chagas' disease
        gambiensis, Gambian B56.0
        rhodesiensis, Rhodesian B56.1
        South American —see Chagas' disease
        where
            African trypanosomiasis is prevalent B56.9
            Chagas' disease is prevalent B57.2
T-shaped incisors K00.2
Tsutsugamushi (disease) (fever) A75.3
Tube, tubal, tubular —see condition
Tubercle —see also Tuberculosis
    brain, solitary A17.81
    Darwin's Q17.8
    Ghon, primary infection A15.7
Tuberculid, tuberculide (indurating,
    subcutaneous) (lichenoid) (miliary)
    (papulonecrotic) (primary) (skin) A18.4
Tuberculoma —see also Tuberculosis
    brain A17.81
    meninges (cerebral) (spinal) A17.1
    spinal cord A17.81
Tuberculosis, tubercular, tuberculous
    (calcification) (calcified) (caseous)
    (chromogenic acid-fast bacilli)
    (degeneration) (fibrocaseous) (fistula)
    (interstitial) (isolated circumscribed
    lesions) (necrosis) (parenchymatous)
    (ulcerative) A15.9
    with pneumoconiosis (any condition in
        J60-J64) J65
    abdomen (lymph gland) A18.39
    abscess (respiratory) A15.9
        bone A18.03
            hip A18.02
            knee A18.02
            sacrum A18.01
            specified site NEC A18.03
            spinal A18.01
            vertebra A18.01
        brain A17.81
        breast A18.89
        Cowper's gland A18.15
        dura (mater) (cerebral) (spinal) A17.81
        epidural (cerebral) (spinal) A17.81
        female pelvis A18.17
        frontal sinus A15.8
        genital organs NEC A18.10
        genitourinary A18.10
        gland (lymphatic) —see Tuberculosis,
            lymph gland
        hip A18.02
        intestine A18.32
        ischiorectal A18.32
        joint NEC A18.02
            hip A18.02
            knee A18.02
            specified NEC A18.02
            vertebral A18.01
        kidney A18.11
        knee A18.02
        latent R76.11
        lumbar (spine) A18.01
        lung —see Tuberculosis, pulmonary
        meninges (cerebral) (spinal) A17.0
        muscle A18.09
        perianal (fistula) A18.32
        perinephritic A18.11
        perirectal A18.32
        rectum A18.32
        retropharyngeal A15.8
        sacrum A18.01

Tuberculosis, tubercular, tuberculous
    (Continued)
    abscess (Continued)
        scrofulous A18.2
        scrotum A18.15
        skin (primary) A18.4
        spinal cord A17.81
        spine or vertebra (column) A18.01
        subdiaphragmatic A18.31
        testis A18.15
        urinary A18.13
        uterus A18.17
    accessory sinus —see Tuberculosis, sinus
    Addison's disease A18.7
    adenitis —see Tuberculosis, lymph gland
    adenoids A15.8
    adenopathy —see Tuberculosis, lymph gland
    adherent pericardium A18.84
    adnexa (uteri) A18.17
    adrenal (capsule) (gland) A18.7
    alimentary canal A18.32
    anemia A18.89
    ankle (joint) (bone) A18.02
    anus A18.32
    apex, apical —see Tuberculosis, pulmonary
    appendicitis, appendix A18.32
    arachnoid A17.0
    artery, arteritis A18.89
        cerebral A18.89
    arthritis (chronic) (synovial) A18.02
        spine or vertebra (column) A18.01
    articular —see Tuberculosis, joint
    ascites A18.31
    asthma —see Tuberculosis, pulmonary
    axilla, axillary (gland) A18.2
    bladder A18.12
    bone A18.03
        hip A18.02
        knee A18.02
        limb NEC A18.03
        sacrum A18.01
        spine or vertebral column A18.01
    bowel (miliary) A18.32
    brain A17.81
    breast A18.89
    broad ligament A18.17
    bronchi, bronchial, bronchus A15.5
        ectasia, ectasis (bronchiectasis) —see
            Tuberculosis, pulmonary
        fistula A15.5
            primary (progressive) A15.7
        gland or node A15.4
            primary (progressive) A15.7
        lymph gland or node A15.4
            primary (progressive) A15.7
    bronchiectasis —see Tuberculosis, pulmonary
    bronchitis A15.5
    bronchopleural A15.6
    bronchopneumonia, bronchopneumonic —see
        Tuberculosis, pulmonary
    bronchorrhagia A15.5
    bronchotracheal A15.5
    bronze disease A18.7
    buccal cavity A18.83
    bulbourethral gland A18.15
    bursa A18.09
    cachexia A15.9
    cardiomyopathy A18.84
    caries —see Tuberculosis, bone
    cartilage A18.02
        intervertebral A18.01
    catarrhal —see Tuberculosis, respiratory
    cecum A18.32
    cellulitis (primary) A18.4
    cerebellum A17.81
    cerebral, cerebrum A17.81
    cerebrospinal A17.81
        meninges A17.0
    cervical (lymph gland or node) A18.2
    cervicitis, cervix (uteri) A18.16
    chest —see Tuberculosis, respiratory

▶ New   ⇒ Revised   ~~deleted~~ Deleted   ● Use Additional Character(s)

Tuberculosis, tubercular, tuberculous
(Continued)
chorioretinitis A18.53
choroid, choroiditis A18.53
ciliary body A18.54
colitis A18.32
collier's J65
colliquativa (primary) A18.4
colon A18.32
complex, primary A15.7
congenital P37.0
conjunctiva A18.59
connective tissue (systemic) A18.89
contact Z20.1
cornea (ulcer) A18.52
Cowper's gland A18.15
coxae A18.02
coxalgia A18.02
cul-de-sac of Douglas A18.17
curvature, spine A18.01
cutis (colliquativa) (primary) A18.4
cyst, ovary A18.18
cystitis A18.12
dactylitis A18.03
diarrhea A18.32
diffuse —*see* Tuberculosis, miliary
digestive tract A18.32
disseminated —*see* Tuberculosis, miliary
duodenum A18.32
dura (mater) (cerebral) (spinal) A17.0
  abscess (cerebral) (spinal) A17.81
dysentery A18.32
ear (inner) (middle) A18.6
  bone A18.03
  external (primary) A18.4
  skin (primary) A18.4
elbow A18.02
emphysema —*see* Tuberculosis, pulmonary
empyema A15.6
encephalitis A17.82
endarteritis A18.89
endocarditis A18.84
  aortic A18.84
  mitral A18.84
  pulmonary A18.84
  tricuspid A18.84
endocrine glands NEC A18.82
endometrium A18.17
enteric, enterica, enteritis A18.32
enterocolitis A18.32
epididymis, epididymitis A18.15
epidural abscess (cerebral) (spinal) A17.81
epiglottis A15.5
episcleritis A18.51
erythema (induratum) (nodosum) (primary)
  A18.4
esophagus A18.83
eustachian tube A18.6
exposure (to) Z20.1
exudative —*see* Tuberculosis, pulmonary
eye A18.50
eyelid (primary) (lupus) A18.4
fallopian tube (acute) (chronic) A18.17
fascia A18.09
fauces A15.8
female pelvic inflammatory disease A18.17
finger A18.03
first infection A15.7
gallbladder A18.83
ganglion A18.09
gastritis A18.83
gastrocolic fistula A18.32
gastroenteritis A18.32
gastrointestinal tract A18.32
general, generalized —*see* Tuberculosis,
  miliary
genital organs A18.10
genitourinary A18.10
genu A18.02
glandula suprarenalis A18.7
glandular, general A18.2

Tuberculosis, tubercular, tuberculous
(Continued)
glottis A15.5
grinder's J65
gum A18.83
hand A18.03
heart A18.84
hematogenous —*see* Tuberculosis, miliary
hemoptysis —*see* Tuberculosis, pulmonary
hemorrhage NEC —*see* Tuberculosis,
  pulmonary
hemothorax A15.6
hepatitis A18.83
hilar lymph nodes A15.4
  primary (progressive) A15.7
hip (joint) (disease) (bone) A18.02
hydropneumothorax A15.6
hydrothorax A15.6
hypoadrenalism A18.7
hypopharynx A15.8
ileocecal (hyperplastic) A18.32
ileocolitis A18.32
ileum A18.32
iliac spine (superior) A18.03
immunological findings only A15.7
indurativa (primary) A18.4
infantile A15.7
infection A15.9
  without clinical manifestations A15.7
infraclavicular gland A18.2
inguinal gland A18.2
inguinalis A18.2
intestine (any part) A18.32
iridocyclitis A18.54
iris, iritis A18.54
ischiorectal A18.32
jaw A18.03
jejunum A18.32
joint A18.02
  vertebral A18.01
keratitis (interstitial) A18.52
keratoconjunctivitis A18.52
kidney A18.11
knee (joint) A18.02
kyphosis, kyphoscoliosis A18.01
laryngitis A15.5
larynx A15.5
latent R76.11
leptomeninges, leptomeningitis (cerebral)
  (spinal) A17.0
lichenoides (primary) A18.4
linguae A18.83
lip A18.83
liver A18.83
lordosis A18.01
lung —*see* Tuberculosis, pulmonary
lupus vulgaris A18.4
lymph gland or node (peripheral) A18.2
  abdomen A18.39
  bronchial A15.4
    primary (progressive) A15.7
  cervical A18.2
  hilar A15.4
    primary (progressive) A15.7
  intrathoracic A15.4
    primary (progressive) A15.7
  mediastinal A15.4
    primary (progressive) A15.7
  mesenteric A18.39
  retroperitoneal A18.39
  tracheobronchial A15.4
    primary (progressive) A15.7
lymphadenitis —*see* Tuberculosis, lymph
  gland
lymphangitis —*see* Tuberculosis, lymph
  gland
lymphatic (gland) (vessel) —*see* Tuberculosis,
  lymph gland
mammary gland A18.89
marasmus A15.9
mastoiditis A18.03

Tuberculosis, tubercular, tuberculous
(Continued)
mediastinal lymph gland or node
  A15.4
  primary (progressive) A15.7
mediastinitis A15.8
  primary (progressive) A15.7
mediastinum A15.8
  primary (progressive) A15.7
medulla A17.81
melanosis, Addisonian A18.7
meninges, meningitis (basilar) (cerebral)
  (cerebrospinal) (spinal) A17.0
meningoencephalitis A17.82
mesentery, mesenteric (gland or node)
  A18.39
miliary A19.9
  acute A19.2
    multiple sites A19.1
    single specified site A19.0
  chronic A19.8
  specified NEC A19.8
millstone makers' J65
miner's J65
molder's J65
mouth A18.83
multiple A19.9
  acute A19.1
  chronic A19.8
muscle A18.09
myelitis A17.82
myocardium, myocarditis A18.84
nasal (passage) (sinus) A15.8
nasopharynx A15.8
neck gland A18.2
nephritis A18.11
nerve (mononeuropathy) A17.83
nervous system A17.9
nose (septum) A15.8
ocular A18.50
omentum A18.31
oophoritis (acute) (chronic) A18.17
optic (nerve trunk) (papilla) A18.59
orbit A18.59
orchitis A18.15
organ, specified NEC A18.89
osseous —*see* Tuberculosis, bone
osteitis —*see* Tuberculosis, bone
osteomyelitis —*see* Tuberculosis, bone
otitis media A18.6
ovary, ovaritis (acute) (chronic) A18.17
oviduct (acute) (chronic) A18.17
pachymeningitis A17.0
palate (soft) A18.83
pancreas A18.83
papulonecrotic (a) (primary) A18.4
parathyroid glands A18.82
paronychia (primary) A18.4
parotid gland or region A18.83
pelvis (bony) A18.03
penis A18.15
peribronchitis A15.5
pericardium, pericarditis A18.84
perichondritis, larynx A15.5
periostitis —*see* Tuberculosis, bone
perirectal fistula A18.32
peritoneum NEC A18.31
peritonitis A18.31
pharynx, pharyngitis A15.8
phlyctenulosis (keratoconjunctivitis) A18.52
phthisis NEC —*see* Tuberculosis, pulmonary
pituitary gland A18.82
pleura, pleural, pleurisy, pleuritis (fibrinous)
  (obliterative) (purulent) (simple plastic)
  (with effusion) A15.6
  primary (progressive) A15.7
pneumonia, pneumonic —*see* Tuberculosis,
  pulmonary
pneumothorax (spontaneous) (tense
  valvular) —*see* Tuberculosis, pulmonary
polyneuropathy A17.89

Tuberculosis, tubercular, tuberculous
(Continued)
polyserositis A19.9
acute A19.1
chronic A19.8
potter's J65
prepuce A18.15
primary (complex) A15.7
proctitis A18.32
prostate, prostatitis A18.14
pulmonalis —see Tuberculosis, pulmonary
pulmonary (cavitated) (fibrotic) (infiltrative)
(nodular) A15.0
childhood type or first infection A15.7
primary (complex) A15.7
pyelitis A18.11
pyelonephritis A18.11
pyemia —see Tuberculosis, miliary
pyonephrosis A18.11
pyopneumothorax A15.6
pyothorax A15.6
rectum (fistula) (with abscess) A18.32
reinfection stage —see Tuberculosis,
pulmonary
renal A18.11
renis A18.11
respiratory A15.9
primary A15.7
specified site NEC A15.8
retina, retinitis A18.53
retroperitoneal (lymph gland or node)
A18.39
rheumatism NEC A18.09
rhinitis A15.8
sacroiliac (joint) A18.01
sacrum A18.01
salivary gland A18.83
salpingitis (acute) (chronic) A18.17
sandblaster's J65
sclera A18.51
scoliosis A18.01
scrofulous A18.2
scrotum A18.15
seminal tract or vesicle A18.15
senile A15.9
septic —see Tuberculosis, miliary
shoulder (joint) A18.02
blade A18.03
sigmoid A18.32
sinus (any nasal) A15.8
bone A18.03
epididymis A18.15
skeletal NEC A18.03
skin (any site) (primary) A18.4
small intestine A18.32
soft palate A18.83
spermatic cord A18.15
spine, spinal (column) A18.01
cord A17.81
medulla A17.81
membrane A17.0
meninges A17.0
spleen, splenitis A18.85
spondylitis A18.01
sternoclavicular joint A18.02
stomach A18.83
stonemason's J65
subcutaneous tissue (cellular) (primary)
A18.4
subcutis (primary) A18.4
subdeltoid bursa A18.83
submaxillary (region) A18.83
supraclavicular gland A18.2
suprarenal (capsule) (gland) A18.7
swelling, joint —see also category M01 (see also
Tuberculosis, joint) A18.02
symphysis pubis A18.02
synovitis A18.09
articular A18.02
spine or vertebra A18.01
systemic —see Tuberculosis, miliary

Tuberculosis, tubercular, tuberculous
(Continued)
tarsitis A18.4
tendon (sheath) —see Tuberculosis,
tenosynovitis
tenosynovitis A18.09
spine or vertebra A18.01
testis A18.15
throat A15.8
thymus gland A18.82
thyroid gland A18.81
tongue A18.83
tonsil, tonsillitis A15.8
trachea, tracheal A15.5
lymph gland or node A15.4
primary (progressive) A15.7
tracheobronchial A15.5
lymph gland or node A15.4
primary (progressive) A15.7
tubal (acute) (chronic) A18.17
tunica vaginalis A18.15
ulcer (skin) (primary) A18.4
bowel or intestine A18.32
specified NEC - code under Tuberculosis,
by site
unspecified site A15.9
ureter A18.11
urethra, urethral (gland) A18.13
urinary organ or tract A18.13
uterus A18.17
uveal tract A18.54
uvula A18.83
vagina A18.18
vas deferens A18.15
verruca, verrucosa (cutis) (primary) A18.4
vertebra (column) A18.01
vesiculitis A18.15
vulva A18.18
wrist (joint) A18.02
Tuberculum
Carabelli —see Note at K00.2
occlusal —see Note at K00.2
paramolare K00.2
Tuberosity, enitre maxillary M26.07
Tuberous sclerosis (brain) Q85.1
Tubo-ovarian —see condition
Tuboplasty, after previous sterilization
Z31.0
aftercare Z31.42
Tubotympanitis, catarrhal (chronic) —see Otitis,
media, nonsuppurative, chronic, serous
Tularemia A21.9
with
conjunctivitis A21.1
pneumonia A21.2
abdominal A21.3
bronchopneumonic A21.2
conjunctivitis A21.1
cryptogenic A21.3
enteric A21.3
gastrointestinal A21.3
generalized A21.7
ingestion A21.3
intestinal A21.3
oculoglandular A21.1
ophthalmic A21.1
pneumonia (any), pneumonic A21.2
pulmonary A21.2
sepsis A21.7
specified NEC A21.8
typhoidal A21.7
ulceroglandular A21.0
Tularensis conjunctivitis A21.1
Tumefaction —see also Swelling
liver —see Hypertrophy, liver
Tumor —see also Neoplasm, unspecified
behavior, by site
acinar cell —see Neoplasm, uncertain
behavior, by site
acinic cell —see Neoplasm, uncertain
behavior, by site

Tumor (Continued)
adenocarcinoid —see Neoplasm, malignant,
by site
adenomatoid —see also Neoplasm, benign,
by site
odontogenic —see Cyst, calcifying
odontogenic
adnexal (skin) —see Neoplasm, skin, benign,
by site
adrenal
cortical (benign) D35.0-●
malignant C74.0-●
rest —see Neoplasm, benign, by site
alpha-cell
malignant
pancreas C25.4
specified site NEC —see Neoplasm,
malignant, by site
unspecified site C25.4
pancreas D13.7
specified site NEC —see Neoplasm, benign,
by site
unspecified site D13.7
aneurysmal —see Aneurysm
aortic body D44.7
malignant C75.5
Askin's —see Neoplasm, connective tissue,
malignant
basal cell —see also Neoplasm, skin, uncertain
behavior D48.5
Bednar —see Neoplasm, skin, malignant
benign (unclassified) —see Neoplasm, benign,
by site
beta-cell
malignant
pancreas C25.4
specified site NEC —see Neoplasm,
malignant, by site
unspecified site C25.4
pancreas D13.7
specified site NEC —see Neoplasm, benign,
by site
unspecified site D13.7
Brenner D27.9
borderline malignancy D39.1-●
malignant C56-●
proliferating D39.1
bronchial alveolar, intravascular D38.1
Brooke's —see Neoplasm, skin, benign
brown fat —see Lipoma
Burkitt —see Lymphoma, Burkitt
calcifying epithelial odontogenic —see Cyst,
calcifying odontogenic
carcinoid
benign D3A.00
appendix D3A.020
ascending colon D3A.022
bronchus (lung) D3A.090
cecum D3A.021
colon D3A.029
descending colon D3A.024
duodenum D3A.010
foregut NOS D3A.094
hindgut NOS D3A.096
ileum D3A.012
jejunum D3A.011
kidney D3A.093
large intestine D3A.029
lung (bronchus) D3A.090
midgut NOS D3A.095
rectum D3A.026
sigmoid colon D3A.025
small intestine D3A.019
specified NEC D3A.098
stomach D3A.092
thymus D3A.091
transverse colon D3A.023
malignant C7A.00
appendix C7A.020
ascending colon C7A.022
bronchus (lung) C7A.090

Tumor *(Continued)*
  carcinoid *(Continued)*
    malignant *(Continued)*
      cecum C7A.021
      colon C7A.029
      descending colon C7A.024
      duodenum C7A.010
      foregut NOS C7A.094
      hindgut NOS C7A.096
      ileum C7A.012
      jejunum C7A.011
      kidney C7A.093
      large intestine C7A.029
      lung (bronchus) C7A.090
      midgut NOS C7A.095
      rectum C7A.026
      sigmoid colon C7A.025
      small intestine C7A.019
      specified NEC C7A.098
      stomach C7A.092
      thymus C7A.091
      transverse colon C7A.023
    mesentary metastasis C7B.04
    secondary C7B.00
      bone C7B.03
      distant lymph nodes C7B.01
      liver C7B.02
      peritoneum C7B.04
      specified NEC C7B.09
  carotid body D44.6
    malignant C75.4
  cells —*see also* Neoplasm, unspecified
    behavior, by site
    benign —*see* Neoplasm, benign,
      by site
    malignant —*see* Neoplasm, malignant,
      by site
    uncertain whether benign or malignant —
      see Neoplasm, uncertain behavior,
      by site
  cervix, in pregnancy or childbirth —*see*
    Pregnancy, complicated by, tumor,
    cervix
  chondromatous giant cell —*see* Neoplasm,
    bone, benign
  Codman's —*see* Neoplasm, bone, benign
  chromaffin —*see also* Neoplasm, benign, by
    site
    malignant —*see* Neoplasm, malignant, by
      site
  Cock's peculiar L72.3
  Codman's —*see* Neoplasm, bone, benign
  dentigerous, mixed —*see* Cyst, calcifying
    odontogenic
  dermoid —*see* Neoplasm, benign,
    by site
    with malignant transformation C56-●
  desmoid (extra-abdominal) —*see also*
    Neoplasm, connective tissue, uncertain
    behavior
    abdominal —*see* Neoplasm, connective
      tissue, uncertain behavior
  embolus —*see* Neoplasm, secondary,
    by site
  embryonal (mixed) —*see also* Neoplasm,
    uncertain behavior, by site
    liver C22.7
  endodermal sinus
    specified site —*see* Neoplasm, malignant,
      by site
    unspecified site
      female C56.-●
      male C62.90
  epithelial
    benign —*see* Neoplasm, benign,
      by site
    malignant —*see* Neoplasm, malignant, by
      site
  Ewing's —*see* Neoplasm, bone, malignant,
    by site
  fatty —*see* Lipoma
  fibroid —*see* Leiomyoma

Tumor *(Continued)*
  G cell
    malignant
      pancreas C25.4
      specified site NEC —*see* Neoplasm,
        malignant, by site
      unspecified site C25.4
    specified site —*see* Neoplasm, uncertain
      behavior, by site
    unspecified site D37.8
  germ cell —*see also* Neoplasm, malignant,
    by site
    mixed —*see* Neoplasm, malignant,
      by site
  ghost cell, odontogenic —*see* Cyst, calcifying
    odontogenic
  giant cell —*see also* Neoplasm, uncertain
    behavior, by site
    bone D48.0
      malignant —*see* Neoplasm, bone,
        malignant
    chondromatous —*see* Neoplasm, bone,
      benign
    malignant —*see* Neoplasm, malignant, by
      site
    soft parts —*see* Neoplasm, connective
      tissue, uncertain behavior
      malignant —*see* Neoplasm, connective
        tissue, malignant
  glomus D18.00
    intra-abdominal D18.03
    intracranial D18.02
    jugulare D44.7
      malignant C75.5
    skin D18.01
    specified site NEC D18.09
  gonadal stromal —*see* Neoplasm, uncertain
    behavior, by site
  granular cell —*see also* Neoplasm, connective
    tissue, benign
    malignant —*see* Neoplasm, connective
      tissue, malignant
  granulosa cell D39.1-●
    juvenile D39.1-●
    malignant C56-●
  granulosa cell-theca cell D39.1-●
    malignant C56-●
  Grawitz's C64-●
  hemorrhoidal —*see* Hemorrhoids
  hilar cell D27-●
  hilus cell D27-●
  Hurthle cell (benign) D34
    malignant C73
  hydatid —*see* Echinococcus
  hypernephroid —*see also* Neoplasm,
    uncertain behavior, by site
  interstitial cell —*see also* Neoplasm, uncertain
    behavior, by site
    benign —*see* Neoplasm, benign, by site
    malignant —*see* Neoplasm, malignant, by
      site
  intravascular bronchial alveolar D38.1
  islet cell —*see* Neoplasm, benign, by site
    malignant —*see* Neoplasm, malignant, by
      site
      pancreas C25.4
      specified site NEC —*see* Neoplasm,
        malignant, by site
      unspecified site C25.4
    pancreas D13.7
    specified site NEC —*see* Neoplasm, benign,
      by site
    unspecified site D13.7
  juxtaglomerular D41.0-●
  Klatskin's C24.0
  Krukenberg's C79.6-●
  Leydig cell —*see* Neoplasm, uncertain
    behavior, by site
    benign —*see* Neoplasm, benign, by site
      specified site —*see* Neoplasm, benign,
        by site

Tumor *(Continued)*
  Leydig cell *(Continued)*
    benign *(Continued)*
      unspecified site
        female D27.9
        male D29.20
    malignant —*see* Neoplasm, malignant, by
      site
      specified site —*see* Neoplasm,
        malignant, by site
      unspecified site
        female C56.9
        male C62.90
    specified site —*see* Neoplasm, uncertain
      behavior, by site
    unspecified site
      female D39.10
      male D40.10
  lipid cell, ovary D27-●
  lipoid cell, ovary D27-●
  malignant —*see also* Neoplasm, malignant, by
    site C80.1
    fusiform cell (type) C80.1
    giant cell (type) C80.1
    localized, plasma cell —*see* Plasmacytoma,
      solitary
    mixed NEC C80.1
    small cell (type) C80.1
    spindle cell (type) C80.1
    unclassified C80.1
  mast cell D47.09
  melanotic, neuroectodermal —*see* Neoplasm,
    benign, by site
  Merkel cell —*see* Carcinoma, Merkel cell
  mesenchymal
    malignant —*see* Neoplasm, connective
      tissue, malignant
    mixed —*see* Neoplasm, connective tissue,
      uncertain behavior
  mesodermal, mixed —*see also* Neoplasm,
    malignant, by site
    liver C22.4
  mesonephric —*see also* Neoplasm, uncertain
    behavior, by site
    malignant —*see* Neoplasm, malignant, by
      site
  metastatic
    from specified site —*see* Neoplasm,
      malignant, by site
    of specified site —*see* Neoplasm,
      malignant, by site
    to specified site —*see* Neoplasm, secondary,
      by site
  mixed NEC —*see also* Neoplasm, benign, by
    site
    malignant —*see* Neoplasm, malignant, by
      site
  mucinous of low malignant potential
    specified site —*see* Neoplasm, malignant,
      by site
    unspecified site C56.9
  mucocarcinoid
    specified site —*see* Neoplasm, malignant,
      by site
    unspecified site C18.1
  mucoepidermoid —*see* Neoplasm, uncertain
    behavior, by site
  Müllerian, mixed
    specified site —*see* Neoplasm, malignant,
      by site
    unspecified site C54.9
  myoepithelial —*see* Neoplasm, benign,
    by site
  neuroectodermal (peripheral) —*see*
    Neoplasm, malignant, by site
    primitive
      specified site —*see* Neoplasm,
        malignant, by site
      unspecified site C71.9

Tumor *(Continued)*
  neuroendocrine D3A.8
    malignant poorly differentiated C7A.1
    secondary NEC C7B.8
    specified NEC C7A.8
  neurogenic olfactory C30.0
  nonencapsulated sclerosing C73
  odontogenic (adenomatoid) (benign)
      (calcifying epithelial) (keratocystic)
      (squamous) —*see* Cyst, calcifying
      odontogenic
    malignant C41.1
      upper jaw (bone) C41.0
  ovarian stromal D39.1-•
  ovary, in pregnancy —*see* Pregnancy,
      complicated by
  pacinian —*see* Neoplasm, skin, benign
  Pancoast's —*see* Pancoast's syndrome
  papillary —*see also* Papilloma
    cystic D37.9
    mucinous of low malignant potential C56-•
      specified site —*see* Neoplasm,
          malignant, by site
      unspecified site C56.9
    serous of low malignant potential
      specified site —*see* Neoplasm,
          malignant, by site
      unspecified site C56.9
  pelvic, in pregnancy or childbirth —*see*
      Pregnancy, complicated by
  phantom F45.8
  phyllodes D48.6-•
    benign D24-•
    malignant —*see* Neoplasm, breast,
        malignant
  Pindborg —*see* Cyst, calcifying odontogenic
  placental site trophoblastic D39.2
  plasma cell (malignant) (localized) —*see*
      Plasmacytoma, solitary
  polyvesicular vitelline
    specified site —*see* Neoplasm, malignant,
        by site
    unspecified site
      female C56.9
      male C62.90
  Pott's puffy —*see* Osteomyelitis, specified NEC
  Rathke's pouch D44.3
  retinal anlage —*see* Neoplasm, benign, by site
  salivary gland type, mixed —*see* Neoplasm,
      salivary gland, benign
    malignant —*see* Neoplasm, salivary gland,
        malignant
  Sampson's N80.1
  Schmincke's —*see* Neoplasm, nasopharynx,
      malignant
  sclerosing stromal D27-•
  sebaceous —*see* Cyst, sebaceous
  secondary —*see* Neoplasm, secondary, by site
    carcinoid C7B.00
      bone C7B.03
      distant lymph nodes C7B.01
      liver C7B.02
      peritoneum C7B.04
      specified NEC C7B.09
    neuroendocrine NEC C7B.8
  serous of low malignant potential
    specified site —*see* Neoplasm, malignant,
        by site
    unspecified site C56.9
  Sertoli cell —*see* Neoplasm, benign, by site
    with lipid storage
      specified site —*see* Neoplasm, benign,
          by site
      unspecified site
        female D27.9
        male D29.20
    specified site —*see* Neoplasm, benign, by
        site
    unspecified site
      female D27.9
      male D29.20

Tumor *(Continued)*
  Sertoli-Leydig cell —*see* Neoplasm, benign,
      by site
    specified site —*see* Neoplasm, benign, by
        site
    unspecified site
      female D27.9
      male D29.20
  sex cord(-stromal) —*see* Neoplasm, uncertain
      behavior, by site
    with annular tubules D39.1-•
  skin appendage —*see* Neoplasm, skin,
      benign
  smooth muscle —*see* Neoplasm, connective
      tissue, uncertain behavior
  soft tissue
    benign —*see* Neoplasm, connective tissue,
        benign
    malignant —*see* Neoplasm, connective
        tissue, malignant
  sternomastoid (congenital) Q68.0
  stromal
    endometrial D39.0
    gastric D48.1
      benign D21.4
      malignant C16.9
      uncertain behavior D48.1
    gastrointestinal C49.A-•
      benign D21.4
      esophagus C49.A1
      large intestine C49.A4
      malignant C49.A0
        colon C49.A4
        duodenum C49.A3
        esophagus C49.A1
        ileum C49.A3
        jejunum C49.A3
        Meckel diverticulum C49.A3
        large intestine C49.A4
        omentum C49.A9
        peritoneum C49.A9
        rectum C49.A5
        small intestine C49.A3
        specified site NEC C49.A9
        stomach C49.A2
      rectum C49.A5
      small intestine C49.A3
      specified site NEC C49.A9
      stomach C49.A2
      uncertain behavior D48.1
    intestine
      benign D21.4
      malignant
        large C49.A4
        small C49.A3
      uncertain behavior D48.1
    ovarian D39.1-•
    stomach C49.A2
      benign D21.4
      malignant C49.A2
      uncertain behavior D48.1
  sweat gland —*see also* Neoplasm, skin,
      uncertain behavior
    benign —*see* Neoplasm, skin, benign
    malignant —*see* Neoplasm, skin,
        malignant
  syphilitic, brain A52.17
  testicular D40.10
  testicular stromal D40.1-•
  theca cell D27.-•
  theca cell-granulosa cell D39.1-•
  Triton, malignant —*see* Neoplasm, nerve,
      malignant
  trophoblastic, placental site D39.2
  turban D23.4
  uterus (body), in pregnancy or childbirth —
      see Pregnancy, complicated by, tumor,
      uterus
  vagina, in pregnancy or childbirth —*see*
      Pregnancy, complicated by
  varicose —*see* Varix

Tumor *(Continued)*
  von Recklinghausen's —*see*
      Neurofibromatosis
  vulva or perineum, in pregnancy or
      childbirth —*see* Pregnancy, complicated
      by
    causing obstructed labor O65.5
  Warthin's —*see* Neoplasm, salivary gland,
      benign
  Wilms' C64-•
  yolk sac —*see* Neoplasm, malignant, by site
    specified site —*see* Neoplasm, malignant,
        by site
    unspecified site
      female C56.9
      male C62.90
Tumor lysis syndrome (following
    antineoplastic chemotherapy)
    (spontaneous) NEC E88.3
Tumorlet —*see* Neoplasm, uncertain behavior,
    by site
Tungiasis B88.1
Tunica vasculosa lentis Q12.2
Turban tumor D23.4
Türck's trachoma J37.0
Turner-Kieser syndrome Q87.2
Turner-like syndrome Q87.1
Turner's
  hypoplasia (tooth) K00.4
  syndrome Q96.9
    specified NEC Q96.8
  tooth K00.4
Turner-Ullrich syndrome Q96.9
Tussis convulsiva —*see* Whooping cough
Twiddler's syndrome (due to)
  automatic implantable defibrillator T82.198
  cardiac pacemaker T82.198
Twilight state
  epileptic F05
  psychogenic F44.89
Twin (newborn) —*see also* Newborn, twin
  conjoined Q89.4
  pregnancy —*see* Pregnancy, twin
Twinning, teeth K00.2
Twist, twisted
  bowel, colon or intestine K56.2
  hair (congenital) Q84.1
  mesentery K56.2
  omentum K56.2
  organ or site, congenital NEC —*see* Anomaly,
      by site
  ovarian pedicle —*see* Torsion, ovary
Twitching R25.3
Tylosis (acquired) L84
  buccalis K13.29
  linguae K13.29
  palmaris et plantaris (congenital) (inherited)
      Q82.8
    acquired L85.1
Tympanism R14.0
Tympanites (abdominal) (intestinal) R14.0
Tympanitis —*see* Myringitis
Tympanosclerosis —*see* subcategory H74.0
Tympanum —*see* condition
Tympany
  abdomen R14.0
  chest R09.89
Type A behavior pattern Z73.1
Typhlitis —*see* Appendicitis
Typhoenteritis —*see* Typhoid
Typhoid (abortive) (ambulant) (any site)
    (clinical) (fever) (hemorrhagic) (infection)
    (intermittent) (malignant) (rheumatic)
    (Widal negative) A01.00
  with pneumonia A01.03
  abdominal A01.09
  arthritis A01.04
  carrier (suspected) of Z22.0
  cholecystitis (current) A01.09
  endocarditis A01.02
  heart involvement A01.02

▶ New   ⟹ Revised   ~~deleted~~ Deleted   • Use Additional Character(s)

Typhoid *(Continued)*
  inoculation reaction —*see* Complications, vaccination
  meningitis A01.01
  mesenteric lymph nodes A01.09
  myocarditis A01.02
  osteomyelitis A01.05
  perichondritis, larynx A01.09
  pneumonia A01.03
  specified NEC A01.09
  spine A01.05
  ulcer (perforating) A01.09
Typhomalaria (fever) —*see* Malaria
Typhomania A01.00
Typhoperitonitis A01.09
Typhus (fever) A75.9
  abdominal, abdominalis —*see* Typhoid
  African tick A77.1
  amarillic A95.9
  brain A75.9 [G94]

Typhus *(Continued)*
  cerebral A75.9 [G94]
  classical A75.0
  due to Rickettsia
    prowazekii A75.0
      recrudescent A75.1
    tsutsugamushi A75.3
    typhi A75.2
  endemic (flea-borne) A75.2
  epidemic (louse-borne) A75.0
  exanthematic NEC A75.0
  exanthematicus SAI A75.0
    brillii SAI A75.1
    mexicanus SAI A75.2
    typhus murinus A75.2
  flea-borne A75.2
  India tick A77.1
  Kenya (tick) A77.1
  louse-borne A75.0
  Mexican A75.2

Typhus *(Continued)*
  mite-borne A75.3
  murine A75.2
  North Asian tick-borne A77.2
  petechial A75.9
  Queensland tick A77.3
  rat A75.2
  recrudescent A75.1
  recurrens —*see* Fever, relapsing
  Sao Paulo A77.0
  scrub (China) (India) (Malaysia) (New Guinea) A75.3
  shop (of Malaysia) A75.2
  Siberian tick A77.2
  tick-borne A77.9
  tropical (mite-borne) A75.3
Tyrosinemia E70.21
  newborn, transitory P74.5
Tyrosinosis E70.21
Tyrosinuria E70.29

U

Uhl's anomaly or disease Q24.8
Ulcer, ulcerated, ulcerating, ulceration, ulcerative
  alveolar process M27.3
  amebic (intestine) A06.1
    skin A06.7
  anastomotic —see Ulcer, gastrojejunal
  anorectal K62.6
  antral —see Ulcer, stomach
  anus (sphincter) (solitary) K62.6
  aorta —see Aneurysm
  aphthous (oral) (recurrent) K12.0
    genital organ(s)
      female N76.6
      male N50.89
  artery I77.2
  atrophic —see Ulcer, skin
    decubitus —see Ulcer, pressure, by site
  back L98.429
    with
      bone involvement without evidence of necrosis L98.426
      bone necrosis L98.424
      exposed fat layer L98.422
      muscle involvement without evidence of necrosis L98.425
      muscle necrosis L98.423
      skin breakdown only L98.421
      specified severity NEC L98.428
  Barrett's (esophagus) K22.10
    with bleeding K22.11
  bile duct (common) (hepatic) K83.8
  bladder (solitary) (sphincter) NEC N32.89
    bilharzial B65.9 [N33]
    in schistosomiasis (bilharzial) B65.9 [N33]
    submucosal —see Cystitis, interstitial
    tuberculous A18.12
  bleeding K27.4
  bone —see Osteomyelitis, specified type NEC
  bowel —see Ulcer, intestine
  breast N61.1
  bronchus J98.09
  buccal (cavity) (traumatic) K12.1
  Buruli A31.1
  buttock L98.419
    with
      bone involvement without evidence of necrosis L98.416
      bone necrosis L98.414
      exposed fat layer L98.412
      muscle involvement without evidence of necrosis L98.415
      muscle necrosis L98.413
      skin breakdown only L98.411
      specified severity NEC L98.418
  cancerous —see Neoplasm, malignant, by site
  cardia K22.10
    with bleeding K22.11
  cardioesophageal (peptic) K22.10
    with bleeding K22.11
  cecum —see Ulcer, intestine
  cervix (uteri) (decubitus) (trophic) N86
    with cervicitis N72
  chancroidal A57
  chiclero B55.1
  chronic (cause unknown) —see Ulcer, skin
  Cochin-China B55.1
  colon —see Ulcer, intestine
  conjunctiva H10.89
  cornea H16.00-•
    with hypopyon H16.03-•
    central H16.01-•
    dendritic (herpes simplex) B00.52
    marginal H16.04-•
    Mooren's H16.05-•
    mycotic H16.06-•
    perforated H16.07-•
    ring H16.02-•
    tuberculous (phlyctenular) A18.52

Ulcer, ulcerated, ulcerating, ulceration, ulcerative (Continued)
  corpus cavernosum (chronic) N48.5
  crural —see Ulcer, lower limb
  Curling's —see Ulcer, peptic, acute
  Cushing's —see Ulcer, peptic, acute
  cystic duct K82.8
  cystitis (interstitial) —see Cystitis, interstitial
  decubitus —see Ulcer, pressure, by site
  dendritic, cornea (herpes simplex) B00.52
  diabetes, diabetic —see Diabetes, ulcer
  Dieulafoy's K25.0
  due to
    infection NEC —see Ulcer, skin
    radiation NEC L59.8
    trophic disturbance (any region) —see Ulcer, skin
    X-ray L58.1
  duodenum, duodenal (eroded) (peptic) K26.9
    with
      hemorrhage K26.4
        and perforation K26.6
      perforation K26.5
    acute K26.3
      with
        hemorrhage K26.0
          and perforation K26.2
        perforation K26.1
    chronic K26.7
      with
        hemorrhage K26.4
          and perforation K26.6
        perforation K26.5
  dysenteric A09
  elusive —see Cystitis, interstitial
  endocarditis (acute) (chronic) (subacute) I28.8
  epiglottis J38.7
  esophagus (peptic) K22.10
    with bleeding K22.11
    due to
      aspirin K22.10
        with bleeding K22.11
      gastrointestinal reflux disease K21.0
      ingestion of chemical or medicament K22.10
        with bleeding K22.11
      fungal K22.10
        with bleeding K22.11
      infective K22.10
        with bleeding K22.11
    varicose —see Varix, esophagus
  eyelid (region) H01.8
  fauces J39.2
  Fenwick (-Hunner) (solitary) —see Cystitis, interstitial
  fistulous —see Ulcer, skin
  foot (indolent) (trophic) —see Ulcer, lower limb
  frambesial, initial A66.0
  frenum (tongue) K14.0
  gallbladder or duct K82.8
  gangrenous —see Gangrene
  gastric —see Ulcer, stomach
  gastrocolic —see Ulcer, gastrojejunal
  gastroduodenal —see Ulcer, peptic
  gastroesophageal —see Ulcer, stomach
  gastrointestinal —see Ulcer, gastrojejunal
  gastrojejunal (peptic) K28.9
    with
      hemorrhage K28.4
        and perforation K28.6
      perforation K28.5
    acute K28.3
      with
        hemorrhage K28.0
          and perforation K28.2
        perforation K28.1
    chronic K28.7
      with
        hemorrhage K28.4
          and perforation K28.6
        perforation K28.5

Ulcer, ulcerated, ulcerating, ulceration, ulcerative (Continued)
  gastrojejunocolic —see Ulcer, gastrojejunal
  gingiva K06.8
  gingivitis K05.10
    nonplaque induced K05.11
    plaque induced K05.10
  glottis J38.7
  granuloma of pudenda A58
  gum K06.8
  gumma, due to yaws A66.4
  heel —see Ulcer, lower limb
  hemorrhoid —see also Hemorrhoids, by degree K64.8
  Hunner's —see Cystitis, interstitial
  hypopharynx J39.2
  hypopyon (chronic) (subacute) —see Ulcer, cornea, with hypopyon
  hypostaticum —see Ulcer, varicose
  ileum —see Ulcer, intestine
  intestine, intestinal K63.3
    with perforation K63.1
    amebic A06.1
    duodenal —see Ulcer, duodenum
    granulocytopenic (with hemorrhage) —see Neutropenia
    marginal —see Ulcer, gastrojejunal
    perforating K63.1
      newborn P78.0
    primary, small intestine K63.3
    rectum K62.6
    stercoraceous, stercoral K63.3
    tuberculous A18.32
    typhoid (fever) —see Typhoid
    varicose I86.8
  jejunum, jejunal —see Ulcer, gastrojejunal
  keratitis —see Ulcer, cornea
  knee —see Ulcer, lower limb
  labium (majus) (minus) N76.6
  laryngitis —see Laryngitis
  larynx (aphthous) (contact) J38.7
    diphtheritic A36.2
  leg —see Ulcer, lower limb
  lip K13.0
  Lipschütz's N76.6
  lower limb (atrophic) (chronic) (neurogenic) (perforating) (pyogenic) (trophic) (tropical) L97.909
    with
      bone involvement without evidence of necrosis L97.906
      bone necrosis L97.904
      exposed fat layer L97.902
      muscle involvement without evidence of necrosis L97.905
      muscle necrosis L97.903
      skin breakdown only L97.901
      specified severity NEC L97.908
    ankle L97.309
      with
        bone involvement without evidence of necrosis L97.306
        bone necrosis L97.304
        exposed fat layer L97.302
        muscle involvement without evidence of necrosis L97.305
        muscle necrosis L97.303
        skin breakdown only L97.301
        specified severity NEC L97.308
      left L97.329
        with
          bone involvement without evidence of necrosis L97.326
          bone necrosis L97.324
          exposed fat layer L97.322
          muscle involvement without evidence of necrosis L97.325
          muscle necrosis L97.323
          skin breakdown only L97.321
          specified severity NEC L97.328

▶ New ⇒ Revised ~~deleted~~ Deleted • Use Additional Character(s)

Ulcer, ulcerated, ulcerating, ulceration, ulcerative *(Continued)*
  lower limb *(Continued)*
    ankle *(Continued)*
      right L97.319
        with
          bone involvement without evidence of necrosis L97.316
          bone necrosis L97.314
          exposed fat layer L97.312
          muscle involvement without evidence of necrosis L97.315
          muscle necrosis L97.313
          skin breakdown only L97.311
          specified severity NEC L97.318
    calf L97.209
      with
        bone involvement without evidence of necrosis L97.206
        bone necrosis L97.204
        exposed fat layer L97.202
        muscle involvement without evidence of necrosis L97.205
        muscle necrosis L97.203
        skin breakdown only L97.201
        specified severity NEC L97.208
      left L97.229
        with
          bone involvement without evidence of necrosis L97.226
          bone necrosis L97.224
          exposed fat layer L97.222
          muscle involvement without evidence of necrosis L97.225
          muscle necrosis L97.223
          skin breakdown only L97.221
          specified severity NEC L97.228
      right L97.219
        with
          bone involvement without evidence of necrosis L97.216
          bone necrosis L97.214
          exposed fat layer L97.212
          muscle involvement without evidence of necrosis L97.215
          muscle necrosis L97.213
          skin breakdown only L97.211
          specified severity NEC L97.218
    decubitus —*see* Ulcer, pressure, by site
    foot specified NEC L97.509
      with
        bone involvement without evidence of necrosis L97.506
        bone necrosis L97.504
        exposed fat layer L97.502
        muscle involvement without evidence of necrosis L97.505
        muscle necrosis L97.503
        skin breakdown only L97.501
        specified severity NEC L97.508
      left L97.529
        with
          bone involvement without evidence of necrosis L97.526
          bone necrosis L97.524
          exposed fat layer L97.522
          muscle involvement without evidence of necrosis L97.525
          muscle necrosis L97.523
          skin breakdown only L97.521
          specified severity NEC L97.528
      right L97.519
        with
          bone involvement without evidence of necrosis L97.516
          bone necrosis L97.514
          exposed fat layer L97.512
          muscle involvement without evidence of necrosis L97.515
          muscle necrosis L97.513
          skin breakdown only L97.511
          specified severity NEC L97.518

Ulcer, ulcerated, ulcerating, ulceration, ulcerative *(Continued)*
  lower limb *(Continued)*
    heel L97.409
      with
        bone involvement without evidence of necrosis L97.406
        bone necrosis L97.404
        exposed fat layer L97.402
        muscle involvement without evidence of necrosis L97.405
        muscle necrosis L97.403
        skin breakdown only L97.401
        specified severity NEC L97.408
      left L97.429
        with
          bone involvement without evidence of necrosis L97.426
          bone necrosis L97.424
          exposed fat layer L97.422
          muscle involvement without evidence of necrosis L97.425
          muscle necrosis L97.423
          skin breakdown only L97.421
          specified severity NEC L97.428
      right L97.419
        with
          bone involvement without evidence of necrosis L97.416
          bone necrosis L97.414
          exposed fat layer L97.412
          muscle involvement without evidence of necrosis L97.415
          muscle necrosis L97.413
          skin breakdown only L97.411
          specified severity NEC L97.418
    left L97.929
      with
        bone involvement without evidence of necrosis L97.926
        bone necrosis L97.924
        exposed fat layer L97.922
        muscle involvement without evidence of necrosis L97.925
        muscle necrosis L97.923
        skin breakdown only L97.921
        specified severity NEC L97.928
    lower leg NOS L97.909
      with
        bone involvement without evidence of necrosis L97.906
        bone necrosis L97.904
        exposed fat layer L97.902
        muscle involvement without evidence of necrosis L97.905
        muscle necrosis L97.903
        skin breakdown only L97.901
        specified severity NEC L97.908
      left L97.929
        with
          bone involvement without evidence of necrosis L97.926
          bone necrosis L97.924
          exposed fat layer L97.922
          muscle involvement without evidence of necrosis L97.925
          muscle necrosis L97.923
          skin breakdown only L97.921
          specified severity NEC L97.928
      right L97.919
        with
          bone involvement without evidence of necrosis L97.916
          bone necrosis L97.914
          exposed fat layer L97.912
          muscle involvement without evidence of necrosis L97.915
          muscle necrosis L97.913
          skin breakdown only L97.911
          specified severity NEC L97.918
      specified site NEC L97.809

Ulcer, ulcerated, ulcerating, ulceration, ulcerative *(Continued)*
  lower limb *(Continued)*
    lower leg NOS *(Continued)*
      specified site NEC *(Continued)*
        with
          bone involvement without evidence of necrosis L97.806
          bone necrosis L97.804
          exposed fat layer L97.802
          muscle involvement without evidence of necrosis L97.805
          muscle necrosis L97.803
          skin breakdown only L97.801
          specified severity NEC L97.808
        left L97.829
          with
            bone involvement without evidence of necrosis L97.826
            bone necrosis L97.824
            exposed fat layer L97.822
            muscle involvement without evidence of necrosis L97.825
            muscle necrosis L97.823
            skin breakdown only L97.821
            specified severity NEC L97.828
        right L97.819
          with
            bone involvement without evidence of necrosis L97.816
            bone necrosis L97.814
            exposed fat layer L97.812
            muscle involvement without evidence of necrosis L97.815
            muscle necrosis L97.813
            skin breakdown only L97.811
            specified severity NEC L97.818
    midfoot L97.409
      with
        bone involvement without evidence of necrosis L97.406
        bone necrosis L97.404
        exposed fat layer L97.402
        muscle involvement without evidence of necrosis L97.405
        muscle necrosis L97.403
        skin breakdown only L97.401
        specified severity NEC L97.408
      left L97.429
        with
          bone involvement without evidence of necrosis L97.426
          bone necrosis L97.424
          exposed fat layer L97.422
          muscle involvement without evidence of necrosis L97.425
          muscle necrosis L97.423
          skin breakdown only L97.421
          specified severity NEC L97.428
      right L97.419
        with
          bone involvement without evidence of necrosis L97.416
          bone necrosis L97.414
          exposed fat layer L97.412
          muscle involvement without evidence of necrosis L97.415
          muscle necrosis L97.413
          skin breakdown only L97.411
          specified severity NEC L97.418
    right L97.919
      with
        bone involvement without evidence of necrosis L97.916
        bone necrosis L97.914
        exposed fat layer L97.912
        muscle involvement without evidence of necrosis L97.915
        muscle necrosis L97.913
        skin breakdown only L97.911
        specified severity NEC L97.918

Ulcer, ulcerated, ulcerating, ulceration, ulcerative (Continued)
  lower limb (Continued)
    thigh L97.109
      with
        bone involvement without evidence of necrosis L97.106
        bone necrosis L97.104
        exposed fat layer L97.102
        muscle involvement without evidence of necrosis L97.105
        muscle necrosis L97.103
        skin breakdown only L97.101
        specified severity NEC L97.108
      left L97.129
        with
          bone involvement without evidence of necrosis L97.126
          bone necrosis L97.124
          exposed fat layer L97.122
          muscle involvement without evidence of necrosis L97.125
          muscle necrosis L97.123
          skin breakdown only L97.121
          specified severity NEC L97.128
      right L97.119
        with
          bone involvement without evidence of necrosis L97.116
          bone necrosis L97.114
          exposed fat layer L97.112
          muscle involvement without evidence of necrosis L97.115
          muscle necrosis L97.113
          skin breakdown only L97.111
          specified severity NEC L97.118
    toe L97.509
      with
        bone involvement without evidence of necrosis L97.506
        bone necrosis L97.504
        exposed fat layer L97.502
        muscle involvement without evidence of necrosis L97.505
        muscle necrosis L97.503
        skin breakdown only L97.501
        specified severity NEC L97.508
      left L97.529
        with
          bone involvement without evidence of necrosis L97.526
          bone necrosis L97.524
          exposed fat layer L97.522
          muscle involvement without evidence of necrosis L97.525
          muscle necrosis L97.523
          skin breakdown only L97.521
          specified severity NEC L97.528
      right L97.519
        with
          bone involvement without evidence of necrosis L97.516
          bone necrosis L97.514
          exposed fat layer L97.512
          muscle involvement without evidence of necrosis L97.515
          muscle necrosis L97.513
          skin breakdown only L97.511
          specified severity NEC L97.518
  leprous A30.1
  syphilitic A52.19
  varicose —see Varix, leg, with, ulcer
  luetic —see Ulcer, syphilitic
  lung J98.4
    tuberculous —see Tuberculosis, pulmonary
  malignant —see Neoplasm, malignant, by site
  marginal NEC —see Ulcer, gastrojejunal
  meatus (urinarius) N34.2
  Meckel's diverticulum Q43.0
    malignant —see Table of Neoplasms, small intestine, malignant

Ulcer, ulcerated, ulcerating, ulceration, ulcerative (Continued)
  Meleney's (chronic undermining) —see Ulcer, skin
  Mooren's (cornea) —see Ulcer, cornea, Mooren's
  mycobacterial (skin) A31.1
  nasopharynx J39.2
  neck, uterus N86
  neurogenic NEC —see Ulcer, skin
  nose, nasal (passage) (infective) (septum) J34.0
    skin —see Ulcer, skin
    spirochetal A69.8
    varicose (bleeding) I86.8
  oral mucosa (traumatic) K12.1
  palate (soft) K12.1
  penis (chronic) N48.5
  peptic (site unspecified) K27.9
    with
      hemorrhage K27.4
        and perforation K27.6
      perforation K27.5
    acute K27.3
      with
        hemorrhage K27.0
          and perforation K27.2
        perforation K27.1
    chronic K27.7
      with
        hemorrhage K27.4
          and perforation K27.6
        perforation K27.5
    esophagus K22.10
      with bleeding K22.11
    newborn P78.82
  perforating K27.5
    skin —see Ulcer, skin
  peritonsillar J35.8
  phagedenic (tropical) —see Ulcer, skin
  pharynx J39.2
  phlebitis —see Phlebitis
  plaster —see Ulcer, pressure, by site
  popliteal space —see Ulcer, lower limb
  postpyloric —see Ulcer, duodenum
  prepuce N47.7
  prepyloric —see Ulcer, stomach
  pressure (pressure area) L89.9-●
    ankle L89.5-●
    back L89.1-●
    buttock L89.3-●
    coccyx L89.15-●
    contiguous site of back, buttock, hip L89.4-●
    elbow L89.0-●
    face L89.81-●
    head L89.81-●
    heel L89.6-●
    hip L89.2-●
    sacral region (tailbone) L89.15-●
    specified site NEC L89.89-●
    stage 1 (healing) (pre-ulcer skin changes limited to persistent focal edema)
      ankle L89.5-●
      back L89.1-●
      buttock L89.3-●
      coccyx L89.15-●
      contiguous site of back, buttock, hip L89.4-●
      elbow L89.0-●
      face L89.81-●
      head L89.81-●
      heel L89.6-●
      hip L89.2-●
      sacral region (tailbone) L89.15-●
      specified site NEC L89.89-●
    stage 2 (healing) (abrasion, blister, partial thickness skin loss involving epidermis and/or dermis)
      ankle L89.5-●
      back L89.1-●
      buttock L89.3-●

Ulcer, ulcerated, ulcerating, ulceration, ulcerative (Continued)
  pressure (Continued)
    stage 2 (Continued)
      coccyx L89.15-●
      contiguous site of back, buttock, hip L89.4-●
      elbow L89.0-●
      face L89.81-●
      head L89.81-●
      heel L89.6-●
      hip L89.2-●
      sacral region (tailbone) L89.15-●
      specified site NEC L89.89-●
    stage 3 (healing) (full thickness skin loss involving damage or necrosis of subcutaneous tissue)
      ankle L89.5-●
      back L89.1-●
      buttock L89.3-●
      coccyx L89.15-●
      contiguous site of back, buttock, hip L89.4-●
      elbow L89.0-●
      face L89.81-●
      head L89.81-●
      heel L89.6-●
      hip L89.2-●
      sacral region (tailbone) L89.15-●
      specified site NEC L89.89-●
    stage 4 (healing) (necrosis of soft tissues through to underlying muscle, tendon, or bone)
      ankle L89.5-●
      back L89.1-●
      buttock L89.3-●
      coccyx L89.15-●
      contiguous site of back, buttock, hip L89.4-●
      elbow L89.0-●
      face L89.81-●
      head L89.81-●
      heel L89.6-●
      hip L89.2-●
      sacral region (tailbone) L89.15-●
      specified site NEC L89.89-●
    unspecified stage
      ankle L89.5-●
      back L89.1-●
      buttock L89.3-●
      coccyx L89.15-●
      contiguous site of back, buttock, hip L89.4-●
      elbow L89.0-●
      face L89.81-●
      head L89.81-●
      heel L89.6-●
      hip L89.2-●
      sacral region (tailbone) L89.15-●
      specified site NEC L89.89-●
    unstageable
      ankle L89.5-●
      back L89.1-●
      buttock L89.3-●
      coccyx L89.15-●
      contiguous site of back, buttock, hip L89.4-●
      elbow L89.0-●
      face L89.81-●
      head L89.81-●
      heel L89.6-●
      hip L89.2-●
      sacral region (tailbone) L89.15-●
      specified site NEC L89.89-●
  primary of intestine K63.3
    with perforation K63.1
  prostate N41.9
  pyloric —see Ulcer, stomach
  rectosigmoid K63.3
    with perforation K63.1
  rectum (sphincter) (solitary) K62.6
    stercoraceous, stercoral K62.6

▶ New   ➡ Revised   ~~deleted~~ Deleted   ● Use Additional Character(s)

Ulcer, ulcerated, ulcerating, ulceration, ulcerative *(Continued)*
retina —*see* Inflammation, chorioretinal
rodent —*see also* Neoplasm, skin, malignant
sclera —*see* Scleritis
scrofulous (tuberculous) A18.2
scrotum N50.89
   tuberculous A18.15
   varicose I86.1
seminal vesicle N50.89
sigmoid —*see* Ulcer, intestine
skin (atrophic) (chronic) (neurogenic) (non-healing) (perforating) (pyogenic) (trophic) (tropical) L98.499
   with gangrene —*see* Gangrene
   amebic A06.7
   back —*see* Ulcer, back
   buttock —*see* Ulcer, buttock
   decubitus —*see* Ulcer, pressure
   lower limb —*see* Ulcer, lower limb
   mycobacterial A31.1
   specified site NEC L98.499
     with
       bone involvement without evidence of necrosis L98.496
       bone necrosis L98.494
       exposed fat layer L98.492
       muscle involvement without evidence of necrosis L98.495
       muscle necrosis L98.493
       skin breakdown only L98.491
       specified severity NEC L98.498
   tuberculous (primary) A18.4
   varicose —*see* Ulcer, varicose
sloughing —*see* Ulcer, skin
solitary, anus or rectum (sphincter) K62.6
sore throat J02.9
   streptococcal J02.0
spermatic cord N50.89
spine (tuberculous) A18.01
stasis (venous) —*see* Varix, leg, with, ulcer
   without varicose veins I87.2
stercoraceous, stercoral K63.3
   with perforation K63.1
   anus or rectum K62.6
stoma, stomal —*see* Ulcer, gastrojejunal
stomach (eroded) (peptic) (round) K25.9
   with
     hemorrhage K25.4
       and perforation K25.6
     perforation K25.5
   acute K25.3
     with
       hemorrhage K25.0
         and perforation K25.2
       perforation K25.1
   chronic K25.7
     with
       hemorrhage K25.4
         and perforation K25.6
       perforation K25.5
stomal —*see* Ulcer, gastrojejunal
stomatitis K12.1
stress —*see* Ulcer, peptic
strumous (tuberculous) A18.2
submucosal, bladder —*see* Cystitis, interstitial
syphilitic (any site) (early) (secondary) A51.39
   late A52.79
   perforating A52.79
     foot A52.11
testis N50.89
thigh —*see* Ulcer, lower limb
throat J39.2
   diphtheritic A36.0
toe —*see* Ulcer, lower limb
tongue (traumatic) K14.0
tonsil J35.8
   diphtheritic A36.0
trachea J39.8
trophic —*see* Ulcer, skin

Ulcer, ulcerated, ulcerating, ulceration, ulcerative *(Continued)*
tropical —*see* Ulcer, skin
tuberculous —*see* Tuberculosis, ulcer
tunica vaginalis N50.89
turbinate J34.89
typhoid (perforating) —*see* Typhoid
unspecified site —*see* Ulcer, skin
urethra (meatus) —*see* Urethritis
uterus N85.8
   cervix N86
     with cervicitis N72
   neck N86
     with cervicitis N72
vagina N76.5
   in Behçet's disease M35.2 *[N77.0]*
   pessary N89.8
valve, heart I33.0
varicose (lower limb, any part) —*see also* Varix, leg, with, ulcer
   broad ligament I86.2
   esophagus —*see* Varix, esophagus
   inflamed or infected —*see* Varix, leg, with ulcer, with inflammation
   nasal septum I86.8
   perineum I86.3
   scrotum I86.1
   specified site NEC I86.8
   sublingual I86.0
   vulva I86.3
vas deferens N50.89
vulva (acute) (infectional) N76.6
   in (due to)
     Behçet's disease M35.2 *[N77.0]*
     herpesviral (herpes simplex) infection A60.04
     tuberculosis A18.18
vulvobuccal, recurring N76.6
X-ray L58.1
yaws A66.4
Ulcerosa scarlatina A38.8
Ulcus —*see also* Ulcer
cutis tuberculosum A18.4
duodeni —*see* Ulcer, duodenum
durum (syphilitic) A51.0
   extragenital A51.2
gastrojejunale —*see* Ulcer, gastrojejunal
hypostaticum —*see* Ulcer, varicose
molle (cutis) (skin) A57
serpens corneae —*see* Ulcer, cornea, central
ventriculi —*see* Ulcer, stomach
Ulegyria Q04.8
Ulerythema
ophryogenes, congenital Q84.2
sycosiforme L73.8
Ullrich(-Bonnevie)(-Turner) syndrome —*see also* Turner's syndrome Q87.1
Ullrich-Feichtiger syndrome Q87.0
Ulnar —*see* condition
Ulorrhagia, ulorrhea K06.8
Umbilicus, umbilical —*see* condition
Unacceptable
contours of tooth K08.54
morphology of tooth K08.54
Unavailability (of)
bed at medical facility Z75.1
health service-related agencies Z75.4
medical facilities (at) Z75.3
   due to
     investigation by social service agency Z75.2
     lack of services at home Z75.0
     remoteness from facility Z75.3
     waiting list Z75.1
   home Z75.0
   outpatient clinic Z75.3
schooling Z55.1
social service agencies Z75.4
Uncinaria americana infestation B76.1
Uncinariasis B76.9
Uncongenial work Z56.5

Unconscious (ness) —*see* Coma
Underachievement in school Z55.3
Underdevelopment —*see also* Undeveloped
nose Q30.1
sexual E30.0
Underdosing —*see also* Table of Drugs and Chemicals, categories T36-T50, with final character 6 Z91.14
intentional NEC Z91.128
   due to financial hardship of patient Z91.120
unintentional NEC Z91.138
   due to patient's age related debility Z91.130
Underfeeding, newborn P92.3
Underfill, endodontic M27.53
Underimmunization status Z28.3
Undernourishment —*see* Malnutrition
Undernutrition —*see* Malnutrition
Under observation —*see* Observation
Underweight R63.6
for gestational age —*see* Light for dates
Underwood's disease P83.0
Undescended —*see also* Malposition, congenital
cecum Q43.3
colon Q43.3
testicle —*see* Cryptorchid
Undeveloped, undevelopment —*see also* Hypoplasia
brain (congenital) Q02
cerebral (congenital) Q02
heart Q24.8
lung Q33.6
testis E29.1
uterus E30.0
Undiagnosed (disease) R69
Undulant fever —*see* Brucellosis
Unemployment, anxiety concerning Z56.0
threatened Z56.2
Unequal length (acquired) (limb) —*see also* Deformity, limb, unequal length
leg —*see also* Deformity, limb, unequal length congenital Q72.9-•
Unextracted dental root K08.3
Unguis incarnatus L60.0
Unhappiness R45.2
Unicornate uterus Q51.4
in pregnancy or childbirth O34.00
Unilateral —*see also* condition
development, breast N64.89
organ or site, congenital NEC —*see* Agenesis, by site
Unilocular heart Q20.8
Union, abnormal —*see also* Fusion
larynx and trachea Q34.8
Universal mesentery Q43.3
Unrepairable overhanging of dental restorative materials K08.52
Unsatisfactory
restoration of tooth K08.50
   specified NEC K08.59
sample of cytologic smear
   anus R85.615
   cervix R87.615
   vagina R87.625
surroundings Z59.1
work Z56.5
Unsoundness of mind —*see* Psychosis
Unstable
back NEC —*see* Instability, joint, spine
hip (congenital) Q65.6
   acquired —*see* Derangement, joint, specified type NEC, hip
joint —*see* Instability, joint
   secondary to removal of joint prosthesis M96.89
lie (mother) O32.0
lumbosacral joint (congenital)
   acquired —*see* subcategory M53.2
sacroiliac —*see* subcategory M53.2
spine NEC —*see* Instability, joint, spine
Unsteadiness on feet R26.81

Untruthfulness, child problem F91.8
Unverricht(-Lundborg) disease or epilepsy —
   see Epilepsy, generalized, idiopathic
Unwanted pregnancy Z64.0
Upbringing, institutional Z62.22
   away from parents NEC Z62.29
   in care of non-parental family member
      Z62.21
   in foster care Z62.21
   in orphanage or group home Z62.22
   in welfare custody Z62.21
Upper respiratory —*see* condition
Upset
   gastric K30
   gastrointestinal K30
      psychogenic F45.8
   intestinal (large) (small) K59.9
      psychogenic F45.8
   menstruation N93.9
   mental F48.9
   stomach K30
      psychogenic F45.8
Urachus —*see also* condition
   patent or persistent Q64.4
Urbach-Oppenheim disease (necrobiosis
      lipoidica diabeticorum) —*see* E08-E13 with
      .620
Urbach's lipoid proteinosis E78.89
Urbach-Wiethe disease E78.89
Urban yellow fever A95.1
Urea
   blood, high —*see* Uremia
   cycle metabolism disorder —*see* Disorder,
      urea cycle metabolism
Uremia, uremic N19
   with
      ectopic or molar pregnancy O08.4
      polyneuropathy N18.9 *[G63]*
   chronic NOS —*see also* Disease, kidney,
      chronic N18.9
      due to hypertension —*see* Hypertensive,
         kidney
   complicating
      ectopic or molar pregnancy O08.4
   congenital P96.0
   extrarenal R39.2
   following ectopic or molar pregnancy O08.4
   newborn P96.0
   prerenal R39.2
Ureter, ureteral —*see* condition
Ureteralgia N23
Ureterectasis —*see* Hydroureter
Ureteritis N28.89
   cystica N28.86
   due to calculus N20.1
      with calculus, kidney N20.2
         with hydronephrosis N13.2
   gonococcal (acute) (chronic) A54.21
   nonspecific N28.89
Ureterocele N28.89
   congenital (orthotopic) Q62.31
      ectopic Q62.32
Ureterolith, ureterolithiasis —*see* Calculus,
      ureter
Ureterostomy
   attention to Z43.6
   status Z93.6
Urethra, urethral —*see* condition
Urethralgia R39.89
Urethritis (anterior) (posterior) N34.2
   calculous N21.1
   candidal B37.41
   chlamydial A56.01
   diplococcal (gonococcal) A54.01
      with abscess (accessory gland)
         (periurethral) A54.1
   gonococcal A54.01
      with abscess (accessory gland)
         (periurethral) A54.1

Urethritis *(Continued)*
   nongonococcal N34.1
      Reiter's —*see* Reiter's disease
   nonspecific N34.1
   nonvenereal N34.1
   postmenopausal N34.2
   puerperal O86.22
   Reiter's —*see* Reiter's disease
   specified NEC N34.2
   trichomonal or due to Trichomonas
      (vaginalis) A59.03
Urethrocele N81.0
   with
      cystocele —*see* Cystocele
      prolapse of uterus —*see* Prolapse, uterus
Urethrolithiasis (with colic or infection) N21.1
Urethrorectal —*see* condition
Urethrorrhagia N36.8
Urethrorrhea R36.9
Urethrostomy
   attention to Z43.6
   status Z93.6
Urethrotrigonitis —*see* Trigonitis
Urethrovaginal —*see* condition
Urgency
   fecal R15.2
   hypertensive —*see* Hypertension
   urinary N39.15
Urhidrosis, uridrosis L74.8
Uric acid in blood (increased) E79.0
Uricacidemia (asymptomatic) E79.0
Uricemia (asymptomatic) E79.0
▶Uricosuria R82.998
Urinary —*see* condition
Urination
   frequent R35.0
   painful R30.9
Urine
   blood in —*see* Hematuria
   discharge, excessive R35.8
   enuresis, nonorganic origin F98.0
   extravasation R39.0
   frequency R35.0
   incontinence R32
      nonorganic origin F98.0
   intermittent stream R39.198
   pus in N39.0
   retention or stasis R33.9
      organic R33.8
         drug-induced R33.0
      psychogenic F45.8
   secretion
      deficient R34
      excessive R35.8
      frequency R35.0
   stream
      intermittent R39.198
      slowing R39.198
      splitting R39.13
      weak R39.12
Urinemia —*see* Uremia
Urinoma, urethra N36.8
Uroarthritis, infectious (Reiter's) —*see* Reiter's
      disease
Urodialysis R34
Urolithiasis —*see* Calculus, urinary
Uronephrosis —*see* Hydronephrosis
Uropathy N39.9
   obstructive N13.9
      specified NEC N13.8
   reflux N13.9
      specified NEC N13.8
   vesicoureteral reflux-associated —*see* Reflux,
      vesicoureteral
Urosepsis — code to condition
Urticaria L50.9
   with angioneurotic edema T78.3
      hereditary D84.1
   allergic L50.0
   cholinergic L50.5
   chronic L50.8

Urticaria *(Continued)*
   cold, familial L50.2
   contact L50.6
   dermatographic L50.3
   due to
      cold or heat L50.2
      drugs L50.0
      food L50.0
      inhalants L50.0
      plants L50.6
      serum —*see also* Reaction, serum T80.69
   factitial L50.3
   familial cold M04.2
   giant T78.3
      hereditary D84.1
   gigantea T78.3
   idiopathic L50.1
   larynx T78.3
      hereditary D84.1
   neonatorum P83.88
   nonallergic L50.1
   papulosa (Hebra) L28.2
   pigmentosa D47.01
      congenital Q82.2
      of neonatal onset Q82.2
      of newborn onset Q82.2
   recurrent periodic L50.8
   serum —*see also* Reaction, serum T80.69
   solar L56.3
   specified type NEC L50.8
   thermal (cold) (heat) L50.2
   vibratory L50.4
   xanthelasmoidea —*see* Urticaria pigmentosa
Use (of)
   alcohol Z72.89
      with
         intoxication F10.929
         sleep disorder F10.982
      harmful —*see* Abuse, alcohol
   amphetamines —*see* Use, stimulant NEC
   caffeine —*see* Use, stimulant NEC
   cannabis F12.90
      with
         anxiety disorder F12.980
         intoxication F12.929
            with
               delirium F12.921
               perceptual disturbance F12.922
            uncomplicated F12.920
         other specified disorder F12.988
         psychosis F12.959
            delusions F12.950
            hallucinations F12.951
         unspecified disorder F12.99
      ▶withdrawal F12.93
   cocaine F14.90
      with
         anxiety disorder F14.980
         intoxication F14.929
            with
               delirium F14.921
               perceptual disturbance F14.922
            uncomplicated F14.920
         other specified disorder F14.988
         psychosis F14.959
            delusions F14.950
            hallucinations F14.951
         sexual dysfunction F14.981
         sleep disorder F14.982
         unspecified disorder F14.99
      harmful —*see* Abuse, drug, cocaine
   drug(s) NEC F19.90
      with sleep disorder F19.982
      harmful —*see* Abuse, drug, by type
   hallucinogen NEC F16.90
      with
         anxiety disorder F16.980
         intoxication F16.929
            with
               delirium F16.921
            uncomplicated F16.920

▶ New   ➡ Revised   ~~deleted~~ Deleted   ● Use Additional Character(s)

Use *(Continued)*
  hallucinogen NEC *(Continued)*
    with *(Continued)*
      mood disorder F16.94
      other specified disorder F16.988
      perception disorder (flashbacks) F16.983
      psychosis F16.959
        delusions F16.950
        hallucinations F16.951
      unspecified disorder F16.99
    harmful —*see* Abuse, drug, hallucinogen NEC
  inhalants F18.90
    with
      anxiety disorder F18.980
      intoxication F18.929
        with delirium F18.921
        uncomplicated F18.920
      mood disorder F18.94
      other specified disorder F18.988
      persisting dementia F18.97
      psychosis F18.959
        delusions F18.950
        hallucinations F18.951
      unspecified disorder F18.99
    harmful —*see* Abuse, drug, inhalant
  methadone —*see* Use, opioid
  nonprescribed drugs F19.90
    harmful —*see* Abuse, non-psychoactive substance
  opioid F11.90
    with
      disorder F11.99
        mood F11.94
        sleep F11.982
        specified type NEC F11.988
      intoxication F11.929
        with
          delirium F11.921
          perceptual disturbance F11.922
        uncomplicated F11.920
      withdrawal F11.93
    harmful —*see* Abuse, drug, opioid
  patent medicines F19.90
    harmful —*see* Abuse, non-psychoactive substance
  psychoactive drug NEC F19.90
    with
      anxiety disorder F19.980

Use *(Continued)*
  psychoactive drug NEC *(Continued)*
    with *(Continued)*
      intoxication F19.929
        with
          delirium F19.921
          perceptual disturbance F19.922
        uncomplicated F19.920
      mood disorder F19.94
      other specified disorder F19.988
      persisting
        amnestic disorder F19.96
        dementia F19.97
      psychosis F19.959
        delusions F19.950
        hallucinations F19.951
      sexual dysfunction F19.981
      sleep disorder F19.982
      unspecified disorder F19.99
      withdrawal F19.939
        with
          delirium F19.931
          perceptual disturbance F19.932
        uncomplicated F19.930
    harmful —*see* Abuse, drug NEC, psychoactive NEC
  sedative, hypnotic, or anxiolytic F13.90
    with
      anxiety disorder F13.980
      intoxication F13.929
        with
          delirium F13.921
        uncomplicated F13.920
      other specified disorder F13.988
      persisting
        amnestic disorder F13.96
        dementia F13.97
      psychosis F13.959
        delusions F13.950
        hallucinations F13.951
      sexual dysfunction F13.981
      sleep disorder F13.982
      unspecified disorder F13.99
    harmful —*see* Abuse, drug, sedative, hypnotic, or anxiolytic
  stimulant NEC F15.90
    with
      anxiety disorder F15.980
      intoxication F15.929
        with
          delirium F15.921
          perceptual disturbance F15.922
        uncomplicated F15.920

Use *(Continued)*
  stimulant NEC *(Continued)*
    with *(Continued)*
      mood disorder F15.94
      other specified disorder F15.988
      psychosis F15.959
        delusions F15.950
        hallucinations F15.951
      sexual dysfunction F15.981
      sleep disorder F15.982
      unspecified disorder F15.99
      withdrawal F15.93
    harmful —*see* Abuse, drug, stimulant NEC
  tobacco Z72.0
    with dependence —*see* Dependence, drug, nicotine
  volatile solvents —*see also* Use, inhalant F18.90
    harmful —*see* Abuse, drug, inhalant
Usher-Senear disease or syndrome L10.4
Uta B55.1
Uteromegaly N85.2
Uterovaginal —*see* condition
Uterovesical —*see* condition
Uveal —*see* condition
Uveitis (anterior) —*see also* Iridocyclitis
  acute —*see* Iridocyclitis, acute
  chronic —*see* Iridocyclitis, chronic
  due to toxoplasmosis (acquired) B58.09
    congenital P37.1
  granulomatous —*see* Iridocyclitis, chronic
  heterochromic —*see* Cyclitis, Fuchs' heterochromic
  lens-induced —*see* Iridocyclitis, lens-induced
  posterior —*see* Chorioretinitis
  sympathetic H44.13-●
  syphilitic (secondary) A51.43
    congenital (early) A50.01
    late A52.71
  tuberculous A18.54
Uveoencephalitis —*see* Inflammation, chorioretinal
Uveokeratitis —*see* Iridocyclitis
Uveoparotitis D86.89
Uvula —*see* condition
Uvulitis (acute) (catarrhal) (chronic) (membranous) (suppurative) (ulcerative) K12.2

V

Vaccination (prophylactic)
  complication or reaction —*see* Complications, vaccination
  delayed Z28.9
  encounter for Z23
  not done —*see* Immunization, not done, because (of)
Vaccinia (generalized) (localized) T88.1
  without vaccination B08.011
  congenital P35.8
Vacuum, in sinus (accessory) (nasal) J34.89
Vagabond, vagabondage Z59.0
Vagabond's disease B85.1
Vagina, vaginal —*see* condition
Vaginalitis (tunica) (testis) N49.1
Vaginismus (reflex) N94.2
  functional F52.5
  nonorganic F52.5
  psychogenic F52.5
  secondary N94.2
Vaginitis (acute) (circumscribed) (diffuse) (emphysematous) (nonvenereal) (ulcerative) N76.0
  with ectopic or molar pregnancy O08.0
  amebic A06.82
  atrophic, postmenopausal N95.2
  bacterial N76.0
  blennorrhagic (gonococcal) A54.02
  candidal B37.3
  chlamydial A56.02
  chronic N76.1
  due to Trichomonas (vaginalis) A59.01
  following ectopic or molar pregnancy O08.0
  gonococcal A54.02
    with abscess (accessory gland) (periurethral) A54.1
  granuloma A58
  in (due to)
    candidiasis B37.3
    herpesviral (herpes simplex) infection A60.04
    pinworm infection B80 [N77.1]
  monilial B37.3
  mycotic (candidal) B37.3
  postmenopausal atrophic N95.2
  puerperal (postpartum) O86.13
  senile (atrophic) N95.2
  subacute or chronic N76.1
  syphilitic (early) A51.0
    late A52.76
  trichomonal A59.01
  tuberculous A18.18
Vaginosis —*see* Vaginitis
Vagotonia G52.2
Vagrancy Z59.0
VAIN —*see* Neoplasia, intraepithelial, vagina
Vallecula —*see* condition
Valley fever B38.0
Valsuani's disease —*see* Anemia, obstetric
Valve, valvular (formation) —*see also* condition
  cerebral ventricle (communicating) in situ Z98.2
  cervix, internal os Q51.828
  congenital NEC —*see* Atresia, by site
  ureter (pelvic junction) (vesical orifice) Q62.39
  urethra (congenital) (posterior) Q64.2
Valvulitis (chronic) —*see* Endocarditis
Valvulopathy —*see* Endocarditis
Van Bogaert's leukoencephalopathy (sclerosing) (subacute) A81.1
Van Bogaert-Scherer-Epstein disease or syndrome E75.5
Van Buchem's syndrome M85.2
Van Creveld-von Gierke disease E74.01
Van der Hoeve (-de Kleyn) syndrome Q78.0
Van der Woude's syndrome Q38.0
Van Neck's disease or osteochondrosis M91.0
Vanishing lung J44.9

Vapor asphyxia or suffocation T59.9
  specified agent —*see* Table of Drugs and Chemicals
Variance, lethal ball, prosthetic heart valve T82.09
Variants, thalassemic D56.8
Variations in hair color L67.1
Varicella B01.9
  with
    complications NEC B01.89
    encephalitis B01.11
    encephalomyelitis B01.11
    meningitis B01.0
    myelitis B01.12
    pneumonia B01.2
  congenital P35.8
Varices —*see* Varix
Varicocele (scrotum) (thrombosed) I86.1
  ovary I86.2
  perineum I86.3
  spermatic cord (ulcerated) I86.1
Varicose
  aneurysm (ruptured) I77.0
  dermatitis —*see* Varix, leg, with, inflammation
  eczema —*see* Varix, leg, with, inflammation
  phlebitis —*see* Varix, with, inflammation
  tumor —*see* Varix
  ulcer (lower limb, any part) —*see also* Varix, leg, with, ulcer
    anus —*see also* Hemorrhoids K64.8
    esophagus —*see* Varix, esophagus
    inflamed or infected —*see* Varix, leg, with ulcer, with inflammation
    nasal septum I86.8
    perineum I86.3
    scrotum I86.1
    specified site NEC I86.8
  vein —*see* Varix
  vessel —*see* Varix, leg
Varicosis, varicosities, varicosity —*see* Varix
Variola (major) (minor) B03
Varioloid B03
Varix (lower limb) (ruptured) I83.90
  with
    edema I83.899
    inflammation I83.10
      with ulcer (venous) I83.209
    pain I83.819
    specified complication NEC I83.899
    stasis dermatitis I83.10
      with ulcer (venous) I83.209
    swelling I83.899
    ulcer I83.009
      with inflammation I83.209
  aneurysmal I77.0
  asymptomatic I83.9-●
  bladder I86.2
  broad ligament I86.2
  complicating
    childbirth (lower extremity) O87.4
      anus or rectum O87.2
      genital (vagina, vulva or perineum) O87.8
    pregnancy (lower extremity) O22.0-●
      anus or rectum O22.4-●
      genital (vagina, vulva or perineum) O22.1-●
    puerperium (lower extremity) O87.4
      anus or rectum O87.2
      genital (vagina, vulva, perineum) O87.8
  congenital (any site) Q27.8
  esophagus (idiopathic) (primary) (ulcerated) I85.00
    bleeding I85.01
    congenital Q27.8
    in (due to)
      alcoholic liver disease I85.10
        bleeding I85.11
      cirrhosis of liver I85.10
        bleeding I85.11

Varix (Continued)
  esophagus (Continued)
    in (Continued)
      portal hypertension I85.10
        bleeding I85.11
      schistosomiasis I85.10
        bleeding I85.11
      toxic liver disease I85.10
        bleeding I85.11
    secondary I85.10
      bleeding I85.11
  gastric I86.4
  inflamed or infected I83.10
    ulcerated I83.209
  labia (majora) I86.3
  leg (asymptomatic) I83.90
    with
      edema I83.899
      inflammation I83.10
        with ulcer —*see* Varix, leg, with, ulcer, with inflammation by site
      pain I83.819
      specified complication NEC I83.899
      swelling I83.899
      ulcer I83.009
        with inflammation I83.209
        ankle I83.003
          with inflammation I83.203
        calf I83.002
          with inflammation I83.202
        foot NEC I83.005
          with inflammation I83.205
        heel I83.004
          with inflammation I83.204
        lower leg NEC I83.008
          with inflammation I83.208
        midfoot I83.004
          with inflammation I83.204
        thigh I83.001
          with inflammation I83.201
    bilateral (asymptomatic) I83.93
      with
        edema I83.893
        pain I83.813
        specified complication NEC I83.893
        swelling I83.893
        ulcer I83.0-●
          with inflammation I83.209
    left (asymptomatic) I83.92
      with
        edema I83.892
        inflammation I83.12
          with ulcer —*see* Varix, leg, with, ulcer, with inflammation by site
        pain I83.812
        specified complication NEC I83.892
        swelling I83.892
        ulcer I83.029
          with inflammation I83.229
          ankle I83.023
            with inflammation I83.223
          calf I83.022
            with inflammation I83.222
          foot NEC I83.025
            with inflammation I83.225
          heel I83.024
            with inflammation I83.224
          lower leg NEC I83.028
            with inflammation I83.228
          midfoot I83.024
            with inflammation I83.224
          thigh I83.021
            with inflammation I83.221
    right (asymptomatic) I83.91
      with
        edema I83.891
        inflammation I83.11
          with ulcer —*see* Varix, leg, with, ulcer, with inflammation by site

▶ New   ⟹ Revised   ~~deleted~~ Deleted   ● Use Additional Character(s)

Virulent bubo A57
Virus, viral —*see also* condition
   as cause of disease classified elsewhere
      B97.89
   cytomegalovirus B25.9
   human immunodeficiency (HIV) —*see*
      Human, immunodeficiency virus (HIV)
      disease
   infection —*see* Infection, virus
   specified NEC B34.8
   swine influenza (viruses that normally cause
      infections in pigs) —*see also* Influenza,
      due to, identified novel influenza A virus
      J09.X2
   West Nile (fever) A92.30
     with
       complications NEC A92.39
       cranial nerve disorders A92.32
       encephalitis A92.31
       encephalomyelitis A92.31
       neurologic manifestation NEC A92.32
       optic neuritis A92.32
       polyradiculitis A92.32
Viscera, visceral —*see* condition
Visceroptosis K63.4
Visible peristalsis R19.2
Vision, visual
   binocular, suppression H53.34
   blurred, blurring H53.8
     hysterical F44.6
   defect, defective NEC H54.7
   disorientation (syndrome) H53.8
   disturbance H53.9
     hysterical F44.6
   double H53.2
   examination Z01.00
     with abnormal findings Z01.01
   field, limitation (defect) —*see* Defect, visual
     field
   hallucinations R44.1
   halos H53.19
   loss —*see* Loss, vision
     sudden —*see* Disturbance, vision,
      subjective, loss, sudden
   low (both eyes) —*see* Low, vision
   perception, simultaneous without fusion
     H53.33
Vitality, lack or want of R53.83
   newborn P96.89
Vitamin deficiency —*see* Deficiency, vitamin
Vitelline duct, persistent Q43.0
Vitiligo L80
   eyelid H02.739
     left H02.736
       lower H02.735
       upper H02.734
     right H02.733
       lower H02.732
       upper H02.731

Vitiligo *(Continued)*
   pinta A67.2
   vulva N90.89
Vitreal corneal syndrome H59.01-•
Vitreoretinopathy, proliferative —*see also*
     Retinopathy, proliferative
   with retinal detachment —*see* Detachment,
     retina, traction
Vitreous —*see also* condition
   touch syndrome —*see* Complication,
     postprocedural, following cataract
     surgery
Vocal cord —*see* condition
Vogt-Koyanagi syndrome H20.82-•
Vogt's disease or syndrome G80.3
Vogt-Spielmeyer amaurotic idiocy or disease
     E75.4
Voice
   change R49.9
     specified NEC R49.8
   loss —*see* Aphonia
Volhynian fever A79.0
Volkmann's ischemic contracture or paralysis
     (complicating trauma) T79.6
Volvulus (bowel) (colon) (intestine) K56.2
   with perforation K56.2
   congenital Q43.8
   duodenum K31.5
   fallopian tube —*see* Torsion, fallopian
     tube
   oviduct —*see* Torsion, fallopian tube
   stomach (due to absence of gastrocolic
     ligament) K31.89
Vomiting R11.10
   with nausea R11.2
   without nausea R11.11
   asphyxia —*see* Foreign body, by site, causing
     asphyxia, gastric contents
   bilious (cause unknown) R11.14
     following gastro-intestinal surgery
      K91.0
     in newborn P92.01
   blood —*see* Hematemesis
   causing asphyxia, choking, or suffocation —
     see Foreign body, by site
   cyclical G43.A0
     with refractory migraine G43.A1
     intractable G43.A1
     not intractable G43.A0
     psychogenic F50.89
     without refractory migraine G43.A0
   fecal mater R11.13
   following gastrointestinal surgery
     K91.0
     psychogenic F50.89
   functional K31.89
   hysterical F50.89

Vomiting *(Continued)*
   nervous F50.89
   neurotic F50.89
   newborn NEC P92.09
     bilious P92.01
   periodic R11.10
     psychogenic F50.89
   projectile R11.12
   psychogenic F50.89
   uremic —*see* Uremia
Vomito negro —*see* Fever, yellow
Von Bezold's abscess —*see* Mastoiditis,
     acute
Von Economo-Cruchet disease A85.8
Von Eulenburg's disease G71.19
Von Gierke's disease E74.01
Von Hippel (-Lindau) disease or syndrome
     Q85.8
Von Jaksch's anemia or disease D64.89
Von Recklinghausen
   disease (neurofibromatosis) Q85.01
     bones E21.0
Von Schroetter's syndrome I82.890
Von Willebrand (-Jurgens)(-Minot) disease or
     syndrome D68.0
Von Zumbusch's disease L40.1
Voyeurism F65.3
Vrolik's disease Q78.0
Vulva —*see* condition
Vulvismus N94.2
Vulvitis (acute) (allergic) (atrophic)
     (hypertrophic) (intertriginous) (senile)
     N76.2
   with ectopic or molar pregnancy O08.0
   adhesive, congenital Q52.79
   blennorrhagic (gonococcal) A54.02
   candidal B37.3
   chlamydial A56.02
   due to Haemophilus ducreyi A57
   following ectopic or molar pregnancy
     O08.0
   gonococcal A54.02
     with abscess (accessory gland)
      (periurethral) A54.1
   herpesviral A60.04
   leukoplakic N90.4
   monilial B37.3
   puerperal (postpartum) O86.19
   subacute or chronic N76.3
   syphilitic (early) A51.0
     late A52.76
   trichomonal A59.01
   tuberculous A18.18
Vulvodynia N94.819
   specified NEC N94.818
Vulvorectal —*see* condition
Vulvovaginitis (acute) —*see* Vaginitis

▶ New   ⇒ Revised   ~~deleted~~ Deleted   • Use Additional Character(s)

W

Waiting list, person on Z75.1
  for organ transplant Z76.82
  undergoing social agency investigation
    Z75.2
Waldenström
  hypergammaglobulinemia D89.0
  syndrome or macroglobulinemia
    C88.0
Waldenström-Kjellberg syndrome
  D50.1
Walking
  difficulty R26.2
    psychogenic F44.4
  sleep F51.3
    hysterical F44.89
Wall, abdominal —see condition
Wallenberg's disease or syndrome G46.3
Wallgren's disease I87.8
Wandering
  gallbladder, congenital Q44.1
  in diseases classified elsewhere Z91.83
  kidney, congenital Q63.8
  organ or site, congenital NEC —see
    Malposition, congenital, by site
  pacemaker (heart) I49.8
  spleen D73.89
War neurosis F48.8
Wart (due to HPV) (filiform) (infectious)
  (viral) B07.9
  anogenital region (venereal) A63.0
  common B07.8
  external genital organs (venereal)
    A63.0
  flat B07.8
  Hassal-Henle's (of cornea) H18.49
  Peruvian A44.1
  plantar B07.0
  prosector (tuberculous) A18.4
  seborrheic L82.1
    inflamed L82.0
  senile (seborrheic) L82.1
    inflamed L82.0
  tuberculous A18.4
  venereal A63.0
Warthin's tumor —see Neoplasm, salivary
  gland, benign
Wassilieff's disease A27.0
Wasting
  disease R64
    due to malnutrition E41
  extreme (due to malnutrition) E41
  muscle NEC —see Atrophy, muscle
Water
  clefts (senile cataract) —see Cataract, senile,
    incipient
  deprivation of T73.1
  intoxication E87.79
  itch B76.9
  lack of T73.1
  loading E87.70
  on
    brain —see Hydrocephalus
    chest J94.8
  poisoning E87.79
Waterbrash R12
Waterhouse(-Friderichsen) syndrome or
  disease (meningococcal) A39.1
Water-losing nephritis N25.89
Watermelon stomach K31.819
  with hemorrhage K31.811
  without hemorrhage K31.819
Watsoniasis B66.8
Wax in ear —see Impaction, cerumen
Weak, weakening, weakness (generalized)
  R53.1
  arches (acquired) —see also Deformity, limb,
    flat foot
  bladder (sphincter) R32

Weak, weakening, weakness (Continued)
  facial R29.810
    following
      cerebrovascular disease I69.992
        cerebral infarction I69.392
        intracerebral hemorrhage I69.192
        nontraumatic intracranial hemorrhage
          NEC I69.292
        specified disease NEC I69.892
        stroke I69.392
        subarachnoid hemorrhage I69.092
  foot (double) —see Weak, arches
  heart, cardiac —see Failure, heart
  mind F70
  muscle M62.81
  myocardium —see Failure, heart
  newborn P96.89
  pelvic fundus N81.89
  pubocervical tissue N81.82
  rectovaginal tissue N81.83
  senile R54
  urinary stream R39.12
  valvular —see Endocarditis
Wear, worn (with normal or routine use)
  articular bearing surface of internal joint
    prosthesis —see Complications, joint
    prosthesis, mechanical, wear of articular
    bearing surfaces, by site
  device, implant or graft —see Complications,
    by site, mechanical complication
  tooth, teeth (approximal) (hard tissues)
    (interproximal) (occlusal) K03.0
Weather, weathered
  effects of
    cold T69.9
      specified effect NEC T69.8
    hot —see Heat
    skin L57.8
Weaver's syndrome Q87.3
Web, webbed (congenital)
  duodenal Q43.8
  esophagus Q39.4
  fingers Q70.1
  larynx (glottic) (subglottic) Q31.0
  neck (pterygium colli) Q18.3
  Paterson-Kelly D50.1
  popliteal syndrome Q87.89
  toes Q70.3
Weber-Christian disease M35.6
Weber-Cockayne syndrome (epidermolysis
  bullosa) Q81.8
Weber-Gubler syndrome G46.3
Weber-Leyden syndrome G46.3
Weber-Osler syndrome I78.0
Weber's paralysis or syndrome G46.3
Wedge-shaped or wedging vertebra —see
  Collapse, vertebra NEC
Wegener's granulomatosis or syndrome
  M31.30
  with
    kidney involvement M31.31
    lung involvement M31.30
      with kidney involvement M31.31
Wegner's disease A50.02
Weight
  1000-2499 grams at birth (low) —see Low,
    birthweight
  999 grams or less at birth (extremely low) —
    see Low, birthweight, extreme
  and length below 10th percentile for
    gestational age P05.1-●
  below but length above 10th percentile for
    gestational age P05.0-●
  gain (abnormal) (excessive) R63.5
    in pregnancy —see Pregnancy, complicated
      by, excessive weight gain
      low —see Pregnancy, complicated by,
        insufficient, weight gain
  loss (abnormal) (cause unknown) R63.4
Weightlessness (effect of) T75.82

Weil (l)-Marchesani syndrome Q87.1
Weil's disease A27.0
Weingarten's syndrome J82
Weir Mitchell's disease I73.81
Weiss-Baker syndrome G90.09
Wells' disease L98.3
Wen —see Cyst, sebaceous
Wenckebach's block or phenomenon I44.1
Werdnig-Hoffmann syndrome (muscular
  atrophy) G12.0
Werlhof's disease D69.3
Werner-His disease A79.0
Wermer's disease or syndrome E31.21
Werner's disease or syndrome E34.8
Wernicke-Korsakoff's syndrome or psychosis
  (alcoholic) F10.96
  with dependence F10.26
  drug-induced
    due to drug abuse —see Abuse, drug, by
      type, with amnestic disorder
    due to drug dependence —see
      Dependence, drug, by type, with
      amnestic disorder
  nonalcoholic F04
Wernicke-Posadas disease B38.9
Wernicke's
  developmental aphasia F80.2
  disease or syndrome E51.2
  encephalopathy E51.2
  polioencephalitis, superior E51.2
West African fever B50.8
Westphal-Strümpell syndrome E83.01
West's syndrome —see Epilepsy, spasms
Wet
  feet, tropical (maceration) (syndrome) —see
    Immersion, foot
  lung (syndrome), newborn P22.1
Wharton's duct —see condition
Wheal —see Urticaria
Wheezing R06.2
Whiplash injury S13.4
Whipple's disease —see also subcategory
  M14.8-● K90.81
Whipworm (disease) (infection) (infestation)
  B79
Whistling face Q87.0
White —see also condition
  kidney, small N03.9
  leg, puerperal, postpartum, childbirth O87.1
  mouth B37.0
  patches of mouth K13.29
  spot lesions, teeth
    chewing surface K02.51
    pit and fissure surface K02.51
    smooth surface K02.61
Whitehead L70.0
Whitlow —see also Cellulitis, digit
  with lymphangitis —see Lymphangitis, acute,
    digit
  herpesviral B00.89
Whitmore's disease or fever —see Melioidosis
Whooping cough A37.90
  with pneumonia A37.91
    due to Bordetella
      bronchiseptica A37.81
      parapertussis A37.11
      pertussis A37.01
    specified organism NEC A37.81
  due to
    Bordetella
      bronchiseptica A37.80
        with pneumonia A37.81
      parapertussis A37.10
        with pneumonia A37.11
      pertussis A37.00
        with pneumonia A37.01
    specified NEC A37.80
      with pneumonia A37.81
Wichman's asthma J38.5
Wide cranial sutures, newborn P96.3

▶ New   ⇒ Revised   ~~deleted~~ Deleted   ● Use Additional Character(s)

Widening aorta —*see* Ectasia, aorta
    with aneurysm —*see* Aneurysm, aorta
Wilkie's disease or syndrome K55.1
Wilkinson-Sneddon disease or syndrome
    L13.1
Willebrand (-Jürgens) thrombopathy D68.0
▶ Williams syndrome Q93.82
Willige-Hunt disease or syndrome G23.1
Wilms' tumor C64.-●
Wilson-Mikity syndrome P27.0
Wilson's
    disease or syndrome E83.01
    hepatolenticular degeneration E83.01
    lichen ruber L43.9
Window —*see also* Imperfect, closure
    aorticopulmonary Q21.4
Winter —*see* condition
Wiskott-Aldrich syndrome D82.0
Withdrawal state —*see also* Dependence, drug
    by type, with withdrawal
    alcohol
        with perceptual disturbances F10.232
        without perceptual disturbances F10.239
    caffeine F15.93
➡ cannabis F12.23
    newborn
        correct therapeutic substance properly
            administered P96.2
        infant of dependent mother P96.1
        therapeutic substance, neonatal P96.2
Witts' anemia D50.8
Witzelsucht F07.0
Woakes' ethmoiditis or syndrome J33.1
Wolff-Hirschorn syndrome Q93.3
Wolff-Parkinson-White syndrome I45.6
Wolhynian fever A79.0
Wolman's disease E75.5
Wood lung or pneumonitis J67.8
Woolly, wooly hair (congenital) (nevus) Q84.1
Woolsorter's disease A22.1
Word
    blindness (congenital) (developmental)
        F81.0
    deafness (congenital) (developmental)
        H93.25
Worm(s) (infection) (infestation) —*see also*
    Infestation, helminth
    guinea B72
    in intestine NEC B82.0
Worm-eaten soles A66.3
Worn out —*see* Exhaustion
    cardiac
        defibrillator (with synchronous cardiac
            pacemaker) Z45.02
        pacemaker
            battery Z45.010
            lead Z45.018
    device, implant or graft —*see* Complications,
        by site, mechanical
Worried well Z71.1
Worries R45.82
Wound check Z48.0-●
    due to injury - code to Injury, by site, using
        appropriate seventh character for
        subsequent encounter
Wound, open T14.8-●
    abdomen, abdominal
        wall S31.109
            with penetration into peritoneal cavity
                S31.609
            bite —*see* Bite, abdomen, wall
            epigastric region S31.102
                with penetration into peritoneal cavity
                    S31.602
                bite —*see* Bite, abdomen, wall,
                    epigastric region
                laceration —*see* Laceration, abdomen,
                    wall, epigastric region
                puncture —*see* Puncture, abdomen,
                    wall, epigastric region

Wound, open *(Continued)*
    abdomen, abdominal *(Continued)*
        wall *(Continued)*
            laceration —*see* Laceration, abdomen, wall
            left
                lower quadrant S31.104
                    with penetration into peritoneal
                      cavity S31.604
                  bite —*see* Bite, abdomen, wall, left,
                    lower quadrant
                  laceration —*see* Laceration, abdomen,
                    wall, left, lower quadrant
                  puncture —*see* Puncture, abdomen,
                    wall, left, lower quadrant
                upper quadrant S31.101
                  with penetration into peritoneal
                      cavity S31.601
                  bite —*see* Bite, abdomen, wall, left,
                    upper quadrant
                  laceration —*see* Laceration,
                    abdomen, wall, left, upper
                    quadrant
                  puncture —*see* Puncture, abdomen,
                    wall, left, upper quadrant
             periumbilic region S31.105
                with penetration into peritoneal cavity
                  S31.605
                bite —*see* Bite, abdomen, wall,
                  periumbilic region
                laceration —*see* Laceration, abdomen,
                  wall, periumbilic region
                puncture —*see* Puncture, abdomen,
                  wall, periumbilic region
            puncture —*see* Puncture, abdomen,
                wall
            right
                lower quadrant S31.103
                  with penetration into peritoneal
                    cavity S31.603
                  bite —*see* Bite, abdomen, wall, right,
                    lower quadrant
                  laceration —*see* Laceration,
                    abdomen, wall, right, lower
                    quadrant
                  puncture —*see* Puncture, abdomen,
                    wall, right, lower quadrant
                upper quadrant S31.100
                  with penetration into peritoneal
                    cavity S31.600
                  bite —*see* Bite, abdomen, wall, right,
                    upper quadrant
                  laceration —*see* Laceration,
                    abdomen, wall, right, upper
                    quadrant
                  puncture —*see* Puncture, abdomen,
                    wall, right, upper quadrant
         alveolar (process) —*see* Wound, open, oral
            cavity
        ankle S91.00-●
            bite —*see* Bite, ankle
            laceration —*see* Laceration, ankle
            puncture —*see* Puncture, ankle
        antecubital space —*see* Wound, open, elbow
        anterior chamber, eye —*see* Wound, open,
            ocular
        anus S31.839
            bite S31.835
            laceration —*see* Laceration, anus
            puncture —*see* Puncture, anus
        arm (upper) S41.10-●
            with amputation —*see* Amputation,
                traumatic, arm
            bite —*see* Bite, arm
            forearm —*see* Wound, open, forearm
            laceration —*see* Laceration, arm
            puncture —*see* Puncture, arm
        auditory canal (external) (meatus) —*see*
            Wound, open, ear
        auricle, ear —*see* Wound, open, ear
        axilla —*see* Wound, open, arm

Wound, open *(Continued)*
    back —*see also* Wound, open, thorax, back
        lower S31.000
            with penetration into retroperitoneal
                space S31.001
            bite —*see* Bite, back, lower
            laceration —*see* Laceration, back, lower
            puncture —*see* Puncture, back, lower
    bite —*see* Bite
    blood vessel —*see* Injury, blood vessel
    breast S21.00-●
        with amputation —*see* Amputation,
            traumatic, breast
        bite —*see* Bite, breast
        laceration —*see* Laceration, breast
        puncture —*see* Puncture, breast
    buttock S31.809
        bite —*see* Bite, buttock
        laceration —*see* Laceration, buttock
        left S31.829
        puncture —*see* Puncture, buttock
        right S31.819
    calf —*see* Wound, open, leg
    canaliculus lacrimalis —*see* Wound, open,
        eyelid
    canthus, eye —*see* Wound, open, eyelid
    cervical esophagus S11.20
        bite S11.25
        laceration —*see* Laceration, esophagus,
            traumatic, cervical
        puncture —*see* Puncture, cervical
            esophagus
    cheek (external) S01.40-●
        bite —*see* Bite, cheek
        internal —*see* Wound, open, oral cavity
        laceration —*see* Laceration, cheek
        puncture —*see* Puncture, cheek
    chest wall —*see* Wound, open, thorax
    chin —*see* Wound, open, head, specified site
        NEC
    choroid —*see* Wound, open, ocular
    ciliary body (eye) —*see* Wound, open,
        ocular
    clitoris S31.40
        with amputation —*see* Amputation,
            traumatic, clitoris
        bite S31.45
        laceration —*see* Laceration, vulva
        puncture —*see* Puncture, vulva
    conjunctiva —*see* Wound, open, ocular
    cornea —*see* Wound, open, ocular
    costal region —*see* Wound, open, thorax
    Descemet's membrane —*see* Wound, open,
        ocular
    digit(s)
        foot —*see* Wound, open, toe
        hand —*see* Wound, open, finger
    ear (canal) (external) S01.30-●
        with amputation —*see* Amputation,
            traumatic, ear
        bite —*see* Bite, ear
        drum S09.2-●
        laceration —*see* Laceration, ear
        puncture —*see* Puncture, ear
    elbow S51.00-●
        bite —*see* Bite, elbow
        laceration —*see* Laceration, elbow
        puncture —*see* Puncture, elbow
    epididymis —*see* Wound, open, testis
    epigastric region S31.102
        with penetration into peritoneal cavity
            S31.602
        bite —*see* Bite, abdomen, wall, epigastric
            region
        laceration —*see* Laceration, abdomen, wall,
            epigastric region
        puncture —*see* Puncture, abdomen, wall,
            epigastric region
    epiglottis —*see* Wound, open, neck, specified
        site NEC

▶ New   ➡ Revised   ~~deleted~~ Deleted   ● Use Additional Character(s)

Wound, open *(Continued)*
  esophagus (thoracic) S27.819
    cervical —*see* Wound, open, cervical
        esophagus
    laceration S27.813
    specified type NEC S27.818
  eye —*see* Wound, open, ocular
  eyeball —*see* Wound, open, ocular
  eyebrow —*see* Wound, open, eyelid
  eyelid S01.10-•
    bite —*see* Bite, eyelid
    laceration —*see* Laceration, eyelid
    puncture —*see* Puncture, eyelid
  face NEC —*see* Wound, open, head, specified
        site NEC
  finger(s) S61.209
    with
        amputation —*see* Amputation,
            traumatic, finger
        damage to nail S61.309
    bite —*see* Bite, finger
    index S61.208
      with
          damage to nail S61.308
      left S61.201
        with
            damage to nail S61.301
      right S61.200
        with
            damage to nail S61.300
    laceration —*see* Laceration, finger
    little S61.208
      with
          damage to nail S61.308
      left S61.207
        with damage to nail S61.307
      right S61.206
        with damage to nail S61.306
    middle S61.208
      with
          damage to nail S61.308
      left S61.203
        with damage to nail S61.303
      right S61.202
        with damage to nail S61.302
    puncture —*see* Puncture, finger
    ring S61.208
      with
          damage to nail S61.308
      left S61.205
        with damage to nail S61.305
      right S61.204
        with damage to nail S61.304
  flank —*see* Wound, open, abdomen, wall
  foot (except toe(s) alone) S91.30-•
    with amputation —*see* Amputation,
        traumatic, foot
    bite —*see* Bite, foot
    laceration —*see* Laceration, foot
    puncture —*see* Puncture, foot
    toe —*see* Wound, open, toe
  forearm S51.80-•
    with
        amputation —*see* Amputation,
            traumatic, forearm
    bite —*see* Bite, forearm
    elbow only —*see* Wound, open, elbow
    laceration —*see* Laceration, forearm
    puncture —*see* Puncture, forearm
  forehead —*see* Wound, open, head, specified
        site NEC
  genital organs, external
    with amputation —*see* Amputation,
        traumatic, genital organs
    bite —*see* Bite, genital organ
    female S31.502
        vagina S31.40
        vulva S31.40
    laceration —*see* Laceration, genital
        organ

Wound, open *(Continued)*
  genital organs, external *(Continued)*
    male S31.501
        penis S31.20
        scrotum S31.30
        testes S31.30
    puncture —*see* Puncture, genital organ
  globe (eye) —*see* Wound, open, ocular
  groin —*see* Wound, open, abdomen, wall
  gum —*see* Wound, open, oral cavity
  hand S61.40-•
    with
        amputation —*see* Amputation,
            traumatic, hand
    bite —*see* Bite, hand
    finger(s) —*see* Wound, open, finger
    laceration —*see* Laceration, hand
    puncture —*see* Puncture, hand
    thumb —*see* Wound, open, thumb
  head S01.90
    bite —*see* Bite, head
    cheek —*see* Wound, open, cheek
    ear —*see* Wound, open, ear
    eyelid —*see* Wound, open, eyelid
    laceration —*see* Laceration, head
    lip —*see* Wound, open, lip
    nose S01.20
    oral cavity —*see* Wound, open, oral
        cavity
    puncture —*see* Puncture, head
    scalp —*see* Wound, open, scalp
    specified site NEC S01.80
    temporomandibular area —*see* Wound,
        open, cheek
  heel —*see* Wound, open, foot
  hip S71.00-•
    with amputation —*see* Amputation,
        traumatic, hip
    bite —*see* Bite, hip
    laceration —*see* Laceration, hip
    puncture —*see* Puncture, hip
  hymen S31.40
    bite —*see* Bite, vulva
    laceration —*see* Laceration, vagina
    puncture —*see* Puncture, vagina
  hypochondrium S31.109
    bite —*see* Bite, hypochondrium
    laceration —*see* Laceration,
        hypochondrium
    puncture —*see* Puncture, hypochondrium
  hypogastric region S31.109
    bite —*see* Bite, hypogastric region
    laceration —*see* Laceration, hypogastric
        region
    puncture —*see* Puncture, hypogastric
        region
  iliac (region) —*see* Wound, open, inguinal
        region
  inguinal region S31.109
    bite —*see* Bite, abdomen, wall, lower
        quadrant
    laceration —*see* Laceration, inguinal
        region
    puncture —*see* Puncture, inguinal
        region
  instep —*see* Wound, open, foot
  interscapular region —*see* Wound, open,
        thorax, back
  intraocular —*see* Wound, open, ocular
  iris —*see* Wound, open, ocular
  jaw —*see* Wound, open, head, specified site
        NEC
  knee S81.00-•
    bite —*see* Bite, knee
    laceration —*see* Laceration, knee
    puncture —*see* Puncture, knee
  labium (majus) (minus) —*see* Wound, open,
        vulva
  laceration —*see* Laceration, by site
  lacrimal duct —*see* Wound, open, eyelid

Wound, open *(Continued)*
  larynx S11.019
    bite —*see* Bite, larynx
    laceration —*see* Laceration, larynx
    puncture —*see* Puncture, larynx
  left
    lower quadrant S31.104
      with penetration into peritoneal cavity
          S31.604
      bite —*see* Bite, abdomen, wall, left, lower
          quadrant
      laceration —*see* Laceration, abdomen,
          wall, left, lower quadrant
      puncture —*see* Puncture, abdomen, wall,
          left, lower quadrant
    upper quadrant S31.101
      with penetration into peritoneal cavity
          S31.601
      bite —*see* Bite, abdomen, wall, left,
          upper quadrant
      laceration —*see* Laceration, abdomen,
          wall, left, upper quadrant
      puncture —*see* Puncture, abdomen, wall,
          left, upper quadrant
  leg (lower) S81.80-•
    with amputation —*see* Amputation,
        traumatic, leg
    ankle —*see* Wound, open, ankle
    bite —*see* Bite, leg
    foot —*see* Wound, open, foot
    knee —*see* Wound, open, knee
    laceration —*see* Laceration, leg
    puncture —*see* Puncture, leg
    toe —*see* Wound, open, toe
    upper —*see* Wound, open, thigh
  lip S01.501
    bite —*see* Bite, lip
    laceration —*see* Laceration, lip
    puncture —*see* Puncture, lip
  loin S31.109
    bite —*see* Bite, abdomen, wall
    laceration —*see* Laceration, loin
    puncture —*see* Puncture, loin
  lower back —*see* Wound, open, back,
        lower
  lumbar region —*see* Wound, open, back,
        lower
  malar region —*see* Wound, open, head,
        specified site NEC
  mammary —*see* Wound, open, breast
  mastoid region —*see* Wound, open, head,
        specified site NEC
  mouth —*see* Wound, open, oral cavity
  nail
    finger —*see* Wound, open, finger, with
        damage to nail
    toe —*see* Wound, open, toe, with damage
        to nail
  nape (neck) —*see* Wound, open, neck
  nasal (septum) (sinus) —*see* Wound, open,
        nose
  nasopharynx —*see* Wound, open, head,
        specified site NEC
  neck S11.90
    bite —*see* Bite, neck
    involving
        cervical esophagus S11.20
        larynx —*see* Wound, open, larynx
        pharynx S11.20
        thyroid S11.10
        trachea (cervical) S11.029
          bite —*see* Bite, trachea
          laceration S11.021
            with foreign body S11.022
          puncture S11.023
            with foreign body S11.024
    laceration —*see* Laceration, neck
    puncture —*see* Puncture, neck
    specified site NEC S11.80
        specified type NEC S11.89

Wound, open (Continued)
  nose (septum) (sinus) S01.20
    with amputation —see Amputation,
      traumatic, nose
    bite —see Bite, nose
    laceration —see Laceration, nose
    puncture —see Puncture, nose
  ocular S05.90
    avulsion (traumatic enucleation) S05.7-●
    eyeball S05.6-●
      with foreign body S05.5-●
    eyelid —see Wound, open, eyelid
    laceration and rupture S05.3-●
      with prolapse or loss of intraocular
        tissue S05.2-●
    orbit (penetrating) (with or without foreign
      body) S05.4-●
    periocular area —see Wound, open, eyelid
    specified NEC S05.8X-●
  oral cavity S01.502
    bite S01.552
    laceration —see Laceration, oral cavity
    puncture —see Puncture, oral cavity
  orbit —see Wound, open, ocular, orbit
  palate —see Wound, open, oral cavity
  palm —see Wound, open, hand
  pelvis, pelvic —see also Wound, open, back,
    lower
    girdle —see Wound, open, hip
  penetrating —see Puncture, by site
  penis S31.20
    with amputation —see Amputation,
      traumatic, penis
    bite S31.25
    laceration —see Laceration, penis
    puncture —see Puncture, penis
  perineum
    bite —see Bite, perineum
    female S31.502
    laceration —see Laceration, perineum
    male S31.501
    puncture —see Puncture, perineum
  periocular area (with or without lacrimal
    passages) —see Wound, open, eyelid
  periumbilic region S31.105
    with penetration into peritoneal cavity
      S31.605
    bite —see Bite, abdomen, wall, periumbilic
      region
    laceration —see Laceration, abdomen, wall,
      periumbilic region
    puncture —see Puncture, abdomen, wall,
      periumbilic region
  phalanges
    finger —see Wound, open, finger
    toe —see Wound, open, toe
  pharynx S11.20
  pinna —see Wound, open, ear
  popliteal space —see Wound, open, knee
  prepuce —see Wound, open, penis
  pubic region —see Wound, open, back, lower
  pudendum —see Wound, open, genital
    organs, external
  puncture wound —see Puncture
  rectovaginal septum —see Wound, open,
    vagina
  right
    lower quadrant S31.103
      with penetration into peritoneal cavity
        S31.603
      bite —see Bite, abdomen, wall, right,
        lower quadrant
      laceration —see Laceration, abdomen,
        wall, right, lower quadrant
      puncture —see Puncture, abdomen, wall,
        right, lower quadrant
    upper quadrant S31.100
      with penetration into peritoneal cavity
        S31.600

Wound, open (Continued)
  right (Continued)
    upper quadrant (Continued)
      bite —see Bite, abdomen, wall, right,
        upper quadrant
      laceration —see Laceration, abdomen,
        wall, right, upper quadrant
      puncture —see Puncture, abdomen, wall,
        right, upper quadrant
  sacral region —see Wound, open, back, lower
  sacroiliac region —see Wound, open, back,
    lower
  salivary gland —see Wound, open, oral cavity
  scalp S01.00
    bite S01.05
    laceration —see Laceration, scalp
    puncture —see Puncture, scalp
  scalpel, newborn (birth injury) P15.8
  scapular region —see Wound, open, shoulder
  sclera —see Wound, open, ocular
  scrotum S31.30
    with amputation —see Amputation,
      traumatic, scrotum
    bite S31.35
    laceration —see Laceration, scrotum
    puncture —see Puncture, scrotum
  shin —see Wound, open, leg
  shoulder S41.00-●
    with amputation —see Amputation,
      traumatic, arm
    bite —see Bite, shoulder
    laceration —see Laceration, shoulder
    puncture —see Puncture, shoulder
  skin NOS T14.8
  spermatic cord —see Wound, open, testis
  sternal region —see Wound, open, thorax,
    front wall
  submaxillary region —see Wound, open,
    head, specified site NEC
  submental region —see Wound, open, head,
    specified site NEC
  subungual
    finger(s) —see Wound, open, finger
    toe(s) —see Wound, open, toe
  supraclavicular region —see Wound, open,
    neck, specified site NEC
  temple, temporal region —see Wound, open,
    head, specified site NEC
  temporomandibular area —see Wound, open,
    cheek
  testis S31.30
    with amputation —see Amputation,
      traumatic, testes
    bite S31.35
    laceration —see Laceration, testis
    puncture —see Puncture, testis
  thigh S71.10-●
    with amputation —see Amputation,
      traumatic, hip
    bite —see Bite, thigh
    laceration —see Laceration, thigh
    puncture —see Puncture, thigh
  thorax, thoracic (wall) S21.90
    back S21.20-●
      with penetration S21.40
    bite —see Bite, thorax
    breast —see Wound, open, breast
    front S21.10-●
      with penetration S21.30
    laceration —see Laceration, thorax
    puncture —see Puncture, thorax
  throat —see Wound, open, neck
  thumb S61.009
    with
      amputation —see Amputation,
        traumatic, thumb
      damage to nail S61.109
    bite —see Bite, thumb
    laceration —see Laceration, thumb

Wound, open (Continued)
  thumb (Continued)
    left S61.002
      with
        damage to nail S61.102
      puncture —see Puncture, thumb
    right S61.001
      with
        damage to nail S61.101
  thyroid (gland) —see Wound, open, neck,
    thyroid
  toe(s) S91.109
    with
      amputation —see Amputation,
        traumatic, toe
      damage to nail S91.209
    bite —see Bite, toe
    great S91.103
      with
        damage to nail S91.203
      left S91.102
        with
          damage to nail S91.202
      right S91.101
        with
          damage to nail S91.201
    laceration —see Laceration, toe
    lesser S91.106
      with
        damage to nail S91.206
      left S91.105
        with
          damage to nail S91.205
      right S91.104
        with
          damage to nail S91.204
    puncture —see Puncture, toe
  tongue —see Wound, open, oral cavity
  trachea (cervical region) —see Wound, open,
    neck, trachea
  tunica vaginalis —see Wound, open, testis
  tympanum, tympanic membrane S09.2-●
    laceration —see Laceration, ear, drum
    puncture —see Puncture, tympanum
  umbilical region —see Wound, open,
    abdomen, wall, periumbilic region
  uvula —see Wound, open, oral cavity
  vagina S31.40
    bite S31.45
    laceration —see Laceration, vagina
    puncture —see Puncture, vagina
  vitreous (humor) —see Wound, open, ocular
  vocal cord S11.039
    bite —see Bite, vocal cord
    laceration S11.031
      with foreign body S11.032
    puncture S11.033
      with foreign body S11.034
  vulva S31.40
    with amputation —see Amputation,
      traumatic, vulva
    bite S31.45
    laceration —see Laceration, vulva
    puncture —see Puncture, vulva
  wrist S61.50-●
    bite —see Bite, wrist
    laceration —see Laceration, wrist
    puncture —see Puncture, wrist
Wound, superficial —see Injury (see also
  specified injury type)
Wright's syndrome G54.0
Wrist —see condition
Wrong drug (by accident) (given in error) —
  see Table of Drugs and Chemicals, by
  drug, poisoning
Wry neck —see Torticollis
Wuchereria (bancrofti) infestation B74.0
Wuchereriasis B74.0
Wuchernde Struma Langhans C73

▶ New   ⇒ Revised   ~~deleted~~ Deleted   ● Use Additional Character(s)

X

Xanthelasma (eyelid) (palpebrarum) H02.60
    left H02.66
        lower H02.65
        upper H02.64
    right H02.63
        lower H02.62
        upper H02.61
Xanthelasmatosis (essential) E78.2
Xanthinuria, hereditary E79.8
Xanthoastrocytoma
    specified site —see Neoplasm, malignant, by
        site
    unspecified site C71.9
Xanthofibroma —see Neoplasm, connective
        tissue, benign
Xanthogranuloma D76.3
Xanthoma(s), xanthomatosis (primary)
        (familial) (hereditary) E75.5
    with
        hyperlipoproteinemia
            Type I E78.3
            Type III E78.2
            Type IV E78.1
            Type V E78.3
    bone (generalisata) C96.5
    cerebrotendinous E75.5
    cutaneotendinous E75.5

Xanthoma(s), xanthomatosis (Continued)
    disseminatum (skin) E78.2
    eruptive E78.2
    hypercholesterinemic E78.00
    hypercholesterolemic E78.00
    hyperlipidemic E78.5
    joint E75.5
    multiple (skin) E78.2
    tendon (sheath) E75.5
    tuberosum E78.2
    tuberous E78.2
    tubo-eruptive E78.2
    verrucous, oral mucosa K13.4
Xanthosis R23.8
Xenophobia F40.10
Xeroderma —see also Ichthyosis
    acquired L85.0
    eyelid H01.149
        left H01.146
            lower H01.145
            upper H01.144
        right H01.143
            lower H01.142
            upper H01.141
    pigmentosum Q82.1
    vitamin A deficiency E50.8
Xerophthalmia (vitamin A deficiency) E50.7
    unrelated to vitamin A deficiency —see
        Keratoconjunctivitis

Xerosis
    conjunctiva H11.14-●
        with Bitot's spots —see also Pigmentation,
            conjunctiva
            vitamin A deficiency E50.1
        vitamin A deficiency E50.0
    cornea H18.89-●
        with ulceration —see Ulcer, cornea
            vitamin A deficiency E50.3
        vitamin A deficiency E50.2
    cutis L85.3
    skin L85.3
Xerostomia K11.7
Xiphopagus Q89.4
XO syndrome Q96.9
X-ray (of)
    abnormal findings —see Abnormal,
        diagnostic imaging
    breast (mammogram) (routine) Z12.31
    chest
        routine (as part of a general medical
            examination) Z00.00
            with abnormal findings Z00.01
    routine (as part of a general medical
        examination) Z00.00
        with abnormal findings Z00.01
XXXXY syndrome Q98.1
XXY syndrome Q98.0

Y

Yaba pox virus disease B08.72
Yatapoxvirus B08.70
  specified NEC B08.79
Yawning R06.89
  psychogenic F45.8
Yaws A66.9
  bone lesions A66.6
  butter A66.1
  chancre A66.0
  cutaneous, less than five years after infection
    A66.2
  early (cutaneous) (macular) (maculopapular)
    (micropapular) (papular) A66.2
    frambeside A66.2
    skin lesions NEC A66.2
  eyelid A66.2
  ganglion A66.6
  gangosis, gangosa A66.5
  gumma, gummata A66.4
    bone A66.6
  gummatous
    frambeside A66.4
    osteitis A66.6
    periostitis A66.6
  hydrarthrosis —see also subcategory
    M14.8-● A66.6
  hyperkeratosis (early) (late) A66.3

Yaws (Continued)
  initial lesions A66.0
  joint lesions —see also subcategory
    M14.8-● A66.6
  juxta-articular nodules A66.7
  late nodular (ulcerated) A66.4
  latent (without clinical manifestations) (with
    positive serology) A66.8
  mother A66.0
  mucosal A66.7
  multiple papillomata A66.1
  nodular, late (ulcerated) A66.4
  osteitis A66.6
  papilloma, plantar or palmar A66.1
  periostitis (hypertrophic) A66.6
  specified NEC A66.7
  ulcers A66.4
  wet crab A66.1
Yeast infection —see also Candidiasis B37.9
Yellow
  atrophy (liver) —see Failure, hepatic
  fever —see Fever, yellow
  jack —see Fever, yellow
  jaundice —see Jaundice
  nail syndrome L60.5
Yersiniosis —see also Infection, Yersinia
  extraintestinal A28.2
  intestinal A04.6

Z

Zahorsky's syndrome (herpangina) B08.5
Zellweger's syndrome Q87.89
Zenker's diverticulum (esophagus) K22.5
Ziehen-Oppenheim disease G24.1
Zieve's syndrome K70.0
Zika NOS A92.5
▶congenital P35.4
Zinc
  deficiency, dietary E60
  metabolism disorder E83.2
Zollinger-Ellison syndrome E16.4
Zona —see Herpes, zoster
Zoophobia F40.218
Zoster (herpes) —see Herpes, zoster
Zygomycosis B46.9
  specified NEC B46.8
Zymotic —see condition

▶ New   ➡ Revised   ~~deleted~~ Deleted   ● Use Additional Character(s)

ICD-10-CM
Table of Neoplasms

	Malignant Primary	Malignant Secondary	Ca in situ	Benign	Uncertain Behavior	Unspecified Behavior

The list below gives the code numbers for neoplasms by anatomical site. For each site there are six possible code numbers according to whether the neoplasm in question is malignant, benign, in situ, of uncertain behavior, or of unspecified nature. The description of the neoplasm will often indicate which of the six columns is appropriate; e.g., malignant melanoma of skin, benign fibroadenoma of breast, carcinoma in situ of cervix uteri.

Where such descriptors are not present, the remainder of the Index should be consulted where guidance is given to the appropriate column for each morphological (histological) variety listed; e.g., Mesonephroma—*see Neoplasm, malignant*; Embryoma—*see also Neoplasm, uncertain behavior*; Disease, Bowen's—*see Neoplasm, skin, in situ*. However, the guidance in the Index can be overridden if one of the descriptors mentioned above is present; e.g., malignant adenoma of colon is coded to C18.9 and not to D12.6 as the adjective "Malignant" overrides the Index entry 'Adenoma—*see also Neoplasm, benign.*'

Codes listed with a dash -, following the code have a required additional character for laterality. The Tablular must be reviewed for the complete code.

	Malignant Primary	Malignant Secondary	Ca in situ	Benign	Uncertain Behavior	Unspecified Behavior
Neoplasm, neoplastic	C80.1	C79.9	D09.9	D36.9	D48.9	D49.9
abdomen, abdominal	C76.2	C79.8-●	D09.8	D36.7	D48.7	D49.89
cavity	C76.2	C79.8-●	D09.8	D36.7	D48.7	D49.89
organ	C76.2	C79.8-●	D09.8	D36.7	D48.7	D49.89
viscera	C76.2	C79.8-●	D09.8	D36.7	D48.7	D49.89
wall—*see also Neoplasm, abdomen, wall, skin*	C44.509	C79.2-●	D04.5	D23.5	D48.5	D49.2
connective tissue	C49.4	C79.8-●	—	D21.4	D48.1	D49.2
skin	C44.509					
basal cell carcinoma	C44.519	—	—	—	—	—
specified type NEC	C44.599	—	—	—	—	—
squamous cell carcinoma	C44.529	—	—	—	—	—
abdominopelvic	C76.8	C79.8-●	—	D36.7	D48.7	D49.89
accessory sinus—*see Neoplasm, sinus*						
acoustic nerve	C72.4-●	C79.49	—	D33.3	D43.3	D49.7
adenoid (pharynx) (tissue)	C11.1	C79.89	D00.08	D10.6	D37.05	D49.0
adipose tissue—*see also Neoplasm, connective tissue*	C49.4	C79.89	—	D21.9	D48.1	D49.2
adnexa (uterine)	C57.4	C79.89	D07.39	D28.7	D39.8	D49.59
adrenal	C74.9-●	C79.7-●	D09.3	D35.0-●	D44.1-●	D49.7
capsule	C74.9-●	C79.7-●	D09.3	D35.0-●	D44.1-●	D49.7
cortex	C74.0-●	C79.7-●	D09.3	D35.0-●	D44.1-●	D49.7
gland	C74.9-●	C79.7-●	D09.3	D35.0-●	D44.1-●	D49.7
medulla	C74.1-●	C79.7-●	D09.3	D35.0-●	D44.1-●	D49.7
ala nasi (external)—*see also Neoplasm, skin, nose*	C44.301	C79.2	D04.39	D23.39	D48.5	D49.2

	Malignant Primary	Malignant Secondary	Ca in situ	Benign	Uncertain Behavior	Unspecified Behavior
alimentary canal or tract NEC	C26.9	C78.80	D01.9	D13.9	D37.9	D49.0
alveolar	C03.9	C79.89	D00.03	D10.39	D37.09	D49.0
mucosa	C03.9	C79.89	D00.03	D10.39	D37.09	D49.0
lower	C03.1	C79.89	D00.03	D10.39	D37.09	D49.0
upper	C03.0	C79.89	D00.03	D10.39	D37.09	D49.0
ridge or process	C41.1	C79.51	—	D16.5-●	D48.0	D49.2
carcinoma	C03.9	C79.8-●	—	—	—	—
lower	C03.1	C79.8-●	—	—	—	—
upper	C03.0	C79.8-●	—	—	—	—
lower	C41.1	C79.51	—	D16.5-●	D48.0	D49.2
mucosa	C03.9	C79.89	D00.03	D10.39	D37.09	D49.0
lower	C03.1	C79.89	D00.03	D10.39	D37.09	D49.0
upper	C03.0	C79.89	D00.03	D10.39	D37.09	D49.0
upper	C41.0	C79.51	—	D16.4-●	D48.0	D49.2
sulcus	C06.1	C79.89	D00.02	D10.39	D37.09	D49.0
alveolus	C03.9	C79.89	D00.03	D10.39	D37.09	D49.0
lower	C03.1	C79.89	D00.03	D10.39	D37.09	D49.0
upper	C03.0	C79.89	D00.03	D10.39	D37.09	D49.0
ampulla of Vater	C24.1	C78.89	D01.5	D13.5	D37.6	D49.0
ankle NEC	C76.5-●	C79.89	D04.7-●	D36.7	D48.7	D49.89
anorectum, anorectal (junction)	C21.8	C78.5	D01.3	D12.9	D37.8	D49.0
antecubital fossa or space	C76.4-●	C79.89	D04.6-●	D36.7	D48.7	D49.89
antrum (Highmore) (maxillary)	C31.0	C78.39	D02.3	D14.0	D38.5	D49.1
pyloric	C16.3	C78.89	D00.2	D13.1	D37.1	D49.0
tympanicum	C30.1	C78.39	D02.3	D14.0	D38.5	D49.1
anus, anal	C21.0	C78.5	D01.3	D12.9	D37.8	D49.0
canal	C21.1	C78.5	D01.3	D12.9	D37.8	D49.0
cloacogenic zone	C21.2	C78.5	D01.3	D12.9	D37.8	D49.0
margin—*see also Neoplasm, anus, skin*	C44.500	C79.2	D04.5	D23.5	D48.5	D49.2
overlapping lesion with rectosigmoid junction or rectum	C21.8	—	—	—	—	—
skin	C44.500	C79.2	D04.5	D23.5	D48.5	D49.2
basal cell carcinoma	C44.510	—	—	—	—	—
specified type NEC	C44.590	—	—	—	—	—
squamous cell carcinoma	C44.520	—	—	—	—	—
sphincter	C21.1	C78.5	D01.3	D12.9	D37.8	D49.0
aorta (thoracic)	C49.3	C79.89	—	D21.3	D48.1	D49.2
abdominal	C49.4	C79.89	—	D21.4	D48.1	D49.2
aortic body	C75.5	C79.89	—	D35.6	D44.7	D49.7
aponeurosis	C49.9	C79.89	—	D21.9	D48.1	D49.2
palmar	C49.1-●	C79.89	—	D21.1-●	D48.1	D49.2
plantar	C49.2-●	C79.89	—	D21.2-●	D48.1	D49.2

◀ New   ◀ Revised   ~~deleted~~ Deleted   ● Use Additional Character(s)

TABLE OF NEOPLASMS

	Malignant Primary	Malignant Secondary	Ca in situ	Benign	Uncertain Behavior	Unspecified Behavior
appendix	C18.1	C78.5	D01.0	D12.1	D37.3	D49.0
arachnoid	C70.9	C79.49	—	D32.9	D42.9	D49.7
cerebral	C70.0	C79.32	—	D32.0	D42.0	D49.7
spinal	C70.1	C79.49	—	D32.1	D42.1	D49.7
areola	C50.0-●	C79.81	D05.-●	D24.-●	D48.6-●	D49.3
arm NEC	C76.4-●	C79.89	D04.6-●	D36.7	D48.7	D49.89
artery — see Neoplasm, connective tissue						
aryepiglottic fold	C13.1	C79.89	D00.08	D10.7	D37.05	D49.0
hypopharyngeal aspect	C13.1	C79.89	D00.08	D10.7	D37.05	D49.0
laryngeal aspect	C32.1	C78.39	D02.0	D14.1	D38.0	D49.1
marginal zone	C13.1	C79.89	D00.08	D10.7	D37.05	D49.0
arytenoid (cartilage)	C32.3	C78.39	D02.0	D14.1	D38.0	D49.1
fold — see Neoplasm, aryepiglottic						
associated with transplanted organ	C80.2	—	—	—	—	—
atlas	C41.2	C79.51	—	D16.6	D48.0	D49.2
atrium, cardiac	C38.0	C79.89	—	D15.1	D48.7	D49.89
auditory						
canal (external) (skin)	C44.20-●	C79.2	D04.2-●	D23.2-●	D48.5	D49.2
internal	C30.1	C78.39	D02.3	D14.0	D38.5	D49.1
nerve	C72.4-●	C79.49	—	D33.3	D43.3	D49.7
tube	C30.1	C78.39	D02.3	D14.0	D38.5	D49.1
opening	C11.2	C79.89	D00.08	D10.6	D37.05	D49.0
auricle, ear — see also Neoplasm, skin, ear	C44.20-●	C79.2	D04.2-●	D23.2-●	D48.5	D49.2
auricular canal (external) — see also Neoplasm, skin, ear	C44.20-●	C79.2	D04.2-●	D23.2-●	D48.5	D49.2
internal	C30.1	C78.39	D02.3	D14.0	D38.5	D49.2
autonomic nerve or nervous system NEC (see Neoplasm, nerve, peripheral)						
axilla, axillary	C76.1	C79.89	D09.8	D36.7	D48.7	D49.89
fold — see also Neoplasm, skin, trunk	C44.509	C79.2	D04.5	D23.5	D48.5	D49.2
back NEC	C76.8	C79.89	D04.5	D36.7	D48.7	D49.89
Bartholin's gland	C51.0	C79.82	D07.1	D28.0	D39.8	D49.59
basal ganglia	C71.0	C79.31	—	D33.0	D43.0	D49.6
basis pedunculi	C71.7	C79.31	—	D33.1	D43.1	D49.6
bile or biliary (tract)	C24.9	C78.89	D01.5	D13.5	D37.6	D49.0
canaliculi (biliferi) (intrahepatic)	C22.1	C78.7	D01.5	D13.4	D37.6	D49.0
canals, interlobular	C22.1	C78.89	D01.5	D13.4	D37.6	D49.0

	Malignant Primary	Malignant Secondary	Ca in situ	Benign	Uncertain Behavior	Unspecified Behavior
bile or biliary (Continued)						
duct or passage (common) (cystic) (extrahepatic)	C24.0	C78.89	D01.5	D13.5	D37.6	D49.0
interlobular	C22.1	C78.89	D01.5	D13.4	D37.6	D49.0
intrahepatic	C22.1	C78.7	D01.5	D13.4	D37.6	D49.0
and extrahepatic	C24.8	C78.89	D01.5	D13.5	D37.6	D49.0
bladder (urinary)	C67.9	C79.11	D09.0	D30.3	D41.4	D49.4
dome	C67.1	C79.11	D09.0	D30.3	D41.4	D49.4
neck	C67.5	C79.11	D09.0	D30.3	D41.4	D49.4
orifice	C67.9	C79.11	D09.0	D30.3	D41.4	D49.4
ureteric	C67.6	C79.11	D09.0	D30.3	D41.4	D49.4
urethral	C67.5	C79.11	D09.0	D30.3	D41.4	D49.4
overlapping lesion	C67.8	—	—	—	—	—
sphincter	C67.8	C79.11	D09.0	D30.3	D41.4	D49.4
trigone	C67.0	C79.11	D09.0	D30.3	D41.4	D49.4
urachus	C67.7	C79.11	D09.0	D30.3	D41.4	D49.4
wall	C67.9	C79.11	D09.0	D30.3	D41.4	D49.4
anterior	C67.3	C79.11	D09.0	D30.3	D41.4	D49.4
lateral	C67.2	C79.11	D09.0	D30.3	D41.4	D49.4
posterior	C67.4	C79.11	D09.0	D30.3	D41.4	D49.4
blood vessel — see Neoplasm, connective tissue						
bone (periosteum)	C41.9	C79.51	—	D16.9-●	D48.0	D49.2
acetabulum	C41.4	C79.51	—	D16.8-●	D48.0	D49.2
ankle	C40.3-●	C79.51	—	D16.3-●	—	—
arm NEC	C40.0-●	C79.51	—	D16.0-●	—	—
astragalus	C40.3-●	C79.51	—	D16.3-●	—	—
atlas	C41.2	C79.51	—	D16.6-●	D48.0	D49.2
axis	C41.2	C79.51	—	D16.6-●	D48.0	D49.2
back NEC	C41.2	C79.51	—	D16.6-●	D48.0	D49.2
calcaneus	C40.3-●	C79.51	—	D16.3-●	—	—
calvarium	C41.0	C79.51	—	D16.4-●	D48.0	D49.2
carpus (any)	C40.1-●	C79.51	—	D16.1-●	—	—
cartilage NEC	C41.9	C79.51	—	D16.9-●	D48.0	D49.2
clavicle	C41.3	C79.51	—	D16.7-●	D48.0	D49.2
clivus	C41.0	C79.51	—	D16.4-●	D48.0	D49.2
coccygeal vertebra	C41.4	C79.51	—	D16.8-●	D48.0	D49.2
coccyx	C41.4	C79.51	—	D16.8-●	D48.0	D49.2
costal cartilage	C41.3	C79.51	—	D16.7-●	D48.0	D49.2
costovertebral joint	C41.3	C79.51	—	D16.7-●	D48.0	D49.2
cranial	C41.0	C79.51	—	D16.4-●	D48.0	D49.2
cuboid	C40.3-●	C79.51	—	D16.3-●	—	—
cuneiform	C41.9	C79.51	—	D16.9-●	D48.0	D49.2
elbow	C40.0-●	C79.51	—	D16.0-●	—	—

◀ New   ◀ Revised   ~~deleted~~ Deleted   ● Use Additional Character(s)

	Malignant Primary	Malignant Secondary	Ca in situ	Benign	Uncertain Behavior	Unspecified Behavior
bone *(Continued)*						
ethmoid (labyrinth)	C41.0	C79.51	—	D16.4-•	D48.0	D49.2
face	C41.0	C79.51	—	D16.4-•	D48.0	D49.2
femur (any part)	C40.2-•	C79.51	—	D16.2-•	—	—
fibula (any part)	C40.2-•	C79.51	—	D16.2-•	—	—
finger (any)	C40.1-•	C79.51	—	D16.1-•	—	—
foot	C40.3-•	C79.51	—	D16.3-•	—	—
forearm	C40.0-•	C79.51	—	D16.0-•	—	—
frontal	C41.0	C79.51	—	D16.4-•	D48.0	D49.2
hand	C40.1-•	C79.51	—	D16.1-•	—	—
heel	C40.3-•	C79.51	—	D16.3-•	—	—
hip	C41.4	C79.51	—	D16.8-•	D48.0	D49.2
humerus (any part)	C40.0-•	C79.51	—	D16.0-•	—	—
hyoid	C41.0	C79.51	—	D16.4-•	D48.0	D49.2
ilium	C41.4	C79.51	—	D16.8-•	D48.0	D49.2
innominate	C41.4	C79.51	—	D16.8-•	D48.0	D49.2
intervertebral cartilage or disc	C41.2	C79.51	—	D16.6-•	D48.0	D49.2
ischium	C41.4	C79.51	—	D16.8-•	D48.0	D49.2
jaw (lower)	C41.1	C79.51	—	D16.5-•	D48.0	D49.2
knee	C40.2-•	C79.51	—	D16.2-•	—	—
leg NEC	C40.2-•	C79.51	—	D16.2-•	—	—
limb NEC	C40.9-•	C79.51	—	D16.9-•	—	—
lower (long bones)	C40.2-•	C79.51	—	D16.2-•	—	—
short bones	C40.3-•	C79.51	—	D16.3-•	—	—
upper (long bones)	C40.0-•	C79.51	—	D16.0-•	—	—
short bones	C40.1-•	C79.51	—	D16.1-•	—	—
malar	C41.0	C79.51	—	D16.4-•	D48.0	D49.2
mandible	C41.1	C79.51	—	D16.5-•	D48.0	D49.2
marrow NEC (any bone)	C96.9	C79.52	—	—	D47.9	D49.89
mastoid	C41.0	C79.51	—	D16.4-•	D48.0	D49.2
maxilla, maxillary (superior)	C41.0	C79.51	—	D16.4-•	D48.0	D49.2
inferior	C41.1	C79.51	—	D16.5-•	D48.0	D49.2
metacarpus (any)	C40.1-•	C79.51	—	D16.1-•	—	—
metatarsus (any)	C40.3-•	C79.51	—	D16.3-•	—	—
overlapping sites	C40.8-•	—	—	—	—	—
navicular						
ankle	C40.3-•	C79.51	—	—	—	—
hand	C40.1-•	C79.51	—	—	—	—
nose, nasal	C41.0	C79.51	—	D16.4-•	D48.0	D49.2
occipital	C41.0	C79.51	—	D16.4-•	D48.0	D49.2
orbit	C41.0	C79.51	—	D16.4-•	D48.0	D49.2
parietal	C41.0	C79.51	—	D16.4-•	D48.0	D49.2
patella	C40.2-•	C79.51	—	—	—	—
pelvic	C41.4	C79.51	—	D16.8	D48.0	D49.2

	Malignant Primary	Malignant Secondary	Ca in situ	Benign	Uncertain Behavior	Unspecified Behavior
bone *(Continued)*						
phalanges						
foot	C40.3-•	C79.51	—	—	—	—
hand	C40.1-•	C79.51	—	—	—	—
pubic	C41.4	C79.51	—	D16.8	D48.0	D49.2
radius (any part)	C40.0-•	C79.51	—	D16.0-•	—	—
rib	C41.3	C79.51	—	D16.7	D48.0	D49.2
sacral vertebra	C41.4	C79.51	—	D16.8	D48.0	D49.2
sacrum	C41.4	C79.51	—	D16.8	D48.0	D49.2
scaphoid				—		—
of ankle	C40.3-•	C79.51	—	—	—	—
of hand	C40.1-•	C79.51	—	—	—	—
scapula (any part)	C40.0-•	C79.51	—	D16.0-•	—	—
sella turcica	C41.0	C79.51	—	D16.4-•	D48.0	D49.2
shoulder	C40.0-•	C79.51	—	D16.0-•	—	—
skull	C41.0	C79.51	—	D16.4-•	D48.0	D49.2
sphenoid	C41.0	C79.51	—	D16.4-•	D48.0	D49.2
spine, spinal (column)	C41.2	C79.51	—	D16.6	D48.0	D49.2
coccyx	C41.4	C79.51	—	D16.8	D48.0	D49.2
sacrum	C41.4	C79.51	—	D16.8	D48.0	D49.2
sternum	C41.3	C79.51	—	D16.7	D48.0	D49.2
tarsus (any)	C40.3-•	C79.51	—	—	—	—
temporal	C41.0	C79.51	—	D16.4-•	D48.0	D49.2
thumb	C40.1-•	C79.51	—	—	—	—
tibia (any part)	C40.2-•	C79.51	—	—	—	—
toe (any)	C40.3-•	C79.51	—	—	—	—
trapezium	C40.1-•	C79.51	—	—	—	—
trapezoid	C40.1-•	C79.51	—	—	—	—
turbinate	C41.0	C79.51	—	D16.4-•	D48.0	D49.2
ulna (any part)	C40.0-•	C79.51	—	D16.0-•	—	—
unciform	C40.1-•	C79.51	—	—	—	—
vertebra (column)	C41.2	C79.51	—	D16.6	D48.0	D49.2
coccyx	C41.4	C79.51	—	D16.8	D48.0	D49.2
sacrum	C41.4	C79.51	—	D16.8	D48.0	D49.2
vomer	C41.0	C79.51	—	D16.4-•	D48.0	D49.2
wrist	C40.1-•	C79.51	—	—	—	—
xiphoid process	C41.3	C79.51	—	D16.7	D48.0	D49.2
zygomatic	C41.0	C79.51	—	D16.4-•	D48.0	D49.2
book-leaf (mouth)	C06.89	C79.89	D00.00	D10.39	D37.09	D49.0
bowel — *see* Neoplasm, intestine						
brachial plexus	C47.1-•	C79.89	—	D36.12	D48.2	D49.2
brain NEC	C71.9	C79.31	—	D33.2	D43.2	D49.6
basal ganglia	C71.0	C79.31	—	D33.0	D43.0	D49.6
cerebellopontine angle	C71.6	C79.31	—	D33.1	D43.1	D49.6

◀ New   ◀ Revised   ~~deleted~~ Deleted   • Use Additional Character(s)

TABLE OF NEOPLASMS

	Malignant Primary	Malignant Secondary	Ca in situ	Benign	Uncertain Behavior	Unspecified Behavior
brain NEC *(Continued)*						
cerebellum NOS	C71.6	C79.31	—	D33.1	D43.1	D49.6
cerebrum	C71.0	C79.31	—	D33.0	D43.0	D49.6
choroid plexus	C71.7	C79.31	—	D33.1	D43.1	D49.6
corpus callosum	C71.8	C79.31	—	D33.2	D43.2	D49.6
corpus striatum	C71.0	C79.31	—	D33.0	D43.0	D49.6
cortex (cerebral)	C71.0	C79.31	—	D33.0	D43.0	D49.6
frontal lobe	C71.1	C79.31	—	D33.0	D43.0	D49.6
globus pallidus	C71.0	C79.31	—	D33.0	D43.0	D49.6
hippocampus	C71.2	C79.31	—	D33.0	D43.0	D49.6
hypothalamus	C71.0	C79.31	—	D33.0	D43.0	D49.6
internal capsule	C71.0	C79.31	—	D33.0	D43.0	D49.6
medulla oblongata	C71.7	C79.31	—	D33.1	D43.1	D49.6
meninges	C70.0	C79.32	—	D32.0	D42.0	D49.7
midbrain	C71.7	C79.31	—	D33.1	D43.1	D49.6
occipital lobe	C71.4	C79.31	—	D33.0	D43.0	D49.6
overlapping lesion	C71.8	C79.31	—	—	—	—
parietal lobe	C71.3	C79.31	—	D33.0	D43.0	D49.6
peduncle	C71.7	C79.31	—	D33.1	D43.1	D49.6
pons	C71.7	C79.31	—	D33.1	D43.1	D49.6
stem	C71.7	C79.31	—	D33.1	D43.1	D49.6
tapetum	C71.8	C79.31	—	D33.2	D43.2	D49.6
temporal lobe	C71.2	C79.31	—	D33.0	D43.0	D49.6
thalamus	C71.0	C79.31	—	D33.0	D43.0	D49.6
uncus	C71.2	C79.31	—	D33.0	D43.0	D49.6
ventricle (floor)	C71.5	C79.31	—	D33.0	D43.0	D49.6
fourth	C71.7	C79.31	—	D33.1	D43.1	D49.6
branchial (cleft) (cyst) (vestiges)	C10.4	C79.89	D00.08	D10.5	D37.05	D49.0
breast (connective tissue) (glandular tissue) (soft parts)	C50.9-●	C79.81	D05.-●	D24.-●	D48.6-●	D49.3
areola	C50.0-●	C79.81	D05.-●	D24.-●	D48.6-●	D49.3
axillary tail	C50.6-●	C79.81	D05.-●	D24.-●	D48.6-●	D49.3
central portion	C50.1-●	C79.81	D05.-●	D24.-●	D48.6-●	D49.3
inner	C50.8-●	C79.81	D05.-●	D24.-●	D48.6-●	D49.3
lower	C50.8-●	C79.81	D05.-●	D24.-●	D48.6-●	D49.3
lower-inner quadrant	C50.3-●	C79.81	D05.-●	D24.-●	D48.6-●	D49.3
lower-outer quadrant	C50.5-●	C79.81	D05.-●	D24.-●	D48.6-●	D49.3
mastectomy site (skin) — *see also Neoplasm, breast, skin*	C44.501	C79.2	—	—	—	—
specified as breast tissue	C50.8-●	C79.81	—	—	—	—
midline	C50.8-●	C79.81	D05.-●	D24.-●	D48.6-●	D49.3
nipple	C50.0-●	C79.81	D05.-●	D24.-●	D48.6-●	D49.3
outer	C50.8-●	C79.81	D05.-●	D24.-●	D48.6-●	D49.3
overlapping lesion	C50.8-●					

	Malignant Primary	Malignant Secondary	Ca in situ	Benign	Uncertain Behavior	Unspecified Behavior
breast *(Continued)*						
skin	C44.501	C79.2	D04.5	D23.5	D48.5	D49.2
basal cell carcinoma	C44.511	—	—	—	—	—
specified type NEC	C44.591	—	—	—	—	—
squamous cell carcinoma	C44.521	—	—	—	—	—
tail (axillary)	C50.6-●	C79.81	D05.-●	D24.-●	D48.6-●	D49.3
upper	C50.8-●	C79.81	D05.-●	D24.-●	D48.6-●	D49.3
upper-inner quadrant	C50.2-●	C79.81	D05.-●	D24.-●	D48.6-●	D49.3
upper-outer quadrant	C50.4-●	C79.81	D05.-●	D24.-●	D48.6-●	D49.3
broad ligament	C57.1	C79.82	D07.39	D28.2	D39.8	D49.59
bronchiogenic, bronchogenic (lung)	C34.9-●	C78.0-●	D02.2-●	D14.3-●	D38.1	D49.1
bronchiole	C34.9-●	C78.0-●	D02.2-●	D14.3-●	D38.1	D49.1
bronchus	C34.9-●	C78.0-●	D02.2-●	D14.3-●	D38.1	D49.1
carina	C34.0-●	C78.0-●	D02.2-●	D14.3-●	D38.1	D49.1
lower lobe of lung	C34.3-●	C78.0-●	D02.2-●	D14.3-●	D38.1	D49.1
main	C34.0-●	C78.0-●	D02.2-●	D14.3-●	D38.1	D49.1
middle lobe of lung	C34.2	C78.0-●	D02.21	D14.31	D38.1	D49.1
overlapping lesion	C34.8-●	—	—	—	—	—
upper lobe of lung	C34.1-●	C78.0-●	D02.2-●	D14.3-●	D38.1	D49.1
brow	C44.309	C79.2	D04.39	D23.39	D48.5	D49.2
basal cell carcinoma	C44.319	—	—	—	—	—
specified type NEC	C44.399	—	—	—	—	—
squamous cell carcinoma	C44.329	—	—	—	—	—
buccal (cavity)	C06.9	C79.89	D00.00	D10.39	D37.09	D49.0
commissure	C06.0	C79.89	D00.02	D10.39	D37.09	D49.0
groove (lower) (upper)	C06.1	C79.89	D00.02	D10.39	D37.09	D49.0
mucosa	C06.0	C79.89	D00.02	D10.39	D37.09	D49.0
sulcus (lower) (upper)	C06.1	C79.89	D00.02	D10.39	D37.09	D49.0
bulbourethral gland	C68.0	C79.19	D09.19	D30.4	D41.3	D49.59
bursa — *see Neoplasm, connective tissue*						
buttock NEC	C76.3	C79.89	D04.5	D36.7	D48.7	D49.89
calf	C76.5-●	C79.89	D04.7-●	D36.7	D48.7	D49.89
calvarium	C41.0	C79.51	—	D16.4-●	D48.0	D49.2
calyx, renal	C65.-●	C79.0-●	D09.19	D30.1-●	D41.1-●	D49.51-●
canal						
anal	C21.1	C78.5	D01.3	D12.9	D37.8	D49.0
auditory (external) — *see also Neoplasm, skin, ear*	C44.20-●	C79.2	D04.2-●	D23.2-●	D48.5	D49.2
auricular (external) — *see also Neoplasm, skin, ear*	C44.20-●	C79.2	D04.2-●	D23.2-●	D48.5	D49.2
canaliculi, biliary (biliferi) (intrahepatic)	C22.1	C78.7	D01.5	D13.4	D37.6	D49.0

◀ New ◀◀ Revised ~~deleted~~ Deleted ● Use Additional Character(s)

	Malignant Primary	Malignant Secondary	Ca in situ	Benign	Uncertain Behavior	Unspecified Behavior
canthus (eye) (inner) (outer)	C44.10-●	C79.2	D04.1-●	D23.1-●	D48.5	D49.2
basal cell carcinoma	C44.11-●	—	—	—	—	—
sebaceous cell	C44.13-●	—	—	—	—	—
specified type NEC	C44.19-●	—	—	—	—	—
squamous cell carcinoma	C44.12-●	—	—	—	—	—
capillary — see Neoplasm, connective tissue						
caput coli	C18.0	C78.5	D01.0	D12.0	D37.4	D49.0
carcinoid — see Tumor, carcinoid						
cardia (gastric)	C16.0	C78.89	D00.2	D13.1	D37.1	D49.0
cardiac orifice (stomach)	C16.0	C78.89	D00.2	D13.1	D37.1	D49.0
cardio-esophageal junction	C16.0	C78.89	D00.2	D13.1	D37.1	D49.0
cardio-esophagus	C16.0	C78.89	D00.2	D13.1	D37.1	D49.0
carina (bronchus)	C34.0-●	C78.0-●	D02.2-●	D14.3-●	D38.1	D49.1
carotid (artery)	C49.0	C79.89	—	D21.0	D48.1	D49.2
body	C75.4	C79.89	—	D35.5	D44.6	D49.7
carpus (any bone)	C40.1-●	C79.51	—	D16.1-●	—	—
cartilage (articular) (joint) NEC — see also Neoplasm, bone	C41.9	C79.51	—	D16.9-●	D48.0	D49.2
arytenoid	C32.3	C78.39	D02.0	D14.1	D38.0	D49.1
auricular	C49.0	C79.89	—	D21.0	D48.1	D49.2
bronchi	C34.0-●	C78.39	—	D14.3-●	D38.1	D49.1
costal	C41.3	C79.51	—	D16.7	D48.0	D49.2
cricoid	C32.3	C78.39	D02.0	D14.1	D38.0	D49.1
cuneiform	C32.3	C78.39	D02.0	D14.1	D38.0	D49.1
ear (external)	C49.0	C79.89	—	D21.0	D48.1	D49.2
ensiform	C41.3	C79.51	—	D16.7	D48.0	D49.2
epiglottis	C32.1	C78.39	D02.0	D14.1	D38.0	D49.1
anterior surface	C10.1	C79.89	D00.08	D10.5	D37.05	D49.0
eyelid	C49.0	C79.89	—	D21.0	D48.1	D49.2
intervertebral	C41.2	C79.51	—	D16.6	D48.0	D49.2
larynx, laryngeal	C32.3	C78.39	D02.0	D14.1	D38.0	D49.1
nose, nasal	C30.0	C78.39	D02.3	D14.0	D38.5	D49.1
pinna	C49.0	C79.89	—	D21.0	D48.1	D49.2
rib	C41.3	C79.51	—	D16.7	D48.0	D49.2
semilunar (knee)	C40.2-●	C79.51	—	D16.2-●	D48.0	D49.2
thyroid	C32.3	C78.39	D02.0	D14.1	D38.0	D49.1
trachea	C33	C78.39	D02.1	D14.2	D38.1	D49.1
cauda equina	C72.1	C79.49	—	D33.4	D43.4	D49.7
cavity						
buccal	C06.9	C79.89	D00.00	D10.30	D37.09	D49.0
nasal	C30.0	C78.39	D02.3	D14.0	D38.5	D49.1
oral	C06.9	C79.89	D00.00	D10.30	D37.09	D49.0

	Malignant Primary	Malignant Secondary	Ca in situ	Benign	Uncertain Behavior	Unspecified Behavior
cavity (Continued)						
peritoneal	C48.2	C78.6	—	D20.1	D48.4	D49.0
tympanic	C30.1	C78.39	D02.3	D14.0	D38.5	D49.1
cecum	C18.0	C78.5	D01.0	D12.0	D37.4	D49.0
central nervous system	C72.9	C79.40	—	—	—	—
cerebellopontine (angle)	C71.6	C79.31	—	D33.1	D43.1	D49.6
cerebellum, cerebellar	C71.6	C79.31	—	D33.1	D43.1	D49.6
cerebrum, cerebral (cortex) (hemisphere) (white matter)	C71.0	C79.31	—	D33.0	D43.0	D49.6
meninges	C70.0	C79.32	—	D32.0	D42.0	D49.7
peduncle	C71.7	C79.31	—	D33.1	D43.1	D49.6
ventricle	C71.5	C79.31	—	D33.0	D43.0	D49.6
fourth	C71.7	C79.31	—	D33.1	D43.1	D49.6
cervical region	C76.0	C79.89	D09.8	D36.7	D48.7	D49.89
cervix (cervical) (uteri) (uterus)	C53.9	C79.82	D06.9	D26.0	D39.0	D49.59
canal	C53.0	C79.82	D06.0	D26.0	D39.0	D49.59
endocervix (canal) (gland)	C53.0	C79.82	D06.0	D26.0	D39.0	D49.59
exocervix	C53.1	C79.82	D06.1	D26.0	D39.0	D49.59
external os	C53.1	C79.82	D06.1	D26.0	D39.0	D49.59
internal os	C53.0	C79.82	D06.0	D26.0	D39.0	D49.59
nabothian gland	C53.0	C79.82	D06.0	D26.0	D39.0	D49.59
overlapping lesion	C53.8	—	—	—	—	—
squamocolumnar junction	C53.8	C79.82	D06.7	D26.0	D39.0	D49.59
stump	C53.8	C79.82	D06.7	D26.0	D39.0	D49.59
cheek	C76.0	C79.89	D09.8	D36.7	D48.7	D49.89
external	C44.309	C79.2	D04.39	D23.39	D48.5	D49.2
basal cell carcinoma	C44.319	—	—	—	—	—
specified type NEC	C44.399	—	—	—	—	—
squamous cell carcinoma	C44.329	—	—	—	—	—
inner aspect	C06.0	C79.89	D00.02	D10.39	D37.09	D49.0
internal	C06.0	C79.89	D00.02	D10.39	D37.09	D49.0
mucosa	C06.0	C79.89	D00.02	D10.39	D37.09	D49.0
chest (wall) NEC	C76.1	C79.89	D09.8	D36.7	D48.7	D49.89
chiasma opticum	C72.3-●	C79.49	—	D33.3	D43.3	D49.7
chin	C44.309	C79.2	D04.39	D23.39	D48.5	D49.2
basal cell carcinoma	C44.319	—	—	—	—	—
specified type NEC	C44.399	—	—	—	—	—
squamous cell carcinoma	C44.329	—	—	—	—	—
choana	C11.3	C79.89	D00.08	D10.6	D37.05	D49.0
cholangiole	C22.1	C78.89	D01.5	D13.4	D37.6	D49.0
choledochal duct	C24.0	C78.89	D01.5	D13.5	D37.6	D49.0
choroid	C69.3-●	C79.49	D09.2-●	D31.3-●	D48.7	D49.81
plexus	C71.5	C79.31	—	D33.0	D43.0	D49.6
ciliary body	C69.4-●	C79.49	D09.2-●	D31.4-●	D48.7	D49.89

TABLE OF NEOPLASMS

	Malignant Primary	Malignant Secondary	Ca in situ	Benign	Uncertain Behavior	Unspecified Behavior
clavicle	C41.3	C79.51	—	D16.7	D48.0	D49.2
clitoris	C51.2	C79.82	D07.1	D28.0	D39.8	D49.59
clivus	C41.0	C79.51	—	D16.4-●	D48.0	D49.2
cloacogenic zone	C21.2	C78.5	D01.3	D12.9	D37.8	D49.0
coccygeal						
body or glomus	C49.5	C79.89	—	D21.5	D48.1	D49.2
vertebra	C41.4	C79.51	—	D16.8	D48.0	D49.2
coccyx	C41.4	C79.51	—	D16.8	D48.0	D49.2
colon—*see also Neoplasm, intestine, large*	C18.9	C78.5	—	—	—	—
with rectum	C19	C78.5	D01.1	D12.7	D37.5	D49.0
column, spinal—*see Neoplasm, spine*						
columnella—*see also Neoplasm, skin, face*	C44.390	C79.2	D04.39	D23.39	D48.5	D49.2
commissure						
labial, lip	C00.6	C79.89	D00.01	D10.39	D37.01	D49.0
laryngeal	C32.0	C78.39	D02.0	D14.1	D38.0	D49.1
common (bile) duct	C24.0	C78.89	D01.5	D13.5	D37.6	D49.0
concha—*see also Neoplasm, skin, ear*	C44.20-●	C79.2	D04.2-●	D23.2-●	D48.5	D49.2
nose	C30.0	C78.39	D02.3	D14.0	D38.5	D49.1
conjunctiva	C69.0-●	C79.49	D09.2-●	D31.0-●	D48.7	D49.89
connective tissue NEC	C49.9	C79.89	—	D21.9	D48.1	D49.2

Note: For neoplasms of connective tissue (blood vessel, bursa, fascia, ligament, muscle, peripheral nerves, sympathetic and parasympathetic nerves and ganglia, synovia, tendon, etc.) or of morphological types that indicate connective tissue, code according to the list under "Neoplasm, connective tissue". For sites that do not appear in this list, code to neoplasm of that site; e.g., fibrosarcoma, pancreas (C25.9)

Note: Morphological types that indicate connective tissue appear in their proper place in the alphabetic index with the instruction "*see Neoplasm, connective tissue ....*"

	Malignant Primary	Malignant Secondary	Ca in situ	Benign	Uncertain Behavior	Unspecified Behavior
abdomen	C49.4	C79.89	—	D21.4	D48.1	D49.2
abdominal wall	C49.4	C79.89	—	D21.4	D48.1	D49.2
ankle	C49.2-●	C79.89	—	D21.2-●	D48.1	D49.2
antecubital fossa or space	C49.1-●	C79.89	—	D21.1-●	D48.1	D49.2
arm	C49.1-●	C79.89	—	D21.1-●	D48.1	D49.2
auricle (ear)	C49.0	C79.89	—	D21.0	D48.1	D49.2
axilla	C49.3	C79.89	—	D21.3	D48.1	D49.2
back	C49.6	C79.89	—	D21.6	D48.1	D49.2
breast—*see Neoplasm, breast*						
buttock	C49.5	C79.89	—	D21.5	D48.1	D49.2
calf	C49.2-●	C79.89	—	D21.2-●	D48.1	D49.2
cervical region	C49.0	C79.89	—	D21.0	D48.1	D49.2

	Malignant Primary	Malignant Secondary	Ca in situ	Benign	Uncertain Behavior	Unspecified Behavior
connective tissue NEC *(Continued)*						
cheek	C49.0	C79.89	—	D21.0	D48.1	D49.2
chest (wall)	C49.3	C79.89	—	D21.3	D48.1	D49.2
chin	C49.0	C79.89	—	D21.0	D48.1	D49.2
diaphragm	C49.3	C79.89	—	D21.3	D48.1	D49.2
ear (external)	C49.0	C79.89	—	D21.0	D48.1	D49.2
elbow	C49.1-●	C79.89	—	D21.1-●	D48.1	D49.2
extrarectal	C49.5	C79.89	—	D21.5	D48.1	D49.2
extremity	C49.9	C79.89	—	D21.9	D48.1	D49.2
lower	C49.2-●	C79.89	—	D21.2-●	D48.1	D49.2
upper	C49.1-●	C79.89	—	D21.1-●	D48.1	D49.2
eyelid	C49.0	C79.89	—	D21.0	D48.1	D49.2
face	C49.0	C79.89	—	D21.0	D48.1	D49.2
finger	C49.1-●	C79.89	—	D21.1-●	D48.1	D49.2
flank	C49.6	C79.89	—	D21.6	D48.1	D49.2
foot	C49.2-●	C79.89	—	D21.2-●	D48.1	D49.2
forearm	C49.1-●	C79.89	—	D21.1-●	D48.1	D49.2
forehead	C49.0	C79.89	—	D21.0	D48.1	D49.2
gastric	C49.4	C79.89	—	D21.4	D48.1	D49.2
gastrointestinal	C49.4	C79.89	—	D21.4	D48.1	D49.2
gluteal region	C49.5	C79.89	—	D21.5	D48.1	D49.2
great vessels NEC	C49.3	C79.89	—	D21.3	D48.1	D49.2
groin	C49.5	C79.89	—	D21.5	D48.1	D49.2
hand	C49.1-●	C79.89	—	D21.1-●	D48.1	D49.2
head	C49.0	C79.89	—	D21.0	D48.1	D49.2
heel	C49.2-●	C79.89	—	D21.2-●	D48.1	D49.2
hip	C49.2-●	C79.89	—	D21.2-●	D48.1	D49.2
hypochondrium	C49.4	C79.89	—	D21.4	D48.1	D49.2
iliopsoas muscle	C49.5	C79.89	—	D21.5	D48.1	D49.2
infraclavicular region	C49.3	C79.89	—	D21.3	D48.1	D49.2
inguinal (canal) (region)	C49.5	C79.89	—	D21.5	D48.1	D49.2
intestinal	C49.4	C79.89	—	D21.4	D48.1	D49.2
intrathoracic	C49.3	C79.89	—	D21.3	D48.1	D49.2
ischiorectal fossa	C49.5	C79.89	—	D21.5	D48.1	D49.2
jaw	C03.9	C79.89	D00.03	D10.39	D48.1	D49.0
knee	C49.2-●	C79.89	—	D21.2-●	D48.1	D49.2
leg	C49.2-●	C79.89	—	D21.2-●	D48.1	D49.2
limb NEC	C49.9	C79.89	—	D21.9	D48.1	D49.2
lower	C49.2-●	C79.89	—	D21.2-●	D48.1	D49.2
upper	C49.1-●	C79.89	—	D21.1-●	D48.1	D49.2
nates	C49.5	C79.89	—	D21.5	D48.1	D49.2
neck	C49.0	C79.89	—	D21.0	D48.1	D49.2
orbit	C69.6-●	C79.49	D09.2-●	D31.6-●	D48.1	D49.89
overlapping lesion	C49.8	—	—	—	—	—

◀ New ◀ Revised deleted Deleted ● Use Additional Character(s)

connective tissue NEC *(Continued)*	Malignant Primary	Malignant Secondary	Ca in situ	Benign	Uncertain Behavior	Unspecified Behavior
pararectal	C49.5	C79.89	—	D21.5	D48.1	D49.2
para-urethral	C49.5	C79.89	—	D21.5	D48.1	D49.2
paravaginal	C49.5	C79.89	—	D21.5	D48.1	D49.2
pelvis (floor)	C49.5	C79.89	—	D21.5	D48.1	D49.2
pelvo-abdominal	C49.8	C79.89	—	D21.6	D48.1	D49.2
perineum	C49.5	C79.89	—	D21.5	D48.1	D49.2
perirectal (tissue)	C49.5	C79.89	—	D21.5	D48.1	D49.2
periurethral (tissue)	C49.5	C79.89	—	D21.5	D48.1	D49.2
popliteal fossa or space	C49.2-●	C79.89	—	D21.2-●	D48.1	D49.2
presacral	C49.5	C79.89	—	D21.5	D48.1	D49.2
psoas muscle	C49.4	C79.89	—	D21.4	D48.1	D49.2
pterygoid fossa	C49.0	C79.89	—	D21.0	D48.1	D49.2
rectovaginal septum or wall	C49.5	C79.89	—	D21.5	D48.1	D49.2
rectovesical	C49.5	C79.89	—	D21.5	D48.1	D49.2
retroperitoneum	C48.0	C78.6	—	D20.0	D48.3	D49.0
sacrococcygeal region	C49.5	C79.89	—	D21.5	D48.1	D49.2
scalp	C49.0	C79.89	—	D21.0	D48.1	D49.2
scapular region	C49.3	C79.89	—	D21.3	D48.1	D49.2
shoulder	C49.1-●	C79.89	—	D21.1-●	D48.1	D49.2
skin (dermis) NEC — *see also* *Neoplasm, skin, by site*	C44.90	C79.2	D04.9	D23.9	D48.5	D49.2
stomach	C49.4	C79.89	—	D21.4	D48.1	D49.2
submental	C49.0	C79.89	—	D21.0	D48.1	D49.2
supraclavicular region	C49.0	C79.89	—	D21.0	D48.1	D49.2
temple	C49.0	C79.89	—	D21.0	D48.1	D49.2
temporal region	C49.0	C79.89	—	D21.0	D48.1	D49.2
thigh	C49.2-●	C79.89	—	D21.2-●	D48.1	D49.2
thoracic (duct) (wall)	C49.3	C79.89	—	D21.3	D48.1	D49.2
thorax	C49.3	C79.89	—	D21.3	D48.1	D49.2
thumb	C49.1-●	C79.89	—	D21.1-●	D48.1	D49.2
toe	C49.2-●	C79.89	—	D21.2-●	D48.1	D49.2
trunk	C49.6	C79.89	—	D21.6	D48.1	D49.2
umbilicus	C49.4	C79.89	—	D21.4	D48.1	D49.2
vesicorectal	C49.5	C79.89	—	D21.5	D48.1	D49.2
wrist	C49.1-●	C79.89	—	D21.1-●	D48.1	D49.2
conus medullaris	C72.0	C79.49	—	D33.4	D43.4	D49.7
cord (true) (vocal)	C32.0	C78.39	D02.0	D14.1	D38.0	D49.1
false	C32.1	C78.39	D02.0	D14.1	D38.0	D49.1
spermatic	C63.1-●	C79.82	D07.69	D29.8	D40.8	D49.59
spinal (cervical) (lumbar) (thoracic)	C72.0	C79.49	—	D33.4	D43.4	D49.7
cornea (limbus)	C69.1-●	C79.49	D09.2-●	D31.1-●	D48.7	D49.89
corpus						

corpus *(Continued)*	Malignant Primary	Malignant Secondary	Ca in situ	Benign	Uncertain Behavior	Unspecified Behavior
albicans	C56.-●	C79.6-●	D07.39	D27.-●	D39.1-●	D49.59
callosum, brain	C71.0	C79.31	—	D33.2	D43.2	D49.6
cavernosum	C60.2	C79.82	D07.4	D29.0	D40.8	D49.59
gastric	C16.2	C78.89	D00.2	D13.1	D37.1	D49.0
overlapping sites	C54.8	—	—	—	—	—
penis	C60.2	C79.82	D07.4	D29.0	D40.8	D49.59
striatum, cerebrum	C71.0	C79.31	—	D33.0	D43.0	D49.6
uteri	C54.9	C79.82	D07.0	D26.1	D39.0	D49.59
isthmus	C54.0	C79.82	D07.0	D26.1	D39.0	D49.59
cortex						
adrenal	C74.0-●	C79.7-●	D09.3	D35.0-●	D44.1-●	D49.7
cerebral	C71.0	C79.31	—	D33.0	D43.0	D49.6
costal cartilage	C41.3	C79.51	—	D16.7	D48.0	D49.2
costovertebral joint	C41.3	C79.51	—	D16.7	D48.0	D49.2
Cowper's gland	C68.0	C79.19	D09.19	D30.4	D41.3	D49.59
cranial (fossa, any)	C71.9	C79.31	—	D33.2	D43.2	D49.6
meninges	C70.0	C79.32	—	D32.0	D42.0	D49.7
nerve	C72.50	C79.49	—	D33.3	D43.3	D49.7
specified NEC	C72.59	C79.49	—	D33.3	D43.3	D49.7
craniobuccal pouch	C75.2	C79.89	D09.3	D35.2	D44.3	D49.7
craniopharyngeal (duct) (pouch)	C75.2	C79.89	D09.3	D35.3	D44.4	D49.7
cricoid	C13.0	C79.89	D00.08	D10.7	D37.05	D49.0
cartilage	C32.3	C78.39	D02.0	D14.1	D38.0	D49.1
cricopharynx	C13.0	C79.89	D00.08	D10.7	D37.05	D49.0
crypt of Morgagni	C21.8	C78.5	D01.3	D12.9	D37.8	D49.0
crystalline lens	C69.4-●	C79.49	D09.2-●	D31.4-●	D48.7	D49.89
cul-de-sac (Douglas')	C48.1	C78.6	—	D20.1	D48.4	D49.0
cuneiform cartilage	C32.3	C78.39	D02.0	D14.1	D38.0	D49.1
cutaneous — *see Neoplasm, skin*						
cutis — *see Neoplasm, skin*						
cystic (bile) duct (common)	C24.0	C78.89	D01.5	D13.5	D37.6	D49.0
dermis — *see Neoplasm, skin*						
diaphragm	C49.3	C79.89	—	D21.3	D48.1	D49.2
digestive organs, system, tube, or tract NEC	C26.9	C78.89	D01.9	D13.9	D37.9	D49.0
disc, intervertebral	C41.2	C79.51	—	D16.6	D48.0	D49.2
disease, generalized	C80.0	—	—	—	—	—
disseminated	C80.0	—	—	—	—	—
Douglas' cul-de-sac or pouch	C48.1	C78.6	—	D20.1	D48.4	D49.0
duodenojejunal junction	C17.8	C78.4	D01.49	D13.39	D37.2	D49.0
duodenum	C17.0	C78.4	D01.49	D13.2	D37.2	D49.0

 ◀ New ◀ Revised ~~deleted~~ Deleted ● Use Additional Character(s)

	Malignant Primary	Malignant Secondary	Ca in situ	Benign	Uncertain Behavior	Unspecified Behavior
dura (cranial) (mater)	C70.9	C79.49	—	D32.9	D42.9	D49.7
cerebral	C70.0	C79.32	—	D32.0	D42.0	D49.7
spinal	C70.1	C79.49	—	D32.1	D42.1	D49.7
ear (external) — see also Neoplasm, skin, ear	C44.20-●	C79.2	D04.2-●	D23.2-●	D48.5	D49.2
auricle or auris — see also Neoplasm, skin, ear	C44.20-●	C79.2	D04.2-●	D23.2-●	D48.5	D49.2
canal, external — see also Neoplasm, skin, ear	C44.20-●	C79.2	D04.2-●	D23.2-●	D48.5	D49.2
cartilage	C49.0	C79.89	—	D21.0	D48.1	D49.2
external meatus — see also Neoplasm, skin, ear	C44.20-●	C79.2	D04.2-●	D23.2-●	D48.5	D49.2
inner	C30.1	C78.39	D02.3	D14.0	D38.5	D49.1
lobule — see also Neoplasm, skin, ear	C44.20-●	C79.2	D04.2-●	D23.2-●	D48.5	D49.2
middle	C30.1	C78.39	D02.3	D14.0	D38.5	D49.1
overlapping lesion with accessory sinuses	C31.8	—	—	—	—	—
skin	C44.20-●	C79.2	D04.2-●	D23.2-●	D48.5	D49.2
basal cell carcinoma	C44.21-●	—	—	—	—	—
specified type NEC	C44.29-●	—	—	—	—	—
squamous cell carcinoma	C44.22-●	—	—	—	—	—
earlobe	C44.20-●	C79.2	D04.2-●	D23.2-●	D48.5	D49.2
basal cell carcinoma	C44.21-●	—	—	—	—	—
specified type NEC	C44.29-●	—	—	—	—	—
squamous cell carcinoma	C44.22-●	—	—	—	—	—
ejaculatory duct	C63.7	C79.82	D07.69	D29.8	D40.8	D49.59
elbow NEC	C76.4-●	C79.89	D04.6-●	D36.7	D48.7	D49.89
endocardium	C38.0	C79.89	—	D15.1	D48.7	D49.89
endocervix (canal) (gland)	C53.0	C79.82	D06.0	D26.0	D39.0	D49.59
endocrine gland NEC	C75.9	C79.89	D09.3	D35.9	D44.9	D49.7
pluriglandular	C75.8	C79.89	D09.3	D35.7	D44.9	D49.7
endometrium (gland) (stroma)	C54.1	C79.82	D07.0	D26.1	D39.0	D49.59
ensiform cartilage	C41.3	C79.51	—	D16.7	D48.0	D49.2
enteric — see Neoplasm, intestine						
ependyma (brain)	C71.5	C79.31	—	D33.0	D43.0	D49.6
fourth ventricle	C71.7	C79.31	—	D33.1	D43.1	D49.6
epicardium	C38.0	C79.89	—	D15.1	D48.7	D49.89
epididymis	C63.0-●	C79.82	D07.69	D29.3-●	D40.8	D49.59
epidural	C72.9	C79.49	—	D33.9	D43.9	D49.7
epiglottis	C32.1	C78.39	D02.0	D14.1	D38.0	D49.1
anterior aspect or surface	C10.1	C79.89	D00.08	D10.5	D37.05	D49.0
cartilage	C32.3	C78.39	D02.0	D14.1	D38.0	D49.1
free border (margin)	C10.1	C79.89	D00.08	D10.5	D37.05	D49.0

	Malignant Primary	Malignant Secondary	Ca in situ	Benign	Uncertain Behavior	Unspecified Behavior
junctional region	C10.8	C79.89	D00.08	D10.5	D37.05	D49.0
posterior (laryngeal) surface	C32.1	C78.39	D02.0	D14.1	D38.0	D49.1
suprahyoid portion	C32.1	C78.39	D02.0	D14.1	D38.0	D49.1
esophagogastric junction	C16.0	C78.89	D00.2	D13.1	D37.1	D49.0
esophagus	C15.9	C78.89	D00.1	D13.0	D37.8	D49.0
abdominal	C15.5	C78.89	D00.1	D13.0	D37.8	D49.0
cervical	C15.3	C78.89	D00.1	D13.0	D37.8	D49.0
distal (third)	C15.5	C78.89	D00.1	D13.0	D37.8	D49.0
lower (third)	C15.5	C78.89	D00.1	D13.0	D37.8	D49.0
middle (third)	C15.4	C78.89	D00.1	D13.0	D37.8	D49.0
overlapping lesion	C15.8	—	—	—	—	—
proximal (third)	C15.3	C78.89	D00.1	D13.0	D37.8	D49.0
thoracic	C15.4	C78.89	D00.1	D13.0	D37.8	D49.0
upper (third)	C15.3	C78.89	D00.1	D13.0	D37.8	D49.0
ethmoid (sinus)	C31.1	C78.39	D02.3	D14.0	D38.5	D49.1
bone or labyrinth	C41.0	C79.51	—	D16.4-●	D48.0	D49.2
eustachian tube	C30.1	C78.39	D02.3	D14.0	D38.5	D49.1
exocervix	C53.1	C79.82	D06.1	D26.0	D39.0	D49.59
external						
meatus (ear) — see also Neoplasm, skin, ear	C44.20-●	C79.2	D04.2-●	D23.2-●	D48.5	D49.2
os, cervix uteri	C53.1	C79.82	D06.1	D26.0	D39.0	D49.59
extradural	C72.9	C79.49	—	D33.9	D43.9	D49.7
extrahepatic (bile) duct	C24.0	C78.89	D01.5	D13.5	D37.6	D49.0
overlapping lesion with gallbladder	C24.8	—	—	—	—	—
extraocular muscle	C69.6-●	C79.49	D09.2-●	D31.6-●	D48.7	D49.89
extrarectal	C76.3	C79.89	D09.8	D36.7	D48.7	D49.89
extremity	C76.8	C79.89	D04.8	D36.7	D48.7	D49.89
lower	C76.5-●	C79.89	D04.7-●	D36.7	D48.7	D49.89
upper	C76.4-●	C79.89	D04.6-●	D36.7	D48.7	D49.89
eye NEC	C69.9-●	C79.49	D09.2	D31.9	D48.7	D49.89
overlapping sites	C69.8	—	—	—	—	—
eyeball	C69.9-●	C79.49	D09.2-●	D31.9-●	D48.7	D49.89
eyebrow	C44.309	C79.2	D04.39	D23.39	D48.5	D49.2
basal cell carcinoma	C44.319	—	—	—	—	—
specified type NEC	C44.399	—	—	—	—	—
squamous cell carcinoma	C44.329	—	—	—	—	—
eyelid (lower) (skin) (upper)	C44.10-●	—	—	—	—	—
basal cell carcinoma	C44.11-●	—	—	—	—	—
cartilage	C49.0	C79.89	—	D21.0	D48.1	D49.2
sebaceous cell	C44.13-●	—	—	—	—	—
specified type NEC	C44.19-●	—	—	—	—	—
squamous cell carcinoma	C44.12-●	—	—	—	—	—

◀ New ◀ Revised ~~deleted~~ Deleted ● Use Additional Character(s)

	Malignant Primary	Malignant Secondary	Ca in situ	Benign	Uncertain Behavior	Unspecified Behavior
face NEC	C76.0	C79.89	D04.39	D36.7	D48.7	D49.89
fallopian tube (accessory)	C57.0-●	C79.82	D07.39	D28.2	D39.8	D49.59
falx (cerebella) (cerebri)	C70.0	C79.32	—	D32.0	D42.0	D49.7
fascia — see also Neoplasm, connective tissue						
palmar	C49.1-●	C79.89	—	D21.1-●	D48.1	D49.2
plantar	C49.2-●	C79.89	—	D21.2-●	D48.1	D49.2
fatty tissue — see Neoplasm, connective tissue						
fauces, faucial NEC	C10.9	C79.89	D00.08	D10.5	D37.05	D49.0
pillars	C09.1	C79.89	D00.08	D10.5	D37.05	D49.0
tonsil	C09.9	C79.89	D00.08	D10.4	D37.05	D49.0
femur (any part)	C40.2-●	—	—	D16.2-●	—	—
fetal membrane	C58	C79.82	D07.0	D26.7	D39.2	D49.59
fibrous tissue — see Neoplasm, connective tissue						
fibula (any part)	C40.2-●	C79.51	—	D16.2-●	—	—
filum terminale	C72.0	C79.49	—	D33.4	D43.4	D49.7
finger NEC	C76.4-●	C79.89	D04.6-●	D36.7	D48.7	D49.89
flank NEC	C76.8	C79.89	D04.5	D36.7	D48.7	D49.89
follicle, nabothian	C53.0	C79.82	D06.0	D26.0	D39.0	D49.59
foot NEC	C76.5-●	C79.89	D04.7-●	D36.7	D48.7	D49.89
forearm NEC	C76.4-●	C79.89	D04.6-●	D36.7	D48.7	D49.89
forehead (skin)	C44.309	C79.2	D04.39	D23.39	D48.5	D49.2
basal cell carcinoma	C44.319	—	—	—	—	—
specified type NEC	C44.399	—	—	—	—	—
squamous cell carcinoma	C44.329	—	—	—	—	—
foreskin	C60.0	C79.82	D07.4	D29.0	D40.8	D49.59
fornix						
pharyngeal	C11.3	C79.89	D00.08	D10.6	D37.05	D49.0
vagina	C52	C79.82	D07.2	D28.1	D39.8	D49.59
fossa (of)						
anterior (cranial)	C71.9	C79.31	—	D33.2	D43.2	D49.6
cranial	C71.9	C79.31	—	D33.2	D43.2	D49.6
ischiorectal	C76.3	C79.89	D09.8	D36.7	D48.7	D49.89
middle (cranial)	C71.9	C79.31	—	D33.2	D43.2	D49.6
piriform	C12	C79.89	D00.08	D10.7	D37.05	D49.0
pituitary	C75.1	C79.89	D09.3	D35.2	D44.3	D49.7
posterior (cranial)	C71.9	C79.31	—	D33.2	D43.2	D49.6
pterygoid	C49.0	C79.89	—	D21.0	D48.1	D49.2
pyriform	C12	C79.89	D00.08	D10.7	D37.05	D49.0
Rosenmuller	C11.2	C79.89	D00.08	D10.6	D37.05	D49.0
tonsillar	C09.0	C79.89	D00.08	D10.5	D37.05	D49.0
fourchette	C51.9	C79.82	D07.1	D28.0	D39.8	D49.59

	Malignant Primary	Malignant Secondary	Ca in situ	Benign	Uncertain Behavior	Unspecified Behavior
frenulum						
labii — see Neoplasm, lip, internal						
linguae	C02.2	C79.89	D00.07	D10.1	D37.02	D49.0
frontal						
bone	C41.0	C79.51	—	D16.4-●	D48.0	D49.2
lobe, brain	C71.1	C79.31	—	D33.0	D43.0	D49.6
pole	C71.1	C79.31	—	D33.0	D43.0	D49.6
sinus	C31.2	C78.39	D02.3	D14.0	D38.5	D49.1
fundus						
stomach	C16.1	C78.89	D00.2	D13.1	D37.1	D49.0
uterus	C54.3	C79.82	D07.0	D26.1	D39.0	D49.59
gall duct (extrahepatic)	C24.0	C78.89	D01.5	D13.5	D37.6	D49.0
intrahepatic	C22.1	C78.7	D01.5	D13.4	D37.6	D49.0
gallbladder	C23	C78.89	D01.5	D13.5	D37.6	D49.0
overlapping lesion with extrahepatic bile ducts	C24.8	—	—	—	—	—
ganglia — see also Neoplasm, nerve, peripheral	C47.9	C79.89	—	D36.10	D48.2	D49.2
basal	C71.0	C79.31	—	D33.0	D43.0	D49.6
cranial nerve	C72.50	C79.49	—	D33.3	D43.3	D49.7
Gartner's duct	C52	C79.82	D07.2	D28.1	D39.8	D49.59
gastric — see Neoplasm, stomach						
gastrocolic	C26.9	C78.89	D01.9	D13.9	D37.9	D49.0
gastroesophageal junction	C16.0	C78.89	D00.2	D13.1	D37.1	D49.0
gastrointestinal (tract) NEC	C26.9	C78.89	D01.9	D13.9	D37.9	D49.0
generalized	C80.0	—	—	—	—	—
genital organ or tract						
female NEC	C57.9	C79.82	D07.30	D28.9	D39.9	D49.59
overlapping lesion	C57.8	—	—	—	—	—
specified site NEC	C57.7	C79.82	D07.39	D28.7	D39.8	D49.59
male NEC	C63.9	C79.82	D07.60	D29.9	D40.9	D49.59
overlapping lesion	C63.8	—	—	—	—	—
specified site NEC	C63.7	C79.82	D07.69	D29.8	D40.8	D49.59
genitourinary tract						
female	C57.9	C79.82	D07.30	D28.9	D39.9	D49.59
male	C63.9	C79.82	D07.60	D29.9	D40.9	D49.59
gingiva (alveolar) (marginal)	C03.9	C79.89	D00.03	D10.39	D37.09	D49.0
lower	C03.1	C79.89	D00.03	D10.39	D37.09	D49.0
mandibular	C03.1	C79.89	D00.03	D10.39	D37.09	D49.0
maxillary	C03.0	C79.89	D00.03	D10.39	D37.09	D49.0
upper	C03.0	C79.89	D00.03	D10.39	D37.09	D49.0

◀ New   ◀ Revised   ~~deleted~~ Deleted   ● Use Additional Character(s)

	Malignant Primary	Malignant Secondary	Ca in situ	Benign	Uncertain Behavior	Unspecified Behavior
gland, glandular (lymphatic) (system) — see also Neoplasm, lymph gland						
endocrine NEC	C75.9	C79.89	D09.3	D35.9	D44.9	D49.7
salivary — see Neoplasm, salivary gland						
glans penis	C60.1	C79.82	D07.4	D29.0	D40.8	D49.59
globus pallidus	C71.0	C79.31	—	D33.0	D43.0	D49.6
glomus						
coccygeal	C49.5	C79.89	—	D21.5	D48.1	D49.2
jugularis	C75.5	C79.89	—	D35.6	D44.7	D49.7
glosso-epiglottic fold(s)	C10.1	C79.89	D00.08	D10.5	D37.05	D49.0
glossopalatine fold	C09.1	C79.89	D00.08	D10.5	D37.05	D49.0
glossopharyngeal sulcus	C09.0	C79.89	D00.08	D10.5	D37.05	D49.0
glottis	C32.0	C78.39	D02.0	D14.1	D38.0	D49.1
gluteal region	C76.3	C79.89	D04.5	D36.7	D48.7	D49.89
great vessels NEC	C49.3	C79.89	—	D21.3	D48.1	D49.2
groin NEC	C76.3	C79.89	D04.5	D36.7	D48.7	D49.89
gum	C03.9	C79.89	D00.03	D10.39	D37.09	D49.0
lower	C03.1	C79.89	D00.03	D10.39	D37.09	D49.0
upper	C03.0	C79.89	D00.03	D10.39	D37.09	D49.0
hand NEC	C76.4-•	C79.89	D04.6-•	D36.7	D48.7	D49.89
head NEC	C76.0	C79.89	D04.4	D36.7	D48.7	D49.89
heart	C38.0	C79.89	—	D15.1	D48.7	D49.89
heel NEC	C76.5-•	C79.89	D04.7-•	D36.7	D48.7	D49.89
helix — see also Neoplasm, skin, ear	C44.20-•	C79.2	D04.2-•	D23.2-•	D48.5	D49.2
hematopoietic, hemopoietic tissue NEC	C96.9	—	—	—	—	—
specified NEC	C96.Z	—	—	—	—	—
hemisphere, cerebral	C71.0	C79.31	—	D33.0	D43.0	D49.6
hemorrhoidal zone	C21.1	C78.5	D01.3	D12.9	D37.8	D49.0
hepatic — see also Index to disease, by histology	C22.9	C78.7	D01.5	D13.4	D37.6	D49.0
duct (bile)	C24.0	C78.89	D01.5	D13.5	D37.6	D49.0
flexure (colon)	C18.3	C78.5	D01.0	D12.3	D37.4	D49.0
primary	C22.8	C78.7	D01.5	D13.4	D37.6	D49.0
hepatobiliary	C24.9	C79.89	D01.5	D13.5	D37.6	D49.0
hepatoblastoma	C22.2	C78.7	D01.5	D13.4	D37.6	D49.0
hepatoma	C22.0	C78.7	D01.5	D13.4	D37.6	D49.0
hilus of lung	C34.0-•	C78.0-•	D02.2-•	D14.3-•	D38.1	D49.1
hip NEC	C76.5-•	C79.89	D04.7-•	D36.7	D48.7	D49.89
hippocampus, brain	C71.2	C79.31	—	D33.0	D43.0	D49.6
humerus (any part)	C40.0-•	C79.51	—	D16.0-•	—	—
hymen	C52	C79.82	D07.2	D28.1	D39.8	D49.59

	Malignant Primary	Malignant Secondary	Ca in situ	Benign	Uncertain Behavior	Unspecified Behavior
hypopharynx, hypopharyngeal NEC	C13.9	C79.89	D00.08	D10.7	D37.05	D49.0
overlapping lesion	C13.8	—	—	—	—	—
postcricoid region	C13.0	C79.89	D00.08	D10.7	D37.05	D49.0
posterior wall	C13.2	C79.89	D00.08	D10.7	D37.05	D49.0
pyriform fossa (sinus)	C12	C79.89	D00.08	D10.7	D37.05	D49.0
hypophysis	C75.1	C79.89	D09.3	D35.2	D44.3	D49.7
hypothalamus	C71.0	C79.31	—	D33.0	D43.0	D49.6
ileocecum, ileocecal (coil) (junction) (valve)	C18.0	C78.5	D01.0	D12.0	D37.4	D49.0
ileum	C17.2	C78.4	D01.49	D13.39	D37.2	D49.0
ilium	C41.4	C79.51	—	D16.8	D48.0	D49.2
immunoproliferative NEC	C88.9	—	—	—	—	—
infraclavicular (region)	C76.1	C79.89	D04.5	D36.7	D48.7	D49.89
inguinal (region)	C76.3	C79.89	D04.5	D36.7	D48.7	D49.89
insula	C71.0	C79.31	—	D33.0	D43.0	D49.6
insular tissue (pancreas)	C25.4	C78.89	D01.7	D13.7	D37.8	D49.0
brain	C71.0	C79.31	—	D33.0	D43.0	D49.6
interarytenoid fold	C13.1	C79.89	D00.08	D10.7	D37.05	D49.0
hypopharyngeal aspect	C13.1	C79.89	D00.08	D10.7	D37.05	D49.0
laryngeal aspect	C32.1	C78.39	D02.0	D14.1	D38.0	D49.1
marginal zone	C13.1	C79.89	D00.08	D10.7	D37.05	D49.0
interdental papillae	C03.9	C79.89	D00.03	D10.39	D37.09	D49.0
lower	C03.1	C79.89	D00.03	D10.39	D37.09	D49.0
upper	C03.0	C79.89	D00.03	D10.39	D37.09	D49.0
internal						
capsule	C71.0	C79.31	—	D33.0	D43.0	D49.6
os (cervix)	C53.0	C79.82	D06.0	D26.0	D39.0	D49.59
intervertebral cartilage or disc	C41.2	C79.51	—	D16.6	D48.0	D49.2
intestine, intestinal	C26.0	C78.80	D01.40	D13.9	D37.8	D49.0
large	C18.9	C78.5	D01.0	D12.6	D37.4	D49.0
appendix	C18.1	C78.5	D01.0	D12.1	D37.3	D49.0
caput coli	C18.0	C78.5	D01.0	D12.0	D37.4	D49.0
cecum	C18.0	C78.5	D01.0	D12.0	D37.4	D49.0
colon	C18.9	C78.5	D01.0	D12.6	D37.4	D49.0
and rectum	C19	C78.5	D01.1	D12.7	D37.5	D49.0
ascending	C18.2	C78.5	D01.0	D12.2	D37.4	D49.0
caput	C18.0	C78.5	D01.0	D12.0	D37.4	D49.0
descending	C18.6	C78.5	D01.0	D12.4	D37.4	D49.0
distal	C18.6	C78.5	D01.0	D12.4	D37.4	D49.0
left	C18.6	C78.5	D01.0	D12.4	D37.4	D49.0
overlapping lesion	C18.8	—	—	—	—	—
pelvic	C18.7	C78.5	D01.0	D12.5	D37.4	D49.0
right	C18.2	C78.5	D01.0	D12.2	D37.4	D49.0

◀ New ◀ Revised ~~deleted~~ Deleted • Use Additional Character(s)

	Malignant Primary	Malignant Secondary	Ca in situ	Benign	Uncertain Behavior	Unspecified Behavior
intestine, intestinal (Continued)						
large (Continued)						
colon (Continued)						
sigmoid (flexure)	C18.7	C78.5	D01.0	D12.5	D37.4	D49.0
transverse	C18.4	C78.5	D01.0	D12.3	D37.4	D49.0
hepatic flexure	C18.3	C78.5	D01.0	D12.3	D37.4	D49.0
ileocecum, ileocecal (coil) (valve)	C18.0	C78.5	D01.0	D12.0	D37.4	D49.0
overlapping lesion	C18.8	—	—	—	—	—
sigmoid flexure (lower) (upper)	C18.7	C78.5	D01.0	D12.5	D37.4	D49.0
splenic flexure	C18.5	C78.5	D01.0	D12.3	D37.4	D49.0
small	C17.9	C78.4	D01.40	D13.30	D37.2	D49.0
duodenum	C17.0	C78.4	D01.49	D13.2	D37.2	D49.0
ileum	C17.2	C78.4	D01.49	D13.39	D37.2	D49.0
jejunum	C17.1	C78.4	D01.49	D13.39	D37.2	D49.0
overlapping lesion	C17.8	—	—	—	—	—
tract NEC	C26.0	C78.89	D01.40	D13.9	D37.8	D49.0
intra-abdominal	C76.2	C79.89	D09.8	D36.7	D48.7	D49.89
intracranial NEC	C71.9	C79.31	—	D33.2	D43.2	D49.6
intrahepatic (bile) duct	C22.1	C78.7	D01.5	D13.4	D37.6	D49.0
intraocular	C69.9-●	C79.49	D09.2-●	D31.9-●	D48.7	D49.89
intraorbital	C69.6-●	C79.49	D09.2-●	D31.6-●	D48.7	D49.89
intrasellar	C75.1	C79.89	D09.3	D35.2	D44.3	D49.7
intrathoracic (cavity) (organs)	C76.1	C79.89	D09.8	D15.9	D48.7	D49.89
specified NEC	C76.1	C79.89	D09.8	D15.7	—	—
iris	C69.4-●	C79.49	D09.2-●	D31.4-●	D48.7	D49.89
ischiorectal (fossa)	C76.3	C79.89	D09.8	D36.7	D48.7	D49.89
ischium	C41.4	C79.51	—	D16.8	D48.0	D49.2
island of Reil	C71.0	C79.31	—	D33.0	D43.0	D49.6
islands or islets of Langerhans	C25.4	C78.89	D01.7	D13.7	D37.8	D49.0
isthmus uteri	C54.0	C79.82	D07.0	D26.1	D39.0	D49.59
jaw	C76.0	C79.89	D09.8	D36.7	D48.7	D49.89
bone	C41.1	C79.51	—	D16.5-●	D48.0	D49.2
lower	C41.1	C79.51	—	D16.5-●	—	—
upper	C41.0	C79.51	—	D16.4-●	—	—
carcinoma (any type) (lower) (upper)	C76.0	C79.89				
skin — see also Neoplasm, skin, face	C44.309	C79.2	D04.39	D23.39	D48.5	D49.2
soft tissues	C03.9	C79.89	D00.03	D10.39	D37.09	D49.0
lower	C03.1	C79.89	D00.03	D10.39	D37.09	D49.0
upper	C03.0	C79.89	D00.03	D10.39	D37.09	D49.0
jejunum	C17.1	C78.4	D01.49	D13.39	D37.2	D49.0

	Malignant Primary	Malignant Secondary	Ca in situ	Benign	Uncertain Behavior	Unspecified Behavior
joint NEC — see also Neoplasm, bone	C41.9	C79.51	—	D16.9-●	D48.0	D49.2
acromioclavicular	C40.0-●	C79.51	—	D16.0-●	—	—
bursa or synovial membrane — see Neoplasm, connective tissue						
costovertebral	C41.3	C79.51	—	D16.7	D48.0	D49.2
sternocostal	C41.3	C79.51	—	D16.7	D48.0	D49.2
temporomandibular	C41.1	C79.51	—	D16.5-●	D48.0	D49.2
junction						
anorectal	C21.8	C78.5	D01.3	D12.9	D37.8	D49.0
cardioesophageal	C16.0	C78.89	D00.2	D13.1	D37.1	D49.0
esophagogastric	C16.0	C78.89	D00.2	D13.1	D37.1	D49.0
gastroesophageal	C16.0	C78.89	D00.2	D13.1	D37.1	D49.0
hard and soft palate	C05.9	C79.89	D00.00	D10.39	D37.09	D49.0
ileocecal	C18.0	C78.5	D01.0	D12.0	D37.4	D49.0
pelvirectal	C19	C78.5	D01.1	D12.7	D37.5	D49.0
pelviureteric	C65.-●	C79.0-●	D09.19	D30.1-●	D41.1-●	D49.59
rectosigmoid	C19	C78.5	D01.1	D12.7	D37.5	D49.0
squamocolumnar, of cervix	C53.8	C79.82	D06.7	D26.0	D39.0	D49.59
Kaposi's sarcoma — see Kaposi's, sarcoma						
kidney (parenchymal)	C64.-●	C79.0-●	D09.19	D30.0-●	D41.0-●	D49.51-●
calyx	C65.-●	C79.0-●	D09.19	D30.1-●	D41.1-●	D49.51-●
hilus	C65.-●	C79.0-●	D09.19	D30.1-●	D41.1-●	D49.51-●
pelvis	C65.-●	C79.0-●	D09.19	D30.1-●	D41.1-●	D49.51-●
knee NEC	C76.5-●	C79.89	D04.7-●	D36.7	D48.7	D49.89
labia (skin)	C51.9	C79.82	D07.1	D28.0	D39.8	D49.59
majora	C51.0	C79.82	D07.1	D28.0	D39.8	D49.59
minora	C51.1	C79.82	D07.1	D28.0	D39.8	D49.59
labial — see also Neoplasm, lip	C00.9	C79.89	D00.01	D10.0	D37.01	D49.0
sulcus (lower) (upper)	C06.1	C79.89	D00.02	D10.39	D37.09	D49.0
labium (skin)	C51.9	C79.82	D07.1	D28.0	D39.8	D49.59
majus	C51.0	C79.82	D07.1	D28.0	D39.8	D49.59
minus	C51.1	C79.82	D07.1	D28.0	D39.8	D49.59
lacrimal						
canaliculi	C69.5-●	C79.49	D09.2-●	D31.5-●	D48.7	D49.89
duct (nasal)	C69.5-●	C79.49	D09.2-●	D31.5-●	D48.7	D49.89
gland	C69.5-●	C79.49	D09.2-●	D31.5-●	D48.7	D49.89
punctum	C69.5-●	C79.49	D09.2-●	D31.5-●	D48.7	D49.89
sac	C69.5-●	C79.49	D09.2-●	D31.5-●	D48.7	D49.89
Langerhans, islands or islets	C25.4	C78.89	D01.7	D13.7	D37.8	D49.0
laryngopharynx	C13.9	C79.89	D00.08	D10.7	D37.05	D49.0

TABLE OF NEOPLASMS

	Malignant Primary	Malignant Secondary	Ca in situ	Benign	Uncertain Behavior	Unspecified Behavior
larynx, laryngeal NEC	C32.9	C78.39	D02.0	D14.1	D38.0	D49.1
aryepiglottic fold	C32.1	C78.39	D02.0	D14.1	D38.0	D49.1
cartilage (arytenoid) (cricoid) (cuneiform) (thyroid)	C32.3	C78.39	D02.0	D14.1	D38.0	D49.1
commissure (anterior) (posterior)	C32.0	C78.39	D02.0	D14.1	D38.0	D49.1
extrinsic NEC	C32.1	C78.39	D02.0	D14.1	D38.0	D49.1
meaning hypopharynx	C13.9	C79.89	D00.08	D10.7	D37.05	D49.0
interarytenoid fold	C32.1	C78.39	D02.0	D14.1	D38.0	D49.1
intrinsic	C32.0	C78.39	D02.0	D14.1	D38.0	D49.1
overlapping lesion	C32.8	—	—	—	—	—
ventricular band	C32.1	C78.39	D02.0	D14.1	D38.0	D49.1
leg NEC	C76.5-●	C79.89	D04.7-●	D36.7	D48.7	D49.89
lens, crystalline	C69.4-●	C79.49	D09.2-●	D31.4-●	D48.7	D49.89
lid (lower) (upper)	C44.10-●	C79.2	D04.1-●	D23.1-●	D48.5	D49.2
basal cell carcinoma	C44.11-●	—	—	—	—	—
sebaceous cell	C44.13-●	—	—	—	—	—
specified type NEC	C44.19-●	—	—	—	—	—
squamous cell carcinoma	C44.12-●	—	—	—	—	—
ligament — see also Neoplasm, connective tissue						
broad	C57.1	C79.82	D07.39	D28.2	D39.8	D49.59
Mackenrodt's	C57.7	C79.82	D07.39	D28.7	D39.8	D49.59
non-uterine — see Neoplasm, connective tissue						
round	C57.2	C79.82	—	D28.2	D39.8	D49.59
sacro-uterine	C57.3	C79.82	—	D28.2	D39.8	D49.59
uterine	C57.3	C79.82	—	D28.2	D39.8	D49.59
utero-ovarian	C57.7	C79.82	D07.39	D28.2	D39.8	D49.59
uterosacral	C57.3	C79.82	—	D28.2	D39.8	D49.59
limb	C76.8	C79.89	D04.8	D36.7	D48.7	D49.89
lower	C76.5-●	C79.89	D04.7-●	D36.7	D48.7	D49.89
upper	C76.4-●	C79.89	D04.6-●	D36.7	D48.7	D49.89
limbus of cornea	C69.1-●	C79.49	D09.2-●	D31.1-●	D48.7	D49.89
lingual NEC — see also Neoplasm, tongue	C02.9	C79.89	D00.07	D10.1	D37.02	D49.0
lingula, lung	C34.1-●	C78.0-●	D02.2-●	D14.3-●	D38.1	D49.1
lip	C00.9	C79.89	D00.01	D10.0	D37.01	D49.0
buccal aspect — see Neoplasm, lip, internal						
commissure	C00.6	C79.89	D00.01	D10.0	D37.01	D49.0
external	C00.2	C79.89	D00.01	D10.0	D37.01	D49.0
lower	C00.1	C79.89	D00.01	D10.0	D37.01	D49.0
upper	C00.0	C79.89	D00.01	D10.0	D37.01	D49.0
frenulum — see Neoplasm, lip, internal						

	Malignant Primary	Malignant Secondary	Ca in situ	Benign	Uncertain Behavior	Unspecified Behavior
lip (Continued)						
inner aspect — see Neoplasm, lip, internal						
internal	C00.5	C79.89	D00.01	D10.0	D37.01	D49.0
lower	C00.4	C79.89	D00.01	D10.0	D37.01	D49.0
upper	C00.3	C79.89	D00.01	D10.0	D37.01	D49.0
lipstick area	C00.2	C79.89	D00.01	D10.0	D37.01	D49.0
lower	C00.1	C79.89	D00.01	D10.0	D37.01	D49.0
upper	C00.0	C79.89	D00.01	D10.0	D37.01	D49.0
lower	C00.1	C79.89	D00.01	D10.0	D37.01	D49.0
internal	C00.4	C79.89	D00.01	D10.0	D37.01	D49.0
mucosa — see Neoplasm, lip, internal						
oral aspect — see Neoplasm, lip, internal						
overlapping lesion	C00.8	—	—	—	—	—
with oral cavity or pharynx	C14.8	—	—	—	—	—
skin (commissure) (lower) (upper)	C44.00	C79.2	D04.0	D23.0	D48.5	D49.2
basal cell carcinoma	C44.01	—	—	—	—	—
specified type NEC	C44.09	—	—	—	—	—
squamous cell carcinoma	C44.02	—	—	—	—	—
upper	C00.0	C79.89	D00.01	D10.0	D37.01	D49.0
internal	C00.3	C79.89	D00.01	D10.0	D37.01	D49.0
vermilion border	C00.2	C79.89	D00.01	D10.0	D37.01	D49.0
lower	C00.1	C79.89	D00.01	D10.0	D37.01	D49.0
upper	C00.0	C79.89	D00.01	D10.0	D37.01	D49.0
lipomatous — see Lipoma, by site						
liver — see also Index to disease, by histology	C22.9	C78.7	D01.5	D13.4	D37.6	D49.0
primary	C22.8	C78.7	D01.5	D13.4	D37.6	D49.0
lumbosacral plexus	C47.5	C79.89	—	D36.16	D48.2	D49.2
lung	C34.9-●	C78.0-●	D02.2-●	D14.3-●	D38.1	D49.1
azygos lobe	C34.1-●	C78.0-●	D02.2-●	D14.3-●	D38.1	D49.1
carina	C34.0-●	C78.0-●	D02.2-●	D14.3-●	D38.1	D49.1
hilus	C34.0-●	C78.0-●	D02.2-●	D14.3-●	D38.1	D49.1
lingula	C34.1-●	C78.0-●	D02.2-●	D14.3-●	D38.1	D49.1
lobe NEC	C34.9-●	C78.0-●	D02.2-●	D14.3-●	D38.1	D49.1
lower lobe	C34.3-●	C78.0-●	D02.2-●	D14.3-●	D38.1	D49.1
main bronchus	C34.0-●	C78.0-●	D02.2-●	D14.3-●	D38.1	D49.1
mesothelioma — see Mesothelioma						
middle lobe	C34.2	C78.0-●	D02.21	D14.31	D38.1	D49.1
overlapping lesion	C34.8-●	—	—	—	—	—
upper lobe	C34.1-●	C78.0-●	D02.2-●	D14.3-●	D38.1	D49.1

◀ New ◀ Revised ~~deleted~~ Deleted ● Use Additional Character(s)

	Malignant Primary	Malignant Secondary	Ca in situ	Benign	Uncertain Behavior	Unspecified Behavior
lymph, lymphatic channel NEC	C49.9	C79.89	—	D21.9	D48.1	D49.2
gland (secondary)	—	C77.9	—	D36.Ø	D48.7	D49.89
abdominal	—	C77.2	—	D36.Ø	D48.7	D49.89
aortic	—	C77.2	—	D36.Ø	D48.7	D49.89
arm	—	C77.3	—	D36.Ø	D48.7	D49.89
auricular (anterior) (posterior)	—	C77.Ø	—	D36.Ø	D48.7	D49.89
axilla, axillary	—	C77.3	—	D36.Ø	D48.7	D49.89
brachial	—	C77.3	—	D36.Ø	D48.7	D49.89
bronchial	—	C77.1	—	D36.Ø	D48.7	D49.89
bronchopulmonary	—	C77.1	—	D36.Ø	D48.7	D49.89
celiac	—	C77.2	—	D36.Ø	D48.7	D49.89
cervical	—	C77.Ø	—	D36.Ø	D48.7	D49.89
cervicofacial	—	C77.Ø	—	D36.Ø	D48.7	D49.89
Cloquet	—	C77.4	—	D36.Ø	D48.7	D49.89
colic	—	C77.2	—	D36.Ø	D48.7	D49.89
common duct	—	C77.2	—	D36.Ø	D48.7	D49.89
cubital	—	C77.3	—	D36.Ø	D48.7	D49.89
diaphragmatic	—	C77.1	—	D36.Ø	D48.7	D49.89
epigastric, inferior	—	C77.1	—	D36.Ø	D48.7	D49.89
epitrochlear	—	C77.3	—	D36.Ø	D48.7	D49.89
esophageal	—	C77.1	—	D36.Ø	D48.7	D49.89
face	—	C77.Ø	—	D36.Ø	D48.7	D49.89
femoral	—	C77.4	—	D36.Ø	D48.7	D49.89
gastric	—	C77.2	—	D36.Ø	D48.7	D49.89
groin	—	C77.4	—	D36.Ø	D48.7	D49.89
head	—	C77.Ø	—	D36.Ø	D48.7	D49.89
hepatic	—	C77.2	—	D36.Ø	D48.7	D49.89
hilar (pulmonary)	—	C77.1	—	D36.Ø	D48.7	D49.89
splenic	—	C77.2	—	D36.Ø	D48.7	D49.89
hypogastric	—	C77.5	—	D36.Ø	D48.7	D49.89
ileocolic	—	C77.2	—	D36.Ø	D48.7	D49.89
iliac	—	C77.5	—	D36.Ø	D48.7	D49.89
infraclavicular	—	C77.3	—	D36.Ø	D48.7	D49.89
inguina, inguinal	—	C77.4	—	D36.Ø	D48.7	D49.89
innominate	—	C77.1	—	D36.Ø	D48.7	D49.89
intercostal	—	C77.1	—	D36.Ø	D48.7	D49.89
intestinal	—	C77.2	—	D36.Ø	D48.7	D49.89
intrabdominal	—	C77.2	—	D36.Ø	D48.7	D49.89
intrapelvic	—	C77.5	—	D36.Ø	D48.7	D49.89
intrathoracic	—	C77.1	—	D36.Ø	D48.7	D49.89
jugular	—	C77.Ø	—	D36.Ø	D48.7	D49.89
leg	—	C77.4	—	D36.Ø	D48.7	D49.89
limb						
lower	—	C77.4	—	D36.Ø	D48.7	D49.89
upper	—	C77.3	—	D36.Ø	D48.7	D49.89

	Malignant Primary	Malignant Secondary	Ca in situ	Benign	Uncertain Behavior	Unspecified Behavior
lymph, lymphatic channel NEC (Continued) gland (Continued)						
lower limb	—	C77.4	—	D36.Ø	D48.7	D49.89
lumbar	—	C77.2	—	D36.Ø	D48.7	D49.89
mandibular	—	C77.Ø	—	D36.Ø	D48.7	D49.89
mediastinal	—	C77.1	—	D36.Ø	D48.7	D49.89
mesenteric (inferior) (superior)	—	C77.2	—	D36.Ø	D48.7	D49.89
midcolic	—	C77.2	—	D36.Ø	D48.7	D49.89
multiple sites in categories C77.Ø - C77.5	—	C77.8	—	D36.Ø	D48.7	D49.89
neck	—	C77.Ø	—	D36.Ø	D48.7	D49.89
obturator	—	C77.5	—	D36.Ø	D48.7	D49.89
occipital	—	C77.Ø	—	D36.Ø	D48.7	D49.89
pancreatic	—	C77.2	—	D36.Ø	D48.7	D49.89
para-aortic	—	C77.2	—	D36.Ø	D48.7	D49.89
paracervical	—	C77.5	—	D36.Ø	D48.7	D49.89
parametrial	—	C77.5	—	D36.Ø	D48.7	D49.89
parasternal	—	C77.1	—	D36.Ø	D48.7	D49.89
parotid	—	C77.Ø	—	D36.Ø	D48.7	D49.89
pectoral	—	C77.3	—	D36.Ø	D48.7	D49.89
pelvic	—	C77.5	—	D36.Ø	D48.7	D49.89
peri-aortic	—	C77.2	—	D36.Ø	D48.7	D49.89
peripancreatic	—	C77.2	—	D36.Ø	D48.7	D49.89
popliteal	—	C77.4	—	D36.Ø	D48.7	D49.89
porta hepatis	—	C77.2	—	D36.Ø	D48.7	D49.89
portal	—	C77.2	—	D36.Ø	D48.7	D49.89
preauricular	—	C77.Ø	—	D36.Ø	D48.7	D49.89
prelaryngeal	—	C77.Ø	—	D36.Ø	D48.7	D49.89
presymphysial	—	C77.5	—	D36.Ø	D48.7	D49.89
pretracheal	—	C77.Ø	—	D36.Ø	D48.7	D49.89
primary (any site) NEC	C96.9	—	—	—	—	—
pulmonary (hiler)	—	C77.1	—	D36.Ø	D48.7	D49.89
pyloric	—	C77.2	—	D36.Ø	D48.7	D49.89
retroperitoneal	—	C77.2	—	D36.Ø	D48.7	D49.89
retropharyngeal	—	C77.Ø	—	D36.Ø	D48.7	D49.89
Rosenmuller's	—	C77.4	—	D36.Ø	D48.7	D49.89
sacral	—	C77.5	—	D36.Ø	D48.7	D49.89
scalene	—	C77.Ø	—	D36.Ø	D48.7	D49.89
site NEC	—	C77.9	—	D36.Ø	D48.7	D49.89
splenic (hilar)	—	C77.2	—	D36.Ø	D48.7	D49.89
subclavicular	—	C77.3	—	D36.Ø	D48.7	D49.89
subinguinal	—	C77.4	—	D36.Ø	D48.7	D49.89

◄ New ◄ Revised ~~deleted~~ Deleted ● Use Additional Character(s)

TABLE OF NEOPLASMS

	Malignant Primary	Malignant Secondary	Ca in situ	Benign	Uncertain Behavior	Unspecified Behavior
lymph, lymphatic channel NEC *(Continued)*						
gland *(Continued)*						
sublingual	—	C77.0	—	D36.0	D48.7	D49.89
submandibular	—	C77.0	—	D36.0	D48.7	D49.89
submaxillary	—	C77.0	—	D36.0	D48.7	D49.89
submental	—	C77.0	—	D36.0	D48.7	D49.89
subscapular	—	C77.3	—	D36.0	D48.7	D49.89
supraclavicular	—	C77.0	—	D36.0	D48.7	D49.89
thoracic	—	C77.1	—	D36.0	D48.7	D49.89
tibial	—	C77.4	—	D36.0	D48.7	D49.89
tracheal	—	C77.1	—	D36.0	D48.7	D49.89
tracheobronchial	—	C77.1	—	D36.0	D48.7	D49.89
upper limb	—	C77.3	—	D36.0	D48.7	D49.89
Virchow's	—	C77.0	—	D36.0	D48.7	D49.89
node — *see also Neoplasm, lymph gland*						
primary NEC	C96.9	—	—	—	—	—
vessel — *see also Neoplasm, connective tissue*	C49.9	C79.89	—	D21.9	D48.1	D49.2
Mackenrodt's ligament	C57.7	C79.82	D07.39	D28.7	D39.8	D49.59
malar	C41.0	C79.51	—	D16.4-●	D48.0	D49.2
region — *see Neoplasm, cheek*						
mammary gland — *see Neoplasm, breast*						
mandible	C41.1	C79.51	—	D16.5-●	D48.0	D49.2
alveolar						
mucosa (carcinoma)	C03.1	C79.89	D00.03	D10.39	D37.09	D49.0
ridge or process	C41.1	C79.51	—	D16.5-●	D48.0	D49.2
marrow (bone) NEC	C96.9	C79.52	—	—	D47.9	D49.89
mastectomy site (skin) — *see also Neoplasm, breast, skin*	C44.501	C79.2	—	—	—	—
specified as breast tissue	C50.8-●	C79.81	—	—	—	—
mastoid (air cells) (antrum) (cavity)	C30.1	C78.39	D02.3	D14.0	D38.5	D49.1
bone or process	C41.0	C79.51	—	D16.4-●	D48.0	D49.2
maxilla, maxillary (superior)	C41.0	C79.51	—	D16.4-●	D48.0	D49.2
alveolar						
mucosa	C03.0	C79.89	D00.03	D10.39	D37.09	D49.0
ridge or process (carcinoma)	C41.0	C79.51	—	D16.4-●	D48.0	D49.2
antrum	C31.0	C78.39	D02.3	D14.0	D38.5	D49.1
carcinoma	C03.0	C79.51	—	—	—	—
inferior — *see Neoplasm, mandible*						
sinus	C31.0	C78.39	D02.3	D14.0	D38.5	D49.1
meatus external (ear) — *see also Neoplasm, skin, ear*	C44.20-●	C79.2	D04.2-●	D23.2-●	D48.5	D49.2
Meckel diverticulum, malignant	C17.3	C78.4	D01.49	D13.39	D37.2	D49.0
mediastinum, mediastinal	C38.3	C78.1	—	D15.2	D38.3	D49.89
anterior	C38.1	C78.1	—	D15.2	D38.3	D49.89
posterior	C38.2	C78.1	—	D15.2	D38.3	D49.89
medulla						
adrenal	C74.1-●	C79.7-●	D09.3	D35.0-●	D44.1-●	D49.7
oblongata	C71.7	C79.31	—	D33.1	D43.1	D49.6
meibomian gland	C44.10-●	C79.2	D04.1-●	D23.1-●	D48.5	D49.2
basal cell carcinoma	C44.11-●	—	—	—	—	—
sebaceous cell	C44.13-●	—	—	—	—	—
specified type NEC	C44.19-●	—	—	—	—	—
squamous cell carcinoma	C44.12-●	—	—	—	—	—
melanoma — *see Melanoma*						
meninges	C70.9	C79.49	—	D32.9	D42.9	D49.7
brain	C70.0	C79.32	—	D32.0	D42.0	D49.7
cerebral	C70.0	C79.32	—	D32.0	D42.0	D49.7
crainial	C70.0	C79.32	—	D32.0	D42.0	D49.7
intracranial	C70.0	C79.32	—	D32.0	D42.0	D49.7
spinal (cord)	C70.1	C79.49	—	D32.1	D42.1	D49.7
meniscus, knee joint (lateral) (medial)	C40.2-●	C79.51	—	D16.2-●	D48.0	D49.2
Merkel cell — *see Carcinoma, Merkel cell*						
mesentery, mesenteric	C48.1	C78.6	—	D20.1	D48.4	D49.0
mesoappendix	C48.1	C78.6	—	D20.1	D48.4	D49.0
mesocolon	C48.1	C78.6	—	D20.1	D48.4	D49.0
mesopharynx — *see Neoplasm, oropharynx*						
mesosalpinx	C57.1	C79.82	D07.39	D28.2	D39.8	D49.59
mesothelial tissue — *see Mesothelioma*						
mesothelioma — *see Mesothelioma*						
mesovarium	C57.1	C79.82	D07.39	D28.2	D39.8	D49.59
metacarpus (any bone)	C40.1-●	C79.51	—	D16.1-●	—	—
metastatic NEC — *see also Neoplasm, by site, secondary*	—	C79.9	—	—	—	—
metatarsus (any bone)	C40.3-●	C79.51	—	D16.3-●	—	—
midbrain	C71.7	C79.31	—	D33.1	D43.1	D49.6
milk duct — *see Neoplasm, breast*						
mons						
pubis	C51.9	C79.82	D07.1	D28.0	D39.8	D49.59
veneris	C51.9	C79.82	D07.1	D28.0	D39.8	D49.59

◀ New   ◀ Revised   ~~deleted~~ Deleted   ● Use Additional Character(s)

	Malignant Primary	Malignant Secondary	Ca in situ	Benign	Uncertain Behavior	Unspecified Behavior
motor tract	C72.9	C79.49	—	D33.9	D43.9	D49.7
brain	C71.9	C79.31	—	D33.2	D43.2	D49.6
cauda equina	C72.1	C79.49	—	D33.4	D43.4	D49.7
spinal	C72.0	C79.49	—	D33.4	D43.4	D49.7
mouth	C06.9	C79.89	D00.00	D10.30	D37.09	D49.0
book-leaf	C06.89	C79.89	—	—	—	—
floor	C04.9	C79.89	D00.06	D10.2	D37.09	D49.0
anterior portion	C04.0	C79.89	D00.06	D10.2	D37.09	D49.0
lateral portion	C04.1	C79.89	D00.06	D10.2	D37.09	D49.0
overlapping lesion	C04.8	—	—	—	—	—
overlapping NEC	C06.80	—	—	—	—	—
roof	C05.9	C79.89	D00.00	D10.39	D37.09	D49.0
specified part NEC	C06.89	C79.89	D00.00	D10.39	D37.09	D49.0
vestibule	C06.1	C79.89	D00.00	D10.39	D37.09	D49.0
mucosa						
alveolar (ridge or process)	C03.9	C79.89	D00.03	D10.39	D37.09	D49.0
lower	C03.1	C79.89	D00.03	D10.39	D37.09	D49.0
upper	C03.0	C79.89	D00.03	D10.39	D37.09	D49.0
buccal	C06.0	C79.89	D00.02	D10.39	D37.09	D49.0
cheek	C06.0	C79.89	D00.02	D10.39	D37.09	D49.0
lip — see Neoplasm, lip, internal						
nasal	C30.0	C78.39	D02.3	D14.0	D38.5	D49.1
oral	C06.0	C79.89	D00.02	D10.39	D37.09	D49.0
Mullerian duct						
female	C57.7	C79.82	D07.39	D28.7	D39.8	D49.59
male	C63.7	C79.82	D07.69	D29.8	D40.8	D49.59
muscle — see also Neoplasm, connective tissue						
extraocular	C69.6-●	C79.49	D09.2-●	D31.6-●	D48.7	D49.89
myocardium	C38.0	C79.89	—	D15.1	D48.7	D49.89
myometrium	C54.2	C79.82	D07.0	D26.1	D39.0	D49.59
myopericardium	C38.0	C79.89	—	D15.1	D48.7	D49.89
nabothian gland (follicle)	C53.0	C79.82	D06.0	D26.0	D39.0	D49.59
nail — see also Neoplasm, skin, limb	C44.90	C79.2	D04.9	D23.9	D48.5	D49.2
finger — see also Neoplasm, skin, limb, upper	C44.60-●	C79.2	D04.6-●	D23.6-●	D48.5	D49.2
toe — see also Neoplasm, skin, limb, lower	C44.70-●	C79.2	D04.7-●	D23.7-●	D48.5	D49.2
nares, naris (anterior) (posterior)	C30.0	C78.39	D02.3	D14.0	D38.5	D49.1
nasal — see Neoplasm, nose						
nasolabial groove — see also Neoplasm, skin, face	C44.309	C79.2	D04.39	D23.39	D48.5	D49.2
nasolacrimal duct	C69.5-●	C79.49	D09.2-●	D31.5-●	D48.7	D49.89

	Malignant Primary	Malignant Secondary	Ca in situ	Benign	Uncertain Behavior	Unspecified Behavior
nasopharynx, nasopharyngeal	C11.9	C79.89	D00.08	D10.6	D37.05	D49.0
floor	C11.3	C79.89	D00.08	D10.6	D37.05	D49.0
overlapping lesion	C11.8	—	—	—	—	—
roof	C11.0	C79.89	D00.08	D10.6	D37.05	D49.0
wall	C11.9	C79.89	D00.08	D10.6	D37.05	D49.0
anterior	C11.3	C79.89	D00.08	D10.6	D37.05	D49.0
lateral	C11.2	C79.89	D00.08	D10.6	D37.05	D49.0
posterior	C11.1	C79.89	D00.08	D10.6	D37.05	D49.0
superior	C11.0	C79.89	D00.08	D10.6	D37.05	D49.0
nates — see also Neoplasm, skin, trunk	C44.509	C79.2	D04.5	D23.5	D48.5	D49.2
neck NEC	C76.0	C79.89	D09.8	D36.7	D48.7	D49.89
skin	C44.40	—	—	—	—	—
basal cell carcinoma	C44.41	—	—	—	—	—
specified type NEC	C44.49	—	—	—	—	—
squamous cell carcinoma	C44.42	—	—	—	—	—
nerve (ganglion)	C47.9	C79.89	—	D36.10	D48.2	D49.2
abducens	C72.59	C79.49	—	D33.3	D43.3	D49.7
accessory (spinal)	C72.59	C79.49	—	D33.3	D43.3	D49.7
acoustic	C72.4-●	C79.49	—	D33.3	D43.3	D49.7
auditory	C72.4-●	C79.49	—	D33.3	D43.3	D49.7
autonomic NEC — see also Neoplasm, nerve, peripheral	C47.9	C79.89	—	D36.10	D48.2	D49.2
brachial	C47.1-●	C79.89	—	D36.12	D48.2	D49.2
cranial	C72.50	C79.49	—	D33.3	D43.3	D49.7
specified NEC	C72.59	C79.49	—	D33.3	D43.3	D49.7
facial	C72.59	C79.49	—	D33.3	D43.3	D49.7
femoral	C47.2-●	C79.89	—	D36.13	D48.2	D49.2
ganglion NEC — see also Neoplasm, nerve, peripheral	C47.9	C79.89	—	D36.10	D48.2	D49.2
glossopharyngeal	C72.59	C79.49	—	D33.3	D43.3	D49.7
hypoglossal	C72.59	C79.49	—	D33.3	D43.3	D49.7
intercostal	C47.3	C79.89	—	D36.14	D48.2	D49.2
lumbar	C47.6	C79.89	—	D36.17	D48.2	D49.2
median	C47.1-●	C79.89	—	D36.12	D48.2	D49.2
obturator	C47.2-●	C79.89	—	D36.13	D48.2	D49.2
oculomotor	C72.59	C79.49	—	D33.3	D43.3	D49.7
olfactory	C47.2-●	C79.49	—	D33.3	D43.3	D49.7
optic	C72.3-●	C79.49	—	D33.3	D43.3	D49.7
parasympathetic NEC	C47.9	C79.89	—	D36.10	D48.2	D49.2
peripheral NEC	C47.9	C79.89	—	D36.10	D48.2	D49.2
abdomen	C47.4	C79.89	—	D36.15	D48.2	D49.2
abdominal wall	C47.4	C79.89	—	D36.15	D48.2	D49.2

◀ New   ◀ Revised   ~~deleted~~ Deleted   ● Use Additional Character(s)

nerve (Continued)	Malignant Primary	Malignant Secondary	Ca in situ	Benign	Uncertain Behavior	Unspecified Behavior
peripheral NEC (Continued)						
ankle	C47.2-●	C79.89	—	D36.13	D48.2	D49.2
antecubital fossa or space	C47.1-●	C79.89	—	D36.12	D48.2	D49.2
arm	C47.1-●	C79.89	—	D36.12	D48.2	D49.2
auricle (ear)	C47.0	C79.89	—	D36.11	D48.2	D49.2
axilla	C47.3	C79.89	—	D36.12	D48.2	D49.2
back	C47.6	C79.89	—	D36.17	D48.2	D49.2
buttock	C47.5	C79.89	—	D36.16	D48.2	D49.2
calf	C47.2-●	C79.89	—	D36.13	D48.2	D49.2
cervical region	C47.0	C79.89	—	D36.11	D48.2	D49.2
cheek	C47.0	C79.89	—	D36.11	D48.2	D49.2
chest (wall)	C47.3	C79.89	—	D36.14	D48.2	D49.2
chin	C47.0	C79.89	—	D36.11	D48.2	D49.2
ear (external)	C47.0	C79.89	—	D36.11	D48.2	D49.2
elbow	C47.1-●	C79.89	—	D36.12	D48.2	D49.2
extrarectal	C47.5	C79.89	—	D36.16	D48.2	D49.2
extremity	C47.9	C79.89	—	D36.10	D48.2	D49.2
lower	C47.2-●	C79.89	—	D36.13	D48.2	D49.2
upper	C47.1-●	C79.89	—	D36.12	D48.2	D49.2
eyelid	C47.0	C79.89	—	D36.11	D48.2	D49.2
face	C47.0	C79.89	—	D36.11	D48.2	D49.2
finger	C47.1-●	C79.89	—	D36.12	D48.2	D49.2
flank	C47.6	C79.89	—	D36.17	D48.2	D49.2
foot	C47.2-●	C79.89	—	D36.13	D48.2	D49.2
forearm	C47.1-●	C79.89	—	D36.12	D48.2	D49.2
forehead	C47.0	C79.89	—	D36.11	D48.2	D49.2
gluteal region	C47.5	C79.89	—	D36.16	D48.2	D49.2
groin	C47.5	C79.89	—	D36.16	D48.2	D49.2
hand	C47.1-●	C79.89	—	D36.12	D48.2	D49.2
head	C47.0	C79.89	—	D36.11	D48.2	D49.2
heel	C47.2-●	C79.89	—	D36.13	D48.2	D49.2
hip	C47.2-●	C79.89	—	D36.13	D48.2	D49.2
infraclavicular region	C47.3	C79.89	—	D36.14	D48.2	D49.2
inguinal (canal) (region)	C47.5	C79.89	—	D36.16	D48.2	D49.2
intrathoracic	C47.3	C79.89	—	D36.14	D48.2	D49.2
ischiorectal fossa	C47.5	C79.89	—	D36.16	D48.2	D49.2
knee	C47.2-●	C79.89	—	D36.13	D48.2	D49.2
leg	C47.2-●	C79.89	—	D36.13	D48.2	D49.2
limb NEC	C47.9	C79.89	—	D36.10	D48.2	D49.2
lower	C47.2-●	C79.89	—	D36.13	D48.2	D49.2
upper	C47.1-●	C79.89	—	D36.12	D48.2	D49.2
nates	C47.5	C79.89	—	D36.16	D48.2	D49.2
neck	C47.0	C79.89	—	D36.11	D48.2	D49.2

nerve (Continued)	Malignant Primary	Malignant Secondary	Ca in situ	Benign	Uncertain Behavior	Unspecified Behavior
peripheral NEC (Continued)						
orbit	C69.6-●	C79.49	—	D31.6-●	D48.7	D49.2
pararectal	C47.5	C79.89	—	D36.16	D48.2	D49.2
paraurethral	C47.5	C79.89	—	D36.16	D48.2	D49.2
paravaginal	C47.5	C79.89	—	D36.16	D48.2	D49.2
pelvis (floor)	C47.5	C79.89	—	D36.16	D48.2	D49.2
pelvoabdominal	C47.8	C79.89	—	D36.17	D48.2	D49.2
perineum	C47.5	C79.89	—	D36.16	D48.2	D49.2
perirectal (tissue)	C47.5	C79.89	—	D36.16	D48.2	D49.2
periurethral (tissue)	C47.5	C79.89	—	D36.16	D48.2	D49.2
popliteal fossa or space	C47.2-●	C79.89	—	D36.13	D48.2	D49.2
presacral	C47.5	C79.89	—	D36.16	D48.2	D49.2
pterygoid fossa	C47.0	C79.89	—	D36.11	D48.2	D49.2
rectovaginal septum or wall	C47.5	C79.89	—	D36.16	D48.2	D49.2
rectovesical	C47.5	C79.89	—	D36.16	D48.2	D49.2
sacrococcygeal region	C47.5	C79.89	—	D36.16	D48.2	D49.2
scalp	C47.0	C79.89	—	D36.11	D48.2	D49.2
scapular region	C47.3	C79.89	—	D36.14	D48.2	D49.2
shoulder	C47.1-●	C79.89	—	D36.12	D48.2	D49.2
submental	C47.0	C79.89	—	D36.11	D48.2	D49.2
supraclavicular region	C47.0	C79.89	—	D36.11	D48.2	D49.2
temple	C47.0	C79.89	—	D36.11	D48.2	D49.2
temporal region	C47.0	C79.89	—	D36.11	D48.2	D49.2
thigh	C47.2-●	C79.89	—	D36.13	D48.2	D49.2
thoracic (duct) (wall)	C47.3	C79.89	—	D36.14	D48.2	D49.2
thorax	C47.3	C79.89	—	D36.14	D48.2	D49.2
thumb	C47.1-●	C79.89	—	D36.12	D48.2	D49.2
toe	C47.2-●	C79.89	—	D36.13	D48.2	D49.2
trunk	C47.6	C79.89	—	D36.17	D48.2	D49.2
umbilicus	C47.4	C79.89	—	D36.15	D48.2	D49.2
vesicorectal	C47.5	C79.89	—	D36.16	D48.2	D49.2
wrist	C47.1-●	C79.89	—	D36.12	D48.2	D49.2
radial	C47.1-●	C79.89	—	D36.12	D48.2	D49.2
sacral	C47.5	C79.89	—	D36.16	D48.2	D49.2
sciatic	C47.2-●	C79.89	—	D36.13	D48.2	D49.2
spinal NEC	C47.9	C79.89	—	D36.10	D48.2	D49.2
accessory	C72.59	C79.49	—	D33.3	D43.3	D49.7
sympathetic NEC—see also Neoplasm, nerve, peripheral	C47.9	C79.89	—	D36.10	D48.2	D49.2
trigeminal	C72.59	C79.49	—	D33.3	D43.3	D49.7
trochlear	C72.59	C79.49	—	D33.3	D43.3	D49.7
ulnar	C47.1-●	C79.89	—	D36.12	D48.2	D49.2
vagus	C72.59	C79.49	—	D33.3	D43.3	D49.7

◀ New   ◀ Revised   ~~deleted~~ Deleted   ● Use Additional Character(s)

	Malignant Primary	Malignant Secondary	Ca in situ	Benign	Uncertain Behavior	Unspecified Behavior
nervous system (central)	C72.9	C79.40	—	D33.9	D43.9	D49.7
autonomic — see Neoplasm, nerve, peripheral						
parasympathetic — see Neoplasm, nerve, peripheral						
specified site NEC	—	C79.49	—	D33.7	D43.8	—
sympathetic — see Neoplasm, nerve, peripheral						
nevus — see Nevus						
nipple	C50.0-●	C79.81	D05.-●	D24.-●	—	—
nose, nasal	C76.0	C79.89	D09.8	D36.7	D48.7	D49.89
ala (external) (nasi) — see also Neoplasm, nose, skin	C44.301	C79.2	D04.39	D23.39	D48.5	D49.2
bone	C41.0	C79.51	—	D16.4-●	D48.0	D49.2
cartilage	C30.0	C78.39	D02.3	D14.0	D38.5	D49.1
cavity	C30.0	C78.39	D02.3	D14.0	D38.5	D49.1
choana	C11.3	C79.89	D00.08	D10.6	D37.05	D49.0
external (skin) — see also Neoplasm, nose, skin	C44.301	C79.2	D04.39	D23.39	D48.5	D49.2
fossa	C30.0	C78.39	D02.3	D14.0	D38.5	D49.1
internal	C30.0	C78.39	D02.3	D14.0	D38.5	D49.1
mucosa	C30.0	C78.39	D02.3	D14.0	D38.5	D49.1
septum	C30.0	C78.39	D02.3	D14.0	D38.5	D49.1
posterior margin	C11.3	C79.89	D00.08	D10.6	D37.05	D49.0
sinus — see Neoplasm, sinus						
skin	C44.301	C79.2	D04.39	D23.39	D48.5	D49.2
basal cell carcinoma	C44.311	—	—	—	—	—
specified type NEC	C44.391	—	—	—	—	—
squamous cell carcinoma	C44.321	—	—	—	—	—
turbinate (mucosa)	C30.0	C78.39	D02.3	D14.0	D38.5	D49.1
bone	C41.0	C79.51	—	D16.4-●	D48.0	D49.2
vestibule	C30.0	C78.39	D02.3	D14.0	D38.5	D49.1
nostril	C30.0	C78.39	D02.3	D14.0	D38.5	D49.1
nucleus pulposus	C41.2	C79.51	—	D16.6	D48.0	D49.2
occipital						
bone	C41.0	C79.51	—	D16.4-●	D48.0	D49.2
lobe or pole, brain	C71.4	C79.31	—	D33.0	D43.0	D49.6
odontogenic — see Neoplasm, jaw bone						
olfactory nerve or bulb	C72.2-●	C79.49	—	D33.3	D43.3	D49.7
olive (brain)	C71.7	C79.31	—	D33.1	D43.1	D49.6
omentum	C48.1	C78.6	—	D20.1	D48.4	D49.0
operculum (brain)	C71.0	C79.31	—	D33.0	D43.0	D49.6
optic nerve, chiasm, or tract	C72.3-●	C79.49	—	D33.3	D43.3	D49.7

	Malignant Primary	Malignant Secondary	Ca in situ	Benign	Uncertain Behavior	Unspecified Behavior
oral (cavity)	C06.9	C79.89	D00.00	D10.30	D37.09	D49.0
ill-defined	C14.8	C79.89	D00.00	D10.30	D37.09	D49.0
mucosa	C06.0	C79.89	D00.02	D10.39	D37.09	D49.0
orbit	C69.6-●	C79.49	D09.2-●	D31.6-●	D48.7	D49.89
autonomic nerve	C69.6-●	C79.49	—	D31.6-●	D48.7	D49.2
bone	C41.0	C79.51	—	D16.4-●	D48.0	D49.2
eye	C69.6-●	C79.49	D09.2-●	D31.6-●	D48.7	D49.89
peripheral nerves	C69.6-●	C79.49	—	D31.6-●	D48.7	D49.2
soft parts	C69.6-●	C79.49	D09.2-●	D31.6-●	D48.7	D49.89
organ of Zuckerkandl	C75.5	C79.89	—	D35.6	D44.7	D49.7
oropharynx	C10.9	C79.89	D00.08	D10.5	D37.05	D49.0
branchial cleft (vestige)	C10.4	C79.89	D00.08	D10.5	D37.05	D49.0
junctional region	C10.8	C79.89	D00.08	D10.5	D37.05	D49.0
lateral wall	C10.2	C79.89	D00.08	D10.5	D37.05	D49.0
overlapping lesion	C10.8	—	—	—	—	—
pillars or fauces	C09.1	C79.89	D00.08	D10.5	D37.05	D49.0
posterior wall	C10.3	C79.89	D00.08	D10.5	D37.05	D49.0
vallecula	C10.0	C79.89	D00.08	D10.5	D37.05	D49.0
os						
external	C53.1	C79.82	D06.1	D26.0	D39.0	D49.59
internal	C53.0	C79.82	D06.0	D26.0	D39.0	D49.59
ovary	C56.-●	C79.6-●	D07.39	D27.-●	D39.1-●	D49.59
oviduct	C57.0-●	C79.82	D07.39	D28.2	D39.8	D49.59
palate	C05.9	C79.89	D00.00	D10.39	D37.09	D49.0
hard	C05.0	C79.89	D00.05	D10.39	D37.09	D49.0
junction of hard and soft palate	C05.9	C79.89	D00.00	D10.39	D37.09	D49.0
overlapping lesions	C05.8	—	—	—	—	—
soft	C05.1	C79.89	D00.04	D10.39	D37.09	D49.0
nasopharyngeal surface	C11.3	C79.89	D00.08	D10.6	D37.05	D49.0
posterior surface	C11.3	C79.89	D00.08	D10.6	D37.05	D49.0
superior surface	C11.3	C79.89	D00.08	D10.6	D37.05	D49.0
palatoglossal arch	C09.1	C79.89	D00.00	D10.5	D37.09	D49.0
palatopharyngeal arch	C09.1	C79.89	D00.00	D10.5	D37.09	D49.0
pallium	C71.0	C79.31	—	D33.0	D43.0	D49.6
palpebra	C44.10-●	C79.2	D04.1-●	D23.1-●	D48.5	D49.2
basal cell carcinoma	C44.11-●	—	—	—	—	—
sebaceous cell	C44.13-●	—	—	—	—	—
specified type NEC	C44.19-●	—	—	—	—	—
squamous cell carcinoma	C44.12-●	—	—	—	—	—
pancreas	C25.9	C78.89	D01.7	D13.6	D37.8	D49.0
body	C25.1	C78.89	D01.7	D13.6	D37.8	D49.0
duct (of Santorini) (of Wirsung)	C25.3	C78.89	D01.7	D13.6	D37.8	D49.0
ectopic tissue	C25.7	C78.89	—	D13.6	D37.8	D49.0
head	C25.0	C78.89	D01.7	D13.6	D37.8	D49.0

◀ New ◀ Revised ~~deleted~~ Deleted ● Use Additional Character(s)

TABLE OF NEOPLASMS

	Malignant Primary	Malignant Secondary	Ca in situ	Benign	Uncertain Behavior	Unspecified Behavior
pancreas *(Continued)*						
islet cells	C25.4	C78.89	D01.7	D13.7	D37.8	D49.0
neck	C25.7	C78.89	D01.7	D13.6	D37.8	D49.0
overlapping lesion	C25.8	—	—	—	—	—
tail	C25.2	C78.89	D01.7	D13.6	D37.8	D49.0
para-aortic body	C75.5	C79.89	—	D35.6	D44.7	D49.7
paraganglion NEC	C75.5	C79.89	—	D35.6	D44.7	D49.7
parametrium	C57.3	C79.82		D28.2	D39.8	D49.59
paranephric	C48.0	C78.6		D20.0	D48.3	D49.0
pararectal	C76.3	C79.89		D36.7	D48.7	D49.89
parasagittal (region)	C76.0	C79.89	D09.8	D36.7	D48.7	D49.89
parasellar	C72.9	C79.49		D33.9	D43.8	D49.7
parathyroid (gland)	C75.0	C79.89	D09.3	D35.1	D44.2	D49.7
paraurethral	C76.3	C79.89		D36.7	D48.7	D49.89
gland	C68.1	C79.19	D09.19	D30.8	D41.8	D49.59
paravaginal	C76.3	C79.89		D36.7	D48.7	D49.89
parenchyma, kidney	C64.-●	C79.0-●	D09.19	D30.0-●	D41.0-●	D49.51-●
parietal						
bone	C41.0	C79.51		D16.4-●	D48.0	D49.2
lobe, brain	C71.3	C79.31		D33.0	D43.0	D49.6
paroophoron	C57.1	C79.82	D07.39	D28.2	D39.8	D49.59
parotid (duct) (gland)	C07	C79.89	D00.00	D11.0	D37.030	D49.0
parovarium	C57.1	C79.82	D07.39	D28.2	D39.8	D49.59
patella	C40.20	C79.51		—	—	—
peduncle, cerebral	C71.7	C79.31	—	D33.1	D43.1	D49.6
pelvirectal junction	C19	C78.5	D01.1	D12.7	D37.5	D49.0
pelvis, pelvic	C76.3	C79.89	D09.8	D36.7	D48.7	D49.89
bone	C41.4	C79.51		D16.8	D48.0	D49.2
floor	C76.3	C79.89	D09.8	D36.7	D48.7	D49.89
renal	C65.-●	C79.0-●	D09.19	D30.1-●	D41.1-●	D49.51-●
viscera	C76.3	C79.89	D09.8	D36.7	D48.7	D49.89
wall	C76.3	C79.89	D09.8	D36.7	D48.7	D49.89
pelvo-abdominal	C76.8	C79.89	D09.8	D36.7	D48.7	D49.89
penis	C60.9	C79.82	D07.4	D29.0	D40.8	D49.59
body	C60.2	C79.82	D07.4	D29.0	D40.8	D49.59
corpus (cavernosum)	C60.2	C79.82	D07.4	D29.0	D40.8	D49.59
glans	C60.1	C79.82	D07.4	D29.0	D40.8	D49.59
overlapping sites	C60.8	—	—	—	—	—
skin NEC	C60.9	C79.82	D07.4	D29.0	D40.8	D49.59
periadrenal (tissue)	C48.0	C78.6		D20.0	D48.3	D49.0
perianal (skin) — *see also Neoplasm, anus, skin*	C44.500	C79.2	D04.5	D23.5	D48.5	D49.2
pericardium	C38.0	C79.89		D15.1	D48.7	D49.89
perinephric	C48.0	C78.6	—	D20.0	D48.3	D49.0

	Malignant Primary	Malignant Secondary	Ca in situ	Benign	Uncertain Behavior	Unspecified Behavior
perineum	C76.3	C79.89	D09.8	D36.7	D48.7	D49.89
periodontal tissue NEC	C03.9	C79.89	D00.03	D10.39	D37.09	D49.0
periosteum — *see Neoplasm, bone*						
peripancreatic	C48.0	C78.6	—	D20.0	D48.3	D49.0
peripheral nerve NEC	C47.9	C79.89	—	D36.10	D48.2	D49.2
perirectal (tissue)	C76.3	C79.89		D36.7	D48.7	D49.89
perirenal (tissue)	C48.0	C78.6		D20.0	D48.3	D49.0
peritoneum, peritoneal (cavity)	C48.2	C78.6	—	D20.1	D48.4	D49.0
benign mesothelial tissue — *see Mesothelioma, benign*						
overlapping lesion	C48.8	—	—	—	—	—
with digestive organs	C26.9	—	—	—	—	—
parietal	C48.1	C78.6	—	D20.1	D48.4	D49.0
pelvic	C48.1	C78.6	—	D20.1	D48.4	D49.0
specified part NEC	C48.1	C78.6	—	D20.1	D48.4	D49.0
peritonsillar (tissue)	C76.0	C79.89	D09.8	D36.7	D48.7	D49.89
periurethral tissue	C76.3	C79.89	—	D36.7	D48.7	D49.89
phalanges						
foot	C40.3-●	C79.51		D16.3-●	—	—
hand	C40.1-●	C79.51	—	D16.1-●	—	—
pharynx, pharyngeal	C14.0	C79.89	D00.08	D10.9	D37.05	D49.0
bursa	C11.1	C79.89	D00.08	D10.6	D37.05	D49.0
fornix	C11.3	C79.89	D00.08	D10.6	D37.05	D49.0
recess	C11.2	C79.89	D00.08	D10.6	D37.05	D49.0
region	C14.0	C79.89	D00.08	D10.9	D37.05	D49.0
tonsil	C11.1	C79.89	D00.08	D10.6	D37.05	D49.0
wall (lateral) (posterior)	C14.0	C79.89	D00.08	D10.9	D37.05	D49.0
pia mater	C70.9	C79.40	—	D32.9	D42.9	D49.7
cerebral	C70.0	C79.32	—	D32.0	D42.0	D49.7
cranial	C70.0	C79.32		D32.0	D42.0	D49.7
spinal	C70.1	C79.49	—	D32.1	D42.1	D49.7
pillars of fauces	C09.1	C79.89	D00.08	D10.5	D37.05	D49.0
pineal (body) (gland)	C75.3	C79.89	D09.3	D35.4	D44.5	D49.7
pinna (ear) NEC — *see also Neoplasm, skin, ear*	C44.20-●	C79.2	D04.2-●	D23.2-●	D48.5	D49.2
piriform fossa or sinus	C12	C79.89	D00.08	D10.7	D37.05	D49.0
pituitary (body) (fossa) (gland) (lobe)	C75.1	C79.89	D09.3	D35.2	D44.3	D49.7
placenta	C58	C79.82	D07.0	D26.7	D39.2	D49.59
pleura, pleural (cavity)	C38.4	C78.2		D19.0	D38.2	D49.1
overlapping lesion with heart or mediastinum	C38.8	—	—	—	—	—
parietal	C38.4	C78.2		D19.0	D38.2	D49.1
visceral	C38.4	C78.2	—	D19.0	D38.2	D49.1

◀ New   ◀◀ Revised   ~~deleted~~ Deleted   ● Use Additional Character(s)

	Malignant Primary	Malignant Secondary	Ca in situ	Benign	Uncertain Behavior	Unspecified Behavior
plexus						
brachial	C47.1-●	C79.89	—	D36.12	D48.2	D49.2
cervical	C47.0	C79.89	—	D36.11	D48.2	D49.2
choroid	C71.5	C79.31	—	D33.0	D43.0	D49.6
lumbosacral	C47.5	C79.89	—	D36.16	D48.2	D49.2
sacral	C47.5	C79.89	—	D36.16	D48.2	D49.2
pluriendocrine	C75.8	C79.89	D09.3	D35.7	D44.9	D49.7
pole						
frontal	C71.1	C79.31	—	D33.0	D43.0	D49.6
occipital	C71.4	C79.31	—	D33.0	D43.0	D49.6
pons (varolii)	C71.7	C79.31	—	D33.1	D43.1	D49.6
popliteal fossa or space	C76.5-●	C79.89	D04.7-●	D36.7	D48.7	D49.89
postcricoid (region)	C13.0	C79.89	D00.08	D10.7	D37.05	D49.0
posterior fossa (cranial)	C71.9	C79.31	—	D33.2	D43.2	D49.6
postnasal space	C11.9	C79.89	D00.08	D10.6	D37.05	D49.0
prepuce	C60.0	C79.82	D07.4	D29.0	D40.8	D49.59
prepylorus	C16.4	C78.89	D00.2	D13.1	D37.1	D49.0
presacral (region)	C76.3	C79.89	—	D36.7	D48.7	D49.89
prostate (gland)	C61	C79.82	D07.5	D29.1	D40.0	D49.59
utricle	C68.0	C79.19	D09.19	D30.4	D41.3	D49.59
pterygoid fossa	C49.0	C79.89	—	D21.0	D48.1	D49.2
pubic bone	C41.4	C79.51	—	D16.8	D48.0	D49.2
pudenda, pudendum (femaie)	C51.9	C79.82	D07.1	D28.0	D39.8	D49.59
pulmonary — see also Neoplasm, lung	C34.9-●	C78.0-●	D02.2-●	D14.3-●	D38.1	D49.1
putamen	C71.0	C79.31	—	D33.0	D43.0	D49.6
pyloric						
antrum	C16.3	C78.89	D00.2	D13.1	D37.1	D49.0
canal	C16.4	C78.89	D00.2	D13.1	D37.1	D49.0
pylorus	C16.4	C78.89	D00.2	D13.1	D37.1	D49.0
pyramid (brain)	C71.7	C79.31	—	D33.1	D43.1	D49.6
pyriform fossa or sinus	C12	C79.89	D00.08	D10.7	D37.05	D49.0
radius (any part)	C40.0-●	C79.51	—	D16.0-●	—	—
Rathke's pouch	C75.1	C79.89	D09.3	D35.2	D44.3	D49.7
rectosigmoid (junction)	C19	C78.5	D01.1	D12.7	D37.5	D49.0
overlapping lesion with anus or rectum	C21.8	—	—	—	—	—
rectouterine pouch	C48.1	C78.6	—	D20.1	D48.4	D49.0
rectovaginal septum or wall	C76.3	C79.89	D09.8	D36.7	D48.7	D49.89
rectovesical septum	C76.3	C79.89	D09.8	D36.7	D48.7	D49.89
rectum (ampulla)	C20	C78.5	D01.2	D12.8	D37.5	D49.0
and colon	C19	C78.5	D01.1	D12.7	D37.5	D49.0
overlapping lesion with anus or rectosigmoid junction	C21.8	—	—	—	—	—
renal	C64.-●	C79.0-●	D09.19	D30.0-●	D41.0-●	D49.51-●
calyx	C65.-●	C79.0-●	D09.19	D30.1-●	D41.1-●	D49.51-●
hilus	C65.-●	C79.0-●	D09.19	D30.1-●	D41.1-●	D49.51-●
parenchyma	C64.-●	C79.0-●	D09.19	D30.0-●	D41.0-●	D49.51-●
pelvis	C65.-●	C79.0-●	D09.19	D30.1-●	D41.1-●	D49.51-●
respiratory						
organs or system NEC	C39.9	C78.30	D02.4	D14.4	D38.6	D49.1
tract NEC	C39.9	C78.30	D02.4	D14.4	D38.5	D49.1
upper	C39.0	C78.30	D02.4	D14.4	D38.5	D49.1
retina	C69.2-●	C79.49	D09.2-●	D31.2-●	D48.7	D49.81
retrobulbar	C69.6-●	C79.49	—	D31.6-●	D48.7	D49.89
retrocecal	C48.0	C78.6	—	D20.0	D48.3	D49.0
retromolar (area) (triangle) (trigone)	C06.2	C79.89	D00.00	D10.39	D37.09	D49.0
retro-orbital	C76.0	C79.89	D09.8	D36.7	D48.7	D49.89
retroperitoneal (space) (tissue)	C48.0	C78.6	—	D20.0	D48.3	D49.0
retroperitoneum	C48.0	C78.6	—	D20.0	D48.3	D49.0
retropharyngeal	C14.0	C79.89	D00.08	D10.9	D37.05	D49.0
retrovesical (septum)	C76.3	C79.89	D09.8	D36.7	D48.7	D49.89
rhinencephalon	C71.0	C79.31	—	D33.0	D43.0	D49.6
rib	C41.3	C79.51	—	D16.7	D48.0	D49.2
Rosenmuller's fossa	C11.2	C79.89	D00.08	D10.6	D37.05	D49.0
round ligament	C57.2	C79.82	—	D28.2	D39.8	D49.59
sacrococcyx, sacrococcygeal	C41.4	C79.51	—	D16.8	D48.0	D49.2
region	C76.3	C79.89	D09.8	D36.7	D48.7	D49.89
sacrouterine ligament	C57.3	C79.82	—	D28.2	D39.8	D49.59
sacrum, sacral (vertebra)	C41.4	C79.51	—	D16.8	D48.0	D49.2
salivary gland or duct (major)	C08.9	C79.89	D00.00	D11.9	D37.039	D49.0
minor NEC	C06.9	C79.89	D00.00	D10.39	D37.04	D49.0
overlapping lesion	C08.9	—	—	—	—	—
parotid	C07	C79.89	D00.00	D11.0	D37.030	D49.0
pluriglandular	C08.9	C79.89	D00.00	D11.9	D37.039	D49.0
sublingual	C08.1	C79.89	D00.00	D11.7	D37.031	D49.0
submandibular	C08.0	C79.89	D00.00	D11.7	D37.032	D49.0
submaxillary	C08.0	C79.89	D00.00	D11.7	D37.032	D49.0
salpinx (uterine)	C57.0-●	C79.82	D07.39	D28.2	D39.8	D49.59
Santorini's duct	C25.3	C78.89	D01.7	D13.6	D37.8	D49.0
scalp	C44.40	C79.2	D04.4	D23.4	D48.5	D49.2
basal cell carcinoma	C44.41	—	—	—	—	—
specified type NEC	C44.49	—	—	—	—	—
squamous cell carcinoma	C44.42	—	—	—	—	—
scapula (any part)	C40.0-●	C79.51	—	D16.0-●	—	—
scapular region	C76.1	C79.89	D09.8	D36.7	D48.7	D49.89

◀ New   ◀ Revised   ~~deleted~~ Deleted   ● Use Additional Character(s)

TABLE OF NEOPLASMS

	Malignant Primary	Malignant Secondary	Ca in situ	Benign	Uncertain Behavior	Unspecified Behavior
scar NEC — *see also Neoplasm, skin, by site*	C44.90	C79.2	D04.9	D23.9	D48.5	D49.2
sciatic nerve	C47.2-●	C79.89	—	D36.13	D48.2	D49.2
sclera	C69.4-●	C79.49	D09.2-●	D31.4-●	D48.7	D49.89
scrotum (skin)	C63.2	C79.82	D07.61	D29.4	D40.8	D49.59
sebaceous gland — *see Neoplasm, skin*						
sella turcica	C75.1	C79.89	D09.3	D35.2	D44.3	D49.7
bone	C41.0	C79.51	—	D16.4-●	D48.0	D49.2
semilunar cartilage (knee)	C40.2-●	C79.51	—	D16.2-●	D48.0	D49.2
seminal vesicle	C63.7	C79.82	D07.69	D29.8	D40.8	D49.59
septum						
nasal	C30.0	C78.39	D02.3	D14.0	D38.5	D49.1
posterior margin	C11.3	C79.89	D00.08	D10.6	D37.05	D49.0
rectovaginal	C76.3	C79.89	D09.8	D36.7	D48.7	D49.89
rectovesical	C76.3	C79.89	D09.8	D36.7	D48.7	D49.89
urethrovaginal	C57.9	C79.82	D07.30	D28.9	D39.9	D49.59
vesicovaginal	C57.9	C79.82	D07.30	D28.9	D39.9	D49.59
shoulder NEC	C76.4-●	C79.89	D04.6-●	D36.7	D48.7	D49.89
sigmoid flexure (lower) (upper)	C18.7	C78.5	D01.0	D12.5	D37.4	D49.0
sinus (accessory)	C31.9	C78.39	D02.3	D14.0	D38.5	D49.1
bone (any)	C41.0	C79.51	—	D16.4-●	D48.0	D49.2
ethmoidal	C31.1	C78.39	D02.3	D14.0	D38.5	D49.1
frontal	C31.2	C78.39	D02.3	D14.0	D38.5	D49.1
maxillary	C31.0	C78.39	D02.3	D14.0	D38.5	D49.1
nasal, paranasal NEC	C31.9	C78.39	D02.3	D14.0	D38.5	D49.1
overlapping lesion	C31.8	—	—	—	—	—
pyriform	C12	C79.89	D00.08	D10.7	D37.05	D49.0
sphenoid	C31.3	C78.39	D02.3	D14.0	D38.5	D49.1
skeleton, skeletal NEC	C41.9	C79.51	—	D16.9-●	D48.0	D49.2
Skene's gland	C68.1	C79.19	D09.19	D30.8	D41.8	D49.59
skin NOS	C44.90	C79.2	D04.9	D23.9	D48.5	D49.2
abdominal wall	C44.509	C79.2	D04.5	D23.5	D48.5	D49.2
basal cell carcinoma	C44.519	—	—	—	—	—
specified type NEC	C44.599	—	—	—	—	—
squamous cell carcinoma	C44.529	—	—	—	—	—
ala nasi — *see also Neoplasm, nose, skin*	C44.301	C79.2	D04.39	D23.39	D48.5	D49.2
ankle — *see also Neoplasm, skin, limb, lower*	C44.70-●	C79.2	D04.7-●	D23.7-●	D48.5	D49.2
antecubital space — *see also Neoplasm, skin, limb, upper*	C44.60-●	C79.2	D04.6-●	D23.6-●	D48.5	D49.2

	Malignant Primary	Malignant Secondary	Ca in situ	Benign	Uncertain Behavior	Unspecified Behavior
skin NOS *(Continued)*						
anus	C44.500	C79.2	D04.5	D23.5	D48.5	D49.2
basal cell carcinoma	C44.510	—	—	—	—	—
specified type NEC	C44.590	—	—	—	—	—
squamous cell carcinoma	C44.520	—	—	—	—	—
arm — *see also Neoplasm, skin, limb, upper*	C44.60-●	C79.2	D04.6-●	D23.6-●	D48.5	D49.2
auditory canal (external) — *see also Neoplasm, skin, ear*	C44.20-●	C79.2	D04.2-●	D23.2-●	D48.5	D49.2
auricle (ear) — *see also Neoplasm, skin, ear*	C44.20-●	C79.2	D04.2-●	D23.2-●	D48.5	D49.2
auricular canal (external) — *see also Neoplasm, skin, ear*	C44.20-●	C79.2	D04.2-●	D23.2-●	D48.5	D49.2
axilla, axillary fold — *see also Neoplasm, skin, trunk*	C44.509	C79.2	D04.5	D23.5	D48.5	D49.2
back — *see also Neoplasm, skin, trunk*	C44.509	C79.2	D04.5	D23.5	D48.5	D49.2
basal cell carcinoma	C44.91					
breast	C44.501	C79.2	D04.5	D23.5	D48.5	D49.2
basal cell carcinoma	C44.511	—	—	—	—	—
specified type NEC	C44.591	—	—	—	—	—
squamous cell carcinoma	C44.521	—	—	—	—	—
brow — *see also Neoplasm, skin, face*	C44.309	C79.2	D04.39	D23.39	D48.5	D49.2
buttock — *see also Neoplasm, skin, trunk*	C44.509	C79.2	D04.5	D23.5	D48.5	D49.2
calf — *see also Neoplasm, skin, limb, lower*	C44.70-●	C79.2	D04.7-●	D23.7-●	D48.5	D49.2
canthus (eye) (inner) (outer)	C44.10-●	C79.2	D04.1-●	D23.1-●	D48.5	D49.2
basal cell carcinoma	C44.11-●	—	—	—	—	—
sebaceous cell	C44.13-●	—	—	—	—	—
specified type NEC	C44.19-●	—	—	—	—	—
squamous cell carcinoma	C44.12-●	—	—	—	—	—
cervical region — *see also Neoplasm, skin, neck*	C44.40	C79.2	D04.4	D23.4	D48.5	D49.2
cheek (external) — *see also Neoplasm, skin, face*	C44.309	C79.2	D04.39	D23.39	D48.5	D49.2
chest (wall) — *see also Neoplasm, skin, trunk*	C44.509	C79.2	D04.5	D23.5	D48.5	D49.2
chin — *see also Neoplasm, skin, face*	C44.309	C79.2	D04.39	D23.39	D48.5	D49.2
clavicular area — *see also Neoplasm, skin, trunk*	C44.509	C79.2	D04.5	D23.5	D48.5	D49.2
clitoris	C51.2	C79.82	D07.1	D28.0	D39.8	D49.59

◀ New   ◀◀ Revised   ~~deleted~~ Deleted   ● Use Additional Character(s)

	Malignant Primary	Malignant Secondary	Ca in situ	Benign	Uncertain Behavior	Unspecified Behavior
skin NOS *(Continued)*						
columnella — *see also Neoplasm, skin, face*	C44.309	C79.2	D04.39	D23.39	D48.5	D49.2
concha — *see also Neoplasm, skin, ear*	C44.20-●	C79.2	D04.2-●	D23.2-●	D48.5	D49.2
ear (external)	C44.20-●	C79.2	D04.2-●	D23.2-●	D48.5	D49.2
basal cell carcinoma	C44.21-●	—	—	—	—	—
specified type NEC	C44.29-●	—	—	—	—	—
squamous cell carcinoma	C44.22-●	—	—	—	—	—
elbow — *see also Neoplasm, skin, limb, upper*	C44.60-●	C79.2	D04.6-●	D23.6-●	D48.5	D49.2
eyebrow — *see also Neoplasm, skin, face*	C44.309	C79.2	D04.39	D23.39	D48.5	D49.2
eyelid	C44.10-●	C79.2	D04.1-●	D23.1-●	D48.5	D49.2
basal cell carcinoma	C44.11-●	—	—	—	—	—
sebaceous cell	C44.13-●	—	—	—	—	—
specified type NEC	C44.19-●	—	—	—	—	—
squamous cell carcinoma	C44.12-●	—	—	—	—	—
face NOS	C44.300	C79.2	D04.30	D23.30	D48.5	D49.2
basal cell carcinoma	C44.310	—	—	—	—	—
specified type NEC	C44.390	—	—	—	—	—
squamous cell carcinoma	C44.320	—	—	—	—	—
female genital organs (external)	C51.9	C79.82	D07.1	D28.0	D39.8	D49.59
clitoris	C51.2	C79.82	D07.1	D28.0	D39.8	D49.59
labium NEC	C51.9	C79.82	D07.1	D28.0	D39.8	D49.59
majus	C51.0	C79.82	D07.1	D28.0	D39.8	D49.59
minus	C51.1	C79.82	D07.1	D28.0	D39.8	D49.59
pudendum	C51.9	C79.82	D07.1	D28.0	D39.8	D49.59
vulva	C51.9	C79.82	D07.1	D28.0	D39.8	D49.59
finger — *see also Neoplasm, skin, limb, upper*	C44.60-●	C79.2	D04.6-●	D23.6-●	D48.5	D49.2
flank — *see also Neoplasm, skin, trunk*	C44.509	C79.2	D04.5	D23.5	D48.5	D49.2
foot — *see also Neoplasm, skin, limb, lower*	C44.70-●	C79.2	D04.7-●	D23.7-●	D48.5	D49.2
forearm — *see also Neoplasm, skin, limb, upper*	C44.60-●	C79.2	D04.6-●	D23.6-●	D48.5	D49.2
forehead — *see also Neoplasm, skin, face*	C44.309	C79.2	D04.39	D23.39	D48.5	D49.2
glabella — *see also Neoplasm, skin, face*	C44.309	C79.2	D04.39	D23.39	D48.5	D49.2
gluteal region — *see also Neoplasm, skin, trunk*	C44.509	C79.2	D04.5	D23.5	D48.5	D49.2
groin — *see also Neoplasm, skin, trunk*	C44.509	C79.2	D04.5	D23.5	D48.5	D49.2

	Malignant Primary	Malignant Secondary	Ca in situ	Benign	Uncertain Behavior	Unspecified Behavior
skin NOS *(Continued)*						
hand — *see also Neoplasm, skin, limb, upper*	C44.60-●	C79.2	D04.6-●	D23.6-●	D48.5	D49.2
head NEC — *see also Neoplasm, skin, scalp*	C44.40	C79.2	D04.4	D23.4	D48.5	D49.2
heel — *see also Neoplasm, skin, limb, lower*	C44.70-●	C79.2	D04.7-●	D23.7-●	D48.5	D49.2
helix — *see also Neoplasm, skin, ear*	C44.20-●	C79.2	D04.2-●	D23.2-●	D48.5	D49.2
hip — *see also Neoplasm, skin, limb, lower*	C44.70-●	C79.2	D04.7-●	D23.7-●	D48.5	D49.2
infraclavicular region — *see also Neoplasm, skin, trunk*	C44.509	C79.2	D04.5	D23.5	D48.5	D49.2
inguinal region — *see also Neoplasm, skin, trunk*	C44.509	C79.2	D04.5	D23.5	D48.5	D49.2
jaw — *see also Neoplasm, skin, face*	C44.309	C79.2	D04.39	D23.39	D48.5	D49.2
Kaposi's sarcoma — *see Kaposi's, sarcoma, skin*						
knee — *see also Neoplasm, skin, limb, lower*	C44.70-●	C79.2	D04.7-●	D23.7-●	D48.5	D49.2
labia						
majora	C51.0	C79.82	D07.1	D28.0	D39.8	D49.59
minora	C51.1	C79.82	D07.1	D28.0	D39.8	D49.59
leg — *see also Neoplasm, skin, limb, lower*	C44.70-●	C79.2	D04.7-●	D23.7-●	D48.5	D49.2
lid (lower) (upper)	C44.10-●	C79.2	D04.1-●	D23.1-●	D48.5	D49.2
basal cell carcinoma	C44.11-●	—	—	—	—	—
sebaceous cell	C44.13-●	—	—	—	—	—
specified type NEC	C44.19-●	—	—	—	—	—
squamous cell carcinoma	C44.12-●	—	—	—	—	—
limb NEC	C44.90	C79.2	D04.9	D23.9	D48.5	D49.2
basal cell carcinoma	C44.91					
lower	C44.70-●	C79.2	D04.7-●	D23.7-●	D48.5	D49.2
basal cell carcinoma	C44.71-●	—	—	—	—	—
specified type NEC	C44.79-●	—	—	—	—	—
squamous cell carcinoma	C44.72-●	—	—	—	—	—
upper	C44.60-●	C79.2	D04.6-●	D23.6-●	D48.5	D49.2
basal cell carcinoma	C44.61-●	—	—	—	—	—
specified type NEC	C44.69-●	—	—	—	—	—
squamous cell carcinoma	C44.62-●	—	—	—	—	—
lip (lower) (upper)	C44.00	C79.2	D04.0	D23.0	D48.5	D49.2
basal cell carcinoma	C44.01	—	—	—	—	—
specified type NEC	C44.09	—	—	/	—	—
squamous cell carcinoma	C44.02	—	—	—	—	—

TABLE OF NEOPLASMS

	Malignant Primary	Malignant Secondary	Ca in situ	Benign	Uncertain Behavior	Unspecified Behavior
skin NOS *(Continued)*						
male genital organs	C63.9	C79.82	D07.60	D29.9	D40.8	D49.59
penis	C60.9	C79.82	D07.4	D29.0	D40.8	D49.59
prepuce	C60.0	C79.82	D07.4	D29.0	D40.8	D49.59
scrotum	C63.2	C79.82	D07.61	D29.4	D40.8	D49.59
mastectomy site (skin) — *see also Neoplasm, skin, breast*	C44.501	C79.2	—	—	—	—
specified as breast tissue	C50.8-●	C79.81	—	—	—	—
meatus, acoustic (external) — *see also Neoplasm, skin, ear*	C44.20-●	C79.2	D04.2-●	D23.2-●	D48.5	D49.2
melanotic — *see Melanoma*						
Merkel cell — *see Carcinoma, Merkel cell*						
nates — *see also Neoplasm, skin, trunk*	C44.509	C79.2	D04.5	D23.5	D48.5	D49.2
neck	C44.40	C79.2	D04.4	D23.4	D48.5	D49.2
basal cell carcinoma	C44.41	—	—	—	—	—
specified type NEC	C44.49	—	—	—	—	—
squamous cell carcinoma	C44.42	—	—	—	—	—
nevus — *see Nevus, skin*						
nose (external) — *see also Neoplasm, nose, skin*	C44.301	C79.2	D04.39	D23.39	D48.5	D49.2
overlapping lesion	C44.80	—	—	—	—	—
basal cell carcinoma	C44.81	—	—	—	—	—
specified type NEC	C44.89	—	—	—	—	—
squamous cell carcinoma	C44.82	—	—	—	—	—
palm — *see also Neoplasm, skin, limb, upper*	C44.60-●	C79.2	D04.6-●	D23.6-●	D48.5	D49.2
palpebra	C44.10-●	C79.2	D04.1-●	D23.1-●	D48.5	D49.2
basal cell carcinoma	C44.11-●	—	—	—	—	—
sebaceous cell	C44.13-●	—	—	—	—	—
specified type NEC	C44.19-●	—	—	—	—	—
squamous cell carcinoma	C44.12-●	—	—	—	—	—
penis NEC	C60.9	C79.82	D07.4	D29.0	D40.8	D49.59
perianal — *see also Neoplasm, skin, anus*	C44.500	C79.2	D04.5	D23.5	D48.5	D49.2
perineum — *see also Neoplasm, skin, anus*	C44.500	C79.2	D04.5	D23.5	D48.5	D49.2
pinna — *see also Neoplasm, skin, ear*	C44.20-●	C79.2	D04.2-●	D23.2-●	D48.5	D49.2
plantar — *see also Neoplasm, skin, limb, lower*	C44.70-●	C79.2	D04.7-●	D23.7-●	D48.5	D49.2
popliteal fossa or space — *see also Neoplasm, skin, limb, lower*	C44.70-●	C79.2	D04.7-●	D23.7-●	D48.5	D49.2

	Malignant Primary	Malignant Secondary	Ca in situ	Benign	Uncertain Behavior	Unspecified Behavior
skin NOS *(Continued)*						
prepuce	C60.0	C79.82	D07.4	D29.0	D40.8	D49.59
pubes — *see also Neoplasm, skin, trunk*	C44.509	C79.2	D04.5	D23.5	D48.5	D49.2
sacrococcygeal region — *see also Neoplasm, skin, trunk*	C44.509	C79.2	D04.5	D23.5	D48.5	D49.2
scalp	C44.40	C79.2	D04.4	D23.4	D48.5	D49.2
basal cell carcinoma	C44.41	—	—	—	—	—
specified type NEC	C44.49	—	—	—	—	—
squamous cell carcinoma	C44.42	—	—	—	—	—
scapular region — *see also Neoplasm, skin, trunk*	C44.509	C79.2	D04.5	D23.5	D48.5	D49.2
scrotum	C63.2	C79.82	D07.61	D29.4	D40.8	D49.59
shoulder — *see also Neoplasm, skin, limb, upper*	C44.60-●	C79.2	D04.6-●	D23.6-●	D48.5	D49.2
sole (foot) — *see also Neoplasm, skin, limb, lower*	C44.70-●	C79.2	D04.7-●	D23.7-●	D48.5	D49.2
specified sites NEC	C44.80	C79.2	D04.8	D23.9	D48.5	D49.2
basal cell carcinoma	C44.81	—	—	—	—	—
specified type NEC	C44.89	—	—	—	—	—
squamous cell carcinoma	C44.82	—	—	—	—	—
specified type NEC	C44.99	—	—	—	—	—
squamous cell carcinoma	C44.92	—	—	—	—	—
submammary fold — *see also Neoplasm, skin, trunk*	C44.509	C79.2	D04.5	D23.5	D48.5	D49.2
supraclavicular region — *see also Neoplasm, skin, neck*	C44.40	C79.2	D04.4	D23.4	D48.5	D49.2
temple — *see also Neoplasm, skin, face*	C44.309	C79.2	D04.39	D23.39	D48.5	D49.2
thigh — *see also Neoplasm, skin, limb, lower*	C44.70-●	C79.2	D04.7-●	D23.7-●	D48.5	D49.2
thoracic wall — *see also Neoplasm, skin, trunk*	C44.509	C79.2	D04.5	D23.5	D48.5	D49.2
thumb — *see also Neoplasm, skin, limb, upper*	C44.60-●	C79.2	D04.6-●	D23.6-●	D48.5	D49.2
toe — *see also Neoplasm, skin, limb, lower*	C44.70-●	C79.2	D04.7-●	D23.7-●	D48.5	D49.2
tragus — *see also Neoplasm, skin, ear*	C44.20-●	C79.2	D04.2-●	D23.2-●	D48.5	D49.2
trunk	C44.509	C79.2	D04.5	D23.5	D48.5	D49.2
basal cell carcinoma	C44.519	—	—	—	—	—
specified type NEC	C44.599	—	—	—	—	—
squamous cell carcinoma	C44.529	—	—	—	—	—
umbilicus — *see also Neoplasm, skin, trunk*	C44.509	C79.2	D04.5	D23.5	D48.5	D49.2

◄ New ◀ Revised ~~deleted~~ Deleted ● Use Additional Character(s)

	Malignant Primary	Malignant Secondary	Ca in situ	Benign	Uncertain Behavior	Unspecified Behavior
skin NOS *(Continued)*						
vulva	C51.9	C79.82	D07.1	D28.0	D39.8	D49.59
overlapping lesion	C51.8	—	—	—	—	—
wrist — *see also Neoplasm, skin, limb, upper*	C44.60-●	C79.2	D04.6-●	D23.6-●	D48.5	D49.2
skull	C41.0	C79.51	—	D16.4-●	D48.0	D49.2
soft parts or tissues — *see Neoplasm, connective tissue*						
specified site NEC	C76.8	C79.89	D09.8	D36.7	D48.7	D49.89
spermatic cord	C63.1-●	C79.82	D07.69	D29.8	D40.8	D49.59
sphenoid	C31.3	C78.39	D02.3	D14.0	D38.5	D49.1
bone	C41.0	C79.51	—	D16.4-●	D48.0	D49.2
sinus	C31.3	C78.39	D02.3	D14.0	D38.5	D49.1
sphincter						
anal	C21.1	C78.5	D01.3	D12.9	D37.8	D49.0
of Oddi	C24.0	C78.89	D01.5	D13.5	D37.6	D49.0
spine, spinal (column)	C41.2	C79.51	—	D16.6	D48.0	D49.2
bulb	C71.7	C79.31	—	D33.1	D43.1	D49.6
coccyx	C41.4	C79.51	—	D16.8	D48.0	D49.2
cord (cervical) (lumbar) (sacral) (thoracic)	C72.0	C79.49	—	D33.4	D43.4	D49.7
dura mater	C70.1	C79.49	—	D32.1	D42.1	D49.7
lumbosacral	C41.2	C79.51	—	D16.6	D48.0	D49.2
marrow NEC	C96.9	C79.52	—	—	D47.9	D49.89
membrane	C70.1	C79.49	—	D32.1	D42.1	D49.7
meninges	C70.1	C79.49	—	D32.1	D42.1	D49.7
nerve (root)	C47.9	C79.89	—	D36.10	D48.2	D49.2
pia mater	C70.1	C79.49	—	D32.1	D42.1	D49.7
root	C47.9	C79.89	—	D36.10	D48.2	D49.2
sacrum	C41.4	C79.51	—	D16.8	D48.0	D49.2
spleen, splenic NEC	C26.1	C78.89	D01.7	D13.9	D37.8	D49.0
flexure (colon)	C18.5	C78.5	D01.0	D12.3	D37.4	D49.0
stem, brain	C71.7	C79.31	—	D33.1	D43.1	D49.6
Stensen's duct	C07	C79.89	D00.00	D11.0	D37.030	D49.0
sternum	C41.3	C79.51	—	D16.7	D48.0	D49.2
stomach	C16.9	C78.89	D00.2	D13.1	D37.1	D49.0
antrum (pyloric)	C16.3	C78.89	D00.2	D13.1	D37.1	D49.0
body	C16.2	C78.89	D00.2	D13.1	D37.1	D49.0
cardia	C16.0	C78.89	D00.2	D13.1	D37.1	D49.0
cardiac orifice	C16.0	C78.89	D00.2	D13.1	D37.1	D49.0
corpus	C16.2	C78.89	D00.2	D13.1	D37.1	D49.0
fundus	C16.1	C78.89	D00.2	D13.1	D37.1	D49.0
greater curvature NEC	C16.6	C78.89	D00.2	D13.1	D37.1	D49.0
lesser curvature NEC	C16.5	C78.89	D00.2	D13.1	D37.1	D49.0

	Malignant Primary	Malignant Secondary	Ca in situ	Benign	Uncertain Behavior	Unspecified Behavior
stomach *(Continued)*						
overlapping lesion	C16.8	—	—	D13.1	—	—
prepylorus	C16.4	C78.89	D00.2	D13.1	D37.1	D49.0
pylorus	C16.4	C78.89	D00.2	D13.1	D37.1	D49.0
wall NEC	C16.9	C78.89	D00.2	D13.1	D37.1	D49.0
anterior NEC	C16.8	C78.89	D00.2	D13.1	D37.1	D49.0
posterior NEC	C16.8	C78.89	D00.2	D13.1	D37.1	D49.0
stroma, endometrial	C54.1	C79.82	D07.0	D26.1	D39.0	D49.59
stump, cervical	C53.8	C79.82	D06.7	D26.0	D39.0	D49.59
subcutaneous (nodule) (tissue) NEC — *see Neoplasm, connective tissue*						
subdural	C70.9	C79.32	—	D32.9	D42.9	D49.7
subglottis, subglottic	C32.2	C78.39	D02.0	D14.1	D38.0	D49.1
sublingual	C04.9	C79.89	D00.06	D10.2	D37.09	D49.0
gland or duct	C08.1	C79.89	D00.00	D11.7	D37.031	D49.0
submandibular gland	C08.0	C79.89	D00.00	D11.7	D37.032	D49.0
submaxillary gland or duct	C08.0	C79.89	D00.00	D11.7	D37.032	D49.0
submental	C76.0	C79.89	D09.8	D36.7	D48.7	D49.89
subpleural	C34.9-●	C78.0-●	D02.2-●	D14.3-●	D38.1	D49.1
substernal	C38.1	C78.1	—	D15.2	D38.3	D49.89
sudoriferous, sudoriparous gland, site unspecified	C44.90	C79.2	D04.9	D23.9	D48.5	D49.2
specified site — *see Neoplasm, skin*						
supraclavicular region	C76.0	C79.89	D09.8	D36.7	D48.7	D49.89
supraglottis	C32.1	C78.39	D02.0	D14.1	D38.0	D49.1
suprarenal	C74.9-●	C79.7-●	D09.3	D35.0-●	D44.1-●	D49.7
capsule	C74.9-●	C79.7-●	D09.3	D35.0-●	D44.1-●	D49.7
cortex	C74.0-●	C79.7-●	D09.3	D35.0-●	D44.1-●	D49.7
gland	C74.9-●	C79.7-●	D09.3	D35.0-●	D44.1-●	D49.7
medulla	C74.1-●	C79.7-●	D09.3	D35.0-●	D44.1-●	D49.7
suprasellar (region)	C71.9	C79.31	—	D33.2	D43.2	D49.6
supratentorial (brain) NEC	C71.0	C79.31	—	D33.0	D43.0	D49.6
sweat gland (apocrine) (eccrine), site unspecified	C44.90	C79.2	D04.9	D23.9	D48.5	D49.2
specified site — *see Neoplasm, skin*						
sympathetic nerve or nervous system NEC	C47.9	C79.89	—	D36.10	D48.2	D49.2
symphysis pubis	C41.4	C79.51	—	D16.8	D48.0	D49.2
synovial membrane — *see Neoplasm, connective tissue*						
tapetum, brain	C71.8	C79.31	—	D33.2	D43.2	D49.6

◀ New   ◀ Revised   ~~deleted~~ Deleted   ● Use Additional Character(s)

	Malignant Primary	Malignant Secondary	Ca in situ	Benign	Uncertain Behavior	Unspecified Behavior
tarsus (any bone)	C40.3-●	C79.51	—	D16.3-●	—	—
temple (skin) — *see also Neoplasm, skin, face*	C44.309	C79.2	D04.39	D23.39	D48.5	D49.2
temporal						
bone	C41.0	C79.51	—	D16.4-●	D48.0	D49.2
lobe or pole	C71.2	C79.31	—	D33.0	D43.0	D49.6
region	C76.0	C79.89	D09.8	D36.7	D48.7	D49.89
skin — *see also Neoplasm, skin, face*	C44.309	C79.2	D04.39	D23.39	D48.5	D49.2
tendon (sheath) — *see Neoplasm, connective tissue*						
tentorium (cerebelli)	C70.0	C79.32	—	D32.0	D42.0	D49.7
testis, testes	C62.9-●	C79.82	D07.69	D29.2-●	D40.1-●	D49.59
descended	C62.1-●	C79.82	D07.69	D29.2-●	D40.1-●	D49.59
ectopic	C62.0-●	C79.82	D07.69	D29.2-●	D40.1-●	D49.59
retained	C62.0-●	C79.82	D07.69	D29.2-●	D40.1-●	D49.59
scrotal	C62.1-●	C79.82	D07.69	D29.2-●	D40.1-●	D49.59
undescended	C62.0-●	C79.82	D07.69	D29.2-●	D40.1-●	D49.59
unspecified whether descended or undescended	C62.9-●	C79.82	D07.69	D29.2-●	D40.1-●	D49.59
thalamus	C71.0	C79.31	—	D33.0	D43.0	D49.6
thigh NEC	C76.5-●	C79.89	D04.7-●	D36.7	D48.7	D49.89
thorax, thoracic (cavity) (organs NEC)	C76.1	C79.89	D09.8	D36.7	D48.7	D49.89
duct	C49.3	C79.89	—	D21.3	D48.1	D49.2
wall NEC	C76.1	C79.89	D09.8	D36.7	D48.7	D49.89
throat	C14.0	C79.89	D00.08	D10.9	D37.05	D49.0
thumb NEC	C76.4-●	C79.89	D04.6-●	D36.7	D48.7	D49.89
thymus (gland)	C37	C79.89	D09.3	D15.0	D38.4	D49.89
thyroglossal duct	C73	C79.89	D09.3	D34	D44.0	D49.7
thyroid (gland)	C73	C79.89	D09.3	D34	D44.0	D49.7
cartilage	C32.3	C78.39	D02.0	D14.1	D38.0	D49.1
tibia (any part)	C40.2-●	C79.51	—	D16.2-●	—	—
toe NEC	C76.5-●	C79.89	D04.7-●	D36.7	D48.7	D49.89
tongue	C02.9	C79.89	D00.07	D10.1	D37.02	D49.0
anterior (two-thirds) NEC	C02.3	C79.89	D00.07	D10.1	D37.02	D49.0
dorsal surface	C02.0	C79.89	D00.07	D10.1	D37.02	D49.0
ventral surface	C02.2	C79.89	D00.07	D10.1	D37.02	D49.0
base (dorsal surface)	C01	C79.89	D00.07	D10.1	D37.02	D49.0
border (lateral)	C02.1	C79.89	D00.07	D10.1	D37.02	D49.0
dorsal surface NEC	C02.0	C79.89	D00.07	D10.1	D37.02	D49.0
fixed part NEC	C01	C79.89	D00.07	D10.1	D37.02	D49.0
foreamen cecum	C02.0	C79.89	D00.07	D10.1	D37.02	D49.0
frenulum linguae	C02.2	C79.89	D00.07	D10.1	D37.02	D49.0

	Malignant Primary	Malignant Secondary	Ca in situ	Benign	Uncertain Behavior	Unspecified Behavior
tongue *(Continued)*						
junctional zone	C02.8	C79.89	D00.07	D10.1	D37.02	D49.0
margin (lateral)	C02.1	C79.89	D00.07	D10.1	D37.02	D49.0
midline NEC	C02.0	C79.89	D00.07	D10.1	D37.02	D49.0
mobile part NEC	C02.3	C79.89	D00.07	D10.1	D37.02	D49.0
overlapping lesion	C02.8	—	—	—	—	—
posterior (third)	C01	C79.89	D00.07	D10.1	D37.02	D49.0
root	C01	C79.89	D00.07	D10.1	D37.02	D49.0
surface (dorsal)	C02.0	C79.89	D00.07	D10.1	D37.02	D49.0
base	C01	C79.89	D00.07	D10.1	D37.02	D49.0
ventral	C02.2	C79.89	D00.07	D10.1	D37.02	D49.0
tip	C02.1	C79.89	D00.07	D10.1	D37.02	D49.0
tonsil	C02.4	C79.89	D00.07	D10.1	D37.02	D49.0
tonsil	C09.9	C79.89	D00.08	D10.4	D37.05	D49.0
fauces, faucial	C09.9	C79.89	D00.08	D10.4	D37.05	D49.0
lingual	C02.4	C79.89	D00.07	D10.1	D37.02	D49.0
overlapping sites	C09.8	—	—	—	—	—
palatine	C09.9	C79.89	D00.08	D10.4	D37.05	D49.0
pharyngeal	C11.1	C79.89	D00.08	D10.6	D37.05	D49.0
pillar (anterior) (posterior)	C09.1	C79.89	D00.08	D10.5	D37.05	D49.0
tonsillar fossa	C09.0	C79.89	D00.08	D10.5	D37.05	D49.0
tooth socket NEC	C03.9	C79.89	D00.03	D10.39	D37.09	D49.0
trachea (cartilage) (mucosa)	C33	C78.39	D02.1	D14.2	D38.1	D49.1
overlapping lesion with bronchus or lung	C34.8-●	—	—	—	—	—
tracheobronchial	C34.8-●	C78.39	D02.1	D14.2	D38.1	D49.1
overlapping lesion with lung	C34.8-●	—	—	—	—	—
tragus — *see also Neoplasm, skin, ear*	C44.20-●	C79.2	D04.2-●	D23.2-●	D48.5	D49.2
trunk NEC	C76.8	C79.89	D04.5	D36.7	D48.7	D49.89
tubo-ovarian	C57.8	C79.82	D07.39	D28.7	D39.8	D49.59
tunica vaginalis	C63.7	C79.82	D07.69	D29.8	D40.8	D49.59
turbinate (bone)	C41.0	C79.51	—	D16.4-●	D48.0	D49.2
nasal	C30.0	C78.39	D02.3	D14.0	D38.5	D49.1
tympanic cavity	C30.1	C78.39	D02.3	D14.0	D38.5	D49.1
ulna (any part)	C40.0-●	C79.51	—	D16.0-●	—	—
umbilicus, umbilical — *see also Neoplasm, skin, trunk*	C44.509	C79.2	D04.5	D23.5	D48.5	D49.2
uncus, brain	C71.2	C79.31	—	D33.0	D43.0	D49.6
unknown site or unspecified	C80.1	C79.9	D09.9	D36.9	D48.9	D49.9
urachus	C67.7	C79.11	D09.0	D30.3	D41.4	D49.4
ureter, ureteral	C66.-●	C79.19	D09.19	D30.2-●	D41.2-●	D49.59
orifice (bladder)	C67.6	C79.11	D09.0	D30.3	D41.4	D49.4
ureter-bladder (junction)	C67.6	C79.11	D09.0	D30.3	D41.4	D49.4

◀ New   ◀ Revised   ~~deleted~~ Deleted   ● Use Additional Character(s)

	Malignant Primary	Malignant Secondary	Ca in situ	Benign	Uncertain Behavior	Unspecified Behavior
urethra, urethral (gland)	C68.0	C79.19	D09.19	D30.4	D41.3	D49.59
orifice, internal	C67.5	C79.11	D09.0	D30.3	D41.4	D49.4
urethrovaginal (septum)	C57.9	C79.82	D07.30	D28.9	D39.8	D49.59
urinary organ or system	C68.9	C79.10	D09.10	D30.9	D41.9	D49.59
bladder — *see Neoplasm, bladder*						
overlapping lesion	C68.8	—	—	—	—	—
specified sites NEC	C68.8	C79.19	D09.19	D30.8	D41.8	D49.59
utero-ovarian	C57.8	C79.82	D07.39	D28.7	D39.8	D49.59
ligament	C57.1	C79.82	D07.39	D28.2	D39.8	D49.59
uterosacral ligament	C57.3	C79.82	—	D28.2	D39.8	D49.59
uterus, uteri, uterine	C55	C79.82	D07.0	D26.9	D39.0	D49.59
adnexa NEC	C57.4	C79.82	D07.39	D28.7	D39.8	D49.59
body	C54.9	C79.82	D07.0	D26.1	D39.0	D49.59
cervix	C53.9	C79.82	D06.9	D26.0	D39.0	D49.59
cornu	C54.9	C79.82	D07.0	D26.1	D39.0	D49.59
corpus	C54.9	C79.82	D07.0	D26.1	D39.0	D49.59
endocervix (canal) (gland)	C53.0	C79.82	D06.0	D26.0	D39.0	D49.59
endometrium	C54.1	C79.82	D07.0	D26.1	D39.0	D49.59
exocervix	C53.1	C79.82	D06.1	D26.0	D39.0	D49.59
external os	C53.1	C79.82	D06.1	D26.0	D39.0	D49.59
fundus	C54.3	C79.82	D07.0	D26.1	D39.0	D49.59
internal os	C53.0	C79.82	D06.0	D26.0	D39.0	D49.59
isthmus	C54.0	C79.82	D07.0	D26.1	D39.0	D49.59
ligament	C57.3	C79.82	—	D28.2	D39.8	D49.59
broad	C57.1	C79.82	D07.39	D28.2	D39.8	D49.59
round	C57.2	C79.82	—	D28.2	D39.8	D49.59
lower segment	C54.0	C79.82	D07.0	D26.1	D39.0	D49.59
myometrium	C54.2	C79.82	D07.0	D26.1	D39.0	D49.59
overlapping sites	C54.8	—	—	—	—	—
squamocolumnar junction	C53.8	C79.82	D06.7	D26.0	D39.0	D49.59
tube	C57.0-•	C79.82	D07.39	D28.2	D39.8	D49.59
utricle, prostatic	C68.0	C79.19	D09.19	D30.4	D41.3	D49.59
uveal tract	C69.4-•	C79.49	D09.2-•	D31.4-•	D48.7	D49.89
uvula	C05.2	C79.89	D00.04	D10.39	D37.09	D49.0
vagina, vaginal (fornix) (vault) (wall)	C52	C79.82	D07.2	D28.1	D39.8	D49.59
vaginovesical	C57.9	C79.82	D07.30	D28.9	D39.9	D49.59
septum	C57.9	C79.82	D07.30	D28.9	D39.9	D49.59
vallecula (epiglottis)	C10.0	C79.89	D00.08	D10.5	D37.05	D49.0
vas deferens	C63.1-•	C79.82	D07.69	D29.8	D40.8	D49.59
vascular — *see Neoplasm, connective tissue*						

	Malignant Primary	Malignant Secondary	Ca in situ	Benign	Uncertain Behavior	Unspecified Behavior
Vater's ampulla	C24.1	C78.89	D01.5	D13.5	D37.6	D49.0
vein, venous — *see Neoplasm, connective tissue*						
vena cava (abdominal) (inferior)	C49.4	C79.89	—	D21.4	D48.1	D49.2
superior	C49.3	C79.89	—	D21.3	D48.1	D49.2
ventricle (cerebral) (floor) (lateral) (third)	C71.5	C79.31	—	D33.0	D43.0	D49.6
cardiac (left) (right)	C38.0	C79.89	—	D15.1	D48.7	D49.89
fourth	C71.7	C79.31	—	D33.1	D43.1	D49.6
ventricular band of larynx	C32.1	C78.39	D02.0	D14.1	D38.0	D49.1
ventriculus — *see Neoplasm, stomach*						
vermillion border — *see Neoplasm, lip*						
vermis, cerebellum	C71.6	C79.31	—	D33.1	D43.1	D49.6
vertebra (column)	C41.2	C79.51	—	D16.6	D48.0	D49.2
coccyx	C41.4	C79.51	—	D16.8-•	D48.0	D49.2
marrow NEC	C96.9	C79.52	—	—	D47.9	D49.89
sacrum	C41.4	C79.51	—	D16.8-•	D48.0	D49.2
vesical — *see Neoplasm, bladder*						
vesicle, seminal	C63.7	C79.82	D07.69	D29.8	D40.8	D49.59
vesicocervical tissue	C57.9	C79.82	D07.30	D28.9	D39.9	D49.59
vesicorectal	C76.3	C79.82	D09.8	D36.7	D48.7	D49.89
vesicovaginal	C57.9	C79.82	D07.30	D28.9	D39.9	D49.59
septum	C57.9	C79.82	D07.30	D28.9	D39.8	D49.59
vessel (blood) — *see Neoplasm, connective tissue*						
vestibular gland, greater	C51.0	C79.82	D07.1	D28.0	D39.8	D49.59
vestibule						
mouth	C06.1	C79.89	D00.00	D10.39	D37.09	D49.0
nose	C30.0	C78.39	D02.3	D14.0	D38.5	D49.1
Virchow's gland	C77.0	C77.0	—	D36.0	D48.7	D49.89
viscera NEC	C76.8	C79.89	D09.8	D36.7	D48.7	D49.89
vocal cords (true)	C32.0	C78.39	D02.0	D14.1	D38.0	D49.1
false	C32.1	C78.39	D02.0	D14.1	D38.0	D49.1
vomer	C41.0	C79.51	—	D16.4-•	D48.0	D49.2
vulva	C51.9	C79.82	D07.1	D28.0	D39.8	D49.59
vulvovaginal gland	C51.0	C79.82	D07.1	D28.0	D39.8	D49.59
Waldeyer's ring	C14.2	C79.89	D00.08	D10.9	D37.05	D49.0
Wharton's duct	C08.0	C79.89	D00.00	D11.7	D37.032	D49.0
white matter (central) (cerebral)	C71.0	C79.31	—	D33.0	D43.0	D49.6
windpipe	C33	C78.39	D02.1	D14.2	D38.1	D49.1

◀ New ◀ Revised ~~deleted~~ Deleted • Use Additional Character(s)

TABLE OF NEOPLASMS

	Malignant Primary	Malignant Secondary	Ca in situ	Benign	Uncertain Behavior	Unspecified Behavior
Wirsung's duct	C25.3	C78.89	DØ1.7	D13.6	D37.8	D49.Ø
wolffian (body) (duct)						
female	C57.7	C79.82	DØ7.39	D28.7	D39.8	D49.59
male	C63.7	C79.82	DØ7.69	D29.8	D4Ø.8	D49.59

	Malignant Primary	Malignant Secondary	Ca in situ	Benign	Uncertain Behavior	Unspecified Behavior
womb — *see Neoplasm, uterus*						
wrist NEC	C76.4-●	C79.89	DØ4.6-●	D36.7	D48.7	D49.89
xiphoid process	C41.3	C79.51	—	D16.7	D48.Ø	D49.2
Zuckerkandl organ	C75.5	C79.89	—	D35.6	D44.7	D49.7

TABLE OF NEOPLASMS

◀ New   ◀ Revised   ~~deleted~~ Deleted   ● Use Additional Character(s)

ICD-10-CM
Table of Drugs and Chemicals

ICD-10-CM
Table of Drugs and Chemicals

Substance	Poisoning, Accidental (Unintentional)	Poisoning, Intentional Self-Harm	Poisoning, Assault	Poisoning, Undetermined	Adverse Effect	Underdosing
#						
1-propanol	T51.3X1	T51.3X2	T51.3X3	T51.3X4	—	—
2-propanol	T51.2X1	T51.2X2	T51.2X3	T51.2X4	—	—
2,4-D (dichlorophen-oxyacetic acid)	T60.3X1	T60.3X2	T60.3X3	T60.3X4	—	—
2,4-toluene diisocyanate	T65.0X1	T65.0X2	T65.0X3	T65.0X4	—	—
2,4,5-T (trichloro-phenoxyacetic acid)	T60.1X1	T60.1X2	T60.1X3	T60.1X4	—	—
3,4-methylenedioxy-methamphetamine	T43.641	T43.642	T43.643	T43.644		
14-hydroxydihydro-morphinone	T40.2X1	T40.2X2	T40.2X3	T40.2X4	T40.2X5	T40.2X6
A						
ABOB	T37.5X1	T37.5X2	T37.5X3	T37.5X4	T37.5X5	T37.5X6
Abrine	T62.2X1	T62.2X2	T62.2X3	T62.2X4	—	—
Abrus (seed)	T62.2X1	T62.2X2	T62.2X3	T62.2X4	—	—
Absinthe	T51.0X1	T51.0X2	T51.0X3	T51.0X4	—	—
beverage	T51.0X1	T51.0X2	T51.0X3	T51.0X4	—	—
Acaricide	T60.8X1	T60.8X2	T60.8X3	T60.8X4	—	—
Acebutolol	T44.7X1	T44.7X2	T44.7X3	T44.7X4	T44.7X5	T44.7X6
Acecarbromal	T42.6X1	T42.6X2	T42.6X3	T42.6X4	T42.6X5	T42.6X6
Aceclidine	T44.1X1	T44.1X2	T44.1X3	T44.1X4	T44.1X5	T44.1X6
Acedapsone	T37.0X1	T37.0X2	T37.0X3	T37.0X4	T37.0X5	T37.0X6
Acefylline piperazine	T48.6X1	T48.6X2	T48.6X3	T48.6X4	T48.6X5	T48.6X6
Acemorphan	T40.2X1	T40.2X2	T40.2X3	T40.2X4	T40.2X5	T40.2X6
Acenocoumarin	T45.511	T45.512	T45.513	T45.514	T45.515	T45.516
Acenocoumarol	T45.511	T45.512	T45.513	T45.514	T45.515	T45.516
Acepifylline	T48.6X1	T48.6X2	T48.6X3	T48.6X4	T48.6X5	T48.6X6
Acepromazine	T43.3X1	T43.3X2	T43.3X3	T43.3X4	T43.3X5	T43.3X6
Acesulfamethoxypyridazine	T37.0X1	T37.0X2	T37.0X3	T37.0X4	T37.0X5	T37.0X6
Acetal	T52.8X1	T52.8X2	T52.8X3	T52.8X4	—	—
Acetaldehyde (vapor)	T52.8X1	T52.8X2	T52.8X3	T52.8X4	—	—
liquid	T65.891	T65.892	T65.893	T65.894	—	—
P-Acetamidophenol	T39.1X1	T39.1X2	T39.1X3	T39.1X4	T39.1X5	T39.1X6
Acetaminophen	T39.1X1	T39.1X2	T39.1X3	T39.1X4	T39.1X5	T39.1X6
Acetaminosalol	T39.1X1	T39.1X2	T39.1X3	T39.1X4	T39.1X5	T39.1X6
Acetanilide	T39.1X1	T39.1X2	T39.1X3	T39.1X4	T39.1X5	T39.1X6
Acetarsol	T37.3X1	T37.3X2	T37.3X3	T37.3X4	T37.3X5	T37.3X6
Acetazolamide	T50.2X1	T50.2X2	T50.2X3	T50.2X4	T50.2X5	T50.2X6
Acetiamine	T45.2X1	T45.2X2	T45.2X3	T45.2X4	T45.2X5	T45.2X6
Acetic						
acid	T54.2X1	T54.2X2	T54.2X3	T54.2X4	—	—
with sodium acetate (ointment)	T49.3X1	T49.3X2	T49.3X3	T49.3X4	T49.3X5	T49.3X6

Substance	Poisoning, Accidental (Unintentional)	Poisoning, Intentional Self-Harm	Poisoning, Assault	Poisoning, Undetermined	Adverse Effect	Underdosing
Acetic *(Continued)*						
acid *(Continued)*						
ester (solvent) (vapor)	T52.8X1	T52.8X2	T52.8X3	T52.8X4	—	—
irrigating solution	T50.3X1	T50.3X2	T50.3X3	T50.3X4	T50.3X5	T50.3X6
medicinal (lotion)	T49.2X1	T49.2X2	T49.2X3	T49.2X4	T49.2X5	T49.2X6
anhydride	T65.891	T65.892	T65.893	T65.894		
ether (vapor)	T52.8X1	T52.8X2	T52.8X3	T52.8X4	—	—
Acetohexamide	T38.3X1	T38.3X2	T38.3X3	T38.3X4	T38.3X5	T38.3X6
Acetohydroxamic acid	T50.991	T50.992	T50.993	T50.994	T50.995	T50.996
Acetomenaphthone	T45.7X1	T45.7X2	T45.7X3	T45.7X4	T45.7X5	T45.7X6
Acetomorphine	T40.1X1	T40.1X2	T40.1X3	T40.1X4	—	—
Acetone (oils)	T52.4X1	T52.4X2	T52.4X3	T52.4X4	—	—
chlorinated	T52.4X1	T52.4X2	T52.4X3	T52.4X4	—	—
vapor	T52.4X1	T52.4X2	T52.4X3	T52.4X4	—	—
Acetonitrile	T52.8X1	T52.8X2	T52.8X3	T52.8X4	—	—
Acetophenazine	T43.3X1	T43.3X2	T43.3X3	T43.3X4	T43.3X5	T43.3X6
Acetophenetedin	T39.1X1	T39.1X2	T39.1X3	T39.1X4	T39.1X5	T39.1X6
Acetophenone	T52.4X1	T52.4X2	T52.4X3	T52.4X4	—	—
Acetorphine	T40.2X1	T40.2X2	T40.2X3	T40.2X4	—	—
Acetosulfone (sodium)	T37.1X1	T37.1X2	T37.1X3	T37.1X4	T37.1X5	T37.1X6
Acetrizoate (sodium)	T50.8X1	T50.8X2	T50.8X3	T50.8X4	T50.8X5	T50.8X6
Acetylcarbromal	T42.6X1	T42.6X2	T42.6X3	T42.6X4	T42.6X5	T42.6X6
Acetrizoic acid	T50.8X1	T50.8X2	T50.8X3	T50.8X4	T50.8X5	T50.8X6
Acetyl						
bromide	T53.6X1	T53.6X2	T53.6X3	T53.6X4	—	—
chloride	T53.6X1	T53.6X2	T53.6X3	T53.6X4	—	—
Acetylcholine						
chloride	T44.1X1	T44.1X2	T44.1X3	T44.1X4	T44.1X5	T44.1X6
derivative	T44.1X1	T44.1X2	T44.1X3	T44.1X4	T44.1X5	T44.1X6
Acetylcysteine	T48.4X1	T48.4X2	T48.4X3	T48.4X4	T48.4X5	T48.4X6
Acetyldigitoxin	T46.0X1	T46.0X2	T46.0X3	T46.0X4	T46.0X5	T46.0X6
Acetyldigoxin	T46.0X1	T46.0X2	T46.0X3	T46.0X4	T46.0X5	T46.0X6
Acetyldihydrocodeine	T40.2X1	T40.2X2	T40.2X3	T40.2X4	—	—
Acetyldihydrocodeinone	T40.2X1	T40.2X2	T40.2X3	T40.2X4	—	—
Acetylene (gas)	T59.891	T59.892	T59.893	T59.894	—	—
dichloride	T53.6X1	T53.6X2	T53.6X3	T53.6X4	—	—
incomplete combustion of	T58.11	T58.12	T58.13	T58.14	—	—
industrial	T59.891	T59.892	T59.893	T59.894	—	—
tetrachloride	T53.6X1	T53.6X2	T53.6X3	T53.6X4	—	—
vapor	T53.6X1	T53.6X2	T53.6X3	T53.6X4	—	—
Acetylphenylhydrazine	T39.8X1	T39.8X2	T39.8X3	T39.8X4	T39.8X5	T39.8X6
Acetylpheneturide	T42.6X1	T42.6X2	T42.6X3	T42.6X4	T42.6X5	T42.6X6

◀ New ◀ Revised ~~deleted~~ Deleted

Substance	External Cause (T-Code)					
	Poisoning, Accidental (Unintentional)	Poisoning, Intentional Self-Harm	Poisoning, Assault	Poisoning, Undetermined	Adverse Effect	Underdosing
Acetylsalicylic acid (salts)	T39.011	T39.012	T39.013	T39.014	T39.015	T39.016
enteric coated	T39.011	T39.012	T39.013	T39.014	T39.015	T39.016
Acetylsulfamethoxypyridazine	T37.0X1	T37.0X2	T37.0X3	T37.0X4	T37.0X5	T37.0X6
Achromycin	T36.4X1	T36.4X2	T36.4X3	T36.4X4	T36.4X5	T36.4X6
ophthalmic preparation	T49.5X1	T49.5X2	T49.5X3	T49.5X4	T49.5X5	T49.5X6
topical NEC	T49.0X1	T49.0X2	T49.0X3	T49.0X4	T49.0X5	T49.0X6
Aciclovir	T37.5X1	T37.5X2	T37.5X3	T37.5X4	T37.5X5	T37.5X6
Acid (corrosive) NEC	T54.2X1	T54.2X2	T54.2X3	T54.2X4	—	—
Acidifying agent NEC	T50.901	T50.902	T50.903	T50.904	T50.905	T50.906
Acipimox	T46.6X1	T46.6X2	T46.6X3	T46.6X4	T46.6X5	T46.6X6
Acitretin	T50.991	T50.992	T50.993	T50.994	T50.995	T50.996
Aclarubicin	T45.1X1	T45.1X2	T45.1X3	T45.1X4	T45.1X5	T45.1X6
Aclatonium napadisilate	T48.1X1	T48.1X2	T48.1X3	T48.1X4	T48.1X5	T48.1X6
Aconite (wild)	T46.991	T46.992	T46.993	T46.994	T46.995	T46.996
Aconitine	T46.991	T46.992	T46.993	T46.994	T46.995	T46.996
Aconitum ferox	T46.991	T46.992	T46.993	T46.994	T46.995	T46.996
Acridine	T65.6X1	T65.6X2	T65.6X3	T65.6X4	—	—
vapor	T59.891	T59.892	T59.893	T59.894	—	—
Acriflavine	T37.91	T37.92	T37.93	T37.94	T37.95	T37.96
Acriflavinium chloride	T49.0X1	T49.0X2	T49.0X3	T49.0X4	T49.0X5	T49.0X6
Acrinol	T49.0X1	T49.0X2	T49.0X3	T49.0X4	T49.0X5	T49.0X6
Acrisorcin	T49.0X1	T49.0X2	T49.0X3	T49.0X4	T49.0X5	T49.0X6
Acrivastine	T45.0X1	T45.0X2	T45.0X3	T45.0X4	T45.0X5	T45.0X6
Acrolein (gas)	T59.891	T59.892	T59.893	T59.894	—	—
liquid	T54.1X1	T54.1X2	T54.1X3	T54.1X4	—	—
Acrylamide	T65.891	T65.892	T65.893	T65.894	—	—
Acrylic resin	T49.3X1	T49.3X2	T49.3X3	T49.3X4	T49.3X5	T49.3X6
Acrylonitrile	T65.891	T65.892	T65.893	T65.894	—	—
Actaea spicata	T62.2X1	T62.2X2	T62.2X3	T62.2X4	—	—
berry	T62.1X1	T62.1X2	T62.1X3	T62.1X4	—	—
Acterol	T37.3X1	T37.3X2	T37.3X3	T37.3X4	T37.3X5	T37.3X6
ACTH	T38.811	T38.812	T38.813	T38.814	T38.815	T38.816
Actinomycin C	T45.1X1	T45.1X2	T45.1X3	T45.1X4	T45.1X5	T45.1X6
Actinomycin D	T45.1X1	T45.1X2	T45.1X3	T45.1X4	T45.1X5	T45.1X6
Activated charcoal — see also Charcoal, medicinal	T47.6X1	T47.6X2	T47.6X3	T47.6X4	T47.6X5	T47.6X6
Acyclovir	T37.5X1	T37.5X2	T37.5X3	T37.5X4	T37.5X5	T37.5X6
Adenine	T45.2X1	T45.2X2	T45.2X3	T45.2X4	T45.2X5	T45.2X6
arabinoside	T37.5X1	T37.5X2	T37.5X3	T37.5X4	T37.5X5	T37.5X6
Adenosine (phosphate)	T46.2X1	T46.2X2	T46.2X3	T46.2X4	T46.2X5	T46.2X6
ADH	T38.891	T38.892	T38.893	T38.894	T38.895	T38.896
Adhesive NEC	T65.891	T65.892	T65.893	T65.894	—	—

Substance	External Cause (T-Code)					
	Poisoning, Accidental (Unintentional)	Poisoning, Intentional Self-Harm	Poisoning, Assault	Poisoning, Undetermined	Adverse Effect	Underdosing
Adicillin	T36.0X1	T36.0X2	T36.0X3	T36.0X4	T36.0X5	T36.0X6
Adiphenine	T44.3X1	T44.3X2	T44.3X3	T44.3X4	T44.3X5	T44.3X6
Adipiodone	T50.8X1	T50.8X2	T50.8X3	T50.8X4	T50.8X5	T50.8X6
Adjunct, pharmaceutical	T50.901	T50.902	T50.903	T50.904	T50.905	T50.906
Adrenal (extract, cortex or medulla) (glucocorticoids) (hormones) (mineralo corticoids)	T38.0X1	T38.0X2	T38.0X3	T38.0X4	T38.0X5	T38.0X6
ENT agent	T49.6X1	T49.6X2	T49.6X3	T49.6X4	T49.6X5	T49.6X6
ophthalmic preparation	T49.5X1	T49.5X2	T49.5X3	T49.5X4	T49.5X5	T49.5X6
topical NEC	T49.0X1	T49.0X2	T49.0X3	T49.0X4	T49.0X5	T49.0X6
Adrenaline	T44.5X1	T44.5X2	T44.5X3	T44.5X4	T44.5X5	T44.5X6
Adrenalin — see Adrenaline						
Adrenergic NEC	T44.901	T44.902	T44.903	T44.904	T44.905	T44.906
blocking agent NEC	T44.8X1	T44.8X2	T44.8X3	T44.8X4	T44.8X5	T44.8X6
beta, heart	T44.7X1	T44.7X2	T44.7X3	T44.7X4	T44.7X5	T44.7X6
specified NEC	T44.991	T44.992	T44.993	T44.994	T44.995	T44.996
Adrenochrome						
(mono) semicarbazone	T46.991	T46.992	T46.993	T46.994	T46.995	T46.996
derivative	T46.991	T46.992	T46.993	T46.994	T46.995	T46.996
Adrenocorticotrophic hormone	T38.811	T38.812	T38.813	T38.814	T38.815	T38.816
Adrenocorticotrophin	T38.811	T38.812	T38.813	T38.814	T38.815	T38.816
Adriamycin	T45.1X1	T45.1X2	T45.1X3	T45.1X4	T45.1X5	T45.1X6
Aerosol spray NEC	T65.91	T65.92	T65.93	T65.94	—	—
Aerosporin	T36.8X1	T36.8X2	T36.8X3	T36.8X4	T36.8X5	T36.8X6
ENT agent	T49.6X1	T49.6X2	T49.6X3	T49.6X4	T49.6X5	T49.6X6
ophthalmic preparation	T49.5X1	T49.5X2	T49.5X3	T49.5X4	T49.5X5	T49.5X6
topical NEC	T49.0X1	T49.0X2	T49.0X3	T49.0X4	T49.0X5	T49.0X6
Aethusa cynapium	T62.2X1	T62.2X2	T62.2X3	T62.2X4	—	—
Afghanistan black	T40.7X1	T40.7X2	T40.7X3	T40.7X4	T40.7X5	T40.7X6
Aflatoxin	T64.01	T64.02	T64.03	T64.04	—	—
Afloqualone	T42.8X1	T42.8X2	T42.8X3	T42.8X4	T42.8X5	T42.8X6
African boxwood	T62.2X1	T62.2X2	T62.2X3	T62.2X4	—	—
Agar	T47.4X1	T47.4X2	T47.4X3	T47.4X4	T47.4X5	T47.4X6
Agonist						
predominantly						
alpha-adrenoreceptor	T44.4X1	T44.4X2	T44.4X3	T44.4X4	T44.4X5	T44.4X6
beta-adrenoreceptor	T44.5X1	T44.5X2	T44.5X3	T44.5X4	T44.5X5	T44.5X6
Agricultural agent NEC	T65.91	T65.92	T65.93	T65.94	—	—
Agrypnal	T42.3X1	T42.3X2	T42.3X3	T42.3X4	T42.3X5	T42.3X6
AHLG	T50.Z11	T50.Z12	T50.Z13	T50.Z14	T50.Z15	T50.Z16
Air contaminant(s), source/type NOS	T65.91	T65.92	T65.93	T65.94	—	—

◄ New   ◀ Revised   ~~deleted~~ Deleted

Substance	Poisoning, Accidental (Unintentional)	Poisoning, Intentional Self-Harm	Poisoning, Assault	Poisoning, Undetermined	Adverse Effect	Underdosing
Ajmaline	T46.2X1	T46.2X2	T46.2X3	T46.2X4	T46.2X5	T46.2X6
Akritoin	T37.8X1	T37.8X2	T37.8X3	T37.8X4	T37.8X5	T37.8X6
Akee	T62.1X1	T62.1X2	T62.1X3	T62.1X4	—	—
Akrinol	T49.0X1	T49.0X2	T49.0X3	T49.0X4	T49.0X5	T49.0X6
Alacepril	T46.4X1	T46.4X2	T46.4X3	T46.4X4	T46.4X5	T46.4X6
Alantolactone	T37.4X1	T37.4X2	T37.4X3	T37.4X4	T37.4X5	T37.4X6
Albamycin	T36.8X1	T36.8X2	T36.8X3	T36.8X4	T36.8X5	T36.8X6
Albendazole	T37.4X1	T37.4X2	T37.4X3	T37.4X4	T37.4X5	T37.4X6
Albumin						
bovine	T45.8X1	T45.8X2	T45.8X3	T45.8X4	T45.8X5	T45.8X6
human serum	T45.8X1	T45.8X2	T45.8X3	T45.8X4	T45.8X5	T45.8X6
salt-poor	T45.8X1	T45.8X2	T45.8X3	T45.8X4	T45.8X5	T45.8X6
normal human serum	T45.8X1	T45.8X2	T45.8X3	T45.8X4	T45.8X5	T45.8X6
Albuterol	T48.6X1	T48.6X2	T48.6X3	T48.6X4	T48.6X5	T48.6X6
Albutoin	T42.0X1	T42.0X2	T42.0X3	T42.0X4	T42.0X5	T42.0X6
Alclometasone	T49.0X1	T49.0X2	T49.0X3	T49.0X4	T49.0X5	T49.0X6
Alcohol	T51.91	T51.92	T51.93	T51.94	—	—
absolute	T51.0X1	T51.0X2	T51.0X3	T51.0X4	—	—
beverage	T51.0X1	T51.0X2	T51.0X3	T51.0X4	—	—
allyl	T51.8X1	T51.8X2	T51.8X3	T51.8X4	—	—
amyl	T51.3X1	T51.3X2	T51.3X3	T51.3X4	—	—
antifreeze	T51.1X1	T51.1X2	T51.1X3	T51.1X4	—	—
beverage	T51.0X1	T51.0X2	T51.0X3	T51.0X4	—	—
butyl	T51.3X1	T51.3X2	T51.3X3	T51.3X4	—	—
dehydrated	T51.0X1	T51.0X2	T51.0X3	T51.0X4	—	—
beverage	T51.0X1	T51.0X2	T51.0X3	T51.0X4	—	—
denatured	T51.0X1	T51.0X2	T51.0X3	T51.0X4	—	—
deterrent NEC	T50.6X1	T50.6X2	T50.6X3	T50.6X4	T50.6X5	T50.6X6
diagnostic (gastric function)	T50.8X1	T50.8X2	T50.8X3	T50.8X4	T50.8X5	T50.8X6
ethyl	T51.0X1	T51.0X2	T51.0X3	T51.0X4	—	—
beverage	T51.0X1	T51.0X2	T51.0X3	T51.0X4	—	—
grain	T51.0X1	T51.0X2	T51.0X3	T51.0X4	—	—
beverage	T51.0X1	T51.0X2	T51.0X3	T51.0X4	—	—
industrial	T51.0X1	T51.0X2	T51.0X3	T51.0X4	—	—
isopropyl	T51.2X1	T51.2X2	T51.2X3	T51.2X4	—	—
methyl	T51.1X1	T51.1X2	T51.1X3	T51.1X4	—	—
preparation for consumption	T51.0X1	T51.0X2	T51.0X3	T51.0X4	—	—
propyl	T51.3X1	T51.3X2	T51.3X3	T51.3X4	—	—
secondary	T51.2X1	T51.2X2	T51.2X3	T51.2X4	—	—
radiator	T51.1X1	T51.1X2	T51.1X3	T51.1X4	—	—
rubbing	T51.2X1	T51.2X2	T51.2X3	T51.2X4	—	—
specified type NEC	T51.8X1	T51.8X2	T51.8X3	T51.8X4	—	—

Substance	Poisoning, Accidental (Unintentional)	Poisoning, Intentional Self-Harm	Poisoning, Assault	Poisoning, Undetermined	Adverse Effect	Underdosing
Alcohol *(Continued)*						
surgical	T51.0X1	T51.0X2	T51.0X3	T51.0X4	—	—
vapor (from any type of Alcohol)	T59.891	T59.892	T59.893	T59.894	—	—
wood	T51.1X1	T51.1X2	T51.1X3	T51.1X4	—	—
Alcuronium (chloride)	T48.1X1	T48.1X2	T48.1X3	T48.1X4	T48.1X5	T48.1X6
Aldactone	T50.0X1	T50.0X2	T50.0X3	T50.0X4	T50.0X5	T50.0X6
Aldesulfone sodium	T37.1X1	T37.1X2	T37.1X3	T37.1X4	T37.1X5	T37.1X6
Aldicarb	T60.0X1	T60.0X2	T60.0X3	T60.0X4	—	—
Aldomet	T46.5X1	T46.5X2	T46.5X3	T46.5X4	T46.5X5	T46.5X6
Aldosterone	T50.0X1	T50.0X2	T50.0X3	T50.0X4	T50.0X5	T50.0X6
Aldrin (dust)	T60.1X1	T60.1X2	T60.1X3	T60.1X4	—	—
Aleve — *see Naproxen*						
Alexitol sodium	T47.1X1	T47.1X2	T47.1X3	T47.1X4	T47.1X5	T47.1X6
Alfacalcidol	T45.2X1	T45.2X2	T45.2X3	T45.2X4	T45.2X5	T45.2X6
Alfadolone	T41.1X1	T41.1X2	T41.1X3	T41.1X4	T41.1X5	T41.1X6
Alfaxalone	T41.1X1	T41.1X2	T41.1X3	T41.1X4	T41.1X5	T41.1X6
Alfentanil	T40.4X1	T40.4X2	T40.4X3	T40.4X4	T40.4X5	T40.4X6
Alfuzosin (hydrochloride)	T44.8X1	T44.8X2	T44.8X3	T44.8X4	T44.8X5	T44.8X6
Algae (harmful) (toxin)	T65.821	T65.822	T65.823	T65.824	—	—
Algeldrate	T47.1X1	T47.1X2	T47.1X3	T47.1X4	T47.1X5	T47.1X6
Algin	T47.8X1	T47.8X2	T47.8X3	T47.8X4	T47.8X5	T47.8X6
Alglucerase	T45.3X1	T45.3X2	T45.3X3	T45.3X4	T45.3X5	T45.3X6
Alidase	T45.3X1	T45.3X2	T45.3X3	T45.3X4	T45.3X5	T45.3X6
Alimemazine	T43.3X1	T43.3X2	T43.3X3	T43.3X4	T43.3X5	T43.3X6
Aliphatic thiocyanates	T65.0X1	T65.0X2	T65.0X3	T65.0X4	—	—
Alizapride	T45.0X1	T45.0X2	T45.0X3	T45.0X4	T45.0X5	T45.0X6
Alkali (caustic)	T54.3X1	T54.3X2	T54.3X3	T54.3X4	—	—
Alkalizing agent NEC	T50.901	T50.902	T50.903	T50.904	T50.905	T50.906
Alkaline antiseptic solution (aromatic)	T49.6X1	T49.6X2	T49.6X3	T49.6X4	T49.6X5	T49.6X6
Alkalinizing agents (medicinal)	T50.901	T50.902	T50.903	T50.904	T50.905	T50.906
Alka-seltzer	T39.011	T39.012	T39.013	T39.014	T39.015	T39.016
Alkavervir	T46.5X1	T46.5X2	T46.5X3	T46.5X4	T46.5X5	T46.5X6
Alkonium (bromide)	T49.0X1	T49.0X2	T49.0X3	T49.0X4	T49.0X5	T49.0X6
Alkylating drug NEC	T45.1X1	T45.1X2	T45.1X3	T45.1X4	T45.1X5	T45.1X6
antimyeloproliferative	T45.1X1	T45.1X2	T45.1X3	T45.1X4	T45.1X5	T45.1X6
lymphatic	T45.1X1	T45.1X2	T45.1X3	T45.1X4	T45.1X5	T45.1X6
Alkylisocyanate	T65.0X1	T65.0X2	T65.0X3	T65.0X4	—	—
Allantoin	T49.411	T49.412	T49.413	T49.414	T49.415	T49.416
Allegron	T43.0X1	T43.0X2	T43.0X3	T43.0X4	T43.0X5	T43.0X6
Allethrin	T49.0X1	T49.0X2	T49.0X3	T49.0X4	T49.0X5	T49.0X6
Allobarbital	T42.3X1	T42.3X2	T42.3X3	T42.3X4	T42.3X5	T42.3X6

◀ New   ◀ Revised   ~~deleted~~ Deleted

TABLE OF DRUGS AND CHEMICALS

Substance	External Cause (T-Code)					
	Poisoning, Accidental (Unintentional)	Poisoning, Intentional Self-Harm	Poisoning, Assault	Poisoning, Undetermined	Adverse Effect	Underdosing
Allopurinol	T50.4X1	T50.4X2	T50.4X3	T50.4X4	T50.4X5	T50.4X6
Allyl						
alcohol	T51.8X1	T51.8X2	T51.8X3	T51.8X4	—	—
disulfide	T46.6X1	T46.6X2	T46.6X3	T46.6X4	T46.6X5	T46.6X6
Allylestrenol	T38.5X1	T38.5X2	T38.5X3	T38.5X4	T38.5X5	T38.5X6
Allylisopropylacetylurea	T42.6X1	T42.6X2	T42.6X3	T42.6X4	T42.6X5	T42.6X6
Allylisopropylmalonylurea	T42.3X1	T42.3X2	T42.3X3	T42.3X4	T42.3X5	T42.3X6
Allylthiourea	T49.3X1	T49.3X2	T49.3X3	T49.3X4	T49.3X5	T49.3X6
Allyltribromide	T42.6X1	T42.6X2	T42.6X3	T42.6X4	T42.6X5	T42.6X6
Allypropymal	T42.3X1	T42.3X2	T42.3X3	T42.3X4	T42.3X5	T42.3X6
Almagate	T47.1X1	T47.1X2	T47.1X3	T47.1X4	T47.1X5	T47.1X6
Almasilate	T47.1X1	T47.1X2	T47.1X3	T47.1X4	T47.1X5	T47.1X6
Almitrine	T50.7X1	T50.7X2	T50.7X3	T50.7X4	T50.7X5	T50.7X6
Aloes	T47.2X1	T47.2X2	T47.2X3	T47.2X4	T47.2X5	T47.2X6
Aloglutamol	T47.1X1	T47.1X2	T47.1X3	T47.1X4	T47.1X5	T47.1X6
Aloin	T47.2X1	T47.2X2	T47.2X3	T47.2X4	T47.2X5	T47.2X6
Aloxidone	T42.2X1	T42.2X2	T42.2X3	T42.2X4	T42.2X5	T42.2X6
Alpha						
acetyldigoxin	T46.0X1	T46.0X2	T46.0X3	T46.0X4	T46.0X5	T46.0X6
adrenergic blocking drug	T44.6X1	T44.6X2	T44.6X3	T44.6X4	T44.6X5	T44.6X6
amylase	T45.3X1	T45.3X2	T45.3X3	T45.3X4	T45.3X5	T45.3X6
tocoferol (acetate)	T45.2X1	T45.2X2	T45.2X3	T45.2X4	T45.2X5	T45.2X6
tocopherol	T45.2X1	T45.2X2	T45.2X3	T45.2X4	T45.2X5	T45.2X6
Alphadolone	T41.1X1	T41.1X2	T41.1X3	T41.1X4	T41.1X5	T41.1X6
Alphaprodine	T40.4X1	T40.4X2	T40.4X3	T40.4X4	T40.4X5	T40.4X6
Alphaxalone	T41.1X1	T41.1X2	T41.1X3	T41.1X4	T41.1X5	T41.1X6
Alprazolam	T42.4X1	T42.4X2	T42.4X3	T42.4X4	T42.4X5	T42.4X6
Alprenolol	T44.7X1	T44.7X2	T44.7X3	T44.7X4	T44.7X5	T44.7X6
Alprostadil	T46.7X1	T46.7X2	T46.7X3	T46.7X4	T46.7X5	T46.7X6
Alsactide	T38.811	T38.812	T38.813	T38.814	T38.815	T38.816
Alseroxylon	T46.5X1	T46.5X2	T46.5X3	T46.5X4	T46.5X5	T46.5X6
Alteplase	T45.611	T45.612	T45.613	T45.614	T45.615	T45.616
Altizide	T50.2X1	T50.2X2	T50.2X3	T50.2X4	T50.2X5	T50.2X6
Altretamine	T45.1X1	T45.1X2	T45.1X3	T45.1X4	T45.1X5	T45.1X6
Alum (medicinal)	T49.4X1	T49.4X2	T49.4X3	T49.4X4	T49.4X5	T49.4X6
nonmedicinal (ammonium) (potassium)	T56.891	T56.892	T56.893	T56.894	—	—
Aluminium, aluminum						
acetate	T49.2X1	T49.2X2	T49.2X3	T49.2X4	T49.2X5	T49.2X6
solution	T49.0X1	T49.0X2	T49.0X3	T49.0X4	T49.0X5	T49.0X6
aspirin	T39.011	T39.012	T39.013	T39.014	T39.015	T39.016
bis (acetylsalicylate)	T39.011	T39.012	T39.013	T39.014	T39.015	T39.016

Substance	External Cause (T-Code)					
	Poisoning, Accidental (Unintentional)	Poisoning, Intentional Self-Harm	Poisoning, Assault	Poisoning, Undetermined	Adverse Effect	Underdosing
Aluminium, aluminum (Continued)						
carbonate (gel, basic)	T47.1X1	T47.1X2	T47.1X3	T47.1X4	T47.1X5	T47.1X6
chlorhydroxide-complex	T47.1X1	T47.1X2	T47.1X3	T47.1X4	T47.1X5	T47.1X6
chloride	T49.2X1	T49.2X2	T49.2X3	T49.2X4	T49.2X5	T49.2X6
clofibrate	T46.6X1	T46.6X2	T46.6X3	T46.6X4	T46.6X5	T46.6X6
diacetate	T49.2X1	T49.2X2	T49.2X3	T49.2X4	T49.2X5	T49.2X6
glycinate	T47.1X1	T47.1X2	T47.1X3	T47.1X4	T47.1X5	T47.1X6
hydroxide (gel)	T47.1X1	T47.1X2	T47.1X3	T47.1X4	T47.1X5	T47.1X6
hydroxide-magnesium carb. gel	T47.1X1	T47.1X2	T47.1X3	T47.1X4	T47.1X5	T47.1X6
magnesium silicate	T47.1X1	T47.1X2	T47.1X3	T47.1X4	T47.1X5	T47.1X6
nicotinate	T46.7X1	T46.7X2	T46.7X3	T46.7X4	T46.7X5	T46.7X6
ointment (surgical) (topical)	T49.3X1	T49.3X2	T49.3X3	T49.3X4	T49.3X5	T49.3X6
phosphate	T47.1X1	T47.1X2	T47.1X3	T47.1X4	T47.1X5	T47.1X6
salicylate	T39.091	T39.092	T39.093	T39.094	T39.095	T39.096
silicate	T47.1X1	T47.1X2	T47.1X3	T47.1X4	T47.1X5	T47.1X6
sodium silicate	T47.1X1	T47.1X2	T47.1X3	T47.1X4	T47.1X5	T47.1X6
subacetate	T49.2X1	T49.2X2	T49.2X3	T49.2X4	T49.2X5	T49.2X6
sulfate	T49.0X1	T49.0X2	T49.0X3	T49.0X4	T49.0X5	T49.0X6
tannate	T47.6X1	T47.6X2	T47.6X3	T47.6X4	T47.6X5	T47.6X6
topical NEC	T49.3X1	T49.3X2	T49.3X3	T49.3X4	T49.3X5	T49.3X6
Alurate	T42.3X1	T42.3X2	T42.3X3	T42.3X4	T42.3X5	T42.3X6
Alverine	T44.3X1	T44.3X2	T44.3X3	T44.3X4	T44.3X5	T44.3X6
Alvodine	T40.2X1	T40.2X2	T40.2X3	T40.2X4	T40.2X5	T40.2X6
Amanita phalloides	T62.0X1	T62.0X2	T62.0X3	T62.0X4	—	—
Amanitine	T62.0X1	T62.0X2	T62.0X3	T62.0X4	—	—
Amantadine	T42.8X1	T42.8X2	T42.8X3	T42.8X4	T42.8X5	T42.8X6
Ambazone	T49.6X1	T49.6X2	T49.6X3	T49.6X4	T49.6X5	T49.6X6
Ambenonium (chloride)	T44.0X1	T44.0X2	T44.0X3	T44.0X4	T44.0X5	T44.0X6
Ambroxol	T48.4X1	T48.4X2	T48.4X3	T48.4X4	T48.4X5	T48.4X6
Ambuphylline	T48.6X1	T48.6X2	T48.6X3	T48.6X4	T48.6X5	T48.6X6
Ambutonium bromide	T44.3X1	T44.3X2	T44.3X3	T44.3X4	T44.3X5	T44.3X6
Amcinonide	T49.0X1	T49.0X2	T49.0X3	T49.0X4	T49.0X5	T49.0X6
Amdinocilline	T36.0X1	T36.0X2	T36.0X3	T36.0X4	T36.0X5	T36.0X6
Ametazole	T50.8X1	T50.8X2	T50.8X3	T50.8X4	T50.8X5	T50.8X6
Amethocaine	T41.3X1	T41.3X2	T41.3X3	T41.3X4	T41.3X5	T41.3X6
regional	T41.3X1	T41.3X2	T41.3X3	T41.3X4	T41.3X5	T41.3X6
spinal	T41.3X1	T41.3X2	T41.3X3	T41.3X4	T41.3X5	T41.3X6
Amethopterin	T45.1X1	T45.1X2	T45.1X3	T45.1X4	T45.1X5	T45.1X6
Amezinium metilsulfate	T44.991	T44.992	T44.993	T44.994	T44.995	T44.996
Amfebutamone	T43.291	T43.292	T43.293	T43.294	T43.295	T43.296
Amfepramone	T50.5X1	T50.5X2	T50.5X3	T50.5X4	T50.5X5	T50.5X6

◀ New ◀ Revised ~~deleted~~ Deleted

Substance	External Cause (T-Code) Poisoning, Accidental (Unintentional)	Poisoning, Intentional Self-Harm	Poisoning, Assault	Poisoning, Undetermined	Adverse Effect	Underdosing
Amfetamine	T43.621	T43.622	T43.623	T43.624	T43.625	T43.626
Amfetaminil	T43.621	T43.622	T43.623	T43.624	T43.625	T43.626
Amfomycin	T36.8X1	T36.8X2	T36.8X3	T36.8X4	T36.8X5	T36.8X6
Amidefrine mesilate	T48.5X1	T48.5X2	T48.5X3	T48.5X4	T48.5X5	T48.5X6
Amidone	T40.3X1	T40.3X2	T40.3X3	T40.3X4	T40.3X5	T40.3X6
Amidopyrine	T39.2X1	T39.2X2	T39.2X3	T39.2X4	T39.2X5	T39.2X6
Amidotrizoate	T50.8X1	T50.8X2	T50.8X3	T50.8X4	T50.8X5	T50.8X6
Amiflamine	T43.1X1	T43.1X2	T43.1X3	T43.1X4	T43.1X5	T43.1X6
Amikacin	T36.5X1	T36.5X2	T36.5X3	T36.5X4	T36.5X5	T36.5X6
Amikhelline	T46.3X1	T46.3X2	T46.3X3	T46.3X4	T46.3X5	T46.3X6
Amiloride	T50.2X1	T50.2X2	T50.2X3	T50.2X4	T50.2X5	T50.2X6
Aminacrine	T49.0X1	T49.0X2	T49.0X3	T49.0X4	T49.0X5	T49.0X6
Amineptine	T43.011	T43.012	T43.013	T43.014	T43.015	T43.016
Aminitrozole	T37.3X1	T37.3X2	T37.3X3	T37.3X4	T37.3X5	T37.3X6
Aminoacetic acid (derivatives)	T50.3X1	T50.3X2	T50.3X3	T50.3X4	T50.3X5	T50.3X6
Amino acids	T50.3X1	T50.3X2	T50.3X3	T50.3X4	T50.3X5	T50.3X6
Aminoacridine	T49.0X1	T49.0X2	T49.0X3	T49.0X4	T49.0X5	T49.0X6
Aminobenzoic acid (-p)	T49.3X1	T49.3X2	T49.3X3	T49.3X4	T49.3X5	T49.3X6
4-Aminobutyric acid	T43.8X1	T43.8X2	T43.8X3	T43.8X4	T43.8X5	T43.8X6
Aminocaproic acid	T45.621	T45.622	T45.623	T45.624	T45.625	T45.626
Aminofenazone	T39.2X1	T39.2X2	T39.2X3	T39.2X4	T39.2X5	T39.2X6
Aminoethylisothiourium	T45.8X1	T45.8X2	T45.8X3	T45.8X4	T45.8X5	T45.8X6
Aminoglutethimide	T45.1X1	T45.1X2	T45.1X3	T45.1X4	T45.1X5	T45.1X6
Aminohippuric acid	T50.8X1	T50.8X2	T50.8X3	T50.8X4	T50.8X5	T50.8X6
Aminomethylbenzoic acid	T45.691	T45.692	T45.693	T45.694	T45.695	T45.696
Aminometradine	T50.2X1	T50.2X2	T50.2X3	T50.2X4	T50.2X5	T50.2X6
Aminopentamide	T44.3X1	T44.3X2	T44.3X3	T44.3X4	T44.3X5	T44.3X6
Aminophenazone	T39.2X1	T39.2X2	T39.2X3	T39.2X4	T39.2X5	T39.2X6
Aminophenol	T54.0X1	T54.0X2	T54.0X3	T54.0X4	—	—
4-Aminophenol derivatives	T39.1X1	T39.1X2	T39.1X3	T39.1X4	T39.1X5	T39.1X6
Aminophenylpyridone	T43.591	T43.592	T43.593	T43.594	T43.595	T43.596
Aminophylline	T48.6X1	T48.6X2	T48.6X3	T48.6X4	T48.6X5	T48.6X6
Aminopterin sodium	T45.1X1	T45.1X2	T45.1X3	T45.1X4	T45.1X5	T45.1X6
Aminopyrine	T39.2X1	T39.2X2	T39.2X3	T39.2X4	T39.2X5	T39.2X6
8-Aminoquinoline drugs	T37.2X1	T37.2X2	T37.2X3	T37.2X4	T37.2X5	T37.2X6
Aminorex	T50.5X1	T50.5X2	T50.5X3	T50.5X4	T50.5X5	T50.5X6
Aminosalicylic acid	T37.1X1	T37.1X2	T37.1X3	T37.1X4	T37.1X5	T37.1X6
Aminosalylum	T37.1X1	T37.1X2	T37.1X3	T37.1X4	T37.1X5	T37.1X6
Amiodarone	T46.2X1	T46.2X2	T46.2X3	T46.2X4	T46.2X5	T46.2X6
Amiphenazole	T50.7X1	T50.7X2	T50.7X3	T50.7X4	T50.7X5	T50.7X6
Amiquinsin	T46.5X1	T46.5X2	T46.5X3	T46.5X4	T46.5X5	T46.5X6
Amisometradine	T50.2X1	T50.2X2	T50.2X3	T50.2X4	T50.2X5	T50.2X6

Substance	External Cause (T-Code) Poisoning, Accidental (Unintentional)	Poisoning, Intentional Self-Harm	Poisoning, Assault	Poisoning, Undetermined	Adverse Effect	Underdosing
Amisulpride	T43.591	T43.592	T43.593	T43.594	T43.595	T43.596
Amitriptyline	T43.021	T43.022	T43.023	T43.024	T43.025	T43.026
Amitriptylinoxide	T43.021	T43.022	T43.023	T43.024	T43.025	T43.026
Amlexanox	T48.6X1	T48.6X2	T48.6X3	T48.6X4	T48.6X5	T48.6X6
Ammonia (fumes) (gas) (vapor)	T59.891	T59.892	T59.893	T59.894	—	—
aromatic spirit	T48.991	T48.992	T48.993	T48.994	T48.995	T48.996
liquid (household)	T54.3X1	T54.3X2	T54.3X3	T54.3X4	—	—
Ammoniated mercury	T49.0X1	T49.0X2	T49.0X3	T49.0X4	T49.0X5	T49.0X6
Ammonium						
acid tartrate	T49.5X1	T49.5X2	T49.5X3	T49.5X4	T49.5X5	T49.5X6
bromide	T42.6X1	T42.6X2	T42.6X3	T42.6X4	T42.6X5	T42.6X6
carbonate	T54.3X1	T54.3X2	T54.3X3	T54.3X4	—	—
chloride	T50.991	T50.992	T50.993	T50.994	T50.995	T50.996
expectorant	T48.4X1	T48.4X2	T48.4X3	T48.4X4	T48.4X5	T48.4X6
compounds (household) NEC	T54.3X1	T54.3X2	T54.3X3	T54.3X4	—	—
fumes (any usage)	T59.891	T59.892	T59.893	T59.894	—	—
industrial	T54.3X1	T54.3X2	T54.3X3	T54.3X4	—	—
ichthyosulronate	T49.4X1	T49.4X2	T49.4X3	T49.4X4	T49.4X5	T49.4X6
mandelate	T37.91	T37.92	T37.93	T37.94	T37.95	T37.96
sulfamate	T60.3X1	T60.3X2	T60.3X3	T60.3X4	—	—
sulfonate resin	T47.8X1	T47.8X2	T47.8X3	T47.8X4	T47.8X5	T47.8X6
Amobarbital (sodium)	T42.3X1	T42.3X2	T42.3X3	T42.3X4	T42.3X5	T42.3X6
Amodiaquine	T37.2X1	T37.2X2	T37.2X3	T37.2X4	T37.2X5	T37.2X6
Amopyroquin(e)	T37.2X1	T37.2X2	T37.2X3	T37.2X4	T37.2X5	T37.2X6
Amoxapine	T43.011	T43.012	T43.013	T43.014	T43.015	T43.016
Amoxicillin	T36.0X1	T36.0X2	T36.0X3	T36.0X4	T36.0X5	T36.0X6
Amperozide	T43.591	T43.592	T43.593	T43.594	T43.595	T43.596
Amphenidone	T43.591	T43.592	T43.593	T43.594	T43.595	T43.596
Amphetamine NEC	T43.621	T43.622	T43.623	T43.624	T43.625	T43.626
Amphomycin	T36.8X1	T36.8X2	T36.8X3	T36.8X4	T36.8X5	T36.8X6
Amphotalide	T37.4X1	T37.4X2	T37.4X3	T37.4X4	T37.4X5	T37.4X6
Amphotericin B	T36.7X1	T36.7X2	T36.7X3	T36.7X4	T36.7X5	T36.7X6
topical	T49.0X1	T49.0X2	T49.0X3	T49.0X4	T49.0X5	T49.0X6
Ampicillin	T36.0X1	T36.0X2	T36.0X3	T36.0X4	T36.0X5	T36.0X6
Amprotropine	T44.3X1	T44.3X2	T44.3X3	T44.3X4	T44.3X5	T44.3X6
Amsacrine	T45.1X1	T45.1X2	T45.1X3	T45.1X4	T45.1X5	T45.1X6
Amygdaline	T62.2X1	T62.2X2	T62.2X3	T62.2X4	—	—
Amyl						
acetate	T52.8X1	T52.8X2	T52.8X3	T52.8X4	—	—
vapor	T59.891	T59.892	T59.893	T59.894	—	—
alcohol	T51.3X1	T51.3X2	T51.3X3	T51.3X4	—	—
chloride	T53.6X1	T53.6X2	T53.6X3	T53.6X4	—	—

◀ New ◀ Revised ~~deleted~~ Deleted

TABLE OF DRUGS AND CHEMICALS

Substance	External Cause (T-Code)					
	Poisoning, Accidental (Unintentional)	Poisoning, Intentional Self-Harm	Poisoning, Assault	Poisoning, Undetermined	Adverse Effect	Underdosing
Amyl (Continued)						
formate	T52.8X1	T52.8X2	T52.8X3	T52.8X4	—	—
nitrite	T46.3X1	T46.3X2	T46.3X3	T46.3X4	T46.3X5	T46.3X6
propionate	T65.891	T65.892	T65.893	T65.894	—	—
Amylase	T47.5X1	T47.5X2	T47.5X3	T47.5X4	T47.5X5	T47.5X6
Amyleine, regional	T41.3X1	T41.3X2	T41.3X3	T41.3X4	T41.3X5	T41.3X6
Amylene						
dichloride	T53.6X1	T53.6X2	T53.6X3	T53.6X4	—	—
hydrate	T51.3X1	T51.3X2	T51.3X3	T51.3X4	—	—
Amylmetacresol	T49.6X1	T49.6X2	T49.6X3	T49.6X4	T49.6X5	T49.6X6
Amylobarbitone	T42.3X1	T42.3X2	T42.3X3	T42.3X4	T42.3X5	T42.3X6
Amylocaine, regional	T41.3X1	T41.3X2	T41.3X3	T41.3X4	T41.3X5	T41.3X6
infiltration (subcutaneous)	T41.3X1	T41.3X2	T41.3X3	T41.3X4	T41.3X5	T41.3X6
nerve block (peripheral) (plexus)	T41.3X1	T41.3X2	T41.3X3	T41.3X4	T41.3X5	T41.3X6
spinal	T41.3X1	T41.3X2	T41.3X3	T41.3X4	T41.3X5	T41.3X6
topical (surface)	T41.3X1	T41.3X2	T41.3X3	T41.3X4	T41.3X5	T41.3X6
Amylopectin	T47.6X1	T47.6X2	T47.6X3	T47.6X4	T47.6X5	T47.6X6
Amytal (sodium)	T42.3X1	T42.3X2	T42.3X3	T42.3X4	T42.3X5	T42.3X6
Anabolic steroid	T38.7X1	T38.7X2	T38.7X3	T38.7X4	T38.7X5	T38.7X6
Analeptic NEC	T50.7X1	T50.7X2	T50.7X3	T50.7X4	T50.7X5	T50.7X6
Analgesic	T39.91	T39.92	T39.93	T39.94	T39.95	T39.96
anti-inflammatory NEC	T39.91	T39.92	T39.93	T39.94	T39.95	T39.96
propionic acid derivative	T39.311	T39.312	T39.313	T39.314	T39.315	T39.316
antirheumatic NEC	T39.4X1	T39.4X2	T39.4X3	T39.4X4	T39.4X5	T39.4X6
aromatic NEC	T39.1X1	T39.1X2	T39.1X3	T39.1X4	T39.1X5	T39.1X6
narcotic NEC	T40.601	T40.602	T40.603	T40.604	T40.605	T40.606
combination	T40.601	T40.602	T40.603	T40.604	T40.605	T40.606
obstetric	T40.601	T40.602	T40.603	T40.604	T40.605	T40.606
non-narcotic NEC	T39.91	T39.92	T39.93	T39.94	T39.95	T39.96
combination	T39.91	T39.92	T39.93	T39.94	T39.95	T39.96
pyrazole	T39.2X1	T39.2X2	T39.2X3	T39.2X4	T39.2X5	T39.2X6
specified NEC	T39.8X1	T39.8X2	T39.8X3	T39.8X4	T39.8X5	T39.8X6
Analgin	T39.2X1	T39.2X2	T39.2X3	T39.2X4	T39.2X5	T39.2X6
Anamirta cocculus	T62.1X1	T62.1X2	T62.1X3	T62.1X4	—	—
Ancillin	T36.0X1	T36.0X2	T36.0X3	T36.0X4	T36.0X5	T36.0X6
Ancrod	T45.691	T45.692	T45.693	T45.694	T45.695	T45.696
Androgen	T38.7X1	T38.7X2	T38.7X3	T38.7X4	T38.7X5	T38.7X6
Androgen-estrogen mixture	T38.7X1	T38.7X2	T38.7X3	T38.7X4	T38.7X5	T38.7X6
Androstalone	T38.7X1	T38.7X2	T38.7X3	T38.7X4	T38.7X5	T38.7X6
Androstanolone	T38.7X1	T38.7X2	T38.7X3	T38.7X4	T38.7X5	T38.7X6
Androsterone	T38.7X1	T38.7X2	T38.7X3	T38.7X4	T38.7X5	T38.7X6

Substance	External Cause (T-Code)					
	Poisoning, Accidental (Unintentional)	Poisoning, Intentional Self-Harm	Poisoning, Assault	Poisoning, Undetermined	Adverse Effect	Underdosing
Anemone pulsatilla	T62.2X1	T62.2X2	T62.2X3	T62.2X4	—	—
Anesthesia						
caudal	T41.3X1	T41.3X2	T41.3X3	T41.3X4	T41.3X5	T41.3X6
endotracheal	T41.0X1	T41.0X2	T41.0X3	T41.0X4	T41.0X5	T41.0X6
epidural	T41.3X1	T41.3X2	T41.3X3	T41.3X4	T41.3X5	T41.3X6
inhalation	T41.0X1	T41.0X2	T41.0X3	T41.0X4	T41.0X5	T41.0X6
local	T41.3X1	T41.3X2	T41.3X3	T41.3X4	T41.3X5	T41.3X6
mucosal	T41.3X1	T41.3X2	T41.3X3	T41.3X4	T41.3X5	T41.3X6
muscle relaxation	T48.1X1	T48.1X2	T48.1X3	T48.1X4	T48.1X5	T48.1X6
nerve blocking	T41.3X1	T41.3X2	T41.3X3	T41.3X4	T41.3X5	T41.3X6
plexus blocking	T41.3X1	T41.3X2	T41.3X3	T41.3X4	T41.3X5	T41.3X6
potentiated	T41.201	T41.202	T41.203	T41.204	T41.205	T41.206
rectal	T41.201	T41.202	T41.203	T41.204	T41.205	T41.206
general	T41.201	T41.202	T41.203	T41.204	T41.205	T41.206
local	T41.3X1	T41.3X2	T41.3X3	T41.3X4	T41.3X5	T41.3X6
regional	T41.3X1	T41.3X2	T41.3X3	T41.3X4	T41.3X5	T41.3X6
surface	T41.3X1	T41.3X2	T41.3X3	T41.3X4	T41.3X5	T41.3X6
Anesthetic NEC — see also Anesthesia	T41.41	T41.42	T41.43	T41.44	T41.45	T41.46
with muscle relaxant	T41.201	T41.202	T41.203	T41.204	T41.205	T41.206
general	T41.201	T41.202	T41.203	T41.204	T41.205	T41.206
local	T41.3X1	T41.3X2	T41.3X3	T41.3X4	T41.3X5	T41.3X6
gaseous NEC	T41.0X1	T41.0X2	T41.0X3	T41.0X4	T41.0X5	T41.0X6
general NEC	T41.201	T41.202	T41.203	T41.204	T41.205	T41.206
halogenated hydrocarbon derivatives NEC	T41.0X1	T41.0X2	T41.0X3	T41.0X4	T41.0X5	T41.0X6
infiltration NEC	T41.3X1	T41.3X2	T41.3X3	T41.3X4	T41.3X5	T41.3X6
intravenous NEC	T41.1X1	T41.1X2	T41.1X3	T41.1X4	T41.1X5	T41.1X6
local NEC	T41.3X1	T41.3X2	T41.3X3	T41.3X4	T41.3X5	T41.3X6
rectal	T41.201	T41.202	T41.203	T41.204	T41.205	T41.206
general	T41.201	T41.202	T41.203	T41.204	T41.205	T41.206
local	T41.3X1	T41.3X2	T41.3X3	T41.3X4	T41.3X5	T41.3X6
regional NEC	T41.3X1	T41.3X2	T41.3X3	T41.3X4	T41.3X5	T41.3X6
spinal NEC	T41.3X1	T41.3X2	T41.3X3	T41.3X4	T41.3X5	T41.3X6
thiobarbiturate	T41.1X1	T41.1X2	T41.1X3	T41.1X4	T41.1X5	T41.1X6
topical	T41.3X1	T41.3X2	T41.3X3	T41.3X4	T41.3X5	T41.3X6
Aneurine	T45.2X1	T45.2X2	T45.2X3	T45.2X4	T45.2X5	T45.2X6
Angio-Conray	T50.8X1	T50.8X2	T50.8X3	T50.8X4	T50.8X5	T50.8X6
Angiotensin	T44.5X1	T44.5X2	T44.5X3	T44.5X4	T44.5X5	T44.5X6
Angiotensinamide	T44.991	T44.992	T44.993	T44.994	T44.995	T44.996
Anhydrohydroxy-progesterone	T38.5X1	T38.5X2	T38.5X3	T38.5X4	T38.5X5	T38.5X6
Anhydron	T50.2X1	T50.2X2	T50.2X3	T50.2X4	T50.2X5	T50.2X6
Anileridine	T40.4X1	T40.4X2	T40.4X3	T40.4X4	T40.4X5	T40.4X6

◄ New ◄ Revised ~~deleted~~ Deleted

Substance	External Cause (T-Code) Poisoning, Accidental (Unintentional)	Poisoning, Intentional Self-Harm	Poisoning, Assault	Poisoning, Undetermined	Adverse Effect	Underdosing
Aniline (dye) (liquid)	T65.3X1	T65.3X2	T65.3X3	T65.3X4	—	—
analgesic	T39.1X1	T39.1X2	T39.1X3	T39.1X4	T39.1X5	T39.1X6
derivatives, therapeutic NEC	T39.1X1	T39.1X2	T39.1X3	T39.1X4	T39.1X5	T39.1X6
vapor	T65.3X1	T65.3X2	T65.3X3	T65.3X4	—	—
Anise oil	T47.5X1	T47.5X2	T47.5X3	T47.5X4	T47.5X5	T47.5X6
Aniscoropine	T44.3X1	T44.3X2	T44.3X3	T44.3X4	T44.3X5	T44.3X6
Anisidine	T65.3X1	T65.3X2	T65.3X3	T65.3X4	—	—
Anisindione	T45.511	T45.512	T45.513	T45.514	T45.515	T45.516
Anisotropine methyl-bromide	T44.3X1	T44.3X2	T44.3X3	T44.3X4	T44.3X5	T44.3X6
Anistreplase	T45.611	T45.612	T45.613	T45.614	T45.615	T45.616
Anorexiant (central)	T50.5X1	T50.5X2	T50.5X3	T50.5X4	T50.5X5	T50.5X6
Anorexic agents	T50.5X1	T50.5X2	T50.5X3	T50.5X4	T50.5X5	T50.5X6
Ansamycin	T36.6X1	T36.6X2	T36.6X3	T36.6X4	T36.6X5	T36.6X6
Ant (bite) (sting)	T63.421	T63.422	T63.423	T63.424	—	—
Antabuse	T50.6X1	T50.6X2	T50.6X3	T50.6X4	T50.6X5	T50.6X6
Ant poison — see Insecticide						
Antacid NEC	T47.1X1	T47.1X2	T47.1X3	T47.1X4	T47.1X5	T47.1X6
Antagonist						
Aldosterone	T50.0X1	T50.0X2	T50.0X3	T50.0X4	T50.0X5	T50.0X6
alpha-adrenoreceptor	T44.6X1	T44.6X2	T44.6X3	T44.6X4	T44.6X5	T44.6X6
anticoagulant	T45.7X1	T45.7X2	T45.7X3	T45.7X4	T45.7X5	T45.7X6
beta-adrenoreceptor	T44.7X1	T44.7X2	T44.7X3	T44.7X4	T44.7X5	T44.7X6
extrapyramidal NEC	T44.3X1	T44.3X2	T44.3X3	T44.3X4	T44.3X5	T44.3X6
folic acid	T45.1X1	T45.1X2	T45.1X3	T45.1X4	T45.1X5	T45.1X6
H2 receptor	T47.0X1	T47.0X2	T47.0X3	T47.0X4	T47.0X5	T47.0X6
heavy metal	T45.8X1	T45.8X2	T45.8X3	T45.8X4	T45.8X5	T45.8X6
narcotic analgesic	T50.7X1	T50.7X2	T50.7X3	T50.7X4	T50.7X5	T50.7X6
opiate	T50.7X1	T50.7X2	T50.7X3	T50.7X4	T50.7X5	T50.7X6
pyrimidine	T45.1X1	T45.1X2	T45.1X3	T45.1X4	T45.1X5	T45.1X6
serotonin	T46.5X1	T46.5X2	T46.5X3	T46.5X4	T46.5X5	T46.5X6
Antazolin(e)	T45.0X1	T45.0X2	T45.0X3	T45.0X4	T45.0X5	T45.0X6
Anterior pituitary hormone NEC	T38.811	T38.812	T38.813	T38.814	T38.815	T38.816
Anthelmintic NEC	T37.4X1	T37.4X2	T37.4X3	T37.4X4	T37.4X5	T37.4X6
Anthiolimine	T37.4X1	T37.4X2	T37.4X3	T37.4X4	T37.4X5	T37.4X6
Anthralin	T49.4X1	T49.4X2	T49.4X3	T49.4X4	T49.4X5	T49.4X6
Anthramycin	T45.1X1	T45.1X2	T45.1X3	T45.1X4	T45.1X5	T45.1X6
Antiadrenergic NEC	T44.8X1	T44.8X2	T44.8X3	T44.8X4	T44.8X5	T44.8X6
Antiallergic NEC	T45.0X1	T45.0X2	T45.0X3	T45.0X4	T45.0X5	T45.0X6
Anti-anemic (drug) (preparation)	T45.8X1	T45.8X2	T45.8X3	T45.8X4	T45.8X5	T45.8X6
Antiandrogen NEC	T38.6X1	T38.6X2	T38.6X3	T38.6X4	T38.6X5	T38.6X6
Antianxiety drug NEC	T43.501	T43.502	T43.503	T43.504	T43.505	T43.506
Antiaris toxicaria	T65.891	T65.892	T65.893	T65.894	—	—

Substance	External Cause (T-Code) Poisoning, Accidental (Unintentional)	Poisoning, Intentional Self-Harm	Poisoning, Assault	Poisoning, Undetermined	Adverse Effect	Underdosing
Antiarteriosclerotic drug	T46.6X1	T46.6X2	T46.6X3	T46.6X4	T46.6X5	T46.6X6
Antiasthmatic drug NEC	T48.6X1	T48.6X2	T48.6X3	T48.6X4	T48.6X5	T48.6X6
Antibiotic NEC	T36.91	T36.92	T36.93	T36.94	T36.95	T36.96
aminoglycoside	T36.5X1	T36.5X2	T36.5X3	T36.5X4	T36.5X5	T36.5X6
anticancer	T45.1X1	T45.1X2	T45.1X3	T45.1X4	T45.1X5	T45.1X6
antifungal	T36.7X1	T36.7X2	T36.7X3	T36.7X4	T36.7X5	T36.7X6
antimycobacterial	T36.5X1	T36.5X2	T36.5X3	T36.5X4	T36.5X5	T36.5X6
antineoplastic	T45.1X1	T45.1X2	T45.1X3	T45.1X4	T45.1X5	T45.1X6
cephalosporin (group)	T36.1X1	T36.1X2	T36.1X3	T36.1X4	T36.1X5	T36.1X6
chloramphenicol (group)	T36.2X1	T36.2X2	T36.2X3	T36.2X4	T36.2X5	T36.2X6
ENT	T49.6X1	T49.6X2	T49.6X3	T49.6X4	T49.6X5	T49.6X6
eye	T49.5X1	T49.5X2	T49.5X3	T49.5X4	T49.5X5	T49.5X6
fungicidal (local)	T49.0X1	T49.0X2	T49.0X3	T49.0X4	T49.0X5	T49.0X6
intestinal	T36.8X1	T36.8X2	T36.8X3	T36.8X4	T36.8X5	T36.8X6
b-lactam NEC	T36.1X1	T36.1X2	T36.1X3	T36.1X4	T36.1X5	T36.1X6
local	T49.0X1	T49.0X2	T49.0X3	T49.0X4	T49.0X5	T49.0X6
macrolides	T36.3X1	T36.3X2	T36.3X3	T36.3X4	T36.3X5	T36.3X6
polypeptide	T36.8X1	T36.8X2	T36.8X3	T36.8X4	T36.8X5	T36.8X6
specified NEC	T36.8X1	T36.8X2	T36.8X3	T36.8X4	T36.8X5	T36.8X6
tetracycline (group)	T36.4X1	T36.4X2	T36.4X3	T36.4X4	T36.4X5	T36.4X6
throat	T49.6X1	T49.6X2	T49.6X3	T49.6X4	T49.6X5	T49.6X6
Anticancer agents NEC	T45.1X1	T45.1X2	T45.1X3	T45.1X4	T45.1X5	T45.1X6
Anticholesterolemic drug NEC	T46.6X1	T46.6X2	T46.6X3	T46.6X4	T46.6X5	T46.6X6
Anticholinergic NEC	T44.3X1	T44.3X2	T44.3X3	T44.3X4	T44.3X5	T44.3X6
Anticholinesterase	T44.0X1	T44.0X2	T44.0X3	T44.0X4	T44.0X5	T44.0X6
organophosphorus	T44.0X1	T44.0X2	T44.0X3	T44.0X4	T44.0X5	T44.0X6
insecticide	T60.0X1	T60.0X2	T60.0X3	T60.0X4	—	—
nerve gas	T59.891	T59.892	T59.893	T59.894	—	—
reversible	T44.0X1	T44.0X2	T44.0X3	T44.0X4	T44.0X5	T44.0X6
ophthalmological	T49.5X1	T49.5X2	T49.5X3	T49.5X4	T49.5X5	T49.5X6
Anticoagulant NEC	T45.511	T45.512	T45.513	T45.514	T45.515	T45.516
Antagonist	T45.7X1	T45.7X2	T45.7X3	T45.7X4	T45.7X5	T45.7X6
Anti-common-cold drug NEC	T48.5X1	T48.5X2	T48.5X3	T48.5X4	T48.5X5	T48.5X6
Anticonvulsant	T42.71	T42.72	T42.73	T42.74	T42.75	T42.76
barbiturate	T42.3X1	T42.3X2	T42.3X3	T42.3X4	T42.3X5	T42.3X6
combination (with barbiturate)	T42.3X1	T42.3X2	T42.3X3	T42.3X4	T42.3X5	T42.3X6
hydantoin	T42.0X1	T42.0X2	T42.0X3	T42.0X4	T42.0X5	T42.0X6
hypnotic NEC	T42.6X1	T42.6X2	T42.6X3	T42.6X4	T42.6X5	T42.6X6
oxazolidinedione	T42.2X1	T42.2X2	T42.2X3	T42.2X4	T42.2X5	T42.2X6
pyrimidinedione	T42.6X1	T42.6X2	T42.6X3	T42.6X4	T42.6X5	T42.6X6
specified NEC	T42.6X1	T42.6X2	T42.6X3	T42.6X4	T42.6X5	T42.6X6
succinimide	T42.2X1	T42.2X2	T42.2X3	T42.2X4	T42.2X5	T42.2X6

◀ New ◀ Revised ~~deleted~~ Deleted

	External Cause (T-Code)					
Substance	Poisoning, Accidental (Unintentional)	Poisoning, Intentional Self-Harm	Poisoning, Assault	Poisoning, Undetermined	Adverse Effect	Underdosing
Anti-D immunoglobulin (human)	T50.Z11	T50.Z12	T50.Z13	T50.Z14	T50.Z15	T50.Z16
Antidepressant NEC	T43.201	T43.202	T43.203	T43.204	T43.205	T43.206
monoamine oxidase inhibitor	T43.1X1	T43.1X2	T43.1X3	T43.1X4	T43.1X5	T43.1X6
selective serotonin norepinephrine reuptake inhibitor	T43.211	T43.212	T43.213	T43.214	T43.215	T43.216
selective serotonin reuptake inhibitor	T43.221	T43.222	T43.223	T43.224	T43.225	T43.226
specified NEC	T43.291	T43.292	T43.293	T43.294	T43.295	T43.296
tetracyclic	T43.021	T43.022	T43.023	T43.024	T43.025	T43.026
triazolopyridine	T43.221	T43.222	T43.223	T43.224	T43.225	T43.226
tricyclic	T43.011	T43.012	T43.013	T43.014	T43.015	T43.016
Antidiabetic NEC	T38.3X1	T38.3X2	T38.3X3	T38.3X4	T38.3X5	T38.3X6
biguanide	T38.3X1	T38.3X2	T38.3X3	T38.3X4	T38.3X5	T38.3X6
and sulfonyl combined	T38.3X1	T38.3X2	T38.3X3	T38.3X4	T38.3X5	T38.3X6
combined	T38.3X1	T38.3X2	T38.3X3	T38.3X4	T38.3X5	T38.3X6
sulfonylurea	T38.3X1	T38.3X2	T38.3X3	T38.3X4	T38.3X5	T38.3X6
Antidiarrheal drug NEC	T47.6X1	T47.6X2	T47.6X3	T47.6X4	T47.6X5	T47.6X6
absorbent	T47.6X1	T47.6X2	T47.6X3	T47.6X4	T47.6X5	T47.6X6
Antidiphtheria serum	T50.Z11	T50.Z12	T50.Z13	T50.Z14	T50.Z15	T50.Z16
Antidiuretic hormone	T38.891	T38.892	T38.893	T38.894	T38.895	T38.896
Antidote NEC	T50.6X1	T50.6X2	T50.6X3	T50.6X4	T50.6X5	T50.6X6
heavy metal	T45.8X1	T45.8X2	T45.8X3	T45.8X4	T45.8X5	T45.8X6
Antidysrhythmic NEC	T46.2X1	T46.2X2	T46.2X3	T46.2X4	T46.2X5	T46.2X6
Antiemetic drug	T45.0X1	T45.0X2	T45.0X3	T45.0X4	T45.0X5	T45.0X6
Antiepilepsy agent	T42.71	T42.72	T42.73	T42.74	T42.75	T42.76
combination	T42.5X1	T42.5X2	T42.5X3	T42.5X4	T42.5X5	T42.5X6
mixed	T42.5X1	T42.5X2	T42.5X3	T42.5X4	T42.5X5	T42.5X6
specified, NEC	T42.6X1	T42.6X2	T42.6X3	T42.6X4	T42.6X5	T42.6X6
Antiestrogen NEC	T38.6X1	T38.6X2	T38.6X3	T38.6X4	T38.6X5	T38.6X6
Antifertility pill	T38.4X1	T38.4X2	T38.4X3	T38.4X4	T38.4X5	T38.4X6
Antifibrinolytic drug	T45.621	T45.622	T45.623	T45.624	T45.625	T45.626
Antifilarial drug	T37.4X1	T37.4X2	T37.4X3	T37.4X4	T37.4X5	T37.4X6
Antiflatulent	T47.5X1	T47.5X2	T47.5X3	T47.5X4	T47.5X5	T47.5X6
Antifreeze	T65.91	T65.92	T65.93	T65.94	—	—
alcohol	T51.1X1	T51.1X2	T51.1X3	T51.1X4	—	—
ethylene glycol	T51.8X1	T51.8X2	T51.8X3	T51.8X4	—	—
Antifungal						
antibiotic (systemic)	T36.7X1	T36.7X2	T36.7X3	T36.7X4	T36.7X5	T36.7X6
anti-infective NEC	T37.91	T37.92	T37.93	T37.94	T37.95	T37.96
disinfectant, local	T49.0X1	T49.0X2	T49.0X3	T49.0X4	T49.0X5	T49.0X6
nonmedicinal (spray)	T60.3X1	T60.3X2	T60.3X3	T60.3X4	—	—
topical	T49.0X1	T49.0X2	T49.0X3	T49.0X4	T49.0X5	T49.0X6

	External Cause (T-Code)					
Substance	Poisoning, Accidental (Unintentional)	Poisoning, Intentional Self-Harm	Poisoning, Assault	Poisoning, Undetermined	Adverse Effect	Underdosing
Anti-gastric-secretion drug NEC	T47.1X1	T47.1X2	T47.1X3	T47.1X4	T47.1X5	T47.1X6
Antigonadotrophin NEC	T38.6X1	T38.6X2	T38.6X3	T38.6X4	T38.6X5	T38.6X6
Antihallucinogen	T43.501	T43.502	T43.503	T43.504	T43.505	T43.506
Antihelmintics	T37.4X1	T37.4X2	T37.4X3	T37.4X4	T37.4X5	T37.4X6
Antihemophilic						
factor	T45.8X1	T45.8X2	T45.8X3	T45.8X4	T45.8X5	T45.8X6
fraction	T45.8X1	T45.8X2	T45.8X3	T45.8X4	T45.8X5	T45.8X6
globulin concentrate	T45.7X1	T45.7X2	T45.7X3	T45.7X4	T45.7X5	T45.7X6
human plasma	T45.8X1	T45.8X2	T45.8X3	T45.8X4	T45.8X5	T45.8X6
plasma, dried	T45.7X1	T45.7X2	T45.7X3	T45.7X4	T45.7X5	T45.7X6
Antihemorrhoidal preparation	T49.2X1	T49.2X2	T49.2X3	T49.2X4	T49.2X5	T49.2X6
Antiheparin drug	T45.7X1	T45.7X2	T45.7X3	T45.7X4	T45.7X5	T45.7X6
Antihistamine	T45.0X1	T45.0X2	T45.0X3	T45.0X4	T45.0X5	T45.0X6
Antihookworm drug	T37.4X1	T37.4X2	T37.4X3	T37.4X4	T37.4X5	T37.4X6
Anti-human lymphocytic globulin	T50.Z11	T50.Z12	T50.Z13	T50.Z14	T50.Z15	T50.Z16
Antihyperlipidemic drug	T46.6X1	T46.6X2	T46.6X3	T46.6X4	T46.6X5	T46.6X6
Antihypertensive drug NEC	T46.5X1	T46.5X2	T46.5X3	T46.5X4	T46.5X5	T46.5X6
Anti-infective NEC	T37.91	T37.92	T37.93	T37.94	T37.95	T37.96
anthelmintic	T37.4X1	T37.4X2	T37.4X3	T37.4X4	T37.4X5	T37.4X6
antibiotics	T36.91	T36.92	T36.93	T36.94	T36.95	T36.96
specified NEC	T36.8X1	T36.8X2	T36.8X3	T36.8X4	T36.8X5	T36.8X6
antimalarial	T37.2X1	T37.2X2	T37.2X3	T37.2X4	T37.2X5	T37.2X6
antimycobacterial NEC	T37.1X1	T37.1X2	T37.1X3	T37.1X4	T37.1X5	T37.1X6
antibiotics	T36.5X1	T36.5X2	T36.5X3	T36.5X4	T36.5X5	T36.5X6
antiprotozoal NEC	T37.3X1	T37.3X2	T37.3X3	T37.3X4	T37.3X5	T37.3X6
blood	T37.2X1	T37.2X2	T37.2X3	T37.2X4	T37.2X5	T37.2X6
antiviral	T37.5X1	T37.5X2	T37.5X3	T37.5X4	T37.5X5	T37.5X6
arsenical	T37.8X1	T37.8X2	T37.8X3	T37.8X4	T37.8X5	T37.8X6
bismuth, local	T49.0X1	T49.0X2	T49.0X3	T49.0X4	T49.0X5	T49.0X6
ENT	T49.6X1	T49.6X2	T49.6X3	T49.6X4	T49.6X5	T49.6X6
eye NEC	T49.5X1	T49.5X2	T49.5X3	T49.5X4	T49.5X5	T49.5X6
heavy metals NEC	T37.8X1	T37.8X2	T37.8X3	T37.8X4	T37.8X5	T37.8X6
local NEC	T49.0X1	T49.0X2	T49.0X3	T49.0X4	T49.0X5	T49.0X6
specified NEC	T49.0X1	T49.0X2	T49.0X3	T49.0X4	T49.0X5	T49.0X6
mixed	T37.91	T37.92	T37.93	T37.94	T37.95	T37.96
ophthalmic preparation	T49.5X1	T49.5X2	T49.5X3	T49.5X4	T49.5X5	T49.5X6
topical NEC	T49.0X1	T49.0X2	T49.0X3	T49.0X4	T49.0X5	T49.0X6
Anti-inflammatory drug NEC	T49.0X1	T49.0X2	T49.0X3	T49.0X4	T49.0X5	T49.0X6
local	T49.0X1	T49.0X2	T49.0X3	T49.0X4	T49.0X5	T49.0X6
nonsteroidal NEC	T39.391	T39.392	T39.393	T39.394	T39.395	T39.396
propionic acid derivative	T39.311	T39.312	T39.313	T39.314	T39.315	T39.316
specified NEC	T39.391	T39.392	T39.393	T39.394	T39.395	T39.396

◀ New ◀ Revised ~~deleted~~ Deleted

	External Cause (T-Code)					
Substance	Poisoning, Accidental (Unintentional)	Poisoning, Intentional Self-Harm	Poisoning, Assault	Poisoning, Undetermined	Adverse Effect	Underdosing
Antikaluretic	T50.3X1	T50.3X2	T50.3X3	T50.3X4	T50.3X5	T50.3X6
Antiknock (tetraethyl lead)	T56.0X1	T56.0X2	T56.0X3	T56.0X4	—	—
Antilipemic drug NEC	T46.6X1	T46.6X2	T46.6X3	T46.6X4	T46.6X5	T46.6X6
Antimalarial	T37.2X1	T37.2X2	T37.2X3	T37.2X4	T37.2X5	T37.2X6
prophylactic NEC	T37.2X1	T37.2X2	T37.2X3	T37.2X4	T37.2X5	T37.2X6
pyrimidine derivative	T37.2X1	T37.2X2	T37.2X3	T37.2X4	T37.2X5	T37.2X6
Antimetabolite	T45.1X1	T45.1X2	T45.1X4	T45.1X4	T45.1X5	T45.1X6
Antimitotic agent	T45.1X1	T45.1X2	T45.1X3	T45.1X4	T45.1X5	T45.1X6
Antimony (compounds) (vapor) NEC	T56.891	T56.892	T56.893	T56.894	—	—
anti-infectives	T37.8X1	T37.8X2	T37.8X3	T37.8X4	T37.8X5	T37.8X6
dimercaptosuccinate	T37.3X1	T37.3X2	T37.3X3	T37.3X4	T37.3X5	T37.3X6
hydride	T56.891	T56.892	T56.893	T56.894	—	—
pesticide (vapor)	T60.8X1	T60.8X2	T60.8X3	T60.8X4	—	—
potassium (sodium) tartrate	T37.8X1	T37.8X2	T37.8X3	T37.8X4	T37.8X5	T37.8X6
sodium dimercaptosuccinate	T37.3X1	T37.3X2	T37.3X3	T37.3X4	T37.3X5	T37.3X6
tartrated	T37.8X1	T37.8X2	T37.8X3	T37.8X4	T37.8X5	T37.8X6
Antimuscarinic NEC	T44.3X1	T44.3X2	T44.3X3	T44.3X4	T44.3X5	T44.3X6
Antimycobacterial drug NEC	T37.1X1	T37.1X2	T37.1X3	T37.1X4	T37.1X5	T37.1X6
antibiotics	T36.5X1	T36.5X2	T36.5X3	T36.5X4	T36.5X5	T36.5X6
combination	T37.1X1	T37.1X2	T37.1X3	T37.1X4	T37.1X5	T37.1X6
Antinausea drug	T45.0X1	T45.0X2	T45.0X3	T45.0X4	T45.0X5	T45.0X6
Antinematode drug	T37.4X1	T37.4X2	T37.4X3	T37.4X4	T37.4X5	T37.4X6
Antineoplastic NEC	T45.1X1	T45.1X2	T45.1X3	T45.1X4	T45.1X5	T45.1X6
alkaloidal	T45.1X1	T45.1X2	T45.1X3	T45.1X4	T45.1X5	T45.1X6
antibiotics	T45.1X1	T45.1X2	T45.1X3	T45.1X4	T45.1X5	T45.1X6
combination	T45.1X1	T45.1X2	T45.1X3	T45.1X4	T45.1X5	T45.1X6
estrogen	T38.5X1	T38.5X2	T38.5X3	T38.5X4	T38.5X5	T38.5X6
steroid	T38.7X1	T38.7X2	T38.7X3	T38.7X4	T38.7X5	T38.7X6
Antiparasitic drug (systemic)	T37.91	T37.92	T37.93	T37.94	T37.95	T37.96
local	T49.0X1	T49.0X2	T49.0X3	T49.0X4	T49.0X5	T49.0X6
specified NEC	T37.8X1	T37.8X2	T37.8X3	T37.8X4	T37.8X5	T37.8X6
Antiparkinsonism drug NEC	T42.8X1	T42.8X2	T42.8X3	T42.8X4	T42.8X5	T42.8X6
Antiperspirant NEC	T49.2X1	T49.2X2	T49.2X3	T49.2X4	T49.2X5	T49.2X6
Antiphlogistic NEC	T39.4X1	T39.4X2	T39.4X3	T39.4X4	T39.4X5	T39.4X6
Antiplatyhelmintic drug	T37.4X1	T37.4X2	T37.4X3	T37.4X4	T37.4X5	T37.4X6
Antiprotozoal drug NEC	T37.3X1	T37.3X2	T37.3X3	T37.3X4	T37.3X5	T37.3X6
blood	T37.2X1	T37.2X2	T37.2X3	T37.2X4	T37.2X5	T37.2X6
local	T49.0X1	T49.0X2	T49.0X3	T49.0X4	T49.0X5	T49.0X6
Antipruritic drug NEC	T49.1X1	T49.1X2	T49.1X3	T49.1X4	T49.1X5	T49.1X6
Antipsychotic drug	T43.501	T43.502	T43.503	T43.504	T43.505	T43.506
specified NEC	T43.591	T43.592	T43.593	T43.594	T43.595	T43.596

	External Cause (T-Code)					
Substance	Poisoning, Accidental (Unintentional)	Poisoning, Intentional Self-Harm	Poisoning, Assault	Poisoning, Undetermined	Adverse Effect	Underdosing
Antipyretic	T39.91	T39.92	T39.93	T39.94	T39.95	T39.96
specified NEC	T39.8X1	T39.8X2	T39.8X3	T39.8X4	T39.8X5	T39.8X6
Antipyrine	T39.2X1	T39.2X2	T39.2X3	T39.2X4	T39.2X5	T39.2X6
Antirabies hyperimmune serum	T50.Z11	T50.Z12	T50.Z13	T50.Z14	T50.Z15	T50.Z16
Antirheumatic NEC	T39.4X1	T39.4X2	T39.4X3	T39.4X4	T39.4X5	T39.4X6
Antirigidity drug NEC	T42.8X1	T42.8X2	T42.8X3	T42.8X4	T42.8X5	T42.8X6
Antischistosomal drug	T37.4X1	T37.4X2	T37.4X3	T37.4X4	T37.4X5	T37.4X6
Antiscorpion sera	T50.Z11	T50.Z12	T50.Z13	T50.Z14	T50.Z15	T50.Z16
Antiseborrheics	T49.4X1	T49.4X2	T49.4X3	T49.4X4	T49.4X5	T49.4X6
Antiseptics (external) (medicinal)	T49.0X1	T49.0X2	T49.0X3	T49.0X4	T49.0X5	T49.0X6
Antistine	T45.0X1	T45.0X2	T45.0X3	T45.0X4	T45.0X5	T45.0X6
Antitapeworm drug	T37.4X1	T37.4X2	T37.4X3	T37.4X4	T37.4X5	T37.4X6
Antitetanus immunoglobulin	T50.Z11	T50.Z12	T50.Z13	T50.Z14	T50.Z15	T50.Z16
Antithrombotic	T45.521	T45.522	T45.523	T45.524	T45.525	T45.526
Antithyroid drug NEC	T38.2X1	T38.2X2	T38.2X3	T38.2X4	T38.2X5	T38.2X6
Antitoxin	T50.Z11	T50.Z12	T50.Z13	T50.Z14	T50.Z15	T50.Z16
diphtheria	T50.Z11	T50.Z12	T50.Z13	T50.Z14	T50.Z15	T50.Z16
gas gangrene	T50.Z11	T50.Z12	T50.Z13	T50.Z14	T50.Z15	T50.Z16
tetanus	T50.Z11	T50.Z12	T50.Z13	T50.Z14	T50.Z15	T50.Z16
Antitoxin, any	T50.901	T50.902	T50.903	T50.904	T50.905	T50.906
Antitrichomonal drug	T37.3X1	T37.3X2	T37.3X3	T37.3X4	T37.3X5	T37.3X6
Antituberculars	T37.1X1	T37.1X2	T37.1X3	T37.1X4	T37.1X5	T37.1X6
antibiotics	T36.5X1	T36.5X2	T36.5X3	T36.5X4	T36.5X5	T36.5X6
Antitussive NEC	T48.3X1	T48.3X2	T48.3X3	T48.3X4	T48.3X5	T48.3X6
codeine mixture	T40.2X1	T40.2X2	T40.2X3	T40.2X4	T40.2X5	T40.2X6
opiate	T40.2X1	T40.2X2	T40.2X3	T40.2X4	T40.2X5	T40.2X6
Antivaricose drug	T46.8X1	T46.8X2	T46.8X3	T46.8X4	T46.8X5	T46.8X6
Antivenin, antivenom (sera)	T50.Z11	T50.Z12	T50.Z13	T50.Z14	T50.Z15	T50.Z16
crotaline	T50.Z11	T50.Z12	T50.Z13	T50.Z14	T50.Z15	T50.Z16
spider bite	T50.Z11	T50.Z12	T50.Z13	T50.Z14	T50.Z15	T50.Z16
Antivertigo drug	T45.0X1	T45.0X2	T45.0X3	T45.0X4	T45.0X5	T45.0X6
Antiviral drug NEC	T37.5X1	T37.5X2	T37.5X3	T37.5X4	T37.5X5	T37.5X6
eye	T49.5X1	T49.5X2	T49.5X3	T49.5X4	T49.5X5	T49.5X6
Antiwhipworm drug	T37.4X1	T37.4X2	T37.4X3	T37.4X4	T37.4X5	T37.4X6
Ant poisons — see Pesticides						
Antrol — see also by specific chemical substance	T60.91	T60.92	T60.93	T60.94		
fungicide	T60.91	T60.92	T60.93	T60.94	—	—
ANTU (alpha naphthylthiourea)	T60.4X1	T60.4X2	T60.4X3	T60.4X4	—	—
Apalcillin	T36.0X1	T36.0X2	T36.0X3	T36.0X4	T36.0X5	T36.0X6
APC	T48.5X1	T48.5X2	T48.5X3	T48.5X4	T48.5X5	T48.5X6
Aplonidine	T44.4X1	T44.4X2	T44.4X3	T44.4X4	T44.4X5	T44.4X6
Apomorphine	T47.7X1	T47.7X2	T47.7X3	T47.7X4	T47.7X5	T47.7X6

Substance	Poisoning, Accidental (Unintentional)	Poisoning, Intentional Self-Harm	Poisoning, Assault	Poisoning, Undetermined	Adverse Effect	Underdosing
Appetite depressants, central	T50.5X1	T50.5X2	T50.5X3	T50.5X4	T50.5X5	T50.5X6
Apraclonidine (hydrochloride)	T44.4X1	T44.4X2	T44.4X3	T44.4X4	T44.4X5	T44.4X6
Apresoline	T46.5X1	T46.5X2	T46.5X3	T46.5X4	T46.5X5	T46.5X6
Aprindine	T46.2X1	T46.2X2	T46.2X3	T46.2X4	T46.2X5	T46.2X6
Aprobarbital	T42.3X1	T42.3X2	T42.3X3	T42.3X4	T42.3X5	T42.3X6
Apronalide	T42.6X1	T42.6X2	T42.6X3	T42.6X4	T42.6X5	T42.6X6
Aprotinin	T45.621	T45.622	T45.623	T45.624	T45.625	T45.626
Aptocaine	T41.3X1	T41.3X2	T41.3X3	T41.3X4	T41.3X5	T41.3X6
Aqua fortis	T54.2X1	T54.2X2	T54.2X3	T54.2X4	—	—
Ara-A	T37.5X1	T37.5X2	T37.5X3	T37.5X4	T37.5X5	T37.5X6
Ara-C	T45.1X1	T45.1X2	T45.1X3	T45.1X4	T45.1X5	T45.1X6
Arachis oil	T49.3X1	T49.3X2	T49.3X3	T49.3X4	T49.3X5	T49.3X6
cathartic	T47.4X1	T47.4X2	T47.4X3	T47.4X4	T47.4X5	T47.4X6
Aralen	T37.2X1	T37.2X2	T37.2X3	T37.2X4	T37.2X5	T37.2X6
Arecoline	T44.1X1	T44.1X2	T44.1X3	T44.1X4	T44.1X5	T44.1X6
Arginine	T50.991	T50.992	T50.993	T50.994	T50.995	T50.996
glutamate	T50.991	T50.992	T50.993	T50.994	T50.995	T50.996
Argyrol	T49.0X1	T49.0X2	T49.0X3	T49.0X4	T49.0X5	T49.0X6
ENT agent	T49.6X1	T49.6X2	T49.6X3	T49.6X4	T49.6X5	T49.6X6
ophthalmic preparation	T49.5X1	T49.5X2	T49.5X3	T49.5X4	T49.5X5	T49.5X6
Aristocort	T38.0X1	T38.0X2	T38.0X3	T38.0X4	T38.0X5	T38.0X6
ENT agent	T49.6X1	T49.6X2	T49.6X3	T49.6X4	T49.6X5	T49.6X6
ophthalmic preparation	T49.5X1	T49.5X2	T49.5X3	T49.5X4	T49.5X5	T49.5X6
topical NEC	T49.0X1	T49.0X2	T49.0X3	T49.0X4	T49.0X5	T49.0X6
Aromatics, corrosive	T54.1X1	T54.1X2	T54.1X3	T54.1X4	—	—
disinfectants	T54.1X1	T54.1X2	T54.1X3	T54.1X4	—	—
Arsenate of lead	T57.0X1	T57.0X2	T57.0X3	T57.0X4	—	—
herbicide	T57.0X1	T57.0X2	T57.0X3	T57.0X4	—	—
Arsenic, arsenicals (compounds) (dust) (vapor) NEC	T57.0X1	T57.0X2	T57.0X3	T57.0X4	—	—
anti-infectives	T37.8X1	T37.8X2	T37.8X3	T37.8X4	T37.8X5	T37.8X6
pesticide (dust) (fumes)	T57.0X1	T57.0X2	T57.0X3	T57.0X4	—	—
Arsine (gas)	T57.0X1	T57.0X2	T57.0X3	T57.0X4	—	—
Arsphenamine (silver)	T37.8X1	T37.8X2	T37.8X3	T37.8X4	T37.8X5	T37.8X6
Arsthinol	T37.3X1	T37.3X2	T37.3X3	T37.3X4	T37.3X5	T37.3X6
Artane	T44.3X1	T44.3X2	T44.3X3	T44.3X4	T44.3X5	T44.3X6
Arthropod (venomous) NEC	T63.481	T63.482	T63.483	T63.484	—	—
Articaine	T41.3X1	T41.3X2	T41.3X3	T41.3X4	T41.3X5	T41.3X6
Asbestos	T57.8X1	T57.8X2	T57.8X3	T57.8X4	—	—
Ascaridole	T37.4X1	T37.4X2	T37.4X3	T37.4X4	T37.4X5	T37.4X6
Ascorbic acid	T45.2X1	T45.2X2	T45.2X3	T45.2X4	T45.2X5	T45.2X6
Asiaticoside	T49.0X1	T49.0X2	T49.0X3	T49.0X4	T49.0X5	T49.0X6

Substance	Poisoning, Accidental (Unintentional)	Poisoning, Intentional Self-Harm	Poisoning, Assault	Poisoning, Undetermined	Adverse Effect	Underdosing
Asparaginase	T45.1X1	T45.1X2	T45.1X3	T45.1X4	T45.1X5	T45.1X6
Aspidium (oleoresin)	T37.4X1	T37.4X2	T37.4X3	T37.4X4	T37.4X5	T37.4X6
Aspirin (aluminum) (soluble)	T39.011	T39.012	T39.013	T39.014	T39.015	T39.016
Aspoxicillin	T36.0X1	T36.0X2	T36.0X3	T36.0X4	T36.0X5	T36.0X6
Astemizole	T45.0X1	T45.0X2	T45.0X3	T45.0X4	T45.0X5	T45.0X6
Astringent (local)	T49.2X1	T49.2X2	T49.2X3	T49.2X4	T49.2X5	T49.2X6
specified NEC	T49.2X1	T49.2X2	T49.2X3	T49.2X4	T49.2X5	T49.2X6
Astromicin	T36.5X1	T36.5X2	T36.5X3	T36.5X4	T36.5X5	T36.5X6
Ataractic drug NEC	T43.501	T43.502	T43.503	T43.504	T43.505	T43.506
Atenolol	T44.7X1	T44.7X2	T44.7X3	T44.7X4	T44.7X5	T44.7X6
Atonia drug, intestinal	T47.4X1	T47.4X2	T47.4X3	T47.4X4	T47.4X5	T47.4X6
Atophan	T50.4X1	T50.4X2	T50.4X3	T50.4X4	T50.4X5	T50.4X6
Atracurium besilate	T48.1X1	T48.1X2	T48.1X3	T48.1X4	T48.1X5	T48.1X6
Atropine	T44.3X1	T44.3X2	T44.3X3	T44.3X4	T44.3X5	T44.3X6
derivative	T44.3X1	T44.3X2	T44.3X3	T44.3X4	T44.3X5	T44.3X6
methonitrate	T44.3X1	T44.3X2	T44.3X3	T44.3X4	T44.3X5	T44.3X6
Attapulgite	T47.6X1	T47.6X2	T47.6X3	T47.6X4	T47.6X5	T47.6X6
Attenuvax	T50.991	T50.992	T50.993	T50.994	T50.995	T50.996
Auramine	T65.891	T65.892	T65.893	T65.894	—	—
dye	T65.6X1	T65.6X2	T65.6X3	T65.6X4	—	—
fungicide	T60.3X1	T60.3X2	T60.3X3	T60.3X4	—	—
Auranofin	T39.4X1	T39.4X2	T39.4X3	T39.4X4	T39.4X5	T39.4X6
Aurantiin	T46.991	T46.992	T46.993	T46.994	T46.995	T46.996
Aureomycin	T36.4X1	T36.4X2	T36.4X3	T36.4X4	T36.4X5	T36.4X6
ophthalmic preparation	T49.5X1	T49.5X2	T49.5X3	T49.5X4	T49.5X5	T49.5X6
topical NEC	T49.0X1	T49.0X2	T49.0X3	T49.0X4	T49.0X5	T49.0X6
Aurothioglucose	T39.4X1	T39.4X2	T39.4X3	T39.4X4	T39.4X5	T39.4X6
Aurothioglycanide	T39.4X1	T39.4X2	T39.4X3	T39.4X4	T39.4X5	T39.4X6
Aurothiomalate sodium	T39.4X1	T39.4X2	T39.4X3	T39.4X4	T39.4X5	T39.4X6
Aurotioprol	T39.4X1	T39.4X2	T39.4X3	T39.4X4	T39.4X5	T39.4X6
Automobile fuel	T52.0X1	T52.0X2	T52.0X3	T52.0X4	—	—
Autonomic nervous system agent NEC	T44.901	T44.902	T44.903	T44.904	T44.905	T44.906
Avlosulfon	T37.1X1	T37.1X2	T37.1X3	T37.1X4	T37.1X5	T37.1X6
Avomine	T42.6X1	T42.6X2	T42.6X3	T42.6X4	T42.6X5	T42.6X6
Axerophthol	T45.2X1	T45.2X2	T45.2X3	T45.2X4	T45.2X5	T45.2X6
Azacitidine	T45.1X1	T45.1X2	T45.1X3	T45.1X4	T45.1X5	T45.1X6
Azacyclonol	T43.591	T43.592	T43.593	T43.594	T43.595	T43.596
Azadirachta	T60.2X1	T60.2X2	T60.2X3	T60.2X4	—	—
Azanidazole	T37.3X1	T37.3X2	T37.3X3	T37.3X4	T37.3X5	T37.3X6
Azapetine	T46.7X1	T46.7X2	T46.7X3	T46.7X4	T46.7X5	T46.7X6
Azapropazone	T39.2X1	T39.2X2	T39.2X3	T39.2X4	T39.2X5	T39.2X6

◀ New　◀◀ Revised　~~deleted~~ Deleted

	External Cause (T-Code)					
Substance	Poisoning, Accidental (Unintentional)	Poisoning, Intentional Self-Harm	Poisoning, Assault	Poisoning, Undetermined	Adverse Effect	Underdosing
Azaribine	T45.1X1	T45.1X2	T45.1X3	T45.1X4	T45.1X5	T45.1X6
Azaserine	T45.1X1	T45.1X2	T45.1X3	T45.1X4	T45.1X5	T45.1X6
Azatadine	T45.0X1	T45.0X2	T45.0X3	T45.0X4	T45.0X5	T45.0X6
Azatepa	T45.1X1	T45.1X2	T45.1X3	T45.1X4	T45.1X5	T45.1X6
Azathioprine	T45.1X1	T45.1X2	T45.1X3	T45.1X4	T45.1X5	T45.1X6
Azelaic acid	T49.0X1	T49.0X2	T49.0X3	T49.0X4	T49.0X5	T49.0X6
Azelastine	T45.0X1	T45.0X2	T45.0X3	T45.0X4	T45.0X5	T45.0X6
Azidocillin	T36.0X1	T36.0X2	T36.0X3	T36.0X4	T36.0X5	T36.0X6
Azidothymidine	T37.5X1	T37.5X2	T37.5X3	T37.5X4	T37.5X5	T37.5X6
Azinphos (ethyl) (methyl)	T60.0X1	T60.0X2	T60.0X3	T60.0X4	—	—
Aziridine (chelating)	T54.1X1	T54.1X2	T54.1X3	T54.1X4	—	—
Azithromycin	T36.3X1	T36.3X2	T36.3X3	T36.3X4	T36.3X5	T36.3X6
Azlocillin	T36.01	T36.02	T36.03	T36.04	T36.05	T36.06
Azobenzene smoke	T65.3X1	T65.3X2	T65.3X3	T65.3X4		
acaricide	T60.8X1	T60.8X2	T60.8X3	T60.8X4	—	—
Azosulfamide	T37.0X1	T37.0X2	T37.0X3	T37.0X4	T37.0X5	T37.0X6
AZT	T37.5X1	T37.5X2	T37.5X3	T37.5X4	T37.5X5	T37.5X6
Aztreonam	T36.1X1	T36.1X2	T36.1X3	T36.1X4	T36.1X5	T36.1X6
Azulfidine	T37.0X1	T37.0X2	T37.0X3	T37.0X4	T37.0X5	T37.0X6
Azuresin	T50.8X1	T50.8X2	T50.8X3	T50.8X4	T50.8X5	T50.8X6
B						
Bacampicillin	T36.0X1	T36.0X2	T36.0X3	T36.0X4	T36.0X5	T36.0X6
Bacillus						
lactobacillus	T47.8X1	T47.8X2	T47.8X3	T47.8X4	T47.8X5	T47.8X6
subtilis	T47.6X1	T47.6X2	T47.6X3	T47.6X4	T47.6X5	T47.6X6
Bacimycin	T49.0X1	T49.0X2	T49.0X3	T49.0X4	T49.0X5	T49.0X6
ophthalmic preparation	T49.5X1	T49.5X2	T49.5X3	T49.5X4	T49.5X5	T49.5X6
Bacitracin zinc	T49.0X1	T49.0X2	T49.0X3	T49.0X4	T49.0X5	T49.0X6
with neomycin	T49.0X1	T49.0X2	T49.0X3	T49.0X4	T49.0X5	T49.0X6
ENT agent	T49.6X1	T49.6X2	T49.6X3	T49.6X4	T49.6X5	T49.6X6
ophthalmic preparation	T49.5X1	T49.5X2	T49.5X3	T49.5X4	T49.5X5	T49.5X6
topical NEC	T49.0X1	T49.0X2	T49.0X3	T49.0X4	T49.0X5	T49.0X6
Baclofen	T42.8X1	T42.8X2	T42.8X3	T42.8X4	T42.8X5	T42.8X6
Baking soda	T50.991	T50.992	T50.993	T50.994	T50.995	T50.996
BAL	T45.8X1	T45.8X2	T45.8X3	T45.8X4	T45.8X5	T45.8X6
Bambuterol	T48.6X1	T48.6X2	T48.6X3	T48.6X4	T48.6X5	T48.6X6
Bamethan (sulfate)	T46.7X1	T46.7X2	T46.7X3	T46.7X4	T46.7X5	T46.7X6
Bamifylline	T48.6X1	T48.6X2	T48.6X3	T48.6X4	T48.6X5	T48.6X6
Bamipine	T45.0X1	T45.0X2	T45.0X3	T45.0X4	T45.0X5	T45.0X6
Baneberry — see Actaea spicata						
Banewort — see Belladonna						

	External Cause (T-Code)					
Substance	Poisoning, Accidental (Unintentional)	Poisoning, Intentional Self-Harm	Poisoning, Assault	Poisoning, Undetermined	Adverse Effect	Underdosing
Barbenyl	T42.3X1	T42.3X2	T42.3X3	T42.3X4	T42.3X5	T42.3X6
Barbexaclone	T42.6X1	T42.6X2	T42.6X3	T42.6X4	T42.6X5	T42.6X6
Barbital	T42.3X1	T42.3X2	T42.3X3	T42.3X4	T42.3X5	T42.3X6
sodium	T42.3X1	T42.3X2	T42.3X3	T42.3X4	T42.3X5	T42.3X6
Barbitone	T42.3X1	T42.3X2	T42.3X3	T42.3X4	T42.3X5	T42.3X6
Barbiturate NEC	T42.3X1	T42.3X2	T42.3X3	T42.3X4	T42.3X5	T42.3X6
with tranquilizer	T42.3X1	T42.3X2	T42.3X3	T42.3X4	T42.3X5	T42.3X6
anesthetic (intravenous)	T41.1X1	T41.1X2	T41.1X3	T41.1X4	T41.1X5	T41.1X6
Barium (carbonate) (chloride) (sulfite)	T57.8X1	T57.8X2	T57.8X3	T57.8X4		
diagnostic agent	T50.8X1	T50.8X2	T50.8X3	T50.8X4	T50.8X5	T50.8X6
pesticide	T60.4X1	T60.4X2	T60.4X3	T60.4X4		
rodenticide	T60.4X1	T60.4X2	T60.4X3	T60.4X4		
sulfate (medicinal)	T50.8X1	T50.8X2	T50.8X3	T50.8X4	T50.8X5	T50.8X6
Barrier cream	T49.3X1	T49.3X2	T49.3X3	T49.3X4	T49.3X5	T49.3X6
Basic fuchsin	T49.0X1	T49.0X2	T49.0X3	T49.0X4	T49.0X5	T49.0X6
Battery acid or fluid	T54.2X1	T54.2X2	T54.2X3	T54.2X4	—	—
Bay rum	T51.8X1	T51.8X2	T51.8X3	T51.8X4	—	—
BCG (vaccine)	T50.A91	T50.A92	T50.A93	T50.A94	T50.A95	T50.A96
BCNU	T45.1X1	T45.1X2	T45.1X3	T45.1X4	T45.1X5	T45.1X6
Bearsfoot	T62.2X1	T62.2X2	T62.2X3	T62.2X4		
Beclamide	T42.6X1	T42.6X2	T42.6X3	T42.6X4	T42.6X5	T42.6X6
Beclomethasone	T44.5X1	T44.5X2	T44.5X3	T44.5X4	T44.5X5	T44.5X6
Bee (sting) (venom)	T63.441	T63.442	T63.443	T63.444	—	—
Befunolol	T49.5X1	T49.5X2	T49.5X3	T49.5X4	T49.5X5	T49.5X6
Bekanamycin	T36.5X1	T36.5X2	T36.5X3	T36.5X4	T36.5X5	T36.5X6
Belladonna — see also Nightshade						
alkaloids	T44.3X1	T44.3X2	T44.3X3	T44.3X4	T44.3X5	T44.3X6
extract	T44.3X1	T44.3X2	T44.3X3	T44.3X4	T44.3X5	T44.3X6
herb	T44.3X1	T44.3X2	T44.3X3	T44.3X4	T44.3X5	T44.3X6
Bemegride	T50.7X1	T50.7X2	T50.7X3	T50.7X4	T50.7X5	T50.7X6
Benactyzine	T44.3X1	T44.3X2	T44.3X3	T44.3X4	T44.3X5	T44.3X6
Benadryl	T45.0X1	T45.0X2	T45.0X3	T45.0X4	T45.0X5	T45.0X6
Benaprizine	T44.3X1	T44.3X2	T44.3X3	T44.3X4	T44.3X5	T44.3X6
Benazepril	T46.4X1	T46.4X2	T46.4X3	T46.4X4	T46.4X5	T46.4X6
Bencyclane	T46.7X1	T46.7X2	T46.7X3	T46.7X4	T46.7X5	T46.7X6
Bendazol	T46.3X1	T46.3X2	T46.3X3	T46.3X4	T46.3X5	T46.3X6
Bendrofluazide	T50.2X1	T50.2X2	T50.2X3	T50.2X4	T50.2X5	T50.2X6
Bendroflumethiazide	T50.2X1	T50.2X2	T50.2X3	T50.2X4	T50.2X5	T50.2X6
Benemid	T50.4X1	T50.4X2	T50.4X3	T50.4X4	T50.4X5	T50.4X6
Benethamine penicillin	T36.0X1	T36.0X2	T36.0X3	T36.0X4	T36.0X5	T36.0X6
Benisone	T49.0X1	T49.0X2	T49.0X3	T49.0X4	T49.0X5	T49.0X6

◀ New   ◀ Revised   ~~deleted~~ Deleted

Substance	External Cause (T-Code)					
	Poisoning, Accidental (Unintentional)	Poisoning, Intentional Self-Harm	Poisoning, Assault	Poisoning, Undetermined	Adverse Effect	Underdosing
Benexate	T47.1X1	T47.1X2	T47.1X3	T47.1X4	T47.1X5	T47.1X6
Benfluorex	T46.6X1	T46.6X2	T46.6X3	T46.6X4	T46.6X5	T46.6X6
Benfotiamine	T45.2X1	T45.2X2	T45.2X3	T45.2X4	T45.2X5	T45.2X6
Benomyl	T60.0X1	T60.0X2	T60.0X3	T60.0X4	—	—
Benoquin	T49.8X1	T49.8X2	T49.8X3	T49.8X4	T49.8X5	T49.8X6
Benoxinate	T41.3X1	T41.3X2	T41.3X3	T41.3X4	T41.3X5	T41.3X6
Benperidol	T43.4X1	T43.4X2	T43.4X3	T43.4X4	T43.4X5	T43.4X6
Benproperine	T48.3X1	T48.3X2	T48.3X3	T48.3X4	T48.3X5	T48.3X6
Benserazide	T42.8X1	T42.8X2	T42.8X3	T42.8X4	T42.8X5	T42.8X6
Bentazepam	T42.4X1	T42.4X2	T42.4X3	T42.4X4	T42.4X5	T42.4X6
Bentiromide	T50.8X1	T50.8X2	T50.8X3	T50.8X4	T50.8X5	T50.8X6
Bentonite	T49.3X1	T49.3X2	T49.3X3	T49.3X4	T49.3X5	T49.3X6
Benzalbutyramide	T46.6X1	T46.6X2	T46.6X3	T46.6X4	T46.6X5	T46.6X6
Benzalkonium (chloride)	T49.0X1	T49.0X2	T49.0X3	T49.0X4	T49.0X5	T49.0X6
ophthalmic preparation	T49.5X1	T49.5X2	T49.5X3	T49.5X4	T49.5X5	T49.5X6
Benzamine	T41.3X1	T41.3X2	T41.3X3	T41.3X4	T41.3X5	T41.3X6
lactate	T49.1X1	T49.1X2	T49.1X3	T49.1X4	T49.1X5	T49.1X6
Benzamidosalicylate (calcium)	T37.1X1	T37.1X2	T37.1X3	T37.1X4	T37.1X5	T37.1X6
Benzamphetamine	T50.5X1	T50.5X2	T50.5X3	T50.5X4	T50.5X5	T50.5X6
Benzapril hydrochloride	T46.5X1	T46.5X2	T46.5X3	T46.5X4	T46.5X5	T46.5X6
Benzathine benzylpenicillin	T36.0X1	T36.0X2	T36.0X3	T36.0X4	T36.0X5	T36.0X6
Benzathine penicillin	T36.0X1	T36.0X2	T36.0X3	T36.0X4	T36.0X5	T36.0X6
Benzatropine	T42.8X1	T42.8X2	T42.8X3	T42.8X4	T42.8X5	T42.8X6
Benzbromarone	T50.4X1	T50.4X2	T50.4X3	T50.4X4	T50.4X5	T50.4X6
Benzcarbimine	T45.1X1	T45.1X2	T45.1X3	T45.1X4	T45.1X5	T45.1X6
Benzedrex	T44.991	T44.992	T44.993	T44.994	T44.995	T44.996
Benzedrine (amphetamine)	T43.621	T43.622	T43.623	T43.624	T43.625	T43.626
Benzenamine	T65.3X1	T65.3X2	T65.3X3	T65.3X4	—	—
Benzene	T52.1X1	T52.1X2	T52.1X3	T52.1X4	—	—
homologues (acetyl) (dimethyl) (methyl) (solvent)	T52.2X1	T52.2X2	T52.2X3	T52.2X4	—	—
Benzethonium (chloride)	T49.0X1	T49.0X2	T49.0X3	T49.0X4	T49.0X5	T49.0X6
Benzfetamine	T50.5X1	T50.5X2	T50.5X3	T50.5X4	T50.5X5	T50.5X6
Benzhexol	T44.3X1	T44.3X2	T44.3X3	T44.3X4	T44.3X5	T44.3X6
Benzhydramine (chloride)	T45.0X1	T45.0X2	T45.0X3	T45.0X4	T45.0X5	T45.0X6
Benzidine	T65.891	T65.892	T65.893	T65.894	—	—
Benzilonium bromide	T44.3X1	T44.3X2	T44.3X3	T44.3X4	T44.3X5	T44.3X6
Benzimidazole	T60.3X1	T60.3X2	T60.3X3	T60.3X4	—	—
Benzin(e) — see Ligroin						
Benziodarone	T46.3X1	T46.3X2	T46.3X3	T46.3X4	T46.3X5	T46.3X6
Benznidazole	T37.3X1	T37.3X2	T37.3X3	T37.3X4	T37.3X5	T37.3X6
Benzocaine	T41.3X1	T41.3X2	T41.3X3	T41.3X4	T41.3X5	T41.3X6

Substance	External Cause (T-Code)					
	Poisoning, Accidental (Unintentional)	Poisoning, Intentional Self-Harm	Poisoning, Assault	Poisoning, Undetermined	Adverse Effect	Underdosing
Benzoctamine	T43.0X1	T43.0X2	T43.0X3	T43.0X4	T43.0X5	T43.0X6
Benzodiapin	T42.4X1	T42.4X2	T42.4X3	T42.4X4	T42.4X5	T42.4X6
Benzodiazepine NEC	T42.4X1	T42.4X2	T42.4X3	T42.4X4	T42.4X5	T42.4X6
Benzoic acid	T49.0X1	T49.0X2	T49.0X3	T49.0X4	T49.0X5	T49.0X6
with salicylic acid	T49.0X1	T49.0X2	T49.0X3	T49.0X4	T49.0X5	T49.0X6
Benzoin (tincture)	T48.5X1	T48.5X2	T48.5X3	T48.5X4	T48.5X5	T48.5X6
Benzol (benzene)	T52.1X1	T52.1X2	T52.1X3	T52.1X4	—	—
vapor	T52.0X1	T52.0X2	T52.0X3	T52.0X4	—	—
Benzomorphan	T40.2X1	T40.2X2	T40.2X3	T40.2X4	T40.2X5	T40.2X6
Benzonatate	T48.3X1	T48.3X2	T48.3X3	T48.3X4	T48.3X5	T48.3X6
Benzophenones	T49.3X1	T49.3X2	T49.3X3	T49.3X4	T49.3X5	T49.3X6
Benzopyrone	T46.991	T46.992	T46.993	T46.994	T46.995	T46.996
Benzothiadiazides	T50.2X1	T50.2X2	T50.2X3	T50.2X4	T50.2X5	T50.2X6
Benzoxonium chloride	T49.0X1	T49.0X2	T49.0X3	T49.0X4	T49.0X5	T49.0X6
Benzoyl peroxide	T49.0X1	T49.0X2	T49.0X3	T49.0X4	T49.0X5	T49.0X6
Benzoylpas calcium	T37.1X1	T37.1X2	T37.1X3	T37.1X4	T37.1X5	T37.1X6
Benzperidin	T43.591	T43.592	T43.593	T43.594	T43.595	T43.596
Benzperidol	T43.591	T43.592	T43.593	T43.594	T43.595	T43.596
Benzphetamine	T50.5X1	T50.5X2	T50.5X3	T50.5X4	T50.5X5	T50.5X6
Benzpyrinium bromide	T44.1X1	T44.1X2	T44.1X3	T44.1X4	T44.1X5	T44.1X6
Benzquinamide	T45.0X1	T45.0X2	T45.0X3	T45.0X4	T45.0X5	T45.0X6
Benzthiazide	T50.2X1	T50.2X2	T50.2X3	T50.2X4	T50.2X5	T50.2X6
Benztropine						
anticholinergic	T44.3X1	T44.3X2	T44.3X3	T44.3X4	T44.3X5	T44.3X6
antiparkinson	T42.8X1	T42.8X2	T42.8X3	T42.8X4	T42.8X5	T42.8X6
Benzydamine	T49.0X1	T49.0X2	T49.0X3	T49.0X4	T49.0X5	T49.0X6
Benzyl						
acetate	T52.8X1	T52.8X2	T52.8X3	T52.8X4	—	—
alcohol	T49.0X1	T49.0X2	T49.0X3	T49.0X4	T49.0X5	T49.0X6
benzoate	T49.0X1	T49.0X2	T49.0X3	T49.0X4	T49.0X5	T49.0X6
Benzoic acid	T49.0X1	T49.0X2	T49.0X3	T49.0X4	T49.0X5	T49.0X6
morphine	T40.2X1	T40.2X2	T40.2X3	T40.2X4	—	—
nicotinate	T46.6X1	T46.6X2	T46.6X3	T46.6X4	T46.6X5	T46.6X6
penicillin	T36.0X1	T36.0X2	T36.0X3	T36.0X4	T36.0X5	T36.0X6
Benzylhydrochlorthia-zide	T50.2X1	T50.2X2	T50.2X3	T50.2X4	T50.2X5	T50.2X6
Benzylpenicillin	T36.0X1	T36.0X2	T36.0X3	T36.0X4	T36.0X5	T36.0X6
Benzylthiouracil	T38.2X1	T38.2X2	T38.2X3	T38.2X4	T38.2X5	T38.2X6
Bephenium hydroxy-naphthoate	T37.4X1	T37.4X2	T37.4X3	T37.4X4	T37.4X5	T37.4X6
Bepridil	T46.1X1	T46.1X2	T46.1X3	T46.1X4	T46.1X5	T46.1X6
Bergamot oil	T65.891	T65.892	T65.893	T65.894	—	—
Bergapten	T50.991	T50.992	T50.993	T50.994	T50.995	T50.996
Berries, poisonous	T62.1X1	T62.1X2	T62.1X3	T62.1X4	—	—

◀ New ◀ Revised deleted Deleted

	External Cause (T-Code)					
Substance	Poisoning, Accidental (Unintentional)	Poisoning, Intentional Self-Harm	Poisoning, Assault	Poisoning, Undetermined	Adverse Effect	Underdosing
Beryllium (compounds)	T56.7X1	T56.7X2	T56.7X3	T56.7X4	—	—
b-acetyldigoxin	T46.0X1	T46.0X2	T46.0X3	T46.0X4	T46.0X5	T46.0X6
beta adrenergic blocking agent, heart	T44.7X1	T44.7X2	T44.7X3	T44.7X4	T44.7X5	T44.7X6
b-benzalbutyramide	T46.6X1	T46.6X2	T46.6X3	T46.6X4	T46.6X5	T46.6X6
Betacarotene	T45.2X1	T45.2X2	T45.2X3	T45.2X4	T45.2X5	T45.2X6
b-eucaine	T49.1X1	T49.1X2	T49.1X3	T49.1X4	T49.1X5	T49.1X6
Beta-Chlor	T42.6X1	T42.6X2	T42.6X3	T42.6X4	T42.6X5	T42.6X6
b-galactosidase	T47.5X1	T47.5X2	T47.5X3	T47.5X4	T47.5X5	T47.5X6
Betahistine	T46.7X1	T46.7X2	T46.7X3	T46.7X4	T46.7X5	T46.7X6
Betaine	T47.5X1	T47.5X2	T47.5X3	T47.5X4	T47.5X5	T47.5X6
Betamethasone	T49.0X1	T49.0X2	T49.0X3	T49.0X4	T49.0X5	T49.0X6
topical	T49.0X1	T49.0X2	T49.0X3	T49.0X4	T49.0X5	T49.0X6
Betamicin	T36.8X1	T36.8X2	T36.8X3	T36.8X4	T36.8X5	T36.8X6
Betanidine	T46.5X1	T46.5X2	T46.5X3	T46.5X4	T46.5X5	T46.5X6
b-sitosterol(s)	T46.6X1	T46.6X2	T46.6X3	T46.6X4	T46.6X5	T46.6X6
Betaxolol	T44.7X1	T44.7X2	T44.7X3	T44.7X4	T44.7X5	T44.7X6
Betazole	T50.8X1	T50.8X2	T50.8X3	T50.8X4	T50.8X5	T50.8X6
Bethanechol	T44.1X1	T44.1X2	T44.1X3	T44.1X4	T44.1X5	T44.1X6
chloride	T44.1X1	T44.1X2	T44.1X3	T44.1X4	T44.1X5	T44.1X6
Bethanidine	T46.5X1	T46.5X2	T46.5X3	T46.5X4	T46.5X5	T46.5X6
Betoxycaine	T41.3X1	T41.3X2	T41.3X3	T41.3X4	T41.3X5	T41.3X6
Betula oil	T49.3X1	T49.3X2	T49.3X3	T49.3X4	T49.3X5	T49.3X6
Bevantolol	T44.7X1	T44.7X2	T44.7X3	T44.7X4	T44.7X5	T44.7X6
Bevonium metilsulfate	T44.3X1	T44.3X2	T44.3X3	T44.3X4	T44.3X5	T44.3X6
Bezafibrate	T46.6X1	T46.6X2	T46.6X3	T46.6X4	T46.6X5	T46.6X6
Bezitramide	T40.4X1	T40.4X2	T40.4X3	T40.4X4	T40.4X5	T40.4X6
BHA	T50.991	T50.992	T50.993	T50.994	T50.995	T50.996
Bhang	T40.7X1	T40.7X2	T40.7X3	T40.7X4	T40.7X5	T40.7X6
BHC (medicinal)	T49.0X1	T49.0X2	T49.0X3	T49.0X4	T49.0X5	T49.0X6
nonmedicinal (vapor)	T53.6X1	T53.6X2	T53.6X3	T53.6X4	—	—
Bialamicol	T37.3X1	T37.3X2	T37.3X3	T37.3X4	T37.3X5	T37.3X6
Bibenzonium bromide	T48.3X1	T48.3X2	T48.3X3	T48.3X4	T48.3X5	T48.3X6
Bibrocathol	T49.5X1	T49.5X2	T49.5X3	T49.5X4	T49.5X5	T49.5X6
Bichloride of mercury — see Mercury, chloride						
Bichromates (calcium) (potassium) (sodium) (crystals)	T57.8X1	T57.8X2	T57.8X3	T57.8X4	—	—
fumes	T56.2X1	T56.2X2	T56.2X3	T56.2X4	—	—
Biclotymol	T49.6X1	T49.6X2	T49.6X3	T49.6X4	T49.6X5	T49.6X6
Bicuculline	T50.7X1	T50.7X2	T50.7X3	T50.7X4	T50.7X5	T50.7X6
Bifemelane	T43.291	T43.292	T43.293	T43.294	T43.295	T43.296
Biguanide derivatives, oral	T38.3X1	T38.3X2	T38.3X3	T38.3X4	T38.3X5	T38.3X6

	External Cause (T-Code)					
Substance	Poisoning, Accidental (Unintentional)	Poisoning, Intentional Self-Harm	Poisoning, Assault	Poisoning, Undetermined	Adverse Effect	Underdosing
Biligrafin	T50.8X1	T50.8X2	T50.8X3	T50.8X4	T50.8X5	T50.8X6
Bile salts	T47.5X1	T47.5X2	T47.5X3	T47.5X4	T47.5X5	T47.5X6
Bilopaque	T50.8X1	T50.8X2	T50.8X3	T50.8X4	T50.8X5	T50.8X6
Binifibrate	T46.6X1	T46.6X2	T46.6X3	T46.6X4	T46.6X5	T46.6X6
Binitrobenzol	T65.3X1	T65.3X2	T65.3X3	T65.3X4	—	—
Bioflavonoid(s)	T46.991	T46.992	T46.993	T46.994	T46.995	T46.996
Biological substance NEC	T50.901	T50.902	T50.903	T50.904	T50.905	T50.906
Biotin	T45.2X1	T45.2X2	T45.2X3	T45.2X4	T45.2X5	T45.2X6
Biperiden	T44.3X1	T44.3X2	T44.3X3	T44.3X4	T44.3X5	T44.3X6
Bisacodyl	T47.2X1	T47.2X2	T47.2X3	T47.2X4	T47.2X5	T47.2X6
Bisbentiamine	T45.2X1	T45.2X2	T45.2X3	T45.2X4	T45.2X5	T45.2X6
Bisbutiamine	T45.2X1	T45.2X2	T45.2X3	T45.2X4	T45.2X5	T45.2X6
Bisdequalinium (salts) (diacetate)	T49.6X1	T49.6X2	T49.6X3	T49.6X4	T49.6X5	T49.6X6
Bishydroxycoumarin	T45.511	T45.512	T45.513	T45.514	T45.515	T45.516
Bismarsen	T37.8X1	T37.8X2	T37.8X3	T37.8X4	T37.8X5	T37.8X6
Bismuth salts	T47.6X1	T47.6X2	T47.6X3	T47.6X4	T47.6X5	T47.6X6
aluminate	T47.1X1	T47.1X2	T47.1X3	T47.1X4	T47.1X5	T47.1X6
anti-infectives	T37.8X1	T37.8X2	T37.8X3	T37.8X4	T37.8X5	T37.8X6
formic iodide	T49.0X1	T49.0X2	T49.0X3	T49.0X4	T49.0X5	T49.0X6
glycolylarsenate	T49.0X1	T49.0X2	T49.0X3	T49.0X4	T49.0X5	T49.0X6
nonmedicinal (compounds) NEC	T65.91	T65.92	T65.93	T65.94	—	—
subcarbonate	T47.6X1	T47.6X2	T47.6X3	T47.6X4	T47.6X5	T47.6X6
subsalicylate	T37.8X1	T37.8X2	T37.8X3	T37.8X4	T37.8X5	T37.8X6
sulfarsphenamine	T37.8X1	T37.8X2	T37.8X3	T37.8X4	T37.8X5	T37.8X6
Bisoprolol	T44.7X1	T44.7X2	T44.7X3	T44.7X4	T44.7X5	T44.7X6
Bisoxatin	T47.2X1	T47.2X2	T47.2X3	T47.2X4	T47.2X5	T47.2X6
Bisulepin (hydrochloride)	T45.0X1	T45.0X2	T45.0X3	T45.0X4	T45.0X5	T45.0X6
Bithionol	T37.8X1	T37.8X2	T37.8X3	T37.8X4	T37.8X5	T37.8X6
anthelminthic	T37.4X1	T37.4X2	T37.4X3	T37.4X4	T37.4X5	T37.4X6
Bitolterol	T48.6X1	T48.6X2	T48.6X3	T48.6X4	T48.6X5	T48.6X6
Bitoscanate	T37.4X1	T37.4X2	T37.4X3	T37.4X4	T37.4X5	T37.4X6
Bitter almond oil	T62.8X1	T62.8X2	T62.8X3	T62.8X4	—	—
Bittersweet	T62.2X1	T62.2X2	T62.2X3	T62.2X4	—	—
Black						
flag	T60.91	T60.92	T60.93	T60.94	—	—
henbane	T62.2X1	T62.2X2	T62.2X3	T62.2X4	—	—
leaf (40)	T60.91	T60.92	T60.93	T60.94	—	—
widow spider (bite)	T63.311	T63.312	T63.313	T63.314	—	—
antivenin	T50.Z11	T50.Z12	T50.Z13	T50.Z14	T50.Z15	T50.Z16
Blast furnace gas (carbon monoxide from)	T58.8X1	T58.8X2	T58.8X3	T58.8X4	—	—
Bleach	T54.91	T54.92	T54.93	T54.94	—	—

◀ New　◀ Revised　deleted Deleted

TABLE OF DRUGS AND CHEMICALS

Substance	External Cause (T-Code)					
	Poisoning, Accidental (Unintentional)	Poisoning, Intentional Self-Harm	Poisoning, Assault	Poisoning, Undetermined	Adverse Effect	Underdosing
Bleaching agent (medicinal)	T49.4X1	T49.4X2	T49.4X3	T49.4X4	T49.4X5	T49.4X6
Bleomycin	T45.1X1	T45.1X2	T45.1X3	T45.1X4	T45.1X5	T45.1X6
Blockain	T41.3X1	T41.3X2	T41.3X3	T41.3X4	T41.3X5	T41.3X6
infiltration (subcutaneous)	T41.3X1	T41.3X2	T41.3X3	T41.3X4	T41.3X5	T41.3X6
nerve block (peripheral) (plexus)	T41.3X1	T41.3X2	T41.3X3	T41.3X4	T41.3X5	T41.3X6
topical (surface)	T41.3X1	T41.3X2	T41.3X3	T41.3X4	T41.3X5	T41.3X6
Blockers, calcium channel	T46.1X1	T46.1X2	T46.1X3	T46.1X4	T46.1X5	T46.1X6
Blood (derivatives) (natural) (plasma) (whole)	T45.8X1	T45.8X2	T45.8X3	T45.8X4	T45.8X5	T45.8X6
dried	T45.8X1	T45.8X2	T45.8X3	T45.8X4	T45.8X5	T45.8X6
drug affecting NEC	T45.91	T45.92	T45.93	T45.94	T45.95	T45.96
expander NEC	T45.8X1	T45.8X2	T45.8X3	T45.8X4	T45.8X5	T45.8X6
fraction NEC	T45.8X1	T45.8X2	T45.8X3	T45.8X4	T45.8X5	T45.8X6
substitute (macromolecular)	T45.8X1	T45.8X2	T45.8X3	T45.8X4	T45.8X5	T45.8X6
Blue velvet	T40.2X1	T40.2X2	T40.2X3	T40.2X4	—	—
Bone meal	T62.8X1	T62.8X2	T62.8X3	T62.8X4	—	—
Bonine	T45.0X1	T45.0X2	T45.0X3	T45.0X4	T45.0X5	T45.0X6
Bopindolol	T44.7X1	T44.7X2	T44.7X3	T44.7X4	T44.7X5	T44.7X6
Boracic acid	T49.0X1	T49.0X2	T49.0X3	T49.0X4	T49.0X5	T49.0X6
ENT agent	T49.6X1	T49.6X2	T49.6X3	T49.6X4	T49.6X5	T49.6X6
ophthalmic preparation	T49.5X1	T49.5X2	T49.5X3	T49.5X4	T49.5X5	T49.5X6
Borane complex	T57.8X1	T57.8X2	T57.8X3	T57.8X4	—	—
Borate(s)	T57.8X1	T57.8X2	T57.8X3	T57.8X4	—	—
buffer	T50.991	T50.992	T50.993	T50.994	T50.995	T50.996
cleanser	T54.91	T54.92	T54.93	T54.94		
sodium	T57.8X1	T57.8X2	T57.8X3	T57.8X4	—	—
Borax (cleanser)	T54.91	T54.92	T54.93	T54.94		
Bordeaux mixture	T60.3X1	T60.3X2	T60.3X3	T60.3X4		
Boric acid	T49.0X1	T49.0X2	T49.0X3	T49.0X4	T49.0X5	T49.0X6
ENT agent	T49.6X1	T49.6X2	T49.6X3	T49.6X4	T49.6X5	T49.6X6
ophthalmic preparation	T49.5X1	T49.5X2	T49.5X3	T49.5X4	T49.5X5	T49.5X6
Bornaprine	T44.3X1	T44.3X2	T44.3X3	T44.3X4	T44.3X5	T44.3X6
Boron	T57.8X1	T57.8X2	T57.8X3	T57.8X4	—	—
hydride NEC	T57.8X1	T57.8X2	T57.8X3	T57.8X4	—	—
fumes or gas	T57.8X1	T57.8X2	T57.8X3	T57.8X4	—	—
trifluoride	T59.891	T59.892	T59.893	T59.894		
Botox	T48.291	T48.292	T48.293	T48.294	T48.295	T48.296
Botulinus anti-toxin (type A, B)	T50.Z11	T50.Z12	T50.Z13	T50.Z14	T50.Z15	T50.Z16
Brake fluid vapor	T59.891	T59.892	T59.893	T59.894		
Brallobarbital	T42.3X1	T42.3X2	T42.3X3	T42.3X4	T42.3X5	T42.3X6
Bran (wheat)	T47.4X1	T47.4X2	T47.4X3	T47.4X4	T47.4X5	T47.4X6
Brass (fumes)	T56.891	T56.892	T56.893	T56.894	—	—

Substance	External Cause (T-Code)					
	Poisoning, Accidental (Unintentional)	Poisoning, Intentional Self-Harm	Poisoning, Assault	Poisoning, Undetermined	Adverse Effect	Underdosing
Brasso	T52.0X1	T52.0X2	T52.0X3	T52.0X4	—	—
Bretylium tosilate	T46.2X1	T46.2X2	T46.2X3	T46.2X4	T46.2X5	T46.2X6
Brevital (sodium)	T41.1X1	T41.1X2	T41.1X3	T41.1X4	T41.1X5	T41.1X6
Brinase	T45.3X1	T45.3X2	T45.3X3	T45.3X4	T45.3X5	T45.3X6
British antilewisite	T45.8X1	T45.8X2	T45.8X3	T45.8X4	T45.8X5	T45.8X6
Brodifacoum	T60.4X1	T60.4X2	T60.4X3	T60.4X4	—	—
Bromal (hydrate)	T42.6X1	T42.6X2	T42.6X3	T42.6X4	T42.6X5	T42.6X6
Bromazepam	T42.4X1	T42.4X2	T42.4X3	T42.4X4	T42.4X5	T42.4X6
Bromazine	T45.0X1	T45.0X2	T45.0X3	T45.0X4	T45.0X5	T45.0X6
Brombenzylcyanide	T59.3X1	T59.3X2	T59.3X3	T59.3X4	—	—
Bromelains	T45.3X1	T45.3X2	T45.3X3	T45.3X4	T45.3X5	T45.3X6
Bromethalin	T60.4X1	T60.4X2	T60.4X3	T60.4X4	—	—
Bromhexine	T48.4X1	T48.4X2	T48.4X3	T48.4X4	T48.4X5	T48.4X6
Bromide salts	T42.6X1	T42.6X2	T42.6X3	T42.6X4	T42.6X5	T42.6X6
Bromindione	T45.511	T45.512	T45.513	T45.514	T45.515	T45.516
Bromine						
compounds (medicinal)	T42.6X1	T42.6X2	T42.6X3	T42.6X4	T42.6X5	T42.6X6
sedative	T42.6X1	T42.6X2	T42.6X3	T42.6X4	T42.6X5	T42.6X6
vapor	T59.891	T59.892	T59.893	T59.894	—	—
Bromisovalum	T42.6X1	T42.6X2	T42.6X3	T42.6X4	T42.6X5	T42.6X6
Bromisoval	T42.6X1	T42.6X2	T42.6X3	T42.6X4	T42.6X5	T42.6X6
Bromobenzylcyanide	T59.3X1	T59.3X2	T59.3X3	T59.3X4	—	—
Bromochlorosalicylani-lide	T49.0X1	T49.0X2	T49.0X3	T49.0X4	T49.0X5	T49.0X6
Bromocriptine	T42.8X1	T42.8X2	T42.8X3	T42.8X4	T42.8X5	T42.8X6
Bromodiphenhydramine	T45.0X1	T45.0X2	T45.0X3	T45.0X4	T45.0X5	T45.0X6
Bromoform	T42.6X1	T42.6X2	T42.6X3	T42.6X4	T42.6X5	T42.6X6
Bromophenol blue reagent	T50.991	T50.992	T50.993	T50.994	T50.995	T50.996
Bromopride	T47.8X1	T47.8X2	T47.8X3	T47.8X4	T47.8X5	T47.8X6
Bromosalicylchloranitide	T49.0X1	T49.0X2	T49.0X3	T49.0X4	T49.0X5	T49.0X6
Bromosalicylhydroxamic acid	T37.1X1	T37.1X2	T37.1X3	T37.1X4	T37.1X5	T37.1X6
Bromo-seltzer	T39.1X1	T39.1X2	T39.1X3	T39.1X4	T39.1X5	T39.1X6
Bromoxynil	T60.3X1	T60.3X2	T60.3X3	T60.3X4	—	—
Bromperidol	T43.4X1	T43.4X2	T43.4X3	T43.4X4	T43.4X5	T43.4X6
Brompheniramine	T45.0X1	T45.0X2	T45.0X3	T45.0X4	T45.0X5	T45.0X6
Bromsulfophthalein	T50.8X1	T50.8X2	T50.8X3	T50.8X4	T50.8X5	T50.8X6
Bromural	T42.6X1	T42.6X2	T42.6X3	T42.6X4	T42.6X5	T42.6X6
Bromvaletone	T42.6X1	T42.6X2	T42.6X3	T42.6X4	T42.6X5	T42.6X6
Bronchodilator NEC	T48.6X1	T48.6X2	T48.6X3	T48.6X4	T48.6X5	T48.6X6
Brotizolam	T42.4X1	T42.4X2	T42.4X3	T42.4X4	T42.4X5	T42.4X6
Brovincamine	T46.7X1	T46.7X2	T46.7X3	T46.7X4	T46.7X5	T46.7X6
Brown spider (bite) (venom)	T63.391	T63.392	T63.393	T63.394	—	—

◀ New ◀ Revised ~~deleted~~ Deleted

Substance	Poisoning, Accidental (Unintentional)	Poisoning, Intentional Self-Harm	Poisoning, Assault	Poisoning, Undetermined	Adverse Effect	Underdosing
Brown recluse spider (bite) (venom)	T63.331	T63.332	T63.333	T63.334	—	—
Broxaterol	T48.6X1	T48.6X2	T48.6X3	T48.6X4	T48.6X5	T48.6X6
Broxuridine	T45.1X1	T45.1X2	T45.1X3	T45.1X4	T45.1X5	T45.1X6
Broxyquinoline	T37.8X1	T37.8X2	T37.8X3	T37.8X4	T37.8X5	T37.8X6
Bruceine	T48.291	T48.292	T48.293	T48.294	T48.295	T48.296
Brucia	T62.2X1	T62.2X2	T62.2X3	T62.2X4	—	—
Brucine	T65.1X1	T65.1X2	T65.1X3	T65.1X4	—	—
Brunswick green — *see Copper*						
Bruten — *see Ibuprofen*						
Bryonia	T47.2X1	T47.2X2	T47.2X3	T47.2X4	T47.2X5	T47.2X6
Buclizine	T45.0X1	T45.0X2	T45.0X3	T45.0X4	T45.0X5	T45.0X6
Buclosamide	T49.0X1	T49.0X2	T49.0X3	T49.0X4	T49.0X5	T49.0X6
Budesonide	T44.5X1	T44.5X2	T44.5X3	T44.5X4	T44.5X5	T44.5X6
Budralazine	T46.5X1	T46.5X2	T46.5X3	T46.5X4	T46.5X5	T46.5X6
Bufferin	T39.011	T39.012	T39.013	T39.014	T39.015	T39.016
Buflomedil	T46.7X1	T46.7X2	T46.7X3	T46.7X4	T46.7X5	T46.7X6
Buformin	T38.3X1	T38.3X2	T38.3X3	T38.3X4	T38.3X5	T38.3X6
Bufotenine	T40.991	T40.992	T40.993	T40.994	—	—
Bufrolin	T48.6X1	T48.6X2	T48.6X3	T48.6X4	T48.6X5	T48.6X6
Bufylline	T48.6X1	T48.6X2	T48.6X3	T48.6X4	T48.6X5	T48.6X6
Bulk filler	T50.5X1	T50.5X2	T50.5X3	T50.5X4	T50.5X5	T50.5X6
cathartic	T47.4X1	T47.4X2	T47.4X3	T47.4X4	T47.4X5	T47.4X6
Bumetanide	T50.1X1	T50.1X2	T50.1X3	T50.1X4	T50.1X5	T50.1X6
Bunaftine	T46.2X1	T46.2X2	T46.2X3	T46.2X4	T46.2X5	T46.2X6
Bunamiodyl	T50.8X1	T50.8X2	T50.8X3	T50.8X4	T50.8X5	T50.8X6
Bunazosin	T44.6X1	T44.6X2	T44.6X3	T44.6X4	T44.6X5	T44.6X6
Bunitrolol	T44.7X1	T44.7X2	T44.7X3	T44.7X4	T44.7X5	T44.7X6
Buphenine	T46.7X1	T46.7X2	T46.7X3	T46.7X4	T46.7X5	T46.7X6
Bupivacaine	T41.3X1	T41.3X2	T41.3X3	T41.3X4	T41.3X5	T41.3X6
infiltration (subcutaneous)	T41.3X1	T41.3X2	T41.3X3	T41.3X4	T41.3X5	T41.3X6
nerve block (peripheral) (plexus)	T41.3X1	T41.3X2	T41.3X3	T41.3X4	T41.3X5	T41.3X6
spinal	T41.3X1	T41.3X2	T41.3X3	T41.3X4	T41.3X5	T41.3X6
Bupranolol	T44.7X1	T44.7X2	T44.7X3	T44.7X4	T44.7X5	T44.7X6
Buprenorphine	T40.4X1	T40.4X2	T40.4X3	T40.4X4	T40.4X5	T40.4X6
Bupropion	T43.291	T43.292	T43.293	T43.294	T43.295	T43.296
Burimamide	T47.1X1	T47.1X2	T47.1X3	T47.1X4	T47.1X5	T47.1X6
Buserelin	T38.891	T38.892	T38.893	T38.894	T38.895	T38.896
Buspirone	T43.591	T43.592	T43.593	T43.594	T43.595	T43.596
Busulfan, busulphan	T45.1X1	T45.1X2	T45.1X3	T45.1X4	T45.1X5	T45.1X6
Butabarbital (sodium)	T42.3X1	T42.3X2	T42.3X3	T42.3X4	T42.3X5	T42.3X6
Butabarbitone	T42.3X1	T42.3X2	T42.3X3	T42.3X4	T42.3X5	T42.3X6

Substance	Poisoning, Accidental (Unintentional)	Poisoning, Intentional Self-Harm	Poisoning, Assault	Poisoning, Undetermined	Adverse Effect	Underdosing
Butabarpal	T42.3X1	T42.3X2	T42.3X3	T42.3X4	T42.3X5	T42.3X6
Butacaine	T41.3X1	T41.3X2	T41.3X3	T41.3X4	T41.3X5	T41.3X6
Butalamine	T46.7X1	T46.7X2	T46.7X3	T46.7X4	T46.7X5	T46.7X6
Butalbital	T42.3X1	T42.3X2	T42.3X3	T42.3X4	T42.3X5	T42.3X6
Butallylonal	T42.3X1	T42.3X2	T42.3X3	T42.3X4	T42.3X5	T42.3X6
Butamben	T41.3X1	T41.3X2	T41.3X3	T41.3X4	T41.3X5	T41.3X6
Butamirate	T48.3X1	T48.3X2	T48.3X3	T48.3X4	T48.3X5	T48.3X6
Butane (distributed in mobile container)	T59.891	T59.892	T59.893	T59.894	—	—
distributed through pipes	T59.891	T59.892	T59.893	T59.894	—	—
incomplete combustion	T58.11	T58.12	T58.13	T58.14	—	—
Butanilicaine	T41.3X1	T41.3X2	T41.3X3	T41.3X4	T41.3X5	T41.3X6
Butanol	T51.3X1	T51.3X2	T51.3X3	T51.3X4		
Butanone, 2-butanone	T52.4X1	T52.4X2	T52.4X3	T52.4X4	—	
Butantrone	T49.4X1	T49.4X2	T49.4X3	T49.4X4	T49.4X5	T49.4X6
Butaperazine	T43.3X1	T43.3X2	T43.3X3	T43.3X4	T43.3X5	T43.3X6
Butazolidin	T39.2X1	T39.2X2	T39.2X3	T39.2X4	T39.2X5	T39.2X6
Butetamate	T48.6X1	T48.6X2	T48.6X3	T48.6X4	T48.6X5	T48.6X6
Butethal	T42.3X1	T42.3X2	T42.3X3	T42.3X4	T42.3X5	T42.3X6
Butethamate	T44.3X1	T44.3X2	T44.3X3	T44.3X4	T44.3X5	T44.3X6
Buthalitone (sodium)	T41.1X1	T41.1X2	T41.1X3	T41.1X4	T41.1X5	T41.1X6
Butisol (sodium)	T42.3X1	T42.3X2	T42.3X3	T42.3X4	T42.3X5	T42.3X6
Butizide	T50.2X1	T50.2X2	T50.2X3	T50.2X4	T50.2X5	T50.2X6
Butobarbital	T42.3X1	T42.3X2	T42.3X3	T42.3X4	T42.3X5	T42.3X6
sodium	T42.3X1	T42.3X2	T42.3X3	T42.3X4	T42.3X5	T42.3X6
Butobarbitone	T42.3X1	T42.3X2	T42.3X3	T42.3X4	T42.3X5	T42.3X6
Butoconazole (nitrate)	T49.0X1	T49.0X2	T49.0X3	T49.0X4	T49.0X5	T49.0X6
Butorphanol	T40.4X1	T40.4X2	T40.4X3	T40.4X4	T40.4X5	T40.4X6
Butriptyline	T43.011	T43.012	T43.013	T43.014	T43.015	T43.016
Butropium bromide	T44.3X1	T44.3X2	T44.3X3	T44.3X4	T44.3X5	T44.3X6
Buttercups	T62.2X1	T62.2X2	T62.2X3	T62.2X4	—	—
Butter of antimony — *see Antimony*						
Butyl						
acetate (secondary)	T52.8X1	T52.8X2	T52.8X3	T52.8X4	—	—
alcohol	T51.3X1	T51.3X2	T51.3X3	T51.3X4	—	—
aminobenzoate	T41.3X1	T41.3X2	T41.3X3	T41.3X4	T41.3X5	T41.3X6
butyrate	T52.8X1	T52.8X2	T52.8X3	T52.8X4		
carbinol	T51.3X1	T51.3X2	T51.3X3	T51.3X4		
carbitol	T52.3X1	T52.3X2	T52.3X3	T52.3X4	—	—
cellosolve	T52.3X1	T52.3X2	T52.3X3	T52.3X4		
chloral (hydrate)	T42.6X1	T42.6X2	T42.6X3	T42.6X4	T42.6X5	T42.6X6
formate	T52.8X1	T52.8X2	T52.8X3	T52.8X4	—	—

◀ New   ◀ Revised   d̶e̶l̶e̶t̶e̶d̶ Deleted

TABLE OF DRUGS AND CHEMICALS

	External Cause (T-Code)					
Substance	Poisoning, Accidental (Unintentional)	Poisoning, Intentional Self-Harm	Poisoning, Assault	Poisoning, Undetermined	Adverse Effect	Underdosing
Butyl *(Continued)*						
lactate	T52.8X1	T52.8X2	T52.8X3	T52.8X4	—	—
propionate	T52.8X1	T52.8X2	T52.8X3	T52.8X4	—	—
scopolamine bromide	T44.3X1	T44.3X2	T44.3X3	T44.3X4	T44.3X5	T44.3X6
thiobarbital sodium	T41.1X1	T41.1X2	T41.1X3	T41.1X4	T41.1X5	T41.1X6
Butylated hydroxy-anisole	T50.991	T50.992	T50.993	T50.994	T50.995	T50.996
Butylchloral hydrate	T42.6X1	T42.6X2	T42.6X3	T42.6X4	T42.6X5	T42.6X6
Butyltoluene	T52.2X1	T52.2X2	T52.2X3	T52.2X4	—	—
Butyn	T41.3X1	T41.3X2	T41.3X3	T41.3X4	T41.3X5	T41.3X6
Butyrophenone (-based tranquilizers)	T43.4X1	T43.4X2	T43.4X3	T43.4X4	T43.4X5	T43.4X6
C						
Cabergoline	T42.8X1	T42.8X2	T42.8X3	T42.8X4	T42.8X5	T42.8X6
Cacodyl, cacodylic acid	T57.0X1	T57.0X2	T57.0X3	T57.0X4	—	—
Cactinomycin	T45.1X1	T45.1X2	T45.1X3	T45.1X4	T45.1X5	T45.1X6
Cade oil	T49.4X1	T49.4X2	T49.4X3	T49.4X4	T49.4X5	T49.4X6
Cadexomer iodine	T49.0X1	T49.0X2	T49.0X3	T49.0X4	T49.0X5	T49.0X6
Cadmium (chloride) (fumes) (oxide)	T56.3X1	T56.3X2	T56.3X3	T56.3X4	—	—
sulfide (medicinal) NEC	T49.4X1	T49.4X2	T49.4X3	T49.4X4	T49.4X5	T49.4X6
Cadralazine	T46.5X1	T46.5X2	T46.5X3	T46.5X4	T46.5X5	T46.5X6
Caffeine	T43.611	T43.612	T43.613	T43.614	T43.615	T43.616
Calabar bean	T62.2X1	T62.2X2	T62.2X3	T62.2X4	—	—
Caladium seguinum	T62.2X1	T62.2X2	T62.2X3	T62.2X4	—	—
Calamine (lotion)	T49.3X1	T49.3X2	T49.3X3	T49.3X4	T49.3X5	T49.3X6
Calcifediol	T45.2X1	T45.2X2	T45.2X3	T45.2X4	T45.2X5	T45.2X6
Calciferol	T45.2X1	T45.2X2	T45.2X3	T45.2X4	T45.2X5	T45.2X6
Calcitonin	T50.991	T50.992	T50.993	T50.994	T50.995	T50.996
Calcitriol	T45.2X1	T45.2X2	T45.2X3	T45.2X4	T45.2X5	T45.2X6
Calcium	T50.3X1	T50.3X2	T50.3X3	T50.3X4	T50.3X5	T50.3X6
actylsalicylate	T39.011	T39.012	T39.013	T39.014	T39.015	T39.016
benzamidosalicylate	T37.1X1	T37.1X2	T37.1X3	T37.1X4	T37.1X5	T37.1X6
bromide	T42.6X1	T42.6X2	T42.6X3	T42.6X4	T42.6X5	T42.6X6
bromolactobionate	T42.6X1	T42.6X2	T42.6X3	T42.6X4	T42.6X5	T42.6X6
carbaspirin	T39.011	T39.012	T39.013	T39.014	T39.015	T39.016
carbimide	T50.6X1	T50.6X2	T50.6X3	T50.6X4	T50.6X5	T50.6X6
carbonate	T47.1X1	T47.1X2	T47.1X3	T47.1X4	T47.1X5	T47.1X6
chloride	T50.991	T50.992	T50.993	T50.994	T50.995	T50.996
anhydrous	T50.991	T50.992	T50.993	T50.994	T50.995	T50.996
cyanide	T57.8X1	T57.8X2	T57.8X3	T57.8X4	—	—
dioctyl sulfosuccinate	T47.4X1	T47.4X2	T47.4X3	T47.4X4	T47.4X5	T47.4X6
disodium edathamil	T45.8X1	T45.8X2	T45.8X3	T45.8X4	T45.8X5	T45.8X6

	External Cause (T-Code)					
Substance	Poisoning, Accidental (Unintentional)	Poisoning, Intentional Self-Harm	Poisoning, Assault	Poisoning, Undetermined	Adverse Effect	Underdosing
Calcium *(Continued)*						
disodium edetate	T45.8X1	T45.8X2	T45.8X3	T45.8X4	T45.8X5	T45.8X6
dobesilate	T46.991	T46.992	T46.993	T46.994	T46.995	T46.996
EDTA	T45.8X1	T45.8X2	T45.8X3	T45.8X4	T45.8X5	T45.8X6
ferrous citrate	T45.4X1	T45.4X2	T45.4X3	T45.4X4	T45.4X5	T45.4X6
folinate	T45.8X1	T45.8X2	T45.8X3	T45.8X4	T45.8X5	T45.8X6
glubionate	T50.3X1	T50.3X2	T50.3X3	T50.3X4	T50.3X5	T50.3X6
gluconate	T50.3X1	T50.3X2	T50.3X3	T50.3X4	T50.3X5	T50.3X6
gluconogalactogluconate	T50.3X1	T50.3X2	T50.3X3	T50.3X4	T50.3X5	T50.3X6
hydrate, hydroxide	T54.3X1	T54.3X2	T54.3X3	T54.3X4	—	—
hypochlorite	T54.3X1	T54.3X2	T54.3X3	T54.3X4	—	—
iodide	T48.4X1	T48.4X2	T48.4X3	T48.4X4	T48.4X5	T48.4X6
ipodate	T50.8X1	T50.8X2	T50.8X3	T50.8X4	T50.8X5	T50.8X6
lactate	T50.3X1	T50.3X2	T50.3X3	T50.3X4	T50.3X5	T50.3X6
leucovorin	T45.8X1	T45.8X2	T45.8X3	T45.8X4	T45.8X5	T45.8X6
mandelate	T37.91	T37.92	T37.93	T37.94	T37.95	T37.96
oxide	T54.3X1	T54.3X2	T54.3X3	T54.3X4	—	—
pantothenate	T45.2X1	T45.2X2	T45.2X3	T45.2X4	T45.2X5	T45.2X6
phosphate	T50.3X1	T50.3X2	T50.3X3	T50.3X4	T50.3X5	T50.3X6
salicylate	T39.091	T39.092	T39.093	T39.094	T39.095	T39.096
salts	T50.3X1	T50.3X2	T50.3X3	T50.3X4	T50.3X5	T50.3X6
Calculus-dissolving drug	T50.991	T50.992	T50.993	T50.994	T50.995	T50.996
Calomel	T49.0X1	T49.0X2	T49.0X3	T49.0X4	T49.0X5	T49.0X6
Caloric agent	T50.3X1	T50.3X2	T50.3X3	T50.3X4	T50.3X5	T50.3X6
Calusterone	T38.7X1	T38.7X2	T38.7X3	T38.7X4	T38.7X5	T38.7X6
Camazepam	T42.4X1	T42.4X2	T42.4X3	T42.4X4	T42.4X5	T42.4X6
Camomile	T49.0X1	T49.0X2	T49.0X3	T49.0X4	T49.0X5	T49.0X6
Camoquin	T37.2X1	T37.2X2	T37.2X3	T37.2X4	T37.2X5	T37.2X6
Camphor						
insecticide	T60.2X1	T60.2X2	T60.2X3	T60.2X4	—	—
medicinal	T49.8X1	T49.8X2	T49.8X3	T49.8X4	T49.8X5	T49.8X6
Camylofin	T44.3X1	T44.3X2	T44.3X3	T44.3X4	T44.3X5	T44.3X6
Cancer chemotherapy drug regimen	T45.1X1	T45.1X2	T45.1X3	T45.1X4	T45.1X5	T45.1X6
Candeptin	T49.0X1	T49.0X2	T49.0X3	T49.0X4	T49.0X5	T49.0X6
Candicidin	T49.0X1	T49.0X2	T49.0X3	T49.0X4	T49.0X5	T49.0X6
Cannabinol	T40.7X1	T40.7X2	T40.7X3	T40.7X4	T40.7X5	T40.7X6
Cannabis (derivatives)	T40.7X1	T40.7X2	T40.7X3	T40.7X4	T40.7X5	T40.7X6
Canned heat	T51.1X1	T51.1X2	T51.1X3	T51.1X4	—	—
Canrenoic acid	T50.0X1	T50.0X2	T50.0X3	T50.0X4	T50.0X5	T50.0X6
Canrenone	T50.0X1	T50.0X2	T50.0X3	T50.0X4	T50.0X5	T50.0X6
Cantharides, cantharidin, cantharis	T49.8X1	T49.8X2	T49.8X3	T49.8X4	T49.8X5	T49.8X6

◀ New ◀ Revised ~~deleted~~ Deleted

Substance	Poisoning, Accidental (Unintentional)	Poisoning, Intentional Self-Harm	Poisoning, Assault	Poisoning, Undetermined	Adverse Effect	Underdosing
Canthaxanthin	T50.991	T50.992	T50.993	T50.994	T50.995	T50.996
Capillary-active drug NEC	T46.901	T46.902	T46.903	T46.904	T46.905	T46.906
Capreomycin	T36.8X1	T36.8X2	T36.8X3	T36.8X4	T36.8X5	T36.8X6
Capsicum	T49.4X1	T49.4X2	T49.4X3	T49.4X4	T49.4X5	T49.4X6
Captafol	T60.3X1	T60.3X2	T60.3X3	T60.3X4	—	—
Captan	T60.3X1	T60.3X2	T60.3X3	T60.3X4	—	—
Captodiame, captodiamine	T43.591	T43.592	T43.593	T43.594	T43.595	T43.596
Captopril	T46.4X1	T46.4X2	T46.4X3	T46.4X4	T46.4X5	T46.4X6
Caramiphen	T44.3X1	T44.3X2	T44.3X3	T44.3X4	T44.3X5	T44.3X6
Carazolol	T44.7X1	T44.7X2	T44.7X3	T44.7X4	T44.7X5	T44.7X6
Carbachol	T44.1X1	T44.1X2	T44.1X3	T44.1X4	T44.1X5	T44.1X6
Carbacrylamine (resin)	T50.3X1	T50.3X2	T50.3X3	T50.3X4	T50.3X5	T50.3X6
Carbamate (insecticide)	T60.0X1	T60.0X2	T60.0X3	T60.0X4	—	—
Carbamate (sedative)	T42.6X1	T42.6X2	T42.6X3	T42.6X4	T42.6X5	T42.6X6
herbicide	T60.0X1	T60.0X2	T60.0X3	T60.0X4	—	—
insecticide	T60.0X1	T60.0X2	T60.0X3	T60.0X4	—	—
Carbamazepine	T42.1X1	T42.1X2	T42.1X3	T42.1X4	T42.1X5	T42.1X6
Carbamide	T47.3X1	T47.3X2	T47.3X3	T47.3X4	T47.3X5	T47.3X6
peroxide	T49.0X1	T49.0X2	T49.0X3	T49.0X4	T49.0X5	T49.0X6
topical	T49.8X1	T49.8X2	T49.8X3	T49.8X4	T49.8X5	T49.8X6
Carbamylcholine chloride	T44.1X1	T44.1X2	T44.1X3	T44.1X4	T44.1X5	T44.1X6
Carbaril	T60.0X1	T60.0X2	T60.0X3	T60.0X4	—	—
Carbarsone	T37.3X1	T37.3X2	T37.3X3	T37.3X4	T37.3X5	T37.3X6
Carbaryl	T60.0X1	T60.0X2	T60.0X3	T60.0X4	—	—
Carbaspirin	T39.011	T39.012	T39.013	T39.014	T39.015	T39.016
Carbazochrome (salicylate) (sodium sulfonate)	T49.4X1	T49.4X2	T49.4X3	T49.4X4	T49.4X5	T49.4X6
Carbenicillin	T36.0X1	T36.0X2	T36.0X3	T36.0X4	T36.0X5	T36.0X6
Carbenoxolone	T47.1X1	T47.1X2	T47.1X3	T47.1X4	T47.1X5	T47.1X6
Carbetapentane	T48.3X1	T48.3X2	T48.3X3	T48.3X4	T48.3X5	T48.3X6
Carbethyl salicylate	T39.091	T39.092	T39.093	T39.094	T39.095	T39.096
Carbidopa (with levodopa)	T42.8X1	T42.8X2	T42.8X3	T42.8X4	T42.8X5	T42.8X6
Carbimazole	T38.2X1	T38.2X2	T38.2X3	T38.2X4	T38.2X5	T38.2X6
Carbinol	T51.1X1	T51.1X2	T51.1X3	T51.1X4	—	—
Carbinoxamine	T45.0X1	T45.0X2	T45.0X3	T45.0X4	T45.0X5	T45.0X6
Carbiphene	T39.8X1	T39.8X2	T39.8X3	T39.8X4	T39.8X5	T39.8X6
Carbitol	T52.3X1	T52.3X2	T52.3X3	T52.3X4	—	—
Carbocaine	T41.3X1	T41.3X2	T41.3X3	T41.3X4	T41.3X5	T41.3X6
infiltration (subcutaneous)	T41.3X1	T41.3X2	T41.3X3	T41.3X4	T41.3X5	T41.3X6
nerve block (peripheral) (plexus)	T41.3X1	T41.3X2	T41.3X3	T41.3X4	T41.3X5	T41.3X6
topical (surface)	T41.3X1	T41.3X2	T41.3X3	T41.3X4	T41.3X5	T41.3X6
Carbo medicinalis	T47.6X1	T47.6X2	T47.6X3	T47.6X4	T47.6X5	T47.6X6

Substance	Poisoning, Accidental (Unintentional)	Poisoning, Intentional Self-Harm	Poisoning, Assault	Poisoning, Undetermined	Adverse Effect	Underdosing
Carbomycin	T36.8X1	T36.8X2	T36.8X3	T36.8X4	T36.8X5	T36.8X6
Carbocisteine	T48.4X1	T48.4X2	T48.4X3	T48.4X4	T48.4X5	T48.4X6
Carbocromen	T46.3X1	T46.3X2	T46.3X3	T46.3X4	T46.3X5	T46.3X6
Carbol fuchsin	T49.0X1	T49.0X2	T49.0X3	T49.0X4	T49.0X5	T49.0X6
Carbolic acid — *see also Phenol*	T54.0X1	T54.0X2	T54.0X3	T54.0X4	—	—
Carbolonium (bromide)	T48.1X1	T48.1X2	T48.1X3	T48.1X4	T48.1X5	T48.1X6
Carbon						
bisulfide (liquid)	T65.4X1	T65.4X2	T65.4X3	T65.4X4	—	—
vapor	T65.4X1	T65.4X2	T65.4X3	T65.4X4	—	—
dioxide (gas)	T59.7X1	T59.7X2	T59.7X3	T59.7X4	—	—
medicinal	T41.5X1	T41.5X2	T41.5X3	T41.5X4	T41.5X5	T41.5X6
nonmedicinal	T59.7X1	T59.7X2	T59.7X3	T59.7X4	—	—
snow	T49.4X1	T49.4X2	T49.4X3	T49.4X4	T49.4X5	T49.4X6
disulfide (liquid)	T65.4X1	T65.4X2	T65.4X3	T65.4X4	—	—
vapor	T65.4X1	T65.4X2	T65.4X3	T65.4X4	—	—
monoxide (from incomplete combustion)	T58.91	T58.92	T58.93	T58.94	—	—
blast furnace gas	T58.8X1	T58.8X2	T58.8X3	T58.8X4	—	—
butane (distributed in mobile container)	T58.11	T58.12	T58.13	T58.14	—	—
distributed through pipes	T58.11	T58.12	T58.13	T58.14	—	—
charcoal fumes	T58.2X1	T58.2X2	T58.2X3	T58.2X4	—	—
coal	T58.2X1	T58.2X2	T58.2X3	T58.2X4	—	—
coke (in domestic stoves, fireplaces)	T58.2X1	T58.2X2	T58.2X3	T58.2X4	—	—
gas (piped)	T58.11	T58.12	T58.13	T58.14	—	—
solid (in domestic stoves, fireplaces)	T58.2X1	T58.2X2	T58.2X3	T58.2X4	—	—
exhaust gas (motor) not in transit	T58.01	T58.02	T58.03	T58.04	—	—
combustion engine, any not in watercraft	T58.01	T58.02	T58.03	T58.04	—	—
farm tractor, not in transit	T58.01	T58.02	T58.03	T58.04	—	—
gas engine	T58.01	T58.02	T58.03	T58.04	—	—
motor pump	T58.01	T58.02	T58.03	T58.04	—	—
motor vehicle, not in transit	T58.01	T58.02	T58.03	T58.04	—	—
fuel (in domestic use)	T58.2X1	T58.2X2	T58.2X3	T58.2X4	—	—
gas (piped)	T58.11	T58.12	T58.13	T58.14	—	—
in mobile container	T58.11	T58.12	T58.13	T58.14	—	—
utility	T58.11	T58.12	T58.13	T58.14	—	—
in mobile container	T58.11	T58.12	T58.13	T58.14	—	—
piped (natural)	T58.11	T58.12	T58.13	T58.14	—	—

TABLE OF DRUGS AND CHEMICALS

Substance	Poisoning, Accidental (Unintentional)	Poisoning, Intentional Self-Harm	Poisoning, Assault	Poisoning, Undetermined	Adverse Effect	Underdosing
Carbon *(Continued)*						
monoxide *(Continued)*						
illuminating gas	T58.11	T58.12	T58.13	T58.14	—	—
industrial fuels or gases, any	T58.8X1	T58.8X2	T58.8X3	T58.8X4	—	—
kerosene (in domestic stoves, fireplaces)	T58.2X1	T58.2X2	T58.2X3	T58.2X4	—	—
kiln gas or vapor	T58.8X1	T58.8X2	T58.8X3	T58.8X4	—	—
motor exhaust gas, not in transit	T58.01	T58.02	T58.03	T58.04	—	—
piped gas (manufactured) (natural)	T58.11	T58.12	T58.13	T58.14	—	—
producer gas	T58.8X1	T58.8X2	T58.8X3	T58.8X4	—	—
propane (distributed in mobile container)	T58.11	T58.12	T58.13	T58.14	—	—
distributed through pipes	T58.11	T58.12	T58.13	T58.14	—	—
specified source NEC	T58.8X1	T58.8X2	T58.8X3	T58.8X4	—	—
stove gas	T58.11	T58.12	T58.13	T58.14	—	—
piped	T58.11	T58.12	T58.13	T58.14	—	—
utility gas	T58.11	T58.12	T58.13	T58.14	—	—
piped	T58.11	T58.12	T58.13	T58.14	—	—
water gas	T58.11	T58.12	T58.13	T58.14	—	—
wood (in domestic stoves, fireplaces)	T58.2X1	T58.2X2	T58.2X3	T58.2X4	—	—
tetrachloride (vapor) NEC	T53.0X1	T53.0X2	T53.0X3	T53.0X4	—	—
liquid (cleansing agent) NEC	T53.0X1	T53.0X2	T53.0X3	T53.0X4	—	—
solvent	T53.0X1	T53.0X2	T53.0X3	T53.0X4	—	—
Carbonic acid gas	T59.7X1	T59.7X2	T59.7X3	T59.7X4	—	—
anhydrase inhibitor NEC	T50.2X1	T50.2X2	T50.2X3	T50.2X4	T50.2X5	T50.2X6
Carbophenothion	T60.0X1	T60.0X2	T60.0X3	T60.0X4	—	—
Carboplatin	T45.1X1	T45.1X2	T45.1X3	T45.1X4	T45.1X5	T45.1X6
Carboprost	T48.0X1	T48.0X2	T48.0X3	T48.0X4	T48.0X5	T48.0X6
Carboquone	T45.1X1	T45.1X2	T45.1X3	T45.1X4	T45.1X5	T45.1X6
Carbowax	T49.3X1	T49.3X2	T49.3X3	T49.3X4	T49.3X5	T49.3X6
Carboxymethyl-cellulose	T47.4X1	T47.4X2	T47.4X3	T47.4X4	T47.4X5	T47.4X6
S-Carboxymethyl-cysteine	T48.4X1	T48.4X2	T48.4X3	T48.4X4	T48.4X5	T48.4X6
Carbrital	T42.3X1	T42.3X2	T42.3X3	T42.3X4	T42.3X5	T42.3X6
Carbromal	T42.6X1	T42.6X2	T42.6X3	T42.6X4	T42.6X5	T42.6X6
Carbutamide	T38.3X1	T38.3X2	T38.3X3	T38.3X4	T38.3X5	T38.3X6
Carbuterol	T48.6X1	T48.6X2	T48.6X3	T48.6X4	T48.6X5	T48.6X6
Cardiac						
depressants	T46.2X1	T46.2X2	T46.2X3	T46.2X4	T46.2X5	T46.2X6
rhythm regulator	T46.2X1	T46.2X2	T46.2X3	T46.2X4	T46.2X5	T46.2X6
specified NEC	T46.2X1	T46.2X2	T46.2X3	T46.2X4	T46.2X5	T46.2X6

Substance	Poisoning, Accidental (Unintentional)	Poisoning, Intentional Self-Harm	Poisoning, Assault	Poisoning, Undetermined	Adverse Effect	Underdosing
Cardiografin	T50.8X1	T50.8X2	T50.8X3	T50.8X4	T50.8X5	T50.8X6
Cardio-green	T50.8X1	T50.8X2	T50.8X3	T50.8X4	T50.8X5	T50.8X6
Cardiotonic (glycoside) NEC	T46.0X1	T46.0X2	T46.0X3	T46.0X4	T46.0X5	T46.0X6
Cardiovascular drug NEC	T46.901	T46.902	T46.903	T46.904	T46.905	T46.906
Cardrase	T50.2X1	T50.2X2	T50.2X3	T50.2X4	T50.2X5	T50.2X6
Carfusin	T49.0X1	T49.0X2	T49.0X3	T49.0X4	T49.0X5	T49.0X6
Carfecillin	T36.0X1	T36.0X2	T36.0X3	T36.0X4	T36.0X5	T36.0X6
Carfenazine	T43.3X1	T43.3X2	T43.3X3	T43.3X4	T43.3X5	T43.3X6
Carindacillin	T36.0X1	T36.0X2	T36.0X3	T36.0X4	T36.0X5	T36.0X6
Carisoprodol	T42.8X1	T42.8X2	T42.8X3	T42.8X4	T42.8X5	T42.8X6
Carmellose	T47.4X1	T47.4X2	T47.4X3	T47.4X4	T47.4X5	T47.4X6
Carminative	T47.5X1	T47.5X2	T47.5X3	T47.5X4	T47.5X5	T47.5X6
Carmofur	T45.1X1	T45.1X2	T45.1X3	T45.1X4	T45.1X5	T45.1X6
Carmustine	T45.1X1	T45.1X2	T45.1X3	T45.1X4	T45.1X5	T45.1X6
Carotene	T45.2X1	T45.2X2	T45.2X3	T45.2X4	T45.2X5	T45.2X6
Carphenazine	T43.3X1	T43.3X2	T43.3X3	T43.3X4	T43.3X5	T43.3X6
Carpipramine	T42.4X1	T42.4X2	T42.4X3	T42.4X4	T42.4X5	T42.4X6
Carprofen	T39.311	T39.312	T39.313	T39.314	T39.315	T39.316
Carpronium chloride	T44.3X1	T44.3X2	T44.3X3	T44.3X4	T44.3X5	T44.3X6
Carrageenan	T47.8X1	T47.8X2	T47.8X3	T47.8X4	T47.8X5	T47.8X6
Carteolol	T44.7X1	T44.7X2	T44.7X3	T44.7X4	T44.7X5	T44.7X6
Carter's Little Pills	T47.2X1	T47.2X2	T47.2X3	T47.2X4	T47.2X5	T47.2X6
Cascara (sagrada)	T47.2X1	T47.2X2	T47.2X3	T47.2X4	T47.2X5	T47.2X6
Cassava	T62.2X1	T62.2X2	T62.2X3	T62.2X4	—	—
Castellani's paint	T49.0X1	T49.0X2	T49.0X3	T49.0X4	T49.0X5	T49.0X6
Castor						
bean	T62.2X1	T62.2X2	T62.2X3	T62.2X4	—	—
oil	T47.2X1	T47.2X2	T47.2X3	T47.2X4	T47.2X5	T47.2X6
Catalase	T45.3X1	T45.3X2	T45.3X3	T45.3X4	T45.3X5	T45.3X6
Caterpillar (sting)	T63.431	T63.432	T63.433	T63.434	—	—
Catha (edulis) (tea)	T43.691	T43.692	T43.693	T43.694	—	—
Cathartic NEC	T47.4X1	T47.4X2	T47.4X3	T47.4X4	T47.4X5	T47.4X6
anthacene derivative	T47.2X1	T47.2X2	T47.2X3	T47.2X4	T47.2X5	T47.2X6
bulk	T47.4X1	T47.4X2	T47.4X3	T47.4X4	T47.4X5	T47.4X6
contact	T47.2X1	T47.2X2	T47.2X3	T47.2X4	T47.2X5	T47.2X6
emollient NEC	T47.4X1	T47.4X2	T47.4X3	T47.4X4	T47.4X5	T47.4X6
irritant NEC	T47.2X1	T47.2X2	T47.2X3	T47.2X4	T47.2X5	T47.2X6
mucilage	T47.4X1	T47.4X2	T47.4X3	T47.4X4	T47.4X5	T47.4X6
saline	T47.3X1	T47.3X2	T47.3X3	T47.3X4	T47.3X5	T47.3X6
vegetable	T47.2X1	T47.2X2	T47.2X3	T47.2X4	T47.2X5	T47.2X6
Cathine	T50.5X1	T50.5X2	T50.5X3	T50.5X4	T50.5X5	T50.5X6
Cathomycin	T36.8X1	T36.8X2	T36.8X3	T36.8X4	T36.8X5	T36.8X6

◀ New ◀ Revised ~~deleted~~ Deleted

Substance	Poisoning, Accidental (Unintentional)	Poisoning, Intentional Self-Harm	Poisoning, Assault	Poisoning, Undetermined	Adverse Effect	Underdosing
Cation exchange resin	T50.3X1	T50.3X2	T50.3X3	T50.3X4	T50.3X5	T50.3X6
Caustic(s) NEC	T54.91	T54.92	T54.93	T54.94	—	—
alkali	T54.3X1	T54.3X2	T54.3X3	T54.3X4	—	—
hydroxide	T54.3X1	T54.3X2	T54.3X3	T54.3X4	—	—
potash	T54.3X1	T54.3X2	T54.3X3	T54.3X4	—	—
soda	T54.3X1	T54.3X2	T54.3X3	T54.3X4	—	—
specified NEC	T54.91	T54.92	T54.93	T54.94	—	—
Ceepryn	T49.0X1	T49.0X2	T49.0X3	T49.0X4	T49.0X5	T49.0X6
ENT agent	T49.6X1	T49.6X2	T49.6X3	T49.6X4	T49.6X5	T49.6X6
lozenges	T49.6X1	T49.6X2	T49.6X3	T49.6X4	T49.6X5	T49.6X6
Cefacetrile	T36.1X1	T36.1X2	T36.1X3	T36.1X4	T36.1X5	T36.1X6
Cefaclor	T36.1X1	T36.1X2	T36.1X3	T36.1X4	T36.1X5	T36.1X6
Cefadroxil	T36.1X1	T36.1X2	T36.1X3	T36.1X4	T36.1X5	T36.1X6
Cefalexin	T36.1X1	T36.1X2	T36.1X3	T36.1X4	T36.1X5	T36.1X6
Cefaloglycin	T36.1X1	T36.1X2	T36.1X3	T36.1X4	T36.1X5	T36.1X6
Cefaloridine	T36.1X1	T36.1X2	T36.1X3	T36.1X4	T36.1X5	T36.1X6
Cefalosporins	T36.1X1	T36.1X2	T36.1X3	T36.1X4	T36.1X5	T36.1X6
Cefalotin	T36.1X1	T36.1X2	T36.1X3	T36.1X4	T36.1X5	T36.1X6
Cefamandole	T36.1X1	T36.1X2	T36.1X3	T36.1X4	T36.1X5	T36.1X6
Cefamycin antibiotic	T36.1X1	T36.1X2	T36.1X3	T36.1X4	T36.1X5	T36.1X6
Cefapirin	T36.1X1	T36.1X2	T36.1X3	T36.1X4	T36.1X5	T36.1X6
Cefatrizine	T36.1X1	T36.1X2	T36.1X3	T36.1X4	T36.1X5	T36.1X6
Cefazedone	T36.1X1	T36.1X2	T36.1X3	T36.1X4	T36.1X5	T36.1X6
Cefazolin	T36.1X1	T36.1X2	T36.1X3	T36.1X4	T36.1X5	T36.1X6
Cefbuperazone	T36.1X1	T36.1X2	T36.1X3	T36.1X4	T36.1X5	T36.1X6
Cefetamet	T36.1X1	T36.1X2	T36.1X3	T36.1X4	T36.1X5	T36.1X6
Cefixime	T36.1X1	T36.1X2	T36.1X3	T36.1X4	T36.1X5	T36.1X6
Cefmenoxime	T36.1X1	T36.1X2	T36.1X3	T36.1X4	T36.1X5	T36.1X6
Cefmetazole	T36.1X1	T36.1X2	T36.1X3	T36.1X4	T36.1X5	T36.1X6
Cefminox	T36.1X1	T36.1X2	T36.1X3	T36.1X4	T36.1X5	T36.1X6
Cefonicid	T36.1X1	T36.1X2	T36.1X3	T36.1X4	T36.1X5	T36.1X6
Cefoperazone	T36.1X1	T36.1X2	T36.1X3	T36.1X4	T36.1X5	T36.1X6
Ceforanide	T36.1X1	T36.1X2	T36.1X3	T36.1X4	T36.1X5	T36.1X6
Cefotaxime	T36.1X1	T36.1X2	T36.1X3	T36.1X4	T36.1X5	T36.1X6
Cefotetan	T36.1X1	T36.1X2	T36.1X3	T36.1X4	T36.1X5	T36.1X6
Cefotiam	T36.1X1	T36.1X2	T36.1X3	T36.1X4	T36.1X5	T36.1X6
Cefoxitin	T36.1X1	T36.1X2	T36.1X3	T36.1X4	T36.1X5	T36.1X6
Cefpimizole	T36.1X1	T36.1X2	T36.1X3	T36.1X4	T36.1X5	T36.1X6
Cefpiramide	T36.1X1	T36.1X2	T36.1X3	T36.1X4	T36.1X5	T36.1X6
Cefradine	T36.1X1	T36.1X2	T36.1X3	T36.1X4	T36.1X5	T36.1X6
Cefroxadine	T36.1X1	T36.1X2	T36.1X3	T36.1X4	T36.1X5	T36.1X6
Cefsulodin	T36.1X1	T36.1X2	T36.1X3	T36.1X4	T36.1X5	T36.1X6

Substance	Poisoning, Accidental (Unintentional)	Poisoning, Intentional Self-Harm	Poisoning, Assault	Poisoning, Undetermined	Adverse Effect	Underdosing
Ceftazidime	T36.1X1	T36.1X2	T36.1X3	T36.1X4	T36.1X5	T36.1X6
Cefteram	T36.1X1	T36.1X2	T36.1X3	T36.1X4	T36.1X5	T36.1X6
Ceftezole	T36.1X1	T36.1X2	T36.1X3	T36.1X4	T36.1X5	T36.1X6
Ceftizoxime	T36.1X1	T36.1X2	T36.1X3	T36.1X4	T36.1X5	T36.1X6
Ceftriaxone	T36.1X1	T36.1X2	T36.1X3	T36.1X4	T36.1X5	T36.1X6
Cefuroxime	T36.1X1	T36.1X2	T36.1X3	T36.1X4	T36.1X5	T36.1X6
Cefuzonam	T36.1X1	T36.1X2	T36.1X3	T36.1X4	T36.1X5	T36.1X6
Celestone	T38.0X1	T38.0X2	T38.0X3	T38.0X4	T38.0X5	T38.0X6
topical	T49.0X1	T49.0X2	T49.0X3	T49.0X4	T49.0X5	T49.0X6
Celiprolol	T44.7X1	T44.7X2	T44.7X3	T44.7X4	T44.7X5	T44.7X6
Cellosolve	T52.91	T52.92	T52.93	T52.94	—	—
Cell stimulants and proliferants	T49.8X1	T49.8X2	T49.8X3	T49.8X4	T49.8X5	T49.8X6
Cellulose						
cathartic	T47.4X1	T47.4X2	T47.4X3	T47.4X4	T47.4X5	T47.4X6
hydroxyethyl	T47.4X1	T47.4X2	T47.4X3	T47.4X4	T47.4X5	T47.4X6
nitrates (topical)	T49.3X1	T49.3X2	T49.3X3	T49.3X4	T49.3X5	T49.3X6
oxidized	T49.4X1	T49.4X2	T49.4X3	T49.4X4	T49.4X5	T49.4X6
Centipede (bite)	T63.411	T63.412	T63.413	T63.414	—	—
Central nervous system						
depressants	T42.71	T42.72	T42.73	T42.74	T42.75	T42.76
anesthetic (general) NEC	T41.201	T41.202	T41.203	T41.204	T41.205	T41.206
gases NEC	T41.0X1	T41.0X2	T41.0X3	T41.0X4	T41.0X5	T41.0X6
intravenous	T41.1X1	T41.1X2	T41.1X3	T41.1X4	T41.1X5	T41.1X6
barbiturates	T42.3X1	T42.3X2	T42.3X3	T42.3X4	T42.3X5	T42.3X6
benzodiazepines	T42.4X1	T42.4X2	T42.4X3	T42.4X4	T42.4X5	T42.4X6
bromides	T42.6X1	T42.6X2	T42.6X3	T42.6X4	T42.6X5	T42.6X6
cannabis sativa	T40.7X1	T40.7X2	T40.7X3	T40.7X4	T40.7X5	T40.7X6
chloral hydrate	T42.6X1	T42.6X2	T42.6X3	T42.6X4	T42.6X5	T42.6X6
ethanol	T51.0X1	T51.0X2	T51.0X3	T51.0X4	—	—
hallucinogenics	T40.901	T40.902	T40.903	T40.904	T40.905	T40.906
hypnotics	T42.71	T42.72	T42.73	T42.74	T42.75	T42.76
specified NEC	T42.6X1	T42.6X2	T42.6X3	T42.6X4	T42.6X5	T42.6X6
muscle relaxants	T42.8X1	T42.8X2	T42.8X3	T42.8X4	T42.8X5	T42.8X6
paraldehyde	T42.6X1	T42.6X2	T42.6X3	T42.6X4	T42.6X5	T42.6X6
sedatives; sedative-hypnotics	T42.71	T42.72	T42.73	T42.74	T42.75	T42.76
mixed NEC	T42.6X1	T42.6X2	T42.6X3	T42.6X4	T42.6X5	T42.6X6
specified NEC	T42.6X1	T42.6X2	T42.6X3	T42.6X4	T42.6X5	T42.6X6
muscle-tone depressants	T42.8X1	T42.8X2	T42.8X3	T42.8X4	T42.8X5	T42.8X6
stimulants	T43.601	T43.602	T43.603	T43.604	T43.605	T43.606
amphetamines	T43.621	T43.622	T43.623	T43.624	T43.625	T43.626
analeptics	T50.7X1	T50.7X2	T50.7X3	T50.7X4	T50.7X5	T50.7X6

◀ New ◀ Revised ~~deleted~~ Deleted

TABLE OF DRUGS AND CHEMICALS

Substance	Poisoning, Accidental (Unintentional)	Poisoning, Intentional Self-Harm	Poisoning, Assault	Poisoning, Undetermined	Adverse Effect	Underdosing
Central nervous system *(Continued)*						
stimulants *(Continued)*						
antidepressants	T43.201	T43.202	T43.203	T43.204	T43.205	T43.206
opiate antagonists	T50.7X1	T50.7X2	T50.7X3	T50.7X4	T50.7X5	T50.7X6
specified NEC	T43.691	T43.692	T43.693	T43.694	T43.695	T43.696
Cephalexin	T36.1X1	T36.1X2	T36.1X3	T36.1X4	T36.1X5	T36.1X6
Cephaloglycin	T36.1X1	T36.1X2	T36.1X3	T36.1X4	T36.1X5	T36.1X6
Cephaloridine	T36.1X1	T36.1X2	T36.1X3	T36.1X4	T36.1X5	T36.1X6
Cephalosporins	T36.1X1	T36.1X2	T36.1X3	T36.1X4	T36.1X5	T36.1X6
N (adicillin)	T36.0X1	T36.0X2	T36.0X3	T36.0X4	T36.0X5	T36.0X6
Cephalothin	T36.1X1	T36.1X2	T36.1X3	T36.1X4	T36.1X5	T36.1X6
Cephalotin	T36.1X1	T36.1X2	T36.1X3	T36.1X4	T36.1X5	T36.1X6
Cephradine	T36.1X1	T36.1X2	T36.1X3	T36.1X4	T36.1X5	T36.1X6
Cerbera (odallam)	T62.2X1	T62.2X2	T62.2X3	T62.2X4	—	—
Cerberin	T46.0X1	T46.0X2	T46.0X3	T46.0X4	T46.0X5	T46.0X6
Cerebral stimulants	T43.601	T43.602	T43.603	T43.604	T43.605	T43.606
psychotherapeutic	T43.601	T43.602	T43.603	T43.604	T43.605	T43.606
specified NEC	T43.691	T43.692	T43.693	T43.694	T43.695	T43.696
Cerium oxalate	T45.0X1	T45.0X2	T45.0X3	T45.0X4	T45.0X5	T45.0X6
Cerous oxalate	T45.0X1	T45.0X2	T45.0X3	T45.0X4	T45.0X5	T45.0X6
Ceruletide	T50.8X1	T50.8X2	T50.8X3	T50.8X4	T50.8X5	T50.8X6
Cetalkonium (chloride)	T49.0X1	T49.0X2	T49.0X3	T49.0X4	T49.0X5	T49.0X6
Cethexonium chloride	T49.0X1	T49.0X2	T49.0X3	T49.0X4	T49.0X5	T49.0X6
Cetiedil	T46.7X1	T46.7X2	T46.7X3	T46.7X4	T46.7X5	T46.7X6
Cetirizine	T45.0X1	T45.0X2	T45.0X3	T45.0X4	T45.0X5	T45.0X6
Cetomacrogol	T50.991	T50.992	T50.993	T50.994	T50.995	T50.996
Cetotiamine	T45.2X1	T45.2X2	T45.2X3	T45.2X4	T45.2X5	T45.2X6
Cetoxime	T45.0X1	T45.0X2	T45.0X3	T45.0X4	T45.0X5	T45.0X6
Cetraxate	T47.1X1	T47.1X2	T47.1X3	T47.1X4	T47.1X5	T47.1X6
Cetrimide	T49.0X1	T49.0X2	T49.0X3	T49.0X4	T49.0X5	T49.0X6
Cetrimonium (bromide)	T49.0X1	T49.0X2	T49.0X3	T49.0X4	T49.0X5	T49.0X6
Cetylpyridinium chloride	T49.0X1	T49.0X2	T49.0X3	T49.0X4	T49.0X5	T49.0X6
ENT agent	T49.6X1	T49.6X2	T49.6X3	T49.6X4	T49.6X5	T49.6X6
lozenges	T49.6X1	T49.6X2	T49.6X3	T49.6X4	T49.6X5	T49.6X6
Cevadillasee Sabadilla						
Cevitamic acid	T45.2X1	T45.2X2	T45.2X3	T45.2X4	T45.2X5	T45.2X6
Chalk, precipitated	T47.1X1	T47.1X2	T47.1X3	T47.1X4	T47.1X5	T47.1X6
Chamomile	T49.0X1	T49.0X2	T49.0X3	T49.0X4	T49.0X5	T49.0X6
Ch'an su	T46.0X1	T46.0X2	T46.0X3	T46.0X4	T46.0X5	T46.0X6
Charcoal	T47.6X1	T47.6X2	T47.6X3	T47.6X4	T47.6X5	T47.6X6
activated — *see also Charcoal, medicinal*	T47.6X1	T47.6X2	T47.6X3	T47.6X4	T47.6X5	T47.6X6

Substance	Poisoning, Accidental (Unintentional)	Poisoning, Intentional Self-Harm	Poisoning, Assault	Poisoning, Undetermined	Adverse Effect	Underdosing
Charcoal *(Continued)*						
fumes (Carbon monoxide)	T58.2X1	T58.2X2	T58.2X3	T58.2X4	—	—
industrial	T58.8X1	T58.8X2	T58.8X3	T58.8X4	—	—
medicinal (activated)	T47.6X1	T47.6X2	T47.6X3	T47.6X4	T47.6X5	T47.6X6
antidiarrheal	T47.6X1	T47.6X2	T47.6X3	T47.6X4	T47.6X5	T47.6X6
poison control	T47.8X1	T47.8X2	T47.8X3	T47.8X4	T47.8X5	T47.8X6
specified use other than for diarrhea	T47.8X1	T47.8X2	T47.8X3	T47.8X4	T47.8X5	T47.8X6
topical	T49.8X1	T49.8X2	T49.8X3	T49.8X4	T49.8X5	T49.8X6
Chaulmosulfone	T37.1X1	T37.1X2	T37.1X3	T37.1X4	T37.1X5	T37.1X6
Chelating agent NEC	T50.6X1	T50.6X2	T50.6X3	T50.6X4	T50.6X5	T50.6X6
Chelidonium majus	T62.2X1	T62.2X2	T62.2X3	T62.2X4	—	—
Chemical substance NEC	T65.91	T65.92	T65.93	T65.94	—	—
Chenodeoxycholic acid	T47.5X1	T47.5X2	T47.5X3	T47.5X4	T47.5X5	T47.5X6
Chenodiol	T47.5X1	T47.5X2	T47.5X3	T47.5X4	T47.5X5	T47.5X6
Chenopodium	T37.4X1	T37.4X2	T37.4X3	T37.4X4	T37.4X5	T37.4X6
Cherry laurel	T62.2X1	T62.2X2	T62.2X3	T62.2X4	—	—
Chinidin(e)	T46.2X1	T46.2X2	T46.2X3	T46.2X4	T46.2X5	T46.2X6
Chiniofon	T37.8X1	T37.8X2	T37.8X3	T37.8X4	T37.8X5	T37.8X6
Chlophedianol	T48.3X1	T48.3X2	T48.3X3	T48.3X4	T48.3X5	T48.3X6
Chloral	T42.6X1	T42.6X2	T42.6X3	T42.6X4	T42.6X5	T42.6X6
derivative	T42.6X1	T42.6X2	T42.6X3	T42.6X4	T42.6X5	T42.6X6
hydrate	T42.6X1	T42.6X2	T42.6X3	T42.6X4	T42.6X5	T42.6X6
Chloralamide	T42.6X1	T42.6X2	T42.6X3	T42.6X4	T42.6X5	T42.6X6
Chloralodol	T42.6X1	T42.6X2	T42.6X3	T42.6X4	T42.6X5	T42.6X6
Chloralose	T60.4X1	T60.4X2	T60.4X3	T60.4X4	—	—
Chlorambucil	T45.1X1	T45.1X2	T45.1X3	T45.1X4	T45.1X5	T45.1X6
Chloramine	T57.8X1	T57.8X2	T57.8X3	T57.8X4	—	—
T	T49.0X1	T49.0X2	T49.0X3	T49.0X4	T49.0X5	T49.0X6
topical	T49.0X1	T49.0X2	T49.0X3	T49.0X4	T49.0X5	T49.0X6
Chloramphenicol	T36.2X1	T36.2X2	T36.2X3	T36.2X4	T36.2X5	T36.2X6
ENT agent	T49.6X1	T49.6X2	T49.6X3	T49.6X4	T49.6X5	T49.6X6
ophthalmic preparation	T49.5X1	T49.5X2	T49.5X3	T49.5X4	T49.5X5	T49.5X6
topical NEC	T49.0X1	T49.0X2	T49.0X3	T49.0X4	T49.0X5	T49.0X6
Chlorate (potassium) (sodium) NEC	T60.3X1	T60.3X2	T60.3X3	T60.3X4		
herbicide	T60.3X1	T60.3X2	T60.3X3	T60.3X4	—	—
Chlorazanil	T50.2X1	T50.2X2	T50.2X3	T50.2X4	T50.2X5	T50.2X6
Chlorbenzene, chlorbenzol	T53.7X1	T53.7X2	T53.7X3	T53.7X4	—	—
Chlorbenzoxamine	T44.3X1	T44.3X2	T44.3X3	T44.3X4	T44.3X5	T44.3X6
Chlorbutol	T42.6X1	T42.6X2	T42.6X3	T42.6X4	T42.6X5	T42.6X6
Chlorcyclizine	T45.0X1	T45.0X2	T45.0X3	T45.0X4	T45.0X5	T45.0X6

◀ New ◀ Revised ~~deleted~~ Deleted

Substance	Poisoning, Accidental (Unintentional)	Poisoning, Intentional Self-Harm	Poisoning, Assault	Poisoning, Undetermined	Adverse Effect	Underdosing
Chlordan(e) (dust)	T60.1X1	T60.1X2	T60.1X3	T60.1X4	—	—
Chlordantoin	T49.0X1	T49.0X2	T49.0X3	T49.0X4	T49.0X5	T49.0X6
Chlordiazepoxide	T42.4X1	T42.4X2	T42.4X3	T42.4X4	T42.4X5	T42.4X6
Chlordiethyl benzamide	T49.3X1	T49.3X2	T49.3X3	T49.3X4	T49.3X5	T49.3X6
Chloresium	T49.8X1	T49.8X2	T49.8X3	T49.8X4	T49.8X5	T49.8X6
Chlorethiazol	T42.6X1	T42.6X2	T42.6X3	T42.6X4	T42.6X5	T42.6X6
Chlorethyl — see Ethyl chloride						
Chloretone	T42.6X1	T42.6X2	T42.6X3	T42.6X4	T42.6X5	T42.6X6
Chlorex	T53.6X1	T53.6X2	T53.6X3	T53.6X4	—	—
insecticide	T60.1X1	T60.1X2	T60.1X3	T60.1X4	—	—
Chlorfenvinphos	T60.0X1	T60.0X2	T60.0X3	T60.0X4	—	—
Chlorhexadol	T42.6X1	T42.6X2	T42.6X3	T42.6X4	T42.6X5	T42.6X6
Chlorhexamide	T45.1X1	T45.1X2	T45.1X3	T45.1X4	T45.1X5	T45.1X6
Chlorhexidine	T49.0X1	T49.0X2	T49.0X3	T49.0X4	T49.0X5	T49.0X6
Chlorhydroxyquinolin	T49.0X1	T49.0X2	T49.0X3	T49.0X4	T49.0X5	T49.0X6
Chloride of lime (bleach)	T54.3X1	T54.3X2	T54.3X3	T54.3X4	—	—
Chlorimipramine	T43.011	T43.012	T43.013	T43.014	T43.015	T43.016
Chlorinated						
camphene	T53.6X1	T53.6X2	T53.6X3	T53.6X4	—	—
diphenyl	T53.7X1	T53.7X2	T53.7X3	T53.7X4	—	—
hydrocarbons NEC	T53.91	T53.92	T53.93	T53.94	—	—
solvents	T53.91	T53.92	T53.93	T53.94	—	—
lime (bleach)	T54.3X1	T54.3X2	T54.3X3	T54.3X4	—	—
and boric acid solution	T49.0X1	T49.0X2	T49.0X3	T49.0X4	T49.0X5	T49.0X6
naphthalene (insecticide)	T60.1X1	T60.1X2	T60.1X3	T60.1X4	—	—
industrial (non-pesticide)	T53.7X1	T53.7X2	T53.7X3	T53.7X4	—	—
pesticide NEC	T60.8X1	T60.8X2	T60.8X3	T60.8X4	—	—
soda — see also sodium hypochlorite						
solution	T49.0X1	T49.0X2	T49.0X3	T49.0X4	T49.0X5	T49.0X6
Chlorine (fumes) (gas)	T59.4X1	T59.4X2	T59.4X3	T59.4X4	—	—
bleach	T54.3X1	T54.3X2	T54.3X3	T54.3X4	—	—
compound gas NEC	T59.4X1	T59.4X2	T59.4X3	T59.4X4	—	—
disinfectant	T59.4X1	T59.4X2	T59.4X3	T59.4X4	—	—
releasing agents NEC	T59.4X1	T59.4X2	T59.4X3	T59.4X4	—	—
Chlorisondamine chloride	T46.991	T46.992	T46.993	T46.994	T46.995	T46.996
Chlormadinone	T38.5X1	T38.5X2	T38.5X3	T38.5X4	T38.5X5	T38.5X6
Chlormephos	T60.0X1	T60.0X2	T60.0X3	T60.0X4	—	—
Chlormerodrin	T50.2X1	T50.2X2	T50.2X3	T50.2X4	T50.2X5	T50.2X6
Chlormethiazole	T42.6X1	T42.6X2	T42.6X3	T42.6X4	T42.6X5	T42.6X6
Chlormethine	T45.1X1	T45.1X2	T45.1X3	T45.1X4	T45.1X5	T45.1X6
Chlormethylenecycline	T36.4X1	T36.4X2	T36.4X3	T36.4X4	T36.4X5	T36.4X6

Substance	Poisoning, Accidental (Unintentional)	Poisoning, Intentional Self-Harm	Poisoning, Assault	Poisoning, Undetermined	Adverse Effect	Underdosing
Chlormezanone	T42.6X1	T42.6X2	T42.6X3	T42.6X4	T42.6X5	T42.6X6
Chloroacetic acid	T60.3X1	T60.3X2	T60.3X3	T60.3X4	—	—
Chloroacetone	T59.3X1	T59.3X2	T59.3X3	T59.3X4	—	—
Chloroacetophenone	T59.3X1	T59.3X2	T59.3X3	T59.3X4	—	—
Chloroaniline	T53.7X1	T53.7X2	T53.7X3	T53.7X4	—	—
Chlorobenzene, chlorobenzol	T53.7X1	T53.7X2	T53.7X3	T53.7X4	—	—
Chlorobromomethane (fire extinguisher)	T53.6X1	T53.6X2	T53.6X3	T53.6X4	—	—
Chlorobutanol	T49.0X1	T49.0X2	T49.0X3	T49.0X4	T49.0X5	T49.0X6
Chlorocresol	T49.0X1	T49.0X2	T49.0X3	T49.0X4	T49.0X5	T49.0X6
Chlorodehydro-methyltestosterone	T38.7X1	T38.7X2	T38.7X3	T38.7X4	T38.7X5	T38.7X6
Chlorodinitrobenzene	T53.7X1	T53.7X2	T53.7X3	T53.7X4	—	—
dust or vapor	T53.7X1	T53.7X2	T53.7X3	T53.7X4	—	—
Chlorodiphenyl	T53.7X1	T53.7X2	T53.7X3	T53.7X4	—	—
Chloroethane — see Ethyl chloride						
Chloroethylene	T53.6X1	T53.6X2	T53.6X3	T53.6X4	—	—
Chlorofluorocarbons	T53.5X1	T53.5X2	T53.5X3	T53.5X4	—	—
Chloroform (fumes) (vapor)	T53.1X1	T53.1X2	T53.1X3	T53.1X4	—	—
anesthetic	T41.0X1	T41.0X2	T41.0X3	T41.0X4	T41.0X5	T41.0X6
solvent	T53.1X1	T53.1X2	T53.1X3	T53.1X4	—	—
water, concentrated	T41.0X1	T41.0X2	T41.0X3	T41.0X4	T41.0X5	T41.0X6
Chloroguanide	T37.2X1	T37.2X2	T37.2X3	T37.2X4	T37.2X5	T37.2X6
Chloromycetin	T36.2X1	T36.2X2	T36.2X3	T36.2X4	T36.2X5	T36.2X6
ENT agent	T49.6X1	T49.6X2	T49.6X3	T49.6X4	T49.6X5	T49.6X6
ophthalmic preparation	T49.5X1	T49.5X2	T49.5X3	T49.5X4	T49.5X5	T49.5X6
otic solution	T49.6X1	T49.6X2	T49.6X3	T49.6X4	T49.6X5	T49.6X6
topical NEC	T49.0X1	T49.0X2	T49.0X3	T49.0X4	T49.0X5	T49.0X6
Chloronitrobenzene	T53.7X1	T53.7X2	T53.7X3	T53.7X4	—	—
dust or vapor	T53.7X1	T53.7X2	T53.7X3	T53.7X4	—	—
Chlorophacinone	T60.4X1	T60.4X2	T60.4X3	T60.4X4	—	—
Chlorophenol	T53.7X1	T53.7X2	T53.7X3	T53.7X4	—	—
Chlorophenothane	T60.1X1	T60.1X2	T60.1X3	T60.1X4	—	—
Chlorophyll	T50.991	T50.992	T50.993	T50.994	T50.995	T50.996
Chloropicrin (fumes)	T53.6X1	T53.6X2	T53.6X3	T53.6X4	—	—
fumigant	T60.8X1	T60.8X2	T60.8X3	T60.8X4	—	—
fungicide	T60.3X1	T60.3X2	T60.3X3	T60.3X4	—	—
pesticide	T60.8X1	T60.8X2	T60.8X3	T60.8X4	—	—
Chloroprocaine	T41.3X1	T41.3X2	T41.3X3	T41.3X4	T41.3X5	T41.3X6
infiltration (subcutaneous)	T41.3X1	T41.3X2	T41.3X3	T41.3X4	T41.3X5	T41.3X6
nerve block (peripheral) (plexus)	T41.3X1	T41.3X2	T41.3X3	T41.3X4	T41.3X5	T41.3X6
spinal	T41.3X1	T41.3X2	T41.3X3	T41.3X4	T41.3X5	T41.3X6

◀ New ◀ Revised ~~deleted~~ Deleted

Substance	Poisoning, Accidental (Unintentional)	Poisoning, Intentional Self-Harm	Poisoning, Assault	Poisoning, Undetermined	Adverse Effect	Underdosing
Chloroptic	T49.5X1	T49.5X2	T49.5X3	T49.5X4	T49.5X5	T49.5X6
Chloropurine	T45.1X1	T45.1X2	T45.1X3	T45.1X4	T45.1X5	T45.1X6
Chloropyramine	T45.0X1	T45.0X2	T45.0X3	T45.0X4	T45.0X5	T45.0X6
Chloropyrifos	T60.0X1	T60.0X2	T60.0X3	T60.0X4	—	—
Chloropyrilene	T45.0X1	T45.0X2	T45.0X3	T45.0X4	T45.0X5	T45.0X6
Chloroquine	T37.2X1	T37.2X2	T37.2X3	T37.2X4	T37.2X5	T37.2X6
Chlorothalonil	T60.3X1	T60.3X2	T60.3X3	T60.3X4	—	—
Chlorothen	T45.0X1	T45.0X2	T45.0X3	T45.0X4	T45.0X5	T45.0X6
Chlorothiazide	T50.2X1	T50.2X2	T50.2X3	T50.2X4	T50.2X5	T50.2X6
Chlorothymol	T49.4X1	T49.4X2	T49.4X3	T49.4X4	T49.4X5	T49.4X6
Chlorotrianisene	T38.5X1	T38.5X2	T38.5X3	T38.5X4	T38.5X5	T38.5X6
Chlorovinyldichloro-arsine, not in war	T57.0X1	T57.0X2	T57.0X3	T57.0X4	—	—
Chloroxine	T49.4X1	T49.4X2	T49.4X3	T49.4X4	T49.4X5	T49.4X6
Chloroxylenol	T49.0X1	T49.0X2	T49.0X3	T49.0X4	T49.0X5	T49.0X6
Chlorphenamine	T45.0X1	T45.0X2	T45.0X3	T45.0X4	T45.0X5	T45.0X6
Chlorphenesin	T42.8X1	T42.8X2	T42.8X3	T42.8X4	T42.8X5	T42.8X6
topical (antifungal)	T49.0X1	T49.0X2	T49.0X3	T49.0X4	T49.0X5	T49.0X6
Chlorpheniramine	T45.0X1	T45.0X2	T45.0X3	T45.0X4	T45.0X5	T45.0X6
Chlorphenoxamine	T45.0X1	T45.0X2	T45.0X3	T45.0X4	T45.0X5	T45.0X6
Chlorphentermine	T50.5X1	T50.5X2	T50.5X3	T50.5X4	T50.5X5	T50.5X6
Chlorprocaine — see Chloroprocaine						
Chlorproguanil	T37.2X1	T37.2X2	T37.2X3	T37.2X4	T37.2X5	T37.2X6
Chlorpromazine	T43.3X1	T43.3X2	T43.3X3	T43.3X4	T43.3X5	T43.3X6
Chlorpropamide	T38.3X1	T38.3X2	T38.3X3	T38.3X4	T38.3X5	T38.3X6
Chlorprothixene	T43.4X1	T43.4X2	T43.4X3	T43.4X4	T43.4X5	T43.4X6
Chlorquinaldol	T49.0X1	T49.0X2	T49.0X3	T49.0X4	T49.0X5	T49.0X6
Chlorquinol	T49.0X1	T49.0X2	T49.0X3	T49.0X4	T49.0X5	T49.0X6
Chlortalidone	T50.2X1	T50.2X2	T50.2X3	T50.2X4	T50.2X5	T50.2X6
Chlortetracycline	T36.4X1	T36.4X2	T36.4X3	T36.4X4	T36.4X5	T36.4X6
Chlorthalidone	T50.2X1	T50.2X2	T50.2X3	T50.2X4	T50.2X5	T50.2X6
Chlorthiophos	T60.0X1	T60.0X2	T60.0X3	T60.0X4	—	—
Chlorotrianisene	T38.5X1	T38.5X2	T38.5X3	T38.5X4	T38.5X5	T38.5X6
Chlor-Trimeton	T45.0X1	T45.0X2	T45.0X3	T45.0X4	T45.0X5	T45.0X6
Chlorthion	T60.0X1	T60.0X2	T60.0X3	T60.0X4	—	—
Chlorzoxazone	T42.8X1	T42.8X2	T42.8X3	T42.8X4	T42.8X5	T42.8X6
Choke damp	T59.7X1	T59.7X2	T59.7X3	T59.7X4		
Cholagogues	T47.5X1	T47.5X2	T47.5X3	T47.5X4	T47.5X5	T47.5X6
Cholebrine	T50.8X1	T50.8X2	T50.8X3	T50.8X4	T50.8X5	T50.8X6
Cholecalciferol	T45.2X1	T45.2X2	T45.2X3	T45.2X4	T45.2X5	T45.2X6
Cholecystokinin	T50.8X1	T50.8X2	T50.8X3	T50.8X4	T50.8X5	T50.8X6
Cholera vaccine	T50.A91	T50.A92	T50.A93	T50.A94	T50.A95	T50.A96

Substance	Poisoning, Accidental (Unintentional)	Poisoning, Intentional Self-Harm	Poisoning, Assault	Poisoning, Undetermined	Adverse Effect	Underdosing
Choleretic	T47.5X1	T47.5X2	T47.5X3	T47.5X4	T47.5X5	T47.5X6
Cholesterol-lowering agents	T46.6X1	T46.6X2	T46.6X3	T46.6X4	T46.6X5	T46.6X6
Cholestyramine (resin)	T46.6X1	T46.6X2	T46.6X3	T46.6X4	T46.6X5	T46.6X6
Cholic acid	T47.5X1	T47.5X2	T47.5X3	T47.5X4	T47.5X5	T47.5X6
Choline	T48.6X1	T48.6X2	T48.6X3	T48.6X4	T48.6X5	T48.6X6
chloride	T50.991	T50.992	T50.993	T50.994	T50.995	T50.996
dihydrogen citrate	T50.991	T50.992	T50.993	T50.994	T50.995	T50.996
salicylate	T39.091	T39.092	T39.093	T39.094	T39.095	T39.096
theophyllinate	T48.6X1	T48.6X2	T48.6X3	T48.6X4	T48.6X5	T48.6X6
Cholinergic (drug) NEC	T44.1X1	T44.1X2	T44.1X3	T44.1X4	T44.1X5	T44.1X6
muscle tone enhancer	T44.1X1	T44.1X2	T44.1X3	T44.1X4	T44.1X5	T44.1X6
organophosphorus	T44.0X1	T44.0X2	T44.0X3	T44.0X4	T44.0X5	T44.0X6
insecticide	T60.0X1	T60.0X2	T60.0X3	T60.0X4	—	—
nerve gas	T59.891	T59.892	T59.893	T59.894	—	—
trimethyl ammonium propanediol	T44.1X1	T44.1X2	T44.1X3	T44.1X4	T44.1X5	T44.1X6
Cholinesterase reactivator	T50.6X1	T50.6X2	T50.6X3	T50.6X4	T50.6X5	T50.6X6
Cholografin	T50.8X1	T50.8X2	T50.8X3	T50.8X4	T50.8X5	T50.8X6
Chorionic gonadotropin	T38.891	T38.892	T38.893	T38.894	T38.895	T38.896
Chromate	T56.2X1	T56.2X2	T56.2X3	T56.2X4	—	—
dust or mist	T56.2X1	T56.2X2	T56.2X3	T56.2X4	—	—
lead — see also lead	T56.0X1	T56.0X2	T56.0X3	T56.0X4	—	—
paint	T56.0X1	T56.0X2	T56.0X3	T56.0X4	—	—
Chromic						
acid	T56.2X1	T56.2X2	T56.2X3	T56.2X4	—	—
dust or mist	T56.2X1	T56.2X2	T56.2X3	T56.2X4	—	—
phosphate 32P	T45.1X1	T45.1X2	T45.1X3	T45.1X4	T45.1X5	T45.1X6
Chromium	T56.2X1	T56.2X2	T56.2X3	T56.2X4	—	—
compounds — see Chromate						
sesquioxide	T50.8X1	T50.8X2	T50.8X3	T50.8X4	T50.8X5	T50.8X6
Chromomycin A3	T45.1X1	T45.1X2	T45.1X3	T45.1X4	T45.1X5	T45.1X6
Chromonar	T46.3X1	T46.3X2	T46.3X3	T46.3X4	T46.3X5	T46.3X6
Chromyl chloride	T56.2X1	T56.2X2	T56.2X3	T56.2X4	—	—
Chrysarobin	T49.4X1	T49.4X2	T49.4X3	T49.4X4	T49.4X5	T49.4X6
Chrysazin	T47.2X1	T47.2X2	T47.2X3	T47.2X4	T47.2X5	T47.2X6
Chymar	T45.3X1	T45.3X2	T45.3X3	T45.3X4	T45.3X5	T45.3X6
ophthalmic preparation	T49.5X1	T49.5X2	T49.5X3	T49.5X4	T49.5X5	T49.5X6
Chymopapain	T45.3X1	T45.3X2	T45.3X3	T45.3X4	T45.3X5	T45.3X6
Chymotrypsin	T45.3X1	T45.3X2	T45.3X3	T45.3X4	T45.3X5	T45.3X6
ophthalmic preparation	T49.5X1	T49.5X2	T49.5X3	T49.5X4	T49.5X5	T49.5X6
Cianidanol	T50.991	T50.992	T50.993	T50.994	T50.995	T50.996
Cianopramine	T43.011	T43.012	T43.013	T43.014	T43.015	T43.016
Cibenzoline	T46.2X1	T46.2X2	T46.2X3	T46.2X4	T46.2X5	T46.2X6

◀ New ◀ Revised ~~deleted~~ Deleted

Substance	Poisoning, Accidental (Unintentional)	Poisoning, Intentional Self-Harm	Poisoning, Assault	Poisoning, Undetermined	Adverse Effect	Underdosing
Ciclacillin	T36.0X1	T36.0X2	T36.0X3	T36.0X4	T36.0X5	T36.0X6
Ciclobarbital — see Hexobarbital						
Ciclonicate	T46.7X1	T46.7X2	T46.7X3	T46.7X4	T46.7X5	T46.7X6
Ciclopirox (olamine)	T49.0X1	T49.0X2	T49.0X3	T49.0X4	T49.0X5	T49.0X6
Ciclosporin	T45.1X1	T45.1X2	T45.1X3	T45.1X4	T45.1X5	T45.1X6
Cicuta maculata or virosa	T62.2X1	T62.2X2	T62.2X3	T62.2X4	—	—
Cicutoxin	T62.2X1	T62.2X2	T62.2X3	T62.2X4	—	—
Cigarette lighter fluid	T52.0X1	T52.0X2	T52.0X3	T52.0X4	—	—
Cigarettes (tobacco)	T65.221	T65.222	T65.223	T65.224		
Ciguatoxin	T61.01	T61.02	T61.03	T61.04	—	—
Cilazapril	T46.4X1	T46.4X2	T46.4X3	T46.4X4	T46.4X5	T46.4X6
Cimetidine	T47.0X1	T47.0X2	T47.0X3	T47.0X4	T47.0X5	T47.0X6
Cimetropium bromide	T44.3X1	T44.3X2	T44.3X3	T44.3X4	T44.3X5	T44.3X6
Cinchocaine	T41.3X1	T41.3X2	T41.3X3	T41.3X4	T41.3X5	T41.3X6
topical (surface)	T41.3X1	T41.3X2	T41.3X3	T41.3X4	T41.3X5	T41.3X6
Cinchona	T37.2X1	T37.2X2	T37.2X3	T37.2X4	T37.2X5	T37.2X6
Cinchonine alkaloids	T37.2X1	T37.2X2	T37.2X3	T37.2X4	T37.2X5	T37.2X6
Cinchophen	T50.4X1	T50.4X2	T50.4X3	T50.4X4	T50.4X5	T50.4X6
Cinepazide	T46.7X1	T46.7X2	T46.7X3	T46.7X4	T46.7X5	T46.7X6
Cinnamedrine	T48.5X1	T48.5X2	T48.5X3	T48.5X4	T48.5X5	T48.5X6
Cinnarizine	T45.0X1	T45.0X2	T45.0X3	T45.0X4	T45.0X5	T45.0X6
Cinoxacin	T37.8X1	T37.8X2	T37.8X3	T37.8X4	T37.8X5	T37.8X6
Ciprofibrate	T46.6X1	T46.6X2	T46.6X3	T46.6X4	T46.6X5	T46.6X6
Ciprofloxacin	T36.8X1	T36.8X2	T36.8X3	T36.8X4	T36.8X5	T36.8X6
Cisapride	T47.8X1	T47.8X2	T47.8X3	T47.8X4	T47.8X5	T47.8X6
Cisplatin	T45.1X1	T45.1X2	T45.1X3	T45.1X4	T45.1X5	T45.1X6
Citalopram	T43.221	T43.222	T43.223	T43.224	T43.225	T43.226
Citanest	T41.3X1	T41.3X2	T41.3X3	T41.3X4	T41.3X5	T41.3X6
infiltration (subcutaneous)	T41.3X1	T41.3X2	T41.3X3	T41.3X4	T41.3X5	T41.3X6
nerve block (peripheral) (plexus)	T41.3X1	T41.3X2	T41.3X3	T41.3X4	T41.3X5	T41.3X6
Citric acid	T47.5X1	T47.5X2	T47.5X3	T47.5X4	T47.5X5	T47.5X6
Citrovorum (factor)	T45.8X1	T45.8X2	T45.8X3	T45.8X4	T45.8X5	T45.8X6
Claviceps purpurea	T62.2X1	T62.2X2	T62.2X3	T62.2X4	—	—
Clavulanic acid	T36.1X1	T36.1X2	T36.1X3	T36.1X4	T36.1X5	T36.1X6
Cleaner, cleansing agent, type not specified	T65.891	T65.892	T65.893	T65.894	—	—
of paint or varnish	T52.91	T52.92	T52.93	T52.94	—	—
specified type NEC	T65.891	T65.892	T65.893	T65.894	—	—
Clebopride	T47.8X1	T47.8X2	T47.8X3	T47.8X4	T47.8X5	T47.8X6
Clefamide	T37.3X1	T37.3X2	T37.3X3	T37.3X4	T37.3X5	T37.3X6
Clemastine	T45.0X1	T45.0X2	T45.0X3	T45.0X4	T45.0X5	T45.0X6
Clematis vitalba	T62.2X1	T62.2X2	T62.2X3	T62.2X4	—	—

Substance	Poisoning, Accidental (Unintentional)	Poisoning, Intentional Self-Harm	Poisoning, Assault	Poisoning, Undetermined	Adverse Effect	Underdosing
Clemizole	T45.0X1	T45.0X2	T45.0X3	T45.0X4	T45.0X5	T45.0X6
penicillin	T36.0X1	T36.0X2	T36.0X3	T36.0X4	T36.0X5	T36.0X6
Clenbuterol	T48.6X1	T48.6X2	T48.6X3	T48.6X4	T48.6X5	T48.6X6
Clidinium bromide	T44.3X1	T44.3X2	T44.3X3	T44.3X4	T44.3X5	T44.3X6
Clindamycin	T36.8X1	T36.8X2	T36.8X3	T36.8X4	T36.8X5	T36.8X6
Clinofibrate	T46.6X1	T46.6X2	T46.6X3	T46.6X4	T46.6X5	T46.6X6
Clioquinol	T37.8X1	T37.8X2	T37.8X3	T37.8X4	T37.8X5	T37.8X6
Cliradon	T40.2X1	T40.2X2	T40.2X3	T40.2X4	—	—
Clobazam	T42.4X1	T42.4X2	T42.4X3	T42.4X4	T42.4X5	T42.4X6
Clobenzorex	T50.5X1	T50.5X2	T50.5X3	T50.5X4	T50.5X5	T50.5X6
Clobetasol	T49.0X1	T49.0X2	T49.0X3	T49.0X4	T49.0X5	T49.0X6
Clobetasone	T49.0X1	T49.0X2	T49.0X3	T49.0X4	T49.0X5	T49.0X6
Clobutinol	T48.3X1	T48.3X2	T48.3X3	T48.3X4	T48.3X5	T48.3X6
Clocapramine	T43.0X1	T43.0X2	T43.0X3	T43.0X4	T43.0X5	T43.0X6
Clocortolone	T38.0X1	T38.0X2	T38.0X3	T38.0X4	T38.0X5	T38.0X6
Clodantoin	T49.0X1	T49.0X2	T49.0X3	T49.0X4	T49.0X5	T49.0X6
Clodronic acid	T50.991	T50.992	T50.993	T50.994	T50.995	T50.996
Clofazimine	T37.1X1	T37.1X2	T37.1X3	T37.1X4	T37.1X5	T37.1X6
Clofedanol	T48.3X1	T48.3X2	T48.3X3	T48.3X4	T48.3X5	T48.3X6
Clofenamide	T50.2X1	T50.2X2	T50.2X3	T50.2X4	T50.2X5	T50.2X6
Clofenotane	T49.0X1	T49.0X2	T49.0X3	T49.0X4	T49.0X5	T49.0X6
Clofezone	T39.2X1	T39.2X2	T39.2X3	T39.2X4	T39.2X5	T39.2X6
Clofibrate	T46.6X1	T46.6X2	T46.6X3	T46.6X4	T46.6X5	T46.6X6
Clofibride	T46.6X1	T46.6X2	T46.6X3	T46.6X4	T46.6X5	T46.6X6
Cloforex	T50.5X1	T50.5X2	T50.5X3	T50.5X4	T50.5X5	T50.5X6
Clomacran	T43.0X1	T43.0X2	T43.0X3	T43.0X4	T43.0X5	T43.0X6
Clomethiazole	T42.6X1	T42.6X2	T42.6X3	T42.6X4	T42.6X5	T42.6X6
Clometocillin	T36.0X1	T36.0X2	T36.0X3	T36.0X4	T36.0X5	T36.0X6
Clomifene	T38.5X1	T38.5X2	T38.5X3	T38.5X4	T38.5X5	T38.5X6
Clomiphene	T38.5X1	T38.5X2	T38.5X3	T38.5X4	T38.5X5	T38.5X6
Clomipramine	T43.011	T43.012	T43.013	T43.014	T43.015	T43.016
Clomocycline	T36.4X1	T36.4X2	T36.4X3	T36.4X4	T36.4X5	T36.4X6
Clonazepam	T42.4X1	T42.4X2	T42.4X3	T42.4X4	T42.4X5	T42.4X6
Clonidine	T46.5X1	T46.5X2	T46.5X3	T46.5X4	T46.5X5	T46.5X6
Clonixin	T39.8X1	T39.8X2	T39.8X3	T39.8X4	T39.8X5	T39.8X6
Clopamide	T50.2X1	T50.2X2	T50.2X3	T50.2X4	T50.2X5	T50.2X6
Clopenthixol	T43.4X1	T43.4X2	T43.4X3	T43.4X4	T43.4X5	T43.4X6
Cloperastine	T48.3X1	T48.3X2	T48.3X3	T48.3X4	T48.3X5	T48.3X6
Clophedianol	T48.3X1	T48.3X2	T48.3X3	T48.3X4	T48.3X5	T48.3X6
Cloponone	T36.2X1	T36.2X2	T36.2X3	T36.2X4	T36.2X5	T36.2X6
Cloprednol	T38.0X1	T38.0X2	T38.0X3	T38.0X4	T38.0X5	T38.0X6
Cloral betaine	T42.6X1	T42.6X2	T42.6X3	T42.6X4	T42.6X5	T42.6X6

◀ New ◀ Revised ~~deleted~~ Deleted

	External Cause (T-Code)					
Substance	Poisoning, Accidental (Unintentional)	Poisoning, Intentional Self-Harm	Poisoning, Assault	Poisoning, Undetermined	Adverse Effect	Underdosing
Cloramfenicol	T36.2X1	T36.2X2	T36.2X3	T36.2X4	T36.2X5	T36.2X6
Clorazepate (dipotassium)	T42.4X1	T42.4X2	T42.4X3	T42.4X4	T42.4X5	T42.4X6
Clorexolone	T50.2X1	T50.2X2	T50.2X3	T50.2X4	T50.2X5	T50.2X6
Clorox (bleach)	T54.91	T54.92	T54.93	T54.94	—	—
Clorfenamine	T45.0X1	T45.0X2	T45.0X3	T45.0X4	T45.0X5	T45.0X6
Clorgiline	T43.1X1	T43.1X2	T43.1X3	T43.1X4	T43.1X5	T43.1X6
Clorotepine	T44.3X1	T44.3X2	T44.3X3	T44.3X4	T44.3X5	T44.3X6
Clorprenaline	T48.6X1	T48.6X2	T48.6X3	T48.6X4	T48.6X5	T48.6X6
Clortermine	T50.5X1	T50.5X2	T50.5X3	T50.5X4	T50.5X5	T50.5X6
Clotiapine	T43.591	T43.592	T43.593	T43.594	T43.595	T43.596
Clotiazepam	T42.4X1	T42.4X2	T42.4X3	T42.4X4	T42.4X5	T42.4X6
Clotibric acid	T46.6X1	T46.6X2	T46.6X3	T46.6X4	T46.6X5	T46.6X6
Clotrimazole	T49.0X1	T49.0X2	T49.0X3	T49.0X4	T49.0X5	T49.0X6
Cloxacillin	T36.0X1	T36.0X2	T36.0X3	T36.0X4	T36.0X5	T36.0X6
Cloxazolam	T42.4X1	T42.4X2	T42.4X3	T42.4X4	T42.4X5	T42.4X6
Cloxiquine	T49.0X1	T49.0X2	T49.0X3	T49.0X4	T49.0X5	T49.0X6
Clozapine	T42.4X1	T42.4X2	T42.4X3	T42.4X4	T42.4X5	T42.4X6
Coagulant NEC	T45.7X1	T45.7X2	T45.7X3	T45.7X4	T45.7X5	T45.7X6
Coal (carbon monoxide from) — see also Carbon, monoxide, coal	T58.2X1	T58.2X2	T58.2X3	T58.2X4	—	—
oil — see Kerosene						
tar	T49.1X1	T49.1X2	T49.1X3	T49.1X4	T49.1X5	T49.1X6
fumes	T59.891	T59.892	T59.893	T59.894	—	—
medicinal (ointment)	T49.4X1	T49.4X2	T49.4X3	T49.4X4	T49.4X5	T49.4X6
analgesics NEC	T39.2X1	T39.2X2	T39.2X3	T39.2X4	T39.2X5	T39.2X6
naphtha (solvent)	T52.0X1	T52.0X2	T52.0X3	T52.0X4		
Cobalamine	T45.2X1	T45.2X2	T45.2X3	T45.2X4	T45.2X5	T45.2X6
Cobalt (nonmedicinal) (fumes) (industrial)	T56.891	T56.892	T56.893	T56.894		
medicinal (trace) (chloride)	T45.8X1	T45.8X2	T45.8X3	T45.8X4	T45.8X5	T45.8X6
Cobra (venom)	T63.041	T63.042	T63.043	T63.044		
Coca (leaf)	T40.5X1	T40.5X2	T40.5X3	T40.5X4	T40.5X5	T40.5X6
Cocaine	T40.5X1	T40.5X2	T40.5X3	T40.5X4	T40.5X5	T40.5X6
topical anesthetic	T41.3X1	T41.3X2	T41.3X3	T41.3X4	T41.3X5	T41.3X6
Cocarboxylase	T45.3X1	T45.3X2	T45.3X3	T45.3X4	T45.3X5	T45.3X6
Coccidioidin	T50.8X1	T50.8X2	T50.8X3	T50.8X4	T50.8X5	T50.8X6
Cocculus indicus	T62.1X1	T62.1X2	T62.1X3	T62.1X4		
Cochineal	T65.6X1	T65.6X2	T65.6X3	T65.6X4		
medicinal products	T50.991	T50.992	T50.993	T50.994	T50.995	T50.996
Codeine	T40.2X1	T40.2X2	T40.2X3	T40.2X4	T40.2X5	T40.2X6
Cod-liver oil	T45.2X1	T45.2X2	T45.2X3	T45.2X4	T45.2X5	T45.2X6

	External Cause (T-Code)					
Substance	Poisoning, Accidental (Unintentional)	Poisoning, Intentional Self-Harm	Poisoning, Assault	Poisoning, Undetermined	Adverse Effect	Underdosing
Coenzyme A	T50.991	T50.992	T50.993	T50.994	T50.995	T50.996
Coffee	T62.8X1	T62.8X2	T62.8X3	T62.8X4	—	—
Cogalactoisomerase	T50.991	T50.992	T50.993	T50.994	T50.995	T50.996
Cogentin	T44.3X1	T44.3X2	T44.3X3	T44.3X4	T44.3X5	T44.3X6
Coke fumes or gas (carbon monoxide)	T58.2X1	T58.2X2	T58.2X3	T58.2X4	—	—
industrial use	T58.8X1	T58.8X2	T58.8X3	T58.8X4	—	—
Colace	T47.4X1	T47.4X2	T47.4X3	T47.4X4	T47.4X5	T47.4X6
Colaspase	T45.1X1	T45.1X2	T45.1X3	T45.1X4	T45.1X5	T45.1X6
Colchicine	T50.4X1	T50.4X2	T50.4X3	T50.4X4	T50.4X5	T50.4X6
Colchicum	T62.2X1	T62.2X2	T62.2X3	T62.2X4	—	—
Cold cream	T49.3X1	T49.3X2	T49.3X3	T49.3X4	T49.3X5	T49.3X6
Colecalciferol	T45.2X1	T45.2X2	T45.2X3	T45.2X4	T45.2X5	T45.2X6
Colestipol	T46.6X1	T46.6X2	T46.6X3	T46.6X4	T46.6X5	T46.6X6
Colestyramine	T46.6X1	T46.6X2	T46.6X3	T46.6X4	T46.6X5	T46.6X6
Colimycin	T36.8X1	T36.8X2	T36.8X3	T36.8X4	T36.8X5	T36.8X6
Colistimethate	T36.8X1	T36.8X2	T36.8X3	T36.8X4	T36.8X5	T36.8X6
Colistin	T36.8X1	T36.8X2	T36.8X3	T36.8X4	T36.8X5	T36.8X6
sulfate (eye preparation)	T49.5X1	T49.5X2	T49.5X3	T49.5X4	T49.5X5	T49.5X6
Collagen	T50.991	T50.992	T50.993	T50.994	T50.995	T50.996
Collagenase	T49.4X1	T49.4X2	T49.4X3	T49.4X4	T49.4X5	T49.4X6
Collodion	T49.3X1	T49.3X2	T49.3X3	T49.3X4	T49.3X5	T49.3X6
Colocynth	T47.2X1	T47.2X2	T47.2X3	T47.2X4	T47.2X5	T47.2X6
Colophony adhesive	T49.3X1	T49.3X2	T49.3X3	T49.3X4	T49.3X5	T49.3X6
Colorant — see also Dye	T50.991	T50.992	T50.993	T50.994	T50.995	T50.996
Coloring matter — see Dye(s)						
Combustion gas (after combustion) — see Carbon, monoxide						
prior to combustion	T59.891	T59.892	T59.893	T59.894	—	—
Compazine	T43.3X1	T43.3X2	T43.3X3	T43.3X4	T43.3X5	T43.3X6
Compound						
42 (warfarin)	T60.4X1	T60.4X2	T60.4X3	T60.4X4		
269 (endrin)	T60.1X1	T60.1X2	T60.1X3	T60.1X4	—	—
497 (dieldrin)	T60.1X1	T60.1X2	T60.1X3	T60.1X4	—	—
1080 (sodium fluoroacetate)	T60.4X1	T60.4X2	T60.4X3	T60.4X4		
3422 (parathion)	T60.0X1	T60.0X2	T60.0X3	T60.0X4		
3911 (phorate)	T60.0X1	T60.0X2	T60.0X3	T60.0X4		
3956 (toxaphene)	T60.1X1	T60.1X2	T60.1X3	T60.1X4	—	—
4049 (malathion)	T60.0X1	T60.0X2	T60.0X3	T60.0X4	—	—
4069 (malathion)	T60.0X1	T60.0X2	T60.0X3	T60.0X4	—	—
4124 (dicapthon)	T60.0X1	T60.0X2	T60.0X3	T60.0X4	—	—

◀ New   ◀ Revised   ~~deleted~~ Deleted

Substance	External Cause (T-Code) Poisoning, Accidental (Unintentional)	Poisoning, Intentional Self-Harm	Poisoning, Assault	Poisoning, Undetermined	Adverse Effect	Underdosing
Compound (*Continued*)						
E (cortisone)	T38.0X1	T38.0X2	T38.0X3	T38.0X4	T38.0X5	T38.0X6
F (hydrocortisone)	T38.0X1	T38.0X2	T38.0X3	T38.0X4	T38.0X5	T38.0X6
Congener, anabolic	T38.7X1	T38.7X2	T38.7X3	T38.7X4	T38.7X5	T38.7X6
Congo red	T50.8X1	T50.8X2	T50.8X3	T50.8X4	T50.8X5	T50.8X6
Coniine, conine	T62.2X1	T62.2X2	T62.2X3	T62.2X4	—	—
Conium (maculatum)	T62.2X1	T62.2X2	T62.2X3	T62.2X4	—	—
Conjugated estrogenic substances	T38.5X1	T38.5X2	T38.5X3	T38.5X4	T38.5X5	T38.5X6
Contac	T48.5X1	T48.5X2	T48.5X3	T48.5X4	T48.5X5	T48.5X6
Contact lens solution	T49.5X1	T49.5X2	T49.5X3	T49.5X4	T49.5X5	T49.5X6
Contraceptive (oral)	T38.4X1	T38.4X2	T38.4X3	T38.4X4	T38.4X5	T38.4X6
vaginal	T49.8X1	T49.8X2	T49.8X3	T49.8X4	T49.8X5	T49.8X6
Contrast medium, radiography	T50.8X1	T50.8X2	T50.8X3	T50.8X4	T50.8X5	T50.8X6
Convallaria glycosides	T46.0X1	T46.0X2	T46.0X3	T46.0X4	T46.0X5	T46.0X6
Convallaria majalis	T62.2X1	T62.2X2	T62.2X3	T62.2X4	—	—
berry	T62.1X1	T62.1X2	T62.1X3	T62.1X4	—	—
Copper (dust) (fumes) (nonmedicinal) NEC	T56.4X1	T56.4X2	T56.4X3	T56.4X4	—	—
arsenate, arsenite	T57.0X1	T57.0X2	T57.0X3	T57.0X4	—	—
insecticide	T60.2X1	T60.2X2	T60.2X3	T60.2X4	—	—
emetic	T47.7X1	T47.7X2	T47.7X3	T47.7X4	T47.7X5	T47.7X6
fungicide	T60.3X1	T60.3X2	T60.3X3	T60.3X4	—	—
gluconate	T49.0X1	T49.0X2	T49.0X3	T49.0X4	T49.0X5	T49.0X6
insecticide	T60.2X1	T60.2X2	T60.2X3	T60.2X4	—	—
medicinal (trace)	T45.8X1	T45.8X2	T45.8X3	T45.8X4	T45.8X5	T45.8X6
oleate	T49.0X1	T49.0X2	T49.0X3	T49.0X4	T49.0X5	T49.0X6
sulfate	T56.4X1	T56.4X2	T56.4X3	T56.4X4		
cupric	T56.4X1	T56.4X2	T56.4X3	T56.4X4		
fungicide	T60.3X1	T60.3X2	T60.3X3	T60.3X4	—	—
medicinal						
ear	T49.6X1	T49.6X2	T49.6X3	T49.6X4	T49.6X5	T49.6X6
emetic	T47.7X1	T47.7X2	T47.7X3	T47.7X4	T47.7X5	T47.7X6
eye	T49.5X1	T49.5X2	T49.5X3	T49.5X4	T49.5X5	T49.5X6
cuprous	T56.4X1	T56.4X2	T56.4X3	T56.4X4	—	—
fungicide	T60.3X1	T60.3X2	T60.3X3	T60.3X4	—	—
medicinal						
ear	T49.6X1	T49.6X2	T49.6X3	T49.6X4	T49.6X5	T49.6X6
emetic	T47.7X1	T47.7X2	T47.7X3	T47.7X4	T47.7X5	T47.7X6
eye	T49.5X1	T49.5X2	T49.5X3	T49.5X4	T49.5X5	T49.5X6
Copperhead snake (bite) (venom)	T63.061	T63.062	T63.063	T63.064	—	—
Coral (sting)	T63.691	T63.692	T63.693	T63.694	—	—
snake (bite) (venom)	T63.021	T63.022	T63.023	T63.024	—	—

Substance	External Cause (T-Code) Poisoning, Accidental (Unintentional)	Poisoning, Intentional Self-Harm	Poisoning, Assault	Poisoning, Undetermined	Adverse Effect	Underdosing
Corbadrine	T49.6X1	T49.6X2	T49.6X3	T49.6X4	T49.6X5	T49.6X6
Cordran	T49.0X1	T49.0X2	T49.0X3	T49.0X4	T49.0X5	T49.0X6
Cordite	T65.891	T65.892	T65.893	T65.894	—	—
vapor	T59.891	T59.892	T59.893	T59.894	—	—
Corn cures	T49.4X1	T49.4X2	T49.4X3	T49.4X4	T49.4X5	T49.4X6
Cornhusker's lotion	T49.3X1	T49.3X2	T49.3X3	T49.3X4	T49.3X5	T49.3X6
Corn starch	T49.3X1	T49.3X2	T49.3X3	T49.3X4	T49.3X5	T49.3X6
Coronary vasodilator NEC	T46.3X1	T46.3X2	T46.3X3	T46.3X4	T46.3X5	T46.3X6
Corrosive NEC	T54.91	T54.92	T54.93	T54.94		
acid NEC	T54.2X1	T54.2X2	T54.2X3	T54.2X4	—	—
aromatics	T54.1X1	T54.1X2	T54.1X3	T54.1X4		
disinfectant	T54.1X1	T54.1X2	T54.1X3	T54.1X4		
fumes NEC	T54.91	T54.92	T54.93	T54.94	—	—
specified NEC	T54.91	T54.92	T54.93	T54.94		
sublimate	T56.1X1	T56.1X2	T56.1X3	T56.1X4	—	—
Cortate	T38.0X1	T38.0X2	T38.0X3	T38.0X4	T38.0X5	T38.0X6
Cort-Dome	T38.0X1	T38.0X2	T38.0X3	T38.0X4	T38.0X5	T38.0X6
ENT agent	T49.6X1	T49.6X2	T49.6X3	T49.6X4	T49.6X5	T49.6X6
ophthalmic preparation	T49.5X1	T49.5X2	T49.5X3	T49.5X4	T49.5X5	T49.5X6
topical NEC	T49.0X1	T49.0X2	T49.0X3	T49.0X4	T49.0X5	T49.0X6
Cortef	T38.0X1	T38.0X2	T38.0X3	T38.0X4	T38.0X5	T38.0X6
ENT agent	T49.6X1	T49.6X2	T49.6X3	T49.6X4	T49.6X5	T49.6X6
ophthalmic preparation	T49.5X1	T49.5X2	T49.5X3	T49.5X4	T49.5X5	T49.5X6
topical NEC	T49.0X1	T49.0X2	T49.0X3	T49.0X4	T49.0X5	T49.0X6
Corticosteroid	T38.0X1	T38.0X2	T38.0X3	T38.0X4	T38.0X5	T38.0X6
ENT agent	T49.6X1	T49.6X2	T49.6X3	T49.6X4	T49.6X5	T49.6X6
mineral	T50.0X1	T50.0X2	T50.0X3	T50.0X4	T50.0X5	T50.0X6
ophthalmic	T49.5X1	T49.5X2	T49.5X3	T49.5X4	T49.5X5	T49.5X6
topical NEC	T49.0X1	T49.0X2	T49.0X3	T49.0X4	T49.0X5	T49.0X6
Corticotropin	T38.811	T38.812	T38.813	T38.814	T38.815	T38.816
Cortisol	T49.0X1	T49.0X2	T49.0X3	T49.0X4	T49.0X5	T49.0X6
ENT agent	T49.6X1	T49.6X2	T49.6X3	T49.6X4	T49.6X5	T49.6X6
ophthalmic preparation	T49.5X1	T49.5X2	T49.5X3	T49.5X4	T49.5X5	T49.5X6
topical NEC	T49.0X1	T49.0X2	T49.0X3	T49.0X4	T49.0X5	T49.0X6
Cortisone (acetate)	T38.0X1	T38.0X2	T38.0X3	T38.0X4	T38.0X5	T38.0X6
ENT agent	T49.6X1	T49.6X2	T49.6X3	T49.6X4	T49.6X5	T49.6X6
ophthalmic preparation	T49.5X1	T49.5X2	T49.5X3	T49.5X4	T49.5X5	T49.5X6
topical NEC	T49.0X1	T49.0X2	T49.0X3	T49.0X4	T49.0X5	T49.0X6
Cortivazol	T38.0X1	T38.0X2	T38.0X3	T38.0X4	T38.0X5	T38.0X6
Cortogen	T38.0X1	T38.0X2	T38.0X3	T38.0X4	T38.0X5	T38.0X6
ENT agent	T49.6X1	T49.6X2	T49.6X3	T49.6X4	T49.6X5	T49.6X6
ophthalmic preparation	T49.5X1	T49.5X2	T49.5X3	T49.5X4	T49.5X5	T49.5X6

◄ New   ◄ Revised   ~~deleted~~ Deleted

	External Cause (T-Code)					
Substance	Poisoning, Accidental (Unintentional)	Poisoning, Intentional Self-Harm	Poisoning, Assault	Poisoning, Undetermined	Adverse Effect	Underdosing
Cortone	T38.0X1	T38.0X2	T38.0X3	T38.0X4	T38.0X5	T38.0X6
ENT agent	T49.6X1	T49.6X2	T49.6X3	T49.6X4	T49.6X5	T49.6X6
ophthalmic preparation	T49.5X1	T49.5X2	T49.5X3	T49.5X4	T49.5X5	T49.5X6
Cortril	T38.0X1	T38.0X2	T38.0X3	T38.0X4	T38.0X5	T38.0X6
ENT agent	T49.6X1	T49.6X2	T49.6X3	T49.6X4	T49.6X5	T49.6X6
ophthalmic preparation	T49.5X1	T49.5X2	T49.5X3	T49.5X4	T49.5X5	T49.5X6
topical NEC	T49.0X1	T49.0X2	T49.0X3	T49.0X4	T49.0X5	T49.0X6
Corynebacterium parvum	T45.1X1	T45.1X2	T45.1X3	T45.1X4	T45.1X5	T45.1X6
Cosmetic preparation	T49.8X1	T49.8X2	T49.8X3	T49.8X4	T49.8X5	T49.8X6
Cosmetics	T49.8X1	T49.8X2	T49.8X3	T49.8X4	T49.8X5	T49.8X6
Cosyntropin	T38.811	T38.812	T38.813	T38.814	T38.815	T38.816
Cotarnine	T45.7X1	T45.7X2	T45.7X3	T45.7X4	T45.7X5	T45.7X6
Co-trimoxazole	T36.8X1	T36.8X2	T36.8X3	T36.8X4	T36.8X5	T36.8X6
Cottonseed oil	T49.3X1	T49.3X2	T49.3X3	T49.3X4	T49.3X5	T49.3X6
Cough mixture (syrup)	T48.4X1	T48.4X2	T48.4X3	T48.4X4	T48.4X5	T48.4X6
containing opiates	T40.2X1	T40.2X2	T40.2X3	T40.2X4	T40.2X5	T40.2X6
expectorants	T48.4X1	T48.4X2	T48.4X3	T48.4X4	T48.4X5	T48.4X6
Coumadin	T45.511	T45.512	T45.513	T45.514	T45.515	T45.516
rodenticide	T60.4X1	T60.4X2	T60.4X3	T60.4X4	—	—
Coumaphos	T60.0X1	T60.0X2	T60.0X3	T60.0X4	—	—
Coumarin	T45.511	T45.512	T45.513	T45.514	T45.515	T45.516
Coumetarol	T45.511	T45.512	T45.513	T45.514	T45.515	T45.516
Cowbane	T62.2X1	T62.2X2	T62.2X3	T62.2X4	—	—
Cozyme	T45.2X1	T45.2X2	T45.2X3	T45.2X4	T45.2X5	T45.2X6
Crack	T40.5X1	T40.5X2	T40.5X3	T40.5X4	—	—
Crataegus extract	T46.0X1	T46.0X2	T46.0X3	T46.0X4	T46.0X5	T46.0X6
Creolin	T54.1X1	T54.1X2	T54.1X3	T54.1X4	—	—
disinfectant	T54.1X1	T54.1X2	T54.1X3	T54.1X4	—	—
Creosol (compound)	T49.0X1	T49.0X2	T49.0X3	T49.0X4	T49.0X5	T49.0X6
Creosote (coal tar) (beechwood)	T49.0X1	T49.0X2	T49.0X3	T49.0X4	T49.0X5	T49.0X6
medicinal (expectorant)	T48.4X1	T48.4X2	T48.4X3	T48.4X4	T48.4X5	T48.4X6
syrup	T48.4X1	T48.4X2	T48.4X3	T48.4X4	T48.4X5	T48.4X6
Cresol(s)	T49.0X1	T49.0X2	T49.0X3	T49.0X4	T49.0X5	T49.0X6
and soap solution	T49.0X1	T49.0X2	T49.0X3	T49.0X4	T49.0X5	T49.0X6
Cresyl acetate	T49.0X1	T49.0X2	T49.0X3	T49.0X4	T49.0X5	T49.0X6
Cresylic acid	T49.0X1	T49.0X2	T49.0X3	T49.0X4	T49.0X5	T49.0X6
Crimidine	T60.4X1	T60.4X2	T60.4X3	T60.4X4	—	—
Croconazole	T37.8X1	T37.8X2	T37.8X3	T37.8X4	T37.8X5	T37.8X6
Cromoglicic acid	T48.6X1	T48.6X2	T48.6X3	T48.6X4	T48.6X5	T48.6X6
Cromolyn	T48.6X1	T48.6X2	T48.6X3	T48.6X4	T48.6X5	T48.6X6
Cromonar	T46.3X1	T46.3X2	T46.3X3	T46.3X4	T46.3X5	T46.3X6

	External Cause (T-Code)					
Substance	Poisoning, Accidental (Unintentional)	Poisoning, Intentional Self-Harm	Poisoning, Assault	Poisoning, Undetermined	Adverse Effect	Underdosing
Cropropamide	T39.8X1	T39.8X2	T39.8X3	T39.8X4	T39.8X5	T39.8X6
with crotethamide	T50.7X1	T50.7X2	T50.7X3	T50.7X4	T50.7X5	T50.7X6
Crotamiton	T49.0X1	T49.0X2	T49.0X3	T49.0X4	T49.0X5	T49.0X6
Crotethamide	T39.8X1	T39.8X2	T39.8X3	T39.8X4	T39.8X5	T39.8X6
with cropropamide	T50.7X1	T50.7X2	T50.7X3	T50.7X4	T50.7X5	T50.7X6
Croton (oil)	T47.2X1	T47.2X2	T47.2X3	T47.2X4	T47.2X5	T47.2X6
chloral	T42.6X1	T42.6X2	T42.6X3	T42.6X4	T42.6X5	T42.6X6
Crude oil	T52.0X1	T52.0X2	T52.0X3	T52.0X4	—	—
Cryogenine	T39.8X1	T39.8X2	T39.8X3	T39.8X4	T39.8X5	T39.8X6
Cryolite (vapor)	T60.1X1	T60.1X2	T60.1X3	T60.1X4	—	—
insecticide	T60.1X1	T60.1X2	T60.1X3	T60.1X4	—	—
Cryptenamine (tannates)	T46.5X1	T46.5X2	T46.5X3	T46.5X4	T46.5X5	T46.5X6
Crystal violet	T49.0X1	T49.0X2	T49.0X3	T49.0X4	T49.0X5	T49.0X6
Cuckoopint	T62.2X1	T62.2X2	T62.2X3	T62.2X4	—	—
Cumetharol	T45.511	T45.512	T45.513	T45.514	T45.515	T45.516
Cupric						
acetate	T60.3X1	T60.3X2	T60.3X3	T60.3X4	—	—
acetoarsenite	T57.0X1	T57.0X2	T57.0X3	T57.0X4	—	—
arsenate	T57.0X1	T57.0X2	T57.0X3	T57.0X4	—	—
gluconate	T49.0X1	T49.0X2	T49.0X3	T49.0X4	T49.0X5	T49.0X6
oleate	T49.0X1	T49.0X2	T49.0X3	T49.0X4	T49.0X5	T49.0X6
sulfate	T56.4X1	T56.4X2	T56.4X3	T56.4X4	—	—
Cuprous sulfate — see also Copper sulfate	T56.4X1	T56.4X2	T56.4X3	T56.4X4	—	—
Curare, curarine	T48.1X1	T48.1X2	T48.1X3	T48.1X4	T48.1X5	T48.1X6
Cyamemazine	T43.3X1	T43.3X2	T43.3X3	T43.3X4	T43.3X5	T43.3X6
Cyamopsis tetragono-loba	T46.6X1	T46.6X2	T46.6X3	T46.6X4	T46.6X5	T46.6X6
Cyanacetyl hydrazide	T37.1X1	T37.1X2	T37.1X3	T37.1X4	T37.1X5	T37.1X6
Cyanic acid (gas)	T59.891	T59.892	T59.893	T59.894	—	—
Cyanide(s) (compounds) (potassium) (sodium) NEC	T65.0X1	T65.0X2	T65.0X3	T65.0X4	—	—
dust or gas (inhalation) NEC	T57.3X1	T57.3X2	T57.3X3	T57.3X4	—	—
fumigant	T65.0X1	T65.0X2	T65.0X3	T65.0X4	—	—
hydrogen	T57.3X1	T57.3X2	T57.3X3	T57.3X4	—	—
mercuric — see Mercury						
pesticide (dust) (fumes)	T65.0X1	T65.0X2	T65.0X3	T65.0X4	—	—
Cyanoacrylate adhesive	T49.3X1	T49.3X2	T49.3X3	T49.3X4	T49.3X5	T49.3X6
Cyanocobalamin	T45.8X1	T45.8X2	T45.8X3	T45.8X4	T45.8X5	T45.8X6
Cyanogen (chloride) (gas) NEC	T59.891	T59.892	T59.893	T59.894	—	—
Cyclacillin	T36.0X1	T36.0X2	T36.0X3	T36.0X4	T36.0X5	T36.0X6
Cyclaine	T41.3X1	T41.3X2	T41.3X3	T41.3X4	T41.3X5	T41.3X6
Cyclamate	T50.991	T50.992	T50.993	T50.994	T50.995	T50.996

◄ New   ◄ Revised   ~~deleted~~ Deleted

	External Cause (T-Code)					
Substance	Poisoning, Accidental (Unintentional)	Poisoning, Intentional Self-Harm	Poisoning, Assault	Poisoning, Undetermined	Adverse Effect	Underdosing
Cyclamen europaeum	T62.2X1	T62.2X2	T62.2X3	T62.2X4	—	—
Cyclandelate	T46.7X1	T46.7X2	T46.7X3	T46.7X4	T46.7X5	T46.7X6
Cyclazocine	T50.7X1	T50.7X2	T50.7X3	T50.7X4	T50.7X5	T50.7X6
Cyclizine	T45.0X1	T45.0X2	T45.0X3	T45.0X4	T45.0X5	T45.0X6
Cyclobarbital	T42.3X1	T42.3X2	T42.3X3	T42.3X4	T42.3X5	T42.3X6
Cyclobarbitone	T42.3X1	T42.3X2	T42.3X3	T42.3X4	T42.3X5	T42.3X6
Cyclobenzaprine	T48.1X1	T48.1X2	T48.1X3	T48.1X4	T48.1X5	T48.1X6
Cyclodrine	T44.3X1	T44.3X2	T44.3X3	T44.3X4	T44.3X5	T44.3X6
Cycloguanil embonate	T37.2X1	T37.2X2	T37.2X3	T37.2X4	T37.2X5	T37.2X6
Cycloheptadiene	T43.291	T43.292	T43.293	T43.294	T43.295	T43.296
Cyclohexane	T52.8X1	T52.8X2	T52.8X3	T52.8X4	—	—
Cyclohexanol	T51.8X1	T51.8X2	T51.8X3	T51.8X4	—	—
Cyclohexanone	T52.4X1	T52.4X2	T52.4X3	T52.4X4	—	—
Cycloheximide	T60.3X1	T60.3X2	T60.3X3	T60.3X4	—	—
Cyclohexyl acetate	T52.8X1	T52.8X2	T52.8X3	T52.8X4	—	—
Cycloleucin	T45.1X1	T45.1X2	T45.1X3	T45.1X4	T45.1X5	T45.1X6
Cyclomethycaine	T41.3X1	T41.3X2	T41.3X3	T41.3X4	T41.3X5	T41.3X6
Cyclopentamine	T44.4X1	T44.4X2	T44.4X3	T44.4X4	T44.4X5	T44.4X6
Cyclopenthiazide	T50.2X1	T50.2X2	T50.2X3	T50.2X4	T50.2X5	T50.2X6
Cyclopentolate	T44.3X1	T44.3X2	T44.3X3	T44.3X4	T44.3X5	T44.3X6
Cyclophosphamide	T45.1X1	T45.1X2	T45.1X3	T45.1X4	T45.1X5	T45.1X6
Cycloplegic drug	T49.5X1	T49.5X2	T49.5X3	T49.5X4	T49.5X5	T49.5X6
Cyclopropane	T41.291	T41.292	T41.293	T41.294	T41.295	T41.296
Cyclopyrabital	T39.8X1	T39.8X2	T39.8X3	T39.8X4	T39.8X5	T39.8X6
Cycloserine	T37.1X1	T37.1X2	T37.1X3	T37.1X4	T37.1X5	T37.1X6
Cyclosporin	T45.1X1	T45.1X2	T45.1X3	T45.1X4	T45.1X5	T45.1X6
Cyclothiazide	T50.2X1	T50.2X2	T50.2X3	T50.2X4	T50.2X5	T50.2X6
Cycrimine	T44.3X1	T44.3X2	T44.3X3	T44.3X4	T44.3X5	T44.3X6
Cyhalothrin	T60.1X1	T60.1X2	T60.1X3	T60.1X4	—	—
Cymarin	T46.0X1	T46.0X2	T46.0X3	T46.0X4	T46.0X5	T46.0X6
Cypermethrin	T60.1X1	T60.1X2	T60.1X3	T60.1X4	—	—
Cyphenothrin	T60.2X1	T60.2X2	T60.2X3	T60.2X4	—	—
Cyproheptadine	T45.0X1	T45.0X2	T45.0X3	T45.0X4	T45.0X5	T45.0X6
Cyprolidol	T43.291	T43.292	T43.293	T43.294	T43.295	T43.296
Cyproterone	T38.6X1	T38.6X2	T38.6X3	T38.6X4	T38.6X5	T38.6X6
Cysteamine	T50.6X1	T50.6X2	T50.6X3	T50.6X4	T50.6X5	T50.6X6
Cytarabine	T45.1X1	T45.1X2	T45.1X3	T45.1X4	T45.1X5	T45.1X6
Cytisus						
laburnum	T62.2X1	T62.2X2	T62.2X3	T62.2X4		
scoparius	T62.2X1	T62.2X2	T62.2X3	T62.2X4	—	—
Cytochrome C	T47.5X1	T47.5X2	T47.5X3	T47.5X4	T47.5X5	T47.5X6
Cytomel	T38.1X1	T38.1X2	T38.1X3	T38.1X4	T38.1X5	T38.1X6

	External Cause (T-Code)					
Substance	Poisoning, Accidental (Unintentional)	Poisoning, Intentional Self-Harm	Poisoning, Assault	Poisoning, Undetermined	Adverse Effect	Underdosing
Cytosine arabinoside	T45.1X1	T45.1X2	T45.1X3	T45.1X4	T45.1X5	T45.1X6
Cytoxan	T45.1X1	T45.1X2	T45.1X3	T45.1X4	T45.1X5	T45.1X6
Cytozyme	T45.7X1	T45.7X2	T45.7X3	T45.7X4	T45.7X5	T45.7X6
2,4-D	T60.3X1	T60.3X2	T60.3X3	T60.3X4	—	—
			D			
Dacarbazine	T45.1X1	T45.1X2	T45.1X3	T45.1X4	T45.1X5	T45.1X6
Dactinomycin	T45.1X1	T45.1X2	T45.1X3	T45.1X4	T45.1X5	T45.1X6
DADPS	T37.1X1	T37.1X2	T37.1X3	T37.1X4	T37.1X5	T37.1X6
Dakin's solution	T49.0X1	T49.0X2	T49.0X3	T49.0X4	T49.0X5	T49.0X6
Dalapon (sodium)	T60.3X1	T60.3X2	T60.3X3	T60.3X4	—	—
Dalmane	T42.4X1	T42.4X2	T42.4X3	T42.4X4	T42.4X5	T42.4X6
Danazol	T38.6X1	T38.6X2	T38.6X3	T38.6X4	T38.6X5	T38.6X6
Danilone	T45.511	T45.512	T45.513	T45.514	T45.515	T45.516
Danthron	T47.2X1	T47.2X2	T47.2X3	T47.2X4	T47.2X5	T47.2X6
Dantrolene	T42.8X1	T42.8X2	T42.8X3	T42.8X4	T42.8X5	T42.8X6
Dantron	T47.2X1	T47.2X2	T47.2X3	T47.2X4	T47.2X5	T47.2X6
Daphne (gnidium) (mezereum)	T62.2X1	T62.2X2	T62.2X3	T62.2X4	—	—
berry	T62.1X1	T62.1X2	T62.1X3	T62.1X4		
Dapsone	T37.1X1	T37.1X2	T37.1X3	T37.1X4	T37.1X5	T37.1X6
Daraprim	T37.2X1	T37.2X2	T37.2X3	T37.2X4	T37.2X5	T37.2X6
Darnel	T62.2X1	T62.2X2	T62.2X3	T62.2X4		
Darvon	T39.8X1	T39.8X2	T39.8X3	T39.8X4	T39.8X5	T39.8X6
Daunomycin	T45.1X1	T45.1X2	T45.1X3	T45.1X4	T45.1X5	T45.1X6
Daunorubicin	T45.1X1	T45.1X2	T45.1X3	T45.1X4	T45.1X5	T45.1X6
DBI	T38.3X1	T38.3X2	T38.3X3	T38.3X4	T38.3X5	T38.3X6
D-Con	T60.91	T60.92	T60.93	T60.94	—	—
insecticide	T60.2X1	T60.2X2	T60.2X3	T60.2X4	—	—
rodenticide	T60.4X1	T60.4X2	T60.4X3	T60.4X4	—	—
DDAVP	T38.891	T38.892	T38.893	T38.894	T38.895	T38.896
DDE (bis(chlorophenyl)-dichloroethylene)	T60.2X1	T60.2X2	T60.2X3	T60.2X4	—	—
DDS	T37.1X1	T37.1X2	T37.1X3	T37.1X4	T37.1X5	T37.1X6
DDT (dust)	T60.1X1	T60.1X2	T60.1X3	T60.1X4	—	—
Deadly nightshade — see also Belladonna	T62.2X1	T62.2X2	T62.2X3	T62.2X4	—	—
berry	T62.1X1	T62.1X2	T62.1X3	T62.1X4		
Deamino-D-arginine vasopressin	T38.891	T38.892	T38.893	T38.894	T38.895	T38.896
Deanol (aceglumate)	T50.991	T50.992	T50.993	T50.994	T50.995	T50.996
Debrisoquine	T46.5X1	T46.5X2	T46.5X3	T46.5X4	T46.5X5	T46.5X6
Decaborane	T57.8X1	T57.8X2	T57.8X3	T57.8X4	—	—
fumes	T59.891	T59.892	T59.893	T59.894	—	—

◀ New   ◀ Revised   ~~deleted~~ Deleted

Substance	External Cause (T-Code)					
	Poisoning, Accidental (Unintentional)	Poisoning, Intentional Self-Harm	Poisoning, Assault	Poisoning, Undetermined	Adverse Effect	Underdosing
Decadron	T38.0X1	T38.0X2	T38.0X3	T38.0X4	T38.0X5	T38.0X6
ENT agent	T49.6X1	T49.6X2	T49.6X3	T49.6X4	T49.6X5	T49.6X6
ophthalmic preparation	T49.5X1	T49.5X2	T49.5X3	T49.5X4	T49.5X5	T49.5X6
topical NEC	T49.0X1	T49.0X2	T49.0X3	T49.0X4	T49.0X5	T49.0X6
Decahydronaphthalene	T52.8X1	T52.8X2	T52.8X3	T52.8X4	—	—
Decalin	T52.8X1	T52.8X2	T52.8X3	T52.8X4	—	—
Decamethonium (bromide)	T48.1X1	T48.1X2	T48.1X3	T48.1X4	T48.1X5	T48.1X6
Decholin	T47.5X1	T47.5X2	T47.5X3	T47.5X4	T47.5X5	T47.5X6
Declomycin	T36.4X1	T36.4X2	T36.4X3	T36.4X4	T36.4X5	T36.4X6
Decongestant, nasal (mucosa)	T48.5X1	T48.5X2	T48.5X3	T48.5X4	T48.5X5	T48.5X6
combination	T48.5X1	T48.5X2	T48.5X3	T48.5X4	T48.5X5	T48.5X6
Deet	T60.8X1	T60.8X2	T60.8X3	T60.8X4	—	—
Deferoxamine	T45.8X1	T45.8X2	T45.8X3	T45.8X4	T45.8X5	T45.8X6
Deflazacort	T38.0X1	T38.0X2	T38.0X3	T38.0X4	T38.0X5	T38.0X6
Deglycyrrhizinized extract of licorice	T48.4X1	T48.4X2	T48.4X3	T48.4X4	T48.4X5	T48.4X6
Dehydrocholic acid	T47.5X1	T47.5X2	T47.5X3	T47.5X4	T47.5X5	T47.5X6
Dehydroemetine	T37.3X1	T37.3X2	T37.3X3	T37.3X4	T37.3X5	T37.3X6
Dekalin	T52.8X1	T52.8X2	T52.8X3	T52.8X4	—	—
Delalutin	T38.5X1	T38.5X2	T38.5X3	T38.5X4	T38.5X5	T38.5X6
Delphinium	T62.2X1	T62.2X2	T62.2X3	T62.2X4	—	—
Deltasone	T38.0X1	T38.0X2	T38.0X3	T38.0X4	T38.0X5	T38.0X6
Deltra	T38.0X1	T38.0X2	T38.0X3	T38.0X4	T38.0X5	T38.0X6
Delvinal	T42.3X1	T42.3X2	T42.3X3	T42.3X4	T42.3X5	T42.3X6
Delorazepam	T42.4X1	T42.4X2	T42.4X3	T42.4X4	T42.4X5	T42.4X6
Deltamethrin	T60.1X1	T60.1X2	T60.1X3	T60.1X4	—	—
Demecarium (bromide)	T49.5X1	T49.5X2	T49.5X3	T49.5X4	T49.5X5	T49.5X6
Demeclocycline	T36.4X1	T36.4X2	T36.4X3	T36.4X4	T36.4X5	T36.4X6
Demecolcine	T45.1X1	T45.1X2	T45.1X3	T45.1X4	T45.1X5	T45.1X6
Demegestone	T38.5X1	T38.5X2	T38.5X3	T38.5X4	T38.5X5	T38.5X6
Demelanizing agents	T49.8X1	T49.8X2	T49.8X3	T49.8X4	T49.8X5	T49.8X6
Demephion -O and -S	T60.0X1	T60.0X2	T60.0X3	T60.0X4	—	—
Demerol	T40.2X1	T40.2X2	T40.2X3	T40.2X4	T40.2X5	T40.2X6
Demethylchlortetracycline	T36.4X1	T36.4X2	T36.4X3	T36.4X4	T36.4X5	T36.4X6
Demethyltetracycline	T36.4X1	T36.4X2	T36.4X3	T36.4X4	T36.4X5	T36.4X6
Demeton -O and -S	T60.0X1	T60.0X2	T60.0X3	T60.0X4	—	—
Demulcent (external)	T49.3X1	T49.3X2	T49.3X3	T49.3X4	T49.3X5	T49.3X6
specified NEC	T49.3X1	T49.3X2	T49.3X3	T49.3X4	T49.3X5	T49.3X6
Demulen	T38.4X1	T38.4X2	T38.4X3	T38.4X4	T38.4X5	T38.4X6
Denatured alcohol	T51.0X1	T51.0X2	T51.0X3	T51.0X4	—	—
Dendrid	T49.5X1	T49.5X2	T49.5X3	T49.5X4	T49.5X5	T49.5X6
Dental drug, topical application NEC	T49.7X1	T49.7X2	T49.7X3	T49.7X4	T49.7X5	T49.7X6

Substance	External Cause (T-Code)					
	Poisoning, Accidental (Unintentional)	Poisoning, Intentional Self-Harm	Poisoning, Assault	Poisoning, Undetermined	Adverse Effect	Underdosing
Dentifrice	T49.7X1	T49.7X2	T49.7X3	T49.7X4	T49.7X5	T49.7X6
Deodorant spray (feminine hygiene)	T49.8X1	T49.8X2	T49.8X3	T49.8X4	T49.8X5	T49.8X6
Deoxycortone	T50.0X1	T50.0X2	T50.0X3	T50.0X4	T50.0X5	T50.0X6
2-Deoxy-5-fluorouridine	T45.1X1	T45.1X2	T45.1X3	T45.1X4	T45.1X5	T45.1X6
5-Deoxy-5-fluorouridine	T45.1X1	T45.1X2	T45.1X3	T45.1X4	T45.1X5	T45.1X6
Deoxyribonuclease (pancreatic)	T45.3X1	T45.3X2	T45.3X3	T45.3X4	T45.3X5	T45.3X6
Depilatory	T49.4X1	T49.4X2	T49.4X3	T49.4X4	T49.4X5	T49.4X6
Deprenalin	T42.8X1	T42.8X2	T42.8X3	T42.8X4	T42.8X5	T42.8X6
Deprenyl	T42.8X1	T42.8X2	T42.8X3	T42.8X4	T42.8X5	T42.8X6
Depressant, appetite	T50.5X1	T50.5X2	T50.5X3	T50.5X4	T50.5X5	T50.5X6
Depressant						
appetite, central	T50.5X1	T50.5X2	T50.5X3	T50.5X4	T50.5X5	T50.5X6
cardiac	T46.2X1	T46.2X2	T46.2X3	T46.2X4	T46.2X5	T46.2X6
central nervous system (anesthetic) — see also Central nervous system, depressants	T42.71	T42.72	T42.73	T42.74	T42.75	T42.76
general anesthetic	T41.201	T41.202	T41.203	T41.204	T41.205	T41.206
muscle tone	T42.8X1	T42.8X2	T42.8X3	T42.8X4	T42.8X5	T42.8X6
muscle tone, central	T42.8X1	T42.8X2	T42.8X3	T42.8X4	T42.8X5	T42.8X6
psychotherapeutic	T43.501	T43.502	T43.503	T43.504	T43.505	T43.506
Deptropine	T45.0X1	T45.0X2	T45.0X3	T45.0X4	T45.0X5	T45.0X6
Dequalinium (chloride)	T49.0X1	T49.0X2	T49.0X3	T49.0X4	T49.0X5	T49.0X6
Derris root	T60.2X1	T60.2X2	T60.2X3	T60.2X4	—	—
Deserpidine	T43.011	T43.012	T43.013	T43.014	T43.015	T43.016
Desferrioxamine	T45.8X1	T45.8X2	T45.8X3	T45.8X4	T45.8X5	T45.8X6
Desipramine	T43.0X1	T43.0X2	T43.0X3	T43.0X4	T43.0X5	T43.0X6
Deslanoside	T46.0X1	T46.0X2	T46.0X3	T46.0X4	T46.0X5	T46.0X6
Desloughing agent	T49.4X1	T49.4X2	T49.4X3	T49.4X4	T49.4X5	T49.4X6
Desmethylimipramine	T43.011	T43.012	T43.013	T43.014	T43.015	T43.016
Desmopressin	T38.891	T38.892	T38.893	T38.894	T38.895	T38.896
Desocodeine	T40.2X1	T40.2X2	T40.2X3	T40.2X4	T40.2X5	T40.2X6
Desogestrel	T38.5X1	T38.5X2	T38.5X3	T38.5X4	T38.5X5	T38.5X6
Desomorphine	T40.2X1	T40.2X2	T40.2X3	T40.2X4	—	—
Desonide	T49.0X1	T49.0X2	T49.0X3	T49.0X4	T49.0X5	T49.0X6
Desoximetasone	T49.0X1	T49.0X2	T49.0X3	T49.0X4	T49.0X5	T49.0X6
Desoxycorticosteroid	T50.0X1	T50.0X2	T50.0X3	T50.0X4	T50.0X5	T50.0X6
Desoxycortone	T50.0X1	T50.0X2	T50.0X3	T50.0X4	T50.0X5	T50.0X6
Desoxyephedrine	T43.621	T43.622	T43.623	T43.624	T43.625	T43.626
Detaxtran	T46.6X1	T46.6X2	T46.6X3	T46.6X4	T46.6X5	T46.6X6
Detergent	T49.2X1	T49.2X2	T49.2X3	T49.2X4	T49.2X5	T49.2X6
external medication	T49.2X1	T49.2X2	T49.2X3	T49.2X4	T49.2X5	T49.2X6
local	T49.2X1	T49.2X2	T49.2X3	T49.2X4	T49.2X5	T49.2X6

◀ New ◀ Revised ~~deleted~~ Deleted

Substance	Poisoning, Accidental (Unintentional)	Poisoning, Intentional Self-Harm	Poisoning, Assault	Poisoning, Undetermined	Adverse Effect	Underdosing
Detergent *(Continued)*						
medicinal	T49.2X1	T49.2X2	T49.2X3	T49.2X4	T49.2X5	T49.2X6
nonmedicinal	T55.1X1	T55.1X2	T55.1X3	T55.1X4	—	—
specified NEC	T55.1X1	T55.1X2	T55.1X3	T55.1X4	T55.1X5	T55.1X6
Deterrent, alcohol	T50.6X1	T50.6X2	T50.6X3	T50.6X4	T50.6X5	T50.6X6
Detoxifying agent	T50.6X1	T50.6X2	T50.6X3	T50.6X4	T50.6X5	T50.6X6
Detrothyronine	T38.1X1	T38.1X2	T38.1X3	T38.1X4	T38.1X5	T38.1X6
Dettol (external medication)	T49.0X1	T49.0X2	T49.0X3	T49.0X4	T49.0X5	T49.0X6
Dexamethasone	T38.0X1	T38.0X2	T38.0X3	T38.0X4	T38.0X5	T38.0X6
ENT agent	T49.6X1	T49.6X2	T49.6X3	T49.6X4	T49.6X5	T49.6X6
ophthalmic preparation	T49.5X1	T49.5X2	T49.5X3	T49.5X4	T49.5X5	T49.5X6
topical NEC	T49.0X1	T49.0X2	T49.0X3	T49.0X4	T49.0X5	T49.0X6
Dexamfetamine	T43.621	T43.622	T43.623	T43.624	T43.625	T43.626
Dexamphetamine	T43.621	T43.622	T43.623	T43.624	T43.625	T43.626
Dexbrompheniramine	T45.0X1	T45.0X2	T45.0X3	T45.0X4	T45.0X5	T45.0X6
Dexchlorpheniramine	T45.0X1	T45.0X2	T45.0X3	T45.0X4	T45.0X5	T45.0X6
Dexedrine	T43.621	T43.622	T43.623	T43.624	T43.625	T43.626
Dexetimide	T44.3X1	T44.3X2	T44.3X3	T44.3X4	T44.3X5	T44.3X6
Dexfenfluramine	T50.5X1	T50.5X2	T50.5X3	T50.5X4	T50.5X5	T50.5X6
Dexpanthenol	T45.2X1	T45.2X2	T45.2X3	T45.2X4	T45.2X5	T45.2X6
Dextran (40) (70) (150)	T45.8X1	T45.8X2	T45.8X3	T45.8X4	T45.8X5	T45.8X6
Dextriferron	T45.4X1	T45.4X2	T45.4X3	T45.4X4	T45.4X5	T45.4X6
Dextroamphetamine	T43.621	T43.622	T43.623	T43.624	T43.625	T43.626
Dextro calcium pantothenate	T45.2X1	T45.2X2	T45.2X3	T45.2X4	T45.2X5	T45.2X6
Dextromethorphan	T48.3X1	T48.3X2	T48.3X3	T48.3X4	T48.3X5	T48.3X6
Dextromoramide	T40.4X1	T40.4X2	T40.4X3	T40.4X4	—	—
topical	T49.8X1	T49.8X2	T49.8X3	T49.8X4	T49.8X5	T49.8X6
Dextro pantothenyl alcohol	T45.2X1	T45.2X2	T45.2X3	T45.2X4	T45.2X5	T45.2X6
Dextropropoxyphene	T40.4X1	T40.4X2	T40.4X3	T40.4X4	T40.4X5	T40.4X6
Dextrorphan	T40.2X1	T40.2X2	T40.2X3	T40.2X4	T40.2X5	T40.2X6
Dextrose	T50.3X1	T50.3X2	T50.3X3	T50.3X4	T50.3X5	T50.3X6
concentrated solution, intravenous	T46.8X1	T46.8X2	T46.8X3	T46.8X4	T46.8X5	T46.8X6
Dextrothyroxin	T38.1X1	T38.1X2	T38.1X3	T38.1X4	T38.1X5	T38.1X6
Dextrothyroxine sodium	T38.1X1	T38.1X2	T38.1X3	T38.1X4	T38.1X5	T38.1X6
DFP	T44.0X1	T44.0X2	T44.0X3	T44.0X4	T44.0X5	T44.0X6
DHE	T37.3X1	T37.3X2	T37.3X3	T37.3X4	T37.3X5	T37.3X6
45	T46.5X1	T46.5X2	T46.5X3	T46.5X4	T46.5X5	T46.5X6
Diabinese	T38.3X1	T38.3X2	T38.3X3	T38.3X4	T38.3X5	T38.3X6
Diacetone alcohol	T52.4X1	T52.4X2	T52.4X3	T52.4X4	—	—
Diacetyl monoxime	T50.991	T50.992	T50.993	T50.994	—	—
Diacetylmorphine	T40.1X1	T40.1X2	T40.1X3	T40.1X4	—	—

Substance	Poisoning, Accidental (Unintentional)	Poisoning, Intentional Self-Harm	Poisoning, Assault	Poisoning, Undetermined	Adverse Effect	Underdosing
Diachylon plaster	T49.4X1	T49.4X2	T49.4X3	T49.4X4	T49.4X5	T49.4X6
Diaethylstilboestrolum	T38.5X1	T38.5X2	T38.5X3	T38.5X4	T38.5X5	T38.5X6
Diagnostic agent NEC	T50.8X1	T50.8X2	T50.8X3	T50.8X4	T50.8X5	T50.8X6
Dial (soap)	T49.2X1	T49.2X2	T49.2X3	T49.2X4	T49.2X5	T49.2X6
sedative	T42.3X1	T42.3X2	T42.3X3	T42.3X4	T42.3X5	T42.3X6
Dialkyl carbonate	T52.91	T52.92	T52.93	T52.94	—	—
Diallylbarbituric acid	T42.3X1	T42.3X2	T42.3X3	T42.3X4	T42.3X5	T42.3X6
Diallymal	T42.3X1	T42.3X2	T42.3X3	T42.3X4	T42.3X5	T42.3X6
Dialysis solution (intraperitoneal)	T50.3X1	T50.3X2	T50.3X3	T50.3X4	T50.3X5	T50.3X6
Diaminodiphenylsulfone	T37.1X1	T37.1X2	T37.1X3	T37.1X4	T37.1X5	T37.1X6
Diamorphine	T40.1X1	T40.1X2	T40.1X3	T40.1X4	—	—
Diamox	T50.2X1	T50.2X2	T50.2X3	T50.2X4	T50.2X5	T50.2X6
Diamthazole	T49.0X1	T49.0X2	T49.0X3	T49.0X4	T49.0X5	T49.0X6
Dianthone	T47.2X1	T47.2X2	T47.2X3	T47.2X4	T47.2X5	T47.2X6
Diaphenylsulfone	T37.0X1	T37.0X2	T37.0X3	T37.0X4	T37.0X5	T37.0X6
Diasone (sodium)	T37.1X1	T37.1X2	T37.1X3	T37.1X4	T37.1X5	T37.1X6
Diastase	T47.5X1	T47.5X2	T47.5X3	T47.5X4	T47.5X5	T47.5X6
Diatrizoate	T50.8X1	T50.8X2	T50.8X3	T50.8X4	T50.8X5	T50.8X6
Diazepam	T42.4X1	T42.4X2	T42.4X3	T42.4X4	T42.4X5	T42.4X6
Diazinon	T60.0X1	T60.0X2	T60.0X3	T60.0X4	—	—
Diazomethane (gas)	T59.891	T59.892	T59.893	T59.894	—	—
Diazoxide	T46.5X1	T46.5X2	T46.5X3	T46.5X4	T46.5X5	T46.5X6
Dibekacin	T36.5X1	T36.5X2	T36.5X3	T36.5X4	T36.5X5	T36.5X6
Dibenamine	T44.6X1	T44.6X2	T44.6X3	T44.6X4	T44.6X5	T44.6X6
Dibenzepin	T43.011	T43.012	T43.013	T43.014	T43.015	T43.016
Dibenzheptropine	T45.0X1	T45.0X2	T45.0X3	T45.0X4	T45.0X5	T45.0X6
Dibenzyline	T44.6X1	T44.6X2	T44.6X3	T44.6X4	T44.6X5	T44.6X6
Diborane (gas)	T59.891	T59.892	T59.893	T59.894	—	—
Dibromochloropropane	T60.8X1	T60.8X2	T60.8X3	T60.8X4	—	—
Dibromodulcitol	T45.1X1	T45.1X2	T45.1X3	T45.1X4	T45.1X5	T45.1X6
Dibromoethane	T53.6X1	T53.6X2	T53.6X3	T53.6X4	—	—
Dibromomannitol	T45.1X1	T45.1X2	T45.1X3	T45.1X4	T45.1X5	T45.1X6
Dibromopropamidine isethionate	T49.0X1	T49.0X2	T49.0X3	T49.0X4	T49.0X5	T49.0X6
Dibrompropamidine	T49.0X1	T49.0X2	T49.0X3	T49.0X4	T49.0X5	T49.0X6
Dibucaine	T41.3X1	T41.3X2	T41.3X3	T41.3X4	T41.3X5	T41.3X6
topical (surface)	T41.3X1	T41.3X2	T41.3X3	T41.3X4	T41.3X5	T41.3X6
Dibunate sodium	T48.3X1	T48.3X2	T48.3X3	T48.3X4	T48.3X5	T48.3X6
Dibutoline sulfate	T44.3X1	T44.3X2	T44.3X3	T44.3X4	T44.3X5	T44.3X6
Dicamba	T60.3X1	T60.3X2	T60.3X3	T60.3X4	—	—
Dicapthon	T60.0X1	T60.0X2	T60.0X3	T60.0X4	—	—
Dichlobenil	T60.3X1	T60.3X2	T60.3X3	T60.3X4	—	—
Dichlone	T60.3X1	T60.3X2	T60.3X3	T60.3X4	—	—

◀ New ◀ Revised ~~deleted~~ Deleted

Substance	Poisoning, Accidental (Unintentional)	Poisoning, Intentional Self-Harm	Poisoning, Assault	Poisoning, Undetermined	Adverse Effect	Underdosing
Dichloralphenozone	T42.6X1	T42.6X2	T42.6X3	T42.6X4	T42.6X5	T42.6X6
Dichlorbenzidine	T65.3X1	T65.3X2	T65.3X3	T65.3X4	—	—
Dichlorhydrin	T52.8X1	T52.8X2	T52.8X3	T52.8X4	—	—
Dichlorhydroxyquinoline	T37.8X1	T37.8X2	T37.8X3	T37.8X4	T37.8X5	T37.8X6
Dichlorobenzene	T53.7X1	T53.7X2	T53.7X3	T53.7X4		
Dichlorobenzyl alcohol	T49.6X1	T49.6X2	T49.6X3	T49.6X4	T49.6X5	T49.6X6
Dichlorodifluoromethane	T53.5X1	T53.5X2	T53.5X3	T53.5X4	—	—
Dichloroethane	T52.8X1	T52.8X2	T52.8X3	T52.8X4	—	—
Sym-Dichloroethyl ether	T53.6X1	T53.6X2	T53.6X3	T53.6X4		
Dichloroethyl sulfide, not in war	T59.891	T59.892	T59.893	T59.894	—	—
Dichloroethylene	T53.6X1	T53.6X2	T53.6X3	T53.6X4		
Dichloroformoxine, not in war	T59.891	T59.892	T59.893	T59.894		
Dichlorohydrin, alpha-dichlorohydrin	T52.8X1	T52.8X2	T52.8X3	T52.8X4	—	—
Dichloromethane (solvent)	T53.4X1	T53.4X2	T53.4X3	T53.4X4	—	—
vapor	T53.4X1	T53.4X2	T53.4X3	T53.4X4	—	—
Dichloronaphthoquinone	T60.3X1	T60.3X2	T60.3X3	T60.3X4	—	—
Dichlorophen	T37.4X1	T37.4X2	T37.4X3	T37.4X4	T37.4X5	T37.4X6
2,4-Dichlorophenoxy-acetic acid	T60.3X1	T60.3X2	T60.3X3	T60.3X4		
Dichloropropene	T60.3X1	T60.3X2	T60.3X3	T60.3X4		
Dichloropropionic acid	T60.3X1	T60.3X2	T60.3X3	T60.3X4	—	—
Dichlorphenamide	T50.2X1	T50.2X2	T50.2X3	T50.2X4	T50.2X5	T50.2X6
Dichlorvos	T60.0X1	T60.0X2	T60.0X3	T60.0X4		
Diclofenac	T39.391	T39.392	T39.393	T39.394	T39.395	T39.396
Diclofenamide	T50.2X1	T50.2X2	T50.2X3	T50.2X4	T50.2X5	T50.2X6
Diclofensine	T43.291	T43.292	T43.293	T43.294	T43.295	T43.296
Diclonixine	T39.8X1	T39.8X2	T39.8X3	T39.8X4	T39.8X5	T39.8X6
Dicloxacillin	T36.0X1	T36.0X2	T36.0X3	T36.0X4	T36.0X5	T36.0X6
Dicophane	T49.0X1	T49.0X2	T49.0X3	T49.0X4	T49.0X5	T49.0X6
Dicoumarol, dicoumarin, dicumarol	T45.511	T45.512	T45.513	T45.514	T45.515	T45.516
Dicrotophos	T60.0X1	T60.0X2	T60.0X3	T60.0X4	—	—
Dicyanogen (gas)	T65.0X1	T65.0X2	T65.0X3	T65.0X4	—	—
Dicyclomine	T44.3X1	T44.3X2	T44.3X3	T44.3X4	T44.3X5	T44.3X6
Dicycloverine	T44.3X1	T44.3X2	T44.3X3	T44.3X4	T44.3X5	T44.3X6
Dideoxycytidine	T37.5X1	T37.5X2	T37.5X3	T37.5X4	T37.5X5	T37.5X6
Dideoxyinosine	T37.5X1	T37.5X2	T37.5X3	T37.5X4	T37.5X5	T37.5X6
Dieldrin (vapor)	T60.1X1	T60.1X2	T60.1X3	T60.1X4	—	—
Diemal	T42.3X1	T42.3X2	T42.3X3	T42.3X4	T42.3X5	T42.3X6
Dienestrol	T38.5X1	T38.5X2	T38.5X3	T38.5X4	T38.5X5	T38.5X6
Dienoestrol	T38.5X1	T38.5X2	T38.5X3	T38.5X4	T38.5X5	T38.5X6
Dietetic drug NEC	T50.901	T50.902	T50.903	T50.904	T50.905	T50.906
Diethazine	T42.8X1	T42.8X2	T42.8X3	T42.8X4	T42.8X5	T42.8X6

Substance	Poisoning, Accidental (Unintentional)	Poisoning, Intentional Self-Harm	Poisoning, Assault	Poisoning, Undetermined	Adverse Effect	Underdosing
Diethyl						
barbituric acid	T42.3X1	T42.3X2	T42.3X3	T42.3X4	T42.3X5	T42.3X6
carbamazine	T37.4X1	T37.4X2	T37.4X3	T37.4X4	T37.4X5	T37.4X6
carbinol	T51.3X1	T51.3X2	T51.3X3	T51.3X4		
carbonate	T52.8X1	T52.8X2	T52.8X3	T52.8X4		
ether (vapor) — see also ether	T41.0X1	T41.0X2	T41.0X3	T41.0X4	T41.0X5	T41.0X6
oxide	T52.8X1	T52.8X2	T52.8X3	T52.8X4		
propion	T50.5X1	T50.5X2	T50.5X3	T50.5X4	T50.5X5	T50.5X6
stilbestrol	T38.5X1	T38.5X2	T38.5X3	T38.5X4	T38.5X5	T38.5X6
toluamide (nonmedicinal)	T60.8X1	T60.8X2	T60.8X3	T60.8X4	—	—
medicinal	T49.3X1	T49.3X2	T49.3X3	T49.3X4	T49.3X5	T49.3X6
Diethylcarbamazine	T37.4X1	T37.4X2	T37.4X3	T37.4X4	T37.4X5	T37.4X6
Diethylene						
dioxide	T52.8X1	T52.8X2	T52.8X3	T52.8X4		
glycol (monoacetate) (monobutyl ether) (monoethyl ether)	T52.3X1	T52.3X2	T52.3X3	T52.3X4		
Diethylhexylphthalate	T65.891	T65.892	T65.893	T65.894	—	—
Diethylpropion	T50.5X1	T50.5X2	T50.5X3	T50.5X4	T50.5X5	T50.5X6
Diethylstilbestrol	T38.5X1	T38.5X2	T38.5X3	T38.5X4	T38.5X5	T38.5X6
Diethylstilboestrol	T38.5X1	T38.5X2	T38.5X3	T38.5X4	T38.5X5	T38.5X6
Diethylsulfone-diethylmethane	T42.6X1	T42.6X2	T42.6X3	T42.6X4	T42.6X5	T42.6X6
Diethyltoluamide	T49.0X1	T49.0X2	T49.0X3	T49.0X4	T49.0X5	T49.0X6
Diethyltryptamine (DET)	T40.991	T40.992	T40.993	T40.994	—	—
Difebarbamate	T42.3X1	T42.3X2	T42.3X3	T42.3X4	T42.3X5	T42.3X6
Difencloxazine	T40.2X1	T40.2X2	T40.2X3	T40.2X4	T40.2X5	T40.2X6
Difenidol	T45.0X1	T45.0X2	T45.0X3	T45.0X4	T45.0X5	T45.0X6
Difenoxin	T47.6X1	T47.6X2	T47.6X3	T47.6X4	T47.6X5	T47.6X6
Difetarsone	T37.3X1	T37.3X2	T37.3X3	T37.3X4	T37.3X5	T37.3X6
Diffusin	T45.3X1	T45.3X2	T45.3X3	T45.3X4	T45.3X5	T45.3X6
Diflorasone	T49.0X1	T49.0X2	T49.0X3	T49.0X4	T49.0X5	T49.0X6
Diflubenzuron	T60.1X1	T60.1X2	T60.1X3	T60.1X4	—	—
Diflos	T44.0X1	T44.0X2	T44.0X3	T44.0X4	T44.0X5	T44.0X6
Diflucortolone	T49.0X1	T49.0X2	T49.0X3	T49.0X4	T49.0X5	T49.0X6
Diflunisal	T39.091	T39.092	T39.093	T39.094	T39.095	T39.096
Difluoromethyldopa	T42.8X1	T42.8X2	T42.8X3	T42.8X4	T42.8X5	T42.8X6
Difluorophate	T44.0X1	T44.0X2	T44.0X3	T44.0X4	T44.0X5	T44.0X6
Digestant NEC	T47.5X1	T47.5X2	T47.5X3	T47.5X4	T47.5X5	T47.5X6
Digitalin(e)	T46.0X1	T46.0X2	T46.0X3	T46.0X4	T46.0X5	T46.0X6
Digitalis (leaf) (glycoside)	T46.0X1	T46.0X2	T46.0X3	T46.0X4	T46.0X5	T46.0X6
lanata	T46.0X1	T46.0X2	T46.0X3	T46.0X4	T46.0X5	T46.0X6
purpurea	T46.0X1	T46.0X2	T46.0X3	T46.0X4	T46.0X5	T46.0X6
Digitoxin	T46.0X1	T46.0X2	T46.0X3	T46.0X4	T46.0X5	T46.0X6

◀ New   ◀ Revised   ~~deleted~~ Deleted

Substance	Poisoning, Accidental (Unintentional)	Poisoning, Intentional Self-Harm	Poisoning, Assault	Poisoning, Undetermined	Adverse Effect	Underdosing
Digitoxose	T46.0X1	T46.0X2	T46.0X3	T46.0X4	T46.0X5	T46.0X6
Digoxin	T46.0X1	T46.0X2	T46.0X3	T46.0X4	T46.0X5	T46.0X6
Digoxine	T46.0X1	T46.0X2	T46.0X3	T46.0X4	T46.0X5	T46.0X6
Dihydralazine	T46.5X1	T46.5X2	T46.5X3	T46.5X4	T46.5X5	T46.5X6
Dihydrazine	T46.5X1	T46.5X2	T46.5X3	T46.5X4	T46.5X5	T46.5X6
Dihydrocodeinone	T40.2X1	T40.2X2	T40.2X3	T40.2X4	T40.2X5	T40.2X6
Dihydroergocornine	T46.7X1	T46.7X2	T46.7X3	T46.7X4	T46.7X5	T46.7X6
Dihydroergocristine (mesilate)	T46.7X1	T46.7X2	T46.7X3	T46.7X4	T46.7X5	T46.7X6
Dihydroergokryptine	T46.7X1	T46.7X2	T46.7X3	T46.7X4	T46.7X5	T46.7X6
Dihydroergotamine	T46.5X1	T46.5X2	T46.5X3	T46.5X4	T46.5X5	T46.5X6
Dihydroergotoxine	T46.7X1	T46.7X2	T46.7X3	T46.7X4	T46.7X5	T46.7X6
mesilate	T46.7X1	T46.7X2	T46.7X3	T46.7X4	T46.7X5	T46.7X6
Dihydrohydroxycodein-one	T40.2X1	T40.2X2	T40.2X3	T40.2X4	T40.2X5	T40.2X6
Dihydrohydroxymorphinone	T40.2X1	T40.2X2	T40.2X3	T40.2X4	T40.2X5	T40.2X6
Dihydroisocodeine	T40.2X1	T40.2X2	T40.2X3	T40.2X4	T40.2X5	T40.2X6
Dihydromorphine	T40.2X1	T40.2X2	T40.2X3	T40.2X4	—	—
Dihydromorphinone	T40.2X1	T40.2X2	T40.2X3	T40.2X4	T40.2X5	T40.2X6
Dihydrostreptomycin	T36.5X1	T36.5X2	T36.5X3	T36.5X4	T36.5X5	T36.5X6
Dihydrotachysterol	T45.2X1	T45.2X2	T45.2X3	T45.2X4	T45.2X5	T45.2X6
Dihydroxyaluminum aminoacetate	T47.1X1	T47.1X2	T47.1X3	T47.1X4	T47.1X5	T47.1X6
Dihydroxyaluminum sodium carbonate	T47.1X1	T47.1X2	T47.1X3	T47.1X4	T47.1X5	T47.1X6
Dihydroxyanthraquinone	T47.2X1	T47.2X2	T47.2X3	T47.2X4	T47.2X5	T47.2X6
Dihydroxycodeinone	T40.2X1	T40.2X2	T40.2X3	T40.2X4	T40.2X5	T40.2X6
Dihydroxypropyl theophylline	T50.2X1	T50.2X2	T50.2X3	T50.2X4	T50.2X5	T50.2X6
Diiodohydroxyquin	T37.8X1	T37.8X2	T37.8X3	T37.8X4	T37.8X5	T37.8X6
topical	T49.0X1	T49.0X2	T49.0X3	T49.0X4	T49.0X5	T49.0X6
Diiodohydroxyquinoline	T37.8X1	T37.8X2	T37.8X3	T37.8X4	T37.8X5	T37.8X6
Diiodotyrosine	T38.2X1	T38.2X2	T38.2X3	T38.2X4	T38.2X5	T38.2X6
Diisopromine	T44.3X1	T44.3X2	T44.3X3	T44.3X4	T44.3X5	T44.3X6
Diisopropylamine	T46.3X1	T46.3X2	T46.3X3	T46.3X4	T46.3X5	T46.3X6
Diisopropylfluorophosphonate	T44.0X1	T44.0X2	T44.0X3	T44.0X4	T44.0X5	T44.0X6
Dilantin	T42.0X1	T42.0X2	T42.0X3	T42.0X4	T42.0X5	T42.0X6
Dilaudid	T40.2X1	T40.2X2	T40.2X3	T40.2X4	T40.2X5	T40.2X6
Dilazep	T46.3X1	T46.3X2	T46.3X3	T46.3X4	T46.3X5	T46.3X6
Dill	T47.5X1	T47.5X2	T47.5X3	T47.5X4	T47.5X5	T47.5X6
Diloxanide	T37.3X1	T37.3X2	T37.3X3	T37.3X4	T37.3X5	T37.3X6
Diltiazem	T46.1X1	T46.1X2	T46.1X3	T46.1X4	T46.1X5	T46.1X6
Dimazole	T49.0X1	T49.0X2	T49.0X3	T49.0X4	T49.0X5	T49.0X6
Dimefline	T50.7X1	T50.7X2	T50.7X3	T50.7X4	T50.7X5	T50.7X6
Dimefox	T60.0X1	T60.0X2	T60.0X3	T60.0X4	—	—
Dimemorfan	T48.3X1	T48.3X2	T48.3X3	T48.3X4	T48.3X5	T48.3X6
Dimenhydrinate	T45.0X1	T45.0X2	T45.0X3	T45.0X4	T45.0X5	T45.0X6
Dimercaprol (British anti-lewisite)	T45.8X1	T45.8X2	T45.8X3	T45.8X4	T45.8X5	T45.8X6
Dimercaptopropanol	T45.8X1	T45.8X2	T45.8X3	T45.8X4	T45.8X5	T45.8X6
Dimestrol	T38.5X1	T38.5X2	T38.5X3	T38.5X4	T38.5X5	T38.5X6
Dimetane	T45.0X1	T45.0X2	T45.0X3	T45.0X4	T45.0X5	T45.0X6
Dimethicone	T47.1X1	T47.1X2	T47.1X3	T47.1X4	T47.1X5	T47.1X6
Dimethindene	T45.0X1	T45.0X2	T45.0X3	T45.0X4	T45.0X5	T45.0X6
Dimethisoquin	T49.1X1	T49.1X2	T49.1X3	T49.1X4	T49.1X5	T49.1X6
Dimethisterone	T38.5X1	T38.5X2	T38.5X3	T38.5X4	T38.5X5	T38.5X6
Dimethoate	T60.0X1	T60.0X2	T60.0X3	T60.0X4	—	—
Dimethocaine	T41.3X1	T41.3X2	T41.3X3	T41.3X4	T41.3X5	T41.3X6
Dimethoxanate	T48.3X1	T48.3X2	T48.3X3	T48.3X4	T48.3X5	T48.3X6
Dimethyl						
arsine, arsinic acid	T57.0X1	T57.0X2	T57.0X3	T57.0X4	—	—
carbinol	T51.2X1	T51.2X2	T51.2X3	T51.2X4	—	—
carbonate	T52.8X1	T52.8X2	T52.8X3	T52.8X4	—	—
diguanide	T38.3X1	T38.3X2	T38.3X3	T38.3X4	T38.3X5	T38.3X6
ketone	T52.4X1	T52.4X2	T52.4X3	T52.4X4	—	—
vapor	T52.4X1	T52.4X2	T52.4X3	T52.4X4	—	—
meperidine	T40.2X1	T40.2X2	T40.2X3	T40.2X4	T40.2X5	T40.2X6
parathion	T60.0X1	T60.0X2	T60.0X3	T60.0X4	—	—
phthlate	T49.3X1	T49.3X2	T49.3X3	T49.3X4	T49.3X5	T49.3X6
polysiloxane	T47.8X1	T47.8X2	T47.8X3	T47.8X4	T47.8X5	T47.8X6
sulfate (fumes)	T59.891	T59.892	T59.893	T59.894	—	—
liquid	T65.891	T65.892		T65.894	—	—
sulfoxide (nonmedicinal)	T52.8X1	T52.8X2	T52.8X3	T52.8X4	—	—
medicinal	T49.4X1	T49.4X2	T49.4X3	T49.4X4	T49.4X5	T49.4X6
tryptamine	T40.991	T40.992	T40.993	T40.994		
tubocurarine	T48.1X1	T48.1X2	T48.1X3	T48.1X4	T48.1X5	T48.1X6
Dimethylamine sulfate	T49.4X1	T49.4X2	T49.4X3	T49.4X4	T49.4X5	T49.4X6
Dimethylformamide	T52.8X1	T52.8X2	T52.8X3	T52.8X4		
Dimethyltubocurarinium chloride	T48.1X1	T48.1X2	T48.1X3	T48.1X4	T48.1X5	T48.1X6
Dimeticone	T47.1X1	T47.1X2	T47.1X3	T47.1X4	T47.1X5	T47.1X6
Dimetilan	T60.0X1	T60.0X2	T60.0X3	T60.0X4	—	—
Dimetindene	T45.0X1	T45.0X2	T45.0X3	T45.0X4	T45.0X5	T45.0X6
Dimetotiazine	T43.3X1	T43.3X2	T43.3X3	T43.3X4	T43.3X5	T43.3X6
Dimorpholamine	T50.7X1	T50.7X2	T50.7X3	T50.7X4	T50.7X5	T50.7X6
Dimoxyline	T46.3X1	T46.3X2	T46.3X3	T46.3X4	T46.3X5	T46.3X6
Dinitrobenzene	T65.3X1	T65.3X2	T65.3X3	T65.3X4	—	—
vapor	T59.891	T59.892	T59.893	T59.894	—	—

◀ New ◀ Revised ~~deleted~~ Deleted

Substance	External Cause (T-Code)					
	Poisoning, Accidental (Unintentional)	Poisoning, Intentional Self-Harm	Poisoning, Assault	Poisoning, Undetermined	Adverse Effect	Underdosing
Dinitrobenzol	T65.3X1	T65.3X2	T65.3X3	T65.3X4	—	—
vapor	T59.891	T59.892	T59.893	T59.894	—	—
Dinitrobutylphenol	T65.3X1	T65.3X2	T65.3X3	T65.3X4	—	—
Dinitro (-ortho-)cresol (pesticide) (spray)	T65.3X1	T65.3X2	T65.3X3	T65.3X4	—	—
Dinitrocyclohexylphenol	T65.3X1	T65.3X2	T65.3X3	T65.3X4	—	—
Dinitrophenol	T65.3X1	T65.3X2	T65.3X3	T65.3X4	—	—
Dinoprost	T48.0X1	T48.0X2	T48.0X3	T48.0X4	T48.0X5	T48.0X6
Dinoprostone	T48.0X1	T48.0X2	T48.0X3	T48.0X4	T48.0X5	T48.0X6
Dinoseb	T60.3X1	T60.3X2	T60.3X3	T60.3X4		
Dioctyl sulfosuccinate (calcium) (sodium)	T47.4X1	T47.4X2	T47.4X3	T47.4X4	T47.4X5	T47.4X6
Diodone	T50.8X1	T50.8X2	T50.8X3	T50.8X4	T50.8X5	T50.8X6
Diodoquin	T37.8X1	T37.8X2	T37.8X3	T37.8X4	T37.8X5	T37.8X6
Dionin	T40.2X1	T40.2X2	T40.2X3	T40.2X4	T40.2X5	T40.2X6
Diosmin	T46.991	T46.992	T46.993	T46.994	T46.995	T46.996
Dioxane	T52.8X1	T52.8X2	T52.8X3	T52.8X4	—	—
Dioxathion	T60.0X1	T60.0X2	T60.0X3	T60.0X4	—	—
Dioxin	T53.7X1	T53.7X2	T53.7X3	T53.7X4	—	—
Dioxopromethazine	T43.3X1	T43.3X2	T43.3X3	T43.3X4	T43.3X5	T43.3X6
Dioxyline	T46.3X1	T46.3X2	T46.3X3	T46.3X4	T46.3X5	T46.3X6
Dipentene	T52.8X1	T52.8X2	T52.8X3	T52.8X4	—	—
Diperodon	T41.3X1	T41.3X2	T41.3X3	T41.3X4	T41.3X5	T41.3X6
Diphacinone	T60.4X1	T60.4X2	T60.4X3	T60.4X4	—	—
Diphemanil	T44.3X1	T44.3X2	T44.3X3	T44.3X4	T44.3X5	T44.3X6
metilsulfate	T44.3X1	T44.3X2	T44.3X3	T44.3X4	T44.3X5	T44.3X6
Diphenadione	T45.511	T45.512	T45.513	T45.514	T45.515	T45.516
rodenticide	T60.4X1	T60.4X2	T60.4X3	T60.4X4	—	—
Diphenhydramine	T45.0X1	T45.0X2	T45.0X3	T45.0X4	T45.0X5	T45.0X6
Diphenidol	T45.0X1	T45.0X2	T45.0X3	T45.0X4	T45.0X5	T45.0X6
Diphenoxylate	T47.6X1	T47.6X2	T47.6X3	T47.6X4	T47.6X5	T47.6X6
Diphenylamine	T65.3X1	T65.3X2	T65.3X3	T65.3X4	—	—
Diphenylbutazone	T39.2X1	T39.2X2	T39.2X3	T39.2X4	T39.2X5	T39.2X6
Diphenylchloroarsine, not in war	T57.0X1	T57.0X2	T57.0X3	T57.0X4	—	—
Diphenylhydantoin	T42.0X1	T42.0X2	T42.0X3	T42.0X4	T42.0X5	T42.0X6
Diphenylmethane dye	T52.1X1	T52.1X2	T52.1X3	T52.1X4	—	—
Diphenylpyraline	T45.0X1	T45.0X2	T45.0X3	T45.0X4	T45.0X5	T45.0X6
Diphtheria						
antitoxin	T50.Z11	T50.Z12	T50.Z13	T50.Z14	T50.Z15	T50.Z16
toxoid	T50.A91	T50.A92	T50.A93	T50.A94	T50.A95	T50.A96
with tetanus toxoid	T50.A21	T50.A22	T50.A23	T50.A24	T50.A25	T50.A26
with pertussis component	T50.A11	T50.A12	T50.A13	T50.A14	T50.A15	T50.A16

Substance	External Cause (T-Code)					
	Poisoning, Accidental (Unintentional)	Poisoning, Intentional Self-Harm	Poisoning, Assault	Poisoning, Undetermined	Adverse Effect	Underdosing
Diphtheria (Continued)						
vaccine (combination)	T50.A91	T50.A92	T50.A93	T50.A94	T50.A95	T50.A96
combination						
including pertussis	T50.A11	T50.A12	T50.A13	T50.A14	T50.A15	T50.A16
without pertussis	T50.A21	T50.A22	T50.A23	T50.A24	T50.A25	T50.A26
Diphylline	T50.2X1	T50.2X2	T50.2X3	T50.2X4	T50.2X5	T50.2X6
Dipipanone	T40.4X1	T40.4X2	T40.4X3	T40.4X4	—	—
Dipivefrine	T49.5X1	T49.5X2	T49.5X3	T49.5X4	T49.5X5	T49.5X6
Diplovax	T50.B91	T50.B92	T50.B93	T50.B94	T50.B95	T50.B96
Diprophylline	T50.2X1	T50.2X2	T50.2X3	T50.2X4	T50.2X5	T50.2X6
Dipropyline	T48.291	T48.292	T48.293	T48.294	T48.295	T48.296
Dipyridamole	T46.3X1	T46.3X2	T46.3X3	T46.3X4	T46.3X5	T46.3X6
Dipyrone	T39.2X1	T39.2X2	T39.2X3	T39.2X4	T39.2X5	T39.2X6
Diquat (dibromide)	T60.3X1	T60.3X2	T60.3X3	T60.3X4	—	—
Disinfectant	T65.891	T65.892	T65.893	T65.894	—	—
alkaline	T54.3X1	T54.3X2	T54.3X3	T54.3X4	—	—
aromatic	T54.1X1	T54.1X2	T54.1X3	T54.1X4	—	—
intestinal	T37.8X1	T37.8X2	T37.8X3	T37.8X4	T37.8X5	T37.8X6
Disipal	T42.8X1	T42.8X2	T42.8X3	T42.8X4	T42.8X5	T42.8X6
Disodium edetate	T50.6X1	T50.6X2	T50.6X3	T50.6X4	T50.6X5	T50.6X6
Disoprofol	T41.291	T41.292	T41.293	T41.294	T41.295	T41.296
Disopyramide	T46.2X1	T46.2X2	T46.2X3	T46.2X4	T46.2X5	T46.2X6
Distigmine (bromide)	T44.0X1	T44.0X2	T44.0X3	T44.0X4	T44.0X5	T44.0X6
Disulfamide	T50.2X1	T50.2X2	T50.2X3	T50.2X4	T50.2X5	T50.2X6
Disulfanilamide	T37.0X1	T37.0X2	T37.0X3	T37.0X4	T37.0X5	T37.0X6
Disulfiram	T50.6X1	T50.6X2	T50.6X3	T50.6X4	T50.6X5	T50.6X6
Disulfoton	T60.0X1	T60.0X2	T60.0X3	T60.0X4	—	—
Dithiazanine iodide	T37.4X1	T37.4X2	T37.4X3	T37.4X4	T37.4X5	T37.4X6
Dithiocarbamate	T60.0X1	T60.0X2	T60.0X3	T60.0X4	—	—
Dithranol	T49.4X1	T49.4X2	T49.4X3	T49.4X4	T49.4X5	T49.4X6
Diucardin	T50.2X1	T50.2X2	T50.2X3	T50.2X4	T50.2X5	T50.2X6
Diupres	T50.2X1	T50.2X2	T50.2X3	T50.2X4	T50.2X5	T50.2X6
Diuretic NEC	T50.2X1	T50.2X2	T50.2X3	T50.2X4	T50.2X5	T50.2X6
benzothiadiazine	T50.2X1	T50.2X2	T50.2X3	T50.2X4	T50.2X5	T50.2X6
carbonic acid anhydrase inhibitors	T50.2X1	T50.2X2	T50.2X3	T50.2X4	T50.2X5	T50.2X6
furfuryl NEC	T50.2X1	T50.2X2	T50.2X3	T50.2X4	T50.2X5	T50.2X6
loop (high-ceiling)	T50.1X1	T50.1X2	T50.1X3	T50.1X4	T50.1X5	T50.1X6
mercurial NEC	T50.2X1	T50.2X2	T50.2X3	T50.2X4	T50.2X5	T50.2X6
osmotic	T50.2X1	T50.2X2	T50.2X3	T50.2X4	T50.2X5	T50.2X6
purine NEC	T50.2X1	T50.2X2	T50.2X3	T50.2X4	T50.2X5	T50.2X6
saluretic NEC	T50.2X1	T50.2X2	T50.2X3	T50.2X4	T50.2X5	T50.2X6

◀ New ◀ Revised ~~deleted~~ Deleted

Substance	External Cause (T-Code) Poisoning, Accidental (Unintentional)	Poisoning, Intentional Self-Harm	Poisoning, Assault	Poisoning, Undetermined	Adverse Effect	Underdosing
Diuretic NEC *(Continued)*						
sulfonamide	T50.2X1	T50.2X2	T50.2X3	T50.2X4	T50.2X5	T50.2X6
thiazide NEC	T50.2X1	T50.2X2	T50.2X3	T50.2X4	T50.2X5	T50.2X6
xanthine	T50.2X1	T50.2X2	T50.2X3	T50.2X4	T50.2X5	T50.2X6
Diurgin	T50.2X1	T50.2X2	T50.2X3	T50.2X4	T50.2X5	T50.2X6
Diuril	T50.2X1	T50.2X2	T50.2X3	T50.2X4	T50.2X5	T50.2X6
Diuron	T60.3X1	T60.3X2	T60.3X3	T60.3X4	—	—
Divalproex	T42.6X1	T42.6X2	T42.6X3	T42.6X4	T42.6X5	T42.6X6
Divinyl ether	T41.0X1	T41.0X2	T41.0X3	T41.0X4	T41.0X5	T41.0X6
Dixanthogen	T49.0X1	T49.0X2	T49.0X3	T49.0X4	T49.0X5	T49.0X6
Dixyrazine	T43.3X1	T43.3X2	T43.3X3	T43.3X4	T43.3X5	T43.3X6
D-lysergic acid diethylamide	T40.8X1	T40.8X2	T40.8X3	T40.8X4	—	—
DMCT	T36.4X1	T36.4X2	T36.4X3	T36.4X4	T36.4X5	T36.4X6
DMSO — *see Dimethyl sulfoxide*						
DNBP	T60.3X1	T60.3X2	T60.3X3	T60.3X4	—	—
DNOC	T65.3X1	T65.3X2	T65.3X3	T65.3X4	—	—
DOCA	T38.0X1	T38.0X2	T38.0X3	T38.0X4	T38.0X5	T38.0X6
Dobutamine	T44.5X1	T44.5X2	T44.5X3	T44.5X4	T44.5X5	T44.5X6
Docusate sodium	T47.4X1	T47.4X2	T47.4X3	T47.4X4	T47.4X5	T47.4X6
Dodicin	T49.0X1	T49.0X2	T49.0X3	T49.0X4	T49.0X5	T49.0X6
Dofamium chloride	T49.0X1	T49.0X2	T49.0X3	T49.0X4	T49.0X5	T49.0X6
Dolophine	T40.3X1	T40.3X2	T40.3X3	T40.3X4	T40.3X5	T40.3X6
Doloxene	T39.8X1	T39.8X2	T39.8X3	T39.8X4	T39.8X5	T39.8X6
Domestic gas (after combustion) — *see Gas, utility*						
prior to combustion	T59.891	T59.892	T59.893	T59.894	—	—
Domiodol	T48.4X1	T48.4X2	T48.4X3	T48.4X4	T48.4X5	T48.4X6
Domiphen (bromide)	T49.0X1	T49.0X2	T49.0X3	T49.0X4	T49.0X5	T49.0X6
Domperidone	T45.0X1	T45.0X2	T45.0X3	T45.0X4	T45.0X5	T45.0X6
Dopa	T42.8X1	T42.8X2	T42.8X3	T42.8X4	T42.8X5	T42.8X6
Dopamine	T44.991	T44.992	T44.993	T44.994	T44.995	T44.996
Doriden	T42.6X1	T42.6X2	T42.6X3	T42.6X4	T42.6X5	T42.6X6
Dormiral	T42.3X1	T42.3X2	T42.3X3	T42.3X4	T42.3X5	T42.3X6
Dormison	T42.6X1	T42.6X2	T42.6X3	T42.6X4	T42.6X5	T42.6X6
Dornase	T48.4X1	T48.4X2	T48.4X3	T48.4X4	T48.4X5	T48.4X6
Dorsacaine	T41.3X1	T41.3X2	T41.3X3	T41.3X4	T41.3X5	T41.3X6
Dosulepin	T43.011	T43.012	T43.013	T43.014	T43.015	T43.016
Dothiepin	T43.011	T43.012	T43.013	T43.014	T43.015	T43.016
Doxantrazole	T48.6X1	T48.6X2	T48.6X3	T48.6X4	T48.6X5	T48.6X6
Doxapram	T50.7X1	T50.7X2	T50.7X3	T50.7X4	T50.7X5	T50.7X6
Doxazosin	T44.6X1	T44.6X2	T44.6X3	T44.6X4	T44.6X5	T44.6X6
Doxepin	T43.011	T43.012	T43.013	T43.014	T43.015	T43.016

Substance	External Cause (T-Code) Poisoning, Accidental (Unintentional)	Poisoning, Intentional Self-Harm	Poisoning, Assault	Poisoning, Undetermined	Adverse Effect	Underdosing
Doxifluridine	T45.1X1	T45.1X2	T45.1X3	T45.1X4	T45.1X5	T45.1X6
Doxorubicin	T45.1X1	T45.1X2	T45.1X3	T45.1X4	T45.1X5	T45.1X6
Doxycycline	T36.4X1	T36.4X2	T36.4X3	T36.4X4	T36.4X5	T36.4X6
Doxylamine	T45.0X1	T45.0X2	T45.0X3	T45.0X4	T45.0X5	T45.0X6
Dramamine	T45.0X1	T45.0X2	T45.0X3	T45.0X4	T45.0X5	T45.0X6
Drano (drain cleaner)	T54.3X1	T54.3X2	T54.3X3	T54.3X4	—	—
Dressing, live pulp	T49.7X1	T49.7X2	T49.7X3	T49.7X4	T49.7X5	T49.7X6
Drocode	T40.2X1	T40.2X2	T40.2X3	T40.2X4	T40.2X5	T40.2X6
Dromoran	T40.2X1	T40.2X2	T40.2X3	T40.2X4	T40.2X5	T40.2X6
Dromostanolone	T38.7X1	T38.7X2	T38.7X3	T38.7X4	T38.7X5	T38.7X6
Dronabinol	T40.7X1	T40.7X2	T40.7X3	T40.7X4	T40.7X5	T40.7X6
Droperidol	T43.591	T43.592	T43.593	T43.594	T43.595	T43.596
Dropropizine	T48.3X1	T48.3X2	T48.3X3	T48.3X4	T48.3X5	T48.3X6
Drostanolone	T38.7X1	T38.7X2	T38.7X3	T38.7X4	T38.7X5	T38.7X6
Drotaverine	T44.3X1	T44.3X2	T44.3X3	T44.3X4	T44.3X5	T44.3X6
Drotrecogin alfa	T45.511	T45.512	T45.513	T45.514	T45.515	T45.516
Drug NEC	T50.901	T50.902	T50.903	T50.904	T50.905	T50.906
specified NEC	T50.991	T50.992	T50.993	T50.994	T50.995	T50.996
DTIC	T45.1X1	T45.1X2	T45.1X3	T45.1X4	T45.1X5	T45.1X6
Duboisine	T44.3X1	T44.3X2	T44.3X3	T44.3X4	T44.3X5	T44.3X6
Dulcolax	T47.2X1	T47.2X2	T47.2X3	T47.2X4	T47.2X5	T47.2X6
Duponol (C) (EP)	T49.2X1	T49.2X2	T49.2X3	T49.2X4	T49.2X5	T49.2X6
Durabolin	T38.7X1	T38.7X2	T38.7X3	T38.7X4	T38.7X5	T38.7X6
Dyclone	T41.3X1	T41.3X2	T41.3X3	T41.3X4	T41.3X5	T41.3X6
Dyclonine	T41.3X1	T41.3X2	T41.3X3	T41.3X4	T41.3X5	T41.3X6
Dydrogesterone	T38.5X1	T38.5X2	T38.5X3	T38.5X4	T38.5X5	T38.5X6
Dye NEC	T65.6X1	T65.6X2	T65.6X3	T65.6X4	—	—
antiseptic	T49.0X1	T49.0X2	T49.0X3	T49.0X4	T49.0X5	T49.0X6
diagnostic agents	T50.8X1	T50.8X2	T50.8X3	T50.8X4	T50.8X5	T50.8X6
pharmaceutical NEC	T50.901	T50.902	T50.903	T50.904	T50.905	T50.906
Dyflos	T44.0X1	T44.0X2	T44.0X3	T44.0X4	T44.0X5	T44.0X6
Dymelor	T38.3X1	T38.3X2	T38.3X3	T38.3X4	T38.3X5	T38.3X6
Dynamite	T65.3X1	T65.3X2	T65.3X3	T65.3X4	—	—
fumes	T59.891	T59.892	T59.893	T59.894	—	—
Dyphylline	T44.3X1	T44.3X2	T44.3X3	T44.3X4	T44.3X5	T44.3X6
E						
Ear drug NEC	T49.6X1	T49.6X2	T49.6X3	T49.6X4	T49.6X5	T49.6X6
Ear preparations	T49.6X1	T49.6X2	T49.6X3	T49.6X4	T49.6X5	T49.6X6
Econazole	T49.0X1	T49.0X2	T49.0X3	T49.0X4	T49.0X5	T49.0X6
Ecothiopate iodide	T49.5X1	T49.5X2	T49.5X3	T49.5X4	T49.5X5	T49.5X6
Echothiophate, echothiopate, ecothiopate	T49.5X1	T49.5X2	T49.5X3	T49.5X4	T49.5X5	T49.5X6

◄ New ◄ Revised ~~deleted~~ Deleted

TABLE OF DRUGS AND CHEMICALS

Substance	External Cause (T-Code)					
	Poisoning, Accidental (Unintentional)	Poisoning, Intentional Self-Harm	Poisoning, Assault	Poisoning, Undetermined	Adverse Effect	Underdosing
Ecstasy	T43.641	T43.642	T43.643	T43.644	—	—
Ectylurea	T42.6X1	T42.6X2	T42.6X3	T42.6X4	T42.6X5	T42.6X6
Edathamil disodium	T45.8X1	T45.8X2	T45.8X3	T45.8X4	T45.8X5	T45.8X6
Edecrin	T50.1X1	T50.1X2	T50.1X3	T50.1X4	T50.1X5	T50.1X6
Edetate, disodium (calcium)	T45.8X1	T45.8X2	T45.8X3	T45.8X4	T45.8X5	T45.8X6
Edoxudine	T49.5X1	T49.5X2	T49.5X3	T49.5X4	T49.5X5	T49.5X6
Edrophonium	T44.0X1	T44.0X2	T44.0X3	T44.0X4	T44.0X5	T44.0X6
chloride	T44.0X1	T44.0X2	T44.0X3	T44.0X4	T44.0X5	T44.0X6
EDTA	T50.6X1	T50.6X2	T50.6X3	T50.6X4	T50.6X5	T50.6X6
Eflornithine	T37.2X1	T37.2X2	T37.2X3	T37.2X4	T37.2X5	T37.2X6
Efloxate	T46.3X1	T46.3X2	T46.3X3	T46.3X4	T46.3X5	T46.3X6
Elase	T49.8X1	T49.8X2	T49.8X3	T49.8X4	T49.8X5	T49.8X6
Elastase	T47.5X1	T47.5X2	T47.5X3	T47.5X4	T47.5X5	T47.5X6
Elaterium	T47.2X1	T47.2X2	T47.2X3	T47.2X4	T47.2X5	T47.2X6
Elcatonin	T50.991	T50.992	T50.993	T50.994	T50.995	T50.996
Elder	T62.2X1	T62.2X2	T62.2X3	T62.2X4	—	—
berry (unripe)	T62.1X1	T62.1X2	T62.1X3	T62.1X4	—	—
Electrolyte balance drug	T50.3X1	T50.3X2	T50.3X3	T50.3X4	T50.3X5	T50.3X6
Electrolytes NEC	T50.3X1	T50.3X2	T50.3X3	T50.3X4	T50.3X5	T50.3X6
Electrolytic agent NEC	T50.3X1	T50.3X2	T50.3X3	T50.3X4	T50.3X5	T50.3X6
Elemental diet	T50.901	T50.902	T50.903	T50.904	T50.905	T50.906
Elliptinium acetate	T45.1X1	T45.1X2	T45.1X3	T45.1X4	T45.1X5	T45.1X6
Embramine	T45.0X1	T45.0X2	T45.0X3	T45.0X4	T45.0X5	T45.0X6
Emepronium (salts)	T44.3X1	T44.3X2	T44.3X3	T44.3X4	T44.3X5	T44.3X6
bromide	T44.3X1	T44.3X2	T44.3X3	T44.3X4	T44.3X5	T44.3X6
Emetic NEC	T47.7X1	T47.7X2	T47.7X3	T47.7X4	T47.7X5	T47.7X6
Emetine	T37.3X1	T37.3X2	T37.3X3	T37.3X4	T37.3X5	T37.3X6
Emollient NEC	T49.3X1	T49.3X2	T49.3X3	T49.3X4	T49.3X5	T49.3X6
Emorfazone	T39.8X1	T39.8X2	T39.8X3	T39.8X4	T39.8X5	T39.8X6
Emylcamate	T43.591	T43.592	T43.593	T43.594	T43.595	T43.596
Enalapril	T46.4X1	T46.4X2	T46.4X3	T46.4X4	T46.4X5	T46.4X6
Enalaprilat	T46.4X1	T46.4X2	T46.4X3	T46.4X4	T46.4X5	T46.4X6
Encainide	T46.2X1	T46.2X2	T46.2X3	T46.2X4	T46.2X5	T46.2X6
Endocaine	T41.3X1	T41.3X2	T41.3X3	T41.3X4	T41.3X5	T41.3X6
Endosulfan	T60.2X1	T60.2X2	T60.2X3	T60.2X4	—	—
Endothall	T60.3X1	T60.3X2	T60.3X3	T60.3X4	—	—
Endralazine	T46.5X1	T46.5X2	T46.5X3	T46.5X4	T46.5X5	T46.5X6
Endrin	T60.1X1	T60.1X2	T60.1X3	T60.1X4	—	—
Enflurane	T41.0X1	T41.0X2	T41.0X3	T41.0X4	T41.0X5	T41.0X6
Enhexymal	T42.3X1	T42.3X2	T42.3X3	T42.3X4	T42.3X5	T42.3X6
Enocitabine	T45.1X1	T45.1X2	T45.1X3	T45.1X4	T45.1X5	T45.1X6
Enovid	T38.4X1	T38.4X2	T38.4X3	T38.4X4	T38.4X5	T38.4X6

Substance	External Cause (T-Code)					
	Poisoning, Accidental (Unintentional)	Poisoning, Intentional Self-Harm	Poisoning, Assault	Poisoning, Undetermined	Adverse Effect	Underdosing
Enoxacin	T36.8X1	T36.8X2	T36.8X3	T36.8X4	T36.8X5	T36.8X6
Enoxaparin (sodium)	T45.511	T45.512	T45.513	T45.514	T45.515	T45.516
Enpiprazole	T43.591	T43.592	T43.593	T43.594	T43.595	T43.596
Enprofylline	T48.6X1	T48.6X2	T48.6X3	T48.6X4	T48.6X5	T48.6X6
Enprostil	T47.1X1	T47.1X2	T47.1X3	T47.1X4	T47.1X5	T47.1X6
ENT preparations (anti-infectives)	T49.6X1	T49.6X2	T49.6X3	T49.6X4	T49.6X5	T49.6X6
Enviomycin	T36.8X1	T36.8X2	T36.8X3	T36.8X4	T36.8X5	T36.8X6
Enzodase	T45.3X1	T45.3X2	T45.3X3	T45.3X4	T45.3X5	T45.3X6
Enzyme NEC	T45.3X1	T45.3X2	T45.3X3	T45.3X4	T45.3X5	T45.3X6
depolymerizing	T49.8X1	T49.8X2	T49.8X3	T49.8X4	T49.8X5	T49.8X6
fibrolytic	T45.3X1	T45.3X2	T45.3X3	T45.3X4	T45.3X5	T45.3X6
gastric	T47.5X1	T47.5X2	T47.5X3	T47.5X4	T47.5X5	T47.5X6
intestinal	T47.5X1	T47.5X2	T47.5X3	T47.5X4	T47.5X5	T47.5X6
local action	T49.4X1	T49.4X2	T49.4X3	T49.4X4	T49.4X5	T49.4X6
proteolytic	T49.4X1	T49.4X2	T49.4X3	T49.4X4	T49.4X5	T49.4X6
thrombolytic	T45.3X1	T45.3X2	T45.3X3	T45.3X4	T45.3X5	T45.3X6
EPAB	T41.3X1	T41.3X2	T41.3X3	T41.3X4	T41.3X5	T41.3X6
Epanutin	T42.0X1	T42.0X2	T42.0X3	T42.0X4	T42.0X5	T42.0X6
Ephedra	T44.991	T44.992	T44.993	T44.994	T44.995	T44.996
Ephedrine	T44.991	T44.992	T44.993	T44.994	T44.995	T44.996
Epichlorhydrin, epichlorohydrin	T52.8X1	T52.8X2	T52.8X3	T52.8X4	—	—
Epicillin	T36.0X1	T36.0X2	T36.0X3	T36.0X4	T36.0X5	T36.0X6
Epiestriol	T38.5X1	T38.5X2	T38.5X3	T38.5X4	T38.5X5	T38.5X6
Epilim — see Sodium valproate						
Epimestrol	T38.5X1	T38.5X2	T38.5X3	T38.5X4	T38.5X5	T38.5X6
Epinephrine	T44.5X1	T44.5X2	T44.5X3	T44.5X4	T44.5X5	T44.5X6
Epirubicin	T45.1X1	T45.1X2	T45.1X3	T45.1X4	T45.1X5	T45.1X6
Epitiostanol	T38.7X1	T38.7X2	T38.7X3	T38.7X4	T38.7X5	T38.7X6
Epitizide	T50.2X1	T50.2X2	T50.2X3	T50.2X4	T50.2X5	T50.2X6
EPN	T60.0X1	T60.0X2	T60.0X3	T60.0X4	—	—
EPO	T45.8X1	T45.8X2	T45.8X3	T45.8X4	T45.8X5	T45.8X6
Epoetin alpha	T45.8X1	T45.8X2	T45.8X3	T45.8X4	T45.8X5	T45.8X6
Epomediol	T50.991	T50.992	T50.993	T50.994	T50.995	T50.996
Epoprostenol	T45.521	T45.522	T45.523	T45.524	T45.525	T45.526
Epoxy resin	T65.891	T65.892	T65.893	T65.894	—	—
Eprazinone	T48.4X1	T48.4X2	T48.4X3	T48.4X4	T48.4X5	T48.4X6
Epsilon amino-caproic acid	T45.621	T45.622	T45.623	T45.624	T45.625	T45.626
Epsom salt	T47.3X1	T47.3X2	T47.3X3	T47.3X4	T47.3X5	T47.3X6
Eptazocine	T40.4X1	T40.4X2	T40.4X3	T40.4X4	T40.4X5	T40.4X6
Equanil	T43.591	T43.592	T43.593	T43.594	T43.595	T43.596
Equisetum	T62.2X1	T62.2X2	T62.2X3	T62.2X4	—	—
diuretic	T50.2X1	T50.2X2	T50.2X3	T50.2X4	T50.2X5	T50.2X6

◀ New ◀◀ Revised ~~deleted~~ Deleted

Substance	Poisoning, Accidental (Unintentional)	Poisoning, Intentional Self-Harm	Poisoning, Assault	Poisoning, Undetermined	Adverse Effect	Underdosing
Ergobasine	T48.0X1	T48.0X2	T48.0X3	T48.0X4	T48.0X5	T48.0X6
Ergocalciferol	T45.2X1	T45.2X2	T45.2X3	T45.2X4	T45.2X5	T45.2X6
Ergoloid mesylates	T46.7X1	T46.7X2	T46.7X3	T46.7X4	T46.7X5	T46.7X6
Ergometrine	T48.0X1	T48.0X2	T48.0X3	T48.0X4	T48.0X5	T48.0X6
Ergonovine	T48.0X1	T48.0X2	T48.0X3	T48.0X4	T48.0X5	T48.0X6
Ergot NEC	T64.81	T64.82	T64.83	T64.84	—	—
derivative	T48.0X1	T48.0X2	T48.0X3	T48.0X4	T48.0X5	T48.0X6
medicinal (alkaloids)	T48.0X1	T48.0X2	T48.0X3	T48.0X4	T48.0X5	T48.0X6
prepared	T48.0X1	T48.0X2	T48.0X3	T48.0X4	T48.0X5	T48.0X6
Ergotamine	T46.5X1	T46.5X2	T46.5X3	T46.5X4	T46.5X5	T46.5X6
Ergotocine	T48.0X1	T48.0X2	T48.0X3	T48.0X4	T48.0X5	T48.0X6
Ergotrate	T48.0X1	T48.0X2	T48.0X3	T48.0X4	T48.0X5	T48.0X6
Eritrityl tetranitrate	T46.3X1	T46.3X2	T46.3X3	T46.3X4	T46.3X5	T46.3X6
Erythrityl tetranitrate	T46.3X1	T46.3X2	T46.3X3	T46.3X4	T46.3X5	T46.3X6
Erythrol tetranitrate	T46.3X1	T46.3X2	T46.3X3	T46.3X4	T46.3X5	T46.3X6
Erythromycin (salts)	T36.3X1	T36.3X2	T36.3X3	T36.3X4	T36.3X5	T36.3X6
ophthalmic preparation	T49.5X1	T49.5X2	T49.5X3	T49.5X4	T49.5X5	T49.5X6
topical NEC	T49.0X1	T49.0X2	T49.0X3	T49.0X4	T49.0X5	T49.0X6
Erythropoietin	T45.8X1	T45.8X2	T45.8X3	T45.8X4	T45.8X5	T45.8X6
human	T45.8X1	T45.8X2	T45.8X3	T45.8X4	T45.8X5	T45.8X6
Escin	T46.991	T46.992	T46.993	T46.994	T46.995	T46.996
Esculin	T45.2X1	T45.2X2	T45.2X3	T45.2X4	T45.2X5	T45.2X6
Esculoside	T45.2X1	T45.2X2	T45.2X3	T45.2X4	T45.2X5	T45.2X6
ESDT (ether-soluble tar distillate)	T49.1X1	T49.1X2	T49.1X3	T49.1X4	T49.1X5	T49.1X6
Eserine	T49.5X1	T49.5X2	T49.5X3	T49.5X4	T49.5X5	T49.5X6
Esflurbiprofen	T39.311	T39.312	T39.313	T39.314	T39.315	T39.316
Eskabarb	T42.3X1	T42.3X2	T42.3X3	T42.3X4	T42.3X5	T42.3X6
Eskalith	T43.8X1	T43.8X2	T43.8X3	T43.8X4	T43.8X5	T43.8X6
Esmolol	T44.7X1	T44.7X2	T44.7X3	T44.7X4	T44.7X5	T44.7X6
Estanozolol	T38.7X1	T38.7X2	T38.7X3	T38.7X4	T38.7X5	T38.7X6
Estazolam	T42.4X1	T42.4X2	T42.4X3	T42.4X4	T42.4X5	T42.4X6
Estradiol	T38.5X1	T38.5X2	T38.5X3	T38.5X4	T38.5X5	T38.5X6
with testosterone	T38.7X1	T38.7X2	T38.7X3	T38.7X4	T38.7X5	T38.7X6
benzoate	T38.5X1	T38.5X2	T38.5X3	T38.5X4	T38.5X5	T38.5X6
Estramustine	T45.1X1	T45.1X2	T45.1X3	T45.1X4	T45.1X5	T45.1X6
Estriol	T38.5X1	T38.5X2	T38.5X3	T38.5X4	T38.5X5	T38.5X6
Estrogen	T38.5X1	T38.5X2	T38.5X3	T38.5X4	T38.5X5	T38.5X6
with progesterone	T38.5X1	T38.5X2	T38.5X3	T38.5X4	T38.5X5	T38.5X6
conjugated	T38.5X1	T38.5X2	T38.5X3	T38.5X4	T38.5X5	T38.5X6
Estrone	T38.5X1	T38.5X2	T38.5X3	T38.5X4	T38.5X5	T38.5X6
Estropipate	T38.5X1	T38.5X2	T38.5X3	T38.5X4	T38.5X5	T38.5X6

Substance	Poisoning, Accidental (Unintentional)	Poisoning, Intentional Self-Harm	Poisoning, Assault	Poisoning, Undetermined	Adverse Effect	Underdosing
Etacrynate sodium	T50.1X1	T50.1X2	T50.1X3	T50.1X4	T50.1X5	T50.1X6
Etacrynic acid	T50.1X1	T50.1X2	T50.1X3	T50.1X4	T50.1X5	T50.1X6
Etafedrine	T48.6X1	T48.6X2	T48.6X3	T48.6X4	T48.6X5	T48.6X6
Etafenone	T46.3X1	T46.3X2	T46.3X3	T46.3X4	T46.3X5	T46.3X6
Etambutol	T37.1X1	T37.1X2	T37.1X3	T37.1X4	T37.1X5	T37.1X6
Etamiphyllin	T48.6X1	T48.6X2	T48.6X3	T48.6X4	T48.6X5	T48.6X6
Etamivan	T50.7X1	T50.7X2	T50.7X3	T50.7X4	T50.7X5	T50.7X6
Etamsylate	T45.7X1	T45.7X2	T45.7X3	T45.7X4	T45.7X5	T45.7X6
Etebenecid	T50.4X1	T50.4X2	T50.4X3	T50.4X4	T50.4X5	T50.4X6
Ethacridine	T49.0X1	T49.0X2	T49.0X3	T49.0X4	T49.0X5	T49.0X6
Ethacrynic acid	T50.1X1	T50.1X2	T50.1X3	T50.1X4	T50.1X5	T50.1X6
Ethadione	T42.2X1	T42.2X2	T42.2X3	T42.2X4	T42.2X5	T42.2X6
Ethambutol	T37.1X1	T37.1X2	T37.1X3	T37.1X4	T37.1X5	T37.1X6
Ethamide	T50.2X1	T50.2X2	T50.2X3	T50.2X4	T50.2X5	T50.2X6
Ethamivan	T50.7X1	T50.7X2	T50.7X3	T50.7X4	T50.7X5	T50.7X6
Ethamsylate	T45.7X1	T45.7X2	T45.7X3	T45.7X4	T45.7X5	T45.7X6
Ethanol	T51.0X1	T51.0X2	T51.0X3	T51.0X4	—	—
beverage	T51.0X1	T51.0X2	T51.0X3	T51.0X4	—	—
Ethanolamine oleate	T46.8X1	T46.8X2	T46.8X3	T46.8X4	T46.8X5	T46.8X6
Ethaverine	T44.3X1	T44.3X2	T44.3X3	T44.3X4	T44.3X5	T44.3X6
Ethchlorvynol	T42.6X1	T42.6X2	T42.6X3	T42.6X4	T42.6X5	T42.6X6
Ethebenecid	T50.4X1	T50.4X2	T50.4X3	T50.4X4	T50.4X5	T50.4X6
Ether (vapor)	T41.0X1	T41.0X2	T41.0X3	T41.0X4	T41.0X5	T41.0X6
anesthetic	T41.0X1	T41.0X2	T41.0X3	T41.0X4	T41.0X5	T41.0X6
divinyl	T41.0X1	T41.0X2	T41.0X3	T41.0X4	T41.0X5	T41.0X6
ethyl (medicinal)	T41.0X1	T41.0X2	T41.0X3	T41.0X4	T41.0X5	T41.0X6
nonmedicinal	T52.8X1	T52.8X2	T52.8X3	T52.8X4	—	—
petroleum—see Ligroin						
solvent	T52.8X1	T52.8X2	T52.8X3	T52.8X4	—	—
Ethiazide	T50.2X1	T50.2X2	T50.2X3	T50.2X4	T50.2X5	T50.2X6
Ethidium chloride (vapor)	T59.891	T59.892	T59.893	T59.894	—	—
Ethinamate	T42.6X1	T42.6X2	T42.6X3	T42.6X4	T42.6X5	T42.6X6
Ethinylestradiol, ethinyloestradiol	T38.5X1	T38.5X2	T38.5X3	T38.5X4	T38.5X5	T38.5X6
with						
levonorgestrel	T38.4X1	T38.4X2	T38.4X3	T38.4X4	T38.4X5	T38.4X6
norethisterone	T38.4X1	T38.4X2	T38.4X3	T38.4X4	T38.4X5	T38.4X6
Ethiodized oil (131 I)	T50.8X1	T50.8X2	T50.8X3	T50.8X4	T50.8X5	T50.8X6
Ethion	T60.0X1	T60.0X2	T60.0X3	T60.0X4	—	—
Ethionamide	T37.1X1	T37.1X2	T37.1X3	T37.1X4	T37.1X5	T37.1X6
Ethioniamide	T37.1X1	T37.1X2	T37.1X3	T37.1X4	T37.1X5	T37.1X6
Ethisterone	T38.5X1	T38.5X2	T38.5X3	T38.5X4	T38.5X5	T38.5X6
Ethobral	T42.3X1	T42.3X2	T42.3X3	T42.3X4	T42.3X5	T42.3X6

◀ New   ◀ Revised   deleted Deleted

Substance	External Cause (T-Code) Poisoning, Accidental (Unintentional)	Poisoning, Intentional Self-Harm	Poisoning, Assault	Poisoning, Undetermined	Adverse Effect	Underdosing
Ethocaine (infiltration) (topical)	T41.3X1	T41.3X2	T41.3X3	T41.3X4	T41.3X5	T41.3X6
nerve block (peripheral) (plexus)	T41.3X1	T41.3X2	T41.3X3	T41.3X4	T41.3X5	T41.3X6
spinal	T41.3X1	T41.3X2	T41.3X3	T41.3X4	T41.3X5	T41.3X6
Ethoheptazine	T40.4X1	T40.4X2	T40.4X3	T40.4X4	T40.4X5	T40.4X6
Ethopropazine	T44.3X1	T44.3X2	T44.3X3	T44.3X4	T44.3X5	T44.3X6
Ethosuximide	T42.2X1	T42.2X2	T42.2X3	T42.2X4	T42.2X5	T42.2X6
Ethotoin	T42.0X1	T42.0X2	T42.0X3	T42.0X4	T42.0X5	T42.0X6
Ethoxazene	T37.91	T37.92	T37.93	T37.94	T37.95	T37.96
Ethoxazorutoside	T46.991	T46.992	T46.993	T46.994	T46.995	T46.996
2-Ethoxyethanol	T52.3X1	T52.3X2	T52.3X3	T52.3X4	—	—
Ethoxzolamide	T50.2X1	T50.2X2	T50.2X3	T50.2X4	T50.2X5	T50.2X6
Ethyl						
acetate	T52.8X1	T52.8X2	T52.8X3	T52.8X4	—	—
alcohol	T51.0X1	T51.0X2	T51.0X3	T51.0X4	—	—
beverage	T51.0X1	T51.0X2	T51.0X3	T51.0X4	—	—
aldehyde (vapor)	T59.891	T59.892	T59.893	T59.894	—	—
liquid	T52.8X1	T52.8X2	T52.8X3	T52.8X4	—	—
aminobenzoate	T41.3X1	T41.3X2	T41.3X3	T41.3X4	T41.3X5	T41.3X6
aminophenothiazine	T43.3X1	T43.3X2	T43.3X3	T43.3X4	T43.3X5	T43.3X6
benzoate	T52.8X1	T52.8X2	T52.8X3	T52.8X4	—	—
biscoumacetate	T45.511	T45.512	T45.513	T45.514	T45.515	T45.516
bromide (anesthetic)	T41.0X1	T41.0X2	T41.0X3	T41.0X4	T41.0X5	T41.0X6
carbamate	T45.1X1	T45.1X2	T45.1X3	T45.1X4	T45.1X5	T45.1X6
carbinol	T51.3X1	T51.3X2	T51.3X3	T51.3X4	—	—
carbonate	T52.8X1	T52.8X2	T52.8X3	T52.8X4	—	—
chaulmoograte	T37.1X1	T37.1X2	T37.1X3	T37.1X4	T37.1X5	T37.1X6
chloride (anesthetic)	T41.0X1	T41.0X2	T41.0X3	T41.0X4	T41.0X5	T41.0X6
anesthetic (local)	T41.3X1	T41.3X2	T41.3X3	T41.3X4	T41.3X5	T41.3X6
inhaled	T41.0X1	T41.0X2	T41.0X3	T41.0X4	T41.0X5	T41.0X6
local	T49.4X1	T49.4X2	T49.4X3	T49.4X4	T49.4X5	T49.4X6
solvent	T53.6X1	T53.6X2	T53.6X3	T53.6X4	—	—
dibunate	T48.3X1	T48.3X2	T48.3X3	T48.3X4	T48.3X5	T48.3X6
dichloroarsine (vapor)	T57.0X1	T57.0X2	T57.0X3	T57.0X4	—	—
estranol	T38.7X1	T38.7X2	T38.7X3	T38.7X4	T38.7X5	T38.7X6
ether — see also ether	T52.8X1	T52.8X2	T52.8X3	T52.8X4	—	—
formate NEC (solvent)	T52.0X1	T52.0X2	T52.0X3	T52.0X4	—	—
fumarate	T49.4X1	T49.4X2	T49.4X3	T49.4X4	T49.4X5	T49.4X6
hydroxyisobutyrate NEC (solvent)	T52.8X1	T52.8X2	T52.8X3	T52.8X4	—	—
iodoacetate	T59.3X1	T59.3X2	T59.3X3	T59.3X4	—	—
lactate NEC (solvent)	T52.8X1	T52.8X2	T52.8X3	T52.8X4	—	—
loflazepate	T42.4X1	T42.4X2	T42.4X3	T42.4X4	T42.4X5	T42.4X6

Substance	External Cause (T-Code) Poisoning, Accidental (Unintentional)	Poisoning, Intentional Self-Harm	Poisoning, Assault	Poisoning, Undetermined	Adverse Effect	Underdosing
Ethyl (Continued)						
mercuric chloride	T56.1X1	T56.1X2	T56.1X3	T56.1X4	—	—
methylcarbinol	T51.8X1	T51.8X2	T51.8X3	T51.8X4	—	—
morphine	T40.2X1	T40.2X2	T40.2X3	T40.2X4	T40.2X5	T40.2X6
noradrenaline	T48.6X1	T48.6X2	T48.6X3	T48.6X4	T48.6X5	T48.6X6
oxybutyrate NEC (solvent)	T52.8X1	T52.8X2	T52.8X3	T52.8X4	—	—
Ethylene (gas)	T59.891	T59.892	T59.893	T59.894	—	—
anesthetic (general)	T41.0X1	T41.0X2	T41.0X3	T41.0X4	T41.0X5	T41.0X6
chlorohydrin	T52.8X1	T52.8X2	T52.8X3	T52.8X4	—	—
vapor	T53.6X1	T53.6X2	T53.6X3	T53.6X4	—	—
dichloride	T52.8X1	T52.8X2	T52.8X3	T52.8X4	—	—
vapor	T53.6X1	T53.6X2	T53.6X3	T53.6X4	—	—
dinitrate	T52.3X1	T52.3X2	T52.3X3	T52.3X4	—	—
glycol(s)	T52.8X1	T52.8X2	T52.8X3	T52.8X4	—	—
dinitrate	T52.3X1	T52.3X2	T52.3X3	T52.3X4	—	—
monobutyl ether	T52.3X1	T52.3X2	T52.3X3	T52.3X4	—	—
imine	T54.1X1	T54.1X2	T54.1X3	T54.1X4	—	—
oxide (fumigant) (nonmedicinal)	T59.891	T59.892	T59.893	T59.894	—	—
medicinal	T49.0X1	T49.0X2	T49.0X3	T49.0X4	T49.0X5	T49.0X6
Ethylenediamine theophylline	T48.6X1	T48.6X2	T48.6X3	T48.6X4	T48.6X5	T48.6X6
Ethylenediaminetetra-acetic acid	T50.6X1	T50.6X2	T50.6X3	T50.6X4	T50.6X5	T50.6X6
Ethylenedinitrilotetra-acetate	T50.6X1	T50.6X2	T50.6X3	T50.6X4	T50.6X5	T50.6X6
Ethylestrenol	T38.7X1	T38.7X2	T38.7X3	T38.7X4	T38.7X5	T38.7X6
Ethylhydroxycellulose	T47.4X1	T47.4X2	T47.4X3	T47.4X4	T47.4X5	T47.4X6
Ethylidene						
chloride NEC	T53.6X1	T53.6X2	T53.6X3	T53.6X4	—	—
diacetate	T60.3X1	T60.3X2	T60.3X3	T60.3X4	—	—
dicoumarin	T45.511	T45.512	T45.513	T45.514	T45.515	T45.516
dicoumarol	T45.511	T45.512	T45.513	T45.514	T45.515	T45.516
diethyl ether	T52.0X1	T52.0X2	T52.0X3	T52.0X4	—	—
Ethylmorphine	T40.2X1	T40.2X2	T40.2X3	T40.2X4	T40.2X5	T40.2X6
Ethylnorepinephrine	T48.6X1	T48.6X2	T48.6X3	T48.6X4	T48.6X5	T48.6X6
Ethylparachlorophen-oxyisobutyrate	T46.6X1	T46.6X2	T46.6X3	T46.6X4	T46.6X5	T46.6X6
Ethynodiol	T38.4X1	T38.4X2	T38.4X3	T38.4X4	T38.4X5	T38.4X6
with mestranol diacetate	T38.4X1	T38.4X2	T38.4X3	T38.4X4	T38.4X5	T38.4X6
Etidocaine	T41.3X1	T41.3X2	T41.3X3	T41.3X4	T41.3X5	T41.3X6
infiltration (subcutaneous)	T41.3X1	T41.3X2	T41.3X3	T41.3X4	T41.3X5	T41.3X6
nerve (peripheral) (plexus)	T41.3X1	T41.3X2	T41.3X3	T41.3X4	T41.3X5	T41.3X6
Etidronate	T50.991	T50.992	T50.993	T50.994	T50.995	T50.996
Etidronic acid (disodium salt)	T50.991	T50.992	T50.993	T50.994	T50.995	T50.996
Etifoxine	T42.6X1	T42.6X2	T42.6X3	T42.6X4	T42.6X5	T42.6X6

◄ New ◄◄ Revised ~~deleted~~ Deleted

Substance	Poisoning, Accidental (Unintentional)	Poisoning, Intentional Self-Harm	Poisoning, Assault	Poisoning, Undetermined	Adverse Effect	Underdosing
Etilefrine	T44.4X1	T44.4X2	T44.4X3	T44.4X4	T44.4X5	T44.4X6
Etilfen	T42.3X1	T42.3X2	T42.3X3	T42.3X4	T42.3X5	T42.3X6
Etinodiol	T38.4X1	T38.4X2	T38.4X3	T38.4X4	T38.4X5	T38.4X6
Etiroxate	T46.6X1	T46.6X2	T46.6X3	T46.6X4	T46.6X5	T46.6X6
Etizolam	T42.4X1	T42.4X2	T42.4X3	T42.4X4	T42.4X5	T42.4X6
Etodolac	T39.391	T39.392	T39.393	T39.394	T39.395	T39.396
Etofamide	T37.3X1	T37.3X2	T37.3X3	T37.3X4	T37.3X5	T37.3X6
Etofibrate	T46.6X1	T46.6X2	T46.6X3	T46.6X4	T46.6X5	T46.6X6
Etofylline	T46.7X1	T46.7X2	T46.7X3	T46.7X4	T46.7X5	T46.7X6
clofibrate	T46.6X1	T46.6X2	T46.6X3	T46.6X4	T46.6X5	T46.6X6
Etoglucid	T45.1X1	T45.1X2	T45.1X3	T45.1X4	T45.1X5	T45.1X6
Etomidate	T41.1X1	T41.1X2	T41.1X3	T41.1X4	T41.1X5	T41.1X6
Etomide	T39.8X1	T39.8X2	T39.8X3	T39.8X4	T39.8X5	T39.8X6
Etomidoline	T44.3X1	T44.3X2	T44.3X3	T44.3X4	T44.3X5	T44.3X6
Etoposide	T45.1X1	T45.1X2	T45.1X3	T45.1X4	T45.1X5	T45.1X6
Etorphine	T40.2X1	T40.2X2	T40.2X3	T40.2X4	T40.2X5	T40.2X6
Etoval	T42.3X1	T42.3X2	T42.3X3	T42.3X4	T42.3X5	T42.3X6
Etozolin	T50.1X1	T50.1X2	T50.1X3	T50.1X4	T50.1X5	T50.1X6
Etretinate	T50.991	T50.992	T50.993	T50.994	T50.995	T50.996
Etryptamine	T43.691	T43.692	T43.693	T43.694	T43.695	T43.696
Etybenzatropine	T44.3X1	T44.3X2	T44.3X3	T44.3X4	T44.3X5	T44.3X6
Etynodiol	T38.4X1	T38.4X2	T38.4X3	T38.4X4	T38.4X5	T38.4X6
Eucaine	T41.3X1	T41.3X2	T41.3X3	T41.3X4	T41.3X5	T41.3X6
Eucalyptus oil	T49.7X1	T49.7X2	T49.7X3	T49.7X4	T49.7X5	T49.7X6
Eucatropine	T49.5X1	T49.5X2	T49.5X3	T49.5X4	T49.5X5	T49.5X6
Eucodal	T40.2X1	T40.2X2	T40.2X3	T40.2X4	T40.2X5	T40.2X6
Euneryl	T42.3X1	T42.3X2	T42.3X3	T42.3X4	T42.3X5	T42.3X6
Euphthalmine	T44.3X1	T44.3X2	T44.3X3	T44.3X4	T44.3X5	T44.3X6
Eurax	T49.0X1	T49.0X2	T49.0X3	T49.0X4	T49.0X5	T49.0X6
Euresol	T49.4X1	T49.4X2	T49.4X3	T49.4X4	T49.4X5	T49.4X6
Euthroid	T38.1X1	T38.1X2	T38.1X3	T38.1X4	T38.1X5	T38.1X6
Evans blue	T50.8X1	T50.8X2	T50.8X3	T50.8X4	T50.8X5	T50.8X6
Evipal	T42.3X1	T42.3X2	T42.3X3	T42.3X4	T42.3X5	T42.3X6
sodium	T41.1X1	T41.1X2	T41.1X3	T41.1X4	T41.1X5	T41.1X6
Evipan	T42.3X1	T42.3X2	T42.3X3	T42.3X4	T42.3X5	T42.3X6
sodium	T41.1X1	T41.1X2	T41.1X3	T41.1X4	T41.1X5	T41.1X6
Exalamide	T49.0X1	T49.0X2	T49.0X3	T49.0X4	T49.0X5	T49.0X6
Exalgin	T39.1X1	T39.1X2	T39.1X3	T39.1X4	T39.1X5	T39.1X6
Excipients, pharmaceutical	T50.901	T50.902	T50.903	T50.904	T50.905	T50.906
Exhaust gas (engine) (motor vehicle)	T58.01	T58.02	T58.03	T58.04	—	—
Ex-Lax (phenolphthalein)	T47.2X1	T47.2X2	T47.2X3	T47.2X4	T47.2X5	T47.2X6
Expectorant NEC	T48.4X1	T48.4X2	T48.4X3	T48.4X4	T48.4X5	T48.4X6

Substance	Poisoning, Accidental (Unintentional)	Poisoning, Intentional Self-Harm	Poisoning, Assault	Poisoning, Undetermined	Adverse Effect	Underdosing
Extended insulin zinc suspension	T38.3X1	T38.3X2	T38.3X3	T38.3X4	T38.3X5	T38.3X6
External medications (skin) (mucous membrane)	T49.91	T49.92	T49.93	T49.94	T49.95	T49.96
dental agent	T49.7X1	T49.7X2	T49.7X3	T49.7X4	T49.7X5	T49.7X6
ENT agent	T49.6X1	T49.6X2	T49.6X3	T49.6X4	T49.6X5	T49.6X6
ophthalmic preparation	T49.5X1	T49.5X2	T49.5X3	T49.5X4	T49.5X5	T49.5X6
specified NEC	T49.8X1	T49.8X2	T49.8X3	T49.8X4	T49.8X5	T49.8X6
Extrapyramidal antagonist NEC	T44.3X1	T44.3X2	T44.3X3	T44.3X4	T44.3X5	T44.3X6
Eye agents (anti-infective)	T49.5X1	T49.5X2	T49.5X3	T49.5X4	T49.5X5	T49.5X6
Eye drug NEC	T49.5X1	T49.5X2	T49.5X3	T49.5X4	T49.5X5	T49.5X6
F						
FAC (fluorouracil + doxorubicin + cyclophosphamide)	T45.1X1	T45.1X2	T45.1X3	T45.1X4	T45.1X5	T45.1X6
Factor						
I (fibrinogen)	T45.8X1	T45.8X2	T45.8X3	T45.8X4	T45.8X5	T45.8X6
III (thromboplastin)	T45.8X1	T45.8X2	T45.8X3	T45.8X4	T45.8X5	T45.8X6
VIII (antihemophilic Factor) (Concentrate)	T45.8X1	T45.8X2	T45.8X3	T45.8X4	T45.8X5	T45.8X6
IX complex	T45.7X1	T45.7X2	T45.7X3	T45.7X4	T45.7X5	T45.7X6
human	T45.8X1	T45.8X2	T45.8X3	T45.8X4	T45.8X5	T45.8X6
Famotidine	T47.0X1	T47.0X2	T47.0X3	T47.0X4	T47.0X5	T47.0X6
Fat suspension, intravenous	T50.991	T50.992	T50.993	T50.994	T50.995	T50.996
Fazadinium bromide	T48.1X1	T48.1X2	T48.1X3	T48.1X4	T48.1X5	T48.1X6
Febarbamate	T42.3X1	T42.3X2	T42.3X3	T42.3X4	T42.3X5	T42.3X6
Fecal softener	T47.4X1	T47.4X2	T47.4X3	T47.4X4	T47.4X5	T47.4X6
Fedrilate	T48.3X1	T48.3X2	T48.3X3	T48.3X4	T48.3X5	T48.3X6
Felodipine	T46.1X1	T46.1X2	T46.1X3	T46.1X4	T46.1X5	T46.1X6
Felypressin	T38.891	T38.892	T38.893	T38.894	T38.895	T38.896
Femoxetine	T43.221	T43.222	T43.223	T43.224	T43.225	T43.226
Fenalcomine	T46.3X1	T46.3X2	T46.3X3	T46.3X4	T46.3X5	T46.3X6
Fenamisal	T37.1X1	T37.1X2	T37.1X3	T37.1X4	T37.1X5	T37.1X6
Fenazone	T39.2X1	T39.2X2	T39.2X3	T39.2X4	T39.2X5	T39.2X6
Fenbendazole	T37.4X1	T37.4X2	T37.4X3	T37.4X4	T37.4X5	T37.4X6
Fenbutrazate	T50.5X1	T50.5X2	T50.5X3	T50.5X4	T50.5X5	T50.5X6
Fencamfamine	T43.691	T43.692	T43.693	T43.694	T43.695	T43.696
Fendiline	T46.1X1	T46.1X2	T46.1X3	T46.1X4	T46.1X5	T46.1X6
Fenetylline	T43.691	T43.692	T43.693	T43.694	T43.695	T43.696
Fenflumizole	T39.391	T39.392	T39.393	T39.394	T39.395	T39.396
Fenfluramine	T50.5X1	T50.5X2	T50.5X3	T50.5X4	T50.5X5	T50.5X6
Fenobarbital	T42.3X1	T42.3X2	T42.3X3	T42.3X4	T42.3X5	T42.3X6
Fenofibrate	T46.6X1	T46.6X2	T46.6X3	T46.6X4	T46.6X5	T46.6X6
Fenoprofen	T39.311	T39.312	T39.313	T39.314	T39.315	T39.316
Fenoterol	T48.6X1	T48.6X2	T48.6X3	T48.6X4	T48.6X5	T48.6X6

◀ New ◀ Revised ~~deleted~~ Deleted

TABLE OF DRUGS AND CHEMICALS

Substance	External Cause (T-Code)					
	Poisoning, Accidental (Unintentional)	Poisoning, Intentional Self-Harm	Poisoning, Assault	Poisoning, Undetermined	Adverse Effect	Underdosing
Fenoverine	T44.3X1	T44.3X2	T44.3X3	T44.3X4	T44.3X5	T44.3X6
Fenoxazoline	T48.5X1	T48.5X2	T48.5X3	T48.5X4	T48.5X5	T48.5X6
Fenproporex	T50.5X1	T50.5X2	T50.5X3	T50.5X4	T50.5X5	T50.5X6
Fenquizone	T50.2X1	T50.2X2	T50.2X3	T50.2X4	T50.2X5	T50.2X6
Fentanyl	T40.4X1	T40.4X2	T40.4X3	T40.4X4	T40.4X5	T40.4X6
Fentazin	T43.3X1	T43.3X2	T43.3X3	T43.3X4	T43.3X5	T43.3X6
Fenthion	T60.0X1	T60.0X2	T60.0X3	T60.0X4	—	—
Fenticlor	T49.0X1	T49.0X2	T49.0X3	T49.0X4	T49.0X5	T49.0X6
Fenylbutazone	T39.2X1	T39.2X2	T39.2X3	T39.2X4	T39.2X5	T39.2X6
Feprazone	T39.2X1	T39.2X2	T39.2X3	T39.2X4	T39.2X5	T39.2X6
Fer de lance (bite) (venom)	T63.061	T63.062	T63.063	T63.064	—	—
Ferric — see also Iron						
chloride	T45.4X1	T45.4X2	T45.4X3	T45.4X4	T45.4X5	T45.4X6
citrate	T45.4X1	T45.4X2	T45.4X3	T45.4X4	T45.4X5	T45.4X6
hydroxide						
colloidal	T45.4X1	T45.4X2	T45.4X3	T45.4X4	T45.4X5	T45.4X6
polymaltose	T45.4X1	T45.4X2	T45.4X3	T45.4X4	T45.4X5	T45.4X6
pyrophosphate	T45.4X1	T45.4X2	T45.4X3	T45.4X4	T45.4X5	T45.4X6
Ferritin	T45.4X1	T45.4X2	T45.4X3	T45.4X4	T45.4X5	T45.4X6
Ferrocholinate	T45.4X1	T45.4X2	T45.4X3	T45.4X4	T45.4X5	T45.4X6
Ferrodextrane	T45.4X1	T45.4X2	T45.4X3	T45.4X4	T45.4X5	T45.4X6
Ferropolimaler	T45.4X1	T45.4X2	T45.4X3	T45.4X4	T45.4X5	T45.4X6
Ferrous — see also Iron						
phosphate	T45.4X1	T45.4X2	T45.4X3	T45.4X4	T45.4X5	T45.4X6
salt	T45.4X1	T45.4X2	T45.4X3	T45.4X4	T45.4X5	T45.4X6
with folic acid	T45.4X1	T45.4X2	T45.4X3	T45.4X4	T45.4X5	T45.4X6
Ferrous fumerate, gluconate, lactate, salt NEC, sulfate (medicinal)	T45.4X1	T45.4X2	T45.4X3	T45.4X4	T45.4X5	T45.4X6
Ferrovanadium (fumes)	T59.891	T59.892	T59.893	T59.894	—	—
Ferrum — see Iron						
Fertilizers NEC	T65.891	T65.892	T65.893	T65.894	—	—
with herbicide mixture	T60.3X1	T60.3X2	T60.3X3	T60.3X4	—	—
Fetoxilate	T47.6X1	T47.6X2	T47.6X3	T47.6X4	T47.6X5	T47.6X6
Fiber, dietary	T47.4X1	T47.4X2	T47.4X3	T47.4X4	T47.4X5	T47.4X6
Fibrinogen (human)	T45.8X1	T45.8X2	T45.8X3	T45.8X4	T45.8X5	T45.8X6
Fibrinolysin (human)	T45.691	T45.692	T45.693	T45.694	T45.695	T45.696
Fibrinolysis						
affecting drug	T45.601	T45.602	T45.603	T45.604	T45.605	T45.606
inhibitor NEC	T45.621	T45.622	T45.623	T45.624	T45.625	T45.626
Fibrinolytic drug	T45.611	T45.612	T45.613	T45.614	T45.615	T45.616
Filix mas	T37.4X1	T37.4X2	T37.4X3	T37.4X4	T37.4X5	T37.4X6
Filtering cream	T49.3X1	T49.3X2	T49.3X3	T49.3X4	T49.3X5	T49.3X6

Substance	External Cause (T-Code)					
	Poisoning, Accidental (Unintentional)	Poisoning, Intentional Self-Harm	Poisoning, Assault	Poisoning, Undetermined	Adverse Effect	Underdosing
Fiorinal	T39.011	T39.012	T39.013	T39.014	T39.015	T39.016
Firedamp	T59.891	T59.892	T59.893	T59.894	—	—
Fish, noxious, nonbacterial	T61.91	T61.92	T61.93	T61.94	—	—
ciguatera	T61.01	T61.02	T61.03	T61.04	—	—
scombroid	T61.11	T61.12	T61.13	T61.14	—	—
shell	T61.781	T61.782	T61.783	T61.784	—	—
specified NEC	T61.771	T61.772	T61.773	T61.774	—	—
Flagyl	T37.3X1	T37.3X2	T37.3X3	T37.3X4	T37.3X5	T37.3X6
Flavine adenine dinucleotide	T45.2X1	T45.2X2	T45.2X3	T45.2X4	T45.2X5	T45.2X6
Flavodic acid	T46.991	T46.992	T46.993	T46.994	T46.995	T46.996
Flavoxate	T44.3X1	T44.3X2	T44.3X3	T44.3X4	T44.3X5	T44.3X6
Flaxedil	T48.1X1	T48.1X2	T48.1X3	T48.1X4	T48.1X5	T48.1X6
Flaxseed (medicinal)	T49.3X1	T49.3X2	T49.3X3	T49.3X4	T49.3X5	T49.3X6
Flecainide	T46.2X1	T46.2X2	T46.2X3	T46.2X4	T46.2X5	T46.2X6
Fleroxacin	T36.8X1	T36.8X2	T36.8X3	T36.8X4	T36.8X5	T36.8X6
Floctafenine	T39.8X1	T39.8X2	T39.8X3	T39.8X4	T39.8X5	T39.8X6
Flomax	T44.6X1	T44.6X2	T44.6X3	T44.6X4	T44.6X5	T44.6X6
Flomoxef	T36.1X1	T36.1X2	T36.1X3	T36.1X4	T36.1X5	T36.1X6
Flopropione	T44.3X1	T44.3X2	T44.3X3	T44.3X4	T44.3X5	T44.3X6
Florantyrone	T47.5X1	T47.5X2	T47.5X3	T47.5X4	T47.5X5	T47.5X6
Floraquin	T37.8X1	T37.8X2	T37.8X3	T37.8X4	T37.8X5	T37.8X6
Florinef	T38.0X1	T38.0X2	T38.0X3	T38.0X4	T38.0X5	T38.0X6
ENT agent	T49.6X1	T49.6X2	T49.6X3	T49.6X4	T49.6X5	T49.6X6
ophthalmic preparation	T49.5X1	T49.5X2	T49.5X3	T49.5X4	T49.5X5	T49.5X6
topical NEC	T49.0X1	T49.0X2	T49.0X3	T49.0X4	T49.0X5	T49.0X6
Flowers of sulfur	T49.4X1	T49.4X2	T49.4X3	T49.4X4	T49.4X5	T49.4X6
Floxuridine	T45.1X1	T45.1X2	T45.1X3	T45.1X4	T45.1X5	T45.1X6
Fluanisone	T43.4X1	T43.4X2	T43.4X3	T43.4X4	T43.4X5	T43.4X6
Flubendazole	T37.4X1	T37.4X2	T37.4X3	T37.4X4	T37.4X5	T37.4X6
Fluclorolone acetonide	T49.0X1	T49.0X2	T49.0X3	T49.0X4	T49.0X5	T49.0X6
Flucloxacillin	T36.0X1	T36.0X2	T36.0X3	T36.0X4	T36.0X5	T36.0X6
Fluconazole	T37.8X1	T37.8X2	T37.8X3	T37.8X4	T37.8X5	T37.8X6
Flucytosine	T37.8X1	T37.8X2	T37.8X3	T37.8X4	T37.8X5	T37.8X6
Fludeoxyglucose (18F)	T50.8X1	T50.8X2	T50.8X3	T50.8X4	T50.8X5	T50.8X6
Fludiazepam	T42.4X1	T42.4X2	T42.4X3	T42.4X4	T42.4X5	T42.4X6
Fludrocortisone	T50.0X1	T50.0X2	T50.0X3	T50.0X4	T50.0X5	T50.0X6
ENT agent	T49.6X1	T49.6X2	T49.6X3	T49.6X4	T49.6X5	T49.6X6
ophthalmic preparation	T49.5X1	T49.5X2	T49.5X3	T49.5X4	T49.5X5	T49.5X6
topical NEC	T49.0X1	T49.0X2	T49.0X3	T49.0X4	T49.0X5	T49.0X6
Fludroxycortide	T49.0X1	T49.0X2	T49.0X3	T49.0X4	T49.0X5	T49.0X6
Flufenamic acid	T39.391	T39.392	T39.393	T39.394	T39.395	T39.396
Fluindione	T45.511	T45.512	T45.513	T45.514	T45.515	T45.516

◄ New ◄ Revised ~~deleted~~ Deleted

	External Cause (T-Code)					
Substance	Poisoning, Accidental (Unintentional)	Poisoning, Intentional Self-Harm	Poisoning, Assault	Poisoning, Undetermined	Adverse Effect	Underdosing
Flumequine	T37.8X1	T37.8X2	T37.8X3	T37.8X4	T37.8X5	T37.8X6
Flumethasone	T49.0X1	T49.0X2	T49.0X3	T49.0X4	T49.0X5	T49.0X6
Flumethiazide	T50.2X1	T50.2X2	T50.2X3	T50.2X4	T50.2X5	T50.2X6
Flumidin	T37.5X1	T37.5X2	T37.5X3	T37.5X4	T37.5X5	T37.5X6
Flunarizine	T46.7X1	T46.7X2	T46.7X3	T46.7X4	T46.7X5	T46.7X6
Flunidazole	T37.8X1	T37.8X2	T37.8X3	T37.8X4	T37.8X5	T37.8X6
Flunisolide	T48.6X1	T48.6X2	T48.6X3	T48.6X4	T48.6X5	T48.6X6
Flunitrazepam	T42.4X1	T42.4X2	T42.4X3	T42.4X4	T42.4X5	T42.4X6
Fluocinolone (acetonide)	T49.0X1	T49.0X2	T49.0X3	T49.0X4	T49.0X5	T49.0X6
Fluocinonide	T49.0X1	T49.0X2	T49.0X3	T49.0X4	T49.0X5	T49.0X6
Fluocortin (butyl)	T49.0X1	T49.0X2	T49.0X3	T49.0X4	T49.0X5	T49.0X6
Fluocortolone	T49.0X1	T49.0X2	T49.0X3	T49.0X4	T49.0X5	T49.0X6
Fluohydrocortisone	T38.0X1	T38.0X2	T38.0X3	T38.0X4	T38.0X5	T38.0X6
ENT agent	T49.6X1	T49.6X2	T49.6X3	T49.6X4	T49.6X5	T49.6X6
ophthalmic preparation	T49.5X1	T49.5X2	T49.5X3	T49.5X4	T49.5X5	T49.5X6
topical NEC	T49.0X1	T49.0X2	T49.0X3	T49.0X4	T49.0X5	T49.0X6
Fluonid	T49.0X1	T49.0X2	T49.0X3	T49.0X4	T49.0X5	T49.0X6
Fluopromazine	T43.3X1	T43.3X2	T43.3X3	T43.3X4	T43.3X5	T43.3X6
Fluoroacetate	T60.8X1	T60.8X2	T60.8X3	T60.8X4	—	—
Fluorescein	T50.8X1	T50.8X2	T50.8X3	T50.8X4	T50.8X5	T50.8X6
Fluorhydrocortisone	T50.0X1	T50.0X2	T50.0X3	T50.0X4	T50.0X5	T50.0X6
Fluoride (nonmedicinal) (pesticide) (sodium) NEC	T60.8X1	T60.8X2	T60.8X3	T60.8X4	—	—
hydrogen — see Hydrofluoric acid						
medicinal NEC	T50.991	T50.992	T50.993	T50.994	T50.995	T50.996
dental use	T49.7X1	T49.7X2	T49.7X3	T49.7X4	T49.7X5	T49.7X6
not pesticide NEC	T54.91	T54.92	T54.93	T54.94	—	—
stannous	T49.7X1	T49.7X2	T49.7X3	T49.7X4	T49.7X5	T49.7X6
Fluorinated corticosteroids	T38.0X1	T38.0X2	T38.0X3	T38.0X4	T38.0X5	T38.0X6
Fluorine (gas)	T59.5X1	T59.5X2	T59.5X3	T59.5X4	—	—
salt — see Fluoride(s)						
Fluoristan	T49.7X1	T49.7X2	T49.7X3	T49.7X4	T49.7X5	T49.7X6
Fluormetholone	T49.0X1	T49.0X2	T49.0X3	T49.0X4	T49.0X5	T49.0X6
Fluoroacetate	T60.8X1	T60.8X2	T60.8X3	T60.8X4	—	—
Fluorocarbon monomer	T53.6X1	T53.6X2	T53.6X3	T53.6X4	—	—
Fluorocytosine	T37.8X1	T37.8X2	T37.8X3	T37.8X4	T37.8X5	T37.8X6
Fluorodeoxyuridine	T45.1X1	T45.1X2	T45.1X3	T45.1X4	T45.1X5	T45.1X6
Fluorometholone	T49.0X1	T49.0X2	T49.0X3	T49.0X4	T49.0X5	T49.0X6
ophthalmic preparation	T49.5X1	T49.5X2	T49.5X3	T49.5X4	T49.5X5	T49.5X6
Fluorophosphate insecticide	T60.0X1	T60.0X2	T60.0X3	T60.0X4	—	—
Fluorosol	T46.3X1	T46.3X2	T46.3X3	T46.3X4	T46.3X5	T46.3X6
Fluorouracil	T45.1X1	T45.1X2	T45.1X3	T45.1X4	T45.1X5	T45.1X6

	External Cause (T-Code)					
Substance	Poisoning, Accidental (Unintentional)	Poisoning, Intentional Self-Harm	Poisoning, Assault	Poisoning, Undetermined	Adverse Effect	Underdosing
Fluorphenylalanine	T49.5X1	T49.5X2	T49.5X3	T49.5X4	T49.5X5	T49.5X6
Fluothane	T41.0X1	T41.0X2	T41.0X3	T41.0X4	T41.0X5	T41.0X6
Fluoxetine	T43.221	T43.222	T43.223	T43.224	T43.225	T43.226
Fluoxymesterone	T38.7X1	T38.7X2	T38.7X3	T38.7X4	T38.7X5	T38.7X6
Flupenthixol	T43.4X1	T43.4X2	T43.4X3	T43.4X4	T43.4X5	T43.4X6
Flupentixol	T43.4X1	T43.4X2	T43.4X3	T43.4X4	T43.4X5	T43.4X6
Fluphenazine	T43.3X1	T43.3X2	T43.3X3	T43.3X4	T43.3X5	T43.3X6
Fluprednidene	T49.0X1	T49.0X2	T49.0X3	T49.0X4	T49.0X5	T49.0X6
Fluprednisolone	T38.0X1	T38.0X2	T38.0X3	T38.0X4	T38.0X5	T38.0X6
Fluradoline	T39.8X1	T39.8X2	T39.8X3	T39.8X4	T39.8X5	T39.8X6
Flurandrenolide	T49.0X1	T49.0X2	T49.0X3	T49.0X4	T49.0X5	T49.0X6
Flurandrenolone	T49.0X1	T49.0X2	T49.0X3	T49.0X4	T49.0X5	T49.0X6
Flurazepam	T42.4X1	T42.4X2	T42.4X3	T42.4X4	T42.4X5	T42.4X6
Flurbiprofen	T39.311	T39.312	T39.313	T39.314	T39.315	T39.316
Flurobate	T49.0X1	T49.0X2	T49.0X3	T49.0X4	T49.0X5	T49.0X6
Flurotyl	T43.291	T43.292	T43.293	T43.294	T43.295	T43.296
Fluroxene	T41.0X1	T41.0X2	T41.0X3	T41.0X4	T41.0X5	T41.0X6
Fluspirilene	T43.591	T43.592	T43.593	T43.594	T43.595	T43.596
Flutamide	T38.6X1	T38.6X2	T38.6X3	T38.6X4	T38.6X5	T38.6X6
Flutazolam	T42.4X1	T42.4X2	T42.4X3	T42.4X4	T42.4X5	T42.4X6
Fluticasone propionate	T38.0X1	T38.0X2	T38.0X3	T38.0X4	T38.0X5	T38.0X6
Flutoprazepam	T42.4X1	T42.4X2	T42.4X3	T42.4X4	T42.4X5	T42.4X6
Flutropium bromide	T48.6X1	T48.6X2	T48.6X3	T48.6X4	T48.6X5	T48.6X6
Fluvoxamine	T43.221	T43.222	T43.223	T43.224	T43.225	T43.226
Folacin	T45.8X1	T45.8X2	T45.8X3	T45.8X4	T45.8X5	T45.8X6
Folic acid	T45.8X1	T45.8X2	T45.8X3	T45.8X4	T45.8X5	T45.8X6
with ferrous salt	T45.2X1	T45.2X2	T45.2X3	T45.2X4	T45.2X5	T45.2X6
antagonist	T45.1X1	T45.1X2	T45.1X3	T45.1X4	T45.1X5	T45.1X6
Folinic acid	T45.8X1	T45.8X2	T45.8X3	T45.8X4	T45.8X5	T45.8X6
Folium stramoniae	T48.6X1	T48.6X2	T48.6X3	T48.6X4	T48.6X5	T48.6X6
Follicle-stimulating hormone, human	T38.811	T38.812	T38.813	T38.814	T38.815	T38.816
Folpet	T60.3X1	T60.3X2	T60.3X3	T60.3X4	—	—
Fominoben	T48.3X1	T48.3X2	T48.3X3	T48.3X4	T48.3X5	T48.3X6
Food, foodstuffs, noxious, nonbacterial, NEC	T62.91	T62.92	T62.93	T62.94		
berries	T62.1X1	T62.1X2	T62.1X3	T62.1X4	—	—
fish — see also Fish	T61.91	T61.92	T61.93	T61.94	—	—
mushrooms	T62.0X1	T62.0X2	T62.0X3	T62.0X4	—	—
plants	T62.2X1	T62.2X2	T62.2X3	T62.2X4	—	—
seafood	T61.91	T61.92	T61.93	T61.94	—	—
specified NEC	T61.8X1	T61.8X2	T61.8X3	T61.8X4	—	—
seeds	T62.2X1	T62.2X2	T62.2X3	T62.2X4	—	—

◀ New ◀ Revised ~~deleted~~ Deleted

Substance	External Cause (T-Code)					
	Poisoning, Accidental (Unintentional)	Poisoning, Intentional Self-Harm	Poisoning, Assault	Poisoning, Undetermined	Adverse Effect	Underdosing
Food, foodstuffs, noxious, nonbacterial, NEC (Continued)						
shellfish	T61.781	T61.782	T61.783	T61.784	—	—
specified NEC	T62.8X1	T62.8X2	T62.8X3	T62.8X4	—	—
Fool's parsley	T62.2X1	T62.2X2	T62.2X3	T62.2X4	—	—
Formaldehyde (solution), gas or vapor	T59.2X1	T59.2X2	T59.2X3	T59.2X4	—	—
fungicide	T60.3X1	T60.3X2	T60.3X3	T60.3X4	—	—
Formalin	T59.2X1	T59.2X2	T59.2X3	T59.2X4	—	—
fungicide	T60.3X1	T60.3X2	T60.3X3	T60.3X4	—	—
vapor	T59.2X1	T59.2X2	T59.2X3	T59.2X4	—	—
Formic acid	T54.2X1	T54.2X2	T54.2X3	T54.2X4	—	—
vapor	T59.891	T59.892	T59.893	T59.894	—	—
Foscarnet sodium	T37.5X1	T37.5X2	T37.5X3	T37.5X4	T37.5X5	T37.5X6
Fosfestrol	T38.5X1	T38.5X2	T38.5X3	T38.5X4	T38.5X5	T38.5X6
Fosfomycin	T36.8X1	T36.8X2	T36.8X3	T36.8X4	T36.8X5	T36.8X6
Fosfonet sodium	T37.5X1	T37.5X2	T37.5X3	T37.5X4	T37.5X5	T37.5X6
Fosinopril	T46.4X1	T46.4X2	T46.4X3	T46.4X4	T46.4X5	T46.4X6
sodium	T46.4X1	T46.4X2	T46.4X3	T46.4X4	T46.4X5	T46.4X6
Fowler's solution	T57.0X1	T57.0X2	T57.0X3	T57.0X4	—	—
Foxglove	T62.2X1	T62.2X2	T62.2X3	T62.2X4	—	—
Framycetin	T36.5X1	T36.5X2	T36.5X3	T36.5X4	T36.5X5	T36.5X6
Frangula	T47.2X1	T47.2X2	T47.2X3	T47.2X4	T47.2X5	T47.2X6
extract	T47.2X1	T47.2X2	T47.2X3	T47.2X4	T47.2X5	T47.2X6
Frei antigen	T50.8X1	T50.8X2	T50.8X3	T50.8X4	T50.8X5	T50.8X6
Freon	T53.5X1	T53.5X2	T53.5X3	T53.5X4	—	—
Fructose	T50.3X1	T50.3X2	T50.3X3	T50.3X4	T50.3X5	T50.3X6
Frusemide	T50.1X1	T50.1X2	T50.1X3	T50.1X4	T50.1X5	T50.1X6
FSH	T38.811	T38.812	T38.813	T38.814	T38.815	T38.816
Ftorafur	T45.1X1	T45.1X2	T45.1X3	T45.1X4	T45.1X5	T45.1X6
Fuel						
automobile	T52.0X1	T52.0X2	T52.0X3	T52.0X4	—	—
exhaust gas, not in transit	T58.01	T58.02	T58.03	T58.04	—	—
vapor NEC	T52.0X1	T52.0X2	T52.0X3	T52.0X4	—	—
gas (domestic use) — see also Carbon, monoxide, fuel, utility	T59.891	T59.892	T59.893	T59.894	—	—
utility	T59.891	T59.892	T59.893	T59.894	—	—
in mobile container	T59.891	T59.892	T59.893	T59.894	—	—
incomplete combustion of — see Carbon, monoxide, fuel, utility						
piped (natural)	T59.891	T59.892	T59.893	T59.894	—	—
industrial, incomplete combustion	T58.8X1	T58.8X2	T58.8X3	T58.8X4	—	—

Substance	External Cause (T-Code)					
	Poisoning, Accidental (Unintentional)	Poisoning, Intentional Self-Harm	Poisoning, Assault	Poisoning, Undetermined	Adverse Effect	Underdosing
Fugillin	T36.8X1	T36.8X2	T36.8X3	T36.8X4	T36.8X5	T36.8X6
Fulminate of mercury	T56.1X1	T56.1X2	T56.1X3	T56.1X4	—	—
Fulvicin	T36.7X1	T36.7X2	T36.7X3	T36.7X4	T36.7X5	T36.7X6
Fumadil	T36.8X1	T36.8X2	T36.8X3	T36.8X4	T36.8X5	T36.8X6
Fumagillin	T36.8X1	T36.8X2	T36.8X3	T36.8X4	T36.8X5	T36.8X6
Fumaric acid	T49.4X1	T49.4X2	T49.4X3	T49.4X4	T49.4X5	T49.4X6
Fumes (from)	T59.91	T59.92	T59.93	T59.94	—	—
carbon monoxide — see Carbon, monoxide						
charcoal (domestic use) — see Charcoal, fumes						
chloroform — see Chloroform						
coke (in domestic stoves, fireplaces) — see Coke, fumes						
corrosive NEC	T54.91	T54.92	T54.93	T54.94	—	—
ether — see ether						
freons	T53.5X1	T53.5X2	T53.5X3	T53.5X4	—	—
hydrocarbons	T59.891	T59.892	T59.893	T59.894	—	—
petroleum (liquefied)	T59.891	T59.892	T59.893	T59.894	—	—
distributed through pipes (pure or mixed with air)	T59.891	T59.892	T59.893	T59.894		
lead — see lead						
metal — see Metals, or the specified metal						
nitrogen dioxide	T59.0X1	T59.0X2	T59.0X3	T59.0X4		
pesticides — see Pesticides						
petroleum (liquefied)	T59.891	T59.892	T59.893	T59.894	—	—
distributed through pipes (pure or mixed with air)	T59.891	T59.892	T59.893	T59.894		
polyester	T59.891	T59.892	T59.893	T59.894		
specified source NEC — see also substance specified	T59.891	T59.892	T59.893	T59.894	—	—
sulfur dioxide	T59.1X1	T59.1X2	T59.1X3	T59.1X4	—	—
Fumigant NEC	T60.91	T60.92	T60.93	T60.94	—	—
Fungi, noxious, used as food	T62.0X1	T62.0X2	T62.0X3	T62.0X4	—	—
Fungicide NEC (nonmedicinal)	T60.3X1	T60.3X2	T60.3X3	T60.3X4	—	—
Fungizone	T36.7X1	T36.7X2	T36.7X3	T36.7X4	T36.7X5	T36.7X6
topical	T49.0X1	T49.0X2	T49.0X3	T49.0X4	T49.0X5	T49.0X6
Furacin	T49.0X1	T49.0X2	T49.0X3	T49.0X4	T49.0X5	T49.0X6
Furadantin	T37.91	T37.92	T37.93	T37.94	T37.95	T37.96
Furazolidone	T37.8X1	T37.8X2	T37.8X3	T37.8X4	T37.8X5	T37.8X6
Furazolium chloride	T49.0X1	T49.0X2	T49.0X3	T49.0X4	T49.0X5	T49.0X6
Furfural	T52.8X1	T52.8X2	T52.8X3	T52.8X4	—	—

◀ New ◀ Revised ~~deleted~~ Deleted

	External Cause (T-Code)					
Substance	Poisoning, Accidental (Unintentional)	Poisoning, Intentional Self-Harm	Poisoning, Assault	Poisoning, Undetermined	Adverse Effect	Underdosing
Furnace (coal burning) (domestic), gas from industrial	T58.2X1	T58.2X2	T58.2X3	T58.2X4	—	—
industrial	T58.8X1	T58.8X2	T58.8X3	T58.8X4	—	—
Furniture polish	T65.891	T65.892	T65.893	T65.894		
Furosemide	T50.1X1	T50.1X2	T50.1X3	T50.1X4	T50.1X5	T50.1X6
Furoxone	T37.91	T37.92	T37.93	T37.94	T37.95	T37.96
Fursultiamine	T45.2X1	T45.2X2	T45.2X3	T45.2X4	T45.2X5	T45.2X6
Fusafungine	T36.8X1	T36.8X2	T36.8X3	T36.8X4	T36.8X5	T36.8X6
Fusel oil (any) (amyl) (butyl) (propyl), vapor	T51.3X1	T51.3X2	T51.3X3	T51.3X4	—	—
Fusidate (ethanolamine) (sodium)	T36.8X1	T36.8X2	T36.8X3	T36.8X4	T36.8X5	T36.8X6
Fusidic acid	T36.8X1	T36.8X2	T36.8X3	T36.8X4	T36.8X5	T36.8X6
Fytic acid, nonasodium	T50.6X1	T50.6X2	T50.6X3	T50.6X4	T50.6X5	T50.6X6
G						
GABA	T43.8X1	T43.8X2	T43.8X3	T43.8X4	T43.8X5	T43.8X6
Gadopentetic acid	T50.8X1	T50.8X2	T50.8X3	T50.8X4	T50.8X5	T50.8X6
Galactose	T50.3X1	T50.3X2	T50.3X3	T50.3X4	T50.3X5	T50.3X6
b-Galactosidase	T47.5X1	T47.5X2	T47.5X3	T47.5X4	T47.5X5	T47.5X6
Galantamine	T44.0X1	T44.0X2	T44.0X3	T44.0X4	T44.0X5	T44.0X6
Gallamine (triethiodide)	T48.1X1	T48.1X2	T48.1X3	T48.1X4	T48.1X5	T48.1X6
Gallium citrate	T50.991	T50.992	T50.993	T50.994	T50.995	T50.996
Gallopamil	T46.1X1	T46.1X2	T46.1X3	T46.1X4	T46.1X5	T46.1X6
Gamboge	T47.2X1	T47.2X2	T47.2X3	T47.2X4	T47.2X5	T47.2X6
Gamimune	T50.Z11	T50.Z12	T50.Z13	T50.Z14	T50.Z15	T50.Z16
Gamma-aminobutyric acid	T43.8X1	T43.8X2	T43.8X3	T43.8X4	T43.8X5	T43.8X6
Gamma-benzene hexachloride (medicinal)	T49.0X1	T49.0X2	T49.0X3	T49.0X4	T49.0X5	T49.0X6
nonmedicinal, vapor	T53.6X1	T53.6X2	T53.6X3	T53.6X4	—	—
Gamma-BHC (medicinal) — see also Gamma-benzene hexachloride	T49.0X1	T49.0X2	T49.0X3	T49.0X4	T49.0X5	T49.0X6
Gamma globulin	T50.Z11	T50.Z12	T50.Z13	T50.Z14	T50.Z15	T50.Z16
Gamulin	T50.Z11	T50.Z12	T50.Z13	T50.Z14	T50.Z15	T50.Z16
Ganciclovir (sodium)	T37.5X1	T37.5X2	T37.5X3	T37.5X4	T37.5X5	T37.5X6
Ganglionic blocking drug NEC	T44.2X1	T44.2X2	T44.2X3	T44.2X4	T44.2X5	T44.2X6
specified NEC	T44.2X1	T44.2X2	T44.2X3	T44.2X4	T44.2X5	T44.2X6
Ganja	T40.7X1	T40.7X2	T40.7X3	T40.7X4	T40.7X5	T40.7X6
Garamycin	T36.5X1	T36.5X2	T36.5X3	T36.5X4	T36.5X5	T36.5X6
ophthalmic preparation	T49.5X1	T49.5X2	T49.5X3	T49.5X4	T49.5X5	T49.5X6
topical NEC	T49.0X1	T49.0X2	T49.0X3	T49.0X4	T49.0X5	T49.0X6
Gardenal	T42.3X1	T42.3X2	T42.3X3	T42.3X4	T42.3X5	T42.3X6
Gardepanyl	T42.3X1	T42.3X2	T42.3X3	T42.3X4	T42.3X5	T42.3X6

	External Cause (T-Code)					
Substance	Poisoning, Accidental (Unintentional)	Poisoning, Intentional Self-Harm	Poisoning, Assault	Poisoning, Undetermined	Adverse Effect	Underdosing
Gas NEC	T59.91	T59.92	T59.93	T59.94	—	—
acetylene	T59.891	T59.892	T59.893	T59.894	—	—
incomplete combustion of	T58.11	T58.12	T58.13	T58.14	—	—
air contaminants, source or type not specified	T59.91	T59.92	T59.93	T59.94	—	—
anesthetic	T41.0X1	T41.0X2	T41.0X3	T41.0X4	T41.0X5	T41.0X6
blast furnace	T58.8X1	T58.8X2	T58.8X3	T58.8X4	—	—
butane — see butane						
carbon monoxide — see Carbon, monoxide						
chlorine	T59.4X1	T59.4X2	T59.4X3	T59.4X4	—	—
coal	T58.2X1	T58.2X2	T58.2X3	T58.2X4	—	—
cyanide	T57.3X1	T57.3X2	T57.3X3	T57.3X4	—	—
dicyanogen	T65.0X1	T65.0X2	T65.0X3	T65.0X4	—	—
domestic — see Domestic gas	T57.91	T57.92	T57.93	T57.94	—	—
exhaust	T57.91	T57.92	T57.93	T57.94	—	—
from utility (for cooking, heating, or lighting) (after combustion) — see Carbon, monoxide, fuel, utility						
prior to combustion	T59.891	T59.892	T59.893	T59.894	—	—
from wood or coal-burning stove or fireplace	T57.91	T57.92	T57.93	T57.94	—	—
fuel (domestic use) (after combustion) — see also Carbon, monoxide, fuel	T57.91	T57.92	T57.93	T57.94	—	—
industrial use	T58.8X1	T58.8X2	T58.8X3	T58.8X4	—	—
prior to combustion	T59.891	T59.892	T59.893	T59.894	—	—
utility	T59.891	T59.892	T59.893	T59.894	—	—
in mobile container	T59.891	T59.892	T59.893	T59.894	—	—
incomplete combustion of — see Carbon, monoxide, fuel, utility						
piped (natural)	T59.891	T59.892	T59.893	T59.894	—	—
garage	T58.01	T58.02	T58.03	T58.04	—	—
hydrocarbon NEC	T59.891	T59.892	T59.893	T59.894	—	—
incomplete combustion of — see Carbon, monoxide, fuel, utility						
liquefied — see butane						
piped	T59.891	T59.892	T59.893	T59.894	—	—
hydrocyanic acid	T65.0X1	T65.0X2	T65.0X3	T65.0X4	—	—

◀ New ◀ Revised ~~deleted~~ Deleted

TABLE OF DRUGS AND CHEMICALS

Substance	External Cause (T-Code)					
	Poisoning, Accidental (Unintentional)	Poisoning, Intentional Self-Harm	Poisoning, Assault	Poisoning, Undetermined	Adverse Effect	Underdosing
Gas (Continued)						
illuminating (after combustion)	T58.11	T58.12	T58.13	T58.14	—	—
prior to combustion	T59.891	T59.892	T59.893	T59.894	—	—
incomplete combustion, any — see Carbon, monoxide						
kiln	T58.8X1	T58.8X2	T58.8X3	T58.8X4	—	—
lacrimogenic	T59.3X1	T59.3X2	T59.3X3	T59.3X4	—	—
liquefied petroleum — see butane						
marsh	T59.891	T59.892	T59.893	T59.894	—	—
motor exhaust, not in transit	T58.01	T58.02	T58.03	T58.04	—	—
mustard, not in war	T59.891	T59.892	T59.893	T59.894	—	—
natural	T59.891	T59.892	T59.893	T59.894	—	—
nerve, not in war	T59.91	T59.92	T59.93	T59.94	—	—
oil	T52.0X1	T52.0X2	T52.0X3	T52.0X4	—	—
petroleum (liquefied) (distributed in mobile containers)	T59.891	T59.892	T59.893	T59.894	—	—
piped (pure or mixed with air)	T59.891	T59.892	T59.893	T59.894	—	—
piped (manufactured) (natural) NEC	T59.891	T59.892	T59.893	T59.894	—	—
producer	T58.8X1	T58.8X2	T58.8X3	T58.8X4	—	—
propane — see propane						
refrigerant (chlorofluoro-carbon)	T53.5X1	T53.5X2	T53.5X3	T53.5X4	—	—
not chlorofluoro-carbon	T59.891	T59.892	T59.893	T59.894	—	—
sewer	T59.91	T59.92	T59.93	T59.94	—	—
specified source NEC	T59.91	T59.92	T59.93	T59.94	—	—
stove (after combustion)	T58.11	T58.12	T58.13	T58.14	—	—
tear	T59.3X1	T59.3X2	T59.3X3	T59.3X4	—	—
therapeutic	T41.5X1	T41.5X2	T41.5X3	T41.5X4	T41.5X5	T41.5X6
utility (for cooking, heating, or lighting) (piped) NEC	T59.891	T59.892	T59.893	T59.894	—	—
in mobile container	T59.891	T59.892	T59.893	T59.894	—	—
incomplete combustion of — see Carbon, monoxide, fuel, utility						
piped (natural)	T59.891	T59.892	T59.893	T59.894	—	—
water	T58.11	T58.12	T58.13	T58.14	—	—
incomplete combustion of — see Carbon, monoxide, fuel, utility						

Substance	External Cause (T-Code)					
	Poisoning, Accidental (Unintentional)	Poisoning, Intentional Self-Harm	Poisoning, Assault	Poisoning, Undetermined	Adverse Effect	Underdosing
Gaseous substance — see Gas						
Gasoline	T52.0X1	T52.0X2	T52.0X3	T52.0X4	—	—
vapor	T52.0X1	T52.0X2	T52.0X3	T52.0X4	—	—
Gastric enzymes	T47.5X1	T47.5X2	T47.5X3	T47.5X4	T47.5X5	T47.5X6
Gastrografin	T50.8X1	T50.8X2	T50.8X3	T50.8X4	T50.8X5	T50.8X6
Gastrointestinal drug	T47.91	T47.92	T47.93	T47.94	T47.95	T47.96
biological	T47.8X1	T47.8X2	T47.8X3	T47.8X4	T47.8X5	T47.8X6
specified NEC	T47.8X1	T47.8X2	T47.8X3	T47.8X4	T47.8X5	T47.8X6
Gaultheria procumbens	T62.2X1	T62.2X2	T62.2X3	T62.2X4	—	—
Gelatin (intravenous)	T45.8X1	T45.8X2	T45.8X3	T45.8X4	T45.8X5	T45.8X6
absorbable (sponge)	T45.7X1	T45.7X2	T45.7X3	T45.7X4	T45.7X5	T45.7X6
Gefarnate	T44.3X1	T44.3X2	T44.3X3	T44.3X4	T44.3X5	T44.3X6
Gelfilm	T49.8X1	T49.8X2	T49.8X3	T49.8X4	T49.8X5	T49.8X6
Gelfoam	T45.7X1	T45.7X2	T45.7X3	T45.7X4	T45.7X5	T45.7X6
Gelsemine	T50.991	T50.992	T50.993	T50.994	T50.995	T50.996
Gelsemium (sempervirens)	T62.2X1	T62.2X2	T62.2X3	T62.2X4	—	—
Gemeprost	T48.0X1	T48.0X2	T48.0X3	T48.0X4	T48.0X5	T48.0X6
Gemfibrozil	T46.6X1	T46.6X2	T46.6X3	T46.6X4	T46.6X5	T46.6X6
Gemonil	T42.3X1	T42.3X2	T42.3X3	T42.3X4	T42.3X5	T42.3X6
Gentamicin	T36.5X1	T36.5X2	T36.5X3	T36.5X4	T36.5X5	T36.5X6
ophthalmic preparation	T49.5X1	T49.5X2	T49.5X3	T49.5X4	T49.5X5	T49.5X6
topical NEC	T49.0X1	T49.0X2	T49.0X3	T49.0X4	T49.0X5	T49.0X6
Gentian	T47.5X1	T47.5X2	T47.5X3	T47.5X4	T47.5X5	T47.5X6
violet	T49.0X1	T49.0X2	T49.0X3	T49.0X4	T49.0X5	T49.0X6
Gepefrine	T44.4X1	T44.4X2	T44.4X3	T44.4X4	T44.4X5	T44.4X6
Gestonorone caproate	T38.5X1	T38.5X2	T38.5X3	T38.5X4	T38.5X5	T38.5X6
Gexane	T49.0X1	T49.0X2	T49.0X3	T49.0X4	T49.0X5	T49.0X6
Gila monster (venom)	T63.111	T63.112	T63.113	T63.114	—	—
Ginger	T47.5X1	T47.5X2	T47.5X3	T47.5X4	T47.5X5	T47.5X6
Jamaica — see Jamaica, ginger						
Gitalin	T46.0X1	T46.0X2	T46.0X3	T46.0X4	T46.0X5	T46.0X6
amorphous	T46.0X1	T46.0X2	T46.0X3	T46.0X4	T46.0X5	T46.0X6
Gitaloxin	T46.0X1	T46.0X2	T46.0X3	T46.0X4	T46.0X5	T46.0X6
Gitoxin	T46.0X1	T46.0X2	T46.0X3	T46.0X4	T46.0X5	T46.0X6
Glafenine	T39.8X1	T39.8X2	T39.8X3	T39.8X4	T39.8X5	T39.8X6
Glandular extract (medicinal) NEC	T50.Z91	T50.Z92	T50.Z93	T50.Z94	T50.Z95	T50.Z96
Glaucarubin	T37.3X1	T37.3X2	T37.3X3	T37.3X4	T37.3X5	T37.3X6
Glibenclamide	T38.3X1	T38.3X2	T38.3X3	T38.3X4	T38.3X5	T38.3X6
Glibornuride	T38.3X1	T38.3X2	T38.3X3	T38.3X4	T38.3X5	T38.3X6
Gliclazide	T38.3X1	T38.3X2	T38.3X3	T38.3X4	T38.3X5	T38.3X6
Glimidine	T38.3X1	T38.3X2	T38.3X3	T38.3X4	T38.3X5	T38.3X6

TABLE OF DRUGS AND CHEMICALS

◀ New　◀ Revised　~~deleted~~ Deleted

Substance	Poisoning, Accidental (Unintentional)	Poisoning, Intentional Self-Harm	Poisoning, Assault	Poisoning, Undetermined	Adverse Effect	Underdosing
	External Cause (T-Code)					
Glipizide	T38.3X1	T38.3X2	T38.3X3	T38.3X4	T38.3X5	T38.3X6
Gliquidone	T38.3X1	T38.3X2	T38.3X3	T38.3X4	T38.3X5	T38.3X6
Glisolamide	T38.3X1	T38.3X2	T38.3X3	T38.3X4	T38.3X5	T38.3X6
Glisoxepide	T38.3X1	T38.3X2	T38.3X3	T38.3X4	T38.3X5	T38.3X6
Globin zinc insulin	T38.3X1	T38.3X2	T38.3X3	T38.3X4	T38.3X5	T38.3X6
Globulin						
antilymphocytic	T50.Z11	T50.Z12	T50.Z13	T50.Z14	T50.Z15	T50.Z16
antirhesus	T50.Z11	T50.Z12	T50.Z13	T50.Z14	T50.Z15	T50.Z16
antivenin	T50.Z11	T50.Z12	T50.Z13	T50.Z14	T50.Z15	T50.Z16
antiviral	T50.Z11	T50.Z12	T50.Z13	T50.Z14	T50.Z15	T50.Z16
Glucagon	T38.3X1	T38.3X2	T38.3X3	T38.3X4	T38.3X5	T38.3X6
Glucocorticoids	T38.0X1	T38.0X2	T38.0X3	T38.0X4	T38.0X5	T38.0X6
Glucocorticosteroid	T38.0X1	T38.0X2	T38.0X3	T38.0X4	T38.0X5	T38.0X6
Gluconic acid	T50.991	T50.992	T50.993	T50.994	T50.995	T50.996
Glucosamine sulfate	T39.4X1	T39.4X2	T39.4X3	T39.4X4	T39.4X5	T39.4X6
Glucose	T50.3X1	T50.3X2	T50.3X3	T50.3X4	T50.3X5	T50.3X6
with sodium chloride	T50.3X1	T50.3X2	T50.3X3	T50.3X4	T50.3X5	T50.3X6
Glucosulfone sodium	T37.1X1	T37.1X2	T37.1X3	T37.1X4	T37.1X5	T37.1X6
Glucurolactone	T47.8X1	T47.8X2	T47.8X3	T47.8X4	T47.8X5	T47.8X6
Glue NEC	T52.8X1	T52.8X2	T52.8X3	T52.8X4	—	—
Glutamic acid	T47.5X1	T47.5X2	T47.5X3	T47.5X4	T47.5X5	T47.5X6
Glutaral (medicinal)	T49.0X1	T49.0X2	T49.0X3	T49.0X4	T49.0X5	T49.0X6
nonmedicinal	T65.891	T65.892	T65.893	T65.894	—	—
Glutaraldehyde (nonmedicinal)	T65.891	T65.892	T65.893	T65.894	—	—
medicinal	T49.0X1	T49.0X2	T49.0X3	T49.0X4	T49.0X5	T49.0X6
Glutathione	T50.6X1	T50.6X2	T50.6X3	T50.6X4	T50.6X5	T50.6X6
Glutethimide	T42.6X1	T42.6X2	T42.6X3	T42.6X4	T42.6X5	T42.6X6
Glyburide	T38.3X1	T38.3X2	T38.3X3	T38.3X4	T38.3X5	T38.3X6
Glycerin	T47.4X1	T47.4X2	T47.4X3	T47.4X4	T47.4X5	T47.4X6
Glycerol	T47.4X1	T47.4X2	T47.4X3	T47.4X4	T47.4X5	T47.4X6
borax	T49.6X1	T49.6X2	T49.6X3	T49.6X4	T49.6X5	T49.6X6
intravenous	T50.3X1	T50.3X2	T50.3X3	T50.3X4	T50.3X5	T50.3X6
iodinated	T48.4X1	T48.4X2	T48.4X3	T48.4X4	T48.4X5	T48.4X6
Glycerophosphate	T50.991	T50.992	T50.993	T50.994	T50.995	T50.996
Glyceryl						
gualacolate	T48.4X1	T48.4X2	T48.4X3	T48.4X4	T48.4X5	T48.4X6
nitrate	T46.3X1	T46.3X2	T46.3X3	T46.3X4	T46.3X5	T46.3X6
triacetate (topical)	T49.0X1	T49.0X2	T49.0X3	T49.0X4	T49.0X5	T49.0X6
trinitrate	T46.3X1	T46.3X2	T46.3X3	T46.3X4	T46.3X5	T46.3X6
Glycine	T50.3X1	T50.3X2	T50.3X3	T50.3X4	T50.3X5	T50.3X6
Glyclopyramide	T38.3X1	T38.3X2	T38.3X3	T38.3X4	T38.3X5	T38.3X6
Glycobiarsol	T37.3X1	T37.3X2	T37.3X3	T37.3X4	T37.3X5	T37.3X6

Substance	Poisoning, Accidental (Unintentional)	Poisoning, Intentional Self-Harm	Poisoning, Assault	Poisoning, Undetermined	Adverse Effect	Underdosing
	External Cause (T-Code)					
Glycols (ether)	T52.3X1	T52.3X2	T52.3X3	T52.3X4	—	—
Glyconiazide	T37.1X1	T37.1X2	T37.1X3	T37.1X4	T37.1X5	T37.1X6
Glycopyrrolate	T44.3X1	T44.3X2	T44.3X3	T44.3X4	T44.3X5	T44.3X6
Glycopyrronium	T44.3X1	T44.3X2	T44.3X3	T44.3X4	T44.3X5	T44.3X6
bromide	T44.3X1	T44.3X2	T44.3X3	T44.3X4	T44.3X5	T44.3X6
Glycoside, cardiac (stimulant)	T46.0X1	T46.0X2	T46.0X3	T46.0X4	T46.0X5	T46.0X6
Glycyclamide	T38.3X1	T38.3X2	T38.3X3	T38.3X4	T38.3X5	T38.3X6
Glycyrrhiza extract	T48.4X1	T48.4X2	T48.4X3	T48.4X4	T48.4X5	T48.4X6
Glycyrrhizic acid	T48.4X1	T48.4X2	T48.4X3	T48.4X4	T48.4X5	T48.4X6
Glycyrrhizinate potassium	T48.4X1	T48.4X2	T48.4X3	T48.4X4	T48.4X5	T48.4X6
Glymidine sodium	T38.3X1	T38.3X2	T38.3X3	T38.3X4	T38.3X5	T38.3X6
Glyphosate	T60.3X1	T60.3X2	T60.3X3	T60.3X4	—	—
Glyphylline	T48.6X1	T48.6X2	T48.6X3	T48.6X4	T48.6X5	T48.6X6
Gold						
colloidal (I98Au)	T45.1X1	T45.1X2	T45.1X3	T45.1X4	T45.1X5	T45.1X6
salts	T39.4X1	T39.4X2	T39.4X3	T39.4X4	T39.4X5	T39.4X6
Golden sulfide of antimony	T56.891	T56.892	T56.893	T56.894	—	—
Goldylocks	T62.2X1	T62.2X2	T62.2X3	T62.2X4	—	—
Gonadal tissue extract	T38.901	T38.902	T38.903	T38.904	T38.905	T38.906
female	T38.5X1	T38.5X2	T38.5X3	T38.5X4	T38.5X5	T38.5X6
male	T38.7X1	T38.7X2	T38.7X3	T38.7X4	T38.7X5	T38.7X6
Gonadorelin	T38.891	T38.892	T38.893	T38.894	T38.895	T38.896
Gonadotropin	T38.891	T38.892	T38.893	T38.894	T38.895	T38.896
chorionic	T38.891	T38.892	T38.893	T38.894	T38.895	T38.896
pituitary	T38.811	T38.812	T38.813	T38.814	T38.815	T38.816
Goserelin	T45.1X1	T45.1X2	T45.1X3	T45.1X4	T45.1X5	T45.1X6
Grain alcohol	T51.0X1	T51.0X2	T51.0X3	T51.0X4	—	—
Gramicidin	T49.0X1	T49.0X2	T49.0X3	T49.0X4	T49.0X5	T49.0X6
Granisetron	T45.0X1	T45.0X2	T45.0X3	T45.0X4	T45.0X5	T45.0X6
Gratiola officinalis	T62.2X1	T62.2X2	T62.2X3	T62.2X4	—	—
Grease	T65.891	T65.892	T65.893	T65.894	—	—
Green hellebore	T62.2X1	T62.2X2	T62.2X3	T62.2X4	—	—
Green soap	T49.2X1	T49.2X2	T49.2X3	T49.2X4	T49.2X5	T49.2X6
Grifulvin	T36.7X1	T36.7X2	T36.7X3	T36.7X4	T36.7X5	T36.7X6
Griseofulvin	T36.7X1	T36.7X2	T36.7X3	T36.7X4	T36.7X5	T36.7X6
Growth hormone	T38.811	T38.812	T38.813	T38.814	T38.815	T38.816
Guaiacol derivatives	T48.4X1	T48.4X2	T48.4X3	T48.4X4	T48.4X5	T48.4X6
Guaiac reagent	T50.991	T50.992	T50.993	T50.994	T50.995	T50.996
Guaifenesin	T48.4X1	T48.4X2	T48.4X3	T48.4X4	T48.4X5	T48.4X6
Guaimesal	T48.4X1	T48.4X2	T48.4X3	T48.4X4	T48.4X5	T48.4X6
Guaiphenesin	T48.4X1	T48.4X2	T48.4X3	T48.4X4	T48.4X5	T48.4X6
Guamecycline	T36.4X1	T36.4X2	T36.4X3	T36.4X4	T36.4X5	T36.4X6

◀ New ◀ Revised ~~deleted~~ Deleted

Substance	Poisoning, Accidental (Unintentional)	Poisoning, Intentional Self-Harm	Poisoning, Assault	Poisoning, Undetermined	Adverse Effect	Underdosing
Guanabenz	T46.5X1	T46.5X2	T46.5X3	T46.5X4	T46.5X5	T46.5X6
Guanacline	T46.5X1	T46.5X2	T46.5X3	T46.5X4	T46.5X5	T46.5X6
Guanadrel	T46.5X1	T46.5X2	T46.5X3	T46.5X4	T46.5X5	T46.5X6
Guanatol	T37.2X1	T37.2X2	T37.2X3	T37.2X4	T37.2X5	T37.2X6
Guanethidine	T46.5X1	T46.5X2	T46.5X3	T46.5X4	T46.5X5	T46.5X6
Guanfacine	T46.5X1	T46.5X2	T46.5X3	T46.5X4	T46.5X5	T46.5X6
Guano	T65.891	T65.892	T65.893	T65.894	—	—
Guanochlor	T46.5X1	T46.5X2	T46.5X3	T46.5X4	T46.5X5	T46.5X6
Guanoclor	T46.5X1	T46.5X2	T46.5X3	T46.5X4	T46.5X5	T46.5X6
Guanoctine	T46.5X1	T46.5X2	T46.5X3	T46.5X4	T46.5X5	T46.5X6
Guanoxabenz	T46.5X1	T46.5X2	T46.5X3	T46.5X4	T46.5X5	T46.5X6
Guanoxan	T46.5X1	T46.5X2	T46.5X3	T46.5X4	T46.5X5	T46.5X6
Guar gum (medicinal)	T46.6X1	T46.6X2	T46.6X3	T46.6X4	T46.6X5	T46.6X6
H						
Hachimycin	T36.7X1	T36.7X2	T36.7X3	T36.7X4	T36.7X5	T36.7X6
Hair						
dye	T49.4X1	T49.4X2	T49.4X3	T49.4X4	T49.4X5	T49.4X6
preparation NEC	T49.4X1	T49.4X2	T49.4X3	T49.4X4	T49.4X5	T49.4X6
Halazepam	T42.4X1	T42.4X2	T42.4X3	T42.4X4	T42.4X5	T42.4X6
Halcinolone	T49.0X1	T49.0X2	T49.0X3	T49.0X4	T49.0X5	T49.0X6
Halcinonide	T49.0X1	T49.0X2	T49.0X3	T49.0X4	T49.0X5	T49.0X6
Halethazole	T49.0X1	T49.0X2	T49.0X3	T49.0X4	T49.0X5	T49.0X6
Hallucinogen NEC	T40.901	T40.902	T40.903	T40.904	T40.905	T40.906
Halofantrine	T37.2X1	T37.2X2	T37.2X3	T37.2X4	T37.2X5	T37.2X6
Halofenate	T46.6X1	T46.6X2	T46.6X3	T46.6X4	T46.6X5	T46.6X6
Halometasone	T49.0X1	T49.0X2	T49.0X3	T49.0X4	T49.0X5	T49.0X6
Haloperidol	T43.4X1	T43.4X2	T43.4X3	T43.4X4	T43.4X5	T43.4X6
Haloprogin	T49.0X1	T49.0X2	T49.0X3	T49.0X4	T49.0X5	T49.0X6
Halotex	T49.0X1	T49.0X2	T49.0X3	T49.0X4	T49.0X5	T49.0X6
Halothane	T41.0X1	T41.0X2	T41.0X3	T41.0X4	T41.0X5	T41.0X6
Haloxazolam	T42.4X1	T42.4X2	T42.4X3	T42.4X4	T42.4X5	T42.4X6
Halquinols	T49.0X1	T49.0X2	T49.0X3	T49.0X4	T49.0X5	T49.0X6
Hamamelis	T49.2X1	T49.2X2	T49.2X3	T49.2X4	T49.2X5	T49.2X6
Haptendextran	T45.8X1	T45.8X2	T45.8X3	T45.8X4	T45.8X5	T45.8X6
Harmonyl	T46.5X1	T46.5X2	T46.5X3	T46.5X4	T46.5X5	T46.5X6
Hartmann's solution	T50.3X1	T50.3X2	T50.3X3	T50.3X4	T50.3X5	T50.3X6
Hashish	T40.7X1	T40.7X2	T40.7X3	T40.7X4	T40.7X5	T40.7X6
Hawaiian Woodrose seeds	T40.991	T40.992	T40.993	T40.994		
HCB	T60.3X1	T60.3X2	T60.3X3	T60.3X4	—	—
HCH	T53.6X1	T53.6X2	T53.6X3	T53.6X4	—	—
medicinal	T49.0X1	T49.0X2	T49.0X3	T49.0X4	T49.0X5	T49.0X6

Substance	Poisoning, Accidental (Unintentional)	Poisoning, Intentional Self-Harm	Poisoning, Assault	Poisoning, Undetermined	Adverse Effect	Underdosing
HCN	T57.3X1	T57.3X2	T57.3X3	T57.3X4	—	—
Headache cures, drugs, powders NEC	T50.901	T50.902	T50.903	T50.904	T50.905	T50.906
Heavenly Blue (morning glory)	T40.991	T40.992	T40.993	T40.994	—	—
Heavy metal antidote	T45.8X1	T45.8X2	T45.8X3	T45.8X4	T45.8X5	T45.8X6
Hedaquinium	T49.0X1	T49.0X2	T49.0X3	T49.0X4	T49.0X5	T49.0X6
Hedge hyssop	T62.2X1	T62.2X2	T62.2X3	T62.2X4	—	—
Heet	T49.8X1	T49.8X2	T49.8X3	T49.8X4	T49.8X5	T49.8X6
Helium	T48.991	T48.992	T48.993	T48.994	T48.995	T48.996
Helenin	T37.4X1	T37.4X2	T37.4X3	T37.4X4	T37.4X5	T37.4X6
Hellebore (black) (green) (white)	T62.2X1	T62.2X2	T62.2X3	T62.2X4	—	—
Helium (nonmedicinal) NEC	T59.891	T59.892	T59.893	T59.894		
medicinal	T48.991	T48.992	T48.993	T48.994	T48.995	T48.996
Hematin	T45.8X1	T45.8X2	T45.8X3	T45.8X4	T45.8X5	T45.8X6
Hematinic preparation	T45.8X1	T45.8X2	T45.8X3	T45.8X4	T45.8X5	T45.8X6
Hemlock	T62.2X1	T62.2X2	T62.2X3	T62.2X4	—	—
Hemostatic	T45.621	T45.622	T45.623	T45.624	T45.625	T45.626
drug, systemic	T45.621	T45.622	T45.623	T45.624	T45.625	T45.626
Hemostyptic	T49.4X1	T49.4X2	T49.4X3	T49.4X4	T49.4X5	T49.4X6
Henbane	T62.2X1	T62.2X2	T62.2X3	T62.2X4	—	—
Heparin (sodium)	T45.511	T45.512	T45.513	T45.514	T45.515	T45.516
action reverser	T45.7X1	T45.7X2	T45.7X3	T45.7X4	T45.7X5	T45.7X6
Heparin-fraction	T45.511	T45.512	T45.513	T45.514	T45.515	T45.516
Heparinoid (systemic)	T45.511	T45.512	T45.513	T45.514	T45.515	T45.516
Hepatic secretion stimulant	T47.8X1	T47.8X2	T47.8X3	T47.8X4	T47.8X5	T47.8X6
Hepatitis B						
immune globulin	T50.Z11	T50.Z12	T50.Z13	T50.Z14	T50.Z15	T50.Z16
vaccine	T50.B91	T50.B92	T50.B93	T50.B94	T50.B95	T50.B96
Hepronicate	T46.7X1	T46.7X2	T46.7X3	T46.7X4	T46.7X5	T46.7X6
Heptabarb	T42.3X1	T42.3X2	T42.3X3	T42.3X4	T42.3X5	T42.3X6
Heptabarbitone	T42.3X1	T42.3X2	T42.3X3	T42.3X4	T42.3X5	T42.3X6
Heptabarbital	T42.3X1	T42.3X2	T42.3X3	T42.3X4	T42.3X5	T42.3X6
Heptachlor	T60.1X1	T60.1X2	T60.1X3	T60.1X4	—	—
Heptalgin	T40.2X1	T40.2X2	T40.2X3	T40.2X4	T40.2X5	T40.2X6
Heptaminol	T46.3X1	T46.3X2	T46.3X3	T46.3X4	T46.3X5	T46.3X6
Herbicide NEC	T60.3X1	T60.3X2	T60.3X3	T60.3X4	—	—
Heroin	T40.1X1	T40.1X2	T40.1X3	T40.1X4	—	—
Herplex	T49.5X1	T49.5X2	T49.5X3	T49.5X4	T49.5X5	T49.5X6
HES	T45.8X1	T45.8X2	T45.8X3	T45.8X4	T45.8X5	T45.8X6
Hesperidin	T46.991	T46.992	T46.993	T46.994	T46.995	T46.996
Hetacillin	T36.0X1	T36.0X2	T36.0X3	T36.0X4	T36.0X5	T36.0X6

◀ New ◀ Revised ~~deleted~~ Deleted

Substance	Poisoning, Accidental (Unintentional)	Poisoning, Intentional Self-Harm	Poisoning, Assault	Poisoning, Undetermined	Adverse Effect	Underdosing
Hetastarch	T45.8X1	T45.8X2	T45.8X3	T45.8X4	T45.8X5	T45.8X6
HETP	T60.0X1	T60.0X2	T60.0X3	T60.0X4	—	—
Hexachlorobenzene (vapor)	T60.3X1	T60.3X2	T60.3X3	T60.3X4	—	—
Hexachlorocyclohexane	T53.6X1	T53.6X2	T53.6X3	T53.6X4	—	—
Hexachlorophene	T49.0X1	T49.0X2	T49.0X3	T49.0X4	T49.0X5	T49.0X6
Hexadiline	T46.3X1	T46.3X2	T46.3X3	T46.3X4	T46.3X5	T46.3X6
Hexadimethrine (bromide)	T45.7X1	T45.7X2	T45.7X3	T45.7X4	T45.7X5	T45.7X6
Hexadylamine	T46.3X1	T46.3X2	T46.3X3	T46.3X4	T46.3X5	T46.3X6
Hexaethyl tetraphosphate	T60.0X1	T60.0X2	T60.0X3	T60.0X4	—	—
Hexafluorenium bromide	T48.1X1	T48.1X2	T48.1X3	T48.1X4	T48.1X5	T48.1X6
Hexafluorodiethyl ether	T43.291	T43.292	T43.293	T43.294	T43.295	T43.296
Hexafluronium (bromide)	T48.1X1	T48.1X2	T48.1X3	T48.1X4	T48.1X5	T48.1X6
Hexahydrobenzol	T52.8X1	T52.8X2	T52.8X3	T52.8X4	—	—
Hexahydrocresol(s)	T51.8X1	T51.8X2	T51.8X3	T51.8X4	—	—
arsenide	T57.0X1	T57.0X2	T57.0X3	T57.0X4	—	—
arseniurated	T57.0X1	T57.0X2	T57.0X3	T57.0X4	—	—
cyanide	T57.3X1	T57.3X2	T57.3X3	T57.3X4	—	—
gas	T59.891	T59.892	T59.893	T59.894	—	—
Fluoride (liquid)	T57.8X1	T57.8X2	T57.8X3	T57.8X4	—	—
vapor	T59.891	T59.892	T59.893	T59.894	—	—
phophorated	T60.0X1	T60.0X2	T60.0X3	T60.0X4	—	—
sulfate	T57.8X1	T57.8X2	T57.8X3	T57.8X4	—	—
sulfide (gas)	T59.6X1	T59.6X2	T59.6X3	T59.6X4	—	—
arseniurated	T57.0X1	T57.0X2	T57.0X3	T57.0X4	—	—
sulfurated	T57.8X1	T57.8X2	T57.8X3	T57.8X4	—	—
Hexahydrophenol	T51.8X1	T51.8X2	T51.8X3	T51.8X4	—	—
Hexa-germ	T49.2X1	T49.2X2	T49.2X3	T49.2X4	T49.2X5	T49.2X6
Hexalen	T51.8X1	T51.8X2	T51.8X3	T51.8X4	—	—
Hexamethonium bromide	T44.2X1	T44.2X2	T44.2X3	T44.2X4	T44.2X5	T44.2X6
Hexamethylene	T52.8X1	T52.8X2	T52.8X3	T52.8X4	—	—
Hexamethylmelamine	T45.1X1	T45.1X2	T45.1X3	T45.1X4	T45.1X5	T45.1X6
Hexamidine	T49.0X1	T49.0X2	T49.0X3	T49.0X4	T49.0X5	T49.0X6
Hexamine (mandelate)	T37.8X1	T37.8X2	T37.8X3	T37.8X4	T37.8X5	T37.8X6
Hexanone, 2-hexanone	T52.4X1	T52.4X2	T52.4X3	T52.4X4	—	—
Hexanuorenium	T48.1X1	T48.1X2	T48.1X3	T48.1X4	T48.1X5	T48.1X6
Hexapropymate	T42.6X1	T42.6X2	T42.6X3	T42.6X4	T42.6X5	T42.6X6
Hexasonium iodide	T44.3X1	T44.3X2	T44.3X3	T44.3X4	T44.3X5	T44.3X6
Hexcarbacholine bromide	T48.1X1	T48.1X2	T48.1X3	T48.1X4	T48.1X5	T48.1X6
Hexemal	T42.3X1	T42.3X2	T42.3X3	T42.3X4	T42.3X5	T42.3X6
Hexestrol	T38.5X1	T38.5X2	T38.5X3	T38.5X4	T38.5X5	T38.5X6
Hexethal (sodium)	T42.3X1	T42.3X2	T42.3X3	T42.3X4	T42.3X5	T42.3X6
Hexetidine	T37.8X1	T37.8X2	T37.8X3	T37.8X4	T37.8X5	T37.8X6

Substance	Poisoning, Accidental (Unintentional)	Poisoning, Intentional Self-Harm	Poisoning, Assault	Poisoning, Undetermined	Adverse Effect	Underdosing
Hexobarbital	T42.3X1	T42.3X2	T42.3X3	T42.3X4	T42.3X5	T42.3X6
rectal	T41.291	T41.292	T41.293	T41.294	T41.295	T41.296
sodium	T41.1X1	T41.1X2	T41.1X3	T41.1X4	T41.1X5	T41.1X6
Hexobendine	T46.3X1	T46.3X2	T46.3X3	T46.3X4	T46.3X5	T46.3X6
Hexocyclium	T44.3X1	T44.3X2	T44.3X3	T44.3X4	T44.3X5	T44.3X6
metilsulfate	T44.3X1	T44.3X2	T44.3X3	T44.3X4	T44.3X5	T44.3X6
Hexoestrol	T38.5X1	T38.5X2	T38.5X3	T38.5X4	T38.5X5	T38.5X6
Hexone	T52.4X1	T52.4X2	T52.4X3	T52.4X4	—	—
Hexoprenaline	T48.6X1	T48.6X2	T48.6X3	T48.6X4	T48.6X5	T48.6X6
Hexylcaine	T41.3X1	T41.3X2	T41.3X3	T41.3X4	T41.3X5	T41.3X6
Hexylresorcinol	T52.2X1	T52.2X2	T52.2X3	T52.2X4	—	—
HGH (human growth hormone)	T38.811	T38.812	T38.813	T38.814	T38.815	T38.816
Hinkle's pills	T47.2X1	T47.2X2	T47.2X3	T47.2X4	T47.2X5	T47.2X6
Histalog	T50.8X1	T50.8X2	T50.8X3	T50.8X4	T50.8X5	T50.8X6
Histamine (phosphate)	T50.8X1	T50.8X2	T50.8X3	T50.8X4	T50.8X5	T50.8X6
Histoplasmin	T50.8X1	T50.8X2	T50.8X3	T50.8X4	T50.8X5	T50.8X6
Holly berries	T62.2X1	T62.2X2	T62.2X3	T62.2X4	—	—
Homatropine	T44.3X1	T44.3X2	T44.3X3	T44.3X4	T44.3X5	T44.3X6
methylbromide	T44.3X1	T44.3X2	T44.3X3	T44.3X4	T44.3X5	T44.3X6
Homochlorcyclizine	T45.0X1	T45.0X2	T45.0X3	T45.0X4	T45.0X5	T45.0X6
Homosalate	T49.3X1	T49.3X2	T49.3X3	T49.3X4	T49.3X5	T49.3X6
Homo-tet	T50.Z11	T50.Z12	T50.Z13	T50.Z14	T50.Z15	T50.Z16
Hormone	T38.801	T38.802	T38.803	T38.804	T38.805	T38.806
adrenal cortical steroids	T38.0X1	T38.0X2	T38.0X3	T38.0X4	T38.0X5	T38.0X6
androgenic	T38.7X1	T38.7X2	T38.7X3	T38.7X4	T38.7X5	T38.7X6
anterior pituitary NEC	T38.811	T38.812	T38.813	T38.814	T38.815	T38.816
antidiabetic agents	T38.3X1	T38.3X2	T38.3X3	T38.3X4	T38.3X5	T38.3X6
antidiuretic	T38.891	T38.892	T38.893	T38.894	T38.895	T38.896
cancer therapy	T45.1X1	T45.1X2	T45.1X3	T45.1X4	T45.1X5	T45.1X6
follicle stimulating	T38.811	T38.812	T38.813	T38.814	T38.815	T38.816
gonadotropic	T38.891	T38.892	T38.893	T38.894	T38.895	T38.896
pituitary	T38.811	T38.812	T38.813	T38.814	T38.815	T38.816
growth	T38.811	T38.812	T38.813	T38.814	T38.815	T38.816
luteinizing	T38.811	T38.812	T38.813	T38.814	T38.815	T38.816
ovarian	T38.5X1	T38.5X2	T38.5X3	T38.5X4	T38.5X5	T38.5X6
oxytocic	T48.0X1	T48.0X2	T48.0X3	T48.0X4	T48.0X5	T48.0X6
parathyroid (derivatives)	T50.991	T50.992	T50.993	T50.994	T50.995	T50.996
pituitary (posterior) NEC	T38.891	T38.892	T38.893	T38.894	T38.895	T38.896
anterior	T38.811	T38.812	T38.813	T38.814	T38.815	T38.816
specified, NEC	T38.891	T38.892	T38.893	T38.894	T38.895	T38.896
thyroid	T38.1X1	T38.1X2	T38.1X3	T38.1X4	T38.1X5	T38.1X6
Hornet (sting)	T63.451	T63.452	T63.453	T63.454	—	—

◀ New ◀ Revised ~~deleted~~ Deleted

TABLE OF DRUGS AND CHEMICALS

Substance	Poisoning, Accidental (Unintentional)	Poisoning, Intentional Self-Harm	Poisoning, Assault	Poisoning, Undetermined	Adverse Effect	Underdosing
Horse anti-human lymphocytic serum	T50.Z11	T50.Z12	T50.Z13	T50.Z14	T50.Z15	T50.Z16
Horticulture agent NEC	T65.91	T65.92	T65.93	T65.94	—	—
with pesticide	T60.91	T60.92	T60.93	T60.94	—	—
Human						
albumin	T45.8X1	T45.8X2	T45.8X3	T45.8X4	T45.8X5	T45.8X6
growth hormone (HGH)	T38.811	T38.812	T38.813	T38.814	T38.815	T38.816
immune serum	T50.Z11	T50.Z12	T50.Z13	T50.Z14	T50.Z15	T50.Z16
Hyaluronidase	T45.3X1	T45.3X2	T45.3X3	T45.3X4	T45.3X5	T45.3X6
Hyazyme	T45.3X1	T45.3X2	T45.3X3	T45.3X4	T45.3X5	T45.3X6
Hycodan	T40.2X1	T40.2X2	T40.2X3	T40.2X4	T40.2X5	T40.2X6
Hydantoin derivative NEC	T42.0X1	T42.0X2	T42.0X3	T42.0X4	T42.0X5	T42.0X6
Hydeltra	T38.0X1	T38.0X2	T38.0X3	T38.0X4	T38.0X5	T38.0X6
Hydergine	T44.6X1	T44.6X2	T44.6X3	T44.6X4	T44.6X5	T44.6X6
Hydrabamine penicillin	T36.0X1	T36.0X2	T36.0X3	T36.0X4	T36.0X5	T36.0X6
Hydralazine	T46.5X1	T46.5X2	T46.5X3	T46.5X4	T46.5X5	T46.5X6
Hydrargaphen	T49.0X1	T49.0X2	T49.0X3	T49.0X4	T49.0X5	T49.0X6
Hydrargyri amino-chloridum	T49.0X1	T49.0X2	T49.0X3	T49.0X4	T49.0X5	T49.0X6
Hydrastine	T48.291	T48.292	T48.293	T48.294	T48.295	T48.296
Hydrazine	T54.1X1	T54.1X2	T54.1X3	T54.1X4	—	—
monoamine oxidase inhibitors	T43.1X1	T43.1X2	T43.1X3	T43.1X4	T43.1X5	T43.1X6
Hydrazoic acid, azides	T54.2X1	T54.2X2	T54.2X3	T54.2X4	—	—
Hydriodic acid	T48.4X1	T48.4X2	T48.4X3	T48.4X4	T48.4X5	T48.4X6
Hydrocarbon gas	T59.891	T59.892	T59.893	T59.894	—	—
incomplete combustion of — see Carbon, monoxide, fuel, utility						
liquefied (mobile container)	T59.891	T59.892	T59.893	T59.894	—	—
piped (natural)	T59.891	T59.892	T59.893	T59.894	—	—
Hydrochloric acid (liquid)	T54.2X1	T54.2X2	T54.2X3	T54.2X4	—	—
medicinal (digestant)	T47.5X1	T47.5X2	T47.5X3	T47.5X4	T47.5X5	T47.5X6
vapor	T59.891	T59.892	T59.893	T59.894	—	—
Hydrochlorothiazide	T50.2X1	T50.2X2	T50.2X3	T50.2X4	T50.2X5	T50.2X6
Hydrocodone	T40.2X1	T40.2X2	T40.2X3	T40.2X4	T40.2X5	T40.2X6
Hydrocortisone (derivatives)	T38.0X1	T38.0X2	T38.0X3	T38.0X4	T38.0X5	T38.0X6
aceponate	T49.0X1	T49.0X2	T49.0X3	T49.0X4	T49.0X5	T49.0X6
ENT agent	T49.6X1	T49.6X2	T49.6X3	T49.6X4	T49.6X5	T49.6X6
ophthalmic preparation	T49.5X1	T49.5X2	T49.5X3	T49.5X4	T49.5X5	T49.5X6
topical NEC	T49.0X1	T49.0X2	T49.0X3	T49.0X4	T49.0X5	T49.0X6
Hydrocortone	T38.0X1	T38.0X2	T38.0X3	T38.0X4	T38.0X5	T38.0X6
ENT agent	T49.6X1	T49.6X2	T49.6X3	T49.6X4	T49.6X5	T49.6X6
ophthalmic preparation	T49.5X1	T49.5X2	T49.5X3	T49.5X4	T49.5X5	T49.5X6
topical NEC	T49.0X1	T49.0X2	T49.0X3	T49.0X4	T49.0X5	T49.0X6

Substance	Poisoning, Accidental (Unintentional)	Poisoning, Intentional Self-Harm	Poisoning, Assault	Poisoning, Undetermined	Adverse Effect	Underdosing
Hydrocyanic acid (liquid)	T57.3X1	T57.3X2	T57.3X3	T57.3X4	—	—
gas	T65.0X1	T65.0X2	T65.0X3	T65.0X4	—	—
Hydroflumethiazide	T50.2X1	T50.2X2	T50.2X3	T50.2X4	T50.2X5	T50.2X6
Hydrofluoric acid (liquid)	T54.2X1	T54.2X2	T54.2X3	T54.2X4	—	—
vapor	T59.891	T59.892	T59.893	T59.894	—	—
Hydrogen	T59.891	T59.892	T59.893	T59.894	—	—
arsenide	T57.0X1	T57.0X2	T57.0X3	T57.0X4	—	—
arseniureted	T57.0X1	T57.0X2	T57.0X3	T57.0X4	—	—
chloride	T57.8X1	T57.8X2	T57.8X3	T57.8X4	—	—
cyanide (salts)	T57.3X1	T57.3X2	T57.3X3	T57.3X4	—	—
gas	T57.3X1	T57.3X2	T57.3X3	T57.3X4	—	—
Fluoride	T59.5X1	T59.5X2	T59.5X3	T59.5X4	—	—
vapor	T59.5X1	T59.5X2	T59.5X3	T59.5X4	—	—
peroxide	T49.0X1	T49.0X2	T49.0X3	T49.0X4	T49.0X5	T49.0X6
phosphureted	T57.1X1	T57.1X2	T57.1X3	T57.1X4	—	—
sulfide	T59.6X1	T59.6X2	T59.6X3	T59.6X4	—	—
arseniureted	T57.0X1	T57.0X2	T57.0X3	T57.0X4	—	—
sulfureted	T59.6X1	T59.6X2	T59.6X3	T59.6X4	—	—
Hydromethylpyridine	T46.7X1	T46.7X2	T46.7X3	T46.7X4	T46.7X5	T46.7X6
Hydromorphinol	T40.2X1	T40.2X2	T40.2X3	T40.2X4	—	—
Hydromorphinone	T40.2X1	T40.2X2	T40.2X3	T40.2X4	T40.2X5	T40.2X6
Hydromorphone	T40.2X1	T40.2X2	T40.2X3	T40.2X4	T40.2X5	T40.2X6
Hydromox	T50.2X1	T50.2X2	T50.2X3	T50.2X4	T50.2X5	T50.2X6
Hydrophilic lotion	T49.3X1	T49.3X2	T49.3X3	T49.3X4	T49.3X5	T49.3X6
Hydroquinidine	T46.2X1	T46.2X2	T46.2X3	T46.2X4	T46.2X5	T46.2X6
Hydroquinone	T52.2X1	T52.2X2	T52.2X3	T52.2X4	—	—
vapor	T59.891	T59.892	T59.893	T59.894	—	—
Hydrosulfuric acid (gas)	T59.6X1	T59.6X2	T59.6X3	T59.6X4	—	—
Hydrotalcite	T47.1X1	T47.1X2	T47.1X3	T47.1X4	T47.1X5	T47.1X6
Hydrous wool fat	T49.3X1	T49.3X2	T49.3X3	T49.3X4	T49.3X5	T49.3X6
Hydroxide, caustic	T54.3X1	T54.3X2	T54.3X3	T54.3X4	—	—
Hydroxocobalamin	T45.8X1	T45.8X2	T45.8X3	T45.8X4	T45.8X5	T45.8X6
Hydroxyamphetamine	T49.5X1	T49.5X2	T49.5X3	T49.5X4	T49.5X5	T49.5X6
Hydroxycarbamide	T45.1X1	T45.1X2	T45.1X3	T45.1X4	T45.1X5	T45.1X6
Hydroxychloroquine	T37.8X1	T37.8X2	T37.8X3	T37.8X4	T37.8X5	T37.8X6
Hydroxydihydrocodeinone	T40.2X1	T40.2X2	T40.2X3	T40.2X4	T40.2X5	T40.2X6
Hydroxyestrone	T38.5X1	T38.5X2	T38.5X3	T38.5X4	T38.5X5	T38.5X6
Hydroxyethyl starch	T45.8X1	T45.8X2	T45.8X3	T45.8X4	T45.8X5	T45.8X6
Hydroxymethylpentanone	T52.4X1	T52.4X2	T52.4X3	T52.4X4	—	—
Hydroxyphenamate	T43.591	T43.592	T43.593	T43.594	T43.595	T43.596
Hydroxyphenylbutazone	T39.2X1	T39.2X2	T39.2X3	T39.2X4	T39.2X5	T39.2X6

◀ New ◀ Revised ~~deleted~~ Deleted

Substance	Poisoning, Accidental (Unintentional)	Poisoning, Intentional Self-Harm	Poisoning, Assault	Poisoning, Undetermined	Adverse Effect	Underdosing
Hydroxyprogesterone	T38.5X1	T38.5X2	T38.5X3	T38.5X4	T38.5X5	T38.5X6
caproate	T38.5X1	T38.5X2	T38.5X3	T38.5X4	T38.5X5	T38.5X6
Hydroxyquinoline (derivatives) NEC	T37.8X1	T37.8X2	T37.8X3	T37.8X4	T37.8X5	T37.8X6
Hydroxystilbamidine	T37.3X1	T37.3X2	T37.3X3	T37.3X4	T37.3X5	T37.3X6
Hydroxytoluene (nonmedicinal)	T54.0X1	T54.0X2	T54.0X3	T54.0X4	—	—
medicinal	T49.0X1	T49.0X2	T49.0X3	T49.0X4	T49.0X5	T49.0X6
Hydroxyurea	T45.1X1	T45.1X2	T45.1X3	T45.1X4	T45.1X5	T45.1X6
Hydroxyzine	T43.591	T43.592	T43.593	T43.594	T43.595	T43.596
Hyoscine	T44.3X1	T44.3X2	T44.3X3	T44.3X4	T44.3X5	T44.3X6
Hyoscyamine	T44.3X1	T44.3X2	T44.3X3	T44.3X4	T44.3X5	T44.3X6
Hyoscyamus	T44.3X1	T44.3X2	T44.3X3	T44.3X4	T44.3X5	T44.3X6
dry extract	T44.3X1	T44.3X2	T44.3X3	T44.3X4	T44.3X5	T44.3X6
Hypaque	T50.8X1	T50.8X2	T50.8X3	T50.8X4	T50.8X5	T50.8X6
Hypertussis	T50.Z11	T50.Z12	T50.Z13	T50.Z14	T50.Z15	T50.Z16
Hypnotic	T42.71	T42.72	T42.73	T42.74	T42.75	T42.76
anticonvulsant	T42.71	T42.72	T42.73	T42.74	T42.75	T42.76
specified NEC	T42.6X1	T42.6X2	T42.6X3	T42.6X4	T42.6X5	T42.6X6
Hypochlorite	T49.0X1	T49.0X2	T49.0X3	T49.0X4	T49.0X5	T49.0X6
Hypophysis, posterior	T38.891	T38.892	T38.893	T38.894	T38.895	T38.896
Hypotensive NEC	T46.5X1	T46.5X2	T46.5X3	T46.5X4	T46.5X5	T46.5X6
Hypromellose	T49.5X1	T49.5X2	T49.5X3	T49.5X4	T49.5X5	T49.5X6

I

Substance	Poisoning, Accidental (Unintentional)	Poisoning, Intentional Self-Harm	Poisoning, Assault	Poisoning, Undetermined	Adverse Effect	Underdosing
Ibacitabine	T37.5X1	T37.5X2	T37.5X3	T37.5X4	T37.5X5	T37.5X6
Ibopamine	T44.991	T44.992	T44.993	T44.994	T44.995	T44.996
Ibufenac	T39.311	T39.312	T39.313	T39.314	T39.315	T39.316
Ibuprofen	T39.311	T39.312	T39.313	T39.314	T39.315	T39.316
Ibuproxam	T39.311	T39.312	T39.313	T39.314	T39.315	T39.316
Ibuterol	T48.6X1	T48.6X2	T48.6X3	T48.6X4	T48.6X5	T48.6X6
Ichthammol	T49.0X1	T49.0X2	T49.0X3	T49.0X4	T49.0X5	T49.0X6
Ichthyol	T49.4X1	T49.4X2	T49.4X3	T49.4X4	T49.4X5	T49.4X6
Idarubicin	T45.1X1	T45.1X2	T45.1X3	T45.1X4	T45.1X5	T45.1X6
Idrocilamide	T42.8X1	T42.8X2	T42.8X3	T42.8X4	T42.8X5	T42.8X6
Ifenprodil	T46.7X1	T46.7X2	T46.7X3	T46.7X4	T46.7X5	T46.7X6
Ifosfamide	T45.1X1	T45.1X2	T45.1X3	T45.1X4	T45.1X5	T45.1X6
Iletin	T38.3X1	T38.3X2	T38.3X3	T38.3X4	T38.3X5	T38.3X6
Ilex	T62.2X1	T62.2X2	T62.2X3	T62.2X4	—	—
Illuminating gas (after combustion)	T58.11	T58.12	T58.13	T58.14	—	—
prior to combustion	T59.891	T59.892	T59.893	T59.894	—	—
Ilopan	T45.2X1	T45.2X2	T45.2X3	T45.2X4	T45.2X5	T45.2X6
Iloprost	T46.7X1	T46.7X2	T46.7X3	T46.7X4	T46.7X5	T46.7X6

Substance	Poisoning, Accidental (Unintentional)	Poisoning, Intentional Self-Harm	Poisoning, Assault	Poisoning, Undetermined	Adverse Effect	Underdosing
Ilotycin	T36.3X1	T36.3X2	T36.3X3	T36.3X4	T36.3X5	T36.3X6
ophthalmic preparation	T49.5X1	T49.5X2	T49.5X3	T49.5X4	T49.5X5	T49.5X6
topical NEC	T49.0X1	T49.0X2	T49.0X3	T49.0X4	T49.0X5	T49.0X6
Imidazole-4-carboxamide	T45.1X1	T45.1X2	T45.1X3	T45.1X4	T45.1X5	T45.1X6
Imipenem	T36.0X1	T36.0X2	T36.0X3	T36.0X4	T36.0X5	T36.0X6
Imipramine	T43.011	T43.012	T43.013	T43.014	T43.015	T43.016
Iminostilbene	T42.1X1	T42.1X2	T42.1X3	T42.1X4	T42.1X5	T42.1X6
Immu-G	T50.Z11	T50.Z12	T50.Z13	T50.Z14	T50.Z15	T50.Z16
Immuglobin	T50.Z11	T50.Z12	T50.Z13	T50.Z14	T50.Z15	T50.Z16
Immune						
globulin	T50.Z11	T50.Z12	T50.Z13	T50.Z14	T50.Z15	T50.Z16
serum globulin	T50.Z11	T50.Z12	T50.Z13	T50.Z14	T50.Z15	T50.Z16
Immunoglobin human (intravenous) (normal)	T50.Z11	T50.Z12	T50.Z13	T50.Z14	T50.Z15	T50.Z16
unmodified	T50.Z11	T50.Z12	T50.Z13	T50.Z14	T50.Z15	T50.Z16
Immunosuppressive drug	T45.1X1	T45.1X2	T45.1X3	T45.1X4	T45.1X5	T45.1X6
Immu-tetanus	T50.Z11	T50.Z12	T50.Z13	T50.Z14	T50.Z15	T50.Z16
Indalpine	T43.221	T43.222	T43.223	T43.224	T43.225	T43.226
Indanazoline	T48.5X1	T48.5X2	T48.5X3	T48.5X4	T48.5X5	T48.5X6
Indandione (derivatives)	T45.511	T45.512	T45.513	T45.514	T45.515	T45.516
Indapamide	T46.5X1	T46.5X2	T46.5X3	T46.5X4	T46.5X5	T46.5X6
Indendione (derivatives)	T45.511	T45.512	T45.513	T45.514	T45.515	T45.516
Indenolol	T44.7X1	T44.7X2	T44.7X3	T44.7X4	T44.7X5	T44.7X6
Inderal	T44.7X1	T44.7X2	T44.7X3	T44.7X4	T44.7X5	T44.7X6
Indian						
hemp	T40.7X1	T40.7X2	T40.7X3	T40.7X4	T40.7X5	T40.7X6
tobacco	T62.2X1	T62.2X2	T62.2X3	T62.2X4	—	—
Indigo carmine	T50.8X1	T50.8X2	T50.8X3	T50.8X4	T50.8X5	T50.8X6
Indobufen	T45.521	T45.522	T45.523	T45.524	T45.525	T45.526
Indocin	T39.2X1	T39.2X2	T39.2X3	T39.2X4	T39.2X5	T39.2X6
Indocyanine green	T50.8X1	T50.8X2	T50.8X3	T50.8X4	T50.8X5	T50.8X6
Indometacin	T39.391	T39.392	T39.393	T39.394	T39.395	T39.396
Indomethacin	T39.391	T39.392	T39.393	T39.394	T39.395	T39.396
farnesil	T39.4X1	T39.4X2	T39.4X3	T39.4X4	T39.4X5	T39.4X6
Indoramin	T44.6X1	T44.6X2	T44.6X3	T44.6X4	T44.6X5	T44.6X6
Industrial						
alcohol	T51.0X1	T51.0X2	T51.0X3	T51.0X4	—	—
fumes	T59.891	T59.892	T59.893	T59.894	—	—
solvents (fumes) (vapors)	T52.91	T52.92	T52.93	T52.94	—	—
Influenza vaccine	T50.B91	T50.B92	T50.B93	T50.B94	T50.B95	T50.B96
Ingested substance NEC	T65.91	T65.92	T65.93	T65.94	—	—
INH	T37.1X1	T37.1X2	T37.1X3	T37.1X4	T37.1X5	T37.1X6

TABLE OF DRUGS AND CHEMICALS

TABLE OF DRUGS AND CHEMICALS

Substance	External Cause (T-Code)					
	Poisoning, Accidental (Unintentional)	Poisoning, Intentional Self-Harm	Poisoning, Assault	Poisoning, Undetermined	Adverse Effect	Underdosing
Inhalation, gas (noxious) — *see* Gas						
Inhibitor						
angiotensin-converting enzyme	T46.4X1	T46.4X2	T46.4X3	T46.4X4	T46.4X5	T46.4X6
carbonic anhydrase	T50.2X1	T50.2X2	T50.2X3	T50.2X4	T50.2X5	T50.2X6
fibrinolysis	T45.621	T45.622	T45.623	T45.624	T45.625	T45.626
monoamine oxidase NEC	T43.1X1	T43.1X2	T43.1X3	T43.1X4	T43.1X5	T43.1X6
hydrazine	T43.1X1	T43.1X2	T43.1X3	T43.1X4	T43.1X5	T43.1X6
postsynaptic	T43.8X1	T43.8X2	T43.8X3	T43.8X4	T43.8X5	T43.8X6
prothrombin synthesis	T45.511	T45.512	T45.513	T45.514	T45.515	T45.516
Ink	T65.891	T65.892	T65.893	T65.894	—	—
Inorganic substance NEC	T57.91	T57.92	T57.93	T57.94	—	—
Inosine pranobex	T37.5X1	T37.5X2	T37.5X3	T37.5X4	T37.5X5	T37.5X6
Inositol	T50.991	T50.992	T50.993	T50.994	T50.995	T50.996
nicotinate	T46.7X1	T46.7X2	T46.7X3	T46.7X4	T46.7X5	T46.7X6
Inproquone	T45.1X1	T45.1X2	T45.1X3	T45.1X4	T45.1X5	T45.1X6
Insect (sting), venomous	T63.481	T63.482	T63.483	T63.484	—	—
ant	T63.421	T63.422	T63.423	T63.424	—	—
bee	T63.441	T63.442	T63.443	T63.444	—	—
caterpillar	T63.431	T63.432	T63.433	T63.434	—	—
hornet	T63.451	T63.452	T63.453	T63.454	—	—
wasp	T63.461	T63.462	T63.463	T63.464	—	—
Insecticide NEC	T60.91	T60.92	T60.93	T60.94	—	—
carbamate	T60.0X1	T60.0X2	T60.0X3	T60.0X4	—	—
chlorinated	T60.1X1	T60.1X2	T60.1X3	T60.1X4	—	—
mixed	T60.91	T60.92	T60.93	T60.94	—	—
organochlorine	T60.1X1	T60.1X2	T60.1X3	T60.1X4	—	—
organophosphorus	T60.0X1	T60.0X2	T60.0X3	T60.0X4	—	—
Insular tissue extract	T38.3X1	T38.3X2	T38.3X3	T38.3X4	T38.3X5	T38.3X6
Insulin (amorphous) (globin) (isophane) (Lente) (NPH) (Semilente) (Ultralente)	T38.3X1	T38.3X2	T38.3X3	T38.3X4	T38.3X5	T38.3X6
defalan	T38.3X1	T38.3X2	T38.3X3	T38.3X4	T38.3X5	T38.3X6
human	T38.3X1	T38.3X2	T38.3X3	T38.3X4	T38.3X5	T38.3X6
injection, soluble	T38.3X1	T38.3X2	T38.3X3	T38.3X4	T38.3X5	T38.3X6
biphasic	T38.3X1	T38.3X2	T38.3X3	T38.3X4	T38.3X5	T38.3X6
intermediate acting	T38.3X1	T38.3X2	T38.3X3	T38.3X4	T38.3X5	T38.3X6
protamine zinc	T38.3X1	T38.3X2	T38.3X3	T38.3X4	T38.3X5	T38.3X6
slow acting	T38.3X1	T38.3X2	T38.3X3	T38.3X4	T38.3X5	T38.3X6
zinc						
protamine injection	T38.3X1	T38.3X2	T38.3X3	T38.3X4	T38.3X5	T38.3X6
suspension (amorphous) (crystalline)	T38.3X1	T38.3X2	T38.3X3	T38.3X4	T38.3X5	T38.3X6

Substance	External Cause (T-Code)					
	Poisoning, Accidental (Unintentional)	Poisoning, Intentional Self-Harm	Poisoning, Assault	Poisoning, Undetermined	Adverse Effect	Underdosing
Interferon (alpha) (beta) (gamma)	T37.5X1	T37.5X2	T37.5X3	T37.5X4	T37.5X5	T37.5X6
Intestinal motility control drug	T47.6X1	T47.6X2	T47.6X3	T47.6X4	T47.6X5	T47.6X6
biological	T47.8X1	T47.8X2	T47.8X3	T47.8X4	T47.8X5	T47.8X6
Intranarcon	T41.1X1	T41.1X2	T41.1X3	T41.1X4	T41.1X5	T41.1X6
Intravenous						
amino acids	T50.991	T50.992	T50.993	T50.994	T50.995	T50.996
fat suspension	T50.991	T50.992	T50.993	T50.994	T50.995	T50.996
Inulin	T50.8X1	T50.8X2	T50.8X3	T50.8X4	T50.8X5	T50.8X6
Invert sugar	T50.3X1	T50.3X2	T50.3X3	T50.3X4	T50.3X5	T50.3X6
Inza — *see* Naproxen						
Iobenzamic acid	T50.8X1	T50.8X2	T50.8X3	T50.8X4	T50.8X5	T50.8X6
Iocarmic acid	T50.8X1	T50.8X2	T50.8X3	T50.8X4	T50.8X5	T50.8X6
Iocetamic acid	T50.8X1	T50.8X2	T50.8X3	T50.8X4	T50.8X5	T50.8X6
Iodamide	T50.8X1	T50.8X2	T50.8X3	T50.8X4	T50.8X5	T50.8X6
Iodide NEC — *see also* Iodine	T49.0X1	T49.0X2	T49.0X3	T49.0X4	T49.0X5	T49.0X6
mercury (ointment)	T49.0X1	T49.0X2	T49.0X3	T49.0X4	T49.0X5	T49.0X6
methylate	T49.0X1	T49.0X2	T49.0X3	T49.0X4	T49.0X5	T49.0X6
potassium (expectorant) NEC	T48.4X1	T48.4X2	T48.4X3	T48.4X4	T48.4X5	T48.4X6
Iodinated						
contrast medium	T50.8X1	T50.8X2	T50.8X3	T50.8X4	T50.8X5	T50.8X6
glycerol	T48.4X1	T48.4X2	T48.4X3	T48.4X4	T48.4X5	T48.4X6
human serum albumin (1311)	T50.8X1	T50.8X2	T50.8X3	T50.8X4	T50.8X5	T50.8X6
Iodine (antiseptic, external) (tincture) NEC	T49.0X1	T49.0X2	T49.0X3	T49.0X4	T49.0X5	T49.0X6
125 — *see also* Radiation sickness, and Exposure to radioactivce isotopes	T50.8X1	T50.8X2	T50.8X3	T50.8X4	T50.8X5	T50.8X6
therapeutic	T50.991	T50.992	T50.993	T50.994	T50.995	T50.996
131 — *see also* Radiation sickness, and Exposure to radioactivce isotopes	T50.8X1	T50.8X2	T50.8X3	T50.8X4	T50.8X5	T50.8X6
therapeutic	T38.2X1	T38.2X2	T38.2X3	T38.2X4	T38.2X5	T38.2X6
diagnostic	T50.8X1	T50.8X2	T50.8X3	T50.8X4	T50.8X5	T50.8X6
for thyroid conditions (antithyroid)	T38.2X1	T38.2X2	T38.2X3	T38.2X4	T38.2X5	T38.2X6
solution	T49.0X1	T49.0X2	T49.0X3	T49.0X4	T49.0X5	T49.0X6
vapor	T59.891	T59.892	T59.893	T59.894	—	—
Iodipamide	T50.8X1	T50.8X2	T50.8X3	T50.8X4	T50.8X5	T50.8X6
Iodized (poppy seed) oil	T50.8X1	T50.8X2	T50.8X3	T50.8X4	T50.8X5	T50.8X6
Iodobismitol	T37.8X1	T37.8X2	T37.8X3	T37.8X4	T37.8X5	T37.8X6
Iodochlorhydroxyquin	T37.8X1	T37.8X2	T37.8X3	T37.8X4	T37.8X5	T37.8X6
topical	T49.0X1	T49.0X2	T49.0X3	T49.0X4	T49.0X5	T49.0X6
Iodochlorhydroxyquino-line	T37.8X1	T37.8X2	T37.8X3	T37.8X4	T37.8X5	T37.8X6
Iodocholesterol (1311)	T50.8X1	T50.8X2	T50.8X3	T50.8X4	T50.8X5	T50.8X6

◀ New ◀ Revised ~~deleted~~ Deleted

Substance	Poisoning, Accidental (Unintentional)	Poisoning, Intentional Self-Harm	Poisoning, Assault	Poisoning, Undetermined	Adverse Effect	Underdosing
Iodoform	T49.0X1	T49.0X2	T49.0X3	T49.0X4	T49.0X5	T49.0X6
Iodohippuric acid	T50.8X1	T50.8X2	T50.8X3	T50.8X4	T50.8X5	T50.8X6
Iodopanoic acid	T50.8X1	T50.8X2	T50.8X3	T50.8X4	T50.8X5	T50.8X6
Iodophthalein (sodium)	T50.8X1	T50.8X2	T50.8X3	T50.8X4	T50.8X5	T50.8X6
Iodopyracet	T50.8X1	T50.8X2	T50.8X3	T50.8X4	T50.8X5	T50.8X6
Iodoquinol	T37.8X1	T37.8X2	T37.8X3	T37.8X4	T37.8X5	T37.8X6
Iodoxamic acid	T50.8X1	T50.8X2	T50.8X3	T50.8X4	T50.8X5	T50.8X6
Iofendylate	T50.8X1	T50.8X2	T50.8X3	T50.8X4	T50.8X5	T50.8X6
Ioglycamic acid	T50.8X1	T50.8X2	T50.8X3	T50.8X4	T50.8X5	T50.8X6
Iohexol	T50.8X1	T50.8X2	T50.8X3	T50.8X4	T50.8X5	T50.8X6
Ion exchange resin						
anion	T47.8X1	T47.8X2	T47.8X3	T47.8X4	T47.8X5	T47.8X6
cation	T50.3X1	T50.3X2	T50.3X3	T50.3X4	T50.3X5	T50.3X6
cholestyramine	T46.6X1	T46.6X2	T46.6X3	T46.6X4	T46.6X5	T46.6X6
intestinal	T47.8X1	T47.8X2	T47.8X3	T47.8X4	T47.8X5	T47.8X6
Iopamidol	T50.8X1	T50.8X2	T50.8X3	T50.8X4	T50.8X5	T50.8X6
Iopanoic acid	T50.8X1	T50.8X2	T50.8X3	T50.8X4	T50.8X5	T50.8X6
Iophenoic acid	T50.8X1	T50.8X2	T50.8X3	T50.8X4	T50.8X5	T50.8X6
Iopodate, sodium	T50.8X1	T50.8X2	T50.8X3	T50.8X4	T50.8X5	T50.8X6
Iopodic acid	T50.8X1	T50.8X2	T50.8X3	T50.8X4	T50.8X5	T50.8X6
Iopromide	T50.8X1	T50.8X2	T50.8X3	T50.8X4	T50.8X5	T50.8X6
Iopydol	T50.8X1	T50.8X2	T50.8X3	T50.8X4	T50.8X5	T50.8X6
Iotalamic acid	T50.8X1	T50.8X2	T50.8X3	T50.8X4	T50.8X5	T50.8X6
Iothalamate	T50.8X1	T50.8X2	T50.8X3	T50.8X4	T50.8X5	T50.8X6
Iothiouracil	T38.2X1	T38.2X2	T38.2X3	T38.2X4	T38.2X5	T38.2X6
Iotrol	T50.8X1	T50.8X2	T50.8X3	T50.8X4	T50.8X5	T50.8X6
Iotrolan	T50.8X1	T50.8X2	T50.8X3	T50.8X4	T50.8X5	T50.8X6
Iotroxate	T50.8X1	T50.8X2	T50.8X3	T50.8X4	T50.8X5	T50.8X6
Iotroxic acid	T50.8X1	T50.8X2	T50.8X3	T50.8X4	T50.8X5	T50.8X6
Ioversol	T50.8X1	T50.8X2	T50.8X3	T50.8X4	T50.8X5	T50.8X6
Ioxaglate	T50.8X1	T50.8X2	T50.8X3	T50.8X4	T50.8X5	T50.8X6
Ioxaglic acid	T50.8X1	T50.8X2	T50.8X3	T50.8X4	T50.8X5	T50.8X6
Ioxitalamic acid	T50.8X1	T50.8X2	T50.8X3	T50.8X4	T50.8X5	T50.8X6
Ipecac	T47.7X1	T47.7X2	T47.7X3	T47.7X4	T47.7X5	T47.7X6
Ipecacuanha	T48.4X1	T48.4X2	T48.4X3	T48.4X4	T48.4X5	T48.4X6
Ipodate, calcium	T50.8X1	T50.8X2	T50.8X3	T50.8X4	T50.8X5	T50.8X6
Ipral	T42.3X1	T42.3X2	T42.3X3	T42.3X4	T42.3X5	T42.3X6
Ipratropium (bromide)	T48.6X1	T48.6X2	T48.6X3	T48.6X4	T48.6X5	T48.6X6
Ipriflavone	T46.3X1	T46.3X2	T46.3X3	T46.3X4	T46.3X5	T46.3X6
Iprindole	T43.011	T43.012	T43.013	T43.014	T43.015	T43.016
Iproclozide	T43.1X1	T43.1X2	T43.1X3	T43.1X4	T43.1X5	T43.1X6
Iprofenin	T50.8X1	T50.8X2	T50.8X3	T50.8X4	T50.8X5	T50.8X6

Substance	Poisoning, Accidental (Unintentional)	Poisoning, Intentional Self-Harm	Poisoning, Assault	Poisoning, Undetermined	Adverse Effect	Underdosing
Iproheptine	T49.2X1	T49.2X2	T49.2X3	T49.2X4	T49.2X5	T49.2X6
Iproniazid	T43.1X1	T43.1X2	T43.1X3	T43.1X4	T43.1X5	T43.1X6
Iproplatin	T45.1X1	T45.1X2	T45.1X3	T45.1X4	T45.1X5	T45.1X6
Iproveratril	T46.1X1	T46.1X2	T46.1X3	T46.1X4	T46.1X5	T46.1X6
Iron (compounds) (medicinal) NEC	T45.4X1	T45.4X2	T45.4X3	T45.4X4	T45.4X5	T45.4X6
ammonium	T45.4X1	T45.4X2	T45.4X3	T45.4X4	T45.4X5	T45.4X6
dextran injection	T45.4X1	T45.4X2	T45.4X3	T45.4X4	T45.4X5	T45.4X6
nonmedicinal	T56.891	T56.892	T56.893	T56.894	—	—
salts	T45.4X1	T45.4X2	T45.4X3	T45.4X4	T45.4X5	T45.4X6
sorbitex	T45.4X1	T45.4X2	T45.4X3	T45.4X4	T45.4X5	T45.4X6
sorbitol citric acid complex	T45.4X1	T45.4X2	T45.4X3	T45.4X4	T45.4X5	T45.4X6
Irrigating fluid (vaginal)	T49.8X1	T49.8X2	T49.8X3	T49.8X4	T49.8X5	T49.8X6
eye	T49.5X1	T49.5X2	T49.5X3	T49.5X4	T49.5X5	T49.5X6
Isepamicin	T36.5X1	T36.5X2	T36.5X3	T36.5X4	T36.5X5	T36.5X6
Isoaminile (citrate)	T48.3X1	T48.3X2	T48.3X3	T48.3X4	T48.3X5	T48.3X6
Isoamyl nitrite	T46.3X1	T46.3X2	T46.3X3	T46.3X4	T46.3X5	T46.3X6
Isobenzan	T60.1X1	T60.1X2	T60.1X3	T60.1X4	—	—
Isobutyl acetate	T52.8X1	T52.8X2	T52.8X3	T52.8X4	—	—
Isocarboxazid	T43.1X1	T43.1X2	T43.1X3	T43.1X4	T43.1X5	T43.1X6
Isoconazole	T49.0X1	T49.0X2	T49.0X3	T49.0X4	T49.0X5	T49.0X6
Isocyanate	T65.0X1	T65.0X2	T65.0X3	T65.0X4	—	—
Isoephedrine	T44.991	T44.992	T44.993	T44.994	T44.995	T44.996
Isoetarine	T48.6X1	T48.6X2	T48.6X3	T48.6X4	T48.6X5	T48.6X6
Isoethadione	T42.2X1	T42.2X2	T42.2X3	T42.2X4	T42.2X5	T42.2X6
Isoetharine	T44.5X1	T44.5X2	T44.5X3	T44.5X4	T44.5X5	T44.5X6
Isoflurane	T41.0X1	T41.0X2	T41.0X3	T41.0X4	T41.0X5	T41.0X6
Isoflurophate	T44.0X1	T44.0X2	T44.0X3	T44.0X4	T44.0X5	T44.0X6
Isomaltose, ferric complex	T45.4X1	T45.4X2	T45.4X3	T45.4X4	T45.4X5	T45.4X6
Isometheptene	T44.3X1	T44.3X2	T44.3X3	T44.3X4	T44.3X5	T44.3X6
Isoniazid	T37.1X1	T37.1X2	T37.1X3	T37.1X4	T37.1X5	T37.1X6
with						
rifampicin	T36.6X1	T36.6X2	T36.6X3	T36.6X4	T36.6X5	T36.6X6
thioacetazone	T37.1X1	T37.1X2	T37.1X3	T37.1X4	T37.1X5	T37.1X6
Isonicotinic acid hydrazide	T37.1X1	T37.1X2	T37.1X3	T37.1X4	T37.1X5	T37.1X6
Isonipecaine	T40.4X1	T40.4X2	T40.4X3	T40.4X4	T40.4X5	T40.4X6
Isopentaquine	T37.2X1	T37.2X2	T37.2X3	T37.2X4	T37.2X5	T37.2X6
Isophane insulin	T38.3X1	T38.3X2	T38.3X3	T38.3X4	T38.3X5	T38.3X6
Isophorone	T65.891	T65.892	T65.893	T65.894	—	—
Isophosphamide	T45.1X1	T45.1X2	T45.1X3	T45.1X4	T45.1X5	T45.1X6
Isopregnenone	T38.5X1	T38.5X2	T38.5X3	T38.5X4	T38.5X5	T38.5X6
Isoprenaline	T48.6X1	T48.6X2	T48.6X3	T48.6X4	T48.6X5	T48.6X6
Isopromethazine	T43.3X1	T43.3X2	T43.3X3	T43.3X4	T43.3X5	T43.3X6

TABLE OF DRUGS AND CHEMICALS

Substance	External Cause (T-Code)					
	Poisoning, Accidental (Unintentional)	Poisoning, Intentional Self-Harm	Poisoning, Assault	Poisoning, Undetermined	Adverse Effect	Underdosing
Isopropamide	T44.3X1	T44.3X2	T44.3X3	T44.3X4	T44.3X5	T44.3X6
iodide	T44.3X1	T44.3X2	T44.3X3	T44.3X4	T44.3X5	T44.3X6
Isopropanol	T51.2X1	T51.2X2	T51.2X3	T51.2X4	—	—
Isopropyl						
acetate	T52.8X1	T52.8X2	T52.8X3	T52.8X4	—	—
alcohol	T51.2X1	T51.2X2	T51.2X3	T51.2X4	—	—
medicinal	T49.4X1	T49.4X2	T49.4X3	T49.4X4	T49.4X5	T49.4X6
ether	T52.8X1	T52.8X2	T52.8X3	T52.8X4	—	—
Isopropylaminophena-zone	T39.2X1	T39.2X2	T39.2X3	T39.2X4	T39.2X5	T39.2X6
Isoproterenol	T48.6X1	T48.6X2	T48.6X3	T48.6X4	T48.6X5	T48.6X6
Isosorbide dinitrate	T46.3X1	T46.3X2	T46.3X3	T46.3X4	T46.3X5	T46.3X6
Isothipendyl	T45.0X1	T45.0X2	T45.0X3	T45.0X4	T45.0X5	T45.0X6
Isotretinoin	T50.991	T50.992	T50.993	T50.994	T50.995	T50.996
Isoxazolyl penicillin	T36.0X1	T36.0X2	T36.0X3	T36.0X4	T36.0X5	T36.0X6
Isoxicam	T39.391	T39.392	T39.393	T39.394	T39.395	T39.396
Isoxsuprine	T46.7X1	T46.7X2	T46.7X3	T46.7X4	T46.7X5	T46.7X6
Ispagula	T47.4X1	T47.4X2	T47.4X3	T47.4X4	T47.4X5	T47.4X6
husk	T47.4X1	T47.4X2	T47.4X3	T47.4X4	T47.4X5	T47.4X6
Isradipine	T46.1X1	T46.1X2	T46.1X3	T46.1X4	T46.1X5	T46.1X6
I-thyroxine sodium	T38.1X1	T38.1X2	T38.1X3	T38.1X4	T38.1X5	T38.1X6
Itraconazole	T37.8X1	T37.8X2	T37.8X3	T37.8X4	T37.8X5	T37.8X6
Itramin tosilate	T46.3X1	T46.3X2	T46.3X3	T46.3X4	T46.3X5	T46.3X6
Ivermectin	T37.4X1	T37.4X2	T37.4X3	T37.4X4	T37.4X5	T37.4X6
Izoniazid	T37.1X1	T37.1X2	T37.1X3	T37.1X4	T37.1X5	T37.1X6
with thioacetazone	T37.1X1	T37.1X2	T37.1X3	T37.1X4	T37.1X5	T37.1X6
J						
Jalap	T47.2X1	T47.2X2	T47.2X3	T47.2X4	T47.2X5	T47.2X6
Jamaica						
dogwood (bark)	T39.8X1	T39.8X2	T39.8X3	T39.8X4	T39.8X5	T39.8X6
ginger	T65.891	T65.892	T65.893	T65.894	—	—
root	T62.2X1	T62.2X2	T62.2X3	T62.2X4	—	—
Jatropha	T62.2X1	T62.2X2	T62.2X3	T62.2X4	—	—
curcas	T62.2X1	T62.2X2	T62.2X3	T62.2X4	—	—
Jectofer	T45.4X1	T45.4X2	T45.4X3	T45.4X4	T45.4X5	T45.4X6
Jellyfish (sting)	T63.621	T63.622	T63.623	T63.624	—	—
Jequirity (bean)	T62.2X1	T62.2X2	T62.2X3	T62.2X4	—	—
Jimson weed (stramonium)	T62.2X1	T62.2X2	T62.2X3	T62.2X4	—	—
seeds	T62.2X1	T62.2X2	T62.2X3	T62.2X4	—	—
Josamycin	T36.3X1	T36.3X2	T36.3X3	T36.3X4	T36.3X5	T36.3X6
Juniper tar	T49.1X1	T49.1X2	T49.1X3	T49.1X4	T49.1X5	T49.1X6

Substance	External Cause (T-Code)					
	Poisoning, Accidental (Unintentional)	Poisoning, Intentional Self-Harm	Poisoning, Assault	Poisoning, Undetermined	Adverse Effect	Underdosing
K						
Kallidinogenase	T46.7X1	T46.7X2	T46.7X3	T46.7X4	T46.7X5	T46.7X6
Kallikrein	T46.7X1	T46.7X2	T46.7X3	T46.7X4	T46.7X5	T46.7X6
Kanamycin	T36.5X1	T36.5X2	T36.5X3	T36.5X4	T36.5X5	T36.5X6
Kantrex	T36.5X1	T36.5X2	T36.5X3	T36.5X4	T36.5X5	T36.5X6
Kaolin	T47.6X1	T47.6X2	T47.6X3	T47.6X4	T47.6X5	T47.6X6
light	T47.6X1	T47.6X2	T47.6X3	T47.6X4	T47.6X5	T47.6X6
Karaya (gum)	T47.4X1	T47.4X2	T47.4X3	T47.4X4	T47.4X5	T47.4X6
Kebuzone	T39.2X1	T39.2X2	T39.2X3	T39.2X4	T39.2X5	T39.2X6
Kelevan	T60.1X1	T60.1X2	T60.1X3	T60.1X4	—	—
Kemithal	T41.1X1	T41.1X2	T41.1X3	T41.1X4	T41.1X5	T41.1X6
Kenacort	T38.0X1	T38.0X2	T38.0X3	T38.0X4	T38.0X5	T38.0X6
Keratolytic drug NEC	T49.4X1	T49.4X2	T49.4X3	T49.4X4	T49.4X5	T49.4X6
anthracene	T49.4X1	T49.4X2	T49.4X3	T49.4X4	T49.4X5	T49.4X6
Keratoplastic NEC	T49.4X1	T49.4X2	T49.4X3	T49.4X4	T49.4X5	T49.4X6
Kerosene, kerosine (fuel) (solvent) NEC	T52.0X1	T52.0X2	T52.0X3	T52.0X4	—	—
insecticide	T52.0X1	T52.0X2	T52.0X3	T52.0X4	—	—
vapor	T52.0X1	T52.0X2	T52.0X3	T52.0X4	—	—
Ketamine	T41.291	T41.292	T41.293	T41.294	T41.295	T41.296
Ketazolam	T42.4X1	T42.4X2	T42.4X3	T42.4X4	T42.4X5	T42.4X6
Ketazon	T39.2X1	T39.2X2	T39.2X3	T39.2X4	T39.2X5	T39.2X6
Ketobemidone	T40.4X1	T40.4X2	T40.4X3	T40.4X4	—	—
Ketoconazole	T49.0X1	T49.0X2	T49.0X3	T49.0X4	T49.0X5	T49.0X6
Ketols	T52.4X1	T52.4X2	T52.4X3	T52.4X4	—	—
Ketone oils	T52.4X1	T52.4X2	T52.4X3	T52.4X4	—	—
Ketoprofen	T39.311	T39.312	T39.313	T39.314	T39.315	T39.316
Ketorolac	T39.8X1	T39.8X2	T39.8X3	T39.8X4	T39.8X5	T39.8X6
Ketotifen	T45.0X1	T45.0X2	T45.0X3	T45.0X4	T45.0X5	T45.0X6
Khat	T43.691	T43.692	T43.693	T43.694	—	—
Khellin	T46.3X1	T46.3X2	T46.3X3	T46.3X4	T46.3X5	T46.3X6
Khelloside	T46.3X1	T46.3X2	T46.3X3	T46.3X4	T46.3X5	T46.3X6
Kiln gas or vapor (carbon monoxide)	T58.8X1	T58.8X2	T58.8X3	T58.8X4	—	—
Kitasamycin	T36.3X1	T36.3X2	T36.3X3	T36.3X4	T36.3X5	T36.3X6
Konsyl	T47.4X1	T47.4X2	T47.4X3	T47.4X4	T47.4X5	T47.4X6
Kosam seed	T62.2X1	T62.2X2	T62.2X3	T62.2X4	—	—
Krait (venom)	T63.091	T63.092	T63.093	T63.094	—	—
Kwell (insecticide)	T60.1X1	T60.1X2	T60.1X3	T60.1X4	—	—
anti-infective (topical)	T49.0X1	T49.0X2	T49.0X3	T49.0X4	T49.0X5	T49.0X6

◀ New ◀◀ Revised ~~deleted~~ Deleted

Substance	External Cause (T-Code)					
	Poisoning, Accidental (Unintentional)	Poisoning, Intentional Self-Harm	Poisoning, Assault	Poisoning, Undetermined	Adverse Effect	Underdosing
L						
Labetalol	T44.8X1	T44.8X2	T44.8X3	T44.8X4	T44.8X5	T44.8X6
Laburnum (seeds)	T62.2X1	T62.2X2	T62.2X3	T62.2X4	—	—
leaves	T62.2X1	T62.2X2	T62.2X3	T62.2X4	—	—
Lachesine	T49.5X1	T49.5X2	T49.5X3	T49.5X4	T49.5X5	T49.5X6
Lacidipine	T46.5X1	T46.5X2	T46.5X3	T46.5X4	T46.5X5	T46.5X6
Lacquer	T65.6X1	T65.6X2	T65.6X3	T65.6X4	—	—
Lacrimogenic gas	T59.3X1	T59.3X2	T59.3X3	T59.3X4		
Lactated potassic saline	T50.3X1	T50.3X2	T50.3X3	T50.3X4	T50.3X5	T50.3X6
Lactic acid	T49.8X1	T49.8X2	T49.8X3	T49.8X4	T49.8X5	T49.8X6
Lactobacillus						
acidophilus	T47.6X1	T47.6X2	T47.6X3	T47.6X4	T47.6X5	T47.6X6
compound	T47.6X1	T47.6X2	T47.6X3	T47.6X4	T47.6X5	T47.6X6
bifidus, lyophilized	T47.6X1	T47.6X2	T47.6X3	T47.6X4	T47.6X5	T47.6X6
bulgaricus	T47.6X1	T47.6X2	T47.6X3	T47.6X4	T47.6X5	T47.6X6
sporogenes	T47.6X1	T47.6X2	T47.6X3	T47.6X4	T47.6X5	T47.6X6
Lactoflavin	T45.2X1	T45.2X2	T45.2X3	T45.2X4	T45.2X5	T45.2X6
Lactose (as excipient)	T50.901	T50.902	T50.903	T50.904	T50.905	T50.906
Lactuca (virosa) (extract)	T42.6X1	T42.6X2	T42.6X3	T42.6X4	T42.6X5	T42.6X6
Lactucarium	T42.6X1	T42.6X2	T42.6X3	T42.6X4	T42.6X5	T42.6X6
Lactulose	T47.3X1	T47.3X2	T47.3X3	T47.3X4	T47.3X5	T47.3X6
Laevo—see Levo-						
Lanatosides	T46.0X1	T46.0X2	T46.0X3	T46.0X4	T46.0X5	T46.0X6
Lanolin	T49.3X1	T49.3X2	T49.3X3	T49.3X4	T49.3X5	T49.3X6
Largactil	T43.3X1	T43.3X2	T43.3X3	T43.3X4	T43.3X5	T43.3X6
Larkspur	T62.2X1	T62.2X2	T62.2X3	T62.2X4	—	—
Laroxyl	T43.011	T43.012	T43.013	T43.014	T43.015	T43.016
Lassar's paste	T49.4X1	T49.4X2	T49.4X3	T49.4X4	T49.4X5	T49.4X6
Lasix	T50.1X1	T50.1X2	T50.1X3	T50.1X4	T50.1X5	T50.1X6
Latamoxef	T36.1X1	T36.1X2	T36.1X3	T36.1X4	T36.1X5	T36.1X6
Latex	T65.811	T65.812	T65.813	T65.814	—	—
Lathyrus (seed)	T62.2X1	T62.2X2	T62.2X3	T62.2X4	—	—
Laudanum	T40.0X1	T40.0X2	T40.0X3	T40.0X4	T40.0X5	T40.0X6
Laudexium	T48.1X1	T48.1X2	T48.1X3	T48.1X4	T48.1X5	T48.1X6
Laughing gas	T41.0X1	T41.0X2	T41.0X3	T41.0X4	T41.0X5	T41.0X6
Laurel, black or cherry	T62.2X1	T62.2X2	T62.2X3	T62.2X4	—	—
Laurolinium	T49.0X1	T49.0X2	T49.0X3	T49.0X4	T49.0X5	T49.0X6
Lauryl sulfoacetate	T49.2X1	T49.2X2	T49.2X3	T49.2X4	T49.2X5	T49.2X6

Substance	External Cause (T-Code)					
	Poisoning, Accidental (Unintentional)	Poisoning, Intentional Self-Harm	Poisoning, Assault	Poisoning, Undetermined	Adverse Effect	Underdosing
Laxative NEC	T47.4X1	T47.4X2	T47.4X3	T47.4X4	T47.4X5	T47.4X6
osmotic	T47.3X1	T47.3X2	T47.3X3	T47.3X4	T47.3X5	T47.3X6
saline	T47.3X1	T47.3X2	T47.3X3	T47.3X4	T47.3X5	T47.3X6
stimulant	T47.2X1	T47.2X2	T47.2X3	T47.2X4	T47.2X5	T47.2X6
L-dopa	T42.8X1	T42.8X2	T42.8X3	T42.8X4	T42.8X5	T42.8X6
Lead (dust) (fumes) (vapor) NEC	T56.0X1	T56.0X2	T56.0X3	T56.0X4	—	—
acetate	T49.2X1	T49.2X2	T49.2X3	T49.2X4	T49.2X5	T49.2X6
alkyl (fuel additive)	T56.0X1	T56.0X2	T56.0X3	T56.0X4		
anti-infectives	T37.8X1	T37.8X2	T37.8X3	T37.8X4	T37.8X5	T37.8X6
antiknock compound (tetraethyl)	T56.0X1	T56.0X2	T56.0X3	T56.0X4	—	—
arsenate, arsenite (dust) (herbicide) (insecticide) (vapor)	T57.0X1	T57.0X2	T57.0X3	T57.0X4	—	—
carbonate	T56.0X1	T56.0X2	T56.0X3	T56.0X4		
paint	T56.0X1	T56.0X2	T56.0X3	T56.0X4	—	—
chromate	T56.0X1	T56.0X2	T56.0X3	T56.0X4		
paint	T56.0X1	T56.0X2	T56.0X3	T56.0X4		
dioxide	T56.0X1	T56.0X2	T56.0X3	T56.0X4	—	—
inorganic	T56.0X1	T56.0X2	T56.0X3	T56.0X4		
iodide	T56.0X1	T56.0X2	T56.0X3	T56.0X4		
pigment (paint)	T56.0X1	T56.0X2	T56.0X3	T56.0X4		
monoxide (dust)	T56.0X1	T56.0X2	T56.0X3	T56.0X4		
paint	T56.0X1	T56.0X2	T56.0X3	T56.0X4		
organic	T56.0X1	T56.0X2	T56.0X3	T56.0X4		
oxide	T56.0X1	T56.0X2	T56.0X3	T56.0X4	—	—
paint	T56.0X1	T56.0X2	T56.0X3	T56.0X4		
paint	T56.0X1	T56.0X2	T56.0X3	T56.0X4	—	—
salts	T56.0X1	T56.0X2	T56.0X3	T56.0X4		
specified compound NEC	T56.0X1	T56.0X2	T56.0X3	T56.0X4		
tetra-ethyl	T56.0X1	T56.0X2	T56.0X3	T56.0X4	—	—
Lebanese red	T40.7X1	T40.7X2	T40.7X3	T40.7X4	T40.7X5	T40.7X6
Lefetamine	T39.8X1	T39.8X2	T39.8X3	T39.8X4	T39.8X5	T39.8X6
Lenperone	T43.4X1	T43.4X2	T43.4X3	T43.4X4	T43.4X5	T43.4X6
Lente lietin (insulin)	T38.3X1	T38.3X2	T38.3X3	T38.3X4	T38.3X5	T38.3X6
Leptazol	T50.7X1	T50.7X2	T50.7X3	T50.7X4	T50.7X5	T50.7X6
Leptophos	T60.0X1	T60.0X2	T60.0X3	T60.0X4	—	—
Leritine	T40.2X1	T40.2X2	T40.2X3	T40.2X4	T40.2X5	T40.2X6
Letosteine	T48.4X1	T48.4X2	T48.4X3	T48.4X4	T48.4X5	T48.4X6
Letter	T38.1X1	T38.1X2	T38.1X3	T38.1X4	T38.1X5	T38.1X6
Lettuce opium	T42.6X1	T42.6X2	T42.6X3	T42.6X4	T42.6X5	T42.6X6
Leucinocaine	T41.3X1	T41.3X2	T41.3X3	T41.3X4	T41.3X5	T41.3X6

TABLE OF DRUGS AND CHEMICALS

Substance	Poisoning, Accidental (Unintentional)	Poisoning, Intentional Self-Harm	Poisoning, Assault	Poisoning, Undetermined	Adverse Effect	Underdosing
Leucocianidol	T46.991	T46.992	T46.993	T46.994	T46.995	T46.996
Leucovorin (factor)	T45.8X1	T45.8X2	T45.8X3	T45.8X4	T45.8X5	T45.8X6
Leukeran	T45.1X1	T45.1X2	T45.1X3	T45.1X4	T45.1X5	T45.1X6
Leuprolide	T38.891	T38.892	T38.893	T38.894	T38.895	T38.896
Levalbuterol	T48.6X1	T48.6X2	T48.6X3	T48.6X4	T48.6X5	T48.6X6
Levallorphan	T50.7X1	T50.7X2	T50.7X3	T50.7X4	T50.7X5	T50.7X6
Levamisole	T37.4X1	T37.4X2	T37.4X3	T37.4X4	T37.4X5	T37.4X6
Levanil	T42.6X1	T42.6X2	T42.6X3	T42.6X4	T42.6X5	T42.6X6
Levarterenol	T44.4X1	T44.4X2	T44.4X3	T44.4X4	T44.4X5	T44.4X6
Levdropropizine	T48.3X1	T48.3X2	T48.3X3	T48.3X4	T48.3X5	T48.3X6
Levobunolol	T49.5X1	T49.5X2	T49.5X3	T49.5X4	T49.5X5	T49.5X6
Levocabastine (hydrochloride)	T45.0X1	T45.0X2	T45.0X3	T45.0X4	T45.0X5	T45.0X6
Levocarnitine	T50.991	T50.992	T50.993	T50.994	T50.995	T50.996
Levodopa	T42.8X1	T42.8X2	T42.8X3	T42.8X4	T42.8X5	T42.8X6
with carbidopa	T42.8X1	T42.8X2	T42.8X3	T42.8X4	T42.8X5	T42.8X6
Levo-dromoran	T40.2X1	T40.2X2	T40.2X3	T40.2X4	T40.2X5	T40.2X6
Levoglutamide	T50.991	T50.992	T50.993	T50.994	T50.995	T50.996
Levoid	T38.1X1	T38.1X2	T38.1X3	T38.1X4	T38.1X5	T38.1X6
Levo-iso-methadone	T40.3X1	T40.3X2	T40.3X3	T40.3X4	T40.3X5	T40.3X6
Levomepromazine	T43.3X1	T43.3X2	T43.3X3	T43.3X4	T43.3X5	T43.3X6
Levonordefrin	T49.6X1	T49.6X2	T49.6X3	T49.6X4	T49.6X5	T49.6X6
Levonorgestrel	T38.4X1	T38.4X2	T38.4X3	T38.4X4	T38.4X5	T38.4X6
with ethinylestradiol	T38.5X1	T38.5X2	T38.5X3	T38.5X4	T38.5X5	T38.5X6
Levopromazine	T43.3X1	T43.3X2	T43.3X3	T43.3X4	T43.3X5	T43.3X6
Levoprome	T42.6X1	T42.6X2	T42.6X3	T42.6X4	T42.6X5	T42.6X6
Levopropoxyphene	T40.4X1	T40.4X2	T40.4X3	T40.4X4	T40.4X5	T40.4X6
Levopropylhexedrine	T50.5X1	T50.5X2	T50.5X3	T50.5X4	T50.5X5	T50.5X6
Levoproxyphylline	T48.6X1	T48.6X2	T48.6X3	T48.6X4	T48.6X5	T48.6X6
Levorphanol	T40.4X1	T40.4X2	T40.4X3	T40.4X4	T40.4X5	T40.4X6
Levothyroxine	T38.1X1	T38.1X2	T38.1X3	T38.1X4	T38.1X5	T38.1X6
sodium	T38.1X1	T38.1X2	T38.1X3	T38.1X4	T38.1X5	T38.1X6
Levsin	T44.3X1	T44.3X2	T44.3X3	T44.3X4	T44.3X5	T44.3X6
Levulose	T50.3X1	T50.3X2	T50.3X3	T50.3X4	T50.3X5	T50.3X6
Lewisite (gas), not in war	T57.0X1	T57.0X2	T57.0X3	T57.0X4	—	—
Librium	T42.4X1	T42.4X2	T42.4X3	T42.4X4	T42.4X5	T42.4X6
Lidex	T49.0X1	T49.0X2	T49.0X3	T49.0X4	T49.0X5	T49.0X6
Lidocaine	T41.3X1	T41.3X2	T41.3X3	T41.3X4	T41.3X5	T41.3X6
regional	T41.3X1	T41.3X2	T41.3X3	T41.3X4	T41.3X5	T41.3X6
spinal	T41.3X1	T41.3X2	T41.3X3	T41.3X4	T41.3X5	T41.3X6
Lidofenin	T50.8X1	T50.8X2	T50.8X3	T50.8X4	T50.8X5	T50.8X6
Lidoflazine	T46.1X1	T46.1X2	T46.1X3	T46.1X4	T46.1X5	T46.1X6
Lighter fluid	T52.0X1	T52.0X2	T52.0X3	T52.0X4	—	—

Substance	Poisoning, Accidental (Unintentional)	Poisoning, Intentional Self-Harm	Poisoning, Assault	Poisoning, Undetermined	Adverse Effect	Underdosing
Lignin hemicellulose	T47.6X1	T47.6X2	T47.6X3	T47.6X4	T47.6X5	T47.6X6
Lignocaine	T41.3X1	T41.3X2	T41.3X3	T41.3X4	T41.3X5	T41.3X6
regional	T41.3X1	T41.3X2	T41.3X3	T41.3X4	T41.3X5	T41.3X6
spinal	T41.3X1	T41.3X2	T41.3X3	T41.3X4	T41.3X5	T41.3X6
Ligroin(e) (solvent)	T52.0X1	T52.0X2	T52.0X3	T52.0X4	—	—
vapor	T59.891	T59.892	T59.893	T59.894	—	—
Ligustrum vulgare	T62.2X1	T62.2X2	T62.2X3	T62.2X4	—	—
Lily of the valley	T62.2X1	T62.2X2	T62.2X3	T62.2X4	—	—
Lime (chloride)	T54.3X1	T54.3X2	T54.3X3	T54.3X4	—	—
Limonene	T52.8X1	T52.8X2	T52.8X3	T52.8X4	—	—
Lincomycin	T36.8X1	T36.8X2	T36.8X3	T36.8X4	T36.8X5	T36.8X6
Lindane (insecticide) (nonmedicinal) (vapor)	T53.6X1	T53.6X2	T53.6X3	T53.6X4	—	—
medicinal	T49.0X1	T49.0X2	T49.0X3	T49.0X4	T49.0X5	T49.0X6
Liniments NEC	T49.91	T49.92	T49.93	T49.94	T49.95	T49.96
Linoleic acid	T46.6X1	T46.6X2	T46.6X3	T46.6X4	T46.6X5	T46.6X6
Linolenic acid	T46.6X1	T46.6X2	T46.6X3	T46.6X4	T46.6X5	T46.6X6
Linseed	T47.4X1	T47.4X2	T47.4X3	T47.4X4	T47.4X5	T47.4X6
Liothyronine	T38.1X1	T38.1X2	T38.1X3	T38.1X4	T38.1X5	T38.1X6
Liotrix	T38.1X1	T38.1X2	T38.1X3	T38.1X4	T38.1X5	T38.1X6
Lipancreatin	T47.5X1	T47.5X2	T47.5X3	T47.5X4	T47.5X5	T47.5X6
Lipo-alprostadil	T46.7X1	T46.7X2	T46.7X3	T46.7X4	T46.7X5	T46.7X6
Lipo-Lutin	T38.5X1	T38.5X2	T38.5X3	T38.5X4	T38.5X5	T38.5X6
Lipotropic drug NEC	T50.901	T50.902	T50.903	T50.904	T50.905	T50.906
Liquefied petroleum gases	T59.891	T59.892	T59.893	T59.894	—	—
piped (pure or mixed with air)	T59.891	T59.892	T59.893	T59.894	—	—
Liquid						
paraffin	T47.4X1	T47.4X2	T47.4X3	T47.4X4	T47.4X5	T47.4X6
petrolatum	T47.4X1	T47.4X2	T47.4X3	T47.4X4	T47.4X5	T47.4X6
topical	T49.3X1	T49.3X2	T49.3X3	T49.3X4	T49.3X5	T49.3X6
specified NEC	T65.891	T65.892	T65.893	T65.894	—	—
substance	T65.91	T65.92	T65.93	T65.94	—	—
Liquor creosolis compositus	T65.891	T65.892	T65.893	T65.894	—	—
Liquorice	T48.4X1	T48.4X2	T48.4X3	T48.4X4	T48.4X5	T48.4X6
extract	T47.8X1	T47.8X2	T47.8X3	T47.8X4	T47.8X5	T47.8X6
Lirugen	T50.991	T50.992	T50.993	T50.994	T50.995	T50.996
Lisinopril	T46.4X1	T46.4X2	T46.4X3	T46.4X4	T46.4X5	T46.4X6
Lisuride	T42.8X1	T42.8X2	T42.8X3	T42.8X4	T42.8X5	T42.8X6
Lithane	T43.8X1	T43.8X2	T43.8X3	T43.8X4	T43.8X5	T43.8X6
Lithium	T56.891	T56.892	T56.893	T56.894	—	—
gluconate	T43.591	T43.592	T43.593	T43.594	T43.595	T43.596
salts (carbonate)	T43.591	T43.592	T43.593	T43.594	T43.595	T43.596

◀ New ◀ Revised ~~deleted~~ Deleted

Substance	External Cause (T-Code)					
	Poisoning, Accidental (Unintentional)	Poisoning, Intentional Self-Harm	Poisoning, Assault	Poisoning, Undetermined	Adverse Effect	Underdosing
Lithonate	T43.8X1	T43.8X2	T43.8X3	T43.8X4	T43.8X5	T43.8X6
Liver						
extract	T45.8X1	T45.8X2	T45.8X3	T45.8X4	T45.8X5	T45.8X6
for parenteral use	T45.8X1	T45.8X2	T45.8X3	T45.8X4	T45.8X5	T45.8X6
fraction 1	T45.8X1	T45.8X2	T45.8X3	T45.8X4	T45.8X5	T45.8X6
hydrolysate	T45.8X1	T45.8X2	T45.8X3	T45.8X4	T45.8X5	T45.8X6
Lizard (bite) (venom)	T63.121	T63.122	T63.123	T63.124	—	—
LMD	T45.8X1	T45.8X2	T45.8X3	T45.8X4	T45.8X5	T45.8X6
Lobelia	T62.2X1	T62.2X2	T62.2X3	T62.2X4	—	—
Lobeline	T50.7X1	T50.7X2	T50.7X3	T50.7X4	T50.7X5	T50.7X6
Local action drug NEC	T49.8X1	T49.8X2	T49.8X3	T49.8X4	T49.8X5	T49.8X6
Locorten	T49.0X1	T49.0X2	T49.0X3	T49.0X4	T49.0X5	T49.0X6
Lofepramine	T43.011	T43.012	T43.013	T43.014	T43.015	T43.016
Lolium temulentum	T62.2X1	T62.2X2	T62.2X3	T62.2X4	—	—
Lomotil	T47.6X1	T47.6X2	T47.6X3	T47.6X4	T47.6X5	T47.6X6
Lomustine	T45.1X1	T45.1X2	T45.1X3	T45.1X4	T45.1X5	T45.1X6
Lonidamine	T45.1X1	T45.1X2	T45.1X3	T45.1X4	T45.1X5	T45.1X6
Loperamide	T47.6X1	T47.6X2	T47.6X3	T47.6X4	T47.6X5	T47.6X6
Loprazolam	T42.4X1	T42.4X2	T42.4X3	T42.4X4	T42.4X5	T42.4X6
Lorajmine	T46.2X1	T46.2X2	T46.2X3	T46.2X4	T46.2X5	T46.2X6
Loratidine	T45.0X1	T45.0X2	T45.0X3	T45.0X4	T45.0X5	T45.0X6
Lorazepam	T42.4X1	T42.4X2	T42.4X3	T42.4X4	T42.4X5	T42.4X6
Lorcainide	T46.2X1	T46.2X2	T46.2X3	T46.2X4	T46.2X5	T46.2X6
Lormetazepam	T42.4X1	T42.4X2	T42.4X3	T42.4X4	T42.4X5	T42.4X6
Lotions NEC	T49.91	T49.92	T49.93	T49.94	T49.95	T49.96
Lotusate	T42.3X1	T42.3X2	T42.3X3	T42.3X4	T42.3X5	T42.3X6
Lovastatin	T46.6X1	T46.6X2	T46.6X3	T46.6X4	T46.6X5	T46.6X6
Loxapine	T43.591	T43.592	T43.593	T43.594	T43.595	T43.596
Lowila	T49.2X1	T49.2X2	T49.2X3	T49.2X4	T49.2X5	T49.2X6
Lozenges (throat)	T49.6X1	T49.6X2	T49.6X3	T49.6X4	T49.6X5	T49.6X6
LSD	T40.8X1	T40.8X2	T40.8X3	T40.8X4	—	—
L-Tryptophan — see amino acid						
Lubricant, eye	T49.5X1	T49.5X2	T49.5X3	T49.5X4	T49.5X5	T49.5X6
Lubricating oil NEC	T52.0X1	T52.0X2	T52.0X3	T52.0X4	—	—
Lucanthone	T37.4X1	T37.4X2	T37.4X3	T37.4X4	T37.4X5	T37.4X6
Luminal	T42.3X1	T42.3X2	T42.3X3	T42.3X4	T42.3X5	T42.3X6
Lung irritant (gas) NEC	T59.91	T59.92	T59.93	T59.94	—	—
Luteinizing hormone	T38.811	T38.812	T38.813	T38.814	T38.815	T38.816
Lutocylol	T38.5X1	T38.5X2	T38.5X3	T38.5X4	T38.5X5	T38.5X6
Lutromone	T38.5X1	T38.5X2	T38.5X3	T38.5X4	T38.5X5	T38.5X6
Lututrin	T48.291	T48.292	T48.293	T48.294	T48.295	T48.296
Lye (Concentrated)	T54.3X1	T54.3X2	T54.3X3	T54.3X4	—	—

Substance	External Cause (T-Code)					
	Poisoning, Accidental (Unintentional)	Poisoning, Intentional Self-Harm	Poisoning, Assault	Poisoning, Undetermined	Adverse Effect	Underdosing
Lygranum (skin test)	T50.8X1	T50.8X2	T50.8X3	T50.8X4	T50.8X5	T50.8X6
Lymecycline	T36.4X1	T36.4X2	T36.4X3	T36.4X4	T36.4X5	T36.4X6
Lymphogranuloma venereum antigen	T50.8X1	T50.8X2	T50.8X3	T50.8X4	T50.8X5	T50.8X6
Lynestrenol	T38.4X1	T38.4X2	T38.4X3	T38.4X4	T38.4X5	T38.4X6
Lypressin	T38.891	T38.892	T38.893	T38.894	T38.895	T38.896
Lyovac Sodium Edecrin	T50.1X1	T50.1X2	T50.1X3	T50.1X4	T50.1X5	T50.1X6
Lysergic acid diethylamide	T40.8X1	T40.8X2	T40.8X3	T40.8X4	—	—
Lysergide	T40.8X1	T40.8X2	T40.8X3	T40.8X4	—	—
Lysine vasopressin	T38.891	T38.892	T38.893	T38.894	T38.895	T38.896
Lysol	T54.1X1	T54.1X2	T54.1X3	T54.1X4	—	—
Lysozyme	T49.0X1	T49.0X2	T49.0X3	T49.0X4	T49.0X5	T49.0X6
Lytta (vitatta)	T49.8X1	T49.8X2	T49.8X3	T49.8X4	T49.8X5	T49.8X6
M						
Mace	T59.3X1	T59.3X2	T59.3X3	T59.3X4	—	—
Macrogol	T50.991	T50.992	T50.993	T50.994	T50.995	T50.996
Macrolide						
anabolic drug	T38.7X1	T38.7X2	T38.7X3	T38.7X4	T38.7X5	T38.7X6
antibiotic	T36.3X1	T36.3X2	T36.3X3	T36.3X4	T36.3X5	T36.3X6
Mafenide	T49.0X1	T49.0X2	T49.0X3	T49.0X4	T49.0X5	T49.0X6
Magaldrate	T47.1X1	T47.1X2	T47.1X3	T47.1X4	T47.1X5	T47.1X6
Magic mushroom	T40.991	T40.992	T40.993	T40.994	—	—
Magnamycin	T36.8X1	T36.8X2	T36.8X3	T36.8X4	T36.8X5	T36.8X6
Magnesia magma	T47.1X1	T47.1X2	T47.1X3	T47.1X4	T47.1X5	T47.1X6
Magnesium NEC	T56.891	T56.892	T56.893	T56.894	—	—
carbonate	T47.1X1	T47.1X2	T47.1X3	T47.1X4	T47.1X5	T47.1X6
citrate	T47.4X1	T47.4X2	T47.4X3	T47.4X4	T47.4X5	T47.4X6
hydroxide	T47.1X1	T47.1X2	T47.1X3	T47.1X4	T47.1X5	T47.1X6
oxide	T47.1X1	T47.1X2	T47.1X3	T47.1X4	T47.1X5	T47.1X6
peroxide	T49.0X1	T49.0X2	T49.0X3	T49.0X4	T49.0X5	T49.0X6
salicylate	T39.091	T39.092	T39.093	T39.094	T39.095	T39.096
silicofluoride	T50.3X1	T50.3X2	T50.3X3	T50.3X4	T50.3X5	T50.3X6
sulfate	T47.4X1	T47.4X2	T47.4X3	T47.4X4	T47.4X5	T47.4X6
thiosulfate	T45.0X1	T45.0X2	T45.0X3	T45.0X4	T45.0X5	T45.0X6
trisilicate	T47.1X1	T47.1X2	T47.1X3	T47.1X4	T47.1X5	T47.1X6
Malathion (medicinal)	T49.0X1	T49.0X2	T49.0X3	T49.0X4	T49.0X5	T49.0X6
insecticide	T60.0X1	T60.0X2	T60.0X3	T60.0X4	—	—
Male fern extract	T37.4X1	T37.4X2	T37.4X3	T37.4X4	T37.4X5	T37.4X6
M-AMSA	T45.1X1	T45.1X2	T45.1X3	T45.1X4	T45.1X5	T45.1X6
Mandelic acid	T37.8X1	T37.8X2	T37.8X3	T37.8X4	T37.8X5	T37.8X6
Manganese (dioxide) (salts)	T57.2X1	T57.2X2	T57.2X3	T57.2X4	—	—
medicinal	T50.991	T50.992	T50.993	T50.994	T50.995	T50.996

TABLE OF DRUGS AND CHEMICALS

	External Cause (T-Code)					
Substance	Poisoning, Accidental (Unintentional)	Poisoning, Intentional Self-Harm	Poisoning, Assault	Poisoning, Undetermined	Adverse Effect	Underdosing
Mannitol	T47.3X1	T47.3X2	T47.3X3	T47.3X4	T47.3X5	T47.3X6
hexanitrate	T46.3X1	T46.3X2	T46.3X3	T46.3X4	T46.3X5	T46.3X6
Mannomustine	T45.1X1	T45.1X2	T45.1X3	T45.1X4	T45.1X5	T45.1X6
MAO inhibitors	T43.1X1	T43.1X2	T43.1X3	T43.1X4	T43.1X5	T43.1X6
Mapharsen	T37.8X1	T37.8X2	T37.8X3	T37.8X4	T37.8X5	T37.8X6
Maphenide	T49.0X1	T49.0X2	T49.0X3	T49.0X4	T49.0X5	T49.0X6
Maprotiline	T43.021	T43.022	T43.023	T43.024	T43.025	T43.026
Marcaine	T41.3X1	T41.3X2	T41.3X3	T41.3X4	T41.3X5	T41.3X6
infiltration (subcutaneous)	T41.3X1	T41.3X2	T41.3X3	T41.3X4	T41.3X5	T41.3X6
nerve block (peripheral) (plexus)	T41.3X1	T41.3X2	T41.3X3	T41.3X4	T41.3X5	T41.3X6
Marezine	T45.0X1	T45.0X2	T45.0X3	T45.0X4	T45.0X5	T45.0X6
Marihuana	T40.7X1	T40.7X2	T40.7X3	T40.7X4	T40.7X5	T40.7X6
Marijuana	T40.7X1	T40.7X2	T40.7X3	T40.7X4	T40.7X5	T40.7X6
Marine (sting)	T63.691	T63.692	T63.693	T63.694	—	—
animals (sting)	T63.691	T63.692	T63.693	T63.694	—	—
plants (sting)	T63.711	T63.712	T63.713	T63.714	—	—
Marplan	T43.1X1	T43.1X2	T43.1X3	T43.1X4	T43.1X5	T43.1X6
Marsh gas	T59.891	T59.892	T59.893	T59.894	—	—
Marsilid	T43.1X1	T43.1X2	T43.1X3	T43.1X4	T43.1X5	T43.1X6
Matulane	T45.1X1	T45.1X2	T45.1X3	T45.1X4	T45.1X5	T45.1X6
Mazindol	T50.5X1	T50.5X2	T50.5X3	T50.5X4	T50.5X5	T50.5X6
MCPA	T60.3X1	T60.3X2	T60.3X3	T60.3X4		
MDMA	T43.641	T43.642	T43.643	T43.644	—	—
Meadow saffron	T62.2X1	T62.2X2	T62.2X3	T62.2X4	—	—
Measles virus vaccine (attenuated)	T50.B91	T50.B92	T50.B93	T50.B94	T50.B95	T50.B96
Meat, noxious	T62.8X1	T62.8X2	T62.8X3	T62.8X4		
Meballymal	T42.3X1	T42.3X2	T42.3X3	T42.3X4	T42.3X5	T42.3X6
Mebanazine	T43.1X1	T43.1X2	T43.1X3	T43.1X4	T43.1X5	T43.1X6
Mebaral	T42.3X1	T42.3X2	T42.3X3	T42.3X4	T42.3X5	T42.3X6
Mebendazole	T37.4X1	T37.4X2	T37.4X3	T37.4X4	T37.4X5	T37.4X6
Mebeverine	T44.3X1	T44.3X2	T44.3X3	T44.3X4	T44.3X5	T44.3X6
Mebhydrolin	T45.0X1	T45.0X2	T45.0X3	T45.0X4	T45.0X5	T45.0X6
Mebumal	T42.3X1	T42.3X2	T42.3X3	T42.3X4	T42.3X5	T42.3X6
Mebutamate	T43.591	T43.592	T43.593	T43.594	T43.595	T43.596
Mecamylamine	T44.2X1	T44.2X2	T44.2X3	T44.2X4	T44.2X5	T44.2X6
Mechlorethamine	T45.1X1	T45.1X2	T45.1X3	T45.1X4	T45.1X5	T45.1X6
Mecillinam	T36.0X1	T36.0X2	T36.0X3	T36.0X4	T36.0X5	T36.0X6
Meclizine (hydrochloride)	T45.0X1	T45.0X2	T45.0X3	T45.0X4	T45.0X5	T45.0X6
Meclocycline	T36.4X1	T36.4X2	T36.4X3	T36.4X4	T36.4X5	T36.4X6
Meclofenamate	T39.391	T39.392	T39.393	T39.394	T39.395	T39.396
Meclofenamic acid	T39.391	T39.392	T39.393	T39.394	T39.395	T39.396

	External Cause (T-Code)					
Substance	Poisoning, Accidental (Unintentional)	Poisoning, Intentional Self-Harm	Poisoning, Assault	Poisoning, Undetermined	Adverse Effect	Underdosing
Meclofenoxate	T43.691	T43.692	T43.693	T43.694	T43.695	T43.696
Meclozine	T45.0X1	T45.0X2	T45.0X3	T45.0X4	T45.0X5	T45.0X6
Mecobalamin	T45.8X1	T45.8X2	T45.8X3	T45.8X4	T45.8X5	T45.8X6
Mecoprop	T60.3X1	T60.3X2	T60.3X3	T60.3X4	—	—
Mecrilate	T49.3X1	T49.3X2	T49.3X3	T49.3X4	T49.3X5	T49.3X6
Mecysteine	T48.4X1	T48.4X2	T48.4X3	T48.4X4	T48.4X5	T48.4X6
Medazepam	T42.4X1	T42.4X2	T42.4X3	T42.4X4	T42.4X5	T42.4X6
Medicament NEC	T50.901	T50.902	T50.903	T50.904	T50.905	T50.906
Medinal	T42.3X1	T42.3X2	T42.3X3	T42.3X4	T42.3X5	T42.3X6
Medomin	T42.3X1	T42.3X2	T42.3X3	T42.3X4	T42.3X5	T42.3X6
Medrogestone	T38.5X1	T38.5X2	T38.5X3	T38.5X4	T38.5X5	T38.5X6
Medroxalol	T44.8X1	T44.8X2	T44.8X3	T44.8X4	T44.8X5	T44.8X6
Medroxyprogesterone acetate (depot)	T38.5X1	T38.5X2	T38.5X3	T38.5X4	T38.5X5	T38.5X6
Medrysone	T49.0X1	T49.0X2	T49.0X3	T49.0X4	T49.0X5	T49.0X6
Mefenamic acid	T39.391	T39.392	T39.393	T39.394	T39.395	T39.396
Mefenorex	T50.5X1	T50.5X2	T50.5X3	T50.5X4	T50.5X5	T50.5X6
Mefloquine	T37.2X1	T37.2X2	T37.2X3	T37.2X4	T37.2X5	T37.2X6
Mefruside	T50.2X1	T50.2X2	T50.2X3	T50.2X4	T50.2X5	T50.2X6
Megahallucinogen	T40.901	T40.902	T40.903	T40.904	T40.905	T40.906
Megestrol	T38.5X1	T38.5X2	T38.5X3	T38.5X4	T38.5X5	T38.5X6
Meglumine						
antimoniate	T37.8X1	T37.8X2	T37.8X3	T37.8X4	T37.8X5	T37.8X6
diatrizoate	T50.8X1	T50.8X2	T50.8X3	T50.8X4	T50.8X5	T50.8X6
iodipamide	T50.8X1	T50.8X2	T50.8X3	T50.8X4	T50.8X5	T50.8X6
iotroxate	T50.8X1	T50.8X2	T50.8X3	T50.8X4	T50.8X5	T50.8X6
MEK (methyl ethyl ketone)	T52.4X1	T52.4X2	T52.4X3	T52.4X4	—	—
Meladrazine	T44.3X1	T44.3X2	T44.3X3	T44.3X4	T44.3X5	T44.3X6
Meladinin	T49.3X1	T49.3X2	T49.3X3	T49.3X4	T49.3X5	T49.3X6
Melaleuca alternifolia oil	T49.0X1	T49.0X2	T49.0X3	T49.0X4	T49.0X5	T49.0X6
Melanizing agents	T49.3X1	T49.3X2	T49.3X3	T49.3X4	T49.3X5	T49.3X6
Melanocyte-stimulating hormone	T38.891	T38.892	T38.893	T38.894	T38.895	T38.896
Melarsonyl potassium	T37.3X1	T37.3X2	T37.3X3	T37.3X4	T37.3X5	T37.3X6
Melarsoprol	T37.3X1	T37.3X2	T37.3X3	T37.3X4	T37.3X5	T37.3X6
Melia azedarach	T62.2X1	T62.2X2	T62.2X3	T62.2X4	—	—
Melitracen	T43.011	T43.012	T43.013	T43.014	T43.015	T43.016
Mellaril	T43.3X1	T43.3X2	T43.3X3	T43.3X4	T43.3X5	T43.3X6
Meloxine	T49.3X1	T49.3X2	T49.3X3	T49.3X4	T49.3X5	T49.3X6
Melperone	T43.4X1	T43.4X2	T43.4X3	T43.4X4	T43.4X5	T43.4X6
Melphalan	T45.1X1	T45.1X2	T45.1X3	T45.1X4	T45.1X5	T45.1X6
Memantine	T43.8X1	T43.8X2	T43.8X3	T43.8X4	T43.8X5	T43.8X6

◄ New ◄ Revised ~~deleted~~ Deleted

Substance	Poisoning, Accidental (Unintentional)	Poisoning, Intentional Self-Harm	Poisoning, Assault	Poisoning, Undetermined	Adverse Effect	Underdosing
Menadiol	T45.7X1	T45.7X2	T45.7X3	T45.7X4	T45.7X5	T45.7X6
sodium sulfate	T45.7X1	T45.7X2	T45.7X3	T45.7X4	T45.7X5	T45.7X6
Menadione	T45.7X1	T45.7X2	T45.7X3	T45.7X4	T45.7X5	T45.7X6
sodium bisulfite	T45.7X1	T45.7X2	T45.7X3	T45.7X4	T45.7X5	T45.7X6
Menaphthone	T45.7X1	T45.7X2	T45.7X3	T45.7X4	T45.7X5	T45.7X6
Menaquinone	T45.7X1	T45.7X2	T45.7X3	T45.7X4	T45.7X5	T45.7X6
Menatetrenone	T45.7X1	T45.7X2	T45.7X3	T45.7X4	T45.7X5	T45.7X6
Meningococcal vaccine	T50.A91	T50.A92	T50.A93	T50.A94	T50.A95	T50.A96
Menningovax (-AC) (-C)	T50.A91	T50.A92	T50.A93	T50.A94	T50.A95	T50.A96
Menotropins	T38.811	T38.812	T38.813	T38.814	T38.815	T38.816
Menthol	T48.5X1	T48.5X2	T48.5X3	T48.5X4	T48.5X5	T48.5X6
Mepacrine	T37.2X1	T37.2X2	T37.2X3	T37.2X4	T37.2X5	T37.2X6
Meparfynol	T42.6X1	T42.6X2	T42.6X3	T42.6X4	T42.6X5	T42.6X6
Mepartricin	T36.7X1	T36.7X2	T36.7X3	T36.7X4	T36.7X5	T36.7X6
Mepazine	T43.3X1	T43.3X2	T43.3X3	T43.3X4	T43.3X5	T43.3X6
Mepenzolate	T44.3X1	T44.3X2	T44.3X3	T44.3X4	T44.3X5	T44.3X6
bromide	T44.3X1	T44.3X2	T44.3X3	T44.3X4	T44.3X5	T44.3X6
Meperidine	T40.4X1	T40.4X2	T40.4X3	T40.4X4	T40.4X5	T40.4X6
Mephebarbital	T42.3X1	T42.3X2	T42.3X3	T42.3X4	T42.3X5	T42.3X6
Mephenamin(e)	T42.8X1	T42.8X2	T42.8X3	T42.8X4	T42.8X5	T42.8X6
Mephenesin	T42.8X1	T42.8X2	T42.8X3	T42.8X4	T42.8X5	T42.8X6
Mephenhydramine	T45.0X1	T45.0X2	T45.0X3	T45.0X4	T45.0X5	T45.0X6
Mephenoxalone	T42.8X1	T42.8X2	T42.8X3	T42.8X4	T42.8X5	T42.8X6
Mephentermine	T44.991	T44.992	T44.993	T44.994	T44.995	T44.996
Mephenytoin	T42.0X1	T42.0X2	T42.0X3	T42.0X4	T42.0X5	T42.0X6
with phenobarbital	T42.3X1	T42.3X2	T42.3X3	T42.3X4	T42.3X5	T42.3X6
Mephobarbital	T42.3X1	T42.3X2	T42.3X3	T42.3X4	T42.3X5	T42.3X6
Mephosfolan	T60.0X1	T60.0X2	T60.0X3	T60.0X4	—	—
Mepindolol	T44.7X1	T44.7X2	T44.7X3	T44.7X4	T44.7X5	T44.7X6
Mepiperphenidol	T44.3X1	T44.3X2	T44.3X3	T44.3X4	T44.3X5	T44.3X6
Mepitiostane	T38.7X1	T38.7X2	T38.7X3	T38.7X4	T38.7X5	T38.7X6
Mepivacaine	T41.3X1	T41.3X2	T41.3X3	T41.3X4	T41.3X5	T41.3X6
epidural	T41.3X1	T41.3X2	T41.3X3	T41.3X4	T41.3X5	T41.3X6
Meprednisone	T38.0X1	T38.0X2	T38.0X3	T38.0X4	T38.0X5	T38.0X6
Meprobam	T43.591	T43.592	T43.593	T43.594	T43.595	T43.596
Meprobamate	T43.591	T43.592	T43.593	T43.594	T43.595	T43.596
Meproscillarin	T46.0X1	T46.0X2	T46.0X3	T46.0X4	T46.0X5	T46.0X6
Meprylcaine	T41.3X1	T41.3X2	T41.3X3	T41.3X4	T41.3X5	T41.3X6
Meptazinol	T39.8X1	T39.8X2	T39.8X3	T39.8X4	T39.8X5	T39.8X6
Mepyramine	T45.0X1	T45.0X2	T45.0X3	T45.0X4	T45.0X5	T45.0X6
Mequitazine	T43.3X1	T43.3X2	T43.3X3	T43.3X4	T43.3X5	T43.3X6
Meralluride	T50.2X1	T50.2X2	T50.2X3	T50.2X4	T50.2X5	T50.2X6

Substance	Poisoning, Accidental (Unintentional)	Poisoning, Intentional Self-Harm	Poisoning, Assault	Poisoning, Undetermined	Adverse Effect	Underdosing
Merbaphen	T50.2X1	T50.2X2	T50.2X3	T50.2X4	T50.2X5	T50.2X6
Merbromin	T49.0X1	T49.0X2	T49.0X3	T49.0X4	T49.0X5	T49.0X6
Mercaptobenzothiazole salts	T49.0X1	T49.0X2	T49.0X3	T49.0X4	T49.0X5	T49.0X6
Mercaptomerin	T50.2X1	T50.2X2	T50.2X3	T50.2X4	T50.2X5	T50.2X6
Mercaptopurine	T45.1X1	T45.1X2	T45.1X3	T45.1X4	T45.1X5	T45.1X6
Mercumatilin	T50.2X1	T50.2X2	T50.2X3	T50.2X4	T50.2X5	T50.2X6
Mercuramide	T50.2X1	T50.2X2	T50.2X3	T50.2X4	T50.2X5	T50.2X6
Mercurochrome	T49.0X1	T49.0X2	T49.0X3	T49.0X4	T49.0X5	T49.0X6
Mercurophylline	T50.2X1	T50.2X2	T50.2X3	T50.2X4	T50.2X5	T50.2X6
Mercury, mercurial, mercuric, mercurous (compounds) (cyanide) (fumes) (nonmedicinal) (vapor) NEC	T56.1X1	T56.1X2	T56.1X3	T56.1X4	—	—
ammoniated	T49.0X1	T49.0X2	T49.0X3	T49.0X4	T49.0X5	T49.0X6
anti-infective						
local	T49.0X1	T49.0X2	T49.0X3	T49.0X4	T49.0X5	T49.0X6
systemic	T37.8X1	T37.8X2	T37.8X3	T37.8X4	T37.8X5	T37.8X6
topical	T49.0X1	T49.0X2	T49.0X3	T49.0X4	T49.0X5	T49.0X6
chloride (ammoniated)	T49.0X1	T49.0X2	T49.0X3	T49.0X4	T49.0X5	T49.0X6
fungicide	T56.1X1	T56.1X2	T56.1X3	T56.1X4	—	—
diuretic NEC	T50.2X1	T50.2X2	T50.2X3	T50.2X4	T50.2X5	T50.2X6
fungicide	T56.1X1	T56.1X2	T56.1X3	T56.1X4	—	—
organic (fungicide)	T56.1X1	T56.1X2	T56.1X3	T56.1X4	—	—
oxide, yellow	T49.0X1	T49.0X2	T49.0X3	T49.0X4	T49.0X5	T49.0X6
Mersalyl	T50.2X1	T50.2X2	T50.2X3	T50.2X4	T50.2X5	T50.2X6
Merthiolate	T49.0X1	T49.0X2	T49.0X3	T49.0X4	T49.0X5	T49.0X6
ophthalmic preparation	T49.5X1	T49.5X2	T49.5X3	T49.5X4	T49.5X5	T49.5X6
Meruvax	T50.B91	T50.B92	T50.B93	T50.B94	T50.B95	T50.B96
Mesalazine	T47.8X1	T47.8X2	T47.8X3	T47.8X4	T47.8X5	T47.8X6
Mescal buttons	T40.991	T40.992	T40.993	T40.994	—	—
Mescaline	T40.991	T40.992	T40.993	T40.994	—	—
Mesna	T48.4X1	T48.4X2	T48.4X3	T48.4X4	T48.4X5	T48.4X6
Mesoglycan	T46.6X1	T46.6X2	T46.6X3	T46.6X4	T46.6X5	T46.6X6
Mesoridazine	T43.3X1	T43.3X2	T43.3X3	T43.3X4	T43.3X5	T43.3X6
Mestanolone	T38.7X1	T38.7X2	T38.7X3	T38.7X4	T38.7X5	T38.7X6
Mesterolone	T38.7X1	T38.7X2	T38.7X3	T38.7X4	T38.7X5	T38.7X6
Mestranol	T38.5X1	T38.5X2	T38.5X3	T38.5X4	T38.5X5	T38.5X6
Mesulergine	T42.8X1	T42.8X2	T42.8X3	T42.8X4	T42.8X5	T42.8X6
Mesulfen	T49.0X1	T49.0X2	T49.0X3	T49.0X4	T49.0X5	T49.0X6
Mesuximide	T42.2X1	T42.2X2	T42.2X3	T42.2X4	T42.2X5	T42.2X6
Metabutethamine	T41.3X1	T41.3X2	T41.3X3	T41.3X4	T41.3X5	T41.3X6
Metactesylacetate	T49.0X1	T49.0X2	T49.0X3	T49.0X4	T49.0X5	T49.0X6

TABLE OF DRUGS AND CHEMICALS

Substance	Poisoning, Accidental (Unintentional)	Poisoning, Intentional Self-Harm	Poisoning, Assault	Poisoning, Undetermined	Adverse Effect	Underdosing
Metacycline	T36.4X1	T36.4X2	T36.4X3	T36.4X4	T36.4X5	T36.4X6
Metaldehyde (snail killer) NEC	T60.8X1	T60.8X2	T60.8X3	T60.8X4	—	—
Metals (heavy) (nonmedicinal)	T56.91	T56.92	T56.93	T56.94	—	—
dust, fumes, or vapor NEC	T56.91	T56.92	T56.93	T56.94	—	—
light NEC	T56.91	T56.92	T56.93	T56.94	—	—
dust, fumes, or vapor NEC	T56.91	T56.92	T56.93	T56.94	—	—
specified NEC	T56.891	T56.892	T56.893	T56.894	—	—
thallium	T56.811	T56.812	T56.813	T56.814	—	—
Metamfetamine	T43.621	T43.622	T43.623	T43.624	T43.625	T43.626
Metamizole sodium	T39.2X1	T39.2X2	T39.2X3	T39.2X4	T39.2X5	T39.2X6
Metampicillin	T36.0X1	T36.0X2	T36.0X3	T36.0X4	T36.0X5	T36.0X6
Metamucil	T47.4X1	T47.4X2	T47.4X3	T47.4X4	T47.4X5	T47.4X6
Metaphen	T49.0X1	T49.0X2	T49.0X3	T49.0X4	T49.0X5	T49.0X6
Metandienone	T38.7X1	T38.7X2	T38.7X3	T38.7X4	T38.7X5	T38.7X6
Metandrostenolone	T38.7X1	T38.7X2	T38.7X3	T38.7X4	T38.7X5	T38.7X6
Metaphos	T60.0X1	T60.0X2	T60.0X3	T60.0X4	—	—
Metapramine	T43.011	T43.012	T43.013	T43.014	T43.015	T43.016
Metaproterenol	T48.291	T48.292	T48.293	T48.294	T48.295	T48.296
Metaraminol	T44.4X1	T44.4X2	T44.4X3	T44.4X4	T44.4X5	T44.4X6
Metaxalone	T42.8X1	T42.8X2	T42.8X3	T42.8X4	T42.8X5	T42.8X6
Metenolone	T38.7X1	T38.7X2	T38.7X3	T38.7X4	T38.7X5	T38.7X6
Metergoline	T42.8X1	T42.8X2	T42.8X3	T42.8X4	T42.8X5	T42.8X6
Metescufylline	T46.991	T46.992	T46.993	T46.994	T46.995	T46.996
Metetoin	T42.0X1	T42.0X2	T42.0X3	T42.0X4	T42.0X5	T42.0X6
Metformin	T38.3X1	T38.3X2	T38.3X3	T38.3X4	T38.3X5	T38.3X6
Methacholine	T44.1X1	T44.1X2	T44.1X3	T44.1X4	T44.1X5	T44.1X6
Methacycline	T36.4X1	T36.4X2	T36.4X3	T36.4X4	T36.4X5	T36.4X6
Methadone	T40.3X1	T40.3X2	T40.3X3	T40.3X4	T40.3X5	T40.3X6
Methallenestril	T38.5X1	T38.5X2	T38.5X3	T38.5X4	T38.5X5	T38.5X6
Methallenoestril	T38.5X1	T38.5X2	T38.5X3	T38.5X4	T38.5X5	T38.5X6
Methamphetamine	T43.621	T43.622	T43.623	T43.624	T43.625	T43.626
Methampyrone	T39.2X1	T39.2X2	T39.2X3	T39.2X4	T39.2X5	T39.2X6
Methandienone	T38.7X1	T38.7X2	T38.7X3	T38.7X4	T38.7X5	T38.7X6
Methandriol	T38.7X1	T38.7X2	T38.7X3	T38.7X4	T38.7X5	T38.7X6
Methandrostenolone	T38.7X1	T38.7X2	T38.7X3	T38.7X4	T38.7X5	T38.7X6
Methane	T59.891	T59.892	T59.893	T59.894	—	—
Methanethiol	T59.891	T59.892	T59.893	T59.894	—	—
Methaniazide	T37.1X1	T37.1X2	T37.1X3	T37.1X4	T37.1X5	T37.1X6
Methanol (vapor)	T51.1X1	T51.1X2	T51.1X3	T51.1X4	—	—
Methantheline	T44.3X1	T44.3X2	T44.3X3	T44.3X4	T44.3X5	T44.3X6
Methanthelinium bromide	T44.3X1	T44.3X2	T44.3X3	T44.3X4	T44.3X5	T44.3X6
Methaphenilene	T45.0X1	T45.0X2	T45.0X3	T45.0X4	T45.0X5	T45.0X6

Substance	Poisoning, Accidental (Unintentional)	Poisoning, Intentional Self-Harm	Poisoning, Assault	Poisoning, Undetermined	Adverse Effect	Underdosing
Methapyrilene	T45.0X1	T45.0X2	T45.0X3	T45.0X4	T45.0X5	T45.0X6
Methaqualone (compound)	T42.6X1	T42.6X2	T42.6X3	T42.6X4	T42.6X5	T42.6X6
Metharbital	T42.3X1	T42.3X2	T42.3X3	T42.3X4	T42.3X5	T42.3X6
Methazolamide	T50.2X1	T50.2X2	T50.2X3	T50.2X4	T50.2X5	T50.2X6
Methdilazine	T43.3X1	T43.3X2	T43.3X3	T43.3X4	T43.3X5	T43.3X6
Methedrine	T43.621	T43.622	T43.623	T43.624	T43.625	T43.626
Methenamine (mandelate)	T37.8X1	T37.8X2	T37.8X3	T37.8X4	T37.8X5	T37.8X6
Methenolone	T38.7X1	T38.7X2	T38.7X3	T38.7X4	T38.7X5	T38.7X6
Methergine	T48.0X1	T48.0X2	T48.0X3	T48.0X4	T48.0X5	T48.0X6
Methetoin	T42.0X1	T42.0X2	T42.0X3	T42.0X4	T42.0X5	T42.0X6
Methiacil	T38.2X1	T38.2X2	T38.2X3	T38.2X4	T38.2X5	T38.2X6
Methicillin	T36.0X1	T36.0X2	T36.0X3	T36.0X4	T36.0X5	T36.0X6
Methimazole	T38.2X1	T38.2X2	T38.2X3	T38.2X4	T38.2X5	T38.2X6
Methiodal sodium	T50.8X1	T50.8X2	T50.8X3	T50.8X4	T50.8X5	T50.8X6
Methionine	T50.991	T50.992	T50.993	T50.994	T50.995	T50.996
Methisazone	T37.5X1	T37.5X2	T37.5X3	T37.5X4	T37.5X5	T37.5X6
Methisoprinol	T37.5X1	T37.5X2	T37.5X3	T37.5X4	T37.5X5	T37.5X6
Methitural	T42.3X1	T42.3X2	T42.3X3	T42.3X4	T42.3X5	T42.3X6
Methixene	T44.3X1	T44.3X2	T44.3X3	T44.3X4	T44.3X5	T44.3X6
Methobarbital, methobarbitone	T42.3X1	T42.3X2	T42.3X3	T42.3X4	T42.3X5	T42.3X6
Methocarbamol	T42.8X1	T42.8X2	T42.8X3	T42.8X4	T42.8X5	T42.8X6
skeletal muscle relaxant	T48.1X1	T48.1X2	T48.1X3	T48.1X4	T48.1X5	T48.1X6
Methohexital	T41.1X1	T41.1X2	T41.1X3	T41.1X4	T41.1X5	T41.1X6
Methohexitone	T41.1X1	T41.1X2	T41.1X3	T41.1X4	T41.1X5	T41.1X6
Methoin	T42.0X1	T42.0X2	T42.0X3	T42.0X4	T42.0X5	T42.0X6
Methopholine	T39.8X1	T39.8X2	T39.8X3	T39.8X4	T39.8X5	T39.8X6
Methopromazine	T43.3X1	T43.3X2	T43.3X3	T43.3X4	T43.3X5	T43.3X6
Methorate	T48.3X1	T48.3X2	T48.3X3	T48.3X4	T48.3X5	T48.3X6
Methoserpidine	T46.5X1	T46.5X2	T46.5X3	T46.5X4	T46.5X5	T46.5X6
Methotrexate	T45.1X1	T45.1X2	T45.1X3	T45.1X4	T45.1X5	T45.1X6
Methotrimeprazine	T43.3X1	T43.3X2	T43.3X3	T43.3X4	T43.3X5	T43.3X6
Methoxa-Dome	T49.3X1	T49.3X2	T49.3X3	T49.3X4	T49.3X5	T49.3X6
Methoxamine	T44.4X1	T44.4X2	T44.4X3	T44.4X4	T44.4X5	T44.4X6
Methoxsalen	T50.991	T50.992	T50.993	T50.994	T50.995	T50.996
Methoxyaniline	T65.3X1	T65.3X2	T65.3X3	T65.3X4	—	—
Methoxybenzyl penicillin	T36.0X1	T36.0X2	T36.0X3	T36.0X4	T36.0X5	T36.0X6
Methoxychlor	T53.7X1	T53.7X2	T53.7X3	T53.7X4	—	—
Methoxy-DDT	T53.7X1	T53.7X2	T53.7X3	T53.7X4	—	—
2-Methoxyethanol	T52.3X1	T52.3X2	T52.3X3	T52.3X4	—	—
Methoxyflurane	T41.0X1	T41.0X2	T41.0X3	T41.0X4	T41.0X5	T41.0X6
Methoxyphenamine	T48.6X1	T48.6X2	T48.6X3	T48.6X4	T48.6X5	T48.6X6
Methoxypromazine	T43.3X1	T43.3X2	T43.3X3	T43.3X4	T43.3X5	T43.3X6

◀ New ◀ Revised ~~deleted~~ Deleted

Substance	External Cause (T-Code) Poisoning, Accidental (Unintentional)	Poisoning, Intentional Self-Harm	Poisoning, Assault	Poisoning, Undetermined	Adverse Effect	Underdosing
5-Methoxypsoralen (5-MOP)	T50.991	T50.992	T50.993	T50.994	T50.995	T50.996
8-Methoxypsoralen (8-MOP)	T50.991	T50.992	T50.993	T50.994	T50.995	T50.996
Methscopolamine bromide	T44.3X1	T44.3X2	T44.3X3	T44.3X4	T44.3X5	T44.3X6
Methsuximide	T42.2X1	T42.2X2	T42.2X3	T42.2X4	T42.2X5	T42.2X6
Methyclothiazide	T50.2X1	T50.2X2	T50.2X3	T50.2X4	T50.2X5	T50.2X6
Methyl						
acetate	T52.4X1	T52.4X2	T52.4X3	T52.4X4	—	—
acetone	T52.4X1	T52.4X2	T52.4X3	T52.4X4	—	—
acrylate	T65.891	T65.892	T65.893	T65.894	—	—
alcohol	T51.1X1	T51.1X2	T51.1X3	T51.1X4	—	—
aminophenol	T65.3X1	T65.3X2	T65.3X3	T65.3X4	—	—
amphetamine	T43.621	T43.622	T43.623	T43.624	T43.625	T43.626
androstanolone	T38.7X1	T38.7X2	T38.7X3	T38.7X4	T38.7X5	T38.7X6
atropine	T44.3X1	T44.3X2	T44.3X3	T44.3X4	T44.3X5	T44.3X6
benzene	T52.2X1	T52.2X2	T52.2X3	T52.2X4	—	—
benzoate	T52.8X1	T52.8X2	T52.8X3	T52.8X4	—	—
benzol	T52.2X1	T52.2X2	T52.2X3	T52.2X4	—	—
bromide (gas)	T59.891	T59.892	T59.893	T59.894	—	—
fumigant	T60.8X1	T60.8X2	T60.8X3	T60.8X4	—	—
butanol	T51.3X1	T51.3X2	T51.3X3	T51.3X4	—	—
carbinol	T51.1X1	T51.1X2	T51.1X3	T51.1X4	—	—
carbonate	T52.8X1	T52.8X2	T52.8X3	T52.8X4	—	—
CCNU	T45.1X1	T45.1X2	T45.1X3	T45.1X4	T45.1X5	T45.1X6
cellosolve	T52.91	T52.92	T52.93	T52.94	—	—
cellulose	T47.4X1	T47.4X2	T47.4X3	T47.4X4	T47.4X5	T47.4X6
chloride (gas)	T59.891	T59.892	T59.893	T59.894	—	—
chloroformate	T59.3X1	T59.3X2	T59.3X3	T59.3X4	—	—
cyclohexane	T52.8X1	T52.8X2	T52.8X3	T52.8X4	—	—
cyclohexanol	T51.8X1	T51.8X2	T51.8X3	T51.8X4	—	—
cyclohexanone	T52.8X1	T52.8X2	T52.8X3	T52.8X4	—	—
cyclohexyl acetate	T52.8X1	T52.8X2	T52.8X3	T52.8X4	—	—
demeton	T60.0X1	T60.0X2	T60.0X3	T60.0X4	—	—
dihydromorphinone	T40.2X1	T40.2X2	T40.2X3	T40.2X4	T40.2X5	T40.2X6
ergometrine	T48.0X1	T48.0X2	T48.0X3	T48.0X4	T48.0X5	T48.0X6
ergonovine	T48.0X1	T48.0X2	T48.0X3	T48.0X4	T48.0X5	T48.0X6
ethyl ketone	T52.4X1	T52.4X2	T52.4X3	T52.4X4	—	—
glucamine antimonate	T37.8X1	T37.8X2	T37.8X3	T37.8X4	T37.8X5	T37.8X6
hydrazine	T65.891	T65.892	T65.893	T65.894	—	—
iodide	T65.891	T65.892	T65.893	T65.894	—	—
isobutyl ketone	T52.4X1	T52.4X2	T52.4X3	T52.4X4	—	—
isothiocyanate	T60.3X1	T60.3X2	T60.3X3	T60.3X4	—	—
mercaptan	T59.891	T59.892	T59.893	T59.894	—	—

Substance	External Cause (T-Code) Poisoning, Accidental (Unintentional)	Poisoning, Intentional Self-Harm	Poisoning, Assault	Poisoning, Undetermined	Adverse Effect	Underdosing
Methyl (Continued)						
morphine NEC	T40.2X1	T40.2X2	T40.2X3	T40.2X4	T40.2X5	T40.2X6
nicotinate	T49.4X1	T49.4X2	T49.4X3	T49.4X4	T49.4X5	T49.4X6
paraben	T49.0X1	T49.0X2	T49.0X3	T49.0X4	T49.0X5	T49.0X6
parafynol	T42.6X1	T42.6X2	T42.6X3	T42.6X4	T42.6X5	T42.6X6
parathion	T60.0X1	T60.0X2	T60.0X3	T60.0X4	—	—
peridol	T43.4X1	T43.4X2	T43.4X3	T43.4X4	T43.4X5	T43.4X6
phenidate	T43.631	T43.632	T43.633	T43.634	T43.635	T43.636
prednisolone	T38.0X1	T38.0X2	T38.0X3	T38.0X4	T38.0X5	T38.0X6
ENT agent	T49.6X1	T49.6X2	T49.6X3	T49.6X4	T49.6X5	T49.6X6
ophthalmic preparation	T49.5X1	T49.5X2	T49.5X3	T49.5X4	T49.5X5	T49.5X6
topical NEC	T49.0X1	T49.0X2	T49.0X3	T49.0X4	T49.0X5	T49.0X6
propylcarbinol	T51.3X1	T51.3X2	T51.3X3	T51.3X4	—	—
rosaniline NEC	T49.0X1	T49.0X2	T49.0X3	T49.0X4	T49.0X5	T49.0X6
salicylate	T49.2X1	T49.2X2	T49.2X3	T49.2X4	T49.2X5	T49.2X6
sulfate (fumes)	T59.891	T59.892	T59.893	T59.894	—	—
liquid	T52.8X1	T52.8X2	T52.8X3	T52.8X4	—	—
sulfonal	T42.6X1	T42.6X2	T42.6X3	T42.6X4	T42.6X5	T42.6X6
testosterone	T38.7X1	T38.7X2	T38.7X3	T38.7X4	T38.7X5	T38.7X6
thiouracil	T38.2X1	T38.2X2	T38.2X3	T38.2X4	T38.2X5	T38.2X6
Methylamphetamine	T43.621	T43.622	T43.623	T43.624	T43.625	T43.626
Methylated spirit	T51.1X1	T51.1X2	T51.1X3	T51.1X4	—	—
Methylatropine nitrate	T44.3X1	T44.3X2	T44.3X3	T44.3X4	T44.3X5	T44.3X6
Methylbenactyzium bromide	T44.3X1	T44.3X2	T44.3X3	T44.3X4	T44.3X5	T44.3X6
Methylbenzethonium chloride	T49.0X1	T49.0X2	T49.0X3	T49.0X4	T49.0X5	T49.0X6
Methylcellulose	T47.4X1	T47.4X2	T47.4X3	T47.4X4	T47.4X5	T47.4X6
laxative	T47.4X1	T47.4X2	T47.4X3	T47.4X4	T47.4X5	T47.4X6
Methylchlorophenoxy-acetic acid	T60.3X1	T60.3X2	T60.3X3	T60.3X4	—	—
Methyldopa	T46.5X1	T46.5X2	T46.5X3	T46.5X4	T46.5X5	T46.5X6
Methyldopate	T46.5X1	T46.5X2	T46.5X3	T46.5X4	T46.5X5	T46.5X6
Methylene						
blue	T50.6X1	T50.6X2	T50.6X3	T50.6X4	T50.6X5	T50.6X6
chloride or dichloride (solvent) NEC	T53.4X1	T53.4X2	T53.4X3	T53.4X4	—	—
Methylenedioxyamphet-amine	T43.621	T43.622	T43.623	T43.624	T43.625	T43.626
Methylenedioxymethamphetamine	T43.641	T43.642	T43.643	T43.644	—	—
Methylergometrine	T48.0X1	T48.0X2	T48.0X3	T48.0X4	T48.0X5	T48.0X6
Methylergonovine	T48.0X1	T48.0X2	T48.0X3	T48.0X4	T48.0X5	T48.0X6
Methylestrenolone	T38.5X1	T38.5X2	T38.5X3	T38.5X4	T38.5X5	T38.5X6
Methylethyl cellulose	T50.991	T50.992	T50.993	T50.994	T50.995	T50.996
Methylhexabital	T42.3X1	T42.3X2	T42.3X3	T42.3X4	T42.3X5	T42.3X6
Methylmorphine	T40.2X1	T40.2X2	T40.2X3	T40.2X4	T40.2X5	T40.2X6

◀ New ◀ Revised ~~deleted~~ Deleted

TABLE OF DRUGS AND CHEMICALS

Substance	External Cause (T-Code)					
	Poisoning, Accidental (Unintentional)	Poisoning, Intentional Self-Harm	Poisoning, Assault	Poisoning, Undetermined	Adverse Effect	Underdosing
Methylparaben (ophthalmic)	T49.5X1	T49.5X2	T49.5X3	T49.5X4	T49.5X5	T49.5X6
Methylparafynol	T42.6X1	T42.6X2	T42.6X3	T42.6X4	T42.6X5	T42.6X6
Methylpentynol, methylpenthynol	T42.6X1	T42.6X2	T42.6X3	T42.6X4	T42.6X5	T42.6X6
Methylphenidate	T43.631	T43.632	T43.633	T43.634	T43.635	T43.636
Methylphenobarbital	T42.3X1	T42.3X2	T42.3X3	T42.3X4	T42.3X5	T42.3X6
Methylpolysiloxane	T47.1X1	T47.1X2	T47.1X3	T47.1X4	T47.1X5	T47.1X6
Methylprednisolone — see Methyl, prednisolone						
Methylrosaniline	T49.0X1	T49.0X2	T49.0X3	T49.0X4	T49.0X5	T49.0X6
Methylrosanilinium chloride	T49.0X1	T49.0X2	T49.0X3	T49.0X4	T49.0X5	T49.0X6
Methyltestosterone	T38.7X1	T38.7X2	T38.7X3	T38.7X4	T38.7X5	T38.7X6
Methylthionine chloride	T50.6X1	T50.6X2	T50.6X3	T50.6X4	T50.6X5	T50.6X6
Methylthioninium chloride	T50.6X1	T50.6X2	T50.6X3	T50.6X4	T50.6X5	T50.6X6
Methylthiouracil	T38.2X1	T38.2X2	T38.2X3	T38.2X4	T38.2X5	T38.2X6
Methyprylon	T42.6X1	T42.6X2	T42.6X3	T42.6X4	T42.6X5	T42.6X6
Methysergide	T46.5X1	T46.5X2	T46.5X3	T46.5X4	T46.5X5	T46.5X6
Metiamide	T47.1X1	T47.1X2	T47.1X3	T47.1X4	T47.1X5	T47.1X6
Meticillin	T36.0X1	T36.0X2	T36.0X3	T36.0X4	T36.0X5	T36.0X6
Meticrane	T50.2X1	T50.2X2	T50.2X3	T50.2X4	T50.2X5	T50.2X6
Metildigoxin	T46.0X1	T46.0X2	T46.0X3	T46.0X4	T46.0X5	T46.0X6
Metipranolol	T49.5X1	T49.5X2	T49.5X3	T49.5X4	T49.5X5	T49.5X6
Metirosine	T46.5X1	T46.5X2	T46.5X3	T46.5X4	T46.5X5	T46.5X6
Metisazone	T37.5X1	T37.5X2	T37.5X3	T37.5X4	T37.5X5	T37.5X6
Metixene	T44.3X1	T44.3X2	T44.3X3	T44.3X4	T44.3X5	T44.3X6
Metizoline	T48.5X1	T48.5X2	T48.5X3	T48.5X4	T48.5X5	T48.5X6
Metoclopramide	T45.0X1	T45.0X2	T45.0X3	T45.0X4	T45.0X5	T45.0X6
Metofenazate	T43.3X1	T43.3X2	T43.3X3	T43.3X4	T43.3X5	T43.3X6
Metofoline	T39.8X1	T39.8X2	T39.8X3	T39.8X4	T39.8X5	T39.8X6
Metolazone	T50.2X1	T50.2X2	T50.2X3	T50.2X4	T50.2X5	T50.2X6
Metopon	T40.2X1	T40.2X2	T40.2X3	T40.2X4	T40.2X5	T40.2X6
Metoprine	T45.1X1	T45.1X2	T45.1X3	T45.1X4	T45.1X5	T45.1X6
Metoprolol	T44.7X1	T44.7X2	T44.7X3	T44.7X4	T44.7X5	T44.7X6
Metrifonate	T60.0X1	T60.0X2	T60.0X3	T60.0X4	—	—
Metrizamide	T50.8X1	T50.8X2	T50.8X3	T50.8X4	T50.8X5	T50.8X6
Metrizoic acid	T50.8X1	T50.8X2	T50.8X3	T50.8X4	T50.8X5	T50.8X6
Metronidazole	T37.8X1	T37.8X2	T37.8X3	T37.8X4	T37.8X5	T37.8X6
Metycaine	T41.3X1	T41.3X2	T41.3X3	T41.3X4	T41.3X5	T41.3X6
infiltration (subcutaneous)	T41.3X1	T41.3X2	T41.3X3	T41.3X4	T41.3X5	T41.3X6
nerve block (peripheral) (plexus)	T41.3X1	T41.3X2	T41.3X3	T41.3X4	T41.3X5	T41.3X6
topical (surface)	T41.3X1	T41.3X2	T41.3X3	T41.3X4	T41.3X5	T41.3X6
Metyrapone	T50.8X1	T50.8X2	T50.8X3	T50.8X4	T50.8X5	T50.8X6
Mevinphos	T60.0X1	T60.0X2	T60.0X3	T60.0X4	—	—

Substance	External Cause (T-Code)					
	Poisoning, Accidental (Unintentional)	Poisoning, Intentional Self-Harm	Poisoning, Assault	Poisoning, Undetermined	Adverse Effect	Underdosing
Mexazolam	T42.4X1	T42.4X2	T42.4X3	T42.4X4	T42.4X5	T42.4X6
Mexenone	T49.3X1	T49.3X2	T49.3X3	T49.3X4	T49.3X5	T49.3X6
Mexiletine	T46.2X1	T46.2X2	T46.2X3	T46.2X4	T46.2X5	T46.2X6
Mezereon	T62.2X1	T62.2X2	T62.2X3	T62.2X4	—	—
berries	T62.1X1	T62.1X2	T62.1X3	T62.1X4	—	—
Mezlocillin	T36.0X1	T36.0X2	T36.0X3	T36.0X4	T36.0X5	T36.0X6
Mianserin	T43.021	T43.022	T43.023	T43.024	T43.025	T43.026
Micatin	T49.0X1	T49.0X2	T49.0X3	T49.0X4	T49.0X5	T49.0X6
Miconazole	T49.0X1	T49.0X2	T49.0X3	T49.0X4	T49.0X5	T49.0X6
Micronomicin	T36.5X1	T36.5X2	T36.5X3	T36.5X4	T36.5X5	T36.5X6
Midazolam	T42.4X1	T42.4X2	T42.4X3	T42.4X4	T42.4X5	T42.4X6
Midecamycin	T36.3X1	T36.3X2	T36.3X3	T36.3X4	T36.3X5	T36.3X6
Mifepristone	T38.6X1	T38.6X2	T38.6X3	T38.6X4	T38.6X5	T38.6X6
Milk of magnesia	T47.1X1	T47.1X2	T47.1X3	T47.1X4	T47.1X5	T47.1X6
Millipede (tropical) (venomous)	T63.411	T63.412	T63.413	T63.414	—	—
Miltown	T43.591	T43.592	T43.593	T43.594	T43.595	T43.596
Milverine	T44.3X1	T44.3X2	T44.3X3	T44.3X4	T44.3X5	T44.3X6
Minaprine	T43.291	T43.292	T43.293	T43.294	T43.295	T43.296
Minaxolone	T41.291	T41.292	T41.293	T41.294	T41.295	T41.296
Mineral						
acids	T54.2X1	T54.2X2	T54.2X3	T54.2X4	—	—
oil (laxative) (medicinal)	T47.4X1	T47.4X2	T47.4X3	T47.4X4	T47.4X5	T47.4X6
emulsion	T47.2X1	T47.2X2	T47.2X3	T47.2X4	T47.2X5	T47.2X6
nonmedicinal	T52.0X1	T52.0X2	T52.0X3	T52.0X4	—	—
topical	T49.3X1	T49.3X2	T49.3X3	T49.3X4	T49.3X5	T49.3X6
salt NEC	T50.3X1	T50.3X2	T50.3X3	T50.3X4	T50.3X5	T50.3X6
spirits	T52.0X1	T52.0X2	T52.0X3	T52.0X4	—	—
Mineralocorticosteroid	T50.0X1	T50.0X2	T50.0X3	T50.0X4	T50.0X5	T50.0X6
Minocycline	T36.4X1	T36.4X2	T36.4X3	T36.4X4	T36.4X5	T36.4X6
Minoxidil	T46.7X1	T46.7X2	T46.7X3	T46.7X4	T46.7X5	T46.7X6
Miokamycin	T36.3X1	T36.3X2	T36.3X3	T36.3X4	T36.3X5	T36.3X6
Miotic drug	T49.5X1	T49.5X2	T49.5X3	T49.5X4	T49.5X5	T49.5X6
Mipafox	T60.0X1	T60.0X2	T60.0X3	T60.0X4	—	—
Mirex	T60.1X1	T60.1X2	T60.1X3	T60.1X4	—	—
Mirtazapine	T43.021	T43.022	T43.023	T43.024	T43.025	T43.026
Misonidazole	T37.3X1	T37.3X2	T37.3X3	T37.3X4	T37.3X5	T37.3X6
Misoprostol	T47.1X1	T47.1X2	T47.1X3	T47.1X4	T47.1X5	T47.1X6
Mithramycin	T45.1X1	T45.1X2	T45.1X3	T45.1X4	T45.1X5	T45.1X6
Mitobronitol	T45.1X1	T45.1X2	T45.1X3	T45.1X4	T45.1X5	T45.1X6
Mitoguazone	T45.1X1	T45.1X2	T45.1X3	T45.1X4	T45.1X5	T45.1X6
Mitolactol	T45.1X1	T45.1X2	T45.1X3	T45.1X4	T45.1X5	T45.1X6
Mitomycin	T45.1X1	T45.1X2	T45.1X3	T45.1X4	T45.1X5	T45.1X6

◀ New ◀ Revised ~~deleted~~ Deleted

TABLE OF DRUGS AND CHEMICALS

Substance	External Cause (T-Code) Poisoning, Accidental (Unintentional)	Poisoning, Intentional Self-Harm	Poisoning, Assault	Poisoning, Undetermined	Adverse Effect	Underdosing
Mitopodozide	T45.1X1	T45.1X2	T45.1X3	T45.1X4	T45.1X5	T45.1X6
Mitotane	T45.1X1	T45.1X2	T45.1X3	T45.1X4	T45.1X5	T45.1X6
Mitoxantrone	T45.1X1	T45.1X2	T45.1X3	T45.1X4	T45.1X5	T45.1X6
Mivacurium chloride	T48.1X1	T48.1X2	T48.1X3	T48.1X4	T48.1X5	T48.1X6
Miyari bacteria	T47.6X1	T47.6X2	T47.6X3	T47.6X4	T47.6X5	T47.6X6
Moclobemide	T43.1X1	T43.1X2	T43.1X3	T43.1X4	T43.1X5	T43.1X6
Moderil	T46.5X1	T46.5X2	T46.5X3	T46.5X4	T46.5X5	T46.5X6
Mofebutazone	T39.2X1	T39.2X2	T39.2X3	T39.2X4	T39.2X5	T39.2X6
Mogadon — see Nitrazepam						
Molindone	T43.591	T43.592	T43.593	T43.594	T43.595	T43.596
Molsidomine	T46.3X1	T46.3X2	T46.3X3	T46.3X4	T46.3X5	T46.3X6
Mometasone	T49.0X1	T49.0X2	T49.0X3	T49.0X4	T49.0X5	T49.0X6
Monistat	T49.0X1	T49.0X2	T49.0X3	T49.0X4	T49.0X5	T49.0X6
Monkshood	T62.2X1	T62.2X2	T62.2X3	T62.2X4	—	—
Monoamine oxidase inhibitor NEC	T43.1X1	T43.1X2	T43.1X3	T43.1X4	T43.1X5	T43.1X6
hydrazine	T43.1X1	T43.1X2	T43.1X3	T43.1X4	T43.1X5	T43.1X6
Monobenzone	T49.4X1	T49.4X2	T49.4X3	T49.4X4	T49.4X5	T49.4X6
Monochloroacetic acid	T60.3X1	T60.3X2	T60.3X3	T60.3X4	—	—
Monochlorobenzene	T53.7X1	T53.7X2	T53.7X3	T53.7X4	—	—
Monoethanolamine	T46.8X1	T46.8X2	T46.8X3	T46.8X4	T46.8X5	T46.8X6
oleate	T46.8X1	T46.8X2	T46.8X3	T46.8X4	T46.8X5	T46.8X6
Monooctanoin	T50.991	T50.992	T50.993	T50.994	T50.995	T50.996
Monophenylbutazone	T39.2X1	T39.2X2	T39.2X3	T39.2X4	T39.2X5	T39.2X6
Monosodium glutamate	T65.891	T65.892	T65.893	T65.894	—	—
Monosulfiram	T49.0X1	T49.0X2	T49.0X3	T49.0X4	T49.0X5	T49.0X6
Monoxide, carbon — see Carbon, monoxide	T57.91	T57.92	T57.93	T57.94	—	—
Monoxidine hydrochloride	T46.1X1	T46.1X2	T46.1X3	T46.1X4	T46.1X5	T46.1X6
Monuron	T60.3X1	T60.3X2	T60.3X3	T60.3X4	—	—
Moperone	T43.4X1	T43.4X2	T43.4X3	T43.4X4	T43.4X5	T43.4X6
Mopidamol	T45.1X1	T45.1X2	T45.1X3	T45.1X4	T45.1X5	T45.1X6
MOPP (mechlorethamine + vincristine + prednisone + procarbazine)	T45.1X1	T45.1X2	T45.1X3	T45.1X4	T45.1X5	T45.1X6
Morfin	T40.2X1	T40.2X2	T40.2X3	T40.2X4	T40.2X5	T40.2X6
Morinamide	T37.1X1	T37.1X2	T37.1X3	T37.1X4	T37.1X5	T37.1X6
Morning glory seeds	T40.991	T40.992	T40.993	T40.994	—	—
Moroxydine	T37.5X1	T37.5X2	T37.5X3	T37.5X4	T37.5X5	T37.5X6
Morphazinamide	T37.1X1	T37.1X2	T37.1X3	T37.1X4	T37.1X5	T37.1X6
Morphine	T40.2X1	T40.2X2	T40.2X3	T40.2X4	T40.2X5	T40.2X6
antagonist	T50.7X1	T50.7X2	T50.7X3	T50.7X4	T50.7X5	T50.7X6
Morpholinylethylmorphine	T40.2X1	T40.2X2	T40.2X3	T40.2X4	—	—
Morsuximide	T42.2X1	T42.2X2	T42.2X3	T42.2X4	T42.2X5	T42.2X6

Substance	External Cause (T-Code) Poisoning, Accidental (Unintentional)	Poisoning, Intentional Self-Harm	Poisoning, Assault	Poisoning, Undetermined	Adverse Effect	Underdosing
Mosapramine	T43.591	T43.592	T43.593	T43.594	T43.595	T43.596
Moth balls — see also Pesticides	T60.2X1	T60.2X2	T60.2X3	T60.2X4	—	—
naphthalene	T60.2X1	T60.2X2	T60.2X3	T60.2X4	—	—
paradichlorobenzene	T60.1X1	T60.1X2	T60.1X3	T60.1X4	—	—
Motor exhaust gas	T58.01	T58.02	T58.03	T58.04	—	—
Mouthwash (antiseptic) (zinc chloride)	T49.6X1	T49.6X2	T49.6X3	T49.6X4	T49.6X5	T49.6X6
Moxastine	T45.0X1	T45.0X2	T45.0X3	T45.0X4	T45.0X5	T45.0X6
Moxaverine	T44.3X1	T44.3X2	T44.3X3	T44.3X4	T44.3X5	T44.3X6
Moxifensine	T43.291	T43.292	T43.293	T43.294	T43.295	T43.296
Moxisylyte	T46.7X1	T46.7X2	T46.7X3	T46.7X4	T46.7X5	T46.7X6
Mucilage, plant	T47.4X1	T47.4X2	T47.4X3	T47.4X4	T47.4X5	T47.4X6
Mucolytic drug	T48.4X1	T48.4X2	T48.4X3	T48.4X4	T48.4X5	T48.4X6
Mucomyst	T48.4X1	T48.4X2	T48.4X3	T48.4X4	T48.4X5	T48.4X6
Mucous membrane agents (external)	T49.91	T49.92	T49.93	T49.94	T49.95	T49.96
specified NEC	T49.8X1	T49.8X2	T49.8X3	T49.8X4	T49.8X5	T49.8X6
Mumps						
immune globulin (human)	T50.Z11	T50.Z12	T50.Z13	T50.Z14	T50.Z15	T50.Z16
skin test antigen	T50.8X1	T50.8X2	T50.8X3	T50.8X4	T50.8X5	T50.8X6
vaccine	T50.B91	T50.B92	T50.B93	T50.B94	T50.B95	T50.B96
Mumpsvax	T50.B91	T50.B92	T50.B93	T50.B94	T50.B95	T50.B96
Mupirocin	T49.0X1	T49.0X2	T49.0X3	T49.0X4	T49.0X5	T49.0X6
Muriatic acid — see Hydrochloric acid						
Muromonab-CD3	T45.1X1	T45.1X2	T45.1X3	T45.1X4	T45.1X5	T45.1X6
Muscle relaxant — see Relaxant, muscle						
Muscle-action drug NEC	T48.201	T48.202	T48.203	T48.204	T48.205	T48.206
Muscle affecting agents NEC	T48.201	T48.202	T48.203	T48.204	T48.205	T48.206
oxytocic	T48.0X1	T48.0X2	T48.0X3	T48.0X4	T48.0X5	T48.0X6
relaxants	T48.201	T48.202	T48.203	T48.204	T48.205	T48.206
central nervous system	T42.8X1	T42.8X2	T42.8X3	T42.8X4	T42.8X5	T42.8X6
skeletal	T48.1X1	T48.1X2	T48.1X3	T48.1X4	T48.1X5	T48.1X6
smooth	T44.3X1	T44.3X2	T44.3X3	T44.3X4	T44.3X5	T44.3X6
Muscle-tone depressant, central NEC	T42.8X1	T42.8X2	T42.8X3	T42.8X4	T42.8X5	T42.8X6
specified NEC	T42.8X1	T42.8X2	T42.8X3	T42.8X4	T42.8X5	T42.8X6
Mushroom, noxious	T62.0X1	T62.0X2	T62.0X3	T62.0X4	—	—
Mussel, noxious	T61.781	T61.782	T61.783	T61.784	—	—
Mustard (emetic)	T47.7X1	T47.7X2	T47.7X3	T47.7X4	T47.7X5	T47.7X6
black	T47.7X1	T47.7X2	T47.7X3	T47.7X4	T47.7X5	T47.7X6
gas, not in war	T59.91	T59.92	T59.93	T59.94	—	—
nitrogen	T45.1X1	T45.1X2	T45.1X3	T45.1X4	T45.1X5	T45.1X6

◀ New ◀ Revised ~~deleted~~ Deleted

TABLE OF DRUGS AND CHEMICALS

Substance	Poisoning, Accidental (Unintentional)	Poisoning, Intentional Self-Harm	Poisoning, Assault	Poisoning, Undetermined	Adverse Effect	Underdosing
Mustine	T45.1X1	T45.1X2	T45.1X3	T45.1X4	T45.1X5	T45.1X6
M-vac	T45.1X1	T45.1X2	T45.1X3	T45.1X4	T45.1X5	T45.1X6
Mycifradin	T36.5X1	T36.5X2	T36.5X3	T36.5X4	T36.5X5	T36.5X6
topical	T49.0X1	T49.0X2	T49.0X3	T49.0X4	T49.0X5	T49.0X6
Mycitracin	T36.8X1	T36.8X2	T36.8X3	T36.8X4	T36.8X5	T36.8X6
ophthalmic preparation	T49.5X1	T49.5X2	T49.5X3	T49.5X4	T49.5X5	T49.5X6
Mycostatin	T36.7X1	T36.7X2	T36.7X3	T36.7X4	T36.7X5	T36.7X6
topical	T49.0X1	T49.0X2	T49.0X3	T49.0X4	T49.0X5	T49.0X6
Mycotoxins	T64.81	T64.82	T64.83	T64.84	—	—
aflatoxin	T64.01	T64.02	T64.03	T64.04	—	—
specified NEC	T64.81	T64.82	T64.83	T64.84	—	—
Mydriacyl	T44.3X1	T44.3X2	T44.3X3	T44.3X4	T44.3X5	T44.3X6
Mydriatic drug	T49.5X1	T49.5X2	T49.5X3	T49.5X4	T49.5X5	T49.5X6
Myelobromal	T45.1X1	T45.1X2	T45.1X3	T45.1X4	T45.1X5	T45.1X6
Myleran	T45.1X1	T45.1X2	T45.1X3	T45.1X4	T45.1X5	T45.1X6
Myochrysin(e)	T39.2X1	T39.2X2	T39.2X3	T39.2X4	T39.2X5	T39.2X6
Myoneural blocking agents	T48.1X1	T48.1X2	T48.1X3	T48.1X4	T48.1X5	T48.1X6
Myralact	T49.0X1	T49.0X2	T49.0X3	T49.0X4	T49.0X5	T49.0X6
Myristica fragrans	T62.2X1	T62.2X2	T62.2X3	T62.2X4	—	—
Myristicin	T65.891	T65.892	T65.893	T65.894	—	—
Mysoline	T42.3X1	T42.3X2	T42.3X3	T42.3X4	T42.3X5	T42.3X6
N						
Nabilone	T40.7X1	T40.7X2	T40.7X3	T40.7X4	T40.7X5	T40.7X6
Nabumetone	T39.391	T39.392	T39.393	T39.394	T39.395	T39.396
Nadolol	T44.7X1	T44.7X2	T44.7X3	T44.7X4	T44.7X5	T44.7X6
Nafcillin	T36.0X1	T36.0X2	T36.0X3	T36.0X4	T36.0X5	T36.0X6
Nafoxidine	T38.6X1	T38.6X2	T38.6X3	T38.6X4	T38.6X5	T38.6X6
Naftazone	T46.991	T46.992	T46.993	T46.994	T46.995	T46.996
Naftidrofuryl (oxalate)	T46.7X1	T46.7X2	T46.7X3	T46.7X4	T46.7X5	T46.7X6
Naftifine	T49.0X1	T49.0X2	T49.0X3	T49.0X4	T49.0X5	T49.0X6
Nail polish remover	T52.91	T52.92	T52.93	T52.94	—	—
Nalbuphine	T40.4X1	T40.4X2	T40.4X3	T40.4X4	T40.4X5	T40.4X6
Naled	T60.0X1	T60.0X2	T60.0X3	T60.0X4	—	—
Nalidixic acid	T37.8X1	T37.8X2	T37.8X3	T37.8X4	T37.8X5	T37.8X6
Nalorphine	T50.7X1	T50.7X2	T50.7X3	T50.7X4	T50.7X5	T50.7X6
Naloxone	T50.7X1	T50.7X2	T50.7X3	T50.7X4	T50.7X5	T50.7X6
Naltrexone	T50.7X1	T50.7X2	T50.7X3	T50.7X4	T50.7X5	T50.7X6
Namenda	T43.8X1	T43.8X2	T43.8X3	T43.8X4	T43.8X5	T43.8X6
Nandrolone	T38.7X1	T38.7X2	T38.7X3	T38.7X4	T38.7X5	T38.7X6
Naphazoline	T48.5X1	T48.5X2	T48.5X3	T48.5X4	T48.5X5	T48.5X6

Substance	Poisoning, Accidental (Unintentional)	Poisoning, Intentional Self-Harm	Poisoning, Assault	Poisoning, Undetermined	Adverse Effect	Underdosing
Naphtha (painters') (petroleum)	T52.0X1	T52.0X2	T52.0X3	T52.0X4	—	—
solvent	T52.0X1	T52.0X2	T52.0X3	T52.0X4	—	—
vapor	T52.0X1	T52.0X2	T52.0X3	T52.0X4	—	—
Naphthalene (non-chlorinated)	T60.2X1	T60.2X2	T60.2X3	T60.2X4	—	—
chlorinated	T60.1X1	T60.1X2	T60.1X3	T60.1X4	—	—
vapor	T60.1X1	T60.1X2	T60.1X3	T60.1X4	—	—
insecticide or moth repellent	T60.2X1	T60.2X2	T60.2X3	T60.2X4	—	—
chlorinated	T60.1X1	T60.1X2	T60.1X3	T60.1X4	—	—
vapor	T60.2X1	T60.2X2	T60.2X3	T60.2X4	—	—
chlorinated	T60.1X1	T60.1X2	T60.1X3	T60.1X4	—	—
Naphthol	T65.891	T65.892	T65.893	T65.894	—	—
Naphthylamine	T65.891	T65.892	T65.893	T65.894	—	—
Naphthylthiourea (ANTU)	T60.4X1	T60.4X2	T60.4X3	T60.4X4	—	—
Naprosyn — see Naproxen						
Naproxen	T39.311	T39.312	T39.313	T39.314	T39.315	T39.316
Narcotic (drug)	T40.601	T40.602	T40.603	T40.604	T40.605	T40.606
analgesic NEC	T40.601	T40.602	T40.603	T40.604	T40.605	T40.606
antagonist	T50.7X1	T50.7X2	T50.7X3	T50.7X4	T50.7X5	T50.7X6
specified NEC	T40.691	T40.692	T40.693	T40.694	T40.695	T40.696
synthetic	T40.4X1	T40.4X2	T40.4X3	T40.4X4	T40.4X5	T40.4X6
Narcotine	T48.3X1	T48.3X2	T48.3X3	T48.3X4	T48.3X5	T48.3X6
Nardil	T43.1X1	T43.1X2	T43.1X3	T43.1X4	T43.1X5	T43.1X6
Nasal drug NEC	T49.6X1	T49.6X2	T49.6X3	T49.6X4	T49.6X5	T49.6X6
Natamycin	T49.0X1	T49.0X2	T49.0X3	T49.0X4	T49.0X5	T49.0X6
Natrium cyanide — see Cyanide(s)						
Natural gas	T59.891	T59.892	T59.893	T59.894	—	—
incomplete combustion	T57.91	T57.92	T57.93	T57.94	—	—
Natural						
blood (product)	T45.8X1	T45.8X2	T45.8X3	T45.8X4	T45.8X5	T45.8X6
gas (piped)	T59.891	T59.892	T59.893	T59.894	—	—
incomplete combustion	T58.11	T58.12	T58.13	T58.14	—	—
Nealbarbital	T42.3X1	T42.3X2	T42.3X3	T42.3X4	T42.3X5	T42.3X6
Nectadon	T48.3X1	T48.3X2	T48.3X3	T48.3X4	T48.3X5	T48.3X6
Nedocromil	T48.6X1	T48.6X2	T48.6X3	T48.6X4	T48.6X5	T48.6X6
Nefopam	T39.8X1	T39.8X2	T39.8X3	T39.8X4	T39.8X5	T39.8X6
Nematocyst (sting)	T63.691	T63.692	T63.693	T63.694	—	—
Nembutal	T42.3X1	T42.3X2	T42.3X3	T42.3X4	T42.3X5	T42.3X6
Nemonapride	T43.591	T43.592	T43.593	T43.594	T43.595	T43.596
Neoarsphenamine	T37.8X1	T37.8X2	T37.8X3	T37.8X4	T37.8X5	T37.8X6

◀ New ◀ Revised ~~deleted~~ Deleted

	External Cause (T-Code)					
Substance	Poisoning, Accidental (Unintentional)	Poisoning, Intentional Self-Harm	Poisoning, Assault	Poisoning, Undetermined	Adverse Effect	Underdosing
Neocinchophen	T50.4X1	T50.4X2	T50.4X3	T50.4X4	T50.4X5	T50.4X6
Neomycin (derivatives)	T36.5X1	T36.5X2	T36.5X3	T36.5X4	T36.5X5	T36.5X6
with						
bacitracin	T49.0X1	T49.0X2	T49.0X3	T49.0X4	T49.0X5	T49.0X6
neostigmine	T44.0X1	T44.0X2	T44.0X3	T44.0X4	T44.0X5	T44.0X6
ENT agent	T49.6X1	T49.6X2	T49.6X3	T49.6X4	T49.6X5	T49.6X6
ophthalmic preparation	T49.5X1	T49.5X2	T49.5X3	T49.5X4	T49.5X5	T49.5X6
topical NEC	T49.0X1	T49.0X2	T49.0X3	T49.0X4	T49.0X5	T49.0X6
Neonal	T42.3X1	T42.3X2	T42.3X3	T42.3X4	T42.3X5	T42.3X6
Neoprontosil	T37.0X1	T37.0X2	T37.0X3	T37.0X4	T37.0X5	T37.0X6
Neosalvarsan	T37.8X1	T37.8X2	T37.8X3	T37.8X4	T37.8X5	T37.8X6
Neosilversalvarsan	T37.8X1	T37.8X2	T37.8X3	T37.8X4	T37.8X5	T37.8X6
Neosporin	T36.8X1	T36.8X2	T36.8X3	T36.8X4	T36.8X5	T36.8X6
ENT agent	T49.6X1	T49.6X2	T49.6X3	T49.6X4	T49.6X5	T49.6X6
opthalmic preparation	T49.5X1	T49.5X2	T49.5X3	T49.5X4	T49.5X5	T49.5X6
topical NEC	T49.0X1	T49.0X2	T49.0X3	T49.0X4	T49.0X5	T49.0X6
Neostigmine bromide	T44.0X1	T44.0X2	T44.0X3	T44.0X4	T44.0X5	T44.0X6
Neraval	T42.3X1	T42.3X2	T42.3X3	T42.3X4	T42.3X5	T42.3X6
Neravan	T42.3X1	T42.3X2	T42.3X3	T42.3X4	T42.3X5	T42.3X6
Nerium oleander	T62.2X1	T62.2X2	T62.2X3	T62.2X4	—	—
Nerve gas, not in war	T59.91	T59.92	T59.93	T59.94	—	—
Nesacaine	T41.3X1	T41.3X2	T41.3X3	T41.3X4	T41.3X5	T41.3X6
infiltration (subcutaneous)	T41.3X1	T41.3X2	T41.3X3	T41.3X4	T41.3X5	T41.3X6
nerve block (peripheral) (plexus)	T41.3X1	T41.3X2	T41.3X3	T41.3X4	T41.3X5	T41.3X6
Netilmicin	T36.5X1	T36.5X2	T36.5X3	T36.5X4	T36.5X5	T36.5X6
Neurobarb	T42.3X1	T42.3X2	T42.3X3	T42.3X4	T42.3X5	T42.3X6
Neuroleptic drug NEC	T43.501	T43.502	T43.503	T43.504	T43.505	T43.506
Neuromuscular blocking drug	T48.1X1	T48.1X2	T48.1X3	T48.1X4	T48.1X5	T48.1X6
Neutral insulin injection	T38.3X1	T38.3X2	T38.3X3	T38.3X4	T38.3X5	T38.3X6
Neutral spirits	T51.0X1	T51.0X2	T51.0X3	T51.0X4	—	—
beverage	T51.0X1	T51.0X2	T51.0X3	T51.0X4	—	—
Niacin	T46.7X1	T46.7X2	T46.7X3	T46.7X4	T46.7X5	T46.7X6
Niacinamide	T45.2X1	T45.2X2	T45.2X3	T45.2X4	T45.2X5	T45.2X6
Nialamide	T43.1X1	T43.1X2	T43.1X3	T43.1X4	T43.1X5	T43.1X6
Niaprazine	T42.6X1	T42.6X2	T42.6X3	T42.6X4	T42.6X5	T42.6X6
Nicametate	T46.7X1	T46.7X2	T46.7X3	T46.7X4	T46.7X5	T46.7X6
Nicardipine	T46.1X1	T46.1X2	T46.1X3	T46.1X4	T46.1X5	T46.1X6
Nicergoline	T46.7X1	T46.7X2	T46.7X3	T46.7X4	T46.7X5	T46.7X6
Nickel (carbonyl) (tetra-carbonyl) (fumes) (vapor)	T56.891	T56.892	T56.893	T56.894	—	—

	External Cause (T-Code)					
Substance	Poisoning, Accidental (Unintentional)	Poisoning, Intentional Self-Harm	Poisoning, Assault	Poisoning, Undetermined	Adverse Effect	Underdosing
Nickelocene	T56.891	T56.892	T56.893	T56.894	—	—
Niclosamide	T37.4X1	T37.4X2	T37.4X3	T37.4X4	T37.4X5	T37.4X6
Nicofuranose	T46.7X1	T46.7X2	T46.7X3	T46.7X4	T46.7X5	T46.7X6
Nicomorphine	T40.2X1	T40.2X2	T40.2X3	T40.2X4	—	—
Nicorandil	T46.3X1	T46.3X2	T46.3X3	T46.3X4	T46.3X5	T46.3X6
Nicotiana (plant)	T62.2X1	T62.2X2	T62.2X3	T62.2X4	—	—
Nicotinamide	T45.2X1	T45.2X2	T45.2X3	T45.2X4	T45.2X5	T45.2X6
Nicotine (insecticide) (spray) (sulfate) NEC	T60.2X1	T60.2X2	T60.2X3	T60.2X4	—	—
from tobacco	T65.291	T65.292	T65.293	T65.294	—	—
cigarettes	T65.221	T65.222	T65.223	T65.224	—	—
not insecticide	T65.291	T65.292	T65.293	T65.294		
Nicotinic acid	T46.7X1	T46.7X2	T46.7X3	T46.7X4	T46.7X5	T46.7X6
Nicotinyl alcohol	T46.7X1	T46.7X2	T46.7X3	T46.7X4	T46.7X5	T46.7X6
Nicoumalone	T45.511	T45.512	T45.513	T45.514	T45.515	T45.516
Nifedipine	T46.1X1	T46.1X2	T46.1X3	T46.1X4	T46.1X5	T46.1X6
Nifenazone	T39.2X1	T39.2X2	T39.2X3	T39.2X4	T39.2X5	T39.2X6
Nifuraldezone	T37.91	T37.92	T37.93	T37.94	T37.95	T37.96
Nifuratel	T37.8X1	T37.8X2	T37.8X3	T37.8X4	T37.8X5	T37.8X6
Nifurtimox	T37.3X1	T37.3X2	T37.3X3	T37.3X4	T37.3X5	T37.3X6
Nifurtoinol	T37.8X1	T37.8X2	T37.8X3	T37.8X4	T37.8X5	T37.8X6
Nightshade, deadly (solanum) — see also Belladonna	T62.2X1	T62.2X2	T62.2X3	T62.2X4	—	—
berry	T62.1X1	T62.1X2	T62.1X3	T62.1X4	—	—
Nikethamide	T50.7X1	T50.7X2	T50.7X3	T50.7X4	T50.7X5	T50.7X6
Nilstat	T36.7X1	T36.7X2	T36.7X3	T36.7X4	T36.7X5	T36.7X6
topical	T49.0X1	T49.0X2	T49.0X3	T49.0X4	T49.0X5	T49.0X6
Nilutamide	T38.6X1	T38.6X2	T38.6X3	T38.6X4	T38.6X5	T38.6X6
Nimesulide	T39.391	T39.392	T39.393	T39.394	T39.395	T39.396
Nimetazepam	T42.4X1	T42.4X2	T42.4X3	T42.4X4	T42.4X5	T42.4X6
Nimodipine	T46.1X1	T46.1X2	T46.1X3	T46.1X4	T46.1X5	T46.1X6
Nimorazole	T37.3X1	T37.3X2	T37.3X3	T37.3X4	T37.3X5	T37.3X6
Nimustine	T45.1X1	T45.1X2	T45.1X3	T45.1X4	T45.1X5	T45.1X6
Niridazole	T37.4X1	T37.4X2	T37.4X3	T37.4X4	T37.4X5	T37.4X6
Nisentil	T40.2X1	T40.2X2	T40.2X3	T40.2X4	T40.2X5	T40.2X6
Nisoldipine	T46.1X1	T46.1X2	T46.1X3	T46.1X4	T46.1X5	T46.1X6
Nitramine	T65.3X1	T65.3X2	T65.3X3	T65.3X4	—	—
Nitrate, organic	T46.3X1	T46.3X2	T46.3X3	T46.3X4	T46.3X5	T46.3X6
Nitrazepam	T42.4X1	T42.4X2	T42.4X3	T42.4X4	T42.4X5	T42.4X6
Nitrefazole	T50.6X1	T50.6X2	T50.6X3	T50.6X4	T50.6X5	T50.6X6
Nitrendipine	T46.1X1	T46.1X2	T46.1X3	T46.1X4	T46.1X5	T46.1X6

◀ New ◀ Revised ~~deleted~~ Deleted

TABLE OF DRUGS AND CHEMICALS

Substance	External Cause (T-Code)					
	Poisoning, Accidental (Unintentional)	Poisoning, Intentional Self-Harm	Poisoning, Assault	Poisoning, Undetermined	Adverse Effect	Underdosing
Nitric						
acid (liquid)	T54.2X1	T54.2X2	T54.2X3	T54.2X4	—	—
vapor	T59.891	T59.892	T59.893	T59.894	—	—
oxide (gas)	T59.0X1	T59.0X2	T59.0X3	T59.0X4	—	—
Nitrimidazine	T37.3X1	T37.3X2	T37.3X3	T37.3X4	T37.3X5	T37.3X6
Nitrite, amyl (medicinal) (vapor)	T46.3X1	T46.3X2	T46.3X3	T46.3X4	T46.3X5	T46.3X6
Nitroaniline	T65.3X1	T65.3X2	T65.3X3	T65.3X4	—	—
vapor	T59.891	T59.892	T59.893	T59.894	—	—
Nitrobenzene, nitrobenzol	T65.3X1	T65.3X2	T65.3X3	T65.3X4	—	—
vapor	T65.3X1	T65.3X2	T65.3X3	T65.3X4	—	—
Nitrocellulose	T65.891	T65.892	T65.893	T65.894	—	—
lacquer	T65.891	T65.892	T65.893	T65.894	—	—
Nitrodiphenyl	T65.3X1	T65.3X2	T65.3X3	T65.3X4	—	—
Nitrofural	T49.0X1	T49.0X2	T49.0X3	T49.0X4	T49.0X5	T49.0X6
Nitrofurantoin	T37.8X1	T37.8X2	T37.8X3	T37.8X4	T37.8X5	T37.8X6
Nitrofurazone	T49.0X1	T49.0X2	T49.0X3	T49.0X4	T49.0X5	T49.0X6
Nitrogen	T59.0X1	T59.0X2	T59.0X3	T59.0X4	—	—
mustard	T45.1X1	T45.1X2	T45.1X3	T45.1X4	T45.1X5	T45.1X6
Nitroglycerin, nitro-glycerol (medicinal)	T46.3X1	T46.3X2	T46.3X3	T46.3X4	T46.3X5	T46.3X6
nonmedicinal	T65.5X1	T65.5X2	T65.5X3	T65.5X4	—	—
fumes	T65.5X1	T65.5X2	T65.5X3	T65.5X4	—	—
Nitroglycol	T52.3X1	T52.3X2	T52.3X3	T52.3X4	—	—
Nitrohydrochloric acid	T54.2X1	T54.2X2	T54.2X3	T54.2X4	—	—
Nitromersol	T49.0X1	T49.0X2	T49.0X3	T49.0X4	T49.0X5	T49.0X6
Nitronaphthalene	T65.891	T65.892	T65.893	T65.894	—	—
Nitrophenol	T54.0X1	T54.0X2	T54.0X3	T54.0X4	—	—
Nitropropane	T52.8X1	T52.8X2	T52.8X3	T52.8X4	—	—
Nitroprusside	T46.5X1	T46.5X2	T46.5X3	T46.5X4	T46.5X5	T46.5X6
Nitrosodimethylamine	T65.3X1	T65.3X2	T65.3X3	T65.3X4	—	—
Nitrothiazol	T37.4X1	T37.4X2	T37.4X3	T37.4X4	T37.4X5	T37.4X6
Nitrotoluene, nitrotoluol	T65.3X1	T65.3X2	T65.3X3	T65.3X4	—	—
vapor	T65.3X1	T65.3X2	T65.3X3	T65.3X4	—	—
Nitrous						
acid (liquid)	T54.2X1	T54.2X2	T54.2X3	T54.2X4	—	—
fumes	T59.891	T59.892	T59.893	T59.894	—	—
ether spirit	T46.3X1	T46.3X2	T46.3X3	T46.3X4	T46.3X5	T46.3X6
oxide	T41.0X1	T41.0X2	T41.0X3	T41.0X4	T41.0X5	T41.0X6
Nitroxoline	T37.8X1	T37.8X2	T37.8X3	T37.8X4	T37.8X5	T37.8X6
Nitrozone	T49.0X1	T49.0X2	T49.0X3	T49.0X4	T49.0X5	T49.0X6
Nizatidine	T47.0X1	T47.0X2	T47.0X3	T47.0X4	T47.0X5	T47.0X6

Substance	External Cause (T-Code)					
	Poisoning, Accidental (Unintentional)	Poisoning, Intentional Self-Harm	Poisoning, Assault	Poisoning, Undetermined	Adverse Effect	Underdosing
Nizofenone	T43.8X1	T43.8X2	T43.8X3	T43.8X4	T43.8X5	T43.8X6
Noctec	T42.6X1	T42.6X2	T42.6X3	T42.6X4	T42.6X5	T42.6X6
Noludar	T42.6X1	T42.6X2	T42.6X3	T42.6X4	T42.6X5	T42.6X6
Noptil	T42.3X1	T42.3X2	T42.3X3	T42.3X4	T42.3X5	T42.3X6
Nomegestrol	T38.5X1	T38.5X2	T38.5X3	T38.5X4	T38.5X5	T38.5X6
Nomifensine	T43.291	T43.292	T43.293	T43.294	T43.295	T43.296
Nonoxinol	T49.8X1	T49.8X2	T49.8X3	T49.8X4	T49.8X5	T49.8X6
Nonylphenoxy (polyethoxy-ethanol)	T49.8X1	T49.8X2	T49.8X3	T49.8X4	T49.8X5	T49.8X6
Noptil	T42.3X1	T42.3X2	T42.3X3	T42.3X4	T42.3X5	T42.3X6
Noradrenaline	T44.4X1	T44.4X2	T44.4X3	T44.4X4	T44.4X5	T44.4X6
Noramidopyrine	T39.2X1	T39.2X2	T39.2X3	T39.2X4	T39.2X5	T39.2X6
methanesulfonate sodium	T39.2X1	T39.2X2	T39.2X3	T39.2X4	T39.2X5	T39.2X6
Norbormide	T60.4X1	T60.4X2	T60.4X3	T60.4X4	—	—
Nordazepam	T42.4X1	T42.4X2	T42.4X3	T42.4X4	T42.4X5	T42.4X6
Norepinephrine	T44.4X1	T44.4X2	T44.4X3	T44.4X4	T44.4X5	T44.4X6
Norethandrolone	T38.7X1	T38.7X2	T38.7X3	T38.7X4	T38.7X5	T38.7X6
Norethindrone	T38.4X1	T38.4X2	T38.4X3	T38.4X4	T38.4X5	T38.4X6
Norethisterone (acetate) (enantate)	T38.4X1	T38.4X2	T38.4X3	T38.4X4	T38.4X5	T38.4X6
with ethinylestradiol	T38.5X1	T38.5X2	T38.5X3	T38.5X4	T38.5X5	T38.5X6
Noretynodrel	T38.5X1	T38.5X2	T38.5X3	T38.5X4	T38.5X5	T38.5X6
Norfenefrine	T44.4X1	T44.4X2	T44.4X3	T44.4X4	T44.4X5	T44.4X6
Norfloxacin	T36.8X1	T36.8X2	T36.8X3	T36.8X4	T36.8X5	T36.8X6
Norgestrel	T38.4X1	T38.4X2	T38.4X3	T38.4X4	T38.4X5	T38.4X6
Norgestrienone	T38.4X1	T38.4X2	T38.4X3	T38.4X4	T38.4X5	T38.4X6
Norlestrin	T38.4X1	T38.4X2	T38.4X3	T38.4X4	T38.4X5	T38.4X6
Norlutin	T38.4X1	T38.4X2	T38.4X3	T38.4X4	T38.4X5	T38.4X6
Normal serum albumin (human), salt-poor	T45.8X1	T45.8X2	T45.8X3	T45.8X4	T45.8X5	T45.8X6
Normethandrone	T38.5X1	T38.5X2	T38.5X3	T38.5X4	T38.5X5	T38.5X6
Normison — see Benzodiazepines						
Normorphine	T40.2X1	T40.2X2	T40.2X3	T40.2X4	—	—
Norpseudoephedrine	T50.5X1	T50.5X2	T50.5X3	T50.5X4	T50.5X5	T50.5X6
Nortestosterone (furanpropionate)	T38.7X1	T38.7X2	T38.7X3	T38.7X4	T38.7X5	T38.7X6
Nortriptyline	T43.011	T43.012	T43.013	T43.014	T43.015	T43.016
Noscapine	T48.3X1	T48.3X2	T48.3X3	T48.3X4	T48.3X5	T48.3X6
Nose preparations	T49.6X1	T49.6X2	T49.6X3	T49.6X4	T49.6X5	T49.6X6
Novobiocin	T36.5X1	T36.5X2	T36.5X3	T36.5X4	T36.5X5	T36.5X6
Novocain (infiltration) (topical)	T41.3X1	T41.3X2	T41.3X3	T41.3X4	T41.3X5	T41.3X6
nerve block (peripheral) (plexus)	T41.3X1	T41.3X2	T41.3X3	T41.3X4	T41.3X5	T41.3X6
spinal	T41.3X1	T41.3X2	T41.3X3	T41.3X4	T41.3X5	T41.3X6

◀ New   ◀ Revised   ~~deleted~~ Deleted

	External Cause (T-Code)					
Substance	Poisoning, Accidental (Unintentional)	Poisoning, Intentional Self-Harm	Poisoning, Assault	Poisoning, Undetermined	Adverse Effect	Underdosing
Noxious foodstuff	T62.91	T62.92	T62.93	T62.94	—	—
specified NEC	T62.8X1	T62.8X2	T62.8X3	T62.8X4	—	—
Noxiptiline	T43.011	T43.012	T43.013	T43.014	T43.015	T43.016
Noxytiolin	T49.0X1	T49.0X2	T49.0X3	T49.0X4	T49.0X5	T49.0X6
NPH Iletin (insulin)	T38.3X1	T38.3X2	T38.3X3	T38.3X4	T38.3X5	T38.3X6
Numorphan	T40.2X1	T40.2X2	T40.2X3	T40.2X4	T40.2X5	T40.2X6
Nunol	T42.3X1	T42.3X2	T42.3X3	T42.3X4	T42.3X5	T42.3X6
Nupercaine (spinal anesthetic)	T41.3X1	T41.3X2	T41.3X3	T41.3X4	T41.3X5	T41.3X6
topical (surface)	T41.3X1	T41.3X2	T41.3X3	T41.3X4	T41.3X5	T41.3X6
Nutmeg oil (liniment)	T49.3X1	T49.3X2	T49.3X3	T49.3X4	T49.3X5	T49.3X6
Nutritional supplement	T50.901	T50.902	T50.903	T50.904	T50.905	T50.906
Nux vomica	T65.1X1	T65.1X2	T65.1X3	T65.1X4	—	—
Nydrazid	T37.1X1	T37.1X2	T37.1X3	T37.1X4	T37.1X5	T37.1X6
Nylidrin	T46.7X1	T46.7X2	T46.7X3	T46.7X4	T46.7X5	T46.7X6
Nystatin	T36.7X1	T36.7X2	T36.7X3	T36.7X4	T36.7X5	T36.7X6
topical	T49.0X1	T49.0X2	T49.0X3	T49.0X4	T49.0X5	T49.0X6
Nytol	T45.0X1	T45.0X2	T45.0X3	T45.0X4	T45.0X5	T45.0X6
O						
Obidoxime chloride	T50.6X1	T50.6X2	T50.6X3	T50.6X4	T50.6X5	T50.6X6
Octafonium (chloride)	T49.3X1	T49.3X2	T49.3X3	T49.3X4	T49.3X5	T49.3X6
Octamethyl pyrophos-phoramide	T60.0X1	T60.0X2	T60.0X3	T60.0X4	—	—
Octanoin	T50.991	T50.992	T50.993	T50.994	T50.995	T50.996
Octatropine methyl-bromide	T44.3X1	T44.3X2	T44.3X3	T44.3X4	T44.3X5	T44.3X6
Octotiamine	T45.2X1	T45.2X2	T45.2X3	T45.2X4	T45.2X5	T45.2X6
Octoxinol (9)	T49.8X1	T49.8X2	T49.8X3	T49.8X4	T49.8X5	T49.8X6
Octreotide	T38.991	T38.992	T38.993	T38.994	T38.995	T38.996
Octyl nitrite	T46.3X1	T46.3X2	T46.3X3	T46.3X4	T46.3X5	T46.3X6
Oestradiol	T38.5X1	T38.5X2	T38.5X3	T38.5X4	T38.5X5	T38.5X6
Oestriol	T38.5X1	T38.5X2	T38.5X3	T38.5X4	T38.5X5	T38.5X6
Oestrogen	T38.5X1	T38.5X2	T38.5X3	T38.5X4	T38.5X5	T38.5X6
Oestrone	T38.5X1	T38.5X2	T38.5X3	T38.5X4	T38.5X5	T38.5X6
Ofloxacin	T36.8X1	T36.8X2	T36.8X3	T36.8X4	T36.8X5	T36.8X6
Oil (of)	T65.891	T65.892	T65.893	T65.894	—	—
bitter almond	T62.8X1	T62.8X2	T62.8X3	T62.8X4	—	—
cloves	T49.7X1	T49.7X2	T49.7X3	T49.7X4	T49.7X5	T49.7X6
colors	T65.6X1	T65.6X2	T65.6X3	T65.6X4	—	—
fumes	T59.891	T59.892	T59.893	T59.894	—	—
lubricating	T52.0X1	T52.0X2	T52.0X3	T52.0X4	—	—
Niobe	T52.8X1	T52.8X2	T52.8X3	T52.8X4	—	—

	External Cause (T-Code)					
Substance	Poisoning, Accidental (Unintentional)	Poisoning, Intentional Self-Harm	Poisoning, Assault	Poisoning, Undetermined	Adverse Effect	Underdosing
Oil (of) (Continued)						
vitriol (liquid)	T54.2X1	T54.2X2	T54.2X3	T54.2X4	—	—
fumes	T54.2X1	T54.2X2	T54.2X3	T54.2X4	—	—
wintergreen (bitter) NEC	T49.3X1	T49.3X2	T49.3X3	T49.3X4	T49.3X5	T49.3X6
Oily preparation (for skin)	T49.3X1	T49.3X2	T49.3X3	T49.3X4	T49.3X5	T49.3X6
Ointment NEC	T49.3X1	T49.3X2	T49.3X3	T49.3X4	T49.3X5	T49.3X6
Olanzapine	T43.591	T43.592	T43.593	T43.594	T43.595	T43.596
Oleander	T62.2X1	T62.2X2	T62.2X3	T62.2X4	—	—
Oleandomycin	T36.3X1	T36.3X2	T36.3X3	T36.3X4	T36.3X5	T36.3X6
Oleandrin	T46.0X1	T46.0X2	T46.0X3	T46.0X4	T46.0X5	T46.0X6
Oleic acid	T46.6X1	T46.6X2	T46.6X3	T46.6X4	T46.6X5	T46.6X6
Oleovitamin A	T45.2X1	T45.2X2	T45.2X3	T45.2X4	T45.2X5	T45.2X6
Oleum ricini	T47.2X1	T47.2X2	T47.2X3	T47.2X4	T47.2X5	T47.2X6
Olive oil (medicinal) NEC	T47.4X1	T47.4X2	T47.4X3	T47.4X4	T47.4X5	T47.4X6
Olivomycin	T45.1X1	T45.1X2	T45.1X3	T45.1X4	T45.1X5	T45.1X6
Olsalazine	T47.8X1	T47.8X2	T47.8X3	T47.8X4	T47.8X5	T47.8X6
Omeprazole	T47.1X1	T47.1X2	T47.1X3	T47.1X4	T47.1X5	T47.1X6
OMPA	T60.0X1	T60.0X2	T60.0X3	T60.0X4	—	—
Ondansetron	T45.0X1	T45.0X2	T45.0X3	T45.0X4	T45.0X5	T45.0X6
Oncovin	T45.1X1	T45.1X2	T45.1X3	T45.1X4	T45.1X5	T45.1X6
Ophthaine	T41.3X1	T41.3X2	T41.3X3	T41.3X4	T41.3X5	T41.3X6
Ophthetic	T41.3X1	T41.3X2	T41.3X3	T41.3X4	T41.3X5	T41.3X6
Opiate NEC	T40.601	T40.602	T40.603	T40.604	T40.605	T40.606
antagonists	T50.7X1	T50.7X2	T50.7X3	T50.7X4	T50.7X5	T50.7X6
Opioid NEC	T40.2X1	T40.2X2	T40.2X3	T40.2X4	T40.2X5	T40.2X6
Opipramol	T43.011	T43.012	T43.013	T43.014	T43.015	T43.016
Opium alkaloids (total)	T40.0X1	T40.0X2	T40.0X3	T40.0X4	T40.0X5	T40.0X6
standardized powdered	T40.0X1	T40.0X2	T40.0X3	T40.0X4	T40.0X5	T40.0X6
tincture (camphorated)	T40.0X1	T40.0X2	T40.0X3	T40.0X4	T40.0X5	T40.0X6
Oracon	T38.4X1	T38.4X2	T38.4X3	T38.4X4	T38.4X5	T38.4X6
Oragrafin	T50.8X1	T50.8X2	T50.8X3	T50.8X4	T50.8X5	T50.8X6
Oral contraceptives	T38.4X1	T38.4X2	T38.4X3	T38.4X4	T38.4X5	T38.4X6
Oral rehydration salts	T50.3X1	T50.3X2	T50.3X3	T50.3X4	T50.3X5	T50.3X6
Orazamide	T50.991	T50.992	T50.993	T50.994	T50.995	T50.996
Orciprenaline	T48.291	T48.292	T48.293	T48.294	T48.295	T48.296
Organidin	T48.4X1	T48.4X2	T48.4X3	T48.4X4	T48.4X5	T48.4X6
Organonitrate NEC	T46.3X1	T46.3X2	T46.3X3	T46.3X4	T46.3X5	T46.3X6
Organophosphates	T60.0X1	T60.0X2	T60.0X3	T60.0X4	—	—
Orimune	T50.B91	T50.B92	T50.B93	T50.B94	T50.B95	T50.B96
Orinase	T38.3X1	T38.3X2	T38.3X3	T38.3X4	T38.3X5	T38.3X6
Ormeloxifene	T38.6X1	T38.6X2	T38.6X3	T38.6X4	T38.6X5	T38.6X6

TABLE OF DRUGS AND CHEMICALS

Substance	External Cause (T-Code)					
	Poisoning, Accidental (Unintentional)	Poisoning, Intentional Self-Harm	Poisoning, Assault	Poisoning, Undetermined	Adverse Effect	Underdosing
Ornidazole	T37.3X1	T37.3X2	T37.3X3	T37.3X4	T37.3X5	T37.3X6
Ornithine aspartate	T50.991	T50.992	T50.993	T50.994	T50.995	T50.996
Ornoprostil	T47.1X1	T47.1X2	T47.1X3	T47.1X4	T47.1X5	T47.1X6
Orphenadrine (hydrochloride)	T42.8X1	T42.8X2	T42.8X3	T42.8X4	T42.8X5	T42.8X6
Ortal (sodium)	T42.3X1	T42.3X2	T42.3X3	T42.3X4	T42.3X5	T42.3X6
Orthoboric acid	T49.0X1	T49.0X2	T49.0X3	T49.0X4	T49.0X5	T49.0X6
ENT agent	T49.6X1	T49.6X2	T49.6X3	T49.6X4	T49.6X5	T49.6X6
ophthalmic preparation	T49.5X1	T49.5X2	T49.5X3	T49.5X4	T49.5X5	T49.5X6
Orthocaine	T41.3X1	T41.3X2	T41.3X3	T41.3X4	T41.3X5	T41.3X6
Orthodichlorobenzene	T53.7X1	T53.7X2	T53.7X3	T53.7X4	—	—
Ortho-Novum	T38.4X1	T38.4X2	T38.4X3	T38.4X4	T38.4X5	T38.4X6
Orthotolidine (reagent)	T54.2X1	T54.2X2	T54.2X3	T54.2X4	—	—
Osmic acid (liquid)	T54.2X1	T54.2X2	T54.2X3	T54.2X4	—	—
fumes	T54.2X1	T54.2X2	T54.2X3	T54.2X4	—	—
Osmotic diuretics	T50.2X1	T50.2X2	T50.2X3	T50.2X4	T50.2X5	T50.2X6
Otilonium bromide	T44.3X1	T44.3X2	T44.3X3	T44.3X4	T44.3X5	T44.3X6
Otorhinolaryngological drug NEC	T49.6X1	T49.6X2	T49.6X3	T49.6X4	T49.6X5	T49.6X6
Ouabain(e)	T46.0X1	T46.0X2	T46.0X3	T46.0X4	T46.0X5	T46.0X6
Ovarian						
hormone	T38.5X1	T38.5X2	T38.5X3	T38.5X4	T38.5X5	T38.5X6
stimulant	T38.5X1	T38.5X2	T38.5X3	T38.5X4	T38.5X5	T38.5X6
Ovral	T38.4X1	T38.4X2	T38.4X3	T38.4X4	T38.4X5	T38.4X6
Ovulen	T38.4X1	T38.4X2	T38.4X3	T38.4X4	T38.4X5	T38.4X6
Oxacillin	T36.0X1	T36.0X2	T36.0X3	T36.0X4	T36.0X5	T36.0X6
Oxalic acid	T54.2X1	T54.2X2	T54.2X3	T54.2X4	—	—
ammonium salt	T50.991	T50.992	T50.993	T50.994	T50.995	T50.996
Oxamniquine	T37.4X1	T37.4X2	T37.4X3	T37.4X4	T37.4X5	T37.4X6
Oxanamide	T43.591	T43.592	T43.593	T43.594	T43.595	T43.596
Oxandrolone	T38.7X1	T38.7X2	T38.7X3	T38.7X4	T38.7X5	T38.7X6
Oxantel	T37.4X1	T37.4X2	T37.4X3	T37.4X4	T37.4X5	T37.4X6
Oxapium iodide	T44.3X1	T44.3X2	T44.3X3	T44.3X4	T44.3X5	T44.3X6
Oxaprotiline	T43.021	T43.022	T43.023	T43.024	T43.025	T43.026
Oxaprozin	T39.311	T39.312	T39.313	T39.314	T39.315	T39.316
Oxatomide	T45.0X1	T45.0X2	T45.0X3	T45.0X4	T45.0X5	T45.0X6
Oxazepam	T42.4X1	T42.4X2	T42.4X3	T42.4X4	T42.4X5	T42.4X6
Oxazimedrine	T50.5X1	T50.5X2	T50.5X3	T50.5X4	T50.5X5	T50.5X6
Oxazolam	T42.4X1	T42.4X2	T42.4X3	T42.4X4	T42.4X5	T42.4X6
Oxazolidine derivatives	T42.2X1	T42.2X2	T42.2X3	T42.2X4	T42.2X5	T42.2X6
Oxazolidinedione (derivative)	T42.2X1	T42.2X2	T42.2X3	T42.2X4	T42.2X5	T42.2X6
Ox bile extract	T47.5X1	T47.5X2	T47.5X3	T47.5X4	T47.5X5	T47.5X6
Oxcarbazepine	T42.1X1	T42.1X2	T42.1X3	T42.1X4	T42.1X5	T42.1X6
Oxedrine	T44.4X1	T44.4X2	T44.4X3	T44.4X4	T44.4X5	T44.4X6

Substance	External Cause (T-Code)					
	Poisoning, Accidental (Unintentional)	Poisoning, Intentional Self-Harm	Poisoning, Assault	Poisoning, Undetermined	Adverse Effect	Underdosing
Oxeladin (citrate)	T48.3X1	T48.3X2	T48.3X3	T48.3X4	T48.3X5	T48.3X6
Oxendolone	T38.5X1	T38.5X2	T38.5X3	T38.5X4	T38.5X5	T38.5X6
Oxetacaine	T41.3X1	T41.3X2	T41.3X3	T41.3X4	T41.3X5	T41.3X6
Oxethazine	T41.3X1	T41.3X2	T41.3X3	T41.3X4	T41.3X5	T41.3X6
Oxetorone	T39.8X1	T39.8X2	T39.8X3	T39.8X4	T39.8X5	T39.8X6
Oxiconazole	T49.0X1	T49.0X2	T49.0X3	T49.0X4	T49.0X5	T49.0X6
Oxidizing agent NEC	T54.91	T54.92	T54.93	T54.94	—	—
Oxipurinol	T50.4X1	T50.4X2	T50.4X3	T50.4X4	T50.4X5	T50.4X6
Oxitriptan	T43.291	T43.292	T43.293	T43.294	T43.295	T43.296
Oxitropium bromide	T48.6X1	T48.6X2	T48.6X3	T48.6X4	T48.6X5	T48.6X6
Oxodipine	T46.1X1	T46.1X2	T46.1X3	T46.1X4	T46.1X5	T46.1X6
Oxolamine	T48.3X1	T48.3X2	T48.3X3	T48.3X4	T48.3X5	T48.3X6
Oxolinic acid	T37.8X1	T37.8X2	T37.8X3	T37.8X4	T37.8X5	T37.8X6
Oxomemazine	T43.3X1	T43.3X2	T43.3X3	T43.3X4	T43.3X5	T43.3X6
Oxophenarsine	T37.3X1	T37.3X2	T37.3X3	T37.3X4	T37.3X5	T37.3X6
Oxprenolol	T44.7X1	T44.7X2	T44.7X3	T44.7X4	T44.7X5	T44.7X6
Oxsoralen	T49.3X1	T49.3X2	T49.3X3	T49.3X4	T49.3X5	T49.3X6
Oxtriphylline	T48.6X1	T48.6X2	T48.6X3	T48.6X4	T48.6X5	T48.6X6
Oxybate sodium	T41.291	T41.292	T41.293	T41.294	T41.295	T41.296
Oxybuprocaine	T41.3X1	T41.3X2	T41.3X3	T41.3X4	T41.3X5	T41.3X6
Oxybutynin	T44.3X1	T44.3X2	T44.3X3	T44.3X4	T44.3X5	T44.3X6
Oxychlorosene	T49.0X1	T49.0X2	T49.0X3	T49.0X4	T49.0X5	T49.0X6
Oxycodone	T40.2X1	T40.2X2	T40.2X3	T40.2X4	T40.2X5	T40.2X6
Oxyfedrine	T46.3X1	T46.3X2	T46.3X3	T46.3X4	T46.3X5	T46.3X6
Oxygen	T41.5X1	T41.5X2	T41.5X3	T41.5X4	T41.5X5	T41.5X6
Oxylone	T49.0X1	T49.0X2	T49.0X3	T49.0X4	T49.0X5	T49.0X6
ophthalmic preparation	T49.5X1	T49.5X2	T49.5X3	T49.5X4	T49.5X5	T49.5X6
Oxymesterone	T38.7X1	T38.7X2	T38.7X3	T38.7X4	T38.7X5	T38.7X6
Oxymetazoline	T48.5X1	T48.5X2	T48.5X3	T48.5X4	T48.5X5	T48.5X6
Oxymetholone	T38.7X1	T38.7X2	T38.7X3	T38.7X4	T38.7X5	T38.7X6
Oxymorphone	T40.2X1	T40.2X2	T40.2X3	T40.2X4	T40.2X5	T40.2X6
Oxypertine	T43.591	T43.592	T43.593	T43.594	T43.595	T43.596
Oxyphenbutazone	T39.2X1	T39.2X2	T39.2X3	T39.2X4	T39.2X5	T39.2X6
Oxyphencyclimine	T44.3X1	T44.3X2	T44.3X3	T44.3X4	T44.3X5	T44.3X6
Oxyphenisatine	T47.2X1	T47.2X2	T47.2X3	T47.2X4	T47.2X5	T47.2X6
Oxyphenonium bromide	T44.3X1	T44.3X2	T44.3X3	T44.3X4	T44.3X5	T44.3X6
Oxypolygelatin	T45.8X1	T45.8X2	T45.8X3	T45.8X4	T45.8X5	T45.8X6
Oxyquinoline (derivatives)	T37.8X1	T37.8X2	T37.8X3	T37.8X4	T37.8X5	T37.8X6
Oxytetracycline	T36.4X1	T36.4X2	T36.4X3	T36.4X4	T36.4X5	T36.4X6
Oxytocic drug NEC	T48.0X1	T48.0X2	T48.0X3	T48.0X4	T48.0X5	T48.0X6
Oxytocin (synthetic)	T48.0X1	T48.0X2	T48.0X3	T48.0X4	T48.0X5	T48.0X6
Ozone	T59.891	T59.892	T59.893	T59.894	—	—

◀ New ◀ Revised ~~deleted~~ Deleted

Substance	Poisoning, Accidental (Unintentional)	Poisoning, Intentional Self-Harm	Poisoning, Assault	Poisoning, Undetermined	Adverse Effect	Underdosing
P						
PABA	T49.3X1	T49.3X2	T49.3X3	T49.3X4	T49.3X5	T49.3X6
Packed red cells	T45.8X1	T45.8X2	T45.8X3	T45.8X4	T45.8X5	T45.8X6
Padimate	T49.3X1	T49.3X2	T49.3X3	T49.3X4	T49.3X5	T49.3X6
Paint NEC	T65.6X1	T65.6X2	T65.6X3	T65.6X4	—	—
cleaner	T52.91	T52.92	T52.93	T52.94	—	—
fumes NEC	T59.891	T59.892	T59.893	T59.894	—	—
lead (fumes)	T56.0X1	T56.0X2	T56.0X3	T56.0X4	—	—
solvent NEC	T52.8X1	T52.8X2	T52.8X3	T52.8X4	—	—
stripper	T52.8X1	T52.8X2	T52.8X3	T52.8X4	—	—
Palfium	T40.2X1	T40.2X2	T40.2X3	T40.2X4		
Palm kernel oil	T50.991	T50.992	T50.993	T50.994	T50.995	T50.996
Paludrine	T37.2X1	T37.2X2	T37.2X3	T37.2X4	T37.2X5	T37.2X6
PAM (pralidoxime)	T50.6X1	T50.6X2	T50.6X3	T50.6X4	T50.6X5	T50.6X6
Pamaquine (naphthoute)	T37.2X1	T37.2X2	T37.2X3	T37.2X4	T37.2X5	T37.2X6
Panadol	T39.1X1	T39.1X2	T39.1X3	T39.1X4	T39.1X5	T39.1X6
Pancreatic						
digestive secretion stimulant	T47.8X1	T47.8X2	T47.8X3	T47.8X4	T47.8X5	T47.8X6
dornase	T45.3X1	T45.3X2	T45.3X3	T45.3X4	T45.3X5	T45.3X6
Pancreatin	T47.5X1	T47.5X2	T47.5X3	T47.5X4	T47.5X5	T47.5X6
Pancrelipase	T47.5X1	T47.5X2	T47.5X3	T47.5X4	T47.5X5	T47.5X6
Pancuronium (bromide)	T48.1X1	T48.1X2	T48.1X3	T48.1X4	T48.1X5	T48.1X6
Pangamic acid	T45.2X1	T45.2X2	T45.2X3	T45.2X4	T45.2X5	T45.2X6
Panthenol	T45.2X1	T45.2X2	T45.2X3	T45.2X4	T45.2X5	T45.2X6
topical	T49.8X1	T49.8X2	T49.8X3	T49.8X4	T49.8X5	T49.8X6
Pantopon	T40.0X1	T40.0X2	T40.0X3	T40.0X4	T40.0X5	T40.0X6
Pantothenic acid	T45.2X1	T45.2X2	T45.2X3	T45.2X4	T45.2X5	T45.2X6
Panwarfin	T45.511	T45.512	T45.513	T45.514	T45.515	T45.516
Papain	T47.5X1	T47.5X2	T47.5X3	T47.5X4	T47.5X5	T47.5X6
digestant	T47.5X1	T47.5X2	T47.5X3	T47.5X4	T47.5X5	T47.5X6
Papaveretum	T40.0X1	T40.0X2	T40.0X3	T40.0X4	T40.0X5	T40.0X6
Papaverine	T44.3X1	T44.3X2	T44.3X3	T44.3X4	T44.3X5	T44.3X6
Para-acetamidophenol	T39.1X1	T39.1X2	T39.1X3	T39.1X4	T39.1X5	T39.1X6
Para-aminobenzoic acid	T49.3X1	T49.3X2	T49.3X3	T49.3X4	T49.3X5	T49.3X6
Para-aminophenol derivatives	T39.1X1	T39.1X2	T39.1X3	T39.1X4	T39.1X5	T39.1X6
Para-aminosalicylic acid	T37.1X1	T37.1X2	T37.1X3	T37.1X4	T37.1X5	T37.1X6
Paracetaldehyde	T42.6X1	T42.6X2	T42.6X3	T42.6X4	T42.6X5	T42.6X6
Paracetamol	T39.1X1	T39.1X2	T39.1X3	T39.1X4	T39.1X5	T39.1X6
Parachlorophenol (camphorated)	T49.0X1	T49.0X2	T49.0X3	T49.0X4	T49.0X5	T49.0X6
Paracodin	T40.2X1	T40.2X2	T40.2X3	T40.2X4	T40.2X5	T40.2X6
Paradione	T42.2X1	T42.2X2	T42.2X3	T42.2X4	T42.2X5	T42.2X6

Substance	Poisoning, Accidental (Unintentional)	Poisoning, Intentional Self-Harm	Poisoning, Assault	Poisoning, Undetermined	Adverse Effect	Underdosing
Paraffin(s) (wax)	T52.0X1	T52.0X2	T52.0X3	T52.0X4	—	—
liquid (medicinal)	T47.4X1	T47.4X2	T47.4X3	T47.4X4	T47.4X5	T47.4X6
nonmedicinal	T52.0X1	T52.0X2	T52.0X3	T52.0X4	—	—
Paraformaldehyde	T60.3X1	T60.3X2	T60.3X3	T60.3X4	—	—
Paraldehyde	T42.6X1	T42.6X2	T42.6X3	T42.6X4	T42.6X5	T42.6X6
Paramethadione	T42.2X1	T42.2X2	T42.2X3	T42.2X4	T42.2X5	T42.2X6
Paramethasone	T38.0X1	T38.0X2	T38.0X3	T38.0X4	T38.0X5	T38.0X6
acetate	T49.0X1	T49.0X2	T49.0X3	T49.0X4	T49.0X5	T49.0X6
Paraoxon	T60.0X1	T60.0X2	T60.0X3	T60.0X4	—	—
Paraquat	T60.3X1	T60.3X2	T60.3X3	T60.3X4	—	—
Parasympatholytic NEC	T44.3X1	T44.3X2	T44.3X3	T44.3X4	T44.3X5	T44.3X6
Parasympathomimetic drug NEC	T44.1X1	T44.1X2	T44.1X3	T44.1X4	T44.1X5	T44.1X6
Parathion	T60.0X1	T60.0X2	T60.0X3	T60.0X4	—	—
Parathormone	T50.991	T50.992	T50.993	T50.994	T50.995	T50.996
Parathyroid extract	T50.991	T50.992	T50.993	T50.994	T50.995	T50.996
Paratyphoid vaccine	T50.A91	T50.A92	T50.A93	T50.A94	T50.A95	T50.A96
Paredrine	T44.4X1	T44.4X2	T44.4X3	T44.4X4	T44.4X5	T44.4X6
Paregoric	T40.0X1	T40.0X2	T40.0X3	T40.0X4	T40.0X5	T40.0X6
Pargyline	T46.5X1	T46.5X2	T46.5X3	T46.5X4	T46.5X5	T46.5X6
Paris green	T57.0X1	T57.0X2	T57.0X3	T57.0X4	—	—
insecticide	T57.0X1	T57.0X2	T57.0X3	T57.0X4	—	—
Parnate	T43.1X1	T43.1X2	T43.1X3	T43.1X4	T43.1X5	T43.1X6
Paromomycin	T36.5X1	T36.5X2	T36.5X3	T36.5X4	T36.5X5	T36.5X6
Paroxypropione	T45.1X1	T45.1X2	T45.1X3	T45.1X4	T45.1X5	T45.1X6
Parzone	T40.2X1	T40.2X2	T40.2X3	T40.2X4	T40.2X5	T40.2X6
PAS	T37.1X1	T37.1X2	T37.1X3	T37.1X4	T37.1X5	T37.1X6
Pasiniazid	T37.1X1	T37.1X2	T37.1X3	T37.1X4	T37.1X5	T37.1X6
PBB (polybrominated biphenyls)	T65.891	T65.892	T65.893	T65.894	—	—
PCB	T65.891	T65.892	T65.893	T65.894	—	—
PCP						
meaning pentachlorophenol	T60.1X1	T60.1X2	T60.1X3	T60.1X4	—	—
fungicide	T60.3X1	T60.3X2	T60.3X3	T60.3X4	—	—
herbicide	T60.3X1	T60.3X2	T60.3X3	T60.3X4	—	—
insecticide	T60.1X1	T60.1X2	T60.1X3	T60.1X4	—	—
meaning phencyclidine	T40.991	T40.992	T40.993	T40.994		
Peach kernel oil (emulsion)	T47.4X1	T47.4X2	T47.4X3	T47.4X4	T47.4X5	T47.4X6
Peanut oil (emulsion) NEC	T47.4X1	T47.4X2	T47.4X3	T47.4X4	T47.4X5	T47.4X6
topical	T49.3X1	T49.3X2	T49.3X3	T49.3X4	T49.3X5	T49.3X6
Pearly Gates (morning glory seeds)	T40.991	T40.992	T40.993	T40.994	—	—
Pecazine	T43.3X1	T43.3X2	T43.3X3	T43.3X4	T43.3X5	T43.3X6
Pectin	T47.6X1	T47.6X2	T47.6X3	T47.6X4	T47.6X5	T47.6X6

◀ New   ◀ Revised   ~~deleted~~ Deleted

TABLE OF DRUGS AND CHEMICALS

Substance	Poisoning, Accidental (Unintentional)	Poisoning, Intentional Self-Harm	Poisoning, Assault	Poisoning, Undetermined	Adverse Effect	Underdosing
Pefloxacin	T37.8X1	T37.8X2	T37.8X3	T37.8X4	T37.8X5	T37.8X6
Pegademase, bovine	T50.Z91	T50.Z92	T50.Z93	T50.Z94	T50.Z95	T50.Z96
Pelletierine tannate	T37.4X1	T37.4X2	T37.4X3	T37.4X4	T37.4X5	T37.4X6
Pemirolast (potassium)	T48.6X1	T48.6X2	T48.6X3	T48.6X4	T48.6X5	T48.6X6
Pemoline	T50.7X1	T50.7X2	T50.7X3	T50.7X4	T50.7X5	T50.7X6
Pempidine	T44.2X1	T44.2X2	T44.2X3	T44.2X4	T44.2X5	T44.2X6
Penamecillin	T36.0X1	T36.0X2	T36.0X3	T36.0X4	T36.0X5	T36.0X6
Penbutolol	T44.7X1	T44.7X2	T44.7X3	T44.7X4	T44.7X5	T44.7X6
Penethamate	T36.0X1	T36.0X2	T36.0X3	T36.0X4	T36.0X5	T36.0X6
Penfluridol	T43.591	T43.592	T43.593	T43.594	T43.595	T43.596
Penflutizide	T50.2X1	T50.2X2	T50.2X3	T50.2X4	T50.2X5	T50.2X6
Pengitoxin	T46.0X1	T46.0X2	T46.0X3	T46.0X4	T46.0X5	T46.0X6
Penicillamine	T50.6X1	T50.6X2	T50.6X3	T50.6X4	T50.6X5	T50.6X6
Penicillin (any)	T36.0X1	T36.0X2	T36.0X3	T36.0X4	T36.0X5	T36.0X6
Penicillinase	T45.3X1	T45.3X2	T45.3X3	T45.3X4	T45.3X5	T45.3X6
Penicilloyl polylysine	T50.8X1	T50.8X2	T50.8X3	T50.8X4	T50.8X5	T50.8X6
Penimepicycline	T36.4X1	T36.4X2	T36.4X3	T36.4X4	T36.4X5	T36.4X6
Pentachloroethane	T53.6X1	T53.6X2	T53.6X3	T53.6X4	—	—
Pentachloronaphthalene	T53.7X1	T53.7X2	T53.7X3	T53.7X4	—	—
Pentachlorophenol (pesticide)	T60.1X1	T60.1X2	T60.1X3	T60.1X4	—	—
fungicide	T60.3X1	T60.3X2	T60.3X3	T60.3X4	—	—
herbicide	T60.3X1	T60.3X2	T60.3X3	T60.3X4	—	—
insecticide	T60.1X1	T60.1X2	T60.1X3	T60.1X4	—	—
Pentaerythritol tetranitrate	T46.3X1	T46.3X2	T46.3X3	T46.3X4	T46.3X5	T46.3X6
Pentaerythritol	T46.3X1	T46.3X2	T46.3X3	T46.3X4	T46.3X5	T46.3X6
chloral	T42.6X1	T42.6X2	T42.6X3	T42.6X4	T42.6X5	T42.6X6
tetranitrate NEC	T46.3X1	T46.3X2	T46.3X3	T46.3X4	T46.3X5	T46.3X6
Pentagastrin	T50.8X1	T50.8X2	T50.8X3	T50.8X4	T50.8X5	T50.8X6
Pentalin	T53.6X1	T53.6X2	T53.6X3	T53.6X4	—	—
Pentamethonium bromide	T44.2X1	T44.2X2	T44.2X3	T44.2X4	T44.2X5	T44.2X6
Pentamidine	T37.3X1	T37.3X2	T37.3X3	T37.3X4	T37.3X5	T37.3X6
Pentanol	T51.3X1	T51.3X2	T51.3X3	T51.3X4	—	—
Pentapyrrolinium (bitartrate)	T44.2X1	T44.2X2	T44.2X3	T44.2X4	T44.2X5	T44.2X6
Pentaquine	T37.2X1	T37.2X2	T37.2X3	T37.2X4	T37.2X5	T37.2X6
Pentazocine	T40.4X1	T40.4X2	T40.4X3	T40.4X4	T40.4X5	T40.4X6
Pentetrazole	T50.7X1	T50.7X2	T50.7X3	T50.7X4	T50.7X5	T50.7X6
Penthienate bromide	T44.3X1	T44.3X2	T44.3X3	T44.3X4	T44.3X5	T44.3X6
Pentifylline	T46.7X1	T46.7X2	T46.7X3	T46.7X4	T46.7X5	T46.7X6
Pentobarbital	T42.3X1	T42.3X2	T42.3X3	T42.3X4	T42.3X5	T42.3X6
sodium	T42.3X1	T42.3X2	T42.3X3	T42.3X4	T42.3X5	T42.3X6
Pentobarbitone	T42.3X1	T42.3X2	T42.3X3	T42.3X4	T42.3X5	T42.3X6
Pentolonium tartrate	T44.2X1	T44.2X2	T44.2X3	T44.2X4	T44.2X5	T44.2X6

Substance	Poisoning, Accidental (Unintentional)	Poisoning, Intentional Self-Harm	Poisoning, Assault	Poisoning, Undetermined	Adverse Effect	Underdosing
Pentosan polysulfate (sodium)	T39.8X1	T39.8X2	T39.8X3	T39.8X4	T39.8X5	T39.8X6
Pentostatin	T45.1X1	T45.1X2	T45.1X3	T45.1X4	T45.1X5	T45.1X6
Pentothal	T41.1X1	T41.1X2	T41.1X3	T41.1X4	T41.1X5	T41.1X6
Pentoxifylline	T46.7X1	T46.7X2	T46.7X3	T46.7X4	T46.7X5	T46.7X6
Pentoxyverine	T48.3X1	T48.3X2	T48.3X3	T48.3X4	T48.3X5	T48.3X6
Pentrinat	T46.3X1	T46.3X2	T46.3X3	T46.3X4	T46.3X5	T46.3X6
Pentylenetetrazole	T50.7X1	T50.7X2	T50.7X3	T50.7X4	T50.7X5	T50.7X6
Pentylsalicylamide	T37.1X1	T37.1X2	T37.1X3	T37.1X4	T37.1X5	T37.1X6
Pentymal	T42.3X1	T42.3X2	T42.3X3	T42.3X4	T42.3X5	T42.3X6
Peplomycin	T45.1X1	T45.1X2	T45.1X3	T45.1X4	T45.1X5	T45.1X6
Peppermint (oil)	T47.5X1	T47.5X2	T47.5X3	T47.5X4	T47.5X5	T47.5X6
Pepsin	T47.5X1	T47.5X2	T47.5X3	T47.5X4	T47.5X5	T47.5X6
digestant	T47.5X1	T47.5X2	T47.5X3	T47.5X4	T47.5X5	T47.5X6
Pepstatin	T47.1X1	T47.1X2	T47.1X3	T47.1X4	T47.1X5	T47.1X6
Peptavlon	T50.8X1	T50.8X2	T50.8X3	T50.8X4	T50.8X5	T50.8X6
Perazine	T43.3X1	T43.3X2	T43.3X3	T43.3X4	T43.3X5	T43.3X6
Percaine (spinal)	T41.3X1	T41.3X2	T41.3X3	T41.3X4	T41.3X5	T41.3X6
topical (surface)	T41.3X1	T41.3X2	T41.3X3	T41.3X4	T41.3X5	T41.3X6
Perchloroethylene	T53.3X1	T53.3X2	T53.3X3	T53.3X4	—	—
medicinal	T37.4X1	T37.4X2	T37.4X3	T37.4X4	T37.4X5	T37.4X6
vapor	T53.3X1	T53.3X2	T53.3X3	T53.3X4	—	—
Percodan	T40.2X1	T40.2X2	T40.2X3	T40.2X4	T40.2X5	T40.2X6
Percogesic — see also acetaminophen	T45.0X1	T45.0X2	T45.0X3	T45.0X4	T45.0X5	T45.0X6
Percorten	T38.0X1	T38.0X2	T38.0X3	T38.0X4	T38.0X5	T38.0X6
Pergolide	T42.8X1	T42.8X2	T42.8X3	T42.8X4	T42.8X5	T42.8X6
Pergonal	T38.811	T38.812	T38.813	T38.814	T38.815	T38.816
Perhexilene	T46.3X1	T46.3X2	T46.3X3	T46.3X4	T46.3X5	T46.3X6
Perhexiline (maleate)	T46.3X1	T46.3X2	T46.3X3	T46.3X4	T46.3X5	T46.3X6
Periactin	T45.0X1	T45.0X2	T45.0X3	T45.0X4	T45.0X5	T45.0X6
Periciazine	T43.3X1	T43.3X2	T43.3X3	T43.3X4	T43.3X5	T43.3X6
Periclor	T42.6X1	T42.6X2	T42.6X3	T42.6X4	T42.6X5	T42.6X6
Perindopril	T46.4X1	T46.4X2	T46.4X3	T46.4X4	T46.4X5	T46.4X6
Perisoxal	T39.8X1	T39.8X2	T39.8X3	T39.8X4	T39.8X5	T39.8X6
Peritrate	T46.3X1	T46.3X2	T46.3X3	T46.3X4	T46.3X5	T46.3X6
Peritoneal dialysis solution	T50.3X1	T50.3X2	T50.3X3	T50.3X4	T50.3X5	T50.3X6
Perlapine	T42.4X1	T42.4X2	T42.4X3	T42.4X4	T42.4X5	T42.4X6
Permanganate	T65.891	T65.892	T65.893	T65.894	—	—
Permethrin	T60.1X1	T60.1X2	T60.1X3	T60.1X4	—	—
Pernocton	T42.3X1	T42.3X2	T42.3X3	T42.3X4	T42.3X5	T42.3X6
Pernoston	T42.3X1	T42.3X2	T42.3X3	T42.3X4	T42.3X5	T42.3X6
Peronine	T40.2X1	T40.2X2	T40.2X3	T40.2X4	—	—
Perphenazine	T43.3X1	T43.3X2	T43.3X3	T43.3X4	T43.3X5	T43.3X6

◀ New   ◀ Revised   ~~deleted~~ Deleted

Substance	External Cause (T-Code)					
	Poisoning, Accidental (Unintentional)	Poisoning, Intentional Self-Harm	Poisoning, Assault	Poisoning, Undetermined	Adverse Effect	Underdosing
Pertofrane	T43.011	T43.012	T43.013	T43.014	T43.015	T43.016
Pertussis						
immune serum (human)	T50.Z11	T50.Z12	T50.Z13	T50.Z14	T50.Z15	T50.Z16
vaccine (with diphtheria toxoid) (with tetanus toxoid)	T50.A11	T50.A12	T50.A13	T50.A14	T50.A15	T50.A16
Peruvian balsam	T49.0X1	T49.0X2	T49.0X3	T49.0X4	T49.0X5	T49.0X6
Peruvoside	T46.0X1	T46.0X2	T46.0X3	T46.0X4	T46.0X5	T46.0X6
Pesticide (dust) (fumes) (vapor) NEC	T60.91	T60.92	T60.93	T60.94	—	—
arsenic	T57.0X1	T57.0X2	T57.0X3	T57.0X4	—	—
chlorinated	T60.1X1	T60.1X2	T60.1X3	T60.1X4	—	—
cyanide	T65.0X1	T65.0X2	T65.0X3	T65.0X4	—	—
kerosene	T52.0X1	T52.0X2	T52.0X3	T52.0X4	—	—
mixture (of compounds)	T60.91	T60.92	T60.93	T60.94	—	—
naphthalene	T60.2X1	T60.2X2	T60.2X3	T60.2X4	—	—
organochlorine (compounds)	T60.1X1	T60.1X2	T60.1X3	T60.1X4	—	—
petroleum (distillate) (products) NEC	T60.8X1	T60.8X2	T60.8X3	T60.8X4	—	—
specified ingredient NEC	T60.8X1	T60.8X2	T60.8X3	T60.8X4	—	—
strychnine	T65.1X1	T65.1X2	T65.1X3	T65.1X4	—	—
thallium	T60.4X1	T60.4X2	T60.4X3	T60.4X4	—	—
Pethidine	T40.4X1	T40.4X2	T40.4X3	T40.4X4	T40.4X5	T40.4X6
Petrichloral	T42.6X1	T42.6X2	T42.6X3	T42.6X4	T42.6X5	T42.6X6
Petrol	T52.0X1	T52.0X2	T52.0X3	T52.0X4	—	—
vapor	T52.0X1	T52.0X2	T52.0X3	T52.0X4	—	—
Petrolatum	T49.3X1	T49.3X2	T49.3X3	T49.3X4	T49.3X5	T49.3X6
hydrophilic	T49.3X1	T49.3X2	T49.3X3	T49.3X4	T49.3X5	T49.3X6
liquid	T47.4X1	T47.4X2	T47.4X3	T47.4X4	T47.4X5	T47.4X6
topical	T49.3X1	T49.3X2	T49.3X3	T49.3X4	T49.3X5	T49.3X6
nonmedicinal	T52.0X1	T52.0X2	T52.0X3	T52.0X4	—	—
red veterinary	T49.3X1	T49.3X2	T49.3X3	T49.3X4	T49.3X5	T49.3X6
white	T49.3X1	T49.3X2	T49.3X3	T49.3X4	T49.3X5	T49.3X6
Petroleum (products) NEC	T52.0X1	T52.0X2	T52.0X3	T52.0X4	—	—
benzine(s) — see Ligroin						
ether — see Ligroin						
jelly — see Petrolatum						
naphtha — see Ligroin						
pesticide	T60.8X1	T60.8X2	T60.8X3	T60.8X4	—	—
solids	T52.0X1	T52.0X2	T52.0X3	T52.0X4	—	—
solvents	T52.0X1	T52.0X2	T52.0X3	T52.0X4	—	—
vapor	T52.0X1	T52.0X2	T52.0X3	T52.0X4	—	—
Peyote	T40.991	T40.992	T40.993	T40.994	—	—
Phanodorm, phanodorn	T42.3X1	T42.3X2	T42.3X3	T42.3X4	T42.3X5	T42.3X6

Substance	External Cause (T-Code)					
	Poisoning, Accidental (Unintentional)	Poisoning, Intentional Self-Harm	Poisoning, Assault	Poisoning, Undetermined	Adverse Effect	Underdosing
Phanquinone	T37.3X1	T37.3X2	T37.3X3	T37.3X4	T37.3X5	T37.3X6
Phanquone	T37.3X1	T37.3X2	T37.3X3	T37.3X4	T37.3X5	T37.3X6
Pharmaceutical						
adjunct NEC	T50.901	T50.902	T50.903	T50.904	T50.905	T50.906
excipient NEC	T50.901	T50.902	T50.903	T50.904	T50.905	T50.906
sweetener	T50.901	T50.902	T50.903	T50.904	T50.905	T50.906
viscous agent	T50.901	T50.902	T50.903	T50.904	T50.905	T50.906
Phemitone	T42.3X1	T42.3X2	T42.3X3	T42.3X4	T42.3X5	T42.3X6
Phenacaine	T41.3X1	T41.3X2	T41.3X3	T41.3X4	T41.3X5	T41.3X6
Phenacemide	T42.6X1	T42.6X2	T42.6X3	T42.6X4	T42.6X5	T42.6X6
Phenacetin	T39.1X1	T39.1X2	T39.1X3	T39.1X4	T39.1X5	T39.1X6
Phenadoxone	T40.2X1	T40.2X2	T40.2X3	T40.2X4	—	—
Phenaglycodol	T43.591	T43.592	T43.593	T43.594	T43.595	T43.596
Phenantoin	T42.0X1	T42.0X2	T42.0X3	T42.0X4	T42.0X5	T42.0X6
Phenaphthazine reagent	T50.991	T50.992	T50.993	T50.994	T50.995	T50.996
Phenazocine	T40.4X1	T40.4X2	T40.4X3	T40.4X4	T40.4X5	T40.4X6
Phenazone	T39.2X1	T39.2X2	T39.2X3	T39.2X4	T39.2X5	T39.2X6
Phenazopyridine	T39.8X1	T39.8X2	T39.8X3	T39.8X4	T39.8X5	T39.8X6
Phenbenicillin	T36.0X1	T36.0X2	T36.0X3	T36.0X4	T36.0X5	T36.0X6
Phenbutrazate	T50.5X1	T50.5X2	T50.5X3	T50.5X4	T50.5X5	T50.5X6
Phencyclidine	T40.991	T40.992	T40.993	T40.994	T40.995	T40.996
Phendimetrazine	T50.5X1	T50.5X2	T50.5X3	T50.5X4	T50.5X5	T50.5X6
Phenelzine	T43.1X1	T43.1X2	T43.1X3	T43.1X4	T43.1X5	T43.1X6
Phenemal	T42.3X1	T42.3X2	T42.3X3	T42.3X4	T42.3X5	T42.3X6
Phenergan	T42.6X1	T42.6X2	T42.6X3	T42.6X4	T42.6X5	T42.6X6
Pheneticillin	T36.0X1	T36.0X2	T36.0X3	T36.0X4	T36.0X5	T36.0X6
Pheneturide	T42.6X1	T42.6X2	T42.6X3	T42.6X4	T42.6X5	T42.6X6
Phenformin	T38.3X1	T38.3X2	T38.3X3	T38.3X4	T38.3X5	T38.3X6
Phenglutarimide	T44.3X1	T44.3X2	T44.3X3	T44.3X4	T44.3X5	T44.3X6
Phenicarbazide	T39.8X1	T39.8X2	T39.8X3	T39.8X4	T39.8X5	T39.8X6
Phenindamine	T45.0X1	T45.0X2	T45.0X3	T45.0X4	T45.0X5	T45.0X6
Phenindione	T45.511	T45.512	T45.513	T45.514	T45.515	T45.516
Pheniprazine	T43.1X1	T43.1X2	T43.1X3	T43.1X4	T43.1X5	T43.1X6
Pheniramine	T45.0X1	T45.0X2	T45.0X3	T45.0X4	T45.0X5	T45.0X6
Phenisatin	T47.2X1	T47.2X2	T47.2X3	T47.2X4	T47.2X5	T47.2X6
Phenmetrazine	T50.5X1	T50.5X2	T50.5X3	T50.5X4	T50.5X5	T50.5X6
Phenobal	T42.3X1	T42.3X2	T42.3X3	T42.3X4	T42.3X5	T42.3X6
Phenobarbital	T42.3X1	T42.3X2	T42.3X3	T42.3X4	T42.3X5	T42.3X6
with						
mephenytoin	T42.3X1	T42.3X2	T42.3X3	T42.3X4	T42.3X5	T42.3X6
phenytoin	T42.3X1	T42.3X2	T42.3X3	T42.3X4	T42.3X5	T42.3X6
sodium	T42.3X1	T42.3X2	T42.3X3	T42.3X4	T42.3X5	T42.3X6

Substance	External Cause (T-Code) Poisoning, Accidental (Unintentional)	Poisoning, Intentional Self-Harm	Poisoning, Assault	Poisoning, Undetermined	Adverse Effect	Underdosing
Phenobarbitone	T42.3X1	T42.3X2	T42.3X3	T42.3X4	T42.3X5	T42.3X6
Phenobutiodil	T50.8X1	T50.8X2	T50.8X3	T50.8X4	T50.8X5	T50.8X6
Phenoctide	T49.0X1	T49.0X2	T49.0X3	T49.0X4	T49.0X5	T49.0X6
Phenol	T49.0X1	T49.0X2	T49.0X3	T49.0X4	T49.0X5	T49.0X6
disinfectant	T54.0X1	T54.0X2	T54.0X3	T54.0X4	—	—
in oil injection	T46.8X1	T46.8X2	T46.8X3	T46.8X4	T46.8X5	T46.8X6
medicinal	T49.1X1	T49.1X2	T49.1X3	T49.1X4	T49.1X5	T49.1X6
nonmedicinal NEC	T54.0X1	T54.0X2	T54.0X3	T54.0X4	—	—
pesticide	T60.8X1	T60.8X2	T60.8X3	T60.8X4	—	—
red	T50.8X1	T50.8X2	T50.8X3	T50.8X4	T50.8X5	T50.8X6
Phenolic preparation	T49.1X1	T49.1X2	T49.1X3	T49.1X4	T49.1X5	T49.1X6
Phenolphthalein	T47.2X1	T47.2X2	T47.2X3	T47.2X4	T47.2X5	T47.2X6
Phenolsulfonphthalein	T50.8X1	T50.8X2	T50.8X3	T50.8X4	T50.8X5	T50.8X6
Phenomorphan	T40.2X1	T40.2X2	T40.2X3	T40.2X4		
Phenonyl	T42.3X1	T42.3X2	T42.3X3	T42.3X4	T42.3X5	T42.3X6
Phenoperidine	T40.4X1	T40.4X2	T40.4X3	T40.4X4	—	—
Phenopyrazone	T46.991	T46.992	T46.993	T46.994	T46.995	T46.996
Phenoquin	T50.4X1	T50.4X2	T50.4X3	T50.4X4	T50.4X5	T50.4X6
Phenothiazine (psychotropic) NEC	T43.3X1	T43.3X2	T43.3X3	T43.3X4	T43.3X5	T43.3X6
insecticide	T60.2X1	T60.2X2	T60.2X3	T60.2X4	—	—
Phenothrin	T49.0X1	T49.0X2	T49.0X3	T49.0X4	T49.0X5	T49.0X6
Phenoxybenzamine	T46.7X1	T46.7X2	T46.7X3	T46.7X4	T46.7X5	T46.7X6
Phenoxyethanol	T49.0X1	T49.0X2	T49.0X3	T49.0X4	T49.0X5	T49.0X6
Phenoxymethyl penicillin	T36.0X1	T36.0X2	T36.0X3	T36.0X4	T36.0X5	T36.0X6
Phenprobamate	T42.8X1	T42.8X2	T42.8X3	T42.8X4	T42.8X5	T42.8X6
Phenprocoumon	T45.511	T45.512	T45.513	T45.514	T45.515	T45.516
Phensuximide	T42.2X1	T42.2X2	T42.2X3	T42.2X4	T42.2X5	T42.2X6
Phentermine	T50.5X1	T50.5X2	T50.5X3	T50.5X4	T50.5X5	T50.5X6
Phenthicillin	T36.0X1	T36.0X2	T36.0X3	T36.0X4	T36.0X5	T36.0X6
Phentolamine	T46.7X1	T46.7X2	T46.7X3	T46.7X4	T46.7X5	T46.7X6
Phenyl						
butazone	T39.2X1	T39.2X2	T39.2X3	T39.2X4	T39.2X5	T39.2X6
enediamine	T65.3X1	T65.3X2	T65.3X3	T65.3X4	—	—
hydrazine	T65.3X1	T65.3X2	T65.3X3	T65.3X4	—	—
antineoplastic	T45.1X1	T45.1X2	T45.1X3	T45.1X4	T45.1X5	T45.1X6
mercuric compounds — see Mercury						
salicylate	T49.3X1	T49.3X2	T49.3X3	T49.3X4	T49.3X5	T49.3X6
Phenylalanine mustard	T45.1X1	T45.1X2	T45.1X3	T45.1X4	T45.1X5	T45.1X6
Phenylbutazone	T39.2X1	T39.2X2	T39.2X3	T39.2X4	T39.2X5	T39.2X6
Phenylenediamine	T65.3X1	T65.3X2	T65.3X3	T65.3X4	—	—
Phenylephrine	T44.4X1	T44.4X2	T44.4X3	T44.4X4	T44.4X5	T44.4X6

Substance	External Cause (T-Code) Poisoning, Accidental (Unintentional)	Poisoning, Intentional Self-Harm	Poisoning, Assault	Poisoning, Undetermined	Adverse Effect	Underdosing
Phenylethylbiguanide	T38.3X1	T38.3X2	T38.3X3	T38.3X4	T38.3X5	T38.3X6
Phenylmercuric						
acetate	T49.0X1	T49.0X2	T49.0X3	T49.0X4	T49.0X5	T49.0X6
borate	T49.0X1	T49.0X2	T49.0X3	T49.0X4	T49.0X5	T49.0X6
nitrate	T49.0X1	T49.0X2	T49.0X3	T49.0X4	T49.0X5	T49.0X6
Phenylmethylbarbitone	T42.3X1	T42.3X2	T42.3X3	T42.3X4	T42.3X5	T42.3X6
Phenylpropanol	T47.5X1	T47.5X2	T47.5X3	T47.5X4	T47.5X5	T47.5X6
Phenylpropanolamine	T44.991	T44.992	T44.993	T44.994	T44.995	T44.996
Phenylsulfthion	T60.0X1	T60.0X2	T60.0X3	T60.0X4	—	—
Phenyltoloxamine	T45.0X1	T45.0X2	T45.0X3	T45.0X4	T45.0X5	T45.0X6
Phenyramidol, phenyramidon	T39.8X1	T39.8X2	T39.8X3	T39.8X4	T39.8X5	T39.8X6
Phenytoin	T42.0X1	T42.0X2	T42.0X3	T42.0X4	T42.0X5	T42.0X6
with Phenobarbital	T42.3X1	T42.3X2	T42.3X3	T42.3X4	T42.3X5	T42.3X6
pHisoHex	T49.2X1	T49.2X2	T49.2X3	T49.2X4	T49.2X5	T49.2X6
Pholcodine	T48.3X1	T48.3X2	T48.3X3	T48.3X4	T48.3X5	T48.3X6
Pholedrine	T46.991	T46.992	T46.993	T46.994	T46.995	T46.996
Phorate	T60.0X1	T60.0X2	T60.0X3	T60.0X4	—	—
Phosdrin	T60.0X1	T60.0X2	T60.0X3	T60.0X4	—	—
Phosfolan	T60.0X1	T60.0X2	T60.0X3	T60.0X4	—	—
Phosgene (gas)	T59.891	T59.892	T59.893	T59.894		
Phosphamidon	T60.0X1	T60.0X2	T60.0X3	T60.0X4	—	—
Phosphate	T65.891	T65.892	T65.893	T65.894		
laxative	T47.4X1	T47.4X2	T47.4X3	T47.4X4	T47.4X5	T47.4X6
organic	T60.0X1	T60.0X2	T60.0X3	T60.0X4	—	—
solvent	T52.91	T52.92	T52.93	T52.94		
tricresyl	T65.891	T65.892	T65.893	T65.894		
Phosphine	T57.1X1	T57.1X2	T57.1X3	T57.1X4	—	
fumigant	T57.1X1	T57.1X2	T57.1X3	T57.1X4		
Phospholine	T49.5X1	T49.5X2	T49.5X3	T49.5X4	T49.5X5	T49.5X6
Phosphoric acid	T54.2X1	T54.2X2	T54.2X3	T54.2X4	—	—
Phosphorus (compound) NEC	T57.1X1	T57.1X2	T57.1X3	T57.1X4	—	—
pesticide	T60.0X1	T60.0X2	T60.0X3	T60.0X4	—	—
Phthalates	T65.891	T65.892	T65.893	T65.894	—	—
Phthalic anhydride	T65.891	T65.892	T65.893	T65.894	—	—
Phthalimidoglutarimide	T42.6X1	T42.6X2	T42.6X3	T42.6X4	T42.6X5	T42.6X6
Phthalylsulfathiazole	T37.0X1	T37.0X2	T37.0X3	T37.0X4	T37.0X5	T37.0X6
Phylloquinone	T45.7X1	T45.7X2	T45.7X3	T45.7X4	T45.7X5	T45.7X6
Physeptone	T40.3X1	T40.3X2	T40.3X3	T40.3X4	T40.3X5	T40.3X6
Physostigma venenosum	T62.2X1	T62.2X2	T62.2X3	T62.2X4	—	—
Physostigmine	T49.5X1	T49.5X2	T49.5X3	T49.5X4	T49.5X5	T49.5X6
Phytolacca decandra	T62.2X1	T62.2X2	T62.2X3	T62.2X4	—	—
berries	T62.1X1	T62.1X2	T62.1X3	T62.1X4	—	—

◀ New ◀ Revised deleted Deleted

Substance	External Cause (T-Code)					
	Poisoning, Accidental (Unintentional)	Poisoning, Intentional Self-Harm	Poisoning, Assault	Poisoning, Undetermined	Adverse Effect	Underdosing
Phytomenadione	T45.7X1	T45.7X2	T45.7X3	T45.7X4	T45.7X5	T45.7X6
Phytonadione	T45.7X1	T45.7X2	T45.7X3	T45.7X4	T45.7X5	T45.7X6
Picoperine	T48.3X1	T48.3X2	T48.3X3	T48.3X4	T48.3X5	T48.3X6
Picosulfate (sodium)	T47.2X1	T47.2X2	T47.2X3	T47.2X4	T47.2X5	T47.2X6
Picric (acid)	T54.2X1	T54.2X2	T54.2X3	T54.2X4	—	—
Picrotoxin	T50.7X1	T50.7X2	T50.7X3	T50.7X4	T50.7X5	T50.7X6
Piketoprofen	T49.0X1	T49.0X2	T49.0X3	T49.0X4	T49.0X5	T49.0X6
Pilocarpine	T44.1X1	T44.1X2	T44.1X3	T44.1X4	T44.1X5	T44.1X6
Pilocarpus (jaborandi) extract	T44.1X1	T44.1X2	T44.1X3	T44.1X4	T44.1X5	T44.1X6
Pilsicainide (hydrochloride)	T46.2X1	T46.2X2	T46.2X3	T46.2X4	T46.2X5	T46.2X6
Pimaricin	T36.7X1	T36.7X2	T36.7X3	T36.7X4	T36.7X5	T36.7X6
Pimeclone	T50.7X1	T50.7X2	T50.7X3	T50.7X4	T50.7X5	T50.7X6
Pimelic ketone	T52.8X1	T52.8X2	T52.8X3	T52.8X4	—	—
Pimethixene	T45.0X1	T45.0X2	T45.0X3	T45.0X4	T45.0X5	T45.0X6
Piminodine	T40.2X1	T40.2X2	T40.2X3	T40.2X4	T40.2X5	T40.2X6
Pimozide	T43.591	T43.592	T43.593	T43.594	T43.595	T43.596
Pinacidil	T46.5X1	T46.5X2	T46.5X3	T46.5X4	T46.5X5	T46.5X6
Pinaverium bromide	T44.3X1	T44.3X2	T44.3X3	T44.3X4	T44.3X5	T44.3X6
Pinazepam	T42.4X1	T42.4X2	T42.4X3	T42.4X4	T42.4X5	T42.4X6
Pindolol	T44.7X1	T44.7X2	T44.7X3	T44.7X4	T44.7X5	T44.7X6
Pindone	T60.4X1	T60.4X2	T60.4X3	T60.4X4	—	—
Pine oil (disinfectant)	T65.891	T65.892	T65.893	T65.894	—	—
Pinkroot	T37.4X1	T37.4X2	T37.4X3	T37.4X4	T37.4X5	T37.4X6
Pipadone	T40.2X1	T40.2X2	T40.2X3	T40.2X4	—	—
Pipamazine	T45.0X1	T45.0X2	T45.0X3	T45.0X4	T45.0X5	T45.0X6
Pipamperone	T43.4X1	T43.4X2	T43.4X3	T43.4X4	T43.4X5	T43.4X6
Pipazetate	T48.3X1	T48.3X2	T48.3X3	T48.3X4	T48.3X5	T48.3X6
Pipemidic acid	T37.8X1	T37.8X2	T37.8X3	T37.8X4	T37.8X5	T37.8X6
Pipenzolate bromide	T44.3X1	T44.3X2	T44.3X3	T44.3X4	T44.3X5	T44.3X6
Piperacetazine	T43.3X1	T43.3X2	T43.3X3	T43.3X4	T43.3X5	T43.3X6
Piperacillin	T36.0X1	T36.0X2	T36.0X3	T36.0X4	T36.0X5	T36.0X6
Piperazine	T37.4X1	T37.4X2	T37.4X3	T37.4X4	T37.4X5	T37.4X6
estrone sulfate	T38.5X1	T38.5X2	T38.5X3	T38.5X4	T38.5X5	T38.5X6
Piper cubeba	T62.2X1	T62.2X2	T62.2X3	T62.2X4	—	—
Piperidione	T48.3X1	T48.3X2	T48.3X3	T48.3X4	—	—
Piperidolate	T44.3X1	T44.3X2	T44.3X3	T44.3X4	T44.3X5	T44.3X6
Piperocaine	T41.3X1	T41.3X2	T41.3X3	T41.3X4	T41.3X5	T41.3X6
infiltration (subcutaneous)	T41.3X1	T41.3X2	T41.3X3	T41.3X4	T41.3X5	T41.3X6
nerve block (peripheral) (plexus)	T41.3X1	T41.3X2	T41.3X3	T41.3X4	T41.3X5	T41.3X6
topical (surface)	T41.3X1	T41.3X2	T41.3X3	T41.3X4	T41.3X5	T41.3X6
Piperonyl butoxide	T60.8X1	T60.8X2	T60.8X3	T60.8X4	—	—
Pipethanate	T44.3X1	T44.3X2	T44.3X3	T44.3X4	T44.3X5	T44.3X6

Substance	External Cause (T-Code)					
	Poisoning, Accidental (Unintentional)	Poisoning, Intentional Self-Harm	Poisoning, Assault	Poisoning, Undetermined	Adverse Effect	Underdosing
Pipobroman	T45.1X1	T45.1X2	T45.1X3	T45.1X4	T45.1X5	T45.1X6
Pipofezine	T43.0X1	T43.0X2	T43.0X3	T43.0X4	T43.0X5	T43.0X6
Pipotiazine	T43.3X1	T43.3X2	T43.3X3	T43.3X4	T43.3X5	T43.3X6
Pipoxizine	T45.0X1	T45.0X2	T45.0X3	T45.0X4	T45.0X5	T45.0X6
Pipradrol	T43.691	T43.692	T43.693	T43.694	T43.695	T43.696
Piprinhydrinate	T45.0X1	T45.0X2	T45.0X3	T45.0X4	T45.0X5	T45.0X6
Pirarubicin	T45.1X1	T45.1X2	T45.1X3	T45.1X4	T45.1X5	T45.1X6
Pirazinamide	T37.1X1	T37.1X2	T37.1X3	T37.1X4	T37.1X5	T37.1X6
Pirbuterol	T48.6X1	T48.6X2	T48.6X3	T48.6X4	T48.6X5	T48.6X6
Pirenzepine	T47.1X1	T47.1X2	T47.1X3	T47.1X4	T47.1X5	T47.1X6
Piretanide	T50.1X1	T50.1X2	T50.1X3	T50.1X4	T50.1X5	T50.1X6
Piribedil	T42.8X1	T42.8X2	T42.8X3	T42.8X4	T42.8X5	T42.8X6
Piridoxilate	T46.3X1	T46.3X2	T46.3X3	T46.3X4	T46.3X5	T46.3X6
Piritramide	T40.4X1	T40.4X2	T40.4X3	T40.4X4	—	—
Pirlindole	T43.0X1	T43.0X2	T43.0X3	T43.0X4	T43.0X5	T43.0X6
Piromidic acid	T37.8X1	T37.8X2	T37.8X3	T37.8X4	T37.8X5	T37.8X6
Piroxicam	T39.391	T39.392	T39.393	T39.394	T39.395	T39.396
beta-cyclodextrin complex	T39.8X1	T39.8X2	T39.8X3	T39.8X4	T39.8X5	T39.8X6
Pirozadil	T46.6X1	T46.6X2	T46.6X3	T46.6X4	T46.6X5	T46.6X6
Piscidia (bark) (erythrina)	T39.8X1	T39.8X2	T39.8X3	T39.8X4	T39.8X5	T39.8X6
Pitch	T65.891	T65.892	T65.893	T65.894	—	—
Pitkin's solution	T41.3X1	T41.3X2	T41.3X3	T41.3X4	T41.3X5	T41.3X6
Pitocin	T48.0X1	T48.0X2	T48.0X3	T48.0X4	T48.0X5	T48.0X6
Pitressin (tannate)	T38.891	T38.892	T38.893	T38.894	T38.895	T38.896
Pituitary extracts (posterior)	T38.891	T38.892	T38.893	T38.894	T38.895	T38.896
anterior	T38.811	T38.812	T38.813	T38.814	T38.815	T38.816
Pituitrin	T38.891	T38.892	T38.893	T38.894	T38.895	T38.896
Pivampicillin	T36.0X1	T36.0X2	T36.0X3	T36.0X4	T36.0X5	T36.0X6
Pivmecillinam	T36.0X1	T36.0X2	T36.0X3	T36.0X4	T36.0X5	T36.0X6
Placental hormone	T38.891	T38.892	T38.893	T38.894	T38.895	T38.896
Placidyl	T42.6X1	T42.6X2	T42.6X3	T42.6X4	T42.6X5	T42.6X6
Plague vaccine	T50.A91	T50.A92	T50.A93	T50.A94	T50.A95	T50.A96
Plant						
food or fertilizer NEC	T65.891	T65.892	T65.893	T65.894	—	—
containing herbicide	T60.3X1	T60.3X2	T60.3X3	T60.3X4	—	—
noxious, used as food	T62.2X1	T62.2X2	T62.2X3	T62.2X4	—	—
berries	T62.1X1	T62.1X2	T62.1X3	T62.1X4	—	—
seeds	T62.2X1	T62.2X2	T62.2X3	T62.2X4	—	—
specified type NEC	T62.2X1	T62.2X2	T62.2X3	T62.2X4	—	—
Plasma	T45.8X1	T45.8X2	T45.8X3	T45.8X4	T45.8X5	T45.8X6
expander NEC	T45.8X1	T45.8X2	T45.8X3	T45.8X4	T45.8X5	T45.8X6
protein fraction (human)	T45.8X1	T45.8X2	T45.8X3	T45.8X4	T45.8X5	T45.8X6

◀ New ◀ Revised ~~deleted~~ Deleted

TABLE OF DRUGS AND CHEMICALS

Substance	External Cause (T-Code)					
	Poisoning, Accidental (Unintentional)	Poisoning, Intentional Self-Harm	Poisoning, Assault	Poisoning, Undetermined	Adverse Effect	Underdosing
Plasmanate	T45.8X1	T45.8X2	T45.8X3	T45.8X4	T45.8X5	T45.8X6
Plasminogen (tissue) activator	T45.611	T45.612	T45.613	T45.614	T45.615	T45.616
Plaster dressing	T49.3X1	T49.3X2	T49.3X3	T49.3X4	T49.3X5	T49.3X6
Plastic dressing	T49.3X1	T49.3X2	T49.3X3	T49.3X4	T49.3X5	T49.3X6
Plegicil	T43.3X1	T43.3X2	T43.3X3	T43.3X4	T43.3X5	T43.3X6
Plicamycin	T45.1X1	T45.1X2	T45.1X3	T45.1X4	T45.1X5	T45.1X6
Podophyllotoxin	T49.8X1	T49.8X2	T49.8X3	T49.8X4	T49.8X5	T49.8X6
Podophyllum (resin)	T49.4X1	T49.4X2	T49.4X3	T49.4X4	T49.4X5	T49.4X6
Poison NEC	T65.91	T65.92	T65.93	T65.94	—	—
Poisonous berries	T62.1X1	T62.1X2	T62.1X3	T62.1X4	—	—
Pokeweed (any part)	T62.2X1	T62.2X2	T62.2X3	T62.2X4	—	—
Poldine metilsulfate	T44.3X1	T44.3X2	T44.3X3	T44.3X4	T44.3X5	T44.3X6
Polidexide (sulfate)	T46.6X1	T46.6X2	T46.6X3	T46.6X4	T46.6X5	T46.6X6
Polidocanol	T46.8X1	T46.8X2	T46.8X3	T46.8X4	T46.8X5	T46.8X6
Poliomyelitis vaccine	T50.B91	T50.B92	T50.B93	T50.B94	T50.B95	T50.B96
Polish (car) (floor) (furniture) (metal) (porcelain) (silver)	T65.891	T65.892	T65.893	T65.894	—	—
abrasive	T65.891	T65.892	T65.893	T65.894	—	—
porcelain	T65.891	T65.892	T65.893	T65.894	—	—
Poloxalkol	T47.4X1	T47.4X2	T47.4X3	T47.4X4	T47.4X5	T47.4X6
Poloxamer	T47.4X1	T47.4X2	T47.4X3	T47.4X4	T47.4X5	T47.4X6
Polyaminostyrene resins	T50.3X1	T50.3X2	T50.3X3	T50.3X4	T50.3X5	T50.3X6
Polycarbophil	T47.4X1	T47.4X2	T47.4X3	T47.4X4	T47.4X5	T47.4X6
Polychlorinated biphenyl	T65.891	T65.892	T65.893	T65.894	—	—
Polycycline	T36.4X1	T36.4X2	T36.4X3	T36.4X4	T36.4X5	T36.4X6
Polyester fumes	T59.891	T59.892	T59.893	T59.894	—	—
Polyester resin hardener	T52.91	T52.92	T52.93	T52.94	—	—
fumes	T59.891	T59.892	T59.893	T59.894	—	—
Polyestradiol phosphate	T38.5X1	T38.5X2	T38.5X3	T38.5X4	T38.5X5	T38.5X6
Polyethanolamine alkyl sulfate	T49.2X1	T49.2X2	T49.2X3	T49.2X4	T49.2X5	T49.2X6
Polyethylene adhesive	T49.3X1	T49.3X2	T49.3X3	T49.3X4	T49.3X5	T49.3X6
Polyferose	T45.4X1	T45.4X2	T45.4X3	T45.4X4	T45.4X5	T45.4X6
Polygeline	T45.8X1	T45.8X2	T45.8X3	T45.8X4	T45.8X5	T45.8X6
Polymyxin	T36.8X1	T36.8X2	T36.8X3	T36.8X4	T36.8X5	T36.8X6
B	T36.8X1	T36.8X2	T36.8X3	T36.8X4	T36.8X5	T36.8X6
ENT agent	T49.6X1	T49.6X2	T49.6X3	T49.6X4	T49.6X5	T49.6X6
ophthalmic preparation	T49.5X1	T49.5X2	T49.5X3	T49.5X4	T49.5X5	T49.5X6
topical NEC	T49.0X1	T49.0X2	T49.0X3	T49.0X4	T49.0X5	T49.0X6
E sulfate (eye preparation)	T49.5X1	T49.5X2	T49.5X3	T49.5X4	T49.5X5	T49.5X6
Polynoxylin	T49.0X1	T49.0X2	T49.0X3	T49.0X4	T49.0X5	T49.0X6
Polyoestradiol phosphate	T38.5X1	T38.5X2	T38.5X3	T38.5X4	T38.5X5	T38.5X6
Polyoxymethyleneurea	T49.0X1	T49.0X2	T49.0X3	T49.0X4	T49.0X5	T49.0X6

Substance	External Cause (T-Code)					
	Poisoning, Accidental (Unintentional)	Poisoning, Intentional Self-Harm	Poisoning, Assault	Poisoning, Undetermined	Adverse Effect	Underdosing
Polysilane	T47.8X1	T47.8X2	T47.8X3	T47.8X4	T47.8X5	T47.8X6
Polytetrafluoroethylene (inhaled)	T59.891	T59.892	T59.893	T59.894	—	—
Polythiazide	T50.2X1	T50.2X2	T50.2X3	T50.2X4	T50.2X5	T50.2X6
Polyvidone	T45.8X1	T45.8X2	T45.8X3	T45.8X4	T45.8X5	T45.8X6
Polyvinylpyrrolidone	T45.8X1	T45.8X2	T45.8X3	T45.8X4	T45.8X5	T45.8X6
Pontocaine (hydrochloride) (infiltration) (topical)	T41.3X1	T41.3X2	T41.3X3	T41.3X4	T41.3X5	T41.3X6
nerve block (peripheral) (plexus)	T41.3X1	T41.3X2	T41.3X3	T41.3X4	T41.3X5	T41.3X6
spinal	T41.3X1	T41.3X2	T41.3X3	T41.3X4	T41.3X5	T41.3X6
Porfiromycin	T45.1X1	T45.1X2	T45.1X3	T45.1X4	T45.1X5	T45.1X6
Posterior pituitary hormone NEC	T38.891	T38.892	T38.893	T38.894	T38.895	T38.896
Pot	T40.7X1	T40.7X2	T40.7X3	T40.7X4	T40.7X5	T40.7X6
Potash (caustic)	T54.3X1	T54.3X2	T54.3X3	T54.3X4	—	—
Potassic saline injection (lactated)	T50.3X1	T50.3X2	T50.3X3	T50.3X4	T50.3X5	T50.3X6
Potassium (salts) NEC	T50.3X1	T50.3X2	T50.3X3	T50.3X4	T50.3X5	T50.3X6
aminobenzoate	T45.8X1	T45.8X2	T45.8X3	T45.8X4	T45.8X5	T45.8X6
aminosalicylate	T37.1X1	T37.1X2	T37.1X3	T37.1X4	T37.1X5	T37.1X6
antimony 'tartrate'	T37.8X1	T37.8X2	T37.8X3	T37.8X4	T37.8X5	T37.8X6
arsenite (solution)	T57.0X1	T57.0X2	T57.0X3	T57.0X4	—	—
bichromate	T56.2X1	T56.2X2	T56.2X3	T56.2X4	—	—
bisulfate	T47.3X1	T47.3X2	T47.3X3	T47.3X4	T47.3X5	T47.3X6
bromide	T42.6X1	T42.6X2	T42.6X3	T42.6X4	T42.6X5	T42.6X6
canrenoate	T50.0X1	T50.0X2	T50.0X3	T50.0X4	T50.0X5	T50.0X6
carbonate	T54.3X1	T54.3X2	T54.3X3	T54.3X4	—	—
chlorate NEC	T65.891	T65.892	T65.893	T65.894	—	—
chloride	T50.3X1	T50.3X2	T50.3X3	T50.3X4	T50.3X5	T50.3X6
citrate	T50.991	T50.992	T50.993	T50.994	T50.995	T50.996
cyanide	T65.0X1	T65.0X2	T65.0X3	T65.0X4	—	—
ferric hexacyanoferrate (medicinal)	T50.6X1	T50.6X2	T50.6X3	T50.6X4	T50.6X5	T50.6X6
nonmedicinal	T65.891	T65.892	T65.893	T65.894	—	—
Fluoride	T57.8X1	T57.8X2	T57.8X3	T57.8X4	—	—
glucaldrate	T47.1X1	T47.1X2	T47.1X3	T47.1X4	T47.1X5	T47.1X6
hydroxide	T54.3X1	T54.3X2	T54.3X3	T54.3X4	—	—
iodate	T49.0X1	T49.0X2	T49.0X3	T49.0X4	T49.0X5	T49.0X6
iodide	T48.4X1	T48.4X2	T48.4X3	T48.4X4	T48.4X5	T48.4X6
nitrate	T57.8X1	T57.8X2	T57.8X3	T57.8X4	—	—
oxalate	T65.891	T65.892	T65.893	T65.894	—	—
perchlorate (nonmedicinal) NEC	T65.891	T65.892	T65.893	T65.894	—	—
antithyroid	T38.2X1	T38.2X2	T38.2X3	T38.2X4	T38.2X5	T38.2X6
medicinal	T38.2X1	T38.2X2	T38.2X3	T38.2X4	T38.2X5	T38.2X6

◀ New ◀|| Revised ~~deleted~~ Deleted

Substance	Poisoning, Accidental (Unintentional)	Poisoning, Intentional Self-Harm	Poisoning, Assault	Poisoning, Undetermined	Adverse Effect	Underdosing
Permanganate (nonmedicinal)	T65.891	T65.892	T65.893	T65.894	—	—
medicinal	T49.0X1	T49.0X2	T49.0X3	T49.0X4	T49.0X5	T49.0X6
sulfate	T47.2X1	T47.2X2	T47.2X3	T47.2X4	T47.2X5	T47.2X6
Potassium-removing resin	T50.3X1	T50.3X2	T50.3X3	T50.3X4	T50.3X5	T50.3X6
Potassium-retaining drug	T50.3X1	T50.3X2	T50.3X3	T50.3X4	T50.3X5	T50.3X6
Povidone	T45.8X1	T45.8X2	T45.8X3	T45.8X4	T45.8X5	T45.8X6
iodine	T49.0X1	T49.0X2	T49.0X3	T49.0X4	T49.0X5	T49.0X6
Practolol	T44.7X1	T44.7X2	T44.7X3	T44.7X4	T44.7X5	T44.7X6
Prajmalium bitartrate	T46.2X1	T46.2X2	T46.2X3	T46.2X4	T46.2X5	T46.2X6
Pralidoxime (iodide)	T50.6X1	T50.6X2	T50.6X3	T50.6X4	T50.6X5	T50.6X6
chloride	T50.6X1	T50.6X2	T50.6X3	T50.6X4	T50.6X5	T50.6X6
Pramiverine	T44.3X1	T44.3X2	T44.3X3	T44.3X4	T44.3X5	T44.3X6
Pramocaine	T49.1X1	T49.1X2	T49.1X3	T49.1X4	T49.1X5	T49.1X6
Pramoxine	T49.1X1	T49.1X2	T49.1X3	T49.1X4	T49.1X5	T49.1X6
Prasterone	T38.7X1	T38.7X2	T38.7X3	T38.7X4	T38.7X5	T38.7X6
Pravastatin	T46.6X1	T46.6X2	T46.6X3	T46.6X4	T46.6X5	T46.6X6
Prazepam	T42.4X1	T42.4X2	T42.4X3	T42.4X4	T42.4X5	T42.4X6
Praziquantel	T37.4X1	T37.4X2	T37.4X3	T37.4X4	T37.4X5	T37.4X6
Prazitone	T43.291	T43.292	T43.293	T43.294	T43.295	T43.296
Prazosin	T44.6X1	T44.6X2	T44.6X3	T44.6X4	T44.6X5	T44.6X6
Prednicarbate	T49.0X1	T49.0X2	T49.0X3	T49.0X4	T49.0X5	T49.0X6
Prednimustine	T45.1X1	T45.1X2	T45.1X3	T45.1X4	T45.1X5	T45.1X6
Prednisolone	T38.0X1	T38.0X2	T38.0X3	T38.0X4	T38.0X5	T38.0X6
ENT agent	T49.6X1	T49.6X2	T49.6X3	T49.6X4	T49.6X5	T49.6X6
ophthalmic preparation	T49.5X1	T49.5X2	T49.5X3	T49.5X4	T49.5X5	T49.5X6
steaglate	T49.0X1	T49.0X2	T49.0X3	T49.0X4	T49.0X5	T49.0X6
topical NEC	T49.0X1	T49.0X2	T49.0X3	T49.0X4	T49.0X5	T49.0X6
Prednisone	T38.0X1	T38.0X2	T38.0X3	T38.0X4	T38.0X5	T38.0X6
Prednylidene	T38.0X1	T38.0X2	T38.0X3	T38.0X4	T38.0X5	T38.0X6
Pregnandiol	T38.5X1	T38.5X2	T38.5X3	T38.5X4	T38.5X5	T38.5X6
Pregneninolone	T38.5X1	T38.5X2	T38.5X3	T38.5X4	T38.5X5	T38.5X6
Preludin	T43.691	T43.692	T43.693	T43.694	T43.695	T43.696
Premarin	T38.5X1	T38.5X2	T38.5X3	T38.5X4	T38.5X5	T38.5X6
Premedication anesthetic	T41.201	T41.202	T41.203	T41.204	T41.205	T41.206
Prenalterol	T44.5X1	T44.5X2	T44.5X3	T44.5X4	T44.5X5	T44.5X6
Prenoxdiazine	T48.3X1	T48.3X2	T48.3X3	T48.3X4	T48.3X5	T48.3X6
Prenylamine	T46.3X1	T46.3X2	T46.3X3	T46.3X4	T46.3X5	T46.3X6
Preparation, local	T49.4X1	T49.4X2	T49.4X3	T49.4X4	T49.4X5	T49.4X6
Preparation H	T49.8X1	T49.8X2	T49.8X3	T49.8X4	T49.8X5	T49.8X6
Preservative (nonmedicinal)	T65.891	T65.892	T65.893	T65.894	—	—
medicinal	T50.901	T50.902	T50.903	T50.904	T50.905	T50.906
wood	T60.91	T60.92	T60.93	T60.94	—	—

Substance	Poisoning, Accidental (Unintentional)	Poisoning, Intentional Self-Harm	Poisoning, Assault	Poisoning, Undetermined	Adverse Effect	Underdosing
Prethcamide	T50.7X1	T50.7X2	T50.7X3	T50.7X4	T50.7X5	T50.7X6
Pride of China	T62.2X1	T62.2X2	T62.2X3	T62.2X4	—	—
Pridinol	T44.3X1	T44.3X2	T44.3X3	T44.3X4	T44.3X5	T44.3X6
Prifinium bromide	T44.3X1	T44.3X2	T44.3X3	T44.3X4	T44.3X5	T44.3X6
Prilocaine	T41.3X1	T41.3X2	T41.3X3	T41.3X4	T41.3X5	T41.3X6
infiltration (subcutaneous)	T41.3X1	T41.3X2	T41.3X3	T41.3X4	T41.3X5	T41.3X6
nerve block (peripheral) (plexus)	T41.3X1	T41.3X2	T41.3X3	T41.3X4	T41.3X5	T41.3X6
regional	T41.3X1	T41.3X2	T41.3X3	T41.3X4	T41.3X5	T41.3X6
Primaquine	T37.2X1	T37.2X2	T37.2X3	T37.2X4	T37.2X5	T37.2X6
Primidone	T42.6X1	T42.6X2	T42.6X3	T42.6X4	T42.6X5	T42.6X6
Primula (veris)	T62.2X1	T62.2X2	T62.2X3	T62.2X4	—	—
Prinadol	T40.2X1	T40.2X2	T40.2X3	T40.2X4	T40.2X5	T40.2X6
Priscol, Priscoline	T44.6X1	T44.6X2	T44.6X3	T44.6X4	T44.6X5	T44.6X6
Pristinamycin	T36.3X1	T36.3X2	T36.3X3	T36.3X4	T36.3X5	T36.3X6
Privet	T62.2X1	T62.2X2	T62.2X3	T62.2X4	—	—
berries	T62.1X1	T62.1X2	T62.1X3	T62.1X4	—	—
Privine	T44.4X1	T44.4X2	T44.3X3	T44.4X4	T44.4X5	T44.4X6
Pro-Banthine	T44.3X1	T44.3X2	T44.3X3	T44.3X4	T44.3X5	T44.3X6
Probarbital	T42.3X1	T42.3X2	T42.3X3	T42.3X4	T42.3X5	T42.3X6
Probenecid	T50.4X1	T50.4X2	T50.4X3	T50.4X4	T50.4X5	T50.4X6
Probucol	T46.6X1	T46.6X2	T46.6X3	T46.6X4	T46.6X5	T46.6X6
Procainamide	T46.2X1	T46.2X2	T46.2X3	T46.2X4	T46.2X5	T46.2X6
Procaine	T41.3X1	T41.3X2	T41.3X3	T41.3X4	T41.3X5	T41.3X6
benzylpenicillin	T36.0X1	T36.0X2	T36.0X3	T36.0X4	T36.0X5	T36.0X6
nerve block (peripheral) (plexus)	T41.3X1	T41.3X2	T41.3X3	T41.3X4	T41.3X5	T41.3X6
penicillin G	T36.0X1	T36.0X2	T36.0X3	T36.0X4	T36.0X5	T36.0X6
regional	T41.3X1	T41.3X2	T41.3X3	T41.3X4	T41.3X5	T41.3X6
spinal	T41.3X1	T41.3X2	T41.3X3	T41.3X4	T41.3X5	T41.3X6
Procalmidol	T43.591	T43.592	T43.593	T43.594	T43.595	T43.596
Procarbazine	T45.1X1	T45.1X2	T45.1X3	T45.1X4	T45.1X5	T45.1X6
Procaterol	T44.5X1	T44.5X2	T44.5X3	T44.5X4	T44.5X5	T44.5X6
Prochlorperazine	T43.3X1	T43.3X2	T43.3X3	T43.3X4	T43.3X5	T43.3X6
Procyclidine	T44.3X1	T44.3X2	T44.3X3	T44.3X4	T44.3X5	T44.3X6
Producer gas	T58.8X1	T58.8X2	T58.8X3	T58.8X4	—	—
Profadol	T40.4X1	T40.4X2	T40.4X3	T40.4X4	T40.4X5	T40.4X6
Profenamine	T44.3X1	T44.3X2	T44.3X3	T44.3X4	T44.3X5	T44.3X6
Profenil	T44.3X1	T44.3X2	T44.3X3	T44.3X4	T44.3X5	T44.3X6
Proflavine	T49.0X1	T49.0X2	T49.0X3	T49.0X4	T49.0X5	T49.0X6
Progabide	T42.6X1	T42.6X2	T42.6X3	T42.6X4	T42.6X5	T42.6X6
Progestin	T38.5X1	T38.5X2	T38.5X3	T38.5X4	T38.5X5	T38.5X6
oral contraceptive	T38.4X1	T38.4X2	T38.4X3	T38.4X4	T38.4X5	T38.4X6

Substance	External Cause (T-Code)					
	Poisoning, Accidental (Unintentional)	Poisoning, Intentional Self-Harm	Poisoning, Assault	Poisoning, Undetermined	Adverse Effect	Underdosing
Progesterone	T38.5X1	T38.5X2	T38.5X3	T38.5X4	T38.5X5	T38.5X6
Progestogen NEC	T38.5X1	T38.5X2	T38.5X3	T38.5X4	T38.5X5	T38.5X6
Progestone	T38.5X1	T38.5X2	T38.5X3	T38.5X4	T38.5X5	T38.5X6
Proglumide	T47.1X1	T47.1X2	T47.1X3	T47.1X4	T47.1X5	T47.1X6
Proguanil	T37.2X1	T37.2X2	T37.2X3	T37.2X4	T37.2X5	T37.2X6
Prolactin	T38.811	T38.812	T38.813	T38.814	T38.815	T38.816
Prolintane	T43.691	T43.692	T43.693	T43.694	T43.695	T43.696
Proloid	T38.1X1	T38.1X2	T38.1X3	T38.1X4	T38.1X5	T38.1X6
Proluton	T38.5X1	T38.5X2	T38.5X3	T38.5X4	T38.5X5	T38.5X6
Promacetin	T37.1X1	T37.1X2	T37.1X3	T37.1X4	T37.1X5	T37.1X6
Promazine	T43.3X1	T43.3X2	T43.3X3	T43.3X4	T43.3X5	T43.3X6
Promedol	T40.2X1	T40.2X2	T40.2X3	T40.2X4	—	—
Promegestone	T38.5X1	T38.5X2	T38.5X3	T38.5X4	T38.5X5	T38.5X6
Promethazine (teoclate)	T43.3X1	T43.3X2	T43.3X3	T43.3X4	T43.3X5	T43.3X6
Promin	T37.1X1	T37.1X2	T37.1X3	T37.1X4	T37.1X5	T37.1X6
Pronase	T45.3X1	T45.3X2	T45.3X3	T45.3X4	T45.3X5	T45.3X6
Pronestyl (hydrochloride)	T46.2X1	T46.2X2	T46.2X3	T46.2X4	T46.2X5	T46.2X6
Pronetalol	T44.7X1	T44.7X2	T44.7X3	T44.7X4	T44.7X5	T44.7X6
Prontosil	T37.0X1	T37.0X2	T37.0X3	T37.0X4	T37.0X5	T37.0X6
Propachlor	T60.3X1	T60.3X2	T60.3X3	T60.3X4	—	—
Propafenone	T46.2X1	T46.2X2	T46.2X3	T46.2X4	T46.2X5	T46.2X6
Propallylonal	T42.3X1	T42.3X2	T42.3X3	T42.3X4	T42.3X5	T42.3X6
Propamidine	T49.0X1	T49.0X2	T49.0X3	T49.0X4	T49.0X5	T49.0X6
Propane (distributed in mobile container)	T59.891	T59.892	T59.893	T59.894	—	—
distributed through pipes	T59.891	T59.892	T59.893	T59.894	—	—
incomplete combustion	T57.11	T57.12	T57.13	T57.14	—	—
Propanidid	T41.291	T41.292	T41.293	T41.294	T41.295	T41.296
Propanil	T60.3X1	T60.3X2	T60.3X3	T60.3X4	—	—
1-Propanol	T51.3X1	T51.3X2	T51.3X3	T51.3X4	—	—
2-Propanol	T51.2X1	T51.2X2	T51.2X3	T51.2X4	—	—
Propantheline	T44.3X1	T44.3X2	T44.3X3	T44.3X4	T44.3X5	T44.3X6
bromide	T44.3X1	T44.3X2	T44.3X3	T44.3X4	T44.3X5	T44.3X6
Proparacaine	T41.3X1	T41.3X2	T41.3X3	T41.3X4	T41.3X5	T41.3X6
Propatylnitrate	T46.3X1	T46.3X2	T46.3X3	T46.3X4	T46.3X5	T46.3X6
Propicillin	T36.0X1	T36.0X2	T36.0X3	T36.0X4	T36.0X5	T36.0X6
Propiolactone	T49.0X1	T49.0X2	T49.0X3	T49.0X4	T49.0X5	T49.0X6
Propiomazine	T45.0X1	T45.0X2	T45.0X3	T45.0X4	T45.0X5	T45.0X6
Propionaldehyde (medicinal)	T42.6X1	T42.6X2	T42.6X3	T42.6X4	T42.6X5	T42.6X6
Propionate (calcium) (sodium)	T49.0X1	T49.0X2	T49.0X3	T49.0X4	T49.0X5	T49.0X6
Propion gel	T49.0X1	T49.0X2	T49.0X3	T49.0X4	T49.0X5	T49.0X6

Substance	External Cause (T-Code)					
	Poisoning, Accidental (Unintentional)	Poisoning, Intentional Self-Harm	Poisoning, Assault	Poisoning, Undetermined	Adverse Effect	Underdosing
Propitocaine	T41.3X1	T41.3X2	T41.3X3	T41.3X4	T41.3X5	T41.3X6
infiltration (subcutaneous)	T41.3X1	T41.3X2	T41.3X3	T41.3X4	T41.3X5	T41.3X6
nerve block (peripheral) (plexus)	T41.3X1	T41.3X2	T41.3X3	T41.3X4	T41.3X5	T41.3X6
Propofol	T41.291	T41.292	T41.293	T41.294	T41.295	T41.296
Propoxur	T60.0X1	T60.0X2	T60.0X3	T60.0X4	—	—
Propoxycaine	T41.3X1	T41.3X2	T41.3X3	T41.3X4	T41.3X5	T41.3X6
infiltration (subcutaneous)	T41.3X1	T41.3X2	T41.3X3	T41.3X4	T41.3X5	T41.3X6
nerve block (peripheral) (plexus)	T41.3X1	T41.3X2	T41.3X3	T41.3X4	T41.3X5	T41.3X6
topical (surface)	T41.3X1	T41.3X2	T41.3X3	T41.3X4	T41.3X5	T41.3X6
Propoxyphene	T40.4X1	T40.4X2	T40.4X3	T40.4X4	T40.4X5	T40.4X6
Propranolol	T44.7X1	T44.7X2	T44.7X3	T44.7X4	T44.7X5	T44.7X6
Propyl						
alcohol	T51.3X1	T51.3X2	T51.3X3	T51.3X4	—	—
carbinol	T51.3X1	T51.3X2	T51.3X3	T51.3X4	—	—
hexadrine	T44.4X1	T44.4X2	T44.4X3	T44.4X4	T44.4X5	T44.4X6
iodone	T50.8X1	T50.8X2	T50.8X3	T50.8X4	T50.8X5	T50.8X6
thiouracil	T38.2X1	T38.2X2	T38.2X3	T38.2X4	T38.2X5	T38.2X6
Propylaminophenothiazine	T43.3X1	T43.3X2	T43.3X3	T43.3X4	T43.3X5	T43.3X6
Propylene	T59.891	T59.892	T59.893	T59.894	—	—
Propylhexedrine	T48.5X1	T48.5X2	T48.5X3	T48.5X4	T48.5X5	T48.5X6
Propyliodone	T50.8X1	T50.8X2	T50.8X3	T50.8X4	T50.8X5	T50.8X6
Propylthiouracil	T38.2X1	T38.2X2	T38.2X3	T38.2X4	T38.2X5	T38.2X6
Propylparaben (ophthalmic)	T49.5X1	T49.5X2	T49.5X3	T49.5X4	T49.5X5	T49.5X6
Propyphenazone	T39.2X1	T39.2X2	T39.2X3	T39.2X4	T39.2X5	T39.2X6
Proquazone	T39.391	T39.392	T39.393	T39.394	T39.395	T39.396
Proscillaridin	T46.0X1	T46.0X2	T46.0X3	T46.0X4	T46.0X5	T46.0X6
Prostacyclin	T45.521	T45.522	T45.523	T45.524	T45.525	T45.526
Prostaglandin (I2)	T45.521	T45.522	T45.523	T45.524	T45.525	T45.526
E1	T46.7X1	T46.7X2	T46.7X3	T46.7X4	T46.7X5	T46.7X6
E2	T48.0X1	T48.0X2	T48.0X3	T48.0X4	T48.0X5	T48.0X6
F2 alpha	T48.0X1	T48.0X2	T48.0X3	T48.0X4	T48.0X5	T48.0X6
Prostigmin	T44.0X1	T44.0X2	T44.0X3	T44.0X4	T44.0X5	T44.0X6
Prosultiamine	T45.2X1	T45.2X2	T45.2X3	T45.2X4	T45.2X5	T45.2X6
Protamine sulfate	T45.7X1	T45.7X2	T45.7X3	T45.7X4	T45.7X5	T45.7X6
zinc insulin	T38.3X1	T38.3X2	T38.3X3	T38.3X4	T38.3X5	T38.3X6
Protease	T47.5X1	T47.5X2	T47.5X3	T47.5X4	T47.5X5	T47.5X6
Protectant, skin NEC	T49.3X1	T49.3X2	T49.3X3	T49.3X4	T49.3X5	T49.3X6
Protein hydrolysate	T50.991	T50.992	T50.993	T50.994	T50.995	T50.996
Prothiaden — see Dothiepin hydrochloride						
Prothionamide	T37.1X1	T37.1X2	T37.1X3	T37.1X4	T37.1X5	T37.1X6

◀ New   ◀◀ Revised   ~~deleted~~ Deleted

Substance	Poisoning, Accidental (Unintentional)	Poisoning, Intentional Self-Harm	Poisoning, Assault	Poisoning, Undetermined	Adverse Effect	Underdosing
Prothipendyl	T43.591	T43.592	T43.593	T43.594	T43.595	T43.596
Prothoate	T60.0X1	T60.0X2	T60.0X3	T60.0X4	—	—
Prothrombin						
activator	T45.7X1	T45.7X2	T45.7X3	T45.7X4	T45.7X5	T45.7X6
synthesis inhibitor	T45.511	T45.512	T45.513	T45.514	T45.515	T45.516
Protionamide	T37.1X1	T37.1X2	T37.1X3	T37.1X4	T37.1X5	T37.1X6
Protirelin	T38.891	T38.892	T38.893	T38.894	T38.895	T38.896
Protokylol	T48.6X1	T48.6X2	T48.6X3	T48.6X4	T48.6X5	T48.6X6
Protopam	T50.6X1	T50.6X2	T50.6X3	T50.6X4	T50.6X5	T50.6X6
Protoveratrine(s) (A) (B)	T46.5X1	T46.5X2	T46.5X3	T46.5X4	T46.5X5	T46.5X6
Protriptyline	T43.011	T43.012	T43.013	T43.014	T43.015	T43.016
Provera	T38.5X1	T38.5X2	T38.5X3	T38.5X4	T38.5X5	T38.5X6
Provitamin A	T45.2X1	T45.2X2	T45.2X3	T45.2X4	T45.2X5	T45.2X6
Proxibarbal	T42.3X1	T42.3X2	T42.3X3	T42.3X4	T42.3X5	T42.3X6
Proxymetacaine	T41.3X1	T41.3X2	T41.3X3	T41.3X4	T41.3X5	T41.3X6
Proxyphylline	T48.6X1	T48.6X2	T48.6X3	T48.6X4	T48.6X5	T48.6X6
Prozac — see Fluoxetine hydrochloride						
Prunus						
laurocerasus	T62.2X1	T62.2X2	T62.2X3	T62.2X4	—	—
virginiana	T62.2X1	T62.2X2	T62.2X3	T62.2X4	—	—
Prussian blue						
commercial	T65.891	T65.892	T65.893	T65.894	—	—
therapeutic	T50.6X1	T50.6X2	T50.6X3	T50.6X4	T50.6X5	T50.6X6
Prussic acid	T65.0X1	T65.0X2	T65.0X3	T65.0X4	—	—
vapor	T57.3X1	T57.3X2	T57.3X3	T57.3X4	—	—
Pseudoephedrine	T44.991	T44.992	T44.993	T44.994	T44.995	T44.996
Psilocin	T40.991	T40.992	T40.993	T40.994	—	—
Psilocybin	T40.991	T40.992	T40.993	T40.994	—	—
Psilocybine	T40.991	T40.992	T40.993	T40.994	—	—
Psoralene (nonmedicinal)	T65.891	T65.892	T65.893	T65.894	—	—
Psoralens (medicinal)	T50.991	T50.992	T50.993	T50.994	T50.995	T50.996
PSP (phenolsulfonphthalein)	T50.8X1	T50.8X2	T50.8X3	T50.8X4	T50.8X5	T50.8X6
Psychodysleptic drug NEC	T40.901	T40.902	T40.903	T40.904	T40.905	T40.906
Psychostimulant	T43.601	T43.602	T43.603	T43.604	T43.605	T43.606
amphetamine	T43.621	T43.622	T43.623	T43.624	T43.625	T43.626
caffeine	T43.611	T43.612	T43.613	T43.614	T43.615	T43.616
methylphenidate	T43.631	T43.632	T43.633	T43.634	T43.635	T43.636
specified NEC	T43.691	T43.692	T43.693	T43.694	T43.695	T43.696
Psychotherapeutic drug NEC	T43.91	T43.92	T43.93	T43.94	T43.95	T43.96
antidepressants — see also Antidepressant	T43.201	T43.202	T43.203	T43.204	T43.205	T43.206

Substance	Poisoning, Accidental (Unintentional)	Poisoning, Intentional Self-Harm	Poisoning, Assault	Poisoning, Undetermined	Adverse Effect	Underdosing
Psychotherapeutic drug NEC (Continued)						
specified NEC	T43.8X1	T43.8X2	T43.8X3	T43.8X4	T43.8X5	T43.8X6
tranquilizers NEC	T43.501	T43.502	T43.503	T43.504	T43.505	T43.506
Psychotomimetic agents	T40.901	T40.902	T40.903	T40.904	T40.905	T40.906
Psychotropic drug NEC	T43.91	T43.92	T43.93	T43.94	T43.95	T43.96
specified NEC	T43.8X1	T43.8X2	T43.8X3	T43.8X4	T43.8X5	T43.8X6
Psyllium hydrophilic mucilloid	T47.4X1	T47.4X2	T47.4X3	T47.4X4	T47.4X5	T47.4X6
Pteroylglutamic acid	T45.8X1	T45.8X2	T45.8X3	T45.8X4	T45.8X5	T45.8X6
Pteroyltriglutamate	T45.1X1	T45.1X2	T45.1X3	T45.1X4	T45.1X5	T45.1X6
PTFE — see Polytetrafluoroethylene						
Pulp						
devitalizing paste	T49.7X1	T49.7X2	T49.7X3	T49.7X4	T49.7X5	T49.7X6
dressing	T49.7X1	T49.7X2	T49.7X3	T49.7X4	T49.7X5	T49.7X6
Pulsatilla	T62.2X1	T62.2X2	T62.2X3	T62.2X4	—	—
Pumpkin seed extract	T37.4X1	T37.4X2	T37.4X3	T37.4X4	T37.4X5	T37.4X6
Purex (bleach)	T54.91	T54.92	T54.93	T54.94	—	—
Purgative NEC — see also Cathartic	T47.4X1	T47.4X2	T47.4X3	T47.4X4	T47.4X5	T47.4X6
Purine analogue (antineoplastic)	T45.1X1	T45.1X2	T45.1X3	T45.1X4	T45.1X5	T45.1X6
Purine diuretics	T50.2X1	T50.2X2	T50.2X3	T50.2X4	T50.2X5	T50.2X6
Purinethol	T45.1X1	T45.1X2	T45.1X3	T45.1X4	T45.1X5	T45.1X6
PVP	T45.8X1	T45.8X2	T45.8X3	T45.8X4	T45.8X5	T45.8X6
Pyrabital	T39.8X1	T39.8X2	T39.8X3	T39.8X4	T39.8X5	T39.8X6
Pyramidon	T39.2X1	T39.2X2	T39.2X3	T39.2X4	T39.2X5	T39.2X6
Pyrantel	T37.4X1	T37.4X2	T37.4X3	T37.4X4	T37.4X5	T37.4X6
Pyrathiazine	T45.0X1	T45.0X2	T45.0X3	T45.0X4	T45.0X5	T45.0X6
Pyrazinamide	T37.1X1	T37.1X2	T37.1X3	T37.1X4	T37.1X5	T37.1X6
Pyrazinoic acid (amide)	T37.1X1	T37.1X2	T37.1X3	T37.1X4	T37.1X5	T37.1X6
Pyrazole (derivatives)	T39.2X1	T39.2X2	T39.2X3	T39.2X4	T39.2X5	T39.2X6
Pyrazolone analgesic NEC	T39.2X1	T39.2X2	T39.2X3	T39.2X4	T39.2X5	T39.2X6
Pyrethrin, pyrethrum (nonmedicinal)	T60.2X1	T60.2X2	T60.2X3	T60.2X4	—	—
Pyrethrum extract	T49.0X1	T49.0X2	T49.0X3	T49.0X4	T49.0X5	T49.0X6
Pyribenzamine	T45.0X1	T45.0X2	T45.0X3	T45.0X4	T45.0X5	T45.0X6
Pyridine	T52.8X1	T52.8X2	T52.8X3	T52.8X4	—	—
aldoxime methiodide	T50.6X1	T50.6X2	T50.6X3	T50.6X4	T50.6X5	T50.6X6
aldoxime methyl chloride	T50.6X1	T50.6X2	T50.6X3	T50.6X4	T50.6X5	T50.6X6
vapor	T59.891	T59.892	T59.893	T59.894	—	—
Pyridium	T39.8X1	T39.8X2	T39.8X3	T39.8X4	T39.8X5	T39.8X6
Pyridostigmine bromide	T44.0X1	T44.0X2	T44.0X3	T44.0X4	T44.0X5	T44.0X6
Pyridoxal phosphate	T45.2X1	T45.2X2	T45.2X3	T45.2X4	T45.2X5	T45.2X6

◀ New   ◀ Revised   deleted Deleted

Substance	Poisoning, Accidental (Unintentional)	Poisoning, Intentional Self-Harm	Poisoning, Assault	Poisoning, Undetermined	Adverse Effect	Underdosing
Pyridoxine	T45.2X1	T45.2X2	T45.2X3	T45.2X4	T45.2X5	T45.2X6
Pyrilamine	T45.0X1	T45.0X2	T45.0X3	T45.0X4	T45.0X5	T45.0X6
Pyrimethamine	T37.2X1	T37.2X2	T37.2X3	T37.2X4	T37.2X5	T37.2X6
with sulfadoxine	T37.2X1	T37.2X2	T37.2X3	T37.2X4	T37.2X5	T37.2X6
Pyrimidine antagonist	T45.1X1	T45.1X2	T45.1X3	T45.1X4	T45.1X5	T45.1X6
Pyriminil	T60.4X1	T60.4X2	T60.4X3	T60.4X4	—	—
Pyrithione zinc	T49.4X1	T49.4X2	T49.4X3	T49.4X4	T49.4X5	T49.4X6
Pyrithyldione	T42.6X1	T42.6X2	T42.6X3	T42.6X4	T42.6X5	T42.6X6
Pyrogallic acid	T49.0X1	T49.0X2	T49.0X3	T49.0X4	T49.0X5	T49.0X6
Pyrogallol	T49.0X1	T49.0X2	T49.0X3	T49.0X4	T49.0X5	T49.0X6
Pyroxylin	T49.3X1	T49.3X2	T49.3X3	T49.3X4	T49.3X5	T49.3X6
Pyrrobutamine	T45.0X1	T45.0X2	T45.0X3	T45.0X4	T45.0X5	T45.0X6
Pyrrolizidine alkaloids	T62.8X1	T62.8X2	T62.8X3	T62.8X4	—	—
Pyrvinium chloride	T37.4X1	T37.4X2	T37.4X3	T37.4X4	T37.4X5	T37.4X6
PZI	T38.3X1	T38.3X2	T38.3X3	T38.3X4	T38.3X5	T38.3X6
Q						
Quaalude	T42.6X1	T42.6X2	T42.6X3	T42.6X4	T42.6X5	T42.6X6
Quarternary ammonium						
anti-infective	T49.0X1	T49.0X2	T49.0X3	T49.0X4	T49.0X5	T49.0X6
ganglion blocking	T44.2X1	T44.2X2	T44.2X3	T44.2X4	T44.2X5	T44.2X6
parasympatholytic	T44.3X1	T44.3X2	T44.3X3	T44.3X4	T44.3X5	T44.3X6
Quazepam	T42.4X1	T42.4X2	T42.4X3	T42.4X4	T42.4X5	T42.4X6
Quicklime	T54.3X1	T54.3X2	T54.3X3	T54.3X4	—	—
Quillaja extract	T48.4X1	T48.4X2	T48.4X3	T48.4X4	T48.4X5	T48.4X6
Quinacrine	T37.2X1	T37.2X2	T37.2X3	T37.2X4	T37.2X5	T37.2X6
Quinaglute	T46.2X1	T46.2X2	T46.2X3	T46.2X4	T46.2X5	T46.2X6
Quinalbarbital	T42.3X1	T42.3X2	T42.3X3	T42.3X4	T42.3X5	T42.3X6
Quinalbarbitone sodium	T42.3X1	T42.3X2	T42.3X3	T42.3X4	T42.3X5	T42.3X6
Quinalphos	T60.0X1	T60.0X2	T60.0X3	T60.0X4	—	—
Quinapril	T46.4X1	T46.4X2	T46.4X3	T46.4X4	T46.4X5	T46.4X6
Quinestradiol	T38.5X1	T38.5X2	T38.5X3	T38.5X4	T38.5X5	T38.5X6
Quinestradol	T38.5X1	T38.5X2	T38.5X3	T38.5X4	T38.5X5	T38.5X6
Quinestrol	T38.5X1	T38.5X2	T38.5X3	T38.5X4	T38.5X5	T38.5X6
Quinethazone	T50.2X1	T50.2X2	T50.2X3	T50.2X4	T50.2X5	T50.2X6
Quingestanol	T38.4X1	T38.4X2	T38.4X3	T38.4X4	T38.4X5	T38.4X6
Quinidine	T46.2X1	T46.2X2	T46.2X3	T46.2X4	T46.2X5	T46.2X6
Quinine	T37.2X1	T37.2X2	T37.2X3	T37.2X4	T37.2X5	T37.2X6
Quiniobine	T37.8X1	T37.8X2	T37.8X3	T37.8X4	T37.8X5	T37.8X6
Quinisocaine	T49.1X1	T49.1X2	T49.1X3	T49.1X4	T49.1X5	T49.1X6
Quinocide	T37.2X1	T37.2X2	T37.2X3	T37.2X4	T37.2X5	T37.2X6
Quinoline (derivatives) NEC	T37.8X1	T37.8X2	T37.8X3	T37.8X4	T37.8X5	T37.8X6

Substance	Poisoning, Accidental (Unintentional)	Poisoning, Intentional Self-Harm	Poisoning, Assault	Poisoning, Undetermined	Adverse Effect	Underdosing
Quinupramine	T43.011	T43.012	T43.013	T43.014	T43.015	T43.016
Quotane	T41.3X1	T41.3X2	T41.3X3	T41.3X4	T41.3X5	T41.3X6
R						
Rabies						
immune globulin (human)	T50.Z11	T50.Z12	T50.Z13	T50.Z14	T50.Z15	T50.Z16
vaccine	T50.B91	T50.B92	T50.B93	T50.B94	T50.B95	T50.B96
Racemoramide	T40.2X1	T40.2X2	T40.2X3	T40.2X4	—	—
Racemorphan	T40.2X1	T40.2X2	T40.2X3	T40.2X4	T40.2X5	T40.2X6
Racepinefrin	T44.5X1	T44.5X2	T44.5X3	T44.5X4	T44.5X5	T44.5X6
Raclopride	T43.591	T43.592	T43.593	T43.594	T43.595	T43.596
Radiator alcohol	T51.1X1	T51.1X2	T51.1X3	T51.1X4	—	—
Radioactive drug NEC	T50.8X1	T50.8X2	T50.8X3	T50.8X4	T50.8X5	T50.8X6
Radio-opaque (drugs) (materials)	T50.8X1	T50.8X2	T50.8X3	T50.8X4	T50.8X5	T50.8X6
Ramifenazone	T39.2X1	T39.2X2	T39.2X3	T39.2X4	T39.2X5	T39.2X6
Ramipril	T46.4X1	T46.4X2	T46.4X3	T46.4X4	T46.4X5	T46.4X6
Ranitidine	T47.0X1	T47.0X2	T47.0X3	T47.0X4	T47.0X5	T47.0X6
Ranunculus	T62.2X1	T62.2X2	T62.2X3	T62.2X4	—	—
Rat poison NEC	T60.4X1	T60.4X2	T60.4X3	T60.4X4	—	—
Rattlesnake (venom)	T63.011	T63.012	T63.013	T63.014	—	—
Raubasine	T46.7X1	T46.7X2	T46.7X3	T46.7X4	T46.7X5	T46.7X6
Raudixin	T46.5X1	T46.5X2	T46.5X3	T46.5X4	T46.5X5	T46.5X6
Rautensin	T46.5X1	T46.5X2	T46.5X3	T46.5X4	T46.5X5	T46.5X6
Rautina	T46.5X1	T46.5X2	T46.5X3	T46.5X4	T46.5X5	T46.5X6
Rautotal	T46.5X1	T46.5X2	T46.5X3	T46.5X4	T46.5X5	T46.5X6
Rauwiloid	T46.5X1	T46.5X2	T46.5X3	T46.5X4	T46.5X5	T46.5X6
Rauwoldin	T46.5X1	T46.5X2	T46.5X3	T46.5X4	T46.5X5	T46.5X6
Rauwolfia (alkaloids)	T46.5X1	T46.5X2	T46.5X3	T46.5X4	T46.5X5	T46.5X6
Razoxane	T45.1X1	T45.1X2	T45.1X3	T45.1X4	T45.1X5	T45.1X6
Realgar	T57.0X1	T57.0X2	T57.0X3	T57.0X4	—	—
Recombinant (R) — *see specific protein*						
Red blood cells, packed	T45.8X1	T45.8X2	T45.8X3	T45.8X4	T45.8X5	T45.8X6
Red squill (scilliroside)	T60.4X1	T60.4X2	T60.4X3	T60.4X4	—	—
Reducing agent, industrial NEC	T65.891	T65.892	T65.893	T65.894		
Refrigerant gas (chlorofluoro-carbon)	T53.5X1	T53.5X2	T53.5X3	T53.5X4	—	—
not chlorofluoro-carbon	T59.891	T59.892	T59.893	T59.894	—	—
Regroton	T50.2X1	T50.2X2	T50.2X3	T50.2X4	T50.2X5	T50.2X6
Rehydration salts (oral)	T50.3X1	T50.3X2	T50.3X3	T50.3X4	T50.3X5	T50.3X6
Rela	T42.8X1	T42.8X2	T42.8X3	T42.8X4	T42.8X5	T42.8X6

◀ New   ◀ Revised   ~~deleted~~ Deleted

Substance	Poisoning, Accidental (Unintentional)	Poisoning, Intentional Self-Harm	Poisoning, Assault	Poisoning, Undetermined	Adverse Effect	Underdosing
Relaxant, muscle						
anesthetic	T48.1X1	T48.1X2	T48.1X3	T48.1X4	T48.1X5	T48.1X6
central nervous system	T42.8X1	T42.8X2	T42.8X3	T42.8X4	T42.8X5	T42.8X6
skeletal NEC	T48.1X1	T48.1X2	T48.1X3	T48.1X4	T48.1X5	T48.1X6
smooth NEC	T44.3X1	T44.3X2	T44.3X3	T44.3X4	T44.3X5	T44.3X6
Remoxipride	T43.591	T43.592	T43.593	T43.594	T43.595	T43.596
Renese	T50.2X1	T50.2X2	T50.2X3	T50.2X4	T50.2X5	T50.2X6
Renografin	T50.8X1	T50.8X2	T50.8X3	T50.8X4	T50.8X5	T50.8X6
Replacement solution	T50.3X1	T50.3X2	T50.3X3	T50.3X4	T50.3X5	T50.3X6
Reproterol	T48.6X1	T48.6X2	T48.6X3	T48.6X4	T48.6X5	T48.6X6
Rescinnamine	T46.5X1	T46.5X2	T46.5X3	T46.5X4	T46.5X5	T46.5X6
Reserpin(e)	T46.5X1	T46.5X2	T46.5X3	T46.5X4	T46.5X5	T46.5X6
Resorcin, resorcinol (nonmedicinal)	T65.891	T65.892	T65.893	T65.894	—	—
medicinal	T49.4X1	T49.4X2	T49.4X3	T49.4X4	T49.4X5	T49.4X6
Respaire	T48.4X1	T48.4X2	T48.4X3	T48.4X4	T48.4X5	T48.4X6
Respiratory drug NEC	T48.901	T48.902	T48.903	T48.904	T48.905	T48.906
antiasthmatic NEC	T48.6X1	T48.6X2	T48.6X3	T48.6X4	T48.6X5	T48.6X6
anti-common-cold NEC	T48.5X1	T48.5X2	T48.5X3	T48.5X4	T48.5X5	T48.5X6
expectorant NEC	T48.4X1	T48.4X2	T48.4X3	T48.4X4	T48.4X5	T48.4X6
stimulant	T48.901	T48.902	T48.903	T48.904	T48.905	T48.906
Retinoic acid	T49.0X1	T49.0X2	T49.0X3	T49.0X4	T49.0X5	T49.0X6
Retinol	T45.2X1	T45.2X2	T45.2X3	T45.2X4	T45.2X5	T45.2X6
Rh (D) immune globulin (human)	T50.Z11	T50.Z12	T50.Z13	T50.Z14	T50.Z15	T50.Z16
Rhodine	T39.011	T39.012	T39.013	T39.014	T39.015	T39.016
RhoGAM	T50.Z11	T50.Z12	T50.Z13	T50.Z14	T50.Z15	T50.Z16
Rhubarb						
dry extract	T47.2X1	T47.2X2	T47.2X3	T47.2X4	T47.2X5	T47.2X6
tincture, compound	T47.2X1	T47.2X2	T47.2X3	T47.2X4	T47.2X5	T47.2X6
Ribavirin	T37.5X1	T37.5X2	T37.5X3	T37.5X4	T37.5X5	T37.5X6
Riboflavin	T45.2X1	T45.2X2	T45.2X3	T45.2X4	T45.2X5	T45.2X6
Ribostamycin	T36.5X1	T36.5X2	T36.5X3	T36.5X4	T36.5X5	T36.5X6
Ricin	T62.2X1	T62.2X2	T62.2X3	T62.2X4	—	—
Ricinus communis	T62.2X1	T62.2X2	T62.2X3	T62.2X4	—	—
Rickettsial vaccine NEC	T50.A91	T50.A92	T50.A93	T50.A94	T50.A95	T50.A96
Rifabutin	T36.6X1	T36.6X2	T36.6X3	T36.6X4	T36.6X5	T36.6X6
Rifamide	T36.6X1	T36.6X2	T36.6X3	T36.6X4	T36.6X5	T36.6X6
Rifampicin	T36.6X1	T36.6X2	T36.6X3	T36.6X4	T36.6X5	T36.6X6
with isoniazid	T37.1X1	T37.1X2	T37.1X3	T37.1X4	T37.1X5	T37.1X6
Rifampin	T36.6X1	T36.6X2	T36.6X3	T36.6X4	T36.6X5	T36.6X6
Rifamycin	T36.6X1	T36.6X2	T36.6X3	T36.6X4	T36.6X5	T36.6X6
Rifaximin	T36.6X1	T36.6X2	T36.6X3	T36.6X4	T36.6X5	T36.6X6
Rimantadine	T37.5X1	T37.5X2	T37.5X3	T37.5X4	T37.5X5	T37.5X6
Rimazolium metilsulfate	T39.8X1	T39.8X2	T39.8X3	T39.8X4	T39.8X5	T39.8X6
Rimifon	T37.1X1	T37.1X2	T37.1X3	T37.1X4	T37.1X5	T37.1X6
Rimiterol	T48.6X1	T48.6X2	T48.6X3	T48.6X4	T48.6X5	T48.6X6
Ringer (lactate) solution	T50.3X1	T50.3X2	T50.3X3	T50.3X4	T50.3X5	T50.3X6
Ristocetin	T36.8X1	T36.8X2	T36.8X3	T36.8X4	T36.8X5	T36.8X6
Ritalin	T43.631	T43.632	T43.633	T43.634	T43.635	T43.636
Ritodrine	T44.5X1	T44.5X2	T44.5X3	T44.5X4	T44.5X5	T44.5X6
Roach killer — see Insecticide						
Rociverine	T44.3X1	T44.3X2	T44.3X3	T44.3X4	T44.3X5	T44.3X6
Rocky Mountain spotted fever vaccine	T50.A91	T50.A92	T50.A93	T50.A94	T50.A95	T50.A96
Rodenticide NEC	T60.4X1	T60.4X2	T60.4X3	T60.4X4	—	—
Rohypnol	T42.4X1	T42.4X2	T42.4X3	T42.4X4	T42.4X5	T42.4X6
Rokitamycin	T36.3X1	T36.3X2	T36.3X3	T36.3X4	T36.3X5	T36.3X6
Rolaids	T47.1X1	T47.1X2	T47.1X3	T47.1X4	T47.1X5	T47.1X6
Rolitetracycline	T36.4X1	T36.4X2	T36.4X3	T36.4X4	T36.4X5	T36.4X6
Romilar	T48.3X1	T48.3X2	T48.3X3	T48.3X4	T48.3X5	T48.3X6
Ronifibrate	T46.6X1	T46.6X2	T46.6X3	T46.6X4	T46.6X5	T46.6X6
Rosaprostol	T47.1X1	T47.1X2	T47.1X3	T47.1X4	T47.1X5	T47.1X6
Rose bengal sodium (131I)	T50.8X1	T50.8X2	T50.8X3	T50.8X4	T50.8X5	T50.8X6
Rose water ointment	T49.3X1	T49.3X2	T49.3X3	T49.3X4	T49.3X5	T49.3X6
Rosoxacin	T37.8X1	T37.8X2	T37.8X3	T37.8X4	T37.8X5	T37.8X6
Rotenone	T60.2X1	T60.2X2	T60.2X3	T60.2X4	—	—
Rotoxamine	T45.0X1	T45.0X2	T45.0X3	T45.0X4	T45.0X5	T45.0X6
Rough-on-rats	T60.4X1	T60.4X2	T60.4X3	T60.4X4	—	—
Roxatidine	T47.0X1	T47.0X2	T47.0X3	T47.0X4	T47.0X5	T47.0X6
Roxithromycin	T36.3X1	T36.3X2	T36.3X3	T36.3X4	T36.3X5	T36.3X6
Rt-PA	T45.611	T45.612	T45.613	T45.614	T45.615	T45.616
Rubbing alcohol	T51.2X1	T51.2X2	T51.2X3	T51.2X4	—	—
Rubefacient	T49.4X1	T49.4X2	T49.4X3	T49.4X4	T49.4X5	T49.4X6
Rubella vaccine	T50.B91	T50.B92	T50.B93	T50.B94	T50.B95	T50.B96
Rubelogen	T50.B91	T50.B92	T50.B93	T50.B94	T50.B95	T50.B96
Rubeovax	T50.991	T50.992	T50.993	T50.994	T50.995	T50.996
Rubidium chloride Rb82	T50.8X1	T50.8X2	T50.8X3	T50.8X4	T50.8X5	T50.8X6
Rubidomycin	T45.1X1	T45.1X2	T45.1X3	T45.1X4	T45.1X5	T45.1X6
Rue	T62.2X1	T62.2X2	T62.2X3	T62.2X4	—	—
Rufocromomycin	T45.1X1	T45.1X2	T45.1X3	T45.1X4	T45.1X5	T45.1X6
Russel's viper venin	T45.7X1	T45.7X2	T45.7X3	T45.7X4	T45.7X5	T45.7X6
Ruta (graveolens)	T62.2X1	T62.2X2	T62.2X3	T62.2X4	—	—
Rutinum	T46.991	T46.992	T46.993	T46.994	T46.995	T46.996
Rutoside	T46.991	T46.992	T46.993	T46.994	T46.995	T46.996

◀ New ◀ Revised ~~deleted~~ Deleted

Substance	External Cause (T-Code)					
	Poisoning, Accidental (Unintentional)	Poisoning, Intentional Self-Harm	Poisoning, Assault	Poisoning, Undetermined	Adverse Effect	Underdosing
S						
Sabadilla (plant)	T62.2X1	T62.2X2	T62.2X3	T62.2X4	—	—
pesticide	T60.2X1	T60.2X2	T60.2X3	T60.2X4	—	—
Saccharated iron oxide	T45.8X1	T45.8X2	T45.8X3	T45.8X4	T45.8X5	T45.8X6
Saccharin	T50.901	T50.902	T50.903	T50.904	T50.905	T50.906
Saccharomyces boulardii	T47.6X1	T47.6X2	T47.6X3	T47.6X4	T47.6X5	T47.6X6
Safflower oil	T46.6X1	T46.6X2	T46.6X3	T46.6X4	T46.6X5	T46.6X6
Safrazine	T43.1X1	T43.1X2	T43.1X3	T43.1X4	T43.1X5	T43.1X6
Salazosulfapyridine	T37.0X1	T37.0X2	T37.0X3	T37.0X4	T37.0X5	T37.0X6
Salbutamol	T48.6X1	T48.6X2	T48.6X3	T48.6X4	T48.6X5	T48.6X6
Salicylamide	T39.091	T39.092	T39.093	T39.094	T39.095	T39.096
Salicylate NEC	T39.091	T39.092	T39.093	T39.094	T39.095	T39.096
methyl	T49.3X1	T49.3X2	T49.3X3	T49.3X4	T49.3X5	T49.3X6
theobromine calcium	T50.2X1	T50.2X2	T50.2X3	T50.2X4	T50.2X5	T50.2X6
Salicylazosulfapyridine	T37.0X1	T37.0X2	T37.0X3	T37.0X4	T37.0X5	T37.0X6
Salicylhydroxamic acid	T49.0X1	T49.0X2	T49.0X3	T49.0X4	T49.0X5	T49.0X6
Salicylic acid	T49.4X1	T49.4X2	T49.4X3	T49.4X4	T49.4X5	T49.4X6
with benzoic acid	T49.4X1	T49.4X2	T49.4X3	T49.4X4	T49.4X5	T49.4X6
congeners	T39.091	T39.092	T39.093	T39.094	T39.095	T39.096
derivative	T39.091	T39.092	T39.093	T39.094	T39.095	T39.096
salts	T39.091	T39.092	T39.093	T39.094	T39.095	T39.096
Salinazid	T37.1X1	T37.1X2	T37.1X3	T37.1X4	T37.1X5	T37.1X6
Salmeterol	T48.6X1	T48.6X2	T48.6X3	T48.6X4	T48.6X5	T48.6X6
Salol	T49.3X1	T49.3X2	T49.3X3	T49.3X4	T49.3X5	T49.3X6
Salsalate	T39.091	T39.092	T39.093	T39.094	T39.095	T39.096
Salt substitute	T50.901	T50.902	T50.903	T50.904	T50.905	T50.906
Salt-replacing drug	T50.901	T50.902	T50.903	T50.904	T50.905	T50.906
Salt-retaining mineralocorticoid	T50.0X1	T50.0X2	T50.0X3	T50.0X4	T50.0X5	T50.0X6
Saluretic NEC	T50.2X1	T50.2X2	T50.2X3	T50.2X4	T50.2X5	T50.2X6
Saluron	T50.2X1	T50.2X2	T50.2X3	T50.2X4	T50.2X5	T50.2X6
Salvarsan 606 (neosilver) (silver)	T37.8X1	T37.8X2	T37.8X3	T37.8X4	T37.8X5	T37.8X6
Sambucus canadensis	T62.2X1	T62.2X2	T62.2X3	T62.2X4	—	—
berry	T62.1X1	T62.1X2	T62.1X3	T62.1X4	—	—
Sandril	T46.5X1	T46.5X2	T46.5X3	T46.5X4	T46.5X5	T46.5X6
Sanguinaria canadensis	T62.2X1	T62.2X2	T62.2X3	T62.2X4	—	—
Saniflush (cleaner)	T54.2X1	T54.2X2	T54.2X3	T54.2X4	—	—
Santonin	T37.4X1	T37.4X2	T37.4X3	T37.4X4	T37.4X5	T37.4X6
Santyl	T49.8X1	T49.8X2	T49.8X3	T49.8X4	T49.8X5	T49.8X6
Saralasin	T46.5X1	T46.5X2	T46.5X3	T46.5X4	T46.5X5	T46.5X6
Sarcolysin	T45.1X1	T45.1X2	T45.1X3	T45.1X4	T45.1X5	T45.1X6
Sarkomycin	T45.1X1	T45.1X2	T45.1X3	T45.1X4	T45.1X5	T45.1X6
Saroten	T43.011	T43.012	T43.013	T43.014	T43.015	T43.016

Substance	External Cause (T-Code)					
	Poisoning, Accidental (Unintentional)	Poisoning, Intentional Self-Harm	Poisoning, Assault	Poisoning, Undetermined	Adverse Effect	Underdosing
Saturnine—see Lead						
Savin (oil)	T49.4X1	T49.4X2	T49.4X3	T49.4X4	T49.4X5	T49.4X6
Scammony	T47.2X1	T47.2X2	T47.2X3	T47.2X4	T47.2X5	T47.2X6
Scarlet red	T49.8X1	T49.8X2	T49.8X3	T49.8X4	T49.8X5	T49.8X6
Scheele's green	T57.0X1	T57.0X2	T57.0X3	T57.0X4		
insecticide	T57.0X1	T57.0X2	T57.0X3	T57.0X4	—	—
Schizontozide (blood) (tissue)	T37.2X1	T37.2X2	T37.2X3	T37.2X4	T37.2X5	T37.2X6
Schradan	T60.0X1	T60.0X2	T60.0X3	T60.0X4		
Schweinfurth green	T57.0X1	T57.0X2	T57.0X3	T57.0X4		
insecticide	T57.0X1	T57.0X2	T57.0X3	T57.0X4	—	—
Scilla, rat poison	T60.4X1	T60.4X2	T60.4X3	T60.4X4		
Scillaren	T60.4X1	T60.4X2	T60.4X3	T60.4X4	—	—
Sclerosing agent	T46.8X1	T46.8X2	T46.8X3	T46.8X4	T46.8X5	T46.8X6
Scombrotoxin	T61.11	T61.12	T61.13	T61.14		
Scopolamine	T44.3X1	T44.3X2	T44.3X3	T44.3X4	T44.3X5	T44.3X6
Scopolia extract	T44.3X1	T44.3X2	T44.3X3	T44.3X4	T44.3X5	T44.3X6
Scouring powder	T65.891	T65.892	T65.893	T65.894	—	—
Sea						
anemone (sting)	T63.631	T63.632	T63.633	T63.634	—	—
cucumber (sting)	T63.691	T63.692	T63.693	T63.694		
snake (bite) (venom)	T63.091	T63.092	T63.093	T63.094	—	—
urchin spine (puncture)	T63.691	T63.692	T63.693	T63.694		
Seafood	T61.91	T61.92	T61.93	T61.94		
specified NEC	T61.8X1	T61.8X2	T61.8X3	T61.8X4	—	—
Secbutabarbital	T42.3X1	T42.3X2	T42.3X3	T42.3X4	T42.3X5	T42.3X6
Secbutabarbitone	T42.3X1	T42.3X2	T42.3X3	T42.3X4	T42.3X5	T42.3X6
Secnidazole	T37.3X1	T37.3X2	T37.3X3	T37.3X4	T37.3X5	T37.3X6
Secobarbital	T42.3X1	T42.3X2	T42.3X3	T42.3X4	T42.3X5	T42.3X6
Seconal	T42.3X1	T42.3X2	T42.3X3	T42.3X4	T42.3X5	T42.3X6
Secretin	T50.8X1	T50.8X2	T50.8X3	T50.8X4	T50.8X5	T50.8X6
Sedative NEC	T42.71	T42.72	T42.73	T42.74	T42.75	T42.76
mixed NEC	T42.6X1	T42.6X2	T42.6X3	T42.6X4	T42.6X5	T42.6X6
Sedormid	T42.6X1	T42.6X2	T42.6X3	T42.6X4	T42.6X5	T42.6X6
Seed disinfectant or dressing	T60.8X1	T60.8X2	T60.8X3	T60.8X4	—	—
Seeds (poisonous)	T62.2X1	T62.2X2	T62.2X3	T62.2X4	—	—
Selegiline	T42.8X1	T42.8X2	T42.8X3	T42.8X4	T42.8X5	T42.8X6
Selenium NEC	T56.891	T56.892	T56.893	T56.894	—	—
disulfide or sulfide	T49.4X1	T49.4X2	T49.4X3	T49.4X4	T49.4X5	T49.4X6
fumes	T59.891	T59.892	T59.893	T59.894	—	—
sulfide	T49.4X1	T49.4X2	T49.4X3	T49.4X4	T49.4X5	T49.4X6
Selenomethionine (75Se)	T50.8X1	T50.8X2	T50.8X3	T50.8X4	T50.8X5	T50.8X6
Selsun	T49.4X1	T49.4X2	T49.4X3	T49.4X4	T49.4X5	T49.4X6

◀ New   ◀ Revised   ~~deleted~~ Deleted

	External Cause (T-Code)					
Substance	Poisoning, Accidental (Unintentional)	Poisoning, Intentional Self-Harm	Poisoning, Assault	Poisoning, Undetermined	Adverse Effect	Underdosing
Semustine	T45.1X1	T45.1X2	T45.1X3	T45.1X4	T45.1X5	T45.1X6
Senega syrup	T48.4X1	T48.4X2	T48.4X3	T48.4X4	T48.4X5	T48.4X6
Senna	T47.2X1	T47.2X2	T47.2X3	T47.2X4	T47.2X5	T47.2X6
Sennoside A+B	T47.2X1	T47.2X2	T47.2X3	T47.2X4	T47.2X5	T47.2X6
Septisol	T49.2X1	T49.2X2	T49.2X3	T49.2X4	T49.2X5	T49.2X6
Seractide	T38.811	T38.812	T38.813	T38.814	T38.815	T38.816
Serax	T42.4X1	T42.4X2	T42.4X3	T42.4X4	T42.4X5	T42.4X6
Serenesil	T42.6X1	T42.6X2	T42.6X3	T42.6X4	T42.6X5	T42.6X6
Serenium (hydrochloride)	T37.91	T37.92	T37.93	T37.94	T37.95	T37.96
Serepax — see Oxazepam						
Sermorelin	T38.891	T38.892	T38.893	T38.894	T38.895	T38.896
Sernyl	T41.1X1	T41.1X2	T41.1X3	T41.1X4	T41.1X5	T41.1X6
Serotonin	T50.991	T50.992	T50.993	T50.994	T50.995	T50.996
Serpasil	T46.5X1	T46.5X2	T46.5X3	T46.5X4	T46.5X5	T46.5X6
Serrapeptase	T45.3X1	T45.3X2	T45.3X3	T45.3X4	T45.3X5	T45.3X6
Serum						
antibotulinus	T50.Z11	T50.Z12	T50.Z13	T50.Z14	T50.Z15	T50.Z16
anticytotoxic	T50.Z11	T50.Z12	T50.Z13	T50.Z14	T50.Z15	T50.Z16
antidiphtheria	T50.Z11	T50.Z12	T50.Z13	T50.Z14	T50.Z15	T50.Z16
antimeningococcus	T50.Z11	T50.Z12	T50.Z13	T50.Z14	T50.Z15	T50.Z16
anti-Rh	T50.Z11	T50.Z12	T50.Z13	T50.Z14	T50.Z15	T50.Z16
anti-snake-bite	T50.Z11	T50.Z12	T50.Z13	T50.Z14	T50.Z15	T50.Z16
antitetanic	T50.Z11	T50.Z12	T50.Z13	T50.Z14	T50.Z15	T50.Z16
antitoxic	T50.Z11	T50.Z12	T50.Z13	T50.Z14	T50.Z15	T50.Z16
complement (inhibitor)	T45.8X1	T45.8X2	T45.8X3	T45.8X4	T45.8X5	T45.8X6
convalescent	T50.Z11	T50.Z12	T50.Z13	T50.Z14	T50.Z15	T50.Z16
hemolytic complement	T45.8X1	T45.8X2	T45.8X3	T45.8X4	T45.8X5	T45.8X6
immune (human)	T50.Z11	T50.Z12	T50.Z13	T50.Z14	T50.Z15	T50.Z16
protective NEC	T50.Z11	T50.Z12	T50.Z13	T50.Z14	T50.Z15	T50.Z16
Setastine	T45.0X1	T45.0X2	T45.0X3	T45.0X4	T45.0X5	T45.0X6
Setoperone	T43.591	T43.592	T43.593	T43.594	T43.595	T43.596
Sewer gas	T59.91	T59.92	T59.93	T59.94	—	—
Shampoo	T55.0X1	T55.0X2	T55.0X3	T55.0X4	—	—
Shellfish, noxious, nonbacterial	T61.781	T61.782	T61.783	T61.784	—	—
Sildenafil	T46.7X1	T46.7X2	T46.7X3	T46.7X4	T46.7X5	T46.7X6
Silibinin	T50.991	T50.992	T50.993	T50.994	T50.995	T50.996
Silicone NEC	T65.891	T65.892	T65.893	T65.894	—	—
medicinal	T49.3X1	T49.3X2	T49.3X3	T49.3X4	T49.3X5	T49.3X6
Silvadene	T49.0X1	T49.0X2	T49.0X3	T49.0X4	T49.0X5	T49.0X6
Silver	T49.0X1	T49.0X2	T49.0X3	T49.0X4	T49.0X5	T49.0X6
anti-infectives	T49.0X1	T49.0X2	T49.0X3	T49.0X4	T49.0X5	T49.0X6
arsphenamine	T37.8X1	T37.8X2	T37.8X3	T37.8X4	T37.8X5	T37.8X6

	External Cause (T-Code)					
Substance	Poisoning, Accidental (Unintentional)	Poisoning, Intentional Self-Harm	Poisoning, Assault	Poisoning, Undetermined	Adverse Effect	Underdosing
Silver (Continued)						
colloidal	T49.0X1	T49.0X2	T49.0X3	T49.0X4	T49.0X5	T49.0X6
nitrate	T49.0X1	T49.0X2	T49.0X3	T49.0X4	T49.0X5	T49.0X6
ophthalmic preparation	T49.5X1	T49.5X2	T49.5X3	T49.5X4	T49.5X5	T49.5X6
toughened (keratolytic)	T49.4X1	T49.4X2	T49.4X3	T49.4X4	T49.4X5	T49.4X6
nonmedicinal (dust)	T56.891	T56.892	T56.893	T56.894	—	—
protein	T49.5X1	T49.5X2	T49.5X3	T49.5X4	T49.5X5	T49.5X6
salvarsan	T37.8X1	T37.8X2	T37.8X3	T37.8X4	T37.8X5	T37.8X6
sulfadiazine	T49.4X1	T49.4X2	T49.4X3	T49.4X4	T49.4X5	T49.4X6
Silymarin	T50.991	T50.992	T50.993	T50.994	T50.995	T50.996
Simaldrate	T47.1X1	T47.1X2	T47.1X3	T47.1X4	T47.1X5	T47.1X6
Simazine	T60.3X1	T60.3X2	T60.3X3	T60.3X4	—	—
Simethicone	T47.1X1	T47.1X2	T47.1X3	T47.1X4	T47.1X5	T47.1X6
Simfibrate	T46.6X1	T46.6X2	T46.6X3	T46.6X4	T46.6X5	T46.6X6
Simvastatin	T46.6X1	T46.6X2	T46.6X3	T46.6X4	T46.6X5	T46.6X6
Sincalide	T50.8X1	T50.8X2	T50.8X3	T50.8X4	T50.8X5	T50.8X6
Sinequan	T43.011	T43.012	T43.013	T43.014	T43.015	T43.016
Singoserp	T46.5X1	T46.5X2	T46.5X3	T46.5X4	T46.5X5	T46.5X6
Sintrom	T45.511	T45.512	T45.513	T45.514	T45.515	T45.516
Sisomicin	T36.5X1	T36.5X2	T36.5X3	T36.5X4	T36.5X5	T36.5X6
Sitosterols	T46.6X1	T46.6X2	T46.6X3	T46.6X4	T46.6X5	T46.6X6
Skeletal muscle relaxants	T48.1X1	T48.1X2	T48.1X3	T48.1X4	T48.1X5	T48.1X6
Skin						
agents (external)	T49.91	T49.92	T49.93	T49.94	T49.95	T49.96
specified NEC	T49.8X1	T49.8X2	T49.8X3	T49.8X4	T49.8X5	T49.8X6
test antigen	T50.8X1	T50.8X2	T50.8X3	T50.8X4	T50.8X5	T50.8X6
Sleep-eze	T45.0X1	T45.0X2	T45.0X3	T45.0X4	T45.0X5	T45.0X6
Sleeping draught, pill	T42.71	T42.72	T42.73	T42.74	T42.75	T42.76
Smallpox vaccine	T50.B11	T50.B12	T50.B13	T50.B14	T50.B15	T50.B16
Smelter fumes NEC	T56.91	T56.92	T56.93	T56.94	—	—
Smog	T59.1X1	T59.1X2	T59.1X3	T59.1X4	—	—
Smoke NEC	T59.811	T59.812	T59.813	T59.814	—	—
Smooth muscle relaxant	T44.3X1	T44.3X2	T44.3X3	T44.3X4	T44.3X5	T44.3X6
Snail killer NEC	T60.8X1	T60.8X2	T60.8X3	T60.8X4	—	—
Snake venom or bite	T63.001	T63.002	T63.003	T63.004	—	—
hemocoagulase	T45.7X1	T45.7X2	T45.7X3	T45.7X4	T45.7X5	T45.7X6
Snuff	T65.211	T65.212	T65.213	T65.214	—	—
Soap (powder) (product)	T55.0X1	T55.0X2	T55.0X3	T55.0X4	—	—
enema	T47.4X1	T47.4X2	T47.4X3	T47.4X4	T47.4X5	T47.4X6
medicinal, soft	T49.2X1	T49.2X2	T49.2X3	T49.2X4	T49.2X5	T49.2X6
superfatted	T49.2X1	T49.2X2	T49.2X3	T49.2X4	T49.2X5	T49.2X6
Sobrerol	T48.4X1	T48.4X2	T48.4X3	T48.4X4	T48.4X5	T48.4X6

TABLE OF DRUGS AND CHEMICALS

Substance	External Cause (T-Code)					
	Poisoning, Accidental (Unintentional)	Poisoning, Intentional Self-Harm	Poisoning, Assault	Poisoning, Undetermined	Adverse Effect	Underdosing
Soda (caustic)	T54.3X1	T54.3X2	T54.3X3	T54.3X4	—	—
bicarb	T47.1X1	T47.1X2	T47.1X3	T47.1X4	T47.1X5	T47.1X6
chlorinated — see Sodium, hypochlorite						
Sodium						
acetosulfone	T37.1X1	T37.1X2	T37.1X3	T37.1X4	T37.1X5	T37.1X6
acetrizoate	T50.8X1	T50.8X2	T50.8X3	T50.8X4	T50.8X5	T50.8X6
acid phosphate	T50.3X1	T50.3X2	T50.3X3	T50.3X4	T50.3X5	T50.3X6
alginate	T47.8X1	T47.8X2	T47.8X3	T47.8X4	T47.8X5	T47.8X6
amidotrizoate	T50.8X1	T50.8X2	T50.8X3	T50.8X4	T50.8X5	T50.8X6
aminopterin	T45.1X1	T45.1X2	T45.1X3	T45.1X4	T45.1X5	T45.1X6
amylosulfate	T47.8X1	T47.8X2	T47.8X3	T47.8X4	T47.8X5	T47.8X6
amytal	T42.3X1	T42.3X2	T42.3X3	T42.3X4	T42.3X5	T42.3X6
antimony gluconate	T37.3X1	T37.3X2	T37.3X3	T37.3X4	T37.3X5	T37.3X6
arsenate	T57.0X1	T57.0X2	T57.0X3	T57.0X4	—	—
aurothiomalate	T39.4X1	T39.4X2	T39.4X3	T39.4X4	T39.4X5	T39.4X6
aurothiosulfate	T39.4X1	T39.4X2	T39.4X3	T39.4X4	T39.4X5	T39.4X6
barbiturate	T42.3X1	T42.3X2	T42.3X3	T42.3X4	T42.3X5	T42.3X6
basic phosphate	T47.4X1	T47.4X2	T47.4X3	T47.4X4	T47.4X5	T47.4X6
bicarbonate	T47.1X1	T47.1X2	T47.1X3	T47.1X4	T47.1X5	T47.1X6
bichromate	T57.8X1	T57.8X2	T57.8X3	T57.8X4	—	—
biphosphate	T50.3X1	T50.3X2	T50.3X3	T50.3X4	T50.3X5	T50.3X6
bisulfate	T65.891	T65.892	T65.893	T65.894	—	—
borate						
cleanser	T57.8X1	T57.8X2	T57.8X3	T57.8X4	—	—
eye	T49.5X1	T49.5X2	T49.5X3	T49.5X4	T49.5X5	T49.5X6
therapeutic	T49.8X1	T49.8X2	T49.8X3	T49.8X4	T49.8X5	T49.8X6
bromide	T42.6X1	T42.6X2	T42.6X3	T42.6X4	T42.6X5	T42.6X6
cacodylate (nonmedicinal) NEC	T50.8X1	T50.8X2	T50.8X3	T50.8X4	T50.8X5	T50.8X6
anti-infective	T37.8X1	T37.8X2	T37.8X3	T37.8X4	T37.8X5	T37.8X6
herbicide	T60.3X1	T60.3X2	T60.3X3	T60.3X4	—	—
calcium edetate	T45.8X1	T45.8X2	T45.8X3	T45.8X4	T45.8X5	T45.8X6
carbonate NEC	T54.3X1	T54.3X2	T54.3X3	T54.3X4	—	—
chlorate NEC	T65.891	T65.892	T65.893	T65.894	—	—
herbicide	T54.91	T54.92	T54.93	T54.94	—	—
chloride	T50.3X1	T50.3X2	T50.3X3	T50.3X4	T50.3X5	T50.3X6
with glucose	T50.3X1	T50.3X2	T50.3X3	T50.3X4	T50.3X5	T50.3X6
chromate	T65.891	T65.892	T65.893	T65.894	—	—
citrate	T50.991	T50.992	T50.993	T50.994	T50.995	T50.996
cromoglicate	T48.6X1	T48.6X2	T48.6X3	T48.6X4	T48.6X5	T48.6X6
cyanide	T65.0X1	T65.0X2	T65.0X3	T65.0X4	—	—
cyclamate	T50.3X1	T50.3X2	T50.3X3	T50.3X4	T50.3X5	T50.3X6

Substance	External Cause (T-Code)					
	Poisoning, Accidental (Unintentional)	Poisoning, Intentional Self-Harm	Poisoning, Assault	Poisoning, Undetermined	Adverse Effect	Underdosing
Sodium (Continued)						
dehydrocholate	T45.8X1	T45.8X2	T45.8X3	T45.8X4	T45.8X5	T45.8X6
diatrizoate	T50.8X1	T50.8X2	T50.8X3	T50.8X4	T50.8X5	T50.8X6
dibunate	T48.4X1	T48.4X2	T48.4X3	T48.4X4	T48.4X5	T48.4X6
dioctyl sulfosuccinate	T47.4X1	T47.4X2	T47.4X3	T47.4X4	T47.4X5	T47.4X6
dipantoyl ferrate	T45.8X1	T45.8X2	T45.8X3	T45.8X4	T45.8X5	T45.8X6
edetate	T45.8X1	T45.8X2	T45.8X3	T45.8X4	T45.8X5	T45.8X6
ethacrynate	T50.1X1	T50.1X2	T50.1X3	T50.1X4	T50.1X5	T50.1X6
feredetate	T45.8X1	T45.8X2	T45.8X3	T45.8X4	T45.8X5	T45.8X6
Fluoride — see Fluoride						
fluoroacetate (dust) (pesticide)	T60.4X1	T60.4X2	T60.4X3	T60.4X4		
free salt	T50.3X1	T50.3X2	T50.3X3	T50.3X4	T50.3X5	T50.3X6
fusidate	T36.8X1	T36.8X2	T36.8X3	T36.8X4	T36.8X5	T36.8X6
glucaldrate	T47.1X1	T47.1X2	T47.1X3	T47.1X4	T47.1X5	T47.1X6
glucosulfone	T37.1X1	T37.1X2	T37.1X3	T37.1X4	T37.1X5	T37.1X6
glutamate	T45.8X1	T45.8X2	T45.8X3	T45.8X4	T45.8X5	T45.8X6
hydrogen carbonate	T50.3X1	T50.3X2	T50.3X3	T50.3X4	T50.3X5	T50.3X6
hydroxide	T54.3X1	T54.3X2	T54.3X3	T54.3X4	—	—
hypochlorite (bleach) NEC	T54.3X1	T54.3X2	T54.3X3	T54.3X4	—	—
disinfectant	T54.3X1	T54.3X2	T54.3X3	T54.3X4	—	—
medicinal (anti-infective) (external)	T49.0X1	T49.0X2	T49.0X3	T49.0X4	T49.0X5	T49.0X6
vapor	T54.3X1	T54.3X2	T54.3X3	T54.3X4	—	—
hyposulfite	T49.0X1	T49.0X2	T49.0X3	T49.0X4	T49.0X5	T49.0X6
indigotin disulfonate	T50.8X1	T50.8X2	T50.8X3	T50.8X4	T50.8X5	T50.8X6
iodide	T50.991	T50.992	T50.993	T50.994	T50.995	T50.996
I-131	T50.8X1	T50.8X2	T50.8X3	T50.8X4	T50.8X5	T50.8X6
therapeutic	T38.2X1	T38.2X2	T38.2X3	T38.2X4	T38.2X5	T38.2X6
iodohippurate (131I)	T50.8X1	T50.8X2	T50.8X3	T50.8X4	T50.8X5	T50.8X6
iopodate	T50.8X1	T50.8X2	T50.8X3	T50.8X4	T50.8X5	T50.8X6
iothalamate	T50.8X1	T50.8X2	T50.8X3	T50.8X4	T50.8X5	T50.8X6
iron edetate	T45.4X1	T45.4X2	T45.4X3	T45.4X4	T45.4X5	T45.4X6
lactate (compound solution)	T45.8X1	T45.8X2	T45.8X3	T45.8X4	T45.8X5	T45.8X6
lauryl (sulfate)	T49.2X1	T49.2X2	T49.2X3	T49.2X4	T49.2X5	T49.2X6
(L)-triiodothyronine	T38.1X1	T38.1X2	T38.1X3	T38.1X4	T38.1X5	T38.1X6
magnesium citrate	T50.991	T50.992	T50.993	T50.994	T50.995	T50.996
mersalate	T50.2X1	T50.2X2	T50.2X3	T50.2X4	T50.2X5	T50.2X6
metasilicate	T65.891	T65.892	T65.893	T65.894	—	—
metrizoate	T50.8X1	T50.8X2	T50.8X3	T50.8X4	T50.8X5	T50.8X6
monofluoroacetate (pesticide)	T60.1X1	T60.1X2	T60.1X3	T60.1X4	—	—
morrhuate	T46.8X1	T46.8X2	T46.8X3	T46.8X4	T46.8X5	T46.8X6
nafcillin	T36.0X1	T36.0X2	T36.0X3	T36.0X4	T36.0X5	T36.0X6

◀ New   ◀ Revised   ~~deleted~~ Deleted

Substance	External Cause (T-Code)					
	Poisoning, Accidental (Unintentional)	Poisoning, Intentional Self-Harm	Poisoning, Assault	Poisoning, Undetermined	Adverse Effect	Underdosing
Sodium *(Continued)*						
nitrate (oxidizing agent)	T65.891	T65.892	T65.893	T65.894	—	—
nitrite	T50.6X1	T50.6X2	T50.6X3	T50.6X4	T50.6X5	T50.6X6
nitroferricyanide	T46.5X1	T46.5X2	T46.5X3	T46.5X4	T46.5X5	T46.5X6
nitroprusside	T46.5X1	T46.5X2	T46.5X3	T46.5X4	T46.5X5	T46.5X6
oxalate	T65.891	T65.892	T65.893	T65.894	—	—
oxide/peroxide	T65.891	T65.892	T65.893	T65.894	—	—
oxybate	T41.291	T41.292	T41.293	T41.294	T41.295	T41.296
para-aminohippurate	T50.8X1	T50.8X2	T50.8X3	T50.8X4	T50.8X5	T50.8X6
perborate (nonmedicinal) NEC	T65.891	T65.892	T65.893	T65.894	—	—
medicinal	T49.0X1	T49.0X2	T49.0X3	T49.0X4	T49.0X5	T49.0X6
soap	T55.0X1	T55.0X2	T55.0X3	T55.0X4	—	—
percarbonate — *see Sodium, perborate*						
pertechnetate Tc99m	T50.8X1	T50.8X2	T50.8X3	T50.8X4	T50.8X5	T50.8X6
phosphate						
cellulose	T45.8X1	T45.8X2	T45.8X3	T45.8X4	T45.8X5	T45.8X6
dibasic	T47.2X1	T47.2X2	T47.2X3	T47.2X4	T47.2X5	T47.2X6
monobasic	T47.2X1	T47.2X2	T47.2X3	T47.2X4	T47.2X5	T47.2X6
phytate	T50.6X1	T50.6X2	T50.6X3	T50.6X4	T50.6X5	T50.6X6
picosulfate	T47.2X1	T47.2X2	T47.2X3	T47.2X4	T47.2X5	T47.2X6
polyhydroxyaluminium monocarbonate	T47.1X1	T47.1X2	T47.1X3	T47.1X4	T47.1X5	T47.1X6
polystyrene sulfonate	T50.3X1	T50.3X2	T50.3X3	T50.3X4	T50.3X5	T50.3X6
propionate	T49.0X1	T49.0X2	T49.0X3	T49.0X4	T49.0X5	T49.0X6
propyl hydroxybenzoate	T50.991	T50.992	T50.993	T50.994	T50.995	T50.996
psylliate	T46.8X1	T46.8X2	T46.8X3	T46.8X4	T46.8X5	T46.8X6
removing resins	T50.3X1	T50.3X2	T50.3X3	T50.3X4	T50.3X5	T50.3X6
salicylate	T39.091	T39.092	T39.093	T39.094	T39.095	T39.096
salt NEC	T50.3X1	T50.3X2	T50.3X3	T50.3X4	T50.3X5	T50.3X6
selenate	T60.2X1	T60.2X2	T60.2X3	T60.2X4	—	—
stibogluconate	T37.3X1	T37.3X2	T37.3X3	T37.3X4	T37.3X5	T37.3X6
sulfate	T47.4X1	T47.4X2	T47.4X3	T47.4X4	T47.4X5	T47.4X6
sulfoxone	T37.1X1	T37.1X2	T37.1X3	T37.1X4	T37.1X5	T37.1X6
tetradecyl sulfate	T46.8X1	T46.8X2	T46.8X3	T46.8X4	T46.8X5	T46.8X6
thiopental	T41.1X1	T41.1X2	T41.1X3	T41.1X4	T41.1X5	T41.1X6
thiosalicylate	T39.091	T39.092	T39.093	T39.094	T39.095	T39.096
thiosulfate	T50.6X1	T50.6X2	T50.6X3	T50.6X4	T50.6X5	T50.6X6
tolbutamide	T38.3X1	T38.3X2	T38.3X3	T38.3X4	T38.3X5	T38.3X6
l-triiodothyronine	T38.1X1	T38.1X2	T38.1X3	T38.1X4	T38.1X5	T38.1X6
tyropanoate	T50.8X1	T50.8X2	T50.8X3	T50.8X4	T50.8X5	T50.8X6
valproate	T42.6X1	T42.6X2	T42.6X3	T42.6X4	T42.6X5	T42.6X6
versenate	T50.6X1	T50.6X2	T50.6X3	T50.6X4	T50.6X5	T50.6X6

Substance	External Cause (T-Code)					
	Poisoning, Accidental (Unintentional)	Poisoning, Intentional Self-Harm	Poisoning, Assault	Poisoning, Undetermined	Adverse Effect	Underdosing
Sodium-free salt	T50.901	T50.902	T50.903	T50.904	T50.905	T50.906
Sodium-removing resin	T50.3X1	T50.3X2	T50.3X3	T50.3X4	T50.3X5	T50.3X6
Soft soap	T55.0X1	T55.0X2	T55.0X3	T55.0X4	—	—
Solanine	T62.2X1	T62.2X2	T62.2X3	T62.2X4	—	—
berries	T62.1X1	T62.1X2	T62.1X3	T62.1X4	—	—
Solanum dulcamara	T62.2X1	T62.2X2	T62.2X3	T62.2X4	—	—
berries	T62.1X1	T62.1X2	T62.1X3	T62.1X4	—	—
Solapsone	T37.1X1	T37.1X2	T37.1X3	T37.1X4	T37.1X5	T37.1X6
Solar lotion	T49.3X1	T49.3X2	T49.3X3	T49.3X4	T49.3X5	T49.3X6
Solasulfone	T37.1X1	T37.1X2	T37.1X3	T37.1X4	T37.1X5	T37.1X6
Soldering fluid	T65.891	T65.892	T65.893	T65.894	—	—
Solid substance	T65.91	T65.92	T65.93	T65.94	—	—
specified NEC	T65.891	T65.892	T65.893	T65.894	—	—
Solvent, industrial NEC	T52.91	T52.92	T52.93	T52.94	—	—
naphtha	T52.0X1	T52.0X2	T52.0X3	T52.0X4	—	—
petroleum	T52.0X1	T52.0X2	T52.0X3	T52.0X4	—	—
specified NEC	T52.8X1	T52.8X2	T52.8X3	T52.8X4	—	—
Soma	T42.8X1	T42.8X2	T42.8X3	T42.8X4	T42.8X5	T42.8X6
Somatorelin	T38.891	T38.892	T38.893	T38.894	T38.895	T38.896
Somatostatin	T38.991	T38.992	T38.993	T38.994	T38.995	T38.996
Somatotropin	T38.811	T38.812	T38.813	T38.814	T38.815	T38.816
Somatrem	T38.811	T38.812	T38.813	T38.814	T38.815	T38.816
Somatropin	T38.811	T38.812	T38.813	T38.814	T38.815	T38.816
Sominex	T45.0X1	T45.0X2	T45.0X3	T45.0X4	T45.0X5	T45.0X6
Somnos	T42.6X1	T42.6X2	T42.6X3	T42.6X4	T42.6X5	T42.6X6
Somonal	T42.3X1	T42.3X2	T42.3X3	T42.3X4	T42.3X5	T42.3X6
Soneryl	T42.3X1	T42.3X2	T42.3X3	T42.3X4	T42.3X5	T42.3X6
Soothing syrup	T50.901	T50.902	T50.903	T50.904	T50.905	T50.906
Sopor	T42.6X1	T42.6X2	T42.6X3	T42.6X4	T42.6X5	T42.6X6
Soporific	T42.71	T42.72	T42.73	T42.74	T42.75	T42.76
Soporific drug	T42.71	T42.72	T42.73	T42.74	T42.75	T42.76
specified type NEC	T42.6X1	T42.6X2	T42.6X3	T42.6X4	T42.6X5	T42.6X6
Sorbide nitrate	T46.3X1	T46.3X2	T46.3X3	T46.3X4	T46.3X5	T46.3X6
Sorbitol	T47.4X1	T47.4X2	T47.4X3	T47.4X4	T47.4X5	T47.4X6
Sotalol	T44.7X1	T44.7X2	T44.7X3	T44.7X4	T44.7X5	T44.7X6
Sotradecol	T46.8X1	T46.8X2	T46.8X3	T46.8X4	T46.8X5	T46.8X6
Soysterol	T46.6X1	T46.6X2	T46.6X3	T46.6X4	T46.6X5	T46.6X6
Spacoline	T44.3X1	T44.3X2	T44.3X3	T44.3X4	T44.3X5	T44.3X6
Spanish fly	T49.8X1	T49.8X2	T49.8X3	T49.8X4	T49.8X5	T49.8X6
Sparine	T43.3X1	T43.3X2	T43.3X3	T43.3X4	T43.3X5	T43.3X6
Sparteine	T48.0X1	T48.0X2	T48.0X3	T48.0X4	T48.0X5	T48.0X6

◀ New   ◀ Revised   ~~deleted~~ Deleted

TABLE OF DRUGS AND CHEMICALS

Substance	External Cause (T-Code)					
	Poisoning, Accidental (Unintentional)	Poisoning, Intentional Self-Harm	Poisoning, Assault	Poisoning, Undetermined	Adverse Effect	Underdosing
Spasmolytic						
anticholinergics	T44.3X1	T44.3X2	T44.3X3	T44.3X4	T44.3X5	T44.3X6
autonomic	T44.3X1	T44.3X2	T44.3X3	T44.3X4	T44.3X5	T44.3X6
bronchial NEC	T48.6X1	T48.6X2	T48.6X3	T48.6X4	T48.6X5	T48.6X6
quaternary ammonium	T44.3X1	T44.3X2	T44.3X3	T44.3X4	T44.3X5	T44.3X6
skeletal muscle NEC	T48.1X1	T48.1X2	T48.1X3	T48.1X4	T48.1X5	T48.1X6
Spectinomycin	T36.5X1	T36.5X2	T36.5X3	T36.5X4	T36.5X5	T36.5X6
Speed	T43.621	T43.622	T43.623	T43.624	T43.625	T43.626
Spermicide	T49.8X1	T49.8X2	T49.8X3	T49.8X4	T49.8X5	T49.8X6
Spider (bite) (venom)	T63.391	T63.392	T63.393	T63.394	—	—
antivenin	T50.Z11	T50.Z12	T50.Z13	T50.Z14	T50.Z15	T50.Z16
Spigelia (root)	T37.4X1	T37.4X2	T37.4X3	T37.4X4	T37.4X5	T37.4X6
Spindle inactivator	T50.4X1	T50.4X2	T50.4X3	T50.4X4	T50.4X5	T50.4X6
Spiperone	T43.4X1	T43.4X2	T43.4X3	T43.4X4	T43.4X5	T43.4X6
Spiramycin	T36.3X1	T36.3X2	T36.3X3	T36.3X4	T36.3X5	T36.3X6
Spirapril	T46.4X1	T46.4X2	T46.4X3	T46.4X4	T46.4X5	T46.4X6
Spirilene	T43.591	T43.592	T43.593	T43.594	T43.595	T43.596
Spirit(s) (neutral) NEC	T51.0X1	T51.0X2	T51.0X3	T51.0X4	—	—
beverage	T51.0X1	T51.0X2	T51.0X3	T51.0X4	—	—
industrial	T51.0X1	T51.0X2	T51.0X3	T51.0X4	—	—
mineral	T52.0X1	T52.0X2	T52.0X3	T52.0X4	—	—
of salt — see Hydrochloric acid						
surgical	T51.0X1	T51.0X2	T51.0X3	T51.0X4	—	—
Spironolactone	T50.0X1	T50.0X2	T50.0X3	T50.0X4	T50.0X5	T50.0X6
Spiroperidol	T43.4X1	T43.4X2	T43.4X3	T43.4X4	T43.4X5	T43.4X6
Sponge, absorbable (gelatin)	T45.7X1	T45.7X2	T45.7X3	T45.7X4	T45.7X5	T45.7X6
Sporostacin	T49.0X1	T49.0X2	T49.0X3	T49.0X4	T49.0X5	T49.0X6
Spray (aerosol)	T65.91	T65.92	T65.93	T65.94	—	—
cosmetic	T65.891	T65.892	T65.893	T65.894	—	—
medicinal NEC	T50.901	T50.902	T50.903	T50.904	T50.905	T50.906
pesticides — see Pesticides						
specified content — see specific substance						
Spurge flax	T62.2X1	T62.2X2	T62.2X3	T62.2X4	—	—
Spurges	T62.2X1	T62.2X2	T62.2X3	T62.2X4	—	—
Sputum viscosity-lowering drug	T48.4X1	T48.4X2	T48.4X3	T48.4X4	T48.4X5	T48.4X6
Squill	T46.0X1	T46.0X2	T46.0X3	T46.0X4	T46.0X5	T46.0X6
rat poison	T60.4X1	T60.4X2	T60.4X3	T60.4X4	—	—
Squirting cucumber (cathartic)	T47.2X1	T47.2X2	T47.2X3	T47.2X4	T47.2X5	T47.2X6
Stains	T65.6X1	T65.6X2	T65.6X3	T65.6X4	—	—
Stannous fluoride	T49.7X1	T49.7X2	T49.7X3	T49.7X4	T49.7X5	T49.7X6
Stanolone	T38.7X1	T38.7X2	T38.7X3	T38.7X4	T38.7X5	T38.7X6

Substance	External Cause (T-Code)					
	Poisoning, Accidental (Unintentional)	Poisoning, Intentional Self-Harm	Poisoning, Assault	Poisoning, Undetermined	Adverse Effect	Underdosing
Stanozolol	T38.7X1	T38.7X2	T38.7X3	T38.7X4	T38.7X5	T38.7X6
Staphisagria or stavesacre (pediculicide)	T49.0X1	T49.0X2	T49.0X3	T49.0X4	T49.0X5	T49.0X6
Starch	T50.901	T50.902	T50.903	T50.904	T50.905	T50.906
Stelazine	T43.3X1	T43.3X2	T43.3X3	T43.3X4	T43.3X5	T43.3X6
Stemetil	T43.3X1	T43.3X2	T43.3X3	T43.3X4	T43.3X5	T43.3X6
Stepronin	T48.4X1	T48.4X2	T48.4X3	T48.4X4	T48.4X5	T48.4X6
Sterculia	T47.4X1	T47.4X2	T47.4X3	T47.4X4	T47.4X5	T47.4X6
Sternutator gas	T59.891	T59.892	T59.893	T59.894	—	—
Steroid	T38.0X1	T38.0X2	T38.0X3	T38.0X4	T38.0X5	T38.0X6
anabolic	T38.7X1	T38.7X2	T38.7X3	T38.7X4	T38.7X5	T38.7X6
androgenic	T38.7X1	T38.7X2	T38.7X3	T38.7X4	T38.7X5	T38.7X6
antineoplastic, hormone	T38.7X1	T38.7X2	T38.7X3	T38.7X4	T38.7X5	T38.7X6
estrogen	T38.5X1	T38.5X2	T38.5X3	T38.5X4	T38.5X5	T38.5X6
ENT agent	T49.6X1	T49.6X2	T49.6X3	T49.6X4	T49.6X5	T49.6X6
ophthalmic preparation	T49.5X1	T49.5X2	T49.5X3	T49.5X4	T49.5X5	T49.5X6
topical NEC	T49.0X1	T49.0X2	T49.0X3	T49.0X4	T49.0X5	T49.0X6
Stibine	T56.891	T56.892	T56.893	T56.894	—	—
Stibogluconate	T37.3X1	T37.3X2	T37.3X3	T37.3X4	T37.3X5	T37.3X6
Stibophen	T37.4X1	T37.4X2	T37.4X3	T37.4X4	T37.4X5	T37.4X6
Stilbamidine (isetionate)	T37.3X1	T37.3X2	T37.3X3	T37.3X4	T37.3X5	T37.3X6
Stilbestrol	T38.5X1	T38.5X2	T38.5X3	T38.5X4	T38.5X5	T38.5X6
Stilboestrol	T38.5X1	T38.5X2	T38.5X3	T38.5X4	T38.5X5	T38.5X6
Stimulant						
central nervous system — see also Psychostimulant	T43.601	T43.602	T43.603	T43.604	T43.605	T43.606
analeptics	T50.7X1	T50.7X2	T50.7X3	T50.7X4	T50.7X5	T50.7X6
opiate antagonist	T50.7X1	T50.7X2	T50.7X3	T50.7X4	T50.7X5	T50.7X6
psychotherapeutic NEC — see also Psychotherapeutic drug	T43.601	T43.602	T43.603	T43.604	T43.605	T43.606
specified NEC	T43.691	T43.692	T43.693	T43.694	T43.695	T43.696
respiratory	T48.901	T48.902	T48.903	T48.904	T48.905	T48.906
Stone-dissolving drug	T50.901	T50.902	T50.903	T50.904	T50.905	T50.906
Storage battery (cells) (acid)	T54.2X1	T54.2X2	T54.2X3	T54.2X4	—	—
Stovaine	T41.3X1	T41.3X2	T41.3X3	T41.3X4	T41.3X5	T41.3X6
infiltration (subcutaneous)	T41.3X1	T41.3X2	T41.3X3	T41.3X4	T41.3X5	T41.3X6
nerve block (peripheral) (plexus)	T41.3X1	T41.3X2	T41.3X3	T41.3X4	T41.3X5	T41.3X6
spinal	T41.3X1	T41.3X2	T41.3X3	T41.3X4	T41.3X5	T41.3X6
topical (surface)	T41.3X1	T41.3X2	T41.3X3	T41.3X4	T41.3X5	T41.3X6
Stovarsal	T37.8X1	T37.8X2	T37.8X3	T37.8X4	T37.8X5	T37.8X6
Stove gas — see Gas, stove	T57.91	T57.92	T57.93	T57.94		

◀ New ◀ Revised ~~deleted~~ Deleted

Substance	Poisoning, Accidental (Unintentional)	Poisoning, Intentional Self-Harm	Poisoning, Assault	Poisoning, Undetermined	Adverse Effect	Underdosing
Stoxil	T49.5X1	T49.5X2	T49.5X3	T49.5X4	T49.5X5	T49.5X6
Stramonium	T48.6X1	T48.6X2	T48.6X3	T48.6X4	T48.6X5	T48.6X6
natural state	T62.2X1	T62.2X2	T62.2X3	T62.2X4	—	—
Streptodornase	T45.3X1	T45.3X2	T45.3X3	T45.3X4	T45.3X5	T45.3X6
Streptoduocin	T36.5X1	T36.5X2	T36.5X3	T36.5X4	T36.5X5	T36.5X6
Streptokinase	T45.611	T45.612	T45.613	T45.614	T45.615	T45.616
Streptomycin (derivative)	T36.5X1	T36.5X2	T36.5X3	T36.5X4	T36.5X5	T36.5X6
Streptonivicin	T36.5X1	T36.5X2	T36.5X3	T36.5X4	T36.5X5	T36.5X6
Streptovarycin	T36.5X1	T36.5X2	T36.5X3	T36.5X4	T36.5X5	T36.5X6
Streptozocin	T45.1X1	T45.1X2	T45.1X3	T45.1X4	T45.1X5	T45.1X6
Streptozotocin	T45.1X1	T45.1X2	T45.1X3	T45.1X4	T45.1X5	T45.1X6
Stripper (paint) (solvent)	T52.8X1	T52.8X2	T52.8X3	T52.8X4	—	—
Strobane	T60.1X1	T60.1X2	T60.1X3	T60.1X4	—	—
Strofantina	T46.0X1	T46.0X2	T46.0X3	T46.0X4	T46.0X5	T46.0X6
Strophanthin (g) (k)	T46.0X1	T46.0X2	T46.0X3	T46.0X4	T46.0X5	T46.0X6
Strophanthus	T46.0X1	T46.0X2	T46.0X3	T46.0X4	T46.0X5	T46.0X6
Strophantin	T46.0X1	T46.0X2	T46.0X3	T46.0X4	T46.0X5	T46.0X6
Strophantin-g	T46.0X1	T46.0X2	T46.0X3	T46.0X4	T46.0X5	T46.0X6
Strychnine (nonmedicinal) (pesticide) (salts)	T65.1X1	T65.1X2	T65.1X3	T65.1X4	—	—
medicinal	T48.291	T48.292	T48.293	T48.294	T48.295	T48.296
Strychnos (ignatii) — see Strychnine						
Styramate	T42.8X1	T42.8X2	T42.8X3	T42.8X4	T42.8X5	T42.8X6
Styrene	T65.891	T65.892	T65.893	T65.894	—	—
Succinimide, antiepileptic or anticonvulsant	T42.2X1	T42.2X2	T42.2X3	T42.2X4	T42.2X5	T42.2X6
mercuric — see Mercury						
Succinylcholine	T48.1X1	T48.1X2	T48.1X3	T48.1X4	T48.1X5	T48.1X6
Succinylsulfathiazole	T37.0X1	T37.0X2	T37.0X3	T37.0X4	T37.0X5	T37.0X6
Sucralfate	T47.1X1	T47.1X2	T47.1X3	T47.1X4	T47.1X5	T47.1X6
Sucrose	T50.3X1	T50.3X2	T50.3X3	T50.3X4	T50.3X5	T50.3X6
Sufentanil	T40.4X1	T40.4X2	T40.4X3	T40.4X4	T40.4X5	T40.4X6
Sulbactam	T36.0X1	T36.0X2	T36.0X3	T36.0X4	T36.0X5	T36.0X6
Sulbenicillin	T36.0X1	T36.0X2	T36.0X3	T36.0X4	T36.0X5	T36.0X6
Sulbentine	T49.0X1	T49.0X2	T49.0X3	T49.0X4	T49.0X5	T49.0X6
Sulfacetamide	T49.0X1	T49.0X2	T49.0X3	T49.0X4	T49.0X5	T49.0X6
ophthalmic preparation	T49.5X1	T49.5X2	T49.5X3	T49.5X4	T49.5X5	T49.5X6
Sulfachlorpyridazine	T37.0X1	T37.0X2	T37.0X3	T37.0X4	T37.0X5	T37.0X6
Sulfacitine	T37.0X1	T37.0X2	T37.0X3	T37.0X4	T37.0X5	T37.0X6
Sulfadiasulfone sodium	T37.0X1	T37.0X2	T37.0X3	T37.0X4	T37.0X5	T37.0X6
Sulfadiazine	T37.0X1	T37.0X2	T37.0X3	T37.0X4	T37.0X5	T37.0X6
silver (topical)	T49.0X1	T49.0X2	T49.0X3	T49.0X4	T49.0X5	T49.0X6

Substance	Poisoning, Accidental (Unintentional)	Poisoning, Intentional Self-Harm	Poisoning, Assault	Poisoning, Undetermined	Adverse Effect	Underdosing
Sulfadimethoxine	T37.0X1	T37.0X2	T37.0X3	T37.0X4	T37.0X5	T37.0X6
Sulfadimidine	T37.0X1	T37.0X2	T37.0X3	T37.0X4	T37.0X5	T37.0X6
Sulfadoxine	T37.0X1	T37.0X2	T37.0X3	T37.0X4	T37.0X5	T37.0X6
with pyrimethamine	T37.2X1	T37.2X2	T37.2X3	T37.2X4	T37.2X5	T37.2X6
Sulfaethidole	T37.0X1	T37.0X2	T37.0X3	T37.0X4	T37.0X5	T37.0X6
Sulfafurazole	T37.0X1	T37.0X2	T37.0X3	T37.0X4	T37.0X5	T37.0X6
Sulfaguanidine	T37.0X1	T37.0X2	T37.0X3	T37.0X4	T37.0X5	T37.0X6
Sulfalene	T37.0X1	T37.0X2	T37.0X3	T37.0X4	T37.0X5	T37.0X6
Sulfaloxate	T37.0X1	T37.0X2	T37.0X3	T37.0X4	T37.0X5	T37.0X6
Sulfaloxic acid	T37.0X1	T37.0X2	T37.0X3	T37.0X4	T37.0X5	T37.0X6
Sulfamazone	T39.2X1	T39.2X2	T39.2X3	T39.2X4	T39.2X5	T39.2X6
Sulfamerazine	T37.0X1	T37.0X2	T37.0X3	T37.0X4	T37.0X5	T37.0X6
Sulfameter	T37.0X1	T37.0X2	T37.0X3	T37.0X4	T37.0X5	T37.0X6
Sulfamethazine	T37.0X1	T37.0X2	T37.0X3	T37.0X4	T37.0X5	T37.0X6
Sulfamethizole	T37.0X1	T37.0X2	T37.0X3	T37.0X4	T37.0X5	T37.0X6
Sulfamethoxazole	T37.0X1	T37.0X2	T37.0X3	T37.0X4	T37.0X5	T37.0X6
with trimethoprim	T36.8X1	T36.8X2	T36.8X3	T36.8X4	T36.8X5	T36.8X6
Sulfamethoxydiazine	T37.0X1	T37.0X2	T37.0X3	T37.0X4	T37.0X5	T37.0X6
Sulfamethoxypyridazine	T37.0X1	T37.0X2	T37.0X3	T37.0X4	T37.0X5	T37.0X6
Sulfamethylthiazole	T37.0X1	T37.0X2	T37.0X3	T37.0X4	T37.0X5	T37.0X6
Sulfametoxydiazine	T37.0X1	T37.0X2	T37.0X3	T37.0X4	T37.0X5	T37.0X6
Sulfamidopyrine	T39.2X1	T39.2X2	T39.2X3	T39.2X4	T39.2X5	T39.2X6
Sulfamonomethoxine	T37.0X1	T37.0X2	T37.0X3	T37.0X4	T37.0X5	T37.0X6
Sulfamoxole	T37.0X1	T37.0X2	T37.0X3	T37.0X4	T37.0X5	T37.0X6
Sulfamylon	T49.0X1	T49.0X2	T49.0X3	T49.0X4	T49.0X5	T49.0X6
Sulfan blue (diagnostic dye)	T50.8X1	T50.8X2	T50.8X3	T50.8X4	T50.8X5	T50.8X6
Sulfanilamide	T37.0X1	T37.0X2	T37.0X3	T37.0X4	T37.0X5	T37.0X6
Sulfanilylguanidine	T37.0X1	T37.0X2	T37.0X3	T37.0X4	T37.0X5	T37.0X6
Sulfaperin	T37.0X1	T37.0X2	T37.0X3	T37.0X4	T37.0X5	T37.0X6
Sulfaphenazole	T37.0X1	T37.0X2	T37.0X3	T37.0X4	T37.0X5	T37.0X6
Sulfaphenylthiazole	T37.0X1	T37.0X2	T37.0X3	T37.0X4	T37.0X5	T37.0X6
Sulfaproxyline	T37.0X1	T37.0X2	T37.0X3	T37.0X4	T37.0X5	T37.0X6
Sulfapyridine	T37.0X1	T37.0X2	T37.0X3	T37.0X4	T37.0X5	T37.0X6
Sulfapyrimidine	T37.0X1	T37.0X2	T37.0X3	T37.0X4	T37.0X5	T37.0X6
Sulfarsphenamine	T37.8X1	T37.8X2	T37.8X3	T37.8X4	T37.8X5	T37.8X6
Sulfasalazine	T37.0X1	T37.0X2	T37.0X3	T37.0X4	T37.0X5	T37.0X6
Sulfasuxidine	T37.0X1	T37.0X2	T37.0X3	T37.0X4	T37.0X5	T37.0X6
Sulfasymazine	T37.0X1	T37.0X2	T37.0X3	T37.0X4	T37.0X5	T37.0X6
Sulfated amylopectin	T47.8X1	T47.8X2	T47.8X3	T47.8X4	T47.8X5	T47.8X6
Sulfathiazole	T37.0X1	T37.0X2	T37.0X3	T37.0X4	T37.0X5	T37.0X6
Sulfatostearate	T49.2X1	T49.2X2	T49.2X3	T49.2X4	T49.2X5	T49.2X6
Sulfinpyrazone	T50.4X1	T50.4X2	T50.4X3	T50.4X4	T50.4X5	T50.4X6

◀ New ◀ Revised ~~deleted~~ Deleted

TABLE OF DRUGS AND CHEMICALS

Substance	Poisoning, Accidental (Unintentional)	Poisoning, Intentional Self-Harm	Poisoning, Assault	Poisoning, Undetermined	Adverse Effect	Underdosing
Sulfiram	T49.0X1	T49.0X2	T49.0X3	T49.0X4	T49.0X5	T49.0X6
Sulfisomidine	T37.0X1	T37.0X2	T37.0X3	T37.0X4	T37.0X5	T37.0X6
Sulfisoxazole	T37.0X1	T37.0X2	T37.0X3	T37.0X4	T37.0X5	T37.0X6
ophthalmic preparation	T49.5X1	T49.5X2	T49.5X3	T49.5X4	T49.5X5	T49.5X6
Sulfobromophthalein (sodium)	T50.8X1	T50.8X2	T50.8X3	T50.8X4	T50.8X5	T50.8X6
Sulfobromphthalein	T50.8X1	T50.8X2	T50.8X3	T50.8X4	T50.8X5	T50.8X6
Sulfogaiacol	T48.4X1	T48.4X2	T48.4X3	T48.4X4	T48.4X5	T48.4X6
Sulfomyxin	T36.8X1	T36.8X2	T36.8X3	T36.8X4	T36.8X5	T36.8X6
Sulfonal	T42.6X1	T42.6X2	T42.6X3	T42.6X4	T42.6X5	T42.6X6
Sulfonamide NEC	T37.0X1	T37.0X2	T37.0X3	T37.0X4	T37.0X5	T37.0X6
eye	T49.5X1	T49.5X2	T49.5X3	T49.5X4	T49.5X5	T49.5X6
Sulfonazide	T37.1X1	T37.1X2	T37.1X3	T37.1X4	T37.1X5	T37.1X6
Sulfones	T37.1X1	T37.1X2	T37.1X3	T37.1X4	T37.1X5	T37.1X6
Sulfonethylmethane	T42.6X1	T42.6X2	T42.6X3	T42.6X4	T42.6X5	T42.6X6
Sulfonmethane	T42.6X1	T42.6X2	T42.6X3	T42.6X4	T42.6X5	T42.6X6
Sulfonphthal, sulfonphthol	T50.8X1	T50.8X2	T50.8X3	T50.8X4	T50.8X5	T50.8X6
Sulfonylurea derivatives, oral	T38.3X1	T38.3X2	T38.3X3	T38.3X4	T38.3X5	T38.3X6
Sulforidazine	T43.3X1	T43.3X2	T43.3X3	T43.3X4	T43.3X5	T43.3X6
Sulfoxone	T37.1X1	T37.1X2	T37.1X3	T37.1X4	T37.1X5	T37.1X6
Sulfur, sulfurated, sulfuric, sulfurous, sulfuryl (compounds NEC) (medicinal)	T49.4X1	T49.4X2	T49.4X3	T49.4X4	T49.4X5	T49.4X6
acid	T54.2X1	T54.2X2	T54.2X3	T54.2X4	—	—
dioxide (gas)	T59.1X1	T59.1X2	T59.1X3	T59.1X4	—	—
ether — see Ether(s)						
hydrogen	T59.6X1	T59.6X2	T59.6X3	T59.6X4	—	—
medicinal (keratolytic) (ointment) NEC	T49.4X1	T49.4X2	T49.4X3	T49.4X4	T49.4X5	T49.4X6
ointment	T49.0X1	T49.0X2	T49.0X3	T49.0X4	T49.0X5	T49.0X6
pesticide (vapor)	T60.91	T60.92	T60.93	T60.94		
vapor NEC	T59.891	T59.892	T59.893	T59.894	—	—
Sulfuric acid	T54.2X1	T54.2X2	T54.2X3	T54.2X4	—	—
Sulglicotide	T47.1X1	T47.1X2	T47.1X3	T47.1X4	T47.1X5	T47.1X6
Sulindac	T39.391	T39.392	T39.393	T39.394	T39.395	T39.396
Sulisatin	T47.2X1	T47.2X2	T47.2X3	T47.2X4	T47.2X5	T47.2X6
Sulisobenzone	T49.3X1	T49.3X2	T49.3X3	T49.3X4	T49.3X5	T49.3X6
Sulkowitch's reagent	T50.8X1	T50.8X2	T50.8X3	T50.8X4	T50.8X5	T50.8X6
Sulmetozine	T44.3X1	T44.3X2	T44.3X3	T44.3X4	T44.3X5	T44.3X6
Suloctidil	T46.7X1	T46.7X2	T46.7X3	T46.7X4	T46.7X5	T46.7X6
Sulph — see also Sulf-						
Sulphadiazine	T37.0X1	T37.0X2	T37.0X3	T37.0X4	T37.0X5	T37.0X6
Sulphadimethoxine	T37.0X1	T37.0X2	T37.0X3	T37.0X4	T37.0X5	T37.0X6
Sulphadimidine	T37.0X1	T37.0X2	T37.0X3	T37.0X4	T37.0X5	T37.0X6
Sulphadione	T37.1X1	T37.1X2	T37.1X3	T37.1X4	T37.1X5	T37.1X6
Sulphafurazole	T37.0X1	T37.0X2	T37.0X3	T37.0X4	T37.0X5	T37.0X6
Sulphamethizole	T37.0X1	T37.0X2	T37.0X3	T37.0X4	T37.0X5	T37.0X6
Sulphamethoxazole	T37.0X1	T37.0X2	T37.0X3	T37.0X4	T37.0X5	T37.0X6
Sulphan blue	T50.8X1	T50.8X2	T50.8X3	T50.8X4	T50.8X5	T50.8X6
Sulphaphenazole	T37.0X1	T37.0X2	T37.0X3	T37.0X4	T37.0X5	T37.0X6
Sulphapyridine	T37.0X1	T37.0X2	T37.0X3	T37.0X4	T37.0X5	T37.0X6
Sulphasalazine	T37.0X1	T37.0X2	T37.0X3	T37.0X4	T37.0X5	T37.0X6
Sulphinpyrazone	T50.4X1	T50.4X2	T50.4X3	T50.4X4	T50.4X5	T50.4X6
Sulpiride	T43.591	T43.592	T43.593	T43.594	T43.595	T43.596
Sulprostone	T48.0X1	T48.0X2	T48.0X3	T48.0X4	T48.0X5	T48.0X6
Sulpyrine	T39.2X1	T39.2X2	T39.2X3	T39.2X4	T39.2X5	T39.2X6
Sultamicillin	T36.0X1	T36.0X2	T36.0X3	T36.0X4	T36.0X5	T36.0X6
Sulthiame	T42.6X1	T42.6X2	T42.6X3	T42.6X4	T42.6X5	T42.6X6
Sultiame	T42.6X1	T42.6X2	T42.6X3	T42.6X4	T42.6X5	T42.6X6
Sultopride	T43.591	T43.592	T43.593	T43.594	T43.595	T43.596
Sumatriptan	T39.8X1	T39.8X2	T39.8X3	T39.8X4	T39.8X5	T39.8X6
Sunflower seed oil	T46.6X1	T46.6X2	T46.6X3	T46.6X4	T46.6X5	T46.6X6
Superinone	T48.4X1	T48.4X2	T48.4X3	T48.4X4	T48.4X5	T48.4X6
Suprofen	T39.311	T39.312	T39.313	T39.314	T39.315	T39.316
Suramin (sodium)	T37.4X1	T37.4X2	T37.4X3	T37.4X4	T37.4X5	T37.4X6
Surfacaine	T41.3X1	T41.3X2	T41.3X3	T41.3X4	T41.3X5	T41.3X6
Surital	T41.1X1	T41.1X2	T41.1X3	T41.1X4	T41.1X5	T41.1X6
Sutilains	T45.3X1	T45.3X2	T45.3X3	T45.3X4	T45.3X5	T45.3X6
Suxamethonium (chloride)	T48.1X1	T48.1X2	T48.1X3	T48.1X4	T48.1X5	T48.1X6
Suxethonium (chloride)	T48.1X1	T48.1X2	T48.1X3	T48.1X4	T48.1X5	T48.1X6
Suxibuzone	T39.2X1	T39.2X2	T39.2X3	T39.2X4	T39.2X5	T39.2X6
Sweet oil (birch)	T49.3X1	T49.3X2	T49.3X3	T49.3X4	T49.3X5	T49.3X6
Sweet niter spirit	T46.3X1	T46.3X2	T46.3X3	T46.3X4	T46.3X5	T46.3X6
Sweetener	T50.901	T50.902	T50.903	T50.904	T50.905	T50.906
Sym-dichloroethyl ether	T53.6X1	T53.6X2	T53.6X3	T53.6X4	—	—
Sympatholytic NEC	T44.8X1	T44.8X2	T44.8X3	T44.8X4	T44.8X5	T44.8X6
haloalkylamine	T44.8X1	T44.8X2	T44.8X3	T44.8X4	T44.8X5	T44.8X6
Sympathomimetic NEC	T44.901	T44.902	T44.903	T44.904	T44.905	T44.906
anti-common-cold	T48.5X1	T48.5X2	T48.5X3	T48.5X4	T48.5X5	T48.5X6
bronchodilator	T48.6X1	T48.6X2	T48.6X3	T48.6X4	T48.6X5	T48.6X6
specified NEC	T44.991	T44.992	T44.993	T44.994	T44.995	T44.996
Synagis	T50.B91	T50.B92	T50.B93	T50.B94	T50.B95	T50.B96
Synalar	T49.0X1	T49.0X2	T49.0X3	T49.0X4	T49.0X5	T49.0X6
Synthroid	T38.1X1	T38.1X2	T38.1X3	T38.1X4	T38.1X5	T38.1X6

◀ New   ◀ Revised   ~~deleted~~ Deleted

Substance	Poisoning, Accidental (Unintentional)	Poisoning, Intentional Self-Harm	Poisoning, Assault	Poisoning, Undetermined	Adverse Effect	Underdosing
Syntocinon	T48.0X1	T48.0X2	T48.0X3	T48.0X4	T48.0X5	T48.0X6
Syrosingopine	T46.5X1	T46.5X2	T46.5X3	T46.5X4	T46.5X5	T46.5X6
Systemic drug	T45.91	T45.92	T45.93	T45.94	T45.95	T45.96
specified NEC	T45.8X1	T45.8X2	T45.8X3	T45.8X4	T45.8X5	T45.8X6
2,4,5-T	T60.3X1	T60.3X2	T60.3X3	T60.3X4	—	—

T

Substance	Poisoning, Accidental (Unintentional)	Poisoning, Intentional Self-Harm	Poisoning, Assault	Poisoning, Undetermined	Adverse Effect	Underdosing
Tablets — *see also specified substance*	T50.901	T50.902	T50.903	T50.904	T50.905	T50.906
Tace	T38.5X1	T38.5X2	T38.5X3	T38.5X4	T38.5X5	T38.5X6
Tacrine	T44.0X1	T44.0X2	T44.0X3	T44.0X4	T44.0X5	T44.0X6
Tadalafil	T46.7X1	T46.7X2	T46.7X3	T46.7X4	T46.7X5	T46.7X6
Talampicillin	T36.0X1	T36.0X2	T36.0X3	T36.0X4	T36.0X5	T36.0X6
Talbutal	T42.3X1	T42.3X2	T42.3X3	T42.3X4	T42.3X5	T42.3X6
Talc powder	T49.3X1	T49.3X2	T49.3X3	T49.3X4	T49.3X5	T49.3X6
Talcum	T49.3X1	T49.3X2	T49.3X3	T49.3X4	T49.3X5	T49.3X6
Taleranol	T38.6X1	T38.6X2	T38.6X3	T38.6X4	T38.6X5	T38.6X6
Tamoxifen	T38.6X1	T38.6X2	T38.6X3	T38.6X4	T38.6X5	T38.6X6
Tamsulosin	T44.6X1	T44.6X2	T44.6X3	T44.6X4	T44.6X5	T44.6X6
Tandearil, tanderil	T39.2X1	T39.2X2	T39.2X3	T39.2X4	T39.2X5	T39.2X6
Tannic acid	T49.2X1	T49.2X2	T49.2X3	T49.2X4	T49.2X5	T49.2X6
medicinal (astringent)	T49.2X1	T49.2X2	T49.2X3	T49.2X4	T49.2X5	T49.2X6
Tannin — *see Tannic acid*						
Tansy	T62.2X1	T62.2X2	T62.2X3	T62.2X4	—	—
TAO	T36.3X1	T36.3X2	T36.3X3	T36.3X4	T36.3X5	T36.3X6
Tapazole	T38.2X1	T38.2X2	T38.2X3	T38.2X4	T38.2X5	T38.2X6
Tar NEC	T52.0X1	T52.0X2	T52.0X3	T52.0X4	—	—
camphor	T60.1X1	T60.1X2	T60.1X3	T60.1X4	—	—
distillate	T49.1X1	T49.1X2	T49.1X3	T49.1X4	T49.1X5	T49.1X6
fumes	T59.891	T59.892	T59.893	T59.894		
medicinal	T49.1X1	T49.1X2	T49.1X3	T49.1X4	T49.1X5	T49.1X6
ointment	T49.1X1	T49.1X2	T49.1X3	T49.1X4	T49.1X5	T49.1X6
Taractan	T43.591	T43.592	T43.593	T43.594	T43.595	T43.596
Tarantula (venomous)	T63.321	T63.322	T63.323	T63.324	—	—
Tartar emetic	T37.8X1	T37.8X2	T37.8X3	T37.8X4	T37.8X5	T37.8X6
Tartaric acid	T65.891	T65.892	T65.893	T65.894		
Tartrated antimony (anti-infective)	T37.8X1	T37.8X2	T37.8X3	T37.8X4	T37.8X5	T37.8X6
Tartrate, laxative	T47.4X1	T47.4X2	T47.4X3	T47.4X4	T47.4X5	T47.4X6
Tauromustine	T45.1X1	T45.1X2	T45.1X3	T45.1X4	T45.1X5	T45.1X6
TCA — *see Trichloroacetic acid*						
TCDD	T53.7X1	T53.7X2	T53.7X3	T53.7X4	—	—
TDI (vapor)	T65.0X1	T65.0X2	T65.0X3	T65.0X4		

Substance	Poisoning, Accidental (Unintentional)	Poisoning, Intentional Self-Harm	Poisoning, Assault	Poisoning, Undetermined	Adverse Effect	Underdosing
Tear						
gas	T59.3X1	T59.3X2	T59.3X3	T59.3X4	—	—
solution	T49.5X1	T49.5X2	T49.5X3	T49.5X4	T49.5X5	T49.5X6
Teclothiazide	T50.2X1	T50.2X2	T50.2X3	T50.2X4	T50.2X5	T50.2X6
Teclozan	T37.3X1	T37.3X2	T37.3X3	T37.3X4	T37.3X5	T37.3X6
Tegafur	T45.1X1	T45.1X2	T45.1X3	T45.1X4	T45.1X5	T45.1X6
Tegretol	T42.1X1	T42.1X2	T42.1X3	T42.1X4	T42.1X5	T42.1X6
Teicoplanin	T36.8X1	T36.8X2	T36.8X3	T36.8X4	T36.8X5	T36.8X6
Telepaque	T50.8X1	T50.8X2	T50.8X3	T50.8X4	T50.8X5	T50.8X6
Tellurium	T56.891	T56.892	T56.893	T56.894		
fumes	T56.891	T56.892	T56.893	T56.894	—	—
TEM	T45.1X1	T45.1X2	T45.1X3	T45.1X4	T45.1X5	T45.1X6
Temazepam	T42.4X1	T42.4X2	T42.4X3	T42.4X4	T42.4X5	T42.4X6
Temocillin	T36.0X1	T36.0X2	T36.0X3	T36.0X4	T36.0X5	T36.0X6
Tenamfetamine	T43.621	T43.622	T43.623	T43.624	T43.625	T43.626
Teniposide	T45.1X1	T45.1X2	T45.1X3	T45.1X4	T45.1X5	T45.1X6
Tenitramine	T46.3X1	T46.3X2	T46.3X3	T46.3X4	T46.3X5	T46.3X6
Tenoglicin	T48.4X1	T48.4X2	T48.4X3	T48.4X4	T48.4X5	T48.4X6
Tenonitrozole	T37.3X1	T37.3X2	T37.3X3	T37.3X4	T37.3X5	T37.3X6
Tenoxicam	T39.391	T39.392	T39.393	T39.394	T39.395	T39.396
TEPA	T45.1X1	T45.1X2	T45.1X3	T45.1X4	T45.1X5	T45.1X6
TEPP	T60.0X1	T60.0X2	T60.0X3	T60.0X4	—	—
Teprotide	T46.5X1	T46.5X2	T46.5X3	T46.5X4	T46.5X5	T46.5X6
Terazosin	T44.6X1	T44.6X2	T44.6X3	T44.6X4	T44.6X5	T44.6X6
Terbufos	T60.0X1	T60.0X2	T60.0X3	T60.0X4	—	—
Terbutaline	T48.6X1	T48.6X2	T48.6X3	T48.6X4	T48.6X5	T48.6X6
Terconazole	T49.0X1	T49.0X2	T49.0X3	T49.0X4	T49.0X5	T49.0X6
Terfenadine	T45.0X1	T45.0X2	T45.0X3	T45.0X4	T45.0X5	T45.0X6
Teriparatide (acetate)	T50.991	T50.992	T50.993	T50.994	T50.995	T50.996
Terizidone	T37.1X1	T37.1X2	T37.1X3	T37.1X4	T37.1X5	T37.1X6
Terlipressin	T38.891	T38.892	T38.893	T38.894	T38.895	T38.896
Terodiline	T46.3X1	T46.3X2	T46.3X3	T46.3X4	T46.3X5	T46.3X6
Teroxalene	T37.4X1	T37.4X2	T37.4X3	T37.4X4	T37.4X5	T37.4X6
Terpin(cis) hydrate	T48.4X1	T48.4X2	T48.4X3	T48.4X4	T48.4X5	T48.4X6
Terramycin	T36.4X1	T36.4X2	T36.4X3	T36.4X4	T36.4X5	T36.4X6
Tertatolol	T44.7X1	T44.7X2	T44.7X3	T44.7X4	T44.7X5	T44.7X6
Tessalon	T48.3X1	T48.3X2	T48.3X3	T48.3X4	T48.3X5	T48.3X6
Testolactone	T38.7X1	T38.7X2	T38.7X3	T38.7X4	T38.7X5	T38.7X6
Testosterone	T38.7X1	T38.7X2	T38.7X3	T38.7X4	T38.7X5	T38.7X6
Tetanus toxoid or vaccine	T50.A91	T50.A92	T50.A93	T50.A94	T50.A95	T50.A96
antitoxin	T50.Z11	T50.Z12	T50.Z13	T50.Z14	T50.Z15	T50.Z16
immune globulin (human)	T50.Z11	T50.Z12	T50.Z13	T50.Z14	T50.Z15	T50.Z16

◀ New   ◀ Revised   ~~deleted~~ Deleted

TABLE OF DRUGS AND CHEMICALS

TABLE OF DRUGS AND CHEMICALS

Substance	External Cause (T-Code)					
	Poisoning, Accidental (Unintentional)	Poisoning, Intentional Self-Harm	Poisoning, Assault	Poisoning, Undetermined	Adverse Effect	Underdosing
Tetanus toxoid or vaccine *(Continued)*						
toxoid	T50.A91	T50.A92	T50.A93	T50.A94	T50.A95	T50.A96
with diphtheria toxoid	T50.A21	T50.A22	T50.A23	T50.A24	T50.A25	T50.A26
with pertussis	T50.A11	T50.A12	T50.A13	T50.A14	T50.A15	T50.A16
Tetrabenazine	T43.591	T43.592	T43.593	T43.594	T43.595	T43.596
Tetracaine	T41.3X1	T41.3X2	T41.3X3	T41.3X4	T41.3X5	T41.3X6
nerve block (peripheral) (plexus)	T41.3X1	T41.3X2	T41.3X3	T41.3X4	T41.3X5	T41.3X6
regional	T41.3X1	T41.3X2	T41.3X3	T41.3X4	T41.3X5	T41.3X6
spinal	T41.3X1	T41.3X2	T41.3X3	T41.3X4	T41.3X5	T41.3X6
Tetrachlorethylene — *see Tetrachloroethylene*						
Tetrachlormethiazide	T50.2X1	T50.2X2	T50.2X3	T50.2X4	T50.2X5	T50.2X6
2,3,7,8-Tetrachlorodibenzo-p-dioxin	T53.7X1	T53.7X2	T53.7X3	T53.7X4	—	—
Tetrachloroethane	T53.6X1	T53.6X2	T53.6X3	T53.6X4	—	—
vapor	T53.6X1	T53.6X2	T53.6X3	T53.6X4	—	—
paint or varnish	T53.6X1	T53.6X2	T53.6X3	T53.6X4	—	—
Tetrachloroethylene (liquid)	T53.3X1	T53.3X2	T53.3X3	T53.3X4	—	—
medicinal	T37.4X1	T37.4X2	T37.4X3	T37.4X4	T37.4X5	T37.4X6
vapor	T53.3X1	T53.3X2	T53.3X3	T53.3X4	—	—
Tetrachloromethane — *see Carbon tetrachloride*						
Tetracosactide	T38.811	T38.812	T38.813	T38.814	T38.815	T38.816
Tetracosactrin	T38.811	T38.812	T38.813	T38.814	T38.815	T38.816
Tetracycline	T36.4X1	T36.4X2	T36.4X3	T36.4X4	T36.4X5	T36.4X6
ophthalmic preparation	T49.5X1	T49.5X2	T49.5X3	T49.5X4	T49.5X5	T49.5X6
topical NEC	T49.0X1	T49.0X2	T49.0X3	T49.0X4	T49.0X5	T49.0X6
Tetradifon	T60.8X1	T60.8X2	T60.8X3	T60.8X4	—	—
Tetradotoxin	T61.771	T61.772	T61.773	T61.774	—	—
Tetraethyl						
lead	T56.0X1	T56.0X2	T56.0X3	T56.0X4	—	—
pyrophosphate	T60.0X1	T60.0X2	T60.0X3	T60.0X4	—	—
Tetraethylammonium chloride	T44.2X1	T44.2X2	T44.2X3	T44.2X4	T44.2X5	T44.2X6
Tetraethylthiuram disulfide	T50.6X1	T50.6X2	T50.6X3	T50.6X4	T50.6X5	T50.6X6
Tetrahydroaminoacridine	T44.0X1	T44.0X2	T44.0X3	T44.0X4	T44.0X5	T44.0X6
Tetrahydrocannabinol	T40.7X1	T40.7X2	T40.7X3	T40.7X4	T40.7X5	T40.7X6
Tetrahydrofuran	T52.8X1	T52.8X2	T52.8X3	T52.8X4	—	—
Tetrahydronaphthalene	T52.8X1	T52.8X2	T52.8X3	T52.8X4	—	—
Tetrahydrozoline	T49.5X1	T49.5X2	T49.5X3	T49.5X4	T49.5X5	T49.5X6
Tetralin	T52.8X1	T52.8X2	T52.8X3	T52.8X4	—	—
Tetramethrin	T60.2X1	T60.2X2	T60.2X3	T60.2X4	—	—

Substance	External Cause (T-Code)					
	Poisoning, Accidental (Unintentional)	Poisoning, Intentional Self-Harm	Poisoning, Assault	Poisoning, Undetermined	Adverse Effect	Underdosing
Tetramethylthiuram (disulfide) NEC	T60.3X1	T60.3X2	T60.3X3	T60.3X4	—	—
medicinal	T49.0X1	T49.0X2	T49.0X3	T49.0X4	T49.0X5	T49.0X6
Tetramisole	T37.4X1	T37.4X2	T37.4X3	T37.4X4	T37.4X5	T37.4X6
Tetranicotinoyl fructose	T46.7X1	T46.7X2	T46.7X3	T46.7X4	T46.7X5	T46.7X6
Tetronal	T42.6X1	T42.6X2	T42.6X3	T42.6X4	T42.6X5	T42.6X6
Tetrazepam	T42.4X1	T42.4X2	T42.4X3	T42.4X4	T42.4X5	T42.4X6
Tetryl	T65.3X1	T65.3X2	T65.3X3	T65.3X4	—	—
Tetrylammonium chloride	T44.2X1	T44.2X2	T44.2X3	T44.2X4	T44.2X5	T44.2X6
Tetryzoline	T49.5X1	T49.5X2	T49.5X3	T49.5X4	T49.5X5	T49.5X6
Thalidomide	T45.1X1	T45.1X2	T45.1X3	T45.1X4	T45.1X5	T45.1X6
Thallium (compounds) (dust) NEC	T56.811	T56.812	T56.813	T56.814	—	—
pesticide	T60.4X1	T60.4X2	T60.4X3	T60.4X4	—	—
THC	T40.7X1	T40.7X2	T40.7X3	T40.7X4	T40.7X5	T40.7X6
Thebacon	T48.3X1	T48.3X2	T48.3X3	T48.3X4	T48.3X5	T48.3X6
Thebaine	T40.2X1	T40.2X2	T40.2X3	T40.2X4	T40.2X5	T40.2X6
Thenoic acid	T49.6X1	T49.6X2	T49.6X3	T49.6X4	T49.6X5	T49.6X6
Thenyldiamine	T45.0X1	T45.0X2	T45.0X3	T45.0X4	T45.0X5	T45.0X6
Theobromine (calcium salicylate)	T48.6X1	T48.6X2	T48.6X3	T48.6X4	T48.6X5	T48.6X6
sodium salicylate	T48.6X1	T48.6X2	T48.6X3	T48.6X4	T48.6X5	T48.6X6
Theophyllamine	T48.6X1	T48.6X2	T48.6X3	T48.6X4	T48.6X5	T48.6X6
Theophylline	T48.6X1	T48.6X2	T48.6X3	T48.6X4	T48.6X5	T48.6X6
aminobenzoic acid	T48.6X1	T48.6X2	T48.6X3	T48.6X4	T48.6X5	T48.6X6
ethylenediamine	T48.6X1	T48.6X2	T48.6X3	T48.6X4	T48.6X5	T48.6X6
piperazine p-amino-benzoate	T48.6X1	T48.6X2	T48.6X3	T48.6X4	T48.6X5	T48.6X6
Thiabendazole	T37.4X1	T37.4X2	T37.4X3	T37.4X4	T37.4X5	T37.4X6
Thialbarbital	T41.1X1	T41.1X2	T41.1X3	T41.1X4	T41.1X5	T41.1X6
Thiamazole	T38.2X1	T38.2X2	T38.2X3	T38.2X4	T38.2X5	T38.2X6
Thiambutosine	T37.1X1	T37.1X2	T37.1X3	T37.1X4	T37.1X5	T37.1X6
Thiamine	T45.2X1	T45.2X2	T45.2X3	T45.2X4	T45.2X5	T45.2X6
Thiamphenicol	T36.2X1	T36.2X2	T36.2X3	T36.2X4	T36.2X5	T36.2X6
Thiamylal	T41.1X1	T41.1X2	T41.1X3	T41.1X4	T41.1X5	T41.1X6
sodium	T41.1X1	T41.1X2	T41.1X3	T41.1X4	T41.1X5	T41.1X6
Thiazesim	T43.291	T43.292	T43.293	T43.294	T43.295	T43.296
Thiazides (diuretics)	T50.2X1	T50.2X2	T50.2X3	T50.2X4	T50.2X5	T50.2X6
Thiazinamium metilsulfate	T43.3X1	T43.3X2	T43.3X3	T43.3X4	T43.3X5	T43.3X6
Thiethylperazine	T43.3X1	T43.3X2	T43.3X3	T43.3X4	T43.3X5	T43.3X6
Thimerosal	T49.0X1	T49.0X2	T49.0X3	T49.0X4	T49.0X5	T49.0X6
ophthalmic preparation	T49.5X1	T49.5X2	T49.5X3	T49.5X4	T49.5X5	T49.5X6
Thioacetazone	T37.1X1	T37.1X2	T37.1X3	T37.1X4	T37.1X5	T37.1X6
with isoniazid	T37.1X1	T37.1X2	T37.1X3	T37.1X4	T37.1X5	T37.1X6
Thiobarbital sodium	T41.1X1	T41.1X2	T41.1X3	T41.1X4	T41.1X5	T41.1X6

◀ New ◀ Revised ~~deleted~~ Deleted

Substance	Poisoning, Accidental (Unintentional)	Poisoning, Intentional Self-Harm	Poisoning, Assault	Poisoning, Undetermined	Adverse Effect	Underdosing
Thiobarbiturate anesthetic	T41.1X1	T41.1X2	T41.1X3	T41.1X4	T41.1X5	T41.1X6
Thiobismol	T37.8X1	T37.8X2	T37.8X3	T37.8X4	T37.8X5	T37.8X6
Thiobutabarbital sodium	T41.1X1	T41.1X2	T41.1X3	T41.1X4	T41.1X5	T41.1X6
Thiocarbamate (insecticide)	T60.0X1	T60.0X2	T60.0X3	T60.0X4	—	—
Thiocarbamide	T38.2X1	T38.2X2	T38.2X3	T38.2X4	T38.2X5	T38.2X6
Thiocarbarsone	T37.8X1	T37.8X2	T37.8X3	T37.8X4	T37.8X5	T37.8X6
Thiocarlide	T37.1X1	T37.1X2	T37.1X3	T37.1X4	T37.1X5	T37.1X6
Thioctamide	T50.991	T50.992	T50.993	T50.994	T50.995	T50.996
Thioctic acid	T50.991	T50.992	T50.993	T50.994	T50.995	T50.996
Thiofos	T60.0X1	T60.0X2	T60.0X3	T60.0X4	—	—
Thioglycolate	T49.4X1	T49.4X2	T49.4X3	T49.4X4	T49.4X5	T49.4X6
Thioglycolic acid	T65.891	T65.892	T65.893	T65.894		
Thioguanine	T45.1X1	T45.1X2	T45.1X3	T45.1X4	T45.1X5	T45.1X6
Thiomercaptomerin	T50.2X1	T50.2X2	T50.2X3	T50.2X4	T50.2X5	T50.2X6
Thiomerin	T50.2X1	T50.2X2	T50.2X3	T50.2X4	T50.2X5	T50.2X6
Thiomersal	T49.0X1	T49.0X2	T49.0X3	T49.0X4	T49.0X5	T49.0X6
Thionazin	T60.0X1	T60.0X2	T60.0X3	T60.0X4	—	—
Thiopental (sodium)	T41.1X1	T41.1X2	T41.1X3	T41.1X4	T41.1X5	T41.1X6
Thiopentone (sodium)	T41.1X1	T41.1X2	T41.1X3	T41.1X4	T41.1X5	T41.1X6
Thiopropazate	T43.3X1	T43.3X2	T43.3X3	T43.3X4	T43.3X5	T43.3X6
Thioproperazine	T43.3X1	T43.3X2	T43.3X3	T43.3X4	T43.3X5	T43.3X6
Thioridazine	T43.3X1	T43.3X2	T43.3X3	T43.3X4	T43.3X5	T43.3X6
Thiosinamine	T49.3X1	T49.3X2	T49.3X3	T49.3X4	T49.3X5	T49.3X6
Thiotepa	T45.1X1	T45.1X2	T45.1X3	T45.1X4	T45.1X5	T45.1X6
Thiothixene	T43.4X1	T43.4X2	T43.4X3	T43.4X4	T43.4X5	T43.4X6
Thiouracil (benzyl) (methyl) (propyl)	T38.2X1	T38.2X2	T38.2X3	T38.2X4	T38.2X5	T38.2X6
Thiourea	T38.2X1	T38.2X2	T38.2X3	T38.2X4	T38.2X5	T38.2X6
Thiphenamil	T44.3X1	T44.3X2	T44.3X3	T44.3X4	T44.3X5	T44.3X6
Thiram	T60.3X1	T60.3X2	T60.3X3	T60.3X4	—	—
medicinal	T49.2X1	T49.2X2	T49.2X3	T49.2X4	T49.2X5	T49.2X6
Thonzylamine (systemic)	T45.0X1	T45.0X2	T45.0X3	T45.0X4	T45.0X5	T45.0X6
mucosal decongestant	T48.5X1	T48.5X2	T48.5X3	T48.5X4	T48.5X5	T48.5X6
Thorazine	T43.3X1	T43.3X2	T43.3X3	T43.3X4	T43.3X5	T43.3X6
Thorium dioxide suspension	T50.8X1	T50.8X2	T50.8X3	T50.8X4	T50.8X5	T50.8X6
Thornapple	T62.2X1	T62.2X2	T62.2X3	T62.2X4	—	—
Throat drug NEC	T49.6X1	T49.6X2	T49.6X3	T49.6X4	T49.6X5	T49.6X6
Thrombin	T45.7X1	T45.7X2	T45.7X3	T45.7X4	T45.7X5	T45.7X6
Thrombolysin	T45.611	T45.612	T45.613	T45.614	T45.615	T45.616
Thromboplastin	T45.7X1	T45.7X2	T45.7X3	T45.7X4	T45.7X5	T45.7X6
Thurfyl nicotinate	T46.7X1	T46.7X2	T46.7X3	T46.7X4	T46.7X5	T46.7X6
Thymol	T49.0X1	T49.0X2	T49.0X3	T49.0X4	T49.0X5	T49.0X6

Substance	Poisoning, Accidental (Unintentional)	Poisoning, Intentional Self-Harm	Poisoning, Assault	Poisoning, Undetermined	Adverse Effect	Underdosing
Thymopentin	T37.5X1	T37.5X2	T37.5X3	T37.5X4	T37.5X5	T37.5X6
Thymoxamine	T46.7X1	T46.7X2	T46.7X3	T46.7X4	T46.7X5	T46.7X6
Thymus extract	T38.891	T38.892	T38.893	T38.894	T38.895	T38.896
Thyreotrophic hormone	T38.811	T38.812	T38.813	T38.814	T38.815	T38.816
Thyroglobulin	T38.1X1	T38.1X2	T38.1X3	T38.1X4	T38.1X5	T38.1X6
Thyroid (hormone)	T38.1X1	T38.1X2	T38.1X3	T38.1X4	T38.1X5	T38.1X6
Thyrolar	T38.1X1	T38.1X2	T38.1X3	T38.1X4	T38.1X5	T38.1X6
Thyrotrophin	T38.811	T38.812	T38.813	T38.814	T38.815	T38.816
Thyrotropic hormone	T38.811	T38.812	T38.813	T38.814	T38.815	T38.816
Thyroxine	T38.1X1	T38.1X2	T38.1X3	T38.1X4	T38.1X5	T38.1X6
Tiabendazole	T37.4X1	T37.4X2	T37.4X3	T37.4X4	T37.4X5	T37.4X6
Tiamizide	T50.2X1	T50.2X2	T50.2X3	T50.2X4	T50.2X5	T50.2X6
Tianeptine	T43.291	T43.292	T43.293	T43.294	T43.295	T43.296
Tiapamil	T46.1X1	T46.1X2	T46.1X3	T46.1X4	T46.1X5	T46.1X6
Tiapride	T43.591	T43.592	T43.593	T43.594	T43.595	T43.596
Tiaprofenic acid	T39.311	T39.312	T39.313	T39.314	T39.315	T39.316
Tiaramide	T39.8X1	T39.8X2	T39.8X3	T39.8X4	T39.8X5	T39.8X6
Ticarcillin	T36.0X1	T36.0X2	T36.0X3	T36.0X4	T36.0X5	T36.0X6
Ticlatone	T49.0X1	T49.0X2	T49.0X3	T49.0X4	T49.0X5	T49.0X6
Ticlopidine	T45.521	T45.522	T45.523	T45.524	T45.525	T45.526
Ticrynafen	T50.1X1	T50.1X2	T50.1X3	T50.1X4	T50.1X5	T50.1X6
Tidiacic	T50.991	T50.992	T50.993	T50.994	T50.995	T50.996
Tiemonium	T44.3X1	T44.3X2	T44.3X3	T44.3X4	T44.3X5	T44.3X6
iodide	T44.3X1	T44.3X2	T44.3X3	T44.3X4	T44.3X5	T44.3X6
Tienilic acid	T50.1X1	T50.1X2	T50.1X3	T50.1X4	T50.1X5	T50.1X6
Tifenamil	T44.3X1	T44.3X2	T44.3X3	T44.3X4	T44.3X5	T44.3X6
Tigan	T45.0X1	T45.0X2	T45.0X3	T45.0X4	T45.0X5	T45.0X6
Tigloidine	T44.3X1	T44.3X2	T44.3X3	T44.3X4	T44.3X5	T44.3X6
Tilactase	T47.5X1	T47.5X2	T47.5X3	T47.5X4	T47.5X5	T47.5X6
Tiletamine	T41.291	T41.292	T41.293	T41.294	T41.295	T41.296
Tilidine	T40.4X1	T40.4X2	T40.4X3	T40.4X4	—	—
Timepidium bromide	T44.3X1	T44.3X2	T44.3X3	T44.3X4	T44.3X5	T44.3X6
Timiperone	T43.4X1	T43.4X2	T43.4X3	T43.4X4	T43.4X5	T43.4X6
Timolol	T44.7X1	T44.7X2	T44.7X3	T44.7X4	T44.7X5	T44.7X6
Tin (chloride) (dust) (oxide) NEC	T56.6X1	T56.6X2	T56.6X3	T56.6X4	—	—
anti-infectives	T37.8X1	T37.8X2	T37.8X3	T37.8X4	T37.8X5	T37.8X6
Tincture, iodine — see Iodine						
Tindal	T43.3X1	T43.3X2	T43.3X3	T43.3X4	T43.3X5	T43.3X6
Tinidazole	T37.3X1	T37.3X2	T37.3X3	T37.3X4	T37.3X5	T37.3X6
Tinoridine	T39.8X1	T39.8X2	T39.8X3	T39.8X4	T39.8X5	T39.8X6
Tiocarlide	T37.1X1	T37.1X2	T37.1X3	T37.1X4	T37.1X5	T37.1X6
Tioclomarol	T45.511	T45.512	T45.513	T45.514	T45.515	T45.516

◀ New   ◀ Revised   deleted Deleted

TABLE OF DRUGS AND CHEMICALS

Substance	Poisoning, Accidental (Unintentional)	Poisoning, Intentional Self-Harm	Poisoning, Assault	Poisoning, Undetermined	Adverse Effect	Underdosing
Tioconazole	T49.0X1	T49.0X2	T49.0X3	T49.0X4	T49.0X5	T49.0X6
Tioguanine	T45.1X1	T45.1X2	T45.1X3	T45.1X4	T45.1X5	T45.1X6
Tiopronin	T50.991	T50.992	T50.993	T50.994	T50.995	T50.996
Tiotixene	T43.4X1	T43.4X2	T43.4X3	T43.4X4	T43.4X5	T43.4X6
Tioxolone	T49.4X1	T49.4X2	T49.4X3	T49.4X4	T49.4X5	T49.4X6
Tipepidine	T48.3X1	T48.3X2	T48.3X3	T48.3X4	T48.3X5	T48.3X6
Tiquizium bromide	T44.3X1	T44.3X2	T44.3X3	T44.3X4	T44.3X5	T44.3X6
Tiratricol	T38.1X1	T38.1X2	T38.1X3	T38.1X4	T38.1X5	T38.1X6
Tisopurine	T50.4X1	T50.4X2	T50.4X3	T50.4X4	T50.4X5	T50.4X6
Titanium (compounds) (vapor)	T56.891	T56.892	T56.893	T56.894	—	—
dioxide	T49.3X1	T49.3X2	T49.3X3	T49.3X4	T49.3X5	T49.3X6
ointment	T49.3X1	T49.3X2	T49.3X3	T49.3X4	T49.3X5	T49.3X6
oxide	T49.3X1	T49.3X2	T49.3X3	T49.3X4	T49.3X5	T49.3X6
tetrachloride	T56.891	T56.892	T56.893	T56.894	—	—
Titanocene	T56.891	T56.892	T56.893	T56.894	—	—
Titroid	T38.1X1	T38.1X2	T38.1X3	T38.1X4	T38.1X5	T38.1X6
Tizanidine	T42.8X1	T42.8X2	T42.8X3	T42.8X4	T42.8X5	T42.8X6
TMTD	T60.3X1	T60.3X2	T60.3X3	T60.3X4	—	—
TNT (fumes)	T65.3X1	T65.3X2	T65.3X3	T65.3X4	—	—
Toadstool	T62.0X1	T62.0X2	T62.0X3	T62.0X4	—	—
Tobacco NEC	T65.291	T65.292	T65.293	T65.294	—	—
cigarettes	T65.221	T65.222	T65.223	T65.224	—	—
Indian	T62.2X1	T62.2X2	T62.2X3	T62.2X4	—	—
smoke, second-hand	T65.221	T65.222	T65.223	T65.224	—	—
Tobramycin	T36.5X1	T36.5X2	T36.5X3	T36.5X4	T36.5X5	T36.5X6
Tocainide	T46.2X1	T46.2X2	T46.2X3	T46.2X4	T46.2X5	T46.2X6
Tocoferol	T45.2X1	T45.2X2	T45.2X3	T45.2X4	T45.2X5	T45.2X6
Tocopherol	T45.2X1	T45.2X2	T45.2X3	T45.2X4	T45.2X5	T45.2X6
acetate	T45.2X1	T45.2X2	T45.2X3	T45.2X4	T45.2X5	T45.2X6
Tocosamine	T48.0X1	T48.0X2	T48.0X3	T48.0X4	T48.0X5	T48.0X6
Todralazine	T46.5X1	T46.5X2	T46.5X3	T46.5X4	T46.5X5	T46.5X6
Tofisopam	T42.4X1	T42.4X2	T42.4X3	T42.4X4	T42.4X5	T42.4X6
Tofranil	T43.011	T43.012	T43.013	T43.014	T43.015	T43.016
Toilet deodorizer	T65.891	T65.892	T65.893	T65.894	—	—
Tolamolol	T44.7X1	T44.7X2	T44.7X3	T44.7X4	T44.7X5	T44.7X6
Tolazamide	T38.3X1	T38.3X2	T38.3X3	T38.3X4	T38.3X5	T38.3X6
Tolazoline	T46.7X1	T46.7X2	T46.7X3	T46.7X4	T46.7X5	T46.7X6
Tolbutamide (sodium)	T38.3X1	T38.3X2	T38.3X3	T38.3X4	T38.3X5	T38.3X6
Tolciclate	T49.0X1	T49.0X2	T49.0X3	T49.0X4	T49.0X5	T49.0X6
Tolmetin	T39.391	T39.392	T39.393	T39.394	T39.395	T39.396
Tolnaftate	T49.0X1	T49.0X2	T49.0X3	T49.0X4	T49.0X5	T49.0X6
Tolonidine	T46.5X1	T46.5X2	T46.5X3	T46.5X4	T46.5X5	T46.5X6
Toloxatone	T42.6X1	T42.6X2	T42.6X3	T42.6X4	T42.6X5	T42.6X6
Tolperisone	T44.3X1	T44.3X2	T44.3X3	T44.3X4	T44.3X5	T44.3X6
Tolserol	T42.8X1	T42.8X2	T42.8X3	T42.8X4	T42.8X5	T42.8X6
Toluene (liquid)	T52.2X1	T52.2X2	T52.2X3	T52.2X4	—	—
diisocyanate	T65.0X1	T65.0X2	T65.0X3	T65.0X4	—	—
Toluidine	T65.891	T65.892	T65.893	T65.894	—	—
vapor	T59.891	T59.892	T59.893	T59.894	—	—
Toluol (liquid)	T52.2X1	T52.2X2	T52.2X3	T52.2X4	—	—
vapor	T52.2X1	T52.2X2	T52.2X3	T52.2X4	—	—
Toluylenediamine	T65.3X1	T65.3X2	T65.3X3	T65.3X4	—	—
Tolylene-2,4-diisocyanate	T65.0X1	T65.0X2	T65.0X3	T65.0X4	—	—
Tonic NEC	T50.901	T50.902	T50.903	T50.904	T50.905	T50.906
Topical action drug NEC	T49.91	T49.92	T49.93	T49.94	T49.95	T49.96
ear, nose or throat	T49.6X1	T49.6X2	T49.6X3	T49.6X4	T49.6X5	T49.6X6
eye	T49.5X1	T49.5X2	T49.5X3	T49.5X4	T49.5X5	T49.5X6
skin	T49.91	T49.92	T49.93	T49.94	T49.95	T49.96
specified NEC	T49.8X1	T49.8X2	T49.8X3	T49.8X4	T49.8X5	T49.8X6
Toquizine	T44.3X1	T44.3X2	T44.3X3	T44.3X4	T44.3X5	T44.3X6
Toremifene	T38.6X1	T38.6X2	T38.6X3	T38.6X4	T38.6X5	T38.6X6
Tosylchloramide sodium	T49.8X1	T49.8X2	T49.8X3	T49.8X4	T49.8X5	T49.8X6
Toxaphene (dust) (spray)	T60.1X1	T60.1X2	T60.1X3	T60.1X4	—	—
Toxin, diphtheria (Schick Test)	T50.8X1	T50.8X2	T50.8X3	T50.8X4	T50.8X5	T50.8X6
Toxoid						
combined	T50.A21	T50.A22	T50.A23	T50.A24	T50.A25	T50.A26
diphtheria	T50.A91	T50.A92	T50.A93	T50.A94	T50.A95	T50.A96
tetanus	T50.A91	T50.A92	T50.A93	T50.A94	T50.A95	T50.A96
Trace element NEC	T45.8X1	T45.8X2	T45.8X3	T45.8X4	T45.8X5	T45.8X6
Tractor fuel NEC	T52.0X1	T52.0X2	T52.0X3	T52.0X4	—	—
Tragacanth	T50.991	T50.992	T50.993	T50.994	T50.995	T50.996
Tramadol	T40.4X1	T40.4X2	T40.4X3	T40.4X4	T40.4X5	T40.4X6
Tramazoline	T48.5X1	T48.5X2	T48.5X3	T48.5X4	T48.5X5	T48.5X6
Tranexamic acid	T45.621	T45.622	T45.623	T45.624	T45.625	T45.626
Tranilast	T45.0X1	T45.0X2	T45.0X3	T45.0X4	T45.0X5	T45.0X6
Tranquilizer NEC	T43.501	T43.502	T43.503	T43.504	T43.505	T43.506
with hypnotic or sedative	T42.6X1	T42.6X2	T42.6X3	T42.6X4	T42.6X5	T42.6X6
benzodiazepine NEC	T42.4X1	T42.4X2	T42.4X3	T42.4X4	T42.4X5	T42.4X6
butyrophenone NEC	T43.4X1	T43.4X2	T43.4X3	T43.4X4	T43.4X5	T43.4X6
carbamate	T43.591	T43.592	T43.593	T43.594	T43.595	T43.596
dimethylamine	T43.3X1	T43.3X2	T43.3X3	T43.3X4	T43.3X5	T43.3X6
ethylamine	T43.3X1	T43.3X2	T43.3X3	T43.3X4	T43.3X5	T43.3X6
hydroxyzine	T43.591	T43.592	T43.593	T43.594	T43.595	T43.596
major NEC	T43.501	T43.502	T43.503	T43.504	T43.505	T43.506

◄ New ◄ Revised ~~deleted~~ Deleted

Substance	Poisoning, Accidental (Unintentional)	Poisoning, Intentional Self-Harm	Poisoning, Assault	Poisoning, Undetermined	Adverse Effect	Underdosing
Tranquilizer NEC *(Continued)*						
penothiazine NEC	T43.3X1	T43.3X2	T43.3X3	T43.3X4	T43.3X5	T43.3X6
phenothiazine-based	T43.3X1	T43.3X2	T43.3X3	T43.3X4	T43.3X5	T43.3X6
piperazine NEC	T43.3X1	T43.3X2	T43.3X3	T43.3X4	T43.3X5	T43.3X6
piperidine	T43.3X1	T43.3X2	T43.3X3	T43.3X4	T43.3X5	T43.3X6
propylamine	T43.3X1	T43.3X2	T43.3X3	T43.3X4	T43.3X5	T43.3X6
specified NEC	T43.591	T43.592	T43.593	T43.594	T43.595	T43.596
thioxanthene NEC	T43.591	T43.592	T43.593	T43.594	T43.595	T43.596
Tranxene	T42.4X1	T42.4X2	T42.4X3	T42.4X4	T42.4X5	T42.4X6
Tranylcypromine	T43.1X1	T43.1X2	T43.1X3	T43.1X4	T43.1X5	T43.1X6
Trapidil	T46.3X1	T46.3X2	T46.3X3	T46.3X4	T46.3X5	T46.3X6
Trasentine	T44.3X1	T44.3X2	T44.3X3	T44.3X4	T44.3X5	T44.3X6
Travert	T50.3X1	T50.3X2	T50.3X3	T50.3X4	T50.3X5	T50.3X6
Trazodone	T43.211	T43.212	T43.213	T43.214	T43.215	T43.216
Trecator	T37.1X1	T37.1X2	T37.1X3	T37.1X4	T37.1X5	T37.1X6
Treosulfan	T45.1X1	T45.1X2	T45.1X3	T45.1X4	T45.1X5	T45.1X6
Tretamine	T45.1X1	T45.1X2	T45.1X3	T45.1X4	T45.1X5	T45.1X6
Tretinoin	T49.0X1	T49.0X2	T49.0X3	T49.0X4	T49.0X5	T49.0X6
Tretoquinol	T48.6X1	T48.6X2	T48.6X3	T48.6X4	T48.6X5	T48.6X6
Triacetin	T49.0X1	T49.0X2	T49.0X3	T49.0X4	T49.0X5	T49.0X6
Triacetoxyanthracene	T49.4X1	T49.4X2	T49.4X3	T49.4X4	T49.4X5	T49.4X6
Triacetyloleandomycin	T36.3X1	T36.3X2	T36.3X3	T36.3X4	T36.3X5	T36.3X6
Triamcinolone	T38.0X1	T38.0X2	T38.0X3	T38.0X4	T38.0X5	T38.0X6
ENT agent	T49.6X1	T49.6X2	T49.6X3	T49.6X4	T49.6X5	T49.6X6
hexacetonide	T49.0X1	T49.0X2	T49.0X3	T49.0X4	T49.0X5	T49.0X6
ophthalmic preparation	T49.5X1	T49.5X2	T49.5X3	T49.5X4	T49.5X5	T49.5X6
topical NEC	T49.0X1	T49.0X2	T49.0X3	T49.0X4	T49.0X5	T49.0X6
Triampyzine	T44.3X1	T44.3X2	T44.3X3	T44.3X4	T44.3X5	T44.3X6
Triamterene	T50.2X1	T50.2X2	T50.2X3	T50.2X4	T50.2X5	T50.2X6
Triazine (herbicide)	T60.3X1	T60.3X2	T60.3X3	T60.3X4	—	—
Triaziquone	T45.1X1	T45.1X2	T45.1X3	T45.1X4	T45.1X5	T45.1X6
Triazolam	T42.4X1	T42.4X2	T42.4X3	T42.4X4	T42.4X5	T42.4X6
Triazole (herbicide)	T60.3X1	T60.3X2	T60.3X3	T60.3X4	—	—
Tribenoside	T46.991	T46.992	T46.993	T46.994	T46.995	T46.996
Tribromacetaldehyde	T42.6X1	T42.6X2	T42.6X3	T42.6X4	T42.6X5	T42.6X6
Tribromoethanol, rectal	T41.291	T41.292	T41.293	T41.294	T41.295	T41.296
Tribromomethane	T42.6X1	T42.6X2	T42.6X3	T42.6X4	T42.6X5	T42.6X6
Trichlorethane	T53.2X1	T53.2X2	T53.2X3	T53.2X4	—	—
Trichlorethylene	T53.2X1	T53.2X2	T53.2X3	T53.2X4	—	—
Trichlorfon	T60.0X1	T60.0X2	T60.0X3	T60.0X4	—	—
Trichlormethiazide	T50.2X1	T50.2X2	T50.2X3	T50.2X4	T50.2X5	T50.2X6
Trichlormethine	T45.1X1	T45.1X2	T45.1X3	T45.1X4	T45.1X5	T45.1X6

Substance	Poisoning, Accidental (Unintentional)	Poisoning, Intentional Self-Harm	Poisoning, Assault	Poisoning, Undetermined	Adverse Effect	Underdosing
Trichloroacetic acid, Trichloroacetic acid	T54.2X1	T54.2X2	T54.2X3	T54.2X4	—	—
medicinal	T49.4X1	T49.4X2	T49.4X3	T49.4X4	T49.4X5	T49.4X6
Trichloroethane	T53.2X1	T53.2X2	T53.2X3	T53.2X4	—	—
Trichloroethanol	T42.6X1	T42.6X2	T42.6X3	T42.6X4	T42.6X5	T42.6X6
Trichloroethylene (liquid) (vapor)	T53.2X1	T53.2X2	T53.2X3	T53.2X4	—	—
anesthetic (gas)	T41.0X1	T41.0X2	T41.0X3	T41.0X4	T41.0X5	T41.0X6
vapor NEC	T53.2X1	T53.2X2	T53.2X3	T53.2X4	—	—
Trichloroethyl phosphate	T42.6X1	T42.6X2	T42.6X3	T42.6X4	T42.6X5	T42.6X6
Trichlorofluoromethane NEC	T53.5X1	T53.5X2	T53.5X3	T53.5X4	—	—
Trichloronate	T60.0X1	T60.0X2	T60.0X3	T60.0X4	—	—
2,4,5-Trichlorophen-oxyacetic acid	T60.3X1	T60.3X2	T60.3X3	T60.3X4	—	—
Trichloropropane	T53.6X1	T53.6X2	T53.6X3	T53.6X4	—	—
Trichlorotriethylamine	T45.1X1	T45.1X2	T45.1X3	T45.1X4	T45.1X5	T45.1X6
Trichomonacides NEC	T37.3X1	T37.3X2	T37.3X3	T37.3X4	T37.3X5	T37.3X6
Trichomycin	T36.7X1	T36.7X2	T36.7X3	T36.7X4	T36.7X5	T36.7X6
Triclobisonium chloride	T49.0X1	T49.0X2	T49.0X3	T49.0X4	T49.0X5	T49.0X6
Triclocarban	T49.0X1	T49.0X2	T49.0X3	T49.0X4	T49.0X5	T49.0X6
Triclofos	T42.6X1	T42.6X2	T42.6X3	T42.6X4	T42.6X5	T42.6X6
Triclosan	T49.0X1	T49.0X2	T49.0X3	T49.0X4	T49.0X5	T49.0X6
Tricresyl phosphate	T65.891	T65.892	T65.893	T65.894	—	—
solvent	T52.91	T52.92	T52.93	T52.94		
Tricyclamol chloride	T44.3X1	T44.3X2	T44.3X3	T44.3X4	T44.3X5	T44.3X6
Tridesilon	T49.0X1	T49.0X2	T49.0X3	T49.0X4	T49.0X5	T49.0X6
Tridihexethyl iodide	T44.3X1	T44.3X2	T44.3X3	T44.3X4	T44.3X5	T44.3X6
Tridione	T42.2X1	T42.2X2	T42.2X3	T42.2X4	T42.2X5	T42.2X6
Trientine	T45.8X1	T45.8X2	T45.8X3	T45.8X4	T45.8X5	T45.8X6
Triethanolamine NEC	T54.3X1	T54.3X2	T54.3X3	T54.3X4	—	—
detergent	T54.3X1	T54.3X2	T54.3X3	T54.3X4	—	—
trinitrate (biphosphate)	T46.3X1	T46.3X2	T46.3X3	T46.3X4	T46.3X5	T46.3X6
Triethanomelamine	T45.1X1	T45.1X2	T45.1X3	T45.1X4	T45.1X5	T45.1X6
Triethylenemelamine	T45.1X1	T45.1X2	T45.1X3	T45.1X4	T45.1X5	T45.1X6
Triethylenephosphoramide	T45.1X1	T45.1X2	T45.1X3	T45.1X4	T45.1X5	T45.1X6
Triethylenethiophosphoramide	T45.1X1	T45.1X2	T45.1X3	T45.1X4	T45.1X5	T45.1X6
Trifluoperazine	T43.3X1	T43.3X2	T43.3X3	T43.3X4	T43.3X5	T43.3X6
Trifluoroethyl vinyl ether	T41.0X1	T41.0X2	T41.0X3	T41.0X4	T41.0X5	T41.0X6
Trifluperidol	T43.4X1	T43.4X2	T43.4X3	T43.4X4	T43.4X5	T43.4X6
Triflupromazine	T43.3X1	T43.3X2	T43.3X3	T43.3X4	T43.3X5	T43.3X6
Trifluridine	T37.5X1	T37.5X2	T37.5X3	T37.5X4	T37.5X5	T37.5X6
Triflusal	T45.521	T45.522	T45.523	T45.524	T45.525	T45.526
Trihexyphenidyl	T44.3X1	T44.3X2	T44.3X3	T44.3X4	T44.3X5	T44.3X6
Triiodothyronine	T38.1X1	T38.1X2	T38.1X3	T38.1X4	T38.1X5	T38.1X6

◀ New ◀ Revised ~~deleted~~ Deleted

	External Cause (T-Code)					
Substance	Poisoning, Accidental (Unintentional)	Poisoning, Intentional Self-Harm	Poisoning, Assault	Poisoning, Undetermined	Adverse Effect	Underdosing
Trilene	T41.0X1	T41.0X2	T41.0X3	T41.0X4	T41.0X5	T41.0X6
Trilostane	T38.991	T38.992	T38.993	T38.994	T38.995	T38.996
Trimebutine	T44.3X1	T44.3X2	T44.3X3	T44.3X4	T44.3X5	T44.3X6
Trimecaine	T41.3X1	T41.3X2	T41.3X3	T41.3X4	T41.3X5	T41.3X6
Trimeprazine (tartrate)	T44.3X1	T44.3X2	T44.3X3	T44.3X4	T44.3X5	T44.3X6
Trimetaphan camsilate	T44.2X1	T44.2X2	T44.2X3	T44.2X4	T44.2X5	T44.2X6
Trimetazidine	T46.7X1	T46.7X2	T46.7X3	T46.7X4	T46.7X5	T46.7X6
Trimethadione	T42.2X1	T42.2X2	T42.2X3	T42.2X4	T42.2X5	T42.2X6
Trimethaphan	T44.2X1	T44.2X2	T44.2X3	T44.2X4	T44.2X5	T44.2X6
Trimethidinium	T44.2X1	T44.2X2	T44.2X3	T44.2X4	T44.2X5	T44.2X6
Trimethobenzamide	T45.0X1	T45.0X2	T45.0X3	T45.0X4	T45.0X5	T45.0X6
Trimethoprim	T37.8X1	T37.8X2	T37.8X3	T37.8X4	T37.8X5	T37.8X6
with sulfamethoxazole	T36.8X1	T36.8X2	T36.8X3	T36.8X4	T36.8X5	T36.8X6
Trimethylcarbinol	T51.3X1	T51.3X2	T51.3X3	T51.3X4	—	—
Trimethylpsoralen	T49.3X1	T49.3X2	T49.3X3	T49.3X4	T49.3X5	T49.3X6
Trimeton	T45.0X1	T45.0X2	T45.0X3	T45.0X4	T45.0X5	T45.0X6
Trimetrexate	T45.1X1	T45.1X2	T45.1X3	T45.1X4	T45.1X5	T45.1X6
Trimipramine	T43.011	T43.012	T43.013	T43.014	T43.015	T43.016
Trimustine	T45.1X1	T45.1X2	T45.1X3	T45.1X4	T45.1X5	T45.1X6
Trinitrine	T46.3X1	T46.3X2	T46.3X3	T46.3X4	T46.3X5	T46.3X6
Trinitrobenzol	T65.3X1	T65.3X2	T65.3X3	T65.3X4	—	—
Trinitrophenol	T65.3X1	T65.3X2	T65.3X3	T65.3X4	—	—
Trinitrotoluene (fumes)	T65.3X1	T65.3X2	T65.3X3	T65.3X4	—	—
Trional	T42.6X1	T42.6X2	T42.6X3	T42.6X4	T42.6X5	T42.6X6
Triorthocresyl phosphate	T65.891	T65.892	T65.893	T65.894		
Trioxide of arsenic	T57.0X1	T57.0X2	T57.0X3	T57.0X4	—	—
Trioxysalen	T49.4X1	T49.4X2	T49.4X3	T49.4X4	T49.4X5	T49.4X6
Tripamide	T50.2X1	T50.2X2	T50.2X3	T50.2X4	T50.2X5	T50.2X6
Triparanol	T46.6X1	T46.6X2	T46.6X3	T46.6X4	T46.6X5	T46.6X6
Tripelennamine	T45.0X1	T45.0X2	T45.0X3	T45.0X4	T45.0X5	T45.0X6
Triperiden	T44.3X1	T44.3X2	T44.3X3	T44.3X4	T44.3X5	T44.3X6
Triperidol	T43.4X1	T43.4X2	T43.4X3	T43.4X4	T43.4X5	T43.4X6
Triphenylphosphate	T65.891	T65.892	T65.893	T65.894	—	—
Triple						
bromides	T42.6X1	T42.6X2	T42.6X3	T42.6X4	T42.6X5	T42.6X6
carbonate	T47.1X1	T47.1X2	T47.1X3	T47.1X4	T47.1X5	T47.1X6
vaccine						
DPT	T50.A11	T50.A12	T50.A13	T50.A14	T50.A15	T50.A16
including pertussis	T50.A11	T50.A12	T50.A13	T50.A14	T50.A15	T50.A16
MMR	T50.B91	T50.B92	—	—	—	—
Triprolidine	T45.0X1	T45.0X2	T45.0X3	T45.0X4	T45.0X5	T45.0X6
Trisodium hydrogen edetate	T50.6X1	T50.6X2	T50.6X3	T50.6X4	T50.6X5	T50.6X6

	External Cause (T-Code)					
Substance	Poisoning, Accidental (Unintentional)	Poisoning, Intentional Self-Harm	Poisoning, Assault	Poisoning, Undetermined	Adverse Effect	Underdosing
Trisoralen	T49.3X1	T49.3X2	T49.3X3	T49.3X4	T49.3X5	T49.3X6
Trisulfapyrimidines	T37.0X1	T37.0X2	T37.0X3	T37.0X4	T37.0X5	T37.0X6
Trithiozine	T44.3X1	T44.3X2	T44.3X3	T44.3X4	T44.3X5	T44.3X6
Tritiozine	T44.3X1	T44.3X2	T44.3X3	T44.3X4	T44.3X5	T44.3X6
Tritoqualine	T45.0X1	T45.0X2	T45.0X3	T45.0X4	T45.0X5	T45.0X6
Trofosfamide	T45.1X1	T45.1X2	T45.1X3	T45.1X4	T45.1X5	T45.1X6
Troleandomycin	T36.3X1	T36.3X2	T36.3X3	T36.3X4	T36.3X5	T36.3X6
Trolnitrate (phosphate)	T46.3X1	T46.3X2	T46.3X3	T46.3X4	T46.3X5	T46.3X6
Tromantadine	T37.5X1	T37.5X2	T37.5X3	T37.5X4	T37.5X5	T37.5X6
Trometamol	T50.2X1	T50.2X2	T50.2X3	T50.2X4	T50.2X5	T50.2X6
Tromethamine	T50.2X1	T50.2X2	T50.2X3	T50.2X4	T50.2X5	T50.2X6
Tronothane	T41.3X1	T41.3X2	T41.3X3	T41.3X4	T41.3X5	T41.3X6
Tropacine	T44.3X1	T44.3X2	T44.3X3	T44.3X4	T44.3X5	T44.3X6
Tropatepine	T44.3X1	T44.3X2	T44.3X3	T44.3X4	T44.3X5	T44.3X6
Tropicamide	T44.3X1	T44.3X2	T44.3X3	T44.3X4	T44.3X5	T44.3X6
Trospium chloride	T44.3X1	T44.3X2	T44.3X3	T44.3X4	T44.3X5	T44.3X6
Troxerutin	T46.991	T46.992	T46.993	T46.994	T46.995	T46.996
Troxidone	T42.2X1	T42.2X2	T42.2X3	T42.2X4	T42.2X5	T42.2X6
Tryparsamide	T37.3X1	T37.3X2	T37.3X3	T37.3X4	T37.3X5	T37.3X6
Trypsin	T45.3X1	T45.3X2	T45.3X3	T45.3X4	T45.3X5	T45.3X6
Tryptizol	T43.011	T43.012	T43.013	T43.014	T43.015	T43.016
TSH	T38.811	T38.812	T38.813	T38.814	T38.815	T38.816
Tuaminoheptane	T48.5X1	T48.5X2	T48.5X3	T48.5X4	T48.5X5	T48.5X6
Tuberculin, purified protein derivative (PPD)	T50.8X1	T50.8X2	T50.8X3	T50.8X4	T50.8X5	T50.8X6
Tubocurare	T48.1X1	T48.1X2	T48.1X3	T48.1X4	T48.1X5	T48.1X6
Tubocurarine (chloride)	T48.1X1	T48.1X2	T48.1X3	T48.1X4	T48.1X5	T48.1X6
Tulobuterol	T48.6X1	T48.6X2	T48.6X3	T48.6X4	T48.6X5	T48.6X6
Turpentine (spirits of)	T52.8X1	T52.8X2	T52.8X3	T52.8X4	—	—
vapor	T52.8X1	T52.8X2	T52.8X3	T52.8X4	—	—
Tybamate	T43.591	T43.592	T43.593	T43.594	T43.595	T43.596
Tyloxapol	T48.4X1	T48.4X2	T48.4X3	T48.4X4	T48.4X5	T48.4X6
Tymazoline	T48.5X1	T48.5X2	T48.5X3	T48.5X4	T48.5X5	T48.5X6
Typhoid-paratyphoid vaccine	T50.A91	T50.A92	T50.A93	T50.A94	T50.A95	T50.A96
Typhus vaccine	T50.A91	T50.A92	T50.A93	T50.A94	T50.A95	T50.A96
Tyropanoate	T50.8X1	T50.8X2	T50.8X3	T50.8X4	T50.8X5	T50.8X6
Tyrothricin	T49.6X1	T49.6X2	T49.6X3	T49.6X4	T49.6X5	T49.6X6
ENT agent	T49.6X1	T49.6X2	T49.6X3	T49.6X4	T49.6X5	T49.6X6
ophthalmic preparation	T49.5X1	T49.5X2	T49.5X3	T49.5X4	T49.5X5	T49.5X6
U						
Ufenamate	T39.391	T39.392	T39.393	T39.394	T39.395	T39.396
Ultraviolet light protectant	T49.3X1	T49.3X2	T49.3X3	T49.3X4	T49.3X5	T49.3X6

◀ New   ◀ Revised   ~~deleted~~ Deleted

Substance	Poisoning, Accidental (Unintentional)	Poisoning, Intentional Self-Harm	Poisoning, Assault	Poisoning, Undetermined	Adverse Effect	Underdosing
Undecenoic acid	T49.0X1	T49.0X2	T49.0X3	T49.0X4	T49.0X5	T49.0X6
Undecoylium	T49.0X1	T49.0X2	T49.0X3	T49.0X4	T49.0X5	T49.0X6
Undecylenic acid (derivatives)	T49.0X1	T49.0X2	T49.0X3	T49.0X4	T49.0X5	T49.0X6
Unna's boot	T49.3X1	T49.3X2	T49.3X3	T49.3X4	T49.3X5	T49.3X6
Unsaturated fatty acid	T46.6X1	T46.6X2	T46.6X3	T46.6X4	T46.6X5	T46.6X6
Uracil mustard	T45.1X1	T45.1X2	T45.1X3	T45.1X4	T45.1X5	T45.1X6
Uramustine	T45.1X1	T45.1X2	T45.1X3	T45.1X4	T45.1X5	T45.1X6
Urapidil	T46.5X1	T46.5X2	T46.5X3	T46.5X4	T46.5X5	T46.5X6
Urari	T48.1X1	T48.1X2	T48.1X3	T48.1X4	T48.1X5	T48.1X6
Urate oxidase	T50.4X1	T50.4X2	T50.4X3	T50.4X4	T50.4X5	T50.4X6
Urea	T47.3X1	T47.3X2	T47.3X3	T47.3X4	T47.3X5	T47.3X6
peroxide	T49.0X1	T49.0X2	T49.0X3	T49.0X4	T49.0X5	T49.0X6
stibamine	T37.4X1	T37.4X2	T37.4X3	T37.4X4	T37.4X5	T37.4X6
topical	T49.8X1	T49.8X2	T49.8X3	T49.8X4	T49.8X5	T49.8X6
Urethane	T45.1X1	T45.1X2	T45.1X3	T45.1X4	T45.1X5	T45.1X6
Urginea (maritima) (scilla) — see Squill						
Uric acid metabolism drug NEC	T50.4X1	T50.4X2	T50.4X3	T50.4X4	T50.4X5	T50.4X6
Uricosuric agent	T50.4X1	T50.4X2	T50.4X3	T50.4X4	T50.4X5	T50.4X6
Urinary anti-infective	T37.8X1	T37.8X2	T37.8X3	T37.8X4	T37.8X5	T37.8X6
Urofollitropin	T38.811	T38.812	T38.813	T38.814	T38.815	T38.816
Urokinase	T45.611	T45.612	T45.613	T45.614	T45.615	T45.616
Urokon	T50.8X1	T50.8X2	T50.8X3	T50.8X4	T50.8X5	T50.8X6
Ursodeoxycholic acid	T50.991	T50.992	T50.993	T50.994	T50.995	T50.996
Ursodiol	T50.991	T50.992	T50.993	T50.994	T50.995	T50.996
Urtica	T62.2X1	T62.2X2	T62.2X3	T62.2X4	—	—
Utility gas — see Gas, utility						
V						
Vaccine NEC	T50.Z91	T50.Z92	T50.Z93	T50.Z94	T50.Z95	T50.Z96
antineoplastic	T50.Z91	T50.Z92	T50.Z93	T50.Z94	T50.Z95	T50.Z96
bacterial NEC	T50.A91	T50.A92	T50.A93	T50.A94	T50.A95	T50.A96
with						
other bacterial component	T50.A91	T50.A92	T50.A93	T50.A94	T50.A95	T50.A96
pertussis component	T50.A91	T50.A92	T50.A93	T50.A94	T50.A95	T50.A96
viral-rickettsial component	T50.A91	T50.A92	T50.A93	T50.A94	T50.A95	T50.A96
mixed NEC	T50.A91	T50.A92	T50.A93	T50.A94	T50.A95	T50.A96
BCG	T50.A91	T50.A92	T50.A93	T50.A94	T50.A95	T50.A96
cholera	T50.A91	T50.A92	T50.A93	T50.A94	T50.A95	T50.A96
diphtheria	T50.A91	T50.A92	T50.A93	T50.A94	T50.A95	T50.A96
with tetanus	T50.A21	T50.A22	T50.A23	T50.A24	T50.A25	T50.A26
and pertussis	T50.A11	T50.A12	T50.A13	T50.A14	T50.A15	T50.A16

Substance	Poisoning, Accidental (Unintentional)	Poisoning, Intentional Self-Harm	Poisoning, Assault	Poisoning, Undetermined	Adverse Effect	Underdosing
Vaccine NEC *(Continued)*						
influenza	T50.B91	T50.B92	T50.B93	T50.B94	T50.B95	T50.B96
measles	T50.B91	T50.B92	T50.B93	T50.B94	T50.B95	T50.B96
with mumps and rubella	T50.B91	T50.B92	T50.B93	T50.B94	T50.B95	T50.B96
meningococcal	T50.A91	T50.A92	T50.A93	T50.A94	T50.A95	T50.A96
mumps	T50.B91	T50.B92	T50.B93	T50.B94	T50.B95	T50.B96
paratyphoid	T50.A91	T50.A92	T50.A93	T50.A94	T50.A95	T50.A96
pertussis	T50.A11	T50.A12	T50.A13	T50.A14	T50.A15	T50.A16
with diphtheria	T50.A11	T50.A12	T50.A13	T50.A14	T50.A15	T50.A16
and tetanus	T50.A11	T50.A12	T50.A13	T50.A14	T50.A15	T50.A16
plague	T50.A91	T50.A92	T50.A93	T50.A94	T50.A95	T50.A96
poliomyelitis	T50.B91	T50.B92	T50.B93	T50.B94	T50.B95	T50.B96
poliovirus	T50.B91	T50.B92	T50.B93	T50.B94	T50.B95	T50.B96
rabies	T50.B91	T50.B92	T50.B93	T50.B94	T50.B95	T50.B96
respiratory syncytial virus	T50.B91	T50.B92	T50.B93	T50.B94	T50.B95	T50.B96
rickettsial NEC	T50.A91	T50.A92	T50.A93	T50.A94	T50.A95	T50.A96
with						
bacterial component	T50.A21	T50.A22	T50.A23	T50.A24	T50.A25	T50.A26
Rocky Mountain spotted fever	T50.A91	T50.A92	T50.A93	T50.A94	T50.A95	T50.A96
rubella	T50.B91	T50.B92	T50.B93	T50.B94	T50.B95	T50.B96
sabin oral	T50.B91	T50.B92	T50.B93	T50.B94	T50.B95	T50.B96
smallpox	T50.B11	T50.B12	T50.B13	T50.B14	T50.B15	T50.B16
TAB	T50.A91	T50.A92	T50.A93	T50.A94	T50.A95	T50.A96
tetanus	T50.A91	T50.A92	T50.A93	T50.A94	T50.A95	T50.A96
typhoid	T50.A91	T50.A92	T50.A93	T50.A94	T50.A95	T50.A96
typhus	T50.A91	T50.A92	T50.A93	T50.A94	T50.A95	T50.A96
viral NEC	T50.B91	T50.B92	T50.B93	T50.B94	T50.B95	T50.B96
yellow fever	T50.B91	T50.B92	T50.B93	T50.B94	T50.B95	T50.B96
Vaccinia immune globulin	T50.Z11	T50.Z12	T50.Z13	T50.Z14	T50.Z15	T50.Z16
Vaginal contraceptives	T49.8X1	T49.8X2	T49.8X3	T49.8X4	T49.8X5	T49.8X6
Valerian						
root	T42.6X1	T42.6X2	T42.6X3	T42.6X4	T42.6X5	T42.6X6
tincture	T42.6X1	T42.6X2	T42.6X3	T42.6X4	T42.6X5	T42.6X6
Valethamate bromide	T44.3X1	T44.3X2	T44.3X3	T44.3X4	T44.3X5	T44.3X6
Valisone	T49.0X1	T49.0X2	T49.0X3	T49.0X4	T49.0X5	T49.0X6
Valium	T42.4X1	T42.4X2	T42.4X3	T42.4X4	T42.4X5	T42.4X6
Valmid	T42.6X1	T42.6X2	T42.6X3	T42.6X4	T42.6X5	T42.6X6
Valnoctamide	T42.6X1	T42.6X2	T42.6X3	T42.6X4	T42.6X5	T42.6X6
Valproate (sodium)	T42.6X1	T42.6X2	T42.6X3	T42.6X4	T42.6X5	T42.6X6
Valproic acid	T42.6X1	T42.6X2	T42.6X3	T42.6X4	T42.6X5	T42.6X6
Valpromide	T42.6X1	T42.6X2	T42.6X3	T42.6X4	T42.6X5	T42.6X6
Vanadium	T56.891	T56.892	T56.893	T56.894	—	—

◄ New   ◄ Revised   deleted Deleted

TABLE OF DRUGS AND CHEMICALS

TABLE OF DRUGS AND CHEMICALS

Substance	External Cause (T-Code)					
	Poisoning, Accidental (Unintentional)	Poisoning, Intentional Self-Harm	Poisoning, Assault	Poisoning, Undetermined	Adverse Effect	Underdosing
Vancomycin	T36.8X1	T36.8X2	T36.8X3	T36.8X4	T36.8X5	T36.8X6
Vapor — see also Gas	T59.91	T59.92	T59.93	T59.94	—	—
kiln (carbon monoxide)	T58.8X1	T58.8X2	T58.8X3	T58.8X4		
lead — see lead						
specified source NEC	T59.891	T59.892	T59.893	T59.894	—	—
Vardenafil	T46.7X1	T46.7X2	T46.7X3	T46.7X4	T46.7X5	T46.7X6
Varicose reduction drug	T46.8X1	T46.8X2	T46.8X3	T46.8X4	T46.8X5	T46.8X6
Varnish	T65.4X1	T65.4X2	T65.4X3	T65.4X4	—	—
cleaner	T52.91	T52.92	T52.93	T52.94	—	—
Vaseline	T49.3X1	T49.3X2	T49.3X3	T49.3X4	T49.3X5	T49.3X6
Vasodilan	T46.7X1	T46.7X2	T46.7X3	T46.7X4	T46.7X5	T46.7X6
Vasodilator						
coronary NEC	T46.3X1	T46.3X2	T46.3X3	T46.3X4	T46.3X5	T46.3X6
peripheral NEC	T46.7X1	T46.7X2	T46.7X3	T46.7X4	T46.7X5	T46.7X6
Vasopressin	T38.891	T38.892	T38.893	T38.894	T38.895	T38.896
Vasopressor drugs	T38.891	T38.892	T38.893	T38.894	T38.895	T38.896
Vecuronium bromide	T48.1X1	T48.1X2	T48.1X3	T48.1X4	T48.1X5	T48.1X6
Vegetable extract, astringent	T49.2X1	T49.2X2	T49.2X3	T49.2X4	T49.2X5	T49.2X6
Venlafaxine	T43.211	T43.212	T43.213	T43.214	T43.215	T43.216
Venom, venomous (bite) (sting)	T63.91	T63.92	T63.93	T63.94	—	—
amphibian NEC	T63.831	T63.832	T63.833	T63.834	—	—
animal NEC	T63.891	T63.892	T63.893	T63.894	—	—
ant	T63.421	T63.422	T63.423	T63.424	—	—
arthropod NEC	T63.481	T63.482	T63.483	T63.484	—	—
bee	T63.441	T63.442	T63.443	T63.444	—	—
centipede	T63.411	T63.412	T63.413	T63.414	—	—
fish	T63.591	T63.592	T63.593	T63.594	—	—
frog	T63.811	T63.812	T63.813	T63.814	—	—
hornet	T63.451	T63.452	T63.453	T63.454	—	—
insect NEC	T63.481	T63.482	T63.483	T63.484	—	—
lizard	T63.121	T63.122	T63.123	T63.124	—	—
marine						
animals	T63.691	T63.692	T63.693	T63.694	—	—
bluebottle	T63.611	T63.612	T63.613	T63.614	—	—
jellyfish NEC	T63.621	T63.622	T63.623	T63.624	—	—
Portugese Man-o-war	T63.611	T63.612	T63.613	T63.614	—	—
sea anemone	T63.631	T63.632	T63.633	T63.634	—	—
specified NEC	T63.691	T63.692	T63.693	T63.694	—	—
fish	T63.591	T63.592	T63.593	T63.594	—	—
plants	T63.711	T63.712	T63.713	T63.714	—	—
sting ray	T63.511	T63.512	T63.513	T63.514	—	—

Substance	External Cause (T-Code)					
	Poisoning, Accidental (Unintentional)	Poisoning, Intentional Self-Harm	Poisoning, Assault	Poisoning, Undetermined	Adverse Effect	Underdosing
Venom, venomous (Continued)						
millipede (tropical)	T63.411	T63.412	T63.413	T63.414	—	—
plant NEC	T63.791	T63.792	T63.793	T63.794	—	—
marine	T63.711	T63.712	T63.713	T63.714	—	—
reptile	T63.191	T63.192	T63.193	T63.194	—	—
gila monster	T63.111	T63.112	T63.113	T63.114	—	—
lizard NEC	T63.121	T63.122	T63.123	T63.124	—	—
scorpion	T63.2X1	T63.2X2	T63.2X3	T63.2X4	—	—
snake	T63.001	T63.002	T63.003	T63.004	—	—
African NEC	T63.081	T63.082	T63.083	T63.084	—	—
American (North) (South) NEC	T63.061	T63.062	T63.063	T63.064	—	—
Asian	T63.081	T63.082	T63.083	T63.084	—	—
Australian	T63.071	T63.072	T63.073	T63.074	—	—
cobra	T63.041	T63.042	T63.043	T63.044	—	—
coral snake	T63.021	T63.022	T63.023	T63.024	—	—
rattlesnake	T63.011	T63.012	T63.013	T63.014	—	—
specified NEC	T63.091	T63.092	T63.093	T63.094	—	—
taipan	T63.031	T63.032	T63.033	T63.034	—	—
specified NEC	T63.891	T63.892	T63.893	T63.894	—	—
spider	T63.301	T63.302	T63.303	T63.304	—	—
black widow	T63.311	T63.312	T63.313	T63.314	—	—
brown recluse	T63.331	T63.332	T63.333	T63.334	—	—
specified NEC	T63.391	T63.392	T63.393	T63.394	—	—
tarantula	T63.321	T63.322	T63.323	T63.324	—	—
sting ray	T63.511	T63.512	T63.513	T63.514	—	—
toad	T63.821	T63.822	T63.823	T63.824	—	—
wasp	T63.461	T63.462	T63.463	T63.464	—	—
Venous sclerosing drug NEC	T46.8X1	T46.8X2	T46.8X3	T46.8X4	T46.8X5	T46.8X6
Ventolin — see Albuterol						
Verapamil	T46.1X1	T46.1X2	T46.1X3	T46.1X4	T46.1X5	T46.1X6
Veramon	T42.3X1	T42.3X2	T42.3X3	T42.3X4	T42.3X5	T42.3X6
Veratrine	T46.5X1	T46.5X2	T46.5X3	T46.5X4	T46.5X5	T46.5X6
Veratrum						
album	T62.2X1	T62.2X2	T62.2X3	T62.2X4	—	—
alkaloids	T46.5X1	T46.5X2	T46.5X3	T46.5X4	T46.5X5	T46.5X6
viride	T62.2X1	T62.2X2	T62.2X3	T62.2X4	—	—
Verdigris	T60.3X1	T60.3X2	T60.3X3	T60.3X4	—	—
Veronal	T42.3X1	T42.3X2	T42.3X3	T42.3X4	T42.3X5	T42.3X6
Veroxil	T37.4X1	T37.4X2	T37.4X3	T37.4X4	T37.4X5	T37.4X6
Versenate	T50.6X1	T50.6X2	T50.6X3	T50.6X4	T50.6X5	T50.6X6

◀ New   ◀ Revised   ~~deleted~~ Deleted

	External Cause (T-Code)					
Substance	Poisoning, Accidental (Unintentional)	Poisoning, Intentional Self-Harm	Poisoning, Assault	Poisoning, Undetermined	Adverse Effect	Underdosing
Versidyne	T39.8X1	T39.8X2	T39.8X3	T39.8X4	T39.8X5	T39.8X6
Vetrabutine	T48.0X1	T48.0X2	T48.0X3	T48.0X4	T48.0X5	T48.0X6
Vidarabine	T37.5X1	T37.5X2	T37.5X3	T37.5X4	T37.5X5	T37.5X6
Vienna						
green	T57.0X1	T57.0X2	T57.0X3	T57.0X4	—	—
insecticide	T60.2X1	T60.2X2	T60.2X3	T60.2X4	—	—
red	T57.0X1	T57.0X2	T57.0X3	T57.0X4	—	—
pharmaceutical dye	T50.991	T50.992	T50.993	T50.994	T50.995	T50.996
Vigabatrin	T42.6X1	T42.6X2	T42.6X3	T42.6X4	T42.6X5	T42.6X6
Viloxazine	T43.291	T43.292	T43.293	T43.294	T43.295	T43.296
Viminol	T39.8X1	T39.8X2	T39.8X3	T39.8X4	T39.8X5	T39.8X6
Vinbarbital, vinbarbitone	T42.3X1	T42.3X2	T42.3X3	T42.3X4	T42.3X5	T42.3X6
Vinblastine	T45.1X1	T45.1X2	T45.1X3	T45.1X4	T45.1X5	T45.1X6
Vinburnine	T46.7X1	T46.7X2	T46.7X3	T46.7X4	T46.7X5	T46.7X6
Vincamine	T45.1X1	T45.1X2	T45.1X3	T45.1X4	T45.1X5	T45.1X6
Vincristine	T45.1X1	T45.1X2	T45.1X3	T45.1X4	T45.1X5	T45.1X6
Vindesine	T45.1X1	T45.1X2	T45.1X3	T45.1X4	T45.1X5	T45.1X6
Vinesthene, vinethene	T41.0X1	T41.0X2	T41.0X3	T41.0X4	T41.0X5	T41.0X6
Vinorelbine tartrate	T45.1X1	T45.1X2	T45.1X3	T45.1X4	T45.1X5	T45.1X6
Vinpocetine	T46.7X1	T46.7X2	T46.7X3	T46.7X4	T46.7X5	T46.7X6
Vinyl						
acetate	T65.891	T65.892	T65.893	T65.894	—	—
bital	T42.3X1	T42.3X2	T42.3X3	T42.3X4	T42.3X5	T42.3X6
bromide	T65.891	T65.892	T65.893	T65.894	—	—
chloride	T59.891	T59.892	T59.893	T59.894	—	—
ether	T41.0X1	T41.0X2	T41.0X3	T41.0X4	T41.0X5	T41.0X6
Vinylbital	T42.3X1	T42.3X2	T42.3X3	T42.3X4	T42.3X5	T42.3X6
Vinylidene chloride	T65.891	T65.892	T65.893	T65.894	—	—
Vioform	T37.8X1	T37.8X2	T37.8X3	T37.8X4	T37.8X5	T37.8X6
topical	T49.0X1	T49.0X2	T49.0X3	T49.0X4	T49.0X5	T49.0X6
Viomycin	T36.8X1	T36.8X2	T36.8X3	T36.8X4	T36.8X5	T36.8X6
Viosterol	T45.2X1	T45.2X2	T45.2X3	T45.2X4	T45.2X5	T45.2X6
Viper (venom)	T63.091	T63.092	T63.093	T63.094	—	—
Viprynium	T37.4X1	T37.4X2	T37.4X3	T37.4X4	T37.4X5	T37.4X6
Viquidil	T46.7X1	T46.7X2	T46.7X3	T46.7X4	T46.7X5	T46.7X6
Viral vaccine NEC	T50.B91	T50.B92	T50.B93	T50.B94	T50.B95	T50.B96
Virginiamycin	T36.8X1	T36.8X2	T36.8X3	T36.8X4	T36.8X5	T36.8X6
Virugon	T37.5X1	T37.5X2	T37.5X3	T37.5X4	T37.5X5	T37.5X6
Viscous agent	T50.901	T50.902	T50.903	T50.904	T50.905	T50.906
Visine	T49.5X1	T49.5X2	T49.5X3	T49.5X4	T49.5X5	T49.5X6
Visnadine	T46.3X1	T46.3X2	T46.3X3	T46.3X4	T46.3X5	T46.3X6

	External Cause (T-Code)					
Substance	Poisoning, Accidental (Unintentional)	Poisoning, Intentional Self-Harm	Poisoning, Assault	Poisoning, Undetermined	Adverse Effect	Underdosing
Vitamin NEC	T45.2X1	T45.2X2	T45.2X3	T45.2X4	T45.2X5	T45.2X6
A	T45.2X1	T45.2X2	T45.2X3	T45.2X4	T45.2X5	T45.2X6
B NEC	T45.2X1	T45.2X2	T45.2X3	T45.2X4	T45.2X5	T45.2X6
nicotinic acid	T46.7X1	T46.7X2	T46.7X3	T46.7X4	T46.7X5	T46.7X6
B1	T45.2X1	T45.2X2	T45.2X3	T45.2X4	T45.2X5	T45.2X6
B2	T45.2X1	T45.2X2	T45.2X3	T45.2X4	T45.2X5	T45.2X6
B6	T45.2X1	T45.2X2	T45.2X3	T45.2X4	T45.2X5	T45.2X6
B12	T45.2X1	T45.2X2	T45.2X3	T45.2X4	T45.2X5	T45.2X6
B15	T45.2X1	T45.2X2	T45.2X3	T45.2X4	T45.2X5	T45.2X6
C	T45.2X1	T45.2X2	T45.2X3	T45.2X4	T45.2X5	T45.2X6
D	T45.2X1	T45.2X2	T45.2X3	T45.2X4	T45.2X5	T45.2X6
D2	T45.2X1	T45.2X2	T45.2X3	T45.2X4	T45.2X5	T45.2X6
D3	T45.2X1	T45.2X2	T45.2X3	T45.2X4	T45.2X5	T45.2X6
E	T45.2X1	T45.2X2	T45.2X3	T45.2X4	T45.2X5	T45.2X6
E acetate	T45.2X1	T45.2X2	T45.2X3	T45.2X4	T45.2X5	T45.2X6
hematopoietic	T45.8X1	T45.8X2	T45.8X3	T45.8X4	T45.8X5	T45.8X6
K NEC	T45.7X1	T45.7X2	T45.7X3	T45.7X4	T45.7X5	T45.7X6
K1	T45.7X1	T45.7X2	T45.7X3	T45.7X4	T45.7X5	T45.7X6
K2	T45.7X1	T45.7X2	T45.7X3	T45.7X4	T45.7X5	T45.7X6
PP	T45.2X1	T45.2X2	T45.2X3	T45.2X4	T45.2X5	T45.2X6
ulceroprotectant	T47.1X1	T47.1X2	T47.1X3	T47.1X4	T47.1X5	T47.1X6
Vleminckx's solution	T49.4X1	T49.4X2	T49.4X3	T49.4X4	T49.4X5	T49.4X6
Voltaren — *see Diclofenac sodium*						
	W					
Warfarin	T45.511	T45.512	T45.513	T45.514	T45.515	T45.516
rodenticide	T60.4X1	T60.4X2	T60.4X3	T60.4X4	—	—
sodium	T45.511	T45.512	T45.513	T45.514	T45.515	T45.516
Wasp (sting)	T63.461	T63.462	T63.463	T63.464	—	—
Water						
balance drug	T50.3X1	T50.3X2	T50.3X3	T50.3X4	T50.3X5	T50.3X6
distilled	T50.3X1	T50.3X2	T50.3X3	T50.3X4	T50.3X5	T50.3X6
gas — *see Gas, water*						
incomplete combustion of — *see Carbon, monoxide, fuel, utility*						
hemlock	T62.2X1	T62.2X2	T62.2X3	T62.2X4	—	—
moccasin (venom)	T63.061	T63.062	T63.063	T63.064	—	—
purified	T50.3X1	T50.3X2	T50.3X3	T50.3X4	T50.3X5	T50.3X6
Wax (paraffin) (petroleum)	T52.0X1	T52.0X2	T52.0X3	T52.0X4	—	—
automobile	T65.891	T65.892	T65.893	T65.894	—	—
floor	T52.0X1	T52.0X2	T52.0X3	T52.0X4	—	—

◀ New ◀ Revised ~~deleted~~ Deleted

Substance	Poisoning, Accidental (Unintentional)	Poisoning, Intentional Self-Harm	Poisoning, Assault	Poisoning, Undetermined	Adverse Effect	Underdosing
Weed killers NEC	T60.3X1	T60.3X2	T60.3X3	T60.3X4	—	—
Welldorm	T42.6X1	T42.6X2	T42.6X3	T42.6X4	T42.6X5	T42.6X6
White						
arsenic	T57.0X1	T57.0X2	T57.0X3	T57.0X4	—	—
hellebore	T62.2X1	T62.2X2	T62.2X3	T62.2X4	—	—
lotion (keratolytic)	T49.4X1	T49.4X2	T49.4X3	T49.4X4	T49.4X5	T49.4X6
spirit	T52.0X1	T52.0X2	T52.0X3	T52.0X4	—	—
Whitewash	T65.891	T65.892	T65.893	T65.894	—	—
Whole blood (human)	T45.8X1	T45.8X2	T45.8X3	T45.8X4	T45.8X5	T45.8X6
Wild						
black cherry	T62.2X1	T62.2X2	T62.2X3	T62.2X4	—	—
poisonous plants NEC	T62.2X1	T62.2X2	T62.2X3	T62.2X4	—	—
Window cleaning fluid	T65.891	T65.892	T65.893	T65.894	—	—
Wintergreen (oil)	T49.3X1	T49.3X2	T49.3X3	T49.3X4	T49.3X5	T49.3X6
Wisterine	T62.2X1	T62.2X2	T62.2X3	T62.2X4	—	—
Witch hazel	T49.2X1	T49.2X2	T49.2X3	T49.2X4	T49.2X5	T49.2X6
Wood alcohol or spirit	T51.1X1	T51.1X2	T51.1X3	T51.1X4	—	—
Wool fat (hydrous)	T49.3X1	T49.3X2	T49.3X3	T49.3X4	T49.3X5	T49.3X6
Woorali	T48.1X1	T48.1X2	T48.1X3	T48.1X4	T48.1X5	T48.1X6
Wormseed, American	T37.4X1	T37.4X2	T37.4X3	T37.4X4	T37.4X5	T37.4X6

X

Substance	Poisoning, Accidental (Unintentional)	Poisoning, Intentional Self-Harm	Poisoning, Assault	Poisoning, Undetermined	Adverse Effect	Underdosing
Xamoterol	T44.5X1	T44.5X2	T44.5X3	T44.5X4	T44.5X5	T44.5X6
Xanthine diuretics	T50.2X1	T50.2X2	T50.2X3	T50.2X4	T50.2X5	T50.2X6
Xanthinol nicotinate	T46.7X1	T46.7X2	T46.7X3	T46.7X4	T46.7X5	T46.7X6
Xanthotoxin	T49.3X1	T49.3X2	T49.3X3	T49.3X4	T49.3X5	T49.3X6
Xantinol nicotinate	T46.7X1	T46.7X2	T46.7X3	T46.7X4	T46.7X5	T46.7X6
Xantocillin	T36.0X1	T36.0X2	T36.0X3	T36.0X4	T36.0X5	T36.0X6
Xenon (127Xe) (133Xe)	T50.8X1	T50.8X2	T50.8X3	T50.8X4	T50.8X5	T50.8X6
Xenysalate	T49.4X1	T49.4X2	T49.4X3	T49.4X4	T49.4X5	T49.4X6
Xibornol	T37.8X1	T37.8X2	T37.8X3	T37.8X4	T37.8X5	T37.8X6
Xigris	T45.511	T45.512	T45.513	T45.514	T45.515	T45.516
Xipamide	T50.2X1	T50.2X2	T50.2X3	T50.2X4	T50.2X5	T50.2X6
Xylene (vapor)	T52.2X1	T52.2X2	T52.2X3	T52.2X4	—	—
Xylocaine (infiltration) (topical)	T41.3X1	T41.3X2	T41.3X3	T41.3X4	T41.3X5	T41.3X6
nerve block (peripheral) (plexus)	T41.3X1	T41.3X2	T41.3X3	T41.3X4	T41.3X5	T41.3X6
spinal	T41.3X1	T41.3X2	T41.3X3	T41.3X4	T41.3X5	T41.3X6
Xylol (vapor)	T52.2X1	T52.2X2	T52.2X3	T52.2X4	—	—
Xylometazoline	T48.5X1	T48.5X2	T48.5X3	T48.5X4	T48.5X5	T48.5X6

Y

Substance	Poisoning, Accidental (Unintentional)	Poisoning, Intentional Self-Harm	Poisoning, Assault	Poisoning, Undetermined	Adverse Effect	Underdosing
Yeast	T45.2X1	T45.2X2	T45.2X3	T45.2X4	T45.2X5	T45.2X6
dried	T45.2X1	T45.2X2	T45.2X3	T45.2X4	T45.2X5	T45.2X6
Yellow						
fever vaccine	T50.B91	T50.B92	T50.B93	T50.B94	T50.B95	T50.B96
jasmine	T62.2X1	T62.2X2	T62.2X3	T62.2X4	—	—
phenolphthalein	T47.2X1	T47.2X2	T47.2X3	T47.2X4	T47.2X5	T47.2X6
Yew	T62.2X1	T62.2X2	T62.2X3	T62.2X4	—	—
Yohimbic acid	T40.991	T40.992	T40.993	T40.994	T40.995	T40.996

Z

Substance	Poisoning, Accidental (Unintentional)	Poisoning, Intentional Self-Harm	Poisoning, Assault	Poisoning, Undetermined	Adverse Effect	Underdosing
Zactane	T39.8X1	T39.8X2	T39.8X3	T39.8X4	T39.8X5	T39.8X6
Zalcitabine	T37.5X1	T37.5X2	T37.5X3	T37.5X4	T37.5X5	T37.5X6
Zaroxolyn	T50.2X1	T50.2X2	T50.2X3	T50.2X4	T50.2X5	T50.2X6
Zephiran (topical)	T49.0X1	T49.0X2	T49.0X3	T49.0X4	T49.0X5	T49.0X6
ophthalmic preparation	T49.5X1	T49.5X2	T49.5X3	T49.5X4	T49.5X5	T49.5X6
Zeranol	T38.7X1	T38.7X2	T38.7X3	T38.7X4	T38.7X5	T38.7X6
Zerone	T51.1X1	T51.1X2	T51.1X3	T51.1X4	—	—
Zidovudine	T37.5X1	T37.5X2	T37.5X3	T37.5X4	T37.5X5	T37.5X6
Zimeldine	T43.221	T43.222	T43.223	T43.224	T43.225	T43.226
Zinc (compounds) (fumes) (vapor) NEC	T56.5X1	T56.5X2	T56.5X3	T56.5X4	—	—
anti-infectives	T49.0X1	T49.0X2	T49.0X3	T49.0X4	T49.0X5	T49.0X6
antivaricose	T46.8X1	T46.8X2	T46.8X3	T46.8X4	T46.8X5	T46.8X6
bacitracin	T49.0X1	T49.0X2	T49.0X3	T49.0X4	T49.0X5	T49.0X6
chloride (mouthwash)	T49.6X1	T49.6X2	T49.6X3	T49.6X4	T49.6X5	T49.6X6
chromate	T56.5X1	T56.5X2	T56.5X3	T56.5X4	—	—
gelatin	T49.3X1	T49.3X2	T49.3X3	T49.3X4	T49.3X5	T49.3X6
oxide	T49.3X1	T49.3X2	T49.3X3	T49.3X4	T49.3X5	T49.3X6
plaster	T49.3X1	T49.3X2	T49.3X3	T49.3X4	T49.3X5	T49.3X6
peroxide	T49.0X1	T49.0X2	T49.0X3	T49.0X4	T49.0X5	T49.0X6
pesticides	T56.5X1	T56.5X2	T56.5X3	T56.5X4	—	—
phosphide	T60.4X1	T60.4X2	T60.4X3	T60.4X4	—	—
pyrithionate	T49.4X1	T49.4X2	T49.4X3	T49.4X4	T49.4X5	T49.4X6
stearate	T49.3X1	T49.3X2	T49.3X3	T49.3X4	T49.3X5	T49.3X6
sulfate	T49.5X1	T49.5X2	T49.5X3	T49.5X4	T49.5X5	T49.5X6
ENT agent	T49.6X1	T49.6X2	T49.6X3	T49.6X4	T49.6X5	T49.6X6
ophthalmic solution	T49.5X1	T49.5X2	T49.5X3	T49.5X4	T49.5X5	T49.5X6
topical NEC	T49.0X1	T49.0X2	T49.0X3	T49.0X4	T49.0X5	T49.0X6
undecylenate	T49.0X1	T49.0X2	T49.0X3	T49.0X4	T49.0X5	T49.0X6

◀ New   ◀ Revised   ~~deleted~~ Deleted

Substance	Poisoning, Accidental (Unintentional)	Poisoning, Intentional Self-Harm	Poisoning, Assault	Poisoning, Undetermined	Adverse Effect	Underdosing
Zineb	T60.0X1	T60.0X2	T60.0X3	T60.0X4	—	—
Zinostatin	T45.1X1	T45.1X2	T45.1X3	T45.1X4	T45.1X5	T45.1X6
Zipeprol	T48.3X1	T48.3X2	T48.3X3	T48.3X4	T48.3X5	T48.3X6
Zofenopril	T46.4X1	T46.4X2	T46.4X3	T46.4X4	T46.4X5	T46.4X6
Zolpidem	T42.6X1	T42.6X2	T42.6X3	T42.6X4	T42.6X5	T42.6X6
Zomepirac	T39.391	T39.392	T39.393	T39.394	T39.395	T39.396
Zopiclone	T42.6X1	T42.6X2	T42.6X3	T42.6X4	T42.6X5	T42.6X6

Substance	Poisoning, Accidental (Unintentional)	Poisoning, Intentional Self-Harm	Poisoning, Assault	Poisoning, Undetermined	Adverse Effect	Underdosing
Zorubicin	T45.1X1	T45.1X2	T45.1X3	T45.1X4	T45.1X5	T45.1X6
Zotepine	T43.591	T43.592	T43.593	T43.594	T43.595	T43.596
Zovant	T45.511	T45.512	T45.513	T45.514	T45.515	T45.516
Zoxazolamine	T42.8X1	T42.8X2	T42.8X3	T42.8X4	T42.8X5	T42.8X6
Zuclopenthixol	T43.4X1	T43.4X2	T43.4X3	T43.4X4	T43.4X5	T43.4X6
Zygadenus (venenosus)	T62.2X1	T62.2X2	T62.2X3	T62.2X4	—	—
Zyprexa	T43.591	T43.592	T43.593	T43.594	T43.595	T43.596

◀ New ◀ Revised ~~deleted~~ Deleted

External Cause of Injuries Index

A

Abandonment (causing exposure to weather conditions) (with intent to injure or kill) NEC X58

Abuse (adult) (child) (mental) (physical) (sexual) X58

Accident (to) X58
  aircraft (in transit) (powered) —see also Accident, transport, aircraft
    due to, caused by cataclysm —see Forces of nature, by type
  animal-drawn vehicle —see Accident, transport, animal-drawn vehicle occupant
  animal-rider —see Accident, transport, animal-rider
  automobile —see Accident, transport, car occupant
  bare foot water skiier V94.4
  boat, boating —see also Accident, watercraft
    striking swimmer
      powered V94.11
      unpowered V94.12
  bus —see Accident, transport, bus occupant
  cable car, not on rails V98.0
    on rails —see Accident, transport, streetcar occupant
  car —see Accident, transport, car occupant
  caused by, due to
    animal NEC W64
    chain hoist W24.0
    cold (excessive) —see Exposure, cold
    corrosive liquid, substance —see Table of Drugs and Chemicals
    cutting or piercing instrument —see Contact, with, by type of instrument
    drive belt W24.0
    electric
      current —see Exposure, electric current
      motor —see also Contact, with, by type of machine W31.3
      current (of) W86.8
    environmental factor NEC X58
    explosive material —see Explosion
    fire, flames —see Exposure, fire
    firearm missile —see Discharge, firearm by type
    heat (excessive) —see Heat
    hot —see Contact, with, hot
    ignition —see Ignition
    lifting device W24.0
    lightning —see subcategory T75.0
      causing fire —see Exposure, fire
    machine, machinery —see Contact, with, by type of machine
    natural factor NEC X58
    pulley (block) W24.0
    radiation —see Radiation
    steam X13.1
      inhalation X13.0
      pipe X16
    thunderbolt —see subcategory T75.0
      causing fire —see Exposure, fire
    transmission device W24.1
  coach —see Accident, transport, bus occupant
  coal car —see Accident, transport, industrial vehicle occupant
  diving —see also Fall, into, water
    with
      drowning or submersion —see Drowning
  forklift —see Accident, transport, industrial vehicle occupant
  heavy transport vehicle NOS —see Accident, transport, truck occupant
  ice yacht V98.2

Accident (Continued)
  in
    medical, surgical procedure
      as, or due to misadventure —see Misadventure
      causing an abnormal reaction or later complication without mention of misadventure —see also Complication of or following, by type of procedure Y84.9
  land yacht V98.1
  late effect of —see W00-X58 with 7th character S
  logging car —see Accident, transport, industrial vehicle occupant
  machine, machinery —see also Contact, with, by type of machine
    on board watercraft V93.69
      explosion —see Explosion, in, watercraft
      fire —see Burn, on board watercraft
      powered craft V93.63
        ferry boat V93.61
        fishing boat V93.62
        jet ski V93.63
        liner V93.61
        merchant ship V93.60
        passenger ship V93.61
        sailboat V93.64
  mine tram —see Accident, transport, industrial vehicle occupant
  mobility scooter (motorized) —see Accident, transport, pedestrian, conveyance, specified type NEC
  motor scooter —see Accident, transport, motorcyclist
  motor vehicle NOS (traffic) —see also Accident, transport V89.2
    nontraffic V89.0
    three-wheeled NOS —see Accident, transport, three-wheeled motor vehicle occupant
  motorcycle NOS —see Accident, transport, motorcyclist
  nonmotor vehicle NOS (nontraffic) —see also Accident, transport V89.1
    traffic NOS V89.3
  nontraffic (victim's mode of transport NOS) V88.9
    collision (between) V88.7
      bus and truck V88.5
      car and:
        bus V88.3
        pickup V88.2
        three-wheeled motor vehicle V88.0
        train V88.6
        truck V88.4
        two-wheeled motor vehicle V88.0
        van V88.2
      specified vehicle NEC and:
        three-wheeled motor vehicle V88.1
        two-wheeled motor vehicle V88.1
    known mode of transport —see Accident, transport, by type of vehicle
    noncollision V88.8
  on board watercraft V93.89
    powered craft V93.83
      ferry boat V93.81
      fishing boat V93.82
      jet ski V93.83
      liner V93.81
      merchant ship V93.80
      passenger ship V93.81
    unpowered craft V93.88
      canoe V93.85
      inflatable V93.86
        in tow
          recreational V94.31
          specified NEC V94.32
      kayak V93.85

Accident (Continued)
  on board watercraft (Continued)
    unpowered craft (Continued)
      sailboat V93.84
      surf-board V93.88
      water skis V93.87
      windsurfer V93.88
  parachutist V97.29
    entangled in object V97.21
    injured on landing V97.22
  pedal cycle —see Accident, transport, pedal cyclist
  pedestrian (on foot)
    with
      another pedestrian W51
        with fall W03
          due to ice or snow W00.0
        on pedestrian conveyance NEC V00.09
      roller skater (in-line) V00.01
      skate boarder V00.02
      transport vehicle —see Accident, transport
    on pedestrian conveyance —see Accident, transport, pedestrian, conveyance
  pick-up truck or van —see Accident, transport, pickup truck occupant
  quarry truck —see Accident, transport, industrial vehicle occupant
  railway vehicle (any) (in motion) —see Accident, transport, railway vehicle occupant
    due to cataclysm —see Forces of nature, by type
  scooter (non-motorized) —see Accident, transport, pedestrian, conveyance, scooter
  sequelae of —see W00-X58 with 7th character S
  skateboard —see Accident, transport, pedestrian, conveyance, skateboard
  ski (ing) —see Accident, transport, pedestrian, conveyance
    lift V98.3
  specified cause NEC X58
  streetcar —see Accident, transport, streetcar occupant
  traffic (victim's mode of transport NOS) V87.9
    collision (between) V87.7
      bus and truck V87.5
      car and:
        bus V87.3
        pickup V87.2
        three-wheeled motor vehicle V87.0
        train V87.6
        truck V87.4
        two-wheeled motor vehicle V87.0
        van V87.2
      specified vehicle NEC and:
        three-wheeled motor vehicle V87.1
        two-wheeled motor vehicle V87.1
    known mode of transport —see Accident, transport, by type of vehicle
    noncollision V87.8
  transport (involving injury to) V99
    18 wheeler —see Accident, transport, truck occupant
    agricultural vehicle occupant (nontraffic) V84.9
      driver V84.5
      hanger-on V84.7
      passenger V84.6
      traffic V84.3
        driver V84.0
        hanger-on V84.2
        passenger V84.1
      while boarding or alighting V84.4

► New   ⇒ Revised   ~~deleted~~ Deleted   ● Use Additional Character(s)

Accident *(Continued)*
transport *(Continued)*
aircraft NEC V97.89
military NEC V97.818
with civilian aircraft V97.810
civilian injured by V97.811
occupant injured (in)
nonpowered craft accident
V96.9
balloon V96.00
collision V96.03
crash V96.01
explosion V96.05
fire V96.04
forced landing V96.02
specified type NEC V96.09
glider V96.20
collision V96.23
crash V96.21
explosion V96.25
fire V96.24
forced landing V96.22
specified type NEC V96.29
hang glider V96.10
collision V96.13
crash V96.11
explosion V96.15
fire V96.14
forced landing V96.12
specified type NEC V96.19
specified craft NEC V96.8
powered craft accident V95.9
fixed wing NEC
commercial V95.30
collision V95.33
crash V95.31
explosion V95.35
fire V95.34
forced landing V95.32
specified type NEC
V95.39
private V95.20
collision V95.23
crash V95.21
explosion V95.25
fire V95.24
forced landing V95.22
specified type NEC
V95.29
glider V95.10
collision V95.13
crash V95.11
explosion V95.15
fire V95.14
forced landing V95.12
specified type NEC V95.19
helicopter V95.00
collision V95.03
crash V95.01
explosion V95.05
fire V95.04
forced landing V95.02
specified type NEC V95.09
spacecraft V95.40
collision V95.43
crash V95.41
explosion V95.45
fire V95.44
forced landing V95.42
specified type NEC V95.49
specified craft NEC V95.8
ultralight V95.10
collision V95.13
crash V95.11
explosion V95.15
fire V95.14
forced landing V95.12
specified type NEC V95.19
specified accident NEC V97.0
while boarding or alighting
V97.1

Accident *(Continued)*
transport *(Continued)*
aircraft NEC *(Continued)*
person (injured by)
falling from, in or on aircraft V97.0
machinery on aircraft V97.89
on ground with aircraft involvement
V97.39
rotating propeller V97.32
struck by object falling from aircraft
V97.31
sucked into aircraft jet V97.33
while boarding or alighting aircraft
V97.1
airport (battery-powered) passenger
vehicle —*see* Accident, transport,
industrial vehicle occupant
all-terrain vehicle occupant (nontraffic)
V86.95
driver V86.55
dune buggy —*see* Accident, transport,
dune buggy occupant
hanger-on V86.75
passenger V86.65
snowmobile —*see* Accident, transport,
snowmobile occupant
specified type NEC V86.99
traffic V86.35
driver V86.05
hanger-on V86.25
passenger V86.15
while boarding or alighting V86.45
ambulance occupant (traffic) V86.31
driver V86.01
hanger-on V86.21
nontraffic V86.91
driver V86.51
hanger-on V86.71
passenger V86.61
passenger V86.11
while boarding or alighting V86.41
animal-drawn vehicle occupant (in)
V80.929
collision (with)
animal V80.12
being ridden V80.711
animal-drawn vehicle V80.721
bus V80.42
car V80.42
fixed or stationary object V80.82
military vehicle V80.920
nonmotor vehicle V80.791
pedal cycle V80.22
pedestrian V80.12
pickup V80.42
railway train or vehicle V80.62
specified motor vehicle NEC V80.52
streetcar V80.731
truck V80.42
two-or three-wheeled motor vehicle
V80.32
van V80.42
noncollision V80.02
specified circumstance NEC V80.928
animal-rider V80.919
collision (with)
animal V80.11
being ridden V80.710
animal-drawn vehicle V80.720
bus V80.41
car V80.41
fixed or stationary object V80.81
military vehicle V80.910
nonmotor vehicle V80.790
pedal cycle V80.21
pedestrian V80.11
pickup V80.41
railway train or vehicle V80.61
specified motor vehicle NEC V80.51
streetcar V80.730
truck V80.41

Accident *(Continued)*
transport *(Continued)*
animal-rider *(Continued)*
collision *(Continued)*
two- or three-wheeled motor vehicle
V80.31
van V80.41
noncollision V80.018
specified as horse rider V80.010
specified circumstance NEC V80.918
armored car —*see* Accident, transport,
truck occupant
battery-powered truck (baggage) (mail) —
see Accident, transport, industrial
vehicle occupant
bus occupant V79.9
collision (with)
animal (traffic) V70.9
being ridden (traffic) V76.9
nontraffic V76.3
while boarding or alighting V76.4
nontraffic V70.3
while boarding or alighting V70.4
animal-drawn vehicle (traffic) V76.9
nontraffic V76.3
while boarding or alighting V76.4
bus (traffic) V74.9
nontraffic V74.3
while boarding or alighting V74.4
car (traffic) V73.9
nontraffic V73.3
while boarding or alighting V73.4
motor vehicle NOS (traffic) V79.60
nontraffic V79.20
specified type NEC (traffic) V79.69
nontraffic V79.29
pedal cycle (traffic) V71.9
nontraffic V71.3
while boarding or alighting V71.4
pickup truck (traffic) V73.9
nontraffic V73.3
while boarding or alighting V73.4
railway vehicle (traffic) V75.9
nontraffic V75.3
while boarding or alighting V75.4
specified vehicle NEC (traffic) V76.9
nontraffic V76.3
while boarding or alighting V76.4
stationary object (traffic) V77.9
nontraffic V77.3
while boarding or alighting V77.4
streetcar (traffic) V76.9
nontraffic V76.3
while boarding or alighting V76.4
three wheeled motor vehicle (traffic)
V72.9
nontraffic V72.3
while boarding or alighting V72.4
truck (traffic) V74.9
nontraffic V74.3
while boarding or alighting V74.4
two wheeled motor vehicle (traffic)
V72.9
nontraffic V72.3
while boarding or alighting V72.4
van (traffic) V73.9
nontraffic V73.3
while boarding or alighting V73.4
driver
collision (with)
animal (traffic) V70.5
being ridden (traffic) V76.5
nontraffic V76.0
nontraffic V70.0
animal-drawn vehicle (traffic)
V76.5
nontraffic V76.0
bus (traffic) V74.5
nontraffic V74.0
car (traffic) V73.5
nontraffic V73.0

Accident (Continued)
  transport (Continued)
    bus occupant (Continued)
      driver (Continued)
        collision (Continued)
          motor vehicle NOS (traffic) V79.40
            nontraffic V79.00
            specified type NEC (traffic)
              V79.49
              nontraffic V79.09
          pedal cycle (traffic) V71.5
            nontraffic V71.0
          pickup truck (traffic) V73.5
            nontraffic V73.0
          railway vehicle (traffic) V75.5
            nontraffic V75.0
          specified vehicle NEC (traffic)
            V76.5
            nontraffic V76.0
          stationary object (traffic) V77.5
            nontraffic V77.0
          streetcar (traffic) V76.5
            nontraffic V76.0
          three wheeled motor vehicle
            (traffic) V72.5
            nontraffic V72.0
          truck (traffic) V74.5
            nontraffic V74.0
          two wheeled motor vehicle (traffic)
            V72.5
            nontraffic V72.0
          van (traffic) V73.5
            nontraffic V73.0
        noncollision accident (traffic) V78.5
          nontraffic V78.0
      hanger-on
        collision (with)
          animal (traffic) V70.7
            being ridden (traffic) V76.7
              nontraffic V76.2
            nontraffic V70.2
          animal-drawn vehicle (traffic) V76.7
            nontraffic V76.2
          bus (traffic) V74.7
            nontraffic V74.2
          car (traffic) V73.7
            nontraffic V73.2
          pedal cycle (traffic) V71.7
            nontraffic V71.2
          pickup truck (traffic) V73.7
            nontraffic V73.2
          railway vehicle (traffic) V75.7
            nontraffic V75.2
          specified vehicle NEC (traffic) V76.7
            nontraffic V76.2
          stationary object (traffic) V77.7
            nontraffic V77.2
          streetcar (traffic) V76.7
            nontraffic V76.2
          three wheeled motor vehicle
            (traffic) V72.7
            nontraffic V72.2
          truck (traffic) V74.7
            nontraffic V74.2
          two wheeled motor vehicle (traffic)
            V72.7
            nontraffic V72.2
          van (traffic) V73.7
            nontraffic V73.2
        noncollision accident (traffic) V78.7
          nontraffic V78.2
      noncollision accident (traffic) V78.9
        nontraffic V78.3
        while boarding or alighting V78.4
      nontraffic V79.3
      passenger
        collision (with)
          animal (traffic) V70.6
            being ridden (traffic) V76.6
              nontraffic V76.1
            nontraffic V70.1

Accident (Continued)
  transport (Continued)
    bus occupant (Continued)
      passenger (Continued)
        collision (Continued)
          animal-drawn vehicle (traffic) V76.6
            nontraffic V76.1
          bus (traffic) V74.6
            nontraffic V74.1
          car (traffic) V73.6
            nontraffic V73.1
          motor vehicle NOS (traffic) V79.50
            nontraffic V79.10
            specified type NEC (traffic)
              V79.59
              nontraffic V79.19
          pedal cycle (traffic) V71.6
            nontraffic V71.1
          pickup truck (traffic) V73.6
            nontraffic V73.1
          railway vehicle (traffic) V75.6
            nontraffic V75.1
          specified vehicle NEC (traffic) V76.6
            nontraffic V76.1
          stationary object (traffic) V77.6
            nontraffic V77.1
          streetcar (traffic) V76.6
            nontraffic V76.1
          three wheeled motor vehicle
            (traffic) V72.6
            nontraffic V72.1
          truck (traffic) V74.6
            nontraffic V74.1
          two wheeled motor vehicle (traffic)
            V72.6
            nontraffic V72.1
          van (traffic) V73.6
            nontraffic V73.1
        noncollision accident (traffic) V78.6
          nontraffic V78.1
      specified type NEC V79.88
      military vehicle V79.81
    cable car, not on rails V98.0
      on rails —see Accident, transport,
        streetcar occupant
    car occupant V49.9
      ambulance occupant —see Accident,
        transport, ambulance occupant
      collision (with)
        animal (traffic) V40.9
          being ridden (traffic) V46.9
            nontraffic V46.3
            while boarding or alighting
              V46.4
          nontraffic V40.3
          while boarding or alighting V40.4
        animal-drawn vehicle (traffic) V46.9
          nontraffic V46.3
          while boarding or alighting V46.4
        bus (traffic) V44.9
          nontraffic V44.3
          while boarding or alighting V44.4
        car (traffic) V43.92
          nontraffic V43.32
          while boarding or alighting V43.42
        motor vehicle NOS (traffic) V49.60
          nontraffic V49.20
          specified type NEC (traffic) V49.69
            nontraffic V49.29
        pedal cycle (traffic) V41.9
          nontraffic V41.3
          while boarding or alighting V41.4
        pickup truck (traffic) V43.93
          nontraffic V43.33
          while boarding or alighting V43.43
        railway vehicle (traffic) V45.9
          nontraffic V45.3
          while boarding or alighting V45.4
        specified vehicle NEC (traffic) V46.9
          nontraffic V46.3
          while boarding or alighting V46.4

Accident (Continued)
  transport (Continued)
    car occupant (Continued)
      collision (Continued)
        sport utility vehicle (traffic) V43.91
          nontraffic V43.31
          while boarding or alighting V43.41
        stationary object (traffic) V47.9
          nontraffic V47.3
          while boarding or alighting V47.4
        streetcar (traffic) V46.9
          nontraffic V46.3
          while boarding or alighting V46.4
        three wheeled motor vehicle (traffic)
          V42.9
          nontraffic V42.3
          while boarding or alighting V42.4
        truck (traffic) V44.9
          nontraffic V44.3
          while boarding or alighting V44.4
        two wheeled motor vehicle (traffic)
          V42.9
          nontraffic V42.3
          while boarding or alighting V42.4
        van (traffic) V43.94
          nontraffic V43.34
          while boarding or alighting V43.44
    driver
      collision (with)
        animal (traffic) V40.5
          being ridden (traffic) V46.5
            nontraffic V46.0
          nontraffic V40.0
        animal-drawn vehicle (traffic) V46.5
          nontraffic V46.0
        bus (traffic) V44.5
          nontraffic V44.0
        car (traffic) V43.52
          nontraffic V43.02
        motor vehicle NOS (traffic) V49.40
          nontraffic V49.00
          specified type NEC (traffic)
            V49.49
            nontraffic V49.09
        pedal cycle (traffic) V41.5
          nontraffic V41.0
        pickup truck (traffic) V43.53
          nontraffic V43.03
        railway vehicle (traffic) V45.5
          nontraffic V45.0
        specified vehicle NEC (traffic) V46.5
          nontraffic V46.0
        sport utility vehicle (traffic) V43.51
          nontraffic V43.01
        stationary object (traffic) V47.5
          nontraffic V47.0
        streetcar (traffic) V46.5
          nontraffic V46.0
        three wheeled motor vehicle
          (traffic) V42.5
          nontraffic V42.0
        truck (traffic) V44.5
          nontraffic V44.0
        two wheeled motor vehicle (traffic)
          V42.5
          nontraffic V42.0
        van (traffic) V43.54
          nontraffic V43.04
      noncollision accident (traffic) V48.5
        nontraffic V48.0
    hanger-on
      collision (with)
        animal (traffic) V40.7
          being ridden (traffic) V46.7
            nontraffic V46.2
          nontraffic V40.2
        animal-drawn vehicle (traffic)
          V46.7
          nontraffic V46.2
        bus (traffic) V44.7
          nontraffic V44.2

▶ New   ⇒ Revised   ~~deleted~~ Deleted   ● Use Additional Character(s)

Accident (Continued)
  transport (Continued)
    car occupant (Continued)
      hanger-on (Continued)
        collision (Continued)
          car (traffic) V43.72
            nontraffic V43.22
          pedal cycle (traffic) V41.7
            nontraffic V41.2
          pickup truck (traffic) V43.73
            nontraffic V43.23
          railway vehicle (traffic) V45.7
            nontraffic V45.2
          specified vehicle NEC (traffic) V46.7
            nontraffic V46.2
          sport utility vehicle (traffic) V43.71
            nontraffic V43.21
          stationary object (traffic) V47.7
            nontraffic V47.2
          streetcar (traffic) V46.7
            nontraffic V46.2
          three wheeled motor vehicle (traffic) V42.7
            nontraffic V42.2
          truck (traffic) V44.7
            nontraffic V44.2
          two wheeled motor vehicle (traffic) V42.7
            nontraffic V42.2
          van (traffic) V43.74
            nontraffic V43.24
        noncollision accident (traffic) V48.7
          nontraffic V48.2
      noncollision accident (traffic) V48.9
        nontraffic V48.3
      while boarding or alighting V48.4
      nontraffic V49.3
      passenger
        collision (with)
          animal (traffic) V40.6
            being ridden (traffic) V46.6
              nontraffic V46.1
            nontraffic V40.1
          animal-drawn vehicle (traffic) V46.6
            nontraffic V46.1
          bus (traffic) V44.6
            nontraffic V44.1
          car (traffic) V43.62
            nontraffic V43.12
          motor vehicle NOS (traffic) V49.50
            nontraffic V49.10
            specified type NEC (traffic) V49.59
              nontraffic V49.19
          pedal cycle (traffic) V41.6
            nontraffic V41.1
          pickup truck (traffic) V43.63
            nontraffic V43.13
          railway vehicle (traffic) V45.6
            nontraffic V45.1
          specified vehicle NEC (traffic) V46.6
            nontraffic V46.1
          sport utility vehicle (traffic) V43.61
            nontraffic V43.11
          stationary object (traffic) V47.6
            nontraffic V47.1
          streetcar (traffic) V46.6
            nontraffic V46.1
          three wheeled motor vehicle (traffic) V42.6
            nontraffic V42.1
          truck (traffic) V44.6
            nontraffic V44.1
          two wheeled motor vehicle (traffic) V42.6
            nontraffic V42.1
          van (traffic) V43.64
            nontraffic V43.14
        noncollision accident (traffic) V48.6
          nontraffic V48.1
      specified type NEC V49.88
      military vehicle V49.81

Accident (Continued)
  transport (Continued)
    coal car —see Accident, transport, industrial vehicle occupant
    construction vehicle occupant (nontraffic) V85.9
      driver V85.5
      hanger-on V85.7
      passenger V85.6
      traffic V85.3
        driver V85.0
        hanger-on V85.2
        passenger V85.1
      while boarding or alighting V85.4
    dirt bike rider (nontraffic) V86.96
      driver V86.56
      hanger-on V86.76
      passenger V86.66
      traffic V86.36
        driver V86.06
        hanger-on V86.26
        passenger V86.16
      while boarding or alighting V86.46
    due to cataclysm —see Forces of nature, by type
    dune buggy occupant (nontraffic) V86.93
      driver V86.53
      hanger-on V86.73
      passenger V86.63
      traffic V86.33
        driver V86.03
        hanger-on V86.23
        passenger V86.13
      while boarding or alighting V86.43
    forklift —see Accident, transport, industrial vehicle occupant
    go cart —see Accident, transport, all-terrain vehicle occupant
    golf cart —see Accident, transport, all-terrain vehicle occupant
    heavy transport vehicle occupant — see Accident, transport, truck occupant
    ice yacht V98.2
    industrial vehicle occupant (nontraffic) V83.9
      driver V83.5
      hanger-on V83.7
      passenger V83.6
      traffic V83.3
        driver V83.0
        hanger-on V83.2
        passenger V83.1
      while boarding or alighting V83.4
    interurban electric car —see Accident, transport, streetcar
    land yacht V98.1
    logging car —see Accident, transport, industrial vehicle occupant
    military vehicle occupant (traffic) V86.34
      driver V86.04
      hanger-on V86.24
      nontraffic V86.94
        driver V86.54
        hanger-on V86.74
        passenger V86.64
      passenger V86.14
      while boarding or alighting V86.44
    mine tram —see Accident, transport, industrial vehicle occupant
    motor vehicle NEC occupant (traffic) V89.2
    motorcoach —see Accident, transport, bus occupant
    motor/cross bike rider —see also Accident, transport, dirt bike rider V86.96
    motorcyclist V29.9
      collision (with)
        animal (traffic) V20.9
          being ridden (traffic) V26.9
            nontraffic V26.2
            while boarding or alighting V26.3
          nontraffic V20.2
          while boarding or alighting V20.3

Accident (Continued)
  transport (Continued)
    motorcyclist (Continued)
      collision (Continued)
        animal-drawn vehicle (traffic) V26.9
          nontraffic V26.2
          while boarding or alighting V26.3
        bus (traffic) V24.9
          nontraffic V24.2
          while boarding or alighting V24.3
        car (traffic) V23.9
          nontraffic V23.2
          while boarding or alighting V23.3
        motor vehicle NOS (traffic) V29.60
          nontraffic V29.20
          specified type NEC (traffic) V29.69
            nontraffic V29.29
        pedal cycle (traffic) V21.9
          nontraffic V21.2
          while boarding or alighting V21.3
        pickup truck (traffic) V23.9
          nontraffic V23.2
          while boarding or alighting V23.3
        railway vehicle (traffic) V25.9
          nontraffic V25.2
          while boarding or alighting V25.3
        specified vehicle NEC (traffic) V26.9
          nontraffic V26.2
          while boarding or alighting V26.3
        stationary object (traffic) V27.9
          nontraffic V27.2
          while boarding or alighting V27.3
        streetcar (traffic) V26.9
          nontraffic V26.2
          while boarding or alighting V26.3
        three wheeled motor vehicle (traffic) V22.9
          nontraffic V22.2
          while boarding or alighting V22.3
        truck (traffic) V24.9
          nontraffic V24.2
          while boarding or alighting V24.3
        two wheeled motor vehicle (traffic) V22.9
          nontraffic V22.2
          while boarding or alighting V22.3
        van (traffic) V23.9
          nontraffic V23.2
          while boarding or alighting V23.3
      driver
        collision (with)
          animal (traffic) V20.4
            being ridden (traffic) V26.4
              nontraffic V26.0
            nontraffic V20.0
          animal-drawn vehicle (traffic) V26.4
            nontraffic V26.0
          bus (traffic) V24.4
            nontraffic V24.0
          car (traffic) V23.4
            nontraffic V23.0
          motor vehicle NOS (traffic) V29.40
            nontraffic V29.00
            specified type NEC (traffic) V29.49
              nontraffic V29.09
          pedal cycle (traffic) V21.4
            nontraffic V21.0
          pickup truck (traffic) V23.4
            nontraffic V23.0
          railway vehicle (traffic) V25.4
            nontraffic V25.0
          specified vehicle NEC (traffic) V26.4
            nontraffic V26.0
          stationary object (traffic) V27.4
            nontraffic V27.0
          streetcar (traffic) V26.4
            nontraffic V26.0
          three wheeled motor vehicle (traffic) V22.4
            nontraffic V22.0

Accident *(Continued)*
  transport *(Continued)*
    motorcyclist *(Continued)*
      driver *(Continued)*
        collision *(Continued)*
          truck (traffic) V24.4
            nontraffic V24.0
          two wheeled motor vehicle (traffic) V22.4
            nontraffic V22.0
          van (traffic) V23.4
            nontraffic V23.0
        noncollision accident (traffic) V28.4
          nontraffic V28.0
      noncollision accident (traffic) V28.9
        nontraffic V28.2
        while boarding or alighting V28.3
      nontraffic V29.3
      passenger
        collision (with)
          animal (traffic) V20.5
            being ridden (traffic) V26.5
              nontraffic V26.1
            nontraffic V20.1
          animal-drawn vehicle (traffic) V26.5
            nontraffic V26.1
          bus (traffic) V24.5
            nontraffic V24.1
          car (traffic) V23.5
            nontraffic V23.1
          motor vehicle NOS (traffic) V29.50
            nontraffic V29.10
            specified type NEC (traffic) V29.59
              nontraffic V29.19
          pedal cycle (traffic) V21.5
            nontraffic V21.1
          pickup truck (traffic) V23.5
            nontraffic V23.1
          railway vehicle (traffic) V25.5
            nontraffic V25.1
          specified vehicle NEC (traffic) V26.5
            nontraffic V26.1
          stationary object (traffic) V27.5
            nontraffic V27.1
          streetcar (traffic) V26.5
            nontraffic V26.1
          three wheeled motor vehicle (traffic) V22.5
            nontraffic V22.1
          truck (traffic) V24.5
            nontraffic V24.1
          two wheeled motor vehicle (traffic) V22.5
            nontraffic V22.1
          van (traffic) V23.5
            nontraffic V23.1
        noncollision accident (traffic) V28.5
          nontraffic V28.1
      specified type NEC V29.88
      military vehicle V29.81
    occupant (of)
      aircraft (powered) V95.9
        fixed wing
          commercial —*see* Accident, transport, aircraft, occupant, powered, fixed wing, commercial
          private —*see* Accident, transport, aircraft, occupant, powered, fixed wing, private
        nonpowered V96.9
        specified NEC V95.8
      airport battery-powered vehicle —*see* Accident, transport, industrial vehicle occupant
      all-terrain vehicle (ATV) —*see* Accident, transport, all-terrain vehicle occupant
      animal-drawn vehicle —*see* Accident, transport, animal-drawn vehicle occupant

Accident *(Continued)*
  transport *(Continued)*
    occupant *(Continued)*
      automobile —*see* Accident, transport, car occupant
      balloon V96.00
      battery-powered vehicle —*see* Accident, transport, industrial vehicle occupant
      bicycle —*see* Accident, transport, pedal cyclist
        motorized —*see* Accident, transport, motorcycle rider
      boat NEC —*see* Accident, watercraft
      bulldozer —*see* Accident, transport, construction vehicle occupant
      bus —*see* Accident, transport, bus occupant
      cable car (on rails) —*see also* Accident, transport, streetcar occupant
        not on rails V98.0
      car —*see also* Accident, transport, car occupant
        cable (on rails) —*see also* Accident, transport, streetcar occupant
          not on rails V98.0
      coach —*see* Accident, transport, bus occupant
      coal-car —*see* Accident, transport, industrial vehicle occupant
      digger —*see* Accident, transport, construction vehicle occupant
      dump truck —*see* Accident, transport, construction vehicle occupant
      earth-leveler —*see* Accident, transport, construction vehicle occupant
      farm machinery (self-propelled) —*see* Accident, transport, agricultural vehicle occupant
      forklift —*see* Accident, transport, industrial vehicle occupant
      glider (unpowered) V96.20
        hang V96.10
        powered (microlight) (ultralight) —*see* Accident, transport, aircraft, occupant, powered, glider
      glider (unpowered) NEC V96.20
      hang-glider V96.10
      harvester —*see* Accident, transport, agricultural vehicle occupant
      heavy (transport) vehicle —*see* Accident, transport, truck occupant
      helicopter —*see* Accident, transport, aircraft, occupant, helicopter
      ice-yacht V98.2
      kite (carrying person) V96.8
      land-yacht V98.1
      logging car —*see* Accident, transport, industrial vehicle occupant
      mechanical shovel —*see* Accident, transport, construction vehicle occupant
      microlight —*see* Accident, transport, aircraft, occupant, powered, glider
      minibus —*see* Accident, transport, pickup truck occupant
      minivan —*see* Accident, transport, pickup truck occupant
      moped —*see* Accident, transport, motorcycle
      motor scooter —*see* Accident, transport, motorcycle
      motorcycle (with sidecar) —*see* Accident, transport, motorcycle
      off-road motor-vehicle —*see also* Accident, transport, all-terrain vehicle occupant V86.99
      pedal cycle —*see also* Accident, transport, pedal cyclist
      pick-up (truck) —*see* Accident, transport, pickup truck occupant

Accident *(Continued)*
  transport *(Continued)*
    occupant *(Continued)*
      railway (train) (vehicle) (subterranean) (elevated) —*see* Accident, transport, railway vehicle occupant
      rickshaw —*see* Accident, transport, pedal cycle
        pedal driven —*see* Accident, transport, pedal cyclist
      road-roller —*see* Accident, transport, construction vehicle occupant
      ship NOS V94.9
      ski-lift (chair) (gondola) V98.3
      snowmobile —*see* Accident, transport, snowmobile occupant
      spacecraft, spaceship —*see* Accident, transport, aircraft, occupant, spacecraft
      sport utility vehicle —*see* Accident, transport, pickup truck occupant
      streetcar (interurban) (operating on public street or highway) —*see* Accident, transport, streetcar occupant
      SUV —*see* Accident, transport, pickup truck occupant
      téléférique V98.0
      three-wheeled vehicle (motorized) —*see also* Accident, transport, three-wheeled motor vehicle occupant
        nonmotorized —*see* Accident, transport, pedal cycle
      tractor (farm) (and trailer) —*see* Accident, transport, agricultural vehicle occupant
      train —*see* Accident, transport, railway vehicle occupant
      tram —*see* Accident, transport, streetcar occupant
        in mine or quarry —*see* Accident, transport, industrial vehicle occupant
      tricycle —*see* Accident, transport, pedal cycle
        motorized —*see* Accident, transport, three-wheeled motor vehicle
      trolley —*see* Accident, transport, streetcar occupant
        in mine or quarry —*see* Accident, transport, industrial vehicle occupant
      tub, in mine or quarry —*see* Accident, transport, industrial vehicle occupant
      ultralight —*see* Accident, transport, aircraft, occupant, powered, glider
      van —*see* Accident, transport, van occupant
      vehicle NEC V89.9
        heavy transport —*see* Accident, transport, truck occupant
        motor (traffic) NEC V89.2
          nontraffic NEC V89.0
      watercraft NOS V94.9
        causing drowning —*see* Drowning, resulting from accident to boat
    off-road motor-vehicle —*see also* Accident, transport, all-terrain vehicle occupant V86.99
    parachutist V97.29
      after accident to aircraft —*see* Accident, transport, aircraft
      entangled in object V97.21
      injured on landing V97.22
    pedal cyclist V19.9
      collision (with)
        animal (traffic) V10.9
          being ridden (traffic) V16.9
            nontraffic V16.2
            while boarding or alighting V16.3

Accident *(Continued)*
  transport *(Continued)*
    pedal cyclist *(Continued)*
      collision *(Continued)*
        animal (traffic) V10.9 *(Continued)*
          nontraffic V10.2
          while boarding or alighting V10.3
        animal-drawn vehicle (traffic) V16.9
          nontraffic V16.2
          while boarding or alighting V16.3
        bus (traffic) V14.9
          nontraffic V14.2
          while boarding or alighting V14.3
        car (traffic) V13.9
          nontraffic V13.2
          while boarding or alighting V13.3
        motor vehicle NOS (traffic) V19.60
          nontraffic V19.20
          specified type NEC (traffic) V19.69
            nontraffic V19.29
        pedal cycle (traffic) V11.9
          nontraffic V11.2
          while boarding or alighting V11.3
        pickup truck (traffic) V13.9
          nontraffic V13.2
          while boarding or alighting V13.3
        railway vehicle (traffic) V15.9
          nontraffic V15.2
          while boarding or alighting V15.3
        specified vehicle NEC (traffic) V16.9
          nontraffic V16.2
          while boarding or alighting V16.3
        stationary object (traffic) V17.9
          nontraffic V17.2
          while boarding or alighting V17.3
        streetcar (traffic) V16.9
          nontraffic V16.2
          while boarding or alighting V16.3
        three wheeled motor vehicle (traffic)
          V12.9
          nontraffic V12.2
          while boarding or alighting V12.3
        truck (traffic) V14.9
          nontraffic V14.2
          while boarding or alighting V14.3
        two wheeled motor vehicle (traffic)
          V12.9
          nontraffic V12.2
          while boarding or alighting V12.3
        van (traffic) V13.9
          nontraffic V13.2
          while boarding or alighting V13.3
      driver
        collision (with)
          animal (traffic) V10.4
            being ridden (traffic) V16.4
              nontraffic V16.0
            nontraffic V10.0
          animal-drawn vehicle (traffic) V16.4
            nontraffic V16.0
          bus (traffic) V14.4
            nontraffic V14.0
          car (traffic) V13.4
            nontraffic V13.0
          motor vehicle NOS (traffic) V19.40
            nontraffic V19.00
            specified type NEC (traffic) V19.49
              nontraffic V19.09
          pedal cycle (traffic) V11.4
            nontraffic V11.0
          pickup truck (traffic) V13.4
            nontraffic V13.0
          railway vehicle (traffic) V15.4
            nontraffic V15.0
          specified vehicle NEC (traffic) V16.4
            nontraffic V16.0
          stationary object (traffic) V17.4
            nontraffic V17.0
          streetcar (traffic) V16.4
            nontraffic V16.0
          three wheeled motor vehicle
            (traffic) V12.4
            nontraffic V12.0

Accident *(Continued)*
  transport *(Continued)*
    pedal cyclist *(Continued)*
      driver *(Continued)*
        collision *(Continued)*
          truck (traffic) V14.4
            nontraffic V14.0
          two wheeled motor vehicle (traffic)
            V12.4
            nontraffic V12.0
          van (traffic) V13.4
            nontraffic V13.0
        noncollision accident (traffic) V18.4
          nontraffic V18.0
      noncollision accident (traffic) V18.9
        nontraffic V18.2
        while boarding or alighting V18.3
      nontraffic V19.3
      passenger
        collision (with)
          animal (traffic) V10.5
            being ridden (traffic) V16.5
              nontraffic V16.1
            nontraffic V10.1
          animal-drawn vehicle (traffic) V16.5
            nontraffic V16.1
          bus (traffic) V14.5
            nontraffic V14.1
          car (traffic) V13.5
            nontraffic V13.1
          motor vehicle NOS (traffic) V19.50
            nontraffic V19.10
            specified type NEC (traffic)
              V19.59
              nontraffic V19.19
          pedal cycle (traffic) V11.5
            nontraffic V11.1
          pickup truck (traffic) V13.5
            nontraffic V13.1
          railway vehicle (traffic) V15.5
            nontraffic V15.1
          specified vehicle NEC (traffic) V16.5
            nontraffic V16.1
          stationary object (traffic) V17.5
            nontraffic V17.1
          streetcar (traffic) V16.5
            nontraffic V16.1
          three wheeled motor vehicle
            (traffic) V12.5
            nontraffic V12.1
          truck (traffic) V14.5
            nontraffic V14.1
          two wheeled motor vehicle (traffic)
            V12.5
            nontraffic V12.1
          van (traffic) V13.5
            nontraffic V13.1
        noncollision accident (traffic) V18.5
          nontraffic V18.1
      specified type NEC V19.88
      military vehicle V19.81
    pedestrian
      conveyance (occupant) V09.9
        baby stroller V00.828
          collision (with) V09.9
            animal being ridden or animal
              drawn vehicle V06.99
              nontraffic V06.09
              traffic V06.19
            bus or heavy transport V04.99
              nontraffic V04.09
              traffic V04.19
            car V03.99
              nontraffic V03.09
              traffic V03.19
            pedal cycle V01.99
              nontraffic V01.09
              traffic V01.19
            pick-up truck or van V03.99
              nontraffic V03.09
              traffic V03.19

Accident *(Continued)*
  transport *(Continued)*
    pedestrian *(Continued)*
      conveyance *(Continued)*
        babystroller *(Continued)*
          collision *(Continued)*
            railway (train) (vehicle) V05.99
              nontraffic V05.09
              traffic V05.19
            stationary object V00.822
            streetcar V06.99
              nontraffic V06.09
              traffic V06.19
            two- or three-wheeled motor
              vehicle V02.99
              nontraffic V02.09
              traffic V02.19
            vehicle V09.9
              animal-drawn V06.99
                nontraffic V06.09
                traffic V06.19
              motor
                nontraffic V09.00
                traffic V09.20
          fall V00.821
          nontraffic V09.1
            involving motor vehicle NEC
              V09.00
          traffic V09.3
            involving motor vehicle NEC
              V09.20
        flat-bottomed NEC V00.388
          collision (with) V09.9
            animal being ridden or animal
              drawn vehicle V06.99
              nontraffic V06.09
              traffic V06.19
            bus or heavy transport V04.99
              nontraffic V04.09
              traffic V04.19
            car V03.99
              nontraffic V03.09
              traffic V03.19
            pedal cycle V01.99
              nontraffic V01.09
              traffic V01.19
            pick-up truck or van V03.99
              nontraffic V03.09
              traffic V03.19
            railway (train) (vehicle) V05.99
              nontraffic V05.09
              traffic V05.19
            stationary object V00.382
            streetcar V06.99
              nontraffic V06.09
              traffic V06.19
            two-or three-wheeled motor
              vehicle V02.99
              nontraffic V02.09
              traffic V02.19
            vehicle V09.9
              animal-drawn V06.99
                nontraffic V06.09
                traffic V06.19
              motor
                nontraffic V09.00
                traffic V09.20
          fall V00.381
          nontraffic V09.1
            involving motor vehicle NEC
              V09.00
          snow
            board —*see* Accident, transport,
              pedestrian, conveyance,
              snow board
            ski —*see* Accident, transport,
              pedestrian, conveyance, skis
              (snow)
          traffic V09.3
            involving motor vehicle NEC
              V09.20

Accident (Continued)
  transport (Continued)
    pedestrian (Continued)
      conveyance (Continued)
        gliding type NEC V00.288
          collision (with) V09.9
            animal being ridden or animal
                drawn vehicle V06.99
              nontraffic V06.09
              traffic V06.19
            bus or heavy transport
                V04.99
              nontraffic V04.09
              traffic V04.19
            car V03.99
              nontraffic V03.09
              traffic V03.19
            pedal cycle V01.99
              nontraffic V01.09
              traffic V01.19
            pick-up truck or van V03.99
              nontraffic V03.09
              traffic V03.19
            railway (train) (vehicle) V05.99
              nontraffic V05.09
              traffic V05.19
            stationary object V00.282
            streetcar V06.99
              nontraffic V06.09
              traffic V06.19
            two- or three-wheeled motor
                vehicle V02.99
              nontraffic V02.09
              traffic V02.19
            vehicle V09.9
              animal-drawn V06.99
                nontraffic V06.09
                traffic V06.19
              motor
                nontraffic V09.00
                traffic V09.20
          fall V00.281
        heelies —see Accident, transport,
            pedestrian, conveyance,
            heelies
        ice skate —see Accident, transport,
            pedestrian, conveyance, ice
            skate
        nontraffic V09.1
          involving motor vehicle NEC
              V09.00
        sled —see Accident, transport,
            pedestrian, conveyance, sled
        traffic V09.3
          involving motor vehicle NEC
              V09.20
            wheelies —see Accident,
                transport, pedestrian,
                conveyance, heelies
        heelies V00.158
          colliding with stationary object
              V00.152
          fall V00.151
        ice skates V00.218
          collision (with) V09.9
            animal being ridden or animal
                drawn vehicle V06.99
              nontraffic V06.09
              traffic V06.19
            bus or heavy transport V04.99
              nontraffic V04.09
              traffic V04.19
            car V03.99
              nontraffic V03.09
              traffic V03.19
            pedal cycle V01.99
              nontraffic V01.09
              traffic V01.19
            pick-up truck or van V03.99
              nontraffic V03.09
              traffic V03.19

Accident (Continued)
  transport (Continued)
    pedestrian (Continued)
      conveyance (Continued)
        ice skates (Continued)
          collision (Continued)
            railway (train) (vehicle)
                V05.99
              nontraffic V05.09
              traffic V05.19
            stationary object V00.212
            streetcar V06.99
              nontraffic V06.09
              traffic V06.19
            two- or three-wheeled motor
                vehicle V02.99
              nontraffic V02.09
              traffic V02.19
            vehicle V09.9
              animal-drawn V06.99
                nontraffic V06.09
                traffic V06.19
              motor
                nontraffic V09.00
                traffic V09.20
          fall V00.211
          nontraffic V09.1
            involving motor vehicle NEC
                V09.00
          traffic V09.3
            involving motor vehicle NEC
                V09.20
        motorized mobility scooter
            V00.838
          collision with stationary object
              V00.832
          fall from V00.831
        nontraffic V09.1
          involving motor vehicle
              V09.00
            military V09.01
            specified type NEC V09.09
        roller skates (non in-line) V00.128
          collision (with) V09.9
            animal being ridden or animal
                drawn vehicle V06.91
              nontraffic V06.01
              traffic V06.11
            bus or heavy transport
                V04.91
              nontraffic V04.01
              traffic V04.11
            car V03.91
              nontraffic V03.01
              traffic V03.11
            pedal cycle V01.91
              nontraffic V01.01
              traffic V01.11
            pick-up truck or van V03.91
              nontraffic V03.01
              traffic V03.11
            railway (train) (vehicle)
                V05.91
              nontraffic V05.01
              traffic V05.11
            stationary object V00.122
            streetcar V06.91
              nontraffic V06.01
              traffic V06.11
            two- or three-wheeled motor
                vehicle V02.91
              nontraffic V02.01
              traffic V02.11
            vehicle V09.9
              animal-drawn V06.91
                nontraffic V06.01
                traffic V06.11
              motor
                nontraffic V09.00
                traffic V09.20
          fall V00.121

Accident (Continued)
  transport (Continued)
    pedestrian (Continued)
      conveyance (Continued)
        roller skates (Continued)
          in-line V00.118
            collision —see also Accident,
                transport, pedestrian,
                conveyance occupant, roller
                skates, collision
              with stationary object
                  V00.112
            fall V00.111
            nontraffic V09.1
              involving motor vehicle NEC
                  V09.00
            traffic V09.3
              involving motor vehicle NEC
                  V09.20
          rolling shoes V00.158
            colliding with stationary object
                V00.152
            fall V00.151
          rolling type NEC V00.188
            collision (with) V09.9
              animal being ridden or animal
                  drawn vehicle V06.99
                nontraffic V06.09
                traffic V06.19
              bus or heavy transport V04.99
                nontraffic V04.09
                traffic V04.19
              car V03.99
                nontraffic V03.09
                traffic V03.19
              pedal cycle V01.99
                nontraffic V01.09
                traffic V01.19
              pick-up truck or van V03.99
                nontraffic V03.09
                traffic V03.19
              railway (train) (vehicle)
                  V05.99
                nontraffic V05.09
                traffic V05.19
              stationary object V00.182
              streetcar V06.99
                nontraffic V06.09
                traffic V06.19
              two- or three-wheeled motor
                  vehicle V02.99
                nontraffic V02.09
                traffic V02.19
              vehicle V09.9
                animal-drawn V06.99
                  nontraffic V06.09
                  traffic V06.19
                motor
                  nontraffic V09.00
                  traffic V09.20
            fall V00.181
          in-line roller skate —see Accident,
              transport, pedestrian,
              conveyance, roller skate,
              in-line
          nontraffic V09.1
            involving motor vehicle NEC
                V09.00
          roller skate —see Accident,
              transport, pedestrian,
              conveyance, roller skate
          scooter (non-motorized) —
              see Accident, transport,
              pedestrian, conveyance,
              scooter
          skateboard —see Accident,
              transport, pedestrian,
              conveyance, skateboard
          traffic V09.3
            involving motor vehicle NEC
                V09.20

▶ New   ⇒ Revised   ~~deleted~~ Deleted   ● Use Additional Character(s)

Accident *(Continued)*
  transport *(Continued)*
    pedestrian *(Continued)*
      conveyance *(Continued)*
        scooter (non-motorized) V00.148
          collision (with) V09.9
            animal being ridden or animal
                drawn vehicle V06.99
              nontraffic V06.09
              traffic V06.19
            bus or heavy transport
                V04.99
              nontraffic V04.09
              traffic V04.19
            car V03.99
              nontraffic V03.09
              traffic V03.19
            pedal cycle V01.99
              nontraffic V01.09
              traffic V01.19
            pick-up truck or van V03.99
              nontraffic V03.09
              traffic V03.19
            railway (train) (vehicle)
                V05.99
              nontraffic V05.09
              traffic V05.19
            stationary object V00.142
            streetcar V06.99
              nontraffic V06.09
              traffic V06.19
            two- or three-wheeled motor
                vehicle V02.99
              nontraffic V02.09
              traffic V02.19
            vehicle V09.9
              animal-drawn V06.99
                nontraffic V06.09
                traffic V06.19
              motor
                nontraffic V09.00
                traffic V09.20
          fall V00.141
          nontraffic V09.1
            involving motor vehicle NEC
                V09.00
          traffic V09.3
            involving motor vehicle NEC
                V09.20
        skate board V00.138
          collision (with) V09.9
            animal being ridden or
                animal drawn vehicle
                V06.92
              nontraffic V06.02
              traffic V06.12
            bus or heavy transport
                V04.92
              nontraffic V04.02
              traffic V04.12
            car V03.92
              nontraffic V03.02
              traffic V03.12
            pedal cycle V01.92
              nontraffic V01.02
              traffic V01.12
            pick-up truck or van V03.92
              nontraffic V03.02
              traffic V03.12
            railway (train) (vehicle)
                V05.92
              nontraffic V05.02
              traffic V05.12
            stationary object V00.132
            streetcar V06.92
              nontraffic V06.02
              traffic V06.12
            two- or three-wheeled motor
                vehicle V02.92
              nontraffic V02.02
              traffic V02.12

Accident *(Continued)*
  transport *(Continued)*
    pedestrian *(Continued)*
      conveyance *(Continued)*
        skate board *(Continued)*
          collision *(Continued)*
            vehicle V09.9
              animal-drawn V06.92
                nontraffic V06.02
                traffic V06.12
              motor
                nontraffic V09.00
                traffic V09.20
          fall V00.131
          nontraffic V09.1
            involving motor vehicle NEC
                V09.00
          traffic V09.3
            involving motor vehicle NEC
                V09.20
        skis (snow) V00.328
          collision (with) V09.9
            animal being ridden or animal
                drawn vehicle V06.99
              nontraffic V06.09
              traffic V06.19
            bus or heavy transport V04.99
              nontraffic V04.09
              traffic V04.19
            car V03.99
              nontraffic V03.09
              traffic V03.19
            pedal cycle V01.99
              nontraffic V01.09
              traffic V01.19
            pick-up truck or van V03.99
              nontraffic V03.09
              traffic V03.19
            railway (train) (vehicle) V05.99
              nontraffic V05.09
              traffic V05.19
            stationary object V00.322
            streetcar V06.99
              nontraffic V06.09
              traffic V06.19
            two- or three-wheeled motor
                vehicle V02.99
              nontraffic V02.09
              traffic V02.19
            vehicle V09.9
              animal-drawn V06.99
                nontraffic V06.09
                traffic V06.19
              motor
                nontraffic V09.00
                traffic V09.20
          fall V00.321
          nontraffic V09.1
            involving motor vehicle NEC
                V09.00
          traffic V09.3
            involving motor vehicle NEC
                V09.20
        sled V00.228
          collision (with) V09.9
            animal being ridden or animal
                drawn vehicle V06.99
              nontraffic V06.09
              traffic V06.19
            bus or heavy transport V04.99
              nontraffic V04.09
              traffic V04.19
            car V03.99
              nontraffic V03.09
              traffic V03.19
            pedal cycle V01.99
              nontraffic V01.09
              traffic V01.19
            pick-up truck or van V03.99
              nontraffic V03.09
              traffic V03.19

Accident *(Continued)*
  transport *(Continued)*
    pedestrian *(Continued)*
      conveyance *(Continued)*
        sled *(Continued)*
          collision *(Continued)*
            railway (train) (vehicle)
                V05.99
              nontraffic V05.09
              traffic V05.19
            stationary object V00.222
            streetcar V06.99
              nontraffic V06.09
              traffic V06.19
            two- or three-wheeled motor
                vehicle V02.99
              nontraffic V02.09
              traffic V02.19
            vehicle V09.9
              animal-drawn V06.99
                nontraffic V06.09
                traffic V06.19
              motor
                nontraffic V09.00
                traffic V09.20
          fall V00.221
          nontraffic V09.1
            involving motor vehicle NEC
                V09.00
          traffic V09.3
            involving motor vehicle NEC
                V09.20
        snow board V00.318
          collision (with) V09.9
            animal being ridden or animal
                drawn vehicle V06.99
              nontraffic V06.09
              traffic V06.19
            bus or heavy transport V04.99
              nontraffic V04.09
              traffic V04.19
            car V03.99
              nontraffic V03.09
              traffic V03.19
            pedal cycle V01.99
              nontraffic V01.09
              traffic V01.19
            pick-up truck or van V03.99
              nontraffic V03.09
              traffic V03.19
            railway (train) (vehicle) V05.99
              nontraffic V05.09
              traffic V05.19
            stationary object V00.312
            streetcar V06.99
              nontraffic V06.09
              traffic V06.19
            two- or three-wheeled motor
                vehicle V02.99
              nontraffic V02.09
              traffic V02.19
            vehicle V09.9
              animal-drawn V06.99
                nontraffic V06.09
                traffic V06.19
              motor
                nontraffic V09.00
                traffic V09.20
          fall V00.311
          nontraffic V09.1
            involving motor vehicle NEC
                V09.00
          traffic V09.3
            involving motor vehicle NEC
                V09.20
        specified type NEC V00.898
          collision (with) V09.9
            animal being ridden or animal
                drawn vehicle V06.99
              nontraffic V06.09
              traffic V06.19

Accident (Continued)
  transport (Continued)
    pedestrian (Continued)
      conveyance (Continued)
        specified type NEC (Continued)
          collision (Continued)
            bus or heavy transport
              V04.99
              nontraffic V04.09
              traffic V04.19
            car V03.99
              nontraffic V03.09
              traffic V03.19
            pedal cycle V01.99
              nontraffic V01.09
              traffic V01.19
            pick-up truck or van V03.99
              nontraffic V03.09
              traffic V03.19
            railway (train) (vehicle)
              V05.99
              nontraffic V05.09
              traffic V05.19
            stationary object V00.892
            streetcar V06.99
              nontraffic V06.09
              traffic V06.19
            two- or three-wheeled motor
              vehicle V02.99
              nontraffic V02.09
              traffic V02.19
            vehicle V09.9
              animal-drawn V06.99
                nontraffic V06.09
                traffic V06.19
              motor
                nontraffic V09.00
                traffic V09.20
          fall V00.891
          nontraffic V09.1
            involving motor vehicle NEC
              V09.00
          traffic V09.3
            involving motor vehicle NEC
              V09.20
        traffic V09.3
          involving motor vehicle V09.20
          military V09.21
          specified type NEC V09.29
      wheelchair (powered) V00.818
        collision (with) V09.9
          animal being ridden or
            animal drawn vehicle
            V06.99
            nontraffic V06.09
            traffic V06.19
          bus or heavy transport
            V04.99
            nontraffic V04.09
            traffic V04.19
          car V03.99
            nontraffic V03.09
            traffic V03.19
          pedal cycle V01.99
            nontraffic V01.09
            traffic V01.19
          pick-up truck or van V03.99
            nontraffic V03.09
            traffic V03.19
          railway (train) (vehicle)
            V05.99
            nontraffic V05.09
            traffic V05.19
          stationary object V00.812
          streetcar V06.99
            nontraffic V06.09
            traffic V06.19
          two- or three-wheeled motor
            vehicle V02.99
            nontraffic V02.09
            traffic V02.19

Accident (Continued)
  transport (Continued)
    pedestrian (Continued)
      conveyance (Continued)
        wheelchair (Continued)
          collision (Continued)
            vehicle V09.9
              animal-drawn V06.99
                nontraffic V06.09
                traffic V06.19
              motor
                nontraffic V09.00
                traffic V09.20
          fall V00.811
          nontraffic V09.1
            involving motor vehicle NEC
              V09.00
          traffic V09.3
            involving motor vehicle NEC
              V09.20
        wheeled shoe V00.158
          colliding with stationary object
            V00.152
          fall V00.151
      on foot —see also Accident, pedestrian
        collision (with)
          animal being ridden or animal
            drawn vehicle V06.90
            nontraffic V06.00
            traffic V06.10
          bus or heavy transport V04.90
            nontraffic V04.00
            traffic V04.10
          car V03.90
            nontraffic V03.00
            traffic V03.10
          pedal cycle V01.90
            nontraffic V01.00
            traffic V01.10
          pick-up truck or van V03.90
            nontraffic V03.00
            traffic V03.10
          railway (train) (vehicle) V05.90
            nontraffic V05.00
            traffic V05.10
          streetcar V06.90
            nontraffic V06.00
            traffic V06.10
          two- or three-wheeled motor
            vehicle V02.90
            nontraffic V02.00
            traffic V02.10
          vehicle V09.9
            animal-drawn V06.90
              nontraffic V06.00
              traffic V06.10
            motor
              nontraffic V09.00
              traffic V09.20
        nontraffic V09.1
         involving motor vehicle V09.00
          military V09.01
          specified type NEC V09.09
        traffic V09.3
         involving motor vehicle V09.20
          military V09.21
          specified type NEC V09.29
    person NEC (unknown way or
      transportation) V99
    collision (between)
      bus (with)
        heavy transport vehicle (traffic)
          V87.5
        nontraffic V88.5
      car (with)
        nontraffic V88.5
        bus (traffic) V87.3
          nontraffic V88.3
        heavy transport vehicle (traffic)
          V87.4
          nontraffic V88.4

Accident (Continued)
  transport (Continued)
    person NEC (Continued)
      collision (Continued)
        car (Continued)
          pick-up truck or van (traffic) V87.2
            nontraffic V88.2
          train or railway vehicle (traffic)
            V87.6
            nontraffic V88.6
          two- or three-wheeled motor
            vehicle (traffic) V87.0
            nontraffic V88.0
          motor vehicle (traffic) NEC V87.7
            nontraffic V88.7
          two- or three-wheeled vehicle (with)
            (traffic)
            motor vehicle NEC V87.1
            nontraffic V88.1
        nonmotor vehicle (collision)
          (noncollision) (traffic) V87.9
          nontraffic V88.9
    pickup truck occupant V59.9
      collision (with)
        animal (traffic) V50.9
          being ridden (traffic) V56.9
            nontraffic V56.3
            while boarding or alighting V56.4
          nontraffic V50.3
          while boarding or alighting V50.4
        animal-drawn vehicle (traffic) V56.9
          nontraffic V56.3
          while boarding or alighting V56.4
        bus (traffic) V54.9
          nontraffic V54.3
          while boarding or alighting V54.4
        car (traffic) V53.9
          nontraffic V53.3
          while boarding or alighting V53.4
        motor vehicle NOS (traffic) V59.60
          nontraffic V59.20
          specified type NEC (traffic) V59.69
            nontraffic V59.29
        pedal cycle (traffic) V51.9
          nontraffic V51.3
          while boarding or alighting V51.4
        pickup truck (traffic) V53.9
          nontraffic V53.3
          while boarding or alighting V53.4
        railway vehicle (traffic) V55.9
          nontraffic V55.3
          while boarding or alighting V55.4
        specified vehicle NEC (traffic) V56.9
          nontraffic V56.3
          while boarding or alighting V56.4
        stationary object (traffic) V57.9
          nontraffic V57.3
          while boarding or alighting V57.4
        streetcar (traffic) V56.9
          nontraffic V56.3
          while boarding or alighting V56.4
        three wheeled motor vehicle (traffic)
          V52.9
          nontraffic V52.3
          while boarding or alighting V52.4
        truck (traffic) V54.9
          nontraffic V54.3
          while boarding or alighting V54.4
        two wheeled motor vehicle (traffic)
          V52.9
          nontraffic V52.3
          while boarding or alighting V52.4
        van (traffic) V53.9
          nontraffic V53.3
          while boarding or alighting V53.4
    driver
      collision (with)
        animal (traffic) V50.5
          being ridden (traffic) V56.5
            nontraffic V56.0
          nontraffic V50.0

▶ New   ⇒ Revised   ~~deleted~~ Deleted   ● Use Additional Character(s)

Accident *(Continued)*
  transport *(Continued)*
    pickup truck occupant *(Continued)*
      driver *(Continued)*
        collision *(Continued)*
          animal-drawn vehicle (traffic)
              V56.5
            nontraffic V56.0
          bus (traffic) V54.5
            nontraffic V54.0
          car (traffic) V53.5
            nontraffic V53.0
          motor vehicle NOS (traffic) V59.40
            nontraffic V59.00
            specified type NEC (traffic)
                V59.49
              nontraffic V59.09
          pedal cycle (traffic) V51.5
            nontraffic V51.0
          pickup truck (traffic) V53.5
            nontraffic V53.0
          railway vehicle (traffic) V55.5
            nontraffic V55.0
          specified vehicle NEC (traffic) V56.5
            nontraffic V56.0
          stationary object (traffic) V57.5
            nontraffic V57.0
          streetcar (traffic) V56.5
            nontraffic V56.0
          three wheeled motor vehicle
              (traffic) V52.5
            nontraffic V52.0
          truck (traffic) V54.5
            nontraffic V54.0
          two wheeled motor vehicle (traffic)
              V52.5
            nontraffic V52.0
          van (traffic) V53.5
            nontraffic V53.0
        noncollision accident (traffic) V58.5
          nontraffic V58.0
      hanger-on
        collision (with)
          animal (traffic) V50.7
            being ridden (traffic) V56.7
              nontraffic V56.2
            nontraffic V50.2
          animal-drawn vehicle (traffic) V56.7
            nontraffic V56.2
          bus (traffic) V54.7
            nontraffic V54.2
          car (traffic) V53.7
            nontraffic V53.2
          pedal cycle (traffic) V51.7
            nontraffic V51.2
          pickup truck (traffic) V53.7
            nontraffic V53.2
          railway vehicle (traffic) V55.7
            nontraffic V55.2
          specified vehicle NEC (traffic) V56.7
            nontraffic V56.2
          stationary object (traffic) V57.7
            nontraffic V57.2
          streetcar (traffic) V56.7
            nontraffic V56.2
          three wheeled motor vehicle
              (traffic) V52.7
            nontraffic V52.2
          truck (traffic) V54.7
            nontraffic V54.2
          two wheeled motor vehicle (traffic)
              V52.7
            nontraffic V52.2
          van (traffic) V53.7
            nontraffic V53.2
        noncollision accident (traffic) V58.7
          nontraffic V58.2
      noncollision accident (traffic) V58.9
        nontraffic V58.3
        while boarding or alighting V58.4
      nontraffic V59.3

Accident *(Continued)*
  transport *(Continued)*
    pickup truck occupant *(Continued)*
      passenger
        collision (with)
          animal (traffic) V50.6
            being ridden (traffic) V56.6
              nontraffic V56.1
            nontraffic V50.1
          animal-drawn vehicle (traffic)
              V56.6
            nontraffic V56.1
          bus (traffic) V54.6
            nontraffic V54.1
          car (traffic) V53.6
            nontraffic V53.1
          motor vehicle NOS (traffic) V59.50
            nontraffic V59.10
            specified type NEC (traffic)
                V59.59
              nontraffic V59.19
          pedal cycle (traffic) V51.6
            nontraffic V51.1
          pickup truck (traffic) V53.6
            nontraffic V53.1
          railway vehicle (traffic) V55.6
            nontraffic V55.1
          specified vehicle NEC (traffic) V56.6
            nontraffic V56.1
          stationary object (traffic) V57.6
            nontraffic V57.1
          streetcar (traffic) V56.6
            nontraffic V56.1
          three wheeled motor vehicle
              (traffic) V52.6
            nontraffic V52.1
          truck (traffic) V54.6
            nontraffic V54.1
          two wheeled motor vehicle (traffic)
              V52.6
            nontraffic V52.1
          van (traffic) V53.6
            nontraffic V53.1
        noncollision accident (traffic) V58.6
          nontraffic V58.1
      specified type NEC V59.88
        military vehicle V59.81
    quarry truck —*see* Accident, transport,
        industrial vehicle occupant
    race car —*see* Accident, transport, motor
        vehicle NEC occupant
    railway vehicle occupant V81.9
      collision (with) V81.3
        motor vehicle (non-military) (traffic)
            V81.1
          military V81.83
          nontraffic V81.0
        rolling stock V81.2
        specified object NEC V81.3
      during derailment V81.7
        with antecedent collision —*see*
            Accident, transport, railway
            vehicle occupant, collision
      explosion V81.81
      fall (in railway vehicle) V81.5
        during derailment V81.7
          with antecedent collision —*see*
              Accident, transport, railway
              vehicle occupant, collision
        from railway vehicle V81.6
          during derailment V81.7
            with antecedent collision —*see*
                Accident, transport,
                railway vehicle occupant,
                collision
        while boarding or alighting V81.4
      fire V81.81
      object falling onto train V81.82
      specified type NEC V81.89
      while boarding or alighting V81.4
    ski lift V98.3

Accident *(Continued)*
  transport *(Continued)*
    snowmobile occupant (nontraffic)
        V86.92
      driver V86.52
      hanger-on V86.72
      passenger V86.62
      traffic V86.32
        driver V86.02
        hanger-on V86.22
        passenger V86.12
      while boarding or alighting V86.42
    specified NEC V98.8
    sport utility vehicle occupant —*see also*
        Accident, transport, pickup truck
        occupant
    streetcar occupant V82.9
      collision (with) V82.3
        motor vehicle (traffic) V82.1
          nontraffic V82.0
        rolling stock V82.2
      during derailment V82.7
        with antecedent collision —*see*
            Accident, transport, streetcar
            occupant, collision
      fall (in streetcar) V82.5
        during derailment V82.7
          with antecedent collision —*see*
              Accident, transport, streetcar
              occupant, collision
        from streetcar V82.6
          during derailment V82.7
            with antecedent collision —*see*
                Accident, transport, streetcar
                occupant, collision
          while boarding or alighting
              V82.4
      while boarding or alighting V82.4
      specified type NEC V82.8
      while boarding or alighting V82.4
    three-wheeled motor vehicle occupant
        V39.9
      collision (with)
        animal (traffic) V30.9
          being ridden (traffic) V36.9
            nontraffic V36.3
            while boarding or alighting
                V36.4
          nontraffic V30.3
          while boarding or alighting
              V30.4
        animal-drawn vehicle (traffic)
            V36.9
          nontraffic V36.3
          while boarding or alighting
              V36.4
        bus (traffic) V34.9
          nontraffic V34.3
          while boarding or alighting
              V34.4
        car (traffic) V33.9
          nontraffic V33.3
          while boarding or alighting
              V33.4
        motor vehicle NOS (traffic) V39.60
          nontraffic V39.20
          specified type NEC (traffic)
              V39.69
            nontraffic V39.29
        pedal cycle (traffic) V31.9
          nontraffic V31.3
          while boarding or alighting
              V31.4
        pickup truck (traffic) V33.9
          nontraffic V33.3
          while boarding or alighting
              V33.4
        railway vehicle (traffic) V35.9
          nontraffic V35.3
          while boarding or alighting
              V35.4

A

Accident (*Continued*)
  transport (*Continued*)
    three-wheeled motor vehicle occupant
    (*Continued*)
      collision (*Continued*)
        specified vehicle NEC (traffic) V36.9
          nontraffic V36.3
          while boarding or alighting V36.4
        stationary object (traffic) V37.9
          nontraffic V37.3
          while boarding or alighting V37.4
        streetcar (traffic) V36.9
          nontraffic V36.3
          while boarding or alighting V36.4
        three wheeled motor vehicle (traffic)
          V32.9
          nontraffic V32.3
          while boarding or alighting V32.4
        truck (traffic) V34.9
          nontraffic V34.3
          while boarding or alighting V34.4
        two wheeled motor vehicle (traffic)
          V32.9
          nontraffic V32.3
          while boarding or alighting V32.4
        van (traffic) V33.9
          nontraffic V33.3
          while boarding or alighting V33.4
      driver
        collision (with)
          animal (traffic) V30.5
            being ridden (traffic) V36.5
              nontraffic V36.0
            nontraffic V30.0
          animal-drawn vehicle (traffic) V36.5
            nontraffic V36.0
          bus (traffic) V34.5
            nontraffic V34.0
          car (traffic) V33.5
            nontraffic V33.0
          motor vehicle NOS (traffic) V39.40
            nontraffic V39.00
            specified type NEC (traffic)
              V39.49
              nontraffic V39.09
          pedal cycle (traffic) V31.5
            nontraffic V31.0
          pickup truck (traffic) V33.5
            nontraffic V33.0
          railway vehicle (traffic) V35.5
            nontraffic V35.0
          specified vehicle NEC (traffic) V36.5
            nontraffic V36.0
          stationary object (traffic) V37.5
            nontraffic V37.0
          streetcar (traffic) V36.5
            nontraffic V36.0
          three wheeled motor vehicle
            (traffic) V32.5
            nontraffic V32.0
          truck (traffic) V34.5
            nontraffic V34.0
          two wheeled motor vehicle (traffic)
            V32.5
            nontraffic V32.0
          van (traffic) V33.5
            nontraffic V33.0
        noncollision accident (traffic) V38.5
          nontraffic V38.0
      hanger-on
        collision (with)
          animal (traffic) V30.7
            being ridden (traffic) V36.7
              nontraffic V36.2
            nontraffic V30.2
          animal-drawn vehicle (traffic) V36.7
            nontraffic V36.2
          bus (traffic) V34.7
            nontraffic V34.2
          car (traffic) V33.7
            nontraffic V33.2

Accident (*Continued*)
  transport (*Continued*)
    three-wheeled motor vehicle occupant
    (*Continued*)
      hanger-on (*Continued*)
        collision (*Continued*)
          pedal cycle (traffic) V31.7
            nontraffic V31.2
          pickup truck (traffic) V33.7
            nontraffic V33.2
          railway vehicle (traffic) V35.7
            nontraffic V35.2
          specified vehicle NEC (traffic) V36.7
            nontraffic V36.2
          stationary object (traffic) V37.7
            nontraffic V37.2
          streetcar (traffic) V36.7
            nontraffic V36.2
          three wheeled motor vehicle
            (traffic) V32.7
            nontraffic V32.2
          truck (traffic) V34.7
            nontraffic V34.2
          two wheeled motor vehicle (traffic)
            V32.7
            nontraffic V32.2
          van (traffic) V33.7
            nontraffic V33.2
        noncollision accident (traffic) V38.7
          nontraffic V38.2
      noncollision accident (traffic) V38.9
        nontraffic V38.3
        while boarding or alighting V38.4
      nontraffic V39.3
      passenger
        collision (with)
          animal (traffic) V30.6
            being ridden (traffic) V36.6
              nontraffic V36.1
            nontraffic V30.1
          animal-drawn vehicle (traffic) V36.6
            nontraffic V36.1
          bus (traffic) V34.6
            nontraffic V34.1
          car (traffic) V33.6
            nontraffic V33.1
          motor vehicle NOS (traffic) V39.50
            nontraffic V39.10
            specified type NEC (traffic)
              V39.59
              nontraffic V39.19
          pedal cycle (traffic) V31.6
            nontraffic V31.1
          pickup truck (traffic) V33.6
            nontraffic V33.1
          railway vehicle (traffic) V35.6
            nontraffic V35.1
          specified vehicle NEC (traffic)
            V36.6
            nontraffic V36.1
          stationary object (traffic) V37.6
            nontraffic V37.1
          streetcar (traffic) V36.6
            nontraffic V36.1
          three wheeled motor vehicle
            (traffic) V32.6
            nontraffic V32.1
          truck (traffic) V34.6
            nontraffic V34.1
          two wheeled motor vehicle (traffic)
            V32.6
            nontraffic V32.1
          van (traffic) V33.6
            nontraffic V33.1
        noncollision accident (traffic) V38.6
          nontraffic V38.1
      specified type NEC V39.89
      military vehicle V39.81
    tractor (farm) (and trailer) —*see* Accident,
      transport, agricultural vehicle
      occupant

Accident (*Continued*)
  transport (*Continued*)
    tram —*see* Accident, transport, streetcar
      in mine or quarry —*see* Accident,
      transport, industrial vehicle
      occupant
    trolley —*see* Accident, transport, streetcar
      in mine or quarry —*see* Accident,
      transport, industrial vehicle
      occupant
    truck (heavy) occupant V69.9
      collision (with)
        animal (traffic) V60.9
          being ridden (traffic) V66.9
            nontraffic V66.3
            while boarding or alighting V66.4
          nontraffic V60.3
          while boarding or alighting V60.4
        animal-drawn vehicle (traffic) V66.9
          nontraffic V66.3
          while boarding or alighting V66.4
        bus (traffic) V64.9
          nontraffic V64.3
          while boarding or alighting V64.4
        car (traffic) V63.9
          nontraffic V63.3
          while boarding or alighting V63.4
        motor vehicle NOS (traffic) V69.60
          nontraffic V69.20
          specified type NEC (traffic) V69.69
            nontraffic V69.29
        pedal cycle (traffic) V61.9
          nontraffic V61.3
          while boarding or alighting V61.4
        pickup truck (traffic) V63.9
          nontraffic V63.3
          while boarding or alighting V63.4
        railway vehicle (traffic) V65.9
          nontraffic V65.3
          while boarding or alighting V65.4
        specified vehicle NEC (traffic) V66.9
          nontraffic V66.3
          while boarding or alighting V66.4
        stationary object (traffic) V67.9
          nontraffic V67.3
          while boarding or alighting V67.4
        streetcar (traffic) V66.9
          nontraffic V66.3
          while boarding or alighting V66.4
        three wheeled motor vehicle (traffic)
          V62.9
          nontraffic V62.3
          while boarding or alighting V62.4
        truck (traffic) V64.9
          nontraffic V64.3
          while boarding or alighting V64.4
        two wheeled motor vehicle (traffic)
          V62.9
          nontraffic V62.3
          while boarding or alighting V62.4
        van (traffic) V63.9
          nontraffic V63.3
          while boarding or alighting V63.4
      driver
        collision (with)
          animal (traffic) V60.5
            being ridden (traffic) V66.5
              nontraffic V66.0
            nontraffic V60.0
          animal-drawn vehicle (traffic)
            V66.5
            nontraffic V66.0
          bus (traffic) V64.5
            nontraffic V64.0
          car (traffic) V63.5
            nontraffic V63.0
          motor vehicle NOS (traffic) V69.40
            nontraffic V69.00
            specified type NEC (traffic)
              V69.49
              nontraffic V69.09

▶ New   ⇒ Revised   ~~deleted~~ Deleted   ● Use Additional Character(s)

Accident (Continued)
transport (Continued)
  truck occupant (Continued)
    driver (Continued)
      collision (Continued)
        pedal cycle (traffic) V61.5
          nontraffic V61.0
        pickup truck (traffic) V63.5
          nontraffic V63.0
        railway vehicle (traffic) V65.5
          nontraffic V65.0
        specified vehicle NEC (traffic) V66.5
          nontraffic V66.0
        stationary object (traffic) V67.5
          nontraffic V67.0
        streetcar (traffic) V66.5
          nontraffic V66.0
        three wheeled motor vehicle
          (traffic) V62.5
          nontraffic V62.0
        truck (traffic) V64.5
          nontraffic V64.0
        two wheeled motor vehicle (traffic)
          V62.5
          nontraffic V62.0
        van (traffic) V63.5
          nontraffic V63.0
      noncollision accident (traffic) V68.5
        nontraffic V68.0
    dump —see Accident, transport,
      construction vehicle occupant
    hanger-on
      collision (with)
        animal (traffic) V60.7
          being ridden (traffic) V66.7
            nontraffic V66.2
          nontraffic V60.2
        animal-drawn vehicle (traffic) V66.7
          nontraffic V66.2
        bus (traffic) V64.7
          nontraffic V64.2
        car (traffic) V63.7
          nontraffic V63.2
        pedal cycle (traffic) V61.7
          nontraffic V61.2
        pickup truck (traffic) V63.7
          nontraffic V63.2
        railway vehicle (traffic) V65.7
          nontraffic V65.2
        specified vehicle NEC (traffic) V66.7
          nontraffic V66.2
        stationary object (traffic) V67.7
          nontraffic V67.2
        streetcar (traffic) V66.7
          nontraffic V66.2
        three wheeled motor vehicle
          (traffic) V62.7
          nontraffic V62.2
        truck (traffic) V64.7
          nontraffic V64.2
        two wheeled motor vehicle (traffic)
          V62.7
          nontraffic V62.2
        van (traffic) V63.7
          nontraffic V63.2
      noncollision accident (traffic) V68.7
        nontraffic V68.2
    noncollision accident (traffic) V68.9
      nontraffic V68.3
      while boarding or alighting V68.4
    nontraffic V69.3
    passenger
      collision (with)
        animal (traffic) V60.6
          being ridden (traffic) V66.6
            nontraffic V66.1
          nontraffic V60.1
        animal-drawn vehicle (traffic) V66.6
          nontraffic V66.1
        bus (traffic) V64.6
          nontraffic V64.1

Accident (Continued)
transport (Continued)
  truck occupant (Continued)
    passenger (Continued)
      collision (Continued)
        car (traffic) V63.6
          nontraffic V63.1
        motor vehicle NOS (traffic) V69.50
          nontraffic V69.10
          specified type NEC (traffic)
            V69.59
            nontraffic V69.19
        pedal cycle (traffic) V61.6
          nontraffic V61.1
        pickup truck (traffic) V63.6
          nontraffic V63.1
        railway vehicle (traffic) V65.6
          nontraffic V65.1
        specified vehicle NEC (traffic)
          V66.6
          nontraffic V66.1
        stationary object (traffic) V67.6
          nontraffic V67.1
        streetcar (traffic) V66.6
          nontraffic V66.1
        three wheeled motor vehicle
          (traffic) V62.6
          nontraffic V62.1
        truck (traffic) V64.6
          nontraffic V64.1
        two wheeled motor vehicle (traffic)
          V62.6
          nontraffic V62.1
        van (traffic) V63.6
          nontraffic V63.1
      noncollision accident (traffic) V68.6
        nontraffic V68.1
    pickup —see Accident, transport, pickup
      truck occupant
    specified type NEC V69.88
      military vehicle V69.81
  van occupant V59.9
    collision (with)
      animal (traffic) V50.9
        being ridden (traffic) V56.9
          nontraffic V56.3
          while boarding or alighting
            V56.4
        nontraffic V50.3
        while boarding or alighting V50.4
      animal-drawn vehicle (traffic) V56.9
        nontraffic V56.3
        while boarding or alighting V56.4
      bus (traffic) V54.9
        nontraffic V54.3
        while boarding or alighting V54.4
      car (traffic) V53.9
        nontraffic V53.3
        while boarding or alighting V53.4
      motor vehicle NOS (traffic) V59.60
        nontraffic V59.20
        specified type NEC (traffic) V59.69
          nontraffic V59.29
      pedal cycle (traffic) V51.9
        nontraffic V51.3
        while boarding or alighting V51.4
      pickup truck (traffic) V53.9
        nontraffic V53.3
        while boarding or alighting V53.4
      railway vehicle (traffic) V55.9
        nontraffic V55.3
        while boarding or alighting V55.4
      specified vehicle NEC (traffic) V56.9
        nontraffic V56.3
        while boarding or alighting V56.4
      stationary object (traffic) V57.9
        nontraffic V57.3
        while boarding or alighting V57.4
      streetcar (traffic) V56.9
        nontraffic V56.3
        while boarding or alighting V56.4

Accident (Continued)
transport (Continued)
  van occupant (Continued)
    collision (Continued)
      three wheeled motor vehicle (traffic)
        V52.9
        nontraffic V52.3
        while boarding or alighting V52.4
      truck (traffic) V54.9
        nontraffic V54.3
        while boarding or alighting V54.4
      two wheeled motor vehicle (traffic)
        V52.9
        nontraffic V52.3
        while boarding or alighting V52.4
      van (traffic) V53.9
        nontraffic V53.3
        while boarding or alighting V53.4
    driver
      collision (with)
        animal (traffic) V50.5
          being ridden (traffic) V56.5
            nontraffic V56.0
          nontraffic V50.0
        animal-drawn vehicle (traffic) V56.5
          nontraffic V56.0
        bus (traffic) V54.5
          nontraffic V54.0
        car (traffic) V53.5
          nontraffic V53.0
        motor vehicle NOS (traffic) V59.40
          nontraffic V59.00
          specified type NEC (traffic)
            V59.49
            nontraffic V59.09
        pedal cycle (traffic) V51.5
          nontraffic V51.0
        pickup truck (traffic) V53.5
          nontraffic V53.0
        railway vehicle (traffic) V55.5
          nontraffic V55.0
        specified vehicle NEC (traffic) V56.5
          nontraffic V56.0
        stationary object (traffic) V57.5
          nontraffic V57.0
        streetcar (traffic) V56.5
          nontraffic V56.0
        three wheeled motor vehicle
          (traffic) V52.5
          nontraffic V52.0
        truck (traffic) V54.5
          nontraffic V54.0
        two wheeled motor vehicle (traffic)
          V52.5
          nontraffic V52.0
        van (traffic) V53.5
          nontraffic V53.0
      noncollision accident (traffic) V58.5
        nontraffic V58.0
    hanger-on
      collision (with)
        animal (traffic) V50.7
          being ridden (traffic) V56.7
            nontraffic V56.2
          nontraffic V50.2
        animal-drawn vehicle (traffic) V56.7
          nontraffic V56.2
        bus (traffic) V54.7
          nontraffic V54.2
        car (traffic) V53.7
          nontraffic V53.2
        pedal cycle (traffic) V51.7
          nontraffic V51.2
        pickup truck (traffic) V53.7
          nontraffic V53.2
        railway vehicle (traffic) V55.7
          nontraffic V55.2
        specified vehicle NEC (traffic) V56.7
          nontraffic V56.2
        stationary object (traffic) V57.7
          nontraffic V57.2

A

▶ New ⇒ Revised ~~deleted~~ Deleted ● Use Additional Character(s)

Activity *(Continued)*
digging
    dirt Y93.H1
dirt digging Y93.H1
dishwashing Y93.G1
diving (platform) (springboard) Y93.12
    underwater Y93.15
dodge ball Y93.6A
downhill skiing Y93.23
drum playing Y93.J2
dumbbells Y93.B3
electronic
    devices NEC Y93.C9
      hand held interactive Y93.C2
    game playing (using) (with)
      interactive device Y93.C2
      keyboard or other stationary device
        Y93.C1
elliptical machine Y93.A1
exercise(s)
    machines ((primarily) for)
      cardiorespiratory conditioning Y93.A1
      muscle strengthening Y93.B1
    muscle strengthening (non-machine) NEC
      Y93.B9
external motion NEC Y93.I9
    rollercoaster Y93.I1
fainting game Y93.85
field hockey Y93.65
figure skating (pairs) (singles) Y93.21
flag football Y93.62
floor mopping and cleaning Y93.E5
food preparation and clean up Y93.G1
football (American) NOS Y93.61
    flag Y93.62
    tackle Y93.61
    touch Y93.62
four square Y93.6A
free weights Y93.B3
frisbee (ultimate) Y93.74
furniture
    building Y93.D3
    finishing Y93.D3
    repair Y93.D3
game playing (electronic)
    using interactive device Y93.C2
    using keyboard or other stationary device
      Y93.C1
gardening Y93.H2
golf Y93.53
grass drills Y93.A6
grilling and smoking food Y93.G2
grooming and shearing an animal Y93.K3
guerilla drills Y93.A6
gymnastics (rhythmic) Y93.43
hand held interactive electronic device Y93.C2
handball Y93.73
handcrafts NEC Y93.D9
hang gliding Y93.35
hiking (on level or elevated terrain) Y93.Ø1
hockey (ice) Y93.22
    field Y93.65
horseback riding Y93.52
household (interior) maintenance NEC Y93.E9
ice NEC Y93.29
    dancing Y93.21
    hockey Y93.22
    skating Y93.21
inline roller skating Y93.51
ironing Y93.E4
judo Y93.75
jumping (off) NEC Y93.39
    BASE (Building, Antenna, Span, Earth)
      Y93.33
    bungee Y93.34
    jacks Y93.A2
    rope Y93.56
jumping jacks Y93.A2
jumping rope Y93.56
karate Y93.75

Activity *(Continued)*
kayaking (in calm and turbulent water) Y93.16
keyboarding (computer) Y93.C1
kickball Y93.6A
knitting Y93.D1
lacrosse Y93.65
land maintenance NEC Y93.H9
landscaping Y93.H2
laundry Y93.E2
machines (exercise)
    primarily for cardiorespiratory
      conditioning Y93.A1
    primarily for muscle strengthening Y93.B1
maintenance
    exterior building NEC Y93.H9
    household (interior) NEC Y93.E9
    land Y93.H9
    property Y93.H9
marching (on level or elevated terrain) Y93.Ø1
martial arts Y93.75
microwave oven Y93.G3
milking an animal Y93.K2
mopping (floor) Y93.E5
mountain climbing Y93.31
muscle strengthening
    exercises (non-machine) NEC Y93.B9
    machines Y93.B1
musical keyboard (electronic) playing Y93.J1
nordic skiing Y93.24
obstacle course Y93.A5
oven (microwave) Y93.G3
packing up and unpacking in moving to a
    new residence Y93.E6
parasailing Y93.19
pass out game Y93.85
percussion instrument playing NEC Y93.J2
personal
    bathing and showering Y93.E1
    hygiene NEC Y93.E8
    showering Y93.E1
physical games generally associated with
    school recess, summer camp and
    children Y93.6A
physical training NEC Y93.A9
piano playing Y93.J1
pilates Y93.B4
platform diving Y93.12
playing musical instrument
    brass instrument Y93.J4
    drum Y93.J2
    musical keyboard (electronic) Y93.J1
    percussion instrument NEC Y93.J2
    piano Y93.J1
    string instrument Y93.J3
    winds instrument Y93.J4
property maintenance
    exterior NEC Y93.H9
    interior NEC Y93.E9
pruning (garden and lawn) Y93.H2
pull-ups Y93.B2
push-ups Y93.B2
racquetball Y93.73
rafting (in calm and turbulent water) Y93.16
raking (leaves) Y93.H1
rappelling Y93.32
refereeing a sports activity Y93.81
residential relocation Y93.E6
rhythmic gymnastics Y93.43
rhythmic movement NEC Y93.49
riding
    horseback Y93.52
    rollercoaster Y93.I1
rock climbing Y93.31
roller skating (inline) Y93.51
rollercoaster riding Y93.I1
rough housing and horseplay Y93.83
rowing (in calm and turbulent water)
    Y93.16
rugby Y93.63
SCUBA diving Y93.15
sewing Y93.D2

Activity *(Continued)*
shoveling Y93.H1
    dirt Y93.H1
    snow Y93.H1
showering (personal) Y93.E1
sit-ups Y93.B2
skateboarding Y93.51
skating (ice) Y93.21
    roller Y93.51
skiing (alpine) (downhill) Y93.23
    cross country Y93.24
    nordic Y93.24
    water Y93.17
sledding (snow) Y93.23
sleeping (sleep) Y93.84
smoking and grilling food Y93.G2
snorkeling Y93.15
snow NEC Y93.29
    boarding Y93.23
    shoveling Y93.H1
    sledding Y93.23
    tubing Y93.23
soccer Y93.66
softball Y93.64
specified NEC Y93.89
spectator at an event Y93.82
sports NEC Y93.79
    sports played as a team or group NEC
      Y93.69
    sports played individually NEC Y93.59
springboard diving Y93.12
squash Y93.73
stationary bike Y93.A1
step (stepping) exercise (class) Y93.A3
stepper machine Y93.A1
stove Y93.G3
string instrument playing Y93.J3
surfing Y93.18
    wind Y93.18
swimming Y93.11
tackle football Y93.61
tap dancing Y93.41
tennis Y93.73
tobogganing Y93.23
touch football Y93.62
track and field events (non-running) Y93.57
    running Y93.Ø2
trampoline Y93.44
treadmill Y93.A1
trimming shrubs Y93.H2
tubing (in calm and turbulent water) Y93.16
    snow Y93.23
ultimate frisbee Y93.74
underwater diving Y93.15
unpacking in moving to a new residence
    Y93.E6
use of stove, oven and microwave oven Y93.
    G3
vacuuming Y93.E3
volleyball (beach) (court) Y93.68
wake boarding Y93.17
walking (on level or elevated terrain) Y93.Ø1
    an animal Y93.K1
walking an animal Y93.K1
wall climbing Y93.31
warm up and cool down exercises Y93.A2
water NEC Y93.19
    aerobics Y93.14
    craft NEC Y93.19
    exercise Y93.14
    polo Y93.13
    skiing Y93.17
    sliding Y93.18
    survival training and testing Y93.19
weeding (garden and lawn) Y93.H2
wind instrument playing Y93.J4
windsurfing Y93.18
wrestling Y93.72
yoga Y93.42
Adverse effect of drugs —*see* Table of Drugs
    and Chemicals

▶ New   ⇒ Revised   ~~deleted~~ Deleted   ● Use Additional Character(s)

Aerosinusitis —see Air, pressure
After-effect, late —see Sequelae
Air
  blast in war operations —see War operations, air blast
  pressure
    change, rapid
      during
        ascent W94.29
          while (in) (surfacing from)
            aircraft W94.23
            deep water diving W94.21
            underground W94.22
        descent W94.39
          in
            aircraft W94.31
            water W94.32
      high, prolonged W94.0
      low, prolonged W94.12
        due to residence or long visit at high altitude W94.11
Alpine sickness W94.11
Altitude sickness W94.11
Anaphylactic shock, anaphylaxis —see Table of Drugs and Chemicals
Andes disease W94.11
Arachnidism, arachnoidism X58
Arson (with intent to injure or kill) X97
Asphyxia, asphyxiation
  by
    food (bone) (seed) —see categories T17 and T18
    gas —see also Table of Drugs and Chemicals
      legal
        execution —see Legal, intervention, gas
        intervention —see Legal, intervention, gas
  from
    fire —see also Exposure, fire
      in war operations —see War operations, fire
    ignition —see Ignition
    vomitus T17.81
  in war operations —see War operations, restriction of airway
Aspiration
  food (any type) (into respiratory tract) (with asphyxia, obstruction respiratory tract, suffocation) —see categories T17 and T18
  foreign body —see Foreign body, aspiration
  vomitus (with asphyxia, obstruction respiratory tract, suffocation) T17.81
Assassination (attempt) —see Assault
Assault (homicidal) (by) (in) Y09
  arson X97
  bite (of human being) Y04.1
  bodily force Y04.8
    bite Y04.1
    bumping into Y04.2
    sexual —see subcategories T74.0, T76.0
    unarmed fight Y04.0

Assault (Continued)
  bomb X96.9
    antipersonnel X96.0
    fertilizer X96.3
    gasoline X96.1
    letter X96.2
    petrol X96.1
    pipe X96.3
    specified NEC X96.8
  brawl (hand) (fists) (foot) (unarmed) Y04.0
  burning, burns (by fire) NEC X97
    acid Y08.89
    caustic, corrosive substance Y08.89
    chemical from swallowing caustic, corrosive substance —see Table of Drugs and Chemicals
    cigarette(s) X97
    hot object X98.9
      fluid NEC X98.2
      household appliance X98.3
      specified NEC X98.8
      steam X98.0
      tap water X98.1
      vapors X98.0
    scalding —see Assault, burning
    steam X98.0
    vitriol Y08.89
  caustic, corrosive substance (gas) Y08.89
  crashing of
    aircraft Y08.81
    motor vehicle Y03.8
      pushed in front of Y02.0
      run over Y03.0
      specified NEC Y03.8
  cutting or piercing instrument X99.9
    dagger X99.2
    glass X99.0
    knife X99.1
    specified NEC X99.8
    sword X99.2
  dagger X99.2
  drowning (in) X92.9
    bathtub X92.0
    natural water X92.3
    specified NEC X92.8
    swimming pool X92.1
      following fall X92.2
  dynamite X96.8
  explosive(s) (material) X96.9
  fight (hand) (fists) (foot) (unarmed) Y04.0
    with weapon —see Assault, by type of weapon
  fire X97
  firearm X95.9
    airgun X95.01
    handgun X93
    hunting rifle X94.1
    larger X94.9
      specified NEC X94.8
    machine gun X94.2
    shotgun X94.0
    specified NEC X95.8

Assault (Continued)
  from high place Y01
  gunshot (wound) NEC —see Assault, firearm, by type
  incendiary device X97
  injury Y09
    to child due to criminal abortion attempt NEC Y08.89
  knife X99.1
  late effect of —see X92-Y08 with 7th character S
  placing before moving object NEC Y02.8
    motor vehicle Y02.0
  poisoning —see categories T36-T65 with 7th character S
  puncture, any part of body —see Assault, cutting or piercing instrument
  pushing
    before moving object NEC Y02.8
      motor vehicle Y02.0
      subway train Y02.1
      train Y02.1
  rape T74.2-●
  scalding —see Assault, burning
  sequelae of —see X92-Y08 with 7th character S
  sexual (by bodily force) T74.2-●
  shooting —see Assault, firearm
  specified means NEC Y08.89
  stab, any part of body —see Assault, cutting or piercing instrument
  steam X98.0
  striking against
    other person Y04.2
    sports equipment Y08.09
      baseball bat Y08.02
      hockey stick Y08.01
  struck by
    sports equipment Y08.09
      baseball bat Y08.02
      hockey stick Y08.01
  submersion —see Assault, drowning
  violence Y09
  weapon Y09
    blunt Y00
    cutting or piercing —see Assault, cutting or piercing instrument
    firearm —see Assault, firearm
  wound Y09
    cutting —see Assault, cutting or piercing instrument
    gunshot —see Assault, firearm
    knife X99.1
    piercing —see Assault, cutting or piercing instrument
    puncture —see Assault, cutting or piercing instrument
    stab —see Assault, cutting or piercing instrument
Attack by mammals NEC W55.89
Avalanche —see Landslide
Aviator's disease —see Air, pressure

▶ New   ⇒ Revised   ~~deleted~~ Deleted   ● Use Additional Character(s)

B

Barotitis, barodontalgia, barosinusitis, barotrauma (otitic) (sinus) —*see* Air, pressure
Battered (baby) (child) (person) (syndrome) X58
Bayonet wound W26.1
  in
    legal intervention —*see* Legal, intervention, sharp object, bayonet
    war operations —*see* War operations, combat
  stated as undetermined whether accidental or intentional Y28.8
  suicide (attempt) X78.2
Bean in nose —*see* categories T17 and T18
Bed set on fire NEC —*see* Exposure, fire, uncontrolled, building, bed
Beheading (by guillotine)
  homicide X99.9
  legal execution —*see* Legal, intervention
Bending, injury in (prolonged) (static) X50.1
Bends —*see* Air, pressure, change
Bite, bitten by
  alligator W58.01
  arthropod (nonvenomous) NEC W57
  bull W55.21
  cat W55.01
  cow W55.21
  crocodile W58.11
  dog W54.0
  goat W55.31
  hoof stock NEC W55.31
  horse W55.11
  human being (accidentally) W50.3
    with intent to injure or kill Y04.1
    as, or caused by, a crowd or human stampede (with fall) W52
    assault Y04.1
    homicide (attempt) Y04.1
    in
      fight Y04.1
  insect (nonvenomous) W57
  lizard (nonvenomous) W59.01
  mammal NEC W55.81
    marine W56.31
  marine animal (nonvenomous) W56.81
  millipede W57
  moray eel W56.51
  mouse W53.01
  person(s) (accidentally) W50.3
    with intent to injure or kill Y04.1
    as, or caused by, a crowd or human stampede (with fall) W52
    assault Y04.1
    homicide (attempt) Y04.1
    in
      fight Y04.1
  pig W55.41
  raccoon W55.51
  rat W53.11
  reptile W59.81
    lizard W59.01
    snake W59.11
    turtle W59.21
      terrestrial W59.81
  rodent W53.81
    mouse W53.01
    rat W53.11
    specified NEC W53.81
    squirrel W53.21
  shark W56.41
  sheep W55.31
  snake (nonvenomous) W59.11
  spider (nonvenomous) W57
  squirrel W53.21
Blast (air) in war operations —*see* War operations, blast
Blizzard X37.2

Blood alcohol level Y90.9
  20-39mg/100ml Y90.1
  40-59mg/100ml Y90.2
  60-79mg/100ml Y90.3
  80-99mg/100ml Y90.4
  100-119mg/100ml Y90.5
  120-199mg/100ml Y90.6
  200-239mg/100ml Y90.7
  less than 20mg/100ml Y90.0
  presence in blood, level not specified Y90.9
Blow X58
  by law-enforcing agent, police (on duty) —*see* Legal, intervention, manhandling
    blunt object —*see* Legal, intervention, blunt object
Blowing up —*see* Explosion
Brawl (hand) (fists) (foot) Y04.0
Breakage (accidental) (part of)
  ladder (causing fall) W11
  scaffolding (causing fall) W12
Broken
  glass, contact with —*see* Contact, with, glass
  power line (causing electric shock) W85
Bumping against, into (accidentally)
  object NEC W22.8
    with fall —*see* Fall, due to, bumping against, object
    caused by crowd or human stampede (with fall) W52
    sports equipment W21.9
  person(s) W51
    with fall W03
      due to ice or snow W00.0
    assault Y04.2
    caused by, a crowd or human stampede (with fall) W52
    homicide (attempt) Y04.2
    sports equipment W21.9
Burn, burned, burning (accidental) (by) (from) (on)
  acid NEC —*see* Table of Drugs and Chemicals
  bed linen —*see* Exposure, fire, uncontrolled, in building, bed
  blowtorch X08.8
    with ignition of clothing NEC X06.2
      nightwear X05
  bonfire, campfire (controlled) —*see also* Exposure, fire, controlled, not in building
    uncontrolled —*see* Exposure, fire, uncontrolled, not in building
  candle X08.8
    with ignition of clothing NEC X06.2
      nightwear X05
  caustic liquid, substance (external) (internal) NEC —*see* Table of Drugs and Chemicals
  chemical (external) (internal) —*see also* Table of Drugs and Chemicals
    in war operations —*see* War operations, fire
  cigar(s) or cigarette(s) X08.8
    with ignition of clothing NEC X06.2
      nightwear X05
  clothes, clothing NEC (from controlled fire) X06.2
    with conflagration —*see* Exposure, fire, uncontrolled, building
    not in building or structure —*see* Exposure, fire, uncontrolled, not in building
  cooker (hot) X15.8
    stated as undetermined whether accidental or intentional Y27.3
    suicide (attempt) X77.3
  electric blanket X16
  engine (hot) X17
  fire, flames —*see* Exposure, fire
  flare, Very pistol —*see* Discharge, firearm NEC

Burn, burned, burning (Continued)
  heat
    from appliance (electrical) (household) X15.8
      cooker X15.8
      hotplate X15.2
      kettle X15.8
      light bulb X15.8
      saucepan X15.3
      skillet X15.3
      stated as undetermined whether accidental or intentional Y27.3
      stove X15.0
      suicide (attempt) X77.3
      toaster X15.1
    in local application or packing during medical or surgical procedure Y63.5
  heating
    appliance, radiator or pipe X16
  homicide (attempt) —*see* Assault, burning
  hot
    air X14.1
    cooker X15.8
    drink X10.0
    engine X17
    fat X10.2
    fluid NEC X12
    food X10.1
    gases X14.1
    heating appliance X16
    household appliance NEC X15.8
    kettle X15.8
    liquid NEC X12
    machinery X17
    metal (molten) (liquid) NEC X18
    object (not producing fire or flames) NEC X19
    oil (cooking) X10.2
    pipe(s) X16
    radiator X16
    saucepan (glass) (metal) X15.3
    stove (kitchen) X15.0
    substance NEC X19
      caustic or corrosive NEC —*see* Table of Drugs and Chemicals
    toaster X15.1
    tool X17
    vapor X13.1
    water (tap) —*see* Contact, with, hot, tap water
  hotplate X15.2
    suicide (attempt) X77.3
  ignition —*see* Ignition
  in war operations —*see* War operations, fire
  inflicted by other person X97
    by hot objects, hot vapor, and steam —*see* Assault, burning, hot object
  internal, from swallowed caustic, corrosive liquid, substance —*see* Table of Drugs and Chemicals
  iron (hot) X15.8
    stated as undetermined whether accidental or intentional Y27.3
    suicide (attempt) X77.3
  kettle (hot) X15.8
    stated as undetermined whether accidental or intentional Y27.3
    suicide (attempt) X77.3
  lamp (flame) X08.8
    with ignition of clothing NEC X06.2
      nightwear X05
  lighter (cigar) (cigarette) X08.8
    with ignition of clothing NEC X06.2
      nightwear X05
  lightning —*see* subcategory T75.0
    causing fire —*see* Exposure, fire
  liquid (boiling) (hot) NEC X12
    stated as undetermined whether accidental or intentional Y27.2
    suicide (attempt) X77.2

Burn, burned, burning *(Continued)*
  local application of externally applied
    substance in medical or surgical care
    Y63.5
  machinery (hot) X17
  matches X08.8
    with ignition of clothing NEC X06.2
      nightwear X05
  mattress —*see* Exposure, fire, uncontrolled,
    building, bed
  medicament, externally applied Y63.5
  metal (hot) (liquid) (molten) NEC X18
  nightwear (nightclothes, nightdress, gown,
    pajamas, robe) X05
  object (hot) NEC X19
  on board watercraft
    due to
      accident to watercraft V91.09
        powered craft V91.03
          ferry boat V91.01
          fishing boat V91.02
          jet ski V91.03
          liner V91.01
          merchant ship V91.00
          passenger ship V91.01
        unpowered craft V91.08
          canoe V91.05
          inflatable V91.06
          kayak V91.05
          sailboat V91.04
          surf-board V91.08
          water skis V91.07
          windsurfer V91.08
      fire on board V93.09
        ferry boat V93.01
        fishing boat V93.02
        jet ski V93.03
        liner V93.01
        merchant ship V93.00
        passenger ship V93.01
        powered craft NEC V93.03
        sailboat V93.04

Burn, burned, burning *(Continued)*
  on board watercraft *(Continued)*
    due to *(Continued)*
      specified heat source NEC on board
        V93.19
        ferry boat V93.11
        fishing boat V93.12
        jet ski V93.13
        liner V93.11
        merchant ship V93.10
        passenger ship V93.11
        powered craft NEC V93.13
        sailboat V93.14
  pipe (hot) X16
    smoking X08.8
      with ignition of clothing NEC X06.2
        nightwear X05
  powder —*see* Powder burn
  radiator (hot) X16
  saucepan (hot) (glass) (metal) X15.3
    stated as undetermined whether
      accidental or intentional
      Y27.3
    suicide (attempt) X77.3
  self-inflicted X76
    stated as undetermined whether
      accidental or intentional
      Y26
  stated as undetermined whether
    accidental or intentional Y27.0
  steam X13.1
    pipe X16
      stated as undetermined whether
        accidental or intentional
        Y27.8
    stated as undetermined whether
      accidental or intentional Y27.0
    suicide (attempt) X77.0
  stove (hot) (kitchen) X15.0
    stated as undetermined whether
      accidental or intentional Y27.3
    suicide (attempt) X77.3

Burn, burned, burning *(Continued)*
  substance (hot) NEC X19
    boiling X12
      stated as undetermined whether
        accidental or intentional Y27.2
      suicide (attempt) X77.2
    molten (metal) X18
  suicide (attempt) NEC X76
    hot
      household appliance X77.3
      object X77.9
  stated as undetermined whether accidental or
    intentional Y27.0
  therapeutic misadventure
    heat in local application or packing during
      medical or surgical procedure Y63.5
    overdose of radiation Y63.2
  toaster (hot) X15.1
    stated as undetermined whether accidental
      or intentional Y27.3
    suicide (attempt) X77.3
  tool (hot) X17
  torch, welding X08.8
    with ignition of clothing NEC X06.2
      nightwear X05
  trash fire (controlled) —*see* Exposure, fire,
    controlled, not in building
    uncontrolled —*see* Exposure, fire,
      uncontrolled, not in building
  vapor (hot) X13.1
    stated as undetermined whether accidental
      or intentional Y27.0
    suicide (attempt) X77.0
  Very pistol —*see* Discharge, firearm NEC
Butted by animal W55.82
  bull W55.22
  cow W55.22
  goat W55.32
  horse W55.12
  pig W55.42
  sheep W55.32

▶ New   ⇒ Revised   ~~deleted~~ Deleted   ● Use Additional Character(s)

C

Caisson disease —*see* Air, pressure, change
Campfire (exposure to) (controlled) —*see also* Exposure, fire, controlled, not in building
   uncontrolled —*see* Exposure, fire, uncontrolled, not in building
Capital punishment (any means) —*see* Legal, intervention
Car sickness T75.3
Casualty (not due to war) NEC X58
   war —*see* War operations
Cat
   bite W55.01
   scratch W55.03
Cataclysm, cataclysmic (any injury) NEC —*see* Forces of nature
Catching fire —*see* Exposure, fire
Caught
   between
      folding object W23.0
      objects (moving) (stationary and moving) W23.0
         and machinery —*see* Contact, with, by type of machine
         stationary W23.1
      sliding door and door frame W23.0
   by, in
      machinery (moving parts of) —*see* Contact, with, by type of machine
      washing-machine wringer W23.0
   under packing crate (due to losing grip) W23.1
Cave-in caused by cataclysmic earth surface movement or eruption —*see* Landslide
Change(s) in air pressure —*see* Air, pressure, change
Choked, choking (on) (any object except food or vomitus)
   food (bone) (seed) —*see* categories T17 and T18
   vomitus T17.81-●
Civil insurrection —*see* War operations
Cloudburst (any injury) X37.8
Cold, exposure to (accidental) (excessive) (extreme) (natural) (place) NEC —*see* Exposure, cold
Collapse
   building W20.1
      burning (uncontrolled fire) X00.2
   dam or man-made structure (causing earth movement) X36.0
   machinery —*see* Contact, with, by type of machine
   structure W20.1
      burning (uncontrolled fire) X00.2
Collision (accidental) NEC —*see also* Accident, transport V89.9
   pedestrian W51
      with fall W03
         due to ice or snow W00.0
         involving pedestrian conveyance —*see* Accident, transport, pedestrian, conveyance
      and
         crowd or human stampede (with fall) W52
         object W22.8
            with fall —*see* Fall, due to, bumping against, object
      person(s) —*see* Collision, pedestrian
   transport vehicle NEC V89.9
      and
         avalanche, fallen or not moving —*see* Accident, transport
            falling or moving —*see* Landslide
         landslide, fallen or not moving —*see* Accident, transport
            falling or moving —*see* Landslide

Collision NEC (*Continued*)
   transport vehicle NEC (*Continued*)
      due to cataclysm —*see* Forces of nature, by type
      intentional, purposeful suicide (attempt) —*see* Suicide, collision
Combustion, spontaneous —*see* Ignition
Complication (delayed) of or following (medical or surgical procedure) Y84.9
   with misadventure —*see* Misadventure
   amputation of limb(s) Y83.5
   anastomosis (arteriovenous) (blood vessel) (gastrojejunal) (tendon) (natural or artificial material) Y83.2
   aspiration (of fluid) Y84.4
      tissue Y84.8
   biopsy Y84.8
   blood
      sampling Y84.7
      transfusion
         procedure Y84.8
   bypass Y83.2
   catheterization (urinary) Y84.6
      cardiac Y84.0
   colostomy Y83.3
   cystostomy Y83.3
   dialysis (kidney) Y84.1
   drug —*see* Table of Drugs and Chemicals
   due to misadventure —*see* Misadventure
   duodenostomy Y83.3
   electroshock therapy Y84.3
   external stoma, creation of Y83.3
   formation of external stoma Y83.3
   gastrostomy Y83.3
   graft Y83.2
   hypothermia (medically-induced) Y84.8
   implant, implantation (of)
      artificial
         internal device (cardiac pacemaker) (electrodes in brain) (heart valve prosthesis) (orthopedic) Y83.1
         material or tissue (for anastomosis or bypass) Y83.2
            with creation of external stoma Y83.3
      natural tissues (for anastomosis or bypass) Y83.2
         with creation of external stoma Y83.3
   infusion
      procedure Y84.8
   injection —*see* Table of Drugs and Chemicals
      procedure Y84.8
   insertion of gastric or duodenal sound Y84.5
   insulin-shock therapy Y84.3
   paracentesis (abdominal) (thoracic) (aspirative) Y84.4
   procedures other than surgical operation —*see* Complication of or following, by type of procedure
   radiological procedure or therapy Y84.2
   removal of organ (partial) (total) NEC Y83.6
   sampling
      blood Y84.7
      fluid NEC Y84.4
      tissue Y84.8
   shock therapy Y84.3
   surgical operation NEC —*see also* Complication of or following, by type of operation Y83.9
      reconstructive NEC Y83.4
         with
            anastomosis, bypass or graft Y83.2
            formation of external stoma Y83.3
      specified NEC Y83.8
   transfusion —*see also* Table of Drugs and Chemicals
      procedure Y84.8
   transplant, transplantation (heart) (kidney) (liver) (whole organ, any) Y83.0
      partial organ Y83.4
   ureterostomy Y83.3

Complication of or following (*Continued*)
   vaccination —*see also* Table of Drugs and Chemicals
      procedure Y84.8
Compression
   divers' squeeze —*see* Air, pressure, change
   trachea by
      food (lodged in esophagus) —*see* categories T17 and T18
      vomitus (lodged in esophagus) T17.81-●
Conflagration —*see* Exposure, fire, uncontrolled
Constriction (external)
   hair W49.01
   jewelry W49.04
   ring W49.04
   rubber band W49.03
   specified item NEC W49.09
   string W49.02
   thread W49.02
Contact (accidental)
   with
      abrasive wheel (metalworking) W31.1
      alligator W58.09
         bite W58.01
         crushing W58.03
         strike W58.02
      amphibian W62.9
         frog W62.0
         toad W62.1
      animal (nonvenomous) NEC W64
         marine W56.89
            bite W56.81
            dolphin —*see* Contact, with, dolphin
            fish NEC —*see* Contact, with, fish
            mammal —*see* Contact, with, mammal, marine
            orca —*see* Contact, with, orca
            sea lion —*see* Contact, with, sea lion
            shark —*see* Contact, with, shark
            strike W56.82
      animate mechanical force NEC W64
      arrow W21.89
         not thrown, projected or falling W45.8
      arthropods (nonvenomous) W57
      axe W27.0
      band-saw (industrial) W31.2
      bayonet —*see* Bayonet wound
      bee(s) X58
      bench-saw (industrial) W31.2
      bird W61.99
         bite W61.91
         chicken —*see* Contact, with, chicken
         duck —*see* Contact, with, duck
         goose —*see* Contact, with, goose
         macaw —*see* Contact, with, macaw
         parrot —*see* Contact, with, parrot
         psittacine —*see* Contact, with, psittacine
         strike W61.92
         turkey —*see* Contact, with, turkey
      blender W29.0
      boiling water X12
         stated as undetermined whether accidental or intentional Y27.2
         suicide (attempt) X77.2
      bore, earth-drilling or mining (land) (seabed) W31.0
      buffalo —*see* Contact, with, hoof stock NEC
      bull W55.29
         bite W55.21
         gored W55.22
         strike W55.22
      bumper cars W31.81
      camel —*see* Contact, with, hoof stock NEC
      can
         lid W26.8
         opener W27.4
            powered W29.0
      cat W55.09
         bite W55.01
         scratch W55.03
      caterpillar (venomous) X58

Contact *(Continued)*
with *(Continued)*
  centipede (venomous) X58
  chain
    hoist W24.0
      agricultural operations W30.89
    saw W29.3
  chicken W61.39
    peck W61.33
    strike W61.32
  chisel W27.0
  circular saw W31.2
  cobra X58
  combine (harvester) W30.0
  conveyer belt W24.1
  cooker (hot) X15.8
    stated as undetermined whether
      accidental or intentional Y27.3
    suicide (attempt) X77.3
  coral X58
  cotton gin W31.82
  cow W55.29
    bite W55.21
    strike W55.22
  crane W24.0
    agricultural operations W30.89
  crocodile W58.19
    bite W58.11
    crushing W58.13
    strike W58.12
  dagger W26.1
    stated as undetermined whether
      accidental or intentional Y28.2
    suicide (attempt) X78.2
  dairy equipment W31.82
  dart W21.89
    not thrown, projected or falling W45.8
  deer —*see* Contact, with, hoof stock
    NEC
  derrick W24.0
    agricultural operations W30.89
      hay W30.2
  dog W54.8
    bite W54.0
    strike W54.1
  dolphin W56.09
    bite W56.01
    strike W56.02
  donkey —*see* Contact, with, hoof stock
    NEC
  drill (powered) W29.8
    earth (land) (seabed) W31.0
    nonpowered W27.8
  drive belt W24.0
    agricultural operations W30.89
  dry ice —*see* Exposure, cold, man-made
  dryer (clothes) (powered) (spin) W29.2
  duck W61.69
    bite W61.61
    strike W61.62
  earth(-)
    drilling machine (industrial) W31.0
    scraping machine in stationary use
      W31.83
  edge of stiff paper W26.2
  electric
    beater W29.0
    blanket X16
    fan W29.2
      commercial W31.82
    knife W29.1
    mixer W29.0
  elevator (building) W24.0
    agricultural operations W30.89
      grain W30.3
  engine(s), hot NEC X17
  excavating machine W31.0
  farm machine W30.9
  feces —*see* Contact, with, by type of
    animal
  fer de lance X58

Contact *(Continued)*
with *(Continued)*
  fish W56.59
    bite W56.51
    shark —*see* Contact, with, shark
    strike W56.52
  flying horses W31.81
  forging (metalworking) machine
    W31.1
  fork W27.4
  forklift (truck) W24.0
    agricultural operations W30.89
  frog W62.0
  garden
    cultivator (powered) W29.3
      riding W30.89
    fork W27.1
  gas turbine W31.3
  Gila monster X58
  giraffe —*see* Contact, with, hoof stock
    NEC
  glass (sharp) (broken) W25
    with subsequent fall W18.02
    assault X99.0
    due to fall —*see* Fall, by type
    stated as undetermined whether
      accidental or intentional Y28. 0
    suicide (attempt) X78.0
  goat W55.39
    bite W55.31
    strike W55.32
  goose W61.59
    bite W61.51
    strike W61.52
  hand
    saw W27.0
    tool (not powered) NEC W27.8
      powered W29.8
  harvester W30.0
  hay-derrick W30.2
  heat NEC X19
    from appliance (electrical)
      (household) —*see* Contact, with,
      hot, household appliance
    heating appliance X16
  heating
    appliance (hot) X16
    pad (electric) X16
  hedge-trimmer (powered) W29.3
  hoe W27.1
  hoist (chain) (shaft) NEC W24.0
    agricultural W30.89
  hoof stock NEC W55.39
    bite W55.31
    strike W55.32
  hornet(s) X58
  horse W55.19
    bite W55.11
    strike W55.12
  hot
    air X14.1
      inhalation X14.0
    cooker X15.8
    drinks X10.0
    engine X17
    fats X10.2
    fluids NEC X12
      assault X98.2
      suicide (attempt) X77.2
      undetermined whether accidental or
        intentional Y27.2
    food X10.1
    gases X14.1
      inhalation X14.0
    heating appliance X16
    household appliance X15.8
      assault X98.3
      cooker X15.8
      hotplate X15.2
      kettle X15.8
      light bulb X15.8

Contact *(Continued)*
with *(Continued)*
  hot *(Continued)*
    household appliance *(Continued)*
      object NEC X19
        assault X98.8
        stated as undetermined whether
          accidental or intentional Y27.9
        suicide (attempt) X77.8
      saucepan X15.3
      skillet X15.3
      stated as undetermined whether
        accidental or intentional Y27.3
      stove X15.0
      suicide (attempt) X77.3
      toaster X15.1
    kettle X15.8
    light bulb X15.8
    liquid NEC —*see also* Burn X12
      drinks X10.0
      stated as undetermined whether
        accidental or intentional Y27.2
      suicide (attempt) X77.2
      tap water X11.8
        stated as undetermined whether
          accidental or intentional Y27.1
        suicide (attempt) X77.1
    machinery X17
    metal (molten) (liquid) NEC X18
    object (not producing fire or flames)
      NEC X19
    oil (cooking) X10.2
    pipe X16
    plate X15.2
    radiator X16
    saucepan (glass) (metal) X15.3
    skillet X15.3
    stove (kitchen) X15.0
    substance NEC X19
    tap-water X11.8
      assault X98.1
      heated on stove X12
        stated as undetermined whether
          accidental or intentional Y27.2
        suicide (attempt) X77.2
      in bathtub X11.0
      running X11.1
      stated as undetermined whether
        accidental or intentional Y27.1
      suicide (attempt) X77.1
    toaster X15.1
    tool X17
    vapors X13.1
      inhalation X13.0
    water (tap) X11.8
      boiling X12
        stated as undetermined whether
          accidental or intentional Y27.2
        suicide (attempt) X77.2
      heated on stove X12
        stated as undetermined whether
          accidental or intentional Y27.2
        suicide (attempt) X77.2
      in bathtub X11.0
      running X11.1
      stated as undetermined whether
        accidental or intentional Y27.1
      suicide (attempt) X77.1
  hotplate X15.2
  ice-pick W27.4
  insect (nonvenomous) NEC W57
  kettle (hot) X15.8
  knife W26.0
    assault X99.1
    electric W29.1
    stated as undetermined whether
      accidental or intentional Y28.1
    suicide (attempt) X78.1
  lathe (metalworking) W31.1
    turnings W45.8
    woodworking W31.2

▶ New   ⇒ Revised   ~~deleted~~ Deleted   ● Use Additional Character(s)

Contact *(Continued)*
  with *(Continued)*
    lawnmower (powered) (ridden) W28
      causing electrocution W86.8
        suicide (attempt) X83.1
      unpowered W27.1
    lift, lifting (devices) W24.0
      agricultural operations W30.89
      shaft W24.0
    liquefied gas —*see* Exposure, cold,
      man-made
    liquid air, hydrogen, nitrogen —*see*
      Exposure, cold, man-made
    lizard (nonvenomous) W59.09
      bite W59.01
      strike W59.02
    llama —*see* Contact, with, hoof stock NEC
    macaw W61.19
      bite W61.11
      strike W61.12
    machine, machinery W31.9
      abrasive wheel W31.1
      agricultural including animal-powered
        W30.9
        combine harvester W30.0
        grain storage elevator W30.3
        hay derrick W30.2
        power take-off device W30.1
        reaper W30.0
        specified NEC W30.89
        thresher W30.0
        transport vehicle, stationary W30.81
      band saw W31.2
      bench saw W31.2
      circular saw W31.2
      commercial NEC W31.82
      drilling, metal (industrial) W31.1
      earth-drilling W31.0
      earthmoving or scraping W31.89
      excavating W31.89
      forging machine W31.1
      gas turbine W31.3
      hot X17
      internal combustion engine W31.3
      land drill W31.0
      lathe W31.1
      lifting (devices) W24.0
      metal drill W31.1
      metalworking (industrial) W31.1
      milling, metal W31.1
      mining W31.0
      molding W31.2
      overhead plane W31.2
      power press, metal W31.1
      prime mover W31.3
      printing W31.89
      radial saw W31.2
      recreational W31.81
      roller-coaster W31.81
      rolling mill, metal W31.1
      sander W31.2
      seabed drill W31.0
      shaft
        hoist W31.0
        lift W31.0
      specified NEC W31.89
      spinning W31.89
      steam engine W31.3
      transmission W24.1
      undercutter W31.0
      water driven turbine W31.3
      weaving W31.89
      woodworking or forming (industrial)
        W31.2
    mammal (feces) (urine) W55.89
      bull —*see* Contact, with, bull
      cat —*see* Contact, with, cat
      cow —*see* Contact, with, cow
      goat —*see* Contact, with, goat
      hoof stock —*see* Contact, with, hoof
        stock

Contact *(Continued)*
  with *(Continued)*
    mammal *(Continued)*
      horse —*see* Contact, with, horse
      marine W56.39
        dolphin —*see* Contact, with, dolphin
        orca —*see* Contact, with, orca
        sea lion —*see* Contact, with, sea lion
        specified NEC W56.39
          bite W56.31
          strike W56.32
      pig —*see* Contact, with, pig
      raccoon —*see* Contact, with, raccoon
      rodent —*see* Contact, with, rodent
      sheep —*see* Contact, with, sheep
      specified NEC W55.89
        bite W55.81
        strike W55.82
    marine
      animal W56.89
        bite W56.81
        dolphin —*see* Contact, with, dolphin
        fish NEC —*see* Contact, with, fish
        mammal —*see* Contact, with,
          mammal, marine
        orca —*see* Contact, with, orca
        sea lion —*see* Contact, with, sea lion
        shark —*see* Contact, with, shark
        strike W56.82
    meat
      grinder (domestic) W29.0
        industrial W31.82
        nonpowered W27.4
      slicer (domestic) W29.0
        industrial W31.82
    merry go round W31.81
    metal, (hot) (liquid) (molten) NEC X18
    millipede W57
    nail W45.0
      gun W29.4
    needle (sewing) W27.3
      hypodermic W46.0
        contaminated W46.1
    object (blunt) NEC
      hot NEC X19
      legal intervention —*see* Legal,
        intervention, blunt object
      sharp NEC W45.8
        inflicted by other person NEC W45.8
          stated as
            intentional homicide (attempt) —
              see Assault, cutting or
              piercing instrument
        legal intervention —*see* Legal,
          intervention, sharp object
        self-inflicted X78.9
    orca W56.29
      bite W56.21
      strike W56.22
    overhead plane W31.2
    paper (as sharp object) W26.2
    paper-cutter W27.5
    parrot W61.09
      bite W61.01
      strike W61.02
    pig W55.49
      bite W55.41
      strike W55.42
    pipe, hot X16
    pitchfork W27.1
    plane (metal) (wood) W27.0
      overhead W31.2
    plant thorns, spines, sharp leaves or other
      mechanisms W60
    powered
      garden cultivator W29.3
      household appliance, implement, or
        machine W29.8
      saw (industrial) W31.2
        hand W29.8
    printing machine W31.89

Contact *(Continued)*
  with *(Continued)*
    psittacine bird W61.29
      bite W61.21
      macaw —*see* Contact, with, macaw
      parrot —*see* Contact, with, parrot
      strike W61.22
    pulley (block) (transmission) W24.0
      agricultural operations W30.89
    raccoon W55.59
      bite W55.51
      strike W55.52
    radial-saw (industrial) W31.2
    radiator (hot) X16
    rake W27.1
    rattlesnake X58
    reaper W30.0
    reptile W59.89
      lizard —*see* Contact, with, lizard
      snake —*see* Contact, with, snake
      specified NEC W59.89
        bite W59.81
        crushing W59.83
        strike W59.82
      turtle —*see* Contact, with, turtle
    rivet gun (powered) W29.4
    road scraper —*see* Accident, transport,
      construction vehicle
    rodent (feces) (urine) W53.89
      bite W53.81
      mouse W53.09
        bite W53.01
      rat W53.19
        bite W53.11
      specified NEC W53.89
        bite W53.81
      squirrel W53.29
        bite W53.21
    roller coaster W31.81
    rope NEC W24.0
      agricultural operations W30.89
    saliva —*see* Contact, with, by type of
      animal
    sander W29.8
      industrial W31.2
    saucepan (hot) (glass) (metal) X15.3
    saw W27.0
      band (industrial) W31.2
      bench (industrial) W31.2
      chain W29.3
      hand W27.0
    sawing machine, metal W31.1
    scissors W27.2
    scorpion X58
    screwdriver W27.0
      powered W29.8
    sea
      anemone, cucumber or urchin (spine)
        X58
      lion W56.19
        bite W56.11
        strike W56.12
    serpent —*see* Contact, with, snake, by type
    sewing-machine (electric) (powered) W29.2
      not powered W27.8
    shaft (hoist) (lift) (transmission) NEC W24.0
      agricultural W30.89
    shark W56.49
      bite W56.41
      strike W56.42
    sharp object(s) W26.9
      specified NEC W26.8
    shears (hand) W27.2
      powered (industrial) W31.1
        domestic W29.2
    sheep W55.39
      bite W55.31
      strike W55.32
    shovel W27.8
      steam —*see* Accident, transport,
        construction vehicle

Contact (*Continued*)
  with (*Continued*)
    snake (nonvenomous) W59.19
      bite W59.11
      crushing W59.13
      strike W59.12
    spade W27.1
    spider (venomous) X58
    spin-drier W29.2
    spinning machine W31.89
    splinter W45.8
    sports equipment W21.9
    staple gun (powered) W29.8
    steam X13.1
      engine W31.3
      inhalation X13.Ø
      pipe X16
      shovel W31.89
    stove (hot) (kitchen) X15.Ø
    substance, hot NEC X19
      molten (metal) X18
    sword W26.1
      assault X99.2
      stated as undetermined whether
        accidental or intentional
        Y28.2
      suicide (attempt) X78.2
    tarantula X58
    thresher W30.Ø
    tin can lid W26.8
    toad W62.1
    toaster (hot) X15.1
    tool W27.8
      hand (not powered) W27.8
        auger W27.Ø
        axe W27.Ø
        can opener W27.4
        chisel W27.Ø
        fork W27.4
        garden W27.1
        handsaw W27.Ø
        hoe W27.1
        ice-pick W27.4
        kitchen utensil W27.4
        manual
          lawn mower W27.1
          sewing machine W27.8
        meat grinder W27.4
        needle (sewing) W27.3
          hypodermic W46.Ø
            contaminated W46.1
        paper cutter W27.5
        pitchfork W27.1
        rake W27.1
        scissors W27.2
        screwdriver W27.Ø
        specified NEC W27.8
        workbench W27.Ø
      hot X17
      powered W29.8
        blender W29.Ø
          commercial W31.82
        can opener W29.Ø
          commercial W31.82
        chainsaw W29.3
        clothes dryer W29.2
          commercial W31.82
        dishwasher W29.2
          commercial W31.82
        edger W29.3
        electric fan W29.2
          commercial W31.82
        electric knife W29.1
        food processor W29.Ø
          commercial W31.82
        garbage disposal W29.Ø
          commercial W31.82

Contact (*Continued*)
  with (*Continued*)
    tool (*Continued*)
      powered (*Continued*)
        garden tool W29.3
        hedge trimmer W29.3
        ice maker W29.Ø
          commercial W31.82
        kitchen appliance W29.Ø
          commercial W31.82
        lawn mower W28
        meat grinder W29.Ø
          commercial W31.82
        mixer W29.Ø
          commercial W31.82
        rototiller W29.3
        sewing machine W29.2
          commercial W31.82
        washing machine W29.2
          commercial W31.82
    transmission device (belt, cable, chain,
      gear, pinion, shaft) W24.1
      agricultural operations W30.89
    turbine (gas) (water-driven) W31.3
    turkey W61.49
      peck W61.43
      strike W61.42
    turtle (nonvenomous) W59.29
      bite W59.21
      strike W59.22
      terrestrial W59.89
        bite W59.81
        crushing W59.83
        strike W59.82
    under-cutter W31.Ø
    urine —*see* Contact, with, by type of animal
    vehicle
      agricultural use (transport) —*see*
        Accident, transport, agricultural
        vehicle
      not on public highway W30.81
      industrial use (transport) —*see*
        Accident, transport, industrial
        vehicle
      not on public highway W31.83
      off-road use (transport) —*see* Accident,
        transport, all-terrain or off-road
        vehicle
      not on public highway W31.83
      special construction use (transport) —*see*
        Accident, transport, construction
        vehicle
      not on public highway W31.83
    venomous
      animal X58
      arthropods X58
      lizard X58
      marine animal NEC X58
      marine plant NEC X58
      millipedes (tropical) X58
      plant(s) X58
      snake X58
      spider X58
    viper X58
    washing-machine (powered) W29.2
    wasp X58
    weaving-machine W31.89
    winch W24.Ø
      agricultural operations W30.89
    wire NEC W24.Ø
      agricultural operations W30.89
    wood slivers W45.8
    yellow jacket X58
    zebra —*see* Contact, with, hoof stock NEC
    pressure X50.9
    stress X50.9
Coup de soleil X32

Crash
  aircraft (in transit) (powered) V95.9
    balloon V96.Ø1
    fixed wing NEC (private) V95.21
      commercial V95.31
    glider V96.21
      hang V96.11
      powered V95.11
    helicopter V95.Ø1
    in war operations —*see* War operations,
      destruction of aircraft
    microlight V95.11
    nonpowered V96.9
      specified NEC V96.8
    powered NEC V95.8
    stated as
      homicide (attempt) YØ8.81
      suicide (attempt) X83.Ø
    ultralight V95.11
  spacecraft V95.41
  transport vehicle NEC —*see also* Accident,
    transport V89.9
    homicide (attempt) YØ3.8
    motor NEC (traffic) V89.2
      homicide (attempt) YØ3.8
      suicide (attempt) —*see* Suicide, collision
Cruelty (mental) (physical) (sexual) X58
Crushed (accidentally) X58
  between objects (moving) (stationary and
    moving) W23.Ø
    stationary W23.1
  by
    alligator W58.Ø3
    avalanche NEC —*see* Landslide
    cave-in W2Ø.Ø
      caused by cataclysmic earth surface
        movement —*see* Landslide
    crocodile W58.13
    crowd or human stampede W52
    falling
      aircraft V97.39
        in war operations —*see* War
          operations, destruction of aircraft
      earth, material W2Ø.Ø
        caused by cataclysmic earth surface
          movement —*see* Landslide
      object NEC W2Ø.8
    landslide NEC —*see* Landslide
    lizard (nonvenomous) W59.Ø9
    machinery —*see* Contact, with, by type of
      machine
    reptile NEC W59.89
    snake (nonvenomous) W59.13
  in
    machinery —*see* Contact, with, by type of
      machine
Cut, cutting (any part of body) (accidental) —
    see also Contact, with, by object or machine
  during medical or surgical treatment as
      misadventure —*see* Index to Diseases
      and Injuries, Complications
  homicide (attempt) —*see* Assault, cutting or
    piercing instrument
  inflicted by other person —*see* Assault,
    cutting or piercing instrument
  legal
    execution —*see* Legal, intervention
    intervention —*see* Legal, intervention,
      sharp object
  machine NEC —*see also* Contact, with, by
    type of machine W31.9
  self-inflicted —*see* Suicide, cutting or piercing
    instrument
  suicide (attempt) —*see* Suicide, cutting or
    piercing instrument
Cyclone (any injury) X37.1

▶ New   ⇒ Revised   ~~deleted~~ Deleted   ● Use Additional Character(s)

D

Decapitation (accidental circumstances)
  NEC X58
  homicide X99.9
  legal execution —*see* Legal, intervention
Dehydration from lack of water X58
Deprivation X58
Derailment (accidental)
  railway (rolling stock) (train) (vehicle)
      (without antecedent collision) V81.7
    with antecedent collision —*see* Accident,
        transport, railway vehicle occupant
  streetcar (without antecedent collision)
      V82.7
    with antecedent collision —*see* Accident,
        transport, streetcar occupant
Descent
  parachute (voluntary) (without accident to
      aircraft) V97.29
    due to accident to aircraft —*see* Accident,
        transport, aircraft
Desertion X58
Destitution X58
Disability, late effect or sequela of injury —*see*
  Sequelae
Discharge (accidental)
  airgun W34.010
    assault X95.01
    homicide (attempt) X95.01
    stated as undetermined whether accidental
        or intentional Y24.0
    suicide (attempt) X74.01
  BB gun —*see* Discharge, airgun
  firearm (accidental) W34.00
    assault X95.9
    handgun (pistol) (revolver) W32.0
      assault X93
      homicide (attempt) X93
      legal intervention —*see* Legal,
          intervention, firearm, handgun
      stated as undetermined whether
          accidental or intentional Y22
      suicide (attempt) X72
    homicide (attempt) X95.9
    hunting rifle W33.02
      assault X94.1
      homicide (attempt) X94.1
      legal intervention
        injuring
          bystander Y35.032
          law enforcement personnel
              Y35.031
          suspect Y35.033
      stated as undetermined whether
          accidental or intentional Y23.1
      suicide (attempt) X73.1
    larger W33.00
      assault X94.9
      homicide (attempt) X94.9
      hunting rifle —*see* Discharge, firearm,
          hunting rifle
      legal intervention —*see* Legal,
          intervention, firearm by type of
          firearm
      machine gun —*see* Discharge, firearm,
          machine gun
      shotgun —*see* Discharge, firearm,
          shotgun
      specified NEC W33.09
        assault X94.8
        homicide (attempt) X94.8
        legal intervention
          injuring
            bystander Y35.092
            law enforcement personnel
                Y35.091
            suspect Y35.093
        stated as undetermined whether
            accidental or intentional Y23.8
        suicide (attempt) X73.8

Discharge (*Continued*)
  firearm (*Continued*)
    larger (*Continued*)
      stated as undetermined whether
          accidental or intentional Y23.9
      suicide (attempt) X73.9
      legal intervention
        injuring
          bystander Y35.002
          law enforcement personnel Y35.001
          suspect Y35.03
        using rubber bullet
          injuring
            bystander Y35.042
            law enforcement personnel
                Y35.041
            suspect Y35.043
      machine gun W33.03
        assault X94.2
        homicide (attempt) X94.2
        legal intervention —*see* Legal,
            intervention, firearm, machine gun
        stated as undetermined whether
            accidental or intentional Y23.3
        suicide (attempt) X73.2
      pellet gun —*see* Discharge, airgun
      shotgun W33.01
        assault X94.0
        homicide (attempt) X94.0
        legal intervention —*see* Legal,
            intervention, firearm, specified NEC
        stated as undetermined whether
            accidental or intentional Y23.0
        suicide (attempt) X73.0
      specified NEC W34.09
        assault X95.8
        homicide (attempt) X95.8
        legal intervention —*see* Legal,
            intervention, firearm, specified NEC
        stated as undetermined whether
            accidental or intentional Y24.8
        suicide (attempt) X74.8
      stated as undetermined whether accidental
          or intentional Y24.9
      suicide (attempt) X74.9
      Very pistol W34.09
        assault X95.8
        homicide (attempt) X95.8
        stated as undetermined whether
            accidental or intentional Y24.8
        suicide (attempt) X74.8
  firework(s) W39
    stated as undetermined whether accidental
        or intentional Y25
  gas-operated gun NEC W34.018
    airgun —*see* Discharge, airgun
    assault X95.09
    homicide (attempt) X95.09
    paintball gun —*see* Discharge, paintball
        gun
    stated as undetermined whether accidental
        or intentional Y24.8
    suicide (attempt) X74.09
  gun NEC —*see also* Discharge, firearm NEC
    air —*see* Discharge, airgun
    BB —*see* Discharge, airgun
    for single hand use —*see* Discharge,
        firearm, handgun
    hand —*see* Discharge, firearm, handgun
    machine —*see* Discharge, firearm, machine
        gun
    other specified —*see* Discharge, firearm
        NEC
    paintball —*see* Discharge, paintball gun
    pellet —*see* Discharge, airgun
  handgun —*see* Discharge, firearm, handgun
  machine gun —*see* Discharge, firearm,
      machine gun
  paintball gun W34.011
    assault X95.02
    homicide (attempt) X95.02

Discharge (*Continued*)
  paintball gun (*Continued*)
    stated as undetermined whether accidental
        or intentional Y24.8
    suicide (attempt) X74.02
  pistol —*see* Discharge, firearm, handgun
    flare —*see* Discharge, firearm, Very pistol
    pellet —*see* Discharge, airgun
    Very —*see* Discharge, firearm, Very pistol
  revolver —*see* Discharge, firearm, handgun
  rifle (hunting) —*see* Discharge, firearm,
      hunting rifle
  shotgun —*see* Discharge, firearm, shotgun
  spring-operated gun NEC W34.018
    assault X95.09
    homicide (attempt) X95.09
    stated as undetermined whether accidental
        or intentional Y24.8
    suicide (attempt) X74.09
Disease
  Andes W94.11
  aviator's —*see* Air, pressure
  range W94.11
Diver's disease, palsy, paralysis, squeeze —*see*
  Air, pressure
Diving (into water) —*see* Accident, diving
Dog bite W54.0
Dragged by transport vehicle NEC —*see also*
  Accident, transport V09.9
Drinking poison (accidental) —*see* Table of
  Drugs and Chemicals
Dropped (accidentally) while being carried or
  supported by other person W04
Drowning (accidental) W74
  assault X92.9
  due to
    accident (to)
      machinery —*see* Contact, with, by type
          of machine
      watercraft V90.89
        burning V90.29
          powered V90.23
            fishing boat V90.22
            jet ski V90.23
            merchant ship V90.20
            passenger ship V90.21
          unpowered V90.28
            canoe V90.25
            inflatable V90.26
            kayak V90.25
            sailboat V90.24
            water skis V90.27
        crushed V90.39
          powered V90.33
            fishing boat V90.32
            jet ski V90.33
            merchant ship V90.30
            passenger ship V90.31
          unpowered V90.38
            canoe V90.35
            inflatable V90.36
            kayak V90.35
            sailboat V90.34
            water skis V90.37
        overturning V90.09
          powered V90.03
            fishing boat V90.02
            jet ski V90.03
            merchant ship V90.00
            passenger ship V90.01
          unpowered V90.08
            canoe V90.05
            inflatable V90.06
            kayak V90.05
            sailboat V90.04
        sinking V90.19
          powered V90.13
            fishing boat V90.12
            jet ski V90.13
            merchant ship V90.10
            passenger ship V90.11

▶ New   ⇒ Revised   ~~deleted~~ Deleted   ● Use Additional Character(s)

E

Earth (surface) movement NEC —*see* Forces of
  nature, earth movement
Earth falling (on) W20.0
  caused by cataclysmic earth surface
    movement or eruption —*see* Landslide
Earthquake (any injury) X34
Effect(s) (adverse) of
  air pressure (any) —*see* Air, pressure
  cold, excessive (exposure to) —*see* Exposure,
    cold
  heat (excessive) —*see* Heat
  hot place (weather) —*see* Heat
  insolation X30
  late —*see* Sequelae
  motion —*see* Motion
  nuclear explosion or weapon in war
    operations —*see* War operations, nuclear
    weapon
  radiation —*see* Radiation
  travel —*see* Travel
Electric shock (accidental) (by) (in) —*see*
  Exposure, electric current
Electrocution (accidental) —*see* Exposure,
  electric current
Endotracheal tube wrongly placed during
  anesthetic procedure Y65.3
Entanglement
  in
    bed linen, causing suffocation —*see*
      category T71
    wheel of pedal cycle V19.88
Entry of foreign body or material —*see* Foreign
  body
Environmental pollution related condition —
  see Z57
Execution, legal (any method) —*see* Legal,
  intervention
Exhaustion
  cold —*see* Exposure, cold
  due to excessive exertion —*see also*
    Overexertion X50.9
  heat —*see* Heat
Explosion (accidental) (of) (with secondary fire)
  W40.9
  acetylene W40.1
  aerosol can W36.1
  air tank (compressed) (in machinery) W36.2
  aircraft (in transit) (powered) NEC V95.9
    balloon V96.05
    fixed wing NEC (private) V95.25
      commercial V95.35
    glider V96.25
      hang V96.15
      powered V95.15
    helicopter V95.05
    in war operations —*see* War operations,
      destruction of aircraft
    microlight V95.15
    nonpowered V96.9
      specified NEC V96.8
    powered NEC V95.8
    stated as
      homicide (attempt) Y03.8
      suicide (attempt) X83.0
    ultralight V95.15
  anesthetic gas in operating room W40.1
  antipersonnel bomb W40.8
    assault X96.0
    homicide (attempt) X96.0
    suicide (attempt) X75
  assault X96.9
  bicycle tire W37.0
  blasting (cap) (materials) W40.0
  boiler (machinery), not on transport vehicle
    W35
    on watercraft —*see* Explosion, in,
      watercraft
  butane W40.1
  caused by other person X96.9
  coal gas W40.1

Explosion (Continued)
  detonator W40.0
  dump (munitions) W40.8
  dynamite W40.0
    in
      assault X96.8
      homicide (attempt) X96.8
      legal intervention
        injuring
          bystander Y35.112
          law enforcement personnel Y35.111
          suspect Y35.113
      suicide (attempt) X75
  explosive (material) W40.9
    gas W40.1
    in blasting operation W40.0
    specified NEC W40.8
      in
        assault X96.8
        homicide (attempt) X96.8
        legal intervention
          injuring
            bystander Y35.192
            law enforcement personnel
              Y35.191
            suspect Y35.193
        suicide (attempt) X75
  factory (munitions) W40.8
  fertilizer bomb W40.8
    assault X96.3
    homicide (attempt) X96.3
    suicide (attempt) X75
  fire-damp W40.1
  firearm (parts) NEC W34.19
    airgun W34.110
    BB gun W34.110
    gas, air or spring-operated gun NEC
      W34.118
    handgun W32.1
    hunting rifle W33.12
    larger firearm W33.10
      specified NEC W33.19
    machine gun W33.13
    paintball gun W34.111
    pellet gun W34.110
    shotgun W33.11
    Very pistol [flare] W34.19
  fireworks W39
  gas (coal) (explosive) W40.1
    cylinder W36.9
      aerosol can W36.1
      air tank W36.2
      pressurized W36.3
      specified NEC W36.8
  gasoline (fumes) (tank) not in moving motor
    vehicle W40.1
    bomb W40.8
      assault X96.1
      homicide (attempt) X96.1
      suicide (attempt) X75
    in motor vehicle —*see* Accident, transport,
      by type of vehicle
  grain store W40.8
  grenade W40.8
    in
      assault X96.8
      homicide (attempt) X96.8
      legal intervention
        injuring
          bystander Y35.192
          law enforcement personnel
            Y35.191
          suspect Y35.193
      suicide (attempt) X75
  handgun (parts) —*see* Explosion, firearm,
    handgun (parts)
  homicide (attempt) X96.9
    antipersonnel bomb —*see* Explosion,
      antipersonnel bomb
    fertilizer bomb —*see* Explosion, fertilizer
      bomb

Explosion (Continued)
  homicide (Continued)
    gasoline bomb —*see* Explosion, gasoline
      bomb
    letter bomb —*see* Explosion, letter bomb
    pipe bomb —*see* Explosion, pipe bomb
    specified NEC X96.8
  hose, pressurized W37.8
  hot water heater, tank (in machinery) W35
    on watercraft —*see* Explosion, in,
      watercraft
  in, on
    dump W40.8
    factory W40.8
    mine (of explosive gases) NEC W40.1
    watercraft V93.59
      powered craft V93.53
        ferry boat V93.51
        fishing boat V93.52
        jet ski V93.53
        liner V93.51
        merchant ship V93.50
        passenger ship V93.51
        sailboat V93.54
  letter bomb W40.8
    assault X96.2
    homicide (attempt) X96.2
    suicide (attempt) X75
  machinery —*see also* Contact, with, by type
    of machine
    on board watercraft —*see* Explosion, in,
      watercraft
    pressure vessel —*see* Explosion, by type
      of vessel
  methane W40.1
  mine W40.1
  missile NEC W40.8
  mortar bomb W40.8
    in
      assault X96.8
      homicide (attempt) X96.8
      legal intervention
        injuring
          bystander Y35.192
          law enforcement personnel
            Y35.191
          suspect Y35.193
      suicide (attempt) X75
  munitions (dump) (factory) W40.8
  pipe, pressurized W37.8
    bomb W40.8
      assault X96.4
      homicide (attempt) X96.4
      suicide (attempt) X75
  pressure, pressurized
    cooker W38
    gas tank (in machinery) W36.3
    hose W37.8
    pipe W37.8
    specified device NEC W38
    tire W37.8
      bicycle W37.0
    vessel (in machinery) W38
  propane W40.1
  self-inflicted X75
  shell (artillery) NEC W40.8
    during war operations —*see* War
      operations, explosion
    in
      legal intervention
        injuring
          bystander Y35.122
          law enforcement personnel Y35.121
          suspect Y35.123
    war —*see* War operations, explosion
  spacecraft V95.45
  stated as undetermined whether accidental or
    intentional Y25
  steam or water lines (in machinery) W37.8
  stove W40.9
  suicide (attempt) X75

Explosion *(Continued)*
 tire, pressurized W37.8
  bicycle W37.0
 undetermined whether accidental or
   intentional Y25
 vehicle tire NEC W37.8
  bicycle W37.0
 war operations —*see* War operations,
   explosion
Exposure (to) X58
 air pressure change —*see* Air, pressure
 cold (accidental) (excessive) (extreme)
   (natural) (place) X31
  assault Y08.89
  due to
   man-made conditions W93.8
    dry ice (contact) W93.01
     inhalation W93.02
    liquid air (contact) (hydrogen)
      (nitrogen) W93.11
     inhalation W93.12
    refrigeration unit (deep freeze)
      W93.2
   suicide (attempt) X83.2
   weather (conditions) X31
  homicide (attempt) Y08.89
  self-inflicted X83.2
 due to abandonment or neglect X58
 electric current W86.8
  appliance (faulty) W86.8
   domestic W86.0
  caused by other person Y08.89
  conductor (faulty) W86.1
  control apparatus (faulty) W86.1
  electric power generating plant,
    distribution station W86.1
  electroshock gun —*see* Exposure, electric
    current, taser
  high-voltage cable W85
  homicide (attempt) Y08.89
  legal execution —*see* Legal, intervention,
    specified means NEC
  lightning —*see* subcategory T75.0
  live rail W86.8
  misadventure in medical or surgical
    procedure in electroshock therapy
    Y63.4
  motor (electric) (faulty) W86.8
   domestic W86.0
  self-inflicted X83.1
  specified NEC W86.8
   domestic W86.0
  stun gun —*see* Exposure, electric current,
    taser
  suicide (attempt) X83.1
  taser W86.8
   assault Y08.89
   legal intervention —*see* category Y35
   self-harm (intentional) X83.8
   undetermined intent Y33
  third rail W86.8
  transformer (faulty) W86.1
  transmission lines W85
 environmental tobacco smoke X58
 excessive
  cold —*see* Exposure, cold
  heat (natural) NEC X30
   man-made W92
 factor(s) NOS X58
  environmental NEC X58
   man-made NEC W99
   natural NEC —*see* Forces of nature
  specified NEC X58
 fire, flames (accidental) X08.8
  assault X97
  campfire —*see* Exposure, fire, controlled,
    not in building
  controlled (in)
   with ignition (of) clothing —*see also*
     Ignition, clothes X06.2
    nightwear X05

Exposure *(Continued)*
 fire, flames *(Continued)*
  controlled *(Continued)*
   bonfire —*see* Exposure, fire, controlled,
     not in building
   brazier (in building or structure) —*see
     also* Exposure, fire, controlled,
     building
    not in building or structure —*see*
      Exposure, fire, controlled, not in
      building
   building or structure X02.0
    with
     fall from building X02.3
     from building X02.5
     injury due to building collapse
       X02.2
     smoke inhalation X02.1
    hit by object from building X02.4
    specified mode of injury NEC X02.8
   fireplace, furnace or stove —*see*
     Exposure, fire, controlled, building
   not in building or structure X03.0
    with
     fall X03.3
     smoke inhalation X03.1
    hit by object X03.4
    specified mode of injury NEC X03.8
   trash —*see* Exposure, fire, controlled, not
     in building
  fireplace —*see* Exposure, fire, controlled,
    building
  fittings or furniture (in building or
    structure) (uncontrolled) —*see*
    Exposure, fire, uncontrolled, building
  forest (uncontrolled) —*see* Exposure, fire,
    uncontrolled, not in building
  grass (uncontrolled) —*see* Exposure, fire,
    uncontrolled, not in building
  hay (uncontrolled) —*see* Exposure, fire,
    uncontrolled, not in building
  homicide (attempt) X97
  ignition of highly flammable material X04
  in, of, on, starting in
   machinery —*see* Contact, with, by type
     of machine
   motor vehicle (in motion) —*see also*
     Accident, transport, occupant by
     type of vehicle V87.8
    with collision —*see* Collision
   railway rolling stock, train, vehicle
     V81.81
    with collision —*see* Accident,
      transport, railway vehicle
      occupant
   street car (in motion) V82.8
    with collision —*see* Accident,
      transport, streetcar occupant
   transport vehicle NEC —*see also*
     Accident, transport
    with collision —*see* Collision
   war operations —*see also* War operations,
     fire
    from nuclear explosion —*see* War
      operations, nuclear weapons
   watercraft (in transit) (not in transit)
     V91.09
    localized —*see* Burn, on board
      watercraft, due to, fire on board
    powered craft V91.03
     ferry boat V91.01
     fishing boat V91.02
     jet skis V91.03
     liner V91.01
     merchant ship V91.00
     passenger ship V91.01
    unpowered craft V91.08
     canoe V91.05
     inflatable V91.06
     kayak V91.05
     sailboat V91.04

Exposure *(Continued)*
 fire, flames *(Continued)*
  in, of, on, starting in *(Continued)*
   watercraft *(Continued)*
    unpowered craft *(Continued)*
     surf-board V91.08
     waterskis V91.07
     windsurfer V91.08
    lumber (uncontrolled) —*see* Exposure, fire,
      uncontrolled, not in building
    mine (uncontrolled) —*see* Exposure, fire,
      uncontrolled, not in building
    prairie (uncontrolled) —*see* Exposure, fire,
      uncontrolled, not in building
    resulting from
     explosion —*see* Explosion
     lightning X08.8
    self-inflicted X76
    specified NEC X08.8
    started by other person X97
    stated as undetermined whether accidental
      or intentional Y26
    stove —*see* Exposure, fire, controlled,
      building
    suicide (attempt) X76
    tunnel (uncontrolled) —*see* Exposure, fire,
      uncontrolled, not in building
    uncontrolled
     in building or structure X00.0
      with
       fall from building X00.3
       injury due to building collapse
         X00.2
       jump from building X00.5
       smoke inhalation X00.1
      bed X08.00
       due to
        cigarette X08.01
        specified material NEC X08.09
      furniture NEC X08.20
       due to
        cigarette X08.21
        specified material NEC X08.29
      hit by object from building X00.4
      sofa X08.10
       due to
        cigarette X08.11
        specified material NEC
          X08.19
      specified mode of injury NEC
        X00.8
     not in building or structure (any)
       X01.0
      with
       fall X01.3
       smoke inhalation X01.1
      hit by object X01.4
      specified mode of injury NEC
        X01.8
    undetermined whether accidental or
      intentional Y26
 forces of nature NEC —*see* Forces of nature
 G-forces (abnormal) W49.9
 gravitational forces (abnormal) W49.9
 heat (natural) NEC —*see* Heat
 high-pressure jet (hydraulic) (pneumatic)
   W49.9
 hydraulic jet W49.9
 inanimate mechanical force W49.9
 jet, high-pressure (hydraulic) (pneumatic)
   W49.9
 lightning —*see* subcategory T75.0
  causing fire —*see* Exposure, fire
 mechanical forces NEC W49.9
  animate NEC W64
  inanimate NEC W49.9
 noise W42.9
  supersonic W42.0
 noxious substance —*see* Table of Drugs and
   Chemicals
 pneumatic jet W49.9

▶ New   ⇒ Revised   ~~deleted~~ Deleted   ● Use Additional Character(s)

Exposure *(Continued)*
  prolonged in deep-freeze unit or refrigerator
    W93.2
  radiation —*see* Radiation
  smoke —*see also* Exposure, fire
    tobacco, second hand Z77.22
  specified factors NEC X58
  sunlight X32
    man-made (sun lamp) W89.8
      tanning bed W89.1
  supersonic waves W42.0
  transmission line(s), electric W85
  vibration W49.9

Exposure *(Continued)*
  waves
    infrasound W49.9
    sound W42.9
    supersonic W42.0
  weather NEC —*see* Forces of nature
External cause status Y99.9
  child assisting in compensated work for
    family Y99.8
  civilian activity done for financial or other
    compensation Y99.0
  civilian activity done for income or pay
    Y99.0

External cause status *(Continued)*
  family member assisting in compensated
    work for other family member Y99.8
  hobby not done for income Y99.8
  leisure activity Y99.8
  military activity Y99.1
  off-duty activity of military personnel Y99.8
  recreation or sport not for income or while a
    student Y99.8
  specified NEC Y99.8
  student activity Y99.8
  volunteer activity Y99.2

F

Factors, supplemental
  alcohol
    blood level
      less than 20mg/100ml Y90.0
      presence in blood, level not specified
        Y90.9
      20-39mg/100ml Y90.1
      40-59mg/100ml Y90.2
      60-79mg/100ml Y90.3
      80-99mg/100ml Y90.4
      100-119mg/100ml Y90.5
      120-199mg/100ml Y90.6
      200-239mg/100ml Y90.7
      240mg/100ml or more Y90.8
    presence in blood, but level not specified
      Y90.9
  environmental-pollution-related condition —
    see Z57
  nosocomial condition Y95
  work-related condition Y99.0
Failure
  in suture or ligature during surgical
    procedure Y65.2
  mechanical, of instrument or apparatus
    (any) (during any medical or surgical
    procedure) Y65.8
  sterile precautions (during medical and
    surgical care) —see Misadventure,
    failure, sterile precautions, by type of
    procedure
  to
    introduce tube or instrument Y65.4
    endotracheal tube during anesthesia Y65.3
    make curve (transport vehicle) NEC —see
      Accident, transport
    remove tube or instrument Y65.4
Fall, falling (accidental) W19
  building W20.1
    burning (uncontrolled fire) X00.3
  down
    embankment W17.81
    escalator W10.0
    hill W17.81
    ladder W11
    ramp W10.2
    stairs, steps W10.9
  due to
    bumping against
      object W18.00
        sharp glass W18.02
        specified NEC W18.09
        sports equipment W18.01
      person W03
        due to ice or snow W00.0
        on pedestrian conveyance —see
          Accident, transport, pedestrian,
          conveyance
    collision with another person W03
      due to ice or snow W00.0
      involving pedestrian conveyance —see
        Accident, transport, pedestrian,
        conveyance
    grocery cart tipping over W17.82
    ice or snow W00.9
      from one level to another W00.2
        on stairs or steps W00.1
      involving pedestrian conveyance —see
        Accident, transport, pedestrian,
        conveyance
      on same level W00.0
    slipping (on moving sidewalk) W01.0
      with subsequent striking against object
        W01.10
        furniture W01.190
        sharp object W01.119
          glass W01.110
          power tool or machine W01.111
          specified NEC W01.118
        specified NEC W01.198

Fall, falling (Continued)
  due to (Continued)
    striking against
      object W18.00
        sharp glass W18.02
        specified NEC W18.09
        sports equipment W18.01
      person W03
        due to ice or snow W00.0
        on pedestrian conveyance —see
          Accident, transport, pedestrian,
          conveyance
  earth (with asphyxia or suffocation (by
    pressure)) —see Earth, falling
  from, off, out of
    aircraft NEC (with accident to aircraft
      NEC) V97.0
      while boarding or alighting V97.1
    balcony W13.0
    bed W06
    boat, ship, watercraft NEC (with
      drowning or submersion) —
      see Drowning, due to, fall
      overboard
      with hitting bottom or object V94.0
    bridge W13.1
    building W13.9
      burning (uncontrolled fire) X00.3
    cavity W17.2
    chair W07
    cherry picker W17.89
    cliff W15
    dock W17.4
    embankment W17.81
    escalator W10.0
    flagpole W13.8
    furniture NEC W08
    grocery cart W17.82
    haystack W17.89
    high place NEC W17.89
      stated as undetermined whether
        accidental or intentional Y30
    hole W17.2
    incline W10.2
    ladder W11
    lifting device W17.89
    machine, machinery —see also Contact,
      with, by type of machine
      not in operation W17.89
    manhole W17.1
    mobile elevated work platform [MEWP]
      W17.89
    motorized mobility scooter W05.2
    one level to another NEC W17.89
      intentional, purposeful, suicide
        (attempt) X80
      stated as undetermined whether
        accidental or intentional Y30
    pit W17.2
    playground equipment W09.8
      jungle gym W09.2
      slide W09.0
      swing W09.1
    quarry W17.89
    railing W13.9
    ramp W10.2
    roof W13.2
    scaffolding W12
    scooter (nonmotorized) W05.1
      motorized mobility W05.2
    sky lift W17.89
    stairs, steps W10.9
      curb W10.1
      due to ice or snow W00.1
      escalator W10.0
      incline W10.2
      ramp W10.2
      sidewalk curb W10.1
      specified NEC W10.8
    stepladder W11
    storm drain W17.1

Fall, falling (Continued)
  from, off, out of (Continued)
    streetcar NEC V82.6
      with antecedent collision —see
        Accident, transport, streetcar
        occupant
      while boarding or alighting V82.4
    structure NEC W13.8
      burning (uncontrolled fire) X00.3
    table W08
    toilet W18.11
      with subsequent striking against object
        W18.12
    train NEC V81.6
      during derailment (without antecedent
        collision) V81.7
        with antecedent collision —see
          Accident, transport, railway
          vehicle occupant
      while boarding or alighting V81.4
    transport vehicle after collision —see
      Accident, transport, by type of
      vehicle, collision
    tree W14
    vehicle (in motion) NEC —see also
      Accident, transport V89.9
      motor NEC —see also Accident,
        transport, occupant, by type of
        vehicle V87.8
      stationary W17.89
        while boarding or alighting —see
          Accident, transport, by type of
          vehicle, while boarding or
          alighting
    viaduct W13.8
    wall W13.8
    watercraft —see also Drowning, due to, fall
      overboard
      with hitting bottom or object V94.0
    well W17.0
    wheelchair, non-moving W05.0
      powered —see Accident, transport,
        pedestrian, conveyance occupant,
        specified type NEC
    window W13.4
  in, on
    aircraft NEC V97.0
      with accident to aircraft V97.0
      while boarding or alighting
        V97.1
    bathtub (empty) W18.2
      filled W16.212
        causing drowning W16.211
    escalator W10.0
    incline W10.2
    ladder W11
    machine, machinery —see Contact, with,
      by type of machine
    object, edged, pointed or sharp (with
      cut) —see Fall, by type
    playground equipment W09.8
      jungle gym W09.2
      slide W09.0
      swing W09.1
    ramp W10.2
    scaffolding W12
    shower W18.2
      causing drowning W16.211
    staircase, stairs, steps W10.9
      curb W10.1
      due to ice or snow W00.1
      escalator W10.0
      incline W10.2
      specified NEC W10.8
    streetcar (without antecedent collision)
      V82.5
      with antecedent collision —see
        Accident, transport, streetcar
        occupant
      while boarding or alighting
        V82.4

▶ New   ⇒ Revised   ~~deleted~~ Deleted   ● Use Additional Character(s)

Forces of nature *(Continued)*
  radiation (natural) X39.Ø8
    radon X39.Ø1
  radon X39.Ø1
  specified force NEC X39.8
  storm surge X37.Ø
  structure collapse causing
      earth movement
      X36.Ø
  sunlight X32
  tidal wave X37.41
    due to
      earthquake X37.41
      landslide X37.43
      storm X37.42
      volcanic eruption X37.41
  tornado X37.1

Forces of nature *(Continued)*
  tsunami X37.41
  twister X37.1
  typhoon X37.Ø
  volcanic eruption X35
Foreign body
  aspiration —*see* Index to Diseases and
    Injuries, Foreign body, respitory
    tract
  embedded in skin W45
  entering through skin W45.8
    can lid W26.2
    nail W45.Ø
    paper W26.2
    specified NEC 45.8
    splinter W45.8

Forest fire (exposure to) —*see* Exposure, fire,
  uncontrolled, not in building
Found injured X58
  from exposure (to) —*see* Exposure
  on
    highway, road(way), street V89.9
    railway right of way V81.9
Fracture (circumstances unknown or
  unspecified) X58
  due to specified cause NEC X58
Freezing —*see* Exposure, cold
Frostbite X31
  due to man-made conditions —*see* Exposure,
    cold, man-made
Frozen —*see* Exposure, cold

G

Gored by bull W55.22
Gunshot wound W34.ØØ

H

Hailstones, injured by X39.8
Hanged herself or himself —*see* Hanging,
  self-inflicted
Hanging (accidental) —*see also* category T71
  legal execution —*see* Legal, intervention,
    specified means NEC
Heat (effects of) (excessive) X30
  due to
    man-made conditions W92
      on board watercraft V93.29
        fishing boat V93.22
        merchant ship V93.2Ø
        passenger ship V93.21
        sailboat V93.24
        specified powered craft NEC V93.23
    weather (conditions) X30

Heat *(Continued)*
  from
    electric heating apparatus causing
      burning X16
    nuclear explosion in war operations —
      see War operations, nuclear
      weapons
  inappropriate in local application or
    packing in medical or surgical
    procedure Y63.5
Hemorrhage
  delayed following medical or surgical
    treatment without mention of
    misadventure —*see* Index to Diseases
    and Injuries, Complication(s)
  during medical or surgical treatment as
    misadventure —*see* Index to Diseases
    and Injuries, Complication(s)

High
  altitude (effects) —*see* Air, pressure, low
  level of radioactivity, effects —*see* Radiation
  pressure (effects) —*see* Air, pressure, high
  temperature, effects —*see* Heat
Hit, hitting (accidental) by —*see* Struck by
Hitting against —*see* Striking against
Homicide (attempt) (justifiable) —*see* Assault
Hot
  place, effects —*see also* Heat
  weather, effects X30
House fire (uncontrolled) —*see* Exposure, fire,
  uncontrolled, building
Humidity, causing problem X39.8
Hunger X58
Hurricane (any injury) X37.Ø
Hypobarism, hypobaropathy —*see* Air,
  pressure, low

▶ New   ⇒ Revised   ~~deleted~~ Deleted   ● Use Additional Character(s)

I

Ictus
  caloris —*see also* Heat
  solaris X3Ø
Ignition (accidental) —*see also* Exposure, fire
    XØ8.8
  anesthetic gas in operating room W4Ø.1
  apparel XØ6.2
    from highly flammable material XØ4
    nightwear XØ5
  bed linen (sheets) (spreads) (pillows)
    (mattress) —*see* Exposure, fire,
    uncontrolled, building, bed
  benzine XØ4
  clothes, clothing NEC (from controlled fire)
    XØ6.2
    from
      highly flammable material XØ4
  ether XØ4
    in operating room W4Ø.1
  explosive material —*see* Explosion
  gasoline XØ4
  jewelry (plastic) (any) XØ6.Ø
  kerosene XØ4
  material
    explosive —*see* Explosion
    highly flammable with secondary
      explosion XØ4
  nightwear XØ5
  paraffin XØ4
  petrol XØ4
Immersion (accidental) —*see also* Drowning
  hand or foot due to cold (excessive) X31
Implantation of quills of porcupine
    W55.89
Inanition (from) (hunger) X58
  thirst X58.8
Inappropriate operation performed
  correct operation on wrong side or body
    part (wrong side) (wrong site)
    Y65.53
  operation intended for another patient done
    on wrong patient Y65.52
  wrong operation performed on correct
    patient Y65.51
Inattention after, at birth (homicidal intent)
    (infanticidal intent) X58
Incident, adverse
  device
    anesthesiology Y7Ø.8
      accessory Y7Ø.2
      diagnostic Y7Ø.Ø
      miscellaneous Y7Ø.8
      monitoring Y7Ø.Ø
      prosthetic Y7Ø.2
      rehabilitative Y7Ø.1
      surgical Y7Ø.3
      therapeutic Y7Ø.1
    cardiovascular Y71.8
      accessory Y71.2
      diagnostic Y71.Ø
      miscellaneous Y71.8
      monitoring Y71.Ø
      prosthetic Y71.2
      rehabilitative Y71.1
      surgical Y71.3
      therapeutic Y71.1
    gastroenterology Y73.8
      accessory Y73.2
      diagnostic Y73.Ø
      miscellaneous Y73.8
      monitoring Y73.Ø
      prosthetic Y73.2
      rehabilitative Y73.1
      surgical Y73.3
      therapeutic Y73.1
    general
      hospital Y74.8
        accessory Y74.2
        diagnostic Y74.Ø

Incident, adverse *(Continued)*
  device *(Continued)*
    general *(Continued)*
      hospital *(Continued)*
        miscellaneous Y74.8
        monitoring Y74.Ø
        prosthetic Y74.2
        rehabilitative Y74.1
        surgical Y74.3
        therapeutic Y74.1
      surgical Y81.8
        accessory Y81.2
        diagnostic Y81.Ø
        miscellaneous Y81.8
        monitoring Y81.Ø
        prosthetic Y81.2
        rehabilitative Y81.1
        surgical Y81.3
        therapeutic Y81.1
    gynecological Y76.8
      accessory Y76.2
      diagnostic Y76.Ø
      miscellaneous Y76.8
      monitoring Y76.Ø
      prosthetic Y76.2
      rehabilitative Y76.1
      surgical Y76.3
      therapeutic Y76.1
    medical Y82.9
      specified type NEC Y82.8
    neurological Y75.8
      accessory Y75.2
      diagnostic Y75.Ø
      miscellaneous Y75.8
      monitoring Y75.Ø
      prosthetic Y75.2
      rehabilitative Y75.1
      surgical Y75.3
      therapeutic Y75.1
    obstetrical Y76.8
      accessory Y76.2
      diagnostic Y76.Ø
      miscellaneous Y76.8
      monitoring Y76.Ø
      prosthetic Y76.2
      rehabilitative Y76.1
      surgical Y76.3
      therapeutic Y76.1
    ophthalmic Y77.8
      accessory Y77.2
      diagnostic Y77.Ø
      miscellaneous Y77.8
      monitoring Y77.Ø
      prosthetic Y77.2
      rehabilitative Y77.1
      surgical Y77.3
      therapeutic Y77.1
    orthopedic Y79.8
      accessory Y79.2
      diagnostic Y79.Ø
      miscellaneous Y79.8
      monitoring Y79.Ø
      prosthetic Y79.2
      rehabilitative Y79.1
      surgical Y79.3
      therapeutic Y79.1
    otorhinolaryngological Y72.8
      accessory Y72.2
      diagnostic Y72.Ø
      miscellaneous Y72.8
      monitoring Y72.Ø
      prosthetic Y72.2
      rehabilitative Y72.1
      surgical Y72.3
      therapeutic Y72.1
    personal use Y74.8
      accessory Y74.2
      diagnostic Y74.Ø
      miscellaneous Y74.8
      monitoring Y74.Ø
      prosthetic Y74.2

Incident, adverse *(Continued)*
  device *(Continued)*
    personal use *(Continued)*
      rehabilitative Y74.1
      surgical Y74.3
      therapeutic Y74.1
    physical medicine Y8Ø.8
      accessory Y8Ø.2
      diagnostic Y8Ø.Ø
      miscellaneous Y8Ø.8
      monitoring Y8Ø.Ø
      prosthetic Y8Ø.2
      rehabilitative Y8Ø.1
      surgical Y8Ø.3
      therapeutic Y8Ø.1
    plastic surgical Y81.8
      accessory Y81.2
      diagnostic Y81.Ø
      miscellaneous Y81.8
      monitoring Y81.Ø
      prosthetic Y81.2
      rehabilitative Y81.1
      surgical Y81.3
      therapeutic Y81.1
    radiological Y78.8
      accessory Y78.2
      diagnostic Y78.Ø
      miscellaneous Y78.8
      monitoring Y78.Ø
      prosthetic Y78.2
      rehabilitative Y78.1
      surgical Y78.3
      therapeutic Y78.1
    urology Y73.8
      accessory Y73.2
      diagnostic Y73.Ø
      miscellaneous Y73.8
      monitoring Y73.Ø
      prosthetic Y73.2
      rehabilitative Y73.1
      surgical Y73.3
      therapeutic Y73.1
Incineration (accidental) —*see* Exposure, fire
Infanticide —*see* Assault
Infrasound waves (causing injury) W49.9
Ingestion
  foreign body (causing injury) (with
    obstruction) —*see* Foreign body,
    alimentary canal
  poisonous
    plant(s) X58
    substance NEC —*see* Table of Drugs and
      Chemicals
Inhalation
  excessively cold substance, man-made —*see*
    Exposure, cold, man-made
  food (any type) (into respiratory tract) (with
    asphyxia, obstruction respiratory tract,
    suffocation) —*see* categories T17 and T18
  foreign body —*see* Foreign body, aspiration
  gastric contents (with asphyxia, obstruction
    respiratory passage, suffocation) T17.81-●
  hot air or gases X14.Ø
  liquid air, hydrogen, nitrogen W93.12
    suicide (attempt) X83.2
  steam X13.Ø
    assault X98.Ø
    stated as undetermined whether accidental
      or intentional Y27.Ø
    suicide (attempt) X77.Ø
  toxic gas —*see* Table of Drugs and
    Chemicals
  vomitus (with asphyxia, obstruction
    respiratory passage, suffocation) T17.81-●
Injury, injured (accidental(ly)) NOS X58
  by, caused by, from
    assault —*see* Assault
    law-enforcing agent, police, in course
      of legal intervention —*see* Legal
      intervention
    suicide (attempt) X83.8

Injury, injured NOS *(Continued)*
due to, in
civil insurrection —*see* War
operations
fight —*see also* Assault, fight
Y04.0
war operations —*see* War
operations
homicide —*see also* Assault Y09
inflicted (by)
in course of arrest (attempted), suppression
of disturbance, maintenance of order,
by law-enforcing agents —*see* Legal
intervention

Injury, injured NOS *(Continued)*
inflicted *(Continued)*
other person
stated as
accidental X58
intentional, homicide (attempt) —*see*
Assault
undetermined whether accidental or
intentional Y33
purposely (inflicted) by other person(s) —*see*
Assault
self-inflicted X83.8
stated as accidental X58
specified cause NEC X58

Injury, injured NOS *(Continued)*
undetermined whether accidental or
intentional Y33
Insolation, effects X30
Insufficient nourishment X58
Interruption of respiration (by)
food (lodged in esophagus) —*see* categories
T17 and T18
vomitus (lodged in esophagus) T17.81-•
Intervention, legal —*see* Legal intervention
Intoxication
drug —*see* Table of Drugs and Chemicals
poison —*see* Table of Drugs and
Chemicals

J

Jammed (accidentally)
between objects (moving) (stationary and
moving) W23.0
stationary W23.1
Jumped, jumping
before moving object NEC X81.8
motor vehicle X81.0
subway train X81.1
train X81.1
undetermined whether accidental or
intentional Y31
from
boat (into water) voluntarily,
without accident (to or on boat)
W16.712
with
accident to or on boat —*see* Accident,
watercraft
drowning or submersion W16.711
suicide (attempt) X71.3

Jumped, jumping *(Continued)*
from *(Continued)*
boat voluntarily, without accident
(Continued)
striking bottom W16.722
causing drowning W16.721
building —*see also* Jumped, from,
high place W13.9
burning (uncontrolled fire)
X00.5
high place NEC W17.89
suicide (attempt) X80
undetermined whether accidental or
intentional Y30
structure —*see also* Jumped, from, high
place W13.9
burning (uncontrolled fire)
X00.5
into water W16.92
causing drowning W16.91
from, off watercraft —*see* Jumped, from,
boat

Jumped, jumping *(Continued)*
into water *(Continued)*
in
natural body W16.612
causing drowning W16.611
striking bottom W16.622
causing drowning W16.621
specified place NEC W16.812
causing drowning W16.811
striking
bottom W16.822
causing drowning W16.821
wall W16.832
causing drowning W16.831
swimming pool W16.512
causing drowning W16.511
striking
bottom W16.522
causing drowning W16.521
wall W16.532
causing drowning W16.531
suicide (attempt) X71.3

K

Kicked by
animal NEC W55.82
person(s) (accidentally) W50.1
with intent to injure or kill Y04.0
as, or caused by, a crowd or human
stampede (with fall) W52
assault Y04.0
homicide (attempt) Y04.0
in
fight Y04.0
legal intervention
injuring
bystander Y35.812
law enforcement personnel
Y35.811
suspect Y35.813

Kicking
against
object W22.8
sports equipment W21.9
stationary W22.09
sports equipment W21.89
person —*see* Striking against, person
sports equipment W21.9
carpet stretcher with knee X50.3
Killed, killing (accidentally) NOS —*see also*
Injury X58
in
action —*see* War operations
brawl, fight (hand) (fists) (foot) Y04.0
by weapon —*see also* Assault
cutting, piercing —*see* Assault, cutting
or piercing instrument
firearm —*see* Discharge, firearm, by
type, homicide

Killed, killing NOS *(Continued)*
self
stated as
accident NOS X58
suicide —*see* Suicide
undetermined whether accidental or
intentional Y33
Kneeling (prolonged) (static) X50.1
Knocked down (accidentally) (by) NOS X58
animal (not being ridden) NEC —*see also*
Struck by, by type of animal
crowd or human stampede W52
person W51
in brawl, fight Y04.0
transport vehicle NEC —*see also* Accident,
transport V09.9

L

Laceration NEC —*see* Injury
Lack of
  care (helpless person) (infant) (newborn) X58
  food except as result of abandonment or
    neglect X58
    due to abandonment or neglect X58
  water except as result of transport accident X58
    due to transport accident —*see* Accident,
      transport, by type
  helpless person, infant, newborn X58
Landslide (falling on transport vehicle) X36.1
  caused by collapse of man-made structure
    X36.0
Late effect —*see* Sequelae
Legal
  execution (any method) —*see* Legal,
    intervention
  intervention (by)
    baton —*see* Legal, intervention, blunt
      object, baton
    bayonet —*see* Legal, intervention, sharp
      object, bayonet
    blow —*see* Legal, intervention,
      manhandling
    blunt object
      baton
        injuring
          bystander Y35.312
          law enforcement personnel Y35.311
          suspect Y35.313
      injuring
        bystander Y35.302
        law enforcement personnel Y35.301
        suspect Y35.303
      specified NEC
        injuring
          bystander Y35.392
          law enforcement personnel Y35.391
          suspect Y35.393
      stave
        injuring
          bystander Y35.392
          law enforcement personnel Y35.391
          suspect Y35.393
    bomb —*see* Legal, intervention, explosive
    cutting or piercing instrument —*see* Legal,
      intervention, sharp object
    dynamite —*see* Legal, intervention,
      explosive, dynamite
    explosive(s)
      dynamite
        injuring
          bystander Y35.112
          law enforcement personnel Y35.111
          suspect Y35.113
      grenade
        injuring
          bystander Y35.192
          law enforcement personnel Y35.191
          suspect Y35.193
      injuring
        bystander Y35.102
        law enforcement personnel Y35.101
        suspect Y35.103

Legal *(Continued)*
  intervention *(Continued)*
    explosive *(Continued)*
      mortar bomb
        injuring
          bystander Y35.192
          law enforcement personnel
            Y35.191
          suspect Y35.193
      shell
        injuring
          bystander Y35.122
          law enforcement personnel Y35.121
          suspect Y35.123
      specified NEC
        injuring
          bystander Y35.192
          law enforcement personnel Y35.191
          suspect Y35.193
    firearm(s) (discharge)
      handgun
        injuring
          bystander Y35.022
          law enforcement personnel Y35.021
          suspect Y35.023
      injuring
        bystander Y35.002
        law enforcement personnel Y35.001
        suspect Y35.003
      machine gun
        injuring
          bystander Y35.012
          law enforcement personnel Y35.011
          suspect Y35.013
      rifle pellet
        injuring
          bystander Y35.032
          law enforcement personnel Y35.031
          suspect Y35.033
      rubber bullet
        injuring
          bystander Y35.042
          law enforcement personnel Y35.041
          suspect Y35.043
      shotgun —*see* Legal, intervention,
        firearm, specified NEC
      specified NEC
        injuring
          bystander Y35.092
          law enforcement personnel Y35.091
          suspect Y35.093
    gas (asphyxiation) (poisoning)
      injuring
        bystander Y35.202
        law enforcement personnel Y35.201
        suspect Y35.203
      specified NEC
        injuring
          bystander Y35.292
          law enforcement personnel Y35.291
          suspect Y35.293
      tear gas
        injuring
          bystander Y35.212
          law enforcement personnel Y35.211
          suspect Y35.213

Legal *(Continued)*
  intervention *(Continued)*
    grenade —*see* Legal, intervention,
      explosive, grenade
    injuring
      bystander Y35.92
      law enforcement personnel Y35.91
      suspect Y35.93
    late effect (of) —*see* with 7th character S
      Y35
    manhandling
      injuring
        bystander Y35.812
        law enforcement personnel Y35.811
        suspect Y35.813
    sequelae (of) —*see* with 7th character S
      Y35
    sharp objects
      bayonet
        injuring
          bystander Y35.412
          law enforcement personnel
            Y35.411
          suspect Y35.413
      injuring
        bystander Y35.402
        law enforcement personnel Y35.401
        suspect Y35.403
      specified NEC
        injuring
          bystander Y35.492
          law enforcement personnel Y35.491
          suspect Y35.493
    specified means NEC
      injuring
        bystander Y35.892
        law enforcement personnel Y35.891
        suspect Y35.893
    stabbing —*see* Legal, intervention, sharp
      object
    stave —*see* Legal, intervention, blunt
      object, stave
    tear gas —*see* Legal, intervention, gas, tear
      gas
    truncheon —*see* Legal, intervention, blunt
      object, stave
Lifting —*see also* Overexertion
  heavy objects X50.0
  weights X50.0
Lightning (shock) (stroke) (struck by) —*see*
  subcategory T75.0
  causing fire —*see* Exposure, fire
Loss of control (transport vehicle) NEC —*see*
  Accident, transport
Lost at sea NOS —*see* Drowning, due to, fall
  overboard
Low
  pressure (effects) —*see* Air, pressure, low
  temperature (effects) —*see* Exposure, cold
Lying before train, vehicle or other moving
  object X81.8
  subway train X81.1
  train X81.1
  undetermined whether accidental or
    intentional Y31
Lynching —*see* Assault

M

Malfunction (mechanism or component) (of)
  firearm
    airgun W34.10
    BB gun W34.110
    gas, air or spring-operated gun NEC
      W34.118
    handgun W32.1
    hunting rifle W33.12
    larger firearm W33.10
      specified NEC W33.19
    machine gun W33.13
    paintball gun W34.111
    pellet gun W34.110
    shotgun W33.11
    specified NEC W34.19
    Very pistol [flare] W34.19
  handgun —see Malfunction, firearm,
    handgun
Maltreatment —see Perpetrator
Mangled (accidentally) NOS X58
Manhandling (in brawl, fight) Y04.0
  legal intervention —see Legal, intervention,
    manhandling
Manslaughter (nonaccidental) —see Assault
Mauled by animal NEC W55.89
Medical procedure, complication of
  (delayed or as an abnormal reaction
    without mention of misadventure) —see
    Complication of or following, by specified
    type of procedure
  due to or as a result of misadventure —see
    Misadventure
Melting (due to fire) —see also Exposure, fire
  apparel NEC X06.3
  clothes, clothing NEC X06.3
    nightwear X05
  fittings or furniture (burning building)
    (uncontrolled fire) X00.8
  nightwear X05
  plastic jewelry X06.1
Mental cruelty X58
Military operations (injuries to military and
  civilians occuring during peacetime on
  military property and during routine
  military exercises and operations) (by)
  (from) (involving) Y37.90-●
  air blast Y37.20-●
  aircraft
    destruction —see Military operations,
      destruction of aircraft
  airway restriction —see Military operations,
    restriction of airways
  asphyxiation —see Military operations,
    restriction of airways
  biological weapons Y37.6X-●
  blast Y37.20-●
  blast fragments Y37.20-●
  blast wave Y37.20-●
  blast wind Y37.20-●
  bomb Y37.20-●
    dirty Y37.50-●
    gasoline Y37.31-●
    incendiary Y37.31-●
    petrol Y37.31-●
  bullet Y37.43-●
    incendiary Y37.32-●
    rubber Y37.41-●
  chemical weapons Y37.7X-●
  combat
    hand to hand (unarmed) combat
      Y37.44-●
    using blunt or piercing object Y37.45-●
  conflagration —see Military operations, fire
  conventional warfare NEC Y37.49-●
  depth-charge Y37.01-●
  destruction of aircraft Y37.10-●
    due to
      air to air missile Y37.11-●
      collision with other aircraft Y37.12-●

Military operations (Continued)
  destruction of aircraft (Continued)
    due to (Continued)
      detonation (accidental) of onboard
        munitions and explosives Y37.14-●
      enemy fire or explosives Y37.11-●
      explosive placed on aircraft Y37.11-●
      onboard fire Y37.13-●
      rocket propelled grenade [RPG] Y37.11-●
      small arms fire Y37.11-●
      surface to air missile Y37.11-●
      specified NEC Y37.19-●
  detonation (accidental) of
    onboard marine weapons Y37.05-●
    own munitions or munitions launch device
      Y37.24-●
  dirty bomb Y37.50-●
  explosion (of) Y37.20-●
    aerial bomb Y37.21-●
    bomb NOS —see also Military operations,
      bomb(s) Y37.20-●
    fragments Y37.20-●
    grenade Y37.29-●
    guided missile Y37.22-●
    improvised explosive device [IED]
      (person-borne) (roadside) (vehicle-
      borne) Y37.23-●
    land mine Y37.29-●
    marine mine (at sea) (in harbor) Y37.02-●
    marine weapon Y37.00-●
      specified NEC Y37.09-●
    own munitions or munitions launch device
      (accidental) Y37.24-●
    sea-based artillery shell Y37.03-●
    specified NEC Y37.29-●
    torpedo Y37.04-●
  fire Y37.30-●
    specified NEC Y37.39-●
  firearms
    discharge Y37.43-●
    pellets Y37.42-●
  flamethrower Y37.33-●
  fragments (from) (of)
    improvised explosive device [IED]
      (person-borne) (roadside) (vehicle-
      borne) Y37.26-●
    munitions Y37.25-●
    specified NEC Y37.29-●
    weapons Y37.27-●
  friendly fire Y37.92-●
  hand to hand (unarmed) combat Y37.44-●
  hot substances —see Military operations, fire
  incendiary bullet Y37.32-●
  nuclear weapon (effects of) Y37.50-●
    acute radiation exposure Y37.54-●
    blast pressure Y37.51-●
    direct blast Y37.51-●
    direct heat Y37.53-●
    fallout exposure Y37.54-●
    fireball Y37.53-●
    indirect blast (struck or crushed by blast
      debris) (being thrown by blast)
      Y37.52-●
    ionizing radiation (immediate exposure)
      Y37.54-●
    nuclear radiation Y37.54-●
    radiation
      ionizing (immediate exposure) Y37.54-●
      nuclear Y37.54-●
      thermal Y37.53-●
    secondary effects Y37.54-●
    specified NEC Y37.59-●
    thermal radiation Y37.53-●
  restriction of air (airway)
    intentional Y37.46-●
    unintentional Y37.47-●
  rubber bullets Y37.41-●
  shrapnel NOS Y37.29-●
  suffocation —see Military operations,
    restriction of airways
  unconventional warfare NEC Y37.7X-●

Military operations (Continued)
  underwater blast NOS Y37.00-●
  warfare
    conventional NEC Y37.49-●
    unconventional NEC Y37.7X-●
  weapon of mass destruction [WMD]
    Y37.91-●
  weapons
    biological weapons Y37.6X-●
    chemical Y37.7X-●
    nuclear (effects of) Y37.50-●
      acute radiation exposure Y37.54-●
      blast pressure Y37.51-●
      direct blast Y37.51-●
      direct heat Y37.53-●
      fallout exposure Y37.54-●
      fireball Y37.53-●
      radiation
        ionizing (immediate exposure)
          Y37.54-●
        nuclear Y37.54-●
        thermal Y37.53-●
      secondary effects Y37.54-●
      specified NEC Y37.59-●
    of mass destruction [WMD] Y37.91-●
Misadventure(s) to patient(s) during surgical
  or medical care Y69
contaminated medical or biological substance
  (blood, drug, fluid) Y64.9
  administered (by) NEC Y64.9
    immunization Y64.1
    infusion Y64.0
    injection Y64.1
    specified means NEC Y64.8
    transfusion Y64.0
    vaccination Y64.1
excessive amount of blood or other fluid
  during transfusion or infusion Y63.0
failure
  in dosage Y63.9
    electroshock therapy Y63.4
    inappropriate temperature (too hot or
      too cold) in local application and
      packing Y63.5
    infusion
      excessive amount of fluid Y63.0
      incorrect dilution of fluid Y63.1
    insulin-shock therapy Y63.4
    nonadministration of necessary drug or
      biological substance Y63.6
    overdose —see Table of Drugs and
      Chemicals
    radiation, in therapy Y63.2
    radiation
      overdose Y63.2
    specified procedure NEC Y63.8
    transfusion
      excessive amount of blood Y63.0
  mechanical, of instrument or apparatus
    (any) (during any procedure) Y65.8
  sterile precautions (during procedure)
    Y62.9
    aspiration of fluid or tissue (by puncture
      or catheterization, except heart)
      Y62.6
    biopsy (except needle aspiration)
      Y62.8
      needle (aspirating) Y62.6
    blood sampling Y62.6
    catheterization Y62.6
      heart Y62.5
    dialysis (kidney) Y62.2
    endoscopic examination Y62.4
    enema Y62.8
    immunization Y62.3
    infusion Y62.1
    injection Y62.3
    needle biopsy Y62.6
    paracentesis (abdominal) (thoracic)
      Y62.6
    perfusion Y62.2

▶ New   ➡ Revised   ~~deleted~~ Deleted   ● Use Additional Character(s)

Misadventure(s) to patient(s) during surgical or medical care *(Continued)*
  failure *(Continued)*
    sterile precautions *(Continued)*
      puncture (lumbar) Y62.6
      removal of catheter or packing Y62.8
      specified procedure NEC Y62.8
      surgical operation Y62.0
      transfusion Y62.1
      vaccination Y62.3
    suture or ligature during surgical procedure Y65.2
    to introduce or to remove tube or instrument —*see* Failure, to
  hemorrhage —*see* Index to Diseases and Injuries, Complication(s)
  inadvertent exposure of patient to radiation Y63.3
  inappropriate
    operation performed —*see* Inappropriate operation performed
    temperature (too hot or too cold) in local application or packing Y63.5

infusion —*see also* Misadventure, by type, infusion Y69
  excessive amount of fluid Y63.0
  incorrect dilution of fluid Y63.1
  wrong fluid Y65.1
mismatched blood in transfusion Y65.0
nonadministration of necessary drug or biological substance Y63.6
overdose —*see* Table of Drugs and Chemicals
  radiation (in therapy) Y63.2
perforation —*see* Index to Diseases and Injuries, Complication(s)
performance of inappropriate operation —*see* Inappropriate operation performed
puncture —*see* Index to Diseases and Injuries, Complication(s)
specified type NEC Y65.8
  failure
    suture or ligature during surgical operation Y65.2
    to introduce or to remove tube or instrument —*see* Failure, to
  infusion of wrong fluid Y65.1

specified type NEC *(Continued)*
  performance of inappropriate operation —*see* Inappropriate operation performed
  transfusion of mismatched blood Y65.0
  wrong
    fluid in infusion Y65.1
    placement of endotracheal tube during anesthetic procedure Y65.3
transfusion —*see* Misadventure, by type, transfusion
  excessive amount of blood Y63.0
  mismatched blood Y65.0
wrong
  drug given in error —*see* Table of Drugs and Chemicals
  fluid in infusion Y65.1
  placement of endotracheal tube during anesthetic procedure Y65.3
Mismatched blood in transfusion Y65.0
Motion sickness T75.3
Mountain sickness W94.11
Mudslide (of cataclysmic nature) —*see* Landslide
Murder (attempt) —*see* Assault

N

Nail
  contact with W45.0
    gun W29.4
  embedded in skin W45.0
Neglect (criminal) (homicidal intent) X58

Noise (causing injury) (pollution) W42.9
  supersonic W42.0
Nonadministration (of)
  drug or biological substance (necessary) Y63.6
  surgical and medical care Y66
Nosocomial condition Y95

O

Object
  falling
    from, in, on, hitting
      machinery —*see* Contact, with, by type of machine
  set in motion by
    accidental explosion or rupture of pressure vessel W38
    firearm —*see* Discharge, firearm, by type
    machine (ry) —*see* Contact, with, by type of machine
Overdose (drug) —*see* Table of Drugs and Chemicals
  radiation Y63.2

Overexertion X50.9
  from
    prolonged static or awkward postures X50.1
    repetitive movements X50.3
    specified strenuous movements or postures NEC X50.9
    strenuous movement or load X50.0
Overexposure (accidental) (to)
  cold —*see also* Exposure, cold X31
    due to man-made conditions —*see* Exposure, cold, man-made
  heat —*see also* Heat X30
  radiation —*see* Radiation
  radioactivity W88.0
  sun (sunburn) X32

Overexposure *(Continued)*
  weather NEC —*see* Forces of nature
  wind NEC —*see* Forces of nature
Overheated —*see* Heat
Overturning (accidental)
  machinery —*see* Contact, with, by type of machine
  transport vehicle NEC —*see also* Accident, transport V89.9
  watercraft (causing drowning, submersion) —*see also* Drowning, due to, accident to, watercraft, overturning
    causing injury except drowning or submersion —*see* Accident, watercraft, causing, injury NEC

M, N, & O

P

Parachute descent (voluntary) (without accident to aircraft) V97.29
  due to accident to aircraft —*see* Accident, transport, aircraft
Pecked by bird W61.99
Perforation during medical or surgical treatment as misadventure —*see* Index to Diseases and Injuries, Complication(s)
Perpetrator, perpetration, of assault, maltreatment and neglect (by) Y07.9
  boyfriend Y07.03
  brother Y07.410
    stepbrother Y07.435
  coach Y07.53
  cousin
    female Y07.491
    male Y07.490
  daycare provider Y07.519
    at-home
      adult care Y07.512
      childcare Y07.510
    care center
      adult care Y07.513
      childcare Y07.511
  family member NEC Y07.499
  father Y07.11
    adoptive Y07.13
    foster Y07.420
    stepfather Y07.430
  foster father Y07.420
  foster mother Y07.421
  girl friend Y07.04
  healthcare provider Y07.529
    mental health Y07.521
    specified NEC Y07.528
  husband Y07.01
  instructor Y07.53
  mother Y07.12
    adoptive Y07.14
    foster Y07.421
    stepmother Y07.433
  nonfamily member Y07.50
    specified NEC Y07.59
  nurse Y07.528
  occupational therapist Y07.528
  partner of parent
    female Y07.434
    male Y07.432
  physical therapist Y07.528
  sister Y07.411
  speech therapist Y07.528
  stepbrother Y07.435
  stepfather Y07.430
  stepmother Y07.433
  stepsister Y07.436
  teacher Y07.53
  wife Y07.02
Piercing —*see* Contact, with, by type of object or machine
Pinched
  between objects (moving) (stationary and moving) W23.0
    stationary W23.1
Pinned under machine (ry) —*see* Contact, with, by type of machine
Place of occurrence Y92.9
  abandoned house Y92.89
  airplane Y92.813
  airport Y92.520
  ambulatory health services establishment NEC Y92.538
  ambulatory surgery center Y92.530
  amusement park Y92.831
  apartment (co-op) —*see* Place of occurrence, residence, apartment
  assembly hall Y92.29
  bank Y92.510
  barn Y92.71
  baseball field Y92.320

Place of occurrence (*Continued*)
  basketball court Y92.310
  beach Y92.832
  boarding house —*see* Place of occurrence, residence, boarding house
  boat Y92.814
  bowling alley Y92.39
  bridge Y92.89
  building under construction Y92.61
  bus Y92.811
    station Y92.521
  cafe Y92.511
  campsite Y92.833
  campus —*see* Place of occurrence, school
  canal Y92.89
  car Y92.810
  casino Y92.59
  children's home —*see* Place of occurrence, residence, institutional, orphanage
  church Y92.22
  cinema Y92.26
  clubhouse Y92.29
  coal pit Y92.64
  college (community) Y92.214
  condominium —*see* Place of occurrence, residence, apartment
  construction area —*see* Place of occurrence, industrial and construction area
  convalescent home —*see* Place of occurrence, residence, institutional, nursing home
  court-house Y92.240
  cricket ground Y92.328
  cultural building Y92.258
    art gallery Y92.250
    museum Y92.251
    music hall Y92.252
    opera house Y92.253
    specified NEC Y92.258
    theater Y92.254
  dancehall Y92.252
  day nursery Y92.210
  dentist office Y92.531
  derelict house Y92.89
  desert Y92.820
  dock NOS Y92.89
  dockyard Y92.62
  doctor's office Y92.531
  dormitory —*see* Place of occurrence, residence, institutional, school dormitory
  dry dock Y92.62
  factory (building) (premises) Y92.63
  farm (land under cultivation) (outbuildings) Y92.79
    barn Y92.71
    chicken coop Y92.72
    field Y92.73
    hen house Y92.72
    house —*see* Place of occurrence, residence, house
    orchard Y92.74
    specified NEC Y92.79
  football field Y92.321
  forest Y92.821
  freeway Y92.411
  gallery Y92.250
  garage (commercial) Y92.59
    boarding house Y92.044
    military base Y92.135
    mobile home Y92.025
    nursing home Y92.124
    orphanage Y92.114
    private house Y92.015
    reform school Y92.155
  gas station Y92.524
  gasworks Y92.69
  golf course Y92.39
  gravel pit Y92.64
  grocery Y92.512
  gymnasium Y92.39
  handball court Y92.318
  harbor Y92.89

Place of occurrence (*Continued*)
  harness racing course Y92.39
  healthcare provider office Y92.531
  highway (interstate) Y92.411
  hill Y92.828
  hockey rink Y92.330
  home —*see* Place of occurrence, residence
  hospice —*see* Place of occurrence, residence, institutional, nursing home
  hospital Y92.239
    cafeteria Y92.233
    corridor Y92.232
    operating room Y92.234
    patient
      bathroom Y92.231
      room Y92.230
    specified NEC Y92.238
  hotel Y92.59
  house —*see also* Place of occurrence, residence
    abandoned Y92.89
    under construction Y92.61
  industrial and construction area (yard) Y92.69
    building under construction Y92.61
    dock Y92.62
    dry dock Y92.62
    factory Y92.63
    gasworks Y92.69
    mine Y92.64
    oil rig Y92.65
    pit Y92.64
    power station Y92.69
    shipyard Y92.62
    specified NEC Y92.69
    tunnel under construction Y92.69
    workshop Y92.69
  kindergarten Y92.211
  lacrosse field Y92.328
  lake Y92.828
  library Y92.241
  mall Y92.59
  market Y92.512
  marsh Y92.828
  military
    base —*see* Place of occurrence, residence, institutional, military base
    training ground Y92.84
  mine Y92.64
  mosque Y92.22
  motel Y92.59
  motorway (interstate) Y92.411
  mountain Y92.828
  movie-house Y92.26
  museum Y92.251
  music-hall Y92.252
  not applicable Y92.9
  nuclear power station Y92.69
  nursing home —*see* Place of occurrence, residence, institutional, nursing home
  office building Y92.59
  offshore installation Y92.65
  oil rig Y92.65
  old people's home —*see* Place of occurrence, residence, institutional, specified NEC
  opera-house Y92.253
  orphanage —*see* Place of occurrence, residence, institutional, orphanage
  outpatient surgery center Y92.530
  park (public) Y92.830
    amusement Y92.831
  parking garage Y92.89
    lot Y92.481
  pavement Y92.480
  physician office Y92.531
  polo field Y92.328
  pond Y92.828
  post office Y92.242
  power station Y92.69
  prairie Y92.828
  prison —*see* Place of occurrence, residence, institutional, prison

► New   ⇒ Revised   ~~deleted~~ Deleted   ● Use Additional Character(s)

Place of occurrence (Continued)
public
  administration building Y92.248
    city hall Y92.243
    courthouse Y92.240
    library Y92.241
    post office Y92.242
    specified NEC Y92.248
  building NEC Y92.29
  hall Y92.29
  place NOS Y92.89
race course Y92.39
radio station Y92.59
railway line (bridge) Y92.85
ranch (outbuildings) —see Place of
  occurrence, farm
recreation area Y92.838
  amusement park Y92.831
  beach Y92.832
  campsite Y92.833
  park (public) Y92.830
  seashore Y92.832
  specified NEC Y92.838
reform school —see Place of occurrence,
  residence, institutional, reform school
religious institution Y92.22
residence (non-institutional) (private) Y92.009
  apartment Y92.039
    bathroom Y92.031
    bedroom Y92.032
    kitchen Y92.030
    specified NEC Y92.038
  bathroom Y92.002
  bedroom Y92.003
  boarding house Y92.049
    bathroom Y92.041
    bedroom Y92.042
    driveway Y92.043
    garage Y92.044
    garden Y92.046
    kitchen Y92.040
    specified NEC Y92.048
    swimming pool Y92.045
    yard Y92.046
  dining room Y92.001
  garden Y92.007
  home Y92.009
  house, single family Y92.019
    bathroom Y92.012
    bedroom Y92.013
    dining room Y92.011
    driveway Y92.014
    garage Y92.015
    garden Y92.017
    kitchen Y92.010
    specified NEC Y92.018
    swimming pool Y92.016
    yard Y92.017
  institutional Y92.10
    children's home —see Place of
      occurrence, residence, institutional,
      orphanage
    hospice —see Place of occurrence,
      residence, institutional, nursing
      home
    military base Y92.139
      barracks Y92.133
      garage Y92.135
      garden Y92.137
      kitchen Y92.130
      mess hall Y92.131
      specified NEC Y92.138
      swimming pool Y92.136
      yard Y92.137
    nursing home Y92.129
      bathroom Y92.121
      bedroom Y92.122
      driveway Y92.123
      garage Y92.124
      garden Y92.126
      kitchen Y92.120

Place of occurrence (Continued)
residence (Continued)
  institutional (Continued)
    nursing home (Continued)
      specified NEC Y92.128
      swimming pool Y92.125
      yard Y92.126
    orphanage Y92.119
      bathroom Y92.111
      bedroom Y92.112
      driveway Y92.113
      garage Y92.114
      garden Y92.116
      kitchen Y92.110
      specified NEC Y92.118
      swimming pool Y92.115
      yard Y92.116
    prison Y92.149
      bathroom Y92.142
      cell Y92.143
      courtyard Y92.147
      dining room Y92.141
      kitchen Y92.140
      specified NEC Y92.148
      swimming pool Y92.146
    reform school Y92.159
      bathroom Y92.152
      bedroom Y92.153
      dining room Y92.151
      driveway Y92.154
      garage Y92.155
      garden Y92.157
      kitchen Y92.150
      specified NEC Y92.158
      swimming pool Y92.156
      yard Y92.157
    school dormitory Y92.169
      bathroom Y92.162
      bedroom Y92.163
      dining room Y92.161
      kitchen Y92.160
      specified NEC Y92.168
    specified NEC Y92.199
      bathroom Y92.192
      bedroom Y92.193
      dining room Y92.191
      driveway Y92.194
      garage Y92.195
      garden Y92.197
      kitchen Y92.190
      specified NEC Y92.198
      swimming pool Y92.196
      yard Y92.197
  kitchen Y92.000
  mobile home Y92.029
    bathroom Y92.022
    bedroom Y92.023
    dining room Y92.021
    driveway Y92.024
    garage Y92.025
    garden Y92.027
    kitchen Y92.020
    specified NEC Y92.028
    swimming pool Y92.026
    yard Y92.027
  specified place in residence NEC Y92.008
  specified residence type NEC Y92.099
    bathroom Y92.091
    bedroom Y92.092
    driveway Y92.093
    garage Y92.094
    garden Y92.096
    kitchen Y92.090
    specified NEC Y92.098
    swimming pool Y92.095
    yard Y92.096
restaurant Y92.511
riding school Y92.39
river Y92.828
road Y92.410
rodeo ring Y92.39

Place of occurrence (Continued)
rugby field Y92.328
same day surgery center Y92.530
sand pit Y92.64
school (private) (public) (state) Y92.219
  college Y92.214
  daycare center Y92.210
  elementary school Y92.211
  high school Y92.213
  kindergarten Y92.211
  middle school Y92.212
  specified NEC Y92.218
  trace school Y92.215
  university Y92.214
  vocational school Y92.215
sea (shore) Y92.832
senior citizen center Y92.29
service area
  airport Y92.520
  bus station Y92.521
  gas station Y92.524
  highway rest stop Y92.523
  railway station Y92.522
shipyard Y92.62
shop(commercial) Y92.513
sidewalk Y92.480
silo Y92.79
skating rink (roller) Y92.331
  ice Y92.330
slaughter house Y92.86
soccer field Y92.322
specified place NEC Y92.89
sports area Y92.39
  athletic
    court Y92.318
      basketball Y92.310
      specified NEC Y92.318
      squash Y92.311
      tennis Y92.312
    field Y92.328
      baseball Y92.320
      cricket ground Y92.328
      football Y92.321
      hockey Y92.328
      soccer Y92.322
      specified NEC Y92.328
  golf course Y92.39
  gymnasium Y92.39
  riding school Y92.39
  skating rink (roller) Y92.331
    ice Y92.330
  stadium Y92.39
  swimming pool Y92.34
squash court Y92.311
stadium Y92.39
steeplechasing course Y92.39
store Y92.512
stream Y92.828
street and highway Y92.410
  bike path Y92.482
  freeway Y92.411
  highway ramp Y92.415
  interstate highway Y92.411
  local residential or business street
    Y92.414
  motorway Y92.411
  parking lot Y92.481
  parkway Y92.412
  sidewalk Y92.480
  specified NEC Y92.488
  state road Y92.413
subway car Y92.816
supermarket Y92.512
swamp Y92.828
swimming pool (public) Y92.34
  private (at) Y92.095
    boarding house Y92.045
    military base Y92.136
    mobile home Y92.026
    nursing home Y92.125
    orphanage Y92.115

Place of occurrence (Continued)
   swimming pool (Continued)
      private (Continued)
         prison Y92.146
         reform school Y92.156
         single family residence Y92.016
   synagogue Y92.22
   television station Y92.59
   tennis court Y92.312
   theater Y92.254
   trade area Y92.59
      bank Y92.510
      cafe Y92.511
      casino Y92.59
      garage Y92.59
      hotel Y92.59
      market Y92.512
      office building Y92.59
      radio station Y92.59
      restaurant Y92.511
      shop Y92.513
      shopping mall Y92.59
      store Y92.512
      supermarket Y92.512
      television station Y92.59
      warehouse Y92.59
   trailer park, residential —see Place of occurrence, residence, mobile home
   trailer site NOS Y92.89
   train Y92.815
      station Y92.522
   truck Y92.812
   tunnel under construction Y92.69
   university Y92.214
   urgent (health) care center Y92.532
   vehicle (transport) Y92.818
      airplane Y92.813
      boat Y92.814
      bus Y92.811
      car Y92.810
      specified NEC Y92.818
      subway car Y92.816
      train Y92.815
      truck Y92.812
   warehouse Y92.59
   water reservoir Y92.89
   wilderness area Y92.828
      desert Y92.820
      forest Y92.821
      marsh Y92.828
      mountain Y92.828
      prairie Y92.828
      specified NEC Y92.828
      swamp Y92.828
   workshop Y92.69
   yard, private Y92.096
      boarding house Y92.046
      mobile home Y92.027
      single family house Y92.017

Place of occurrence (Continued)
   youth center Y92.29
   zoo (zoological garden) Y92.834
Plumbism —see Table of Drugs and Chemicals, lead
Poisoning (accidental) (by) —see also Table of Drugs and Chemicals
   by plant, thorns, spines, sharp leaves or other mechanisms NEC X58
   carbon monoxide
      generated by
         motor vehicle —see Accident, transport
         watercraft (in transit) (not in transit) V93.89
            ferry boat V93.81
            fishing boat V93.82
            jet skis V93.83
            liner V93.81
            merchant ship V93.80
            passenger ship V93.81
            powered craft NEC V93.83
   caused by injection of poisons into skin by plant thorns, spines, sharp leaves X58
      marine or sea plants (venomous) X58
   exhaust gas
      generated by
         motor vehicle —see Accident, transport
         watercraft (in transit) (not in transit) V93.89
            ferry boat V93.81
            fishing boat V93.82
            jet skis V93.83
            liner V93.81
            merchant ship V93.80
            passenger ship V93.81
            powered craft NEC V93.83
   fumes or smoke due to
      explosion —see also Explosion W40.9
      fire —see Exposure, fire
      ignition —see Ignition
   gas
      in legal intervention —see Legal, intervention, gas
      legal execution —see Legal, intervention, gas
   in war operations —see War operations
   legal
   execution —see Legal, intervention, gas
   intervention
         by gas —see Legal, intervention, gas
         other specified means —see Legal, intervention, specified means NEC
Powder burn (by) (from)
   airgun W34.110
   BB gun W34.110
   firearm NEC W34.19
   gas, air or spring-operated gun NEC W34.118
   handgun W32.1
   hunting rifle W33.12

Powder burn (Continued)
   larger firearm W33.10
      specified NEC W33.19
   machine gun W33.13
   paintball gun W34.111
   pellet gun W34.110
   shotgun W33.11
   Very pistol [flare] W34.19
Premature cessation (of) surgical and medical care Y66
Privation (food) (water) X58
Procedure (operation)
   correct, on wrong side or body part (wrong side) (wrong site) Y65.53
   intended for another patient done on wrong patient Y65.52
   performed on patient not scheduled for surgery Y65.52
   performed on wrong patient Y65.52
   wrong, performed on correct patient Y65.51
Prolonged
   sitting in transport vehicle —see Travel, by type of vehicle
   stay in
      high altitude as cause of anoxia, barodontalgia, barotitis or hypoxia W94.11
      weightless environment X52
Pulling, excessive —see also Overexertion X50.9
Puncture, puncturing —see also Contact, with, by type of object or machine
   by
      plant thorns, spines, sharp leaves or other mechanisms NEC W60
   during medical or surgical treatment as misadventure —see Index to Diseases and Injuries, Complication(s)
Pushed, pushing (accidental) (injury in)
   by other person(s) (accidental) W51
      with fall W03
         due to ice or snow W00.0
      as, or caused by, a crowd or human stampede (with fall) W52
      before moving object NEC Y02.8
         motor vehicle Y02.0
         subway train Y02.1
         train Y02.1
      from
         high place NEC
            in accidental circumstances W17.89
            stated as
               intentional, homicide (attempt) Y01
               undetermined whether accidental or intentional Y30
         transport vehicle NEC —see also Accident, transport V89.9
            stated as
               intentional, homicide (attempt) Y08.89
   overexertion X50.9

▶ New   ⇒ Revised   ~~deleted~~ Deleted   ● Use Additional Character(s)

R

Radiation (exposure to)
  arc lamps W89.0
  atomic power plant (malfunction) NEC
    W88.1
  complication of or abnormal reaction to
    medical radiotherapy Y84.2
  electromagnetic, ionizing W88.0
  gamma rays W88.1
  in
    war operations (from or following
      nuclear explosion) —see also War
      operations
  inadvertent exposure of patient (receiving
    test or therapy) Y63.3
  infrared (heaters and lamps) W90.1
    excessive heat from W92
  ionized, ionizing (particles, artificially
    accelerated)
    radioisotopes W88.1
    specified NEC W88.8
    x-rays W88.0
  isotopes, radioactive —see Radiation,
    radioactive isotopes
  laser(s) W90.2
    in war operations —see War operations
    misadventure in medical care Y63.2
  light sources (man-made visible and
    ultraviolet) W89.9
    natural X32
    specified NEC W89.8
    tanning bed W89.1
    welding light W89.0
  man-made visible light W89.9
    specified NEC W89.8
    tanning bed W89.1
    welding light W89.0
  microwave W90.8
  misadventure in medical or surgical
    procedure Y63.2

Radiation (Continued)
  natural NEC X39.08
    radon X39.01
  overdose (in medical or surgical procedure)
    Y63.2
  radar W90.0
  radioactive isotopes (any) W88.1
    atomic power plant malfunction W88.1
    misadventure in medical or surgical
      treatment Y63.2
  radiofrequency W90.0
  radium NEC W88.1
  sun X32
  ultraviolet (light) (man-made) W89.9
    natural X32
    specified NEC W89.8
    tanning bed W89.1
    welding light W89.0
  welding arc, torch, or light W89.0
    excessive heat from W92
  x-rays (hard) (soft) W88.0
Range disease W94.11
Rape (attempted) T74.2-●
Rat bite W53.11
Reaching (prolonged) (static) X50.1
Reaction, abnormal to medical procedure —see
    also Complication of or following, by type
    of procedure Y84.9
  with misadventure —see Misadventure
  biologicals —see Table of Drugs and
    Chemicals
  drugs —see Table of Drugs and Chemicals
  vaccine —see Table of Drugs and
    Chemicals
Recoil
  airgun W34.110
  BB gun W34.110
  firearm NEC W34.19
  gas, air or spring-operated gun NEC W34.118

Recoil (Continued)
  handgun W32.1
  hunting rifle W33.12
  larger firearm W33.10
    specified NEC W33.19
  machine gun W33.13
  paintball gun W34.111
  pellet W34.110
  shotgun W33.11
  Very pistol [flare] W34.19
Reduction in
  atmospheric pressure —see Air, pressure,
    change
Rock falling on or hitting (accidentally)
    (person) W20.8
  in cave-in W20.0
Run over (accidentally) (by)
  animal (not being ridden) NEC W55.89
  machinery —see Contact, with, by specified
    type of machine
  transport vehicle NEC —see also Accident,
    transport V09.9
    intentional homicide (attempt) Y03.0
    motor NEC V09.20
      intentional homicide (attempt) Y03.0
Running
  before moving object X81.8
    motor vehicle X81.0
Running off, away
  animal (being ridden) —see also Accident,
    transport V80.918
    not being ridden W55.89
  animal-drawn vehicle NEC —see also
    Accident, transport V80.928
  highway, road(way), street
    transport vehicle NEC —see also Accident,
      transport V89.9
Rupture pressurized devices —see Explosion,
    by type of device

S

Saturnism —see Table of Drugs and Chemicals, lead
Scald, scalding (accidental) (by) (from) (in) X19
  air (hot) X14.1
  gases (hot) X14.1
  homicide (attempt) —see Assault, burning, hot object
  inflicted by other person
    stated as intentional, homicide (attempt) —see Assault, burning, hot object
  liquid (boiling) (hot) NEC X12
    stated as undetermined whether accidental or intentional Y27.2
    suicide (attempt) X77.2
  local application of externally applied substance in medical or surgical care Y63.5
  metal (molten) (liquid) (hot) NEC X18
  self-inflicted X77.9
    stated as undetermined whether accidental or intentional Y27.8
  steam X13.1
    assault X98.0
    stated as undetermined whether accidental or intentional Y27.0
    suicide (attempt) X77.0
  suicide (attempt) X77.9
  vapor (hot) X13.1
    assault X98.0
    stated as undetermined whether accidental or intentional Y27.0
    suicide (attempt) X77.0
Scratched by
  cat W55.03
  person(s) (accidentally) W50.4
    with intent to injure or kill Y04.0
    as, or caused by, a crowd or human stampede (with fall) W52
    assault Y04.0
    homicide (attempt) Y04.0
    in
      fight Y04.0
      legal intervention
        injuring
          bystander Y35.892
          law enforcement personnel Y35.891
          suspect Y35.893
Seasickness T75.3
Self-harm NEC —see also External cause by type, undetermined whether accidental or intentional
  intentional —see Suicide
  poisoning NEC —see Table of drugs and biologicals, accident
Self-inflicted (injury) NEC —see also External cause by type, undetermined whether accidental or intentional
  intentional —see Suicide
  poisoning NEC —see Table of drugs and biologicals, accident
Sequelae (of)
  accident NEC —see W00-X58 with 7th character S
  assault (homicidal) (any means) —see X92-Y08 with 7th character S
  homicide, attempt (any means) —see X92-Y08 with 7th character S
  injury undetermined whether accidentally or purposely inflicted —see Y21-Y33 with 7th character S
  intentional self-harm (classifiable to X71-X83) —see X71-X83 with 7th character S
  legal intervention (see with 7th character S Y35)
  motor vehicle accident —see V00-V99 with 7th character S
  suicide, attempt (any means) —see X71-X83 with 7th character S

Sequelae (Continued)
  transport accident —see V00-V99 with 7th character S
  war operations —see War operations
Shock
  electric —see Exposure, electric current
  from electric appliance (any) (faulty) W86.8
    domestic W86.0
    suicide (attempt) X83.1
Shooting, shot (accidental (ly)) —see also Discharge, firearm, by type
  herself or himself —see Discharge, firearm by type, self-inflicted
  homicide (attempt) —see Discharge, firearm by type, homicide
  in war operations —see War operations
  inflicted by other person —see Discharge, firearm by type, homicide
    accidental —see Discharge, firearm, by type of firearm
  legal
    execution —see Legal, intervention, firearm
    intervention —see Legal, intervention, firearm
  self-inflicted —see Discharge, firearm by type, suicide
    accidental —see Discharge, firearm, by type of firearm
  suicide (attempt) —see Discharge, firearm by type, suicide
Shoving (accidentally) by other person —see Pushed, by other person
Sickness
  alpine W94.11
  motion —see Motion
  mountain W94.11
Sinking (accidental)
  watercraft (causing drowning, submersion) —see also Drowning, due to, accident to, watercraft, sinking
    causing injury except drowning or submersion —see Accident, watercraft, causing, injury NEC
Siriasis X32
Sitting (prolonged) (static) X50.1
Slashed wrists —see Cut, self-inflicted
Slipping (accidental) (on same level) (with fall) W01.0
  without fall W18.40
    due to
      specified NEC W18.49
      stepping from one level to another W18.43
      stepping into hole or opening W18.42
      stepping on object W18.41
  on
    ice W00.0
      with skates —see Accident, transport, pedestrian, conveyance
    mud W01.0
    oil W01.0
    snow W00.0
      with skis —see Accident, transport, pedestrian, conveyance
    surface (slippery) (wet) NEC W01.0
Sliver, wood, contact with W45.8
Smoldering (due to fire) —see Exposure, fire
Sodomy (attempted) by force T74.2-●
Sound waves (causing injury) W42.9
  supersonic W42.0
Splinter, contact with W45.8
Stab, stabbing —see Cut
Standing (prolonged) (static) X50.1
Starvation X58
Status of external cause Y99.9
  child assisting in compensated work for family Y99.8
  civilian activity done for financial or other compensation Y99.0
  civilian activity done for income or pay Y99.0

Status of external cause (Continued)
  family member assisting in compensated work for other family member Y99.8
  hobby not done for income Y99.8
  leisure activity Y99.8
  military activity Y99.1
  off-duty activity of military personnel Y99.8
  recreation or sport not for income or while a student Y99.8
  specified NEC Y99.8
  student activity Y99.8
  volunteer activity Y99.2
Stepped on
  by
    animal (not being ridden) NEC W55.89
    crowd or human stampede W52
    person W50.0
Stepping on
  object W22.8
    with fall W18.31
      sports equipment W21.9
    stationary W22.09
      sports equipment W21.89
  person W51
    by crowd or human stampede W52
  sports equipment W21.9
Sting
  arthropod, nonvenomous W57
  insect, nonvenomous W57
Storm (cataclysmic) —see Forces of nature, cataclysmic storm
Straining, excessive —see also Overexertion X50.9
Strangling —see Strangulation
Strangulation (accidental) —see category T71
Strenuous movements —see also Overexertion X50.9
Striking against
  airbag (automobile) W22.10
    driver side W22.11
    front passenger side W22.12
    specified NEC W22.19
  bottom when
    diving or jumping into water (in) W16.822
      causing drowning W16.821
      from boat W16.722
        causing drowning W16.721
      natural body W16.622
        causing drowning W16.821
      swimming pool W16.522
        causing drowning W16.521
    falling into water (in) W16.322
      causing drowning W16.321
      fountain —see Striking against, bottom when, falling into water, specified NEC
      natural body W16.122
        causing drowning W16.121
      reservoir —see Striking against, bottom when, falling into water, specified NEC
      specified NEC W16.322
        causing drowning W16.321
      swimming pool W16.022
        causing drowning W16.021
  diving board (swimming-pool) W21.4
  object W22.8
    with
      drowning or submersion —see Drowning
      fall —see Fall, due to, bumping against, object
    caused by crowd or human stampede (with fall) W52
    furniture W22.03
    lamppost W22.02
    sports equipment W21.9
    stationary W22.09
      sports equipment W21.89
    wall W22.01

▶ New   ⇒ Revised   ~~deleted~~ Deleted   ● Use Additional Character(s)

Striking against *(Continued)*
  person(s) W51
    with fall W03
      due to ice or snow W00.0
      as, or caused by, a crowd or human
        stampede (with fall) W52
    assault Y04.2
    homicide (attempt) Y04.2
  sports equipment W21.9
  wall (when) W22.01
    diving or jumping into water (in) W16.832
      causing drowning W16.831
      swimming pool W16.532
        causing drowning W16.531
    falling into water (in) W16.332
      causing drowning W16.331
      fountain —*see* Striking against, wall
        when, falling into water, specified
        NEC
      natural body W16.132
        causing drowning W16.131
      reservoir —*see* Striking against, wall
        when, falling into water, specified
        NEC
      specified NEC W16.332
        causing drowning W16.331
      swimming pool W16.032
        causing drowning W16.031
    swimming pool (when) W22.042
      causing drowning W22.041
      diving or jumping into water W16.532
        causing drowning W16.531
      falling into water W16.032
        causing drowning W16.031
Struck (accidentally) by
  airbag (automobile) W22.10
    driver side W22.11
    front passenger side W22.12
    specified NEC W22.19
  alligator W58.02
  animal (not being ridden) NEC W55.89
  avalanche —*see* Landslide
  ball (hit) (thrown) W21.00
    assault Y08.09
    baseball W21.03
    basketball W21.05
    football W21.01
    golf ball W21.04
    football W21.01
    soccer W21.02
    softball W21.07
    specified NEC W21.09
    volleyball W21.06
  bat or racquet
    baseball bat W21.11
      assault Y08.02
    golf club W21.13
      assault Y08.09
    specified NEC W21.19
      assault Y08.09
    tennis racquet W21.12
      assault Y08.09
  bullet —*see also* Discharge, firearm by type
    in war operations —*see* War operations
  crocodile W58.12
  dog W54.1
  flare, Very pistol —*see* Discharge, firearm
    NEC
  hailstones X39.8
  hockey (ice)
    field
      puck W21.221
      stick W21.211
    puck W21.220
    stick W21.210
      assault Y08.01
  landslide —*see* Landslide
  law-enforcement agent (on duty) —*see* Legal,
    intervention, manhandling
    with blunt object —*see* Legal, intervention,
      blunt object

Struck by *(Continued)*
  lightning —*see* subcategory T75.0
    causing fire —*see* Exposure, fire
  machine —*see* Contact, with, by type of
    machine
  mammal NEC W55.89
    marine W56.32
  marine animal W56.82
  missile
    firearm —*see* Discharge, firearm by type
    in war operations —*see* War operations,
      missile
  object W22.8
    blunt W22.8
      assault Y00
      suicide (attempt) X79
      undetermined whether accidental or
        intentional Y29
    falling W20.8
      from, in, on
        building W20.1
          burning (uncontrolled fire) X00.4
        cataclysmic
          earth surface movement NEC —*see*
            Landslide
          storm —*see* Forces of nature,
            cataclysmic storm
        cave-in W20.0
        earthquake X34
        machine (in operation) —*see* Contact,
          with, by type of machine
        structure W20.1
          burning X00.4
        transport vehicle (in motion) —*see*
          Accident, transport, by type of
          vehicle
        watercraft V93.49
          due to
            accident to craft V91.39
              powered craft V91.33
                ferry boat V91.31
                fishing boat V91.32
                jet ski V91.33
                liner V91.31
                merchant ship V91.30
                passenger ship V91.31
              unpowered craft V91.38
                canoe V91.35
                inflatable V91.36
                kayak V91.35
                sailboat V91.34
                surf-board V91.38
                windsurfer V91.38
          powered craft V93.43
            ferry boat V93.41
            fishing boat V93.42
            jet ski V93.43
            liner V93.41
            merchant ship V93.40
            passenger ship V93.41
          unpowered craft V93.48
            sailboat V93.44
            surf-board V93.48
            windsurfer V93.48
    moving NEC W20.8
    projected W20.8
      assault Y00
      in sports W21.9
        assault Y08.09
        ball W21.00
          baseball W21.03
          basketball W21.05
          football W21.01
          golf ball W21.04
          soccer W21.02
          softball W21.07
          specified NEC W21.09
          volleyball W21.06
        bat or racquet
          baseball bat W21.11
            assault Y08.02

Struck by *(Continued)*
  object *(Continued)*
    projected *(Continued)*
      in sports *(Continued)*
        bat or racquet *(Continued)*
          golf club W21.13
            assault Y08.09-●
          specified NEC W21.19
            assault Y08.09
          tennis racquet W21.12
            assault Y08.09
        hockey (ice)
          field
            puck W21.221
            stick W21.211
          puck W21.220
          stick W21.210
            assault Y08.01
        specified NEC W21.89
    set in motion by explosion —*see* Explosion
    thrown W20.8
      assault Y00
      in sports W21.9
        assault Y08.09
        ball W21.00
          baseball W21.03
          basketball W21.05
          football W21.01
          golf ball W21.04
          soccer W21.02
          soft ball W21.07
          specified NEC W21.09
          volleyball W21.06
        bat or racquet
          baseball bat W21.11
            assault Y08.02
          golf club W21.13
            assault Y08.09
          specified NEC W21.19
            assault Y08.09
          tennis racquet W21.12
            assault Y08.09
        hockey (ice)
          field
            puck W21.221
            stick W21.211
          puck W21.220
          stick W21.210
            assault Y08.01
        specified NEC W21.89
  other person(s) W50.0
    with
      blunt object W22.8
        intentional, homicide (attempt) Y00
        sports equipment W21.9
        undetermined whether accidental or
          intentional Y29
      fall W03
        due to ice or snow W00.0
      as, or caused by, a crowd or human
        stampede (with fall) W52
      assault Y04.2
      homicide (attempt) Y04.2
      in legal intervention
        injuring
          bystander Y35.812
          law enforcement personnel Y35.811
          suspect Y35.813
      sports equipment W21.9
  police (on duty) —*see* Legal, intervention,
    manhandling
    with blunt object —*see* Legal, intervention,
      blunt object
  sports equipment W21.9
    assault Y08.09
    ball W21.00
      baseball W21.03
      basketball W21.05
      football W21.01
      golf ball W21.04
      soccer W21.02

Struck by (Continued)
  sports equipment (Continued)
    ball (Continued)
      soft ball W21.07
      specified NEC W21.09
      volleyball W21.06
    bat or racquet
      baseball bat W21.11
        assault Y08.02
      golf club W21.13
        assault Y08.09
      specified NEC W21.19
      tennis racquet W21.12
        assault Y08.09
    cleats (shoe) W21.31
    foot wear NEC W21.39
    football helmet W21.81
    hockey (ice)
      field
        puck W21.221
        stick W21.211
      puck W21.220
      stick W21.210
        assault Y08.01
    skate blades W21.32
    specified NEC W21.89
      assault Y08.09
  thunderbolt —see subcategory
    T75.0
  causing fire —see Exposure, fire
  transport vehicle NEC —see also Accident,
    transport V09.9
    intentional, homicide (attempt) Y03.0
    motor NEC —see also Accident, transport
      V09.20
      homicide Y03.0
  vehicle (transport) NEC —see Accident,
    transport, by type of vehicle
    stationary (falling from jack,
      hydraulic lift, ramp)
      W20.8
Stumbling
  without fall W18.40
    due to
      specified NEC W18.49
      stepping from one level to another
        W18.43
      stepping into hole or opening W18.42
      stepping on object W18.41
  over
    animal NEC W01.0
      with fall W18.09
    carpet, rug or (small) object W22.8
      with fall W18.09
    person W51
      with fall W03
        due to ice or snow W00.0

Submersion (accidental) —see Drowning
Suffocation (accidental) (by external means)
  (by pressure) (mechanical) —see also
    category T71
  due to, by
    avalanche —see Landslide
    explosion —see Explosion
    fire —see Exposure, fire
    food, any type (aspiration) (ingestion)
      (inhalation) —see categories T17 and
      T18
    ignition —see Ignition
    landslide —see Landslide
    machine (ry) —see Contact, with, by type
      of machine
    vomitus (aspiration) (inhalation)
      T17.81-•
  in
    burning building X00.8
Suicide, suicidal (attempted) (by) X83.8
  blunt object X79
  burning, burns X76
    hot object X77.9
      fluid NEC X77.2
      household appliance X77.3
      specified NEC X77.8
      steam X77.0
      tap water X77.1
      vapors X77.0
  caustic substance —see Table of Drugs and
    Chemicals
  cold, extreme X83.2
  collision of motor vehicle with
    motor vehicle X82.0
    specified NEC X82.8
    train X82.1
    tree X82.2
  crashing of aircraft X83.0
  cut (any part of body) X78.9
  cutting or piercing instrument X78.9
    dagger X78.2
    glass X78.0
    knife X78.1
    specified NEC X78.8
    sword X78.2
  drowning (in) X71.9
    bathtub X71.0
    natural water X71.3
    specified NEC X71.8
    swimming pool X71.1
      following fall X71.2
  electrocution X83.1
  explosive(s) (material) X75
  fire, flames X76
  firearm X74.9
    airgun X74.01
    handgun X72

Suicide, suicidal (Continued)
  firearm (Continued)
    hunting rifle X73.1
    larger X73.9
      specified NEC X73.8
    machine gun X73.2
    shotgun X73.0
    specified NEC X74.8
  hanging X83.8
  hot object —see Suicide, burning, hot object
  jumping
    before moving object X81.8
      motor vehicle X81.0
      subway train X81.1
      train X81.1
    from high place X80
  late effect of attempt —see X71-X83 with 7th
    character S
  lying before moving object, train, vehicle X81.8
  poisoning —see Table of Drugs and
    Chemicals
  puncture (any part of body) —see Suicide,
    cutting or piercing instrument
  scald —see Suicide, burning, hot object
  sequelae of attempt —see X71-X83 with 7th
    character S
  sharp object (any) —see Suicide, cutting or
    piercing instrument
  shooting —see Suicide, firearm
  specified means NEC X83.8
  stab (any part of body) —see Suicide, cutting
    or piercing instrument
  steam, hot vapors X77.0
  strangulation X83.8
  submersion —see Suicide, drowning
  suffocation X83.8
  wound NEC X83.8
Sunstroke X32
Supersonic waves (causing injury) W42.0
Surgical procedure, complication of (delayed
  or as an abnormal reaction without
  mention of misadventure) —see also
  Complication of or following, by type of
  procedure
  due to or as a result of misadventure —see
    Misadventure
Swallowed, swallowing
  foreign body —see Foreign body, alimentary
    canal
  poison —see Table of Drugs and Chemicals
  substance
    caustic or corrosive —see Table of Drugs
      and Chemicals
    poisonous —see Table of Drugs and
      Chemicals

▶ New   ⟹ Revised   ~~deleted~~ Deleted   • Use Additional Character(s)

T

Tackle in sport W03
Terrorism (involving) Y38.80
  biological weapons Y38.6X-●
  chemical weapons Y38.7X-●
  conflagration Y38.3X-●
  drowning and submersion Y38.89-●
  explosion Y38.2X-●
    destruction of aircraft Y38.1X-●
    marine weapons Y38.0X-●
  fire Y38.3X-●
  firearms Y38.4X-●
  hot substances Y38.3X-●
  lasers Y38.89-●
  nuclear weapons Y38.5X-●
  piercing or stabbing instruments
    Y38.89-●
  secondary effects Y38.9X-●
  specified method NEC Y38.89-●
  suicide bomber Y38.81-●
Thirst X58
Threat to breathing
  aspiration —*see* Aspiration
  due to cave-in, falling earth or substance
    NEC —*see* category T71
Thrown (accidentally)
  against part (any) of or object in transport
    vehicle (in motion) NEC —*see also*
    Accident, transport

Thrown *(Continued)*
  from
    high place, homicide (attempt) Y01
    machinery —*see* Contact, with, by type of
      machine
    transport vehicle NEC —*see also* Accident,
      transport V89.9
  off —*see* Thrown, from
Thunderbolt —*see* subcategory T75.0
  causing fire —*see* Exposure, fire
Tidal wave (any injury) NEC —*see* Forces of
  nature, tidal wave
Took
  overdose (drug) —*see* Table of Drugs and
    Chemicals
  poison —*see* Table of Drugs and
    Chemicals
Tornado (any injury) X37.1
Torrential rain (any injury) X37.8
Torture X58
Trampled by animal NEC W55.89
Trapped (accidentally)
  between objects (moving) (stationary and
    moving) —*see* Caught
  by part (any) of
    motorcycle V29.88
    pedal cycle V19.88
    transport vehicle NEC —*see also* Accident,
      transport V89.9
Travel (effects) (sickness) T75.3

Tree falling on or hitting (accidentally)
  (person) W20.8
Tripping
  without fall W18.40
    due to
      specified NEC W18.49
      stepping from one level to another
        W18.43
      stepping into hole or opening
        W18.42
      stepping on object W18.41
  over
    animal W01.0
      with fall W01.0
    carpet, rug or (small) object W22.8
      with fall W18.09
    person W51
      with fall W03
        due to ice or snow W00.0
Twisted by person(s) (accidentally) W50.2
  with intent to injure or kill Y04.0
  as, or caused by, a crowd or human stampede
    (with fall) W52
  assault Y04.0
  homicide (attempt) Y04.0
  in
    fight Y04.0
    legal intervention —*see* Legal, intervention,
      manhandling
Twisting (prolonged) (static) X50.1

U

Underdosing of necessary drugs, medicaments
  or biological substances Y63.6
Undetermined intent (contact)
  (exposure)
  automobile collision Y32
  blunt object Y29
  drowning (submersion) (in) Y21.9
    bathtub Y21.0
      after fall Y21.1
    natural water (lake) (ocean) (pond) (river)
      (stream) Y21.4
    specified place NEC Y21.8
    swimming pool Y21.2
      after fall Y21.3
  explosive material Y25
  fall, jump or push from high place Y30
  falling, lying or running before moving object
    Y31
  fire Y26

Undetermined intent *(Continued)*
  firearm discharge Y24.9
    airgun (BB) (pellet) Y24.0
    handgun (pistol) (revolver)
      Y22
    hunting rifle Y23.1
    larger Y23.9
      hunting rifle Y23.1
      machine gun Y23.3
      military Y23.2
      shotgun Y23.0
      specified type NEC Y23.8
    machine gun Y23.3
    military Y23.2
    shotgun Y23.0
    specified type NEC Y24.8
    Very pistol Y24.8
  hot object Y27.9
    fluid NEC Y27.2
    household appliance Y27.3
    specified object NEC Y27.8

Undetermined intent *(Continued)*
  hot object *(Continued)*
    steam Y27.0
    tap water Y27.1
    vapor Y27.0
  jump, fall or push from high place Y30
  lying, falling or running before moving object
    Y31
  motor vehicle crash Y32
  push, fall or jump from high place Y30
  running, falling or lying before moving object
    Y31
  sharp object Y28.9
    dagger Y28.2
    glass Y28.0
    knife Y28.1
    specified object NEC Y28.8
    sword Y28.2
  smoke Y26
  specified event NEC Y33
Use of hand as hammer X50.3

V

Vibration (causing injury) W49.9
Victim (of)
  avalanche —*see* Landslide
  earth movements NEC —*see* Forces of nature,
    earth movement
  earthquake X34

Victim *(Continued)*
  flood —*see* Flood
  landslide —*see* Landslide
  lightning —*see* subcategory T75.0
    causing fire —*see* Exposure, fire
  storm (cataclysmic) NEC —*see* Forces of
    nature, cataclysmic storm
  volcanic eruption X35

Volcanic eruption (any injury) X35
Vomitus, gastric contents in air passages (with
  asphyxia, obstruction or
  suffocation) T17.81-●

▶ New   ⇒ Revised   ~~deleted~~ Deleted   ● Use Additional Character(s)

W

Walked into stationary object (any) W22.09
  furniture W22.03
  lamppost W22.02
  wall W22.01
War operations (injuries to military personnel
  and civilians during war, civil insurrection
  and peacekeeping missions) (by) (from)
  (involving) Y36.90-●
  after cessation of hostilities Y36.89-●
    explosion (of)
      bomb placed during war operations
        Y36.82-●
      mine placed during war operations
        Y36.81-●
    specified NEC Y36.88-●
  air blast Y36.20-●
  aircraft
    destruction —*see* War operations,
      destruction of aircraft
  airway restriction —*see* War operations,
    restriction of airways
  asphyxiation —*see* War operations, restriction
    of airways
  biological weapons Y36.6X-●
  blast Y36.20-●
  blast fragments Y36.20-●
  blast wave Y36.20-●
  blast wind Y36.20-●
  bomb Y36.20-●
    dirty Y36.50-●
    gasoline Y36.31-●
    incendiary Y36.31-●
    petrol Y36.31-●
  bullet Y36.43-●
    incendiary Y36.32-●
    rubber Y36.41-●
  chemical weapons Y36.7X-●
  combat
    hand to hand (unarmed) combat Y36.44-●
    using blunt or piercing object Y36.45-●
  conflagration —*see* War operations, fire
  conventional warfare NEC Y36.49-●
  depth-charge Y36.01-●
  destruction of aircraft Y36.10-●
    due to
      air to air missile Y36.11-●
      collision with other aircraft Y36.12-●
      detonation (accidental) of onboard
        munitions and explosives Y36.14-●
      enemy fire or explosives Y36.11-●
      explosive placed on aircraft Y36.11-●
      onboard fire Y36.13-●
      rocket propelled grenade [RPG] Y36.11-●
      small arms fire Y36.11-●
      surface to air missile Y36.11-●
    specified NEC Y36.19-●
  detonation (accidental) of
    onboard marine weapons Y36.05-●
    own munitions or munitions launch device
      Y36.24-●

War operations (*Continued*)
  dirty bomb Y36.50-●
  explosion (of) Y36.20-●
    aerial bomb Y36.21-●
    after cessation of hostilities
      bomb placed during war operations
        Y36.82-●
      mine placed during war operations
        Y36.81-●
    bomb NOS —*see also* War operations,
      bomb(s) Y36.20-●
    fragments Y36.20-●
    grenade Y36.29-●
    guided missile Y36.22-●
    improvised explosive device [IED]
      (person-borne) (roadside)
      (vehicle-borne) Y36.23-●
    land mine Y36.29-●
    marine mine (at sea) (in harbor)
      Y36.02-●
    marine weapon Y36.00-●
      specified NEC Y36.09-●
    own munitions or munitions launch
      device (accidental) Y36.24-●
    sea-based artillery shell Y36.03-●
    specified NEC Y36.29-●
    torpedo Y36.04-●
  fire Y36.30-●
    specified NEC Y36.39-●
  firearms
    discharge Y36.43-●
    pellets Y36.42-●
  flamethrower Y36.33-●
  fragments (from) (of)
    improvised explosive device [IED]
      (person-borne) (roadside)
      (vehicle-borne) Y36.26-●
    munitions Y36.25-●
    specified NEC Y36.29-●
    weapons Y36.27-●
  friendly fire Y36.92
  hand to hand (unarmed) combat
    Y36.44-●
  hot substances —*see* War operations,
    fire
  incendiary bullet Y36.32-●
  nuclear weapon (effects of) Y36.50-●
    acute radiation exposure Y36.54-●
    blast pressure Y36.51-●
    direct blast Y36.51-●
    direct heat Y36.53-●
    fallout exposure Y36.54-●
    fireball Y36.53-●
    indirect blast (struck or crushed by blast
      debris) (being thrown by blast)
      Y36.52-●
    ionizing radiation (immediate exposure)
      Y36.54-●
    nuclear radiation Y36.54-●
    radiation
      ionizing (immediate exposure)
        Y36.54-●

War operations (*Continued*)
  nuclear weapon (*Continued*)
    radiation (*Continued*)
      nuclear Y36.54-●
      thermal Y36.53-●
    secondary effects Y36.54-●
    specified NEC Y36.59-●
    thermal radiation Y36.53-●
  restriction of air (airway)
    intentional Y36.46-●
    unintentional Y36.47-●
  rubber bullets Y36.41-●
  shrapnel NOS Y36.29-●
  suffocation —*see* War operations, restriction
    of airways
  unconventional warfare NEC Y36.7X-●
  underwater blast NOS Y36.00-●
  warfare
    conventional NEC Y36.49-●
    unconventional NEC Y36.7X-●
  weapon of mass destruction [WMD] Y36.91
  weapons
    biological weapons Y36.6X-●
    chemical Y36.7X-●
    nuclear (effects of) Y36.50-●
      acute radiation exposure Y36.54-●
      blast pressure Y36.51-●
      direct blast Y36.51-●
      direct heat Y36.53-●
      fallout exposure Y36.54-●
      fireball Y36.53-●
      radiation
        ionizing (immediate exposure)
          Y36.54-●
        nuclear Y36.54-●
        thermal Y36.53-●
      secondary effects Y36.54-●
      specified NEC Y36.59-●
    of mass destruction [WMD] Y36.91-●
Washed
  away by flood —*see* Flood
  off road by storm (transport vehicle) —*see*
    Forces of nature, cataclysmic storm
Weather exposure NEC —*see* Forces of nature
Weightlessness (causing injury) (effects of) (in
  spacecraft, real or simulated) X52
Work related condition Y99.0
Wound (accidental) NEC —*see also* Injury X58
  battle —*see also* War operations Y36.90
  gunshot —*see* Discharge, firearm by type
Wreck transport vehicle NEC —*see also*
  Accident, transport V89.9
Wrong
  device implanted into correct surgical site
    Y65.51
  fluid in infusion Y65.1
  patient, procedure performed on Y65.52
  procedure (operation) on correct patient
    Y65.51

▶ New   ⇒ Revised   ~~deleted~~ Deleted   ● Use Additional Character(s)

PART III

ICD-10-CM Tabular List of Diseases and Injuries

CHAPTER 1

CERTAIN INFECTIOUS AND PARASITIC DISEASES (A00-B99)

OGCR Chapter-Specific Coding Guidelines

1. **Chapter 1: Certain Infectious and Parasitic Diseases (A00-B99)**

   a. **Human Immunodeficiency Virus (HIV) Infections**

      1) **Code only confirmed cases**

      Code only confirmed cases of HIV infection/illness. This is an exception to the hospital inpatient guideline Section II, H.

      In this context, "confirmation" does not require documentation of positive serology or culture for HIV; the provider's diagnostic statement that the patient is HIV positive, or has an HIV-related illness is sufficient.

      2) **Selection and sequencing of HIV codes**

         (a) **Patient admitted for HIV-related condition**

         If a patient is admitted for an HIV-related condition, the principal diagnosis should be B20, Human immunodeficiency virus [HIV] disease followed by additional diagnosis codes for all reported HIV-related conditions.

         (b) **Patient with HIV disease admitted for unrelated condition**

         If a patient with HIV disease is admitted for an unrelated condition (such as a traumatic injury), the code for the unrelated condition (e.g., the nature of injury code) should be the principal diagnosis. Other diagnoses would be B20 followed by additional diagnosis codes for all reported HIV-related conditions.

         (c) **Whether the patient is newly diagnosed**

         Whether the patient is newly diagnosed or has had previous admissions/encounters for HIV conditions is irrelevant to the sequencing decision.

         (d) **Asymptomatic human immunodeficiency virus**

         Z21, Asymptomatic human immunodeficiency virus [HIV] infection status, is to be applied when the patient without any documentation of symptoms is listed as being "HIV positive," "known HIV," "HIV test positive," or similar terminology. Do not use this code if the term "AIDS" is used or if the patient is treated for any HIV-related illness or is described as having any condition(s) resulting from his/her HIV positive status; use B20 in these cases.

         (e) **Patients with inconclusive HIV serology**

         Patients with inconclusive HIV serology, but no definitive diagnosis or manifestations of the illness, may be assigned code R75, Inconclusive laboratory evidence of human immunodeficiency virus [HIV].

         (f) **Previously diagnosed HIV-related illness**

         Patients with any known prior diagnosis of an HIV-related illness should be coded to B20. Once a patient has developed an HIV-related illness, the patient should always be assigned code B20 on every subsequent admission/encounter. Patients previously diagnosed with any HIV illness (B20) should never be assigned to R75 or Z21, Asymptomatic human immunodeficiency virus [HIV] infection status.

         (g) **HIV Infection in Pregnancy, Childbirth and the Puerperium**

         During pregnancy, childbirth or the puerperium, a patient admitted (or presenting for a health care encounter) because of an HIV-related illness should receive a principal diagnosis code of O98.7-, Human immunodeficiency [HIV] disease complicating pregnancy, childbirth and the puerperium, followed by B20 and the code(s) for the HIV-related illness(es). Codes from Chapter 15 always take sequencing priority.

         Patients with asymptomatic HIV infection status admitted (or presenting for a health care encounter) during pregnancy, childbirth, or the puerperium should receive codes of O98.7- and Z21.

         (h) **Encounters for testing for HIV**

         If a patient is being seen to determine his/her HIV status, use code Z11.4, Encounter for screening for human immunodeficiency virus [HIV]. Use additional codes for any associated high risk behavior.

         If a patient with signs or symptoms is being seen for HIV testing, code the signs and symptoms. An additional counseling code Z71.7, Human immunodeficiency virus [HIV] counseling, may be used if counseling is provided during the encounter for the test.

         When a patient returns to be informed of his/her HIV test results and the test result is negative, use code Z71.7, Human immunodeficiency virus [HIV] counseling.

         If the results are positive, see previous guidelines and assign codes as appropriate.

   b. **Infectious agents as the cause of diseases classified to other chapters**

   Certain infections are classified in chapters other than Chapter 1 and no organism is identified as part of the infection code. In these instances, it is necessary to use an additional code from Chapter 1 to identify the organism. A code from category B95, Streptococcus, Staphylococcus, and Enterococcus as the cause of diseases classified to other chapters, B96, Other bacterial agents as the cause of diseases classified to other chapters, or B97, Viral agents as the cause of diseases classified to other chapters, is to be used as an additional code to identify the organism. An instructional note will be found at the infection code advising that an additional organism code is required.

   c. **Infections resistant to antibiotics**

   Many bacterial infections are resistant to current antibiotics. It is necessary to identify all infections documented as antibiotic resistant. Assign a code from category Z16, Resistance to antimicrobial drugs, following the infection code only if the infection code does not identify drug resistance.

   d. **Sepsis, Severe Sepsis, and Septic Shock**

      1) **Coding of Sepsis and Severe Sepsis**

         (a) **Sepsis**

         For a diagnosis of sepsis, assign the appropriate code for the underlying systemic infection. If the type of infection or causal organism is not further specified, assign code A41.9, Sepsis, unspecified organism.

         A code from subcategory R65.2, Severe sepsis, should not be assigned unless severe sepsis or an associated acute organ dysfunction is documented.

         (i) Negative or inconclusive blood cultures and sepsis

         Negative or inconclusive blood cultures do not preclude a diagnosis of sepsis in patients with clinical evidence of the condition, however, the provider should be queried.

         (ii) Urosepsis

         The term urosepsis is a nonspecific term. It is not to be considered synonymous with sepsis. It has no default code in the Alphabetic Index. Should a provider use this term, he/she must be queried for clarification.

         (iii) Sepsis with organ dysfunction

         If a patient has sepsis and associated acute organ dysfunction or multiple organ dysfunction (MOD), follow the instructions for coding severe sepsis.

         (iv) Acute organ dysfunction that is not clearly associated with the sepsis

         If a patient has sepsis and an acute organ dysfunction, but the medical record documentation indicates that the acute organ dysfunction is related to a medical condition other than the sepsis, do not assign a code from subcategory R65.2, Severe sepsis. An acute organ dysfunction must be associated with the sepsis in order to assign the severe sepsis code. If the documentation is not clear as to whether an acute organ dysfunction is related to the sepsis or another medical condition, query the provider.

         (b) **Severe sepsis**

         The coding of severe sepsis requires a minimum of 2 codes: first a code for the underlying systemic infection, followed by a code from subcategory R65.2, Severe sepsis. If the causal organism is not documented, assign code A41.9, Sepsis, unspecified organism, for the infection. Additional code(s) for the associated acute organ dysfunction are also required.

         Due to the complex nature of severe sepsis, some cases may require querying the provider prior to assignment of the codes.

      2) **Septic shock**

         (a) Septic shock generally refers to circulatory failure associated with severe sepsis, and therefore, it represents a type of acute organ dysfunction.

         For all cases of septic shock, the code for the systemic infection should be sequenced first, followed by code R65.21, Severe sepsis with septic shock or code T81.12, Postprocedural septic shock.

Any additional codes for the other acute organ dysfunctions should also be assigned. As noted in the sequencing instructions in the Tabular List, the code for septic shock cannot be assigned as a principal diagnosis.

3) Sequencing of severe sepsis

If severe sepsis is present on admission, and meets the definition of principal diagnosis, the underlying systemic infection should be assigned as principal diagnosis followed by the appropriate code from subcategory R65.2 as required by the sequencing rules in the Tabular List. A code from subcategory R65.2 can never be assigned as a principal diagnosis.

When severe sepsis develops during an encounter (it was not present on admission) the underlying systemic infection and the appropriate code from subcategory R65.2 should be assigned as secondary diagnoses.

Severe sepsis may be present on admission but the diagnosis may not be confirmed until sometime after admission. If the documentation is not clear whether severe sepsis was present on admission, the provider should be queried.

4) Sepsis and severe sepsis with a localized infection

If the reason for admission is both sepsis or severe sepsis and a localized infection, such as pneumonia or cellulitis, a code(s) for the underlying systemic infection should be assigned first and the code for the localized infection should be assigned as a secondary diagnosis. If the patient has severe sepsis, a code from subcategory R65.2 should also be assigned as a secondary diagnosis. If the patient is admitted with a localized infection, such as pneumonia, and sepsis/severe sepsis doesn't develop until after admission, the localized infection should be assigned first, followed by the appropriate sepsis/severe sepsis codes.

5) Sepsis due to a postprocedural infection

(a) Documentation of causal relationship

As with all postprocedural complications, code assignment is based on the provider's documentation of the relationship between the infection and the procedure.

(b) Sepsis due to a postprocedural infection

For **infections following a procedure, a code from T81.40, to T81.43.** Infection following a procedure, or O86.00 to O86.03, Infection of obstetric surgical wound, **that identifies the site of the infection should be coded first, if known. Assign an additional code for sepsis following a procedure (T81.44) or sepsis following an obstetrical procedure (O86.04). Use an additional code to identify the infectious agent.** If the patient has severe sepsis the appropriate code from subcategory R65.2 should also be assigned with the additional code(s) for any acute organ dysfunction.

For infections following infusion, transfusion, therapeutic injection, or immunization, a code from subcategory T80.2, Infections following infusion, transfusion, and therapeutic injection, or code T88.0-, Infection following immunization, should be coded first, followed by the code for the specific infection. If the patient has severe sepsis, the appropriate code from subcategory R65.2 should also be assigned, with the additional codes(s) for any acute organ dysfunction.

(c) Postprocedural infection and postprocedural septic shock

If a postprocedural infection has resulted in postprocedural septic shock, **assign the codes indicated above for sepsis due to a postprocedural infection, followed by code T81.12-, Postprocedural septic shock. Do not assign code R65.21, Severe sepsis with septic shock. Additional code(s) should be assigned for any acute organ dysfunction.**

6) Sepsis and severe sepsis associated with a noninfectious process (condition)

In some cases a noninfectious process (condition), such as trauma, may lead to an infection which can result in sepsis or severe sepsis. If sepsis or severe sepsis is documented as associated with a noninfectious condition, such as a burn or serious injury, and this condition meets the definition for principal diagnosis, the code for the noninfectious condition should be sequenced first, followed by the code for the resulting infection. If severe sepsis is present, a code from subcategory R65.2 should also be assigned with any associated organ dysfunction(s) codes. It is not necessary to assign a code from subcategory R65.1, Systemic inflammatory response syndrome (SIRS) of non-infectious origin, for these cases.

If the infection meets the definition of principal diagnosis it should be sequenced before the non-infectious condition. When both the associated non-infectious condition and the infection meet the definition of principal diagnosis either may be assigned as principal diagnosis.

Only one code from category R65, Symptoms and signs specifically associated with systemic inflammation and infection, should be assigned. Therefore, when a non-infectious condition leads to an infection resulting in severe sepsis, assign the appropriate code from subcategory R65.2, Severe sepsis. Do not additionally assign a code from subcategory R65.1, Systemic inflammatory response syndrome (SIRS) of non-infectious origin.
See Section I.C.18. SIRS due to non-infectious process

7) Sepsis and septic shock complicating abortion, pregnancy, childbirth, and the puerperium

See Section I.C.15. Sepsis and septic shock complicating abortion, pregnancy, childbirth and the puerperium

8) Newborn sepsis

See Section I.C.16. f. Bacterial sepsis of Newborn

e. Methicillin Resistant Staphylococcus aureus (MRSA) Conditions

1) Selection and sequencing of MRSA codes

(a) Combination codes for MRSA infection

When a patient is diagnosed with an infection that is due to methicillin resistant *Staphylococcus aureus* (MRSA), and that infection has a combination code that includes the causal organism (e.g., sepsis, pneumonia) assign the appropriate combination code for the condition (e.g., code A41.02, Sepsis due to Methicillin resistant Staphylococcus aureus or code J15.212, Pneumonia due to Methicillin resistant Staphylococcus aureus). Do not assign code B95.62, Methicillin resistant Staphylococcus aureus infection as the cause of diseases classified elsewhere, as an additional code because the combination code includes the type of infection and the MRSA organism. Do not assign a code from subcategory Z16.11, Resistance to penicillins, as an additional diagnosis.
See Section C.1. for instructions on coding and sequencing of sepsis and severe sepsis.

(b) Other codes for MRSA infection

When there is documentation of a current infection (e.g., wound infection, stitch abscess, urinary tract infection) due to MRSA, and that infection does not have a combination code that includes the causal organism, assign the appropriate code to identify the condition along with code B95.62, Methicillin resistant Staphylococcus aureus infection as the cause of diseases classified elsewhere for the MRSA infection. Do not assign a code from subcategory Z16.11, Resistance to penicillins.

(c) Methicillin susceptible Staphylococcus aureus (MSSA) and MRSA colonization

The condition or state of being colonized or carrying MSSA or MRSA is called colonization or carriage, while an individual person is described as being colonized or being a carrier. Colonization means that MSSA or MSRA is present on or in the body without necessarily causing illness. A positive MRSA colonization test might be documented by the provider as "MRSA screen positive" or "MRSA nasal swab positive".

Assign code Z22.322, Carrier or suspected carrier of Methicillin resistant Staphylococcus aureus, for patients documented as having MRSA colonization. Assign code Z22.321, Carrier or suspected carrier of Methicillin susceptible Staphylococcus aureus, for patient documented as having MSSA colonization. Colonization is not necessarily indicative of a disease process or as the cause of a specific condition the patient may have unless documented as such by the provider.

(d) MRSA colonization and infection

If a patient is documented as having both MRSA colonization and infection during a hospital admission, code Z22.322, Carrier or suspected carrier of Methicillin resistant Staphylococcus aureus, and a code for the MRSA infection may both be assigned.

f. Zika virus infections

1) Code only confirmed cases

Code only a confirmed diagnosis of Zika virus (A92.5, Zika virus disease) as documented by the provider. This is an exception to the hospital inpatient guideline Section II, H.

In this context, "confirmation" does not require documentation of the type of test performed; the physician's diagnostic statement that the condition is confirmed is sufficient. This code should be assigned regardless of the stated mode of transmission.

If the provider documents "suspected", "possible" or "probable" Zika, do not assign code A92.5. Assign a code(s) explaining the reason for encounter (such as fever, rash, or joint pain) or Z20.821, Contact with and (suspected) exposure to Zika virus.

CHAPTER 1 (A00-B99)

CHAPTER 1

CERTAIN INFECTIOUS AND PARASITIC DISEASES (A00-B99)

Includes diseases generally recognized as communicable or transmissible

Use additional code to identify resistance to antimicrobial drugs (Z16.-)

Excludes1 certain localized infections - see body system-related chapters

Excludes2 carrier or suspected carrier of infectious disease (Z22.-)

infectious and parasitic diseases complicating pregnancy, childbirth and the puerperium (O98.-)

infectious and parasitic diseases specific to the perinatal period (P35-P39)

influenza and other acute respiratory infections (J00-J22)

This chapter contains the following blocks:

A00-A09	Intestinal infectious diseases
A15-A19	Tuberculosis
A20-A28	Certain zoonotic bacterial diseases
A30-A49	Other bacterial diseases
A50-A64	Infections with a predominantly sexual mode of transmission
A65-A69	Other spirochetal diseases
A70-A74	Other diseases caused by chlamydiae
A75-A79	Rickettsioses
A80-A89	Viral and prion infections of the central nervous system
A90-A99	Arthropod-borne viral fevers and viral hemorrhagic fevers
B00-B09	Viral infections characterized by skin and mucous membrane lesions
B10	Other human herpesviruses
B15-B19	Viral hepatitis
B20	Human immunodeficiency virus [HIV] disease
B25-B34	Other viral diseases
B35-B49	Mycoses
B50-B64	Protozoal diseases
B65-B83	Helminthiases
B85-B89	Pediculosis, acariasis and other infestations
B90-B94	Sequelae of infectious and parasitic diseases
B95-B97	Bacterial and viral infectious agents
B99	Other infectious diseases

INTESTINAL INFECTIOUS DISEASES (A00-A09)

● **A00 Cholera**
A serious, often deadly, infectious disease of the small intestine

A00.0 Cholera due to Vibrio cholerae 01, biovar cholerae
Classical cholera

A00.1 Cholera due to Vibrio cholerae 01, biovar eltor
Cholera eltor

A00.9 Cholera, unspecified

● **A01 Typhoid and paratyphoid fevers**
Caused by Salmonella typhi and Salmonella paratyphi A, B, and C bacteria

● **A01.0 Typhoid fever**
Infection due to Salmonella typhi

A01.00 Typhoid fever, unspecified

A01.01 Typhoid meningitis

A01.02 Typhoid fever with heart involvement
Typhoid endocarditis
Typhoid myocarditis

A01.03 Typhoid pneumonia

A01.04 Typhoid arthritis

A01.05 Typhoid osteomyelitis

A01.09 Typhoid fever with other complications

A01.1 Paratyphoid fever A

A01.2 Paratyphoid fever B

A01.3 Paratyphoid fever C

A01.4 Paratyphoid fever, unspecified
Infection due to Salmonella paratyphi NOS

● **A02 Other salmonella infections**
Includes infection or foodborne intoxication due to any Salmonella species other than S. typhi and S. paratyphi

A02.0 Salmonella enteritis
Salmonellosis

A02.1 Salmonella sepsis

● **A02.2 Localized salmonella infections**

A02.20 Localized salmonella infection, unspecified
Specified in the documentation as localized, but unspecified as to type

A02.21 Salmonella meningitis
Specified as localized in the meninges

A02.22 Salmonella pneumonia
Specified as localized in the lungs

A02.23 Salmonella arthritis
Specified as localized in the joints

A02.24 Salmonella osteomyelitis
Specified as localized in bone

A02.25 Salmonella pyelonephritis
Salmonella tubulo-interstitial nephropathy

A02.29 Salmonella with other localized infection
Specified as localized (because it is still under localized heading) but does not assign into any of the above codes

A02.8 Other specified salmonella infections
Any specified salmonella infection which does NOT assign into any of the above codes (not specified as localized)

A02.9 Salmonella infection, unspecified
Unspecified in the documentation as to specific type of salmonella

● **A03 Shigellosis**
An infectious disease caused by bacteria (Shigella)

A03.0 Shigellosis due to Shigella dysenteriae
Group A shigellosis [Shiga-Kruse dysentery]

A03.1 Shigellosis due to Shigella flexneri
Group B shigellosis

A03.2 Shigellosis due to Shigella boydii
Group C shigellosis

A03.3 Shigellosis due to Shigella sonnei
Group D shigellosis

A03.8 Other shigellosis

A03.9 Shigellosis, unspecified
Bacillary dysentery NOS

Item 1-1 Salmonella is a bacterium that lives in the intestines of fowl and mammals and can spread to humans through improper food preparation and cooking. Salmonellosis is an infection with the bacterium. Symptoms include diarrhea, fever, and abdominal cramps 12 to 72 hours after infection. The illness usually lasts 4 to 7 days, and most persons recover without treatment. The diarrhea may be so severe that the patient needs to be hospitalized. Patients with immunocompromised systems in chronic, ill health are more likely to have the infection invade their bloodstream with life-threatening results. For example, patients with sickle cell disease are more prone to salmonella osteomyelitis than others.

▶ New   ⇒ Revised   ~~deleted~~ Deleted   Excludes 1   Excludes 2   Includes   Use additional   Code first   Code also   Key words

OGCR Official Guidelines   X Assign placeholder X   ● Use Additional Character(s)   ▶ Manifestation Code   Coding Clinic

CHAPTER 1 (A00-B99)

Figure 1-1 Electron micrograph of escherichia coli (E. coli) expressing P fimbriae. (Getty Image)

Item 1-2 *Escherichia coli [E. coli]* is a gram-negative bacterium found in the intestinal tracts of humans and animals and is usually nonpathogenic. Pathogenic strains can cause diarrhea or pyogenic (pus-producing) infections. Can be a threat to food safety.

● **A04   Other bacterial intestinal infections**

> **Excludes1**   bacterial foodborne intoxications, NEC (A05.-)
> tuberculous enteritis (A18.32)

A04.0   Enteropathogenic Escherichia coli infection
Pertaining to or producing intestinal disease

A04.1   Enterotoxigenic Escherichia coli infection
Producing or containing intestinal toxin

A04.2   Enteroinvasive Escherichia coli infection
Capable of penetrating and spreading through intestinal mucosal epithelium

A04.3   Enterohemorrhagic Escherichia coli infection
Causing bloody diarrhea, resulting from microorganisms

A04.4   Other intestinal Escherichia coli infections
Escherichia coli enteritis NOS

A04.5   Campylobacter enteritis
Spiral shaped bacterium

A04.6   Enteritis due to Yersinia enterocolitica

> **Excludes1**   extraintestinal yersiniosis (A28.2)

Transmitted by infected food /water and person-to-person contact, affecting intestinal tract

● **A04.7   Enterocolitis due to Clostridium difficile**
Foodborne intoxication by Clostridium difficile
Pseudomembraneous colitis
Marked by fibrinous deposit (false membrane) with enmeshed necrotic cells

A04.71   Enterocolitis due to Clostridium difficile, recurrent

A04.72   Enterocolitis due to Clostridium difficile, not specified as recurrent

A04.8   Other specified bacterial intestinal infections

A04.9   Bacterial intestinal infection, unspecified
Bacterial enteritis NOS

● **A05   Other bacterial foodborne intoxications, not elsewhere classified**

> **Excludes1**   Clostridium difficile foodborne intoxication and infection (A04.7-)
> Escherichia coli infection (A04.0-A04.4)
> listeriosis (A32.-)
> salmonella foodborne intoxication and infection (A02.-)
> toxic effect of noxious foodstuffs (T61-T62)

A05.0   Foodborne staphylococcal intoxication

A05.1   Botulism food poisoning
Botulism NOS
Classical foodborne intoxication due to Clostridium botulinum

> **Excludes1**   infant botulism (A48.51)
> wound botulism (A48.52)

A05.2   Foodborne Clostridium perfringens [Clostridium welchii] intoxication
Type A causes gas gangrene and necrotizing colitis; major cause of food poisoning in humans
Enteritis necroticans
Pig-bel

A05.3   Foodborne Vibrio parahaemolyticus intoxication
Organism that survives only in high salt environment (halophilic), major cause of gastroenteritis due to consumption of raw or improperly cooked fish/seafood

A05.4   Foodborne Bacillus cereus intoxication
Spore-forming species commonly found in soil, causes food poisoning from formation of intestinal toxins in contaminated foods

A05.5   Foodborne Vibrio vulnificus intoxication
Species that survives in high salt environment (halophilic) with infection by eating raw seafood causes septicemia and cellulitis

A05.8   Other specified bacterial foodborne intoxications

A05.9   Bacterial foodborne intoxication, unspecified

● **A06   Amebiasis**
An intestinal illness caused by the microscopic parasite Entamoeba histolytica

> **Includes**   infection due to Entamoeba histolytica
> **Excludes1**   other protozoal intestinal diseases (A07.-)
> **Excludes2**   acanthamebiasis (B60.1-)
> Naegleriasis (B60.2)

A06.0   Acute amebic dysentery
Acute amebiasis
Intestinal amebiasis NOS

A06.1   Chronic intestinal amebiasis

A06.2   Amebic nondysenteric colitis
Pertaining to single cell microorganism

A06.3   Ameboma of intestine
Tumorlike mass produced by localized inflammation often in intestine
Ameboma NOS

A06.4   Amebic liver abscess
Hepatic amebiasis

A06.5   Amebic lung abscess
Amebic abscess of lung (and liver)

A06.6   Amebic brain abscess
Amebic abscess of brain (and liver) (and lung)

A06.7   Cutaneous amebiasis

● **A06.8   Amebic infection of other sites**

A06.81   Amebic cystitis

A06.82   Other amebic genitourinary infections
Amebic balanitis
Amebic vesiculitis
Amebic vulvovaginitis

A06.89   Other amebic infections
Amebic appendicitis
Amebic splenic abscess

A06.9   Amebiasis, unspecified

● **A07   Other protozoal intestinal diseases**

A07.0   Balantidiasis
Balantidial dysentery
Infection by protozoa that may cause diarrhea and dysentery, with ulceration of colonic mucous membranes

A07.1   Giardiasis [lambliasis]
Common infection in small intestine spread by contaminated food, water, or direct person-to-person contact

A07.2   Cryptosporidiosis
Human infection with protozoa usually seen as self-limited diarrhea in those who work with cattle

A07.3   Isosporiasis
Human intestinal disease caused by protozoa
Infection due to Isospora belli and Isospora hominis
Intestinal coccidiosis
Isosporosis

A07.4   Cyclosporiasis
Infection by protozoa with most common species infecting humans being C cayetanensis

A07.8   Other specified protozoal intestinal diseases
Intestinal microsporidiosis
Intestinal trichomoniasis
Sarcocystosis
Sarcosporidiosis

A07.9   Protozoal intestinal disease, unspecified
Flagellate diarrhea
Protozoal colitis
Protozoal diarrhea
Protozoal dysentery

● **A08   Viral and other specified intestinal infections**
> **Excludes1**   influenza with involvement of gastrointestinal tract (J09.X3, J10.2, J11.2)

A08.0   Rotaviral enteritis

● **A08.1   Acute gastroenteropathy due to Norwalk agent and other small round viruses**

A08.11   Acute gastroenteropathy due to Norwalk agent
Acute gastroenteropathy due to Norovirus
Acute gastroenteropathy due to Norwalk-like agent

A08.19   Acute gastroenteropathy due to other small round viruses
Acute gastroenteropathy due to small round virus [SRV] NOS

A08.2   Adenoviral enteritis

● **A08.3   Other viral enteritis**

A08.31   Calicivirus enteritis

A08.32   Astrovirus enteritis

A08.39   Other viral enteritis
Coxsackie virus enteritis
Echovirus enteritis
Enterovirus enteritis NEC
Torovirus enteritis

A08.4   Viral intestinal infection, unspecified
Viral enteritis NOS
Viral gastroenteritis NOS
Viral gastroenteropathy NOS
Coding Clinic: 2016, Q3, P12

A08.8   Other specified intestinal infections

A09   Infectious gastroenteritis and colitis, unspecified
Infectious colitis NOS
Infectious enteritis NOS
Infectious gastroenteritis NOS
> **Excludes1**   colitis NOS (K52.9)
> diarrhea NOS (R19.7)
> enteritis NOS (K52.9)
> gastroenteritis NOS (K52.9)
> noninfective gastroenteritis and colitis, unspecified (K52.9)

Figure 1-2 Far advanced bilateral pulmonary tuberculosis before and after 8 months of treatment with streptomycin, PAS, and isoniazid. (Getty Image)

Item 1–3 Tuberculosis is a common and deadly infectious disease caused by the *Mycobacterium tuberculosis* organism. The first tuberculosis infection is called the **primary infection** and most commonly attacks the lungs but can affect the central nervous system, lymphatic system, circulatory system, genitourinary system, bones, joints, and even the skin. A **Ghon** lesion is the **initial lesion.** A **secondary lesion** occurs when the tubercle bacilli are carried to other areas.

Item 1–4 Although it primarily affects the lungs, the bacteria *Mycobacterium tuberculosis* can travel from the pulmonary circulation to virtually any organ in the body, much as a cancer metastasizes to a secondary site. If the immune system becomes compromised by age or disease, what would otherwise be a self-limiting primary tuberculosis in the lungs will develop in other organs. These are known as extrapulmonary sites.

TUBERCULOSIS (A15-A19)

> **Includes**   infections due to Mycobacterium tuberculosis and Mycobacterium bovis
> **Excludes1**   congenital tuberculosis (P37.0)
> nonspecific reaction to test for tuberculosis without active tuberculosis (R76.1-)
> pneumoconiosis associated with tuberculosis, any type in A15 (J65)
> positive PPD (R76.11)
> positive tuberculin skin test without active tuberculosis (R76.11)
> sequelae of tuberculosis (B90.-)
> silicotuberculosis (J65)

● **A15   Respiratory tuberculosis**

A15.0   Tuberculosis of lung
Tuberculous bronchiectasis
Chronic dilatation of bronchi
Tuberculous fibrosis of lung
Tuberculous pneumonia
Tuberculous pneumothorax

A15.4   Tuberculosis of intrathoracic lymph nodes
Tuberculosis of hilar lymph nodes
Tuberculosis of mediastinal lymph nodes
Tuberculosis of tracheobronchial lymph nodes
> **Excludes1**   tuberculosis specified as primary (A15.7)

A15.5   Tuberculosis of larynx, trachea and bronchus
Tuberculosis of bronchus
Tuberculosis of glottis
Tuberculosis of larynx
Tuberculosis of trachea

A15.6   Tuberculous pleurisy
Tuberculosis of pleura
Tuberculous empyema
> **Excludes1**   primary respiratory tuberculosis (A15.7)

A15.7   Primary respiratory tuberculosis

A15.8   Other respiratory tuberculosis
Mediastinal tuberculosis
Nasopharyngeal tuberculosis
Tuberculosis of nose
Tuberculosis of sinus [any nasal]

A15.9   Respiratory tuberculosis unspecified

▶ New   ➡ Revised   ~~deleted~~ Deleted   Excludes 1   Excludes 2   Includes   Use additional   Code first   Code also   Key words

OGCR Official Guidelines   X Assign placeholder X   ● Use Additional Character(s)   ▶ Manifestation Code   **Coding Clinic**

● **A17 Tuberculosis of nervous system**

   A17.0 Tuberculous meningitis
       Tuberculosis of meninges (cerebral) (spinal)
       Tuberculous leptomeningitis
       > **Excludes1** tuberculous meningoencephalitis
       >   (A17.82)

   A17.1 Meningeal tuberculoma
       Tuberculoma of meninges (cerebral) (spinal)
       > **Excludes2** tuberculoma of brain and spinal cord
       >   (A17.81)

● **A17.8 Other tuberculosis of nervous system**

   A17.81 Tuberculoma of brain and spinal cord
       Tuberculous abscess of brain and spinal cord

   A17.82 Tuberculous meningoencephalitis
       Inflammation of brain and meninges; AKA
           cerebromeningitis and encephalomeningitis
       Tuberculous myelitis

   A17.83 Tuberculous neuritis
       Tuberculous mononeuropathy

   A17.89 Other tuberculosis of nervous system
       Tuberculous polyneuropathy

   A17.9 Tuberculosis of nervous system, unspecified

● **A18 Tuberculosis of other organs**

● **A18.0 Tuberculosis of bones and joints**

   A18.01 Tuberculosis of spine
       Pott's disease or curvature of spine
       Tuberculous arthritis
       Tuberculous osteomyelitis of spine
       Tuberculous spondylitis

   A18.02 Tuberculous arthritis of other joints
       Tuberculosis of hip (joint)
       Tuberculosis of knee (joint)

   A18.03 Tuberculosis of other bones
       Tuberculous mastoiditis
       Tuberculous osteomyelitis

   A18.09 Other musculoskeletal tuberculosis
       Tuberculous myositis
       Tuberculous synovitis
       Tuberculous tenosynovitis

● **A18.1 Tuberculosis of genitourinary system**

   **A18.10 Tuberculosis of genitourinary system,
             unspecified**

   A18.11 Tuberculosis of kidney and ureter

   A18.12 Tuberculosis of bladder

   A18.13 Tuberculosis of other urinary organs
       Tuberculous urethritis

   A18.14 Tuberculosis of prostate ♂   A

   A18.15 Tuberculosis of other male genital organs ♂

   A18.16 Tuberculosis of cervix ♀

   **A18.17 Tuberculous female pelvic inflammatory
             disease** ♀
       Tuberculous endometritis
       Tuberculous oophoritis and salpingitis
       Oophoritis = inflammation of ovary
       Salpingitis = inflammation of fallopian tube

   A18.18 Tuberculosis of other female genital organs ♀
       Tuberculous ulceration of vulva

   A18.2 Tuberculous peripheral lymphadenopathy
       Tuberculous adenitis
       > **Excludes2** tuberculosis of bronchial and mediastinal
       >   lymph nodes (A15.4)
       >   tuberculosis of mesenteric and
       >   retroperitoneal lymph nodes
       >   (A18.39)
       >   tuberculous tracheobronchial adenopathy
       >   (A15.4)

● **A18.3 Tuberculosis of intestines, peritoneum and mesenteric
          glands**

   A18.31 Tuberculous peritonitis
       Tuberculous ascites

   A18.32 Tuberculous enteritis
       Tuberculosis of anus and rectum
       Tuberculosis of intestine (large) (small)

   A18.39 Retroperitoneal tuberculosis
       Tuberculosis of mesenteric glands
       Tuberculosis of retroperitoneal (lymph glands)

   A18.4 Tuberculosis of skin and subcutaneous tissue
       Erythema induratum, tuberculous
       Lupus excedens
       Lupus vulgaris NOS
       Lupus vulgaris of eyelid
           Cutaneous tuberculosis characterized by reddish brown
           plaque on skin surrounded by papules and nodules
       Scrofuloderma
           Type of cutaneous tuberculosis, with direct extension of
           tuberculosis into skin from underlying structures;
           AKA tuberculosis colliquativa
       Tuberculosis of external ear
       > **Excludes2** lupus erythematosus (L93.-)
       >   lupus NOS (M32.9)
       >   systemic (M32.-)

● **A18.5 Tuberculosis of eye**
       > **Excludes2** lupus vulgaris of eyelid (A18.4)

   A18.50 Tuberculosis of eye, unspecified

   A18.51 Tuberculous episcleritis
       Inflammation of episclera and adjacent tissues

   A18.52 Tuberculous keratitis
       Tuberculous interstitial keratitis
       Tuberculous keratoconjunctivitis (interstitial)
           (phlyctenular)
       Inflammation of cornea and conjunctiva

   A18.53 Tuberculous chorioretinitis
       Inflammation of choroid and retina;
           retinochoroiditis

   A18.54 Tuberculous iridocyclitis
       Inflammation of iris and ciliary body

   A18.59 Other tuberculosis of eye
       Tuberculous conjunctivitis

   A18.6 Tuberculosis of (inner) (middle) ear
       Tuberculous otitis media
       > **Excludes2** tuberculosis of external ear (A18.4)
       >   tuberculous mastoiditis (A18.03)

   A18.7 Tuberculosis of adrenal glands
       Tuberculous Addison's disease

● **A18.8 Tuberculosis of other specified organs**

   A18.81 Tuberculosis of thyroid gland

   A18.82 Tuberculosis of other endocrine glands
       Tuberculosis of pituitary gland
       Tuberculosis of thymus gland

   **A18.83 Tuberculosis of digestive tract organs, not
             elsewhere classified**
       > **Excludes1** tuberculosis of intestine (A18.32)

   A18.84 Tuberculosis of heart
       Tuberculous cardiomyopathy
       Tuberculous endocarditis
       Tuberculous myocarditis
       Tuberculous pericarditis

   A18.85 Tuberculosis of spleen

   A18.89 Tuberculosis of other sites
       Tuberculosis of muscle
       Tuberculous cerebral arteritis

CHAPTER 1 (A00-B99)

Item 1-5   Miliary tuberculosis can be a life-threatening condition. If a tuberculous lesion enters a blood vessel, immense dissemination of tuberculous organisms can occur if the immune system is weak. High-risk populations—children under 4 years of age, the elderly, or the immunocompromised—are particularly prone to this type of infection. The lesions will have a millet seedlike appearance on chest x-ray. Bronchial washings and biopsy may aid in diagnosis.

● **A19   Miliary tuberculosis**

     Includes   disseminated tuberculosis
                  generalized tuberculosis
                  tuberculous polyserositis

     A19.0   Acute miliary tuberculosis of a single specified site

     A19.1   Acute miliary tuberculosis of multiple sites

     A19.2   Acute miliary tuberculosis, unspecified

     A19.8   Other miliary tuberculosis

     A19.9   Miliary tuberculosis, unspecified

CERTAIN ZOONOTIC BACTERIAL DISEASES (A20-A28)

● **A20   Plague**
     Infectious disease caused by a Yersinia pestis bacterium, transmitted by a rodent flea bite or handling of infected animal

     Includes   infection due to Yersinia pestis

     A20.0   Bubonic plague

     A20.1   Cellulocutaneous plague
          Skin and subcutaneous tissue plague

     A20.2   Pneumonic plague

     A20.3   Plague meningitis

     A20.7   Septicemic plague

     A20.8   Other forms of plague
          Abortive plague
          Asymptomatic plague
          Pestis minor
             Systemic bacterial disease

     A20.9   Plague, unspecified

● **A21   Tularemia**
     Caused by Francisella tularensis bacterium found in rodents, rabbits, and hares and transmitted to humans by contact with infected animal tissues or by ticks, biting flies, or mosquitoes

     Includes   deer-fly fever
                  infection due to Francisella tularensis
                  rabbit fever
     Coding Clinic: 2016, Q4, P25

     A21.0   Ulceroglandular tularemia
          Most common form of tularemia in humans is painful, swollen, erythematous papule at point of inoculation that ruptures to form shallow ulcer

     A21.1   Oculoglandular tularemia
          Primary site of entry is conjunctival sac, results in granulomatous corneal lesions
          Ophthalmic tularemia

     A21.2   Pulmonary tularemia

     A21.3   Gastrointestinal tularemia
          Abdominal tularemia

     A21.7   Generalized tularemia

     A21.8   Other forms of tularemia

     A21.9   Tularemia, unspecified

Item 1-6   Brucellosis: An infectious disease caused by the bacterium Brucella. Humans are infected by contact with contaminated animals or animal products. In humans brucellosis symptoms that are similar to the flu include fever, sweats, headaches, back pains, and physical weakness. Severe infections of the central nervous system or lining of the heart may occur. Brucellosis can also cause chronic symptoms that include recurrent fevers, joint pain, and fatigue.

● **A22   Anthrax**
     An acute infectious disease caused by the spore-forming Bacillus anthracis; occurs in humans exposed to infected animals or tissue from infected animals

     Includes   infection due to Bacillus anthracis

     A22.0   Cutaneous anthrax
          Malignant carbuncle
          Malignant pustule

     A22.1   Pulmonary anthrax
          Inhalation anthrax
          Ragpicker's disease
          Woolsorter's disease

     A22.2   Gastrointestinal anthrax

     A22.7   Anthrax sepsis
          Infectious bacterial disease

     A22.8   Other forms of anthrax
          Anthrax meningitis

     A22.9   Anthrax, unspecified

● **A23   Brucellosis**

     Includes   Malta fever
                  Mediterranean fever
                  undulant fever

     A23.0   Brucellosis due to Brucella melitensis
          Resulting in flu-like symptoms that may lead to chronic symptoms that include recurrent fevers, joint pain, and fatigue

     A23.1   Brucellosis due to Brucella abortus
          Most common cause of brucellosis in humans; AKA Bang bacillus

     A23.2   Brucellosis due to Brucella suis
          Species found primarily in pigs, rabbits, and reindeer

     A23.3   Brucellosis due to Brucella canis
          Species that causes respiratory tract infection in humans

     A23.8   Other brucellosis

     A23.9   Brucellosis, unspecified

● **A24   Glanders and melioidosis**
     Infection, usually of rodents, which spreads to other animals and humans, caused by Burkholderia pseudomallei through break in skin contaminated with infested soil or water

     A24.0   Glanders
          Infection due to Pseudomonas mallei
          Malleus

     A24.1   Acute and fulminating melioidosis
          Melioidosis pneumonia
          Melioidosis sepsis

     A24.2   Subacute and chronic melioidosis

     A24.3   Other melioidosis

     A24.9   Melioidosis, unspecified
          Infection due to Pseudomonas pseudomallei NOS
          Whitmore's disease

▶ New   ⇒ Revised   ~~deleted~~ Deleted   Excludes 1   Excludes 2   Includes   Use additional   Code first   Code also   Key words

OGCR Official Guidelines   X Assign placeholder X   ● Use Additional Character(s)   ▷ Manifestation Code   **Coding Clinic**

● **A25   Rat-bite fevers**
RBF, infectious disease caused by Streptobacillus moniliformis or Spirillum minus.

     A25.0   Spirillosis
         Any disease condition caused by spirilla
         Sodoku

     A25.1   Streptobacillosis
         Acute, febrile human illness caused by bacteria transmitted by rats in most cases, passed from rodent to human via rodent's urine or mucous secretions; AKA rat fever
         Epidemic arthritic erythema
         Haverhill fever
         Streptobacillary rat-bite fever

     A25.9   Rat-bite fever, unspecified

● **A26   Erysipeloid**
Infection with Erysipelothrix rhusiopathiae, occurring often as occupational disease resulting from handling infected fish, shellfish, meat, or poultry

     A26.0   Cutaneous erysipeloid
         Erythema migrans

     A26.7   Erysipelothrix sepsis

     A26.8   Other forms of erysipeloid

     A26.9   Erysipeloid, unspecified

● **A27   Leptospirosis**
Occurs most commonly in the tropics

     A27.0   Leptospirosis icterohemorrhagica
         Leptospiral or spirochetal jaundice (hemorrhagic)
         Weil's disease

     ● **A27.8   Other forms of leptospirosis**
         A27.81   Aseptic meningitis in leptospirosis
         A27.89   Other forms of leptospirosis

     A27.9   Leptospirosis, unspecified

● **A28   Other zoonotic bacterial diseases, not elsewhere classified**

     A28.0   Pasteurellosis
         Infection of humans or other animals by species of Pasteurella

     A28.1   Cat-scratch disease
         Cat-scratch fever

     A28.2   Extraintestinal yersiniosis
         Infection from Yersinia enterocolitica; AKA enteric yersiniosis, intestinal yersiniosis, Yersinia enteritis
         Excludes1   enteritis due to Yersinia enterocolitica (A04.6)
                    plague (A20.-)

     A28.8   Other specified zoonotic bacterial diseases, not elsewhere classified

     A28.9   Zoonotic bacterial disease, unspecified

OTHER BACTERIAL DISEASES (A30-A49)

● **A30   Leprosy [Hansen's disease]**
Chronic infectious disease attacking the skin, peripheral nerves, and mucous membranes

     Includes   infection due to Mycobacterium leprae
     Excludes1   sequelae of leprosy (B92)

     A30.0   Indeterminate leprosy
         I leprosy

     A30.1   Tuberculoid leprosy
         TT leprosy

     A30.2   Borderline tuberculoid leprosy
         BT leprosy

     A30.3   Borderline leprosy
         BB leprosy

     A30.4   Borderline lepromatous leprosy
         BL leprosy

     A30.5   Lepromatous leprosy
         LL leprosy

     A30.8   Other forms of leprosy

     A30.9   Leprosy, unspecified

● **A31   Infection due to other mycobacteria**
     Excludes2   leprosy (A30.-)
                tuberculosis (A15-A19)

     A31.0   Pulmonary mycobacterial infection
         Infection due to Mycobacterium avium
         Infection due to Mycobacterium intracellulare [Battey bacillus]
         Infection due to Mycobacterium kansasii

     A31.1   Cutaneous mycobacterial infection
         Buruli ulcer
         Infection due to Mycobacterium marinum
         Infection due to Mycobacterium ulcerans

     A31.2   Disseminated mycobacterium avium-intracellulare complex (DMAC)
         MAC sepsis

     A31.8   Other mycobacterial infections

     A31.9   Mycobacterial infection, unspecified
         Atypical mycobacterial infection NOS
         Mycobacteriosis NOS

● **A32   Listeriosis**
Infection caused by Listeria monocytogenes

     Includes   listerial foodborne infection
     Excludes1   neonatal (disseminated) listeriosis (P37.2)

     A32.0   Cutaneous listeriosis

     ● **A32.1   Listerial meningitis and meningoencephalitis**
         A32.11   Listerial meningitis
         A32.12   Listerial meningoencephalitis

     A32.7   Listerial sepsis

     ● **A32.8   Other forms of listeriosis**
         A32.81   Oculoglandular listeriosis
             Primary infection site is conjunctival sac, which if untreated may result in perforation of cornea and optic atrophy

         A32.82   Listerial endocarditis
             Exudative and proliferative inflammatory condition of endocardium caused by listeria bacteria

         A32.89   Other forms of listeriosis
             Listerial cerebral arteritis

     A32.9   Listeriosis, unspecified

A33   Tetanus neonatorum   N
Neonate = newborn

A34   Obstetrical tetanus ♀   M

A35   Other tetanus
     Tetanus NOS
     Excludes1   tetanus neonatorum (A33)
                    obstetrical tetanus (A34)

● **A36   Diphtheria**

     A36.0   Pharyngeal diphtheria
         Diphtheritic membranous angina
         Tonsillar diphtheria

     A36.1   Nasopharyngeal diphtheria

     A36.2   Laryngeal diphtheria
         Diphtheritic laryngotracheitis

     A36.3   Cutaneous diphtheria
         Excludes2   erythrasma (L08.1)

Item 1-7 Diptheria: A highly contagious bacterial disease that results in the formation of an adherent membrane in the throat that may lead to suffocation. In its most poisonous form, it attacks the heart and lungs. It is spread by direct physical contact or breathing the aerosolized secretions of infected individuals. The exact location is specified in the codes.

- **A36.8   Other diphtheria**
  - **A36.81   Diphtheritic cardiomyopathy**
    - Diphtheritic myocarditis
  - **A36.82   Diphtheritic radiculomyelitis**
  - **A36.83   Diphtheritic polyneuritis**
  - **A36.84   Diphtheritic tubulo-interstitial nephropathy**
  - **A36.85   Diphtheritic cystitis**
  - **A36.86   Diphtheritic conjunctivitis**
  - **A36.89   Other diphtheritic complications**
    - Diphtheritic peritonitis
- **A36.9   Diphtheria, unspecified**
- **A37   Whooping cough**
  - *Pertussis is a highly contagious disease caused by the bacterium Bordetella pertussis and results in a whooping sounding cough.*
  - **A37.0   Whooping cough due to Bordetella pertussis**
    - **A37.00   Whooping cough due to Bordetella pertussis without pneumonia**
    - **A37.01   Whooping cough due to Bordetella pertussis with pneumonia**
  - **A37.1   Whooping cough due to Bordetella parapertussis**
    - **A37.10   Whooping cough due to Bordetella parapertussis without pneumonia**
    - **A37.11   Whooping cough due to Bordetella parapertussis with pneumonia**
  - **A37.8   Whooping cough due to other Bordetella species**
    - **A37.80   Whooping cough due to other Bordetella species without pneumonia**
    - **A37.81   Whooping cough due to other Bordetella species with pneumonia**
  - **A37.9   Whooping cough, unspecified species**
    - **A37.90   Whooping cough, unspecified species without pneumonia**
    - **A37.91   Whooping cough, unspecified species with pneumonia**
- **A38   Scarlet fever**
  - *Most commonly caused by the bacteria Streptococcus pneumoniae and Neisseria meningitides*
  - **Includes**   scarlatina
  - **Excludes2**   streptococcal sore throat (J02.0)
  - **A38.0   Scarlet fever with otitis media**
  - **A38.1   Scarlet fever with myocarditis**
  - **A38.8   Scarlet fever with other complications**
  - **A38.9   Scarlet fever, uncomplicated**
    - Scarlet fever, NOS
- **A39   Meningococcal infection**
  - *Most commonly caused by the bacteria Streptococcus pneumoniae and Neisseria meningitides*
  - **A39.0   Meningococcal meningitis**
  - **A39.1   Waterhouse-Friderichsen syndrome**
    - *Fulminating complication of meningococcemia*
    - Meningococcal hemorrhagic adrenalitis
    - Meningococcic adrenal syndrome
  - **A39.2   Acute meningococcemia**
  - **A39.3   Chronic meningococcemia**
  - **A39.4   Meningococcemia, unspecified**
  - **A39.5   Meningococcal heart disease**
    - **A39.50   Meningococcal carditis, unspecified**
    - **A39.51   Meningococcal endocarditis**
    - **A39.52   Meningococcal myocarditis**
    - **A39.53   Meningococcal pericarditis**

- **A39.8   Other meningococcal infections**
  - **A39.81   Meningococcal encephalitis**
  - **A39.82   Meningococcal retrobulbar neuritis**
    - *Optic neuritis in portion of optic nerve posterior to eyeball; AKA postocular optic neuritis*
  - **A39.83   Meningococcal arthritis**
  - **A39.84   Postmeningococcal arthritis**
  - **A39.89   Other meningococcal infections**
    - Meningococcal conjunctivitis
- **A39.9   Meningococcal infection, unspecified**
  - Meningococcal disease NOS
- **A40   Streptococcal sepsis**
  - *Code first*
    - postprocedural streptococcal sepsis (T81.44)
    - streptococcal sepsis during labor (O75.3)
    - streptococcal sepsis following abortion or ectopic or molar pregnancy (O03-O07, O08.0)
    - streptococcal sepsis following immunization (T88.0)
    - streptococcal sepsis following infusion, transfusion or therapeutic injection (T80.2-)
  - **Excludes1**   neonatal (P36.0-P36.1)
    - puerperal sepsis (O85)
    - sepsis due to Streptococcus, group D (A41.81)
  - **A40.0   Sepsis due to streptococcus, group A**
  - **A40.1   Sepsis due to streptococcus, group B**
  - **A40.3   Sepsis due to Streptococcus pneumoniae**
    - Pneumococcal sepsis
  - **A40.8   Other streptococcal sepsis**
  - **A40.9   Streptococcal sepsis, unspecified**
- **A41   Other sepsis**
  - *Code first*
    - postprocedural sepsis (T81.44)
    - sepsis during labor (O75.3)
    - sepsis following abortion, ectopic or molar pregnancy (O03-O07, O08.0)
    - sepsis following immunization (T88.0)
    - sepsis following infusion, transfusion or therapeutic injection (T80.2-)
  - **Excludes1**   bacteremia NOS (R78.81)
    - neonatal (P36.-)
    - puerperal sepsis (O85)
    - streptococcal sepsis (A40.-)
  - **Excludes2**   sepsis (due to) (in) actinomycotic (A42.7)
    - sepsis (due to) (in) anthrax (A22.7)
    - sepsis (due to) (in) candidal (B37.7)
    - sepsis (due to) (in) Erysipelothrix (A26.7)
    - sepsis (due to) (in) extraintestinal yersiniosis (A28.2)
    - sepsis (due to) (in) gonococcal (A54.86)
    - sepsis (due to) (in) herpesviral (B00.7)
    - sepsis (due to) (in) listerial (A32.7)
    - sepsis (due to) (in) melioidosis (A24.1)
    - sepsis (due to) (in) meningococcal (A39.2-A39.4)
    - sepsis (due to) (in) plague (A20.7)
    - sepsis (due to) (in) tularemia (A21.7)
    - toxic shock syndrome (A48.3)
  - **Coding Clinic: 2016, Q1, P39**
  - **A41.0   Sepsis due to Staphylococcus aureus**
    - **A41.01   Sepsis due to Methicillin susceptible Staphylococcus aureus**
      - MSSA sepsis
      - Staphylococcus aureus sepsis NOS
    - **A41.02   Sepsis due to Methicillin resistant Staphylococcus aureus**
  - **A41.1   Sepsis due to other specified staphylococcus**
    - Coagulase negative staphylococcus sepsis
  - **A41.2   Sepsis due to unspecified staphylococcus**
  - **A41.3   Sepsis due to Hemophilus influenzae**
  - **A41.4   Sepsis due to anaerobes**
    - **Excludes1**   gas gangrene (A48.0)

▶ New   ⇒ Revised   ~~deleted~~ Deleted   Excludes 1   Excludes 2   Includes   Use additional   Code first   Code also   Key words

644   OGCR Official Guidelines   X Assign placeholder X   ● Use Additional Character(s)   ▷ Manifestation Code   **Coding Clinic**

● **A41.5   Sepsis due to other Gram-negative organisms**

    A41.50   Gram-negative sepsis, unspecified
        Gram-negative sepsis NOS

    A41.51   Sepsis due to Escherichia coli [E. coli]
        Coding Clinic: 2018, Q1, P16

    A41.52   Sepsis due to Pseudomonas
        Pseudomonas aeroginosa

    A41.53   Sepsis due to Serratia

    A41.59   Other Gram-negative sepsis

● **A41.8   Other specified sepsis**

    A41.81   Sepsis due to Enterococcus

    A41.89   Other specified sepsis
        Coding Clinic: 2016, Q3, P8-14

  A41.9   Sepsis, unspecified organism
    Septicemia NOS

● **A42   Actinomycosis**

    Excludes1   actinomycetoma (B47.1)

  A42.0   Pulmonary actinomycosis

  A42.1   Abdominal actinomycosis

  A42.2   Cervicofacial actinomycosis

  A42.7   Actinomycotic sepsis

● **A42.8   Other forms of actinomycosis**

    A42.81   Actinomycotic meningitis

    A42.82   Actinomycotic encephalitis

    A42.89   Other forms of actinomycosis

  A42.9   Actinomycosis, unspecified

● **A43   Nocardiosis**

  A43.0   Pulmonary nocardiosis

  A43.1   Cutaneous nocardiosis

  A43.8   Other forms of nocardiosis

  A43.9   Nocardiosis, unspecified

● **A44   Bartonellosis**

  A44.0   Systemic bartonellosis
    Oroya fever

  A44.1   Cutaneous and mucocutaneous bartonellosis
    Verruga peruana

  A44.8   Other forms of bartonellosis

  A44.9   Bartonellosis, unspecified

  A46   Erysipelas

    Excludes1   postpartum or puerperal erysipelas (O86.89)

● **A48   Other bacterial diseases, not elsewhere classified**

    Excludes1   actinomycetoma (B47.1)

  A48.0   Gas gangrene
    Clostridial cellulitis
    Clostridial myonecrosis
    Coding Clinic: 2017, Q4, P102

  A48.1   Legionnaires' disease

  A48.2   Nonpneumonic Legionnaires' disease [Pontiac fever]

  A48.3   Toxic shock syndrome
    Use additional code to identify the organism (B95, B96)

    Excludes1   endotoxic shock NOS (R57.8)
        sepsis NOS (A41.9)

  A48.4   Brazilian purpuric fever
    Systemic Hemophilus aegyptius infection

● **A48.5   Other specified botulism**
    Non-foodborne intoxication due to toxins of
        Clostridium botulinum [C. botulinum]

    Excludes1   food poisoning due to toxins of
        Clostridium botulinum (A05.1)

  A48.51   Infant botulism   P

  A48.52   Wound botulism
    Non-foodborne botulism NOS
    Use additional code for associated wound

  A48.8   Other specified bacterial diseases

● **A49   Bacterial infection of unspecified site**

    Excludes1   bacterial agents as the cause of diseases classified
        elsewhere (B95-B96)
        chlamydial infection NOS (A74.9)
        meningococcal infection NOS (A39.9)
        rickettsial infection NOS (A79.9)
        spirochetal infection NOS (A69.9)

● **A49.0   Staphylococcal infection, unspecified site**

    A49.01   Methicillin susceptible Staphylococcus aureus infection, unspecified site
        Methicillin susceptible Staphylococcus aureus
        (MSSA) infection
        Staphylococcus aureus infection NOS

    A49.02   Methicillin resistant Staphylococcus aureus infection, unspecified site
        Methicillin resistant Staphylococcus aureus
        (MRSA) infection

  A49.1   Streptococcal infection, unspecified site

  A49.2   Hemophilus influenzae infection, unspecified site
    Any of seven bacterium of genus Haemophilus

  A49.3   Mycoplasma infection, unspecified site
    Bacterium of class Mollicutes, unusual group of bacteria distinguished by absence of cell wall

  A49.8   Other bacterial infections of unspecified site

  A49.9   Bacterial infection, unspecified

    Excludes1   bacteremia NOS (R78.81)

INFECTIONS WITH A PREDOMINANTLY SEXUAL MODE OF TRANSMISSION (A50-A64)

    Excludes1   human immunodeficiency virus [HIV] disease
        (B20)
        nonspecific and nongonococcal urethritis (N34.1)
        Reiter's disease (M02.3-)

● **A50   Congenital syphilis**

● **A50.0   Early congenital syphilis, symptomatic**
    Any congenital syphilitic condition specified as early or
    manifest less than two years after birth

    A50.01   Early congenital syphilitic oculopathy

    A50.02   Early congenital syphilitic osteochondropathy

    A50.03   Early congenital syphilitic pharyngitis
        Early congenital syphilitic laryngitis

    A50.04   Early congenital syphilitic pneumonia

    A50.05   Early congenital syphilitic rhinitis

    A50.06   Early cutaneous congenital syphilis

    A50.07   Early mucocutaneous congenital syphilis

    A50.08   Early visceral congenital syphilis

    A50.09   Other early congenital syphilis, symptomatic

  A50.1   Early congenital syphilis, latent
    Congenital syphilis without clinical manifestations,
        with positive serological reaction and negative
        spinal fluid test, less than two years after birth

  A50.2   Early congenital syphilis, unspecified
    Congenital syphilis NOS less than two years after birth

Item 1–8   Gas gangrene is a necrotizing subcutaneous infection that will cause tissue death. Patients with poor circulation (e.g., diabetes, peripheral nephropathy) will have low oxygen content in their tissues (hypoxia), which allows the Clostridium bacteria to flourish. Gas gangrene often occurs at the site of a surgical wound or trauma. Onset is sudden and dramatic. Treatment can include debridement, amputation, and/or hyperbaric oxygen treatments.

CHAPTER 1 (A00-B99)

Figure 1-3 Chancre of primary syphilis. (From James WD, Berger TG, Elston DM: Andrews' Diseases of the Skin: Clinical Dermatology, Philadelphia, Saunders Elsevier, 2006)

Item 1–9 **Syphilis,** also known as lues, is the most serious of the venereal diseases caused by *Treponema pallidum*. The **primary** stage is characterized by an ulceration known as **chancre,** which usually appears on the genitals but can also develop on the anus, lips, tonsils, breasts, or fingers. Syphilis is easy to cure in its early stages. A single intramuscular injection of penicillin will usually cure a person who has had syphilis for less than a year.

The **secondary** stage is characterized by a rash that can affect any area of the body. **Latent** syphilis is divided into **early,** which is diagnosed within two years of infection, and **late,** which is diagnosed two years or more after infection. Additional doses of penicillin or another antibiotic are needed to treat someone who has had syphilis for longer than a year. For those allergic to penicillin, there are other antibiotic treatments. **Congenital** syphilis is also labeled **early** or **late** based on the time of diagnosis.

● **A50.3** Late congenital syphilitic oculopathy
    Excludes1 Hutchinson's triad (A50.53)
    A50.30 Late congenital syphilitic oculopathy, unspecified
    A50.31 Late congenital syphilitic interstitial keratitis
    A50.32 Late congenital syphilitic chorioretinitis
    A50.39 Other late congenital syphilitic oculopathy
● **A50.4** Late congenital neurosyphilis [juvenile neurosyphilis]
    Use additional code to identify any associated mental disorder
    Excludes1 Hutchinson's triad (A50.53)
    A50.40 Late congenital neurosyphilis, unspecified
        Juvenile neurosyphilis NOS
    A50.41 Late congenital syphilitic meningitis
    A50.42 Late congenital syphilitic encephalitis
    A50.43 Late congenital syphilitic polyneuropathy
    A50.44 Late congenital syphilitic optic nerve atrophy
    A50.45 Juvenile general paresis
        Dementia paralytica juvenilis
        Juvenile tabetoparetic neurosyphilis
    A50.49 Other late congenital neurosyphilis
        Juvenile tabes dorsalis
● **A50.5** Other late congenital syphilis, symptomatic
    Any congenital syphilitic condition specified as late or manifest two years or more after birth
    A50.51 Clutton's joints
    A50.52 Hutchinson's teeth
    A50.53 Hutchinson's triad
    A50.54 Late congenital cardiovascular syphilis
    A50.55 Late congenital syphilitic arthropathy
    A50.56 Late congenital syphilitic osteochondropathy
    A50.57 Syphilitic saddle nose
    A50.59 Other late congenital syphilis, symptomatic
A50.6 Late congenital syphilis, latent
    Congenital syphilis without clinical manifestations, with positive serological reaction and negative spinal fluid test, two years or more after birth.
A50.7 Late congenital syphilis, unspecified
    Congenital syphilis NOS two years or more after birth.
A50.9 Congenital syphilis, unspecified

● **A51** Early syphilis
    A51.0 Primary genital syphilis
        Syphilitic chancre NOS
    A51.1 Primary anal syphilis
    A51.2 Primary syphilis of other sites
  ● **A51.3** Secondary syphilis of skin and mucous membranes
        A51.31 Condyloma latum
        A51.32 Syphilitic alopecia
        A51.39 Other secondary syphilis of skin
            Syphilitic leukoderma
            Syphilitic mucous patch
            Excludes1 late syphilitic leukoderma (A52.79)
  ● **A51.4** Other secondary syphilis
        A51.41 Secondary syphilitic meningitis
        A51.42 Secondary syphilitic female pelvic disease ♀
        A51.43 Secondary syphilitic oculopathy
            Secondary syphilitic chorioretinitis
            Secondary syphilitic iridocyclitis, iritis
            Secondary syphilitic uveitis
        A51.44 Secondary syphilitic nephritis
        A51.45 Secondary syphilitic hepatitis
        A51.46 Secondary syphilitic osteopathy
        A51.49 Other secondary syphilitic conditions
            Secondary syphilitic lymphadenopathy
            Secondary syphilitic myositis
    A51.5 Early syphilis, latent
        Syphilis (acquired) without clinical manifestations, with positive serological reaction and negative spinal fluid test, less than two years after infection.
    A51.9 Early syphilis, unspecified

● **A52** Late syphilis
  ● **A52.0** Cardiovascular and cerebrovascular syphilis
        A52.00 Cardiovascular syphilis, unspecified
        A52.01 Syphilitic aneurysm of aorta
        A52.02 Syphilitic aortitis
        A52.03 Syphilitic endocarditis
            Syphilitic aortic valve incompetence or stenosis
            Syphilitic mitral valve stenosis
            Syphilitic pulmonary valve regurgitation
        A52.04 Syphilitic cerebral arteritis
        A52.05 Other cerebrovascular syphilis
            Syphilitic cerebral aneurysm (ruptured) (non-ruptured)
            Syphilitic cerebral thrombosis
        A52.06 Other syphilitic heart involvement
            Syphilitic coronary artery disease
            Syphilitic myocarditis
            Syphilitic pericarditis
        A52.09 Other cardiovascular syphilis
  ● **A52.1** Symptomatic neurosyphilis
        A52.10 Symptomatic neurosyphilis, unspecified
        A52.11 Tabes dorsalis
            Cognitive decline with progressive degeneration of posterior columns, roots, and ganglia of spinal cord, occur 15-20 years after initial infection of syphilis; AKA Duchenne disease
            Locomotor ataxia (progressive)
            Tabetic neurosyphilis
        A52.12 Other cerebrospinal syphilis
        A52.13 Late syphilitic meningitis
        A52.14 Late syphilitic encephalitis

CHAPTER 1 (A00-B99)

▶ New   ⇒ Revised   ~~deleted~~ Deleted   Excludes 1   Excludes 2   Includes   Use additional   Code first   Code also   Key words

OGCR Official Guidelines   X Assign placeholder X   ● Use Additional Character(s)   ▶ Manifestation Code   **Coding Clinic**

A52.15   **Late syphilitic neuropathy**
      Late syphilitic acoustic neuritis
      Late syphilitic optic (nerve) atrophy
      Late syphilitic polyneuropathy
      Late syphilitic retrobulbar neuritis

A52.16   **Charcôt's arthropathy (tabetic)**
      Progressive musculoskeletal condition characterized by joint dislocation, fractures, and deformities, results in progressive destruction of bone and soft tissue of weight-bearing joints

A52.17   **General paresis**
      Chronic meningoencephalitis results in loss of cortical function, or progressive dementia and generalized paralysis, occurring 10-20 years after initial infection of syphilis; AKA Bayle disease, dementia paralytica, paralytic dementiaparetic neurosyphilis, syphilitic meningoencephalitis
      Dementia paralytica

A52.19   **Other symptomatic neurosyphilis**
      Syphilitic parkinsonism

A52.2   **Asymptomatic neurosyphilis**

A52.3   **Neurosyphilis, unspecified**
      Gumma (syphilitic)
      Destructive lesions of syphilis
      Syphilis (late)
      Syphiloma

● **A52.7**   **Other symptomatic late syphilis**

A52.71   **Late syphilitic oculopathy**
      Late syphilitic chorioretinitis
      Late syphilitic episcleritis

A52.72   **Syphilis of lung and bronchus**

A52.73   **Symptomatic late syphilis of other respiratory organs**

A52.74   **Syphilis of liver and other viscera**
      Late syphilitic peritonitis

A52.75   **Syphilis of kidney and ureter**
      Syphilitic glomerular disease

A52.76   **Other genitourinary symptomatic late syphilis**
      Late syphilitic female pelvic inflammatory disease

A52.77   **Syphilis of bone and joint**

A52.78   **Syphilis of other musculoskeletal tissue**
      Late syphilitic bursitis
      Syphilis [stage unspecified] of bursa
      Syphilis [stage unspecified] of muscle
      Syphilis [stage unspecified] of synovium
      Syphilis [stage unspecified] of tendon

A52.79   **Other symptomatic late syphilis**
      Late syphilitic leukoderma
      Syphilis of adrenal gland
      Syphilis of pituitary gland
      Syphilis of thyroid gland
      Syphilitic splenomegaly
      Excludes1   syphilitic leukoderma (secondary) (A51.39)

A52.8   **Late syphilis, latent**
      Syphilis (acquired) without clinical manifestations, with positive serological reaction and negative spinal fluid test, two years or more after infection

A52.9   **Late syphilis, unspecified**

● **A53**   **Other and unspecified syphilis**

A53.0   **Latent syphilis, unspecified as early or late**
      Latent syphilis NOS
      Positive serological reaction for syphilis

A53.9   **Syphilis, unspecified**
      Infection due to Treponema pallidum NOS
      Syphilis (acquired) NOS
      Excludes1   syphilis NOS under two years of age (A50.2)

Item 1-10 An STD (sexually transmitted disease) caused by **Neisseria gonorrhoeae** that flourishes in the warm, moist areas of the reproductive tract. Untreated gonorrhea spreads to other parts of the body, causing inflammation of the testes or prostate or pelvic inflammatory disease (PID).

● **A54**   **Gonococcal infection**

● **A54.0**   **Gonococcal infection of lower genitourinary tract without periurethral or accessory gland abscess**
      Excludes1   gonococcal infection with genitourinary gland abscess (A54.1)
          gonococcal infection with periurethral abscess (A54.1)

A54.00   **Gonococcal infection of lower genitourinary tract, unspecified**

A54.01   **Gonococcal cystitis and urethritis, unspecified**

A54.02   **Gonococcal vulvovaginitis, unspecified** ♀

A54.03   **Gonococcal cervicitis, unspecified** ♀

A54.09   **Other gonococcal infection of lower genitourinary tract**

A54.1   **Gonococcal infection of lower genitourinary tract with periurethral and accessory gland abscess**
      Gonococcal Bartholin's gland abscess

● **A54.2**   **Gonococcal pelviperitonitis and other gonococcal genitourinary infection**

A54.21   **Gonococcal infection of kidney and ureter**

A54.22   **Gonococcal prostatitis** ♂

A54.23   **Gonococcal infection of other male genital organs** ♂
      Gonococcal epididymitis
      Gonococcal orchitis

A54.24   **Gonococcal female pelvic inflammatory disease** ♀
      Gonococcal pelviperitonitis
      Excludes1   gonococcal peritonitis (A54.85)

A54.29   **Other gonococcal genitourinary infections**

● **A54.3**   **Gonococcal infection of eye**

A54.30   **Gonococcal infection of eye, unspecified**

A54.31   **Gonococcal conjunctivitis**
      Form of bacterial conjunctivitis contracted by newborns during delivery; AKA neonatal conjunctivitis
      Ophthalmia neonatorum due to gonococcus

A54.32   **Gonococcal iridocyclitis**
      Inflammation of iris and of ciliary body due to gonococcal infection

A54.33   **Gonococcal keratitis**
      Inflammation of cornea due to gonococcal infection; AKA keratoconjunctivitis, keratopathy

A54.39   **Other gonococcal eye infection**
      Gonococcal endophthalmia

● **A54.4**   **Gonococcal infection of musculoskeletal system**

A54.40   **Gonococcal infection of musculoskeletal system, unspecified**

A54.41   **Gonococcal spondylopathy**
      Disorder of vertebrae due to gonococcal infection; AKA rachiopathy

A54.42   **Gonococcal arthritis**
      Excludes2   gonococcal infection of spine (A54.41)

A54.43   **Gonococcal osteomyelitis**
      Excludes2   gonococcal infection of spine (A54.41)

A54.49   **Gonococcal infection of other musculoskeletal tissue**
      Gonococcal bursitis
      Gonococcal myositis
      Gonococcal synovitis
      Gonococcal tenosynovitis

CHAPTER 1 (A00-B99)

- A54.5   Gonococcal pharyngitis
- A54.6   Gonococcal infection of anus and rectum
- ● A54.8   Other gonococcal infections
  - A54.81   Gonococcal meningitis
  - A54.82   Gonococcal brain abscess
  - A54.83   Gonococcal heart infection
    - Gonococcal endocarditis
    - Gonococcal myocarditis
    - Gonococcal pericarditis
  - A54.84   Gonococcal pneumonia
  - A54.85   Gonococcal peritonitis
    - **Excludes1**   gonococcal pelviperitonitis (A54.24)
  - A54.86   Gonococcal sepsis
  - A54.89   Other gonococcal infections
    - Gonococcal keratoderma
    - Gonococcal lymphadenitis
- A54.9   Gonococcal infection, unspecified

A55   Chlamydial lymphogranuloma (venereum)
- Climatic or tropical bubo
- Durand-Nicolas-Favre disease
- Esthiomene
- Lymphogranuloma inguinale

● A56   Other sexually transmitted chlamydial diseases

     Includes   sexually transmitted diseases due to Chlamydia trachomatis

     Excludes1   neonatal chlamydial conjunctivitis (P39.1)
neonatal chlamydial pneumonia (P23.1)

     Excludes2   chlamydial lymphogranuloma (A55)
conditions classified to A74.-

- ● A56.0   Chlamydial infection of lower genitourinary tract
  - A56.00   Chlamydial infection of lower genitourinary tract, unspecified
  - A56.01   Chlamydial cystitis and urethritis
  - A56.02   Chlamydial vulvovaginitis ♀
  - A56.09   Other chlamydial infection of lower genitourinary tract
    - Chlamydial cervicitis
- ● A56.1   Chlamydial infection of pelviperitoneum and other genitourinary organs
  - A56.11   Chlamydial female pelvic inflammatory disease ♀
  - A56.19   Other chlamydial genitourinary infection
    - Chlamydial epididymitis
    - Chlamydial orchitis
- A56.2   Chlamydial infection of genitourinary tract, unspecified
- A56.3   Chlamydial infection of anus and rectum
- A56.4   Chlamydial infection of pharynx
- A56.8   Sexually transmitted chlamydial infection of other sites

A57   Chancroid
- Ulcus molle
- *Sexually transmitted infection caused by bacteria, Haemophilus ducreyi*

A58   Granuloma inguinale
- *Chronic, progressive, ulcerative granulomatous disease*
- Donovanosis

● A59   Trichomoniasis

     Excludes2   intestinal trichomoniasis (A07.8)

     A common STD caused by a parasite, Trichomonas vaginalis

- ● A59.0   Urogenital trichomoniasis
  - A59.00   Urogenital trichomoniasis, unspecified
    - Fluor (vaginalis) due to Trichomonas
    - Leukorrhea (vaginalis) due to Trichomonas
  - A59.01   Trichomonal vulvovaginitis ♀
  - A59.02   Trichomonal prostatitis ♂
  - A59.03   Trichomonal cystitis and urethritis
  - A59.09   Other urogenital trichomoniasis
    - *Common sexually transmitted disease (STD) caused by single-celled protozoan parasite; AKA trich*
    - Trichomonas cervicitis
- A59.8   Trichomoniasis of other sites
- A59.9   Trichomoniasis, unspecified

● A60   Anogenital herpesviral [herpes simplex] infections
- ● A60.0   Herpesviral infection of genitalia and urogenital tract
  - A60.00   Herpesviral infection of urogenital system, unspecified
  - A60.01   Herpesviral infection of penis ♂
  - A60.02   Herpesviral infection of other male genital organs ♂
  - A60.03   Herpesviral cervicitis ♀
  - A60.04   Herpesviral vulvovaginitis ♀
    - Herpesviral [herpes simplex] ulceration
    - Herpesviral [herpes simplex] vaginitis
    - Herpesviral [herpes simplex] vulvitis
  - A60.09   Herpesviral infection of other urogenital tract
- A60.1   Herpesviral infection of perianal skin and rectum
- A60.9   Anogenital herpesviral infection, unspecified

● A63   Other predominantly sexually transmitted diseases, not elsewhere classified

     Excludes2   molluscum contagiosum (B08.1)
papilloma of cervix (D26.0)

- A63.0   Anogenital (venereal) warts
  - Anogenital warts due to (human) papillomavirus [HPV]
  - Condyloma acuminatum
- A63.8   Other specified predominantly sexually transmitted diseases

A64   Unspecified sexually transmitted disease

OTHER SPIROCHETAL DISEASES (A65-A69)

     Excludes2   leptospirosis (A27.-)
syphilis (A50-A53)

A65   Nonvenereal syphilis
- Bejel
- Endemic syphilis
- Njovera

● A66   Yaws

     Endemic, infectious, tropical disease caused by spirochete, spread by direct contact; AKA frambesia, framboesia, frambesia tropica

     Includes   bouba
frambesia (tropica)
pian

- A66.0   Initial lesions of yaws
  - Chancre of yaws
  - Frambesia, initial or primary
  - Initial frambesial ulcer
  - Mother yaw
- A66.1   Multiple papillomata and wet crab yaws
  - Frambesioma
  - Pianoma
  - Plantar or palmar papilloma of yaws

▶ New   ⇥ Revised   ~~deleted~~ Deleted   Excludes 1   Excludes 2   Includes   Use additional   Code first   Code also   Key words

OGCR Official Guidelines   X Assign placeholder X   ● Use Additional Character(s)   ▶ Manifestation Code   **Coding Clinic**

A66.2   **Other early skin lesions** of yaws
     Cutaneous yaws, less than five years after infection
     Early yaws (cutaneous)(macular)(maculopapular)
        (micropapular)(papular)
     Frambeside of early yaws

A66.3   **Hyperkeratosis** of yaws
     Hypertrophy of stratum corneum of skin in which there are
       small, hard, verrucous scales
     Ghoul hand
     Hyperkeratosis, palmar or plantar (early) (late) due to
       yaws
     Worm-eaten soles

A66.4   **Gummata and ulcers** of yaws
     Small, rubbery granuloma with necrotic center and inflamed
       characteristic of advanced stage of syphilis; AKA
       syphiloma
     Gummatous frambeside
     Nodular late yaws (ulcerated)

A66.5   **Gangosa**
     Manifestation of yaws that develops in the soft palate and
       spreads eroding bone, cartilage, and soft tissue
     Rhinopharyngitis mutilans

A66.6   **Bone and joint lesions** of yaws
     Yaws ganglion
     Yaws goundou
     Yaws gumma, bone
     Yaws gummatous osteitis or periostitis
     Yaws hydrarthrosis
     Yaws osteitis
     Yaws periostitis (hypertrophic)

A66.7   **Other manifestations** of yaws
     Juxta-articular nodules of yaws
     Mucosal yaws

A66.8   **Latent yaws**
     Yaws without clinical manifestations, with positive
       serology

A66.9   **Yaws, unspecified**

● **A67**   **Pinta [carate]**
     Group of nonvenereal diseases caused by Treponema species

A67.0   **Primary lesions** of pinta
     Chancre (primary) of pinta
     Papule (primary) of pinta

A67.1   **Intermediate lesions** of pinta
     Erythematous plaques of pinta
     Hyperchromic lesions of pinta
     Hyperkeratosis of pinta
     Pintids

A67.2   **Late lesions** of pinta
     Achromic skin lesions of pinta
     Cicatricial skin lesions of pinta
     Dyschromic skin lesions of pinta

A67.3   **Mixed lesions** of pinta
     Achromic with hyperchromic skin lesions of pinta
       [carate]

A67.9   **Pinta, unspecified**

● **A68**   **Relapsing fevers**
     Includes   recurrent fever
     Excludes2   Lyme disease (A69.2-)

A68.0   **Louse-borne relapsing fever**
     Relapsing fever due to Borrelia recurrentis

A68.1   **Tick-borne relapsing fever**
     Relapsing fever due to any Borrelia species other than
       Borrelia recurrentis

A68.9   **Relapsing fever, unspecified**

Item 1-11   Cancrum oris, also known as **noma** or **gangrenous stomatitis,** begins as an ulcer of the gingiva and results in a progressive gangrenous process.

● **A69**   **Other spirochetal infections**

A69.0   **Necrotizing ulcerative stomatitis**
     Cancrum oris
     Fusospirochetal gangrene
     Noma
     Stomatitis gangrenosa

A69.1   **Other Vincent's infections**
     Fusospirochetal pharyngitis
     Necrotizing ulcerative (acute) gingivitis
     Necrotizing ulcerative (acute) gingivostomatitis
     Spirochetal stomatitis
     Trench mouth
     Vincent's angina
     Vincent's gingivitis

● **A69.2**   **Lyme disease**
     Erythema chronicum migrans due to Borrelia
       burgdorferi

     A69.20   **Lyme disease, unspecified**
     A69.21   **Meningitis due to Lyme disease**
     A69.22   **Other neurologic disorders** in Lyme disease
         Cranial neuritis
         Meningoencephalitis
         Polyneuropathy
     A69.23   **Arthritis due to Lyme disease**
     A69.29   **Other conditions** associated with Lyme disease
         Myopericarditis due to Lyme disease
         Coding Clinic: 2016, Q3, P12

A69.8   **Other specified** spirochetal infections
A69.9   **Spirochetal infection, unspecified**

OTHER DISEASES CAUSED BY CHLAMYDIAE (A70-A74)

     Excludes1   sexually transmitted chlamydial diseases
       (A55-A56)

A70   **Chlamydia psittaci infections**
     Ornithosis
     Parrot fever
     Psittacosis

● **A71**   **Trachoma**
     Excludes1   sequelae of trachoma (B94.0)

A71.0   **Initial stage** of trachoma
     Trachoma dubium

A71.1   **Active stage** of trachoma
     Granular conjunctivitis (trachomatous)
     Trachomatous follicular conjunctivitis
     Trachomatous pannus

A71.9   **Trachoma, unspecified**

● **A74**   **Other diseases caused by chlamydiae**
     Excludes1   neonatal chlamydial conjunctivitis (P39.1)
       neonatal chlamydial pneumonia (P23.1)
       Reiter's disease (M02.3-)
       sexually transmitted chlamydial diseases
       (A55-A56)
     Excludes2   chlamydial pneumonia (J16.0)

A74.0   **Chlamydial conjunctivitis**
     Paratrachoma

● **A74.8**   **Other chlamydial diseases**
     A74.81   **Chlamydial peritonitis**
     A74.89   **Other chlamydial diseases**

A74.9   **Chlamydial infection, unspecified**
     Chlamydiosis NOS

Item 1-12 Rickettsioses are diseases spread from ticks, lice, fleas, or mites to humans.

Typhus is spread to humans chiefly by the fleas of rats.

Endemic identifies a disease as being present in low numbers of humans at all times, whereas **epidemic** identifies a disease as being present in high numbers of humans at a specific time. Morbidity (death) is higher in epidemic diseases.

Brill's disease, also known as **Brill-Zinsser disease,** is spread from human to human by body lice and also from the lice of flying squirrels. **Scrub typhus** is spread in the same ways as Brill's disease.

Malaria is spread to humans by mosquitoes.

RICKETTSIOSES (A75-A79)

● **A75 Typhus fever**

> **Excludes1**   rickettsiosis due to Ehrlichia sennetsu (A79.81)

A75.0 Epidemic louse-borne typhus fever due to Rickettsia prowazekii
Organisms transmitted between humans via louse
Classical typhus (fever)
Epidemic (louse-borne) typhus

A75.1 Recrudescent typhus [Brill's disease]
Brill-Zinsser disease

A75.2 Typhus fever due to Rickettsia typhi
Murine (flea-borne) typhus

A75.3 Typhus fever due to Rickettsia tsutsugamushi
Scrub (mite-borne) typhus
Tsutsugamushi fever

A75.9 Typhus fever, unspecified
Typhus (fever) NOS

● **A77 Spotted fever [tick-borne rickettsioses]**

A77.0 Spotted fever due to Rickettsia rickettsii
Rocky Mountain spotted fever
Sao Paulo fever

A77.1 Spotted fever due to Rickettsia conorii
African tick typhus
Boutonneuse fever
India tick typhus
Kenya tick typhus
Marseilles fever
Mediterranean tick fever

A77.2 Spotted fever due to Rickettsia siberica
North Asian tick fever
Siberian tick typhus

A77.3 Spotted fever due to Rickettsia australis
Queensland tick typhus

● **A77.4 Ehrlichiosis**
Type of tick-borne fever caused by bacteria infection

> **Excludes1**   Rickettsiosis due to Ehrlichia sennetsu (A79.81)

A77.40 Ehrlichiosis, unspecified

A77.41 Ehrlichiosis chafeensis [E. chafeensis]

A77.49 Other ehrlichiosis

A77.8 Other spotted fevers

A77.9 Spotted fever, unspecified
Tick-borne typhus NOS

A78 Q fever
Infection due to Coxiella burnetii
Nine Mile fever
Quadrilateral fever

● **A79 Other rickettsioses**

A79.0 Trench fever
Quintan fever
Wolhynian fever

A79.1 Rickettsialpox due to Rickettsia akari
Kew Garden fever
Vesicular rickettsiosis

● **A79.8 Other specified rickettsioses**

A79.81 Rickettsiosis due to Ehrlichia sennetsu

A79.89 Other specified rickettsioses

A79.9 Rickettsiosis, unspecified
Rickettsial infection NOS

Item 1-13 Acute Poliomyelitis: Also called infantile paralysis and is caused by the poliovirus, which enters the body orally and infects the intestinal wall and then enters the blood stream and central nervous system, causing muscle weakness and paralysis. This disease has been nearly eradicated with the polio vaccine.

VIRAL AND PRION INFECTIONS OF THE CENTRAL NERVOUS SYSTEM (A80-A89)

> **Excludes1**   postpolio syndrome (G14)
> sequelae of poliomyelitis (B91)
> sequelae of viral encephalitis (B94.1)

● **A80 Acute poliomyelitis**

A80.0 Acute paralytic poliomyelitis, vaccine-associated

A80.1 Acute paralytic poliomyelitis, wild virus, imported

A80.2 Acute paralytic poliomyelitis, wild virus, indigenous

● **A80.3 Acute paralytic poliomyelitis, other and unspecified**

A80.30 Acute paralytic poliomyelitis, unspecified

A80.39 Other acute paralytic poliomyelitis

A80.4 Acute nonparalytic poliomyelitis

A80.9 Acute poliomyelitis, unspecified

● **A81 Atypical virus infections of central nervous system**

> **Includes**   diseases of the central nervous system caused by prions

Use additional code to identify:
dementia with behavioral disturbance (F02.81)
dementia without behavioral disturbance (F02.80)

● **A81.0 Creutzfeldt-Jakob disease**

A81.00 Creutzfeldt-Jakob disease, unspecified
Jakob-Creutzfeldt disease, unspecified

A81.01 Variant Creutzfeldt-Jakob disease
vCJD

A81.09 Other Creutzfeldt-Jakob disease
CJD
Familial Creutzfeldt-Jakob disease
Iatrogenic Creutzfeldt-Jakob disease
Sporadic Creutzfeldt-Jakob disease
Subacute spongiform encephalopathy (with dementia)

A81.1 Subacute sclerosing panencephalitis
Type of viral encephalitis that causes parenchymatous lesions in gray and white matter of brain
Dawson's inclusion body encephalitis
Van Bogaert's sclerosing leukoencephalopathy

A81.2 Progressive multifocal leukoencephalopathy
Group of diseases affecting white matter of brain
Multifocal leukoencephalopathy NOS

● **A81.8 Other atypical virus infections of central nervous system**

A81.81 Kuru

A81.82 Gerstmann-Sträussler-Scheinker syndrome
GSS syndrome

A81.83 Fatal familial insomnia
FFI

A81.89 Other atypical virus infections of central nervous system

A81.9 Atypical virus infection of central nervous system, unspecified
Prion diseases of the central nervous system NOS

● **A82 Rabies**
Viral disease affecting the central nervous system and transmitted from infected mammals to man.

A82.0 Sylvatic rabies

A82.1 Urban rabies

A82.9 Rabies, unspecified

▶ New   ⇒ Revised   ~~deleted~~ Deleted   Excludes 1   Excludes 2   Includes   Use additional   Code first   Code also   Key words

OGCR Official Guidelines   X Assign placeholder X   ● Use Additional Character(s)   ▶ Manifestation Code   **Coding Clinic**

Item 1-14 Encephalitis is an inflammation of the brain most often caused by a virus but may also be caused by a bacteria and most commonly transmitted by a mosquito. **Myelitis** is an inflammation of the spinal cord that may disrupt CNS function. Untreated myelitis may rapidly lead to permanent damage to the spinal cord. **Encephalomyelitis** is a general term for an inflammation of the brain and spinal cord.

● **A83   Mosquito-borne viral encephalitis**
Inflammation of the brain caused most commonly by Herpes Simplex virus.

Includes	mosquito-borne viral meningoencephalitis
Excludes2	Venezuelan equine encephalitis (A92.2)
	West Nile fever (A92.3-)
	West Nile virus (A92.3-)

A83.0 **Japanese encephalitis**

A83.1 **Western equine encephalitis**

A83.2 **Eastern equine encephalitis**

A83.3 **St. Louis encephalitis**

A83.4 **Australian encephalitis**
     Kunjin virus disease

A83.5 **California encephalitis**
     California meningoencephalitis
     La Crosse encephalitis

A83.6 **Rocio virus disease**
     Mosquito-borne virus

A83.8 **Other mosquito-borne viral encephalitis**

A83.9 **Mosquito-borne viral encephalitis, unspecified**

● **A84   Tick-borne viral encephalitis**

| **Includes** | tick-borne viral meningoencephalitis |

A84.0 **Far Eastern tick-borne encephalitis [Russian spring-summer encephalitis]**

A84.1 **Central European tick-borne encephalitis**

A84.8 **Other tick-borne viral encephalitis**
     Louping ill
     Powassan virus disease

A84.9 **Tick-borne viral encephalitis, unspecified**

● **A85   Other viral encephalitis, not elsewhere classified**

Includes	specified viral encephalomyelitis NEC
	specified viral meningoencephalitis NEC
Excludes1	benign myalgic encephalomyelitis (G93.3)
	encephalitis due to cytomegalovirus (B25.8)
	encephalitis due to herpesvirus NEC (B10.0-)
	encephalitis due to herpesvirus [herpes simplex] (B00.4)
	encephalitis due to measles virus (B05.0)
	encephalitis due to mumps virus (B26.2)
	encephalitis due to poliomyelitis virus (A80.-)
	encephalitis due to zoster (B02.0)
	lymphocytic choriomeningitis (A87.2)

A85.0 **Enteroviral encephalitis**
     Enteroviral encephalomyelitis

A85.1 **Adenoviral encephalitis**
     Adenoviral meningoencephalitis

A85.2 **Arthropod-borne viral encephalitis, unspecified**

| **Excludes1** | West nile virus with encephalitis (A92.31) |

A85.8 **Other specified viral encephalitis**
     Encephalitis lethargica
     Von Economo-Cruchet disease

● **A86   Unspecified viral encephalitis**
     Viral encephalomyelitis NOS
     Viral meningoencephalitis NOS

● **A87   Viral meningitis**

Excludes1	meningitis due to herpesvirus [herpes simplex] (B00.3)
	meningitis due to measles virus (B05.1)
	meningitis due to mumps virus (B26.1)
	meningitis due to poliomyelitis virus (A80.-)
	meningitis due to zoster (B02.1)

A87.0 **Enteroviral meningitis**
     Group of common viruses responsible for the majority of viral meningitis
     Coxsackievirus meningitis
     Echovirus meningitis

A87.1 **Adenoviral meningitis**

A87.2 **Lymphocytic choriomeningitis**
     Lymphocytic meningoencephalitis

A87.8 **Other viral meningitis**

A87.9 **Viral meningitis, unspecified**

● **A88   Other viral infections of central nervous system, not elsewhere classified**

| **Excludes1** | viral encephalitis NOS (A86) |
| | viral meningitis NOS (A87.9) |

A88.0 **Enteroviral exanthematous fever [Boston exanthem]**
     Infectious skin eruption

A88.1 **Epidemic vertigo**

A88.8 **Other specified viral infections of central nervous system**

A89   Unspecified viral infection of central nervous system

ARTHROPOD-BORNE VIRAL FEVERS AND VIRAL HEMORRHAGIC FEVERS (A90-A99)

A90   Dengue fever [classical dengue]
Acute, self-limited disease, characterized by fever, prostration, severe muscle pains, headache, rash, lymphadenopathy, and leukopenia, caused by dengue virus; AKA breakbone, dandy

| **Excludes1** | dengue hemorrhagic fever (A91) |

Coding Clinic: 2016, Q3, P13

A91   Dengue hemorrhagic fever
Serious follow-up to regular dengue, with symptoms of hemorrhage

● **A92   Other mosquito-borne viral fevers**

| **Excludes1** | Ross River disease (B33.1) |

A92.0 **Chikungunya virus disease**
     Transmitted by mosquitoes
     Chikungunya (hemorrhagic) fever

A92.1 **O'nyong-nyong fever**
     Acute, nonfatal febrile disease transmitted by mosquitoes, which clinically resembles dengue and chikungunya

A92.2 **Venezuelan equine fever**
     Venezuelan equine encephalitis
     Venezuelan equine encephalomyelitis virus disease

● A92.3 **West Nile virus infection**
     West Nile fever

     A92.30 **West Nile virus infection, unspecified**
          West Nile fever NOS
          West Nile fever without complications
          West Nile virus NOS

     A92.31 **West Nile virus infection with encephalitis**
          West Nile encephalitis
          West Nile encephalomyelitis
          Coding Clinic: 2016, Q3, P13

     A92.32 **West Nile virus infection with other neurologic manifestation**
          Use additional code to specify the neurologic manifestation

     A92.39 **West Nile virus infection with other complications**
          Use additional code to specify the other conditions

CHAPTER 1 (A00-B99)

OGCR Section I. C.1.f.

Certain Infectious and Parasitic Diseases (A00-B99)

Zika virus infections

Code only confirmed cases

Code only a confirmed diagnosis of Zika virus (A92.5, Zika virus disease) as documented by the provider. This is an exception to the hospital inpatient guideline Section II, H.

In this context, "confirmation" does not require documentation of the type of test performed; the physician's diagnostic statement that the condition is confirmed is sufficient. This code should be assigned regardless of the stated mode of transmission.

If the provider documents "suspected", "possible" or "probable" Zika, do not assign code A92.5. Assign a code(s) explaining the reason for encounter (such as fever, rash, or joint pain) or Z20.828, Contact with and (suspected) exposure to other viral communicable diseases.

A92.4 **Rift Valley fever**

A92.5 **Zika virus disease**
Zika virus fever
Zika virus infection
Zika NOS
▶ **Excludes1** congenital Zika virus disease (P35.4)
Coding Clinic: 2016, Q4, P4-7, 121

A92.8 **Other specified mosquito-borne viral fevers**

A92.9 **Mosquito-borne viral fever, unspecified**

● **A93** **Other arthropod-borne viral fevers, not elsewhere classified**

A93.0 **Oropouche virus disease**
Tropical viral infection
Oropouche fever

A93.1 **Sandfly fever**
Pappataci fever
Phlebotomus fever

A93.2 **Colorado tick fever**

A93.8 **Other specified arthropod-borne viral fevers**
Piry virus disease
Vesicular stomatitis virus disease [Indiana fever]

A94 **Unspecified arthropod-borne viral fever**
Arboviral fever NOS
Arbovirus infection NOS

● **A95** **Yellow fever**
Acute infectious disease transmitted by mosquitoes

A95.0 **Sylvatic yellow fever**
Jungle yellow fever

A95.1 **Urban yellow fever**

A95.9 **Yellow fever, unspecified**

● **A96** **Arenaviral hemorrhagic fever**
Virus that causes various hemorrhagic fevers

A96.0 **Junin hemorrhagic fever**
Argentinian hemorrhagic fever

A96.1 **Machupo hemorrhagic fever**
Transmitted by contact with infected rodents
Bolivian hemorrhagic fever

A96.2 **Lassa fever**
Acute type of hemorrhagic fever caused by contact with disease carrying mouse or person

A96.8 **Other arenaviral hemorrhagic fevers**

A96.9 **Arenaviral hemorrhagic fever, unspecified**

● **A98** **Other viral hemorrhagic fevers, not elsewhere classified**
Excludes1 chikungunya hemorrhagic fever (A92.0)
dengue hemorrhagic fever (A91)

A98.0 **Crimean-Congo hemorrhagic fever**
Virus transmitted by ticks and contact with blood, secretions, or fluids from infected humans or animals
Central Asian hemorrhagic fever

A98.1 **Omsk hemorrhagic fever**
Transmitted to humans by bites of infected ticks or contact with infected muskrats

A98.2 **Kyasanur Forest disease**
Transmitted via infected monkeys, voles, ticks

A98.3 **Marburg virus disease**
Rare, acute, often fatal type of hemorrhagic fever

A98.4 **Ebola virus disease**

A98.5 **Hemorrhagic fever with renal syndrome**
Epidemic hemorrhagic fever
Korean hemorrhagic fever
Russian hemorrhagic fever
Hantaan virus disease
Hantavirus disease with renal manifestations
Nephropathia epidemica
Songo fever
Excludes1 hantavirus (cardio)-pulmonary syndrome (B33.4)

A98.8 **Other specified viral hemorrhagic fevers**

A99 **Unspecified viral hemorrhagic fever**

VIRAL INFECTIONS CHARACTERIZED BY SKIN AND MUCOUS MEMBRANE LESIONS (B00-B09)

● **B00** **Herpesviral [herpes simplex] infections**
Excludes1 congenital herpesviral infections (P35.2)
Excludes2 anogenital herpesviral infection (A60.-)
gammaherpesviral mononucleosis (B27.0-)
herpangina (B08.5)

B00.0 **Eczema herpeticum**
Cutaneous eruption caused by herpes simplex virus (HSV) type 1, HSV-2, coxsackievirus A16, or vaccinia virus
Kaposi's varicelliform eruption

B00.1 **Herpesviral vesicular dermatitis**
Vesicle formation; characteristics include formation of blisters and scabs on feet and legs
Herpes simplex facialis
Herpes simplex labialis
Herpes simplex otitis externa
Vesicular dermatitis of ear
Vesicular dermatitis of lip

B00.2 **Herpesviral gingivostomatitis and pharyngotonsillitis**
Inflammation involving both gingivae and oral mucosa
Herpesviral pharyngitis
Inflammation of pharynx and tonsils; AKA tonsillopharyngitis

B00.3 **Herpesviral meningitis**

B00.4 **Herpesviral encephalitis**
Herpesviral meningoencephalitis
Simian B disease
Excludes1 herpesviral encephalitis due to herpesvirus 6 and 7 (B10.01, B10.09)
non-simplex herpesviral encephalitis (B10.0-)

● **B00.5** **Herpesviral ocular disease**

B00.50 **Herpesviral ocular disease, unspecified**

B00.51 **Herpesviral iridocyclitis**
Herpesviral iritis
Herpesviral uveitis, anterior

B00.52 **Herpesviral keratitis**
Herpesviral keratoconjunctivitis

B00.53 **Herpesviral conjunctivitis**

B00.59 **Other herpesviral disease of eye**
Herpesviral dermatitis of eyelid

Figure 1-4 Primary herpes simplex in and around the mouth. The infection is usually acquired from siblings or parents and is readily transmitted to other direct contacts. (Getty Image)

Item 1-15 **Herpes** is a viral disease for which there is no cure. There are two types of the herpes simplex virus: **Type I** causes **cold sores** or **fever blisters,** and **Type II** causes **genital herpes.** The virus can be spread from a sore on the lips to the genitals or from the genitals to the lips.

▶ New   ⇒ Revised   ~~deleted~~ Deleted   Excludes 1   Excludes 2   Includes   Use additional   Code first   Code also   Key words

OGCR Official Guidelines   X Assign placeholder X   ● Use Additional Character(s)   ▌ Manifestation Code   **Coding Clinic**

B00.7 **Disseminated** herpesviral disease
Herpesviral sepsis

● **B00.8** **Other** forms of herpesviral infections

B00.81 **Herpesviral hepatitis**

B00.82 **Herpes simplex myelitis**

B00.89 **Other** herpesviral infection
Herpesviral whitlow

B00.9 **Herpesviral** infection, **unspecified**
Herpes simplex infection NOS

● **B01** Varicella [chickenpox]
Very contagious disease caused by the varicella zoster virus that results in an itchy outbreak of skin blisters (varicella). The same virus causes shingles (zoster).

B01.0 **Varicella meningitis**

● **B01.1** **Varicella encephalitis,** myelitis and encephalomyelitis
Postchickenpox encephalitis, myelitis and encephalomyelitis

B01.11 **Varicella encephalitis** and **encephalomyelitis**
Postchickenpox encephalitis and encephalomyelitis

B01.12 **Varicella myelitis**
Postchickenpox myelitis

B01.2 **Varicella pneumonia**

● **B01.8** **Varicella with other** complications

B01.81 **Varicella keratitis**

B01.89 **Other** varicella complications

B01.9 **Varicella without complication**
Varicella NOS

● **B02** Zoster [herpes zoster]

Includes shingles
zona

B02.0 **Zoster encephalitis**
Zoster meningoencephalitis

B02.1 **Zoster meningitis**

● **B02.2** **Zoster with other nervous system** involvement

B02.21 **Postherpetic geniculate ganglionitis**

B02.22 **Postherpetic trigeminal neuralgia**

B02.23 **Postherpetic polyneuropathy**

B02.24 **Postherpetic myelitis**
Herpes zoster myelitis

B02.29 **Other** postherpetic nervous system involvement
Postherpetic radiculopathy

● **B02.3** **Zoster ocular disease**

B02.30 **Zoster ocular disease, unspecified**

B02.31 **Zoster conjunctivitis**

B02.32 **Zoster iridocyclitis**

B02.33 **Zoster keratitis**
Herpes zoster keratoconjunctivitis

B02.34 **Zoster scleritis**

B02.39 **Other** herpes zoster eye disease
Zoster blepharitis

B02.7 **Disseminated zoster**

B02.8 **Zoster with other complications**
Herpes zoster otitis externa

B02.9 **Zoster without complications**
Zoster NOS

Figure 1-5 Photograph of eyelids with marginal blepharitis. (From Hoyt CS, Taylor D: Pediatric Ophthalmology and Strabismus, London, Elsevier Saunders, 2005)

Item 1–17 Blepharitis is a common condition in which the eyelid is swollen and yellow scaling and conjunctivitis develop. Usually the hair on the scalp and brow is involved.

B03 Smallpox
Note: In 1980 the 33rd World Health Assembly declared that smallpox had been eradicated. The classification is maintained for surveillance purposes.

B04 Monkeypox
Disease occurring in captive monkeys and other mammals that may be transmitted to humans, clinically similar to smallpox

● **B05** Measles

Includes morbilli

Excludes1 subacute sclerosing panencephalitis (A81.1)

B05.0 **Measles complicated by encephalitis**
Postmeasles encephalitis

B05.1 **Measles complicated by meningitis**
Postmeasles meningitis

B05.2 **Measles complicated by pneumonia**
Postmeasles pneumonia

B05.3 **Measles complicated by otitis media**
Postmeasles otitis media

B05.4 **Measles with intestinal complications**

● **B05.8** **Measles with other complications**

B05.81 **Measles keratitis and keratoconjunctivitis**

B05.89 **Other** measles complications

B05.9 **Measles without complication**
Measles NOS

● **B06** Rubella [German measles]

Excludes1 congenital rubella (P35.0)

● **B06.0** **Rubella with neurological complications**

B06.00 **Rubella** with neurological complication, **unspecified**

B06.01 **Rubella encephalitis**
Rubella meningoencephalitis

B06.02 **Rubella meningitis**

B06.09 **Other** neurological complications of **rubella**

● **B06.8** **Rubella with other complications**

B06.81 **Rubella pneumonia**

B06.82 **Rubella arthritis**

B06.89 **Other** rubella complications

B06.9 **Rubella without complication**
Rubella NOS

● **B07** **Viral warts**

Includes verruca simplex
verruca vulgaris
viral warts due to human papillomavirus

Excludes2 anogenital (venereal) warts (A63.0)
papilloma of bladder (D41.4)
papilloma of cervix (D26.0)
papilloma larynx (D14.1)

B07.0 **Plantar wart**
Verruca plantaris

B07.8 **Other viral warts**
Common wart
Flat wart
Verruca plana

B07.9 **Viral wart, unspecified**

Item 1-16 Zoster: Also known as ***shingles*** and is caused by the same virus as chickenpox. After exposure, the virus lies dormant in nerve tissue and is activated by factors including aging, stress, suppression of the immune system, and certain medication. It begins as a unilateral rash that leads to blisters and sores on the skin. It may involve the nerve pathways of the eye, forehead, nose, and eyelids and may be very painful with long-term systemic effects.

N Newborn Age: 0   **P** Pediatric Age: 0–17   **M** Maternity DX: 12–55   **A** Adult Age: 15–124   ♀ Females Only   ♂ Males Only

653

CHAPTER 1 (A00-B99)

● **B08** **Other viral infections characterized by skin and mucous membrane lesions, not elsewhere classified**
> Excludes1   vesicular stomatitis virus disease (A93.8)

● **B08.0** **Other orthopoxvirus infections**
> Excludes2   monkeypox (B04)

  ● **B08.01** **Cowpox and vaccinia not from vaccine**

    B08.010 **Cowpox**

    B08.011 **Vaccinia not from vaccine**
> Excludes1   vaccinia (from vaccination) (generalized) (T88.1)

  B08.02 **Orf virus disease**
Contagious pustular dermatitis
Ecthyma contagiosum

  B08.03 **Pseudocowpox [milker's node]**

  B08.04 **Paravaccinia, unspecified**

  B08.09 **Other orthopoxvirus infections**
Orthopoxvirus infection NOS

B08.1 **Molluscum contagiosum**
Various skin diseases characterized by soft, rounded, cutaneous lesions

● **B08.2** **Exanthema subitum [sixth disease] Roseola infantum**
Acute, short-lived high fever in infants and young children followed by a rash mainly on the trunk, caused by human herpesvirus 6

  B08.20 **Exanthema subitum [sixth disease], unspecified Roseola infantum, unspecified**   P

  B08.21 **Exanthema subitum [sixth disease] due to human herpesvirus 6 Roseola infantum due to human herpesvirus 6**   P
Virus results in sudden rash; infection results in lifelong persistence

  B08.22 **Exanthema subitum [sixth disease] due to human herpesvirus 7 Roseola infantum due to human herpesvirus 7**   P

B08.3 **Erythema infectiosum [fifth disease]**
Moderately contagious, epidemic disease in children caused by B19 virus; onset of rash that begins as redness of cheeks, later there is rash on trunk and limbs; when this fades, there may be central clearing that leaves lacelike pattern

B08.4 **Enteroviral vesicular stomatitis with exanthem**
Hand, foot and mouth disease
Check your documentation—this code is HAND, foot, and mouth disease. Code B08.8 is foot and mouth disease.

B08.5 **Enteroviral vesicular pharyngitis**
Herpangina

● **B08.6** **Parapoxvirus infections**

  B08.60 **Parapoxvirus infection, unspecified**

  B08.61 **Bovine stomatitis**

  B08.62 **Sealpox**

  B08.69 **Other parapoxvirus infections**

● **B08.7** **Yatapoxvirus infections**

  B08.70 **Yatapoxvirus infection, unspecified**

  B08.71 **Tanapox virus disease**

  B08.72 **Yaba pox virus disease**
Yaba monkey tumor disease

  B08.79 **Other yatapoxvirus infections**

B08.8 **Other specified viral infections characterized by skin and mucous membrane lesions**
Enteroviral lymphonodular pharyngitis
Foot-and-mouth disease
Check your documentation. Code B08.4 is for HAND, foot, and mouth disease.
Poxvirus NEC

B09 **Unspecified viral infection characterized by skin and mucous membrane lesions**
Viral enanthema NOS
Viral exanthema NOS

OTHER HUMAN HERPESVIRUSES (B10)

● **B10** **Other human herpesviruses**
> Excludes2   cytomegalovirus (B25.9)
> Epstein-Barr virus (B27.0-)
> herpes NOS (B00.9)
> herpes simplex (B00.-)
> herpes zoster (B02.-)
> human herpesvirus NOS (B00.-)
> human herpesvirus 1 and 2 (B00.-)
> human herpesvirus 3 (B01.-, B02.-)
> human herpesvirus 4 (B27.0-)
> human herpesvirus 5 (B25.-)
> varicella (B01.-)
> zoster (B02.-)

● **B10.0** **Other human herpesvirus encephalitis**
> Excludes2   herpes encephalitis NOS (B00.4)
> herpes simplex encephalitis (B00.4)
> human herpesvirus encephalitis (B00.4)
> simian B herpes virus encephalitis (B00.4)

  B10.01 **Human herpesvirus 6 encephalitis**
Sudden rash or roseola

  B10.09 **Other human herpesvirus encephalitis**
Human herpesvirus 7 encephalitis
Virus closely related to human herpesvirus 6, but not known to cause any disease

● **B10.8** **Other human herpesvirus infection**

  B10.81 **Human herpesvirus 6 infection**
Causative agent of exanthema subitum that results in sudden rash

  B10.82 **Human herpesvirus 7 infection**
Closely related to human herpesvirus 6, but not known cause any disease

  B10.89 **Other human herpesvirus infection**
Human herpesvirus 8 infection
May be the cause of Kaposi sarcoma, a malignant tumor
Kaposi's sarcoma-associated herpesvirus infection

VIRAL HEPATITIS (B15-B19)

> Excludes1   sequelae of viral hepatitis (B94.2)
> Excludes2   cytomegaloviral hepatitis (B25.1)
> herpesviral [herpes simplex] hepatitis (B00.81)

● **B15** **Acute hepatitis A**

B15.0 **Hepatitis A with hepatic coma**

B15.9 **Hepatitis A without hepatic coma**
Hepatitis A (acute) (viral) NOS

Figure 1-6 Hepatitis B viral infection. **A.** Liver parenchyma showing hepatocytes with diffuse granular cytoplasm, so-called ground glass hepatocytes (H&E). **B.** Immunoperoxidase stains from the same case, showing cytoplasmic inclusions of viral particles. (From Kumar: Robbins and Cotran: Pathologic Basis of Disease, ed 8, Saunders, An Imprint of Elsevier, 2009)

Item 1–18 Hepatitis A (HAV) was formerly called epidemic, infectious, short-incubation, or acute catarrhal jaundice hepatitis. The primary transmission mode is the oral–fecal route. **Hepatitis B (HBV)** was formerly called long-incubation period, serum, or homologous serum hepatitis. Transmission modes are through blood from infected persons and from body fluids of infected mother to neonate. **Hepatitis C (HCV),** caused by the hepatitis C virus, is primarily transfusion associated. **Hepatitis D (HDV),** also called delta hepatitis, is caused by the hepatitis D virus in patients formerly or currently infected with hepatitis B. **Hepatitis E (HEV)** is also called enterically transmitted non-A, non-B hepatitis. The primary transmission mode is the oral–fecal route, usually through contaminated water.

▶ New   ⇒ Revised   ~~deleted~~ Deleted   Excludes 1   Excludes 2   Includes   Use additional   Code first   Code also   Key words
OGCR Official Guidelines   X Assign placeholder X   ● Use Additional Character(s)   ▷ Manifestation Code   **Coding Clinic**

● **B16**   **Acute hepatitis B**
    B16.0   **Acute hepatitis B with delta-agent with hepatic coma**
    B16.1   **Acute hepatitis B with delta-agent without hepatic coma**
    B16.2   **Acute hepatitis B without delta-agent with hepatic coma**
    B16.9   **Acute hepatitis B without delta-agent and without hepatic coma**
       Hepatitis B (acute) (viral) NOS
       Coding Clinic: 2016, Q3, P13

● **B17**   **Other acute viral hepatitis**
    B17.0   **Acute delta-(super) infection of hepatitis B carrier**
   ● B17.1   **Acute hepatitis C**
      B17.10   **Acute hepatitis C without hepatic coma**
         Acute hepatitis C NOS
      B17.11   **Acute hepatitis C with hepatic coma**
    B17.2   **Acute hepatitis E**
    B17.8   **Other specified acute viral hepatitis**
       Hepatitis non-A non-B (acute) (viral) NEC
    B17.9   **Acute viral hepatitis, unspecified**
       Acute hepatitis NOS
       Acute infectious hepatitis NOS

● **B18**   **Chronic viral hepatitis**
     Includes   Carrier of viral hepatitis
    B18.0   **Chronic viral hepatitis B with delta-agent**
    B18.1   **Chronic viral hepatitis B without delta-agent**
       Carrier of viral hepatitis B
       Chronic (viral) hepatitis B
    B18.2   **Chronic viral hepatitis C**
       Carrier of viral hepatitis C
       Coding Clinic: 2018, Q1, P4; 2017, Q1, P41
    B18.8   **Other chronic viral hepatitis**
       Carrier of other viral hepatitis
    B18.9   **Chronic viral hepatitis, unspecified**
       Carrier of unspecified viral hepatitis

● **B19**   **Unspecified viral hepatitis**
    B19.0   **Unspecified viral hepatitis with hepatic coma**
   ● B19.1   **Unspecified viral hepatitis B**
      B19.10   **Unspecified viral hepatitis B without hepatic coma**
         Unspecified viral hepatitis B NOS
      B19.11   **Unspecified viral hepatitis B with hepatic coma**
   ● B19.2   **Unspecified viral hepatitis C**
      B19.20   **Unspecified viral hepatitis C without hepatic coma**
         Viral hepatitis C NOS
      B19.21   **Unspecified viral hepatitis C with hepatic coma**
    B19.9   **Unspecified viral hepatitis without hepatic coma**
       Viral hepatitis NOS

Figure 1-7   Kaposi's sarcoma. There are large confluent hyperpigmented patch-stage lesions with lymphedema. (From Kanski, JJ: Clinical Diagnosis in Ophthalmology, London, Elsevier Mosby, 2006)

Item 1–19   **AIDS** (acquired immune deficiency syndrome) is caused by **HIV** (human immunodeficiency virus). HIV affects certain white blood cells (T-4 lymphocytes) and destroys the ability of the cells to fight infections, making patients susceptible to a host of infectious diseases (e.g., ***Pneumocystis carinii pneumonia (PCP), Kaposi's sarcoma,*** and **lymphoma**). ***AIDS-related complex (ARC)*** is an early stage of AIDS in which tests for HIV are positive but the symptoms are mild.

OGCR   Section I. C.1.a.

Certain Infectious and Parasitic Diseases (A00-B99)
  a.   Human Immunodeficiency Virus (HIV) Infections
    1)   Code only confirmed cases
       Code only confirmed cases of HIV infection illness. This is an exception to the hospital inpatient guideline Section II, H.
       In this context, "confirmation" does not require documentation of positive serology or culture for HIV; the provider's diagnostic statement that the patient is HIV positive or has an HIV-related illness is sufficient.

HUMAN IMMUNODEFICIENCY VIRUS [HIV] DISEASE (B20)

B20   **Human immunodeficiency virus [HIV] disease**
     Includes   acquired immune deficiency syndrome [AIDS]
            AIDS-related complex [ARC]
            HIV infection, symptomatic
     Code first Human immunodeficiency virus [HIV] disease complicating pregnancy, childbirth and the puerperium, if applicable (O98.7-)
     Use additional code(s) to identify all manifestations of HIV infection
     Excludes1   asymptomatic human immunodeficiency virus [HIV] infection status (Z21)
            exposure to HIV virus (Z20.6)
            inconclusive serologic evidence of HIV (R75)

OTHER VIRAL DISEASES (B25-B34)

● **B25**   **Cytomegaloviral disease**
     AKA: HCMV or Human Herpesvirus 5 (HHV-5)
     Excludes1   congenital cytomegalovirus infection (P35.1)
            cytomegaloviral mononucleosis (B27.1-)
    B25.0   **Cytomegaloviral pneumonitis**
    B25.1   **Cytomegaloviral hepatitis**
    B25.2   **Cytomegaloviral pancreatitis**
    B25.8   **Other cytomegaloviral diseases**
       Cytomegaloviral encephalitis
    B25.9   **Cytomegaloviral disease, unspecified**

● **B26**   **Mumps**
     Includes   epidemic parotitis
            infectious parotitis
     Acute, contagious, viral disease
    B26.0   **Mumps orchitis** ♂
    B26.1   **Mumps meningitis**
    B26.2   **Mumps encephalitis**
    B26.3   **Mumps pancreatitis**
   ● B26.8   **Mumps with other complications**
      B26.81   **Mumps hepatitis**
      B26.82   **Mumps myocarditis**
      B26.83   **Mumps nephritis**
      B26.84   **Mumps polyneuropathy**
      B26.85   **Mumps arthritis**
      B26.89   **Other mumps complications**
    B26.9   **Mumps without complication**
       Mumps NOS
       Mumps parotitis NOS

CHAPTER 1 (A00-B99)

CHAPTER 1 (A00-B99)

● **B27**   **Infectious mononucleosis**
    Includes   glandular fever
           monocytic angina
           Pfeiffer's disease

● **B27.0**   **Gammaherpesviral mononucleosis**
    AKA: Pfeiffer's disease, infective mononucleosis
    Mononucleosis due to Epstein-Barr virus

    B27.00   **Gammaherpesviral mononucleosis without complication**
       Infective mononucleosis

    B27.01   **Gammaherpesviral mononucleosis with polyneuropathy**

    B27.02   **Gammaherpesviral mononucleosis with meningitis**

    B27.09   **Gammaherpesviral mononucleosis with other complications**
       Hepatomegaly in gammaherpesviral mononucleosis

● **B27.1**   **Cytomegaloviral mononucleosis**
    Infectious disease resembling infectious mononucleosis

    B27.10   **Cytomegaloviral mononucleosis without complications**

    B27.11   **Cytomegaloviral mononucleosis with polyneuropathy**

    B27.12   **Cytomegaloviral mononucleosis with meningitis**

    B27.19   **Cytomegaloviral mononucleosis with other complication**
       Hepatomegaly in cytomegaloviral mononucleosis

● **B27.8**   **Other infectious mononucleosis**

    B27.80   **Other infectious mononucleosis without complication**

    B27.81   **Other infectious mononucleosis with polyneuropathy**

    B27.82   **Other infectious mononucleosis with meningitis**

    B27.89   **Other infectious mononucleosis with other complication**
       Hepatomegaly in other infectious mononucleosis

● **B27.9**   **Infectious mononucleosis, unspecified**

    B27.90   **Infectious mononucleosis, unspecified without complication**

    B27.91   **Infectious mononucleosis, unspecified with polyneuropathy**

    B27.92   **Infectious mononucleosis, unspecified with meningitis**

    B27.99   **Infectious mononucleosis, unspecified with other complication**
       Hepatomegaly in unspecified infectious mononucleosis

● **B30**   **Viral conjunctivitis**
    Excludes1   herpesviral [herpes simplex] ocular disease (B00.5)
           ocular zoster (B02.3)

    B30.0   **Keratoconjunctivitis due to adenovirus**
       Epidemic keratoconjunctivitis
       Shipyard eye

    B30.1   **Conjunctivitis due to adenovirus**
       Acute adenoviral follicular conjunctivitis
       Swimming-pool conjunctivitis

    B30.2   **Viral pharyngoconjunctivitis**

    B30.3   **Acute epidemic hemorrhagic conjunctivitis (enteroviral)**
       Conjunctivitis due to coxsackievirus 24
       Conjunctivitis due to enterovirus 70
       Hemorrhagic conjunctivitis (acute)(epidemic)

    B30.8   **Other viral conjunctivitis**
       Newcastle conjunctivitis

    B30.9   **Viral conjunctivitis, unspecified**

● **B33**   **Other viral diseases, not elsewhere classified**

    B33.0   **Epidemic myalgia**
       Acute infectious disease, caused by group A coxsackie viruses or other enteroviruses with symptoms that include sudden pain in chest or upper abdomen with fever
       Bornholm disease

    B33.1   **Ross River disease**
       Epidemic polyarthritis and exanthema
       Ross River fever

●   **B33.2**   **Viral carditis**
       Coxsackie (virus) carditis

    B33.20   **Viral carditis, unspecified**
    B33.21   **Viral endocarditis**
    B33.22   **Viral myocarditis**
    B33.23   **Viral pericarditis**
    B33.24   **Viral cardiomyopathy**

    B33.3   **Retrovirus infections, not elsewhere classified**
       Retrovirus infection NOS

    B33.4   **Hantavirus (cardio)-pulmonary syndrome [HPS] [HCPS]**
       Hantavirus disease with pulmonary manifestations
       Sin nombre virus disease
       Use additional code to identify any associated acute kidney failure (N17.9)
       Excludes1   hantavirus disease with renal manifestations (A98.5)
           hemorrhagic fever with renal manifestations (A98.5)

    B33.8   **Other specified viral diseases**
       Excludes1   anogenital human papillomavirus infection (A63.0)
           viral warts due to human papillomavirus infection (B07)

● **B34**   **Viral infection of unspecified site**
    Excludes1   anogenital human papillomavirus infection (A63.0)
           cytomegaloviral disease NOS (B25.9)
           herpesvirus [herpes simplex] infection NOS (B00.9)
           retrovirus infection NOS (B33.3)
           viral agents as the cause of diseases classified elsewhere (B97.-)
           viral warts due to human papillomavirus infection (B07)

    B34.0   **Adenovirus infection, unspecified**
    B34.1   **Enterovirus infection, unspecified**
       Intestinal tract infection
       Coxsackievirus infection NOS
       Echovirus infection NOS

    B34.2   **Coronavirus infection, unspecified**
       Excludes1   pneumonia due to SARS-associated coronavirus (J12.81)

    B34.3   **Parvovirus infection, unspecified**
    B34.4   **Papovavirus infection, unspecified**
    B34.8   **Other viral infections of unspecified site**
    B34.9   **Viral infection, unspecified**
       Viremia NOS
       Coding Clinic: 2016, Q3, P10

▶ New   ⇒ Revised   ~~deleted~~ Deleted   Excludes 1   Excludes 2   Includes   Use additional   Code first   Code also   Key words

OGCR Official Guidelines   X Assign placeholder X   ● Use Additional Character(s)   ▶ Manifestation Code   **Coding Clinic**

MYCOSES (B35-B49)

Excludes2   hypersensitivity pneumonitis due to organic dust (J67.-)

mycosis fungoides (C84.0-)

● **B35**   **Dermatophytosis**

AKA tinea or ringworm

Includes   favus

infections due to species of Epidermophyton, Micro-sporum and Trichophyton

tinea, any type except those in B36.-

B35.0   **Tinea barbae and tinea capitis**

Beard ringworm

Kerion

Scalp ringworm

Sycosis, mycotic

B35.1   **Tinea unguium**

White patches or pits on surface or edges of nails, followed by infection under nail plate

Dermatophytic onychia

Dermatophytosis of nail

Onychomycosis

Ringworm of nails

B35.2   **Tinea manuum**

Tinea of hands

Dermatophytosis of hand

Hand ringworm

B35.3   **Tinea pedis**

Tinea affecting feet

Athlete's foot

Dermatophytosis of foot

Foot ringworm

B35.4   **Tinea corporis**

Infecting skin areas other than hands

Ringworm of the body

B35.5   **Tinea imbricata**

Chronic tropical tinea corporis; AKA Oriental ringworm, tinea inguinalis, tinea cruris

Tokelau

B35.6   **Tinea cruris**

In groin or perineal area, spreading to adjacent regions; AKA jock itch, eczema marginatum, ringworm of groin, or t inguinalis

Dhobi itch

Groin ringworm

Jock itch

B35.8   **Other dermatophytoses**

Disseminated dermatophytosis

Granulomatous dermatophytosis

B35.9   **Dermatophytosis, unspecified**

Ringworm NOS

● **B36**   **Other superficial mycoses**

B36.0   **Pityriasis versicolor**

Common, chronic, symptomless disorder that includes macular patches of various sizes and shapes; AKA liver spots

Tinea flava

Tinea versicolor

B36.1   **Tinea nigra**

Minor fungal infection, with dark lesions, usually on skin of hands

Keratomycosis nigricans palmaris

Microsporosis nigra

Pityriasis nigra

B36.2   **White piedra**

White to light brown nodules on hair of beard, axilla, or groin; AKA trichosporosis

Tinea blanca

B36.3   **Black piedra**

Characterized by small black or brown nodules on shafts of scalp hair

B36.8   **Other specified superficial mycoses**

B36.9   **Superficial mycosis, unspecified**

Figure 1-8   Oral candidiasis (thrush). (From James WD, Berger T, Elston D: Andrews' Diseases of the Skin: Clinical Dermatology, 11e, Saunders, 2011)

Item 1–20   **Candidiasis,** also called oidiomycosis or moniliasis, is a fungal infection. It most often appears on moist cutaneous areas of the body but can also be responsible for a variety of systemic infections such as endocarditis, meningitis, arthritis, and myositis. Antifungal medications cure most yeast infections.

● **B37**   **Candidiasis**

Includes   candidosis

moniliasis

Excludes1   neonatal candidiasis (P37.5)

B37.0   **Candidal stomatitis**

Oral thrush

B37.1   **Pulmonary candidiasis**

Candidal bronchitis

Candidal pneumonia

B37.2   **Candidiasis of skin and nail**

Candidal onychia

Candidal paronychia

Excludes2   diaper dermatitis (L22)

B37.3   **Candidiasis of vulva and vagina ♀**

Candidal vulvovaginitis

Monilial vulvovaginitis

Vaginal thrush

● **B37.4**   **Candidiasis of other urogenital sites**

B37.41   **Candidal cystitis and urethritis**

B37.42   **Candidal balanitis ♂**

Male condition only

B37.49   **Other urogenital candidiasis**

Candidal pyelonephritis

B37.5   **Candidal meningitis**

B37.6   **Candidal endocarditis**

B37.7   **Candidal sepsis**

Disseminated candidiasis systemic candidiasis

● **B37.8**   **Candidiasis of other sites**

B37.81   **Candidal esophagitis**

B37.82   **Candidal enteritis**

Candidal proctitis

B37.83   **Candidal cheilitis**

Inflammation affecting lip

B37.84   **Candidal otitis externa**

Inflammation of external auditory canal

B37.89   **Other sites of candidiasis**

Infection manifested by invasive candidiasis

Candidal osteomyelitis

B37.9   **Candidiasis, unspecified**

Thrush NOS

● **B38**   **Coccidioidomycosis**

Fungal disease; AKA coccidioidosis, coccidioidal granuloma, Posadas, or Posadas-Wernicke disease

B38.0   **Acute pulmonary coccidioidomycosis**

B38.1   **Chronic pulmonary coccidioidomycosis**

B38.2   **Pulmonary coccidioidomycosis, unspecified**

B38.3   **Cutaneous coccidioidomycosis**

B38.4   **Coccidioidomycosis meningitis**

B38.7   **Disseminated coccidioidomycosis**

Generalized coccidioidomycosis

● **B38.8**   **Other forms of coccidioidomycosis**

B38.81   **Prostatic coccidioidomycosis ♂**

B38.89   **Other forms of coccidioidomycosis**

B38.9   **Coccidioidomycosis, unspecified**

CHAPTER 1 (A00-B99)

Item 1–21 Bird and bat droppings that fall into the soil give rise to a fungus that can spread airborne spores. When inhaled into the lungs, these spores divide and multiply into lesions. Histoplasmosis capsulatum takes three forms: primary (lodged in the lungs only), chronic (resembles TB), and disseminated (infection has moved to other organs). This is an opportunistic infection in immunosuppressed patients.

● B39   **Histoplasmosis**
> *Infection resulting from inhalation or ingestion of spores; AKA Darling disease*
>
> Code first *associated AIDS (B2Ø)*
>
> Use additional code for any associated manifestations, such as:
> endocarditis (I39)
> meningitis (GØ2)
> pericarditis (I32)
> ⇒ retinitis (H32)

    B39.Ø   **Acute pulmonary histoplasmosis capsulati**

    B39.1   **Chronic pulmonary histoplasmosis capsulati**

    B39.2   **Pulmonary histoplasmosis capsulati, unspecified**

    B39.3   **Disseminated histoplasmosis capsulati**
         Generalized histoplasmosis capsulati

    B39.4   **Histoplasmosis capsulati, unspecified**
         American histoplasmosis

    B39.5   **Histoplasmosis duboisii**
         African histoplasmosis

    B39.9   **Histoplasmosis, unspecified**

● B40   **Blastomycosis**
> *Rare and potentially fatal infection caused by inhaling fungus found in moist soil in temperate climates.*
>
> **Excludes1**   Brazilian blastomycosis (B41.-)
> keloidal blastomycosis (B48.Ø)

    B40.Ø   **Acute pulmonary blastomycosis**

    B40.1   **Chronic pulmonary blastomycosis**

    B40.2   **Pulmonary blastomycosis, unspecified**

    B40.3   **Cutaneous blastomycosis**

    B40.7   **Disseminated blastomycosis**
         Generalized blastomycosis

   ● B40.8   **Other forms of blastomycosis**

       B40.81   **Blastomycotic meningoencephalitis**
          Meningomyelitis due to blastomycosis

       B40.89   **Other forms of blastomycosis**

    B40.9   **Blastomycosis, unspecified**

● B41   **Paracoccidioidomycosis**
> *Fungal infection usually chronic that begins in lungs, spreads to mucocutaneous areas which may extend to skin, tonsils, gastrointestinal lymphatics, liver, and spleen; AKA Almeida or Lutz-Splendore-Almeida disease, Brazilian or South American blastomycosis, or paracoccidioidal granuloma*
>
> **Includes**   Brazilian blastomycosis
> Lutz' disease

    B41.Ø   **Pulmonary paracoccidioidomycosis**

    B41.7   **Disseminated paracoccidioidomycosis**
         Generalized paracoccidioidomycosis

    B41.8   **Other forms of paracoccidioidomycosis**

    B41.9   **Paracoccidioidomycosis, unspecified**

● B42   **Sporotrichosis**
> *Chronic fungal infection with nodular lesions*

    B42.Ø   **Pulmonary sporotrichosis**

    B42.1   **Lymphocutaneous sporotrichosis**

    B42.7   **Disseminated sporotrichosis**
         Generalized sporotrichosis

   ● B42.8   **Other forms of sporotrichosis**

       B42.81   **Cerebral sporotrichosis**
          Meningitis due to sporotrichosis

       B42.82   **Sporotrichosis arthritis**

       B42.89   **Other forms of sporotrichosis**

    B42.9   **Sporotrichosis, unspecified**

● B43   **Chromomycosis and pheomycotic abscess**
> *Chronic fungal infection of skin, initiated at site of puncture affecting lower limb or foot (mossy foot)*

    B43.Ø   **Cutaneous chromomycosis**
         Dermatitis verrucosa

    B43.1   **Pheomycotic brain abscess**
         Cerebral chromomycosis

    B43.2   **Subcutaneous pheomycotic abscess and cyst**

    B43.8   **Other forms of chromomycosis**

    B43.9   **Chromomycosis, unspecified**

● B44   **Aspergillosis**
> *Infection marked by inflammatory lesions in skin, ear, orbit, nasal sinuses, lungs, and occasionally bones and meninges*
>
> **Includes**   aspergilloma

    B44.Ø   **Invasive pulmonary aspergillosis**

    B44.1   **Other pulmonary aspergillosis**

    B44.2   **Tonsillar aspergillosis**

    B44.7   **Disseminated aspergillosis**
         Generalized aspergillosis

   ● B44.8   **Other forms of aspergillosis**

       B44.81   **Allergic bronchopulmonary aspergillosis**

       B44.89   **Other forms of aspergillosis**

    B44.9   **Aspergillosis, unspecified**

● B45   **Cryptococcosis**
> *Infection in the immunocompromised and fatal if left untreated; AKA torulosis, Buschke, or Busse-Buschke disease*

    B45.Ø   **Pulmonary cryptococcosis**

    B45.1   **Cerebral cryptococcosis**
         Cryptococcal meningitis
         Cryptococcosis meningocerebralis

    B45.2   **Cutaneous cryptococcosis**

    B45.3   **Osseous cryptococcosis**

    B45.7   **Disseminated cryptococcosis**
         Generalized cryptococcosis

    B45.8   **Other forms of cryptococcosis**

    B45.9   **Cryptococcosis, unspecified**

● B46   **Zygomycosis**
> *Fungal infections including subcutaneous lesions and infection of sinuses, brain, or lungs*

    B46.Ø   **Pulmonary mucormycosis**
         Fungal infection affecting lung

    B46.1   **Rhinocerebral mucormycosis**

    B46.2   **Gastrointestinal mucormycosis**

    B46.3   **Cutaneous mucormycosis**
         Subcutaneous mucormycosis

    B46.4   **Disseminated mucormycosis**
         Generalized mucormycosis

    B46.5   **Mucormycosis, unspecified**

    B46.8   **Other zygomycoses**
         Entomophthoromycosis

    B46.9   **Zygomycosis, unspecified**
         Phycomycosis NOS

● B47   **Mycetoma**
> *Slow progressive, destructive fungal infection of cutaneous and subcutaneous tissues, fascia, and bone, primarily seen in foot (Madura foot) or leg*

    B47.Ø   **Eumycetoma**
         Madura foot, mycotic Maduromycosis

    B47.1   **Actinomycetoma**

    B47.9   **Mycetoma, unspecified**
         Madura foot NOS

CHAPTER 1 (AØØ-B99)

▶ New   ⇒ Revised   ~~deleted~~ Deleted   Excludes 1   Excludes 2   Includes   Use additional   Code first   Code also   Key words

OGCR Official Guidelines   X Assign placeholder X   ● Use Additional Character(s)   ▶ Manifestation Code   **Coding Clinic**

● **B48   Other mycoses, not elsewhere classified**
     B48.0   Lobomycosis
         Infection with symptoms of red, smooth, hard cutaneous
             nodules resembling keloids
         Keloidal blastomycosis
         Lobo's disease

     B48.1   Rhinosporidiosis
         Chronic, localized granulomatous fungal infection, affecting
             mucocutaneous tissues, usually of nose characterized by
             polyps, papillomas, and wartlike lesions

     B48.2   Allescheriasis
         Fungal infection
         Infection due to Pseudallescheria boydii
         Excludes1   eumycetoma (B47.0)

     B48.3   Geotrichosis
         Fungal infection usually of bronchi, lungs, mouth, or
             intestinal tract
         Geotrichum stomatitis

     B48.4   Penicillosis
         Fungal infection

     B48.8   Other specified mycoses
         Adiaspiromycosis
         Infection of tissue and organs by Alternaria
         Infection of tissue and organs by Drechslera
         Infection of tissue and organs by Fusarium
         Infection of tissue and organs by saprophytic fungi
         NEC

B49   Unspecified mycosis
     Fungemia NOS

PROTOZOAL DISEASES (B50-B64)

     Excludes1   amebiasis (A06.-)
                 other protozoal intestinal diseases (A07.-)

● **B50   Plasmodium falciparum malaria**
     Severe form of malaria that can be fatal
     Includes   mixed infections of Plasmodium falciparum with
                any other Plasmodium species

     B50.0   Plasmodium falciparum malaria with cerebral complications
         Cerebral malaria NOS

     B50.8   Other severe and complicated Plasmodium falciparum malaria
         Severe or complicated Plasmodium falciparum malaria
             NOS

     B50.9   Plasmodium falciparum malaria, unspecified

● **B51   Plasmodium vivax malaria**
     Includes   mixed infections of Plasmodium vivax with other
                Plasmodium species, except Plasmodium
                falciparum
  ⇒ **Excludes1**   plasmodium vivax with Plasmodium falciparum
                 (B50.-)

     B51.0   Plasmodium vivax malaria with rupture of spleen
     B51.8   Plasmodium vivax malaria with other complications
     B51.9   Plasmodium vivax malaria without complication
         Plasmodium vivax malaria NOS

● **B52   Plasmodium malariae malaria**
     Causes fever that recurs at approximately three-day intervals (quartan
         fever), longer than two-day (tertian) intervals of other malarial
         parasites
     Includes   mixed infections of Plasmodium malariae
                with other Plasmodium species, except
                Plasmodium falciparum and Plasmodium
                vivax
     Excludes1   plasmodium falciparum (B50.-)
                 plasmodium vivax (B51.-)

     B52.0   Plasmodium malariae malaria with nephropathy
     B52.8   Plasmodium malariae malaria with other complications
     B52.9   Plasmodium malariae malaria without complication
         Plasmodium malariae malaria NOS

● **B53   Other specified malaria**
     B53.0   Plasmodium ovale malaria
         Least diagnosed type of malaria spread by female mosquitoes
             of rare species
         Excludes1   plasmodium ovale with Plasmodium
                 falciparum (B50.-)
                 plasmodium ovale with Plasmodium
                 malariae (B52.-)
                 plasmodium ovale with Plasmodium
                 vivax (B51.-)

     B53.1   Malaria due to simian plasmodia
         Malaria-like disease (parasite infection)
         Excludes1   malaria due to simian plasmodia with
                 Plasmodium falciparum (B50.-)
                 malaria due to simian plasmodia with
                 Plasmodium malariae (B52.-)
                 malaria due to simian plasmodia with
                 Plasmodium ovale (B53.0)
                 malaria due to simian plasmodia with
                 Plasmodium vivax (B51.-)

     B53.8   Other malaria, not elsewhere classified

  B54   Unspecified malaria

● **B55   Leishmaniasis**
     Protozoal infection
     B55.0   Visceral leishmaniasis
         Kala-azar
         Post-kala-azar dermal leishmaniasis

     B55.1   Cutaneous leishmaniasis
     B55.2   Mucocutaneous leishmaniasis
     B55.9   Leishmaniasis, unspecified

● **B56   African trypanosomiasis**
     Human African trypanosomiasis (HAT) is transmitted by fly bites
     B56.0   Gambiense trypanosomiasis
         Infection due to Trypanosoma brucei gambiense
         West African sleeping sickness

     B56.1   Rhodesiense trypanosomiasis
         East African sleeping sickness
         Infection due to Trypanosoma brucei rhodesiense

     B56.9   African trypanosomiasis, unspecified
         Sleeping sickness NOS

● **B57   Chagas' disease**
     Tropical parasitic disease
     Includes   American trypanosomiasis
                infection due to Trypanosoma cruzi

     B57.0   Acute Chagas' disease with heart involvement
         Acute Chagas' disease with myocarditis

     B57.1   Acute Chagas' disease without heart involvement
         Acute Chagas' disease NOS

     B57.2   Chagas' disease (chronic) with heart involvement
         American trypanosomiasis NOS
         Chagas' disease (chronic) NOS
         Chagas' disease (chronic) with myocarditis
         Trypanosomiasis NOS

●   **B57.3   Chagas' disease (chronic) with digestive system involvement**
         B57.30   Chagas' disease with digestive system involvement, unspecified
         B57.31   Megaesophagus in Chagas' disease
         B57.32   Megacolon in Chagas' disease
         B57.39   Other digestive system involvement in Chagas' disease

●   **B57.4   Chagas' disease (chronic) with nervous system involvement**
         B57.40   Chagas' disease with nervous system involvement, unspecified
         B57.41   Meningitis in Chagas' disease
         B57.42   Meningoencephalitis in Chagas' disease
         B57.49   Other nervous system involvement in Chagas' disease

     B57.5   Chagas' disease (chronic) with other organ involvement

Item 1-22 Toxoplasmosis is caused by the protozoa **Toxoplasma gondii,** of which the house cat can be a host. Human infection occurs when contact is made with materials containing the pathogen, such as feces, contaminated soil, or ingestion of infected lamb, goat, or pork. Of the infected, very few have symptoms because a healthy person's immune system keeps the parasite from causing illness. When the immune system is compromised, symptoms may occur. Clinical symptoms include flu-like symptoms, but the disease progresses to include the eyes and the brain in babies.

● **B58 Toxoplasmosis**
  Infection by protozoon transmitted in cysts in feces of cats
      Includes infection due to Toxoplasma gondii
      Excludes1 congenital toxoplasmosis (P37.1)
  ● **B58.0 Toxoplasma oculopathy**
      B58.00 Toxoplasma oculopathy, unspecified
      B58.01 Toxoplasma chorioretinitis
      B58.09 Other toxoplasma oculopathy
          Toxoplasma uveitis
    B58.1 Toxoplasma hepatitis
    B58.2 Toxoplasma meningoencephalitis
    B58.3 Pulmonary toxoplasmosis
  ● **B58.8 Toxoplasmosis with other organ involvement**
      B58.81 Toxoplasma myocarditis
      B58.82 Toxoplasma myositis
      B58.83 Toxoplasma tubulo-interstitial nephropathy
          Toxoplasma pyelonephritis
      B58.89 Toxoplasmosis with other organ involvement
    B58.9 Toxoplasmosis, unspecified

  B59 Pneumocystosis
      Caused by fungus
      Pneumonia due to Pneumocystis carinii
      Pneumonia due to Pneumocystis jiroveci

● **B60 Other protozoal diseases, not elsewhere classified**
      Excludes1 cryptosporidiosis (A07.2)
          intestinal microsporidiosis (A07.8)
          isosporiasis (A07.3)
    B60.0 Babesiosis
        Tickborne disease caused by microscopic organisms
        Piroplasmosis
  ● **B60.1 Acanthamebiasis**
      B60.10 Acanthamebiasis, unspecified
      B60.11 Meningoencephalitis due to Acanthamoeba (culbertsoni)
      B60.12 Conjunctivitis due to Acanthamoeba
      B60.13 Keratoconjunctivitis due to Acanthamoeba
      B60.19 Other acanthamebic disease
    B60.2 Naegleriasis
        Infection with microscopic organisms
        Primary amebic meningoencephalitis
    B60.8 Other specified protozoal diseases
        Microsporidiosis

  B64 Unspecified protozoal disease

HELMINTHIASES (B65-B83)

Diseases or infestations caused by parasitic worms

● **B65 Schistosomiasis [bilharziasis]**
    Infection with flukes (flat parasitic worms)
      Includes snail fever
    B65.0 Schistosomiasis due to Schistosoma haematobium [urinary schistosomiasis]
    B65.1 Schistosomiasis due to Schistosoma mansoni [intestinal schistosomiasis]
    B65.2 Schistosomiasis due to Schistosoma japonicum
        Asiatic schistosomiasis

    B65.3 Cercarial dermatitis
        Swimmer's itch
    B65.8 Other schistosomiasis
        Infection due to Schistosoma intercalatum
        Infection due to Schistosoma mattheei
        Infection due to Schistosoma mekongi
    B65.9 Schistosomiasis, unspecified
● **B66 Other fluke infections**
      Trematode (parasitic worms)
    B66.0 Opisthorchiasis
        Infection due to cat liver fluke
        Infection due to Opisthorchis (felineus)(viverrini)
    B66.1 Clonorchiasis
        Chinese liver fluke disease
        Infection due to Clonorchis sinensis
        Oriental liver fluke disease
    B66.2 Dicroceliasis
        Liver fluke
        Infection due to Dicrocoelium dendriticum
        Lancet fluke infection
    B66.3 Fascioliasis
        Infection due to Fasciola gigantica
        Infection due to Fasciola hepatica
        Infection due to Fasciola indica
        Sheep liver fluke disease
    B66.4 Paragonimiasis
        Infection due to Paragonimus species
        Lung fluke disease
        Pulmonary distomiasis
    B66.5 Fasciolopsiasis
        Largest intestinal fluke in humans
        Infection due to Fasciolopsis buski
        Intestinal distomiasis
    B66.8 Other specified fluke infections
        Echinostomiasis
        Heterophyiasis
        Metagonimiasis
        Nanophyetiasis
        Watsoniasis
    B66.9 Fluke infection, unspecified
● **B67 Echinococcosis**
      Larval forms of tapeworms usually of liver or lungs
      Includes hydatidosis
    B67.0 Echinococcus granulosus infection of liver
    B67.1 Echinococcus granulosus infection of lung
    B67.2 Echinococcus granulosus infection of bone
  ● **B67.3 Echinococcus granulosus infection, other and multiple sites**
      B67.31 Echinococcus granulosus infection, thyroid gland
      B67.32 Echinococcus granulosus infection, multiple sites
      B67.39 Echinococcus granulosus infection, other sites
    B67.4 Echinococcus granulosus infection, unspecified
        Dog tapeworm (infection)
    B67.5 Echinococcus multilocularis infection of liver
  ● **B67.6 Echinococcus multilocularis infection, other and multiple sites**
      B67.61 Echinococcus multilocularis infection, multiple sites
      B67.69 Echinococcus multilocularis infection, other sites

Item 1-23 Echinococcosis: Also known as hydatid disease; is caused by Echinococcus granulosus, E. multilocularis, and E. vogeli tapeworms; and is contracted from infected food. Found in southern South America, the Mediterranean, the Middle East, central Asia, and Africa and uncommon in the United States but has been reported in California, New Mexico, Arizona and Utah. The disease is treated with medication over a long course, as it is resistive.

▶ New ⇒ Revised ~~deleted~~ Deleted Excludes 1 Excludes 2 Includes Use additional Code first Code also Key words
OGCR Official Guidelines X Assign placeholder X ● Use Additional Character(s) ▷ Manifestation Code **Coding Clinic**

B67.7   Echinococcus multilocularis infection, unspecified

B67.8   Echinococcosis, unspecified, of liver

● B67.9   Echinococcosis, other and unspecified

   B67.90   Echinococcosis, unspecified
            Echinococcosis NOS

   B67.99   Other echinococcosis

● B68   Taeniasis
   Intestinal tapeworm (cestode) infection from raw or undercooked meat of infected animal

   Excludes1   cysticercosis (B69.-)

   B68.0   Taenia solium taeniasis
           Pork tapeworm (infection)

   B68.1   Taenia saginata taeniasis
           Beef tapeworm (infection)
           Infection due to adult tapeworm Taenia saginata

   B68.9   Taeniasis, unspecified

● B69   Cysticercosis
   Systemic illness caused by the larvae of pork tapeworm

   Includes   cysticerciasis infection due to larval form of Taenia solium

   B69.0   Cysticercosis of central nervous system

   B69.1   Cysticercosis of eye

● B69.8   Cysticercosis of other sites

   B69.81   Myositis in cysticercosis

   B69.89   Cysticercosis of other sites

   B69.9   Cysticercosis, unspecified

● B70   Diphyllobothriasis and sparganosis
   Infection with tapeworms seen most often from inadequately cooked fish

   B70.0   Diphyllobothriasis
           Diphyllobothrium (adult) (latum) (pacificum) infection
           Fish tapeworm (infection)

           Excludes2   larval diphyllobothriasis (B70.1)

   B70.1   Sparganosis
           Infection with migrating tapeworm larvae, which invade subcutaneous tissues, causing inflammation and fibrosis that resembles cellulitis
           Infection due to Sparganum (mansoni) (proliferum)
           Infection due to Spirometra larva
           Larval diphyllobothriasis
           Spirometrosis

● B71   Other cestode infections

   B71.0   Hymenolepiasis
           Intestinal infestation with tapeworms
           Dwarf tapeworm infection
           Rat tapeworm (infection)

   B71.1   Dipylidiasis
           Infection with tapeworm common to dogs and cats and seen in children having close contact with infected pets

   B71.8   Other specified cestode infections
           Infection by the larval stage of a tapeworm, usually through fruit or vegetables
           Coenurosis

   B71.9   Cestode infection, unspecified
           Tapeworm (infection) NOS

B72   Dracunculiasis
   Infection with roundworms

   Includes   guinea worm infection
                  infection due to Dracunculus medinensis

● B73   Onchocerciasis
   Infection with parasitic worm

   Includes   onchocerca volvulus infection
                  onchocercosis
                  river blindness

● B73.0   Onchocerciasis with eye disease

   B73.00   Onchocerciasis with eye involvement, unspecified

   B73.01   Onchocerciasis with endophthalmitis

   B73.02   Onchocerciasis with glaucoma

   B73.09   Onchocerciasis with other eye involvement
            Infestation of eyelid due to onchocerciasis

   B73.1   Onchocerciasis without eye disease

● B74   Filariasis
   Infestation with slender threadlike worms

   Excludes2   onchocerciasis (B73)
                   tropical (pulmonary) eosinophilia NOS (J82)

   B74.0   Filariasis due to Wuchereria bancrofti
           Bancroftian elephantiasis
           Bancroftian filariasis

   B74.1   Filariasis due to Brugia malayi

   B74.2   Filariasis due to Brugia timori

   B74.3   Loiasis
           Infection with round worms growing in subcutaneous connective tissue
           Calabar swelling
           Eyeworm disease of Africa
           Loa loa infection

   B74.4   Mansonelliasis
           Infection with filarial parasite
           Infection due to Mansonella ozzardi
           Infection due to Mansonella perstans
           Infection due to Mansonella streptocerca

   B74.8   Other filariases
           Dirofilariasis

   B74.9   Filariasis, unspecified

B75   Trichinellosis
   Infestation with parasitic roundworms ingested in undercooked contaminated meat

   Includes   infection due to Trichinella species trichiniasis

● B76   Hookworm diseases
   Occurs in hot, humid parts of world where larvae are soil borne, enter digestive tract through skin of feet/legs or in contaminated food/water; AKA ground itch

   Includes   uncinariasis

   B76.0   Ancylostomiasis
           Infection due to Ancylostoma species

   B76.1   Necatoriasis
           Infection due to Necator americanus

   B76.8   Other hookworm diseases

   B76.9   Hookworm disease, unspecified
           Cutaneous larva migrans NOS

● B77   Ascariasis
   Infection by roundworm in small intestine

   Includes   ascaridiasis
                  roundworm infection

   B77.0   Ascariasis with intestinal complications

● B77.8   Ascariasis with other complications

   B77.81   Ascariasis pneumonia

   B77.89   Ascariasis with other complications

   B77.9   Ascariasis, unspecified

CHAPTER 1 (A00-B99)

● **B78** **Strongyloidiasis**
Infection with adult female roundworms
> **Excludes1**   trichostrongyliasis (B81.2)

    B78.0 **Intestinal strongyloidiasis**
    B78.1 **Cutaneous strongyloidiasis**
    B78.7 **Disseminated strongyloidiasis**
    B78.9 **Strongyloidiasis, unspecified**

 B79 **Trichuriasis**
Intestinal infection with roundworms
> **Includes**   trichocephaliasis
>   whipworm (disease)(infection)

 B80 **Enterobiasis**
Intestinal infection with pinworms
> **Includes**   oxyuriasis
>   pinworm infection
>   threadworm infection

● **B81** **Other intestinal helminthiases, not elsewhere classified**
Diseases or infestations caused by parasitic worms
> **Excludes1**   angiostrongyliasis due to:
>   Angiostrongylus cantonensis (B83.2)
>   Parastrongylus cantonensis (B83.2)

    B81.0 **Anisakiasis**
Roundworm infection via contaminated undercooked infected fish or marine mammals
Infection due to Anisakis larva

    B81.1 **Intestinal capillariasis**
Infestation with of parasites (nematodes)
Capillariasis NOS
Infection due to Capillaria philippinensis
> **Excludes2**   hepatic capillariasis (B83.8)

    B81.2 **Trichostrongyliasis**
    B81.3 **Intestinal angiostrongyliasis**
Angiostrongyliasis due to:
    Angiostrongylus costaricensis (B83.2)
    Parastrongylus costaricensis (B83.2)

    B81.4 **Mixed intestinal helminthiases**
Infection due to intestinal helminths classified to more than one of the categories B65.0-B81.3 and B81.8
Mixed helminthiasis NOS

    B81.8 **Other specified intestinal helminthiases**
Infection due to Oesophagostomum species [esophagostomiasis]
Infection due to Ternidens diminutus [ternidensiasis]

● **B82** **Unspecified intestinal parasitism**
    B82.0 **Intestinal helminthiasis, unspecified**
Infected with worms
    B82.9 **Intestinal parasitism, unspecified**

● **B83** **Other helminthiases**
Caused by parasitic worms
> **Excludes1**   capillariasis NOS (B81.1)
> **Excludes2**   intestinal capillariasis (B81.1)

    B83.0 **Visceral larva migrans**
Prolonged migration of nematode larvae
Toxocariasis

    B83.1 **Gnathostomiasis**
Infection with nematode occurring from ingested undercooked fish contaminated with larvae; larvae migrate to subcutaneous tissue or deeper tissues, results are abscesses
Wandering swelling

    B83.2 **Angiostrongyliasis due to Parastrongylus cantonensis**
Nematode infection caused by eating contaminated raw snails, slugs, or paratenic hosts such as prawns or crabs; larval worms migrate to central nervous system resulting in eosinophilic meningitis
Eosinophilic meningoencephalitis due to Parastrongylus cantonensis
> **Excludes2**   intestinal angiostrongyliasis (B81.3)

    B83.3 **Syngamiasis**
Infestation with gapeworm from turkey, pheasant, guinea fowl, goose, and wild birds
Syngamosis

    B83.4 **Internal hirudiniasis**
Infestation by leeches
> **Excludes2**   external hirudiniasis (B88.3)

    B83.8 **Other specified helminthiases**
Parasitic worm infestation
Acanthocephaliasis
Gongylonemiasis
Hepatic capillariasis
Metastrongyliasis
Thelaziasis

    B83.9 **Helminthiasis, unspecified**
Worms NOS
> **Excludes1**   intestinal helminthiasis NOS (B82.0)

PEDICULOSIS, ACARIASIS AND OTHER INFESTATIONS (B85-B89)

● **B85** **Pediculosis and phthiriasis**
Infestation of lice
    B85.0 **Pediculosis due to Pediculus humanus capitis**
Head-louse infestation
    B85.1 **Pediculosis due to Pediculus humanus corporis**
Body-louse infestation
    B85.2 **Pediculosis, unspecified**
    B85.3 **Phthiriasis**
Crab or pubic lice
Infestation by crab-louse
Infestation by Phthirus pubis
    B85.4 **Mixed pediculosis and phthiriasis**
Infestation classifiable to more than one of the categories B85.0-B85.3

 B86 **Scabies**
Contagious dermatitis caused by mites
Sarcoptic itch

● **B87** **Myiasis**
Infestation by fly maggots
> **Includes**   infestation by larva of flies

    B87.0 **Cutaneous myiasis**
Creeping myiasis
    B87.1 **Wound myiasis**
Traumatic myiasis
    B87.2 **Ocular myiasis**
    B87.3 **Nasopharyngeal myiasis**
Laryngeal myiasis
    B87.4 **Aural myiasis**
●   **B87.8** **Myiasis of other sites**
       B87.81 **Genitourinary myiasis**
       B87.82 **Intestinal myiasis**
       B87.89 **Myiasis of other sites**
    B87.9 **Myiasis, unspecified**

● **B88   Other infestations**

    B88.0   Other acariasis
        Acarine dermatitis
        Dermatitis due to Demodex species
        Dermatitis due to Dermanyssus gallinae
        Dermatitis due to Liponyssoides sanguineus
        Trombiculosis
        Excludes2   scabies (B86)

    B88.1   Tungiasis [sandflea infestation]
        Inflammatory skin disease caused by infestation of fleas

    B88.2   Other arthropod infestations
        Scarabiasis

    B88.3   External hirudiniasis
        Leech infestation NOS
        Excludes2   internal hirudiniasis (B83.4)

    B88.8   Other specified infestations
        Infection of topical fresh water fish parasite
        Ichthyoparasitism due to Vandellia cirrhosa
        Linguatulosis
        Porocephaliasis

    B88.9   Infestation, unspecified
        Infestation (skin) NOS
        Infestation by mites NOS
        Skin parasites NOS

B89   Unspecified parasitic disease

SEQUELAE OF INFECTIOUS AND PARASITIC DISEASES (B90-B94)

Note: Categories B90-B94 are to be used to indicate conditions in categories A00-B89 as the cause of sequelae, which are themselves classified elsewhere. The 'sequelae' include conditions specified as such; they also include residuals of diseases classifiable to the above categories if there is evidence that the disease itself is no longer present. Codes from these categories are not to be used for chronic infections. Code chronic current infections to active infectious disease as appropriate.

Code first condition resulting from (sequela) the infectious or parasitic disease

● **B90   Sequelae of tuberculosis**
    Condition resulting from tuberculosis

    B90.0   Sequelae of central nervous system tuberculosis
    B90.1   Sequelae of genitourinary tuberculosis
    B90.2   Sequelae of tuberculosis of bones and joints
    B90.8   Sequelae of tuberculosis of other organs
        Excludes2   sequelae of respiratory tuberculosis (B90.9)

    B90.9   Sequelae of respiratory and unspecified tuberculosis
        Sequelae of tuberculosis NOS

B91   Sequelae of poliomyelitis
    Excludes1   postpolio syndrome (G14)

B92   Sequelae of leprosy

● **B94   Sequelae of other and unspecified infectious and parasitic diseases**
    B94.0   Sequelae of trachoma
    B94.1   Sequelae of viral encephalitis
    B94.2   Sequelae of viral hepatitis
    B94.8   Sequelae of other specified infectious and parasitic diseases
    B94.9   Sequelae of unspecified infectious and parasitic disease
        Coding Clinic: 2017, Q4, P109

OGCR Section I.C.1.b.

Certain infectious and parasitic diseases

Infectious agents as the cause of diseases classified to other chapters

Certain infections are classified in chapters other than Chapter 1 and no organism is identified as part of the infection code. In these instances, it is necessary to use an additional code from Chapter 1 to identify the organism. A code from category B95, Streptococcus, Staphylococcus, and Enterococcus as the cause of diseases classified to other chapters, B96, Other bacterial agents as the cause of diseases classified to other chapters, or B97, Viral agents as the cause of diseases classified to other chapters, is to be used as an additional code to identify the organism. An instructional note will be found at the infection code advising that an additional organism code is required.

BACTERIAL AND VIRAL INFECTIOUS AGENTS (B95-B97)

Note: These categories are provided for use as supplementary or additional codes to identify the infectious agent(s) in diseases classified elsewhere.
Code the disease first, then the bacterium. Do not report codes from B95-B97 for sepsis.

● **B95   Streptococcus, Staphylococcus, and Enterococcus as the cause of diseases classified elsewhere**

    B95.0   Streptococcus, group A, as the cause of diseases classified elsewhere
    B95.1   Streptococcus, group B, as the cause of diseases classified elsewhere
    B95.2   Enterococcus as the cause of diseases classified elsewhere
    B95.3   Streptococcus pneumoniae as the cause of diseases classified elsewhere
    B95.4   Other streptococcus as the cause of diseases classified elsewhere
    B95.5   Unspecified streptococcus as the cause of diseases classified elsewhere
●   **B95.6   Staphylococcus aureus as the cause of diseases classified elsewhere**

        B95.61   Methicillin susceptible Staphylococcus aureus infection as the cause of diseases classified elsewhere
            Methicillin susceptible Staphylococcus aureus (MSSA) infection as the cause of diseases classified elsewhere
            Staphylococcus aureus infection NOS as the cause of diseases classified elsewhere

        B95.62   Methicillin resistant Staphylococcus aureus infection as the cause of diseases classified elsewhere
            Methicillin resistant staphylococcus aureus (MRSA) infection as the cause of diseases classified elsewhere
            Coding Clinic: 2016, Q1, P13

    B95.7   Other staphylococcus as the cause of diseases classified elsewhere
    B95.8   Unspecified staphylococcus as the cause of diseases classified elsewhere

● **B96   Other bacterial agents as the cause of diseases classified elsewhere**

    B96.0   Mycoplasma pneumoniae [M. pneumoniae] as the cause of diseases classified elsewhere
        Pleuro-pneumonia-like-organism [PPLO]

    B96.1   Klebsiella pneumoniae [K. pneumoniae] as the cause of diseases classified elsewhere

●   **B96.2   Escherichia coli [E. coli] as the cause of diseases classified elsewhere**

        B96.20   Unspecified Escherichia coli [E. coli] as the cause of diseases classified elsewhere
            Escherichia coli [E. coli] NOS
            Coding Clinic: 2018, Q1, P16

CHAPTER 1 (A00-B99)

B96.21 **Shiga toxin-producing Escherichia coli [E. coli] (STEC) O157 as the cause of diseases classified elsewhere**
E. coli O157:H- (nonmotile) with confirmation of Shiga toxin
E. coli O157 with confirmation of Shiga toxin when H antigen is unknown, or is not H7
O157:H7 Escherichia coli [E.coli] with or without confirmation of Shiga toxin-production
Shiga toxin-producing Escherichia coli [E.coli] O157:H7 with or without confirmation of Shiga toxin-production
STEC O157:H7 with or without confirmation of Shiga toxin-production

B96.22 **Other specified Shiga toxin-producing Escherichia coli [E. coli] (STEC) as the cause of diseases classified elsewhere**
Non-O157 Shiga toxin-producing Escherichia coli [E.coli]
Non-O157 Shiga toxin-producing Escherichia coli [E.coli] with known O group

B96.23 **Unspecified Shiga toxin-producing Escherichia coli [E. coli] (STEC) as the cause of diseases classified elsewhere**
Shiga toxin-producing Escherichia coli [E. coli] with unspecified O group
STEC NOS

B96.29 **Other Escherichia coli [E. coli] as the cause of diseases classified elsewhere**
Non-Shiga toxin-producing E. coli

B96.3 **Hemophilus influenzae [H. influenzae] as the cause of diseases classified elsewhere**

B96.4 **Proteus (mirabilis) (morganii) as the cause of diseases classified elsewhere**

B96.5 **Pseudomonas (aeruginosa) (mallei) (pseudomallei) as the cause of diseases classified elsewhere**
Coding Clinic: 2015, Q1, P18

B96.6 **Bacteroides fragilis [B. fragilis] as the cause of diseases classified elsewhere**

B96.7 **Clostridium perfringens [C. perfringens] as the cause of diseases classified elsewhere**

B96.8 Other specified bacterial agents as the cause of diseases classified elsewhere
B96.81 **Helicobacter pylori [H. pylori] as the cause of diseases classified elsewhere**
B96.82 **Vibrio vulnificus as the cause of diseases classified elsewhere**
B96.89 **Other specified bacterial agents as the cause of diseases classified elsewhere**

B97 Viral agents as the cause of diseases classified elsewhere
B97.0 **Adenovirus as the cause of diseases classified elsewhere**
B97.1 Enterovirus as the cause of diseases classified elsewhere
B97.10 **Unspecified enterovirus as the cause of diseases classified elsewhere**
B97.11 **Coxsackievirus as the cause of diseases classified elsewhere**
B97.12 **Echovirus as the cause of diseases classified elsewhere**
B97.19 **Other enterovirus as the cause of diseases classified elsewhere**

Item 1–24 Retrovirus develops by copying its RNA, genetic materials, into the DNA, which then produces new virus particles. It is from the Retroviridae virus family. **Human T-cell lymphotropic virus, Type I (HTLV-I),** is also called human T-cell leukemia virus, Type I, and is a retrovirus thought to cause T-cell leukemia/lymphoma. **Human T-cell lymphotropic virus, Type II (HTLV-II),** is also called human T-cell leukemia virus, Type II, and is a retrovirus associated with hematologic disorders.
HIV-2 is one of the serotypes of HIV and is usually confined to West Africa, whereas **HIV-1** is found worldwide.

B97.2 **Coronavirus as the cause of diseases classified elsewhere**
B97.21 **SARS-associated coronavirus as the cause of diseases classified elsewhere**
Excludes1 pneumonia due to SARS-associated coronavirus (J12.81)
B97.29 **Other coronavirus as the cause of diseases classified elsewhere**

B97.3 **Retrovirus as the cause of diseases classified elsewhere**
Excludes1 human immunodeficiency virus [HIV] disease (B20)
B97.30 **Unspecified retrovirus as the cause of diseases classified elsewhere**
B97.31 **Lentivirus as the cause of diseases classified elsewhere**
B97.32 **Oncovirus as the cause of diseases classified elsewhere**
B97.33 **Human T-cell lymphotrophic virus, type I [HTLV-I] as the cause of diseases classified elsewhere**
B97.34 **Human T-cell lymphotrophic virus, type II [HTLV-II] as the cause of diseases classified elsewhere**
B97.35 **Human immunodeficiency virus, type 2 [HIV 2] as the cause of diseases classified elsewhere**
B97.39 **Other retrovirus as the cause of diseases classified elsewhere**

B97.4 **Respiratory syncytial virus as the cause of diseases classified elsewhere**
B97.5 **Reovirus as the cause of diseases classified elsewhere**
B97.6 **Parvovirus as the cause of diseases classified elsewhere**
B97.7 **Papillomavirus as the cause of diseases classified elsewhere**
B97.8 Other viral agents as the cause of diseases classified elsewhere
B97.81 **Human metapneumovirus as the cause of diseases classified elsewhere**
B97.89 **Other viral agents as the cause of diseases classified elsewhere**
Coding Clinic: 2016, Q3, P8-10, 14

OTHER INFECTIOUS DISEASES (B99)

B99 Other and unspecified infectious diseases
B99.8 **Other infectious disease**
B99.9 **Unspecified infectious disease**

CHAPTER 2

NEOPLASMS (C00-D49)

OGCR Chapter-Specific Coding Guidelines

2. **Chapter 2: Neoplasms (C00-D49)**
   General guidelines
   Chapter 2 of the ICD-10-CM contains the codes for most benign and all malignant neoplasms. Certain benign neoplasms, such as prostatic adenomas, may be found in the specific body system chapters. To properly code a neoplasm it is necessary to determine from the record if the neoplasm is benign, in-situ, malignant, or of uncertain histologic behavior. If malignant, any secondary (metastatic) sites should also be determined.

   Primary malignant neoplasms overlapping site boundaries
   A primary malignant neoplasm that overlaps two or more contiguous (next to each other) sites should be classified to the subcategory/code .8 ('overlapping lesion'), unless the combination is specifically indexed elsewhere. For multiple neoplasms of the same site that are not contiguous such as tumors in different quadrants of the same breast, codes for each site should be assigned.

   Malignant neoplasm of ectopic tissue
   Malignant neoplasms of ectopic tissue are to be coded to the site of origin mentioned, e.g., ectopic pancreatic malignant neoplasms involving the stomach are coded to malignant neoplasm of pancreas, unspecified (C25.9).

   The neoplasm table in the Alphabetic Index should be referenced first. However, if the histological term is documented, that term should be referenced first, rather than going immediately to the Neoplasm Table, in order to determine which column in the Neoplasm Table is appropriate. For example, if the documentation indicates "adenoma," refer to the term in the Alphabetic Index to review the entries under this term and the instructional note to "see also neoplasm, by site, benign." The table provides the proper code based on the type of neoplasm and the site. It is important to select the proper column in the table that corresponds to the type of neoplasm. The Tabular List should then be referenced to verify that the correct code has been selected from the table and that a more specific site code does not exist.

   See Section I.C.21. Factors influencing health status and contact with health services, Status, for information regarding Z15.0, codes for genetic susceptibility to cancer.

   a. **Treatment directed at the malignancy**
   If the treatment is directed at the malignancy, designate the malignancy as the principal diagnosis.
   The only exception to this guideline is if a patient admission/encounter is solely for the administration of chemotherapy, immunotherapy or external beam radiation therapy, assign the appropriate Z51.— code as the first-listed or principal diagnosis, and the diagnosis or problem for which the service is being performed as a secondary diagnosis.

   b. **Treatment of secondary site**
   When a patient is admitted because of a primary neoplasm with metastasis and treatment is directed toward the secondary site only, the secondary neoplasm is designated as the principal diagnosis even though the primary malignancy is still present.

   c. **Coding and sequencing of complications**
   Coding and sequencing of complications associated with the malignancies or with the therapy thereof are subject to the following guidelines:

   1) **Anemia associated with malignancy**
   When admission/encounter is for management of an anemia associated with the malignancy, and the treatment is only for anemia, the appropriate code for the malignancy is sequenced as the principal or first-listed diagnosis followed by the appropriate code for the anemia (such as code D63.0, Anemia in neoplastic disease).

   2) **Anemia associated with chemotherapy, immunotherapy and radiation therapy**
   When the admission/encounter is for management of an anemia associated with an adverse effect of the administration of chemotherapy or immunotherapy and the only treatment is for the anemia, the anemia code is sequenced first followed by the appropriate codes for the neoplasm and the adverse effect (T45.1X5, Adverse effect of antineoplastic and immunosuppressive drugs).
   When the admission/encounter is for management of an anemia associated with an adverse effect of radiotherapy, the anemia code should be sequenced first, followed by the appropriate neoplasm code and code Y84.2, Radiological procedure and radiotherapy as the cause of abnormal reaction of the patient, or of later complication, without mention of misadventure at the time of the procedure.

   3) **Management of dehydration due to the malignancy**
   When the admission/encounter is for management of dehydration due to the malignancy and only the dehydration is being treated (intravenous rehydration), the dehydration is sequenced first, followed by the code(s) for the malignancy.

   4) **Treatment of a complication resulting from a surgical procedure**
   When the admission/encounter is for treatment of a complication resulting from a surgical procedure, designate the complication as the principal or first-listed diagnosis if treatment is directed at resolving the complication.

   d. **Primary malignancy previously excised**
   When a primary malignancy has been previously excised or eradicated from its site and there is no further treatment directed to that site and there is no evidence of any existing primary malignancy *at that site*, a code from category Z85, Personal history of malignant neoplasm, should be used to indicate the former site of the malignancy. Any mention of extension, invasion, or metastasis to another site is coded as a secondary malignant neoplasm to that site. The secondary site may be the principal or first-listed with the Z85 code used as a secondary code.

   e. **Admissions/Encounters involving chemotherapy, immunotherapy and radiation therapy**

   1) **Episode of care involves surgical removal of neoplasm**
   When an episode of care involves the surgical removal of a neoplasm, primary or secondary site, followed by adjunct chemotherapy or radiation treatment during the same episode of care, the code for the neoplasm should be assigned as principal or first-listed diagnosis.

   2) **Patient admission/encounter solely for administration of chemotherapy, immunotherapy and radiation therapy**
   If a patient admission/encounter is solely for the administration of chemotherapy, immunotherapy or external beam radiation therapy assign code Z51.0, Encounter for antineoplastic radiation therapy, or Z51.11, Encounter for antineoplastic chemotherapy, or Z51.12, Encounter for antineoplastic immunotherapy as the first-listed or principal diagnosis. If a patient receives more than one of these therapies during the same admission more than one of these codes may be assigned, in any sequence.
   The malignancy for which the therapy is being administered should be assigned as a secondary diagnosis.
   If a patient admission/encounter is for the insertion or implantation of radioactive elements (e.g., brachytherapy) the appropriate code for the malignancy is sequenced as the principal or first-listed diagnosis. Code Z51.0 should not be assigned.

   3) **Patient admitted for radiation therapy, chemotherapy or immunotherapy and develops complications**
   When a patient is admitted for the purpose of external beam radiotherapy, immunotherapy or chemotherapy and develops complications such as uncontrolled nausea and vomiting or dehydration, the principal or first-listed diagnosis is Z51.0, Encounter for antineoplastic radiation therapy, or Z51.11, Encounter for antineoplastic chemotherapy, or Z51.12, Encounter for antineoplastic immunotherapy followed by any codes for the complications.
   When a patient is admitted for the purpose of insertion or implantation of radioactive elements (e.g., brachytherapy) and develops complications such as uncontrolled nausea and vomiting or dehydration, the principal or first-listed diagnosis is the appropriate code for the malignancy followed by any codes for the complications.

   f. **Admission/encounter to determine extent of malignancy**
   When the reason for admission/encounter is to determine the extent of the malignancy, or for a procedure such as paracentesis

or thoracentesis, the primary malignancy or appropriate metastatic site is designated as the principal or first-listed diagnosis, even though chemotherapy or radiotherapy is administered.

g. Symptoms, signs, and abnormal findings listed in Chapter 18 associated with neoplasms

Symptoms, signs, and ill-defined conditions listed in Chapter 18 characteristic of, or associated with, an existing primary or secondary site malignancy cannot be used to replace the malignancy as principal or first-listed diagnosis, regardless of the number of admissions or encounters for treatment and care of the neoplasm.

See Section I.C.21. Factors influencing health status and contact with health services, Encounter for prophylactic organ removal.

h. Admission/encounter for pain control/management

See Section I.C.6. for information on coding admission/encounter for pain control/management.

i. Malignancy in two or more noncontiguous sites

A patient may have more than one malignant tumor in the same organ. These tumors may represent different primaries or metastatic disease, depending on the site. Should the documentation be unclear, the provider should be queried as to the status of each tumor so that the correct codes can be assigned.

j. Disseminated malignant neoplasm, unspecified

Code C80.0, Disseminated malignant neoplasm, unspecified, is for use only in those cases where the patient has advanced metastatic disease and no known primary or secondary sites are specified. It should not be used in place of assigning codes for the primary site and all known secondary sites.

k. Malignant neoplasm without specification of site

Code C80.1, Malignant (primary) neoplasm, unspecified, equates to Cancer, unspecified. This code should only be used when no determination can be made as to the primary site of a malignancy. This code should rarely be used in the inpatient setting.

l. Sequencing of neoplasm codes

1) Encounter for treatment of primary malignancy

If the reason for the encounter is for treatment of a primary malignancy, assign the malignancy as the principal/first-listed diagnosis. The primary site is to be sequenced first, followed by any metastatic sites.

2) Encounter for treatment of secondary malignancy

When an encounter is for a primary malignancy with metastasis and treatment is directed toward the metastatic (secondary) site(s) only, the metastatic site(s) is designated as the principal/first-listed diagnosis. The primary malignancy is coded as an additional code.

3) Malignant neoplasm in a pregnant patient

When a pregnant woman has a malignant neoplasm, a code from subcategory O9A.1-, Malignant neoplasm complicating pregnancy, childbirth, and the puerperium, should be sequenced first, followed by the appropriate code from Chapter 2 to indicate the type of neoplasm.

4) Encounter for complication associated with a neoplasm

When an encounter is for management of a complication associated with a neoplasm, such as dehydration, and the treatment is only for the complication, the complication is coded first, followed by the appropriate code(s) for the neoplasm.

The exception to this guideline is anemia. When the admission/encounter is for management of an anemia associated with the malignancy, and the treatment is only for anemia, the appropriate code for the malignancy is sequenced as the principal or first-listed diagnosis followed by code D63.0, Anemia in neoplastic disease.

5) Complication from surgical procedure for treatment of a neoplasm

When an encounter is for treatment of a complication resulting from a surgical procedure performed for the treatment of the neoplasm, designate the complication as the principal/first-listed diagnosis. See guideline regarding the coding of a current malignancy versus personal history to determine if the code for the neoplasm should also be assigned.

6) Pathologic fracture due to a neoplasm

When an encounter is for a pathological fracture due to a neoplasm, and the focus of treatment is the fracture, a code from subcategory M84.5, Pathological fracture in neoplastic disease, should be sequenced first, followed by the code for the neoplasm.

If the focus of treatment is the neoplasm with an associated pathological fracture, the neoplasm code should be sequenced first, followed by a code from M84.5 for the pathological fracture.

m. Current malignancy versus personal history of malignancy

When a primary malignancy has been excised but further treatment, such as an additional surgery for the malignancy, radiation therapy or chemotherapy is directed to that site, the primary malignancy code should be used until treatment is completed.

When a primary malignancy has been previously excised or eradicated from its site, there is no further treatment (of the malignancy) directed to that site, and there is no evidence of any existing primary malignancy **at that site**, a code from category Z85, Personal history of malignant neoplasm, should be used to indicate the former site of the malignancy.

Subcategories Z85.0–Z85.7 should only be assigned for the former site of a primary malignancy, not the site of a secondary malignancy. Codes from subcategory Z85.8-, may be assigned for the former site(s) of either a primary or secondary malignancy included in this subcategory.

See Section I.C.21. Factors influencing health status and contact with health services, History (of)

n. Leukemia, Multiple Myeloma, and Malignant Plasma Cell Neoplasms in remission versus personal history

The categories for leukemia, and category C90, Multiple myeloma and malignant plasma cell neoplasms, have codes indicating whether or not the leukemia has achieved remission. There are also codes Z85.6, Personal history of leukemia, and Z85.79, Personal history of other malignant neoplasms of lymphoid, hematopoietic and related tissues. If the documentation is unclear, as to whether the leukemia has achieved remission, the provider should be queried.

See Section I.C.21. Factors influencing health status and contact with health services, History (of)

o. Aftercare following surgery for neoplasm

See Section I.C.21. Factors influencing health status and contact with health services, Aftercare

p. Follow-up care for completed treatment of a malignancy

See Section I.C.21. Factors influencing health status and contact with health services, Follow-up

q. Prophylactic organ removal for prevention of malignancy

See Section I.C. 21, Factors influencing health status and contact with health services, Prophylactic organ removal

r. Malignant neoplasm associated with transplanted organ

A malignant neoplasm of a transplanted organ should be coded as a transplant complication. Assign first the appropriate code from category T86.-, Complications of transplanted organs and tissue, followed by code C80.2, Malignant neoplasm associated with transplanted organ. Use an additional code for the specific malignancy.

Item 2–1 Neoplasm: Neo = new, plasm = growth, development, formation. This new growth (mass, tumor) can be malignant or benign, which is confirmed by the pathology report. Do not assign a code to a neoplasm until you review the pathology report. Certain CPT codes will specify benign or malignant lesion, so be certain the diagnosis code supports the procedure code.

CHAPTER 2

NEOPLASMS (C00-D49)

This chapter contains the following blocks:

C00-C14	Malignant neoplasms of lip, oral cavity and pharynx
C15-C26	Malignant neoplasms of digestive organs
C30-C39	Malignant neoplasms of respiratory and intrathoracic organs
C40-C41	Malignant neoplasms of bone and articular cartilage
C43-C44	Melanoma and other malignant neoplasms of skin
C45-C49	Malignant neoplasms of mesothelial and soft tissue
C50	Malignant neoplasms of breast
C51-C58	Malignant neoplasms of female genital organs
C60-C63	Malignant neoplasms of male genital organs
C64-C68	Malignant neoplasms of urinary tract
C69-C72	Malignant neoplasms of eye, brain and other parts of central nervous system
C73-C75	Malignant neoplasms of thyroid and other endocrine glands
C7A	Malignant neuroendocrine tumors
C7B	Secondary neuroendocrine tumors
C76-C80	Malignant neoplasms of ill-defined, other secondary and unspecified sites
C81-C96	Malignant neoplasms of lymphoid, hematopoietic and related tissue
D00-D09	In situ neoplasms
D10-D36	Benign neoplasms, except benign neuroendocrine tumors
D3A	Benign neuroendocrine tumors
D37-D48	Neoplasms of uncertain behavior, polycythemia vera and myelodysplastic syndromes
D49	Neoplasms of unspecified behavior

Notes: Functional activity

All neoplasms are classified in this chapter, whether they are functionally active or not. An additional code from Chapter 4 may be used, to identify functional activity associated with any neoplasm.

Morphology [Histology]

Chapter 2 classifies neoplasms primarily by site (topography), with broad groupings for behavior, malignant, in situ, benign, etc. The Table of Neoplasms should be used to identify the correct topography code. In a few cases, such as for malignant melanoma and certain neuroendocrine tumors, the morphology (histologic type) is included in the category and codes.

Primary malignant neoplasms overlapping site boundaries

A primary malignant neoplasm that overlaps two or more contiguous (next to each other) sites should be classified to the subcategory/code .8 ("overlapping lesion"), unless the combination is specifically indexed elsewhere. For multiple neoplasms of the same site that are not contiguous, such as tumors in different quadrants of the same breast, codes for each site should be assigned.

Malignant neoplasm of ectopic tissue

Malignant neoplasms of ectopic tissue are to be coded to the site mentioned, e.g., ectopic pancreatic malignant neoplasms are coded to pancreas, unspecified (C25.9).

MALIGNANT NEOPLASMS (C00-C96)

MALIGNANT NEOPLASMS, STATED OR PRESUMED TO BE PRIMARY (OF SPECIFIED SITES), AND CERTAIN SPECIFIED HISTOLOGIES, EXCEPT NEUROENDOCRINE, AND OF LYMPHOID, HEMATOPOIETIC AND RELATED TISSUE (C00-C75)

MALIGNANT NEOPLASMS OF LIP, ORAL CAVITY AND PHARYNX (C00-C14)

● **C00   Malignant neoplasm of lip**

Use additional code to identify:
 alcohol abuse and dependence (F10.-)
 history of tobacco dependence (Z87.891)
 tobacco dependence (F17.-)
 tobacco use (Z72.0)

Excludes1 malignant melanoma of lip (C43.0)
 Merkel cell carcinoma of lip (C4A.0)
 other and unspecified malignant neoplasm of skin of lip (C44.0-)

C00.0 Malignant neoplasm of external upper lip
 Malignant neoplasm of lipstick area of upper lip
 Malignant neoplasm of upper lip NOS
 Malignant neoplasm of vermilion border of upper lip

C00.1 Malignant neoplasm of external lower lip
 Malignant neoplasm of lower lip NOS
 Malignant neoplasm of lipstick area of lower lip
 Malignant neoplasm of vermilion border of lower lip

C00.2 Malignant neoplasm of external lip, unspecified
 Malignant neoplasm of vermilion border of lip NOS

C00.3 Malignant neoplasm of upper lip, inner aspect
 Malignant neoplasm of buccal aspect of upper lip
 Malignant neoplasm of frenulum of upper lip
 Malignant neoplasm of mucosa of upper lip
 Malignant neoplasm of oral aspect of upper lip

C00.4 Malignant neoplasm of lower lip, inner aspect
 Malignant neoplasm of buccal aspect of lower lip
 Malignant neoplasm of frenulum of lower lip
 Malignant neoplasm of mucosa of lower lip
 Malignant neoplasm of oral aspect of lower lip

C00.5 Malignant neoplasm of lip, unspecified, inner aspect
 Malignant neoplasm of buccal aspect of lip, unspecified
 Malignant neoplasm of frenulum of lip, unspecified
 Malignant neoplasm of mucosa of lip, unspecified
 Malignant neoplasm of oral aspect of lip, unspecified

C00.6 Malignant neoplasm of commissure of lip, unspecified
 Commissure: Site of union of corresponding parts

C00.8 Malignant neoplasm of overlapping sites of lip

C00.9 Malignant neoplasm of lip, unspecified

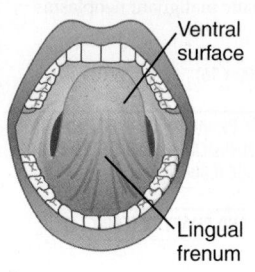

Transitional or vermilion surfaces

Lips are connected to
A   the gums by frenulum

Ventral surface

Lingual frenum

C

Figure 2-1 Anatomical structures of the mouth and lips. **A.** Transitional or vermilion borders. Lips are connected to the gums by frenulum. **B.** Dorsal surface. **C.** Ventral surface.

CHAPTER 2 (C00-D49)

C01   Malignant neoplasm of base of tongue
Malignant neoplasm of dorsal surface of base of tongue
Malignant neoplasm of fixed part of tongue NOS
Malignant neoplasm of posterior third of tongue

Use additional code to identify:
alcohol abuse and dependence (F10.-)
history of tobacco dependence (Z87.891)
tobacco dependence (F17.-)
tobacco use (Z72.0)

● **C02   Malignant neoplasm of other and unspecified parts of tongue**
Use additional code to identify:
alcohol abuse and dependence (F10.-)
history of tobacco dependence (Z87.891)
tobacco dependence (F17.-)
tobacco use (Z72.0)

C02.0   Malignant neoplasm of dorsal surface of tongue
Malignant neoplasm of anterior two-thirds of tongue, dorsal surface

     Excludes2   malignant neoplasm of dorsal surface of base of tongue (C01)

C02.1   Malignant neoplasm of border of tongue
Malignant neoplasm of tip of tongue

C02.2   Malignant neoplasm of ventral surface of tongue
Malignant neoplasm of anterior two-thirds of tongue, ventral surface
Malignant neoplasm of frenulum linguae

C02.3   Malignant neoplasm of anterior two-thirds of tongue, part unspecified
Malignant neoplasm of middle third of tongue NOS
Malignant neoplasm of mobile part of tongue NOS

C02.4   Malignant neoplasm of lingual tonsil
Lingual tonsil: Aggregation of lymph follicles at root of tongue

     Excludes2   malignant neoplasm of tonsil NOS (C09.9)

C02.8   Malignant neoplasm of overlapping sites of tongue
Malignant neoplasm of two or more contiguous sites of tongue

C02.9   Malignant neoplasm of tongue, unspecified

● **C03   Malignant neoplasm of gum**
     Includes   malignant neoplasm of alveolar (ridge) mucosa
                  malignant neoplasm of gingiva

Use additional code to identify:
alcohol abuse and dependence (F10.-)
history of tobacco dependence (Z87.891)
tobacco dependence (F17.-)
tobacco use (Z72.0)

     Excludes2   malignant odontogenic neoplasms (C41.0-C41.1)

C03.0   Malignant neoplasm of upper gum

C03.1   Malignant neoplasm of lower gum

C03.9   Malignant neoplasm of gum, unspecified

● **C04   Malignant neoplasm of floor of mouth**
Use additional code to identify:
alcohol abuse and dependence (F10.-)
history of tobacco dependence (Z87.891)
tobacco dependence (F17.-)
tobacco use (Z72.0)

C04.0   Malignant neoplasm of anterior floor of mouth
Malignant neoplasm of anterior to the premolar-canine junction

C04.1   Malignant neoplasm of lateral floor of mouth

C04.8   Malignant neoplasm of overlapping sites of floor of mouth

C04.9   Malignant neoplasm of floor of mouth, unspecified

● **C05   Malignant neoplasm of palate**
Use additional code to identify:
alcohol abuse and dependence (F10.-)
history of tobacco dependence (Z87.891)
tobacco dependence (F17.-)
tobacco use (Z72.0)

     Excludes1   Kaposi's sarcoma of palate (C46.2)

C05.0   Malignant neoplasm of hard palate

C05.1   Malignant neoplasm of soft palate
     Excludes2   malignant neoplasm of nasopharyngeal surface of soft palate (C11.3)

C05.2   Malignant neoplasm of uvula

C05.8   Malignant neoplasm of overlapping sites of palate

C05.9   Malignant neoplasm of palate, unspecified
Malignant neoplasm of roof of mouth

● **C06   Malignant neoplasm of other and unspecified parts of mouth**
Use additional code to identify:
alcohol abuse and dependence (F10.-)
history of tobacco dependence (Z87.891)
tobacco dependence (F17.-)
tobacco use (Z72.0)

C06.0   Malignant neoplasm of cheek mucosa
Malignant neoplasm of buccal mucosa NOS
Malignant neoplasm of internal cheek

C06.1   Malignant neoplasm of vestibule of mouth
Malignant neoplasm of buccal sulcus (upper) (lower)
Malignant neoplasm of labial sulcus (upper) (lower)

C06.2   Malignant neoplasm of retromolar area

● **C06.8   Malignant neoplasm of overlapping sites of other and unspecified parts of mouth**

C06.80   Malignant neoplasm of overlapping sites of unspecified parts of mouth

C06.89   Malignant neoplasm of overlapping sites of other parts of mouth
'book leaf' neoplasm [ventral surface of tongue and floor of mouth]

C06.9   Malignant neoplasm of mouth, unspecified
Malignant neoplasm of minor salivary gland, unspecified site
Malignant neoplasm of oral cavity NOS

▶ New   ⟹ Revised   ~~deleted~~ Deleted   Excludes 1   Excludes 2   Includes   Use additional   Code first   Code also   Key words
OGCR Official Guidelines   X Assign placeholder X   ● Use Additional Character(s)   ▌ Manifestation Code   **Coding Clinic**

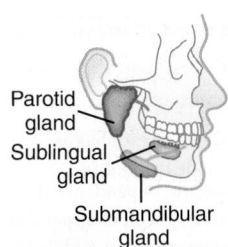

Parotid gland
Sublingual gland
Submandibular gland

Figure 2-2   Major salivary glands.

C07   Malignant neoplasm of parotid gland
Use additional code to identify:
alcohol abuse and dependence (F10.-)
exposure to environmental tobacco smoke (Z77.22)
exposure to tobacco smoke in the perinatal period (P96.81)
history of tobacco dependence (Z87.891)
occupational exposure to environmental tobacco smoke (Z57.31)
tobacco dependence (F17.-)
tobacco use (Z72.0)

● **C08   Malignant neoplasm of other and unspecified major salivary glands**
Includes   malignant neoplasm of salivary ducts
Use additional code to identify:
alcohol abuse and dependence (F10.-)
exposure to environmental tobacco smoke (Z77.22)
exposure to tobacco smoke in the perinatal period (P96.81)
history of tobacco dependence (Z87.891)
occupational exposure to environmental tobacco smoke (Z57.31)
tobacco dependence (F17.-)
tobacco use (Z72.0)
Excludes1   malignant neoplasms of specified minor salivary glands which are classified according to their anatomical location
Excludes2   malignant neoplasms of minor salivary glands NOS (C06.9)
malignant neoplasm of parotid gland (C07)

C08.0   Malignant neoplasm of submandibular gland
Malignant neoplasm of submaxillary gland

C08.1   Malignant neoplasm of sublingual gland

C08.9   Malignant neoplasm of major salivary gland, unspecified
Malignant neoplasm of salivary gland (major) NOS

★ **(See Plate 61 on page 73.)**

● **C09   Malignant neoplasm of tonsil**
Use additional code to identify:
alcohol abuse and dependence (F10.-)
exposure to environmental tobacco smoke (Z77.22)
exposure to tobacco smoke in the perinatal period (P96.81)
history of tobacco dependence (Z87.891)
occupational exposure to environmental tobacco smoke (Z57.31)
tobacco dependence (F17.-)
tobacco use (Z72.0)
Excludes2   malignant neoplasm of lingual tonsil (C02.4)
malignant neoplasm of pharyngeal tonsil (C11.1)

C09.0   Malignant neoplasm of tonsillar fossa
Surface of palatine (two masses of lymphatic tissue on sides of throat) tonsils

C09.1   Malignant neoplasm of tonsillar pillar (anterior) (posterior)
Extension from palatine (two masses of lymphatic tissue on sides of throat) tonsils

C09.8   Malignant neoplasm of overlapping sites of tonsil

C09.9   Malignant neoplasm of tonsil, unspecified
Malignant neoplasm of tonsil NOS
Malignant neoplasm of faucial tonsils
Malignant neoplasm of palatine tonsils

● **C10   Malignant neoplasm of oropharynx**
Area of throat at back of mouth
Use additional code to identify:
alcohol abuse and dependence (F10.-)
exposure to environmental tobacco smoke (Z77.22)
exposure to tobacco smoke in the perinatal period (P96.81)
history of tobacco dependence (Z87.891)
occupational exposure to environmental tobacco smoke (Z57.31)
tobacco dependence (F17.-)
tobacco use (Z72.0)
Excludes2   malignant neoplasm of tonsil (C09.-)

C10.0   Malignant neoplasm of vallecula
Vallecula, depression or furrow

C10.1   Malignant neoplasm of anterior surface of epiglottis
Malignant neoplasm of epiglottis, free border [margin]
Malignant neoplasm of glossoepiglottic fold(s)
Excludes2   malignant neoplasm of epiglottis (suprahyoid portion) NOS (C32.1)

C10.2   Malignant neoplasm of lateral wall of oropharynx

C10.3   Malignant neoplasm of posterior wall of oropharynx

C10.4   Malignant neoplasm of branchial cleft
Congenital slitlike openings formed between branchial arches pharyngeal groove
Malignant neoplasm of branchial cyst [site of neoplasm]

C10.8   Malignant neoplasm of overlapping sites of oropharynx
Malignant neoplasm of junctional region of oropharynx

C10.9   Malignant neoplasm of oropharynx, unspecified

● **C11   Malignant neoplasm of nasopharynx**
Use additional code to identify:
exposure to environmental tobacco smoke (Z77.22)
exposure to tobacco smoke in the perinatal period (P96.81)
history of tobacco dependence (Z87.891)
occupational exposure to environmental tobacco smoke (Z57.31)
tobacco dependence (F17.-)
tobacco use (Z72.0)

C11.0   Malignant neoplasm of superior wall of nasopharynx
Part of pharynx that lies above soft palate
Malignant neoplasm of roof of nasopharynx

C11.1   Malignant neoplasm of posterior wall of nasopharynx
Malignant neoplasm of adenoid
Malignant neoplasm of pharyngeal tonsil

C11.2   Malignant neoplasm of lateral wall of nasopharynx
Malignant neoplasm of fossa of Rosenmüller
Malignant neoplasm of opening of auditory tube
Malignant neoplasm of pharyngeal recess

C11.3   Malignant neoplasm of anterior wall of nasopharynx
Malignant neoplasm of floor of nasopharynx
Malignant neoplasm of nasopharyngeal (anterior) (posterior) surface of soft palate
Malignant neoplasm of posterior margin of nasal choana
Malignant neoplasm of posterior margin of nasal septum

C11.8   Malignant neoplasm of overlapping sites of nasopharynx

C11.9   Malignant neoplasm of nasopharynx, unspecified
Malignant neoplasm of nasopharyngeal wall NOS

C12   Malignant neoplasm of pyriform sinus
Malignant neoplasm of pyriform fossa
Use additional code to identify:
exposure to environmental tobacco smoke (Z77.22)
exposure to tobacco smoke in the perinatal period (P96.81)
history of tobacco dependence (Z87.891)
occupational exposure to environmental tobacco smoke (Z57.31)
tobacco dependence (F17.-)
tobacco use (Z72.0)

CHAPTER 2 (C00-D49)

CHAPTER 2 (C00-D49)

● **C13**   Malignant neoplasm of hypopharynx
>Use additional code to identify:
>>exposure to environmental tobacco smoke (Z77.22)
>>exposure to tobacco smoke in the perinatal period (P96.81)
>>history of tobacco dependence (Z87.891)
>>occupational exposure to environmental tobacco smoke (Z57.31)
>>tobacco dependence (F17.-)
>>tobacco use (Z72.0)
>
>**Excludes2**   malignant neoplasm of pyriform sinus (C12)

C13.0   Malignant neoplasm of postcricoid region
>*Behind the cricoid cartilage of neck*

C13.1   Malignant neoplasm of aryepiglottic fold, hypopharyngeal aspect
>*Arytenoepiglottic fold, triangular opening between side of epiglottis and apex of arytenoid cartilage*
>Malignant neoplasm of aryepiglottic fold, marginal zone
>Malignant neoplasm of aryepiglottic fold NOS
>Malignant neoplasm of interarytenoid fold, marginal zone
>Malignant neoplasm of interarytenoid fold NOS
>>**Excludes2**   malignant neoplasm of aryepiglottic fold or interarytenoid fold, laryngeal aspect (C32.1)

C13.2   Malignant neoplasm of posterior wall of hypopharynx

C13.8   Malignant neoplasm of overlapping sites of hypopharynx

C13.9   Malignant neoplasm of hypopharynx, unspecified
>Malignant neoplasm of hypopharyngeal wall NOS

● **C14**   Malignant neoplasm of other and ill-defined sites in the lip, oral cavity and pharynx
>Use additional code to identify:
>>alcohol abuse and dependence (F10.-)
>>exposure to environmental tobacco smoke (Z77.22)
>>exposure to tobacco smoke in the perinatal period (P96.81)
>>history of tobacco dependence (Z87.891)
>>occupational exposure to environmental tobacco smoke (Z57.31)
>>tobacco dependence (F17.-)
>>tobacco use (Z72.0)
>
>**Excludes1**   malignant neoplasm of oral cavity NOS (C06.9)

C14.0   Malignant neoplasm of pharynx, unspecified

C14.2   Malignant neoplasm of Waldeyer's ring

C14.8   Malignant neoplasm of overlapping sites of lip, oral cavity and pharynx
>Primary malignant neoplasm of two or more contiguous sites of lip, oral cavity and pharynx
>>**Excludes1**   'book leaf' neoplasm [ventral surface of tongue and floor of mouth] (C06.89)

MALIGNANT NEOPLASM OF DIGESTIVE ORGANS (C15-C26)

>**Excludes1**   Kaposi's sarcoma of gastrointestinal sites (C46.4)
>
>**Excludes2**   gastrointestinal stromal tumors (C49.A-)

● **C15**   Malignant neoplasms of esophagus
>Use additional code to identify:
>>alcohol abuse and dependence (F10.-)

C15.3   Malignant neoplasm of upper third of esophagus

C15.4   Malignant neoplasm of middle third of esophagus

C15.5   Malignant neoplasm of lower third of esophagus
>>**Excludes1**   malignant neoplasm of cardio-esophageal junction (C16.0)

C15.8   Malignant neoplasm of overlapping sites of esophagus

C15.9   Malignant neoplasm of esophagus, unspecified

● **C16**   Malignant neoplasm of stomach
>Use additional code to identify:
>>alcohol abuse and dependence (F10.-)
>
>**Excludes2**   malignant carcinoid tumor of the stomach (C7A.092)

C16.0   Malignant neoplasm of cardia
>Malignant neoplasm of cardiac orifice
>Malignant neoplasm of cardio-esophageal junction
>Malignant neoplasm of esophagus and stomach
>Malignant neoplasm of gastro-esophageal junction

C16.1   Malignant neoplasm of fundus of stomach

C16.2   Malignant neoplasm of body of stomach

C16.3   Malignant neoplasm of pyloric antrum
>Malignant neoplasm of gastric antrum

C16.4   Malignant neoplasm of pylorus
>Malignant neoplasm of prepylorus
>Malignant neoplasm of pyloric canal

C16.5   Malignant neoplasm of lesser curvature of stomach, unspecified
>Malignant neoplasm of lesser curvature of stomach, not classifiable to C16.1-C16.4

C16.6   Malignant neoplasm of greater curvature of stomach, unspecified
>Malignant neoplasm of greater curvature of stomach, not classifiable to C16.0-C16.4

C16.8   Malignant neoplasm of overlapping sites of stomach

C16.9   Malignant neoplasm of stomach, unspecified
>Gastric cancer NOS

Figure 2-3 The esophagus is the muscular tube that connects the pharynx and the stomach. The 10 inch (25 cm) long esophagus is divided into three parts: **cervical, thoracic,** and **abdominal.**

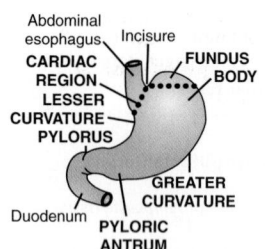

Figure 2-4 Parts of the stomach.

Item 2-2 The esophagus opens into the stomach through the **cardiac orifice,** also called the **cardioesophageal junction.** The **cardia** is adjacent to the cardiac orifice. The stomach widens into the **greater** and **lesser** curvatures. The **pyloric antrum** precedes the **pylorus,** which opens to the duodenum.

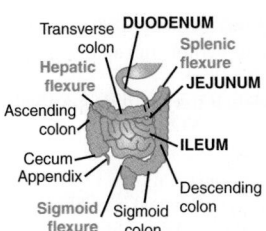

Figure 2-5 Small intestine and colon.

● **C17** Malignant neoplasm of small intestine
> **Excludes1** malignant carcinoid tumor of the small intestine (C7A.Ø1)

C17.Ø **Malignant neoplasm of duodenum**
> *First or proximal portion of small intestine, extending from pylorus to jejunum*

C17.1 **Malignant neoplasm of jejunum**
> *Second section of small intestine, extending from duodenum to ileum*

C17.2 **Malignant neoplasm of ileum**
> *Distal and longest portion of small intestine, extending from jejunum to cecum*
> > **Excludes1** malignant neoplasm of ileocecal valve (C18.Ø)

C17.3 **Meckel's diverticulum, malignant**
> *Appendage of ileum*
> > **Excludes1** Meckel's diverticulum, congenital (Q43.Ø)

C17.8 **Malignant neoplasm of overlapping sites of small intestine**

C17.9 **Malignant neoplasm of small intestine, unspecified**

● **C18** Malignant neoplasm of colon
> **Excludes1** malignant carcinoid tumors of the colon (C7A.Ø2)

C18.Ø **Malignant neoplasm of cecum**
> *First section of large intestine*
> Malignant neoplasm of ileocecal valve

C18.1 **Malignant neoplasm of appendix**
> *Blind ended tube connected to the cecum; AKA vermiform appendix*

C18.2 **Malignant neoplasm of ascending colon**
> *Ascending colon is between cecum and right colic flexure*

C18.3 **Malignant neoplasm of hepatic flexure**
> *A flexure is a bending in a structure or organ. Note the three flexures illustrated in Figure 2–5.*

C18.4 **Malignant neoplasm of transverse colon**
> *Portion of colon that runs transversely across upper part of abdomen, between right and left colic flexures*

C18.5 **Malignant neoplasm of splenic flexure**
> *Bend at junction of transverse and descending colon*

C18.6 **Malignant neoplasm of descending colon**
> *Portion between left colic flexure and sigmoid colon at pelvic brim; AKA iliac colon*

C18.7 **Malignant neoplasm of sigmoid colon**
> *S-shaped part of colon extending from pelvic brim to third segment of sacrum*
> Malignant neoplasm of sigmoid (flexure)
> > **Excludes1** malignant neoplasm of rectosigmoid junction (C19)

C18.8 **Malignant neoplasm of overlapping sites of colon**

C18.9 **Malignant neoplasm of colon, unspecified**
> Malignant neoplasm of large intestine NOS

C19 **Malignant neoplasm of rectosigmoid junction**
> Malignant neoplasm of colon with rectum
> Malignant neoplasm of rectosigmoid (colon)
> > **Excludes1** malignant carcinoid tumors of the colon (C7A.Ø2-)

C2Ø **Malignant neoplasm of rectum**
> Malignant neoplasm of rectal ampulla
> > **Excludes1** malignant carcinoid tumor of the rectum (C7A.Ø26)

● **C21** Malignant neoplasm of anus and anal canal
> **Excludes2** malignant carcinoid tumors of the colon (C7A.Ø2-)
> malignant melanoma of anal margin (C43.51)
> malignant melanoma of anal skin (C43.51)
> malignant melanoma of perianal skin (C43.51)
> other and unspecified malignant neoplasm of anal margin (C44.5ØØ, C44.51Ø, C44.52Ø, C44.59Ø)
> other and unspecified malignant neoplasm of anal skin (C44.5ØØ, C44.51Ø, C44.52Ø, C44.59Ø)
> other and unspecified malignant neoplasm of perianal skin (C44.5ØØ, C44.51Ø, C44.52Ø, C44.59Ø)

C21.Ø **Malignant neoplasm of anus, unspecified**

C21.1 **Malignant neoplasm of anal canal**
> *Terminal part of large intestine*
> Malignant neoplasm of anal sphincter

C21.2 **Malignant neoplasm of cloacogenic zone**

C21.8 **Malignant neoplasm of overlapping sites of rectum, anus and anal canal**
> Malignant neoplasm of anorectal junction
> Malignant neoplasm of anorectum
> Primary malignant neoplasm of two or more contiguous sites of rectum, anus and anal canal

● **C22** Malignant neoplasm of liver and intrahepatic bile ducts
> *Intrahepatic: Within liver*
> Use additional code to identify:
> alcohol abuse and dependence (F1Ø.-)
> hepatitis B (B16.-, B18.Ø-B18.1) hepatitis C (B17.1-, B18.2)
> > **Excludes1** malignant neoplasm of biliary tract NOS (C24.9)
> > secondary malignant neoplasm of liver and intrahepatic bile duct (C78.7)

C22.Ø **Liver cell carcinoma**
> Hepatocellular carcinoma
> Hepatoma

C22.1 **Intrahepatic bile duct carcinoma**
> Cholangiocarcinoma
> *Adenocarcinoma (cancer that originates in glandular tissue) arising from epithelium of intrahepatic bile ducts*
> > **Excludes1** malignant neoplasm of hepatic duct (C24.Ø)

C22.2 **Hepatoblastoma**
> *Malignant intrahepatic tumor*

C22.3 **Angiosarcoma of liver**
> Kupffer cell sarcoma

C22.4 **Other sarcomas of liver**

C22.7 **Other specified carcinomas of liver**

C22.8 **Malignant neoplasm of liver, primary, unspecified as to type**

C22.9 **Malignant neoplasm of liver, not specified as primary or secondary**

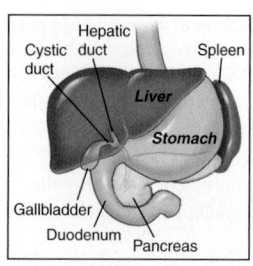

Figure 2-6 Diagram of liver, gallbladder, hepatic duct, pancreas, and spleen. (From Thibodeau and Patton: Anatomy and Physiology, ed 7, Mosby, 2010)

C23   **Malignant neoplasm of gallbladder**

● C24   **Malignant neoplasm of other and unspecified parts of biliary tract**

  Excludes1   malignant neoplasm of intrahepatic bile duct (C22.1)

  C24.0   **Malignant neoplasm of extrahepatic bile duct**
    Extrahepatic = outside the liver
    Malignant neoplasm of biliary duct or passage NOS
    Malignant neoplasm of common bile duct
    Malignant neoplasm of cystic duct
    Malignant neoplasm of hepatic duct

  C24.1   **Malignant neoplasm of ampulla of Vater**
    Union of pancreatic duct and common bile duct

  C24.8   **Malignant neoplasm of overlapping sites of biliary tract**
    Malignant neoplasm involving both intrahepatic and extrahepatic bile ducts
    Primary malignant neoplasm of two or more contiguous sites of biliary tract

  C24.9   **Malignant neoplasm of biliary tract, unspecified**

● C25   **Malignant neoplasm of pancreas**
    Check documentation for specific site.
    Code also exocrine pancreatic insufficiency (K86.81)
    Use additional code to identify:
      alcohol abuse and dependence (F10.-)

  C25.0   **Malignant neoplasm of head of pancreas**
  C25.1   **Malignant neoplasm of body of pancreas**
  C25.2   **Malignant neoplasm of tail of pancreas**
  C25.3   **Malignant neoplasm of pancreatic duct**
  C25.4   **Malignant neoplasm of endocrine pancreas**
    Malignant neoplasm of islets of Langerhans
    That part of the pancreas that acts as endocrine gland and consists of islets of Langerhans
      Use additional code to identify any functional activity.

  C25.7   **Malignant neoplasm of other parts of pancreas**
    Malignant neoplasm of neck of pancreas
  C25.8   **Malignant neoplasm of overlapping sites of pancreas**
  C25.9   **Malignant neoplasm of pancreas, unspecified**

Item 2–3   Islets of Langerhans (endocrine producing cells comprising 1% to 2% of the pancreatic mass) make and secrete hormones that regulate the body's production of insulin, glucagon, and stomach acid. Breakdown of the insulin-producing cells can cause diabetes mellitus. Islet cell tumors can be benign or malignant and include glucagonomas, insulinomas, gastrinomas, and neuroendocrine tumor. The neoplasm table must be consulted for the correct neoplasm code.

Figure 2-7 Paranasal sinuses. (From Buck CJ: Step-by-Step Medical Coding, ed 2016, St. Louis, Elsevier, 2016)

● C26   **Malignant neoplasm of other and ill-defined digestive organs**

  Excludes1   malignant neoplasm of peritoneum and retroperitoneum (C48.-)

  C26.0   **Malignant neoplasm of intestinal tract, part unspecified**
    Malignant neoplasm of intestine NOS

  C26.1   **Malignant neoplasm of spleen**

    Excludes1   Hodgkin lymphoma (C81.-)
      non-Hodgkin lymphoma (C82-C85)

  C26.9   **Malignant neoplasm of ill-defined sites within the digestive system**
    Malignant neoplasm of alimentary canal or tract NOS
    Malignant neoplasm of gastrointestinal tract NOS

    Excludes1   malignant neoplasm of abdominal NOS (C76.2)
      malignant neoplasm of intra-abdominal NOS (C76.2)

MALIGNANT NEOPLASMS OF RESPIRATORY AND INTRATHORACIC ORGANS (C30-C39)

  Includes   malignant neoplasm of middle ear
  Excludes1   mesothelioma (C45.-)

● C30   **Malignant neoplasm of nasal cavity and middle ear**

  C30.0   **Malignant neoplasm of nasal cavity**
    Malignant neoplasm of cartilage of nose
    Malignant neoplasm of nasal concha
    Malignant neoplasm of internal nose
    Malignant neoplasm of septum of nose
    Malignant neoplasm of vestibule of nose
    Anterior part of nasal cavity

    Excludes1   malignant neoplasm of nasal bone (C41.0)
      malignant neoplasm of nose NOS (C76.0)
      malignant neoplasm of olfactory bulb (C72.2-)
      malignant neoplasm of posterior margin of nasal septum and choana (C11.3)
      malignant melanoma of skin of nose (C43.31)
      malignant neoplasm of turbinates (C41.0)
      other and unspecified malignant neoplasm of skin of nose C44.301, C44.311, C44.321, C44.391

  C30.1   **Malignant neoplasm of middle ear**
    Malignant neoplasm of antrum tympanicum
    Boney cavity or chamber
    Malignant neoplasm of auditory tube
    Malignant neoplasm of eustachian tube
    Malignant neoplasm of inner ear
    Malignant neoplasm of mastoid air cells
    Malignant neoplasm of tympanic cavity

    Excludes1   malignant neoplasm of auricular canal (external) (C43.2-, C44.2-)
      malignant neoplasm of bone of ear (meatus) (C41.0)
      malignant neoplasm of cartilage of ear (C49.0)
      malignant melanoma of skin of (external) ear (C43.2-)
      other and unspecified malignant neoplasm of skin of (external) ear (C44.2-)

● C31   **Malignant neoplasm of accessory sinuses**
    Paired sinuses in bones of face

  C31.0   **Malignant neoplasm of maxillary sinus**
    Malignant neoplasm of antrum (Highmore) (maxillary)

  C31.1   **Malignant neoplasm of ethmoidal sinus**
  C31.2   **Malignant neoplasm of frontal sinus**
  C31.3   **Malignant neoplasm of sphenoid sinus**
  C31.8   **Malignant neoplasm of overlapping sites of accessory sinuses**
  C31.9   **Malignant neoplasm of accessory sinus, unspecified**

▶ New   ⮕ Revised   ~~deleted~~ Deleted   Excludes 1   Excludes 2   Includes   Use additional   Code first   Code also   Key words

OGCR Official Guidelines   X Assign placeholder X   ● Use Additional Character(s)   ▷ Manifestation Code   **Coding Clinic**

● **C32**   **Malignant neoplasm of larynx**

Use additional code to identify:
- alcohol abuse and dependence (F10.-)
- exposure to environmental tobacco smoke (Z77.22)
- exposure to tobacco smoke in the perinatal period (P96.81)
- history of tobacco dependence (Z87.891)
- occupational exposure to environmental tobacco smoke (Z57.31)
- tobacco dependence (F17.-)
- tobacco use (Z72.0)

C32.0   **Malignant neoplasm of glottis**

Vocal apparatus of larynx, consisting of true vocal cords (plicae vocales) and opening between them (rima glottidis)

Malignant neoplasm of intrinsic larynx

Malignant neoplasm of laryngeal commissure (anterior) (posterior)

Malignant neoplasm of vocal cord (true) NOS

*True vocal cords ("lower vocal folds") produce vocalization when air from the lungs passes between them. Check your documentation. Code C32.1 is for malignant neoplasm of the **false** vocal cords.*

C32.1   **Malignant neoplasm of supraglottis**

Area of pharynx above glottis

Malignant neoplasm of aryepiglottic fold or interarytenoid fold, laryngeal aspect

Malignant neoplasm of epiglottis (suprahyoid portion) NOS

Malignant neoplasm of extrinsic larynx

Malignant neoplasm of false vocal cord

False vocal cords ("upper vocal folds") are not involved in vocalization. Check your documentation. Code C32.0 is for true vocal cords.

Malignant neoplasm of posterior (laryngeal) surface of epiglottis

Malignant neoplasm of ventricular bands

Excludes2   malignant neoplasm of anterior surface of epiglottis (C10.1)

malignant neoplasm of aryepiglottic fold or interarytenoid fold, hypopharyngeal aspect (C13.1)

malignant neoplasm of aryepiglottic fold or interarytenoid fold, marginal zone (C13.1)

malignant neoplasm of aryepiglottic fold or interarytenoid fold NOS (C13.1)

C32.2   **Malignant neoplasm of subglottis**

Lowest part of larynx from just below vocal cords down to top of trachea

C32.3   **Malignant neoplasm of laryngeal cartilage**

Cartilages of larynx, including cricoid, thyroid, and epiglottic, and two each of arytenoid, corniculate, and cuneiform

C32.8   **Malignant neoplasm of overlapping sites of larynx**

C32.9   **Malignant neoplasm of larynx, unspecified**

C33   **Malignant neoplasm of trachea**

Use additional code to identify:
- exposure to environmental tobacco smoke (Z77.22)
- exposure to tobacco smoke in the perinatal period (P96.81)
- history of tobacco dependence (Z87.891)
- occupational exposure to environmental tobacco smoke (Z57.31)
- tobacco dependence (F17.-)
- tobacco use (Z72.0)

● **C34**   **Malignant neoplasm of bronchus and lung**

Use additional code to identify:
- exposure to environmental tobacco smoke (Z77.22)
- exposure to tobacco smoke in the perinatal period (P96.81)
- history of tobacco dependence (Z87.891)
- occupational exposure to environmental tobacco smoke (Z57.31)
- tobacco dependence (F17.-)
- tobacco use (Z72.0)

Excludes1   Kaposi's sarcoma of lung (C46.5-)

malignant carcinoid tumor of the bronchus and lung (C7A.090)

● **C34.0**   **Malignant neoplasm of main bronchus**

Malignant neoplasm of carina

Ridgelike structure

Malignant neoplasm of hilus (of lung)

Anatomic depression or pit

    C34.00   **Malignant neoplasm of unspecified main bronchus**

    C34.01   **Malignant neoplasm of right main bronchus**

    C34.02   **Malignant neoplasm of left main bronchus**

● **C34.1**   **Malignant neoplasm of upper lobe, bronchus or lung**

    C34.10   **Malignant neoplasm of unspecified bronchus or lung**

    C34.11   **Malignant neoplasm of upper lobe, right bronchus or lung**

    C34.12   **Malignant neoplasm of upper lobe, left bronchus or lung**

C34.2   **Malignant neoplasm of middle lobe, bronchus or lung**

● **C34.3**   **Malignant neoplasm of lower lobe, bronchus or lung**

    C34.30   **Malignant neoplasm of lower lobe, unspecified bronchus or lung**

    C34.31   **Malignant neoplasm of lower lobe, right bronchus or lung**

    C34.32   **Malignant neoplasm of lower lobe, left bronchus or lung**

● **C34.8**   **Malignant neoplasm of overlapping sites of bronchus and lung**

    C34.80   **Malignant neoplasm of overlapping sites of unspecified bronchus and lung**

    C34.81   **Malignant neoplasm of overlapping sites of right bronchus and lung**

    C34.82   **Malignant neoplasm of overlapping sites of left bronchus and lung**

● **C34.9**   **Malignant neoplasm of unspecified part of bronchus or lung**

    C34.90   **Malignant neoplasm of unspecified part of unspecified bronchus or lung**

Lung cancer NOS

    C34.91   **Malignant neoplasm of unspecified part of right bronchus or lung**

    C34.92   **Malignant neoplasm of unspecified part of left bronchus or lung**

C37   **Malignant neoplasm of thymus**

Excludes1   malignant carcinoid tumor of the thymus (C7A.091)

CHAPTER 2 (C00-D49)

● **C38 Malignant neoplasm of heart, mediastinum and pleura**

> **Excludes1** mesothelioma (C45.-)

C38.0 Malignant neoplasm of heart
Malignant neoplasm of pericardium
> **Excludes1** malignant neoplasm of great vessels (C49.3)

C38.1 Malignant neoplasm of anterior mediastinum
C38.2 Malignant neoplasm of posterior mediastinum
C38.3 Malignant neoplasm of mediastinum, part unspecified
C38.4 Malignant neoplasm of pleura
C38.8 Malignant neoplasm of overlapping sites of heart, mediastinum and pleura
Pleura are comprised of serous membrane that lines the thoracic cavity (parietal) and covers the lungs (visceral).

● **C39 Malignant neoplasm of other and ill-defined sites in the respiratory system and intrathoracic organs**
Intrathoracic: within thorax/chest
Use additional code to identify:
exposure to environmental tobacco smoke (Z77.22)
exposure to tobacco smoke in the perinatal period (P96.81)
history of tobacco dependence (Z87.891)
occupational exposure to environmental tobacco smoke (Z57.31)
tobacco dependence (F17.-)
tobacco use (Z72.0)
> **Excludes1** intrathoracic malignant neoplasm NOS (C76.1)
> thoracic malignant neoplasm NOS (C76.1)

C39.0 Malignant neoplasm of upper respiratory tract, part unspecified
C39.9 Malignant neoplasm of lower respiratory tract, part unspecified
Malignant neoplasm of respiratory tract NOS

MALIGNANT NEOPLASMS OF BONE AND ARTICULAR CARTILAGE (C40-C41)

> **Includes** malignant neoplasm of cartilage (articular) (joint)
> malignant neoplasm of periosteum
> **Excludes1** malignant neoplasm of bone marrow NOS (C96.9)
> malignant neoplasm of synovia (C49.-)

● **C40 Malignant neoplasm of bone and articular cartilage of limbs**
Use additional code to identify major osseous defect, if applicable (M89.7-)

● **C40.0 Malignant neoplasm of scapula and long bones of upper limb**
C40.00 Malignant neoplasm of scapula and long bones of unspecified upper limb
C40.01 Malignant neoplasm of scapula and long bones of right upper limb
C40.02 Malignant neoplasm of scapula and long bones of left upper limb

● **C40.1 Malignant neoplasm of short bones of upper limb**
C40.10 Malignant neoplasm of short bones of unspecified upper limb
C40.11 Malignant neoplasm of short bones of right upper limb
C40.12 Malignant neoplasm of short bones of left upper limb

● **C40.2 Malignant neoplasm of long bones of lower limb**
C40.20 Malignant neoplasm of long bones of unspecified lower limb
C40.21 Malignant neoplasm of long bones of right lower limb
C40.22 Malignant neoplasm of long bones of left lower limb

Figure 2-8 Diagram of skeleton of trunk and limbs with bones labeled. (From Thibodeau and Patton: Anatomy and Physiology, ed 7, Mosby, 2010)

● **C40.3 Malignant neoplasm of short bones of lower limb**
C40.30 Malignant neoplasm of short bones of unspecified lower limb
C40.31 Malignant neoplasm of short bones of right lower limb
C40.32 Malignant neoplasm of short bones of left lower limb

● **C40.8 Malignant neoplasm of overlapping sites of bone and articular cartilage of limb**
C40.80 Malignant neoplasm of overlapping sites of bone and articular cartilage of unspecified limb
C40.81 Malignant neoplasm of overlapping sites of bone and articular cartilage of right limb
C40.82 Malignant neoplasm of overlapping sites of bone and articular cartilage of left limb

● **C40.9 Malignant neoplasm of unspecified bones and articular cartilage of limb**
C40.90 Malignant neoplasm of unspecified bones and articular cartilage of unspecified limb
C40.91 Malignant neoplasm of unspecified bones and articular cartilage of right limb
C40.92 Malignant neoplasm of unspecified bones and articular cartilage of left limb

● **C41 Malignant neoplasm of bone and articular cartilage of other and unspecified sites**
> **Excludes1** malignant neoplasm of bones of limbs (C40.-)
> malignant neoplasm of cartilage of ear (C49.0)
> malignant neoplasm of cartilage of eyelid (C49.0)
> malignant neoplasm of cartilage of larynx (C32.3)
> malignant neoplasm of cartilage of limbs (C40.-)
> malignant neoplasm of cartilage of nose (C30.0)

C41.0 Malignant neoplasm of bones of skull and face
Malignant neoplasm of maxilla (superior)
Malignant neoplasm of orbital bone
> **Excludes2** carcinoma, any type except intraosseous or odontogenic of:
> maxillary sinus (C31.0)
> upper jaw (C03.0)
> malignant neoplasm of jaw bone (lower) (C41.1)

▶ New ⇒ Revised ~~deleted~~ Deleted | Excludes 1 | Excludes 2 | Includes | Use additional | Code first | Code also | Key words
OGCR Official Guidelines X Assign placeholder X ● Use Additional Character(s) ▮ Manifestation Code **Coding Clinic**

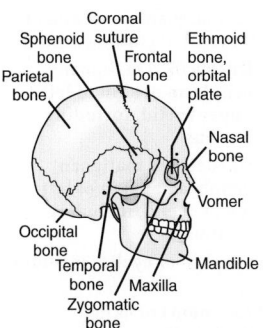

Figure 2-9 Bones of the skull.

Figure 2-10 Malignant melanoma of skin. (Getty Image)

Item 2-4   Malignant melanoma is a serious form of skin cancer that affects the melanocytes (pigment-forming cells) and is caused by ultraviolet (UV) rays from the sun that damage skin. It is most commonly seen in the 40- to 60-year-olds with fair skin, blue or green eyes, and red or blond hair who sunburn easily.

Melanoma can spread very rapidly and is the most deadly form of skin cancer. It is less common than other types of skin cancer. The rate of melanoma is increasing and currently is the leading cause of death from skin disease.

C41.1 **Malignant neoplasm of mandible**
Malignant neoplasm of inferior maxilla
Malignant neoplasm of lower jaw bone
> **Excludes2**   carcinoma, any type except intraosseous or odontogenic of:
> jaw NOS (C03.9)
> lower (C03.1)
> malignant neoplasm of upper jaw bone (C41.0)

C41.2 **Malignant neoplasm of vertebral column**
> **Excludes1**   malignant neoplasm of sacrum and coccyx (C41.4)

C41.3 **Malignant neoplasm of ribs, sternum and clavicle**

C41.4 **Malignant neoplasm of pelvic bones, sacrum and coccyx**

C41.9 **Malignant neoplasm of bone and articular cartilage, unspecified**

MELANOMA AND OTHER MALIGNANT NEOPLASMS OF SKIN (C43-C44)

● **C43** **Malignant melanoma of skin**
> **Excludes1**   melanoma in situ (D03.-)
> **Excludes2**   malignant melanoma of skin of genital organs (C51-C52, C60.-, C63.-)
> Merkel cell carcinoma (C4A.-)
> sites other than skin-code to malignant neoplasm of the site

C43.0 **Malignant melanoma of lip**
> **Excludes1**   malignant neoplasm of vermilion border of lip (C00.0-C00.2)

● **C43.1** **Malignant melanoma of eyelid, including canthus**
Canthus: Either corner of eye where upper and lower eyelids meet
   C43.10 **Malignant melanoma of unspecified eyelid, including canthus**
   C43.11 **Malignant melanoma of right eyelid, including canthus**
     ▶ **C43.111** **Malignant melanoma of right upper eyelid, including canthus**
     ▶ **C43.112** **Malignant melanoma of right lower eyelid, including canthus**
   C43.12 **Malignant melanoma of left eyelid, including canthus**
     ▶ **C43.121** **Malignant melanoma of left upper eyelid, including canthus**
     ▶ **C43.122** **Malignant melanoma of left lower eyelid, including canthus**

● **C43.2** **Malignant melanoma of ear and external auricular canal**
   C43.20 **Malignant melanoma of unspecified ear and external auricular canal**
   C43.21 **Malignant melanoma of right ear and external auricular canal**
   C43.22 **Malignant melanoma of left ear and external auricular canal**

● **C43.3** **Malignant melanoma of other and unspecified parts of face**
   C43.30 **Malignant melanoma of unspecified part of face**
   C43.31 **Malignant melanoma of nose**
   C43.39 **Malignant melanoma of other parts of face**

C43.4 **Malignant melanoma of scalp and neck**

● **C43.5** **Malignant melanoma of trunk**
> **Excludes2**   malignant neoplasm of anus NOS (C21.0)
> malignant neoplasm of scrotum (C63.2)

   C43.51 **Malignant melanoma of anal skin**
Malignant melanoma of anal margin
Malignant melanoma of perianal skin
   C43.52 **Malignant melanoma of skin of breast**
   C43.59 **Malignant melanoma of other part of trunk**

● **C43.6** **Malignant melanoma of upper limb, including shoulder**
   C43.60 **Malignant melanoma of upper limb, including shoulder, unspecified side**
   C43.61 **Malignant melanoma of right upper limb, including shoulder**
   C43.62 **Malignant melanoma of left upper limb, including shoulder**

● **C43.7** **Malignant melanoma of lower limb, including hip**
   C43.70 **Malignant melanoma of unspecified lower limb, including hip**
   C43.71 **Malignant melanoma of right lower limb, including hip**
   C43.72 **Malignant melanoma of left lower limb, including hip**

C43.8 **Malignant melanoma of overlapping sites of skin**

C43.9 **Malignant melanoma of skin, unspecified**
Malignant melanoma of unspecified site of skin
Melanoma (malignant) NOS

● **C4A** **Merkel cell carcinoma**
C4A.0 **Merkel cell carcinoma of lip**
> **Excludes1**   malignant neoplasm of vermilion border of lip (C00.0-C00.2)

● **C4A.1** **Merkel cell carcinoma of eyelid, including canthus**
   C4A.10 **Merkel cell carcinoma of unspecified eyelid, including canthus**
   C4A.11 **Merkel cell carcinoma of right eyelid, including canthus**
     ▶ **C4A.111** **Merkel cell carcinoma of right upper eyelid, including canthus**
     ▶ **C4A.112** **Merkel cell carcinoma of right lower eyelid, including canthus**
   C4A.12 **Merkel cell carcinoma of left eyelid, including canthus**
     ▶ **C4A.121** **Merkel cell carcinoma of left upper eyelid, including canthus**
     ▶ **C4A.122** **Merkel cell carcinoma of left lower eyelid, including canthus**

CHAPTER 2 (C00-D49)

● C4A.2   Merkel cell carcinoma of ear and external auricular canal

    C4A.20   Merkel cell carcinoma of unspecified ear and external auricular canal

    C4A.21   Merkel cell carcinoma of right ear and external auricular canal

    C4A.22   Merkel cell carcinoma of left ear and external auricular canal

● C4A.3   Merkel cell carcinoma of other and unspecified parts of face

    C4A.30   Merkel cell carcinoma of unspecified part of face

    C4A.31   Merkel cell carcinoma of nose

    C4A.39   Merkel cell carcinoma of other parts of face

C4A.4   Merkel cell carcinoma of scalp and neck

● C4A.5   Merkel cell carcinoma of trunk

    Excludes2   malignant neoplasm of anus NOS (C21.0)
               malignant neoplasm of scrotum (C63.2)

    C4A.51   Merkel cell carcinoma of anal skin
          Merkel cell carcinoma of anal margin
          Merkel cell carcinoma of perianal skin

    C4A.52   Merkel cell carcinoma of skin of breast

    C4A.59   Merkel cell carcinoma of other part of trunk

● C4A.6   Merkel cell carcinoma of upper limb, including shoulder

    C4A.60   Merkel cell carcinoma of unspecified upper limb, including shoulder

    C4A.61   Merkel cell carcinoma of right upper limb, including shoulder

    C4A.62   Merkel cell carcinoma of left upper limb, including shoulder

● C4A.7   Merkel cell carcinoma of lower limb, including hip

    C4A.70   Merkel cell carcinoma of unspecified lower limb, including hip

    C4A.71   Merkel cell carcinoma of right lower limb, including hip

    C4A.72   Merkel cell carcinoma of left lower limb, including hip

C4A.8   Merkel cell carcinoma of overlapping sites

C4A.9   Merkel cell carcinoma, unspecified
      Merkel cell carcinoma of unspecified site
      Merkel cell carcinoma NOS

● C44   Other and unspecified malignant neoplasm of skin

    Includes   malignant neoplasm of sebaceous glands
               malignant neoplasm of sweat glands

    Excludes1   Kaposi's sarcoma of skin (C46.0)
               malignant melanoma of skin (C43.-)
               malignant neoplasm of skin of genital organs (C51-C52, C60.-, C63.2)
               Merkel cell carcinoma (C4A.-)

● C44.0   Other and unspecified malignant neoplasm of skin of lip

    Excludes1   malignant neoplasm of lip (C00.-)

    C44.00   Unspecified malignant neoplasm of skin of lip

    C44.01   Basal cell carcinoma of skin of lip

    C44.02   Squamous cell carcinoma of skin of lip

    C44.09   Other specified malignant neoplasm of skin of lip

● C44.1   Other and unspecified malignant neoplasm of skin of eyelid, including canthus

    Excludes1   connective tissue of eyelid (C49.0)

  ● C44.10   Unspecified malignant neoplasm of skin of eyelid, including canthus

      C44.101   Unspecified malignant neoplasm of skin of unspecified eyelid, including canthus

      C44.102   Unspecified malignant neoplasm of skin of right eyelid, including canthus

      ▶ C44.1021   Unspecified malignant neoplasm of skin of right upper eyelid, including canthus

      ▶ C44.1022   Unspecified malignant neoplasm of skin of right lower eyelid, including canthus

      C44.109   Unspecified malignant neoplasm of skin of left eyelid, including canthus

      ▶ C44.1091   Unspecified malignant neoplasm of skin of left upper eyelid, including canthus

      ▶ C44.1092   Unspecified malignant neoplasm of skin of left lower eyelid, including canthus

  ● C44.11   Basal cell carcinoma of skin of eyelid, including canthus

      C44.111   Basal cell carcinoma of skin of unspecified eyelid, including canthus

      C44.112   Basal cell carcinoma of skin of right eyelid, including canthus

      ▶ C44.1121   Basal cell carcinoma of skin of right upper eyelid, including canthus

      ▶ C44.1122   Basal cell carcinoma of skin of right lower eyelid, including canthus

      C44.119   Basal cell carcinoma of skin of left eyelid, including canthus

      ▶ C44.1191   Basal cell carcinoma of skin of left upper eyelid, including canthus

      ▶ C44.1192   Basal cell carcinoma of skin of left lower eyelid, including canthus

  ● C44.12   Squamous cell carcinoma of skin of eyelid, including canthus

      C44.121   Squamous cell carcinoma of skin of unspecified eyelid, including canthus

      C44.122   Squamous cell carcinoma of skin of right eyelid, including canthus

      ▶ C44.1221   Squamous cell carcinoma of skin of right upper eyelid, including canthus

      ▶ C44.1222   Squamous cell carcinoma of skin of right lower eyelid, including canthus

      C44.129   Squamous cell carcinoma of skin of left eyelid, including canthus

      ▶ C44.1291   Squamous cell carcinoma of skin of left upper eyelid, including canthus

      ▶ C44.1292   Squamous cell carcinoma of skin of left lower eyelid, including canthus

▶● C44.13   Sebaceous cell carcinoma of skin of eyelid, including canthus

  ▶ C44.131   Sebaceous cell carcinoma of skin of unspecified eyelid, including canthus

  ▶ C44.132   Sebaceous cell carcinoma of skin of right eyelid, including canthus

    ▶ C44.1321   Sebaceous cell carcinoma of skin of right upper eyelid, including canthus

    ▶ C44.1322   Sebaceous cell carcinoma of skin of right lower eyelid, including canthus

  ▶ C44.139   Sebaceous cell carcinoma of skin of left eyelid, including canthus

    ▶ C44.1391   Sebaceous cell carcinoma of skin of left upper eyelid, including canthus

    ▶ C44.1392   Sebaceous cell carcinoma of skin of left lower eyelid, including canthus

▶ New   ⇒ Revised   ~~deleted~~ Deleted   Excludes 1   Excludes 2   Includes   Use additional   Code first   Code also   Key words

OGCR Official Guidelines   X Assign placeholder X   ● Use Additional Character(s)   ▶ Manifestation Code   **Coding Clinic**

● **C44.19** Other specified malignant neoplasm of skin of eyelid, including canthus

    C44.191 Other specified malignant neoplasm of skin of unspecified eyelid, including canthus

    C44.192 Other specified malignant neoplasm of skin of right eyelid, including canthus

       ▶ **C44.1921** Other specified malignant neoplasm of skin of right upper eyelid, including canthus

       ▶ **C44.1922** Other specified malignant neoplasm of skin of right lower eyelid, including canthus

    C44.199 Other specified malignant neoplasm of skin of left eyelid, including canthus

       ▶ **C44.1991** Other specified malignant neoplasm of skin of left upper eyelid, including canthus

       ▶ **C44.1992** Other specified malignant neoplasm of skin of left lower eyelid, including canthus

● **C44.2** Other and unspecified malignant neoplasm of skin of ear and external auricular canal

    Excludes1   connective tissue of ear (C49.0)

● **C44.20** Unspecified malignant neoplasm of skin of ear and external auricular canal

    C44.201 Unspecified malignant neoplasm of skin of unspecified ear and external auricular canal

    C44.202 Unspecified malignant neoplasm of skin of right ear and external auricular canal

    C44.209 Unspecified malignant neoplasm of skin of left ear and external auricular canal

● **C44.21** Basal cell carcinoma of skin of ear and external auricular canal

    C44.211 Basal cell carcinoma of skin of unspecified ear and external auricular canal

    C44.212 Basal cell carcinoma of skin of right ear and external auricular canal

    C44.219 Basal cell carcinoma of skin of left ear and external auricular canal

● **C44.22** Squamous cell carcinoma of skin of ear and external auricular canal

    C44.221 Squamous cell carcinoma of skin of unspecified ear and external auricular canal

    C44.222 Squamous cell carcinoma of skin of right ear and external auricular canal

    C44.229 Squamous cell carcinoma of skin of left ear and external auricular canal

● **C44.29** Other specified malignant neoplasm of skin of ear and external auricular canal

    C44.291 Other specified malignant neoplasm of skin of unspecified ear and external auricular canal

    C44.292 Other specified malignant neoplasm of skin of right ear and external auricular canal

    C44.299 Other specified malignant neoplasm of skin of left ear and external auricular canal

● **C44.3** Other and unspecified malignant neoplasm of skin of other and unspecified parts of face

● **C44.30** Unspecified malignant neoplasm of skin of other and unspecified parts of face

    C44.300 Unspecified malignant neoplasm of skin of unspecified part of face

    C44.301 Unspecified malignant neoplasm of skin of nose

    C44.309 Unspecified malignant neoplasm of skin of other parts of face

● **C44.31** Basal cell carcinoma of skin of other and unspecified parts of face

    C44.310 Basal cell carcinoma of skin of unspecified parts of face

    C44.311 Basal cell carcinoma of skin of nose

    C44.319 Basal cell carcinoma of skin of other parts of face

       Coding Clinic: 2017, Q1, P4

● **C44.32** Squamous cell carcinoma of skin of other and unspecified parts of face

    C44.320 Squamous cell carcinoma of skin of unspecified parts of face

    C44.321 Squamous cell carcinoma of skin of nose

    C44.329 Squamous cell carcinoma of skin of other parts of face

● **C44.39** Other specified malignant neoplasm of skin of other and unspecified parts of face

    C44.390 Other specified malignant neoplasm of skin of unspecified parts of face

    C44.391 Other specified malignant neoplasm of skin of nose

    C44.399 Other specified malignant neoplasm of skin of other parts of face

● **C44.4** Other and unspecified malignant neoplasm of skin of scalp and neck

    C44.40 Unspecified malignant neoplasm of skin of scalp and neck

    C44.41 Basal cell carcinoma of skin of scalp and neck

    C44.42 Squamous cell carcinoma of skin of scalp and neck

    C44.49 Other specified malignant neoplasm of skin of scalp and neck

● **C44.5** Other and unspecified malignant neoplasm of skin of trunk

    Excludes1   anus NOS (C21.0)
                scrotum (C63.2)

● **C44.50** Unspecified malignant neoplasm of skin of trunk

    C44.500 Unspecified malignant neoplasm of anal skin
           Unspecified malignant neoplasm of anal margin
           Unspecified malignant neoplasm of perianal skin

    C44.501 Unspecified malignant neoplasm of skin of breast

    C44.509 Unspecified malignant neoplasm of skin of other part of trunk

● **C44.51** Basal cell carcinoma of skin of trunk

    C44.510 Basal cell carcinoma of anal skin
           Basal cell carcinoma of anal margin
           Basal cell carcinoma of perianal skin

    C44.511 Basal cell carcinoma of skin of breast

    C44.519 Basal cell carcinoma of skin of other part of trunk

CHAPTER 2 (C00-D49)

● **C44.52** Squamous cell carcinoma of skin of trunk

    C44.520 Squamous cell carcinoma of anal skin

        Squamous cell carcinoma of anal margin

        Squamous cell carcinoma of perianal skin

    C44.521 Squamous cell carcinoma of skin of breast

    C44.529 Squamous cell carcinoma of skin of other part of trunk

● **C44.59** Other specified malignant neoplasm of skin of trunk

    C44.590 Other specified malignant neoplasm of anal skin

        Other specified malignant neoplasm of anal margin

        Other specified malignant neoplasm of perianal skin

    C44.591 Other specified malignant neoplasm of skin of breast

    C44.599 Other specified malignant neoplasm of skin of other part of trunk

● **C44.6** Other and unspecified malignant neoplasm of skin of upper limb, including shoulder

  ● **C44.60** Unspecified malignant neoplasm of skin of upper limb, including shoulder

    C44.601 Unspecified malignant neoplasm of skin of unspecified upper limb, including shoulder

    C44.602 Unspecified malignant neoplasm of skin of right upper limb, including shoulder

    C44.609 Unspecified malignant neoplasm of skin of left upper limb, including shoulder

  ● **C44.61** Basal cell carcinoma of skin of upper limb, including shoulder

    C44.611 Basal cell carcinoma of skin of unspecified upper limb, including shoulder

    C44.612 Basal cell carcinoma of skin of right upper limb, including shoulder

    C44.619 Basal cell carcinoma of skin of left upper limb, including shoulder

  ● **C44.62** Squamous cell carcinoma of skin of upper limb, including shoulder

    C44.621 Squamous cell carcinoma of skin of unspecified upper limb, including shoulder

    C44.622 Squamous cell carcinoma of skin of right upper limb, including shoulder

    C44.629 Squamous cell carcinoma of skin of left upper limb, including shoulder

  ● **C44.69** Other specified malignant neoplasm of skin of upper limb, including shoulder

    C44.691 Other specified malignant neoplasm of skin of unspecified upper limb, including shoulder

    C44.692 Other specified malignant neoplasm of skin of right upper limb, including shoulder

    C44.699 Other specified malignant neoplasm of skin of left upper limb, including shoulder

● **C44.7** Other and unspecified malignant neoplasm of skin of lower limb, including hip

  ● **C44.70** Unspecified malignant neoplasm of skin of lower limb, including hip

    C44.701 Unspecified malignant neoplasm of skin of unspecified lower limb, including hip

    C44.702 Unspecified malignant neoplasm of skin of right lower limb, including hip

    C44.709 Unspecified malignant neoplasm of skin of left lower limb, including hip

  ● **C44.71** Basal cell carcinoma of skin of lower limb, including hip

    C44.711 Basal cell carcinoma of skin of unspecified lower limb, including hip

    C44.712 Basal cell carcinoma of skin of right lower limb, including hip

    C44.719 Basal cell carcinoma of skin of left lower limb, including hip

  ● **C44.72** Squamous cell carcinoma of skin of lower limb, including hip

    C44.721 Squamous cell carcinoma of skin of unspecified lower limb, including hip

    C44.722 Squamous cell carcinoma of skin of right lower limb, including hip

    C44.729 Squamous cell carcinoma of skin of left lower limb, including hip

  ● **C44.79** Other specified malignant neoplasm of skin of lower limb, including hip

    C44.791 Other specified malignant neoplasm of skin of unspecified lower limb, including hip

    C44.792 Other specified malignant neoplasm of skin of right lower limb, including hip

    C44.799 Other specified malignant neoplasm of skin of left lower limb, including hip

● **C44.8** Other and unspecified malignant neoplasm of overlapping sites of skin

  C44.80 Unspecified malignant neoplasm of overlapping sites of skin

  C44.81 Basal cell carcinoma of overlapping sites of skin

  C44.82 Squamous cell carcinoma of overlapping sites of skin

  C44.89 Other specified malignant neoplasm of overlapping sites of skin

● **C44.9** Other and unspecified malignant neoplasm of skin, unspecified

  C44.90 Unspecified malignant neoplasm of skin, unspecified

    Malignant neoplasm of unspecified site of skin

  C44.91 Basal cell carcinoma of skin, unspecified

  C44.92 Squamous cell carcinoma of skin, unspecified

  C44.99 Other specified malignant neoplasm of skin, unspecified

▶ New   ⇒ Revised   ~~deleted~~ Deleted   Excludes 1   Excludes 2   Includes   Use additional   Code first   Code also   Key words

OGCR Official Guidelines   X Assign placeholder X   ● Use Additional Character(s)   ▶ Manifestation Code   **Coding Clinic**

MALIGNANT NEOPLASMS OF MESOTHELIAL AND SOFT TISSUE (C45-C49)

● **C45   Mesothelioma**
Malignant cells develop in protective lining that covers internal organs (mesothelium) caused by exposure to asbestos

    C45.0   Mesothelioma of pleura
       Excludes1   other malignant neoplasm of pleura (C38.4)
       Coding Clinic: 2017, Q2, P11

    C45.1   Mesothelioma of peritoneum
       Mesothelioma of cul-de-sac
       Mesothelioma of mesentery
       Mesothelioma of mesocolon
       Mesothelioma of omentum
       Mesothelioma of peritoneum (parietal) (pelvic)
       Excludes1   other malignant neoplasm of soft tissue of peritoneum (C48.-)

    C45.2   Mesothelioma of pericardium
       Excludes1   other malignant neoplasm of pericardium (C38.0)

    C45.7   Mesothelioma of other sites
    C45.9   Mesothelioma, unspecified

● **C46   Kaposi's sarcoma**
Code first any human immunodeficiency virus [HIV] disease (B20)

    C46.0   Kaposi's sarcoma of skin
    C46.1   Kaposi's sarcoma of soft tissue
       Kaposi's sarcoma of blood vessel
       Kaposi's sarcoma of connective tissue
       Kaposi's sarcoma of fascia
       Kaposi's sarcoma of ligament
       Kaposi's sarcoma of lymphatic(s) NEC
       Kaposi's sarcoma of muscle
       Excludes2   Kaposi's sarcoma of lymph glands and nodes (C46.3)

    C46.2   Kaposi's sarcoma of palate
    C46.3   Kaposi's sarcoma of lymph nodes
    C46.4   Kaposi's sarcoma of gastrointestinal sites
  ● **C46.5   Kaposi's sarcoma of lung**
       C46.50   Kaposi's sarcoma of unspecified lung
       C46.51   Kaposi's sarcoma of right lung
       C46.52   Kaposi's sarcoma of left lung

    C46.7   Kaposi's sarcoma of other sites
    C46.9   Kaposi's sarcoma, unspecified
       Kaposi's sarcoma of unspecified site

● **C47   Malignant neoplasm of peripheral nerves and autonomic nervous system**
       Includes   malignant neoplasm of sympathetic and parasympathetic nerves and ganglia
       Excludes1   Kaposi's sarcoma of soft tissue (C46.1)

    C47.0   Malignant neoplasm of peripheral nerves of head, face and neck
       Excludes1   malignant neoplasm of peripheral nerves of orbit (C69.6-)

  ● **C47.1   Malignant neoplasm of peripheral nerves of upper limb, including shoulder**
       C47.10   Malignant neoplasm of peripheral nerves of unspecified upper limb, including shoulder
       C47.11   Malignant neoplasm of peripheral nerves of right upper limb, including shoulder
       C47.12   Malignant neoplasm of peripheral nerves of left upper limb, including shoulder

  ● **C47.2   Malignant neoplasm of peripheral nerves of lower limb, including hip**
       C47.20   Malignant neoplasm of peripheral nerves of unspecified lower limb, including hip
       C47.21   Malignant neoplasm of peripheral nerves of right lower limb, including hip
       C47.22   Malignant neoplasm of peripheral nerves of left lower limb, including hip

    C47.3   Malignant neoplasm of peripheral nerves of thorax
    C47.4   Malignant neoplasm of peripheral nerves of abdomen
    C47.5   Malignant neoplasm of peripheral nerves of pelvis
    C47.6   Malignant neoplasm of peripheral nerves of trunk, unspecified
       Malignant neoplasm of peripheral nerves of unspecified part of trunk

    C47.8   Malignant neoplasm of overlapping sites of peripheral nerves and autonomic nervous system
    C47.9   Malignant neoplasm of peripheral nerves and autonomic nervous system, unspecified
       Malignant neoplasm of unspecified site of peripheral nerves and autonomic nervous system

● **C48   Malignant neoplasm of retroperitoneum and peritoneum**
       Excludes1   Kaposi's sarcoma of connective tissue (C46.1)
             mesothelioma (C45.-)

    C48.0   Malignant neoplasm of retroperitoneum
       Behind/outside of peritoneum

    C48.1   Malignant neoplasm of specified parts of peritoneum
       Serous membrane lining abdominopelvic walls and covering viscera
       Malignant neoplasm of cul-de-sac
       Malignant neoplasm of mesentery
       Malignant neoplasm of mesocolon
       Malignant neoplasm of omentum
       Malignant neoplasm of parietal peritoneum
       Malignant neoplasm of pelvic peritoneum

    C48.2   Malignant neoplasm of peritoneum, unspecified
    C48.8   Malignant neoplasm of overlapping sites of retroperitoneum and peritoneum

CHAPTER 2 (C00-D49)

Figure 2-11 Kaposi's sarcoma. There are large confluent hyperpigmented patch-stage lesions with lymphedema. (From Goldman L, Ausiello D, Arend W, Armitage J, Clemmons D, Drazen J, Griggs R, et al: Cecil Medicine: Expert Consult, 23e, Saunders, 2007)

Item 2–5   Kaposi's sarcoma is a cancer that causes patches of abnormal tissue to grow under the skin; in the lining of the mouth, nose, and throat; or in other organs, often beginning and spreading to other organs. Patients who have had organ transplants or patients with AIDS are at high risk for this malignancy.

● **C49   Malignant neoplasm of other connective and soft tissue**

Includes   malignant neoplasm of blood vessel
malignant neoplasm of bursa
malignant neoplasm of cartilage
malignant neoplasm of fascia
malignant neoplasm of fat
malignant neoplasm of ligament, except uterine
malignant neoplasm of lymphatic vessel
malignant neoplasm of muscle
malignant neoplasm of synovia
malignant neoplasm of tendon (sheath)

Excludes1   malignant neoplasm of cartilage (of):
    articular (C40-C41)
    larynx (C32.3)
    nose (C30.0)
malignant neoplasm of connective tissue of breast (C50.-)

Excludes2   Kaposi's sarcoma of soft tissue (C46.1)
malignant neoplasm of heart (C38.0)
malignant neoplasm of peripheral nerves and autonomic nervous system (C47.-)
malignant neoplasm of peritoneum (C48.2)
malignant neoplasm of retroperitoneum (C48.0)
malignant neoplasm of uterine ligament (C57.3)
mesothelioma (C45.-)

C49.0   Malignant neoplasm of connective and soft tissue of head, face and neck
Malignant neoplasm of connective tissue of ear
Malignant neoplasm of connective tissue of eyelid

     Excludes1   connective tissue of orbit (C69.6-)

● **C49.1   Malignant neoplasm of connective and soft tissue of upper limb, including shoulder**

C49.10   Malignant neoplasm of connective and soft tissue of unspecified upper limb, including shoulder

C49.11   Malignant neoplasm of connective and soft tissue of right upper limb, including shoulder

C49.12   Malignant neoplasm of connective and soft tissue of left upper limb, including shoulder

● **C49.2   Malignant neoplasm of connective and soft tissue of lower limb, including hip**

C49.20   Malignant neoplasm of connective and soft tissue of unspecified lower limb, including hip

C49.21   Malignant neoplasm of connective and soft tissue of right lower limb, including hip

C49.22   Malignant neoplasm of connective and soft tissue of left lower limb, including hip

C49.3   Malignant neoplasm of connective and soft tissue of thorax
Malignant neoplasm of axilla
Malignant neoplasm of diaphragm
Malignant neoplasm of great vessels

     Excludes1   malignant neoplasm of breast (C50.-)
malignant neoplasm of heart (C38.0)
malignant neoplasm of mediastinum (C38.1-C38.3)
malignant neoplasm of thymus (C37)
Coding Clinic: 2015, Q3, P19

C49.4   Malignant neoplasm of connective and soft tissue of abdomen
Malignant neoplasm of abdominal wall
Malignant neoplasm of hypochondrium

C49.5   Malignant neoplasm of connective and soft tissue of pelvis
Malignant neoplasm of buttock
Malignant neoplasm of groin
Malignant neoplasm of perineum

C49.6   Malignant neoplasm of connective and soft tissue of trunk, unspecified
Malignant neoplasm of back NOS

C49.8   Malignant neoplasm of overlapping sites of connective and soft tissue
Primary malignant neoplasm of two or more contiguous sites of connective and soft tissue

C49.9   Malignant neoplasm of connective and soft tissue, unspecified

● **C49.A   Gastrointestinal stromal tumor**
Coding Clinic: 2016, Q4, P8

C49.A0   Gastrointestinal stromal tumor, unspecified site

C49.A1   Gastrointestinal stromal tumor of esophagus

C49.A2   Gastrointestinal stromal tumor of stomach

C49.A3   Gastrointestinal stromal tumor of small intestine

C49.A4   Gastrointestinal stromal tumor of large intestine

C49.A5   Gastrointestinal stromal tumor of rectum

C49.A9   Gastrointestinal stromal tumor of other sites

MALIGNANT NEOPLASMS OF BREAST (C50)

● **C50   Malignant neoplasm of breast**

Includes   connective tissue of breast
Paget's disease of breast
Paget's disease of nipple
Intraductal carcinoma of breast characterized by eczema-like inflammatory skin changes

Use additional code to identify estrogen receptor status (Z17.0, Z17.1)

Excludes1   skin of breast (C44.501, C44.511, C44.521, C44.591)

● **C50.0   Malignant neoplasm of nipple and areola**

● **C50.01   Malignant neoplasm of nipple and areola, female**

C50.011   Malignant neoplasm of nipple and areola, right female breast ♀

C50.012   Malignant neoplasm of nipple and areola, left female breast ♀

C50.019   Malignant neoplasm of nipple and areola, unspecified female breast ♀

● **C50.02   Malignant neoplasm of nipple and areola, male**

C50.021   Malignant neoplasm of nipple and areola, right male breast ♂

C50.022   Malignant neoplasm of nipple and areola, left male breast ♂

C50.029   Malignant neoplasm of nipple and areola, unspecified male breast ♂

● **C50.1   Malignant neoplasm of central portion of breast**

● **C50.11   Malignant neoplasm of central portion of breast, female**

C50.111   Malignant neoplasm of central portion of right female breast ♀

C50.112   Malignant neoplasm of central portion of left female breast ♀

C50.119   Malignant neoplasm of central portion of unspecified female breast ♀

● **C50.12   Malignant neoplasm of central portion of breast, male**

C50.121   Malignant neoplasm of central portion of right male breast ♂

C50.122   Malignant neoplasm of central portion of left male breast ♂

C50.129   Malignant neoplasm of central portion of unspecified male breast ♂

● **C50.2   Malignant neoplasm of upper-inner quadrant of breast**

● **C50.21   Malignant neoplasm of upper-inner quadrant of breast, female**

C50.211   Malignant neoplasm of upper-inner quadrant of right female breast ♀

C50.212   Malignant neoplasm of upper-inner quadrant of left female breast ♀

C50.219   Malignant neoplasm of upper-inner quadrant of unspecified female breast ♀

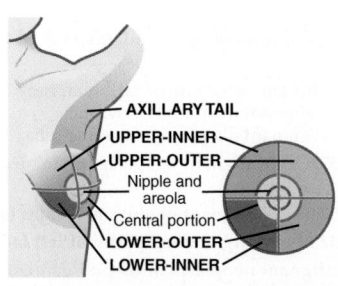

Figure 2-12 Female breast quadrants and axillary tail.

● C50.22   Malignant neoplasm of upper-inner quadrant of breast, male

    C50.221   Malignant neoplasm of upper-inner quadrant of right male breast ♂

    C50.222   Malignant neoplasm of upper-inner quadrant of left male breast ♂

    C50.229   Malignant neoplasm of upper-inner quadrant of unspecified male breast ♂

● C50.3   Malignant neoplasm of lower-inner quadrant of breast

  ● C50.31   Malignant neoplasm of lower-inner quadrant of breast, female

    C50.311   Malignant neoplasm of lower-inner quadrant of right female breast ♀

    C50.312   Malignant neoplasm of lower-inner quadrant of left female breast ♀

    C50.319   Malignant neoplasm of lower-inner quadrant of unspecified female breast ♀

  ● C50.32   Malignant neoplasm of lower-inner quadrant of breast, male

    C50.321   Malignant neoplasm of lower-inner quadrant of right male breast ♂

    C50.322   Malignant neoplasm of lower-inner quadrant of left male breast ♂

    C50.329   Malignant neoplasm of lower-inner quadrant of unspecified male breast ♂

● C50.4   Malignant neoplasm of upper-outer quadrant of breast

  ● C50.41   Malignant neoplasm of upper-outer quadrant of breast, female

    C50.411   Malignant neoplasm of upper-outer quadrant of right female breast ♀

    C50.412   Malignant neoplasm of upper-outer quadrant of left female breast ♀

    C50.419   Malignant neoplasm of upper-outer quadrant of unspecified female breast ♀

  ● C50.42   Malignant neoplasm of upper-outer quadrant of breast, male

    C50.421   Malignant neoplasm of upper-outer quadrant of right male breast ♂

    C50.422   Malignant neoplasm of upper-outer quadrant of left male breast ♂

    C50.429   Malignant neoplasm of upper-outer quadrant of unspecified male breast ♂

● C50.5   Malignant neoplasm of lower-outer quadrant of breast

  ● C50.51   Malignant neoplasm of lower-outer quadrant of breast, female

    C50.511   Malignant neoplasm of lower-outer quadrant of right female breast ♀

    C50.512   Malignant neoplasm of lower-outer quadrant of left female breast ♀

    C50.519   Malignant neoplasm of lower-outer quadrant of unspecified female breast ♀

● C50.52   Malignant neoplasm of lower-outer quadrant of breast, male

    C50.521   Malignant neoplasm of lower-outer quadrant of right male breast ♂

    C50.522   Malignant neoplasm of lower-outer quadrant of left male breast ♂

    C50.529   Malignant neoplasm of lower-outer quadrant of unspecified male breast ♂

● C50.6   Malignant neoplasm of axillary tail of breast

  ● C50.61   Malignant neoplasm of axillary tail of breast, female

    C50.611   Malignant neoplasm of axillary tail of right female breast ♀

    C50.612   Malignant neoplasm of axillary tail of left female breast ♀

    C50.619   Malignant neoplasm of axillary tail of unspecified female breast ♀

  ● C50.62   Malignant neoplasm of axillary tail of breast, male

    C50.621   Malignant neoplasm of axillary tail of right male breast ♂

    C50.622   Malignant neoplasm of axillary tail of left male breast ♂

    C50.629   Malignant neoplasm of axillary tail of unspecified male breast ♂

● C50.8   Malignant neoplasm of overlapping sites of breast

  ● C50.81   Malignant neoplasm of overlapping sites of breast, female

    C50.811   Malignant neoplasm of overlapping sites of right female breast ♀

    C50.812   Malignant neoplasm of overlapping sites of left female breast ♀

    C50.819   Malignant neoplasm of overlapping sites of unspecified female breast ♀

  ● C50.82   Malignant neoplasm of overlapping sites of breast, male

    C50.821   Malignant neoplasm of overlapping sites of right male breast ♂

    C50.822   Malignant neoplasm of overlapping sites of left male breast ♂

    C50.829   Malignant neoplasm of overlapping sites of unspecified male breast ♂

● C50.9   Malignant neoplasm of breast of unspecified site

  ● C50.91   Malignant neoplasm of breast of unspecified site, female

    C50.911   Malignant neoplasm of unspecified site of right female breast ♀

    C50.912   Malignant neoplasm of unspecified site of left female breast ♀

    C50.919   Malignant neoplasm of unspecified site of unspecified female breast ♀

  ● C50.92   Malignant neoplasm of breast of unspecified site, male

    C50.921   Malignant neoplasm of unspecified site of right male breast ♂

    C50.922   Malignant neoplasm of unspecified site of left male breast ♂

    C50.929   Malignant neoplasm of unspecified site of unspecified male breast ♂

CHAPTER 2 (C00-D49)

MALIGNANT NEOPLASMS OF FEMALE GENITAL ORGANS (C51-C58)

> **Includes**   malignant neoplasm of skin of female genital organs

● **C51   Malignant neoplasm of vulva**

> **Excludes1**   carcinoma in situ of vulva (D07.1)

> **C51.0   Malignant neoplasm of labium majus ♀**
> *Outer folds of skin external female genitalia*
> Malignant neoplasm of Bartholin's [greater vestibular] gland

> **C51.1   Malignant neoplasm of labium minus ♀**
> *Two inner folds surrounding vulva in female genitalia*

> **C51.2   Malignant neoplasm of clitoris ♀**

> **C51.8   Malignant neoplasm of overlapping sites of vulva ♀**

> **C51.9   Malignant neoplasm of vulva, unspecified ♀**
> Malignant neoplasm of external female genitalia NOS
> Malignant neoplasm of pudendum

C52   Malignant neoplasm of vagina ♀

> **Excludes1**   carcinoma in situ of vagina (D07.2)

● **C53   Malignant neoplasm of cervix uteri**

> **Excludes1**   carcinoma in situ of cervix uteri (D06.-)

> **C53.0   Malignant neoplasm of endocervix ♀**
> *Inside the cervix*

> **C53.1   Malignant neoplasm of exocervix ♀**
> *Outside the cervix*

> **C53.8   Malignant neoplasm of overlapping sites of cervix uteri ♀**

> **C53.9   Malignant neoplasm of cervix uteri, unspecified ♀**
> **Coding Clinic: 2017, Q4, P103**

● **C54   Malignant neoplasm of corpus uteri**

> **C54.0   Malignant neoplasm of isthmus uteri ♀**
> *Constricted part of uterus between cervix and body*
> Malignant neoplasm of lower uterine segment

> **C54.1   Malignant neoplasm of endometrium ♀**
> *Lining of uterus*

> **C54.2   Malignant neoplasm of myometrium ♀**
> *Middle layer of uterine wall consisting of smooth muscle supporting stromal and vascular tissue*

> **C54.3   Malignant neoplasm of fundus uteri ♀**
> *Top rounded portion of uterus*

> **C54.8   Malignant neoplasm of overlapping sites of corpus uteri ♀**
> *Main body of uterus*

> **C54.9   Malignant neoplasm of corpus uteri, unspecified ♀**

C55   Malignant neoplasm of uterus, part unspecified ♀

● **C56   Malignant neoplasm of ovary**
> Use additional code to identify any functional activity

> **C56.1   Malignant neoplasm of right ovary ♀**
> **C56.2   Malignant neoplasm of left ovary ♀**
> **C56.9   Malignant neoplasm of unspecified ovary ♀**

● **C57   Malignant neoplasm of other and unspecified female genital organs**

> ● **C57.0   Malignant neoplasm of fallopian tube**
> Malignant neoplasm of oviduct
> Malignant neoplasm of uterine tube

>> **C57.00   Malignant neoplasm of unspecified fallopian tube ♀**
>> **C57.01   Malignant neoplasm of right fallopian tube ♀**
>> **C57.02   Malignant neoplasm of left fallopian tube ♀**

> ● **C57.1   Malignant neoplasm of broad ligament**
>> **C57.10   Malignant neoplasm of unspecified broad ligament ♀**
>> **C57.11   Malignant neoplasm of right broad ligament ♀**
>> **C57.12   Malignant neoplasm of left broad ligament ♀**

> ● **C57.2   Malignant neoplasm of round ligament**
>> **C57.20   Malignant neoplasm of unspecified round ligament ♀**
>> **C57.21   Malignant neoplasm of right round ligament ♀**
>> **C57.22   Malignant neoplasm of left round ligament ♀**

> **C57.3   Malignant neoplasm of parametrium ♀**
> Malignant neoplasm of uterine ligament NOS

> **C57.4   Malignant neoplasm of uterine adnexa, unspecified ♀**

> **C57.7   Malignant neoplasm of other specified female genital organs ♀**
> Malignant neoplasm of wolffian body or duct

> **C57.8   Malignant neoplasm of overlapping sites of female genital organs ♀**
> Primary malignant neoplasm of two or more contiguous sites of the female genital organs whose point of origin cannot be determined
> Primary tubo-ovarian malignant neoplasm whose point of origin cannot be determined
> Primary utero-ovarian malignant neoplasm whose point of origin cannot be determined

> **C57.9   Malignant neoplasm of female genital organ, unspecified ♀**
> Malignant neoplasm of female genitourinary tract NOS

C58   Malignant neoplasm of placenta ♀   M

> **Includes**   choriocarcinoma NOS
> chorionepithelioma NOS

> **Excludes1**   chorioadenoma (destruens) (D39.2)
> hydatidiform mole NOS (O01.9)
> invasive hydatidiform mole (D39.2)
> male choriocarcinoma NOS (C62.9-)
> malignant hydatidiform mole (D39.2)

MALIGNANT NEOPLASMS OF MALE GENITAL ORGANS (C60-C63)

> **Includes**   malignant neoplasm of skin of male genital organs

● **C60   Malignant neoplasm of penis**

> **C60.0   Malignant neoplasm of prepuce ♂**
> Malignant neoplasm of foreskin

> **C60.1   Malignant neoplasm of glans penis ♂**

> **C60.2   Malignant neoplasm of body of penis ♂**
> Malignant neoplasm of corpus cavernosum

> **C60.8   Malignant neoplasm of overlapping sites of penis ♂**

> **C60.9   Malignant neoplasm of penis, unspecified ♂**
> Malignant neoplasm of skin of penis NOS

C61   Malignant neoplasm of prostate ♂
> Use additional code to identify:
> hormone sensitivity status (Z19.1-Z19.2)
> rising PSA following treatment for malignant neoplasm of prostate (R97.21)

> **Excludes1**   malignant neoplasm of seminal vesicle (C63.7)

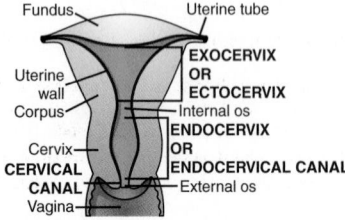

Fundus — Uterine tube
Uterine wall
Corpus
EXOCERVIX OR ECTOCERVIX
Internal os
ENDOCERVIX OR ENDOCERVICAL CANAL
Cervix
CERVICAL CANAL
External os
Vagina

Figure 2-13   Cervix uteri.

Figure 2-14 Penis and other male genital organs.

● C62   Malignant neoplasm of testis
    Use additional code to identify any functional activity.
  ● C62.0   Malignant neoplasm of undescended testis
      Malignant neoplasm of ectopic testis
      Malignant neoplasm of retained testis
    C62.00   Malignant neoplasm of unspecified undescended testis ♂
    C62.01   Malignant neoplasm of undescended right testis ♂
    C62.02   Malignant neoplasm of undescended left testis ♂
  ● C62.1   Malignant neoplasm of descended testis
      Malignant neoplasm of scrotal testis
    C62.10   Malignant neoplasm of unspecified descended testis, unspecified side ♂
    C62.11   Malignant neoplasm of descended right testis ♂
    C62.12   Malignant neoplasm of descended left testis ♂
  ● C62.9   Malignant neoplasm of testis, unspecified whether descended or undescended
    C62.90   Malignant neoplasm of unspecified testis, unspecified whether descended or undescended ♂
      Malignant neoplasm of testis NOS
    C62.91   Malignant neoplasm of right testis, unspecified whether descended or undescended ♂
    C62.92   Malignant neoplasm of left testis, unspecified whether descended or undescended ♂

● C63   Malignant neoplasm of other and unspecified male genital organs
  ● C63.0   Malignant neoplasm of epididymis
    C63.00   Malignant neoplasm of unspecified epididymis ♂
    C63.01   Malignant neoplasm of right epididymis ♂
    C63.02   Malignant neoplasm of left epididymis ♂
  ● C63.1   Malignant neoplasm of spermatic cord
    C63.10   Malignant neoplasm of unspecified spermatic cord ♂
    C63.11   Malignant neoplasm of right spermatic cord ♂
    C63.12   Malignant neoplasm of left spermatic cord ♂
  C63.2   Malignant neoplasm of scrotum ♂
      Malignant neoplasm of skin of scrotum
  C63.7   Malignant neoplasm of other specified male genital organs ♂
      Malignant neoplasm of seminal vesicle
      Malignant neoplasm of tunica vaginalis
  C63.8   Malignant neoplasm of overlapping sites of male genital organs ♂
      Primary malignant neoplasm of two or more contiguous sites of male genital organs whose point of origin cannot be determined
  C63.9   Malignant neoplasm of male genital organ, unspecified ♂
      Malignant neoplasm of male genitourinary tract NOS

MALIGNANT NEOPLASMS OF URINARY TRACT (C64-C68)

● C64   Malignant neoplasm of kidney, except renal pelvis
    Excludes1   malignant carcinoid tumor of the kidney (C7A.093)
      malignant neoplasm of renal calyces (C65.-)
      malignant neoplasm of renal pelvis (C65.-)
  C64.1   Malignant neoplasm of right kidney, except renal pelvis
  C64.2   Malignant neoplasm of left kidney, except renal pelvis
  C64.9   Malignant neoplasm of unspecified kidney, except renal pelvis

● C65   Malignant neoplasm of renal pelvis
    Includes   malignant neoplasm of pelviureteric junction
      malignant neoplasm of renal calyces
  C65.1   Malignant neoplasm of right renal pelvis
  C65.2   Malignant neoplasm of left renal pelvis
  C65.9   Malignant neoplasm of unspecified renal pelvis

● C66   Malignant neoplasm of ureter
    Excludes1   malignant neoplasm of ureteric orifice of bladder (C67.6)
  C66.1   Malignant neoplasm of right ureter
  C66.2   Malignant neoplasm of left ureter
  C66.9   Malignant neoplasm of unspecified ureter

● C67   Malignant neoplasm of bladder
  C67.0   Malignant neoplasm of trigone of bladder
    Triangular area formed by three openings in the floor of urinary bladder
  C67.1   Malignant neoplasm of dome of bladder
    Vaulted roof
  C67.2   Malignant neoplasm of lateral wall of bladder
    Side walls
  C67.3   Malignant neoplasm of anterior wall of bladder
    Front wall
  C67.4   Malignant neoplasm of posterior wall of bladder
    Back wall
  C67.5   Malignant neoplasm of bladder neck
    Joining of bladder and urethra
    Malignant neoplasm of internal urethral orifice
  C67.6   Malignant neoplasm of ureteric orifice
    Opening from bladder to ureters
  C67.7   Malignant neoplasm of urachus
    Embryonic canal that connects the urinary bladder with the structure that forms the umbilical cord (allantois)
  C67.8   Malignant neoplasm of overlapping sites of bladder
  C67.9   Malignant neoplasm of bladder, unspecified
    Coding Clinic: 2017, Q1, P6; 2016, Q1, P19

● C68   Malignant neoplasm of other and unspecified urinary organs
    Excludes1   malignant neoplasm of female genitourinary tract NOS (C57.9)
      malignant neoplasm of male genitourinary tract NOS (C63.9)
  C68.0   Malignant neoplasm of urethra
    Excludes1   malignant neoplasm of urethral orifice of bladder (C67.5)
  C68.1   Malignant neoplasm of paraurethral glands
    Group of glands of female urethra drained by paraurethral ducts; AKA Skene glands, female prostate
  C68.8   Malignant neoplasm of overlapping sites of urinary organs
    Primary malignant neoplasm of two or more contiguous sites of urinary organs whose point of origin cannot be determined
  C68.9   Malignant neoplasm of urinary organ, unspecified
    Malignant neoplasm of urinary system NOS

MALIGNANT NEOPLASMS OF EYE, BRAIN AND OTHER PARTS OF CENTRAL NERVOUS SYSTEM (C69-C72)

● **C69**   **Malignant neoplasm of eye and adnexa**

> **Excludes1**   malignant neoplasm of connective tissue of eyelid (C49.0)
> malignant neoplasm of eyelid (skin) (C43.1-, C44.1-)
> malignant neoplasm of optic nerve (C72.3-)

   ● **C69.0**   **Malignant neoplasm of conjunctiva**

     C69.00   Malignant neoplasm of unspecified conjunctiva

     C69.01   Malignant neoplasm of right conjunctiva

     C69.02   Malignant neoplasm of left conjunctiva

   ● **C69.1**   **Malignant neoplasm of cornea**

     C69.10   Malignant neoplasm of unspecified cornea

     C69.11   Malignant neoplasm of right cornea

     C69.12   Malignant neoplasm of left cornea

   ● **C69.2**   **Malignant neoplasm of retina**

> **Excludes1**   dark area on retina (D49.81)
> neoplasm of unspecified behavior of retina and choroid (D49.81)
> retinal freckle (D49.81)

     C69.20   Malignant neoplasm of unspecified retina

     C69.21   Malignant neoplasm of right retina

     C69.22   Malignant neoplasm of left retina

   ● **C69.3**   **Malignant neoplasm of choroid**

     C69.30   Malignant neoplasm of unspecified choroid

     C69.31   Malignant neoplasm of right choroid

     C69.32   Malignant neoplasm of left choroid

   ● **C69.4**   **Malignant neoplasm of ciliary body**

     C69.40   Malignant neoplasm of unspecified ciliary body

     C69.41   Malignant neoplasm of right ciliary body

     C69.42   Malignant neoplasm of left ciliary body

   ● **C69.5**   **Malignant neoplasm of lacrimal gland and duct**
Malignant neoplasm of lacrimal sac
Malignant neoplasm of nasolacrimal duct

     C69.50   Malignant neoplasm of unspecified lacrimal gland and duct

     C69.51   Malignant neoplasm of right lacrimal gland and duct

     C69.52   Malignant neoplasm of left lacrimal gland and duct

   ● **C69.6**   **Malignant neoplasm of orbit**
Malignant neoplasm of connective tissue of orbit
Malignant neoplasm of extraocular muscle
Malignant neoplasm of peripheral nerves of orbit
Malignant neoplasm of retrobulbar tissue
Malignant neoplasm of retro-ocular tissue

> **Excludes1**   malignant neoplasm of orbital bone (C41.0)

     C69.60   Malignant neoplasm of unspecified orbit

     C69.61   Malignant neoplasm of right orbit

     C69.62   Malignant neoplasm of left orbit

   ● **C69.8**   **Malignant neoplasm of overlapping sites of eye and adnexa**

     C69.80   Malignant neoplasm of overlapping sites of unspecified eye and adnexa

     C69.81   Malignant neoplasm of overlapping sites of right eye and adnexa

     C69.82   Malignant neoplasm of overlapping sites of left eye and adnexa

   ● **C69.9**   **Malignant neoplasm of unspecified site of eye**
Malignant neoplasm of eyeball

     C69.90   Malignant neoplasm of unspecified site of unspecified eye

     C69.91   Malignant neoplasm of unspecified site of right eye

     C69.92   Malignant neoplasm of unspecified site of left eye

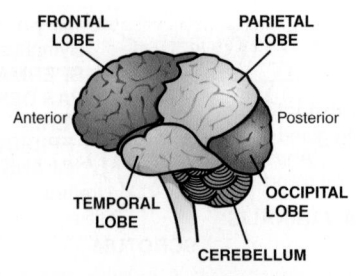

Figure 2-15   The brain.

● **C70**   **Malignant neoplasm of meninges**

     C70.0   Malignant neoplasm of cerebral meninges

     C70.1   Malignant neoplasm of spinal meninges

     C70.9   Malignant neoplasm of meninges, unspecified

● **C71**   **Malignant neoplasm of brain**

> **Excludes1**   malignant neoplasm of cranial nerves (C72.2-C72.5)
> retrobulbar malignant neoplasm (C69.6-)

     C71.0   **Malignant neoplasm of cerebrum, except lobes and ventricles**
Malignant neoplasm of supratentorial NOS

     C71.1   Malignant neoplasm of frontal lobe

     C71.2   Malignant neoplasm of temporal lobe

     C71.3   Malignant neoplasm of parietal lobe

     C71.4   Malignant neoplasm of occipital lobe

     C71.5   Malignant neoplasm of cerebral ventricle

> **Excludes1**   malignant neoplasm of fourth cerebral ventricle (C71.7)

     C71.6   Malignant neoplasm of cerebellum

     C71.7   Malignant neoplasm of brain stem
Malignant neoplasm of fourth cerebral ventricle
Infratentorial malignant neoplasm NOS

     C71.8   Malignant neoplasm of overlapping sites of brain

     C71.9   Malignant neoplasm of brain, unspecified

● **C72**   **Malignant neoplasm of spinal cord, cranial nerves and other parts of central nervous system**

> **Excludes1**   malignant neoplasm of meninges (C70.-)
> malignant neoplasm of peripheral nerves and autonomic nervous system (C47.-)

     C72.0   Malignant neoplasm of spinal cord

     C72.1   Malignant neoplasm of cauda equina
Lower end of spinal column

   ● **C72.2**   **Malignant neoplasm of olfactory nerve**
Malignant neoplasm of olfactory bulb

     C72.20   Malignant neoplasm of unspecified olfactory nerve

     C72.21   Malignant neoplasm of right olfactory nerve

     C72.22   Malignant neoplasm of left olfactory nerve

   ● **C72.3**   **Malignant neoplasm of optic nerve**

     C72.30   Malignant neoplasm of unspecified optic nerve

     C72.31   Malignant neoplasm of right optic nerve

     C72.32   Malignant neoplasm of left optic nerve

   ● **C72.4**   **Malignant neoplasm of acoustic nerve**

     C72.40   Malignant neoplasm of unspecified acoustic nerve

     C72.41   Malignant neoplasm of right acoustic nerve

     C72.42   Malignant neoplasm of left acoustic nerve

   ● **C72.5**   **Malignant neoplasm of other and unspecified cranial nerves**

     C72.50   Malignant neoplasm of unspecified cranial nerve
Malignant neoplasm of cranial nerve NOS

     C72.59   Malignant neoplasm of other cranial nerves

▶ New   ⇒ Revised   ~~deleted~~ Deleted   Excludes 1   Excludes 2   Includes   Use additional   Code first   Code also   Key words

684   OGCR Official Guidelines   X Assign placeholder X   ● Use Additional Character(s)   ▷ Manifestation Code   **Coding Clinic**

C72.9   Malignant neoplasm of central nervous system, unspecified
> Malignant neoplasm of unspecified site of central nervous system
> Malignant neoplasm of nervous system NOS

MALIGNANT NEOPLASMS OF THYROID AND OTHER ENDOCRINE GLANDS (C73-C75)

C73   Malignant neoplasm of thyroid gland
> Use additional code to identify any functional activity

● **C74**   Malignant neoplasm of adrenal gland
   ● **C74.0**   Malignant neoplasm of cortex of adrenal gland
     C74.00   Malignant neoplasm of cortex of unspecified adrenal gland
     C74.01   Malignant neoplasm of cortex of right adrenal gland
     C74.02   Malignant neoplasm of cortex of left adrenal gland
   ● **C74.1**   Malignant neoplasm of medulla of adrenal gland
     Pair of glands situated on top of or above each kidney ("suprarenal")
     C74.10   Malignant neoplasm of medulla of unspecified adrenal gland
     C74.11   Malignant neoplasm of medulla of right adrenal gland
     C74.12   Malignant neoplasm of medulla of left adrenal gland
   ● **C74.9**   Malignant neoplasm of unspecified part of adrenal gland
     C74.90   Malignant neoplasm of unspecified part of unspecified adrenal gland
     C74.91   Malignant neoplasm of unspecified part of right adrenal gland
     C74.92   Malignant neoplasm of unspecified part of left adrenal gland

● **C75**   Malignant neoplasm of other endocrine glands and related structures
   Excludes1   malignant carcinoid tumors (C7A.0-)
     malignant neoplasm of adrenal gland (C74.-)
     malignant neoplasm of endocrine pancreas (C25.4)
     malignant neoplasm of islets of Langerhans (C25.4)
     malignant neoplasm of ovary (C56.-)
     malignant neoplasm of testis (C62.-)
     malignant neoplasm of thymus (C37)
     malignant neoplasm of thyroid gland (C73)
     malignant neuroendocrine tumors (C7A.-)
   C75.0   Malignant neoplasm of parathyroid gland
   C75.1   Malignant neoplasm of pituitary gland
   C75.2   Malignant neoplasm of craniopharyngeal duct
   C75.3   Malignant neoplasm of pineal gland
   C75.4   Malignant neoplasm of carotid body
   C75.5   Malignant neoplasm of aortic body and other paraganglia
   C75.8   Malignant neoplasm with pluriglandular involvement, unspecified
   C75.9   Malignant neoplasm of endocrine gland, unspecified

MALIGNANT NEUROENDOCRINE TUMORS (C7A)

● **C7A**   Malignant neuroendocrine tumors
> Code also any associated multiple endocrine neoplasia [MEN] syndromes (E31.2-)
> Use additional code to identify any associated endocrine syndrome, such as:
> carcinoid syndrome (E34.0)
   Excludes2   malignant pancreatic islet cell tumors (C25.4)
     Merkel cell carcinoma (C4A.-)
   ● **C7A.0**   Malignant carcinoid tumors
     C7A.00   Malignant carcinoid tumor of unspecified site
     ● **C7A.01**   Malignant carcinoid tumors of the small intestine
       C7A.010   Malignant carcinoid tumor of the duodenum
       C7A.011   Malignant carcinoid tumor of the jejunum
       C7A.012   Malignant carcinoid tumor of the ileum
       C7A.019   Malignant carcinoid tumor of the small intestine, unspecified portion
     ● **C7A.02**   Malignant carcinoid tumors of the appendix, large intestine, and rectum
       C7A.020   Malignant carcinoid tumor of the appendix
       C7A.021   Malignant carcinoid tumor of the cecum
       C7A.022   Malignant carcinoid tumor of the ascending colon
       C7A.023   Malignant carcinoid tumor of the transverse colon
       C7A.024   Malignant carcinoid tumor of the descending colon
       C7A.025   Malignant carcinoid tumor of the sigmoid colon
       C7A.026   Malignant carcinoid tumor of the rectum
       C7A.029   Malignant carcinoid tumor of the large intestine, unspecified portion
         Malignant carcinoid tumor of the colon NOS
     ● **C7A.09**   Malignant carcinoid tumors of other sites
       C7A.090   Malignant carcinoid tumor of the bronchus and lung
       C7A.091   Malignant carcinoid tumor of the thymus
       C7A.092   Malignant carcinoid tumor of the stomach
       C7A.093   Malignant carcinoid tumor of the kidney
       C7A.094   Malignant carcinoid tumor of the foregut, unspecified
       C7A.095   Malignant carcinoid tumor of the midgut, unspecified
       C7A.096   Malignant carcinoid tumor of the hindgut, unspecified
       C7A.098   Malignant carcinoid tumors of other sites
   C7A.1   Malignant poorly differentiated neuroendocrine tumors
     Malignant poorly differentiated neuroendocrine tumor NOS
     Malignant poorly differentiated neuroendocrine carcinoma, any site
     High grade neuroendocrine carcinoma, any site
   C7A.8   Other malignant neuroendocrine tumors
     Secondary neuroendocrine tumors (C7B)

CHAPTER 2 (C00-D49)

SECONDARY NEUROENDOCRINE TUMORS (C7B)

● **C7B** Secondary neuroendocrine tumors
Use additional code to identify any functional activity

  ● **C7B.0** Secondary carcinoid tumors

    C7B.00 Secondary carcinoid tumors, unspecified site

    C7B.01 Secondary carcinoid tumors of distant lymph nodes

    C7B.02 Secondary carcinoid tumors of liver

    C7B.03 Secondary carcinoid tumors of bone

    C7B.04 Secondary carcinoid tumors of peritoneum
      Mesentary metastasis of carcinoid tumor

    C7B.09 Secondary carcinoid tumors of other sites

  C7B.1 Secondary Merkel cell carcinoma
    Merkel cell carcinoma nodal presentation
    Merkel cell carcinoma visceral metastatic presentation

  C7B.8 Other secondary neuroendocrine tumors

MALIGNANT NEOPLASMS OF ILL-DEFINED, OTHER SECONDARY AND UNSPECIFIED SITES (C76-C80)

● **C76** Malignant neoplasm of other and ill-defined sites
  Excludes1 malignant neoplasm of female genitourinary tract NOS (C57.9)
    malignant neoplasm of male genitourinary tract NOS (C63.9)
    malignant neoplasm of lymphoid, hematopoietic and related tissue (C81-C96)
    malignant neoplasm of skin (C44.-)
    malignant neoplasm of unspecified site NOS (C80.1)

  C76.0 Malignant neoplasm of head, face and neck
    Malignant neoplasm of cheek NOS
    Malignant neoplasm of nose NOS

  C76.1 Malignant neoplasm of thorax
    Intrathoracic malignant neoplasm NOS
    Malignant neoplasm of axilla NOS
    Thoracic malignant neoplasm NOS

  C76.2 Malignant neoplasm of abdomen

  C76.3 Malignant neoplasm of pelvis
    Malignant neoplasm of groin NOS
    Malignant neoplasm of sites overlapping systems within the pelvis
    Rectovaginal (septum) malignant neoplasm
      Between rectum and vagina
    Rectovesical (septum) malignant neoplasm
      Between rectum and urinary bladder; AKA vesicorectal

  ● **C76.4** Malignant neoplasm of upper limb

    C76.40 Malignant neoplasm of unspecified upper limb

    C76.41 Malignant neoplasm of right upper limb

    C76.42 Malignant neoplasm of left upper limb

  ● **C76.5** Malignant neoplasm of lower limb

    C76.50 Malignant neoplasm of unspecified lower limb

    C76.51 Malignant neoplasm of right lower limb

    C76.52 Malignant neoplasm of left lower limb

  C76.8 Malignant neoplasm of other specified ill-defined sites
    Malignant neoplasm of overlapping ill-defined sites

● **C77** Secondary and unspecified malignant neoplasm of lymph nodes
  Excludes1 malignant neoplasm of lymph nodes, specified as primary (C81-C86, C88, C96.-)
    mesentary metastasis of carcinoid tumor (C7B.04)
    secondary carcinoid tumors of distant lymph nodes (C7B.01)

  C77.0 Secondary and unspecified malignant neoplasm of lymph nodes of head, face and neck
    Secondary and unspecified malignant neoplasm of supraclavicular lymph nodes

  C77.1 Secondary and unspecified malignant neoplasm of intrathoracic lymph nodes

  C77.2 Secondary and unspecified malignant neoplasm of intra-abdominal lymph nodes

  C77.3 Secondary and unspecified malignant neoplasm of axilla and upper limb lymph nodes
    Secondary and unspecified malignant neoplasm of pectoral lymph nodes

  C77.4 Secondary and unspecified malignant neoplasm of inguinal and lower limb lymph nodes

  C77.5 Secondary and unspecified malignant neoplasm of intrapelvic lymph nodes

  C77.8 Secondary and unspecified malignant neoplasm of lymph nodes of multiple regions

  C77.9 Secondary and unspecified malignant neoplasm of lymph node, unspecified

● **C78** Secondary malignant neoplasm of respiratory and digestive organs
  Excludes1 secondary carcinoid tumors of liver (C7B.02)
    secondary carcinoid tumors of peritoneum (C7B.04)
  Excludes2 lymph node metastases (C77.0)

  ● **C78.0** Secondary malignant neoplasm of lung

    C78.00 Secondary malignant neoplasm of unspecified lung

    C78.01 Secondary malignant neoplasm of right lung

    C78.02 Secondary malignant neoplasm of left lung

  C78.1 Secondary malignant neoplasm of mediastinum
    Thoracic cavity between pleural cavities

  C78.2 Secondary malignant neoplasm of pleura
    Serous membrane covering lungs and lining thoracic cavity

  ● **C78.3** Secondary malignant neoplasm of other and unspecified respiratory organs

    C78.30 Secondary malignant neoplasm of unspecified respiratory organ

    C78.39 Secondary malignant neoplasm of other respiratory organs

  C78.4 Secondary malignant neoplasm of small intestine

  C78.5 Secondary malignant neoplasm of large intestine and rectum

  C78.6 Secondary malignant neoplasm of retroperitoneum and peritoneum
    Coding Clinic: 2017, Q2, P12

  C78.7 Secondary malignant neoplasm of liver and intrahepatic bile duct

  ● **C78.8** Secondary malignant neoplasm of other and unspecified digestive organs

    C78.80 Secondary malignant neoplasm of unspecified digestive organ

    C78.89 Secondary malignant neoplasm of other digestive organs
      Code also exocrine pancreatic insufficiency (K86.81)

● **C79** Secondary malignant neoplasm of other and unspecified sites
  Excludes1 secondary carcinoid tumors (C7B.-)
    secondary neuroendocrine tumors (C7B.-)

  ● **C79.0** Secondary malignant neoplasm of kidney and renal pelvis

    C79.00 Secondary malignant neoplasm of unspecified kidney and renal pelvis

    C79.01 Secondary malignant neoplasm of right kidney and renal pelvis

    C79.02 Secondary malignant neoplasm of left kidney and renal pelvis

Item 2–6 The adrenal glands are a pair of glands situated on top of or above each kidney ("suprarenal") and chiefly responsible for regulating the stress response through the synthesis of corticosteroids and catecholamines, including cortisol and adrenaline.

▶ New   ⇒ Revised   ~~deleted~~ Deleted   Excludes 1   Excludes 2   Includes   Use additional   Code first   Code also   Key words

OGCR Official Guidelines   X Assign placeholder X   ● Use Additional Character(s)   ▶ Manifestation Code   Coding Clinic

● **C79.1** **Secondary malignant neoplasm of bladder and other and unspecified urinary organs**
     C79.10 **Secondary malignant neoplasm of unspecified urinary organs**
     C79.11 **Secondary malignant neoplasm of bladder**
         Excludes2   lymph node metastases (C77.0)
     C79.19 **Secondary malignant neoplasm of other urinary organs**

● **C79.2** **Secondary malignant neoplasm of skin**
     Excludes1   secondary Merkel cell carcinoma (C7B.1)

● **C79.3** **Secondary malignant neoplasm of brain and cerebral meninges**
     C79.31 **Secondary malignant neoplasm of brain**
     C79.32 **Secondary malignant neoplasm of cerebral meninges**

● **C79.4** **Secondary malignant neoplasm of other and unspecified parts of nervous system**
     C79.40 **Secondary malignant neoplasm of unspecified part of nervous system**
     C79.49 **Secondary malignant neoplasm of other parts of nervous system**

● **C79.5** **Secondary malignant neoplasm of bone and bone marrow**
     Excludes1   secondary carcinoid tumors of bone (C7B.03)
     C79.51 **Secondary malignant neoplasm of bone**
     C79.52 **Secondary malignant neoplasm of bone marrow**

● **C79.6** **Secondary malignant neoplasm of ovary**
     C79.60 **Secondary malignant neoplasm of unspecified ovary** ♀
     C79.61 **Secondary malignant neoplasm of right ovary** ♀
     C79.62 **Secondary malignant neoplasm of left ovary** ♀

● **C79.7** **Secondary malignant neoplasm of adrenal gland**
     C79.70 **Secondary malignant neoplasm of unspecified adrenal gland**
     C79.71 **Secondary malignant neoplasm of right adrenal gland**
     C79.72 **Secondary malignant neoplasm of left adrenal gland**

● **C79.8** **Secondary malignant neoplasm of other specified sites**
     C79.81 **Secondary malignant neoplasm of breast**
     C79.82 **Secondary malignant neoplasm of genital organs**
     C79.89 **Secondary malignant neoplasm of other specified sites**
         Coding Clinic: 2017, Q2, P11

     C79.9 **Secondary malignant neoplasm of unspecified site**
     Metastatic cancer NOS
     Metastatic disease NOS
         Excludes1   carcinomatosis NOS (C80.0)
                 generalized cancer NOS (C80.0)
                 malignant (primary) neoplasm of unspecified site (C80.1)

OGCR Section I.C.2.j and k

Disseminated malignant neoplasm, unspecified

j. Code C80.0, Disseminated malignant neoplasm, unspecified, is for use only in those cases where the patient has advanced metastatic disease and no known primary or secondary sites are specified. It should not be used in place of assigning codes for the primary site and all known secondary sites.

Malignant neoplasm without specification of site

k. Code C80.1, Malignant (primary) neoplasm, unspecified, equates to Cancer, unspecified. This code should only be used when no determination can be made as to the primary site of a malignancy. This code should rarely be used in the inpatient setting.

● **C80** **Malignant neoplasm without specification of site**
     Excludes1   malignant carcinoid tumor of unspecified site (C7A.00)
                 malignant neoplasm of specified multiple sites- code to each site

     C80.0 **Disseminated malignant neoplasm, unspecified**
     Carcinomatosis NOS
     Generalized cancer, unspecified site (primary) (secondary)
     Generalized malignancy, unspecified site (primary) (secondary)

     C80.1 **Malignant (primary) neoplasm, unspecified**
     Cancer NOS
     Cancer unspecified site (primary)
     Carcinoma unspecified site (primary)
     Malignancy unspecified site (primary)
         Excludes1   secondary malignant neoplasm of unspecified site (C79.9)

     C80.2 **Malignant neoplasm associated with transplanted organ**
     Code first complication of transplanted organ (T86.-)
     Use additional code to identify the specific malignancy

★ **(See Plate 315 on page 49.)**

MALIGNANT NEOPLASMS OF LYMPHOID, HEMATOPOIETIC AND RELATED TISSUE (C81-C96)

     Excludes2   Kaposi's sarcoma of lymph nodes (C46.3)
                 secondary and unspecified neoplasm of lymph nodes (C77.-)
                 secondary neoplasm of bone marrow (C79.52)
                 secondary neoplasm of spleen (C78.89)

● **C81** **Hodgkin lymphoma**
     Form of malignant lymphoma with four types, nodular sclerosis, mixed cellularity, lymphocyte depleted, and lymphocyte predominant
     Excludes1   personal history of Hodgkin lymphoma (Z85.71)

● **C81.0** **Nodular lymphocyte predominant Hodgkin lymphoma**
     Least aggressive, least common, typically no symptoms
     Lymphocytic-histiocytic predominance Hodgkin's disease
     C81.00 **Nodular lymphocyte predominant Hodgkin lymphoma, unspecified site**
     C81.01 **Nodular lymphocyte predominant Hodgkin lymphoma, lymph nodes of head, face, and neck**
     C81.02 **Nodular lymphocyte predominant Hodgkin lymphoma, intrathoracic lymph nodes**
     C81.03 **Nodular lymphocyte predominant Hodgkin lymphoma, intra-abdominal lymph nodes**
     C81.04 **Nodular lymphocyte predominant Hodgkin lymphoma, lymph nodes of axilla and upper limb**
     C81.05 **Nodular lymphocyte predominant Hodgkin lymphoma, lymph nodes of inguinal region and lower limb**
     C81.06 **Nodular lymphocyte predominant Hodgkin lymphoma, intrapelvic lymph nodes**
     C81.07 **Nodular lymphocyte predominant Hodgkin lymphoma, spleen**
     C81.08 **Nodular lymphocyte predominant Hodgkin lymphoma, lymph nodes of multiple sites**
     C81.09 **Nodular lymphocyte predominant Hodgkin lymphoma, extranodal and solid organ sites**

CHAPTER 2 (C00-D49)

● **C81.1**   **Nodular sclerosis Hodgkin lymphoma**
     Nodular sclerosis classical Hodgkin lymphoma
     Moderately aggressive; most common in young adults

    C81.10   Nodular sclerosis Hodgkin lymphoma, unspecified site

    C81.11   Nodular sclerosis Hodgkin lymphoma, lymph nodes of head, face, and neck

    C81.12   Nodular sclerosis Hodgkin lymphoma, intrathoracic lymph nodes

    C81.13   Nodular sclerosis Hodgkin lymphoma, intra-abdominal lymph nodes

    C81.14   Nodular sclerosis Hodgkin lymphoma, lymph nodes of axilla and upper limb

    C81.15   Nodular sclerosis Hodgkin lymphoma, lymph nodes of inguinal region and lower limb

    C81.16   Nodular sclerosis Hodgkin lymphoma, intrapelvic lymph nodes

    C81.17   Nodular sclerosis Hodgkin lymphoma, spleen

    C81.18   Nodular sclerosis Hodgkin lymphoma, lymph nodes of multiple sites

    C81.19   Nodular sclerosis Hodgkin lymphoma, extranodal and solid organ sites

● **C81.2**   **Mixed cellularity Hodgkin lymphoma**
     Mixed cellularity classical Hodgkin lymphoma
     A type of Hodgkin's that is moderately aggressive with mixed cell types

    C81.20   Mixed cellularity Hodgkin lymphoma, unspecified site

    C81.21   Mixed cellularity Hodgkin lymphoma, lymph nodes of head, face, and neck

    C81.22   Mixed cellularity Hodgkin lymphoma, intrathoracic lymph nodes

    C81.23   Mixed cellularity Hodgkin lymphoma, intra-abdominal lymph nodes

    C81.24   Mixed cellularity Hodgkin lymphoma, lymph nodes of axilla and upper limb

    C81.25   Mixed cellularity Hodgkin lymphoma, lymph nodes of inguinal region and lower limb

    C81.26   Mixed cellularity Hodgkin lymphoma, intrapelvic lymph nodes

    C81.27   Mixed cellularity Hodgkin lymphoma, spleen

    C81.28   Mixed cellularity Hodgkin lymphoma, lymph nodes of multiple sites

    C81.29   Mixed cellularity Hodgkin lymphoma, extranodal and solid organ sites

● **C81.3**   **Lymphocyte depleted Hodgkin lymphoma**
     Lymphocyte depleted classical Hodgkin lymphoma
     Most aggressive type with poor prognosis

    C81.30   Lymphocyte depleted Hodgkin lymphoma, unspecified site

    C81.31   Lymphocyte depleted Hodgkin lymphoma, lymph nodes of head, face, and neck

    C81.32   Lymphocyte depleted Hodgkin lymphoma, intrathoracic lymph nodes

    C81.33   Lymphocyte depleted Hodgkin lymphoma, intra-abdominal lymph nodes

    C81.34   Lymphocyte depleted Hodgkin lymphoma, lymph nodes of axilla and upper limb

    C81.35   Lymphocyte depleted Hodgkin lymphoma, lymph nodes of inguinal region and lower limb

    C81.36   Lymphocyte depleted Hodgkin lymphoma, intrapelvic lymph nodes

    C81.37   Lymphocyte depleted Hodgkin lymphoma, spleen

    C81.38   Lymphocyte depleted Hodgkin lymphoma, lymph nodes of multiple sites

    C81.39   Lymphocyte depleted Hodgkin lymphoma, extranodal and solid organ sites

● **C81.4**   **Lymphocyte-rich Hodgkin lymphoma**
     Lymphocyte-rich classical Hodgkin lymphoma

    Excludes1   nodular lymphocyte predominant Hodgkin lymphoma (C81.0-)

    C81.40   Lymphocyte-rich Hodgkin lymphoma, unspecified site

    C81.41   Lymphocyte-rich Hodgkin lymphoma, lymph nodes of head, face, and neck

    C81.42   Lymphocyte-rich Hodgkin lymphoma, intrathoracic lymph nodes

    C81.43   Lymphocyte-rich Hodgkin lymphoma, intra-abdominal lymph nodes

    C81.44   Lymphocyte-rich Hodgkin lymphoma, lymph nodes of axilla and upper limb

    C81.45   Lymphocyte-rich Hodgkin lymphoma, lymph nodes of inguinal region and lower limb

    C81.46   Lymphocyte-rich Hodgkin lymphoma, intrapelvic lymph nodes

    C81.47   Lymphocyte-rich Hodgkin lymphoma, spleen

    C81.48   Lymphocyte-rich Hodgkin lymphoma, lymph nodes of multiple sites

    C81.49   Lymphocyte-rich Hodgkin lymphoma, extranodal and solid organ sites

● **C81.7**   **Other Hodgkin lymphoma**
     Classical Hodgkin lymphoma NOS
     Other classical Hodgkin lymphoma

    C81.70   Other Hodgkin lymphoma, unspecified site

    C81.71   Other Hodgkin lymphoma, lymph nodes of head, face, and neck

    C81.72   Other Hodgkin lymphoma, intrathoracic lymph nodes

    C81.73   Other Hodgkin lymphoma, intra-abdominal lymph nodes

    C81.74   Other Hodgkin lymphoma, lymph nodes of axilla and upper limb

    C81.75   Other Hodgkin lymphoma, lymph nodes of inguinal region and lower limb

    C81.76   Other Hodgkin lymphoma, intrapelvic lymph nodes

    C81.77   Other Hodgkin lymphoma, spleen

    C81.78   Other Hodgkin lymphoma, lymph nodes of multiple sites

    C81.79   Other Hodgkin lymphoma, extranodal and solid organ sites

● **C81.9**   **Hodgkin lymphoma, unspecified**

    C81.90   Hodgkin lymphoma, unspecified, unspecified site

    C81.91   Hodgkin lymphoma, unspecified, lymph nodes of head, face, and neck

    C81.92   Hodgkin lymphoma, unspecified, intrathoracic lymph nodes

    C81.93   Hodgkin lymphoma, unspecified, intra-abdominal lymph nodes

    C81.94   Hodgkin lymphoma, unspecified, lymph nodes of axilla and upper limb

    C81.95   Hodgkin lymphoma, unspecified, lymph nodes of inguinal region and lower limb

    C81.96   Hodgkin lymphoma, unspecified, intrapelvic lymph nodes

    C81.97   Hodgkin lymphoma, unspecified, spleen

    C81.98   Hodgkin lymphoma, unspecified, lymph nodes of multiple sites

    C81.99   Hodgkin lymphoma, unspecified, extranodal and solid organ sites

▶ New   ⇒ Revised   ~~deleted~~ Deleted   Excludes 1   Excludes 2   Includes   Use additional   Code first   Code also   Key words

OGCR Official Guidelines   X Assign placeholder X   ● Use Additional Character(s)   ▶ Manifestation Code   **Coding Clinic**

● **C82 Follicular lymphoma**
  Group of malignant lymphomas
  Includes follicular lymphoma with or without diffuse areas
  Excludes1 mature T/NK-cell lymphomas (C84.-)
    personal history of non-Hodgkin lymphoma (Z85.72)

● **C82.0 Follicular lymphoma grade I**
  C82.00 Follicular lymphoma grade I, unspecified site
  C82.01 Follicular lymphoma grade I, lymph nodes of head, face, and neck
  C82.02 Follicular lymphoma grade I, intrathoracic lymph nodes
  C82.03 Follicular lymphoma grade I, intra-abdominal lymph nodes
  C82.04 Follicular lymphoma grade I, lymph nodes of axilla and upper limb
  C82.05 Follicular lymphoma grade I, lymph nodes of inguinal region and lower limb
  C82.06 Follicular lymphoma grade I, intrapelvic lymph nodes
  C82.07 Follicular lymphoma grade I, spleen
  C82.08 Follicular lymphoma grade I, lymph nodes of multiple sites
  C82.09 Follicular lymphoma grade I, extranodal and solid organ sites

● **C82.1 Follicular lymphoma grade II**
  C82.10 Follicular lymphoma grade II, unspecified site
  C82.11 Follicular lymphoma grade II, lymph nodes of head, face, and neck
  C82.12 Follicular lymphoma grade II, intrathoracic lymph nodes
  C82.13 Follicular lymphoma grade II, intra-abdominal lymph nodes
  C82.14 Follicular lymphoma grade II, lymph nodes of axilla and upper limb
  C82.15 Follicular lymphoma grade II, lymph nodes of inguinal region and lower limb
  C82.16 Follicular lymphoma grade II, intrapelvic lymph nodes
  C82.17 Follicular lymphoma grade II, spleen
  C82.18 Follicular lymphoma grade II, lymph nodes of multiple sites
  C82.19 Follicular lymphoma grade II, extranodal and solid organ sites

● **C82.2 Follicular lymphoma grade III, unspecified**
  C82.20 Follicular lymphoma grade III, unspecified, unspecified site
  C82.21 Follicular lymphoma grade III, unspecified, lymph nodes of head, face, and neck
  C82.22 Follicular lymphoma grade III, unspecified, intrathoracic lymph nodes
  C82.23 Follicular lymphoma grade III, unspecified, intra-abdominal lymph nodes
  C82.24 Follicular lymphoma grade III, unspecified, lymph nodes of axilla and upper limb
  C82.25 Follicular lymphoma grade III, unspecified, lymph nodes of inguinal region and lower limb
  C82.26 Follicular lymphoma grade III, unspecified, intrapelvic lymph nodes
  C82.27 Follicular lymphoma grade III, unspecified, spleen
  C82.28 Follicular lymphoma grade III, unspecified, lymph nodes of multiple sites
  C82.29 Follicular lymphoma grade III, unspecified, extranodal and solid organ sites

● **C82.3 Follicular lymphoma grade IIIa**
  C82.30 Follicular lymphoma grade IIIa, unspecified site
  C82.31 Follicular lymphoma grade IIIa, lymph nodes of head, face, and neck
  C82.32 Follicular lymphoma grade IIIa, intrathoracic lymph nodes
  C82.33 Follicular lymphoma grade IIIa, intra-abdominal lymph nodes
  C82.34 Follicular lymphoma grade IIIa, lymph nodes of axilla and upper limb
  C82.35 Follicular lymphoma grade IIIa, lymph nodes of inguinal region and lower limb
  C82.36 Follicular lymphoma grade IIIa, intrapelvic lymph nodes
  C82.37 Follicular lymphoma grade IIIa, spleen
  C82.38 Follicular lymphoma grade IIIa, lymph nodes of multiple sites
  C82.39 Follicular lymphoma grade IIIa, extranodal and solid organ sites

● **C82.4 Follicular lymphoma grade IIIb**
  C82.40 Follicular lymphoma grade IIIb, unspecified site
  C82.41 Follicular lymphoma grade IIIb, lymph nodes of head, face, and neck
  C82.42 Follicular lymphoma grade IIIb, intrathoracic lymph nodes
  C82.43 Follicular lymphoma grade IIIb, intra-abdominal lymph nodes
  C82.44 Follicular lymphoma grade IIIb, lymph nodes of axilla and upper limb
  C82.45 Follicular lymphoma grade IIIb, lymph nodes of inguinal region and lower limb
  C82.46 Follicular lymphoma grade IIIb, intrapelvic lymph nodes
  C82.47 Follicular lymphoma grade IIIb, spleen
  C82.48 Follicular lymphoma grade IIIb, lymph nodes of multiple sites
  C82.49 Follicular lymphoma grade IIIb, extranodal and solid organ sites

● **C82.5 Diffuse follicle center lymphoma**
  C82.50 Diffuse follicle center lymphoma, unspecified site
  C82.51 Diffuse follicle center lymphoma, lymph nodes of head, face, and neck
  C82.52 Diffuse follicle center lymphoma, intrathoracic lymph nodes
  C82.53 Diffuse follicle center lymphoma, intra-abdominal lymph nodes
  C82.54 Diffuse follicle center lymphoma, lymph nodes of axilla and upper limb
  C82.55 Diffuse follicle center lymphoma, lymph nodes of inguinal region and lower limb
  C82.56 Diffuse follicle center lymphoma, intrapelvic lymph nodes
  C82.57 Diffuse follicle center lymphoma, spleen
  C82.58 Diffuse follicle center lymphoma, lymph nodes of multiple sites
  C82.59 Diffuse follicle center lymphoma, extranodal and solid organ sites

● **C82.6 Cutaneous follicle center lymphoma**
  C82.60 Cutaneous follicle center lymphoma, unspecified site
  C82.61 Cutaneous follicle center lymphoma, lymph nodes of head, face, and neck
  C82.62 Cutaneous follicle center lymphoma, intrathoracic lymph nodes
  C82.63 Cutaneous follicle center lymphoma, intra-abdominal lymph nodes

CHAPTER 2 (C00–D49)

C82.64   Cutaneous follicle center lymphoma, lymph nodes of axilla and upper limb

C82.65   Cutaneous follicle center lymphoma, lymph nodes of inguinal region and lower limb

C82.66   Cutaneous follicle center lymphoma, intrapelvic lymph nodes

C82.67   Cutaneous follicle center lymphoma, spleen

C82.68   Cutaneous follicle center lymphoma, lymph nodes of multiple sites

C82.69   Cutaneous follicle center lymphoma, extranodal and solid organ sites

● C82.8   Other types of follicular lymphoma

C82.80   Other types of follicular lymphoma, unspecified site

C82.81   Other types of follicular lymphoma, lymph nodes of head, face, and neck

C82.82   Other types of follicular lymphoma, intrathoracic lymph nodes

C82.83   Other types of follicular lymphoma, intra-abdominal lymph nodes

C82.84   Other types of follicular lymphoma, lymph nodes of axilla and upper limb

C82.85   Other types of follicular lymphoma, lymph nodes of inguinal region and lower limb

C82.86   Other types of follicular lymphoma, intrapelvic lymph nodes

C82.87   Other types of follicular lymphoma, spleen

C82.88   Other types of follicular lymphoma, lymph nodes of multiple sites

C82.89   Other types of follicular lymphoma, extranodal and solid organ sites

● C82.9   Follicular lymphoma, unspecified

C82.90   Follicular lymphoma, unspecified, unspecified site

C82.91   Follicular lymphoma, unspecified, lymph nodes of head, face, and neck

C82.92   Follicular lymphoma, unspecified, intrathoracic lymph nodes

C82.93   Follicular lymphoma, unspecified, intra-abdominal lymph nodes

C82.94   Follicular lymphoma, unspecified, lymph nodes of axilla and upper limb

C82.95   Follicular lymphoma, unspecified, lymph nodes of inguinal region and lower limb

C82.96   Follicular lymphoma, unspecified, intrapelvic lymph nodes

C82.97   Follicular lymphoma, unspecified, spleen

C82.98   Follicular lymphoma, unspecified, lymph nodes of multiple sites

C82.99   Follicular lymphoma, unspecified, extranodal and solid organ sites

● C83   Non-follicular lymphoma

> **Excludes1**   personal history of non-Hodgkin lymphoma (Z85.72)

● C83.0   Small cell B-cell lymphoma
Lymphoplasmacytic lymphoma
Nodal marginal zone lymphoma
Non-leukemic variant of B-CLL
Splenic marginal zone lymphoma

> **Excludes1**   chronic lymphocytic leukemia (C91.1)
> mature T/NK-cell lymphomas (C84.-)
> Waldenström macroglobulinemia (C88.0)

C83.00   Small cell B-cell lymphoma, unspecified site

C83.01   Small cell B-cell lymphoma, lymph nodes of head, face, and neck

C83.02   Small cell B-cell lymphoma, intrathoracic lymph nodes

C83.03   Small cell B-cell lymphoma, intra-abdominal lymph nodes

C83.04   Small cell B-cell lymphoma, lymph nodes of axilla and upper limb

C83.05   Small cell B-cell lymphoma, lymph nodes of inguinal region and lower limb

C83.06   Small cell B-cell lymphoma, intrapelvic lymph nodes

C83.07   Small cell B-cell lymphoma, spleen

C83.08   Small cell B-cell lymphoma, lymph nodes of multiple sites

C83.09   Small cell B-cell lymphoma, extranodal and solid organ sites

● C83.1   Mantle cell lymphoma
Centrocytic lymphoma
Malignant lymphomatous polyposis

C83.10   Mantle cell lymphoma, unspecified site

C83.11   Mantle cell lymphoma, lymph nodes of head, face, and neck

C83.12   Mantle cell lymphoma, intrathoracic lymph nodes

C83.13   Mantle cell lymphoma, intra-abdominal lymph nodes

C83.14   Mantle cell lymphoma, lymph nodes of axilla and upper limb

C83.15   Mantle cell lymphoma, lymph nodes of inguinal region and lower limb

C83.16   Mantle cell lymphoma, intrapelvic lymph nodes

C83.17   Mantle cell lymphoma, spleen

C83.18   Mantle cell lymphoma, lymph nodes of multiple sites

C83.19   Mantle cell lymphoma, extranodal and solid organ sites

● C83.3   Diffuse large B-cell lymphoma
Anaplastic diffuse large B-cell lymphoma
CD30-positive diffuse large B-cell lymphoma
Centroblastic diffuse large B-cell lymphoma
Diffuse large B-cell lymphoma, subtype not specified
Immunoblastic diffuse large B-cell lymphoma
Plasmablastic diffuse large B-cell lymphoma
Diffuse large B-cell lymphoma, subtype not specified
T-cell rich diffuse large B-cell lymphoma

> **Excludes1**   mediastinal (thymic) large B-cell lymphoma (C85.2-)
> mature T/NK-cell lymphomas (C84.-)

C83.30   Diffuse large B-cell lymphoma, unspecified site

C83.31   Diffuse large B-cell lymphoma, lymph nodes of head, face, and neck

C83.32   Diffuse large B-cell lymphoma, intrathoracic lymph nodes

C83.33   Diffuse large B-cell lymphoma, intra-abdominal lymph nodes

C83.34   Diffuse large B-cell lymphoma, lymph nodes of axilla and upper limb

C83.35   Diffuse large B-cell lymphoma, lymph nodes of inguinal region and lower limb

C83.36   Diffuse large B-cell lymphoma, intrapelvic lymph nodes

C83.37   Diffuse large B-cell lymphoma, spleen

C83.38   Diffuse large B-cell lymphoma, lymph nodes of multiple sites

C83.39   Diffuse large B-cell lymphoma, extranodal and solid organ sites

---

▶ New   ⇒ Revised   ~~deleted~~ Deleted   Excludes 1   Excludes 2   Includes   Use additional   Code first   Code also   Key words

OGCR Official Guidelines   X Assign placeholder X   ● Use Additional Character(s)   ▌ Manifestation Code   **Coding Clinic**

● **C83.5**   **Lymphoblastic (diffuse) lymphoma**
Highly malignant type of non-Hodgkin lymphoma with
diffuse infiltration
B-precursor lymphoma
Lymphoblastic B-cell lymphoma
Lymphoblastic lymphoma NOS
Lymphoblastic T-cell lymphoma
T-precursor lymphoma

    C83.50   Lymphoblastic (diffuse) lymphoma, unspecified site

    C83.51   Lymphoblastic (diffuse) lymphoma, lymph nodes of head, face, and neck

    C83.52   Lymphoblastic (diffuse) lymphoma, intrathoracic lymph nodes

    C83.53   Lymphoblastic (diffuse) lymphoma, intra-abdominal lymph nodes

    C83.54   Lymphoblastic (diffuse) lymphoma, lymph nodes of axilla and upper limb

    C83.55   Lymphoblastic (diffuse) lymphoma, lymph nodes of inguinal region and lower limb

    C83.56   Lymphoblastic (diffuse) lymphoma, intrapelvic lymph nodes

    C83.57   Lymphoblastic (diffuse) lymphoma, spleen

    C83.58   Lymphoblastic (diffuse) lymphoma, lymph nodes of multiple sites

    C83.59   Lymphoblastic (diffuse) lymphoma, extranodal and solid organ sites

● **C83.7**   **Burkitt lymphoma**
Form of small cell lymphoma
Atypical Burkitt lymphoma
Burkitt-like lymphoma

    Excludes1   mature B-cell leukemia Burkitt type (C91.A-)

    C83.70   Burkitt lymphoma, unspecified site

    C83.71   Burkitt lymphoma, lymph nodes of head, face, and neck

    C83.72   Burkitt lymphoma, intrathoracic lymph nodes

    C83.73   Burkitt lymphoma, intra-abdominal lymph nodes

    C83.74   Burkitt lymphoma, lymph nodes of axilla and upper limb

    C83.75   Burkitt lymphoma, lymph nodes of inguinal region and lower limb

    C83.76   Burkitt lymphoma, intrapelvic lymph nodes

    C83.77   Burkitt lymphoma, spleen

    C83.78   Burkitt lymphoma, lymph nodes of multiple sites

    C83.79   Burkitt lymphoma, extranodal and solid organ sites

● **C83.8**   **Other non-follicular lymphoma**
Intravascular large B-cell lymphoma
Lymphoid granulomatosis
Primary effusion B-cell lymphoma

    Excludes1   mediastinal (thymic) large B-cell lymphoma (C85.2-)
                  T-cell rich B-cell lymphoma (C83.3-)

    C83.80   Other non-follicular lymphoma, unspecified site

    C83.81   Other non-follicular lymphoma, lymph nodes of head, face, and neck

    C83.82   Other non-follicular lymphoma, intrathoracic lymph nodes

    C83.83   Other non-follicular lymphoma, intra-abdominal lymph nodes

    C83.84   Other non-follicular lymphoma, lymph nodes of axilla and upper limb

    C83.85   Other non-follicular lymphoma, lymph nodes of inguinal region and lower limb

    C83.86   Other non-follicular lymphoma, intrapelvic lymph nodes

    C83.87   Other non-follicular lymphoma, spleen

    C83.88   Other non-follicular lymphoma, lymph nodes of multiple sites

    C83.89   Other non-follicular lymphoma, extranodal and solid organ sites

● **C83.9**   **Non-follicular (diffuse) lymphoma, unspecified**

    C83.90   Non-follicular (diffuse) lymphoma, unspecified, unspecified site

    C83.91   Non-follicular (diffuse) lymphoma, unspecified, lymph nodes of head, face, and neck

    C83.92   Non-follicular (diffuse) lymphoma, unspecified, intrathoracic lymph nodes

    C83.93   Non-follicular (diffuse) lymphoma, unspecified, intra-abdominal lymph nodes

    C83.94   Non-follicular (diffuse) lymphoma, unspecified, lymph nodes of axilla and upper limb

    C83.95   Non-follicular (diffuse) lymphoma, unspecified, lymph nodes of inguinal region and lower limb

    C83.96   Non-follicular (diffuse) lymphoma, unspecified, intrapelvic lymph nodes

    C83.97   Non-follicular (diffuse) lymphoma, unspecified, spleen

    C83.98   Non-follicular (diffuse) lymphoma, unspecified, lymph nodes of multiple sites

    C83.99   Non-follicular (diffuse) lymphoma, unspecified, extranodal and solid organ sites

● **C84**   **Mature T/NK-cell lymphomas**

    Excludes1   personal history of non-Hodgkin lymphoma (Z85.72)

● **C84.0**   **Mycosis fungoides**
Chronic or rapidly progressive form of cutaneous T-cell
lymphoma; AKA granuloma fungoides

    Excludes1   peripheral T-cell lymphoma, not classified (C84.4-)

    C84.00   Mycosis fungoides, unspecified site

    C84.01   Mycosis fungoides, lymph nodes of head, face, and neck

    C84.02   Mycosis fungoides, intrathoracic lymph nodes

    C84.03   Mycosis fungoides, intra-abdominal lymph nodes

    C84.04   Mycosis fungoides, lymph nodes of axilla and upper limb

    C84.05   Mycosis fungoides, lymph nodes of inguinal region and lower limb

    C84.06   Mycosis fungoides, intrapelvic lymph nodes

    C84.07   Mycosis fungoides, spleen

    C84.08   Mycosis fungoides, lymph nodes of multiple sites

    C84.09   Mycosis fungoides, extranodal and solid organ sites

● **C84.1**   **Sézary disease**
Type of cutaneous lymphoma affecting T-cells

    C84.10   Sézary disease, unspecified site

    C84.11   Sézary disease, lymph nodes of head, face, and neck

    C84.12   Sézary disease, intrathoracic lymph nodes

    C84.13   Sézary disease, intra-abdominal lymph nodes

    C84.14   Sézary disease, lymph nodes of axilla and upper limb

    C84.15   Sézary disease, lymph nodes of inguinal region and lower limb

    C84.16   Sézary disease, intrapelvic lymph nodes

    C84.17   Sézary disease, spleen

    C84.18   Sézary disease, lymph nodes of multiple sites

    C84.19   Sézary disease, extranodal and solid organ sites

CHAPTER 2 (C00-D49)

● **C84.4**   **Peripheral T-cell lymphoma, not classified**
Diverse group of blood carcinomas originating from T-cells, requiring aggressive chemotherapy
Lennert's lymphoma
Lymphoepithelioid lymphoma
Mature T-cell lymphoma, not elsewhere classified

     C84.40   Peripheral T-cell lymphoma, not classified, unspecified site

     C84.41   Peripheral T-cell lymphoma, not classified, lymph nodes of head, face, and neck

     C84.42   Peripheral T-cell lymphoma, not classified, intrathoracic lymph nodes

     C84.43   Peripheral T-cell lymphoma, not classified, intra-abdominal lymph nodes

     C84.44   Peripheral T-cell lymphoma, not classified, lymph nodes of axilla and upper limb

     C84.45   Peripheral T-cell lymphoma, not classified, lymph nodes of inguinal region and lower limb

     C84.46   Peripheral T-cell lymphoma, not classified, intrapelvic lymph nodes

     C84.47   Peripheral T-cell lymphoma, not classified, spleen

     C84.48   Peripheral T-cell lymphoma, not classified, lymph nodes of multiple sites

     C84.49   Peripheral T-cell lymphoma, not classified, extranodal and solid organ sites

● **C84.6**   **Anaplastic large cell lymphoma, ALK-positive**
Anaplastic large cell lymphoma, CD30-positive

     C84.60   Anaplastic large cell lymphoma, ALK-positive, unspecified site

     C84.61   Anaplastic large cell lymphoma, ALK-positive, lymph nodes of head, face, and neck

     C84.62   Anaplastic large cell lymphoma, ALK-positive, intrathoracic lymph nodes

     C84.63   Anaplastic large cell lymphoma, ALK-positive, intra-abdominal lymph nodes

     C84.64   Anaplastic large cell lymphoma, ALK-positive, lymph nodes of axilla and upper limb

     C84.65   Anaplastic large cell lymphoma, ALK-positive, lymph nodes of inguinal region and lower limb

     C84.66   Anaplastic large cell lymphoma, ALK-positive, intrapelvic lymph nodes

     C84.67   Anaplastic large cell lymphoma, ALK-positive, spleen

     C84.68   Anaplastic large cell lymphoma, ALK-positive, lymph nodes of multiple sites

     C84.69   Anaplastic large cell lymphoma, ALK-positive, extranodal and solid organ sites

● **C84.7**   **Anaplastic large cell lymphoma, ALK-negative**

     Excludes1   primary cutaneous CD30-positive T-cell proliferations (C86.6-)

     C84.70   Anaplastic large cell lymphoma, ALK-negative, unspecified site

     C84.71   Anaplastic large cell lymphoma, ALK-negative, lymph nodes of head, face, and neck

     C84.72   Anaplastic large cell lymphoma, ALK-negative, intrathoracic lymph nodes

     C84.73   Anaplastic large cell lymphoma, ALK-negative, intra-abdominal lymph nodes

     C84.74   Anaplastic large cell lymphoma, ALK-negative, lymph nodes of axilla and upper limb

     C84.75   Anaplastic large cell lymphoma, ALK-negative, lymph nodes of inguinal region and lower limb

     C84.76   Anaplastic large cell lymphoma, ALK-negative, intrapelvic lymph nodes

     C84.77   Anaplastic large cell lymphoma, ALK-negative, spleen

     C84.78   Anaplastic large cell lymphoma, ALK-negative, lymph nodes of multiple sites

     C84.79   Anaplastic large cell lymphoma, ALK-negative, extranodal and solid organ sites

Item 2-7   Lymphosarcoma, also known as malignant lymphoma, is a cancer of the lymph system exhibiting abnormal cells encompassing an entire lymph node creating a diffuse pattern without any definite organization. Diffuse pattern lymphoma has a more unfavorable survival outlook than those with a follicular or nodular pattern. Reticulosarcoma is the most common aggressive form of non-Hodgkin's lymphoma.

● **C84.A**   **Cutaneous T-cell lymphoma, unspecified**

     C84.A0   Cutaneous T-cell lymphoma, unspecified, unspecified site

     C84.A1   Cutaneous T-cell lymphoma, unspecified lymph nodes of head, face, and neck

     C84.A2   Cutaneous T-cell lymphoma, unspecified, intrathoracic lymph nodes

     C84.A3   Cutaneous T-cell lymphoma, unspecified, intra-abdominal lymph nodes

     C84.A4   Cutaneous T-cell lymphoma, unspecified, lymph nodes of axilla and upper limb

     C84.A5   Cutaneous T-cell lymphoma, unspecified, lymph nodes of inguinal region and lower limb

     C84.A6   Cutaneous T-cell lymphoma, unspecified, intrapelvic lymph nodes

     C84.A7   Cutaneous T-cell lymphoma, unspecified, spleen

     C84.A8   Cutaneous T-cell lymphoma, unspecified, lymph nodes of multiple sites

     C84.A9   Cutaneous T-cell lymphoma, unspecified, extranodal and solid organ sites

● **C84.Z**   **Other mature T/NK-cell lymphomas**

     Note: If T-cell lineage or involvement is mentioned in conjunction with a specific lymphoma, code to the more specific description.

     Excludes1   angioimmunoblastic T-cell lymphoma (C86.5)
               blastic NK-cell lymphoma (C86.4)
               enteropathy-type T-cell lymphoma (C86.2)
               extranodal NK-cell lymphoma, nasal type (C86.0)
               hepatosplenic T-cell lymphoma (C86.1)
               primary cutaneous CD30-positive T-cell proliferations (C86.6)
               subcutaneous panniculitis-like T-cell lymphoma (C86.3)
               T-cell leukemia (C91.1-)

     C84.Z0   Other mature T/NK-cell lymphomas, unspecified site

     C84.Z1   Other mature T/NK-cell lymphomas, lymph nodes of head, face, and neck

     C84.Z2   Other mature T/NK-cell lymphomas, intrathoracic lymph nodes

     C84.Z3   Other mature T/NK-cell lymphomas, intra-abdominal lymph nodes

     C84.Z4   Other mature T/NK-cell lymphomas, lymph nodes of axilla and upper limb

     C84.Z5   Other mature T/NK-cell lymphomas, lymph nodes of inguinal region and lower limb

     C84.Z6   Other mature T/NK-cell lymphomas, intrapelvic lymph nodes

     C84.Z7   Other mature T/NK-cell lymphomas, spleen

     C84.Z8   Other mature T/NK-cell lymphomas, lymph nodes of multiple sites

     C84.Z9   Other mature T/NK-cell lymphomas, extranodal and solid organ sites

● **C84.9**   **Mature T/NK-cell lymphomas, unspecified**
NK/T cell lymphoma NOS

     Excludes1   mature T-cell lymphoma, not elsewhere classified (C84.4-)

     C84.90   Mature T/NK-cell lymphomas, unspecified, unspecified site

     C84.91   Mature T/NK-cell lymphomas, unspecified, lymph nodes of head, face, and neck

▶ New   ⇒ Revised   ~~deleted~~ Deleted   Excludes 1   Excludes 2   Includes   Use additional   Code first   Code also   Key words

OGCR Official Guidelines   X Assign placeholder X   ● Use Additional Character(s)   ▶ Manifestation Code   **Coding Clinic**

692

C84.92 Mature T/NK-cell lymphomas, unspecified, intrathoracic lymph nodes

C84.93 Mature T/NK-cell lymphomas, unspecified, intra-abdominal lymph nodes

C84.94 Mature T/NK-cell lymphomas, unspecified, lymph nodes of axilla and upper limb

C84.95 Mature T/NK-cell lymphomas, unspecified, lymph nodes of inguinal region and lower limb

C84.96 Mature T/NK-cell lymphomas, unspecified, intrapelvic lymph nodes

C84.97 Mature T/NK-cell lymphomas, unspecified, spleen

C84.98 Mature T/NK-cell lymphomas, unspecified, lymph nodes of multiple sites

C84.99 Mature T/NK-cell lymphomas, unspecified, extranodal and solid organ sites

● **C85** Other specified and unspecified types of non-Hodgkin lymphoma

     Excludes1   other specified types of T/NK-cell lymphoma (C86.-)
                     personal history of non-Hodgkin lymphoma (Z85.72)

● **C85.1** Unspecified B-cell lymphoma

     Note: If B-cell lineage or involvement is mentioned in conjunction with a specific lymphoma, code to the more specific description.

C85.10 Unspecified B-cell lymphoma, unspecified site

C85.11 Unspecified B-cell lymphoma, lymph nodes of head, face, and neck

C85.12 Unspecified B-cell lymphoma, intrathoracic lymph nodes

C85.13 Unspecified B-cell lymphoma, intra-abdominal lymph nodes

C85.14 Unspecified B-cell lymphoma, lymph nodes of axilla and upper limb

C85.15 Unspecified B-cell lymphoma, lymph nodes of inguinal region and lower limb

C85.16 Unspecified B-cell lymphoma, intrapelvic lymph nodes

C85.17 Unspecified B-cell lymphoma, spleen

C85.18 Unspecified B-cell lymphoma, lymph nodes of multiple sites

C85.19 Unspecified B-cell lymphoma, extranodal and solid organ sites

● **C85.2** Mediastinal (thymic) large B-cell lymphoma

C85.20 Mediastinal (thymic) large B-cell lymphoma, unspecified site

C85.21 Mediastinal (thymic) large B-cell lymphoma, lymph nodes of head, face, and neck

C85.22 Mediastinal (thymic) large B-cell lymphoma, intrathoracic lymph nodes

C85.23 Mediastinal (thymic) large B-cell lymphoma, intra-abdominal lymph nodes

C85.24 Mediastinal (thymic) large B-cell lymphoma, lymph nodes of axilla and upper limb

C85.25 Mediastinal (thymic) large B-cell lymphoma, lymph nodes of inguinal region and lower limb

C85.26 Mediastinal (thymic) large B-cell lymphoma, intrapelvic lymph nodes

C85.27 Mediastinal (thymic) large B-cell lymphoma, spleen

C85.28 Mediastinal (thymic) large B-cell lymphoma, lymph nodes of multiple sites

C85.29 Mediastinal (thymic) large B-cell lymphoma, extranodal and solid organ sites

● **C85.8** Other specified types of non-Hodgkin lymphoma

C85.80 Other specified types of non-Hodgkin lymphoma, unspecified site

C85.81 Other specified types of non-Hodgkin lymphoma, lymph nodes of head, face, and neck

C85.82 Other specified types of non-Hodgkin lymphoma, intrathoracic lymph nodes

C85.83 Other specified types of non-Hodgkin lymphoma, intra-abdominal lymph nodes

C85.84 Other specified types of non-Hodgkin lymphoma, lymph nodes of axilla and upper limb

C85.85 Other specified types of non-Hodgkin lymphoma, lymph nodes of inguinal region and lower limb

C85.86 Other specified types of non-Hodgkin lymphoma, intrapelvic lymph nodes

C85.87 Other specified types of non-Hodgkin lymphoma, spleen

C85.88 Other specified types of non-Hodgkin lymphoma, lymph nodes of multiple sites

C85.89 Other specified types of non-Hodgkin lymphoma, extranodal and solid organ sites

● **C85.9** Non-Hodgkin lymphoma, unspecified
     Lymphoma NOS
     Malignant lymphoma NOS
     Non-Hodgkin lymphoma NOS

C85.90 Non-Hodgkin lymphoma, unspecified, unspecified site

C85.91 Non-Hodgkin lymphoma, unspecified, lymph nodes of head, face, and neck

C85.92 Non-Hodgkin lymphoma, unspecified, intrathoracic lymph nodes

C85.93 Non-Hodgkin lymphoma, unspecified, intra-abdominal lymph nodes

C85.94 Non-Hodgkin lymphoma, unspecified, lymph nodes of axilla and upper limb

C85.95 Non-Hodgkin lymphoma, unspecified, lymph nodes of inguinal region and lower limb

C85.96 Non-Hodgkin lymphoma, unspecified, intrapelvic lymph nodes

C85.97 Non-Hodgkin lymphoma, unspecified, spleen

C85.98 Non-Hodgkin lymphoma, unspecified, lymph nodes of multiple sites

C85.99 Non-Hodgkin lymphoma, unspecified, extranodal and solid organ sites

● **C86** Other specified types of T/NK-cell lymphoma

     Excludes1   anaplastic large cell lymphoma, ALK negative (C84.7-)
                     anaplastic large cell lymphoma, ALK positive (C84.6-)
                     mature T/NK-cell lymphomas (C84.-)
                     other specified types of non-Hodgkin lymphoma (C85.8-)

C86.0 Extranodal NK/T-cell lymphoma, nasal type

C86.1 Hepatosplenic T-cell lymphoma
     Alpha-beta and gamma delta types

C86.2 Enteropathy-type (intestinal) T-cell lymphoma
     Enteropathy associated T-cell lymphoma

C86.3 Subcutaneous panniculitis-like T-cell lymphoma

C86.4 Blastic NK-cell lymphoma
     Blastic plasmacytoid dendritic cell neoplasm (BPDCN)

C86.5 Angioimmunoblastic T-cell lymphoma
     Angioimmunoblastic lymphadenopathy with dysproteinemia (AILD)

C86.6 Primary cutaneous CD30-positive T-cell proliferations
     Lymphomatoid papulosis
     Primary cutaneous anaplastic large cell lymphoma
     Primary cutaneous CD30-positive large T-cell lymphoma

CHAPTER 2 (C00-D49)

● C88 Malignant immunoproliferative diseases and certain other B-cell lymphomas
Diseases involving immune system
> **Excludes1**   B-cell lymphoma, unspecified (C85.1-)
> personal history of other malignant neoplasms of lymphoid, hematopoietic and related tissues (Z85.79)

C88.0 Waldenström's macroglobulinemia
Lymphoplasmacytic lymphoma with IgM-production
Macroglobulinemia (idiopathic) (primary)
> **Excludes1**   small cell B-cell lymphoma (C83.0)

C88.2 Heavy chain disease
Franklin disease
Gamma heavy chain disease
Mu heavy chain disease

C88.3 Immunoproliferative small intestinal disease
Alpha heavy chain disease
Mediterranean lymphoma

C88.4 Extranodal marginal zone B-cell lymphoma of mucosa-associated lymphoid tissue [MALT-lymphoma]
Lymphoma of skin-associated lymphoid tissue [SALT-lymphoma]
Lymphoma of bronchial-associated lymphoid tissue [BALT-lymphoma]
> **Excludes1**   high malignant (diffuse large B-cell) lymphoma (C83.3-)

C88.8 Other malignant immunoproliferative diseases

C88.9 Malignant immunoproliferative disease, unspecified
Immunoproliferative disease NOS

● C90 Multiple myeloma and malignant plasma cell neoplasms
> **Excludes1**   personal history of other malignant neoplasms of lymphoid, hematopoietic and related tissues (Z85.79)

● C90.0 Multiple myeloma
Kahler's disease
Medullary plasmacytoma
Myelomatosis
Plasma cell myeloma
> **Excludes1**   solitary myeloma (C90.3-)
> solitary plasmacytoma (C90.3-)

C90.00 Multiple myeloma not having achieved remission
Multiple myeloma with failed remission
Multiple myeloma NOS

C90.01 Multiple myeloma in remission

C90.02 Multiple myeloma in relapse

● C90.1 Plasma cell leukemia
Rare type of acute leukemia
Plasmacytic leukemia

C90.10 Plasma cell leukemia not having achieved remission
Plasma cell leukemia with failed remission
Plasma cell leukemia NOS

C90.11 Plasma cell leukemia in remission

C90.12 Plasma cell leukemia in relapse

● C90.2 Extramedullary plasmacytoma
Malignant monoclonal plasma cell tumor growing in soft tissue; AKA plasma cell dyscrasias

C90.20 Extramedullary plasmacytoma not having achieved remission
Extramedullary plasmacytoma with failed remission
Extramedullary plasmacytoma NOS

C90.21 Extramedullary plasmacytoma in remission

C90.22 Extramedullary plasmacytoma in relapse

Item 2-8   Multiple myeloma is a cancer of a plasma cell (a type of white blood cell) and is an incurable but treatable disease. Immunoproliferative neoplasm is a term for diseases (mostly cancers) in which the immune system cells proliferate.

● C90.3 Solitary plasmacytoma
Localized malignant plasma cell tumor NOS
Plasmacytoma NOS
Solitary myeloma

C90.30 Solitary plasmacytoma not having achieved remission
Solitary plasmacytoma with failed remission
Solitary plasmacytoma NOS

C90.31 Solitary plasmacytoma in remission

C90.32 Solitary plasmacytoma in relapse

● C91 Lymphoid leukemia
Type of leukemia affecting circulating cells of lymphoid origin
> **Excludes1**   personal history of leukemia (Z85.6)

● C91.0 Acute lymphoblastic leukemia [ALL]
> **Note:** Code C91.0 should only be used for T-cell and B-cell precursor leukemia

C91.00 Acute lymphoblastic leukemia not having achieved remission
Acute lymphoblastic leukemia with failed remission
Acute lymphoblastic leukemia NOS

C91.01 Acute lymphoblastic leukemia, in remission

C91.02 Acute lymphoblastic leukemia, in relapse

● C91.1 Chronic lymphocytic leukemia of B-cell type
Lymphoplasmacytic leukemia
Richter syndrome
> **Excludes1**   lymphoplasmacytic lymphoma (C83.0-)

C91.10 Chronic lymphocytic leukemia of B-cell type not having achieved remission
Chronic lymphocytic leukemia of B-cell type with failed remission
Chronic lymphocytic leukemia of B-cell type NOS

C91.11 Chronic lymphocytic leukemia of B-cell type in remission

C91.12 Chronic lymphocytic leukemia of B-cell type in relapse

● C91.3 Prolymphocytic leukemia of B-cell type
Chronic leukemia with symptoms of large number of circulating lymphocytes

C91.30 Prolymphocytic leukemia of B-cell type not having achieved remission
Prolymphocytic leukemia of B-cell type with failed remission
Prolymphocytic leukemia of B-cell type NOS

C91.31 Prolymphocytic leukemia of B-cell type, in remission

C91.32 Prolymphocytic leukemia of B-cell type, in relapse

● C91.4 Hairy cell leukemia
Chronic leukemia with splenomegaly and excessive number of abnormal large mononuclear cells covered by hairlike villi
Leukemic reticuloendotheliosis

C91.40 Hairy cell leukemia not having achieved remission
Hairy cell leukemia with failed remission
Hairy cell leukemia NOS

C91.41 Hairy cell leukemia, in remission

C91.42 Hairy cell leukemia, in relapse

▶ New   ⮕ Revised   ~~deleted~~ Deleted   Excludes 1   Excludes 2   Includes   Use additional   Code first   Code also   Key words

694   **OGCR** Official Guidelines   X Assign placeholder X   ● Use Additional Character(s)   ▶ Manifestation Code   **Coding Clinic**

Item 2–9 *Leukemia is a cancer (acute or chronic) of the blood-forming tissues of the bone marrow. Blood cells all start out as stem cells. They mature and become red cells, white cells, or platelets. There are three main types of leukocytes (white cells that fight infection): monocytes, lymphocytes, and granulocytes.* **Acute monocytic leukemia** *(AML) affects monocytes.* **Acute lymphoid leukemia** *(ALL) affects lymphocytes, and* **acute myeloid leukemia** *(AML) affects cells that typically develop into white blood cells (not lymphocytes), though it may develop in other blood cells.*

● **C91.5   Adult T-cell lymphoma/leukemia (HTLV-1-associated)**
     Acute variant of adult T-cell lymphoma/leukemia (HTLV-1-associated)
     Chronic variant of adult T-cell lymphoma/leukemia (HTLV-1-associated)
     Lymphomatoid variant of adult T-cell lymphoma/leukemia (HTLV-1-associated)
     Smouldering variant of adult T-cell lymphoma/leukemia (HTLV-1-associated)

     C91.50   Adult T-cell lymphoma/leukemia (HTLV-1-associated) not having achieved remission   A
         Adult T-cell lymphoma/leukemia (HTLV-1-associated) with failed remission
         Adult T-cell lymphoma/leukemia (HTLV-1-associated) NOS

     C91.51   Adult T-cell lymphoma/leukemia (HTLV-1-associated), in remission   A

     C91.52   Adult T-cell lymphoma/leukemia (HTLV-1-associated), in relapse   A

● **C91.6   Prolymphocytic leukemia of T-cell type**

     C91.60   Prolymphocytic leukemia of T-cell type not having achieved remission
         Prolymphocytic leukemia of T-cell type with failed remission
         Prolymphocytic leukemia of T-cell type NOS

     C91.61   Prolymphocytic leukemia of T-cell type, in remission

     C91.62   Prolymphocytic leukemia of T-cell type, in relapse

● **C91.A   Mature B-cell leukemia Burkitt-type**

     Excludes1   Burkitt lymphoma (C83.7-)

     C91.A0   Mature B-cell leukemia Burkitt-type not having achieved remission
         Mature B-cell leukemia Burkitt-type with failed remission
         Mature B-cell leukemia Burkitt-type NOS

     C91.A1   Mature B-cell leukemia Burkitt-type, in remission

     C91.A2   Mature B-cell leukemia Burkitt-type, in relapse

● **C91.Z   Other lymphoid leukemia**
     T-cell large granular lymphocytic leukemia (associated with rheumatoid arthritis)

     C91.Z0   Other lymphoid leukemia not having achieved remission
         Other lymphoid leukemia with failed remission
         Other lymphoid leukemia NOS

     C91.Z1   Other lymphoid leukemia, in remission

     C91.Z2   Other lymphoid leukemia, in relapse

● **C91.9   Lymphoid leukemia, unspecified**

     C91.90   Lymphoid leukemia, unspecified not having achieved remission
         Lymphoid leukemia with failed remission
         Lymphoid leukemia NOS

     C91.91   Lymphoid leukemia, unspecified, in remission

     C91.92   Lymphoid leukemia, unspecified, in relapse

● **C92   Myeloid leukemia**

     Includes   granulocytic leukemia
               myelogenous leukemia

     Excludes1   personal history of leukemia (Z85.6)

● **C92.0   Acute myeloblastic leukemia**
     Acute myeloblastic leukemia, minimal differentiation
     Acute myeloblastic leukemia (with maturation)
     Acute myeloblastic leukemia 1/ETO
     Acute myeloblastic leukemia M0
     Acute myeloblastic leukemia M1
     Acute myeloblastic leukemia M2
     Acute myeloblastic leukemia with t(8;21)
     Acute myeloblastic leukemia (without a FAB classification) NOS
     Refractory anemia with excess blasts in transformation [RAEB T]

     Excludes1   acute exacerbation of chronic myeloid leukemia (C92.10)
               refractory anemia with excess of blasts not in transformation (D46.2-)

     C92.00   Acute myeloblastic leukemia, not having achieved remission
         Acute myeloblastic leukemia with failed remission
         Acute myeloblastic leukemia NOS

     C92.01   Acute myeloblastic leukemia, in remission

     C92.02   Acute myeloblastic leukemia, in relapse

● **C92.1   Chronic myeloid leukemia, BCR/ABL-positive**
     Chronic myelogenous leukemia, Philadelphia chromosome (Ph1) positive
     Chronic myelogenous leukemia, t(9;22) (q34;q11)
     Chronic myelogenous leukemia with crisis of blast cells

     Excludes1   atypical chronic myeloid leukemia BCR/ABL-negative (C92.2-)
               chronic myelomonocytic leukemia (C93.1-)
               chronic myeloproliferative disease (D47.1)

     C92.10   Chronic myeloid leukemia, BCR/ABL-positive, not having achieved remission
         Chronic myeloid leukemia, BCR/ABL-positive with failed remission
         Chronic myeloid leukemia, BCR/ABL-positive NOS
         Coding Clinic: 2017, Q1, P7

     C92.11   Chronic myeloid leukemia, BCR/ABL-positive, in remission

     C92.12   Chronic myeloid leukemia, BCR/ABL-positive, in relapse

● **C92.2   Atypical chronic myeloid leukemia, BCR/ABL-negative**

     C92.20   Atypical chronic myeloid leukemia, BCR/ABL-negative, not having achieved remission
         Atypical chronic myeloid leukemia, BCR/ABL-negative with failed remission
         Atypical chronic myeloid leukemia, BCR/ABL-negative NOS

     C92.21   Atypical chronic myeloid leukemia, BCR/ABL-negative, in remission

     C92.22   Atypical chronic myeloid leukemia, BCR/ABL-negative, in relapse

CHAPTER 2 (C00-D49)

CHAPTER 2 (C00-D49)

● **C92.3   Myeloid sarcoma**
    A malignant tumor of immature myeloid cells
    Chloroma
    Granulocytic sarcoma

    C92.30   Myeloid sarcoma, not having achieved remission
        Myeloid sarcoma with failed remission
        Myeloid sarcoma NOS

    C92.31   Myeloid sarcoma, in remission

    C92.32   Myeloid sarcoma, in relapse

● **C92.4   Acute promyelocytic leukemia**
    AML M3
    AML Me with t(15;17) and variants

    C92.40   Acute promyelocytic leukemia, not having achieved remission
        Acute promyelocytic leukemia with failed remission
        Acute promyelocytic leukemia NOS

    C92.41   Acute promyelocytic leukemia, in remission

    C92.42   Acute promyelocytic leukemia, in relapse

● **C92.5   Acute myelomonocytic leukemia**
    AML M4
    AML M4 Eo with inv(16) or t(16;16)

    C92.50   Acute myelomonocytic leukemia, not having achieved remission
        Acute myelomonocytic leukemia with failed remission
        Acute myelomonocytic leukemia NOS

    C92.51   Acute myelomonocytic leukemia, in remission

    C92.52   Acute myelomonocytic leukemia, in relapse

● **C92.6   Acute myeloid leukemia with 11q23-abnormality**
    Acute myeloid leukemia with variation of MLL-gene

    C92.60   Acute myeloid leukemia with 11q23-abnormality not having achieved remission
        Acute myeloid leukemia with 11q23-abnormality with failed remission
        Acute myeloid leukemia with 11q23-abnormality NOS

    C92.61   Acute myeloid leukemia with 11q23-abnormality in remission

    C92.62   Acute myeloid leukemia with 11q23-abnormality in relapse

● **C92.A   Acute myeloid leukemia with multilineage dysplasia**
    Acute myeloid leukemia with dysplasia of remaining hematopoesis and/or myelodysplastic disease in its history

    C92.A0   Acute myeloid leukemia with multilineage dysplasia, not having achieved remission
        Acute myeloid leukemia with multilineage dysplasia with failed remission
        Acute myeloid leukemia with multilineage dysplasia NOS

    C92.A1   Acute myeloid leukemia with multilineage dysplasia, in remission

    C92.A2   Acute myeloid leukemia with multilineage dysplasia, in relapse

● **C92.Z   Other myeloid leukemia**

    C92.Z0   Other myeloid leukemia not having achieved remission
        Myeloid leukemia NEC with failed remission
        Myeloid leukemia NEC

    C92.Z1   Other myeloid leukemia, in remission

    C92.Z2   Other myeloid leukemia, in relapse

● **C92.9   Myeloid leukemia, unspecified**

    C92.90   Myeloid leukemia, unspecified, not having achieved remission
        Myeloid leukemia, unspecified with failed remission
        Myeloid leukemia, unspecified NOS

    C92.91   Myeloid leukemia, unspecified in remission

    C92.92   Myeloid leukemia, unspecified in relapse

● **C93   Monocytic leukemia**
    Includes   monocytoid leukemia
    Excludes1   personal history of leukemia (Z85.6)

● **C93.0   Acute monoblastic/monocytic leukemia**
    AML M5
    AML M5a
    AML M5b

    C93.00   Acute monoblastic/monocytic leukemia, not having achieved remission
        Acute monoblastic/monocytic leukemia with failed remission
        Acute monoblastic/monocytic leukemia NOS

    C93.01   Acute monoblastic/monocytic leukemia, in remission

    C93.02   Acute monoblastic/monocytic leukemia, in relapse

● **C93.1   Chronic myelomonocytic leukemia**
    Chronic monocytic leukemia
    CMML-1
    CMML-2
    CMML with eosinophilia

    C93.10   Chronic myelomonocytic leukemia not having achieved remission
        Chronic myelomonocytic leukemia with failed remission
        Chronic myelomonocytic leukemia NOS

    C93.11   Chronic myelomonocytic leukemia, in remission

    C93.12   Chronic myelomonocytic leukemia, in relapse

● **C93.3   Juvenile myelomonocytic leukemia**

    C93.30   Juvenile myelomonocytic leukemia, not having achieved remission   P
        Juvenile myelomonocytic leukemia with failed remission
        Juvenile myelomonocytic leukemia NOS

    C93.31   Juvenile myelomonocytic leukemia, in remission   P

    C93.32   Juvenile myelomonocytic leukemia, in relapse P

● **C93.Z   Other monocytic leukemia**

    C93.Z0   Other monocytic leukemia, not having achieved remission
        Other monocytic leukemia NOS

    C93.Z1   Other monocytic leukemia, in remission

    C93.Z2   Other monocytic leukemia, in relapse

● **C93.9   Monocytic leukemia, unspecified**

    C93.90   Monocytic leukemia, unspecified, not having achieved remission
        Monocytic leukemia, unspecified with failed remission
        Monocytic leukemia, unspecified NOS

    C93.91   Monocytic leukemia, unspecified in remission

    C93.92   Monocytic leukemia, unspecified in relapse

● **C94   Other leukemias of specified cell type**
    Excludes1   leukemic reticuloendotheliosis (C91.4-)
        myelodysplastic syndromes (D46.-)
        personal history of leukemia (Z85.6)
        plasma cell leukemia (C90.1-)

● **C94.0   Acute erythroid leukemia**
    Acute myeloid leukemia M6(a)(b)
    Erythroleukemia

    C94.00   Acute erythroid leukemia, not having achieved remission
        Acute erythroid leukemia with failed remission
        Acute erythroid leukemia NOS

    C94.01   Acute erythroid leukemia, in remission

    C94.02   Acute erythroid leukemia, in relapse

▶ New   ➧ Revised   ~~deleted~~ Deleted   Excludes 1   Excludes 2   Includes   Use additional   Code first   Code also   Key words
OGCR Official Guidelines   X Assign placeholder X   ● Use Additional Character(s)   ▶ Manifestation Code   **Coding Clinic**

● **C94.2   Acute megakaryoblastic leukemia**
Acute myeloid leukemia M7
Acute megakaryocytic leukemia

     C94.20   Acute megakaryoblastic leukemia not having achieved remission
Acute megakaryoblastic leukemia with failed remission
Acute megakaryoblastic leukemia NOS

     C94.21   Acute megakaryoblastic leukemia, in remission

     C94.22   Acute megakaryoblastic leukemia, in relapse

● **C94.3   Mast cell leukemia**

     C94.30   Mast cell leukemia not having achieved remission
Mast cell leukemia with failed remission
Mast cell leukemia NOS

     C94.31   Mast cell leukemia, in remission

     C94.32   Mast cell leukemia, in relapse

● **C94.4   Acute panmyelosis with myelofibrosis**
Acute myelofibrosis

     Excludes1   myelofibrosis NOS (D75.81)
secondary myelofibrosis NOS (D75.81)

     C94.40   Acute panmyelosis with myelofibrosis not having achieved remission
Acute myelofibrosis NOS
Acute panmyelosis with myelofibrosis with failed remission
Acute panmyelosis NOS

     C94.41   Acute panmyelosis with myelofibrosis, in remission

     C94.42   Acute panmyelosis with myelofibrosis, in relapse

   C94.6   Myelodysplastic disease, not classified
Myeloproliferative disease, not classified

● **C94.8   Other specified leukemias**
Aggressive NK-cell leukemia
Acute basophilic leukemia

     C94.80   Other specified leukemias not having achieved remission
Other specified leukemia with failed remission
Other specified leukemias NOS

     C94.81   Other specified leukemias, in remission

     C94.82   Other specified leukemias, in relapse

● **C95   Leukemia of unspecified cell type**

     Excludes1   personal history of leukemia (Z85.6)

● **C95.0   Acute leukemia of unspecified cell type**
Acute bilineal leukemia
Acute mixed lineage leukemia
Biphenotypic acute leukemia
Stem cell leukemia of unclear lineage

     Excludes1   acute exacerbation of unspecified chronic leukemia (C95.10)

     C95.00   Acute leukemia of unspecified cell type not having achieved remission
Acute leukemia of unspecified cell type with failed remission
Acute leukemia NOS

     C95.01   Acute leukemia of unspecified cell type, in remission

     C95.02   Acute leukemia of unspecified cell type, in relapse

● **C95.1   Chronic leukemia of unspecified cell type**

     C95.10   Chronic leukemia of unspecified cell type not having achieved remission
Chronic leukemia of unspecified cell type with failed remission
Chronic leukemia NOS

     C95.11   Chronic leukemia of unspecified cell type, in remission

     C95.12   Chronic leukemia of unspecified cell type, in relapse

● **C95.9   Leukemia, unspecified**

     C95.90   Leukemia, unspecified not having achieved remission
Leukemia, unspecified with failed remission
Leukemia NOS

     C95.91   Leukemia, unspecified, in remission

     C95.92   Leukemia, unspecified, in relapse

● **C96   Other and unspecified malignant neoplasms of lymphoid, hematopoietic and related tissue**

     Excludes1   personal history of other malignant neoplasms of lymphoid, hematopoietic and related tissues (Z85.79)

   C96.0   Multifocal and multisystemic (disseminated) Langerhans-cell histiocytosis
Histiocytosis X, multisystemic
Letterer-Siwe disease

     Excludes1   adult pulmonary Langerhans cell histiocytosis (J84.82)
multifocal and unisystemic Langerhans-cell histiocytosis (C96.5)
unifocal Langerhans-cell histiocytosis (C96.6)

   C96.2   Malignant mast cell neoplasm

     Excludes1   indolent mastocytosis (D47.02)
mast cell leukemia (C94.30)
mastocytosis (congenital) (cutaneous) (Q82.2)

     C96.20   Malignant mast cell neoplasm, unspecified

     C96.21   Aggressive systemic mastocytosis

     C96.22   Mast cell sarcoma

     C96.29   Other malignant mast cell neoplasm

   C96.4   Sarcoma of dendritic cells (accessory cells)
Follicular dendritic cell sarcoma
Interdigitating dendritic cell sarcoma
Langerhans cell sarcoma

   C96.5   Multifocal and unisystemic Langerhans-cell histiocytosis
Hand-Schüller-Christian disease
Histiocytosis X, multifocal

     Excludes1   multifocal and multisystemic (disseminated) Langerhans-cell histiocytosis (C96.0)
unifocal Langerhans-cell histiocytosis (C96.6)

   C96.6   Unifocal Langerhans-cell histiocytosis
Eosinophilic granuloma
Histiocytosis X, unifocal
Histiocytosis X NOS
Langerhans-cell histiocytosis NOS

     Excludes1   multifocal and multisysemic (disseminated) Langerhans-cell histiocytosis (C96.0)
multifocal and unisystemic Langerhans-cell histiocytosis (C96.5)

   C96.A   Histiocytic sarcoma
Malignant histiocytosis

   C96.Z   Other specified malignant neoplasms of lymphoid, hematopoietic and related tissue

   C96.9   Malignant neoplasm of lymphoid, hematopoietic and related tissue, unspecified

CHAPTER 2 (C00-D49)

IN SITU NEOPLASMS (D00-D09)

In situ is carcinoma involving cells in localized tissues that has not spread to nearby tissues

Includes   Bowen's disease
erythroplasia
grade III intraepithelial neoplasia
Queyrat's erythroplasia

● **D00   Carcinoma in situ of oral cavity, esophagus and stomach**
     Excludes1   melanoma in situ (D03.-)

● **D00.0   Carcinoma in situ of lip, oral cavity and pharynx**
       Use additional code to identify:
       exposure to environmental tobacco smoke (Z77.22)
       exposure to tobacco smoke in the perinatal period (P96.81)
       history of tobacco dependence (Z87.891)
       occupational exposure to environmental tobacco smoke (Z57.31)
       tobacco dependence (F17.-)
       tobacco use (Z72.0)
       Excludes1   carcinoma in situ of aryepiglottic fold or interarytenoid fold, laryngeal aspect (D02.0)
                 carcinoma in situ of epiglottis NOS (D02.0)
                 carcinoma in situ of epiglottis suprahyoid portion (D02.0)
                 carcinoma in situ of skin of lip (D03.0, D04.0)

       D00.00   Carcinoma in situ of oral cavity, unspecified site
       D00.01   Carcinoma in situ of labial mucosa and vermilion border
       D00.02   Carcinoma in situ of buccal mucosa
       D00.03   Carcinoma in situ of gingiva and edentulous alveolar ridge
       D00.04   Carcinoma in situ of soft palate
       D00.05   Carcinoma in situ of hard palate
       D00.06   Carcinoma in situ of floor of mouth
       D00.07   Carcinoma in situ of tongue
       D00.08   Carcinoma in situ of pharynx
           Carcinoma in situ of aryepiglottic fold NOS
           Carcinoma in situ of hypopharyngeal aspect of aryepiglottic fold
           Carcinoma in situ of marginal zone of aryepiglottic fold

     D00.1   Carcinoma in situ of esophagus
     D00.2   Carcinoma in situ of stomach

● **D01   Carcinoma in situ of other and unspecified digestive organs**
     Excludes1   melanoma in situ (D03.-)
     D01.0   Carcinoma in situ of colon
       Excludes1   carcinoma in situ of rectosigmoid junction (D01.1)
     D01.1   Carcinoma in situ of rectosigmoid junction
     D01.2   Carcinoma in situ of rectum
     D01.3   Carcinoma in situ of anus and anal canal
       Anal intraepithelial neoplasia III [AIN III]
       Severe dysplasia of anus
       Excludes1   anal intraepithelial neoplasia I and II [AIN I and AIN II] (K62.82)
                 carcinoma in situ of anal margin (D04.5)
                 carcinoma in situ of anal skin (D04.5)
                 carcinoma in situ of perianal skin (D04.5)
● **D01.4   Carcinoma in situ of other and unspecified parts of intestine**
       Excludes1   carcinoma in situ of ampulla of Vater (D01.5)
       D01.40   Carcinoma in situ of unspecified part of intestine
       D01.49   Carcinoma in situ of other parts of intestine

     D01.5   Carcinoma in situ of liver, gallbladder and bile ducts
       Carcinoma in situ of ampulla of Vater
     D01.7   Carcinoma in situ of other specified digestive organs
       Carcinoma in situ of pancreas
     D01.9   Carcinoma in situ of digestive organ, unspecified

● **D02   Carcinoma in situ of middle ear and respiratory system**
       Use additional code to identify:
       exposure to environmental tobacco smoke (Z77.22)
       exposure to tobacco smoke in the perinatal period (P96.81)
       history of tobacco dependence (Z87.891)
       occupational exposure to environmental tobacco smoke (Z57.31)
       tobacco dependence (F17.-)
       tobacco use (Z72.0)
       Excludes1   melanoma in situ (D03.-)

     D02.0   Carcinoma in situ of larynx
       Carcinoma in situ of aryepiglottic fold or interarytenoid fold, laryngeal aspect
       Carcinoma in situ of epiglottis (suprahyoid portion)
       Excludes1   carcinoma in situ of aryepiglottic fold or interarytenoid fold NOS (D00.08)
                 carcinoma in situ of hypopharyngeal aspect (D00.08)
                 carcinoma in situ of marginal zone (D00.08)
     D02.1   Carcinoma in situ of trachea
● **D02.2   Carcinoma in situ of bronchus and lung**
       D02.20   Carcinoma in situ of unspecified bronchus and lung
       D02.21   Carcinoma in situ of right bronchus and lung
       D02.22   Carcinoma in situ of left bronchus and lung
     D02.3   Carcinoma in situ of other parts of respiratory system
       Carcinoma in situ of accessory sinuses
       Carcinoma in situ of middle ear
       Carcinoma in situ of nasal cavities
       Excludes1   carcinoma in situ of ear (external) (skin) (D04.2-)
                 carcinoma in situ of nose NOS (D09.8)
                 carcinoma in situ of skin of nose (D04.3)
     D02.4   Carcinoma in situ of respiratory system, unspecified

● **D03   Melanoma in situ**
     D03.0   Melanoma in situ of lip
● **D03.1   Melanoma in situ of eyelid, including canthus**
       D03.10   Melanoma in situ of unspecified eyelid, including canthus
       D03.11   Melanoma in situ of right eyelid, including canthus
        ▶ **D03.111   Melanoma in situ of right upper eyelid, including canthus**
        ▶ **D03.112   Melanoma in situ of right lower eyelid, including canthus**
       D03.12   Melanoma in situ of left eyelid, including canthus
        ▶ **D03.121   Melanoma in situ of left upper eyelid, including canthus**
        ▶ **D03.122   Melanoma in situ of left lower eyelid, including canthus**
● **D03.2   Melanoma in situ of ear and external auricular canal**
       D03.20   Melanoma in situ of unspecified ear and external auricular canal
       D03.21   Melanoma in situ of right ear and external auricular canal
       D03.22   Melanoma in situ of left ear and external auricular canal
● **D03.3   Melanoma in situ of other and unspecified parts of face**
       D03.30   Melanoma in situ of unspecified part of face
       D03.39   Melanoma in situ of other parts of face

▶ New   ⇒ Revised   ~~deleted~~ Deleted   Excludes 1   Excludes 2   Includes   Use additional   Code first   Code also   Key words
OGCR Official Guidelines   X Assign placeholder X   ● Use Additional Character(s)   ▷ Manifestation Code   **Coding Clinic**

D03.4   Melanoma in situ of scalp and neck

● D03.5   Melanoma in situ of trunk

     D03.51   Melanoma in situ of anal skin
         Melanoma in situ of anal margin
         Melanoma in situ of perianal skin

     D03.52   Melanoma in situ of breast (skin) (soft tissue)

     D03.59   Melanoma in situ of other part of trunk

● D03.6   Melanoma in situ of upper limb, including shoulder

     D03.60   Melanoma in situ of unspecified upper limb, including shoulder

     D03.61   Melanoma in situ of right upper limb, including shoulder

     D03.62   Melanoma in situ of left upper limb, including shoulder

● D03.7   Melanoma in situ of lower limb, including hip

     D03.70   Melanoma in situ of unspecified lower limb, including hip

     D03.71   Melanoma in situ of right lower limb, including hip

     D03.72   Melanoma in situ of left lower limb, including hip

D03.8   Melanoma in situ of other sites
     Melanoma in situ of scrotum
     Excludes1   carcinoma in situ of scrotum (D07.61)

D03.9   Melanoma in situ, unspecified

● D04   **Carcinoma in situ of skin**
     Excludes1   erythroplasia of Queyrat (penis) NOS (D07.4)
         melanoma in situ (D03.-)

D04.0   **Carcinoma in situ of skin of lip**
     Excludes1   carcinoma in situ of vermilion border of lip (D00.01)

● D04.1   Carcinoma in situ of skin of eyelid, including canthus

     D04.10   Carcinoma in situ of skin of unspecified eyelid, including canthus

     D04.11   Carcinoma in situ of skin of right eyelid, including canthus

         ▸ D04.111   Carcinoma in situ of skin of right upper eyelid, including canthus

         ▸ D04.112   Carcinoma in situ of skin of right lower eyelid, including canthus

     D04.12   Carcinoma in situ of skin of left eyelid, including canthus

         ▸ D04.121   Carcinoma in situ of skin of left upper eyelid, including canthus

         ▸ D04.122   Carcinoma in situ of skin of left lower eyelid, including canthus

● D04.2   Carcinoma in situ of skin of ear and external auricular canal

     D04.20   Carcinoma in situ of skin of unspecified ear and external auricular canal

     D04.21   Carcinoma in situ of skin of right ear and external auricular canal

     D04.22   Carcinoma in situ of skin of left ear and external auricular canal

● D04.3   Carcinoma in situ of skin of other and unspecified parts of face

     D04.30   Carcinoma in situ of skin of unspecified part of face

     D04.39   Carcinoma in situ of skin of other parts of face

D04.4   Carcinoma in situ of skin of scalp and neck

D04.5   Carcinoma in situ of skin of trunk
     Carcinoma in situ of anal margin
     Carcinoma in situ of anal skin
     Carcinoma in situ of perianal skin
     Carcinoma in situ of skin of breast
     Excludes1   carcinoma in situ of anus NOS (D01.3)
         carcinoma in situ of scrotum (D07.61)
         carcinoma in situ of skin of genital organs (D07.-)

● D04.6   Carcinoma in situ of skin of upper limb, including shoulder

     D04.60   Carcinoma in situ of skin of unspecified upper limb, including shoulder

     D04.61   Carcinoma in situ of skin of right upper limb, including shoulder

     D04.62   Carcinoma in situ of skin of left upper limb, including shoulder

● D04.7   Carcinoma in situ of skin of lower limb, including hip

     D04.70   Carcinoma in situ of skin of unspecified lower limb, including hip

     D04.71   Carcinoma in situ of skin of right lower limb, including hip

     D04.72   Carcinoma in situ of skin of left lower limb, including hip

D04.8   Carcinoma in situ of skin of other sites

D04.9   Carcinoma in situ of skin, unspecified

● D05   **Carcinoma in situ of breast**
     Excludes1   carcinoma in situ of skin of breast (D04.5)
         melanoma in situ of breast (skin) (D03.5)
         Paget's disease of breast or nipple (C50.-)

● D05.0   Lobular carcinoma in situ of breast

     D05.00   Lobular carcinoma in situ of unspecified breast

     D05.01   Lobular carcinoma in situ of right breast

     D05.02   Lobular carcinoma in situ of left breast

● D05.1   Intraductal carcinoma in situ of breast

     D05.10   Intraductal carcinoma in situ of unspecified breast

     D05.11   Intraductal carcinoma in situ of right breast

     D05.12   Intraductal carcinoma in situ of left breast

● D05.8   Other specified type of carcinoma in situ of breast

     D05.80   Other specified type of carcinoma in situ of unspecified breast

     D05.81   Other specified type of carcinoma in situ of right breast

     D05.82   Other specified type of carcinoma in situ of left breast

● D05.9   Unspecified type of carcinoma in situ of breast

     D05.90   Unspecified type of carcinoma in situ of unspecified breast

     D05.91   Unspecified type of carcinoma in situ of right breast

     D05.92   Unspecified type of carcinoma in situ of left breast

● D06   **Carcinoma in situ of cervix uteri**
     Includes   cervical adenocarcinoma in situ
         cervical intraepithelial glandular neoplasia
         cervical intraepithelial neoplasia III [CIN III]
         severe dysplasia of cervix uteri
     Excludes1   cervical intraepithelial neoplasia II [CIN II] (N87.1)
         cytologic evidence of malignancy of cervix without histologic confirmation (R87.614)
         high grade squamous intraepithelial lesion (HGSIL) of cervix (R87.613)
         melanoma in situ of cervix (D03.5)
         moderate cervical dysplasia (N87.1)

D06.0   Carcinoma in situ of endocervix ♀

D06.1   Carcinoma in situ of exocervix ♀

D06.7   Carcinoma in situ of other parts of cervix ♀

D06.9   Carcinoma in situ of cervix, unspecified ♀

CHAPTER 2 (C00-D49)

● **D07** **Carcinoma in situ of** other and unspecified genital organs
    Excludes1 melanoma in situ of trunk (D03.5)
  D07.0 **Carcinoma in situ of** endometrium ♀
  D07.1 **Carcinoma in situ of** vulva ♀
    Severe dysplasia of vulva
    Vulvar intraepithelial neoplasia III [VIN III]
    Excludes1 moderate dysplasia of vulva (N90.1)
        vulvar intraepithelial neoplasia II [VIN II] (N90.1)
  D07.2 **Carcinoma in situ of** vagina ♀
    Severe dysplasia of vagina
    Vaginal intraepithelial neoplasia III [VIN III]
    Excludes1 moderate dysplasia of vagina (N89.1)
        vaginal intraepithelial neoplasia II [VIN II] (N89.1)
● **D07.3** **Carcinoma in situ of** other and unspecified female genital organs
    D07.30 **Carcinoma in situ of** unspecified female genital organs ♀
    D07.39 **Carcinoma in situ of** other female genital organs ♀
  D07.4 **Carcinoma in situ of** penis ♂
    Erythroplasia of Queyrat NOS
  D07.5 **Carcinoma in situ of** prostate ♂
    Prostatic intraepithelial neoplasia III (PIN III)
    Severe dysplasia of prostate
    Excludes1 dysplasia (mild) (moderate) of prostate (N42.3-)
        prostatic intraepithelial neoplasia II [PIN II] (N42.3-)
● **D07.6** **Carcinoma in situ of** other and unspecified male genital organs
    D07.60 **Carcinoma in situ of** unspecified male genital organs ♂
    D07.61 **Carcinoma in situ of** scrotum ♂
    D07.69 **Carcinoma in situ of** other male genital organs ♂

● **D09** **Carcinoma in situ of** other and unspecified sites
    Excludes1 melanoma in situ (D03.-)
  D09.0 **Carcinoma in situ of** bladder
● **D09.1** **Carcinoma in situ of** other and unspecified urinary organs
    D09.10 **Carcinoma in situ of** unspecified urinary organ
    D09.19 **Carcinoma in situ of** other urinary organs
● **D09.2** **Carcinoma in situ of** eye
    Excludes1 carcinoma in situ of skin of eyelid (D04.1-)
    D09.20 **Carcinoma in situ of** unspecified eye
    D09.21 **Carcinoma in situ of** right eye
    D09.22 **Carcinoma in situ of** left eye
  D09.3 **Carcinoma in situ of** thyroid and other endocrine glands
    Excludes1 carcinoma in situ of endocrine pancreas (D01.7)
        carcinoma in situ of ovary (D07.39)
        carcinoma in situ of testis (D07.69)
  D09.8 **Carcinoma in situ of** other specified sites
  D09.9 **Carcinoma in situ,** unspecified

Figure 2-16 The esophagus is the muscular tube that connects the pharynx and the stomach. The 10 inch (25 cm) long esophagus is divided into three parts: **cervical, thoracic,** and **abdominal.**

BENIGN NEOPLASMS, EXCEPT BENIGN NEUROENDOCRINE TUMORS (D10-D36)

● **D10** **Benign neoplasm of** mouth and pharynx
  D10.0 **Benign neoplasm of** lip
    Benign neoplasm of lip (frenulum) (inner aspect) (mucosa) (vermilion border)
    Excludes1 benign neoplasm of skin of lip (D22.0, D23.0)
  D10.1 **Benign neoplasm of** tongue
    Benign neoplasm of lingual tonsil
  D10.2 **Benign neoplasm of** floor of mouth
● **D10.3** **Benign neoplasm of** other and unspecified parts of mouth
    D10.30 **Benign neoplasm of** unspecified part of mouth
    D10.39 **Benign neoplasm of** other parts of mouth
    Benign neoplasm of minor salivary gland NOS
    Excludes1 benign odontogenic neoplasms (D16.4-D16.5)
        benign neoplasm of mucosa of lip (D10.0)
        benign neoplasm of nasopharyngeal surface of soft palate (D10.6)
  D10.4 **Benign neoplasm of** tonsil
    Benign neoplasm of tonsil (faucial) (palatine)
    Excludes1 benign neoplasm of lingual tonsil (D10.1)
        benign neoplasm of pharyngeal tonsil (D10.6)
        benign neoplasm of tonsillar fossa (D10.5)
        benign neoplasm of tonsillar pillars (D10.5)
  D10.5 **Benign neoplasm of** other parts of oropharynx
    Division of pharynx lying between soft palate and upper edge of epiglottis
    Benign neoplasm of epiglottis, anterior aspect
    Benign neoplasm of tonsillar fossa
    Benign neoplasm of tonsillar pillars
    Benign neoplasm of vallecula
    Excludes1 benign neoplasm of epiglottis NOS (D14.1)
        benign neoplasm of epiglottis, suprahyoid portion (D14.1)
  D10.6 **Benign neoplasm of** nasopharynx
    Segment of pharynx that lies above soft palate
    Benign neoplasm of pharyngeal tonsil
    Benign neoplasm of posterior margin of septum and choanae
  D10.7 **Benign neoplasm of** hypopharynx
    Segment of pharynx that lies below upper edge of epiglottis and opens into larynx and esophagus
  D10.9 **Benign neoplasm of** pharynx, unspecified

CHAPTER 2 (C00-D49)

● **D11 Benign neoplasm of major salivary glands**

> **Excludes1**   benign neoplasms of specified minor salivary
> glands which are classified according to their
> anatomical location
> benign neoplasms of minor salivary glands NOS
> (D10.39)

D11.0 Benign neoplasm of parotid gland

D11.7 Benign neoplasm of other major salivary glands
Benign neoplasm of sublingual salivary gland
Benign neoplasm of submandibular salivary gland

D11.9 Benign neoplasm of major salivary gland, unspecified

● **D12 Benign neoplasm of colon, rectum, anus and anal canal**

> **Excludes1**   benign carcinoid tumors of the large intestine,
> and rectum (D3A.02-)

Coding Clinic: 2017, Q1, P15; 2015, Q2, P14

D12.0 Benign neoplasm of cecum
Benign neoplasm of ileocecal valve

D12.1 Benign neoplasm of appendix

> **Excludes1**   benign carcinoid tumor of the appendix
> (D3A.020)

D12.2 Benign neoplasm of ascending colon
Coding Clinic: 2018, Q2, P14; 2017, Q1, P15

D12.3 Benign neoplasm of transverse colon
Benign neoplasm of hepatic flexure
Benign neoplasm of splenic flexure
*Flexure is a bending in a structure or organ. Note the
three flexures illustrated in Figure 2–17. Hepatic =
liver, sigmoid = colon, splenic = spleen.*
Coding Clinic: 2017, Q1, P16

D12.4 Benign neoplasm of descending colon
Coding Clinic: 2015, Q2, P14

D12.5 Benign neoplasm of sigmoid colon

D12.6 Benign neoplasm of colon, unspecified
Adenomatosis of colon
Benign neoplasm of large intestine NOS
Polyposis (hereditary) of colon

> **Excludes1**   inflammatory polyp of colon (K51.4-)
> polyp of colon NOS (K63.5)

Coding Clinic: 2017, Q1, P8-9

D12.7 Benign neoplasm of rectosigmoid junction
Angle where sigmoid colon becomes rectum

D12.8 Benign neoplasm of rectum

> **Excludes1**   benign carcinoid tumor of the rectum
> (D3A.026)

Coding Clinic: 2018, Q1, P7

D12.9 Benign neoplasm of anus and anal canal
Benign neoplasm of anus NOS

> **Excludes1**   benign neoplasm of anal margin (D22.5,
> D23.5)
> benign neoplasm of anal skin (D22.5,
> D23.5)
> benign neoplasm of perianal skin (D22.5,
> D23.5)

● **D13 Benign neoplasm of other and ill-defined parts of digestive system**

> **Excludes1**   benign stromal tumors of digestive system
> (D21.4)

D13.0 Benign neoplasm of esophagus

D13.1 Benign neoplasm of stomach

> **Excludes1**   benign carcinoid tumor of the stomach
> (D3A.092)

D13.2 Benign neoplasm of duodenum

> **Excludes1**   benign carcinoid tumor of the duodenum
> (D3A.010)

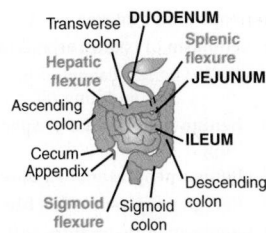

Figure 2-17 Small intestine and colon.

● **D13.3 Benign neoplasm of other and unspecified parts of small intestine**

> **Excludes1**   benign carcinoid tumors of the small
> intestine (D3A.01-)
> benign neoplasm of ileocecal valve
> (D12.0)

D13.30 Benign neoplasm of unspecified part of small intestine

D13.39 Benign neoplasm of other parts of small intestine

D13.4 Benign neoplasm of liver
Benign neoplasm of intrahepatic bile ducts

D13.5 Benign neoplasm of extrahepatic bile ducts
*Extensions of common hepatic bile duct (tube that collects
bile from liver)*

D13.6 Benign neoplasm of pancreas

> **Excludes1**   benign neoplasm of endocrine pancreas
> (D13.7)

D13.7 Benign neoplasm of endocrine pancreas
Pancreatic islets: Cells scattered throughout pancreas
Islet cell tumor
Benign neoplasm of islets of Langerhans
Use additional code to identify any functional activity.

D13.9 Benign neoplasm of ill-defined sites within the digestive system
Benign neoplasm of digestive system NOS
Benign neoplasm of intestine NOS
Benign neoplasm of spleen

● **D14 Benign neoplasm of middle ear and respiratory system**

D14.0 Benign neoplasm of middle ear, nasal cavity and accessory sinuses
Benign neoplasm of cartilage of nose

> **Excludes1**   benign neoplasm of auricular canal
> (external) (D22.2-, D23.2-)
> benign neoplasm of bone of ear (D16.4)
> benign neoplasm of bone of nose (D16.4)
> benign neoplasm of cartilage of ear
> (D21.0)
> benign neoplasm of ear (external) (skin)
> (D22.2-, D23.2-)
> benign neoplasm of nose NOS (D36.7)
> benign neoplasm of skin of nose (D22.39,
> D23.39)
> benign neoplasm of olfactory bulb (D33.3)
> benign neoplasm of posterior margin of
> septum and choanae (D10.6)
> polyp of accessory sinus (J33.8)
> polyp of ear (middle) (H74.4)
> polyp of nasal (cavity) (J33.-)

D14.1 Benign neoplasm of larynx
Adenomatous polyp of larynx
Benign neoplasm of epiglottis (suprahyoid portion)
*Horseshoe shaped bone in anterior midline of neck between
chin and thyroid cartilage*

> **Excludes1**   benign neoplasm of epiglottis, anterior
> aspect (D10.5)
> polyp (nonadenomatous) of vocal cord or
> larynx (J38.1)

CHAPTER 2 (C00-D49)

D14.2   Benign neoplasm of trachea

● **D14.3**   Benign neoplasm of bronchus and lung

> **Excludes1**   benign carcinoid tumor of the bronchus and lung (D3A.Ø9Ø)

  D14.3Ø   Benign neoplasm of unspecified bronchus and lung

  D14.31   Benign neoplasm of right bronchus and lung

  D14.32   Benign neoplasm of left bronchus and lung

D14.4   Benign neoplasm of respiratory system, unspecified

● **D15**   Benign neoplasm of other and unspecified intrathoracic organs

> **Excludes1**   benign neoplasm of mesothelial tissue (D19.-)

  D15.Ø   Benign neoplasm of thymus

> **Excludes1**   benign carcinoid tumor of the thymus (D3A.Ø91)

  D15.1   Benign neoplasm of heart

> **Excludes1**   benign neoplasm of great vessels (D21.3)

  D15.2   Benign neoplasm of mediastinum

  D15.7   Benign neoplasm of other specified intrathoracic organs

  D15.9   Benign neoplasm of intrathoracic organ, unspecified

● **D16**   Benign neoplasm of bone and articular cartilage

> **Excludes1**   benign neoplasm of connective tissue of ear (D21.Ø)
> benign neoplasm of connective tissue of eyelid (D21.Ø)
> benign neoplasm of connective tissue of larynx (D14.1)
> benign neoplasm of connective tissue of nose (D14.Ø)
> benign neoplasm of synovia (D21.-)

● **D16.Ø**   Benign neoplasm of scapula and long bones of upper limb

  D16.ØØ   Benign neoplasm of scapula and long bones of unspecified upper limb

  D16.Ø1   Benign neoplasm of scapula and long bones of right upper limb

  D16.Ø2   Benign neoplasm of scapula and long bones of left upper limb

● **D16.1**   Benign neoplasm of short bones of upper limb

  D16.1Ø   Benign neoplasm of short bones of unspecified upper limb

  D16.11   Benign neoplasm of short bones of right upper limb

  D16.12   Benign neoplasm of short bones of left upper limb

● **D16.2**   Benign neoplasm of long bones of lower limb

  D16.2Ø   Benign neoplasm of long bones of unspecified lower limb

  D16.21   Benign neoplasm of long bones of right lower limb

  D16.22   Benign neoplasm of long bones of left lower limb

● **D16.3**   Benign neoplasm of short bones of lower limb

  D16.3Ø   Benign neoplasm of short bones of unspecified lower limb

  D16.31   Benign neoplasm of short bones of right lower limb

  D16.32   Benign neoplasm of short bones of left lower limb

D16.4   Benign neoplasm of bones of skull and face
Benign neoplasm of maxilla (superior)
Benign neoplasm of orbital bone
Cavity or socket of skull in which eye and its appendages are located
Keratocyst of maxilla
Keratocystic odontogenic tumor of maxilla

> **Excludes2**   benign neoplasm of lower jaw bone (D16.5)

D16.5   Benign neoplasm of lower jaw bone
Keratocyst of mandible
Keratocystic odontogenic tumor of mandible

D16.6   Benign neoplasm of vertebral column

> **Excludes1**   benign neoplasm of sacrum and coccyx (D16.8)

D16.7   Benign neoplasm of ribs, sternum and clavicle

D16.8   Benign neoplasm of pelvic bones, sacrum and coccyx

D16.9   Benign neoplasm of bone and articular cartilage, unspecified

● **D17**   Benign lipomatous neoplasm
Slow-growing benign tumors (rubbery masses) of mature fat cells enclosed in a thin fibrous capsule

D17.Ø   Benign lipomatous neoplasm of skin and subcutaneous tissue of head, face and neck

D17.1   Benign lipomatous neoplasm of skin and subcutaneous tissue of trunk

● **D17.2**   Benign lipomatous neoplasm of skin and subcutaneous tissue of limb

  D17.2Ø   Benign lipomatous neoplasm of skin and subcutaneous tissue of unspecified limb

  D17.21   Benign lipomatous neoplasm of skin and subcutaneous tissue of right arm

  D17.22   Benign lipomatous neoplasm of skin and subcutaneous tissue of left arm

  D17.23   Benign lipomatous neoplasm of skin and subcutaneous tissue of right leg

  D17.24   Benign lipomatous neoplasm of skin and subcutaneous tissue of left leg

● **D17.3**   Benign lipomatous neoplasm of skin and subcutaneous tissue of other and unspecified sites

  D17.3Ø   Benign lipomatous neoplasm of skin and subcutaneous tissue of unspecified sites

  D17.39   Benign lipomatous neoplasm of skin and subcutaneous tissue of other sites

D17.4   Benign lipomatous neoplasm of intrathoracic organs

D17.5   Benign lipomatous neoplasm of intra-abdominal organs

> **Excludes1**   benign lipomatous neoplasm of peritoneum and retroperitoneum (D17.79)

D17.6   Benign lipomatous neoplasm of spermatic cord ♂

● **D17.7**   Benign lipomatous neoplasm of other sites

  D17.71   Benign lipomatous neoplasm of kidney

  D17.72   Benign lipomatous neoplasm of other genitourinary organ

  D17.79   Benign lipomatous neoplasm of other sites
Benign lipomatous neoplasm of peritoneum
Benign lipomatous neoplasm of retroperitoneum

D17.9   Benign lipomatous neoplasm, unspecified
Lipoma NOS

● **D18**   Hemangioma and lymphangioma, any site

> **Excludes1**   benign neoplasm of glomus jugulare (D35.6)
> blue or pigmented nevus (D22.-)
> nevus NOS (D22.-)
> vascular nevus (Q82.5)

● **D18.Ø**   Hemangioma
Common type of vascular malformation
Angioma NOS
Cavernous nevus

  D18.ØØ   Hemangioma unspecified site

  D18.Ø1   Hemangioma of skin and subcutaneous tissue

  D18.Ø2   Hemangioma of intracranial structures

  D18.Ø3   Hemangioma of intra-abdominal structures

  D18.Ø9   Hemangioma of other sites

D18.1   Lymphangioma, any site
Coding Clinic: 2Ø18, Q2, P13

▶ New   ⇒ Revised   ~~deleted~~ Deleted   Excludes 1   Excludes 2   Includes   Use additional   Code first   Code also   Key words

OGCR Official Guidelines   X Assign placeholder X   ● Use Additional Character(s)   ▷ Manifestation Code   **Coding Clinic**

Figure 2-18 Hemangioma of skin and subcutaneous tissue. (Getty Image)

Item 2-10 Hemangiomas are abnormally dense collections of dilated capillaries that occur on the skin or in internal organs. Hemangiomas are both deep and superficial and undergo a rapid growth phase when the size increases rapidly, followed by a rest phase, in which the tumor changes very little, followed by an involutional phase in which the tumor begins to and can disappear altogether. **Lymphangiomas** or cystic hygroma are benign collections of overgrown lymph vessels and, although rare, may occur anywhere but most commonly on the head and neck of children and infants. Visceral organs, lungs, and gastrointestinal tract may also be involved.

● **D19   Benign neoplasm of mesothelial tissue**
    Mesothelial tissue is the membrane lining several body cavities

    D19.0   Benign neoplasm of mesothelial tissue of pleura

    D19.1   Benign neoplasm of mesothelial tissue of peritoneum

    D19.7   Benign neoplasm of mesothelial tissue of other sites

    D19.9   Benign neoplasm of mesothelial tissue, unspecified
           Benign mesothelioma NOS

● **D20   Benign neoplasm of soft tissue of retroperitoneum and peritoneum**
    Excludes1   benign lipomatous neoplasm of peritoneum and
               retroperitoneum (D17.79)
               benign neoplasm of mesothelial tissue (D19.-)

    D20.0   Benign neoplasm of soft tissue of retroperitoneum

    D20.1   Benign neoplasm of soft tissue of peritoneum

● **D21   Other benign neoplasms of connective and other soft tissue**
    Includes   benign neoplasm of blood vessel
               benign neoplasm of bursa
               benign neoplasm of cartilage
               benign neoplasm of fascia
               benign neoplasm of fat
               benign neoplasm of ligament, except uterine
               benign neoplasm of lymphatic channel
               benign neoplasm of muscle
               benign neoplasm of synovia
               benign neoplasm of tendon (sheath)
               benign stromal tumors

    Excludes1   benign neoplasm of articular cartilage (D16.-)
               benign neoplasm of cartilage of larynx (D14.1)
               benign neoplasm of cartilage of nose (D14.0)
               benign neoplasm of connective tissue of breast
                   (D24.-)
               benign neoplasm of peripheral nerves and
                   autonomic nervous system (D36.1-)
               benign neoplasm of peritoneum (D20.1)
               benign neoplasm of retroperitoneum (D20.0)
               benign neoplasm of uterine ligament, any (D28.2)
               benign neoplasm of vascular tissue (D18.-)
               hemangioma (D18.0-)
               lipomatous neoplasm (D17.-)
               lymphangioma (D18.1)
               uterine leiomyoma (D25.-)

    D21.0   Benign neoplasm of connective and other soft tissue of head, face and neck
           Benign neoplasm of connective tissue of ear
           Benign neoplasm of connective tissue of eyelid
           Excludes1   benign neoplasm of connective tissue of
                       orbit (D31.6-)

● **D21.1   Benign neoplasm of connective and other soft tissue of upper limb, including shoulder**

    D21.10   Benign neoplasm of connective and other soft tissue of unspecified upper limb, including shoulder

    D21.11   Benign neoplasm of connective and other soft tissue of right upper limb, including shoulder

    D21.12   Benign neoplasm of connective and other soft tissue of left upper limb, including shoulder

● **D21.2   Benign neoplasm of connective and other soft tissue of lower limb, including hip**

    D21.20   Benign neoplasm of connective and other soft tissue of unspecified lower limb, including hip

    D21.21   Benign neoplasm of connective and other soft tissue of right lower limb, including hip

    D21.22   Benign neoplasm of connective and other soft tissue of left lower limb, including hip

    D21.3   Benign neoplasm of connective and other soft tissue of thorax
           Benign neoplasm of axilla
           Benign neoplasm of diaphragm
           Benign neoplasm of great vessels
           Excludes1   benign neoplasm of heart (D15.1)
                       benign neoplasm of mediastinum (D15.2)
                       benign neoplasm of thymus (D15.0)

    D21.4   Benign neoplasm of connective and other soft tissue of abdomen
           Benign stromal tumors of abdomen

    D21.5   Benign neoplasm of connective and other soft tissue of pelvis
           Excludes1   benign neoplasm of any uterine ligament
                       (D28.2)
                       uterine leiomyoma (D25.-)

    D21.6   Benign neoplasm of connective and other soft tissue of trunk, unspecified
           Benign neoplasm of back NOS

    D21.9   Benign neoplasm of connective and other soft tissue, unspecified

● **D22   Melanocytic nevi**
    Includes   atypical nevus
               blue hairy pigmented nevus
               nevus NOS

    D22.0   Melanocytic nevi of lip
           Skin lesions composed of nests of nevus cells with macules/ papules

● **D22.1   Melanocytic nevi of eyelid, including canthus**

    D22.10   Melanocytic nevi of unspecified eyelid, including canthus

    D22.11   Melanocytic nevi of right eyelid, including canthus

    ▶ **D22.111   Melanocytic nevi of right upper eyelid, including canthus**

    ▶ **D22.112   Melanocytic nevi of right lower eyelid, including canthus**

    D22.12   Melanocytic nevi of left eyelid, including canthus

    ▶ **D22.121   Melanocytic nevi of left upper eyelid, including canthus**

    ▶ **D22.122   Melanocytic nevi of left lower eyelid, including canthus**

● **D22.2   Melanocytic nevi of ear and external auricular canal**

    D22.20   Melanocytic nevi of unspecified ear and external auricular canal

    D22.21   Melanocytic nevi of right ear and external auricular canal

    D22.22   Melanocytic nevi of left ear and external auricular canal

CHAPTER 2 (C00-D49)

● **D22.3**　Melanocytic nevi of other and unspecified parts of face
　　D22.30　Melanocytic nevi of unspecified part of face
　　D22.39　Melanocytic nevi of other parts of face
D22.4　Melanocytic nevi of scalp and neck
D22.5　Melanocytic nevi of trunk
　　Melanocytic nevi of anal margin
　　Melanocytic nevi of anal skin
　　Melanocytic nevi of perianal skin
　　Melanocytic nevi of skin of breast
● **D22.6**　Melanocytic nevi of upper limb, including shoulder
　　D22.60　Melanocytic nevi of unspecified upper limb, including shoulder
　　D22.61　Melanocytic nevi of right upper limb, including shoulder
　　D22.62　Melanocytic nevi of left upper limb, including shoulder
● **D22.7**　Melanocytic nevi of lower limb, including hip
　　D22.70　Melanocytic nevi of unspecified lower limb, including hip
　　D22.71　Melanocytic nevi of right lower limb, including hip
　　D22.72　Melanocytic nevi of left lower limb, including hip
D22.9　Melanocytic nevi, unspecified

● **D23**　Other benign neoplasms of skin
　　Includes　benign neoplasm of hair follicles
　　　　benign neoplasm of sebaceous glands
　　　　benign neoplasm of sweat glands
　　Excludes1　benign lipomatous neoplasms of skin (D17.0-D17.3)
　　　　melanocytic nevi (D22.-)
D23.0　Other benign neoplasm of skin of lip
　　Excludes1　benign neoplasm of vermilion border of lip (D10.0)
● **D23.1**　Other benign neoplasm of skin of eyelid, including canthus
　　D23.10　Other benign neoplasm of skin unspecified of eyelid, including canthus
　　D23.11　Other benign neoplasm of skin of right eyelid, including canthus
　　　▶ **D23.111**　Other benign neoplasm of skin of right upper eyelid, including canthus
　　　▶ **D23.112**　Other benign neoplasm of skin of right lower eyelid, including canthus
　　D23.12　Other benign neoplasm of skin of left eyelid, including canthus
　　　▶ **D23.121**　Other benign neoplasm of skin of left upper eyelid, including canthus
　　　▶ **D23.122**　Other benign neoplasm of skin of left lower eyelid, including canthus
● **D23.2**　Other benign neoplasm of skin of ear and external auricular canal
　　D23.20　Other benign neoplasm of skin of unspecified ear and external auricular canal
　　D23.21　Other benign neoplasm of skin of right ear and external auricular canal
　　D23.22　Other benign neoplasm of skin of left ear and external auricular canal
● **D23.3**　Other benign neoplasm of skin of other and unspecified parts of face
　　D23.30　Other benign neoplasm of skin of unspecified part of face
　　D23.39　Other benign neoplasm of skin of other parts of face

D23.4　Other benign neoplasm of skin of scalp and neck
D23.5　Other benign neoplasm of skin of trunk
　　Other benign neoplasm of anal margin
　　Other benign neoplasm of anal skin
　　Other benign neoplasm of perianal skin
　　Other benign neoplasm of skin of breast
　　Excludes1　benign neoplasm of anus NOS (D12.9)
● **D23.6**　Other benign neoplasm of skin of upper limb, including shoulder
　　D23.60　Other benign neoplasm of skin of unspecified upper limb, including shoulder
　　D23.61　Other benign neoplasm of skin of right upper limb, including shoulder
　　D23.62　Other benign neoplasm of skin of left upper limb, including shoulder
● **D23.7**　Other benign neoplasm of skin of lower limb, including hip
　　D23.70　Other benign neoplasm of skin of unspecified lower limb, including hip
　　D23.71　Other benign neoplasm of skin of right lower limb, including hip
　　D23.72　Other benign neoplasm of skin of left lower limb, including hip
D23.9　Other benign neoplasm of skin, unspecified

● **D24**　Benign neoplasm of breast
　　Includes　benign neoplasm of connective tissue of breast
　　　　benign neoplasm of soft parts of breast
　　　　fibroadenoma of breast
　　Excludes2　adenofibrosis of breast (N60.2)
　　　　benign cyst of breast (N60.-)
　　　　benign mammary dysplasia (N60.-)
　　　　benign neoplasm of skin of breast (D22.5, D23.5)
　　　　fibrocystic disease of breast (N60.-)
D24.1　Benign neoplasm of right breast
　　Coding Clinic: 2017, Q1, P5
D24.2　Benign neoplasm of left breast
D24.9　Benign neoplasm of unspecified breast

● **D25**　Leiomyoma of uterus
　　Benign tumors or nodules of the uterine wall
　　Includes　uterine fibroid
　　　　uterine fibromyoma
　　　　uterine myoma
D25.0　Submucous leiomyoma of uterus ♀
D25.1　Intramural leiomyoma of uterus ♀
　　Interstitial leiomyoma of uterus
D25.2　Subserosal leiomyoma of uterus ♀
　　Subperitoneal leiomyoma of uterus
D25.9　Leiomyoma of uterus, unspecified ♀

● **D26**　Other benign neoplasms of uterus
D26.0　Other benign neoplasm of cervix uteri ♀
D26.1　Other benign neoplasm of corpus uteri ♀
D26.7　Other benign neoplasm of other parts of uterus ♀
D26.9　Other benign neoplasm of uterus, unspecified ♀

● **D27**　Benign neoplasm of ovary
　　Use additional code to identify any functional activity.
　　Excludes2　corpus albicans cyst (N83.2-)
　　　　corpus luteum cyst (N83.1-)
　　　　endometrial cyst (N80.1)
　　　　follicular (atretic) cyst (N83.0-)
　　　　graafian follicle cyst (N83.0-)
　　　　ovarian cyst NEC (N83.2-)
　　　　ovarian retention cyst (N83.2-)
D27.0　Benign neoplasm of right ovary ♀
D27.1　Benign neoplasm of left ovary ♀
D27.9　Benign neoplasm of unspecified ovary ♀
　　Ovarian teratoma

▶ New　⇒ Revised　~~deleted~~ Deleted　Excludes 1　Excludes 2　Includes　Use additional　Code first　Code also　Key words
OGCR Official Guidelines　X Assign placeholder X　● Use Additional Character(s)　▶ Manifestation Code　Coding Clinic

Item 2-11 Teratoma: terat = monster, oma = mass, tumor. Alternate terms: dermoid cyst of the ovary, ovarian teratoma. Teratomas are neoplasms and arise from germ cells (ovaries in female and testes in male) and can be benign or malignant. Teratomas have been known to contain hair, nails, and teeth, giving them a bizarre ("monster") appearance.

● **D28   Benign neoplasm of other and unspecified female genital organs**

　　Includes　adenomatous polyp
　　　　　　　benign neoplasm of skin of female genital organs
　　　　　　　benign teratoma

　　Excludes1　epoophoron cyst (Q50.5)
　　　　　　　fimbrial cyst (Q50.4)
　　　　　　　Gartner's duct cyst (Q52.4)
　　　　　　　parovarian cyst (Q50.5)

　D28.0   Benign neoplasm of vulva ♀

　D28.1   Benign neoplasm of vagina ♀

　D28.2   Benign neoplasm of uterine tubes and ligaments ♀
　　　　Benign neoplasm of fallopian tube
　　　　Benign neoplasm of uterine ligament (broad) (round)

　D28.7   Benign neoplasm of other specified female genital organs ♀

　D28.9   Benign neoplasm of female genital organ, unspecified ♀

● **D29   Benign neoplasm of male genital organs**

　　Includes　benign neoplasm of skin of male genital organs

　D29.0   Benign neoplasm of penis ♂

　D29.1   Benign neoplasm of prostate ♂

　　Excludes1　enlarged prostate (N40.-)

● **D29.2   Benign neoplasm of testis**
　　　Use additional code to identify any functional activity.

　　D29.20   Benign neoplasm of unspecified testis ♂

　　D29.21   Benign neoplasm of right testis ♂

　　D29.22   Benign neoplasm of left testis ♂

● **D29.3   Benign neoplasm of epididymis**

　　D29.30   Benign neoplasm of unspecified epididymis ♂

　　D29.31   Benign neoplasm of right epididymis ♂

　　D29.32   Benign neoplasm of left epididymis ♂

　D29.4   Benign neoplasm of scrotum ♂
　　　Benign neoplasm of skin of scrotum

　D29.8   Benign neoplasm of other specified male genital organs ♂
　　　Benign neoplasm of seminal vesicle
　　　Benign neoplasm of spermatic cord
　　　Benign neoplasm of tunica vaginalis

　D29.9   Benign neoplasm of male genital organ, unspecified ♂

● **D30   Benign neoplasm of urinary organs**

● **D30.0   Benign neoplasm of kidney**

　　Excludes1　benign carcinoid tumor of the kidney (D3A.093)
　　　　　　　benign neoplasm of renal calyces (D30.1-)
　　　　　　　benign neoplasm of renal pelvis (D30.1-)

　　D30.00   Benign neoplasm of unspecified kidney

　　D30.01   Benign neoplasm of right kidney

　　D30.02   Benign neoplasm of left kidney

● **D30.1   Benign neoplasm of renal pelvis**

　　D30.10   Benign neoplasm of unspecified renal pelvis

　　D30.11   Benign neoplasm of right renal pelvis

　　D30.12   Benign neoplasm of left renal pelvis

● **D30.2   Benign neoplasm of ureter**

　　Excludes1　benign neoplasm of ureteric orifice of bladder (D30.3)

　　D30.20   Benign neoplasm of unspecified ureter

　　D30.21   Benign neoplasm of right ureter

　　D30.22   Benign neoplasm of left ureter

　D30.3   Benign neoplasm of bladder
　　　Benign neoplasm of ureteric orifice of bladder
　　　Benign neoplasm of urethral orifice of bladder

　D30.4   Benign neoplasm of urethra

　　Excludes1　benign neoplasm of urethral orifice of bladder (D30.3)

　D30.8   Benign neoplasm of other specified urinary organs
　　　Benign neoplasm of paraurethral glands

　D30.9   Benign neoplasm of urinary organ, unspecified
　　　Benign neoplasm of urinary system NOS

● **D31   Benign neoplasm of eye and adnexa**

　　Excludes1　benign neoplasm of connective tissue of eyelid (D21.0)
　　　　　　　benign neoplasm of optic nerve (D33.3)
　　　　　　　benign neoplasm of skin of eyelid (D22.1-, D23.1-)

● **D31.0   Benign neoplasm of conjunctiva**

　　D31.00   Benign neoplasm of unspecified conjunctiva

　　D31.01   Benign neoplasm of right conjunctiva

　　D31.02   Benign neoplasm of left conjunctiva

● **D31.1   Benign neoplasm of cornea**

　　D31.10   Benign neoplasm of unspecified cornea

　　D31.11   Benign neoplasm of right cornea

　　D31.12   Benign neoplasm of left cornea

● **D31.2   Benign neoplasm of retina**

　　Excludes1　dark area on retina (D49.81)
　　　　　　　hemangioma of retina (D49.81)
　　　　　　　neoplasm of unspecified behavior of retina and choroid (D49.81)
　　　　　　　retinal freckle (D49.81)

　　D31.20   Benign neoplasm of unspecified retina

　　D31.21   Benign neoplasm of right retina

　　D31.22   Benign neoplasm of left retina

● **D31.3   Benign neoplasm of choroid**

　　D31.30   Benign neoplasm of unspecified choroid

　　D31.31   Benign neoplasm of right choroid

　　D31.32   Benign neoplasm of left choroid

● **D31.4   Benign neoplasm of ciliary body**

　　D31.40   Benign neoplasm of unspecified ciliary body

　　D31.41   Benign neoplasm of right ciliary body

　　D31.42   Benign neoplasm of left ciliary body

● **D31.5   Benign neoplasm of lacrimal gland and duct**
　　　Benign neoplasm of lacrimal sac
　　　Benign neoplasm of nasolacrimal duct

　　D31.50   Benign neoplasm of unspecified lacrimal gland and duct

　　D31.51   Benign neoplasm of right lacrimal gland and duct

　　D31.52   Benign neoplasm of left lacrimal gland and duct

● **D31.6   Benign neoplasm of unspecified site of orbit**
　　　Benign neoplasm of connective tissue of orbit
　　　Benign neoplasm of extraocular muscle
　　　Benign neoplasm of peripheral nerves of orbit
　　　Benign neoplasm of retrobulbar tissue
　　　Benign neoplasm of retro-ocular tissue

　　Excludes1　benign neoplasm of orbital bone (D16.4)

　　D31.60   Benign neoplasm of unspecified site of unspecified orbit

　　D31.61   Benign neoplasm of unspecified site of right orbit

　　D31.62   Benign neoplasm of unspecified site of left orbit

● **D31.9   Benign neoplasm of unspecified part of eye**
　　　Benign neoplasm of eyeball

　　D31.90   Benign neoplasm of unspecified part of unspecified eye

　　D31.91   Benign neoplasm of unspecified part of right eye

　　D31.92   Benign neoplasm of unspecified part of left eye

CHAPTER 2 (C00-D49)

● **D32 Benign neoplasm of meninges**

D32.0 Benign neoplasm of cerebral meninges

D32.1 Benign neoplasm of spinal meninges

D32.9 Benign neoplasm of meninges, unspecified
Meningioma NOS

● **D33 Benign neoplasm of brain and other parts of central nervous system**

Excludes1 angioma (D18.0-)
benign neoplasm of meninges (D32.-)
benign neoplasm of peripheral nerves and
autonomic nervous system (D36.1-)
hemangioma (D18.0-)
neurofibromatosis (Q85.0-)
retro-ocular benign neoplasm (D31.6-)

D33.0 Benign neoplasm of brain, supratentorial
Benign neoplasm of cerebral ventricle
Benign neoplasm of cerebrum
Benign neoplasm of frontal lobe
Benign neoplasm of occipital lobe
Benign neoplasm of parietal lobe
Benign neoplasm of temporal lobe

Excludes1 benign neoplasm of fourth ventricle
(D33.1)

D33.1 Benign neoplasm of brain, infratentorial
Benign neoplasm of brain stem
Benign neoplasm of cerebellum
Benign neoplasm of fourth ventricle

D33.2 Benign neoplasm of brain, unspecified

D33.3 Benign neoplasm of cranial nerves
Benign neoplasm of olfactory bulb

D33.4 Benign neoplasm of spinal cord

D33.7 Benign neoplasm of other specified parts of central nervous system

D33.9 Benign neoplasm of central nervous system, unspecified
Benign neoplasm of nervous system (central) NOS

D34 Benign neoplasm of thyroid gland
Use additional code to identify any functional activity.

● **D35 Benign neoplasm of other and unspecified endocrine glands**
Use additional code to identify any functional activity.

Excludes1 benign neoplasm of endocrine pancreas (D13.7)
benign neoplasm of ovary (D27.-)
benign neoplasm of testis (D29.2.-)
benign neoplasm of thymus (D15.0)

● **D35.0** Benign neoplasm of adrenal gland

D35.00 Benign neoplasm of unspecified adrenal gland

D35.01 Benign neoplasm of right adrenal gland

D35.02 Benign neoplasm of left adrenal gland

D35.1 Benign neoplasm of parathyroid gland

D35.2 Benign neoplasm of pituitary gland

D35.3 Benign neoplasm of craniopharyngeal duct

D35.4 Benign neoplasm of pineal gland

D35.5 Benign neoplasm of carotid body

D35.6 Benign neoplasm of aortic body and other paraganglia
Benign tumor of glomus jugulare

D35.7 Benign neoplasm of other specified endocrine glands

D35.9 Benign neoplasm of endocrine gland, unspecified
Benign neoplasm of unspecified endocrine gland

● **D36 Benign neoplasm of other and unspecified sites**

D36.0 Benign neoplasm of lymph nodes

Excludes1 lymphangioma (D18.1)

● **D36.1** Benign neoplasm of peripheral nerves and autonomic nervous system

Excludes1 benign neoplasm of peripheral nerves of
orbit (D31.6-)
neurofibromatosis (Q85.0-)

D36.10 Benign neoplasm of peripheral nerves and autonomic nervous system, unspecified

D36.11 Benign neoplasm of peripheral nerves and autonomic nervous system of face, head, and neck

D36.12 Benign neoplasm of peripheral nerves and autonomic nervous system, upper limb, including shoulder

D36.13 Benign neoplasm of peripheral nerves and autonomic nervous system of lower limb, including hip

D36.14 Benign neoplasm of peripheral nerves and autonomic nervous system of thorax

D36.15 Benign neoplasm of peripheral nerves and autonomic nervous system of abdomen

D36.16 Benign neoplasm of peripheral nerves and autonomic nervous system of pelvis

D36.17 Benign neoplasm of peripheral nerves and autonomic nervous system of trunk, unspecified

D36.7 Benign neoplasm of other specified sites
Benign neoplasm of nose NOS

D36.9 Benign neoplasm, unspecified site

BENIGN NEUROENDOCRINE TUMORS (D3A)

● **D3A Benign neuroendocrine tumors**
Code also any associated multiple endocrine neoplasia [MEN]
syndromes (E31.2-)
Use additional code to identify any associated endocrine
syndrome, such as:
carcinoid syndrome (E34.0)

Excludes2 benign pancreatic islet cell tumors (D13.7)

● **D3A.0** Benign carcinoid tumors

D3A.00 Benign carcinoid tumor of unspecified site
Carcinoid tumor NOS

● **D3A.01** Benign carcinoid tumors of the small intestine

D3A.010 Benign carcinoid tumor of the
duodenum

D3A.011 Benign carcinoid tumor of the
jejunum

D3A.012 Benign carcinoid tumor of the ileum

D3A.019 Benign carcinoid tumor of the small
intestine, unspecified portion

● **D3A.02** Benign carcinoid tumors of the appendix, large
intestine, and rectum

D3A.020 Benign carcinoid tumor of the
appendix

D3A.021 Benign carcinoid tumor of the cecum

D3A.022 Benign carcinoid tumor of the
ascending colon

D3A.023 Benign carcinoid tumor of the
transverse colon

D3A.024 Benign carcinoid tumor of the
descending colon

D3A.025 Benign carcinoid tumor of the
sigmoid colon

D3A.026 Benign carcinoid tumor of the rectum

D3A.029 Benign carcinoid tumor of the large
intestine, unspecified portion
Benign carcinoid tumor of the colon
NOS

● **D3A.09 Benign carcinoid tumors of** other sites

  D3A.090 Benign carcinoid tumor of the bronchus and lung

  D3A.091 Benign carcinoid tumor of the thymus

  D3A.092 Benign carcinoid tumor of the stomach

  D3A.093 Benign carcinoid tumor of the kidney

  D3A.094 Benign carcinoid tumor of the foregut, unspecified

  D3A.095 Benign carcinoid tumor of the midgut, unspecified

  D3A.096 Benign carcinoid tumor of the hindgut, unspecified

  D3A.098 Benign carcinoid tumors of other sites

D3A.8 Other benign neuroendocrine tumors
   Neuroendocrine tumor NOS

NEOPLASMS OF UNCERTAIN BEHAVIOR, POLYCYTHEMIA VERA AND MYELODYSPLASTIC SYNDROMES (D37-D48)

Note: Categories D37-D44, and D48 classify by site neoplasms of uncertain behavior, i.e., histologic confirmation whether the neoplasm is malignant or benign cannot be made.

Excludes1   neoplasms of unspecified behavior (D49.-)

● **D37 Neoplasm of uncertain behavior of oral cavity and digestive organs**

  Excludes1   stromal tumors of uncertain behavior of digestive system (D48.1)

● **D37.0 Neoplasm of uncertain behavior of** lip, oral cavity and **pharynx**

  Excludes1   neoplasm of uncertain behavior of aryepiglottic fold or interarytenoid fold, laryngeal aspect (D38.0)
  neoplasm of uncertain behavior of epiglottis NOS (D38.0)
  neoplasm of uncertain behavior of skin of lip (D48.5)
  neoplasm of uncertain behavior of suprahyoid portion of epiglottis (D38.0)

  D37.01 Neoplasm of uncertain behavior of lip
     Neoplasm of uncertain behavior of vermilion border of lip

  D37.02 Neoplasm of uncertain behavior of tongue

● **D37.03 Neoplasm of uncertain behavior of the** major **salivary glands**

  D37.030 Neoplasm of uncertain behavior of the parotid **salivary glands**

  D37.031 Neoplasm of uncertain behavior of the sublingual **salivary glands**

  D37.032 Neoplasm of uncertain behavior of the submandibular salivary glands

  D37.039 Neoplasm of uncertain behavior of the major salivary glands, unspecified

D37.04 Neoplasm of uncertain behavior of the minor **salivary glands**
   Neoplasm of uncertain behavior of submucosal salivary glands of lip
   Neoplasm of uncertain behavior of submucosal salivary glands of cheek
   Neoplasm of uncertain behavior of submucosal salivary glands of hard palate
   Neoplasm of uncertain behavior of submucosal salivary glands of soft palate

D37.05 Neoplasm of uncertain behavior of pharynx
   Neoplasm of uncertain behavior of aryepiglottic fold of pharynx NOS
   Neoplasm of uncertain behavior of hypopharyngeal aspect of aryepiglottic fold of pharynx
   Neoplasm of uncertain behavior of marginal zone of aryepiglottic fold of pharynx

D37.09 Neoplasm of uncertain behavior of other **specified sites of the oral cavity**

D37.1 Neoplasm of uncertain behavior of stomach

D37.2 Neoplasm of uncertain behavior of small intestine

D37.3 Neoplasm of uncertain behavior of appendix

D37.4 Neoplasm of uncertain behavior of colon

D37.5 Neoplasm of uncertain behavior of rectum
   Neoplasm of uncertain behavior of rectosigmoid junction
   Rectosigmoid junction: Angle where sigmoid colon becomes rectum

D37.6 Neoplasm of uncertain behavior of liver, gallbladder **and bile ducts**
   Neoplasm of uncertain behavior of ampulla of Vater
   Ampulla of Vater: Enlarged segment of ducts from liver and pancreas at entry point to small intestine

D37.8 Neoplasm of uncertain behavior of other specified **digestive organs**
   Neoplasm of uncertain behavior of anal canal
   Neoplasm of uncertain behavior of anal sphincter
   Neoplasm of uncertain behavior of anus NOS
   Neoplasm of uncertain behavior of esophagus
   Neoplasm of uncertain behavior of intestine NOS
   Neoplasm of uncertain behavior of pancreas

   Excludes1   neoplasm of uncertain behavior of anal margin (D48.5)
   neoplasm of uncertain behavior of anal skin (D48.5)
   neoplasm of uncertain behavior of perianal skin (D48.5)

D37.9 Neoplasm of uncertain behavior of digestive organ, unspecified

CHAPTER 2 (C00-D49)

Figure 2-19 Major salivary glands.

Parotid gland
Sublingual gland
Submandibular gland

● **D38 Neoplasm of uncertain behavior of middle ear and respiratory and intrathoracic organs**

     Excludes1   neoplasm of uncertain behavior of heart (D48.7)

     D38.0 Neoplasm of uncertain behavior of larynx

         Neoplasm of uncertain behavior of aryepiglottic fold or interarytenoid fold, laryngeal aspect

         Neoplasm of uncertain behavior of epiglottis (suprahyoid portion)

         Excludes1   neoplasm of uncertain behavior of aryepiglottic fold or interarytenoid fold NOS (D37.05)

                 neoplasm of uncertain behavior of hypopharyngeal aspect of aryepiglottic fold (D37.05)

                 neoplasm of uncertain behavior of marginal zone of aryepiglottic fold (D37.05)

     D38.1 Neoplasm of uncertain behavior of trachea, bronchus and lung

     D38.2 Neoplasm of uncertain behavior of pleura

     D38.3 Neoplasm of uncertain behavior of mediastinum

     D38.4 Neoplasm of uncertain behavior of thymus

     D38.5 Neoplasm of uncertain behavior of other respiratory organs

         Neoplasm of uncertain behavior of accessory sinuses

         Neoplasm of uncertain behavior of cartilage of nose

         Neoplasm of uncertain behavior of middle ear

         Neoplasm of uncertain behavior of nasal cavities

         Excludes1   neoplasm of uncertain behavior of ear (external) (skin) (D48.5)

                 neoplasm of uncertain behavior of nose NOS (D48.7)

                 neoplasm of uncertain behavior of skin of nose (D48.5)

     D38.6 Neoplasm of uncertain behavior of respiratory organ, unspecified

● **D39 Neoplasm of uncertain behavior of female genital organs**

     D39.0 Neoplasm of uncertain behavior of uterus ♀

●   **D39.1 Neoplasm of uncertain behavior of ovary**

         Use additional code to identify any functional activity.

         D39.10 Neoplasm of uncertain behavior of unspecified ovary ♀

         D39.11 Neoplasm of uncertain behavior of right ovary ♀

         D39.12 Neoplasm of uncertain behavior of left ovary ♀

     D39.2 Neoplasm of uncertain behavior of placenta ♀   **M**

         Chorioadenoma destruens

         Invasive hydatidiform mole

         Malignant hydatidiform mole

         Excludes1   hydatidiform mole NOS (O01.9)

     D39.8 Neoplasm of uncertain behavior of other specified female genital organs ♀

         Neoplasm of uncertain behavior of skin of female genital organs

     D39.9 Neoplasm of uncertain behavior of female genital organ, unspecified ♀

● **D40 Neoplasm of uncertain behavior of male genital organs**

     D40.0 Neoplasm of uncertain behavior of prostate ♂

●   **D40.1 Neoplasm of uncertain behavior of testis**

         D40.10 Neoplasm of uncertain behavior of unspecified testis ♂

         D40.11 Neoplasm of uncertain behavior of right testis ♂

         D40.12 Neoplasm of uncertain behavior of left testis ♂

     D40.8 Neoplasm of uncertain behavior of other specified male genital organs ♂

         Neoplasm of uncertain behavior of skin of male genital organs

     D40.9 Neoplasm of uncertain behavior of male genital organ, unspecified ♂

● **D41 Neoplasm of uncertain behavior of urinary organs**

●   **D41.0 Neoplasm of uncertain behavior of kidney**

         Excludes1   neoplasm of uncertain behavior of renal pelvis (D41.1-)

         D41.00 Neoplasm of uncertain behavior of unspecified kidney

         D41.01 Neoplasm of uncertain behavior of right kidney

         D41.02 Neoplasm of uncertain behavior of left kidney

●   **D41.1 Neoplasm of uncertain behavior of renal pelvis**

         D41.10 Neoplasm of uncertain behavior of unspecified renal pelvis

         D41.11 Neoplasm of uncertain behavior of right renal pelvis

         D41.12 Neoplasm of uncertain behavior of left renal pelvis

●   **D41.2 Neoplasm of uncertain behavior of ureter**

         D41.20 Neoplasm of uncertain behavior of unspecified ureter

         D41.21 Neoplasm of uncertain behavior of right ureter

         D41.22 Neoplasm of uncertain behavior of left ureter

     D41.3 Neoplasm of uncertain behavior of urethra

     D41.4 Neoplasm of uncertain behavior of bladder

     D41.8 Neoplasm of uncertain behavior of other specified urinary organs

     D41.9 Neoplasm of uncertain behavior of unspecified urinary organ

● **D42 Neoplasm of uncertain behavior of meninges**

     D42.0 Neoplasm of uncertain behavior of cerebral meninges

     D42.1 Neoplasm of uncertain behavior of spinal meninges

     D42.9 Neoplasm of uncertain behavior of meninges, unspecified

● **D43 Neoplasm of uncertain behavior of brain and central nervous system**

     Excludes1   neoplasm of uncertain behavior of peripheral nerves and autonomic nervous system (D48.2)

     D43.0 Neoplasm of uncertain behavior of brain, supratentorial

         Superior to tentorium of cerebellum

         Neoplasm of uncertain behavior of cerebral ventricle

         Neoplasm of uncertain behavior of cerebrum

         Neoplasm of uncertain behavior of frontal lobe

         Neoplasm of uncertain behavior of occipital lobe

         Neoplasm of uncertain behavior of parietal lobe

         Neoplasm of uncertain behavior of temporal lobe

         Excludes1   neoplasm of uncertain behavior of fourth ventricle (D43.1)

     D43.1 Neoplasm of uncertain behavior of brain, infratentorial

         Beneath the tentorium of cerebellum

         Neoplasm of uncertain behavior of brain stem

         Neoplasm of uncertain behavior of cerebellum

         Neoplasm of uncertain behavior of fourth ventricle

     D43.2 Neoplasm of uncertain behavior of brain, unspecified

     D43.3 Neoplasm of uncertain behavior of cranial nerves

     D43.4 Neoplasm of uncertain behavior of spinal cord

     D43.8 Neoplasm of uncertain behavior of other specified parts of central nervous system

     D43.9 Neoplasm of uncertain behavior of central nervous system, unspecified

         Neoplasm of uncertain behavior of nervous system (central) NOS

CHAPTER 2 (C00-D49)

▶ New   ⇒ Revised   ~~deleted~~ Deleted   Excludes 1   Excludes 2   Includes   Use additional   Code first   Code also   Key words

OGCR Official Guidelines   X Assign placeholder X   ● Use Additional Character(s)   ▌ Manifestation Code   **Coding Clinic**

● **D44 Neoplasm of uncertain behavior of endocrine glands**

> **Excludes1** multiple endocrine adenomatosis (E31.2-)
> multiple endocrine neoplasia (E31.2-)
> neoplasm of uncertain behavior of endocrine pancreas (D37.8)
> neoplasm of uncertain behavior of ovary (D39.1-)
> neoplasm of uncertain behavior of testis (D40.1-)
> neoplasm of uncertain behavior of thymus (D38.4)

D44.0 Neoplasm of uncertain behavior of thyroid gland

● **D44.1 Neoplasm of uncertain behavior of adrenal gland**
> Use additional code to identify any functional activity.

> **D44.10 Neoplasm of uncertain behavior of unspecified adrenal gland**

> **D44.11 Neoplasm of uncertain behavior of right adrenal gland**

> **D44.12 Neoplasm of uncertain behavior of left adrenal gland**

D44.2 Neoplasm of uncertain behavior of parathyroid gland

D44.3 Neoplasm of uncertain behavior of pituitary gland
> Use additional code to identify any functional activity.

D44.4 Neoplasm of uncertain behavior of craniopharyngeal duct

D44.5 Neoplasm of uncertain behavior of pineal gland

D44.6 Neoplasm of uncertain behavior of carotid body

D44.7 Neoplasm of uncertain behavior of aortic body and other paraganglia
> **Coding Clinic: 2016, Q4, P26**

D44.9 Neoplasm of uncertain behavior of unspecified endocrine gland

D45 Polycythemia vera

> **Excludes1** familial polycythemia (D75.0)
> secondary polycythemia (D75.1)

> *Primary polycythemia. Secondary polycythemia is D75.1. Check your documentation. Polycythemia is caused by too many red blood cells, which increase the thickness of blood (viscosity). This can cause engorgement of the spleen (splenomegaly) with extra RBCs and potential clot formation.*

● **D46 Myelodysplastic syndromes**

> Use additional code for adverse effect, if applicable, to identify drug (T36-T50 with fifth or sixth character 5)

> **Excludes2** drug-induced aplastic anemia (D61.1)

D46.0 Refractory anemia without ring sideroblasts, so stated
> Refractory anemia without sideroblasts, without excess of blasts

D46.1 Refractory anemia with ring sideroblasts RARS

● **D46.2 Refractory anemia with excess of blasts [RAEB]**
> *Form of myelodysplasia with increased immature white blood cells (blasts) in bone marrow*

> **D46.20 Refractory anemia with excess of blasts, unspecified RAEB NOS**

> **D46.21 Refractory anemia with excess of blasts 1 RAEB 1**
> > *Bone marrow disease which results in insufficient RBCs (anemia) in which level of blasts is less than 10%*

> **D46.22 Refractory anemia with excess of blasts 2 RAEB 2**
> > *Bone marrow disease manifested by insufficient numbers of RBCs (anemia) with level of blasts 10-20%*

D46.A Refractory cytopenia with multilineage dysplasia

D46.B Refractory cytopenia with multilineage dysplasia and ring sideroblasts
> RCMD RS

D46.C Myelodysplastic syndrome with isolated del(5q) chromosomal abnormality
> Myelodysplastic syndrome with 5q deletion
> 5q minus syndrome NOS

D46.4 Refractory anemia, unspecified

D46.Z Other myelodysplastic syndromes
> **Excludes1** chronic myelomonocytic leukemia (C93.1-)

D46.9 Myelodysplastic syndrome, unspecified
> Myelodysplasia NOS

● **D47 Other neoplasms of uncertain behavior of lymphoid, hematopoietic and related tissue**

● **D47.0 Mast cell neoplasms of uncertain behavior**

> ⇒ **Excludes1** congenital cutaneous mastocytosis (Q82.2)
> histiocytic neoplasms of uncertain behavior (D47.Z9)
> malignant mast cell neoplasm (C96.2-)

D47.01 Cutaneous mastocytosis
> Diffuse cutaneous mastocytosis
> Maculopapular cutaneous mastocytosis
> Solitary mastocytoma
> Telangiectasia macularis eruptiva perstans
> Urticaria pigmentosa

> **Excludes1** congenital (diffuse) (maculopapular) cutaneous mastocytosis (Q82.2)
> congenital urticaria pigmentosa (Q82.2)
> extracutaneous mastocytoma (D47.09)

D47.02 Systemic mastocytosis
> Indolent systemic mastocytosis
> Isolated bone marrow mastocytosis
> Smoldering systemic mastocytosis
> Systemic mastocytosis, with an associated hematological non-mast cell lineage disease (SM-AHNMD)

> Code also if applicable, any associated hematological non-mast cell lineage disease, such as:
> acute myeloid leukemia (C92.6-, C92.A-)
> chronic myelomonocytic leukemia (C93.1-)
> essential thrombocytosis (D47.3)
> hypereosinophilic syndrome (D72.1)
> myelodysplastic syndrome (D46.9)
> myeloproliferative syndrome (D47.1)
> non-Hodgkin lymphoma (C82-C85)
> plasma cell myeloma (C90.0-)
> polycythemia vera (D45)

> **Excludes1** aggressive systemic mastocytosis (C96.21)
> mast cell leukemia (C94.3-)

D47.09 Other mast cell neoplasms of uncertain behavior
> Extracutaneous mastocytoma
> Mast cell tumor NOS
> Mastocytoma NOS
> Mastocytosis NOS

D47.1 Chronic myeloproliferative disease
> Chronic neutrophilic leukemia
> Myeloproliferative disease, unspecified

> **Excludes1** atypical chronic myeloid leukemia BCR/ABL-negative (C92.2-)
> chronic myeloid leukemia BCR/ABL-positive (C92.1-)
> myelofibrosis NOS (D75.81)
> myelophthisic anemia (D61.82)
> myelophthisis (D61.82)
> secondary myelofibrosis NOS (D75.81)

CHAPTER 2 (C00-D49)

D47.2   Monoclonal gammopathy
Monoclonal gammopathy of undetermined significance [MGUS]

D47.3   Essential (hemorrhagic) thrombocythemia
Essential thrombocytosis
Idiopathic hemorrhagic thrombocythemia

D47.4   Osteomyelofibrosis
Chronic idiopathic myelofibrosis
Myelofibrosis (idiopathic) (with myeloid metaplasia)
Myelosclerosis (megakaryocytic) with myeloid metaplasia
Secondary myelofibrosis in myeloproliferative disease
Excludes1   acute myelofibrosis (C94.4-)

● **D47.Z   Other specified neoplasms of uncertain behavior of lymphoid, hematopoietic and related tissue**

D47.Z1   Post-transplant lymphoproliferative disorder (PTLD)
Code first complications of transplanted organs and tissue (T86.-)

D47.Z2   Castleman disease
Code also if applicable human herpesvirus 8 infection (B10.89)
Excludes2   Kaposi's sarcoma (C46-)
Coding Clinic: 2016, Q4, P8

D47.Z9   Other specified neoplasms of uncertain behavior of lymphoid, hematopoietic and related tissue
Histiocytic tumors of uncertain behavior

D47.9   Neoplasm of uncertain behavior of lymphoid, hematopoietic and related tissue, unspecified
Lymphoproliferative disease NOS

● **D48   Neoplasm of uncertain behavior of other and unspecified sites**
Excludes1   neurofibromatosis (nonmalignant) (Q85.0-)

D48.0   Neoplasm of uncertain behavior of bone and articular cartilage
Excludes1   neoplasm of uncertain behavior of cartilage of ear (D48.1)
neoplasm of uncertain behavior of cartilage of larynx (D38.0)
neoplasm of uncertain behavior of cartilage of nose (D38.5)
neoplasm of uncertain behavior of connective tissue of eyelid (D48.1)
neoplasm of uncertain behavior of synovia (D48.1)

D48.1   Neoplasm of uncertain behavior of connective and other soft tissue
Neoplasm of uncertain behavior of connective tissue of ear
Neoplasm of uncertain behavior of connective tissue of eyelid
Stromal tumors of uncertain behavior of digestive system
Excludes1   neoplasm of uncertain behavior of articular cartilage (D48.0)
neoplasm of uncertain behavior of cartilage of larynx (D38.0)
neoplasm of uncertain behavior of cartilage of nose (D38.5)
neoplasm of uncertain behavior of connective tissue of breast (D48.6-)

D48.2   Neoplasm of uncertain behavior of peripheral nerves and autonomic nervous system
Excludes1   neoplasm of uncertain behavior of peripheral nerves of orbit (D48.7)

D48.3   Neoplasm of uncertain behavior of retroperitoneum

D48.4   Neoplasm of uncertain behavior of peritoneum

D48.5   Neoplasm of uncertain behavior of skin
Neoplasm of uncertain behavior of anal margin
Neoplasm of uncertain behavior of anal skin
Neoplasm of uncertain behavior of perianal skin
Neoplasm of uncertain behavior of skin of breast
Excludes1   neoplasm of uncertain behavior of anus NOS (D37.8)
neoplasm of uncertain behavior of skin of genital organs (D39.8, D40.8)
neoplasm of uncertain behavior of vermilion border of lip (D37.0)

● **D48.6   Neoplasm of uncertain behavior of breast**
Neoplasm of uncertain behavior of connective tissue of breast
Cystosarcoma phyllodes
Excludes1   neoplasm of uncertain behavior of skin of breast (D48.5)

D48.60   Neoplasm of uncertain behavior of unspecified breast

D48.61   Neoplasm of uncertain behavior of right breast

D48.62   Neoplasm of uncertain behavior of left breast

D48.7   Neoplasm of uncertain behavior of other specified sites
Neoplasm of uncertain behavior of eye
Neoplasm of uncertain behavior of heart
Neoplasm of uncertain behavior of peripheral nerves of orbit
Excludes1   neoplasm of uncertain behavior of connective tissue (D48.1)
neoplasm of uncertain behavior of skin of eyelid (D48.5)

D48.9   Neoplasm of uncertain behavior, unspecified

● **D49   Neoplasms of unspecified behavior**
Note: Category D49 classifies by site neoplasms of unspecified morphology and behavior. The term 'mass,' unless otherwise stated, is not to be regarded as a neoplastic growth.
Includes   'growth' NOS
neoplasm NOS
new growth NOS
tumor NOS
Excludes1   neoplasms of uncertain behavior (D37-D44, D48)

D49.0   Neoplasm of unspecified behavior of digestive system
Excludes1   neoplasm of unspecified behavior of margin of anus (D49.2)
neoplasm of unspecified behavior of perianal skin (D49.2)
neoplasm of unspecified behavior of skin of anus (D49.2)

D49.1   Neoplasm of unspecified behavior of respiratory system

D49.2   Neoplasm of unspecified behavior of bone, soft tissue, and skin
Excludes1   neoplasm of unspecified behavior of anal canal (D49.0)
neoplasm of unspecified behavior of anus NOS (D49.0)
neoplasm of unspecified behavior of bone marrow (D49.89)
neoplasm of unspecified behavior of cartilage of larynx (D49.1)
neoplasm of unspecified behavior of cartilage of nose (D49.1)
neoplasm of unspecified behavior of connective tissue of breast (D49.3)
neoplasm of unspecified behavior of skin of genital organs (D49.59)
neoplasm of unspecified behavior of vermilion border of lip (D49.0)

▶ New   ⇒ Revised   ~~deleted~~ Deleted   Excludes 1   Excludes 2   Includes   Use additional   Code first   Code also   Key words
OGCR Official Guidelines   X Assign placeholder X   ● Use Additional Character(s)   ▷ Manifestation Code   **Coding Clinic**

D49.3   Neoplasm of unspecified behavior of breast
    Excludes1   neoplasm of unspecified behavior of skin
        of breast (D49.2)

D49.4   Neoplasm of unspecified behavior of bladder

● D49.5   Neoplasm of unspecified behavior of other
    genitourinary organs

    ● D49.51   Neoplasm of unspecified behavior of kidney

        D49.511   Neoplasm of unspecified behavior of
            right kidney
             Coding Clinic: 2016, Q4, P9

        D49.512   Neoplasm of unspecified behavior of
            left kidney
             Coding Clinic: 2016, Q4, P9

        D49.519   Neoplasm of unspecified behavior of
            unspecified kidney
             Coding Clinic: 2016, Q4, P9

    D49.59   Neoplasm of unspecified behavior of other
        genitourinary organ
        Coding Clinic: 2016, Q4, P9

D49.6   Neoplasm of unspecified behavior of brain
    Excludes1   neoplasm of unspecified behavior of
        cerebral meninges (D49.7)
        neoplasm of unspecified behavior of
        cranial nerves (D49.7)

D49.7   Neoplasm of unspecified behavior of endocrine glands
and other parts of nervous system
    Excludes1   neoplasm of unspecified behavior
        of peripheral, sympathetic, and
        parasympathetic nerves and ganglia
        (D49.2)

● D49.8   Neoplasm of unspecified behavior of other specified
sites
    Excludes1   neoplasm of unspecified behavior of
        eyelid (skin) (D49.2)
        neoplasm of unspecified behavior of
        eyelid cartilage (D49.2)
        neoplasm of unspecified behavior of great
        vessels (D49.2)
        neoplasm of unspecified behavior of optic
        nerve (D49.7)

    D49.81   Neoplasm of unspecified behavior of retina and
        choroid
        Dark area on retina
        Retinal freckle

    D49.89   Neoplasm of unspecified behavior of other
        specified sites

D49.9   Neoplasm of unspecified behavior of unspecified site

CHAPTER 2 (C00-D49)

OGCR Chapter-Specific Coding Guidelines

3. Chapter 3: Disease of the blood and blood-forming organs and certain disorders involving the immune mechanism (D50-D89)
Reserved for future guideline expansion

CHAPTER 3

DISEASES OF THE BLOOD AND BLOOD-FORMING ORGANS AND CERTAIN DISORDERS INVOLVING THE IMMUNE MECHANISM (D50-D89)

Excludes2   autoimmune disease (systemic) NOS (M35.9)
certain conditions originating in the perinatal period (P00-P96)
complications of pregnancy, childbirth and the puerperium (O00-O9A)
congenital malformations, deformations and chromosomal abnormalities (Q00-Q99)
endocrine, nutritional and metabolic diseases (E00-E88)
human immunodeficiency virus [HIV] disease (B20)
injury, poisoning and certain other consequences of external causes (S00-T88)
neoplasms (C00-D49)
symptoms, signs and abnormal clinical and laboratory findings, not elsewhere classified (R00-R94)

This chapter contains the following blocks:

D50-D53	Nutritional anemias
D55-D59	Hemolytic anemias
D60-D64	Aplastic and other anemias and other bone marrow failure syndromes
D65-D69	Coagulation defects, purpura and other hemorrhagic conditions
D70-D77	Other disorders of blood and blood-forming organs
D78	Intraoperative and postprocedural complications of the spleen
D80-D89	Certain disorders involving the immune mechanism

NUTRITIONAL ANEMIAS (D50-D53)

● **D50**   **Iron deficiency anemia**
A disease characterized by a decrease in the number of red cells (hemoglobin) in the blood.

    Includes   asiderotic anemia
hypochromic anemia

    D50.0   **Iron deficiency anemia secondary to blood loss (chronic)**
Posthemorrhagic anemia (chronic)

       Excludes1   acute posthemorrhagic anemia (D62)
congenital anemia from fetal blood loss (P61.3)

    D50.1   **Sideropenic dysphagia**
Web-like growth of membranes in throat that makes swallowing difficult
Kelly-Paterson syndrome
Plummer-Vinson syndrome

    D50.8   **Other iron deficiency anemias**
Iron deficiency anemia due to inadequate dietary iron intake

    D50.9   **Iron deficiency anemia, unspecified**

● **D51**   **Vitamin B12 deficiency anemia**

    Excludes1   vitamin B12 deficiency (E53.8)

    D51.0   **Vitamin B12 deficiency anemia due to intrinsic factor deficiency**
Addison anemia
Biermer anemia
Pernicious (congenital) anemia
Congenital intrinsic factor deficiency

    D51.1   **Vitamin B12 deficiency anemia due to selective vitamin B12 malabsorption with proteinuria**
Imerslund (Gräsbeck) syndrome
Megaloblastic hereditary anemia

    D51.2   **Transcobalamin II deficiency**

    D51.3   **Other dietary vitamin B12 deficiency anemia**
Vegan anemia

    D51.8   **Other vitamin B12 deficiency anemias**

    D51.9   **Vitamin B12 deficiency anemia, unspecified**

● **D52**   **Folate deficiency anemia**

    Excludes1   folate deficiency without anemia (E53.8)

    D52.0   **Dietary folate deficiency anemia**
Nutritional megaloblastic anemia

    D52.1   **Drug-induced folate deficiency anemia**
Use additional code for adverse effect, if applicable, to identify drug (T36-T50 with fifth or sixth character 5)

    D52.8   **Other folate deficiency anemias**

    D52.9   **Folate deficiency anemia, unspecified**
Folic acid deficiency anemia NOS

● **D53**   **Other nutritional anemias**

    Includes   megaloblastic anemia unresponsive to vitamin B12 or folate therapy

    D53.0   **Protein deficiency anemia**
Amino-acid deficiency anemia
Orotaciduric anemia

       Excludes1   Lesch-Nyhan syndrome (E79.1)

    D53.1   **Other megaloblastic anemias, not elsewhere classified**
Megaloblastic anemia NOS

       Excludes1   Di Guglielmo's disease (C94.0)

    D53.2   **Scorbutic anemia**
Anemia resulting from deficiency of ascorbic acid (vitamin C)

       Excludes1   scurvy (E54)

    D53.8   **Other specified nutritional anemias**
Anemia associated with deficiency of copper
Anemia associated with deficiency of molybdenum
Anemia associated with deficiency of zinc

       Excludes1   nutritional deficiencies without anemia, such as:
copper deficiency NOS (E61.0)
molybdenum deficiency NOS (E61.5)
zinc deficiency NOS (E60)

    D53.9   **Nutritional anemia, unspecified**
Simple chronic anemia

       Excludes1   anemia NOS (D64.9)

▶ New   ⇒ Revised   ~~deleted~~ Deleted   Excludes 1   Excludes 2   Includes   Use additional   Code first   Code also   Key words
OGCR Official Guidelines   X Assign placeholder X   ● Use Additional Character(s)   ▶ Manifestation Code   **Coding Clinic**

HEMOLYTIC ANEMIAS (D55-D59)

● **D55** **Anemia due to enzyme disorders**
   Excludes1 drug-induced enzyme deficiency anemia (D59.2)

   D55.0 **Anemia due to glucose-6-phosphate dehydrogenase [G6PD] deficiency**
   Favism
   G6PD deficiency anemia

   D55.1 **Anemia due to other disorders of glutathione metabolism**
   Anemia (due to) enzyme deficiencies, except G6PD, related to the hexose monophosphate [HMP] shunt pathway
   Anemia (due to) hemolytic nonspherocytic (hereditary), type I

   D55.2 **Anemia due to disorders of glycolytic enzymes**
   Hemolytic nonspherocytic (hereditary) anemia, type II
   Hexokinase deficiency anemia
   Pyruvate kinase [PK] deficiency anemia
   Triose-phosphate isomerase deficiency anemia
   Excludes1 disorders of glycolysis not associated with anemia (E74.8)

   D55.3 **Anemia due to disorders of nucleotide metabolism**

   D55.8 **Other anemias due to enzyme disorders**

   D55.9 **Anemia due to enzyme disorder, unspecified**

● **D56** **Thalassemia**
   Hereditary disorders characterized by low production of hemoglobin or excessive destruction of red blood cells
   Excludes1 sickle-cell thalassemia (D57.4-)

   D56.0 **Alpha thalassemia**
   Alpha thalassemia major
   Hemoglobin H Constant Spring
   Hemoglobin H disease
   Hydrops fetalis due to alpha thalassemia
   Severe alpha thalassemia
   Triple gene defect alpha thalassemia
   Use additional code, if applicable, for hydrops fetalis due to alpha thalassemia (P56.99)
   Excludes1 alpha thalassemia trait or minor (D56.3)
   asymptomatic alpha thalassemia (D56.3)
   hydrops fetalis due to isoimmunization (P56.0)
   hydrops fetalis not due to immune hemolysis (P83.2)

   D56.1 **Beta thalassemia**
   Beta thalassemia major
   Cooley's anemia
   Homozygous beta thalassemia
   Severe beta thalassemia
   Thalassemia intermedia
   Thalassemia major
   Excludes1 beta thalassemia minor (D56.3)
   beta thalassemia trait (D56.3)
   delta-beta thalassemia (D56.2)
   hemoglobin E-beta thalassemia (D56.5)
   sickle-cell beta thalassemia (D57.4-)

   D56.2 **Delta-beta thalassemia**
   Homozygous delta-beta thalassemia
   Excludes1 delta-beta thalassemia minor (D56.3)
   delta-beta thalassemia trait (D56.3)

   D56.3 **Thalassemia minor**
   Genetic disorders that have in common defective production of hemoglobin
   Alpha thalassemia minor
   Alpha thalassemia silent carrier
   Alpha thalassemia trait
   Beta thalassemia minor
   Beta thalassemia trait
   Delta-beta thalassemia minor
   Delta-beta thalassemia trait
   Thalassemia trait NOS
   Excludes1 alpha thalassemia (D56.0)
   beta thalassemia (D56.1)
   delta-beta thalassemia (D56.2)
   hemoglobin E-beta thalassemia (D56.5)
   sickle-cell trait (D57.3)

   D56.4 **Hereditary persistence of fetal hemoglobin [HPFH]**
   Persistent production of hemoglobin

   D56.5 **Hemoglobin E-beta thalassemia**
   Excludes1 beta thalassemia (D56.1)
   beta thalassemia minor (D56.3)
   beta thalassemia trait (D56.3)
   delta-beta thalassemia (D56.2)
   delta-beta thalassemia trait (D56.3)
   hemoglobin E disease (D58.2)
   other hemoglobinopathies (D58.2)
   sickle-cell beta thalassemia (D57.4-)

   D56.8 **Other thalassemias**
   Dominant thalassemia
   Hemoglobin C thalassemia
   Mixed thalassemia
   Thalassemia with other hemoglobinopathy
   Excludes1 hemoglobin C disease (D58.2)
   hemoglobin E disease (D58.2)
   other hemoglobinopathies (D58.2)
   sickle cell anemia (D57.-)
   sickle-cell thalassemia (D57.4)

   D56.9 **Thalassemia, unspecified**
   Mediterranean anemia (with other hemoglobinopathy)

● **D57** **Sickle-cell disorders**
   Inherited disease in which red blood cells, normally disc-shaped, become crescent shaped
   Use additional code for any associated fever (R50.81)
   Excludes1 other hemoglobinopathies (D58.-)

● **D57.0** **Hb-SS disease with crisis**
   Sickle-cell disease NOS with crisis
   Hb-SS disease with vasoocclusive pain

   D57.00 **Hb-SS disease with crisis, unspecified**

   D57.01 **Hb-SS disease with acute chest syndrome**

   D57.02 **Hb-SS disease with splenic sequestration**

   D57.1 **Sickle-cell disease without crisis Hb-SS disease without crisis**
   Sickle-cell anemia NOS
   Sickle-cell disease NOS
   Sickle-cell disorder NOS

● **D57.2** **Sickle-cell/Hb-C disease**
   Hb-SC disease
   Hb-S/Hb-C disease

   D57.20 **Sickle-cell/Hb-C disease without crisis**

● **D57.21** **Sickle-cell/Hb-C disease with crisis**

   D57.211 **Sickle-cell/Hb-C disease with acute chest syndrome**

   D57.212 **Sickle-cell/Hb-C disease with splenic sequestration**

   D57.219 **Sickle-cell/Hb-C disease with crisis, unspecified**
   Sickle-cell/Hb-C disease with crisis NOS

CHAPTER 3 (D50-D89)

CHAPTER 3 (D50-D89)

D57.3 Sickle-cell trait
Hb-S trait
Heterozygous hemoglobin S

● **D57.4 Sickle-cell thalassemia**
Sickle-cell beta thalassemia
Thalassemia Hb-S disease

  D57.40 Sickle-cell thalassemia without crisis
Microdrepanocytosis
Sickle-cell thalassemia NOS

  ● **D57.41 Sickle-cell thalassemia with crisis**
Sickle-cell "crisis" is precipitated when abnormally crescent-shaped red blood cells form clots and interrupt blood flow to major organs, causing severe pain and organ damage.
Sickle-cell thalassemia with vasoocclusive pain

    D57.411 Sickle-cell thalassemia with acute chest syndrome

    D57.412 Sickle-cell thalassemia with splenic sequestration

    D57.419 Sickle-cell thalassemia with crisis, unspecified
Sickle-cell thalassemia with crisis NOS

● **D57.8 Other sickle-cell disorders**
Hb-SD disease
Hb-SE disease

  D57.80 Other sickle-cell disorders without crisis

  ● **D57.81 Other sickle-cell disorders with crisis**

    D57.811 Other sickle-cell disorders with acute chest syndrome

    D57.812 Other sickle-cell disorders with splenic sequestration

    D57.819 Other sickle-cell disorders with crisis, unspecified
Other sickle-cell disorders with crisis NOS

● **D58 Other hereditary hemolytic anemias**
Genetic condition in which bone marrow is unable to compensate for premature destruction of red blood cells

  Excludes1 hemolytic anemia of the newborn (P55.-)

D58.0 Hereditary spherocytosis
Presence of spherocytes (spherically shaped red blood cells)
Acholuric (familial) jaundice
Congenital (spherocytic) hemolytic icterus
Minkowski-Chauffard syndrome

D58.1 Hereditary elliptocytosis
Presence of large numbers of elliptocytes in blood
Elliptocytosis (congenital)
Ovalocytosis (congenital) (hereditary)

D58.2 Other hemoglobinopathies
Abnormal hemoglobin NOS
Congenital Heinz body anemia
Hb-C disease
Hb-D disease
Hb-E disease
Hemoglobinopathy NOS
Unstable hemoglobin hemolytic disease

  Excludes1 familial polycythemia (D75.0)
Hb-M disease (D74.0)
hemoglobin E-beta thalassemia (D56.5)
hereditary persistence of fetal hemoglobin [HPFH] (D56.4)
high-altitude polycythemia (D75.1)
methemoglobinemia (D74.-)
other hemoglobinopathies with thalassemia (D56.8)

D58.8 Other specified hereditary hemolytic anemias
Stomatocytosis

D58.9 Hereditary hemolytic anemia, unspecified

● **D59 Acquired hemolytic anemia**

D59.0 Drug-induced autoimmune hemolytic anemia
Use additional code for adverse effect, if applicable, to identify drug (T36-T50 with fifth or sixth character 5)

D59.1 Other autoimmune hemolytic anemias
Autoimmune hemolytic disease (cold type) (warm type)
Chronic cold hemagglutinin disease
Cold agglutinin disease
Cold agglutinin hemoglobinuria
Cold type (secondary) (symptomatic) hemolytic anemia
Warm type (secondary) (symptomatic) hemolytic anemia

  Excludes1 Evans syndrome (D69.41)
hemolytic disease of newborn (P55.-)
paroxysmal cold hemoglobinuria (D59.6)

D59.2 Drug-induced nonautoimmune hemolytic anemia
Drug-induced enzyme deficiency anemia
Use additional code for adverse effect, if applicable, to identify drug (T36-T50 with fifth or sixth character 5)

D59.3 Hemolytic-uremic syndrome
Use additional code to identify associated:
E. coli infection (B96.2-)
Pneumococcal pneumonia (J13)
Shigella dysenteriae (A03.9)

D59.4 Other nonautoimmune hemolytic anemias
Mechanical hemolytic anemia
Microangiopathic hemolytic anemia
Toxic hemolytic anemia

D59.5 Paroxysmal nocturnal hemoglobinuria [Marchiafava-Micheli]

  Excludes1 hemoglobinuria NOS (R82.3)

D59.6 Hemoglobinuria due to hemolysis from other external causes
Hemoglobinuria from exertion
March hemoglobinuria
Paroxysmal cold hemoglobinuria
Use additional code (Chapter 20) to identify external cause

  Excludes1 hemoglobinuria NOS (R82.3)

D59.8 Other acquired hemolytic anemias

D59.9 Acquired hemolytic anemia, unspecified
Idiopathic hemolytic anemia, chronic

APLASTIC AND OTHER ANEMIAS AND OTHER BONE MARROW FAILURE SYNDROMES (D60-D64)

● **D60 Acquired pure red cell aplasia [erythroblastopenia]**
Deficiency of erythroblasts

  Includes red cell aplasia (acquired) (adult) (with thymoma)
  Excludes1 congenital red cell aplasia (D61.01)

D60.0 Chronic acquired pure red cell aplasia
Lack of development of blood cell

D60.1 Transient acquired pure red cell aplasia

D60.8 Other acquired pure red cell aplasias

D60.9 Acquired pure red cell aplasia, unspecified

● **D61 Other aplastic anemias and other bone marrow failure syndromes**

  Excludes1 neutropenia (D70.-)

● **D61.0 Constitutional aplastic anemia**
Condition where bone marrow is unable to produce blood cells

D61.01 Constitutional (pure) red blood cell aplasia
Blackfan-Diamond syndrome
Congenital (pure) red cell aplasia
Familial hypoplastic anemia
Primary (pure) red cell aplasia
Red cell (pure) aplasia of infants

  Excludes1 acquired red cell aplasia (D60.9)

D61.09 Other constitutional aplastic anemia
Fanconi's anemia
Pancytopenia with malformations

▶ New   ⇒ Revised   ~~deleted~~ Deleted   Excludes 1   Excludes 2   Includes   Use additional   Code first   Code also   Key words

OGCR Official Guidelines   X Assign placeholder X   ● Use Additional Character(s)   ▶ Manifestation Code   **Coding Clinic**

D61.1   **Drug-induced aplastic anemia**
Use additional code for adverse effect, if applicable, to identify drug (T36-T50 with fifth or sixth character 5)

D61.2   **Aplastic anemia due to other external agents**
Code first, if applicable, toxic effects of substances chiefly nonmedicinal as to source (T51-T65)

D61.3   **Idiopathic aplastic anemia**

● **D61.8**   **Other specified aplastic anemias and other bone marrow failure syndromes**

● **D61.81**   **Pancytopenia**
Marked deficiency of all the blood elements: Red blood cells (erythrocytes), white blood cells (leukocytes), and platelets (thrombocytes). Check laboratory results.

Excludes1   pancytopenia (due to) (with) aplastic anemia (D61.9)
pancytopenia (due to) (with) bone marrow infiltration (D61.82)
pancytopenia (due to) (with) congenital (pure) red cell aplasia (D61.01)
pancytopenia (due to) (with) hairy cell leukemia (C91.4-)
pancytopenia (due to) (with) human immunodeficiency virus disease (B20.-)
pancytopenia (due to) (with) leukoerythroblastic anemia (D61.82)
pancytopenia (due to) (with) myeloproliferative disease (D47.1)

Excludes2   pancytopenia (due to) (with) myelodysplastic syndromes (D46.-)

D61.810   **Antineoplastic chemotherapy induced pancytopenia**
Excludes2   aplastic anemia due to antineoplastic chemotherapy (D61.1)

D61.811   **Other drug-induced pancytopenia**
Excludes2   aplastic anemia due to drugs (D61.1)

D61.818   **Other pancytopenia**

D61.82   **Myelophthisis**
Leukoerythroblastic anemia
Myelophthisic anemia
Panmyelophthisis
Code also the underlying disorder, such as: malignant neoplasm of breast (C50.-)
tuberculosis (A15.-)

Excludes1   idiopathic myelofibrosis (D47.1)
myelofibrosis NOS (D75.81)
myelofibrosis with myeloid metaplasia (D47.4)
primary myelofibrosis (D47.1)
secondary myelofibrosis (D75.81)

D61.89   **Other specified aplastic anemias and other bone marrow failure syndromes**

D61.9   **Aplastic anemia, unspecified**
Hypoplastic anemia NOS
Medullary hypoplasia

D62   **Acute posthemorrhagic anemia**
Excludes1   anemia due to chronic blood loss (D50.0)
blood loss anemia NOS (D50.0)
congenital anemia from fetal blood loss (P61.3)

● **D63**   **Anemia in chronic diseases classified elsewhere**
▶ **D63.0**   *Anemia in neoplastic disease*
Code first neoplasm (C00-D49)
Excludes1   aplastic anemia due to antineoplastic chemotherapy (D61.1)
Excludes2   anemia due to antineoplastic chemotherapy (D64.81)

OGCR   Section I.C.2.e.2.
2) Anemia associated with chemotherapy, immunotherapy and radiation therapy
When the admission/encounter is for management of an anemia associated with an adverse effect of the administration of chemotherapy or immunotherapy and the only treatment is for the anemia, the anemia code is sequenced first followed by the appropriate codes for the neoplasm and the adverse effect (T45.1X5, Adverse effect of antineoplastic and immunosuppressive drugs).

▶ **D63.1**   *Anemia in chronic kidney disease*
Erythropoietin resistant anemia (EPO resistant anemia)
Code first underlying chronic kidney disease (CKD) (N18.-)

▶ **D63.8**   *Anemia in other chronic diseases classified elsewhere*
Code first underlying disease, such as:
diphyllobothriasis (B70.0)
hookworm disease (B76.0-B76.9)
hypothyroidism (E00.0-E03.9)
malaria (B50.0-B54)
symptomatic late syphilis (A52.79)
tuberculosis (A18.89)

● **D64**   **Other anemias**
Excludes1   refractory anemia (D46.-)
refractory anemia with excess blasts in transformation [RAEB T] (C92.0-)

D64.0   **Hereditary sideroblastic anemia**
Abnormal production RBCs (erythrocytes)
Sex-linked hypochromic sideroblastic anemia

▶ **D64.1**   *Secondary sideroblastic anemia due to disease*
Code first underlying disease

D64.2   **Secondary sideroblastic anemia due to drugs and toxins**
Code first poisoning due to drug or toxin, if applicable (T36-T65 with fifth or sixth character 1-4 or 6)
Use additional code for adverse effect, if applicable, to identify drug (T36-T50 with fifth or sixth character 5)

D64.3   **Other sideroblastic anemias**
Sideroblastic anemia NOS
Pyridoxine-responsive sideroblastic anemia NEC

D64.4   **Congenital dyserythropoietic anemia**
Any of several rare hereditary anemias, mostly types of macrocytic anemia
Dyshematopoietic anemia (congenital)
Excludes1   Blackfan-Diamond syndrome (D61.01)
Di Guglielmo's disease (C94.0)

● **D64.8**   **Other specified anemias**
D64.81   **Anemia due to antineoplastic chemotherapy**
Antineoplastic chemotherapy induced anemia
Excludes1   aplastic anemia due to antineoplastic chemotherapy (D61.1)
Excludes2   anemia in neoplastic disease (D63.0)

D64.89   **Other specified anemias**
Infantile pseudoleukemia

D64.9   **Anemia, unspecified**
Coding Clinic: 2017, Q1, P7

CHAPTER 3 (D50-D89)

COAGULATION DEFECTS, PURPURA AND OTHER HEMORRHAGIC CONDITIONS (D65-D69)

D65   Disseminated intravascular coagulation [defibrination syndrome]
Blood clots form and consume all coagulation proteins and platelets and disrupt normal coagulation, resulting in abnormal bleeding
Afibrinogenemia, acquired
Consumption coagulopathy
Diffuse or disseminated intravascular coagulation [DIC]
Fibrinolytic hemorrhage, acquired
Fibrinolytic purpura
Purpura fulminans

> **Excludes1**   disseminated intravascular coagulation (complicating):
> abortion or ectopic or molar pregnancy (O00-O07, O08.1)
> in newborn (P60)
> pregnancy, childbirth and the puerperium (O45.0, O46.0, O67.0, O72.3)

D66   Hereditary factor VIII deficiency
Inherited coagulation disorder carried by females but most often affecting males
Classical hemophilia
Deficiency factor VIII (with functional defect)
Hemophilia NOS
Hemophilia A

> **Excludes1**   factor VIII deficiency with vascular defect (D68.0)

D67   Hereditary factor IX deficiency
Christmas disease
Factor IX deficiency (with functional defect)
Hemophilia B
Plasma thromboplastin component [PTC] deficiency

● **D68   Other coagulation defects**

> **Excludes1**   abnormal coagulation profile (R79.1)
> coagulation defects complicating abortion or ectopic or molar pregnancy (O00-O07, O08.1)
> coagulation defects complicating pregnancy, childbirth and the puerperium (O45.0, O46.0, O67.0, O72.3)

Coding Clinic: 2016, Q1, P14

D68.0   Von Willebrand's disease
Congenital bleeding disorder
Angiohemophilia
Factor VIII deficiency with vascular defect
Vascular hemophilia

> **Excludes1**   capillary fragility (hereditary) (D69.8)
> factor VIII deficiency NOS (D66)
> factor VIII deficiency with functional defect (D66)

D68.1   Hereditary factor XI deficiency
Deficiency of blood coagulation resulting in systemic blood-clotting defect
Hemophilia C
Plasma thromboplastin antecedent [PTA] deficiency
Rosenthal's disease

D68.2   Hereditary deficiency of other clotting factors
Blood clotting disorders caused by hereditary deficiencies of one or more clotting factors
AC globulin deficiency
Congenital afibrinogenemia
Deficiency of factor I [fibrinogen]
Deficiency of factor II [prothrombin]
Deficiency of factor V [labile]
Deficiency of factor VII [stable]
Deficiency of factor X [Stuart-Prower]
Deficiency of factor XII [Hageman]
Deficiency of factor XIII [fibrin stabilizing]
Dysfibrinogenemia (congenital)
Hypoproconvertinemia
Owren's disease
Proaccelerin deficiency

● **D68.3   Hemorrhagic disorder due to circulating anticoagulants**
Blood clotting disorders caused by anticoagulants (warfarin and heparin)

● **D68.31   Hemorrhagic disorder due to intrinsic circulating anticoagulants, antibodies, or inhibitors**

     D68.311   Acquired hemophilia
Autoimmune hemophilia
Autoimmune inhibitors to clotting factors
Secondary hemophilia

     D68.312   Antiphospholipid antibody with hemorrhagic disorder
Lupus anticoagulant (LAC) with hemorrhagic disorder
Systemic lupus erythematosus [SLE] inhibitor with hemorrhagic disorder

> **Excludes1**   antiphospholipid antibody, finding without diagnosis (R76.0)
> antiphospholipid antibody syndrome (D68.61)
> antiphospholipid antibody with hypercoagulable state (D68.61)
> lupus anticoagulant (LAC) finding without diagnosis (R76.0)
> lupus anticoagulant (LAC) with hypercoagulable state (D68.62)
> systemic lupus erythematosus [SLE] inhibitor finding without diagnosis (R76.0)
> systemic lupus erythematosus [SLE] inhibitor with hypercoagulable state (D68.62)

     D68.318   Other hemorrhagic disorder due to intrinsic circulating anticoagulants, antibodies, or inhibitors
Antithromboplastinemia
Antithromboplastinogenemia
Hemorrhagic disorder due to intrinsic increase in antithrombin
Hemorrhagic disorder due to intrinsic increase in anti-VIIIa
Hemorrhagic disorder due to intrinsic increase in anti-IXa
Hemorrhagic disorder due to intrinsic increase in anti-XIa

     D68.32   Hemorrhagic disorder due to extrinsic circulating anticoagulants
Drug-induced hemorrhagic disorder
Hemorrhagic disorder due to increase in anti-IIa
Hemorrhagic disorder due to increase in anti-Xa
Hyperheparinemia

> Use additional code for adverse effect, if applicable, to identify drug (T45.515, T45.525)

Coding Clinic: 2016, Q1, P14-15

▶ New   ⇒ Revised   ~~deleted~~ Deleted   Excludes 1   Excludes 2   Includes   Use additional   Code first   Code also   Key words

OGCR Official Guidelines   **X** Assign placeholder X   ● Use Additional Character(s)   ▌ Manifestation Code   **Coding Clinic**

D68.4   Acquired coagulation factor deficiency
Deficiency of coagulation factor due to liver disease
Deficiency of coagulation factor due to vitamin K deficiency

> **Excludes1**   vitamin K deficiency of newborn (P53)

● **D68.5   Primary thrombophilia**
AKA idiopathic thrombocytopenia, may be acquired or congenital and is a common cause of coagulation disorders.
Primary hypercoagulable states

> **Excludes1**   antiphospholipid syndrome (D68.61)
> lupus anticoagulant (D68.62)
> secondary activated protein C resistance (D68.69)
> secondary antiphospholipid antibody syndrome (D68.69)
> secondary lupus anticoagulant with hypercoagulable state (D68.69)
> secondary systemic lupus erythematosus [SLE] inhibitor with hypercoagulable state (D68.69)
> systemic lupus erythematosus [SLE] inhibitor finding without diagnosis (R76.0)
> systemic lupus erythematosus [SLE] inhibitor with hemorrhagic disorder (D68.312)
> thrombotic thrombocytopenic purpura (M31.1)

D68.51   Activated protein C resistance
Factor V Leiden mutation

D68.52   Prothrombin gene mutation

D68.59   Other primary thrombophilia
Antithrombin III deficiency
Hypercoagulable state NOS
Primary hypercoagulable state NEC
Primary thrombophilia NEC
Protein C deficiency
Protein S deficiency
Thrombophilia NOS

● **D68.6   Other thrombophilia**
Other hypercoagulable states

> **Excludes1**   diffuse or disseminated intravascular coagulation [DIC] (D65)
> heparin induced thrombocytopenia (HIT) (D75.82)
> hyperhomocysteinemia (E72.11)

D68.61   Antiphospholipid syndrome
Anticardiolipin syndrome
Antiphospholipid antibody syndrome

> **Excludes1**   anti-phospholipid antibody, finding without diagnosis (R76.0)
> anti-phospholipid antibody with hemorrhagic disorder (D68.312)
> lupus anticoagulant syndrome (D68.62)

D68.62   Lupus anticoagulant syndrome
Lupus anticoagulant
Presence of systemic lupus erythematosus [SLE] inhibitor

> **Excludes1**   anticardiolipin syndrome (D68.61)
> antiphospholipid syndrome (D68.61)
> lupus anticoagulant (LAC) finding without diagnosis (R76.0)
> lupus anticoagulant (LAC) with hemorrhagic disorder (D68.312)

D68.69   Other thrombophilia
Hypercoagulable states NEC
Secondary hypercoagulable state NOS

D68.8   Other specified coagulation defects

> **Excludes1**   hemorrhagic disease of newborn (P53)

D68.9   Coagulation defect, unspecified

● **D69   Purpura and other hemorrhagic conditions**
Group of conditions characterized by small hemorrhages in skin, mucous membranes, or serosal surfaces

> **Excludes1**   benign hypergammaglobulinemic purpura (D89.0)
> cryoglobulinemic purpura (D89.1)
> essential (hemorrhagic) thrombocythemia (D47.3)
> hemorrhagic thrombocythemia (D47.3)
> purpura fulminans (D65)
> thrombotic thrombocytopenic purpura (M31.1)
> Waldenström hypergammaglobulinemic purpura (D89.0)

D69.0   Allergic purpura
Allergic vasculitis
Nonthrombocytopenic hemorrhagic purpura
Nonthrombocytopenic idiopathic purpura
Purpura anaphylactoid
Purpura Henoch(-Schönlein)
Purpura rheumatica
Vascular purpura

> **Excludes1**   thrombocytopenic hemorrhagic purpura (D69.3)

D69.1   Qualitative platelet defects
Bernard-Soulier [giant platelet] syndrome
Glanzmann's disease
Grey platelet syndrome
Thromboasthenia (hemorrhagic) (hereditary)
Thrombocytopathy

> **Excludes1**   von Willebrand's disease (D68.0)

D69.2   Other nonthrombocytopenic purpura
Purpura NOS
Purpura simplex
Senile purpura

D69.3   Immune thrombocytopenic purpura
Hemorrhagic (thrombocytopenic) purpura
Idiopathic thrombocytopenic purpura
Tidal platelet dysgenesis

● **D69.4   Other primary thrombocytopenia**

> **Excludes1**   transient neonatal thrombocytopenia (P61.0)
> Wiskott-Aldrich syndrome (D82.0)

D69.41   Evans syndrome
Acquired hemolytic anemia and thrombocytopenia

D69.42   Congenital and hereditary thrombocytopenia purpura
Congenital thrombocytopenia
Hereditary thrombocytopenia

> *Code first congenital or hereditary disorder, such as:*
> thrombocytopenia with absent radius (TAR syndrome) (Q87.2)

D69.49   Other primary thrombocytopenia
Megakaryocytic hypoplasia
Primary thrombocytopenia NOS

● **D69.5   Secondary thrombocytopenia**
Acquired reduction of number of platelets required for blood clotting

> **Excludes1**   heparin induced thrombocytopenia (HIT) (D75.82)
> transient thrombocytopenia of newborn (P61.0)

D69.51   Posttransfusion purpura
Posttransfusion purpura from whole blood (fresh) or blood products PTP

D69.59   Other secondary thrombocytopenia

D69.6   Thrombocytopenia, unspecified

D69.8   Other specified hemorrhagic conditions
Capillary fragility (hereditary)
Vascular pseudohemophilia

D69.9   Hemorrhagic condition, unspecified

CHAPTER 3 (D50-D89)

OTHER DISORDERS OF BLOOD AND BLOOD-FORMING ORGANS (D70-D77)

● **D70   Neutropenia**
Decrease in number of neutrophils (type of white blood cell)

> **Includes**   agranulocytosis
> decreased absolute neurophile count (ANC)

Use additional code for any associated:
fever (R50.81)
mucositis (J34.81, K12.3-, K92.81, N76.81)

> **Excludes1**   neutropenic splenomegaly (D73.81)
> transient neonatal neutropenia (P61.5)

D70.0   Congenital agranulocytosis
Reduced numbers of neutrophils (type of white blood cell)
Congenital neutropenia
Infantile genetic agranulocytosis
Kostmann's disease

D70.1   Agranulocytosis secondary to cancer chemotherapy
Decreased numbers of granulocytes (type of white blood cell)
Code also *underlying neoplasm*
Use additional code for adverse effect, if applicable, to identify drug (T45.1X5)

D70.2   Other drug-induced agranulocytosis
Use additional code for adverse effect, if applicable, to identify drug (T36-T50 with fifth or sixth character 5)

D70.3   Neutropenia due to infection

D70.4   Cyclic neutropenia
Chronic neutropenia (low number of type of white blood cell)
Cyclic hematopoiesis
Periodic neutropenia

D70.8   Other neutropenia

D70.9   Neutropenia, unspecified

D71   Functional disorders of polymorphonuclear neutrophils
Polymorphonuclear: varying shapes of nucleus; AKA PMNs
Cell membrane receptor complex [CR3] defect
Chronic (childhood) granulomatous disease
Congenital dysphagocytosis
Progressive septic granulomatosis

● **D72   Other disorders of white blood cells**

> **Excludes1**   basophilia (D72.824)
> immunity disorders (D80-D89)
> neutropenia (D70)
> preleukemia (syndrome) (D46.9)

D72.0   Genetic anomalies of leukocytes
Alder (granulation) (granulocyte) anomaly
Alder syndrome
Hereditary leukocytic hypersegmentation
Hereditary leukocytic hyposegmentation
Hereditary leukomelanopathy
May-Hegglin (granulation) (granulocyte) anomaly
May-Hegglin syndrome
Pelger-Huët (granulation) (granulocyte) anomaly
Pelger-Huët syndrome

> **Excludes1**   Chédiak (-Steinbrinck)-Higashi syndrome (E70.330)

D72.1   Eosinophilia
Formation and accumulation of high number of white cells in blood/tissue
Allergic eosinophilia
Hereditary eosinophilia

> **Excludes1**   Löffler's syndrome (J82)
> pulmonary eosinophilia (J82)

● **D72.8   Other specified disorders of white blood cells**

> **Excludes1**   leukemia (C91-C95)

● **D72.81   Decreased white blood cell count**

> **Excludes1**   neutropenia (D70.-)

D72.810   Lymphocytopenia
Decreased lymphocytes
Reduction in number of lympho cytes in blood

D72.818   Other decreased white blood cell count
Basophilic leukopenia
Eosinophilic leukopenia
Monocytopenia
Other decreased leukocytes
Plasmacytopenia

D72.819   Decreased white blood cell count, unspecified
Decreased leukocytes, unspecified
Leukocytopenia, unspecified
Leukopenia

> **Excludes1**   malignant leukopenia (D70.9)

● **D72.82   Elevated white blood cell count**

> **Excludes1**   eosinophilia (D72.1)

D72.820   Lymphocytosis (symptomatic)
Elevated lymphocytes
Excess of normal lymphocytes

D72.821   Monocytosis (symptomatic)

> **Excludes1**   infectious mononucleosis (B27.-)

D72.822   Plasmacytosis
Presence of excess plasma cells

D72.823   Leukemoid reaction
Basophilic leukemoid reaction
Leukemoid reaction NOS
Lymphocytic leukemoid reaction
Monocytic leukemoid reaction
Myelocytic leukemoid reaction
Neutrophilic leukemoid reaction

D72.824   Basophilia
Increase of basophils in blood

D72.825   Bandemia
Bandemia without diagnosis of specific infection
Excess number of band cells (immature white blood cells) released by bone marrow

> **Excludes1**   confirmed infection -code to infection
> leukemia (C91.-, C92.-, C93.-, C94.-, C95.-)

D72.828   Other elevated white blood cell count

D72.829   Elevated white blood cell count, unspecified
Elevated leukocytes, unspecified
Leukocytosis, unspecified

D72.89   Other specified disorders of white blood cells
Abnormality of white blood cells NEC

D72.9   Disorder of white blood cells, unspecified
Abnormal leukocyte differential NOS

▶ New   ⇒ Revised   ~~deleted~~ Deleted   Excludes 1   Excludes 2   Includes   Use additional   Code first   Code also   Key words
OGCR Official Guidelines   X Assign placeholder X   ● Use Additional Character(s)   ▸ Manifestation Code   **Coding Clinic**

● **D73   Diseases of spleen**

    D73.0   Hyposplenism
        Diminished functioning of spleen
        Atrophy of spleen
        Excludes1   asplenia (congenital) (Q89.01)
                    postsurgical absence of spleen (Z90.81)

    D73.1   Hypersplenism
        Accelerated function of spleen
        Excludes1   neutropenic splenomegaly (D73.81)
                    primary splenic neutropenia (D73.81)
                    splenitis, splenomegaly in late syphilis (A52.79)
                    splenitis, splenomegaly in tuberculosis (A18.85)
                    splenomegaly NOS (R16.1)
                    splenomegaly congenital (Q89.0)

    D73.2   Chronic congestive splenomegaly
        Enlargement of spleen

    D73.3   Abscess of spleen

    D73.4   Cyst of spleen

    D73.5   Infarction of spleen
        Splenic rupture, nontraumatic
        Torsion of spleen
        Excludes1   rupture of spleen due to Plasmodium vivax malaria (B51.0)
                    traumatic rupture of spleen (S36.03-)

● **D73.8   Other diseases of spleen**

        D73.81   Neutropenic splenomegaly
            Werner-Schultz disease
            Enlarged spleen responding to inadequate number of neutrophils

        D73.89   Other diseases of spleen
            Fibrosis of spleen NOS
            Perisplenitis
            Splenitis NOS

    D73.9   Disease of spleen, unspecified

● **D74   Methemoglobinemia**
    Excessive methemoglobin (form of hemoglobin)

    D74.0   Congenital methemoglobinemia
        Congenital NADH-methemoglobin reductase deficiency
        Hemoglobin-M [Hb-M] disease
        Methemoglobinemia, hereditary

    D74.8   Other methemoglobinemias
        Acquired methemoglobinemia (with sulfhemoglobinemia)
        Toxic methemoglobinemia

    D74.9   Methemoglobinemia, unspecified

● **D75   Other and unspecified diseases of blood and blood-forming organs**
    Excludes2   acute lymphadenitis (L04.-)
                chronic lymphadenitis (I88.1)
                enlarged lymph nodes (R59.-)
                hypergammaglobulinemia NOS (D89.2)
                lymphadenitis NOS (I88.9)
                mesenteric lymphadenitis (acute) (chronic) (I88.0)

    D75.0   Familial erythrocytosis
        Genetic mutation of gene that results in increased circulating RBCs
        Benign polycythemia
        Familial polycythemia
        Excludes1   hereditary ovalocytosis (D58.1)

    D75.1   Secondary polycythemia
        Increase in total red cell mass
        Acquired polycythemia
        Emotional polycythemia
        Erythrocytosis NOS
        Hypoxemic polycythemia
        Nephrogenous polycythemia
        Polycythemia due to erythropoietin
        Polycythemia due to fall in plasma volume
        Polycythemia due to high altitude
        Polycythemia due to stress
        Polycythemia NOS
        Relative polycythemia
        Excludes1   polycythemia neonatorum (P61.1)
                    polycythemia vera (D45)

● **D75.8   Other specified diseases of blood and blood-forming organs**

    ▸ **D75.81   *Myelofibrosis***
        Replacing bone marrow by fibrous tissue
        Myelofibrosis NOS
        Secondary myelofibrosis NOS
        Code first the underlying disorder, such as:
            malignant neoplasm of breast (C50.-)
        Use additional code, if applicable, for associated therapy-related myelodysplastic syndrome (D46.-)
        Use additional code for adverse effect, if applicable, to identify drug (T45.1X5)
        Excludes1   acute myelofibrosis (C94.4-)
                    idiopathic myelofibrosis (D47.1)
                    leukoerythroblastic anemia (D61.82)
                    myelofibrosis with myeloid metaplasia (D47.4)
                    myelophthisic anemia (D61.82)
                    myelophthisis (D61.82)
                    primary myelofibrosis (D47.1)

        D75.82   Heparin induced thrombocytopenia (HIT)

        D75.89   Other specified diseases of blood and blood-forming organs

    D75.9   Disease of blood and blood-forming organs, unspecified

● **D76   Other specified diseases with participation of lymphoreticular and reticulohistiocytic tissue**
    Excludes1   (Abt-) Letterer-Siwe disease (C96.0)
                eosinophilic granuloma (C96.6)
                Hand-Schüller-Christian disease (C96.5)
                histiocytic medullary reticulosis (C96.9)
                histiocytic sarcoma (C96.A)
                histiocytosis X, multifocal (C96.5)
                histiocytosis X, unifocal (C96.6)
                Langerhans-cell histiocytosis, multifocal (C96.5)
                Langerhans-cell histiocytosis NOS (C96.6)
                Langerhans-cell histiocytosis, unifocal (C96.6)
                leukemic reticuloendotheliosis (C91.4-)
                lipomelanotic reticulosis (I89.8)
                malignant histiocytosis (C96.A)
                malignant reticulosis (C86.0)
                nonlipid reticuloendotheliosis (C96.0)

    D76.1   Hemophagocytic lymphohistiocytosis
        Familial hemophagocytic reticulosis
        Histiocytoses of mononuclear phagocytes

    D76.2   Hemophagocytic syndrome, infection-associated
        Use additional code to identify infectious agent or disease.

    D76.3   Other histiocytosis syndromes
        Reticulohistiocytoma (giant-cell)
        Sinus histiocytosis with massive lymphadenopathy
        Xanthogranuloma

CHAPTER 3 (D50-D89)

▶ **D77 Other disorders of blood and blood-forming organs in diseases classified elsewhere**

Code first underlying disease, such as:
amyloidosis (E85.-)
congenital early syphilis (A50.0)
echinococcosis (B67.0-B67.9)
malaria (B50.0-B54)
schistosomiasis [bilharziasis] (B65.0-B65.9)
vitamin C deficiency (E54)

Excludes1 rupture of spleen due to Plasmodium vivax malaria (B51.0)
splenitis, splenomegaly in late syphilis (A52.79)
splenitis, splenomegaly in tuberculosis (A18.85)

INTRAOPERATIVE AND POSTPROCEDURAL COMPLICATIONS OF THE SPLEEN (D78)

● **D78 Intraoperative and postprocedural complications of the spleen**
Coding Clinic: 2016, Q4, P9

● **D78.0 Intraoperative hemorrhage and hematoma of the spleen complicating a procedure**

Excludes1 intraoperative hemorrhage and hematoma of the spleen due to accidental puncture or laceration during a procedure (D78.1-)

D78.01 Intraoperative hemorrhage and hematoma of the spleen complicating a procedure on the spleen

D78.02 Intraoperative hemorrhage and hematoma of the spleen complicating other procedure

● **D78.1 Accidental puncture and laceration of the spleen during a procedure**

D78.11 Accidental puncture and laceration of the spleen during a procedure on the spleen

D78.12 Accidental puncture and laceration of the spleen during other procedure

● **D78.2 Postprocedural hemorrhage of the spleen following a procedure**

D78.21 Postprocedural hemorrhage of the spleen following a procedure on the spleen

D78.22 Postprocedural hemorrhage of the spleen following other procedure

● **D78.3 Postprocedural hematoma and seroma of the spleen following a procedure**

D78.31 Postprocedural hematoma of the spleen following a procedure on the spleen

D78.32 Postprocedural hematoma of the spleen following other procedure

D78.33 Postprocedural seroma of the spleen following a procedure on the spleen

D78.34 Postprocedural seroma of the spleen following other procedure

● **D78.8 Other intraoperative and postprocedural complications of the spleen**

Use additional code, if applicable, to further specify disorder

D78.81 Other intraoperative complications of the spleen

D78.89 Other postprocedural complications of the spleen

CERTAIN DISORDERS INVOLVING THE IMMUNE MECHANISM (D80-D89)

Includes defects in the complement system
immunodeficiency disorders, except human immunodeficiency virus [HIV] disease
sarcoidosis

Excludes1 autoimmune disease (systemic) NOS (M35.9)
functional disorders of polymorphonuclear neutrophils (D71)
human immunodeficiency virus [HIV] disease (B20)

● **D80 Immunodeficiency with predominantly antibody defects**

D80.0 **Hereditary hypogammaglobulinemia**
Autosomal recessive agammaglobulinemia (Swiss type)
X-linked agammaglobulinemia [Bruton] (with growth hormone deficiency)

D80.1 **Nonfamilial hypogammaglobulinemia**
Abnormally low levels of all classes of immunoglobulins
Agammaglobulinemia with immunoglobulin-bearing B-lymphocytes
Common variable agammaglobulinemia [CVAgamma]
Hypogammaglobulinemia NOS

D80.2 Selective deficiency of immunoglobulin A [IgA]

D80.3 Selective deficiency of immunoglobulin G [IgG] subclasses

D80.4 Selective deficiency of immunoglobulin M [IgM]

D80.5 Immunodeficiency with increased immunoglobulin M [IgM]

D80.6 Antibody deficiency with near-normal immunoglobulins or with hyperimmunoglobulinemia
Abnormally high levels of immunoglobulins in serum

D80.7 Transient hypogammaglobulinemia of infancy

D80.8 Other immunodeficiencies with predominantly antibody defects
Kappa light chain deficiency

D80.9 Immunodeficiency with predominantly antibody defects, unspecified

● **D81 Combined immunodeficiencies**

Excludes1 autosomal recessive agammaglobulinemia (Swiss type) (D80.0)

D81.0 Severe combined immunodeficiency [SCID] with reticular dysgenesis

D81.1 Severe combined immunodeficiency [SCID] with low T- and B-cell numbers

D81.2 Severe combined immunodeficiency [SCID] with low or normal B-cell numbers

D81.3 Adenosine deaminase [ADA] deficiency

D81.4 Nezelof's syndrome

D81.5 Purine nucleoside phosphorylase [PNP] deficiency

D81.6 Major histocompatibility complex class I deficiency
Bare lymphocyte syndrome

D81.7 Major histocompatibility complex class II deficiency

● **D81.8   Other combined immunodeficiencies**
    ● **D81.81   Biotin-dependent carboxylase deficiency**
          Multiple carboxylase deficiency

          Excludes1   biotin-dependent carboxylase deficiency due to dietary deficiency of biotin (E53.8)

       D81.810   Biotinidase deficiency

       D81.818   Other biotin-dependent carboxylase deficiency
          Holocarboxylase synthetase deficiency
          Other multiple carboxylase deficiency

       D81.819   Biotin-dependent carboxylase deficiency, unspecified
          Multiple carboxylase deficiency, unspecified

    D81.89   Other combined immunodeficiencies

   D81.9   Combined immunodeficiency, unspecified
      Severe combined immunodeficiency disorder [SCID] NOS

● **D82   Immunodeficiency associated with other major defects**
    Excludes1   ataxia telangiectasia [Louis-Bar] (G11.3)

   D82.0   Wiskott-Aldrich syndrome
      X-linked immunodeficiency
      Immunodeficiency with thrombocytopenia and eczema

   D82.1   Di George's syndrome
      Congenital disorder with defective development of third and fourth pharyngeal pouches
      Pharyngeal pouch syndrome
      Thymic alymphoplasia
      Thymic aplasia or hypoplasia with immunodeficiency

   D82.2   Immunodeficiency with short-limbed stature

   D82.3   Immunodeficiency following hereditary defective response to Epstein-Barr virus
      X-linked lymphoproliferative disease

   D82.4   Hyperimmunoglobulin E [IgE] syndrome
      Suspected genetic defect that produces high levels of antibody immunoglobulin (IgE) that causes skin and lung infections and eczema

   D82.8   Immunodeficiency associated with other specified major defects

   D82.9   Immunodeficiency associated with major defect, unspecified

● **D83   Common variable immunodeficiency**

   D83.0   Common variable immunodeficiency with predominant abnormalities of B-cell numbers and function

   D83.1   Common variable immunodeficiency with predominant immunoregulatory T-cell disorders

   D83.2   Common variable immunodeficiency with autoantibodies to B- or T-cells

   D83.8   Other common variable immunodeficiencies

   D83.9   Common variable immunodeficiency, unspecified

● **D84   Other immunodeficiencies**

   D84.0   Lymphocyte function antigen-1 [LFA-1] defect

   D84.1   Defects in the complement system
      C1 esterase inhibitor [C1-INH] deficiency

   D84.8   Other specified immunodeficiencies

   D84.9   Immunodeficiency, unspecified

Item 3-1 Sarcoidosis: A symptom of an inflammation producing tiny lumps of cells (granulomas) in various organs, most commonly the lungs and lymph nodes, that affect organ function. Cause is unknown occurring primarily in 20- to 40-year-olds, African-American, especially women, and those of Asian, German, Irish, Scandinavian, and Puerto Rican heritage.

● **D86   Sarcoidosis**

   D86.0   Sarcoidosis of lung

   D86.1   Sarcoidosis of lymph nodes

   D86.2   Sarcoidosis of lung with sarcoidosis of lymph nodes

   D86.3   Sarcoidosis of skin

   ● **D86.8   Sarcoidosis of other sites**

       D86.81   Sarcoid meningitis

       D86.82   Multiple cranial nerve palsies in sarcoidosis

       D86.83   Sarcoid iridocyclitis
          Rare large tumor with irregular surface of iris

       D86.84   Sarcoid pyelonephritis
          Systemic disease of unknown etiology characterized by chronic granulomatous inflammation with tissue destruction of pelvis kidney
          Tubulo-interstitial nephropathy in sarcoidosis

       D86.85   Sarcoid myocarditis

       D86.86   Sarcoid arthropathy
          Polyarthritis in sarcoidosis

       D86.87   Sarcoid myositis
          Granumloma of muscle

       D86.89   Sarcoidosis of other sites
          Hepatic granuloma
          Uveoparotid fever [Heerfordt]

   D86.9   Sarcoidosis, unspecified

● **D89   Other disorders involving the immune mechanism, not elsewhere classified**
    Excludes1   hyperglobulinemia NOS (R77.1)
          monoclonal gammopathy (of undetermined significance) (D47.2)

    Excludes2   transplant failure and rejection (T86.-)

   D89.0   Polyclonal hypergammaglobulinemia
      Benign hypergammaglobulinemic purpura
      Polyclonal gammopathy NOS

   D89.1   Cryoglobulinemia
      Cryoglobulin (proteins) in blood that precipitate temperatures below 98.6° F; usually symptomatic of underlying disease
      Cryoglobulinemic purpura
      Cryoglobulinemic vasculitis
      Essential cryoglobulinemia
      Idiopathic cryoglobulinemia
      Mixed cryoglobulinemia
      Primary cryoglobulinemia
      Secondary cryoglobulinemia

   D89.2   Hypergammaglobulinemia, unspecified

   D89.3   Immune reconstitution syndrome
      Immune reconstitution inflammatory syndrome [IRIS]
      Use additional code for adverse effect, if applicable, to identify drug (T36-T50 with fifth or sixth character 5)

CHAPTER 3 (D50-D89)

● **D89.4   Mast cell activation syndrome and related disorders**

     Excludes1   aggressive systemic mastocytosis (C96.21)

                   congenital cutaneous mastocytosis (Q82.2)

                   (non-congenital) cutaneous mastocytosis (D47.01)

                   (indolent) systemic mastocytosis (D47.02)

                   malignant mast cell neoplasm (C96.2-)

                   malignant mastocytoma (C96.29)

                   mast cell leukemia (C94.3-)

                   mast cell sarcoma (C96.22)

                   mastocytoma NOS (D47.09)

                   other mast cell neoplasms of uncertain behavior (D47.09)

                   systemic mastocytosis associated with a clonal hematologic non-mast cell lineage disease (SM-AHNMD) (D47.02)

     Coding Clinic: 2016, Q4, P11

D89.40   Mast cell activation, unspecified

     Mast cell activation disorder, unspecified

     Mast cell activation syndrome, NOS

D89.41   Monoclonal mast cell activation syndrome

     Coding Clinic: 2016, Q4, P11

D89.42   Idiopathic mast cell activation syndrome

     Coding Clinic: 2016, Q4, P11

D89.43   Secondary mast cell activation

     Secondary mast cell activation syndrome

     Code also underlying etiology, if known

     Coding Clinic: 2016, Q4, P11

D89.49   Other mast cell activation disorder

     Other mast cell activation syndrome

     Coding Clinic: 2016, Q4, P11

● **D89.8   Other specified disorders involving the immune mechanism, not elsewhere classified**

● **D89.81   Graft-versus-host disease**

     Code first underlying cause, such as:

       complications of transplanted organs and tissue (T86.-)

       complications of blood transfusion (T80.89)

     Use additional code to identify associated manifestations, such as:

     desquamative dermatitis (L30.8)

     diarrhea (R19.7)

     elevated bilirubin (R17)

     hair loss (L65.9)

     D89.810   Acute graft-versus-host disease

     D89.811   Chronic graft-versus-host disease

     D89.812   Acute on chronic graft-versus-host disease

     D89.813   Graft-versus-host disease, unspecified

D89.82   Autoimmune lymphoproliferative syndrome [ALPS]

D89.89   Other specified disorders involving the immune mechanism, not elsewhere classified

     Excludes1   human immunodeficiency virus disease (B20)

     Coding Clinic: 2017, Q4, P109

D89.9   Disorder involving the immune mechanism, unspecified

     Immune disease NOS

     Coding Clinic: 2015, Q3, P22

CHAPTER 4

ENDOCRINE, NUTRITIONAL AND METABOLIC DISEASES (E00-E89)

OGCR Chapter-Specific Coding Guidelines

4. Chapter 4: Endocrine, Nutritional, and Metabolic Diseases (E00-E89)

a. Diabetes mellitus

The diabetes mellitus codes are combination codes that include the type of diabetes mellitus, the body system affected, and the complications affecting that body system. As many codes within a particular category as are necessary to describe all of the complications of the disease may be used. They should be sequenced based on the reason for a particular encounter. Assign as many codes from categories E08 – E13 as needed to identify all of the associated conditions that the patient has.

1) Type of diabetes

The age of a patient is not the sole determining factor, though most type 1 diabetics develop the condition before reaching puberty. For this reason type 1 diabetes mellitus is also referred to as juvenile diabetes.

2) Type of diabetes mellitus not documented

If the type of diabetes mellitus is not documented in the medical record the default is E11.-, Type 2 diabetes mellitus.

3) Diabetes mellitus and the use of insulin oral hypoglycemics

If the documentation in a medical record does not indicate the type of diabetes but does indicate that the patient uses insulin, code E11, Type 2 diabetes mellitus, should be assigned. An additional code should be assigned from category Z79 to identify the long-term (current) use of insulin or oral hypoglycemic drugs. If the patient is treated with both oral medications and insulin, only the code for long-term (current) use of insulin should be assigned. Code Z79.4 should not be assigned if insulin is given temporarily to bring a type 2 patient's blood sugar under control during an encounter.

4) Diabetes mellitus in pregnancy and gestational diabetes

See Section I.C.15. Diabetes mellitus in pregnancy.
See Section I.C.15. Gestational (pregnancy induced) diabetes

5) Complications due to insulin pump malfunction

(a) Underdose of insulin due to insulin pump failure

An underdose of insulin due to an insulin pump failure should be assigned to a code from subcategory T85.6, Mechanical complication of other specified internal and external prosthetic devices, implants and grafts, that specifies the type of pump malfunction, as the principal or first-listed code, followed by code T38.3X6-, Underdosing of insulin and oral hypoglycemic

[antidiabetic] drugs. Additional codes for the type of diabetes mellitus and any associated complications due to the underdosing should also be assigned.

(b) Overdose of insulin due to insulin pump failure

The principal or first-listed code for an encounter due to an insulin pump malfunction resulting in an overdose of insulin, should also be T85.6-, Mechanical complication of other specified internal and external prosthetic devices, implants and grafts, followed by code T38.3X1-, Poisoning by insulin and oral hypoglycemic [antidiabetic] drugs, accidental (unintentional).

6) Secondary diabetes mellitus

Codes under categories E08, Diabetes mellitus due to underlying condition, E09, Drug or chemical induced diabetes mellitus and E13, Other specified diabetes mellitus, identify complications/ manifestations associated with secondary diabetes mellitus. Secondary diabetes is always caused by another condition or event (e.g., cystic fibrosis, malignant neoplasm of pancreas, pancreatectomy, adverse effect of drug, or poisoning).

(a) Secondary diabetes mellitus and the use of insulin or hypoglycemic drugs

For patients with secondary diabetes mellitus who routinely use insulin or oral hypoglycemic drugs, an additional code from category Z79 should be assigned to identify the long-term (current) use of insulin or oral hypoglycemic drugs. If the patient is treated with both oral medications and insulin, only the code for long-term (current) use of insulin should be assigned. Code Z79.4 should not be assigned if insulin is given temporarily to bring a type 2 patient's blood sugar under control during an encounter.

(b) Assigning and sequencing secondary diabetes codes and its causes

The sequencing of the secondary diabetes codes in relationship to codes for the cause of the diabetes is based on the Tabular List instructions for categories E08, E09 and E13.

(i) Secondary diabetes mellitus due to pancreatectomy
For postpancreatectomy diabetes mellitus (lack of insulin due to the surgical removal of all or part of the pancreas), assign code E89.1, Postprocedural hypoinsulinemia. Assign a code from category E13 and a code from subcategory Z90.41-, Acquired absence of pancreas, as additional codes.

(ii) Secondary diabetes due to drugs
Secondary diabetes may be caused by an adverse effect of correctly administered medications, poisoning or sequela of poisoning.

See Section I.C.19.e for coding of adverse effects and poisoning, and Section I.C.20 for external cause code reporting.

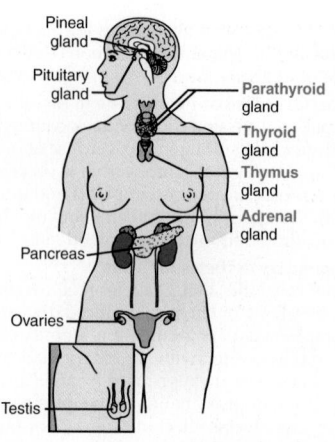

Figure 4-1 The endocrine system. (From Buck CJ: Step-by-Step Medical Coding, ed 2016, St. Louis, Elsevier, 2016)

CHAPTER 4

ENDOCRINE, NUTRITIONAL AND METABOLIC DISEASES (E00-E89)

All neoplasms, whether functionally active or not, are classified in Chapter 2. Appropriate codes in this chapter (i.e., E05.8, E07.0, E16-E31, E34.-) may be used as additional codes to indicate either functional activity by neoplasms and ectopic endocrine tissue or hyperfunction and hypofunction of endocrine glands associated with neoplasms and other conditions classified elsewhere.

Excludes1 transitory endocrine and metabolic disorders specific to newborn (P70-P74)

This chapter contains the following blocks:

E00-E07	Disorders of thyroid gland
E08-E13	Diabetes mellitus
E15-E16	Other disorders of glucose regulation and pancreatic internal secretion
E20-E35	Disorders of other endocrine glands
E36	Intraoperative complications of endocrine system
E40-E46	Malnutrition
E50-E64	Other nutritional deficiencies
E65-E68	Overweight, obesity and other hyperalimentation
E70-E88	Metabolic disorders
E89	Postprocedural endocrine and metabolic complications and disorders, not elsewhere classified

DISORDERS OF THYROID GLAND (E00-E07)

● **E00**   **Congenital iodine-deficiency syndrome**

Use additional code (F70-F79) to identify associated intellectual disabilities.

Excludes1 subclinical iodine-deficiency hypothyroidism (E02)

E00.0   **Congenital iodine-deficiency syndrome, neurological type**
Endemic cretinism, neurological type

E00.1   **Congenital iodine-deficiency syndrome, myxedematous type**
Dry, waxy type of swelling (nonpitting edema) with abnormal deposits of mucin in skin (mucinosis) and other tissues
Endemic hypothyroid cretinism
Endemic cretinism, myxedematous type

E00.2   **Congenital iodine-deficiency syndrome, mixed type**
Endemic cretinism, mixed type

E00.9   **Congenital iodine-deficiency syndrome, unspecified**
Congenital iodine-deficiency hypothyroidism NOS
Endemic cretinism NOS

Figure 4-2 Goiter is an enlargement of the thyroid gland.

Item 4–1 Simple goiter indicates no nodules are present. The most common type of goiter is a **diffuse colloidal,** also called a **nontoxic** or **endemic** goiter.

● **E01**   **Iodine-deficiency related thyroid disorders and allied conditions**

Excludes1 congenital iodine-deficiency syndrome (E00.-)
subclinical iodine-deficiency hypothyroidism (E02)

E01.0   **Iodine-deficiency related diffuse (endemic) goiter**
Thyroid gland is enlarged

E01.1   **Iodine-deficiency related multinodular (endemic) goiter**
Iodine-deficiency related nodular goiter

E01.2   **Iodine-deficiency related (endemic) goiter, unspecified**
Endemic goiter NOS

E01.8   **Other iodine-deficiency related thyroid disorders and allied conditions**
Acquired iodine-deficiency hypothyroidism NOS

E02   **Subclinical iodine-deficiency hypothyroidism**

● **E03**   **Other hypothyroidism**

Excludes1 iodine-deficiency related hypothyroidism (E00-E02)
postprocedural hypothyroidism (E89.0)

E03.0   **Congenital hypothyroidism with diffuse goiter**
Congenital parenchymatous goiter (nontoxic)
Congenital goiter (nontoxic) NOS

Excludes1 transitory congenital goiter with normal function (P72.0)

E03.1   **Congenital hypothyroidism without goiter**
Aplasia of thyroid (with myxedema)
Congenital atrophy of thyroid
Congenital hypothyroidism NOS

E03.2   **Hypothyroidism due to medicaments and other exogenous substances**
Code first poisoning due to drug or toxin, if applicable (T36-T65 with fifth or sixth character 1-4 or 6)
Use additional code for adverse effect, if applicable, to identify drug (T36-T50 with fifth or sixth character 5)

E03.3   **Postinfectious hypothyroidism**

E03.4   **Atrophy of thyroid (acquired)**
Excludes1 congenital atrophy of thyroid (E03.1)

E03.5   **Myxedema coma**
Often fatal complication of long-term hypothyroidism

E03.8   **Other specified hypothyroidism**

E03.9   **Hypothyroidism, unspecified**
Myxedema NOS

Item 4–2 Hypothyroidism is a condition in which there are insufficient levels of thyroxine. **Cretinism** is congenital hypothyroidism, which can result in mental and physical retardation.

● **E04** **Other nontoxic goiter**

    Excludes1 congenital goiter (NOS) (diffuse)
                    (parenchymatous) (E03.0)
                    iodine-deficiency related goiter (E00-E02)

  E04.0 **Nontoxic diffuse goiter**
        Thyroid gland is enlarged
        Diffuse (colloid) nontoxic goiter
        Simple nontoxic goiter

  E04.1 **Nontoxic single thyroid nodule**
        Colloid nodule (cystic) (thyroid)
        Nontoxic uninodular goiter
        Thyroid (cystic) nodule NOS

  E04.2 **Nontoxic multinodular goiter**
        Enlarged thyroid gland with multiple nodules
        Cystic goiter NOS
        Multinodular (cystic) goiter NOS

  E04.8 **Other specified nontoxic goiter**

  E04.9 **Nontoxic goiter, unspecified**
        Goiter NOS
        Nodular goiter (nontoxic) NOS

● **E05** **Thyrotoxicosis [hyperthyroidism]**
    Enlarged thyroid gland with multiple nodules

    Excludes1 chronic thyroiditis with transient thyrotoxicosis
                    (E06.2)
                    neonatal thyrotoxicosis (P72.1)

● **E05.0** **Thyrotoxicosis with diffuse goiter**
        Exophthalmic or toxic goiter NOS
        Graves' disease
        Toxic diffuse goiter

    E05.00 **Thyrotoxicosis with diffuse goiter without
                 thyrotoxic crisis or storm**

    E05.01 **Thyrotoxicosis with diffuse goiter with
                 thyrotoxic crisis or storm**

● **E05.1** **Thyrotoxicosis with toxic single thyroid nodule**
        Thyrotoxicosis with toxic uninodular goiter

    E05.10 **Thyrotoxicosis with toxic single thyroid nodule
                 without thyrotoxic crisis or storm**

    E05.11 **Thyrotoxicosis with toxic single thyroid nodule
                 with thyrotoxic crisis or storm**

● **E05.2** **Thyrotoxicosis with toxic multinodular goiter**
        Toxic nodular goiter NOS

    E05.20 **Thyrotoxicosis with toxic multinodular goiter
                 without thyrotoxic crisis or storm**

    E05.21 **Thyrotoxicosis with toxic multinodular goiter
                 with thyrotoxic crisis or storm**

● **E05.3** **Thyrotoxicosis from ectopic thyroid tissue**

    E05.30 **Thyrotoxicosis from ectopic thyroid tissue
                 without thyrotoxic crisis or storm**

    E05.31 **Thyrotoxicosis from ectopic thyroid tissue with
                 thyrotoxic crisis or storm**

● **E05.4** **Thyrotoxicosis factitia**

    E05.40 **Thyrotoxicosis factitia without thyrotoxic crisis
                 or storm**

    E05.41 **Thyrotoxicosis factitia with thyrotoxic crisis or
                 storm**

● **E05.8** **Other thyrotoxicosis**
        Overproduction of thyroid-stimulating hormone

    E05.80 **Other thyrotoxicosis without thyrotoxic crisis or
                 storm**

    E05.81 **Other thyrotoxicosis with thyrotoxic crisis or
                 storm**

● **E05.9** **Thyrotoxicosis, unspecified**
        Hyperthyroidism NOS

    E05.90 **Thyrotoxicosis, unspecified without thyrotoxic
                 crisis or storm**

    E05.91 **Thyrotoxicosis, unspecified with thyrotoxic
                 crisis or storm**

● **E06** **Thyroiditis**
    *An inflammation of the thyroid gland which results in an inability to
    convert iodine into thyroid hormone*

    Excludes1 postpartum thyroiditis (O90.5)

  E06.0 **Acute thyroiditis**
        Abscess of thyroid
        Pyogenic thyroiditis
        Suppurative thyroiditis
        Use additional code (B95-B97) to identify infectious
            agent.

  E06.1 **Subacute thyroiditis**
        *Inflammation of thyroid gland following viral upper
           respiratory infection*
        de Quervain thyroiditis
        Giant-cell thyroiditis
        Granulomatous thyroiditis
        Nonsuppurative thyroiditis
        Viral thyroiditis

      Excludes1 autoimmune thyroiditis (E06.3)

  E06.2 **Chronic thyroiditis with transient thyrotoxicosis**
        *Chronic inflammation of thyroid gland with intermittent
           overproduction of thyroid hormone*

      Excludes1 autoimmune thyroiditis (E06.3)

  E06.3 **Autoimmune thyroiditis**
        Hashimoto's thyroiditis
        Hashitoxicosis (transient)
        Lymphadenoid goiter
        Lymphocytic thyroiditis
        Struma lymphomatosa

  E06.4 **Drug-induced thyroiditis**
        Use additional code for adverse effect, if applicable,
           to identify drug (T36-T50 with fifth or sixth
           character 5)

  E06.5 **Other chronic thyroiditis**
        Chronic fibrous thyroiditis
        Chronic thyroiditis NOS
        Ligneous thyroiditis
        Riedel thyroiditis

  E06.9 **Thyroiditis, unspecified**

● **E07** **Other disorders of thyroid**

  E07.0 **Hypersecretion of calcitonin**
        C-cell hyperplasia of thyroid
        Hypersecretion of thyrocalcitonin

  E07.1 **Dyshormogenetic goiter**
        *Group of several types of goiter resulting from enzyme defects
           in hormone synthesis*
        Familial dyshormogenetic goiter
        Pendred's syndrome

      Excludes1 transitory congenital goiter with normal
                    function (P72.0)

● **E07.8** **Other specified disorders of thyroid**

    E07.81 **Sick-euthyroid syndrome**
            Euthyroid sick-syndrome

    E07.89 **Other specified disorders of thyroid**
            Abnormality of thyroid-binding globulin
            Hemorrhage of thyroid
            Infarction of thyroid

  E07.9 **Disorder of thyroid, unspecified**

Figure 4-3 **Graves' disease.** In Graves' disease, exophthalmos often looks more pronounced than it actually is because of the extreme lid retraction that may occur. This patient, for instance, had minimal proptosis of the left eye but marked lid retraction. (From Lissauer T, Clayden G, and Craft A: Illustrated Textbook of Paediatrics, Edinburgh, Mosby, 2015)

Item 4-3 **Thyrotoxicosis** is a condition caused by excessive amounts of the thyroid hormone thyroxine production or hyperthyroidism. **Graves' disease is associated with hyperthyroidism** (known as **Basedow's disease** in Europe).

CHAPTER 4 (E00-E90)

OGCR Section I.C.4.a.

Diabetes mellitus

The diabetes mellitus codes are combination codes that include the type of diabetes mellitus, body system affected, and the complications affecting that body system. As many codes within a particular category as are necessary to describe all of the complications of the disease may be used. They should be sequenced based on the reason for a particular visit. Assign as many codes from categories E08–E13 as needed to identify all of the associated conditions that the patient has.

DIABETES MELLITUS (E08-E13)

A metabolic disease that results in persistent hyperglycemia.
Coding Clinic: 2016, Q4, P142

● **E08**   **Diabetes mellitus due to underlying condition**

     Code first the underlying condition, such as:
         congenital rubella (P35.0)
         Cushing's syndrome (E24.-)
         cystic fibrosis (E84.-)
         malignant neoplasm (C00-C96)
         malnutrition (E40-E46)
         pancreatitis and other diseases of the pancreas (K85-K86.-)

     Use additional code to identify control using:
         insulin (Z79.4)
         oral antidiabetic drugs (Z79.84)
         oral hypoglycemic drugs (Z79.84)

     Excludes1   drug or chemical induced diabetes mellitus
                     (E09.-)
                gestational diabetes (O24.4-)
                neonatal diabetes mellitus (P70.2)
                postpancreatectomy diabetes mellitus (E13.-)
                postprocedural diabetes mellitus (E13.-)
                secondary diabetes mellitus NEC (E13.-)
                type 1 diabetes mellitus (E10.-)
                type 2 diabetes mellitus (E11.-)

● **E08.0**   **Diabetes mellitus due to underlying condition with hyperosmolarity**

   ▶ *E08.00*   *Diabetes mellitus due to underlying condition with hyperosmolarity without nonketotic hyperglycemic-hyperosmolar coma (NKHHC)*

   ▶ *E08.01*   *Diabetes mellitus due to underlying condition with hyperosmolarity with coma*

● **E08.1**   **Diabetes mellitus due to underlying condition with ketoacidosis**

   ▶ *E08.10*   *Diabetes mellitus due to underlying condition with ketoacidosis without coma*

   ▶ *E08.11*   *Diabetes mellitus due to underlying condition with ketoacidosis with coma*

● **E08.2**   **Diabetes mellitus due to underlying condition with kidney complications**

   ▶ *E08.21*   *Diabetes mellitus due to underlying condition with diabetic nephropathy*
             Diabetes mellitus due to underlying condition with intercapillary glomerulosclerosis
             Diabetes mellitus due to underlying condition with intracapillary glomerulonephrosis
             Diabetes mellitus due to underlying condition with Kimmelstiel-Wilson disease

   ▶ *E08.22*   *Diabetes mellitus due to underlying condition with diabetic chronic kidney disease*
             Use additional code to identify stage of chronic kidney disease (N18.1-N18.6)

   ▶ *E08.29*   *Diabetes mellitus due to underlying condition with other diabetic kidney complication*
             Renal tubular degeneration in diabetes mellitus due to underlying condition

● **E08.3**   **Diabetes mellitus due to underlying condition with ophthalmic complications**
     Changes in blood vessels of retina in which blood vessels swell and leak fluid into retinal surface.
     Coding Clinic: 2016, Q4, P11

   ● **E08.31**   **Diabetes mellitus due to underlying condition with unspecified diabetic retinopathy**

     ▶ *E08.311*   *Diabetes mellitus due to underlying condition with unspecified diabetic retinopathy with macular edema*

     ▶ *E08.319*   *Diabetes mellitus due to underlying condition with unspecified diabetic retinopathy without macular edema*

   ● **E08.32**   **Diabetes mellitus due to underlying condition with mild nonproliferative diabetic retinopathy**
     Diabetes mellitus due to underlying condition with nonproliferative diabetic retinopathy NOS

     One of the following 7th characters is to be assigned to codes in subcategory E08.32 to designate laterality of the disease:

1	right eye
2	left eye
3	bilateral
9	unspecified eye

   ●▶ *E08.321*   *Diabetes mellitus due to underlying condition with mild nonproliferative diabetic retinopathy with macular edema*

   ●▶ *E08.329*   *Diabetes mellitus due to underlying condition with mild nonproliferative diabetic retinopathy without macular edema*

   ● **E08.33**   **Diabetes mellitus due to underlying condition with moderate nonproliferative diabetic retinopathy**

     One of the following 7th characters is to be assigned to codes in subcategory E08.33 to designate laterality of the disease:

1	right eye
2	left eye
3	bilateral
9	unspecified eye

   ●▶ *E08.331*   *Diabetes mellitus due to underlying condition with moderate nonproliferative diabetic retinopathy with macular edema*

   ●▶ *E08.339*   *Diabetes mellitus due to underlying condition with moderate nonproliferative diabetic retinopathy without macular edema*

   ● **E08.34**   **Diabetes mellitus due to underlying condition with severe nonproliferative diabetic retinopathy**

     One of the following 7th characters is to be assigned to codes in subcategory E08.34 to designate laterality of the disease:

1	right eye
2	left eye
3	bilateral
9	unspecified eye

   ●▶ *E08.341*   *Diabetes mellitus due to underlying condition with severe nonproliferative diabetic retinopathy with macular edema*

   ●▶ *E08.349*   *Diabetes mellitus due to underlying condition with severe nonproliferative diabetic retinopathy without macular edema*

▶ New   ⇒ Revised   ~~deleted~~ Deleted   Excludes 1   Excludes 2   Includes   Use additional   Code first   Code also   Key words

OGCR Official Guidelines   X Assign placeholder X   ● Use Additional Character(s)   ▶ Manifestation Code   **Coding Clinic**

● **E08.35 Diabetes mellitus due to underlying condition with proliferative diabetic retinopathy**

One of the following 7th characters is to be assigned to codes in subcategory E08.35 to designate laterality of the disease:

1	right eye
2	left eye
3	bilateral
9	unspecified eye

● *E08.351 Diabetes mellitus due to underlying condition with proliferative diabetic retinopathy with macular edema*

● *E08.352 Diabetes mellitus due to underlying condition with proliferative diabetic retinopathy with traction retinal detachment involving the macula*

● *E08.353 Diabetes mellitus due to underlying condition with proliferative diabetic retinopathy with traction retinal detachment not involving the macula*

● *E08.354 Diabetes mellitus due to underlying condition with proliferative diabetic retinopathy with combined traction retinal detachment and rhegmatogenous retinal detachment*

● *E08.355 Diabetes mellitus due to underlying condition with stable proliferative diabetic retinopathy*

● *E08.359 Diabetes mellitus due to underlying condition with proliferative diabetic retinopathy without macular edema*

▮ *E08.36 Diabetes mellitus due to underlying condition with diabetic cataract*

X ● *E08.37 Diabetes mellitus due to underlying condition with diabetic macular edema, resolved following treatment*

One of the following 7th characters is to be assigned to code E08.37 to designate laterality of the disease:

1	right eye
2	left eye
3	bilateral
9	unspecified eye

▮ *E08.39 Diabetes mellitus due to underlying condition with other diabetic ophthalmic complication*

Use additional code to identify manifestation, such as:
diabetic glaucoma (H40-H42)

● **E08.4 Diabetes mellitus due to underlying condition with neurological complications**

▮ *E08.40 Diabetes mellitus due to underlying condition with diabetic neuropathy, unspecified*

▮ *E08.41 Diabetes mellitus due to underlying condition with diabetic mononeuropathy*

▮ *E08.42 Diabetes mellitus due to underlying condition with diabetic polyneuropathy*
Diabetes mellitus due to underlying condition with diabetic neuralgia

▮ *E08.43 Diabetes mellitus due to underlying condition with diabetic autonomic (poly)neuropathy*
Diabetes mellitus due to underlying condition with diabetic gastroparesis

▮ *E08.44 Diabetes mellitus due to underlying condition with diabetic amyotrophy*

▮ *E08.49 Diabetes mellitus due to underlying condition with other diabetic neurological complication*

● **E08.5 Diabetes mellitus due to underlying condition with circulatory complications**

▮ *E08.51 Diabetes mellitus due to underlying condition with diabetic peripheral angiopathy without gangrene*

▮ *E08.52 Diabetes mellitus due to underlying condition with diabetic peripheral angiopathy with gangrene*
Diabetes mellitus due to underlying condition with diabetic gangrene

▮ *E08.59 Diabetes mellitus due to underlying condition with other circulatory complications*

● **E08.6 Diabetes mellitus due to underlying condition with other specified complications**

● **E08.61 Diabetes mellitus due to underlying condition with diabetic arthropathy**

▮ *E08.610 Diabetes mellitus due to underlying condition with diabetic neuropathic arthropathy*
Diabetes mellitus due to underlying condition with Charcôt's joints

▮ *E08.618 Diabetes mellitus due to underlying condition with other diabetic arthropathy*

● **E08.62 Diabetes mellitus due to underlying condition with skin complications**

▮ *E08.620 Diabetes mellitus due to underlying condition with diabetic dermatitis*
Diabetes mellitus due to underlying condition with diabetic necrobiosis lipoidica

▮ *E08.621 Diabetes mellitus due to underlying condition with foot ulcer*
Use additional code to identify site of ulcer (L97.4-, L97.5-)

▮ *E08.622 Diabetes mellitus due to underlying condition with other skin ulcer*
Use additional code to identify site of ulcer (L97.1-L97.9, L98.41-L98.49)

▮ *E08.628 Diabetes mellitus due to underlying condition with other skin complications*

● **E08.63 Diabetes mellitus due to underlying condition with oral complications**

▮ *E08.630 Diabetes mellitus due to underlying condition with periodontal disease*

▮ *E08.638 Diabetes mellitus due to underlying condition with other oral complications*

● **E08.64 Diabetes mellitus due to underlying condition with hypoglycemia**

▮ *E08.641 Diabetes mellitus due to underlying condition with hypoglycemia with coma*

▮ *E08.649 Diabetes mellitus due to underlying condition with hypoglycemia without coma*

▮ *E08.65 Diabetes mellitus due to underlying condition with hyperglycemia*

▮ *E08.69 Diabetes mellitus due to underlying condition with other specified complication*
Use additional code to identify complication

▮ *E08.8 Diabetes mellitus due to underlying condition with unspecified complications*

▮ *E08.9 Diabetes mellitus due to underlying condition without complications*

CHAPTER 4 (E00-E90)

● **E09**   **Drug or chemical induced diabetes mellitus**

Code first poisoning due to drug or toxin, if applicable (T36-T65 with fifth or sixth character 1-4 or 6)

Use additional code for adverse effect, if applicable, to identify drug (T36-T50 with fifth or sixth character 5)

Use additional code to identify control using:
insulin (Z79.4)
oral antidiabetic drugs (Z79.84)
oral hypoglycemic drugs (Z79.84)

Excludes1   diabetes mellitus due to underlying condition (E08.-)
gestational diabetes (O24.4-)
neonatal diabetes mellitus (P70.2)
postpancreatectomy diabetes mellitus (E13.-)
postprocedural diabetes mellitus (E13.-)
secondary diabetes mellitus NEC (E13.-)
type 1 diabetes mellitus (E10.-)
type 2 diabetes mellitus (E11.-)

● **E09.0**   **Drug or chemical induced diabetes mellitus with hyperosmolarity**

    E09.00   **Drug or chemical induced diabetes mellitus with hyperosmolarity without nonketotic hyperglycemic-hyperosmolar coma (NKHHC)**

    E09.01   **Drug or chemical induced diabetes mellitus with hyperosmolarity with coma**

● **E09.1**   **Drug or chemical induced diabetes mellitus with ketoacidosis**

    E09.10   **Drug or chemical induced diabetes mellitus with ketoacidosis without coma**

    E09.11   **Drug or chemical induced diabetes mellitus with ketoacidosis with coma**

● **E09.2**   **Drug or chemical induced diabetes mellitus with kidney complications**

    E09.21   **Drug or chemical induced diabetes mellitus with diabetic nephropathy**
Drug or chemical induced diabetes mellitus with intercapillary glomerulosclerosis
Drug or chemical induced diabetes mellitus with intracapillary glomerulonephrosis
Drug or chemical induced diabetes mellitus with Kimmelstiel-Wilson disease

    E09.22   **Drug or chemical induced diabetes mellitus with diabetic chronic kidney disease**
Use additional code to identify stage of chronic kidney disease (N18.1-N18.6)

    E09.29   **Drug or chemical induced diabetes mellitus with other diabetic kidney complication**
Drug or chemical induced diabetes mellitus with renal tubular degeneration

● **E09.3**   **Drug or chemical induced diabetes mellitus with ophthalmic complications**
Coding Clinic: 2016, Q4, P11

  ● **E09.31**   **Drug or chemical induced diabetes mellitus with unspecified diabetic retinopathy**

      E09.311   **Drug or chemical induced diabetes mellitus with unspecified diabetic retinopathy with macular edema**

      E09.319   **Drug or chemical induced diabetes mellitus with unspecified diabetic retinopathy without macular edema**

● **E09.32**   **Drug or chemical induced diabetes mellitus with mild nonproliferative diabetic retinopathy**
Drug or chemical induced diabetes mellitus with nonproliferative diabetic retinopathy NOS

One of the following 7th characters is to be assigned to codes in subcategory E09.32 to designate laterality of the disease:

1	right eye
2	left eye
3	bilateral
9	unspecified eye

  ● **E09.321**   **Drug or chemical induced diabetes mellitus with mild nonproliferative diabetic retinopathy with macular edema**

  ● **E09.329**   **Drug or chemical induced diabetes mellitus with mild nonproliferative diabetic retinopathy without macular edema**

● **E09.33**   **Drug or chemical induced diabetes mellitus with moderate nonproliferative diabetic retinopathy**

One of the following 7th characters is to be assigned to codes in subcategory E09.33 to designate laterality of the disease:

1	right eye
2	left eye
3	bilateral
9	unspecified eye

  ● **E09.331**   **Drug or chemical induced diabetes mellitus with moderate nonproliferative diabetic retinopathy with macular edema**

  ● **E09.339**   **Drug or chemical induced diabetes mellitus with moderate nonproliferative diabetic retinopathy without macular edema**

● **E09.34**   **Drug or chemical induced diabetes mellitus with severe nonproliferative diabetic retinopathy**

One of the following 7th characters is to be assigned to codes in subcategory E09.34 to designate laterality of the disease:

1	right eye
2	left eye
3	bilateral
9	unspecified eye

  ● **E09.341**   **Drug or chemical induced diabetes mellitus with severe nonproliferative diabetic retinopathy with macular edema**

  ● **E09.349**   **Drug or chemical induced diabetes mellitus with severe nonproliferative diabetic retinopathy without macular edema**

▶ New   ⇛ Revised   ~~deleted~~ Deleted   Excludes 1   Excludes 2   Includes   Use additional   Code first   Code also   Key words

OGCR Official Guidelines   X Assign placeholder X   ● Use Additional Character(s)   ▶ Manifestation Code   **Coding Clinic**

● **E09.35**   **Drug or chemical induced diabetes mellitus with proliferative diabetic retinopathy**

One of the following 7th characters is to be assigned to codes in subcategory E09.35 to designate laterality of the disease:

1	right eye
2	left eye
3	bilateral
9	unspecified eye

  ● **E09.351**   **Drug or chemical induced diabetes mellitus with proliferative diabetic retinopathy with macular edema**

  ● **E09.352**   **Drug or chemical induced diabetes mellitus with proliferative diabetic retinopathy with traction retinal detachment involving the macula**

  ● **E09.353**   **Drug or chemical induced diabetes mellitus with proliferative diabetic retinopathy with traction retinal detachment not involving the macula**

  ● **E09.354**   **Drug or chemical induced diabetes mellitus with proliferative diabetic retinopathy with combined traction retinal detachment and rhegmatogenous retinal detachment**

  ● **E09.355**   **Drug or chemical induced diabetes mellitus with stable proliferative diabetic retinopathy**

  ● **E09.359**   **Drug or chemical induced diabetes mellitus with proliferative diabetic retinopathy without macular edema**

  E09.36   **Drug or chemical induced diabetes mellitus with diabetic cataract**

X ● **E09.37**   **Drug or chemical induced diabetes mellitus with diabetic macular edema, resolved following treatment**

One of the following 7th characters is to be assigned to code E09.37 to designate laterality of the disease:

1	right eye
2	left eye
3	bilateral
9	unspecified eye

  E09.39   **Drug or chemical induced diabetes mellitus with other diabetic ophthalmic complication**

Use additional code to identify manifestation, such as:
    diabetic glaucoma (H40-H42)

● **E09.4**   **Drug or chemical induced diabetes mellitus with neurological complications**

  E09.40   **Drug or chemical induced diabetes mellitus with neurological complications with diabetic neuropathy, unspecified**

  E09.41   **Drug or chemical induced diabetes mellitus with neurological complications with diabetic mononeuropathy**

  E09.42   **Drug or chemical induced diabetes mellitus with neurological complications with diabetic polyneuropathy**

Drug or chemical induced diabetes mellitus with diabetic neuralgia

  E09.43   **Drug or chemical induced diabetes mellitus with neurological complications with diabetic autonomic (poly)neuropathy**

Drug or chemical induced diabetes mellitus with diabetic gastroparesis

  E09.44   **Drug or chemical induced diabetes mellitus with neurological complications with diabetic amyotrophy**

  E09.49   **Drug or chemical induced diabetes mellitus with neurological complications with other diabetic neurological complication**

● **E09.5**   **Drug or chemical induced diabetes mellitus with circulatory complications**

  E09.51   **Drug or chemical induced diabetes mellitus with diabetic peripheral angiopathy without gangrene**

  E09.52   **Drug or chemical induced diabetes mellitus with diabetic peripheral angiopathy with gangrene**

Drug or chemical induced diabetes mellitus with diabetic gangrene

  E09.59   **Drug or chemical induced diabetes mellitus with other circulatory complications**

● **E09.6**   **Drug or chemical induced diabetes mellitus with other specified complications**

  ● **E09.61**   **Drug or chemical induced diabetes mellitus with diabetic arthropathy**

    E09.610   **Drug or chemical induced diabetes mellitus with diabetic neuropathic arthropathy**

Drug or chemical induced diabetes mellitus with Charcôt's joints

Progressive degeneration of weight-bearing joint

    E09.618   **Drug or chemical induced diabetes mellitus with other diabetic arthropathy**

  ● **E09.62**   **Drug or chemical induced diabetes mellitus with skin complications**

    E09.620   **Drug or chemical induced diabetes mellitus with diabetic dermatitis**

Drug or chemical induced diabetes mellitus with diabetic necrobiosis lipoidica

Necrotizing skin condition

    E09.621   **Drug or chemical induced diabetes mellitus with foot ulcer**

Use additional code to identify site of ulcer (L97.4-, L97.5-)

    E09.622   **Drug or chemical induced diabetes mellitus with other skin ulcer**

Use additional code to identify site of ulcer (L97.1-L97.9, L98.41-L98.49)

    E09.628   **Drug or chemical induced diabetes mellitus with other skin complications**

  ● **E09.63**   **Drug or chemical induced diabetes mellitus with oral complications**

    E09.630   **Drug or chemical induced diabetes mellitus with periodontal disease**

    E09.638   **Drug or chemical induced diabetes mellitus with other oral complications**

  ● **E09.64**   **Drug or chemical induced diabetes mellitus with hypoglycemia**

    E09.641   **Drug or chemical induced diabetes mellitus with hypoglycemia with coma**

    E09.649   **Drug or chemical induced diabetes mellitus with hypoglycemia without coma**

    E09.65   **Drug or chemical induced diabetes mellitus with hyperglycemia**

    E09.69   **Drug or chemical induced diabetes mellitus with other specified complication**

Use additional code to identify complication

  E09.8   **Drug or chemical induced diabetes mellitus with unspecified complications**

  E09.9   **Drug or chemical induced diabetes mellitus without complications**

● **E10**   **Type 1 diabetes mellitus**

     Includes   brittle diabetes (mellitus)
                   diabetes (mellitus) due to autoimmune process
                   diabetes (mellitus) due to immune mediated
                      pancreatic islet beta-cell destruction
                   idiopathic diabetes (mellitus)
                   juvenile onset diabetes (mellitus)
                   ketosis-prone diabetes (mellitus)

     Excludes1   diabetes mellitus due to underlying condition
                      (E08.-)
                   drug or chemical induced diabetes mellitus (E09.-)
                   gestational diabetes (O24.4-)
                   hyperglycemia NOS (R73.9)
                   neonatal diabetes mellitus (P70.2)
                   postpancreatectomy diabetes mellitus (E13.-)
                   postprocedural diabetes mellitus (E13.-)
                   secondary diabetes mellitus NEC (E13.-)
                   type 2 diabetes mellitus (E11.-)

● **E10.1**   **Type 1 diabetes mellitus with ketoacidosis**
           Acidosis accompanied by accumulation of ketone bodies
           (ketosis) in body tissues and fluids

     E10.10   **Type 1 diabetes mellitus with ketoacidosis without coma**
                Coding Clinic: 2013, Q3, P20

     E10.11   **Type 1 diabetes mellitus with ketoacidosis with coma**

● **E10.2**   **Type 1 diabetes mellitus with kidney complications**

     E10.21   **Type 1 diabetes mellitus with diabetic nephropathy**
                Type 1 diabetes mellitus with intercapillary
                   glomerulosclerosis
                Type 1 diabetes mellitus with intracapillary
                   glomerulonephrosis
                Type 1 diabetes mellitus with Kimmelstiel-
                   Wilson disease

     E10.22   **Type 1 diabetes mellitus with diabetic chronic kidney disease**
                Use additional code to identify stage of chronic
                   kidney disease (N18.1-N18.6)

     E10.29   **Type 1 diabetes mellitus with other diabetic kidney complication**
                Type 1 diabetes mellitus with renal tubular
                   degeneration
                Coding Clinic: 2016, Q1, P13

● **E10.3**   **Type 1 diabetes mellitus with ophthalmic complications**
           Coding Clinic: 2016, Q4, P11

   ● **E10.31**   **Type 1 diabetes mellitus with unspecified diabetic retinopathy**

     E10.311   **Type 1 diabetes mellitus with unspecified diabetic retinopathy with macular edema**

     E10.319   **Type 1 diabetes mellitus with unspecified diabetic retinopathy without macular edema**

   ● **E10.32**   **Type 1 diabetes mellitus with mild nonproliferative diabetic retinopathy**
                Type 1 diabetes mellitus with nonproliferative
                   diabetic retinopathy NOS

                One of the following 7th characters is to be
                   assigned to codes in subcategory E10.32 to
                   designate laterality of the disease:

1	right eye
2	left eye
3	bilateral
9	unspecified eye

   ● **E10.321**   **Type 1 diabetes mellitus with mild nonproliferative diabetic retinopathy with macular edema**

   ● **E10.329**   **Type 1 diabetes mellitus with mild nonproliferative diabetic retinopathy without macular edema**

● **E10.33**   **Type 1 diabetes mellitus with moderate nonproliferative diabetic retinopathy**
           One of the following 7th characters is to be
              assigned to codes in subcategory E10.33 to
              designate laterality of the disease:

1	right eye
2	left eye
3	bilateral
9	unspecified eye

   ● **E10.331**   **Type 1 diabetes mellitus with moderate nonproliferative diabetic retinopathy with macular edema**

   ● **E10.339**   **Type 1 diabetes mellitus with moderate nonproliferative diabetic retinopathy without macular edema**

● **E10.34**   **Type 1 diabetes mellitus with severe nonproliferative diabetic retinopathy**
           One of the following 7th characters is to be
              assigned to codes in subcategory E10.34 to
              designate laterality of the disease:

1	right eye
2	left eye
3	bilateral
9	unspecified eye

   ● **E10.341**   **Type 1 diabetes mellitus with severe nonproliferative diabetic retinopathy with macular edema**

   ● **E10.349**   **Type 1 diabetes mellitus with severe nonproliferative diabetic retinopathy without macular edema**

● **E10.35**   **Type 1 diabetes mellitus with proliferative diabetic retinopathy**
           One of the following 7th characters is to be
              assigned to codes in subcategory E10.35 to
              designate laterality of the disease:

1	right eye
2	left eye
3	bilateral
9	unspecified eye

   ● **E10.351**   **Type 1 diabetes mellitus with proliferative diabetic retinopathy with macular edema**

   ● **E10.352**   **Type 1 diabetes mellitus with proliferative diabetic retinopathy with traction retinal detachment involving the macula**

   ● **E10.353**   **Type 1 diabetes mellitus with proliferative diabetic retinopathy with traction retinal detachment not involving the macula**

   ● **E10.354**   **Type 1 diabetes mellitus with proliferative diabetic retinopathy with combined traction retinal detachment and rhegmatogenous retinal detachment**

   ● **E10.355**   **Type 1 diabetes mellitus with stable proliferative diabetic retinopathy**

   ● **E10.359**   **Type 1 diabetes mellitus with proliferative diabetic retinopathy without macular edema**

E10.36   Type 1 diabetes mellitus with diabetic cataract

X● E10.37   Type 1 diabetes mellitus with diabetic macular edema, resolved following treatment

One of the following 7th characters is to be assigned to code E10.37 to designate laterality of the disease:

> 1   right eye
> 2   left eye
> 3   bilateral
> 9   unspecified eye

E10.39   Type 1 diabetes mellitus with other diabetic ophthalmic complication

Use additional code to identify manifestation, such as:
diabetic glaucoma (H40-H42)

● E10.4   Type 1 diabetes mellitus with neurological complications

E10.40   Type 1 diabetes mellitus with diabetic neuropathy, unspecified

E10.41   Type 1 diabetes mellitus with diabetic mononeuropathy

E10.42   Type 1 diabetes mellitus with diabetic polyneuropathy
Type 1 diabetes mellitus with diabetic neuralgia

E10.43   Type 1 diabetes mellitus with diabetic autonomic (poly)neuropathy
Type 1 diabetes mellitus with diabetic gastroparesis

E10.44   Type 1 diabetes mellitus with diabetic amyotrophy

E10.49   Type 1 diabetes mellitus with other diabetic neurological complication

● E10.5   Type 1 diabetes mellitus with circulatory complications

E10.51   Type 1 diabetes mellitus with diabetic peripheral angiopathy without gangrene

E10.52   Type 1 diabetes mellitus with diabetic peripheral angiopathy with gangrene
Type 1 diabetes mellitus with diabetic gangrene

E10.59   Type 1 diabetes mellitus with other circulatory complications

● E10.6   Type 1 diabetes mellitus with other specified complications

● E10.61   Type 1 diabetes mellitus with diabetic arthropathy

E10.610   Type 1 diabetes mellitus with diabetic neuropathic arthropathy
Type 1 diabetes mellitus with Charcôt's joints

E10.618   Type 1 diabetes mellitus with other diabetic arthropathy

● E10.62   Type 1 diabetes mellitus with skin complications

E10.620   Type 1 diabetes mellitus with diabetic dermatitis
Type 1 diabetes mellitus with diabetic necrobiosis lipoidica

E10.621   Type 1 diabetes mellitus with foot ulcer
Use additional code to identify site of ulcer (L97.4-, L97.5-)

E10.622   Type 1 diabetes mellitus with other skin ulcer
Use additional code to identify site of ulcer (L97.1-L97.9, L98.41-L98.49)

E10.628   Type 1 diabetes mellitus with other skin complications

● E10.63   Type 1 diabetes mellitus with oral complications

E10.630   Type 1 diabetes mellitus with periodontal disease

E10.638   Type 1 diabetes mellitus with other oral complications

● E10.64   Type 1 diabetes mellitus with hypoglycemia

E10.641   Type 1 diabetes mellitus with hypoglycemia with coma

E10.649   Type 1 diabetes mellitus with hypoglycemia without coma
Coding Clinic: 2016, Q1, P13

E10.65   Type 1 diabetes mellitus with hyperglycemia
Coding Clinic: 2013, Q3, P20

E10.69   Type 1 diabetes mellitus with other specified complication
Use additional code to identify complication

E10.8   Type 1 diabetes mellitus with unspecified complications

E10.9   Type 1 diabetes mellitus without complications

● E11   Type 2 diabetes mellitus

Includes   diabetes (mellitus) due to insulin secretory defect
diabetes NOS
insulin resistant diabetes (mellitus)

Use additional code to identify control using:
insulin (Z79.4)
oral antidiabetic drugs (Z79.84)
oral hypoglycemic drugs (Z79.84)

Excludes1   diabetes mellitus due to underlying condition (E08.-)
drug or chemical induced diabetes mellitus (E09.-)
gestational diabetes (O24.4-)
neonatal diabetes mellitus (P70.2)
postpancreatectomy diabetes mellitus (E13.-)
postprocedural diabetes mellitus (E13.-)
secondary diabetes mellitus NEC (E13.-)
type 1 diabetes mellitus (E10.-)

Coding Clinic: 2016, Q4, P121, Q2, P10

● E11.0   Type 2 diabetes mellitus with hyperosmolarity

E11.00   Type 2 diabetes mellitus with hyperosmolarity without nonketotic hyperglycemic-hyperosmolar coma (NKHHC)

E11.01   Type 2 diabetes mellitus with hyperosmolarity with coma

● E11.1   Type 2 diabetes mellitus with ketoacidosis

E11.10   Type 2 diabetes mellitus with ketoacidosis without coma
Coding Clinic: 2017, Q4, P6

E11.11   Type 2 diabetes mellitus with ketoacidosis with coma

● E11.2   Type 2 diabetes mellitus with kidney complications

E11.21   Type 2 diabetes mellitus with diabetic nephropathy
Type 2 diabetes mellitus with intercapillary glomerulosclerosis
Type 2 diabetes mellitus with intracapillary glomerulonephrosis
Type 2 diabetes mellitus with Kimmelstiel-Wilson disease

E11.22   Type 2 diabetes mellitus with diabetic chronic kidney disease
Use additional code to identify stage of chronic kidney disease (N18.1-N18.6)
Coding Clinic: 2016, Q2, P36, Q1, P13

E11.29   Type 2 diabetes mellitus with other diabetic kidney complication
Type 2 diabetes mellitus with renal tubular degeneration

● **E11.3** Type 2 diabetes mellitus with ophthalmic complications
Coding Clinic: 2016, Q4, P11

● **E11.31** Type 2 diabetes mellitus with unspecified diabetic retinopathy

E11.311 Type 2 diabetes mellitus with unspecified diabetic retinopathy with macular edema

E11.319 Type 2 diabetes mellitus with unspecified diabetic retinopathy without macular edema
Coding Clinic: 2013, Q3, P20

● **E11.32** Type 2 diabetes mellitus with mild nonproliferative diabetic retinopathy

Type 2 diabetes mellitus with nonproliferative diabetic retinopathy NOS

One of the following 7th characters is to be assigned to codes in subcategory E11.32 to designate laterality of the disease:

1	right eye
2	left eye
3	bilateral
9	unspecified eye

● **E11.321** Type 2 diabetes mellitus with mild nonproliferative diabetic retinopathy with macular edema

● **E11.329** Type 2 diabetes mellitus with mild nonproliferative diabetic retinopathy without macular edema

● **E11.33** Type 2 diabetes mellitus with moderate nonproliferative diabetic retinopathy

One of the following 7th characters is to be assigned to codes in subcategory E11.33 to designate laterality of the disease:

1	right eye
2	left eye
3	bilateral
9	unspecified eye

● **E11.331** Type 2 diabetes mellitus with moderate nonproliferative diabetic retinopathy with macular edema

● **E11.339** Type 2 diabetes mellitus with moderate nonproliferative diabetic retinopathy without macular edema

● **E11.34** Type 2 diabetes mellitus with severe nonproliferative diabetic retinopathy

One of the following 7th characters is to be assigned to codes in subcategory E11.34 to designate laterality of the disease:

1	right eye
2	left eye
3	bilateral
9	unspecified eye

● **E11.341** Type 2 diabetes mellitus with severe nonproliferative diabetic retinopathy with macular edema

● **E11.349** Type 2 diabetes mellitus with severe nonproliferative diabetic retinopathy without macular edema

● **E11.35** Type 2 diabetes mellitus with proliferative diabetic retinopathy

One of the following 7th characters is to be assigned to codes in subcategory E11.35 to designate laterality of the disease:

1	right eye
2	left eye
3	bilateral
9	unspecified eye

● **E11.351** Type 2 diabetes mellitus with proliferative diabetic retinopathy with macular edema

● **E11.352** Type 2 diabetes mellitus with proliferative diabetic retinopathy with traction retinal detachment involving the macula

● **E11.353** Type 2 diabetes mellitus with proliferative diabetic retinopathy with traction retinal detachment not involving the macula

● **E11.354** Type 2 diabetes mellitus with proliferative diabetic retinopathy with combined traction retinal detachment and rhegmatogenous retinal detachment

● **E11.355** Type 2 diabetes mellitus with stable proliferative diabetic retinopathy

● **E11.359** Type 2 diabetes mellitus with proliferative diabetic retinopathy without macular edema

E11.36 Type 2 diabetes mellitus with diabetic cataract
Coding Clinic: 2016, Q2, P36

X ● **E11.37** Type 2 diabetes mellitus with diabetic macular edema, resolved following treatment

One of the following 7th characters is to be assigned to code E11.37 to designate laterality of the disease:

1	right eye
2	left eye
3	bilateral
9	unspecified eye

E11.39 Type 2 diabetes mellitus with other diabetic ophthalmic complication

Use additional code to identify manifestation, such as:
diabetic glaucoma (H40-H42)

● **E11.4** Type 2 diabetes mellitus with neurological complications

E11.40 Type 2 diabetes mellitus with diabetic neuropathy, unspecified

E11.41 Type 2 diabetes mellitus with diabetic mononeuropathy

E11.42 Type 2 diabetes mellitus with diabetic polyneuropathy

Type 2 diabetes mellitus with diabetic neuralgia
Coding Clinic: 2016, Q1, P13

E11.43 Type 2 diabetes mellitus with diabetic autonomic (poly)neuropathy

Type 2 diabetes mellitus with diabetic gastroparesis
Coding Clinic: 2016, Q2, P36

E11.44 Type 2 diabetes mellitus with diabetic amyotrophy
Coding Clinic: 2016, Q2, P36

E11.49 Type 2 diabetes mellitus with other diabetic neurological complication

▶ New ⇒ Revised ~~deleted~~ Deleted | Excludes 1 | Excludes 2 | Includes | Use additional | Code first | Code also | Key words

OGCR Official Guidelines X Assign placeholder X ● Use Additional Character(s) ▷ Manifestation Code **Coding Clinic**

● **E11.5 Type 2 diabetes mellitus with circulatory complications**

   E11.51 Type 2 diabetes mellitus with diabetic peripheral angiopathy without gangrene

   E11.52 Type 2 diabetes mellitus with diabetic peripheral angiopathy with gangrene
       Type 2 diabetes mellitus with diabetic gangrene
       Coding Clinic: 2017, Q4, P102

   E11.59 Type 2 diabetes mellitus with other circulatory complications

● **E11.6 Type 2 diabetes mellitus with other specified complications**

  ● **E11.61** Type 2 diabetes mellitus with diabetic arthropathy

     E11.610 Type 2 diabetes mellitus with diabetic neuropathic arthropathy
         Type 2 diabetes mellitus with Charcôt's joints
         Coding Clinic: 2016, Q2, P36

     E11.618 Type 2 diabetes mellitus with other diabetic arthropathy
         Coding Clinic: 2018, Q2, P7; 2016, Q2, P36

  ● **E11.62** Type 2 diabetes mellitus with skin complications

     E11.620 Type 2 diabetes mellitus with diabetic dermatitis
         Type 2 diabetes mellitus with diabetic necrobiosis lipoidica

     E11.621 Type 2 diabetes mellitus with foot ulcer
         Use additional code to identify site of ulcer (L97.4-, L97.5-)
         Coding Clinic: 2016, Q1, P12

     E11.622 Type 2 diabetes mellitus with other skin ulcer
         Use additional code to identify site of ulcer (L97.1-L97.9, L98.41-L98.49)
         Coding Clinic: 2017, Q4, P17

     E11.628 Type 2 diabetes mellitus with other skin complications

  ● **E11.63** Type 2 diabetes mellitus with oral complications

     E11.630 Type 2 diabetes mellitus with periodontal disease

     E11.638 Type 2 diabetes mellitus with other oral complications

  ● **E11.64** Type 2 diabetes mellitus with hypoglycemia

     E11.641 Type 2 diabetes mellitus with hypoglycemia with coma

     E11.649 Type 2 diabetes mellitus with hypoglycemia without coma
         Coding Clinic: 2016, Q3, P42; 2015, Q3, P21

   E11.65 Type 2 diabetes mellitus with hyperglycemia
       Coding Clinic: 2013, Q3, P20

   E11.69 Type 2 diabetes mellitus with other specified complication
       Use additional code to identify complication
       Coding Clinic: 2016, Q4, P142

E11.8 Type 2 diabetes mellitus with unspecified complications

E11.9 Type 2 diabetes mellitus without complications
    Coding Clinic: 2016, Q4, P142, Q2, P36

● **E13 Other specified diabetes mellitus**

  Includes   diabetes mellitus due to genetic defects of beta-cell function
           diabetes mellitus due to genetic defects in insulin action
           postpancreatectomy diabetes mellitus
           postprocedural diabetes mellitus
           secondary diabetes mellitus NEC

Use additional code to identify control using:
    insulin (Z79.4)
    oral antidiabetic drugs (Z79.84)
    oral hypoglycemic drugs (Z79.84)

  Excludes1   diabetes (mellitus) due to autoimmune process (E10.-)
            diabetes (mellitus) due to immune mediated pancreatic islet beta-cell destruction (E10.-)
            diabetes mellitus due to underlying condition (E08.-)
            drug or chemical induced diabetes mellitus (E09.-)
            gestational diabetes (O24.4-)
            neonatal diabetes mellitus (P70.2)
            type 1 diabetes mellitus (E10.-)

● **E13.0 Other specified diabetes mellitus with hyperosmolarity**

   E13.00 Other specified diabetes mellitus with hyperosmolarity without nonketotic hyperglycemic-hyperosmolar coma (NKHHC)
         Excludes2   type 2 diabetes mellitus (E11.-)

   E13.01 Other specified diabetes mellitus with hyperosmolarity with coma

● **E13.1 Other specified diabetes mellitus with ketoacidosis**

   E13.10 Other specified diabetes mellitus with ketoacidosis without coma
       Coding Clinic: 2016, Q2, P10; 2013, Q1, P26

   E13.11 Other specified diabetes mellitus with ketoacidosis with coma

● **E13.2 Other specified diabetes mellitus with kidney complications**

   E13.21 Other specified diabetes mellitus with diabetic nephropathy
       Other specified diabetes mellitus with intercapillary glomerulosclerosis
       Other specified diabetes mellitus with intracapillary glomerulonephrosis
       Other specified diabetes mellitus with Kimmelstiel-Wilson disease

   E13.22 Other specified diabetes mellitus with diabetic chronic kidney disease
       Use additional code to identify stage of chronic kidney disease (N18.1-N18.6)

   E13.29 Other specified diabetes mellitus with other diabetic kidney complication
       Other specified diabetes mellitus with renal tubular degeneration

● **E13.3 Other specified diabetes mellitus with ophthalmic complications**
    Coding Clinic: 2016, Q4, P11

  ● **E13.31** Other specified diabetes mellitus with unspecified diabetic retinopathy

     E13.311 Other specified diabetes mellitus with unspecified diabetic retinopathy with macular edema

     E13.319 Other specified diabetes mellitus with unspecified diabetic retinopathy without macular edema

CHAPTER 4 (E00-E90)

● **E13.32**   Other specified diabetes mellitus with **mild nonproliferative** diabetic retinopathy
Other specified diabetes mellitus with nonproliferative diabetic retinopathy NOS
One of the following 7th characters is to be assigned to codes in subcategory E13.32 to designate laterality of the disease:

1	right eye
2	left eye
3	bilateral
9	unspecified eye

● **E13.321**   Other specified diabetes mellitus with mild nonproliferative diabetic retinopathy **with macular edema**

● **E13.329**   Other specified diabetes mellitus with mild nonproliferative diabetic retinopathy **without macular edema**

● **E13.33**   Other specified diabetes mellitus with **moderate nonproliferative** diabetic retinopathy
One of the following 7th characters is to be assigned to codes in subcategory E13.33 to designate laterality of the disease:

1	right eye
2	left eye
3	bilateral
9	unspecified eye

● **E13.331**   Other specified diabetes mellitus with moderate nonproliferative diabetic retinopathy **with macular edema**

● **E13.339**   Other specified diabetes mellitus with moderate nonproliferative diabetic retinopathy **without macular edema**

● **E13.34**   Other specified diabetes mellitus with **severe nonproliferative** diabetic retinopathy
One of the following 7th characters is to be assigned to codes in subcategory E13.34 to designate laterality of the disease:

1	right eye
2	left eye
3	bilateral
9	unspecified eye

● **E13.341**   Other specified diabetes mellitus with severe nonproliferative diabetic retinopathy **with macular edema**

● **E13.349**   Other specified diabetes mellitus with severe nonproliferative diabetic retinopathy **without macular edema**

● **E13.35**   Other specified diabetes mellitus with **proliferative** diabetic retinopathy
One of the following 7th characters is to be assigned to codes in subcategory E13.35 to designate laterality of the disease:

1	right eye
2	left eye
3	bilateral
9	unspecified eye

● **E13.351**   Other specified diabetes mellitus with proliferative diabetic retinopathy **with macular edema**

● **E13.352**   Other specified diabetes mellitus with proliferative diabetic retinopathy **with traction retinal detachment involving the macula**

● **E13.353**   Other specified diabetes mellitus with proliferative diabetic retinopathy **with traction retinal detachment not involving the macula**

● **E13.354**   Other specified diabetes mellitus with proliferative diabetic retinopathy **with combined traction retinal detachment and rhegmatogenous retinal detachment**

● **E13.355**   Other specified diabetes mellitus with **stable proliferative diabetic retinopathy**

● **E13.359**   Other specified diabetes mellitus with proliferative diabetic retinopathy **without macular edema**

E13.36   Other specified diabetes mellitus with diabetic cataract

X ● **E13.37**   Other specified diabetes mellitus with diabetic **macular edema, resolved following treatment**
One of the following 7th characters is to be assigned to code E13.37 to designate laterality of the disease:

1	right eye
2	left eye
3	bilateral
9	unspecified eye

E13.39   Other specified diabetes mellitus with **other** diabetic ophthalmic complication
Use additional code to identify manifestation, such as:
diabetic glaucoma (H40-H42)

● **E13.4**   Other specified diabetes mellitus **with neurological complications**

E13.40   Other specified diabetes mellitus with diabetic neuropathy, unspecified

E13.41   Other specified diabetes mellitus with diabetic mononeuropathy

E13.42   Other specified diabetes mellitus with diabetic polyneuropathy
Other specified diabetes mellitus with diabetic neuralgia

E13.43   Other specified diabetes mellitus with diabetic autonomic (poly)neuropathy
Other specified diabetes mellitus with diabetic gastroparesis

E13.44   Other specified diabetes mellitus with diabetic amyotrophy

E13.49   Other specified diabetes mellitus with **other** diabetic neurological complication

● **E13.5**   Other specified diabetes mellitus **with circulatory complications**

E13.51   Other specified diabetes mellitus with diabetic peripheral angiopathy without gangrene

E13.52   Other specified diabetes mellitus with diabetic peripheral angiopathy with gangrene
Other specified diabetes mellitus with diabetic gangrene

E13.59   Other specified diabetes mellitus with other circulatory complications

● **E13.6**   Other specified diabetes mellitus with **other specified complications**

● **E13.61**   Other specified diabetes mellitus with diabetic arthropathy

E13.610   Other specified diabetes mellitus with diabetic **neuropathic** arthropathy
Other specified diabetes mellitus with Charcôt's joints

E13.618   Other specified diabetes mellitus with **other** diabetic arthropathy

▶ New   ⇒ Revised   ~~deleted~~ Deleted   Excludes 1   Excludes 2   Includes   Use additional   Code first   Code also   Key words
OGCR Official Guidelines   X Assign placeholder X   ● Use Additional Character(s)   ▶ Manifestation Code   **Coding Clinic**

● **E13.62** **Other specified diabetes mellitus with skin complications**

    E13.620 **Other specified diabetes mellitus with diabetic dermatitis**
        Other specified diabetes mellitus with diabetic necrobiosis lipoidica

    E13.621 **Other specified diabetes mellitus with foot ulcer**
        Use additional code to identify site of ulcer (L97.4-, L97.5-)

    E13.622 **Other specified diabetes mellitus with other skin ulcer**
        Use additional code to identify site of ulcer (L97.1-L97.9, L98.41-L98.49)

    E13.628 **Other specified diabetes mellitus with other skin complications**

● **E13.63** **Other specified diabetes mellitus with oral complications**

    E13.630 **Other specified diabetes mellitus with periodontal disease**

    E13.638 **Other specified diabetes mellitus with other oral complications**

● **E13.64** **Other specified diabetes mellitus with hypoglycemia**

    E13.641 **Other specified diabetes mellitus with hypoglycemia with coma**

    E13.649 **Other specified diabetes mellitus with hypoglycemia without coma**

  E13.65 **Other specified diabetes mellitus with hyperglycemia**

  E13.69 **Other specified diabetes mellitus with other specified complication**
    Use additional code to identify complication

  E13.8 **Other specified diabetes mellitus with unspecified complications**

  E13.9 **Other specified diabetes mellitus without complications**

OTHER DISORDERS OF GLUCOSE REGULATION AND PANCREATIC INTERNAL SECRETION (E15-E16)

E15 **Nondiabetic hypoglycemic coma**
    Includes drug-induced insulin coma in nondiabetic
        hyperinsulinism with hypoglycemic coma
        hypoglycemic coma NOS

● **E16** **Other disorders of pancreatic internal secretion**

  E16.0 **Drug-induced hypoglycemia without coma**
    Excludes1 diabetes with hypoglycemia without coma (E09.649)

    Use additional code for adverse effect, if applicable, to identify drug (T36-T50 with fifth or sixth character 5)

  E16.1 **Other hypoglycemia**
    Functional hyperinsulinism
    Functional nonhyperinsulinemic hypoglycemia
    Hyperinsulinism NOS
    Hyperplasia of pancreatic islet beta cells NOS
    Excludes1 diabetes with hypoglycemia (E08.649, E10.649, E11.649, E13.649)
        hypoglycemia in infant of diabetic mother (P70.1)
        neonatal hypoglycemia (P70.4)

  E16.2 **Hypoglycemia, unspecified**
    Excludes1 diabetes with hypoglycemia (E08.649, E10.649, E11.649, E13.649)
    Coding Clinic: 2016, Q3, P42

  E16.3 **Increased secretion of glucagon**
    Hyperplasia of pancreatic endocrine cells with glucagon excess

  E16.4 **Increased secretion of gastrin**
    Hypergastrinemia
    Hyperplasia of pancreatic endocrine cells with gastrin excess
    Zollinger-Ellison syndrome

  E16.8 **Other specified disorders of pancreatic internal secretion**
    Increased secretion from endocrine pancreas of growth hormone-releasing hormone
    Increased secretion from endocrine pancreas of pancreatic polypeptide
    Increased secretion from endocrine pancreas of somatostatin
    Increased secretion from endocrine pancreas of vasoactive-intestinal polypeptide

  E16.9 **Disorder of pancreatic internal secretion, unspecified**
    Islet-cell hyperplasia NOS
    Pancreatic endocrine cell hyperplasia NOS

DISORDERS OF OTHER ENDOCRINE GLANDS (E20-E35)

  Excludes1 galactorrhea (N64.3)
        gynecomastia (N62)

● **E20** **Hypoparathyroidism**
  Greatly reduced function of parathyroid glands; AKA parathyroid insufficiency
    Excludes1 Di George's syndrome (D82.1)
        postprocedural hypoparathyroidism (E89.2)
        tetany NOS (R29.0)
        transitory neonatal hypoparathyroidism (P71.4)

  E20.0 **Idiopathic hypoparathyroidism**
    Rare condition, unknown cause; short dwarf-like with round face

  E20.1 **Pseudohypoparathyroidism**
    Hereditary condition resembling hypoparathyroidism, but caused by inability to respond to parathyroid hormone

  E20.8 **Other hypoparathyroidism**

  E20.9 **Hypoparathyroidism, unspecified**
    Parathyroid tetany

● **E21** **Hyperparathyroidism and other disorders of parathyroid gland**
    Excludes1 adult osteomalacia (M83.-)
        ectopic hyperparathyroidism (E34.2)
        familial hypocalciuric hypercalcemia (E83.52)
        hungry bone syndrome (E83.81)
        infantile and juvenile osteomalacia (E55.0)

  E21.0 **Primary hyperparathyroidism**
    Hyperplasia of parathyroid
    Osteitis fibrosa cystica generalisata [von Recklinghausen's disease of bone]

  E21.1 **Secondary hyperparathyroidism, not elsewhere classified**
    Excludes1 secondary hyperparathyroidism of renal origin (N25.81)

  E21.2 **Other hyperparathyroidism**
    Tertiary hyperparathyroidism
    Excludes1 familial hypocalciuric hypercalcemia (E83.52)

  E21.3 **Hyperparathyroidism, unspecified**

  E21.4 **Other specified disorders of parathyroid gland**

  E21.5 **Disorder of parathyroid gland, unspecified**

Item 4-4 **Hyperparathyroidism** is an overactive parathyroid gland that secretes excessive parathormone, causing increased levels of circulating calcium. This results in a loss of calcium in the bone (osteoporosis).

    Hypoparathyroidism is an underactive parathyroid gland that results in decreased levels of circulating calcium. The primary manifestation is **tetany,** a continuous muscle spasm.

Figure 4-4 **Tetany** caused by hypoparathyroidism.

Item 4–5 Hyperadrenalism is overactivity of the adrenal cortex, which secretes corticosteroid hormones. Excessive glucocorticoid hormone results in hyperglycemia **(Cushing's syndrome),** and excessive aldosterone results in **Conn's syndrome. Adrenogenital syndrome** is the result of excessive secretion of androgens, male hormones, which stimulates premature sexual development. **Hypoadrenalism, Addison's disease,** is a condition in which the adrenal glands atrophy.

Figure 4-5 Centripetal and generalized obesity and dorsal kyphosis in a woman with Cushing's disease. (From Salvo SG: Mosby's Pathology for Massage Therapists, St. Louis, MO: Mosby/Elsevier, 2009)

● **E22   Hyperfunction of pituitary gland**

> **Excludes1**   Cushing's syndrome (E24.-)
> Nelson's syndrome (E24.1)
> overproduction of ACTH not associated with Cushing's disease (E27.0)
> overproduction of pituitary ACTH (E24.0)
> overproduction of thyroid-stimulating hormone (E05.8-)

E22.0   Acromegaly and pituitary gigantism
Chronic disease caused by hypersecretion of growth hormone
Overproduction of growth hormone

> **Excludes1**   constitutional gigantism (E34.4)
> constitutional tall stature (E34.4)
> increased secretion from endocrine pancreas of growth hormone-releasing hormone (E16.8)

E22.1   Hyperprolactinemia
Increased levels of prolactin

> Use additional code for adverse effect, if applicable, to identify drug (T36-T50 with fifth or sixth character 5)

E22.2   Syndrome of inappropriate secretion of antidiuretic hormone

E22.8   Other hyperfunction of pituitary gland
Central precocious puberty

E22.9   Hyperfunction of pituitary gland, unspecified

● **E23   Hypofunction and other disorders of the pituitary gland**

> **Includes**   the listed conditions whether the disorder is in the pituitary or the hypothalamus

> **Excludes1**   postprocedural hypopituitarism (E89.3)

E23.0   Hypopituitarism
Fertile eunuch syndrome
Hypogonadotropic hypogonadism
Idiopathic growth hormone deficiency
Isolated deficiency of gonadotropin
Isolated deficiency of growth hormone
Isolated deficiency of pituitary hormone
Kallmann's syndrome
Lorain-Levi short stature
Necrosis of pituitary gland (postpartum)
Panhypopituitarism
Pituitary cachexia
Pituitary insufficiency NOS
Pituitary short stature
Sheehan's syndrome
Simmonds' disease

E23.1   Drug-induced hypopituitarism

> Use additional code for adverse effect, if applicable, to identify drug (T36-T50 with fifth or sixth character 5)

E23.2   Diabetes insipidus

> **Excludes1**   nephrogenic diabetes insipidus (N25.1)

E23.3   Hypothalamic dysfunction, not elsewhere classified

> **Excludes1**   Prader-Willi syndrome (Q87.1)
> Russell-Silver syndrome (Q87.1)

E23.6   Other disorders of pituitary gland
Abscess of pituitary
Adiposogenital dystrophy

E23.7   Disorder of pituitary gland, unspecified

● **E24   Cushing's syndrome**

> **Excludes1**   congenital adrenal hyperplasia (E25.0)

E24.0   Pituitary-dependent Cushing's disease
Overproduction of pituitary ACTH
Pituitary-dependent hypercorticalism

E24.1   Nelson's syndrome

E24.2   Drug-induced Cushing's syndrome

> Use additional code for adverse effect, if applicable, to identify drug (T36-T50 with fifth or sixth character 5)

E24.3   Ectopic ACTH syndrome

E24.4   Alcohol-induced pseudo-Cushing's syndrome

E24.8   Other Cushing's syndrome

E24.9   Cushing's syndrome, unspecified

● **E25   Adrenogenital disorders**
Disorder of production of steroid hormone in adrenal gland

> **Includes**   adrenogenital syndromes, virilizing or feminizing, whether acquired or due to adrenal hyperplasia consequent on inborn enzyme defects in hormone synthesis
> female adrenal pseudohermaphroditism
> female heterosexual precocious pseudopuberty
> male isosexual precocious pseudopuberty
> male macrogenitosomia praecox
> male sexual precocity with adrenal hyperplasia
> male virilization (female)

> **Excludes1**   indeterminate sex and pseudohermaphroditism (Q56)
> chromosomal abnormalities (Q90-Q99)

E25.0   Congenital adrenogenital disorders associated with enzyme deficiency
Congenital adrenal hyperplasia
21-Hydroxylase deficiency
Salt-losing congenital adrenal hyperplasia

E25.8   Other adrenogenital disorders
Idiopathic adrenogenital disorder

> Use additional code for adverse effect, if applicable, to identify drug (T36-T50 with fifth or sixth character 5)

E25.9   Adrenogenital disorder, unspecified
Adrenogenital syndrome NOS

● **E26   Hyperaldosteronism**
Abnormality of electrolyte metabolism caused by excessive secretion of aldosterone

● **E26.0   Primary hyperaldosteronism**

E26.01   Conn's syndrome
Code also adrenal adenoma (D35.0-)

E26.02   Glucocorticoid-remediable aldosteronism
Familial aldosteronism type I

E26.09   Other primary hyperaldosteronism
Primary aldosteronism due to adrenal hyperplasia (bilateral)

E26.1   Secondary hyperaldosteronism

● **E26.8   Other hyperaldosteronism**

E26.81   Bartter's syndrome

E26.89   Other hyperaldosteronism

E26.9   Hyperaldosteronism, unspecified
Aldosteronism NOS
Hyperaldosteronism NOS

▶ New   ⇒ Revised   ~~deleted~~ Deleted   Excludes 1   Excludes 2   Includes   Use additional   Code first   Code also   Key words

OGCR Official Guidelines   X Assign placeholder X   ● Use Additional Character(s)   ▷ Manifestation Code   **Coding Clinic**

● **E27**   **Other disorders of adrenal gland**

    E27.0   **Other adrenocortical overactivity**
        Overproduction of ACTH, not associated with
          Cushing's disease
        Premature adrenarche
        Excludes1   Cushing's syndrome (E24.-)

    E27.1   **Primary adrenocortical insufficiency**
        Addison's disease
        Autoimmune adrenalitis
        Excludes1   Addison only phenotype
                   adrenoleukodystrophy (E71.528)
               amyloidosis (E85.-)
               tuberculous Addison's disease (A18.7)
               Waterhouse-Friderichsen syndrome
                   (A39.1)

    E27.2   **Addisonian crisis**
        Acute onset of adrenocortical insufficiency
        Adrenal crisis
        Adrenocortical crisis

    E27.3   **Drug-induced adrenocortical insufficiency**
        Use additional code for adverse effect, if applicable,
          to identify drug (T36-T50 with fifth or sixth
          character 5)

●   **E27.4**   **Other and unspecified adrenocortical insufficiency**
        Excludes1   adrenoleukodystrophy [Addison-
                   Schilder] (E71.528)
               Waterhouse-Friderichsen syndrome
                   (A39.1)

       E27.40   **Unspecified adrenocortical insufficiency**
            Adrenocortical insufficiency NOS
            Hypoaldosteronism

       E27.49   **Other adrenocortical insufficiency**
            Adrenal hemorrhage
            Adrenal infarction

    E27.5   **Adrenomedullary hyperfunction**
        Adrenomedullary hyperplasia
        Catecholamine hypersecretion

    E27.8   **Other specified disorders of adrenal gland**
        Abnormality of cortisol-binding globulin

    E27.9   **Disorder of adrenal gland, unspecified**

● **E28**   **Ovarian dysfunction**

        Excludes1   isolated gonadotropin deficiency (E23.0)
                 postprocedural ovarian failure (E89.4-)

    E28.0   **Estrogen excess** ♀
        Use additional code for adverse effect, if applicable,
          to identify drug (T36-T50 with fifth or sixth
          character 5)

    E28.1   **Androgen excess** ♀
        Hypersecretion of ovarian androgens
        Use additional code for adverse effect, if applicable,
          to identify drug (T36-T50 with fifth or sixth
          character 5)

    E28.2   **Polycystic ovarian syndrome** ♀
        Sclerocystic ovary syndrome
        Stein-Leventhal syndrome

●   **E28.3**   **Primary ovarian failure**
        Excludes1   pure gonadal dysgenesis (Q99.1)
                 Turner's syndrome (Q96.-)

   ●   **E28.31**   **Premature menopause**
          E28.310   **Symptomatic premature**
                 menopause ♀   A
                 Symptoms such as flushing,
                   sleeplessness, headache, lack of
                   concentration, associated with
                   premature menopause

          E28.319   **Asymptomatic premature**
                 menopause ♀   A
                 Premature menopause NOS

       E28.39   **Other primary ovarian failure** ♀
            Decreased estrogen
            Resistant ovary syndrome

    E28.8   **Other ovarian dysfunction** ♀
        Ovarian hyperfunction NOS
        Excludes1   postprocedural ovarian failure (E89.4-)

    E28.9   **Ovarian dysfunction, unspecified** ♀

● **E29**   **Testicular dysfunction**

        Excludes1   androgen insensitivity syndrome (E34.5-)
                 azoospermia or oligospermia NOS (N46.0-N46.1)
                 isolated gonadotropin deficiency (E23.0)
                 Klinefelter's syndrome (Q98.0-Q98.1, Q98.4)

    E29.0   **Testicular hyperfunction** ♂
        Hypersecretion of testicular hormones

    E29.1   **Testicular hypofunction** ♂
        Defective biosynthesis of testicular androgen NOS
        5-delta-Reductase deficiency (with male
          pseudohermaphroditism)
        Testicular hypogonadism NOS
        Use additional code for adverse effect, if applicable,
          to identify drug (T36-T50 with fifth or sixth
          character 5)
        Excludes1   postprocedural testicular hypofunction
                 (E89.5)

    E29.8   **Other testicular dysfunction** ♂

    E29.9   **Testicular dysfunction, unspecified** ♂

● **E30**   **Disorders of puberty, not elsewhere classified**

    E30.0   **Delayed puberty**
        Constitutional delay of puberty
        Delayed sexual development

    E30.1   **Precocious puberty**   P
        Sexual maturation at earlier age than normal, or before age
          8 in girls and 9 in boys, usually hormonal; AKA sexual
          precocity or pubertas praecox
        Precocious menstruation
        Excludes1   Albright (-McCune) (-Sternberg)
                 syndrome (Q78.1)
               central precocious puberty (E22.8)
               congenital adrenal hyperplasia (E25.0)
               female heterosexual precocious
                 pseudopuberty (E25.-)
               male isosexual precocious pseudopuberty
                 (E25.-)

    E30.8   **Other disorders of puberty**   P
        Premature thelarche

    E30.9   **Disorder of puberty, unspecified**

● **E31**   **Polyglandular dysfunction**

        Excludes1   ataxia telangiectasia [Louis-Bar] (G11.3)
                 dystrophia myotonica [Steinert] (G71.11)
                 pseudohypoparathyroidism (E20.1)

    E31.0   **Autoimmune polyglandular failure**
        Schmidt's syndrome

    E31.1   **Polyglandular hyperfunction**
        Excludes1   multiple endocrine adenomatosis (E31.2-)
                 multiple endocrine neoplasia (E31.2-)

●   **E31.2**   **Multiple endocrine neoplasia [MEN] syndromes**
        Adenomatous hyperplasia and malignant tumors in
          endocrine glands
        Multiple endocrine adenomatosis
        Code also any associated malignancies and other
          conditions associated with the syndromes

       E31.20   **Multiple endocrine neoplasia [MEN]**
            syndrome, unspecified
            Multiple endocrine adenomatosis NOS
            Multiple endocrine neoplasia [MEN]
              syndrome NOS

       E31.21   **Multiple endocrine neoplasia [MEN] type I**
            Wermer's syndrome

       E31.22   **Multiple endocrine neoplasia [MEN] type IIA**
            Sipple's syndrome

       E31.23   **Multiple endocrine neoplasia [MEN] type IIB**

    E31.8   **Other polyglandular dysfunction**

    E31.9   **Polyglandular dysfunction, unspecified**

● **E32   Diseases of thymus**
> **Excludes1**   aplasia or hypoplasia of thymus with immunodeficiency (D82.1)
> myasthenia gravis (G70.0)

E32.0   Persistent hyperplasia of thymus
> Hypertrophy of thymus

E32.1   Abscess of thymus

E32.8   Other diseases of thymus
> **Excludes1**   aplasia or hypoplasia with immunodeficiency (D82.1)
> thymoma (D15.0)

E32.9   Disease of thymus, unspecified

● **E34   Other endocrine disorders**
> **Excludes1**   pseudohypoparathyroidism (E20.1)

E34.0   Carcinoid syndrome
> **Note:** May be used as an additional code to identify functional activity associated with a carcinoid tumor.

E34.1   Other hypersecretion of intestinal hormones

E34.2   Ectopic hormone secretion, not elsewhere classified
> **Excludes1**   ectopic ACTH syndrome (E24.3)

E34.3   Short stature due to endocrine disorder
> Constitutional short stature
> Laron-type short stature
> **Excludes1**   achondroplastic short stature (Q77.4)
> hypochondroplastic short stature (Q77.4)
> nutritional short stature (E45)
> pituitary short stature (E23.0)
> progeria (E34.8)
> renal short stature (N25.0)
> Russell-Silver syndrome (Q87.1)
> short-limbed stature with immunodeficiency (D82.2)
> short stature in specific dysmorphic syndromes - code to syndrome - see Alphabetical Index
> short stature NOS (R62.52)

E34.4   Constitutional tall stature
> Constitutional gigantism

● **E34.5   Androgen insensitivity syndrome**
> **E34.50   Androgen insensitivity syndrome, unspecified**
> Androgen insensitivity NOS

> **E34.51   Complete androgen insensitivity syndrome**
> Complete androgen insensitivity
> de Quervain syndrome
> Goldberg-Maxwell syndrome

> **E34.52   Partial androgen insensitivity syndrome**
> Partial androgen insensitivity
> Reifenstein syndrome

E34.8   Other specified endocrine disorders
> Pineal gland dysfunction
> Progeria
> **Excludes2**   pseudohypoparathyroidism (E20.1)

E34.9   Endocrine disorder, unspecified
> Endocrine disturbance NOS
> Hormone disturbance NOS

▷ **E35   *Disorders of endocrine glands in diseases classified elsewhere***
> *Code first* underlying disease, such as:
> late congenital syphilis of thymus gland [Dubois disease] (A50.5)
> ⇒ Use additional code, if applicable, to identify:
> sequelae of tuberculosis of other organs (B90.8)
> **Excludes1**   Echinococcus granulosus infection of thyroid gland (B67.3)
> meningococcal hemorrhagic adrenalitis (A39.1)
> syphilis of endocrine gland (A52.79)
> tuberculosis of adrenal gland, except calcification (A18.7)
> tuberculosis of endocrine gland NEC (A18.82)
> tuberculosis of thyroid gland (A18.81)
> Waterhouse-Friderichsen syndrome (A39.1)

INTRAOPERATIVE COMPLICATIONS OF ENDOCRINE SYSTEM (E36)

● **E36   Intraoperative complications of endocrine system**
> **Excludes2**   postprocedural endocrine and metabolic complications and disorders, not elsewhere classified (E89.-)

● **E36.0   Intraoperative hemorrhage and hematoma of an endocrine system organ or structure complicating a procedure**
> **Excludes1**   intraoperative hemorrhage and hematoma of an endocrine system organ or structure due to accidental puncture or laceration during a procedure (E36.1-)

> **E36.01   Intraoperative hemorrhage and hematoma of an endocrine system organ or structure complicating an endocrine system procedure**

> **E36.02   Intraoperative hemorrhage and hematoma of an endocrine system organ or structure complicating other procedure**

● **E36.1   Accidental puncture and laceration of an endocrine system organ or structure during a procedure**
> **E36.11   Accidental puncture and laceration of an endocrine system organ or structure during an endocrine system procedure**

> **E36.12   Accidental puncture and laceration of an endocrine system organ or structure during other procedure**

E36.8   Other intraoperative complications of endocrine system
> Use additional code, if applicable, to further specify disorder

MALNUTRITION (E40-E46)

> **Excludes1**   intestinal malabsorption (K90.-)
> sequelae of protein-calorie malnutrition (E64.0)
> **Excludes2**   nutritional anemias (D50-D53)
> starvation (T73.0)

E40   Kwashiorkor
> *Malnutrition produced by severe protein deficiency*
> Severe malnutrition with nutritional edema with dyspigmentation of skin and hair
> **Excludes1**   marasmic kwashiorkor (E42)
> **Coding Clinic:** 22017, Q3, P25

E41   Nutritional marasmus
> Severe malnutrition with marasmus
> **Excludes1**   marasmic kwashiorkor (E42)
> **Coding Clinic:** 2017, Q3, P24-25

E42   Marasmic kwashiorkor
> *Severe protein malnutrition*
> Intermediate form severe protein-calorie malnutrition
> Severe protein-calorie malnutrition with signs of both kwashiorkor and marasmus
> **Coding Clinic:** 2017, Q3, P25

E43   Unspecified severe protein-calorie malnutrition
> Starvation edema
> **Coding Clinic:** 2017, Q4, P108-109; 2017, Q3, P25

● **E44   Protein-calorie malnutrition of moderate and mild degree**
> **E44.0   Moderate protein-calorie malnutrition**
> **E44.1   Mild protein-calorie malnutrition**

E45   Retarded development following protein-calorie malnutrition
> Nutritional short stature
> Nutritional stunting
> Physical retardation due to malnutrition

E46   Unspecified protein-calorie malnutrition
> Malnutrition NOS
> Protein-calorie imbalance NOS
> **Excludes1**   nutritional deficiency NOS (E63.9)
> **Coding Clinic:** 2017, Q3, P25

▶ New   ⇒ Revised   ~~deleted~~ Deleted   Excludes 1   Excludes 2   Includes   Use additional   Code first   Code also   Key words

OGCR Official Guidelines   X Assign placeholder X   ● Use Additional Character(s)   ▷ Manifestation Code   **Coding Clinic**

Item 4–6 **Bitot's spots** are the result of a buildup of keratin debris found on the superficial surface the conjunctiva; oval, triangular, or irregular in shape; and a sign of vitamin A deficiency and associated with night blindness. The disease may progress to **keratomalacia,** which can result in eventual prolapse of the iris and loss of the lens.

Figure 4-6   Bitot's spot on the conjunctiva.

OTHER NUTRITIONAL DEFICIENCIES (E50-E64)

Excludes2   nutritional anemias (D50-D53)

● **E50**   **Vitamin A deficiency**

     Excludes1   sequelae of vitamin A deficiency (E64.1)

   E50.0   **Vitamin A deficiency with conjunctival xerosis**

   E50.1   **Vitamin A deficiency with Bitot's spot and conjunctival xerosis**
         Bitot's spot in the young child

   E50.2   **Vitamin A deficiency with corneal xerosis**

   E50.3   **Vitamin A deficiency with corneal ulceration and xerosis**

   E50.4   **Vitamin A deficiency with keratomalacia**
         Eye disorder that results in dry cornea caused by vitamin A deficiency

   E50.5   **Vitamin A deficiency with night blindness**

   E50.6   **Vitamin A deficiency with xerophthalmic scars of cornea**
         Abnormal dryness and thickening of conjunctiva and cornea due to vitamin A deficiency

   E50.7   **Other ocular manifestations of vitamin A deficiency**
         Xerophthalmia NOS

   E50.8   **Other manifestations of vitamin A deficiency**
         Follicular keratosis
         Xeroderma

   E50.9   **Vitamin A deficiency, unspecified**
         Hypovitaminosis A NOS

● **E51**   **Thiamine deficiency**

     Excludes1   sequelae of thiamine deficiency (E64.8)

   ● **E51.1**   **Beriberi**

     E51.11   **Dry beriberi**
           Thiamine deficiency with nervous system manifestation most often caused by excessive alcohol consumption
           Beriberi NOS
           Beriberi with polyneuropathy

     E51.12   **Wet beriberi**
           Thiamine deficiency with cardiovascular manifestation most often caused by excessive alcohol consumption
           Beriberi with cardiovascular manifestations
           Cardiovascular beriberi
           Shoshin disease

   E51.2   **Wernicke's encephalopathy**
         Acute disease of brain due to thiamine deficiency most often associated with excessive alcohol consumption

   E51.8   **Other manifestations of thiamine deficiency**

   E51.9   **Thiamine deficiency, unspecified**

Figure 4-7   The sharply demarcated, characteristic scaling dermatitis of pellagra. (From James WD, Berger TG, Elston DM: Andrews' Diseases of the Skin: Clinical Dermatology, Philadelphia, Saunders Elsevier, 2006)

Item 4–7 **Pellagra** is associated with a deficiency of niacin and its precursor, **tryptophan.** Characteristics of the condition include diarrhea, dermatitis on exposed skin surfaces, dementia, and death. It is prevalent in developing countries where nutrition is inadequate. **Beriberi** is associated with thiamine deficiency.

   E52   **Niacin deficiency [pellagra]**
         Niacin (-tryptophan) deficiency
         Nicotinamide deficiency
         Pellagra (alcoholic)

     Excludes1   sequelae of niacin deficiency (E64.8)

● **E53**   **Deficiency of other B group vitamins**

     Excludes1   sequelae of vitamin B deficiency (E64.8)

   E53.0   **Riboflavin deficiency**
         Ariboflavinosis
         Vitamin B2 deficiency

   E53.1   **Pyridoxine deficiency**
         Vitamin B6 deficiency

     Excludes1   pyridoxine-responsive sideroblastic anemia (D64.3)

   E53.8   **Deficiency of other specified B group vitamins**
         Biotin deficiency
         Cyanocobalamin deficiency
         Folate deficiency
         Folic acid deficiency
         Pantothenic acid deficiency
         Vitamin B12 deficiency

     Excludes1   folate deficiency anemia (D52.-)
           vitamin B12 deficiency anemia (D51.-)

   E53.9   **Vitamin B deficiency, unspecified**

   E54   **Ascorbic acid deficiency**
         Deficiency of vitamin C
         Scurvy

     Excludes1   scorbutic anemia (D53.2)
           sequelae of vitamin C deficiency (E64.2)

● **E55**   **Vitamin D deficiency**

     Excludes1   adult osteomalacia (M83.-)
           osteoporosis (M80.-)
           sequelae of rickets (E64.3)

   E55.0   **Rickets, active**
         Infantile osteomalacia
         Juvenile osteomalacia
         Softening of bone

     Excludes1   celiac rickets (K90.0)
           Crohn's rickets (K50.-)
           hereditary vitamin D-dependent rickets (E83.32)
           inactive rickets (E64.3)
           renal rickets (N25.0)
           sequelae of rickets (E64.3)
           vitamin D-resistant rickets (E83.31)

   E55.9   **Vitamin D deficiency, unspecified**
         Avitaminosis D

CHAPTER 4 (E00-E90)

CHAPTER 4 (E00-E90)

● **E56**   **Other vitamin deficiencies**
    Excludes1   sequelae of other vitamin deficiencies (E64.8)
    E56.0   **Deficiency of vitamin E**
    E56.1   **Deficiency of vitamin K**
        Excludes1   deficiency of coagulation factor due to vitamin K deficiency (D68.4)
                         vitamin K deficiency of newborn (P53)
    E56.8   **Deficiency of other vitamins**
    E56.9   **Vitamin deficiency, unspecified**

  E58   **Dietary calcium deficiency**
    Excludes1   disorders of calcium metabolism (E83.5-)
                  sequelae of calcium deficiency (E64.8)

  E59   **Dietary selenium deficiency**
    Keshan disease
    Excludes1   sequelae of selenium deficiency (E64.8)

  E60   **Dietary zinc deficiency**

● **E61**   **Deficiency of other nutrient elements**
    Use additional code for adverse effect, if applicable, to identify drug (T36-T50 with fifth or sixth character 5)
    Excludes1   disorders of mineral metabolism (E83.-)
                  iodine deficiency related thyroid disorders (E00-E02)
                  sequelae of malnutrition and other nutritional deficiencies (E64.-)
    E61.0   **Copper deficiency**
    E61.1   **Iron deficiency**
        Excludes1   iron deficiency anemia (D50.-)
    E61.2   **Magnesium deficiency**
    E61.3   **Manganese deficiency**
    E61.4   **Chromium deficiency**
    E61.5   **Molybdenum deficiency**
    E61.6   **Vanadium deficiency**
    E61.7   **Deficiency of multiple nutrient elements**
    E61.8   **Deficiency of other specified nutrient elements**
    E61.9   **Deficiency of nutrient element, unspecified**

● **E63**   **Other nutritional deficiencies**
    Excludes1   dehydration (E86.0)
                  failure to thrive, adult (R62.7)
                  failure to thrive, child (R62.51)
                  feeding problems in newborn (P92.-)
                  sequelae of malnutrition and other nutritional deficiencies (E64.-)
    E63.0   **Essential fatty acid [EFA] deficiency**
    E63.1   **Imbalance of constituents of food intake**
    E63.8   **Other specified nutritional deficiencies**
    E63.9   **Nutritional deficiency, unspecified**

● **E64**   **Sequelae of malnutrition and other nutritional deficiencies**
    Pathological condition resulting from disease, injury, or other trauma
    Note: This category is to be used to indicate conditions in categories E43, E44, E46, E50-E63 as the cause of sequelae, which are themselves classified elsewhere. The "sequelae" include conditions specified as such; they also include the late effects of diseases classifiable to the above categories if the disease itself is no longer present
    Code first condition resulting from (sequela) of malnutrition and other nutritional deficiencies
    E64.0   **Sequelae of protein-calorie malnutrition**
        Excludes2   retarded development following protein-calorie malnutrition (E45)
    E64.1   **Sequelae of vitamin A deficiency**
    E64.2   **Sequelae of vitamin C deficiency**
    E64.3   **Sequelae of rickets**
    E64.8   **Sequelae of other nutritional deficiencies**
    E64.9   **Sequelae of unspecified nutritional deficiency**

OVERWEIGHT, OBESITY AND OTHER HYPERALIMENTATION (E65-E68)

  E65   **Localized adiposity**
    Fat pad

● **E66**   **Overweight and obesity**
    Code first obesity complicating pregnancy, childbirth and the puerperium, if applicable (O99.21-)
    Use additional code to identify body mass index (BMI), if known (Z68.-)
    Excludes1   adiposogenital dystrophy (E23.6)
                  lipomatosis NOS (E88.2)
                  lipomatosis dolorosa [Dercum] (E88.2)
                  Prader-Willi syndrome (Q87.1)
    ● **E66.0**   **Obesity due to excess calories**
        E66.01   **Morbid (severe) obesity due to excess calories**
            Excludes1   morbid (severe) obesity with alveolar hypoventilation (E66.2)
        E66.09   **Other obesity due to excess calories**
    E66.1   **Drug-induced obesity**
        Use additional code for adverse effect, if applicable, to identify drug (T36-T50 with fifth or sixth character 5)
    E66.2   **Morbid (severe) obesity with alveolar hypoventilation**
        Uncommon condition of unknown cause leading to inadequate ventilation in lungs, even though lungs and airways are normal
        Obesity hypoventilation syndrome (OHS)
        Pickwickian syndrome
    E66.3   **Overweight**
    E66.8   **Other obesity**
    E66.9   **Obesity, unspecified**
        Obesity NOS

● **E67**   **Other hyperalimentation**
    Ingestion of more than optimal amount of nutrients
    Excludes1   hyperalimentation NOS (R63.2)
                  sequelae of hyperalimentation (E68)
    E67.0   **Hypervitaminosis A**
➠   **E67.1**   **Hypercarotenemia**
    E67.2   **Megavitamin-B6 syndrome**
    E67.3   **Hypervitaminosis D**
    E67.8   **Other specified hyperalimentation**

  E68   **Sequelae of hyperalimentation**
    Code first condition resulting from (sequela) of hyperalimentation

METABOLIC DISORDERS (E70-E88)

    Excludes1   androgen insensitivity syndrome (E34.5-)
                  congenital adrenal hyperplasia (E25.0)
                  Ehlers-Danlos syndrome (Q79.6)
                  hemolytic anemias attributable to enzyme disorders (D55.-)
                  Marfan's syndrome (Q87.4)
                  5-alpha-reductase deficiency (E29.1)

● **E70**   **Disorders of aromatic amino-acid metabolism**
    E70.0   **Classical phenylketonuria**
        Inherited disorder that increases to harmful levels amino acid phenylalanine
    E70.1   **Other hyperphenylalaninemias**
  ● **E70.2**   **Disorders of tyrosine metabolism**
        Excludes1   transitory tyrosinemia of newborn (P74.5)
        E70.20   **Disorder of tyrosine metabolism, unspecified**
            Tyrosine: Nonessential amino acid occurring in most proteins
        E70.21   **Tyrosinemia**
            Congenital amino acid metabolism
            Hypertyrosinemia
        E70.29   **Other disorders of tyrosine metabolism**
            Alkaptonuria
            Ochronosis

▶ New   ➠ Revised   ~~deleted~~ Deleted   Excludes 1   Excludes 2   Includes   Use additional   Code first   Code also   Key words
OGCR Official Guidelines   X Assign placeholder X   ● Use Additional Character(s)   ▌Manifestation Code   **Coding Clinic**

● **E70.3**   **Albinism**
      Congenital condition of reduced or absent pigment in eyes,
      skin, and hair
      E70.30   **Albinism, unspecified**
●   **E70.31**   **Ocular albinism**
        E70.310   **X-linked ocular albinism**
        E70.311   **Autosomal recessive ocular albinism**
        E70.318   **Other ocular albinism**
        E70.319   **Ocular albinism, unspecified**
●   **E70.32**   **Oculocutaneous albinism**
        Partial or total lack of melanin pigment in eyes

        Excludes1   Chediak-Higashi syndrome
                  (E70.330)
                  Hermansky-Pudlak syndrome
                  (E70.331)

        E70.320   **Tyrosinase negative oculocutaneous albinism**
              Albinism I
              Oculocutaneous albinism ty-neg
        E70.321   **Tyrosinase positive oculocutaneous albinism**
              Albinism II
              Oculocutaneous albinism ty-pos
        E70.328   **Other oculocutaneous albinism**
              Cross syndrome
        E70.329   **Oculocutaneous albinism, unspecified**
●   **E70.33**   **Albinism with hematologic abnormality**
        E70.330   **Chediak-Higashi syndrome**
        E70.331   **Hermansky-Pudlak syndrome**
        E70.338   **Other albinism with hematologic abnormality**
        E70.339   **Albinism with hematologic abnormality, unspecified**
      E70.39   **Other specified albinism**
           Piebaldism
● **E70.4**   **Disorders of histidine metabolism**
      E70.40   **Disorders of histidine metabolism, unspecified**
      E70.41   **Histidinemia**
      E70.49   **Other disorders of histidine metabolism**
   E70.5   **Disorders of tryptophan metabolism**
   E70.8   **Other disorders of aromatic amino-acid metabolism**
   E70.9   **Disorder of aromatic amino-acid metabolism, unspecified**

● **E71**   **Disorders of branched-chain amino-acid metabolism and fatty-acid metabolism**
      E71.0   **Maple-syrup-urine disease**
        Due to defect in amino acid catabolism, causing severe
        ketoacidosis with smell of maple syrup in urine and on
        body
●   **E71.1**   **Other disorders of branched-chain amino-acid metabolism**
●   **E71.11**   **Branched-chain organic acidurias**
        E71.110   **Isovaleric acidemia**
        E71.111   **3-methylglutaconic aciduria**
        E71.118   **Other branched-chain organic acidurias**
●   **E71.12**   **Disorders of propionate metabolism**
        E71.120   **Methylmalonic acidemia**
        E71.121   **Propionic acidemia**
        E71.128   **Other disorders of propionate metabolism**
      E71.19   **Other disorders of branched-chain amino-acid metabolism**
           Hyperleucine-isoleucinemia
           Hypervalinemia

   E71.2   **Disorder of branched-chain amino-acid metabolism, unspecified**
●   **E71.3**   **Disorders of fatty-acid metabolism**

        Excludes1   peroxisomal disorders (E71.5)
                  Refsum's disease (G60.1)
                  Schilder's disease (G37.0)

        Excludes2   carnitine deficiency due to inborn error of
                  metabolism (E71.42)

      E71.30   **Disorder of fatty-acid metabolism, unspecified**
●   **E71.31**   **Disorders of fatty-acid oxidation**
        E71.310   **Long chain/very long chain acyl CoA dehydrogenase deficiency**
              LCAD
              VLCAD
        E71.311   **Medium chain acyl CoA dehydrogenase deficiency**
              MCAD
        E71.312   **Short chain acyl CoA dehydrogenase deficiency**
              SCAD
        E71.313   **Glutaric aciduria type II**
              Glutaric aciduria type II A
              Glutaric aciduria type II B
              Glutaric aciduria type II C

          Excludes1   glutaric aciduria (type
                   1) NOS (E72.3)

        E71.314   **Muscle carnitine palmitoyltransferase deficiency**
        E71.318   **Other disorders of fatty-acid oxidation**
      E71.32   **Disorders of ketone metabolism**
      E71.39   **Other disorders of fatty-acid metabolism**
●   **E71.4**   **Disorders of carnitine metabolism**

        Excludes1   muscle carnitine palmitoyltransferase
                  deficiency (E71.314)

      E71.40   **Disorder of carnitine metabolism, unspecified**
      E71.41   **Primary carnitine deficiency**
      E71.42   **Carnitine deficiency due to inborn errors of metabolism**

           Code also associated inborn error or
              metabolism

      E71.43   **Iatrogenic carnitine deficiency**
           Iatrogenic: Outcomes from activity of physicians
           Carnitine deficiency due to hemodialysis
           Carnitine deficiency due to Valproic acid
              therapy
●   **E71.44**   **Other secondary carnitine deficiency**
        E71.440   **Ruvalcaba-Myhre-Smith syndrome**
        E71.448   **Other secondary carnitine deficiency**
●   **E71.5**   **Peroxisomal disorders**
       Class of conditions which lead to disorders of lipid
       metabolism

        Excludes1   Schilder's disease (G37.0)

      E71.50   **Peroxisomal disorder, unspecified**
●   **E71.51**   **Disorders of peroxisome biogenesis**
          Group 1 peroxisomal disorders

        Excludes1   Refsum's disease (G60.1)

        E71.510   **Zellweger syndrome**
        E71.511   **Neonatal adrenoleukodystrophy**

          Excludes1   X-linked adrenoleuko-
                   dystrophy
                   (E71.42-)

        E71.518   **Other disorders of peroxisome biogenesis**

CHAPTER 4 (E00-E90)

● **E71.52**   **X-linked adrenoleukodystrophy**

    E71.520   Childhood cerebral X-linked adrenoleukodystrophy

    E71.521   Adolescent X-linked adrenoleukodystrophy

    E71.522   Adrenomyeloneuropathy

    E71.528   Other X-linked adrenoleukodystrophy
       Addison only phenotype adrenoleukodystrophy
       Addison-Schilder adrenoleukodystrophy

    E71.529   X-linked adrenoleukodystrophy, unspecified type

   E71.53   Other group 2 peroxisomal disorders

● **E71.54**   Other peroxisomal disorders

    E71.540   Rhizomelic chondrodysplasia punctata
       Rare, severe, inherited disorder with limb shortening, bone and cartilage abnormalities, abnormal facial appearance, severe mental retardation, psychomotor retardation, and cataracts

       Excludes1   chondrodysplasia punctata NOS (Q77.3)

    E71.541   Zellweger-like syndrome

    E71.542   Other group 3 peroxisomal disorders

    E71.548   Other peroxisomal disorders

● **E72**   **Other disorders of amino-acid metabolism**

   Excludes1   disorders of:
      aromatic amino-acid metabolism (E70.-)
      branched-chain amino-acid metabolism (E71.0-E71.2)
      fatty-acid metabolism (E71.3)
      purine and pyrimidine metabolism (E79.-)
      gout (M1A.-, M10.-)

● **E72.0**   **Disorders of amino-acid transport**

   Excludes1   disorders of tryptophan metabolism (E70.5)

   E72.00   Disorders of amino-acid transport, unspecified

   E72.01   Cystinuria
      Hereditary aminoaciduria due to impairment of renal transport with predominant symptom of urinary cystine calculi

   E72.02   Hartnup's disease
      Inborn error of metabolism

   E72.03   Lowe's syndrome
      X-linked disorder with rickets, hydrophthalmia, congenital glaucoma, cataracts, mental retardation, and renal tubule dysfunction

      Use additional code for associated glaucoma (H42)

   E72.04   Cystinosis
      Genetic disease with excessive depostits of amino acid cystine in cells
      Fanconi (-de Toni) (-Debré) syndrome with cystinosis

      Excludes1   Fanconi (-de Toni) (-Debré) syndrome without cystinosis (E72.09)

   E72.09   Other disorders of amino-acid transport
      Fanconi (-de Toni) (-Debré) syndrome, unspecified

● **E72.1**   **Disorders of sulfur-bearing amino-acid metabolism**

   Excludes1   cystinosis (E72.04)
      cystinuria (E72.01)
      transcobalamin II deficiency (D51.2)

   E72.10   Disorders of sulfur-bearing amino-acid metabolism, unspecified

   E72.11   Homocystinuria
      Cystathionine synthase deficiency

   E72.12   Methylenetetrahydrofolate reductase deficiency

   E72.19   Other disorders of sulfur-bearing amino-acid metabolism
      Cystathioninuria
      Methioninemia
      Sulfite oxidase deficiency

● **E72.2**   **Disorders of urea cycle metabolism**

   Excludes1   disorders of ornithine metabolism (E72.4)

   E72.20   Disorder of urea cycle metabolism, unspecified
      Hyperammonemia
      Elevated levels of ammonia

      Excludes1   hyperammonemia-hyperornithinemia-homocitrullinemia syndrome E72.4
       transient hyperammonemia of newborn (P74.6)

   E72.21   Argininemia
      Disorder in which deficiency of enzyme arginase causes build up of arginine and ammonia in blood

   E72.22   Arginosuccinic aciduria
      Gene disorder of urea cycle resulting accumulation of ammonia

   E72.23   Citrullinemia
      Urea cycle disorder that causes ammonia and other toxic substances to accumulate in blood

   E72.29   Other disorders of urea cycle metabolism

   E72.3   **Disorders of lysine and hydroxylysine metabolism**
      Glutaric aciduria NOS
      Glutaric aciduria (type I)
      Hydroxylysinemia
      Hyperlysinemia

      Excludes1   glutaric aciduria type II (E71.313)
       Refsum's disease (G60.1)
       Zellweger syndrome (E71.510)

   E72.4   **Disorders of ornithine metabolism**
      Hyperammonemia-Hyperornithinemia-Homocitrullinemia syndrome
      Ornithinemia (types I, II)
      Ornithine transcarbamylase deficiency

      Excludes1   hereditary choroidal dystrophy (H31.2-)

● **E72.5**   **Disorders of glycine metabolism**

   E72.50   Disorder of glycine metabolism, unspecified

   E72.51   Non-ketotic hyperglycinemia

   E72.52   Trimethylaminuria

⮕ **E72.53**   Primary hyperoxaluria
      Oxalosis
      Oxaluria

   E72.59   Other disorders of glycine metabolism
      D-glycericacidemia
      Hyperhydroxyprolinemia
      Hyperprolinemia (types I, II)
      Sarcosinemia

▶ New   ⮕ Revised   ~~deleted~~ Deleted   Excludes 1   Excludes 2   Includes   Use additional   Code first   Code also   Key words

OGCR Official Guidelines   X Assign placeholder X   ● Use Additional Character(s)   ▶ Manifestation Code   **Coding Clinic**

742

E72.8   **Other specified disorders of amino-acid metabolism**
~~Disorders of beta-amino-acid metabolism~~
~~Disorders of gamma-glutamyl cycle~~

▶ E72.81   **Disorders of gamma aminobutyric acid metabolism**
▶4-hydroxybutyric aciduria
▶Disorders of GABA metabolism
▶GABA metabolic defect
▶GABA transaminase deficiency
▶GABA-T deficiency
▶Gamma-hydroxybutyric aciduria
▶SSADHD
▶Succinic semialdehyde dehydrogenase deficiency

▶ E72.89   **Other specified disorders of amino-acid metabolism**
▶Disorders of beta-amino-acid metabolism
▶Disorders of gamma-glutamyl cycle

E72.9   **Disorder of amino-acid metabolism, unspecified**

● E73   **Lactose intolerance**
Intolerance for lactose, due to inherited deficiency of lactase activity in intestinal mucosa

E73.0   **Congenital lactase deficiency**
E73.1   **Secondary lactase deficiency**
E73.8   **Other lactose intolerance**
E73.9   **Lactose intolerance, unspecified**

● E74   **Other disorders of carbohydrate metabolism**
Excludes1   diabetes mellitus (E08-E13)
hypoglycemia NOS (E16.2)
increased secretion of glucagon (E16.3)
mucopolysaccharidosis (E76.0-E76.3)

● E74.0   **Glycogen storage disease**
E74.00   **Glycogen storage disease, unspecified**
E74.01   **von Gierke's disease**
Type I glycogen storage disease
E74.02   **Pompe disease**
Cardiac glycogenosis
Type II glycogen storage disease
E74.03   **Cori disease**
Forbes' disease
Type III glycogen storage disease
E74.04   **McArdle disease**
Type V glycogen storage disease
E74.09   **Other glycogen storage disease**
Andersen disease
Hers disease
Tauri disease
Glycogen storage disease, types 0, IV, VI-XI
Liver phosphorylase deficiency
Muscle phosphofructokinase deficiency

● E74.1   **Disorders of fructose metabolism**
Excludes1   muscle phosphofructokinase deficiency (E74.09)
E74.10   **Disorder of fructose metabolism, unspecified**
E74.11   **Essential fructosuria**
Fructokinase deficiency
E74.12   **Hereditary fructose intolerance**
Fructosemia
E74.19   **Other disorders of fructose metabolism**
Fructose-1, 6-diphosphatase deficiency

● E74.2   **Disorders of galactose metabolism**
E74.20   **Disorders of galactose metabolism, unspecified**
E74.21   **Galactosemia**
Genetic disorders resulting from defective simple sugar (galactose) metabolism
E74.29   **Other disorders of galactose metabolism**
Galactokinase deficiency

● E74.3   **Other disorders of intestinal carbohydrate absorption**
Excludes2   lactose intolerance (E73.-)
E74.31   **Sucrase-isomaltase deficiency**
Deficiency in metabolism in intestinal mucosa results in malabsorption of sucrose and starch
E74.39   **Other disorders of intestinal carbohydrate absorption**
Disorder of intestinal carbohydrate absorption NOS
Glucose-galactose malabsorption
Sucrase deficiency

● E74.4   **Disorders of pyruvate metabolism and gluconeogenesis**
Deficiency of phosphoenolpyruvate carboxykinase
Deficiency of pyruvate carboxylase
Deficiency of pyruvate dehydrogenase
Excludes1   disorders of pyruvate metabolism and gluconeogenesis with anemia (D55.-)
Leigh's syndrome (G31.82)

● E74.8   **Other specified disorders of carbohydrate metabolism**
Essential pentosuria
Renal glycosuria

E74.9   **Disorder of carbohydrate metabolism, unspecified**

● E75   **Disorders of sphingolipid metabolism and other lipid storage disorders**
Excludes1   mucolipidosis, types I-III (E77.0-E77.1)
Refsum's disease (G60.1)

● E75.0   **GM2 gangliosidosis**
Rare metabolic disorder that causes destruction of nerve cells of brain and spinal cord
E75.00   **GM2 gangliosidosis, unspecified**
E75.01   **Sandhoff disease**
E75.02   **Tay-Sachs disease**
E75.09   **Other GM2 gangliosidosis**
Adult GM2 gangliosidosis
Juvenile GM2 gangliosidosis

● E75.1   **Other and unspecified gangliosidosis**
E75.10   **Unspecified gangliosidosis**
Gangliosidosis NOS
E75.11   **Mucolipidosis IV**
Disorder with symptoms of psychomotor retardation and severe visual impairment
E75.19   **Other gangliosidosis**
GM1 gangliosidosis
GM3 gangliosidosis

● E75.2   **Other sphingolipidosis**
Lysosomal (a particle in a cytoplasm cell that contains digestive enzymes) storage diseases with symptoms of abnormal storage of amino acids
Excludes1   adrenoleukodystrophy [Addison-Schilder] (E71.528)
E75.21   **Fabry (-Anderson) disease**
E75.22   **Gaucher disease**
E75.23   **Krabbe disease**
● E75.24   **Niemann-Pick disease**
E75.240   **Niemann-Pick disease type A**
E75.241   **Niemann-Pick disease type B**
E75.242   **Niemann-Pick disease type C**
E75.243   **Niemann-Pick disease type D**
E75.248   **Other Niemann-Pick disease**
E75.249   **Niemann-Pick disease, unspecified**
E75.25   **Metachromatic leukodystrophy**
▶ E75.26   **Sulfatase deficiency**
▶Multiple sulfatase deficiency (MSD)
E75.29   **Other sphingolipidosis**
Farber's syndrome
~~Sulfatase deficiency~~
Sulfatide lipidosis

Item 4-8 Leukodystrophy is characterized by degeneration and/or failure of the myelin formation of the central nervous system and sometimes of the peripheral nervous system. The disease is inherited and progressive.

CHAPTER 4 (E00-E90)

CHAPTER 4 (E00-E90)

E75.3   Sphingolipidosis, unspecified

E75.4   Neuronal ceroid lipofuscinosis
      Batten disease
      Bielschowsky-Jansky disease
      Kufs disease
      Spielmeyer-Vogt disease

E75.5   Other lipid storage disorders
      Cerebrotendinous cholesterosis [van Bogaert-Scherer-Epstein]
      Wolman's disease

E75.6   Lipid storage disorder, unspecified

● E76   Disorders of glycosaminoglycan metabolism

  ● E76.0   Mucopolysaccharidosis, type I
     Inborn metabolic disorder of enzymes that break down carbohydrates

    E76.01   Hurler's syndrome

    E76.02   Hurler-Scheie syndrome

    E76.03   Scheie's syndrome

  E76.1   Mucopolysaccharidosis, type II
     Inborn metabolic disorder of enzymes that break down carbohydrates occurs in 2-4 year old males
     Hunter's syndrome

  ● E76.2   Other mucopolysaccharides

    ● E76.21   Morquio mucopolysaccharidoses

      E76.210   Morquio A mucopolysaccharidoses
        Classic Morquio syndrome
        Morquio syndrome A
        Mucopolysaccharidosis, type IVA

      E76.211   Morquio B mucopolysaccharidoses
        Morquio-like mucopolysaccharidoses
        Morquio-like syndrome
        Morquio syndrome B
        Mucopolysaccharidosis, type IVB

      E76.219   Morquio mucopolysaccharidoses, unspecified
        Morquio syndrome
        Mucopolysaccharidosis, type IV

    E76.22   Sanfilippo mucopolysaccharidoses
      Mucopolysaccharidosis, type III (A) (B) (C) (D)
      Sanfilippo A syndrome
      Sanfilippo B syndrome
      Sanfilippo C syndrome
      Sanfilippo D syndrome

    E76.29   Other mucopolysaccharidoses
      beta-Glucuronidase deficiency
      Maroteaux-Lamy (mild) (severe) syndrome
      Mucopolysaccharidosis, types VI, VII

  E76.3   Mucopolysaccharidosis, unspecified

  E76.8   Other disorders of glucosaminoglycan metabolism

  E76.9   Glucosaminoglycan metabolism disorder, unspecified

● E77   Disorders of glycoprotein metabolism

  E77.0   Defects in post-translational modification of lysosomal enzymes
      Mucolipidosis II [I-cell disease]
      Mucolipidosis III [pseudo-Hurler polydystrophy]

  E77.1   Defects in glycoprotein degradation
      Aspartylglucosaminuria
      Fucosidosis
      Mannosidosis
      Sialidosis [mucolipidosis I]

  E77.8   Other disorders of glycoprotein metabolism

  E77.9   Disorder of glycoprotein metabolism, unspecified

● E78   Disorders of lipoprotein metabolism and other lipidemias
    Excludes1   sphingolipidosis (E75.0-E75.3)

  ● E78.0   Pure hypercholesterolemia
     Coding Clinic: 2016, Q4, P13

    E78.00   Pure hypercholesterolemia, unspecified
      Fredrickson's hyperlipoproteinemia, type IIa
      Hyperbetalipoproteinemia
      Low-density-lipoprotein-type [LDL] hyperlipoproteinemia
      (Pure) hypercholesterolemia NOS
     Coding Clinic: 2016, Q4, P13

    E78.01   Familial hypercholesterolemia
     Coding Clinic: 2016, Q4, P13

  E78.1   Pure hyperglyceridemia
      Elevated fasting triglycerides
      Endogenous hyperglyceridemia
      Fredrickson's hyperlipoproteinemia, type IV
      Hyperlipidemia, group B
      Hyperprebetalipoproteinemia
      Very-low-density-lipoprotein-type [VLDL] hyperlipoproteinemia

  E78.2   Mixed hyperlipidemia
      Broad- or floating-betalipoproteinemia
      Combined hyperlipidemia NOS
      Elevated cholesterol with elevated triglycerides NEC
      Fredrickson's hyperlipoproteinemia, type IIb or III
      Hyperbetalipoproteinemia with prebetalipoproteinemia
      Hypercholesteremia with endogenous hyperglyceridemia
      Hyperlipidemia, group C
      Tubo-eruptive xanthoma
      Xanthoma tuberosum

    Excludes1   cerebrotendinous cholesterosis [van Bogaert-Scherer-Epstein] (E75.5)
    ➡ familial combined hyperlipidemia (E78.49)

  E78.3   Hyperchylomicronemia
      Chylomicron retention disease
      Fredrickson's hyperlipoproteinemia, type I or V
      Hyperlipidemia, group D
      Mixed hyperglyceridemia

  E78.4   Other hyperlipidemia
      ~~Familial combined hyperlipidemia~~

    ▶ E78.41   Elevated Lipoprotein(a)
      ▶ Elevated Lp(a)

    ▶ E78.49   Other hyperlipidemia
      ▶ Familial combined hyperlipidemia

  E78.5   Hyperlipidemia, unspecified

  E78.6   Lipoprotein deficiency
      Abetalipoproteinemia
      Depressed HDL cholesterol
      High-density lipoprotein deficiency
      Hypoalphalipoproteinemia
      Hypobetalipoproteinemia (familial)
      Lecithin cholesterol acyltransferase deficiency
      Tangier disease

  ● E78.7   Disorders of bile acid and cholesterol metabolism
    Excludes1   Niemann-Pick disease type C (E75.242)

    E78.70   Disorder of bile acid and cholesterol metabolism, unspecified

    E78.71   Barth syndrome

    E78.72   Smith-Lemli-Opitz syndrome

    E78.79   Other disorders of bile acid and cholesterol metabolism

  ● E78.8   Other disorders of lipoprotein metabolism

    E78.81   Lipoid dermatoarthritis

    E78.89   Other lipoprotein metabolism disorders

  E78.9   Disorder of lipoprotein metabolism, unspecified

▶ New   ⇒ Revised   ~~deleted~~ Deleted   Excludes 1   Excludes 2   Includes   Use additional   Code first   Code also   Key words
OGCR Official Guidelines   X Assign placeholder X   ● Use Additional Character(s)   ▷ Manifestation Code   Coding Clinic

● **E79**   **Disorders of purine and pyrimidine metabolism**
Purines, along with pyrimidines, signal RNA and DNA production

> **Excludes1**   Ataxia-telangiectasia (Q87.1)
> Bloom's syndrome (Q82.8)
> Cockayne's syndrome (Q87.1)
> calculus of kidney (N20.0)
> combined immunodeficiency disorders (D81.-)
> Fanconi's anemia (D61.09)
> gout (M1A.-, M10.-)
> orotaciduric anemia (D53.0)
> progeria (E34.8)
> Werner's syndrome (E34.8)
> xeroderma pigmentosum (Q82.1)

E79.0   **Hyperuricemia without signs of inflammatory arthritis and tophaceous disease**
Asymptomatic hyperuricemia

E79.1   **Lesch-Nyhan syndrome**
HGPRT deficiency

E79.2   **Myoadenylate deaminase deficiency**

E79.8   **Other disorders of purine and pyrimidine metabolism**
Hereditary xanthinuria

E79.9   **Disorder of purine and pyrimidine metabolism, unspecified**

● **E80**   **Disorders of porphyrin and bilirubin metabolism**
Group of chemical compounds in RBCs that combine with iron to form heme

> **Includes**   defects of catalase and peroxidase

E80.0   **Hereditary erythropoietic porphyria**
Congenital erythropoietic porphyria
Erythropoietic protoporphyria

E80.1   **Porphyria cutanea tarda**

● **E80.2**   **Other and unspecified porphyria**

     E80.20   **Unspecified porphyria**
        Porphyria NOS

     E80.21   **Acute intermittent (hepatic) porphyria**

     E80.29   **Other porphyria**
        Hereditary coproporphyria

E80.3   **Defects of catalase and peroxidase**
Acatalasia [Takahara]

E80.4   **Gilbert syndrome**

E80.5   **Crigler-Najjar syndrome**

E80.6   **Other disorders of bilirubin metabolism**
Dubin-Johnson syndrome
Rotor's syndrome

E80.7   **Disorder of bilirubin metabolism, unspecified**

● **E83**   **Disorders of mineral metabolism**

> **Excludes1**   dietary mineral deficiency (E58-E61)
> parathyroid disorders (E20-E21)
> vitamin D deficiency (E55.-)

● **E83.0**   **Disorders of copper metabolism**

     E83.00   **Disorder of copper metabolism, unspecified**

     E83.01   **Wilson's disease**
        Code also associated Kayser Fleischer ring (H18.04-)

     E83.09   **Other disorders of copper metabolism**
        Menkes' (kinky hair) (steely hair) disease

● **E83.1**   **Disorders of iron metabolism**

> **Excludes1**   iron deficiency anemia (D50.-)
> sideroblastic anemia (D64.0-D64.3)

     E83.10   **Disorder of iron metabolism, unspecified**

●   **E83.11**   **Hemochromatosis**

>   **Excludes1**   GALD (P78.84)
> Gestational alloimmune liver disease (P78.84)
> Neonatal hemochromatosis (P78.84)

        E83.110   **Hereditary hemochromatosis**
           Bronzed diabetes
           Pigmentary cirrhosis (of liver)
           Primary (hereditary) hemochromatosis

        E83.111   **Hemochromatosis due to repeated red blood cell transfusions**
           Iron overload due to repeated red blood cell transfusions
           Transfusion (red blood cell) associated hemochromatosis

        E83.118   **Other hemochromatosis**

        E83.119   **Hemochromatosis, unspecified**

     E83.19   **Other disorders of iron metabolism**
        Use additional code, if applicable, for idiopathic pulmonary hemosiderosis (J84.03)

E83.2   **Disorders of zinc metabolism**
Acrodermatitis enteropathica

● **E83.3**   **Disorders of phosphorus metabolism and phosphatases**

> **Excludes1**   adult osteomalacia (M83.-)
> osteoporosis (M80.-)

     E83.30   **Disorder of phosphorus metabolism, unspecified**

     E83.31   **Familial hypophosphatemia**
        Vitamin D-resistant osteomalacia
        Vitamin D-resistant rickets

>   **Excludes1**   vitamin D-deficiency rickets (E55.0)

     E83.32   **Hereditary vitamin D-dependent rickets (type 1) (type 2)**
        25-hydroxyvitamin D 1-alpha-hydroxylase deficiency
        Pseudovitamin D deficiency
        Vitamin D receptor defect

     E83.39   **Other disorders of phosphorus metabolism**
        Acid phosphatase deficiency
        Hypophosphatasia

● **E83.4**   **Disorders of magnesium metabolism**

     E83.40   **Disorders of magnesium metabolism, unspecified**

     E83.41   **Hypermagnesemia**
        Coding Clinic: 2016, Q4, P55

     E83.42   **Hypomagnesemia**

     E83.49   **Other disorders of magnesium metabolism**

● **E83.5**   **Disorders of calcium metabolism**

> **Excludes1**   chondrocalcinosis (M11.1-M11.2)
> hungry bone syndrome (E83.81)
> hyperparathyroidism (E21.0-E21.3)

     E83.50   **Unspecified disorder of calcium metabolism**

     E83.51   **Hypocalcemia**

     E83.52   **Hypercalcemia**
        Familial hypocalciuric hypercalcemia

     E83.59   **Other disorders of calcium metabolism**
        Idiopathic hypercalciuria

● **E83.8**   **Other disorders of mineral metabolism**

     E83.81   **Hungry bone syndrome**

     E83.89   **Other disorders of mineral metabolism**

E83.9   **Disorder of mineral metabolism, unspecified**

● **E84**   **Cystic fibrosis**

     Includes   mucoviscidosis

     Code also exocrine pancreatic insufficiency (K86.81)

   E84.0   **Cystic fibrosis with pulmonary manifestations**

       Use additional code to identify any infectious organism present, such as:

         Pseudomonas (B96.5)

● **E84.1**   **Cystic fibrosis with intestinal manifestations**

     E84.11   **Meconium ileus in cystic fibrosis**   N

         Excludes1   meconium ileus not due to cystic fibrosis (P76.0)

     E84.19   **Cystic fibrosis with other intestinal manifestations**

         Distal intestinal obstruction syndrome

   E84.8   **Cystic fibrosis with other manifestations**

   E84.9   **Cystic fibrosis, unspecified**

● **E85**   **Amyloidosis**

     A disorder resulting from the abnormal deposition of a particular protein (amyloid) into tissues of the body

     Excludes2   Alzheimer's disease (G30.0-)

   E85.0   **Non-neuropathic heredofamilial amyloidosis**

       Hereditary amyloid nephropathy

       Code also associated disorders, such as:

         autoinflammatory syndromes (M04.-)

     Excludes2   Transthyretin-related (ATTR) familial amyloid cardiomyopathy (E85.4)

   E85.1   **Neuropathic heredofamilial amyloidosis**

       Amyloid polyneuropathy (Portuguese)

       Transthyretin-related (ATTR) familial amyloid polyneuropathy

       Coding Clinic: 2012, Q4, P100

   E85.2   **Heredofamilial amyloidosis, unspecified**

   E85.3   **Secondary systemic amyloidosis**

       Hemodialysis-associated amyloidosis

   E85.4   **Organ-limited amyloidosis**

       Localized amyloidosis

       Transthyretin-related (ATTR) familial amyloid cardiomyopathy

● **E85.8**   **Other amyloidosis**

     E85.81   **Light chain (AL) amyloidosis**

     E85.82   **Wild-type transthyretin-related (ATTR) amyloidosis**

         Senile systemic amyloidosis (SSA)

     E85.89   **Other amyloidosis**

   E85.9   **Amyloidosis, unspecified**

● **E86**   **Volume depletion**

     Excludes1   dehydration of newborn (P74.1)

         hypovolemic shock NOS (R57.1)

         postprocedural hypovolemic shock (T81.19)

         traumatic hypovolemic shock (T79.4)

     Use additional code(s) for any associated disorders of electrolyte and acid-base balance (E87.-)

   E86.0   **Dehydration**

       Excessive loss of body water

   E86.1   **Hypovolemia**

       Diminished volume of circulating blood

       Depletion of volume of plasma

   E86.9   **Volume depletion, unspecified**

● **E87**   **Other disorders of fluid, electrolyte and acid-base balance**

     Excludes1   diabetes insipidus (E23.2)

         electrolyte imbalance associated with hyperemesis gravidarum (O21.1)

         electrolyte imbalance following ectopic or molar pregnancy (O08.5)

         familial periodic paralysis (G72.3)

   E87.0   **Hyperosmolality and hypernatremia**

       Sodium [Na] excess

       Sodium [Na] overload

       Coding Clinic: 2018, Q2, P6

   E87.1   **Hypo-osmolality and hyponatremia**

       Sodium [Na] deficiency

     Excludes1   syndrome of inappropriate secretion of antidiuretic hormone (E22.2)

       Coding Clinic: 2018, Q2, P6

   E87.2   **Acidosis**

       Acidosis NOS

       Lactic acidosis

       Metabolic acidosis

       Respiratory acidosis

     Excludes1   diabetic acidosis - see categories E08-E10, E13 with ketoacidosis

   E87.3   **Alkalosis**

       Alkalosis NOS

       Metabolic alkalosis

       Respiratory alkalosis

   E87.4   **Mixed disorder of acid-base balance**

   E87.5   **Hyperkalemia**

       Potassium [K] excess

       Potassium [K] overload

   E87.6   **Hypokalemia**

       Potassium [K] deficiency

● **E87.7**   **Fluid overload**

     Excludes1   edema NOS (R60.9)

         fluid retention (R60.9)

     E87.70   **Fluid overload, unspecified**

     E87.71   **Transfusion associated circulatory overload**

         Fluid overload due to transfusion (blood) (blood components) TACO

     E87.79   **Other fluid overload**

   E87.8   **Other disorders of electrolyte and fluid balance, not elsewhere classified**

       Electrolyte imbalance NOS

       Hyperchloremia

       Hypochloremia

Item 4–9   Circulating fluid volume is regulated by the amount of water and sodium ingested, excreted by the kidneys into the urine, and lost through the gastrointestinal tract, lungs, and skin. To maintain blood volume within a normal range, the kidneys regulate the amount of water and sodium lost into the urine. Too much (**fluid overload**) or too little fluid volume (**volume depletion**) will affect blood pressure. Severe cases of vomiting, diarrhea, bleeding, and burns (fluid loss through exposed burn surface area) can contribute to fluid loss. Internal body environment must maintain a precise balance (homeostasis) between too much fluid and too little fluid. This complex balancing mechanism is critical to good health.

▶ New   ⇢ Revised   ~~deleted~~ Deleted   Excludes 1   Excludes 2   Includes   Use additional   Code first   Code also   Key words

746   **OGCR** Official Guidelines   X Assign placeholder X   ● Use Additional Character(s)   ▮ Manifestation Code   **Coding Clinic**

● **E88   Other and unspecified metabolic disorders**
    Use additional codes for associated conditions
      Excludes1   histiocytosis X (chronic) (C96.6)
  ● **E88.0   Disorders of plasma-protein metabolism, not elsewhere classified**
      Excludes1   disorder of lipoprotein metabolism (E78.-)
              monoclonal gammopathy (of undetermined significance) (D47.2)
              polyclonal hypergammaglobulinemia (D89.0)
              Waldenström macroglobulinemia (C88.0)
    E88.01   Alpha-1-antitrypsin deficiency AAT deficiency
  ▶ **E88.02   Plasminogen deficiency**
      ▶Dysplasminogenemia
      ▶Hypoplasminogenemia
      ▶Type 1 plasminogen deficiency
      ▶Type 2 plasminogen deficiency
      ▶ Code also, if applicable, ligneous conjunctivitis (H10.51)
      ▶Use additional code for associated findings, such as:
        ▶hydrocephalus (G91.4)
        ▶ligneous conjunctivitis (H10.51)
        ▶otitis media (H67.-)
        ▶respiratory disorder related to plasminogen deficiency (J99)
    E88.09   Other disorders of plasma-protein metabolism, not elsewhere classified
      Bisalbuminemia
  E88.1   Lipodystrophy, not elsewhere classified
    Defective fat metabolism resulting in absence of subcutaneous fat
    Lipodystrophy NOS
      Excludes1   Whipple's disease (K90.81)
  E88.2   Lipomatosis, not elsewhere classified
    Abnormal tumorlike accumulations of fat in tissue
    Lipomatosis NOS
    Lipomatosis (Check) dolorosa [Dercum]
  E88.3   Tumor lysis syndrome
    Tumor lysis syndrome (spontaneous)
    Tumor lysis syndrome following antineoplastic drug chemotherapy
    Use additional code for adverse effect, if applicable, to identify drug (T45.1X5)
  ● **E88.4   Mitochondrial metabolism disorders**
    Congenital disorder of metabolism
      Excludes1   disorders of pyruvate metabolism (E74.4)
              Kearns-Sayre syndrome (H49.81)
              Leber's disease (H47.22)
              Leigh's encephalopathy (G31.82)
              Mitochondrial myopathy, NEC (G71.3)
              Reye's syndrome (G93.7)
    E88.40   Mitochondrial metabolism disorder, unspecified
    E88.41   MELAS syndrome
      Mitochondrial myopathy, encephalopathy, lactic acidosis and stroke-like episodes
    E88.42   MERRF syndrome
      Myoclonic epilepsy associated with ragged-red fibers
      Code also progressive myoclonic epilepsy (G40.3-)
    E88.49   Other mitochondrial metabolism disorders
  ● **E88.8   Other specified metabolic disorders**
    E88.81   Metabolic syndrome
      Dysmetabolic syndrome X
      Use additional codes for associated manifestations, such as:
      obesity (E66.-)
    E88.89   Other specified metabolic disorders
      Launois-Bensaude adenolipomatosis
      Excludes1   adult pulmonary Langerhans cell histiocytosis (J84.82)
  E88.9   Metabolic disorder, unspecified

POSTPROCEDURAL ENDOCRINE AND METABOLIC COMPLICATIONS AND DISORDERS, NOT ELSEWHERE CLASSIFIED (E89)

● **E89   Postprocedural endocrine and metabolic complications and disorders, not elsewhere classified**
      Excludes2   intraoperative complications of endocrine system organ or structure (E36.0-, E36.1-, E36.8)
  E89.0   Postprocedural hypothyroidism
    Postirradiation hypothyroidism
    Postsurgical hypothyroidism
  E89.1   Postprocedural hypoinsulinemia
    Postpancreatectomy hyperglycemia
    Postsurgical hypoinsulinemia
    Use additional code, if applicable, to identify:
      acquired absence of pancreas (Z90.41-)
      diabetes mellitus (postpancreatectomy) (postprocedural) (E13.-)
      insulin use (Z79.4)
      Excludes1   transient postprocedural hyperglycemia (R73.9)
              transient postprocedural hypoglycemia (E16.2)
  E89.2   Postprocedural hypoparathyroidism
    Parathyroprival tetany
  E89.3   Postprocedural hypopituitarism
    Postirradiation hypopituitarism
  ● **E89.4   Postprocedural ovarian failure**
    E89.40   Asymptomatic postprocedural ovarian failure ♀
      Postprocedural ovarian failure NOS
    E89.41   Symptomatic postprocedural ovarian failure ♀
      Symptoms such as flushing, sleeplessness, headache, lack of concentration, associated with postprocedural menopause
  E89.5   Postprocedural testicular hypofunction ♂
  E89.6   Postprocedural adrenocortical (-medullary) hypofunction
  ● **E89.8   Other postprocedural endocrine and metabolic complications and disorders**
    Coding Clinic: 2016, Q4, P9
  ● **E89.81   Postprocedural hemorrhage of an endocrine system organ or structure following a procedure**
    E89.810   Postprocedural hemorrhage of an endocrine system organ or structure following an endocrine system procedure
    E89.811   Postprocedural hemorrhage of an endocrine system organ or structure following other procedure
  ● **E89.82   Postprocedural hematoma and seroma of an endocrine system organ or structure**
    E89.820   Postprocedural hematoma of an endocrine system organ or structure following an endocrine system procedure
    E89.821   Postprocedural hematoma of an endocrine system organ or structure following other procedure
    E89.822   Postprocedural seroma of an endocrine system organ or structure following an endocrine system procedure
    E89.823   Postprocedural seroma of an endocrine system organ or structure following other procedure
    E89.89   Other postprocedural endocrine and metabolic complications and disorders
      Use additional code, if applicable, to further specify disorder

CHAPTER 4 (E00-E90)

CHAPTER 5

MENTAL, BEHAVIORAL AND NEURODEVELOPMENTAL DISORDERS (F01-F99)

OGCR Chapter-Specific Coding Guidelines

5. **Chapter 5: Mental, Behavioral and Neurodevelopmental disorders (F01 – F99)**

   a. Pain disorders related to psychological factors
   Assign code F45.41, for pain that is exclusively related to psychological disorders. As indicated by the Excludes 1 note under category G89, a code from category G89 should not be assigned with code F45.41

   Code F45.42, Pain disorders with related psychological factors, should be used with a code from category G89, Pain, not elsewhere classified, if there is documentation of a psychological component for a patient with acute or chronic pain.
   See Section I.C.6. Pain

   b. Mental and behavioral disorders due to psychoactive substance use

   1) In Remission
   Selection of codes for "in remission" for categories F10-F19, Mental and behavioral disorders due to psychoactive substance use (categories F10-F19 with -11, -.21) requires the provider's clinical judgment. The appropriate codes for "in remission" are assigned only on the basis of provider documentation (as defined in the Official Guidelines for Coding and Reporting), unless otherwise instructed by the classification.

   Mild substance use disorders in early or sustained remission are classified to the appropriate codes for substance abuse in remission, and moderate or severe substance use disorders in early or sustained remission are classified to the appropriate codes for substance dependence in remission.

   2) Psychoactive Substance Use, Abuse and Dependence
   When the provider documentation refers to use, abuse and dependence of the same substance (e.g. alcohol, opioid, cannabis, etc.), only one code should be assigned to identify the pattern of use based on the following hierarchy:
   - If both use and abuse are documented, assign only the code for abuse
   - If both abuse and dependence are documented, assign only the code for dependence
   - If use, abuse and dependence are all documented, assign only the code for dependence
   - If both use and dependence are documented, assign only the code for dependence.

   3) Psychoactive Substance Use, *Unspecified*
   As with all other **unspecified** diagnoses, the codes for **unspecified** psychoactive substance use disorders (F10.9-, F11.9-, F12.9-, F13.9-, F14.9-, F15.9-, F16.9-, **F19.9-, F19.9-**) should only be assigned based on provider documentation and when they meet the definition of a reportable diagnosis (see Section III, Reporting Additional Diagnoses). These codes are to be used only when the psychoactive substance use is associated with a physical, mental or behavioral disorder, and such a relationship is documented by the provider.

   c. Factitious Disorder
   Factitious disorder imposed on self or Munchausen's syndrome is a disorder in which a person falsely reports or causes his or her own physical or psychological signs or symptoms. For patients with documented factitious disorder on self or Munchausen's syndrome, assign the appropriate code from subcategory F68.1-, Factitious disorder imposed on self.

   Munchausen's syndrome by proxy (MSBP) is a disorder in which a caregiver (perpetrator) falsely reports or causes an illness or injury in another person (victim) under his or her care, such as a child, an elderly adult, or a person who has a disability. The condition is also referred to as "factitious disorder imposed on another" or "factitious disorder by proxy." The perpetrator, not the victim, receives this diagnosis. Assign code F68.A, Factitious disorder imposed on another, to the perpetrator's record. For the victim of a patient suffering from MSBP, assign the appropriate code from categories T74, Adult and child abuse, neglect and other maltreatment, confirmed, or T76, Adult and child abuse, neglect and other maltreatment, suspected.

   See Section I.C.19.f. Adult and child abuse, neglect and other maltreatment

CHAPTER 5

MENTAL, BEHAVIORAL AND NEURODEVELOPMENTAL DISORDERS (F01-F99)

| **Includes** | disorders of psychological development |
| **Excludes2** | symptoms, signs and abnormal clinical laboratory findings, not elsewhere classified (R00-R99) |

This chapter contains the following blocks:

F01-F09	Mental disorders due to known physiological conditions
F10-F19	Mental and behavioral disorders due to psychoactive substance use
F20-F29	Schizophrenia, schizotypal, delusional, and other non-mood psychotic disorders
F30-F39	Mood [affective] disorders
F40-F48	Anxiety, dissociative, stress-related, somatoform and other nonpsychotic mental disorders
F50-F59	Behavioral syndromes associated with physiological disturbances and physical factors
F60-F69	Disorders of adult personality and behavior
F70-F79	Intellectual disabilities
F80-F89	Pervasive and specific developmental disorders
F90-F98	Behavioral and emotional disorders with onset usually occurring in childhood and adolescence
F99	Unspecified mental disorder

MENTAL DISORDERS DUE TO KNOWN PHYSIOLOGICAL CONDITIONS (F01-F09)

This block comprises a range of mental disorders grouped together on the basis of their having in common a demonstrable etiology in cerebral disease, brain injury, or other insult leading to cerebral dysfunction. The dysfunction may be primary, as in diseases, injuries, and insults that affect the brain directly and selectively; or secondary, as in systemic diseases and disorders that attack the brain only as one of the multiple organs or systems of the body that are involved.

● **F01   Vascular dementia**
Vascular dementia as a result of infarction of the brain due to vascular disease, including hypertensive cerebrovascular disease.

| **Includes** | arteriosclerotic dementia |

Code first the underlying physiological condition or sequelae of cerebrovascular disease.

● **F01.5   Vascular dementia**

F01.50   Vascular dementia without behavioral disturbance   A
Major neurocognitive disorder without behavioral disturbance

F01.51   Vascular dementia with behavioral disturbance   A
Major neurocognitive disorder due to vascular disease, with behavioral disturbance
Major neurocognitive disorder with aggressive behavior
Major neurocognitive disorder with combative behavior
Major neurocognitive disorder with violent behavior
Vascular dementia with aggressive behavior
Vascular dementia with combative behavior
Vascular dementia with violent behavior

Use additional code, if applicable, to identify wandering in vascular dementia (Z91.83)

▶ New   ▦ Revised   ~~deleted~~ Deleted   Excludes 1   Excludes 2   Includes   Use additional   Code first   Code also   Key words

OGCR Official Guidelines   X Assign placeholder X   ● Use Additional Character(s)   ▮ Manifestation Code   **Coding Clinic**

● **F02**   **Dementia in other diseases classified elsewhere**

Code first the underlying physiological condition, such as:

Alzheimer's (G30.-)
cerebral lipidosis (E75.4)
Creutzfeldt-Jakob disease (A81.0-)
dementia with Lewy bodies (G31.83)
dementia with Parkinsonism (G31.83)
epilepsy and recurrent seizures (G40.-)
frontotemporal dementia (G31.09)
hepatolenticular degeneration (E83.0)
human immunodeficiency virus [HIV] disease (B20)
Huntington's disease (G10)
hypercalcemia (E83.52)
hypothyroidism, acquired (E00-E03.-)
intoxications (T36-T65)
Jakob-Creutzfeldt disease (A81.0-)
multiple sclerosis (G35)
neurosyphilis (A52.17)
niacin deficiency [pellagra] (E52)
Parkinson's disease (G20)
Pick's disease (G31.01)
polyarteritis nodosa (M30.0)
prion disease (A81.9)
systemic lupus erythematosus (M32.-)
traumatic brain injury (S06.-)
trypanosomiasis (B56.-, B57.-)
vitamin B deficiency (E53.8)

Includes   Major neurocognitive disorder in other diseases classified elsewhere

Excludes2   dementia in alcohol and psychoactive substance disorders (F10-F19, with .17, .27, .97)
vascular dementia (F01.5-)

Coding Clinic: 2016, Q4, P141

● **F02.8**   **Dementia in other diseases classified elsewhere**

▷ **F02.80**   *Dementia in other diseases classified elsewhere without behavioral disturbance*
Dementia in other diseases classified elsewhere NOS
Major neurocognitive disorder in other diseases classified elsewhere
Coding Clinic: 2017, Q1, P43; 2016, Q2, P6

▷ **F02.81**   *Dementia in other diseases classified elsewhere with behavioral disturbance*
Dementia in other diseases classified elsewhere with aggressive behavior
Dementia in other diseases classified elsewhere with combative behavior
Dementia in other diseases classified elsewhere with violent behavior
Major neurocognitive disorder in other diseases classified elsewhere with aggressive behavior
Major neurocognitive disorder in other diseases classified elsewhere with combative behavior
Major neurocognitive disorder in other diseases classified elsewhere with violent behavior
Use additional code, if applicable, to identify wandering in dementia in conditions classified elsewhere (Z91.83)
Coding Clinic: 2017, Q2, P8, Q1, P43

Item 5-1 Psychosis was a term formerly applied to any mental disorder but is now restricted to disturbances of a great magnitude in which there is a personality disintegration and loss of contact with reality.

● **F03**   **Unspecified dementia**
Presenile dementia NOS
Presenile psychosis NOS
Primary degenerative dementia NOS
Senile dementia NOS
Senile dementia depressed or paranoid type
Senile psychosis NOS

Excludes1   senility NOS (R41.81)

Excludes2   mild memory disturbance due to known physiological condition (F06.8)
senile dementia with delirium or acute confusional state (F05)

● **F03.9**   **Unspecified dementia**

F03.90   **Unspecified dementia without behavioral disturbance**   A
Dementia NOS
Coding Clinic: 2012, Q4, P92

F03.91   **Unspecified dementia with behavioral disturbance**   A
Unspecified dementia with aggressive behavior
Unspecified dementia with combative behavior
Unspecified dementia with violent behavior
Use additional code, if applicable, to identify wandering in unspecified dementia (Z91.83)

F04   **Amnestic disorder due to known physiological condition**
Korsakov's psychosis or syndrome, nonalcoholic

Code first the underlying physiological condition

Excludes1   amnesia NOS (R41.3)
anterograde amnesia (R41.1)
dissociative amnesia (F44.0)
retrograde amnesia (R41.2)

Excludes2   alcohol-induced or unspecified Korsakov's syndrome (F10.26, F10.96)
Korsakov's syndrome induced by other psychoactive substances (F13.26, F13.96, F19.16, F19.26, F19.96)

F05   **Delirium due to known physiological condition**
Acute or subacute brain syndrome
Acute or subacute confusional state (nonalcoholic)
Acute or subacute infective psychosis
Acute or subacute organic reaction
Acute or subacute psycho-organic syndrome
Delirium of mixed etiology
Delirium superimposed on dementia
Sundowning

Code first the underlying physiological condition

Excludes1   delirium NOS (R41.0)

Excludes2   delirium tremens alcohol-induced or unspecified (F10.231, F10.921)

● **F06   Other mental disorders due to known physiological condition**

    Includes   mental disorders due to endocrine disorder
                mental disorders due to exogenous hormone
                mental disorders due to exogenous toxic substance
                mental disorders due to primary cerebral disease
                mental disorders due to somatic illness
                mental disorders due to systemic disease affecting the brain

    Code first the underlying physiological condition

    Excludes1   unspecified dementia (F03)

    Excludes2   delirium due to known physiological condition (F05)
                dementia as classified in F01-F02
                other mental disorders associated with alcohol and other psychoactive substances (F10-F19)

    F06.0   Psychotic disorder with hallucinations due to known physiological condition
         Organic hallucinatory state (nonalcoholic)

        Excludes2   hallucinations and perceptual disturbance induced by alcohol and other psychoactive substances (F10-F19 with .151, .251, .951)
                    schizophrenia (F20.-)

    F06.1   Catatonic disorder due to known physiological condition
         Catatonia associated with another mental disorder
         Catatonia NOS

        Excludes1   catatonic stupor (R40.1)
                    stupor NOS (R40.1)

        Excludes2   catatonic schizophrenia (F20.2)
                    dissociative stupor (F44.2)

    F06.2   Psychotic disorder with delusions due to known physiological condition
         Paranoid and paranoid-hallucinatory organic states
         Schizophrenia-like psychosis in epilepsy

        Excludes2   alcohol and drug-induced psychotic disorder (F10-F19 with .150, .250, .950)
                    brief psychotic disorder (F23)
                    delusional disorder (F22)
                    schizophrenia (F20.-)

●   **F06.3   Mood disorder due to known physiological condition**

        Excludes2   mood disorders due to alcohol and other psychoactive substances (F10-F19 with .14, .24, .94)
                    mood disorders, not due to known physiological condition or unspecified (F30-F39)

    F06.30   Mood disorder due to known physiological condition, unspecified

    F06.31   Mood disorder due to known physiological condition with depressive features
         Depressive disorder due to known physiological condition, with depressive features

    F06.32   Mood disorder due to known physiological condition with major depressive-like episode
         Depressive disorder due to known physiological condition, with major depressive-like episode

    F06.33   Mood disorder due to known physiological condition with manic features
         Bipolar and related disorder due to a known physiological condition, with manic features
         Bipolar and related disorder due to known physiological condition, with manic- or hypomanic-like episodes

    F06.34   Mood disorder due to known physiological condition with mixed features
         Bipolar and related disorder due to known physiological condition, with mixed features
         Depressive disorder due to known physiological condition, with mixed features

    F06.4   Anxiety disorder due to known physiological condition

        Excludes2   anxiety disorders due to alcohol and other psychoactive substances (F10-F19 with .180, .280, .980)
                    anxiety disorders, not due to known physiological condition or unspecified (F40.-, F41.-)

    F06.8   Other specified mental disorders due to known physiological condition
         Epileptic psychosis NOS
         Obsessive-compulsive and related disorder due to a known physiological condition
         Organic dissociative disorder
         Organic emotionally labile [asthenic] disorder

● **F07   Personality and behavioral disorders due to known physiological condition**

    Code first the underlying physiological condition

    F07.0   Personality change due to known physiological condition
         Frontal lobe syndrome
         Limbic epilepsy personality syndrome
         Lobotomy syndrome
         Organic personality disorder
         Organic pseudopsychopathic personality
         Organic pseudoretarded personality
         Postleucotomy syndrome

        Code first underlying physiological condition

        Excludes1   mild cognitive impairment (G31.84)
                    postconcussional syndrome (F07.81)
                    postencephalitic syndrome (F07.89)
                    signs and symptoms involving emotional state (R45.-)

        Excludes2   specific personality disorder (F60.-)

●   **F07.8   Other personality and behavioral disorders due to known physiological condition**

    F07.81   Postconcussional syndrome
         Postcontusional syndrome (encephalopathy)
         Post-traumatic brain syndrome, nonpsychotic

         Use additional code to identify associated post-traumatic headache, if applicable (G44.3-)

        Excludes1   current concussion (brain) (S06.0-)
                    postencephalitic syndrome (F07.89)

    F07.89   Other personality and behavioral disorders due to known physiological condition
         Postencephalitic syndrome
         Damage to temporal brain lobes with memory loss and abnormal behavior
         Right hemispheric organic affective disorder

    F07.9   Unspecified personality and behavioral disorder due to known physiological condition
         Organic psychosyndrome
         Due to exposure to organic solvents

F09   Unspecified mental disorder due to known physiological condition
     Mental disorder NOS due to known physiological condition
     Organic brain syndrome NOS
     Organic mental disorder NOS
     Organic psychosis NOS
     Symptomatic psychosis NOS

    Code first the underlying physiological condition

    Excludes1   psychosis NOS (F29)

▶ New   ⇒ Revised   ~~deleted~~ Deleted   Excludes 1   Excludes 2   Includes   Use additional   Code first   Code also   Key words

OGCR Official Guidelines   X Assign placeholder X   ● Use Additional Character(s)   ▶ Manifestation Code   **Coding Clinic**

MENTAL AND BEHAVIORAL DISORDERS DUE TO PSYCHOACTIVE SUBSTANCE USE (F10-F19)

● **F10**   Alcohol related disorders

Use additional code for blood alcohol level, if applicable (Y90.-)

● **F10.1**   **Alcohol abuse**

    Excludes1   alcohol dependence (F10.2-)
                      alcohol use, unspecified (F10.9-)

   F10.10   **Alcohol abuse, uncomplicated**
            Alcohol use disorder, mild

   F10.11   **Alcohol abuse, in remission**
            Alcohol use disorder, mild, in early remission
            Alcohol use disorder, mild, in sustained remission

●   **F10.12**   **Alcohol abuse with intoxication**

      F10.120   **Alcohol abuse with intoxication, uncomplicated**

      F10.121   **Alcohol abuse with intoxication, delirium**

      F10.129   **Alcohol abuse with intoxication, unspecified**

   F10.14   **Alcohol abuse with alcohol-induced mood disorder**
            Alcohol use disorder, mild, with alcohol-induced bipolar or related disorder
            Alcohol use disorder, mild, with alcohol-induced depressive disorder

●   **F10.15**   **Alcohol abuse with alcohol-induced psychotic disorder**

      F10.150   **Alcohol abuse with alcohol-induced psychotic disorder with delusions**

      F10.151   **Alcohol abuse with alcohol-induced psychotic disorder with hallucinations**

      F10.159   **Alcohol abuse with alcohol-induced psychotic disorder, unspecified**

●   **F10.18**   **Alcohol abuse with other alcohol-induced disorders**

      F10.180   **Alcohol abuse with alcohol-induced anxiety disorder**

      F10.181   **Alcohol abuse with alcohol-induced sexual dysfunction**

      F10.182   **Alcohol abuse with alcohol-induced sleep disorder**

      F10.188   **Alcohol abuse with other alcohol-induced disorder**

   F10.19   **Alcohol abuse with unspecified alcohol-induced disorder**

● **F10.2**   **Alcohol dependence**

    Excludes1   alcohol abuse (F10.1-)
                      alcohol use, unspecified (F10.9-)

    Excludes2   toxic effect of alcohol (T51.0-)

   F10.20   **Alcohol dependence, uncomplicated**
            Alcohol use disorder, moderate
            Alcohol use disorder, severe

   F10.21   **Alcohol dependence, in remission**
            Alcohol use disorder, moderate, in early remission
            Alcohol use disorder, moderate, in sustained remission
            Alcohol use disorder, severe, in early remission
            Alcohol use disorder, severe, in sustained remission

● **F10.22**   **Alcohol dependence with intoxication**
            Acute drunkenness (in alcoholism)

    Excludes2   alcohol dependence with withdrawal (F10.23-)

   F10.220   **Alcohol dependence with intoxication, uncomplicated**

   F10.221   **Alcohol dependence with intoxication delirium**

   F10.229   **Alcohol dependence with intoxication, unspecified**

● **F10.23**   **Alcohol dependence with withdrawal**

    Excludes2   alcohol dependence with intoxication (F10.22-)

   F10.230   **Alcohol dependence with withdrawal, uncomplicated**

   F10.231   **Alcohol dependence with withdrawal delirium**

   F10.232   **Alcohol dependence with withdrawal with perceptual disturbance**

   F10.239   **Alcohol dependence with withdrawal, unspecified**
            Coding Clinic: 2015, Q2, P15

   F10.24   **Alcohol dependence with alcohol-induced mood disorder**
            Alcohol use disorder, moderate, with alcohol-induced bipolar or related disorder
            Alcohol use disorder, moderate, with alcohol-induced depressive disorder
            Alcohol use disorder, severe, with alcohol-induced bipolar or related disorder
            Alcohol use disorder, severe, with alcohol-induced depressive disorder

● **F10.25**   **Alcohol dependence with alcohol-induced psychotic disorder**

   F10.250   **Alcohol dependence with alcohol-induced psychotic disorder with delusions**

   F10.251   **Alcohol dependence with alcohol-induced psychotic disorder with hallucinations**

   F10.259   **Alcohol dependence with alcohol-induced psychotic disorder, unspecified**

   F10.26   **Alcohol dependence with alcohol-induced persisting amnestic disorder**
            Alcohol use disorder, moderate, with alcohol-induced major neurocognitive disorder, amnestic-confabulatory type
            Alcohol use disorder, severe, with alcohol-induced major neurocognitive disorder, amnestic-confabulatory type

   F10.27   **Alcohol dependence with alcohol-induced persisting dementia**
            Alcohol use disorder, moderate, with alcohol-induced major neurocognitive disorder, nonamnestic-confabulatory type
            Alcohol use disorder, severe, with alcohol-induced major neurocognitive disorder, nonamnestic-confabulatory type

CHAPTER 5 (F01-F99)

● F10.28   **Alcohol dependence with other alcohol-induced disorders**
   F10.280   **Alcohol dependence with alcohol-induced anxiety disorder**
   F10.281   **Alcohol dependence with alcohol-induced sexual dysfunction**
   F10.282   **Alcohol dependence with alcohol-induced sleep disorder**
   F10.288   **Alcohol dependence with other alcohol-induced disorder**
             Alcohol use disorder, moderate, with alcohol-induced mild neurocognitive disorder
             Alcohol use disorder, severe, with alcohol-induced mild neurocognitive disorder
   F10.29   **Alcohol dependence with unspecified alcohol-induced disorder**
● F10.9   **Alcohol use, unspecified**
           Excludes1   alcohol abuse (F10.1-)
                           alcohol dependence (F10.2-)
   ● F10.92 **Alcohol use, unspecified with intoxication**
      F10.920   **Alcohol use, unspecified with intoxication, uncomplicated**
      F10.921   **Alcohol use, unspecified with intoxication delirium**
      F10.929   **Alcohol use, unspecified with intoxication, unspecified**
   F10.94   **Alcohol use, unspecified with alcohol-induced mood disorder**
             Alcohol-induced bipolar or related disorder, without use disorder
             Alcohol-induced depressive disorder, without use disorder
   ● F10.95 **Alcohol use, unspecified with alcohol-induced psychotic disorder**
      F10.950   **Alcohol use, unspecified with alcohol-induced psychotic disorder with delusions**
      F10.951   **Alcohol use, unspecified with alcohol-induced psychotic disorder with hallucinations**
      F10.959   **Alcohol use, unspecified with alcohol-induced psychotic disorder, unspecified**
                Alcohol-induced psychotic disorder without use disorder
   F10.96   **Alcohol use, unspecified with alcohol-induced persisting amnestic disorder**
             Alcohol-induced major neurocognitive disorder, amnestic-confabulatory type, without use disorder
   F10.97   **Alcohol use, unspecified with alcohol-induced persisting dementia**
             Alcohol-induced major neurocognitive disorder, nonamnestic-confabulatory type, without use disorder
   ● F10.98 **Alcohol use, unspecified with other alcohol-induced disorders**
      F10.980   **Alcohol use, unspecified with alcohol-induced anxiety disorder**
                Alcohol-induced anxiety disorder, without use disorder
      F10.981   **Alcohol use, unspecified with alcohol-induced sexual dysfunction**
                Alcohol-induced sexual dysfunction, without use disorder

   F10.982   **Alcohol use, unspecified with alcohol-induced sleep disorder**
             Alcohol-induced sleep disorder, without use disorder
   F10.988   **Alcohol use, unspecified with other alcohol-induced disorder**
             Alcohol-induced mild neurocognitive disorder, without use disorder
   F10.99   **Alcohol use, unspecified with unspecified alcohol-induced disorder**
● F11   **Opioid related disorders**
   ● F11.1   **Opioid abuse**
             Excludes1   opioid dependence (F11.2-)
                             opioid use, unspecified (F11.9-)
      F11.10   **Opioid abuse, uncomplicated**
                Opioid use disorder, mild
      F11.11   **Opioid abuse, in remission**
                Opioid use disorder, mild, in early remission
                Opioid use disorder, mild, in sustained remission
      ● F11.12 **Opioid abuse with intoxication**
         F11.120   **Opioid abuse with intoxication, uncomplicated**
         F11.121   **Opioid abuse with intoxication delirium**
         F11.122   **Opioid abuse with intoxication with perceptual disturbance**
         F11.129   **Opioid abuse with intoxication, unspecified**
      F11.14   **Opioid abuse with opioid-induced mood disorder**
                Opioid use disorder, mild, with opioid-induced depressive disorder
      ● F11.15 **Opioid abuse with opioid-induced psychotic disorder**
         F11.150   **Opioid abuse with opioid-induced psychotic disorder with delusions**
         F11.151   **Opioid abuse with opioid-induced psychotic disorder with hallucinations**
         F11.159   **Opioid abuse with opioid-induced psychotic disorder, unspecified**
      ● F11.18 **Opioid abuse with other opioid-induced disorder**
         F11.181   **Opioid abuse with opioid-induced sexual dysfunction**
         F11.182   **Opioid abuse with opioid-induced sleep disorder**
         F11.188   **Opioid abuse with other opioid-induced disorder**
      F11.19   **Opioid abuse with unspecified opioid-induced disorder**
   ● F11.2   **Opioid dependence**
             Excludes1   opioid abuse (F11.1-)
                             opioid use, unspecified (F11.9-)
             Excludes2   opioid poisoning (T40.0--T40.2-)
      F11.20   **Opioid dependence, uncomplicated**
                Opioid use disorder, moderate
                Opioid use disorder, severe
      F11.21   **Opioid dependence, in remission**
                Opioid use disorder, moderate, in early remission
                Opioid use disorder, moderate, in sustained remission
                Opioid use disorder, severe, in early remission
                Opioid use disorder, severe, in sustained remission

▶ New   ⇒ Revised   ~~deleted~~ Deleted   Excludes 1   Excludes 2   Includes   Use additional   Code first   Code also   Key words
OGCR Official Guidelines   X Assign placeholder X   ● Use Additional Character(s)   ▶ Manifestation Code   **Coding Clinic**

● **F11.22**   **Opioid dependence with intoxication**

     Excludes1   opioid dependence with withdrawal (F11.23)

     F11.220   **Opioid dependence with intoxication, uncomplicated**

     F11.221   **Opioid dependence with intoxication delirium**

     F11.222   **Opioid dependence with intoxication with perceptual disturbance**

     F11.229   **Opioid dependence with intoxication, unspecified**

   F11.23   **Opioid dependence with withdrawal**

     Excludes1   opioid dependence with intoxication (F11.22-)

   F11.24   **Opioid dependence with opioid-induced mood disorder**

     Opioid use disorder, moderate, with opioid-induced depressive disorder

● **F11.25**   **Opioid dependence with opioid-induced psychotic disorder**

     F11.250   **Opioid dependence with opioid-induced psychotic disorder with delusions**

     F11.251   **Opioid dependence with opioid-induced psychotic disorder with hallucinations**

     F11.259   **Opioid dependence with opioid-induced psychotic disorder, unspecified**

● **F11.28**   **Opioid dependence with other opioid-induced disorder**

     F11.281   **Opioid dependence with opioid-induced sexual dysfunction**

     F11.282   **Opioid dependence with opioid-induced sleep disorder**

     F11.288   **Opioid dependence with other opioid-induced disorder**

   F11.29   **Opioid dependence with unspecified opioid-induced disorder**

● **F11.9**   **Opioid use, unspecified**

     Excludes1   opioid abuse (F11.1-)
              opioid dependence (F11.2-)

   F11.90   **Opioid use, unspecified, uncomplicated**

● **F11.92**   **Opioid use, unspecified with intoxication**

     Excludes1   opioid use, unspecified with withdrawal (F11.93)

     F11.920   **Opioid use, unspecified with intoxication, uncomplicated**

     F11.921   **Opioid use, unspecified with intoxication delirium**
         Opioid-induced delirium

     F11.922   **Opioid use, unspecified with intoxication with perceptual disturbance**

     F11.929   **Opioid use, unspecified with intoxication, unspecified**

   F11.93   **Opioid use, unspecified with withdrawal**

     Excludes1   opioid use, unspecified with intoxication (F11.92-)

   F11.94   **Opioid use, unspecified with opioid-induced mood disorder**

     Opioid-induced depressive disorder, without use disorder

● **F11.95**   **Opioid use, unspecified with opioid-induced psychotic disorder**

     F11.950   **Opioid use, unspecified with opioid-induced psychotic disorder with delusions**

     F11.951   **Opioid use, unspecified with opioid-induced psychotic disorder with hallucinations**

     F11.959   **Opioid use, unspecified with opioid-induced psychotic disorder, unspecified**

● **F11.98**   **Opioid use, unspecified with other specified opioid-induced disorder**

     F11.981   **Opioid use, unspecified with opioid-induced sexual dysfunction**
         Opioid-induced sexual dysfunction, without use disorder

     F11.982   **Opioid use, unspecified with opioid-induced sleep disorder**
         Opioid-induced sleep disorder, without use disorder

     F11.988   **Opioid use, unspecified with other opioid-induced disorder**
         Opioid-induced anxiety disorder, without use disorder

   F11.99   **Opioid use, unspecified with unspecified opioid-induced disorder**

● **F12**   **Cannabis related disorders**

     Includes   marijuana

● **F12.1**   **Cannabis abuse**

     Excludes1   cannabis dependence (F12.2-)
              cannabis use, unspecified (F12.9-)

   F12.10   **Cannabis abuse, uncomplicated**
     Cannabis use disorder, mild

   F12.11   **Cannabis abuse, in remission**
     Cannabis use disorder, mild, in early remission
     Cannabis use disorder, mild, in sustained remission

● **F12.12**   **Cannabis abuse with intoxication**

     F12.120   **Cannabis abuse with intoxication, uncomplicated**

     F12.121   **Cannabis abuse with intoxication delirium**

     F12.122   **Cannabis abuse with intoxication with perceptual disturbance**

     F12.129   **Cannabis abuse with intoxication, unspecified**

● **F12.15**   **Cannabis abuse with psychotic disorder**

     F12.150   **Cannabis abuse with psychotic disorder with delusions**

     F12.151   **Cannabis abuse with psychotic disorder with hallucinations**

     F12.159   **Cannabis abuse with psychotic disorder, unspecified**

● **F12.18**   **Cannabis abuse with other cannabis-induced disorder**

     F12.180   **Cannabis abuse with cannabis-induced anxiety disorder**

     F12.188   **Cannabis abuse with other cannabis-induced disorder**
         Cannabis use disorder, mild, with cannabis-induced sleep disorder

   F12.19   **Cannabis abuse with unspecified cannabis-induced disorder**

● F12.2   **Cannabis dependence**
       Excludes1   cannabis abuse (F12.1-)
                        cannabis use, unspecified (F12.9-)
       Excludes2   cannabis poisoning (T40.7-)

    F12.20   **Cannabis dependence, uncomplicated**
               Cannabis use disorder, moderate
               Cannabis use disorder, severe

    F12.21   **Cannabis dependence, in remission**
               Cannabis use disorder, moderate, in early
                  remission
               Cannabis use disorder, moderate, in sustained
                  remission
               Cannabis use disorder, severe, in early
                  remission
               Cannabis use disorder, severe, in sustained
                  remission

● F12.22   **Cannabis dependence with intoxication**
    F12.220   **Cannabis dependence with**
               intoxication, uncomplicated
    F12.221   **Cannabis dependence with**
               intoxication delirium
    F12.222   **Cannabis dependence with**
               intoxication with perceptual
               disturbance
    F12.229   **Cannabis dependence with**
               intoxication, unspecified

▶ F12.23   **Cannabis dependence with withdrawal**

● F12.25   **Cannabis dependence with psychotic disorder**
    F12.250   **Cannabis dependence with psychotic**
               disorder with delusions
    F12.251   **Cannabis dependence with psychotic**
               disorder with hallucinations
    F12.259   **Cannabis dependence with psychotic**
               disorder, unspecified

● F12.28   **Cannabis dependence with other cannabis-induced disorder**
    F12.280   **Cannabis dependence with cannabis-induced anxiety disorder**
    F12.288   **Cannabis dependence with other cannabis-induced disorder**
               Cannabis use disorder, moderate,
                  with cannabis-induced sleep
                  disorder
               Cannabis use disorder, severe, with
                  cannabis-induced sleep
                  disorder
               ~~Cannabis withdrawal~~

    F12.29   **Cannabis dependence with unspecified cannabis-induced disorder**

● F12.9   **Cannabis use, unspecified**
       Excludes1   cannabis abuse (F12.1-)
                        cannabis dependence (F12.2-)

    F12.90   **Cannabis use, unspecified, uncomplicated**
● F12.92   **Cannabis use, unspecified with intoxication**
    F12.920   **Cannabis use, unspecified with**
               intoxication, uncomplicated
    F12.921   **Cannabis use, unspecified with**
               intoxication delirium
    F12.922   **Cannabis use, unspecified with**
               intoxication with perceptual
               disturbance
    F12.929   **Cannabis use, unspecified with**
               intoxication, unspecified

▶ F12.93   **Cannabis use, unspecified with withdrawal**

● F12.95   **Cannabis use, unspecified with psychotic disorder**
    F12.950   **Cannabis use, unspecified with**
               psychotic disorder with delusions
    F12.951   **Cannabis use, unspecified**
               with psychotic disorder with
               hallucinations
    F12.959   **Cannabis use, unspecified with**
               psychotic disorder, unspecified
               Cannabis-induced psychotic disorder,
                  without use disorder

● F12.98   **Cannabis use, unspecified with other cannabis-induced disorder**
    F12.980   **Cannabis use, unspecified with anxiety disorder**
               Cannabis-induced anxiety disorder,
                  without use disorder
    F12.988   **Cannabis use, unspecified with other cannabis-induced disorder**
               Cannabis-induced sleep disorder,
                  without use disorder

    F12.99   **Cannabis use, unspecified with unspecified cannabis-induced disorder**

● F13   **Sedative, hypnotic, or anxiolytic related disorders**
   ● F13.1   **Sedative, hypnotic or anxiolytic-related abuse**
         Excludes1   sedative, hypnotic or anxiolytic-related
                        dependence (F13.2-)
                        sedative, hypnotic, or anxiolytic use,
                        unspecified (F13.9-)

      F13.10   **Sedative, hypnotic or anxiolytic abuse, uncomplicated**
               Sedative, hypnotic, or anxiolytic use disorder,
                  mild

      F13.11   **Sedative, hypnotic or anxiolytic abuse, in remission**
               Sedative, hypnotic or anxiolytic use disorder,
                  mild, in early remission
               Sedative, hypnotic or anxiolytic use disorder,
                  mild, in sustained remission

   ● F13.12   **Sedative, hypnotic or anxiolytic abuse with intoxication**
      F13.120   **Sedative, hypnotic or anxiolytic abuse with intoxication, uncomplicated**
      F13.121   **Sedative, hypnotic or anxiolytic abuse with intoxication delirium**
      F13.129   **Sedative, hypnotic or anxiolytic abuse with intoxication, unspecified**

      F13.14   **Sedative, hypnotic or anxiolytic abuse with sedative, hypnotic or anxiolytic-induced mood disorder**
               Sedative, hypnotic, or anxiolytic use disorder,
                  mild, with sedative, hypnotic, or anxiolytic-
                  induced bipolar or related disorder
               Sedative, hypnotic, or anxiolytic use disorder,
                  mild, with sedative, hypnotic, or
                  anxiolytic-induced depressive disorder

   ● F13.15   **Sedative, hypnotic or anxiolytic abuse with sedative, hypnotic or anxiolytic-induced psychotic disorder**
      F13.150   **Sedative, hypnotic or anxiolytic abuse with sedative, hypnotic or anxiolytic-induced psychotic disorder with delusions**
      F13.151   **Sedative, hypnotic or anxiolytic abuse with sedative, hypnotic or anxiolytic-induced psychotic disorder with hallucinations**
      F13.159   **Sedative, hypnotic or anxiolytic abuse with sedative, hypnotic or anxiolytic-induced psychotic disorder, unspecified**

● **F13.18**　Sedative, hypnotic or anxiolytic abuse with other sedative, hypnotic or anxiolytic-induced disorders

　　F13.180　Sedative, hypnotic or anxiolytic abuse with sedative, hypnotic or anxiolytic-induced anxiety disorder

　　F13.181　Sedative, hypnotic or anxiolytic abuse with sedative, hypnotic or anxiolytic-induced sexual dysfunction

　　F13.182　Sedative, hypnotic or anxiolytic abuse with sedative, hypnotic or anxiolytic-induced sleep disorder

　　F13.188　Sedative, hypnotic or anxiolytic abuse with other sedative, hypnotic or anxiolytic-induced disorder

　F13.19　Sedative, hypnotic or anxiolytic abuse with unspecified sedative, hypnotic or anxiolytic-induced disorder

● **F13.2**　Sedative, hypnotic or anxiolytic-related dependence

　　Excludes1　sedative, hypnotic or anxiolytic-related abuse (F13.1-)
　　　　　　　sedative, hypnotic, or anxiolytic use, unspecified (F13.9-)

　　Excludes2　sedative, hypnotic, or anxiolytic poisoning (T42.-)

　F13.20　Sedative, hypnotic or anxiolytic dependence, uncomplicated

　F13.21　Sedative, hypnotic or anxiolytic dependence, in remission
　　　　Sedative, hypnotic or anxiolytic use disorder, moderate, in early remission
　　　　Sedative, hypnotic or anxiolytic use disorder, moderate, in sustained remission
　　　　Sedative, hypnotic or anxiolytic use disorder, severe, in early remission
　　　　Sedative, hypnotic or anxiolytic use disorder, severe, in sustained remission

● **F13.22**　Sedative, hypnotic or anxiolytic dependence with intoxication

　　Excludes1　sedative, hypnotic or anxiolytic dependence with withdrawal (F13.23-)

　　F13.220　Sedative, hypnotic or anxiolytic dependence with intoxication, uncomplicated

　　F13.221　Sedative, hypnotic or anxiolytic dependence with intoxication delirium

　　F13.229　Sedative, hypnotic or anxiolytic dependence with intoxication, unspecified

● **F13.23**　Sedative, hypnotic or anxiolytic dependence with withdrawal
　　　　Sedative, hypnotic, or anxiolytic use disorder, moderate
　　　　Sedative, hypnotic, or anxiolytic use disorder, severe

　　Excludes1　sedative, hypnotic or anxiolytic dependence with intoxication (F13.22-)

　　F13.230　Sedative, hypnotic or anxiolytic dependence with withdrawal, uncomplicated

　　F13.231　Sedative, hypnotic or anxiolytic dependence with withdrawal delirium

　　F13.232　Sedative, hypnotic or anxiolytic dependence with withdrawal with perceptual disturbance
　　　　　　Sedative, hypnotic, or anxiolytic withdrawal with perceptual disturbances

　　F13.239　Sedative, hypnotic or anxiolytic dependence with withdrawal, unspecified
　　　　　　Sedative, hypnotic, or anxiolytic withdrawal without perceptual disturbances

　F13.24　Sedative, hypnotic or anxiolytic dependence with sedative, hypnotic or anxiolytic-induced mood disorder
　　　　Sedative, hypnotic, or anxiolytic use disorder, moderate, with sedative, hypnotic, or anxiolytic-induced bipolar or related disorder
　　　　Sedative, hypnotic, or anxiolytic use disorder, moderate, with sedative, hypnotic, or anxiolytic-induced depressive disorder
　　　　Sedative, hypnotic, or anxiolytic use disorder, severe, with sedative, hypnotic, or anxiolytic-induced bipolar or related disorder
　　　　Sedative, hypnotic, or anxiolytic use disorder, severe, with sedative, hypnotic, or anxiolytic-induced depressive disorder

● **F13.25**　Sedative, hypnotic or anxiolytic dependence with sedative, hypnotic or anxiolytic-induced psychotic disorder

　　F13.250　Sedative, hypnotic or anxiolytic dependence with sedative, hypnotic or anxiolytic-induced psychotic disorder with delusions

　　F13.251　Sedative, hypnotic or anxiolytic dependence with sedative, hypnotic or anxiolytic-induced psychotic disorder with hallucinations

　　F13.259　Sedative, hypnotic or anxiolytic dependence with sedative, hypnotic or anxiolytic-induced psychotic disorder, unspecified

　F13.26　Sedative, hypnotic or anxiolytic dependence with sedative, hypnotic or anxiolytic-induced persisting amnestic disorder

　F13.27　Sedative, hypnotic or anxiolytic dependence with sedative, hypnotic or anxiolytic-induced persisting dementia
　　　　Sedative, hypnotic, or anxiolytic use disorder, moderate, with sedative, hypnotic, or anxiolytic-induced major neurocognitive disorder
　　　　Sedative, hypnotic, or anxiolytic use disorder, severe, with sedative, hypnotic, or anxiolytic-induced major neurocognitive disorder

● **F13.28**　Sedative, hypnotic or anxiolytic dependence with other sedative, hypnotic or anxiolytic-induced disorders

　　F13.280　Sedative, hypnotic or anxiolytic dependence with sedative, hypnotic or anxiolytic-induced anxiety disorder

　　F13.281　Sedative, hypnotic or anxiolytic dependence with sedative, hypnotic or anxiolytic-induced sexual dysfunction

CHAPTER 5 (F01-F99)

F13.282 Sedative, hypnotic or anxiolytic dependence with sedative, hypnotic or anxiolytic-induced sleep disorder

F13.288 Sedative, hypnotic or anxiolytic dependence with other sedative, hypnotic or anxiolytic-induced disorder

> Sedative, hypnotic, or anxiolytic use disorder, moderate, with sedative, hypnotic, or anxiolytic-induced mild neurocognitive disorder
>
> Sedative, hypnotic, or anxiolytic use disorder, severe, with sedative, hypnotic, or anxiolytic-induced mild neurocognitive disorder

F13.29 Sedative, hypnotic or anxiolytic dependence with unspecified sedative, hypnotic or anxiolytic-induced disorder

● F13.9 Sedative, hypnotic or anxiolytic-related use, unspecified

   Excludes1 sedative, hypnotic or anxiolytic-related abuse (F13.1-)
            sedative, hypnotic or anxiolytic-related dependence (F13.2-)

F13.90 Sedative, hypnotic, or anxiolytic use, unspecified, uncomplicated

● F13.92 Sedative, hypnotic or anxiolytic use, unspecified with intoxication

   Excludes1 sedative, hypnotic or anxiolytic use, unspecified with withdrawal (F13.93-)

F13.920 Sedative, hypnotic or anxiolytic use, unspecified with intoxication, uncomplicated

F13.921 Sedative, hypnotic or anxiolytic use, unspecified with intoxication delirium

> Sedative, hypnotic, or anxiolytic-induced delirium

F13.929 Sedative, hypnotic or anxiolytic use, unspecified with intoxication, unspecified

● F13.93 Sedative, hypnotic or anxiolytic use, unspecified with withdrawal

   Excludes1 sedative, hypnotic or anxiolytic use, unspecified with intoxication (F13.92-)

F13.930 Sedative, hypnotic or anxiolytic use, unspecified with withdrawal, uncomplicated

F13.931 Sedative, hypnotic or anxiolytic use, unspecified with withdrawal delirium

F13.932 Sedative, hypnotic or anxiolytic use, unspecified with withdrawal with perceptual disturbances

F13.939 Sedative, hypnotic or anxiolytic use, unspecified with withdrawal, unspecified

F13.94 Sedative, hypnotic or anxiolytic use, unspecified with sedative, hypnotic or anxiolytic-induced mood disorder

> Sedative, hypnotic, or anxiolytic-induced bipolar or related disorder, without use disorder
>
> Sedative, hypnotic, or anxiolytic-induced depressive disorder, without use disorder

● F13.95 Sedative, hypnotic or anxiolytic use, unspecified with sedative, hypnotic or anxiolytic-induced psychotic disorder

F13.950 Sedative, hypnotic or anxiolytic use, unspecified with sedative, hypnotic or anxiolytic-induced psychotic disorder with delusions

F13.951 Sedative, hypnotic or anxiolytic use, unspecified with sedative, hypnotic or anxiolytic-induced psychotic disorder with hallucinations

F13.959 Sedative, hypnotic or anxiolytic use, unspecified with sedative, hypnotic or anxiolytic-induced psychotic disorder, unspecified

> Sedative, hypnotic, or anxiolytic-induced psychotic disorder, without use disorder

F13.96 Sedative, hypnotic or anxiolytic use, unspecified with sedative, hypnotic or anxiolytic-induced persisting amnestic disorder

F13.97 Sedative, hypnotic or anxiolytic use, unspecified with sedative, hypnotic or anxiolytic-induced persisting dementia

> Sedative, hypnotic, or anxiolytic-induced major neurocognitive disorder, without use disorder

● F13.98 Sedative, hypnotic or anxiolytic use, unspecified with other sedative, hypnotic or anxiolytic-induced disorders

F13.980 Sedative, hypnotic or anxiolytic use, unspecified with sedative, hypnotic or anxiolytic-induced anxiety disorder

> Sedative, hypnotic, or anxiolytic-induced anxiety disorder, without use disorder

F13.981 Sedative, hypnotic or anxiolytic use, unspecified with sedative, hypnotic or anxiolytic-induced sexual dysfunction

> Sedative, hypnotic, or anxiolytic-induced sexual dysfunction disorder, without use disorder

F13.982 Sedative, hypnotic or anxiolytic use, unspecified with sedative, hypnotic or anxiolytic-induced sleep disorder

> Sedative, hypnotic, or anxiolytic-induced sleep disorder, without use disorder

F13.988 Sedative, hypnotic or anxiolytic use, unspecified with other sedative, hypnotic or anxiolytic-induced disorder

> Sedative, hypnotic, or anxiolytic-induced mild neurocognitive disorder

F13.99 Sedative, hypnotic or anxiolytic use, unspecified with unspecified sedative, hypnotic or anxiolytic-induced disorder

▶ New ⇒ Revised ~~deleted~~ Deleted Excludes 1 Excludes 2 Includes Use additional Code first Code also Key words
OGCR Official Guidelines X Assign placeholder X ● Use Additional Character(s) ▷ Manifestation Code **Coding Clinic**

● **F14** **Cocaine related disorders**
  Excludes2   other stimulant-related disorders (F15.-)
  ● **F14.1** **Cocaine abuse**
    Excludes1   cocaine dependence (F14.2-)
                    cocaine use, unspecified (F14.9-)
    F14.10   **Cocaine abuse, uncomplicated**
               Cocaine use disorder, mild
    F14.11   **Cocaine abuse, in remission**
               Cocaine use disorder, mild, in early remission
               Cocaine use disorder, mild, in sustained remission
    ● **F14.12**   **Cocaine abuse with intoxication**
      F14.120   **Cocaine abuse with intoxication, uncomplicated**
      F14.121   **Cocaine abuse with intoxication with delirium**
      F14.122   **Cocaine abuse with intoxication with perceptual disturbance**
      F14.129   **Cocaine abuse with intoxication, unspecified**
    F14.14   **Cocaine abuse with cocaine-induced mood disorder**
               Cocaine use disorder, mild, with cocaine-induced bipolar or related disorder
               Cocaine use disorder, mild, with cocaine-induced depressive disorder
    ● **F14.15**   **Cocaine abuse with cocaine-induced psychotic disorder**
      F14.150   **Cocaine abuse with cocaine-induced psychotic disorder with delusions**
      F14.151   **Cocaine abuse with cocaine-induced psychotic disorder with hallucinations**
      F14.159   **Cocaine abuse with cocaine-induced psychotic disorder, unspecified**
    ● **F14.18**   **Cocaine abuse with other cocaine-induced disorder**
      F14.180   **Cocaine abuse with cocaine-induced anxiety disorder**
      F14.181   **Cocaine abuse with cocaine-induced sexual dysfunction**
      F14.182   **Cocaine abuse with cocaine-induced sleep disorder**
      F14.188   **Cocaine abuse with other cocaine-induced disorder**
                 Cocaine use disorder, mild, with cocaine-induced obsessive-compulsive or related disorder
    F14.19   **Cocaine abuse with unspecified cocaine-induced disorder**
  ● **F14.2** **Cocaine dependence**
    Excludes1   cocaine abuse (F14.1-)
                    cocaine use, unspecified (F14.9-)
    Excludes2   cocaine poisoning (T40.5-)
    F14.20   **Cocaine dependence, uncomplicated**
               Cocaine use disorder, moderate
               Cocaine use disorder, severe
    F14.21   **Cocaine dependence, in remission**
               Cocaine use disorder, moderate, in early remission
               Cocaine use disorder, moderate, in sustained remission
               Cocaine use disorder, severe, in early remission
               Cocaine use disorder, severe, in sustained remission
               Coding Clinic: 2017, Q2, P27

  ● **F14.22** **Cocaine dependence with intoxication**
    Excludes1   cocaine dependence with withdrawal (F14.23)
    F14.220   **Cocaine dependence with intoxication, uncomplicated**
    F14.221   **Cocaine dependence with intoxication delirium**
    F14.222   **Cocaine dependence with intoxication with perceptual disturbance**
    F14.229   **Cocaine dependence with intoxication, unspecified**
  F14.23 **Cocaine dependence with withdrawal**
    Excludes1   cocaine dependence with intoxication (F14.22-)
  F14.24 **Cocaine dependence with cocaine-induced mood disorder**
             Cocaine use disorder, moderate, with cocaine-induced bipolar or related disorder
             Cocaine use disorder, moderate, with cocaine-induced depressive disorder
             Cocaine use disorder, severe, with cocaine-induced bipolar or related disorder
             Cocaine use disorder, severe, with cocaine-induced depressive disorder
  ● **F14.25** **Cocaine dependence with cocaine-induced psychotic disorder**
    F14.250   **Cocaine dependence with cocaine-induced psychotic disorder with delusions**
    F14.251   **Cocaine dependence with cocaine-induced psychotic disorder with hallucinations**
    F14.259   **Cocaine dependence with cocaine-induced psychotic disorder, unspecified**
  ● **F14.28** **Cocaine dependence with other cocaine-induced disorder**
    F14.280   **Cocaine dependence with cocaine-induced anxiety disorder**
    F14.281   **Cocaine dependence with cocaine-induced sexual dysfunction**
    F14.282   **Cocaine dependence with cocaine-induced sleep disorder**
    F14.288   **Cocaine dependence with other cocaine-induced disorder**
                 Cocaine use disorder, moderate, with cocaine-induced obsessive-compulsive or related disorder
                 Cocaine use disorder, severe, with cocaine-induced obsessive-compulsive or related disorder
  F14.29 **Cocaine dependence with unspecified cocaine-induced disorder**
● **F14.9** **Cocaine use, unspecified**
  Excludes1   cocaine abuse (F14.1-)
                  cocaine dependence (F14.2-)
  F14.90   **Cocaine use, unspecified, uncomplicated**
             Coding Clinic: 2018, Q2, P11
  ● **F14.92** **Cocaine use, unspecified with intoxication**
    F14.920   **Cocaine use, unspecified with intoxication, uncomplicated**
    F14.921   **Cocaine use, unspecified with intoxication delirium**
    F14.922   **Cocaine use, unspecified with intoxication with perceptual disturbance**
    F14.929   **Cocaine use, unspecified with intoxication, unspecified**

CHAPTER 5 (F01-F99)

CHAPTER 5 (F01-F99)

F14.94   Cocaine use, unspecified with cocaine-induced mood disorder
Cocaine-induced bipolar or related disorder, without use disorder
Cocaine-induced depressive disorder, without use disorder

● **F14.95**   Cocaine use, unspecified with cocaine-induced psychotic disorder

   F14.950   Cocaine use, unspecified with cocaine-induced psychotic disorder with delusions

   F14.951   Cocaine use, unspecified with cocaine-induced psychotic disorder with hallucinations

   F14.959   Cocaine use, unspecified with cocaine-induced psychotic disorder, unspecified
Cocaine-induced psychotic disorder, without use disorder

● **F14.98**   Cocaine use, unspecified with other specified cocaine-induced disorder

   F14.980   Cocaine use, unspecified with cocaine-induced anxiety disorder
Cocaine-induced anxiety disorder, without use disorder

   F14.981   Cocaine use, unspecified with cocaine-induced sexual dysfunction
Cocaine-induced sexual dysfunction, without use disorder

   F14.982   Cocaine use, unspecified with cocaine-induced sleep disorder
Cocaine-induced sleep disorder, without use disorder

   F14.988   Cocaine use, unspecified with other cocaine-induced disorder
Cocaine-induced obsessive-compulsive or related disorder

   F14.99   Cocaine use, unspecified with unspecified cocaine-induced disorder

● **F15**   **Other stimulant related disorders**
   Includes   amphetamine-related disorders
            caffeine
   Excludes2   cocaine-related disorders (F14.-)

● **F15.1**   Other stimulant abuse
   Excludes1   other stimulant dependence (F15.2-)
            other stimulant use, unspecified (F15.9-)

   F15.10   Other stimulant abuse, uncomplicated
Amphetamine type substance use disorder, mild
Other or unspecified stimulant use disorder, mild

   F15.11   Other stimulant abuse, in remission
Amphetamine type substance use disorder, mild, in early remission
Amphetamine type substance use disorder, mild, in sustained remission
Other or unspecified stimulant use disorder, mild, in early remission
Other or unspecified stimulant use disorder, mild, in sustained remission

● **F15.12**   Other stimulant abuse with intoxication

   F15.120   Other stimulant abuse with intoxication, uncomplicated

   F15.121   Other stimulant abuse with intoxication delirium

   F15.122   Other stimulant abuse with intoxication with perceptual disturbance
Amphetamine or other stimulant use disorder, mild, with amphetamine or other stimulant intoxication, with perceptual disturbances

   F15.129   Other stimulant abuse with intoxication, unspecified
Amphetamine or other stimulant use disorder, mild, with amphetamine or other stimulant intoxication, without perceptual disturbances

   F15.14   Other stimulant abuse with stimulant-induced mood disorder
Amphetamine or other stimulant use disorder, mild, with amphetamine or other stimulant-induced bipolar or related disorder
Amphetamine or other stimulant use disorder, mild, with amphetamine or other stimulant-induced depressive disorder

● **F15.15**   Other stimulant abuse with stimulant-induced psychotic disorder

   F15.150   Other stimulant abuse with stimulant-induced psychotic disorder with delusions

   F15.151   Other stimulant abuse with stimulant-induced psychotic disorder with hallucinations

   F15.159   Other stimulant abuse with stimulant-induced psychotic disorder, unspecified

● **F15.18**   Other stimulant abuse with other stimulant-induced disorder

   F15.180   Other stimulant abuse with stimulant-induced anxiety disorder

   F15.181   Other stimulant abuse with stimulant-induced sexual dysfunction

   F15.182   Other stimulant abuse with stimulant-induced sleep disorder

   F15.188   Other stimulant abuse with other stimulant-induced disorder
Amphetamine or other stimulant use disorder, mild, with amphetamine or other stimulant-induced obsessive-compulsive or related disorder

   F15.19   Other stimulant abuse with unspecified stimulant-induced disorder

● **F15.2**   Other stimulant dependence
   Excludes1   other stimulant abuse (F15.1-)
            other stimulant use, unspecified (F15.9-)

   F15.20   Other stimulant dependence, uncomplicated
Amphetamine type substance use disorder, moderate
Amphetamine type substance use disorder, severe
Other or unspecified stimulant use disorder, moderate
Other or unspecified stimulant use disorder, severe

F15.21   Other stimulant dependence, in remission
          Amphetamine type substance use disorder,
              moderate, in early remission
          Amphetamine type substance use disorder,
              moderate, in sustained remission
          Amphetamine type substance use disorder,
              severe, in early remission
          Amphetamine type substance use disorder,
              severe, in sustained remission
          Other or unspecified stimulant use disorder,
              moderate, in early remission
          Other or unspecified stimulant use disorder,
              moderate, in sustained remission
          Other or unspecified stimulant use disorder,
              severe, in early remission
          Other or unspecified stimulant use disorder,
              severe, in sustained remission

● F15.22   Other stimulant dependence with intoxication
          Excludes1   other stimulant dependence with
                       withdrawal (F15.23)

    F15.220   Other stimulant dependence with
              intoxication, uncomplicated

    F15.221   Other stimulant dependence with
              intoxication delirium

    F15.222   Other stimulant dependence
              with intoxication with perceptual
              disturbance
              Amphetamine or other stimulant
                  use disorder, moderate, with
                  amphetamine or other
                  stimulant intoxication, with
                  perceptual disturbances
              Amphetamine or other stimulant
                  use disorder, severe, with
                  amphetamine or other
                  stimulant intoxication, with
                  perceptual disturbances

    F15.229   Other stimulant dependence with
              intoxication, unspecified
              Amphetamine or other stimulant
                  use disorder, moderate, with
                  amphetamine or other
                  stimulant intoxication, without
                  perceptual disturbances
              Amphetamine or other stimulant
                  use disorder, severe, with
                  amphetamine or other
                  stimulant intoxication, without
                  perceptual disturbances

F15.23   Other stimulant dependence with withdrawal
          Amphetamine or other stimulant withdrawal
          Excludes1   other stimulant dependence with
                       intoxication (F15.22-)

F15.24   Other stimulant dependence with stimulant-
          induced mood disorder
          Amphetamine or other stimulant use disorder,
              moderate, with amphetamine or other
              stimulant-induced bipolar or related
              disorder
          Amphetamine or other stimulant use disorder,
              moderate, with amphetamine or other
              stimulant-induced depressive disorder
          Amphetamine or other stimulant use disorder,
              severe, with amphetamine or other
              stimulant-induced bipolar or related
              disorder
          Amphetamine or other stimulant use disorder,
              severe, with amphetamine or other
              stimulant-induced depressive disorder

● F15.25   Other stimulant dependence with stimulant-
          induced psychotic disorder

    F15.250   Other stimulant dependence with
              stimulant-induced psychotic disorder
              with delusions

    F15.251   Other stimulant dependence with
              stimulant-induced psychotic disorder
              with hallucinations

    F15.259   Other stimulant dependence
              with stimulant-induced psychotic
              disorder, unspecified

● F15.28   Other stimulant dependence with other
          stimulant-induced disorder

    F15.280   Other stimulant dependence with
              stimulant-induced anxiety disorder

    F15.281   Other stimulant dependence with
              stimulant-induced sexual dysfunction

    F15.282   Other stimulant dependence with
              stimulant-induced sleep disorder

    F15.288   Other stimulant dependence with
              other stimulant-induced disorder
              Amphetamine or other stimulant
                  use disorder, moderate, with
                  amphetamine or other
                  stimulant-induced obsessive-
                  compulsive or related
                  disorder
              Amphetamine or other stimulant
                  use disorder, severe, with
                  amphetamine or other stimulant-
                  induced obsessive-compulsive
                  or related disorder

F15.29   Other stimulant dependence with unspecified
          stimulant-induced disorder

● F15.9   Other stimulant use, unspecified
          Excludes1   other stimulant abuse (F15.1-)
                       other stimulant dependence (F15.2-)

    F15.90   Other stimulant use, unspecified, uncomplicated

● F15.92   Other stimulant use, unspecified with
          intoxication
          Excludes1   other stimulant use, unspecified
                       with withdrawal (F15.93)

    F15.920   Other stimulant use, unspecified with
              intoxication, uncomplicated

    F15.921   Other stimulant use, unspecified with
              intoxication delirium
              Amphetamine or other stimulant-
                  induced delirium

    F15.922   Other stimulant use, unspecified
              with intoxication with perceptual
              disturbance

    F15.929   Other stimulant use, unspecified with
              intoxication, unspecified
              Caffeine intoxication

F15.93   Other stimulant use, unspecified with
          withdrawal
          Caffeine withdrawal
          Excludes1   other stimulant use, unspecified
                       with intoxication (F15.92-)

F15.94   Other stimulant use, unspecified with
          stimulant-induced mood disorder
          Amphetamine or other stimulant-induced
              bipolar or related disorder, without use
              disorder
          Amphetamine or other stimulant-induced
              depressive disorder, without use
              disorder

CHAPTER 5 (F01-F99)

● F15.95   Other stimulant use, unspecified with stimulant-induced psychotic disorder

     F15.950   Other stimulant use, unspecified with stimulant-induced psychotic disorder with delusions

     F15.951   Other stimulant use, unspecified with stimulant-induced psychotic disorder with hallucinations

     F15.959   Other stimulant use, unspecified with stimulant-induced psychotic disorder, unspecified

        Amphetamine or other stimulant-induced psychotic disorder, without use disorder

● F15.98   Other stimulant use, unspecified with other stimulant-induced disorder

     F15.980   Other stimulant use, unspecified with stimulant-induced anxiety disorder

        Amphetamine or other stimulant-induced anxiety disorder, without use disorder

        Caffeine-induced anxiety disorder, without use disorder

     F15.981   Other stimulant use, unspecified with stimulant-induced sexual dysfunction

        Amphetamine or other stimulant-induced sexual dysfunction, without use disorder

     F15.982   Other stimulant use, unspecified with stimulant-induced sleep disorder

        Amphetamine or other stimulant-induced sleep disorder, without use disorder

        Caffeine-induced sleep disorder, without use disorder

     F15.988   Other stimulant use, unspecified with other stimulant-induced disorder

        Amphetamine or other stimulant-induced obsessive-compulsive or related disorder, without use disorder

     F15.99   Other stimulant use, unspecified with unspecified stimulant-induced disorder

● F16   Hallucinogen related disorders

    Includes   ecstasy
              PCP
              phencyclidine

● F16.1   Hallucinogen abuse

    Excludes1   hallucinogen dependence (F16.2-)
               hallucinogen use, unspecified (F16.9-)

     F16.10   Hallucinogen abuse, uncomplicated

        Other hallucinogen use disorder, mild

        Phencyclidine use disorder, mild

     F16.11   Hallucinogen abuse, in remission

        Other hallucinogen use disorder, mild, in early remission

        Other hallucinogen use disorder, mild, in sustained remission

        Phencyclidine use disorder, mild, in early remission

        Phencyclidine use disorder, mild, in sustained remission

● F16.12   Hallucinogen abuse with intoxication

     F16.120   Hallucinogen abuse with intoxication, uncomplicated

     F16.121   Hallucinogen abuse with intoxication with delirium

     F16.122   Hallucinogen abuse with intoxication with perceptual disturbance

     F16.129   Hallucinogen abuse with intoxication, unspecified

     F16.14   Hallucinogen abuse with hallucinogen-induced mood disorder

        Other hallucinogen use disorder, mild, with other hallucinogen-induced bipolar or related disorder

        Other hallucinogen use disorder, mild, with other hallucinogen-induced depressive disorder

        Phencyclidine use disorder, mild, with phencyclidine-induced bipolar or related disorder

        Phencyclidine use disorder, mild, with phencyclidine-induced depressive disorder

● F16.15   Hallucinogen abuse with hallucinogen-induced psychotic disorder

     F16.150   Hallucinogen abuse with hallucinogen-induced psychotic disorder with delusions

     F16.151   Hallucinogen abuse with hallucinogen-induced psychotic disorder with hallucinations

     F16.159   Hallucinogen abuse with hallucinogen-induced psychotic disorder, unspecified

● F16.18   Hallucinogen abuse with other hallucinogen-induced disorder

     F16.180   Hallucinogen abuse with hallucinogen-induced anxiety disorder

     F16.183   Hallucinogen abuse with hallucinogen persisting perception disorder (flashbacks)

     F16.188   Hallucinogen abuse with other hallucinogen-induced disorder

     F16.19   Hallucinogen abuse with unspecified hallucinogen-induced disorder

● F16.2   Hallucinogen dependence

    Excludes1   hallucinogen abuse (F16.1-)
               hallucinogen use, unspecified (F16.9-)

     F16.20   Hallucinogen dependence, uncomplicated

        Other hallucinogen use disorder, moderate

        Other hallucinogen use disorder, severe

        Phencyclidine use disorder, moderate

        Phencyclidine use disorder, severe

     F16.21   Hallucinogen dependence, in remission

        Other hallucinogen use disorder, moderate, in early remission

        Other hallucinogen use disorder, moderate, in sustained remission

        Other hallucinogen use disorder, severe, in early remission

        Other hallucinogen use disorder, severe, in sustained remission

        Phencyclidine use disorder, moderate, in early remission

        Phencyclidine use disorder, moderate, in sustained remission

        Phencyclidine use disorder, severe, in early remission

        Phencyclidine use disorder, severe, in sustained remission

● F16.22   Hallucinogen dependence with intoxication

     F16.220   Hallucinogen dependence with intoxication, uncomplicated

     F16.221   Hallucinogen dependence with intoxication with delirium

     F16.229   Hallucinogen dependence with intoxication, unspecified

▶ New   ⇒ Revised   ~~deleted~~ Deleted   Excludes 1   Excludes 2   Includes   Use additional   Code first   Code also   Key words

OGCR Official Guidelines   X Assign placeholder X   ● Use Additional Character(s)   ▶ Manifestation Code   **Coding Clinic**

F16.24　Hallucinogen dependence with hallucinogen-induced mood disorder
> Other hallucinogen use disorder, moderate, with other hallucinogen-induced bipolar or related disorder
> Other hallucinogen use disorder, moderate, with other hallucinogen-induced depressive disorder
> Other hallucinogen use disorder, severe, with other hallucinogen-induced bipolar or related disorder
> Other hallucinogen use disorder, severe, with other hallucinogen-induced depressive disorder
> Phencyclidine use disorder, moderate, with phencyclidine-induced bipolar or related disorder
> Phencyclidine use disorder, moderate, with phencyclidine-induced depressive disorder
> Phencyclidine use disorder, severe, with phencyclidine-induced bipolar or related disorder
> Phencyclidine use disorder, severe, with phencyclidine-induced depressive disorder

● F16.25　Hallucinogen dependence with hallucinogen-induced psychotic disorder

F16.250　Hallucinogen dependence with hallucinogen-induced psychotic disorder with delusions

F16.251　Hallucinogen dependence with hallucinogen-induced psychotic disorder with hallucinations

F16.259　Hallucinogen dependence with hallucinogen-induced psychotic disorder, unspecified

● F16.28　Hallucinogen dependence with other hallucinogen-induced disorder

F16.280　Hallucinogen dependence with hallucinogen-induced anxiety disorder

F16.283　Hallucinogen dependence with hallucinogen persisting perception disorder (flashbacks)

F16.288　Hallucinogen dependence with other hallucinogen-induced disorder

F16.29　Hallucinogen dependence with unspecified hallucinogen-induced disorder

● F16.9　Hallucinogen use, unspecified

> **Excludes1**　hallucinogen abuse (F16.1-)
> hallucinogen dependence (F16.2-)

F16.90　Hallucinogen use, unspecified, uncomplicated

● F16.92　Hallucinogen use, unspecified with intoxication

F16.920　Hallucinogen use, unspecified with intoxication, uncomplicated

F16.921　Hallucinogen use, unspecified with intoxication with delirium
> Other hallucinogen intoxication delirium

F16.929　Hallucinogen use, unspecified with intoxication, unspecified

F16.94　Hallucinogen use, unspecified with hallucinogen-induced mood disorder
> Other hallucinogen-induced bipolar or related disorder, without use disorder
> Other hallucinogen-induced depressive disorder, without use disorder
> Phencyclidine-induced bipolar or related disorder, without use disorder
> Phencyclidine-induced depressive disorder, without use disorder

● F16.95　Hallucinogen use, unspecified with hallucinogen-induced psychotic disorder

F16.950　Hallucinogen use, unspecified with hallucinogen-induced psychotic disorder with delusions

F16.951　Hallucinogen use, unspecified with hallucinogen-induced psychotic disorder with hallucinations

F16.959　Hallucinogen use, unspecified with hallucinogen-induced psychotic disorder, unspecified
> Other hallucinogen-induced psychotic disorder, without use disorder
> Phencyclidine-induced psychotic disorder, without use disorder

● F16.98　Hallucinogen use, unspecified with other specified hallucinogen-induced disorder

F16.980　Hallucinogen use, unspecified with hallucinogen-induced anxiety disorder
> Other hallucinogen-induced anxiety disorder, without use disorder
> Phencyclidine-induced anxiety disorder, without use disorder

F16.983　Hallucinogen use, unspecified with hallucinogen persisting perception disorder (flashbacks)

F16.988　Hallucinogen use, unspecified with other hallucinogen-induced disorder

F16.99　Hallucinogen use, unspecified with unspecified hallucinogen-induced disorder

● F17　Nicotine dependence

> **Excludes1**　history of tobacco dependence (Z87.891)
> tobacco use NOS (Z72.0)

> **Excludes2**　tobacco use (smoking) during pregnancy, childbirth and the puerperium (O99.33-)
> toxic effect of nicotine (T65.2-)

● F17.2　Nicotine dependence

● F17.20　Nicotine dependence, unspecified

F17.200　Nicotine dependence, unspecified, uncomplicated
> Tobacco use disorder, mild
> Tobacco use disorder, moderate
> Tobacco use disorder, severe
> **Coding Clinic: 2016, Q1, P37**

F17.201　Nicotine dependence, unspecified, in remission
> Tobacco use disorder, mild, in early remission
> Tobacco use disorder, mild, in sustained remission
> Tobacco use disorder, moderate, in early remission
> Tobacco use disorder, moderate, in sustained remission
> Tobacco use disorder, severe, in early remission
> Tobacco use disorder, severe, in sustained remission

F17.203　Nicotine dependence unspecified, with withdrawal
> Tobacco withdrawal

F17.208　Nicotine dependence, unspecified, with other nicotine-induced disorders

F17.209　Nicotine dependence, unspecified, with unspecified nicotine-induced disorders

CHAPTER 5 (F01-F99)

● F17.21   Nicotine dependence, cigarettes
  F17.210   Nicotine dependence, cigarettes, uncomplicated
            Coding Clinic: 2017, Q2, P28-29
  F17.211   Nicotine dependence, cigarettes, in remission
            Tobacco use disorder, cigarettes, mild, in early remission
            Tobacco use disorder, cigarettes, mild, in sustained remission
            Tobacco use disorder, cigarettes, moderate, in early remission
            Tobacco use disorder, cigarettes, moderate, in sustained remission
            Tobacco use disorder, cigarettes, severe, in early remission
            Tobacco use disorder, cigarettes, severe, in sustained remission
  F17.213   Nicotine dependence, cigarettes, with withdrawal
  F17.218   Nicotine dependence, cigarettes, with other nicotine-induced disorders
  F17.219   Nicotine dependence, cigarettes, with unspecified nicotine-induced disorders
● F17.22   Nicotine dependence, chewing tobacco
  F17.220   Nicotine dependence, chewing tobacco, uncomplicated
  F17.221   Nicotine dependence, chewing tobacco, in remission
            Tobacco use disorder, chewing tobacco, mild, in early remission
            Tobacco use disorder, chewing tobacco, mild, in sustained remission
            Tobacco use disorder, chewing tobacco, moderate, in early remission
            Tobacco use disorder, chewing tobacco, moderate, in sustained remission
            Tobacco use disorder, chewing tobacco, severe, in early remission
            Tobacco use disorder, chewing tobacco, severe, in sustained remission
  F17.223   Nicotine dependence, chewing tobacco, with withdrawal
  F17.228   Nicotine dependence, chewing tobacco, with other nicotine-induced disorders
  F17.229   Nicotine dependence, chewing tobacco, with unspecified nicotine-induced disorders
● F17.29   Nicotine dependence, other tobacco product
  F17.290   Nicotine dependence, other tobacco product, uncomplicated
            Coding Clinic: 2017, Q2, P28-29
  F17.291   Nicotine dependence, other tobacco product, in remission
            Tobacco use disorder, other tobacco product, mild, in early remission
            Tobacco use disorder, other tobacco product, mild, in sustained remission
            Tobacco use disorder, other tobacco product, moderate, in early remission
            Tobacco use disorder, other tobacco product, moderate, in sustained remission
            Tobacco use disorder, other tobacco product, severe, in early remission
            Tobacco use disorder, other tobacco product, severe, in sustained remission

  F17.293   Nicotine dependence, other tobacco product, with withdrawal
  F17.298   Nicotine dependence, other tobacco product, with other nicotine-induced disorders
  F17.299   Nicotine dependence, other tobacco product, with unspecified nicotine-induced disorders

● F18   Inhalant related disorders
        Includes   volatile solvents
  ● F18.1   Inhalant abuse
            Excludes1   inhalant dependence (F18.2-)
                        inhalant use, unspecified (F18.9-)
      F18.10   Inhalant abuse, uncomplicated
               Inhalant use disorder, mild
      F18.11   Inhalant abuse, in remission
               Inhalant use disorder, mild, in early remission
               Inhalant use disorder, mild, in sustained remission
    ● F18.12   Inhalant abuse with intoxication
      F18.120   Inhalant abuse with intoxication, uncomplicated
      F18.121   Inhalant abuse with intoxication delirium
      F18.129   Inhalant abuse with intoxication, unspecified
      F18.14   Inhalant abuse with inhalant-induced mood disorder
               Inhalant use disorder, mild, with inhalant-induced depressive disorder
    ● F18.15   Inhalant abuse with inhalant-induced psychotic disorder
      F18.150   Inhalant abuse with inhalant-induced psychotic disorder with delusions
      F18.151   Inhalant abuse with inhalant-induced psychotic disorder with hallucinations
      F18.159   Inhalant abuse with inhalant-induced psychotic disorder, unspecified
      F18.17   Inhalant abuse with inhalant-induced dementia
               Inhalant use disorder, mild, with inhalant-induced major neurocognitive disorder
    ● F18.18   Inhalant abuse with other inhalant-induced disorders
      F18.180   Inhalant abuse with inhalant-induced anxiety disorder
      F18.188   Inhalant abuse with other inhalant-induced disorder
               Inhalant use disorder, mild, with inhalant-induced mild neurocognitive disorder
      F18.19   Inhalant abuse with unspecified inhalant-induced disorder
  ● F18.2   Inhalant dependence
            Excludes1   inhalant abuse (F18.1-)
                        inhalant use, unspecified (F18.9-)
      F18.20   Inhalant dependence, uncomplicated
               Inhalant use disorder, moderate
               Inhalant use disorder, severe
      F18.21   Inhalant dependence, in remission
               Inhalant use disorder, moderate, in early remission
               Inhalant use disorder, moderate, in sustained remission
               Inhalant use disorder, severe, in early remission
               Inhalant use disorder, severe, in sustained remission

▶ New   ⮚ Revised   ~~deleted~~ Deleted   Excludes 1   Excludes 2   Includes   Use additional   Code first   Code also   Key words
OGCR Official Guidelines   X Assign placeholder X   ● Use Additional Character(s)   ▶ Manifestation Code   Coding Clinic

● F18.22   Inhalant dependence with intoxication

    F18.220   Inhalant dependence with intoxication, uncomplicated

    F18.221   Inhalant dependence with intoxication delirium

    F18.229   Inhalant dependence with intoxication, unspecified

  F18.24   Inhalant dependence with inhalant-induced mood disorder

      Inhalant use disorder, moderate, with inhalant-induced depressive disorder

      Inhalant use disorder, severe, with inhalant-induced depressive disorder

● F18.25   Inhalant dependence with inhalant-induced psychotic disorder

    F18.250   Inhalant dependence with inhalant-induced psychotic disorder with delusions

    F18.251   Inhalant dependence with inhalant-induced psychotic disorder with hallucinations

    F18.259   Inhalant dependence with inhalant-induced psychotic disorder, unspecified

  F18.27   Inhalant dependence with inhalant-induced dementia

      Inhalant use disorder, moderate, with inhalant-induced major neurocognitive disorder

      Inhalant use disorder, severe, with inhalant-induced major neurocognitive disorder

● F18.28   Inhalant dependence with other inhalant-induced disorders

    F18.280   Inhalant dependence with inhalant-induced anxiety disorder

    F18.288   Inhalant dependence with other inhalant-induced disorder

       Inhalant use disorder, moderate, with inhalant-induced mild neurocognitive disorder

       Inhalant use disorder, severe, with inhalant-induced mild neurocognitive disorder

  F18.29   Inhalant dependence with unspecified inhalant-induced disorder

● F18.9   Inhalant use, unspecified

    Excludes1   inhalant abuse (F18.1-)

               inhalant dependence (F18.2-)

  F18.90   Inhalant use, unspecified, uncomplicated

● F18.92   Inhalant use, unspecified with intoxication

    F18.920   Inhalant use, unspecified with intoxication, uncomplicated

    F18.921   Inhalant use, unspecified with intoxication with delirium

    F18.929   Inhalant use, unspecified with intoxication, unspecified

  F18.94   Inhalant use, unspecified with inhalant-induced mood disorder

      Inhalant-induced depressive disorder

● F18.95   Inhalant use, unspecified with inhalant-induced psychotic disorder

    F18.950   Inhalant use, unspecified with inhalant-induced psychotic disorder with delusions

    F18.951   Inhalant use, unspecified with inhalant-induced psychotic disorder with hallucinations

    F18.959   Inhalant use, unspecified with inhalant-induced psychotic disorder, unspecified

  F18.97   Inhalant use, unspecified with inhalant-induced persisting dementia

      Inhalant-induced major neurocognitive disorder

● F18.98   Inhalant use, unspecified with other inhalant-induced disorders

    F18.980   Inhalant use, unspecified with inhalant-induced anxiety disorder

    F18.988   Inhalant use, unspecified with other inhalant-induced disorder

       Inhalant-induced mild neurocognitive disorder

  F18.99   Inhalant use, unspecified with unspecified inhalant-induced disorder

● F19   Other psychoactive substance related disorders

    Includes   polysubstance drug use (indiscriminate drug use)

● F19.1   Other psychoactive substance abuse

    Excludes1   other psychoactive substance dependence (F19.2-)

               other psychoactive substance use, unspecified (F19.9-)

  F19.10   Other psychoactive substance abuse, uncomplicated

      Other (or unknown) substance use disorder, mild

  F19.11   Other psychoactive substance abuse, in remission

      Other (or unknown) substance use disorder, mild, in early remission

      Other (or unknown) substance use disorder, mild, in sustained remission

● F19.12   Other psychoactive substance abuse with intoxication

    F19.120   Other psychoactive substance abuse with intoxication, uncomplicated

    F19.121   Other psychoactive substance abuse with intoxication delirium

    F19.122   Other psychoactive substance abuse with intoxication with perceptual disturbances

    F19.129   Other psychoactive substance abuse with intoxication, unspecified

  F19.14   Other psychoactive substance abuse with psychoactive substance-induced mood disorder

      Other (or unknown) substance use disorder, mild, with other (or unknown) substance-induced bipolar or related disorder

      Other (or unknown) substance use disorder, mild, with other (or unknown) substance-induced depressive disorder

● F19.15   Other psychoactive substance abuse with psychoactive substance-induced psychotic disorder

    F19.150   Other psychoactive substance abuse with psychoactive substance-induced psychotic disorder with delusions

    F19.151   Other psychoactive substance abuse with psychoactive substance-induced psychotic disorder with hallucinations

    F19.159   Other psychoactive substance abuse with psychoactive substance-induced psychotic disorder, unspecified

  F19.16   Other psychoactive substance abuse with psychoactive substance-induced persisting amnestic disorder

  F19.17   Other psychoactive substance abuse with psychoactive substance-induced persisting dementia

      Other (or unknown) substance use disorder, mild, with other (or unknown) substance-induced major neurocognitive disorder

CHAPTER 5 (F01-F99)

● **F19.18**   **Other psychoactive substance abuse with other psychoactive substance-induced disorders**

     F19.180   Other psychoactive substance abuse with psychoactive substance-induced anxiety disorder

     F19.181   Other psychoactive substance abuse with psychoactive substance-induced sexual dysfunction

     F19.182   Other psychoactive substance abuse with psychoactive substance-induced sleep disorder

     F19.188   Other psychoactive substance abuse with other psychoactive substance-induced disorder

         Other (or unknown) substance use disorder, mild, with other (or unknown) substance-induced mild neurocognitive disorder

         Other (or unknown) substance use disorder, mild, with other (or unknown) substance-induced obsessive-compulsive or related disorder

   F19.19   Other psychoactive substance abuse with unspecified psychoactive substance-induced disorder

● **F19.2**   **Other psychoactive substance dependence**

     Excludes1   other psychoactive substance abuse (F19.1-)

         other psychoactive substance use, unspecified (F19.9-)

   F19.20   Other psychoactive substance dependence, uncomplicated

         Other (or unknown) substance use disorder, moderate

         Other (or unknown) substance use disorder, severe

   F19.21   Other psychoactive substance dependence, in remission

         Other (or unknown) substance use disorder, moderate, in early remission

         Other (or unknown) substance use disorder, moderate, in sustained remission

         Other (or unknown) substance use disorder, severe, in early remission

       ⇒ Other (or unknown) substance use disorder, severe, in sustained remission

● **F19.22**   **Other psychoactive substance dependence with intoxication**

     Excludes1   other psychoactive substance dependence with withdrawal (F19.23-)

     F19.220   Other psychoactive substance dependence with intoxication, uncomplicated

     F19.221   Other psychoactive substance dependence with intoxication delirium

     F19.222   Other psychoactive substance dependence with intoxication with perceptual disturbance

     F19.229   Other psychoactive substance dependence with intoxication, unspecified

● **F19.23**   **Other psychoactive substance dependence with withdrawal**

     Excludes1   other psychoactive substance dependence with intoxication (F19.22-)

     F19.230   Other psychoactive substance dependence with withdrawal, uncomplicated

     F19.231   Other psychoactive substance dependence with withdrawal delirium

     F19.232   Other psychoactive substance dependence with withdrawal with perceptual disturbance

     F19.239   Other psychoactive substance dependence with withdrawal, unspecified

   F19.24   Other psychoactive substance dependence with psychoactive substance-induced mood disorder

         Other (or unknown) substance use disorder, moderate, with other (or unknown) substance-induced bipolar or related disorder

         Other (or unknown) substance use disorder, moderate, with other (or unknown) substance-induced depressive disorder

         Other (or unknown) substance use disorder, severe, with other (or unknown) substance-induced bipolar or related disorder

         Other (or unknown) substance use disorder, severe, with other (or unknown) substance-induced depressive disorder

● **F19.25**   **Other psychoactive substance dependence with psychoactive substance-induced psychotic disorder**

     F19.250   Other psychoactive substance dependence with psychoactive substance-induced psychotic disorder with delusions

     F19.251   Other psychoactive substance dependence with psychoactive substance-induced psychotic disorder with hallucinations

     F19.259   Other psychoactive substance dependence with psychoactive substance-induced psychotic disorder, unspecified

   F19.26   Other psychoactive substance dependence with psychoactive substance-induced persisting amnestic disorder

   F19.27   Other psychoactive substance dependence with psychoactive substance-induced persisting dementia

         Other (or unknown) substance use disorder, moderate, with other (or unknown) substance-induced major neurocognitive disorder

         Other (or unknown) substance use disorder, severe, with other (or unknown) substance-induced major neurocognitive disorder

● **F19.28**   **Other psychoactive substance dependence with other psychoactive substance-induced disorders**

     F19.280   Other psychoactive substance dependence with psychoactive substance-induced anxiety disorder

     F19.281   Other psychoactive substance dependence with psychoactive substance-induced sexual dysfunction

     F19.282   Other psychoactive substance dependence with psychoactive substance-induced sleep disorder

▶ New   ⇒ Revised   ~~deleted~~ Deleted   Excludes 1   Excludes 2   Includes   Use additional   Code first   Code also   Key words

OGCR Official Guidelines   X Assign placeholder X   ● Use Additional Character(s)   ▶ Manifestation Code   **Coding Clinic**

F19.288   Other psychoactive substance dependence with other psychoactive substance-induced disorder
  Other (or unknown) substance use disorder, moderate, with other (or unknown) substance-induced mild neurocognitive disorder
  Other (or unknown) substance use disorder, severe, with other (or unknown) substance-induced mild neurocognitive disorder
  Other (or unknown) substance use disorder, moderate, with other (or unknown) substance-induced obsessive-compulsive or related disorder
  Other (or unknown) substance use disorder, severe, with other (or unknown) substance-induced obsessive-compulsive or related disorder

F19.29   Other psychoactive substance dependence with unspecified psychoactive substance-induced disorder

● F19.9   Other psychoactive substance use, unspecified
  Excludes1   other psychoactive substance abuse (F19.1-)
    other psychoactive substance dependence (F19.2-)

F19.90   Other psychoactive substance use, unspecified, uncomplicated

● F19.92   Other psychoactive substance use, unspecified with intoxication
  Excludes1   other psychoactive substance use, unspecified with withdrawal (F19.93)

  F19.920   Other psychoactive substance use, unspecified with intoxication, uncomplicated

  F19.921   Other psychoactive substance use, unspecified with intoxication with delirium
    Other (or unknown) substance-induced delirium

  F19.922   Other psychoactive substance use, unspecified with intoxication with perceptual disturbance

  F19.929   Other psychoactive substance use, unspecified with intoxication, unspecified

● F19.93   Other psychoactive substance use, unspecified with withdrawal
  Excludes1   other psychoactive substance use, unspecified with intoxication (F19.92-)

  F19.930   Other psychoactive substance use, unspecified with withdrawal, uncomplicated

  F19.931   Other psychoactive substance use, unspecified with withdrawal delirium

  F19.932   Other psychoactive substance use, unspecified with withdrawal with perceptual disturbance

  F19.939   Other psychoactive substance use, unspecified with withdrawal, unspecified

F19.94   Other psychoactive substance use, unspecified with psychoactive substance-induced mood disorder
  Other (or unknown) substance-induced bipolar or related disorder, without use disorder
  Other (or unknown) substance-induced depressive disorder, without use disorder

● F19.95   Other psychoactive substance use, unspecified with psychoactive substance-induced psychotic disorder

  F19.950   Other psychoactive substance use, unspecified with psychoactive substance-induced psychotic disorder with delusions

  F19.951   Other psychoactive substance use, unspecified with psychoactive substance-induced psychotic disorder with hallucinations

  F19.959   Other psychoactive substance use, unspecified with psychoactive substance-induced psychotic disorder, unspecified
    Other or unknown substance-induced psychotic disorder, without use disorder

F19.96   Other psychoactive substance use, unspecified with psychoactive substance-induced persisting amnestic disorder

F19.97   Other psychoactive substance use, unspecified with psychoactive substance-induced persisting dementia
  Other (or unknown) substance-induced major neurocognitive disorder, without use disorder

● F19.98   Other psychoactive substance use, unspecified with other psychoactive substance-induced disorders

  F19.980   Other psychoactive substance use, unspecified with psychoactive substance-induced anxiety disorder
    Other (or unknown) substance-induced anxiety disorder, without use disorder

  F19.981   Other psychoactive substance use, unspecified with psychoactive substance-induced sexual dysfunction
    Other (or unknown) substance-induced sexual dysfunction, without use disorder

  F19.982   Other psychoactive substance use, unspecified with psychoactive substance-induced sleep disorder
    Other (or unknown) substance-induced sleep disorder, without use disorder

  F19.988   Other psychoactive substance use, unspecified with other psychoactive substance-induced disorder
    Other (or unknown) substance-induced mild neurocognitive disorder, without use disorder
    Other (or unknown) substance-induced obsessive-compulsive or related disorder, without use disorder

F19.99   Other psychoactive substance use, unspecified with unspecified psychoactive substance-induced disorder

CHAPTER 5 (F01-F99)

SCHIZOPHRENIA, SCHIZOTYPAL, DELUSIONAL, AND OTHER NON-MOOD PSYCHOTIC DISORDERS (F20-F29)

● **F20 Schizophrenia**
Personality disorders characterized by multiple mental and behavioral irregularities (may exhibit disorganized thinking, delusions, and auditory hallucinations)

    Excludes1 brief psychotic disorder (F23)
                cyclic schizophrenia (F25.0)
                mood [affective] disorders with psychotic symptoms (F30.2, F31.2, F31.5, F31.64, F32.3, F33.3)
                schizoaffective disorder (F25.-)
                schizophrenic reaction NOS (F23)

    Excludes2 schizophrenic reaction in:
                alcoholism (F10.15-, F10.25-, F10.95-)
                brain disease (F06.2)
                epilepsy (F06.2)
                psychoactive drug use (F11-F19 with .15, .25, .95)
                schizotypal disorder (F21)

  F20.0 Paranoid schizophrenia
      Paraphrenic schizophrenia
      Excludes1 involutional paranoid state (F22)
                  paranoia (F22)

  F20.1 Disorganized schizophrenia
      Hebephrenic schizophrenia
      Hebephrenia

  F20.2 Catatonic schizophrenia
      Schizophrenic catalepsy
      Schizophrenic catatonia
      Schizophrenic flexibilitas cerea
      Excludes1 catatonic stupor (R40.1)

  F20.3 Undifferentiated schizophrenia
      Atypical schizophrenia
      Excludes1 acute schizophrenia-like psychotic disorder (F23)
      Excludes2 post-schizophrenic depression (F32.89)

  F20.5 Residual schizophrenia
      Restzustand (schizophrenic)
      Schizophrenic residual state

● **F20.8 Other schizophrenia**
    F20.81 Schizophreniform disorder
          Schizophreniform psychosis NOS
    F20.89 Other schizophrenia
          Cenesthopathic schizophrenia
          Simple schizophrenia

  F20.9 Schizophrenia, unspecified

F21 Schizotypal disorder
Personality disorder characterized by need for social isolation, odd behavior and thinking, and often unconventional beliefs
    Borderline schizophrenia
    Latent schizophrenia
    Latent schizophrenic reaction
    Prepsychotic schizophrenia
    Prodromal schizophrenia
    Pseudoneurotic schizophrenia
    Pseudopsychopathic schizophrenia
    Schizotypal personality disorder
    Excludes2 Asperger's syndrome (F84.5)
                schizoid personality disorder (F60.1)

F22 Delusional disorders
    Delusional dysmorphophobia
    Involutional paranoid state
    Paranoia
    Paranoia querulans
    Paranoid psychosis
    Paranoid state
    Paraphrenia (late)
    Sensitiver Beziehungswahn
    Excludes1 mood [affective] disorders with psychotic symptoms (F30.2, F31.2, F31.5, F31.64, F32.3, F33.3)
                paranoid schizophrenia (F20.0)
    Excludes2 paranoid personality disorder (F60.0)
                paranoid psychosis, psychogenic (F23)
                paranoid reaction (F23)

F23 Brief psychotic disorder
    Paranoid reaction
    Psychogenic paranoid psychosis
    Excludes2 mood [affective] disorders with psychotic symptoms (F30.2, F31.2, F31.5, F31.64, F32.3, F33.3)

F24 Shared psychotic disorder
    Folie à deux
    Induced paranoid disorder
    Induced psychotic disorder

● **F25 Schizoaffective disorders**
Mental disorder exhibiting major depressive episode, manic episode, or mixed episode occurs with symptoms of schizophrenia, and mood disorder
    Excludes1 mood [affective] disorders with psychotic symptoms (F30.2, F31.2, F31.5, F31.64, F32.3, F33.3)
                schizophrenia (F20.-)

  F25.0 Schizoaffective disorder, bipolar type
      Cyclic schizophrenia
      Schizoaffective disorder, manic type
      Schizoaffective disorder, mixed type
      Schizoaffective psychosis, bipolar type

  F25.1 Schizoaffective disorder, depressive type
      Schizoaffective psychosis, depressive type

  F25.8 Other schizoaffective disorders

  F25.9 Schizoaffective disorder, unspecified
      Schizoaffective psychosis NOS

F28 Other psychotic disorder not due to a substance or known physiological condition
    Chronic hallucinatory psychosis
    Other specified schizophrenia spectrum and other psychotic disorder

F29 Unspecified psychosis not due to a substance or known physiological condition
    Psychosis NOS
    Unspecified schizophrenia spectrum and other psychotic disorder
    Excludes1 mental disorder NOS (F99)
                unspecified mental disorder due to known physiological condition (F09)

▶ New ⇒ Revised ~~deleted~~ Deleted **Excludes 1** **Excludes 2** **Includes** **Use additional** **Code first** **Code also** **Key words**
OGCR Official Guidelines **X** Assign placeholder X ● Use Additional Character(s) ▶ Manifestation Code **Coding Clinic**

MOOD [AFFECTIVE] DISORDERS (F30-F39)

● **F30 Manic episode**
  Elevated, expansive, or irritable mood

  Includes   bipolar disorder, single manic episode
                     mixed affective episode

  Excludes1   bipolar disorder (F31.-)
                   major depressive disorder, single episode (F32.-)
                   major depressive disorder, recurrent (F33.-)

● **F30.1 Manic episode without psychotic symptoms**

  F30.10 Manic episode without psychotic symptoms, unspecified

  F30.11 Manic episode without psychotic symptoms, mild

  F30.12 Manic episode without psychotic symptoms, moderate

  F30.13 Manic episode, severe, without psychotic symptoms

  F30.2 Manic episode, severe with psychotic symptoms
        Manic stupor
        Mania with mood-congruent psychotic symptoms
        Mania with mood-incongruent psychotic symptoms

  F30.3 Manic episode in partial remission

  F30.4 Manic episode in full remission

  F30.8 Other manic episodes
        Abnormality of mood resembling mania but less intense
        Hypomania

  F30.9 Manic episode, unspecified
        Mania NOS

● **F31 Bipolar disorder**
  Mood disorders with history of manic, mixed, or hypomanic episodes

  Includes   bipolar I disorder
                   bipolar type I disorder
                   manic-depressive illness
                   manic-depressive psychosis
                   manic-depressive reaction

  Excludes1   bipolar disorder, single manic episode (F30.-)
                   major depressive disorder, single episode (F32.-)
                   major depressive disorder, recurrent (F33.-)

  Excludes2   cyclothymia (F34.0)

  F31.0 Bipolar disorder, current episode hypomanic

● **F31.1 Bipolar disorder, current episode manic without psychotic features**

  F31.10 Bipolar disorder, current episode manic without psychotic features, unspecified

  F31.11 Bipolar disorder, current episode manic without psychotic features, mild

  F31.12 Bipolar disorder, current episode manic without psychotic features, moderate

  F31.13 Bipolar disorder, current episode manic without psychotic features, severe

  F31.2 Bipolar disorder, current episode manic severe with psychotic features
        Bipolar disorder, current episode manic with mood-congruent psychotic symptoms
        Bipolar disorder, current episode manic with mood-incongruent psychotic symptoms
        Bipolar I disorder, current or most recent episode manic with psychotic features

● **F31.3 Bipolar disorder, current episode depressed, mild or moderate severity**

  F31.30 Bipolar disorder, current episode depressed, mild or moderate severity, unspecified

  F31.31 Bipolar disorder, current episode depressed, mild

  F31.32 Bipolar disorder, current episode depressed, moderate

  F31.4 Bipolar disorder, current episode depressed, severe, without psychotic features

  F31.5 Bipolar disorder, current episode depressed, severe, with psychotic features
        Bipolar disorder, current episode depressed with mood-incongruent psychotic symptoms
        Bipolar disorder, current episode depressed with mood-congruent psychotic symptoms
        Bipolar I disorder, current or most recent episode depressed, with psychotic features

● **F31.6 Bipolar disorder, current episode mixed**

  F31.60 Bipolar disorder, current episode mixed, unspecified

  F31.61 Bipolar disorder, current episode mixed, mild

  F31.62 Bipolar disorder, current episode mixed, moderate

  F31.63 Bipolar disorder, current episode mixed, severe, without psychotic features

  F31.64 Bipolar disorder, current episode mixed, severe, with psychotic features
        Bipolar disorder, current episode mixed with mood-congruent psychotic symptoms
        Bipolar disorder, current episode mixed with mood-incongruent psychotic symptoms

● **F31.7 Bipolar disorder, currently in remission**

  F31.70 Bipolar disorder, currently in remission, most recent episode unspecified

  F31.71 Bipolar disorder, in partial remission, most recent episode hypomanic

  F31.72 Bipolar disorder, in full remission, most recent episode hypomanic

  F31.73 Bipolar disorder, in partial remission, most recent episode manic

  F31.74 Bipolar disorder, in full remission, most recent episode manic

  F31.75 Bipolar disorder, in partial remission, most recent episode depressed

  F31.76 Bipolar disorder, in full remission, most recent episode depressed

  F31.77 Bipolar disorder, in partial remission, most recent episode mixed

  F31.78 Bipolar disorder, in full remission, most recent episode mixed

  F31.8 Other bipolar disorders

  F31.81 Bipolar II disorder
        Bipolar disorder, type 2

  F31.89 Other bipolar disorder
        Recurrent manic episodes NOS

  F31.9 Bipolar disorder, unspecified
        Manic depression

● **F32 Major depressive disorder, single episode**

  Includes   single episode of agitated depression
                   single episode of depressive reaction
                   single episode of major depression
                   single episode of psychogenic depression
                   single episode of reactive depression
                   single episode of vital depression

  Excludes1   bipolar disorder (F31.-)
                   manic episode (F30.-)
                   recurrent depressive disorder (F33.-)

  Excludes2   adjustment disorder (F43.2)

  F32.0 Major depressive disorder, single episode, mild

  F32.1 Major depressive disorder, single episode, moderate

  F32.2 Major depressive disorder, single episode, severe without psychotic features

CHAPTER 5 (F01-F99)

F32.3 Major depressive disorder, single episode, severe with psychotic features
 Single episode of major depression with mood-congruent psychotic symptoms
 Single episode of major depression with mood-incongruent psychotic symptoms
 Single episode of major depression with psychotic symptoms
 Single episode of psychogenic depressive psychosis
 Single episode of psychotic depression
 Single episode of reactive depressive psychosis

F32.4 Major depressive disorder, single episode, in partial remission

F32.5 Major depressive disorder, single episode, in full remission

● **F32.8** Other depressive episodes
 F32.81 Premenstrual dysphoric disorder ♀
  Excludes1 premenstrual tension syndrome (N94.3)
  Coding Clinic: 2016, Q4, P14
 F32.89 Other specified depressive episodes
  Atypical depression
  Post-schizophrenic depression
  Single episode of 'masked' depression NOS
  Coding Clinic: 2016, Q4, P14

F32.9 Major depressive disorder, single episode, unspecified
 Depression NOS
 Depressive disorder NOS
 Major depression NOS

● **F33** Major depressive disorder, recurrent
 Includes recurrent episodes of depressive reaction
  recurrent episodes of endogenous depression
  recurrent episodes of major depression
  recurrent episodes of psychogenic depression
  recurrent episodes of reactive depression
  recurrent episodes of seasonal depressive disorder
  recurrent episodes of vital depression
 Excludes1 bipolar disorder (F31.-)
  manic episode (F30.-)

F33.0 Major depressive disorder, recurrent, mild
F33.1 Major depressive disorder, recurrent, moderate
F33.2 Major depressive disorder, recurrent severe without psychotic features
F33.3 Major depressive disorder, recurrent, severe with psychotic symptoms
 Endogenous depression with psychotic symptoms
 Major depressive disorder, recurrent, with psychotic features
 Recurrent severe episodes of major depression with mood-congruent psychotic symptoms
 Recurrent severe episodes of major depression with mood-incongruent psychotic symptoms
 Recurrent severe episodes of major depression with psychotic symptoms
 Recurrent severe episodes of psychogenic depressive psychosis
 Recurrent severe episodes of psychotic depression
 Recurrent severe episodes of reactive depressive psychosis

● **F33.4** Major depressive disorder, recurrent, in remission
 F33.40 Major depressive disorder, recurrent, in remission, unspecified
 F33.41 Major depressive disorder, recurrent, in partial remission
 F33.42 Major depressive disorder, recurrent, in full remission

F33.8 Other recurrent depressive disorders
 Recurrent brief depressive episodes
F33.9 Major depressive disorder, recurrent, unspecified
 Monopolar depression NOS

Figure 5-1 PET scan of depressed individual's brain before and after recovery. (From Fortinash KM: Psychiatric Mental Health Nursing, ed 4, St. Louis, Mosby, 2008)

● **F34** Persistent mood [affective] disorders
 F34.0 Cyclothymic disorder
  Affective personality disorder
  Cycloid personality
  Cyclothymia
  Cyclothymic personality
 F34.1 Dysthymic disorder
  Depressive neurosis
  Depressive personality disorder
  Dysthymia
  Neurotic depression
  Persistent anxiety depression
  Persistent depressive disorder
  Excludes2 anxiety depression (mild or not persistent) (F41.8)

● **F34.8** Other persistent mood [affective] disorders
 F34.81 Disruptive mood dysregulation disorder
  Coding Clinic: 2016, Q4, P14
 F34.89 Other specified persistent mood disorders
  Coding Clinic: 2016, Q4, P14

F34.9 Persistent mood [affective] disorder, unspecified

F39 Unspecified mood [affective] disorder
 Affective psychosis NOS

ANXIETY, DISSOCIATIVE, STRESS-RELATED, SOMATOFORM AND OTHER NONPSYCHOTIC MENTAL DISORDERS (F40-F48)

● **F40** Phobic anxiety disorders
 Irrational fear with avoidance of the feared subject, activity, or situation even though the individual knows that the reaction is excessive
● **F40.0** Agoraphobia
  Intense, irrational fear of open spaces
 F40.00 Agoraphobia, unspecified
 F40.01 Agoraphobia with panic disorder
  Panic disorder with agoraphobia
  Excludes1 panic disorder without agoraphobia (F41.0)
 F40.02 Agoraphobia without panic disorder
● **F40.1** Social phobias
  Anthropophobia
  Social anxiety disorder
  Social anxiety disorder of childhood
  Social neurosis
 F40.10 Social phobia, unspecified
 F40.11 Social phobia, generalized

► New ⇒ Revised ~~deleted~~ Deleted Excludes 1 Excludes 2 Includes Use additional Code first Code also Key words
OGCR Official Guidelines X Assign placeholder X ● Use Additional Character(s) ▍ Manifestation Code Coding Clinic

● **F40.2**   **Specific (isolated) phobias**
     Excludes2   dysmorphophobia (nondelusional)
                    (F45.22)
                    nosophobia (F45.22)

   ● **F40.21**   **Animal type phobia**
       F40.210   **Arachnophobia**
                 Fear of spiders
       F40.218   **Other animal type phobia**

   ● **F40.22**   **Natural environment type phobia**
       F40.220   **Fear of thunderstorms**
       F40.228   **Other natural environment type phobia**

   ● **F40.23**   **Blood, injection, injury type phobia**
       F40.230   **Fear of blood**
       F40.231   **Fear of injections and transfusions**
       F40.232   **Fear of other medical care**
       F40.233   **Fear of injury**

   ● **F40.24**   **Situational type phobia**
       F40.240   **Claustrophobia**
                 Fear of closed spaces
       F40.241   **Acrophobia**
                 Fear of heights
       F40.242   **Fear of bridges**
       F40.243   **Fear of flying**
       F40.248   **Other situational type phobia**

   ● **F40.29**   **Other specified phobia**
       F40.290   **Androphobia**
                 Fear of men
       F40.291   **Gynephobia**
                 Fear of women
       F40.298   **Other specified phobia**

  F40.8   **Other phobic anxiety disorders**
       Phobic anxiety disorder of childhood

  F40.9   **Phobic anxiety disorder, unspecified**
       Phobia NOS
       Phobic state NOS

● **F41**   **Other anxiety disorders**
     Excludes2   anxiety in:
                acute stress reaction (F43.0)
                transient adjustment reaction (F43.2)
                neurasthenia (F48.8)
                psychophysiologic disorders (F45.-)
                separation anxiety (F93.0)

  F41.0   **Panic disorder [episodic paroxysmal anxiety]**
       Panic attack
       Panic state
       Excludes1   panic disorder with agoraphobia (F40.01)

  F41.1   **Generalized anxiety disorder**
       Anxiety neurosis
       Anxiety reaction
       Anxiety state
       Overanxious disorder
       Excludes2   neurasthenia (F48.8)

  F41.3   **Other mixed anxiety disorders**

  F41.8   **Other specified anxiety disorders**
       Anxiety depression (mild or not persistent)
       Anxiety hysteria
       Mixed anxiety and depressive disorder

  F41.9   **Anxiety disorder, unspecified**
       Anxiety NOS

● **F42**   **Obsessive-compulsive disorder**
     Anxiety disorder with recurrent obsessions or compulsions
     Excludes2   obsessive-compulsive personality (disorder)
                (F60.5)
                obsessive-compulsive symptoms occurring in
                   depression (F32-F33)
                obsessive-compulsive symptoms occurring in
                   schizophrenia (F20.-)

  F42.2   **Mixed obsessional thoughts and acts**
       Coding Clinic: 2016, Q4, P15

  F42.3   **Hoarding disorder**
       Coding Clinic: 2016, Q4, P14-15

  F42.4   **Excoriation (skin-picking) disorder**
       Excludes1   factitial dermatitis (L98.1)
                other specified behavioral and emotional
                   disorders with onset usually
                   occurring in early childhood and
                   adolescence (F98.8)
       Coding Clinic: 2016, Q4, P14-15

  F42.8   **Other obsessive-compulsive disorder**
       Anancastic neurosis
       Obsessive-compulsive neurosis
       Coding Clinic: 2016, Q4, P15

  F42.9   **Obsessive-compulsive disorder, unspecified**
       Coding Clinic: 2016, Q4, P15

● **F43**   **Reaction to severe stress and adjustment disorders**
  F43.0   **Acute stress reaction**
       Acute crisis reaction
       Acute reaction to stress
       Combat and operational stress reaction
       Combat fatigue
       Crisis state
       Psychic shock

   ● **F43.1**   **Post-traumatic stress disorder (PTSD)**
       Traumatic neurosis
       F43.10   **Post-traumatic stress disorder, unspecified**
       F43.11   **Post-traumatic stress disorder, acute**
       F43.12   **Post-traumatic stress disorder, chronic**

   ● **F43.2**   **Adjustment disorders**
       Culture shock
       Grief reaction
       Hospitalism in children
       Excludes2   separation anxiety disorder of childhood
                (F93.0)
       F43.20   **Adjustment disorder, unspecified**
       F43.21   **Adjustment disorder with depressed mood**
       F43.22   **Adjustment disorder with anxiety**
       F43.23   **Adjustment disorder with mixed anxiety and depressed mood**
       F43.24   **Adjustment disorder with disturbance of conduct**
       F43.25   **Adjustment disorder with mixed disturbance of emotions and conduct**
       F43.29   **Adjustment disorder with other symptoms**

  F43.8   **Other reactions to severe stress**
       Other specified trauma and stressor-related disorder

  F43.9   **Reaction to severe stress, unspecified**
       Trauma and stressor-related disorder, NOS

CHAPTER 5 (F01-F99)

● **F44   Dissociative and conversion disorders**

     Includes   conversion hysteria
                    conversion reaction
                    hysteria
                    hysterical psychosis

     Excludes2   malingering [conscious simulation] (Z76.5)

F44.0   Dissociative amnesia
     Sudden loss of memory for personal information

       Excludes1   amnesia NOS (R41.3)
                   anterograde amnesia (R41.1)
                   dissociative amnesia with dissociative fugue (F44.1)
                   retrograde amnesia (R41.2)

       Excludes2   alcohol-or other psychoactive substance-induced amnestic disorder (F10, F13, F19 with .26, .96)
                   amnestic disorder due to known physiological condition (F04)
                   postictal amnesia in epilepsy (G40.-)

F44.1   Dissociative fugue
     Characterized by episode of sudden, unexpected travel with amnesia for past and partial to total confusion about identity or assumption of new identity
     Dissociative amnesia with dissociative fugue

       Excludes2   postictal fugue in epilepsy (G40.-)

F44.2   Dissociative stupor
     Profound diminution or absence of voluntary movement and responsiveness to external stimuli

       Excludes1   catatonic stupor (R40.1)
                   stupor NOS (R40.1)

       Excludes2   catatonic disorder due to known physiological condition (F06.1)
                   depressive stupor (F32, F33)
                   manic stupor (F30, F31)

F44.4   Conversion disorder with motor symptom or deficit
     Conversion disorder with abnormal movement
     Conversion disorder with speech symptoms
     Conversion disorder with swallowing symptoms
     Conversion disorder with weakness/paralysis
     Dissociative motor disorders
     Psychogenic aphonia
     Psychogenic dysphonia

F44.5   Conversion disorder with seizures or convulsions
     Conversion disorder with attacks or seizures
     Dissociative convulsions

F44.6   Conversion disorder with sensory symptom or deficit
     Conversion disorder with anesthesia or sensory loss
     Conversion disorder with special sensory symptoms
     Dissociative anesthesia and sensory loss
     Psychogenic deafness

F44.7   Conversion disorder with mixed symptom presentation

● **F44.8   Other dissociative and conversion disorders**

     F44.81   Dissociative identity disorder
               Multiple personality disorder

     F44.89   Other dissociative and conversion disorders
               Ganser's syndrome
               Psychogenic confusion
               Psychogenic twilight state
               Trance and possession disorders

F44.9   Dissociative and conversion disorder, unspecified
     Dissociative disorder NOS

OGCR   Section I.C.5.a.

Pain disorders related to psychological factors

Assign code F45.41, for pain that is exclusively related to psychological disorders. As indicated by the Excludes 1 note under category G89, a code from category G89 should not be assigned with code F45.41 Code F45.42, Pain disorders with related psychological factors, should be used with a code from category G89, Pain, not elsewhere classified, if there is documentation of a psychological component for a patient with acute or chronic pain.

See Section I.C.6. Pain

● **F45   Somatoform disorders**
     Mental disorders characterized by symptoms suggesting general medical condition

     Excludes2   dissociative and conversion disorders (F44.-)
                 ⇒ factitious disorders (F68.1-, F68.A)
                 hair-plucking (F63.3)
                 lalling (F80.0)
                 lisping (F80.0)
                 malingering [conscious simulation] (Z76.5)
                 nail-biting (F98.8)
                 psychological or behavioral factors associated with disorders or diseases classified elsewhere (F54)
                 sexual dysfunction, not due to a substance or known physiological condition (F52.-)
                 thumb-sucking (F98.8)
                 tic disorders (in childhood and adolescence) (F95.-)
                 Tourette's syndrome (F95.2)
                 trichotillomania (F63.3)

F45.0   Somatization disorder
     Briquet's disorder
     Multiple psychosomatic disorder

F45.1   Undifferentiated somatoform disorder
     Somatic symptom disorder
     Undifferentiated psychosomatic disorder

● **F45.2   Hypochondriacal disorders**
     Persistent, unrealistic preoccupation with possibility of having serious disease

     Excludes2   delusional dysmorphophobia (F22)
                 fixed delusions about bodily functions or shape (F22)

     F45.20   Hypochondriacal disorder, unspecified

     F45.21   Hypochondriasis
               Hypochondriacal neurosis
               Illness anxiety disorder

     F45.22   Body dysmorphic disorder
               Dysmorphophobia (nondelusional)
               Nosophobia

     F45.29   Other hypochondriacal disorders

● **F45.4   Pain disorders related to psychological factors**

     Excludes1   pain NOS (R52)

     F45.41   Pain disorder exclusively related to psychological factors
               Somatoform pain disorder (persistent)

     F45.42   Pain disorder with related psychological factors
               Code also associated acute or chronic pain (G89.-)

F45.8   Other somatoform disorders
     Psychogenic dysmenorrhea
     Psychogenic dysphagia, including 'globus hystericus'
     Psychogenic pruritus
     Psychogenic torticollis
     Somatoform autonomic dysfunction
     Teeth grinding

     Excludes1   sleep related teeth grinding (G47.63)
     Coding Clinic: 2016, Q4, P118

F45.9   Somatoform disorder, unspecified
     Psychosomatic disorder NOS

▶ New   ⇒ Revised   ~~deleted~~ Deleted   Excludes 1   Excludes 2   Includes   Use additional   Code first   Code also   Key words

OGCR Official Guidelines   X Assign placeholder X   ● Use Additional Character(s)   ▶ Manifestation Code   **Coding Clinic**

- **F48** **Other nonpsychotic mental disorders**
  - **F48.1** **Depersonalization-derealization syndrome**
  - **F48.2** **Pseudobulbar affect**
    Involuntary emotional expression disorder
    Code first underlying cause, if known, such as:
    amyotrophic lateral sclerosis (G12.21)
    multiple sclerosis (G35)
    sequelae of cerebrovascular disease (I69.-)
    sequelae of traumatic intracranial injury (S06.-)
  - **F48.8** **Other specified nonpsychotic mental disorders**
    Dhat syndrome
    Neurasthenia
    Occupational neurosis, including writer's cramp
    Psychasthenia
    Psychasthenic neurosis
    Psychogenic syncope
  - **F48.9** **Nonpsychotic mental disorder, unspecified**
    Neurosis NOS

BEHAVIORAL SYNDROMES ASSOCIATED WITH PHYSIOLOGICAL DISTURBANCES AND PHYSICAL FACTORS (F50-F59)

- **F50** **Eating disorders**
  - **Excludes1** anorexia NOS (R63.0)
    feeding difficulties (R63.3)
    feeding problems of newborn (P92.-)
    polyphagia (R63.2)
  - **Excludes2** feeding disorder in infancy or childhood (F98.2-)
  - **F50.0** **Anorexia nervosa**
    - **Excludes1** loss of appetite (R63.0)
      psychogenic loss of appetite (F50.89)
    - **F50.00** **Anorexia nervosa, unspecified**
    - **F50.01** **Anorexia nervosa, restricting type**
    - **F50.02** **Anorexia nervosa, binge eating/purging type**
      - **Excludes1** bulimia nervosa (F50.2)
  - **F50.2** **Bulimia nervosa**
    Bulimia NOS
    Hyperorexia nervosa
    - **Excludes1** anorexia nervosa, binge eating/purging type (F50.02)
  - **F50.8** **Other eating disorders**
    - **Excludes2** pica of infancy and childhood (F98.3)
    - **F50.81** **Binge eating disorder**
      Coding Clinic: 2016, Q4, P15
    - **F50.82** **Avoidant/restrictive food intake disorder**
    - **F50.89** **Other specified eating disorder**
      Pica in adults
      Psychogenic loss of appetite
      Coding Clinic: 2016, Q4, P16
  - **F50.9** **Eating disorder, unspecified**
    Atypical anorexia nervosa
    Atypical bulimia nervosa
    Feeding or eating disorder, unspecified
    Other specified feeding disorder

- **F51** **Sleep disorders not due to a substance or known physiological condition**
  - **Excludes2** organic sleep disorders (G47.-)
  - **F51.0** **Insomnia not due to a substance or known physiological condition**
    - **Excludes2** alcohol related insomnia (F10.182, F10.282, F10.982)
      drug-related insomnia (F11.182, F11.282, F11.982, F13.182, F13.282, F13.982, F14.182, F14.282, F14.982, F15.182, F15.282, F15.982, F19.182, F19.282, F19.982)
      insomnia NOS (G47.0-)
      insomnia due to known physiological condition (G47.0-)
      organic insomnia (G47.0-)
      sleep deprivation (Z72.820)
    - **F51.01** **Primary insomnia**
      Idiopathic insomnia
    - **F51.02** **Adjustment insomnia**
    - **F51.03** **Paradoxical insomnia**
    - **F51.04** **Psychophysiologic insomnia**
    - **F51.05** **Insomnia due to other mental disorder**
      Code also associated mental disorder
    - **F51.09** **Other insomnia not due to a substance or known physiological condition**
  - **F51.1** **Hypersomnia not due to a substance or known physiological condition**
    Hypersomnia: Excessive sleeping/sleepiness
    - **Excludes2** alcohol related hypersomnia (F10.182, F10.282, F10.982)
      drug-related hypersomnia (F11.182, F11.282, F11.982, F13.182, F13.282, F13.982, F14.182, F14.282, F14.982, F15.182, F15.282, F15.982, F19.182, F19.282, F19.982)
      hypersomnia NOS (G47.10)
      hypersomnia due to known physiological condition (G47.10)
      idiopathic hypersomnia (G47.11, G47.12)
      narcolepsy (G47.4-)
    - **F51.11** **Primary hypersomnia**
    - **F51.12** **Insufficient sleep syndrome**
      - **Excludes1** sleep deprivation (Z72.820)
    - **F51.13** **Hypersomnia due to other mental disorder**
      Code also associated mental disorder
    - **F51.19** **Other hypersomnia not due to a substance or known physiological condition**
  - **F51.3** **Sleepwalking [somnambulism]**
    Non-rapid eye movement sleep arousal disorders, sleepwalking type
  - **F51.4** **Sleep terrors [night terrors]**
    Non-rapid eye movement sleep arousal disorders, sleep terror type
  - **F51.5** **Nightmare disorder**
    Dream anxiety disorder
  - **F51.8** **Other sleep disorders not due to a substance or known physiological condition**
  - **F51.9** **Sleep disorder not due to a substance or known physiological condition, unspecified**
    Emotional sleep disorder NOS

- **F52 Sexual dysfunction not due to a substance or known physiological condition**
  - **Excludes2** Dhat syndrome (F48.8)
  - **F52.0 Hypoactive sexual desire disorder**
    - *Total loss of feeling of sexual pleasure*
    - Lack or loss of sexual desire
    - Male hypoactive sexual desire disorder
    - Sexual anhedonia
    - **Excludes1** decreased libido (R68.82)
  - **F52.1 Sexual aversion disorder**
    - Sexual aversion and lack of sexual enjoyment
  - **F52.2 Sexual arousal disorders**
    - Failure of genital response
    - **F52.21 Male erectile disorder ♂**
      - Erectile disorder
      - Psychogenic impotence
      - **Excludes1** impotence of organic origin (N52.-)
        - impotence NOS (N52.-)
    - **F52.22 Female sexual arousal disorder ♀**
      - Female sexual interest/arousal disorder
  - **F52.3 Orgasmic disorder**
    - Inhibited orgasm
    - Psychogenic anorgasmy
    - **F52.31 Female orgasmic disorder ♀**
    - **F52.32 Male orgasmic disorder ♂**
      - Delayed ejaculation
  - **F52.4 Premature ejaculation ♂**
  - **F52.5 Vaginismus not due to a substance or known physiological condition ♀**
    - Psychogenic vaginismus
    - **Excludes2** vaginismus (due to a known physiological condition) (N94.2)
  - **F52.6 Dyspareunia not due to a substance or known physiological condition**
    - *Dyspareunia: Difficult or painful sexual intercourse*
    - Genito-pelvic pain penetration disorder
    - Psychogenic dyspareunia
    - **Excludes2** dyspareunia (due to a known physiological condition) (N94.1-)
  - **F52.8 Other sexual dysfunction not due to a substance or known physiological condition**
    - Excessive sexual drive
    - Nymphomania
    - Satyriasis
  - **F52.9 Unspecified sexual dysfunction not due to a substance or known physiological condition**
    - Sexual dysfunction NOS

- **F53 Mental and behavioral disorders associated with the puerperium, not elsewhere classified ♀**   M
  - ~~Postpartum depression~~
  - *Acute mental illness with sudden onset following childbirth with symptoms of affective psychosis, disorientation, and confusion are prevalent*
  - **Excludes1** mood disorders with psychotic features (F30.2, F31.2, F31.5, F31.64, F32.3, F33.3)
    - postpartum dysphoria (O90.6)
    - psychosis in schizophrenia, schizotypal, delusional, and other psychotic disorders (F20-F29)
  - **F53.0 Postpartum depression**
    - Postnatal depression, NOS
    - Postpartum depression, NOS
  - **F53.1 Puerperal psychosis**
    - Postpartum psychosis
    - Puerperal psychosis, NOS

- **F54 Psychological and behavioral factors associated with disorders or diseases classified elsewhere**
  - Psychological factors affecting physical conditions
  - *Code first the associated physical disorder, such as:*
    - asthma (J45.-)
    - dermatitis (L23-L25)
    - gastric ulcer (K25.-)
    - mucous colitis (K58.-)
    - ulcerative colitis (K51.-)
    - urticaria (L50.-)
  - **Excludes2** tension-type headache (G44.2)

- **F55 Abuse of non-psychoactive substances**
  - **Excludes2** abuse of psychoactive substances (F10-F19)
  - **F55.0 Abuse of antacids**
  - **F55.1 Abuse of herbal or folk remedies**
  - **F55.2 Abuse of laxatives**
  - **F55.3 Abuse of steroids or hormones**
  - **F55.4 Abuse of vitamins**
  - **F55.8 Abuse of other non-psychoactive substances**

- **F59 Unspecified behavioral syndromes associated with physiological disturbances and physical factors**
  - Psychogenic physiological dysfunction NOS

DISORDERS OF ADULT PERSONALITY AND BEHAVIOR (F60-F69)

- **F60 Specific personality disorders**
  - *Long-term patterns of thoughts and behaviors causing serious problems with relationships and work.*
  - **F60.0 Paranoid personality disorder**
    - *Hostile, devious, and combative response to disappointments*
    - Expansive paranoid personality (disorder)
    - Fanatic personality (disorder)
    - Querulant personality (disorder)
    - Paranoid personality (disorder)
    - Sensitive paranoid personality (disorder)
    - **Excludes2** paranoia (F22)
      - paranoia querulans (F22)
      - paranoid psychosis (F22)
      - paranoid schizophrenia (F20.0)
      - paranoid state (F22)
  - **F60.1 Schizoid personality disorder**
    - *Detachment from social relationships with minimal emotional experiences and expressions*
    - **Excludes2** Asperger's syndrome (F84.5)
      - delusional disorder (F22)
      - schizoid disorder of childhood (F84.5)
      - schizophrenia (F20.-)
      - schizotypal disorder (F21)
  - **F60.2 Antisocial personality disorder**
    - *Continuous and chronic antisocial behavior*
    - Amoral personality (disorder)
    - Asocial personality (disorder)
    - Dissocial personality disorder
    - Psychopathic personality (disorder)
    - Sociopathic personality (disorder)
    - **Excludes1** conduct disorders (F91.-)
    - **Excludes2** borderline personality disorder (F60.3)
  - **F60.3 Borderline personality disorder**
    - *Instability of mood, self-image or sense of self, and interpersonal relationships*
    - Aggressive personality (disorder)
    - Emotionally unstable personality disorder
    - Explosive personality (disorder)
    - **Excludes2** antisocial personality disorder (F60.2)
  - **F60.4 Histrionic personality disorder**
    - *Personality disorder with excessive emotional and attention-seeking behavior*
    - Hysterical personality (disorder)
    - Psychoinfantile personality (disorder)

F60.5 Obsessive-compulsive personality disorder
Anankastic personality (disorder)
Compulsive personality (disorder)
Obsessional personality (disorder)
> **Excludes2**   obsessive-compulsive disorder (F42-)

F60.6 Avoidant personality disorder
Anxious personality disorder

F60.7 Dependent personality disorder
Asthenic personality (disorder)
Inadequate personality (disorder)
Passive personality (disorder)

● **F60.8 Other specific personality disorders**

     F60.81 Narcissistic personality disorder
Vanity, conceit, egotism or indifference to plight of others

     F60.89 Other specific personality disorders
Eccentric personality disorder
'Haltlose' type personality disorder
Immature personality disorder
Passive-aggressive personality disorder
Psychoneurotic personality disorder
Self-defeating personality disorder

F60.9 Personality disorder, unspecified
Character disorder NOS
Character neurosis NOS
Pathological personality NOS

● **F63 Impulse disorders**
> **Excludes2**   habitual excessive use of alcohol or psychoactive substances (F10-F19)
> impulse disorders involving sexual behavior (F65.-)

F63.0 Pathological gambling
Compulsive gambling
Gambling disorder
> **Excludes1**   gambling and betting NOS (Z72.6)
> **Excludes2**   excessive gambling by manic patients (F30, F31)
> gambling in antisocial personality disorder (F60.2)

F63.1 Pyromania
Pathological fire-setting
> **Excludes2**   fire-setting (by) (in):
> adult with antisocial personality disorder (F60.2)
> alcohol or psychoactive substance intoxication (F10-F19)
> conduct disorders (F91.-)
> mental disorders due to known physiological condition (F01-F09)
> schizophrenia (F20.-)

F63.2 Kleptomania
Pathological stealing
> **Excludes1**   shoplifting as the reason for observation for suspected mental disorder (Z03.8)
> **Excludes2**   depressive disorder with stealing (F31-F33)
> stealing due to underlying mental condition-code to mental condition
> stealing in mental disorders due to known physiological condition (F01-F09)

F63.3 Trichotillomania
Hair plucking
> **Excludes2**   other stereotyped movement disorder (F98.4)

● **F63.8 Other impulse disorders**

     F63.81 Intermittent explosive disorder

     F63.89 Other impulse disorders

F63.9 Impulse disorder, unspecified
Impulse control disorder NOS

● **F64 Gender identity disorders**

F64.0 Transsexualism
Gender identity disorder in adolescence and adulthood
Gender dysphoria in adolescents and adults
Coding Clinic: 2016, Q4, P16

F64.1 Dual role transvestism
Use additional code to identify sex reassignment status (Z87.890)
> **Excludes1**   gender identity disorder in childhood (F64.2)
> **Excludes2**   fetishistic transvestism (F65.1)
Coding Clinic: 2016, Q4, P16

F64.2 Gender identity disorder of childhood   P
Gender dysphoria in children
> **Excludes1**   gender identity disorder in adolescence and adulthood (F64.0)
> **Excludes2**   sexual maturation disorder (F66)

F64.8 Other gender identity disorders
Other specified gender dysphoria

F64.9 Gender identity disorder, unspecified
Gender dysphoria, unspecified
Gender-role disorder NOS

● **F65 Paraphilias**

F65.0 Fetishism
Intense sexual urges and arousing fantasies using inanimate objects
Fetishistic disorder

F65.1 Transvestic fetishism
Intense sexual urges, arousal, or orgasm associated with fantasized/actual cross-dressing
Fetishistic transvestism
Transvestic disorder

F65.2 Exhibitionism
Exhibitionistic disorder

F65.3 Voyeurism
Sexual urges or arousal involving real or fantasized observation of unsuspecting people who are naked, disrobing, or engaging in sexual activity
Voyeuristic disorder

F65.4 Pedophilia
Pedophilic disorder

● **F65.5 Sadomasochism**

     F65.50 Sadomasochism, unspecified

     F65.51 Sexual masochism
Sexual masochism disorder

     F65.52 Sexual sadism
Sexual sadism disorder

● **F65.8 Other paraphilias**

     F65.81 Frotteurism
Sexual arousal or orgasm is achieved by rubbing up against another person (or fantasies of), in crowded place with unsuspecting victim
Frotteuristic disorder

     F65.89 Other paraphilias
Necrophilia
Other specified paraphilic disorder

F65.9 Paraphilia, unspecified
Paraphilic disorder, unspecified
Sexual deviation NOS

CHAPTER 5 (F01-F99)

F66   **Other sexual disorders**
          Sexual maturation disorder
          Sexual relationship disorder

● F68   **Other disorders of adult personality and behavior**
   ⇒ ● **F68.1   Factitious disorder imposed on self**
                  Compensation neurosis
                  Elaboration of physical symptoms for psychological
                     reasons
                  Hospital hopper syndrome
                  Münchhausen's syndrome
                  Peregrinating patient
                  Excludes2   factitial dermatitis (L98.1)
                                person feigning illness (with obvious
                                   motivation) (Z76.5)
      ⇒ **F68.10   Factitious disorder imposed on self, unspecified**
      ⇒ **F68.11   Factitious disorder imposed on self with
                  predominantly psychological signs and
                  symptoms**
      ⇒ **F68.12   Factitious disorder imposed on self with
                  predominantly physical signs and symptoms**
      ⇒ **F68.13   Factitious disorder imposed on self with
                  combined psychological and physical signs and
                  symptoms**
      **F68.8   Other specified disorders of adult personality and
                  behavior**
   ▶ **F68.A   Factitious disorder imposed on another**
                  ▶ Factitious disorder by proxy
                  ▶ Münchausen's by proxy

F69   **Unspecified disorder of adult personality and behavior**   A

INTELLECTUAL DISABILITIES (F70-F79)

Code first any associated physical or developmental disorders
   Excludes1   borderline intellectual functioning, IQ above
                  70 to 84 (R41.83)

F70   **Mild intellectual disabilities**
          IQ level 50-55 to approximately 70
          Mild mental subnormality

F71   **Moderate intellectual disabilities**
          IQ level 35-40 to 50-55
          Moderate mental subnormality

F72   **Severe intellectual disabilities**
          IQ 20-25 to 35-40
          Severe mental subnormality

F73   **Profound intellectual disabilities**
          IQ level below 20-25
          Profound mental subnormality

F78   **Other intellectual disabilities**

F79   **Unspecified intellectual disabilities**
          Mental deficiency NOS
          Mental subnormality NOS

PERVASIVE AND SPECIFIC DEVELOPMENTAL DISORDERS (F80-F89)

● F80   **Specific developmental disorders of speech and language**
   F80.0   Phonological disorder
                  *Communication disorder of unknown cause, characterized by
                     failure to use age-appropriate sounds*
                  Dyslalia
                  Functional speech articulation disorder
                  Lalling
                  Lisping
                  Phonological developmental disorder
                  Speech articulation developmental disorder
                  Speech-sound disorder
                  Excludes1   speech articulation impairment due to
                                   aphasia NOS (R47.01)
                                speech articulation impairment due to
                                   apraxia (R48.2)
                  Excludes2   speech articulation impairment due to
                                   hearing loss (F80.4)
                                speech articulation impairment due to
                                   intellectual disabilities (F70-F79)
                                speech articulation impairment with
                                   expressive language developmental
                                   disorder (F80.1)
                                speech articulation impairment with
                                   mixed receptive expressive language
                                   developmental disorder (F80.2)
   F80.1   Expressive language disorder
                  Developmental dysphasia or aphasia, expressive type
                  Excludes1   mixed receptive-expressive language
                                   disorder (F80.2)
                                dysphasia and aphasia NOS (R47.-)
                  Excludes2   acquired aphasia with epilepsy [Landau-
                                   Kleffner] (G40.80-)
                                intellectual disabilities (F70-F79)
                                pervasive developmental disorders
                                   (F84.-)
                                selective mutism (F94.0)
   F80.2   Mixed receptive-expressive language disorder
                  Developmental dysphasia or aphasia, receptive type
                  Developmental Wernicke's aphasia
                  Excludes1   central auditory processing disorder
                                   (H93.25)
                                dysphasia or aphasia NOS (R47.-)
                                expressive language disorder (F80.1)
                                expressive type dysphasia or aphasia
                                   (F80.1)
                                word deafness (H93.25)
                  Excludes2   acquired aphasia with epilepsy [Landau-
                                   Kleffner] (G40.80-)
                                intellectual disabilities (F70-F79)
                                pervasive developmental disorders
                                   (F84.-)
                                selective mutism (F94.0)
   **F80.4   Speech and language development delay due to hearing
             loss**
                  Code also type of hearing loss (H90.-, H91.-)
● **F80.8   Other developmental disorders of speech or language**
   F80.81   Childhood onset fluency disorder
                  Cluttering NOS
                  Stuttering NOS
                  Excludes1   adult onset fluency disorder
                                   (F98.5)
                                fluency disorder in conditions
                                   classified elsewhere (R47.82)
                                fluency disorder (stuttering)
                                   following cerebrovascular
                                   disease (I69. with final
                                   characters -23)

CHAPTER 5 (F01-F99)

F80.82 Social pragmatic communication disorder
> **Excludes1** Asperger's syndrome (F84.5)
>   autistic disorder (F84.0)
> Coding Clinic: 2016, Q4, P16

F80.89 Other developmental disorders of speech and language
> Coding Clinic: 2017, Q1, P27

F80.9 Developmental disorder of speech and language, unspecified
> Communication disorder NOS
> Language disorder NOS

● **F81 Specific developmental disorders of scholastic skills**

F81.0 Specific reading disorder
> 'Backward reading'
> Developmental dyslexia
> Specific learning disorder, with impairment in reading
> Specific reading retardation
> **Excludes1** alexia NOS (R48.0)
>   dyslexia NOS (R48.0)

F81.2 Mathematics disorder
> Developmental acalculia
> Developmental arithmetical disorder
> Developmental Gerstmann's syndrome
> Specific learning disorder, with impairment in mathematics
> **Excludes1** acalculia NOS (R48.8)
> **Excludes2** arithmetical difficulties associated with a reading disorder (F81.0)
>   arithmetical difficulties associated with a spelling disorder (F81.81)
>   arithmetical difficulties due to inadequate teaching (Z55.8)

● **F81.8 Other developmental disorders of scholastic skills**

F81.81 Disorder of written expression
> Specific learning disorder, with impairment in written expression
> Specific spelling disorder

F81.89 Other developmental disorders of scholastic skills

F81.9 Developmental disorder of scholastic skills, unspecified
> Knowledge acquisition disability NOS
> Learning disability NOS
> Learning disorder NOS

F82 Specific developmental disorder of motor function
> Clumsy child syndrome
> Developmental coordination disorder
> Developmental dyspraxia
> **Excludes1** abnormalities of gait and mobility (R26.-)
>   lack of coordination (R27.-)
> **Excludes2** lack of coordination secondary to intellectual disabilities (F70-F79)

● **F84 Pervasive developmental disorders**
> Use additional code to identify any associated medical condition and intellectual disabilities.

F84.0 Autistic disorder
> Autism spectrum disorder
> Infantile autism
> Infantile psychosis
> Kanner's syndrome
> **Excludes1** Asperger's syndrome (F84.5)
> Coding Clinic: 2017, Q1, P27

F84.2 Rett's syndrome
> *Neurodevelopmental disorder*
> **Excludes1** Asperger's syndrome (F84.5)
>   Autistic disorder (F84.0)
>   other childhood disintegrative disorder (F84.3)

F84.3 Other childhood disintegrative disorder   P
> Dementia infantilis
> *At least two years of normal development followed by significant loss of language abilities, social skills, bowel/bladder control, motor skills*
> Disintegrative psychosis
> Heller's syndrome
> *At least two years of normal development followed by significant loss of language abilities, social skills, bowel/bladder control, motor skills*
> Symbiotic psychosis
> *Abnormal relationship to mothering figure, characterized by intense separation anxiety, severe regression, giving up of useful speech, and autism*
> Use additional code to identify any associated neurological condition.
> **Excludes1** Asperger's syndrome (F84.5)
>   Autistic disorder (F84.0)
>   Rett's syndrome (F84.2)

F84.5 Asperger's syndrome
> *Developmental disorder*
> Asperger's disorder
> Autistic psychopathy
> Schizoid disorder of childhood

F84.8 Other pervasive developmental disorders
> Overactive disorder associated with intellectual disabilities and stereotyped movements

F84.9 Pervasive developmental disorder, unspecified
> Atypical autism

F88 Other disorders of psychological development
> Developmental agnosia
> Global developmental delay
> Other specified neurodevelopmental disorder

F89 Unspecified disorder of psychological development
> Developmental disorder NOS
> Neurodevelopmental disorder NOS

BEHAVIORAL AND EMOTIONAL DISORDERS WITH ONSET USUALLY OCCURRING IN CHILDHOOD AND ADOLESCENCE (F90-F98)

Note: Codes within categories F90-F98 may be used regardless of the age of a patient. These disorders generally have onset within the childhood or adolescent years, but may continue throughout life or not be diagnosed until adulthood.

● **F90 Attention-deficit hyperactivity disorders**
> *Attention deficit disorder with hyperactivity=ADHD*
> **Includes** attention deficit disorder with hyperactivity
>   attention deficit syndrome with hyperactivity
> **Excludes2** anxiety disorders (F40.-, F41.-)
>   mood [affective] disorders (F30-F39)
>   pervasive developmental disorders (F84.-)
>   schizophrenia (F20.-)

F90.0 Attention-deficit hyperactivity disorder, predominantly inattentive type
> Attention-deficit/hyperactivity disorder, predominantly inattentive presentation

F90.1 Attention-deficit hyperactivity disorder, predominantly hyperactive type
> Attention-deficit/hyperactivity disorder, predominantly hyperactive impulsive presentation

F90.2 Attention-deficit hyperactivity disorder, combined type
> Attention-deficit/hyperactivity disorder, combined presentation

F90.8 Attention-deficit hyperactivity disorder, other type

F90.9 Attention-deficit hyperactivity disorder, unspecified type
> Attention-deficit hyperactivity disorder of childhood or adolescence NOS
> Attention-deficit hyperactivity disorder NOS

CHAPTER 5 (F01-F99)

● **F91**   **Conduct disorders**
Childhood/adolescence disruptive behavior disorder

> **Excludes1**   antisocial behavior (Z72.81-)
> antisocial personality disorder (F60.2)

> **Excludes2**   conduct problems associated with attention-deficit hyperactivity disorder (F90.-)
> mood [affective] disorders (F30-F39)
> pervasive developmental disorders (F84.-)
> schizophrenia (F20.-)

   F91.0   **Conduct disorder confined to family context**

   F91.1   **Conduct disorder, childhood-onset type**
     Unsocialized conduct disorder
     Conduct disorder, solitary aggressive type
     Unsocialized aggressive disorder

   F91.2   **Conduct disorder, adolescent-onset type**
     Socialized conduct disorder
     Conduct disorder, group type

   F91.3   **Oppositional defiant disorder**

   F91.8   **Other conduct disorders**
     Other specified conduct disorder
     Other specified disruptive disorder

   F91.9   **Conduct disorder, unspecified**
     Behavioral disorder NOS
     Conduct disorder NOS
     Disruptive behavior disorder NOS
     Disruptive disorder NOS

● **F93**   **Emotional disorders with onset specific to childhood**

   F93.0   **Separation anxiety disorder of childhood**

> **Excludes2**   mood [affective] disorders (F30-F39)
> nonpsychotic mental disorders (F40-F48)
> phobic anxiety disorder of childhood (F40.8)
> social phobia (F40.1)

   F93.8   **Other childhood emotional disorders**
     Identity disorder

> **Excludes2**   gender identity disorder of childhood (F64.2)

   F93.9   **Childhood emotional disorder, unspecified**

● **F94**   **Disorders of social functioning with onset specific to childhood and adolescence**

   F94.0   **Selective mutism**
     Elective mutism

> **Excludes2**   pervasive developmental disorders (F84.-)
> schizophrenia (F20.-)
> specific developmental disorders of speech and language (F80.-)
> transient mutism as part of separation anxiety in young children (F93.0)

   F94.1   **Reactive attachment disorder of childhood**
     Use additional code to identify any associated failure to thrive or growth retardation

> **Excludes1**   disinhibited attachment disorder of childhood (F94.2)
> normal variation in pattern of selective attachment

> **Excludes2**   Asperger's syndrome (F84.5)
> maltreatment syndromes (T74.-)
> sexual or physical abuse in childhood, resulting in psychosocial problems (Z62.81-)

   F94.2   **Disinhibited attachment disorder of childhood**
     Affectionless psychopathy
     Institutional syndrome

> **Excludes1**   reactive attachment disorder of childhood (F94.1)

> **Excludes2**   Asperger's syndrome (F84.5)
> attention-deficit hyperactivity disorders (F90.-)
> hospitalism in children (F43.2-)

   F94.8   **Other childhood disorders of social functioning**

   F94.9   **Childhood disorder of social functioning, unspecified**

● **F95**   **Tic disorder**
Involuntary twitch

   F95.0   **Transient tic disorder**
     Provisional tic disorder

   F95.1   **Chronic motor or vocal tic disorder**

   F95.2   **Tourette's disorder**
     Combined vocal and multiple motor tic disorder [de la Tourette]
     Tourette's syndrome

   F95.8   **Other tic disorders**

   F95.9   **Tic disorder, unspecified**
     Tic NOS

● **F98**   **Other behavioral and emotional disorders with onset usually occurring in childhood and adolescence**

> **Excludes2**   breath-holding spells (R06.89)
> gender identity disorder of childhood (F64.2)
> Kleine-Levin syndrome (G47.13)
> obsessive-compulsive disorder (F42-)
> sleep disorders not due to a substance or known physiological condition (F51.-)

   F98.0   **Enuresis not due to a substance or known physiological condition**
     Enuresis: Urinary incontinence
     Enuresis (primary) (secondary) of nonorganic origin
     Functional enuresis
     Psychogenic enuresis
     Urinary incontinence of nonorganic origin

> **Excludes1**   enuresis NOS (R32)

   F98.1   **Encopresis not due to a substance or known physiological condition**
     Encopresis: Fecal incontinence
     Functional encopresis
     Incontinence of feces of nonorganic origin
     Psychogenic encopresis
     Use additional code to identify the cause of any coexisting constipation.

> **Excludes1**   encopresis NOS (R15.-)

● **F98.2**   **Other feeding disorders of infancy and childhood**

> **Excludes1**   feeding difficulties (R63.3)

> **Excludes2**   anorexia nervosa and other eating disorders (F50.-)
> feeding problems of newborn (P92.-)
> pica of infancy or childhood (F98.3)

   F98.21   **Rumination disorder of infancy**

   F98.29   **Other feeding disorders of infancy and early childhood**

   F98.3   **Pica of infancy and childhood**
     Craving and eating substances such as paint, clay, or dirt to replace a nutritional deficit in the body.

   F98.4   **Stereotyped movement disorders**
     Stereotype/habit disorder

> **Excludes1**   abnormal involuntary movements (R25.-)

> **Excludes2**   compulsions in obsessive-compulsive disorder (F42-)
> hair plucking (F63.3)
> movement disorders of organic origin (G20-G25)
> nail-biting (F98.8)
> nose-picking (F98.8)
> stereotypies that are part of a broader psychiatric condition (F01-F95)
> thumb-sucking (F98.8)
> tic disorders (F95.-)
> trichotillomania (F63.3)

Item 5–2 Enuresis: Bed wetting by children at night. Causes can be either psychological or medical (diabetes, urinary tract infections, or abnormalities). **Encopresis:** Overflow incontinence of bowels sometimes resulting from chronic constipation or fecal impaction. Check the documentation for additional diagnoses.

▶ New   ⇛ Revised   ~~deleted~~ Deleted   Excludes 1   Excludes 2   Includes   Use additional   Code first   Code also   Key words
OGCR Official Guidelines   X Assign placeholder X   ● Use Additional Character(s)   ▶ Manifestation Code   **Coding Clinic**

F98.5   **Adult onset fluency disorder**

> **Excludes1**   childhood onset fluency disorder (F80.81)
> dysphasia (R47.02)
> fluency disorder in conditions classified elsewhere (R47.82)
> fluency disorder (stuttering) following cerebrovascular disease (I69. with final characters -23)
> tic disorders (F95.-)

F98.8   **Other specified behavioral and emotional disorders with onset usually occurring in childhood and adolescence**

> Excessive masturbation
> Nail-biting
> Nose-picking
> Thumb-sucking

F98.9   **Unspecified behavioral and emotional disorders with onset usually occurring in childhood and adolescence**

UNSPECIFIED MENTAL DISORDER (F99)

F99   **Mental disorder, not otherwise specified**

> Mental illness NOS
>
> **Excludes1**   unspecified mental disorder due to known physiological condition (F09)

CHAPTER 5 (F01-F99)

CHAPTER 6

DISEASES OF THE NERVOUS SYSTEM (G00-G99)

OGCR Chapter-Specific Coding Guidelines

6. Chapter 6: Diseases of the Nervous System (G00-G99)

a. Dominant/nondominant side

Codes from category G81, Hemiplegia and hemiparesis, and subcategories, G83.1, Monoplegia of lower limb, G83.2, Monoplegia of upper limb, and G83.3, Monoplegia, unspecified, identify whether the dominant or nondominant side is affected. Should the affected side be documented, but not specified as dominant or nondominant, and the classification system does not indicate a default, code selection is as follows:

- For ambidextrous patients, the default should be dominant.
- If the left side is affected, the default is non-dominant.
- If the right side is affected, the default is dominant.

b. Pain - Category G89

1) General coding information

Codes in category G89, Pain, not elsewhere classified, may be used in conjunction with codes from other categories and chapters to provide more detail about acute or chronic pain and neoplasm-related pain, unless otherwise indicated below.

If the pain is not specified as acute or chronic, post-thoracotomy, postprocedural, or neoplasm-related, do not assign codes from category G89.

A code from category G89 should not be assigned if the underlying (definitive) diagnosis is known, unless the reason for the encounter is pain control/management and not management of the underlying condition.

When an admission or encounter is for a procedure aimed at treating the underlying condition (e.g., spinal fusion, kyphoplasty), a code for the underlying condition (e.g., vertebral fracture, spinal stenosis) should be assigned as the principal diagnosis. No code from category G89 should be assigned.

(a) Category G89 Codes as Principal or First-Listed Diagnosis

Category G89 codes are acceptable as principal diagnosis or the first-listed code:

- When pain control or pain management is the reason for the admission/encounter (e.g., a patient with displaced intervertebral disc, nerve impingement and severe back pain presents for injection of steroid into the spinal canal). The underlying cause of the pain should be reported as an additional diagnosis, if known.
- When a patient is admitted for the insertion of a neurostimulator for pain control, assign the appropriate pain code as the principal or first-listed diagnosis. When an admission or encounter is for a procedure aimed at treating the underlying condition and a neurostimulator is inserted for pain control during the same admission/encounter, a code for the underlying condition should be assigned as the principal diagnosis and the appropriate pain code should be assigned as a secondary diagnosis.

(b) Use of Category G89 Codes in Conjunction with Site Specific Pain Codes

(i) Assigning Category G89 and Site-Specific Pain Codes

Codes from category G89 may be used in conjunction with codes that identify the site of pain (including codes from chapter 18) if the category G89 code provides additional information. For example, if the code describes the site of the pain, but does not fully describe whether the pain is acute or chronic, then both codes should be assigned.

(ii) Sequencing of Category G89 Codes with Site-Specific Pain Codes

The sequencing of category G89 codes with site-specific pain codes (including chapter 18 codes), is dependent on the circumstances of the encounter/admission as follows:

- If the encounter is for pain control or pain management, assign the code from category G89 followed by the code identifying the specific site of pain (e.g., encounter for pain management for acute neck pain from trauma is assigned code G89.11, Acute pain due to trauma, followed by code M54.2, Cervicalgia, to identify the site of pain).
- If the encounter is for any other reason except pain control or pain management, and a related definitive diagnosis has not been established (confirmed) by the provider, assign the code for the specific site of pain first, followed by the appropriate code from category G89.

2) Pain due to devices, implants and grafts

See Section I.C.19. Pain due to medical devices

3) Postoperative Pain

The provider's documentation should be used to guide the coding of postoperative pain, as well as Section III. Reporting Additional Diagnoses and Section IV. Diagnostic Coding and Reporting in the Outpatient Setting.

The default for post-thoracotomy and other postoperative pain not specified as acute or chronic is the code for the acute form.

Routine or expected postoperative pain immediately after surgery should not be coded.

(a) Postoperative pain not associated with specific postoperative complication

Postoperative pain not associated with a specific postoperative complication is assigned to the appropriate postoperative pain code in category G89.

(b) Postoperative pain associated with specific postoperative complication

Postoperative pain associated with a specific postoperative complication (such as painful wire sutures) is assigned to the appropriate code(s) found in Chapter 19, Injury, poisoning, and certain other consequences of external causes. If appropriate, use additional code(s) from category G89 to identify acute or chronic pain (G89.18 or G89.28).

4) Chronic pain

Chronic pain is classified to subcategory G89.2. There is no time frame defining when pain becomes chronic pain. The provider's documentation should be used to guide use of these codes.

5) Neoplasm Related Pain

Code G89.3 is assigned to pain documented as being related, associated or due to cancer, primary or secondary malignancy, or tumor. This code is assigned regardless of whether the pain is acute or chronic.

This code may be assigned as the principal or first-listed code when the stated reason for the admission/encounter is documented as pain control/pain management. The underlying neoplasm should be reported as an additional diagnosis.

When the reason for the admission/encounter is management of the neoplasm and the pain associated with the neoplasm is also documented, code G89.3 may be assigned as an additional diagnosis. It is not necessary to assign an additional code for the site of the pain.

See Section I.C.2 for instructions on the sequencing of neoplasms for all other stated reasons for the admission/encounter (except for pain control/pain management).

6) Chronic pain syndrome

Central pain syndrome (G89.0) and chronic pain syndrome (G89.4) are different than the term "chronic pain," and therefore codes should only be used when the provider has specifically documented this condition.

See Section I.C.5. Pain disorders related to psychological factors

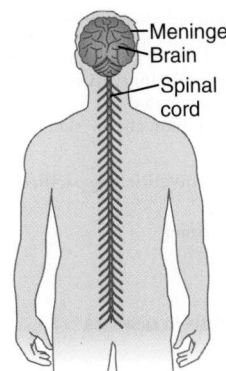

Meninges
Brain
Spinal
cord

Figure 6-1 The brain and spinal cord make up the central nervous system.

Item 6-1 The two major classifications of the nervous system are the peripheral nervous system and the central nervous system (CNS). The central nervous system is comprised of the brain and the spinal cord. The peripheral nervous system is comprised of the parasympathetic and sympathetic systems. **Encephalitis** is the swelling of the brain. **Meningitis** is swelling of the covering of the brain, the meninges. Types and causes of brain infections are:

Type	Cause
purulent	bacterial
aseptic/abacterial	viral
chronic meningitis	mycobacterial and fungal

CHAPTER 6

DISEASES OF THE NERVOUS SYSTEM (G00-G99)

Excludes2   certain conditions originating in the perinatal period (P04-P96)
certain infectious and parasitic diseases (A00-B99)
complications of pregnancy, childbirth and the puerperium (O00-O9A)
congenital malformations, deformations, and chromosomal abnormalities (Q00-Q99)
endocrine, nutritional and metabolic diseases (E00-E88)
injury, poisoning and certain other consequences of external causes (S00-T88)
neoplasms (C00-D49)
symptoms, signs and abnormal clinical and laboratory findings, not elsewhere classified (R00-R94)

This chapter contains the following blocks:

G00-G09	Inflammatory diseases of the central nervous system
G10-G14	Systemic atrophies primarily affecting the central nervous system
G20-G26	Extrapyramidal and movement disorders
G30-G32	Other degenerative diseases of the nervous system
G35-G37	Demyelinating diseases of the central nervous system
G40-G47	Episodic and paroxysmal disorders
G50-G59	Nerve, nerve root and plexus disorders
G60-G65	Polyneuropathies and other disorders of the peripheral nervous system
G70-G73	Diseases of myoneural junction and muscle
G80-G83	Cerebral palsy and other paralytic syndromes
G89-G99	Other disorders of the nervous system

INFLAMMATORY DISEASES OF THE CENTRAL NERVOUS SYSTEM (G00-G09)

● **G00**   **Bacterial meningitis, not elsewhere classified**
An infection of the cerebrospinal fluid surrounding the spinal cord and brain.

    Includes   bacterial arachnoiditis
bacterial leptomeningitis
bacterial meningitis
bacterial pachymeningitis

    Excludes1   bacterial meningoencephalitis (G04.2)
bacterial meningomyelitis (G04.2)

    G00.0   **Hemophilus meningitis**
Meningitis due to Hemophilus influenzae

    G00.1   **Pneumococcal meningitis**
Meningitis due to Streptococcal pneumoniae

    G00.2   **Streptococcal meningitis**
Use additional code to further identify organism (B95.0-B95.5)

    G00.3   **Staphylococcal meningitis**
Use additional code to further identify organism (B95.61-B95.8)

    G00.8   **Other bacterial meningitis**
Meningitis due to Escherichia coli
Meningitis due to Friedländer bacillus
Meningitis due to Klebsiella
Use additional code to further identify organism (B96.-)

    G00.9   **Bacterial meningitis, unspecified**
Meningitis due to gram-negative bacteria, unspecified
Purulent meningitis NOS
Pyogenic meningitis NOS
Suppurative meningitis NOS

▶ **G01**   *Meningitis in bacterial diseases classified elsewhere*
Code first underlying disease

    Excludes1   meningitis (in):
gonococcal (A54.81)
leptospirosis (A27.81)
listeriosis (A32.11)
Lyme disease (A69.21)
meningococcal (A39.0)
neurosyphilis (A52.13)
tuberculosis (A17.0)
meningoencephalitis and meningomyelitis in bacterial diseases classified elsewhere (G05)

▶ **G02**   *Meningitis in other infectious and parasitic diseases classified elsewhere*
Code first underlying disease, such as:
African trypanosomiasis (B56.-)
poliovirus infection (A80.-)

    Excludes1   candidal meningitis (B37.5)
coccidioidomycosis meningitis (B38.4)
cryptococcal meningitis (B45.1)
herpesviral [herpes simplex] meningitis (B00.3)
infectious mononucleosis complicated by meningitis (B27.- with fourth character 2)
measles complicated by meningitis (B05.1)
meningoencephalitis and meningomyelitis in other infectious and parasitic diseases classified elsewhere (G05)
mumps meningitis (B26.1)
rubella meningitis (B06.02)
varicella [chickenpox] meningitis (B01.0)
zoster meningitis (B02.1)

G03   Meningitis due to other and unspecified causes

Includes   arachnoiditis NOS
leptomeningitis NOS
meningitis NOS
pachymeningitis NOS

Excludes1   meningoencephalitis (G04.-)
meningomyelitis (G04.-)

G03.0   Nonpyogenic meningitis
Aseptic meningitis
Nonbacterial meningitis

G03.1   Chronic meningitis

G03.2   Benign recurrent meningitis [Mollaret]

G03.8   Meningitis due to other specified causes

G03.9   Meningitis, unspecified
Arachnoiditis (spinal) NOS

G04   Encephalitis, myelitis and encephalomyelitis

Includes   acute ascending myelitis
meningoencephalitis
meningomyelitis

Excludes1   encephalopathy NOS (G93.40)
other noninfectious acute disseminated
encephalomyelitis (noninfectious ADEM)
(G04.81)

Excludes2   acute transverse myelitis (G37.3-)
alcoholic encephalopathy (G31.2)
benign myalgic encephalomyelitis (G93.3)
multiple sclerosis (G35)
subacute necrotizing myelitis (G37.4)
toxic encephalitis (G92)
toxic encephalopathy (G92)

G04.0   Acute disseminated encephalitis and encephalomyelitis (ADEM)

Excludes1   acute necrotizing hemorrhagic
encephalopathy (G04.3-)

G04.00   Acute disseminated encephalitis and encephalomyelitis, unspecified

▶ *G04.01   Postinfectious acute disseminated encephalitis
and encephalomyelitis (postinfectious ADEM)*

Excludes1   post chickenpox encephalitis
(B01.1)
post measles encephalitis (B05.0)
post measles myelitis (B05.1)

**G04.02   Postimmunization acute disseminated
encephalitis, myelitis and encephalomyelitis**
Encephalitis, post immunization
Encephalomyelitis, post immunization

Use additional code to identify the vaccine
(T50.A-, T50.B-, T50.Z-)

G04.1   Tropical spastic paraplegia

**G04.2   Bacterial meningoencephalitis and meningomyelitis, not
elsewhere classified**

G04.3   Acute necrotizing hemorrhagic encephalopathy
*Sudden and severe CNS disease with pathology of
hemorrhages and necrosis of white matter*

Excludes1   acute disseminated encephalitis and
encephalomyelitis (G04.0-)

**G04.30   Acute necrotizing hemorrhagic
encephalopathy, unspecified**

**G04.31   Postinfectious acute necrotizing hemorrhagic
encephalopathy**

**G04.32   Postimmunization acute necrotizing
hemorrhagic encephalopathy**

Use additional code to identify vaccine
(T50.A-, T50.B-, T50.Z-)

**G04.39   Other acute necrotizing hemorrhagic
encephalopathy**

Code also underlying etiology, if applicable

G04.8   Other encephalitis, myelitis and encephalomyelitis
Code also any associated seizure (G40.-, R56.9)

G04.81   Other encephalitis and encephalomyelitis
Noninfectious acute disseminated
encephalomyelitis (noninfectious ADEM)

G04.89   Other myelitis

G04.9   Encephalitis, myelitis and encephalomyelitis, unspecified

**G04.90   Encephalitis and
encephalomyelitis, unspecified**
Ventriculitis (cerebral) NOS

G04.91   Myelitis, unspecified

**G05   Encephalitis, myelitis and encephalomyelitis in diseases
classified elsewhere**

Code first underlying disease, such as:
human immunodeficiency virus [HIV] disease (B20)
poliovirus (A80.-)
suppurative otitis media (H66.01-H66.4)
trichinellosis (B75)

Excludes1   adenoviral encephalitis, myelitis and
encephalomyelitis (A85.1)
congenital toxoplasmosis encephalitis, myelitis
and encephalomyelitis (P37.1)
cytomegaloviral encephalitis, myelitis and
encephalomyelitis (B25.8)
encephalitis, myelitis and encephalomyelitis (in)
measles (B05.0)
encephalitis, myelitis and encephalomyelitis (in)
systemic lupus erythematosus (M32.19)
enteroviral encephalitis, myelitis and
encephalomyelitis (A85.0)
eosinophilic meningoencephalitis (B83.2)
herpesviral [herpes simplex] encephalitis,
myelitis and encephalomyelitis (B00.4)
listerial encephalitis, myelitis and
encephalomyelitis (A32.12)
meningococcal encephalitis, myelitis and
encephalomyelitis (A39.81)
mumps encephalitis, myelitis and
encephalomyelitis (B26.2)
postchickenpox encephalitis, myelitis and
encephalomyelitis (B01.1-)
rubella encephalitis, myelitis and
encephalomyelitis (B06.01)
toxoplasmosis encephalitis, myelitis and
encephalomyelitis (B58.2)
zoster encephalitis, myelitis and
encephalomyelitis (B02.0)

▶ *G05.3   Encephalitis and encephalomyelitis in diseases classified
elsewhere*
Meningoencephalitis in diseases classified elsewhere

▶ *G05.4   Myelitis in diseases classified elsewhere*
Meningomyelitis in diseases classified elsewhere

G06   Intracranial and intraspinal abscess and granuloma
An accumulation of pus in either the brain or spinal cord

Use additional code (B95-B97) to identify infectious agent.

G06.0   Intracranial abscess and granuloma
Brain [any part] abscess (embolic)
Cerebellar abscess (embolic)
Cerebral abscess (embolic)
Intracranial epidural abscess or granuloma
Intracranial extradural abscess or granuloma
Intracranial subdural abscess or granuloma
Otogenic abscess (embolic)

Excludes1   tuberculous intracranial abscess and
granuloma (A17.81)

G06.1   Intraspinal abscess and granuloma
Abscess (embolic) of spinal cord [any part]
Intraspinal epidural abscess or granuloma
Intraspinal extradural abscess or granuloma
Intraspinal subdural abscess or granuloma

Excludes1   tuberculous intraspinal abscess and
granuloma (A17.81)

G06.2   Extradural and subdural abscess, unspecified

▶ *G07 Intracranial and intraspinal abscess and granuloma in diseases classified elsewhere*

  Code first underlying disease, such as:
  schistosomiasis granuloma of brain (B65.-)

  Excludes1 abscess of brain:
              amebic (A06.6)
              chromomycotic (B43.1)
              gonococcal (A54.82)
              tuberculous (A17.81)
              tuberculoma of meninges (A17.1)

G08 **Intracranial and intraspinal phlebitis and thrombophlebitis**
  Septic embolism of intracranial or intraspinal venous sinuses and veins
  Septic endophlebitis of intracranial or intraspinal venous sinuses and veins
  Septic phlebitis of intracranial or intraspinal venous sinuses and veins
  Septic thrombophlebitis of intracranial or intraspinal venous sinuses and veins
  Septic thrombosis of intracranial or intraspinal venous sinuses and veins

  Excludes1 intracranial phlebitis and thrombophlebitis complicating:
              abortion, ectopic or molar pregnancy (O00-O07, O08.7)
              pregnancy, childbirth and the puerperium (O22.5, O87.3)
              nonpyogenic intracranial phlebitis and thrombophlebitis (I67.6)

  Excludes2 intracranial phlebitis and thrombophlebitis complicating nonpyogenic intraspinal phlebitis and thrombophlebitis (G95.1)

G09 **Sequelae of inflammatory diseases of central nervous system**
  Note: Category G09 is to be used to indicate conditions whose primary classification is to G00-G08 as the cause of sequelae, themselves classifiable elsewhere. The 'sequelae' include conditions specified as residuals.

  Code first condition resulting from (sequela) of inflammatory diseases of central nervous system

SYSTEMIC ATROPHIES PRIMARILY AFFECTING THE CENTRAL NERVOUS SYSTEM (G10-G14)

G10 **Huntington's disease**
  Genetic disease with degeneration of cells of the nervous system, including brain
  Huntington's chorea
  Huntington's dementia
  Code also dementia in other diseases classified elsewhere without behavioral disturbance (F02.80)

● G11 **Hereditary ataxia**
  Genetic neurological disorder affecting coordination
  Excludes2 cerebral palsy (G80.-)
              hereditary and idiopathic neuropathy (G60.-)
              metabolic disorders (E70-E88)

  G11.0 **Congenital nonprogressive ataxia**
  G11.1 **Early-onset cerebellar ataxia**
      Early-onset cerebellar ataxia with essential tremor
      Early-onset cerebellar ataxia with myoclonus [Hunt's ataxia]
      Early-onset cerebellar ataxia with retained tendon reflexes
      Friedreich's ataxia (autosomal recessive)
      X-linked recessive spinocerebellar ataxia
  G11.2 **Late-onset cerebellar ataxia**   A

  G11.3 **Cerebellar ataxia with defective DNA repair**
      Ataxia telangiectasia [Louis-Bar]
      Excludes2 Cockayne's syndrome (Q87.1)
                  other disorders of purine and pyrimidine metabolism (E79.-)
                  xeroderma pigmentosum (Q82.1)
  G11.4 **Hereditary spastic paraplegia**
  G11.8 **Other hereditary ataxias**
  G11.9 **Hereditary ataxia, unspecified**
      Hereditary cerebellar ataxia NOS
      Hereditary cerebellar degeneration
      Hereditary cerebellar disease
      Hereditary cerebellar syndrome

● G12 **Spinal muscular atrophy and related syndromes**
  G12.0 **Infantile spinal muscular atrophy, type I [Werdnig-Hoffman]**
  G12.1 **Other inherited spinal muscular atrophy**
      Adult form spinal muscular atrophy
      Childhood form, type II spinal muscular atrophy
      Distal spinal muscular atrophy
      Juvenile form, type III spinal muscular atrophy [Kugelberg-Welander]
      Progressive bulbar palsy of childhood [Fazio-Londe]
      Scapuloperoneal form spinal muscular atrophy
  ● G12.2 **Motor neuron disease**
      Progressive disease of motor neurons that carry impulses to muscles to move
      G12.20 **Motor neuron disease, unspecified**
      G12.21 **Amyotrophic lateral sclerosis**   A
              Lou Gehrig's disease (ALS)
      G12.22 **Progressive bulbar palsy**
      G12.23 **Primary lateral sclerosis**
      G12.24 **Familial motor neuron disease**
      G12.25 **Progressive spinal muscle atrophy**
      G12.29 **Other motor neuron disease**
  G12.8 **Other spinal muscular atrophies and related syndromes**
  G12.9 **Spinal muscular atrophy, unspecified**

● G13 **Systemic atrophies primarily affecting central nervous system in diseases classified elsewhere**
  ▶ *G13.0 Paraneoplastic neuromyopathy and neuropathy*
      Carcinomatous neuromyopathy
      Sensorial paraneoplastic neuropathy [Denny Brown]
      Code first underlying neoplasm (C00-D49)
  ▶ *G13.1 Other systemic atrophy primarily affecting central nervous system in neoplastic disease*
      Paraneoplastic limbic encephalopathy
      Code first underlying neoplasm (C00-D49)
  ▶ *G13.2 Systemic atrophy primarily affecting the central nervous system in myxedema*
      Code first underlying disease, such as:
      hypothyroidism (E03.-)
      myxedematous congenital iodine deficiency (E00.1)
  ▶ *G13.8 Systemic atrophy primarily affecting central nervous system in other diseases classified elsewhere*
      Code first underlying disease

G14 **Postpolio syndrome**
  Includes Postpolio myelitic syndrome
  Excludes1 sequelae of poliomyelitis (B91)

Item 6–2 Huntington's chorea is an inherited degenerative disorder of the central nervous system and is characterized by ceaseless, jerky movements and progressive cognitive and behavioral deterioration.

N Newborn Age: 0   **P** Pediatric Age: 0–17   **M** Maternity DX: 12–55   **A** Adult Age: 15–124   ♀ Females Only   ♂ Males Only

781

CHAPTER 6 (G00-G99)

EXTRAPYRAMIDAL AND MOVEMENT DISORDERS (G20-G26)

G20 Parkinson's disease
Progressive disease of the nervous system that affects muscle coordination
Hemiparkinsonism
Idiopathic Parkinsonism or Parkinson's disease
Paralysis agitans
Parkinsonism or Parkinson's disease NOS
Primary Parkinsonism or Parkinson's disease
> **Excludes1** dementia with Parkinsonism (G31.83)

> **Coding Clinic: 2017, Q2, P7-8; 2016, Q2, P7**

● **G21 Secondary parkinsonism**
Symptoms of Parkinson's caused by medicines, illness, or other nervous system disorder
> **Excludes1** dementia with Parkinsonism (G31.83)
> Huntington's disease (G10)
> Shy-Drager syndrome (G90.3)
> syphilitic Parkinsonism (A52.19)

G21.0 Malignant neuroleptic syndrome
Use additional code for adverse effect, if applicable, to identify drug (T43.3X5, T43.4X5, T43.505, T43.595)
> **Excludes1** neuroleptic induced parkinsonism (G21.11)

● **G21.1 Other drug-induced secondary parkinsonism**
G21.11 Neuroleptic induced parkinsonism
Use additional code for adverse effect, if applicable, to identify drug (T43.3X5, T43.4X5, T43.505, T43.595)
> **Excludes1** malignant neuroleptic syndrome (G21.0)

G21.19 Other drug induced secondary parkinsonism
Other medication-induced parkinsonism
Use additional code for adverse effect, if applicable, to identify drug (T36-T50 with fifth or sixth character 5)

G21.2 Secondary parkinsonism due to other external agents
Code first (T51-T65) to identify external agent

G21.3 Postencephalitic parkinsonism

G21.4 Vascular parkinsonism

G21.8 Other secondary parkinsonism

G21.9 Secondary parkinsonism, unspecified

● **G23 Other degenerative diseases of basal ganglia**
> **Excludes2** multi-system degeneration of the autonomic nervous system (G90.3)

G23.0 Hallervorden-Spatz disease
Pigmentary pallidal degeneration

G23.1 Progressive supranuclear ophthalmoplegia [Steele-Richardson-Olszewski]
Progressive supranuclear palsy

G23.2 Striatonigral degeneration

G23.8 Other specified degenerative diseases of basal ganglia
Calcification of basal ganglia

G23.9 Degenerative disease of basal ganglia, unspecified

● **G24 Dystonia**
Involuntary movements
> **Includes** dyskinesia
> **Excludes2** athetoid cerebral palsy (G80.3)

● **G24.0 Drug induced dystonia**
➡ Use additional code for adverse effect, if applicable, to identify drug (T36-T50 with fifth or sixth character 5)

G24.01 Drug induced subacute dyskinesia
Drug induced blepharospasm
Drug induced orofacial dyskinesia
Neuroleptic induced tardive dyskinesia
Tardive dyskinesia

G24.02 Drug induced acute dystonia
Acute dystonic reaction to drugs
Neuroleptic induced acute dystonia

G24.09 Other drug induced dystonia

G24.1 Genetic torsion dystonia
Dystonia deformans progressiva
Dystonia musculorum deformans
Familial torsion dystonia
Idiopathic familial dystonia
Idiopathic (torsion) dystonia NOS
(Schwalbe-) Ziehen-Oppenheim disease

G24.2 Idiopathic nonfamilial dystonia

G24.3 Spasmodic torticollis
Head tilts toward one side and chin is elevated and turned toward opposite side (wry neck)
> **Excludes1** congenital torticollis (Q68.0)
> hysterical torticollis (F44.4)
> ocular torticollis (R29.891)
> psychogenic torticollis (F45.8)
> torticollis NOS (M43.6)
> traumatic recurrent torticollis (S13.4)

G24.4 Idiopathic orofacial dystonia
Orofacial dyskinesia
> **Excludes1** drug induced orofacial dyskinesia (G24.01)

G24.5 Blepharospasm
Tonic spasm of orbicularis oculi muscle, producing closure of eyelids
> **Excludes1** drug induced blepharospasm (G24.01)

G24.8 Other dystonia
Acquired torsion dystonia NOS

G24.9 Dystonia, unspecified
Dyskinesia NOS

● **G25 Other extrapyramidal and movement disorders**
Extrapyramidal: Other than pyramidal tracts
> **Excludes2** sleep related movement disorders (G47.6-)

G25.0 Essential tremor
Familial tremor
> **Excludes1** tremor NOS (R25.1)

G25.1 Drug-induced tremor
Use additional code for adverse effect, if applicable, to identify drug (T36-T50 with fifth or sixth character 5)

G25.2 Other specified forms of tremor
Intention tremor

G25.3 Myoclonus
Shocklike contractions muscle(s)
Drug-induced myoclonus
Palatal myoclonus
Use additional code for adverse effect, if applicable, to identify drug (T36-T50 with fifth or sixth character 5)
> **Excludes1** facial myokymia (G51.4)
> myoclonic epilepsy (G40.-)

G25.4 Drug-induced chorea
Use additional code for adverse effect, if applicable, to identify drug (T36-T50 with fifth or sixth character 5)

G25.5 Other chorea
Continual, involuntary, jerky, movements
Chorea NOS
> **Excludes1** chorea NOS with heart involvement (I02.0)
> Huntington's chorea (G10)
> rheumatic chorea (I02.-)
> Sydenham's chorea (I02.-)

▶ New   ➡ Revised   ~~deleted~~ Deleted   [Excludes 1]   [Excludes 2]   [Includes]   [Use additional]   [Code first]   [Code also]   [Key words]
OGCR Official Guidelines   X Assign placeholder X   ● Use Additional Character(s)   ▷ Manifestation Code   **Coding Clinic**

● G25.6 **Drug induced tics and other tics of organic origin**

    G25.61 **Drug induced tics**

        Use additional code for adverse effect, if applicable, to identify drug (T36-T50 with fifth or sixth character 5)

    G25.69 **Other tics of organic origin**

        Excludes1 habit spasm (F95.9)
                  tic NOS (F95.9)
                  Tourette's syndrome (F95.2)

● G25.7 **Other and unspecified drug induced movement disorders**

    Use additional code for adverse effect, if applicable, to identify drug (T36-T50 with fifth or sixth character 5)

    G25.70 **Drug induced movement disorder, unspecified**

    G25.71 **Drug induced akathisia**
        Drug induced acathisia
        Neuroleptic induced acute akathisia
        Tardive akathisia

    G25.79 **Other drug induced movement disorders**

● G25.8 **Other specified extrapyramidal and movement disorders**

    G25.81 **Restless legs syndrome**

    G25.82 **Stiff-man syndrome**

    G25.83 **Benign shuddering attacks**

    G25.89 **Other specified extrapyramidal and movement disorders**

    G25.9 **Extrapyramidal and movement disorder, unspecified**

▷ G26 *Extrapyramidal and movement disorders in diseases classified elsewhere*

    Code first underlying disease

OTHER DEGENERATIVE DISEASES OF THE NERVOUS SYSTEM (G30-G32)

● G30 **Alzheimer's disease**

    Progressive central neurodegenerative disorder

    Includes Alzheimer's dementia senile and presenile forms

    Use additional code to identify:
      delirium, if applicable (F05)
      dementia with behavioral disturbance (F02.81)
      dementia without behavioral disturbance (F02.80)

    Excludes1 senile degeneration of brain NEC (G31.1)
                senile dementia NOS (F03)
                senility NOS (R41.81)

    G30.0 **Alzheimer's disease with early onset**

    G30.1 **Alzheimer's disease with late onset**   A

    G30.8 **Other Alzheimer's disease**

    G30.9 **Alzheimer's disease, unspecified**
        Coding Clinic: 2017, Q1, P43; 2016, Q2, P6; 2012, Q4, P95

● G31 **Other degenerative diseases of nervous system, not elsewhere classified**

    Use additional code to identify:
      dementia with behavioral disturbance (F02.81)
      dementia without behavioral disturbance (F02.80)

    Excludes2 Reye's syndrome (G93.7)

● G31.0 **Frontotemporal dementia**

    G31.01 **Pick's disease**
        Primary progressive aphasia
        Progressive isolated aphasia

    G31.09 **Other frontotemporal dementia**
        Frontal dementia

    G31.1 **Senile degeneration of brain, not elsewhere classified**

        Excludes1 Alzheimer's disease (G30.-)
                  senility NOS (R41.81)

● G31.2 **Degeneration of nervous system due to alcohol**
    Alcoholic cerebellar ataxia
    Alcoholic cerebellar degeneration
    Alcoholic cerebral degeneration
    Alcoholic encephalopathy
    Dysfunction of the autonomic nervous system due to alcohol

    Code also associated alcoholism (F10.-)

● G31.8 **Other specified degenerative diseases of nervous system**

    G31.81 **Alpers' disease**
        Rare neuronal degeneration of cerebral cortex disease of young children
        Grey-matter degeneration
        Coding Clinic: 2017, Q2, P7

    G31.82 **Leigh's disease**
        Rare neurometabolic disorder that affects central nervous system
        Subacute necrotizing encephalopathy

    G31.83 **Dementia with Lewy bodies**
        Closely allied to Parkinson's Disease
        Dementia with Parkinsonism
        Lewy body dementia
        Lewy body disease
        Coding Clinic: 2017, Q2, P7; 2016, Q4, P141

    G31.84 **Mild cognitive impairment, so stated**
        Mild neurocognitive disorder

        Excludes1 age related cognitive decline (R41.81)
                  altered mental status (R41.82)
                  cerebral degeneration (G31.9)
                  change in mental status (R41.82)
                  cognitive deficits following (sequelae of) cerebral hemorrhage or infarction (I69.01-, I69.11-, I69.21-, I69.31-, I69.81-, I69.91-)
                  cognitive impairment due to intracranial or head injury (S06.-)
                  dementia (F01.-, F02.-, F03)
                  mild memory disturbance (F06.8)
                  neurologic neglect syndrome (R41.4)
                  personality change, nonpsychotic (F68.8)

    G31.85 **Corticobasal degeneration**

    G31.89 **Other specified degenerative diseases of nervous system**

    G31.9 **Degenerative disease of nervous system, unspecified**

● G32 **Other degenerative disorders of nervous system in diseases classified elsewhere**

  ▷ G32.0 *Subacute combined degeneration of spinal cord in diseases classified elsewhere*
      Dana-Putnam syndrome
      Sclerosis of spinal cord (combined) (dorsolateral) (posterolateral)

      Code first underlying disease, such as:
        anemia (D51.9)
        dietary (D51.3)
        pernicious (D51.0)
        vitamin B12 deficiency (E53.8)

      Excludes1 syphilitic combined degeneration of spinal cord (A52.11)

● **G32.8** **Other specified degenerative disorders of nervous system in diseases classified elsewhere**
Code first underlying disease, such as:
    amyloidosis cerebral degeneration (E85.-)
    cerebral degeneration (due to) hypothyroidism (E00.0-E03.9)
    cerebral degeneration (due to) neoplasm (C00-D49)
    cerebral degeneration (due to) vitamin B deficiency, except thiamine (E52-E53.-)

     Excludes1   superior hemorrhagic polioencephalitis [Wernicke's encephalopathy] (E51.2)

▷ **G32.81** *Cerebellar ataxia in diseases classified elsewhere*
Code first underlying disease, such as:
    celiac disease (with gluten ataxia) (K90.0)
    cerebellar ataxia (in) neoplastic disease (paraneoplastic cerebellar degeneration) (C00-D49)
    non-celiac gluten ataxia (M35.9)

     Excludes1   systemic atrophy primarily affecting the central nervous system in alcoholic cerebellar ataxia (G31.2)
         systemic atrophy primarily affecting the central nervous system in myxedema (G13.2)

▷ **G32.89** *Other specified degenerative disorders of nervous system in diseases classified elsewhere*
Degenerative encephalopathy in diseases classified elsewhere

DEMYELINATING DISEASES OF THE CENTRAL NERVOUS SYSTEM (G35-G37)

G35 **Multiple sclerosis**
Destruction of central nervous system; four types: relapsing remitting, secondary progressive, primary progressive, and progressive relapsing
Disseminated multiple sclerosis
Generalized multiple sclerosis
Multiple sclerosis NOS
Multiple sclerosis of brain stem
Multiple sclerosis of cord

● **G36** **Other acute disseminated demyelination**
     Excludes1   postinfectious encephalitis and encephalomyelitis NOS (G04.01)

  G36.0 **Neuromyelitis optica [Devic]**
Inflammatory disorder in which immune system attacks optic nerves and spinal cord producing inflammation of optic nerve (optic neuritis) and spinal cord (myelitis)
Demyelination in optic neuritis
     Excludes1   optic neuritis NOS (H46)

  G36.1 **Acute and subacute hemorrhagic leukoencephalitis [Hurst]**

  G36.8 **Other specified acute disseminated demyelination**

  G36.9 **Acute disseminated demyelination, unspecified**

● **G37** **Other demyelinating diseases of central nervous system**
Destruction of central nervous system

  G37.0 **Diffuse sclerosis of central nervous system**
Periaxial encephalitis
Schilder's disease
     Excludes1   X linked adrenoleukodystrophy (E71.52-)

  G37.1 **Central demyelination of corpus callosum**

  G37.2 **Central pontine myelinolysis**

Item 6–3 **Multiple sclerosis** (MS) is a nervous system disease affecting the brain and spinal cord by damaging the myelin sheath surrounding and protecting nerve cells. The damage slows down/blocks messages between the brain and body. Symptoms are visual disturbances, muscle weakness, coordination and balance issues, numbness, prickling, thinking and memory problems. The cause is unknown, though it is thought that it may be an autoimmune disease. It affects women more than men, between 20 and 40 years of age. MS can be mild, but it may cause the loss of ability to write, walk, and speak. There is no cure, but medication may slow or control symptoms.

  G37.3 **Acute transverse myelitis in demyelinating disease of central nervous system**
Acute transverse myelitis NOS
Acute transverse myelopathy
     Excludes1   multiple sclerosis (G35)
         neuromyelitis optica [Devic] (G36.0)

  G37.4 **Subacute necrotizing myelitis of central nervous system**

  G37.5 **Concentric sclerosis [Baló] of central nervous system**

  G37.8 **Other specified demyelinating diseases of central nervous system**

  G37.9 **Demyelinating disease of central nervous system, unspecified**

EPISODIC AND PAROXYSMAL DISORDERS (G40-G47)

● **G40** **Epilepsy and recurrent seizures**
Note: The following terms are to be considered equivalent to intractable: pharmacoresistant (pharmacologically resistant), treatment resistant, refractory (medically) and poorly controlled

     Excludes1   conversion disorder with seizures (F44.5)
         convulsions NOS (R56.9)
         post traumatic seizures (R56.1)
         seizure (convulsive) NOS (R56.9)
         seizure of newborn (P90)

     Excludes2   hippocampal sclerosis (G93.81)
         mesial temporal sclerosis (G93.81)
         temporal sclerosis (G93.81)
         Todd's paralysis (G83.84)

● **G40.0** **Localization-related (focal) (partial) idiopathic epilepsy and epileptic syndromes with seizures of localized onset**
Benign childhood epilepsy with centrotemporal EEG spikes
Childhood epilepsy with occipital EEG paroxysms
     Excludes1   adult onset localization-related epilepsy (G40.1-, G40.2-)

● **G40.00** **Localization-related (focal) (partial) idiopathic epilepsy and epileptic syndromes with seizures of localized onset, not intractable**
Localization-related (focal) (partial) idiopathic epilepsy and epileptic syndromes with seizures of localized onset without intractability

    G40.001 **Localization-related (focal) (partial) idiopathic epilepsy and epileptic syndromes with seizures of localized onset, not intractable, with status epilepticus**

    G40.009 **Localization-related (focal) (partial) idiopathic epilepsy and epileptic syndromes with seizures of localized onset, not intractable, without status epilepticus**
Localization-related (focal) (partial) idiopathic epilepsy and epileptic syndromes with seizures of localized onset NOS

● **G40.01** **Localization-related (focal) (partial) idiopathic epilepsy and epileptic syndromes with seizures of localized onset, intractable**

    G40.011 **Localization-related (focal) (partial) idiopathic epilepsy and epileptic syndromes with seizures of localized onset, intractable, with status epilepticus**

    G40.019 **Localization-related (focal) (partial) idiopathic epilepsy and epileptic syndromes with seizures of localized onset, intractable, without status epilepticus**

▶ New   ⇒ Revised   ~~deleted~~ Deleted   Excludes 1   Excludes 2   Includes   Use additional   Code first   Code also   Key words
OGCR Official Guidelines   X Assign placeholder X   ● Use Additional Character(s)   ▷ Manifestation Code   **Coding Clinic**

● G40.1 **Localization-related (focal) (partial) symptomatic epilepsy and epileptic syndromes with simple partial seizures**
> Attacks without alteration of consciousness
> Epilepsia partialis continua [Kozhevnikof]
> Simple partial seizures developing into secondarily generalized seizures

● G40.10 **Localization-related (focal) (partial) symptomatic epilepsy and epileptic syndromes with simple partial seizures, not intractable**
> Localization-related (focal) (partial) symptomatic epilepsy and epileptic syndromes with simple partial seizures without intractability

G40.101 **Localization-related (focal) (partial) symptomatic epilepsy and epileptic syndromes with simple partial seizures, not intractable, with status epilepticus**

G40.109 **Localization-related (focal) (partial) symptomatic epilepsy and epileptic syndromes with simple partial seizures, not intractable, without status epilepticus**
> Localization-related (focal) (partial) symptomatic epilepsy and epileptic syndromes with simple partial seizures NOS

● G40.11 **Localization-related (focal) (partial) symptomatic epilepsy and epileptic syndromes with simple partial seizures, intractable**

G40.111 **Localization-related (focal) (partial) symptomatic epilepsy and epileptic syndromes with simple partial seizures, intractable, with status epilepticus**

G40.119 **Localization-related (focal) (partial) symptomatic epilepsy and epileptic syndromes with simple partial seizures, intractable, without status epilepticus**

● G40.2 **Localization-related (focal) (partial) symptomatic epilepsy and epileptic syndromes with complex partial seizures**
> Attacks with alteration of consciousness, often with automatisms
> Complex partial seizures developing into secondarily generalized seizures

● G40.20 **Localization-related (focal) (partial) symptomatic epilepsy and epileptic syndromes with complex partial seizures, not intractable**
> Localization-related (focal) (partial) symptomatic epilepsy and epileptic syndromes with complex partial seizures without intractability

G40.201 **Localization-related (focal) (partial) symptomatic epilepsy and epileptic syndromes with complex partial seizures, not intractable, with status epilepticus**

G40.209 **Localization-related (focal) (partial) symptomatic epilepsy and epileptic syndromes with complex partial seizures, not intractable, without status epilepticus**
> Localization-related (focal) (partial) symptomatic epilepsy and epileptic syndromes with complex partial seizures NOS

● G40.21 **Localization-related (focal) (partial) symptomatic epilepsy and epileptic syndromes with complex partial seizures, intractable**

G40.211 **Localization-related (focal) (partial) symptomatic epilepsy and epileptic syndromes with complex partial seizures, intractable, with status epilepticus**

G40.219 **Localization-related (focal) (partial) symptomatic epilepsy and epileptic syndromes with complex partial seizures, intractable, without status epilepticus**

● G40.3 **Generalized idiopathic epilepsy and epileptic syndromes**
> Code also MERRF syndrome, if applicable (E88.42)

● G40.30 **Generalized idiopathic epilepsy and epileptic syndromes, not intractable**
> Generalized idiopathic epilepsy and epileptic syndromes without intractability

G40.301 **Generalized idiopathic epilepsy and epileptic syndromes, not intractable, with status epilepticus**

G40.309 **Generalized idiopathic epilepsy and epileptic syndromes, not intractable, without status epilepticus**
> Generalized idiopathic epilepsy and epileptic syndromes NOS

● G40.31 **Generalized idiopathic epilepsy and epileptic syndromes, intractable**

G40.311 **Generalized idiopathic epilepsy and epileptic syndromes, intractable, with status epilepticus**

G40.319 **Generalized idiopathic epilepsy and epileptic syndromes, intractable, without status epilepticus**

● G40.A **Absence epileptic syndrome**
> Childhood absence epilepsy [pyknolepsy]
> Juvenile absence epilepsy
> Absence epileptic syndrome, NOS

● G40.A0 **Absence epileptic syndrome, not intractable**

G40.A01 **Absence epileptic syndrome, not intractable, with status epilepticus**

G40.A09 **Absence epileptic syndrome, not intractable, without status epilepticus**

● G40.A1 **Absence epileptic syndrome, intractable**

G40.A11 **Absence epileptic syndrome, intractable, with status epilepticus**

G40.A19 **Absence epileptic syndrome, intractable, without status epilepticus**

● G40.B **Juvenile myoclonic epilepsy [impulsive petit mal]**

● G40.B0 **Juvenile myoclonic epilepsy, not intractable**

G40.B01 **Juvenile myoclonic epilepsy, not intractable, with status epilepticus**

G40.B09 **Juvenile myoclonic epilepsy, not intractable, without status epilepticus**

● G40.B1 **Juvenile myoclonic epilepsy, intractable**

G40.B11 **Juvenile myoclonic epilepsy, intractable, with status epilepticus**

G40.B19 **Juvenile myoclonic epilepsy, intractable, without status epilepticus**

CHAPTER 6 (G00-G99)

● **G40.4   Other generalized epilepsy and epileptic syndromes**
Epilepsy with grand mal seizures on awakening
Epilepsy with myoclonic absences
Epilepsy with myoclonic-astatic seizures
Grand mal seizure NOS
Nonspecific atonic epileptic seizures
Nonspecific clonic epileptic seizures
Nonspecific myoclonic epileptic seizures
Nonspecific tonic epileptic seizures
Nonspecific tonic-clonic epileptic seizures
Symptomatic early myoclonic encephalopathy

  ● **G40.40   Other generalized epilepsy and epileptic syndromes, not intractable**
     Other generalized epilepsy and epileptic syndromes without intractability
     Other generalized epilepsy and epileptic syndromes NOS

    G40.401   Other generalized epilepsy and epileptic syndromes, not intractable, with status epilepticus

    G40.409   Other generalized epilepsy and epileptic syndromes, not intractable, without status epilepticus

  ● **G40.41   Other generalized epilepsy and epileptic syndromes, intractable**

    G40.411   Other generalized epilepsy and epileptic syndromes, intractable, with status epilepticus

    G40.419   Other generalized epilepsy and epileptic syndromes, intractable, without status epilepticus

● **G40.5   Epileptic seizures related to external causes**
Epileptic seizures related to alcohol
Epileptic seizures related to drugs
Epileptic seizures related to hormonal changes
Epileptic seizures related to sleep deprivation
Epileptic seizures related to stress

  Code also, if applicable, associated epilepsy and recurrent seizures (G40.-)

  Use additional code for adverse effect, if applicable, to identify drug (T36-T50 with fifth or sixth character 5)

  ● **G40.50   Epileptic seizures related to external causes, not intractable**

    G40.501   Epileptic seizures related to external causes, not intractable, with status epilepticus

    G40.509   Epileptic seizures related to external causes, not intractable, without status epilepticus
       Epileptic seizures related to external causes, NOS

● **G40.8   Other epilepsy and recurrent seizures**
Epilepsies and epileptic syndromes undetermined as to whether they are focal or generalized
Landau-Kleffner syndrome

  ● **G40.80   Other epilepsy**

    G40.801   Other epilepsy, not intractable, with status epilepticus
       Other epilepsy without intractability with status epilepticus

    G40.802   Other epilepsy, not intractable, without status epilepticus
       Other epilepsy NOS
       Other epilepsy without intractability without status epilepticus

    G40.803   Other epilepsy, intractable, with status epilepticus

    G40.804   Other epilepsy, intractable, without status epilepticus

  ● **G40.81   Lennox-Gastaut syndrome**

    G40.811   Lennox-Gastaut syndrome, not intractable, with status epilepticus

    G40.812   Lennox-Gastaut syndrome, not intractable, without status epilepticus

    G40.813   Lennox-Gastaut syndrome, intractable, with status epilepticus

    G40.814   Lennox-Gastaut syndrome, intractable, without status epilepticus

  ● **G40.82   Epileptic spasms**
     Infantile spasms
     Salaam attacks
     West's syndrome

    G40.821   Epileptic spasms, not intractable, with status epilepticus

    G40.822   Epileptic spasms, not intractable, without status epilepticus

    G40.823   Epileptic spasms, intractable, with status epilepticus

    G40.824   Epileptic spasms, intractable, without status epilepticus

  G40.89   Other seizures
    Excludes1   post traumatic seizures (R56.1)
               recurrent seizures NOS (G40.909)
               seizure NOS (R56.9)

● **G40.9   Epilepsy, unspecified**

  ● **G40.90   Epilepsy, unspecified, not intractable**
     Epilepsy, unspecified, without intractability

    G40.901   Epilepsy, unspecified, not intractable, with status epilepticus

    G40.909   Epilepsy, unspecified, not intractable, without status epilepticus
       Epilepsy NOS
       Epileptic convulsions NOS
       Epileptic fits NOS
       Epileptic seizures NOS
       Recurrent seizures NOS
       Seizure disorder NOS

  ● **G40.91   Epilepsy, unspecified, intractable**
     Intractable seizure disorder NOS

    G40.911   Epilepsy, unspecified, intractable, with status epilepticus

    G40.919   Epilepsy, unspecified, intractable, without status epilepticus

● **G43   Migraine**
  Note: The following terms are to be considered equivalent to intractable: pharmacoresistant (pharmacologically resistant), treatment resistant, refractory (medically) and poorly controlled

  Use additional code for adverse effect, if applicable, to identify drug (T36-T50 with fifth or sixth character 5)

  Excludes1   headache NOS (R51)
               lower half migraine (G44.00)

  Excludes2   headache syndromes (G44.-)

● **G43.0   Migraine without aura**
  Neurological disorder, generally recurring headaches without early symptom (aura)
  Common migraine

  Excludes1   chronic migraine without aura (G43.7-)

  ● **G43.00   Migraine without aura, not intractable**
     Neurological disorder, generally recurring headaches without early symptom (aura); resistant to cure, relief, or control
     Migraine without aura without mention of refractory migraine

    G43.001   Migraine without aura, not intractable, with status migrainosus

    G43.009   Migraine without aura, not intractable, without status migrainosus
       Migraine without aura NOS

▶ New   ⇒ Revised   ~~deleted~~ Deleted   Excludes 1   Excludes 2   Includes   Use additional   Code first   Code also   Key words
OGCR Official Guidelines   X Assign placeholder X   ● Use Additional Character(s)   ▶ Manifestation Code   **Coding Clinic**

Item 6–4 Migraine headache is described as an intense pulsing or throbbing pain in one area of the head. It can be accompanied by extreme sensitivity to light (photophobic) and sound and is three times more common in women than in men. Symptoms include nausea and vomiting. Research indicates migraine headaches are caused by inherited abnormalities in genes that control the activities of certain cell populations in the brain.

● **G43.01 Migraine without aura, intractable**
　　Intractable migraine: Not easily cured or managed; relentless pain from a migraine
　　Migraine without aura with refractory migraine
　　G43.011 Migraine without aura, intractable, with status migrainosus
　　G43.019 Migraine without aura, intractable, without status migrainosus

● **G43.1 Migraine with aura**
　　Basilar migraine
　　Classical migraine
　　Migraine equivalents
　　Migraine preceded or accompanied by transient focal neurological phenomena
　　Migraine triggered seizures
　　Migraine with acute-onset aura
　　Migraine with aura without headache (migraine equivalents)
　　Migraine with prolonged aura
　　Migraine with typical aura
　　Retinal migraine
　　Code also any associated seizure (G40.-, R56.9)
　　Excludes1　persistent migraine aura (G43.5-, G43.6-)
● **G43.10 Migraine with aura, not intractable**
　　Migraine with aura without mention of refractory migraine
　　G43.101 Migraine with aura, not intractable, with status migrainosus
　　G43.109 Migraine with aura, not intractable, without status migrainosus
　　　　Migraine with aura NOS
● **G43.11 Migraine with aura, intractable**
　　Migraine with aura with refractory migraine
　　G43.111 Migraine with aura, intractable, with status migrainosus
　　G43.119 Migraine with aura, intractable, without status migrainosus

● **G43.4 Hemiplegic migraine**
　　Inherited migraine disorder causing temporary paralysis of one side of body followed by severe headache and nausea
　　Familial migraine
　　Sporadic migraine
● **G43.40 Hemiplegic migraine, not intractable**
　　Hemiplegic migraine without refractory migraine
　　G43.401 Hemiplegic migraine, not intractable, with status migrainosus
　　G43.409 Hemiplegic migraine, not intractable, without status migrainosus
　　　　Hemiplegic migraine NOS
● **G43.41 Hemiplegic migraine, intractable**
　　Hemiplegic migraine with refractory migraine
　　G43.411 Hemiplegic migraine, intractable, with status migrainosus
　　G43.419 Hemiplegic migraine, intractable, without status migrainosus

● **G43.5 Persistent migraine aura without cerebral infarction**
● **G43.50 Persistent migraine aura without cerebral infarction, not intractable**
　　Persistent migraine aura without cerebral infarction, without refractory migraine
　　G43.501 Persistent migraine aura without cerebral infarction, not intractable, with status migrainosus
　　G43.509 Persistent migraine aura without cerebral infarction, not intractable, without status migrainosus
　　　　Persistent migraine aura NOS
● **G43.51 Persistent migraine aura without cerebral infarction, intractable**
　　Persistent migraine aura without cerebral infarction, with refractory migraine
　　G43.511 Persistent migraine aura without cerebral infarction, intractable, with status migrainosus
　　G43.519 Persistent migraine aura without cerebral infarction, intractable, without status migrainosus

● **G43.6 Persistent migraine aura with cerebral infarction**
　　Visual, motor, or psychic disturbances, paresthesias, and related neurologic abnormalities accompanying migraine
　　Code also the type of cerebral infarction (I63.-)
● **G43.60 Persistent migraine aura with cerebral infarction, not intractable**
　　Persistent migraine aura with cerebral infarction, without refractory migraine
　　G43.601 Persistent migraine aura with cerebral infarction, not intractable, with status migrainosus
　　G43.609 Persistent migraine aura with cerebral infarction, not intractable, without status migrainosus
● **G43.61 Persistent migraine aura with cerebral infarction, intractable**
　　Persistent migraine aura with cerebral infarction, with refractory migraine
　　G43.611 Persistent migraine aura with cerebral infarction, intractable, with status migrainosus
　　G43.619 Persistent migraine aura with cerebral infarction, intractable, without status migrainosus

● **G43.7 Chronic migraine without aura**
　　Transformed migraine
　　Excludes1　migraine without aura (G43.0-)
● **G43.70 Chronic migraine without aura, not intractable**
　　Chronic migraine without aura, without refractory migraine
　　G43.701 Chronic migraine without aura, not intractable, with status migrainosus
　　G43.709 Chronic migraine without aura, not intractable, without status migrainosus
　　　　Chronic migraine without aura NOS
● **G43.71 Chronic migraine without aura, intractable**
　　Chronic migraine without aura, with refractory migraine
　　G43.711 Chronic migraine without aura, intractable, with status migrainosus
　　G43.719 Chronic migraine without aura, intractable, without status migrainosus

CHAPTER 6 (G00-G99)

- G43.A Cyclical vomiting
  - G43.A0 Cyclical vomiting, not intractable
    Cyclical vomiting, without refractory migraine
  - G43.A1 Cyclical vomiting, intractable
    Cyclical vomiting, with refractory migraine
- G43.B Ophthalmoplegic migraine
  - G43.B0 Ophthalmoplegic migraine, not intractable
    Ophthalmoplegic migraine, without refractory migraine
  - G43.B1 Ophthalmoplegic migraine, intractable
    Ophthalmoplegic migraine, with refractory migraine
- G43.C Periodic headache syndromes in child or adult
  - G43.C0 Periodic headache syndromes in child or adult, not intractable
    Periodic headache syndromes in child or adult, without refractory migraine
  - G43.C1 Periodic headache syndromes in child or adult, intractable
    Periodic headache syndromes in child or adult, with refractory migraine
- G43.D Abdominal migraine
  - G43.D0 Abdominal migraine, not intractable
    Abdominal migraine, without refractory migraine
  - G43.D1 Abdominal migraine, intractable
    Abdominal migraine, with refractory migraine
- G43.8 Other migraine
  - G43.80 Other migraine, not intractable
    Other migraine, without refractory migraine
    - G43.801 Other migraine, not intractable, with status migrainosus
    - G43.809 Other migraine, not intractable, without status migrainosus
  - G43.81 Other migraine, intractable
    Other migraine, with refractory migraine
    - G43.811 Other migraine, intractable, with status migrainosus
    - G43.819 Other migraine, intractable, without status migrainosus
  - G43.82 Menstrual migraine, not intractable
    Menstrual headache, not intractable
    Menstrual migraine, without refractory migraine
    Menstrually related migraine, not intractable
    Pre-menstrual headache, not intractable
    Pre-menstrual migraine, not intractable
    Pure menstrual migraine, not intractable
    Code also associated premenstrual tension syndrome (N94.3)
    - G43.821 Menstrual migraine, not intractable, with status migrainosus ♀
    - G43.829 Menstrual migraine, not intractable, without status migrainosus ♀
      Menstrual migraine NOS
  - G43.83 Menstrual migraine, intractable
    Menstrual headache, intractable
    Menstrual migraine, with refractory migraine
    Menstrually related migraine, intractable
    Pre-menstrual headache, intractable
    Pre-menstrual migraine, intractable
    Pure menstrual migraine, intractable
    Code also associated premenstrual tension syndrome (N94.3)
    - G43.831 Menstrual migraine, intractable, with status migrainosus ♀
    - G43.839 Menstrual migraine, intractable, without status migrainosus ♀

- G43.9 Migraine, unspecified
  - G43.90 Migraine, unspecified, not intractable
    Migraine, unspecified, without refractory migraine
    - G43.901 Migraine, unspecified, not intractable, with status migrainosus
      Status migrainosus NOS
    - G43.909 Migraine, unspecified, not intractable, without status migrainosus
      Migraine NOS
  - G43.91 Migraine, unspecified, intractable
    Migraine, unspecified, with refractory migraine
    - G43.911 Migraine, unspecified, intractable, with status migrainosus
    - G43.919 Migraine, unspecified, intractable, without status migrainosus

- G44 Other headache syndromes
  - **Excludes1** headache NOS (R51)
  - **Excludes2** atypical facial pain (G50.1)
    headache due to lumbar puncture (G97.1)
    migraines (G43.-)
    trigeminal neuralgia (G50.0)
  - G44.0 Cluster headaches and other trigeminal autonomic cephalgias (TAC)
    - G44.00 Cluster headache syndrome, unspecified
      Ciliary neuralgia
      Cluster headache NOS
      Histamine cephalgia
      Lower half migraine
      Migrainous neuralgia
      - G44.001 Cluster headache syndrome, unspecified, intractable
      - G44.009 Cluster headache syndrome, unspecified, not intractable
        Cluster headache syndrome NOS
    - G44.01 Episodic cluster headache
      - G44.011 Episodic cluster headache, intractable
      - G44.019 Episodic cluster headache, not intractable
        Episodic cluster headache NOS
    - G44.02 Chronic cluster headache
      - G44.021 Chronic cluster headache, intractable
      - G44.029 Chronic cluster headache, not intractable
        Chronic cluster headache NOS
    - G44.03 Episodic paroxysmal hemicrania
      Paroxysmal hemicrania NOS
      - G44.031 Episodic paroxysmal hemicrania, intractable
      - G44.039 Episodic paroxysmal hemicrania, not intractable
        Episodic paroxysmal hemicrania NOS
    - G44.04 Chronic paroxysmal hemicrania
      Unilateral headache
      - G44.041 Chronic paroxysmal hemicrania, intractable
      - G44.049 Chronic paroxysmal hemicrania, not intractable
        Chronic paroxysmal hemicrania NOS

● **G44.05** **Short lasting unilateral** neuralgiform headache with conjunctival injection and tearing (SUNCT)

   G44.051 Short lasting unilateral neuralgiform headache with conjunctival injection and tearing (SUNCT), **intractable**

   G44.059 Short lasting unilateral neuralgiform headache with conjunctival injection and tearing (SUNCT), **not intractable**
    Short lasting unilateral neuralgiform headache with conjunctival injection and tearing (SUNCT) NOS

● **G44.09** **Other trigeminal autonomic cephalgias (TAC)**
   Cluster headaches

   G44.091 Other trigeminal autonomic cephalgias (TAC), **intractable**

   G44.099 Other trigeminal autonomic cephalgias (TAC), **not intractable**

G44.1 **Vascular** headache, not elsewhere classified

  Excludes2   cluster headache (G44.0)
    complicated headache syndromes (G44.5-)
    drug-induced headache (G44.4-)
    migraine (G43.-)
    other specified headache syndromes (G44.8-)
    post-traumatic headache (G44.3-)
    tension-type headache (G44.2-)

● **G44.2** **Tension-type headache**

  ● **G44.20** **Tension-type headache, unspecified**

   G44.201 Tension-type headache, unspecified, **intractable**

   G44.209 Tension-type headache, unspecified, **not intractable**
    Tension headache NOS

  ● **G44.21** **Episodic** tension-type headache

   G44.211 Episodic tension-type headache, **intractable**

   G44.219 Episodic tension-type headache, **not intractable**
    Episodic tension-type headache NOS

  ● **G44.22** **Chronic** tension-type headache

   G44.221 Chronic tension-type headache, **intractable**

   G44.229 Chronic tension-type headache, **not intractable**
    Chronic tension-type headache NOS

● **G44.3** **Post-traumatic** headache

  ● **G44.30** **Post-traumatic headache, unspecified**

   G44.301 Post-traumatic headache, unspecified, **intractable**

   G44.309 Post-traumatic headache, unspecified, **not intractable**
    Post-traumatic headache NOS

  ● **G44.31** **Acute** post-traumatic headache

   G44.311 Acute post-traumatic headache, **intractable**

   G44.319 Acute post-traumatic headache, **not intractable**
    Acute post-traumatic headache NOS

  ● **G44.32** **Chronic** post-traumatic headache

   G44.321 Chronic post-traumatic headache, **intractable**

   G44.329 Chronic post-traumatic headache, **not intractable**
    Chronic post-traumatic headache NOS

● **G44.4** **Drug-induced** headache, not elsewhere classified
   Medication overuse headache
   Use additional code for adverse effect, if applicable, to identify drug (T36-T50 with fifth or sixth character 5)

   G44.40 Drug-induced headache, not elsewhere classified, **not intractable**

   G44.41 Drug-induced headache, not elsewhere classified, **intractable**

● **G44.5** **Complicated** headache syndromes

   G44.51 Hemicrania continua
    Persistent unilateral headache

   G44.52 New daily persistent headache (NDPH)

   G44.53 Primary thunderclap headache

   G44.59 Other complicated headache syndrome

● **G44.8** **Other specified** headache syndromes

   G44.81 **Hypnic** headache
    Benign primary headaches

   G44.82 Headache associated with **sexual activity**
    Orgasmic headache
    Preorgasmic headache

   G44.83 Primary **cough** headache

   G44.84 Primary **exertional** headache

   G44.85 Primary **stabbing** headache

   G44.89 **Other** headache syndrome

● **G45** **Transient cerebral ischemic attacks and related syndromes**

  Excludes1   neonatal cerebral ischemia (P91.0)
    transient retinal artery occlusion (H34.0-)

  Coding Clinic: 2018, Q2, P9

  G45.0 Vertebro-basilar artery syndrome

  G45.1 Carotid artery syndrome (hemispheric)

  G45.2 Multiple and bilateral precerebral artery syndromes

  G45.3 Amaurosis fugax
   Transient visual loss in one eye

  G45.4 Transient global amnesia
   Episode of short-term memory loss, nonrecurrent, lasting few hours

   Excludes1   amnesia NOS (R41.3)

  G45.8 Other transient cerebral ischemic attacks and related syndromes

  G45.9 Transient cerebral ischemic attack, **unspecified**
   Spasm of cerebral artery
   TIA
   Transient cerebral ischemia NOS

● **G46** **Vascular syndromes of brain in cerebrovascular diseases**
  Code first underlying cerebrovascular disease (I60-I69)

  G46.0 **Middle** cerebral artery syndrome

  G46.1 **Anterior** cerebral artery syndrome

  G46.2 **Posterior** cerebral artery syndrome

  G46.3 **Brain stem stroke** syndrome
   Benedikt syndrome
   Claude syndrome
   Foville syndrome
   Millard-Gubler syndrome
   Wallenberg syndrome
   Weber syndrome

  G46.4 **Cerebellar stroke** syndrome

  G46.5 **Pure motor lacunar** syndrome
   Occlusion of single deep penetrating artery

  G46.6 **Pure sensory lacunar** syndrome

  G46.7 **Other lacunar** syndromes

  G46.8 **Other vascular syndromes** of brain in cerebrovascular diseases

- ● **G47 Sleep disorders**
  - **Excludes2** nightmares (F51.5)
    - nonorganic sleep disorders (F51.-)
    - sleep terrors (F51.4)
    - sleepwalking (F51.3)
  - ● **G47.0 Insomnia**
    - **Excludes2** alcohol related insomnia (F10.182, F10.282, F10.982)
      - drug-related insomnia (F11.182, F11.282, F11.982, F13.182, F13.282, F13.982, F14.182, F14.282, F14.982, F15.182, F15.282, F15.982, F19.182, F19.282, F19.982)
      - idiopathic insomnia (F51.01)
      - insomnia due to a mental disorder (F51.05)
      - insomnia not due to a substance or known physiological condition (F51.0-)
      - nonorganic insomnia (F51.0-)
      - primary insomnia (F51.01)
      - sleep apnea (G47.3-)
    - **G47.00 Insomnia, unspecified**
      - Insomnia NOS
    - **G47.01 Insomnia due to medical condition**
      - Code also associated medical condition
    - **G47.09 Other insomnia**
  - ● **G47.1 Hypersomnia**
    - **Excludes2** alcohol-related hypersomnia (F10.182, F10.282, F10.982)
      - drug-related hypersomnia (F11.182, F11.282, F11.982, F13.182, F13.282, F13.982, F14.182, F14.282, F14.982, F15.182, F15.282, F15.982, F19.182, F19.282, F19.982)
      - hypersomnia due to a mental disorder (F51.13)
      - hypersomnia not due to a substance or known physiological condition (F51.1-)
      - primary hypersomnia (F51.11)
      - sleep apnea (G47.3-)
    - **G47.10 Hypersomnia, unspecified**
      - Hypersomnia NOS
    - **G47.11 Idiopathic hypersomnia with long sleep time**
      - Idiopathic hypersomnia NOS
    - **G47.12 Idiopathic hypersomnia without long sleep time**
    - **G47.13 Recurrent hypersomnia**
      - Kleine-Levin syndrome
      - Menstrual related hypersomnia
    - **G47.14 Hypersomnia due to medical condition**
      - Code also associated medical condition
    - **G47.19 Other hypersomnia**
  - ● **G47.2 Circadian rhythm sleep disorders**
    - Disorders of the sleep wake schedule
    - Inversion of nyctohemeral rhythm
    - Inversion of sleep rhythm
    - **G47.20 Circadian rhythm sleep disorder, unspecified type**
      - Sleep wake schedule disorder NOS
    - **G47.21 Circadian rhythm sleep disorder, delayed sleep phase type**
      - Delayed sleep phase syndrome
    - **G47.22 Circadian rhythm sleep disorder, advanced sleep phase type**
    - **G47.23 Circadian rhythm sleep disorder, irregular sleep wake type**
      - Irregular sleep-wake pattern
    - **G47.24 Circadian rhythm sleep disorder, free running type**
      - Circadian rhythm sleep disorder, non-24-hour sleep-wake type
    - **G47.25 Circadian rhythm sleep disorder, jet lag type**
  - **G47.26 Circadian rhythm sleep disorder, shift work type**
  - ▶ *G47.27 Circadian rhythm sleep disorder in conditions classified elsewhere*
    - *Code first underlying condition*
  - **G47.29 Other circadian rhythm sleep disorder**
  - ● **G47.3 Sleep apnea**
    - *Characterized by episodes in which breathing stops during sleep*
    - Code also any associated underlying condition
    - **Excludes1** apnea NOS (R06.81)
      - Cheyne-Stokes breathing (R06.3)
      - pickwickian syndrome (E66.2)
      - sleep apnea of newborn (P28.3)
    - **G47.30 Sleep apnea, unspecified**
      - Sleep apnea NOS
    - **G47.31 Primary central sleep apnea**
      - Idiopathic central sleep apnea
    - **G47.32 High altitude periodic breathing**
    - **G47.33 Obstructive sleep apnea (adult) (pediatric)**
      - Obstructive sleep apnea hypopnea
      - **Excludes1** obstructive sleep apnea of newborn (P28.3)
    - **G47.34 Idiopathic sleep related nonobstructive alveolar hypoventilation**
      - Sleep related hypoxia
    - **G47.35 Congenital central alveolar hypoventilation syndrome**
    - ▶ *G47.36 Sleep related hypoventilation in conditions classified elsewhere*
      - Sleep related hypoxemia in conditions classified elsewhere
      - *Code first underlying condition*
    - ▶ *G47.37 Central sleep apnea in conditions classified elsewhere*
      - *Code first underlying condition*
    - **G47.39 Other sleep apnea**
  - ● **G47.4 Narcolepsy and cataplexy**
    - *Cataplexy is a disorder evidenced by seizures including minor slacking of the facial muscles to complete collapse and often affects people who have narcolepsy, a disorder in which there is great difficulty remaining awake during the daytime.*
    - ● **G47.41 Narcolepsy**
      - **G47.411 Narcolepsy with cataplexy**
      - **G47.419 Narcolepsy without cataplexy**
        - Narcolepsy NOS
    - ● **G47.42 Narcolepsy in conditions classified elsewhere**
      - *Code first underlying condition*
      - ▶ *G47.421 Narcolepsy in conditions classified elsewhere with cataplexy*
      - ▶ *G47.429 Narcolepsy in conditions classified elsewhere without cataplexy*
  - ● **G47.5 Parasomnia**
    - **Excludes1** alcohol induced parasomnia (F10.182, F10.282, F10.982)
      - drug induced parasomnia (F11.182, F11.282, F11.982, F13.182, F13.282, F13.982, F14.182, F14.282, F14.982, F15.182, F15.282, F15.982, F19.182, F19.282, F19.982)
      - parasomnia not due to a substance or known physiological condition (F51.8)
    - **G47.50 Parasomnia, unspecified**
      - Parasomnia NOS
    - **G47.51 Confusional arousals**
    - **G47.52 REM sleep behavior disorder**
    - **G47.53 Recurrent isolated sleep paralysis**
    - ▶ *G47.54 Parasomnia in conditions classified elsewhere*
      - *Code first underlying condition*
    - **G47.59 Other parasomnia**

▶ New   ⇒ Revised   ~~deleted~~ Deleted   Excludes 1   Excludes 2   Includes   Use additional   Code first   Code also   Key words
OGCR Official Guidelines   X Assign placeholder X   ● Use Additional Character(s)   ▶ Manifestation Code   **Coding Clinic**

● **G47.6**   Sleep related movement disorders
     Excludes2   restless legs syndrome (G25.81)
   G47.61   Periodic limb movement disorder
   G47.62   Sleep related leg cramps
   G47.63   Sleep related bruxism
     Excludes1   psychogenic bruxism (F45.8)
     Coding Clinic: 2016, Q4, P118
   G47.69   Other sleep related movement disorders
  G47.8   Other sleep disorders
     Other specified sleep-wake disorder
  G47.9   Sleep disorder, unspecified
     Sleep disorder NOS
     Unspecified sleep-wake disorder

★ **(See Plate 118 on page 54.)**

NERVE, NERVE ROOT AND PLEXUS DISORDERS (G50-G59)

   Excludes1   current traumatic nerve, nerve root and plexus
     disorders - see Injury, nerve by body region
     neuralgia NOS (M79.2)
     neuritis NOS (M79.2)
     peripheral neuritis in pregnancy (O26.82-)
     radiculitis NOS (M54.1-)

● **G50**   Disorders of trigeminal nerve
     Includes   disorders of 5th cranial nerve
  G50.0   Trigeminal neuralgia
     Syndrome of paroxysmal facial pain
     Tic douloureux
  G50.1   Atypical facial pain
  G50.8   Other disorders of trigeminal nerve
  G50.9   Disorder of trigeminal nerve, unspecified
● **G51**   Facial nerve disorders
     Includes   disorders of 7th cranial nerve
  G51.0   Bell's palsy
     Facial palsy
  G51.1   Geniculate ganglionitis
     Rare disorder with symptoms of severe pain deep in ear,
     spreading to ear canal, outer ear, mastoid or eye regions
     Excludes1   postherpetic geniculate ganglionitis
     (B02.21)
  G51.2   Melkersson's syndrome
     Melkersson-Rosenthal syndrome
  G51.3   Clonic hemifacial spasm
 ▶ **G51.31**   Clonic hemifacial spasm, right
 ▶ **G51.32**   Clonic hemifacial spasm, left
 ▶ **G51.33**   Clonic hemifacial spasm, bilateral
 ▶ **G51.39**   Clonic hemifacial spasm, unspecified
  G51.4   Facial myokymia
     Involuntary facial muscle movement
  G51.8   Other disorders of facial nerve
  G51.9   Disorder of facial nerve, unspecified

● **G52**   Disorders of other cranial nerves
     Excludes2   disorders of acoustic [8th] nerve (H93.3)
     disorders of optic [2nd] nerve (H46, H47.0)
     paralytic strabismus due to nerve palsy
     (H49.0-H49.2)
  G52.0   Disorders of olfactory nerve
     Disorders of 1st cranial nerve
  G52.1   Disorders of glossopharyngeal nerve
     Disorder of 9th cranial nerve
     Glossopharyngeal neuralgia
  G52.2   Disorders of vagus nerve
     Disorders of pneumogastric [10th] nerve
  G52.3   Disorders of hypoglossal nerve
     Disorders of 12th cranial nerve
  G52.7   Disorders of multiple cranial nerves
     Polyneuritis cranialis
  G52.8   Disorders of other specified cranial nerves
  G52.9   Cranial nerve disorder, unspecified

▸ **G53**   *Cranial nerve disorders in diseases classified elsewhere*
     Code first underlying disease, such as:
     neoplasm (C00-D49)
     Excludes1   multiple cranial nerve palsy in sarcoidosis (D86.82)
     multiple cranial nerve palsy in syphilis (A52.15)
     postherpetic geniculate ganglionitis (B02.21)
     postherpetic trigeminal neuralgia (B02.22)

● **G54**   Nerve root and plexus disorders
     Radiculopathy (nerve root disorder) caused by pressure on nerve root,
     most common cause is herniation of intervertebral disk. Plexus
     disorders (plexopathies) are due to compression or injury.
     Excludes1   current traumatic nerve root and plexus disorders
     - see nerve injury by body region
     intervertebral disc disorders (M50-M51)
     neuralgia or neuritis NOS (M79.2)
     neuritis or radiculitis brachial NOS (M54.13)
     neuritis or radiculitis lumbar NOS (M54.16)
     neuritis or radiculitis lumbosacral NOS (M54.17)
     neuritis or radiculitis thoracic NOS (M54.14)
     radiculitis NOS (M54.10)
     radiculopathy NOS (M54.10)
     spondylosis (M47.-)
  G54.0   Brachial plexus disorders
     Thoracic outlet syndrome
  G54.1   Lumbosacral plexus disorders
  G54.2   Cervical root disorders, not elsewhere classified
  G54.3   Thoracic root disorders, not elsewhere classified
  G54.4   Lumbosacral root disorders, not elsewhere classified
  G54.5   Neuralgic amyotrophy
     Parsonage-Aldren-Turner syndrome
     Shoulder-girdle neuritis
     Excludes1   neuralgic amyotrophy in diabetes
     mellitus (E08-E13 with .44)
  G54.6   Phantom limb syndrome with pain
     Sensations (cramping, itching) in a limb that no longer
     exists
  G54.7   Phantom limb syndrome without pain
     Phantom limb syndrome NOS
  G54.8   Other nerve root and plexus disorders
  G54.9   Nerve root and plexus disorder, unspecified

CHAPTER 6 (G00-G99)

Item 6–5   **Trigeminal neuralgia,** tic douloureux, is a pain syndrome diagnosed from the patient's history alone. The condition is characterized by pain and a brief facial spasm or tic. Pain is unilateral and follows the sensory distribution of cranial nerve V, typically radiating to the maxillary (V2) or mandibular (V3) area.

Item 6–6   The most common facial nerve disorder is **Bell's Palsy,** which occurs suddenly and results in facial drooping unilaterally. This disorder is the result of a reaction to a virus that causes the facial nerve in the ear to swell, resulting in pressure in the bony canal.

▶ **G55** *Nerve root and plexus compressions in diseases classified elsewhere*

> *Code first underlying disease, such as:*
> neoplasm (C00-D49)
>
> **Excludes1**   nerve root compression (due to) (in) ankylosing spondylitis (M45.-)
> nerve root compression (due to) (in)dorsopathies (M53.-, M54.-)
> nerve root compression (due to) (in)intervertebral disc disorders (M50.1.-, M51.1.-)
> nerve root compression (due to) (in) spondylopathies (M46.-, M48.-)

★ **(See Plates 472 and 473 on pages 56 and 57.)**

● **G56** Mononeuropathies of upper limb

> **Excludes1**   current traumatic nerve disorder - see nerve injury by body region

● **G56.0** Carpal tunnel syndrome

- **G56.00** Carpal tunnel syndrome, unspecified upper limb
- **G56.01** Carpal tunnel syndrome, right upper limb
- **G56.02** Carpal tunnel syndrome, left upper limb
- **G56.03** Carpal tunnel syndrome, bilateral upper limbs
  Coding Clinic: 2016, Q4, P17

● **G56.1** Other lesions of median nerve

- **G56.10** Other lesions of median nerve, unspecified side
- **G56.11** Other lesions of median nerve, right upper limb
- **G56.12** Other lesions of median nerve, left upper limb
- **G56.13** Other lesions of median nerve, bilateral upper limbs
  Coding Clinic: 2016, Q4, P17

● **G56.2** Lesion of ulnar nerve
  Tardy ulnar nerve palsy

- **G56.20** Lesion of ulnar nerve, unspecified upper limb
- **G56.21** Lesion of ulnar nerve, right upper limb
- **G56.22** Lesion of ulnar nerve, left upper limb
- **G56.23** Lesion of ulnar nerve, bilateral upper limbs
  Coding Clinic: 2016, Q4, P17

● **G56.3** Lesion of radial nerve

- **G56.30** Lesion of radial nerve, unspecified upper limb
- **G56.31** Lesion of radial nerve, right upper limb
- **G56.32** Lesion of radial nerve, left upper limb
- **G56.33** Lesion of radial nerve, bilateral upper limbs
  Coding Clinic: 2016, Q4, P17

● **G56.4** Causalgia of upper limb
  Intense burning pain and sensitivity to slight touch
  Complex regional pain syndrome II of upper limb

> **Excludes1**   complex regional pain syndrome I of lower limb (G90.52-)
> complex regional pain syndrome I of upper limb (G90.51-)
> complex regional pain syndrome II of lower limb (G57.7-)
> reflex sympathetic dystrophy of lower limb (G90.52-)
> reflex sympathetic dystrophy (G90.51-)

- **G56.40** Causalgia of unspecified upper limb
- **G56.41** Causalgia of right upper limb
- **G56.42** Causalgia of left upper limb
- **G56.43** Causalgia of bilateral upper limbs
  Coding Clinic: 2016, Q4, P17

● **G56.8** Other specified mononeuropathies of upper limb
  Disease of a single nerve
  Interdigital neuroma of upper limb

- **G56.80** Other specified mononeuropathies of unspecified upper limb
- **G56.81** Other specified mononeuropathies of right upper limb
- **G56.82** Other specified mononeuropathies of left upper limb
- **G56.83** Other specified mononeuropathies of bilateral upper limbs
  Coding Clinic: 2016, Q4, P17

● **G56.9** Unspecified mononeuropathy of upper limb
  Disease of a single nerve

- **G56.90** Unspecified mononeuropathy of unspecified upper limb
- **G56.91** Unspecified mononeuropathy of right upper limb
- **G56.92** Unspecified mononeuropathy of left upper limb
- **G56.93** Unspecified mononeuropathy of bilateral upper limbs
  Coding Clinic: 2016, Q4, P17

● **G57** Mononeuropathies of lower limb

> **Excludes1**   current traumatic nerve disorder - see nerve injury by body region

★ **(See Plates 544 and 545 on pages 58 and 59.)**

● **G57.0** Lesion of sciatic nerve

> **Excludes1**   sciatica NOS (M54.3-)
> **Excludes2**   sciatica attributed to intervertebral disc disorder (M51.1.-)

- **G57.00** Lesion of sciatic nerve, unspecified lower limb
- **G57.01** Lesion of sciatic nerve, right lower limb
- **G57.02** Lesion of sciatic nerve, left lower limb
- **G57.03** Lesion of sciatic nerve, bilateral lower limbs
  Coding Clinic: 2016, Q4, P1

● **G57.1** Meralgia paresthetica
  Numbness or pain in outer thigh caused by injury to nerve
  Lateral cutaneous nerve of thigh syndrome

- **G57.10** Meralgia paresthetica, unspecified lower limb
- **G57.11** Meralgia paresthetica, right lower limb
- **G57.12** Meralgia paresthetica, left lower limb
- **G57.13** Meralgia paresthetica, bilateral lower limbs
  Coding Clinic: 2016, Q4, P1

● **G57.2** Lesion of femoral nerve

- **G57.20** Lesion of femoral nerve, unspecified lower limb
- **G57.21** Lesion of femoral nerve, right lower limb
- **G57.22** Lesion of femoral nerve, left lower limb
- **G57.23** Lesion of femoral nerve, bilateral lower limbs
  Coding Clinic: 2016, Q4, P1

● **G57.3** Lesion of lateral popliteal nerve
  Peroneal nerve palsy

- **G57.30** Lesion of lateral popliteal nerve, unspecified lower limb
- **G57.31** Lesion of lateral popliteal nerve, right lower limb
- **G57.32** Lesion of lateral popliteal nerve, left lower limb
- **G57.33** Lesion of lateral popliteal nerve, bilateral lower limbs
  Coding Clinic: 2016, Q4, P1

CHAPTER 6 (G00-G99)

● G57.4   Lesion of medial popliteal nerve
    G57.40   Lesion of medial popliteal nerve, unspecified lower limb
    G57.41   Lesion of medial popliteal nerve, right lower limb
    G57.42   Lesion of medial popliteal nerve, left lower limb
    G57.43   Lesion of medial popliteal nerve, bilateral lower limbs
        Coding Clinic: 2016, Q4, P1

● G57.5   Tarsal tunnel syndrome
    G57.50   Tarsal tunnel syndrome, unspecified lower limb
    G57.51   Tarsal tunnel syndrome, right lower limb
    G57.52   Tarsal tunnel syndrome, left lower limb
    G57.53   Tarsal tunnel syndrome, bilateral lower limbs
        Coding Clinic: 2016, Q4, P1

● G57.6   Lesion of plantar nerve
    Morton's metatarsalgia
    G57.60   Lesion of plantar nerve, unspecified lower limb
    G57.61   Lesion of plantar nerve, right lower limb
    G57.62   Lesion of plantar nerve, left lower limb
    G57.63   Lesion of plantar nerve, bilateral lower limbs
        Coding Clinic: 2016, Q4, P1

● G57.7   Causalgia of lower limb
    Complex regional pain syndrome II of lower limb

    Excludes1   complex regional pain syndrome I of lower limb (G90.52-)
                complex regional pain syndrome I of upper limb (G90.51-)
                complex regional pain syndrome II of upper limb (G56.4-)
                reflex sympathetic dystrophy of lower limb (G90.52-)
                reflex sympathetic dystrophy of upper limb (G90.51-)

    G57.70   Causalgia of unspecified lower limb
    G57.71   Causalgia of right lower limb
    G57.72   Causalgia of left lower limb
    G57.73   Causalgia of bilateral lower limbs
        Coding Clinic: 2016, Q4, P1

● G57.8   Other specified mononeuropathies of lower limb
    Interdigital neuroma of lower limb
    G57.80   Other specified mononeuropathies of unspecified lower limb
    G57.81   Other specified mononeuropathies of right lower limb
    G57.82   Other specified mononeuropathies of left lower limb
    G57.83   Other specified mononeuropathies of bilateral lower limbs
        Coding Clinic: 2016, Q4, P17

● G57.9   Unspecified mononeuropathy of lower limb
    G57.90   Unspecified mononeuropathy of unspecified lower limb
    G57.91   Unspecified mononeuropathy of right lower limb
    G57.92   Unspecified mononeuropathy of left lower limb
    G57.93   Unspecified mononeuropathy of bilateral lower limbs
        Coding Clinic: 2016, Q4, P17

● G58   Other mononeuropathies
    G58.0   Intercostal neuropathy
    G58.7   Mononeuritis multiplex
    G58.8   Other specified mononeuropathies
    G58.9   Mononeuropathy, unspecified

▶ G59   Mononeuropathy in diseases classified elsewhere
    Code first underlying disease
    Excludes1   diabetic mononeuropathy (E08-E13 with .41)
                syphilitic nerve paralysis (A52.19)
                syphilitic neuritis (A52.15)
                tuberculous mononeuropathy (A17.83)

POLYNEUROPATHIES AND OTHER DISORDERS OF THE PERIPHERAL NERVOUS SYSTEM (G60-G65)

    Excludes1   neuralgia NOS (M79.2)
                neuritis NOS (M79.2)
                peripheral neuritis in pregnancy (O26.82-)
                radiculitis NOS (M54.10)

● G60   Hereditary and idiopathic neuropathy
    G60.0   Hereditary motor and sensory neuropathy
        Charcot-Marie-Tooth disease
        Déjerine-Sottas disease
        Hereditary motor and sensory neuropathy, types I-IV
        Hypertrophic neuropathy of infancy
        Peroneal muscular atrophy (axonal type) (hypertrophic type)
        Roussy-Lévy syndrome

    G60.1   Refsum's disease
        Genetic disorder affecting fatty acid metabolism
        Infantile Refsum disease

    G60.2   Neuropathy in association with hereditary ataxia
    G60.3   Idiopathic progressive neuropathy
    G60.8   Other hereditary and idiopathic neuropathies
        Dominantly inherited sensory neuropathy
        Morvan's disease
        Nelaton's syndrome
        Recessively inherited sensory neuropathy

    G60.9   Hereditary and idiopathic neuropathy, unspecified

Figure 6-2 Actions of parasympathetic and sympathetic nerves. (From Chabner: The Language of Medicine, ed 9, St. Louis, Saunders, 2011)

Item 6–7 The **peripheral nervous system** consists of 31 pairs of spinal nerves, 12 pairs of cranial nerves, and the autonomic nerves, which are divided into the parasympathetic and sympathetic nerves. The cranial nerves are: olfactory (I), optic (II), oculomotor (III), trochlear (IV), trigeminal (V), abducens (VI), facial (VII), vestibulocochlear (VIII), glossopharyngeal (IX), vagus (X), accessory (XI), and hypoglossal (XII).

- **G61   Inflammatory polyneuropathy**
  - **G61.0   Guillain-Barré syndrome**
    - *Autoimmune disease affecting peripheral nervous system*
    - Acute (post-)infective polyneuritis
    - Miller Fisher Syndrome
  - **G61.1   Serum neuropathy**
    - Use additional code for adverse effect, if applicable, to identify serum (T50.-)
  - **G61.8   Other inflammatory polyneuropathies**
    - **G61.81   Chronic inflammatory demyelinating polyneuritis**
    - **G61.82   Multifocal motor neuropathy**
      - MMN
    - **G61.89   Other inflammatory polyneuropathies**
  - **G61.9   Inflammatory polyneuropathy, unspecified**

- **G62   Other and unspecified polyneuropathies**
  - **G62.0   Drug-induced polyneuropathy**
    - Use additional code for adverse effect, if applicable, to identify drug (T36-T50 with fifth or sixth character 5)
  - **G62.1   Alcoholic polyneuropathy**
    - *Malfunction of many peripheral nerves throughout the body*
  - **G62.2   Polyneuropathy due to other toxic agents**
    - *Code first (T51-T65) to identify toxic agent*
  - **G62.8   Other specified polyneuropathies**
    - **G62.81   Critical illness polyneuropathy**
      - Acute motor neuropathy
    - **G62.82   Radiation-induced polyneuropathy**
      - Use additional external cause code (W88-W90, X39.0-) to identify cause
      - **Coding Clinic: 2016, Q4, P18**
    - **G62.89   Other specified polyneuropathies**
      - **Coding Clinic: 2016, Q2, P11**
  - **G62.9   Polyneuropathy, unspecified**
    - Neuropathy NOS

- ▷ *G63   Polyneuropathy in diseases classified elsewhere*
  - *Code first underlying disease, such as:*
    - amyloidosis (E85.-)
    - endocrine disease, except diabetes (E00-E07, E15-E16, E20-E34)
    - metabolic diseases (E70-E88)
    - neoplasm (C00-D49)
    - nutritional deficiency (E40-E64)
  - **Excludes1**   polyneuropathy (in):
    - diabetes mellitus (E08-E13 with .42)
    - diphtheria (A36.83)
    - infectious mononucleosis (B27.0-B27.9 with 1)
    - Lyme disease (A69.22)
    - mumps (B26.84)
    - postherpetic (B02.23)
    - rheumatoid arthritis (M05.33)
    - scleroderma (M34.83)
    - systemic lupus erythematosus (M32.19)
  - **Coding Clinic: 2012, Q4, P100**

- **G64   Other disorders of peripheral nervous system**
  - Disorder of peripheral nervous system NOS

- **G65   Sequelae of inflammatory and toxic polyneuropathies**
  - *Code first condition resulting from (sequela) of inflammatory and toxic polyneuropathies*
  - **G65.0   Sequelae of Guillain-Barré syndrome**
  - **G65.1   Sequelae of other inflammatory polyneuropathy**
  - **G65.2   Sequelae of toxic polyneuropathy**

DISEASES OF MYONEURAL JUNCTION AND MUSCLE (G70-G73)

- **G70   Myasthenia gravis and other myoneural disorders**
  - **Excludes1**   botulism (A05.1, A48.51-A48.52)
    - transient neonatal myasthenia gravis (P94.0)
  - **G70.0   Myasthenia gravis**
    - *Acquired and results in fatigable muscle weakness exacerbated by activity and improved with rest*
    - **G70.00   Myasthenia gravis without (acute) exacerbation**
      - Myasthenia gravis NOS
    - **G70.01   Myasthenia gravis with (acute) exacerbation**
      - Myasthenia gravis in crisis
  - **G70.1   Toxic myoneural disorders**
    - *Dysfunction at junction of muscle and motor nerve (myoneural junction)*
    - *Code first (T51-T65) to identify toxic agent*
  - **G70.2   Congenital and developmental myasthenia**
  - **G70.8   Other specified myoneural disorders**
    - **G70.80   Lambert-Eaton syndrome, unspecified**
      - Lambert-Eaton syndrome NOS
    - ▷ *G70.81   Lambert-Eaton syndrome in disease classified elsewhere*
      - *Code first underlying disease*
      - **Excludes1**   Lambert-Eaton syndrome in neoplastic disease (G73.1)
    - **G70.89   Other specified myoneural disorders**
  - **G70.9   Myoneural disorder, unspecified**

- **G71   Primary disorders of muscles**
  - **Excludes2**   arthrogryposis multiplex congenita (Q74.3)
    - metabolic disorders (E70-E88)
    - myositis (M60.-)
  - **G71.0   Muscular dystrophy**
    - ▶ **G71.00   Muscular dystrophy, unspecified**
    - ▶ **G71.01   Duchenne or Becker muscular dystrophy**
      - ▶ Autosomal recessive, childhood type, muscular dystrophy resembling Duchenne or Becker muscular dystrophy
      - ▶ Benign [Becker] muscular dystrophy
      - ▶ Severe [Duchenne] muscular dystrophy
    - ▶ **G71.02   Facioscapulohumeral muscular dystrophy**
      - ▶ Scapulohumeral muscular dystrophy
    - ▶ **G71.09   Other specified muscular dystrophies**
      - ▶ Benign scapuloperoneal muscular dystrophy with early contractures [Emery-Dreifuss]
      - ▶ Congenital muscular dystrophy NOS
      - ▶ Congenital muscular dystrophy with specific morphological abnormalities of the muscle fiber
      - ▶ Distal muscular dystrophy
      - ▶ Limb-girdle muscular dystrophy
      - ▶ Ocular muscular dystrophy
      - ▶ Oculopharyngeal muscular dystrophy
      - ▶ Scapuloperoneal muscular dystrophy
      - ~~Autosomal recessive, childhood type, muscular dystrophy resembling Duchenne or Becker muscular dystrophy~~
      - ~~Benign [Becker] muscular dystrophy~~
      - ~~Benign scapuloperoneal muscular dystrophy with early contractures [Emery-Dreifuss]~~
      - ~~Congenital muscular dystrophy NOS~~
      - ~~Congenital muscular dystrophy with specific morphological abnormalities of the muscle fiber~~
      - ~~Distal muscular dystrophy~~
      - ~~Facioscapulohumeral muscular dystrophy~~
      - ~~Limb-girdle muscular dystrophy~~
      - ~~Ocular muscular dystrophy~~
      - ~~Oculopharyngeal muscular dystrophy~~
      - ~~Scapuloperoneal muscular dystrophy~~
      - ~~Severe [Duchenne] muscular dystrophy~~

▶ New   ⇒ Revised   ~~deleted~~ Deleted   Excludes 1   Excludes 2   Includes   Use additional   Code first   Code also   Key words

OGCR Official Guidelines   X Assign placeholder X   ● Use Additional Character(s)   ▷ Manifestation Code   **Coding Clinic**

● **G71.1   Myotonic disorders**
Inherited disorder that affects muscles tone

    G71.11   Myotonic muscular dystrophy
Dystrophia myotonica [Steinert]
Myotonia atrophica
Myotonic dystrophy
Proximal myotonic myopathy (PROMM)
Steinert disease

    G71.12   Myotonia congenita
Acetazolamide responsive myotonia congenita
Dominant myotonia congenita [Thomsen disease]
Myotonia levior
Recessive myotonia congenita [Becker disease]

    G71.13   Myotonic chondrodystrophy
Chondrodystrophic myotonia
Congenital myotonic chondrodystrophy
Schwartz-Jampel disease

    G71.14   Drug induced myotonia
Use additional code for adverse effect, if applicable, to identify drug (T36-T50 with fifth or sixth character 5)

    G71.19   Other specified myotonic disorders
Myotonia fluctuans
Myotonia permanens
Neuromyotonia [Isaacs]
Paramyotonia congenita (of von Eulenburg)
Pseudomyotonia
Symptomatic myotonia

G71.2   Congenital myopathies
Central core disease
Fiber-type disproportion
Minicore disease
Multicore disease
Myotubular (centronuclear) myopathy
Nemaline myopathy
    Excludes1   arthrogryposis multiplex congenita (Q74.3)

G71.3   Mitochondrial myopathy, not elsewhere classified
Myopathies associated with increased number of enlarged, often abnormal, mitochondria in muscle fibers
    Excludes1   Kearns-Sayre syndrome (H49.81)
Leber's disease (H47.21)
Leigh's encephalopathy (G31.82)
mitochondrial metabolism disorders (E88.4.-)
Reye's syndrome (G93.7)

G71.8   Other primary disorders of muscles

G71.9   Primary disorder of muscle, unspecified
Hereditary myopathy NOS

● **G72   Other and unspecified myopathies**
    Excludes1   arthrogryposis multiplex congenita (Q74.3)
dermatopolymyositis (M33.-)
ischemic infarction of muscle (M62.2-)
myositis (M60.-)
polymyositis (M33.2.-)

G72.0   Drug-induced myopathy
Use additional code for adverse effect, if applicable, to identify drug (T36-T50 with fifth or sixth character 5)

G72.1   Alcoholic myopathy
Use additional code to identify alcoholism (F10.-)

G72.2   Myopathy due to other toxic agents
Code first (T51-T65) to identify toxic agent

G72.3   Periodic paralysis
Familial periodic paralysis
Hyperkalemic periodic paralysis (familial)
Hypokalemic periodic paralysis (familial)
Myotonic periodic paralysis (familial)
Normokalemic paralysis (familial)
Potassium sensitive periodic paralysis
    Excludes1   paramyotonia congenita (of von Eulenburg) (G71.19)

● **G72.4   Inflammatory and immune myopathies, not elsewhere classified**

    G72.41   Inclusion body myositis [IBM]

    G72.49   Other inflammatory and immune myopathies, not elsewhere classified
Inflammatory myopathy NOS

● **G72.8   Other specified myopathies**

    G72.81   Critical illness myopathy
Acute necrotizing myopathy
Acute quadriplegic myopathy
Intensive care (ICU) myopathy
Myopathy of critical illness

    G72.89   Other specified myopathies

G72.9   Myopathy, unspecified

● **G73   Disorders of myoneural junction and muscle in diseases classified elsewhere**

    ▷ *G73.1   Lambert-Eaton syndrome in neoplastic disease*
Rare autoimmune disorder affecting calcium channels of nerve-muscle (neuromuscular) junction
Code first underlying neoplasm (C00-D49)
    Excludes1   Lambert-Eaton syndrome not associated with neoplasm (G70.80-G70.81)

    ▷ *G73.3   Myasthenic syndromes in other diseases classified elsewhere*
Code first underlying disease, such as:
neoplasm (C00-D49)
thyrotoxicosis (E05.-)

    ▷ *G73.7   Myopathy in diseases classified elsewhere*
Code first underlying disease, such as:
hyperparathyroidism (E21.0, E21.3)
hypoparathyroidism (E20.-)
glycogen storage disease (E74.0)
lipid storage disorders (E75.-)
    Excludes1   myopathy in:
rheumatoid arthritis (M05.32)
sarcoidosis (D86.87)
scleroderma (M34.82)
sicca syndrome [Sjögren] (M35.03)
systemic lupus erythematosus (M32.19)

CEREBRAL PALSY AND OTHER PARALYTIC SYNDROMES (G80-G83)

● **G80   Cerebral palsy**
    Excludes1   hereditary spastic paraplegia (G11.4)

G80.0   Spastic quadriplegic cerebral palsy
Congenital spastic paralysis (cerebral)

G80.1   Spastic diplegic cerebral palsy
Spastic cerebral palsy NOS

G80.2   Spastic hemiplegic cerebral palsy

G80.3   Athetoid cerebral palsy
Result of damage to cerebellum or basal ganglia responsible for processing neuromuscular signals
Double athetosis (syndrome)
Dyskinetic cerebral palsy
Dystonic cerebral palsy
Vogt disease

G80.4   Ataxic cerebral palsy
Poor muscle tone and coordination

G80.8   Other cerebral palsy
Mixed cerebral palsy syndromes

G80.9   Cerebral palsy, unspecified
Cerebral palsy NOS

Item 6-8   Muscular dystrophies (MD) are a group of rare inherited muscle diseases. Voluntary muscles become progressively weaker. In the late stages of MD, fat and connective tissue replace muscle fibers. In some types of muscular dystrophy, heart muscles, other involuntary muscles, and other organs are affected. **Myopathies** is a general term for neuromuscular diseases in which the muscle fibers dysfunction for any one of many reasons, resulting in muscular weakness.

CHAPTER 6 (G00-G99)

OGCR Section I.C.6.a.

Dominant/nondominant side

Codes from category G81, Hemiplegia and hemiparesis, and subcategories, G83.1, Monoplegia of lower limb, G83.2, Monoplegia of upper limb, and G83.3, Monoplegia, unspecified, identify whether the dominant and nondominant side is affected. Should the affected side be documented, but not specified as dominant or nondominant, and the classification system does not indicate a default, code selection is as follows:

- For ambidextrous patients, the default should be dominant.
- If the left side is affected, the default is nondominant.
- If the right side is affected, the default is dominant.

G81   Hemiplegia and hemiparesis

Note: This category is to be used only when hemiplegia (complete)(incomplete) is reported without further specification, or is stated to be old or longstanding but of unspecified cause. The category is also for use in multiple coding to identify these types of hemiplegia resulting from any cause.

Excludes1   congenital cerebral palsy (G80.-)
hemiplegia and hemiparesis due to sequela of cerebrovascular disease (I69.05-, I69.15-, I69.25-, I69.35-, I69.85-, I69.95-)

Coding Clinic: 2012, Q4, P106

G81.0   Flaccid hemiplegia
Paralysis of half of body with loss of tone of muscles of paralyzed part and absence of tendon reflexes

G81.00   Flaccid hemiplegia affecting unspecified side

G81.01   Flaccid hemiplegia affecting right dominant side

G81.02   Flaccid hemiplegia affecting left dominant side

G81.03   Flaccid hemiplegia affecting right nondominant side

G81.04   Flaccid hemiplegia affecting left nondominant side

G81.1   Spastic hemiplegia
Paralysis of half of body with spasticity of muscles of paralyzed part and increased tendon reflexes

G81.10   Spastic hemiplegia affecting unspecified side

G81.11   Spastic hemiplegia affecting right dominant side

G81.12   Spastic hemiplegia affecting left dominant side

G81.13   Spastic hemiplegia affecting right nondominant side

G81.14   Spastic hemiplegia affecting left nondominant side

G81.9   Hemiplegia, unspecified

G81.90   Hemiplegia, unspecified affecting unspecified side

G81.91   Hemiplegia, unspecified affecting right dominant side

G81.92   Hemiplegia, unspecified affecting left dominant side

G81.93   Hemiplegia, unspecified affecting right nondominant side

G81.94   Hemiplegia, unspecified affecting left nondominant side
Coding Clinic: 2015, Q1, P26

Item 6–9   **Hemiplegia** is complete paralysis of one side of the body—arm, leg, and trunk. **Hemiparesis** is a generalized weakness or incomplete paralysis of one side of the body. If most activities (eating, writing) are performed with the right hand, the right is the dominant side, and the left is the nondominant side. **Quadriplegia,** also called tetraplegia, is the complete paralysis of all four limbs. **Quadriparesis** is the incomplete paralysis of all four limbs. Nerve damage in C1–C4 is associated with lower limb paralysis, and C5–C7 damage is associated with upper limb paralysis. **Diplegia** is the paralysis of the upper limbs. **Monoplegia** is the complete paralysis of one limb.

G82   Paraplegia (paraparesis) and quadriplegia (quadriparesis)

Note: This category is to be used only when the listed conditions are reported without further specification, or are stated to be old or longstanding but of unspecified cause. The category is also for use in multiple coding to identify these conditions resulting from any cause.

Excludes1   congenital cerebral palsy (G80.-)
functional quadriplegia (R53.2)
hysterical paralysis (F44.4)

G82.2   Paraplegia
Paralysis of both lower limbs NOS
Paraparesis (lower) NOS
Paraplegia (lower) NOS

G82.20   Paraplegia, unspecified
Coding Clinic: 2017, Q3, P3

G82.21   Paraplegia, complete

G82.22   Paraplegia, incomplete

G82.5   Quadriplegia
Paralysis of all limbs; AKA tetraplegia

G82.50   Quadriplegia, unspecified

G82.51   Quadriplegia, C1-C4 complete

G82.52   Quadriplegia, C1-C4 incomplete

G82.53   Quadriplegia, C5-C7 complete

G82.54   Quadriplegia, C5-C7 incomplete

G83   Other paralytic syndromes

Note: This category is to be used only when the listed conditions are reported without further specification, or are stated to be old or longstanding but of unspecified cause. The category is also for use in multiple coding to identify these conditions resulting from any cause.

Includes   paralysis (complete) (incomplete), except as in G80-G82

G83.0   Diplegia of upper limbs
Paralysis affecting limbs on both sides; AKA bilateral paralysis
Diplegia (upper)
Paralysis of both upper limbs

G83.1   Monoplegia of lower limb
Paralysis of limb on one side
Paralysis of lower limb

Excludes1   monoplegia of lower limbs due to sequela of cerebrovascular disease (I69.04-, I69.14-, I69.24-, I69.34-, I69.84-, I69.94-)

Coding Clinic: 2012, Q4, P106

G83.10   Monoplegia of lower limb affecting unspecified side

G83.11   Monoplegia of lower limb affecting right dominant side

G83.12   Monoplegia of lower limb affecting left dominant side

G83.13   Monoplegia of lower limb affecting right nondominant side

G83.14   Monoplegia of lower limb affecting left nondominant side

G83.2   Monoplegia of upper limb
Paralysis of upper limb

Excludes1   monoplegia of upper limbs due to sequela of cerebrovascular disease (I69.03-, I69.13-, I69.23-, I69.33-, I69.83-, I69.93-)

Coding Clinic: 2012, Q4, P106

G83.20   Monoplegia of upper limb affecting unspecified side

G83.21   Monoplegia of upper limb affecting right dominant side

G83.22   Monoplegia of upper limb affecting left dominant side

G83.23   Monoplegia of upper limb affecting right nondominant side

G83.24   Monoplegia of upper limb affecting left nondominant side

▶ New   ⟹ Revised   ~~deleted~~ Deleted   Excludes 1   Excludes 2   Includes   Use additional   Code first   Code also   Key words

OGCR Official Guidelines   X Assign placeholder X   ● Use Additional Character(s)   ▸ Manifestation Code   **Coding Clinic**

● **G83.3** Monoplegia, unspecified
Coding Clinic: 2012, Q4, P106

　　G83.30 Monoplegia, unspecified affecting unspecified side

　　G83.31 Monoplegia, unspecified affecting right dominant side

　　G83.32 Monoplegia, unspecified affecting left dominant side

　　G83.33 Monoplegia, unspecified affecting right nondominant side

　　G83.34 Monoplegia, unspecified affecting left nondominant side

G83.4 Cauda equina syndrome
　　Aching pain due to compression of spinal nerve roots
　　Neurogenic bladder due to cauda equina syndrome

　　　Excludes1　cord bladder NOS (G95.89)
　　　　　　　　　neurogenic bladder NOS (N31.9)

G83.5 Locked-in state

● **G83.8** Other specified paralytic syndromes

　　　Excludes1　paralytic syndromes due to current spinal cord injury-code to spinal cord injury (S14, S24, S34)

　　G83.81 Brown-Séquard syndrome

　　G83.82 Anterior cord syndrome

　　G83.83 Posterior cord syndrome

　　G83.84 Todd's paralysis (postepileptic)

　　G83.89 Other specified paralytic syndromes

G83.9 Paralytic syndrome, unspecified

OTHER DISORDERS OF THE NERVOUS SYSTEM (G89-G99)

● **G89** Pain, not elsewhere classified
　　Code also related psychological factors associated with pain (F45.42)

　　　Excludes1　generalized pain NOS (R52)
　　　　　　　　　pain disorders exclusively related to psychological factors (F45.41)
　　　　　　　　　pain NOS (R52)

　　　Excludes2　atypical face pain (G50.1)
　　　　　　　　　headache syndromes (G44.-)
　　　　　　　　　localized pain, unspecified type - code to pain by site, such as:
　　　　　　　　　　abdomen pain (R10.-)
　　　　　　　　　　back pain (M54.9)
　　　　　　　　　　breast pain (N64.4)
　　　　　　　　　　chest pain (R07.1-R07.9)
　　　　　　　　　　ear pain (H92.0-)
　　　　　　　　　　eye pain (H57.1)
　　　　　　　　　　headache (R51)
　　　　　　　　　　joint pain (M25.5-)
　　　　　　　　　　limb pain (M79.6-)
　　　　　　　　　　lumbar region pain (M54.5)
　　　　　　　　　　painful urination (R30.9)
　　　　　　　　　　pelvic and perineal pain (R10.2)
　　　　　　　　　　shoulder pain (M25.51-)
　　　　　　　　　　spine pain (M54.-)
　　　　　　　　　　throat pain (R07.0)
　　　　　　　　　　tongue pain (K14.6)
　　　　　　　　　　tooth pain (K08.8)
　　　　　　　　　renal colic (N23)
　　　　　　　　　migraines (G43.-)
　　　　　　　⇒myalgia (M79.1-)
　　　　　　　　　pain from prosthetic devices, implants, and grafts (T82.84, T83.84, T84.84, T85.84-)
　　　　　　　　　phantom limb syndrome with pain (G54.6)
　　　　　　　　　vulvar vestibulitis (N94.810)
　　　　　　　　　vulvodynia (N94.81-)

G89.0 Central pain syndrome
　　Neurological condition causing intractable pain resulting from damage to CNS
　　Déjérine-Roussy syndrome
　　Myelopathic pain syndrome
　　Thalamic pain syndrome (hyperesthetic)

G89.1 Acute pain, not elsewhere classified

　　G89.11 Acute pain due to trauma

　　G89.12 Acute post-thoracotomy pain
　　　　　Post-thoracotomy pain NOS

　　G89.18 Other acute postprocedural pain
　　　　　Postoperative pain NOS
　　　　　Postprocedural pain NOS

● **G89.2** Chronic pain, not elsewhere classified

　　　Excludes1　causalgia, lower limb (G57.7-)
　　　　　　　　　causalgia, upper limb (G56.4-)
　　　　　　　　　central pain syndrome (G89.0)
　　　　　　　　　chronic pain syndrome (G89.4)
　　　　　　　　　complex regional pain syndrome II, lower limb (G57.7-)
　　　　　　　　　complex regional pain syndrome II, upper limb (G56.4-)
　　　　　　　　　neoplasm related chronic pain (G89.3)
　　　　　　　　　reflex sympathetic dystrophy (G90.5-)

　　G89.21 Chronic pain due to trauma

　　G89.22 Chronic post-thoracotomy pain

　　G89.28 Other chronic postprocedural pain
　　　　　Other chronic postoperative pain

　　G89.29 Other chronic pain

G89.3 Neoplasm related pain (acute) (chronic)
　　Cancer associated pain
　　Pain due to malignancy (primary) (secondary)
　　Tumor associated pain

G89.4 Chronic pain syndrome
　　Chronic pain associated with significant psychosocial dysfunction

● **G90** Disorders of autonomic nervous system

　　　Excludes1　dysfunction of the autonomic nervous system due to alcohol (G31.2)

● **G90.0** Idiopathic peripheral autonomic neuropathy

　　G90.01 Carotid sinus syncope
　　　　　Carotid sinus syndrome

　　G90.09 Other idiopathic peripheral autonomic neuropathy
　　　　　Idiopathic peripheral autonomic neuropathy NOS

G90.1 Familial dysautonomia [Riley-Day]
　　Inherited disorder that affects nerve function

G90.2 Horner's syndrome
　　Due to damage of the sympathetic nervous system
　　Bernard(-Horner) syndrome
　　Cervical sympathetic dystrophy or paralysis

G90.3 Multi-system degeneration of the autonomic nervous system
　　Neurogenic orthostatic hypotension [Shy-Drager]
　　　Excludes1　orthostatic hypotension NOS (I95.1)

G90.4 Autonomic dysreflexia
　　Syndrome resulting from lesions of spinal cord
　　Use additional code to identify the cause, such as:
　　　fecal impaction (K56.41)
　　　pressure ulcer (pressure area) (L89.-)
　　　urinary tract infection (N39.0)

● **G90.5** Complex regional pain syndrome I (CRPS I)
　　Reflex sympathetic dystrophy
　　　Excludes1　causalgia of lower limb (G57.7-)
　　　　　　　　　causalgia of upper limb (G56.4-)
　　　　　　　　　complex regional pain syndrome II of lower limb (G57.7-)
　　　　　　　　　complex regional pain syndrome II of upper limb (G56.4-)

　　G90.50 Complex regional pain syndrome I, unspecified

● **G90.51** Complex regional pain syndrome I of upper limb

　　　G90.511 Complex regional pain syndrome I of right upper limb

　　　G90.512 Complex regional pain syndrome I of left upper limb

G90.513   Complex regional pain syndrome I of upper limb, bilateral

G90.519   Complex regional pain syndrome I of unspecified upper limb

G90.52   Complex regional pain syndrome I of lower limb

G90.521   Complex regional pain syndrome I of right lower limb

G90.522   Complex regional pain syndrome I of left lower limb

G90.523   Complex regional pain syndrome I of lower limb, bilateral

G90.529   Complex regional pain syndrome I of unspecified lower limb

G90.59   Complex regional pain syndrome I of other specified site

G90.8   Other disorders of autonomic nervous system

G90.9   Disorder of the autonomic nervous system, unspecified

G91   Hydrocephalus

Dilatation of cerebral ventricles, accompanied by accumulation of cerebrospinal fluid

Includes   acquired hydrocephalus

Excludes1   Arnold-Chiari syndrome with hydrocephalus (Q07.-)

congenital hydrocephalus (Q03.-)

spina bifida with hydrocephalus (Q05.-)

G91.0   Communicating hydrocephalus

Secondary normal pressure hydrocephalus

G91.1   Obstructive hydrocephalus

G91.2   (Idiopathic) normal pressure hydrocephalus

Normal pressure hydrocephalus NOS

G91.3   Post-traumatic hydrocephalus, unspecified

G91.4   *Hydrocephalus in diseases classified elsewhere*

Code first underlying condition, such as:

congenital syphilis (A50.4-)

neoplasm (C00-D49)

plasminogen deficiency (E88.02)

Excludes1   hydrocephalus due to congenital toxoplasmosis (P37.1)

G91.8   Other hydrocephalus

G91.9   Hydrocephalus, unspecified

G92   Toxic encephalopathy

Disorder or disease of brain caused by chemicals

Toxic encephalitis

Toxic metabolic encephalopathy

Code first if applicable, drug induced (T36-T50) (T51-T65) to identify toxic agent

Coding Clinic: 2017, Q1, P39-40

G93   Other disorders of brain

G93.0   Cerebral cysts

Arachnoid cyst

Porencephalic cyst, acquired

Excludes1   acquired periventricular cysts of newborn (P91.1)

congenital cerebral cysts (Q04.6)

G93.1   Anoxic brain damage, not elsewhere classified

Permanent brain damage by lack of oxygen perfusion through brain tissues.

Excludes1   cerebral anoxia due to anesthesia during labor and delivery (O74.3)

cerebral anoxia due to anesthesia during the puerperium (O89.2)

neonatal anoxia (P84)

G93.2   Benign intracranial hypertension

Excludes1   hypertensive encephalopathy (I67.4)

G93.3   Postviral fatigue syndrome

Benign myalgic encephalomyelitis

Excludes1   chronic fatigue syndrome NOS (R53.82)

G93.4   Other and unspecified encephalopathy

Excludes1   alcoholic encephalopathy (G31.2)

encephalopathy in diseases classified elsewhere (G94)

hypertensive encephalopathy (I67.4)

toxic (metabolic) encephalopathy (G92)

Coding Clinic: 2017, Q2, P9

G93.40   Encephalopathy, unspecified

G93.41   Metabolic encephalopathy

Septic encephalopathy

Coding Clinic: 2017, Q2, P8; 2016, Q3, P42; 2015, Q3, P21

G93.49   Other encephalopathy

Encephalopathy NEC

Coding Clinic: 2018, Q2, P22; 2017, Q2, P9

G93.5   Compression of brain

Arnold-Chiari type 1 compression of brain

Compression of brain (stem)

Herniation of brain (stem)

Excludes1   diffuse traumatic compression of brain (S06.2-)

focal traumatic compression of brain (S06.3-)

G93.6   Cerebral edema

Excludes1   cerebral edema due to birth injury (P11.0)

traumatic cerebral edema (S06.1-)

G93.7   Reye's syndrome   P

Life-threatening neurological condition, usually follows viral illness

Code first (poisoning due to salicylates, if applicable (T39.0-, with sixth character 1-4)

Use additional code for adverse effect due to salicylates, if applicable (T39.0-, with sixth character 5)

G93.8   Other specified disorders of brain

G93.81   Temporal sclerosis

Hippocampal sclerosis

Mesial temporal sclerosis

G93.82   Brain death

G93.89   Other specified disorders of brain

Postradiation encephalopathy

Coding Clinic: 2016, Q4, P7

G93.9   Disorder of brain, unspecified

G94   *Other disorders of brain in diseases classified elsewhere*

Code first underlying disease

Excludes1   encephalopathy in congenital syphilis (A50.49)

encephalopathy in influenza (J09.X9, J10.81, J11.81)

encephalopathy in syphilis (A52.19)

hydrocephalus in diseases classified elsewhere (G91.4)

Coding Clinic: 2018, Q2, P22; 2017, Q2, P8

G95   Other and unspecified diseases of spinal cord

Excludes2   myelitis (G04.-)

G95.0   Syringomyelia and syringobulbia

G95.1   Vascular myelopathies

Excludes2   intraspinal phlebitis and thrombophlebitis, except non-pyogenic (G08)

G95.11   Acute infarction of spinal cord (embolic) (nonembolic)

Anoxia of spinal cord

Arterial thrombosis of spinal cord

G95.19   Other vascular myelopathies

Edema of spinal cord

Hematomyelia

Nonpyogenic intraspinal phlebitis and thrombophlebitis

Subacute necrotic myelopathy

▶ New   ⟹ Revised   ~~deleted~~ Deleted   Excludes 1   Excludes 2   Includes   Use additional   Code first   Code also   Key words

OGCR Official Guidelines   X Assign placeholder X   ● Use Additional Character(s)   ▷ Manifestation Code   Coding Clinic

● **G95.2**   **Other and unspecified cord compression**
     G95.20   Unspecified cord compression
     G95.29   Other cord compression

● **G95.8**   **Other specified diseases of spinal cord**
     Excludes1   neurogenic bladder NOS (N31.9)
                  neurogenic bladder due to cauda equina syndrome (G83.4)
                  neuromuscular dysfunction of bladder without spinal cord lesion (N31.-)

     G95.81   Conus medullaris syndrome
            Damage to gray matter and/or nerve roots in lower end of spinal cord

     G95.89   Other specified diseases of spinal cord
            Cord bladder NOS
            Drug-induced myelopathy
            Radiation-induced myelopathy
            Excludes1   myelopathy NOS (G95.9)

   G95.9   **Disease of spinal cord, unspecified**
          Myelopathy NOS

● **G96**   **Other disorders of central nervous system**
     G96.0   **Cerebrospinal fluid leak**
         Excludes1   cerebrospinal fluid leak from spinal puncture (G97.0)
         Coding Clinic: 2018, Q2, P13

     G96.1   **Disorders of meninges, not elsewhere classified**
         G96.11   Dural tear
            Excludes1   accidental puncture or laceration of dura during a procedure (G97.41)

         G96.12   Meningeal adhesions (cerebral) (spinal)
         G96.19   Other disorders of meninges, not elsewhere classified

     G96.8   **Other specified disorders of central nervous system**
     G96.9   **Disorder of central nervous system, unspecified**

● **G97**   **Intraoperative and postprocedural complications and disorders of nervous system, not elsewhere classified**
     Excludes2   intraoperative and postprocedural cerebrovascular infarction (I97.81-, I97.82-)
     Coding Clinic: 2016, Q4, P9

     G97.0   **Cerebrospinal fluid leak from spinal puncture**
     G97.1   **Other reaction to spinal and lumbar puncture**
          Headache due to lumbar puncture
     G97.2   **Intracranial hypotension following ventricular shunting**

●   **G97.3**   **Intraoperative hemorrhage and hematoma of a nervous system organ or structure complicating a procedure**
         Excludes1   intraoperative hemorrhage and hematoma of a nervous system organ or structure due to accidental puncture and laceration during a procedure (G97.4-)

     G97.31   Intraoperative hemorrhage and hematoma of a nervous system organ or structure complicating a nervous system procedure
     G97.32   Intraoperative hemorrhage and hematoma of a nervous system organ or structure complicating other procedure

●   **G97.4**   **Accidental puncture and laceration of a nervous system organ or structure during a procedure**
     G97.41   Accidental puncture or laceration of dura during a procedure
            Incidental (inadvertent) durotomy
     G97.48   Accidental puncture and laceration of other nervous system organ or structure during a nervous system procedure
     G97.49   Accidental puncture and laceration of other nervous system organ or structure during other procedure

● **G97.5**   **Postprocedural hemorrhage of a nervous system organ or structure following a procedure**
     G97.51   Postprocedural hemorrhage of a nervous system organ or structure following a nervous system procedure
     G97.52   Postprocedural hemorrhage of a nervous system organ or structure following other procedure

● **G97.6**   **Postprocedural hematoma and seroma of a nervous system organ or structure following a procedure**
     G97.61   Postprocedural hematoma of a nervous system organ or structure following a nervous system procedure
     G97.62   Postprocedural hematoma of a nervous system organ or structure following other procedure
     G97.63   Postprocedural seroma of a nervous system organ or structure following a nervous system procedure
     G97.64   Postprocedural seroma of a nervous system organ or structure following other procedure

● **G97.8**   **Other intraoperative and postprocedural complications and disorders of nervous system**
     Use additional code to further specify disorder
     G97.81   Other intraoperative complications of nervous system
     G97.82   Other postprocedural complications and disorders of nervous system

● **G98**   **Other disorders of nervous system not elsewhere classified**
     Includes   nervous system disorder NOS
     G98.0   **Neurogenic arthritis, not elsewhere classified**
         Nonsyphilitic neurogenic arthropathy NEC
         Nonsyphilitic neurogenic spondylopathy NEC
         Excludes1   spondylopathy (in):
                  syringomyelia and syringobulbia (G95.0)
                tabes dorsalis (A52.11)

     G98.8   **Other disorders of nervous system**
         Nervous system disorder NOS

● **G99**   **Other disorders of nervous system in diseases classified elsewhere**
▸ **G99.0**   *Autonomic neuropathy in diseases classified elsewhere*
     Code first underlying disease, such as:
         amyloidosis (E85.-)
         gout (M1A.-, M10.-)
         hyperthyroidism (E05.-)
     Excludes1   diabetic autonomic neuropathy (E08-E13 with .43)

▸ **G99.2**   *Myelopathy in diseases classified elsewhere*
     Code first underlying disease, such as:
         neoplasm (C00-D49)
     Excludes1   myelopathy in:
                 intervertebral disease (M50.0-, M51.0-)
                 spondylosis (M47.0-, M47.1-)

▸ **G99.8**   *Other specified disorders of nervous system in diseases classified elsewhere*
     Code first underlying disorder, such as:
         amyloidosis (E85.-)
         avitaminosis (E56.9)
     Excludes1   nervous system involvement in:
                 cysticercosis (B69.0)
                 rubella (B06.0-)
                 syphilis (A52.1-)

CHAPTER 6 (G00-G99)

CHAPTER 7

DISEASES OF THE EYE AND ADNEXA (H00-H59)

OGCR Chapter-Specific Coding Guidelines

7. Chapter 7: Diseases of the Eye and Adnexa (H00-H59)

a. Glaucoma

1) Assigning Glaucoma Codes

Assign as many codes from category H40, Glaucoma, as needed to identify the type of glaucoma, the affected eye, and the glaucoma stage.

2) Bilateral glaucoma with same type and stage

When a patient has bilateral glaucoma and both eyes are documented as being the same type and stage, and there is a code for bilateral glaucoma, report only the code for the type of glaucoma, bilateral, with the seventh character for the stage.

When a patient has bilateral glaucoma and both eyes are documented as being the same type and stage, and the classification does not provide a code for bilateral glaucoma (i.e., subcategories H40.10, H40.11, and H40.20) report only one code for the type of glaucoma with the appropriate seventh character for the stage.

3) Bilateral glaucoma stage with different types or stages

When a patient has bilateral glaucoma and each eye is documented as having a different type or stage, and the classification distinguishes laterality, assign the appropriate code for each eye rather than the code for bilateral glaucoma.

When a patient has bilateral glaucoma and each eye is documented as having a different type, and the classification does not distinguish laterality (i.e., subcategories H40.10, H40.11 and H40.20), assign one code for each type of glaucoma with the appropriate seventh character for the stage.

When a patient has bilateral glaucoma and each eye is documented as having the same type, but different stage, and the classification does not distinguish laterality (i.e., subcategories H40.10, H40.11, and H40.20), assign a code for the type of glaucoma for each eye with the seventh character for the specific glaucoma stage documented for each eye.

4) Patient admitted with glaucoma and stage evolves during the admission

If a patient is admitted with glaucoma and the stage progresses during the admission, assign the code for highest stage documented.

5) Indeterminate stage glaucoma

Assignment of the seventh character "4" for "indeterminate stage" should be based on the clinical documentation. The seventh character "4" is used for glaucomas whose stage cannot be clinically determined. This seventh character should not be confused with the seventh character "0", unspecified, which should be assigned when there is no documentation regarding the stage of the glaucoma.

b. Blindness

If "blindness" or "low vision" of both eyes is documented but the visual impairment category is not documented, assign code H54.3, Unqualified visual loss, both eyes. If "blindness" or "low vision" in one eye is documented but the visual impairment category is not documented, assign a code from H54.6-, Unqualified visual loss, one eye. If "blindness" or "visual loss" is documented without any information about whether one or both eyes are affected, assign code H54.7, Unspecified visual loss.

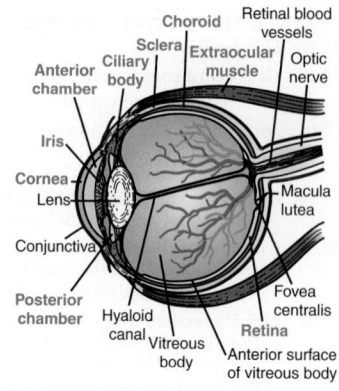

Figure 7-1 Eye and ocular adnexa. (From Buck CJ: Step-by-Step Medical Coding, ed 2016, St. Louis, Elsevier, 2016)

★ **(See Plate 87 on page 63.)**

CHAPTER 7

DISEASES OF THE EYE AND ADNEXA (H00-H59)

Note: Use an external cause code following the code for the eye condition, if applicable, to identify the cause of the eye condition

Excludes2 certain conditions originating in the perinatal period (P04-P96)

certain infectious and parasitic diseases (A00-B99)

complications of pregnancy, childbirth and the puerperium (O00-O9A)

congenital malformations, deformations, and chromosomal abnormalities (Q00-Q99)

diabetes mellitus related eye conditions (E09.3-, E10.3-, E11.3-, E13.3-)

endocrine, nutritional and metabolic diseases (E00-E88)

injury (trauma) of eye and orbit (S05.-)

injury, poisoning and certain other consequences of external causes (S00-T88)

neoplasms (C00-D49)

symptoms, signs and abnormal clinical and laboratory findings, not elsewhere classified (R00-R94)

syphilis related eye disorders (A50.01, A50.3-, A51.43, A52.71)

This chapter contains the following blocks:

H00-H05	Disorders of eyelid, lacrimal system and orbit
H10-H11	Disorders of conjunctiva
H15-H22	Disorders of sclera, cornea, iris and ciliary body
H25-H28	Disorders of lens
H30-H36	Disorders of choroid and retina
H40-H42	Glaucoma
H43-H44	Disorders of vitreous body and globe
H46-H47	Disorders of optic nerve and visual pathways
H49-H52	Disorders of ocular muscles, binocular movement, accommodation and refraction
H53-H54	Visual disturbances and blindness
H55-H57	Other disorders of eye and adnexa
H59	Intraoperative and postprocedural complications and disorders of eye and adnexa, not elsewhere classified

▶ New ⟹ Revised ~~deleted~~ Deleted Excludes 1 Excludes 2 Includes Use additional Code first Code also Key words

OGCR Official Guidelines X Assign placeholder X ● Use Additional Character(s) ▶ Manifestation Code **Coding Clinic**

DISORDERS OF EYELID, LACRIMAL SYSTEM AND ORBIT (H00-H05)

Excludes2   open wound of eyelid (S01.1-)
superficial injury of eyelid (S00.1-, S00.2-)

● **H00**   **Hordeolum and chalazion**
Hordeolum: inflammatory staphylococcal infection of sebaceous glands of eyelids; AKA stye. Chalazion: eyelid mass

● **H00.0**   **Hordeolum (externum) (internum) of eyelid**
Bacterial infection (staphylococcus) of the sebaceous gland of the eyelid (stye)

● **H00.01**   **Hordeolum externum**
Hordeolum NOS
Stye

H00.011   Hordeolum externum right upper eyelid

H00.012   Hordeolum externum right lower eyelid

H00.013   Hordeolum externum right eye, unspecified eyelid

H00.014   Hordeolum externum left upper eyelid

H00.015   Hordeolum externum left lower eyelid

H00.016   Hordeolum externum left eye, unspecified eyelid

H00.019   Hordeolum externum unspecified eye, unspecified eyelid

● **H00.02**   **Hordeolum internum**
Infection of meibomian gland

H00.021   Hordeolum internum right upper eyelid

H00.022   Hordeolum internum right lower eyelid

H00.023   Hordeolum internum right eye, unspecified eyelid

H00.024   Hordeolum internum left upper eyelid

H00.025   Hordeolum internum left lower eyelid

H00.026   Hordeolum internum left eye, unspecified eyelid

H00.029   Hordeolum internum unspecified eye, unspecified eyelid

● **H00.03**   **Abscess of eyelid**
Furuncle of eyelid

H00.031   Abscess of right upper eyelid

H00.032   Abscess of right lower eyelid

H00.033   Abscess of eyelid right eye, unspecified eyelid

H00.034   Abscess of left upper eyelid

H00.035   Abscess of left lower eyelid

H00.036   Abscess of eyelid left eye, unspecified eyelid

H00.039   Abscess of eyelid unspecified eye, unspecified eyelid

● **H00.1**   **Chalazion**
Often caused by accumulation of meibomian gland secretions resulting from a blockage of duct.
Meibomian (gland) cyst

Excludes2   infected meibomian gland (H00.02-)

H00.11   Chalazion right upper eyelid

H00.12   Chalazion right lower eyelid

H00.13   Chalazion right eye, unspecified eyelid

H00.14   Chalazion left upper eyelid

H00.15   Chalazion left lower eyelid

H00.16   Chalazion left eye, unspecified eyelid

H00.19   Chalazion unspecified eye, unspecified eyelid

● **H01**   **Other inflammation of eyelid**

● **H01.0**   **Blepharitis**
Inflammation of eyelids

Excludes1   blepharoconjunctivitis (H10.5-)

● **H01.00**   **Unspecified blepharitis**

H01.001   Unspecified blepharitis right upper eyelid

H01.002   Unspecified blepharitis right lower eyelid

H01.003   Unspecified blepharitis right eye, unspecified eyelid

H01.004   Unspecified blepharitis left upper eyelid

H01.005   Unspecified blepharitis left lower eyelid

H01.006   Unspecified blepharitis left eye, unspecified eyelid

H01.009   Unspecified blepharitis unspecified eye, unspecified eyelid

▶ H01.00A   Unspecified blepharitis right eye, upper and lower eyelids

▶ H01.00B   Unspecified blepharitis left eye, upper and lower eyelids

● **H01.01**   **Ulcerative blepharitis**

H01.011   Ulcerative blepharitis right upper eyelid

H01.012   Ulcerative blepharitis right lower eyelid

H01.013   Ulcerative blepharitis right eye, unspecified eyelid

H01.014   Ulcerative blepharitis left upper eyelid

H01.015   Ulcerative blepharitis left lower eyelid

H01.016   Ulcerative blepharitis left eye, unspecified eyelid

H01.019   Ulcerative blepharitis unspecified eye, unspecified eyelid

▶ H01.01A   Ulcerative blepharitis right eye, upper and lower eyelids

▶ H01.01B   Ulcerative blepharitis left eye, upper and lower eyelids

● **H01.02**   **Squamous blepharitis**

H01.021   Squamous blepharitis right upper eyelid

H01.022   Squamous blepharitis right lower eyelid

H01.023   Squamous blepharitis right eye, unspecified eyelid

H01.024   Squamous blepharitis left upper eyelid

H01.025   Squamous blepharitis left lower eyelid

H01.026   Squamous blepharitis left eye, unspecified eyelid

H01.029   Squamous blepharitis unspecified eye, unspecified eyelid

▶ H01.02A   Squamous blepharitis right eye, upper and lower eyelids

▶ H01.02B   Squamous blepharitis left eye, upper and lower eyelids

CHAPTER 7 (H00–H59)

- **H01.1** Noninfectious dermatoses of eyelid
  - **H01.11** Allergic dermatitis of eyelid
    Contact dermatitis of eyelid
    - H01.111 Allergic dermatitis of right upper eyelid
    - H01.112 Allergic dermatitis of right lower eyelid
    - H01.113 Allergic dermatitis of right eye, unspecified eyelid
    - H01.114 Allergic dermatitis of left upper eyelid
    - H01.115 Allergic dermatitis of left lower eyelid
    - H01.116 Allergic dermatitis of left eye, unspecified eyelid
    - H01.119 Allergic dermatitis of unspecified eye, unspecified eyelid
  - **H01.12** Discoid lupus erythematosus of eyelid
    - H01.121 Discoid lupus erythematosus of right upper eyelid
    - H01.122 Discoid lupus erythematosus of right lower eyelid
    - H01.123 Discoid lupus erythematosus of right eye, unspecified eyelid
    - H01.124 Discoid lupus erythematosus of left upper eyelid
    - H01.125 Discoid lupus erythematosus of left lower eyelid
    - H01.126 Discoid lupus erythematosus of left eye, unspecified eyelid
    - H01.129 Discoid lupus erythematosus of unspecified eye, unspecified eyelid
  - **H01.13** Eczematous dermatitis of eyelid
    - H01.131 Eczematous dermatitis of right upper eyelid
    - H01.132 Eczematous dermatitis of right lower eyelid
    - H01.133 Eczematous dermatitis of right eye, unspecified eyelid
    - H01.134 Eczematous dermatitis of left upper eyelid
    - H01.135 Eczematous dermatitis of left lower eyelid
    - H01.136 Eczematous dermatitis of left eye, unspecified eyelid
    - H01.139 Eczematous dermatitis of unspecified eye, unspecified eyelid
  - **H01.14** Xeroderma of eyelid
    Abnormally dry
    - H01.141 Xeroderma of right upper eyelid
    - H01.142 Xeroderma of right lower eyelid
    - H01.143 Xeroderma of right eye, unspecified eyelid
    - H01.144 Xeroderma of left upper eyelid
    - H01.145 Xeroderma of left lower eyelid
    - H01.146 Xeroderma of left eye, unspecified eyelid
    - H01.149 Xeroderma of unspecified eye, unspecified eyelid
- **H01.8** Other specified inflammations of eyelid
- **H01.9** Unspecified inflammation of eyelid
  Inflammation of eyelid NOS

Figure 7-2 Right lower eyelid entropion. Note the inward rotation of the tarsal plate about the horizontal axis and the resultant contact between the mucocutaneous junction and ocular surface. (From Glynn M, Drake WM, Hutchison R: Hutchison's Clinical Methods: An Integrated Approach to Clinical Practice, Edinburgh, Saunders/Elsevier, 2012)

- **H02** Other disorders of eyelid
  Turning inward (inversion) of eyelid margin and ingrowing eyelashes
  Excludes1 congenital malformations of eyelid (Q10.0-Q10.3)
  - **H02.0** Entropion and trichiasis of eyelid
    - **H02.00** Unspecified entropion of eyelid
      - H02.001 Unspecified entropion of right upper eyelid
      - H02.002 Unspecified entropion of right lower eyelid
      - H02.003 Unspecified entropion of right eye, unspecified eyelid
      - H02.004 Unspecified entropion of left upper eyelid
      - H02.005 Unspecified entropion of left lower eyelid
      - H02.006 Unspecified entropion of left eye, unspecified eyelid
      - H02.009 Unspecified entropion of unspecified eye, unspecified eyelid
    - **H02.01** Cicatricial entropion of eyelid
      Scar
      - H02.011 Cicatricial entropion of right upper eyelid
      - H02.012 Cicatricial entropion of right lower eyelid
      - H02.013 Cicatricial entropion of right eye, unspecified eyelid
      - H02.014 Cicatricial entropion of left upper eyelid
      - H02.015 Cicatricial entropion of left lower eyelid
      - H02.016 Cicatricial entropion of left eye, unspecified eyelid
      - H02.019 Cicatricial entropion of unspecified eye, unspecified eyelid
    - **H02.02** Mechanical entropion of eyelid
      Turning inward (inversion) of eyelid margin due to lack of support
      - H02.021 Mechanical entropion of right upper eyelid
      - H02.022 Mechanical entropion of right lower eyelid
      - H02.023 Mechanical entropion of right eye, unspecified eyelid
      - H02.024 Mechanical entropion of left upper eyelid
      - H02.025 Mechanical entropion of left lower eyelid
      - H02.026 Mechanical entropion of left eye, unspecified eyelid
      - H02.029 Mechanical entropion of unspecified eye, unspecified eyelid

● **H02.03**   Senile entropion of eyelid
*Turning inward (inversion) of eyelid margin due
to aging*

    H02.031   Senile entropion of right upper eyelid
                 A

    H02.032   Senile entropion of right lower eyelid
                 A

    H02.033   Senile entropion of right eye,
unspecified eyelid   A

    H02.034   Senile entropion of left upper eyelid A

    H02.035   Senile entropion of left lower eyelid A

    H02.036   Senile entropion of left eye,
unspecified eyelid   A

    H02.039   Senile entropion of unspecified eye,
unspecified eyelid   A

● **H02.04**   Spastic entropion of eyelid
*Turning inward (inversion) of eyelid margin caused
by spasm of muscle*

    H02.041   Spastic entropion of right upper
eyelid

    H02.042   Spastic entropion of right lower
eyelid

    H02.043   Spastic entropion of right eye,
unspecified eyelid

    H02.044   Spastic entropion of left upper eyelid

    H02.045   Spastic entropion of left lower eyelid

    H02.046   Spastic entropion of left eye,
unspecified eyelid

    H02.049   Spastic entropion of unspecified eye,
unspecified eyelid

● **H02.05**   Trichiasis without entropion
Ingrowing hairs of eyelashes

    H02.051   Trichiasis without entropion right
upper eyelid

    H02.052   Trichiasis without entropion right
lower eyelid

    H02.053   Trichiasis without entropion right
eye, unspecified eyelid

    H02.054   Trichiasis without entropion left
upper eyelid

    H02.055   Trichiasis without entropion left
lower eyelid

    H02.056   Trichiasis without entropion left eye,
unspecified eyelid

    H02.059   Trichiasis without entropion
unspecified eye, unspecified eyelid

● **H02.1**   Ectropion of eyelid
Eversion (pulling away) of eyelid

  ● **H02.10**   Unspecified ectropion of eyelid

    H02.101   Unspecified ectropion of right upper
eyelid

    H02.102   Unspecified ectropion of right lower
eyelid

    H02.103   Unspecified ectropion of right eye,
unspecified eyelid

    H02.104   Unspecified ectropion of left upper
eyelid

    H02.105   Unspecified ectropion of left lower
eyelid

    H02.106   Unspecified ectropion of left eye,
unspecified eyelid

    H02.109   Unspecified ectropion of unspecified
eye, unspecified eyelid

● **H02.11**   Cicatricial ectropion of eyelid
*Pulling of eyelid down and away from eye due to
scar or tightening*

    H02.111   Cicatricial ectropion of right upper
eyelid

    H02.112   Cicatricial ectropion of right lower
eyelid

    H02.113   Cicatricial ectropion of right eye,
unspecified eyelid

    H02.114   Cicatricial ectropion of left upper
eyelid

    H02.115   Cicatricial ectropion of left lower
eyelid

    H02.116   Cicatricial ectropion of left eye,
unspecified eyelid

    H02.119   Cicatricial ectropion of unspecified
eye, unspecified eyelid

● **H02.12**   Mechanical ectropion of eyelid
*Eversion (pulling away) of eyelid due to lack of
support*

    H02.121   Mechanical ectropion of right upper
eyelid

    H02.122   Mechanical ectropion of right lower
eyelid

    H02.123   Mechanical ectropion of right eye,
unspecified eyelid

    H02.124   Mechanical ectropion of left upper
eyelid

    H02.125   Mechanical ectropion of left lower
eyelid

    H02.126   Mechanical ectropion of left eye,
unspecified eyelid

    H02.129   Mechanical ectropion of unspecified
eye, unspecified eyelid

● **H02.13**   Senile ectropion of eyelid
Eversion (pulling away) of eyelid due to age

    H02.131   Senile ectropion of right upper eyelid
                 A

    H02.132   Senile ectropion of right lower eyelid
                 A

    H02.133   Senile ectropion of right eye,
unspecified eyelid   A

    H02.134   Senile ectropion of left upper eyelid A

    H02.135   Senile ectropion of left lower eyelid A

    H02.136   Senile ectropion of left eye,
unspecified eyelid   A

    H02.139   Senile ectropion of unspecified eye,
unspecified eyelid   A

● **H02.14**   Spastic ectropion of eyelid
*Eversion (pulling away) of eyelid due to tonic
muscle spasm*

    H02.141   Spastic ectropion of right upper
eyelid

    H02.142   Spastic ectropion of right lower
eyelid

    H02.143   Spastic ectropion of right eye,
unspecified eyelid

    H02.144   Spastic ectropion of left upper eyelid

    H02.145   Spastic ectropion of left lower eyelid

    H02.146   Spastic ectropion of left eye,
unspecified eyelid

    H02.149   Spastic ectropion of unspecified eye,
unspecified eyelid

CHAPTER 7 (H00-H59)

- H02.15 Paralytic ectropion of eyelid
  - H02.151 Paralytic ectropion of right upper eyelid
  - H02.152 Paralytic ectropion of right lower eyelid
  - H02.153 Paralytic ectropion of right eye, unspecified eyelid
  - H02.154 Paralytic ectropion of left upper eyelid
  - H02.155 Paralytic ectropion of left lower eyelid
  - H02.156 Paralytic ectropion of left eye, unspecified eyelid
  - H02.159 Paralytic ectropion of unspecified eye, unspecified eyelid
- H02.2 **Lagophthalmos**
  - *Condition in which eye cannot completely close*
  - H02.20 **Unspecified** lagophthalmos
    - H02.201 Unspecified lagophthalmos right upper eyelid
    - H02.202 Unspecified lagophthalmos right lower eyelid
    - H02.203 Unspecified lagophthalmos right eye, unspecified eyelid
    - H02.204 Unspecified lagophthalmos left upper eyelid
    - H02.205 Unspecified lagophthalmos left lower eyelid
    - H02.206 Unspecified lagophthalmos left eye, unspecified eyelid
    - H02.209 Unspecified lagophthalmos unspecified eye, unspecified eyelid
    - H02.20A Unspecified lagophthalmos right eye, upper and lower eyelids
    - H02.20B Unspecified lagophthalmos left eye, upper and lower eyelids
    - H02.20C Unspecified lagophthalmos, bilateral, upper and lower eyelids
  - H02.21 **Cicatricial lagophthalmos**
    - *Upper or lower eyelid does not close due to scar or tightening*
    - H02.211 Cicatricial lagophthalmos right upper eyelid
    - H02.212 Cicatricial lagophthalmos right lower eyelid
    - H02.213 Cicatricial lagophthalmos right eye, unspecified eyelid
    - H02.214 Cicatricial lagophthalmos left upper eyelid
    - H02.215 Cicatricial lagophthalmos left lower eyelid
    - H02.216 Cicatricial lagophthalmos left eye, unspecified eyelid
    - H02.219 Cicatricial lagophthalmos unspecified eye, unspecified eyelid
    - H02.21A Cicatricial lagophthalmos right eye, upper and lower eyelids
    - H02.21B Cicatricial lagophthalmos left eye, upper and lower eyelids
    - H02.21C Cicatricial lagophthalmos, bilateral, upper and lower eyelids
  - H02.22 **Mechanical lagophthalmos**
    - *Inability to close lids due to structural disorder*
    - H02.221 Mechanical lagophthalmos right upper eyelid
    - H02.222 Mechanical lagophthalmos right lower eyelid
    - H02.223 Mechanical lagophthalmos right eye, unspecified eyelid

- H02.224 Mechanical lagophthalmos left upper eyelid
- H02.225 Mechanical lagophthalmos left lower eyelid
- H02.226 Mechanical lagophthalmos left eye, unspecified eyelid
- H02.229 Mechanical lagophthalmos unspecified eye, unspecified eyelid
- H02.22A Mechanical lagophthalmos right eye, upper and lower eyelids [new]
- H02.22B Mechanical lagophthalmos left eye, upper and lower eyelids
- H02.22C Mechanical lagophthalmos, bilateral, upper and lower eyelids
- H02.23 **Paralytic lagophthalmos**
  - *Eyelids do not close due to paralysis*
  - H02.231 Paralytic lagophthalmos right upper eyelid
  - H02.232 Paralytic lagophthalmos right lower eyelid
  - H02.233 Paralytic lagophthalmos right eye, unspecified eyelid
  - H02.234 Paralytic lagophthalmos left upper eyelid
  - H02.235 Paralytic lagophthalmos left lower eyelid
  - H02.236 Paralytic lagophthalmos left eye, unspecified eyelid
  - H02.239 Paralytic lagophthalmos unspecified eye, unspecified eyelid
  - H02.23A Paralytic lagophthalmos right eye, upper and lower eyelids
  - H02.23B Paralytic lagophthalmos left eye, upper and lower eyelids
  - H02.23C Paralytic lagophthalmos, bilateral, upper and lower eyelids

★ **(See Plate 81, middle, on page 65.)**

- H02.3 **Blepharochalasis**
  - *Relaxation of skin of eyelid, due to atrophy of intercellular tissue*
  - Pseudoptosis
  - H02.30 Blepharochalasis unspecified eye, unspecified eyelid
  - H02.31 Blepharochalasis right upper eyelid
  - H02.32 Blepharochalasis right lower eyelid
  - H02.33 Blepharochalasis right eye, unspecified eyelid
  - H02.34 Blepharochalasis left upper eyelid
  - H02.35 Blepharochalasis left lower eyelid
  - H02.36 Blepharochalasis left eye, unspecified eyelid
- H02.4 **Ptosis of eyelid**
  - *Falling forward, drooping, sagging of eyelid*
  - H02.40 **Unspecified** ptosis of eyelid
    - H02.401 Unspecified ptosis of right eyelid
    - H02.402 Unspecified ptosis of left eyelid
    - H02.403 Unspecified ptosis of bilateral eyelids
    - H02.409 Unspecified ptosis of unspecified eyelid

Figure 7-3 Ptosis of eyelid. (From Kanski JJ: Clinical Diagnosis in Ophthalmology, London, Elsevier Mosby, 2006)

Item 7-1 Ptosis of eyelid is drooping of the upper eyelid over the pupil when the eyes are fully opened resulting from nerve or muscle damage, which may require surgical correction.

▶ New ⇒ Revised ~~deleted~~ Deleted Excludes 1 Excludes 2 Includes Use additional Code first Code also Key words
OGCR Official Guidelines X Assign placeholder X ● Use Additional Character(s) ▷ Manifestation Code **Coding Clinic**

● **H02.41 Mechanical ptosis of eyelid**
   H02.411 Mechanical ptosis of right eyelid
   H02.412 Mechanical ptosis of left eyelid
   H02.413 Mechanical ptosis of bilateral eyelids
   H02.419 Mechanical ptosis of unspecified eyelid

● **H02.42 Myogenic ptosis of eyelid**
   H02.421 Myogenic ptosis of right eyelid
   H02.422 Myogenic ptosis of left eyelid
   H02.423 Myogenic ptosis of bilateral eyelids
   H02.429 Myogenic ptosis of unspecified eyelid

● **H02.43 Paralytic ptosis of eyelid**
   Neurogenic ptosis of eyelid
   H02.431 Paralytic ptosis of right eyelid
   H02.432 Paralytic ptosis of left eyelid
   H02.433 Paralytic ptosis of bilateral eyelids
   H02.439 Paralytic ptosis unspecified eyelid

● **H02.5 Other disorders affecting eyelid function**
   Excludes2 blepharospasm (G24.5)
                  organic tic (G25.69)
                  psychogenic tic (F95.-)

● **H02.51 Abnormal innervation syndrome**
   H02.511 Abnormal innervation syndrome right upper eyelid
   H02.512 Abnormal innervation syndrome right lower eyelid
   H02.513 Abnormal innervation syndrome right eye, unspecified eyelid
   H02.514 Abnormal innervation syndrome left upper eyelid
   H02.515 Abnormal innervation syndrome left lower eyelid
   H02.516 Abnormal innervation syndrome left eye, unspecified eyelid
   H02.519 Abnormal innervation syndrome unspecified eye, unspecified eyelid

● **H02.52 Blepharophimosis**
   Drooping of eyelid with reduced lid size
   Ankyloblepharon
   H02.521 Blepharophimosis right upper eyelid
   H02.522 Blepharophimosis right lower eyelid
   H02.523 Blepharophimosis right eye, unspecified eyelid
   H02.524 Blepharophimosis left upper eyelid
   H02.525 Blepharophimosis left lower eyelid
   H02.526 Blepharophimosis left eye, unspecified eyelid
   H02.529 Blepharophimosis unspecified eye, unspecified lid

● **H02.53 Eyelid retraction**
   Eyelid lag
   H02.531 Eyelid retraction right upper eyelid
   H02.532 Eyelid retraction right lower eyelid
   H02.533 Eyelid retraction right eye, unspecified eyelid
   H02.534 Eyelid retraction left upper eyelid
   H02.535 Eyelid retraction left lower eyelid
   H02.536 Eyelid retraction left eye, unspecified eyelid
   H02.539 Eyelid retraction unspecified eye, unspecified lid

   H02.59 Other disorders affecting eyelid function
   Deficient blink reflex
   Sensory disorders

● **H02.6 Xanthelasma of eyelid**
   Yellow-to-orange patches or pimples clustered together on eyelid
   H02.60 Xanthelasma of unspecified eye, unspecified eyelid
   H02.61 Xanthelasma of right upper eyelid
   H02.62 Xanthelasma of right lower eyelid
   H02.63 Xanthelasma of right eye, unspecified eyelid
   H02.64 Xanthelasma of left upper eyelid
   H02.65 Xanthelasma of left lower eyelid
   H02.66 Xanthelasma of left eye, unspecified eyelid

● **H02.7 Other and unspecified degenerative disorders of eyelid and periocular area**
   H02.70 Unspecified degenerative disorders of eyelid and periocular area

● **H02.71 Chloasma of eyelid and periocular area**
   Dyspigmentation of eyelid
   Hyperpigmentation of eyelid
   H02.711 Chloasma of right upper eyelid and periocular area
   H02.712 Chloasma of right lower eyelid and periocular area
   H02.713 Chloasma of right eye, unspecified eyelid and periocular area
   H02.714 Chloasma of left upper eyelid and periocular area
   H02.715 Chloasma of left lower eyelid and periocular area
   H02.716 Chloasma of left eye, unspecified eyelid and periocular area
   H02.719 Chloasma of unspecified eye, unspecified eyelid and periocular area

● **H02.72 Madarosis of eyelid and periocular area**
   Loss of eyelashes and/or eyebrows
   Hypotrichosis of eyelid
   H02.721 Madarosis of right upper eyelid and periocular area
   H02.722 Madarosis of right lower eyelid and periocular area
   H02.723 Madarosis of right eye, unspecified eyelid and periocular area
   H02.724 Madarosis of left upper eyelid and periocular area
   H02.725 Madarosis of left lower eyelid and periocular area
   H02.726 Madarosis of left eye, unspecified eyelid and periocular area
   H02.729 Madarosis of unspecified eye, unspecified eyelid and periocular area

● **H02.73 Vitiligo of eyelid and periocular area**
   Skin pigmentation disease characterized by white patches
   Hypopigmentation of eyelid
   H02.731 Vitiligo of right upper eyelid and periocular area
   H02.732 Vitiligo of right lower eyelid and periocular area
   H02.733 Vitiligo of right eye, unspecified eyelid and periocular area
   H02.734 Vitiligo of left upper eyelid and periocular area
   H02.735 Vitiligo of left lower eyelid and periocular area
   H02.736 Vitiligo of left eye, unspecified eyelid and periocular area
   H02.739 Vitiligo of unspecified eye, unspecified eyelid and periocular area

   H02.79 Other degenerative disorders of eyelid and periocular area

CHAPTER 7 (H00-H59)

● **H02.8   Other specified disorders of eyelid**

● **H02.81   Retained foreign body in eyelid**

Use additional code to identify the type of retained foreign body (Z18.-)

> **Excludes1**   laceration of eyelid with foreign body (S01.12-)
> retained intraocular foreign body (H44.6-, H44.7-)
> superficial foreign body of eyelid and periocular area (S00.25-)

H02.811   Retained foreign body in right upper eyelid

H02.812   Retained foreign body in right lower eyelid

H02.813   Retained foreign body in right eye, unspecified eyelid

H02.814   Retained foreign body in left upper eyelid

H02.815   Retained foreign body in left lower eyelid

H02.816   Retained foreign body in left eye, unspecified eyelid

H02.819   Retained foreign body in unspecified eye, unspecified eyelid

● **H02.82   Cysts of eyelid**

Sebaceous cyst of eyelid

H02.821   Cysts of right upper eyelid

H02.822   Cysts of right lower eyelid

H02.823   Cysts of right eye, unspecified eyelid

H02.824   Cysts of left upper eyelid

H02.825   Cysts of left lower eyelid

H02.826   Cysts of left eye, unspecified eyelid

H02.829   Cysts of unspecified eye, unspecified eyelid

● **H02.83   Dermatochalasis of eyelid**

Skin is inelastic and hangs loosely in folds

H02.831   Dermatochalasis of right upper eyelid

H02.832   Dermatochalasis of right lower eyelid

H02.833   Dermatochalasis of right eye, unspecified eyelid

H02.834   Dermatochalasis of left upper eyelid

H02.835   Dermatochalasis of left lower eyelid

H02.836   Dermatochalasis of left eye, unspecified eyelid

H02.839   Dermatochalasis of unspecified eye, unspecified eyelid

● **H02.84   Edema of eyelid**

Hyperemia of eyelid

H02.841   Edema of right upper eyelid

H02.842   Edema of right lower eyelid

H02.843   Edema of right eye, unspecified eyelid

H02.844   Edema of left upper eyelid

H02.845   Edema of left lower eyelid

H02.846   Edema of left eye, unspecified eyelid

H02.849   Edema of unspecified eye, unspecified eyelid

● **H02.85   Elephantiasis of eyelid**

Massive secondary lymphedema with hypertrophy of skin and subcutaneous tissues (pachyderma)

H02.851   Elephantiasis of right upper eyelid

H02.852   Elephantiasis of right lower eyelid

H02.853   Elephantiasis of right eye, unspecified eyelid

H02.854   Elephantiasis of left upper eyelid

H02.855   Elephantiasis of left lower eyelid

H02.856   Elephantiasis of left eye, unspecified eyelid

H02.859   Elephantiasis of unspecified eye, unspecified eyelid

● **H02.86   Hypertrichosis of eyelid**

Excessive growth of hair

H02.861   Hypertrichosis of right upper eyelid

H02.862   Hypertrichosis of right lower eyelid

H02.863   Hypertrichosis of right eye, unspecified eyelid

H02.864   Hypertrichosis of left upper eyelid

H02.865   Hypertrichosis of left lower eyelid

H02.866   Hypertrichosis of left eye, unspecified eyelid

H02.869   Hypertrichosis of unspecified eye, unspecified eyelid

● **H02.87   Vascular anomalies of eyelid**

H02.871   Vascular anomalies of right upper eyelid

H02.872   Vascular anomalies of right lower eyelid

H02.873   Vascular anomalies of right eye, unspecified eyelid

H02.874   Vascular anomalies of left upper eyelid

H02.875   Vascular anomalies of left lower eyelid

H02.876   Vascular anomalies of left eye, unspecified eyelid

H02.879   Vascular anomalies of unspecified eye, unspecified eyelid

▶● **H02.88   Meibomian gland dysfunction of eyelid**

▶ H02.881   Meibomian gland dysfunction right upper eyelid

▶ H02.882   Meibomian gland dysfunction right lower eyelid

▶ H02.883   Meibomian gland dysfunction of right eye, unspecified eyelid

▶ H02.884   Meibomian gland dysfunction left upper eyelid

▶ H02.885   Meibomian gland dysfunction left lower eyelid

▶ H02.886   Meibomian gland dysfunction of left eye, unspecified eyelid

▶ H02.889   Meibomian gland dysfunction of unspecified eye, unspecified eyelid

▶ H02.88A   Meibomian gland dysfunction right eye, upper and lower eyelids

▶ H02.88B   Meibomian gland dysfunction left eye, upper and lower eyelids

H02.89   Other specified disorders of eyelid

Hemorrhage of eyelid

H02.9   Unspecified disorder of eyelid

Disorder of eyelid NOS

● **H04   Disorders of lacrimal system**

> **Excludes1**   congenital malformations of lacrimal system (Q10.4-Q10.6)

● **H04.0   Dacryoadenitis**

Inflammation of lacrimal gland

● **H04.00   Unspecified dacryoadenitis**

H04.001   Unspecified dacryoadenitis, right lacrimal gland

H04.002   Unspecified dacryoadenitis, left lacrimal gland

H04.003   Unspecified dacryoadenitis, bilateral lacrimal glands

H04.009   Unspecified dacryoadenitis, unspecified lacrimal gland

▶ New   ⇒ Revised   ~~deleted~~ Deleted   Excludes 1   Excludes 2   Includes   Use additional   Code first   Code also   Key words

OGCR Official Guidelines   X Assign placeholder X   ● Use Additional Character(s)   ▌ Manifestation Code   **Coding Clinic**

● H04.01   Acute dacryoadenitis
    H04.011   Acute dacryoadenitis, right lacrimal gland
    H04.012   Acute dacryoadenitis, left lacrimal gland
    H04.013   Acute dacryoadenitis, bilateral lacrimal glands
    H04.019   Acute dacryoadenitis, unspecified lacrimal gland

★ **(See Plate 82 on page 67.)**

● H04.02   Chronic dacryoadenitis
    H04.021   Chronic dacryoadenitis, right lacrimal gland
    H04.022   Chronic dacryoadenitis, left lacrimal gland
    H04.023   Chronic dacryoadenitis, bilateral lacrimal gland
    H04.029   Chronic dacryoadenitis, unspecified lacrimal gland

● H04.03   Chronic enlargement of lacrimal gland
    H04.031   Chronic enlargement of right lacrimal gland
    H04.032   Chronic enlargement of left lacrimal gland
    H04.033   Chronic enlargement of bilateral lacrimal glands
    H04.039   Chronic enlargement of unspecified lacrimal gland

● H04.1   Other disorders of lacrimal gland
  ● H04.11   Dacryops
     Watery eye or distention of lacrimal duct due to fluid
    H04.111   Dacryops of right lacrimal gland
    H04.112   Dacryops of left lacrimal gland
    H04.113   Dacryops of bilateral lacrimal glands
    H04.119   Dacryops of unspecified lacrimal gland

  ● H04.12   Dry eye syndrome
     Tear film insufficiency, NOS
    H04.121   Dry eye syndrome of right lacrimal gland
    H04.122   Dry eye syndrome of left lacrimal gland
    H04.123   Dry eye syndrome of bilateral lacrimal glands
    H04.129   Dry eye syndrome of unspecified lacrimal gland

  ● H04.13   Lacrimal cyst
     Lacrimal cystic degeneration
    H04.131   Lacrimal cyst right lacrimal gland
    H04.132   Lacrimal cyst left lacrimal gland
    H04.133   Lacrimal cyst bilateral lacrimal glands
    H04.139   Lacrimal cyst unspecified lacrimal gland

● H04.14   Primary lacrimal gland atrophy
    H04.141   Primary lacrimal gland atrophy, right lacrimal gland
    H04.142   Primary lacrimal gland atrophy, left lacrimal gland
    H04.143   Primary lacrimal gland atrophy, bilateral lacrimal glands
    H04.149   Primary lacrimal gland atrophy, unspecified lacrimal gland

● H04.15   Secondary lacrimal gland atrophy
    H04.151   Secondary lacrimal gland atrophy, right lacrimal gland
    H04.152   Secondary lacrimal gland atrophy, left lacrimal gland
    H04.153   Secondary lacrimal gland atrophy, bilateral lacrimal glands
    H04.159   Secondary lacrimal gland atrophy, unspecified lacrimal gland

● H04.16   Lacrimal gland dislocation
    H04.161   Lacrimal gland dislocation, right lacrimal gland
    H04.162   Lacrimal gland dislocation, left lacrimal gland
    H04.163   Lacrimal gland dislocation, bilateral lacrimal glands
    H04.169   Lacrimal gland dislocation, unspecified lacrimal gland

H04.19   Other specified disorders of lacrimal gland

● H04.2   Epiphora
    Overflow of tears due to stricture of lacrimal passages; AKA lacrimation
  ● H04.20   Unspecified epiphora
    ➡ H04.201   Unspecified epiphora, right side
    ➡ H04.202   Unspecified epiphora, left side
    ➡ H04.203   Unspecified epiphora, bilateral
    ➡ H04.209   Unspecified epiphora, unspecified side

  ● H04.21   Epiphora due to excess lacrimation
    H04.211   Epiphora due to excess lacrimation, right lacrimal gland
    H04.212   Epiphora due to excess lacrimation, left lacrimal gland
    H04.213   Epiphora due to excess lacrimation, bilateral lacrimal glands
    H04.219   Epiphora due to excess lacrimation, unspecified lacrimal gland

  ● H04.22   Epiphora due to insufficient drainage
    ➡ H04.221   Epiphora due to insufficient drainage, right side
    ➡ H04.222   Epiphora due to insufficient drainage, left side
    ➡ H04.223   Epiphora due to insufficient drainage, bilateral
    ➡ H04.229   Epiphora due to insufficient drainage, unspecified side

● H04.3   Acute and unspecified inflammation of lacrimal passages
    Excludes 1   neonatal dacryocystitis (P39.1)
  ● H04.30   Unspecified dacryocystitis
    H04.301   Unspecified dacryocystitis of right lacrimal passage
    H04.302   Unspecified dacryocystitis of left lacrimal passage
    H04.303   Unspecified dacryocystitis of bilateral lacrimal passages
    H04.309   Unspecified dacryocystitis of unspecified lacrimal passage

Figure 7-4   Lacrimal apparatus. (From Buck CJ: Step-by-Step Medical Coding, 2016, St. Louis, Elsevier, 2016)

CHAPTER 7 (HØØ-H59)

CHAPTER 7 (H00-H59)

● H04.31   **Phlegmonous** dacryocystitis
       Cellulitis of lacrimal sac
     H04.311   Phlegmonous dacryocystitis of **right** lacrimal passage
     H04.312   Phlegmonous dacryocystitis of **left** lacrimal passage
     H04.313   Phlegmonous dacryocystitis of **bilateral** lacrimal passages
     H04.319   Phlegmonous dacryocystitis of **unspecified** lacrimal passage

● H04.32   **Acute** dacryocystitis
       Acute dacryopericystitis
     H04.321   Acute dacryocystitis of **right** lacrimal passage
     H04.322   Acute dacryocystitis of **left** lacrimal passage
     H04.323   Acute dacryocystitis of **bilateral** lacrimal passages
     H04.329   Acute dacryocystitis of **unspecified** lacrimal passage

● H04.33   Acute lacrimal **canaliculitis**
     H04.331   Acute lacrimal canaliculitis of **right** lacrimal passage
     H04.332   Acute lacrimal canaliculitis of **left** lacrimal passage
     H04.333   Acute lacrimal canaliculitis of **bilateral** lacrimal passages
     H04.339   Acute lacrimal canaliculitis of **unspecified** lacrimal passage

● H04.4   **Chronic inflammation** of lacrimal passages
   ● H04.41   Chronic **dacryocystitis**
       Inflammation of lacrimal sac
     H04.411   Chronic dacryocystitis of **right** lacrimal passage
     H04.412   Chronic dacryocystitis of **left** lacrimal passage
     H04.413   Chronic dacryocystitis of **bilateral** lacrimal passages
     H04.419   Chronic dacryocystitis of **unspecified** lacrimal passage

   ● H04.42   Chronic lacrimal **canaliculitis**
       Inflammation of lacrimal ducts
     H04.421   Chronic lacrimal canaliculitis of **right** lacrimal passage
     H04.422   Chronic lacrimal canaliculitis of **left** lacrimal passage
     H04.423   Chronic lacrimal canaliculitis of **bilateral** lacrimal passages
     H04.429   Chronic lacrimal canaliculitis of **unspecified** lacrimal passage

   ● H04.43   Chronic lacrimal **mucocele**
       Accumulation of mucous secretion
     H04.431   Chronic lacrimal mucocele of **right** lacrimal passage
     H04.432   Chronic lacrimal mucocele of **left** lacrimal passage
     H04.433   Chronic lacrimal mucocele of **bilateral** lacrimal passages
     H04.439   Chronic lacrimal mucocele of **unspecified** lacrimal passage

● H04.5   **Stenosis and insufficiency** of lacrimal passages
   ● H04.51   **Dacryolith**
       Concretion in lacrimal sac/duct; AKA lacrimal calculus
     H04.511   Dacryolith of **right** lacrimal passage
     H04.512   Dacryolith of **left** lacrimal passage
     H04.513   Dacryolith of **bilateral** lacrimal passages
     H04.519   Dacryolith of **unspecified** lacrimal passage

● H04.52   **Eversion** of lacrimal **punctum**
       Turning out of lacrimal drainage opening
     H04.521   Eversion of **right** lacrimal punctum
     H04.522   Eversion of **left** lacrimal punctum
     H04.523   Eversion of **bilateral** lacrimal punctum
     H04.529   Eversion of **unspecified** lacrimal punctum

● H04.53   **Neonatal obstruction** of nasolacrimal duct
     Excludes1   congenital stenosis and stricture of lacrimal duct (Q10.5)
     H04.531   Neonatal obstruction of **right** nasolacrimal duct   N
     H04.532   Neonatal obstruction of **left** nasolacrimal duct   N
     H04.533   Neonatal obstruction of **bilateral** nasolacrimal duct   N
     H04.539   Neonatal obstruction of **unspecified** nasolacrimal duct   N

● H04.54   Stenosis of lacrimal **canaliculi**
     H04.541   Stenosis of **right** lacrimal canaliculi
     H04.542   Stenosis of **left** lacrimal canaliculi
     H04.543   Stenosis of **bilateral** lacrimal canaliculi
     H04.549   Stenosis of **unspecified** lacrimal canaliculi

● H04.55   Acquired stenosis of nasolacrimal duct
     H04.551   Acquired stenosis of **right** nasolacrimal duct
     H04.552   Acquired stenosis of **left** nasolacrimal duct
     H04.553   Acquired stenosis of **bilateral** nasolacrimal duct
     H04.559   Acquired stenosis of **unspecified** nasolacrimal duct

● H04.56   Stenosis of lacrimal **punctum**
     H04.561   Stenosis of **right** lacrimal punctum
     H04.562   Stenosis of **left** lacrimal punctum
     H04.563   Stenosis of **bilateral** lacrimal punctum
     H04.569   Stenosis of **unspecified** lacrimal punctum

● H04.57   Stenosis of lacrimal sac
     H04.571   Stenosis of **right** lacrimal sac
     H04.572   Stenosis of **left** lacrimal sac
     H04.573   Stenosis of **bilateral** lacrimal sac
     H04.579   Stenosis of **unspecified** lacrimal sac

● H04.6   Other changes of lacrimal passages
   ● H04.61   Lacrimal **fistula**
     H04.611   Lacrimal fistula **right** lacrimal passage
     H04.612   Lacrimal fistula **left** lacrimal passage
     H04.613   Lacrimal fistula **bilateral** lacrimal passages
     H04.619   Lacrimal fistula **unspecified** lacrimal passage
     H04.69   Other changes of lacrimal passages

● H04.8   Other disorders of lacrimal system
   ● H04.81   Granuloma of lacrimal passages
       Inflammatory response due to infectious or noninfectious agents
     H04.811   Granuloma of **right** lacrimal passage
     H04.812   Granuloma of **left** lacrimal passage
     H04.813   Granuloma of **bilateral** lacrimal passages
     H04.819   Granuloma of **unspecified** lacrimal passage
     H04.89   Other disorders of lacrimal system
   H04.9   Disorder of lacrimal system, **unspecified**

▶ New   ⇒ Revised   ~~deleted~~ Deleted   Excludes 1   Excludes 2   Includes   Use additional   Code first   Code also   Key words
OGCR Official Guidelines   X Assign placeholder X   ● Use Additional Character(s)   ▷ Manifestation Code   **Coding Clinic**

● **H05**   **Disorders of orbit**
     Excludes1   congenital malformation of orbit (Q10.7)
   ● **H05.0**   **Acute inflammation of orbit**
     H05.00   **Unspecified acute inflammation of orbit**
     ● **H05.01**   **Cellulitis of orbit**
        Infection of soft tissue of orbit
        Abscess of orbit
        H05.011   **Cellulitis of right orbit**
        H05.012   **Cellulitis of left orbit**
        H05.013   **Cellulitis of bilateral orbits**
        H05.019   **Cellulitis of unspecified orbit**
     ● **H05.02**   **Osteomyelitis of orbit**
        Infection of boney orbit of eye
        H05.021   **Osteomyelitis of right orbit**
        H05.022   **Osteomyelitis of left orbit**
        H05.023   **Osteomyelitis of bilateral orbits**
        H05.029   **Osteomyelitis of unspecified orbit**
     ● **H05.03**   **Periostitis of orbit**
        Inflammation of periosteum (membrane covering bone surface)
        H05.031   **Periostitis of right orbit**
        H05.032   **Periostitis of left orbit**
        H05.033   **Periostitis of bilateral orbits**
        H05.039   **Periostitis of unspecified orbit**
     ● **H05.04**   **Tenonitis of orbit**
        Inflammation of tenon capsule (space enclosing fascia of Tenon between eyeball and fat of orbit)
        H05.041   **Tenonitis of right orbit**
        H05.042   **Tenonitis of left orbit**
        H05.043   **Tenonitis of bilateral orbits**
        H05.049   **Tenonitis of unspecified orbit**
   ● **H05.1**   **Chronic inflammatory disorders of orbit**
     H05.10   **Unspecified chronic inflammatory disorders of orbit**
     ● **H05.11**   **Granuloma of orbit**
        Pseudotumor (inflammatory) of orbit
        H05.111   **Granuloma of right orbit**
        H05.112   **Granuloma of left orbit**
        H05.113   **Granuloma of bilateral orbits**
        H05.119   **Granuloma of unspecified orbit**
     ● **H05.12**   **Orbital myositis**
        Inflammation of extraocular muscles of orbit
        H05.121   **Orbital myositis, right orbit**
        H05.122   **Orbital myositis, left orbit**
        H05.123   **Orbital myositis, bilateral**
        H05.129   **Orbital myositis, unspecified orbit**
   ● **H05.2**   **Exophthalmic conditions**
        Bulging eyes
     H05.20   **Unspecified exophthalmos**
     ● **H05.21**   **Displacement (lateral) of globe**
        H05.211   **Displacement (lateral) of globe, right eye**
        H05.212   **Displacement (lateral) of globe, left eye**
        H05.213   **Displacement (lateral) of globe, bilateral**
        H05.219   **Displacement (lateral) of globe, unspecified eye**
     ● **H05.22**   **Edema of orbit**
        Orbital congestion
        H05.221   **Edema of right orbit**
        H05.222   **Edema of left orbit**
        H05.223   **Edema of bilateral orbit**
        H05.229   **Edema of unspecified orbit**

Figure 7-5   Exophthalmos. (From Black JM, Hokanson JH: Medical-Surgical Nursing: Clinical Management for Positive Outcomes, St. Louis, Saunders Elsevier, 2009)

     ● **H05.23**   **Hemorrhage of orbit**
        H05.231   **Hemorrhage of right orbit**
        H05.232   **Hemorrhage of left orbit**
        H05.233   **Hemorrhage of bilateral orbit**
        H05.239   **Hemorrhage of unspecified orbit**
     ● **H05.24**   **Constant exophthalmos**
        Constant bulging eyes, often symptom of Graves disease
        H05.241   **Constant exophthalmos, right eye**
        H05.242   **Constant exophthalmos, left eye**
        H05.243   **Constant exophthalmos, bilateral**
        H05.249   **Constant exophthalmos, unspecified eye**
     ● **H05.25**   **Intermittent exophthalmos**
        Intermittent bulging eye occurring with bending forward or sharp turning of head
        H05.251   **Intermittent exophthalmos, right eye**
        H05.252   **Intermittent exophthalmos, left eye**
        H05.253   **Intermittent exophthalmos, bilateral**
        H05.259   **Intermittent exophthalmos, unspecified eye**
     ● **H05.26**   **Pulsating exophthalmos**
        Bulging eyes with pulsation and bruit, often due to aneurysm pushing eye forward
        H05.261   **Pulsating exophthalmos, right eye**
        H05.262   **Pulsating exophthalmos, left eye**
        H05.263   **Pulsating exophthalmos, bilateral**
        H05.269   **Pulsating exophthalmos, unspecified eye**
   ● **H05.3**   **Deformity of orbit**
     Excludes1   congenital deformity of orbit (Q10.7)
                    hypertelorism (Q75.2)
     H05.30   **Unspecified deformity of orbit**
     ● **H05.31**   **Atrophy of orbit**
        H05.311   **Atrophy of right orbit**
        H05.312   **Atrophy of left orbit**
        H05.313   **Atrophy of bilateral orbit**
        H05.319   **Atrophy of unspecified orbit**
     ● **H05.32**   **Deformity of orbit due to bone disease**
        Code also associated bone disease
        H05.321   **Deformity of right orbit due to bone disease**
        H05.322   **Deformity of left orbit due to bone disease**
        H05.323   **Deformity of bilateral orbits due to bone disease**
        H05.329   **Deformity of unspecified orbit due to bone disease**

CHAPTER 7 (H00-H59)

● H05.33   Deformity of orbit due to trauma or surgery
     H05.331   Deformity of right orbit due to trauma or surgery
     H05.332   Deformity of left orbit due to trauma or surgery
     H05.333   Deformity of bilateral orbits due to trauma or surgery
     H05.339   Deformity of unspecified orbit due to trauma or surgery

● H05.34   Enlargement of orbit
     H05.341   Enlargement of right orbit
     H05.342   Enlargement of left orbit
     H05.343   Enlargement of bilateral orbits
     H05.349   Enlargement of unspecified orbit

● H05.35   Exostosis of orbit
     H05.351   Exostosis of right orbit
     H05.352   Exostosis of left orbit
     H05.353   Exostosis of bilateral orbits
     H05.359   Exostosis of unspecified orbit

● H05.4   Enophthalmos
     Recessed eyeball into orbit

● H05.40   Unspecified enophthalmos
     H05.401   Unspecified enophthalmos, right eye
     H05.402   Unspecified enophthalmos, left eye
     H05.403   Unspecified enophthalmos, bilateral
     H05.409   Unspecified enophthalmos, unspecified eye

● H05.41   Enophthalmos due to atrophy of orbital tissue
     H05.411   Enophthalmos due to atrophy of orbital tissue, right eye
     H05.412   Enophthalmos due to atrophy of orbital tissue, left eye
     H05.413   Enophthalmos due to atrophy of orbital tissue, bilateral
     H05.419   Enophthalmos due to atrophy of orbital tissue, unspecified eye

● H05.42   Enophthalmos due to trauma or surgery
     H05.421   Enophthalmos due to trauma or surgery, right eye
     H05.422   Enophthalmos due to trauma or surgery, left eye
     H05.423   Enophthalmos due to trauma or surgery, bilateral
     H05.429   Enophthalmos due to trauma or surgery, unspecified eye

● H05.5   Retained (old) foreign body following penetrating wound of orbit
     Retrobulbar foreign body
     Use additional code to identify the type of retained foreign body (Z18.-)

     Excludes1   current penetrating wound of orbit (S05.4-)

     Excludes2   retained foreign body of eyelid (H02.81-) retained intraocular foreign body (H44.6-, H44.7-)

     H05.50   Retained (old) foreign body following penetrating wound of unspecified orbit
     H05.51   Retained (old) foreign body following penetrating wound of right orbit
     H05.52   Retained (old) foreign body following penetrating wound of left orbit
     H05.53   Retained (old) foreign body following penetrating wound of bilateral orbits

● H05.8   Other disorders of orbit
   ● H05.81   Cyst of orbit
     Encephalocele of orbit
     H05.811   Cyst of right orbit
     H05.812   Cyst of left orbit
     H05.813   Cyst of bilateral orbits
     H05.819   Cyst of unspecified orbit

   ● H05.82   Myopathy of extraocular muscles
     Weakness of muscles of eye
     H05.821   Myopathy of extraocular muscles, right orbit
     H05.822   Myopathy of extraocular muscles, left orbit
     H05.823   Myopathy of extraocular muscles, bilateral
     H05.829   Myopathy of extraocular muscles, unspecified orbit

   H05.89   Other disorders of orbit
   H05.9   Unspecified disorder of orbit

DISORDERS OF CONJUNCTIVA (H10-H11)

★ **(See Plate 81, upper, on page 66.)**

● H10   Conjunctivitis
     Inflammation of membrane of the inside of the eyelid or on surface of eye (conjunctiva)

     Excludes1   keratoconjunctivitis (H16.2-)

● H10.0   Mucopurulent conjunctivitis
   ● H10.01   Acute follicular conjunctivitis
     H10.011   Acute follicular conjunctivitis, right eye
     H10.012   Acute follicular conjunctivitis, left eye
     H10.013   Acute follicular conjunctivitis, bilateral
     H10.019   Acute follicular conjunctivitis, unspecified eye

   ● H10.02   Other mucopurulent conjunctivitis
     H10.021   Other mucopurulent conjunctivitis, right eye
     H10.022   Other mucopurulent conjunctivitis, left eye
     H10.023   Other mucopurulent conjunctivitis, bilateral
     H10.029   Other mucopurulent conjunctivitis, unspecified eye

● H10.1   Acute atopic conjunctivitis
     Acute papillary conjunctivitis
     H10.10   Acute atopic conjunctivitis, unspecified eye
     H10.11   Acute atopic conjunctivitis, right eye
     H10.12   Acute atopic conjunctivitis, left eye
     H10.13   Acute atopic conjunctivitis, bilateral

● H10.2   Other acute conjunctivitis
   ● H10.21   Acute toxic conjunctivitis
     Acute chemical conjunctivitis
     Code first (T51-T65) to identify chemical and intent

     Excludes1   burn and corrosion of eye and adnexa (T26.-)

     H10.211   Acute toxic conjunctivitis, right eye
     H10.212   Acute toxic conjunctivitis, left eye
     H10.213   Acute toxic conjunctivitis, bilateral
     H10.219   Acute toxic conjunctivitis, unspecified eye

▶ New   ⮕ Revised   ~~deleted~~ Deleted   Excludes 1   Excludes 2   Includes   Use additional   Code first   Code also   Key words
OGCR Official Guidelines   X Assign placeholder X   ● Use Additional Character(s)   ▶ Manifestation Code   **Coding Clinic**

● H10.22   Pseudomembranous conjunctivitis

    H10.221   Pseudomembranous conjunctivitis, right eye

    H10.222   Pseudomembranous conjunctivitis, left eye

    H10.223   Pseudomembranous conjunctivitis, bilateral

    H10.229   Pseudomembranous conjunctivitis, unspecified eye

● H10.23   Serous conjunctivitis, except viral

    Excludes 1   viral conjunctivitis (B30.-)

    H10.231   Serous conjunctivitis, except viral, right eye

    H10.232   Serous conjunctivitis, except viral, left eye

    H10.233   Serous conjunctivitis, except viral, bilateral

    H10.239   Serous conjunctivitis, except viral, unspecified eye

● H10.3   Unspecified acute conjunctivitis

    Excludes 1   ophthalmia neonatorum NOS (P39.1)

    H10.30   Unspecified acute conjunctivitis, unspecified eye

    H10.31   Unspecified acute conjunctivitis, right eye

    H10.32   Unspecified acute conjunctivitis, left eye

    H10.33   Unspecified acute conjunctivitis, bilateral

● H10.4   Chronic conjunctivitis

● H10.40   Unspecified chronic conjunctivitis

    H10.401   Unspecified chronic conjunctivitis, right eye

    H10.402   Unspecified chronic conjunctivitis, left eye

    H10.403   Unspecified chronic conjunctivitis, bilateral

    H10.409   Unspecified chronic conjunctivitis, unspecified eye

● H10.41   Chronic giant papillary conjunctivitis

    Inflammation of membrane of the inside of the eyelid or on surface of eye often associated with contact lens wear

    H10.411   Chronic giant papillary conjunctivitis, right eye

    H10.412   Chronic giant papillary conjunctivitis, left eye

    H10.413   Chronic giant papillary conjunctivitis, bilateral

    H10.419   Chronic giant papillary conjunctivitis, unspecified eye

● H10.42   Simple chronic conjunctivitis

    H10.421   Simple chronic conjunctivitis, right eye

    H10.422   Simple chronic conjunctivitis, left eye

    H10.423   Simple chronic conjunctivitis, bilateral

    H10.429   Simple chronic conjunctivitis, unspecified eye

● H10.43   Chronic follicular conjunctivitis

    Inflammation of membrane of the inside of the eyelid or on surface of eye due to topical medications or infection

    H10.431   Chronic follicular conjunctivitis, right eye

    H10.432   Chronic follicular conjunctivitis, left eye

    H10.433   Chronic follicular conjunctivitis, bilateral

    H10.439   Chronic follicular conjunctivitis, unspecified eye

H10.44   Vernal conjunctivitis

    Affecting children, especially boys in which there are flattened papules with thick, gelatinous exudate on conjunctivae on inside of upper lid

    Excludes 1   vernal keratoconjunctivitis with limbar and corneal involvement (H16.26-)

H10.45   Other chronic allergic conjunctivitis

● H10.5   Blepharoconjunctivitis

    Inflammation of eyelids and conjunctiva

● H10.50   Unspecified blepharoconjunctivitis

    H10.501   Unspecified blepharoconjunctivitis, right eye

    H10.502   Unspecified blepharoconjunctivitis, left eye

    H10.503   Unspecified blepharoconjunctivitis, bilateral

    H10.509   Unspecified blepharoconjunctivitis, unspecified eye

● H10.51   Ligneous conjunctivitis

    ▶Code also underlying condition if known, such as:

      ▶plasminogen deficiency (E88.02)

    H10.511   Ligneous conjunctivitis, right eye

    H10.512   Ligneous conjunctivitis, left eye

    H10.513   Ligneous conjunctivitis, bilateral

    H10.519   Ligneous conjunctivitis, unspecified eye

● H10.52   Angular blepharoconjunctivitis

    H10.521   Angular blepharoconjunctivitis, right eye

    H10.522   Angular blepharoconjunctivitis, left eye

    H10.523   Angular blepharoconjunctivitis, bilateral

    H10.529   Angular blepharoconjunctivitis, unspecified eye

● H10.53   Contact blepharoconjunctivitis

    H10.531   Contact blepharoconjunctivitis, right eye

    H10.532   Contact blepharoconjunctivitis, left eye

    H10.533   Contact blepharoconjunctivitis, bilateral

    H10.539   Contact blepharoconjunctivitis, unspecified eye

● H10.8   Other conjunctivitis

● H10.81   Pingueculitis

    Inflammation of a yellow, raised thickening on the white of the eye associated with chronic dry eyes

    Excludes 1   pinguecula (H11.15-)

    H10.811   Pingueculitis, right eye

    H10.812   Pingueculitis, left eye

    H10.813   Pingueculitis, bilateral

    H10.819   Pingueculitis, unspecified eye

▶ H10.82   Rosacea conjunctivitis

    ▶ *Code first underlying rosacea dermatitis (L71.-)*

    ▶ H10.821   Rosacea conjunctivitis, right eye

    ▶ H10.822   Rosacea conjunctivitis, left eye

    ▶ H10.823   Rosacea conjunctivitis, bilateral

    ▶ H10.829   Rosacea conjunctivitis, unspecified eye

    H10.89   Other conjunctivitis

H10.9   Unspecified conjunctivitis

CHAPTER 7 (H00-H59)

CHAPTER 7 (H00-H59)

● **H11 Other disorders of conjunctiva**
    Excludes1 keratoconjunctivitis (H16.2-)
  ● **H11.0 Pterygium of eye**
      Excludes1 pseudopterygium (H11.81-)
    ● **H11.00 Unspecified pterygium of eye**
        H11.001 Unspecified pterygium of right eye
        H11.002 Unspecified pterygium of left eye
        H11.003 Unspecified pterygium of eye, bilateral
        H11.009 Unspecified pterygium of unspecified eye
    ● **H11.01 Amyloid pterygium**
        H11.011 Amyloid pterygium of right eye
        H11.012 Amyloid pterygium of left eye
        H11.013 Amyloid pterygium of eye, bilateral
        H11.019 Amyloid pterygium of unspecified eye
    ● **H11.02 Central pterygium of eye**
        H11.021 Central pterygium of right eye
        H11.022 Central pterygium of left eye
        H11.023 Central pterygium of eye, bilateral
        H11.029 Central pterygium of unspecified eye
    ● **H11.03 Double pterygium of eye**
        H11.031 Double pterygium of right eye
        H11.032 Double pterygium of left eye
        H11.033 Double pterygium of eye, bilateral
        H11.039 Double pterygium of unspecified eye
    ● **H11.04 Peripheral pterygium of eye, stationary**
        H11.041 Peripheral pterygium, stationary, right eye
        H11.042 Peripheral pterygium, stationary, left eye
        H11.043 Peripheral pterygium, stationary, bilateral
        H11.049 Peripheral pterygium, stationary, unspecified eye
    ● **H11.05 Peripheral pterygium of eye, progressive**
        H11.051 Peripheral pterygium, progressive, right eye
        H11.052 Peripheral pterygium, progressive, left eye
        H11.053 Peripheral pterygium, progressive, bilateral
        H11.059 Peripheral pterygium, progressive, unspecified eye
    ● **H11.06 Recurrent pterygium of eye**
        H11.061 Recurrent pterygium of right eye
        H11.062 Recurrent pterygium of left eye
        H11.063 Recurrent pterygium of eye, bilateral
        H11.069 Recurrent pterygium of unspecified eye

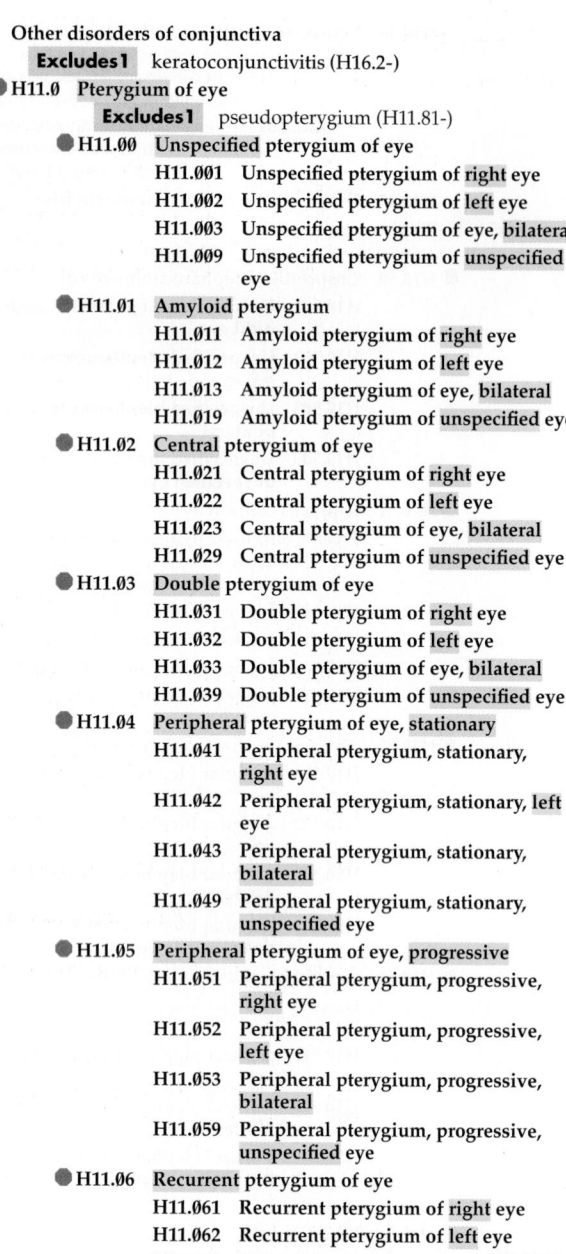

Figure 7-6 Double pterygium. Note both nasal and temporal pterygia in a 57-year-old farmer. (From Brightbill FS, McDonnell PJ: Corneal Surgery: Theory, Technique and Tissue, S.l., Mosby Elsevier, 2009)

Item 7-2 Pterygium is Greek for batlike. The condition is characterized by a membrane that extends from the limbus to the center of the cornea and resembles a wing.

● **H11.1 Conjunctival degenerations and deposits**
    Excludes2 pseudopterygium (H11.81)
    H11.10 Unspecified conjunctival degenerations
  ● **H11.11 Conjunctival deposits**
      H11.111 Conjunctival deposits, right eye
      H11.112 Conjunctival deposits, left eye
      H11.113 Conjunctival deposits, bilateral
      H11.119 Conjunctival deposits, unspecified eye
  ● **H11.12 Conjunctival concretions**
      White to yellow nodules within or beneath conjunctiva
      H11.121 Conjunctival concretions, right eye
      H11.122 Conjunctival concretions, left eye
      H11.123 Conjunctival concretions, bilateral
      H11.129 Conjunctival concretions, unspecified eye
  ● **H11.13 Conjunctival pigmentations**
      Conjunctival argyrosis [argyria]
      H11.131 Conjunctival pigmentations, right eye
      H11.132 Conjunctival pigmentations, left eye
      H11.133 Conjunctival pigmentations, bilateral
      H11.139 Conjunctival pigmentations, unspecified eye
  ● **H11.14 Conjunctival xerosis, unspecified**
      Excludes1 xerosis of conjunctiva due to vitamin A deficiency (E50.0, E50.1)
      H11.141 Conjunctival xerosis, unspecified, right eye
      H11.142 Conjunctival xerosis, unspecified, left eye
      H11.143 Conjunctival xerosis, unspecified, bilateral
      H11.149 Conjunctival xerosis, unspecified, unspecified eye
  ● **H11.15 Pinguecula**
      Yellowish spot near sclerocorneal junction, usually on nasal side; associated with aging
      Excludes1 pingueculitis (H10.81-)
      H11.151 Pinguecula, right eye
      H11.152 Pinguecula, left eye
      H11.153 Pinguecula, bilateral
      H11.159 Pinguecula, unspecified eye
● **H11.2 Conjunctival scars**
  ● **H11.21 Conjunctival adhesions and strands (localized)**
      H11.211 Conjunctival adhesions and strands (localized), right eye
      H11.212 Conjunctival adhesions and strands (localized), left eye
      H11.213 Conjunctival adhesions and strands (localized), bilateral
      H11.219 Conjunctival adhesions and strands (localized), unspecified eye
  ● **H11.22 Conjunctival granuloma**
      H11.221 Conjunctival granuloma, right eye
      H11.222 Conjunctival granuloma, left eye
      H11.223 Conjunctival granuloma, bilateral
      H11.229 Conjunctival granuloma, unspecified
  ● **H11.23 Symblepharon**
      Adhesion between tarsal conjunctiva and bulbar conjunctiva
      H11.231 Symblepharon, right eye
      H11.232 Symblepharon, left eye
      H11.233 Symblepharon, bilateral
      H11.239 Symblepharon, unspecified eye

▶ New ⇨ Revised ~~deleted~~ Deleted Excludes 1 Excludes 2 Includes Use additional Code first Code also Key words
OGCR Official Guidelines X Assign placeholder X ● Use Additional Character(s) ▷ Manifestation Code **Coding Clinic**

● H11.24   Scarring of conjunctiva
    H11.241   Scarring of conjunctiva, right eye
    H11.242   Scarring of conjunctiva, left eye
    H11.243   Scarring of conjunctiva, bilateral
    H11.249   Scarring of conjunctiva, unspecified eye

● H11.3   Conjunctival hemorrhage
    Subconjunctival hemorrhage
    H11.30   Conjunctival hemorrhage, unspecified eye
    H11.31   Conjunctival hemorrhage, right eye
    H11.32   Conjunctival hemorrhage, left eye
    H11.33   Conjunctival hemorrhage, bilateral

● H11.4   Other conjunctival vascular disorders and cysts
    ● H11.41   Vascular abnormalities of conjunctiva
      Conjunctival aneurysm
      H11.411   Vascular abnormalities of conjunctiva, right eye
      H11.412   Vascular abnormalities of conjunctiva, left eye
      H11.413   Vascular abnormalities of conjunctiva, bilateral
      H11.419   Vascular abnormalities of conjunctiva, unspecified eye

    ● H11.42   Conjunctival edema
      H11.421   Conjunctival edema, right eye
      H11.422   Conjunctival edema, left eye
      H11.423   Conjunctival edema, bilateral
      H11.429   Conjunctival edema, unspecified eye

    ● H11.43   Conjunctival hyperemia
      H11.431   Conjunctival hyperemia, right eye
      H11.432   Conjunctival hyperemia, left eye
      H11.433   Conjunctival hyperemia, bilateral
      H11.439   Conjunctival hyperemia, unspecified eye

    ● H11.44   Conjunctival cysts
      H11.441   Conjunctival cysts, right eye
      H11.442   Conjunctival cysts, left eye
      H11.443   Conjunctival cysts, bilateral
      H11.449   Conjunctival cysts, unspecified eye

● H11.8   Other specified disorders of conjunctiva
    ● H11.81   Pseudopterygium of conjunctiva
      Conjunctival scar attached to cornea
      H11.811   Pseudopterygium of conjunctiva, right eye
      H11.812   Pseudopterygium of conjunctiva, left eye
      H11.813   Pseudopterygium of conjunctiva, bilateral
      H11.819   Pseudopterygium of conjunctiva, unspecified eye

    ● H11.82   Conjunctivochalasis
      Conjunctiva bulges over eyelid margin or covers lower punctum
      H11.821   Conjunctivochalasis, right eye
      H11.822   Conjunctivochalasis, left eye
      H11.823   Conjunctivochalasis, bilateral
      H11.829   Conjunctivochalasis, unspecified eye
    H11.89   Other specified disorders of conjunctiva
● H11.9   Unspecified disorder of conjunctiva

DISORDERS OF SCLERA, CORNEA, IRIS AND CILIARY BODY (H15-H22)

● H15   Disorders of sclera
    ● H15.0   Scleritis
      Inflammation of the white (sclera and episclera) of the eye.
      ● H15.00   Unspecified scleritis
        H15.001   Unspecified scleritis, right eye
        H15.002   Unspecified scleritis, left eye
        H15.003   Unspecified scleritis, bilateral
        H15.009   Unspecified scleritis, unspecified eye

      ● H15.01   Anterior scleritis
        H15.011   Anterior scleritis, right eye
        H15.012   Anterior scleritis, left eye
        H15.013   Anterior scleritis, bilateral
        H15.019   Anterior scleritis, unspecified eye

      ● H15.02   Brawny scleritis
        Swelling around the cornea that is gelantinous in appearance
        H15.021   Brawny scleritis, right eye
        H15.022   Brawny scleritis, left eye
        H15.023   Brawny scleritis, bilateral
        H15.029   Brawny scleritis, unspecified eye

      ● H15.03   Posterior scleritis
        Sclerotenonitis
        H15.031   Posterior scleritis, right eye
        H15.032   Posterior scleritis, left eye
        H15.033   Posterior scleritis, bilateral
        H15.039   Posterior scleritis, unspecified eye

      ● H15.04   Scleritis with corneal involvement
        H15.041   Scleritis with corneal involvement, right eye
        H15.042   Scleritis with corneal involvement, left eye
        H15.043   Scleritis with corneal involvement, bilateral
        H15.049   Scleritis with corneal involvement, unspecified eye

      ● H15.05   Scleromalacia perforans
        Necrotic without inflammation; usually associated with rheumatoid arthritis
        H15.051   Scleromalacia perforans, right eye
        H15.052   Scleromalacia perforans, left eye
        H15.053   Scleromalacia perforans, bilateral
        H15.059   Scleromalacia perforans, unspecified eye

      ● H15.09   Other scleritis
        Scleral abscess
        H15.091   Other scleritis, right eye
        H15.092   Other scleritis, left eye
        H15.093   Other scleritis, bilateral
        H15.099   Other scleritis, unspecified eye

    ● H15.1   Episcleritis
      Inflammation of the white (sclera and episclera) of the eye.
      ● H15.10   Unspecified episcleritis
        H15.101   Unspecified episcleritis, right eye
        H15.102   Unspecified episcleritis, left eye
        H15.103   Unspecified episcleritis, bilateral
        H15.109   Unspecified episcleritis, unspecified eye

      ● H15.11   Episcleritis periodica fugax
        Transient, recurrent inflammation of portion of episclera (connective tissue on the surface of the sclera)
        H15.111   Episcleritis periodica fugax, right eye
        H15.112   Episcleritis periodica fugax, left eye
        H15.113   Episcleritis periodica fugax, bilateral
        H15.119   Episcleritis periodica fugax, unspecified eye

CHAPTER 7 (H00-H59)

● **H15.12** Nodular episcleritis
Characterized by tender, localized, moveable nodule within inflamed area
     H15.121   Nodular episcleritis, **right eye**
     H15.122   Nodular episcleritis, **left eye**
     H15.123   Nodular episcleritis, **bilateral**
     H15.129   Nodular episcleritis, **unspecified** eye

● **H15.8** Other disorders of sclera
     Excludes2   blue sclera (Q13.5)
                 degenerative myopia (H44.2-)

● **H15.81** Equatorial staphyloma
     H15.811   Equatorial staphyloma, **right eye**
     H15.812   Equatorial staphyloma, **left eye**
     H15.813   Equatorial staphyloma, **bilateral**
     H15.819   Equatorial staphyloma, **unspecified eye**

● **H15.82** Localized anterior staphyloma
     H15.821   Localized anterior staphyloma, **right eye**
     H15.822   Localized anterior staphyloma, **left eye**
     H15.823   Localized anterior staphyloma, **bilateral**
     H15.829   Localized anterior staphyloma, **unspecified eye**

● **H15.83** Staphyloma posticum
     H15.831   Staphyloma posticum, **right eye**
     H15.832   Staphyloma posticum, **left eye**
     H15.833   Staphyloma posticum, **bilateral**
     H15.839   Staphyloma posticum, **unspecified eye**

● **H15.84** Scleral ectasia
     H15.841   Scleral ectasia, **right eye**
     H15.842   Scleral ectasia, **left eye**
     H15.843   Scleral ectasia, **bilateral**
     H15.849   Scleral ectasia, **unspecified eye**

● **H15.85** Ring staphyloma
     H15.851   Ring staphyloma, **right eye**
     H15.852   Ring staphyloma, **left eye**
     H15.853   Ring staphyloma, **bilateral**
     H15.859   Ring staphyloma, **unspecified eye**

   H15.89 Other disorders of sclera
   H15.9 Unspecified disorder of sclera

● **H16** Keratitis
   ● **H16.0** Corneal ulcer
     ● **H16.00** Unspecified corneal ulcer
       H16.001   Unspecified corneal ulcer, **right eye**
       H16.002   Unspecified corneal ulcer, **left eye**
       H16.003   Unspecified corneal ulcer, **bilateral**
       H16.009   Unspecified corneal ulcer, **unspecified eye**

     ● **H16.01** Central corneal ulcer
       H16.011   Central corneal ulcer, **right eye**
       H16.012   Central corneal ulcer, **left eye**
       H16.013   Central corneal ulcer, **bilateral**
       H16.019   Central corneal ulcer, **unspecified eye**

     ● **H16.02** Ring corneal ulcer
       H16.021   Ring corneal ulcer, **right eye**
       H16.022   Ring corneal ulcer, **left eye**
       H16.023   Ring corneal ulcer, **bilateral**
       H16.029   Ring corneal ulcer, **unspecified eye**

     ● **H16.03** Corneal ulcer with hypopyon
       H16.031   Corneal ulcer with hypopyon, **right eye**
       H16.032   Corneal ulcer with hypopyon, **left eye**
       H16.033   Corneal ulcer with hypopyon, **bilateral**
       H16.039   Corneal ulcer with hypopyon, **unspecified eye**

Figure 7-7   Corneal ulcers: marginal, ring, central corneal, rosacea, and Mooren's.

Item 7-3   An infected ulcer is usually called a **serpiginous** or **hypopyon** ulcer which is a pus sac in the anterior chamber of the eye. **Marginal** ulcers are usually asymptomatic, not primary, and are often superficial and simple. More severe marginal ulcers spread to form a ring ulcer. **Ring** ulcers can extend around the entire corneal periphery. **Central corneal** ulcers develop when there is an abrasion to the epithelium and an infection develops in the eroded area. The **pyocyaneal** ulcer is the most serious corneal infection, which, if left untreated, can lead to loss of the eye.

● **H16.04** **Marginal** corneal ulcer
     H16.041   Marginal corneal ulcer, **right eye**
     H16.042   Marginal corneal ulcer, **left eye**
     H16.043   Marginal corneal ulcer, **bilateral**
     H16.049   Marginal corneal ulcer, **unspecified eye**

● **H16.05** Mooren's corneal ulcer
     H16.051   Mooren's corneal ulcer, **right eye**
     H16.052   Mooren's corneal ulcer, **left eye**
     H16.053   Mooren's corneal ulcer, **bilateral**
     H16.059   Mooren's corneal ulcer, **unspecified eye**

● **H16.06** Mycotic corneal ulcer
     H16.061   Mycotic corneal ulcer, **right eye**
     H16.062   Mycotic corneal ulcer, **left eye**
     H16.063   Mycotic corneal ulcer, **bilateral**
     H16.069   Mycotic corneal ulcer, **unspecified eye**

● **H16.07** Perforated corneal ulcer
     H16.071   Perforated corneal ulcer, **right eye**
     H16.072   Perforated corneal ulcer, **left eye**
     H16.073   Perforated corneal ulcer, **bilateral**
     H16.079   Perforated corneal ulcer, **unspecified eye**

● **H16.1** Other and unspecified superficial keratitis without conjunctivitis
   ● **H16.10** Unspecified superficial keratitis
     H16.101   Unspecified superficial keratitis, **right eye**
     H16.102   Unspecified superficial keratitis, **left eye**
     H16.103   Unspecified superficial keratitis, **bilateral**
     H16.109   Unspecified superficial keratitis, **unspecified eye**

   ● **H16.11** Macular keratitis
     Areolar keratitis
     Nummular keratitis
     Stellate keratitis
     Striate keratitis
     H16.111   Macular keratitis, **right eye**
     H16.112   Macular keratitis, **left eye**
     H16.113   Macular keratitis, **bilateral**
     H16.119   Macular keratitis, **unspecified eye**

   ● **H16.12** Filamentary keratitis
     H16.121   Filamentary keratitis, **right eye**
     H16.122   Filamentary keratitis, **left eye**
     H16.123   Filamentary keratitis, **bilateral**
     H16.129   Filamentary keratitis, **unspecified eye**

▶ New   ⇒ Revised   ~~deleted~~ Deleted   Excludes 1   Excludes 2   Includes   Use additional   Code first   Code also   Key words

OGCR Official Guidelines   X Assign placeholder X   ● Use Additional Character(s)   ▶ Manifestation Code   **Coding Clinic**

● **H16.13**   **Photokeratitis**
Snow blindness
Welders' keratitis

     H16.131   Photokeratitis, right eye
     H16.132   Photokeratitis, left eye
     H16.133   Photokeratitis, bilateral
     H16.139   Photokeratitis, unspecified eye

● **H16.14**   **Punctate keratitis**

     H16.141   Punctate keratitis, right eye
     H16.142   Punctate keratitis, left eye
     H16.143   Punctate keratitis, bilateral
     H16.149   Punctate keratitis, unspecified eye

● **H16.2**   **Keratoconjunctivitis**

● **H16.20**   **Unspecified keratoconjunctivitis**
Superficial keratitis with conjunctivitis NOS

     H16.201   Unspecified keratoconjunctivitis, right eye
     H16.202   Unspecified keratoconjunctivitis, left eye
     H16.203   Unspecified keratoconjunctivitis, bilateral
     H16.209   Unspecified keratoconjunctivitis, unspecified eye

● **H16.21**   **Exposure keratoconjunctivitis**

     H16.211   Exposure keratoconjunctivitis, right eye
     H16.212   Exposure keratoconjunctivitis, left eye
     H16.213   Exposure keratoconjunctivitis, bilateral
     H16.219   Exposure keratoconjunctivitis, unspecified eye

● **H16.22**   **Keratoconjunctivitis sicca, not specified as Sjögren's**

     Excludes1   Sjogren's syndrome (M35.01)

     H16.221   Keratoconjunctivitis sicca, not specified as Sjögren's, right eye
     H16.222   Keratoconjunctivitis sicca, not specified as Sjögren's, left eye
     H16.223   Keratoconjunctivitis sicca, not specified as Sjögren's, bilateral
     H16.229   Keratoconjunctivitis sicca, not specified as Sjögren's, unspecified eye

● **H16.23**   **Neurotrophic keratoconjunctivitis**

     H16.231   Neurotrophic keratoconjunctivitis, right eye
     H16.232   Neurotrophic keratoconjunctivitis, left eye
     H16.233   Neurotrophic keratoconjunctivitis, bilateral
     H16.239   Neurotrophic keratoconjunctivitis, unspecified eye

● **H16.24**   **Ophthalmia nodosa**

     H16.241   Ophthalmia nodosa, right eye
     H16.242   Ophthalmia nodosa, left eye
     H16.243   Ophthalmia nodosa, bilateral
     H16.249   Ophthalmia nodosa, unspecified eye

● **H16.25**   **Phlyctenular keratoconjunctivitis**

     H16.251   Phlyctenular keratoconjunctivitis, right eye
     H16.252   Phlyctenular keratoconjunctivitis, left eye
     H16.253   Phlyctenular keratoconjunctivitis, bilateral
     H16.259   Phlyctenular keratoconjunctivitis, unspecified eye

● **H16.26**   **Vernal keratoconjunctivitis, with limbar and corneal involvement**

     Excludes1   vernal conjunctivitis without limbar and corneal involvement (H10.44)

     H16.261   Vernal keratoconjunctivitis, with limbar and corneal involvement, right eye
     H16.262   Vernal keratoconjunctivitis, with limbar and corneal involvement, left eye
     H16.263   Vernal keratoconjunctivitis, with limbar and corneal involvement, bilateral
     H16.269   Vernal keratoconjunctivitis, with limbar and corneal involvement, unspecified eye

● **H16.29**   **Other keratoconjunctivitis**

     H16.291   Other keratoconjunctivitis, right eye
     H16.292   Other keratoconjunctivitis, left eye
     H16.293   Other keratoconjunctivitis, bilateral
     H16.299   Other keratoconjunctivitis, unspecified eye

● **H16.3**   **Interstitial and deep keratitis**

● **H16.30**   **Unspecified interstitial keratitis**

     H16.301   Unspecified interstitial keratitis, right eye
     H16.302   Unspecified interstitial keratitis, left eye
     H16.303   Unspecified interstitial keratitis, bilateral
     H16.309   Unspecified interstitial keratitis, unspecified eye

● **H16.31**   **Corneal abscess**

     H16.311   Corneal abscess, right eye
     H16.312   Corneal abscess, left eye
     H16.313   Corneal abscess, bilateral
     H16.319   Corneal abscess, unspecified eye

● **H16.32**   **Diffuse interstitial keratitis**
Cogan's syndrome

     H16.321   Diffuse interstitial keratitis, right eye
     H16.322   Diffuse interstitial keratitis, left eye
     H16.323   Diffuse interstitial keratitis, bilateral
     H16.329   Diffuse interstitial keratitis, unspecified eye

● **H16.33**   **Sclerosing keratitis**

     H16.331   Sclerosing keratitis, right eye
     H16.332   Sclerosing keratitis, left eye
     H16.333   Sclerosing keratitis, bilateral
     H16.339   Sclerosing keratitis, unspecified eye

● **H16.39**   **Other interstitial and deep keratitis**

     H16.391   Other interstitial and deep keratitis, right eye
     H16.392   Other interstitial and deep keratitis, left eye
     H16.393   Other interstitial and deep keratitis, bilateral
     H16.399   Other interstitial and deep keratitis, unspecified eye

● **H16.4**   **Corneal neovascularization**

● **H16.40**   **Unspecified corneal neovascularization**

     H16.401   Unspecified corneal neovascularization, right eye
     H16.402   Unspecified corneal neovascularization, left eye
     H16.403   Unspecified corneal neovascularization, bilateral
     H16.409   Unspecified corneal neovascularization, unspecified eye

CHAPTER 7 (H00-H59)

- H16.41 **Ghost vessels** (corneal)
  - H16.411 Ghost vessels (corneal), **right** eye
  - H16.412 Ghost vessels (corneal), **left** eye
  - H16.413 Ghost vessels (corneal), **bilateral**
  - H16.419 Ghost vessels (corneal), **unspecified** eye
- H16.42 **Pannus** (corneal)
  - H16.421 Pannus (corneal), **right** eye
  - H16.422 Pannus (corneal), **left** eye
  - H16.423 Pannus (corneal), **bilateral**
  - H16.429 Pannus (corneal), **unspecified** eye
- H16.43 **Localized vascularization** of cornea
  - H16.431 Localized vascularization of cornea, **right** eye
  - H16.432 Localized vascularization of cornea, **left** eye
  - H16.433 Localized vascularization of cornea, **bilateral**
  - H16.439 Localized vascularization of cornea, **unspecified** eye
- H16.44 **Deep vascularization** of cornea
  - H16.441 Deep vascularization of cornea, **right** eye
  - H16.442 Deep vascularization of cornea, **left** eye
  - H16.443 Deep vascularization of cornea, **bilateral**
  - H16.449 Deep vascularization of cornea, **unspecified** eye
- H16.8 **Other keratitis**
- H16.9 **Unspecified keratitis**

- H17 **Corneal scars and opacities**
  - H17.0 **Adherent leukoma**
    - H17.00 Adherent leukoma, **unspecified** eye
    - H17.01 Adherent leukoma, **right** eye
    - H17.02 Adherent leukoma, **left** eye
    - H17.03 Adherent leukoma, **bilateral**
  - H17.1 **Central corneal opacity**
    - H17.10 Central corneal opacity, **unspecified** eye
    - H17.11 Central corneal opacity, **right** eye
    - H17.12 Central corneal opacity, **left** eye
    - H17.13 Central corneal opacity, **bilateral**
  - H17.8 **Other corneal scars and opacities**
    - H17.81 **Minor** opacity of cornea
      Corneal nebula
      - H17.811 Minor opacity of cornea, **right** eye
      - H17.812 Minor opacity of cornea, **left** eye
      - H17.813 Minor opacity of cornea, **bilateral**
      - H17.819 Minor opacity of cornea, **unspecified** eye
    - H17.82 **Peripheral** opacity of cornea
      - H17.821 Peripheral opacity of cornea, **right** eye
      - H17.822 Peripheral opacity of cornea, **left** eye
      - H17.823 Peripheral opacity of cornea, **bilateral**
      - H17.829 Peripheral opacity of cornea, **unspecified** eye
    - H17.89 Other corneal scars and opacities
  - H17.9 **Unspecified** corneal scar and opacity

- H18 **Other disorders of cornea**
  - H18.0 **Corneal pigmentations and deposits**
    - H18.00 **Unspecified** corneal deposit
      - H18.001 Unspecified corneal deposit, **right** eye
      - H18.002 Unspecified corneal deposit, **left** eye
      - H18.003 Unspecified corneal deposit, **bilateral**
      - H18.009 Unspecified corneal deposit, **unspecified** eye
    - H18.01 **Anterior corneal pigmentations**
      Staehli's line
      - H18.011 Anterior corneal pigmentations, **right** eye
      - H18.012 Anterior corneal pigmentations, **left** eye
      - H18.013 Anterior corneal pigmentations, **bilateral**
      - H18.019 Anterior corneal pigmentations, **unspecified** eye
    - H18.02 **Argentous corneal deposits**
      - H18.021 Argentous corneal deposits, **right** eye
      - H18.022 Argentous corneal deposits, **left** eye
      - H18.023 Argentous corneal deposits, **bilateral**
      - H18.029 Argentous corneal deposits, **unspecified** eye
    - H18.03 **Corneal deposits in metabolic disorders**
      Code also associated metabolic disorder
      - H18.031 Corneal deposits in metabolic disorders, **right** eye
      - H18.032 Corneal deposits in metabolic disorders, **left** eye
      - H18.033 Corneal deposits in metabolic disorders, **bilateral**
      - H18.039 Corneal deposits in metabolic disorders, **unspecified** eye
    - H18.04 **Kayser-Fleischer ring**
      Code also associated Wilson's disease (E83.01)
      - H18.041 Kayser-Fleischer ring, **right** eye
      - H18.042 Kayser-Fleischer ring, **left** eye
      - H18.043 Kayser-Fleischer ring, **bilateral**
      - H18.049 Kayser-Fleischer ring, **unspecified** eye
    - H18.05 **Posterior** corneal pigmentations
      Krukenberg's spindle
      - H18.051 Posterior corneal pigmentations, **right** eye
      - H18.052 Posterior corneal pigmentations, **left** eye
      - H18.053 Posterior corneal pigmentations, **bilateral**
      - H18.059 Posterior corneal pigmentations, **unspecified** eye
    - H18.06 **Stromal corneal pigmentations**
      Hematocornea
      - H18.061 Stromal corneal pigmentations, **right** eye
      - H18.062 Stromal corneal pigmentations, **left** eye
      - H18.063 Stromal corneal pigmentations, **bilateral**
      - H18.069 Stromal corneal pigmentations, **unspecified** eye
  - H18.1 **Bullous keratopathy**
    - H18.10 Bullous keratopathy, **unspecified** eye
    - H18.11 Bullous keratopathy, **right** eye
    - H18.12 Bullous keratopathy, **left** eye
    - H18.13 Bullous keratopathy, **bilateral**
  - H18.2 **Other and unspecified corneal edema**
    - H18.20 Unspecified corneal edema
    - H18.21 **Corneal edema secondary to contact lens**
      Excludes2 other corneal disorders due to contact lens (H18.82-)
      - H18.211 Corneal edema secondary to contact lens, **right** eye
      - H18.212 Corneal edema secondary to contact lens, **left** eye

H18.213   Corneal edema secondary to contact lens, bilateral

H18.219   Corneal edema secondary to contact lens, unspecified eye

● H18.22   Idiopathic corneal edema

H18.221   Idiopathic corneal edema, right eye

H18.222   Idiopathic corneal edema, left eye

H18.223   Idiopathic corneal edema, bilateral

H18.229   Idiopathic corneal edema, unspecified eye

● H18.23   Secondary corneal edema

H18.231   Secondary corneal edema, right eye

H18.232   Secondary corneal edema, left eye

H18.233   Secondary corneal edema, bilateral

H18.239   Secondary corneal edema, unspecified eye

● H18.3   Changes of corneal membranes

H18.30   Unspecified corneal membrane change

● H18.31   Folds and rupture in Bowman's membrane

H18.311   Folds and rupture in Bowman's membrane, right eye

H18.312   Folds and rupture in Bowman's membrane, left eye

H18.313   Folds and rupture in Bowman's membrane, bilateral

H18.319   Folds and rupture in Bowman's membrane, unspecified eye

● H18.32   Folds in Descemet's membrane

H18.321   Folds in Descemet's membrane, right eye

H18.322   Folds in Descemet's membrane, left eye

H18.323   Folds in Descemet's membrane, bilateral

H18.329   Folds in Descemet's membrane, unspecified eye

● H18.33   Rupture in Descemet's membrane

H18.331   Rupture in Descemet's membrane, right eye

H18.332   Rupture in Descemet's membrane, left eye

H18.333   Rupture in Descemet's membrane, bilateral

H18.339   Rupture in Descemet's membrane, unspecified eye

● H18.4   Corneal degeneration

Excludes1   Mooren's ulcer (H16.0-)
recurrent erosion of cornea (H18.83-)

H18.40   Unspecified corneal degeneration

● H18.41   Arcus senilis
Senile corneal changes

H18.411   Arcus senilis, right eye

H18.412   Arcus senilis, left eye

H18.413   Arcus senilis, bilateral

H18.419   Arcus senilis, unspecified eye

● H18.42   Band keratopathy

H18.421   Band keratopathy, right eye

H18.422   Band keratopathy, left eye

H18.423   Band keratopathy, bilateral

H18.429   Band keratopathy, unspecified eye

H18.43   Other calcerous corneal degeneration

● H18.44   Keratomalacia

Excludes1   keratomalacia due to vitamin A deficiency (E50.4)

H18.441   Keratomalacia, right eye

H18.442   Keratomalacia, left eye

H18.443   Keratomalacia, bilateral

H18.449   Keratomalacia, unspecified eye

● H18.45   Nodular corneal degeneration

H18.451   Nodular corneal degeneration, right eye

H18.452   Nodular corneal degeneration, left eye

H18.453   Nodular corneal degeneration, bilateral

H18.459   Nodular corneal degeneration, unspecified eye

● H18.46   Peripheral corneal degeneration

H18.461   Peripheral corneal degeneration, right eye

H18.462   Peripheral corneal degeneration, left eye

H18.463   Peripheral corneal degeneration, bilateral

H18.469   Peripheral corneal degeneration, unspecified eye

H18.49   Other corneal degeneration

● H18.5   Hereditary corneal dystrophies

H18.50   Unspecified hereditary corneal dystrophies

H18.51   Endothelial corneal dystrophy
Fuchs' dystrophy

H18.52   Epithelial (juvenile) corneal dystrophy

H18.53   Granular corneal dystrophy

H18.54   Lattice corneal dystrophy

H18.55   Macular corneal dystrophy

H18.59   Other hereditary corneal dystrophies

● H18.6   Keratoconus

● H18.60   Keratoconus, unspecified

H18.601   Keratoconus, unspecified, right eye

H18.602   Keratoconus, unspecified, left eye

H18.603   Keratoconus, unspecified, bilateral

H18.609   Keratoconus, unspecified, unspecified eye

● H18.61   Keratoconus, stable

H18.611   Keratoconus, stable, right eye

H18.612   Keratoconus, stable, left eye

H18.613   Keratoconus, stable, bilateral

H18.619   Keratoconus, stable, unspecified eye

● H18.62   Keratoconus, unstable
Acute hydrops

H18.621   Keratoconus, unstable, right eye

H18.622   Keratoconus, unstable, left eye

H18.623   Keratoconus, unstable, bilateral

H18.629   Keratoconus, unstable, unspecified eye

Figure 7-8 Lateral view of the displacement of the cone apex in keratoconus. (From Yanoff: Ophthalmology, ed 3, Mosby, Inc., 2008)

Item 7–4 Keratoconus results in corneal degeneration that begins in childhood, gradually changes the cornea from a round to cone shape, decreasing visual acuity. Treatment includes contact lenses. In severe cases the need for corneal transplant may be the treatment of choice; however, newer technologies may use high-frequency radio energy to shrink the edges of the cornea, pulling the central area back to a more normal shape. It can help delay or avoid the need for a corneal transplantation.

● **H18.7   Other and unspecified corneal deformities**

     Excludes1   congenital malformations of cornea (Q13.3-Q13.4)

     H18.70   Unspecified corneal deformity

●   H18.71   Corneal ectasia

       H18.711   Corneal ectasia, right eye

       H18.712   Corneal ectasia, left eye

       H18.713   Corneal ectasia, bilateral

       H18.719   Corneal ectasia, unspecified eye

●   H18.72   Corneal staphyloma

       H18.721   Corneal staphyloma, right eye

       H18.722   Corneal staphyloma, left eye

       H18.723   Corneal staphyloma, bilateral

       H18.729   Corneal staphyloma, unspecified eye

●   H18.73   Descemetocele

       H18.731   Descemetocele, right eye

       H18.732   Descemetocele, left eye

       H18.733   Descemetocele, bilateral

       H18.739   Descemetocele, unspecified eye

●   H18.79   Other corneal deformities

       H18.791   Other corneal deformities, right eye

       H18.792   Other corneal deformities, left eye

       H18.793   Other corneal deformities, bilateral

       H18.799   Other corneal deformities, unspecified eye

● **H18.8   Other specified disorders of cornea**

●   H18.81   Anesthesia and hypoesthesia of cornea

       H18.811   Anesthesia and hypoesthesia of cornea, right eye

       H18.812   Anesthesia and hypoesthesia of cornea, left eye

       H18.813   Anesthesia and hypoesthesia of cornea, bilateral

       H18.819   Anesthesia and hypoesthesia of cornea, unspecified eye

●   H18.82   Corneal disorder due to contact lens

       Excludes2   corneal edema due to contact lens (H18.21-)

       H18.821   Corneal disorder due to contact lens, right eye

       H18.822   Corneal disorder due to contact lens, left eye

       H18.823   Corneal disorder due to contact lens, bilateral

       H18.829   Corneal disorder due to contact lens, unspecified eye

●   H18.83   Recurrent erosion of cornea

       H18.831   Recurrent erosion of cornea, right eye

       H18.832   Recurrent erosion of cornea, left eye

       H18.833   Recurrent erosion of cornea, bilateral

       H18.839   Recurrent erosion of cornea, unspecified eye

●   H18.89   Other specified disorders of cornea

       H18.891   Other specified disorders of cornea, right eye

       H18.892   Other specified disorders of cornea, left eye

       H18.893   Other specified disorders of cornea, bilateral

       H18.899   Other specified disorders of cornea, unspecified eye

H18.9   Unspecified disorder of cornea

● **H20   Iridocyclitis**

● **H20.0   Acute and subacute iridocyclitis**

     Acute anterior uveitis

     Acute cyclitis

     Acute iritis

     Subacute anterior uveitis

     Subacute cyclitis

     Subacute iritis

     Excludes1   iridocyclitis, iritis, uveitis (due to) (in) diabetes mellitus (E08-E13 with .39)

            iridocyclitis, iritis, uveitis (due to) (in) diphtheria (A36.89)

            iridocyclitis, iritis, uveitis (due to) (in) gonococcal (A54.32)

            iridocyclitis, iritis, uveitis (due to) (in) herpes (simplex) (B00.51)

            iridocyclitis, iritis, uveitis (due to) (in) herpes zoster (B02.32)

            iridocyclitis, iritis, uveitis (due to) (in) late congenital syphilis (A50.39)

            iridocyclitis, iritis, uveitis (due to) (in) late syphilis (A52.71)

            iridocyclitis, iritis, uveitis (due to) (in) sarcoidosis (D86.83)

            iridocyclitis, iritis, uveitis (due to) (in) syphilis (A51.43)

            iridocyclitis, iritis, uveitis (due to) (in) toxoplasmosis (B58.09)

            iridocyclitis, iritis, uveitis (due to) (in) tuberculosis (A18.54)

     H20.00   Unspecified acute and subacute iridocyclitis

●   H20.01   Primary iridocyclitis

       H20.011   Primary iridocyclitis, right eye

       H20.012   Primary iridocyclitis, left eye

       H20.013   Primary iridocyclitis, bilateral

       H20.019   Primary iridocyclitis, unspecified eye

●   H20.02   Recurrent acute iridocyclitis

       H20.021   Recurrent acute iridocyclitis, right eye

       H20.022   Recurrent acute iridocyclitis, left eye

       H20.023   Recurrent acute iridocyclitis, bilateral

       H20.029   Recurrent acute iridocyclitis, unspecified eye

●   H20.03   Secondary infectious iridocyclitis

       H20.031   Secondary infectious iridocyclitis, right eye

       H20.032   Secondary infectious iridocyclitis, left eye

       H20.033   Secondary infectious iridocyclitis, bilateral

       H20.039   Secondary infectious iridocyclitis, unspecified eye

●   H20.04   Secondary noninfectious iridocyclitis

       H20.041   Secondary noninfectious iridocyclitis, right eye

       H20.042   Secondary noninfectious iridocyclitis, left eye

       H20.043   Secondary noninfectious iridocyclitis, bilateral

       H20.049   Secondary noninfectious iridocyclitis, unspecified eye

●   H20.05   Hypopyon

       H20.051   Hypopyon, right eye

       H20.052   Hypopyon, left eye

       H20.053   Hypopyon, bilateral

       H20.059   Hypopyon, unspecified eye

▶ New   ⇒ Revised   ~~deleted~~ Deleted   Excludes 1   Excludes 2   Includes   Use additional   Code first   Code also   Key words

OGCR Official Guidelines   X Assign placeholder X   ● Use Additional Character(s)   ▶ Manifestation Code   **Coding Clinic**

● **H20.1** Chronic iridocyclitis
> Use additional code for any associated cataract (H26.21-)
> **Excludes2** posterior cyclitis (H30.2-)

　H20.10 Chronic iridocyclitis, unspecified eye
　H20.11 Chronic iridocyclitis, right eye
　H20.12 Chronic iridocyclitis, left eye
　H20.13 Chronic iridocyclitis, bilateral

● **H20.2** Lens-induced iridocyclitis
　H20.20 Lens-induced iridocyclitis, unspecified eye
　H20.21 Lens-induced iridocyclitis, right eye
　H20.22 Lens-induced iridocyclitis, left eye
　H20.23 Lens-induced iridocyclitis, bilateral

● **H20.8** Other iridocyclitis
> **Excludes2** glaucomatocyclitis crises (H40.4-)
> posterior cyclitis (H30.2-)
> sympathetic uveitis (H44.13-)

　● **H20.81** Fuchs' heterochromic cyclitis
　　H20.811 Fuchs' heterochromic cyclitis, right eye
　　H20.812 Fuchs' heterochromic cyclitis, left eye
　　H20.813 Fuchs' heterochromic cyclitis, bilateral
　　H20.819 Fuchs' heterochromic cyclitis, unspecified eye

　● **H20.82** Vogt-Koyanagi syndrome
　　H20.821 Vogt-Koyanagi syndrome, right eye
　　H20.822 Vogt-Koyanagi syndrome, left eye
　　H20.823 Vogt-Koyanagi syndrome, bilateral
　　H20.829 Vogt-Koyanagi syndrome, unspecified eye

　H20.9 Unspecified iridocyclitis
> Uveitis NOS

● **H21** Other disorders of iris and ciliary body
> **Excludes2** sympathetic uveitis (H44.1-)

● **H21.0** Hyphema
> **Excludes1** traumatic hyphema (S05.1-)

　H21.00 Hyphema, unspecified eye
　H21.01 Hyphema, right eye
　H21.02 Hyphema, left eye
　H21.03 Hyphema, bilateral

● **H21.1** Other vascular disorders of iris and ciliary body
> Neovascularization of iris or ciliary body
> Rubeosis iridis
> Rubeosis of iris

　● **H21.1X** Other vascular disorders of iris and ciliary body
　　H21.1X1 Other vascular disorders of iris and ciliary body, right eye
　　H21.1X2 Other vascular disorders of iris and ciliary body, left eye
　　H21.1X3 Other vascular disorders of iris and ciliary body, bilateral
　　H21.1X9 Other vascular disorders of iris and ciliary body, unspecified eye

● **H21.2** Degeneration of iris and ciliary body
　● **H21.21** Degeneration of chamber angle
　　H21.211 Degeneration of chamber angle, right eye
　　H21.212 Degeneration of chamber angle, left eye
　　H21.213 Degeneration of chamber angle, bilateral
　　H21.219 Degeneration of chamber angle, unspecified eye

● **H21.22** Degeneration of ciliary body
　H21.221 Degeneration of ciliary body, right eye
　H21.222 Degeneration of ciliary body, left eye
　H21.223 Degeneration of ciliary body, bilateral
　H21.229 Degeneration of ciliary body, unspecified eye

● **H21.23** Degeneration of iris (pigmentary)
> Translucency of iris

　H21.231 Degeneration of iris (pigmentary), right eye
　H21.232 Degeneration of iris (pigmentary), left eye
　H21.233 Degeneration of iris (pigmentary), bilateral
　H21.239 Degeneration of iris (pigmentary), unspecified eye

● **H21.24** Degeneration of pupillary margin
　H21.241 Degeneration of pupillary margin, right eye
　H21.242 Degeneration of pupillary margin, left eye
　H21.243 Degeneration of pupillary margin, bilateral
　H21.249 Degeneration of pupillary margin, unspecified eye

● **H21.25** Iridoschisis
　H21.251 Iridoschisis, right eye
　H21.252 Iridoschisis, left eye
　H21.253 Iridoschisis, bilateral
　H21.259 Iridoschisis, unspecified eye

● **H21.26** Iris atrophy (essential) (progressive)
　H21.261 Iris atrophy (essential) (progressive), right eye
　H21.262 Iris atrophy (essential) (progressive), left eye
　H21.263 Iris atrophy (essential) (progressive), bilateral
　H21.269 Iris atrophy (essential) (progressive), unspecified eye

● **H21.27** Miotic pupillary cyst
　H21.271 Miotic pupillary cyst, right eye
　H21.272 Miotic pupillary cyst, left eye
　H21.273 Miotic pupillary cyst, bilateral
　H21.279 Miotic pupillary cyst, unspecified eye

　H21.29 Other iris atrophy

● **H21.3** Cyst of iris, ciliary body and anterior chamber
> **Excludes2** miotic pupillary cyst (H21.27-)

● **H21.30** Idiopathic cysts of iris, ciliary body or anterior chamber
> Cyst of iris, ciliary body or anterior chamber NOS

　H21.301 Idiopathic cysts of iris, ciliary body or anterior chamber, right eye
　H21.302 Idiopathic cysts of iris, ciliary body or anterior chamber, left eye
　H21.303 Idiopathic cysts of iris, ciliary body or anterior chamber, bilateral
　H21.309 Idiopathic cysts of iris, ciliary body or anterior chamber, unspecified eye

● **H21.31** Exudative cysts of iris or anterior chamber
　H21.311 Exudative cysts of iris or anterior chamber, right eye
　H21.312 Exudative cysts of iris or anterior chamber, left eye
　H21.313 Exudative cysts of iris or anterior chamber, bilateral
　H21.319 Exudative cysts of iris or anterior chamber, unspecified eye

CHAPTER 7 (H00–H59)

CHAPTER 7 (HØØ-H59)

● **H21.32**   Implantation cysts of iris, ciliary body or anterior chamber
    H21.321   Implantation cysts of iris, ciliary body or anterior chamber, **right eye**
    H21.322   Implantation cysts of iris, ciliary body or anterior chamber, **left eye**
    H21.323   Implantation cysts of iris, ciliary body or anterior chamber, **bilateral**
    H21.329   Implantation cysts of iris, ciliary body or anterior chamber, **unspecified eye**

● **H21.33**   Parasitic cyst of iris, ciliary body or anterior chamber
    H21.331   Parasitic cyst of iris, ciliary body or anterior chamber, **right eye**
    H21.332   Parasitic cyst of iris, ciliary body or anterior chamber, **left eye**
    H21.333   Parasitic cyst of iris, ciliary body or anterior chamber, **bilateral**
    H21.339   Parasitic cyst of iris, ciliary body or anterior chamber, **unspecified eye**

● **H21.34**   Primary cyst of pars plana
    H21.341   Primary cyst of pars plana, **right eye**
    H21.342   Primary cyst of pars plana, **left eye**
    H21.343   Primary cyst of pars plana, **bilateral**
    H21.349   Primary cyst of pars plana, **unspecified eye**

● **H21.35**   Exudative cyst of pars plana
    H21.351   Exudative cyst of pars plana, **right eye**
    H21.352   Exudative cyst of pars plana, **left eye**
    H21.353   Exudative cyst of pars plana, **bilateral**
    H21.359   Exudative cyst of pars plana, **unspecified eye**

● **H21.4**   Pupillary membranes
    Iris bombé
    Pupillary occlusion
    Pupillary seclusion
    Excludes1   congenital pupillary membranes (Q13.8)
    H21.40   Pupillary membranes, **unspecified eye**
    H21.41   Pupillary membranes, **right eye**
    H21.42   Pupillary membranes, **left eye**
    H21.43   Pupillary membranes, **bilateral**

● **H21.5**   Other and unspecified adhesions and disruptions of iris and ciliary body
    Excludes1   corectopia (Q13.2)
    ● **H21.50**   Unspecified adhesions of iris
      Synechia (iris) NOS
      H21.501   Unspecified adhesions of iris, **right eye**
      H21.502   Unspecified adhesions of iris, **left eye**
      H21.503   Unspecified adhesions of iris, **bilateral**
      H21.509   Unspecified adhesions of iris and ciliary body, **unspecified eye**
    ● **H21.51**   Anterior synechiae (iris)
      H21.511   Anterior synechiae (iris), **right eye**
      H21.512   Anterior synechiae (iris), **left eye**
      H21.513   Anterior synechiae (iris), **bilateral**
      H21.519   Anterior synechiae (iris), **unspecified eye**
    ● **H21.52**   Goniosynechiae
      H21.521   Goniosynechiae, **right eye**
      H21.522   Goniosynechiae, **left eye**
      H21.523   Goniosynechiae, **bilateral**
      H21.529   Goniosynechiae, **unspecified eye**

● **H21.53**   Iridodialysis
    H21.531   Iridodialysis, **right eye**
    H21.532   Iridodialysis, **left eye**
    H21.533   Iridodialysis, **bilateral**
    H21.539   Iridodialysis, **unspecified eye**

● **H21.54**   Posterior synechiae (iris)
    H21.541   Posterior synechiae (iris), **right eye**
    H21.542   Posterior synechiae (iris), **left eye**
    H21.543   Posterior synechiae (iris), **bilateral**
    H21.549   Posterior synechiae (iris), **unspecified eye**

● **H21.55**   Recession of chamber angle
    H21.551   Recession of chamber angle, **right eye**
    H21.552   Recession of chamber angle, **left eye**
    H21.553   Recession of chamber angle, **bilateral**
    H21.559   Recession of chamber angle, **unspecified eye**

● **H21.56**   Pupillary abnormalities
    Deformed pupil
    Ectopic pupil
    Rupture of sphincter, pupil
    Excludes1   congenital deformity of pupil (Q13.2-)
    H21.561   Pupillary abnormality, **right eye**
    H21.562   Pupillary abnormality, **left eye**
    H21.563   Pupillary abnormality, **bilateral**
    H21.569   Pupillary abnormality, **unspecified eye**

● **H21.8**   Other specified disorders of iris and ciliary body
    H21.81   Floppy iris syndrome
      Intraoperative floppy iris syndrome (IFIS)
      Use additional code for adverse effect, if applicable, to identify drug (T36-T50 with fifth or sixth character 5)
    H21.82   Plateau iris syndrome (post-iridectomy) (postprocedural)
    H21.89   Other specified disorders of iris and ciliary body

H21.9   Unspecified disorder of iris and ciliary body

▷ **H22**   *Disorders of iris and ciliary body in diseases classified elsewhere*
    Code first underlying disease, such as:
    gout (M1A.-, M10.-)
    leprosy (A30.-)
    parasitic disease (B89)

DISORDERS OF LENS (H25-H28)

● **H25**   Age-related cataract
    Senile cataract
    Excludes2   capsular glaucoma with pseudoexfoliation of lens (H40.1-)
    ● **H25.0**   Age-related incipient cataract
      ● **H25.01**   Cortical age-related cataract
        H25.011   Cortical age-related cataract, **right eye**   A
        H25.012   Cortical age-related cataract, **left eye**   A
        H25.013   Cortical age-related cataract, **bilateral**   A
        H25.019   Cortical age-related cataract, **unspecified eye**   A
      ● **H25.03**   Anterior subcapsular polar age-related cataract
        H25.031   Anterior subcapsular polar age-related cataract, **right eye**   A
        H25.032   Anterior subcapsular polar age-related cataract, **left eye**   A
        H25.033   Anterior subcapsular polar age-related cataract, **bilateral**   A
        H25.039   Anterior subcapsular polar age-related cataract, **unspecified eye**   A

Figure 7-9 Age-related cataract.
Nuclear sclerosis and cortical lens opacities are present. (From Ignatavicius DD, Workman ML: Medical-Surgical Nursing: Patient-Centered Collaborative Care, St. Louis, MO, Saunders/ Elsevier, 2010)

Item 7–5 Senile cataracts are linked to the aging process. The most common area for the formation of a cataract is the cortical area of the lens. **Polar cataracts** can be either anterior or posterior. **Anterior polar cataracts** are more common and are small, white, capsular cataracts located on the anterior portion of the lens. **Total cataracts,** also called **complete** or **mature,** cause an opacity of all fibers of the lens. **Hypermature** describes a mature cataract with a swollen, milky cortex that covers the entire lens. **Immature,** also called **incipient,** cataracts have a clear cortex and are only slightly opaque. Treatment for all cataracts is the removal of the lens.

- **H25.04 Posterior subcapsular polar age-related cataract**
  - H25.041   Posterior subcapsular polar age-related cataract, **right eye**   A
  - H25.042   Posterior subcapsular polar age-related cataract, **left eye**   A
  - H25.043   Posterior subcapsular polar age-related cataract, **bilateral**   A
  - H25.049   Posterior subcapsular polar age-related cataract, **unspecified** eye   A
- **H25.09 Other age-related incipient cataract**
  Coronary age-related cataract
  Punctate age-related cataract
  Water clefts
  - H25.091   Other age-related incipient cataract, **right eye**   A
  - H25.092   Other age-related incipient cataract, **left eye**   A
  - H25.093   Other age-related incipient cataract, **bilateral**   A
  - H25.099   Other age-related incipient cataract, **unspecified eye**   A
- **H25.1 Age-related nuclear cataract**
  Cataracta brunescens
  Nuclear sclerosis cataract
  - H25.10   Age-related nuclear cataract, **unspecified eye**   A
  - H25.11   Age-related nuclear cataract, **right eye**   A
  - H25.12   Age-related nuclear cataract, **left eye**   A
    Coding Clinic: 2016, Q1, P33
  - H25.13   Age-related nuclear cataract, **bilateral**   A
    Coding Clinic: 2016, Q1, P32
- **H25.2 Age-related cataract, morgagnian type**
  Age-related hypermature cataract
  - H25.20   Age-related cataract, morgagnian type, **unspecified eye**   A
  - H25.21   Age-related cataract, morgagnian type, **right eye**   A
  - H25.22   Age-related cataract, morgagnian type, **left eye**   A
  - H25.23   Age-related cataract, morgagnian type, **bilateral**   A
- **H25.8 Other age-related cataract**
  - **H25.81 Combined forms of age-related cataract**
    - H25.811   Combined forms of age-related cataract, **right eye**   A
    - H25.812   Combined forms of age-related cataract, **left eye**   A
    - H25.813   Combined forms of age-related cataract, **bilateral**   A
    - H25.819   Combined forms of age-related cataract, **unspecified eye**   A
  - **H25.89 Other age-related cataract**   A
- **H25.9 Unspecified age-related cataract**   A

- **H26 Other cataract**
  - **Excludes1**   congenital cataract (Q12.0)
  - **H26.0 Infantile and juvenile cataract**
    - **H26.00 Unspecified infantile and juvenile cataract**
      - H26.001   Unspecified infantile and juvenile cataract, **right eye**   P
      - H26.002   Unspecified infantile and juvenile cataract, **left eye**   P
      - H26.003   Unspecified infantile and juvenile cataract, **bilateral**   P
      - H26.009   Unspecified infantile and juvenile cataract, **unspecified eye**   P
    - **H26.01 Infantile and juvenile cortical, lamellar, or zonular cataract**
      - H26.011   Infantile and juvenile cortical, lamellar, or zonular cataract, **right eye**   P
      - H26.012   Infantile and juvenile cortical, lamellar, or zonular cataract, **left eye**   P
      - H26.013   Infantile and juvenile cortical, lamellar, or zonular cataract, **bilateral**   P
      - H26.019   Infantile and juvenile cortical, lamellar, or zonular cataract, **unspecified eye**   P
    - **H26.03 Infantile and juvenile nuclear cataract**
      - H26.031   Infantile and juvenile nuclear cataract, **right eye**   P
      - H26.032   Infantile and juvenile nuclear cataract, **left eye**   P
      - H26.033   Infantile and juvenile nuclear cataract, **bilateral**   P
      - H26.039   Infantile and juvenile nuclear cataract, **unspecified eye**   P
    - **H26.04 Anterior subcapsular polar infantile and juvenile cataract**
      - H26.041   Anterior subcapsular polar infantile and juvenile cataract, **right eye**   P
      - H26.042   Anterior subcapsular polar infantile and juvenile cataract, **left eye**   P
      - H26.043   Anterior subcapsular polar infantile and juvenile cataract, **bilateral**   P
      - H26.049   Anterior subcapsular polar infantile and juvenile cataract, **unspecified** eye   P
    - **H26.05 Posterior subcapsular polar infantile and juvenile cataract**
      - H26.051   Posterior subcapsular polar infantile and juvenile cataract, **right eye**   P
      - H26.052   Posterior subcapsular polar infantile and juvenile cataract, **left eye**   P
      - H26.053   Posterior subcapsular polar infantile and juvenile cataract, **bilateral**   P
      - H26.059   Posterior subcapsular polar infantile and juvenile cataract, **unspecified** eye   P
    - **H26.06 Combined forms of infantile and juvenile cataract**
      - H26.061   Combined forms of infantile and juvenile cataract, **right eye**   P
      - H26.062   Combined forms of infantile and juvenile cataract, **left eye**   P
      - H26.063   Combined forms of infantile and juvenile cataract **bilateral**   P
      - H26.069   Combined forms of infantile and juvenile cataract, **unspecified eye**   P
    - **H26.09 Other infantile and juvenile cataract**   P

CHAPTER 7 (H00-H59)

CHAPTER 7 (H00-H59)

● **H26.1**   **Traumatic cataract**

Use additional code (Chapter 20) to identify external cause

● **H26.10**   Unspecified traumatic cataract

    H26.101   Unspecified traumatic cataract, right eye

    H26.102   Unspecified traumatic cataract, left eye

    H26.103   Unspecified traumatic cataract, bilateral

    H26.109   Unspecified traumatic cataract, unspecified eye

● **H26.11**   Localized traumatic opacities

    H26.111   Localized traumatic opacities, right eye

    H26.112   Localized traumatic opacities, left eye

    H26.113   Localized traumatic opacities, bilateral

    H26.119   Localized traumatic opacities, unspecified eye

● **H26.12**   Partially resolved traumatic cataract

    H26.121   Partially resolved traumatic cataract, right eye

    H26.122   Partially resolved traumatic cataract, left eye

    H26.123   Partially resolved traumatic cataract, bilateral

    H26.129   Partially resolved traumatic cataract, unspecified eye

● **H26.13**   Total traumatic cataract

    H26.131   Total traumatic cataract, right eye

    H26.132   Total traumatic cataract, left eye

    H26.133   Total traumatic cataract, bilateral

    H26.139   Total traumatic cataract, unspecified eye

● **H26.2**   **Complicated cataract**

    H26.20   Unspecified complicated cataract

       Cataracta complicata NOS

● **H26.21**   Cataract with neovascularization

Code also associated condition, such as: chronic iridocyclitis (H20.1-)

    H26.211   Cataract with neovascularization, right eye

    H26.212   Cataract with neovascularization, left eye

    H26.213   Cataract with neovascularization, bilateral

    H26.219   Cataract with neovascularization, unspecified eye

● **H26.22**   Cataract secondary to ocular disorders (degenerative) (inflammatory)

Code also associated ocular disorder

    H26.221   Cataract secondary to ocular disorders (degenerative) (inflammatory), right eye

    H26.222   Cataract secondary to ocular disorders (degenerative) (inflammatory), left eye

    H26.223   Cataract secondary to ocular disorders (degenerative) (inflammatory), bilateral

    H26.229   Cataract secondary to ocular disorders (degenerative) (inflammatory), unspecified eye

● **H26.23**   Glaucomatous flecks (subcapsular)

Code first underlying glaucoma (H40-H42)

    H26.231   Glaucomatous flecks (subcapsular), right eye

    H26.232   Glaucomatous flecks (subcapsular), left eye

    H26.233   Glaucomatous flecks (subcapsular), bilateral

    H26.239   Glaucomatous flecks (subcapsular), unspecified eye

● **H26.3**   **Drug-induced cataract**

Toxic cataract

Use additional code for adverse effect, if applicable, to identify drug (T36-T50 with fifth or sixth character 5)

    H26.30   Drug-induced cataract, unspecified eye

    H26.31   Drug-induced cataract, right eye

    H26.32   Drug-induced cataract, left eye

    H26.33   Drug-induced cataract, bilateral

● **H26.4**   **Secondary cataract**

    Coding Clinic: 2018, Q2, P14

    H26.40   Unspecified secondary cataract

● **H26.41**   Soemmering's ring

    H26.411   Soemmering's ring, right eye

    H26.412   Soemmering's ring, left eye

    H26.413   Soemmering's ring, bilateral

    H26.419   Soemmering's ring, unspecified eye

● **H26.49**   Other secondary cataract

    H26.491   Other secondary cataract, right eye

    H26.492   Other secondary cataract, left eye

       Coding Clinic: 2018, Q2, P13

    H26.493   Other secondary cataract, bilateral

    H26.499   Other secondary cataract, unspecified eye

   H26.8   Other specified cataract

   H26.9   Unspecified cataract

● **H27**   **Other disorders of lens**

    Excludes1   congenital lens malformations (Q12.-)

                mechanical complications of intraocular lens implant (T85.2)

                pseudophakia (Z96.1)

● **H27.0**   **Aphakia**

Acquired absence of lens

Acquired aphakia

Aphakia due to trauma

    Excludes1   cataract extraction status (Z98.4-)

                congenital absence of lens (Q12.3)

                congenital aphakia (Q12.3)

    H27.00   Aphakia, unspecified eye

    H27.01   Aphakia, right eye

    H27.02   Aphakia, left eye

    H27.03   Aphakia, bilateral

● **H27.1**   **Dislocation of lens**

    H27.10   Unspecified dislocation of lens

● **H27.11**   Subluxation of lens

    H27.111   Subluxation of lens, right eye

    H27.112   Subluxation of lens, left eye

    H27.113   Subluxation of lens, bilateral

    H27.119   Subluxation of lens, unspecified eye

● **H27.12**   Anterior dislocation of lens

    H27.121   Anterior dislocation of lens, right eye

    H27.122   Anterior dislocation of lens, left eye

    H27.123   Anterior dislocation of lens, bilateral

    H27.129   Anterior dislocation of lens, unspecified eye

▶ New   ⇒ Revised   ~~deleted~~ Deleted   Excludes 1   Excludes 2   Includes   Use additional   Code first   Code also   Key words

OGCR Official Guidelines   X Assign placeholder X   ● Use Additional Character(s)   ▷ Manifestation Code   **Coding Clinic**

● H27.13   Posterior dislocation of lens

     H27.131   Posterior dislocation of lens, right eye

     H27.132   Posterior dislocation of lens, left eye

     H27.133   Posterior dislocation of lens, bilateral

     H27.139   Posterior dislocation of lens, unspecified eye

H27.8   Other specified disorders of lens

H27.9   Unspecified disorder of lens

◗ *H28*   *Cataract in diseases classified elsewhere*

     Code first underlying disease, such as:
       hypoparathyroidism (E20.-)
       myotonia (G71.1-)
       myxedema (E03.-)
       protein-calorie malnutrition (E40-E46)

     Excludes1   cataract in diabetes mellitus (E08.36, E09.36, E10.36, E11.36, E13.36)

DISORDERS OF CHOROID AND RETINA (H30-H36)

★ **(See Plate 90 on page 64.)**

● H30   Chorioretinal inflammation

   ● H30.0   Focal chorioretinal inflammation
       Focal chorioretinitis
       Focal choroiditis
       Focal retinitis
       Focal retinochoroiditis

     ● H30.00   Unspecified focal chorioretinal inflammation
         Focal chorioretinitis NOS
         Focal choroiditis NOS
         Focal retinitis NOS
         Focal retinochoroiditis NOS

       H30.001   Unspecified focal chorioretinal inflammation, right eye

       H30.002   Unspecified focal chorioretinal inflammation, left eye

       H30.003   Unspecified focal chorioretinal inflammation, bilateral

       H30.009   Unspecified focal chorioretinal inflammation, unspecified eye

     ● H30.01   Focal chorioretinal inflammation, juxtapapillary

       H30.011   Focal chorioretinal inflammation, juxtapapillary, right eye

       H30.012   Focal chorioretinal inflammation, juxtapapillary, left eye

       H30.013   Focal chorioretinal inflammation, juxtapapillary, bilateral

       H30.019   Focal chorioretinal inflammation, juxtapapillary, unspecified eye

     ● H30.02   Focal chorioretinal inflammation of posterior pole

       H30.021   Focal chorioretinal inflammation of posterior pole, right eye

       H30.022   Focal chorioretinal inflammation of posterior pole, left eye

       H30.023   Focal chorioretinal inflammation of posterior pole, bilateral

       H30.029   Focal chorioretinal inflammation of posterior pole, unspecified eye

     ● H30.03   Focal chorioretinal inflammation, peripheral

       H30.031   Focal chorioretinal inflammation, peripheral, right eye

       H30.032   Focal chorioretinal inflammation, peripheral, left eye

       H30.033   Focal chorioretinal inflammation, peripheral, bilateral

       H30.039   Focal chorioretinal inflammation, peripheral, unspecified eye

     ● H30.04   Focal chorioretinal inflammation, macular or paramacular

       H30.041   Focal chorioretinal inflammation, macular or paramacular, right eye

       H30.042   Focal chorioretinal inflammation, macular or paramacular, left eye

       H30.043   Focal chorioretinal inflammation, macular or paramacular, bilateral

       H30.049   Focal chorioretinal inflammation, macular or paramacular, unspecified eye

   ● H30.1   Disseminated chorioretinal inflammation
       Disseminated chorioretinitis
       Disseminated choroiditis
       Disseminated retinitis
       Disseminated retinochoroiditis

     Excludes2   exudative retinopathy (H35.02-)

     ● H30.10   Unspecified disseminated chorioretinal inflammation
         Disseminated chorioretinitis NOS
         Disseminated choroiditis NOS
         Disseminated retinitis NOS
         Disseminated retinochoroiditis NOS

       H30.101   Unspecified disseminated chorioretinal inflammation, right eye

       H30.102   Unspecified disseminated chorioretinal inflammation, left eye

       H30.103   Unspecified disseminated chorioretinal inflammation, bilateral

       H30.109   Unspecified disseminated chorioretinal inflammation, unspecified eye

     ● H30.11   Disseminated chorioretinal inflammation of posterior pole

       H30.111   Disseminated chorioretinal inflammation of posterior pole, right eye

       H30.112   Disseminated chorioretinal inflammation of posterior pole, left eye

       H30.113   Disseminated chorioretinal inflammation of posterior pole, bilateral

       H30.119   Disseminated chorioretinal inflammation of posterior pole, unspecified eye

     ● H30.12   Disseminated chorioretinal inflammation, peripheral

       H30.121   Disseminated chorioretinal inflammation, peripheral right eye

       H30.122   Disseminated chorioretinal inflammation, peripheral, left eye

       H30.123   Disseminated chorioretinal inflammation, peripheral, bilateral

       H30.129   Disseminated chorioretinal inflammation, peripheral, unspecified eye

     ● H30.13   Disseminated chorioretinal inflammation, generalized

       H30.131   Disseminated chorioretinal inflammation, generalized, right eye

       H30.132   Disseminated chorioretinal inflammation, generalized, left eye

       H30.133   Disseminated chorioretinal inflammation, generalized, bilateral

       H30.139   Disseminated chorioretinal inflammation, generalized, unspecified eye

CHAPTER 7 (H00-H59)

- **H30.14   Acute posterior multifocal placoid pigment epitheliopathy**
  - H30.141   Acute posterior multifocal placoid pigment epitheliopathy, right eye
  - H30.142   Acute posterior multifocal placoid pigment epitheliopathy, left eye
  - H30.143   Acute posterior multifocal placoid pigment epitheliopathy, bilateral
  - H30.149   Acute posterior multifocal placoid pigment epitheliopathy, unspecified eye
- **H30.2   Posterior cyclitis**
  - Pars planitis
  - H30.20   Posterior cyclitis, unspecified eye
  - H30.21   Posterior cyclitis, right eye
  - H30.22   Posterior cyclitis, left eye
  - H30.23   Posterior cyclitis, bilateral
- **H30.8   Other chorioretinal inflammations**
  - **H30.81   Harada's disease**
    - H30.811   Harada's disease, right eye
    - H30.812   Harada's disease, left eye
    - H30.813   Harada's disease, bilateral
    - H30.819   Harada's disease, unspecified eye
  - **H30.89   Other chorioretinal inflammations**
    - H30.891   Other chorioretinal inflammations, right eye
    - H30.892   Other chorioretinal inflammations, left eye
    - H30.893   Other chorioretinal inflammations, bilateral
    - H30.899   Other chorioretinal inflammations, unspecified eye
- **H30.9   Unspecified chorioretinal inflammation**
  - Chorioretinitis NOS
  - Choroiditis NOS
  - Neuroretinitis NOS
  - Retinitis NOS
  - Retinochoroiditis NOS
  - H30.90   Unspecified chorioretinal inflammation, unspecified eye
  - H30.91   Unspecified chorioretinal inflammation, right eye
  - H30.92   Unspecified chorioretinal inflammation, left eye
  - H30.93   Unspecified chorioretinal inflammation, bilateral

- **H31   Other disorders of choroid**
  - **H31.0   Chorioretinal scars**
    - **Excludes2**   postsurgical chorioretinal scars (H59.81-)
    - **H31.00   Unspecified chorioretinal scars**
      - H31.001   Unspecified chorioretinal scars, right eye
      - H31.002   Unspecified chorioretinal scars, left eye
      - H31.003   Unspecified chorioretinal scars, bilateral
      - H31.009   Unspecified chorioretinal scars, unspecified eye
    - **H31.01   Macula scars of posterior pole (postinflammatory) (post-traumatic)**
      - **Excludes1**   postprocedural chorioretinal scar (H59.81-)
      - H31.011   Macula scars of posterior pole (postinflammatory) (post-traumatic), right eye
      - H31.012   Macula scars of posterior pole (postinflammatory) (post-traumatic), left eye

  - H31.013   Macula scars of posterior pole (postinflammatory) (post-traumatic), bilateral
  - H31.019   Macula scars of posterior pole (postinflammatory) (post-traumatic), unspecified eye
  - **H31.02   Solar retinopathy**
    - H31.021   Solar retinopathy, right eye
    - H31.022   Solar retinopathy, left eye
    - H31.023   Solar retinopathy, bilateral
    - H31.029   Solar retinopathy, unspecified eye
  - **H31.09   Other chorioretinal scars**
    - H31.091   Other chorioretinal scars, right eye
    - H31.092   Other chorioretinal scars, left eye
    - H31.093   Other chorioretinal scars, bilateral
    - H31.099   Other chorioretinal scars, unspecified eye
- **H31.1   Choroidal degeneration**
  - **Excludes2**   angioid streaks of macula (H35.33)
  - **H31.10   Unspecified choroidal degeneration**
    - Choroidal sclerosis NOS
    - H31.101   Choroidal degeneration, unspecified, right eye
    - H31.102   Choroidal degeneration, unspecified, left eye
    - H31.103   Choroidal degeneration, unspecified, bilateral
    - H31.109   Choroidal degeneration, unspecified, unspecified eye
  - **H31.11   Age-related choroidal atrophy**
    - H31.111   Age-related choroidal atrophy, right eye   A
    - H31.112   Age-related choroidal atrophy, left eye   A
    - H31.113   Age-related choroidal atrophy, bilateral   A
    - H31.119   Age-related choroidal atrophy, unspecified eye   A
  - **H31.12   Diffuse secondary atrophy of choroid**
    - H31.121   Diffuse secondary atrophy of choroid, right eye
    - H31.122   Diffuse secondary atrophy of choroid, left eye
    - H31.123   Diffuse secondary atrophy of choroid, bilateral
    - H31.129   Diffuse secondary atrophy of choroid, unspecified eye
- **H31.2   Hereditary choroidal dystrophy**
  - **Excludes2**   hyperornithinemia (E72.4)
    - ornithinemia (E72.4)
  - H31.20   Hereditary choroidal dystrophy, unspecified
  - H31.21   Choroideremia
  - H31.22   Choroidal dystrophy (central areolar) (generalized) (peripapillary)
  - H31.23   Gyrate atrophy, choroid
  - H31.29   Other hereditary choroidal dystrophy
- **H31.3   Choroidal hemorrhage and rupture**
  - **H31.30   Unspecified choroidal hemorrhage**
    - H31.301   Unspecified choroidal hemorrhage, right eye
    - H31.302   Unspecified choroidal hemorrhage, left eye
    - H31.303   Unspecified choroidal hemorrhage, bilateral
    - H31.309   Unspecified choroidal hemorrhage, unspecified eye

---

▶ New   ⟹ Revised   ~~deleted~~ Deleted   Excludes 1   Excludes 2   Includes   Use additional   Code first   Code also   Key words

   OGCR Official Guidelines   X Assign placeholder X   ● Use Additional Character(s)   ▶ Manifestation Code   **Coding Clinic**

● H31.31   Expulsive choroidal hemorrhage
     H31.311   Expulsive choroidal hemorrhage, right eye
     H31.312   Expulsive choroidal hemorrhage, left eye
     H31.313   Expulsive choroidal hemorrhage, bilateral
     H31.319   Expulsive choroidal hemorrhage, unspecified eye

● H31.32   Choroidal rupture
     H31.321   Choroidal rupture, right eye
     H31.322   Choroidal rupture, left eye
     H31.323   Choroidal rupture, bilateral
     H31.329   Choroidal rupture, unspecified eye

● H31.4   Choroidal detachment
   ● H31.40   Unspecified choroidal detachment
     H31.401   Unspecified choroidal detachment, right eye
     H31.402   Unspecified choroidal detachment, left eye
     H31.403   Unspecified choroidal detachment, bilateral
     H31.409   Unspecified choroidal detachment, unspecified eye

   ● H31.41   Hemorrhagic choroidal detachment
     H31.411   Hemorrhagic choroidal detachment, right eye
     H31.412   Hemorrhagic choroidal detachment, left eye
     H31.413   Hemorrhagic choroidal detachment, bilateral
     H31.419   Hemorrhagic choroidal detachment, unspecified eye

   ● H31.42   Serous choroidal detachment
     H31.421   Serous choroidal detachment, right eye
     H31.422   Serous choroidal detachment, left eye
     H31.423   Serous choroidal detachment, bilateral
     H31.429   Serous choroidal detachment, unspecified eye

   H31.8   Other specified disorders of choroid
   H31.9   Unspecified disorder of choroid

▷ *H32*   *Chorioretinal disorders in diseases classified elsewhere*
    Code first underlying disease, such as:
     congenital toxoplasmosis (P37.1)
     histoplasmosis (B39.-)
     leprosy (A30.-)
    Excludes1   chorioretinitis (in):
       toxoplasmosis (acquired) (B58.01)
       tuberculosis (A18.53)

● H33   Retinal detachments and breaks
    Excludes1   detachment of retinal pigment epithelium (H35.72-, H35.73-)
   ● H33.0   Retinal detachment with retinal break
     Rhegmatogenous retinal detachment
     Excludes1   serous retinal detachment (without retinal break) (H33.2-)
    ● H33.00   Unspecified retinal detachment with retinal break
     H33.001   Unspecified retinal detachment with retinal break, right eye
     H33.002   Unspecified retinal detachment with retinal break, left eye
     H33.003   Unspecified retinal detachment with retinal break, bilateral
     H33.009   Unspecified retinal detachment with retinal break, unspecified eye

NON-RHEGMATOGENOUS RETINAL DETACHMENT
— Vitreous
— Retina
— Protein-rich fluid in sub-retinal space
Retinal pigment epithelium

VITREOUS DETACHMENT
— Vitreous
— Posterior hyaloid
— Internal limiting membrane

RHEGMATOGENOUS RETINAL DETACHMENT
Blood
— Vitreous
— Posterior hyaloid
— Retina
— Retinal tear
— Liquified vitreous
Retinal pigment epithelium

Figure 7-10   Retinal detachment. (From Kumar: Robbins and Cotran: Pathologic Basis of Disease, ed 7, Saunders, 2005)

Item 7–6   Retinal detachments and defects are conditions of the eye in which the retina separates from the underlying tissue. Initial detachment may be localized, requiring rapid treatment (medical emergency) to avoid the entire retina from detaching, which leads to vision loss and blindness.

   ● H33.01   Retinal detachment with single break
     H33.011   Retinal detachment with single break, right eye
     H33.012   Retinal detachment with single break, left eye
     H33.013   Retinal detachment with single break, bilateral
     H33.019   Retinal detachment with single break, unspecified eye

   ● H33.02   Retinal detachment with multiple breaks
     H33.021   Retinal detachment with multiple breaks, right eye
     H33.022   Retinal detachment with multiple breaks, left eye
     H33.023   Retinal detachment with multiple breaks, bilateral
     H33.029   Retinal detachment with multiple breaks, unspecified eye

   ● H33.03   Retinal detachment with giant retinal tear
     H33.031   Retinal detachment with giant retinal tear, right eye
     H33.032   Retinal detachment with giant retinal tear, left eye
     H33.033   Retinal detachment with giant retinal tear, bilateral
     H33.039   Retinal detachment with giant retinal tear, unspecified eye

CHAPTER 7 (H00-H59)

● H33.04 **Retinal detachment with retinal dialysis**
    H33.041 Retinal detachment with retinal dialysis, right eye
    H33.042 Retinal detachment with retinal dialysis, left eye
    H33.043 Retinal detachment with retinal dialysis, bilateral
    H33.049 Retinal detachment with retinal dialysis, unspecified eye

● H33.05 **Total retinal detachment**
    H33.051 Total retinal detachment, right eye
    H33.052 Total retinal detachment, left eye
    H33.053 Total retinal detachment, bilateral
    H33.059 Total retinal detachment, unspecified eye

● H33.1 **Retinoschisis and retinal cysts**
    Excludes1 congenital retinoschisis (Q14.1)
        microcystoid degeneration of retina (H35.42-)

● H33.10 **Unspecified retinoschisis**
    H33.101 Unspecified retinoschisis, right eye
    H33.102 Unspecified retinoschisis, left eye
    H33.103 Unspecified retinoschisis, bilateral
    H33.109 Unspecified retinoschisis, unspecified eye

● H33.11 **Cyst of ora serrata**
    H33.111 Cyst of ora serrata, right eye
    H33.112 Cyst of ora serrata, left eye
    H33.113 Cyst of ora serrata, bilateral
    H33.119 Cyst of ora serrata, unspecified eye

● H33.12 **Parasitic cyst of retina**
    H33.121 Parasitic cyst of retina, right eye
    H33.122 Parasitic cyst of retina, left eye
    H33.123 Parasitic cyst of retina, bilateral
    H33.129 Parasitic cyst of retina, unspecified eye

● H33.19 **Other retinoschisis and retinal cysts**
    Pseudocyst of retina
    H33.191 Other retinoschisis and retinal cysts, right eye
    H33.192 Other retinoschisis and retinal cysts, left eye
    H33.193 Other retinoschisis and retinal cysts, bilateral
    H33.199 Other retinoschisis and retinal cysts, unspecified eye

● H33.2 **Serous retinal detachment**
    Retinal detachment NOS
    Retinal detachment without retinal break
    Excludes1 central serous chorioretinopathy (H35.71-)
    H33.20 Serous retinal detachment, unspecified eye
    H33.21 Serous retinal detachment, right eye
    H33.22 Serous retinal detachment, left eye
    H33.23 Serous retinal detachment, bilateral

● H33.3 **Retinal breaks without detachment**
    Excludes1 chorioretinal scars after surgery for detachment (H59.81-)
        peripheral retinal degeneration without break (H35.4-)

● H33.30 **Unspecified retinal break**
    H33.301 Unspecified retinal break, right eye
    H33.302 Unspecified retinal break, left eye
    H33.303 Unspecified retinal break, bilateral
    H33.309 Unspecified retinal break, unspecified eye

● H33.31 **Horseshoe tear of retina without detachment**
    Operculum of retina without detachment
    H33.311 Horseshoe tear of retina without detachment, right eye
    H33.312 Horseshoe tear of retina without detachment, left eye
    H33.313 Horseshoe tear of retina without detachment, bilateral
    H33.319 Horseshoe tear of retina without detachment, unspecified eye

● H33.32 **Round hole of retina without detachment**
    H33.321 Round hole, right eye
    H33.322 Round hole, left eye
    H33.323 Round hole, bilateral
    H33.329 Round hole, unspecified eye

● H33.33 **Multiple defects of retina without detachment**
    H33.331 Multiple defects of retina without detachment, right eye
    H33.332 Multiple defects of retina without detachment, left eye
    H33.333 Multiple defects of retina without detachment, bilateral
    H33.339 Multiple defects of retina without detachment, unspecified eye

● H33.4 **Traction detachment of retina**
    Proliferative vitreo-retinopathy with retinal detachment
    H33.40 Traction detachment of retina, unspecified eye
    H33.41 Traction detachment of retina, right eye
    H33.42 Traction detachment of retina, left eye
    H33.43 Traction detachment of retina, bilateral

    H33.8 **Other retinal detachments**

● H34 **Retinal vascular occlusions**
    Blockage in vessel of the retina
    Excludes1 amaurosis fugax (G45.3)

● H34.0 **Transient retinal artery occlusion**
    H34.00 Transient retinal artery occlusion, unspecified eye
    H34.01 Transient retinal artery occlusion, right eye
    H34.02 Transient retinal artery occlusion, left eye
    H34.03 Transient retinal artery occlusion, bilateral

● H34.1 **Central retinal artery occlusion**
    H34.10 Central retinal artery occlusion, unspecified eye
    H34.11 Central retinal artery occlusion, right eye
    H34.12 Central retinal artery occlusion, left eye
    H34.13 Central retinal artery occlusion, bilateral

    H34.2 **Other retinal artery occlusions**

● H34.21 **Partial retinal artery occlusion**
    Hollenhorst's plaque
    Retinal microembolism
    H34.211 Partial retinal artery occlusion, right eye
    H34.212 Partial retinal artery occlusion, left eye
    H34.213 Partial retinal artery occlusion, bilateral
    H34.219 Partial retinal artery occlusion, unspecified eye

● H34.23 **Retinal artery branch occlusion**
    H34.231 Retinal artery branch occlusion, right eye
    H34.232 Retinal artery branch occlusion, left eye
    H34.233 Retinal artery branch occlusion, bilateral
    H34.239 Retinal artery branch occlusion, unspecified eye

▶ New   ⇛ Revised   ~~deleted~~ Deleted   Excludes 1   Excludes 2   Includes   Use additional   Code first   Code also   Key words
OGCR Official Guidelines   X Assign placeholder X   ● Use Additional Character(s)   ▮ Manifestation Code   **Coding Clinic**

- H34.8 Other retinal vascular occlusions
  Coding Clinic: 2016, Q4, P19
  - H34.81 Central retinal vein occlusion
    One of the following 7th characters is to be assigned to codes in subcategory H34.81 to designate the severity of the occlusion:

0	with macular edema
1	with retinal neovascularization
2	stable
	Old central retinal vein occlusion

    - H34.811 Central retinal vein occlusion, **right** eye
    - H34.812 Central retinal vein occlusion, **left** eye
    - H34.813 Central retinal vein occlusion, **bilateral**
    - H34.819 Central retinal vein occlusion, **unspecified** eye
  - H34.82 Venous **engorgement**
    Incipient retinal vein occlusion
    Partial retinal vein occlusion
    - H34.821 Venous engorgement, **right** eye
    - H34.822 Venous engorgement, **left** eye
    - H34.823 Venous engorgement, **bilateral**
    - H34.829 Venous engorgement, **unspecified** eye
  - H34.83 **Tributary (branch) retinal vein occlusion**
    One of the following 7th characters is to be assigned to codes in subcategory H34.83 to designate the severity of the occlusion:

0	with macular edema
1	with retinal neovascularization
2	stable
	Old tributary (branch) retinal vein occlusion

    - H34.831 Tributary (branch) retinal vein occlusion, **right** eye
    - H34.832 Tributary (branch) retinal vein occlusion, **left** eye
    - H34.833 Tributary (branch) retinal vein occlusion, **bilateral**
    - H34.839 Tributary (branch) retinal vein occlusion, **unspecified** eye
- H34.9 **Unspecified** retinal vascular occlusion

- H35 Other retinal disorders
  Excludes2 diabetic retinal disorders (E08.311-E08.359, E09.311-E09.359, E10.311-E10.359, E11.311-E11.359, E13.311-E13.359)
  - H35.0 Background retinopathy and retinal vascular changes
    Code also any associated hypertension (I10.-)
    OGCR Section I. C.9.a.5.

    Hypertensive Retinopathy
    Subcategory H35.0, Background retinopathy and retinal vascular changes, should be used with a code from category I10–I15, Hypertensive disease to include the systemic hypertension. The sequencing is based on the reason for the encounter.

    - H35.00 **Unspecified** background retinopathy
    - H35.01 Changes in retinal vascular appearance
      Retinal vascular sheathing
      - H35.011 Changes in retinal vascular appearance, **right** eye
      - H35.012 Changes in retinal vascular appearance, **left** eye
      - H35.013 Changes in retinal vascular appearance, **bilateral**
      - H35.019 Changes in retinal vascular appearance, **unspecified** eye
  - H35.02 Exudative retinopathy
    Coats retinopathy
    - H35.021 Exudative retinopathy, **right** eye
    - H35.022 Exudative retinopathy, **left** eye
    - H35.023 Exudative retinopathy, **bilateral**
    - H35.029 Exudative retinopathy, **unspecified** eye
  - H35.03 Hypertensive retinopathy
    - H35.031 Hypertensive retinopathy, **right** eye
    - H35.032 Hypertensive retinopathy, **left** eye
    - H35.033 Hypertensive retinopathy, **bilateral**
    - H35.039 Hypertensive retinopathy, **unspecified** eye
  - H35.04 Retinal **micro-aneurysms, unspecified**
    - H35.041 Retinal micro-aneurysms, unspecified, **right** eye
    - H35.042 Retinal micro-aneurysms, unspecified, **left** eye
    - H35.043 Retinal micro-aneurysms, unspecified, **bilateral**
    - H35.049 Retinal micro-aneurysms, unspecified, **unspecified** eye
  - H35.05 Retinal **neovascularization, unspecified**
    - H35.051 Retinal neovascularization, unspecified, **right** eye
    - H35.052 Retinal neovascularization, unspecified, **left** eye
    - H35.053 Retinal neovascularization, unspecified, **bilateral**
    - H35.059 Retinal neovascularization, unspecified, **unspecified** eye
  - H35.06 Retinal **vasculitis**
    Eales disease
    Retinal perivasculitis
    - H35.061 Retinal vasculitis, **right** eye
    - H35.062 Retinal vasculitis, **left** eye
    - H35.063 Retinal vasculitis, **bilateral**
    - H35.069 Retinal vasculitis, **unspecified** eye
  - H35.07 Retinal **telangiectasis**
    - H35.071 Retinal telangiectasis, **right** eye
    - H35.072 Retinal telangiectasis, **left** eye
    - H35.073 Retinal telangiectasis, **bilateral**
    - H35.079 Retinal telangiectasis, **unspecified** eye
  - H35.09 **Other intraretinal microvascular abnormalities**
    Retinal varices
  - H35.1 Retinopathy of prematurity
    - H35.10 Retinopathy of prematurity, **unspecified**
      Retinopathy of prematurity NOS
      - H35.101 Retinopathy of prematurity, unspecified, **right** eye
      - H35.102 Retinopathy of prematurity, unspecified, **left** eye
      - H35.103 Retinopathy of prematurity, unspecified, **bilateral**
      - H35.109 Retinopathy of prematurity, unspecified, **unspecified** eye
    - H35.11 Retinopathy of prematurity, **stage 0**
      - H35.111 Retinopathy of prematurity, stage 0, **right** eye
      - H35.112 Retinopathy of prematurity, stage 0, **left** eye
      - H35.113 Retinopathy of prematurity, stage 0, **bilateral**
      - H35.119 Retinopathy of prematurity, stage 0, **unspecified** eye

CHAPTER 7 (H00-H59)

● **H35.12**   **Retinopathy of prematurity, stage 1**
    H35.121   Retinopathy of prematurity, stage 1, right eye
    H35.122   Retinopathy of prematurity, stage 1, left eye
    H35.123   Retinopathy of prematurity, stage 1, bilateral
    H35.129   Retinopathy of prematurity, stage 1, unspecified eye

● **H35.13**   **Retinopathy of prematurity, stage 2**
    H35.131   Retinopathy of prematurity, stage 2, right eye
    H35.132   Retinopathy of prematurity, stage 2, left eye
    H35.133   Retinopathy of prematurity, stage 2, bilateral
    H35.139   Retinopathy of prematurity, stage 2, unspecified eye

● **H35.14**   **Retinopathy of prematurity, stage 3**
    H35.141   Retinopathy of prematurity, stage 3, right eye
    H35.142   Retinopathy of prematurity, stage 3, left eye
    H35.143   Retinopathy of prematurity, stage 3, bilateral
    H35.149   Retinopathy of prematurity, stage 3, unspecified eye

● **H35.15**   **Retinopathy of prematurity, stage 4**
    H35.151   Retinopathy of prematurity, stage 4, right eye
    H35.152   Retinopathy of prematurity, stage 4, left eye
    H35.153   Retinopathy of prematurity, stage 4, bilateral
    H35.159   Retinopathy of prematurity, stage 4, unspecified eye

● **H35.16**   **Retinopathy of prematurity, stage 5**
    H35.161   Retinopathy of prematurity, stage 5, right eye
    H35.162   Retinopathy of prematurity, stage 5, left eye
    H35.163   Retinopathy of prematurity, stage 5, bilateral
    H35.169   Retinopathy of prematurity, stage 5, unspecified eye

● **H35.17**   **Retrolental fibroplasia**
    H35.171   Retrolental fibroplasia, right eye
    H35.172   Retrolental fibroplasia, left eye
    H35.173   Retrolental fibroplasia, bilateral
    H35.179   Retrolental fibroplasia, unspecified eye

● **H35.2**   **Other non-diabetic proliferative retinopathy**
    Proliferative vitreo-retinopathy

    Excludes1   proliferative vitreo-retinopathy with retinal detachment (H33.4-)

    H35.20   Other non-diabetic proliferative retinopathy, unspecified eye
    H35.21   Other non-diabetic proliferative retinopathy, right eye
    H35.22   Other non-diabetic proliferative retinopathy, left eye
    H35.23   Other non-diabetic proliferative retinopathy, bilateral

Item 7-7   *Macular degeneration is typically age-related, chronic, and is evidenced by deterioration of the macula (the part of the retina that provides for central field vision), resulting in blurred vision or a blind spot in the center of visual field while not affecting peripheral vision.*

● **H35.3**   **Degeneration of macula and posterior pole**
    H35.30   Unspecified macular degeneration   A
      Age-related macular degeneration

● **H35.31**   Nonexudative age-related macular degeneration
      Atrophic age-related macular degeneration
      Dry age-related macular degeneration

      One of the following 7th characters is to be assigned to codes in subcategory H35.31 to designate the stage of the disease:

0	stage unspecified
1	early dry stage
2	intermediate dry stage
3	advanced atrophic without subfoveal involvement
	advanced dry stage
4	advanced atrophic with subfoveal involvement

   ● H35.311   Nonexudative age-related macular degeneration, right eye   A
        Coding Clinic: 2016, Q4, P20-21
   ● H35.312   Nonexudative age-related macular degeneration, left eye   A
        Coding Clinic: 2016, Q4, P20-21
   ● H35.313   Nonexudative age-related macular degeneration, bilateral   A
        Coding Clinic: 2016, Q4, P20
   ● H35.319   Nonexudative age-related macular degeneration, unspecified eye   A
        Coding Clinic: 2016, Q4, P20

● **H35.32**   Exudative age-related macular degeneration
      Wet age-related macular degeneration

      One of the following 7th characters is to be assigned to codes in subcategory H35.32 to designate the stage of the disease:

0	stage unspecified
1	with active choroidal neovascularization
2	with inactive choroidal neovascularization
	with involuted or regressed neovascularization
3	with inactive scar

      Coding Clinic: 2016, Q4, P20
   ● H35.321   Exudative age-related macular degeneration, right eye   A
   ● H35.322   Exudative age-related macular degeneration, left eye   A
   ● H35.323   Exudative age-related macular degeneration, bilateral   A
   ● H35.329   Exudative age-related macular degeneration, unspecified eye   A

   H35.33   Angioid streaks of macula

● **H35.34**   Macular cyst, hole, or pseudohole
    H35.341   Macular cyst, hole, or pseudohole, right eye
    H35.342   Macular cyst, hole, or pseudohole, left eye
    H35.343   Macular cyst, hole, or pseudohole, bilateral
    H35.349   Macular cyst, hole, or pseudohole, unspecified eye

● **H35.35**   Cystoid macular degeneration
     Excludes1   cystoid macular edema following cataract surgery (H59.Ø3-)
    H35.351   Cystoid macular degeneration, **right eye**
    H35.352   Cystoid macular degeneration, **left eye**
    H35.353   Cystoid macular degeneration, **bilateral**
    H35.359   Cystoid macular degeneration, **unspecified** eye

● **H35.36**   Drusen (degenerative) of macula
    H35.361   Drusen (degenerative) of macula, **right eye**
        Coding Clinic: 2Ø16, Q4, P21
    H35.362   Drusen (degenerative) of macula, **left eye**
        Coding Clinic: 2Ø16, Q4, P21
    H35.363   Drusen (degenerative) of macula, **bilateral**
        Coding Clinic: 2Ø17, Q1, P51
    H35.369   Drusen (degenerative) of macula, **unspecified** eye

● **H35.37**   Puckering of macula
    H35.371   Puckering of macula, **right eye**
    H35.372   Puckering of macula, **left eye**
    H35.373   Puckering of macula, **bilateral**
    H35.379   Puckering of macula, **unspecified eye**

● **H35.38**   Toxic maculopathy
     Code first poisoning due to drug or toxin, if applicable (T36-T65 with fifth or sixth character 1-4 or 6)
     Use additional code for adverse effect, if applicable, to identify drug (T36-T5Ø with fifth or sixth character 5)
    H35.381   Toxic maculopathy, **right eye**
    H35.382   Toxic maculopathy, **left eye**
    H35.383   Toxic maculopathy, **bilateral**
    H35.389   Toxic maculopathy, **unspecified eye**

● **H35.4**   Peripheral retinal degeneration
     Excludes1   hereditary retinal degeneration (dystrophy) (H35.5-)
               peripheral retinal degeneration with retinal break (H33.3-)
    H35.4Ø   **Unspecified peripheral retinal degeneration**
●   H35.41   **Lattice degeneration of retina**
       Palisade degeneration of retina
    H35.411   Lattice degeneration of retina, **right eye**
    H35.412   Lattice degeneration of retina, **left eye**
    H35.413   Lattice degeneration of retina, **bilateral**
    H35.419   Lattice degeneration of retina, **unspecified eye**
●   H35.42   **Microcystoid degeneration of retina**
    H35.421   Microcystoid degeneration of retina, **right eye**
    H35.422   Microcystoid degeneration of retina, **left eye**
    H35.423   Microcystoid degeneration of retina, **bilateral**
    H35.429   Microcystoid degeneration of retina, **unspecified eye**

● **H35.43**   Paving stone degeneration of retina
    H35.431   Paving stone degeneration of retina, **right eye**
    H35.432   Paving stone degeneration of retina, **left eye**
    H35.433   Paving stone degeneration of retina, **bilateral**
    H35.439   Paving stone degeneration of retina, **unspecified** eye

● **H35.44**   Age-related reticular degeneration of retina
    H35.441   Age-related reticular degeneration of retina, **right eye**   A
    H35.442   Age-related reticular degeneration of retina, **left eye**   A
    H35.443   Age-related reticular degeneration of retina, **bilateral**   A
    H35.449   Age-related reticular degeneration of retina, **unspecified** eye   A

● **H35.45**   Secondary pigmentary degeneration
    H35.451   Secondary pigmentary degeneration, **right eye**
    H35.452   Secondary pigmentary degeneration, **left eye**
    H35.453   Secondary pigmentary degeneration, **bilateral**
    H35.459   Secondary pigmentary degeneration, **unspecified** eye

● **H35.46**   Secondary vitreoretinal degeneration
    H35.461   Secondary vitreoretinal degeneration, **right eye**
    H35.462   Secondary vitreoretinal degeneration, **left eye**
    H35.463   Secondary vitreoretinal degeneration, **bilateral**
    H35.469   Secondary vitreoretinal degeneration, **unspecified** eye

● **H35.5**   Hereditary retinal dystrophy
     Excludes1   dystrophies primarily involving Bruch's membrane (H31.1-)
    H35.5Ø   **Unspecified hereditary retinal dystrophy**
    H35.51   **Vitreoretinal dystrophy**
    H35.52   **Pigmentary retinal dystrophy**
       Albipunctate retinal dystrophy
       Retinitis pigmentosa
       Tapetoretinal dystrophy
    H35.53   **Other dystrophies primarily involving the sensory retina**
       Stargardt's disease
    H35.54   **Dystrophies primarily involving the retinal pigment epithelium**
       Vitelliform retinal dystrophy

● **H35.6**   Retinal hemorrhage
    H35.6Ø   Retinal hemorrhage, **unspecified eye**
    H35.61   Retinal hemorrhage, **right eye**
    H35.62   Retinal hemorrhage, **left eye**
    H35.63   Retinal hemorrhage, **bilateral**

● **H35.7**   Separation of retinal layers
     Excludes1   retinal detachment (serous) (H33.2-)
               rhegmatogenous retinal detachment (H33.Ø-)
    H35.7Ø   **Unspecified separation of retinal layers**
●   H35.71   **Central serous chorioretinopathy**
    H35.711   Central serous chorioretinopathy, **right eye**
    H35.712   Central serous chorioretinopathy, **left eye**
    H35.713   Central serous chorioretinopathy, **bilateral**
    H35.719   Central serous chorioretinopathy, **unspecified** eye

CHAPTER 7 (HØØ-H59)

CHAPTER 7 (H00-H59)

- **H35.72 Serous detachment of retinal pigment epithelium**
  - H35.721 Serous detachment of retinal pigment epithelium, **right eye**
  - H35.722 Serous detachment of retinal pigment epithelium, **left eye**
  - H35.723 Serous detachment of retinal pigment epithelium, **bilateral**
  - H35.729 Serous detachment of retinal pigment epithelium, **unspecified** eye
- **H35.73 Hemorrhagic detachment of retinal pigment epithelium**
  - H35.731 Hemorrhagic detachment of retinal pigment epithelium, **right eye**
  - H35.732 Hemorrhagic detachment of retinal pigment epithelium, **left eye**
  - H35.733 Hemorrhagic detachment of retinal pigment epithelium, **bilateral**
  - H35.739 Hemorrhagic detachment of retinal pigment epithelium, **unspecified eye**
- **H35.8 Other specified retinal disorders**
  - **Excludes2** retinal hemorrhage (H35.6-)
  - H35.81 **Retinal edema**
    - Retinal cotton wool spots
  - H35.82 **Retinal ischemia**
  - H35.89 Other specified retinal disorders
- **H35.9 Unspecified retinal disorder**

- *H36 Retinal disorders in diseases classified elsewhere*
  - *Code first underlying disease, such as:*
    - lipid storage disorders (E75.-)
    - sickle-cell disorders (D57.-)
  - **Excludes1** arteriosclerotic retinopathy (H35.0-)
    - diabetic retinopathy (E08.3-, E09.3-, E10.3-, E11.3-, E13.3-)

GLAUCOMA (H40-H42)

- **H40 Glaucoma**
  - *Intraocular pressure (IOP) that is too high results from too much aqueous humor and because of excess production or inadequate drainage, optic nerve damage and vision loss may occur.*
  - **Excludes1** absolute glaucoma (H44.51-)
    - congenital glaucoma (Q15.0)
    - traumatic glaucoma due to birth injury (P15.3)
- **H40.0 Glaucoma suspect**
  - **H40.00 Preglaucoma, unspecified**
    - H40.001 Preglaucoma, unspecified, **right eye**
    - H40.002 Preglaucoma, unspecified, **left eye**
    - H40.003 Preglaucoma, unspecified, **bilateral**
    - H40.009 Preglaucoma, unspecified, **unspecified** eye
  - **H40.01 Open angle with borderline findings, low risk**
    - Open angle, low risk
    - H40.011 Open angle with borderline findings, low risk, **right eye**
    - H40.012 Open angle with borderline findings, low risk, **left eye**
    - H40.013 Open angle with borderline findings, low risk, **bilateral**
    - H40.019 Open angle with borderline findings, low risk, **unspecified** eye
  - **H40.02 Open angle with borderline findings, high risk**
    - Open angle, high risk
    - H40.021 Open angle with borderline findings, high risk, **right eye**
    - H40.022 Open angle with borderline findings, high risk, **left eye**
    - H40.023 Open angle with borderline findings, high risk, **bilateral**
    - H40.029 Open angle with borderline findings, high risk, **unspecified** eye
  - **H40.03 Anatomical narrow angle**
    - Primary angle closure suspect
    - H40.031 Anatomical narrow angle, **right eye**
    - H40.032 Anatomical narrow angle, **left eye**
    - H40.033 Anatomical narrow angle, **bilateral**
    - H40.039 Anatomical narrow angle, **unspecified** eye
  - **H40.04 Steroid responder**
    - H40.041 Steroid responder, **right eye**
    - H40.042 Steroid responder, **left eye**
    - H40.043 Steroid responder, **bilateral**
    - H40.049 Steroid responder, **unspecified** eye
  - **H40.05 Ocular hypertension**
    - H40.051 Ocular hypertension, **right eye**
    - H40.052 Ocular hypertension, **left eye**
    - H40.053 Ocular hypertension, **bilateral**
    - H40.059 Ocular hypertension, **unspecified** eye
  - **H40.06 Primary angle closure without glaucoma damage**
    - H40.061 Primary angle closure without glaucoma damage, **right eye**
    - H40.062 Primary angle closure without glaucoma damage, **left eye**
    - H40.063 Primary angle closure without glaucoma damage, **bilateral**
    - H40.069 Primary angle closure without glaucoma damage, **unspecified** eye
- **H40.1 Open-angle glaucoma**
  - X **H40.10 Unspecified open-angle glaucoma**
    - One of the following 7th characters is to be assigned to code H40.10 to designate the stage of glaucoma

0	stage unspecified
1	mild stage
2	moderate stage
3	severe stage
4	indeterminate stage

  - **H40.11 Primary open-angle glaucoma**
    - Chronic simple glaucoma
    - One of the following 7th characters is to be assigned to each code in subcategory H40.11 to designate the stage of glaucoma

0	stage unspecified
1	mild stage
2	moderate stage
3	severe stage
4	indeterminate stage

    Coding Clinic: 2016, Q4, P22
    - H40.111 Primary open-angle glaucoma, **right eye**
    - H40.112 Primary open-angle glaucoma, **left eye**
    - H40.113 Primary open-angle glaucoma, **bilateral**
    - H40.119 Primary open-angle glaucoma, **unspecified eye**

▶ New ⟹ Revised ~~deleted~~ Deleted | Excludes 1 | Excludes 2 | Includes | Use additional | Code first | Code also | Key words
OGCR Official Guidelines   X Assign placeholder X   ● Use Additional Character(s)   ▷ Manifestation Code   **Coding Clinic**

● **H40.12   Low-tension glaucoma**

> One of the following 7th characters is to be assigned to each code in subcategory H40.12 to designate the stage of glaucoma

> | | |
> |---|---|
> | Ø | stage unspecified |
> | 1 | mild stage |
> | 2 | moderate stage |
> | 3 | severe stage |
> | 4 | indeterminate stage |

> ● H40.121   Low-tension glaucoma, right eye
> ● H40.122   Low-tension glaucoma, left eye
> ● H40.123   Low-tension glaucoma, bilateral
> ● H40.129   Low-tension glaucoma, unspecified eye

● **H40.13   Pigmentary glaucoma**

> One of the following 7th characters is to be assigned to each code in subcategory H40.13 to designate the stage of glaucoma

> | | |
> |---|---|
> | Ø | stage unspecified |
> | 1 | mild stage |
> | 2 | moderate stage |
> | 3 | severe stage |
> | 4 | indeterminate stage |

> ● H40.131   Pigmentary glaucoma, right eye
> ● H40.132   Pigmentary glaucoma, left eye
> ● H40.133   Pigmentary glaucoma, bilateral
> ● H40.139   Pigmentary glaucoma, unspecified eye

● **H40.14   Capsular glaucoma with pseudoexfoliation of lens**

> One of the following 7th characters is to be assigned to each code in subcategory H40.14 to designate the stage of glaucoma

> | | |
> |---|---|
> | Ø | stage unspecified |
> | 1 | mild stage |
> | 2 | moderate stage |
> | 3 | severe stage |
> | 4 | indeterminate stage |

> ● H40.141   Capsular glaucoma with pseudoexfoliation of lens, right eye
> ● H40.142   Capsular glaucoma with pseudoexfoliation of lens, left eye
> ● H40.143   Capsular glaucoma with pseudoexfoliation of lens, bilateral
> ● H40.149   Capsular glaucoma with pseudoexfoliation of lens, unspecified eye

● **H40.15   Residual stage of open-angle glaucoma**
> H40.151   Residual stage of open-angle glaucoma, right eye
> H40.152   Residual stage of open-angle glaucoma, left eye
> H40.153   Residual stage of open-angle glaucoma, bilateral
> H40.159   Residual stage of open-angle glaucoma, unspecified eye

● **H40.2   Primary angle-closure glaucoma**

> **Excludes1**   aqueous misdirection (H40.83-)
> malignant glaucoma (H40.83-)

X ● **H40.20   Unspecified primary angle-closure glaucoma**

> One of the following 7th characters is to be assigned to code H40.20 to designate the stage of glaucoma

> | | |
> |---|---|
> | Ø | stage unspecified |
> | 1 | mild stage |
> | 2 | moderate stage |
> | 3 | severe stage |
> | 4 | indeterminate stage |

● **H40.21   Acute angle-closure glaucoma**
> Acute angle-closure glaucoma attack
> Acute angle-closure glaucoma crisis

> H40.211   Acute angle-closure glaucoma, right eye
> H40.212   Acute angle-closure glaucoma, left eye
> H40.213   Acute angle-closure glaucoma, bilateral
> H40.219   Acute angle-closure glaucoma, unspecified eye

● **H40.22   Chronic angle-closure glaucoma**
> Chronic primary angle closure glaucoma

> One of the following 7th characters is to be assigned to each code in subcategory H40.22 to designate the stage of glaucoma

> | | |
> |---|---|
> | Ø | stage unspecified |
> | 1 | mild stage |
> | 2 | moderate stage |
> | 3 | severe stage |
> | 4 | indeterminate stage |

> ● H40.221   Chronic angle-closure glaucoma, right eye
> ● H40.222   Chronic angle-closure glaucoma, left eye
> ● H40.223   Chronic angle-closure glaucoma, bilateral
> ● H40.229   Chronic angle-closure glaucoma, unspecified eye

● **H40.23   Intermittent angle-closure glaucoma**
> H40.231   Intermittent angle-closure glaucoma, right eye
> H40.232   Intermittent angle-closure glaucoma, left eye
> H40.233   Intermittent angle-closure glaucoma, bilateral
> H40.239   Intermittent angle-closure glaucoma, unspecified eye

● **H40.24   Residual stage of angle-closure glaucoma**
> H40.241   Residual stage of angle-closure glaucoma, right eye
> H40.242   Residual stage of angle-closure glaucoma, left eye
> H40.243   Residual stage of angle-closure glaucoma, bilateral
> H40.249   Residual stage of angle-closure glaucoma, unspecified eye

CHAPTER 7 (H00-H59)

● **H40.3** Glaucoma secondary to eye trauma

Code also underlying condition

One of the following 7th characters is to be assigned to each code in subcategory H40.3 to designate the stage of glaucoma

0	stage unspecified
1	mild stage
2	moderate stage
3	severe stage
4	indeterminate stage

X ● **H40.30** Glaucoma secondary to eye trauma, unspecified eye

X ● **H40.31** Glaucoma secondary to eye trauma, right eye

X ● **H40.32** Glaucoma secondary to eye trauma, left eye

X ● **H40.33** Glaucoma secondary to eye trauma, bilateral

● **H40.4** Glaucoma secondary to eye inflammation

Code also underlying condition

One of the following 7th characters is to be assigned to each code in subcategory H40.4 to designate the stage of glaucoma

0	stage unspecified
1	mild stage
2	moderate stage
3	severe stage
4	indeterminate stage

X ● **H40.40** Glaucoma secondary to eye inflammation, unspecified eye

X ● **H40.41** Glaucoma secondary to eye inflammation, right eye

X ● **H40.42** Glaucoma secondary to eye inflammation, left eye

X ● **H40.43** Glaucoma secondary to eye inflammation, bilateral

● **H40.5** Glaucoma secondary to other eye disorders

Code also underlying eye disorder

One of the following 7th characters is to be assigned to each code in subcategory H40.5 to designate the stage of glaucoma

0	stage unspecified
1	mild stage
2	moderate stage
3	severe stage
4	indeterminate stage

X ● **H40.50** Glaucoma secondary to other eye disorders, unspecified eye

X ● **H40.51** Glaucoma secondary to other eye disorders, right eye

X ● **H40.52** Glaucoma secondary to other eye disorders, left eye

X ● **H40.53** Glaucoma secondary to other eye disorders, bilateral

● **H40.6** Glaucoma secondary to drugs

Use additional code for adverse effect, if applicable, to identify drug (T36-T50 with fifth or sixth character 5)

One of the following 7th characters is to be assigned to each code in subcategory H40.6 to designate the stage of glaucoma

0	stage unspecified
1	mild stage
2	moderate stage
3	severe stage
4	indeterminate stage

X ● **H40.60** Glaucoma secondary to drugs, unspecified eye

X ● **H40.61** Glaucoma secondary to drugs, right eye

X ● **H40.62** Glaucoma secondary to drugs, left eye

X ● **H40.63** Glaucoma secondary to drugs, bilateral

● **H40.8** Other glaucoma

● **H40.81** Glaucoma with increased episcleral venous pressure

H40.811 Glaucoma with increased episcleral venous pressure, right eye

H40.812 Glaucoma with increased episcleral venous pressure, left eye

H40.813 Glaucoma with increased episcleral venous pressure, bilateral

H40.819 Glaucoma with increased episcleral venous pressure, unspecified eye

● **H40.82** Hypersecretion glaucoma

H40.821 Hypersecretion glaucoma, right eye

H40.822 Hypersecretion glaucoma, left eye

H40.823 Hypersecretion glaucoma, bilateral

H40.829 Hypersecretion glaucoma, unspecified eye

● **H40.83** Aqueous misdirection

Malignant glaucoma

H40.831 Aqueous misdirection, right eye

H40.832 Aqueous misdirection, left eye

H40.833 Aqueous misdirection, bilateral

H40.839 Aqueous misdirection, unspecified eye

H40.89 Other specified glaucoma

H40.9 Unspecified glaucoma

▷ *H42* *Glaucoma in diseases classified elsewhere*

Code first underlying condition, such as:
amyloidosis (E85.-)
aniridia (Q13.1)
glaucoma (in) diabetes mellitus (E08.39, E09.39, E10.39, E11.39, E13.39)
Lowe's syndrome (E72.03)
Reiger's anomaly (Q13.81)
specified metabolic disorder (E70-E88)

Excludes1   glaucoma (in) onchocerciasis (B73.02)
glaucoma (in) syphilis (A52.71)
glaucoma (in) tuberculous (A18.59)

DISORDERS OF VITREOUS BODY AND GLOBE (H43-H44)

● **H43** Disorders of vitreous body

● **H43.0** Vitreous prolapse

Excludes1   vitreous syndrome following cataract surgery (H59.0-)
traumatic vitreous prolapse (S05.2-)

H43.00 Vitreous prolapse, unspecified eye

H43.01 Vitreous prolapse, right eye

H43.02 Vitreous prolapse, left eye

H43.03 Vitreous prolapse, bilateral

● **H43.1** Vitreous hemorrhage

H43.10 Vitreous hemorrhage, unspecified eye

H43.11 Vitreous hemorrhage, right eye

H43.12 Vitreous hemorrhage, left eye

H43.13 Vitreous hemorrhage, bilateral

● **H43.2** Crystalline deposits in vitreous body

H43.20 Crystalline deposits in vitreous body, unspecified eye

H43.21 Crystalline deposits in vitreous body, right eye

H43.22 Crystalline deposits in vitreous body, left eye

H43.23 Crystalline deposits in vitreous body, bilateral

▶ New   ⟴ Revised   ~~deleted~~ Deleted | Excludes 1 | | Excludes 2 | | Includes | | Use additional | | Code first | | Code also | | Key words |

OGCR Official Guidelines   X Assign placeholder X   ● Use Additional Character(s)   ▷ Manifestation Code   **Coding Clinic**

● **H43.3   Other vitreous opacities**
  ● **H43.31   Vitreous membranes and strands**
    H43.311   Vitreous membranes and strands, right eye
    H43.312   Vitreous membranes and strands, left eye
    H43.313   Vitreous membranes and strands, bilateral
    H43.319   Vitreous membranes and strands, unspecified eye
  ● **H43.39   Other vitreous opacities**
    Vitreous floaters
    Small clumps of cells that float in the vitreous of the eye, appearing as black specks or dots in the field of vision and common in the aging eye.
    H43.391   Other vitreous opacities, right eye
    H43.392   Other vitreous opacities, left eye
    H43.393   Other vitreous opacities, bilateral
    H43.399   Other vitreous opacities, unspecified eye

● **H43.8   Other disorders of vitreous body**
    Excludes1   proliferative vitreo-retinopathy with retinal detachment (H33.4)
    Excludes2   vitreous abscess (H44.02-)
  ● **H43.81   Vitreous degeneration**
    Vitreous detachment
    H43.811   Vitreous degeneration, right eye
    H43.812   Vitreous degeneration, left eye
    H43.813   Vitreous degeneration, bilateral
    H43.819   Vitreous degeneration, unspecified eye
  ● **H43.82   Vitreomacular adhesion**
    Vitreomacular traction
    H43.821   Vitreomacular adhesion, right eye   A
    H43.822   Vitreomacular adhesion, left eye   A
    H43.823   Vitreomacular adhesion, bilateral   A
    H43.829   Vitreomacular adhesion, unspecified eye   A
    H43.89   Other disorders of vitreous body
    H43.9   Unspecified disorder of vitreous body

● **H44   Disorders of globe**
    Includes   disorders affecting multiple structures of eye
  ● **H44.0   Purulent endophthalmitis**
    Use additional code to identify organism
    Excludes1   bleb associated endophthalmitis (H59.4-)
  ● **H44.00   Unspecified purulent endophthalmitis**
    H44.001   Unspecified purulent endophthalmitis, right eye
    H44.002   Unspecified purulent endophthalmitis, left eye
    H44.003   Unspecified purulent endophthalmitis, bilateral
    H44.009   Unspecified purulent endophthalmitis, unspecified eye
  ● **H44.01   Panophthalmitis (acute)**
    H44.011   Panophthalmitis (acute), right eye
    H44.012   Panophthalmitis (acute), left eye
    H44.013   Panophthalmitis (acute), bilateral
    H44.019   Panophthalmitis (acute), unspecified eye
  ● **H44.02   Vitreous abscess (chronic)**
    H44.021   Vitreous abscess (chronic), right eye
    H44.022   Vitreous abscess (chronic), left eye
    H44.023   Vitreous abscess (chronic), bilateral
    H44.029   Vitreous abscess (chronic), unspecified eye

● **H44.1   Other endophthalmitis**
    Excludes1   bleb associated endophthalmitis (H59.4-)
    Excludes2   ophthalmia nodosa (H16.2-)
  ● **H44.11   Panuveitis**
    H44.111   Panuveitis, right eye
    H44.112   Panuveitis, left eye
    H44.113   Panuveitis, bilateral
    H44.119   Panuveitis, unspecified eye
  ● **H44.12   Parasitic endophthalmitis, unspecified**
    H44.121   Parasitic endophthalmitis, unspecified, right eye
    H44.122   Parasitic endophthalmitis, unspecified, left eye
    H44.123   Parasitic endophthalmitis, unspecified, bilateral
    H44.129   Parasitic endophthalmitis, unspecified, unspecified eye
  ● **H44.13   Sympathetic uveitis**
    H44.131   Sympathetic uveitis, right eye
    H44.132   Sympathetic uveitis, left eye
    H44.133   Sympathetic uveitis, bilateral
    H44.139   Sympathetic uveitis, unspecified eye
    H44.19   Other endophthalmitis

● **H44.2   Degenerative myopia**
    Malignant myopia
    H44.20   Degenerative myopia, unspecified eye
    H44.21   Degenerative myopia, right eye
    H44.22   Degenerative myopia, left eye
    H44.23   Degenerative myopia, bilateral
  ● **H44.2A   Degenerative myopia with choroidal neovascularization**
    Use Additional code for any associated choroid disorders (H31.-)
    H44.2A1   Degenerative myopia with choroidal neovascularization, right eye
    H44.2A2   Degenerative myopia with choroidal neovascularization, left eye
    H44.2A3   Degenerative myopia with choroidal neovascularization, bilateral eye
    H44.2A9   Degenerative myopia with choroidal neovascularization, unspecified eye
  ● **H44.2B   Degenerative myopia with macular hole**
    H44.2B1   Degenerative myopia with macular hole, right eye
    H44.2B2   Degenerative myopia with macular hole, left eye
    H44.2B3   Degenerative myopia with macular hole, bilateral eye
    H44.2B9   Degenerative myopia with macular hole, unspecified eye
  ● **H44.2C   Degenerative myopia with retinal detachment**
    Use Additional code to identify the retinal detachment (H33.-)
    H44.2C1   Degenerative myopia with retinal detachment, right eye
    H44.2C2   Degenerative myopia with retinal detachment, left eye
    H44.2C3   Degenerative myopia with retinal detachment, bilateral eye
    H44.2C9   Degenerative myopia with retinal detachment, unspecified eye

CHAPTER 7 (H00–H59)

● H44.2D Degenerative myopia with foveoschisis
    H44.2D1 Degenerative myopia with foveoschisis, right eye
    H44.2D2 Degenerative myopia with foveoschisis, left eye
    H44.2D3 Degenerative myopia with foveoschisis, bilateral eye
    H44.2D9 Degenerative myopia with foveoschisis, unspecified eye
● H44.2E Degenerative myopia with other maculopathy
    H44.2E1 Degenerative myopia with other maculopathy, right eye
    H44.2E2 Degenerative myopia with other maculopathy, left eye
    H44.2E3 Degenerative myopia with other maculopathy, bilateral eye
    H44.2E9 Degenerative myopia with other maculopathy, unspecified eye

● H44.3 Other and unspecified degenerative disorders of globe
    H44.30 Unspecified degenerative disorder of globe
● H44.31 Chalcosis
    H44.311 Chalcosis, right eye
    H44.312 Chalcosis, left eye
    H44.313 Chalcosis, bilateral
    H44.319 Chalcosis, unspecified eye
● H44.32 Siderosis of eye
    H44.321 Siderosis of eye, right eye
    H44.322 Siderosis of eye, left eye
    H44.323 Siderosis of eye, bilateral
    H44.329 Siderosis of eye, unspecified eye
● H44.39 Other degenerative disorders of globe
    H44.391 Other degenerative disorders of globe, right eye
    H44.392 Other degenerative disorders of globe, left eye
    H44.393 Other degenerative disorders of globe, bilateral
    H44.399 Other degenerative disorders of globe, unspecified eye

● H44.4 Hypotony of eye
    H44.40 Unspecified hypotony of eye
● H44.41 Flat anterior chamber hypotony of eye
    H44.411 Flat anterior chamber hypotony of right eye
    H44.412 Flat anterior chamber hypotony of left eye
    H44.413 Flat anterior chamber hypotony of eye, bilateral
    H44.419 Flat anterior chamber hypotony of unspecified eye
● H44.42 Hypotony of eye due to ocular fistula
    H44.421 Hypotony of right eye due to ocular fistula
    H44.422 Hypotony of left eye due to ocular fistula
    H44.423 Hypotony of eye due to ocular fistula, bilateral
    H44.429 Hypotony of unspecified eye due to ocular fistula
● H44.43 Hypotony of eye due to other ocular disorders
    H44.431 Hypotony of eye due to other ocular disorders, right eye
    H44.432 Hypotony of eye due to other ocular disorders, left eye
    H44.433 Hypotony of eye due to other ocular disorders, bilateral
    H44.439 Hypotony of eye due to other ocular disorders, unspecified eye

● H44.44 Primary hypotony of eye
    H44.441 Primary hypotony of right eye
    H44.442 Primary hypotony of left eye
    H44.443 Primary hypotony of eye, bilateral
    H44.449 Primary hypotony of unspecified eye
● H44.5 Degenerated conditions of globe
    H44.50 Unspecified degenerated conditions of globe
● H44.51 Absolute glaucoma
    H44.511 Absolute glaucoma, right eye
    H44.512 Absolute glaucoma, left eye
    H44.513 Absolute glaucoma, bilateral
    H44.519 Absolute glaucoma, unspecified eye
● H44.52 Atrophy of globe
    Phthisis bulbi
    H44.521 Atrophy of globe, right eye
    H44.522 Atrophy of globe, left eye
    H44.523 Atrophy of globe, bilateral
    H44.529 Atrophy of globe, unspecified eye
● H44.53 Leucocoria
    H44.531 Leucocoria, right eye
    H44.532 Leucocoria, left eye
    H44.533 Leucocoria, bilateral
    H44.539 Leucocoria, unspecified eye

● H44.6 Retained (old) intraocular foreign body, magnetic
Use additional code to identify magnetic foreign body (Z18.11)

    Excludes1 current intraocular foreign body (S05.-)
    Excludes2 retained foreign body in eyelid (H02.81-)
              retained (old) foreign body following penetrating wound of orbit (H05.5-)
              retained (old) intraocular foreign body, nonmagnetic (H44.7-)

● H44.60 Unspecified retained (old) intraocular foreign body, magnetic
    H44.601 Unspecified retained (old) intraocular foreign body, magnetic, right eye
    H44.602 Unspecified retained (old) intraocular foreign body, magnetic, left eye
    H44.603 Unspecified retained (old) intraocular foreign body, magnetic, bilateral
    H44.609 Unspecified retained (old) intraocular foreign body, magnetic, unspecified eye
● H44.61 Retained (old) magnetic foreign body in anterior chamber
    H44.611 Retained (old) magnetic foreign body in anterior chamber, right eye
    H44.612 Retained (old) magnetic foreign body in anterior chamber, left eye
    H44.613 Retained (old) magnetic foreign body in anterior chamber, bilateral
    H44.619 Retained (old) magnetic foreign body in anterior chamber, unspecified eye
● H44.62 Retained (old) magnetic foreign body in iris or ciliary body
    H44.621 Retained (old) magnetic foreign body in iris or ciliary body, right eye
    H44.622 Retained (old) magnetic foreign body in iris or ciliary body, left eye
    H44.623 Retained (old) magnetic foreign body in iris or ciliary body, bilateral
    H44.629 Retained (old) magnetic foreign body in iris or ciliary body, unspecified eye

▶ New   ⇒ Revised   ~~deleted~~ Deleted   Excludes 1   Excludes 2   Includes   Use additional   Code first   Code also   Key words
OGCR Official Guidelines   X Assign placeholder X   ● Use Additional Character(s)   ▷ Manifestation Code   **Coding Clinic**

● H44.63   Retained (old) magnetic foreign body in lens

    H44.631   Retained (old) magnetic foreign body in lens, right eye

    H44.632   Retained (old) magnetic foreign body in lens, left eye

    H44.633   Retained (old) magnetic foreign body in lens, bilateral

    H44.639   Retained (old) magnetic foreign body in lens, unspecified eye

● H44.64   Retained (old) magnetic foreign body in posterior wall of globe

    H44.641   Retained (old) magnetic foreign body in posterior wall of globe, right eye

    H44.642   Retained (old) magnetic foreign body in posterior wall of globe, left eye

    H44.643   Retained (old) magnetic foreign body in posterior wall of globe, bilateral

    H44.649   Retained (old) magnetic foreign body in posterior wall of globe, unspecified eye

● H44.65   Retained (old) magnetic foreign body in vitreous body

    H44.651   Retained (old) magnetic foreign body in vitreous body, right eye

    H44.652   Retained (old) magnetic foreign body in vitreous body, left eye

    H44.653   Retained (old) magnetic foreign body in vitreous body, bilateral

    H44.659   Retained (old) magnetic foreign body in vitreous body, unspecified eye

● H44.69   Retained (old) intraocular foreign body, magnetic, in other or multiple sites

    H44.691   Retained (old) intraocular foreign body, magnetic, in other or multiple sites, right eye

    H44.692   Retained (old) intraocular foreign body, magnetic, in other or multiple sites, left eye

    H44.693   Retained (old) intraocular foreign body, magnetic, in other or multiple sites, bilateral

    H44.699   Retained (old) intraocular foreign body, magnetic, in other or multiple sites, unspecified eye

● H44.7   Retained (old) intraocular foreign body, nonmagnetic

    Use additional code to identify nonmagnetic foreign body (Z18.01-Z18.10, Z18.12, Z18.2-Z18.9)

    Excludes1   current intraocular foreign body (S05.-)

    Excludes2   retained foreign body in eyelid (H02.81-)
               retained (old) foreign body following penetrating wound of orbit (H05.5-)
               retained (old) intraocular foreign body, magnetic (H44.6-)

● H44.70   Unspecified retained (old) intraocular foreign body, nonmagnetic

    H44.701   Unspecified retained (old) intraocular foreign body, nonmagnetic, right eye

    H44.702   Unspecified retained (old) intraocular foreign body, nonmagnetic, left eye

    H44.703   Unspecified retained (old) intraocular foreign body, nonmagnetic, bilateral

    H44.709   Unspecified retained (old) intraocular foreign body, nonmagnetic, unspecified eye

        Retained (old) intraocular foreign body NOS

● H44.71   Retained (nonmagnetic) (old) foreign body in anterior chamber

    H44.711   Retained (nonmagnetic) (old) foreign body in anterior chamber, right eye

    H44.712   Retained (nonmagnetic) (old) foreign body in anterior chamber, left eye

    H44.713   Retained (nonmagnetic) (old) foreign body in anterior chamber, bilateral

    H44.719   Retained (nonmagnetic) (old) foreign body in anterior chamber, unspecified eye

● H44.72   Retained (nonmagnetic) (old) foreign body in iris or ciliary body

    H44.721   Retained (nonmagnetic) (old) foreign body in iris or ciliary body, right eye

    H44.722   Retained (nonmagnetic) (old) foreign body in iris or ciliary body, left eye

    H44.723   Retained (nonmagnetic) (old) foreign body in iris or ciliary body, bilateral

    H44.729   Retained (nonmagnetic) (old) foreign body in iris or ciliary body, unspecified eye

● H44.73   Retained (nonmagnetic) (old) foreign body in lens

    H44.731   Retained (nonmagnetic) (old) foreign body in lens, right eye

    H44.732   Retained (nonmagnetic) (old) foreign body in lens, left eye

    H44.733   Retained (nonmagnetic) (old) foreign body in lens, bilateral

    H44.739   Retained (nonmagnetic) (old) foreign body in lens, unspecified eye

● H44.74   Retained (nonmagnetic) (old) foreign body in posterior wall of globe

    H44.741   Retained (nonmagnetic) (old) foreign body in posterior wall of globe, right eye

    H44.742   Retained (nonmagnetic) (old) foreign body in posterior wall of globe, left eye

    H44.743   Retained (nonmagnetic) (old) foreign body in posterior wall of globe, bilateral

    H44.749   Retained (nonmagnetic) (old) foreign body in posterior wall of globe, unspecified eye

● H44.75   Retained (nonmagnetic) (old) foreign body in vitreous body

    H44.751   Retained (nonmagnetic) (old) foreign body in vitreous body, right eye

    H44.752   Retained (nonmagnetic) (old) foreign body in vitreous body, left eye

    H44.753   Retained (nonmagnetic) (old) foreign body in vitreous body, bilateral

    H44.759   Retained (nonmagnetic) (old) foreign body in vitreous body, unspecified eye

● H44.79   Retained (old) intraocular foreign body, nonmagnetic, in other or multiple sites

    H44.791   Retained (old) intraocular foreign body, nonmagnetic, in other or multiple sites, right eye

    H44.792   Retained (old) intraocular foreign body, nonmagnetic, in other or multiple sites, left eye

    H44.793   Retained (old) intraocular foreign body, nonmagnetic, in other or multiple sites, bilateral

    H44.799   Retained (old) intraocular foreign body, nonmagnetic, in other or multiple sites, unspecified eye

CHAPTER 7 (H00-H59)

- **H44.8   Other disorders of globe**
  - **H44.81   Hemophthalmos**
    - H44.811   Hemophthalmos, right eye
    - H44.812   Hemophthalmos, left eye
    - H44.813   Hemophthalmos, bilateral
    - H44.819   Hemophthalmos, unspecified eye
  - **H44.82   Luxation of globe**
    - H44.821   Luxation of globe, right eye
    - H44.822   Luxation of globe, left eye
    - H44.823   Luxation of globe, bilateral
    - H44.829   Luxation of globe, unspecified eye
  - **H44.89   Other disorders of globe**
- **H44.9   Unspecified disorder of globe**

★ **(See Plate 86 on page 55.)**

DISORDERS OF OPTIC NERVE AND VISUAL PATHWAYS (H46-H47)

- **H46   Optic neuritis**
  - **Excludes2**   ischemic optic neuropathy (H47.01-)
  - neuromyelitis optica [Devic] (G36.0)
  - **H46.0   Optic papillitis**
    - H46.00   Optic papillitis, unspecified eye
    - H46.01   Optic papillitis, right eye
    - H46.02   Optic papillitis, left eye
    - H46.03   Optic papillitis, bilateral
  - **H46.1   Retrobulbar neuritis**
    - Retrobulbar neuritis NOS
    - **Excludes1**   syphilitic retrobulbar neuritis (A52.15)
    - H46.10   Retrobulbar neuritis, unspecified eye
    - H46.11   Retrobulbar neuritis, right eye
    - H46.12   Retrobulbar neuritis, left eye
    - H46.13   Retrobulbar neuritis, bilateral
  - **H46.2   Nutritional optic neuropathy**
  - **H46.3   Toxic optic neuropathy**
    - *Code first (T51-T65) to identify cause*
  - **H46.8   Other optic neuritis**
  - **H46.9   Unspecified optic neuritis**
- **H47   Other disorders of optic [2nd] nerve and visual pathways**
  - **H47.0   Disorders of optic nerve, not elsewhere classified**
    - **H47.01   Ischemic optic neuropathy**
      - H47.011   Ischemic optic neuropathy, right eye
      - H47.012   Ischemic optic neuropathy, left eye
      - H47.013   Ischemic optic neuropathy, bilateral
      - H47.019   Ischemic optic neuropathy, unspecified eye
    - **H47.02   Hemorrhage in optic nerve sheath**
      - H47.021   Hemorrhage in optic nerve sheath, right eye
      - H47.022   Hemorrhage in optic nerve sheath, left eye
      - H47.023   Hemorrhage in optic nerve sheath, bilateral
      - H47.029   Hemorrhage in optic nerve sheath, unspecified eye
    - **H47.03   Optic nerve hypoplasia**
      - H47.031   Optic nerve hypoplasia, right eye
      - H47.032   Optic nerve hypoplasia, left eye
      - H47.033   Optic nerve hypoplasia, bilateral
      - H47.039   Optic nerve hypoplasia, unspecified eye

Figure 7-11   *Stages of papilledema according to the Frisén grading scale.* **A,** Very eary papilledema (Frisén stage 1). **B,** Early papilledema (Frisén stage 2). **C,** Moderate papilledema (Frisén stage 3). **D,** Marked papilledema (Frisén stage 4). **E,** Severe papilledema. (From Youmans JR, Winn HR: Youmans Neurological Surgery, Philadelphia, PA, Elsevier/Saunders, 2011)

Item 7–8   Papilledema is swelling of the optic disc caused by increased intracranial pressure. It is most often bilateral and occurs quickly (hours) or over weeks of time. It is a common symptom of a brain tumor. The term should not be used to describe optic disc swelling with underlying infectious, infiltrative, or inflammatory etiologies.

- **H47.09   Other disorders of optic nerve, not elsewhere classified**
  - Compression of optic nerve
  - H47.091   Other disorders of optic nerve, not elsewhere classified, right eye
  - H47.092   Other disorders of optic nerve, not elsewhere classified, left eye
  - H47.093   Other disorders of optic nerve, not elsewhere classified, bilateral
  - H47.099   Other disorders of optic nerve, not elsewhere classified, unspecified eye
- **H47.1   Papilledema**
  - H47.10   Unspecified papilledema
  - H47.11   Papilledema associated with increased intracranial pressure
  - H47.12   Papilledema associated with decreased ocular pressure
  - H47.13   Papilledema associated with retinal disorder
  - **H47.14   Foster-Kennedy syndrome**
    - H47.141   Foster-Kennedy syndrome, right eye
    - H47.142   Foster-Kennedy syndrome, left eye
    - H47.143   Foster-Kennedy syndrome, bilateral
    - H47.149   Foster-Kennedy syndrome, unspecified eye
- **H47.2   Optic atrophy**
  - H47.20   Unspecified optic atrophy
  - **H47.21   Primary optic atrophy**
    - H47.211   Primary optic atrophy, right eye
    - H47.212   Primary optic atrophy, left eye
    - H47.213   Primary optic atrophy, bilateral
    - H47.219   Primary optic atrophy, unspecified eye
  - **H47.22   Hereditary optic atrophy**
    - Leber's optic atrophy
  - **H47.23   Glaucomatous optic atrophy**
    - H47.231   Glaucomatous optic atrophy, right eye
    - H47.232   Glaucomatous optic atrophy, left eye
    - H47.233   Glaucomatous optic atrophy, bilateral
    - H47.239   Glaucomatous optic atrophy, unspecified eye

▶ New   ⇒ Revised   ~~deleted~~ Deleted   Excludes 1   Excludes 2   Includes   Use additional   Code first   Code also   Key words
OGCR Official Guidelines   X Assign placeholder X   ● Use Additional Character(s)   ▌ Manifestation Code   **Coding Clinic**

● **H47.29**   Other optic atrophy
     Temporal pallor of optic disc
     H47.291   Other optic atrophy, right eye
     H47.292   Other optic atrophy, left eye
     H47.293   Other optic atrophy, bilateral
     H47.299   Other optic atrophy, unspecified eye

● **H47.3**   Other disorders of optic disc

  ● **H47.31**   Coloboma of optic disc
     H47.311   Coloboma of optic disc, right eye
     H47.312   Coloboma of optic disc, left eye
     H47.313   Coloboma of optic disc, bilateral
     H47.319   Coloboma of optic disc, unspecified eye

  ● **H47.32**   Drusen of optic disc
     H47.321   Drusen of optic disc, right eye
     H47.322   Drusen of optic disc, left eye
     H47.323   Drusen of optic disc, bilateral
     H47.329   Drusen of optic disc, unspecified eye

  ● **H47.33**   Pseudopapilledema of optic disc
     H47.331   Pseudopapilledema of optic disc, right eye
     H47.332   Pseudopapilledema of optic disc, left eye
     H47.333   Pseudopapilledema of optic disc, bilateral
     H47.339   Pseudopapilledema of optic disc, unspecified eye

  ● **H47.39**   Other disorders of optic disc
     H47.391   Other disorders of optic disc, right eye
     H47.392   Other disorders of optic disc, left eye
     H47.393   Other disorders of optic disc, bilateral
     H47.399   Other disorders of optic disc, unspecified eye

● **H47.4**   Disorders of optic chiasm
     Code also underlying condition
   H47.41   Disorders of optic chiasm in (due to) inflammatory disorders
   H47.42   Disorders of optic chiasm in (due to) neoplasm
   H47.43   Disorders of optic chiasm in (due to) vascular disorders
   H47.49   Disorders of optic chiasm in (due to) other disorders

● **H47.5**   Disorders of other visual pathways
     Disorders of optic tracts, geniculate nuclei and optic radiations
     Code also underlying condition

  ● **H47.51**   Disorders of visual pathways in (due to) inflammatory disorders
     H47.511   Disorders of visual pathways in (due to) inflammatory disorders, right side
     H47.512   Disorders of visual pathways in (due to) inflammatory disorders, left side
     H47.519   Disorders of visual pathways in (due to) inflammatory disorders, unspecified side

  ● **H47.52**   Disorders of visual pathways in (due to) neoplasm
     H47.521   Disorders of visual pathways in (due to) neoplasm, right side
     H47.522   Disorders of visual pathways in (due to) neoplasm, left side
     H47.529   Disorders of visual pathways in (due to) neoplasm, unspecified side

  ● **H47.53**   Disorders of visual pathways in (due to) vascular disorders
     H47.531   Disorders of visual pathways in (due to) vascular disorders, right side
     H47.532   Disorders of visual pathways in (due to) vascular disorders, left side
     H47.539   Disorders of visual pathways in (due to) vascular disorders, unspecified side

● **H47.6**   Disorders of visual cortex
     Code also underlying condition
     Excludes1   injury to visual cortex S04.04

  ● **H47.61**   Cortical blindness
     H47.611   Cortical blindness, right side of brain
     H47.612   Cortical blindness, left side of brain
     H47.619   Cortical blindness, unspecified side of brain

  ● **H47.62**   Disorders of visual cortex in (due to) inflammatory disorders
     H47.621   Disorders of visual cortex in (due to) inflammatory disorders, right side of brain
     H47.622   Disorders of visual cortex in (due to) inflammatory disorders, left side of brain
     H47.629   Disorders of visual cortex in (due to) inflammatory disorders, unspecified side of brain

  ● **H47.63**   Disorders of visual cortex in (due to) neoplasm
     H47.631   Disorders of visual cortex in (due to) neoplasm, right side of brain
     H47.632   Disorders of visual cortex in (due to) neoplasm, left side of brain
     H47.639   Disorders of visual cortex in (due to) neoplasm, unspecified side of brain

  ● **H47.64**   Disorders of visual cortex in (due to) vascular disorders
     H47.641   Disorders of visual cortex in (due to) vascular disorders, right side of brain
     H47.642   Disorders of visual cortex in (due to) vascular disorders, left side of brain
     H47.649   Disorders of visual cortex in (due to) vascular disorders, unspecified side of brain

  H47.9   Unspecified disorder of visual pathways

DISORDERS OF OCULAR MUSCLES, BINOCULAR MOVEMENT, ACCOMMODATION AND REFRACTION (H49-H52)

  Excludes2   nystagmus and other irregular eye movements (H55)

● **H49**   Paralytic strabismus
     Excludes2   internal ophthalmoplegia (H52.51-)
                internuclear ophthalmoplegia (H51.2-)
                progressive supranuclear ophthalmoplegia (G23.1)

  ● **H49.0**   Third [oculomotor] nerve palsy
     H49.00   Third [oculomotor] nerve palsy, unspecified eye
     H49.01   Third [oculomotor] nerve palsy, right eye
     H49.02   Third [oculomotor] nerve palsy, left eye
     H49.03   Third [oculomotor] nerve palsy, bilateral

  ● **H49.1**   Fourth [trochlear] nerve palsy
     H49.10   Fourth [trochlear] nerve palsy, unspecified eye
     H49.11   Fourth [trochlear] nerve palsy, right eye
     H49.12   Fourth [trochlear] nerve palsy, left eye
     H49.13   Fourth [trochlear] nerve palsy, bilateral

CHAPTER 7 (H00-H59)

- H49.2 Sixth [abducent] nerve palsy
  - H49.20 Sixth [abducent] nerve palsy, unspecified eye
  - H49.21 Sixth [abducent] nerve palsy, right eye
  - H49.22 Sixth [abducent] nerve palsy, left eye
  - H49.23 Sixth [abducent] nerve palsy, bilateral
- H49.3 Total (external) ophthalmoplegia
  - H49.30 Total (external) ophthalmoplegia, unspecified eye
  - H49.31 Total (external) ophthalmoplegia, right eye
  - H49.32 Total (external) ophthalmoplegia, left eye
  - H49.33 Total (external) ophthalmoplegia, bilateral
- H49.4 Progressive external ophthalmoplegia
  - **Excludes1** Kearns-Sayre syndrome (H49.81-)
  - H49.40 Progressive external ophthalmoplegia, unspecified eye
  - H49.41 Progressive external ophthalmoplegia, right eye
  - H49.42 Progressive external ophthalmoplegia, left eye
  - H49.43 Progressive external ophthalmoplegia, bilateral
- H49.8 Other paralytic strabismus
  - H49.81 Kearns-Sayre syndrome
    Progressive external ophthalmoplegia with pigmentary retinopathy
    Use additional code for other manifestation, such as:
    heart block (I45.9)
    - H49.811 Kearns-Sayre syndrome, right eye
    - H49.812 Kearns-Sayre syndrome, left eye
    - H49.813 Kearns-Sayre syndrome, bilateral
    - H49.819 Kearns-Sayre syndrome, unspecified eye
  - H49.88 Other paralytic strabismus
    External ophthalmoplegia NOS
    - H49.881 Other paralytic strabismus, right eye
    - H49.882 Other paralytic strabismus, left eye
    - H49.883 Other paralytic strabismus, bilateral
    - H49.889 Other paralytic strabismus, unspecified eye
  - H49.9 Unspecified paralytic strabismus

- H50 Other strabismus
  - H50.0 Esotropia
    Convergent concomitant strabismus
    - **Excludes1** intermittent esotropia (H50.31-, H50.32)
    - H50.00 Unspecified esotropia
    - H50.01 Monocular esotropia
      - H50.011 Monocular esotropia, right eye
      - H50.012 Monocular esotropia, left eye

- H50.02 Monocular esotropia with A pattern
  - H50.021 Monocular esotropia with A pattern, right eye
  - H50.022 Monocular esotropia with A pattern, left eye
- H50.03 Monocular esotropia with V pattern
  - H50.031 Monocular esotropia with V pattern, right eye
  - H50.032 Monocular esotropia with V pattern, left eye
- H50.04 Monocular esotropia with other noncomitancies
  - H50.041 Monocular esotropia with other noncomitancies, right eye
  - H50.042 Monocular esotropia with other noncomitancies, left eye
  - H50.05 Alternating esotropia
  - H50.06 Alternating esotropia with A pattern
  - H50.07 Alternating esotropia with V pattern
  - H50.08 Alternating esotropia with other noncomitancies
- H50.1 Exotropia
  Misalignment in which one eye deviates outward (away from nose) while the other fixates normally
  Divergent concomitant strabismus
  - **Excludes1** intermittent exotropia (H50.33-, H50.34)
  - H50.10 Unspecified exotropia
  - H50.11 Monocular exotropia
    - H50.111 Monocular exotropia, right eye
    - H50.112 Monocular exotropia, left eye
  - H50.12 Monocular exotropia with A pattern
    - H50.121 Monocular exotropia with A pattern, right eye
    - H50.122 Monocular exotropia with A pattern, left eye
  - H50.13 Monocular exotropia with V pattern
    - H50.131 Monocular exotropia with V pattern, right eye
    - H50.132 Monocular exotropia with V pattern, left eye
  - H50.14 Monocular exotropia with other noncomitancies
    - H50.141 Monocular exotropia with other noncomitancies, right eye
    - H50.142 Monocular exotropia with other noncomitancies, left eye
    - H50.15 Alternating exotropia
    - H50.16 Alternating exotropia with A pattern
    - H50.17 Alternating exotropia with V pattern
    - H50.18 Alternating exotropia with other noncomitancies
- H50.2 Vertical strabismus
  Hypertropia
  - H50.21 Vertical strabismus, right eye
  - H50.22 Vertical strabismus, left eye
- H50.3 Intermittent heterotropia
  Displacement of an organ or part of an organ from its normal position
  - H50.30 Unspecified intermittent heterotropia
  - H50.31 Intermittent monocular esotropia
    - H50.311 Intermittent monocular esotropia, right eye
    - H50.312 Intermittent monocular esotropia, left eye
  - H50.32 Intermittent alternating esotropia
  - H50.33 Intermittent monocular exotropia
    - H50.331 Intermittent monocular exotropia, right eye
    - H50.332 Intermittent monocular exotropia, left eye
  - H50.34 Intermittent alternating exotropia

Item 7–9 Strabismus or esotropia (crossed eyes) is a condition of the extraocular eye muscles, resulting in an inability of the eyes to focus and also affects depth perception.

Figure 7-12 A. Image of strabismus. **B.** Exotropia. (**A** from Yanoff: Ophthalmology, ed 3, Mosby, Inc., 2008. **B** from Zitelli BJ, Davis HW, Pediatric Physical Diagnosis: Atlas of Pediatric Physical Diagnosis, Philadelphia, Elsevier Saunders, 2012)

▶ New   ⇒ Revised   ~~deleted~~ Deleted   Excludes 1   Excludes 2   Includes   Use additional   Code first   Code also   Key words
OGCR Official Guidelines   X Assign placeholder X   ● Use Additional Character(s)   ▶ Manifestation Code   **Coding Clinic**

● H50.4   Other and unspecified heterotropia
     H50.40   Unspecified heterotropia
     ● H50.41   Cyclotropia
         H50.411   Cyclotropia, right eye
         H50.412   Cyclotropia, left eye
     H50.42   Monofixation syndrome
     H50.43   Accommodative component in esotropia
● H50.5   Heterophoria
     One or both eyes wander away from the position where both
     eyes are looking together in the same direction
     H50.50   Unspecified heterophoria
     H50.51   Esophoria
         Eye deviates inward (toward the nose)
     H50.52   Exophoria
         Eye deviates outward (toward the ear)
     H50.53   Vertical heterophoria
     H50.54   Cyclophoria
     H50.55   Alternating heterophoria
● H50.6   Mechanical strabismus
     H50.60   Mechanical strabismus, unspecified
     ● H50.61   Brown's sheath syndrome
         H50.611   Brown's sheath syndrome, right eye
         H50.612   Brown's sheath syndrome, left eye
     H50.69   Other mechanical strabismus
         Strabismus due to adhesions
         Traumatic limitation of duction of eye muscle
● H50.8   Other specified strabismus
     ● H50.81   Duane's syndrome
         H50.811   Duane's syndrome, right eye
         H50.812   Duane's syndrome, left eye
     H50.89   Other specified strabismus
     H50.9   Unspecified strabismus

● H51   Other disorders of binocular movement
     H51.0   Palsy (spasm) of conjugate gaze
     ● H51.1   Convergence insufficiency and excess
         H51.11   Convergence insufficiency
         H51.12   Convergence excess
     ● H51.2   Internuclear ophthalmoplegia
         H51.20   Internuclear ophthalmoplegia, unspecified eye
         H51.21   Internuclear ophthalmoplegia, right eye
         H51.22   Internuclear ophthalmoplegia, left eye
         H51.23   Internuclear ophthalmoplegia, bilateral
     H51.8   Other specified disorders of binocular movement
     H51.9   Unspecified disorder of binocular movement

● H52   Disorders of refraction and accommodation
     ● H52.0   Hypermetropia
         H52.00   Hypermetropia, unspecified eye
         H52.01   Hypermetropia, right eye
         H52.02   Hypermetropia, left eye
         H52.03   Hypermetropia, bilateral
     ● H52.1   Myopia
         Excludes1   degenerative myopia (H44.2-)
         H52.10   Myopia, unspecified eye
         H52.11   Myopia, right eye
         H52.12   Myopia, left eye
         H52.13   Myopia, bilateral

Item 7-10 Disorders of refraction: **Hypermetropia,** or farsightedness, means focus at a distance is adequate but not on close objects. **Myopia** is near-sightedness or short-sightedness and means the focus on nearby objects is clear but distant objects appear blurred. **Astigmatism** is warping of the curvature of the cornea so light rays entering do not meet at a single focal point, resulting in a distorted image. **Anisometropia** is unequal refractive power in which one eye may be myopic (near-sighted) and the other hyperopic (far-sighted). **Presbyopia** is the loss of focus on near objects, which occurs with age because the lens loses elasticity.

● H52.2   Astigmatism
     ● H52.20   Unspecified astigmatism
         H52.201   Unspecified astigmatism, right eye
         H52.202   Unspecified astigmatism, left eye
         H52.203   Unspecified astigmatism, bilateral
         H52.209   Unspecified astigmatism, unspecified eye
     ● H52.21   Irregular astigmatism
         H52.211   Irregular astigmatism, right eye
         H52.212   Irregular astigmatism, left eye
         H52.213   Irregular astigmatism, bilateral
         H52.219   Irregular astigmatism, unspecified eye
     ● H52.22   Regular astigmatism
         H52.221   Regular astigmatism, right eye
         H52.222   Regular astigmatism, left eye
         H52.223   Regular astigmatism, bilateral
         H52.229   Regular astigmatism, unspecified eye
● H52.3   Anisometropia and aniseikonia
     H52.31   Anisometropia
     H52.32   Aniseikonia
     H52.4   Presbyopia
● H52.5   Disorders of accommodation
     ● H52.51   Internal ophthalmoplegia (complete) (total)
         H52.511   Internal ophthalmoplegia (complete) (total), right eye
         H52.512   Internal ophthalmoplegia (complete) (total), left eye
         H52.513   Internal ophthalmoplegia (complete) (total), bilateral
         H52.519   Internal ophthalmoplegia (complete) (total), unspecified eye
     ● H52.52   Paresis of accommodation
         H52.521   Paresis of accommodation, right eye
         H52.522   Paresis of accommodation, left eye
         H52.523   Paresis of accommodation, bilateral
         H52.529   Paresis of accommodation, unspecified eye
     ● H52.53   Spasm of accommodation
         H52.531   Spasm of accommodation, right eye
         H52.532   Spasm of accommodation, left eye
         H52.533   Spasm of accommodation, bilateral
         H52.539   Spasm of accommodation, unspecified eye
     H52.6   Other disorders of refraction
     H52.7   Unspecified disorder of refraction

VISUAL DISTURBANCES AND BLINDNESS (H53-H54)

● H53   Visual disturbances
     ● H53.0   Amblyopia ex anopsia
         Excludes1   amblyopia due to vitamin A deficiency (E50.5)
     ● H53.00   Unspecified amblyopia
         H53.001   Unspecified amblyopia, right eye
         H53.002   Unspecified amblyopia, left eye
         H53.003   Unspecified amblyopia, bilateral
         H53.009   Unspecified amblyopia, unspecified eye
     ● H53.01   Deprivation amblyopia
         H53.011   Deprivation amblyopia, right eye
         H53.012   Deprivation amblyopia, left eye
         H53.013   Deprivation amblyopia, bilateral
         H53.019   Deprivation amblyopia, unspecified eye

CHAPTER 7 (H00-H59)

● H53.02 Refractive amblyopia
    H53.021 Refractive amblyopia, right eye
    H53.022 Refractive amblyopia, left eye
    H53.023 Refractive amblyopia, bilateral
    H53.029 Refractive amblyopia, unspecified eye

● H53.03 Strabismic amblyopia
    Excludes1 strabismus (H50.-)
    H53.031 Strabismic amblyopia, right eye
    H53.032 Strabismic amblyopia, left eye
    H53.033 Strabismic amblyopia, bilateral
    H53.039 Strabismic amblyopia, unspecified eye

● H53.04 Amblyopia suspect
    Coding Clinic: 2016, Q4, P22
    H53.041 Amblyopia suspect, right eye
    H53.042 Amblyopia suspect, left eye
    H53.043 Amblyopia suspect, bilateral
    H53.049 Amblyopia suspect, unspecified eye

● H53.1 Subjective visual disturbances
    Excludes1 subjective visual disturbances due to vitamin A deficiency (E50.5)
                   visual hallucinations (R44.1)
    H53.10 Unspecified subjective visual disturbances
    H53.11 Day blindness
        Hemeralopia

● H53.12 Transient visual loss
    Scintillating scotoma
    Excludes1 amaurosis fugax (G45.3-)
              transient retinal artery occlusion (H34.0-)
    H53.121 Transient visual loss, right eye
    H53.122 Transient visual loss, left eye
    H53.123 Transient visual loss, bilateral
    H53.129 Transient visual loss, unspecified eye

● H53.13 Sudden visual loss
    H53.131 Sudden visual loss, right eye
    H53.132 Sudden visual loss, left eye
    H53.133 Sudden visual loss, bilateral
    H53.139 Sudden visual loss, unspecified eye

● H53.14 Visual discomfort
    Asthenopia
    Photophobia
    H53.141 Visual discomfort, right eye
    H53.142 Visual discomfort, left eye
    H53.143 Visual discomfort, bilateral
    H53.149 Visual discomfort, unspecified

    H53.15 Visual distortions of shape and size
        Metamorphopsia
    H53.16 Psychophysical visual disturbances
    H53.19 Other subjective visual disturbances
        Visual halos

H53.2 Diplopia
    Double vision

● H53.3 Other and unspecified disorders of binocular vision
    H53.30 Unspecified disorder of binocular vision
    H53.31 Abnormal retinal correspondence
    H53.32 Fusion with defective stereopsis
    H53.33 Simultaneous visual perception without fusion
    H53.34 Suppression of binocular vision

● H53.4 Visual field defects
    H53.40 Unspecified visual field defects
● H53.41 Scotoma involving central area
    Central scotoma
    H53.411 Scotoma involving central area, right eye
    H53.412 Scotoma involving central area, left eye
    H53.413 Scotoma involving central area, bilateral
    H53.419 Scotoma involving central area, unspecified eye

● H53.42 Scotoma of blind spot area
    Enlarged blind spot
    H53.421 Scotoma of blind spot area, right eye
    H53.422 Scotoma of blind spot area, left eye
    H53.423 Scotoma of blind spot area, bilateral
    H53.429 Scotoma of blind spot area, unspecified eye

● H53.43 Sector or arcuate defects
    Arcuate scotoma
    Bjerrum scotoma
    H53.431 Sector or arcuate defects, right eye
    H53.432 Sector or arcuate defects, left eye
    H53.433 Sector or arcuate defects, bilateral
    H53.439 Sector or arcuate defects, unspecified eye

● H53.45 Other localized visual field defect
    Peripheral visual field defect
    Ring scotoma NOS
    Scotoma NOS
    H53.451 Other localized visual field defect, right eye
    H53.452 Other localized visual field defect, left eye
    H53.453 Other localized visual field defect, bilateral
    H53.459 Other localized visual field defect, unspecified eye

● H53.46 Homonymous bilateral field defects
    Homonymous hemianopia
    Homonymous hemianopsia
    Quadrant anopia
    Quadrant anopsia
    H53.461 Homonymous bilateral field defects, right side
    H53.462 Homonymous bilateral field defects, left side
    H53.469 Homonymous bilateral field defects, unspecified side
        Homonymous bilateral field defects NOS

H53.47 Heteronymous bilateral field defects
    Heteronymous hemianop(s)ia

● H53.48 Generalized contraction of visual field
    H53.481 Generalized contraction of visual field, right eye
    H53.482 Generalized contraction of visual field, left eye
    H53.483 Generalized contraction of visual field, bilateral
    H53.489 Generalized contraction of visual field, unspecified eye

▶ New   ⇒ Revised   ~~deleted~~ Deleted   Excludes 1   Excludes 2   Includes   Use additional   Code first   Code also   Key words
OGCR Official Guidelines   X Assign placeholder X   ● Use Additional Character(s)   ▷ Manifestation Code   Coding Clinic

- H53.5   **Color vision deficiencies**
  Color blindness
  Excludes2   day blindness (H53.11)
  - H53.50   **Unspecified color vision deficiencies**
    Color blindness NOS
  - H53.51   **Achromatopsia**
  - H53.52   **Acquired color vision deficiency**
  - H53.53   **Deuteranomaly**
    Deuteranopia
  - H53.54   **Protanomaly**
    Protanopia
  - H53.55   **Tritanomaly**
    Tritanopia
  - H53.59   **Other color vision deficiencies**
- H53.6   **Night blindness**
  Excludes1   night blindness due to vitamin A deficiency (E50.5)
  - H53.60   **Unspecified night blindness**
  - H53.61   **Abnormal dark adaptation curve**
  - H53.62   **Acquired night blindness**
  - H53.63   **Congenital night blindness**
  - H53.69   **Other night blindness**
- H53.7   **Vision sensitivity deficiencies**
  - H53.71   **Glare sensitivity**
  - H53.72   **Impaired contrast sensitivity**
- H53.8   **Other visual disturbances**
- H53.9   **Unspecified visual disturbance**

- H54   **Blindness and low vision**
  Note: For definition of visual impairment categories see table below.
  Code first any associated underlying cause of the blindness
  Excludes1   amaurosis fugax (G45.3)
  - H54.0   **Blindness, both eyes**
    Visual impairment categories 3, 4, 5 in both eyes.
    - H54.0X   **Blindness, both eyes, different category levels**
      - H54.0X3   Blindness right eye, category 3
        - H54.0X33   Blindness right eye category 3, blindness left eye category 3
        - H54.0X34   Blindness right eye category 3, blindness left eye category 4
        - H54.0X35   Blindness right eye category 3, blindness left eye category 5
      - H54.0X4   Blindness right eye, category 4
        - H54.0X43   Blindness right eye category 4, blindness left eye category 3
        - H54.0X44   Blindness right eye category 4, blindness left eye category 4
        - H54.0X45   Blindness right eye category 4, blindness left eye category 5
      - H54.0X5   Blindness right eye, category 5
        - H54.0X53   Blindness right eye category 5, blindness left eye category 3
        - H54.0X54   Blindness right eye category 5, blindness left eye category 4
        - H54.0X55   Blindness right eye category 5, blindness left eye category 5

- H54.1   **Blindness, one eye, low vision other eye**
  Visual impairment categories 3, 4, 5 in one eye, with categories 1 or 2 in the other eye.
  - H54.10   **Blindness, one eye, low vision other eye, unspecified eyes**
  - H54.11   **Blindness, right eye, low vision left eye**
    - H54.113   Blindness right eye category 3, low vision left eye
      - H54.1131   Blindness right eye category 3, low vision left eye category 1
      - H54.1132   Blindness right eye category 3, low vision left eye category 2
    - H54.114   Blindness right eye category 4, low vision left eye
      - H54.1141   Blindness right eye category 4, low vision left eye category 1
      - H54.1142   Blindness right eye category 4, low vision left eye category 2
    - H54.115   Blindness right eye category 5, low vision left eye
      - H54.1151   Blindness right eye category 5, low vision left eye category 1
      - H54.1152   Blindness right eye category 5, low vision left eye category 2
  - H54.12   Blindness, left eye, low vision right eye
    - H54.121   Low vision right eye category 1, blindness left eye
      - H54.1213   Low vision right eye category 1, blindness left eye category 3
      - H54.1214   Low vision right eye category 1, blindness left eye category 4
      - H54.1215   Low vision right eye category 1, blindness left eye category 5
    - H54.122   Low vision right eye category 2, blindness left eye
      - H54.1223   Low vision right eye category 2, blindness left eye category 3
      - H54.1224   Low vision right eye category 2, blindness left eye category 4
      - H54.1225   Low vision right eye category 2, blindness left eye category 5
- H54.2   **Low vision, both eyes**
  Visual impairment categories 1 or 2 in both eyes.
  - H54.2X   **Low vision, both eyes, different category levels**
    - H54.2X1   Low vision, right eye, category 1
      - H54.2X11   Low vision right eye category 1, low vision left eye category 1
      - H54.2X12   Low vision right eye category 1, low vision left eye category 2
    - H54.2X2   Low vision, right eye, category 2
      - H54.2X21   Low vision right eye category 2, low vision left eye category 1
      - H54.2X22   Low vision right eye category 2, low vision left eye category 2

CHAPTER 7 (H00–H59)

OGCR Section I.C.7.b.

> **Blindness**
>
> If "blindness" or "low vision" of both eyes is documented but the visual impairment category is not documented, assign code H54.3, Unqualified visual loss, both eyes. If "blindness" or "low vision" in one eye is documented but the visual impairment category is not documented, assign a code from H54.6-, Unqualified visual loss, one eye. If "blindness" or "visual loss" is documented without any information about whether one or both eyes are affected, assign code H54.7, Unspecified visual loss.

H54.3 Unqualified visual loss, both eyes
Visual impairment category 9 in both eyes.

● **H54.4 Blindness, one eye**
Visual impairment categories 3, 4, 5 in one eye [normal vision in other eye]

     H54.40 Blindness, one eye, unspecified eye

     ● **H54.41 Blindness, right eye, normal vision left eye**

         ● **H54.413 Blindness, right eye, category 3**

             H54.413A Blindness right eye category 3, normal vision left eye

         ● **H54.414 Blindness, right eye, category 4**

             H54.414A Blindness right eye category 4, normal vision left eye

         ● **H54.415 Blindness, right eye, category 5**

             H54.415A Blindness right eye category 5, normal vision left eye

     ● **H54.42 Blindness, left eye, normal vision right eye**

         ● **H54.42A Blindness, left eye, category 3-5**

             H54.42A3 Blindness left eye category 3, normal vision right eye

             H54.42A4 Blindness left eye category 4, normal vision right eye

             H54.42A5 Blindness left eye category 5, normal vision right eye

● **H54.5 Low vision, one eye**
Visual impairment categories 1 or 2 in one eye [normal vision in other eye].

     H54.50 Low vision, one eye, unspecified eye

     ● **H54.51 Low vision, right eye, normal vision left eye**

         ● **H54.511 Low vision, right eye, category 1-2**

             H54.511A Low vision right eye category 1, normal vision left eye

             H54.512A Low vision right eye category 2, normal vision left eye

     ● **H54.52 Low vision, left eye, normal vision right eye**

         ● **H54.52A Low vision, left eye, category 1-2**

             H54.52A1 Low vision left eye category 1, normal vision right eye

             H54.52A2 Low vision left eye category 2, normal vision right eye

● **H54.6 Unqualified visual loss, one eye**
Visual impairment category 9 in one eye [normal vision in other eye].

     H54.60 Unqualified visual loss, one eye, unspecified

     H54.61 Unqualified visual loss, right eye, normal vision left eye

     H54.62 Unqualified visual loss, left eye, normal vision right eye

H54.7 Unspecified visual loss
Visual impairment category 9 NOS

H54.8 Legal blindness, as defined in USA
Blindness NOS according to USA definition

     Excludes1   legal blindness with specification of impairment level (H54.0-H54.7)

Note: The table below gives a classification of severity of visual impairment recommended by a WHO Study Group on the Prevention of Blindness, Geneva, 6-10 November 1972.

The term "low vision" in category H54 comprises categories 1 and 2 of the table, the term "blindness" categories 3, 4, and 5, and the term "unqualified visual loss" category 9.

If the extent of the visual field is taken into account, patients with a field no greater than 10 but greater than 5 around central fixation should be placed in category 3 and patients with a field no greater than 5 around central fixation should be placed in category 4, even if the central acuity is not impaired.

(Document 508 compliance requires all cells in the following table to be filled.)

Category of visual impairment	Visual acuity with best possible correction	
	Maximum less than:	**Minimum equal to or better than:**
—	6/18	6/60
3/10 (0.3)	1/10 (0.1)	—
20/70	20/200	—
—	6/60	3/60
1/10 (0.1)	1/20 (0.05)	—
20/200	20/400	—
—	3/60	1/60 (finger counting at one meter)
1/20 (0.05)	1/50 (0.02)	—
20/400	5/300 (20/1200)	—
—	1/60 (finger counting at one meter)	Light perception
1/50 (0.02)	—	—
5/300	—	—
—	No light perception	
—	Undetermined or unspecified	

OTHER DISORDERS OF EYE AND ADNEXA (H55-H57)

● **H55 Nystagmus and other irregular eye movements**

     ● **H55.0 Nystagmus**
         Rapid, involuntary movements of the eyes in the horizontal or vertical direction

         H55.00 Unspecified nystagmus

         H55.01 Congenital nystagmus

         H55.02 Latent nystagmus

         H55.03 Visual deprivation nystagmus

         H55.04 Dissociated nystagmus

         H55.09 Other forms of nystagmus

     ● **H55.8 Other irregular eye movements**

         H55.81 Saccadic eye movements

         H55.89 Other irregular eye movements

▶ New   ⇒ Revised   ~~deleted~~ Deleted   Excludes 1   Excludes 2   Includes   Use additional   Code first   Code also   Key words

OGCR Official Guidelines   X Assign placeholder X   ● Use Additional Character(s)   ▶ Manifestation Code   **Coding Clinic**

- **H57** **Other disorders of eye and adnexa**
  - **H57.0** **Anomalies of pupillary function**
    - H57.00   Unspecified anomaly of pupillary function
    - H57.01   Argyll Robertson pupil, atypical
      - **Excludes1**   syphilitic Argyll Robertson pupil (A52.19)
    - H57.02   Anisocoria
    - H57.03   Miosis
    - H57.04   Mydriasis
    - **H57.05**   Tonic pupil
      - H57.051   Tonic pupil, right eye
      - H57.052   Tonic pupil, left eye
      - H57.053   Tonic pupil, bilateral
      - H57.059   Tonic pupil, unspecified eye
    - H57.09   Other anomalies of pupillary function
  - **H57.1** **Ocular pain**
    - H57.10   Ocular pain, unspecified eye
    - H57.11   Ocular pain, right eye
    - H57.12   Ocular pain, left eye
    - H57.13   Ocular pain, bilateral
  - **H57.8** **Other specified disorders of eye and adnexa**
    - ▶ **H57.81**   Brow ptosis
      - ▶ H57.811   Brow ptosis, right
      - ▶ H57.812   Brow ptosis, left
      - ▶ H57.813   Brow ptosis, bilateral
      - ▶ H57.819   Brow ptosis, unspecified
    - ▶ H57.89   Other specified disorders of eye and adnexa
  - **H57.9**   Unspecified disorder of eye and adnexa

INTRAOPERATIVE AND POSTPROCEDURAL COMPLICATIONS AND DISORDERS OF EYE AND ADNEXA, NOT ELSEWHERE CLASSIFIED (H59)

- **H59** **Intraoperative and postprocedural complications and disorders of eye and adnexa, not elsewhere classified**
  - **Excludes1**   mechanical complication of intraocular lens (T85.2)
    - mechanical complication of other ocular prosthetic devices, implants and grafts (T85.3)
    - pseudophakia (Z96.1)
    - secondary cataracts (H26.4-)
  - **H59.0** **Disorders of the eye following cataract surgery**
    - **H59.01**   Keratopathy (bullous aphakic) following cataract surgery
      - Vitreal corneal syndrome
      - Vitreous (touch) syndrome
      - H59.011   Keratopathy (bullous aphakic) following cataract surgery, right eye
      - H59.012   Keratopathy (bullous aphakic) following cataract surgery, left eye
      - H59.013   Keratopathy (bullous aphakic) following cataract surgery, bilateral
      - H59.019   Keratopathy (bullous aphakic) following cataract surgery, unspecified eye
    - **H59.02**   Cataract (lens) fragments in eye following cataract surgery
      - H59.021   Cataract (lens) fragments in eye following cataract surgery, right eye
      - H59.022   Cataract (lens) fragments in eye following cataract surgery, left eye
      - H59.023   Cataract (lens) fragments in eye following cataract surgery, bilateral
      - H59.029   Cataract (lens) fragments in eye following cataract surgery, unspecified eye

- **H59.03**   Cystoid macular edema following cataract surgery
  - H59.031   Cystoid macular edema following cataract surgery, right eye
  - H59.032   Cystoid macular edema following cataract surgery, left eye
  - H59.033   Cystoid macular edema following cataract surgery, bilateral
  - H59.039   Cystoid macular edema following cataract surgery, unspecified eye
- **H59.09**   Other disorders of the eye following cataract surgery
  - H59.091   Other disorders of the right eye following cataract surgery
  - H59.092   Other disorders of the left eye following cataract surgery
  - H59.093   Other disorders of the eye following cataract surgery, bilateral
  - H59.099   Other disorders of unspecified eye following cataract surgery
- **H59.1** **Intraoperative hemorrhage and hematoma of eye and adnexa complicating a procedure**
  - **Excludes1**   intraoperative hemorrhage and hematoma of eye and adnexa due to accidental puncture or laceration during a procedure (H59.2-)
  - **H59.11**   Intraoperative hemorrhage and hematoma of eye and adnexa complicating an ophthalmic procedure
    - H59.111   Intraoperative hemorrhage and hematoma of right eye and adnexa complicating an ophthalmic procedure
    - H59.112   Intraoperative hemorrhage and hematoma of left eye and adnexa complicating an ophthalmic procedure
    - H59.113   Intraoperative hemorrhage and hematoma of eye and adnexa complicating an ophthalmic procedure, bilateral
    - H59.119   Intraoperative hemorrhage and hematoma of unspecified eye and adnexa complicating an ophthalmic procedure
  - **H59.12**   Intraoperative hemorrhage and hematoma of eye and adnexa complicating other procedure
    - H59.121   Intraoperative hemorrhage and hematoma of right eye and adnexa complicating other procedure
    - H59.122   Intraoperative hemorrhage and hematoma of left eye and adnexa complicating other procedure
    - H59.123   Intraoperative hemorrhage and hematoma of eye and adnexa complicating other procedure, bilateral
    - H59.129   Intraoperative hemorrhage and hematoma of unspecified eye and adnexa complicating other procedure
- **H59.2** **Accidental puncture and laceration of eye and adnexa during a procedure**
  - **H59.21**   Accidental puncture and laceration of eye and adnexa during an ophthalmic procedure
    - H59.211   Accidental puncture and laceration of right eye and adnexa during an ophthalmic procedure
    - H59.212   Accidental puncture and laceration of left eye and adnexa during an ophthalmic procedure
    - H59.213   Accidental puncture and laceration of eye and adnexa during an ophthalmic procedure, bilateral
    - H59.219   Accidental puncture and laceration of unspecified eye and adnexa during an ophthalmic procedure

CHAPTER 7 (H00-H59)

● H59.22   Accidental puncture and laceration of eye and adnexa during other procedure

    H59.221   Accidental puncture and laceration of right eye and adnexa during other procedure

    H59.222   Accidental puncture and laceration of left eye and adnexa during other procedure

    H59.223   Accidental puncture and laceration of eye and adnexa during other procedure, bilateral

    H59.229   Accidental puncture and laceration of unspecified eye and adnexa during other procedure

● H59.3   Postprocedural hemorrhage, hematoma, and seroma of eye and adnexa following other procedure

    Coding Clinic: 2016, Q4, P10

● H59.31   Postprocedural hemorrhage of eye and adnexa following an ophthalmic procedure

    H59.311   Postprocedural hemorrhage of right eye and adnexa following an ophthalmic procedure

    H59.312   Postprocedural hemorrhage of left eye and adnexa following an ophthalmic procedure

    H59.313   Postprocedural hemorrhage of eye and adnexa following an ophthalmic procedure, bilateral

    H59.319   Postprocedural hemorrhage of unspecified eye and adnexa following an ophthalmic procedure

● H59.32   Postprocedural hemorrhage of eye and adnexa following other procedure

    H59.321   Postprocedural hemorrhage of right eye and adnexa following other procedure

    H59.322   Postprocedural hemorrhage of left eye and adnexa following other procedure

    H59.323   Postprocedural hemorrhage of eye and adnexa following other procedure, bilateral

    H59.329   Postprocedural hemorrhage of unspecified eye and adnexa following other procedure

● H59.33   Postprocedural hematoma of eye and adnexa following an ophthalmic procedure

    H59.331   Postprocedural hematoma of right eye and adnexa following an ophthalmic procedure

    H59.332   Postprocedural hematoma of left eye and adnexa following an ophthalmic procedure

    H59.333   Postprocedural hematoma of eye and adnexa following an ophthalmic procedure, bilateral

    H59.339   Postprocedural hematoma of unspecified eye and adnexa following an ophthalmic procedure

● H59.34   Postprocedural hematoma of eye and adnexa following other procedure

    H59.341   Postprocedural hematoma of right eye and adnexa following other procedure

    H59.342   Postprocedural hematoma of left eye and adnexa following other procedure

    H59.343   Postprocedural hematoma of eye and adnexa following other procedure, bilateral

    H59.349   Postprocedural hematoma of unspecified eye and adnexa following other procedure

● H59.35   Postprocedural seroma of eye and adnexa following an ophthalmic procedure

    H59.351   Postprocedural seroma of right eye and adnexa following an ophthalmic procedure

    H59.352   Postprocedural seroma of left eye and adnexa following an ophthalmic procedure

    H59.353   Postprocedural seroma of eye and adnexa following an ophthalmic procedure, bilateral

    H59.359   Postprocedural seroma of unspecified eye and adnexa following an ophthalmic procedure

● H59.36   Postprocedural seroma of eye and adnexa following other procedure

    H59.361   Postprocedural seroma of right eye and adnexa following other procedure

    H59.362   Postprocedural seroma of left eye and adnexa following other procedure

    H59.363   Postprocedural seroma of eye and adnexa following other procedure, bilateral

    H59.369   Postprocedural seroma of unspecified eye and adnexa following other procedure

● H59.4   Inflammation (infection) of postprocedural bleb

    Postprocedural blebitis

    Excludes1   filtering (vitreous) bleb after glaucoma surgery status (Z98.83)

    H59.40   Inflammation (infection) of postprocedural bleb, unspecified

    H59.41   Inflammation (infection) of postprocedural bleb, stage 1

    H59.42   Inflammation (infection) of postprocedural bleb, stage 2

    H59.43   Inflammation (infection) of postprocedural bleb, stage 3

        Bleb endophthalmitis

● H59.8   Other intraoperative and postprocedural complications and disorders of eye and adnexa, not elsewhere classified

● H59.81   Chorioretinal scars after surgery for detachment

    H59.811   Chorioretinal scars after surgery for detachment, right eye

    H59.812   Chorioretinal scars after surgery for detachment, left eye

    H59.813   Chorioretinal scars after surgery for detachment, bilateral

    H59.819   Chorioretinal scars after surgery for detachment, unspecified eye 🔖

    H59.88   Other intraoperative complications of eye and adnexa, not elsewhere classified 🔖

    H59.89   Other postprocedural complications and disorders of eye and adnexa, not elsewhere classified 🔖

CHAPTER 8

DISEASES OF THE EAR AND MASTOID PROCESS (H60-H95)

OGCR Chapter-Specific Coding Guidelines

8. Chapter 8: Diseases of the Ear and Mastoid Process (H60-H95)
Reserved for future guideline expansion

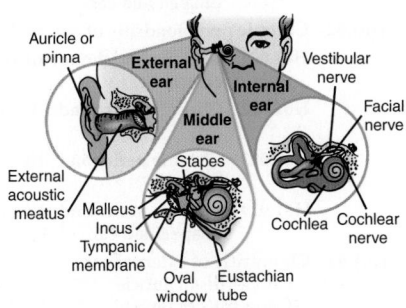

Figure 8-1 Auditory system. (From Buck CJ: Step-by-Step Medical Coding, ed 2016, St. Louis, Elsevier, 2016)

★**(See Plate 92 on page 68.)**

CHAPTER 8

DISEASES OF THE EAR AND MASTOID PROCESS (H60-H95)

Note: Use an external cause code following the code for the ear condition, if applicable, to identify the cause of the ear condition

Excludes2 certain conditions originating in the perinatal period (P04-P96)
certain infectious and parasitic diseases (A00-B99)
complications of pregnancy, childbirth and the puerperium (O00-O9A)
congenital malformations, deformations and chromosomal abnormalities (Q00-Q99)
endocrine, nutritional and metabolic diseases (E00-E88)
injury, poisoning and certain other consequences of external causes (S00-T88)
neoplasms (C00-D49)
symptoms, signs and abnormal clinical and laboratory findings, not elsewhere classified (R00-R94)

This chapter contains the following blocks:

H60-H62	Diseases of external ear
H65-H75	Diseases of middle ear and mastoid
H80-H83	Diseases of inner ear
H90-H94	Other disorders of ear
H95	Intraoperative and postprocedural complications and disorders of ear and mastoid process, not elsewhere classified

DISEASES OF EXTERNAL EAR (H60-H62)

● **H60 Otitis externa**

● **H60.0 Abscess of external ear**
Boil of external ear
Carbuncle of auricle or external auditory canal
Furuncle of external ear

H60.00 Abscess of external ear, unspecified ear
H60.01 Abscess of right external ear
H60.02 Abscess of left external ear
H60.03 Abscess of external ear, bilateral

● **H60.1 Cellulitis of external ear**
Cellulitis of auricle
Cellulitis of external auditory canal

H60.10 Cellulitis of external ear, unspecified ear
H60.11 Cellulitis of right external ear
H60.12 Cellulitis of left external ear
H60.13 Cellulitis of external ear, bilateral

● **H60.2 Malignant otitis externa**
H60.20 Malignant otitis externa, unspecified ear
H60.21 Malignant otitis externa, right ear
H60.22 Malignant otitis externa, left ear
H60.23 Malignant otitis externa, bilateral

● **H60.3 Other infective otitis externa**

● **H60.31 Diffuse otitis externa**
H60.311 Diffuse otitis externa, right ear
H60.312 Diffuse otitis externa, left ear
H60.313 Diffuse otitis externa, bilateral
H60.319 Diffuse otitis externa, unspecified ear

● **H60.32 Hemorrhagic otitis externa**
H60.321 Hemorrhagic otitis externa, right ear
H60.322 Hemorrhagic otitis externa, left ear
H60.323 Hemorrhagic otitis externa, bilateral
H60.329 Hemorrhagic otitis externa, unspecified ear

● **H60.33 Swimmer's ear**
H60.331 Swimmer's ear, right ear
H60.332 Swimmer's ear, left ear
H60.333 Swimmer's ear, bilateral
H60.339 Swimmer's ear, unspecified ear

● **H60.39 Other infective otitis externa**
H60.391 Other infective otitis externa, right ear
H60.392 Other infective otitis externa, left ear
H60.393 Other infective otitis externa, bilateral
H60.399 Other infective otitis externa, unspecified ear

● **H60.4 Cholesteatoma of external ear**
Keratosis obturans of external ear (canal)

Excludes2 cholesteatoma of middle ear (H71.-)
recurrent cholesteatoma of postmastoidectomy cavity (H95.0-)

H60.40 Cholesteatoma of external ear, unspecified ear
H60.41 Cholesteatoma of right external ear
H60.42 Cholesteatoma of left external ear
H60.43 Cholesteatoma of external ear, bilateral

● **H60.5 Acute noninfective otitis externa**

● **H60.50 Unspecified acute noninfective otitis externa**
Acute otitis externa NOS

H60.501 Unspecified acute noninfective otitis externa, right ear
H60.502 Unspecified acute noninfective otitis externa, left ear
H60.503 Unspecified acute noninfective otitis externa, bilateral
H60.509 Unspecified acute noninfective otitis externa, unspecified ear

● **H60.51 Acute actinic otitis externa**
H60.511 Acute actinic otitis externa, right ear
H60.512 Acute actinic otitis externa, left ear
H60.513 Acute actinic otitis externa, bilateral
H60.519 Acute actinic otitis externa, unspecified ear

H60.52 Acute chemical otitis externa

H60.521 Acute chemical otitis externa, right ear

H60.522 Acute chemical otitis externa, left ear

H60.523 Acute chemical otitis externa, bilateral

H60.529 Acute chemical otitis externa, unspecified ear

H60.53 Acute contact otitis externa

H60.531 Acute contact otitis externa, right ear

H60.532 Acute contact otitis externa, left ear

H60.533 Acute contact otitis externa, bilateral

H60.539 Acute contact otitis externa, unspecified ear

H60.54 Acute eczematoid otitis externa

H60.541 Acute eczematoid otitis externa, right ear

H60.542 Acute eczematoid otitis externa, left ear

H60.543 Acute eczematoid otitis externa, bilateral

H60.549 Acute eczematoid otitis externa, unspecified ear

H60.55 Acute reactive otitis externa

H60.551 Acute reactive otitis externa, right ear

H60.552 Acute reactive otitis externa, left ear

H60.553 Acute reactive otitis externa, bilateral

H60.559 Acute reactive otitis externa, unspecified ear

H60.59 Other noninfective acute otitis externa

H60.591 Other noninfective acute otitis externa, right ear

H60.592 Other noninfective acute otitis externa, left ear

H60.593 Other noninfective acute otitis externa, bilateral

H60.599 Other noninfective acute otitis externa, unspecified ear

H60.6 Unspecified chronic otitis externa

H60.60 Unspecified chronic otitis externa, unspecified ear

H60.61 Unspecified chronic otitis externa, right ear

H60.62 Unspecified chronic otitis externa, left ear

H60.63 Unspecified chronic otitis externa, bilateral

H60.8 Other otitis externa

H60.8X Other otitis externa

H60.8X1 Other otitis externa, right ear

H60.8X2 Other otitis externa, left ear

H60.8X3 Other otitis externa, bilateral

H60.8X9 Other otitis externa, unspecified ear

H60.9 Unspecified otitis externa

H60.90 Unspecified otitis externa, unspecified ear

H60.91 Unspecified otitis externa, right ear

H60.92 Unspecified otitis externa, left ear

H60.93 Unspecified otitis externa, bilateral

H61 Other disorders of external ear

H61.0 Chondritis and perichondritis of external ear

Chondrodermatitis nodularis chronica helicis
Perichondritis of auricle
Perichondritis of pinna

H61.00 Unspecified perichondritis of external ear

H61.001 Unspecified perichondritis of right external ear

H61.002 Unspecified perichondritis of left external ear

H61.003 Unspecified perichondritis of external ear, bilateral

H61.009 Unspecified perichondritis of external ear, unspecified ear

H61.01 Acute perichondritis of external ear

H61.011 Acute perichondritis of right external ear

H61.012 Acute perichondritis of left external ear

H61.013 Acute perichondritis of external ear, bilateral

H61.019 Acute perichondritis of external ear, unspecified ear

H61.02 Chronic perichondritis of external ear

H61.021 Chronic perichondritis of right external ear

H61.022 Chronic perichondritis of left external ear

H61.023 Chronic perichondritis of external ear, bilateral

H61.029 Chronic perichondritis of external ear, unspecified ear

H61.03 Chondritis of external ear

Chondritis of auricle
Chondritis of pinna

H61.031 Chondritis of right external ear

H61.032 Chondritis of left external ear
Coding Clinic: 2015, Q1, P18

H61.033 Chondritis of external ear, bilateral

H61.039 Chondritis of external ear, unspecified ear

H61.1 Noninfective disorders of pinna

Excludes2   cauliflower ear (M95.1-)
gouty tophi of ear (M1A.-)

H61.10 Unspecified noninfective disorders of pinna

Disorder of pinna NOS

H61.101 Unspecified noninfective disorders of pinna, right ear

H61.102 Unspecified noninfective disorders of pinna, left ear

H61.103 Unspecified noninfective disorders of pinna, bilateral

H61.109 Unspecified noninfective disorders of pinna, unspecified ear

H61.11 Acquired deformity of pinna

Acquired deformity of auricle

Excludes2   cauliflower ear (M95.1-)

H61.111 Acquired deformity of pinna, right ear

H61.112 Acquired deformity of pinna, left ear

H61.113 Acquired deformity of pinna, bilateral

H61.119 Acquired deformity of pinna, unspecified ear

H61.12 Hematoma of pinna

Hematoma of auricle

H61.121 Hematoma of pinna, right ear

H61.122 Hematoma of pinna, left ear

H61.123 Hematoma of pinna, bilateral

H61.129 Hematoma of pinna, unspecified ear

H61.19 Other noninfective disorders of pinna

H61.191 Noninfective disorders of pinna, right ear

H61.192 Noninfective disorders of pinna, left ear

H61.193 Noninfective disorders of pinna, bilateral

H61.199 Noninfective disorders of pinna, unspecified ear

▶ New   ⇒ Revised   ~~deleted~~ Deleted   Excludes 1   Excludes 2   Includes   Use additional   Code first   Code also   Key words

OGCR Official Guidelines   X Assign placeholder X   ● Use Additional Character(s)   ❱ Manifestation Code   **Coding Clinic**

● **H61.2 Impacted cerumen**
Wax in ear

    H61.20 Impacted cerumen, unspecified ear

    H61.21 Impacted cerumen, right ear

    H61.22 Impacted cerumen, left ear

    H61.23 Impacted cerumen, bilateral

● **H61.3 Acquired stenosis of external ear canal**
Collapse of external ear canal

> **Excludes1** postprocedural stenosis of external ear canal (H95.81-)

  ● **H61.30 Acquired stenosis of external ear canal, unspecified**

    H61.301 Acquired stenosis of right external ear canal, unspecified

    H61.302 Acquired stenosis of left external ear canal, unspecified

    H61.303 Acquired stenosis of external ear canal, unspecified, bilateral

    H61.309 Acquired stenosis of external ear canal, unspecified, unspecified ear

  ● **H61.31 Acquired stenosis of external ear canal secondary to trauma**

    H61.311 Acquired stenosis of right external ear canal secondary to trauma

    H61.312 Acquired stenosis of left external ear canal secondary to trauma

    H61.313 Acquired stenosis of external ear canal secondary to trauma, bilateral

    H61.319 Acquired stenosis of external ear canal secondary to trauma, unspecified ear

  ● **H61.32 Acquired stenosis of external ear canal secondary to inflammation and infection**

    H61.321 Acquired stenosis of right external ear canal secondary to inflammation and infection

    H61.322 Acquired stenosis of left external ear canal secondary to inflammation and infection

    H61.323 Acquired stenosis of external ear canal secondary to inflammation and infection, bilateral

    H61.329 Acquired stenosis of external ear canal secondary to inflammation and infection, unspecified ear

  ● **H61.39 Other acquired stenosis of external ear canal**

    H61.391 Other acquired stenosis of right external ear canal

    H61.392 Other acquired stenosis of left external ear canal

    H61.393 Other acquired stenosis of external ear canal, bilateral

    H61.399 Other acquired stenosis of external ear canal, unspecified ear

● **H61.8 Other specified disorders of external ear**

  ● **H61.81 Exostosis of external canal**

    H61.811 Exostosis of right external canal

    H61.812 Exostosis of left external canal

    H61.813 Exostosis of external canal, bilateral

    H61.819 Exostosis of external canal, unspecified ear

  ● **H61.89 Other specified disorders of external ear**

    H61.891 Other specified disorders of right external ear

    H61.892 Other specified disorders of left external ear

    H61.893 Other specified disorders of external ear, bilateral

    H61.899 Other specified disorders of external ear, unspecified ear

● **H61.9 Disorder of external ear, unspecified**

    H61.90 Disorder of external ear, unspecified, unspecified ear

    H61.91 Disorder of right external ear, unspecified

    H61.92 Disorder of left external ear, unspecified

    H61.93 Disorder of external ear, unspecified, bilateral

● **H62 Disorders of external ear in diseases classified elsewhere**

  ● **H62.4 Otitis externa in other diseases classified elsewhere**

> *Code first* underlying disease, such as:
> erysipelas (A46)
> impetigo (L01.0)

> **Excludes1** otitis externa (in):
> candidiasis (B37.84)
> herpes viral [herpes simplex] (B00.1)
> herpes zoster (B02.8)

    ▷ *H62.40 Otitis externa in other diseases classified elsewhere, unspecified ear*

    ▷ *H62.41 Otitis externa in other diseases classified elsewhere, right ear*

    ▷ *H62.42 Otitis externa in other diseases classified elsewhere, left ear*

    ▷ *H62.43 Otitis externa in other diseases classified elsewhere, bilateral*

  ● **H62.8 Other disorders of external ear in diseases classified elsewhere**

> *Code first* underlying disease, such as:
> gout (M1A.-, M10.-)

  ● **H62.8X Other disorders of external ear in diseases classified elsewhere**

    ▷ *H62.8X1 Other disorders of right external ear in diseases classified elsewhere*

    ▷ *H62.8X2 Other disorders of left external ear in diseases classified elsewhere*

    ▷ *H62.8X3 Other disorders of external ear in diseases classified elsewhere, bilateral*

    ▷ *H62.8X9 Other disorders of external ear in diseases classified elsewhere, unspecified ear*

DISEASES OF MIDDLE EAR AND MASTOID (H65-H75)

★ **(See Plate 94 on page 69.)**

● **H65 Nonsuppurative otitis media**
Bacterial or viral infection or inflammation of the middle ear; may result in fluid accumulation with pain and temporary hearing loss.

> **Includes** nonsuppurative otitis media with myringitis

Use additional code for any associated perforated tympanic membrane (H72.-)

Use additional code to identify:
exposure to environmental tobacco smoke (Z77.22)
exposure to tobacco smoke in the perinatal period (P96.81)
history of tobacco dependence (Z87.891)
occupational exposure to environmental tobacco smoke (Z57.31)
tobacco dependence (F17.-)
tobacco use (Z72.0)

● **H65.0 Acute serous otitis media**
Acute and subacute secretory otitis

    H65.00 Acute serous otitis media, unspecified ear

    H65.01 Acute serous otitis media, right ear

    H65.02 Acute serous otitis media, left ear

    H65.03 Acute serous otitis media, bilateral

    H65.04 Acute serous otitis media, recurrent, right ear

    H65.05 Acute serous otitis media, recurrent, left ear

    H65.06 Acute serous otitis media, recurrent, bilateral

    H65.07 Acute serous otitis media, recurrent, unspecified ear

● **H65.1   Other acute nonsuppurative otitis media**

> **Excludes1**   otitic barotrauma (T70.0)
> otitis media (acute) NOS (H66.9)

● **H65.11   Acute and subacute allergic otitis media (mucoid) (sanguinous) (serous)**

    H65.111   Acute and subacute allergic otitis media (mucoid) (sanguinous) (serous), right ear

    H65.112   Acute and subacute allergic otitis media (mucoid) (sanguinous) (serous), left ear

    H65.113   Acute and subacute allergic otitis media (mucoid) (sanguinous) (serous), bilateral

    H65.114   Acute and subacute allergic otitis media (mucoid) (sanguinous) (serous), recurrent, right ear

    H65.115   Acute and subacute allergic otitis media (mucoid) (sanguinous) (serous), recurrent, left ear

    H65.116   Acute and subacute allergic otitis media (mucoid) (sanguinous) (serous), recurrent, bilateral

    H65.117   Acute and subacute allergic otitis media (mucoid) (sanguinous) (serous), recurrent, unspecified ear

    H65.119   Acute and subacute allergic otitis media (mucoid) (sanguinous) (serous), unspecified ear

● **H65.19   Other acute nonsuppurative otitis media**
Acute and subacute mucoid otitis media
Acute and subacute nonsuppurative otitis media NOS
Acute and subacute sanguinous otitis media
Acute and subacute seromucinous otitis media

    H65.191   Other acute nonsuppurative otitis media, right ear

    H65.192   Other acute nonsuppurative otitis media, left ear

    H65.193   Other acute nonsuppurative otitis media, bilateral

    H65.194   Other acute nonsuppurative otitis media, recurrent, right ear

    H65.195   Other acute nonsuppurative otitis media, recurrent, left ear

    H65.196   Other acute nonsuppurative otitis media, recurrent, bilateral

    H65.197   Other acute nonsuppurative otitis media recurrent, unspecified ear

    H65.199   Other acute nonsuppurative otitis media, unspecified ear

● **H65.2   Chronic serous otitis media**
Chronic tubotympanal catarrh

H65.20   Chronic serous otitis media, unspecified ear

H65.21   Chronic serous otitis media, right ear

H65.22   Chronic serous otitis media, left ear

H65.23   Chronic serous otitis media, bilateral

● **H65.3   Chronic mucoid otitis media**
Chronic mucinous otitis media
Chronic secretory otitis media
Chronic transudative otitis media
Glue ear

> **Excludes1**   adhesive middle ear disease (H74.1)

H65.30   Chronic mucoid otitis media, unspecified ear

H65.31   Chronic mucoid otitis media, right ear

H65.32   Chronic mucoid otitis media, left ear

H65.33   Chronic mucoid otitis media, bilateral

● **H65.4   Other chronic nonsuppurative otitis media**

● **H65.41   Chronic allergic otitis media**

    H65.411   Chronic allergic otitis media, right ear

    H65.412   Chronic allergic otitis media, left ear

    H65.413   Chronic allergic otitis media, bilateral

    H65.419   Chronic allergic otitis media, unspecified ear

● **H65.49   Other chronic nonsuppurative otitis media**
Chronic exudative otitis media
Chronic nonsuppurative otitis media NOS
Chronic otitis media with effusion (nonpurulent)
Chronic seromucinous otitis media

    H65.491   Other chronic nonsuppurative otitis media, right ear

    H65.492   Other chronic nonsuppurative otitis media, left ear

    H65.493   Other chronic nonsuppurative otitis media, bilateral

    H65.499   Other chronic nonsuppurative otitis media, unspecified ear

● **H65.9   Unspecified nonsuppurative otitis media**
Allergic otitis media NOS
Catarrhal otitis media NOS
Exudative otitis media NOS
Mucoid otitis media NOS
Otitis media with effusion (nonpurulent) NOS
Secretory otitis media NOS
Seromucinous otitis media NOS
Serous otitis media NOS
Transudative otitis media NOS

H65.90   Unspecified nonsuppurative otitis media, unspecified ear

H65.91   Unspecified nonsuppurative otitis media, right ear

H65.92   Unspecified nonsuppurative otitis media, left ear

H65.93   Unspecified nonsuppurative otitis media, bilateral

● **H66   Suppurative and unspecified otitis media**
Suppurative: Discharging pus

> **Includes**   suppurative and unspecified otitis media with myringitis

Use additional code to identify:
exposure to environmental tobacco smoke (Z77.22)
exposure to tobacco smoke in the perinatal period (P96.81)
history of tobacco dependence (Z87.891)
occupational exposure to environmental tobacco smoke (Z57.31)
tobacco dependence (F17.-)
tobacco use (Z72.0)

● **H66.0   Acute suppurative otitis media**

● **H66.00   Acute suppurative otitis media without spontaneous rupture of ear drum**

    H66.001   Acute suppurative otitis media without spontaneous rupture of ear drum, right ear
       Coding Clinic: 2016, Q1, P34

    H66.002   Acute suppurative otitis media without spontaneous rupture of ear drum, left ear

    H66.003   Acute suppurative otitis media without spontaneous rupture of ear drum, bilateral

    H66.004   Acute suppurative otitis media without spontaneous rupture of ear drum, recurrent, right ear

    H66.005   Acute suppurative otitis media without spontaneous rupture of ear drum, recurrent, left ear

    H66.006   Acute suppurative otitis media without spontaneous rupture of ear drum, recurrent, bilateral

H66.007   Acute suppurative otitis media without spontaneous rupture of ear drum, recurrent, unspecified ear

H66.009   Acute suppurative otitis media without spontaneous rupture of ear drum, unspecified ear

● H66.01   Acute suppurative otitis media with spontaneous rupture of ear drum

H66.011   Acute suppurative otitis media with spontaneous rupture of ear drum, right ear

H66.012   Acute suppurative otitis media with spontaneous rupture of ear drum, left ear

H66.013   Acute suppurative otitis media with spontaneous rupture of ear drum, bilateral

H66.014   Acute suppurative otitis media with spontaneous rupture of ear drum, recurrent, right ear

H66.015   Acute suppurative otitis media with spontaneous rupture of ear drum, recurrent, left ear

H66.016   Acute suppurative otitis media with spontaneous rupture of ear drum, recurrent, bilateral

H66.017   Acute suppurative otitis media with spontaneous rupture of ear drum, recurrent, unspecified ear

H66.019   Acute suppurative otitis media with spontaneous rupture of ear drum, unspecified ear

● H66.1   Chronic tubotympanic suppurative otitis media

Benign chronic suppurative otitis media
Chronic tubotympanic disease

Use additional code for any associated perforated tympanic membrane (H72.-)

H66.10   Chronic tubotympanic suppurative otitis media, unspecified

H66.11   Chronic tubotympanic suppurative otitis media, right ear

H66.12   Chronic tubotympanic suppurative otitis media, left ear

H66.13   Chronic tubotympanic suppurative otitis media, bilateral

● H66.2   Chronic atticoantral suppurative otitis media

Chronic atticoantral disease

Use additional code for any associated perforated tympanic membrane (H72.-)

H66.20   Chronic atticoantral suppurative otitis media, unspecified ear

H66.21   Chronic atticoantral suppurative otitis media, right ear

H66.22   Chronic atticoantral suppurative otitis media, left ear

H66.23   Chronic atticoantral suppurative otitis media, bilateral

● H66.3   Other chronic suppurative otitis media

Chronic suppurative otitis media NOS

Use additional code for any associated perforated tympanic membrane (H72.-)

Excludes1   tuberculous otitis media (A18.6)

● H66.3X   Other chronic suppurative otitis media

H66.3X1   Other chronic suppurative otitis media, right ear

H66.3X2   Other chronic suppurative otitis media, left ear

H66.3X3   Other chronic suppurative otitis media, bilateral

H66.3X9   Other chronic suppurative otitis media, unspecified ear

● H66.4   Suppurative otitis media, unspecified

Purulent otitis media NOS

Use additional code for any associated perforated tympanic membrane (H72.-)

H66.40   Suppurative otitis media, unspecified, unspecified ear

H66.41   Suppurative otitis media, unspecified, right ear

H66.42   Suppurative otitis media, unspecified, left ear

H66.43   Suppurative otitis media, unspecified, bilateral

● H66.9   Otitis media, unspecified

Otitis media NOS
Acute otitis media NOS
Chronic otitis media NOS

Use additional code for any associated perforated tympanic membrane (H72.-)

H66.90   Otitis media, unspecified, unspecified ear

H66.91   Otitis media, unspecified, right ear

H66.92   Otitis media, unspecified, left ear

H66.93   Otitis media, unspecified, bilateral

● H67   Otitis media in diseases classified elsewhere

Code first underlying disease, such as:
▶ plasminogen deficiency (E88.02)
viral disease NEC (B00-B34)

Use additional code for any associated perforated tympanic membrane (H72.-)

Excludes1   otitis media in:
     influenza (J09.X9, J10.83, J11.83)
     measles (B05.3)
     scarlet fever (A38.0)
     tuberculosis (A18.6)

▷ *H67.1*   *Otitis media in diseases classified elsewhere, right ear*

▷ *H67.2*   *Otitis media in diseases classified elsewhere, left ear*

▷ *H67.3*   *Otitis media in diseases classified elsewhere, bilateral*

▷ *H67.9*   *Otitis media in diseases classified elsewhere, unspecified ear*

● H68   Eustachian salpingitis and obstruction

● H68.0   Eustachian salpingitis

● H68.00   Unspecified Eustachian salpingitis

H68.001   Unspecified Eustachian salpingitis, right ear

H68.002   Unspecified Eustachian salpingitis, left ear

H68.003   Unspecified Eustachian salpingitis, bilateral

H68.009   Unspecified Eustachian salpingitis, unspecified ear

● H68.01   Acute Eustachian salpingitis

H68.011   Acute Eustachian salpingitis, right ear

H68.012   Acute Eustachian salpingitis, left ear

H68.013   Acute Eustachian salpingitis, bilateral

H68.019   Acute Eustachian salpingitis, unspecified ear

● H68.02   Chronic Eustachian salpingitis

H68.021   Chronic Eustachian salpingitis, right ear

H68.022   Chronic Eustachian salpingitis, left ear

H68.023   Chronic Eustachian salpingitis, bilateral

H68.029   Chronic Eustachian salpingitis, unspecified ear

CHAPTER 8 (H60-H95)

● **H68.1**   **Obstruction of Eustachian tube**
     Stenosis of Eustachian tube
     Stricture of Eustachian tube

   ● **H68.10**   **Unspecified obstruction of Eustachian tube**

     H68.101   Unspecified obstruction of Eustachian tube, **right** ear

     H68.102   Unspecified obstruction of Eustachian tube, **left** ear

     H68.103   Unspecified obstruction of Eustachian tube, **bilateral**

     H68.109   Unspecified obstruction of Eustachian tube, **unspecified** ear

   ● **H68.11**   **Osseous** obstruction of Eustachian tube

     H68.111   Osseous obstruction of Eustachian tube, **right** ear

     H68.112   Osseous obstruction of Eustachian tube, **left** ear

     H68.113   Osseous obstruction of Eustachian tube, **bilateral**

     H68.119   Osseous obstruction of Eustachian tube, **unspecified** ear

   ● **H68.12**   **Intrinsic cartilagenous** obstruction of Eustachian tube

     H68.121   Intrinsic cartilagenous obstruction of Eustachian tube, **right** ear

     H68.122   Intrinsic cartilagenous obstruction of Eustachian tube, **left** ear

     H68.123   Intrinsic cartilagenous obstruction of Eustachian tube, **bilateral**

     H68.129   Intrinsic cartilagenous obstruction of Eustachian tube, **unspecified** ear

   ● **H68.13**   **Extrinsic cartilagenous** obstruction of Eustachian tube
     Compression of Eustachian tube

     H68.131   Extrinsic cartilagenous obstruction of Eustachian tube, **right** ear

     H68.132   Extrinsic cartilagenous obstruction of Eustachian tube, **left** ear

     H68.133   Extrinsic cartilagenous obstruction of Eustachian tube, **bilateral**

     H68.139   Extrinsic cartilagenous obstruction of Eustachian tube, **unspecified** ear

● **H69**   **Other and unspecified disorders of Eustachian tube**

   ● **H69.0**   **Patulous** Eustachian tube

     H69.00   Patulous Eustachian tube, **unspecified** ear

     H69.01   Patulous Eustachian tube, **right** ear

     H69.02   Patulous Eustachian tube, **left** ear

     H69.03   Patulous Eustachian tube, **bilateral**

   ● **H69.8**   **Other specified** disorders of Eustachian tube

     H69.80   Other specified disorders of Eustachian tube, **unspecified** ear

     H69.81   Other specified disorders of Eustachian tube, **right** ear

     H69.82   Other specified disorders of Eustachian tube, **left** ear

     H69.83   Other specified disorders of Eustachian tube, **bilateral**

   ● **H69.9**   **Unspecified** Eustachian tube disorder

     H69.90   Unspecified Eustachian tube disorder, **unspecified** ear

     H69.91   Unspecified Eustachian tube disorder, **right** ear

     H69.92   Unspecified Eustachian tube disorder, **left** ear

     H69.93   Unspecified Eustachian tube disorder, **bilateral**

● **H70**   **Mastoiditis and related conditions**

   ● **H70.0**   **Acute mastoiditis**
     Abscess of mastoid
     Empyema of mastoid

   ● **H70.00**   **Acute mastoiditis without complications**

     H70.001   Acute mastoiditis without complications, **right** ear

     H70.002   Acute mastoiditis without complications, **left** ear

     H70.003   Acute mastoiditis without complications, **bilateral**

     H70.009   Acute mastoiditis without complications, **unspecified** ear

   ● **H70.01**   **Subperiosteal abscess** of mastoid

     H70.011   Subperiosteal abscess of mastoid, **right** ear

     H70.012   Subperiosteal abscess of mastoid, **left** ear

     H70.013   Subperiosteal abscess of mastoid, **bilateral**

     H70.019   Subperiosteal abscess of mastoid, **unspecified** ear

   ● **H70.09**   **Acute mastoiditis with other complications**

     H70.091   Acute mastoiditis with other complications, **right** ear

     H70.092   Acute mastoiditis with other complications, **left** ear

     H70.093   Acute mastoiditis with other complications, **bilateral**

     H70.099   Acute mastoiditis with other complications, **unspecified** ear

   ● **H70.1**   **Chronic mastoiditis**
     Caries of mastoid
     Fistula of mastoid

     Excludes1   tuberculous mastoiditis (A18.03)

     H70.10   Chronic mastoiditis, **unspecified** ear

     H70.11   Chronic mastoiditis, **right** ear

     H70.12   Chronic mastoiditis, **left** ear

     H70.13   Chronic mastoiditis, **bilateral**

   ● **H70.2**   **Petrositis**
     Inflammation of petrous bone

   ● **H70.20**   **Unspecified petrositis**

     H70.201   Unspecified petrositis, **right** ear

     H70.202   Unspecified petrositis, **left** ear

     H70.203   Unspecified petrositis, **bilateral**

     H70.209   Unspecified petrositis, **unspecified** ear

   ● **H70.21**   **Acute petrositis**

     H70.211   Acute petrositis, **right** ear

     H70.212   Acute petrositis, **left** ear

     H70.213   Acute petrositis, **bilateral**

     H70.219   Acute petrositis, **unspecified** ear

   ● **H70.22**   **Chronic petrositis**

     H70.221   Chronic petrositis, **right** ear

     H70.222   Chronic petrositis, **left** ear

     H70.223   Chronic petrositis, **bilateral**

     H70.229   Chronic petrositis, **unspecified** ear

   ● **H70.8**   **Other mastoiditis and related conditions**

     Excludes1   preauricular sinus and cyst (Q18.1)
                 sinus, fistula, and cyst of branchial cleft (Q18.0)

   ● **H70.81**   **Postauricular fistula**

     H70.811   Postauricular fistula, **right** ear

     H70.812   Postauricular fistula, **left** ear

     H70.813   Postauricular fistula, **bilateral**

     H70.819   Postauricular fistula, **unspecified** ear

▶ New   ⇒ Revised   ~~deleted~~ Deleted   Excludes 1   Excludes 2   Includes   Use additional   Code first   Code also   Key words
     OGCR Official Guidelines   X Assign placeholder X   ● Use Additional Character(s)   ▶ Manifestation Code   **Coding Clinic**

Item 8-1   Mastoiditis is an infection of the portion of the temporal bone of the skull that is behind the ear (mastoid process) caused by an untreated otitis media, leading to an infection of the surrounding structures which may include the brain.

- ● H70.89   Other mastoiditis and related conditions
  - H70.891   Other mastoiditis and related conditions, **right** ear
  - H70.892   Other mastoiditis and related conditions, **left** ear
  - H70.893   Other mastoiditis and related conditions, bilateral
  - H70.899   Other mastoiditis and related conditions, **unspecified** ear
- ● H70.9   Unspecified mastoiditis
  - H70.90   Unspecified mastoiditis, **unspecified** ear
  - H70.91   Unspecified mastoiditis, **right** ear
  - H70.92   Unspecified mastoiditis, **left** ear
  - H70.93   Unspecified mastoiditis, **bilateral**
- ● H71   Cholesteatoma of middle ear
  - **Excludes2**   cholesteatoma of external ear (H60.4-)
    - recurrent cholesteatoma of postmastoidectomy cavity (H95.0-)
- ● H71.0   Cholesteatoma of **attic**
  - H71.00   Cholesteatoma of attic, **unspecified** ear
  - H71.01   Cholesteatoma of attic, **right** ear
  - H71.02   Cholesteatoma of attic, **left** ear
  - H71.03   Cholesteatoma of attic, **bilateral**
- ● H71.1   Cholesteatoma of **tympanum**
  - H71.10   Cholesteatoma of tympanum, **unspecified** ear
  - H71.11   Cholesteatoma of tympanum, **right** ear
  - H71.12   Cholesteatoma of tympanum, **left** ear
  - H71.13   Cholesteatoma of tympanum, **bilateral**
- ● H71.2   Cholesteatoma of **mastoid**
  - H71.20   Cholesteatoma of mastoid, **unspecified** ear
  - H71.21   Cholesteatoma of mastoid, **right** ear
  - H71.22   Cholesteatoma of mastoid, **left** ear
  - H71.23   Cholesteatoma of mastoid, **bilateral**
- ● H71.3   **Diffuse** cholesteatosis
  - H71.30   Diffuse cholesteatosis, **unspecified** ear
  - H71.31   Diffuse cholesteatosis, **right** ear
  - H71.32   Diffuse cholesteatosis, **left** ear
  - H71.33   Diffuse cholesteatosis, **bilateral**
- ● H71.9   Unspecified cholesteatoma
  - H71.90   Unspecified cholesteatoma, **unspecified** ear
  - H71.91   Unspecified cholesteatoma, **right** ear
  - H71.92   Unspecified cholesteatoma, **left** ear
  - H71.93   Unspecified cholesteatoma, **bilateral**

★ **(See Plate 93 on page 69.)**

- ● H72   Perforation of tympanic membrane
  - *Hole or rupture in ear drum*
  - **Includes**   persistent post-traumatic perforation of ear drum
    - postinflammatory perforation of ear drum
  - *Code first any associated otitis media (H65.-, H66.1-, H66.2-, H66.3-, H66.4-, H66.9-, H67.-)*
  - **Excludes1**   acute suppurative otitis media with rupture of the tympanic membrane (H66.01-)
    - traumatic rupture of ear drum (S09.2-)
- ● H72.0   **Central** perforation of tympanic membrane
  - H72.00   Central perforation of tympanic membrane, **unspecified** ear
  - H72.01   Central perforation of tympanic membrane, **right** ear

- H72.02   Central perforation of tympanic membrane, **left** ear
- H72.03   Central perforation of tympanic membrane, **bilateral**
- ● H72.1   Attic perforation of tympanic membrane
  - Perforation of pars flaccida
  - H72.10   Attic perforation of tympanic membrane, **unspecified** ear
  - H72.11   Attic perforation of tympanic membrane, **right** ear
  - H72.12   Attic perforation of tympanic membrane, **left** ear
  - H72.13   Attic perforation of tympanic membrane, **bilateral**
- ● H72.2   Other marginal perforations of tympanic membrane
  - ● H72.2X   Other marginal perforations of tympanic membrane
    - H72.2X1   Other marginal perforations of tympanic membrane, **right** ear
    - H72.2X2   Other marginal perforations of tympanic membrane, **left** ear
    - H72.2X3   Other marginal perforations of tympanic membrane, **bilateral**
    - H72.2X9   Other marginal perforations of tympanic membrane, **unspecified** ear
- ● H72.8   Other perforations of tympanic membrane
  - ● H72.81   Multiple perforations of tympanic membrane
    - H72.811   Multiple perforations of tympanic membrane, **right** ear
    - H72.812   Multiple perforations of tympanic membrane, **left** ear
    - H72.813   Multiple perforations of tympanic membrane, **bilateral**
    - H72.819   Multiple perforations of tympanic membrane, **unspecified** ear
  - ● H72.82   Total perforations of tympanic membrane
    - H72.821   Total perforations of tympanic membrane, **right** ear
    - H72.822   Total perforations of tympanic membrane, **left** ear
    - H72.823   Total perforations of tympanic membrane, **bilateral**
    - H72.829   Total perforations of tympanic membrane, **unspecified** ear
- ● H72.9   Unspecified perforation of tympanic membrane
  - H72.90   Unspecified perforation of tympanic membrane, **unspecified** ear
  - H72.91   Unspecified perforation of tympanic membrane, **right** ear
  - H72.92   Unspecified perforation of tympanic membrane, **left** ear
  - H72.93   Unspecified perforation of tympanic membrane, **bilateral**
- ● H73   Other disorders of tympanic membrane
  - ● H73.0   Acute myringitis
    - **Excludes1**   acute myringitis with otitis media (H65, H66)
    - ● H73.00   Unspecified acute myringitis
      - Acute tympanitis NOS
      - H73.001   Acute myringitis, **right** ear
      - H73.002   Acute myringitis, **left** ear
      - H73.003   Acute myringitis, **bilateral**
      - H73.009   Acute myringitis, **unspecified** ear
    - ● H73.01   Bullous myringitis
      - H73.011   Bullous myringitis, **right** ear
      - H73.012   Bullous myringitis, **left** ear
      - H73.013   Bullous myringitis, **bilateral**
      - H73.019   Bullous myringitis, **unspecified** ear

CHAPTER 8 (H60-H95)

CHAPTER 8 (H60-H95)

● H73.09   Other acute myringitis
    H73.091   Other acute myringitis, right ear
    H73.092   Other acute myringitis, left ear
    H73.093   Other acute myringitis, bilateral
    H73.099   Other acute myringitis, unspecified
              ear
● H73.1   Chronic myringitis
    Chronic tympanitis
    Excludes1   chronic myringitis with otitis media (H65,
                    H66)
    H73.10   Chronic myringitis, unspecified ear
    H73.11   Chronic myringitis, right ear
    H73.12   Chronic myringitis, left ear
    H73.13   Chronic myringitis, bilateral
● H73.2   Unspecified myringitis
    H73.20   Unspecified myringitis, unspecified ear
    H73.21   Unspecified myringitis, right ear
    H73.22   Unspecified myringitis, left ear
    H73.23   Unspecified myringitis, bilateral
● H73.8   Other specified disorders of tympanic membrane
    ● H73.81   Atrophic flaccid tympanic membrane
        H73.811   Atrophic flaccid tympanic membrane,
                  right ear
        H73.812   Atrophic flaccid tympanic membrane,
                  left ear
        H73.813   Atrophic flaccid tympanic membrane,
                  bilateral
        H73.819   Atrophic flaccid tympanic membrane,
                  unspecified ear
    ● H73.82   Atrophic nonflaccid tympanic membrane
        H73.821   Atrophic nonflaccid tympanic
                  membrane, right ear
        H73.822   Atrophic nonflaccid tympanic
                  membrane, left ear
        H73.823   Atrophic nonflaccid tympanic
                  membrane, bilateral
        H73.829   Atrophic nonflaccid tympanic
                  membrane, unspecified ear
    ● H73.89   Other specified disorders of tympanic
               membrane
        H73.891   Other specified disorders of tympanic
                  membrane, right ear
        H73.892   Other specified disorders of tympanic
                  membrane, left ear
        H73.893   Other specified disorders of tympanic
                  membrane, bilateral
        H73.899   Other specified disorders of tympanic
                  membrane, unspecified ear
● H73.9   Unspecified disorder of tympanic membrane
    H73.90   Unspecified disorder of tympanic membrane,
             unspecified ear
    H73.91   Unspecified disorder of tympanic membrane,
             right ear
    H73.92   Unspecified disorder of tympanic membrane,
             left ear
    H73.93   Unspecified disorder of tympanic membrane,
             bilateral
● H74   Other disorders of middle ear mastoid
    Excludes2   mastoiditis (H70.-)
    ● H74.0   Tympanosclerosis
        H74.01   Tympanosclerosis, right ear
        H74.02   Tympanosclerosis, left ear
        H74.03   Tympanosclerosis, bilateral
        H74.09   Tympanosclerosis, unspecified ear

● H74.1   Adhesive middle ear disease
    Adhesive otitis
    Excludes1   glue ear (H65.3-)
    H74.11   Adhesive right middle ear disease
    H74.12   Adhesive left middle ear disease
    H74.13   Adhesive middle ear disease, bilateral
    H74.19   Adhesive middle ear disease, unspecified ear
● H74.2   Discontinuity and dislocation of ear ossicles
    H74.20   Discontinuity and dislocation of ear ossicles,
             unspecified ear
    H74.21   Discontinuity and dislocation of right ear
             ossicles
    H74.22   Discontinuity and dislocation of left ear
             ossicles
    H74.23   Discontinuity and dislocation of ear ossicles,
             bilateral
● H74.3   Other acquired abnormalities of ear ossicles
    ● H74.31   Ankylosis of ear ossicles
        H74.311   Ankylosis of ear ossicles, right ear
        H74.312   Ankylosis of ear ossicles, left ear
        H74.313   Ankylosis of ear ossicles, bilateral
        H74.319   Ankylosis of ear ossicles, unspecified
                  ear
    ● H74.32   Partial loss of ear ossicles
        H74.321   Partial loss of ear ossicles, right ear
        H74.322   Partial loss of ear ossicles, left ear
        H74.323   Partial loss of ear ossicles, bilateral
        H74.329   Partial loss of ear ossicles, unspecified
                  ear
    ● H74.39   Other acquired abnormalities of ear ossicles
        H74.391   Other acquired abnormalities of right
                  ear ossicles
        H74.392   Other acquired abnormalities of left
                  ear ossicles
        H74.393   Other acquired abnormalities of ear
                  ossicles, bilateral
        H74.399   Other acquired abnormalities of ear
                  ossicles, unspecified ear
● H74.4   Polyp of middle ear
    H74.40   Polyp of middle ear, unspecified ear
    H74.41   Polyp of right middle ear
    H74.42   Polyp of left middle ear
    H74.43   Polyp of middle ear, bilateral
● H74.8   Other specified disorders of middle ear and mastoid
    ● H74.8X   Other specified disorders of middle ear and
               mastoid
        H74.8X1   Other specified disorders of right
                  middle ear and mastoid
        H74.8X2   Other specified disorders of left
                  middle ear and mastoid
        H74.8X3   Other specified disorders of middle
                  ear and mastoid, bilateral
        H74.8X9   Other specified disorders of middle
                  ear and mastoid, unspecified ear
● H74.9   Unspecified disorder of middle ear and mastoid
    H74.90   Unspecified disorder of middle ear and
             mastoid, unspecified ear
    H74.91   Unspecified disorder of right middle ear and
             mastoid
    H74.92   Unspecified disorder of left middle ear and
             mastoid
    H74.93   Unspecified disorder of middle ear and
             mastoid, bilateral

▶ New   ⇒ Revised   ~~deleted~~ Deleted   Excludes 1   Excludes 2   Includes   Use additional   Code first   Code also   Key words
OGCR Official Guidelines   X Assign placeholder X   ● Use Additional Character(s)   ▷ Manifestation Code   **Coding Clinic**

● H75   Other disorders of middle ear and mastoid in diseases classified elsewhere
> *Code first underlying disease*

● H75.0   **Mastoiditis in infectious and parasitic diseases classified elsewhere**
>   **Excludes1**   mastoiditis (in):
>   syphilis (A52.77)
>   tuberculosis (A18.03)

▷ *H75.00*   *Mastoiditis in infectious and parasitic diseases classified elsewhere, unspecified ear*

▷ *H75.01*   *Mastoiditis in infectious and parasitic diseases classified elsewhere, right ear*

▷ *H75.02*   *Mastoiditis in infectious and parasitic diseases classified elsewhere, left ear*

▷ *H75.03*   *Mastoiditis in infectious and parasitic diseases classified elsewhere, bilateral*

● H75.8   Other specified disorders of middle ear and mastoid in diseases classified elsewhere

▷ *H75.80*   *Other specified disorders of middle ear and mastoid in diseases classified elsewhere, unspecified ear*

▷ *H75.81*   *Other specified disorders of right middle ear and mastoid in diseases classified elsewhere*

▷ *H75.82*   *Other specified disorders of left middle ear and mastoid in diseases classified elsewhere*

▷ *H75.83*   *Other specified disorders of middle ear and mastoid in diseases classified elsewhere, bilateral*

DISEASES OF INNER EAR (H80-H83)

★ **(See Plate 95 on page 69.)**

● H80   Otosclerosis
> *Inherited middle ear spongelike bone growth causing hearing loss*
>   **Includes**   Otospongiosis

● H80.0   Otosclerosis involving oval window, nonobliterative

H80.00   Otosclerosis involving oval window, nonobliterative, unspecified ear

H80.01   Otosclerosis involving oval window, nonobliterative, right ear

H80.02   Otosclerosis involving oval window, nonobliterative, left ear

H80.03   Otosclerosis involving oval window, nonobliterative, bilateral

● H80.1   Otosclerosis involving oval window, obliterative

H80.10   Otosclerosis involving oval window, obliterative, unspecified ear

H80.11   Otosclerosis involving oval window, obliterative, right ear

H80.12   Otosclerosis involving oval window, obliterative, left ear

H80.13   Otosclerosis involving oval window, obliterative, bilateral

● H80.2   Cochlear otosclerosis
> Otosclerosis involving otic capsule
> Otosclerosis involving round window

H80.20   Cochlear otosclerosis, unspecified ear

H80.21   Cochlear otosclerosis, right ear

H80.22   Cochlear otosclerosis, left ear

H80.23   Cochlear otosclerosis, bilateral

● H80.8   Other otosclerosis

H80.80   Other otosclerosis, unspecified ear

H80.81   Other otosclerosis, right ear

H80.82   Other otosclerosis, left ear

H80.83   Other otosclerosis, bilateral

● H80.9   Unspecified otosclerosis

H80.90   Unspecified otosclerosis, unspecified ear

H80.91   Unspecified otosclerosis, right ear

H80.92   Unspecified otosclerosis, left ear

H80.93   Unspecified otosclerosis, bilateral

● H81   Disorders of vestibular function
>   **Excludes1**   epidemic vertigo (A88.1)
>   vertigo NOS (R42)

● H81.0   Ménière's disease
> *Vestibular disorder that produces recurring symptoms including severe and intermittent hearing loss including the feeling of ear pressure or pain*
> Labyrinthine hydrops
> Ménière's syndrome or vertigo

H81.01   Ménière's disease, right ear

H81.02   Ménière's disease, left ear

H81.03   Ménière's disease, bilateral

H81.09   Ménière's disease, unspecified ear

● H81.1   Benign paroxysmal vertigo

H81.10   Benign paroxysmal vertigo, unspecified ear

H81.11   Benign paroxysmal vertigo, right ear

H81.12   Benign paroxysmal vertigo, left ear

H81.13   Benign paroxysmal vertigo, bilateral

● H81.2   Vestibular neuronitis

H81.20   Vestibular neuronitis, unspecified ear

H81.21   Vestibular neuronitis, right ear

H81.22   Vestibular neuronitis, left ear

H81.23   Vestibular neuronitis, bilateral

● H81.3   Other peripheral vertigo

● H81.31   Aural vertigo

H81.311   Aural vertigo, right ear

H81.312   Aural vertigo, left ear

H81.313   Aural vertigo, bilateral

H81.319   Aural vertigo, unspecified ear

● H81.39   Other peripheral vertigo
> Lermoyez' syndrome
> Otogenic vertigo
> Peripheral vertigo NOS

H81.391   Other peripheral vertigo, right ear

H81.392   Other peripheral vertigo, left ear

H81.393   Other peripheral vertigo, bilateral

H81.399   Other peripheral vertigo, unspecified ear

● H81.4   Vertigo of central origin
> Central positional nystagmus

H81.41   Vertigo of central origin, right ear

H81.42   Vertigo of central origin, left ear

H81.43   Vertigo of central origin, bilateral

H81.49   Vertigo of central origin, unspecified ear

● H81.8   Other disorders of vestibular function

● H81.8X   Other disorders of vestibular function

H81.8X1   Other disorders of vestibular function, right ear

H81.8X2   Other disorders of vestibular function, left ear

H81.8X3   Other disorders of vestibular function, bilateral

H81.8X9   Other disorders of vestibular function, unspecified ear

● H81.9   Unspecified disorder of vestibular function
> Vertiginous syndrome NOS

H81.90   Unspecified disorder of vestibular function, unspecified ear

H81.91   Unspecified disorder of vestibular function, right ear

H81.92   Unspecified disorder of vestibular function, left ear

H81.93   Unspecified disorder of vestibular function, bilateral

CHAPTER 8 (H60-H95)

CHAPTER 8 (H60-H95)

● H82   **Vertiginous syndromes in diseases classified elsewhere**
        Code first underlying disease
        Excludes1   epidemic vertigo (A88.1)
   ▷ *H82.1*   *Vertiginous syndromes in diseases classified elsewhere, right ear*
   ▷ *H82.2*   *Vertiginous syndromes in diseases classified elsewhere, left ear*
   ▷ *H82.3*   *Vertiginous syndromes in diseases classified elsewhere, bilateral*
   ▷ *H82.9*   *Vertiginous syndromes in diseases classified elsewhere, unspecified ear*

● H83   **Other diseases of inner ear**
   ● H83.0   **Labyrinthitis**
             Balance disorder that follows URI or head injury
             H83.01   Labyrinthitis, **right** ear
             H83.02   Labyrinthitis, **left** ear
             H83.03   Labyrinthitis, **bilateral**
             H83.09   Labyrinthitis, **unspecified** ear
   ● H83.1   Labyrinthine fistula
             H83.11   Labyrinthine fistula, **right** ear
             H83.12   Labyrinthine fistula, **left** ear
             H83.13   Labyrinthine fistula, **bilateral**
             H83.19   Labyrinthine fistula, **unspecified** ear
   ● H83.2   Labyrinthine dysfunction
             Labyrinthine hypersensitivity
             Labyrinthine hypofunction
             Labyrinthine loss of function
      ● H83.2X   Labyrinthine dysfunction
                 H83.2X1   Labyrinthine dysfunction, **right** ear
                 H83.2X2   Labyrinthine dysfunction, **left** ear
                 H83.2X3   Labyrinthine dysfunction, **bilateral**
                 H83.2X9   Labyrinthine dysfunction, **unspecified** ear
   ● H83.3   Noise effects on inner ear
             Acoustic trauma of inner ear
             Noise-induced hearing loss of inner ear
      ● H83.3X   Noise effects on inner ear
                 H83.3X1   Noise effects on **right** inner ear
                 H83.3X2   Noise effects on **left** inner ear
                 H83.3X3   Noise effects on inner ear, **bilateral**
                 H83.3X9   Noise effects on inner ear, **unspecified** ear
   ● H83.8   Other specified diseases of inner ear
      ● H83.8X   Other specified diseases of inner ear
                 H83.8X1   Other specified diseases of **right** inner ear
                 H83.8X2   Other specified diseases of **left** inner ear
                 H83.8X3   Other specified diseases of inner ear, **bilateral**
                 H83.8X9   Other specified diseases of inner ear, **unspecified** ear
   ● H83.9   **Unspecified** disease of inner ear
             H83.90   Unspecified disease of inner ear, **unspecified** ear
             H83.91   Unspecified disease of **right** inner ear
             H83.92   Unspecified disease of **left** inner ear
             H83.93   Unspecified disease of inner ear, **bilateral**

OTHER DISORDERS OF EAR (H90-H94)

● H90   **Conductive and sensorineural hearing loss**
        Excludes1   deaf nonspeaking NEC (H91.3)
                        deafness NOS (H91.9-)
                        hearing loss NOS (H91.9-)
                        noise-induced hearing loss (H83.3-)
                        ototoxic hearing loss (H91.0-)
                        sudden (idiopathic) hearing loss (H91.2-)
   H90.0   **Conductive** hearing loss, **bilateral**
   ● H90.1   **Conductive** hearing loss, **unilateral** with unrestricted hearing on the contralateral side
             H90.11   Conductive hearing loss, unilateral, **right ear**, with unrestricted hearing on the contralateral side
             H90.12   Conductive hearing loss, unilateral, **left ear**, with unrestricted hearing on the contralateral side
   H90.2   **Conductive** hearing loss, **unspecified**
           Conductive deafness NOS
   H90.3   **Sensorineural** hearing loss, **bilateral**
   ● H90.4   **Sensorineural** hearing loss, **unilateral** with unrestricted hearing on the contralateral side
             H90.41   Sensorineural hearing loss, unilateral, **right ear**, with unrestricted hearing on the contralateral side
             H90.42   Sensorineural hearing loss, unilateral, **left ear**, with unrestricted hearing on the contralateral side
   H90.5   **Unspecified sensorineural** hearing loss
           Central hearing loss NOS
           Congenital deafness NOS
           Neural hearing loss NOS
           Perceptive hearing loss NOS
           Sensorineural deafness NOS
           Sensory hearing loss NOS
           Excludes1   abnormal auditory perception (H93.2-)
                           psychogenic deafness (F44.6)
   H90.6   **Mixed conductive and sensorineural hearing loss, bilateral**
           Coding Clinic: 2015, Q2, P7
   ● H90.7   **Mixed conductive and sensorineural hearing loss, unilateral** with unrestricted hearing on the contralateral side
             H90.71   Mixed conductive and sensorineural hearing loss, unilateral, **right ear**, with unrestricted hearing on the contralateral side
             H90.72   Mixed conductive and sensorineural hearing loss, unilateral, **left ear**, with unrestricted hearing on the contralateral side
   H90.8   **Mixed conductive and sensorineural hearing loss, unspecified**
   ● H90.A   Conductive and sensorineural hearing loss with **restricted hearing on the contralateral side**
             Coding Clinic: 2016, Q4, P23-24
      ● H90.A1   **Conductive** hearing loss, **unilateral**, with restricted hearing on the contralateral side
                 H90.A11   Conductive hearing loss, unilateral, **right** ear with restricted hearing on the contralateral side
                 H90.A12   Conductive hearing loss, unilateral, **left** ear with restricted hearing on the contralateral side
                           Coding Clinic: 2016, Q4, P25

854

▶ New   ⇒ Revised   ~~deleted~~ Deleted   Excludes 1   Excludes 2   Includes   Use additional   Code first   Code also   Key words
OGCR Official Guidelines   X Assign placeholder X   ● Use Additional Character(s)   ▷ Manifestation Code   Coding Clinic

● **H90.A2** Sensorineural hearing loss, unilateral, with restricted hearing on the contralateral side

     H90.A21 Sensorineural hearing loss, unilateral, right ear, with restricted hearing on the contralateral side

     H90.A22 Sensorineural hearing loss, unilateral, left ear, with restricted hearing on the contralateral side

● **H90.A3** Mixed conductive and sensorineural hearing loss, unilateral with restricted hearing on the contralateral side

     H90.A31 Mixed conductive and sensorineural hearing loss, unilateral, right ear with restricted hearing on the contralateral side

     H90.A32 Mixed conductive and sensorineural hearing loss, unilateral, left ear with restricted hearing on the contralateral side

● **H91**   Other and unspecified hearing loss

     Excludes1   abnormal auditory perception (H93.2-)
                 hearing loss as classified in H90.-
                 impacted cerumen (H61.2-)
                 noise-induced hearing loss (H83.3-)
                 psychogenic deafness (F44.6)
                 transient ischemic deafness (H93.01-)

● **H91.0**   Ototoxic hearing loss

     Code first poisoning due to drug or toxin, if applicable (T36-T65 with fifth or sixth character 1-4 or 6)

     Use additional code for adverse effect, if applicable, to identify drug (T36-T50 with fifth or sixth character 5)

     H91.01 Ototoxic hearing loss, right ear
     H91.02 Ototoxic hearing loss, left ear
     H91.03 Ototoxic hearing loss, bilateral
     H91.09 Ototoxic hearing loss, unspecified ear

● **H91.1**   Presbycusis
     Presbyacusia

     H91.10 Presbycusis, unspecified ear
     H91.11 Presbycusis, right ear
     H91.12 Presbycusis, left ear
     H91.13 Presbycusis, bilateral

● **H91.2**   Sudden idiopathic hearing loss
     Sudden hearing loss NOS

     H91.20 Sudden idiopathic hearing loss, unspecified ear
     H91.21 Sudden idiopathic hearing loss, right ear
     H91.22 Sudden idiopathic hearing loss, left ear
     H91.23 Sudden idiopathic hearing loss, bilateral

   H91.3   Deaf nonspeaking, not elsewhere classified

● **H91.8**   Other specified hearing loss

    ● **H91.8X** Other specified hearing loss

     H91.8X1 Other specified hearing loss, right ear
     H91.8X2 Other specified hearing loss, left ear
     H91.8X3 Other specified hearing loss, bilateral
     H91.8X9 Other specified hearing loss, unspecified ear

● **H91.9**   Unspecified hearing loss
     Deafness NOS
     High frequency deafness
     Low frequency deafness

     H91.90 Unspecified hearing loss, unspecified ear
     H91.91 Unspecified hearing loss, right ear
     H91.92 Unspecified hearing loss, left ear
     H91.93 Unspecified hearing loss, bilateral

● **H92**   Otalgia and effusion of ear

   ● **H92.0**   Otalgia
     H92.01 Otalgia, right ear
     H92.02 Otalgia, left ear
     H92.03 Otalgia, bilateral
     H92.09 Otalgia, unspecified ear

   ● **H92.1**   Otorrhea
     Excludes1   leakage of cerebrospinal fluid through ear (G96.0)

     H92.10 Otorrhea, unspecified ear
     H92.11 Otorrhea, right ear
     H92.12 Otorrhea, left ear
     H92.13 Otorrhea, bilateral

   ● **H92.2**   Otorrhagia
     Excludes1   traumatic otorrhagia - code to injury

     H92.20 Otorrhagia, unspecified ear
     H92.21 Otorrhagia, right ear
     H92.22 Otorrhagia, left ear
     H92.23 Otorrhagia, bilateral

● **H93**   Other disorders of ear, not elsewhere classified

   ● **H93.0**   Degenerative and vascular disorders of ear
     Excludes1   presbycusis (H91.1)

    ● **H93.01** Transient ischemic deafness
     H93.011 Transient ischemic deafness, right ear
     H93.012 Transient ischemic deafness, left ear
     H93.013 Transient ischemic deafness, bilateral
     H93.019 Transient ischemic deafness, unspecified ear

    ● **H93.09** Unspecified degenerative and vascular disorders of ear
     H93.091 Unspecified degenerative and vascular disorders of right ear
     H93.092 Unspecified degenerative and vascular disorders of left ear
     H93.093 Unspecified degenerative and vascular disorders of ear, bilateral
     H93.099 Unspecified degenerative and vascular disorders of unspecified ear

   ● **H93.1**   Tinnitus
     Perception of sound (ringing, buzzing, humming, whistling tunes, or singing)

     H93.11 Tinnitus, right ear
     H93.12 Tinnitus, left ear
     H93.13 Tinnitus, bilateral
     H93.19 Tinnitus, unspecified ear

   ● **H93.A**   Pulsatile tinnitus
     Coding Clinic: 2016, Q4, P25

     H93.A1 Pulsatile tinnitus, right ear
         Coding Clinic: 2016, Q4, P26
     H93.A2 Pulsatile tinnitus, left ear
     H93.A3 Pulsatile tinnitus, bilateral
     H93.A9 Pulsatile tinnitus, unspecified ear

   ● **H93.2**   Other abnormal auditory perceptions
     Excludes2   auditory hallucinations (R44.0)

    ● **H93.21** Auditory recruitment
     H93.211 Auditory recruitment, right ear
     H93.212 Auditory recruitment, left ear
     H93.213 Auditory recruitment, bilateral
     H93.219 Auditory recruitment, unspecified ear

    ● **H93.22** Diplacusis
     H93.221 Diplacusis, right ear
     H93.222 Diplacusis, left ear
     H93.223 Diplacusis, bilateral
     H93.229 Diplacusis, unspecified ear

CHAPTER 8 (H60-H95)

● H93.23   Hyperacusis
     H93.231   Hyperacusis, right ear
     H93.232   Hyperacusis, left ear
     H93.233   Hyperacusis, bilateral
     H93.239   Hyperacusis, unspecified ear

● H93.24   Temporary auditory threshold shift
     H93.241   Temporary auditory threshold shift, right ear
     H93.242   Temporary auditory threshold shift, left ear
     H93.243   Temporary auditory threshold shift, bilateral
     H93.249   Temporary auditory threshold shift, unspecified ear

H93.25   Central auditory processing disorder
     Congenital auditory imperception
     Word deafness
     Excludes1   mixed receptive-expressive language disorder (F80.2)

● H93.29   Other abnormal auditory perceptions
     H93.291   Other abnormal auditory perceptions, right ear
     H93.292   Other abnormal auditory perceptions, left ear
     H93.293   Other abnormal auditory perceptions, bilateral
     H93.299   Other abnormal auditory perceptions, unspecified ear

● H93.3   Disorders of acoustic nerve
     Disorder of 8th cranial nerve
     Excludes1   acoustic neuroma (D33.3)
            syphilitic acoustic neuritis (A52.15)

● H93.3X   Disorders of acoustic nerve
     H93.3X1   Disorders of right acoustic nerve
     H93.3X2   Disorders of left acoustic nerve
     H93.3X3   Disorders of bilateral acoustic nerves
     H93.3X9   Disorders of unspecified acoustic nerve

● H93.8   Other specified disorders of ear
● H93.8X   Other specified disorders of ear
     H93.8X1   Other specified disorders of right ear
     H93.8X2   Other specified disorders of left ear
     H93.8X3   Other specified disorders of ear, bilateral
     H93.8X9   Other specified disorders of ear, unspecified ear

● H93.9   Unspecified disorder of ear
     H93.90   Unspecified disorder of ear, unspecified ear
     H93.91   Unspecified disorder of right ear
     H93.92   Unspecified disorder of left ear
     H93.93   Unspecified disorder of ear, bilateral

● H94   Other disorders of ear in diseases classified elsewhere
● H94.0   Acoustic neuritis in infectious and parasitic diseases classified elsewhere
     Code first underlying disease, such as:
        parasitic disease (B65-B89)
     Excludes1   acoustic neuritis (in):
            herpes zoster (B02.29)
            syphilis (A52.15)
    ▌ *H94.00   Acoustic neuritis in infectious and parasitic diseases classified elsewhere, unspecified ear*
    ▌ *H94.01   Acoustic neuritis in infectious and parasitic diseases classified elsewhere, right ear*
    ▌ *H94.02   Acoustic neuritis in infectious and parasitic diseases classified elsewhere, left ear*
    ▌ *H94.03   Acoustic neuritis in infectious and parasitic diseases classified elsewhere, bilateral*

● H94.8   Other specified disorders of ear in diseases classified elsewhere
     Code first underlying disease, such as:
        congenital syphilis (A50.0)
     Excludes1   aural myiasis (B87.4)
            syphilitic labyrinthitis (A52.79)
    ▌ *H94.80   Other specified disorders of ear in diseases classified elsewhere, unspecified ear*
    ▌ *H94.81   Other specified disorders of right ear in diseases classified elsewhere*
    ▌ *H94.82   Other specified disorders of left ear in diseases classified elsewhere*
    ▌ *H94.83   Other specified disorders of ear in diseases classified elsewhere, bilateral*

INTRAOPERATIVE AND POSTPROCEDURAL COMPLICATIONS AND DISORDERS OF EAR AND MASTOID PROCESS, NOT ELSEWHERE CLASSIFIED (H95)

● H95   Intraoperative and postprocedural complications and disorders of ear and mastoid process, not elsewhere classified
     Coding Clinic: 2016, Q4, P10

● H95.0   Recurrent cholesteatoma of postmastoidectomy cavity
     H95.00   Recurrent cholesteatoma of postmastoidectomy cavity, unspecified ear
     H95.01   Recurrent cholesteatoma of postmastoidectomy cavity, right ear
     H95.02   Recurrent cholesteatoma of postmastoidectomy cavity, left ear
     H95.03   Recurrent cholesteatoma of postmastoidectomy cavity, bilateral ears

● H95.1   Other disorders of ear and mastoid process following mastoidectomy
● H95.11   Chronic inflammation of postmastoidectomy cavity
     H95.111   Chronic inflammation of postmastoidectomy cavity, right ear
     H95.112   Chronic inflammation of postmastoidectomy cavity, left ear
     H95.113   Chronic inflammation of postmastoidectomy cavity, bilateral ears
     H95.119   Chronic inflammation of postmastoidectomy cavity, unspecified ear

● H95.12   Granulation of postmastoidectomy cavity
     H95.121   Granulation of postmastoidectomy cavity, right ear
     H95.122   Granulation of postmastoidectomy cavity, left ear
     H95.123   Granulation of postmastoidectomy cavity, bilateral ears
     H95.129   Granulation of postmastoidectomy cavity, unspecified ear

● H95.13   Mucosal cyst of postmastoidectomy cavity
     H95.131   Mucosal cyst of postmastoidectomy cavity, right ear
     H95.132   Mucosal cyst of postmastoidectomy cavity, left ear
     H95.133   Mucosal cyst of postmastoidectomy cavity, bilateral ears
     H95.139   Mucosal cyst of postmastoidectomy cavity, unspecified ear

▶ New   ⇒ Revised   ~~deleted~~ Deleted   Excludes 1   Excludes 2   Includes   Use additional   Code first   Code also   Key words
OGCR Official Guidelines   X Assign placeholder X   ● Use Additional Character(s)   ▌ Manifestation Code   Coding Clinic

● **H95.19   Other disorders following mastoidectomy**

     H95.191   Other disorders following mastoidectomy, right ear

     H95.192   Other disorders following mastoidectomy, left ear

     H95.193   Other disorders following mastoidectomy, bilateral ears

     H95.199   Other disorders following mastoidectomy, unspecified ear

● **H95.2   Intraoperative hemorrhage and hematoma of ear and mastoid process complicating a procedure**

     Excludes1   intraoperative hemorrhage and hematoma of ear and mastoid process due to accidental puncture or laceration during a procedure (H95.3-)

     H95.21   Intraoperative hemorrhage and hematoma of ear and mastoid process complicating a procedure on the ear and mastoid process

     H95.22   Intraoperative hemorrhage and hematoma of ear and mastoid process complicating other procedure

● **H95.3   Accidental puncture and laceration of ear and mastoid process during a procedure**

     H95.31   Accidental puncture and laceration of the ear and mastoid process during a procedure on the ear and mastoid process

     H95.32   Accidental puncture and laceration of the ear and mastoid process during other procedure

● **H95.4   Postprocedural hemorrhage of ear and mastoid process following a procedure**

     H95.41   Postprocedural hemorrhage of ear and mastoid process following a procedure on the ear and mastoid process

     H95.42   Postprocedural hemorrhage of ear and mastoid process following other procedure

● **H95.5   Postprocedural hematoma and seroma of ear and mastoid process following a procedure**

     H95.51   Postprocedural hematoma of ear and mastoid process following a procedure on the ear and mastoid process

     H95.52   Postprocedural hematoma of ear and mastoid process following other procedure

     H95.53   Postprocedural seroma of ear and mastoid process following a procedure on the ear and mastoid process

     H95.54   Postprocedural seroma of ear and mastoid process following other procedure

● **H95.8   Other intraoperative and postprocedural complications and disorders of the ear and mastoid process, not elsewhere classified**

     Excludes2   postprocedural complications and disorders following mastoidectomy (H95.0-, H95.1-)

● **H95.81   Postprocedural stenosis of external ear canal**

     H95.811   Postprocedural stenosis of right external ear canal

     H95.812   Postprocedural stenosis of left external ear canal

     H95.813   Postprocedural stenosis of external ear canal, bilateral

     H95.819   Postprocedural stenosis of unspecified external ear canal

     H95.88   Other intraoperative complications and disorders of the ear and mastoid process, not elsewhere classified

        Use additional code, if applicable, to further specify disorder

     H95.89   Other postprocedural complications and disorders of the ear and mastoid process, not elsewhere classified

        Use additional code, if applicable, to further specify disorder

CHAPTER 8 (H60–H95)

CHAPTER 9

DISEASES OF THE CIRCULATORY SYSTEM (I00-I99)

OGCR Chapter-Specific Coding Guidelines

9. Chapter 9: Diseases of the Circulatory System (I00-I99)

a. Hypertension

The classification presumes a causal relationship between hypertension and heart involvement and between hypertension and kidney involvement, as the two conditions are linked by the term "with" in the Alphabetic Index. These conditions should be coded as related even in the absence of provider documentation explicitly linking them, unless the documentation clearly states the conditions are unrelated.

For hypertension and conditions not specifically linked by relational terms such as "with," "associated with" or "due to" in the classification, provider documentation must link the conditions in order to code them as related.

1) Hypertension with Heart Disease

Hypertension with heart conditions classified to I50.- or **I51.4-I51.7, I51.89, I51.9,** are assigned to, a code from category I11, Hypertensive heart disease. Use additional code(s) from category I50, Heart failure, to identify the type(s) of heart failure in those patients with heart failure.

The same heart conditions (I50.-, **I51.4-I51.7, I51.89, I51.9**) with hypertension, are coded separately if the provider has **documented they are unrelated to the hypertension.** Sequence according to the circumstances of the admission/encounter.

2) Hypertensive Chronic Kidney Disease

Assign codes from category I12, Hypertensive chronic kidney disease, when both hypertension and a condition classifiable to category N18, Chronic kidney disease (CKD), are present. CKD should not be coded as hypertension if the **provider indicates the CKD is not related to the hypertension.**

The appropriate code from category N18 should be used as a secondary code with a code from category I12 to identify the stage of chronic kidney disease.

See Section I.C.14. Chronic kidney disease.

If a patient has hypertensive chronic kidney disease and acute renal failure, an additional code for the acute renal failure is required.

3) Hypertensive Heart and Chronic Kidney Disease

Assign codes from combination category I13, Hypertensive heart and chronic kidney disease, when there is hypertension with both heart and kidney involvement. If heart failure is present, assign an additional code from category I50 to identify the type of heart failure.

The appropriate code from category N18, Chronic kidney disease, should be used as a secondary code with a code from category I13 to identify the stage of chronic kidney disease.

See Section I.C.14. Chronic kidney disease.

The codes in category I13, Hypertensive heart and chronic kidney disease, are combination codes that include hypertension, heart disease and chronic kidney disease. The Includes note at I13 specifies that the conditions included at I11 and I12 are included together in I13. If a patient has hypertension, heart disease and chronic kidney disease then a code from I13 should be used, not individual codes for hypertension, heart disease and chronic kidney disease, or codes from I11 or I12.

For patients with both acute renal failure and chronic kidney disease an additional code for acute renal failure is required.

4) Hypertensive Cerebrovascular Disease

For hypertensive cerebrovascular disease, first assign the appropriate code from categories I60-I69, followed by the appropriate hypertension code.

5) Hypertensive Retinopathy

Subcategory H35.0, Background retinopathy and retinal vascular changes, should be used with a code from category I10 – I15, Hypertensive disease to include the systemic hypertension. The sequencing is based on the reason for the encounter.

6) Hypertension, Secondary

Secondary hypertension is due to an underlying condition. Two codes are required: one to identify the underlying etiology and one from category I15 to identify the hypertension. Sequencing of codes is determined by the reason for admission/encounter.

7) Hypertension, Transient

Assign code R03.0, Elevated blood pressure reading without diagnosis of hypertension, unless patient has an established diagnosis of hypertension. Assign code O13.-, Gestational [pregnancy-induced] hypertension without significant proteinuria, or O14.-, Pre-eclampsia, for transient hypertension of pregnancy.

8) Hypertension, Controlled

This diagnostic statement usually refers to an existing state of hypertension under control by therapy. Assign the appropriate code from categories I10-I15, Hypertensive diseases.

9) Hypertension, Uncontrolled

Uncontrolled hypertension may refer to untreated hypertension or hypertension not responding to current therapeutic regimen. In either case, assign the appropriate code from categories I10-I15, Hypertensive diseases.

10) Hypertensive Crisis

Assign a code from category I16, Hypertensive crisis, for documented hypertensive urgency, hypertensive emergency or unspecified hypertensive crisis. Code also any identified hypertensive disease (I10-I15). The sequencing is based on the reason for the encounter.

11) Pulmonary Hypertension

Pulmonary hypertension is classified to category I27, Other pulmonary heart diseases. For secondary pulmonary hypertension (I27.1, I27.2-), code also any associated conditions or adverse effects of drugs or toxins. The sequencing is based on the reason for the encounter, **except for adverse effects of drugs.**

See Section I.C.19.e

b. Atherosclerotic Coronary Artery Disease and Angina

ICD-10-CM has combination codes for atherosclerotic heart disease with angina pectoris. The subcategories for these codes are I25.11, Atherosclerotic heart disease of native coronary artery with angina pectoris and I25.7, Atherosclerosis of coronary artery bypass graft(s) and coronary artery of transplanted heart with angina pectoris.

When using one of these combination codes it is not necessary to use an additional code for angina pectoris. A causal relationship can be assumed in a patient with both atherosclerosis and angina pectoris, unless the documentation indicates the angina is due to something other than the atherosclerosis.

If a patient with coronary artery disease is admitted due to an acute myocardial infarction (AMI), the AMI should be sequenced before the coronary artery disease.

See Section I.C.9. Acute myocardial infarction (AMI)

c. Intraoperative and Postprocedural Cerebrovascular Accident

Medical record documentation should clearly specify the cause-and-effect relationship between the medical intervention and the cerebrovascular accident in order to assign a code for intraoperative or postprocedural cerebrovascular accident.

Proper code assignment depends on whether it was an infarction or hemorrhage and whether it occurred intraoperatively or postoperatively. If it was a cerebral hemorrhage, code assignment depends on the type of procedure performed.

d. Sequelae of Cerebrovascular Disease

1) Category I69, Sequelae of Cerebrovascular disease

Category I69 is used to indicate conditions classifiable to categories I60-I67 as the causes of sequela (neurologic deficits), themselves classified elsewhere. These "late effects" include neurologic deficits that persist after initial onset of conditions classifiable to categories I60-I67. The neurologic deficits caused by cerebrovascular disease may be present from the onset or may arise at any time after the onset of the condition classifiable to categories I60-I67.

Codes from category I69, Sequelae of cerebrovascular disease, that specify hemiplegia, hemiparesis and monoplegia identify whether the dominant or nondominant side is affected. Should the affected side be documented, but not specified as dominant or nondominant, and the classification system does not indicate a default, code selection is as follows:

- For ambidextrous patients, the default should be dominant.
- If the left side is affected, the default is non-dominant.
- If the right side is affected, the default is dominant.

2) Codes from category I69 with codes from I60-I67

Codes from category I69 may be assigned on a health care record with codes from I60-I67, if the patient has a current cerebrovascular disease and deficits from an old cerebrovascular disease.

3) Codes from category I69 and Personal history of transient ischemic attack (TIA) and cerebral infarction (Z86.73)

Codes from category I69 should not be assigned if the patient does not have neurologic deficits.

See Section I.C.21. 4. History (of) for use of personal history codes

e. **Acute myocardial infarction (AMI)**

1) **Type 1 ST elevation myocardial infarction (STEMI) and non ST elevation myocardial infarction (NSTEMI)**

The ICD-10-CM codes for acute type 1 myocardial infarction (AMI) identify the site, such as anterolateral wall or true posterior wall. Subcategories I21.0-I21.2 and code I21.3 are used for type 1 ST elevation myocardial infarction (STEMI). Code I21.4, Non-ST elevation (NSTEMI) myocardial infarction, is used for type 1 non ST elevation myocardial infarction (NSTEMI) and nontransmural MIs.

If a type 1 NSTEMI evolves to STEMI, assign the STEMI code. If a type 1 STEMI converts to NSTEMI due to thrombolytic therapy, it is still coded as STEMI.

For encounters occurring while the myocardial infarction is equal to, or less than, four weeks old, including transfers to another acute setting or a postacute setting, and the myocardial infarction meets the definition for "other diagnoses" (see Section III, Reporting Additional Diagnoses), codes from category I21 may continue to be reported. For encounters after the 4 week time frame and the patient is still receiving care related to the myocardial infarction, the appropriate aftercare code should be assigned, rather than a code from category I21. For old or healed myocardial infarctions not requiring further care, code I25.2, Old myocardial infarction, may be assigned.

2) **Acute myocardial infarction, unspecified**

Code I21.9, Acute myocardial infarction, unspecified, is the default for unspecified acute myocardial infarction or unspecified type. If only type 1 STEMI or transmural MI without the site is documented, assign code I21.3, ST elevation (STEMI) myocardial infarction of unspecified site.

3) **AMI documented as nontransmural or subendocardial but site provided**

If an AMI is documented as nontransmural or subendocardial, but the site is provided, it is still coded as a subendocardial AMI.

See Section I.C.21.3 for information on coding status post administration of tPA in a different facility within the last 24 hours.

4) **Subsequent acute myocardial infarction**

A code from category I22, Subsequent ST elevation (STEMI) and non ST elevation (NSTEMI) myocardial infarction, is to be used when a patient who has suffered a type 1 or unspecified AMI has a new AMI within the 4-week time frame of the initial AMI. A code from category I22 must be used in conjunction with a code from category I21. The sequencing of the I22 and I21 codes depends on the circumstances of the encounter.

Do not assign code I22 for subsequent myocardial infarctions other than type 1 or unspecified. For subsequent type 2 AMI assign only code I21.A1. For subsequent type 4 or type 5 AMI, assign only code I21.A9.

If a subsequent myocardial infarction of one type occurs within 4 weeks of a myocardial infarction of a different type, assign the appropriate codes from category I21 to identify each type. Do not assign a code from category I22. Codes from category I22 should only be assigned if both the initial and subsequent myocardial infarctions are type 1 or unspecified.

5) **Other Types of Myocardial Infarction**

The ICD-10-CM provides codes for different types of myocardial infarction. Type 1 myocardial infarctions are assigned to codes I21.0-I21.4 **and I21.9.**

Type 2 myocardial infarction, and myocardial infarction due to demand ischemia or secondary to ischemic balance, is assigned to code I21.A1, Myocardial infarction type 2 with a code for the underlying cause. Do not assign code I24.8, Other forms of acute ischemic heart disease for the demand ischemia. Sequencing of type 2 AMI or the underlying cause is dependent on the circumstances of admission. When a type 2 AMI code is described as NSTEMI or STEMI, only assign code I21.A1. Codes I21.01-I21.4 should not be assigned for type 1 AMIs.

Acute myocardial infarctions type 3, 4a, 4b, 4c, and 5 are assigned to code I21.A9, Other myocardial infarction type.

The "Code also" and "Code first" notes should be followed related to complications, and for coding of postprocedural myocardial infarctions during or following cardiac surgery.

Figure 9-1 Cardiovascular valves.

Item 9–1 Rheumatic fever is the inflammation of the valve(s) of the heart, usually the mitral or aortic, which leads to valve damage. Rheumatic heart inflammations are usually **pericarditis** (sac surrounding heart), **endocarditis** (heart cavity), or **myocarditis** (heart muscle).

CHAPTER 9

DISEASES OF THE CIRCULATORY SYSTEM (I00-I99)

Excludes2	certain conditions originating in the perinatal period (P04-P96)
	certain infectious and parasitic diseases (A00-B99)
	complications of pregnancy, childbirth and the puerperium (O00-O9A)
	congenital malformations, deformations, and chromosomal abnormalities (Q00-Q99)
	endocrine, nutritional and metabolic diseases (E00-E88)
	injury, poisoning and certain other consequences of external causes (S00-T88)
	neoplasms (C00-D49)
	symptoms, signs and abnormal clinical and laboratory findings, not elsewhere classified (R00-R94)
	systemic connective tissue disorders (M30-M36)
	transient cerebral ischemic attacks and related syndromes (G45.-)

This chapter contains the following blocks:

I00-I02	Acute rheumatic fever
I05-I09	Chronic rheumatic heart diseases
I10-I16	Hypertensive diseases
I20-I25	Ischemic heart diseases
I26-I28	Pulmonary heart disease and diseases of pulmonary circulation
I30-I52	Other forms of heart disease
I60-I69	Cerebrovascular diseases
I70-I79	Diseases of arteries, arterioles and capillaries
I80-I89	Diseases of veins, lymphatic vessels and lymph nodes, not elsewhere classified
I95-I99	Other and unspecified disorders of the circulatory system

ACUTE RHEUMATIC FEVER (I00-I02)

I00   **Rheumatic fever without heart involvement**

Includes	arthritis, rheumatic, acute or subacute
Excludes1	rheumatic fever with heart involvement (I01.0-I01.9)

● **I01**   **Rheumatic fever with heart involvement**

Excludes1	chronic diseases of rheumatic origin (I05-I09) unless rheumatic fever is also present or there is evidence of reactivation or activity of the rheumatic process.

I01.0   **Acute rheumatic pericarditis**

Any condition in I00 with pericarditis
Rheumatic pericarditis (acute)

Excludes1	acute pericarditis not specified as rheumatic (I30.-)

I01.1   **Acute rheumatic endocarditis**

Any condition in I00 with endocarditis or valvulitis
Acute rheumatic valvulitis

Item 9-2 Rheumatic chorea, also called Sydenham's, juvenile, minor, simple, or St. Vitus' dance, is a major symptom of rheumatic fever and is characterized by ceaseless, involuntary, jerky, purposeless movements.

I01.2 Acute rheumatic myocarditis
Any condition in I00 with myocarditis

I01.8 Other acute rheumatic heart disease
Any condition in I00 with other or multiple types of heart involvement
Acute rheumatic pancarditis

I01.9 Acute rheumatic heart disease, unspecified
Any condition in I00 with unspecified type of heart involvement
Rheumatic carditis, acute
Rheumatic heart disease, active or acute

● **I02 Rheumatic chorea**
Includes Sydenham's chorea
Excludes1 chorea NOS (G25.5)
Huntington's chorea (G10)

I02.0 Rheumatic chorea with heart involvement
Chorea NOS with heart involvement
Rheumatic chorea with heart involvement of any type classifiable under I01.-

I02.9 Rheumatic chorea without heart involvement
Rheumatic chorea NOS

CHRONIC RHEUMATIC HEART DISEASES (I05-I09)

● **I05 Rheumatic mitral valve diseases**
Includes conditions classifiable to both I05.0 and I05.2-I05.9, whether specified as rheumatic or not
Excludes1 mitral valve disease specified as nonrheumatic (I34.-)
mitral valve disease with aortic and/or tricuspid valve involvement (I08.-)

I05.0 Rheumatic mitral stenosis
Mitral (valve) obstruction (rheumatic)

I05.1 Rheumatic mitral insufficiency
Rheumatic mitral incompetence
Rheumatic mitral regurgitation
Excludes1 mitral insufficiency not specified as rheumatic (I34.0)

I05.2 Rheumatic mitral stenosis with insufficiency
Rheumatic mitral stenosis with incompetence or regurgitation

I05.8 Other rheumatic mitral valve diseases
Rheumatic mitral (valve) failure

I05.9 Rheumatic mitral valve disease, unspecified
Rheumatic mitral (valve) disorder (chronic) NOS

● **I06 Rheumatic aortic valve diseases**
Excludes1 aortic valve disease not specified as rheumatic (I35.-)
aortic valve disease with mitral and/or tricuspid valve involvement (I08.-)

I06.0 Rheumatic aortic stenosis
Rheumatic aortic (valve) obstruction

I06.1 Rheumatic aortic insufficiency
Rheumatic aortic incompetence
Rheumatic aortic regurgitation

★**(See Plate 244 on page 78.)**

Item 9-4 Aortic stenosis is the narrowing of the aortic valve located between the left ventricle and the aorta. **Aortic insufficiency** is the improper closure of the aortic valve which may lead to enlargement (hypertrophy) of the left ventricle.

I06.2 Rheumatic aortic stenosis with insufficiency
Rheumatic aortic stenosis with incompetence or regurgitation

I06.8 Other rheumatic aortic valve diseases

I06.9 Rheumatic aortic valve disease, unspecified
Rheumatic aortic (valve) disease NOS

● **I07 Rheumatic tricuspid valve diseases**
Includes rheumatic tricuspid valve diseases specified as rheumatic or unspecified
Excludes1 tricuspid valve disease specified as nonrheumatic (I36.-)
tricuspid valve disease with aortic and/or mitral valve involvement (I08.-)

I07.0 Rheumatic tricuspid stenosis
Tricuspid (valve) stenosis (rheumatic)

I07.1 Rheumatic tricuspid insufficiency
Tricuspid (valve) insufficiency (rheumatic)

I07.2 Rheumatic tricuspid stenosis and insufficiency

I07.8 Other rheumatic tricuspid valve diseases

I07.9 Rheumatic tricuspid valve disease, unspecified
Rheumatic tricuspid valve disorder NOS

● **I08 Multiple valve diseases**
Includes multiple valve diseases specified as rheumatic or unspecified
Excludes1 endocarditis, valve unspecified (I38)
multiple valve disease specified a nonrheumatic (I34.-, I35.-, I36.-, I37.-, I38.-, Q22.-, Q23.-, Q24.8-)
rheumatic valve disease NOS (I09.1)

I08.0 Rheumatic disorders of both mitral and aortic valves
Involvement of both mitral and aortic valves specified as rheumatic or unspecified

I08.1 Rheumatic disorders of both mitral and tricuspid valves

I08.2 Rheumatic disorders of both aortic and tricuspid valves

I08.3 Combined rheumatic disorders of mitral, aortic and tricuspid valves

I08.8 Other rheumatic multiple valve diseases

I08.9 Rheumatic multiple valve disease, unspecified

● **I09 Other rheumatic heart diseases**
I09.0 Rheumatic myocarditis
Excludes1 myocarditis not specified as rheumatic (I51.4)

I09.1 Rheumatic diseases of endocardium, valve unspecified
Rheumatic endocarditis (chronic)
Rheumatic valvulitis (chronic)
Excludes1 endocarditis, valve unspecified (I38)

I09.2 Chronic rheumatic pericarditis
Adherent pericardium, rheumatic
Chronic rheumatic mediastinopericarditis
Chronic rheumatic myopericarditis
Excludes1 chronic pericarditis not specified as rheumatic (I31.-)

● **I09.8 Other specified rheumatic heart diseases**
I09.81 Rheumatic heart failure
Use additional code to identify type of heart failure (I50.-)

I09.89 Other specified rheumatic heart diseases
Rheumatic disease of pulmonary valve

● **I09.9 Rheumatic heart disease, unspecified**
Rheumatic carditis
Excludes1 rheumatoid carditis (M05.31)

Item 9-3 Mitral stenosis is the narrowing of the mitral valve separating the left atrium from the left ventricle. **Mitral insufficiency** is the improper closure of the mitral valve which may lead to enlargement (hypertrophy) of the left atrium.

▶ New ⇒ Revised ~~deleted~~ Deleted Excludes 1 Excludes 2 Includes Use additional Code first Code also Key words
OGCR Official Guidelines X Assign placeholder X ● Use Additional Character(s) ▷ Manifestation Code Coding Clinic

Item 9–5 Hypertension is caused by high arterial blood pressure in the arteries. **Essential, primary,** or **idiopathic** hypertension occurs without identifiable organic cause. **Secondary** hypertension is that which has an organic cause. **Malignant** hypertension is severely elevated blood pressure. **Benign** hypertension is mildly elevated blood pressure.

HYPERTENSIVE DISEASES (I10-I16)

Use additional code to identify:
exposure to environmental tobacco smoke (Z77.22)
history of tobacco dependence (Z87.891)
occupational exposure to environmental tobacco smoke (Z57.31)
tobacco dependence (F17.-)
tobacco use (Z72.0)

Excludes1	neonatal hypertension (P29.2)
	primary pulmonary hypertension (I27.0)
Excludes2	hypertensive disease complicating pregnancy, childbirth and the puerperium (O10-O11, O13-O16)

I10   **Essential (primary) hypertension**

Includes	high blood pressure
	hypertension (arterial) (benign) (essential) (malignant) (primary) (systemic)
Excludes1	hypertensive disease complicating pregnancy, childbirth and the puerperium (O10-O11, O13-O16)
Excludes2	essential (primary) hypertension involving vessels of brain (I60-I69)
	essential (primary) hypertension involving vessels of eye (H35.0-)

● **I11**   **Hypertensive heart disease**

| **Includes** | any condition in I50.-, I51.4-I51.9 due to hypertension |

    I11.0   **Hypertensive heart disease with heart failure**
       Hypertensive heart failure
        Use additional code to identify type of heart failure (I50.-)
        Coding Clinic: 2017, Q1, P47

    I11.9   **Hypertensive heart disease without heart failure**
       Hypertensive heart disease NOS

OGCR Section I.C.9.a.2.

Hypertensive Chronic Kidney Disease

Assign codes from category I12, Hypertensive chronic kidney disease, when both hypertension and a condition classifiable to category N18, Chronic kidney disease (CKD), are present. **CKD should not be coded as hypertensive if the physician has specifically documented a different cause.**

The appropriate code from category N18 should be used as a secondary code with a code from category I12 to identify the stage of chronic kidney disease.

See Section I.C.14. Chronic kidney disease.

If a patient has hypertensive chronic kidney disease and acute renal failure, an additional code for the acute renal failure is required.

● **I12**   **Hypertensive chronic kidney disease**

Includes	any condition in N18 and N26 - due to hypertension
	arteriosclerosis of kidney
	arteriosclerotic nephritis (chronic) (interstitial)
	hypertensive nephropathy
	nephrosclerosis
Excludes1	hypertension due to kidney disease (I15.0, I15.1)
	renovascular hypertension (I15.0)
	secondary hypertension (I15.-)
Excludes2	acute kidney failure (N17.-)

Coding Clinic: 2016, Q4, P123

    I12.0   **Hypertensive chronic kidney disease with stage 5 chronic kidney disease or end stage renal disease**
       Use additional code to identify the stage of chronic kidney disease (N18.5, N18.6)
        Coding Clinic: 2016, Q3, P23

    I12.9   **Hypertensive chronic kidney disease with stage 1 through stage 4 chronic kidney disease, or unspecified chronic kidney disease**
       Hypertensive chronic kidney disease NOS
       Hypertensive renal disease NOS
        Use additional code to identify the stage of chronic kidney disease (N18.1-N18.4, N18.9)

OGCR Section I.c.9.a.3.

Hypertensive Heart and Chronic Kidney Disease

Assign codes from combination category I13, Hypertensive heart and chronic kidney disease, when **there is hypertension with both heart and kidney involvement.** If heart failure is present, assign an additional code from category I50 to identify the type of heart failure.

The appropriate code from category N18, Chronic kidney disease, should be used as a secondary code with a code from category I13 to identify the stage of chronic kidney disease. *See Section I.C.14. Chronic kidney disease.*

The codes in category I13, Hypertensive heart and chronic kidney disease, are combination codes that include hypertension, heart disease and chronic kidney disease. The Includes note at I13 specifies that the conditions included at I11 and I12 are included together in I13. If a patient has hypertension, heart disease and chronic kidney disease then a code from I13 should be used, not individual codes for hypertension, heart disease and chronic kidney disease, or codes from I11 or I12.

For patients with both acute renal failure and chronic kidney disease an additional code for acute renal failure is required.

● **I13**   **Hypertensive heart and chronic kidney disease**

Includes	any condition in I11.- with any condition in I12.-
	cardiorenal disease
	cardiovascular renal disease

Coding Clinic: 2016, Q4, P123

    I13.0   **Hypertensive heart and chronic kidney disease with heart failure and stage 1 through stage 4 chronic kidney disease, or unspecified chronic kidney disease**
       Use additional code to identify type of heart failure (I50.-)
       Use additional code to identify stage of chronic kidney disease (N18.1-N18.4, N18.9)

●   **I13.1**   **Hypertensive heart and chronic kidney disease without heart failure**

      I13.10   **Hypertensive heart and chronic kidney disease without heart failure, with stage 1 through stage 4 chronic kidney disease, or unspecified chronic kidney disease**
        Hypertensive heart disease and hypertensive chronic kidney disease NOS
         Use additional code to identify the stage of chronic kidney disease (N18.1-N18.4, N18.9)

      I13.11   **Hypertensive heart and chronic kidney disease without heart failure, with stage 5 chronic kidney disease, or end stage renal disease**
        Use additional code to identify the stage of chronic kidney disease (N18.5, N18.6)

    I13.2   **Hypertensive heart and chronic kidney disease with heart failure and with stage 5 chronic kidney disease, or end stage renal disease**
       Use additional code to identify type of heart failure (I50.-)
       Use additional code to identify the stage of chronic kidney disease (N18.5, N18.6)

Hypertension, Secondary
Secondary hypertension is due to an underlying condition. Two codes are required: one to identify the underlying etiology and one from category I15 to identify the hypertension. Sequencing of codes is determined by the reason for admission/encounter.

I15   Secondary hypertension
Code also underlying condition
Excludes1   postprocedural hypertension (I97.3)
Excludes2   secondary hypertension involving vessels of brain (I60-I69)
secondary hypertension involving vessels of eye (H35.0-)

I15.0   Renovascular hypertension

I15.1   Hypertension secondary to other renal disorders
Coding Clinic: 2016, Q3, P23

I15.2   Hypertension secondary to endocrine disorders

I15.8   Other secondary hypertension

I15.9   Secondary hypertension, unspecified

I16   Hypertensive crisis
Code also any identified hypertensive disease (I10-I15)
Coding Clinic: 2016, Q4, P26-27, 123

I16.0   Hypertensive urgency

I16.1   Hypertensive emergency

I16.9   Hypertensive crisis, unspecified

ISCHEMIC HEART DISEASES (I20-I25)
Use additional code to identify presence of hypertension (I10-I16)

I20   Angina pectoris
Chest pain/discomfort due to lack of oxygen to the heart muscle. Principal symptom of myocardial infarction.
Use additional code to identify:
exposure to environmental tobacco smoke (Z77.22)
history of tobacco dependence (Z87.891)
occupational exposure to environmental tobacco smoke (Z57.31)
tobacco dependence (F17.-)
tobacco use (Z72.0)
Excludes1   angina pectoris with atherosclerotic heart disease of native coronary arteries (I25.1-)
atherosclerosis of coronary artery bypass graft(s) and coronary artery of transplanted heart with angina pectoris (I25.7-)
postinfarction angina (I23.7)

I20.0   Unstable angina
Accelerated angina
Crescendo angina
De novo effort angina
Intermediate coronary syndrome
Preinfarction syndrome
Worsening effort angina

I20.1   Angina pectoris with documented spasm
Angiospastic angina
Prinzmetal angina
Spasm-induced angina
Variant angina

I20.8   Other forms of angina pectoris
Angina equivalent
Angina of effort
Coronary slow flow syndrome
Stable angina
Stenocardia
Use additional code(s) for symptoms associated with angina equivalent

I20.9   Angina pectoris, unspecified
Angina NOS
Anginal syndrome
Cardiac angina
Ischemic chest pain

I21   Acute myocardial infarction
Includes   cardiac infarction
coronary (artery) embolism
coronary (artery) occlusion
coronary (artery) rupture
coronary (artery) thrombosis
infarction of heart, myocardium, or ventricle
myocardial infarction specified as acute or with a stated duration of 4 weeks (28 days) or less from onset
Use additional code, if applicable, to identify:
exposure to environmental tobacco smoke (Z77.22)
history of tobacco dependence (Z87.891)
occupational exposure to environmental tobacco smoke (Z57.31)
status post administration of tPA (rtPA) in a different facility within the last 24 hours prior to admission to current facility (Z92.82)
tobacco dependence (F17.-)
tobacco use (Z72.0)
Excludes2   old myocardial infarction (I25.2)
postmyocardial infarction syndrome (I24.1)
subsequent type 1 myocardial infarction (I22.-)
Coding Clinic: 2016, Q4, P140; 2013, Q1, P25-26; 2012, Q4, P103

I21.0   ST elevation (STEMI) myocardial infarction of anterior wall
Type 1 ST elevation myocardial infarction of anterior wall
Coding Clinic: 2013, Q1, P26

I21.01   ST elevation (STEMI) myocardial infarction involving left main coronary artery

I21.02   ST elevation (STEMI) myocardial infarction involving left anterior descending coronary artery
ST elevation (STEMI) myocardial infarction involving diagonal coronary artery
Coding Clinic: 2013, Q1, P26

I21.09   ST elevation (STEMI) myocardial infarction involving other coronary artery of anterior wall
Acute transmural myocardial infarction of anterior wall
Anteroapical transmural (Q wave) infarction (acute)
Anterolateral transmural (Q wave) infarction (acute)
Anteroseptal transmural (Q wave) infarction (acute)
Transmural (Q wave) infarction (acute) (of) anterior (wall) NOS
Coding Clinic: 2012, Q4, P102, 104

I21.1   ST elevation (STEMI) myocardial infarction of inferior wall
Type 1 ST elevation myocardial infarction of inferior wall
Coding Clinic: 2013, Q1, P26

I21.11   ST elevation (STEMI) myocardial infarction involving right coronary artery
Inferoposterior transmural (Q wave) infarction (acute)

I21.19   ST elevation (STEMI) myocardial infarction involving other coronary artery of inferior wall
Acute transmural myocardial infarction of inferior wall
Inferolateral transmural (Q wave) infarction (acute)
Transmural (Q wave) infarction (acute) (of) diaphragmatic wall
Transmural (Q wave) infarction (acute) (of) inferior (wall) NOS
Excludes2   ST elevation (STEMI) myocardial infarction involving left circumflex coronary artery (I21.21)
Coding Clinic: 2012, Q4, P97

New   Revised   ~~deleted~~ Deleted   Excludes 1   Excludes 2   Includes   Use additional   Code first   Code also   Key words
OGCR Official Guidelines   X Assign placeholder X   Use Additional Character(s)   Manifestation Code   Coding Clinic

●**I21.2   ST elevation (STEMI) myocardial infarction of other sites**

Type 1 ST elevation myocardial infarction of other sites
Coding Clinic: 2013, Q1, P26

I21.21   ST elevation (STEMI) myocardial infarction involving left circumflex coronary artery
ST elevation (STEMI) myocardial infarction involving oblique marginal coronary artery

I21.29   ST elevation (STEMI) myocardial infarction involving other sites
Acute transmural myocardial infarction of other sites
Apical-lateral transmural (Q wave) infarction (acute)
Basal-lateral transmural (Q wave) infarction (acute)
High lateral transmural (Q wave) infarction (acute)
Lateral (wall) NOS transmural (Q wave) infarction (acute)
Posterior (true) transmural (Q wave) infarction (acute)
Posterobasal transmural (Q wave) infarction (acute)
Posterolateral transmural (Q wave) infarction (acute)
Posteroseptal transmural (Q wave) infarction (acute)
Septal transmural (Q wave) infarction (acute) NOS

OGCR Section I.c.9.e.2.

Acute myocardial infarction, unspecified

Code I21.9, Acute myocardial infarction, unspecified, is the default for unspecified acute myocardial infarction or unspecified type. If only type 1 STEMI or transmural MI without the site is documented, assign I21.3, ST elevation (STEMI) myocardial infarction of unspecified site.

I21.3   ST elevation (STEMI) myocardial infarction of unspecified site
Acute transmural myocardial infarction of unspecified site
Transmural (Q wave) myocardial infarction NOS
Type 1 ST elevation myocardial infarction of unspecified site
Coding Clinic: 2013, Q1, P26

I21.4   Non-ST elevation (NSTEMI) myocardial infarction
Acute subendocardial myocardial infarction
Non-Q wave myocardial infarction NOS
Nontransmural myocardial infarction NOS
Type 1 non-ST elevation myocardial infarction
Coding Clinic: 2017, Q1, P44; 2015, Q2, P16; 2013, Q1, P26

I21.9   Acute myocardial infarction, unspecified
Myocardial infarction (acute) NOS

●**I21.A   Other type of myocardial infarction**

I21.A1   Myocardial infarction type 2
Myocardial infarction due to demand ischemia
Myocardial infarction secondary to ischemic imbalance

Code also the underlying cause, if known and applicable, such as:
anemia (D50.0-D64.9)
chronic obstructive pulmonary disease (J44.-)
heart failure (I50.-)
paroxysmal tachycardia (I47.0-I47.9)
renal failure (N17.0-N19)
shock (R57.0-R57.9)
Coding Clinic: 2017, Q4, P13-14

I21.A9   Other myocardial infarction type
Myocardial infarction associated with revascularization procedure
Myocardial infarction type 3
Myocardial infarction type 4a
Myocardial infarction type 4b
Myocardial infarction type 4c
Myocardial infarction type 5

Code first, if applicable, postprocedural myocardial infarction following cardiac surgery (I97.190), or postprocedural myocardial infarction during cardiac surgery (I97.790)

Code also complication, if known and applicable, such as:
(acute) stent occlusion (T82.897-)
(acute) stent stenosis (T82.857-)
(acute) stent thrombosis (T82.867-)
cardiac arrest due to underlying cardiac condition (I46.2)
complication of percutaneous coronary intervention (PCI) (I97.89)
occlusion of coronary artery bypass graft (T82.218-)

●**I22   Subsequent ST elevation (STEMI) and non-ST elevation (NSTEMI) myocardial infarction**

Includes   acute myocardial infarction occurring within four weeks (28 days) of a previous acute myocardial infarction, regardless of site
cardiac infarction
coronary (artery) embolism
coronary (artery) occlusion
coronary (artery) rupture
coronary (artery) thrombosis
infarction of heart, myocardium, or ventricle
recurrent myocardial infarction
reinfarction of myocardium
rupture of heart, myocardium, or ventricle
subsequent type 1 myocardial infarction

Excludes1   subsequent myocardial infarction, type 2 (I21.A1)
subsequent myocardial infarction of other type (type 3) (type 4) (type 5) (I21.A9)

Use additional code, if applicable, to identify:
exposure to environmental tobacco smoke (Z77.22)
history of tobacco dependence (Z87.891)
occupational exposure to environmental tobacco smoke (Z57.31)
status post administration of tPA (rtPA) in a different facility within the last 24 hours prior to admission to current facility (Z92.82)
tobacco dependence (F17.-)
tobacco use (Z72.0)
Coding Clinic: 2017, Q4, P14; 2013, Q1, P25; 2012, Q4, P103

I22.0   Subsequent ST elevation (STEMI) myocardial infarction of anterior wall
Subsequent acute transmural myocardial infarction of anterior wall
Subsequent transmural (Q wave) infarction (acute)(of) anterior (wall) NOS
Subsequent anteroapical transmural (Q wave) infarction (acute)
Subsequent anterolateral transmural (Q wave) infarction (acute)
Subsequent anteroseptal transmural (Q wave) infarction (acute)

I22.1   Subsequent ST elevation (STEMI) myocardial infarction of inferior wall
Subsequent acute transmural myocardial infarction of inferior wall
Subsequent transmural (Q wave) infarction (acute)(of) diaphragmatic wall
Subsequent transmural (Q wave) infarction (acute)(of) inferior (wall) NOS
Subsequent inferolateral transmural (Q wave) infarction (acute)
Subsequent inferoposterior transmural (Q wave) infarction (acute)
Coding Clinic: 2012, Q4, P97, 102, 104

CHAPTER 9 (I00-I99)

I22.2   **Subsequent non-ST elevation (NSTEMI) myocardial infarction**
     Subsequent acute subendocardial myocardial infarction
     Subsequent non-Q wave myocardial infarction NOS
     Subsequent nontransmural myocardial infarction NOS

I22.8   **Subsequent ST elevation (STEMI) myocardial infarction of other sites**
     Subsequent acute transmural myocardial infarction of other sites
     Subsequent apical-lateral transmural (Q wave) myocardial infarction (acute)
     Subsequent basal-lateral transmural (Q wave) myocardial infarction (acute)
     Subsequent high lateral transmural (Q wave) myocardial infarction (acute)
     Subsequent transmural (Q wave) myocardial infarction (acute)(of) lateral (wall) NOS
     ⟹Subsequent posterior (true) transmural (Q wave) myocardial infarction (acute)
     Subsequent posterobasal transmural (Q wave) myocardial infarction (acute)
     Subsequent posterolateral transmural (Q wave) myocardial infarction (acute)
     Subsequent posteroseptal transmural (Q wave) myocardial infarction (acute)
     Subsequent septal NOS transmural (Q wave) myocardial infarction (acute)

I22.9   **Subsequent ST elevation (STEMI) myocardial infarction of unspecified site**
     Subsequent acute myocardial infarction of unspecified site
     Subsequent myocardial infarction (acute) NOS

● I23   **Certain current complications following ST elevation (STEMI) and non-ST elevation (NSTEMI) myocardial infarction (within the 28 day period)**
     Coding Clinic: 2017, Q2, P11

I23.0   **Hemopericardium as current complication following acute myocardial infarction**   A
     Excludes1   hemopericardium not specified as current complication following acute myocardial infarction (I31.2)

I23.1   **Atrial septal defect as current complication following acute myocardial infarction**   A
     Excludes1   acquired atrial septal defect not specified as current complication following acute myocardial infarction (I51.0)

I23.2   **Ventricular septal defect as current complication following acute myocardial infarction**   A
     Excludes1   acquired ventricular septal defect not specified as current complication following acute myocardial infarction (I51.0)

I23.3   **Rupture of cardiac wall without hemopericardium as current complication following acute myocardial infarction**   A
     Coding Clinic: 2017, Q2, P11

I23.4   **Rupture of chordae tendineae as current complication following acute myocardial infarction**
     Excludes1   rupture of chordae tendineae not specified as current complication following acute myocardial infarction (I51.1)

I23.5   **Rupture of papillary muscle as current complication following acute myocardial infarction**
     Excludes1   rupture of papillary muscle not specified as current complication following acute myocardial infarction (I51.2)

I23.6   **Thrombosis of atrium, auricular appendage, and ventricle as current complications following acute myocardial infarction**   A
     Excludes1   thrombosis of atrium, auricular appendage, and ventricle not specified as current complication following acute myocardial infarction (I51.3)

I23.7   **Postinfarction angina**   A
     Coding Clinic: 2015, Q2, P16-17

I23.8   **Other current complications following acute myocardial infarction**   A

● I24   **Other acute ischemic heart diseases**
     Excludes1   angina pectoris (I20.-)
                transient myocardial ischemia in newborn (P29.4)

I24.0   **Acute coronary thrombosis not resulting in myocardial infarction**
     Acute coronary (artery) (vein) embolism not resulting in myocardial infarction
     Acute coronary (artery) (vein) occlusion not resulting in myocardial infarction
     Acute coronary (artery) (vein) thromboembolism not resulting in myocardial infarction
     Excludes1   atherosclerotic heart disease (I25.1-)
     Coding Clinic: 2013, Q1, P24

I24.1   **Dressler's syndrome**
     Postmyocardial infarction syndrome
     Excludes1   postinfarction angina (I23.7)

I24.8   **Other forms of acute ischemic heart disease**
     Excludes1   myocardial infarction due to demand ischemia (I21.A1)
     Coding Clinic: 2017, Q4, P13

I24.9   **Acute ischemic heart disease, unspecified**
     Excludes1   ischemic heart disease (chronic) NOS (I25.9)

● I25   **Chronic ischemic heart disease**
     Use additional code to identify:
       chronic total occlusion of coronary artery (I25.82)
       exposure to environmental tobacco smoke (Z77.22)
       history of tobacco dependence (Z87.891)
       occupational exposure to environmental tobacco smoke (Z57.31)
       tobacco dependence (F17.-)
       tobacco use (Z72.0)

⭐ **(See Plates 218 and 219 on pages 74 and 75.)**

● I25.1   **Atherosclerotic heart disease of native coronary artery**
     Disease in which fatty deposits form on the walls of arteries
     Atherosclerotic cardiovascular disease
     Coronary (artery) atheroma
     Coronary (artery) atherosclerosis
     Coronary (artery) disease
     Coronary (artery) sclerosis
     Use additional code, if applicable, to identify:
       coronary atherosclerosis due to calcified coronary lesion (I25.84)
       coronary atherosclerosis due to lipid rich plaque (I25.83)
     Excludes2   atheroembolism (I75.-)
                atherosclerosis of coronary artery bypass graft(s) and transplanted heart (I25.7-)

I25.10   **Atherosclerotic heart disease of native coronary artery without angina pectoris**   A
     Atherosclerotic heart disease NOS
     Coding Clinic: 2015, Q2, P17; 2012, Q4, P92

Item 9–6   Classification is based on the location of the atherosclerosis. **"Of native coronary artery"** indicates the atherosclerosis is within an original heart artery. **"Of autologous vein bypass graft"** indicates that the atherosclerosis is within a vein graft that was taken from within the patient. **"Of nonautologous biological bypass graft"** indicates the atherosclerosis is within a vessel grafted from other than the patient. **"Of artery bypass graft"** indicates the atherosclerosis is within an artery that was grafted from within the patient.

▶ New   ⟹ Revised   ~~deleted~~ Deleted   Excludes 1   Excludes 2   Includes   Use additional   Code first   Code also   Key words
OGCR Official Guidelines   X Assign placeholder X   ● Use Additional Character(s)   ▶ Manifestation Code   Coding Clinic

Figure 9-2   Atherosclerotic plaque.

Atherosclerotic plaque (atheromas)

OGCR See Section I.9.b.

Atherosclerotic Coronary Artery Disease and Angina

ICD-10-CM has combination codes for atherosclerotic heart disease with angina pectoris. The subcategories for these codes are I25.11, Atherosclerotic heart disease of native coronary artery with angina pectoris and I25.7, Atherosclerosis of coronary artery bypass graft(s) and coronary artery of transplanted heart with angina pectoris.

When using one of these combination codes it is not necessary to use an additional code for angina pectoris. A causal relationship can be assumed in a patient with both atherosclerosis and angina pectoris, unless the documentation indicates the angina is due to something other than the atherosclerosis.

If a patient with coronary artery disease is admitted due to an acute myocardial infarction (AMI), the AMI should be sequenced before the coronary artery disease.

See Section I.C.9. Acute myocardial infarction (AMI)

● **I25.11**   **Atherosclerotic heart disease of native coronary artery with angina pectoris**

     I25.110   **Atherosclerotic heart disease of native coronary artery with unstable angina pectoris**   A

         Excludes1   unstable angina without atherosclerotic heart disease (I20.0)

     I25.111   **Atherosclerotic heart disease of native coronary artery with angina pectoris with documented spasm**   A

         Excludes1   angina pectoris with documented spasm without atherosclerotic heart disease (I20.1)

     I25.118   **Atherosclerotic heart disease of native coronary artery with other forms of angina pectoris**   A

         Excludes1   other forms of angina pectoris without atherosclerotic heart disease (I20.8)

         Coding Clinic: 2015, Q2, P16-17

     I25.119   **Atherosclerotic heart disease of native coronary artery with unspecified angina pectoris**   A

         Atherosclerotic heart disease with angina NOS
         Atherosclerotic heart disease with ischemic chest pain

         Excludes1   unspecified angina pectoris without atherosclerotic heart disease (I20.9)

I25.2   **Old myocardial infarction**
     Healed myocardial infarction
     Past myocardial infarction diagnosed by ECG or other investigation, but currently presenting no symptoms

I25.3   **Aneurysm of heart**
     Mural aneurysm
     Ventricular aneurysm

● **I25.4**   **Coronary artery aneurysm and dissection**

     I25.41   **Coronary artery aneurysm**
         Coronary arteriovenous fistula, acquired
         Excludes1   congenital coronary (artery) aneurysm (Q24.5)

     I25.42   **Coronary artery dissection**

I25.5   **Ischemic cardiomyopathy**
     Excludes2   coronary atherosclerosis (I25.1-, I25.7-)

I25.6   **Silent myocardial ischemia**

● **I25.7**   **Atherosclerosis of coronary artery bypass graft(s) and coronary artery of transplanted heart with angina pectoris**

     Use additional code, if applicable, to identify:
     coronary atherosclerosis due to calcified coronary lesion (I25.84)
     coronary atherosclerosis due to lipid rich plaque (I25.83)

     Excludes1   atherosclerosis of bypass graft(s) of transplanted heart without angina pectoris (I25.812)
         atherosclerosis of coronary artery bypass graft(s) without angina pectoris (I25.810)
         atherosclerosis of native coronary artery of transplanted heart without angina pectoris (I25.811)

● **I25.70**   **Atherosclerosis of coronary artery bypass graft(s), unspecified, with angina pectoris**

     I25.700   **Atherosclerosis of coronary artery bypass graft(s), unspecified, with unstable angina pectoris**   A

         Excludes1   unstable angina pectoris without atherosclerosis of coronary artery bypass graft (I20.0)

     I25.701   **Atherosclerosis of coronary artery bypass graft(s), unspecified, with angina pectoris with documented spasm**   A

         Excludes1   angina pectoris with documented spasm without atherosclerosis of coronary artery bypass graft (I20.1)

     I25.708   **Atherosclerosis of coronary artery bypass graft(s), unspecified, with other forms of angina pectoris**   A

         Excludes1   other forms of angina pectoris without atherosclerosis of coronary artery bypass graft (I20.8)

     I25.709   **Atherosclerosis of coronary artery bypass graft(s), unspecified, with unspecified angina pectoris**   A

         Excludes1   unspecified angina pectoris without atherosclerosis of coronary artery bypass graft (I20.9)

CHAPTER 9 (I00-I99)

● **I25.71 Atherosclerosis of autologous vein coronary artery bypass graft(s) with angina pectoris**

    I25.710 **Atherosclerosis of autologous vein coronary artery bypass graft(s) with unstable angina pectoris** A

        Excludes1   unstable angina without atherosclerosis of autologous vein coronary artery bypass graft(s) (I20.0)

        Excludes2   embolism or thrombus of coronary artery bypass graft(s) (T82.8-)

    I25.711 **Atherosclerosis of autologous vein coronary artery bypass graft(s) with angina pectoris with documented spasm** A

        Excludes1   angina pectoris with documented spasm without atherosclerosis of autologous vein coronary artery bypass graft(s) (I20.1)

    I25.718 **Atherosclerosis of autologous vein coronary artery bypass graft(s) with other forms of angina pectoris** A

        Excludes1   other forms of angina pectoris without atherosclerosis of autologous vein coronary artery bypass graft(s) (I20.8)

    I25.719 **Atherosclerosis of autologous vein coronary artery bypass graft(s) with unspecified angina pectoris** A

        Excludes1   unspecified angina pectoris without atherosclerosis of autologous vein coronary artery bypass graft(s) (I20.9)

● **I25.72 Atherosclerosis of autologous artery coronary artery bypass graft(s) with angina pectoris**

    Atherosclerosis of internal mammary artery graft with angina pectoris

    I25.720 **Atherosclerosis of autologous artery coronary artery bypass graft(s) with unstable angina pectoris** A

        Excludes1   unstable angina without atherosclerosis of autologous artery coronary artery bypass graft(s) (I20.0)

    I25.721 **Atherosclerosis of autologous artery coronary artery bypass graft(s) with angina pectoris with documented spasm** A

        Excludes1   angina pectoris with documented spasm without atherosclerosis of autologous artery coronary artery bypass graft(s) (I20.1)

    I25.728 **Atherosclerosis of autologous artery coronary artery bypass graft(s) with other forms of angina pectoris** A

        Excludes1   other forms of angina pectoris without atherosclerosis of autologous artery coronary artery bypass graft(s) (I20.8)

    I25.729 **Atherosclerosis of autologous artery coronary artery bypass graft(s) with unspecified angina pectoris** A

        Excludes1   unspecified angina pectoris without atherosclerosis of autologous artery coronary artery bypass graft(s) (I20.9)

● **I25.73 Atherosclerosis of nonautologous biological coronary artery bypass graft(s) with angina pectoris**

    I25.730 **Atherosclerosis of nonautologous biological coronary artery bypass graft(s) with unstable angina pectoris** A

        Excludes1   unstable angina without atherosclerosis of nonautologous biological coronary artery bypass graft(s) (I20.0)

    I25.731 **Atherosclerosis of nonautologous biological coronary artery bypass graft(s) with angina pectoris with documented spasm** A

        Excludes1   angina pectoris with documented spasm without atherosclerosis of nonautologous biological coronary artery bypass graft(s) (I20.1)

    I25.738 **Atherosclerosis of nonautologous biological coronary artery bypass graft(s) with other forms of angina pectoris** A

        Excludes1   other forms of angina pectoris without atherosclerosis of nonautologous biological coronary artery bypass graft(s) (I20.8)

    I25.739 **Atherosclerosis of nonautologous biological coronary artery bypass graft(s) with unspecified angina pectoris** A

        Excludes1   unspecified angina pectoris without atherosclerosis of nonautologous biological coronary artery bypass graft(s) (I20.9)

▶ New   ⇒ Revised   ~~deleted~~ Deleted   Excludes 1   Excludes 2   Includes   Use additional   Code first   Code also   Key words

OGCR Official Guidelines   X Assign placeholder X   ● Use Additional Character(s)   ▷ Manifestation Code   **Coding Clinic**

● **I25.75** **Atherosclerosis of native coronary artery of transplanted heart with angina pectoris**

> **Excludes1** atherosclerosis of native coronary artery of transplanted heart without angina pectoris (I25.811)

I25.750 **Atherosclerosis of native coronary artery of transplanted heart with unstable angina**

I25.751 **Atherosclerosis of native coronary artery of transplanted heart with angina pectoris with documented spasm**

I25.758 **Atherosclerosis of native coronary artery of transplanted heart with other forms of angina pectoris**

I25.759 **Atherosclerosis of native coronary artery of transplanted heart with unspecified angina pectoris**

● **I25.76** **Atherosclerosis of bypass graft of coronary artery of transplanted heart with angina pectoris**

> **Excludes1** atherosclerosis of bypass graft of coronary artery of transplanted heart without angina pectoris (I25.812)

I25.760 **Atherosclerosis of bypass graft of coronary artery of transplanted heart with unstable angina** A

I25.761 **Atherosclerosis of bypass graft of coronary artery of transplanted heart with angina pectoris with documented spasm** A

I25.768 **Atherosclerosis of bypass graft of coronary artery of transplanted heart with other forms of angina pectoris** A

I25.769 **Atherosclerosis of bypass graft of coronary artery of transplanted heart with unspecified angina pectoris** A

● **I25.79** **Atherosclerosis of other coronary artery bypass graft(s) with angina pectoris** A

I25.790 **Atherosclerosis of other coronary artery bypass graft(s) with unstable angina pectoris**

> **Excludes1** unstable angina without atherosclerosis of other coronary artery bypass graft(s) (I20.0)

I25.791 **Atherosclerosis of other coronary artery bypass graft(s) with angina pectoris with documented spasm** A

> **Excludes1** angina pectoris with documented spasm without atherosclerosis of other coronary artery bypass graft(s) (I20.1)

I25.798 **Atherosclerosis of other coronary artery bypass graft(s) with other forms of angina pectoris** A

> **Excludes1** other forms of angina pectoris without atherosclerosis of other coronary artery bypass graft(s) (I20.8)

I25.799 **Atherosclerosis of other coronary artery bypass graft(s) with unspecified angina pectoris** A

> **Excludes1** unspecified angina pectoris without atherosclerosis of other coronary artery bypass graft(s) (I20.9)

● **I25.8** **Other forms of chronic ischemic heart disease**

● **I25.81** **Atherosclerosis of other coronary vessels without angina pectoris**

> Use additional code, if applicable, to identify:
> coronary atherosclerosis due to calcified coronary lesion (I25.84)
> coronary atherosclerosis due to lipid rich plaque (I25.83)

> **Excludes1** atherosclerotic heart disease of native coronary artery without angina pectoris (I25.10)

I25.810 **Atherosclerosis of coronary artery bypass graft(s) without angina pectoris** A

> Atherosclerosis of coronary artery bypass graft NOS

> **Excludes1** atherosclerosis of coronary bypass graft(s) with angina pectoris (I25.70- -I25.73-, I25.79-)

> **Coding Clinic: 2016, Q4, P86**

I25.811 **Atherosclerosis of native coronary artery of transplanted heart without angina pectoris**

> Atherosclerosis of native coronary artery of transplanted heart NOS

> **Excludes1** atherosclerosis of native coronary artery of transplanted heart with angina pectoris (I25.75-)

I25.812 **Atherosclerosis of bypass graft of coronary artery of transplanted heart without angina pectoris** A

> Atherosclerosis of bypass graft of transplanted heart NOS

> **Excludes1** atherosclerosis of bypass graft of transplanted heart with angina pectoris (I25.76)

CHAPTER 9 (I00-I99)

I25.82 **Chronic total occlusion of coronary artery**
Complete occlusion of coronary artery
Total occlusion of coronary artery

Code first coronary atherosclerosis (I25.1-, I25.7-, I25.81-)

Excludes1   acute coronary occlusion with myocardial infarction (I21.0-I21.9, I22.-)
acute coronary occlusion without myocardial infarction (I24.0)

I25.83 **Coronary atherosclerosis due to lipid rich plaque**   A

Code first coronary atherosclerosis (I25.1-, I25.7-, I25.81-)

I25.84 **Coronary atherosclerosis due to calcified coronary lesion**
Coronary atherosclerosis due to severely calcified coronary lesion

Code first coronary atherosclerosis (I25.1-, I25.7-, I25.81-)

I25.89 **Other forms of chronic ischemic heart disease**

I25.9   **Chronic ischemic heart disease, unspecified**
Ischemic heart disease (chronic) NOS

PULMONARY HEART DISEASE AND DISEASES OF PULMONARY CIRCULATION (I26-I28)

● I26   **Pulmonary embolism**

Includes   pulmonary (acute)(artery)(vein) infarction
pulmonary (acute)(artery)(vein) thromboembolism
pulmonary (acute)(artery)(vein) thrombosis

Excludes2   chronic pulmonary embolism (I27.82)
personal history of pulmonary embolism (Z86.711)
pulmonary embolism due to trauma (T79.0, T79.1)
pulmonary embolism due to complications of surgical and medical care (T80.0, T81.7-, T82.8-)
pulmonary embolism complicating abortion, ectopic or molar pregnancy (O00-O07, O08.2)
pulmonary embolism complicating pregnancy, childbirth and the puerperium (O88.-)
septic (non-pulmonary) arterial embolism (I76)

● I26.0   **Pulmonary embolism with acute cor pulmonale**

I26.01 **Septic pulmonary embolism with acute cor pulmonale**

Code first underlying infection

I26.02 **Saddle embolus of pulmonary artery with acute cor pulmonale**

I26.09 **Other pulmonary embolism with acute cor pulmonale**
Acute cor pulmonale NOS

● I26.9   **Pulmonary embolism without acute cor pulmonale**

I26.90 **Septic pulmonary embolism without acute cor pulmonale**

Code first underlying infection

I26.92 **Saddle embolus of pulmonary artery without acute cor pulmonale**

I26.99 **Other pulmonary embolism without acute cor pulmonale**
Acute pulmonary embolism NOS
Pulmonary embolism NOS

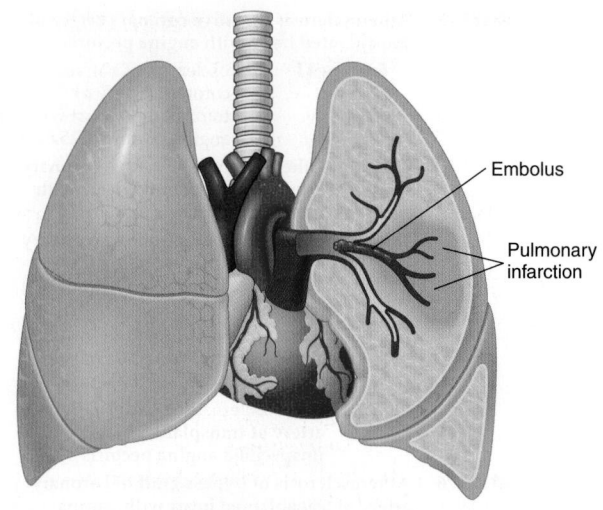

Figure 9-3   Pulmonary embolism. (From Chabner: The Language of Medicine, ed 8, St. Louis, Saunders, 2007)

Item 9–7   Pulmonary heart disease or **cor pulmonale** is right ventricle hypertrophy or RVH as a result of a respiratory disorder increasing back flow pressure to the right ventricle. Left untreated, cor pulmonale leads to right-heart failure and death.

● I27   **Other pulmonary heart diseases**

I27.0   **Primary pulmonary hypertension**
Heritable pulmonary arterial hypertension
Idiopathic pulmonary arterial hypertension
Primary group 1 pulmonary hypertension
Primary pulmonary arterial hypertension

Excludes1   persistent pulmonary hypertension of newborn (P29.30)
pulmonary hypertension NOS (I27.20)
secondary pulmonary arterial hypertension (I27.21)
secondary pulmonary hypertension (I27.29)

I27.1   **Kyphoscoliotic heart disease**

● I27.2   **Other secondary pulmonary hypertension**
Code also associated underlying condition

Excludes1   Eisenmenger's syndrome (I27.83)

Coding Clinic: 2016, Q2, P8

I27.20 **Pulmonary hypertension, unspecified**
Pulmonary hypertension NOS

I27.21 **Secondary pulmonary arterial hypertension**
(Associated) (drug-induced) (toxin-induced) pulmonary arterial hypertension NOS
(Associated) (drug-induced) (toxin-induced) (secondary) group 1 pulmonary hypertension

Code also associated conditions if applicable, or adverse effects of drugs or toxins, such as:
adverse effect of appetite depressants (T50.5X5)
congenital heart disease (Q20-Q28)
human immunodeficiency virus [HIV] disease (B20)
polymyositis (M33.2-)
portal hypertension (K76.6)
rheumatoid arthritis (M05.-)
schistosomiasis (B65.-)
Sjögren syndrome (M35.0-)
systemic sclerosis (M34.-)

I27.22   **Pulmonary hypertension due to left heart disease**
  Group 2 pulmonary hypertension
  Code also associated left heart disease, if known, such as:
    multiple valve disease (I08.-)
    rheumatic mitral valve diseases (I05.-)
    rheumatic aortic valve diseases (I06.-)

I27.23   **Pulmonary hypertension due to lung diseases and hypoxia**
  Group 3 pulmonary hypertension
  Code also associated lung disease, if known, such as:
    bronchiectasis (J47.-)
    cystic fibrosis with pulmonary manifestations (E84.0)
    interstitial lung disease (J84.-)
    pleural effusion (J90)
    sleep apnea (G47.3-)

I27.24   **Chronic thromboembolic pulmonary hypertension**
  Group 4 pulmonary hypertension
  Code also associated pulmonary embolism, if applicable (I26.-, I27.82)

I27.29   **Other secondary pulmonary hypertension**
  Group 5 pulmonary hypertension
  Pulmonary hypertension with unclear multifactorial mechanisms
  Pulmonary hypertension due to hematologic disorders
  Pulmonary hypertension due to metabolic disorders
  Pulmonary hypertension due to other systemic disorders
  Code also other associated disorders, if known, such as:
    chronic myeloid leukemia (C92.10- C92.22)
    essential thrombocythemia (D47.3)
    Gaucher disease (E75.22)
    ⇒hypertensive chronic kidney disease with end stage renal disease (I12.0, I13.11,I13.2)
    hyperthyroidism (E05.-)
    hypothyroidism (E00-E03)
    polycythemia vera (D45)
    sarcoidosis (D86.-)

● **I27.8**   **Other specified pulmonary heart diseases**

I27.81   **Cor pulmonale (chronic)**
  Cor pulmonale NOS
  Excludes1   acute cor pulmonale (I26.0-)

I27.82   **Chronic pulmonary embolism**
  Use additional code, if applicable, for associated long-term (current) use of anticoagulants (Z79.01)
  Excludes1   personal history of pulmonary embolism (Z86.711)

I27.83   **Eisenmenger's syndrome**
  Eisenmenger's complex
  (Irreversible) Eisenmenger's disease
  Pulmonary hypertension with right to left shunt related to congenital heart disease
  Code also underlying heart defect, if known, such as:
    atrial septal defect (Q21.1)
    Eisenmenger's defect (Q21.8)
    patent ductus arteriosus (Q25.0)
    ventricular septal defect (Q21.0)

I27.89   **Other specified pulmonary heart diseases**

I27.9   **Pulmonary heart disease, unspecified**
  Chronic cardiopulmonary disease

● **I28**   **Other diseases of pulmonary vessels**

I28.0   **Arteriovenous fistula of pulmonary vessels**
  Excludes1   congenital arteriovenous fistula (Q25.72)

I28.1   **Aneurysm of pulmonary artery**
  Excludes1   congenital aneurysm (Q25.79)
    congenital arteriovenous aneurysm (Q25.72)

I28.8   **Other diseases of pulmonary vessels**
  Pulmonary arteritis
  Pulmonary endarteritis
  Rupture of pulmonary vessels
  Stenosis of pulmonary vessels
  Stricture of pulmonary vessels

I28.9   **Disease of pulmonary vessels, unspecified**

OTHER FORMS OF HEART DISEASE (I30-I52)

● **I30**   **Acute pericarditis**
  Inflammation of pericardium (sac surrounding the heart) caused by an infection
  Includes   acute mediastinopericarditis
    acute myopericarditis
    acute pericardial effusion
    acute pleuropericarditis
    acute pneumopericarditis
  Excludes1   Dressler's syndrome (I24.1)
    rheumatic pericarditis (acute) (I01.0)
    viral pericarditis due to Coxsakie virus (B33.23)

I30.0   **Acute nonspecific idiopathic pericarditis**

I30.1   **Infective pericarditis**
  Pneumococcal pericarditis
  Pneumopyopericardium
  Purulent pericarditis
  Pyopericarditis
  Pyopericardium
  Pyopneumopericardium
  Staphylococcal pericarditis
  Streptococcal pericarditis
  Suppurative pericarditis
  Viral pericarditis
    Use additional code (B95-B97) to identify infectious agent

I30.8   **Other forms of acute pericarditis**

I30.9   **Acute pericarditis, unspecified**

● **I31**   **Other diseases of pericardium**
  Excludes1   diseases of pericardium specified as rheumatic (I09.2)
    postcardiotomy syndrome (I97.0)
    traumatic injury to pericardium (S26.-)

I31.0   **Chronic adhesive pericarditis**
  Accretio cordis
  Adherent pericardium
  Adhesive mediastinopericarditis

I31.1   **Chronic constrictive pericarditis**
  Concretio cordis
  Pericardial calcification

I31.2   **Hemopericardium, not elsewhere classified**
  Excludes1   hemopericardium as current complication following acute myocardial infarction (I23.0)

I31.3   **Pericardial effusion (noninflammatory)**
  Chylopericardium
  Excludes1   acute pericardial effusion (I30.9)

I31.4   **Cardiac tamponade**
  Code first underlying cause

I31.8   **Other specified diseases of pericardium**
  Epicardial plaques
  Focal pericardial adhesions

I31.9   **Disease of pericardium, unspecified**
  Pericarditis (chronic) NOS

CHAPTER 9 (I00-I99)

▶ **I32**   *Pericarditis in diseases classified elsewhere*

     Code first underlying disease

     Excludes1   pericarditis (in):
- coxsackie (virus) (B33.23)
- gonococcal (A54.83)
- meningococcal (A39.53)
- rheumatoid (arthritis) (M05.31)
- syphilitic (A52.06)
- systemic lupus erythematosus (M32.12)
- tuberculosis (A18.84)

● **I33**   **Acute and subacute endocarditis**

     Inflammation/infection of lining of heart, affecting heart valves including replacement valves and is usually caused by a bacterial infection

     Excludes1   acute rheumatic endocarditis (I01.1)

                endocarditis NOS (I38)

    I33.0   **Acute and subacute infective endocarditis**
- Bacterial endocarditis (acute) (subacute)
- Infective endocarditis (acute) (subacute) NOS
- Endocarditis lenta (acute) (subacute)
- Malignant endocarditis (acute) (subacute)
- Purulent endocarditis (acute) (subacute)
- Septic endocarditis (acute) (subacute)
- Ulcerative endocarditis (acute) (subacute)
- Vegetative endocarditis (acute) (subacute)

       Use additional code (B95-B97) to identify infectious agent

    I33.9   **Acute and subacute endocarditis, unspecified**
- Acute endocarditis NOS
- Acute myoendocarditis NOS
- Acute periendocarditis NOS
- Subacute endocarditis NOS
- Subacute myoendocarditis NOS
- Subacute periendocarditis NOS

● **I34**   **Nonrheumatic mitral valve disorders**

     Excludes1   mitral valve disease (I05.9)
- mitral valve failure (I05.8)
- mitral valve stenosis (I05.0)
- mitral valve disorder of unspecified cause with diseases of aortic and/or tricuspid valve(s) (I08.-)
- mitral valve disorder of unspecified cause with mitral stenosis or obstruction (I05.0)
- mitral valve disorder specified as congenital (Q23.2, Q23.9)
- mitral valve disorder specified as rheumatic (I05.-)

    I34.0   **Nonrheumatic mitral (valve) insufficiency**
- Nonrheumatic mitral (valve) incompetence NOS
- Nonrheumatic mitral (valve) regurgitation NOS

    I34.1   **Nonrheumatic mitral (valve) prolapse**
- Floppy nonrheumatic mitral valve syndrome

       Excludes1   Marfan's syndrome (Q87.4-)

    I34.2   **Nonrheumatic mitral (valve) stenosis**

    I34.8   **Other nonrheumatic mitral valve disorders**

    I34.9   **Nonrheumatic mitral valve disorder, unspecified**

● **I35**   **Nonrheumatic aortic valve disorders**

     Excludes1   aortic valve disorder of unspecified cause but with diseases of mitral and/or tricuspid valve(s) (I08.-)
- aortic valve disorder specified as congenital (Q23.0, Q23.1)
- aortic valve disorder specified as rheumatic (I06.-)
- hypertrophic subaortic stenosis (I42.1)

    I35.0   **Nonrheumatic aortic (valve) stenosis**

    I35.1   **Nonrheumatic aortic (valve) insufficiency**
- Nonrheumatic aortic (valve) incompetence NOS
- Nonrheumatic aortic (valve) regurgitation NOS

    I35.2   **Nonrheumatic aortic (valve) stenosis with insufficiency**

    I35.8   **Other nonrheumatic aortic valve disorders**

    I35.9   **Nonrheumatic aortic valve disorder, unspecified**

● **I36**   **Nonrheumatic tricuspid valve disorders**

     Excludes1   tricuspid valve disorders of unspecified cause (I07.-)
- tricuspid valve disorders specified as congenital (Q22.4, Q22.8, Q22.9)
- tricuspid valve disorders specified as rheumatic (I07.-)
- tricuspid valve disorders with aortic and/or mitral valve involvement (I08.-)

    I36.0   **Nonrheumatic tricuspid (valve) stenosis**

    I36.1   **Nonrheumatic tricuspid (valve) insufficiency**
- Nonrheumatic tricuspid (valve) incompetence
- Nonrheumatic tricuspid (valve) regurgitation

    I36.2   **Nonrheumatic tricuspid (valve) stenosis with insufficiency**

    I36.8   **Other nonrheumatic tricuspid valve disorders**

    I36.9   **Nonrheumatic tricuspid valve disorder, unspecified**

● **I37**   **Nonrheumatic pulmonary valve disorders**

     Excludes1   pulmonary valve disorder specified as congenital (Q22.1, Q22.2, Q22.3)
- pulmonary valve disorder specified as rheumatic (I09.89)

    I37.0   **Nonrheumatic pulmonary valve stenosis**

    I37.1   **Nonrheumatic pulmonary valve insufficiency**
- Nonrheumatic pulmonary valve incompetence
- Nonrheumatic pulmonary valve regurgitation

    I37.2   **Nonrheumatic pulmonary valve stenosis with insufficiency**

    I37.8   **Other nonrheumatic pulmonary valve disorders**

    I37.9   **Nonrheumatic pulmonary valve disorder, unspecified**

   I38   **Endocarditis, valve unspecified**

     Includes   endocarditis (chronic) NOS
- valvular incompetence NOS
- valvular insufficiency NOS
- valvular regurgitation NOS
- valvular stenosis NOS
- valvulitis (chronic) NOS

     Excludes1   congenital insufficiency of cardiac valve NOS (Q24.8)
- congenital stenosis of cardiac valve NOS (Q24.8)
- endocardial fibroelastosis (I42.4)
- endocarditis specified as rheumatic (I09.1)

▶ **I39**   *Endocarditis and heart valve disorders in diseases classified elsewhere*

     Code first underlying disease, such as:

     Q fever (A78)

     Excludes1   endocardial involvement in:
- candidiasis (B37.6)
- gonococcal infection (A54.83)
- Libman-Sacks disease (M32.11)
- listerosis (A32.82)
- meningococcal infection (A39.51)
- rheumatoid arthritis (M05.31)
- syphilis (A52.03)
- tuberculosis (A18.84)
- typhoid fever (A01.02)

● **I40**   **Acute myocarditis**

     Inflammation of heart muscle due to infection (viral/bacterial)

     Includes   subacute myocarditis

     Excludes1   acute rheumatic myocarditis (I01.2)

    I40.0   **Infective myocarditis**
- Septic myocarditis

       Use additional code (B95-B97) to identify infectious agent

    I40.1   **Isolated myocarditis**
- Fiedler's myocarditis
- Giant cell myocarditis
- Idiopathic myocarditis

    I40.8   **Other acute myocarditis**

    I40.9   **Acute myocarditis, unspecified**

▶ New   ⇒ Revised   ~~deleted~~ Deleted   Excludes 1   Excludes 2   Includes   Use additional   Code first   Code also   Key words

OGCR Official Guidelines   X Assign placeholder X   ● Use Additional Character(s)   ▶ Manifestation Code   **Coding Clinic**

▶ **I41**   *Myocarditis in diseases classified elsewhere*

     Code first underlying disease, such as:
         typhus (A75.0-A75.9)

     Excludes1   myocarditis (in):
                Chagas' disease (chronic) (B57.2)
                acute (B57.0)
                coxsackie (virus) infection (B33.22)
                diphtheritic (A36.81)
                gonococcal (A54.83)
                influenzal (J09.X9, J10.82, J11.82)
                meningococcal (A39.52)
                mumps (B26.82)
                rheumatoid arthritis (M05.31)
                sarcoid (D86.85)
                syphilis (A52.06)
                toxoplasmosis (B58.81)
                tuberculous (A18.84)

● **I42**   **Cardiomyopathy**

     Disease of the heart muscle resulting in an abnormally enlarged, weakened, thickened, and/or stiffened muscles

     Includes   myocardiopathy

     Code first pre-existing cardiomyopathy complicating pregnancy and puerperium (O99.4)

     Excludes2   ischemic cardiomyopathy (I25.5)
                  peripartum cardiomyopathy (O90.3)
                  ventricular hypertrophy (I51.7)

   I42.0   **Dilated cardiomyopathy**
         Congestive cardiomyopathy

   I42.1   **Obstructive hypertrophic cardiomyopathy**
         Hypertrophic subaortic stenosis (idiopathic)

   I42.2   **Other hypertrophic cardiomyopathy**
         Nonobstructive hypertrophic cardiomyopathy

   I42.3   **Endomyocardial (eosinophilic) disease**
         Endomyocardial (tropical) fibrosis
         Löffler's endocarditis

   I42.4   **Endocardial fibroelastosis**
         Congenital cardiomyopathy
         Elastomyofibrosis

   I42.5   **Other restrictive cardiomyopathy**
         Constrictive cardiomyopathy NOS

   I42.6   **Alcoholic cardiomyopathy**
         Code also presence of alcoholism (F10.-)

   I42.7   **Cardiomyopathy due to drug and external agent**
         Code first poisoning due to drug or toxin, if applicable (T36-T65 with fifth or sixth character 1-4 or 6)
         Use additional code for adverse effect, if applicable, to identify drug (T36-T50 with fifth or sixth character 5)

   I42.8   **Other cardiomyopathies**

   I42.9   **Cardiomyopathy, unspecified**
         Cardiomyopathy (primary) (secondary) NOS

▶ **I43**   *Cardiomyopathy in diseases classified elsewhere*

     Code first underlying disease, such as:
         amyloidosis (E85.-)
         glycogen storage disease (E74.0)
         gout (M10.0-)
         thyrotoxicosis (E05.0-E05.9-)

     Excludes1   cardiomyopathy (in):
                coxsackie (virus) (B33.24)
                diphtheria (A36.81)
                sarcoidosis (D86.85)
                tuberculosis (A18.84)

● **I44**   **Atrioventricular and left bundle-branch block**

     Conduction problem resulting in arrhythmias/dysrhythmias due to a lack of electrical impulses being transmitted normally through the heart

   I44.0   **Atrioventricular block, first degree**

   I44.1   **Atrioventricular block, second degree**
         Atrioventricular block, type I and II
         ➥Möbitz block, type I and II
         Second degree block, type I and II
         Wenckebach's block

   I44.2   **Atrioventricular block, complete**
         Complete heart block NOS
         Third degree block

   ●**I44.3**   **Other and unspecified atrioventricular block**
         Atrioventricular block NOS

       I44.30   **Unspecified atrioventricular block**

       I44.39   **Other atrioventricular block**

   I44.4   **Left anterior fascicular block**

   I44.5   **Left posterior fascicular block**

   ●**I44.6**   **Other and unspecified fascicular block**

       I44.60   **Unspecified fascicular block**
              Left bundle-branch hemiblock NOS

       I44.69   **Other fascicular block**

   I44.7   **Left bundle-branch block, unspecified**

● **I45**   **Other conduction disorders**

   I45.0   **Right fascicular block**

   ●**I45.1**   **Other and unspecified right bundle-branch block**

       I45.10   **Unspecified right bundle-branch block**
              Right bundle-branch block NOS

       I45.19   **Other right bundle-branch block**

   I45.2   **Bifascicular block**

   I45.3   **Trifascicular block**

   I45.4   **Nonspecific intraventricular block**
         Bundle-branch block NOS

   I45.5   **Other specified heart block**
         Sinoatrial block
         Sinoauricular block

       Excludes1   heart block NOS (I45.9)

   I45.6   **Pre-excitation syndrome**
         Accelerated atrioventricular conduction
         Accessory atrioventricular conduction
         Anomalous atrioventricular excitation
         Lown-Ganong-Levine syndrome
         Pre-excitation atrioventricular conduction
         Wolff-Parkinson-White syndrome

   ●**I45.8**   **Other specified conduction disorders**

       I45.81   **Long QT syndrome**

       I45.89   **Other specified conduction disorders**
              Atrioventricular [AV] dissociation
              Interference dissociation
              Isorhythmic dissociation
              Nonparoxysmal AV nodal tachycardia
              Coding Clinic: 2013, Q2, P32

   I45.9   **Conduction disorder, unspecified**
         Heart block NOS
         Stokes-Adams syndrome

● **I46**   **Cardiac arrest**

     Excludes1   cardiogenic shock (R57.0)

   I46.2   **Cardiac arrest due to underlying cardiac condition**
         Code first underlying cardiac condition

   I46.8   **Cardiac arrest due to other underlying condition**
         Code first underlying condition

   I46.9   **Cardiac arrest, cause unspecified**

CHAPTER 9 (I00-I99)

● **I47   Paroxysmal tachycardia**

Code first tachycardia complicating:
    abortion or ectopic or molar pregnancy (O00-O07, O08.8)
    obstetric surgery and procedures (O75.4)

> **Excludes1**   tachycardia NOS (R00.0)
>   sinoauricular tachycardia NOS (R00.0)
>   sinus [sinusal] tachycardia NOS (R00.0)

I47.0   Re-entry ventricular arrhythmia

I47.1   Supraventricular tachycardia
    Atrial (paroxysmal) tachycardia
    Atrioventricular [AV] (paroxysmal) tachycardia
    Atrioventricular re-entrant (nodal) tachycardia
       [AVNRT] [AVRT]
    Junctional (paroxysmal) tachycardia
    Nodal (paroxysmal) tachycardia

I47.2   Ventricular tachycardia
    Coding Clinic: 2013, Q3, P23

I47.9   Paroxysmal tachycardia, unspecified
    Bouveret (-Hoffman) syndrome

● **I48   Atrial fibrillation and flutter**

*Most common abnormal heart rhythm (arrhythmia) presenting
as irregular, rapid beating (tachycardia) of the heart's upper
chamber.*

I48.0   Paroxysmal atrial fibrillation

I48.1   Persistent atrial fibrillation
    Rapid contractions of the upper heart chamber

I48.2   Chronic atrial fibrillation
    Permanent atrial fibrillation

I48.3   Typical atrial flutter
    Type I atrial flutter

I48.4   Atypical atrial flutter
    Type II atrial flutter

● **I48.9   Unspecified atrial fibrillation and atrial flutter**
    I48.91   Unspecified atrial fibrillation
    I48.92   Unspecified atrial flutter

● **I49   Other cardiac arrhythmias**

Code first cardiac arrhythmia complicating:
    abortion or ectopic or molar pregnancy (O00-O07, O08.8)
    obstetric surgery and procedures (O75.4)

> **Excludes1**   neonatal dysrhythmia (P29.1-)
>   sinoatrial bradycardia (R00.1)
>   sinus bradycardia (R00.1)
>   vagal bradycardia (R00.1)

> **Excludes2**   bradycardia NOS (R00.1)

● **I49.0   Ventricular fibrillation and flutter**
    I49.01   Ventricular fibrillation
    I49.02   Ventricular flutter

I49.1   Atrial premature depolarization
    Atrial premature beats

I49.2   Junctional premature depolarization

I49.3   Ventricular premature depolarization

● **I49.4   Other and unspecified premature depolarization**
    I49.40   Unspecified premature depolarization
         Premature beats NOS
    I49.49   Other premature depolarization
         Ectopic beats
         Extrasystoles
         Extrasystolic arrhythmias
         Premature contractions

I49.5   Sick sinus syndrome
    Tachycardia-bradycardia syndrome

I49.8   Other specified cardiac arrhythmias
    Brugada syndrome
    Coronary sinus rhythm disorder
    Ectopic rhythm disorder
    Nodal rhythm disorder

I49.9   Cardiac arrhythmia, unspecified
    Arrhythmia (cardiac) NOS

Item 9–8 Congestive heart failure (CHF) is a condition in which the left ventricle of the heart cannot pump enough blood to the body. The blood flow from the heart slows or returns to the heart from the venous system (back flow) resulting in congestion (fluid accumulation) particularly in the abdomen. Most commonly, fluid collects in the lungs and results in shortness of breath, especially when in a reclining position.

● **I50   Heart failure**

Code first heart failure complicating abortion or ectopic or molar
    pregnancy (O00-O07, O08.8)
    heart failure due to hypertension (I11.0)
    heart failure due to hypertension with chronic kidney disease
      (I13.-)
    heart failure following surgery (I97.13-)
    obstetric surgery and procedures (O75.4)
    rheumatic heart failure (I09.81)

> **Excludes1**   neonatal cardiac failure (P29.0)

> **Excludes2**   cardiac arrest (I46.-)

Coding Clinic: 2017, Q1, P47; 2016, Q4, P122-123, Q1, P38; 2015, Q2, P15

I50.1   Left ventricular failure, unspecified
    Cardiac asthma
    Edema of lung with heart disease NOS
    Edema of lung with heart failure
    Left heart failure
    Pulmonary edema with heart disease NOS
    Pulmonary edema with heart failure

> **Excludes1**   edema of lung without heart disease or
>   heart failure (J81.-)
>   pulmonary edema without heart disease
>   or failure (J81.-)

● **I50.2   Systolic (congestive) heart failure**
    Heart failure with reduced ejection fraction [HFrEF]
    Systolic left ventricular heart failure

    Code also end stage heart failure, if applicable (I50.84)

> **Excludes1**   combined systolic (congestive) and
>   diastolic (congestive) heart failure
>   (I50.4-)

    I50.20   Unspecified systolic (congestive) heart failure

    I50.21   Acute systolic (congestive) heart failure
         Presenting a short and relatively severe episode

    I50.22   Chronic systolic (congestive) heart failure
         Long-lasting, presenting over time

    I50.23   Acute on chronic systolic (congestive) heart failure
         *Combination code. What was a chronic condition
         now has an acute exacerbation (to make more
         severe).*
         Coding Clinic: 2013, Q2, P33

● **I50.3   Diastolic (congestive) heart failure**
    Diastolic left ventricular heart failure
    Heart failure with normal ejection fraction
    Heart failure with preserved ejection fraction [HFpEF]

    Code also end stage heart failure, if applicable (I50.84)

> **Excludes1**   combined systolic (congestive) and
>   diastolic (congestive) heart failure
>   (I50.4-)

    I50.30   Unspecified diastolic (congestive) heart failure

    I50.31   Acute diastolic (congestive) heart failure
         Coding Clinic: 2017, Q1, P46

    I50.32   Chronic diastolic (congestive) heart failure

    I50.33   Acute on chronic diastolic (congestive) heart failure

---

● **I50.4**   **Combined systolic (congestive) and diastolic (congestive) heart failure**
Combined systolic and diastolic left ventricular heart failure
Heart failure with reduced ejection fraction and diastolic dysfunction
Code also end stage heart failure, if applicable (I50.84)

    I50.40   **Unspecified combined systolic (congestive) and diastolic (congestive) heart failure**

    I50.41   **Acute combined systolic (congestive) and diastolic (congestive) heart failure**

    I50.42   **Chronic combined systolic (congestive) and diastolic (congestive) heart failure**

    I50.43   **Acute on chronic combined systolic (congestive) and diastolic (congestive) heart failure**

● **I50.8**   **Other heart failure**

   ● **I50.81**   **Right heart failure**
Right ventricular failure

     I50.810   **Right heart failure, unspecified**
Right heart failure without mention of left heart failure
Right ventricular failure NOS

     I50.811   **Acute right heart failure**
Acute isolated right heart failure
Acute (isolated) right ventricular failure

     I50.812   **Chronic right heart failure**
Chronic isolated right heart failure
Chronic (isolated) right ventricular failure

     I50.813   **Acute on chronic right heart failure**
Acute on chronic isolated right heart failure
Acute on chronic (isolated) right ventricular failure
Acute decompensation of chronic (isolated) right ventricular failure
Acute exacerbation of chronic (isolated) right ventricular failure

     I50.814   **Right heart failure due to left heart failure**
Right ventricular failure secondary to left ventricular failure
Code also the type of left ventricular failure, if known (I50.2-I50.43)

      Excludes1   Right heart failure with but not due to left heart failure (I50.82)

   I50.82   **Biventricular heart failure**
Code also the type of left ventricular failure as systolic, diastolic, or combined, if known (I50.2-I50.43)

   I50.83   **High output heart failure**

   I50.84   **End stage heart failure**
Stage D heart failure
Code also the type of heart failure as systolic, diastolic, or combined, if known (I50.2-I50.43)

   I50.89   **Other heart failure**

● **I50.9**   **Heart failure, unspecified**
Cardiac, heart or myocardial failure NOS
Congestive heart disease
Congestive heart failure NOS

    Excludes2   fluid overload (E87.70)
    Coding Clinic: 2017, Q1, P45-46; 2015, Q2, P15; 2012, Q4, P92

● **I51**   **Complications and ill-defined descriptions of heart disease**

   Excludes1   any condition in I51.4-I51.9 due to hypertension (I11.-)
any condition in I51.4-I51.9 due to hypertension and chronic kidney disease (I13.-)
heart disease specified as rheumatic (I00-I09)

  I51.0   **Cardiac septal defect, acquired**   A
Acquired septal atrial defect (old)
Acquired septal auricular defect (old)
Acquired septal ventricular defect (old)

    Excludes1   cardiac septal defect as current complication following acute myocardial infarction (I23.1, I23.2)

  I51.1   **Rupture of chordae tendineae, not elsewhere classified**

    Excludes1   rupture of chordae tendineae as current complication following acute myocardial infarction (I23.4)

  I51.2   **Rupture of papillary muscle, not elsewhere classified**

    Excludes1   rupture of papillary muscle as current complication following acute myocardial infarction (I23.5)

  I51.3   **Intracardiac thrombosis, not elsewhere classified**
Apical thrombosis (old)
Atrial thrombosis (old)
Auricular thrombosis (old)
Mural thrombosis (old)
Ventricular thrombosis (old)

    Excludes1   intracardiac thrombosis as current complication following acute myocardial infarction (I23.6)
    Coding Clinic: 2013, Q1, P24

  I51.4   **Myocarditis, unspecified**
Chronic (interstitial) myocarditis
Myocardial fibrosis
Myocarditis NOS

    Excludes1   acute or subacute myocarditis (I40.-)
    Coding Clinic: 2016, Q4, P122

  I51.5   **Myocardial degeneration**
Fatty degeneration of heart or myocardium
Myocardial disease
Senile degeneration of heart or myocardium
    Coding Clinic: 2016, Q4, P122

  I51.7   **Cardiomegaly**
Cardiac dilatation
Cardiac hypertrophy
Ventricular dilatation
    Coding Clinic: 2016, Q4, P122

● **I51.8**   **Other ill-defined heart diseases**
    Coding Clinic: 2016, Q4, P122

   I51.81   **Takotsubo syndrome**
Reversible left ventricular dysfunction following sudden emotional stress
Stress induced cardiomyopathy
Takotsubo cardiomyopathy
Transient left ventricular apical ballooning syndrome

   I51.89   **Other ill-defined heart diseases**
Carditis (acute)(chronic)
Pancarditis (acute)(chronic)

  I51.9   **Heart disease, unspecified**
    Coding Clinic: 2016, Q4, P122

▶ *I52*   *Other heart disorders in diseases classified elsewhere*
Code first underlying disease, such as:
congenital syphilis (A50.5)
mucopolysaccharidosis (E76.3)
schistosomiasis (B65.0-B65.9)

    Excludes1   heart disease (in):
gonococcal infection (A54.83)
meningococcal infection (A39.50)
rheumatoid arthritis (M05.31)
syphilis (A52.06)

CEREBROVASCULAR DISEASES (I60-I69)

Use additional code to identify presence of:
   alcohol abuse and dependence (F10.-)
   exposure to environmental tobacco smoke (Z77.22)
   history of tobacco dependence (Z87.891)
➡ hypertension (I10-I16)
   occupational exposure to environmental tobacco smoke
      (Z57.31)
   tobacco dependence (F17.-)
   tobacco use (Z72.0)

Excludes1   traumatic intracranial hemorrhage (S06.-)

Coding Clinic: 2015, Q4, P40

● I60   Nontraumatic subarachnoid hemorrhage

Excludes1   syphilitic ruptured cerebral aneurysm (A52.05)

Excludes2   sequelae of subarachnoid hemorrhage (I69.0-)

● I60.0   Nontraumatic subarachnoid hemorrhage from carotid
   siphon and bifurcation

   I60.00   Nontraumatic subarachnoid hemorrhage from
      unspecified carotid siphon and bifurcation

   I60.01   Nontraumatic subarachnoid hemorrhage from
      right carotid siphon and bifurcation

   I60.02   Nontraumatic subarachnoid hemorrhage from
      left carotid siphon and bifurcation

● I60.1   Nontraumatic subarachnoid hemorrhage from middle
   cerebral artery

   I60.10   Nontraumatic subarachnoid hemorrhage from
      unspecified middle cerebral artery

   I60.11   Nontraumatic subarachnoid hemorrhage from
      right middle cerebral artery

   I60.12   Nontraumatic subarachnoid hemorrhage from
      left middle cerebral artery

I60.2   Nontraumatic subarachnoid hemorrhage from anterior
   communicating artery

● I60.3   Nontraumatic subarachnoid hemorrhage from posterior
   communicating artery

   I60.30   Nontraumatic subarachnoid hemorrhage from
      unspecified posterior communicating artery

   I60.31   Nontraumatic subarachnoid hemorrhage from
      right posterior communicating artery

   I60.32   Nontraumatic subarachnoid hemorrhage from
      left posterior communicating artery

I60.4   Nontraumatic subarachnoid hemorrhage from basilar
   artery

● I60.5   Nontraumatic subarachnoid hemorrhage from vertebral
   artery

   I60.50   Nontraumatic subarachnoid hemorrhage from
      unspecified vertebral artery

   I60.51   Nontraumatic subarachnoid hemorrhage from
      right vertebral artery

   I60.52   Nontraumatic subarachnoid hemorrhage from
      left vertebral artery

I60.6   Nontraumatic subarachnoid hemorrhage from other
   intracranial arteries

I60.7   Nontraumatic subarachnoid hemorrhage from
   unspecified intracranial artery
      Ruptured (congenital) berry aneurysm
      Ruptured (congenital) cerebral aneurysm
      Subarachnoid hemorrhage (nontraumatic) from cerebral
         artery NOS
      Subarachnoid hemorrhage (nontraumatic) from
         communicating artery NOS

      Excludes1   berry aneurysm, nonruptured (I67.1)

I60.8   Other nontraumatic subarachnoid hemorrhage
      Meningeal hemorrhage
      Rupture of cerebral arteriovenous malformation

I60.9   Nontraumatic subarachnoid hemorrhage, unspecified

● I61   Nontraumatic intracerebral hemorrhage

Excludes2   sequelae of intracerebral hemorrhage (I69.1-)

Coding Clinic: 2017, Q2, P10

   I61.0   Nontraumatic intracerebral hemorrhage in hemisphere,
      subcortical
         Deep intracerebral hemorrhage (nontraumatic)
         Coding Clinic: 2016, Q4, P27

   I61.1   Nontraumatic intracerebral hemorrhage in hemisphere,
      cortical
         Cerebral lobe hemorrhage (nontraumatic)
         Superficial intracerebral hemorrhage (nontraumatic)
         Coding Clinic: 2016, Q4, P28

   I61.2   Nontraumatic intracerebral hemorrhage in hemisphere,
      unspecified

   I61.3   Nontraumatic intracerebral hemorrhage in brain stem

   I61.4   Nontraumatic intracerebral hemorrhage in cerebellum

   I61.5   Nontraumatic intracerebral hemorrhage, intraventricular

   I61.6   Nontraumatic intracerebral hemorrhage, multiple
      localized

   I61.8   Other nontraumatic intracerebral hemorrhage

   I61.9   Nontraumatic intracerebral hemorrhage, unspecified

● I62   Other and unspecified nontraumatic intracranial hemorrhage

Excludes2   sequelae of intracranial hemorrhage (I69.2)

● I62.0   Nontraumatic subdural hemorrhage

   I62.00   Nontraumatic subdural hemorrhage,
      unspecified

   I62.01   Nontraumatic acute subdural hemorrhage

   I62.02   Nontraumatic subacute subdural hemorrhage

   I62.03   Nontraumatic chronic subdural hemorrhage

I62.1   Nontraumatic extradural hemorrhage
      Nontraumatic epidural hemorrhage

I62.9   Nontraumatic intracranial hemorrhage, unspecified

★ **(See Plate 141 on page 76.)**

● I63   Cerebral infarction

Includes   occlusion and stenosis of cerebral and precerebral
   arteries, resulting in cerebral infarction

Use additional code, if applicable, to identify status post
   administration of tPA (rtPA) in a different facility within
   the last 24 hours prior to admission to current facility
   (Z92.82)

Use additional code, if known, to indicate National Institutes of
   Health Stroke Scale (NIHSS) score (R29.7-)

Excludes2   sequelae of cerebral infarction (I69.3-)

Coding Clinic: 2016, Q4, P28, 61, 127

● I63.0   Cerebral infarction due to thrombosis of precerebral
   arteries

   I63.00   Cerebral infarction due to thrombosis of
      unspecified precerebral artery

   ● I63.01   Cerebral infarction due to thrombosis of
      vertebral artery

      I63.011   Cerebral infarction due to thrombosis
         of right vertebral artery

      I63.012   Cerebral infarction due to thrombosis
         of left vertebral artery

      I63.013   Cerebral infarction due to thrombosis
         of bilateral vertebral arteries

      I63.019   Cerebral infarction due to thrombosis
         of unspecified vertebral artery

   I63.02   Cerebral infarction due to thrombosis of basilar
      artery

▶ New   ➡ Revised   ~~deleted~~ Deleted   Excludes 1   Excludes 2   Includes   Use additional   Code first   Code also   Key words
OGCR Official Guidelines   X Assign placeholder X   ● Use Additional Character(s)   ▷ Manifestation Code   Coding Clinic

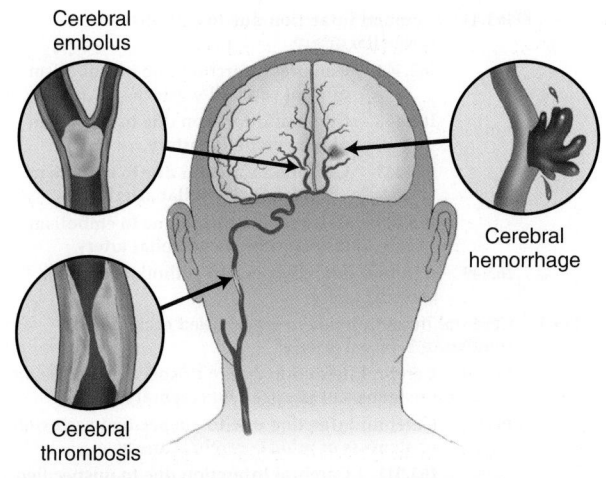

Cerebral embolus

Cerebral hemorrhage

Cerebral thrombosis

Figure 9-4 Events causing a stroke. (From Shiland: Mastering Healthcare Terminology, ed 1, St. Louis, Mosby, 2003)

● I63.03   Cerebral infarction due to thrombosis of carotid artery
   I63.031   Cerebral infarction due to thrombosis of right carotid artery
   I63.032   Cerebral infarction due to thrombosis of left carotid artery
   I63.033   Cerebral infarction due to thrombosis of bilateral carotid arteries
   I63.039   Cerebral infarction due to thrombosis of unspecified carotid artery
 I63.09   Cerebral infarction due to thrombosis of other precerebral artery
● I63.1   Cerebral infarction due to embolism of precerebral arteries
 I63.10   Cerebral infarction due to embolism of unspecified precerebral artery
● I63.11   Cerebral infarction due to embolism of vertebral artery
   I63.111   Cerebral infarction due to embolism of right vertebral artery
   I63.112   Cerebral infarction due to embolism of left vertebral artery
   I63.113   Cerebral infarction due to embolism of bilateral vertebral arteries
   I63.119   Cerebral infarction due to embolism of unspecified vertebral artery
 I63.12   Cerebral infarction due to embolism of basilar artery
● I63.13   Cerebral infarction due to embolism of carotid artery
   I63.131   Cerebral infarction due to embolism of right carotid artery
   I63.132   Cerebral infarction due to embolism of left carotid artery
   I63.133   Cerebral infarction due to embolism of bilateral carotid arteries
   I63.139   Cerebral infarction due to embolism of unspecified carotid artery
 I63.19   Cerebral infarction due to embolism of other precerebral artery

● I63.2   Cerebral infarction due to unspecified occlusion or stenosis of precerebral arteries
 I63.20   Cerebral infarction due to unspecified occlusion or stenosis of unspecified precerebral arteries
● I63.21   Cerebral infarction due to unspecified occlusion or stenosis of vertebral arteries
   I63.211   Cerebral infarction due to unspecified occlusion or stenosis of right vertebral artery
   I63.212   Cerebral infarction due to unspecified occlusion or stenosis of left vertebral artery
   I63.213   Cerebral infarction due to unspecified occlusion or stenosis of bilateral vertebral arteries
➠ I63.219   Cerebral infarction due to unspecified occlusion or stenosis of unspecified vertebral artery
 I63.22   Cerebral infarction due to unspecified occlusion or stenosis of basilar artery
● I63.23   Cerebral infarction due to unspecified occlusion or stenosis of carotid arteries
   I63.231   Cerebral infarction due to unspecified occlusion or stenosis of right carotid arteries
   I63.232   Cerebral infarction due to unspecified occlusion or stenosis of left carotid arteries
   I63.233   Cerebral infarction due to unspecified occlusion or stenosis of bilateral carotid arteries
➠ I63.239   Cerebral infarction due to unspecified occlusion or stenosis of unspecified carotid artery
 I63.29   Cerebral infarction due to unspecified occlusion or stenosis of other precerebral arteries
● I63.3   Cerebral infarction due to thrombosis of cerebral arteries
 I63.30   Cerebral infarction due to thrombosis of unspecified cerebral artery
● I63.31   Cerebral infarction due to thrombosis of middle cerebral artery
   I63.311   Cerebral infarction due to thrombosis of right middle cerebral artery
   I63.312   Cerebral infarction due to thrombosis of left middle cerebral artery
   I63.313   Cerebral infarction due to thrombosis of bilateral middle cerebral arteries
   I63.319   Cerebral infarction due to thrombosis of unspecified middle cerebral artery
● I63.32   Cerebral infarction due to thrombosis of anterior cerebral artery
   I63.321   Cerebral infarction due to thrombosis of right anterior cerebral artery
   I63.322   Cerebral infarction due to thrombosis of left anterior cerebral artery
   I63.323   Cerebral infarction due to thrombosis of bilateral anterior cerebral arteries
   I63.329   Cerebral infarction due to thrombosis of unspecified anterior cerebral artery

CHAPTER 9 (I00-I99)

CHAPTER 9 (I00-I99)

● **I63.33**   **Cerebral infarction due to thrombosis of posterior cerebral artery**

    I63.331   Cerebral infarction due to thrombosis of **right** posterior cerebral artery

    I63.332   Cerebral infarction due to thrombosis of **left** posterior cerebral artery

➡ I63.333   Cerebral infarction due to thrombosis of **bilateral** posterior cerebral arteries

    I63.339   Cerebral infarction due to thrombosis of **unspecified** posterior cerebral artery

● **I63.34**   **Cerebral infarction due to thrombosis of cerebellar artery**

    I63.341   Cerebral infarction due to thrombosis of **right** cerebellar artery

    I63.342   Cerebral infarction due to thrombosis of **left** cerebellar artery

➡ I63.343   Cerebral infarction due to thrombosis of **bilateral** cerebellar arteries

    I63.349   Cerebral infarction due to thrombosis of **unspecified** cerebellar artery

  I63.39   Cerebral infarction due to thrombosis of **other** cerebral artery

● **I63.4**   **Cerebral infarction due to embolism of cerebral arteries**

  I63.40   Cerebral infarction due to embolism of **unspecified** cerebral artery

● **I63.41**   **Cerebral infarction due to embolism of middle cerebral artery**

    I63.411   Cerebral infarction due to embolism of **right** middle cerebral artery

    I63.412   Cerebral infarction due to embolism of **left** middle cerebral artery

    I63.413   Cerebral infarction due to embolism of **bilateral** middle cerebral arteries

    I63.419   Cerebral infarction due to embolism of **unspecified** middle cerebral artery

● **I63.42**   **Cerebral infarction due to embolism of anterior cerebral artery**

    I63.421   Cerebral infarction due to embolism of **right** anterior cerebral artery

    I63.422   Cerebral infarction due to embolism of **left** anterior cerebral artery

    I63.423   Cerebral infarction due to embolism of **bilateral** anterior cerebral arteries

    I63.429   Cerebral infarction due to embolism of **unspecified** anterior cerebral artery

● **I63.43**   **Cerebral infarction due to embolism of posterior cerebral artery**

    I63.431   Cerebral infarction due to embolism of **right** posterior cerebral artery

    I63.432   Cerebral infarction due to embolism of **left** posterior cerebral artery

    I63.433   Cerebral infarction due to embolism of **bilateral** posterior cerebral arteries

    I63.439   Cerebral infarction due to embolism of **unspecified** posterior cerebral artery

● **I63.44**   **Cerebral infarction due to embolism of cerebellar artery**

    I63.441   Cerebral infarction due to embolism of **right** cerebellar artery

    I63.442   Cerebral infarction due to embolism of **left** cerebellar artery

    I63.443   Cerebral infarction due to embolism of **bilateral** cerebellar arteries

    I63.449   Cerebral infarction due to embolism of **unspecified** cerebellar artery

  I63.49   Cerebral infarction due to embolism of **other** cerebral artery

● **I63.5**   **Cerebral infarction due to unspecified occlusion or stenosis of cerebral arteries**

  I63.50   Cerebral infarction due to unspecified occlusion or stenosis of **unspecified** cerebral artery

● **I63.51**   **Cerebral infarction due to unspecified occlusion or stenosis of middle cerebral artery**

    I63.511   Cerebral infarction due to unspecified occlusion or stenosis of **right** middle cerebral artery

    I63.512   Cerebral infarction due to unspecified occlusion or stenosis of **left** middle cerebral artery

    I63.513   Cerebral infarction due to unspecified occlusion or stenosis of **bilateral** middle cerebral arteries

    I63.519   Cerebral infarction due to unspecified occlusion or stenosis of **unspecified** middle cerebral artery

● **I63.52**   **Cerebral infarction due to unspecified occlusion or stenosis of anterior cerebral artery**

    I63.521   Cerebral infarction due to unspecified occlusion or stenosis of **right** anterior cerebral artery

    I63.522   Cerebral infarction due to unspecified occlusion or stenosis of **left** anterior cerebral artery

    I63.523   Cerebral infarction due to unspecified occlusion or stenosis of **bilateral** anterior cerebral arteries

    I63.529   Cerebral infarction due to unspecified occlusion or stenosis of **unspecified** anterior cerebral artery

● **I63.53**   **Cerebral infarction due to unspecified occlusion or stenosis of posterior cerebral artery**

    I63.531   Cerebral infarction due to unspecified occlusion or stenosis of **right** posterior cerebral artery

    I63.532   Cerebral infarction due to unspecified occlusion or stenosis of **left** posterior cerebral artery
         Coding Clinic: 2017, Q2, P10

    I63.533   Cerebral infarction due to unspecified occlusion or stenosis of **bilateral** posterior cerebral arteries

    I63.539   Cerebral infarction due to unspecified occlusion or stenosis of **unspecified** posterior cerebral artery

---

▶ New   ➡ Revised   ~~deleted~~ Deleted   Excludes 1   Excludes 2   Includes   Use additional   Code first   Code also   Key words

OGCR Official Guidelines   X Assign placeholder X   ● Use Additional Character(s)   ▷ Manifestation Code   **Coding Clinic**

● **I63.54** **Cerebral infarction due to unspecified occlusion or stenosis of cerebellar artery**

    I63.541 Cerebral infarction due to unspecified occlusion or stenosis of right cerebellar artery

    I63.542 Cerebral infarction due to unspecified occlusion or stenosis of left cerebellar artery

    I63.543 Cerebral infarction due to unspecified occlusion or stenosis of bilateral cerebellar arteries

    I63.549 Cerebral infarction due to unspecified occlusion or stenosis of unspecified cerebellar artery

  I63.59 Cerebral infarction due to unspecified occlusion or stenosis of other cerebral artery

I63.6 Cerebral infarction due to cerebral venous thrombosis, nonpyogenic

I63.8 Other cerebral infarction

  ▶ **I63.81** Other cerebral infarction due to occlusion or stenosis of small artery
    ▶ Lacunar infarction

  ▶ **I63.89** Other cerebral infarction
    Coding Clinic: 2017, Q2, P9

I63.9 Cerebral infarction, unspecified
  Stroke NOS

  Excludes2 transient cerebral ischemic attacks and related syndromes (G45.-)
  Coding Clinic: 2016, Q4, P62; 2015, Q1, P26

● **I65** **Occlusion and stenosis of precerebral arteries, not resulting in cerebral infarction**

  Includes embolism of precerebral artery
    narrowing of precerebral artery
    obstruction (complete) (partial) of precerebral artery
    thrombosis of precerebral artery

  Excludes1 insufficiency, NOS, of precerebral artery (G45.-)
    insufficiency of precerebral arteries causing cerebral infarction (I63.0-I63.2)

 ● **I65.0** Occlusion and stenosis of vertebral artery

  I65.01 Occlusion and stenosis of right vertebral artery

  I65.02 Occlusion and stenosis of left vertebral artery

  I65.03 Occlusion and stenosis of bilateral vertebral arteries

  I65.09 Occlusion and stenosis of unspecified vertebral artery

 I65.1 Occlusion and stenosis of basilar artery

 ● **I65.2** Occlusion and stenosis of carotid artery

  I65.21 Occlusion and stenosis of right carotid artery

  I65.22 Occlusion and stenosis of left carotid artery

  I65.23 Occlusion and stenosis of bilateral carotid arteries

  I65.29 Occlusion and stenosis of unspecified carotid artery

 I65.8 Occlusion and stenosis of other precerebral arteries

 I65.9 Occlusion and stenosis of unspecified precerebral artery
  Occlusion and stenosis of precerebral artery NOS

● **I66** **Occlusion and stenosis of cerebral arteries, not resulting in cerebral infarction**

  Includes embolism of cerebral artery
    narrowing of cerebral artery
    obstruction (complete) (partial) of cerebral artery
    thrombosis of cerebral artery

  Excludes1 occlusion and stenosis of cerebral artery causing cerebral infarction (I63.3-I63.5)

 ● **I66.0** Occlusion and stenosis of middle cerebral artery

  I66.01 Occlusion and stenosis of right middle cerebral artery

  I66.02 Occlusion and stenosis of left middle cerebral artery

  I66.03 Occlusion and stenosis of bilateral middle cerebral arteries

  I66.09 Occlusion and stenosis of unspecified middle cerebral artery

 ● **I66.1** Occlusion and stenosis of anterior cerebral artery

  I66.11 Occlusion and stenosis of right anterior cerebral artery

  I66.12 Occlusion and stenosis of left anterior cerebral artery

  I66.13 Occlusion and stenosis of bilateral anterior cerebral arteries

  I66.19 Occlusion and stenosis of unspecified anterior cerebral artery

 ● **I66.2** Occlusion and stenosis of posterior cerebral artery

  I66.21 Occlusion and stenosis of right posterior cerebral artery

  I66.22 Occlusion and stenosis of left posterior cerebral artery

  I66.23 Occlusion and stenosis of bilateral posterior cerebral arteries

  I66.29 Occlusion and stenosis of unspecified posterior cerebral artery

 I66.3 Occlusion and stenosis of cerebellar arteries

 I66.8 Occlusion and stenosis of other cerebral arteries
  Occlusion and stenosis of perforating arteries

 I66.9 Occlusion and stenosis of unspecified cerebral artery

● **I67** **Other cerebrovascular diseases**

  Excludes2 sequelae of the listed conditions (I69.8)

 I67.0 Dissection of cerebral arteries, nonruptured

  Excludes1 ruptured cerebral arteries (I60.7)

 I67.1 Cerebral aneurysm, nonruptured
  Cerebral aneurysm NOS
  Cerebral arteriovenous fistula, acquired
  Internal carotid artery aneurysm, intracranial portion
  Internal carotid artery aneurysm, NOS

  Excludes1 congenital cerebral aneurysm, nonruptured (Q28.-)
    ruptured cerebral aneurysm (I60.7)

 I67.2 Cerebral atherosclerosis   A
  Atheroma of cerebral and precerebral arteries

 I67.3 Progressive vascular leukoencephalopathy
  Binswanger's disease

 I67.4 Hypertensive encephalopathy

  Excludes2 insufficiency, NOS, of precerebral arteries (G45.2)

 I67.5 Moyamoya disease

 I67.6 Nonpyogenic thrombosis of intracranial venous system
  Nonpyogenic thrombosis of cerebral vein
  Nonpyogenic thrombosis of intracranial venous sinus

  Excludes1 nonpyogenic thrombosis of intracranial venous system causing infarction (I63.6)

 I67.7 Cerebral arteritis, not elsewhere classified
  Granulomatous angiitis of the nervous system

  Excludes1 allergic granulomatous angiitis (M30.1)

CHAPTER 9 (I00-I99)

CHAPTER 9 (I00-I99)

● **I67.8**   **Other specified cerebrovascular diseases**

     I67.81   **Acute cerebrovascular insufficiency**
         Acute cerebrovascular insufficiency unspecified as to location or reversibility

     I67.82   **Cerebral ischemia**
         Chronic cerebral ischemia

     I67.83   **Posterior reversible encephalopathy syndrome**
         PRES

     ● **I67.84**   **Cerebral vasospasm and vasoconstriction**

         I67.841   **Reversible cerebrovascular vasoconstriction syndrome**
            Call-Fleming syndrome

            Code first underlying condition, if applicable, such as eclampsia (O15.00-O15.9)

         I67.848   **Other cerebrovascular vasospasm and vasoconstriction**

     ▶● **I67.85**   **Hereditary cerebrovascular diseases**

         ▶ **I67.850**   **Cerebral autosomal dominant arteriopathy with subcortical infarcts and leukoencephalopathy**
            ▶CADASIL

            ▶*Code also any associated diagnoses, such as:*
                ▶epilepsy (G40.-), stroke (I63.-)
                ▶vascular dementia (F01.-)

         ▶ **I67.858**   **Other hereditary cerebrovascular disease**

     I67.89   **Other cerebrovascular disease**

   I67.9   **Cerebrovascular disease, unspecified**

● **I68**   **Cerebrovascular disorders in diseases classified elsewhere**

   ▷ *I68.0*   *Cerebral amyloid angiopathy*
       Code first underlying amyloidosis (E85.-)

   ▷ *I68.2*   *Cerebral arteritis in other diseases classified elsewhere*
       Code first underlying disease
       Excludes1   cerebral arteritis (in):
            listerosis (A32.89)
            systemic lupus erythematosus (M32.19)
            syphilis (A52.04)
            tuberculosis (A18.89)

   ▷ *I68.8*   *Other cerebrovascular disorders in diseases classified elsewhere*
       Code first underlying disease
       Excludes1   syphilitic cerebral aneurysm (A52.05)

OGCR Section I.c.9.d.

Sequelae of Cerebrovascular Disease

1) Category I69, Sequelae of Cerebrovascular disease

Category I69 is used to indicate conditions classifiable to categories I60-I67 as the causes of sequela (neurologic deficits), themselves classified elsewhere. These "late effects" include neurologic deficits that persist after initial onset of conditions classifiable to categories I60-I67. The neurologic deficits caused by cerebrovascular disease may be present from the onset of may arise at any time after the onset of the condition classifiable to categories I60-I67.

Codes from category I69, Sequelae of cerebrovascular disease, that specify hemiplegia, hemiparesis and monoplegia identify whether the dominant or nondominant side is affected. Should the affected side be documented, but not specified as dominant or nondominant, and the classification system does not indicate a default, code selection is as follows:

For ambidextrous patients, the default should be dominant.

If the left side is affected, the default is non-dominant.

If the right side is affected, the default is dominant.

2) Codes from category I69 with codes from I60-I67

Codes from category I69 may be assigned on a health care record with codes from I60-I67, if the patient has a current cerebrovascular disease and deficits from an old cerebrovascular disease.

● **I69**   **Sequelae of cerebrovascular disease**

     Note: Category I69 is to be used to indicate conditions in I60-I67 as the cause of sequelae. The 'sequelae' include conditions specified as such or as residuals which may occur at any time after the onset of the causal condition.

     Excludes1   personal history of cerebral infarction without residual deficit (Z86.73)
            personal history of prolonged reversible ischemic neurologic deficit (PRIND) (Z86.73)
            personal history of reversible ischemic neurologcial deficit (RIND) (Z86.73)
            sequelae of traumatic intracranial injury (S06.-)

     Coding Clinic: 2016, Q4, P28; 2015, Q4, P40; 2012, Q4, P107

● **I69.0**   **Sequelae of nontraumatic subarachnoid hemorrhage**

     I69.00   **Unspecified sequelae of nontraumatic subarachnoid hemorrhage**

     ● **I69.01**   **Cognitive deficits following nontraumatic subarachnoid hemorrhage**

         I69.010   **Attention and concentration deficit** following nontraumatic subarachnoid hemorrhage

         I69.011   **Memory deficit following** nontraumatic subarachnoid hemorrhage

         I69.012   **Visuospatial deficit and spatial neglect** following nontraumatic subarachnoid hemorrhage

         I69.013   **Psychomotor deficit following** nontraumatic subarachnoid hemorrhage

         I69.014   **Frontal lobe and executive function deficit** following nontraumatic subarachnoid hemorrhage

         I69.015   **Cognitive social or emotional deficit** following nontraumatic subarachnoid hemorrhage

         I69.018   **Other symptoms and signs** involving cognitive functions following nontraumatic subarachnoid hemorrhage

         I69.019   **Unspecified** symptoms and signs involving cognitive functions following nontraumatic subarachnoid hemorrhage

     ● **I69.02**   **Speech and language deficits** following nontraumatic subarachnoid hemorrhage

         I69.020   **Aphasia following** nontraumatic subarachnoid hemorrhage

         I69.021   **Dysphasia following** nontraumatic subarachnoid hemorrhage

         I69.022   **Dysarthria following** nontraumatic subarachnoid hemorrhage

         I69.023   **Fluency disorder following** nontraumatic subarachnoid hemorrhage
            Stuttering following nontraumatic subarachnoid hemorrhage

         I69.028   **Other speech and language deficits** following nontraumatic subarachnoid hemorrhage

▶ New   ⇒ Revised   ~~deleted~~ Deleted   Excludes 1   Excludes 2   Includes   Use additional   Code first   Code also   Key words

OGCR Official Guidelines   X Assign placeholder X   ● Use Additional Character(s)   ▷ Manifestation Code   **Coding Clinic**

● I69.03 Monoplegia of upper limb following nontraumatic subarachnoid hemorrhage

    I69.031 Monoplegia of upper limb following nontraumatic subarachnoid hemorrhage affecting right dominant side

    I69.032 Monoplegia of upper limb following nontraumatic subarachnoid hemorrhage affecting left dominant side

    I69.033 Monoplegia of upper limb following nontraumatic subarachnoid hemorrhage affecting right non-dominant side

    I69.034 Monoplegia of upper limb following nontraumatic subarachnoid hemorrhage affecting left non-dominant side

    I69.039 Monoplegia of upper limb following nontraumatic subarachnoid hemorrhage affecting unspecified side

● I69.04 Monoplegia of lower limb following nontraumatic subarachnoid hemorrhage

    I69.041 Monoplegia of lower limb following nontraumatic subarachnoid hemorrhage affecting right dominant side

    I69.042 Monoplegia of lower limb following nontraumatic subarachnoid hemorrhage affecting left dominant side

    I69.043 Monoplegia of lower limb following nontraumatic subarachnoid hemorrhage affecting right non-dominant side

    I69.044 Monoplegia of lower limb following nontraumatic subarachnoid hemorrhage affecting left non-dominant side

    I69.049 Monoplegia of lower limb following nontraumatic subarachnoid hemorrhage affecting unspecified side

● I69.05 Hemiplegia and hemiparesis following nontraumatic subarachnoid hemorrhage

    I69.051 Hemiplegia and hemiparesis following nontraumatic subarachnoid hemorrhage affecting right dominant side

    I69.052 Hemiplegia and hemiparesis following nontraumatic subarachnoid hemorrhage affecting left dominant side

    I69.053 Hemiplegia and hemiparesis following nontraumatic subarachnoid hemorrhage affecting right non-dominant side

    I69.054 Hemiplegia and hemiparesis following nontraumatic subarachnoid hemorrhage affecting left non-dominant side

    I69.059 Hemiplegia and hemiparesis following nontraumatic subarachnoid hemorrhage affecting unspecified side

● I69.06 Other paralytic syndrome following nontraumatic subarachnoid hemorrhage

Use additional code to identify type of paralytic syndrome, such as:
locked-in state (G83.5)
quadriplegia (G82.5-)

Excludes1 hemiplegia/hemiparesis following nontraumatic subarachnoid hemorrhage (I69.05-)
monoplegia of lower limb following nontraumatic subarachnoid hemorrhage (I69.04-)
monoplegia of upper limb following nontraumatic subarachnoid hemorrhage (I69.03-)

    I69.061 Other paralytic syndrome following nontraumatic subarachnoid hemorrhage affecting right dominant side

    I69.062 Other paralytic syndrome following nontraumatic subarachnoid hemorrhage affecting left dominant side

    I69.063 Other paralytic syndrome following nontraumatic subarachnoid hemorrhage affecting right non-dominant side

    I69.064 Other paralytic syndrome following nontraumatic subarachnoid hemorrhage affecting left non-dominant side

    I69.065 Other paralytic syndrome following nontraumatic subarachnoid hemorrhage, bilateral

    I69.069 Other paralytic syndrome following nontraumatic subarachnoid hemorrhage affecting unspecified side

● I69.09 Other sequelae of nontraumatic subarachnoid hemorrhage

    I69.090 Apraxia following nontraumatic subarachnoid hemorrhage

    I69.091 Dysphagia following nontraumatic subarachnoid hemorrhage

Use additional code to identify the type of dysphagia, if known (R13.1-)

    I69.092 Facial weakness following nontraumatic subarachnoid hemorrhage

Facial droop following nontraumatic subarachnoid hemorrhage

    I69.093 Ataxia following nontraumatic subarachnoid hemorrhage

    I69.098 Other sequelae following nontraumatic subarachnoid hemorrhage

Alterations of sensation following nontraumatic subarachnoid hemorrhage

Disturbance of vision following nontraumatic subarachnoid hemorrhage

Use additional code to identify the sequelae

N Newborn Age: 0   **P** Pediatric Age: 0–17   **M** Maternity DX: 12–55   **A** Adult Age: 15–124   ♀ Females Only   ♂ Males Only

CHAPTER 9 (I00-I99)

879

CHAPTER 9 (I00-I99)

● **I69.1**   Sequelae of nontraumatic intracerebral hemorrhage

     I69.10   Unspecified sequelae of nontraumatic intracerebral hemorrhage

●   **I69.11**   Cognitive deficits following nontraumatic intracerebral hemorrhage

         I69.110   Attention and concentration deficit following nontraumatic intracerebral hemorrhage

         I69.111   Memory deficit following nontraumatic intracerebral hemorrhage

         I69.112   Visuospatial deficit and spatial neglect following nontraumatic intracerebral hemorrhage

         I69.113   Psychomotor deficit following nontraumatic intracerebral hemorrhage

         I69.114   Frontal lobe and executive function deficit following nontraumatic intracerebral hemorrhage

         I69.115   Cognitive social or emotional deficit following nontraumatic intracerebral hemorrhage

         I69.118   Other symptoms and signs involving cognitive functions following nontraumatic intracerebral hemorrhage

         I69.119   Unspecified symptoms and signs involving cognitive functions following nontraumatic intracerebral hemorrhage

●   **I69.12**   Speech and language deficits following nontraumatic intracerebral hemorrhage

         I69.120   Aphasia following nontraumatic intracerebral hemorrhage

         I69.121   Dysphasia following nontraumatic intracerebral hemorrhage

         I69.122   Dysarthria following nontraumatic intracerebral hemorrhage

         I69.123   Fluency disorder following nontraumatic intracerebral hemorrhage
               Stuttering following nontraumatic intracerebral hemorrhage

         I69.128   Other speech and language deficits following nontraumatic intracerebral hemorrhage

●   **I69.13**   Monoplegia of upper limb following nontraumatic intracerebral hemorrhage

         I69.131   Monoplegia of upper limb following nontraumatic intracerebral hemorrhage affecting right dominant side

         I69.132   Monoplegia of upper limb following nontraumatic intracerebral hemorrhage affecting left dominant side

         I69.133   Monoplegia of upper limb following nontraumatic intracerebral hemorrhage affecting right non-dominant side

         I69.134   Monoplegia of upper limb following nontraumatic intracerebral hemorrhage affecting left non-dominant side

         I69.139   Monoplegia of upper limb following nontraumatic intracerebral hemorrhage affecting unspecified side

● **I69.14**   Monoplegia of lower limb following nontraumatic intracerebral hemorrhage

         I69.141   Monoplegia of lower limb following nontraumatic intracerebral hemorrhage affecting right dominant side

         I69.142   Monoplegia of lower limb following nontraumatic intracerebral hemorrhage affecting left dominant side

         I69.143   Monoplegia of lower limb following nontraumatic intracerebral hemorrhage affecting right non-dominant side

         I69.144   Monoplegia of lower limb following nontraumatic intracerebral hemorrhage affecting left non-dominant side

         I69.149   Monoplegia of lower limb following nontraumatic intracerebral hemorrhage affecting unspecified side

● **I69.15**   Hemiplegia and hemiparesis following nontraumatic intracerebral hemorrhage

         I69.151   Hemiplegia and hemiparesis following nontraumatic intracerebral hemorrhage affecting right dominant side

         I69.152   Hemiplegia and hemiparesis following nontraumatic intracerebral hemorrhage affecting left dominant side

         I69.153   Hemiplegia and hemiparesis following nontraumatic intracerebral hemorrhage affecting right non-dominant side

         I69.154   Hemiplegia and hemiparesis following nontraumatic intracerebral hemorrhage affecting left non-dominant side

         I69.159   Hemiplegia and hemiparesis following nontraumatic intracerebral hemorrhage affecting unspecified side

● **I69.16**   Other paralytic syndrome following nontraumatic intracerebral hemorrhage

     Use additional code to identify type of paralytic syndrome, such as:
       locked-in state (G83.5)
       quadriplegia (G82.5-)

     Excludes1   hemiplegia/hemiparesis following nontraumatic intracerebral hemorrhage (I69.15-)
               monoplegia of lower limb following nontraumatic intracerebral hemorrhage (I69.14-)
               monoplegia of upper limb following nontraumatic intracerebral hemorrhage (I69.13-)

         I69.161   Other paralytic syndrome following nontraumatic intracerebral hemorrhage affecting right dominant side

         I69.162   Other paralytic syndrome following nontraumatic intracerebral hemorrhage affecting left dominant side

         I69.163   Other paralytic syndrome following nontraumatic intracerebral hemorrhage affecting right non-dominant side

         I69.164   Other paralytic syndrome following nontraumatic intracerebral hemorrhage affecting left non-dominant side

▶ New   ⇒ Revised   ~~deleted~~ Deleted   Excludes 1   Excludes 2   Includes   Use additional   Code first   Code also   Key words
OGCR Official Guidelines   X Assign placeholder X   ● Use Additional Character(s)   ▷ Manifestation Code   **Coding Clinic**

I69.165 Other paralytic syndrome following nontraumatic intracerebral hemorrhage, bilateral

I69.169 Other paralytic syndrome following nontraumatic intracerebral hemorrhage affecting unspecified side

● I69.19 Other sequelae of nontraumatic intracerebral hemorrhage

I69.190 Apraxia following nontraumatic intracerebral hemorrhage

I69.191 Dysphagia following nontraumatic intracerebral hemorrhage
Use additional code to identify the type of dysphagia, if known (R13.1-)

I69.192 Facial weakness following nontraumatic intracerebral hemorrhage
Facial droop following nontraumatic intracerebral hemorrhage

I69.193 Ataxia following nontraumatic intracerebral hemorrhage

I69.198 Other sequelae of nontraumatic intracerebral hemorrhage
Alteration of sensations following nontraumatic intracerebral hemorrhage
Disturbance of vision following nontraumatic intracerebral hemorrhage
Use additional code to identify the sequelae

● I69.2 Sequelae of other nontraumatic intracranial hemorrhage

I69.20 Unspecified sequelae of other nontraumatic intracranial hemorrhage

● I69.21 Cognitive deficits following other nontraumatic intracranial hemorrhage

I69.210 Attention and concentration deficit following other nontraumatic intracranial hemorrhage

I69.211 Memory deficit following other nontraumatic intracranial hemorrhage

I69.212 Visuospatial deficit and spatial neglect following other nontraumatic intracranial hemorrhage

I69.213 Psychomotor deficit following other nontraumatic intracranial hemorrhage

I69.214 Frontal lobe and executive function deficit following other nontraumatic intracranial hemorrhage

I69.215 Cognitive social or emotional deficit following other nontraumatic intracranial hemorrhage

I69.218 Other symptoms and signs involving cognitive functions following other nontraumatic intracranial hemorrhage

I69.219 Unspecified symptoms and signs involving cognitive functions following other nontraumatic intracranial hemorrhage

● I69.22 Speech and language deficits following other nontraumatic intracranial hemorrhage

I69.220 Aphasia following other nontraumatic intracranial hemorrhage

I69.221 Dysphasia following other nontraumatic intracranial hemorrhage

I69.222 Dysarthria following other nontraumatic intracranial hemorrhage

I69.223 Fluency disorder following other nontraumatic intracranial hemorrhage
Stuttering following other nontraumatic intracranial hemorrhage

I69.228 Other speech and language deficits following other nontraumatic intracranial hemorrhage

● I69.23 Monoplegia of upper limb following other nontraumatic intracranial hemorrhage

I69.231 Monoplegia of upper limb following other nontraumatic intracranial hemorrhage affecting right dominant side

I69.232 Monoplegia of upper limb following other nontraumatic intracranial hemorrhage affecting left dominant side

I69.233 Monoplegia of upper limb following other nontraumatic intracranial hemorrhage affecting right non-dominant side

I69.234 Monoplegia of upper limb following other nontraumatic intracranial hemorrhage affecting left non-dominant side

I69.239 Monoplegia of upper limb following other nontraumatic intracranial hemorrhage affecting unspecified side

● I69.24 Monoplegia of lower limb following other nontraumatic intracranial hemorrhage

I69.241 Monoplegia of lower limb following other nontraumatic intracranial hemorrhage affecting right dominant side

I69.242 Monoplegia of lower limb following other nontraumatic intracranial hemorrhage affecting left dominant side

I69.243 Monoplegia of lower limb following other nontraumatic intracranial hemorrhage affecting right non-dominant side

I69.244 Monoplegia of lower limb following other nontraumatic intracranial hemorrhage affecting left non-dominant side

I69.249 Monoplegia of lower limb following other nontraumatic intracranial hemorrhage affecting unspecified side

● I69.25 Hemiplegia and hemiparesis following other nontraumatic intracranial hemorrhage

I69.251 Hemiplegia and hemiparesis following other nontraumatic intracranial hemorrhage affecting right dominant side

I69.252 Hemiplegia and hemiparesis following other nontraumatic intracranial hemorrhage affecting left dominant side

I69.253 Hemiplegia and hemiparesis following other nontraumatic intracranial hemorrhage affecting right non-dominant side

I69.254 Hemiplegia and hemiparesis following other nontraumatic intracranial hemorrhage affecting left non-dominant side

I69.259 Hemiplegia and hemiparesis following other nontraumatic intracranial hemorrhage affecting unspecified side

● **I69.26** **Other paralytic syndrome following other nontraumatic intracranial hemorrhage**

Use additional code to identify type of paralytic syndrome, such as:
locked-in state (G83.5)
quadriplegia (G82.5-)

Excludes1 hemiplegia/hemiparesis following other nontraumatic intracranial hemorrhage (I69.25-)
monoplegia of lower limb following other nontraumatic intracranial hemorrhage (I69.24-)
monoplegia of upper limb following other nontraumatic intracranial hemorrhage (I69.23-)

I69.261 Other paralytic syndrome following other nontraumatic intracranial hemorrhage affecting right dominant side

I69.262 Other paralytic syndrome following other nontraumatic intracranial hemorrhage affecting left dominant side

I69.263 Other paralytic syndrome following other nontraumatic intracranial hemorrhage affecting right non-dominant side

I69.264 Other paralytic syndrome following other nontraumatic intracranial hemorrhage affecting left non-dominant side

I69.265 Other paralytic syndrome following other nontraumatic intracranial hemorrhage, bilateral

I69.269 Other paralytic syndrome following other nontraumatic intracranial hemorrhage affecting unspecified side

● **I69.29** **Other sequelae of other nontraumatic intracranial hemorrhage**

I69.290 Apraxia following other nontraumatic intracranial hemorrhage

I69.291 Dysphagia following other nontraumatic intracranial hemorrhage

Use additional code to identify the type of dysphagia, if known (R13.1-)

I69.292 Facial weakness following other nontraumatic intracranial hemorrhage
Facial droop following other nontraumatic intracranial hemorrhage

I69.293 Ataxia following other nontraumatic intracranial hemorrhage

I69.298 Other sequelae of other nontraumatic intracranial hemorrhage
Alteration of sensation following other nontraumatic intracranial hemorrhage
Disturbance of vision following other nontraumatic intracranial hemorrhage
Use additional code to identify the sequelae

● **I69.3** **Sequelae of cerebral infarction**
Sequelae of stroke NOS
Coding Clinic: 2012, Q4, P92, 95

I69.30 Unspecified sequelae of cerebral infarction

● **I69.31** **Cognitive deficits following cerebral infarction**

I69.310 Attention and concentration deficit following cerebral infarction

I69.311 Memory deficit following cerebral infarction

I69.312 Visuospatial deficit and spatial neglect following cerebral infarction

I69.313 Psychomotor deficit following cerebral infarction

I69.314 Frontal lobe and executive function deficit following cerebral infarction

I69.315 Cognitive social or emotional deficit following cerebral infarction

I69.318 Other symptoms and signs involving cognitive functions following cerebral infarction

I69.319 Unspecified symptoms and signs involving cognitive functions following cerebral infarction

● **I69.32** **Speech and language deficits following cerebral infarction**

I69.320 Aphasia following cerebral infarction

I69.321 Dysphasia following cerebral infarction
Coding Clinic: 2012, Q4, P91

I69.322 Dysarthria following cerebral infarction

Excludes2 transient ischemic attack (TIA) (G45.9)

I69.323 Fluency disorder following cerebral infarction
Stuttering following cerebral infarction

I69.328 Other speech and language deficits following cerebral infarction

● **I69.33** **Monoplegia of upper limb following cerebral infarction**
Coding Clinic: 2017, Q1, P47

I69.331 Monoplegia of upper limb following cerebral infarction affecting right dominant side

I69.332 Monoplegia of upper limb following cerebral infarction affecting left dominant side

I69.333 Monoplegia of upper limb following cerebral infarction affecting right non-dominant side

I69.334 Monoplegia of upper limb following cerebral infarction affecting left non-dominant side

I69.339 Monoplegia of upper limb following cerebral infarction affecting unspecified side

● **I69.34** **Monoplegia of lower limb following cerebral infarction**
Coding Clinic: 2017, Q1, P47

I69.341 Monoplegia of lower limb following cerebral infarction affecting right dominant side

I69.342 Monoplegia of lower limb following cerebral infarction affecting left dominant side

I69.343 Monoplegia of lower limb following cerebral infarction affecting right non-dominant side

I69.344　Monoplegia of lower limb following cerebral infarction affecting left non-dominant side

I69.349　Monoplegia of lower limb following cerebral infarction affecting unspecified side

● I69.35　Hemiplegia and hemiparesis following cerebral infarction

I69.351　Hemiplegia and hemiparesis following cerebral infarction affecting right dominant side

　　Excludes2　transient ischemic attack (TIA) (G45.9)
　　Coding Clinic: 2015, Q1, P25

I69.352　Hemiplegia and hemiparesis following cerebral infarction affecting left dominant side

I69.353　Hemiplegia and hemiparesis following cerebral infarction affecting right non-dominant side

I69.354　Hemiplegia and hemiparesis following cerebral infarction affecting left non-dominant side
　　Coding Clinic: 2012, Q4, P91

I69.359　Hemiplegia and hemiparesis following cerebral infarction affecting unspecified side

● I69.36　Other paralytic syndrome following cerebral infarction

Use additional code to identify type of paralytic syndrome, such as:
locked-in state (G83.5)
quadriplegia (G82.5-)

　　Excludes1　hemiplegia/hemiparesis following cerebral infarction (I69.35-)
monoplegia of lower limb following cerebral infarction (I69.34-)
monoplegia of upper limb following cerebral infarction (I69.33-)

I69.361　Other paralytic syndrome following cerebral infarction affecting right dominant side

I69.362　Other paralytic syndrome following cerebral infarction affecting left dominant side

I69.363　Other paralytic syndrome following cerebral infarction affecting right non-dominant side

I69.364　Other paralytic syndrome following cerebral infarction affecting left non-dominant side

I69.365　Other paralytic syndrome following cerebral infarction, bilateral

I69.369　Other paralytic syndrome following cerebral infarction affecting unspecified side

● I69.39　Other sequelae of cerebral infarction

I69.390　Apraxia following cerebral infarction

I69.391　Dysphagia following cerebral infarction
Use additional code to identify the type of dysphagia, if known (R13.1-)

I69.392　Facial weakness following cerebral infarction
Facial droop following cerebral infarction

I69.393　Ataxia following cerebral infarction

I69.398　Other sequelae of cerebral infarction
Alteration of sensation following cerebral infarction
Disturbance of vision following cerebral infarction
Use additional code to identify the sequelae

● I69.8　Sequelae of other cerebrovascular diseases

　　Excludes1　sequelae of traumatic intracranial injury (S06.-)

I69.80　Unspecified sequelae of other cerebrovascular disease

● I69.81　Cognitive deficits following other cerebrovascular disease

I69.810　Attention and concentration deficit following other cerebrovascular disease

I69.811　Memory deficit following other cerebrovascular disease

I69.812　Visuospatial deficit and spatial neglect following other cerebrovascular disease

I69.813　Psychomotor deficit following other cerebrovascular disease

I69.814　Frontal lobe and executive function deficit following other cerebrovascular disease

I69.815　Cognitive social or emotional deficit following other cerebrovascular disease

I69.818　Other symptoms and signs involving cognitive functions following other cerebrovascular disease

I69.819　Unspecified symptoms and signs involving cognitive functions following other cerebrovascular disease

● I69.82　Speech and language deficits following other cerebrovascular disease

I69.820　Aphasia following other cerebrovascular disease

I69.821　Dysphasia following other cerebrovascular disease

I69.822　Dysarthria following other cerebrovascular disease

I69.823　Fluency disorder following other cerebrovascular disease
Stuttering following other cerebrovascular disease

I69.828　Other speech and language deficits following other cerebrovascular disease

● I69.83　Monoplegia of upper limb following other cerebrovascular disease

I69.831　Monoplegia of upper limb following other cerebrovascular disease affecting right dominant side

I69.832　Monoplegia of upper limb following other cerebrovascular disease affecting left dominant side

I69.833　Monoplegia of upper limb following other cerebrovascular disease affecting right non-dominant side

I69.834　Monoplegia of upper limb following other cerebrovascular disease affecting left non-dominant side

I69.839　Monoplegia of upper limb following other cerebrovascular disease affecting unspecified side

CHAPTER 9 (I00-I99)

● **I69.84**   **Monoplegia of lower limb** following other cerebrovascular disease

     I69.841   Monoplegia of lower limb following other cerebrovascular disease affecting **right dominant side**

     I69.842   Monoplegia of lower limb following other cerebrovascular disease affecting **left dominant side**

     I69.843   Monoplegia of lower limb following other cerebrovascular disease affecting **right non-dominant side**

     I69.844   Monoplegia of lower limb following other cerebrovascular disease affecting **left non-dominant side**

     I69.849   Monoplegia of lower limb following other cerebrovascular disease affecting **unspecified** side

● **I69.85**   **Hemiplegia and hemiparesis** following other cerebrovascular disease

     I69.851   Hemiplegia and hemiparesis following other cerebrovascular disease affecting **right dominant side**

     I69.852   Hemiplegia and hemiparesis following other cerebrovascular disease affecting **left dominant side**

     I69.853   Hemiplegia and hemiparesis following other cerebrovascular disease affecting **right non-dominant side**

     I69.854   Hemiplegia and hemiparesis following other cerebrovascular disease affecting **left non-dominant side**

     I69.859   Hemiplegia and hemiparesis following other cerebrovascular disease affecting **unspecified** side

● **I69.86**   **Other paralytic syndrome** following other cerebrovascular disease

     Use additional code to identify type of paralytic syndrome, such as:
     locked-in state (G83.5)
     quadriplegia (G82.5-)

     Excludes1   hemiplegia/hemiparesis following other cerebrovascular disease (I69.85-)
         monoplegia of lower limb following other cerebrovascular disease (I69.84-)
         monoplegia of upper limb following other cerebrovascular disease (I69.83-)

     I69.861   Other paralytic syndrome following other cerebrovascular disease affecting **right dominant side**

     I69.862   Other paralytic syndrome following other cerebrovascular disease affecting **left dominant side**

     I69.863   Other paralytic syndrome following other cerebrovascular disease affecting **right non-dominant side**

     I69.864   Other paralytic syndrome following other cerebrovascular disease affecting **left non-dominant side**

     I69.865   Other paralytic syndrome following other cerebrovascular disease, **bilateral**

     I69.869   Other paralytic syndrome following other cerebrovascular disease affecting **unspecified** side

● **I69.89**   **Other sequelae** of other cerebrovascular disease

     I69.890   **Apraxia** following other cerebrovascular disease

     I69.891   **Dysphagia** following other cerebrovascular disease

         Use additional code to identify the type of dysphagia, if known (R13.1-)

     I69.892   **Facial weakness** following other cerebrovascular disease
         Facial droop following other cerebrovascular disease

     I69.893   **Ataxia** following other cerebrovascular disease

     I69.898   **Other sequelae** of other cerebrovascular disease
         Alteration of sensation following other cerebrovascular disease
         Disturbance of vision following other cerebrovascular disease
         Use additional code to identify the sequelae

● **I69.9**   **Sequelae of unspecified cerebrovascular diseases**

     Excludes1   sequelae of stroke (I69.3)
         sequelae of traumatic intracranial injury (S06.-)

     I69.90   **Unspecified** sequelae of unspecified cerebrovascular disease

● **I69.91**   **Cognitive deficits** following **unspecified** cerebrovascular disease

     I69.910   **Attention and concentration** deficit following unspecified cerebrovascular disease

     I69.911   **Memory** deficit following unspecified cerebrovascular disease

     I69.912   **Visuospatial** deficit and spatial neglect following unspecified cerebrovascular disease

     I69.913   **Psychomotor** deficit following unspecified cerebrovascular disease

     I69.914   **Frontal lobe and executive function** deficit following unspecified cerebrovascular disease

     I69.915   **Cognitive social or emotional** deficit following unspecified cerebrovascular disease

     I69.918   **Other** symptoms and signs involving cognitive functions following unspecified cerebrovascular disease

     I69.919   **Unspecified** symptoms and signs involving cognitive functions following unspecified cerebrovascular disease

● **I69.92**   **Speech and language** deficits following **unspecified** cerebrovascular disease

     I69.920   **Aphasia** following unspecified cerebrovascular disease

     I69.921   **Dysphasia** following unspecified cerebrovascular disease

     I69.922   **Dysarthria** following unspecified cerebrovascular disease

     I69.923   **Fluency disorder** following unspecified cerebrovascular disease
         Stuttering following unspecified cerebrovascular disease

     I69.928   **Other speech and language deficits** following unspecified cerebrovascular disease

● I69.93   **Monoplegia of upper limb following unspecified cerebrovascular disease**

     I69.931   Monoplegia of upper limb following unspecified cerebrovascular disease affecting right dominant side

     I69.932   Monoplegia of upper limb following unspecified cerebrovascular disease affecting left dominant side

     I69.933   Monoplegia of upper limb following unspecified cerebrovascular disease affecting right non-dominant side

     I69.934   Monoplegia of upper limb following unspecified cerebrovascular disease affecting left non-dominant side

     I69.939   Monoplegia of upper limb following unspecified cerebrovascular disease affecting unspecified side

● I69.94   **Monoplegia of lower limb following unspecified cerebrovascular disease**

     I69.941   Monoplegia of lower limb following unspecified cerebrovascular disease affecting right dominant side

     I69.942   Monoplegia of lower limb following unspecified cerebrovascular disease affecting left dominant side

     I69.943   Monoplegia of lower limb following unspecified cerebrovascular disease affecting right non-dominant side

     I69.944   Monoplegia of lower limb following unspecified cerebrovascular disease affecting left non-dominant side

     I69.949   Monoplegia of lower limb following unspecified cerebrovascular disease affecting unspecified side

● I69.95   **Hemiplegia and hemiparesis following unspecified cerebrovascular disease**

     I69.951   Hemiplegia and hemiparesis following unspecified cerebrovascular disease affecting right dominant side

     I69.952   Hemiplegia and hemiparesis following unspecified cerebrovascular disease affecting left dominant side

     I69.953   Hemiplegia and hemiparesis following unspecified cerebrovascular disease affecting right non-dominant side

     I69.954   Hemiplegia and hemiparesis following unspecified cerebrovascular disease affecting left non-dominant side

     I69.959   Hemiplegia and hemiparesis following unspecified cerebrovascular disease affecting unspecified side

● I69.96   **Other paralytic syndrome following unspecified cerebrovascular disease**

Use additional code to identify type of paralytic syndrome, such as:
locked-in state (G83.5)
quadriplegia (G82.5-)

Excludes1   hemiplegia/hemiparesis following unspecified cerebrovascular disease (I69.95-)
monoplegia of lower limb following unspecified cerebrovascular disease (I69.94-)
monoplegia of upper limb following unspecified cerebrovascular disease (I69.93-)

     I69.961   Other paralytic syndrome following unspecified cerebrovascular disease affecting right dominant side

     I69.962   Other paralytic syndrome following unspecified cerebrovascular disease affecting left dominant side

     I69.963   Other paralytic syndrome following unspecified cerebrovascular disease affecting right non-dominant side

     I69.964   Other paralytic syndrome following unspecified cerebrovascular disease affecting left non-dominant side

     I69.965   Other paralytic syndrome following unspecified cerebrovascular disease, bilateral

     I69.969   Other paralytic syndrome following unspecified cerebrovascular disease affecting unspecified side

● I69.99   **Other sequelae of unspecified cerebrovascular disease**

     I69.990   **Apraxia following unspecified cerebrovascular disease**

     I69.991   **Dysphagia following unspecified cerebrovascular disease**
Use additional code to identify the type of dysphagia, if known (R13.1-)

     I69.992   **Facial weakness following unspecified cerebrovascular disease**
Facial droop following unspecified cerebrovascular disease

     I69.993   **Ataxia following unspecified cerebrovascular disease**

     I69.998   **Other sequelae following unspecified cerebrovascular disease**
Alteration in sensation following unspecified cerebrovascular disease
Disturbance of vision following unspecified cerebrovascular disease
Use additional code to identify the sequelae

DISEASES OF ARTERIES, ARTERIOLES AND CAPILLARIES (I70-I79)

● I70   **Atherosclerosis**

   Includes   arteriolosclerosis
arterial degeneration
arteriosclerosis
arteriosclerotic vascular disease
arteriovascular degeneration
atheroma
endarteritis deformans or obliterans
senile arteritis
senile endarteritis
vascular degeneration

Use additional code to identify:
exposure to environmental tobacco smoke (Z77.22)
history of tobacco dependence (Z87.891)
occupational exposure to environmental tobacco smoke (Z57.31)
tobacco dependence (F17.-)
tobacco use (Z72.0)

   Excludes2   arteriosclerotic cardiovascular disease (I25.1-)
arteriosclerotic heart disease (I25.1-)
atheroembolism (I75.-)
cerebral atherosclerosis (I67.2)
coronary atherosclerosis (I25.1-)
mesenteric atherosclerosis (K55.1)
precerebral atherosclerosis (I67.2)
primary pulmonary atherosclerosis (I27.0)

I70.0   **Atherosclerosis of aorta**   A

I70.1   **Atherosclerosis of renal artery**   A
Goldblatt's kidney

   Excludes2   atherosclerosis of renal arterioles (I12.-)

★ **(See Plates 500, 501, and 502 on pages 60 – 62.)**

● **I70.2** **Atherosclerosis of native arteries of the extremities**
Mönckeberg's (medial) sclerosis
Use additional code, if applicable, to identify chronic total occlusion of artery of extremity (I70.92)
Excludes2   atherosclerosis of bypass graft of extremities (I70.30-I70.79)

● **I70.20** **Unspecified atherosclerosis of native arteries of extremities**
I70.201   Unspecified atherosclerosis of native arteries of extremities, right leg   A
I70.202   Unspecified atherosclerosis of native arteries of extremities, left leg   A
I70.203   Unspecified atherosclerosis of native arteries of extremities, bilateral legs   A
I70.208   Unspecified atherosclerosis of native arteries of extremities, other extremity   A
I70.209   Unspecified atherosclerosis of native arteries of extremities, unspecified extremity   A

● **I70.21** **Atherosclerosis of native arteries of extremities with intermittent claudication**
I70.211   Atherosclerosis of native arteries of extremities with intermittent claudication, right leg   A
I70.212   Atherosclerosis of native arteries of extremities with intermittent claudication, left leg   A
I70.213   Atherosclerosis of native arteries of extremities with intermittent claudication, bilateral legs   A
I70.218   Atherosclerosis of native arteries of extremities with intermittent claudication, other extremity   A
I70.219   Atherosclerosis of native arteries of extremities with intermittent claudication, unspecified extremity   A

● **I70.22** **Atherosclerosis of native arteries of extremities with rest pain**
Includes   any condition classifiable to I70.21-
I70.221   Atherosclerosis of native arteries of extremities with rest pain, right leg   A
I70.222   Atherosclerosis of native arteries of extremities with rest pain, left leg   A
I70.223   Atherosclerosis of native arteries of extremities with rest pain, bilateral legs   A
I70.228   Atherosclerosis of native arteries of extremities with rest pain, other extremity   A
I70.229   Atherosclerosis of native arteries of extremities with rest pain, unspecified extremity   A

● **I70.23** **Atherosclerosis of native arteries of right leg with ulceration**
Includes   any condition classifiable to I70.211 and I70.221
Use additional code to identify severity of ulcer (L97.-)
I70.231   Atherosclerosis of native arteries of right leg with ulceration of thigh   A
I70.232   Atherosclerosis of native arteries of right leg with ulceration of calf   A
I70.233   Atherosclerosis of native arteries of right leg with ulceration of ankle   A

I70.234   Atherosclerosis of native arteries of right leg with ulceration of heel and midfoot   A
Atherosclerosis of native arteries of right leg with ulceration of plantar surface of midfoot
I70.235   Atherosclerosis of native arteries of right leg with ulceration of other part of foot   A
Atherosclerosis of native arteries of right leg extremities with ulceration of toe
I70.238   Atherosclerosis of native arteries of right leg with ulceration of other part of lower right leg   A
I70.239   Atherosclerosis of native arteries of right leg with ulceration of unspecified site   A

● **I70.24** **Atherosclerosis of native arteries of left leg with ulceration**
Includes   any condition classifiable to I70.212 and I70.222
Use additional code to identify severity of ulcer (L97.-)
I70.241   Atherosclerosis of native arteries of left leg with ulceration of thigh   A
I70.242   Atherosclerosis of native arteries of left leg with ulceration of calf   A
I70.243   Atherosclerosis of native arteries of left leg with ulceration of ankle   A
I70.244   Atherosclerosis of native arteries of left leg with ulceration of heel and midfoot   A
Atherosclerosis of native arteries of left leg with ulceration of plantar surface of midfoot
I70.245   Atherosclerosis of native arteries of left leg with ulceration of other part of foot   A
Atherosclerosis of native arteries of left leg extremities with ulceration of toe
I70.248   Atherosclerosis of native arteries of left leg with ulceration of other part of lower left leg   A
I70.249   Atherosclerosis of native arteries of left leg with ulceration of unspecified site   A

I70.25 **Atherosclerosis of native arteries of other extremities with ulceration**   A
Includes   any condition classifiable to I70.218 and I70.228
Use additional code to identify the severity of the ulcer (L98.49-)

● **I70.26** **Atherosclerosis of native arteries of extremities with gangrene**
Includes   any condition classifiable to I70.21-, I70.22-, I70.23-, I70.24-, and I70.25-
Use additional code to identify the severity of any ulcer (L97.-, L98.49-), if applicable
I70.261   Atherosclerosis of native arteries of extremities with gangrene, right leg   A
I70.262   Atherosclerosis of native arteries of extremities with gangrene, left leg   A
I70.263   Atherosclerosis of native arteries of extremities with gangrene, bilateral legs   A
I70.268   Atherosclerosis of native arteries of extremities with gangrene, other extremity   A
I70.269   Atherosclerosis of native arteries of extremities with gangrene, unspecified extremity   A

▶ New   ⇒ Revised   ~~deleted~~ Deleted   Excludes 1   Excludes 2   Includes   Use additional   Code first   Code also   Key words
OGCR Official Guidelines   X Assign placeholder X   ● Use Additional Character(s)   ▶ Manifestation Code   **Coding Clinic**

● I70.29 Other atherosclerosis of native arteries of extremities

    I70.291 Other atherosclerosis of native arteries of extremities, right leg   A

    I70.292 Other atherosclerosis of native arteries of extremities, left leg   A

    I70.293 Other atherosclerosis of native arteries of extremities, bilateral legs   A

    I70.298 Other atherosclerosis of native arteries of extremities, other extremity   A

    I70.299 Other atherosclerosis of native arteries of extremities, unspecified extremity   A

● I70.3 Atherosclerosis of unspecified type of bypass graft(s) of the extremities

    Use additional code, if applicable, to identify chronic total occlusion of artery of extremity (I70.92)

    Excludes1 embolism or thrombus of bypass graft(s) of extremities (T82.8-)

● I70.30 Unspecified atherosclerosis of unspecified type of bypass graft(s) of the extremities

    70.301 Unspecified atherosclerosis of unspecified type of bypass graft(s) of the extremities, right leg   A

    I70.302 Unspecified atherosclerosis of unspecified type of bypass graft(s) of the extremities, left leg   A

    I70.303 Unspecified atherosclerosis of unspecified type of bypass graft(s) of the extremities, bilateral legs   A

    I70.308 Unspecified atherosclerosis of unspecified type of bypass graft(s) of the extremities, other extremity   A

    I70.309 Unspecified atherosclerosis of unspecified type of bypass graft(s) of the extremities, unspecified extremity   A

● I70.31 Atherosclerosis of unspecified type of bypass graft(s) of the extremities with intermittent claudication

    I70.311 Atherosclerosis of unspecified type of bypass graft(s) of the extremities with intermittent claudication, right leg   A

    I70.312 Atherosclerosis of unspecified type of bypass graft(s) of the extremities with intermittent claudication, left leg   A

    I70.313 Atherosclerosis of unspecified type of bypass graft(s) of the extremities with intermittent claudication, bilateral legs   A

    I70.318 Atherosclerosis of unspecified type of bypass graft(s) of the extremities with intermittent claudication, other extremity   A

    I70.319 Atherosclerosis of unspecified type of bypass graft(s) of the extremities with intermittent claudication, unspecified extremity   A

● I70.32 Atherosclerosis of unspecified type of bypass graft(s) of the extremities with rest pain

    Includes any condition classifiable to I70.31-

    I70.321 Atherosclerosis of unspecified type of bypass graft(s) of the extremities with rest pain, right leg   A

    I70.322 Atherosclerosis of unspecified type of bypass graft(s) of the extremities with rest pain, left leg   A

    I70.323 Atherosclerosis of unspecified type of bypass graft(s) of the extremities with rest pain, bilateral legs   A

    I70.328 Atherosclerosis of unspecified type of bypass graft(s) of the extremities with rest pain, other extremity   A

    I70.329 Atherosclerosis of unspecified type of bypass graft(s) of the extremities with rest pain, unspecified extremity   A

● I70.33 Atherosclerosis of unspecified type of bypass graft(s) of the right leg with ulceration

    Includes any condition classifiable to I70.311 and I70.321

    Use additional code to identify severity of ulcer (L97.-)

    I70.331 Atherosclerosis of unspecified type of bypass graft(s) of the right leg with ulceration of thigh   A

    I70.332 Atherosclerosis of unspecified type of bypass graft(s) of the right leg with ulceration of calf   A

    I70.333 Atherosclerosis of unspecified type of bypass graft(s) of the right leg with ulceration of ankle   A

    I70.334 Atherosclerosis of unspecified type of bypass graft(s) of the right leg with ulceration of heel and midfoot   A

        Atherosclerosis of unspecified type of bypass graft(s) of right leg with ulceration of plantar surface of midfoot

    I70.335 Atherosclerosis of unspecified type of bypass graft(s) of the right leg with ulceration of other part of foot   A

        Atherosclerosis of unspecified type of bypass graft(s) of the right leg with ulceration of toe

    I70.338 Atherosclerosis of unspecified type of bypass graft(s) of the right leg with ulceration of other part of lower leg   A

    I70.339 Atherosclerosis of unspecified type of bypass graft(s) of the right leg with ulceration of unspecified site   A

● I70.34 Atherosclerosis of unspecified type of bypass graft(s) of the left leg with ulceration

    Includes any condition classifiable to I70.312 and I70.322

    Use additional code to identify severity of ulcer (L97.-)

    I70.341 Atherosclerosis of unspecified type of bypass graft(s) of the left leg with ulceration of thigh   A

    I70.342 Atherosclerosis of unspecified type of bypass graft(s) of the left leg with ulceration of calf   A

    I70.343 Atherosclerosis of unspecified type of bypass graft(s) of the left leg with ulceration of ankle   A

    I70.344 Atherosclerosis of unspecified type of bypass graft(s) of the left leg with ulceration of heel and midfoot   A

        Atherosclerosis of unspecified type of bypass graft(s) of left leg with ulceration of plantar surface of midfoot

    I70.345 Atherosclerosis of unspecified type of bypass graft(s) of the left leg with ulceration of other part of foot   A

        Atherosclerosis of unspecified type of bypass graft(s) of the left leg with ulceration of toe

    I70.348 Atherosclerosis of unspecified type of bypass graft(s) of the left leg with ulceration of other part of lower leg   A

    I70.349 Atherosclerosis of unspecified type of bypass graft(s) of the left leg with ulceration of unspecified site   A

CHAPTER 9 (I00-I99)

I70.35 Atherosclerosis of unspecified type of bypass graft(s) of other extremity with ulceration   A

> **Includes**   any condition classifiable to I70.318 and I70.328

> Use additional code to identify severity of ulcer (L98.49-)

● **I70.36** Atherosclerosis of unspecified type of bypass graft(s) of the extremities with gangrene

> **Includes**   any condition classifiable to I70.31-, I70.32-, I70.33-, I70.34-, I70.35

> Use additional code to identify the severity of any ulcer (L97.-, L98.49-), if applicable

     I70.361 Atherosclerosis of unspecified type of bypass graft(s) of the extremities with gangrene, right leg   A

     I70.362 Atherosclerosis of unspecified type of bypass graft(s) of the extremities with gangrene, left leg   A

     I70.363 Atherosclerosis of unspecified type of bypass graft(s) of the extremities with gangrene, bilateral legs   A

     I70.368 Atherosclerosis of unspecified type of bypass graft(s) of the extremities with gangrene, other extremity   A

     I70.369 Atherosclerosis of unspecified type of bypass graft(s) of the extremities with gangrene, unspecified extremity   A

● **I70.39** Other atherosclerosis of unspecified type of bypass graft(s) of the extremities

     I70.391 Other atherosclerosis of unspecified type of bypass graft(s) of the extremities, right leg   A

     I70.392 Other atherosclerosis of unspecified type of bypass graft(s) of the extremities, left leg   A

     I70.393 Other atherosclerosis of unspecified type of bypass graft(s) of the extremities, bilateral legs   A

     I70.398 Other atherosclerosis of unspecified type of bypass graft(s) of the extremities, other extremity   A

     I70.399 Other atherosclerosis of unspecified type of bypass graft(s) of the extremities, unspecified extremity   A

● **I70.4** Atherosclerosis of autologous vein bypass graft(s) of the extremities

> Use additional code, if applicable, to identify chronic total occlusion of artery of extremity (I70.92)

● **I70.40** Unspecified atherosclerosis of autologous vein bypass graft(s) of the extremities

     I70.401 Unspecified atherosclerosis of autologous vein bypass graft(s) of the extremities, right leg   A

     I70.402 Unspecified atherosclerosis of autologous vein bypass graft(s) of the extremities, left leg   A

     I70.403 Unspecified atherosclerosis of autologous vein bypass graft(s) of the extremities, bilateral legs   A

     I70.408 Unspecified atherosclerosis of autologous vein bypass graft(s) of the extremities, other extremity   A

     I70.409 Unspecified atherosclerosis of autologous vein bypass graft(s) of the extremities, unspecified extremity   A

● **I70.41** Atherosclerosis of autologous vein bypass graft(s) of the extremities with intermittent claudication

     I70.411 Atherosclerosis of autologous vein bypass graft(s) of the extremities with intermittent claudication, right leg   A

     I70.412 Atherosclerosis of autologous vein bypass graft(s) of the extremities with intermittent claudication, left leg   A

     I70.413 Atherosclerosis of autologous vein bypass graft(s) of the extremities with intermittent claudication, bilateral legs   A

     I70.418 Atherosclerosis of autologous vein bypass graft(s) of the extremities with intermittent claudication, other extremity   A

     I70.419 Atherosclerosis of autologous vein bypass graft(s) of the extremities with intermittent claudication, unspecified extremity   A

● **I70.42** Atherosclerosis of autologous vein bypass graft(s) of the extremities with rest pain

> **Includes**   any condition classifiable to I70.41-

     I70.421 Atherosclerosis of autologous vein bypass graft(s) of the extremities with rest pain, right leg   A

     I70.422 Atherosclerosis of autologous vein bypass graft(s) of the extremities with rest pain, left leg   A

     I70.423 Atherosclerosis of autologous vein bypass graft(s) of the extremities with rest pain, bilateral legs   A

     I70.428 Atherosclerosis of autologous vein bypass graft(s) of the extremities with rest pain, other extremity   A

     I70.429 Atherosclerosis of autologous vein bypass graft(s) of the extremities with rest pain, unspecified extremity   A

● **I70.43** Atherosclerosis of autologous vein bypass graft(s) of the right leg with ulceration

> **Includes**   any condition classifiable to I70.411 and I70.421

> Use additional code to identify severity of ulcer (L97.-)

     I70.431 Atherosclerosis of autologous vein bypass graft(s) of the right leg with ulceration of thigh   A

     I70.432 Atherosclerosis of autologous vein bypass graft(s) of the right leg with ulceration of calf   A

     I70.433 Atherosclerosis of autologous vein bypass graft(s) of the right leg with ulceration of ankle   A

     I70.434 Atherosclerosis of autologous vein bypass graft(s) of the right leg with ulceration of heel and midfoot   A

> Atherosclerosis of autologous vein bypass graft(s) of right leg with ulceration of plantar surface of midfoot

     I70.435 Atherosclerosis of autologous vein bypass graft(s) of the right leg with ulceration of other part of foot   A

> Atherosclerosis of autologous vein bypass graft(s) of right leg with ulceration of toe

▶ New   ⇒ Revised   ~~deleted~~ Deleted   Excludes 1   Excludes 2   Includes   Use additional   Code first   Code also   Key words

OGCR Official Guidelines   X Assign placeholder X   ● Use Additional Character(s)   ▶ Manifestation Code   **Coding Clinic**

I70.438 Atherosclerosis of autologous vein bypass graft(s) of the right leg with ulceration of other part of lower leg A

I70.439 Atherosclerosis of autologous vein bypass graft(s) of the right leg with ulceration of unspecified site A

● I70.44 Atherosclerosis of autologous vein bypass graft(s) of the left leg with ulceration

Includes any condition classifiable to I70.412 and I70.422

Use additional code to identify severity of ulcer (L97.-)

I70.441 Atherosclerosis of autologous vein bypass graft(s) of the left leg with ulceration of thigh A

I70.442 Atherosclerosis of autologous vein bypass graft(s) of the left leg with ulceration of calf A

I70.443 Atherosclerosis of autologous vein bypass graft(s) of the left leg with ulceration of ankle A

I70.444 Atherosclerosis of autologous vein bypass graft(s) of the left leg with ulceration of heel and midfoot A
Atherosclerosis of autologous vein bypass graft(s) of left leg with ulceration of plantar surface of midfoot

I70.445 Atherosclerosis of autologous vein bypass graft(s) of the left leg with ulceration of other part of foot A
Atherosclerosis of autologous vein bypass graft(s) of left leg with ulceration of toe

I70.448 Atherosclerosis of autologous vein bypass graft(s) of the left leg with ulceration of other part of lower leg A

I70.449 Atherosclerosis of autologous vein bypass graft(s) of the left leg with ulceration of unspecified site A

I70.45 Atherosclerosis of autologous vein bypass graft(s) of other extremity with ulceration A

Includes any condition classifiable to I70.418, I70.428, and I70.438

Use additional code to identify severity of ulcer (L98.49-)

● I70.46 Atherosclerosis of autologous vein bypass graft(s) of the extremities with gangrene

Includes any condition classifiable to I70.41-, I70.42-, and I70.43-, I70.44-, I70.45

Use additional code to identify the severity of any ulcer (L97.-, L98.49-), if applicable

I70.461 Atherosclerosis of autologous vein bypass graft(s) of the extremities with gangrene, right leg A

I70.462 Atherosclerosis of autologous vein bypass graft(s) of the extremities with gangrene, left leg A

I70.463 Atherosclerosis of autologous vein bypass graft(s) of the extremities with gangrene, bilateral legs A

I70.468 Atherosclerosis of autologous vein bypass graft(s) of the extremities with gangrene, other extremity A

I70.469 Atherosclerosis of autologous vein bypass graft(s) of the extremities with gangrene, unspecified extremity A

● I70.49 Other atherosclerosis of autologous vein bypass graft(s) of the extremities

I70.491 Other atherosclerosis of autologous vein bypass graft(s) of the extremities, right leg A

I70.492 Other atherosclerosis of autologous vein bypass graft(s) of the extremities, left leg A

I70.493 Other atherosclerosis of autologous vein bypass graft(s) of the extremities, bilateral legs A

I70.498 Other atherosclerosis of autologous vein bypass graft(s) of the extremities, other extremity A

I70.499 Other atherosclerosis of autologous vein bypass graft(s) of the extremities, unspecified extremity A

● I70.5 Atherosclerosis of nonautologous biological bypass graft(s) of the extremities

Use additional code, if applicable, to identify chronic total occlusion of artery of extremity (I70.92)

● I70.50 Unspecified atherosclerosis of nonautologous biological bypass graft(s) of the extremities

I70.501 Unspecified atherosclerosis of nonautologous biological bypass graft(s) of the extremities, right leg A

I70.502 Unspecified atherosclerosis of nonautologous biological bypass graft(s) of the extremities, left leg A

I70.503 Unspecified atherosclerosis of nonautologous biological bypass graft(s) of the extremities, bilateral legs A

I70.508 Unspecified atherosclerosis of nonautologous biological bypass graft(s) of the extremities, other extremity A

I70.509 Unspecified atherosclerosis of nonautologous biological bypass graft(s) of the extremities, unspecified extremity A

● I70.51 Atherosclerosis of nonautologous biological bypass graft(s) of the extremities intermittent claudication

I70.511 Atherosclerosis of nonautologous biological bypass graft(s) of the extremities with intermittent claudication, right leg A

I70.512 Atherosclerosis of nonautologous biological bypass graft(s) of the extremities with intermittent claudication, left leg A

I70.513 Atherosclerosis of nonautologous biological bypass graft(s) of the extremities with intermittent claudication, bilateral legs A

I70.518 Atherosclerosis of nonautologous biological bypass graft(s) of the extremities with intermittent claudication, other extremity A

I70.519 Atherosclerosis of nonautologous biological bypass graft(s) of the extremities with intermittent claudication, unspecified extremity A

CHAPTER 9 (I00-I99)

● **I70.52**   Atherosclerosis of nonautologous biological
bypass graft(s) of the extremities with rest pain
> **Includes**   any condition classifiable to
> I70.51-

I70.521   Atherosclerosis of nonautologous
biological bypass graft(s) of the
extremities with rest pain, right leg   A

I70.522   Atherosclerosis of nonautologous
biological bypass graft(s) of the
extremities with rest pain, left leg   A

I70.523   Atherosclerosis of nonautologous
biological bypass graft(s) of the
extremities with rest pain, bilateral
legs   A

I70.528   Atherosclerosis of nonautologous
biological bypass graft(s) of the
extremities with rest pain, other
extremity   A

I70.529   Atherosclerosis of nonautologous
biological bypass graft(s) of the
extremities with rest pain, unspecified
extremity   A

● **I70.53**   Atherosclerosis of nonautologous biological
bypass graft(s) of the right leg with ulceration
> **Includes**   any condition classifiable to
> I70.511 and I70.521

Use additional code to identify severity of
ulcer (L97.-)

I70.531   Atherosclerosis of nonautologous
biological bypass graft(s) of the right
leg with ulceration of thigh   A

I70.532   Atherosclerosis of nonautologous
biological bypass graft(s) of the right
leg with ulceration of calf   A

I70.533   Atherosclerosis of nonautologous
biological bypass graft(s) of the right
leg with ulceration of ankle   A

I70.534   Atherosclerosis of nonautologous
biological bypass graft(s) of the
right leg with ulceration of heel and
midfoot   A
> Atherosclerosis of nonautologous
> biological bypass graft(s) of
> right leg with ulceration of
> plantar surface of midfoot

I70.535   Atherosclerosis of nonautologous
biological bypass graft(s) of the right
leg with ulceration of other part of
foot   A
> Atherosclerosis of nonautologous
> biological bypass graft(s) of the
> right leg with ulceration of toe

I70.538   Atherosclerosis of nonautologous
biological bypass graft(s) of the right
leg with ulceration of other part of
lower leg   A

I70.539   Atherosclerosis of nonautologous
biological bypass graft(s) of the right
leg with ulceration of unspecified
site   A

● **I70.54**   Atherosclerosis of nonautologous biological
bypass graft(s) of the left leg with ulceration
> **Includes**   any condition classifiable to
> I70.512 and I70.522

Use additional code to identify severity of
ulcer (L97.-)

I70.541   Atherosclerosis of nonautologous
biological bypass graft(s) of the left
leg with ulceration of thigh   A

I70.542   Atherosclerosis of nonautologous
biological bypass graft(s) of the left
leg with ulceration of calf   A

I70.543   Atherosclerosis of nonautologous
biological bypass graft(s) of the left
leg with ulceration of ankle   A

I70.544   Atherosclerosis of nonautologous
biological bypass graft(s) of the
left leg with ulceration of heel and
midfoot   A
> Atherosclerosis of nonautologous
> biological bypass graft(s) of left
> leg with ulceration of plantar
> surface of midfoot

I70.545   Atherosclerosis of nonautologous
biological bypass graft(s) of the left
leg with ulceration of other part of
foot   A
> Atherosclerosis of nonautologous
> biological bypass graft(s) of the
> left leg with ulceration of toe

I70.548   Atherosclerosis of nonautologous
biological bypass graft(s) of the left
leg with ulceration of other part of
lower leg   A

I70.549   Atherosclerosis of nonautologous
biological bypass graft(s) of the left
leg with ulceration of unspecified
site   A

I70.55   Atherosclerosis of nonautologous biological
bypass graft(s) of other extremity with
ulceration   A
> **Includes**   any condition classifiable to
> I70.518, I70.528, and I70.538

Use additional code to identify severity of
ulcer (L98.49)

● **I70.56**   Atherosclerosis of nonautologous biological
bypass graft(s) of the extremities with gangrene
> **Includes**   any condition classifiable to
> I70.51-, I70.52-, and I70.53-,
> I70.54-, I70.55

Use additional code to identify the severity of
any ulcer (L97.-, L98.49-), if applicable

I70.561   Atherosclerosis of nonautologous
biological bypass graft(s) of the
extremities with gangrene, right leg   A

I70.562   Atherosclerosis of nonautologous
biological bypass graft(s) of the
extremities with gangrene, left leg   A

I70.563   Atherosclerosis of nonautologous
biological bypass graft(s) of the
extremities with gangrene, bilateral
legs   A

I70.568   Atherosclerosis of nonautologous
biological bypass graft(s) of the
extremities with gangrene, other
extremity   A

I70.569   Atherosclerosis of nonautologous
biological bypass graft(s) of
the extremities with gangrene,
unspecified extremity   A

● **I70.59**   Other atherosclerosis of nonautologous
biological bypass graft(s) of the extremities

I70.591   Other atherosclerosis of
nonautologous biological bypass
graft(s) of the extremities, right leg   A

I70.592   Other atherosclerosis of
nonautologous biological bypass
graft(s) of the extremities, left leg   A

I70.593   Other atherosclerosis of
nonautologous biological bypass
graft(s) of the extremities, bilateral
legs   A

▶ New   ⇒ Revised   deleted Deleted   Excludes 1   Excludes 2   Includes   Use additional   Code first   Code also   Key words

OGCR Official Guidelines   X Assign placeholder X   ● Use Additional Character(s)   ⟩ Manifestation Code   **Coding Clinic**

I70.598   Other atherosclerosis of nonautologous biological bypass graft(s) of the extremities, other extremity A

I70.599   Other atherosclerosis of nonautologous biological bypass graft(s) of the extremities, unspecified extremity A

● **I70.6** Atherosclerosis of nonbiological bypass graft(s) of the extremities

    Use additional code, if applicable, to identify chronic total occlusion of artery of extremity (I70.92)

● **I70.60** Unspecified atherosclerosis of nonbiological bypass graft(s) of the extremities

    I70.601   Unspecified atherosclerosis of nonbiological bypass graft(s) of the extremities, right leg A

    I70.602   Unspecified atherosclerosis of nonbiological bypass graft(s) of the extremities, left leg A

    I70.603   Unspecified atherosclerosis of nonbiological bypass graft(s) of the extremities, bilateral legs A

    I70.608   Unspecified atherosclerosis of nonbiological bypass graft(s) of the extremities, other extremity A

    I70.609   Unspecified atherosclerosis of nonbiological bypass graft(s) of the extremities, unspecified extremity A

● **I70.61** Atherosclerosis of nonbiological bypass graft(s) of the extremities with intermittent claudication

    I70.611   Atherosclerosis of nonbiological bypass graft(s) of the extremities with intermittent claudication, right leg A

    I70.612   Atherosclerosis of nonbiological bypass graft(s) of the extremities with intermittent claudication, left leg A

    I70.613   Atherosclerosis of nonbiological bypass graft(s) of the extremities with intermittent claudication, bilateral legs A

    I70.618   Atherosclerosis of nonbiological bypass graft(s) of the extremities with intermittent claudication, other extremity A

    I70.619   Atherosclerosis of nonbiological bypass graft(s) of the extremities with intermittent claudication, unspecified extremity A

● **I70.62** Atherosclerosis of nonbiological bypass graft(s) of the extremities with rest pain

    Includes   any condition classifiable to I70.61-

    I70.621   Atherosclerosis of nonbiological bypass graft(s) of the extremities with rest pain, right leg A

    I70.622   Atherosclerosis of nonbiological bypass graft(s) of the extremities with rest pain, left leg A

    I70.623   Atherosclerosis of nonbiological bypass graft(s) of the extremities with rest pain, bilateral legs A

    I70.628   Atherosclerosis of nonbiological bypass graft(s) of the extremities with rest pain, other extremity A

    I70.629   Atherosclerosis of nonbiological bypass graft(s) of the extremities with rest pain, unspecified extremity A

● **I70.63** Atherosclerosis of nonbiological bypass graft(s) of the right leg with ulceration

    Includes   any condition classifiable to I70.611 and I70.621

    Use additional code to identify severity of ulcer (L97.-)

    I70.631   Atherosclerosis of nonbiological bypass graft(s) of the right leg with ulceration of thigh A

    I70.632   Atherosclerosis of nonbiological bypass graft(s) of the right leg with ulceration of calf A

    I70.633   Atherosclerosis of nonbiological bypass graft(s) of the right leg with ulceration of ankle A

    I70.634   Atherosclerosis of nonbiological bypass graft(s) of the right leg with ulceration of heel and midfoot A

        Atherosclerosis of nonbiological bypass graft(s) of right leg with ulceration of plantar surface of midfoot

    I70.635   Atherosclerosis of nonbiological bypass graft(s) of the right leg with ulceration of other part of foot A

        Atherosclerosis of nonbiological bypass graft(s) of the right leg with ulceration of toe

    I70.638   Atherosclerosis of nonbiological bypass graft(s) of the right leg with ulceration of other part of lower leg A

    I70.639   Atherosclerosis of nonbiological bypass graft(s) of the right leg with ulceration of unspecified site A

● **I70.64** Atherosclerosis of nonbiological bypass graft(s) of the left leg with ulceration

    Includes   any condition classifiable to I70.612 and I70.622

    Use additional code to identify severity of ulcer (L97.-)

    I70.641   Atherosclerosis of nonbiological bypass graft(s) of the left leg with ulceration of thigh A

    I70.642   Atherosclerosis of nonbiological bypass graft(s) of the left leg with ulceration of calf A

    I70.643   Atherosclerosis of nonbiological bypass graft(s) of the left leg with ulceration of ankle A

    I70.644   Atherosclerosis of nonbiological bypass graft(s) of the left leg with ulceration of heel and midfoot A

        Atherosclerosis of nonbiological bypass graft(s) of left leg with ulceration of plantar surface of midfoot

    I70.645   Atherosclerosis of nonbiological bypass graft(s) of the left leg with ulceration of other part of foot A

        Atherosclerosis of nonbiological bypass graft(s) of the left leg with ulceration of toe

    I70.648   Atherosclerosis of nonbiological bypass graft(s) of the left leg with ulceration of other part of lower leg A

    I70.649   Atherosclerosis of nonbiological bypass graft(s) of the left leg with ulceration of unspecified site A

CHAPTER 9 (I00-I99)

I70.65   **Atherosclerosis of nonbiological bypass graft(s) of other extremity with ulceration**   A
>   **Includes**   any condition classifiable to I70.618 and I70.628
>
>   Use additional code to identify severity of ulcer (L98.49-)

● **I70.66**   **Atherosclerosis of nonbiological bypass graft(s) of the extremities with gangrene**
>   **Includes**   any condition classifiable to I70.61-, I70.62-, I70.63-, I70.64-, I70.65
>
>   Use additional code to identify the severity of any ulcer (L97.-, L98.49-), if applicable

    I70.661   Atherosclerosis of nonbiological bypass graft(s) of the extremities with gangrene, right leg   A

    I70.662   Atherosclerosis of nonbiological bypass graft(s) of the extremities with gangrene, left leg   A

    I70.663   Atherosclerosis of nonbiological bypass graft(s) of the extremities with gangrene, bilateral legs   A

    I70.668   Atherosclerosis of nonbiological bypass graft(s) of the extremities with gangrene, other extremity   A

    I70.669   Atherosclerosis of nonbiological bypass graft(s) of the extremities with gangrene, unspecified extremity   A

● **I70.69**   **Other atherosclerosis of nonbiological bypass graft(s) of the extremities**

    I70.691   Other atherosclerosis of nonbiological bypass graft(s) of the extremities, right leg   A

    I70.692   Other atherosclerosis of nonbiological bypass graft(s) of the extremities, left leg   A

    I70.693   Other atherosclerosis of nonbiological bypass graft(s) of the extremities, bilateral legs   A

    I70.698   Other atherosclerosis of nonbiological bypass graft(s) of the extremities, other extremity   A

    I70.699   Other atherosclerosis of nonbiological bypass graft(s) of the extremities, unspecified extremity   A

● **I70.7**   **Atherosclerosis of other type of bypass graft(s) of the extremities**
>   Use additional code, if applicable, to identify chronic total occlusion of artery of extremity (I70.92)

● **I70.70**   **Unspecified atherosclerosis of other type of bypass graft(s) of the extremities**

    I70.701   Unspecified atherosclerosis of other type of bypass graft(s) of the extremities, right leg   A

    I70.702   Unspecified atherosclerosis of other type of bypass graft(s) of the extremities, left leg   A

    I70.703   Unspecified atherosclerosis of other type of bypass graft(s) of the extremities, bilateral legs   A

    I70.708   Unspecified atherosclerosis of other type of bypass graft(s) of the extremities, other extremity   A

    I70.709   Unspecified atherosclerosis of other type of bypass graft(s) of the extremities, unspecified extremity   A

● **I70.71**   **Atherosclerosis of other type of bypass graft(s) of the extremities with intermittent claudication**

    I70.711   Atherosclerosis of other type of bypass graft(s) of the extremities with intermittent claudication, right leg   A

    I70.712   Atherosclerosis of other type of bypass graft(s) of the extremities with intermittent claudication, left leg   A

    I70.713   Atherosclerosis of other type of bypass graft(s) of the extremities with intermittent claudication, bilateral legs   A

    I70.718   Atherosclerosis of other type of bypass graft(s) of the extremities with intermittent claudication, other extremity   A

    I70.719   Atherosclerosis of other type of bypass graft(s) of the extremities with intermittent claudication, unspecified extremity   A

● **I70.72**   **Atherosclerosis of other type of bypass graft(s) of the extremities with rest pain**
>   **Includes**   any condition classifiable to I70.71-

    I70.721   Atherosclerosis of other type of bypass graft(s) of the extremities with rest pain, right leg   A

    I70.722   Atherosclerosis of other type of bypass graft(s) of the extremities with rest pain, left leg   A

    I70.723   Atherosclerosis of other type of bypass graft(s) of the extremities with rest pain, bilateral legs   A

    I70.728   Atherosclerosis of other type of bypass graft(s) of the extremities with rest pain, other extremity   A

    I70.729   Atherosclerosis of other type of bypass graft(s) of the extremities with rest pain, unspecified extremity   A

● **I70.73**   **Atherosclerosis of other type of bypass graft(s) of the right leg with ulceration**
>   **Includes**   any condition classifiable to I70.711 and I70.721
>
>   Use additional code to identify severity of ulcer (L97.-)

    I70.731   Atherosclerosis of other type of bypass graft(s) of the right leg with ulceration of thigh   A

    I70.732   Atherosclerosis of other type of bypass graft(s) of the right leg with ulceration of calf   A

    I70.733   Atherosclerosis of other type of bypass graft(s) of the right leg with ulceration of ankle   A

    I70.734   Atherosclerosis of other type of bypass graft(s) of the right leg with ulceration of heel and midfoot   A
>   Atherosclerosis of other type of bypass graft(s) of right leg with ulceration of plantar surface of midfoot

    I70.735   Atherosclerosis of other type of bypass graft(s) of the right leg with ulceration of other part of foot   A
>   Atherosclerosis of other type of bypass graft(s) of right leg with ulceration of toe

    I70.738   Atherosclerosis of other type of bypass graft(s) of the right leg with ulceration of other part of lower leg   A

    I70.739   Atherosclerosis of other type of bypass graft(s) of the right leg with ulceration of unspecified site   A

▶ New   ⇒ Revised   ~~deleted~~ Deleted   Excludes 1   Excludes 2   Includes   Use additional   Code first   Code also   Key words
OGCR Official Guidelines   X Assign placeholder X   ● Use Additional Character(s)   ▶ Manifestation Code   **Coding Clinic**

● **I70.74** **Atherosclerosis of other type of bypass graft(s) of the left leg with ulceration**

> **Includes**   any condition classifiable to I70.712 and I70.722

Use additional code to identify severity of ulcer (L97.-)

I70.741   **Atherosclerosis of other type of bypass graft(s) of the left leg with ulceration of thigh**   A

I70.742   **Atherosclerosis of other type of bypass graft(s) of the left leg with ulceration of calf**   A

I70.743   **Atherosclerosis of other type of bypass graft(s) of the left leg with ulceration of ankle**   A

I70.744   **Atherosclerosis of other type of bypass graft(s) of the left leg with ulceration of heel and midfoot**   A

> Atherosclerosis of other type of bypass graft(s) of left leg with ulceration of plantar surface of midfoot

I70.745   **Atherosclerosis of other type of bypass graft(s) of the left leg with ulceration of other part of foot**   A

> Atherosclerosis of other type of bypass graft(s) of left leg with ulceration of toe

I70.748   **Atherosclerosis of other type of bypass graft(s) of the left leg with ulceration of other part of lower leg**   A

I70.749   **Atherosclerosis of other type of bypass graft(s) of the left leg with ulceration of unspecified site**   A

I70.75   **Atherosclerosis of other type of bypass graft(s) of other extremity with ulceration**   A

> **Includes**   any condition classifiable to I70.718 and I70.728

Use additional code to identify severity of ulcer (L98.49)

● **I70.76** **Atherosclerosis of other type of bypass graft(s) of the extremities with gangrene**

> **Includes**   any condition classifiable to I70.71-, I70.72-, I70.73-, I70.74-, I70.75

Use additional code to identify the severity of any ulcer (L97.-, L98.49-), if applicable

I70.761   **Atherosclerosis of other type of bypass graft(s) of the extremities with gangrene, right leg**   A

I70.762   **Atherosclerosis of other type of bypass graft(s) of the extremities with gangrene, left leg**   A

I70.763   **Atherosclerosis of other type of bypass graft(s) of the extremities with gangrene, bilateral legs**   A

I70.768   **Atherosclerosis of other type of bypass graft(s) of the extremities with gangrene, other extremity**   A

I70.769   **Atherosclerosis of other type of bypass graft(s) of the extremities with gangrene, unspecified extremity**   A

● **I70.79** **Other atherosclerosis of other type of bypass graft(s) of the extremities**

I70.791   **Other atherosclerosis of other type of bypass graft(s) of the extremities, right leg**   A

I70.792   **Other atherosclerosis of other type of bypass graft(s) of the extremities, left leg**   A

I70.793   **Other atherosclerosis of other type of bypass graft(s) of the extremities, bilateral legs**   A

I70.798   **Other atherosclerosis of other type of bypass graft(s) of the extremities, other extremity**   A

I70.799   **Other atherosclerosis of other type of bypass graft(s) of the extremities, unspecified extremity**   A

I70.8   **Atherosclerosis of other arteries**   A

● **I70.9** **Other and unspecified atherosclerosis**

I70.90   **Unspecified atherosclerosis**   A

I70.91   **Generalized atherosclerosis**   A

I70.92   **Chronic total occlusion of artery of the extremities**   A

> Complete occlusion of artery of the extremities
> Total occlusion of artery of the extremities
>
> *Code first atherosclerosis of arteries of the extremities (I70.2-, I70.3-, I70.4-, I70.5-, I70.6-, I70.7-)*

● **I71** **Aortic aneurysm and dissection**

> **Excludes1**   aortic ectasia (I77.81-)
> syphilitic aortic aneurysm (A52.01)
> traumatic aortic aneurysm (S25.09, S35.09)

● **I71.0** **Dissection of aorta**

I71.00   **Dissection of unspecified site of aorta**

I71.01   **Dissection of thoracic aorta**

I71.02   **Dissection of abdominal aorta**

I71.03   **Dissection of thoracoabdominal aorta**

I71.1   **Thoracic aortic aneurysm, ruptured**

I71.2   **Thoracic aortic aneurysm, without rupture**

I71.3   **Abdominal aortic aneurysm, ruptured**

I71.4   **Abdominal aortic aneurysm, without rupture**

I71.5   **Thoracoabdominal aortic aneurysm, ruptured**

I71.6   **Thoracoabdominal aortic aneurysm, without rupture**

I71.8   **Aortic aneurysm of unspecified site, ruptured**

> Rupture of aorta NOS

I71.9   **Aortic aneurysm of unspecified site, without rupture**

> Aneurysm of aorta
> Dilatation of aorta
> Hyaline necrosis of aorta

● **I72** **Other aneurysm**

> **Includes**   aneurysm (cirsoid) (false) (ruptured)
>
> **Excludes2**   acquired aneurysm (I77.0)
> aneurysm (of) aorta (I71.-)
> aneurysm (of) arteriovenous NOS (Q27.3-)
> carotid artery dissection (I77.71)
> cerebral (nonruptured) aneurysm (I67.1)
> coronary aneurysm (I25.4)
> coronary artery dissection (I25.42)
> dissection of artery NEC (I77.79)
> dissection of precerebral artery, congenital (nonruptured) (Q28.1)
> heart aneurysm (I25.3)
> iliac artery dissection (I77.72)
> precerebral artery, congential (nonruptured) (Q28.1)
> pulmonary artery aneurysm (I28.1)
> renal artery dissection (I77.73)
> retinal aneurysm (H35.0)
> ruptured cerebral aneurysm (I60.7)
> varicose aneurysm (I77.0)
> vertebral artery dissection (I77.74)

I72.0   **Aneurysm of carotid artery**

> Aneurysm of common carotid artery
> Aneurysm of external carotid artery
> Aneurysm of internal carotid artery, extracranial portion

> **Excludes1**   aneurysm of internal carotid artery, intracranial portion (I67.1)
> aneurysm of internal carotid artery NOS (I67.1)

I72.1   **Aneurysm of artery of upper extremity**

I72.2   **Aneurysm of renal artery**

I72.3   **Aneurysm of iliac artery**

I72.4   **Aneurysm of artery of lower extremity**

CHAPTER 9 (I00–I99)

I72.5   **Aneurysm of other precerebral arteries**
Aneurysm of basilar artery (trunk)

     Excludes2   aneurysm of carotid artery (I72.0)
                   aneurysm of vertebral artery (I72.6)
                   dissection of carotid artery (I77.71)
                   dissection of other precerebral arteries
                      (I77.75)
                   dissection of vertebral artery (I77.74)

Coding Clinic 2016, Q4, P28

I72.6   **Aneurysm of vertebral artery**

     Excludes2   dissection of vertebral artery (I77.74)

Coding Clinic 2016, Q4, P28

I72.8   **Aneurysm of other specified arteries**

I72.9   **Aneurysm of unspecified site**

● **I73**   **Other peripheral vascular diseases**

     Excludes2   chilblains (T69.1)
                   frostbite (T33-T34)
                   immersion hand or foot (T69.0-)
                   spasm of cerebral artery (G45.9)

● **I73.0**   **Raynaud's syndrome**
*Diminishing oxygen supply to fingers, toes, nose, and ears
when exposed to temperature changes or stress*
Raynaud's disease
Raynaud's phenomenon (secondary)

   I73.00   **Raynaud's syndrome without gangrene**

   I73.01   **Raynaud's syndrome with gangrene**

I73.1   **Thromboangiitis obliterans [Buerger's disease]**
*Inflammatory occlusive disease resulting in poor circulation
to the legs, feet, and sometimes the hands due to
progressive inflammatory narrowing and eventually
obliteration of the small arteries*

● **I73.8**   **Other specified peripheral vascular diseases**

     Excludes1   diabetic (peripheral) angiopathy
                      (E08-E13 with .51-.52)

   I73.81   **Erythromelalgia**

   I73.89   **Other specified peripheral vascular diseases**
Acrocyanosis
Erythrocyanosis
Simple acroparesthesia [Schultze's type]
Vasomotor acroparesthesia [Nothnagel's type]

I73.9   **Peripheral vascular disease, unspecified**
Intermittent claudication
Peripheral angiopathy NOS
Spasm of artery

     Excludes1   atherosclerosis of the extremities
                      (I70.2--I70.7-)

● **I74**   **Arterial embolism and thrombosis**

     Includes   embolic infarction
                embolic occlusion
                thrombotic infarction
                thrombotic occlusion

Code first embolism and thrombosis complicating abortion or
ectopic or molar pregnancy (O00-O07, O08.2)
embolism and thrombosis complicating pregnancy, childbirth
and the puerperium (O88.-)

     Excludes2   atheroembolism (I75.-)
                   basilar embolism and thrombosis (I63.0-I63.2,
                      I65.1)
                   carotid embolism and thrombosis (I63.0-I63.2,
                      I65.2)
                   cerebral embolism and thrombosis (I63.3-I63.5,
                      I66.-)
                   coronary embolism and thrombosis (I21-I25)
                   mesenteric embolism and thrombosis (K55.0-)
                   ophthalmic embolism and thrombosis (H34.-)
                   precerebral embolism and thrombosis NOS
                      (I63.0-I63.2, I65.9)
                   pulmonary embolism and thrombosis (I26.-)
                   renal embolism and thrombosis (N28.0)
                   retinal embolism and thrombosis (H34.-)
                   septic embolism and thrombosis (I76)
                   vertebral embolism and thrombosis (I63.0-I63.2,
                      I65.0)

● **I74.0**   **Embolism and thrombosis of abdominal aorta**

   I74.01   **Saddle embolus of abdominal aorta**

   I74.09   **Other arterial embolism and thrombosis of
abdominal aorta**
Aortic bifurcation syndrome
Aortoiliac obstruction
Leriche's syndrome

● **I74.1**   **Embolism and thrombosis of other and unspecified parts
of aorta**

   I74.10   **Embolism and thrombosis of unspecified parts
of aorta**

   I74.11   **Embolism and thrombosis of thoracic aorta**

   I74.19   **Embolism and thrombosis of other parts of
aorta**

I74.2   **Embolism and thrombosis of arteries of the upper
extremities**

I74.3   **Embolism and thrombosis of arteries of the lower
extremities**

I74.4   **Embolism and thrombosis of arteries of extremities,
unspecified**
Peripheral arterial embolism NOS

I74.5   **Embolism and thrombosis of iliac artery**

I74.8   **Embolism and thrombosis of other arteries**

I74.9   **Embolism and thrombosis of unspecified artery**

Figure 9-5   Raynaud's syndrome. (From Hallett: Comprehensive Vascular
and Endovascular Surgery, ed 2, Philadelphia, Mosby Ltd., 2010)

Item 9–9   An **embolus** is a mass of undissolved matter present in the blood
that is transported by the blood current. A **thrombus** is a blood clot that occludes
or shuts off a vessel. When a thrombus is dislodged, it becomes an embolus.

Embolus

Figure 9-6   An arterial embolus.

▶ New   ⇒ Revised   ~~deleted~~ Deleted   Excludes 1   Excludes 2   Includes   Use additional   Code first   Code also   Key words

OGCR Official Guidelines   X Assign placeholder X   ● Use Additional Character(s)   ▶ Manifestation Code   **Coding Clinic**

● **I75**   **Atheroembolism**

     Includes   atherothrombotic microembolism
                  cholesterol embolism

   ● **I75.0**   **Atheroembolism of extremities**

     ● **I75.01**   **Atheroembolism of upper extremity**

         I75.011   **Atheroembolism of right upper extremity**

         I75.012   **Atheroembolism of left upper extremity**

         I75.013   **Atheroembolism of bilateral upper extremities**

         I75.019   **Atheroembolism of unspecified upper extremity**

     ● **I75.02**   **Atheroembolism of lower extremity**

         I75.021   **Atheroembolism of right lower extremity**

         I75.022   **Atheroembolism of left lower extremity**

         I75.023   **Atheroembolism of bilateral lower extremities**

         I75.029   **Atheroembolism of unspecified lower extremity**

   ● **I75.8**   **Atheroembolism of other sites**

         I75.81   **Atheroembolism of kidney**

             Use additional code for any associated acute kidney failure and chronic kidney disease (N17.-, N18.-)

         I75.89   **Atheroembolism of other site**

I76   **Septic arterial embolism**

     Code first underlying infection, such as:
       infective endocarditis (I33.0)
       lung abscess (J85.-)

     Use additional code to identify the site of the embolism (I74.-)

     Excludes2   septic pulmonary embolism (I26.01, I26.90)

● **I77**   **Other disorders of arteries and arterioles**

     Excludes2   collagen (vascular) diseases (M30-M36)
                 hypersensitivity angiitis (M31.0)
                 pulmonary artery (I28.-)

   I77.0   **Arteriovenous fistula, acquired**

       Aneurysmal varix
       Arteriovenous aneurysm, acquired

     Excludes1   arteriovenous aneurysm NOS (Q27.3-)
                 presence of arteriovenous shunt (fistula) for dialysis (Z99.2)
                 traumatic - see injury of blood vessel by body region

     Excludes2   cerebral (I67.1)
                 coronary (I25.4)

   I77.1   **Stricture of artery**
       Narrowing of artery

   I77.2   **Rupture of artery**
       Erosion of artery
       Fistula of artery
       Ulcer of artery

     Excludes1   traumatic rupture of artery - see injury of blood vessel by body region

   I77.3   **Arterial fibromuscular dysplasia**
       Fibromuscular hyperplasia (of) carotid artery
       Fibromuscular hyperplasia (of) renal artery

   I77.4   **Celiac artery compression syndrome**

   I77.5   **Necrosis of artery**

   I77.6   **Arteritis, unspecified**
       Aortitis NOS
       Endarteritis NOS

     Excludes1   arteritis or endarteritis:
                 aortic arch (M31.4)
                 cerebral NEC (I67.7)
                 coronary (I25.89)
                 deformans (I70.-)
                 ⟾giant cell (M31.5, M31.6)
                 obliterans (I70.-)
                 senile (I70.-)

   ● **I77.7**   **Other arterial dissection**

     Excludes2   dissection of aorta (I71.0-)
                 dissection of coronary artery (I25.42)

     I77.70   **Dissection of unspecified artery**
         Coding Clinic 2016, Q4, P28

     I77.71   **Dissection of carotid artery**

     I77.72   **Dissection of iliac artery**

     I77.73   **Dissection of renal artery**

     I77.74   **Dissection of vertebral artery**

         Excludes2   aneurysm of vertebral artery (I72.6)

     I77.75   **Dissection of other precerebral arteries**
         Dissection of basilar artery (trunk)

         Excludes2   aneurysm of carotid artery (I72.0)
                 aneurysm of other precerebral arteries (I72.5)
                 aneurysm of vertebral artery (I72.6) dissection of carotid artery (I77.71)
                 dissection of vertebral artery (I77.74)

         Coding Clinic 2016, Q4, P28

     I77.76   **Dissection of artery of upper extremity**
         Coding Clinic 2016, Q4, P28

     I77.77   **Dissection of artery of lower extremity**
         Coding Clinic 2016, Q4, P28

     I77.79   **Dissection of other specified artery**
         Coding Clinic 2016, Q4, P28

   ● **I77.8**   **Other specified disorders of arteries and arterioles**

     I77.81   **Aortic ectasia**
         Ectasis aorta

         Excludes1   aortic aneurysm and dissection (I71.0-)

         I77.810   **Thoracic aortic ectasia**
         I77.811   **Abdominal aortic ectasia**
         I77.812   **Thoracoabdominal aortic ectasia**
         I77.819   **Aortic ectasia, unspecified site**

     I77.89   **Other specified disorders of arteries and arterioles**

   I77.9   **Disorder of arteries and arterioles, unspecified**

● **I78**   **Diseases of capillaries**

   I78.0   **Hereditary hemorrhagic telangiectasia**
       Rendu-Osler-Weber disease

   I78.1   **Nevus, non-neoplastic**

       Araneus nevus   Spider nevus
       Senile nevus   Stellar nevus

     Excludes1   nevus NOS (D22.-)
                 vascular NOS (Q82.5)

     Excludes2   blue nevus (D22.-)
                 flammeus nevus (Q82.5)
                 hairy nevus (D22.-)
                 melanocytic nevus (D22.-)
                 pigmented nevus (D22.-)
                 portwine nevus (Q82.5)
                 sanguineous nevus (Q82.5)
                 strawberry nevus (Q82.5)
                 verrucous nevus (Q82.5)

   I78.8   **Other diseases of capillaries**

   I78.9   **Disease of capillaries, unspecified**

CHAPTER 9 (I00-I99)

● **I79   Disorders of arteries, arterioles and capillaries in diseases classified elsewhere**

▷ *I79.0   Aneurysm of aorta in diseases classified elsewhere*
     Code first underlying disease
     Excludes1   syphilitic aneurysm (A52.01)

▷ *I79.1   Aortitis in diseases classified elsewhere*
     Code first underlying disease
     Excludes1   syphilitic aortitis (A52.02)

▷ *I79.8   Other disorders of arteries, arterioles and capillaries in diseases classified elsewhere*
     Code first underlying disease, such as:
         amyloidosis (E85.-)
     Excludes1   diabetic (peripheral) angiopathy
                 (E08-E13 with .51-.52)
                 syphilitic endarteritis (A52.09)
                 tuberculous endarteritis (A18.89)

DISEASES OF VEINS, LYMPHATIC VESSELS AND LYMPH NODES, NOT ELSEWHERE CLASSIFIED (I80-I89)

● **I80   Phlebitis and thrombophlebitis**
     Inflammation of a vein with infiltration of walls (phlebitis).
     Includes   endophlebitis
                 inflammation, vein
                 periphlebitis
                 suppurative phlebitis
     Code first phlebitis and thrombophlebitis complicating
         abortion, ectopic or molar pregnancy (O00-O07, O08.7)
         phlebitis and thrombophlebitis complicating pregnancy,
             childbirth and the puerperium (O22.-, O87.-)
     Excludes1   venous embolism and thrombosis of lower
                 extremities (I82.4-, I82.5-, I82.81-)

● **I80.0   Phlebitis and thrombophlebitis of superficial vessels of lower extremities**
     Phlebitis and thrombophlebitis of femoropopliteal vein

     I80.00   Phlebitis and thrombophlebitis of superficial vessels of unspecified lower extremity

     I80.01   Phlebitis and thrombophlebitis of superficial vessels of right lower extremity

     I80.02   Phlebitis and thrombophlebitis of superficial vessels of left lower extremity

     I80.03   Phlebitis and thrombophlebitis of superficial vessels of lower extremities, bilateral

● **I80.1   Phlebitis and thrombophlebitis of femoral vein**

     I80.10   Phlebitis and thrombophlebitis of unspecified femoral vein

     I80.11   Phlebitis and thrombophlebitis of right femoral vein

     I80.12   Phlebitis and thrombophlebitis of left femoral vein

     I80.13   Phlebitis and thrombophlebitis of femoral vein, bilateral

● **I80.2   Phlebitis and thrombophlebitis of other and unspecified deep vessels of lower extremities**

● I80.20   Phlebitis and thrombophlebitis of unspecified deep vessels of lower extremities

     I80.201   Phlebitis and thrombophlebitis of unspecified deep vessels of right lower extremity

     I80.202   Phlebitis and thrombophlebitis of unspecified deep vessels of left lower extremity

     I80.203   Phlebitis and thrombophlebitis of unspecified deep vessels of lower extremities, bilateral

     I80.209   Phlebitis and thrombophlebitis of unspecified deep vessels of unspecified lower extremity

● I80.21   Phlebitis and thrombophlebitis of iliac vein

     I80.211   Phlebitis and thrombophlebitis of right iliac vein

     I80.212   Phlebitis and thrombophlebitis of left iliac vein

     I80.213   Phlebitis and thrombophlebitis of iliac vein, bilateral

     I80.219   Phlebitis and thrombophlebitis of unspecified iliac vein

● I80.22   Phlebitis and thrombophlebitis of popliteal vein

     I80.221   Phlebitis and thrombophlebitis of right popliteal vein

     I80.222   Phlebitis and thrombophlebitis of left popliteal vein

     I80.223   Phlebitis and thrombophlebitis of popliteal vein, bilateral

     I80.229   Phlebitis and thrombophlebitis of unspecified popliteal vein

● I80.23   Phlebitis and thrombophlebitis of tibial vein

     I80.231   Phlebitis and thrombophlebitis of right tibial vein

     I80.232   Phlebitis and thrombophlebitis of left tibial vein

     I80.233   Phlebitis and thrombophlebitis of tibial vein, bilateral

     I80.239   Phlebitis and thrombophlebitis of unspecified tibial vein

● I80.29   Phlebitis and thrombophlebitis of other deep vessels of lower extremities

     I80.291   Phlebitis and thrombophlebitis of other deep vessels of right lower extremity

     I80.292   Phlebitis and thrombophlebitis of other deep vessels of left lower extremity

     I80.293   Phlebitis and thrombophlebitis of other deep vessels of lower extremity, bilateral

     I80.299   Phlebitis and thrombophlebitis of other deep vessels of unspecified lower extremity

I80.3   Phlebitis and thrombophlebitis of lower extremities, unspecified

I80.8   Phlebitis and thrombophlebitis of other sites

I80.9   Phlebitis and thrombophlebitis of unspecified site

● **I81   Portal vein thrombosis**
     Portal (vein) obstruction
     Excludes2   hepatic vein thrombosis (I82.0)
                 phlebitis of portal vein (K75.1)

● **I82   Other venous embolism and thrombosis**
     Code first venous embolism and thrombosis complicating:
         abortion, ectopic or molar pregnancy (O00-O07, O08.7)
         pregnancy, childbirth and the puerperium (O22.-, O87.-)
     Excludes2   venous embolism and thrombosis (of):
                 cerebral (I63.6, I67.6)
                 coronary (I21-I25)
                 intracranial and intraspinal, septic or NOS
                     (G08)
                 intracranial, nonpyogenic (I67.6)
                 intraspinal, nonpyogenic (G95.1)
                 mesenteric (K55.0-)
                 portal (I81)
                 pulmonary (I26.-)

I82.0   **Budd-Chiari syndrome**
     Hepatic vein thrombosis

I82.1   **Thrombophlebitis migrans**
     "White leg" is the other term to describe a migrating thrombus.

▶ New   ⟹ Revised   ~~deleted~~ Deleted   Excludes 1   Excludes 2   Includes   Use additional   Code first   Code also   Key words
OGCR Official Guidelines   X Assign placeholder X   ● Use Additional Character(s)   ▷ Manifestation Code   **Coding Clinic**

● **I82.2**   **Embolism and thrombosis of vena cava and other thoracic veins**

  ● **I82.21**   **Embolism and thrombosis of superior vena cava**

     I82.210   **Acute embolism and thrombosis of superior vena cava**
       Embolism and thrombosis of superior vena cava NOS

     I82.211   **Chronic embolism and thrombosis of superior vena cava**

  ● **I82.22**   **Embolism and thrombosis of inferior vena cava**

     I82.220   **Acute embolism and thrombosis of inferior vena cava**
       Embolism and thrombosis of inferior vena cava NOS

     I82.221   **Chronic embolism and thrombosis of inferior vena cava**

  ● **I82.29**   **Embolism and thrombosis of other thoracic veins**
     Embolism and thrombosis of brachiocephalic (innominate) vein

     I82.290   **Acute embolism and thrombosis of other thoracic veins**

     I82.291   **Chronic embolism and thrombosis of other thoracic veins**

   I82.3   **Embolism and thrombosis of renal vein**

● **I82.4**   **Acute embolism and thrombosis of deep veins of lower extremity**

    I82.40   **Acute embolism and thrombosis of unspecified deep veins of lower extremity**
     Deep vein thrombosis NOS
     DVT NOS

     Excludes1   acute embolism and thrombosis of unspecified deep veins of distal lower extremity (I82.4Z-)
       acute embolism and thrombosis of unspecified deep veins of proximal lower extremity (I82.4Y-)

     I82.401   **Acute embolism and thrombosis of unspecified deep veins of right lower extremity**

     I82.402   **Acute embolism and thrombosis of unspecified deep veins of left lower extremity**

     I82.403   **Acute embolism and thrombosis of unspecified deep veins of lower extremity, bilateral**

     I82.409   **Acute embolism and thrombosis of unspecified deep veins of unspecified lower extremity**

  ● **I82.41**   **Acute embolism and thrombosis of femoral vein**

     I82.411   **Acute embolism and thrombosis of right femoral vein**

     I82.412   **Acute embolism and thrombosis of left femoral vein**

     I82.413   **Acute embolism and thrombosis of femoral vein, bilateral**

     I82.419   **Acute embolism and thrombosis of unspecified femoral vein**

  ● **I82.42**   **Acute embolism and thrombosis of iliac vein**

     I82.421   **Acute embolism and thrombosis of right iliac vein**

     I82.422   **Acute embolism and thrombosis of left iliac vein**

     I82.423   **Acute embolism and thrombosis of iliac vein, bilateral**

     I82.429   **Acute embolism and thrombosis of unspecified iliac vein**

● **I82.43**   **Acute embolism and thrombosis of popliteal vein**

     I82.431   **Acute embolism and thrombosis of right popliteal vein**

     I82.432   **Acute embolism and thrombosis of left popliteal vein**

     I82.433   **Acute embolism and thrombosis of popliteal vein, bilateral**

     I82.439   **Acute embolism and thrombosis of unspecified popliteal vein**

● **I82.44**   **Acute embolism and thrombosis of tibial vein**

     I82.441   **Acute embolism and thrombosis of right tibial vein**

     I82.442   **Acute embolism and thrombosis of left tibial vein**

     I82.443   **Acute embolism and thrombosis of tibial vein, bilateral**

     I82.449   **Acute embolism and thrombosis of unspecified tibial vein**

● **I82.49**   **Acute embolism and thrombosis of other specified deep vein of lower extremity**

     I82.491   **Acute embolism and thrombosis of other specified deep vein of right lower extremity**

     I82.492   **Acute embolism and thrombosis of other specified deep vein of left lower extremity**

     I82.493   **Acute embolism and thrombosis of other specified deep vein of lower extremity, bilateral**

     I82.499   **Acute embolism and thrombosis of other specified deep vein of unspecified lower extremity**

● **I82.4Y**   **Acute embolism and thrombosis of unspecified deep veins of proximal lower extremity**
     Acute embolism and thrombosis of deep vein of thigh NOS
     Acute embolism and thrombosis of deep vein of upper leg NOS

     I82.4Y1   **Acute embolism and thrombosis of unspecified deep veins of right proximal lower extremity**

     I82.4Y2   **Acute embolism and thrombosis of unspecified deep veins of left proximal lower extremity**

     I82.4Y3   **Acute embolism and thrombosis of unspecified deep veins of proximal lower extremity, bilateral**

     I82.4Y9   **Acute embolism and thrombosis of unspecified deep veins of unspecified proximal lower extremity**

● **I82.4Z**   **Acute embolism and thrombosis of unspecified deep veins of distal lower extremity**
     Acute embolism and thrombosis of deep vein of calf NOS
     Acute embolism and thrombosis of deep vein of lower leg NOS

     I82.4Z1   **Acute embolism and thrombosis of unspecified deep veins of right distal lower extremity**

     I82.4Z2   **Acute embolism and thrombosis of unspecified deep veins of left distal lower extremity**

     I82.4Z3   **Acute embolism and thrombosis of unspecified deep veins of distal lower extremity, bilateral**

     I82.4Z9   **Acute embolism and thrombosis of unspecified deep veins of unspecified distal lower extremity**

CHAPTER 9 (I00–I99)

● **I82.5**   Chronic embolism and thrombosis of deep veins of lower extremity

     Use additional code, if applicable, for associated long-term (current) use of anticoagulants (Z79.01)

     Excludes1   personal history of venous embolism and thrombosis (Z86.718)

● **I82.50**   Chronic embolism and thrombosis of unspecified deep veins of lower extremity

     Excludes1   chronic embolism and thrombosis of unspecified deep veins of distal lower extremity (I82.5Z-)
         chronic embolism and thrombosis of unspecified deep veins of proximal lower extremity (I82.5Y-)

     I82.501   Chronic embolism and thrombosis of unspecified deep veins of right lower extremity

     I82.502   Chronic embolism and thrombosis of unspecified deep veins of left lower extremity

     I82.503   Chronic embolism and thrombosis of unspecified deep veins of lower extremity, bilateral

     I82.509   Chronic embolism and thrombosis of unspecified deep veins of unspecified lower extremity

● **I82.51**   Chronic embolism and thrombosis of femoral vein

     I82.511   Chronic embolism and thrombosis of right femoral vein

     I82.512   Chronic embolism and thrombosis of left femoral vein

     I82.513   Chronic embolism and thrombosis of femoral vein, bilateral

     I82.519   Chronic embolism and thrombosis of unspecified femoral vein

● **I82.52**   Chronic embolism and thrombosis of iliac vein

     I82.521   Chronic embolism and thrombosis of right iliac vein

     I82.522   Chronic embolism and thrombosis of left iliac vein

     I82.523   Chronic embolism and thrombosis of iliac vein, bilateral

     I82.529   Chronic embolism and thrombosis of unspecified iliac vein

● **I82.53**   Chronic embolism and thrombosis of popliteal vein

     I82.531   Chronic embolism and thrombosis of right popliteal vein

     I82.532   Chronic embolism and thrombosis of left popliteal vein

     I82.533   Chronic embolism and thrombosis of popliteal vein, bilateral

     I82.539   Chronic embolism and thrombosis of unspecified popliteal vein

● **I82.54**   Chronic embolism and thrombosis of tibial vein

     I82.541   Chronic embolism and thrombosis of right tibial vein

     I82.542   Chronic embolism and thrombosis of left tibial vein

     I82.543   Chronic embolism and thrombosis of tibial vein, bilateral

     I82.549   Chronic embolism and thrombosis of unspecified tibial vein

● **I82.59**   Chronic embolism and thrombosis of other specified deep vein of lower extremity

     I82.591   Chronic embolism and thrombosis of other specified deep vein of right lower extremity

     I82.592   Chronic embolism and thrombosis of other specified deep vein of left lower extremity

     I82.593   Chronic embolism and thrombosis of other specified deep vein of lower extremity, bilateral

     I82.599   Chronic embolism and thrombosis of other specified deep vein of unspecified lower extremity

● **I82.5Y**   Chronic embolism and thrombosis of unspecified deep veins of proximal lower extremity

     Chronic embolism and thrombosis of deep veins of thigh NOS
     Chronic embolism and thrombosis of deep veins of upper leg NOS

     I82.5Y1   Chronic embolism and thrombosis of unspecified deep veins of right proximal lower extremity

     I82.5Y2   Chronic embolism and thrombosis of unspecified deep veins of left proximal lower extremity

     I82.5Y3   Chronic embolism and thrombosis of unspecified deep veins of proximal lower extremity, bilateral

     I82.5Y9   Chronic embolism and thrombosis of unspecified deep veins of unspecified proximal lower extremity

● **I82.5Z**   Chronic embolism and thrombosis of unspecified deep veins of distal lower extremity

     Chronic embolism and thrombosis of deep veins of calf NOS
     Chronic embolism and thrombosis of deep veins of lower leg NOS

     I82.5Z1   Chronic embolism and thrombosis of unspecified deep veins of right distal lower extremity

     I82.5Z2   Chronic embolism and thrombosis of unspecified deep veins of left distal lower extremity

     I82.5Z3   Chronic embolism and thrombosis of unspecified deep veins of distal lower extremity, bilateral

     I82.5Z9   Chronic embolism and thrombosis of unspecified deep veins of unspecified distal lower extremity

---

Item 9–10   Varicose/Varicosities (varix = singular, varices = plural): Enlarged, engorged, tortuous, twisted vascular vessels (veins, arteries, lymphatics). As such, the condition can present in various parts of the body, although the most familiar locations are the lower extremities. A common complication of varices is thrombophlebitis. Varicosities of the anus and rectum are called hemorrhoids.

Figure 9-7   Varicose veins of the legs. (Getty Image)

▶ New   ⇒ Revised   ~~deleted~~ Deleted   Excludes 1   Excludes 2   Includes   Use additional   Code first   Code also   Key words

OGCR Official Guidelines   X Assign placeholder X   ● Use Additional Character(s)   ▶ Manifestation Code   **Coding Clinic**

● **I82.6**   **Acute embolism and thrombosis of veins of upper extremity**

    ● **I82.60**   Acute embolism and thrombosis of unspecified veins of upper extremity

       I82.601   Acute embolism and thrombosis of unspecified veins of right upper extremity

       I82.602   Acute embolism and thrombosis of unspecified veins of left upper extremity

       I82.603   Acute embolism and thrombosis of unspecified veins of upper extremity, bilateral

       I82.609   Acute embolism and thrombosis of unspecified veins of unspecified upper extremity

    ● **I82.61**   Acute embolism and thrombosis of superficial veins of upper extremity

       Acute embolism and thrombosis of antecubital vein

       Acute embolism and thrombosis of basilic vein

       Acute embolism and thrombosis of cephalic vein

       I82.611   Acute embolism and thrombosis of superficial veins of right upper extremity

       I82.612   Acute embolism and thrombosis of superficial veins of left upper extremity

       I82.613   Acute embolism and thrombosis of superficial veins of upper extremity, bilateral

       I82.619   Acute embolism and thrombosis of superficial veins of unspecified upper extremity

    ● **I82.62**   Acute embolism and thrombosis of deep veins of upper extremity

       Acute embolism and thrombosis of brachial vein

       Acute embolism and thrombosis of radial vein

       Acute embolism and thrombosis of ulnar vein

       I82.621   Acute embolism and thrombosis of deep veins of right upper extremity

       I82.622   Acute embolism and thrombosis of deep veins of left upper extremity

       I82.623   Acute embolism and thrombosis of deep veins of upper extremity, bilateral

       I82.629   Acute embolism and thrombosis of deep veins of unspecified upper extremity

● **I82.7**   **Chronic embolism and thrombosis of veins of upper extremity**

    Use additional code, if applicable, for associated long-term (current) use of anticoagulants (Z79.01)

    Excludes1   personal history of venous embolism and thrombosis (Z86.718)

    ● **I82.70**   Chronic embolism and thrombosis of unspecified veins of upper extremity

       I82.701   Chronic embolism and thrombosis of unspecified veins of right upper extremity

       I82.702   Chronic embolism and thrombosis of unspecified veins of left upper extremity

       I82.703   Chronic embolism and thrombosis of unspecified veins of upper extremity, bilateral

       I82.709   Chronic embolism and thrombosis of unspecified veins of unspecified upper extremity

● **I82.71**   Chronic embolism and thrombosis of superficial veins of upper extremity

    Chronic embolism and thrombosis of antecubital vein

    Chronic embolism and thrombosis of basilic vein

    Chronic embolism and thrombosis of cephalic vein

       I82.711   Chronic embolism and thrombosis of superficial veins of right upper extremity

       I82.712   Chronic embolism and thrombosis of superficial veins of left upper extremity

       I82.713   Chronic embolism and thrombosis of superficial veins of upper extremity, bilateral

       I82.719   Chronic embolism and thrombosis of superficial veins of unspecified upper extremity

● **I82.72**   Chronic embolism and thrombosis of deep veins of upper extremity

    Chronic embolism and thrombosis of brachial vein

    Chronic embolism and thrombosis of radial vein

    Chronic embolism and thrombosis of ulnar vein

       I82.721   Chronic embolism and thrombosis of deep veins of right upper extremity

       I82.722   Chronic embolism and thrombosis of deep veins of left upper extremity

       I82.723   Chronic embolism and thrombosis of deep veins of upper extremity, bilateral

       I82.729   Chronic embolism and thrombosis of deep veins of unspecified upper extremity

● **I82.A**   Embolism and thrombosis of axillary vein

    ● **I82.A1**   Acute embolism and thrombosis of axillary vein

       I82.A11   Acute embolism and thrombosis of right axillary vein

       I82.A12   Acute embolism and thrombosis of left axillary vein

       I82.A13   Acute embolism and thrombosis of axillary vein, bilateral

       I82.A19   Acute embolism and thrombosis of unspecified axillary vein

    ● **I82.A2**   Chronic embolism and thrombosis of axillary vein

       I82.A21   Chronic embolism and thrombosis of right axillary vein

       I82.A22   Chronic embolism and thrombosis of left axillary vein

       I82.A23   Chronic embolism and thrombosis of axillary vein, bilateral

       I82.A29   Chronic embolism and thrombosis of unspecified axillary vein

● **I82.B**   Embolism and thrombosis of subclavian vein

    ● **I82.B1**   Acute embolism and thrombosis of subclavian vein

       I82.B11   Acute embolism and thrombosis of right subclavian vein

       I82.B12   Acute embolism and thrombosis of left subclavian vein

       I82.B13   Acute embolism and thrombosis of subclavian vein, bilateral

       I82.B19   Acute embolism and thrombosis of unspecified subclavian vein

CHAPTER 9 (I00–I99)

● **I82.B2**   Chronic embolism and thrombosis of subclavian vein

     I82.B21   Chronic embolism and thrombosis of right subclavian vein

     I82.B22   Chronic embolism and thrombosis of left subclavian vein

     I82.B23   Chronic embolism and thrombosis of subclavian vein, bilateral

     I82.B29   Chronic embolism and thrombosis of unspecified subclavian vein

● **I82.C**   Embolism and thrombosis of internal jugular vein

   ● **I82.C1**   Acute embolism and thrombosis of internal jugular vein

     I82.C11   Acute embolism and thrombosis of right internal jugular vein

     I82.C12   Acute embolism and thrombosis of left internal jugular vein

     I82.C13   Acute embolism and thrombosis of internal jugular vein, bilateral

     I82.C19   Acute embolism and thrombosis of unspecified internal jugular vein

   ● **I82.C2**   Chronic embolism and thrombosis of internal jugular vein

     I82.C21   Chronic embolism and thrombosis of right internal jugular vein

     I82.C22   Chronic embolism and thrombosis of left internal jugular vein

     I82.C23   Chronic embolism and thrombosis of internal jugular vein, bilateral

     I82.C29   Chronic embolism and thrombosis of unspecified internal jugular vein

● **I82.8**   Embolism and thrombosis of other specified veins

     Use additional code, if applicable, for associated long-term (current) use of anticoagulants (Z79.01)

   ● **I82.81**   Embolism and thrombosis of superficial veins of lower extremities

     Embolism and thrombosis of saphenous vein (greater) (lesser)

     I82.811   Embolism and thrombosis of superficial veins of right lower extremity

     I82.812   Embolism and thrombosis of superficial veins of left lower extremity

     I82.813   Embolism and thrombosis of superficial veins of lower extremities, bilateral

     I82.819   Embolism and thrombosis of superficial veins of unspecified lower extremity

   ● **I82.89**   Embolism and thrombosis of other specified veins

     I82.890   Acute embolism and thrombosis of other specified veins

     I82.891   Chronic embolism and thrombosis of other specified veins

● **I82.9**   Embolism and thrombosis of unspecified vein

     I82.90   Acute embolism and thrombosis of unspecified vein

     Embolism of vein NOS
     Thrombosis (vein) NOS

     I82.91   Chronic embolism and thrombosis of unspecified vein

● **I83**   Varicose veins of lower extremities

   Excludes1   varicose veins complicating pregnancy (O22.0-)
     varicose veins complicating the puerperium (O87.4)

● **I83.0**   Varicose veins of lower extremities with ulcer

     Use additional code to identify severity of ulcer (L97.-)

   ● **I83.00**   Varicose veins of unspecified lower extremity with ulcer

     I83.001   Varicose veins of unspecified lower extremity with ulcer of thigh   A

     I83.002   Varicose veins of unspecified lower extremity with ulcer of calf   A

     I83.003   Varicose veins of unspecified lower extremity with ulcer of ankle   A

     I83.004   Varicose veins of unspecified lower extremity with ulcer of heel and midfoot   A

       Varicose veins of unspecified lower extremity with ulcer of plantar surface of midfoot

     I83.005   Varicose veins of unspecified lower extremity with ulcer other part of foot   A

       Varicose veins of unspecified lower extremity with ulcer of toe

     I83.008   Varicose veins of unspecified lower extremity with ulcer other part of lower leg   A

     I83.009   Varicose veins of unspecified lower extremity with ulcer of unspecified site   A

   ● **I83.01**   Varicose veins of right lower extremity with ulcer

     I83.011   Varicose veins of right lower extremity with ulcer of thigh   A

     I83.012   Varicose veins of right lower extremity with ulcer of calf   A

     I83.013   Varicose veins of right lower extremity with ulcer of ankle   A

     I83.014   Varicose veins of right lower extremity with ulcer of heel and midfoot   A

       Varicose veins of right lower extremity with ulcer of plantar surface of midfoot

     I83.015   Varicose veins of right lower extremity with ulcer other part of foot   A

       Varicose veins of right lower extremity with ulcer of toe

     I83.018   Varicose veins of right lower extremity with ulcer other part of lower leg   A

     I83.019   Varicose veins of right lower extremity with ulcer of unspecified site   A

   ● **I83.02**   Varicose veins of left lower extremity with ulcer

     I83.021   Varicose veins of left lower extremity with ulcer of thigh   A

     I83.022   Varicose veins of left lower extremity with ulcer of calf   A

     I83.023   Varicose veins of left lower extremity with ulcer of ankle   A

     I83.024   Varicose veins of left lower extremity with ulcer of heel and midfoot   A

       Varicose veins of left lower extremity with ulcer of plantar surface of midfoot

▶ New   ⇒ Revised   ~~deleted~~ Deleted   Excludes 1   Excludes 2   Includes   Use additional   Code first   Code also   Key words

OGCR Official Guidelines   X Assign placeholder X   ● Use Additional Character(s)   ▶ Manifestation Code   **Coding Clinic**

I83.025   Varicose veins of left lower extremity with ulcer other part of foot   A
     Varicose veins of left lower extremity with ulcer of toe

I83.028   Varicose veins of left lower extremity with ulcer other part of lower leg   A

I83.029   Varicose veins of left lower extremity with ulcer of unspecified site   A

● I83.1   Varicose veins of lower extremities with inflammation

I83.10   Varicose veins of unspecified lower extremity with inflammation   A

I83.11   Varicose veins of right lower extremity with inflammation   A

I83.12   Varicose veins of left lower extremity with inflammation   A

● I83.2   Varicose veins of lower extremities with both ulcer and inflammation
     Use additional code to identify severity of ulcer (L97.-)

   ● I83.20   Varicose veins of unspecified lower extremity with both ulcer and inflammation

I83.201   Varicose veins of unspecified lower extremity with both ulcer of thigh and inflammation   A

I83.202   Varicose veins of unspecified lower extremity with both ulcer of calf and inflammation   A

I83.203   Varicose veins of unspecified lower extremity with both ulcer of ankle and inflammation   A

I83.204   Varicose veins of unspecified lower extremity with both ulcer of heel and midfoot and inflammation   A
     Varicose veins of unspecified lower extremity with both ulcer of plantar surface of midfoot and inflammation

I83.205   Varicose veins of unspecified lower extremity with both ulcer other part of foot and inflammation   A
     Varicose veins of unspecified lower extremity with both ulcer of toe and inflammation

I83.208   Varicose veins of unspecified lower extremity with both ulcer of other part of lower extremity and inflammation   A

I83.209   Varicose veins of unspecified lower extremity with both ulcer of unspecified site and inflammation   A

   ● I83.21   Varicose veins of right lower extremity with both ulcer and inflammation

I83.211   Varicose veins of right lower extremity with both ulcer of thigh and inflammation   A

I83.212   Varicose veins of right lower extremity with both ulcer of calf and inflammation   A

I83.213   Varicose veins of right lower extremity with both ulcer of ankle and inflammation   A

I83.214   Varicose veins of right lower extremity with both ulcer of heel and midfoot and inflammation   A
     Varicose veins of right lower extremity with both ulcer of plantar surface of midfoot and inflammation

I83.215   Varicose veins of right lower extremity with both ulcer other part of foot and inflammation   A
     Varicose veins of right lower extremity with both ulcer of toe and inflammation

I83.218   Varicose veins of right lower extremity with both ulcer of other part of lower extremity and inflammation   A

I83.219   Varicose veins of right lower extremity with both ulcer of unspecified site and inflammation   A

● I83.22   Varicose veins of left lower extremity with both ulcer and inflammation

I83.221   Varicose veins of left lower extremity with both ulcer of thigh and inflammation   A

I83.222   Varicose veins of left lower extremity with both ulcer of calf and inflammation   A

I83.223   Varicose veins of left lower extremity with both ulcer of ankle and inflammation   A

I83.224   Varicose veins of left lower extremity with both ulcer of heel and midfoot and inflammation   A
     Varicose veins of left lower extremity with both ulcer of plantar surface of midfoot and inflammation

I83.225   Varicose veins of left lower extremity with both ulcer other part of foot and inflammation   A
     Varicose veins of left lower extremity with both ulcer of toe and inflammation

I83.228   Varicose veins of left lower extremity with both ulcer of other part of lower extremity and inflammation   A

I83.229   Varicose veins of left lower extremity with both ulcer of unspecified site and inflammation   A

● I83.8   Varicose veins of lower extremities with other complications

   ● I83.81   Varicose veins of lower extremities with pain

I83.811   Varicose veins of right lower extremity with pain   A

I83.812   Varicose veins of left lower extremity with pain   A

I83.813   Varicose veins of bilateral lower extremities with pain   A

I83.819   Varicose veins of unspecified lower extremity with pain   A

   ● I83.89   Varicose veins of lower extremities with other complications
     Varicose veins of lower extremities with edema
     Varicose veins of lower extremities with swelling

I83.891   Varicose veins of right lower extremity with other complications   A

I83.892   Varicose veins of left lower extremity with other complications   A

I83.893   Varicose veins of bilateral lower extremities with other complications   A

I83.899   Varicose veins of unspecified lower extremity with other complications   A

CHAPTER 9 (I00-I99)

ICD-10-CM

● **I83.9** **Asymptomatic varicose veins of lower extremities**
Phlebectasia of lower extremities
Varicose veins of lower extremities
Varix of lower extremities

I83.90 **Asymptomatic varicose veins of unspecified lower extremity** A
Varicose veins NOS

I83.91 **Asymptomatic varicose veins of right lower extremity** A

I83.92 **Asymptomatic varicose veins of left lower extremity** A

I83.93 **Asymptomatic varicose veins of bilateral lower extremities** A

● **I85** **Esophageal varices**
Use additional code to identify:
alcohol abuse and dependence (F10.-)

● **I85.0** **Esophageal varices**
Idiopathic esophageal varices
Primary esophageal varices

I85.00 **Esophageal varices without bleeding**
Esophageal varices NOS

I85.01 **Esophageal varices with bleeding**

● **I85.1** **Secondary esophageal varices**
Esophageal varices secondary to alcoholic liver disease
Esophageal varices secondary to cirrhosis of liver
Esophageal varices secondary to schistosomiasis
Esophageal varices secondary to toxic liver disease
Code first underlying disease

I85.10 **Secondary esophageal varices without bleeding**

I85.11 **Secondary esophageal varices with bleeding**

● **I86** **Varicose veins of other sites**
Excludes1 varicose veins of unspecified site (I83.9-)
Excludes2 retinal varices (H35.0-)

I86.0 **Sublingual varices**

I86.1 **Scrotal varices** ♂
Varicocele

I86.2 **Pelvic varices**

I86.3 **Vulval varices** ♀
Excludes1 vulval varices complicating childbirth and the puerperium (O87.8)
vulval varices complicating pregnancy (O22.1-)

I86.4 **Gastric varices**

I86.8 **Varicose veins of other specified sites** A
Varicose ulcer of nasal septum

● **I87** **Other disorders of veins**

● **I87.0** **Postthrombotic syndrome**
Chronic venous hypertension due to deep vein thrombosis
Postphlebitic syndrome
Excludes1 chronic venous hypertension without deep vein thrombosis (I87.3-)

● **I87.00** **Postthrombotic syndrome without complications**
Asymptomatic Postthrombotic syndrome

I87.001 **Postthrombotic syndrome without complications of right lower extremity**

I87.002 **Postthrombotic syndrome without complications of left lower extremity**

I87.003 **Postthrombotic syndrome without complications of bilateral lower extremity**

I87.009 **Postthrombotic syndrome without complications of unspecified extremity**
Postthrombotic syndrome NOS

● **I87.01** **Postthrombotic syndrome with ulcer**
Use additional code to specify site and severity of ulcer (L97.-)

I87.011 **Postthrombotic syndrome with ulcer of right lower extremity**

I87.012 **Postthrombotic syndrome with ulcer of left lower extremity**

I87.013 **Postthrombotic syndrome with ulcer of bilateral lower extremity**

I87.019 **Postthrombotic syndrome with ulcer of unspecified lower extremity**

● **I87.02** **Postthrombotic syndrome with inflammation**

I87.021 **Postthrombotic syndrome with inflammation of right lower extremity**

I87.022 **Postthrombotic syndrome with inflammation of left lower extremity**

I87.023 **Postthrombotic syndrome with inflammation of bilateral lower extremity**

I87.029 **Postthrombotic syndrome with inflammation of unspecified lower extremity**

● **I87.03** **Postthrombotic syndrome with ulcer and inflammation**
Use additional code to specify site and severity of ulcer (L97.-)

I87.031 **Postthrombotic syndrome with ulcer and inflammation of right lower extremity**

I87.032 **Postthrombotic syndrome with ulcer and inflammation of left lower extremity**

I87.033 **Postthrombotic syndrome with ulcer and inflammation of bilateral lower extremity**

I87.039 **Postthrombotic syndrome with ulcer and inflammation of unspecified lower extremity**

● **I87.09** **Postthrombotic syndrome with other complications**

I87.091 **Postthrombotic syndrome with other complications of right lower extremity**

I87.092 **Postthrombotic syndrome with other complications of left lower extremity**

I87.093 **Postthrombotic syndrome with other complications of bilateral lower extremity**

I87.099 **Postthrombotic syndrome with other complications of unspecified lower extremity**

I87.1 **Compression of vein**
Stricture of vein
Vena cava syndrome (inferior) (superior)
Excludes2 compression of pulmonary vein (I28.8)

I87.2 **Venous insufficiency (chronic) (peripheral)**
Stasis dermatitis
Excludes1 stasis dermatitis with varicose veins of lower extremities (I83.1-, I83.2-)

● **I87.3   Chronic venous hypertension (idiopathic)**
Stasis edema
> **Excludes1**   chronic venous hypertension due to deep vein thrombosis (I87.0-)
> varicose veins of lower extremities (I83.-)

● **I87.30   Chronic venous hypertension (idiopathic) without complications**
Asymptomatic chronic venous hypertension (idiopathic)

I87.301   Chronic venous hypertension (idiopathic) without complications of right lower extremity

I87.302   Chronic venous hypertension (idiopathic) without complications of left lower extremity

I87.303   Chronic venous hypertension (idiopathic) without complications of bilateral lower extremity

I87.309   Chronic venous hypertension (idiopathic) without complications of unspecified lower extremity
Chronic venous hypertension NOS

● **I87.31   Chronic venous hypertension (idiopathic) with ulcer**
Use additional code to specify site and severity of ulcer (L97.-)

I87.311   Chronic venous hypertension (idiopathic) with ulcer of right lower extremity

I87.312   Chronic venous hypertension (idiopathic) with ulcer of left lower extremity

I87.313   Chronic venous hypertension (idiopathic) with ulcer of bilateral lower extremity

I87.319   Chronic venous hypertension (idiopathic) with ulcer of unspecified lower extremity

● **I87.32   Chronic venous hypertension (idiopathic) with inflammation**

I87.321   Chronic venous hypertension (idiopathic) with inflammation of right lower extremity

I87.322   Chronic venous hypertension (idiopathic) with inflammation of left lower extremity

I87.323   Chronic venous hypertension (idiopathic) with inflammation of bilateral lower extremity

I87.329   Chronic venous hypertension (idiopathic) with inflammation of unspecified lower extremity

● **I87.33   Chronic venous hypertension (idiopathic) with ulcer and inflammation**
Use additional code to specify site and severity of ulcer (L97.-)

I87.331   Chronic venous hypertension (idiopathic) with ulcer and inflammation of right lower extremity

I87.332   Chronic venous hypertension (idiopathic) with ulcer and inflammation of left lower extremity

I87.333   Chronic venous hypertension (idiopathic) with ulcer and inflammation of bilateral lower extremity

I87.339   Chronic venous hypertension (idiopathic) with ulcer and inflammation of unspecified lower extremity

● **I87.39   Chronic venous hypertension (idiopathic) with other complications**

I87.391   Chronic venous hypertension (idiopathic) with other complications of right lower extremity

I87.392   Chronic venous hypertension (idiopathic) with other complications of left lower extremity

I87.393   Chronic venous hypertension (idiopathic) with other complications of bilateral lower extremity

I87.399   Chronic venous hypertension (idiopathic) with other complications of unspecified lower extremity

I87.8   Other specified disorders of veins
Phlebosclerosis
Venofibrosis

I87.9   Disorder of vein, unspecified

● **I88   Nonspecific lymphadenitis**
> **Excludes1**   acute lymphadenitis, except mesenteric (L04.-)
> enlarged lymph nodes NOS (R59.-)
> human immunodeficiency virus [HIV] disease resulting in generalized lymphadenopathy (B20)

I88.0   Nonspecific mesenteric lymphadenitis
Mesenteric lymphadenitis (acute)(chronic)

I88.1   Chronic lymphadenitis, except mesenteric
Adenitis
Lymphadenitis

I88.8   Other nonspecific lymphadenitis

I88.9   Nonspecific lymphadenitis, unspecified
Lymphadenitis NOS

● **I89   Other noninfective disorders of lymphatic vessels and lymph nodes**
> **Excludes1**   chylocele, tunica vaginalis (nonfilarial) NOS (N50.89)
> enlarged lymph nodes NOS (R59.-)
> filarial chylocele (B74.-)
> hereditary lymphedema (Q82.0)

I89.0   Lymphedema, not elsewhere classified
Elephantiasis (nonfilarial) NOS
Lymphangiectasis
Obliteration, lymphatic vessel
Praecox lymphedema
Secondary lymphedema
> **Excludes1**   postmastectomy lymphedema (I97.2)

I89.1   Lymphangitis
Chronic lymphangitis
Lymphangitis NOS
Subacute lymphangitis
> **Excludes1**   acute lymphangitis (L03.-)

I89.8   Other specified noninfective disorders of lymphatic vessels and lymph nodes
Chylocele (nonfilarial)
Chylous ascites
Chylous cyst
Lipomelanotic reticulosis
Lymph node or vessel fistula
Lymph node or vessel infarction
Lymph node or vessel rupture

I89.9   Noninfective disorder of lymphatic vessels and lymph nodes, unspecified
Disease of lymphatic vessels NOS

CHAPTER 9 (I00-I99)

OTHER AND UNSPECIFIED DISORDERS OF THE CIRCULATORY SYSTEM (I95-I99)

● **I95**   **Hypotension**
     Subnormal arterial blood pressure
     Excludes1   cardiovascular collapse (R57.9)
                  maternal hypotension syndrome (O26.5-)
                  nonspecific low blood pressure reading NOS
                     (R03.1)

   I95.0   **Idiopathic hypotension**

   I95.1   **Orthostatic hypotension**
       Hypotension, postural
         Moving from a sitting or reclining position to a standing
           position precipitates a sudden drop in blood pressure
           (hypotension).
         Excludes1   neurogenic orthostatic hypotension [Shy-
                     Drager] (G90.3)
                   orthostatic hypotension due to drugs
                     (I95.2)

   I95.2   **Hypotension due to drugs**
       Orthostatic hypotension due to drugs
       Use additional code for adverse effect, if applicable,
          to identify drug (T36-T50 with fifth or sixth
          character 5)

   I95.3   **Hypotension of hemodialysis**
       Intra-dialytic hypotension

●   **I95.8**   **Other hypotension**
     I95.81   **Postprocedural hypotension**
     I95.89   **Other hypotension**
         Chronic hypotension

   I95.9   **Hypotension, unspecified**

I96   **Gangrene, not elsewhere classified**
     Gangrenous cellulitis
     Excludes1   gangrene in atherosclerosis of native arteries of
                 the extremities (I70.26)
                gangrene of certain specified sites - *see*
                 Alphabetical Index
                gangrene in hernia (K40.1, K40.4, K41.1, K41.4,
                 K42.1, K43.1-, K44.1, K45.1, K46.1)
                gangrene in other peripheral vascular diseases
                 (I73.-)
                gas gangrene (A48.0)
                pyoderma gangrenosum (L88)
     Excludes2   gangrene in diabetes mellitus (E08-E13 with .52)
     Coding Clinic: 2017, Q3, P6; 2013, Q2, P35

● **I97**   **Intraoperative and postprocedural complications and disorders**
     of circulatory system, not elsewhere classified
     Excludes2   postprocedural shock (T81.1-)

   I97.0   **Postcardiotomy syndrome**

●   **I97.1**   **Other postprocedural cardiac functional disturbances**
     Excludes2   acute pulmonary insufficiency following
                 thoracic surgery (J95.1)
                intraoperative cardiac functional
                 disturbances (I97.7-)

●   **I97.11**   **Postprocedural cardiac insufficiency**
       I97.110   **Postprocedural cardiac insufficiency**
            following cardiac surgery
       I97.111   **Postprocedural cardiac insufficiency**
            following other surgery

●   **I97.12**   **Postprocedural cardiac arrest**
       I97.120   **Postprocedural cardiac arrest**
            following cardiac surgery
       I97.121   **Postprocedural cardiac arrest**
            following other surgery

●   **I97.13**   **Postprocedural heart failure**
       Use additional code to identify the heart
         failure (I50.-)
       I97.130   **Postprocedural heart failure**
            following cardiac surgery
       I97.131   **Postprocedural heart failure**
            following other surgery

●   **I97.19**   **Other postprocedural cardiac functional**
       disturbances
       Use additional code, if applicable, to further
         specify disorder
       I97.190   **Other postprocedural cardiac**
            functional disturbances following
            cardiac surgery
            Use Additional code, if applicable,
               for type 4 or type 5 myocardial
               infarction, to further specify
               disorder
       I97.191   **Other postprocedural cardiac**
            functional disturbances following
            other surgery

   I97.2   **Postmastectomy lymphedema syndrome**   A
       Elephantiasis due to mastectomy
       Obliteration of lymphatic vessels

   I97.3   **Postprocedural hypertension**

●   **I97.4**   **Intraoperative hemorrhage and hematoma of a**
     circulatory system organ or structure complicating a
     procedure
     Excludes1   intraoperative hemorrhage and
                 hematoma of a circulatory system
                 organ or structure due to accidental
                 puncture and laceration during a
                 procedure (I97.5-)
     Excludes2   intraoperative cerebrovascular
                 hemorrhage complicating a
                 procedure (G97.3-)

●   **I97.41**   **Intraoperative hemorrhage and hematoma**
       of a circulatory system organ or structure
       complicating a circulatory system procedure
       I97.410   **Intraoperative hemorrhage and**
            hematoma of a circulatory system
            organ or structure complicating a
            cardiac catheterization
       I97.411   **Intraoperative hemorrhage and**
            hematoma of a circulatory system
            organ or structure complicating a
            cardiac bypass
       I97.418   **Intraoperative hemorrhage and**
            hematoma of a circulatory system
            organ or structure complicating other
            circulatory system procedure

    I97.42   **Intraoperative hemorrhage and hematoma**
       of a circulatory system organ or structure
       complicating other procedure
       Coding Clinic: 2016, Q4, P100

●   **I97.5**   **Accidental puncture and laceration of a circulatory**
     system organ or structure during a procedure
     Excludes2   accidental puncture and laceration of
                 brain during a procedure (G97.4-)

    I97.51   **Accidental puncture and laceration of a**
       circulatory system organ or structure during a
       circulatory system procedure

    I97.52   **Accidental puncture and laceration of a**
       circulatory system organ or structure during
       other procedure

▶ New   ⇒ Revised   ~~deleted~~ Deleted   Excludes 1   Excludes 2   Includes   Use additional   Code first   Code also   Key words
OGCR Official Guidelines   X Assign placeholder X   ● Use Additional Character(s)   ▷ Manifestation Code   **Coding Clinic**

● **I97.6** **Postprocedural hemorrhage, hematoma and seroma of a circulatory system organ or structure following a procedure**

  Excludes2 postprocedural cerebrovascular hemorrhage complicating a procedure (G97.5-)

  Coding Clinic: 2016, Q4, P10

● **I97.61** Postprocedural hemorrhage of a circulatory system organ or structure following a circulatory system procedure

    I97.610 Postprocedural hemorrhage of a circulatory system organ or structure following a cardiac catheterization

    I97.611 Postprocedural hemorrhage of a circulatory system organ or structure following cardiac bypass

    I97.618 Postprocedural hemorrhage of a circulatory system organ or structure following other circulatory system procedure

● **I97.62** Postprocedural hemorrhage, hematoma and seroma of a circulatory system organ or structure following other procedure

    I97.620 Postprocedural hemorrhage of a circulatory system organ or structure following other procedure

    I97.621 Postprocedural hematoma of a circulatory system organ or structure following other procedure

    I97.622 Postprocedural seroma of a circulatory system organ or structure following other procedure

● **I97.63** Postprocedural hematoma of a circulatory system organ or structure following a circulatory system procedure

    I97.630 Postprocedural hematoma of a circulatory system organ or structure following a cardiac catheterization

    I97.631 Postprocedural hematoma of a circulatory system organ or structure following cardiac bypass

    I97.638 Postprocedural hematoma of a circulatory system organ or structure following other circulatory system procedure

● **I97.64** Postprocedural seroma of a circulatory system organ or structure following a circulatory system procedure

    I97.640 Postprocedural seroma of a circulatory system organ or structure following a cardiac catheterization

    I97.641 Postprocedural seroma of a circulatory system organ or structure following cardiac bypass

    I97.648 Postprocedural seroma of a circulatory system organ or structure following other circulatory system procedure

● **I97.7** **Intraoperative cardiac functional disturbances**

  Excludes2 acute pulmonary insufficiency following thoracic surgery (J95.1)
  postprocedural cardiac functional disturbances (I97.1-)

● **I97.71** Intraoperative cardiac arrest

    I97.710 Intraoperative cardiac arrest during cardiac surgery

    I97.711 Intraoperative cardiac arrest during other surgery

● **I97.79** Other intraoperative cardiac functional disturbances

    Use additional code, if applicable, to further specify disorder

    I97.790 Other intraoperative cardiac functional disturbances during cardiac surgery

    I97.791 Other intraoperative cardiac functional disturbances during other surgery

● **I97.8** **Other intraoperative and postprocedural complications and disorders of the circulatory system, not elsewhere classified**

    Use additional code, if applicable, to further specify disorder

● **I97.81** Intraoperative cerebrovascular infarction

    I97.810 Intraoperative cerebrovascular infarction during cardiac surgery

    I97.811 Intraoperative cerebrovascular infarction during other surgery

● **I97.82** Postprocedural cerebrovascular infarction

    I97.820 Postprocedural cerebrovascular infarction following cardiac surgery

    I97.821 Postprocedural cerebrovascular v

    I97.88 Other intraoperative complications of the circulatory system, not elsewhere classified

    I97.89 Other postprocedural complications and disorders of the circulatory system, not elsewhere classified

● **I99** **Other and unspecified disorders of circulatory system**

  I99.8 Other disorder of circulatory system

  I99.9 Unspecified disorder of circulatory system

CHAPTER 9 (I00-I99)

CHAPTER 10

DISEASES OF THE RESPIRATORY SYSTEM (J00-J99)

OGCR Chapter-Specific Coding Guidelines

10. Chapter 10: Diseases of the Respiratory System (J00-J99)

a. **Chronic Obstructive Pulmonary Disease [COPD] and Asthma**

1) **Acute exacerbation of chronic obstructive bronchitis and asthma**

The codes in categories J44 and J45 distinguish between uncomplicated cases and those in acute exacerbation. An acute exacerbation is a worsening or a decompensation of a chronic condition. An acute exacerbation is not equivalent to an infection superimposed on a chronic condition, though an exacerbation may be triggered by an infection.

b. **Acute Respiratory Failure**

1) **Acute respiratory failure as principal diagnosis**

A code from subcategory J96.0, Acute respiratory failure, or subcategory J96.2, Acute and chronic respiratory failure, may be assigned as a principal diagnosis when it is the condition established after study to be chiefly responsible for occasioning the admission to the hospital, and the selection is supported by the Alphabetic Index and Tabular List. However, chapter-specific coding guidelines (such as obstetrics, poisoning, HIV, newborn) that provide sequencing direction take precedence.

2) **Acute respiratory failure as secondary diagnosis**

Respiratory failure may be listed as a secondary diagnosis if it occurs after admission, or if it is present on admission, but does not meet the definition of principal diagnosis.

3) **Sequencing of acute respiratory failure and another acute condition**

When a patient is admitted with respiratory failure and another acute condition (e.g., myocardial infarction, cerebrovascular accident, aspiration pneumonia), the principal diagnosis will not be the same in every situation. This applies whether the other acute condition is a respiratory or nonrespiratory condition. Selection of the principal diagnosis will be dependent on the circumstances of admission. If both the respiratory failure and the other acute condition are equally responsible for occasioning the admission to the hospital, and there are no chapter-specific sequencing rules, the guideline regarding two or more diagnoses that equally meet the definition for principal diagnosis (*Section II, C.*) may be applied in these situations.

If the documentation is not clear as to whether acute respiratory failure and another condition are equally responsible for occasioning the admission, query the provider for clarification.

c. **Influenza due to certain identified influenza viruses**

Code only confirmed cases of influenza due to certain identified influenza viruses (category J09), and due to other identified influenza virus (category J10). This is an exception to the hospital inpatient guideline Section II, H. (Uncertain Diagnosis).

In this context, "confirmation" does not require documentation of positive laboratory testing specific for avian or other novel influenza A or other identified influenza virus. However, coding should be based on the provider's diagnostic statement that the patient has avian influenza, or other novel influenza A, for category J09, or has another particular identified strain of influenza, such as H1N1 or H3N2, but not identified as novel or variant, for category J10.

If the provider records "suspected" or "possible" or "probable" avian influenza, or novel influenza, or other identified influenza, then the appropriate influenza code from category J11, Influenza due to unidentified influenza virus, should be assigned. A code from category J09, Influenza due to certain identified influenza viruses, should not be assigned nor should a code from category J10, Influenza due to other identified influenza virus.

d. **Ventilator associated Pneumonia**

1) **Documentation of Ventilator associated Pneumonia**

As with all procedural or postprocedural complications, code assignment is based on the provider's documentation of the relationship between the condition and the procedure.

Code J95.851, Ventilator associated pneumonia, should be assigned only when the provider has documented ventilator associated pneumonia (VAP). An additional code to identify the organism (e.g., Pseudomonas aeruginosa, code B96.5) should also be assigned. Do not assign an additional code from categories J12-J18 to identify the type of pneumonia.

Code J95.851 should not be assigned for cases where the patient has pneumonia and is on a mechanical ventilator and the provider has not specifically stated that the pneumonia is ventilator-associated pneumonia. If the documentation is unclear as to whether the patient has a pneumonia that is a complication attributable to the mechanical ventilator, query the provider.

2) **Ventilator associated Pneumonia Develops after Admission**

A patient may be admitted with one type of pneumonia (e.g., code J13, Pneumonia due to Streptococcus pneumonia) and subsequently develop VAP. In this instance, the principal diagnosis would be the appropriate code from categories J12-J18 for the pneumonia diagnosed at the time of admission. Code J95.851, Ventilator associated pneumonia, would be assigned as an additional diagnosis when the provider has also documented the presence of ventilator associated pneumonia.

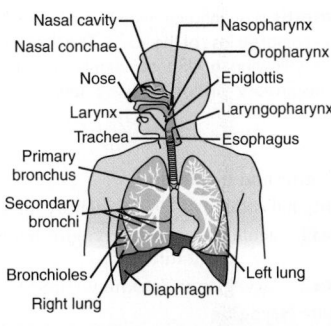

Figure 10-1 Respiratory system. (From Buck CJ: Step-by-Step Medical Coding, ed 2016, St. Louis, Elsevier, 2016)

Figure 10-2 Paranasal sinuses. (From Buck CJ: Step-by-Step Medical Coding, ed 2016, St. Louis, Elsevier, 2016)

Item 10-1 Pharyngitis is painful inflammation of the pharynx (sore throat). Ninety percent of the infections are caused by a virus with the remaining being bacterial and rarely a fungus (candidiasis). Other irritants such as pollutants, chemicals, or smoke may cause similar symptoms.

CHAPTER 10

DISEASES OF THE RESPIRATORY SYSTEM (J00-J99)

Note: When a respiratory condition is described as occurring in more than one site and is not specifically indexed, it should be classified to the lower anatomic site (e.g., tracheobronchitis to bronchitis in J40).

Use additional code, where applicable, to identify:
  exposure to environmental tobacco smoke (Z77.22)
  exposure to tobacco smoke in the perinatal period (P96.81)
  history of tobacco dependence (Z87.891)
  occupational exposure to environmental tobacco smoke (Z57.31)
  tobacco dependence (F17.-)
  tobacco use (Z72.0)

Excludes2   certain conditions originating in the perinatal period (P04-P96)
  certain infectious and parasitic diseases (A00-B99)
  complications of pregnancy, childbirth and the puerperium (O00-O99A)
  congenital malformations, deformations and chromosomal abnormalities (Q00-Q99)
  endocrine, nutritional and metabolic diseases (E00-E88)
  injury, poisoning and certain other consequences of external causes (S00-T88)
  neoplasms (C00-D49)
  smoke inhalation (T59.81-)
  symptoms, signs and abnormal clinical and laboratory findings, not elsewhere classified (R00-R94)

This chapter contains the following blocks:

J00-J06	Acute upper respiratory infections
J09-J18	Influenza and pneumonia
J20-J22	Other acute lower respiratory infections
J30-J39	Other diseases of upper respiratory tract
J40-J47	Chronic lower respiratory diseases
J60-J70	Lung diseases due to external agents
J80-J84	Other respiratory diseases principally affecting the interstitium
J85-J86	Suppurative and necrotic conditions of the lower respiratory tract
J90-J94	Other diseases of the pleura
J95	Intraoperative and postprocedural complications and disorders of respiratory system, not elsewhere classified
J96-J99	Other diseases of the respiratory system

ACUTE UPPER RESPIRATORY INFECTIONS (J00-J06)

Excludes1   chronic obstructive pulmonary disease with acute lower respiratory infection (J44.0)
  influenza virus with other respiratory manifestations (J09.X2, J10.1, J11.1)

J00   Acute nasopharyngitis [common cold]
  Acute rhinitis
  Coryza (acute)
  Infective nasopharyngitis NOS
  Infective rhinitis
  Nasal catarrh, acute
  Nasopharyngitis NOS

    Excludes1   acute pharyngitis (J02.-)
  acute sore throat NOS (J02.9)
  pharyngitis NOS (J02.9)
  rhinitis NOS (J31.0)
  sore throat NOS (J02.9)

    Excludes2   allergic rhinitis (J30.1-J30.9)
  chronic pharyngitis (J31.2)
  chronic rhinitis (J31.0)
  chronic sore throat (J31.2)
  nasopharyngitis, chronic (J31.1)
  vasomotor rhinitis (J30.0)

★**(See Plate 49 on page 72.)**

● **J01   Acute sinusitis**
    Includes   acute abscess of sinus
  acute empyema of sinus
  acute infection of sinus
  acute inflammation of sinus
  acute suppuration of sinus

    Use additional code (B95-B97) to identify infectious agent.
    Excludes1   sinusitis NOS (J32.9)
    Excludes2   chronic sinusitis (J32.0-J32.8)

● **J01.0   Acute maxillary sinusitis**
  Acute antritis
    J01.00   Acute maxillary sinusitis, unspecified
    J01.01   Acute recurrent maxillary sinusitis

● **J01.1   Acute frontal sinusitis**
    J01.10   Acute frontal sinusitis, unspecified
    J01.11   Acute recurrent frontal sinusitis

● **J01.2   Acute ethmoidal sinusitis**
    J01.20   Acute ethmoidal sinusitis, unspecified
    J01.21   Acute recurrent ethmoidal sinusitis

● **J01.3   Acute sphenoidal sinusitis**
    J01.30   Acute sphenoidal sinusitis, unspecified
    J01.31   Acute recurrent sphenoidal sinusitis

● **J01.4   Acute pansinusitis**
    J01.40   Acute pansinusitis, unspecified
    J01.41   Acute recurrent pansinusitis

● **J01.8**   **Other acute sinusitis**
- **J01.80**   **Other** acute sinusitis
  - Acute sinusitis involving more than one sinus but not pansinusitis
- **J01.81**   **Other** acute **recurrent** sinusitis
  - Acute recurrent sinusitis involving more than one sinus but not pansinusitis

● **J01.9**   **Acute sinusitis, unspecified**
- **J01.90**   **Acute sinusitis, unspecified**
- **J01.91**   **Acute recurrent sinusitis, unspecified**

● **J02**   **Acute pharyngitis**
- **Includes**   acute sore throat
- **Excludes1**   acute laryngopharyngitis (J06.0)
  - peritonsillar abscess (J36)
  - pharyngeal abscess (J39.1)
  - retropharyngeal abscess (J39.0)
- **Excludes2**   chronic pharyngitis (J31.2)

J02.0   **Streptococcal pharyngitis**
- Septic pharyngitis
- Streptococcal sore throat
  - **Excludes2**   scarlet fever (A38.-)

J02.8   **Acute pharyngitis due to other specified organisms**
- Use additional code (B95-B97) to identify infectious agent
  - **Excludes1**   pharyngitis due to coxsackie virus (B08.5)
    - pharyngitis due to gonococcus (A54.5)
    - acute pharyngitis due to herpes [simplex] virus (B00.2)
    - acute pharyngitis due to infectious mononucleosis (B27.-)
    - enteroviral vesicular pharyngitis (B08.5)

J02.9   **Acute pharyngitis, unspecified**
- Gangrenous pharyngitis (acute)
- Infective pharyngitis (acute) NOS
- Pharyngitis (acute) NOS
- Sore throat (acute) NOS
- Suppurative pharyngitis (acute)
- Ulcerative pharyngitis (acute)

● **J03**   **Acute tonsillitis**
Inflammation of pharyngeal tonsils caused by virus or bacteria
- **Excludes1**   acute sore throat (J02.-)
  - hypertrophy of tonsils (J35.1)
  - peritonsillar abscess (J36)
  - sore throat NOS (J02.9)
  - streptococcal sore throat (J02.0)
- **Excludes2**   chronic tonsillitis (J35.0)

● **J03.0**   **Streptococcal tonsillitis**
- **J03.00**   **Acute streptococcal tonsillitis, unspecified**
- **J03.01**   **Acute recurrent streptococcal tonsillitis**

● **J03.8**   **Acute tonsillitis due to other specified organisms**
- Use additional code (B95-B97) to identify infectious agent.
  - **Excludes1**   diphtheritic tonsillitis (A36.0)
    - herpesviral pharyngotonsillitis (B00.2)
    - streptococcal tonsillitis (J03.0)
    - tuberculous tonsillitis (A15.8)
    - Vincent's tonsillitis (A69.1)
- **J03.80**   **Acute tonsillitis due to other specified organisms**
- **J03.81**   **Acute recurrent tonsillitis due to other specified organisms**

● **J03.9**   **Acute tonsillitis, unspecified**
- Follicular tonsillitis (acute)
- Gangrenous tonsillitis (acute)
- Infective tonsillitis (acute)
- Tonsillitis (acute) NOS
- Ulcerative tonsillitis (acute)
- **J03.90**   **Acute tonsillitis, unspecified**
- **J03.91**   **Acute recurrent tonsillitis, unspecified**

Item 10–2   **Laryngitis** is an inflammation of the larynx (voice box) resulting in hoarse voice or the complete loss of the voice. **Tracheitis** is an inflammation of the trachea (often following a URI) commonly caused by *staphylococcus aureus* resulting in inspiratory stridor (crowing sound on inspiration) and a croup like cough.

● **J04**   **Acute laryngitis and tracheitis**
- Use additional code (B95-B97) to identify infectious agent.
  - **Excludes1**   acute obstructive laryngitis [croup] and epiglottitis (J05.-)
  - **Excludes2**   laryngismus (stridulus) (J38.5)

J04.0   **Acute laryngitis**
- Edematous laryngitis (acute)
- Laryngitis (acute) NOS
- Subglottic laryngitis (acute)
- Suppurative laryngitis (acute)
- Ulcerative laryngitis (acute)
  - **Excludes1**   acute obstructive laryngitis (J05.0)
  - **Excludes2**   chronic laryngitis (J37.0)

● **J04.1**   **Acute tracheitis**
- Acute viral tracheitis
- Catarrhal tracheitis (acute)
- Tracheitis (acute) NOS
  - **Excludes2**   chronic tracheitis (J42)
- **J04.10**   **Acute tracheitis without obstruction**
- **J04.11**   **Acute tracheitis with obstruction**

J04.2   **Acute laryngotracheitis**
- Laryngotracheitis NOS
- Tracheitis (acute) with laryngitis (acute)
  - **Excludes1**   acute obstructive laryngotracheitis (J05.0)
  - **Excludes2**   chronic laryngotracheitis (J37.1)

● **J04.3**   **Supraglottitis, unspecified**
- **J04.30**   **Supraglottitis, unspecified, without obstruction**
- **J04.31**   **Supraglottitis, unspecified, with obstruction**

● **J05**   **Acute obstructive laryngitis [croup] and epiglottitis**
- Use additional code (B95-B97) to identify infectious agent.

J05.0   **Acute obstructive laryngitis [croup]**
- Obstructive laryngitis (acute) NOS
- Obstructive laryngotracheitis NOS

● **J05.1**   **Acute epiglottitis**
- **Excludes2**   epiglottitis, chronic (J37.0)
- **J05.10**   **Acute epiglottitis without obstruction**
  - Epiglottitis NOS
- **J05.11**   **Acute epiglottitis with obstruction**

● **J06**   **Acute upper respiratory infections of multiple and unspecified sites**
- **Excludes1**   acute respiratory infection NOS (J22)
  - streptococcal pharyngitis (J02.0)
- **J06.0**   **Acute laryngopharyngitis**
- **J06.9**   **Acute upper respiratory infection, unspecified**
  - Upper respiratory disease, acute
  - Upper respiratory infection NOS

▶ New   ⇒ Revised   ~~deleted~~ Deleted   Excludes 1   Excludes 2   Includes   Use additional   Code first   Code also   Key words
OGCR Official Guidelines   X Assign placeholder X   ● Use Additional Character(s)   ▷ Manifestation Code   **Coding Clinic**

INFLUENZA AND PNEUMONIA (J09-J18)

Excludes2　allergic or eosinophilic pneumonia (J82)
aspiration pneumonia NOS (J69.0)
meconium pneumonia (P24.01)
neonatal aspiration pneumonia (P24.-)
pneumonia due to solids and liquids (J69.-)
congenital pneumonia (P23.9)
lipid pneumonia (J69.1)
rheumatic pneumonia (I00)
ventilator associated pneumonia (J95.851)

● **J09**　**Influenza due to certain identified influenza viruses**

　　Excludes1　influenza A/H1N1 (J10.-)
influenza due to other influenza viruses (J10.-)
influenza due to unidentified influenza virus
　　(J11.-)
seasonal influenza due to other identified
　　influenza virus (J10.-)
seasonal influenza due to unidentified influenza
　　virus (J11.-)

● **J09.X**　**Influenza due to identified novel influenza A virus**
Avian influenza
Bird influenza
Influenza A/H5N1
Influenza of other animal origin, not bird or swine
Swine influenza virus (viruses that normally cause
　　infections in pigs)
Coding Clinic: 2016, Q3, P11

　　J09.X1　**Influenza due to identified novel influenza A virus with pneumonia**
Code also , if applicable, associated:
　　lung abscess (J85.1)
　　other specified type of pneumonia

　　J09.X2　**Influenza due to identified novel influenza A virus with other respiratory manifestations**
Influenza due to identified novel influenza A
　　virus NOS
Influenza due to identified novel influenza A
　　virus with laryngitis
Influenza due to identified novel influenza A
　　virus with pharyngitis
Influenza due to identified novel influenza A
　　virus with upper respiratory symptoms
Use additional code, if applicable, for
　　associated:
　　pleural effusion (J91.8)
　　sinusitis (J01.-)

　　J09.X3　**Influenza due to identified novel influenza A virus with gastrointestinal manifestations**
Influenza due to identified novel influenza A
　　virus gastroenteritis
　　Excludes1　'intestinal flu' [viral
　　　　　　gastroenteritis] (A08.-)

　　J09.X9　**Influenza due to identified novel influenza A virus with other manifestations**
Influenza due to identified novel influenza A
　　virus with encephalopathy
Influenza due to identified novel influenza A
　　virus with myocarditis
Influenza due to identified novel influenza A
　　virus with otitis media
Use additional code to identify manifestation

● **J10**　**Influenza due to other identified influenza virus**

　　Excludes1　influenza due to avian influenza virus (J09.X-)
influenza due to swine flu (J09.X-)
influenza due to unidentified influenza virus
　　(J11.-)

● **J10.0**　**Influenza due to other identified influenza virus with pneumonia**
Code also associated lung abscess, if applicable (J85.1)

　　J10.00　**Influenza due to other identified influenza virus with unspecified type of pneumonia**

　　J10.01　**Influenza due to other identified influenza virus with the same other identified influenza virus pneumonia**

　　J10.08　**Influenza due to other identified influenza virus with other specified pneumonia**
Code also other specified type of pneumonia
Coding Clinic: 2017, Q4, P96

　　J10.1　**Influenza due to other identified influenza virus with other respiratory manifestations**
Influenza due to other identified influenza virus NOS
Influenza due to other identified influenza virus with
　　laryngitis
Influenza due to other identified influenza virus with
　　pharyngitis
Influenza due to other identified influenza virus with
　　upper respiratory symptoms
Use additional code for associated pleural effusion, if
　　applicable (J91.8)
Use additional code for associated sinusitis, if
　　applicable (J01.-)
Coding Clinic: 2016, Q3, P11

　　J10.2　**Influenza due to other identified influenza virus with gastrointestinal manifestations**
Influenza due to other identified influenza virus
　　gastroenteritis
　　Excludes1　'intestinal flu' [viral gastroenteritis]
　　　　　　(A08.-)

● **J10.8**　**Influenza due to other identified influenza virus with other manifestations**

　　J10.81　**Influenza due to other identified influenza virus with encephalopathy**

　　J10.82　**Influenza due to other identified influenza virus with myocarditis**

　　J10.83　**Influenza due to other identified influenza virus with otitis media**
Use additional code for any associated
　　perforated tympanic membrane (H72.-)

　　J10.89　**Influenza due to other identified influenza virus with other manifestations**
Use additional codes to identify the
　　manifestations

● **J11**　**Influenza due to unidentified influenza virus**

● **J11.0**　**Influenza due to unidentified influenza virus with pneumonia**
Code also associated lung abscess, if applicable (J85.1)

　　J11.00　**Influenza due to unidentified influenza virus with unspecified type of pneumonia**
Influenza with pneumonia NOS
Coding Clinic: 2016, Q3, P12

　　J11.08　**Influenza due to unidentified influenza virus with specified pneumonia**
Code also other specified type of pneumonia

J11.1 Influenza due to unidentified influenza virus with other respiratory manifestations
Influenza NOS
Influenzal laryngitis NOS
Influenzal pharyngitis NOS
Influenza with upper respiratory symptoms NOS
Use additional code for associated pleural effusion, if applicable (J91.8)
Use additional code for associated sinusitis, if applicable (J01.-)

J11.2 Influenza due to unidentified influenza virus with gastrointestinal manifestations
Influenza gastroenteritis NOS
Excludes1 'intestinal flu' [viral gastroenteritis] (A08.-)

● **J11.8 Influenza due to unidentified influenza virus with other manifestations**

J11.81 Influenza due to unidentified influenza virus with encephalopathy
Influenzal encephalopathy NOS

J11.82 Influenza due to unidentified influenza virus with myocarditis
Influenzal myocarditis NOS

J11.83 Influenza due to unidentified influenza virus with otitis media
Influenzal otitis media NOS
Use additional code for any associated perforated tympanic membrane (H72.-)

J11.89 Influenza due to unidentified influenza virus with other manifestations
Use additional codes to identify the manifestations

● **J12 Viral pneumonia, not elsewhere classified**
Includes bronchopneumonia due to viruses other than influenza viruses
Code first associated influenza, if applicable (J09.X1, J10.0-, J11.0-)
Code also associated abscess, if applicable (J85.1)
Excludes1 aspiration pneumonia due to anesthesia during labor and delivery (O74.0)
aspiration pneumonia due to anesthesia during pregnancy (O29)
aspiration pneumonia due to anesthesia during puerperium (O89.0)
aspiration pneumonia due to solids and liquids (J69.-)
aspiration pneumonia NOS (J69.0)
congenital pneumonia (P23.0)
congenital rubella pneumonitis (P35.0)
interstitial pneumonia NOS (J84.9)
lipid pneumonia (J69.1)
neonatal aspiration pneumonia (P24.-)

J12.0 Adenoviral pneumonia
J12.1 Respiratory syncytial virus pneumonia
J12.2 Parainfluenza virus pneumonia
J12.3 Human metapneumovirus pneumonia
● **J12.8 Other viral pneumonia**
J12.81 Pneumonia due to SARS-associated coronavirus
Severe acute respiratory syndrome NOS
J12.89 Other viral pneumonia
J12.9 Viral pneumonia, unspecified

Item 10–3 Pneumonia is an infection of the lungs, caused by a variety of microorganisms, including viruses, most commonly the Streptococcus pneumoniae (pneumococcus) bacteria, fungi, and parasites. Pneumonia occurs when the immune system is weakened, often by a URI or influenza.

J13 Pneumonia due to Streptococcus pneumoniae
Bronchopneumonia due to S. pneumoniae
Code first associated influenza, if applicable (J09.X1, J10.0-, J11.0-)
Code also associated abscess, if applicable (J85.1)
Excludes1 congenital pneumonia due to S. pneumoniae (P23.6)
lobar pneumonia, unspecified organism (J18.1)
pneumonia due to other streptococci (J15.3-J15.4)

J14 Pneumonia due to Hemophilus influenzae
Bronchopneumonia due to H. influenzae
Code first associated influenza, if applicable (J09.X1, J10.0-, J11.0-)
Code also associated abscess, if applicable (J85.1)
Excludes1 congenital pneumonia due to H. influenzae (P23.6)

● **J15 Bacterial pneumonia, not elsewhere classified**
Includes bronchopneumonia due to bacteria other than S. pneumoniae and H. influenzae
Code first associated influenza, if applicable (J09.X1, J10.0-, J11.0-)
Code also associated abscess, if applicable (J85.1)
Excludes1 chlamydial pneumonia (J16.0)
congenital pneumonia (P23.-)
Legionnaires' disease (A48.1)
spirochetal pneumonia (A69.8)

J15.0 Pneumonia due to Klebsiella pneumoniae
J15.1 Pneumonia due to Pseudomonas
● **J15.2 Pneumonia due to staphylococcus**
J15.20 Pneumonia due to staphylococcus, unspecified
● **J15.21 Pneumonia due to staphylococcus aureus**
J15.211 Pneumonia due to Methicillin susceptible Staphylococcus aureus
MSSA pneumonia
Pneumonia due to Staphylococcus aureus NOS
J15.212 Pneumonia due to Methicillin resistant Staphylococcus aureus
J15.29 Pneumonia due to other staphylococcus
J15.3 Pneumonia due to streptococcus, group B
J15.4 Pneumonia due to other streptococci
Excludes1 pneumonia due to streptococcus, group B (J15.3)
pneumonia due to Streptococcus pneumoniae (J13)
J15.5 Pneumonia due to Escherichia coli
J15.6 Pneumonia due to other Gram-negative bacteria
Pneumonia due to other aerobic Gram-negative bacteria
Pneumonia due to Serratia marcescens
J15.7 Pneumonia due to Mycoplasma pneumoniae
J15.8 Pneumonia due to other specified bacteria
J15.9 Unspecified bacterial pneumonia
Pneumonia due to gram-positive bacteria
Coding Clinic: 2017, Q4, P96

CHAPTER 10 (J00-J99)

● J16 **Pneumonia due to other infectious organisms, not elsewhere classified**

Code first associated influenza, if applicable (J09.X1, J10.0-, J11.0-)

Code also associated abscess, if applicable (J85.1)

Excludes1   congenital pneumonia (P23.-)
ornithosis (A70)
pneumocystosis (B59)
pneumonia NOS (J18.9)

J16.0   **Chlamydial pneumonia**

J16.8   **Pneumonia due to other specified infectious organisms**

◗ J17 *Pneumonia in diseases classified elsewhere*

Code first underlying disease, such as:
Q fever (A78)
rheumatic fever (I00)
schistosomiasis (B65.0-B65.9)

Excludes1   candidial pneumonia (B37.1)
chlamydial pneumonia (J16.0)
gonorrheal pneumonia (A54.84)
histoplasmosis pneumonia (B39.0-B39.2)
measles pneumonia (B05.2)
nocardiosis pneumonia (A43.0)
pneumocystosis (B59)
pneumonia due to Pneumocystis carinii (B59)
pneumonia due to Pneumocystis jiroveci (B59)
pneumonia in actinomycosis (A42.0)
pneumonia in anthrax (A22.1)
pneumonia in ascariasis (B77.81)
pneumonia in aspergillosis (B44.0-B44.1)
pneumonia in coccidioidomycosis (B38.0-B38.2)
pneumonia in cytomegalovirus disease (B25.0)
pneumonia in toxoplasmosis (B58.3)
rubella pneumonia (B06.81)
salmonella pneumonia (A02.22)
spirochetal infection NEC with pneumonia (A69.8)
tularemia pneumonia (A21.2)
typhoid fever with pneumonia (A01.03)
varicella pneumonia (B01.2)
whooping cough with pneumonia (A37 with fifth-character 1)

● J18 **Pneumonia, unspecified organism**

Code first associated influenza, if applicable (J09.X1, J10.0-, J11.0-)

Excludes1   abscess of lung with pneumonia (J85.1)
aspiration pneumonia due to anesthesia during labor and delivery (O74.0)
aspiration pneumonia due to anesthesia during pregnancy (O29)
aspiration pneumonia due to anesthesia during puerperium (O89.0)
aspiration pneumonia due to solids and liquids (J69.-)
aspiration pneumonia NOS (J69.0)
congenital pneumonia (P23.0)
drug-induced interstitial lung disorder (J70.2-J70.4)
interstitial pneumonia NOS (J84.9)
lipid pneumonia (J69.1)
neonatal aspiration pneumonia (P24.-)
pneumonitis due to external agents (J67-J70)
pneumonitis due to fumes and vapors (J68.0)
usual interstitial pneumonia (J84.17)

J18.0   **Bronchopneumonia, unspecified organism**

Excludes1   hypostatic bronchopneumonia (J18.2)
lipid pneumonia (J69.1)

Excludes2   acute bronchiolitis (J21.-)
chronic bronchiolitis (J44.9)

J18.1   **Lobar pneumonia, unspecified organism**
Coding Clinic: 2016, Q3, P15

J18.2   **Hypostatic pneumonia, unspecified organism**
Hypostatic bronchopneumonia
Passive pneumonia

J18.8   **Other pneumonia, unspecified organism**

J18.9   **Pneumonia, unspecified organism**
Coding Clinic: 2016, Q3, P15; 2012, Q4, P94

OTHER ACUTE LOWER RESPIRATORY INFECTIONS (J20-J22)

Excludes2   chronic obstructive pulmonary disease with acute lower respiratory infection (J44.0)

● J20   **Acute bronchitis**
Inflammation/irritation of the bronchial tubes lasting 2-3 weeks, most commonly caused by a virus

Includes   acute and subacute bronchitis (with) bronchospasm
acute and subacute bronchitis (with) tracheitis
acute and subacute bronchitis (with) tracheobronchitis, acute
acute and subacute fibrinous bronchitis
acute and subacute membranous bronchitis
acute and subacute purulent bronchitis
acute and subacute septic bronchitis

Excludes1   bronchitis NOS (J40)
tracheobronchitis NOS (J40)

Excludes2   acute bronchitis with bronchiectasis (J47.0)
acute bronchitis with chronic obstructive asthma (J44.0)
acute bronchitis with chronic obstructive pulmonary disease (J44.0)
allergic bronchitis NOS (J45.909-)
bronchitis due to chemicals, fumes and vapors (J68.0)
chronic bronchitis NOS (J42)
chronic mucopurulent bronchitis (J41.1)
chronic obstructive bronchitis (J44.-)
chronic obstructive tracheobronchitis (J44.-)
chronic simple bronchitis (J41.0)
chronic tracheobronchitis (J42)

J20.0   **Acute bronchitis due to Mycoplasma pneumoniae**

J20.1   **Acute bronchitis due to Hemophilus influenzae**

J20.2   **Acute bronchitis due to streptococcus**

J20.3   **Acute bronchitis due to coxsackievirus**

J20.4   **Acute bronchitis due to parainfluenza virus**

J20.5   **Acute bronchitis due to respiratory syncytial virus**

J20.6   **Acute bronchitis due to rhinovirus**
Coding Clinic: 2016, Q3, P10

J20.7   **Acute bronchitis due to echovirus**

J20.8   **Acute bronchitis due to other specified organisms**
Coding Clinic: 2016, Q3, P11

J20.9   **Acute bronchitis, unspecified**
Coding Clinic: 2016, Q3, P16

● J21   **Acute bronchiolitis**
Bronchiolitis obliterans with organizing pneumonia (BOOP) inflammation of bronchioles and surrounding tissue in lung

Includes   acute bronchiolitis with bronchospasm

Excludes2   respiratory bronchiolitis interstitial lung disease (J84.115)

J21.0   **Acute bronchiolitis due to respiratory syncytial virus**

J21.1   **Acute bronchiolitis due to human metapneumovirus**

J21.8   **Acute bronchiolitis due to other specified organisms**

J21.9   **Acute bronchiolitis, unspecified**
Bronchiolitis (acute)

Excludes1   chronic bronchiolitis (J44.-)

J22   **Unspecified acute lower respiratory infection**
Acute (lower) respiratory (tract) infection NOS

Excludes1   upper respiratory infection (acute) (J06.9)

OTHER DISEASES OF UPPER RESPIRATORY TRACT (J30-J39)

● **J30   Vasomotor and allergic rhinitis**

> **Includes**   spasmodic rhinorrhea
>
> **Excludes1**   allergic rhinitis with asthma (bronchial) (J45.909)
> rhinitis NOS (J31.0)

J30.0   Vasomotor rhinitis

J30.1   Allergic rhinitis due to pollen
> Allergy NOS due to pollen
> Hay fever
> Pollinosis

J30.2   Other seasonal allergic rhinitis

J30.5   Allergic rhinitis due to food

● **J30.8   Other allergic rhinitis**

> **J30.81   Allergic rhinitis due to animal (cat) (dog) hair and dander**
>
> **J30.89   Other allergic rhinitis**
> > Perennial allergic rhinitis

J30.9   Allergic rhinitis, unspecified

● **J31   Chronic rhinitis, nasopharyngitis and pharyngitis**

> Use additional code to identify:
> exposure to environmental tobacco smoke (Z77.22)
> exposure to tobacco smoke in the perinatal period (P96.81)
> history of tobacco dependence (Z87.891)
> occupational exposure to environmental tobacco smoke (Z57.31)
> tobacco dependence (F17.-)
> tobacco use (Z72.0)

J31.0   Chronic rhinitis
> Atrophic rhinitis (chronic)
> Granulomatous rhinitis (chronic)
> Hypertrophic rhinitis (chronic)
> Obstructive rhinitis (chronic)
> Ozena
> Purulent rhinitis (chronic)
> Rhinitis (chronic) NOS
> Ulcerative rhinitis (chronic)
>
> > **Excludes1**   allergic rhinitis (J30.1-J30.9)
> > vasomotor rhinitis (J30.0)

J31.1   Chronic nasopharyngitis
> > **Excludes2**   acute nasopharyngitis (J00)

J31.2   Chronic pharyngitis
> Chronic sore throat
> Atrophic pharyngitis (chronic)
> Granular pharyngitis (chronic)
> Hypertrophic pharyngitis (chronic)
>
> > **Excludes2**   acute pharyngitis (J02.9)

● **J32   Chronic sinusitis**

> **Includes**   sinus abscess
> sinus empyema
> sinus infection
> sinus suppuration
>
> Use additional code to identify:
> exposure to environmental tobacco smoke (Z77.22)
> exposure to tobacco smoke in the perinatal period (P96.81)
> history of tobacco dependence (Z87.891)
> infectious agent (B95-B97)
> occupational exposure to environmental tobacco smoke (Z57.31)
> tobacco dependence (F17.-)
> tobacco use (Z72.0)
>
> **Excludes2**   acute sinusitis (J01.-)

J32.0   Chronic maxillary sinusitis
> Antritis (chronic)
> Maxillary sinusitis NOS

J32.1   Chronic frontal sinusitis
> Frontal sinusitis NOS

Item 10-4   Nasal polyps are an abnormal growth of tissue (tumor) projecting from a mucous membrane and attached to the surface by a narrow elongated stalk (pedunculated). Nasal polyps usually originate in the ethmoid sinus but also may occur in the maxillary sinus. Symptoms are nasal block, sinusitis, anosmia, and secondary infections.

J32.2   Chronic ethmoidal sinusitis
> Ethmoidal sinusitis NOS
>
> > **Excludes1**   Woakes' ethmoiditis (J33.1)

J32.3   Chronic sphenoidal sinusitis
> Sphenoidal sinusitis NOS

J32.4   Chronic pansinusitis
> Pansinusitis NOS

J32.8   Other chronic sinusitis
> Sinusitis (chronic) involving more than one sinus but not pansinusitis

J32.9   Chronic sinusitis, unspecified
> Sinusitis (chronic) NOS

● **J33   Nasal polyp**

> Use additional code to identify:
> exposure to environmental tobacco smoke (Z77.22)
> exposure to tobacco smoke in the perinatal period (P96.81)
> history of tobacco dependence (Z87.891)
> occupational exposure to environmental tobacco smoke (Z57.31)
> tobacco dependence (F17.-)
> tobacco use (Z72.0)
>
> **Excludes1**   adenomatous polyps (D14.0)

J33.0   Polyp of nasal cavity
> Choanal polyp
> Nasopharyngeal polyp

J33.1   Polypoid sinus degeneration
> Woakes' syndrome or ethmoiditis

J33.8   Other polyp of sinus
> Accessory polyp of sinus
> Ethmoidal polyp of sinus
> Maxillary polyp of sinus
> Sphenoidal polyp of sinus

J33.9   Nasal polyp, unspecified

● **J34   Other and unspecified disorders of nose and nasal sinuses**

> **Excludes2**   varicose ulcer of nasal septum (I86.8)

J34.0   Abscess, furuncle and carbuncle of nose
> Cellulitis of nose
> Necrosis of nose
> Ulceration of nose

J34.1   Cyst and mucocele of nose and nasal sinus

J34.2   Deviated nasal septum
> Deflection or deviation of septum (nasal) (acquired)
>
> > **Excludes1**   congenital deviated nasal septum (Q67.4)

J34.3   Hypertrophy of nasal turbinates

Deviated septal cartilage

Figure 10-3 Deviated nasal septum.

Item 10-5   A **deviated nasal septum** is the displacement of the septal cartilage that separates the nares. This displacement causes obstructed air flow through the nasal passages. A child can be born with this displacement (congenital), or the condition may be acquired through trauma, such as a sports injury. Symptoms include nasal block, sinusitis, and related secondary infections. Septoplasty is surgical repair of this condition.

▶ New   ⇒ Revised   ~~deleted~~ Deleted   Excludes 1   Excludes 2   Includes   Use additional   Code first   Code also   Key words

OGCR Official Guidelines   X Assign placeholder X   ● Use Additional Character(s)   ▷ Manifestation Code   **Coding Clinic**

● **J34.8** **Other specified disorders of nose and nasal sinuses**

     J34.81 **Nasal mucositis (ulcerative)**

         Code also type of associated therapy, such as:
             antineoplastic and immunosuppressive
                 drugs (T45.1X-)
             radiological procedure and radiotherapy
                 (Y84.2)

         Excludes2 gastrointestinal mucositis
                   (ulcerative) (K92.81)
                   mucositis (ulcerative) of vagina
                      and vulva (N76.81)
                   oral mucositis (ulcerative)
                      (K12.3-)

     J34.89 **Other specified disorders of nose and nasal sinuses**
         Perforation of nasal septum NOS
         Rhinolith

   J34.9 **Unspecified disorder of nose and nasal sinuses**

● **J35** **Chronic diseases of tonsils and adenoids**

   Use additional code to identify:
     exposure to environmental tobacco smoke (Z77.22)
     exposure to tobacco smoke in the perinatal period (P96.81)
     history of tobacco dependence (Z87.891)
     occupational exposure to environmental tobacco smoke
       (Z57.31)
     tobacco dependence (F17.-)
     tobacco use (Z72.0)

● **J35.0** **Chronic tonsillitis and adenoiditis**

     Excludes2 acute tonsillitis (J03.-)

     J35.01 **Chronic tonsillitis**

     J35.02 **Chronic adenoiditis**

     J35.03 **Chronic tonsillitis and adenoiditis**

   J35.1 **Hypertrophy of tonsils**
     Enlargement of tonsils

     Excludes1 hypertrophy of tonsils with tonsillitis
              (J35.0-)

   J35.2 **Hypertrophy of adenoids**
     Enlargement of adenoids

     Excludes1 hypertrophy of adenoids with adenoiditis
              (J35.0-)

   J35.3 **Hypertrophy of tonsils with hypertrophy of adenoids**

     Excludes1 hypertrophy of tonsils and adenoids with
              tonsillitis and adenoiditis (J35.03)

   J35.8 **Other chronic diseases of tonsils and adenoids**
     Adenoid vegetations
     Amygdalolith
     Calculus, tonsil
     Cicatrix of tonsil (and adenoid)
     Tonsillar tag
     Ulcer of tonsil

   J35.9 **Chronic disease of tonsils and adenoids, unspecified**
     Disease (chronic) of tonsils and adenoids NOS

J36 **Peritonsillar abscess**

   Includes abscess of tonsil
          peritonsillar cellulitis
          quinsy

   Use additional code (B95-B97) to identify infectious agent.

   Excludes1 acute tonsillitis (J03.-)
           chronic tonsillitis (J35.0)
           retropharyngeal abscess (J39.0)
           tonsillitis NOS (J03.9-)

● **J37** **Chronic laryngitis and laryngotracheitis**

   Use additional code to identify:
     exposure to environmental tobacco smoke (Z77.22)
     exposure to tobacco smoke in the perinatal period (P96.81)
     history of tobacco dependence (Z87.891)
     infectious agent (B95-B97)
     occupational exposure to environmental tobacco smoke
       (Z57.31)
     tobacco dependence (F17.-)
     tobacco use (Z72.0)

   J37.0 **Chronic laryngitis**
     Catarrhal laryngitis
     Hypertrophic laryngitis
     Sicca laryngitis

     Excludes2 acute laryngitis (J04.0)
           obstructive (acute) laryngitis (J05.0)

   J37.1 **Chronic laryngotracheitis**
     Laryngitis, chronic, with tracheitis (chronic)
     Tracheitis, chronic, with laryngitis

     Excludes1 chronic tracheitis (J42)
     Excludes2 acute laryngotracheitis (J04.2)
           acute tracheitis (J04.1)

● **J38** **Diseases of vocal cords and larynx, not elsewhere classified**

   Use additional code to identify:
     exposure to environmental tobacco smoke (Z77.22)
     exposure to tobacco smoke in the perinatal period (P96.81)
     history of tobacco dependence (Z87.891)
     occupational exposure to environmental tobacco smoke
       (Z57.31)
     tobacco dependence (F17.-)
     tobacco use (Z72.0)

     Excludes1 congenital laryngeal stridor (P28.89)
           obstructive laryngitis (acute) (J05.0)
           postprocedural subglottic stenosis (J95.5)
           stridor (R06.1)
           ulcerative laryngitis (J04.0)

● **J38.0** **Paralysis of vocal cords and larynx**
     Laryngoplegia
     Paralysis of glottis

     J38.00 **Paralysis of vocal cords and larynx, unspecified**

     J38.01 **Paralysis of vocal cords and larynx, unilateral**

     J38.02 **Paralysis of vocal cords and larynx, bilateral**

   J38.1 **Polyp of vocal cord and larynx**

     Excludes1 adenomatous polyps (D14.1)

   J38.2 **Nodules of vocal cords**
     Chorditis (fibrinous)(nodosa)(tuberosa)
     Singer's nodes
     Teacher's nodes

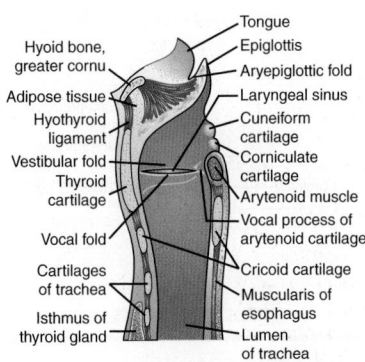

Figure 10-4 Coronal section of the larynx.

Item 10-6 The **larynx** extends from the tongue to the trachea and is divided into an upper and lower portion separated by folds. The framework of the larynx is cartilage composed of the single cricoid, thyroid, and epiglottic cartilages, and the paired arytenoid, cuneiform, and corniculate cartilages.

J38.3   Other diseases of vocal cords
Abscess of vocal cords
Cellulitis of vocal cords
Granuloma of vocal cords
Leukokeratosis of vocal cords
Leukoplakia of vocal cords

J38.4   Edema of larynx
Edema (of) glottis
Subglottic edema
Supraglottic edema
> **Excludes1**   acute obstructive laryngitis [croup] (J05.0)
> edematous laryngitis (J04.0)

J38.5   Laryngeal spasm
Laryngismus (stridulus)

J38.6   Stenosis of larynx

J38.7   Other diseases of larynx
Abscess of larynx
Cellulitis of larynx
Disease of larynx NOS
Necrosis of larynx
Pachyderma of larynx
Perichondritis of larynx
Ulcer of larynx

● **J39   Other diseases of upper respiratory tract**
> **Excludes1**   acute respiratory infection NOS (J22)
> acute upper respiratory infection (J06.9)
> upper respiratory inflammation due to chemicals,
> gases, fumes or vapors (J68.2)

J39.0   Retropharyngeal and parapharyngeal abscess
Peripharyngeal abscess
> **Excludes1**   peritonsillar abscess (J36)

J39.1   Other abscess of pharynx
Cellulitis of pharynx
Nasopharyngeal abscess

J39.2   Other diseases of pharynx
Cyst of pharynx
Edema of pharynx
> **Excludes2**   chronic pharyngitis (J31.2)
> ulcerative pharyngitis (J02.9)

J39.3   Upper respiratory tract hypersensitivity reaction, site unspecified
> **Excludes1**   hypersensitivity reaction of upper
> respiratory tract, such as:
> extrinsic allergic alveolitis (J67.9)
> pneumoconiosis (J60-J67.9)

J39.8   Other specified diseases of upper respiratory tract

J39.9   Disease of upper respiratory tract, unspecified

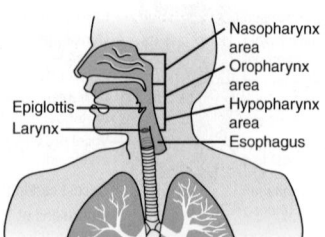

Figure 10-5   The pharynx.

Item 10–7   The **pharynx** is the passage for both food and air between the mouth and the esophagus and is divided into three areas: nasopharynx, oropharynx, and hypopharynx. The hypopharynx branches into the esophagus and the voice box.

Item 10–8   Chronic bronchitis is usually defined as being present in any patient who has persistent cough with sputum production for at least three months in at least two consecutive years. **Simple chronic bronchitis** is marked by a productive cough but no pathological airflow obstruction. **Chronic obstructive pulmonary disease (COPD)** is a group of conditions— bronchitis, emphysema, asthma, bronchiectasis, allergic alveolitis—marked by dyspnea. **Catarrhal** bronchitis is an acute form of bronchitis marked by profuse mucus and pus production (**mucopurulent** discharge). **Croupous** bronchitis, also known as pseudomembranous, fibrinous, plastic, exudative, or membranous, is marked by a violent cough and dyspnea.

CHRONIC LOWER RESPIRATORY DISEASES (J40-J47)

> **Excludes1**   bronchitis due to chemicals, gases, fumes and
> vapors (J68.0)
> **Excludes2**   cystic fibrosis (E84.-)

J40   Bronchitis, not specified as acute or chronic
Bronchitis NOS
Catarrhal bronchitis
Bronchitis with tracheitis NOS
Tracheobronchitis NOS
Use additional code to identify:
exposure to environmental tobacco smoke (Z77.22)
exposure to tobacco smoke in the perinatal period (P96.81)
history of tobacco dependence (Z87.891)
occupational exposure to environmental tobacco smoke (Z57.31)
tobacco dependence (F17.-)
tobacco use (Z72.0)
> **Excludes1**   acute bronchitis (J20.-)
> allergic bronchitis NOS (J45.909-)
> asthmatic bronchitis NOS (J45.9-)
> bronchitis due to chemicals, fumes and
> vapors (J68.0)

● **J41   Simple and mucopurulent chronic bronchitis**
Use additional code to identify:
exposure to environmental tobacco smoke (Z77.22)
exposure to tobacco smoke in the perinatal period (P96.81)
history of tobacco dependence (Z87.891)
occupational exposure to environmental tobacco smoke (Z57.31)
tobacco dependence (F17.-)
tobacco use (Z72.0)
> **Excludes1**   chronic bronchitis NOS (J42)
> chronic obstructive bronchitis (J44.-)

J41.0   Simple chronic bronchitis

J41.1   Mucopurulent chronic bronchitis

J41.8   Mixed simple and mucopurulent chronic bronchitis

J42   Unspecified chronic bronchitis
Chronic bronchitis NOS
Chronic tracheitis
Chronic tracheobronchitis
Use additional code to identify:
exposure to environmental tobacco smoke (Z77.22)
exposure to tobacco smoke in the perinatal period (P96.81)
history of tobacco dependence (Z87.891)
occupational exposure to environmental tobacco smoke (Z57.31)
tobacco dependence (F17.-)
tobacco use (Z72.0)
> **Excludes1**   chronic asthmatic bronchitis (J44.-)
> chronic bronchitis with airways obstruction (J44.-)
> chronic emphysematous bronchitis (J44.-)
> chronic obstructive pulmonary disease NOS
> (J44.9)
> simple and mucopurulent chronic bronchitis
> (J41.-)

● **J43   Emphysema**
     Use additional code to identify:
         exposure to environmental tobacco smoke (Z77.22)
         history of tobacco dependence (Z87.891)
         occupational exposure to environmental tobacco smoke
            (Z57.31)
         tobacco dependence (F17.-)
         tobacco use (Z72.Ø)

     Excludes1   compensatory emphysema (J98.3)
                   emphysema due to inhalation of chemicals, gases,
                     fumes or vapors (J68.4)
                   emphysema with chronic (obstructive) bronchitis
                     (J44.-)
                   emphysematous (obstructive) bronchitis (J44.-)
                   interstitial emphysema (J98.2)
                   mediastinal emphysema (J98.2)
                   neonatal interstitial emphysema (P25.Ø)
                   surgical (subcutaneous) emphysema (T81.82)
                   traumatic subcutaneous emphysema (T79.7)

   J43.Ø   Unilateral pulmonary emphysema [MacLeod's
         syndrome]
         Swyer-James syndrome
         Unilateral emphysema
         Unilateral hyperlucent lung
         Unilateral pulmonary artery functional hypoplasia
         Unilateral transparency of lung

   J43.1   Panlobular emphysema
         Panacinar emphysema

   J43.2   Centrilobular emphysema

   J43.8   Other emphysema

   J43.9   Emphysema, unspecified
         Bullous emphysema (lung)(pulmonary)
         Emphysema (lung)(pulmonary) NOS
         Emphysematous bleb
         Vesicular emphysema (lung)(pulmonary)
         Coding Clinic: 2017, Q4, P97-98

● **J44   Other chronic obstructive pulmonary disease**
     Includes   asthma with chronic obstructive pulmonary
                   disease
                   chronic asthmatic (obstructive) bronchitis
                   chronic bronchitis with airways obstruction
                   chronic bronchitis with emphysema
                   chronic emphysematous bronchitis
                   chronic obstructive asthma
                   chronic obstructive bronchitis
                   chronic obstructive tracheobronchitis

     Code also type of asthma, if applicable (J45.-)
     Use additional code to identify:
         exposure to environmental tobacco smoke (Z77.22)
         history of tobacco dependence (Z87.891)
         occupational exposure to environmental tobacco smoke
            (Z57.31)
         tobacco dependence (F17.-)
         tobacco use (Z72.Ø)

     Excludes1   bronchiectasis (J47.-)
                   chronic bronchitis NOS (J42)
                   chronic simple and mucopurulent bronchitis (J41.-)
                   chronic tracheitis (J42)
                   chronic tracheobronchitis (J42)
                   emphysema without chronic bronchitis (J43.-)
    Coding Clinic: 22017, Q4, P97; 2017, Q1, P25; 2016, Q3, P16

   J44.Ø   Chronic obstructive pulmonary disease with acute lower
         respiratory infection
           Code also to identify the infection
           Coding Clinic: 2017, Q4, P96; 2017, Q2, P30, Q1, P24-25;
             2016, Q3, P15-16

Figure 10-6   Emphysema. (From Shiland, BJ: Medical Terminology &
Anatomy for ICD-10 Coding, ed 2, Mosby, 2015)

   J44.1   Chronic obstructive pulmonary disease with (acute)
         exacerbation
         Decompensated COPD
         Decompensated COPD with (acute) exacerbation

         Excludes2   chronic obstructive pulmonary disease
                        [COPD] with acute bronchitis (J44.Ø)
                      lung diseases due to external agents
                        (J60-J70)
         Coding Clinic: 2017, Q4, P96; 2017, Q1, P26; 2016, Q3, P15-16, Q1, P36

   J44.9   Chronic obstructive pulmonary disease, unspecified
         Chronic obstructive airway disease NOS
         Chronic obstructive lung disease NOS

         Excludes2   lung diseases due to external agents
                        (J60-J70)
         Coding Clinic: 2017, Q4, P96-97; 2017, Q1, P24-25; 2016, Q1, P37

● **J45   Asthma**
     Allergic (predominantly) asthma
     Allergic bronchitis NOS
     Allergic rhinitis with asthma
     Atopic asthma
     Extrinsic allergic asthma
     Hay fever with asthma
     Idiosyncratic asthma
     Intrinsic nonallergic asthma
     Nonallergic asthma

     Use additional code to identify:
         exposure to environmental tobacco smoke (Z77.22)
         exposure to tobacco smoke in the perinatal period (P96.81)
         history of tobacco dependence (Z87.891)
         occupational exposure to environmental tobacco smoke (Z57.31)
         tobacco dependence (F17.-)
         tobacco use (Z72.Ø)

     Excludes1   detergent asthma (J69.8)
                   eosinophilic asthma (J82)
                   miner's asthma (J60)
                   wheezing NOS (RØ6.2)
                   wood asthma (J67.8)

     Excludes2   asthma with chronic obstructive pulmonary
                   disease (J44.9)
                   chronic asthmatic (obstructive) bronchitis (J44.9)
                   chronic obstructive asthma (J44.9)
     Coding Clinic: 2017, Q1, P25

● **J45.2   Mild intermittent asthma**
       J45.2Ø   Mild intermittent asthma, uncomplicated
               Mild intermittent asthma NOS

       J45.21   Mild intermittent asthma with (acute)
            exacerbation

       J45.22   Mild intermittent asthma with status
            asthmaticus

Item 10–9   Asthma is a bronchial condition marked by airway obstruction, hyper-responsiveness, and inflammation. **Extrinsic** asthma, also known as allergic asthma, is characterized by the same symptoms that occur with exposure to allergens and is divided into the following types: **atopic, occupational,** and **allergic bronchopulmonary aspergillosis. Intrinsic** asthma occurs in patients who have no history of allergy or sensitivities to allergens and is divided into the following types: **nonreaginic** and **pharmacologic. Status asthmaticus** is the most severe form of asthma attack and can last for days or weeks.

CHAPTER 1Ø (JØØ-J99)

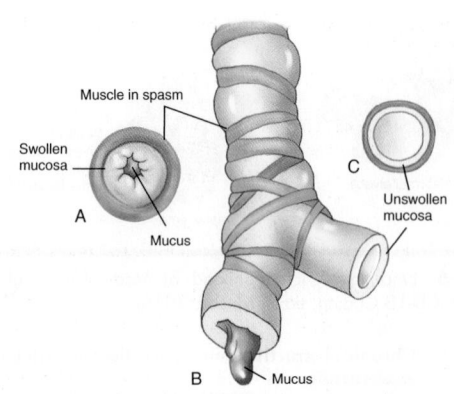

Figure 10-7 Factors causing expiratory obstruction in asthma. **A.** Cross section of a bronchiole occluded by muscle spasm, swollen mucosa, and mucus. **B.** Longitudinal section of an obstructed bronchiole. **C.** Cross-section of a clear bronchiole. (From Shiland: Mastering Healthcare Terminology, ed 1, St. Louis, Mosby, 2003)

● **J45.3**   Mild persistent asthma

    J45.30   Mild persistent asthma, uncomplicated
          Mild persistent asthma NOS

    J45.31   Mild persistent asthma with (acute) exacerbation
          Coding Clinic: 2016, Q1, P35

    J45.32   Mild persistent asthma with status asthmaticus

● **J45.4**   Moderate persistent asthma

    J45.40   Moderate persistent asthma, uncomplicated
          Moderate persistent asthma NOS

    J45.41   Moderate persistent asthma with (acute) exacerbation
          Coding Clinic: 2017, Q1, P26

    J45.42   Moderate persistent asthma with status asthmaticus

● **J45.5**   Severe persistent asthma

    J45.50   Severe persistent asthma, uncomplicated
          Severe persistent asthma NOS

    J45.51   Severe persistent asthma with (acute) exacerbation

    J45.52   Severe persistent asthma with status asthmaticus

● **J45.9**   Other and unspecified asthma

    ● **J45.90**   Unspecified asthma
          Asthmatic bronchitis NOS
          Childhood asthma NOS
          Late onset asthma

       J45.901   Unspecified asthma with (acute) exacerbation
             Coding Clinic: 2017, Q4, P96

       J45.902   Unspecified asthma with status asthmaticus

       J45.909   Unspecified asthma, uncomplicated
             Asthma NOS

          Excludes2   lung diseases due to external agents (J60-J70)
                 Coding Clinic: 2017, Q4, P96; 2017, Q1, P25

    ● **J45.99**   Other asthma

       J45.990   Exercise induced bronchospasm

       J45.991   Cough variant asthma

       J45.998   Other asthma

● **J47**   Bronchiectasis

    Includes   bronchiolectasis

    Use additional code to identify:
       exposure to environmental tobacco smoke (Z77.22)
       exposure to tobacco smoke in the perinatal period (P96.81)
       history of tobacco dependence (Z87.891)
       occupational exposure to environmental tobacco smoke (Z57.31)
       tobacco dependence (F17.-)
       tobacco use (Z72.0)

    Excludes1   congenital bronchiectasis (Q33.4)
              tuberculous bronchiectasis (current disease) (A15.0)

    J47.0   Bronchiectasis with acute lower respiratory infection
          Bronchiectasis with acute bronchitis
            Use additional code to identify the infection

    J47.1   Bronchiectasis with (acute) exacerbation

    J47.9   Bronchiectasis, uncomplicated
          Bronchiectasis NOS

LUNG DISEASES DUE TO EXTERNAL AGENTS (J60-J70)

    Excludes2   asthma (J45.-)
              malignant neoplasm of bronchus and lung (C34.-)

J60   Coalworker's pneumoconiosis   A
    Anthracosilicosis
    Anthracosis
    Black lung disease
    Coalworker's lung

    Excludes1   coalworker pneumoconiosis with tuberculosis, any type in A15 (J65)

J61   Pneumoconiosis due to asbestos and other mineral fibers   A
    Asbestosis

    Excludes1   pleural plaque with asbestosis (J92.0)
              pneumoconiosis with tuberculosis, any type in A15 (J65)

● **J62**   Pneumoconiosis due to dust containing silica

    Includes   silicotic fibrosis (massive) of lung

    Excludes1   pneumoconiosis with tuberculosis, any type in A15 (J65)

    J62.0   Pneumoconiosis due to talc dust

    J62.8   Pneumoconiosis due to other dust containing silica
          Silicosis NOS

● **J63**   Pneumoconiosis due to other inorganic dusts

    Excludes1   pneumoconiosis with tuberculosis, any type in A15 (J65)

    J63.0   Aluminosis (of lung)

    J63.1   Bauxite fibrosis (of lung)

    J63.2   Berylliosis

    J63.3   Graphite fibrosis (of lung)

    J63.4   Siderosis

    J63.5   Stannosis

    J63.6   Pneumoconiosis due to other specified inorganic dusts

Figure 10-8 Progressive massive fibrosis superimposed on coal workers' pneumoconiosis. The large, blackened scars are located principally in the upper lobe. (From Frazier MS, Drzymkowski JW: Essentials of Human Diseases and Conditions, St. Louis, MO, Saunders, 2004)

Item 10–10 Pneumoconiosis refers to a lung condition resulting from exposure to inorganic or organic airborne particles, such as coal dust or moldy hay, as well as chemical fumes and vapors, such as insecticides. In this condition, the lungs retain the airborne particles.

▶ New   ⇒ Revised   ~~deleted~~ Deleted   Excludes 1   Excludes 2   Includes   Use additional   Code first   Code also   Key words

OGCR Official Guidelines   X Assign placeholder X   ● Use Additional Character(s)   ▶ Manifestation Code   **Coding Clinic**

J64   **Unspecified pneumoconiosis**

> **Excludes1**   pneumonoconiosis with tuberculosis, any type in A15 (J65)

J65   **Pneumoconiosis associated with tuberculosis**

> Any condition in J60-J64 with tuberculosis, any type in A15
> Silicotuberculosis

● **J66**   **Airway disease due to specific organic dust**

> **Excludes2**   allergic alveolitis (J67.-)
> asbestosis (J61)
> bagassosis (J67.1)
> farmer's lung (J67.0)
> hypersensitivity pneumonitis due to organic dust (J67.-)
> reactive airways dysfunction syndrome (J68.3)

J66.0   **Byssinosis**
> Airway disease due to cotton dust

J66.1   **Flax-dressers' disease**

J66.2   **Cannabinosis**

J66.8   **Airway disease due to other specific organic dusts**

● **J67**   **Hypersensitivity pneumonitis due to organic dust**

> **Includes**   allergic alveolitis and pneumonitis due to inhaled organic dust and particles of fungal, actinomycetic or other origin

> **Excludes1**   pneumonitis due to inhalation of chemicals, gases, fumes or vapors (J68.0)

J67.0   **Farmer's lung**
> Harvester's lung
> Haymaker's lung
> Moldy hay disease

J67.1   **Bagassosis**
> Bagasse disease
> Bagasse pneumonitis

J67.2   **Bird fancier's lung**
> Budgerigar fancier's disease or lung
> Pigeon fancier's disease or lung

J67.3   **Suberosis**
> Corkhandler's disease or lung
> Corkworker's disease or lung

J67.4   **Maltworker's lung**
> Alveolitis due to Aspergillus clavatus

J67.5   **Mushroom-worker's lung**

J67.6   **Maple-bark-stripper's lung**
> Alveolitis due to Cryptostroma corticale
> Cryptostromosis

J67.7   **Air conditioner and humidifier lung**
> Allergic alveolitis due to fungal, thermophilic actinomycetes and other organisms growing in ventilation [air conditioning] systems

J67.8   **Hypersensitivity pneumonitis due to other organic dusts**
> Cheese-washer's lung
> Coffee-worker's lung
> Fish-meal worker's lung
> Furrier's lung
> Sequoiosis

J67.9   **Hypersensitivity pneumonitis due to unspecified organic dust**
> Allergic alveolitis (extrinsic) NOS
> Hypersensitivity pneumonitis NOS

● **J68**   **Respiratory conditions due to inhalation of chemicals, gases, fumes and vapors**

> *Code first (T51-T65) to identify cause*
> Use additional code to identify associated respiratory conditions, such as:
> acute respiratory failure (J96.0-)

J68.0   **Bronchitis and pneumonitis due to chemicals, gases, fumes and vapors**
> Chemical bronchitis (acute)

J68.1   **Pulmonary edema due to chemicals, gases, fumes and vapors**
> Chemical pulmonary edema (acute) (chronic)
> > **Excludes1**   pulmonary edema (acute) (chronic) NOS (J81.-)

J68.2   **Upper respiratory inflammation due to chemicals, gases, fumes and vapors, not elsewhere classified**

J68.3   **Other acute and subacute respiratory conditions due to chemicals, gases, fumes and vapors**
> Reactive airways dysfunction syndrome

J68.4   **Chronic respiratory conditions due to chemicals, gases, fumes and vapors**
> Emphysema (diffuse) (chronic) due to inhalation of chemicals, gases, fumes and vapors
> Obliterative bronchiolitis (chronic) (subacute) due to inhalation of chemicals, gases, fumes and vapors
> Pulmonary fibrosis (chronic) due to inhalation of chemicals, gases, fumes and vapors
> > **Excludes1**   chronic pulmonary edema due to chemicals, gases, fumes and vapors (J68.1)

J68.8   **Other respiratory conditions due to chemicals, gases, fumes and vapors**

J68.9   **Unspecified respiratory condition due to chemicals, gases, fumes and vapors**

● **J69**   **Pneumonitis due to solids and liquids**

> **Excludes1**   neonatal aspiration syndromes (P24.-)
> postprocedural pneumonitis (J95.4)

J69.0   **Pneumonitis due to inhalation of food and vomit**
> Aspiration pneumonia NOS
> Aspiration pneumonia (due to) food (regurgitated)
> Aspiration pneumonia (due to) gastric secretions
> Aspiration pneumonia (due to) milk
> Aspiration pneumonia (due to) vomit
>
> Code also any associated foreign body in respiratory tract (T17.-)
> > **Excludes1**   chemical pneumonitis due to anesthesia (J95.4)
> > obstetric aspiration pneumonitis (O74.0)
>
> **Coding Clinic: 2017, Q1, P24**

J69.1   **Pneumonitis due to inhalation of oils and essences**
> Exogenous lipoid pneumonia
> Lipid pneumonia NOS
> *Code first (T51-T65) to identify substance*
> > **Excludes1**   endogenous lipoid pneumonia (J84.89)

J69.8   **Pneumonitis due to inhalation of other solids and liquids**
> Pneumonitis due to aspiration of blood
> Pneumonitis due to aspiration of detergent
> *Code first (T51-T65) to identify substance*

CHAPTER 10 (J00-J99)

● **J70**   **Respiratory conditions due to other external agents**

    J70.0   **Acute pulmonary manifestations due to radiation**
        Radiation pneumonitis
        Use additional code (W88-W90, X39.0-) to identify the external cause

    J70.1   **Chronic and other pulmonary manifestations due to radiation**
        Fibrosis of lung following radiation
        Use additional code (W88-W90, X39.0-) to identify the external cause

    J70.2   **Acute drug-induced interstitial lung disorders**
        Use additional code for adverse effect, if applicable, to identify drug (T36-T50 with fifth or sixth character 5)
        Excludes1   interstitial pneumonia NOS (J84.9)
                      lymphoid interstitial pneumonia (J84.2)

    J70.3   **Chronic drug-induced interstitial lung disorders**
        Use additional code for adverse effect, if applicable, to identify drug (T36-T50 with fifth or sixth character 5)
        Excludes1   interstitial pneumonia NOS (J84.9)
                      lymphoid interstitial pneumonia (J84.2)

    J70.4   **Drug-induced interstitial lung disorders, unspecified**
        Use additional code for adverse effect, if applicable, to identify drug (T36-T50 with fifth or sixth character 5)
        Excludes1   interstitial pneumonia NOS (J84.9)
                      lymphoid interstitial pneumonia (J84.2)

    J70.5   **Respiratory conditions due to smoke inhalation**
        Smoke inhalation NOS
        Excludes1   smoke inhalation due to chemicals, gases, fumes and vapors (J68.9)

    J70.8   **Respiratory conditions due to other specified external agents**
        Code first (T51-T65) to identify the external agent

    J70.9   **Respiratory conditions due to unspecified external agent**
        Code first (T51-T65) to identify the external agent

OTHER RESPIRATORY DISEASES PRINCIPALLY AFFECTING THE INTERSTITIUM (J80-J84)

J80   **Acute respiratory distress syndrome**
        Acute respiratory distress syndrome in adult or child
        Adult hyaline membrane disease
        Excludes1   respiratory distress syndrome in newborn (perinatal) (P22.0)
        Coding Clinic: 2017, Q1, P26-27

● **J81**   **Pulmonary edema**
        Use additional code to identify:
        exposure to environmental tobacco smoke (Z77.22)
        history of tobacco dependence (Z87.891)
        occupational exposure to environmental tobacco smoke (Z57.31)
        tobacco dependence (F17.-)
        tobacco use (Z72.0)
        Excludes1   chemical (acute) pulmonary edema (J68.1)
                      hypostatic pneumonia (J18.2)
                      passive pneumonia (J18.2)
                      pulmonary edema due to external agents (J60-J70)
                      pulmonary edema with heart disease NOS (I50.1)
                      pulmonary edema with heart failure (I50.1)

    J81.0   **Acute pulmonary edema**
        Acute edema of lung
        Coding Clinic: 2017, Q1, P26

    J81.1   **Chronic pulmonary edema**
        Pulmonary congestion (chronic) (passive)
        Pulmonary edema NOS

Figure 10-9   Bullous emphysema with large subpleural bullae *(upper left)*. (From Kumar: Robbins and Cotran: Pathologic Basis of Disease, ed 8, Saunders, An Imprint of Elsevier, 2009)

J82   **Pulmonary eosinophilia, not elsewhere classified**
        Allergic pneumonia
        Eosinophilic asthma
        Eosinophilic pneumonia
        Löffler's pneumonia
        Tropical (pulmonary) eosinophilia NOS
        Excludes1   pulmonary eosinophilia due to aspergillosis (B44.-)
                      pulmonary eosinophilia due to drugs (J70.2-J70.4)
                      pulmonary eosinophilia due to specified parasitic infection (B50-B83)
                      pulmonary eosinophilia due to systemic connective tissue disorders (M30-M36)
                      pulmonary infiltrate NOS (R91.8)

● **J84**   **Other interstitial pulmonary diseases**
        Excludes1   drug-induced interstitial lung disorders (J70.2-J70.4)
                      interstitial emphysema (J98.2)
        Excludes2   lung diseases due to external agents (J60-J70)

    ● **J84.0**   **Alveolar and parieto-alveolar conditions**
        J84.01   **Alveolar proteinosis**
        J84.02   **Pulmonary alveolar microlithiasis**
        ▷ **J84.03**   *Idiopathic pulmonary hemosiderosis*
               Essential brown induration of lung
               Code first underlying disease, such as:
               disorders of iron metabolism (E83.1-)
               Excludes1   acute idiopathic pulmonary hemorrhage in infants [AIPHI] (R04.81)
        J84.09   **Other alveolar and parieto-alveolar conditions**

    ● **J84.1**   **Other interstitial pulmonary diseases with fibrosis**
        Excludes1   pulmonary fibrosis (chronic) due to inhalation of chemicals, gases, fumes or vapors (J68.4)
                      pulmonary fibrosis (chronic) following radiation (J70.1)
        J84.10   **Pulmonary fibrosis, unspecified**
            Capillary fibrosis of lung
            Cirrhosis of lung (chronic) NOS
            Fibrosis of lung (atrophic) (chronic) (confluent) (massive) (perialveolar) (peribronchial) NOS
            Induration of lung (chronic) NOS
            Postinflammatory pulmonary fibrosis

▶ New   ⇒ Revised   ~~deleted~~ Deleted   Excludes 1   Excludes 2   Includes   Use additional   Code first   Code also   Key words

OGCR Official Guidelines   X Assign placeholder X   ● Use Additional Character(s)   ▷ Manifestation Code   **Coding Clinic**

● **J84.11**   **Idiopathic interstitial pneumonia**

     Excludes1   lymphoid interstitial pneumonia (J84.2)

                     pneumocystis pneumonia (B59)

   J84.111   **Idiopathic interstitial pneumonia, not otherwise specified**

   J84.112   **Idiopathic pulmonary fibrosis**

            Cryptogenic fibrosing alveolitis

            Idiopathic fibrosing alveolitis

   J84.113   **Idiopathic non-specific interstitial pneumonitis**

       Excludes1   non-specific interstitial pneumonia NOS, or due to known underlying cause (J84.89)

   J84.114   **Acute interstitial pneumonitis**

            Hamman-Rich syndrome

       Excludes1   pneumocystis pneumonia (B59)

   J84.115   **Respiratory bronchiolitis interstitial lung disease**

   J84.116   **Cryptogenic organizing pneumonia**

       Excludes1   organizing pneumonia NOS, or due to known underlying cause (J84.89)

   J84.117   **Desquamative interstitial pneumonia**

▷ *J84.17*   *Other interstitial pulmonary diseases with fibrosis in diseases classified elsewhere*

     Interstitial pneumonia (nonspecific) (usual) due to collagen vascular disease

     Interstitial pneumonia (nonspecific) (usual) in diseases classified elsewhere

     Organizing pneumonia due to collagen vascular disease

     Organizing pneumonia in diseases classified elsewhere

     Code first underlying disease, such as:

       progressive systemic sclerosis (M34.0)

       rheumatoid arthritis (M05.00-M06.9)

       systemic lupus erythematosis (M32.0-M32.9)

J84.2   **Lymphoid interstitial pneumonia**

     Lymphoid interstitial pneumonitis

● **J84.8**   **Other specified interstitial pulmonary diseases**

     Excludes1   exogenous lipoid pneumonia (J69.1)

                  unspecified lipoid pneumonia (J69.1)

   J84.81   **Lymphangioleiomyomatosis**

            Lymphangiomyomatosis

   J84.82   **Adult pulmonary Langerhans cell histiocytosis**   A

            Adult PLCH

   J84.83   **Surfactant mutations of the lung**

● **J84.84**   **Other interstitial lung diseases of childhood**

   J84.841   **Neuroendocrine cell hyperplasia of infancy**

   J84.842   **Pulmonary interstitial glycogenosis**

   J84.843   **Alveolar capillary dysplasia with vein misalignment**

   J84.848   **Other interstitial lung diseases of childhood**

J84.89   **Other specified interstitial pulmonary diseases**

     Endogenous lipoid pneumonia

     Interstitial pneumonitis

     Non-specific interstitial pneumonitis NOS

     Organizing pneumonia NOS

     Code first, if applicable:

       poisoning due to drug or toxin (T51-T65 with fifth or sixth character to indicate intent), for toxic pneumonopathy

       underlying cause of pneumonopathy, if known

     Use additional code, for adverse effect, to identify drug (T36-T50 with fifth or sixth character 5), if drug-induced

       Excludes1   cryptogenic organizing pneumonia (J84.116)

                  idiopathic non-specific interstitial pneumonitis (J84.113)

                  lipoid pneumonia, exogenous or unspecified (J69.1)

                  lymphoid interstitial pneumonia (J84.2)

J84.9   **Interstitial pulmonary disease, unspecified**

     Interstitial pneumonia NOS

SUPPURATIVE AND NECROTIC CONDITIONS OF THE LOWER RESPIRATORY TRACT (J85-J86)

● **J85**   **Abscess of lung and mediastinum**

     Use additional code (B95-B97) to identify infectious agent.

   J85.0   **Gangrene and necrosis of lung**

   J85.1   **Abscess of lung with pneumonia**

       Code also the type of pneumonia

   J85.2   **Abscess of lung without pneumonia**

       Abscess of lung NOS

   J85.3   **Abscess of mediastinum**

Item 10–11   **Empyema** is a condition in which pus accumulates in a body cavity. Empyema **with fistula** occurs when the pus passes from one cavity to another organ or structure.

● **J86**   **Pyothorax**

     Use additional code (B95-B97) to identify infectious agent.

     Excludes1   abscess of lung (J85.-)

                 pyothorax due to tuberculosis (A15.6)

   J86.0   **Pyothorax with fistula**

       Bronchocutaneous fistula

       Bronchopleural fistula

       Hepatopleural fistula

       Mediastinal fistula

       Pleural fistula

       Thoracic fistula

       Any condition classifiable to J86.9 with fistula

   J86.9   **Pyothorax without fistula**

       Abscess of pleura

       Abscess of thorax

       Empyema (chest) (lung) (pleura)

       Fibrinopurulent pleurisy

       Purulent pleurisy

       Pyopneumothorax

       Septic pleurisy

       Seropurulent pleurisy

       Suppurative pleurisy

CHAPTER 10 (J00-J99)

CHAPTER 10 (J00-J99)

OTHER DISEASES OF THE PLEURA (J90-J94)

J90   Pleural effusion, not elsewhere classified
Encysted pleurisy
Pleural effusion NOS
Pleurisy with effusion (exudative) (serous)

Excludes1   chylous (pleural) effusion (J94.0)
malignant pleural effusion (J91.0))
pleurisy NOS (R09.1)
tuberculous pleural effusion (A15.6)
Coding Clinic: 2015, Q2, P16

● **J91   Pleural effusion in conditions classified elsewhere**

Excludes2   pleural effusion in heart failure (I50.-)
pleural effusion in systemic lupus erythematosus (M32.13)

▸ *J91.0   Malignant pleural effusion*
Code first underlying neoplasm

▸ *J91.8   Pleural effusion in other conditions classified elsewhere*
Code first underlying disease, such as:
filariasis (B74.0-B74.9)
influenza (J09.X2, J10.1, J11.1)
Coding Clinic: 2015, Q2, P16

● **J92   Pleural plaque**
Includes   pleural thickening

J92.0   Pleural plaque with presence of asbestos

J92.9   Pleural plaque without asbestos
Pleural plaque NOS

● **J93   Pneumothorax and air leak**
Collapsed lung

Excludes1   congenital or perinatal pneumothorax (P25.1)
postprocedural air leak (J95.812)
postprocedural pneumothorax (J95.811)
traumatic pneumothorax (S27.0)
tuberculous (current disease) pneumothorax (A15.-)
pyopneumothorax (J86.-)

J93.0   Spontaneous tension pneumothorax
Tension pneumothorax (most serious type) occurs when air (positive pressure) collects in the pleural space

● **J93.1   Other spontaneous pneumothorax**

J93.11   Primary spontaneous pneumothorax

J93.12   Secondary spontaneous pneumothorax
Code first underlying condition, such as:
catamenial pneumothorax due to endometriosis (N80.8)
cystic fibrosis (E84.-)
eosinophilic pneumonia (J82)
lymphangioleiomyomatosis (J84.81)
malignant neoplasm of bronchus and lung (C34.-)
Marfan's syndrome (Q87.4)
pneumonia due to Pneumocystis carinii (B59)
secondary malignant neoplasm of lung (C78.0-)
spontaneous rupture of the esophagus (K22.3)

● **J93.8   Other pneumothorax and air leak**

J93.81   Chronic pneumothorax

J93.82   Other air leak
Persistent air leak

J93.83   Other pneumothorax
Acute pneumothorax
Spontaneous pneumothorax NOS

J93.9   Pneumothorax, unspecified
Pneumothorax NOS

● **J94   Other pleural conditions**

Excludes1   pleurisy NOS (R09.1)
traumatic hemopneumothorax (S27.2)
traumatic hemothorax (S27.1)
tuberculous pleural conditions (current disease) (A15.-)

J94.0   Chylous effusion
Chyliform effusion

J94.1   Fibrothorax

J94.2   Hemothorax
Hemopneumothorax

J94.8   Other specified pleural conditions
Hydropneumothorax
Hydrothorax

J94.9   Pleural condition, unspecified

INTRAOPERATIVE AND POSTPROCEDURAL COMPLICATIONS AND DISORDERS OF RESPIRATORY SYSTEM, NOT ELSEWHERE CLASSIFIED (J95)

● **J95   Intraoperative and postprocedural complications and disorders of respiratory system, not elsewhere classified**

Excludes2   aspiration pneumonia (J69.-)
emphysema (subcutaneous) resulting from a procedure (T81.82)
hypostatic pneumonia (J18.2)
pulmonary manifestations due to radiation (J70.0- J70.1)

● **J95.0   Tracheostomy complications**

J95.00   Unspecified tracheostomy complication

J95.01   Hemorrhage from tracheostomy stoma

J95.02   Infection of tracheostomy stoma
Use additional code to identify type of infection, such as:
cellulitis of neck (L03.221)
sepsis (A40, A41.-)

J95.03   Malfunction of tracheostomy stoma
Mechanical complication of tracheostomy stoma
Obstruction of tracheostomy airway
Tracheal stenosis due to tracheostomy

J95.04   Tracheo-esophageal fistula following tracheostomy

J95.09   Other tracheostomy complication

J95.1   Acute pulmonary insufficiency following thoracic surgery

Excludes2   functional disturbances following cardiac surgery (I97.0, I97.1-)

J95.2   Acute pulmonary insufficiency following nonthoracic surgery

Excludes2   functional disturbances following cardiac surgery (I97.0, I97.1-)

J95.3   Chronic pulmonary insufficiency following surgery

Excludes2   functional disturbances following cardiac surgery (I97.0, I97.1-)

J95.4   Chemical pneumonitis due to anesthesia
Mendelson's syndrome
Postprocedural aspiration pneumonia
Use additional code for adverse effect, if applicable, to identify drug (T41.- with fifth or sixth character 5)

Excludes1   aspiration pneumonitis due to anesthesia complicating labor and delivery (O74.0)
aspiration pneumonitis due to anesthesia complicating pregnancy (O29)
aspiration pneumonitis due to anesthesia complicating the puerperium (O89.01)

J95.5   Postprocedural subglottic stenosis

▶ New   ⇒ Revised   ~~deleted~~ Deleted   Excludes 1   Excludes 2   Includes   Use additional   Code first   Code also   Key words
OGCR Official Guidelines   X Assign placeholder X   ● Use Additional Character(s)   ▸ Manifestation Code   Coding Clinic

● **J95.6**   **Intraoperative hemorrhage and hematoma** of a **respiratory system organ or structure complicating a procedure**

     Excludes1   intraoperative hemorrhage and hematoma of a respiratory system organ or structure due to accidental puncture and laceration during procedure (J95.7-)

     J95.61   Intraoperative hemorrhage and hematoma of a respiratory system organ or structure complicating a respiratory system procedure

     J95.62   Intraoperative hemorrhage and hematoma of a respiratory system organ or structure complicating other procedure

● **J95.7**   **Accidental puncture and laceration** of a respiratory system organ or structure during a procedure

     Excludes2   postprocedural pneumothorax (J95.811)

     J95.71   Accidental puncture and laceration of a respiratory system organ or structure during a respiratory system procedure

     J95.72   Accidental puncture and laceration of a respiratory system organ or structure during other procedure

● **J95.8**   **Other intraoperative and postprocedural complications and disorders of respiratory system, not elsewhere classified**

     Coding Clinic: 2016, Q4, P10

     ● **J95.81**   **Postprocedural pneumothorax and air leak**

         J95.811   Postprocedural **pneumothorax**

         J95.812   Postprocedural **air leak**

     ● **J95.82**   **Postprocedural respiratory failure**

         Excludes1   Respiratory failure in other conditions (J96.-)

         J95.821   **Acute** postprocedural respiratory failure

             Postprocedural respiratory failure NOS

         J95.822   **Acute and chronic** postprocedural respiratory failure

     ● **J95.83**   **Postprocedural hemorrhage of a respiratory system organ or structure following a procedure**

         J95.830   Postprocedural hemorrhage of a respiratory system organ or structure following a respiratory system procedure

         J95.831   Postprocedural hemorrhage of a respiratory system organ or structure following other procedure

     J95.84   **Transfusion-related acute lung injury (TRALI)**

     ● **J95.85**   **Complication of respirator [ventilator]**

         J95.850   **Mechanical complication of respirator**

             Excludes1   encounter for respirator [ventilator] dependence during power failure (Z99.12)

         J95.851   **Ventilator associated pneumonia**

             Ventilator associated pneumonitis

             Use additional code to identify the organism, if known (B95.-, B96.-, B97.-)

             Excludes1   ventilator lung in newborn (P27.8)

             Coding Clinic: 2017, Q1, P25

         J95.859   **Other complication of respirator [ventilator]**

● **J95.86**   **Postprocedural hematoma and seroma** of a respiratory system organ or structure following a procedure

     J95.860   Postprocedural **hematoma** of a respiratory system organ or structure following a respiratory system procedure

     J95.861   Postprocedural **hematoma** of a respiratory system organ or structure following other procedure

     J95.862   Postprocedural **seroma** of a respiratory system organ or structure following a respiratory system procedure

     J95.863   Postprocedural **seroma** of a respiratory system organ or structure following other procedure

J95.88   **Other intraoperative** complications of respiratory system, not elsewhere classified

J95.89   **Other postprocedural** complications and disorders of respiratory system, not elsewhere classified

     Use additional code to identify disorder, such as:

         aspiration pneumonia (J69.-)

         bacterial or viral pneumonia (J12-J18)

     Excludes2   acute pulmonary insufficiency following thoracic surgery (J95.1)

               postprocedural subglottic stenosis (J95.5)

OTHER DISEASES OF THE RESPIRATORY SYSTEM (J96-J99)

● **J96**   **Respiratory failure, not elsewhere classified**

     Excludes1   acute respiratory distress syndrome (J80)

               cardiorespiratory failure (R09.2)

               newborn respiratory distress syndrome (P22.0)

               postprocedural respiratory failure (J95.82-)

               respiratory arrest (R09.2)

               respiratory arrest of newborn (P28.81)

               respiratory failure of newborn (P28.5)

     ● **J96.0**   **Acute respiratory failure**

         J96.00   **Acute respiratory failure, unspecified whether with hypoxia or hypercapnia**

             Coding Clinic: 2016, Q3, P14

         J96.01   Acute respiratory failure with **hypoxia**

         J96.02   Acute respiratory failure with **hypercapnia**

     ● **J96.1**   **Chronic respiratory failure**

         J96.10   Chronic respiratory failure, **unspecified whether with hypoxia or hypercapnia**

             Coding Clinic: 2016, Q1, P38; 2015, Q1, P21

         J96.11   Chronic respiratory failure with **hypoxia**

         J96.12   Chronic respiratory failure with **hypercapnia**

     ● **J96.2**   **Acute and chronic respiratory failure**

         Acute on chronic respiratory failure

         J96.20   Acute and chronic respiratory failure, **unspecified** whether with hypoxia or hypercapnia

         J96.21   Acute and chronic respiratory failure with **hypoxia**

         J96.22   Acute and chronic respiratory failure with **hypercapnia**

     ● **J96.9**   **Respiratory failure, unspecified**

         J96.90   Respiratory failure, unspecified, **unspecified** whether with hypoxia or hypercapnia

         J96.91   Respiratory failure, unspecified with **hypoxia**

         J96.92   Respiratory failure, unspecified with **hypercapnia**

● **J98   Other respiratory disorders**

Use additional code to identify:
exposure to environmental tobacco smoke (Z77.22)
exposure to tobacco smoke in the perinatal period (P96.81)
history of tobacco dependence (Z87.891)
occupational exposure to environmental tobacco smoke (Z57.31)
tobacco dependence (F17.-)
tobacco use (Z72.0)

Excludes1   newborn apnea (P28.4)
newborn sleep apnea (P28.3)

Excludes2   apnea NOS (R06.81)
sleep apnea (G47.3-)

● **J98.0   Diseases of bronchus, not elsewhere classified**

J98.01   Acute bronchospasm

Excludes1   acute bronchiolitis with bronchospasm (J21.-)
acute bronchitis with bronchospasm (J20.-)
asthma (J45.-)
exercise induced bronchospasm (J45.990)

J98.09   Other diseases of bronchus, not elsewhere classified
Broncholithiasis
Calcification of bronchus
Stenosis of bronchus
Tracheobronchial collapse
Tracheobronchial dyskinesia
Ulcer of bronchus

● **J98.1   Pulmonary collapse**

Excludes1   therapeutic collapse of lung status (Z98.3)

J98.11   Atelectasis

Excludes1   newborn atelectasis
tuberculous atelectasis (current disease) (A15)

J98.19   Other pulmonary collapse

J98.2   Interstitial emphysema
Mediastinal emphysema

Excludes1   emphysema NOS (J43.9)
emphysema in newborn (P25.0)
surgical emphysema (subcutaneous) (T81.82)
traumatic subcutaneous emphysema (T79.7)

J98.3   Compensatory emphysema

J98.4   Other disorders of lung
Calcification of lung
Cystic lung disease (acquired)
Lung disease NOS
Pulmolithiasis

Excludes1   acute interstitial pneumonitis (J84.114)
pulmonary insufficiency following surgery (J95.1-J95.2)

● **J98.5   Diseases of mediastinum, not elsewhere classified**

Excludes2   abscess of mediastinum (J85.3)

Coding Clinic: 2016, Q4, P29

J98.51   Mediastinitis
Code first underlying condition, if applicable, such as postoperative mediastinitis (T81.-)

J98.59   Other diseases of mediastinum, not elsewhere classified
Fibrosis of mediastinum
Hernia of mediastinum
Retraction of mediastinum

J98.6   Disorders of diaphragm
Diaphragmatitis
Paralysis of diaphragm
Relaxation of diaphragm

Excludes1   congenital malformation of diaphragm NEC (Q79.1)
congenital diaphragmatic hernia (Q79.0)

Excludes2   diaphragmatic hernia (K44.-)

J98.8   Other specified respiratory disorders

J98.9   Respiratory disorder, unspecified
Respiratory disease (chronic) NOS

▷ *J99   Respiratory disorders in diseases classified elsewhere*

Code first underlying disease, such as:
amyloidosis (E85.-)
ankylosing spondylitis (M45)
congenital syphilis (A50.5)
cryoglobulinemia (D89.1)
early congenital syphilis (A50.0)
▷ plasminogen deficiency (E88.02)
schistosomiasis (B65.0-B65.9)

Excludes1   respiratory disorders in:
amebiasis (A06.5)
blastomycosis (B40.0-B40.2)
candidiasis (B37.1)
coccidioidomycosis (B38.0-B38.2)
cystic fibrosis with pulmonary manifestations (E84.0)
dermatomyositis (M33.01, M33.11)
histoplasmosis (B39.0-B39.2)
late syphilis (A52.72, A52.73)
polymyositis (M33.21)
sicca syndrome (M35.02)
systemic lupus erythematosus (M32.13)
systemic sclerosis (M34.81)
Wegener's granulomatosis (M31.30-M31.31)

▶ New   ⇒ Revised   ~~deleted~~ Deleted   Excludes 1   Excludes 2   Includes   Use additional   Code first   Code also   Key words
OGCR Official Guidelines   X Assign placeholder X   ● Use Additional Character(s)   ▷ Manifestation Code   **Coding Clinic**

CHAPTER 11

DISEASES OF THE DIGESTIVE SYSTEM
(K00-K95)

OGCR Chapter-Specific Coding Guidelines

> 11. **Chapter 11: Diseases of the Digestive System (K00-K95)**
> Reserved for future guideline expansion

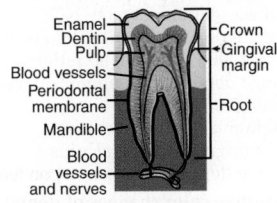

Figure 11-1 Anatomy of a tooth.

Item 11-1 **Anodontia** is the congenital absence of teeth. **Hypodontia** is partial anodontia. **Oligodontia** is the congenital absence of some teeth, whereas **supernumerary** is having more teeth than the normal number. **Mesiodens** are small extra teeth that often appear in pairs, although single small teeth are not uncommon.

CHAPTER 11

DISEASES OF THE DIGESTIVE SYSTEM
(K00-K95)

> **Excludes2** certain conditions originating in the perinatal period (P04-P96)
> certain infectious and parasitic diseases (A00-B99)
> complications of pregnancy, childbirth and the puerperium (O00-O9A)
> congenital malformations, deformations and chromosomal abnormalities (Q00-Q99)
> endocrine, nutritional and metabolic diseases (E00-E88)
> injury, poisoning and certain other consequences of external causes (S00-T88)
> neoplasms (C00-D49)
> symptoms, signs and abnormal clinical and laboratory findings, not elsewhere classified (R00-R94)

This chapter contains the following blocks:

K00-K14	Diseases of oral cavity and salivary glands
K20-K31	Diseases of esophagus, stomach and duodenum
K35-K38	Diseases of appendix
K40-K46	Hernia
K50-K52	Noninfective enteritis and colitis
K55-K64	Other diseases of intestines
K65-K68	Diseases of peritoneum and retroperitoneum
K70-K77	Diseases of liver
K80-K87	Disorders of gallbladder, biliary tract and pancreas
K90-K95	Other diseases of the digestive system

DISEASES OF ORAL CAVITY AND SALIVARY GLANDS (K00-K14)

● **K00** **Disorders of tooth development and eruption**
> **Excludes2** embedded and impacted teeth (K01.-)

    K00.0 **Anodontia**
        Hypodontia
        Oligodontia
> **Excludes1** acquired absence of teeth (K08.1-)

    K00.1 **Supernumerary teeth**
        Distomolar
        Fourth molar
        Mesiodens
        Paramolar
        Supplementary teeth
> **Excludes2** supernumerary roots (K00.2)

    K00.2 **Abnormalities of size and form of teeth**
        Concrescence of teeth
        Fusion of teeth
        Gemination of teeth
        Dens evaginatus
        Dens in dente
        Dens invaginatus
        Enamel pearls
        Macrodontia
        Microdontia
        Peg-shaped [conical] teeth
        Supernumerary roots
        Taurodontism
        Tuberculum paramolare
> **Excludes1** abnormalities of teeth due to congenital syphilis (A50.5)
> tuberculum Carabelli, which is regarded as a normal variation and should not be coded

    K00.3 **Mottled teeth**
        Dental fluorosis
        Mottling of enamel
        Nonfluoride enamel opacities
> **Excludes2** deposits [accretions] on teeth (K03.6)

    K00.4 **Disturbances in tooth formation**
        Aplasia and hypoplasia of cementum
        Dilaceration of tooth
        Enamel hypoplasia (neonatal) (postnatal) (prenatal)
        Regional odontodysplasia
        Turner's tooth
> **Excludes1** Hutchinson's teeth and mulberry molars in congenital syphilis (A50.5)
> **Excludes2** mottled teeth (K00.3)

    K00.5 **Hereditary disturbances in tooth structure, not elsewhere classified**
        Amelogenesis imperfecta
        Dentinogenesis imperfecta
        Odontogenesis imperfecta
        Dentinal dysplasia
        Shell teeth

    K00.6 **Disturbances in tooth eruption**
        Dentia praecox
        Natal tooth
        Neonatal tooth
        Premature eruption of tooth
        Premature shedding of primary [deciduous] tooth
        Prenatal teeth
        Retained [persistent] primary tooth
> **Excludes2** embedded and impacted teeth (K01.-)

    K00.7 **Teething syndrome**

    K00.8 **Other disorders of tooth development**
        Color changes during tooth formation
        Intrinsic staining of teeth NOS
> **Excludes2** posteruptive color changes (K03.7)

    K00.9 **Disorder of tooth development, unspecified**
        Disorder of odontogenesis NOS

● **K01** **Embedded and impacted teeth**
> **Excludes1** abnormal position of fully erupted teeth (M26.3-)

    K01.0 **Embedded teeth**
    K01.1 **Impacted teeth**

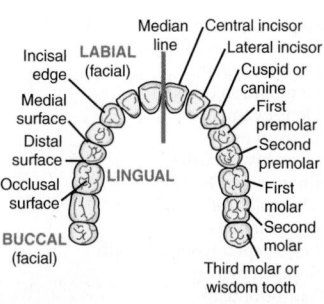

Figure 11-2 The permanent teeth within the dental arch.

Item 11-2 Each dental arch (jaw) normally contains 16 teeth. Tooth decay or **dental caries** is a disease of the enamel, dentin, and cementum of the tooth and can result in a cavity.

● **K02   Dental caries**

　　Includes   caries of dentine
　　　　　　　　dental cavities
　　　　　　　　early childhood caries
　　　　　　　　pre-eruptive caries
　　　　　　　　recurrent caries (dentino enamel junction)
　　　　　　　　　(enamel) (to the pulp)
　　　　　　　　tooth decay

　　K02.3   Arrested dental caries
　　　　　Arrested coronal and root caries

● **K02.5   Dental caries on pit and fissure surface**
　　　　　Dental caries on chewing surface of tooth

　　　　K02.51   Dental caries on pit and fissure surface limited to enamel
　　　　　　　　White spot lesions [initial caries] on pit and fissure surface of tooth

　　　　K02.52   Dental caries on pit and fissure surface penetrating into dentin
　　　　　　　　Primary dental caries, cervical origin

　　　　K02.53   Dental caries on pit and fissure surface penetrating into pulp

● **K02.6   Dental caries on smooth surface**

　　　　K02.61   Dental caries on smooth surface limited to enamel
　　　　　　　　White spot lesions [initial caries] on smooth surface of tooth

　　　　K02.62   Dental caries on smooth surface penetrating into dentin

　　　　K02.63   Dental caries on smooth surface penetrating into pulp

　　K02.7   Dental root caries

　　K02.9   Dental caries, unspecified

● **K03   Other diseases of hard tissues of teeth**

　　Excludes2   bruxism (F45.8)
　　　　　　　　dental caries (K02.-)
　　　　　　　　teeth-grinding NOS (F45.8)

　　K03.0   Excessive attrition of teeth
　　　　　Approximal wear of teeth
　　　　　Occlusal wear of teeth

　　K03.1   Abrasion of teeth
　　　　　Dentifrice abrasion of teeth
　　　　　Habitual abrasion of teeth
　　　　　Occupational abrasion of teeth
　　　　　Ritual abrasion of teeth
　　　　　Traditional abrasion of teeth
　　　　　Wedge defect NOS

　　K03.2   Erosion of teeth
　　　　　Erosion of teeth due to diet
　　　　　Erosion of teeth due to drugs and medicaments
　　　　　Erosion of teeth due to persistent vomiting
　　　　　Erosion of teeth NOS
　　　　　Idiopathic erosion of teeth
　　　　　Occupational erosion of teeth

　　K03.3   Pathological resorption of teeth
　　　　　Internal granuloma of pulp
　　　　　Resorption of teeth (external)

　　K03.4   Hypercementosis
　　　　　Cementation hyperplasia

　　K03.5   Ankylosis of teeth

　　K03.6   Deposits [accretions] on teeth
　　　　　Betel deposits [accretions] on teeth
　　　　　Black deposits [accretions] on teeth
　　　　　Extrinsic staining of teeth NOS
　　　　　Green deposits [accretions] on teeth
　　　　　Materia alba deposits [accretions] on teeth
　　　　　Orange deposits [accretions] on teeth
　　　　　Staining of teeth NOS
　　　　　Subgingival dental calculus
　　　　　Supragingival dental calculus
　　　　　Tobacco deposits [accretions] on teeth

　　K03.7   Posteruptive color changes of dental hard tissues
　　　　Excludes2   deposits [accretions] on teeth (K03.6)

● **K03.8   Other specified diseases of hard tissues of teeth**
　　　　K03.81   Cracked tooth
　　　　　　Excludes1   asymptomatic craze lines in enamel - omit code
　　　　　　　　　　　　broken or fractured tooth due to trauma (S02.5)

　　　　K03.89   Other specified diseases of hard tissues of teeth

　　K03.9   Disease of hard tissues of teeth, unspecified

● **K04   Diseases of pulp and periapical tissues**
　　Coding Clinic: 2016, Q4, P29

● **K04.0   Pulpitis**
　　　　　Acute pulpitis
　　　　　Chronic (hyperplastic) (ulcerative) pulpitis

　　　　K04.01   Reversible pulpitis

　　　　K04.02   Irreversible pulpitis

　　K04.1   Necrosis of pulp
　　　　　Pulpal gangrene

　　K04.2   Pulp degeneration
　　　　　Denticles
　　　　　Pulpal calcifications
　　　　　Pulpal stones

　　K04.3   Abnormal hard tissue formation in pulp
　　　　　Secondary or irregular dentine

　　K04.4   Acute apical periodontitis of pulpal origin
　　　　　Acute apical periodontitis NOS
　　　　Excludes1   acute periodontitis (K05.2-)

　　K04.5   Chronic apical periodontitis
　　　　　Apical or periapical granuloma
　　　　　Apical periodontitis NOS
　　　　Excludes1   chronic periodontitis (K05.3-)

　　K04.6   Periapical abscess with sinus
　　　　　Dental abscess with sinus
　　　　　Dentoalveolar abscess with sinus

　　K04.7   Periapical abscess without sinus
　　　　　Dental abscess without sinus
　　　　　Dentoalveolar abscess without sinus

　　K04.8   Radicular cyst
　　　　　Apical (periodontal) cyst
　　　　　Periapical cyst
　　　　　Residual radicular cyst
　　　　Excludes2   lateral periodontal cyst (K09.0)

● **K04.9   Other and unspecified diseases of pulp and periapical tissues**
　　　　K04.90   Unspecified diseases of pulp and periapical tissues

　　　　K04.99   Other diseases of pulp and periapical tissues

▶ New　⇒ Revised　~~deleted~~ Deleted　Excludes 1　Excludes 2　Includes　Use additional　Code first　Code also　Key words
OGCR Official Guidelines　X Assign placeholder X　● Use Additional Character(s)　▶ Manifestation Code　**Coding Clinic**

CHAPTER 11 (K00-K95)

Item 11–3 Acute gingivitis, also known as orilitis or ulitis, is the short-term, severe inflammation of the gums (gingiva) caused by bacteria. **Chronic gingivitis** is persistent inflammation of the gums. When the gingivitis moves into the periodontium it is called periodontitis, also known as paradentitis.

● **K05   Gingivitis and periodontal diseases**
    Use additional code to identify:
      alcohol abuse and dependence (F10.-)
      exposure to environmental tobacco smoke (Z77.22)
      exposure to tobacco smoke in the perinatal period (P96.81)
      history of tobacco dependence (Z87.891)
      occupational exposure to environmental tobacco smoke (Z57.31)
      tobacco dependence (F17.-)
      tobacco use (Z72.0)
    Coding Clinic: 2016, Q4, P29

● **K05.0   Acute gingivitis**
      Excludes1   acute necrotizing ulcerative gingivitis (A69.1)
                  herpesviral [herpes simplex] gingivostomatitis (B00.2)

    K05.00   Acute gingivitis, plaque induced
        Acute gingivitis NOS
        Plaque induced gingival disease

    K05.01   Acute gingivitis, non-plaque induced

● **K05.1   Chronic gingivitis**
      Desquamative gingivitis (chronic)
      Gingivitis (chronic) NOS
      Hyperplastic gingivitis (chronic)
      Pregnancy associated gingivitis
      Simple marginal gingivitis (chronic)
      Ulcerative gingivitis (chronic)
      Code first, if applicable, diseases of the digestive system complicating pregnancy (O99.61-)

    K05.10   Chronic gingivitis, plaque induced
        Chronic gingivitis NOS
        Gingivitis NOS

    K05.11   Chronic gingivitis, non-plaque induced

● **K05.2   Aggressive periodontitis**
      Acute pericoronitis
      Excludes1   acute apical periodontitis (K04.4)
                  periapical abscess (K04.7)
                  periapical abscess with sinus (K04.6)

    K05.20   Aggressive periodontitis, unspecified
●   **K05.21   Aggressive periodontitis, localized**
        Periodontal abscess

       K05.211   Aggressive periodontitis, localized, slight
       K05.212   Aggressive periodontitis, localized, moderate
       K05.213   Aggressive periodontitis, localized, severe
       K05.219   Aggressive periodontitis, localized, unspecified severity

●   **K05.22   Aggressive periodontitis, generalized**
       K05.221   Aggressive periodontitis, generalized, slight
       K05.222   Aggressive periodontitis, generalized, moderate
       K05.223   Aggressive periodontitis, generalized, severe
       K05.229   Aggressive periodontitis, generalized, unspecified severity

● **K05.3   Chronic periodontitis**
      Chronic pericoronitis
      Complex periodontitis
      Periodontitis NOS
      Simplex periodontitis
      Excludes1   chronic apical periodontitis (K04.5)

    K05.30   Chronic periodontitis, unspecified
●   **K05.31   Chronic periodontitis, localized**
       K05.311   Chronic periodontitis, localized, slight
       K05.312   Chronic periodontitis, localized, moderate
       K05.313   Chronic periodontitis, localized, severe
       K05.319   Chronic periodontitis, localized, unspecified severity

●   **K05.32   Chronic periodontitis, generalized**
       K05.321   Chronic periodontitis, generalized, slight
       K05.322   Chronic periodontitis, generalized, moderate
       K05.323   Chronic periodontitis, generalized, severe
       K05.329   Chronic periodontitis, generalized, unspecified severity

  K05.4   Periodontosis
      Juvenile periodontosis

  K05.5   Other periodontal diseases
      Combined periodontic-endodontic lesion
      Narrow gingival width (of periodontal soft tissue)
      Excludes2   leukoplakia of gingiva (K13.21)

  K05.6   Periodontal disease, unspecified

● **K06   Other disorders of gingiva and edentulous alveolar ridge**
      Excludes2   acute gingivitis (K05.0)
                  atrophy of edentulous alveolar ridge (K08.2)
                  chronic gingivitis (K05.1)
                  gingivitis NOS (K05.1)
    Coding Clinic: 2016, Q4, P29

● **K06.0   Gingival recession**
      Gingival recession (postinfective) (postprocedural)
●   **K06.01   Gingival recession, localized**
       K06.010   Localized gingival recession, unspecified
           Localized gingival recession, NOS
       K06.011   Localized gingival recession, minimal
       K06.012   Localized gingival recession, moderate
       K06.013   Localized gingival recession, severe

●   **K06.02   Gingival recession, generalized**
       K06.020   Generalized gingival recession, unspecified
           Generalized gingival recession, NOS
       K06.021   Generalized gingival recession, minimal
       K06.022   Generalized gingival recession, moderate
       K06.023   Generalized gingival recession, severe

  K06.1   Gingival enlargement
      Gingival fibromatosis

  K06.2   Gingival and edentulous alveolar ridge lesions associated with trauma
      Irritative hyperplasia of edentulous ridge [denture hyperplasia]
      Use additional code (Chapter 20) to identify external cause or denture status (Z97.2)

CHAPTER 11 (K00-K95)

K06.3 Horizontal alveolar bone loss

K06.8 Other specified disorders of gingiva and edentulous alveolar ridge
Fibrous epulis
Flabby alveolar ridge
Giant cell epulis
Peripheral giant cell granuloma of gingiva
Pyogenic granuloma of gingiva
Vertical ridge deficiency
> **Excludes2** gingival cyst (K09.0)

K06.9 Disorder of gingiva and edentulous alveolar ridge, unspecified

● **K08** Other disorders of teeth and supporting structures
> **Excludes2** dentofacial anomalies [including malocclusion] (M26.-)
> disorders of jaw (M27.-)
> Coding Clinic: 2016, Q4, P29

K08.0 Exfoliation of teeth due to systemic causes
Code also underlying systemic condition

● **K08.1** Complete loss of teeth
Acquired loss of teeth, complete
> **Excludes1** congenital absence of teeth (K00.0)
> exfoliation of teeth due to systemic causes (K08.0)
> partial loss of teeth (K08.4-)

● **K08.10** Complete loss of teeth, unspecified cause

K08.101 Complete loss of teeth, unspecified cause, class I

K08.102 Complete loss of teeth, unspecified cause, class II

K08.103 Complete loss of teeth, unspecified cause, class III

K08.104 Complete loss of teeth, unspecified cause, class IV

K08.109 Complete loss of teeth, unspecified cause, unspecified class
Edentulism NOS

● **K08.11** Complete loss of teeth due to trauma

K08.111 Complete loss of teeth due to trauma, class I

K08.112 Complete loss of teeth due to trauma, class II

K08.113 Complete loss of teeth due to trauma, class III

K08.114 Complete loss of teeth due to trauma, class IV

K08.119 Complete loss of teeth due to trauma, unspecified class

● **K08.12** Complete loss of teeth due to periodontal diseases

K08.121 Complete loss of teeth due to periodontal diseases, class I

K08.122 Complete loss of teeth due to periodontal diseases, class II

K08.123 Complete loss of teeth due to periodontal diseases, class III

K08.124 Complete loss of teeth due to periodontal diseases, class IV

K08.129 Complete loss of teeth due to periodontal diseases, unspecified class

● **K08.13** Complete loss of teeth due to caries

K08.131 Complete loss of teeth due to caries, class I

K08.132 Complete loss of teeth due to caries, class II

K08.133 Complete loss of teeth due to caries, class III

K08.134 Complete loss of teeth due to caries, class IV

K08.139 Complete loss of teeth due to caries, unspecified class

● **K08.19** Complete loss of teeth due to other specified cause

K08.191 Complete loss of teeth due to other specified cause, class I

K08.192 Complete loss of teeth due to other specified cause, class II

K08.193 Complete loss of teeth due to other specified cause, class III

K08.194 Complete loss of teeth due to other specified cause, class IV

K08.199 Complete loss of teeth due to other specified cause, unspecified class

● **K08.2** Atrophy of edentulous alveolar ridge

K08.20 Unspecified atrophy of edentulous alveolar ridge
Atrophy of the mandible NOS
Atrophy of the maxilla NOS

K08.21 Minimal atrophy of the mandible
Minimal atrophy of the edentulous mandible

K08.22 Moderate atrophy of the mandible
Moderate atrophy of the edentulous mandible

K08.23 Severe atrophy of the mandible
Severe atrophy of the edentulous mandible

K08.24 Minimal atrophy of maxilla
Minimal atrophy of the edentulous maxilla

K08.25 Moderate atrophy of the maxilla
Moderate atrophy of the edentulous maxilla

K08.26 Severe atrophy of the maxilla
Severe atrophy of the edentulous maxilla

K08.3 Retained dental root

● **K08.4** Partial loss of teeth
Acquired loss of teeth, partial
> **Excludes1** complete loss of teeth (K08.1-)
> congenital absence of teeth (K00.0)
> **Excludes2** exfoliation of teeth due to systemic causes (K08.0)

● **K08.40** Partial loss of teeth, unspecified cause

K08.401 Partial loss of teeth, unspecified cause, class I

K08.402 Partial loss of teeth, unspecified cause, class II

K08.403 Partial loss of teeth, unspecified cause, class III

K08.404 Partial loss of teeth, unspecified cause, class IV

K08.409 Partial loss of teeth, unspecified cause, unspecified class
Tooth extraction status NOS

● **K08.41** Partial loss of teeth due to trauma

K08.411 Partial loss of teeth due to trauma, class I

K08.412 Partial loss of teeth due to trauma, class II

K08.413 Partial loss of teeth due to trauma, class III

K08.414 Partial loss of teeth due to trauma, class IV

K08.419 Partial loss of teeth due to trauma, unspecified class

● **K08.42** Partial loss of teeth due to periodontal diseases

K08.421 Partial loss of teeth due to periodontal diseases, class I

K08.422 Partial loss of teeth due to periodontal diseases, class II

K08.423 Partial loss of teeth due to periodontal diseases, class III

K08.424 Partial loss of teeth due to periodontal diseases, class IV

K08.429 Partial loss of teeth due to periodontal diseases, unspecified class

▶ New　　⇒ Revised　　deleted Deleted　　Excludes 1　　Excludes 2　　Includes　　Use additional　　Code first　　Code also　　Key words
OGCR Official Guidelines　　X Assign placeholder X　　● Use Additional Character(s)　　▶ Manifestation Code　　Coding Clinic

● **K08.43**   Partial loss of teeth due to caries

    K08.431   Partial loss of teeth due to caries, class I

    K08.432   Partial loss of teeth due to caries, class II

    K08.433   Partial loss of teeth due to caries, class III

    K08.434   Partial loss of teeth due to caries, class IV

    K08.439   Partial loss of teeth due to caries, unspecified class

● **K08.49**   Partial loss of teeth due to other specified cause

    K08.491   Partial loss of teeth due to other specified cause, class I

    K08.492   Partial loss of teeth due to other specified cause, class II

    K08.493   Partial loss of teeth due to other specified cause, class III

    K08.494   Partial loss of teeth due to other specified cause, class IV

    K08.499   Partial loss of teeth due to other specified cause, unspecified class

● **K08.5**   Unsatisfactory restoration of tooth
    Defective bridge, crown, filling
    Defective dental restoration

    Excludes1   dental restoration status (Z98.811)

    Excludes2   endosseous dental implant failure (M27.6-)
         unsatisfactory endodontic treatment (M27.5-)

    K08.50   Unsatisfactory restoration of tooth, unspecified
       Defective dental restoration NOS

    K08.51   Open restoration margins of tooth
       Dental restoration failure of marginal integrity
       Open margin on tooth restoration
       Poor gingival margin to tooth restoration

    K08.52   Unrepairable overhanging of dental restorative materials
       Overhanging of tooth restoration

●   **K08.53**   Fractured dental restorative material

       Excludes1   cracked tooth (K03.81)
           traumatic fracture of tooth (S02.5)

       K08.530   Fractured dental restorative material without loss of material

       K08.531   Fractured dental restorative material with loss of material

       K08.539   Fractured dental restorative material, unspecified

    K08.54   Contour of existing restoration of tooth biologically incompatible with oral health
       Dental restoration failure of periodontal anatomical integrity
       Unacceptable contours of existing restoration of tooth
       Unacceptable morphology of existing restoration of tooth

    K08.55   Allergy to existing dental restorative material
       Use additional code to identify the specific type of allergy

    K08.56   Poor aesthetic of existing restoration of tooth
       Dental restoration aesthetically inadequate or displeasing

    K08.59   Other unsatisfactory restoration of tooth
       Other defective dental restoration

● **K08.8**   Other specified disorders of teeth and supporting structures

    K08.81   Primary occlusal trauma

    K08.82   Secondary occlusal trauma

    K08.89   Other specified disorders of teeth and supporting structures
       Enlargement of alveolar ridge NOS
       Insufficient anatomic crown height
       Insufficient clinical crown length
       Irregular alveolar process
       Toothache NOS

    K08.9   Disorder of teeth and supporting structures, unspecified

● **K09**   Cysts of oral region, not elsewhere classified

    Includes   lesions showing histological features both of aneurysmal cyst and of another fibro-osseous lesion

    Excludes2   cysts of jaw (M27.0-, M27.4-)
           radicular cyst (K04.8)

    K09.0   Developmental odontogenic cysts
       Dentigerous cyst
       Eruption cyst
       Follicular cyst
       Gingival cyst
       Lateral periodontal cyst
       Primordial cyst

       Excludes2   keratocysts (D16.4, D16.5)
           odontogenic keratocystic tumors (D16.4, D16.5)

    K09.1   Developmental (nonodontogenic) cysts of oral region
       Cyst (of) incisive canal
       Cyst (of) palatine of papilla
       Globulomaxillary cyst
       Median palatal cyst
       Nasoalveolar cyst
       Nasolabial cyst
       Nasopalatine duct cyst

    K09.8   Other cysts of oral region, not elsewhere classified
       Dermoid cyst
       Epidermoid cyst
       Lymphoepithelial cyst
       Epstein's pearl

    K09.9   Cyst of oral region, unspecified

★ **(See Plate 61 on page 73.)**

● **K11**   Diseases of salivary glands
    Use additional code to identify:
       alcohol abuse and dependence (F10.-)
       exposure to environmental tobacco smoke (Z77.22)
       exposure to tobacco smoke in the perinatal period (P96.81)
       history of tobacco dependence (Z87.891)
       occupational exposure to environmental tobacco smoke (Z57.31)
       tobacco dependence (F17.-)
       tobacco use (Z72.0)

    K11.0   Atrophy of salivary gland

    K11.1   Hypertrophy of salivary gland

Item 11–4 Atrophy is wasting away of a tissue or organ, whereas **hypertrophy** is overdevelopment or enlargement of a tissue or organ. **Sialoadenitis** is salivary gland inflammation. **Parotitis** is the inflammation of the parotid gland. In the epidemic form, parotitis is also known as mumps. **Sialolithiasis** is the formation of calculus within a salivary gland. **Mucocele** is a polyp composed of mucus.

Figure 11-3   Major salivary glands.

Parotid gland
Sublingual gland
Submandibular gland

CHAPTER 11 (K00-K95)

● **K11.2 Sialoadenitis**
Parotitis
Excludes1 epidemic parotitis (B26.-)
mumps (B26.-)
uveoparotid fever [Heerfordt] (D86.89)

K11.20 Sialoadenitis, unspecified
K11.21 Acute sialoadenitis
Excludes1 acute recurrent sialoadenitis (K11.22)
K11.22 Acute recurrent sialoadenitis
K11.23 Chronic sialoadenitis

K11.3 Abscess of salivary gland
K11.4 Fistula of salivary gland
Excludes1 congenital fistula of salivary gland (Q38.4)

K11.5 Sialolithiasis
Calculus of salivary gland or duct
Stone of salivary gland or duct

K11.6 Mucocele of salivary gland
Mucous extravasation cyst of salivary gland
Mucous retention cyst of salivary gland
Ranula

K11.7 Disturbances of salivary secretion
Hypoptyalism
Ptyalism
Xerostomia
Excludes2 dry mouth NOS (R68.2)

K11.8 Other diseases of salivary glands
Benign lymphoepithelial lesion of salivary gland
Mikulicz' disease
Necrotizing sialometaplasia
Sialectasia
Stenosis of salivary duct
Stricture of salivary duct
Excludes1 sicca syndrome [Sjögren] (M35.0-)

K11.9 Disease of salivary gland, unspecified
Sialoadenopathy NOS

● **K12 Stomatitis and related lesions**
Use additional code to identify:
alcohol abuse and dependence (F10.-)
exposure to environmental tobacco smoke (Z77.22)
exposure to tobacco smoke in the perinatal period (P96.81)
history of tobacco dependence (Z87.891)
occupational exposure to environmental tobacco smoke (Z57.31)
tobacco dependence (F17.-)
tobacco use (Z72.0)
Excludes1 cancrum oris (A69.0)
cheilitis (K13.0)
gangrenous stomatitis (A69.0)
herpesviral [herpes simplex] gingivostomatitis (B00.2)
noma (A69.0)

K12.0 Recurrent oral aphthae
Aphthous stomatitis (major) (minor)
Bednar's aphthae
Periadenitis mucosa necrotica recurrens
Recurrent aphthous ulcer
Stomatitis herpetiformis

K12.1 Other forms of stomatitis
Stomatitis NOS
Denture stomatitis
Ulcerative stomatitis
Vesicular stomatitis
Excludes1 acute necrotizing ulcerative stomatitis (A69.1)
Vincent's stomatitis (A69.1)

K12.2 Cellulitis and abscess of mouth
Cellulitis of mouth (floor)
Submandibular abscess
Excludes2 abscess of salivary gland (K11.3)
abscess of tongue (K14.0)
periapical abscess (K04.6-K04.7)
periodontal abscess (K05.21)
peritonsillar abscess (J36)

● **K12.3 Oral mucositis (ulcerative)**
Mucositis (oral) (oropharyneal)
Excludes2 gastrointestinal mucositis (ulcerative) (K92.81)
mucositis (ulcerative) of vagina and vulva (N76.81)
nasal mucositis (ulcerative) (J34.81)

K12.30 Oral mucositis (ulcerative), unspecified
K12.31 Oral mucositis (ulcerative) due to antineoplastic therapy
Use additional code for adverse effect, if applicable, to identify antineoplastic and immunosuppressive drugs (T45.1X5)
Use additional code for other antineoplastic therapy, such as:
radiological procedure and radiotherapy (Y84.2)
K12.32 Oral mucositis (ulcerative) due to other drugs
Use additional code for adverse effect, if applicable, to identify drug (T36-T50 with fifth or sixth character 5)
K12.33 Oral mucositis (ulcerative) due to radiation
Use additional external cause code (W88-W90, X39.0-) to identify cause
K12.39 Other oral mucositis (ulcerative)
Viral oral mucositis (ulcerative)

● **K13 Other diseases of lip and oral mucosa**
Includes epithelial disturbances of tongue
Use additional code to identify:
alcohol abuse and dependence (F10.-)
exposure to environmental tobacco smoke (Z77.22)
exposure to tobacco smoke in the perinatal period (P96.81)
history of tobacco dependence (Z87.891)
occupational exposure to environmental tobacco smoke (Z57.31)
tobacco dependence (F17.-)
tobacco use (Z72.0)
Excludes2 certain disorders of gingiva and edentulous alveolar ridge (K05-K06)
cysts of oral region (K09.-)
diseases of tongue (K14.-)
stomatitis and related lesions (K12.-)

K13.0 Diseases of lips

Abscess of lips	Exfoliative cheilitis
Angular cheilitis	Fistula of lips
Cellulitis of lips	Glandular cheilitis
Cheilitis NOS	Hypertrophy of lips
Cheilodynia	Perlèche NEC
Cheilosis	

Excludes1 ariboflavinosis (E53.0)
cheilitis due to radiation-related disorders (L55-L59)
congenital fistula of lips (Q38.0)
congenital hypertrophy of lips (Q18.6)
Perlèche due to candidiasis (B37.83)
Perlèche due to riboflavin deficiency (E53.0)

K13.1 Cheek and lip biting

Item 11-5 Stomatitis is the inflammation of the oral mucosa. **Mucositis** is the inflammation of the mucous membranes lining the digestive tract from the mouth to the anus. It is a common side effect of chemotherapy and of radiotherapy that involves any part of the digestive tract.

▶ New ⇒ Revised ~~deleted~~ Deleted Excludes 1 Excludes 2 Includes Use additional Code first Code also Key words
OGCR Official Guidelines X Assign placeholder X ● Use Additional Character(s) ▷ Manifestation Code **Coding Clinic**

CHAPTER 11 (K00-K95)

Figure 11-4 Oral leukoplakia and associated. (From Swartz MH: Textbook of Physical Diagnosis: History and Examination, Philadelphia, PA, Saunders/Elsevier, 2010)

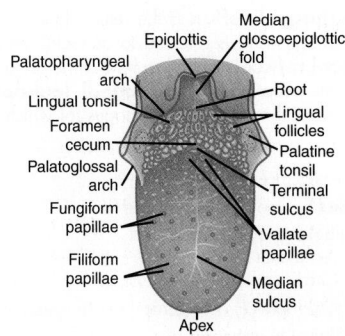

Figure 11-5 Structure of the tongue.

● **K13.2 Leukoplakia and other disturbances of oral epithelium, including tongue**

> **Excludes1** carcinoma in situ of oral epithelium (D00.0-)
> hairy leukoplakia (K13.3)

K13.21 Leukoplakia of oral mucosa, including tongue
Considered precancerous and evidenced by thickened white patches of epithelium on mucous membranes
Leukokeratosis of oral mucosa
Leukoplakia of gingiva, lips, tongue
> **Excludes1** hairy leukoplakia (K13.3)
> leukokeratosis nicotina palati (K13.24)

K13.22 Minimal keratinized residual ridge mucosa
Minimal keratinization of alveolar ridge mucosa

K13.23 Excessive keratinized residual ridge mucosa
Excessive keratinization of alveolar ridge mucosa

K13.24 Leukokeratosis nicotina palati
Smoker's palate

K13.29 Other disturbances of oral epithelium, including tongue
Erythroplakia of mouth or tongue
Focal epithelial hyperplasia of mouth or tongue
Leukoedema of mouth or tongue
Other oral epithelium disturbances

K13.3 Hairy leukoplakia

K13.4 Granuloma and granuloma-like lesions of oral mucosa
Eosinophilic granuloma
Granuloma pyogenicum
Verrucous xanthoma

K13.5 Oral submucous fibrosis
Submucous fibrosis of tongue

K13.6 Irritative hyperplasia of oral mucosa
> **Excludes2** irritative hyperplasia of edentulous ridge [denture hyperplasia] (K06.2)

● **K13.7 Other and unspecified lesions of oral mucosa**
K13.70 Unspecified lesions of oral mucosa
K13.79 Other lesions of oral mucosa
Focal oral mucinosis

★ **(See Plate 58 on page 71.)**

● **K14 Diseases of tongue**
Use additional code to identify:
alcohol abuse and dependence (F10.-)
exposure to environmental tobacco smoke (Z77.22)
history of tobacco dependence (Z87.891)
occupational exposure to environmental tobacco smoke (Z57.31)
tobacco dependence (F17.-)
tobacco use (Z72.0)
> **Excludes2** erythroplakia (K13.29)
> focal epithelial hyperplasia (K13.29)
> leukedema of tongue (K13.29)
> leukoplakia of tongue (K13.21)
> hairy leukoplakia (K13.3)
> macroglossia (congenital) (Q38.2)
> submucous fibrosis of tongue (K13.5)

K14.0 Glossitis
Abscess of tongue
Ulceration (traumatic) of tongue
> **Excludes1** atrophic glossitis (K14.4)

K14.1 Geographic tongue
Benign migratory glossitis
Glossitis areata exfoliativa

K14.2 Median rhomboid glossitis

K14.3 Hypertrophy of tongue papillae
Black hairy tongue
Coated tongue
Hypertrophy of foliate papillae
Lingua villosa nigra

K14.4 Atrophy of tongue papillae
Atrophic glossitis

K14.5 Plicated tongue
Fissured tongue   Scrotal tongue
Furrowed tongue
> **Excludes1** fissured tongue, congenital (Q38.3)

K14.6 Glossodynia
Glossopyrosis   Painful tongue

K14.8 Other diseases of tongue
Atrophy of tongue   Glossocele
Crenated tongue   Glossoptosis
Enlargement of tongue   Hypertrophy of tongue

K14.9 Disease of tongue, unspecified
Glossopathy NOS

DISEASES OF ESOPHAGUS, STOMACH AND DUODENUM (K20-K31)

> **Excludes2** hiatus hernia (K44.-)

● **K20 Esophagitis**
Use additional code to identify:
alcohol abuse and dependence (F10.-)
> **Excludes1** erosion of esophagus (K22.1-)
> esophagitis with gastro-esophageal reflux disease (K21.0)
> reflux esophagitis (K21.0)
> ulcerative esophagitis (K22.1-)
> **Excludes2** eosinophilic gastritis or gastroenteritis (K52.81)

K20.0 Eosinophilic esophagitis

K20.8 Other esophagitis
Abscess of esophagus

K20.9 Esophagitis, unspecified
Esophagitis NOS

● **K21 Gastro-esophageal reflux disease**
> **Excludes1** newborn esophageal reflux (P78.83)

K21.0 Gastro-esophageal reflux disease with esophagitis
Reflux esophagitis

K21.9 Gastro-esophageal reflux disease without esophagitis
Esophageal reflux NOS
Coding Clinic: 2016, Q1, P18

CHAPTER 11 (K00-K95)

Item 11–6   **Esophageal reflux** is the return flow of the contents of the stomach to the esophagus and is referred to as GERD and/or "heartburn." **Gastroesophageal reflux** is the return flow of the contents of the stomach and duodenum to the esophagus. **Esophageal leukoplakia** are white areas on the mucous membrane of the esophagus for which no specific cause can be identified.

- **K22**   **Other diseases of esophagus**
  - **Excludes2**   esophageal varices (I85.-)
  - **K22.0**   **Achalasia of cardia**
    - Achalasia NOS
    - Cardiospasm
    - **Excludes1**   congenital cardiospasm (Q39.5)
  - **K22.1**   **Ulcer of esophagus**
    - Barrett's ulcer
    - Erosion of esophagus
    - Fungal ulcer of esophagus
    - Peptic ulcer of esophagus
    - Ulcer of esophagus due to ingestion of chemicals
    - Ulcer of esophagus due to ingestion of drugs and medicaments
    - Ulcerative esophagitis
    - *Code first* poisoning due to drug or toxin, if applicable (T36-T65 with fifth or sixth character 1-4 or 6)
    - Use additional code for adverse effect, if applicable, to identify drug (T36-T50 with fifth or sixth character 5)
    - **Excludes1**   Barrett's esophagus (K22.87-)
    - **K22.10**   **Ulcer of esophagus without bleeding**
      - Ulcer of esophagus NOS
    - **K22.11**   **Ulcer of esophagus with bleeding**
      - **Excludes2**   bleeding esophageal varices (I85.01, I85.11)
  - **K22.2**   **Esophageal obstruction**
    - Compression of esophagus
    - Constriction of esophagus
    - Stenosis of esophagus
    - Stricture of esophagus
    - **Excludes1**   congenital stenosis or stricture of esophagus (Q39.3)
  - **K22.3**   **Perforation of esophagus**
    - Rupture of esophagus
    - **Excludes1**   traumatic perforation of (thoracic) esophagus (S27.8-)
  - **K22.4**   **Dyskinesia of esophagus**
    - *Difficulty in moving*
    - Corkscrew esophagus
    - Diffuse esophageal spasm
    - Spasm of esophagus
    - **Excludes1**   cardiospasm (K22.0)
  - **K22.5**   **Diverticulum of esophagus, acquired**
    - Esophageal pouch, acquired
    - **Excludes1**   diverticulum of esophagus (congenital) (Q39.6)
  - **K22.6**   **Gastro-esophageal laceration-hemorrhage syndrome**
    - Mallory-Weiss syndrome

Item 11–7   **Achalasia** is a condition in which the smooth muscle fibers of the esophagus do not relax. Most frequently, this condition occurs at the esophagogastric sphincter. **Cardiospasm,** also known as **megaesophagus,** is achalasia of the thoracic esophagus.

- **K22.7**   **Barrett's esophagus**
  - Barrett's disease
  - Barrett's syndrome
  - **Excludes1**   Barrett's ulcer (K22.1)
    - malignant neoplasm of esophagus (C15.-)
  - **K22.70**   **Barrett's esophagus without dysplasia**
    - Barrett's esophagus NOS
  - **K22.71**   **Barrett's esophagus with dysplasia**
    - **K22.710**   **Barrett's esophagus with low grade dysplasia**
    - **K22.711**   **Barrett's esophagus with high grade dysplasia**
    - **K22.719**   **Barrett's esophagus with dysplasia, unspecified**
- **K22.8**   **Other specified diseases of esophagus**
  - Hemorrhage of esophagus NOS
  - **Excludes2**   esophageal varices (I85.-)
    - Paterson-Kelly syndrome (D50.1)
- **K22.9**   **Disease of esophagus, unspecified**

- **K23**   *Disorders of esophagus in diseases classified elsewhere*
  - *Code first* underlying disease, such as:
    - congenital syphilis (A50.5)
  - **Excludes1**   late syphilis (A52.79)
    - megaesophagus due to Chagas' disease (B57.31)
    - tuberculosis (A18.83)

- **K25**   **Gastric ulcer**
  - **Includes**   erosion (acute) of stomach
    - pylorus ulcer (peptic)
    - stomach ulcer (peptic)
  - Use additional code to identify:
    - alcohol abuse and dependence (F10.-)
  - **Excludes1**   acute gastritis (K29.0-)
    - peptic ulcer NOS (K27.-)
  - **K25.0**   **Acute gastric ulcer with hemorrhage**
  - **K25.1**   **Acute gastric ulcer with perforation**
  - **K25.2**   **Acute gastric ulcer with both hemorrhage and perforation**
  - **K25.3**   **Acute gastric ulcer without hemorrhage or perforation**
  - **K25.4**   **Chronic or unspecified gastric ulcer with hemorrhage**
    - **Coding Clinic: 2017, Q3, P27**
  - **K25.5**   **Chronic or unspecified gastric ulcer with perforation**
  - **K25.6**   **Chronic or unspecified gastric ulcer with both hemorrhage and perforation**
  - **K25.7**   **Chronic gastric ulcer without hemorrhage or perforation**
  - **K25.9**   **Gastric ulcer, unspecified as acute or chronic, without hemorrhage or perforation**

CERVICAL ESOPHAGUS
Left subclavian artery
First rib
Arch of aorta
THORACIC ESOPHAGUS
Diaphragm
ABDOMINAL ESOPHAGUS
Stomach

Figure 11-6   The esophagus is the muscular tube that connects the pharynx and the stomach. The 10-inch (25 cm) long esophagus is divided into three parts: **cervical, thoracic,** and **abdominal.**

▶ New   ⇒ Revised   ~~deleted~~ Deleted   Excludes 1   Excludes 2   Includes   Use additional   Code first   Code also   Key words

OGCR Official Guidelines   X Assign placeholder X   ● Use Additional Character(s)   ▷ Manifestation Code   **Coding Clinic**

Figure 11-7 **A.** Ulcer. **B.** Perforated ulcer. **C.** Laparoscopic view of a perforated duodenal ulcer *(arrow)* with fibrinous exudate on the adjacent peritoneum. (**C** from Feldman: Sleisenger & Fordtran's Gastrointestinal and Liver Disease, ed 8, Saunders, An Imprint of Elsevier, 2006)

Item 11-8 · **Gastric ulcers** are lesions of the stomach that result in the death of the tissue and a defect of the surface. **Perforated ulcers** are those in which the lesion penetrates the gastric wall, leaving a hole. **Peptic ulcers** are lesions of the stomach or the duodenum. **Peptic** refers to the gastric juice, pepsin.

● **K26**   **Duodenal ulcer**

    Includes   erosion (acute) of duodenum
                       duodenum ulcer (peptic)
                       postpyloric ulcer (peptic)

    Use additional code to identify:
        alcohol abuse and dependence (F10.-)

    Excludes1   peptic ulcer NOS (K27.-)

    K26.0   Acute duodenal ulcer with hemorrhage
    K26.1   Acute duodenal ulcer with perforation
    K26.2   Acute duodenal ulcer with both hemorrhage and perforation
    K26.3   Acute duodenal ulcer without hemorrhage or perforation
    K26.4   Chronic or unspecified duodenal ulcer with hemorrhage
           Coding Clinic: 2016, Q1, P14
    K26.5   Chronic or unspecified duodenal ulcer with perforation
    K26.6   Chronic or unspecified duodenal ulcer with both hemorrhage and perforation
    K26.7   Chronic duodenal ulcer without hemorrhage or perforation
    K26.9   Duodenal ulcer, unspecified as acute or chronic, without hemorrhage or perforation

● **K27**   **Peptic ulcer, site unspecified**

    Includes   gastroduodenal ulcer NOS
                       peptic ulcer NOS

    Use additional code to identify:
        alcohol abuse and dependence (F10.-)

    Excludes1   peptic ulcer of newborn (P78.82)

    K27.0   Acute peptic ulcer, site unspecified, with hemorrhage
    K27.1   Acute peptic ulcer, site unspecified, with perforation
    K27.2   Acute peptic ulcer, site unspecified, with both hemorrhage and perforation
    K27.3   Acute peptic ulcer, site unspecified, without hemorrhage or perforation
    K27.4   Chronic or unspecified peptic ulcer, site unspecified, with hemorrhage
    K27.5   Chronic or unspecified peptic ulcer, site unspecified, with perforation
    K27.6   Chronic or unspecified peptic ulcer, site unspecified, with both hemorrhage and perforation
    K27.7   Chronic peptic ulcer, site unspecified, without hemorrhage or perforation
    K27.9   Peptic ulcer, site unspecified, unspecified as acute or chronic, without hemorrhage or perforation

● **K28**   **Gastrojejunal ulcer**

    Includes   anastomotic ulcer (peptic) or erosion
                       gastrocolic ulcer (peptic) or erosion
                       gastrointestinal ulcer (peptic) or erosion
                       gastrojejunal ulcer (peptic) or erosion
                       jejunal ulcer (peptic) or erosion
                       marginal ulcer (peptic) or erosion
                       stomal ulcer (peptic) or erosion

    Use additional code to identify:
        alcohol abuse and dependence (F10.-)

    Excludes1   primary ulcer of small intestine (K63.3)

    K28.0   Acute gastrojejunal ulcer with hemorrhage
    K28.1   Acute gastrojejunal ulcer with perforation
    K28.2   Acute gastrojejunal ulcer with both hemorrhage and perforation
    K28.3   Acute gastrojejunal ulcer without hemorrhage or perforation
    K28.4   Chronic or unspecified gastrojejunal ulcer with hemorrhage
    K28.5   Chronic or unspecified gastrojejunal ulcer with perforation
    K28.6   Chronic or unspecified gastrojejunal ulcer with both hemorrhage and perforation
    K28.7   Chronic gastrojejunal ulcer without hemorrhage or perforation
    K28.9   Gastrojejunal ulcer, unspecified as acute or chronic, without hemorrhage or perforation

● **K29**   **Gastritis and duodenitis**

    Excludes1   eosinophilic gastritis or gastroenteritis (K52.81)
                       Zollinger-Ellison syndrome (E16.4)

●   **K29.0**   Acute gastritis

        Use additional code to identify:
            alcohol abuse and dependence (F10.-)

        Excludes1   erosion (acute) of stomach (K25.-)

        K29.00   Acute gastritis without bleeding
        K29.01   Acute gastritis with bleeding

●   **K29.2**   Alcoholic gastritis

        Use additional code to identify:
            alcohol abuse and dependence (F10.-)

        K29.20   Alcoholic gastritis without bleeding
        K29.21   Alcoholic gastritis with bleeding

●   **K29.3**   Chronic superficial gastritis

        K29.30   Chronic superficial gastritis without bleeding
        K29.31   Chronic superficial gastritis with bleeding

●   **K29.4**   Chronic atrophic gastritis
        Gastric atrophy

        K29.40   Chronic atrophic gastritis without bleeding
        K29.41   Chronic atrophic gastritis with bleeding

●   **K29.5**   Unspecified chronic gastritis
        Chronic antral gastritis
        Chronic fundal gastritis

        K29.50   Unspecified chronic gastritis without bleeding
        K29.51   Unspecified chronic gastritis with bleeding

●   **K29.6**   Other gastritis
        Giant hypertrophic gastritis
        Granulomatous gastritis
        Ménétrier's disease

        K29.60   Other gastritis without bleeding
        K29.61   Other gastritis with bleeding

●   **K29.7**   Gastritis, unspecified

        K29.70   Gastritis, unspecified, without bleeding
        K29.71   Gastritis, unspecified, with bleeding

●   **K29.8**   Duodenitis

        K29.80   Duodenitis without bleeding
        K29.81   Duodenitis with bleeding

●   **K29.9**   Gastroduodenitis, unspecified

        K29.90   Gastroduodenitis, unspecified, without bleeding
        K29.91   Gastroduodenitis, unspecified, with bleeding

CHAPTER 11 (K00-K95)

Item 11–9 Gastritis is a severe inflammation of the stomach. **Atrophic gastritis** is a chronic inflammation of the stomach that results in destruction of the cells of the mucosa of the stomach. Duodenitis is an inflammation of the duodenum, the first section of the small intestine.

K30 Functional dyspepsia
Indigestion
Excludes1   dyspepsia NOS (R10.13)
heartburn (R12)
nervous dyspepsia (F45.8)
neurotic dyspepsia (F45.8)
psychogenic dyspepsia (F45.8)

● **K31 Other diseases of stomach and duodenum**
Includes   functional disorders of stomach
Excludes2   diabetic gastroparesis (E08.43, E09.43, E10.43,
E11.43, E13.43)
diverticulum of duodenum (K57.00-K57.13)

K31.0 Acute dilatation of stomach
Acute distention of stomach

K31.1 Adult hypertrophic pyloric stenosis   A
Pyloric stenosis NOS
Excludes1   congenital or infantile pyloric stenosis
(Q40.0)

K31.2 Hourglass stricture and stenosis of stomach
Excludes1   congenital hourglass stomach (Q40.2)
hourglass contraction of stomach (K31.89)

K31.3 Pylorospasm, not elsewhere classified
Excludes1   congenital or infantile pylorospasm
(Q40.0)
neurotic pylorospasm (F45.8)
psychogenic pylorospasm (F45.8)

K31.4 Gastric diverticulum
Excludes1   congenital diverticulum of stomach
(Q40.2)

K31.5 Obstruction of duodenum
Constriction of duodenum
Duodenal ileus (chronic)
Stenosis of duodenum
Narrowing
Stricture of duodenum
Narrowing
Volvulus of duodenum
Twisting/knotting
Excludes1   congenital stenosis of duodenum (Q41.0)

K31.6 Fistula of stomach and duodenum
Gastrocolic fistula
Gastrojejunocolic fistula

K31.7 Polyp of stomach and duodenum
Excludes1   adenomatous polyp of stomach (D13.1)

● **K31.8 Other specified diseases of stomach and duodenum**
● **K31.81 Angiodysplasia of stomach and duodenum**
**K31.811 Angiodysplasia of stomach and
duodenum with bleeding**
**K31.819 Angiodysplasia of stomach and
duodenum without bleeding**
Angiodysplasia of stomach and
duodenum NOS

**K31.82 Dieulafoy lesion (hemorrhagic) of stomach and
duodenum**
Excludes2   Dieulafoy lesion of intestine
(K63.81)

K31.83 Achlorhydria

K31.84 Gastroparesis
Gastroparalysis
Code first underlying disease, if known, such as:
anorexia nervosa (F50.0-)
diabetes mellitus (E08.43, E09.43, E10.43,
E11.43, E13.43)
scleroderma (M34.-)

K31.89 Other diseases of stomach and duodenum
Coding Clinic: 2017, Q1, P28

K31.9 Disease of stomach and duodenum, unspecified

Item 11–10 Achlorhydria, also known as gastric anacidity, is the absence of gastric acid.

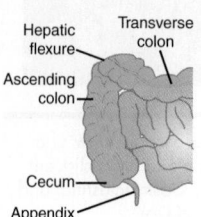
Hepatic flexure
Transverse colon
Ascending colon
Cecum
Appendix

Figure 11-8 Acute appendicitis is the inflammation of the appendix, usually associated with obstruction. Most often this is a disease of adolescents and young adults.

DISEASES OF APPENDIX (K35-K38)

● **K35 Acute appendicitis**
● **K35.2 Acute appendicitis with generalized peritonitis**
Appendicitis (acute) with generalized (diffuse)
peritonitis following rupture or perforation of
appendix
~~Perforated appendix NOS~~
~~Ruptured appendix NOS~~

▶ **K35.20 Acute appendicitis with generalized peritonitis,
without abscess (Acute) appendicitis with
generalized peritonitis NOS**

▶ **K35.21 Acute appendicitis with generalized peritonitis,
with abscess**

● **K35.3 Acute appendicitis with localized peritonitis**
~~Acute appendicitis with or without perforation or
rupture with peritonitis NOS~~
~~Acute appendicitis with or without perforation or
rupture with localized peritonitis~~
~~Acute appendicitis with peritoneal abscess~~

▶ **K35.30 Acute appendicitis with localized peritonitis,
without perforation or gangrene**
▶ Acute appendicitis with localized peritonitis
NOS

▶ **K35.31 Acute appendicitis with localized peritonitis
and gangrene, without perforation**

▶ **K35.32 Acute appendicitis with perforation and
localized peritonitis, without abscess**
▶ (Acute) appendicitis with perforation NOS
▶ Perforated appendix NOS
▶ Ruptured appendix (with localized peritonitis)
NOS

▶ **K35.33 Acute appendicitis with perforation and
localized peritonitis, with abscess**
▶ (Acute) appendicitis with (peritoneal) abscess
NOS
▶ Ruptured appendix with localized peritonitis
and abscess

● **K35.8 Other and unspecified acute appendicitis**
K35.80 Unspecified acute appendicitis
Acute appendicitis NOS
Acute appendicitis without (localized)
(generalized) peritonitis

K35.89 Other acute appendicitis
▶ **K35.890 Other acute appendicitis without
perforation or gangrene**
▶ **K35.891 Other acute appendicitis without
perforation, with gangrene**
▶ (Acute) appendicitis with gangrene
NOS

K36 Other appendicitis
Chronic appendicitis
Recurrent appendicitis

K37 Unspecified appendicitis
⇛ **Excludes1**   unspecified appendicitis with peritonitis
(K35.2-, K35.3)

▶ New   ⇛ Revised   ~~deleted~~ Deleted   Excludes 1   Excludes 2   Includes   Use additional   Code first   Code also   Key words
OGCR Official Guidelines   X Assign placeholder X   ● Use Additional Character(s)   ▌ Manifestation Code   **Coding Clinic**

CHAPTER 11 (K00-K95)

● **K38　Other diseases of appendix**

　　K38.Ø　Hyperplasia of appendix

　　K38.1　Appendicular concretions
　　　　　Fecalith of appendix
　　　　　Stercolith of appendix

　　K38.2　Diverticulum of appendix

　　K38.3　Fistula of appendix

　　K38.8　Other specified diseases of appendix
　　　　　Intussusception of appendix

　　K38.9　Disease of appendix, unspecified

HERNIA (K4Ø-K46)

　　Note:　Hernia with both gangrene and obstruction is classified
　　　　　to hernia with gangrene.

　　　Includes　　acquired hernia
　　　　　　　congenital [except diaphragmatic or hiatus]
　　　　　　　　hernia
　　　　　　　recurrent hernia

● **K4Ø　Inguinal hernia**

　　　Includes　　bubonocele
　　　　　　　direct inguinal hernia
　　　　　　　double inguinal hernia
　　　　　　　indirect inguinal hernia
　　　　　　　inguinal hernia NOS
　　　　　　　oblique inguinal hernia
　　　　　　　scrotal hernia

● **K4Ø.Ø　Bilateral inguinal hernia, with obstruction, without gangrene**
　　　　Inguinal hernia (bilateral) causing obstruction without
　　　　　gangrene
　　　　Incarcerated inguinal hernia (bilateral) without
　　　　　gangrene
　　　　Irreducible inguinal hernia (bilateral) without gangrene
　　　　Strangulated inguinal hernia (bilateral) without
　　　　　gangrene

　　K4Ø.ØØ　Bilateral inguinal hernia, with obstruction, without gangrene, not specified as recurrent
　　　　　Bilateral inguinal hernia, with obstruction,
　　　　　　without gangrene NOS

　　K4Ø.Ø1　Bilateral inguinal hernia, with obstruction, without gangrene, recurrent

● **K4Ø.1　Bilateral inguinal hernia, with gangrene**

　　K4Ø.1Ø　Bilateral inguinal hernia, with gangrene, not specified as recurrent
　　　　　Bilateral inguinal hernia, with gangrene NOS

　　K4Ø.11　Bilateral inguinal hernia, with gangrene, recurrent

● **K4Ø.2　Bilateral inguinal hernia, without obstruction or gangrene**

　　K4Ø.2Ø　Bilateral inguinal hernia, without obstruction or gangrene, not specified as recurrent
　　　　　Bilateral inguinal hernia NOS

　　K4Ø.21　Bilateral inguinal hernia, without obstruction or gangrene, recurrent

● **K4Ø.3　Unilateral inguinal hernia, with obstruction, without gangrene**
　　　　Inguinal hernia (unilateral) causing obstruction without
　　　　　gangrene
　　　　Incarcerated inguinal hernia (unilateral) without
　　　　　gangrene
　　　　Irreducible inguinal hernia (unilateral) without gangrene
　　　　Strangulated inguinal hernia (unilateral) without
　　　　　gangrene

　　K4Ø.3Ø　Unilateral inguinal hernia, with obstruction, without gangrene, not specified as recurrent
　　　　　Inguinal hernia, with obstruction NOS
　　　　　Unilateral inguinal hernia, with obstruction,
　　　　　　without gangrene NOS

　　K4Ø.31　Unilateral inguinal hernia, with obstruction, without gangrene, recurrent

Item 11-11　Hernias of the groin are the most common type, accounting for 8Ø percent of all hernias. There are two major types of inguinal hernias: indirect (oblique) affecting men only and direct. **Indirect inguinal hernias** result when the intestines emerge through the abdominal wall in an indirect fashion through the inguinal canal. **Direct inguinal hernias** penetrate through the abdominal wall in a direct fashion. **Femoral hernias** occur at the femoral ring where the femoral vessels enter the thigh and is most common in women. An abdominal wall hernia is also called a ventral or epigastric hernia and occurs in both sexes. Classification is based on location of the hernia and whether there is obstruction or gangrene.

　　Ventral, epigastric, or incisional hernia occurs on the abdominal surface caused by musculature weakness or a tear at a previous surgical site and is evidenced by a bulge that changes in size, becoming larger with exertion. An **incarcerated** hernia is one in which the intestines become trapped in the hernia. A **strangulated** hernia is one in which the blood supply to the intestines is lost. **Hiatal hernia** occurs when a loop of the stomach protrudes upward through the small opening in the diaphragm through which the esophagus passes, leaving the abdominal cavity and entering the chest. It occurs in both sexes.

Figure 11-9　Inguinal hernias are those that are located in the inguinal or iliac areas of the abdomen.

● **K4Ø.4　Unilateral inguinal hernia, with gangrene**

　　K4Ø.4Ø　Unilateral inguinal hernia, with gangrene, not specified as recurrent
　　　　　Inguinal hernia with gangrene NOS
　　　　　Unilateral inguinal hernia with gangrene NOS

　　K4Ø.41　Unilateral inguinal hernia, with gangrene, recurrent

● **K4Ø.9　Unilateral inguinal hernia, without obstruction or gangrene**

　　K4Ø.9Ø　Unilateral inguinal hernia, without obstruction or gangrene, not specified as recurrent
　　　　　Inguinal hernia NOS
　　　　　Unilateral inguinal hernia NOS

　　K4Ø.91　Unilateral inguinal hernia, without obstruction or gangrene, recurrent

● **K41　Femoral hernia**

● **K41.Ø　Bilateral femoral hernia, with obstruction, without gangrene**
　　　　Femoral hernia (bilateral) causing obstruction, without
　　　　　gangrene
　　　　Incarcerated femoral hernia (bilateral), without
　　　　　gangrene
　　　　Irreducible femoral hernia (bilateral), without gangrene
　　　　Strangulated femoral hernia (bilateral), without
　　　　　gangrene

　　K41.ØØ　Bilateral femoral hernia, with obstruction, without gangrene, not specified as recurrent
　　　　　Bilateral femoral hernia, with obstruction,
　　　　　　without gangrene NOS

　　K41.Ø1　Bilateral femoral hernia, with obstruction, without gangrene, recurrent

● **K41.1**   **Bilateral** femoral hernia, **with gangrene**

     K41.10   Bilateral femoral hernia, with gangrene, **not specified as recurrent**
          Bilateral femoral hernia, with gangrene NOS

     K41.11   Bilateral femoral hernia, with gangrene, **recurrent**

● **K41.2**   **Bilateral** femoral hernia, **without obstruction or gangrene**

     K41.20   Bilateral femoral hernia, without obstruction or gangrene, **not specified as recurrent**
          Bilateral femoral hernia NOS

     K41.21   Bilateral femoral hernia, without obstruction or gangrene, **recurrent**

● **K41.3**   **Unilateral** femoral hernia, **with obstruction, without gangrene**
      Femoral hernia (unilateral) causing obstruction, without gangrene
      Incarcerated femoral hernia (unilateral), without gangrene
      Irreducible femoral hernia (unilateral), without gangrene
      Strangulated femoral hernia (unilateral), without gangrene

     K41.30   Unilateral femoral hernia, with obstruction, without gangrene, **not specified as recurrent**
          Femoral hernia, with obstruction NOS
          Unilateral femoral hernia, with obstruction NOS

     K41.31   Unilateral femoral hernia, with obstruction, without gangrene, **recurrent**

● **K41.4**   **Unilateral** femoral hernia, **with gangrene**

     K41.40   Unilateral femoral hernia, with gangrene, **not specified as recurrent**
          Femoral hernia, with gangrene NOS
          Unilateral femoral hernia, with gangrene NOS

     K41.41   Unilateral femoral hernia, with gangrene, **recurrent**

● **K41.9**   **Unilateral** femoral hernia, **without obstruction or gangrene**

     K41.90   Unilateral femoral hernia, without obstruction or gangrene, **not specified as recurrent**
          Femoral hernia NOS
          Unilateral femoral hernia NOS

     K41.91   Unilateral femoral hernia, without obstruction or gangrene, **recurrent**

● **K42**   **Umbilical hernia**

     Includes   paraumbilical hernia
     Excludes1   omphalocele (Q79.2)

     K42.0   **Umbilical hernia with obstruction, without gangrene**
        Umbilical hernia causing obstruction, without gangrene
        Incarcerated umbilical hernia, without gangrene
        Irreducible umbilical hernia, without gangrene
        Strangulated umbilical hernia, without gangrene

     K42.1   **Umbilical hernia with gangrene**
        Gangrenous umbilical hernia

     K42.9   **Umbilical hernia without obstruction or gangrene**
        Umbilical hernia NOS

● **K43**   **Ventral hernia**

     K43.0   **Incisional hernia with obstruction, without gangrene**
        Incisional hernia causing obstruction, without gangrene
        Incarcerated incisional hernia, without gangrene
        Irreducible incisional hernia, without gangrene
        Strangulated incisional hernia, without gangrene

     K43.1   **Incisional hernia with gangrene**
        Gangrenous incisional hernia

     K43.2   **Incisional hernia without obstruction or gangrene**
        Incisional hernia NOS

     K43.3   **Parastomal hernia with obstruction, without gangrene**
        Incarcerated parastomal hernia, without gangrene
        Irreducible parastomal hernia, without gangrene
        Parastomal hernia causing obstruction, without gangrene
        Strangulated parastomal hernia, without gangrene

     K43.4   **Parastomal hernia with gangrene**
        Gangrenous parastomal hernia

     K43.5   **Parastomal hernia without obstruction or gangrene**
        Parastomal hernia NOS

     K43.6   **Other and unspecified ventral hernia with obstruction, without gangrene**
        Epigastric hernia causing obstruction, without gangrene
        Hypogastric hernia causing obstruction, without gangrene
        Incarcerated epigastric hernia without gangrene
        Incarcerated hypogastric hernia without gangrene
        Incarcerated midline hernia without gangrene
        Incarcerated spigelian hernia without gangrene
        Incarcerated subxiphoid hernia without gangrene
        Irreducible epigastric hernia without gangrene
        Irreducible hypogastric hernia without gangrene
        Irreducible midline hernia without gangrene
        Irreducible spigelian hernia without gangrene
        Irreducible subxiphoid hernia without gangrene
        Midline hernia causing obstruction, without gangrene
        Spigelian hernia causing obstruction, without gangrene
        Strangulated epigastric hernia without gangrene
        Strangulated hypogastric hernia without gangrene
        Strangulated midline hernia without gangrene
        Strangulated spigelian hernia without gangrene
        Strangulated subxiphoid hernia without gangrene
        Subxiphoid hernia causing obstruction, without gangrene

     K43.7   **Other and unspecified ventral hernia with gangrene**
        Any condition listed under K43.6 specified as gangrenous

     K43.9   **Ventral hernia without obstruction or gangrene**
        Epigastric hernia
        Ventral hernia NOS

● **K44**   **Diaphragmatic hernia**

     Includes   hiatus hernia (esophageal) (sliding)
          paraesophageal hernia
     Excludes1   congenital diaphragmatic hernia (Q79.0)
          congenital hiatus hernia (Q40.1)

     K44.0   **Diaphragmatic hernia with obstruction, without gangrene**
        Diaphragmatic hernia causing obstruction
        Incarcerated diaphragmatic hernia
        Irreducible diaphragmatic hernia
        Strangulated diaphragmatic hernia

     K44.1   **Diaphragmatic hernia with gangrene**
        Gangrenous diaphragmatic hernia

     K44.9   **Diaphragmatic hernia without obstruction or gangrene**
        Diaphragmatic hernia NOS
        Coding Clinic: 2017, Q1, P7

● **K45**   **Other abdominal hernia**

     Includes   abdominal hernia, specified site NEC
          lumbar hernia
          obturator hernia
          pudendal hernia
          retroperitoneal hernia
          sciatic hernia

     K45.0   **Other specified abdominal hernia with obstruction, without gangrene**
        Other specified abdominal hernia causing obstruction
        Other specified incarcerated abdominal hernia
        Other specified irreducible abdominal hernia
        Other specified strangulated abdominal hernia

     K45.1   **Other specified abdominal hernia with gangrene**
        Any condition listed under K45 specified as gangrenous

     K45.8   **Other specified abdominal hernia without obstruction or gangrene**

● **K46**   **Unspecified abdominal hernia**

    Includes   enterocele
                       epiplocele
                       hernia NOS
                       interstitial hernia
                       intestinal hernia
                       intra-abdominal hernia

    Excludes1   vaginal enterocele (N81.5)

   K46.0   **Unspecified abdominal hernia with obstruction, without gangrene**
           Unspecified abdominal hernia causing obstruction
           Unspecified incarcerated abdominal hernia
           Unspecified irreducible abdominal hernia
           Unspecified strangulated abdominal hernia

   K46.1   **Unspecified abdominal hernia with gangrene**
           Any condition listed under K46 specified as gangrenous

   K46.9   **Unspecified abdominal hernia without obstruction or gangrene**
           Abdominal hernia NOS

★ **(See Plate 284 on page 77.)**

NONINFECTIVE ENTERITIS AND COLITIS (K50-K52)

    Includes   noninfective inflammatory bowel disease
    Excludes1   irritable bowel syndrome (K58.-)
                   megacolon (K59.3-)

● **K50**   **Crohn's disease [regional enteritis]**

    Includes   granulomatous enteritis

    Use additional code to identify manifestations, such as:
       pyoderma gangrenosum (L88)

    Excludes1   ulcerative colitis (K51.-)

● **K50.0**   **Crohn's disease of small intestine**
           Crohn's disease [regional enteritis] of duodenum
           Crohn's disease [regional enteritis] of ileum
           Crohn's disease [regional enteritis] of jejunum
           Regional ileitis
           Terminal ileitis

     Excludes1   Crohn's disease of both small and large intestine (K50.8-)

    K50.00   **Crohn's disease of small intestine without complications**

●   **K50.01**   **Crohn's disease of small intestine with complications**

      K50.011   Crohn's disease of small intestine with **rectal bleeding**

      K50.012   Crohn's disease of small intestine with **intestinal obstruction**

      K50.013   Crohn's disease of small intestine with **fistula**

      K50.014   Crohn's disease of small intestine with **abscess**
               Coding Clinic: 2012, Q4, P104

      K50.018   Crohn's disease of small intestine with **other complication**

      K50.019   Crohn's disease of small intestine with **unspecified complications**

● **K50.1**   **Crohn's disease of large intestine**
           Crohn's disease [regional enteritis] of colon
           Crohn's disease [regional enteritis] of large bowel
           Crohn's disease [regional enteritis] of rectum
           Granulomatous colitis
           Regional colitis

     Excludes1   Crohn's disease of both small and large intestine (K50.8)

    K50.10   **Crohn's disease of large intestine without complications**

●   **K50.11**   **Crohn's disease of large intestine with complications**

      K50.111   Crohn's disease of large intestine with **rectal bleeding**

      K50.112   Crohn's disease of large intestine with **intestinal obstruction**

      K50.113   Crohn's disease of large intestine with **fistula**

      K50.114   Crohn's disease of large intestine with **abscess**
               Coding Clinic: 2012, Q4, P104

      K50.118   Crohn's disease of large intestine with **other complication**

      K50.119   Crohn's disease of large intestine with **unspecified complications**

● **K50.8**   **Crohn's disease of both small and large intestine**

    K50.80   **Crohn's disease of both small and large intestine without complications**

●   **K50.81**   **Crohn's disease of both small and large intestine with complications**

      K50.811   Crohn's disease of both small and large intestine with **rectal bleeding**

      K50.812   Crohn's disease of both small and large intestine with **intestinal obstruction**

      K50.813   Crohn's disease of both small and large intestine with **fistula**

      K50.814   Crohn's disease of both small and large intestine with **abscess**
               Coding Clinic: 2012, Q4, P104

      K50.818   Crohn's disease of both small and large intestine with **other complication**

      K50.819   Crohn's disease of both small and large intestine with **unspecified complications**

Figure 11-10   Small and large intestines.

Item 11-12 Crohn's disease, also known as **regional enteritis,** is a chronic inflammatory disease of the intestines. Classification is based on location in the small (duodenum, ileum, jejunum) or large (cecum, colon, rectum, anal canal) intestine.

● **K50.9   Crohn's disease, unspecified**
   K50.90   Crohn's disease, unspecified, without complications
     Crohn's disease NOS
     Regional enteritis NOS
  ● **K50.91   Crohn's disease, unspecified, with complications**
    K50.911   Crohn's disease, unspecified, with rectal bleeding
    K50.912   Crohn's disease, unspecified, with intestinal obstruction
    K50.913   Crohn's disease, unspecified, with fistula
    K50.914   Crohn's disease, unspecified, with abscess
      Coding Clinic: 2012, Q4, P104
    K50.918   Crohn's disease, unspecified, with other complication
    K50.919   Crohn's disease, unspecified, with unspecified complications

● **K51   Ulcerative colitis**
  Use additional code to identify manifestations, such as: pyoderma gangrenosum (L88)
  Excludes1   Crohn's disease [regional enteritis] (K50.-)

 ● **K51.0   Ulcerative (chronic) pancolitis**
   Backwash ileitis
   K51.00   Ulcerative (chronic) pancolitis without complications
    Ulcerative (chronic) pancolitis NOS
  ● **K51.01   Ulcerative (chronic) pancolitis with complications**
    K51.011   Ulcerative (chronic) pancolitis with rectal bleeding
    K51.012   Ulcerative (chronic) pancolitis with intestinal obstruction
    K51.013   Ulcerative (chronic) pancolitis with fistula
    K51.014   Ulcerative (chronic) pancolitis with abscess
    K51.018   Ulcerative (chronic) pancolitis with other complication
    K51.019   Ulcerative (chronic) pancolitis with unspecified complications
 ● **K51.2   Ulcerative (chronic) proctitis**
   K51.20   Ulcerative (chronic) proctitis without complications
    Ulcerative (chronic) proctitis NOS
  ● **K51.21   Ulcerative (chronic) proctitis with complications**
    K51.211   Ulcerative (chronic) proctitis with rectal bleeding
    K51.212   Ulcerative (chronic) proctitis with intestinal obstruction
    K51.213   Ulcerative (chronic) proctitis with fistula
    K51.214   Ulcerative (chronic) proctitis with abscess
    K51.218   Ulcerative (chronic) proctitis with other complication
    K51.219   Ulcerative (chronic) proctitis with unspecified complications

● **K51.3   Ulcerative (chronic) rectosigmoiditis**
   K51.30   Ulcerative (chronic) rectosigmoiditis without complications
    Ulcerative (chronic) rectosigmoiditis NOS
  ● **K51.31   Ulcerative (chronic) rectosigmoiditis with complications**
    K51.311   Ulcerative (chronic) rectosigmoiditis with rectal bleeding
    K51.312   Ulcerative (chronic) rectosigmoiditis with intestinal obstruction
    K51.313   Ulcerative (chronic) rectosigmoiditis with fistula
    K51.314   Ulcerative (chronic) rectosigmoiditis with abscess
    K51.318   Ulcerative (chronic) rectosigmoiditis with other complication
    K51.319   Ulcerative (chronic) rectosigmoiditis with unspecified complications
● **K51.4   Inflammatory polyps of colon**
  Excludes1   adenomatous polyp of colon (D12.6)
    polyposis of colon (D12.6)
    polyps of colon NOS (K63.5)
   K51.40   Inflammatory polyps of colon without complications
    Inflammatory polyps of colon NOS
  ● **K51.41   Inflammatory polyps of colon with complications**
    K51.411   Inflammatory polyps of colon with rectal bleeding
    K51.412   Inflammatory polyps of colon with intestinal obstruction
    K51.413   Inflammatory polyps of colon with fistula
    K51.414   Inflammatory polyps of colon with abscess
    K51.418   Inflammatory polyps of colon with other complication
    K51.419   Inflammatory polyps of colon with unspecified complications
● **K51.5   Left sided colitis**
   Left hemicolitis
   K51.50   Left sided colitis without complications
    Left sided colitis NOS
  ● **K51.51   Left sided colitis with complications**
    K51.511   Left sided colitis with rectal bleeding
    K51.512   Left sided colitis with intestinal obstruction
    K51.513   Left sided colitis with fistula
    K51.514   Left sided colitis with abscess
    K51.518   Left sided colitis with other complication
    K51.519   Left sided colitis with unspecified complications
● **K51.8   Other ulcerative colitis**
   K51.80   Other ulcerative colitis without complications
  ● **K51.81   Other ulcerative colitis with complications**
    K51.811   Other ulcerative colitis with rectal bleeding
    K51.812   Other ulcerative colitis with intestinal obstruction
    K51.813   Other ulcerative colitis with fistula
    K51.814   Other ulcerative colitis with abscess
    K51.818   Other ulcerative colitis with other complication
    K51.819   Other ulcerative colitis with unspecified complications

Item 11–13   Ulcerative colitis attacks the colonic mucosa and forms abscesses. The disease involves the intestines. Classification is based on the location:
• Enterocolitis: large and small intestine
• Ileocolitis: ileum and colon
• Proctitis: rectum
• Proctosigmoiditis: sigmoid colon and rectum

▶ New ⮕ Revised ~~deleted~~ Deleted Excludes 1 Excludes 2 Includes Use additional Code first Code also Key words
OGCR Official Guidelines   X Assign placeholder X   ● Use Additional Character(s)   ▮ Manifestation Code   Coding Clinic

● **K51.9   Ulcerative colitis, unspecified**
     K51.90   Ulcerative colitis, unspecified, without complications
     ● **K51.91   Ulcerative colitis, unspecified, with complications**
         K51.911   Ulcerative colitis, unspecified with rectal bleeding
         K51.912   Ulcerative colitis, unspecified with intestinal obstruction
         K51.913   Ulcerative colitis, unspecified with fistula
         K51.914   Ulcerative colitis, unspecified with abscess
         K51.918   Ulcerative colitis, unspecified with other complication
         K51.919   Ulcerative colitis, unspecified with unspecified complications

● **K52   Other and unspecified noninfective gastroenteritis and colitis**
     K52.0   Gastroenteritis and colitis due to radiation
     K52.1   Toxic gastroenteritis and colitis
         Drug-induced gastroenteritis and colitis
         Code first (T51-T65) to identify toxic agent
         Use additional code for adverse effect, if applicable, to identify drug (T36-T50 with fifth or sixth character 5)
     ● **K52.2   Allergic and dietetic gastroenteritis and colitis**
         Food hypersensitivity gastroenteritis or colitis
         Use additional code to identify type of food allergy (Z91.01-, Z91.02-)
         Excludes2   allergic eosinophilic colitis (K52.82)
             allergic eosinophilic esophagitis (K20.0)
             allergic eosinophilic gastritis (K52.81)
             allergic eosinophilic gastroenteritis (K52.81)
             food protein-induced proctocolitis (K52.82)
         Coding Clinic: 2016, Q4, P30-31
         K52.21   Food protein-induced enterocolitis syndrome
             ▶FPIES
             Use additional code for hypovolemic shock, if present (R57.1)
         K52.22   Food protein-induced enteropathy
         K52.29   Other allergic and dietetic gastroenteritis and colitis
             Food hypersensitivity gastroenteritis or colitis
             Immediate gastrointestinal hypersensitivity
     K52.3   Indeterminate colitis
         Colonic inflammatory bowel disease unclassified (IBDU)
         Excludes1   unspecified colitis (K52.9)
     ● **K52.8   Other specified noninfective gastroenteritis and colitis**
         K52.81   Eosinophilic gastritis or gastroenteritis
             Eosinophilic enteritis
             Excludes2   eosinophilic esophagitis (K20.0)
         K52.82   Eosinophilic colitis
             Allergic proctocolitis
             Food-induced eosinophilic proctocolitis
             Food protein-induced proctocolitis
             Milk protein-induced proctocolitis
     ● **K52.83   Microscopic colitis**
         Coding Clinic: 2016, Q4, P30-31
         K52.831   Collagenous colitis
         K52.832   Lymphocytic colitis
         K52.838   Other microscopic colitis
         K52.839   Microscopic colitis, unspecified
         K52.89   Other specified noninfective gastroenteritis and colitis

K52.9   Noninfective gastroenteritis and colitis, unspecified

Colitis NOS	Ileitis NOS
Enteritis NOS	Jejunitis NOS
Gastroenteritis NOS	Sigmoiditis NOS

     Excludes1   diarrhea NOS (R19.7)
         functional diarrhea (K59.1)
         infectious gastroenteritis and colitis NOS (A09)
         neonatal diarrhea (noninfective) (P78.3)
         psychogenic diarrhea (F45.8)

OTHER DISEASES OF INTESTINES (K55-K64)

● **K55   Vascular disorders of intestine**
     Excludes1   necrotizing enterocolitis of newborn (P77.-)
     ● **K55.0   Acute vascular disorders of intestine**
         Infarction of appendices epiploicae
         Mesenteric (artery) (vein) embolism
         Mesenteric (artery) (vein) infarction
         Mesenteric (artery) (vein) thrombosis
     ● **K55.01   Acute (reversible) ischemia of small intestine**
         Coding Clinic: 2016, Q4, P32
         K55.011   Focal (segmental) acute (reversible) ischemia of small intestine
         K55.012   Diffuse acute (reversible) ischemia of small intestine
         K55.019   Acute (reversible) ischemia of small intestine, extent unspecified
     ● **K55.02   Acute infarction of small intestine**
         Gangrene of small intestine
         Necrosis of small intestine
         Coding Clinic: 2016, Q4, P32
         K55.021   Focal (segmental) acute infarction of small intestine
         K55.022   Diffuse acute infarction of small intestine
         K55.029   Acute infarction of small intestine, extent unspecified
     ● **K55.03   Acute (reversible) ischemia of large intestine**
         Acute fulminant ischemic colitis
         Subacute ischemic colitis
         Coding Clinic: 2016, Q4, P32
         K55.031   Focal (segmental) acute (reversible) ischemia of large intestine
         K55.032   Diffuse acute (reversible) ischemia of large intestine
         K55.039   Acute (reversible) ischemia of large intestine, extent unspecified
     ● **K55.04   Acute infarction of large intestine**
         Gangrene of large intestine
         Necrosis of large intestine
         Coding Clinic: 2016, Q4, P32
         K55.041   Focal (segmental) acute infarction of large intestine
         K55.042   Diffuse acute infarction of large intestine
         K55.049   Acute infarction of large intestine, extent unspecified
     ● **K55.05   Acute (reversible) ischemia of intestine, part unspecified**
         K55.051   Focal (segmental) acute (reversible) ischemia of intestine, part unspecified
         K55.052   Diffuse acute (reversible) ischemia of intestine, part unspecified
         K55.059   Acute (reversible) ischemia of intestine, part and extent unspecified

● **K55.06** **Acute infarction of intestine, part unspecified**
  Acute intestinal infarction
  Gangrene of intestine
  Necrosis of intestine

  K55.061 **Focal (segmental) acute infarction of intestine, part unspecified**

  K55.062 **Diffuse acute infarction of intestine, part unspecified**

  K55.069 **Acute infarction of intestine, part and extent unspecified**

K55.1 **Chronic vascular disorders of intestine**
  Chronic ischemic colitis
  Chronic ischemic enteritis
  Chronic ischemic enterocolitis
  Ischemic stricture of intestine
  Mesenteric atherosclerosis
  Mesenteric vascular insufficiency

● **K55.2** **Angiodysplasia of colon**

  K55.20 **Angiodysplasia of colon without hemorrhage**

  K55.21 **Angiodysplasia of colon with hemorrhage**

● **K55.3** **Necrotizing enterocolitis**

  Excludes1 necrotizing enterocolitis of newborn (P77.-)

  Excludes2 necrotizing enterocolitis due to Clostridium difficile (A04.7-)

  K55.30 **Necrotizing enterocolitis, unspecified**
    Necrotizing enterocolitis, NOS

  K55.31 **Stage 1 necrotizing enterocolitis**
    Necrotizing enterocolitis without pneumatosis, without perforation
    Coding Clinic: 2016, Q4, P32

  K55.32 **Stage 2 necrotizing enterocolitis**
    Necrotizing enterocolitis with pneumatosis, without perforation
    Coding Clinic: 2016, Q4, P32

  K55.33 **Stage 3 necrotizing enterocolitis**
    Necrotizing enterocolitis with perforation
    Necrotizing enterocolitis with pneumatosis and perforation
    Coding Clinic: 2016, Q4, P32

K55.8 **Other vascular disorders of intestine**

K55.9 **Vascular disorder of intestine, unspecified**
  Ischemic colitis
  Ischemic enteritis
  Ischemic enterocolitis

● **K56** **Paralytic ileus and intestinal obstruction without hernia**

  Excludes1 congenital stricture or stenosis of intestine (Q41-Q42)
    cystic fibrosis with meconium ileus (E84.11)
    ischemic stricture of intestine (K55.1)
    meconium ileus NOS (P76.0)
    neonatal intestinal obstructions classifiable to P76.-
    obstruction of duodenum (K31.5)
    postprocedural intestinal obstruction (K91.3-)
    stenosis of anus or rectum (K62.4)

K56.0 **Paralytic ileus**
  Paralysis of bowel
  Paralysis of colon
  Paralysis of intestine

  Excludes1 gallstone ileus (K56.3)
    ileus NOS (K56.7)
    obstructive ileus NOS (K56.69-)

K56.1 **Intussusception**
  Intussusception or invagination of bowel
  Intussusception or invagination of colon
  Intussusception or invagination of intestine
  Intussusception or invagination of rectum

  Excludes2 intussusception of appendix (K38.8)

Figure 11-11   Types of intussusception.

Item 11–14   **Intussusception** is the prolapse (telescoping) of a part of the intestine into another adjacent part of the intestine. Intussusception may be enteric (ileoileal, jejunoileal, jejunojejunal), colic (colocolic), or intracolic (ileocecal, ileocolic).

Item 11–15   **Volvulus** is the twisting of a segment of the intestine, resulting in obstruction. Paralytic ileus is paralysis of the intestine. It need not be a complete paralysis, but it must prohibit the passage of food through the intestine and lead to intestinal blockage. It is a common aftermath of some types of surgery.

K56.2 **Volvulus**
  Strangulation of colon or intestine
  Torsion of colon or intestine
  Twist of colon or intestine

  Excludes2 volvulus of duodenum (K31.5)

K56.3 **Gallstone ileus**
  Obstruction of intestine by gallstone

● **K56.4** **Other impaction of intestine**

  K56.41 **Fecal impaction**

    Excludes1 constipation (K59.0-)
      incomplete defecation (R15.0)

  K56.49 **Other impaction of intestine**

● **K56.5** **Intestinal adhesions [bands] with obstruction (postinfection)**
  Abdominal hernia due to adhesions with obstruction
  Peritoneal adhesions [bands] with intestinal obstruction (postinfection)

  K56.50 **Intestinal adhesions [bands], unspecified as to partial versus complete obstruction**
    Intestinal adhesions with obstruction NOS

  K56.51 **Intestinal adhesions [bands], with partial obstruction**
    Intestinal adhesions with incomplete obstruction

  K56.52 **Intestinal adhesions [bands] with complete obstruction**

● **K56.6** **Other and unspecified intestinal obstruction**

  ● **K56.60** **Unspecified intestinal obstruction**

    Excludes1 intestinal obstruction due to specified condition-code to condition
      Coding Clinic: 2017, Q2, P12

    K56.600 **Partial intestinal obstruction, unspecified as to cause**
      Incomplete intestinal obstruction, NOS

    K56.601 **Complete intestinal obstruction, unspecified as to cause**

    K56.609 **Unspecified intestinal obstruction, unspecified as to partial versus complete obstruction**
      Intestinal obstruction NOS

▶ New   ⇒ Revised   ~~deleted~~ Deleted   Excludes 1   Excludes 2   Includes   Use additional   Code first   Code also   Key words
OGCR Official Guidelines   X Assign placeholder X   ● Use Additional Character(s)   ▶ Manifestation Code   **Coding Clinic**

● **K56.69   Other intestinal obstruction**
Enterostenosis NOS
Obstructive ileus NOS
Occlusion of colon or intestine NOS
Stenosis of colon or intestine NOS
Stricture of colon or intestine NOS

     Excludes1   intestinal obstruction due to specified condition-code to condition
     Coding Clinic: 2017, Q2, P12

   K56.690   Other partial intestinal obstruction
Other incomplete intestinal obstruction

   K56.691   Other complete intestinal obstruction

   K56.699   Other intestinal obstruction unspecified as to partial versus complete obstruction
Other intestinal obstruction, NEC

● **K56.7   Ileus, unspecified**

     Excludes1   obstructive ileus (K56.69-)

     Excludes2   intestinal obstruction with hernia (K40-K46)

     Coding Clinic: 2017, Q1, P41

● **K57   Diverticular disease of intestine**
▶ Code also if applicable peritonitis K65.-

     Excludes1   congenital diverticulum of intestine (Q43.8)
Meckel's diverticulum (Q43.0)

     Excludes2   diverticulum of appendix (K38.2)

● **K57.0   Diverticulitis of small intestine with perforation and abscess**
Diverticulitis of small intestine with peritonitis

     Excludes1   diverticulitis of both small and large intestine with perforation and abscess (K57.4-)

   K57.00   Diverticulitis of small intestine with perforation and abscess without bleeding

   K57.01   Diverticulitis of small intestine with perforation and abscess with bleeding

● **K57.1   Diverticular disease of small intestine without perforation or abscess**

     Excludes1   diverticular disease of both small and large intestine without perforation or abscess (K57.5-)

   K57.10   Diverticulosis of small intestine without perforation or abscess without bleeding
Diverticular disease of small intestine NOS

   K57.11   Diverticulosis of small intestine without perforation or abscess with bleeding

   K57.12   Diverticulitis of small intestine without perforation or abscess without bleeding

   K57.13   Diverticulitis of small intestine without perforation or abscess with bleeding

● **K57.2   Diverticulitis of large intestine with perforation and abscess**
Diverticulitis of colon with peritonitis

     Excludes1   diverticulitis of both small and large intestine with perforation and abscess (K57.4-)

   K57.20   Diverticulitis of large intestine with perforation and abscess without bleeding

   K57.21   Diverticulitis of large intestine with perforation and abscess with bleeding

Figure 11-12   Diverticulosis. (From Shiland: Mastering Healthcare Terminology, ed 4, St. Louis, Mosby, 2012)

Item 11–16   Diverticula of the intestines are acquired herniations of the mucosa. Diverticulum (singular): Pocket or pouch that bulges outward through a weak spot (herniation) in the colon. Diverticula (plural). **Diverticulosis** is the condition of having diverticula. **Diverticulitis** is inflammation of these pouches or herniations. Classification is based on location (small intestine or colon) and whether it occurs with or without hemorrhage.

● **K57.3   Diverticular disease of large intestine without perforation or abscess**

     Excludes1   diverticular disease of both small and large intestine without perforation or abscess (K57.5-)

   K57.30   Diverticulosis of large intestine without perforation or abscess without bleeding
Diverticular disease of colon NOS

   K57.31   Diverticulosis of large intestine without perforation or abscess with bleeding

   K57.32   Diverticulitis of large intestine without perforation or abscess without bleeding

   K57.33   Diverticulitis of large intestine without perforation or abscess with bleeding

● **K57.4   Diverticulitis of both small and large intestine with perforation and abscess**
Diverticulitis of both small and large intestine with peritonitis

   K57.40   Diverticulitis of both small and large intestine with perforation and abscess without bleeding

   K57.41   Diverticulitis of both small and large intestine with perforation and abscess with bleeding

● **K57.5   Diverticular disease of both small and large intestine without perforation or abscess**

   K57.50   Diverticulosis of both small and large intestine without perforation or abscess without bleeding
Diverticular disease of both small and large intestine NOS

   K57.51   Diverticulosis of both small and large intestine without perforation or abscess with bleeding

   K57.52   Diverticulitis of both small and large intestine without perforation or abscess without bleeding

   K57.53   Diverticulitis of both small and large intestine without perforation or abscess with bleeding

● **K57.8   Diverticulitis of intestine, part unspecified, with perforation and abscess**
Diverticulitis of intestine NOS with peritonitis

   K57.80   Diverticulitis of intestine, part unspecified, with perforation and abscess without bleeding

   K57.81   Diverticulitis of intestine, part unspecified, with perforation and abscess with bleeding

CHAPTER 11 (K00-K95)

● **K57.9**   **Diverticular disease of intestine, part unspecified, without perforation or abscess**

    K57.90   **Diverticulosis of intestine, part unspecified, without perforation or abscess without bleeding**
       Diverticular disease of intestine NOS

    K57.91   **Diverticulosis of intestine, part unspecified, without perforation or abscess with bleeding**

    K57.92   **Diverticulitis of intestine, part unspecified, without perforation or abscess without bleeding**

    K57.93   **Diverticulitis of intestine, part unspecified, without perforation or abscess with bleeding**

● **K58**   **Irritable bowel syndrome**

    Includes   irritable colon
               spastic colon

    K58.0   **Irritable bowel syndrome with diarrhea**

    K58.1   **Irritable bowel syndrome with constipation**
       Coding Clinic: 2016, Q4, P32

    K58.2   **Mixed irritable bowel syndrome**
       Coding Clinic: 2016, Q4, P32

    K58.8   **Other irritable bowel syndrome**
       Coding Clinic: 2016, Q4, P32

    K58.9   **Irritable bowel syndrome without diarrhea**
       Irritable bowel syndrome NOS

● **K59**   **Other functional intestinal disorders**

    Excludes1   change in bowel habit NOS (R19.4)
               intestinal malabsorption (K90.-)
               psychogenic intestinal disorders (F45.8)

    Excludes2   functional disorders of stomach (K31.-)

● **K59.0**   **Constipation**

       Use additional code for adverse effect, if applicable, to identify drug (T36-T50 with fifth or sixth character 5)

    Excludes1   fecal impaction (K56.41)
               incomplete defecation (R15.0)

    K59.00   **Constipation, unspecified**

    K59.01   **Slow transit constipation**

    K59.02   **Outlet dysfunction constipation**

    K59.03   **Drug induced constipation**

       Use additional code for adverse effect, if applicable, to identify drug (T36-T50 with fifth or sixth character 5)
       Coding Clinic: 2016, Q4, P33

    K59.04   **Chronic idiopathic constipation**
       Functional constipation
       Coding Clinic: 2016, Q4, P33

    K59.09   **Other constipation**
       Chronic constipation

    K59.1   **Functional diarrhea**

    Excludes1   diarrhea NOS (R19.7)
               irritable bowel syndrome with diarrhea (K58.0)

    K59.2   **Neurogenic bowel, not elsewhere classified**

● **K59.3**   **Megacolon, not elsewhere classified**
       Dilatation of colon

       Code first, if applicable (T51-T65) to identify toxic agent

    Excludes1   congenital megacolon (aganglionic) (Q43.1)
               megacolon (due to) (in) Chagas' disease (B57.32)
               megacolon (due to) (in) Clostridium difficile (A04.7-)
               megacolon (due to) (in) Hirschsprung's disease (Q43.1)
       Coding Clinic: 2016, Q4, P33

    K59.31   **Toxic megacolon**

    K59.39   **Other megacolon**
       Megacolon NOS

Item 11–17   A **fissure** is a groove in the surface, whereas a **fistula** is an abnormal passage. An **abscess** is an accumulation of pus in a tissue cavity resulting from a bacterial or parasitic infection.

    K59.4   **Anal spasm**
       Proctalgia fugax

    K59.8   **Other specified functional intestinal disorders**
       Atony of colon Pseudo-obstruction (acute) (chronic) of intestine

    K59.9   **Functional intestinal disorder, unspecified**

● **K60**   **Fissure and fistula of anal and rectal regions**

    Excludes1   fissure and fistula of anal and rectal regions with abscess or cellulitis (K61.-)

    Excludes2   anal sphincter tear (healed) (nontraumatic) (old) (K62.81)

    K60.0   **Acute anal fissure**

    K60.1   **Chronic anal fissure**

    K60.2   **Anal fissure, unspecified**

    K60.3   **Anal fistula**

    K60.4   **Rectal fistula**
       Fistula of rectum to skin

    Excludes1   rectovaginal fistula (N82.3)
               vesicorectal fistula (N32.1)

    K60.5   **Anorectal fistula**

● **K61**   **Abscess of anal and rectal regions**

    Includes   abscess of anal and rectal regions
              cellulitis of anal and rectal regions

    K61.0   **Anal abscess**
       Perianal abscess
       ~~**Excludes1**   intrasphincteric abscess (K61.4)~~

    ▶ **Excludes2**   intrasphincteric abscess (K61.4)

    K61.1   **Rectal abscess**
       Perirectal abscess

    ⇒ **Excludes1**   ischiorectal abscess (K61.39)
       Coding Clinic: 2012, Q4, P104

    K61.2   **Anorectal abscess**

    K61.3   **Ischiorectal abscess**

    ▶ **K61.31**   **Horseshoe abscess**

    ▶ **K61.39**   **Other ischiorectal abscess**
       ▶Abscess of ischiorectal fossa
       ▶Ischiorectal abscess, NOS
       ~~Abscess of ischiorectal fossa~~

    K61.4   **Intrasphincteric abscess**
       ▶Intersphincteric abscess

    ▶ **K61.5**   **Supralevator abscess**

● **K62**   **Other diseases of anus and rectum**

    Includes   anal canal

    Excludes2   colostomy and enterostomy malfunction (K94.0-, K91.4-)
               fecal incontinence (R15.-)
               hemorrhoids (K64.-)

    K62.0   **Anal polyp**
       Coding Clinic: 2018, Q1, P7

    K62.1   **Rectal polyp**

    Excludes1   adenomatous polyp (D12.8)
       Coding Clinic: 2018, Q1, P7

    K62.2   **Anal prolapse**
       Prolapse of anal canal

    K62.3   **Rectal prolapse**
       Prolapse of rectal mucosa

    K62.4   **Stenosis of anus and rectum**
       Stricture of anus (sphincter)

    K62.5   **Hemorrhage of anus and rectum**

    Excludes1   gastrointestinal bleeding NOS (K92.2)
               melena (K92.1)
               neonatal rectal hemorrhage (P54.2)

▶ New   ⇒ Revised   ~~deleted~~ Deleted   Excludes 1   Excludes 2   Includes   Use additional   Code first   Code also   Key words

940   OGCR Official Guidelines   X Assign placeholder X   ● Use Additional Character(s)   ▶ Manifestation Code   **Coding Clinic**

K62.6   **Ulcer of anus and rectum**
Solitary ulcer of anus and rectum
Stercoral ulcer of anus and rectum
> **Excludes1**   fissure and fistula of anus and rectum (K60.-)
> ulcerative colitis (K51.-)

K62.7   **Radiation proctitis**
Use additional code to identify the type of radiation (W90.-)

● **K62.8**   **Other specified diseases of anus and rectum**
> **Excludes2**   ulcerative proctitis (K51.2)

    K62.81   **Anal sphincter tear (healed) (nontraumatic) (old)**
Tear of anus, nontraumatic
Use additional code for any associated fecal incontinence (R15.-)
> **Excludes2**   anal fissure (K60.-)
> anal sphincter tear (healed) (old) complicating delivery (O34.7-)
> traumatic tear of anal sphincter (S31.831)

    K62.82   **Dysplasia of anus**
Anal intraepithelial neoplasia I and II (AIN I and II) (histologically confirmed)
Dysplasia of anus NOS
Mild and moderate dysplasia of anus (histologically confirmed)
> **Excludes1**   abnormal results from anal cytologic examination without histologic confirmation (R85.61-)
> anal intraepithelial neoplasia III (D01.3)
> carcinoma in situ of anus (D01.3)
> HGSIL of anus (R85.613)
> severe dysplasia of anus (D01.3)

    K62.89   **Other specified diseases of anus and rectum**
Proctitis NOS
Use additional code for any associated fecal incontinence (R15.-)

K62.9   **Disease of anus and rectum, unspecified**

● **K63**   **Other diseases of intestine**

    K63.0   **Abscess of intestine**
> **Excludes1**   abscess of intestine with Crohn's disease (K50.014, K50.114, K50.814, K50.914)
> abscess of intestine with diverticular disease (K57.0, K57.2, K57.4, K57.8)
> abscess of intestine with ulcerative colitis (K51.014, K51.214, K51.314, K51.414, K51.514, K51.814, K51.914)
> **Excludes2**   abscess of anal and rectal regions (K61.-)
> ⇒ abscess of appendix (K35.3-)

    K63.1   **Perforation of intestine (nontraumatic)**
Perforation (nontraumatic) of rectum
> **Excludes1**   perforation (nontraumatic) of duodenum (K26.-)
> perforation (nontraumatic) of intestine with diverticular disease (K57.0, K57.2, K57.4, K57.8)
> ⇒ **Excludes2**   perforation (nontraumatic) of appendix (K35.2-, K35.3)

    K63.2   **Fistula of intestine**
> **Excludes1**   fistula of duodenum (K31.6)
> fistula of intestine with Crohn's disease (K50.013, K50.113, K50.813, K50.913)
> fistula of intestine with ulcerative colitis (K51.013, K51.213, K51.313, K51.413, K51.513, K51.813, K51.913)
> **Excludes2**   fistula of anal and rectal regions (K60.-)
> fistula of appendix (K38.3)
> intestinal-genital fistula, female (N82.2-N82.4)
> vesicointestinal fistula (N32.1)
> Coding Clinic: 2017, Q3, P4

    K63.3   **Ulcer of intestine**
Primary ulcer of small intestine
> **Excludes1**   duodenal ulcer (K26.-)
> gastrointestinal ulcer (K28.-)
> gastrojejunal ulcer (K28.-)
> jejunal ulcer (K28.-)
> peptic ulcer, site unspecified (K27.-)
> ulcer of intestine with perforation (K63.1)
> ulcer of anus or rectum (K62.6)
> ulcerative colitis (K51.-)

    K63.4   **Enteroptosis**

    K63.5   **Polyp of colon**
> **Excludes1**   adenomatous polyp of colon (D12.6)
> inflammatory polyp of colon (K51.4-)
> polyposis of colon (D12.6)
> Coding Clinic: 2017, Q1, P15-16; 2015, Q2, P14

● **K63.8**   **Other specified diseases of intestine**

    K63.81   **Dieulafoy lesion of intestine**
> **Excludes2**   Dieulafoy lesion of stomach and duodenum (K31.82)

    K63.89   **Other specified diseases of intestine**
> Coding Clinic: 2013, Q2, P31

    K63.9   **Disease of intestine, unspecified**

● **K64**   **Hemorrhoids and perianal venous thrombosis**
> **Includes**   piles
> **Excludes1**   hemorrhoids complicating childbirth and the puerperium (O87.2)
> hemorrhoids complicating pregnancy (O22.4)

    K64.0   **First degree hemorrhoids**
Grade/stage I hemorrhoids
Hemorrhoids (bleeding) without prolapse outside of anal canal

    K64.1   **Second degree hemorrhoids**
Grade/stage II hemorrhoids
Hemorrhoids (bleeding) that prolapse with straining, but retract spontaneously

    K64.2   **Third degree hemorrhoids**
Grade/stage III hemorrhoids
Hemorrhoids (bleeding) that prolapse with straining and require manual replacement back inside anal canal

    K64.3   **Fourth degree hemorrhoids**
Grade/stage IV hemorrhoids
Hemorrhoids (bleeding) with prolapsed tissue that cannot be manually replaced

    K64.4   **Residual hemorrhoidal skin tags**
External hemorrhoids, NOS
Skin tags of anus

    K64.5   **Perianal venous thrombosis**
External hemorrhoids with thrombosis
Perianal hematoma
Thrombosed hemorrhoids NOS

    K64.8   **Other hemorrhoids**
Internal hemorrhoids, without mention of degree
Prolapsed hemorrhoids, degree not specified

    K64.9   **Unspecified hemorrhoids**
Hemorrhoids (bleeding) NOS
Hemorrhoids (bleeding) without mention of degree

Item 11–18   **Peritonitis** is an inflammation of the lining (peritoneum) of the abdominal cavity and surface of the intestines.

DISEASES OF PERITONEUM AND RETROPERITONEUM (K65-K68)

● **K65   Peritonitis**
> ⇒ Use additional code (B95-B97), to identify infectious agent, if known
> ▶ Code also if applicable diverticular disease of intestine (K57.-)
> ⇒ **Excludes1**   acute appendicitis with generalized peritonitis (K35.2-)
>   aseptic peritonitis (T81.6)
>   benign paroxysmal peritonitis (E85.Ø)
>   chemical peritonitis (T81.6)
>   ~~diverticulitis of both small and large intestine with peritonitis (K57.4-)~~
>   ~~diverticulitis of colon with peritonitis (K57.2-)~~
>   ~~diverticulitis of intestine, NOS, with peritonitis (K57.8-)~~
>   ~~diverticulitis of small intestine with peritonitis (K57.Ø-)~~
>   gonococcal peritonitis (A54.85)
>   neonatal peritonitis (P78.Ø-P78.1)
>   pelvic peritonitis, female (N73.3-N73.5)
>   periodic familial peritonitis (E85.Ø)
>   peritonitis due to talc or other foreign substance (T81.6)
>   peritonitis in chlamydia (A74.81)
>   peritonitis in diphtheria (A36.89)
>   peritonitis in syphilis (late) (A52.74)
>   peritonitis in tuberculosis (A18.31)
>   peritonitis with or following abortion or ectopic or molar pregnancy (OØØ-OØ7, OØ8.Ø)
>   peritonitis with or following appendicitis (K35.-)
>   ~~peritonitis with or following diverticular disease of intestine (K57.-)~~
>   puerperal peritonitis (O85)
>   retroperitoneal infections (K68.-)

   K65.Ø   Generalized (acute) peritonitis
> Pelvic peritonitis (acute), male
> Subphrenic peritonitis (acute)
> Suppurative peritonitis (acute)

   K65.1   Peritoneal abscess
> Abdominopelvic abscess
> Abscess (of) omentum
> Abscess (of) peritoneum
> Mesenteric abscess
> Retrocecal abscess
> Subdiaphragmatic abscess
> Subhepatic abscess
> Subphrenic abscess

   K65.2   Spontaneous bacterial peritonitis
> **Excludes1**   bacterial peritonitis NOS (K65.9)

   K65.3   Choleperitonitis
> Peritonitis due to bile

   K65.4   Sclerosing mesenteritis
> Fat necrosis of peritoneum
> (Idiopathic) sclerosing mesenteric fibrosis
> Mesenteric lipodystrophy
> Mesenteric panniculitis
> Retractile mesenteritis

   K65.8   Other peritonitis
> Chronic proliferative peritonitis
> Peritonitis due to urine

   K65.9   Peritonitis, unspecified
> Bacterial peritonitis NOS
> **Coding Clinic: 2Ø13, Q2, P31**

Item 11–19   **Retroperitoneal infections** occur between the posterior parietal peritoneum and posterior abdominal wall where the kidneys, adrenal glands, ureters, duodenum, ascending colon, descending colon, pancreas, and the large vessels and nerves are located.

● **K66   Other disorders of peritoneum**
> **Excludes2**   ascites (R18.-)
>   peritoneal effusion (chronic) (R18.8)

   K66.Ø   Peritoneal adhesions (postprocedural) (postinfection)
> Adhesions (of) abdominal (wall)
> Adhesions (of) diaphragm
> Adhesions (of) intestine
> Adhesions (of) male pelvis
> Adhesions (of) omentum
> Adhesions (of) stomach
> Adhesive bands
> Mesenteric adhesions
> > **Excludes1**   female pelvic adhesions [bands] (N73.6)
> >   peritoneal adhesions with intestinal obstruction (K56.5-)

   K66.1   Hemoperitoneum
> **Excludes1**   traumatic hemoperitoneum (S36.8-)

   K66.8   Other specified disorders of peritoneum

   K66.9   Disorder of peritoneum, unspecified

▶ *K67   Disorders of peritoneum in infectious diseases classified elsewhere*
> ⇒ *Code first underlying disease, such as:*
>   congenital syphilis (A5Ø.Ø)
>   helminthiasis (B65.Ø-B83.9)
> > **Excludes1**   peritonitis in chlamydia (A74.81)
> >   peritonitis in diphtheria (A36.89)
> >   peritonitis in gonococcal (A54.85)
> >   peritonitis in syphilis (late) (A52.74)
> >   peritonitis in tuberculosis (A18.31)

● **K68   Disorders of retroperitoneum**
> ● **K68.1   Retroperitoneal abscess**
> > **K68.11   Postprocedural retroperitoneal abscess**
> > > ▶ **Excludes2**   infection following procedure (T81.44)
> > **K68.12   Psoas muscle abscess**
> > **K68.19   Other retroperitoneal abscess**
> **K68.9   Other disorders of retroperitoneum**

DISEASES OF LIVER (K7Ø-K77)

> **Excludes1**   jaundice NOS (R17)
>
> **Excludes2**   hemochromatosis (E83.11-)
>   Reye's syndrome (G93.7)
>   viral hepatitis (B15-B19)
>   Wilson's disease (E83.Ø)

● **K7Ø   Alcoholic liver disease**
> Use additional code to identify:
>   alcohol abuse and dependence (F1Ø.-)

   K7Ø.Ø   Alcoholic fatty liver   A

● **K7Ø.1   Alcoholic hepatitis**
> **K7Ø.1Ø   Alcoholic hepatitis without ascites**   A
> **K7Ø.11   Alcoholic hepatitis with ascites**   A

   K7Ø.2   Alcoholic fibrosis and sclerosis of liver   A

● **K7Ø.3   Alcoholic cirrhosis of liver**
> Alcoholic cirrhosis NOS
> **K7Ø.3Ø   Alcoholic cirrhosis of liver without ascites**   A
> **K7Ø.31   Alcoholic cirrhosis of liver with ascites**   A
>   **Coding Clinic: 2Ø18, Q1, P5**

▶ New   ⇒ Revised   ~~deleted~~ Deleted   Excludes 1   Excludes 2   Includes   Use additional   Code first   Code also   Key words

OGCR Official Guidelines   X Assign placeholder X   ● Use Additional Character(s)   ▌Manifestation Code   Coding Clinic

Item 11–20 **Cirrhosis** is the progressive fibrosis of the liver resulting in loss of liver function. The main causes of cirrhosis of the liver are alcohol abuse, chronic hepatitis (inflammation of the liver), biliary disease, and excessive amounts of iron. **Alcoholic cirrhosis of the liver** is also called portal, Laënnec's, or fatty nutritional cirrhosis.

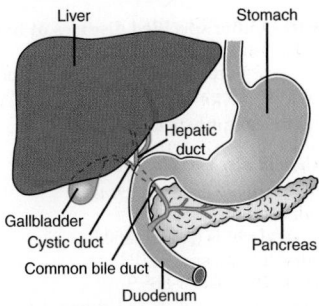

Figure 11-13   Liver and bile ducts.

● **K70.4**   **Alcoholic hepatic failure**
     Acute alcoholic hepatic failure
     Alcoholic hepatic failure NOS
     Chronic alcoholic hepatic failure
     Subacute alcoholic hepatic failure

     K70.40   Alcoholic hepatic failure without coma   A

     K70.41   Alcoholic hepatic failure with coma   A

   K70.9   Alcoholic liver disease, unspecified   A

● **K71**   **Toxic liver disease**
     Includes   drug-induced idiosyncratic (unpredictable) liver disease
                 drug-induced toxic (predictable) liver disease

     Code first poisoning due to drug or toxin, if applicable (T36-T65 with fifth or sixth character 1-4 or 6)

     Use additional code for adverse effect, if applicable, to identify drug (T36-T50 with fifth or sixth character 5)

     Excludes2   alcoholic liver disease (K70.-)
                   Budd-Chiari syndrome (I82.0)

   K71.0   Toxic liver disease with cholestasis
         Cholestasis with hepatocyte injury
         'Pure' cholestasis

● **K71.1**   Toxic liver disease with hepatic necrosis
         Hepatic failure (acute) (chronic) due to drugs

     K71.10   Toxic liver disease with hepatic necrosis, without coma

     K71.11   Toxic liver disease with hepatic necrosis, with coma

   K71.2   Toxic liver disease with acute hepatitis

   K71.3   Toxic liver disease with chronic persistent hepatitis

   K71.4   Toxic liver disease with chronic lobular hepatitis

● **K71.5**   Toxic liver disease with chronic active hepatitis
         Toxic liver disease with lupoid hepatitis

     K71.50   Toxic liver disease with chronic active hepatitis without ascites

     K71.51   Toxic liver disease with chronic active hepatitis with ascites
             Coding Clinic: 2018, Q1, P4

   K71.6   Toxic liver disease with hepatitis, not elsewhere classified

   K71.7   Toxic liver disease with fibrosis and cirrhosis of liver

   K71.8   Toxic liver disease with other disorders of liver
         Toxic liver disease with focal nodular hyperplasia
         Toxic liver disease with hepatic granulomas
         Toxic liver disease with peliosis hepatis
         Toxic liver disease with veno-occlusive disease of liver

   K71.9   Toxic liver disease, unspecified

● **K72**   **Hepatic failure, not elsewhere classified**
     Includes   fulminant hepatitis NEC, with hepatic failure
                 hepatic encephalopathy NOS
                 liver (cell) necrosis with hepatic failure
                 malignant hepatitis NEC, with hepatic failure
                 yellow liver atrophy or dystrophy

     Excludes1   alcoholic hepatic failure (K70.4)
                 hepatic failure with toxic liver disease (K71.1-)
                 icterus of newborn (P55-P59)
                 postprocedural hepatic failure (K91.82)

     Excludes2   hepatic failure complicating abortion or ectopic or molar pregnancy (O00-O07, O08.8)
                 hepatic failure complicating pregnancy, childbirth and the puerperium (O26.6-)
                 viral hepatitis with hepatic coma (B15-B19)

● **K72.0**   **Acute and subacute hepatic failure**
         Acute non-viral hepatitis NOS
         Coding Clinic: 2015, Q2, P17

     K72.00   Acute and subacute hepatic failure without coma
             Coding Clinic: 2015, Q2, P17

     K72.01   Acute and subacute hepatic failure with coma

● **K72.1**   Chronic hepatic failure

     K72.10   Chronic hepatic failure without coma
             Coding Clinic: 2017, Q1, P41

     K72.11   Chronic hepatic failure with coma

● **K72.9**   Hepatic failure, unspecified

     K72.90   Hepatic failure, unspecified without coma

     K72.91   Hepatic failure, unspecified with coma
            Hepatic coma NOS
            Coding Clinic: 2016, Q2, P35

● **K73**   **Chronic hepatitis, not elsewhere classified**
     Excludes1   alcoholic hepatitis (chronic) (K70.1-)
                 drug-induced hepatitis (chronic) (K71.-)
                 granulomatous hepatitis (chronic) NEC (K75.3)
                 reactive, nonspecific hepatitis (chronic) (K75.2)
                 viral hepatitis (chronic) (B15-B19)

   K73.0   Chronic persistent hepatitis, not elsewhere classified

   K73.1   Chronic lobular hepatitis, not elsewhere classified

   K73.2   Chronic active hepatitis, not elsewhere classified

   K73.8   Other chronic hepatitis, not elsewhere classified

   K73.9   Chronic hepatitis, unspecified

● **K74**   **Fibrosis and cirrhosis of liver**
     Code also, if applicable, viral hepatitis (acute) (chronic) (B15-B19)

     Excludes1   alcoholic cirrhosis (of liver) (K70.3)
                 alcoholic fibrosis of liver (K70.2)
                 cardiac sclerosis of liver (K76.1)
                 cirrhosis (of liver) with toxic liver disease (K71.7)
                 congenital cirrhosis (of liver) (P78.81)
                 pigmentary cirrhosis (of liver) (E83.110)

   K74.0   Hepatic fibrosis

   K74.1   Hepatic sclerosis

   K74.2   Hepatic fibrosis with hepatic sclerosis

   K74.3   Primary biliary cirrhosis
         Chronic nonsuppurative destructive cholangitis
         ▶Primary biliary cholangitis

     ▶ **Excludes2**   primary sclerosing cholangitis (K83.01)

   K74.4   Secondary biliary cirrhosis

   K74.5   Biliary cirrhosis, unspecified

● **K74.6**   Other and unspecified cirrhosis of liver

     K74.60   Unspecified cirrhosis of liver
            Cirrhosis (of liver) NOS
            Coding Clinic: 2018, Q1, P4

     K74.69   Other cirrhosis of liver
            Cryptogenic cirrhosis (of liver)
            Macronodular cirrhosis (of liver)
            Micronodular cirrhosis (of liver)
            Mixed type cirrhosis (of liver)
            Portal cirrhosis (of liver)
            Postnecrotic cirrhosis (of liver)

CHAPTER 11 (K00-K95)

● **K75**   **Other inflammatory liver diseases**

> **Excludes2**   toxic liver disease (K71.-)

K75.0   **Abscess of liver**
> Cholangitic hepatic abscess
> Hematogenic hepatic abscess
> Hepatic abscess NOS
> Lymphogenic hepatic abscess
> Pylephlebitic hepatic abscess
>> **Excludes1**   amebic liver abscess (A06.4)
>> ⇒ cholangitis without liver abscess (K83.09)
>> pylephlebitis without liver abscess (K75.1)
>> **Excludes2**   acute or subacute hepatitis NOS (B17.9)
>> acute or subacute non-viral hepatitis (K72.0)
>> chronic hepatitis NEC (K73.8)

K75.1   **Phlebitis of portal vein**
> Pylephlebitis
>> **Excludes1**   pylephlebitic liver abscess (K75.0)

K75.2   **Nonspecific reactive hepatitis**
>> **Excludes1**   acute or subacute hepatitis (K72.0-)
>> chronic hepatitis NEC (K73.-)
>> viral hepatitis (B15-B19)

K75.3   **Granulomatous hepatitis, not elsewhere classified**
>> **Excludes1**   acute or subacute hepatitis (K72.0-)
>> chronic hepatitis NEC (K73.-)
>> viral hepatitis (B15-B19)

K75.4   **Autoimmune hepatitis**
> Lupoid hepatitis NEC

● **K75.8**   **Other specified inflammatory liver diseases**
> **K75.81**   **Nonalcoholic steatohepatitis (NASH)**
> **K75.89**   **Other specified inflammatory liver diseases**

K75.9   **Inflammatory liver disease, unspecified**
> Hepatitis NOS
>> **Excludes1**   acute or subacute hepatitis (K72.0-)
>> chronic hepatitis NEC (K73.-)
>> viral hepatitis (B15-B19)
> **Coding Clinic: 2015, Q2, P17**

● **K76**   **Other diseases of liver**
> **Excludes2**   alcoholic liver disease (K70.-)
> amyloid degeneration of liver (E85.-)
> cystic disease of liver (congenital) (Q44.6)
> hepatic vein thrombosis (I82.0)
> hepatomegaly NOS (R16.0)
> pigmentary cirrhosis (of liver) (E83.110)
> portal vein thrombosis (I81)
> toxic liver disease (K71.-)

K76.0   **Fatty (change of) liver, not elsewhere classified**
> Nonalcoholic fatty liver disease (NAFLD)
>> **Excludes1**   nonalcoholic steatohepatitis (NASH) (K75.81)

K76.1   **Chronic passive congestion of liver**
> Cardiac cirrhosis
> Cardiac sclerosis

K76.2   **Central hemorrhagic necrosis of liver**
>> **Excludes1**   liver necrosis with hepatic failure (K72.-)

K76.3   **Infarction of liver**

K76.4   **Peliosis hepatis**
> Hepatic angiomatosis

K76.5   **Hepatic veno-occlusive disease**
>> **Excludes1**   Budd-Chiari syndrome (I82.0)

K76.6   **Portal hypertension**
> Use additional code for any associated complications, such as:
> portal hypertensive gastropathy (K31.89)

K76.7   **Hepatorenal syndrome**
>> **Excludes1**   hepatorenal syndrome following labor and delivery (O90.4)
>> postprocedural hepatorenal syndrome (K91.83)

● **K76.8**   **Other specified diseases of liver**
> **K76.81**   **Hepatopulmonary syndrome**
>> *Code first underlying liver disease, such as:*
>> alcoholic cirrhosis of liver (K70.3-)
>> cirrhosis of liver without mention of alcohol (K74.6-)
> **K76.89**   **Other specified diseases of liver**
>> Cyst (simple) of liver
>> Focal nodular hyperplasia of liver
>> Hepatoptosis

K76.9   **Liver disease, unspecified**

▷ **K77**   *Liver disorders in diseases classified elsewhere*
> *Code first underlying disease, such as:*
> amyloidosis (E85.-)
> congenital syphilis (A50.0, A50.5)
> congenital toxoplasmosis (P37.1)
> schistosomiasis (B65.0-B65.9)
>> **Excludes1**   alcoholic hepatitis (K70.1-)
>> alcoholic liver disease (K70.-)
>> cytomegaloviral hepatitis (B25.1)
>> herpesviral [herpes simplex] hepatitis (B00.81)
>> infectious mononucleosis with liver disease (B27.0-B27.9 with .9)
>> mumps hepatitis (B26.81)
>> sarcoidosis with liver disease (D86.89)
>> secondary syphilis with liver disease (A51.45)
>> syphilis (late) with liver disease (A52.74)
>> toxoplasmosis (acquired) hepatitis (B58.1)
>> tuberculosis with liver disease (A18.83)

DISORDERS OF GALLBLADDER, BILIARY TRACT AND PANCREAS (K80–K87)

● **K80**   **Cholelithiasis**
> *Presence or formation of gallstones*
>> **Excludes1**   retained cholelithiasis following cholecystectomy (K91.86)

● **K80.0**   **Calculus of gallbladder with acute cholecystitis**
> Any condition listed in K80.2 with acute cholecystitis
> ▷ Use additional code if applicable for associated gangrene of gallbladder (K82.A1), or perforation of gallbladder (K82.A2)
> *Check documentation for acute/chronic gallbladder/common bile duct either with or without obstruction.*
> **K80.00**   **Calculus of gallbladder with acute cholecystitis without obstruction**
> **K80.01**   **Calculus of gallbladder with acute cholecystitis with obstruction**

● **K80.1**   **Calculus of gallbladder with other cholecystitis**
> ▷ Use additional code if applicable for associated gangrene of gallbladder (K82.A1), or perforation of gallbladder (K82.A2)
> **K80.10**   **Calculus of gallbladder with chronic cholecystitis without obstruction**
>> Cholelithiasis with cholecystitis NOS
> **K80.11**   **Calculus of gallbladder with chronic cholecystitis with obstruction**
> **K80.12**   **Calculus of gallbladder with acute and chronic cholecystitis without obstruction**
> **K80.13**   **Calculus of gallbladder with acute and chronic cholecystitis with obstruction**

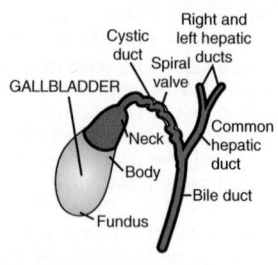

Figure 11-14   Gallbladder and bile ducts.

▷ New   ⇒ Revised   ~~deleted~~ Deleted   Excludes 1   Excludes 2   Includes   Use additional   Code first   Code also   Key words
OGCR Official Guidelines   X Assign placeholder X   ● Use Additional Character(s)   ▷ Manifestation Code   Coding Clinic

K80.18   Calculus of gallbladder with other cholecystitis without obstruction

K80.19   Calculus of gallbladder with other cholecystitis with obstruction

● K80.2   Calculus of gallbladder without cholecystitis
Cholecystolithiasis without cholecystitis
Cholelithiasis (without cholecystitis)
Colic (recurrent) of gallbladder (without cholecystitis)
Gallstone (impacted) of cystic duct (without cholecystitis)
Gallstone (impacted) of gallbladder (without cholecystitis)

K80.20   Calculus of gallbladder without cholecystitis without obstruction

K80.21   Calculus of gallbladder without cholecystitis with obstruction

● K80.3   Calculus of bile duct with cholangitis
Any condition listed in K80.5 with cholangitis

K80.30   Calculus of bile duct with cholangitis, unspecified, without obstruction

K80.31   Calculus of bile duct with cholangitis, unspecified, with obstruction

K80.32   Calculus of bile duct with acute cholangitis without obstruction

K80.33   Calculus of bile duct with acute cholangitis with obstruction

K80.34   Calculus of bile duct with chronic cholangitis without obstruction

K80.35   Calculus of bile duct with chronic cholangitis with obstruction

K80.36   Calculus of bile duct with acute and chronic cholangitis without obstruction

K80.37   Calculus of bile duct with acute and chronic cholangitis with obstruction

● K80.4   Calculus of bile duct with cholecystitis
Any condition listed in K80.5 with cholecystitis (with cholangitis)
▶ Use additional code if applicable for associated gangrene of gallbladder (K82.A1), or perforation of gallbladder (K82.A2)

K80.40   Calculus of bile duct with cholecystitis, unspecified, without obstruction

K80.41   Calculus of bile duct with cholecystitis, unspecified, with obstruction

K80.42   Calculus of bile duct with acute cholecystitis without obstruction

K80.43   Calculus of bile duct with acute cholecystitis with obstruction

K80.44   Calculus of bile duct with chronic cholecystitis without obstruction

K80.45   Calculus of bile duct with chronic cholecystitis with obstruction

K80.46   Calculus of bile duct with acute and chronic cholecystitis without obstruction

K80.47   Calculus of bile duct with acute and chronic cholecystitis with obstruction

● K80.5   Calculus of bile duct without cholangitis or cholecystitis
Choledocholithiasis (without cholangitis or cholecystitis)
Gallstone (impacted) of bile duct NOS (without cholangitis or cholecystitis)
Gallstone (impacted) of common duct (without cholangitis or cholecystitis)
Gallstone (impacted) of hepatic duct (without cholangitis or cholecystitis)
Hepatic cholelithiasis (without cholangitis or cholecystitis)
Hepatic colic (recurrent) (without cholangitis or cholecystitis)

K80.50   Calculus of bile duct without cholangitis or cholecystitis without obstruction

K80.51   Calculus of bile duct without cholangitis or cholecystitis with obstruction

● K80.6   Calculus of gallbladder and bile duct with cholecystitis
▶ Use additional code if applicable for associated gangrene of gallbladder (K82.A1), or perforation of gallbladder (K82.A2)

K80.60   Calculus of gallbladder and bile duct with cholecystitis, unspecified, without obstruction

K80.61   Calculus of gallbladder and bile duct with cholecystitis, unspecified, with obstruction

K80.62   Calculus of gallbladder and bile duct with acute cholecystitis without obstruction

K80.63   Calculus of gallbladder and bile duct with acute cholecystitis with obstruction

K80.64   Calculus of gallbladder and bile duct with chronic cholecystitis without obstruction

K80.65   Calculus of gallbladder and bile duct with chronic cholecystitis with obstruction

K80.66   Calculus of gallbladder and bile duct with acute and chronic cholecystitis without obstruction

K80.67   Calculus of gallbladder and bile duct with acute and chronic cholecystitis with obstruction

● K80.7   Calculus of gallbladder and bile duct without cholecystitis

K80.70   Calculus of gallbladder and bile duct without cholecystitis without obstruction

K80.71   Calculus of gallbladder and bile duct without cholecystitis with obstruction

● K80.8   Other cholelithiasis

K80.80   Other cholelithiasis without obstruction

K80.81   Other cholelithiasis with obstruction

● K81   Cholecystitis
Chronic or acute inflammation of the gallbladder
▶ Use additional code if applicable for associated gangrene of gallbladder (K82.A1), or perforation of gallbladder (K82.A2)
Excludes1   cholecystitis with cholelithiasis (K80.-)

K81.0   Acute cholecystitis
Abscess of gallbladder
Angiocholecystitis
Emphysematous (acute) cholecystitis
Empyema of gallbladder
Gangrene of gallbladder
Gangrenous cholecystitis
Suppurative cholecystitis

K81.1   Chronic cholecystitis

K81.2   Acute cholecystitis with chronic cholecystitis

K81.9   Cholecystitis, unspecified

● K82   Other diseases of gallbladder
Excludes1   nonvisualization of gallbladder (R93.2)
postcholecystectomy syndrome (K91.5)

K82.0   Obstruction of gallbladder
Occlusion of cystic duct or gallbladder without cholelithiasis
Stenosis of cystic duct or gallbladder without cholelithiasis
Stricture of cystic duct or gallbladder without cholelithiasis
Excludes1   obstruction of gallbladder with cholelithiasis (K80.-)

K82.1   Hydrops of gallbladder
Mucocele of gallbladder

K82.2   Perforation of gallbladder
Rupture of cystic duct or gallbladder
▶ **Excludes1**   Perforation of gallbladder in cholecystitis (K82.A2)

K82.3   Fistula of gallbladder
Cholecystocolic fistula
Cholecystoduodenal fistula

CHAPTER 11 (K00-K95)

K82.4 Cholesterolosis of gallbladder
Strawberry gallbladder
  Excludes1 cholesterolosis of gallbladder with
  cholecystitis (K81.-)
  cholesterolosis of gallbladder with
  cholelithiasis (K80.-)

K82.8 Other specified diseases of gallbladder
Adhesions of cystic duct or gallbladder
Atrophy of cystic duct or gallbladder
Cyst of cystic duct or gallbladder
Dyskinesia of cystic duct or gallbladder
Hypertrophy of cystic duct or gallbladder
Nonfunctioning of cystic duct or gallbladder
Ulcer of cystic duct or gallbladder

K82.9 Disease of gallbladder, unspecified

K82.A Disorders of gallbladder in diseases classified elsewhere
  ▶ *Code first the type of cholecystitis (K81.-), or cholelithiasis
    with cholecystitis (K80.00-K80.19, K80.40-K80.47,
    K80.60-K80.67)*

  ▶ **K82.A1 Gangrene of gallbladder in cholecystitis**

  ▶ **K82.A2 Perforation of gallbladder in cholecystitis**

K83 Other diseases of biliary tract
  Excludes1 postcholecystectomy syndrome (K91.5)
  Excludes2 conditions involving the gallbladder (K81-K82)
  conditions involving the cystic duct (K81-K82)

  K83.0 Cholangitis
  ~~Ascending cholangitis~~   ~~Sclerosing cholangitis~~
  ~~Cholangitis NOS~~   ~~Secondary cholangitis~~
  ~~Primary cholangitis~~   ~~Stenosing cholangitis~~
  ~~Recurrent cholangitis~~   ~~Suppurative cholangitis~~
    Excludes1 cholangitic liver abscess (K75.0)
    cholangitis with choledocholithiasis
    (K80.3-, K80.4-)
    ~~chronic nonsuppurative destructive~~
    ~~cholangitis (K74.3)~~
    Excludes2 chronic nonsuppurative destructive
    cholangitis (K74.3)
      ▶ primary biliary cholangitis (K74.3)
      ▶ primary biliary cirrhosis (K74.3)

  ▶ **K83.01 Primary sclerosing cholangitis**

  ▶ **K83.09 Other cholangitis**
      ▶ Ascending cholangitis
      ▶ Cholangitis NOS
      ▶ Primary cholangitis
      ▶ Recurrent cholangitis
      ▶ Sclerosing cholangitis
      ▶ Secondary cholangitis
      ▶ Stenosing cholangitis
      ▶ Suppurative cholangitis

  K83.1 Obstruction of bile duct
  Occlusion of bile duct without cholelithiasis
  Stenosis of bile duct without cholelithiasis
  Stricture of bile duct without cholelithiasis
    Excludes1 congenital obstruction of bile duct (Q44.3)
    obstruction of bile duct with cholelithiasis
    (K80.-)
    Coding Clinic: 2016, Q1, P18

  K83.2 Perforation of bile duct
  Rupture of bile duct

  K83.3 Fistula of bile duct
  Choledochoduodenal fistula

  K83.4 Spasm of sphincter of Oddi

  K83.5 Biliary cyst

  K83.8 Other specified diseases of biliary tract
  Adhesions of biliary tract
  Atrophy of biliary tract
  Hypertrophy of biliary tract
  Ulcer of biliary tract

  K83.9 Disease of biliary tract, unspecified

K85 Acute pancreatitis
  Inflammatory process in which pancreatic enzymes autodigest the gland
  Includes acute (recurrent) pancreatitis
  subacute pancreatitis
  Coding Clinic: 2016, Q4, P34

  K85.0 Idiopathic acute pancreatitis
    **K85.00 Idiopathic acute pancreatitis without necrosis
    or infection**
    **K85.01 Idiopathic acute pancreatitis with uninfected
    necrosis**
    **K85.02 Idiopathic acute pancreatitis with infected
    necrosis**

  K85.1 Biliary acute pancreatitis
  Gallstone pancreatitis
    **K85.10 Biliary acute pancreatitis without necrosis or
    infection**
    **K85.11 Biliary acute pancreatitis with uninfected
    necrosis**
    K85.12 Biliary acute pancreatitis with infected necrosis

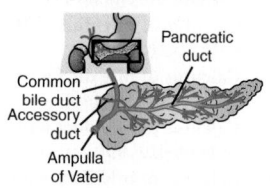

Figure 11-15 Pancreatic ductal system.

  K85.2 Alcohol induced acute pancreatitis
    Excludes2 alcohol induced chronic pancreatitis (K86.0)
    **K85.20 Alcohol induced acute pancreatitis without
    necrosis or infection**
    **K85.21 Alcohol induced acute pancreatitis with
    uninfected necrosis**
    **K85.22 Alcohol induced acute pancreatitis with
    infected necrosis**

  K85.3 Drug induced acute pancreatitis
  Use additional code for adverse effect, if applicable,
  to identify drug (T36-T50 with fifth or sixth
  character 5)
  Use additional code to identify drug abuse and
  dependence (F11.-F17.-)
    **K85.30 Drug induced acute pancreatitis without
    necrosis or infection**
    **K85.31 Drug induced acute pancreatitis with
    uninfected necrosis**
    **K85.32 Drug induced acute pancreatitis with infected
    necrosis**

  K85.8 Other acute pancreatitis
    **K85.80 Other acute pancreatitis without necrosis or
    infection**
    **K85.81 Other acute pancreatitis with uninfected
    necrosis**
    K85.82 Other acute pancreatitis with infected necrosis

  K85.9 Acute pancreatitis, unspecified
  Pancreatitis NOS
    **K85.90 Acute pancreatitis without necrosis or infection,
    unspecified**
    **K85.91 Acute pancreatitis with uninfected necrosis,
    unspecified**
    **K85.92 Acute pancreatitis with infected necrosis,
    unspecified**

▶ New   ⇒ Revised   ~~deleted~~ Deleted   Excludes 1   Excludes 2   Includes   Use additional   Code first   Code also   Key words
OGCR Official Guidelines   X Assign placeholder X   ● Use Additional Character(s)   ▷ Manifestation Code   Coding Clinic

● **K86**   **Other diseases of pancreas**

> **Excludes2**   fibrocystic disease of pancreas (E84.-)
> islet cell tumor (of pancreas) (D13.7)
> pancreatic steatorrhea (K90.3)

K86.0   **Alcohol-induced chronic pancreatitis**
> Use additional code to identify:
> alcohol abuse and dependence (F10.-)
>
> Code also exocrine pancreatic insufficiency (K86.81)
>
> **Excludes2**   alcohol induced acute pancreatitis (K85.2-)

K86.1   **Other chronic pancreatitis**
> Chronic pancreatitis NOS
> Infectious chronic pancreatitis
> Recurrent chronic pancreatitis
> Relapsing chronic pancreatitis
>
> Code also exocrine pancreatic insufficiency (K86.81)

K86.2   **Cyst of pancreas**

K86.3   **Pseudocyst of pancreas**

● **K86.8**   **Other specified diseases of pancreas**
> Coding Clinic: 2016, Q4, P34

     K86.81   **Exocrine pancreatic insufficiency**

     K86.89   **Other specified diseases of pancreas**
> Aseptic pancreatic necrosis, unrelated to acute pancreatitis
> Atrophy of pancreas
> Calculus of pancreas
> Cirrhosis of pancreas
> Fibrosis of pancreas
> Pancreatic fat necrosis, unrelated to acute pancreatitis
> Pancreatic infantilism
> Pancreatic necrosis NOS, unrelated to acute pancreatitis

K86.9   **Disease of pancreas, unspecified**

▶ **K87**   *Disorders of gallbladder, biliary tract and pancreas in diseases classified elsewhere*

> *Code first underlying disease*
>
> ⇒ **Excludes1**   cytomegaloviral pancreatitis (B25.2)
> mumps pancreatitis (B26.3)
> syphilitic gallbladder (A52.74)
> syphilitic pancreas (A52.74)
> tuberculosis of gallbladder (A18.83)
> tuberculosis of pancreas (A18.83)

OTHER DISEASES OF THE DIGESTIVE SYSTEM (K90-K95)

● **K90**   **Intestinal malabsorption**

> **Excludes1**   intestinal malabsorption following gastrointestinal surgery (K91.2)

K90.0   **Celiac disease**
> Celiac disease with steatorrhea
> Celiac gluten-sensitive enteropathy
> Nontropical sprue
>
> Use additional code for associated disorders including:
> dermatitis herpetiformis (L13.0)
> gluten ataxia (G32.81)
>
> Code also exocrine pancreatic insufficiency (K86.81)

K90.1   **Tropical sprue**
> Sprue NOS
> Tropical steatorrhea

K90.2   **Blind loop syndrome, not elsewhere classified**
> Blind loop syndrome NOS
>
> **Excludes1**   congenital blind loop syndrome (Q43.8)
> postsurgical blind loop syndrome (K91.2)

K90.3   **Pancreatic steatorrhea**

● **K90.4**   **Other malabsorption due to intolerance**
> **Excludes2**   celiac gluten-sensitive enteropathy (K90.0)
> lactose intolerance (E73.-)
>
> Coding Clinic: 2016, Q4, P35-36

     K90.41   **Non-celiac gluten sensitivity**
> Gluten sensitivity NOS
> Non-celiac gluten sensitive enteropathy

     K90.49   **Malabsorption due to intolerance, not elsewhere classified**
> Malabsorption due to intolerance to carbohydrate
> Malabsorption due to intolerance to fat
> Malabsorption due to intolerance to protein
> Malabsorption due to intolerance to starch

● **K90.8**   **Other intestinal malabsorption**

     K90.81   **Whipple's disease**

     K90.89   **Other intestinal malabsorption**

K90.9   **Intestinal malabsorption, unspecified**
> Coding Clinic: 2017, Q4, P108-109

● **K91**   **Intraoperative and postprocedural complications and disorders of digestive system, not elsewhere classified**

> **Excludes2**   complications of artificial opening of digestive system (K94.-)
> complications of bariatric procedures (K95.-)
> gastrojejunal ulcer (K28.-)
> postprocedural (radiation) retroperitoneal abscess (K68.11)
> radiation colitis (K52.0)
> radiation gastroenteritis (K52.0)
> radiation proctitis (K62.7)
>
> Coding Clinic: 2016, Q4, P10

K91.0   **Vomiting following gastrointestinal surgery**

K91.1   **Postgastric surgery syndromes**
> Dumping syndrome
> Postgastrectomy syndrome
> Postvagotomy syndrome

K91.2   **Postsurgical malabsorption, not elsewhere classified**
> Postsurgical blind loop syndrome
>
> **Excludes1**   malabsorption osteomalacia in adults (M83.2)
> malabsorption osteoporosis, postsurgical (M80.8-, M81.8)

● **K91.3**   **Postprocedural intestinal obstruction**
> Coding Clinic: 2017, Q1, P40-41

     K91.30   **Postprocedural intestinal obstruction, unspecified as to partial versus complete**
> Postprocedural intestinal obstruction NOS

     K91.31   **Postprocedural partial intestinal obstruction**
> Postprocedural incomplete intestinal obstruction

     K91.32   **Postprocedural complete intestinal obstruction**

K91.5   **Postcholecystectomy syndrome**

● **K91.6**   **Intraoperative hemorrhage and hematoma of a digestive system organ or structure complicating a procedure**
> **Excludes1**   intraoperative hemorrhage and hematoma of a digestive system organ or structure due to accidental puncture and laceration during a procedure (K91.7-)

     K91.61   **Intraoperative hemorrhage and hematoma of a digestive system organ or structure complicating a digestive system procedure**

     K91.62   **Intraoperative hemorrhage and hematoma of a digestive system organ or structure complicating other procedure**

● **K91.7**   **Accidental puncture and laceration of a digestive system organ or structure during a procedure**

     K91.71   **Accidental puncture and laceration of a digestive system organ or structure during a digestive system procedure**

     K91.72   **Accidental puncture and laceration of a digestive system organ or structure during other procedure**

● **K91.8**   **Other intraoperative and postprocedural complications and disorders of digestive system**

     K91.81   **Other intraoperative complications of digestive system**

     K91.82   **Postprocedural hepatic failure**

     K91.83   **Postprocedural hepatorenal syndrome**

● K91.84 **Postprocedural hemorrhage** of a digestive system organ or structure following a procedure

    K91.840 Postprocedural hemorrhage of a digestive system organ or structure following a **digestive system procedure**
        Coding Clinic: 2016, Q1, P15

    K91.841 Postprocedural hemorrhage of a digestive system organ or structure following **other procedure**

● K91.85 Complications of **intestinal pouch**

    K91.850 **Pouchitis**
        Inflammation of internal ileoanal pouch

    K91.858 Other complications of intestinal pouch

K91.86 **Retained cholelithiasis** following cholecystectomy

● K91.87 Postprocedural **hematoma** and **seroma** of a digestive system organ or structure following a procedure

    K91.870 Postprocedural **hematoma** of a digestive system organ or structure following a **digestive system procedure**

    K91.871 Postprocedural **hematoma** of a digestive system organ or structure following **other procedure**

    K91.872 Postprocedural **seroma** of a digestive system organ or structure following a **digestive system procedure**

    K91.873 Postprocedural **seroma** of a digestive system organ or structure following **other procedure**

K91.89 Other postprocedural complications and disorders of digestive system
    Use additional code, if applicable, to further specify disorder
    Excludes2 postprocedural retroperitoneal abscess (K68.11)
    Coding Clinic: 2017, Q1, P41

● K92 **Other diseases of digestive system**
    Excludes1 neonatal gastrointestinal hemorrhage (P54.0-P54.3)

K92.0 **Hematemesis**

K92.1 **Melena**
    Excludes1 occult blood in feces (R19.5)

K92.2 **Gastrointestinal hemorrhage, unspecified**
    Gastric hemorrhage NOS
    Intestinal hemorrhage NOS
    Excludes1 acute hemorrhagic gastritis (K29.01)
        hemorrhage of anus and rectum (K62.5)
        angiodysplasia of stomach with hemorrhage (K31.811)
        diverticular disease with hemorrhage (K57.-)
        gastritis and duodenitis with hemorrhage (K29.-)
        peptic ulcer with hemorrhage (K25-K28)

● K92.8 Other specified diseases of the digestive system

    K92.81 Gastrointestinal mucositis (ulcerative)
        Code also type of associated therapy, such as:
        antineoplastic and immunosuppressive drugs (T45.1X-)
        radiological procedure and radiotherapy (Y84.2)
        Excludes2 mucositis (ulcerative) of vagina and vulva (N76.81)
            nasal mucositis (ulcerative) (J34.81)
            oral mucositis (ulcerative) (K12.3-)

    K92.89 Other specified diseases of the digestive system

K92.9 Disease of digestive system, **unspecified**

● K94 Complications of artificial openings of the digestive system
  ● K94.0 **Colostomy** complications

    K94.00 Colostomy complication, **unspecified**
    K94.01 Colostomy **hemorrhage**
    K94.02 Colostomy **infection**
        Use additional code to specify type of infection, such as:
        cellulitis of abdominal wall (L03.311)
        sepsis (A40.-, A41.-)
    K94.03 Colostomy **malfunction**
        Mechanical complication of colostomy
    K94.09 Other complications of colostomy

  ● K94.1 **Enterostomy** complications
    K94.10 Enterostomy complication, **unspecified**
    K94.11 Enterostomy **hemorrhage**
    K94.12 Enterostomy **infection**
        Use additional code to specify type of infection, such as:
        cellulitis of abdominal wall (L03.311)
        sepsis (A40.-, A41.-)
    K94.13 Enterostomy **malfunction**
        Mechanical complication of enterostomy
    K94.19 Other complications of enterostomy

  ● K94.2 **Gastrostomy** complications
    K94.20 Gastrostomy complication, **unspecified**
    K94.21 Gastrostomy **hemorrhage**
    K94.22 Gastrostomy **infection**
        Use additional code to specify type of infection, such as:
        cellulitis of abdominal wall (L03.311)
        sepsis (A40.-, A41.-)
    K94.23 Gastrostomy **malfunction**
        Mechanical complication of gastrostomy
    K94.29 Other complications of gastrostomy

  ● K94.3 **Esophagostomy** complications
    K94.30 Esophagostomy complications, **unspecified**
    K94.31 Esophagostomy **hemorrhage**
    K94.32 Esophagostomy **infection**
        Use additional code to identify the infection
    K94.33 Esophagostomy **malfunction**
        Mechanical complication of esophagostomy
    K94.39 Other complications of esophagostomy

● K95 **Complications of bariatric procedures**
  ● K95.0 Complications of **gastric band procedure**
    K95.01 **Infection** due to gastric band procedure
        Use additional code to specify type of infection or organism, such as:
        bacterial and viral infectious agents (B95.-, B96.-)
        cellulitis of abdominal wall (L03.311)
        sepsis (A40.-, A41.-)
    K95.09 Other complications of gastric band procedure
        Use additional code, if applicable, to further specify complication

  ● K95.8 Complications of **other bariatric procedure**
    Excludes1 complications of gastric band surgery (K95.0-)
    K95.81 **Infection** due to other bariatric procedure
        Use additional code to specify type of infection or organism, such as:
        bacterial and viral infectious agents (B95.-, B96.-)
        cellulitis of abdominal wall (L03.311)
        sepsis (A40.-, A41.-)
    K95.89 Other complications of other bariatric procedure
        Use additional code, if applicable, to further specify complication

▶ New   ⇒ Revised   ~~deleted~~ Deleted   Excludes 1   Excludes 2   Includes   Use additional   Code first   Code also   Key words

OGCR Official Guidelines   X Assign placeholder X   Use Additional Character(s)   Manifestation Code   Coding Clinic

CHAPTER 12

DISEASES OF THE SKIN AND SUBCUTANEOUS TISSUE (L00-L99)

OGCR Chapter-Specific Coding Guidelines

12. Chapter 12: Diseases of the Skin and Subcutaneous Tissue (L00-L99)

a. Pressure ulcer stage codes

1) **Pressure ulcer stages**
Codes from category L89, Pressure ulcer, identify the site of the pressure ulcer as well as the stage of the ulcer.

The ICD-10-CM classifies pressure ulcer stages based on severity, which is designated by stages 1-4, unspecified stage and unstageable.

Assign as many codes from category L89 as needed to identify all the pressure ulcers the patient has, if applicable.

See Section I.B.14 for pressure ulcer stage documentation by clinicians other than patient's provider

2) **Unstageable pressure ulcers**
Assignment of the code for unstageable pressure ulcer (L89.--0) should be based on the clinical documentation. These codes are used for pressure ulcers whose stage cannot be clinically determined (e.g., the ulcer is covered by eschar or has been treated with a skin or muscle graft) and pressure ulcers that are documented as deep tissue injury but not documented as due to trauma. This code should not be confused with the codes for unspecified stage (L89.--9). When there is no documentation regarding the stage of the pressure ulcer, assign the appropriate code for unspecified stage (L89.--9).

3) **Documented pressure ulcer stage**
Assignment of the pressure ulcer stage code should be guided by clinical documentation of the stage or documentation of the terms found in the Alphabetic Index. For clinical terms describing the stage that are not found in the Alphabetic Index, and there is no documentation of the stage, the provider should be queried.

4) **Patients admitted with pressure ulcers documented as healed**
No code is assigned if the documentation states that the pressure ulcer is completely healed.

5) **Patients admitted with pressure ulcers documented as healing**
Pressure ulcers described as healing should be assigned the appropriate pressure ulcer stage code based on the documentation in the medical record. If the documentation does not provide information about the stage of the healing pressure ulcer, assign the appropriate code for unspecified stage.

If the documentation is unclear as to whether the patient has a current (new) pressure ulcer or if the patient is being treated for a healing pressure ulcer, query the provider.

For ulcers that were present on admission but healed at the time of discharge, assign the code for the site and stage of the pressure ulcer at the time of admission.

6) **Patient admitted with pressure ulcer evolving into another stage during the admission**
If a patient is admitted to an inpatient hospital with a pressure ulcer at one stage and it progresses to a higher stage, two separate codes should be assigned: one code for the site and stage of the ulcer on admission and a second code for the same ulcer site and the highest stage reported during the stay.

b. Non-Pressure Chronic Ulcers

1) **Patients admitted with non-pressure ulcers documented as healed**
No code is assigned if the documentation states that the non-pressure ulcer is completely healed.

2) **Patients admitted with non-pressure ulcers documented as healing**
Non-pressure ulcers described as healing should be assigned the appropriate non-pressure ulcer code based on the documentation in the medical record. If the documentation does not provide information about the severity of the healing non-pressure ulcer, assign the appropriate code for unspecified severity.

If the documentation is unclear as to whether the patient has a current (new) non-pressure ulcer or if the patient is being treated for a healing non-pressure ulcer, query the provider.

For ulcers that were present on admission but healed at the time of discharge, assign the code for the site and severity of the non-pressure ulcer at the time of admission.

3) **Patient admitted with non-pressure ulcer that progresses to another severity level during the admission**
If a patient is admitted to an inpatient hospital with a non-pressure ulcer at one severity level and it progresses to a higher severity level, two separate codes should be assigned: one code for the site and severity level of the ulcer on admission and a second code for the same ulcer site and the highest severity level reported during the stay.

See Section I.B.14 for pressure ulcer stage documentation by clinicians other than patient's provider

Figure 12-1 Furuncle, also known as a boil, is a staphylococcal infection. The organism enters the body through a hair follicle and so furuncles usually appear in hairy areas of the body. A cluster of furuncles is known as a carbuncle and involves infection into the deep subcutaneous fascia. These usually appear on the back and neck. (**B** from Habif TP, Binnick AN, Meyerson LB: Clinical Dermatology: A Color Guide to Diagnosis and Therapy, S.l., Mosby Elsevier, 2010)

CHAPTER 12

DISEASES OF THE SKIN AND SUBCUTANEOUS TISSUE (L00-L99)

Excludes2 certain conditions originating in the perinatal period (P04-P96)
certain infectious and parasitic diseases (A00-B99)
complications of pregnancy, childbirth and the puerperium (O00-O9A)
congenital malformations, deformations, and chromosomal abnormalities (Q00-Q99)
endocrine, nutritional and metabolic diseases (E00-E88)
lipomelanotic reticulosis (I89.8)
neoplasms (C00-D49)
symptoms, signs and abnormal clinical and laboratory findings, not elsewhere classified (R00-R94)
systemic connective tissue disorders (M30-M36)
viral warts (B07.-)

This chapter contains the following blocks:

L00-L08	Infections of the skin and subcutaneous tissue
L10-L14	Bullous disorders
L20-L30	Dermatitis and eczema
L40-L45	Papulosquamous disorders
L49-L54	Urticaria and erythema
L55-L59	Radiation-related disorders of the skin and subcutaneous tissue
L60-L75	Disorders of skin appendages
L76	Intraoperative and postprocedural complications of skin and subcutaneous tissue
L80-L99	Other disorders of the skin and subcutaneous tissue

INFECTIONS OF THE SKIN AND SUBCUTANEOUS TISSUE (L00-L08)

Use additional code (B95-B97) to identify infectious agent.

> **Excludes2**   hordeolum (H00.0)
> infective dermatitis (L30.3)
> local infections of skin classified in Chapter 1
> lupus panniculitis (L93.2)
> panniculitis NOS (M79.3)
> panniculitis of neck and back (M54.0-)
> Perlèche NOS (K13.0)
> Perlèche due to candidiasis (B37.0)
> Perlèche due to riboflavin deficiency (E53.0)
> pyogenic granuloma (L98.0)
> relapsing panniculitis [Weber-Christian] (M35.6)
> viral warts (B07.-)
> zoster (B02.-)

L00   **Staphylococcal scalded skin syndrome**
     Ritter's disease

     Use additional code to identify percentage of skin exfoliation (L49.-)

> **Excludes1**   bullous impetigo (L01.03)
> pemphigus neonatorum (L01.03)
> toxic epidermal necrolysis [Lyell] (L51.2)

● L01   **Impetigo**
     Contagious skin infection caused by a streptococcus or staphylococcus aureus, common skin infections among children

> **Excludes1**   impetigo herpetiformis (L40.1)

   ● L01.0   **Impetigo**
       Impetigo contagiosa
       Impetigo vulgaris

     L01.00   **Impetigo, unspecified**
         Impetigo NOS

     L01.01   **Non-bullous impetigo**

     L01.02   **Bockhart's impetigo**
         Impetigo follicularis
         Perifolliculitis NOS
         Superficial pustular perifolliculitis

     L01.03   **Bullous impetigo**
         Impetigo neonatorum
         Pemphigus neonatorum
           Neonate = newborn

     L01.09   **Other impetigo**
         Ulcerative impetigo

   L01.1   **Impetiginization of other dermatoses**

● L02   **Cutaneous abscess, furuncle and carbuncle**
     Use additional code to identify organism (B95-B96)

> **Excludes2**   abscess of anus and rectal regions (K61.-)
> abscess of female genital organs (external) (N76.4)
> abscess of male genital organs (external) (N48.2, N49.-)

   ● L02.0   **Cutaneous abscess, furuncle and carbuncle of face**

> **Excludes2**   abscess of ear, external (H60.0)
> abscess of eyelid (H00.0)
> abscess of head [any part, except face] (L02.8)
> abscess of lacrimal gland (H04.0)
> abscess of lacrimal passages (H04.3)
> abscess of mouth (K12.2)
> abscess of nose (J34.0)
> abscess of orbit (H05.0)
> submandibular abscess (K12.2)

     L02.01   **Cutaneous abscess of face**

     L02.02   **Furuncle of face**
         Boil of face
         Folliculitis of face

     L02.03   **Carbuncle of face**

   ● L02.1   **Cutaneous abscess, furuncle and carbuncle of neck**

     L02.11   **Cutaneous abscess of neck**

     L02.12   **Furuncle of neck**
         Boil of neck
         Folliculitis of neck

     L02.13   **Carbuncle of neck**

   ● L02.2   **Cutaneous abscess, furuncle and carbuncle of trunk**

> **Excludes1**   non-newborn omphalitis (L08.82)
> omphalitis of newborn (P38.-)

> **Excludes2**   abscess of breast (N61.1)
> abscess of buttocks (L02.3)
> abscess of female external genital organs (N76.4)
> abscess of male external genital organs (N48.2, N49.-)
> abscess of hip (L02.4)

   ● L02.21   **Cutaneous abscess of trunk**

     L02.211   **Cutaneous abscess of abdominal wall**

     L02.212   **Cutaneous abscess of back [any part, except buttock]**

     L02.213   **Cutaneous abscess of chest wall**

     L02.214   **Cutaneous abscess of groin**

     L02.215   **Cutaneous abscess of perineum**

     L02.216   **Cutaneous abscess of umbilicus**

     L02.219   **Cutaneous abscess of trunk, unspecified**

   ● L02.22   **Furuncle of trunk**
       Boil of trunk
       Folliculitis of trunk

     L02.221   **Furuncle of abdominal wall**

     L02.222   **Furuncle of back [any part, except buttock]**

     L02.223   **Furuncle of chest wall**

     L02.224   **Furuncle of groin**

     L02.225   **Furuncle of perineum**

     L02.226   **Furuncle of umbilicus**

     L02.229   **Furuncle of trunk, unspecified**

   ● L02.23   **Carbuncle of trunk**

     L02.231   **Carbuncle of abdominal wall**

     L02.232   **Carbuncle of back [any part, except buttock]**

     L02.233   **Carbuncle of chest wall**

     L02.234   **Carbuncle of groin**

     L02.235   **Carbuncle of perineum**

     L02.236   **Carbuncle of umbilicus**

     L02.239   **Carbuncle of trunk, unspecified**

   ● L02.3   **Cutaneous abscess, furuncle and carbuncle of buttock**

> **Excludes1**   pilonidal cyst with abscess (L05.01)

     L02.31   **Cutaneous abscess of buttock**
         Cutaneous abscess of gluteal region

     L02.32   **Furuncle of buttock**
         Boil of buttock
         Folliculitis of buttock
         Furuncle of gluteal region

     L02.33   **Carbuncle of buttock**
         Carbuncle of gluteal region

Figure 12-2   Impetigo. A thick, honey-yellow adherent crust covers the entire eroded surface. (From James WD, Elston DM, Berger TG, Andrews GC: Andrews' Diseases of the Skin: Clinical Dermatology, London, Saunders/Elsevier, 2011)

▶ New   ⇒ Revised   ~~deleted~~ Deleted   Excludes 1   Excludes 2   Includes   Use additional   Code first   Code also   Key words

OGCR Official Guidelines   X Assign placeholder X   ● Use Additional Character(s)   ▌ Manifestation Code   **Coding Clinic**

● **L02.4** **Cutaneous abscess, furuncle and carbuncle of limb**
 Excludes2   Cutaneous abscess, furuncle and
                carbuncle of groin (L02.214, L02.224,
                L02.234)
                Cutaneous abscess, furuncle and
                carbuncle of hand (L02.5-)
                Cutaneous abscess, furuncle and
                carbuncle of foot (L02.6-)
 ● **L02.41** **Cutaneous abscess of limb**
    L02.411   Cutaneous abscess of right axilla
    L02.412   Cutaneous abscess of left axilla
    L02.413   Cutaneous abscess of right upper
                 limb
    L02.414   Cutaneous abscess of left upper limb
    L02.415   Cutaneous abscess of right lower
                 limb
    L02.416   Cutaneous abscess of left lower limb
    L02.419   Cutaneous abscess of limb,
                 unspecified
 ● **L02.42** **Furuncle of limb**
                 Boil of limb
                 Folliculitis of limb
    L02.421   Furuncle of right axilla
    L02.422   Furuncle of left axilla
    L02.423   Furuncle of right upper limb
    L02.424   Furuncle of left upper limb
    L02.425   Furuncle of right lower limb
    L02.426   Furuncle of left lower limb
    L02.429   Furuncle of limb, unspecified
 ● **L02.43** **Carbuncle of limb**
    L02.431   Carbuncle of right axilla
    L02.432   Carbuncle of left axilla
    L02.433   Carbuncle of right upper limb
    L02.434   Carbuncle of left upper limb
    L02.435   Carbuncle of right lower limb
    L02.436   Carbuncle of left lower limb
    L02.439   Carbuncle of limb, unspecified
● **L02.5** **Cutaneous abscess, furuncle and carbuncle of hand**
 ● **L02.51** **Cutaneous abscess of hand**
    L02.511   Cutaneous abscess of right hand
    L02.512   Cutaneous abscess of left hand
    L02.519   Cutaneous abscess of unspecified
                 hand
 ● **L02.52** **Furuncle hand**
                 Boil of hand
                 Folliculitis of hand
    L02.521   Furuncle right hand
    L02.522   Furuncle left hand
    L02.529   Furuncle unspecified hand
 ● **L02.53** **Carbuncle of hand**
    L02.531   Carbuncle of right hand
    L02.532   Carbuncle of left hand
    L02.539   Carbuncle of unspecified hand
● **L02.6** **Cutaneous abscess, furuncle and carbuncle of foot**
 ● **L02.61** **Cutaneous abscess of foot**
    L02.611   Cutaneous abscess of right foot
    L02.612   Cutaneous abscess of left foot
    L02.619   Cutaneous abscess of unspecified foot
 ● **L02.62** **Furuncle of foot**
                 Boil of foot
                 Folliculitis of foot
    L02.621   Furuncle of right foot
    L02.622   Furuncle of left foot
    L02.629   Furuncle of unspecified foot

 ● **L02.63** **Carbuncle of foot**
    L02.631   Carbuncle of right foot
    L02.632   Carbuncle of left foot
    L02.639   Carbuncle of unspecified foot
● **L02.8** **Cutaneous abscess, furuncle and carbuncle of other sites**
 ● **L02.81** **Cutaneous abscess of other sites**
    L02.811   Cutaneous abscess of head [any part,
                 except face]
    L02.818   Cutaneous abscess of other sites
 ● **L02.82** **Furuncle of other sites**
                 Boil of other sites
                 Folliculitis of other sites
    L02.821   Furuncle of head [any part, except face]
    L02.828   Furuncle of other sites
 ● **L02.83** **Carbuncle of other sites**
    L02.831   Carbuncle of head [any part, except
                 face]
    L02.838   Carbuncle of other sites
● **L02.9** **Cutaneous abscess, furuncle and carbuncle, unspecified**
    L02.91   **Cutaneous abscess, unspecified**
    L02.92   **Furuncle, unspecified**
                 Boil NOS
                 Furunculosis NOS
    L02.93   **Carbuncle, unspecified**
● **L03** **Cellulitis and acute lymphangitis**
 Excludes2   cellulitis of anal and rectal region (K61.-)
                cellulitis of external auditory canal (H60.1)
                cellulitis of eyelid (H00.0)
                cellulitis of female external genital organs (N76.4)
                cellulitis of lacrimal apparatus (H04.3)
                cellulitis of male external genital organs (N48.2,
                N49.-)
                cellulitis of mouth (K12.2)
                cellulitis of nose (J34.0)
                eosinophilic cellulitis [Wells] (L98.3)
                febrile neutrophilic dermatosis [Sweet] (L98.2)
                lymphangitis (chronic) (subacute) (I89.1)
● **L03.0** **Cellulitis and acute lymphangitis of finger and toe**
                 Infection of nail
                 Onychia
                 Paronychia
                 Perionychia
 ● **L03.01** **Cellulitis of finger**
                 Felon
                 Whitlow
        Excludes1   herpetic whitlow (B00.89)
    L03.011   Cellulitis of right finger
    L03.012   Cellulitis of left finger
    L03.019   Cellulitis of unspecified finger
 ● **L03.02** **Acute lymphangitis of finger**
                 Hangnail with lymphangitis of finger
    L03.021   Acute lymphangitis of right finger
    L03.022   Acute lymphangitis of left finger
    L03.029   Acute lymphangitis of unspecified
                 finger
 ● **L03.03** **Cellulitis of toe**
    L03.031   Cellulitis of right toe
    L03.032   Cellulitis of left toe
    L03.039   Cellulitis of unspecified toe
 ● **L03.04** **Acute lymphangitis of toe**
                 Hangnail with lymphangitis of toe
    L03.041   Acute lymphangitis of right toe
    L03.042   Acute lymphangitis of left toe
    L03.049   Acute lymphangitis of unspecified toe

Item 12-1 **Onychia** is an inflammation of the tissue surrounding the nail with pus accumulation and loss of the nail, resulting from microscopic pathogens entering through small wounds. **Paronychia** is a nail disease also known as felon or whitlow and is a bacterial or fungal infection.

CHAPTER 12 (L00-L99)

CHAPTER 12 (L00-L99)

Item 12-2 **Cellulitis** is an acute spreading bacterial infection below the surface of the skin characterized by redness (erythema), warmth, swelling, pain, fever, chills, and enlarged lymph nodes ("swollen glands").

- **L03.1** Cellulitis and acute lymphangitis of **other parts of limb**
  - **L03.11** Cellulitis of other parts of limb

    Excludes2 cellulitis of fingers (L03.01-)
    cellulitis of toes (L03.03-)
    groin (L03.314)

    L03.111 Cellulitis of **right axilla**
    L03.112 Cellulitis of **left axilla**
    L03.113 Cellulitis of **right upper limb**
    L03.114 Cellulitis of **left upper limb**
    L03.115 Cellulitis of **right lower limb**
    L03.116 Cellulitis of **left lower limb**
    L03.119 Cellulitis of **unspecified** part of limb
  - **L03.12** Acute lymphangitis of other parts of limb

    Excludes2 acute lymphangitis of fingers (L03.2-)
    acute lymphangitis of toes (L03.04-)
    acute lymphangitis of groin (L03.324)

    L03.121 Acute lymphangitis of **right axilla**
    L03.122 Acute lymphangitis of **left axilla**
    L03.123 Acute lymphangitis of **right upper limb**
    L03.124 Acute lymphangitis of **left upper limb**
    L03.125 Acute lymphangitis of **right lower limb**
    L03.126 Acute lymphangitis of **left lower limb**
    L03.129 Acute lymphangitis of **unspecified** part of limb
- **L03.2** Cellulitis and acute lymphangitis of **face and neck**
  - **L03.21** Cellulitis and acute lymphangitis of **face**
    L03.211 Cellulitis of face

    Excludes2 abscess of orbit (H05.01-)
    cellulitis of ear (H60.1-)
    cellulitis of eyelid (H00.0-)
    cellulitis of head (L03.81)
    cellulitis of lacrimal apparatus (H04.3)
    cellulitis of lip (K13.0)
    cellulitis of mouth (K12.2)
    cellulitis of nose (internal) (J34.0)
    cellulitis of orbit (H05.01-)
    cellulitis of scalp (L03.81)

    L03.212 Acute lymphangitis of face
    L03.213 **Periorbital cellulitis**
    Preseptal cellulitis
    Coding Clinic: 2016, Q4, P36
  - **L03.22** Cellulitis and acute lymphangitis of **neck**
    L03.221 Cellulitis of neck
    L03.222 Acute lymphangitis of neck

- **L03.3** Cellulitis and acute lymphangitis of **trunk**
  - **L03.31** **Cellulitis of trunk**

    Excludes2 cellulitis of anal and rectal regions (K61.-)
    cellulitis of breast NOS (N61.0)
    cellulitis of female external genital organs (N76.4)
    cellulitis of male external genital organs (N48.2, N49.-)
    omphalitis of newborn (P38.-)
    puerperal cellulitis of breast (O91.2)

    L03.311 Cellulitis of **abdominal wall**

    Excludes2 cellulitis of umbilicus (L03.316)
    cellulitis of groin (L03.314)

    L03.312 Cellulitis of **back** [any part except buttock]
    L03.313 Cellulitis of **chest wall**
    L03.314 Cellulitis of **groin**
    L03.315 Cellulitis of **perineum**
    L03.316 Cellulitis of **umbilicus**
    L03.317 Cellulitis of **buttock**
    L03.319 Cellulitis of trunk, **unspecified**
  - **L03.32** Acute lymphangitis of trunk
    L03.321 Acute lymphangitis of **abdominal wall**
    L03.322 Acute lymphangitis of **back** [any part except buttock]
    L03.323 Acute lymphangitis of **chest wall**
    L03.324 Acute lymphangitis of **groin**
    L03.325 Acute lymphangitis of **perineum**
    L03.326 Acute lymphangitis of **umbilicus**
    L03.327 Acute lymphangitis of **buttock**
    L03.329 Acute lymphangitis of trunk, **unspecified**
- **L03.8** Cellulitis and acute lymphangitis of **other sites**
  - **L03.81** **Cellulitis of other sites**
    L03.811 Cellulitis of **head** [any part, except face]
    Cellulitis of scalp

    Excludes2 cellulitis of face (L03.211)

    L03.818 Cellulitis of **other sites**
  - **L03.89** Acute lymphangitis of other sites
    L03.891 Acute lymphangitis of **head** [any part, except face]
    L03.898 Acute lymphangitis of **other sites**
- **L03.9** Cellulitis and acute lymphangitis, **unspecified**
  - **L03.90** **Cellulitis, unspecified**
  - **L03.91** **Acute lymphangitis, unspecified**

    Excludes1 lymphangitis NOS (I89.1)

▶ New   ⟳ Revised   ~~deleted~~ Deleted   Excludes 1   Excludes 2   Includes   Use additional   Code first   Code also   Key words
OGCR Official Guidelines   X Assign placeholder X   ● Use Additional Character(s)   ▷ Manifestation Code   Coding Clinic

Item 12–3 **Abscess** is a localized collection of pus in tissues or organs and is a sign of infection resulting in swelling and inflammation.

Item 12–4 **Pilonidal cyst,** also called a coccygeal cyst, is the result of a disorder called pilonidal disease. The cyst usually contains hair and pus.

● **L04** **Acute lymphadenitis**
Short-term inflammation of lymph nodes which can be regionalized to involve a given area of the lymph system or systemic involving much of the body

Includes abscess (acute) of lymph nodes, except mesenteric
acute lymphadenitis, except mesenteric

Excludes1 chronic or subacute lymphadenitis, except mesenteric (I88.1)
enlarged lymph nodes (R59.-)
human immunodeficiency virus [HIV] disease resulting in generalized lymphadenopathy (B20)
lymphadenitis NOS (I88.9)
nonspecific mesenteric lymphadenitis (I88.0)

L04.0 **Acute lymphadenitis of face, head and neck**
L04.1 **Acute lymphadenitis of trunk**
L04.2 **Acute lymphadenitis of upper limb**
Acute lymphadenitis of axilla
Acute lymphadenitis of shoulder
L04.3 **Acute lymphadenitis of lower limb**
Acute lymphadenitis of hip
Excludes2 acute lymphadenitis of groin (L04.1)
L04.8 **Acute lymphadenitis of other sites**
L04.9 **Acute lymphadenitis, unspecified**

● **L05** **Pilonidal cyst and sinus**
● **L05.0** **Pilonidal cyst and sinus with abscess**
L05.01 **Pilonidal cyst with abscess**
Pilonidal abscess
Pilonidal dimple with abscess
Postanal dimple with abscess
Excludes2 congenital sacral dimple (Q82.6)
parasacral dimple (Q82.6)
L05.02 **Pilonidal sinus with abscess**
Coccygeal fistula with abscess
Coccygeal sinus with abscess
Pilonidal fistula with abscess
● **L05.9** **Pilonidal cyst and sinus without abscess**
L05.91 **Pilonidal cyst without abscess**
Pilonidal dimple
Postanal dimple
Pilonidal cyst NOS
Excludes2 congenital sacral dimple (Q82.6)
parasacral dimple (Q82.6)
L05.92 **Pilonidal sinus without abscess**
Coccygeal fistula
Coccygeal sinus without abscess
Pilonidal fistula

● **L08** **Other local infections of skin and subcutaneous tissue**
L08.0 **Pyoderma**
Dermatitis gangrenosa
Purulent dermatitis
Septic dermatitis
Suppurative dermatitis
Excludes1 pyoderma gangrenosum (L88)
pyoderma vegetans (L08.81)
L08.1 **Erythrasma**

● **L08.8** **Other specified local infections of the skin and subcutaneous tissue**
L08.81 **Pyoderma vegetans**
Excludes1 pyoderma gangrenosum (L88)
pyoderma NOS (L08.0)
L08.82 **Omphalitis not of newborn**
Excludes1 omphalitis of newborn (P38.-)
L08.89 **Other specified local infections of the skin and subcutaneous tissue**
L08.9 **Local infection of the skin and subcutaneous tissue, unspecified**

BULLOUS DISORDERS (L10-L14)

Excludes1 benign familial pemphigus [Hailey-Hailey] (Q82.8)
staphylococcal scalded skin syndrome (L00)
toxic epidermal necrolysis [Lyell] (L51.2)

● **L10** **Pemphigus**
Excludes1 pemphigus neonatorum (L01.03)
L10.0 **Pemphigus vulgaris**
L10.1 **Pemphigus vegetans**
L10.2 **Pemphigus foliaceous**
L10.3 **Brazilian pemphigus [fogo selvagem]**
L10.4 **Pemphigus erythematosus**
Senear-Usher syndrome
L10.5 **Drug-induced pemphigus**
Use additional code for adverse effect, if applicable, to identify drug (T36-T50 with fifth or sixth character 5)
● **L10.8** **Other pemphigus**
L10.81 **Paraneoplastic pemphigus**
L10.89 **Other pemphigus**
L10.9 **Pemphigus, unspecified**

● **L11** **Other acantholytic disorders**
L11.0 **Acquired keratosis follicularis**
Excludes1 keratosis follicularis (congenital) [Darier-White] (Q82.8)
L11.1 **Transient acantholytic dermatosis [Grover]**
L11.8 **Other specified acantholytic disorders**
L11.9 **Acantholytic disorder, unspecified**

● **L12** **Pemphigoid**
Excludes1 herpes gestationis (O26.4-)
impetigo herpetiformis (L40.1)
L12.0 **Bullous pemphigoid**
L12.1 **Cicatricial pemphigoid**
Benign mucous membrane pemphigoid
L12.2 **Chronic bullous disease of childhood** P
Juvenile dermatitis herpetiformis
● **L12.3** **Acquired epidermolysis bullosa**
Excludes1 epidermolysis bullosa (congenital) (Q81.-)
L12.30 **Acquired epidermolysis bullosa, unspecified**
L12.31 **Epidermolysis bullosa due to drug**
Use additional code for adverse effect, if applicable, to identify drug (T36-T50 with fifth or sixth character 5)
L12.35 **Other acquired epidermolysis bullosa**
L12.8 **Other pemphigoid**
L12.9 **Pemphigoid, unspecified**

CHAPTER 12 (L00-L99)

Item 12–5 Dermatitis herpetiformis, also known as Duhring's disease, is a systemic disease characterized by small blisters (3 to 5 mm) and occasionally large bullae (> 5 mm).

Figure 12-3 Dermatitis herpetiformis. (From Terhorst D: BASICS Dermatologie, München, Elsevier, Urban & Fischer, 2011)

Item 12–7 Atopic dermatitis, also known as atopic eczema, infantile eczema, disseminated neuro dermatitis, flexural eczema, and *prurigo diathesique* (Besnier), is characterized by intense itching and is often hereditary.

Figure 12-5 Atopic dermatitis. (From Chabner D-E: The Language of Medicine, St. Louis, MO, Saunders/Elsevier, 2007)

● **L13 Other bullous disorders**

L13.0 Dermatitis herpetiformis
Duhring's disease
Hydroa herpetiformis
Excludes1 juvenile dermatitis herpetiformis (L12.2)
senile dermatitis herpetiformis (L12.0)

L13.1 Subcorneal pustular dermatitis
Sneddon-Wilkinson disease

L13.8 Other specified bullous disorders

L13.9 Bullous disorder, unspecified

▷ **L14 Bullous disorders in diseases classified elsewhere**
Code first underlying disease

DERMATITIS AND ECZEMA (L20-L30)

Note: In this block the terms dermatitis and eczema are used synonymously and interchangeably.

Excludes2 chronic (childhood) granulomatous disease (D71)
dermatitis gangrenosa (L08.0)
dermatitis herpetiformis (L13.0)
dry skin dermatitis (L85.3)
factitial dermatitis (L98.1)
perioral dermatitis (L71.0)
radiation-related disorders of the skin and subcutaneous tissue (L55-L59)
stasis dermatitis (I87.2)

● **L20 Atopic dermatitis**

L20.0 Besnier's prurigo

● **L20.8 Other atopic dermatitis**
Excludes2 circumscribed neurodermatitis (L28.0)

L20.81 Atopic neurodermatitis
Diffuse neurodermatitis

L20.82 Flexural eczema

L20.83 Infantile (acute) (chronic) eczema P

L20.84 Intrinsic (allergic) eczema

L20.89 Other atopic dermatitis

L20.9 Atopic dermatitis, unspecified

● **L21 Seborrheic dermatitis**
Excludes2 infective dermatitis (L30.3)
seborrheic keratosis (L82.-)

L21.0 Seborrhea capitis
Cradle cap
Coding Clinic: 2018, Q1, P6

L21.1 Seborrheic infantile dermatitis P

L21.8 Other seborrheic dermatitis

L21.9 Seborrheic dermatitis, unspecified
Seborrhea NOS

L22 Diaper dermatitis
Diaper erythema
Diaper rash
Psoriasiform diaper rash

● **L23 Allergic contact dermatitis**
Excludes1 allergy NOS (T78.40)
contact dermatitis NOS (L25.9)
dermatitis NOS (L30.9)

Excludes2 dermatitis due to substances taken internally (L27.-)
dermatitis of eyelid (H01.1-)
diaper dermatitis (L22)
eczema of external ear (H60.5-)
irritant contact dermatitis (L24.-)
perioral dermatitis (L71.0)
radiation-related disorders of the skin and subcutaneous tissue (L55-L59)

L23.0 Allergic contact dermatitis due to metals
Allergic contact dermatitis due to chromium
Allergic contact dermatitis due to nickel

L23.1 Allergic contact dermatitis due to adhesives

L23.2 Allergic contact dermatitis due to cosmetics

L23.3 Allergic contact dermatitis due to drugs in contact with skin
Use additional code for adverse effect, if applicable, to identify drug (T36-T50 with fifth or sixth character 5)
Excludes2 dermatitis due to ingested drugs and medicaments (L27.0-L27.1)

L23.4 Allergic contact dermatitis due to dyes

L23.5 Allergic contact dermatitis due to other chemical products
Allergic contact dermatitis due to cement
Allergic contact dermatitis due to insecticide
Allergic contact dermatitis due to plastic
Allergic contact dermatitis due to rubber

L23.6 Allergic contact dermatitis due to food in contact with the skin
Excludes2 dermatitis due to ingested food (L27.2)

L23.7 Allergic contact dermatitis due to plants, except food
Excludes2 allergy NOS due to pollen (J30.1)

● **L23.8 Allergic contact dermatitis due to other agents**

L23.81 Allergic contact dermatitis due to animal (cat) (dog) dander
Allergic contact dermatitis due to animal (cat) (dog) hair

L23.89 Allergic contact dermatitis due to other agents

L23.9 Allergic contact dermatitis, unspecified cause
Allergic contact eczema NOS

Item 12–6 Seborrheic dermatitis is characterized by greasy, scaly, red patches and is associated with oily skin and scalp.

Figure 12-4 Seborrheic dermatitis. (Getty Image)

▶ New ⇒ Revised ~~deleted~~ Deleted Excludes 1 Excludes 2 Includes Use additional Code first Code also Key words
OGCR Official Guidelines X Assign placeholder X ● Use Additional Character(s) ▷ Manifestation Code **Coding Clinic**

● **L24**   **Irritant contact dermatitis**

     Excludes1   allergy NOS (T78.40)
                   contact dermatitis NOS (L25.9)
                   dermatitis NOS (L30.9)

     Excludes2   allergic contact dermatitis (L23.-)
                   dermatitis due to substances taken internally
                       (L27.-)
                   dermatitis of eyelid (H01.1-)
                   diaper dermatitis (L22)
                   eczema of external ear (H60.5-)
                   perioral dermatitis (L71.0)
                   radiation-related disorders of the skin and
                       subcutaneous tissue (L55-L59)

   L24.0   **Irritant contact dermatitis due to detergents**

   L24.1   **Irritant contact dermatitis due to oils and greases**

   L24.2   **Irritant contact dermatitis due to solvents**
          Irritant contact dermatitis due to chlorocompound
          Irritant contact dermatitis due to cyclohexane
          Irritant contact dermatitis due to ester
          Irritant contact dermatitis due to glycol
          Irritant contact dermatitis due to hydrocarbon
          Irritant contact dermatitis due to ketone

   L24.3   **Irritant contact dermatitis due to cosmetics**

   L24.4   **Irritant contact dermatitis due to drugs in contact with skin**
          Use additional code for adverse effect, if applicable, to identify drug (T36-T50 with fifth or sixth character 5)

   L24.5   **Irritant contact dermatitis due to other chemical products**
          Irritant contact dermatitis due to cement
          Irritant contact dermatitis due to insecticide
          Irritant contact dermatitis due to plastic
          Irritant contact dermatitis due to rubber

   L24.6   **Irritant contact dermatitis due to food in contact with skin**

     Excludes2   dermatitis due to ingested food (L27.2)

   L24.7   **Irritant contact dermatitis due to plants, except food**

     Excludes2   allergy NOS to pollen (J30.1)

●   **L24.8**   **Irritant contact dermatitis due to other agents**

     L24.81   **Irritant contact dermatitis due to metals**
             Irritant contact dermatitis due to chromium
             Irritant contact dermatitis due to nickel

     L24.89   **Irritant contact dermatitis due to other agents**
             Irritant contact dermatitis due to dyes

   L24.9   **Irritant contact dermatitis, unspecified cause**
          Irritant contact eczema NOS

● **L25**   **Unspecified contact dermatitis**

     Excludes1   allergic contact dermatitis (L23.-)
                   allergy NOS (T78.40)
                   dermatitis NOS (L30.9)
                   irritant contact dermatitis (L24.-)

     Excludes2   dermatitis due to ingested substances (L27.-)
                   dermatitis of eyelid (H01.1-)
                   eczema of external ear (H60.5-)
                   perioral dermatitis (L71.0)
                   radiation-related disorders of the skin and
                       subcutaneous tissue (L55-L59)

   L25.0   **Unspecified contact dermatitis due to cosmetics**

   L25.1   **Unspecified contact dermatitis due to drugs in contact with skin**
          Use additional code for adverse effect, if applicable, to identify drug (T36-T50 with fifth or sixth character 5)

     Excludes2   dermatitis due to ingested drugs and medicaments (L27.0-L27.1)

   L25.2   **Unspecified contact dermatitis due to dyes**

   L25.3   **Unspecified contact dermatitis due to other chemical products**
          Unspecified contact dermatitis due to cement
          Unspecified contact dermatitis due to insecticide

   L25.4   **Unspecified contact dermatitis due to food in contact with skin**

     Excludes2   dermatitis due to ingested food (L27.2)

   L25.5   **Unspecified contact dermatitis due to plants, except food**

     Excludes1   nettle rash (L50.9)

     Excludes2   allergy NOS due to pollen (J30.1)

   L25.8   **Unspecified contact dermatitis due to other agents**

   L25.9   **Unspecified contact dermatitis, unspecified cause**
          Contact dermatitis (occupational) NOS
          Contact eczema (occupational) NOS

  L26   **Exfoliative dermatitis**
          Hebra's pityriasis

     Excludes1   Ritter's disease (L00)

● **L27**   **Dermatitis due to substances taken internally**

     Excludes1   allergy NOS (T78.40)

     Excludes2   adverse food reaction, except dermatitis
                       (T78.0-T78.1)
                   contact dermatitis (L23-L25)
                   drug photoallergic response (L56.1)
                   drug phototoxic response (L56.0)
                   urticaria (L50.-)

   L27.0   **Generalized skin eruption due to drugs and medicaments taken internally**
          Use additional code for adverse effect, if applicable, to identify drug (T36-T50 with fifth or sixth character 5)

   L27.1   **Localized skin eruption due to drugs and medicaments taken internally**
          Use additional code for adverse effect, if applicable, to identify drug (T36-T50 with fifth or sixth character 5)

   L27.2   **Dermatitis due to ingested food**

     Excludes2   dermatitis due to food in contact with skin (L23.6, L24.6, L25.4)

   L27.8   **Dermatitis due to other substances taken internally**

   L27.9   **Dermatitis due to unspecified substance taken internally**

● **L28**   **Lichen simplex chronicus and prurigo**

   L28.0   **Lichen simplex chronicus**
          Circumscribed neurodermatitis
          Lichen NOS

   L28.1   **Prurigo nodularis**

   L28.2   **Other prurigo**
          Prurigo NOS   Prurigo mitis
          Prurigo Hebra   Urticaria papulosa

● **L29**   **Pruritus**

     Excludes1   neurotic excoriation (L98.1)
                   psychogenic pruritus (F45.8)

   L29.0   **Pruritus ani**

   L29.1   **Pruritus scroti** ♂

   L29.2   **Pruritus vulvae** ♀

   L29.3   **Anogenital pruritus, unspecified**

   L29.8   **Other pruritus**

   L29.9   **Pruritus, unspecified**
          Itch NOS

CHAPTER 12 (L00-L99)

● **L30** **Other and unspecified dermatitis**

    Excludes2 contact dermatitis (L23-L25)
                 dry skin dermatitis (L85.3)
                 small plaque parapsoriasis (L41.3)
                 stasis dermatitis (I87.2)

    L30.0 **Nummular dermatitis**

    L30.1 **Dyshidrosis [pompholyx]**

    L30.2 **Cutaneous autosensitization**
          Candidid [levurid]   Eczematid
          Dermatophytid

    L30.3 **Infective dermatitis**
          Infectious eczematoid dermatitis

    L30.4 **Erythema intertrigo**

    L30.5 **Pityriasis alba**
          Coding Clinic: 2018, Q1, P6

    L30.8 **Other specified dermatitis**

    L30.9 **Dermatitis, unspecified**
          Eczema NOS

PAPULOSQUAMOUS DISORDERS (L40-L45)

● **L40** **Psoriasis**

    L40.0 **Psoriasis vulgaris**
          Nummular psoriasis   Plaque psoriasis

    L40.1 **Generalized pustular psoriasis**
          Impetigo herpetiformis
          Von Zumbusch's disease

    L40.2 **Acrodermatitis continua**

    L40.3 **Pustulosis palmaris et plantaris**

    L40.4 **Guttate psoriasis**

  ● **L40.5** **Arthropathic psoriasis**

        L40.50 **Arthropathic psoriasis, unspecified**

        L40.51 **Distal interphalangeal psoriatic arthropathy**

        L40.52 **Psoriatic arthritis mutilans**

        L40.53 **Psoriatic spondylitis**

        L40.54 **Psoriatic juvenile arthropathy**

        L40.59 **Other psoriatic arthropathy**

    L40.8 **Other psoriasis**
          Flexural psoriasis

    L40.9 **Psoriasis, unspecified**

● **L41** **Parapsoriasis**

    Excludes1 poikiloderma vasculare atrophicans (L94.5)

    L41.0 **Pityriasis lichenoides et varioliformis acuta**
          Mucha-Habermann disease

    L41.1 **Pityriasis lichenoides chronica**

    L41.3 **Small plaque parapsoriasis**

    L41.4 **Large plaque parapsoriasis**

    L41.5 **Retiform parapsoriasis**

    L41.8 **Other parapsoriasis**

    L41.9 **Parapsoriasis, unspecified**

  L42 **Pityriasis rosea**

● **L43** **Lichen planus**

    Excludes1 lichen planopilaris (L66.1)

    L43.0 **Hypertrophic lichen planus**

    L43.1 **Bullous lichen planus**

    L43.2 **Lichenoid drug reaction**
          Use additional code for adverse effect, if applicable, to
            identify drug (T36-T50 with fifth or sixth character 5)

    L43.3 **Subacute (active) lichen planus**
          Lichen planus tropicus

    L43.8 **Other lichen planus**

    L43.9 **Lichen planus, unspecified**

Item 12-8 Psoriasis is a chronic, recurrent inflammatory skin disease characterized by small patches covered with thick silvery scales. **Parapsoriasis** is a treatment-resistant erythroderma. **Pityriasis rosea** is characterized by a herald patch that is a single large lesion and that usually appears on the trunk and is followed by scattered, smaller lesions.

● **L44** **Other papulosquamous disorders**

    L44.0 **Pityriasis rubra pilaris**

    L44.1 **Lichen nitidus**

    L44.2 **Lichen striatus**

    L44.3 **Lichen ruber moniliformis**

    L44.4 **Infantile papular acrodermatitis [Gianotti-Crosti]** P

    L44.8 **Other specified papulosquamous disorders**

    L44.9 **Papulosquamous disorder, unspecified**

▶ **L45** *Papulosquamous disorders in diseases classified elsewhere*
        Code first underlying disease

URTICARIA AND ERYTHEMA (L49-L54)

    Excludes1 Lyme disease (A69.2-)
                 rosacea (L71.-)

● **L49** **Exfoliation due to erythematous conditions according to extent of body surface involved**

    Code first erythematous condition causing exfoliation, such as:
        Ritter's disease (L00)
        (Staphylococcal) scalded skin syndrome (L00)
        Stevens-Johnson syndrome (L51.1)
        Stevens-Johnson syndrome-toxic epidermal necrolysis overlap syndrome (L51.3)
        Toxic epidermal necrolysis (L51.2)

    L49.0 **Exfoliation due to erythematous condition involving less than 10 percent of body surface**
          Exfoliation due to erythematous condition NOS

    L49.1 **Exfoliation due to erythematous condition involving 10-19 percent of body surface**

    L49.2 **Exfoliation due to erythematous condition involving 20-29 percent of body surface**

    L49.3 **Exfoliation due to erythematous condition involving 30-39 percent of body surface**

    L49.4 **Exfoliation due to erythematous condition involving 40-49 percent of body surface**

    L49.5 **Exfoliation due to erythematous condition involving 50-59 percent of body surface**

    L49.6 **Exfoliation due to erythematous condition involving 60-69 percent of body surface**

    L49.7 **Exfoliation due to erythematous condition involving 70-79 percent of body surface**

    L49.8 **Exfoliation due to erythematous condition involving 80-89 percent of body surface**

    L49.9 **Exfoliation due to erythematous condition involving 90 or more percent of body surface**

Figure 12-6 Erythematous plaques with silvery scales in a patient with psoriasis. (Getty Image)

▶ New   ⇒ Revised   ~~deleted~~ Deleted   Excludes 1   Excludes 2   Includes   Use additional   Code first   Code also   Key words

OGCR Official Guidelines   X Assign placeholder X   ● Use Additional Character(s)   ▶ Manifestation Code   **Coding Clinic**

Figure 12-7 Urticaria (hives). *(Courtesy of David Effron, MD.)* (Getty Image)

Item 12–9　Urticaria is a vascular reaction in which wheals surrounded by a red halo appear and cause severe itching. The causes of urticaria or hives are extensive and varied (e.g., food, heat, cold, drugs, stress, infections).

● **L50　Urticaria**
>　**Excludes1**　allergic contact dermatitis (L23.-)
>　　　　　　　angioneurotic edema (T78.3)
>　　　　　　　giant urticaria (T78.3)
>　　　　　　　hereditary angio-edema (D84.1)
>　　　　　　　Quincke's edema (T78.3)
>　　　　　　　serum urticaria (T80.6-)
>　　　　　　　solar urticaria (L56.3)
>　　　　　　　urticaria neonatorum (P83.8)
>　　　　　　　urticaria papulosa (L28.2)
>　　　　　　　urticaria pigmentosa (Q82.2)

　L50.0　Allergic urticaria
　L50.1　Idiopathic urticaria
　L50.2　Urticaria due to cold and heat
>　　　**Excludes2**　familial cold urticaria (M04.2)

　L50.3　Dermatographic urticaria
　L50.4　Vibratory urticaria
　L50.5　Cholinergic urticaria
　L50.6　Contact urticaria
　L50.8　Other urticaria
　　　　　Chronic urticaria
　　　　　Recurrent periodic urticaria
　L50.9　Urticaria, unspecified

● **L51　Erythema multiforme**
>　Use additional code for adverse effect, if applicable, to identify drug (T36-T50 with fifth or sixth character 5)
>　Use additional code to identify associated manifestations, such as:
>　　arthropathy associated with dermatological disorders (M14.8-)
>　　conjunctival edema (H11.42)
>　　conjunctivitis (H10.22-)
>　　corneal scars and opacities (H17.-)
>　　corneal ulcer (H16.0-)
>⟹　edema of eyelid (H02.84-)
>　　inflammation of eyelid (H01.8)
>　　keratoconjunctivitis sicca (H16.22-)
>　　mechanical lagophthalmos (H02.22-)
>　　stomatitis (K12.-)
>　　symblepharon (H11.23-)
>　Use additional code to identify percentage of skin exfoliation (L49.-)
>　**Excludes1**　staphylococcal scalded skin syndrome (L00)
>　　　　　　　Ritter's disease (L00)

　L51.0　Nonbullous erythema multiforme
　L51.1　Stevens-Johnson syndrome
　L51.2　Toxic epidermal necrolysis [Lyell]
　L51.3　Stevens-Johnson syndrome-toxic epidermal necrolysis overlap syndrome
　　　　　SJS-TEN overlap syndrome
　L51.8　Other erythema multiforme
　L51.9　Erythema multiforme, unspecified
　　　　　Erythema iris
　　　　　Erythema multiforme major NOS
　　　　　Erythema multiforme minor NOS
　　　　　Herpes iris

　L52　Erythema nodosum
>　　**Excludes1**　tuberculous erythema nodosum (A18.4)

● **L53　Other erythematous conditions**
>　**Excludes1**　erythema ab igne (L59.0)
>　　　　　　　erythema due to external agents in contact with skin (L23-L25)
>　　　　　　　erythema intertrigo (L30.4)

　L53.0　Toxic erythema
>　　*Code first poisoning due to drug or toxin, if applicable (T36-T65 with fifth or sixth character 1-4 or 6)*
>　　Use additional code for adverse effect, if applicable, to identify drug (T36-T50 with fifth or sixth character 5)
>　　**Excludes1**　neonatal erythema toxicum (P83.1)

　L53.1　Erythema annulare centrifugum
　L53.2　Erythema marginatum
　L53.3　Other chronic figurate erythema
　L53.8　Other specified erythematous conditions
　L53.9　Erythematous condition, unspecified
　　　　　Erythema NOS
　　　　　Erythroderma NOS

▸ **L54　*Erythema in diseases classified elsewhere***
>　　*Code first underlying disease*

RADIATION-RELATED DISORDERS OF THE SKIN AND SUBCUTANEOUS TISSUE (L55-L59)

● **L55　Sunburn**
　L55.0　Sunburn of first degree
　L55.1　Sunburn of second degree
　L55.2　Sunburn of third degree
　L55.9　Sunburn, unspecified

● **L56　Other acute skin changes due to ultraviolet radiation**
>　Use additional code to identify the source of the ultraviolet radiation (W89, X32)

　L56.0　Drug phototoxic response
>　　Use additional code for adverse effect, if applicable, to identify drug (T36-T50 with fifth or sixth character 5)

　L56.1　Drug photoallergic response
>　　Use additional code for adverse effect, if applicable, to identify drug (T36-T50 with fifth or sixth character 5)

　L56.2　Photocontact dermatitis [berloque dermatitis]
　L56.3　Solar urticaria
　L56.4　Polymorphous light eruption
　L56.5　Disseminated superficial actinic porokeratosis (DSAP)
　L56.8　Other specified acute skin changes due to ultraviolet radiation
　L56.9　Acute skin change due to ultraviolet radiation, unspecified

● **L57　Skin changes due to chronic exposure to nonionizing radiation**
>　Use additional code to identify the source of the ultraviolet radiation (W89)

　L57.0　Actinic keratosis
　　　　　Keratosis NOS　　　　Solar keratosis
　　　　　Senile keratosis
　L57.1　Actinic reticuloid
　L57.2　Cutis rhomboidalis nuchae
　L57.3　Poikiloderma of Civatte
　L57.4　Cutis laxa senilis
　　　　　Elastosis senilis
　L57.5　Actinic granuloma
　L57.8　Other skin changes due to chronic exposure to nonionizing radiation
　　　　　Farmer's skin　　　　Solar dermatitis
　　　　　Sailor's skin
　L57.9　Skin changes due to chronic exposure to nonionizing radiation, unspecified

● **L58**   **Radiodermatitis**

Use additional code to identify the source of the radiation (W88, W90)

L58.0   Acute radiodermatitis

L58.1   Chronic radiodermatitis

L58.9   Radiodermatitis, unspecified

● **L59**   **Other disorders of skin and subcutaneous tissue related to radiation**

L59.0   Erythema ab igne [dermatitis ab igne]

L59.8   Other specified disorders of the skin and subcutaneous tissue related to radiation
     Coding Clinic: 2017, Q1, P34

L59.9   Disorder of the skin and subcutaneous tissue related to radiation, unspecified

DISORDERS OF SKIN APPENDAGES (L60-L75)

Excludes1   congenital malformations of integument (Q84.-)

● **L60**   **Nail disorders**

Excludes2   clubbing of nails (R68.3)
                 onychia and paronychia (L03.0-)

L60.0   Ingrowing nail

L60.1   Onycholysis

L60.2   Onychogryphosis

L60.3   Nail dystrophy

L60.4   Beau's lines

L60.5   Yellow nail syndrome

L60.8   Other nail disorders

L60.9   Nail disorder, unspecified

◗ *L62*   *Nail disorders in diseases classified elsewhere*

Code first *underlying disease, such as:*
     pachydermoperiostosis (M89.4-)

● **L63**   **Alopecia areata**

L63.0   Alopecia (capitis) totalis

L63.1   Alopecia universalis

L63.2   Ophiasis

L63.8   Other alopecia areata

L63.9   Alopecia areata, unspecified

● **L64**   **Androgenic alopecia**

Includes   male-pattern baldness

L64.0   Drug-induced androgenic alopecia

Use additional code for adverse effect, if applicable, to identify drug (T36-T50 with fifth or sixth character 5)

L64.8   Other androgenic alopecia

L64.9   Androgenic alopecia, unspecified

● **L65**   **Other nonscarring hair loss**

Use additional code for adverse effect, if applicable, to identify drug (T36-T50 with fifth or sixth character 5)

Excludes1   trichotillomania (F63.3)

L65.0   Telogen effluvium

L65.1   Anagen effluvium

L65.2   Alopecia mucinosa

L65.8   Other specified nonscarring hair loss

L65.9   Nonscarring hair loss, unspecified
     Alopecia NOS

● **L66**   **Cicatricial alopecia [scarring hair loss]**

L66.0   Pseudopelade

L66.1   Lichen planopilaris
     Follicular lichen planus

L66.2   Folliculitis decalvans

L66.3   Perifolliculitis capitis abscedens

L66.4   Folliculitis ulerythematosa reticulata

L66.8   Other cicatricial alopecia
     Coding Clinic: 2015, Q1, P19

L66.9   Cicatricial alopecia, unspecified

● **L67**   **Hair color and hair shaft abnormalities**

Excludes1   monilethrix (Q84.1)
                 pili annulati (Q84.1)
                 telogen effluvium (L65.0)

L67.0   Trichorrhexis nodosa

L67.1   Variations in hair color
     Canities
     Greyness, hair (premature)
     Heterochromia of hair
     Poliosis circumscripta, acquired
     Poliosis NOS

L67.8   Other hair color and hair shaft abnormalities
     Fragilitas crinium

L67.9   Hair color and hair shaft abnormality, unspecified

● **L68**   **Hypertrichosis**

Includes   excess hair

Excludes1   congenital hypertrichosis (Q84.2)
                 persistent lanugo (Q84.2)

L68.0   Hirsutism
     Excessive growth of hair

L68.1   Acquired hypertrichosis lanuginosa

L68.2   Localized hypertrichosis

L68.3   Polytrichia

L68.8   Other hypertrichosis

L68.9   Hypertrichosis, unspecified

Item 12–10   **Alopecia** is lack of hair and takes many forms. The most common is male pattern alopecia, also known as **androgenetic alopecia.** **Telogen effluvium** is early and excessive loss of hair resulting from a trauma to the hair follicle (fever, drugs, surgery, etc.).

Figure 12-8   Male pattern alopecia.

▶ New   ⇒ Revised   ~~deleted~~ Deleted   Excludes 1   Excludes 2   Includes   Use additional   Code first   Code also   Key words

OGCR Official Guidelines   X Assign placeholder X   ● Use Additional Character(s)   ◗ Manifestation Code   **Coding Clinic**

● **L70   Acne**

   Excludes2   acne keloid (L73.0)

   L70.0   Acne vulgaris

   L70.1   Acne conglobata

   L70.2   Acne varioliformis
            Acne necrotica miliaris

   L70.3   Acne tropica

   L70.4   Infantile acne   P

   L70.5   Acné excoriée
            Acné excoriée des jeunes filles
            Picker's acne

   L70.8   Other acne

   L70.9   Acne, unspecified

● **L71   Rosacea**

   Use additional code for adverse effect, if applicable, to identify
      drug (T36-T50 with fifth or sixth character 5)

   L71.0   Perioral dermatitis

   L71.1   Rhinophyma

   L71.8   Other rosacea

   L71.9   Rosacea, unspecified

● **L72   Follicular cysts of skin and subcutaneous tissue**

   L72.0   Epidermal cyst

 ● L72.1   Pilar and trichodermal cyst

            L72.11   Pilar cyst

            L72.12   Trichodermal cyst
                      Trichilemmal (proliferating) cyst

   L72.3   Sebaceous cyst

            Excludes2   pilar cyst (L72.11)
                             trichilemmal (proliferating) cyst (L72.12)

   L72.2   Steatocystoma multiplex

   L72.8   Other follicular cysts of the skin and subcutaneous
            tissue

   L72.9   Follicular cyst of the skin and subcutaneous tissue,
            unspecified

● **L73   Other follicular disorders**

   L73.0   Acne keloid

   L73.1   Pseudofolliculitis barbae

   L73.2   Hidradenitis suppurativa

   L73.8   Other specified follicular disorders
            Sycosis barbae

   L73.9   Follicular disorder, unspecified

● **L74   Eccrine sweat disorders**

   Excludes2   generalized hyperhidrosis (R61)

   L74.0   Miliaria rubra

   L74.1   Miliaria crystallina

   L74.2   Miliaria profunda
            Miliaria tropicalis

   L74.3   Miliaria, unspecified

   L74.4   Anhidrosis
            Hypohidrosis

 ● L74.5   Focal hyperhidrosis

   ● L74.51   Primary focal hyperhidrosis

               L74.510   Primary focal hyperhidrosis, axilla

               L74.511   Primary focal hyperhidrosis, face

               L74.512   Primary focal hyperhidrosis, palms

               L74.513   Primary focal hyperhidrosis, soles

               L74.519   Primary focal hyperhidrosis,
                          unspecified

      L74.52   Secondary focal hyperhidrosis
                Frey's syndrome

   L74.8   Other eccrine sweat disorders

   L74.9   Eccrine sweat disorder, unspecified
            Sweat gland disorder NOS

● **L75   Apocrine sweat disorders**

   Excludes1   dyshidrosis (L30.1)
                    hidradenitis suppurativa (L73.2)

   L75.0   Bromhidrosis

   L75.1   Chromhidrosis

   L75.2   Apocrine miliaria
            Fox-Fordyce disease

   L75.8   Other apocrine sweat disorders

   L75.9   Apocrine sweat disorder, unspecified
            Intraoperative and postprocedural complications of
            skin and subcutaneous tissue (L76)

INTRAOPERATIVE AND POSTPROCEDURAL COMPLICATIONS OF SKIN AND SUBCUTANEOUS TISSUE (L76)

● **L76   Intraoperative and postprocedural complications of skin and
            subcutaneous tissue**
            Coding Clinic: 2016, Q4, P10

 ● L76.0   Intraoperative hemorrhage and hematoma of skin and
            subcutaneous tissue complicating a procedure

            Excludes1   intraoperative hemorrhage and hematoma
                             of skin and subcutaneous tissue due
                             to accidental puncture and laceration
                             during a procedure (L76.1-)

            L76.01   Intraoperative hemorrhage and hematoma of
                      skin and subcutaneous tissue complicating a
                      dermatologic procedure

            L76.02   Intraoperative hemorrhage and hematoma of
                      skin and subcutaneous tissue complicating
                      other procedure

 ● L76.1   Accidental puncture and laceration of skin and
            subcutaneous tissue during a procedure

            L76.11   Accidental puncture and laceration of skin and
                      subcutaneous tissue during a dermatologic
                      procedure

            L76.12   Accidental puncture and laceration of skin and
                      subcutaneous tissue during other procedure

 ● L76.2   Postprocedural hemorrhage of skin and subcutaneous
            tissue following a procedure

            L76.21   Postprocedural hemorrhage of skin and
                      subcutaneous tissue following a dermatologic
                      procedure

            L76.22   Postprocedural hemorrhage of skin and
                      subcutaneous tissue following other
                      procedure

 ● L76.3   Postprocedural hematoma and seroma of skin and
            subcutaneous tissue following a procedure

            L76.31   Postprocedural hematoma of skin and
                      subcutaneous tissue following a dermatologic
                      procedure

            L76.32   Postprocedural hematoma of skin and
                      subcutaneous tissue following other
                      procedure

            L76.33   Postprocedural seroma of skin and
                      subcutaneous tissue following a dermatologic
                      procedure

            L76.34   Postprocedural seroma of skin and
                      subcutaneous tissue following other
                      procedure

 ● L76.8   Other intraoperative and postprocedural complications
            of skin and subcutaneous tissue

            Use additional code, if applicable, to further specify
               disorder

            L76.81   Other intraoperative complications of skin and
                      subcutaneous tissue

            L76.82   Other postprocedural complications of skin and
                      subcutaneous tissue
                      Coding Clinic: 2017, Q3, P6

CHAPTER 12 (L00-L99)

CHAPTER 12 (L00-L99)

OTHER DISORDERS OF THE SKIN AND SUBCUTANEOUS TISSUE (L80-L99)

L80   Vitiligo
> **Excludes2**   vitiligo of eyelids (H02.73-)
> vitiligo of vulva (N90.89)

● **L81   Other disorders of pigmentation**
> **Excludes1**   birthmark NOS (Q82.5)
> Peutz-Jeghers syndrome (Q85.8)
>
> **Excludes2**   nevus - see Alphabetical Index

L81.0   Postinflammatory hyperpigmentation

L81.1   Chloasma

L81.2   Freckles

L81.3   Café au lait spots

L81.4   Other melanin hyperpigmentation
> Lentigo

L81.5   Leukoderma, not elsewhere classified

L81.6   Other disorders of diminished melanin formation

L81.7   Pigmented purpuric dermatosis
> Angioma serpiginosum

L81.8   Other specified disorders of pigmentation
> Iron pigmentation
> Tattoo pigmentation

L81.9   Disorder of pigmentation, unspecified

● **L82   Seborrheic keratosis**
> **Includes**   basal cell papilloma
> dermatosis papulosa nigra
> Leser-Trélat disease
>
> **Excludes2**   seborrheic dermatitis (L21.-)

L82.0   Inflamed seborrheic keratosis

L82.1   Other seborrheic keratosis
> Seborrheic keratosis NOS

L83   Acanthosis nigricans
> Confluent and reticulated papillomatosis

L84   Corns and callosities
> Callus
> Clavus

● **L85   Other epidermal thickening**
> **Excludes2**   hypertrophic disorders of the skin (L91.-)

L85.0   Acquired ichthyosis
> **Excludes1**   congenital ichthyosis (Q80.-)

L85.1   Acquired keratosis [keratoderma] palmaris et plantaris
> **Excludes1**   inherited keratosis palmaris et plantaris (Q82.8)

L85.2   Keratosis punctata (palmaris et plantaris)

L85.3   Xerosis cutis
> Dry skin dermatitis

L85.8   Other specified epidermal thickening
> Cutaneous horn

L85.9   Epidermal thickening, unspecified

▷ *L86   Keratoderma in diseases classified elsewhere*
> *Firm horny papules that have a cobblestone appearance.*
>
> *Code first underlying disease, such as:*
> Reiter's disease (M02.3-)
>
> **Excludes1**   gonococcal keratoderma (A54.89)
> gonococcal keratosis (A54.89)
> keratoderma due to vitamin A deficiency (E50.8)
> keratosis due to vitamin A deficiency (E50.8)
> xeroderma due to vitamin A deficiency (E50.8)

● **L87   Transepidermal elimination disorders**
> **Excludes1**   granuloma annulare (perforating) (L92.0)

L87.0   Keratosis follicularis et parafollicularis in cutem penetrans
> Kyrle disease
> Hyperkeratosis follicularis penetrans

L87.1   Reactive perforating collagenosis

L87.2   Elastosis perforans serpiginosa

L87.8   Other transepidermal elimination disorders

L87.9   Transepidermal elimination disorder, unspecified

L88   Pyoderma gangrenosum
> Phagedenic pyoderma
>
> **Excludes1**   dermatitis gangrenosa (L08.0)

> **OGCR**   Section I.B.14.
>
> General Coding Guidelines
>
> Documentation for BMI, *Depth of* Non-pressure ulcers, Pressure Ulcer Stages, **Coma Scale, and** *NIH Stroke Scale*
>
> For the Body Mass Index (BMI), depth of non-pressure chronic ulcers, pressure ulcer stage, **coma scale, and NIH stroke scale (NIHSS) codes,** code assignment may be based on medical record documentation from clinicians who are not the patient's provider (i.e., physician or other qualified healthcare practitioner legally accountable for establishing the patient's diagnosis), since this information is typically documented by other clinicians involved in the care of the patient (e.g., a dietitian often documents the BMI, a nurse often documents the pressure ulcer stages, **and an emergency medical technician often documents the coma scale).** However, the associated diagnosis (such as overweight, obesity, **acute stroke,** or pressure ulcer) must be documented by the patient's provider. If there is conflicting medical record documentation, either from the same clinician or different clinicians, the patient's attending provider should be queried for clarification.
>
> The BMI, **coma scale, and NHSS** codes should only be reported as secondary diagnoses.

● **L89   Pressure ulcer**

Includes	bed sore	pressure area
	decubitus ulcer	pressure sore
	plaster ulcer	

> *Code first any associated gangrene (I96)*
>
> **Excludes2**   decubitus (trophic) ulcer of cervix (uteri) (N86)
> diabetic ulcers (E08.621, E08.622, E09.621,
>   E09.622, E10.621, E10.622, E11.621, E11.622,
>   E13.621, E13.622)
> non-pressure chronic ulcer of skin (L97.-)
> skin infections (L00-L08)
> varicose ulcer (I83.0, I83.2)
>
> Coding Clinic: 2018, Q2, P22; 2016, Q4, P124

● **L89.0   Pressure ulcer of elbow**

● **L89.00   Pressure ulcer of unspecified elbow**

L89.000   Pressure ulcer of unspecified elbow, unstageable

L89.001   Pressure ulcer of unspecified elbow, stage 1
> Healing pressure ulcer of unspecified elbow, stage 1
> Pressure pre-ulcer skin changes limited to persistent focal edema, unspecified elbow

L89.002   Pressure ulcer of unspecified elbow, stage 2
> Healing pressure ulcer of unspecified elbow, stage 2
> Pressure ulcer with abrasion, blister, partial thickness skin loss involving epidermis and/or dermis, unspecified elbow

▶ New   ⇒ Revised   ~~deleted~~ Deleted   Excludes 1   Excludes 2   Includes   Use additional   Code first   Code also   Key words

OGCR Official Guidelines   X Assign placeholder X   ● Use Additional Character(s)   ▷ Manifestation Code   **Coding Clinic**

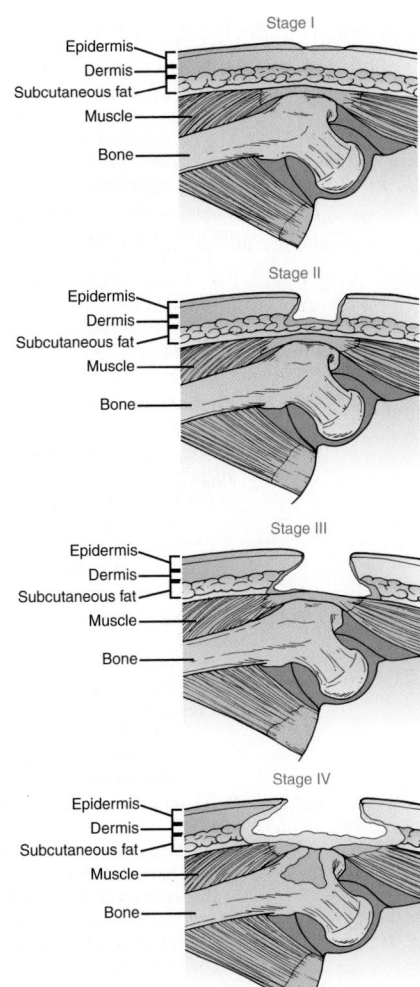

Stage I

Epidermis
Dermis
Subcutaneous fat
Muscle
Bone

Stage II

Epidermis
Dermis
Subcutaneous fat
Muscle
Bone

Stage III

Epidermis
Dermis
Subcutaneous fat
Muscle
Bone

Stage IV

Epidermis
Dermis
Subcutaneous fat
Muscle
Bone

Figure 12-9 Stage I, II, III, and IV of pressure ulcers.

L89.003   **Pressure ulcer of unspecified elbow, stage 3**
Healing pressure ulcer of unspecified elbow, stage 3
Pressure ulcer with full thickness skin loss involving damage or necrosis of subcutaneous tissue, unspecified elbow

L89.004   **Pressure ulcer of unspecified elbow, stage 4**
Healing pressure ulcer of unspecified elbow, stage 4
Pressure ulcer with necrosis of soft tissues through to underlying muscle, tendon, or bone, unspecified elbow

L89.009   **Pressure ulcer of unspecified elbow, unspecified stage**
Healing pressure ulcer of elbow NOS
Healing pressure ulcer of unspecified elbow, unspecified stage

● **L89.01   Pressure ulcer of right elbow**
L89.010   **Pressure ulcer of right elbow, unstageable**
L89.011   **Pressure ulcer of right elbow, stage 1**
Healing pressure ulcer of right elbow, stage 1
Pressure pre-ulcer skin changes limited to persistent focal edema, right elbow
L89.012   **Pressure ulcer of right elbow, stage 2**
Healing pressure ulcer of right elbow, stage 2
Pressure ulcer with abrasion, blister, partial thickness skin loss involving epidermis and/or dermis, right elbow
L89.013   **Pressure ulcer of right elbow, stage 3**
Healing pressure ulcer of right elbow, stage 3
Pressure ulcer with full thickness skin loss involving damage or necrosis of subcutaneous tissue, right elbow
L89.014   **Pressure ulcer of right elbow, stage 4**
Healing pressure ulcer of right elbow, stage 4
Pressure ulcer with necrosis of soft tissues through to underlying muscle, tendon, or bone, right elbow
L89.019   **Pressure ulcer of right elbow, unspecified stage**
Healing pressure right of elbow NOS
Healing pressure ulcer of right elbow, unspecified stage

● **L89.02   Pressure ulcer of left elbow**
L89.020   **Pressure ulcer of left elbow, unstageable**
L89.021   **Pressure ulcer of left elbow, stage 1**
Healing pressure ulcer of left elbow, stage 1
Pressure pre-ulcer skin changes limited to persistent focal edema, left elbow
L89.022   **Pressure ulcer of left elbow, stage 2**
Healing pressure ulcer of left elbow, stage 2
Pressure ulcer with abrasion, blister, partial thickness skin loss involving epidermis and/or dermis, left elbow
L89.023   **Pressure ulcer of left elbow, stage 3**
Healing pressure ulcer of left elbow, stage 3
Pressure ulcer with full thickness skin loss involving damage or necrosis of subcutaneous tissue, left elbow
L89.024   **Pressure ulcer of left elbow, stage 4**
Healing pressure ulcer of left elbow, stage 4
Pressure ulcer with necrosis of soft tissues through to underlying muscle, tendon, or bone, left elbow
L89.029   **Pressure ulcer of left elbow, unspecified stage**
Healing pressure ulcer of left of elbow NOS
Healing pressure ulcer of left elbow, unspecified stage

CHAPTER 12 (LØØ-L99)

● **L89.1   Pressure ulcer of back**
  ● **L89.10   Pressure ulcer of unspecified part of back**
      L89.100   Pressure ulcer of unspecified part of back, unstageable
      L89.101   Pressure ulcer of unspecified part of back, stage 1
              Healing pressure ulcer of unspecified part of back, stage 1
              Pressure pre-ulcer skin changes limited to persistent focal edema, unspecified part of back
      L89.102   Pressure ulcer of unspecified part of back, stage 2
              Healing pressure ulcer of unspecified part of back, stage 2
              Pressure ulcer with abrasion, blister, partial thickness skin loss involving epidermis and/or dermis, unspecified part of back
      L89.103   Pressure ulcer of unspecified part of back, stage 3
              Healing pressure ulcer of unspecified part of back, stage 3
              Pressure ulcer with full thickness skin loss involving damage or necrosis of subcutaneous tissue, unspecified part of back
      L89.104   Pressure ulcer of unspecified part of back, stage 4
              Healing pressure ulcer of unspecified part of back, stage 4
              Pressure ulcer with necrosis of soft tissues through to underlying muscle, tendon, or bone, unspecified part of back
      L89.109   Pressure ulcer of unspecified part of back, unspecified stage
              Healing pressure ulcer of unspecified part of back NOS
              Healing pressure ulcer of unspecified part of back, unspecified stage
  ● **L89.11   Pressure ulcer of right upper back**
          Pressure ulcer of right shoulder blade
      L89.110   Pressure ulcer of right upper back, unstageable
      L89.111   Pressure ulcer of right upper back, stage 1
              Healing pressure ulcer of right upper back, stage 1
              Pressure pre-ulcer skin changes limited to persistent focal edema, right upper back
      L89.112   Pressure ulcer of right upper back, stage 2
              Healing pressure ulcer of right upper back, stage 2
              Pressure ulcer with abrasion, blister, partial thickness skin loss involving epidermis and/or dermis, right upper back
      L89.113   Pressure ulcer of right upper back, stage 3
              Healing pressure ulcer of right upper back, stage 3
              Pressure ulcer with full thickness skin loss involving damage or necrosis of subcutaneous tissue, right upper back

      L89.114   Pressure ulcer of right upper back, stage 4
              Healing pressure ulcer of right upper back, stage 4
              Pressure ulcer with necrosis of soft tissues through to underlying muscle, tendon, or bone, right upper back
      L89.119   Pressure ulcer of right upper back, unspecified stage
              Healing pressure ulcer of right upper back NOS
              Healing pressure ulcer of right upper back, unspecified stage
  ● **L89.12   Pressure ulcer of left upper back**
          Pressure ulcer of left shoulder blade
      L89.120   Pressure ulcer of left upper back, unstageable
      L89.121   Pressure ulcer of left upper back, stage 1
              Healing pressure ulcer of left upper back, stage 1
              Pressure pre-ulcer skin changes limited to persistent focal edema, left upper back
      L89.122   Pressure ulcer of left upper back, stage 2
              Healing pressure ulcer of left upper back, stage 2
              Pressure ulcer with abrasion, blister, partial thickness skin loss involving epidermis and/or dermis, left upper back
      L89.123   Pressure ulcer of left upper back, stage 3
              Healing pressure ulcer of left upper back, stage 3
              Pressure ulcer with full thickness skin loss involving damage or necrosis of subcutaneous tissue, left upper back
      L89.124   Pressure ulcer of left upper back, stage 4
              Healing pressure ulcer of left upper back, stage 4
              Pressure ulcer with necrosis of soft tissues through to underlying muscle, tendon, or bone, left upper back
      L89.129   Pressure ulcer of left upper back, unspecified stage
              Healing pressure ulcer of left upper back NOS
              Healing pressure ulcer of left upper back, unspecified stage
  ● **L89.13   Pressure ulcer of right lower back**
      L89.130   Pressure ulcer of right lower back, unstageable
      L89.131   Pressure ulcer of right lower back, stage 1
              Healing pressure ulcer of right lower back, stage 1
              Pressure pre-ulcer skin changes limited to persistent focal edema, right lower back
      L89.132   Pressure ulcer of right lower back, stage 2
              Healing pressure ulcer of right lower back, stage 2
              Pressure ulcer with abrasion, blister, partial thickness skin loss involving epidermis and/or dermis, right lower back

L89.133 **Pressure ulcer of right lower back, stage 3**
Healing pressure ulcer of right lower back, stage 3
Pressure ulcer with full thickness skin loss involving damage or necrosis of subcutaneous tissue, right lower back

L89.134 **Pressure ulcer of right lower back, stage 4**
Healing pressure ulcer of right lower back, stage 4
Pressure ulcer with necrosis of soft tissues through to underlying muscle, tendon, or bone, right lower back

L89.139 **Pressure ulcer of right lower back, unspecified stage**
Healing pressure ulcer of right lower back NOS
Healing pressure ulcer of right lower back, unspecified stage

● **L89.14 Pressure ulcer of left lower back**

L89.140 **Pressure ulcer of left lower back, unstageable**

L89.141 **Pressure ulcer of left lower back, stage 1**
Healing pressure ulcer of left lower back, stage 1
Pressure pre-ulcer skin changes limited to persistent focal edema, left lower back

L89.142 **Pressure ulcer of left lower back, stage 2**
Healing pressure ulcer of left lower back, stage 2
Pressure ulcer with abrasion, blister, partial thickness skin loss involving epidermis and/or dermis, left lower back

L89.143 **Pressure ulcer of left lower back, stage 3**
Healing pressure ulcer of left lower back, stage 3
Pressure ulcer with full thickness skin loss involving damage or necrosis of subcutaneous tissue, left lower back

L89.144 **Pressure ulcer of left lower back, stage 4**
Healing pressure ulcer of left lower back, stage 4
Pressure ulcer with necrosis of soft tissues through to underlying muscle, tendon, or bone, left lower back

L89.149 **Pressure ulcer of left lower back, unspecified stage**
Healing pressure ulcer of left lower back NOS
Healing pressure ulcer of left lower back, unspecified stage

● **L89.15 Pressure ulcer of sacral region**
Pressure ulcer of coccyx
Pressure ulcer of tailbone

L89.150 **Pressure ulcer of sacral region, unstageable**

L89.151 **Pressure ulcer of sacral region, stage 1**
Healing pressure ulcer of sacral region, stage 1
Pressure pre-ulcer skin changes limited to persistent focal edema, sacral region

L89.152 **Pressure ulcer of sacral region, stage 2**
Healing pressure ulcer of sacral region, stage 2
Pressure ulcer with abrasion, blister, partial thickness skin loss involving epidermis and/or dermis, sacral region

L89.153 **Pressure ulcer of sacral region, stage 3**
Healing pressure ulcer of sacral region, stage 3
Pressure ulcer with full thickness skin loss involving damage or necrosis of subcutaneous tissue, sacral region

L89.154 **Pressure ulcer of sacral region, stage 4**
Healing pressure ulcer of sacral region, stage 4
Pressure ulcer with necrosis of soft tissues through to underlying muscle, tendon, or bone, sacral region

L89.159 **Pressure ulcer of sacral region, unspecified stage**
Healing pressure ulcer of sacral region NOS
Healing pressure ulcer of sacral region, unspecified stage

● **L89.2 Pressure ulcer of hip**

● **L89.20 Pressure ulcer of unspecified hip**

L89.200 **Pressure ulcer of unspecified hip, unstageable**

L89.201 **Pressure ulcer of unspecified hip, stage 1**
Healing pressure ulcer of unspecified hip back, stage 1
Pressure pre-ulcer skin changes limited to persistent focal edema, unspecified hip

L89.202 **Pressure ulcer of unspecified hip, stage 2**
Healing pressure ulcer of unspecified hip, stage 2
Pressure ulcer with abrasion, blister, partial thickness skin loss involving epidermis and/or dermis, unspecified hip

L89.203 **Pressure ulcer of unspecified hip, stage 3**
Healing pressure ulcer of unspecified hip, stage 3
Pressure ulcer with full thickness skin loss involving damage or necrosis of subcutaneous tissue, unspecified hip

L89.204 **Pressure ulcer of unspecified hip, stage 4**
Healing pressure ulcer of unspecified hip, stage 4
Pressure ulcer with necrosis of soft tissues through to underlying muscle, tendon, or bone, unspecified hip

L89.209 **Pressure ulcer of unspecified hip, unspecified stage**
Healing pressure ulcer of unspecified hip NOS
Healing pressure ulcer of unspecified hip, unspecified stage

CHAPTER 12 (L00-L99)

● **L89.21 Pressure ulcer of right hip**

   L89.210 **Pressure ulcer of right hip, unstageable**

   L89.211 **Pressure ulcer of right hip, stage 1**
      Healing pressure ulcer of right hip back, stage 1
      Pressure pre-ulcer skin changes limited to persistent focal edema, right hip

   L89.212 **Pressure ulcer of right hip, stage 2**
      Healing pressure ulcer of right hip, stage 2
      Pressure ulcer with abrasion, blister, partial thickness skin loss involving epidermis and/or dermis, right hip

   L89.213 **Pressure ulcer of right hip, stage 3**
      Healing pressure ulcer of right hip, stage 3
      Pressure ulcer with full thickness skin loss involving damage or necrosis of subcutaneous tissue, right hip

   L89.214 **Pressure ulcer of right hip, stage 4**
      Healing pressure ulcer of right hip, stage 4
      Pressure ulcer with necrosis of soft tissues through to underlying muscle, tendon, or bone, right hip

   L89.219 **Pressure ulcer of right hip, unspecified stage**
      Healing pressure ulcer of right hip NOS
      Healing pressure ulcer of right hip, unspecified stage

● **L89.22 Pressure ulcer of left hip**

   L89.220 **Pressure ulcer of left hip, unstageable**

   L89.221 **Pressure ulcer of left hip, stage 1**
      Healing pressure ulcer of left hip back, stage 1
      Pressure pre-ulcer skin changes limited to persistent focal edema, left hip

   L89.222 **Pressure ulcer of left hip, stage 2**
      Healing pressure ulcer of left hip, stage 2
      Pressure ulcer with abrasion, blister, partial thickness skin loss involving epidermis and/or dermis, left hip

   L89.223 **Pressure ulcer of left hip, stage 3**
      Healing pressure ulcer of left hip, stage 3
      Pressure ulcer with full thickness skin loss involving damage or necrosis of subcutaneous tissue, left hip

   L89.224 **Pressure ulcer of left hip, stage 4**
      Healing pressure ulcer of left hip, stage 4
      Pressure ulcer with necrosis of soft tissues through to underlying muscle, tendon, or bone, left hip

   L89.229 **Pressure ulcer of left hip, unspecified stage**
      Healing pressure ulcer of left hip NOS
      Healing pressure ulcer of left hip, unspecified stage

● **L89.3 Pressure ulcer of buttock**

 ● **L89.30 Pressure ulcer of unspecified buttock**

   L89.300 **Pressure ulcer of unspecified buttock, unstageable**

   L89.301 **Pressure ulcer of unspecified buttock, stage 1**
      Healing pressure ulcer of unspecified buttock, stage 1
      Pressure pre-ulcer skin changes limited to persistent focal edema, unspecified buttock

   L89.302 **Pressure ulcer of unspecified buttock, stage 2**
      Healing pressure ulcer of unspecified buttock, stage 2
      Pressure ulcer with abrasion, blister, partial thickness skin loss involving epidermis and/or dermis, unspecified buttock

   L89.303 **Pressure ulcer of unspecified buttock, stage 3**
      Healing pressure ulcer of unspecified buttock, stage 3
      Pressure ulcer with full thickness skin loss involving damage or necrosis of subcutaneous tissue, unspecified buttock

   L89.304 **Pressure ulcer of unspecified buttock, stage 4**
      Healing pressure ulcer of unspecified buttock, stage 4
      Pressure ulcer with necrosis of soft tissues through to underlying muscle, tendon, or bone, unspecified buttock

   L89.309 **Pressure ulcer of unspecified buttock, unspecified stage**
      Healing pressure ulcer of unspecified buttock NOS
      Healing pressure ulcer of unspecified buttock, unspecified stage

 ● **L89.31 Pressure ulcer of right buttock**

   L89.310 **Pressure ulcer of right buttock, unstageable**

   L89.311 **Pressure ulcer of right buttock, stage 1**
      Healing pressure ulcer of right buttock, stage 1
      Pressure pre-ulcer skin changes limited to persistent focal edema, right buttock

   L89.312 **Pressure ulcer of right buttock, stage 2**
      Healing pressure ulcer of right buttock, stage 2
      Pressure ulcer with abrasion, blister, partial thickness skin loss involving epidermis and/or dermis, right buttock

   L89.313 **Pressure ulcer of right buttock, stage 3**
      Healing pressure ulcer of right buttock, stage 3
      Pressure ulcer with full thickness skin loss involving damage or necrosis of subcutaneous tissue, right buttock

CHAPTER 12 (L00-L99)

▶ New   ⇒ Revised   ~~deleted~~ Deleted   Excludes 1   Excludes 2   Includes   Use additional   Code first   Code also   Key words
OGCR Official Guidelines   X Assign placeholder X   ● Use Additional Character(s)   ▶ Manifestation Code   **Coding Clinic**

L89.314   **Pressure ulcer of right buttock, stage 4**
> Healing pressure ulcer of right buttock, stage 4
> Pressure ulcer with necrosis of soft tissues through to underlying muscle, tendon, or bone, right buttock

L89.319   **Pressure ulcer of right buttock, unspecified stage**
> Healing pressure ulcer of right buttock NOS
> Healing pressure ulcer of right buttock, unspecified stage

● **L89.32**   Pressure ulcer of **left buttock**

L89.320   **Pressure ulcer of left buttock, unstageable**

L89.321   **Pressure ulcer of left buttock, stage 1**
> Healing pressure ulcer of left buttock, stage 1
> Pressure pre-ulcer skin changes limited to persistent focal edema, left buttock

L89.322   **Pressure ulcer of left buttock, stage 2**
> Healing pressure ulcer of left buttock, stage 2
> Pressure ulcer with abrasion, blister, partial thickness skin loss involving epidermis and/or dermis, left buttock

L89.323   **Pressure ulcer of left buttock, stage 3**
> Healing pressure ulcer of left buttock, stage 3
> Pressure ulcer with full thickness skin loss involving damage or necrosis of subcutaneous tissue, left buttock

L89.324   **Pressure ulcer of left buttock, stage 4**
> Healing pressure ulcer of left buttock, stage 4
> Pressure ulcer with necrosis of soft tissues through to underlying muscle, tendon, or bone, left buttock

L89.329   **Pressure ulcer of left buttock, unspecified stage**
> Healing pressure ulcer of left buttock NOS
> Healing pressure ulcer of left buttock, unspecified stage

● **L89.4**   Pressure ulcer of **contiguous site of back, buttock and hip**

L89.40   **Pressure ulcer of contiguous site of back, buttock and hip, unspecified stage**
> Healing pressure ulcer of contiguous site of back, buttock and hip NOS
> Healing pressure ulcer of contiguous site of back, buttock and hip, unspecified stage

L89.41   **Pressure ulcer of contiguous site of back, buttock and hip, stage 1**
> Healing pressure ulcer of contiguous site of back, buttock and hip, stage 1
> Pressure pre-ulcer skin changes limited to persistent focal edema, contiguous site of back, buttock and hip

L89.42   **Pressure ulcer of contiguous site of back, buttock and hip, stage 2**
> Healing pressure ulcer of contiguous site of back, buttock and hip, stage 2
> Pressure ulcer with abrasion, blister, partial thickness skin loss involving epidermis and/or dermis, contiguous site of back, buttock and hip

L89.43   **Pressure ulcer of contiguous site of back, buttock and hip, stage 3**
> Healing pressure ulcer of contiguous site of back, buttock and hip, stage 3
> Pressure ulcer with full thickness skin loss involving damage or necrosis of subcutaneous tissue, contiguous site of back, buttock and hip

L89.44   **Pressure ulcer of contiguous site of back, buttock and hip, stage 4**
> Healing pressure ulcer of contiguous site of back, buttock and hip, stage 4
> Pressure ulcer with necrosis of soft tissues through to underlying muscle, tendon, or bone, contiguous site of back, buttock and hip

L89.45   **Pressure ulcer of contiguous site of back, buttock and hip, unstageable**

● **L89.5**   Pressure ulcer of **ankle**

   ● **L89.50**   Pressure ulcer of **unspecified ankle**

L89.500   **Pressure ulcer of unspecified ankle, unstageable**

L89.501   **Pressure ulcer of unspecified ankle, stage 1**
> Healing pressure ulcer of unspecified ankle, stage 1
> Pressure pre-ulcer skin changes limited to persistent focal edema, unspecified ankle

L89.502   **Pressure ulcer of unspecified ankle, stage 2**
> Healing pressure ulcer of unspecified ankle, stage 2
> Pressure ulcer with abrasion, blister, partial thickness skin loss involving epidermis and/or dermis, unspecified ankle

L89.503   **Pressure ulcer of unspecified ankle, stage 3**
> Healing pressure ulcer of unspecified ankle, stage 3
> Pressure ulcer with full thickness skin loss involving damage or necrosis of subcutaneous tissue, unspecified ankle

L89.504   **Pressure ulcer of unspecified ankle, stage 4**
> Healing pressure ulcer of unspecified ankle, stage 4
> Pressure ulcer with necrosis of soft tissues through to underlying muscle, tendon, or bone, unspecified ankle

L89.509   **Pressure ulcer of unspecified ankle, unspecified stage**
> Healing pressure ulcer of unspecified ankle NOS
> Healing pressure ulcer of unspecified ankle, unspecified stage

CHAPTER 12 (L00-L99)

● L89.51   Pressure ulcer of right ankle

L89.510   Pressure ulcer of right ankle, unstageable

L89.511   Pressure ulcer of right ankle, stage 1
Healing pressure ulcer of right ankle, stage 1
Pressure pre-ulcer skin changes limited to persistent focal edema, right ankle

L89.512   Pressure ulcer of right ankle, stage 2
Healing pressure ulcer of right ankle, stage 2
Pressure ulcer with abrasion, blister, partial thickness skin loss involving epidermis and/or dermis, right ankle

L89.513   Pressure ulcer of right ankle, stage 3
Healing pressure ulcer of right ankle, stage 3
Pressure ulcer with full thickness skin loss involving damage or necrosis of subcutaneous tissue, right ankle

L89.514   Pressure ulcer of right ankle, stage 4
Healing pressure ulcer of right ankle, stage 4
Pressure ulcer with necrosis of soft tissues through to underlying muscle, tendon, or bone, right ankle

L89.519   Pressure ulcer of right ankle, unspecified stage
Healing pressure ulcer of right ankle NOS
Healing pressure ulcer of right ankle, unspecified stage

● L89.52   Pressure ulcer of left ankle

L89.520   Pressure ulcer of left ankle, unstageable

L89.521   Pressure ulcer of left ankle, stage 1
Healing pressure ulcer of left ankle, stage 1
Pressure pre-ulcer skin changes limited to persistent focal edema, left ankle

L89.522   Pressure ulcer of left ankle, stage 2
Healing pressure ulcer of left ankle, stage 2
Pressure ulcer with abrasion, blister, partial thickness skin loss involving epidermis and/or dermis, left ankle

L89.523   Pressure ulcer of left ankle, stage 3
Healing pressure ulcer of left ankle, stage 3
Pressure ulcer with full thickness skin loss involving damage or necrosis of subcutaneous tissue, left ankle

L89.524   Pressure ulcer of left ankle, stage 4
Healing pressure ulcer of left ankle, stage 4
Pressure ulcer with necrosis of soft tissues through to underlying muscle, tendon, or bone, left ankle

L89.529   Pressure ulcer of left ankle, unspecified stage
Healing pressure ulcer of left ankle NOS
Healing pressure ulcer of left ankle, unspecified stage

● L89.6   Pressure ulcer of heel

● L89.60   Pressure ulcer of unspecified heel

L89.600   Pressure ulcer of unspecified heel, unstageable

L89.601   Pressure ulcer of unspecified heel, stage 1
Healing pressure ulcer of unspecified heel, stage 1
Pressure pre-ulcer skin changes limited to persistent focal edema, unspecified heel

L89.602   Pressure ulcer of unspecified heel, stage 2
Healing pressure ulcer of unspecified heel, stage 2
Pressure ulcer with abrasion, blister, partial thickness skin loss involving epidermis and/or dermis, unspecified heel

L89.603   Pressure ulcer of unspecified heel, stage 3
Healing pressure ulcer of unspecified heel, stage 3
Pressure ulcer with full thickness skin loss involving damage or necrosis of subcutaneous tissue, unspecified heel

L89.604   Pressure ulcer of unspecified heel, stage 4
Healing pressure ulcer of unspecified heel, stage 4
Pressure ulcer with necrosis of soft tissues through to underlying muscle, tendon, or bone, unspecified heel

L89.609   Pressure ulcer of unspecified heel, unspecified stage
Healing pressure ulcer of unspecified heel NOS
Healing pressure ulcer of unspecified heel, unspecified stage

● L89.61   Pressure ulcer of right heel

L89.610   Pressure ulcer of right heel, unstageable

L89.611   Pressure ulcer of right heel, stage 1
Healing pressure ulcer of right heel, stage 1
Pressure pre-ulcer skin changes limited to persistent focal edema, right heel

L89.612   Pressure ulcer of right heel, stage 2
Healing pressure ulcer of right heel, stage 2
Pressure ulcer with abrasion, blister, partial thickness skin loss involving epidermis and/or dermis, right heel

L89.613   Pressure ulcer of right heel, stage 3
Healing pressure ulcer of right heel, stage 3
Pressure ulcer with full thickness skin loss involving damage or necrosis of subcutaneous tissue, right heel

L89.614   Pressure ulcer of right heel, stage 4
Healing pressure ulcer of right heel, stage 4
Pressure ulcer with necrosis of soft tissues through to underlying muscle, tendon, or bone, right heel

L89.619   Pressure ulcer of right heel, unspecified stage
Healing pressure ulcer of right heel NOS
Healing pressure ulcer of right heel, unspecified stage

▶ New   ⇒ Revised   ~~deleted~~ Deleted   Excludes 1   Excludes 2   Includes   Use additional   Code first   Code also   Key words
OGCR Official Guidelines   X Assign placeholder X   ● Use Additional Character(s)   ▶ Manifestation Code   Coding Clinic

● **L89.62**   Pressure ulcer of left heel

    L89.620   Pressure ulcer of left heel, unstageable

    L89.621   Pressure ulcer of left heel, stage 1
       Healing pressure ulcer of left heel, stage 1
       Pressure pre-ulcer skin changes limited to persistent focal edema, left heel

    L89.622   Pressure ulcer of left heel, stage 2
       Healing pressure ulcer of left heel, stage 2
       Pressure ulcer with abrasion, blister, partial thickness skin loss involving epidermis and/or dermis, left heel
       Coding Clinic: 2016, Q4, P142

    L89.623   Pressure ulcer of left heel, stage 3
       Healing pressure ulcer of left heel, stage 3
       Pressure ulcer with full thickness skin loss involving damage or necrosis of subcutaneous tissue, left heel
       Coding Clinic: 2016, Q4, P142

    L89.624   Pressure ulcer of left heel, stage 4
       Healing pressure ulcer of left heel, stage 4
       Pressure ulcer with necrosis of soft tissues through to underlying muscle, tendon, or bone, left heel

    L89.629   Pressure ulcer of left heel, unspecified stage
       Healing pressure ulcer of left heel NOS
       Healing pressure ulcer of left heel, unspecified stage

● **L89.8**   Pressure ulcer of other site

   ● **L89.81**   Pressure ulcer of head
      Pressure ulcer of face

    L89.810   Pressure ulcer of head, unstageable

    L89.811   Pressure ulcer of head, stage 1
       Healing pressure ulcer of head, stage 1
       Pressure pre-ulcer skin changes limited to persistent focal edema, head

    L89.812   Pressure ulcer of head, stage 2
       Healing pressure ulcer of head, stage 2
       Pressure ulcer with abrasion, blister, partial thickness skin loss involving epidermis and/or dermis, head

    L89.813   Pressure ulcer of head, stage 3
       Healing pressure ulcer of head, stage 3
       Pressure ulcer with full thickness skin loss involving damage or necrosis of subcutaneous tissue, head

    L89.814   Pressure ulcer of head, stage 4
       Healing pressure ulcer of head, stage 4
       Pressure ulcer with necrosis of soft tissues through to underlying muscle, tendon, or bone, head

    L89.819   Pressure ulcer of head, unspecified stage
       Healing pressure ulcer of head NOS
       Healing pressure ulcer of head, unspecified stage

● **L89.89**   Pressure ulcer of other site

    L89.890   Pressure ulcer of other site, unstageable

    L89.891   Pressure ulcer of other site, stage 1
       Healing pressure ulcer of other site, stage 1
       Pressure pre-ulcer skin changes limited to persistent focal edema, other site

    L89.892   Pressure ulcer of other site, stage 2
       Healing pressure ulcer of other site, stage 2
       Pressure ulcer with abrasion, blister, partial thickness skin loss involving epidermis and/or dermis, other site

    L89.893   Pressure ulcer of other site, stage 3
       Healing pressure ulcer of other site, stage 3
       Pressure ulcer with full thickness skin loss involving damage or necrosis of subcutaneous tissue, other site

    L89.894   Pressure ulcer of other site, stage 4
       Healing pressure ulcer of other site, stage 4
       Pressure ulcer with necrosis of soft tissues through to underlying muscle, tendon, or bone, other site

    L89.899   Pressure ulcer of other site, unspecified stage
       Healing pressure ulcer of other site NOS
       Healing pressure ulcer of other site, unspecified stage

● **L89.9**   Pressure ulcer of unspecified site

    L89.90   Pressure ulcer of unspecified site, unspecified stage
       Healing pressure ulcer of unspecified site NOS
       Healing pressure ulcer of unspecified site, unspecified stage

    L89.91   Pressure ulcer of unspecified site, stage 1
       Healing pressure ulcer of unspecified site, stage 1
       Pressure pre-ulcer skin changes limited to persistent focal edema, unspecified site

    L89.92   Pressure ulcer of unspecified site, stage 2
       Healing pressure ulcer of unspecified site, stage 2
       Pressure ulcer with abrasion, blister, partial thickness skin loss involving epidermis and/or dermis, unspecified site

    L89.93   Pressure ulcer of unspecified site, stage 3
       Healing pressure ulcer of unspecified site, stage 3
       Pressure ulcer with full thickness skin loss involving damage or necrosis of subcutaneous tissue, unspecified site

    L89.94   Pressure ulcer of unspecified site, stage 4
       Healing pressure ulcer of unspecified site, stage 4
       Pressure ulcer with necrosis of soft tissues through to underlying muscle, tendon, or bone, unspecified site

    L89.95   Pressure ulcer of unspecified site, unstageable

CHAPTER 12 (L00-L99)

- **L90** **Atrophic disorders of skin**
  - **L90.0** **Lichen sclerosus et atrophicus**
    - **Excludes2**   lichen sclerosus of external female genital organs (N90.4)
      - lichen sclerosus of external male genital organs (N48.0)
  - **L90.1** **Anetoderma of Schweninger-Buzzi**
  - **L90.2** **Anetoderma of Jadassohn-Pellizzari**
  - **L90.3** **Atrophoderma of Pasini and Pierini**
  - **L90.4** **Acrodermatitis chronica atrophicans**
  - **L90.5** **Scar conditions and fibrosis of skin**
    - Adherent scar (skin)
    - Cicatrix
    - Disfigurement of skin due to scar
    - Fibrosis of skin NOS
    - Scar NOS
    - **Excludes2**   hypertrophic scar (L91.0)
      - keloid scar (L91.0)
    - **Coding Clinic: 2016, Q2, P5; 2015, Q1, P19**
  - **L90.6** **Striae atrophicae**
  - **L90.8** **Other atrophic disorders of skin**
  - **L90.9** **Atrophic disorder of skin, unspecified**

- **L91** **Hypertrophic disorders of skin**
  - **L91.0** **Keloid scar**
    - Hypertrophic scar
    - Keloid
    - **Excludes2**   acne keloid (L73.0)
      - scar NOS (L90.5)
  - **L91.8** **Other hypertrophic disorders of the skin**
  - **L91.9** **Hypertrophic disorder of the skin, unspecified**

- **L92** **Granulomatous disorders of skin and subcutaneous tissue**
  - **Excludes2**   actinic granuloma (L57.5)
  - **L92.0** **Granuloma annulare**
    - Perforating granuloma annulare
  - **L92.1** **Necrobiosis lipoidica, not elsewhere classified**
    - **Excludes1**   necrobiosis lipoidica associated with diabetes mellitus (E08-E13 with .620)
  - **L92.2** **Granuloma faciale [eosinophilic granuloma of skin]**
  - **L92.3** **Foreign body granuloma of the skin and subcutaneous tissue**
    - Use additional code to identify the type of retained foreign body (Z18.-)
  - **L92.8** **Other granulomatous disorders of the skin and subcutaneous tissue**
  - **L92.9** **Granulomatous disorder of the skin and subcutaneous tissue, unspecified**
    - **Excludes2**   umbilical granuloma (P83.81)

- **L93** **Lupus erythematosus**
  - Use additional code for adverse effect, if applicable, to identify drug (T36-T50 with fifth or sixth character 5)
  - **Excludes1**   lupus exedens (A18.4)
    - lupus vulgaris (A18.4)
    - scleroderma (M34.-)
    - systemic lupus erythematosus (M32.-)
  - **L93.0** **Discoid lupus erythematosus**
    - Lupus erythematosus NOS
  - **L93.1** **Subacute cutaneous lupus erythematosus**
  - **L93.2** **Other local lupus erythematosus**
    - Lupus erythematosus profundus
    - Lupus panniculitis

- **L94** **Other localized connective tissue disorders**
  - **Excludes1**   systemic connective tissue disorders (M30-M36)
  - **L94.0** **Localized scleroderma [morphea]**
    - Circumscribed scleroderma
  - **L94.1** **Linear scleroderma**
    - En coup de sabre lesion
  - **L94.2** **Calcinosis cutis**
  - **L94.3** **Sclerodactyly**
  - **L94.4** **Gottron's papules**
  - **L94.5** **Poikiloderma vasculare atrophicans**
  - **L94.6** **Ainhum**
  - **L94.8** **Other specified localized connective tissue disorders**
  - **L94.9** **Localized connective tissue disorder, unspecified**

- **L95** **Vasculitis limited to skin, not elsewhere classified**
  - **Excludes1**   angioma serpiginosum (L81.7)
    - Henoch(-Schönlein) purpura (D69.0)
    - hypersensitivity angiitis (M31.0)
    - lupus panniculitis (L93.2)
    - panniculitis NOS (M79.3)
    - panniculitis of neck and back (M54.0-)
    - polyarteritis nodosa (M30.0)
    - relapsing panniculitis (M35.6)
    - rheumatoid vasculitis (M05.2)
    - serum sickness (T80.6-)
    - urticaria (L50.-)
    - Wegener's granulomatosis (M31.3-)
  - **L95.0** **Livedoid vasculitis**
    - Atrophie blanche (en plaque)
  - **L95.1** **Erythema elevatum diutinum**
  - **L95.8** **Other vasculitis limited to the skin**
  - **L95.9** **Vasculitis limited to the skin, unspecified**

- **L97** **Non-pressure chronic ulcer of lower limb, not elsewhere classified**
  - **Includes**   chronic ulcer of skin of lower limb NOS
    - non-healing ulcer of skin
    - non-infected sinus of skin
    - trophic ulcer NOS
    - tropical ulcer NOS
    - ulcer of skin of lower limb NOS
  - *Code first any associated underlying condition, such as:*
    - any associated gangrene (I96)
    - atherosclerosis of the lower extremities (I70.23-, I70.24-, I70.33-, I70.34-, I70.43-, I70.44-, I70.53-, I70.54-, I70.63-, I70.64-, I70.73-, I70.74-)
    - chronic venous hypertension (I87.31-, I87.33-)
    - diabetic ulcers (E08.621, E08.622, E09.621, E09.622, E10.621, E10.622, E11.621, E11.622, E13.621, E13.622)
    - postphlebitic syndrome (I87.01-, I87.03-)
    - postthrombotic syndrome (I87.01-, I87.03-)
    - varicose ulcer (I83.0-, I83.2-)
  - **Excludes2**   pressure ulcer (pressure area) (L89.-)
    - skin infections (L00-L08)
    - specific infections classified to A00-B99
  - **L97.1** **Non-pressure chronic ulcer of thigh**
    - **L97.10** **Non-pressure chronic ulcer of unspecified thigh**
      - **L97.101** **Non-pressure chronic ulcer of unspecified thigh limited to breakdown of skin**
      - **L97.102** **Non-pressure chronic ulcer of unspecified thigh with fat layer exposed**
      - **L97.103** **Non-pressure chronic ulcer of unspecified thigh with necrosis of muscle**
      - **L97.104** **Non-pressure chronic ulcer of unspecified thigh with necrosis of bone**
      - **L97.105** **Non-pressure chronic ulcer of unspecified thigh with muscle involvement without evidence of necrosis**

Item 12-11   **Scleroderma** means hard skin. It is a group of diseases that causes abnormal growth of connective tissues that support the skin and organs. There are two types: localized scleroderma affecting the skin and systemic scleroderma affecting blood vessels and internal organs and the skin.

▶ New   ⇒ Revised   ~~deleted~~ Deleted   Excludes 1   Excludes 2   Includes   Use additional   Code first   Code also   Key words

OGCR Official Guidelines   X Assign placeholder X   ● Use Additional Character(s)   ▷ Manifestation Code   **Coding Clinic**

L97.106   Non-pressure chronic ulcer of unspecified thigh with bone involvement without evidence of necrosis

L97.108   Non-pressure chronic ulcer of unspecified thigh with other specified severity

L97.109   Non-pressure chronic ulcer of unspecified thigh with unspecified severity

● L97.11   Non-pressure chronic ulcer of right thigh

L97.111   Non-pressure chronic ulcer of right thigh limited to breakdown of skin

L97.112   Non-pressure chronic ulcer of right thigh with fat layer exposed

L97.113   Non-pressure chronic ulcer of right thigh with necrosis of muscle

L97.114   Non-pressure chronic ulcer of right thigh with necrosis of bone

L97.115   Non-pressure chronic ulcer of right thigh with muscle involvement without evidence of necrosis

L97.116   Non-pressure chronic ulcer of right thigh with bone involvement without evidence of necrosis

L97.118   Non-pressure chronic ulcer of right thigh with other specified severity

L97.119   Non-pressure chronic ulcer of right thigh with unspecified severity

● L97.12   Non-pressure chronic ulcer of left thigh

L97.121   Non-pressure chronic ulcer of left thigh limited to breakdown of skin

L97.122   Non-pressure chronic ulcer of left thigh with fat layer exposed

L97.123   Non-pressure chronic ulcer of left thigh with necrosis of muscle

L97.124   Non-pressure chronic ulcer of left thigh with necrosis of bone

L97.125   Non-pressure chronic ulcer of left thigh with muscle involvement without evidence of necrosis

L97.126   Non-pressure chronic ulcer of left thigh with bone involvement without evidence of necrosis

L97.128   Non-pressure chronic ulcer of left thigh with other specified severity

L97.129   Non-pressure chronic ulcer of left thigh with unspecified severity

● L97.2   Non-pressure chronic ulcer of calf

● L97.20   Non-pressure chronic ulcer of unspecified calf

L97.201   Non-pressure chronic ulcer of unspecified calf limited to breakdown of skin

L97.202   Non-pressure chronic ulcer of unspecified calf with fat layer exposed

L97.203   Non-pressure chronic ulcer of unspecified calf with necrosis of muscle

L97.204   Non-pressure chronic ulcer of unspecified calf with necrosis of bone

L97.205   Non-pressure chronic ulcer of unspecified calf with muscle involvement without evidence of necrosis

L97.206   Non-pressure chronic ulcer of unspecified calf with bone involvement without evidence of necrosis

L97.208   Non-pressure chronic ulcer of unspecified calf with other specified severity

L97.209   Non-pressure chronic ulcer of unspecified calf with unspecified severity

● L97.21   Non-pressure chronic ulcer of right calf

L97.211   Non-pressure chronic ulcer of right calf limited to breakdown of skin

L97.212   Non-pressure chronic ulcer of right calf with fat layer exposed

L97.213   Non-pressure chronic ulcer of right calf with necrosis of muscle

L97.214   Non-pressure chronic ulcer of right calf with necrosis of bone

L97.215   Non-pressure chronic ulcer of right calf with muscle involvement without evidence of necrosis

L97.216   Non-pressure chronic ulcer of right calf with bone involvement without evidence of necrosis

L97.218   Non-pressure chronic ulcer of right calf with other specified severity

L97.219   Non-pressure chronic ulcer of right calf with unspecified severity

● L97.22   Non-pressure chronic ulcer of left calf

L97.221   Non-pressure chronic ulcer of left calf limited to breakdown of skin

L97.222   Non-pressure chronic ulcer of left calf with fat layer exposed

L97.223   Non-pressure chronic ulcer of left calf with necrosis of muscle

L97.224   Non-pressure chronic ulcer of left calf with necrosis of bone

L97.225   Non-pressure chronic ulcer of left calf with muscle involvement without evidence of necrosis

L97.226   Non-pressure chronic ulcer of left calf with bone involvement without evidence of necrosis

L97.228   Non-pressure chronic ulcer of left calf with other specified severity

L97.229   Non-pressure chronic ulcer of left calf with unspecified severity

● L97.3   Non-pressure chronic ulcer of ankle

● L97.30   Non-pressure chronic ulcer of unspecified ankle

L97.301   Non-pressure chronic ulcer of unspecified ankle limited to breakdown of skin

L97.302   Non-pressure chronic ulcer of unspecified ankle with fat layer exposed

L97.303   Non-pressure chronic ulcer of unspecified ankle with necrosis of muscle

L97.304   Non-pressure chronic ulcer of unspecified ankle with necrosis of bone

L97.305   Non-pressure chronic ulcer of unspecified ankle with muscle involvement without evidence of necrosis

L97.306   Non-pressure chronic ulcer of unspecified ankle with bone involvement without evidence of necrosis

L97.308   Non-pressure chronic ulcer of unspecified ankle with other specified severity

L97.309   Non-pressure chronic ulcer of unspecified ankle with unspecified severity

CHAPTER 12 (L00-L99)

CHAPTER 12 (L00-L99)

● **L97.31**   **Non-pressure chronic ulcer of right ankle**

    L97.311   Non-pressure chronic ulcer of right ankle limited to breakdown of skin

    L97.312   Non-pressure chronic ulcer of right ankle with fat layer exposed

    L97.313   Non-pressure chronic ulcer of right ankle with necrosis of muscle

    L97.314   Non-pressure chronic ulcer of right ankle with necrosis of bone

    L97.315   Non-pressure chronic ulcer of right ankle with muscle involvement without evidence of necrosis
             Coding Clinic: 2017, Q4, P17

    L97.316   Non-pressure chronic ulcer of right ankle with bone involvement without evidence of necrosis

    L97.318   Non-pressure chronic ulcer of right ankle with other specified severity

    L97.319   Non-pressure chronic ulcer of right ankle with unspecified severity

● **L97.32**   **Non-pressure chronic ulcer of left ankle**

    L97.321   Non-pressure chronic ulcer of left ankle limited to breakdown of skin

    L97.322   Non-pressure chronic ulcer of left ankle with fat layer exposed

    L97.323   Non-pressure chronic ulcer of left ankle with necrosis of muscle

    L97.324   Non-pressure chronic ulcer of left ankle with necrosis of bone

    L97.325   Non-pressure chronic ulcer of left ankle with muscle involvement without evidence of necrosis

    L97.326   Non-pressure chronic ulcer of left ankle with bone involvement without evidence of necrosis

    L97.328   Non-pressure chronic ulcer of left ankle with other specified severity

    L97.329   Non-pressure chronic ulcer of left ankle with unspecified severity

● **L97.4**   **Non-pressure chronic ulcer of heel and midfoot**
     Non-pressure chronic ulcer of plantar surface of midfoot

   ● **L97.40**   **Non-pressure chronic ulcer of unspecified heel and midfoot**

    L97.401   Non-pressure chronic ulcer of unspecified heel and midfoot limited to breakdown of skin

    L97.402   Non-pressure chronic ulcer of unspecified heel and midfoot with fat layer exposed

    L97.403   Non-pressure chronic ulcer of unspecified heel and midfoot with necrosis of muscle

    L97.404   Non-pressure chronic ulcer of unspecified heel and midfoot with necrosis of bone

    L97.405   Non-pressure chronic ulcer of unspecified heel and midfoot with muscle involvement without evidence of necrosis

    L97.406   Non-pressure chronic ulcer of unspecified heel and midfoot with bone involvement without evidence of necrosis

    L97.408   Non-pressure chronic ulcer of unspecified heel and midfoot with other specified severity

    L97.409   Non-pressure chronic ulcer of unspecified heel and midfoot with unspecified severity

● **L97.41**   **Non-pressure chronic ulcer of right heel and midfoot**

    L97.411   Non-pressure chronic ulcer of right heel and midfoot limited to breakdown of skin

    L97.412   Non-pressure chronic ulcer of right heel and midfoot with fat layer exposed

    L97.413   Non-pressure chronic ulcer of right heel and midfoot with necrosis of muscle

    L97.414   Non-pressure chronic ulcer of right heel and midfoot with necrosis of bone

    L97.415   Non-pressure chronic ulcer of right heel and midfoot with muscle involvement without evidence of necrosis

    L97.416   Non-pressure chronic ulcer of right heel and midfoot with bone involvement without evidence of necrosis

    L97.418   Non-pressure chronic ulcer of right heel and midfoot with other specified severity

    L97.419   Non-pressure chronic ulcer of right heel and midfoot with unspecified severity

● **L97.42**   **Non-pressure chronic ulcer of left heel and midfoot**

    L97.421   Non-pressure chronic ulcer of left heel and midfoot limited to breakdown of skin
             Coding Clinic: 2016, Q1, P13

    L97.422   Non-pressure chronic ulcer of left heel and midfoot with fat layer exposed

    L97.423   Non-pressure chronic ulcer of left heel and midfoot with necrosis of muscle

    L97.424   Non-pressure chronic ulcer of left heel and midfoot with necrosis of bone

    L97.425   Non-pressure chronic ulcer of left heel and midfoot with muscle involvement without evidence of necrosis

    L97.426   Non-pressure chronic ulcer of left heel and midfoot with bone involvement without evidence of necrosis

    L97.428   Non-pressure chronic ulcer of left heel and midfoot with other specified severity

    L97.429   Non-pressure chronic ulcer of left heel and midfoot with unspecified severity

● **L97.5**   **Non-pressure chronic ulcer of other part of foot**
     Non-pressure chronic ulcer of toe

   ● **L97.50**   **Non-pressure chronic ulcer of other part of unspecified foot**

    L97.501   Non-pressure chronic ulcer of other part of unspecified foot limited to breakdown of skin

    L97.502   Non-pressure chronic ulcer of other part of unspecified foot with fat layer exposed

▶ New   ⟾ Revised   ~~deleted~~ Deleted   Excludes 1   Excludes 2   Includes   Use additional   Code first   Code also   Key words
     OGCR Official Guidelines   X Assign placeholder X   ● Use Additional Character(s)   ▶ Manifestation Code   **Coding Clinic**

L97.503   Non-pressure chronic ulcer of other part of unspecified foot with necrosis of muscle

L97.504   Non-pressure chronic ulcer of other part of unspecified foot with necrosis of bone

L97.505   Non-pressure chronic ulcer of other part of unspecified foot with muscle involvement without evidence of necrosis

L97.506   Non-pressure chronic ulcer of other part of unspecified foot with bone involvement without evidence of necrosis

L97.508   Non-pressure chronic ulcer of other part of unspecified foot with other specified severity

L97.509   Non-pressure chronic ulcer of other part of unspecified foot with unspecified severity

● L97.51   Non-pressure chronic ulcer of other part of right foot

L97.511   Non-pressure chronic ulcer of other part of right foot limited to breakdown of skin

L97.512   Non-pressure chronic ulcer of other part of right foot with fat layer exposed

L97.513   Non-pressure chronic ulcer of other part of right foot with necrosis of muscle

L97.514   Non-pressure chronic ulcer of other part of right foot with necrosis of bone

L97.515   Non-pressure chronic ulcer of other part of right foot with muscle involvement without evidence of necrosis

L97.516   Non-pressure chronic ulcer of other part of right foot with bone involvement without evidence of necrosis

L97.518   Non-pressure chronic ulcer of other part of right foot with other specified severity

L97.519   Non-pressure chronic ulcer of other part of right foot with unspecified severity

● L97.52   Non-pressure chronic ulcer of other part of left foot

L97.521   Non-pressure chronic ulcer of other part of left foot limited to breakdown of skin

L97.522   Non-pressure chronic ulcer of other part of left foot with fat layer exposed

L97.523   Non-pressure chronic ulcer of other part of left foot with necrosis of muscle

L97.524   Non-pressure chronic ulcer of other part of left foot with necrosis of bone

L97.525   Non-pressure chronic ulcer of other part of left foot with muscle involvement without evidence of necrosis

L97.526   Non-pressure chronic ulcer of other part of left foot with bone involvement without evidence of necrosis

L97.528   Non-pressure chronic ulcer of other part of left foot with other specified severity

L97.529   Non-pressure chronic ulcer of other part of left foot with unspecified severity

● L97.8   Non-pressure chronic ulcer of other part of lower leg

● L97.80   Non-pressure chronic ulcer of other part of unspecified lower leg

L97.801   Non-pressure chronic ulcer of other part of unspecified lower leg limited to breakdown of skin

L97.802   Non-pressure chronic ulcer of other part of unspecified lower leg with fat layer exposed

L97.803   Non-pressure chronic ulcer of other part of unspecified lower leg with necrosis of muscle

L97.804   Non-pressure chronic ulcer of other part of unspecified lower leg with necrosis of bone

L97.805   Non-pressure chronic ulcer of other part of unspecified lower leg with muscle involvement without evidence of necrosis

L97.806   Non-pressure chronic ulcer of other part of unspecified lower leg with bone involvement without evidence of necrosis

L97.808   Non-pressure chronic ulcer of other part of unspecified lower leg with other specified severity

L97.809   Non-pressure chronic ulcer of other part of unspecified lower leg with unspecified severity

● L97.81   Non-pressure chronic ulcer of other part of right lower leg

L97.811   Non-pressure chronic ulcer of other part of right lower leg limited to breakdown of skin

L97.812   Non-pressure chronic ulcer of other part of right lower leg with fat layer exposed

L97.813   Non-pressure chronic ulcer of other part of right lower leg with necrosis of muscle

L97.814   Non-pressure chronic ulcer of other part of right lower leg with necrosis of bone

L97.815   Non-pressure chronic ulcer of other part of right lower leg with muscle involvement without evidence of necrosis

L97.816   Non-pressure chronic ulcer of other part of right lower leg with bone involvement without evidence of necrosis

L97.818   Non-pressure chronic ulcer of other part of right lower leg with other specified severity

L97.819   Non-pressure chronic ulcer of other part of right lower leg with unspecified severity

CHAPTER 12 (L00-L99)

● **L97.82**   Non-pressure chronic ulcer of other part of left lower leg

     L97.821   Non-pressure chronic ulcer of other part of left lower leg limited to breakdown of skin

     L97.822   Non-pressure chronic ulcer of other part of left lower leg with fat layer exposed

     L97.823   Non-pressure chronic ulcer of other part of left lower leg with necrosis of muscle

     L97.824   Non-pressure chronic ulcer of other part of left lower leg with necrosis of bone

     L97.825   Non-pressure chronic ulcer of other part of left lower leg with muscle involvement without evidence of necrosis

     L97.826   Non-pressure chronic ulcer of other part of left lower leg with bone involvement without evidence of necrosis

     L97.828   Non-pressure chronic ulcer of other part of left lower leg with other specified severity

     L97.829   Non-pressure chronic ulcer of other part of left lower leg with unspecified severity

● **L97.9**   Non-pressure chronic ulcer of unspecified part of lower leg

   ● **L97.90**   Non-pressure chronic ulcer of unspecified part of unspecified lower leg

     L97.901   Non-pressure chronic ulcer of unspecified part of unspecified lower leg limited to breakdown of skin

     L97.902   Non-pressure chronic ulcer of unspecified part of unspecified lower leg with fat layer exposed

     L97.903   Non-pressure chronic ulcer of unspecified part of unspecified lower leg with necrosis of muscle

     L97.904   Non-pressure chronic ulcer of unspecified part of unspecified lower leg with necrosis of bone

     L97.905   Non-pressure chronic ulcer of unspecified part of unspecified lower leg with muscle involvement without evidence of necrosis

     L97.906   Non-pressure chronic ulcer of unspecified part of unspecified lower leg with bone involvement without evidence of necrosis

     L97.908   Non-pressure chronic ulcer of unspecified part of unspecified lower leg with other specified severity

     L97.909   Non-pressure chronic ulcer of unspecified part of unspecified lower leg with unspecified severity

   ● **L97.91**   Non-pressure chronic ulcer of unspecified part of right lower leg

     L97.911   Non-pressure chronic ulcer of unspecified part of right lower leg limited to breakdown of skin

     L97.912   Non-pressure chronic ulcer of unspecified part of right lower leg with fat layer exposed

     L97.913   Non-pressure chronic ulcer of unspecified part of right lower leg with necrosis of muscle

     L97.914   Non-pressure chronic ulcer of unspecified part of right lower leg with necrosis of bone

     L97.915   Non-pressure chronic ulcer of unspecified part of right lower leg with muscle involvement without evidence of necrosis

     L97.916   Non-pressure chronic ulcer of unspecified part of right lower leg with bone involvement without evidence of necrosis

     L97.918   Non-pressure chronic ulcer of unspecified part of right lower leg with other specified severity

     L97.919   Non-pressure chronic ulcer of unspecified part of right lower leg with unspecified severity

● **L97.92**   Non-pressure chronic ulcer of unspecified part of left lower leg

     L97.921   Non-pressure chronic ulcer of unspecified part of left lower leg limited to breakdown of skin

     L97.922   Non-pressure chronic ulcer of unspecified part of left lower leg with fat layer exposed

     L97.923   Non-pressure chronic ulcer of unspecified part of left lower leg with necrosis of muscle

     L97.924   Non-pressure chronic ulcer of unspecified part of left lower leg with necrosis of bone

     L97.925   Non-pressure chronic ulcer of unspecified part of left lower leg with muscle involvement without evidence of necrosis

     L97.926   Non-pressure chronic ulcer of unspecified part of left lower leg with bone involvement without evidence of necrosis

     L97.928   Non-pressure chronic ulcer of unspecified part of left lower leg with other specified severity

     L97.929   Non-pressure chronic ulcer of unspecified part of left lower leg with unspecified severity

● **L98**   Other disorders of skin and subcutaneous tissue, not elsewhere classified

L98.0   Pyogenic granuloma

   Excludes2   pyogenic granuloma of gingiva (K06.8)
                 pyogenic granuloma of maxillary alveolar ridge (K04.5)
                 pyogenic granuloma of oral mucosa (K13.4)

L98.1   Factitial dermatitis
     Neurotic excoriation

   Excludes1   Excoriation (skin-picking) disorder (F42.4)

   Coding Clinic: 2016, Q4, P15

L98.2   Febrile neutrophilic dermatosis [Sweet]

L98.3   Eosinophilic cellulitis [Wells]

▶ New   ⇒ Revised   ~~deleted~~ Deleted   Excludes 1   Excludes 2   Includes   Use additional   Code first   Code also   Key words

OGCR Official Guidelines   X Assign placeholder X   ● Use Additional Character(s)   ▶ Manifestation Code   **Coding Clinic**

● **L98.4**   **Non-pressure chronic ulcer of skin, not elsewhere classified**
Chronic ulcer of skin NOS
Tropical ulcer NOS
Ulcer of skin NOS

> **Excludes2**   pressure ulcer (pressure area) (L89.-)
> gangrene (I96)
> skin infections (L00-L08)
> specific infections classified to A00-B99
> ulcer of lower limb NEC (L97.-)
> varicose ulcer (I83.0-I82.2)

● **L98.41**   **Non-pressure chronic ulcer of buttock**

   L98.411   Non-pressure chronic ulcer of buttock limited to breakdown of skin

   L98.412   Non-pressure chronic ulcer of buttock with fat layer exposed

   L98.413   Non-pressure chronic ulcer of buttock with necrosis of muscle

   L98.414   Non-pressure chronic ulcer of buttock with necrosis of bone

   L98.415   Non-pressure chronic ulcer of buttock with muscle involvement without evidence of necrosis

   L98.416   Non-pressure chronic ulcer of buttock with bone involvement without evidence of necrosis

   L98.418   Non-pressure chronic ulcer of buttock with other specified severity

   L98.419   Non-pressure chronic ulcer of buttock with unspecified severity

● **L98.42**   **Non-pressure chronic ulcer of back**

   L98.421   Non-pressure chronic ulcer of back limited to breakdown of skin

   L98.422   Non-pressure chronic ulcer of back with fat layer exposed

   L98.423   Non-pressure chronic ulcer of back with necrosis of muscle

   L98.424   Non-pressure chronic ulcer of back with necrosis of bone

   L98.425   Non-pressure chronic ulcer of back with muscle involvement without evidence of necrosis

   L98.426   Non-pressure chronic ulcer of back with bone involvement without evidence of necrosis

   L98.428   Non-pressure chronic ulcer of back with other specified severity

   L98.429   Non-pressure chronic ulcer of back with unspecified severity

● **L98.49**   **Non-pressure chronic ulcer of skin of other sites**
Non-pressure chronic ulcer of skin NOS

   L98.491   Non-pressure chronic ulcer of skin of other sites limited to breakdown of skin

   L98.492   Non-pressure chronic ulcer of skin of other sites with fat layer exposed

   L98.493   Non-pressure chronic ulcer of skin of other sites with necrosis of muscle

   L98.494   Non-pressure chronic ulcer of skin of other sites with necrosis of bone

➡ **L98.495**   Non-pressure chronic ulcer of skin of other sites with muscle involvement without evidence of necrosis

➡ **L98.496**   Non-pressure chronic ulcer of skin of other sites with bone involvement without evidence of necrosis

➡ **L98.498**   Non-pressure chronic ulcer of skin of other sites with other specified severity

   L98.499   Non-pressure chronic ulcer of skin of other sites with unspecified severity

L98.5   **Mucinosis of the skin**
Focal mucinosis
Lichen myxedematosus
Reticular erythematous mucinosis

> **Excludes1**   focal oral mucinosis (K13.79)
> myxedema (E03.9)

L98.6   **Other infiltrative disorders of the skin and subcutaneous tissue**

> **Excludes1**   hyalinosis cutis et mucosae (E78.89)

L98.7   **Excessive and redundant skin and subcutaneous tissue**
Loose or sagging skin following bariatric surgery weight loss
Loose or sagging skin following dietary weight loss
Loose or sagging skin, NOS

> **Excludes2**   acquired excess or redundant skin of eyelid (H02.3-)
> congenital excess or redundant skin of eyelid (Q10.3)
> skin changes due to chronic exposure to nonionizing radiation (L57.-)

Coding Clinic: 2016, Q4, P36

L98.8   **Other specified disorders of the skin and subcutaneous tissue**

Coding Clinic: 2013, Q2, P32

L98.9   **Disorder of the skin and subcutaneous tissue, unspecified**

▶ *L99*   *Other disorders of skin and subcutaneous tissue in diseases classified elsewhere*

> *Code first underlying disease, such as:*
> amyloidosis (E85.-)

> **Excludes1**   skin disorders in diabetes (E08-E13 with .62)
> skin disorders in gonorrhea (A54.89)
> skin disorders in syphilis (A51.31, A52.79)

CHAPTER 12 (L00-L99)

CHAPTER 13

DISEASES OF THE MUSCULOSKELETAL SYSTEM AND CONNECTIVE TISSUE (M00-M99)

OGCR Chapter-Specific Coding Guidelines

13. **Chapter 13: Diseases of the Musculoskeletal System and Connective Tissue (M00-M99)**

   a. Site and laterality
   Most of the codes within Chapter 13 have site and laterality designations. The site represents the bone, joint or the muscle involved. For some conditions where more than one bone, joint or muscle is usually involved, such as osteoarthritis, there is a "multiple sites" code available. For categories where no multiple site code is provided and more than one bone, joint or muscle is involved, multiple codes should be used to indicate the different sites involved.

   1) Bone versus joint
   For certain conditions, the bone may be affected at the upper or lower end, (e.g., avascular necrosis of bone, M87, Osteoporosis, M80, M81). Though the portion of the bone affected may be at the joint, the site designation will be the bone, not the joint.

   b. Acute traumatic versus chronic or recurrent musculoskeletal conditions
   Many musculoskeletal conditions are a result of previous injury or trauma to a site, or are recurrent conditions. Bone, joint or muscle conditions that are the result of a healed injury are usually found in Chapter 13. Recurrent bone, joint or muscle conditions are also usually found in Chapter 13. Any current, acute injury should be coded to the appropriate injury code from Chapter 19. Chronic or recurrent conditions should generally be coded with a code from Chapter 13. If it is difficult to determine from the documentation in the record which code is best to describe a condition, query the provider.

   c. Coding of Pathologic Fractures
   7th character A is for use as long as the patient is receiving active treatment for the fracture. While the patient may be seen by a new or different provider over the course of treatment for a pathological fracture, assignment of the 7th character is based on whether the patient is undergoing active treatment and not whether the provider is seeing the patient for the first time.
      7th character, D is to be used for encounters after the patient has completed active treatment for the fracture and is receiving routine care for the fracture during the healing or recovery phase. The other 7th characters, listed under each subcategory in the Tabular List, are to be used for subsequent encounters for treatment of problems associated with the healing, such as malunions, nonunions, and sequelae.
      Care for complications of surgical treatment for fracture repairs during the healing or recovery phase should be coded with the appropriate complication codes.
      See Section I.C.19. Coding of traumatic fractures.

   d. Osteoporosis
   Osteoporosis is a systemic condition, meaning that all bones of the musculoskeletal system are affected. Therefore, site is not a component of the codes under category M81, Osteoporosis without current pathological fracture. The site codes under category M80, Osteoporosis with current pathological fracture, identify the site of the fracture, not the osteoporosis.

   1) Osteoporosis without pathological fracture
   Category M81, Osteoporosis without current pathological fracture, is for use for patients with osteoporosis who do not currently have a pathologic fracture due to the osteoporosis, even if they have had a fracture in the past. For patients with a history of osteoporosis fractures, status code Z87.310, Personal history of (healed) osteoporosis fracture, should follow the code from M81.

   2) Osteoporosis with current pathological fracture
   Category M80, Osteoporosis with current pathological fracture, is for patients who have a current pathologic fracture at the time of an encounter. The codes under M80 identify the site of the fracture. A code from category M80, not a traumatic fracture code, should be used for any patient with known osteoporosis who suffers a fracture, even if the patient had a minor fall or trauma, if that fall or trauma would not usually break a normal, healthy bone.

CHAPTER 13

DISEASES OF THE MUSCULOSKELETAL SYSTEM AND CONNECTIVE TISSUE (M00-M99)

Note: Use an external cause code following the code for the musculoskeletal condition, if applicable, to identify the cause of the musculoskeletal condition

Excludes2 arthropathic psoriasis (L40.5-)
   certain conditions originating in the perinatal period (P04-P96)
   certain infectious and parasitic diseases (A00-B99)
   compartment syndrome (traumatic) (T79.A-)
   complications of pregnancy, childbirth and the puerperium (O00-O9A)
   congenital malformations, deformations, and chromosomal abnormalities (Q00-Q99)
   endocrine, nutritional and metabolic diseases (E00-E88)
   injury, poisoning and certain other consequences of external causes (S00-T88)
   neoplasms (C00-D49)
   symptoms, signs and abnormal clinical and laboratory findings, not elsewhere classified (R00-R94)

This chapter contains the following blocks:

M00-M02	Infectious arthropathies
▶ M04	Autoinflammatory syndromes
M05-M14	Inflammatory polyarthropathies
M15-M19	Osteoarthritis
M20-M25	Other joint disorders
M26-M27	Dentofacial anomalies [including malocclusion] and other disorders of jaw
M30-M36	Systemic connective tissue disorders
M40-M43	Deforming dorsopathies
M45-M49	Spondylopathies
M50-M54	Other dorsopathies
M60-M63	Disorders of muscles
M65-M67	Disorders of synovium and tendon
M70-M79	Other soft tissue disorders
M80-M85	Disorders of bone density and structure
M86-M90	Other osteopathies
M91-M94	Chondropathies
M95	Other disorders of the musculoskeletal system and connective tissue
M96	Intraoperative and postprocedural complications and disorders of musculoskeletal system, not elsewhere classified
▶ M97	Periprosthetic fracture around internal prosthetic joint
M99	Biomechanical lesions, not elsewhere classified

Coding Clinic: 2016, Q4, P124

ARTHROPATHIES (M00-M25)

Includes Disorders affecting predominantly peripheral (limb) joints

INFECTIOUS ARTHROPATHIES (M00-M02)

Note: This block comprises arthropathies due to microbiological agents.

   Distinction is made between the following types of etiological relationship:

   a) direct infection of joint, where organisms invade synovial tissue and microbial antigen is present in the joint;

   b) indirect infection, which may be of two types: a reactive arthropathy, where microbial infection of the body is established but neither organisms nor antigens can be identified in the joint, and a postinfective arthropathy, where microbial antigen is present but recovery of an organism is inconstant and evidence of local multiplication is lacking.

▶ New ⇒ Revised ~~deleted~~ Deleted | Excludes 1 | | Excludes 2 | | Includes | | Use additional | | Code first | | Code also | | Key words |

OGCR Official Guidelines X Assign placeholder X ● Use Additional Character(s) ▶ Manifestation Code **Coding Clinic**

● **M00**   Pyogenic arthritis

   ● **M00.0**   Staphylococcal arthritis and polyarthritis

      Use additional code (B95.61-B95.8) to identify bacterial agent

      Excludes2   infection and inflammatory reaction due to internal joint prosthesis (T84.5-)

      M00.00   Staphylococcal arthritis, unspecified joint

     ● **M00.01**   Staphylococcal arthritis, shoulder

        M00.011   Staphylococcal arthritis, right shoulder

        M00.012   Staphylococcal arthritis, left shoulder

        M00.019   Staphylococcal arthritis, unspecified shoulder

     ● **M00.02**   Staphylococcal arthritis, elbow

        M00.021   Staphylococcal arthritis, right elbow

        M00.022   Staphylococcal arthritis, left elbow

        M00.029   Staphylococcal arthritis, unspecified elbow

     ● **M00.03**   Staphylococcal arthritis, wrist

        Staphylococcal arthritis of carpal bones

        M00.031   Staphylococcal arthritis, right wrist

        M00.032   Staphylococcal arthritis, left wrist

        M00.039   Staphylococcal arthritis, unspecified wrist

     ● **M00.04**   Staphylococcal arthritis, hand

        Staphylococcal arthritis of metacarpus and phalanges

        M00.041   Staphylococcal arthritis, right hand

        M00.042   Staphylococcal arthritis, left hand

        M00.049   Staphylococcal arthritis, unspecified hand

     ● **M00.05**   Staphylococcal arthritis, hip

        M00.051   Staphylococcal arthritis, right hip

        M00.052   Staphylococcal arthritis, left hip

        M00.059   Staphylococcal arthritis, unspecified hip

     ● **M00.06**   Staphylococcal arthritis, knee

        M00.061   Staphylococcal arthritis, right knee

        M00.062   Staphylococcal arthritis, left knee

        M00.069   Staphylococcal arthritis, unspecified knee

     ● **M00.07**   Staphylococcal arthritis, ankle and foot

        Staphylococcal arthritis, tarsus, metatarsus and phalanges

        M00.071   Staphylococcal arthritis, right ankle and foot

        M00.072   Staphylococcal arthritis, left ankle and foot

        M00.079   Staphylococcal arthritis, unspecified ankle and foot

      M00.08   Staphylococcal arthritis, vertebrae

      M00.09   Staphylococcal polyarthritis

   ● **M00.1**   Pneumococcal arthritis and polyarthritis

      M00.10   Pneumococcal arthritis, unspecified joint

     ● **M00.11**   Pneumococcal arthritis, shoulder

        M00.111   Pneumococcal arthritis, right shoulder

        M00.112   Pneumococcal arthritis, left shoulder

        M00.119   Pneumococcal arthritis, unspecified shoulder

     ● **M00.12**   Pneumococcal arthritis, elbow

        M00.121   Pneumococcal arthritis, right elbow

        M00.122   Pneumococcal arthritis, left elbow

        M00.129   Pneumococcal arthritis, unspecified elbow

     ● **M00.13**   Pneumococcal arthritis, wrist

        Pneumococcal arthritis of carpal bones

        M00.131   Pneumococcal arthritis, right wrist

        M00.132   Pneumococcal arthritis, left wrist

        M00.139   Pneumococcal arthritis, unspecified wrist

     ● **M00.14**   Pneumococcal arthritis, hand

        Pneumococcal arthritis of metacarpus and phalanges

        M00.141   Pneumococcal arthritis, right hand

        M00.142   Pneumococcal arthritis, left hand

        M00.149   Pneumococcal arthritis, unspecified hand

     ● **M00.15**   Pneumococcal arthritis, hip

        M00.151   Pneumococcal arthritis, right hip

        M00.152   Pneumococcal arthritis, left hip

        M00.159   Pneumococcal arthritis, unspecified hip

     ● **M00.16**   Pneumococcal arthritis, knee

        M00.161   Pneumococcal arthritis, right knee

        M00.162   Pneumococcal arthritis, left knee

        M00.169   Pneumococcal arthritis, unspecified knee

     ● **M00.17**   Pneumococcal arthritis, ankle and foot

        Pneumococcal arthritis, tarsus, metatarsus and phalanges

        M00.171   Pneumococcal arthritis, right ankle and foot

        M00.172   Pneumococcal arthritis, left ankle and foot

        M00.179   Pneumococcal arthritis, unspecified ankle and foot

      M00.18   Pneumococcal arthritis, vertebrae

      M00.19   Pneumococcal polyarthritis

   ● **M00.2**   Other streptococcal arthritis and polyarthritis

      Use additional code (B95.0-B95.2, B95.4-B95.5) to identify bacterial agent

      M00.20   Other streptococcal arthritis, unspecified joint

     ● **M00.21**   Other streptococcal arthritis, shoulder

        M00.211   Other streptococcal arthritis, right shoulder

        M00.212   Other streptococcal arthritis, left shoulder

        M00.219   Other streptococcal arthritis, unspecified shoulder

     ● **M00.22**   Other streptococcal arthritis, elbow

        M00.221   Other streptococcal arthritis, right elbow

        M00.222   Other streptococcal arthritis, left elbow

        M00.229   Other streptococcal arthritis, unspecified elbow

     ● **M00.23**   Other streptococcal arthritis, wrist

        Other streptococcal arthritis of carpal bones

        M00.231   Other streptococcal arthritis, right wrist

        M00.232   Other streptococcal arthritis, left wrist

        M00.239   Other streptococcal arthritis, unspecified wrist

     ● **M00.24**   Other streptococcal arthritis, hand

        Other streptococcal arthritis metacarpus and phalanges

        M00.241   Other streptococcal arthritis, right hand

        M00.242   Other streptococcal arthritis, left hand

        M00.249   Other streptococcal arthritis, unspecified hand

CHAPTER 13 (M00-M99)

● M00.25 Other streptococcal arthritis, **hip**
　　　M00.251 Other streptococcal arthritis, **right hip**
　　　M00.252 Other streptococcal arthritis, **left hip**
　　　M00.259 Other streptococcal arthritis, **unspecified hip**
● M00.26 Other streptococcal arthritis, **knee**
　　　M00.261 Other streptococcal arthritis, **right knee**
　　　M00.262 Other streptococcal arthritis, **left knee**
　　　M00.269 Other streptococcal arthritis, **unspecified knee**
● M00.27 Other streptococcal arthritis, **ankle and foot**
　　　Other streptococcal arthritis, tarsus, metatarsus and phalanges
　　　M00.271 Other streptococcal arthritis, **right ankle and foot**
　　　M00.272 Other streptococcal arthritis, **left ankle and foot**
　　　M00.279 Other streptococcal arthritis, **unspecified ankle and foot**
　M00.28 Other streptococcal arthritis, **vertebrae**
　M00.29 Other streptococcal polyarthritis
● M00.8 Arthritis and polyarthritis **due to other bacteria**
　　　Use additional code (B96) to identify bacteria
　M00.80 Arthritis due to other bacteria, **unspecified joint**
● M00.81 Arthritis due to other bacteria, **shoulder**
　　　M00.811 Arthritis due to other bacteria, **right shoulder**
　　　M00.812 Arthritis due to other bacteria, **left shoulder**
　　　M00.819 Arthritis due to other bacteria, **unspecified shoulder**
● M00.82 Arthritis due to other bacteria, **elbow**
　　　M00.821 Arthritis due to other bacteria, **right elbow**
　　　M00.822 Arthritis due to other bacteria, **left elbow**
　　　M00.829 Arthritis due to other bacteria, **unspecified elbow**
● M00.83 Arthritis due to other bacteria, **wrist**
　　　Arthritis due to other bacteria, carpal bones
　　　M00.831 Arthritis due to other bacteria, **right wrist**
　　　M00.832 Arthritis due to other bacteria, **left wrist**
　　　M00.839 Arthritis due to other bacteria, **unspecified wrist**
● M00.84 Arthritis due to other bacteria, **hand**
　　　Arthritis due to other bacteria, metacarpus and phalanges
　　　M00.841 Arthritis due to other bacteria, **right hand**
　　　M00.842 Arthritis due to other bacteria, **left hand**
　　　M00.849 Arthritis due to other bacteria, **unspecified hand**
● M00.85 Arthritis due to other bacteria, **hip**
　　　M00.851 Arthritis due to other bacteria, **right hip**
　　　M00.852 Arthritis due to other bacteria, **left hip**
　　　M00.859 Arthritis due to other bacteria, **unspecified hip**

● M00.86 Arthritis due to other bacteria, **knee**
　　　M00.861 Arthritis due to other bacteria, **right knee**
　　　M00.862 Arthritis due to other bacteria, **left knee**
　　　M00.869 Arthritis due to other bacteria, **unspecified knee**
● M00.87 Arthritis due to other bacteria, **ankle and foot**
　　　Arthritis due to other bacteria, tarsus, metatarsus, and phalanges
　　　M00.871 Arthritis due to other bacteria, **right ankle and foot**
　　　M00.872 Arthritis due to other bacteria, **left ankle and foot**
　　　M00.879 Arthritis due to other bacteria, **unspecified ankle and foot**
　M00.88 Arthritis due to other bacteria, **vertebrae**
　M00.89 Polyarthritis due to other bacteria
　M00.9 Pyogenic arthritis, **unspecified**
　　　Infective arthritis NOS

● M01 Direct infections of joint in infectious and parasitic diseases classified elsewhere
　　　Code first underlying disease, such as:
　　　leprosy [Hansen's disease] (A30.-)
　　　mycoses (B35-B49)
　　　O'nyong-nyong fever (A92.1)
　　　paratyphoid fever (A01.1-A01.4)

　　Excludes1 arthropathy in Lyme disease (A69.23)
　　　　　　gonococcal arthritis (A54.42)
　　　　　　meningococcal arthritis (A39.83)
　　　　　　mumps arthritis (B26.85)
　　　　　　postinfective arthropathy (M02.-)
　　　　　　postmeningococcal arthritis (A39.84)
　　　　　　reactive arthritis (M02.3)
　　　　　　rubella arthritis (B06.82)
　　　　　　sarcoidosis arthritis (D86.86)
　　　　　　typhoid fever arthritis (A01.04)
　　　　　　tuberculosis arthritis (A18.01-A18.02)

● M01.X Direct infection of joint in infectious and parasitic diseases classified elsewhere
　▷ *M01.X0 Direct infection of unspecified joint in infectious and parasitic diseases classified elsewhere*
　● M01.X1 Direct infection of **shoulder** joint in infectious and parasitic diseases classified elsewhere
　　▷ *M01.X11 Direct infection of right shoulder in infectious and parasitic diseases classified elsewhere*
　　▷ *M01.X12 Direct infection of left shoulder in infectious and parasitic diseases classified elsewhere*
　　▷ *M01.X19 Direct infection of unspecified shoulder in infectious and parasitic diseases classified elsewhere*
　● M01.X2 Direct infection of **elbow** in infectious and parasitic diseases classified elsewhere
　　▷ *M01.X21 Direct infection of right elbow in infectious and parasitic diseases classified elsewhere*
　　▷ *M01.X22 Direct infection of left elbow in infectious and parasitic diseases classified elsewhere*
　　▷ *M01.X29 Direct infection of unspecified elbow in infectious and parasitic diseases classified elsewhere*

▶ New　⇒ Revised　~~deleted~~ Deleted　Excludes 1　Excludes 2　Includes　Use additional　Code first　Code also　Key words
OGCR Official Guidelines　X Assign placeholder X　● Use Additional Character(s)　▷ Manifestation Code　**Coding Clinic**

● **M01.X3** Direct infection of wrist in infectious and parasitic diseases classified elsewhere

    Direct infection of carpal bones in infectious and parasitic diseases classified elsewhere

    ▷ *M01.X31* *Direct infection of right wrist in infectious and parasitic diseases classified elsewhere*

    ▷ *M01.X32* *Direct infection of left wrist in infectious and parasitic diseases classified elsewhere*

    ▷ *M01.X39* *Direct infection of unspecified wrist in infectious and parasitic diseases classified elsewhere*

● **M01.X4** Direct infection of hand in infectious and parasitic diseases classified elsewhere

    Direct infection of metacarpus and phalanges in infectious and parasitic diseases classified elsewhere

    ▷ *M01.X41* *Direct infection of right hand in infectious and parasitic diseases classified elsewhere*

    ▷ *M01.X42* *Direct infection of left hand in infectious and parasitic diseases classified elsewhere*

    ▷ *M01.X49* *Direct infection of unspecified hand in infectious and parasitic diseases classified elsewhere*

● **M01.X5** Direct infection of hip in infectious and parasitic diseases classified elsewhere

    ▷ *M01.X51* *Direct infection of right hip in infectious and parasitic diseases classified elsewhere*

    ▷ *M01.X52* *Direct infection of left hip in infectious and parasitic diseases classified elsewhere*

    ▷ *M01.X59* *Direct infection of unspecified hip in infectious and parasitic diseases classified elsewhere*

● **M01.X6** Direct infection of knee in infectious and parasitic diseases classified elsewhere

    ▷ *M01.X61* *Direct infection of right knee in infectious and parasitic diseases classified elsewhere*

    ▷ *M01.X62* *Direct infection of left knee in infectious and parasitic diseases classified elsewhere*

    ▷ *M01.X69* *Direct infection of unspecified knee in infectious and parasitic diseases classified elsewhere*

● **M01.X7** Direct infection of ankle and foot in infectious and parasitic diseases classified elsewhere

    Direct infection of tarsus, metatarsus and phalanges in infectious and parasitic diseases classified elsewhere

    ▷ *M01.X71* *Direct infection of right ankle and foot in infectious and parasitic diseases classified elsewhere*

    ▷ *M01.X72* *Direct infection of left ankle and foot in infectious and parasitic diseases classified elsewhere*

    ▷ *M01.X79* *Direct infection of unspecified ankle and foot in infectious and parasitic diseases classified elsewhere*

▷ *M01.X8* *Direct infection of vertebrae in infectious and parasitic diseases classified elsewhere*

▷ *M01.X9* *Direct infection of multiple joints in infectious and parasitic diseases classified elsewhere*

● **M02** Postinfective and reactive arthropathies

    Code first *underlying disease, such as:*

    congenital syphilis [Clutton's joints] (A50.5)

    enteritis due to Yersinia enterocolitica (A04.6)

    infective endocarditis (I33.0)

    viral hepatitis (B15-B19)

    Excludes1 Behçet's disease (M35.2)

        direct infections of joint in infectious and parasitic diseases classified elsewhere (M01.-)

        postmeningococcal arthritis (A39.84)

        mumps arthritis (B26.85)

        rubella arthritis (B06.82)

        syphilis arthritis (late) (A52.77)

        rheumatic fever (I00)

        tabetic arthropathy [Charcôt's] (A52.16)

● **M02.0** Arthropathy following intestinal bypass

    M02.00 Arthropathy following intestinal bypass, unspecified site

    ● **M02.01** Arthropathy following intestinal bypass, shoulder

        M02.011 Arthropathy following intestinal bypass, right shoulder

        M02.012 Arthropathy following intestinal bypass, left shoulder

        M02.019 Arthropathy following intestinal bypass, unspecified shoulder

    ● **M02.02** Arthropathy following intestinal bypass, elbow

        M02.021 Arthropathy following intestinal bypass, right elbow

        M02.022 Arthropathy following intestinal bypass, left elbow

        M02.029 Arthropathy following intestinal bypass, unspecified elbow

    ● **M02.03** Arthropathy following intestinal bypass, wrist

        Arthropathy following intestinal bypass, carpal bones

        M02.031 Arthropathy following intestinal bypass, right wrist

        M02.032 Arthropathy following intestinal bypass, left wrist

        M02.039 Arthropathy following intestinal bypass, unspecified wrist

    ● **M02.04** Arthropathy following intestinal bypass, hand

        Arthropathy following intestinal bypass, metacarpals and phalanges

        M02.041 Arthropathy following intestinal bypass, right hand

        M02.042 Arthropathy following intestinal bypass, left hand

        M02.049 Arthropathy following intestinal bypass, unspecified hand

    ● **M02.05** Arthropathy following intestinal bypass, hip

        M02.051 Arthropathy following intestinal bypass, right hip

        M02.052 Arthropathy following intestinal bypass, left hip

        M02.059 Arthropathy following intestinal bypass, unspecified hip

    ● **M02.06** Arthropathy following intestinal bypass, knee

        M02.061 Arthropathy following intestinal bypass, right knee

        M02.062 Arthropathy following intestinal bypass, left knee

        M02.069 Arthropathy following intestinal bypass, unspecified knee

CHAPTER 13 (M00-M99)

CHAPTER 13 (M00-M99)

● **M02.07**   Arthropathy following intestinal bypass, ankle and foot
       Arthropathy following intestinal bypass, tarsus, metatarsus and phalanges
      M02.071   Arthropathy following intestinal bypass, right ankle and foot
      M02.072   Arthropathy following intestinal bypass, left ankle and foot
      M02.079   Arthropathy following intestinal bypass, unspecified ankle and foot
   M02.08   Arthropathy following intestinal bypass, vertebrae
   M02.09   Arthropathy following intestinal bypass, multiple sites

● **M02.1**   Postdysenteric arthropathy
   M02.10   Postdysenteric arthropathy, unspecified site
● M02.11   Postdysenteric arthropathy, shoulder
      M02.111   Postdysenteric arthropathy, right shoulder
      M02.112   Postdysenteric arthropathy, left shoulder
      M02.119   Postdysenteric arthropathy, unspecified shoulder
● M02.12   Postdysenteric arthropathy, elbow
      M02.121   Postdysenteric arthropathy, right elbow
      M02.122   Postdysenteric arthropathy, left elbow
      M02.129   Postdysenteric arthropathy, unspecified elbow
● M02.13   Postdysenteric arthropathy, wrist
       Postdysenteric arthropathy, carpal bones
      M02.131   Postdysenteric arthropathy, right wrist
      M02.132   Postdysenteric arthropathy, left wrist
      M02.139   Postdysenteric arthropathy, unspecified wrist
● M02.14   Postdysenteric arthropathy, hand
       Postdysenteric arthropathy, metacarpus and phalanges
      M02.141   Postdysenteric arthropathy, right hand
      M02.142   Postdysenteric arthropathy, left hand
      M02.149   Postdysenteric arthropathy, unspecified hand
● M02.15   Postdysenteric arthropathy, hip
      M02.151   Postdysenteric arthropathy, right hip
      M02.152   Postdysenteric arthropathy, left hip
      M02.159   Postdysenteric arthropathy, unspecified hip
● M02.16   Postdysenteric arthropathy, knee
      M02.161   Postdysenteric arthropathy, right knee
      M02.162   Postdysenteric arthropathy, left knee
      M02.169   Postdysenteric arthropathy, unspecified knee
● M02.17   Postdysenteric arthropathy, ankle and foot
       Postdysenteric arthropathy, tarsus, metatarsus and phalanges
      M02.171   Postdysenteric arthropathy, right ankle and foot
      M02.172   Postdysenteric arthropathy, left ankle and foot
      M02.179   Postdysenteric arthropathy, unspecified ankle and foot
   M02.18   Postdysenteric arthropathy, vertebrae
   M02.19   Postdysenteric arthropathy, multiple sites

● **M02.2**   Postimmunization arthropathy
   M02.20   Postimmunization arthropathy, unspecified site
● M02.21   Postimmunization arthropathy, shoulder
      M02.211   Postimmunization arthropathy, right shoulder
      M02.212   Postimmunization arthropathy, left shoulder
      M02.219   Postimmunization arthropathy, unspecified shoulder
● M02.22   Postimmunization arthropathy, elbow
      M02.221   Postimmunization arthropathy, right elbow
      M02.222   Postimmunization arthropathy, left elbow
      M02.229   Postimmunization arthropathy, unspecified elbow
● M02.23   Postimmunization arthropathy, wrist
       Postimmunization arthropathy, carpal bones
      M02.231   Postimmunization arthropathy, right wrist
      M02.232   Postimmunization arthropathy, left wrist
      M02.239   Postimmunization arthropathy, unspecified wrist
● M02.24   Postimmunization arthropathy, hand
       Postimmunization arthropathy, metacarpus and phalanges
      M02.241   Postimmunization arthropathy, right hand
      M02.242   Postimmunization arthropathy, left hand
      M02.249   Postimmunization arthropathy, unspecified hand
● M02.25   Postimmunization arthropathy, hip
      M02.251   Postimmunization arthropathy, right hip
      M02.252   Postimmunization arthropathy, left hip
      M02.259   Postimmunization arthropathy, unspecified hip
● M02.26   Postimmunization arthropathy, knee
      M02.261   Postimmunization arthropathy, right knee
      M02.262   Postimmunization arthropathy, left knee
      M02.269   Postimmunization arthropathy, unspecified knee
● M02.27   Postimmunization arthropathy, ankle and foot
       Postimmunization arthropathy, tarsus, metatarsus and phalanges
      M02.271   Postimmunization arthropathy, right ankle and foot
      M02.272   Postimmunization arthropathy, left ankle and foot
      M02.279   Postimmunization arthropathy, unspecified ankle and foot
   M02.28   Postimmunization arthropathy, vertebrae
   M02.29   Postimmunization arthropathy, multiple sites

● **M02.3**   Reiter's disease
       Reactive arthritis
   M02.30   Reiter's disease, unspecified site
● M02.31   Reiter's disease, shoulder
      M02.311   Reiter's disease, right shoulder
      M02.312   Reiter's disease, left shoulder
      M02.319   Reiter's disease, unspecified shoulder

▶ New   ⇒ Revised   ~~deleted~~ Deleted   Excludes 1   Excludes 2   Includes   Use additional   Code first   Code also   Key words
OGCR Official Guidelines   X Assign placeholder X   ● Use Additional Character(s)   ▶ Manifestation Code   **Coding Clinic**

● M02.32   Reiter's disease, elbow
     M02.321   Reiter's disease, right elbow
     M02.322   Reiter's disease, left elbow
     M02.329   Reiter's disease, unspecified elbow

● M02.33   Reiter's disease, wrist
     Reiter's disease, carpal bones
     M02.331   Reiter's disease, right wrist
     M02.332   Reiter's disease, left wrist
     M02.339   Reiter's disease, unspecified wrist

● M02.34   Reiter's disease, hand
     Reiter's disease, metacarpus and phalanges
     M02.341   Reiter's disease, right hand
     M02.342   Reiter's disease, left hand
     M02.349   Reiter's disease, unspecified hand

● M02.35   Reiter's disease, hip
     M02.351   Reiter's disease, right hip
     M02.352   Reiter's disease, left hip
     M02.359   Reiter's disease, unspecified hip

● M02.36   Reiter's disease, knee
     M02.361   Reiter's disease, right knee
     M02.362   Reiter's disease, left knee
     M02.369   Reiter's disease, unspecified knee

● M02.37   Reiter's disease, ankle and foot
     Reiter's disease, tarsus, metatarsus and phalanges
     M02.371   Reiter's disease, right ankle and foot
     M02.372   Reiter's disease, left ankle and foot
     M02.379   Reiter's disease, unspecified ankle and foot

     M02.38   Reiter's disease, vertebrae
     M02.39   Reiter's disease, multiple sites

● M02.8   Other reactive arthropathies
     �; M02.80   Other reactive arthropathies, unspecified site
     ● M02.81   Other reactive arthropathies, shoulder
       ▸ M02.811   Other reactive arthropathies, right shoulder
       ▸ M02.812   Other reactive arthropathies, left shoulder
       ▸ M02.819   Other reactive arthropathies, unspecified shoulder

     ● M02.82   Other reactive arthropathies, elbow
       ▸ M02.821   Other reactive arthropathies, right elbow
       ▸ M02.822   Other reactive arthropathies, left elbow
       ▸ M02.829   Other reactive arthropathies, unspecified elbow

     ● M02.83   Other reactive arthropathies, wrist
       Other reactive arthropathies, carpal bones
       ▸ M02.831   Other reactive arthropathies, right wrist
       ▸ M02.832   Other reactive arthropathies, left wrist
       ▸ M02.839   Other reactive arthropathies, unspecified wrist

     ● M02.84   Other reactive arthropathies, hand
       Other reactive arthropathies, metacarpus and phalanges
       ▸ M02.841   Other reactive arthropathies, right hand
       ▸ M02.842   Other reactive arthropathies, left hand
       ▸ M02.849   Other reactive arthropathies, unspecified hand

     ● M02.85   Other reactive arthropathies, hip
       ▸ M02.851   Other reactive arthropathies, right hip
       ▸ M02.852   Other reactive arthropathies, left hip
       ▸ M02.859   Other reactive arthropathies, unspecified hip

● M02.86   Other reactive arthropathies, knee
     ▸ M02.861   Other reactive arthropathies, right knee
     ▸ M02.862   Other reactive arthropathies, left knee
     ▸ M02.869   Other reactive arthropathies, unspecified knee

● M02.87   Other reactive arthropathies, ankle and foot
     Other reactive arthropathies, tarsus, metatarsus and phalanges
     ▸ M02.871   Other reactive arthropathies, right ankle and foot
     ▸ M02.872   Other reactive arthropathies, left ankle and foot
     ▸ M02.879   Other reactive arthropathies, unspecified ankle and foot

     ▸ M02.88   Other reactive arthropathies, vertebrae
     ▸ M02.89   Other reactive arthropathies, multiple sites
   ▸ M02.9   Reactive arthropathy, unspecified

AUTOINFLAMMATORY SYNDROMES (M04)

● M04   Autoinflammatory syndromes
     Excludes2   Crohn's disease (K50.-)
     Coding Clinic: 2016, Q4, P37

     M04.1   Periodic fever syndromes
       Familial Mediterranean fever
       Hyperimmunoglobin D syndrome
       Mevalonate kinase deficiency
       Tumor necrosis factor receptor associated periodic syndrome [TRAPS]

     M04.2   Cryopyrin-associated periodic syndromes
       Chronic infantile neurological, cutaneous and articular syndrome [CINCA]
       Familial cold autoinflammatory syndrome
       Familial cold urticaria
       Muckle-Wells syndrome
       Neonatal onset multisystemic inflammatory disorder [NOMID]

     M04.8   Other autoinflammatory syndromes
       Blau syndrome
       Deficiency of interleukin 1 receptor antagonist [DIRA]
       Majeed syndrome
       Periodic fever, aphthous stomatitis, pharyngitis, and adenopathy syndrome [PFAPA]
       Pyogenic arthritis, pyoderma gangrenosum, and acne syndrome [PAPA]

     M04.9   Autoinflammatory syndrome, unspecified

INFLAMMATORY POLYARTHROPATHIES (M05-M14)

● M05   Rheumatoid arthritis with rheumatoid factor
     Excludes1   rheumatic fever (I00)
       juvenile rheumatoid arthritis (M08.-)
       rheumatoid arthritis of spine (M45.-)

     ● M05.0   Felty's syndrome
       Rheumatoid arthritis with splenoadenomegaly and leukopenia
       M05.00   Felty's syndrome, unspecified site
       ● M05.01   Felty's syndrome, shoulder
         M05.011   Felty's syndrome, right shoulder
         M05.012   Felty's syndrome, left shoulder
         M05.019   Felty's syndrome, unspecified shoulder
       ● M05.02   Felty's syndrome, elbow
         M05.021   Felty's syndrome, right elbow
         M05.022   Felty's syndrome, left elbow
         M05.029   Felty's syndrome, unspecified elbow

CHAPTER 13 (M00-M99)

Item 13-1   **Rheumatoid arthritis** (RA) is a chronic systemic inflammatory autoimmune disease of undetermined etiology involving primarily the synovial membranes and articular structures of multiple joints. It can also affect other organs, including the eyes, blood vessels, heart, and lungs. The disease is often progressive. In late stages, deformity, ankylosis, and other **inflammatory polyarthropathies** develop.

● **M05.03** **Felty's syndrome, wrist**
       Felty's syndrome, carpal bones
       M05.031 Felty's syndrome, right wrist
       M05.032 Felty's syndrome, left wrist
       M05.039 Felty's syndrome, unspecified wrist

● **M05.04** **Felty's syndrome, hand**
       Felty's syndrome, metacarpus and phalanges
       M05.041 Felty's syndrome, right hand
       M05.042 Felty's syndrome, left hand
       M05.049 Felty's syndrome, unspecified hand

● **M05.05** **Felty's syndrome, hip**
       M05.051 Felty's syndrome, right hip
       M05.052 Felty's syndrome, left hip
       M05.059 Felty's syndrome, unspecified hip

● **M05.06** **Felty's syndrome, knee**
       M05.061 Felty's syndrome, right knee
       M05.062 Felty's syndrome, left knee
       M05.069 Felty's syndrome, unspecified knee

● **M05.07** **Felty's syndrome, ankle and foot**
       Felty's syndrome, tarsus, metatarsus and phalanges
       M05.071 Felty's syndrome, right ankle and foot
       M05.072 Felty's syndrome, left ankle and foot
       M05.079 Felty's syndrome, unspecified ankle and foot

    M05.09 Felty's syndrome, multiple sites

● **M05.1** **Rheumatoid lung disease with rheumatoid arthritis**
    M05.10 Rheumatoid lung disease with rheumatoid arthritis of unspecified site

● **M05.11** Rheumatoid lung disease with rheumatoid arthritis of shoulder
       M05.111 Rheumatoid lung disease with rheumatoid arthritis of right shoulder
       M05.112 Rheumatoid lung disease with rheumatoid arthritis of left shoulder
       M05.119 Rheumatoid lung disease with rheumatoid arthritis of unspecified shoulder

● **M05.12** Rheumatoid lung disease with rheumatoid arthritis of elbow
       M05.121 Rheumatoid lung disease with rheumatoid arthritis of right elbow
       M05.122 Rheumatoid lung disease with rheumatoid arthritis of left elbow
       M05.129 Rheumatoid lung disease with rheumatoid arthritis of unspecified elbow

● **M05.13** Rheumatoid lung disease with rheumatoid arthritis of wrist
       Rheumatoid lung disease with rheumatoid arthritis, carpal bones
       M05.131 Rheumatoid lung disease with rheumatoid arthritis of right wrist
       M05.132 Rheumatoid lung disease with rheumatoid arthritis of left wrist
       M05.139 Rheumatoid lung disease with rheumatoid arthritis of unspecified wrist

● **M05.14** Rheumatoid lung disease with rheumatoid arthritis of hand
       Rheumatoid lung disease with rheumatoid arthritis, metacarpus and phalanges
       M05.141 Rheumatoid lung disease with rheumatoid arthritis of right hand
       M05.142 Rheumatoid lung disease with rheumatoid arthritis of left hand
       M05.149 Rheumatoid lung disease with rheumatoid arthritis of unspecified hand

● **M05.15** Rheumatoid lung disease with rheumatoid arthritis of hip
       M05.151 Rheumatoid lung disease with rheumatoid arthritis of right hip
       M05.152 Rheumatoid lung disease with rheumatoid arthritis of left hip
       M05.159 Rheumatoid lung disease with rheumatoid arthritis of unspecified hip

● **M05.16** Rheumatoid lung disease with rheumatoid arthritis of knee
       M05.161 Rheumatoid lung disease with rheumatoid arthritis of right knee
       M05.162 Rheumatoid lung disease with rheumatoid arthritis of left knee
       M05.169 Rheumatoid lung disease with rheumatoid arthritis of unspecified knee

● **M05.17** Rheumatoid lung disease with rheumatoid arthritis of ankle and foot
       Rheumatoid lung disease with rheumatoid arthritis, tarsus, metatarsus and phalanges
       M05.171 Rheumatoid lung disease with rheumatoid arthritis of right ankle and foot
       M05.172 Rheumatoid lung disease with rheumatoid arthritis of left ankle and foot
       M05.179 Rheumatoid lung disease with rheumatoid arthritis of unspecified ankle and foot

    M05.19 Rheumatoid lung disease with rheumatoid arthritis of multiple sites

● **M05.2** **Rheumatoid vasculitis with rheumatoid arthritis**
    M05.20 Rheumatoid vasculitis with rheumatoid arthritis of unspecified site

● **M05.21** Rheumatoid vasculitis with rheumatoid arthritis of shoulder
       M05.211 Rheumatoid vasculitis with rheumatoid arthritis of right shoulder
       M05.212 Rheumatoid vasculitis with rheumatoid arthritis of left shoulder
       M05.219 Rheumatoid vasculitis with rheumatoid arthritis of unspecified shoulder

● **M05.22** Rheumatoid vasculitis with rheumatoid arthritis of elbow
       M05.221 Rheumatoid vasculitis with rheumatoid arthritis of right elbow
       M05.222 Rheumatoid vasculitis with rheumatoid arthritis of left elbow
       M05.229 Rheumatoid vasculitis with rheumatoid arthritis of unspecified elbow

▶ New   ⇒ Revised   ~~deleted~~ Deleted   Excludes 1   Excludes 2   Includes   Use additional   Code first   Code also   Key words

OGCR Official Guidelines   X Assign placeholder X   ● Use Additional Character(s)   ▶ Manifestation Code   **Coding Clinic**

● **M05.23** Rheumatoid vasculitis with rheumatoid arthritis of wrist
    Rheumatoid vasculitis with rheumatoid arthritis, carpal bones

    M05.231 Rheumatoid vasculitis with rheumatoid arthritis of right wrist

    M05.232 Rheumatoid vasculitis with rheumatoid arthritis of left wrist

    M05.239 Rheumatoid vasculitis with rheumatoid arthritis of unspecified wrist

● **M05.24** Rheumatoid vasculitis with rheumatoid arthritis of hand
    Rheumatoid vasculitis with rheumatoid arthritis, metacarpus and phalanges

    M05.241 Rheumatoid vasculitis with rheumatoid arthritis of right hand

    M05.242 Rheumatoid vasculitis with rheumatoid arthritis of left hand

    M05.249 Rheumatoid vasculitis with rheumatoid arthritis of unspecified hand

● **M05.25** Rheumatoid vasculitis with rheumatoid arthritis of hip

    M05.251 Rheumatoid vasculitis with rheumatoid arthritis of right hip

    M05.252 Rheumatoid vasculitis with rheumatoid arthritis of left hip

    M05.259 Rheumatoid vasculitis with rheumatoid arthritis of unspecified hip

● **M05.26** Rheumatoid vasculitis with rheumatoid arthritis of knee

    M05.261 Rheumatoid vasculitis with rheumatoid arthritis of right knee

    M05.262 Rheumatoid vasculitis with rheumatoid arthritis of left knee

    M05.269 Rheumatoid vasculitis with rheumatoid arthritis of unspecified knee

● **M05.27** Rheumatoid vasculitis with rheumatoid arthritis of ankle and foot
    Rheumatoid vasculitis with rheumatoid arthritis, tarsus, metatarsus and phalanges

    M05.271 Rheumatoid vasculitis with rheumatoid arthritis of right ankle and foot

    M05.272 Rheumatoid vasculitis with rheumatoid arthritis of left ankle and foot

    M05.279 Rheumatoid vasculitis with rheumatoid arthritis of unspecified ankle and foot

  M05.29 Rheumatoid vasculitis with rheumatoid arthritis of multiple sites

● **M05.3** Rheumatoid heart disease with rheumatoid arthritis
    Rheumatoid carditis
    Rheumatoid endocarditis
    Rheumatoid myocarditis
    Rheumatoid pericarditis

  M05.30 Rheumatoid heart disease with rheumatoid arthritis of unspecified site

● **M05.31** Rheumatoid heart disease with rheumatoid arthritis of shoulder

    M05.311 Rheumatoid heart disease with rheumatoid arthritis of right shoulder

    M05.312 Rheumatoid heart disease with rheumatoid arthritis of left shoulder

    M05.319 Rheumatoid heart disease with rheumatoid arthritis of unspecified shoulder

● **M05.32** Rheumatoid heart disease with rheumatoid arthritis of elbow

    M05.321 Rheumatoid heart disease with rheumatoid arthritis of right elbow

    M05.322 Rheumatoid heart disease with rheumatoid arthritis of left elbow

    M05.329 Rheumatoid heart disease with rheumatoid arthritis of unspecified elbow

● **M05.33** Rheumatoid heart disease with rheumatoid arthritis of wrist
    Rheumatoid heart disease with rheumatoid arthritis, carpal bones

    M05.331 Rheumatoid heart disease with rheumatoid arthritis of right wrist

    M05.332 Rheumatoid heart disease with rheumatoid arthritis of left wrist

    M05.339 Rheumatoid heart disease with rheumatoid arthritis of unspecified wrist

● **M05.34** Rheumatoid heart disease with rheumatoid arthritis of hand
    Rheumatoid heart disease with rheumatoid arthritis, metacarpus and phalanges

    M05.341 Rheumatoid heart disease with rheumatoid arthritis of right hand

    M05.342 Rheumatoid heart disease with rheumatoid arthritis of left hand

    M05.349 Rheumatoid heart disease with rheumatoid arthritis of unspecified hand

● **M05.35** Rheumatoid heart disease with rheumatoid arthritis of hip

    M05.351 Rheumatoid heart disease with rheumatoid arthritis of right hip

    M05.352 Rheumatoid heart disease with rheumatoid arthritis of left hip

    M05.359 Rheumatoid heart disease with rheumatoid arthritis of unspecified hip

● **M05.36** Rheumatoid heart disease with rheumatoid arthritis of knee

    M05.361 Rheumatoid heart disease with rheumatoid arthritis of right knee

    M05.362 Rheumatoid heart disease with rheumatoid arthritis of left knee

    M05.369 Rheumatoid heart disease with rheumatoid arthritis of unspecified knee

● **M05.37** Rheumatoid heart disease with rheumatoid arthritis of ankle and foot
    Rheumatoid heart disease with rheumatoid arthritis, tarsus, metatarsus and phalanges

    M05.371 Rheumatoid heart disease with rheumatoid arthritis of right ankle and foot

    M05.372 Rheumatoid heart disease with rheumatoid arthritis of left ankle and foot

    M05.379 Rheumatoid heart disease with rheumatoid arthritis of unspecified ankle and foot

  M05.39 Rheumatoid heart disease with rheumatoid arthritis of multiple sites

CHAPTER 13 (M00-M99)

● **M05.4** Rheumatoid myopathy with rheumatoid arthritis

    M05.40 Rheumatoid myopathy with rheumatoid arthritis of unspecified site

● **M05.41** Rheumatoid myopathy with rheumatoid arthritis of shoulder

        M05.411 Rheumatoid myopathy with rheumatoid arthritis of right shoulder

        M05.412 Rheumatoid myopathy with rheumatoid arthritis of left shoulder

        M05.419 Rheumatoid myopathy with rheumatoid arthritis of unspecified shoulder

● **M05.42** Rheumatoid myopathy with rheumatoid arthritis of elbow

        M05.421 Rheumatoid myopathy with rheumatoid arthritis of right elbow

        M05.422 Rheumatoid myopathy with rheumatoid arthritis of left elbow

        M05.429 Rheumatoid myopathy with rheumatoid arthritis of unspecified elbow

● **M05.43** Rheumatoid myopathy with rheumatoid arthritis of wrist

       Rheumatoid myopathy with rheumatoid arthritis, carpal bones

        M05.431 Rheumatoid myopathy with rheumatoid arthritis of right wrist

        M05.432 Rheumatoid myopathy with rheumatoid arthritis of left wrist

        M05.439 Rheumatoid myopathy with rheumatoid arthritis of unspecified wrist

● **M05.44** Rheumatoid myopathy with rheumatoid arthritis of hand

       Rheumatoid myopathy with rheumatoid arthritis, metacarpus and phalanges

        M05.441 Rheumatoid myopathy with rheumatoid arthritis of right hand

        M05.442 Rheumatoid myopathy with rheumatoid arthritis of left hand

        M05.449 Rheumatoid myopathy with rheumatoid arthritis of unspecified hand

● **M05.45** Rheumatoid myopathy with rheumatoid arthritis of hip

        M05.451 Rheumatoid myopathy with rheumatoid arthritis of right hip

        M05.452 Rheumatoid myopathy with rheumatoid arthritis of left hip

        M05.459 Rheumatoid myopathy with rheumatoid arthritis of unspecified hip

● **M05.46** Rheumatoid myopathy with rheumatoid arthritis of knee

        M05.461 Rheumatoid myopathy with rheumatoid arthritis of right knee

        M05.462 Rheumatoid myopathy with rheumatoid arthritis of left knee

        M05.469 Rheumatoid myopathy with rheumatoid arthritis of unspecified knee

● **M05.47** Rheumatoid myopathy with rheumatoid arthritis of ankle and foot

       Rheumatoid myopathy with rheumatoid arthritis, tarsus, metatarsus and phalanges

        M05.471 Rheumatoid myopathy with rheumatoid arthritis of right ankle and foot

        M05.472 Rheumatoid myopathy with rheumatoid arthritis of left ankle and foot

        M05.479 Rheumatoid myopathy with rheumatoid arthritis of unspecified ankle and foot

    M05.49 Rheumatoid myopathy with rheumatoid arthritis of multiple sites

● **M05.5** Rheumatoid polyneuropathy with rheumatoid arthritis

    M05.50 Rheumatoid polyneuropathy with rheumatoid arthritis of unspecified site

● **M05.51** Rheumatoid polyneuropathy with rheumatoid arthritis of shoulder

        M05.511 Rheumatoid polyneuropathy with rheumatoid arthritis of right shoulder

        M05.512 Rheumatoid polyneuropathy with rheumatoid arthritis of left shoulder

        M05.519 Rheumatoid polyneuropathy with rheumatoid arthritis of unspecified shoulder

● **M05.52** Rheumatoid polyneuropathy with rheumatoid arthritis of elbow

        M05.521 Rheumatoid polyneuropathy with rheumatoid arthritis of right elbow

        M05.522 Rheumatoid polyneuropathy with rheumatoid arthritis of left elbow

        M05.529 Rheumatoid polyneuropathy with rheumatoid arthritis of unspecified elbow

● **M05.53** Rheumatoid polyneuropathy with rheumatoid arthritis of wrist

       Rheumatoid polyneuropathy with rheumatoid arthritis, carpal bones

        M05.531 Rheumatoid polyneuropathy with rheumatoid arthritis of right wrist

        M05.532 Rheumatoid polyneuropathy with rheumatoid arthritis of left wrist

        M05.539 Rheumatoid polyneuropathy with rheumatoid arthritis of unspecified wrist

● **M05.54** Rheumatoid polyneuropathy with rheumatoid arthritis of hand

       Rheumatoid polyneuropathy with rheumatoid arthritis, metacarpus and phalanges

        M05.541 Rheumatoid polyneuropathy with rheumatoid arthritis of right hand

        M05.542 Rheumatoid polyneuropathy with rheumatoid arthritis of left hand

        M05.549 Rheumatoid polyneuropathy with rheumatoid arthritis of unspecified hand

● **M05.55** Rheumatoid polyneuropathy with rheumatoid arthritis of hip

        M05.551 Rheumatoid polyneuropathy with rheumatoid arthritis of right hip

        M05.552 Rheumatoid polyneuropathy with rheumatoid arthritis of left hip

        M05.559 Rheumatoid polyneuropathy with rheumatoid arthritis of unspecified hip

▶ New   ⇒ Revised   ~~deleted~~ Deleted   Excludes 1   Excludes 2   Includes   Use additional   Code first   Code also   Key words

OGCR Official Guidelines   X Assign placeholder X   ● Use Additional Character(s)   ▷ Manifestation Code   **Coding Clinic**

● **M05.56   Rheumatoid polyneuropathy with rheumatoid arthritis of knee**
  M05.561   Rheumatoid polyneuropathy with rheumatoid arthritis of right knee
  M05.562   Rheumatoid polyneuropathy with rheumatoid arthritis of left knee
  M05.569   Rheumatoid polyneuropathy with rheumatoid arthritis of unspecified knee

● **M05.57   Rheumatoid polyneuropathy with rheumatoid arthritis of ankle and foot**
  Rheumatoid polyneuropathy with rheumatoid arthritis, tarsus, metatarsus and phalanges
  M05.571   Rheumatoid polyneuropathy with rheumatoid arthritis of right ankle and foot
  M05.572   Rheumatoid polyneuropathy with rheumatoid arthritis of left ankle and foot
  M05.579   Rheumatoid polyneuropathy with rheumatoid arthritis of unspecified ankle and foot

  M05.59   Rheumatoid polyneuropathy with rheumatoid arthritis of multiple sites

● **M05.6   Rheumatoid arthritis with involvement of other organs and systems**
  M05.60   Rheumatoid arthritis of unspecified site with involvement of other organs and systems

● **M05.61   Rheumatoid arthritis of shoulder with involvement of other organs and systems**
  M05.611   Rheumatoid arthritis of right shoulder with involvement of other organs and systems
  M05.612   Rheumatoid arthritis of left shoulder with involvement of other organs and systems
  M05.619   Rheumatoid arthritis of unspecified shoulder with involvement of other organs and systems

● **M05.62   Rheumatoid arthritis of elbow with involvement of other organs and systems**
  M05.621   Rheumatoid arthritis of right elbow with involvement of other organs and systems
  M05.622   Rheumatoid arthritis of left elbow with involvement of other organs and systems
  M05.629   Rheumatoid arthritis of unspecified elbow with involvement of other organs and systems

● **M05.63   Rheumatoid arthritis of wrist with involvement of other organs and systems**
  Rheumatoid arthritis of carpal bones with involvement of other organs and systems
  M05.631   Rheumatoid arthritis of right wrist with involvement of other organs and systems
  M05.632   Rheumatoid arthritis of left wrist with involvement of other organs and systems
  M05.639   Rheumatoid arthritis of unspecified wrist with involvement of other organs and systems

● **M05.64   Rheumatoid arthritis of hand with involvement of other organs and systems**
  Rheumatoid arthritis of metacarpus and phalanges with involvement of other organs and systems
  M05.641   Rheumatoid arthritis of right hand with involvement of other organs and systems
  M05.642   Rheumatoid arthritis of left hand with involvement of other organs and systems
  M05.649   Rheumatoid arthritis of unspecified hand with involvement of other organs and systems

● **M05.65   Rheumatoid arthritis of hip with involvement of other organs and systems**
  M05.651   Rheumatoid arthritis of right hip with involvement of other organs and systems
  M05.652   Rheumatoid arthritis of left hip with involvement of other organs and systems
  M05.659   Rheumatoid arthritis of unspecified hip with involvement of other organs and systems

● **M05.66   Rheumatoid arthritis of knee with involvement of other organs and systems**
  M05.661   Rheumatoid arthritis of right knee with involvement of other organs and systems
  M05.662   Rheumatoid arthritis of left knee with involvement of other organs and systems
  M05.669   Rheumatoid arthritis of unspecified knee with involvement of other organs and systems

● **M05.67   Rheumatoid arthritis of ankle and foot with involvement of other organs and systems**
  Rheumatoid arthritis of tarsus, metatarsus and phalanges with involvement of other organs and systems
  M05.671   Rheumatoid arthritis of right ankle and foot with involvement of other organs and systems
  M05.672   Rheumatoid arthritis of left ankle and foot with involvement of other organs and systems
  M05.679   Rheumatoid arthritis of unspecified ankle and foot with involvement of other organs and systems

  M05.69   Rheumatoid arthritis of multiple sites with involvement of other organs and systems

● **M05.7   Rheumatoid arthritis with rheumatoid factor without organ or systems involvement**
  M05.70   Rheumatoid arthritis with rheumatoid factor of unspecified site without organ or systems involvement

● **M05.71   Rheumatoid arthritis with rheumatoid factor of shoulder without organ or systems involvement**
  M05.711   Rheumatoid arthritis with rheumatoid factor of right shoulder without organ or systems involvement
  M05.712   Rheumatoid arthritis with rheumatoid factor of left shoulder without organ or systems involvement
  M05.719   Rheumatoid arthritis with rheumatoid factor of unspecified shoulder without organ or systems involvement

● M05.72　Rheumatoid arthritis with rheumatoid factor of elbow without organ or systems involvement

　　M05.721　Rheumatoid arthritis with rheumatoid factor of right elbow without organ or systems involvement

　　M05.722　Rheumatoid arthritis with rheumatoid factor of left elbow without organ or systems involvement

　　M05.729　Rheumatoid arthritis with rheumatoid factor of unspecified elbow without organ or systems involvement

● M05.73　Rheumatoid arthritis with rheumatoid factor of wrist without organ or systems involvement

　　M05.731　Rheumatoid arthritis with rheumatoid factor of right wrist without organ or systems involvement

　　M05.732　Rheumatoid arthritis with rheumatoid factor of left wrist without organ or systems involvement

　　M05.739　Rheumatoid arthritis with rheumatoid factor of unspecified wrist without organ or systems involvement

● M05.74　Rheumatoid arthritis with rheumatoid factor of hand without organ or systems involvement

　　M05.741　Rheumatoid arthritis with rheumatoid factor of right hand without organ or systems involvement

　　M05.742　Rheumatoid arthritis with rheumatoid factor of left hand without organ or systems involvement

　　M05.749　Rheumatoid arthritis with rheumatoid factor of unspecified hand without organ or systems involvement

● M05.75　Rheumatoid arthritis with rheumatoid factor of hip without organ or systems involvement

　　M05.751　Rheumatoid arthritis with rheumatoid factor of right hip without organ or systems involvement

　　M05.752　Rheumatoid arthritis with rheumatoid factor of left hip without organ or systems involvement

　　M05.759　Rheumatoid arthritis with rheumatoid factor of unspecified hip without organ or systems involvement

● M05.76　Rheumatoid arthritis with rheumatoid factor of knee without organ or systems involvement

　　M05.761　Rheumatoid arthritis with rheumatoid factor of right knee without organ or systems involvement

　　M05.762　Rheumatoid arthritis with rheumatoid factor of left knee without organ or systems involvement

　　M05.769　Rheumatoid arthritis with rheumatoid factor of unspecified knee without organ or systems involvement

● M05.77　Rheumatoid arthritis with rheumatoid factor of ankle and foot without organ or systems involvement

　　M05.771　Rheumatoid arthritis with rheumatoid factor of right ankle and foot without organ or systems involvement

　　M05.772　Rheumatoid arthritis with rheumatoid factor of left ankle and foot without organ or systems involvement

　　M05.779　Rheumatoid arthritis with rheumatoid factor of unspecified ankle and foot without organ or systems involvement

　　M05.79　Rheumatoid arthritis with rheumatoid factor of multiple sites without organ or systems involvement

● M05.8　Other rheumatoid arthritis with rheumatoid factor

　　M05.80　Other rheumatoid arthritis with rheumatoid factor of unspecified site

● M05.81　Other rheumatoid arthritis with rheumatoid factor of shoulder

　　M05.811　Other rheumatoid arthritis with rheumatoid factor of right shoulder

　　M05.812　Other rheumatoid arthritis with rheumatoid factor of left shoulder

　　M05.819　Other rheumatoid arthritis with rheumatoid factor of unspecified shoulder

● M05.82　Other rheumatoid arthritis with rheumatoid factor of elbow

　　M05.821　Other rheumatoid arthritis with rheumatoid factor of right elbow

　　M05.822　Other rheumatoid arthritis with rheumatoid factor of left elbow

　　M05.829　Other rheumatoid arthritis with rheumatoid factor of unspecified elbow

● M05.83　Other rheumatoid arthritis with rheumatoid factor of wrist

　　M05.831　Other rheumatoid arthritis with rheumatoid factor of right wrist

　　M05.832　Other rheumatoid arthritis with rheumatoid factor of left wrist

　　M05.839　Other rheumatoid arthritis with rheumatoid factor of unspecified wrist

● M05.84　Other rheumatoid arthritis with rheumatoid factor of hand

　　M05.841　Other rheumatoid arthritis with rheumatoid factor of right hand

　　M05.842　Other rheumatoid arthritis with rheumatoid factor of left hand

　　M05.849　Other rheumatoid arthritis with rheumatoid factor of unspecified hand

● M05.85　Other rheumatoid arthritis with rheumatoid factor of hip

　　M05.851　Other rheumatoid arthritis with rheumatoid factor of right hip

　　M05.852　Other rheumatoid arthritis with rheumatoid factor of left hip

　　M05.859　Other rheumatoid arthritis with rheumatoid factor of unspecified hip

▶ New　⇒ Revised　deleted Deleted　Excludes 1　Excludes 2　Includes　Use additional　Code first　Code also　Key words
OGCR Official Guidelines　X Assign placeholder X　● Use Additional Character(s)　▷ Manifestation Code　Coding Clinic

● **M05.86** Other rheumatoid arthritis with rheumatoid factor of knee

     M05.861 Other rheumatoid arthritis with rheumatoid factor of right knee

     M05.862 Other rheumatoid arthritis with rheumatoid factor of left knee

     M05.869 Other rheumatoid arthritis with rheumatoid factor of unspecified knee

● **M05.87** Other rheumatoid arthritis with rheumatoid factor of ankle and foot

     M05.871 Other rheumatoid arthritis with rheumatoid factor of right ankle and foot

     M05.872 Other rheumatoid arthritis with rheumatoid factor of left ankle and foot

     M05.879 Other rheumatoid arthritis with rheumatoid factor of unspecified ankle and foot

     M05.89 Other rheumatoid arthritis with rheumatoid factor of multiple sites

   M05.9 Rheumatoid arthritis with rheumatoid factor, unspecified

● **M06** Other rheumatoid arthritis

   ● **M06.0** Rheumatoid arthritis without rheumatoid factor

     M06.00 Rheumatoid arthritis without rheumatoid factor, unspecified site

     ● M06.01 Rheumatoid arthritis without rheumatoid factor, shoulder

       M06.011 Rheumatoid arthritis without rheumatoid factor, right shoulder

       M06.012 Rheumatoid arthritis without rheumatoid factor, left shoulder

       M06.019 Rheumatoid arthritis without rheumatoid factor, unspecified shoulder

     ● M06.02 Rheumatoid arthritis without rheumatoid factor, elbow

       M06.021 Rheumatoid arthritis without rheumatoid factor, right elbow

       M06.022 Rheumatoid arthritis without rheumatoid factor, left elbow

       M06.029 Rheumatoid arthritis without rheumatoid factor, unspecified elbow

     ● M06.03 Rheumatoid arthritis without rheumatoid factor, wrist

       M06.031 Rheumatoid arthritis without rheumatoid factor, right wrist

       M06.032 Rheumatoid arthritis without rheumatoid factor, left wrist

       M06.039 Rheumatoid arthritis without rheumatoid factor, unspecified wrist

     ● M06.04 Rheumatoid arthritis without rheumatoid factor, hand

       M06.041 Rheumatoid arthritis without rheumatoid factor, right hand

       M06.042 Rheumatoid arthritis without rheumatoid factor, left hand

       M06.049 Rheumatoid arthritis without rheumatoid factor, unspecified hand

     ● M06.05 Rheumatoid arthritis without rheumatoid factor, hip

       M06.051 Rheumatoid arthritis without rheumatoid factor, right hip

       M06.052 Rheumatoid arthritis without rheumatoid factor, left hip

       M06.059 Rheumatoid arthritis without rheumatoid factor, unspecified hip

● **M06.06** Rheumatoid arthritis without rheumatoid factor, knee

     M06.061 Rheumatoid arthritis without rheumatoid factor, right knee

     M06.062 Rheumatoid arthritis without rheumatoid factor, left knee

     M06.069 Rheumatoid arthritis without rheumatoid factor, unspecified knee

● **M06.07** Rheumatoid arthritis without rheumatoid factor, ankle and foot

     M06.071 Rheumatoid arthritis without rheumatoid factor, right ankle and foot

     M06.072 Rheumatoid arthritis without rheumatoid factor, left ankle and foot

     M06.079 Rheumatoid arthritis without rheumatoid factor, unspecified ankle and foot

   M06.08 Rheumatoid arthritis without rheumatoid factor, vertebrae

   M06.09 Rheumatoid arthritis without rheumatoid factor, multiple sites

   M06.1 Adult-onset Still's disease   A

     Excludes1   Still's disease NOS (M08.2-)

● **M06.2** Rheumatoid bursitis

   M06.20 Rheumatoid bursitis, unspecified site

   ● M06.21 Rheumatoid bursitis, shoulder

     M06.211 Rheumatoid bursitis, right shoulder

     M06.212 Rheumatoid bursitis, left shoulder

     M06.219 Rheumatoid bursitis, unspecified shoulder

   ● M06.22 Rheumatoid bursitis, elbow

     M06.221 Rheumatoid bursitis, right elbow

     M06.222 Rheumatoid bursitis, left elbow

     M06.229 Rheumatoid bursitis, unspecified elbow

   ● M06.23 Rheumatoid bursitis, wrist

     M06.231 Rheumatoid bursitis, right wrist

     M06.232 Rheumatoid bursitis, left wrist

     M06.239 Rheumatoid bursitis, unspecified wrist

   ● M06.24 Rheumatoid bursitis, hand

     M06.241 Rheumatoid bursitis, right hand

     M06.242 Rheumatoid bursitis, left hand

     M06.249 Rheumatoid bursitis, unspecified hand

   ● M06.25 Rheumatoid bursitis, hip

     M06.251 Rheumatoid bursitis, right hip

     M06.252 Rheumatoid bursitis, left hip

     M06.259 Rheumatoid bursitis, unspecified hip

   ● M06.26 Rheumatoid bursitis, knee

     M06.261 Rheumatoid bursitis, right knee

     M06.262 Rheumatoid bursitis, left knee

     M06.269 Rheumatoid bursitis, unspecified knee

   ● M06.27 Rheumatoid bursitis, ankle and foot

     M06.271 Rheumatoid bursitis, right ankle and foot

     M06.272 Rheumatoid bursitis, left ankle and foot

     M06.279 Rheumatoid bursitis, unspecified ankle and foot

   M06.28 Rheumatoid bursitis, vertebrae

   M06.29 Rheumatoid bursitis, multiple sites

CHAPTER 13 (M00-M99)

● **M06.3 Rheumatoid nodule**
    M06.30 Rheumatoid nodule, unspecified site
   ● M06.31 Rheumatoid nodule, shoulder
      M06.311 Rheumatoid nodule, right shoulder
      M06.312 Rheumatoid nodule, left shoulder
      M06.319 Rheumatoid nodule, unspecified shoulder
   ● M06.32 Rheumatoid nodule, elbow
      M06.321 Rheumatoid nodule, right elbow
      M06.322 Rheumatoid nodule, left elbow
      M06.329 Rheumatoid nodule, unspecified elbow
   ● M06.33 Rheumatoid nodule, wrist
      M06.331 Rheumatoid nodule, right wrist
      M06.332 Rheumatoid nodule, left wrist
      M06.339 Rheumatoid nodule, unspecified wrist
   ● M06.34 Rheumatoid nodule, hand
      M06.341 Rheumatoid nodule, right hand
      M06.342 Rheumatoid nodule, left hand
      M06.349 Rheumatoid nodule, unspecified hand
   ● M06.35 Rheumatoid nodule, hip
      M06.351 Rheumatoid nodule, right hip
      M06.352 Rheumatoid nodule, left hip
      M06.359 Rheumatoid nodule, unspecified hip
   ● M06.36 Rheumatoid nodule, knee
      M06.361 Rheumatoid nodule, right knee
      M06.362 Rheumatoid nodule, left knee
      M06.369 Rheumatoid nodule, unspecified knee
   ● M06.37 Rheumatoid nodule, ankle and foot
      M06.371 Rheumatoid nodule, right ankle and foot
      M06.372 Rheumatoid nodule, left ankle and foot
      M06.379 Rheumatoid nodule, unspecified ankle and foot
    M06.38 Rheumatoid nodule, vertebrae
    M06.39 Rheumatoid nodule, multiple sites
  M06.4 **Inflammatory polyarthropathy**
    Excludes1 polyarthritis NOS (M13.0)
● **M06.8 Other specified rheumatoid arthritis**
    M06.80 Other specified rheumatoid arthritis, unspecified site
   ● M06.81 Other specified rheumatoid arthritis, shoulder
      M06.811 Other specified rheumatoid arthritis, right shoulder
      M06.812 Other specified rheumatoid arthritis, left shoulder
      M06.819 Other specified rheumatoid arthritis, unspecified shoulder
   ● M06.82 Other specified rheumatoid arthritis, elbow
      M06.821 Other specified rheumatoid arthritis, right elbow
      M06.822 Other specified rheumatoid arthritis, left elbow
      M06.829 Other specified rheumatoid arthritis, unspecified elbow
   ● M06.83 Other specified rheumatoid arthritis, wrist
      M06.831 Other specified rheumatoid arthritis, right wrist
      M06.832 Other specified rheumatoid arthritis, left wrist
      M06.839 Other specified rheumatoid arthritis, unspecified wrist

   ● M06.84 Other specified rheumatoid arthritis, hand
      M06.841 Other specified rheumatoid arthritis, right hand
      M06.842 Other specified rheumatoid arthritis, left hand
      M06.849 Other specified rheumatoid arthritis, unspecified hand
   ● M06.85 Other specified rheumatoid arthritis, hip
      M06.851 Other specified rheumatoid arthritis, right hip
      M06.852 Other specified rheumatoid arthritis, left hip
      M06.859 Other specified rheumatoid arthritis, unspecified hip
   ● M06.86 Other specified rheumatoid arthritis, knee
      M06.861 Other specified rheumatoid arthritis, right knee
      M06.862 Other specified rheumatoid arthritis, left knee
      M06.869 Other specified rheumatoid arthritis, unspecified knee
   ● M06.87 Other specified rheumatoid arthritis, ankle and foot
      M06.871 Other specified rheumatoid arthritis, right ankle and foot
      M06.872 Other specified rheumatoid arthritis, left ankle and foot
      M06.879 Other specified rheumatoid arthritis, unspecified ankle and foot
    M06.88 Other specified rheumatoid arthritis, vertebrae
    M06.89 Other specified rheumatoid arthritis, multiple sites
  M06.9 Rheumatoid arthritis, unspecified

● **M07 Enteropathic arthropathies**
    Code also associated enteropathy, such as:
      regional enteritis [Crohn's disease] (K50.-)
      ulcerative colitis (K51.-)
    Excludes1 psoriatic arthropathies (L40.5-)
 ● **M07.6 Enteropathic arthropathies**
    M07.60 Enteropathic arthropathies, unspecified site
   ● M07.61 Enteropathic arthropathies, shoulder
      M07.611 Enteropathic arthropathies, right shoulder
      M07.612 Enteropathic arthropathies, left shoulder
      M07.619 Enteropathic arthropathies, unspecified shoulder
   ● M07.62 Enteropathic arthropathies, elbow
      M07.621 Enteropathic arthropathies, right elbow
      M07.622 Enteropathic arthropathies, left elbow
      M07.629 Enteropathic arthropathies, unspecified elbow
   ● M07.63 Enteropathic arthropathies, wrist
      M07.631 Enteropathic arthropathies, right wrist
      M07.632 Enteropathic arthropathies, left wrist
      M07.639 Enteropathic arthropathies, unspecified wrist
   ● M07.64 Enteropathic arthropathies, hand
      M07.641 Enteropathic arthropathies, right hand
      M07.642 Enteropathic arthropathies, left hand
      M07.649 Enteropathic arthropathies, unspecified hand

▶ New   ⇒ Revised   ~~deleted~~ Deleted   Excludes 1   Excludes 2   Includes   Use additional   Code first   Code also   Key words
OGCR Official Guidelines   X Assign placeholder X   ● Use Additional Character(s)   ▶ Manifestation Code   **Coding Clinic**

● **M07.65** Enteropathic arthropathies, hip

　　M07.651 Enteropathic arthropathies, right hip

　　M07.652 Enteropathic arthropathies, left hip

　　M07.659 Enteropathic arthropathies, unspecified hip

● **M07.66** Enteropathic arthropathies, knee

　　M07.661 Enteropathic arthropathies, right knee

　　M07.662 Enteropathic arthropathies, left knee

　　M07.669 Enteropathic arthropathies, unspecified knee

● **M07.67** Enteropathic arthropathies, ankle and foot

　　M07.671 Enteropathic arthropathies, right ankle and foot

　　M07.672 Enteropathic arthropathies, left ankle and foot

　　M07.679 Enteropathic arthropathies, unspecified ankle and foot

　M07.68 Enteropathic arthropathies, vertebrae

　M07.69 Enteropathic arthropathies, multiple sites

● **M08** Juvenile arthritis

Code also any associated underlying condition, such as:
regional enteritis [Crohn's disease] (K50.-)
ulcerative colitis (K51.-)

Excludes1　arthropathy in Whipple's disease (M14.8)
Felty's syndrome (M05.0)
juvenile dermatomyositis (M33.0-)
psoriatic juvenile arthropathy (L40.54)

● **M08.0** Unspecified juvenile rheumatoid arthritis
Juvenile rheumatoid arthritis with or without rheumatoid factor

　　M08.00 Unspecified juvenile rheumatoid arthritis of unspecified site

● **M08.01** Unspecified juvenile rheumatoid arthritis, shoulder

　　M08.011 Unspecified juvenile rheumatoid arthritis, right shoulder

　　M08.012 Unspecified juvenile rheumatoid arthritis, left shoulder

　　M08.019 Unspecified juvenile rheumatoid arthritis, unspecified shoulder

● **M08.02** Unspecified juvenile rheumatoid arthritis of elbow

　　M08.021 Unspecified juvenile rheumatoid arthritis, right elbow

　　M08.022 Unspecified juvenile rheumatoid arthritis, left elbow

　　M08.029 Unspecified juvenile rheumatoid arthritis, unspecified elbow

● **M08.03** Unspecified juvenile rheumatoid arthritis, wrist

　　M08.031 Unspecified juvenile rheumatoid arthritis, right wrist

　　M08.032 Unspecified juvenile rheumatoid arthritis, left wrist

　　M08.039 Unspecified juvenile rheumatoid arthritis, unspecified wrist

● **M08.04** Unspecified juvenile rheumatoid arthritis, hand

　　M08.041 Unspecified juvenile rheumatoid arthritis, right hand

　　M08.042 Unspecified juvenile rheumatoid arthritis, left hand

　　M08.049 Unspecified juvenile rheumatoid arthritis, unspecified hand

● **M08.05** Unspecified juvenile rheumatoid arthritis, hip

　　M08.051 Unspecified juvenile rheumatoid arthritis, right hip

　　M08.052 Unspecified juvenile rheumatoid arthritis, left hip

　　M08.059 Unspecified juvenile rheumatoid arthritis, unspecified hip

● **M08.06** Unspecified juvenile rheumatoid arthritis, knee

　　M08.061 Unspecified juvenile rheumatoid arthritis, right knee

　　M08.062 Unspecified juvenile rheumatoid arthritis, left knee

　　M08.069 Unspecified juvenile rheumatoid arthritis, unspecified knee

● **M08.07** Unspecified juvenile rheumatoid arthritis, ankle and foot

　　M08.071 Unspecified juvenile rheumatoid arthritis, right ankle and foot

　　M08.072 Unspecified juvenile rheumatoid arthritis, left ankle and foot

　　M08.079 Unspecified juvenile rheumatoid arthritis, unspecified ankle and foot

　M08.08 Unspecified juvenile rheumatoid arthritis, vertebrae

　M08.09 Unspecified juvenile rheumatoid arthritis, multiple sites

M08.1 Juvenile ankylosing spondylitis

Excludes1　ankylosing spondylitis in adults (M45.0-)

● **M08.2** Juvenile rheumatoid arthritis with systemic onset
Still's disease NOS

Excludes1　adult-onset Still's disease (M06.1-)

　M08.20 Juvenile rheumatoid arthritis with systemic onset, unspecified site

● **M08.21** Juvenile rheumatoid arthritis with systemic onset, shoulder

　　M08.211 Juvenile rheumatoid arthritis with systemic onset, right shoulder

　　M08.212 Juvenile rheumatoid arthritis with systemic onset, left shoulder

　　M08.219 Juvenile rheumatoid arthritis with systemic onset, unspecified shoulder

● **M08.22** Juvenile rheumatoid arthritis with systemic onset, elbow

　　M08.221 Juvenile rheumatoid arthritis with systemic onset, right elbow

　　M08.222 Juvenile rheumatoid arthritis with systemic onset, left elbow

　　M08.229 Juvenile rheumatoid arthritis with systemic onset, unspecified elbow

● **M08.23** Juvenile rheumatoid arthritis with systemic onset, wrist

　　M08.231 Juvenile rheumatoid arthritis with systemic onset, right wrist

　　M08.232 Juvenile rheumatoid arthritis with systemic onset, left wrist

　　M08.239 Juvenile rheumatoid arthritis with systemic onset, unspecified wrist

● **M08.24** Juvenile rheumatoid arthritis with systemic onset, hand

　　M08.241 Juvenile rheumatoid arthritis with systemic onset, right hand

　　M08.242 Juvenile rheumatoid arthritis with systemic onset, left hand

　　M08.249 Juvenile rheumatoid arthritis with systemic onset, unspecified hand

● **M08.25** Juvenile rheumatoid arthritis with systemic onset, hip

　　M08.251 Juvenile rheumatoid arthritis with systemic onset, right hip

　　M08.252 Juvenile rheumatoid arthritis with systemic onset, left hip

　　M08.259 Juvenile rheumatoid arthritis with systemic onset, unspecified hip

CHAPTER 13 (M00-M99)

CHAPTER 13 (M00-M99)

● M08.26   Juvenile rheumatoid arthritis with systemic onset, knee

     M08.261   Juvenile rheumatoid arthritis with systemic onset, right knee

     M08.262   Juvenile rheumatoid arthritis with systemic onset, left knee

     M08.269   Juvenile rheumatoid arthritis with systemic onset, unspecified knee

● M08.27   Juvenile rheumatoid arthritis with systemic onset, ankle and foot

     M08.271   Juvenile rheumatoid arthritis with systemic onset, right ankle and foot

     M08.272   Juvenile rheumatoid arthritis with systemic onset, left ankle and foot

     M08.279   Juvenile rheumatoid arthritis with systemic onset, unspecified ankle and foot

   M08.28   Juvenile rheumatoid arthritis with systemic onset, vertebrae

   M08.29   Juvenile rheumatoid arthritis with systemic onset, multiple sites

  M08.3   Juvenile rheumatoid polyarthritis (seronegative)

● M08.4   Pauciarticular juvenile rheumatoid arthritis

   M08.40   Pauciarticular juvenile rheumatoid arthritis, unspecified site

● M08.41   Pauciarticular juvenile rheumatoid arthritis, shoulder

     M08.411   Pauciarticular juvenile rheumatoid arthritis, right shoulder

     M08.412   Pauciarticular juvenile rheumatoid arthritis, left shoulder

     M08.419   Pauciarticular juvenile rheumatoid arthritis, unspecified shoulder

● M08.42   Pauciarticular juvenile rheumatoid arthritis, elbow

     M08.421   Pauciarticular juvenile rheumatoid arthritis, right elbow

     M08.422   Pauciarticular juvenile rheumatoid arthritis, left elbow

     M08.429   Pauciarticular juvenile rheumatoid arthritis, unspecified elbow

● M08.43   Pauciarticular juvenile rheumatoid arthritis, wrist

     M08.431   Pauciarticular juvenile rheumatoid arthritis, right wrist

     M08.432   Pauciarticular juvenile rheumatoid arthritis, left wrist

     M08.439   Pauciarticular juvenile rheumatoid arthritis, unspecified wrist

● M08.44   Pauciarticular juvenile rheumatoid arthritis, hand

     M08.441   Pauciarticular juvenile rheumatoid arthritis, right hand

     M08.442   Pauciarticular juvenile rheumatoid arthritis, left hand

     M08.449   Pauciarticular juvenile rheumatoid arthritis, unspecified hand

● M08.45   Pauciarticular juvenile rheumatoid arthritis, hip

     M08.451   Pauciarticular juvenile rheumatoid arthritis, right hip

     M08.452   Pauciarticular juvenile rheumatoid arthritis, left hip

     M08.459   Pauciarticular juvenile rheumatoid arthritis, unspecified hip

● M08.46   Pauciarticular juvenile rheumatoid arthritis, knee

     M08.461   Pauciarticular juvenile rheumatoid arthritis, right knee

     M08.462   Pauciarticular juvenile rheumatoid arthritis, left knee

     M08.469   Pauciarticular juvenile rheumatoid arthritis, unspecified knee

● M08.47   Pauciarticular juvenile rheumatoid arthritis, ankle and foot

     M08.471   Pauciarticular juvenile rheumatoid arthritis, right ankle and foot

     M08.472   Pauciarticular juvenile rheumatoid arthritis, left ankle and foot

     M08.479   Pauciarticular juvenile rheumatoid arthritis, unspecified ankle and foot

   M08.48   Pauciarticular juvenile rheumatoid arthritis, vertebrae

● M08.8   Other juvenile arthritis

   M08.80   Other juvenile arthritis, unspecified site

● M08.81   Other juvenile arthritis, shoulder

     M08.811   Other juvenile arthritis, right shoulder

     M08.812   Other juvenile arthritis, left shoulder

     M08.819   Other juvenile arthritis, unspecified shoulder

● M08.82   Other juvenile arthritis, elbow

     M08.821   Other juvenile arthritis, right elbow

     M08.822   Other juvenile arthritis, left elbow

     M08.829   Other juvenile arthritis, unspecified elbow

● M08.83   Other juvenile arthritis, wrist

     M08.831   Other juvenile arthritis, right wrist

     M08.832   Other juvenile arthritis, left wrist

     M08.839   Other juvenile arthritis, unspecified wrist

● M08.84   Other juvenile arthritis, hand

     M08.841   Other juvenile arthritis, right hand

     M08.842   Other juvenile arthritis, left hand

     M08.849   Other juvenile arthritis, unspecified hand

● M08.85   Other juvenile arthritis, hip

     M08.851   Other juvenile arthritis, right hip

     M08.852   Other juvenile arthritis, left hip

     M08.859   Other juvenile arthritis, unspecified hip

● M08.86   Other juvenile arthritis, knee

     M08.861   Other juvenile arthritis, right knee

     M08.862   Other juvenile arthritis, left knee

     M08.869   Other juvenile arthritis, unspecified knee

● M08.87   Other juvenile arthritis, ankle and foot

     M08.871   Other juvenile arthritis, right ankle and foot

     M08.872   Other juvenile arthritis, left ankle and foot

     M08.879   Other juvenile arthritis, unspecified ankle and foot

   M08.88   Other juvenile arthritis, other specified site

         Other juvenile arthritis, vertebrae

   M08.89   Other juvenile arthritis, multiple sites

▶ New   ⇒ Revised   ~~deleted~~ Deleted   Excludes 1   Excludes 2   Includes   Use additional   Code first   Code also   Key words

OGCR Official Guidelines   X Assign placeholder X   ● Use Additional Character(s)   ▷ Manifestation Code   **Coding Clinic**

● **M08.9**   Juvenile arthritis, unspecified

     Excludes1   juvenile rheumatoid arthritis, unspecified (M08.0-)

    M08.90   Juvenile arthritis, unspecified, unspecified site

● M08.91   Juvenile arthritis, unspecified, shoulder

     M08.911   Juvenile arthritis, unspecified, right shoulder

     M08.912   Juvenile arthritis, unspecified, left shoulder

     M08.919   Juvenile arthritis, unspecified, unspecified shoulder

● M08.92   Juvenile arthritis, unspecified, elbow

     M08.921   Juvenile arthritis, unspecified, right elbow

     M08.922   Juvenile arthritis, unspecified, left elbow

     M08.929   Juvenile arthritis, unspecified, unspecified elbow

● M08.93   Juvenile arthritis, unspecified, wrist

     M08.931   Juvenile arthritis, unspecified, right wrist

     M08.932   Juvenile arthritis, unspecified, left wrist

     M08.939   Juvenile arthritis, unspecified, unspecified wrist

● M08.94   Juvenile arthritis, unspecified, hand

     M08.941   Juvenile arthritis, unspecified, right hand

     M08.942   Juvenile arthritis, unspecified, left hand

     M08.949   Juvenile arthritis, unspecified, unspecified hand

● M08.95   Juvenile arthritis, unspecified, hip

     M08.951   Juvenile arthritis, unspecified, right hip

     M08.952   Juvenile arthritis, unspecified, left hip

     M08.959   Juvenile arthritis, unspecified, unspecified hip

● M08.96   Juvenile arthritis, unspecified, knee

     M08.961   Juvenile arthritis, unspecified, right knee

     M08.962   Juvenile arthritis, unspecified, left knee

     M08.969   Juvenile arthritis, unspecified, unspecified knee

● M08.97   Juvenile arthritis, unspecified, ankle and foot

     M08.971   Juvenile arthritis, unspecified, right ankle and foot

     M08.972   Juvenile arthritis, unspecified, left ankle and foot

     M08.979   Juvenile arthritis, unspecified, unspecified ankle and foot

    M08.98   Juvenile arthritis, unspecified, vertebrae

    M08.99   Juvenile arthritis, unspecified, multiple sites

● **M1A**   Chronic gout

    Use additional code to identify:

     Autonomic neuropathy in diseases classified elsewhere (G99.0)

     Calculus of urinary tract in diseases classified elsewhere (N22)

     Cardiomyopathy in diseases classified elsewhere (I43)

     Disorders of external ear in diseases classified elsewhere (H61.1-, H62.8-)

     Disorders of iris and ciliary body in diseases classified elsewhere (H22)

     Glomerular disorders in diseases classified elsewhere (N08)

    Excludes1   gout NOS (M10.-)

    Excludes2   acute gout (M10.-)

    The appropriate 7th character is to be added to each code from category M1A

Ø	without tophus (tophi)
1	with tophus (tophi)

● **M1A.0**   Idiopathic chronic gout

     Chronic gouty bursitis

     Primary chronic gout

X ● M1A.00   Idiopathic chronic gout, unspecified site

● M1A.01   Idiopathic chronic gout, shoulder

     ● M1A.011   Idiopathic chronic gout, right shoulder

     ● M1A.012   Idiopathic chronic gout, left shoulder

     ● M1A.019   Idiopathic chronic gout, unspecified shoulder

● M1A.02   Idiopathic chronic gout, elbow

     ● M1A.021   Idiopathic chronic gout, right elbow

     ● M1A.022   Idiopathic chronic gout, left elbow

     ● M1A.029   Idiopathic chronic gout, unspecified elbow

● M1A.03   Idiopathic chronic gout, wrist

     ● M1A.031   Idiopathic chronic gout, right wrist

     ● M1A.032   Idiopathic chronic gout, left wrist

     ● M1A.039   Idiopathic chronic gout, unspecified wrist

● M1A.04   Idiopathic chronic gout, hand

     ● M1A.041   Idiopathic chronic gout, right hand

     ● M1A.042   Idiopathic chronic gout, left hand

     ● M1A.049   Idiopathic chronic gout, unspecified hand

● M1A.05   Idiopathic chronic gout, hip

     ● M1A.051   Idiopathic chronic gout, right hip

     ● M1A.052   Idiopathic chronic gout, left hip

     ● M1A.059   Idiopathic chronic gout, unspecified hip

● M1A.06   Idiopathic chronic gout, knee

     ● M1A.061   Idiopathic chronic gout, right knee

     ● M1A.062   Idiopathic chronic gout, left knee

     ● M1A.069   Idiopathic chronic gout, unspecified knee

● M1A.07   Idiopathic chronic gout, ankle and foot

     ● M1A.071   Idiopathic chronic gout, right ankle and foot

     ● M1A.072   Idiopathic chronic gout, left ankle and foot

     ● M1A.079   Idiopathic chronic gout, unspecified ankle and foot

X ● M1A.08   Idiopathic chronic gout, vertebrae

X ● M1A.09   Idiopathic chronic gout, multiple sites

- ● M1A.1 Lead-induced chronic gout
    - *Code first toxic effects of lead and its compounds (T56.0-)*
    - X ● M1A.10 Lead-induced chronic gout, unspecified site
    - ● M1A.11 Lead-induced chronic gout, shoulder
        - ● M1A.111 Lead-induced chronic gout, right shoulder
        - ● M1A.112 Lead-induced chronic gout, left shoulder
        - ● M1A.119 Lead-induced chronic gout, unspecified shoulder
    - ● M1A.12 Lead-induced chronic gout, elbow
        - ● M1A.121 Lead-induced chronic gout, right elbow
        - ● M1A.122 Lead-induced chronic gout, left elbow
        - ● M1A.129 Lead-induced chronic gout, unspecified elbow
    - ● M1A.13 Lead-induced chronic gout, wrist
        - ● M1A.131 Lead-induced chronic gout, right wrist
        - ● M1A.132 Lead-induced chronic gout, left wrist
        - ● M1A.139 Lead-induced chronic gout, unspecified wrist
    - ● M1A.14 Lead-induced chronic gout, hand
        - ● M1A.141 Lead-induced chronic gout, right hand
        - ● M1A.142 Lead-induced chronic gout, left hand
        - ● M1A.149 Lead-induced chronic gout, unspecified hand
    - ● M1A.15 Lead-induced chronic gout, hip
        - ● M1A.151 Lead-induced chronic gout, right hip
        - ● M1A.152 Lead-induced chronic gout, left hip
        - ● M1A.159 Lead-induced chronic gout, unspecified hip
    - ● M1A.16 Lead-induced chronic gout, knee
        - ● M1A.161 Lead-induced chronic gout, right knee
        - ● M1A.162 Lead-induced chronic gout, left knee
        - ● M1A.169 Lead-induced chronic gout, unspecified knee
    - ● M1A.17 Lead-induced chronic gout, ankle and foot
        - ● M1A.171 Lead-induced chronic gout, right ankle and foot
        - ● M1A.172 Lead-induced chronic gout, left ankle and foot
        - ● M1A.179 Lead-induced chronic gout, unspecified ankle and foot
    - X ● M1A.18 Lead-induced chronic gout, vertebrae
    - X ● M1A.19 Lead-induced chronic gout, multiple sites
- ● M1A.2 Drug-induced chronic gout
    - Use additional code for adverse effect, if applicable, to identify drug (T36-T50 with fifth or sixth character 5)
    - X ● M1A.20 Drug-induced chronic gout, unspecified site
    - ● M1A.21 Drug-induced chronic gout, shoulder
        - ● M1A.211 Drug-induced chronic gout, right shoulder
        - ● M1A.212 Drug-induced chronic gout, left shoulder
        - ● M1A.219 Drug-induced chronic gout, unspecified shoulder
    - ● M1A.22 Drug-induced chronic gout, elbow
        - ● M1A.221 Drug-induced chronic gout, right elbow
        - ● M1A.222 Drug-induced chronic gout, left elbow
        - ● M1A.229 Drug-induced chronic gout, unspecified elbow
- ● M1A.23 Drug-induced chronic gout, wrist
    - ● M1A.231 Drug-induced chronic gout, right wrist
    - ● M1A.232 Drug-induced chronic gout, left wrist
    - ● M1A.239 Drug-induced chronic gout, unspecified wrist
- ● M1A.24 Drug-induced chronic gout, hand
    - ● M1A.241 Drug-induced chronic gout, right hand
    - ● M1A.242 Drug-induced chronic gout, left hand
    - ● M1A.249 Drug-induced chronic gout, unspecified hand
- ● M1A.25 Drug-induced chronic gout, hip
    - ● M1A.251 Drug-induced chronic gout, right hip
    - ● M1A.252 Drug-induced chronic gout, left hip
    - ● M1A.259 Drug-induced chronic gout, unspecified hip
- ● M1A.26 Drug-induced chronic gout, knee
    - ● M1A.261 Drug-induced chronic gout, right knee
    - ● M1A.262 Drug-induced chronic gout, left knee
    - ● M1A.269 Drug-induced chronic gout, unspecified knee
- ● M1A.27 Drug-induced chronic gout, ankle and foot
    - ● M1A.271 Drug-induced chronic gout, right ankle and foot
    - ● M1A.272 Drug-induced chronic gout, left ankle and foot
    - ● M1A.279 Drug-induced chronic gout, unspecified ankle and foot
- X ● M1A.28 Drug-induced chronic gout, vertebrae
- X ● M1A.29 Drug-induced chronic gout, multiple sites
- ● M1A.3 Chronic gout due to renal impairment
    - *Code first associated renal disease*
    - X ● M1A.30 Chronic gout due to renal impairment, unspecified site
    - ● M1A.31 Chronic gout due to renal impairment, shoulder
        - ● M1A.311 Chronic gout due to renal impairment, right shoulder
        - ● M1A.312 Chronic gout due to renal impairment, left shoulder
        - ● M1A.319 Chronic gout due to renal impairment, unspecified shoulder
    - ● M1A.32 Chronic gout due to renal impairment, elbow
        - ● M1A.321 Chronic gout due to renal impairment, right elbow
        - ● M1A.322 Chronic gout due to renal impairment, left elbow
        - ● M1A.329 Chronic gout due to renal impairment, unspecified elbow
    - ● M1A.33 Chronic gout due to renal impairment, wrist
        - ● M1A.331 Chronic gout due to renal impairment, right wrist
        - ● M1A.332 Chronic gout due to renal impairment, left wrist
        - ● M1A.339 Chronic gout due to renal impairment, unspecified wrist
    - ● M1A.34 Chronic gout due to renal impairment, hand
        - ● M1A.341 Chronic gout due to renal impairment, right hand
        - ● M1A.342 Chronic gout due to renal impairment, left hand
        - ● M1A.349 Chronic gout due to renal impairment, unspecified hand

▶ New   ⇒ Revised   ~~deleted~~ Deleted   Excludes 1   Excludes 2   Includes   Use additional   Code first   Code also   Key words

OGCR Official Guidelines   X Assign placeholder X   ● Use Additional Character(s)   ▷ Manifestation Code   **Coding Clinic**

● **M1A.35** Chronic gout due to renal impairment, hip

     ● **M1A.351** Chronic gout due to renal impairment, right hip

     ● **M1A.352** Chronic gout due to renal impairment, left hip

     ● **M1A.359** Chronic gout due to renal impairment, unspecified hip

● **M1A.36** Chronic gout due to renal impairment, knee

     ● **M1A.361** Chronic gout due to renal impairment, right knee

     ● **M1A.362** Chronic gout due to renal impairment, left knee

     ● **M1A.369** Chronic gout due to renal impairment, unspecified knee

● **M1A.37** Chronic gout due to renal impairment, ankle and foot

     ● **M1A.371** Chronic gout due to renal impairment, right ankle and foot

     ● **M1A.372** Chronic gout due to renal impairment, left ankle and foot

     ● **M1A.379** Chronic gout due to renal impairment, unspecified ankle and foot

X ● **M1A.38** Chronic gout due to renal impairment, vertebrae

X ● **M1A.39** Chronic gout due to renal impairment, multiple sites

● **M1A.4** Other secondary chronic gout

     Code first associated condition

X ● **M1A.40** Other secondary chronic gout, unspecified site

● **M1A.41** Other secondary chronic gout, shoulder

     ● **M1A.411** Other secondary chronic gout, right shoulder

     ● **M1A.412** Other secondary chronic gout, left shoulder

     ● **M1A.419** Other secondary chronic gout, unspecified shoulder

● **M1A.42** Other secondary chronic gout, elbow

     ● **M1A.421** Other secondary chronic gout, right elbow

     ● **M1A.422** Other secondary chronic gout, left elbow

     ● **M1A.429** Other secondary chronic gout, unspecified elbow

● **M1A.43** Other secondary chronic gout, wrist

     ● **M1A.431** Other secondary chronic gout, right wrist

     ● **M1A.432** Other secondary chronic gout, left wrist

     ● **M1A.439** Other secondary chronic gout, unspecified wrist

● **M1A.44** Other secondary chronic gout, hand

     ● **M1A.441** Other secondary chronic gout, right hand

     ● **M1A.442** Other secondary chronic gout, left hand

     ● **M1A.449** Other secondary chronic gout, unspecified hand

● **M1A.45** Other secondary chronic gout, hip

     ● **M1A.451** Other secondary chronic gout, right hip

     ● **M1A.452** Other secondary chronic gout, left hip

     ● **M1A.459** Other secondary chronic gout, unspecified hip

● **M1A.46** Other secondary chronic gout, knee

     ● **M1A.461** Other secondary chronic gout, right knee

     ● **M1A.462** Other secondary chronic gout, left knee

     ● **M1A.469** Other secondary chronic gout, unspecified knee

● **M1A.47** Other secondary chronic gout, ankle and foot

     ● **M1A.471** Other secondary chronic gout, right ankle and foot

     ● **M1A.472** Other secondary chronic gout, left ankle and foot

     ● **M1A.479** Other secondary chronic gout, unspecified ankle and foot

X ● **M1A.48** Other secondary chronic gout, vertebrae

X ● **M1A.49** Other secondary chronic gout, multiple sites

X ● **M1A.9** Chronic gout, unspecified

● **M10**   Gout

     Accumulation of uric acid that results in swollen, red, hot, painful, stiff joints

     Acute gout

     Gout attack

     Gout flare

     Podagra

     Use additional code to identify:

         Autonomic neuropathy in diseases classified elsewhere (G99.0)

         Calculus of urinary tract in diseases classified elsewhere (N22)

         Cardiomyopathy in diseases classified elsewhere (I43)

         Disorders of external ear in diseases classified elsewhere (H61.1-, H62.8-)

         Disorders of iris and ciliary body in diseases classified elsewhere (H22)

         Glomerular disorders in diseases classified elsewhere (N08)

     Excludes2   chronic gout (M1A.-)

● **M10.0**   Idiopathic gout

     Gouty bursitis

     Primary gout

     M10.00 Idiopathic gout, unspecified site

     ● **M10.01** Idiopathic gout, shoulder

         M10.011 Idiopathic gout, right shoulder

         M10.012 Idiopathic gout, left shoulder

         M10.019 Idiopathic gout, unspecified shoulder

     ● **M10.02** Idiopathic gout, elbow

         M10.021 Idiopathic gout, right elbow

         M10.022 Idiopathic gout, left elbow

         M10.029 Idiopathic gout, unspecified elbow

     ● **M10.03** Idiopathic gout, wrist

         M10.031 Idiopathic gout, right wrist

         M10.032 Idiopathic gout, left wrist

         M10.039 Idiopathic gout, unspecified wrist

     ● **M10.04** Idiopathic gout, hand

         M10.041 Idiopathic gout, right hand

         M10.042 Idiopathic gout, left hand

         M10.049 Idiopathic gout, unspecified hand

     ● **M10.05** Idiopathic gout, hip

         M10.051 Idiopathic gout, right hip

         M10.052 Idiopathic gout, left hip

         M10.059 Idiopathic gout, unspecified hip

     ● **M10.06** Idiopathic gout, knee

         M10.061 Idiopathic gout, right knee

         M10.062 Idiopathic gout, left knee

         M10.069 Idiopathic gout, unspecified knee

CHAPTER 13 (M00-M99)

● M10.07   Idiopathic gout, ankle and foot
    M10.071   Idiopathic gout, right ankle and foot
    M10.072   Idiopathic gout, left ankle and foot
    M10.079   Idiopathic gout, unspecified ankle and foot
M10.08   Idiopathic gout, vertebrae
M10.09   Idiopathic gout, multiple sites

● M10.1   Lead-induced gout
    Code first toxic effects of lead and its compounds (T56.0-)
    M10.10   Lead-induced gout, unspecified site
● M10.11   Lead-induced gout, shoulder
    M10.111   Lead-induced gout, right shoulder
    M10.112   Lead-induced gout, left shoulder
    M10.119   Lead-induced gout, unspecified shoulder
● M10.12   Lead-induced gout, elbow
    M10.121   Lead-induced gout, right elbow
    M10.122   Lead-induced gout, left elbow
    M10.129   Lead-induced gout, unspecified elbow
● M10.13   Lead-induced gout, wrist
    M10.131   Lead-induced gout, right wrist
    M10.132   Lead-induced gout, left wrist
    M10.139   Lead-induced gout, unspecified wrist
● M10.14   Lead-induced gout, hand
    M10.141   Lead-induced gout, right hand
    M10.142   Lead-induced gout, left hand
    M10.149   Lead-induced gout, unspecified hand
● M10.15   Lead-induced gout, hip
    M10.151   Lead-induced gout, right hip
    M10.152   Lead-induced gout, left hip
    M10.159   Lead-induced gout, unspecified hip
● M10.16   Lead-induced gout, knee
    M10.161   Lead-induced gout, right knee
    M10.162   Lead-induced gout, left knee
    M10.169   Lead-induced gout, unspecified knee
● M10.17   Lead-induced gout, ankle and foot
    M10.171   Lead-induced gout, right ankle and foot
    M10.172   Lead-induced gout, left ankle and foot
    M10.179   Lead-induced gout, unspecified ankle and foot
M10.18   Lead-induced gout, vertebrae
M10.19   Lead-induced gout, multiple sites

● M10.2   Drug-induced gout
    Use additional code for adverse effect, if applicable, to identify drug (T36-T50 with fifth or sixth character 5)
    M10.20   Drug-induced gout, unspecified site
● M10.21   Drug-induced gout, shoulder
    M10.211   Drug-induced gout, right shoulder
    M10.212   Drug-induced gout, left shoulder
    M10.219   Drug-induced gout, unspecified shoulder
● M10.22   Drug-induced gout, elbow
    M10.221   Drug-induced gout, right elbow
    M10.222   Drug-induced gout, left elbow
    M10.229   Drug-induced gout, unspecified elbow
● M10.23   Drug-induced gout, wrist
    M10.231   Drug-induced gout, right wrist
    M10.232   Drug-induced gout, left wrist
    M10.239   Drug-induced gout, unspecified wrist

● M10.24   Drug-induced gout, hand
    M10.241   Drug-induced gout, right hand
    M10.242   Drug-induced gout, left hand
    M10.249   Drug-induced gout, unspecified hand
● M10.25   Drug-induced gout, hip
    M10.251   Drug-induced gout, right hip
    M10.252   Drug-induced gout, left hip
    M10.259   Drug-induced gout, unspecified hip
● M10.26   Drug-induced gout, knee
    M10.261   Drug-induced gout, right knee
    M10.262   Drug-induced gout, left knee
    M10.269   Drug-induced gout, unspecified knee
● M10.27   Drug-induced gout, ankle and foot
    M10.271   Drug-induced gout, right ankle and foot
    M10.272   Drug-induced gout, left ankle and foot
    M10.279   Drug-induced gout, unspecified ankle and foot
M10.28   Drug-induced gout, vertebrae
M10.29   Drug-induced gout, multiple sites

● M10.3   Gout due to renal impairment
    Code also associated renal disease
    M10.30   Gout due to renal impairment, unspecified site
● M10.31   Gout due to renal impairment, shoulder
    M10.311   Gout due to renal impairment, right shoulder
    M10.312   Gout due to renal impairment, left shoulder
    M10.319   Gout due to renal impairment, unspecified shoulder
● M10.32   Gout due to renal impairment, elbow
    M10.321   Gout due to renal impairment, right elbow
    M10.322   Gout due to renal impairment, left elbow
    M10.329   Gout due to renal impairment, unspecified elbow
● M10.33   Gout due to renal impairment, wrist
    M10.331   Gout due to renal impairment, right wrist
    M10.332   Gout due to renal impairment, left wrist
    M10.339   Gout due to renal impairment, unspecified wrist
● M10.34   Gout due to renal impairment, hand
    M10.341   Gout due to renal impairment, right hand
    M10.342   Gout due to renal impairment, left hand
    M10.349   Gout due to renal impairment, unspecified hand
● M10.35   Gout due to renal impairment, hip
    M10.351   Gout due to renal impairment, right hip
    M10.352   Gout due to renal impairment, left hip
    M10.359   Gout due to renal impairment, unspecified hip
● M10.36   Gout due to renal impairment, knee
    M10.361   Gout due to renal impairment, right knee
    M10.362   Gout due to renal impairment, left knee
    M10.369   Gout due to renal impairment, unspecified knee

● **M10.37** Gout due to renal impairment, ankle and foot
    M10.371   Gout due to renal impairment, right ankle and foot
    M10.372   Gout due to renal impairment, left ankle and foot
    M10.379   Gout due to renal impairment, unspecified ankle and foot
   M10.38   Gout due to renal impairment, vertebrae
   M10.39   Gout due to renal impairment, multiple sites

● **M10.4**   Other secondary gout
    Code first associated condition
   M10.40   Other secondary gout, unspecified site
● **M10.41**   Other secondary gout, shoulder
    M10.411   Other secondary gout, right shoulder
    M10.412   Other secondary gout, left shoulder
    M10.419   Other secondary gout, unspecified shoulder
● **M10.42**   Other secondary gout, elbow
    M10.421   Other secondary gout, right elbow
    M10.422   Other secondary gout, left elbow
    M10.429   Other secondary gout, unspecified elbow
● **M10.43**   Other secondary gout, wrist
    M10.431   Other secondary gout, right wrist
    M10.432   Other secondary gout, left wrist
    M10.439   Other secondary gout, unspecified wrist
● **M10.44**   Other secondary gout, hand
    M10.441   Other secondary gout, right hand
    M10.442   Other secondary gout, left hand
    M10.449   Other secondary gout, unspecified hand
● **M10.45**   Other secondary gout, hip
    M10.451   Other secondary gout, right hip
    M10.452   Other secondary gout, left hip
    M10.459   Other secondary gout, unspecified hip
● **M10.46**   Other secondary gout, knee
    M10.461   Other secondary gout, right knee
    M10.462   Other secondary gout, left knee
    M10.469   Other secondary gout, unspecified knee
● **M10.47**   Other secondary gout, ankle and foot
    M10.471   Other secondary gout, right ankle and foot
    M10.472   Other secondary gout, left ankle and foot
    M10.479   Other secondary gout, unspecified ankle and foot
   M10.48   Other secondary gout, vertebrae
   M10.49   Other secondary gout, multiple sites
  M10.9   Gout, unspecified
    Gout NOS

● **M11**   Other crystal arthropathies
● **M11.0**   Hydroxyapatite deposition disease
   M11.00   Hydroxyapatite deposition disease, unspecified site
● **M11.01**   Hydroxyapatite deposition disease, shoulder
    M11.011   Hydroxyapatite deposition disease, right shoulder
    M11.012   Hydroxyapatite deposition disease, left shoulder
    M11.019   Hydroxyapatite deposition disease, unspecified shoulder

● **M11.02**   Hydroxyapatite deposition disease, elbow
    M11.021   Hydroxyapatite deposition disease, right elbow
    M11.022   Hydroxyapatite deposition disease, left elbow
    M11.029   Hydroxyapatite deposition disease, unspecified elbow
● **M11.03**   Hydroxyapatite deposition disease, wrist
    M11.031   Hydroxyapatite deposition disease, right wrist
    M11.032   Hydroxyapatite deposition disease, left wrist
    M11.039   Hydroxyapatite deposition disease, unspecified wrist
● **M11.04**   Hydroxyapatite deposition disease, hand
    M11.041   Hydroxyapatite deposition disease, right hand
    M11.042   Hydroxyapatite deposition disease, left hand
    M11.049   Hydroxyapatite deposition disease, unspecified hand
● **M11.05**   Hydroxyapatite deposition disease, hip
    M11.051   Hydroxyapatite deposition disease, right hip
    M11.052   Hydroxyapatite deposition disease, left hip
    M11.059   Hydroxyapatite deposition disease, unspecified hip
● **M11.06**   Hydroxyapatite deposition disease, knee
    M11.061   Hydroxyapatite deposition disease, right knee
    M11.062   Hydroxyapatite deposition disease, left knee
    M11.069   Hydroxyapatite deposition disease, unspecified knee
● **M11.07**   Hydroxyapatite deposition disease, ankle and foot
    M11.071   Hydroxyapatite deposition disease, right ankle and foot
    M11.072   Hydroxyapatite deposition disease, left ankle and foot
    M11.079   Hydroxyapatite deposition disease, unspecified ankle and foot
   M11.08   Hydroxyapatite deposition disease, vertebrae
   M11.09   Hydroxyapatite deposition disease, multiple sites
● **M11.1**   Familial chondrocalcinosis
   M11.10   Familial chondrocalcinosis, unspecified site
● **M11.11**   Familial chondrocalcinosis, shoulder
    M11.111   Familial chondrocalcinosis, right shoulder
    M11.112   Familial chondrocalcinosis, left shoulder
    M11.119   Familial chondrocalcinosis, unspecified shoulder
● **M11.12**   Familial chondrocalcinosis, elbow
    M11.121   Familial chondrocalcinosis, right elbow
    M11.122   Familial chondrocalcinosis, left elbow
    M11.129   Familial chondrocalcinosis, unspecified elbow
● **M11.13**   Familial chondrocalcinosis, wrist
    M11.131   Familial chondrocalcinosis, right wrist
    M11.132   Familial chondrocalcinosis, left wrist
    M11.139   Familial chondrocalcinosis, unspecified wrist

CHAPTER 13 (M00-M99)

● M11.14 Familial chondrocalcinosis, hand
  M11.141 Familial chondrocalcinosis, right hand
  M11.142 Familial chondrocalcinosis, left hand
  M11.149 Familial chondrocalcinosis, unspecified hand
● M11.15 Familial chondrocalcinosis, hip
  M11.151 Familial chondrocalcinosis, right hip
  M11.152 Familial chondrocalcinosis, left hip
  M11.159 Familial chondrocalcinosis, unspecified hip
● M11.16 Familial chondrocalcinosis, knee
  M11.161 Familial chondrocalcinosis, right knee
  M11.162 Familial chondrocalcinosis, left knee
  M11.169 Familial chondrocalcinosis, unspecified knee
● M11.17 Familial chondrocalcinosis, ankle and foot
  M11.171 Familial chondrocalcinosis, right ankle and foot
  M11.172 Familial chondrocalcinosis, left ankle and foot
  M11.179 Familial chondrocalcinosis, unspecified ankle and foot
  M11.18 Familial chondrocalcinosis, vertebrae
  M11.19 Familial chondrocalcinosis, multiple sites
● M11.2 Other chondrocalcinosis
    Chondrocalcinosis NOS
  M11.20 Other chondrocalcinosis, unspecified site
● M11.21 Other chondrocalcinosis, shoulder
  M11.211 Other chondrocalcinosis, right shoulder
  M11.212 Other chondrocalcinosis, left shoulder
  M11.219 Other chondrocalcinosis, unspecified shoulder
● M11.22 Other chondrocalcinosis, elbow
  M11.221 Other chondrocalcinosis, right elbow
  M11.222 Other chondrocalcinosis, left elbow
  M11.229 Other chondrocalcinosis, unspecified elbow
● M11.23 Other chondrocalcinosis, wrist
  M11.231 Other chondrocalcinosis, right wrist
  M11.232 Other chondrocalcinosis, left wrist
  M11.239 Other chondrocalcinosis, unspecified wrist
● M11.24 Other chondrocalcinosis, hand
  M11.241 Other chondrocalcinosis, right hand
  M11.242 Other chondrocalcinosis, left hand
  M11.249 Other chondrocalcinosis, unspecified hand
● M11.25 Other chondrocalcinosis, hip
  M11.251 Other chondrocalcinosis, right hip
  M11.252 Other chondrocalcinosis, left hip
  M11.259 Other chondrocalcinosis, unspecified hip
● M11.26 Other chondrocalcinosis, knee
  M11.261 Other chondrocalcinosis, right knee
  M11.262 Other chondrocalcinosis, left knee
  M11.269 Other chondrocalcinosis, unspecified knee

● M11.27 Other chondrocalcinosis, ankle and foot
  M11.271 Other chondrocalcinosis, right ankle and foot
  M11.272 Other chondrocalcinosis, left ankle and foot
  M11.279 Other chondrocalcinosis, unspecified ankle and foot
  M11.28 Other chondrocalcinosis, vertebrae
  M11.29 Other chondrocalcinosis, multiple sites
● M11.8 Other specified crystal arthropathies
  M11.80 Other specified crystal arthropathies, unspecified site
● M11.81 Other specified crystal arthropathies, shoulder
  M11.811 Other specified crystal arthropathies, right shoulder
  M11.812 Other specified crystal arthropathies, left shoulder
  M11.819 Other specified crystal arthropathies, unspecified shoulder
● M11.82 Other specified crystal arthropathies, elbow
  M11.821 Other specified crystal arthropathies, right elbow
  M11.822 Other specified crystal arthropathies, left elbow
  M11.829 Other specified crystal arthropathies, unspecified elbow
● M11.83 Other specified crystal arthropathies, wrist
  M11.831 Other specified crystal arthropathies, right wrist
  M11.832 Other specified crystal arthropathies, left wrist
  M11.839 Other specified crystal arthropathies, unspecified wrist
● M11.84 Other specified crystal arthropathies, hand
  M11.841 Other specified crystal arthropathies, right hand
  M11.842 Other specified crystal arthropathies, left hand
  M11.849 Other specified crystal arthropathies, unspecified hand
● M11.85 Other specified crystal arthropathies, hip
  M11.851 Other specified crystal arthropathies, right hip
  M11.852 Other specified crystal arthropathies, left hip
  M11.859 Other specified crystal arthropathies, unspecified hip
● M11.86 Other specified crystal arthropathies, knee
  M11.861 Other specified crystal arthropathies, right knee
  M11.862 Other specified crystal arthropathies, left knee
  M11.869 Other specified crystal arthropathies, unspecified knee
● M11.87 Other specified crystal arthropathies, ankle and foot
  M11.871 Other specified crystal arthropathies, right ankle and foot
  M11.872 Other specified crystal arthropathies, left ankle and foot
  M11.879 Other specified crystal arthropathies, unspecified ankle and foot
  M11.88 Other specified crystal arthropathies, vertebrae
  M11.89 Other specified crystal arthropathies, multiple sites
  M11.9 Crystal arthropathy, unspecified

▶ New   ⇒ Revised   ~~deleted~~ Deleted   Excludes 1   Excludes 2   Includes   Use additional   Code first   Code also   Key words
OGCR Official Guidelines   X Assign placeholder X   ● Use Additional Character(s)   ▸ Manifestation Code   Coding Clinic

● **M12 Other and unspecified arthropathy**

　　Excludes1　arthrosis (M15-M19)
　　　　　　　　cricoarytenoid arthropathy (J38.7)

● M12.0　Chronic postrheumatic arthropathy [Jaccoud]

　　M12.00　Chronic postrheumatic arthropathy [Jaccoud], unspecified site

　● M12.01　Chronic postrheumatic arthropathy [Jaccoud], shoulder

　　　M12.011　Chronic postrheumatic arthropathy [Jaccoud], right shoulder

　　　M12.012　Chronic postrheumatic arthropathy [Jaccoud], left shoulder

　　　M12.019　Chronic postrheumatic arthropathy [Jaccoud], unspecified shoulder

　● M12.02　Chronic postrheumatic arthropathy [Jaccoud], elbow

　　　M12.021　Chronic postrheumatic arthropathy [Jaccoud], right elbow

　　　M12.022　Chronic postrheumatic arthropathy [Jaccoud], left elbow

　　　M12.029　Chronic postrheumatic arthropathy [Jaccoud], unspecified elbow

　● M12.03　Chronic postrheumatic arthropathy [Jaccoud], wrist

　　　M12.031　Chronic postrheumatic arthropathy [Jaccoud], right wrist

　　　M12.032　Chronic postrheumatic arthropathy [Jaccoud], left wrist

　　　M12.039　Chronic postrheumatic arthropathy [Jaccoud], unspecified wrist

　● M12.04　Chronic postrheumatic arthropathy [Jaccoud], hand

　　　M12.041　Chronic postrheumatic arthropathy [Jaccoud], right hand

　　　M12.042　Chronic postrheumatic arthropathy [Jaccoud], left hand

　　　M12.049　Chronic postrheumatic arthropathy [Jaccoud], unspecified hand

　● M12.05　Chronic postrheumatic arthropathy [Jaccoud], hip

　　　M12.051　Chronic postrheumatic arthropathy [Jaccoud], right hip

　　　M12.052　Chronic postrheumatic arthropathy [Jaccoud], left hip

　　　M12.059　Chronic postrheumatic arthropathy [Jaccoud], unspecified hip

　● M12.06　Chronic postrheumatic arthropathy [Jaccoud], knee

　　　M12.061　Chronic postrheumatic arthropathy [Jaccoud], right knee

　　　M12.062　Chronic postrheumatic arthropathy [Jaccoud], left knee

　　　M12.069　Chronic postrheumatic arthropathy [Jaccoud], unspecified knee

　● M12.07　Chronic postrheumatic arthropathy [Jaccoud], ankle and foot

　　　M12.071　Chronic postrheumatic arthropathy [Jaccoud], right ankle and foot

　　　M12.072　Chronic postrheumatic arthropathy [Jaccoud], left ankle and foot

　　　M12.079　Chronic postrheumatic arthropathy [Jaccoud], unspecified ankle and foot

　　M12.08　Chronic postrheumatic arthropathy [Jaccoud], other specified site

　　　　　Chronic postrheumatic arthropathy [Jaccoud], vertebrae

　　M12.09　Chronic postrheumatic arthropathy [Jaccoud], multiple sites

● M12.1　Kaschin-Beck disease

　　Osteochondroarthrosis deformans endemica

　　M12.10　Kaschin-Beck disease, unspecified site

　● M12.11　Kaschin-Beck disease, shoulder

　　　M12.111　Kaschin-Beck disease, right shoulder

　　　M12.112　Kaschin-Beck disease, left shoulder

　　　M12.119　Kaschin-Beck disease, unspecified shoulder

　● M12.12　Kaschin-Beck disease, elbow

　　　M12.121　Kaschin-Beck disease, right elbow

　　　M12.122　Kaschin-Beck disease, left elbow

　　　M12.129　Kaschin-Beck disease, unspecified elbow

　● M12.13　Kaschin-Beck disease, wrist

　　　M12.131　Kaschin-Beck disease, right wrist

　　　M12.132　Kaschin-Beck disease, left wrist

　　　M12.139　Kaschin-Beck disease, unspecified wrist

　● M12.14　Kaschin-Beck disease, hand

　　　M12.141　Kaschin-Beck disease, right hand

　　　M12.142　Kaschin-Beck disease, left hand

　　　M12.149　Kaschin-Beck disease, unspecified hand

　● M12.15　Kaschin-Beck disease, hip

　　　M12.151　Kaschin-Beck disease, right hip

　　　M12.152　Kaschin-Beck disease, left hip

　　　M12.159　Kaschin-Beck disease, unspecified hip

　● M12.16　Kaschin-Beck disease, knee

　　　M12.161　Kaschin-Beck disease, right knee

　　　M12.162　Kaschin-Beck disease, left knee

　　　M12.169　Kaschin-Beck disease, unspecified knee

　● M12.17　Kaschin-Beck disease, ankle and foot

　　　M12.171　Kaschin-Beck disease, right ankle and foot

　　　M12.172　Kaschin-Beck disease, left ankle and foot

　　　M12.179　Kaschin-Beck disease, unspecified ankle and foot

　　M12.18　Kaschin-Beck disease, vertebrae

　　M12.19　Kaschin-Beck disease, multiple sites

● M12.2　Villonodular synovitis (pigmented)

　　M12.20　Villonodular synovitis (pigmented), unspecified site

　● M12.21　Villonodular synovitis (pigmented), shoulder

　　　M12.211　Villonodular synovitis (pigmented), right shoulder

　　　M12.212　Villonodular synovitis (pigmented), left shoulder

　　　M12.219　Villonodular synovitis (pigmented), unspecified shoulder

　● M12.22　Villonodular synovitis (pigmented), elbow

　　　M12.221　Villonodular synovitis (pigmented), right elbow

　　　M12.222　Villonodular synovitis (pigmented), left elbow

　　　M12.229　Villonodular synovitis (pigmented), unspecified elbow

　● M12.23　Villonodular synovitis (pigmented), wrist

　　　M12.231　Villonodular synovitis (pigmented), right wrist

　　　M12.232　Villonodular synovitis (pigmented), left wrist

　　　M12.239　Villonodular synovitis (pigmented), unspecified wrist

CHAPTER 13 (M00-M99)

● M12.24   Villonodular synovitis (pigmented), hand
     M12.241   Villonodular synovitis (pigmented), right hand
     M12.242   Villonodular synovitis (pigmented), left hand
     M12.249   Villonodular synovitis (pigmented), unspecified hand
● M12.25   Villonodular synovitis (pigmented), hip
     M12.251   Villonodular synovitis (pigmented), right hip
     M12.252   Villonodular synovitis (pigmented), left hip
     M12.259   Villonodular synovitis (pigmented), unspecified hip
● M12.26   Villonodular synovitis (pigmented), knee
     M12.261   Villonodular synovitis (pigmented), right knee
     M12.262   Villonodular synovitis (pigmented), left knee
     M12.269   Villonodular synovitis (pigmented), unspecified knee
● M12.27   Villonodular synovitis (pigmented), ankle and foot
     M12.271   Villonodular synovitis (pigmented), right ankle and foot
     M12.272   Villonodular synovitis (pigmented), left ankle and foot
     M12.279   Villonodular synovitis (pigmented), unspecified ankle and foot
   M12.28   Villonodular synovitis (pigmented), other specified site
        Villonodular synovitis (pigmented), vertebrae
   M12.29   Villonodular synovitis (pigmented), multiple sites
● M12.3   Palindromic rheumatism
   M12.30   Palindromic rheumatism, unspecified site
● M12.31   Palindromic rheumatism, shoulder
     M12.311   Palindromic rheumatism, right shoulder
     M12.312   Palindromic rheumatism, left shoulder
     M12.319   Palindromic rheumatism, unspecified shoulder
● M12.32   Palindromic rheumatism, elbow
     M12.321   Palindromic rheumatism, right elbow
     M12.322   Palindromic rheumatism, left elbow
     M12.329   Palindromic rheumatism, unspecified elbow
● M12.33   Palindromic rheumatism, wrist
     M12.331   Palindromic rheumatism, right wrist
     M12.332   Palindromic rheumatism, left wrist
     M12.339   Palindromic rheumatism, unspecified wrist
● M12.34   Palindromic rheumatism, hand
     M12.341   Palindromic rheumatism, right hand
     M12.342   Palindromic rheumatism, left hand
     M12.349   Palindromic rheumatism, unspecified hand
● M12.35   Palindromic rheumatism, hip
     M12.351   Palindromic rheumatism, right hip
     M12.352   Palindromic rheumatism, left hip
     M12.359   Palindromic rheumatism, unspecified hip

● M12.36   Palindromic rheumatism, knee
     M12.361   Palindromic rheumatism, right knee
     M12.362   Palindromic rheumatism, left knee
     M12.369   Palindromic rheumatism, unspecified knee
● M12.37   Palindromic rheumatism, ankle and foot
     M12.371   Palindromic rheumatism, right ankle and foot
     M12.372   Palindromic rheumatism, left ankle and foot
     M12.379   Palindromic rheumatism, unspecified ankle and foot
   M12.38   Palindromic rheumatism, other specified site
        Palindromic rheumatism, vertebrae
   M12.39   Palindromic rheumatism, multiple sites
● M12.4   Intermittent hydrarthrosis
   M12.40   Intermittent hydrarthrosis, unspecified site
● M12.41   Intermittent hydrarthrosis, shoulder
     M12.411   Intermittent hydrarthrosis, right shoulder
     M12.412   Intermittent hydrarthrosis, left shoulder
     M12.419   Intermittent hydrarthrosis, unspecified shoulder
● M12.42   Intermittent hydrarthrosis, elbow
     M12.421   Intermittent hydrarthrosis, right elbow
     M12.422   Intermittent hydrarthrosis, left elbow
     M12.429   Intermittent hydrarthrosis, unspecified elbow
● M12.43   Intermittent hydrarthrosis, wrist
     M12.431   Intermittent hydrarthrosis, right wrist
     M12.432   Intermittent hydrarthrosis, left wrist
     M12.439   Intermittent hydrarthrosis, unspecified wrist
● M12.44   Intermittent hydrarthrosis, hand
     M12.441   Intermittent hydrarthrosis, right hand
     M12.442   Intermittent hydrarthrosis, left hand
     M12.449   Intermittent hydrarthrosis, unspecified hand
● M12.45   Intermittent hydrarthrosis, hip
     M12.451   Intermittent hydrarthrosis, right hip
     M12.452   Intermittent hydrarthrosis, left hip
     M12.459   Intermittent hydrarthrosis, unspecified hip
● M12.46   Intermittent hydrarthrosis, knee
     M12.461   Intermittent hydrarthrosis, right knee
     M12.462   Intermittent hydrarthrosis, left knee
     M12.469   Intermittent hydrarthrosis, unspecified knee
● M12.47   Intermittent hydrarthrosis, ankle and foot
     M12.471   Intermittent hydrarthrosis, right ankle and foot
     M12.472   Intermittent hydrarthrosis, left ankle and foot
     M12.479   Intermittent hydrarthrosis, unspecified ankle and foot
   M12.48   Intermittent hydrarthrosis, other site
   M12.49   Intermittent hydrarthrosis, multiple sites

▶ New   ⇒ Revised   ~~deleted~~ Deleted   Excludes 1   Excludes 2   Includes   Use additional   Code first   Code also   Key words
OGCR Official Guidelines   X Assign placeholder X   ● Use Additional Character(s)   ▶ Manifestation Code   **Coding Clinic**

● M12.5   **Traumatic arthropathy**
     Excludes1   current injury–see Alphabetic Index
             post-traumatic osteoarthritis of first
                carpometacarpal joint (M18.2-M18.3)
             post-traumatic osteoarthritis of hip
                (M16.4-M16.5)
             post-traumatic osteoarthritis of knee
                (M17.2-M17.3)
             post-traumatic osteoarthritis NOS
                (M19.1-)
             post-traumatic osteoarthritis of other
                single joints (M19.1-)

     M12.50   Traumatic arthropathy, unspecified site
● M12.51   Traumatic arthropathy, shoulder
         M12.511   Traumatic arthropathy, right shoulder
         M12.512   Traumatic arthropathy, left shoulder
         M12.519   Traumatic arthropathy, unspecified
                  shoulder
● M12.52   Traumatic arthropathy, elbow
         M12.521   Traumatic arthropathy, right elbow
         M12.522   Traumatic arthropathy, left elbow
         M12.529   Traumatic arthropathy, unspecified
                  elbow
● M12.53   Traumatic arthropathy, wrist
         M12.531   Traumatic arthropathy, right wrist
         M12.532   Traumatic arthropathy, left wrist
         M12.539   Traumatic arthropathy, unspecified
                  wrist
● M12.54   Traumatic arthropathy, hand
         M12.541   Traumatic arthropathy, right hand
         M12.542   Traumatic arthropathy, left hand
         M12.549   Traumatic arthropathy, unspecified
                  hand
● M12.55   Traumatic arthropathy, hip
         M12.551   Traumatic arthropathy, right hip
         M12.552   Traumatic arthropathy, left hip
                 Coding Clinic: 2015, Q1, P17
         M12.559   Traumatic arthropathy, unspecified
                  hip
● M12.56   Traumatic arthropathy, knee
         M12.561   Traumatic arthropathy, right knee
         M12.562   Traumatic arthropathy, left knee
         M12.569   Traumatic arthropathy, unspecified
                  knee
● M12.57   Traumatic arthropathy, ankle and foot
         M12.571   Traumatic arthropathy, right ankle
                  and foot
         M12.572   Traumatic arthropathy, left ankle and
                  foot
         M12.579   Traumatic arthropathy, unspecified
                  ankle and foot
     M12.58   Traumatic arthropathy, other specified site
             Traumatic arthropathy, vertebrae
     M12.59   Traumatic arthropathy, multiple sites
● M12.8   Other specific arthropathies, not elsewhere classified
         Transient arthropathy
     M12.80   Other specific arthropathies, not elsewhere
             classified, unspecified site
● M12.81   Other specific arthropathies, not elsewhere
         classified, shoulder
         M12.811   Other specific arthropathies, not
                  elsewhere classified, right shoulder
         M12.812   Other specific arthropathies, not
                  elsewhere classified, left shoulder
         M12.819   Other specific arthropathies, not
                  elsewhere classified, unspecified
                  shoulder

● M12.82   Other specific arthropathies, not elsewhere
         classified, elbow
         M12.821   Other specific arthropathies, not
                  elsewhere classified, right elbow
         M12.822   Other specific arthropathies, not
                  elsewhere classified, left elbow
         M12.829   Other specific arthropathies, not
                  elsewhere classified, unspecified
                  elbow
● M12.83   Other specific arthropathies, not elsewhere
         classified, wrist
         M12.831   Other specific arthropathies, not
                  elsewhere classified, right wrist
         M12.832   Other specific arthropathies, not
                  elsewhere classified, left wrist
         M12.839   Other specific arthropathies, not
                  elsewhere classified, unspecified wrist
● M12.84   Other specific arthropathies, not elsewhere
         classified, hand
         M12.841   Other specific arthropathies, not
                  elsewhere classified, right hand
         M12.842   Other specific arthropathies, not
                  elsewhere classified, left hand
         M12.849   Other specific arthropathies, not
                  elsewhere classified, unspecified hand
● M12.85   Other specific arthropathies, not elsewhere
         classified, hip
         M12.851   Other specific arthropathies, not
                  elsewhere classified, right hip
         M12.852   Other specific arthropathies, not
                  elsewhere classified, left hip
         M12.859   Other specific arthropathies, not
                  elsewhere classified, unspecified hip
● M12.86   Other specific arthropathies, not elsewhere
         classified, knee
         M12.861   Other specific arthropathies, not
                  elsewhere classified, right knee
         M12.862   Other specific arthropathies, not
                  elsewhere classified, left knee
         M12.869   Other specific arthropathies, not
                  elsewhere classified, unspecified knee
● M12.87   Other specific arthropathies, not elsewhere
         classified, ankle and foot
         M12.871   Other specific arthropathies, not
                  elsewhere classified, right ankle and
                  foot
         M12.872   Other specific arthropathies, not
                  elsewhere classified, left ankle and
                  foot
         M12.879   Other specific arthropathies, not
                  elsewhere classified, unspecified
                  ankle and foot
     M12.88   Other specific arthropathies, not elsewhere
         classified, other specified site
             Other specific arthropathies, not elsewhere
                classified, vertebrae
     M12.89   Other specific arthropathies, not elsewhere
         classified, multiple sites

M12.9   Arthropathy, unspecified

CHAPTER 13 (MØØ-M99)

●M13　Other arthritis
　　Excludes1　arthrosis (M15-M19)
　　　　　　　　osteoarthritis (M15-M19)
　　M13.0　Polyarthritis, unspecified
●M13.1　Monoarthritis, not elsewhere classified
　　M13.10　Monoarthritis, not elsewhere classified, unspecified site
　●M13.11　Monoarthritis, not elsewhere classified, shoulder
　　　M13.111　Monoarthritis, not elsewhere classified, right shoulder
　　　M13.112　Monoarthritis, not elsewhere classified, left shoulder
　　　M13.119　Monoarthritis, not elsewhere classified, unspecified shoulder
　●M13.12　Monoarthritis, not elsewhere classified, elbow
　　　M13.121　Monoarthritis, not elsewhere classified, right elbow
　　　M13.122　Monoarthritis, not elsewhere classified, left elbow
　　　M13.129　Monoarthritis, not elsewhere classified, unspecified elbow
　●M13.13　Monoarthritis, not elsewhere classified, wrist
　　　M13.131　Monoarthritis, not elsewhere classified, right wrist
　　　M13.132　Monoarthritis, not elsewhere classified, left wrist
　　　M13.139　Monoarthritis, not elsewhere classified, unspecified wrist
　●M13.14　Monoarthritis, not elsewhere classified, hand
　　　M13.141　Monoarthritis, not elsewhere classified, right hand
　　　M13.142　Monoarthritis, not elsewhere classified, left hand
　　　M13.149　Monoarthritis, not elsewhere classified, unspecified hand
　●M13.15　Monoarthritis, not elsewhere classified, hip
　　　M13.151　Monoarthritis, not elsewhere classified, right hip
　　　M13.152　Monoarthritis, not elsewhere classified, left hip
　　　M13.159　Monoarthritis, not elsewhere classified, unspecified hip
　●M13.16　Monoarthritis, not elsewhere classified, knee
　　　M13.161　Monoarthritis, not elsewhere classified, right knee
　　　M13.162　Monoarthritis, not elsewhere classified, left knee
　　　M13.169　Monoarthritis, not elsewhere classified, unspecified knee
　●M13.17　Monoarthritis, not elsewhere classified, ankle and foot
　　　M13.171　Monoarthritis, not elsewhere classified, right ankle and foot
　　　M13.172　Monoarthritis, not elsewhere classified, left ankle and foot
　　　M13.179　Monoarthritis, not elsewhere classified, unspecified ankle and foot
●M13.8　Other specified arthritis
　　Allergic arthritis
　　Excludes1　osteoarthritis (M15-M19)
　　M13.80　Other specified arthritis, unspecified site
●M13.81　Other specified arthritis, shoulder
　　　M13.811　Other specified arthritis, right shoulder
　　　M13.812　Other specified arthritis, left shoulder
　　　M13.819　Other specified arthritis, unspecified shoulder

●M13.82　Other specified arthritis, elbow
　　　M13.821　Other specified arthritis, right elbow
　　　M13.822　Other specified arthritis, left elbow
　　　M13.829　Other specified arthritis, unspecified elbow
●M13.83　Other specified arthritis, wrist
　　　M13.831　Other specified arthritis, right wrist
　　　M13.832　Other specified arthritis, left wrist
　　　M13.839　Other specified arthritis, unspecified wrist
●M13.84　Other specified arthritis, hand
　　　M13.841　Other specified arthritis, right hand
　　　M13.842　Other specified arthritis, left hand
　　　M13.849　Other specified arthritis, unspecified hand
●M13.85　Other specified arthritis, hip
　　　M13.851　Other specified arthritis, right hip
　　　M13.852　Other specified arthritis, left hip
　　　M13.859　Other specified arthritis, unspecified hip
●M13.86　Other specified arthritis, knee
　　　M13.861　Other specified arthritis, right knee
　　　M13.862　Other specified arthritis, left knee
　　　M13.869　Other specified arthritis, unspecified knee
●M13.87　Other specified arthritis, ankle and foot
　　　M13.871　Other specified arthritis, right ankle and foot
　　　M13.872　Other specified arthritis, left ankle and foot
　　　M13.879　Other specified arthritis, unspecified ankle and foot
　　M13.88　Other specified arthritis, other site
　　M13.89　Other specified arthritis, multiple sites

●M14　Arthropathies in other diseases classified elsewhere
　　Excludes1　arthropathy in:
　　　　　　　　diabetes mellitus (E08-E13 with .61-)
　　　　　　　　hematological disorders (M36.2-M36.3)
　　　　　　　　hypersensitivity reactions (M36.4)
　　　　　　　　neoplastic disease (M36.1)
　　　　　　　　neurosyphillis (A52.16)
　　　　　　　　sarcoidosis (D86.86)
　　　　　　　enteropathic arthropathies (M07.0-)
　　　　　　　juvenile psoriatic arthropathy (L40.54)
　　　　　　　lipoid dermatoarthritis (E78.81)
●M14.6　Charcôt's joint
　　Neuropathic arthropathy
　　Excludes1　Charcôt's joint in diabetes mellitus (E08-E13 with .610)
　　　　　　　　Charcôt's joint in tabes dorsalis (A52.16)
　　M14.60　Charcôt's joint, unspecified site
●M14.61　Charcôt's joint, shoulder
　　　M14.611　Charcôt's joint, right shoulder
　　　M14.612　Charcôt's joint, left shoulder
　　　M14.619　Charcôt's joint, unspecified shoulder
●M14.62　Charcôt's joint, elbow
　　　M14.621　Charcôt's joint, right elbow
　　　M14.622　Charcôt's joint, left elbow
　　　M14.629　Charcôt's joint, unspecified elbow
●M14.63　Charcôt's joint, wrist
　　　M14.631　Charcôt's joint, right wrist
　　　M14.632　Charcôt's joint, left wrist
　　　M14.639　Charcôt's joint, unspecified wrist

▶ New　⇒ Revised　~~deleted~~ Deleted　Excludes 1　Excludes 2　Includes　Use additional　Code first　Code also　Key words
OGCR Official Guidelines　X Assign placeholder X　● Use Additional Character(s)　▶ Manifestation Code　Coding Clinic

● **M14.64** Charcôt's joint, hand

    M14.641 Charcôt's joint, right hand

    M14.642 Charcôt's joint, left hand

    M14.649 Charcôt's joint, unspecified hand

● **M14.65** Charcôt's joint, hip

    M14.651 Charcôt's joint, right hip

    M14.652 Charcôt's joint, left hip

    M14.659 Charcôt's joint, unspecified hip

● **M14.66** Charcôt's joint, knee

    M14.661 Charcôt's joint, right knee

    M14.662 Charcôt's joint, left knee

    M14.669 Charcôt's joint, unspecified knee

● **M14.67** Charcôt's joint, ankle and foot

    M14.671 Charcôt's joint, right ankle and foot

    M14.672 Charcôt's joint, left ankle and foot

    M14.679 Charcôt's joint, unspecified ankle and foot

    M14.68 Charcôt's joint, vertebrae

    M14.69 Charcôt's joint, multiple sites

● **M14.8** Arthropathies in other specified diseases classified elsewhere

    Code first underlying disease, such as:
        amyloidosis (E85.-)
        erythema multiforme (L51.-)
        erythema nodosum (L52)
        hemochromatosis (E83.11-)
        hyperparathyroidism (E21.-)
        hypothyroidism (E00-E03)
        sickle-cell disorders (D57.-)
        thyrotoxicosis [hyperthyroidism] (E05.-)
        Whipple's disease (K90.81)

   ▸ *M14.80* *Arthropathies in other specified diseases classified elsewhere, unspecified site*

  ● **M14.81** Arthropathies in other specified diseases classified elsewhere, shoulder

    ▸ *M14.811* *Arthropathies in other specified diseases classified elsewhere, right shoulder*

    ▸ *M14.812* *Arthropathies in other specified diseases classified elsewhere, left shoulder*

    ▸ *M14.819* *Arthropathies in other specified diseases classified elsewhere, unspecified shoulder*

  ● **M14.82** Arthropathies in other specified diseases classified elsewhere, elbow

    ▸ *M14.821* *Arthropathies in other specified diseases classified elsewhere, right elbow*

    ▸ *M14.822* *Arthropathies in other specified diseases classified elsewhere, left elbow*

    ▸ *M14.829* *Arthropathies in other specified diseases classified elsewhere, unspecified elbow*

  ● **M14.83** Arthropathies in other specified diseases classified elsewhere, wrist

    ▸ *M14.831* *Arthropathies in other specified diseases classified elsewhere, right wrist*

    ▸ *M14.832* *Arthropathies in other specified diseases classified elsewhere, left wrist*

    ▸ *M14.839* *Arthropathies in other specified diseases classified elsewhere, unspecified wrist*

● **M14.84** Arthropathies in other specified diseases classified elsewhere, hand

    ▸ *M14.841* *Arthropathies in other specified diseases classified elsewhere, right hand*

    ▸ *M14.842* *Arthropathies in other specified diseases classified elsewhere, left hand*

    ▸ *M14.849* *Arthropathies in other specified diseases classified elsewhere, unspecified hand*

● **M14.85** Arthropathies in other specified diseases classified elsewhere, hip

    ▸ *M14.851* *Arthropathies in other specified diseases classified elsewhere, right hip*

    ▸ *M14.852* *Arthropathies in other specified diseases classified elsewhere, left hip*

    ▸ *M14.859* *Arthropathies in other specified diseases classified elsewhere, unspecified hip*

● **M14.86** Arthropathies in other specified diseases classified elsewhere, knee

    ▸ *M14.861* *Arthropathies in other specified diseases classified elsewhere, right knee*

    ▸ *M14.862* *Arthropathies in other specified diseases classified elsewhere, left knee*

    ▸ *M14.869* *Arthropathies in other specified diseases classified elsewhere, unspecified knee*

● **M14.87** Arthropathies in other specified diseases classified elsewhere, ankle and foot

    ▸ *M14.871* *Arthropathies in other specified diseases classified elsewhere, right ankle and foot*

    ▸ *M14.872* *Arthropathies in other specified diseases classified elsewhere, left ankle and foot*

    ▸ *M14.879* *Arthropathies in other specified diseases classified elsewhere, unspecified ankle and foot*

  ▸ *M14.88* *Arthropathies in other specified diseases classified elsewhere, vertebrae*

  ▸ *M14.89* *Arthropathies in other specified diseases classified elsewhere, multiple sites*

OSTEOARTHRITIS (M15-M19)

Osteoarthritis is the most common degenerative joint disease and form of arthritis that breaks down the cartilage causing pain, swelling, and reduced motion in the joints.

    Excludes2   osteoarthritis of spine (M47.-)

● **M15** Polyosteoarthritis

    Includes   arthritis of multiple sites

    Excludes1   bilateral involvement of single joint (M16-M19)

    M15.0 Primary generalized (osteo)arthritis

    M15.1 Heberden's nodes (with arthropathy)
        Interphalangeal distal osteoarthritis

    M15.2 Bouchard's nodes (with arthropathy)
        Juxtaphalangeal distal osteoarthritis

    M15.3 Secondary multiple arthritis
        Post-traumatic polyosteoarthritis

    M15.4 Erosive (osteo)arthritis

    M15.8 Other polyosteoarthritis

    M15.9 Polyosteoarthritis, unspecified
        Generalized osteoarthritis NOS

CHAPTER 13 (M00-M99)

CHAPTER 13 (M00-M99)

● M16 **Osteoarthritis of hip**

    M16.0 **Bilateral primary osteoarthritis of hip**
             Coding Clinic: 2018, Q2, P15; 2016, Q4, P146

  ● M16.1 **Unilateral primary osteoarthritis of hip**
            Primary osteoarthritis of hip NOS

       M16.10 Unilateral primary osteoarthritis, unspecified hip

       M16.11 Unilateral primary osteoarthritis, right hip

       M16.12 Unilateral primary osteoarthritis, left hip

    M16.2 **Bilateral osteoarthritis resulting from hip dysplasia**

  ● M16.3 **Unilateral osteoarthritis resulting from hip dysplasia**
            Dysplastic osteoarthritis of hip NOS

       M16.30 Unilateral osteoarthritis resulting from hip dysplasia, unspecified hip

       M16.31 Unilateral osteoarthritis resulting from hip dysplasia, right hip

       M16.32 Unilateral osteoarthritis resulting from hip dysplasia, left hip

    M16.4 **Bilateral post-traumatic osteoarthritis of hip**

  ● M16.5 **Unilateral post-traumatic osteoarthritis of hip**
            Post-traumatic osteoarthritis of hip NOS

       M16.50 Unilateral post-traumatic osteoarthritis, unspecified hip

       M16.51 Unilateral post-traumatic osteoarthritis, right hip

       M16.52 Unilateral post-traumatic osteoarthritis, left hip

    M16.6 **Other bilateral secondary osteoarthritis of hip**

    M16.7 **Other unilateral secondary osteoarthritis of hip**
            Secondary osteoarthritis of hip NOS

    M16.9 **Osteoarthritis of hip, unspecified**

● M17 **Osteoarthritis of knee**

    M17.0 **Bilateral primary osteoarthritis of knee**

  ● M17.1 **Unilateral primary osteoarthritis of knee**
            Primary osteoarthritis of knee NOS

       M17.10 Unilateral primary osteoarthritis, unspecified knee
              Coding Clinic: 2016, Q4, P147

       M17.11 Unilateral primary osteoarthritis, right knee

       M17.12 Unilateral primary osteoarthritis, left knee
              Coding Clinic: 2016, Q4, P146

    M17.2 **Bilateral post-traumatic osteoarthritis of knee**

  ● M17.3 **Unilateral post-traumatic osteoarthritis of knee**
            Post-traumatic osteoarthritis of knee NOS

       M17.30 Unilateral post-traumatic osteoarthritis, unspecified knee

       M17.31 Unilateral post-traumatic osteoarthritis, right knee

       M17.32 Unilateral post-traumatic osteoarthritis, left knee

    M17.4 **Other bilateral secondary osteoarthritis of knee**

    M17.5 **Other unilateral secondary osteoarthritis of knee**
            Secondary osteoarthritis of knee NOS

    M17.9 **Osteoarthritis of knee, unspecified**
            Coding Clinic: 2016, Q4, P146

● M18 **Osteoarthritis of first carpometacarpal joint**

    M18.0 **Bilateral primary osteoarthritis of first carpometacarpal joints**

  ● M18.1 **Unilateral primary osteoarthritis of first carpometacarpal joint**
            Primary osteoarthritis of first carpometacarpal joint NOS

       M18.10 Unilateral primary osteoarthritis of first carpometacarpal joint, unspecified hand

       M18.11 Unilateral primary osteoarthritis of first carpometacarpal joint, right hand

       M18.12 Unilateral primary osteoarthritis of first carpometacarpal joint, left hand

    M18.2 **Bilateral post-traumatic osteoarthritis of first carpometacarpal joints**

  ● M18.3 **Unilateral post-traumatic osteoarthritis of first carpometacarpal joint**
            Post-traumatic osteoarthritis of first carpometacarpal joint NOS

       M18.30 Unilateral post-traumatic osteoarthritis of first carpometacarpal joint, unspecified hand

       M18.31 Unilateral post-traumatic osteoarthritis of first carpometacarpal joint, right hand

       M18.32 Unilateral post-traumatic osteoarthritis of first carpometacarpal joint, left hand

    M18.4 **Other bilateral secondary osteoarthritis of first carpometacarpal joints**

  ● M18.5 **Other unilateral secondary osteoarthritis of first carpometacarpal joint**
            Secondary osteoarthritis of first carpometacarpal joint NOS

       M18.50 Other unilateral secondary osteoarthritis of first carpometacarpal joint, unspecified hand

       M18.51 Other unilateral secondary osteoarthritis of first carpometacarpal joint, right hand

       M18.52 Other unilateral secondary osteoarthritis of first carpometacarpal joint, left hand

    M18.9 **Osteoarthritis of first carpometacarpal joint, unspecified**

● M19 **Other and unspecified osteoarthritis**

    Excludes1   polyarthritis (M15.-)

    Excludes2   arthrosis of spine (M47.-)
                hallux rigidus (M20.2)
                osteoarthritis of spine (M47.-)

  ● M19.0 **Primary osteoarthritis of other joints**

    ● M19.01 Primary osteoarthritis, shoulder

        M19.011 Primary osteoarthritis, right shoulder
               Coding Clinic: 2016, Q4, P145

        M19.012 Primary osteoarthritis, left shoulder

        M19.019 Primary osteoarthritis, unspecified shoulder

    ● M19.02 Primary osteoarthritis, elbow

        M19.021 Primary osteoarthritis, right elbow

        M19.022 Primary osteoarthritis, left elbow

        M19.029 Primary osteoarthritis, unspecified elbow

    ● M19.03 Primary osteoarthritis, wrist

        M19.031 Primary osteoarthritis, right wrist

        M19.032 Primary osteoarthritis, left wrist

        M19.039 Primary osteoarthritis, unspecified wrist

    ● M19.04 Primary osteoarthritis, hand

        Excludes2   primary osteoarthritis of first carpometacarpal joint (M18.0-, M18.1-)

        M19.041 Primary osteoarthritis, right hand

        M19.042 Primary osteoarthritis, left hand

        M19.049 Primary osteoarthritis, unspecified hand

    ● M19.07 Primary osteoarthritis ankle and foot

        M19.071 Primary osteoarthritis, right ankle and foot

        M19.072 Primary osteoarthritis, left ankle and foot

        M19.079 Primary osteoarthritis, unspecified ankle and foot

● **M19.1** Post-traumatic osteoarthritis of other joints

  ● **M19.11** Post-traumatic osteoarthritis, shoulder

     M19.111 Post-traumatic osteoarthritis, right shoulder

     M19.112 Post-traumatic osteoarthritis, left shoulder

     M19.119 Post-traumatic osteoarthritis, unspecified shoulder

  ● **M19.12** Post-traumatic osteoarthritis, elbow

     M19.121 Post-traumatic osteoarthritis, right elbow

     M19.122 Post-traumatic osteoarthritis, left elbow

     M19.129 Post-traumatic osteoarthritis, unspecified elbow

  ● **M19.13** Post-traumatic osteoarthritis, wrist

     M19.131 Post-traumatic osteoarthritis, right wrist

     M19.132 Post-traumatic osteoarthritis, left wrist

     M19.139 Post-traumatic osteoarthritis, unspecified wrist

  ● **M19.14** Post-traumatic osteoarthritis, hand

     Excludes2   post-traumatic osteoarthritis of first carpometacarpal joint (M18.2-, M18.3-)

     M19.141 Post-traumatic osteoarthritis, right hand

     M19.142 Post-traumatic osteoarthritis, left hand

     M19.149 Post-traumatic osteoarthritis, unspecified hand

  ● **M19.17** Post-traumatic osteoarthritis, ankle and foot

     M19.171 Post-traumatic osteoarthritis, right ankle and foot

     M19.172 Post-traumatic osteoarthritis, left ankle and foot

     M19.179 Post-traumatic osteoarthritis, unspecified ankle and foot

● **M19.2** Secondary osteoarthritis of other joints

  ● **M19.21** Secondary osteoarthritis, shoulder

     M19.211 Secondary osteoarthritis, right shoulder

     M19.212 Secondary osteoarthritis, left shoulder

     M19.219 Secondary osteoarthritis, unspecified shoulder

  ● **M19.22** Secondary osteoarthritis, elbow

     M19.221 Secondary osteoarthritis, right elbow

     M19.222 Secondary osteoarthritis, left elbow

     M19.229 Secondary osteoarthritis, unspecified elbow

  ● **M19.23** Secondary osteoarthritis, wrist

     M19.231 Secondary osteoarthritis, right wrist

     M19.232 Secondary osteoarthritis, left wrist

     M19.239 Secondary osteoarthritis, unspecified wrist

  ● **M19.24** Secondary osteoarthritis, hand

     M19.241 Secondary osteoarthritis, right hand

     M19.242 Secondary osteoarthritis, left hand

     M19.249 Secondary osteoarthritis, unspecified hand

  ● **M19.27** Secondary osteoarthritis, ankle and foot

     M19.271 Secondary osteoarthritis, right ankle and foot

     M19.272 Secondary osteoarthritis, left ankle and foot

     M19.279 Secondary osteoarthritis, unspecified ankle and foot

● **M19.9** Osteoarthritis, unspecified site

   M19.90 Unspecified osteoarthritis, unspecified site
     Arthrosis NOS
     Arthritis NOS
     Osteoarthritis NOS
     Coding Clinic: 2016, Q4, P147

   M19.91 Primary osteoarthritis, unspecified site
     Primary osteoarthritis NOS

   M19.92 Post-traumatic osteoarthritis, unspecified site
     Post-traumatic osteoarthritis NOS

   M19.93 Secondary osteoarthritis, unspecified site
     Secondary osteoarthritis NOS

OTHER JOINT DISORDERS (M20-M25)

   Excludes2   joints of the spine (M40-M54)

● **M20** Acquired deformities of fingers and toes

   Excludes1   acquired absence of fingers and toes (Z89.-)
     congenital absence of fingers and toes (Q71.3-, Q72.3-)
     congenital deformities and malformations of fingers and toes (Q66.-, Q68-Q70, Q74.-)

  ● **M20.0** Deformity of finger(s)

     Excludes1   clubbing of fingers (R68.3)
      palmar fascial fibromatosis [Dupuytren] (M72.0)
      trigger finger (M65.3)

    ● **M20.00** Unspecified deformity of finger(s)

      M20.001 Unspecified deformity of right finger(s)

      M20.002 Unspecified deformity of left finger(s)

      M20.009 Unspecified deformity of unspecified finger(s)

    ● **M20.01** Mallet finger

      M20.011 Mallet finger of right finger(s)

      M20.012 Mallet finger of left finger(s)

      M20.019 Mallet finger of unspecified finger(s)

    ● **M20.02** Boutonnière deformity

      M20.021 Boutonnière deformity of right finger(s)

      M20.022 Boutonnière deformity of left finger(s)

      M20.029 Boutonnière deformity of unspecified finger(s)

    ● **M20.03** Swan-neck deformity

      M20.031 Swan-neck deformity of right finger(s)

      M20.032 Swan-neck deformity of left finger(s)

      M20.039 Swan-neck deformity of unspecified finger(s)

    ● **M20.09** Other deformity of finger(s)

      M20.091 Other deformity of right finger(s)

      M20.092 Other deformity of left finger(s)

      M20.099 Other deformity of finger(s), unspecified finger(s)

  ● **M20.1** Hallux valgus (acquired)

     Excludes2   bunion (M21.6-)
     Coding Clinic: 2016, Q4, P38

     M20.10 Hallux valgus (acquired), unspecified foot

     M20.11 Hallux valgus (acquired), right foot

     M20.12 Hallux valgus (acquired), left foot

  ● **M20.2** Hallux rigidus

     M20.20 Hallux rigidus, unspecified foot

     M20.21 Hallux rigidus, right foot

     M20.22 Hallux rigidus, left foot

CHAPTER 13 (M00-M99)

Figure 13-1 Hallux valgus.

Item 13-2 Hallux valgus is a sometimes painful structural deformity caused by an inflammation of the bursal sac at the base of the metatarsophalangeal joint (big toe). **Hallus varus** is a deviation of the great toe to the inner side of the foot or away from the next toe.

- M20.3 Hallux varus (acquired)
  - M20.30 Hallux varus (acquired), unspecified foot
  - M20.31 Hallux varus (acquired), right foot
  - M20.32 Hallux varus (acquired), left foot
- M20.4 Other hammer toe(s) (acquired)
  - M20.40 Other hammer toe(s) (acquired), unspecified foot
  - M20.41 Other hammer toe(s) (acquired), right foot
  - M20.42 Other hammer toe(s) (acquired), left foot
- M20.5 Other deformities of toe(s) (acquired)
  - M20.5X Other deformities of toe(s) (acquired)
    - M20.5X1 Other deformities of toe(s) (acquired), right foot
    - M20.5X2 Other deformities of toe(s) (acquired), left foot
    - M20.5X9 Other deformities of toe(s) (acquired), unspecified foot
- M20.6 Acquired deformities of toe(s), unspecified
  - M20.60 Acquired deformities of toe(s), unspecified, unspecified foot
  - M20.61 Acquired deformities of toe(s), unspecified, right foot
  - M20.62 Acquired deformities of toe(s), unspecified, left foot

- M21 Other acquired deformities of limbs
  - Excludes1 acquired absence of limb (Z89.-)
    congenital absence of limbs (Q71-Q73)
    congenital deformities and malformations of limbs (Q65-Q66, Q68-Q74)
  - Excludes2 acquired deformities of fingers or toes (M20.-)
    coxa plana (M91.2)
  - M21.0 Valgus deformity, not elsewhere classified
    - Excludes1 metatarsus valgus (Q66.6)
      talipes calcaneovalgus (Q66.4)
    - M21.00 Valgus deformity, not elsewhere classified, unspecified site
    - M21.02 Valgus deformity, not elsewhere classified, elbow
      Cubitus valgus
      - M21.021 Valgus deformity, not elsewhere classified, right elbow
      - M21.022 Valgus deformity, not elsewhere classified, left elbow
      - M21.029 Valgus deformity, not elsewhere classified, unspecified elbow

Item 13-3 Cubitus valgus is a deformity of the elbow resulting in an increased carrying angle in which the arm extends at the side and the palm faces forward, which results in the forearm and hand extended at a greater than 15 degrees.

Item 13-4 Cubitus varus is a deformity of the elbow resulting in the arm extended at the side and the palm facing forward so that the forearm and hand are held at less than 5 degrees, decreasing the carrying angle.

- M21.05 Valgus deformity, not elsewhere classified, hip
  - M21.051 Valgus deformity, not elsewhere classified, right hip
  - M21.052 Valgus deformity, not elsewhere classified, left hip
  - M21.059 Valgus deformity, not elsewhere classified, unspecified hip
- M21.06 Valgus deformity, not elsewhere classified, knee
  Genu valgum
  Knock knee
  - M21.061 Valgus deformity, not elsewhere classified, right knee
  - M21.062 Valgus deformity, not elsewhere classified, left knee
  - M21.069 Valgus deformity, not elsewhere classified, unspecified knee
- M21.07 Valgus deformity, not elsewhere classified, ankle
  - M21.071 Valgus deformity, not elsewhere classified, right ankle
  - M21.072 Valgus deformity, not elsewhere classified, left ankle
  - M21.079 Valgus deformity, not elsewhere classified, unspecified ankle
- M21.1 Varus deformity, not elsewhere classified
  - Excludes1 metatarsus varus (Q66.22)
    tibia vara (M92.5)
  - M21.10 Varus deformity, not elsewhere classified, unspecified site
  - M21.12 Varus deformity, not elsewhere classified, elbow
    Cubitus varus, elbow
    - M21.121 Varus deformity, not elsewhere classified, right elbow
    - M21.122 Varus deformity, not elsewhere classified, left elbow
    - M21.129 Varus deformity, not elsewhere classified, unspecified elbow
  - M21.15 Varus deformity, not elsewhere classified, hip
    - M21.151 Varus deformity, not elsewhere classified, right hip
    - M21.152 Varus deformity, not elsewhere classified, left hip
    - M21.159 Varus deformity, not elsewhere classified, unspecified
  - M21.16 Varus deformity, not elsewhere classified, knee
    Bow leg
    Genu varum
    - M21.161 Varus deformity, not elsewhere classified, right knee
    - M21.162 Varus deformity, not elsewhere classified, left knee
    - M21.169 Varus deformity, not elsewhere classified, unspecified knee
  - M21.17 Varus deformity, not elsewhere classified, ankle
    - M21.171 Varus deformity, not elsewhere classified, right ankle
    - M21.172 Varus deformity, not elsewhere classified, left ankle
    - M21.179 Varus deformity, not elsewhere classified, unspecified ankle

▶ New ⟹ Revised deleted Deleted Excludes 1 Excludes 2 Includes Use additional Code first Code also Key words
OGCR Official Guidelines X Assign placeholder X ▸ Use Additional Character(s) ▸ Manifestation Code **Coding Clinic**

● M21.2   Flexion deformity
   M21.20   Flexion deformity, unspecified site
  ● M21.21   Flexion deformity, shoulder
     M21.211   Flexion deformity, right shoulder
     M21.212   Flexion deformity, left shoulder
     M21.219   Flexion deformity, unspecified shoulder
  ● M21.22   Flexion deformity, elbow
     M21.221   Flexion deformity, right elbow
     M21.222   Flexion deformity, left elbow
     M21.229   Flexion deformity, unspecified elbow
  ● M21.23   Flexion deformity, wrist
     M21.231   Flexion deformity, right wrist
     M21.232   Flexion deformity, left wrist
     M21.239   Flexion deformity, unspecified wrist
  ● M21.24   Flexion deformity, finger joints
     M21.241   Flexion deformity, right finger joints
     M21.242   Flexion deformity, left finger joints
     M21.249   Flexion deformity, unspecified finger joints
  ● M21.25   Flexion deformity, hip
     M21.251   Flexion deformity, right hip
     M21.252   Flexion deformity, left hip
     M21.259   Flexion deformity, unspecified hip
  ● M21.26   Flexion deformity, knee
     M21.261   Flexion deformity, right knee
     M21.262   Flexion deformity, left knee
     M21.269   Flexion deformity, unspecified knee
  ● M21.27   Flexion deformity, ankle and toes
     M21.271   Flexion deformity, right ankle and toes
     M21.272   Flexion deformity, left ankle and toes
     M21.279   Flexion deformity, unspecified ankle and toes
● M21.3   Wrist or foot drop (acquired)
  ● M21.33   Wrist drop (acquired)
     M21.331   Wrist drop, right wrist
     M21.332   Wrist drop, left wrist
     M21.339   Wrist drop, unspecified wrist
  ● M21.37   Foot drop (acquired)
     M21.371   Foot drop, right foot
     M21.372   Foot drop, left foot
     M21.379   Foot drop, unspecified foot
● M21.4   Flat foot [pes planus] (acquired)
    Excludes1   congenital pes planus (Q66.5-)
   M21.40   Flat foot [pes planus] (acquired), unspecified foot
   M21.41   Flat foot [pes planus] (acquired), right foot
   M21.42   Flat foot [pes planus] (acquired), left foot
● M21.5   Acquired clawhand, clubhand, clawfoot and clubfoot
    Excludes1   clubfoot, not specified as acquired (Q66.89)
  ● M21.51   Acquired clawhand
     M21.511   Acquired clawhand, right hand
     M21.512   Acquired clawhand, left hand
     M21.519   Acquired clawhand, unspecified hand
  ● M21.52   Acquired clubhand
     M21.521   Acquired clubhand, right hand
     M21.522   Acquired clubhand, left hand
     M21.529   Acquired clubhand, unspecified hand
  ● M21.53   Acquired clawfoot
     M21.531   Acquired clawfoot, right foot
     M21.532   Acquired clawfoot, left foot
     M21.539   Acquired clawfoot, unspecified foot

● M21.54   Acquired clubfoot
     M21.541   Acquired clubfoot, right foot
     M21.542   Acquired clubfoot, left foot
     M21.549   Acquired clubfoot, unspecified foot
● M21.6   Other acquired deformities of foot
    Excludes2   deformities of toe (acquired) (M20.1-M20.6-)
  ● M21.61   Bunion
     Coding Clinic: 2016, Q4, P38
     M21.611   Bunion of right foot
     M21.612   Bunion of left foot
     M21.619   Bunion of unspecified foot
  ● M21.62   Bunionette
     Coding Clinic: 2016, Q4, P38
     M21.621   Bunionette of right foot
     M21.622   Bunionette of left foot
     M21.629   Bunionette of unspecified foot
  ● M21.6X   Other acquired deformities of foot
     M21.6X1   Other acquired deformities of right foot
     M21.6X2   Other acquired deformities of left foot
     M21.6X9   Other acquired deformities of unspecified foot
● M21.7   Unequal limb length (acquired)
    Note: The site used should correspond to the shorter limb.
   M21.70   Unequal limb length (acquired), unspecified site
  ● M21.72   Unequal limb length (acquired), humerus
     M21.721   Unequal limb length (acquired), right humerus
     M21.722   Unequal limb length (acquired), left humerus
     M21.729   Unequal limb length (acquired), unspecified humerus
  ● M21.73   Unequal limb length (acquired), ulna and radius
     M21.731   Unequal limb length (acquired), right ulna
     M21.732   Unequal limb length (acquired), left ulna
     M21.733   Unequal limb length (acquired), right radius
     M21.734   Unequal limb length (acquired), left radius
     M21.739   Unequal limb length (acquired), unspecified ulna and radius
  ● M21.75   Unequal limb length (acquired), femur
     M21.751   Unequal limb length (acquired), right femur
     M21.752   Unequal limb length (acquired), left femur
     M21.759   Unequal limb length (acquired), unspecified femur
  ● M21.76   Unequal limb length (acquired), tibia and fibula
     M21.761   Unequal limb length (acquired), right tibia
     M21.762   Unequal limb length (acquired), left tibia
     M21.763   Unequal limb length (acquired), right fibula
     M21.764   Unequal limb length (acquired), left fibula
     M21.769   Unequal limb length (acquired), unspecified tibia and fibula

CHAPTER 13 (M00-M99)

● **M21.8   Other specified acquired deformities of limbs**
>   **Excludes2**   coxa plana (M91.2)
>
> M21.80   Other specified acquired deformities of unspecified limb

● M21.82   Other specified acquired deformities of upper arm
> M21.821   Other specified acquired deformities of right upper arm
> M21.822   Other specified acquired deformities of left upper arm
> M21.829   Other specified acquired deformities of unspecified upper arm

● M21.83   Other specified acquired deformities of forearm
> M21.831   Other specified acquired deformities of right forearm
> M21.832   Other specified acquired deformities of left forearm
> M21.839   Other specified acquired deformities of unspecified forearm

● M21.85   Other specified acquired deformities of thigh
> M21.851   Other specified acquired deformities of right thigh
> M21.852   Other specified acquired deformities of left thigh
> M21.859   Other specified acquired deformities of unspecified thigh

● M21.86   Other specified acquired deformities of lower leg
> M21.861   Other specified acquired deformities of right lower leg
> M21.862   Other specified acquired deformities of left lower leg
> M21.869   Other specified acquired deformities of unspecified lower leg

● **M21.9   Unspecified acquired deformity of limb and hand**
> M21.90   Unspecified acquired deformity of unspecified limb

● M21.92   Unspecified acquired deformity of upper arm
> M21.921   Unspecified acquired deformity of right upper arm
> M21.922   Unspecified acquired deformity of left upper arm
> M21.929   Unspecified acquired deformity of unspecified upper arm

● M21.93   Unspecified acquired deformity of forearm
> M21.931   Unspecified acquired deformity of right forearm
> M21.932   Unspecified acquired deformity of left forearm
> M21.939   Unspecified acquired deformity of unspecified forearm

● M21.94   Unspecified acquired deformity of hand
> M21.941   Unspecified acquired deformity of hand, right hand
> M21.942   Unspecified acquired deformity of hand, left hand
> M21.949   Unspecified acquired deformity of hand, unspecified hand

● M21.95   Unspecified acquired deformity of thigh
> M21.951   Unspecified acquired deformity of right thigh
> M21.952   Unspecified acquired deformity of left thigh
> M21.959   Unspecified acquired deformity of unspecified thigh

● M21.96   Unspecified acquired deformity of lower leg
> M21.961   Unspecified acquired deformity of right lower leg
> M21.962   Unspecified acquired deformity of left lower leg
> M21.969   Unspecified acquired deformity of unspecified lower leg

● **M22   Disorder of patella**
>   **Excludes1**   traumatic dislocation of patella (S83.0-)

● **M22.0   Recurrent dislocation of patella**
> M22.00   Recurrent dislocation of patella, unspecified knee
> M22.01   Recurrent dislocation of patella, right knee
> M22.02   Recurrent dislocation of patella, left knee

● **M22.1   Recurrent subluxation of patella**
> Incomplete dislocation of patella
>
> M22.10   Recurrent subluxation of patella, unspecified knee
> M22.11   Recurrent subluxation of patella, right knee
> M22.12   Recurrent subluxation of patella, left knee

● **M22.2   Patellofemoral disorders**
> ● M22.2X   Patellofemoral disorders
> > M22.2X1   Patellofemoral disorders, right knee
> > M22.2X2   Patellofemoral disorders, left knee
> > M22.2X9   Patellofemoral disorders, unspecified knee

● **M22.3   Other derangements of patella**
> ● M22.3X   Other derangements of patella
> > M22.3X1   Other derangements of patella, right knee
> > M22.3X2   Other derangements of patella, left knee
> > M22.3X9   Other derangements of patella, unspecified knee

● **M22.4   Chondromalacia patellae**
> M22.40   Chondromalacia patellae, unspecified knee
> M22.41   Chondromalacia patellae, right knee
> M22.42   Chondromalacia patellae, left knee

● **M22.8   Other disorders of patella**
> ● M22.8X   Other disorders of patella
> > M22.8X1   Other disorders of patella, right knee
> > M22.8X2   Other disorders of patella, left knee
> > M22.8X9   Other disorders of patella, unspecified knee

● **M22.9   Unspecified disorder of patella**
> M22.90   Unspecified disorder of patella, unspecified knee
> M22.91   Unspecified disorder of patella, right knee
> M22.92   Unspecified disorder of patella, left knee

▶ New   ⇒ Revised   ~~deleted~~ Deleted   Excludes 1   Excludes 2   Includes   Use additional   Code first   Code also   Key words

OGCR Official Guidelines   X Assign placeholder X   ● Use Additional Character(s)   ▌ Manifestation Code   **Coding Clinic**

● **M23   Internal derangement of knee**

     Excludes1   ankylosis (M24.66)

                    current injury - see injury of knee and lower leg (S80-S89)

                    deformity of knee (M21.-)

                    osteochondritis dissecans (M93.2)

                    recurrent dislocation or subluxation of joints (M24.4)

                    recurrent dislocation or subluxation of patella (M22.0-M22.1)

● **M23.0   Cystic meniscus**

   ● **M23.00   Cystic meniscus, unspecified meniscus**

          Cystic meniscus, unspecified lateral meniscus

          Cystic meniscus, unspecified medial meniscus

       M23.000   Cystic meniscus, unspecified lateral meniscus, right knee

       M23.001   Cystic meniscus, unspecified lateral meniscus, left knee

       M23.002   Cystic meniscus, unspecified lateral meniscus, unspecified knee

       M23.003   Cystic meniscus, unspecified medial meniscus, right knee

       M23.004   Cystic meniscus, unspecified medial meniscus, left knee

       M23.005   Cystic meniscus, unspecified medial meniscus, unspecified knee

       M23.006   Cystic meniscus, unspecified meniscus, right knee

       M23.007   Cystic meniscus, unspecified meniscus, left knee

       M23.009   Cystic meniscus, unspecified meniscus, unspecified knee

   ● **M23.01   Cystic meniscus, anterior horn of medial meniscus**

       M23.011   Cystic meniscus, anterior horn of medial meniscus, right knee

       M23.012   Cystic meniscus, anterior horn of medial meniscus, left knee

       M23.019   Cystic meniscus, anterior horn of medial meniscus, unspecified knee

   ● **M23.02   Cystic meniscus, posterior horn of medial meniscus**

       M23.021   Cystic meniscus, posterior horn of medial meniscus, right knee

       M23.022   Cystic meniscus, posterior horn of medial meniscus, left knee

       M23.029   Cystic meniscus, posterior horn of medial meniscus, unspecified knee

   ● **M23.03   Cystic meniscus, other medial meniscus**

       M23.031   Cystic meniscus, other medial meniscus, right knee

       M23.032   Cystic meniscus, other medial meniscus, left knee

       M23.039   Cystic meniscus, other medial meniscus, unspecified knee

   ● **M23.04   Cystic meniscus, anterior horn of lateral meniscus**

       M23.041   Cystic meniscus, anterior horn of lateral meniscus, right knee

       M23.042   Cystic meniscus, anterior horn of lateral meniscus, left knee

       M23.049   Cystic meniscus, anterior horn of lateral meniscus, unspecified knee

● **M23.05   Cystic meniscus, posterior horn of lateral meniscus**

       M23.051   Cystic meniscus, posterior horn of lateral meniscus, right knee

       M23.052   Cystic meniscus, posterior horn of lateral meniscus, left knee

       M23.059   Cystic meniscus, posterior horn of lateral meniscus, unspecified knee

● **M23.06   Cystic meniscus, other lateral meniscus**

       M23.061   Cystic meniscus, other lateral meniscus, right knee

       M23.062   Cystic meniscus, other lateral meniscus, left knee

       M23.069   Cystic meniscus, other lateral meniscus, unspecified knee

★ **(See Plate 509 on page 79.)**

   ● **M23.2   Derangement of meniscus due to old tear or injury**

       Old bucket-handle tear

   ● **M23.20   Derangement of unspecified meniscus due to old tear or injury**

          Derangement of unspecified lateral meniscus due to old tear or injury

          Derangement of unspecified medial meniscus due to old tear or injury

       M23.200   Derangement of unspecified lateral meniscus due to old tear or injury, right knee

       M23.201   Derangement of unspecified lateral meniscus due to old tear or injury, left knee

       M23.202   Derangement of unspecified lateral meniscus due to old tear or injury, unspecified knee

       M23.203   Derangement of unspecified medial meniscus due to old tear or injury, right knee

       M23.204   Derangement of unspecified medial meniscus due to old tear or injury, left knee

       M23.205   Derangement of unspecified medial meniscus due to old tear or injury, unspecified knee

       M23.206   Derangement of unspecified meniscus due to old tear or injury, right knee

       M23.207   Derangement of unspecified meniscus due to old tear or injury, left knee

       M23.209   Derangement of unspecified meniscus due to old tear or injury, unspecified knee

   ● **M23.21   Derangement of anterior horn of medial meniscus due to old tear or injury**

       M23.211   Derangement of anterior horn of medial meniscus due to old tear or injury, right knee

       M23.212   Derangement of anterior horn of medial meniscus due to old tear or injury, left knee

       M23.219   Derangement of anterior horn of medial meniscus due to old tear or injury, unspecified knee

CHAPTER 13 (M00-M99)

● M23.22   Derangement of posterior horn of medial meniscus due to old tear or injury

   M23.221   Derangement of posterior horn of medial meniscus due to old tear or injury, right knee

   M23.222   Derangement of posterior horn of medial meniscus due to old tear or injury, left knee

   M23.229   Derangement of posterior horn of medial meniscus due to old tear or injury, unspecified knee

● M23.23   Derangement of other medial meniscus due to old tear or injury

   M23.231   Derangement of other medial meniscus due to old tear or injury, right knee

   M23.232   Derangement of other medial meniscus due to old tear or injury, left knee

   M23.239   Derangement of other medial meniscus due to old tear or injury, unspecified knee

● M23.24   Derangement of anterior horn of lateral meniscus due to old tear or injury

   M23.241   Derangement of anterior horn of lateral meniscus due to old tear or injury, right knee

   M23.242   Derangement of anterior horn of lateral meniscus due to old tear or injury, left knee

   M23.249   Derangement of anterior horn of lateral meniscus due to old tear or injury, unspecified knee

● M23.25   Derangement of posterior horn of lateral meniscus due to old tear or injury

   M23.251   Derangement of posterior horn of lateral meniscus due to old tear or injury, right knee

   M23.252   Derangement of posterior horn of lateral meniscus due to old tear or injury, left knee

   M23.259   Derangement of posterior horn of lateral meniscus due to old tear or injury, unspecified knee

● M23.26   Derangement of other lateral meniscus due to old tear or injury

   M23.261   Derangement of other lateral meniscus due to old tear or injury, right knee

   M23.262   Derangement of other lateral meniscus due to old tear or injury, left knee

   M23.269   Derangement of other lateral meniscus due to old tear or injury, unspecified knee

● M23.3   Other meniscus derangements
         Degenerate meniscus
         Detached meniscus
         Retained meniscus

● M23.30   Other meniscus derangements, unspecified meniscus
         Other meniscus derangements, unspecified lateral meniscus
         Other meniscus derangements, unspecified medial meniscus

   M23.300   Other meniscus derangements, unspecified lateral meniscus, right knee

   M23.301   Other meniscus derangements, unspecified lateral meniscus, left knee

   M23.302   Other meniscus derangements, unspecified lateral meniscus, unspecified knee

   M23.303   Other meniscus derangements, unspecified medial meniscus, right knee

   M23.304   Other meniscus derangements, unspecified medial meniscus, left knee

   M23.305   Other meniscus derangements, unspecified medial meniscus, unspecified knee

   M23.306   Other meniscus derangements, unspecified meniscus, right knee

   M23.307   Other meniscus derangements, unspecified meniscus, left knee

   M23.309   Other meniscus derangements, unspecified meniscus, unspecified knee

● M23.31   Other meniscus derangements, anterior horn of medial meniscus

   M23.311   Other meniscus derangements, anterior horn of medial meniscus, right knee

   M23.312   Other meniscus derangements, anterior horn of medial meniscus, left knee

   M23.319   Other meniscus derangements, anterior horn of medial meniscus, unspecified knee

● M23.32   Other meniscus derangements, posterior horn of medial meniscus

   M23.321   Other meniscus derangements, posterior horn of medial meniscus, right knee

   M23.322   Other meniscus derangements, posterior horn of medial meniscus, left knee

   M23.329   Other meniscus derangements, posterior horn of medial meniscus, unspecified knee

● M23.33   Other meniscus derangements, other medial meniscus

   M23.331   Other meniscus derangements, other medial meniscus, right knee

   M23.332   Other meniscus derangements, other medial meniscus, left knee

   M23.339   Other meniscus derangements, other medial meniscus, unspecified knee

● M23.34   Other meniscus derangements, anterior horn of lateral meniscus

   M23.341   Other meniscus derangements, anterior horn of lateral meniscus, right knee

   M23.342   Other meniscus derangements, anterior horn of lateral meniscus, left knee

   M23.349   Other meniscus derangements, anterior horn of lateral meniscus, unspecified knee

● M23.35   Other meniscus derangements, posterior horn of lateral meniscus

   M23.351   Other meniscus derangements, posterior horn of lateral meniscus, right knee

   M23.352   Other meniscus derangements, posterior horn of lateral meniscus, left knee

   M23.359   Other meniscus derangements, posterior horn of lateral meniscus, unspecified knee

▶ New   ⇒ Revised   deleted Deleted   Excludes 1   Excludes 2   Includes   Use additional   Code first   Code also   Key words
OGCR Official Guidelines   X Assign placeholder X   ● Use Additional Character(s)   ▶ Manifestation Code   Coding Clinic

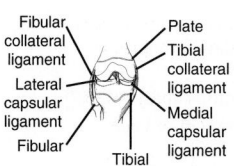

Fibular collateral ligament
Plate
Tibial collateral ligament
Lateral capsular ligament
Medial capsular ligament
Fibular
Tibial

Figure 13-2 Collateral and cruciate ligament of knee. (From DeLee: DeLee and Drez's Orthopaedic Sports Medicine, ed 3, Saunders, 2009)

● M23.36 Other meniscus derangements, other lateral meniscus
    M23.361 Other meniscus derangements, other lateral meniscus, right knee
    M23.362 Other meniscus derangements, other lateral meniscus, left knee
    M23.369 Other meniscus derangements, other lateral meniscus, unspecified knee
● M23.4 Loose body in knee
    M23.40 Loose body in knee, unspecified knee
    M23.41 Loose body in knee, right knee
    M23.42 Loose body in knee, left knee
● M23.5 Chronic instability of knee
    M23.50 Chronic instability of knee, unspecified knee
    M23.51 Chronic instability of knee, right knee
    M23.52 Chronic instability of knee, left knee
● M23.6 Other spontaneous disruption of ligament(s) of knee
  ● M23.60 Other spontaneous disruption of unspecified ligament of knee
    M23.601 Other spontaneous disruption of unspecified ligament of right knee
    M23.602 Other spontaneous disruption of unspecified ligament of left knee
    M23.609 Other spontaneous disruption of unspecified ligament of unspecified knee
  ● M23.61 Other spontaneous disruption of anterior cruciate ligament of knee
    M23.611 Other spontaneous disruption of anterior cruciate ligament of right knee
    M23.612 Other spontaneous disruption of anterior cruciate ligament of left knee
    M23.619 Other spontaneous disruption of anterior cruciate ligament of unspecified knee
  ● M23.62 Other spontaneous disruption of posterior cruciate ligament of knee
    M23.621 Other spontaneous disruption of posterior cruciate ligament of right knee
    M23.622 Other spontaneous disruption of posterior cruciate ligament of left knee
    M23.629 Other spontaneous disruption of posterior cruciate ligament of unspecified knee
  ● M23.63 Other spontaneous disruption of medial collateral ligament of knee
    M23.631 Other spontaneous disruption of medial collateral ligament of right knee
    M23.632 Other spontaneous disruption of medial collateral ligament of left knee
    M23.639 Other spontaneous disruption of medial collateral ligament of unspecified knee

● M23.64 Other spontaneous disruption of lateral collateral ligament of knee
    M23.641 Other spontaneous disruption of lateral collateral ligament of right knee
    M23.642 Other spontaneous disruption of lateral collateral ligament of left knee
    M23.649 Other spontaneous disruption of lateral collateral ligament of unspecified knee
● M23.67 Other spontaneous disruption of capsular ligament of knee
    M23.671 Other spontaneous disruption of capsular ligament of right knee
    M23.672 Other spontaneous disruption of capsular ligament of left knee
    M23.679 Other spontaneous disruption of capsular ligament of unspecified knee
● M23.8 Other internal derangements of knee
    Laxity of ligament of knee
    Snapping knee
  ● M23.8X Other internal derangements of knee
    M23.8X1 Other internal derangements of right knee
    M23.8X2 Other internal derangements of left knee
    M23.8X9 Other internal derangements of unspecified knee
● M23.9 Unspecified internal derangement of knee
    M23.90 Unspecified internal derangement of unspecified knee
    M23.91 Unspecified internal derangement of right knee
    M23.92 Unspecified internal derangement of left knee
● M24 Other specific joint derangements
    Excludes1 current injury - see injury of joint by body region
    Excludes2 ganglion (M67.4)
      snapping knee (M23.8-)
      temporomandibular joint disorders (M26.6-)
● M24.0 Loose body in joint
    Excludes2 loose body in knee (M23.4)
    M24.00 Loose body in unspecified joint
  ● M24.01 Loose body in shoulder
    M24.011 Loose body in right shoulder
    M24.012 Loose body in left shoulder
    M24.019 Loose body in unspecified shoulder
  ● M24.02 Loose body in elbow
    M24.021 Loose body in right elbow
    M24.022 Loose body in left elbow
    M24.029 Loose body in unspecified elbow
  ● M24.03 Loose body in wrist
    M24.031 Loose body in right wrist
    M24.032 Loose body in left wrist
    M24.039 Loose body in unspecified wrist
  ● M24.04 Loose body in finger joints
    M24.041 Loose body in right finger joint(s)
    M24.042 Loose body in left finger joint(s)
    M24.049 Loose body in unspecified finger joint(s)
  ● M24.05 Loose body in hip
    M24.051 Loose body in right hip
    M24.052 Loose body in left hip
    M24.059 Loose body in unspecified hip

CHAPTER 13 (M00-M99)

- M24.07 Loose body in ankle and toe joints
  - M24.071 Loose body in right ankle
  - M24.072 Loose body in left ankle
  - M24.073 Loose body in unspecified ankle
  - M24.074 Loose body in right toe joint(s)
  - M24.075 Loose body in left toe joint(s)
  - M24.076 Loose body in unspecified toe joints
  - M24.08 Loose body, other site
- M24.1 Other articular cartilage disorders
  - **Excludes2** chondrocalcinosis (M11.1, M11.2-)
    internal derangement of knee (M23.-)
    metastatic calcification (E83.5)
    ochronosis (E70.2)
  - M24.10 Other articular cartilage disorders, unspecified site
  - M24.11 Other articular cartilage disorders, shoulder
    - M24.111 Other articular cartilage disorders, right shoulder
    - M24.112 Other articular cartilage disorders, left shoulder
    - M24.119 Other articular cartilage disorders, unspecified shoulder
  - M24.12 Other articular cartilage disorders, elbow
    - M24.121 Other articular cartilage disorders, right elbow
    - M24.122 Other articular cartilage disorders, left elbow
    - M24.129 Other articular cartilage disorders, unspecified elbow
  - M24.13 Other articular cartilage disorders, wrist
    - M24.131 Other articular cartilage disorders, right wrist
    - M24.132 Other articular cartilage disorders, left wrist
    - M24.139 Other articular cartilage disorders, unspecified wrist
  - M24.14 Other articular cartilage disorders, hand
    - M24.141 Other articular cartilage disorders, right hand
    - M24.142 Other articular cartilage disorders, left hand
    - M24.149 Other articular cartilage disorders, unspecified hand
  - M24.15 Other articular cartilage disorders, hip
    - M24.151 Other articular cartilage disorders, right hip
    - M24.152 Other articular cartilage disorders, left hip
    - M24.159 Other articular cartilage disorders, unspecified hip
  - M24.17 Other articular cartilage disorders, ankle and foot
    - M24.171 Other articular cartilage disorders, right ankle
    - M24.172 Other articular cartilage disorders, left ankle
    - M24.173 Other articular cartilage disorders, unspecified ankle
    - M24.174 Other articular cartilage disorders, right foot
    - M24.175 Other articular cartilage disorders, left foot
    - M24.176 Other articular cartilage disorders, unspecified foot

- M24.2 Disorder of ligament
  Instability secondary to old ligament injury
  Ligamentous laxity NOS
  - **Excludes1** familial ligamentous laxity (M35.7)
  - **Excludes2** internal derangement of knee (M23.5-M23.89)
  - M24.20 Disorder of ligament, unspecified site
  - M24.21 Disorder of ligament, shoulder
    - M24.211 Disorder of ligament, right shoulder
    - M24.212 Disorder of ligament, left shoulder
    - M24.219 Disorder of ligament, unspecified shoulder
  - M24.22 Disorder of ligament, elbow
    - M24.221 Disorder of ligament, right elbow
    - M24.222 Disorder of ligament, left elbow
    - M24.229 Disorder of ligament, unspecified elbow
  - M24.23 Disorder of ligament, wrist
    - M24.231 Disorder of ligament, right wrist
    - M24.232 Disorder of ligament, left wrist
    - M24.239 Disorder of ligament, unspecified wrist
  - M24.24 Disorder of ligament, hand
    - M24.241 Disorder of ligament, right hand
    - M24.242 Disorder of ligament, left hand
    - M24.249 Disorder of ligament, unspecified hand
  - M24.25 Disorder of ligament, hip
    - M24.251 Disorder of ligament, right hip
    - M24.252 Disorder of ligament, left hip
    - M24.259 Disorder of ligament, unspecified hip
  - M24.27 Disorder of ligament, ankle and foot
    - M24.271 Disorder of ligament, right ankle
    - M24.272 Disorder of ligament, left ankle
    - M24.273 Disorder of ligament, unspecified ankle
    - M24.274 Disorder of ligament, right foot
    - M24.275 Disorder of ligament, left foot
    - M24.276 Disorder of ligament, unspecified foot
  - M24.28 Disorder of ligament, vertebrae
- M24.3 Pathological dislocation of joint, not elsewhere classified
  - **Excludes1** congenital dislocation or displacement of joint - see congenital malformations and deformations of the musculoskeletal system (Q65-Q79)
    current injury - see injury of joints and ligaments by body region
    recurrent dislocation of joint (M24.4-)
  - M24.30 Pathological dislocation of unspecified joint, not elsewhere classified
  - M24.31 Pathological dislocation of shoulder, not elsewhere classified
    - M24.311 Pathological dislocation of right shoulder, not elsewhere classified
    - M24.312 Pathological dislocation of left shoulder, not elsewhere classified
    - M24.319 Pathological dislocation of unspecified shoulder, not elsewhere classified
  - M24.32 Pathological dislocation of elbow, not elsewhere classified
    - M24.321 Pathological dislocation of right elbow, not elsewhere classified
    - M24.322 Pathological dislocation of left elbow, not elsewhere classified
    - M24.329 Pathological dislocation of unspecified elbow, not elsewhere classified

● **M24.33** Pathological dislocation of wrist, not elsewhere classified

    M24.331 Pathological dislocation of right wrist, not elsewhere classified

    M24.332 Pathological dislocation of left wrist, not elsewhere classified

    M24.339 Pathological dislocation of unspecified wrist, not elsewhere classified

● **M24.34** Pathological dislocation of hand, not elsewhere classified

    M24.341 Pathological dislocation of right hand, not elsewhere classified

    M24.342 Pathological dislocation of left hand, not elsewhere classified

    M24.349 Pathological dislocation of unspecified hand, not elsewhere classified

● **M24.35** Pathological dislocation of hip, not elsewhere classified

    M24.351 Pathological dislocation of right hip, not elsewhere classified

    M24.352 Pathological dislocation of left hip, not elsewhere classified

    M24.359 Pathological dislocation of unspecified hip, not elsewhere classified

● **M24.36** Pathological dislocation of knee, not elsewhere classified

    M24.361 Pathological dislocation of right knee, not elsewhere classified

    M24.362 Pathological dislocation of left knee, not elsewhere classified

    M24.369 Pathological dislocation of unspecified knee, not elsewhere classified

● **M24.37** Pathological dislocation of ankle and foot, not elsewhere classified

    M24.371 Pathological dislocation of right ankle, not elsewhere classified

    M24.372 Pathological dislocation of left ankle, not elsewhere classified

    M24.373 Pathological dislocation of unspecified ankle, not elsewhere classified

    M24.374 Pathological dislocation of right foot, not elsewhere classified

    M24.375 Pathological dislocation of left foot, not elsewhere classified

    M24.376 Pathological dislocation of unspecified foot, not elsewhere classified

● **M24.4** Recurrent dislocation of joint

    Recurrent subluxation of joint

    Excludes2   recurrent dislocation of patella (M22.0-M22.1)

                recurrent vertebral dislocation (M43.3-, M43.4, M43.5-)

    M24.40 Recurrent dislocation, unspecified joint

●   M24.41 Recurrent dislocation, shoulder

    M24.411 Recurrent dislocation, right shoulder

    M24.412 Recurrent dislocation, left shoulder

    M24.419 Recurrent dislocation, unspecified shoulder

●   M24.42 Recurrent dislocation, elbow

    M24.421 Recurrent dislocation, right elbow

    M24.422 Recurrent dislocation, left elbow

    M24.429 Recurrent dislocation, unspecified elbow

● **M24.43** Recurrent dislocation, wrist

    M24.431 Recurrent dislocation, right wrist

    M24.432 Recurrent dislocation, left wrist

    M24.439 Recurrent dislocation, unspecified wrist

● **M24.44** Recurrent dislocation, hand and finger(s)

    M24.441 Recurrent dislocation, right hand

    M24.442 Recurrent dislocation, left hand

    M24.443 Recurrent dislocation, unspecified hand

    M24.444 Recurrent dislocation, right finger

    M24.445 Recurrent dislocation, left finger

    M24.446 Recurrent dislocation, unspecified finger

● **M24.45** Recurrent dislocation, hip

    M24.451 Recurrent dislocation, right hip

    M24.452 Recurrent dislocation, left hip

    M24.459 Recurrent dislocation, unspecified hip

● **M24.46** Recurrent dislocation, knee

    M24.461 Recurrent dislocation, right knee

    M24.462 Recurrent dislocation, left knee

    M24.469 Recurrent dislocation, unspecified knee

● **M24.47** Recurrent dislocation, ankle, foot and toes

    M24.471 Recurrent dislocation, right ankle

    M24.472 Recurrent dislocation, left ankle

    M24.473 Recurrent dislocation, unspecified ankle

    M24.474 Recurrent dislocation, right foot

    M24.475 Recurrent dislocation, left foot

    M24.476 Recurrent dislocation, unspecified foot

    M24.477 Recurrent dislocation, right toe(s)

    M24.478 Recurrent dislocation, left toe(s)

    M24.479 Recurrent dislocation, unspecified toe(s)

● **M24.5** Contracture of joint

    Excludes1   contracture of muscle without contracture of joint (M62.4-)

                contracture of tendon (sheath) without contracture of joint (M62.4-)

                Dupuytren's contracture (M72.0)

    Excludes2   acquired deformities of limbs (M20-M21)

    M24.50 Contracture, unspecified joint

●   M24.51 Contracture, shoulder

    M24.511 Contracture, right shoulder

    M24.512 Contracture, left shoulder

    M24.519 Contracture, unspecified shoulder

●   M24.52 Contracture, elbow

    M24.521 Contracture, right elbow

    M24.522 Contracture, left elbow

    M24.529 Contracture, unspecified elbow

●   M24.53 Contracture, wrist

    M24.531 Contracture, right wrist

    M24.532 Contracture, left wrist

    M24.539 Contracture, unspecified wrist

●   M24.54 Contracture, hand

    M24.541 Contracture, right hand

    M24.542 Contracture, left hand

    M24.549 Contracture, unspecified hand

●   M24.55 Contracture, hip

    M24.551 Contracture, right hip
        Coding Clinic: 2016, Q2, P6

    M24.552 Contracture, left hip
        Coding Clinic: 2016, Q2, P6

    M24.559 Contracture, unspecified hip

CHAPTER 13 (M00-M99)

● M24.56   Contracture, knee
     M24.561   Contracture, right knee
          Coding Clinic: 2016, Q2, P6
     M24.562   Contracture, left knee
          Coding Clinic: 2016, Q2, P6
     M24.569   Contracture, unspecified knee
● M24.57   Contracture, ankle and foot
     M24.571   Contracture, right ankle
     M24.572   Contracture, left ankle
     M24.573   Contracture, unspecified ankle
     M24.574   Contracture, right foot
     M24.575   Contracture, left foot
     M24.576   Contracture, unspecified foot
● M24.6   Ankylosis of joint
     Excludes1   stiffness of joint without ankylosis (M25.6-)
     Excludes2   spine (M43.2-)
   M24.60   Ankylosis, unspecified joint
● M24.61   Ankylosis, shoulder
     M24.611   Ankylosis, right shoulder
     M24.612   Ankylosis, left shoulder
     M24.619   Ankylosis, unspecified shoulder
● M24.62   Ankylosis, elbow
     M24.621   Ankylosis, right elbow
     M24.622   Ankylosis, left elbow
     M24.629   Ankylosis, unspecified elbow
● M24.63   Ankylosis, wrist
     M24.631   Ankylosis, right wrist
     M24.632   Ankylosis, left wrist
     M24.639   Ankylosis, unspecified wrist
● M24.64   Ankylosis, hand
     M24.641   Ankylosis, right hand
     M24.642   Ankylosis, left hand
     M24.649   Ankylosis, unspecified hand
● M24.65   Ankylosis, hip
     M24.651   Ankylosis, right hip
     M24.652   Ankylosis, left hip
     M24.659   Ankylosis, unspecified hip
● M24.66   Ankylosis, knee
     M24.661   Ankylosis, right knee
     M24.662   Ankylosis, left knee
     M24.669   Ankylosis, unspecified knee
● M24.67   Ankylosis, ankle and foot
     M24.671   Ankylosis, right ankle
     M24.672   Ankylosis, left ankle
     M24.673   Ankylosis, unspecified ankle
     M24.674   Ankylosis, right foot
     M24.675   Ankylosis, left foot
     M24.676   Ankylosis, unspecified foot

M24.7   Protrusio acetabuli
● M24.8   Other specific joint derangements, not elsewhere classified
     Excludes2   iliotibial band syndrome (M76.3)
   M24.80   Other specific joint derangements of unspecified joint, not elsewhere classified
● M24.81   Other specific joint derangements of shoulder, not elsewhere classified
     M24.811   Other specific joint derangements of right shoulder, not elsewhere classified
     M24.812   Other specific joint derangements of left shoulder, not elsewhere classified
     M24.819   Other specific joint derangements of unspecified shoulder, not elsewhere classified
● M24.82   Other specific joint derangements of elbow, not elsewhere classified
     M24.821   Other specific joint derangements of right elbow, not elsewhere classified
     M24.822   Other specific joint derangements of left elbow, not elsewhere classified
     M24.829   Other specific joint derangements of unspecified elbow, not elsewhere classified
● M24.83   Other specific joint derangements of wrist, not elsewhere classified
     M24.831   Other specific joint derangements of right wrist, not elsewhere classified
     M24.832   Other specific joint derangements of left wrist, not elsewhere classified
     M24.839   Other specific joint derangements of unspecified wrist, not elsewhere classified
● M24.84   Other specific joint derangements of hand, not elsewhere classified
     M24.841   Other specific joint derangements of right hand, not elsewhere classified
     M24.842   Other specific joint derangements of left hand, not elsewhere classified
     M24.849   Other specific joint derangements of unspecified hand, not elsewhere classified
● M24.85   Other specific joint derangements of hip, not elsewhere classified
     Irritable hip
     M24.851   Other specific joint derangements of right hip, not elsewhere classified
     M24.852   Other specific joint derangements of left hip, not elsewhere classified
     M24.859   Other specific joint derangements of unspecified hip, not elsewhere classified
● M24.87   Other specific joint derangements of ankle and foot, not elsewhere classified
     M24.871   Other specific joint derangements of right ankle, not elsewhere classified
     M24.872   Other specific joint derangements of left ankle, not elsewhere classified
     M24.873   Other specific joint derangements of unspecified ankle, not elsewhere classified
     M24.874   Other specific joint derangements of right foot, not elsewhere classified
     M24.875   Other specific joint derangements left foot, not elsewhere classified
     M24.876   Other specific joint derangements of unspecified foot, not elsewhere classified
M24.9   Joint derangement, unspecified

Item 13–5   **Ankylosis** or arthrokleisis is a consolidation of a joint due to disease, injury, or surgical procedure. Spondylosis is the degeneration of the vertebral processes and formation of osteophytes and commonly occurs with age. **Spondylitis** or ankylosing spondylitis is a type of arthritis that affects the spine or backbone, causing back pain and stiffness.

▶ New   ⇒ Revised   ~~deleted~~ Deleted   Excludes 1   Excludes 2   Includes   Use additional   Code first   Code also   Key words

OGCR Official Guidelines   X Assign placeholder X   ● Use Additional Character(s)   ▷ Manifestation Code   **Coding Clinic**

● **M25 Other joint disorder, not elsewhere classified**
    Excludes2   abnormality of gait and mobility (R26.-)
                acquired deformities of limb (M20-M21)
                calcification of bursa (M71.4-)
                calcification of shoulder (joint) (M75.3)
                calcification of tendon (M65.2-)
                difficulty in walking (R26.2)
                temporomandibular joint disorder (M26.6-)

● **M25.0 Hemarthrosis**
    Excludes1   current injury - see injury of joint by body
                       region
                hemophilic arthropathy (M36.2)

    M25.00 Hemarthrosis, unspecified joint
●   M25.01 Hemarthrosis, shoulder
        M25.011 Hemarthrosis, right shoulder
        M25.012 Hemarthrosis, left shoulder
        M25.019 Hemarthrosis, unspecified shoulder
●   M25.02 Hemarthrosis, elbow
        M25.021 Hemarthrosis, right elbow
        M25.022 Hemarthrosis, left elbow
        M25.029 Hemarthrosis, unspecified elbow
●   M25.03 Hemarthrosis, wrist
        M25.031 Hemarthrosis, right wrist
        M25.032 Hemarthrosis, left wrist
        M25.039 Hemarthrosis, unspecified wrist
●   M25.04 Hemarthrosis, hand
        M25.041 Hemarthrosis, right hand
        M25.042 Hemarthrosis, left hand
        M25.049 Hemarthrosis, unspecified hand
●   M25.05 Hemarthrosis, hip
        M25.051 Hemarthrosis, right hip
        M25.052 Hemarthrosis, left hip
        M25.059 Hemarthrosis, unspecified hip
●   M25.06 Hemarthrosis, knee
        M25.061 Hemarthrosis, right knee
        M25.062 Hemarthrosis, left knee
        M25.069 Hemarthrosis, unspecified knee
●   M25.07 Hemarthrosis, ankle and foot
        M25.071 Hemarthrosis, right ankle
        M25.072 Hemarthrosis, left ankle
        M25.073 Hemarthrosis, unspecified ankle
        M25.074 Hemarthrosis, right foot
        M25.075 Hemarthrosis, left foot
        M25.076 Hemarthrosis, unspecified foot
    M25.08 Hemarthrosis, other specified site
            Hemarthrosis, vertebrae

● **M25.1 Fistula of joint**
    M25.10 Fistula, unspecified joint
●   M25.11 Fistula, shoulder
        M25.111 Fistula, right shoulder
        M25.112 Fistula, left shoulder
        M25.119 Fistula, unspecified shoulder
●   M25.12 Fistula, elbow
        M25.121 Fistula, right elbow
        M25.122 Fistula, left elbow
        M25.129 Fistula, unspecified elbow
●   M25.13 Fistula, wrist
        M25.131 Fistula, right wrist
        M25.132 Fistula, left wrist
        M25.139 Fistula, unspecified wrist
●   M25.14 Fistula, hand
        M25.141 Fistula, right hand
        M25.142 Fistula, left hand
        M25.149 Fistula, unspecified hand

●   M25.15 Fistula, hip
        M25.151 Fistula, right hip
        M25.152 Fistula, left hip
        M25.159 Fistula, unspecified hip
●   M25.16 Fistula, knee
        M25.161 Fistula, right knee
        M25.162 Fistula, left knee
        M25.169 Fistula, unspecified knee
●   M25.17 Fistula, ankle and foot
        M25.171 Fistula, right ankle
        M25.172 Fistula, left ankle
        M25.173 Fistula, unspecified ankle
        M25.174 Fistula, right foot
        M25.175 Fistula, left foot
        M25.176 Fistula, unspecified foot
    M25.18 Fistula, other specified site
            Fistula, vertebrae

● **M25.2 Flail joint**
    M25.20 Flail joint, unspecified joint
●   M25.21 Flail joint, shoulder
        M25.211 Flail joint, right shoulder
        M25.212 Flail joint, left shoulder
        M25.219 Flail joint, unspecified shoulder
●   M25.22 Flail joint, elbow
        M25.221 Flail joint, right elbow
        M25.222 Flail joint, left elbow
        M25.229 Flail joint, unspecified elbow
●   M25.23 Flail joint, wrist
        M25.231 Flail joint, right wrist
        M25.232 Flail joint, left wrist
        M25.239 Flail joint, unspecified wrist
●   M25.24 Flail joint, hand
        M25.241 Flail joint, right hand
        M25.242 Flail joint, left hand
        M25.249 Flail joint, unspecified hand
●   M25.25 Flail joint, hip
        M25.251 Flail joint, right hip
        M25.252 Flail joint, left hip
        M25.259 Flail joint, unspecified hip
●   M25.26 Flail joint, knee
        M25.261 Flail joint, right knee
        M25.262 Flail joint, left knee
        M25.269 Flail joint, unspecified knee
●   M25.27 Flail joint, ankle and foot
        M25.271 Flail joint, right ankle and foot
        M25.272 Flail joint, left ankle and foot
        M25.279 Flail joint, unspecified ankle and foot
    M25.28 Flail joint, other site

● **M25.3 Other instability of joint**
    Excludes1   instability of joint secondary to old
                     ligament injury (M24.2-)
                instability of joint secondary to removal
                     of joint prosthesis (M96.8-)
    Excludes2   spinal instabilities (M53.2-)
    M25.30 Other instability, unspecified joint
●   M25.31 Other instability, shoulder
        M25.311 Other instability, right shoulder
        M25.312 Other instability, left shoulder
        M25.319 Other instability, unspecified
                   shoulder
●   M25.32 Other instability, elbow
        M25.321 Other instability, right elbow
        M25.322 Other instability, left elbow
        M25.329 Other instability, unspecified elbow

● M25.33　Other instability, wrist
　　　　M25.331　Other instability, right wrist
　　　　M25.332　Other instability, left wrist
　　　　M25.339　Other instability, unspecified wrist
● M25.34　Other instability, hand
　　　　M25.341　Other instability, right hand
　　　　M25.342　Other instability, left hand
　　　　M25.349　Other instability, unspecified hand
● M25.35　Other instability, hip
　　　　M25.351　Other instability, right hip
　　　　M25.352　Other instability, left hip
　　　　M25.359　Other instability, unspecified hip
● M25.36　Other instability, knee
　　　　M25.361　Other instability, right knee
　　　　M25.362　Other instability, left knee
　　　　M25.369　Other instability, unspecified knee
● M25.37　Other instability, ankle and foot
　　　　M25.371　Other instability, right ankle
　　　　M25.372　Other instability, left ankle
　　　　M25.373　Other instability, unspecified ankle
　　　　M25.374　Other instability, right foot
　　　　M25.375　Other instability, left foot
　　　　M25.376　Other instability, unspecified foot
● M25.4　Effusion of joint
　　　Excludes1　hydrarthrosis in yaws (A66.6)
　　　　　　　　　intermittent hydrarthrosis (M12.4-)
　　　　　　　　　other infective (teno)synovitis (M65.1-)
　　M25.40　Effusion, unspecified joint
● M25.41　Effusion, shoulder
　　　　M25.411　Effusion, right shoulder
　　　　M25.412　Effusion, left shoulder
　　　　M25.419　Effusion, unspecified shoulder
● M25.42　Effusion, elbow
　　　　M25.421　Effusion, right elbow
　　　　M25.422　Effusion, left elbow
　　　　M25.429　Effusion, unspecified elbow
● M25.43　Effusion, wrist
　　　　M25.431　Effusion, right wrist
　　　　M25.432　Effusion, left wrist
　　　　M25.439　Effusion, unspecified wrist
● M25.44　Effusion, hand
　　　　M25.441　Effusion, right hand
　　　　M25.442　Effusion, left hand
　　　　M25.449　Effusion, unspecified hand
● M25.45　Effusion, hip
　　　　M25.451　Effusion, right hip
　　　　M25.452　Effusion, left hip
　　　　M25.459　Effusion, unspecified hip
● M25.46　Effusion, knee
　　　　M25.461　Effusion, right knee
　　　　M25.462　Effusion, left knee
　　　　M25.469　Effusion, unspecified knee
● M25.47　Effusion, ankle and foot
　　　　M25.471　Effusion, right ankle
　　　　M25.472　Effusion, left ankle
　　　　M25.473　Effusion, unspecified ankle
　　　　M25.474　Effusion, right foot
　　　　M25.475　Effusion, left foot
　　　　M25.476　Effusion, unspecified foot
　　M25.48　Effusion, other site

● M25.5　Pain in joint
　　　Excludes2　pain in hand (M79.64-)
　　　　　　　　　pain in fingers (M79.64-)
　　　　　　　　　pain in foot (M79.67-)
　　　　　　　　　pain in limb (M79.6-)
　　　　　　　　　pain in toes (M79.67-)
　　M25.50　Pain in unspecified joint
● M25.51　Pain in shoulder
　　　　M25.511　Pain in right shoulder
　　　　M25.512　Pain in left shoulder
　　　　M25.519　Pain in unspecified shoulder
● M25.52　Pain in elbow
　　　　M25.521　Pain in right elbow
　　　　M25.522　Pain in left elbow
　　　　M25.529　Pain in unspecified elbow
● M25.53　Pain in wrist
　　　　M25.531　Pain in right wrist
　　　　M25.532　Pain in left wrist
　　　　M25.539　Pain in unspecified wrist
● M25.54　Pain in joints of hand
　　　　Coding Clinic: 2016, Q4, P38
　　　　M25.541　Pain in joints of right hand
　　　　M25.542　Pain in joints of left hand
　　　　M25.549　Pain in joints of unspecified hand
　　　　　　　　　　Pain in joints of hand NOS
● M25.55　Pain in hip
　　　　M25.551　Pain in right hip
　　　　M25.552　Pain in left hip
　　　　M25.559　Pain in unspecified hip
● M25.56　Pain in knee
　　　　M25.561　Pain in right knee
　　　　M25.562　Pain in left knee
　　　　M25.569　Pain in unspecified knee
● M25.57　Pain in ankle and joints of foot
　　　　M25.571　Pain in right ankle and joints of right foot
　　　　M25.572　Pain in left ankle and joints of left foot
　　　　M25.579　Pain in unspecified ankle and joints of unspecified foot
● M25.6　Stiffness of joint, not elsewhere classified
　　　Excludes1　ankylosis of joint (M24.6-)
　　　　　　　　　contracture of joint (M24.5-)
　　M25.60　Stiffness of unspecified joint, not elsewhere classified
● M25.61　Stiffness of shoulder, not elsewhere classified
　　　　M25.611　Stiffness of right shoulder, not elsewhere classified
　　　　M25.612　Stiffness of left shoulder, not elsewhere classified
　　　　M25.619　Stiffness of unspecified shoulder, not elsewhere classified
● M25.62　Stiffness of elbow, not elsewhere classified
　　　　M25.621　Stiffness of right elbow, not elsewhere classified
　　　　M25.622　Stiffness of left elbow, not elsewhere classified
　　　　M25.629　Stiffness of unspecified elbow, not elsewhere classified
● M25.63　Stiffness of wrist, not elsewhere classified
　　　　M25.631　Stiffness of right wrist, not elsewhere classified
　　　　M25.632　Stiffness of left wrist, not elsewhere classified
　　　　M25.639　Stiffness of unspecified wrist, not elsewhere classified

● M25.64 Stiffness of hand, not elsewhere classified
    M25.641 Stiffness of right hand, not elsewhere classified
    M25.642 Stiffness of left hand, not elsewhere classified
    M25.649 Stiffness of unspecified hand, not elsewhere classified
● M25.65 Stiffness of hip, not elsewhere classified
    M25.651 Stiffness of right hip, not elsewhere classified
    M25.652 Stiffness of left hip, not elsewhere classified
    M25.659 Stiffness of unspecified hip, not elsewhere classified
● M25.66 Stiffness of knee, not elsewhere classified
    M25.661 Stiffness of right knee, not elsewhere classified
    M25.662 Stiffness of left knee, not elsewhere classified
    M25.669 Stiffness of unspecified knee, not elsewhere classified
● M25.67 Stiffness of ankle and foot, not elsewhere classified
    M25.671 Stiffness of right ankle, not elsewhere classified
    M25.672 Stiffness of left ankle, not elsewhere classified
    M25.673 Stiffness of unspecified ankle, not elsewhere classified
    M25.674 Stiffness of right foot, not elsewhere classified
    M25.675 Stiffness of left foot, not elsewhere classified
    M25.676 Stiffness of unspecified foot, not elsewhere classified
● M25.7 Osteophyte
    M25.70 Osteophyte, unspecified joint
● M25.71 Osteophyte, shoulder
    M25.711 Osteophyte, right shoulder
    M25.712 Osteophyte, left shoulder
    M25.719 Osteophyte, unspecified shoulder
● M25.72 Osteophyte, elbow
    M25.721 Osteophyte, right elbow
    M25.722 Osteophyte, left elbow
    M25.729 Osteophyte, unspecified elbow
● M25.73 Osteophyte, wrist
    M25.731 Osteophyte, right wrist
    M25.732 Osteophyte, left wrist
    M25.739 Osteophyte, unspecified wrist
● M25.74 Osteophyte, hand
    M25.741 Osteophyte, right hand
    M25.742 Osteophyte, left hand
    M25.749 Osteophyte, unspecified hand
● M25.75 Osteophyte, hip
    M25.751 Osteophyte, right hip
    M25.752 Osteophyte, left hip
    M25.759 Osteophyte, unspecified hip
● M25.76 Osteophyte, knee
    M25.761 Osteophyte, right knee
    M25.762 Osteophyte, left knee
    M25.769 Osteophyte, unspecified knee

● M25.77 Osteophyte, ankle and foot
    M25.771 Osteophyte, right ankle
    M25.772 Osteophyte, left ankle
    M25.773 Osteophyte, unspecified ankle
    M25.774 Osteophyte, right foot
    M25.775 Osteophyte, left foot
    M25.776 Osteophyte, unspecified foot
    M25.78 Osteophyte, vertebrae
● M25.8 Other specified joint disorders
    M25.80 Other specified joint disorders, unspecified joint
● M25.81 Other specified joint disorders, shoulder
    M25.811 Other specified joint disorders, right shoulder
    M25.812 Other specified joint disorders, left shoulder
    M25.819 Other specified joint disorders, unspecified shoulder
● M25.82 Other specified joint disorders, elbow
    M25.821 Other specified joint disorders, right elbow
    M25.822 Other specified joint disorders, left elbow
    M25.829 Other specified joint disorders, unspecified elbow
● M25.83 Other specified joint disorders, wrist
    M25.831 Other specified joint disorders, right wrist
    M25.832 Other specified joint disorders, left wrist
    M25.839 Other specified joint disorders, unspecified wrist
● M25.84 Other specified joint disorders, hand
    M25.841 Other specified joint disorders, right hand
    M25.842 Other specified joint disorders, left hand
    M25.849 Other specified joint disorders, unspecified hand
● M25.85 Other specified joint disorders, hip
    M25.851 Other specified joint disorders, right hip
    M25.852 Other specified joint disorders, left hip
    M25.859 Other specified joint disorders, unspecified hip
● M25.86 Other specified joint disorders, knee
    M25.861 Other specified joint disorders, right knee
    M25.862 Other specified joint disorders, left knee
    M25.869 Other specified joint disorders, unspecified knee
● M25.87 Other specified joint disorders, ankle and foot
    M25.871 Other specified joint disorders, right ankle and foot
    M25.872 Other specified joint disorders, left ankle and foot
    M25.879 Other specified joint disorders, unspecified ankle and foot
    M25.9 Joint disorder, unspecified

CHAPTER 13 (M00-M99)

Figure 13-3 Dentofacial malocclusion.

Item 13–6 **Hyperplasia** is a condition of overdevelopment, whereas **hypoplasia** is a condition of underdevelopment. **Macrogenia** is overdevelopment of the chin, whereas **microgenia** is underdevelopment of the chin.

DENTOFACIAL ANOMALIES [INCLUDING MALOCCLUSION] AND OTHER DISORDERS OF JAW (M26-M27)

> **Excludes1**   hemifacial atrophy or hypertrophy (Q67.4)
> unilateral condylar hyperplasia or hypoplasia (M27.8)

● **M26   Dentofacial anomalies [including malocclusion]**
  ● **M26.0   Major anomalies of jaw size**
    > **Excludes1**   acromegaly (E22.0)
                    Robin's syndrome (Q87.0)
     M26.00   **Unspecified** anomaly of jaw size
     M26.01   **Maxillary hyperplasia**
     M26.02   **Maxillary hypoplasia**
     M26.03   **Mandibular hyperplasia**
     M26.04   **Mandibular hypoplasia**
     M26.05   **Macrogenia**
     M26.06   **Microgenia**
     M26.07   **Excessive tuberosity of jaw**
           Entire maxillary tuberosity
     M26.09   **Other specified anomalies of jaw size**
  ● **M26.1   Anomalies of jaw-cranial base relationship**
     M26.10   **Unspecified** anomaly of jaw-cranial base relationship
     M26.11   **Maxillary asymmetry**
     M26.12   **Other jaw asymmetry**
     M26.19   **Other specified anomalies of jaw-cranial base relationship**
  ● **M26.2   Anomalies of dental arch relationship**
     M26.20   **Unspecified** anomaly of dental arch relationship
    ● M26.21   **Malocclusion, Angle's class**
       M26.211   **Malocclusion, Angle's class I**
              Neutro-occlusion
       M26.212   **Malocclusion, Angle's class II**
              Disto-occlusion Division I
              Disto-occlusion Division II
       M26.213   **Malocclusion, Angle's class III**
              Mesio-occlusion
       M26.219   **Malocclusion, Angle's class, unspecified**
    ● M26.22   **Open occlusal relationship**
       M26.220   **Open anterior occlusal relationship**
           ➠ Anterior open bite
       M26.221   **Open posterior occlusal relationship**
           ➠ Posterior open bite
     M26.23   **Excessive horizontal overlap**
           Excessive horizontal overjet
     M26.24   **Reverse articulation**
           Crossbite (anterior) (posterior)
     M26.25   **Anomalies of interarch distance**
     M26.29   **Other anomalies of dental arch relationship**
           Midline deviation of dental arch
           Overbite (excessive) deep
           Overbite (excessive) horizontal
           Overbite (excessive) vertical
           Posterior lingual occlusion of mandibular teeth

● **M26.3   Anomalies of tooth position of fully erupted tooth or teeth**
  > **Excludes2**   embedded and impacted teeth (K01.-)
   M26.30   **Unspecified anomaly of tooth position of fully erupted tooth or teeth**
        Abnormal spacing of fully erupted tooth or teeth NOS
        Displacement of fully erupted tooth or teeth NOS
        Transposition of fully erupted tooth or teeth NOS
   M26.31   **Crowding of fully erupted teeth**
   M26.32   **Excessive spacing of fully erupted teeth**
        Diastema of fully erupted tooth or teeth NOS
   M26.33   **Horizontal displacement of fully erupted tooth or teeth**
        Tipped tooth or teeth
        Tipping of fully erupted tooth
   M26.34   **Vertical displacement of fully erupted tooth or teeth**
        Extruded tooth
        Infraeruption of tooth or teeth
        Supraeruption of tooth or teeth
   M26.35   **Rotation of fully erupted tooth or teeth**
   M26.36   **Insufficient interocclusal distance of fully erupted teeth (ridge)**
        Lack of adequate intermaxillary vertical dimension of fully erupted teeth
   M26.37   **Excessive interocclusal distance of fully erupted teeth**
        Excessive intermaxillary vertical dimension of fully erupted teeth
        Loss of occlusal vertical dimension of fully erupted teeth
   M26.39   **Other anomalies of tooth position of fully erupted tooth or teeth**
● **M26.4   Malocclusion, unspecified**
● **M26.5   Dentofacial functional abnormalities**
  > **Excludes1**   bruxism (F45.8)
              teeth-grinding NOS (F45.8)
   M26.50   **Dentofacial functional abnormalities, unspecified**
   M26.51   **Abnormal jaw closure**
   M26.52   **Limited mandibular range of motion**
   M26.53   **Deviation in opening and closing of the mandible**
   M26.54   **Insufficient anterior guidance**
        Insufficient anterior occlusal guidance
   M26.55   **Centric occlusion maximum intercuspation discrepancy**
     > **Excludes1**   centric occlusion NOS (M26.59)
   M26.56   **Non-working side interference**
        Balancing side interference
   M26.57   **Lack of posterior occlusal support**
   M26.59   **Other dentofacial functional abnormalities**
        Centric occlusion (of teeth) NOS
        Malocclusion due to abnormal swallowing
        Malocclusion due to mouth breathing
        Malocclusion due to tongue, lip or finger habits

▶ New   ➠ Revised   ~~deleted~~ Deleted   Excludes 1   Excludes 2   Includes   Use additional   Code first   Code also   Key words

1014   OGCR Official Guidelines   X Assign placeholder X   ● Use Additional Character(s)   ▸ Manifestation Code   **Coding Clinic**

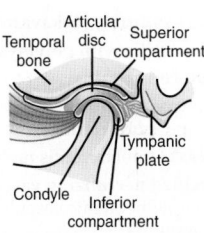

Figure 13-4 Temporomandibular joint.

Item 13–7 Dysfunction of the temporomandibular joint is termed **temporomandibular joint (TMJ) syndrome** and is characterized by pain and tenderness/spasm of the muscles of mastication, joint noise, and in the later stages, limited mandibular movement.

● M26.6 **Temporomandibular joint disorders**
     Excludes2   current temporomandibular joint dislocation (S03.0)
                   current temporomandibular joint sprain (S03.4)
     Coding Clinic: 2016, Q4, P38-39

  ● M26.60 **Temporomandibular joint disorder, unspecified**
      M26.601 **Right temporomandibular joint disorder, unspecified**
      M26.602 **Left temporomandibular joint disorder, unspecified**
      M26.603 **Bilateral temporomandibular joint disorder, unspecified**
      M26.609 **Unspecified temporomandibular joint disorder, unspecified side**
            Temporomandibular joint disorder NOS

  ● M26.61 **Adhesions and ankylosis of temporomandibular joint**
      M26.611 **Adhesions and ankylosis of right temporomandibular joint**
      M26.612 **Adhesions and ankylosis of left temporomandibular joint**
      M26.613 **Adhesions and ankylosis of bilateral temporomandibular joint**
      M26.619 **Adhesions and ankylosis of temporomandibular joint, unspecified side**

  ● M26.62 **Arthralgia of temporomandibular joint**
      M26.621 **Arthralgia of right temporomandibular joint**
      M26.622 **Arthralgia of left temporomandibular joint**
      M26.623 **Arthralgia of bilateral temporomandibular joint**
      M26.629 **Arthralgia of temporomandibular joint, unspecified side**

  ● M26.63 **Articular disc disorder of temporomandibular joint**
      M26.631 **Articular disc disorder of right temporomandibular joint**
      M26.632 **Articular disc disorder of left temporomandibular joint**
      M26.633 **Articular disc disorder of bilateral temporomandibular joint**
      M26.639 **Articular disc disorder of temporomandibular joint, unspecified side**

    M26.69 **Other specified disorders of temporomandibular joint**

● M26.7 **Dental alveolar anomalies**
    M26.70 **Unspecified alveolar anomaly**
    M26.71 **Alveolar maxillary hyperplasia**
    M26.72 **Alveolar mandibular hyperplasia**
    M26.73 **Alveolar maxillary hypoplasia**
    M26.74 **Alveolar mandibular hypoplasia**
    M26.79 **Other specified alveolar anomalies**

● M26.8 **Other dentofacial anomalies**
    M26.81 **Anterior soft tissue impingement**
         Anterior soft tissue impingement on teeth
    M26.82 **Posterior soft tissue impingement**
         Posterior soft tissue impingement on teeth
    M26.89 **Other dentofacial anomalies**

  M26.9 **Dentofacial anomaly, unspecified**

● M27 **Other diseases of jaws**
  M27.0 **Developmental disorders of jaws**
      Latent bone cyst of jaw
      Stafne's cyst
      Torus mandibularis
      Torus palatinus

  M27.1 **Giant cell granuloma, central**
      Giant cell granuloma NOS
     Excludes1   peripheral giant cell granuloma (K06.8)

  M27.2 **Inflammatory conditions of jaws**
      Osteitis of jaw(s)
      Osteomyelitis (neonatal) jaw(s)
      Osteoradionecrosis jaw(s)
      Periostitis jaw(s)
      Sequestrum of jaw bone
      Use additional code (W88-W90, X39.0) to identify radiation, if radiation-induced
     Excludes2   osteonecrosis of jaw due to drug (M87.180)

  M27.3 **Alveolitis of jaws**
      Alveolar osteitis
      Dry socket

● M27.4 **Other and unspecified cysts of jaw**
     Excludes1   cysts of oral region (K09.-)
               latent bone cyst of jaw (M27.0)
               Stafne's cyst (M27.0)
    M27.40 **Unspecified cyst of jaw**
         Cyst of jaw NOS
    M27.49 **Other cysts of jaw**
         Aneurysmal cyst of jaw
         Hemorrhagic cyst of jaw
         Traumatic cyst of jaw

● M27.5 **Periradicular pathology associated with previous endodontic treatment**
    M27.51 **Perforation of root canal space due to endodontic treatment**
    M27.52 **Endodontic overfill**
    M27.53 **Endodontic underfill**
    M27.59 **Other periradicular pathology associated with previous endodontic treatment**

● M27.6 **Endosseous dental implant failure**
    M27.61 **Osseointegration failure of dental implant**
         Hemorrhagic complications of dental implant placement
         Iatrogenic osseointegration failure of dental implant
         Osseointegration failure of dental implant due to complications of systemic disease
         Osseointegration failure of dental implant due to poor bone quality
         Pre-integration failure of dental implant NOS
         Pre-osseointegration failure of dental implant

CHAPTER 13 (M00-M99)

M27.62   Post-osseointegration biological failure of dental implant
Failure of dental implant due to lack of attached gingiva
Failure of dental implant due to occlusal trauma (caused by poor prosthetic design)
Failure of dental implant due to parafunctional habits
Failure of dental implant due to periodontal infection (peri–implantitis)
Failure of dental implant due to poor oral hygiene
Iatrogenic post-osseointegration failure of dental implant
Post-osseointegration failure of dental implant due to complications of systemic disease

M27.63   Post-osseointegration mechanical failure of dental implant
Failure of dental prosthesis causing loss of dental implant
Fracture of dental implant
> **Excludes2**   cracked tooth (K03.81)
> fractured dental restorative material with loss of material (K08.531)
> fractured dental restorative material without loss of material (K08.530)
> fractured tooth (S02.5)

M27.69   Other endosseous dental implant failure
Dental implant failure NOS

M27.8   Other specified diseases of jaws
Cherubism
Exostosis
Fibrous dysplasia
Unilateral condylar hyperplasia
Unilateral condylar hypoplasia
> **Excludes1**   jaw pain (R68.84)

M27.9   Disease of jaws, unspecified

SYSTEMIC CONNECTIVE TISSUE DISORDERS (M30-M36)

> **Includes**   autoimmune disease NOS
> collagen (vascular) disease NOS
> systemic autoimmune disease
> systemic collagen (vascular) disease

> **Excludes1**   autoimmune disease, single organ or single cell-type - code to relevant condition category

● M30   Polyarteritis nodosa and related conditions
> **Excludes1**   microscopic polyarteritis (M31.7)

M30.0   Polyarteritis nodosa

M30.1   Polyarteritis with lung involvement [Churg-Strauss]
Allergic granulomatous angiitis

M30.2   Juvenile polyarteritis

M30.3   Mucocutaneous lymph node syndrome [Kawasaki]

M30.8   Other conditions related to polyarteritis nodosa
Polyangiitis overlap syndrome

● M31   Other necrotizing vasculopathies

M31.0   Hypersensitivity angiitis
Goodpasture's syndrome

M31.1   Thrombotic microangiopathy
Thrombotic thrombocytopenic purpura

M31.2   Lethal midline granuloma

● M31.3   Wegener's granulomatosis
Necrotizing respiratory granulomatosis
   M31.30   Wegener's granulomatosis without renal involvement
     Wegener's granulomatosis NOS
   M31.31   Wegener's granulomatosis with renal involvement

M31.4   Aortic arch syndrome [Takayasu]

M31.5   Giant cell arteritis with polymyalgia rheumatica

M31.6   Other giant cell arteritis

M31.7   Microscopic polyangiitis
Microscopic polyarteritis
> **Excludes1**   polyarteritis nodosa (M30.0)

M31.8   Other specified necrotizing vasculopathies
Hypocomplementemic vasculitis
Septic vasculitis

M31.9   Necrotizing vasculopathy, unspecified

● M32   Systemic lupus erythematosus (SLE)
Autoimmune inflammatory connective tissue disease of unknown cause that occurs most often in women
> **Excludes1**   lupus erythematosus (discoid) (NOS) (L93.0)

M32.0   Drug-induced systemic lupus erythematosus
Use additional code for adverse effect, if applicable, to identify drug (T36-T50 with fifth or sixth character 5)

● M32.1   Systemic lupus erythematosus with organ or system involvement
   M32.10   Systemic lupus erythematosus, organ or system involvement unspecified
   M32.11   Endocarditis in systemic lupus erythematosus
     Libman-Sacks disease
   M32.12   Pericarditis in systemic lupus erythematosus
     Lupus pericarditis
   M32.13   Lung involvement in systemic lupus erythematosus
     Pleural effusion due to systemic lupus erythematosus
   M32.14   Glomerular disease in systemic lupus erythematosus
     Lupus renal disease NOS
   M32.15   Tubulo-interstitial nephropathy in systemic lupus erythematosus
   M32.19   Other organ or system involvement in systemic lupus erythematosus

M32.8   Other forms of systemic lupus erythematosus

M32.9   Systemic lupus erythematosus, unspecified
SLE NOS
Systemic lupus erythematosus NOS
Systemic lupus erythematosus without organ involvement

● M33   Dermatopolymyositis

● M33.0   Juvenile dermatomyositis
   M33.00   Juvenile dermatomyositis, organ involvement unspecified
   M33.01   Juvenile dermatomyositis with respiratory involvement
   M33.02   Juvenile dermatomyositis with myopathy
   M33.03   Juvenile dermatomyositis without myopathy
   M33.09   Juvenile dermatomyositis with other organ involvement

● M33.1   Other dermatomyositis
Adult dermatomyositis
   M33.10   Other dermatomyositis, organ involvement unspecified
   M33.11   Other dermatomyositis with respiratory involvement
   M33.12   Other dermatomyositis with myopathy
   M33.13   Other dermatomyositis without myopathy
     Dermatomyositis NOS
   M33.19   Other dermatomyositis with other organ involvement

Item 13–8 Polymyalgia rheumatica is a syndrome characterized by aching and morning stiffness and is related to aging and hereditary predisposition.

- **M33.2 Polymyositis**
  - M33.20 Polymyositis, organ involvement unspecified
  - M33.21 Polymyositis with respiratory involvement
  - M33.22 Polymyositis with myopathy
  - M33.29 Polymyositis with other organ involvement
- **M33.9 Dermatopolymyositis, unspecified**
  - M33.90 Dermatopolymyositis, unspecified, organ involvement unspecified
  - M33.91 Dermatopolymyositis, unspecified with respiratory involvement
  - M33.92 Dermatopolymyositis, unspecified with myopathy
  - M33.93 Dermatopolymyositis, unspecified without myopathy
  - M33.99 Dermatopolymyositis, unspecified with other organ involvement
- **M34 Systemic sclerosis [scleroderma]**
  - **Excludes1**   circumscribed scleroderma (L94.0)
    neonatal scleroderma (P83.8)
  - M34.0 Progressive systemic sclerosis
  - M34.1 CR(E)ST syndrome
    Combination of calcinosis, Raynaud's phenomenon, esophageal dysfunction, sclerodactyly, telangiectasia
  - M34.2 Systemic sclerosis induced by drug and chemical
    Code first poisoning due to drug or toxin, if applicable (T36-T65 with fifth or sixth character 1-4 or 6)
    Use additional code for adverse effect, if applicable, to identify drug (T36-T50 with fifth or sixth character 5)
  - **M34.8 Other forms of systemic sclerosis**
    - M34.81 Systemic sclerosis with lung involvement
    - M34.82 Systemic sclerosis with myopathy
    - M34.83 Systemic sclerosis with polyneuropathy
    - M34.89 Other systemic sclerosis
  - M34.9 Systemic sclerosis, unspecified
- **M35 Other systemic involvement of connective tissue**
  - **Excludes1**   reactive perforating collagenosis (L87.1)
  - **M35.0 Sicca syndrome [Sjögren]**
    - M35.00 Sicca syndrome, unspecified
    - M35.01 Sicca syndrome with keratoconjunctivitis
    - M35.02 Sicca syndrome with lung involvement
    - M35.03 Sicca syndrome with myopathy
    - M35.04 Sicca syndrome with tubulo-interstitial nephropathy
      Renal tubular acidosis in sicca syndrome
    - M35.09 Sicca syndrome with other organ involvement
  - M35.1 Other overlap syndromes
    Mixed connective tissue disease
    - **Excludes1**   polyangiitis overlap syndrome (M30.8)
  - M35.2 Behçet's disease
  - M35.3 Polymyalgia rheumatica
    - **Excludes1**   polymyalgia rheumatica with giant cell arteritis (M31.5)

M35.4 Diffuse (eosinophilic) fasciitis

M35.5 Multifocal fibrosclerosis

M35.6 Relapsing panniculitis [Weber-Christian]
- **Excludes1**   lupus panniculitis (L93.2)
  panniculitis NOS (M79.3-)

M35.7 Hypermobility syndrome
Familial ligamentous laxity
- **Excludes1**   Ehlers-Danlos syndrome (Q79.6)
  ligamentous laxity, NOS (M24.2-)

M35.8 Other specified systemic involvement of connective tissue

M35.9 Systemic involvement of connective tissue, unspecified
Autoimmune disease (systemic) NOS
Collagen (vascular) disease NOS

- **M36 Systemic disorders of connective tissue in diseases classified elsewhere**
  - **Excludes2**   arthropathies in diseases classified elsewhere (M14.-)
  - *M36.0 Dermato(poly)myositis in neoplastic disease*
    Code first underlying neoplasm (C00-D49)
  - *M36.1 Arthropathy in neoplastic disease*
    Code first underlying neoplasm, such as:
    leukemia (C91-C95)
    malignant histiocytosis (C96.A)
    multiple myeloma (C90.0)
  - *M36.2 Hemophilic arthropathy*
    Hemarthrosis in hemophilic arthropathy
    Code first underlying disease, such as:
    factor VIII deficiency (D66)
    with vascular defect (D68.0)
    factor IX deficiency (D67)
    hemophilia (classical) (D66)
    hemophilia B (D67)
    hemophilia C (D68.1)
  - *M36.3 Arthropathy in other blood disorders*
  - *M36.4 Arthropathy in hypersensitivity reactions classified elsewhere*
    Code first underlying disease, such as:
    Henoch (-Schönlein) purpura (D69.0)
    serum sickness (T80.6-)
  - *M36.8 Systemic disorders of connective tissue in other diseases classified elsewhere*
    Code first underlying disease, such as:
    alkaptonuria (E70.2)
    hypogammaglobulinemia (D80.-)
    ochronosis (E70.2)

DORSOPATHIES (M40-M54)

DEFORMING DORSOPATHIES (M40-M43)

- **M40 Kyphosis and lordosis**
  - **Excludes1**   congenital kyphosis and lordosis (Q76.4)
    kyphoscoliosis (M41.-)
    postprocedural kyphosis and lordosis (M96.-)
  - **M40.0 Postural kyphosis**
    - **Excludes1**   osteochondrosis of spine (M42.-)
    - M40.00 Postural kyphosis, site unspecified
    - M40.03 Postural kyphosis, cervicothoracic region
    - M40.04 Postural kyphosis, thoracic region
    - M40.05 Postural kyphosis, thoracolumbar region

CHAPTER 13 (M00-M99)

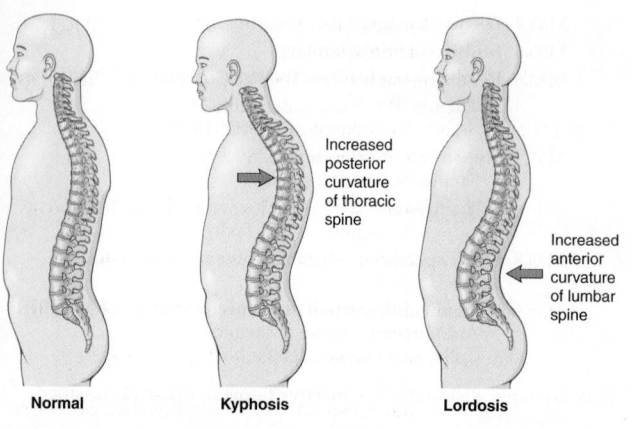

Increased posterior curvature of thoracic spine

Increased anterior curvature of lumbar spine

Normal   Kyphosis   Lordosis

Figure 13-5 Kyphosis, Lordosis, Scoliosis. (From Chabner: The Language of Medicine, ed 8, St. Louis, Saunders, 2007)

Item 13–9 Kyphosis is an abnormal curvature of the spine. **Senile kyphosis** is a result of disc degeneration causing ossification (turning to bone). **Adolescent** or **juvenile** kyphosis is also known as **Scheuermann's disease,** a condition in which the discs of the lower thoracic spine herniate, causing the disc space to narrow and the spine to tilt forward. This condition is attributed to poor posture. **Lordosis or swayback** is an abnormal curvature of the spine resulting in an inward curve of the lumbar spine just above the buttocks. **Scoliosis** causes a sideways curve to the spine. The curves are S- or C-shaped, and it is most commonly acquired in late childhood and early teen years, when growth is fast.

● **M40.1** Other secondary kyphosis
     M40.10   Other secondary kyphosis, site unspecified
     M40.12   Other secondary kyphosis, cervical region
     M40.13   Other secondary kyphosis, cervicothoracic region
     M40.14   Other secondary kyphosis, thoracic region
     M40.15   Other secondary kyphosis, thoracolumbar region

● **M40.2** Other and unspecified kyphosis
     ● **M40.20** Unspecified kyphosis
         M40.202   Unspecified kyphosis, cervical region
         M40.203   Unspecified kyphosis, cervicothoracic region
         M40.204   Unspecified kyphosis, thoracic region
         M40.205   Unspecified kyphosis, thoracolumbar region
         M40.209   Unspecified kyphosis, site unspecified
     ● **M40.29** Other kyphosis
         M40.292   Other kyphosis, cervical region
         M40.293   Other kyphosis, cervicothoracic region
         M40.294   Other kyphosis, thoracic region
         M40.295   Other kyphosis, thoracolumbar region
         M40.299   Other kyphosis, site unspecified

● **M40.3** Flatback syndrome
     M40.30   Flatback syndrome, site unspecified
     M40.35   Flatback syndrome, thoracolumbar region
     M40.36   Flatback syndrome, lumbar region
     M40.37   Flatback syndrome, lumbosacral region

● **M40.4** Postural lordosis
     Abnormal increase in the normal curvature of the lumbar spine (sway back)
     Acquired lordosis
     M40.40   Postural lordosis, site unspecified
     M40.45   Postural lordosis, thoracolumbar region
     M40.46   Postural lordosis, lumbar region
     M40.47   Postural lordosis, lumbosacral region

● **M40.5** Lordosis, unspecified
     M40.50   Lordosis, unspecified, site unspecified
     M40.55   Lordosis, unspecified, thoracolumbar region
     M40.56   Lordosis, unspecified, lumbar region
     M40.57   Lordosis, unspecified, lumbosacral region

● **M41** Scoliosis

Includes	kyphoscoliosis
Excludes1	congenital scoliosis NOS (Q67.5)
	congenital scoliosis due to bony malformation (Q76.3)
	postural congenital scoliosis (Q67.5)
	kyphoscoliotic heart disease (I27.1)
	postprocedural scoliosis (M96.-)

● **M41.0** Infantile idiopathic scoliosis
     M41.00   Infantile idiopathic scoliosis, site unspecified
     M41.02   Infantile idiopathic scoliosis, cervical region
     M41.03   Infantile idiopathic scoliosis, cervicothoracic region
     M41.04   Infantile idiopathic scoliosis, thoracic region
     M41.05   Infantile idiopathic scoliosis, thoracolumbar region
     M41.06   Infantile idiopathic scoliosis, lumbar region
     M41.07   Infantile idiopathic scoliosis, lumbosacral region
     M41.08   Infantile idiopathic scoliosis, sacral and sacrococcygeal region

● **M41.1** Juvenile and adolescent idiopathic scoliosis
     ● **M41.11** Juvenile idiopathic scoliosis
         M41.112   Juvenile idiopathic scoliosis, cervical region
         M41.113   Juvenile idiopathic scoliosis, cervicothoracic region
         M41.114   Juvenile idiopathic scoliosis, thoracic region
         M41.115   Juvenile idiopathic scoliosis, thoracolumbar region
         M41.116   Juvenile idiopathic scoliosis, lumbar region
         M41.117   Juvenile idiopathic scoliosis, lumbosacral region
         M41.119   Juvenile idiopathic scoliosis, site unspecified
     ● **M41.12** Adolescent scoliosis
         M41.122   Adolescent idiopathic scoliosis, cervical region
         M41.123   Adolescent idiopathic scoliosis, cervicothoracic region
         M41.124   Adolescent idiopathic scoliosis, thoracic region
         M41.125   Adolescent idiopathic scoliosis, thoracolumbar region
         M41.126   Adolescent idiopathic scoliosis, lumbar region
         M41.127   Adolescent idiopathic scoliosis, lumbosacral region
         M41.129   Adolescent idiopathic scoliosis, site unspecified

CHAPTER 13 (M00-M99)

▶ New   ⇒ Revised   ~~deleted~~ Deleted   Excludes 1   Excludes 2   Includes   Use additional   Code first   Code also   Key words
OGCR Official Guidelines   X Assign placeholder X   ● Use Additional Character(s)   ❱ Manifestation Code   **Coding Clinic**

● **M41.2** Other idiopathic scoliosis

    M41.20 Other idiopathic scoliosis, site unspecified

    M41.22 Other idiopathic scoliosis, cervical region

    M41.23 Other idiopathic scoliosis, cervicothoracic region

    M41.24 Other idiopathic scoliosis, thoracic region

    M41.25 Other idiopathic scoliosis, thoracolumbar region

    M41.26 Other idiopathic scoliosis, lumbar region

    M41.27 Other idiopathic scoliosis, lumbosacral region

● **M41.3** Thoracogenic scoliosis

    M41.30 Thoracogenic scoliosis, site unspecified

    M41.34 Thoracogenic scoliosis, thoracic region

    M41.35 Thoracogenic scoliosis, thoracolumbar region

● **M41.4** Neuromuscular scoliosis

    Scoliosis secondary to cerebral palsy, Friedreich's ataxia, poliomyelitis and other neuromuscular disorders

    Code also underlying condition

    M41.40 Neuromuscular scoliosis, site unspecified

    M41.41 Neuromuscular scoliosis, occipito-atlanto-axial region

    M41.42 Neuromuscular scoliosis, cervical region

    M41.43 Neuromuscular scoliosis, cervicothoracic region

    M41.44 Neuromuscular scoliosis, thoracic region

    M41.45 Neuromuscular scoliosis, thoracolumbar region

    M41.46 Neuromuscular scoliosis, lumbar region

    M41.47 Neuromuscular scoliosis, lumbosacral region

● **M41.5** Other secondary scoliosis

    M41.50 Other secondary scoliosis, site unspecified

    M41.52 Other secondary scoliosis, cervical region

    M41.53 Other secondary scoliosis, cervicothoracic region

    M41.54 Other secondary scoliosis, thoracic region

    M41.55 Other secondary scoliosis, thoracolumbar region

    M41.56 Other secondary scoliosis, lumbar region

    M41.57 Other secondary scoliosis, lumbosacral region

● **M41.8** Other forms of scoliosis

    M41.80 Other forms of scoliosis, site unspecified

    M41.82 Other forms of scoliosis, cervical region

    M41.83 Other forms of scoliosis, cervicothoracic region

    M41.84 Other forms of scoliosis, thoracic region

    M41.85 Other forms of scoliosis, thoracolumbar region

    M41.86 Other forms of scoliosis, lumbar region

    M41.87 Other forms of scoliosis, lumbosacral region

  M41.9 Scoliosis, unspecified

● **M42** Spinal osteochondrosis

  ● **M42.0** Juvenile osteochondrosis of spine

    Calvé's disease

    Scheuermann's disease

    Excludes1 postural kyphosis (M40.0)

    M42.00 Juvenile osteochondrosis of spine, site unspecified

    M42.01 Juvenile osteochondrosis of spine, occipito-atlanto-axial region

    M42.02 Juvenile osteochondrosis of spine, cervical region

    M42.03 Juvenile osteochondrosis of spine, cervicothoracic region

    M42.04 Juvenile osteochondrosis of spine, thoracic region

    M42.05 Juvenile osteochondrosis of spine, thoracolumbar region

    M42.06 Juvenile osteochondrosis of spine, lumbar region

    M42.07 Juvenile osteochondrosis of spine, lumbosacral region

    M42.08 Juvenile osteochondrosis of spine, sacral and sacrococcygeal region

    M42.09 Juvenile osteochondrosis of spine, multiple sites in spine

  ● **M42.1** Adult osteochondrosis of spine

    M42.10 Adult osteochondrosis of spine, site unspecified   A

    M42.11 Adult osteochondrosis of spine, occipitoatlanto-axial region   A

    M42.12 Adult osteochondrosis of spine, cervical region   A

    M42.13 Adult osteochondrosis of spine, cervicothoracic region   A

    M42.14 Adult osteochondrosis of spine, thoracic region   A

    M42.15 Adult osteochondrosis of spine, thoracolumbar region   A

    M42.16 Adult osteochondrosis of spine, lumbar region   A

    M42.17 Adult osteochondrosis of spine, lumbosacral region   A

    M42.18 Adult osteochondrosis of spine, sacral and sacrococcygeal region   A

    M42.19 Adult osteochondrosis of spine, multiple sites in spine   A

  M42.9 Spinal osteochondrosis, unspecified

● **M43** Other deforming dorsopathies

    Excludes1 congenital spondylolysis and spondylolisthesis (Q76.2)

        hemivertebra (Q76.3-Q76.4)

        Klippel-Feil syndrome (Q76.1)

        lumbarization and sacralization (Q76.4)

        platyspondylisis (Q76.4)

        spina bifida occulta (Q76.0)

        spinal curvature in osteoporosis (M80.-)

        spinal curvature in Paget's disease of bone [osteitis deformans] (M88.-)

  ● **M43.0** Spondylolysis

    Excludes1 congenital spondylolysis (Q76.2)

        spondylolisthesis (M43.1)

    M43.00 Spondylolysis, site unspecified

    M43.01 Spondylolysis, occipito-atlanto-axial region

    M43.02 Spondylolysis, cervical region

    M43.03 Spondylolysis, cervicothoracic region

    M43.04 Spondylolysis, thoracic region

    M43.05 Spondylolysis, thoracolumbar region

    M43.06 Spondylolysis, lumbar region

    M43.07 Spondylolysis, lumbosacral region

    M43.08 Spondylolysis, sacral and sacrococcygeal region

    M43.09 Spondylolysis, multiple sites in spine

  ● **M43.1** Spondylolisthesis

    Excludes1 acute traumatic of lumbosacral region (S33.1)

        acute traumatic of sites other than lumbosacral - code to Fracture, vertebra, by region

        congenital spondylolisthesis (Q76.2)

    M43.10 Spondylolisthesis, site unspecified

    M43.11 Spondylolisthesis, occipito-atlanto-axial region

    M43.12 Spondylolisthesis, cervical region

    M43.13 Spondylolisthesis, cervicothoracic region

    M43.14 Spondylolisthesis, thoracic region

    M43.15 Spondylolisthesis, thoracolumbar region

    M43.16 Spondylolisthesis, lumbar region

    M43.17 Spondylolisthesis, lumbosacral region

    M43.18 Spondylolisthesis, sacral and sacrococcygeal region

    M43.19 Spondylolisthesis, multiple sites in spine

CHAPTER 13 (M00-M99)

Item 13–10 Spondylolisthesis is a condition caused by the slipping forward of one disc over another.

● **M43.2 Fusion of spine**
Ankylosis of spinal joint

Excludes1 ankylosing spondylitis (M45.0-)
congenital fusion of spine (Q76.4)

Excludes2 arthrodesis status (Z98.1)
pseudoarthrosis after fusion or arthrodesis (M96.0)

M43.20 Fusion of spine, site unspecified
M43.21 Fusion of spine, occipito-atlanto-axial region
M43.22 Fusion of spine, cervical region
M43.23 Fusion of spine, cervicothoracic region
M43.24 Fusion of spine, thoracic region
M43.25 Fusion of spine, thoracolumbar region
M43.26 Fusion of spine, lumbar region
M43.27 Fusion of spine, lumbosacral region
M43.28 Fusion of spine, sacral and sacrococcygeal region

M43.3 Recurrent atlantoaxial dislocation with myelopathy
M43.4 Other recurrent atlantoaxial dislocation

● M43.5 Other recurrent vertebral dislocation

Excludes1 biomechanical lesions NEC (M99.-)

● M43.5X Other recurrent vertebral dislocation

M43.5X2 Other recurrent vertebral dislocation, cervical region
M43.5X3 Other recurrent vertebral dislocation, cervicothoracic region
M43.5X4 Other recurrent vertebral dislocation, thoracic region
M43.5X5 Other recurrent vertebral dislocation, thoracolumbar region
M43.5X6 Other recurrent vertebral dislocation, lumbar region
M43.5X7 Other recurrent vertebral dislocation, lumbosacral region
M43.5X8 Other recurrent vertebral dislocation, sacral and sacrococcygeal region
M43.5X9 Other recurrent vertebral dislocation, site unspecified

M43.6 Torticollis

Excludes1 congenital (sternomastoid) torticollis (Q68.0)
current injury - see Injury, of spine, by body region ocular torticollis (R29.891)
psychogenic torticollis (F45.8)
spasmodic torticollis (G24.3)
torticollis due to birth injury (P15.2)

● M43.8 Other specified deforming dorsopathies

Excludes2 kyphosis and lordosis (M40.-)
scoliosis (M41.-)

● M43.8X Other specified deforming dorsopathies

M43.8X1 Other specified deforming dorsopathies, occipito-atlanto-axial region
M43.8X2 Other specified deforming dorsopathies, cervical region
M43.8X3 Other specified deforming dorsopathies, cervicothoracic region
M43.8X4 Other specified deforming dorsopathies, thoracic region
M43.8X5 Other specified deforming dorsopathies, thoracolumbar region
M43.8X6 Other specified deforming dorsopathies, lumbar region
M43.8X7 Other specified deforming dorsopathies, lumbosacral region
M43.8X8 Other specified deforming dorsopathies, sacral and sacrococcygeal region
M43.8X9 Other specified deforming dorsopathies, site unspecified

M43.9 Deforming dorsopathy, unspecified
Curvature of spine NOS

SPONDYLOPATHIES (M45-M49)

● M45 Ankylosing spondylitis
Rheumatoid arthritis of spine

Excludes1 arthropathy in Reiter's disease (M02.3-)
juvenile (ankylosing) spondylitis (M08.1)

Excludes2 Behçet's disease (M35.2)

M45.0 Ankylosing spondylitis of multiple sites in spine
M45.1 Ankylosing spondylitis of occipito-atlanto-axial region
M45.2 Ankylosing spondylitis of cervical region
M45.3 Ankylosing spondylitis of cervicothoracic region
M45.4 Ankylosing spondylitis of thoracic region
M45.5 Ankylosing spondylitis of thoracolumbar region
M45.6 Ankylosing spondylitis lumbar region
M45.7 Ankylosing spondylitis of lumbosacral region
M45.8 Ankylosing spondylitis sacral and sacrococcygeal region
M45.9 Ankylosing spondylitis of unspecified sites in spine

● M46 Other inflammatory spondylopathies

● M46.0 Spinal enthesopathy
Disorder of ligamentous or muscular attachments of spine

M46.00 Spinal enthesopathy, site unspecified
M46.01 Spinal enthesopathy, occipito-atlanto-axial region
M46.02 Spinal enthesopathy, cervical region
M46.03 Spinal enthesopathy, cervicothoracic region
M46.04 Spinal enthesopathy, thoracic region
M46.05 Spinal enthesopathy, thoracolumbar region
M46.06 Spinal enthesopathy, lumbar region
M46.07 Spinal enthesopathy, lumbosacral region
M46.08 Spinal enthesopathy, sacral and sacrococcygeal region
M46.09 Spinal enthesopathy, multiple sites in spine

M46.1 Sacroiliitis, not elsewhere classified

● M46.2 Osteomyelitis of vertebra

M46.20 Osteomyelitis of vertebra, site unspecified
M46.21 Osteomyelitis of vertebra, occipito-atlanto-axial region
M46.22 Osteomyelitis of vertebra, cervical region
M46.23 Osteomyelitis of vertebra, cervicothoracic region
M46.24 Osteomyelitis of vertebra, thoracic region
M46.25 Osteomyelitis of vertebra, thoracolumbar region
M46.26 Osteomyelitis of vertebra, lumbar region
M46.27 Osteomyelitis of vertebra, lumbosacral region
M46.28 Osteomyelitis of vertebra, sacral and sacrococcygeal region

▶ New ⇒ Revised ~~deleted~~ Deleted Excludes 1 Excludes 2 Includes Use additional Code first Code also Key words
OGCR Official Guidelines X Assign placeholder X ● Use Additional Character(s) ▌ Manifestation Code Coding Clinic

● **M46.3 Infection of intervertebral disc (pyogenic)**
    Use additional code (B95-B97) to identify infectious agent

   M46.30   Infection of intervertebral disc (pyogenic), site unspecified

   M46.31   Infection of intervertebral disc (pyogenic), occipito-atlanto-axial region

   M46.32   Infection of intervertebral disc (pyogenic), cervical region

   M46.33   Infection of intervertebral disc (pyogenic), cervicothoracic region

   M46.34   Infection of intervertebral disc (pyogenic), thoracic region

   M46.35   Infection of intervertebral disc (pyogenic), thoracolumbar region

   M46.36   Infection of intervertebral disc (pyogenic), lumbar region

   M46.37   Infection of intervertebral disc (pyogenic), lumbosacral region

   M46.38   Infection of intervertebral disc (pyogenic), sacral and sacrococcygeal region

   M46.39   Infection of intervertebral disc (pyogenic), multiple sites in spine

● **M46.4 Discitis, unspecified**

   M46.40   Discitis, unspecified, site unspecified

   M46.41   Discitis, unspecified, occipito-atlanto-axial region

   M46.42   Discitis, unspecified, cervical region

   M46.43   Discitis, unspecified, cervicothoracic region

   M46.44   Discitis, unspecified, thoracic region

   M46.45   Discitis, unspecified, thoracolumbar region

   M46.46   Discitis, unspecified, lumbar region

   M46.47   Discitis, unspecified, lumbosacral region

   M46.48   Discitis, unspecified, sacral and sacrococcygeal region

   M46.49   Discitis, unspecified, multiple sites in spine

● **M46.5 Other infective spondylopathies**

   M46.50   Other infective spondylopathies, site unspecified

   M46.51   Other infective spondylopathies, occipitoatlanto-axial region

   M46.52   Other infective spondylopathies, cervical region

   M46.53   Other infective spondylopathies, cervicothoracic region

   M46.54   Other infective spondylopathies, thoracic region

   M46.55   Other infective spondylopathies, thoracolumbar region

   M46.56   Other infective spondylopathies, lumbar region

   M46.57   Other infective spondylopathies, lumbosacral region

   M46.58   Other infective spondylopathies, sacral and sacrococcygeal region

   M46.59   Other infective spondylopathies, multiple sites in spine

● **M46.8 Other specified inflammatory spondylopathies**

   M46.80   Other specified inflammatory spondylopathies, site unspecified

   M46.81   Other specified inflammatory spondylopathies, occipito-atlanto-axial region

   M46.82   Other specified inflammatory spondylopathies, cervical region

   M46.83   Other specified inflammatory spondylopathies, cervicothoracic region

   M46.84   Other specified inflammatory spondylopathies, thoracic region

   M46.85   Other specified inflammatory spondylopathies, thoracolumbar region

   M46.86   Other specified inflammatory spondylopathies, lumbar region

   M46.87   Other specified inflammatory spondylopathies, lumbosacral region

   M46.88   Other specified inflammatory spondylopathies, sacral and sacrococcygeal region

   M46.89   Other specified inflammatory spondylopathies, multiple sites in spine

● **M46.9 Unspecified inflammatory spondylopathy**

   M46.90   Unspecified inflammatory spondylopathy, site unspecified

   M46.91   Unspecified inflammatory spondylopathy, occipito-atlanto-axial region

   M46.92   Unspecified inflammatory spondylopathy, cervical region

   M46.93   Unspecified inflammatory spondylopathy, cervicothoracic region

   M46.94   Unspecified inflammatory spondylopathy, thoracic region

   M46.95   Unspecified inflammatory spondylopathy, thoracolumbar region

   M46.96   Unspecified inflammatory spondylopathy, lumbar region

   M46.97   Unspecified inflammatory spondylopathy, lumbosacral region

   M46.98   Unspecified inflammatory spondylopathy, sacral and sacrococcygeal region

   M46.99   Unspecified inflammatory spondylopathy, multiple sites in spine

● **M47 Spondylosis**

   Includes   arthrosis or osteoarthritis of spine
                  degeneration of facet joints

● **M47.0 Anterior spinal and vertebral artery compression syndromes**

   ● **M47.01 Anterior spinal artery compression syndromes**

     M47.011   Anterior spinal artery compression syndromes, occipito-atlanto-axial region

     M47.012   Anterior spinal artery compression syndromes, cervical region

     M47.013   Anterior spinal artery compression syndromes, cervicothoracic region

     M47.014   Anterior spinal artery compression syndromes, thoracic region

     M47.015   Anterior spinal artery compression syndromes, thoracolumbar region

     M47.016   Anterior spinal artery compression syndromes, lumbar region

     M47.019   Anterior spinal artery compression syndromes, site unspecified

   ● **M47.02 Vertebral artery compression syndromes**

     M47.021   Vertebral artery compression syndromes, occipito-atlanto-axial region

     M47.022   Vertebral artery compression syndromes, cervical region

     M47.029   Vertebral artery compression syndromes, site unspecified

CHAPTER 13 (M00-M99)

CHAPTER 13 (M00-M99)

● M47.1   Other spondylosis with myelopathy
Spondylogenic compression of spinal cord
Excludes1   vertebral subluxation (M43.3-M43.59)

M47.10   Other spondylosis with myelopathy, site unspecified

M47.11   Other spondylosis with myelopathy, occipito-atlanto-axial region

M47.12   Other spondylosis with myelopathy, cervical region

M47.13   Other spondylosis with myelopathy, cervicothoracic region

M47.14   Other spondylosis with myelopathy, thoracic region

M47.15   Other spondylosis with myelopathy, thoracolumbar region

M47.16   Other spondylosis with myelopathy, lumbar region

● M47.2   Other spondylosis with radiculopathy

M47.20   Other spondylosis with radiculopathy, site unspecified

M47.21   Other spondylosis with radiculopathy, occipito-atlanto-axial region

M47.22   Other spondylosis with radiculopathy, cervical region

M47.23   Other spondylosis with radiculopathy, cervicothoracic region

M47.24   Other spondylosis with radiculopathy, thoracic region

M47.25   Other spondylosis with radiculopathy, thoracolumbar region

M47.26   Other spondylosis with radiculopathy, lumbar region

M47.27   Other spondylosis with radiculopathy, lumbosacral region

M47.28   Other spondylosis with radiculopathy, sacral and sacrococcygeal region

● M47.8   Other spondylosis

   ● M47.81   Spondylosis without myelopathy or radiculopathy

M47.811   Spondylosis without myelopathy or radiculopathy, occipito-atlanto-axial region

M47.812   Spondylosis without myelopathy or radiculopathy, cervical region
Coding Clinic: 2018, Q2, P15

M47.813   Spondylosis without myelopathy or radiculopathy, cervicothoracic region

M47.814   Spondylosis without myelopathy or radiculopathy, thoracic region

M47.815   Spondylosis without myelopathy or radiculopathy, thoracolumbar region

M47.816   Spondylosis without myelopathy or radiculopathy, lumbar region

M47.817   Spondylosis without myelopathy or radiculopathy, lumbosacral region

M47.818   Spondylosis without myelopathy or radiculopathy, sacral and sacrococcygeal region

M47.819   Spondylosis without myelopathy or radiculopathy, site unspecified

● M47.89   Other spondylosis

M47.891   Other spondylosis, occipito-atlanto-axial region

M47.892   Other spondylosis, cervical region

M47.893   Other spondylosis, cervicothoracic region

M47.894   Other spondylosis, thoracic region

M47.895   Other spondylosis, thoracolumbar region

M47.896   Other spondylosis, lumbar region

M47.897   Other spondylosis, lumbosacral region

M47.898   Other spondylosis, sacral and sacrococcygeal region

M47.899   Other spondylosis, site unspecified

M47.9   Spondylosis, unspecified

● M48   Other spondylopathies

   ● M48.0   Spinal stenosis
Caudal stenosis

M48.00   Spinal stenosis, site unspecified

M48.01   Spinal stenosis, occipito-atlanto-axial region

M48.02   Spinal stenosis, cervical region

M48.03   Spinal stenosis, cervicothoracic region

M48.04   Spinal stenosis, thoracic region

M48.05   Spinal stenosis, thoracolumbar region

   ● M48.06   Spinal stenosis, lumbar region
Coding Clinic: 2017, Q3, P24

M48.061   Spinal stenosis, lumbar region without neurogenic claudication
Spinal stenosis, lumbar region NOS

M48.062   Spinal stenosis, lumbar region with neurogenic claudication
Coding Clinic: 2017, Q4, P19

M48.07   Spinal stenosis, lumbosacral region

M48.08   Spinal stenosis, sacral and sacrococcygeal region

● M48.1   Ankylosing hyperostosis [Forestier]
Diffuse idiopathic skeletal hyperostosis [DISH]

M48.10   Ankylosing hyperostosis [Forestier], site unspecified

M48.11   Ankylosing hyperostosis [Forestier], occipito-atlanto-axial region

M48.12   Ankylosing hyperostosis [Forestier], cervical region

M48.13   Ankylosing hyperostosis [Forestier], cervicothoracic region

M48.14   Ankylosing hyperostosis [Forestier], thoracic region

M48.15   Ankylosing hyperostosis [Forestier], thoracolumbar region

M48.16   Ankylosing hyperostosis [Forestier], lumbar region

M48.17   Ankylosing hyperostosis [Forestier], lumbosacral region

M48.18   Ankylosing hyperostosis [Forestier], sacral and sacrococcygeal region

M48.19   Ankylosing hyperostosis [Forestier], multiple sites in spine

▶ New   ⇒ Revised   ~~deleted~~ Deleted   Excludes 1   Excludes 2   Includes   Use additional   Code first   Code also   Key words
OGCR Official Guidelines   X Assign placeholder X   ● Use Additional Character(s)   ▶ Manifestation Code   **Coding Clinic**

● **M48.2** **Kissing spine**
    M48.20 **Kissing spine, site unspecified**
    M48.21 **Kissing spine, occipito-atlanto-axial region**
    M48.22 **Kissing spine, cervical region**
    M48.23 **Kissing spine, cervicothoracic region**
    M48.24 **Kissing spine, thoracic region**
    M48.25 **Kissing spine, thoracolumbar region**
    M48.26 **Kissing spine, lumbar region**
    M48.27 **Kissing spine, lumbosacral region**

● **M48.3** **Traumatic spondylopathy**
    M48.30 **Traumatic spondylopathy, site unspecified**
    M48.31 **Traumatic spondylopathy, occipito-atlanto-axial region**
    M48.32 **Traumatic spondylopathy, cervical region**
    M48.33 **Traumatic spondylopathy, cervicothoracic region**
    M48.34 **Traumatic spondylopathy, thoracic region**
    M48.35 **Traumatic spondylopathy, thoracolumbar region**
    M48.36 **Traumatic spondylopathy, lumbar region**
    M48.37 **Traumatic spondylopathy, lumbosacral region**
    M48.38 **Traumatic spondylopathy, sacral and sacrococcygeal region**

● **M48.4** **Fatigue fracture of vertebra**
    Stress fracture of vertebra
    Excludes1   pathological fracture NOS (M84.4-)
               pathological fracture of vertebra due to neoplasm (M84.58)
               pathological fracture of vertebra due to other diagnosis (M84.68)
               pathological fracture of vertebra due to osteoporosis (M80.-)
               traumatic fracture of vertebrae (S12.0-S12.3-, S22.0-, S32.0-)

The appropriate 7th character is to be added to each code from subcategory M48.4:

A	initial encounter for fracture
D	subsequent encounter for fracture with routine healing
G	subsequent encounter for fracture with delayed healing
S	sequela of fracture

X ● **M48.40** **Fatigue fracture of vertebra, site unspecified**
X ● **M48.41** **Fatigue fracture of vertebra, occipitoatlanto-axial region**
X ● **M48.42** **Fatigue fracture of vertebra, cervical region**
X ● **M48.43** **Fatigue fracture of vertebra, cervicothoracic region**
X ● **M48.44** **Fatigue fracture of vertebra, thoracic region**
X ● **M48.45** **Fatigue fracture of vertebra, thoracolumbar region**
X ● **M48.46** **Fatigue fracture of vertebra, lumbar region**
X ● **M48.47** **Fatigue fracture of vertebra, lumbosacral region**
X ● **M48.48** **Fatigue fracture of vertebra, sacral and sacrococcygeal region**

● **M48.5** **Collapsed vertebra, not elsewhere classified**
    Collapsed vertebra NOS
    Compression fracture of vertebra NOS
    Wedging of vertebra NOS
    Excludes1   current injury - see Injury of spine, by body region
               fatigue fracture of vertebra (M48.4)
               pathological fracture of vertebra due to neoplasm (M84.58)
               pathological fracture of vertebra due to other diagnosis (M84.68)
               pathological fracture of vertebra due to osteoporosis (M80.-)
               pathological fracture NOS (M84.4-)
               stress fracture of vertebra (M48.4-)
               traumatic fracture of vertebra (S12.-, S22.-, S32.-)

The appropriate 7th character is to be added to each code from subcategory M48.5:

A	initial encounter for fracture
D	subsequent encounter for fracture with routine healing
G	subsequent encounter for fracture with delayed healing
S	sequela of fracture

X ● **M48.50** **Collapsed vertebra, not elsewhere classified, site unspecified**
X ● **M48.51** **Collapsed vertebra, not elsewhere classified, occipito-atlanto-axial region**
X ● **M48.52** **Collapsed vertebra, not elsewhere classified, cervical region**
X ● **M48.53** **Collapsed vertebra, not elsewhere classified, cervicothoracic region**
X ● **M48.54** **Collapsed vertebra, not elsewhere classified, thoracic region**
X ● **M48.55** **Collapsed vertebra, not elsewhere classified, thoracolumbar region**
X ● **M48.56** **Collapsed vertebra, not elsewhere classified, lumbar region**
X ● **M48.57** **Collapsed vertebra, not elsewhere classified, lumbosacral region**
X ● **M48.58** **Collapsed vertebra, not elsewhere classified, sacral and sacrococcygeal region**

● **M48.8** **Other specified spondylopathies**
    Ossification of posterior longitudinal ligament
    ● **M48.8X** **Other specified spondylopathies**
        M48.8X1 **Other specified spondylopathies, occipito-atlanto-axial region**
        M48.8X2 **Other specified spondylopathies, cervical region**
        M48.8X3 **Other specified spondylopathies, cervicothoracic region**
        M48.8X4 **Other specified spondylopathies, thoracic region**
        M48.8X5 **Other specified spondylopathies, thoracolumbar region**
        M48.8X6 **Other specified spondylopathies, lumbar region**
        M48.8X7 **Other specified spondylopathies, lumbosacral region**
        M48.8X8 **Other specified spondylopathies, sacral and sacrococcygeal region**
        M48.8X9 **Other specified spondylopathies, site unspecified**

M48.9 **Spondylopathy, unspecified**

CHAPTER 13 (M00-M99)

● **M49 Spondylopathies in diseases classified elsewhere**

Includes   curvature of spine in diseases classified elsewhere
deformity of spine in diseases classified elsewhere
kyphosis in diseases classified elsewhere
scoliosis in diseases classified elsewhere
spondylopathy in diseases classified elsewhere

Code first underlying disease, such as:
brucellosis (A23.-)
Charcot-Marie-Tooth disease (G60.0)
enterobacterial infections (A01-A04)
osteitis fibrosa cystica (E21.0)

Excludes1   curvature of spine in tuberculosis [Pott's] (A18.01)
enteropathic arthropathies (M07.-)
gonococcal spondylitis (A54.41)
neuropathic [tabes dorsalis] spondylitis (A52.11)
neuropathic spondylopathy in syringomyelia (G95.0)
neuropathic spondylopathy in tabes dorsalis (A52.11)
nonsyphilitic neuropathic spondylopathy NEC (G98.0)
spondylitis in syphilis (acquired) (A52.77)
tuberculous spondylitis (A18.01)
typhoid fever spondylitis (A01.05)

● **M49.8 Spondylopathy in diseases classified elsewhere**

▷ *M49.80 Spondylopathy in diseases classified elsewhere, site unspecified*

▷ *M49.81 Spondylopathy in diseases classified elsewhere, occipito-atlanto-axial region*

▷ *M49.82 Spondylopathy in diseases classified elsewhere, cervical region*

▷ *M49.83 Spondylopathy in diseases classified elsewhere, cervicothoracic region*

▷ *M49.84 Spondylopathy in diseases classified elsewhere, thoracic region*

▷ *M49.85 Spondylopathy in diseases classified elsewhere, thoracolumbar region*

▷ *M49.86 Spondylopathy in diseases classified elsewhere, lumbar region*

▷ *M49.87 Spondylopathy in diseases classified elsewhere, lumbosacral region*

▷ *M49.88 Spondylopathy in diseases classified elsewhere, sacral and sacrococcygeal region*

▷ *M49.89 Spondylopathy in diseases classified elsewhere, multiple sites in spine*

OTHER DORSOPATHIES (M50-M54)

Excludes1   current injury - see injury of spine by body region
discitis NOS (M46.4-)

● **M50 Cervical disc disorders**

Note: Code to the most superior level of disorder.

Includes   cervicothoracic disc disorders with cervicalgia
cervicothoracic disc disorders

Coding Clinic: 2016, Q1, P17

● **M50.0 Cervical disc disorder with myelopathy**

   M50.00   Cervical disc disorder with myelopathy, unspecified cervical region

   M50.01   Cervical disc disorder with myelopathy, high cervical region
C2-C3 disc disorder with myelopathy
C3-C4 disc disorder with myelopathy
Coding Clinic: 2016, Q1, P17

● M50.02   Cervical disc disorder with myelopathy, mid-cervical region
Coding Clinic: 2016, Q4, P39-40

   M50.020   Cervical disc disorder with myelopathy, mid-cervical region, unspecified level

   M50.021   Cervical disc disorder at C4-C5 level with myelopathy
C4-C5 disc disorder with myelopathy

   M50.022   Cervical disc disorder at C5-C6 level with myelopathy
C5-C6 disc disorder with myelopathy

   M50.023   Cervical disc disorder at C6-C7 level with myelopathy
C6-C7 disc disorder with myelopathy

   M50.03   Cervical disc disorder with myelopathy, cervicothoracic region
C7-T1 disc disorder with myelopathy

● **M50.1 Cervical disc disorder with radiculopathy**

Excludes2   brachial radiculitis NOS (M54.13)

   M50.10   Cervical disc disorder with radiculopathy, unspecified cervical region

   M50.11   Cervical disc disorder with radiculopathy, high cervical region
C2-C3 disc disorder with radiculopathy
C3 radiculopathy due to disc disorder
C3-C4 disc disorder with radiculopathy
C4 radiculopathy due to disc disorder

● M50.12   Cervical disc disorder with radiculopathy, mid-cervical region
Coding Clinic: 2016, Q4, P39-40

   M50.120   Mid-cervical disc disorder, unspecified

   M50.121   Cervical disc disorder at C4-C5 level with radiculopathy
C4-C5 disc disorder with radiculopathy
C5 radiculopathy due to disc disorder

   M50.122   Cervical disc disorder at C5-C6 level with radiculopathy
C5-C6 disc disorder with radiculopathy
C6 radiculopathy due to disc disorder

   M50.123   Cervical disc disorder at C6-C7 level with radiculopathy
C6-C7 disc disorder with radiculopathy
C7 radiculopathy due to disc disorder

   M50.13   Cervical disc disorder with radiculopathy, cervicothoracic region
C7-T1 disc disorder with radiculopathy
C8 radiculopathy due to disc disorder

● **M50.2 Other cervical disc displacement**
Coding Clinic: 2016, Q4, P40

   M50.20   Other cervical disc displacement, unspecified cervical region

   M50.21   Other cervical disc displacement, high cervical region
Other C2-C3 cervical disc displacement
Other C3-C4 cervical disc displacement

● M50.22   Other cervical disc displacement, mid-cervical region

    M50.220   Other cervical disc displacement, mid-cervical region, unspecified level

    M50.221   Other cervical disc displacement at C4-C5 level
        Other C4-C5 cervical disc displacement

    M50.222   Other cervical disc displacement at C5-C6 level
        Other C5-C6 cervical disc displacement

    M50.223   Other cervical disc displacement at C6-C7 level
        Other C6-C7 cervical disc displacement

   M50.23   Other cervical disc displacement, cervicothoracic region
      Other C7-T1 cervical disc displacement

● M50.3   Other cervical disc degeneration
    Coding Clinic: 2016, Q4, P40

   M50.30   Other cervical disc degeneration, unspecified cervical region

   M50.31   Other cervical disc degeneration, high cervical region
      Other C2-C3 cervical disc degeneration
      Other C3-C4 cervical disc degeneration

● M50.32   Other cervical disc degeneration, mid-cervical region

    M50.320   Other cervical disc degeneration, mid-cervical region, unspecified level

    M50.321   Other cervical disc degeneration at C4-C5 level
        Other C4-C5 cervical disc degeneration

    M50.322   Other cervical disc degeneration at C5-C6 level
        Other C5-C6 cervical disc degeneration

    M50.323   Other cervical disc degeneration at C6-C7 level
        Other C6-C7 cervical disc degeneration

   M50.33   Other cervical disc degeneration, cervicothoracic region
      Other C7-T1 cervical disc degeneration

● M50.8   Other cervical disc disorders
    Coding Clinic: 2016, Q4, P40

   M50.80   Other cervical disc disorders, unspecified cervical region

   M50.81   Other cervical disc disorders, high cervical region
      Other C2-C3 cervical disc disorders
      Other C3-C4 cervical disc disorders

● M50.82   Other cervical disc disorders, mid-cervical region

    M50.820   Other cervical disc disorders, mid-cervical region, unspecified level

    M50.821   Other cervical disc disorders at C4-C5 level
        Other C4-C5 cervical disc disorders

    M50.822   Other cervical disc disorders at C5-C6 level
        Other C5-C6 cervical disc disorders

    M50.823   Other cervical disc disorders at C6-C7 level
        Other C6-C7 cervical disc disorders

   M50.83   Other cervical disc disorders, cervicothoracic region
      Other C7-T1 cervical disc disorders

● M50.9   Cervical disc disorder, unspecified
    Coding Clinic: 2016, Q4, P40

   M50.90   Cervical disc disorder, unspecified, unspecified cervical region

   M50.91   Cervical disc disorder, unspecified, high cervical region
      C2-C3 cervical disc disorder, unspecified
      C3-C4 cervical disc disorder, unspecified

● M50.92   Cervical disc disorder, unspecified, mid-cervical region

    M50.920   Unspecified cervical disc disorder, mid-cervical region, unspecified level

    M50.921   Unspecified cervical disc disorder at C4-C5 level
        Unspecified C4-C5 cervical disc disorder

    M50.922   Unspecified cervical disc disorder at C5-C6 level
        Unspecified C5-C6 cervical disc disorder

    M50.923   Unspecified cervical disc disorder at C6-C7 level
        Unspecified C6-C7 cervical disc disorder

   M50.93   Cervical disc disorder, unspecified, cervicothoracic region
      C7-T1 cervical disc disorder, unspecified

● M51   Thoracic, thoracolumbar, and lumbosacral intervertebral disc disorders

    Excludes2   cervical and cervicothoracic disc disorders (M50.-)
             sacral and sacrococcygeal disorders (M53.3)

● M51.0   Thoracic, thoracolumbar and lumbosacral intervertebral disc disorders with myelopathy

   M51.04   Intervertebral disc disorders with myelopathy, thoracic region

   M51.05   Intervertebral disc disorders with myelopathy, thoracolumbar region

   M51.06   Intervertebral disc disorders with myelopathy, lumbar region

● M51.1   Thoracic, thoracolumbar and lumbosacral intervertebral disc disorders with radiculopathy
    Sciatica due to intervertebral disc disorder

    Excludes1   lumbar radiculitis NOS (M54.16)
             sciatica NOS (M54.3)

   M51.14   Intervertebral disc disorders with radiculopathy, thoracic region

   M51.15   Intervertebral disc disorders with radiculopathy, thoracolumbar region

   M51.16   Intervertebral disc disorders with radiculopathy, lumbar region

   M51.17   Intervertebral disc disorders with radiculopathy, lumbosacral region

CHAPTER 13 (M00-M99)

- M51.2 **Other** thoracic, thoracolumbar and lumbosacral intervertebral disc **displacement**
  Lumbago due to displacement of intervertebral disc
  - M51.24 Other intervertebral disc displacement, **thoracic** region
  - M51.25 Other intervertebral disc displacement, **thoracolumbar region**
  - M51.26 Other intervertebral disc displacement, **lumbar** region
  - M51.27 Other intervertebral disc displacement, **lumbosacral region**
- M51.3 **Other** thoracic, thoracolumbar and lumbosacral intervertebral disc **degeneration**
  Coding Clinic: 2013, Q3, P22
  - M51.34 Other intervertebral disc degeneration, **thoracic** region
  - M51.35 Other intervertebral disc degeneration, **thoracolumbar region**
  - M51.36 Other intervertebral disc degeneration, **lumbar** region
    Coding Clinic: 2018, Q2, P15
  - M51.37 Other intervertebral disc degeneration, **lumbosacral region**
- M51.4 Schmorl's nodes
  - M51.44 Schmorl's nodes, **thoracic region**
  - M51.45 Schmorl's nodes, **thoracolumbar region**
  - M51.46 Schmorl's nodes, **lumbar region**
  - M51.47 Schmorl's nodes, **lumbosacral region**
- M51.8 **Other** thoracic, thoracolumbar and lumbosacral intervertebral disc **disorders**
  - M51.84 Other intervertebral disc disorders, **thoracic** region
  - M51.85 Other intervertebral disc disorders, **thoracolumbar region**
  - M51.86 Other intervertebral disc disorders, **lumbar** region
  - M51.87 Other intervertebral disc disorders, **lumbosacral** region
  - M51.9 **Unspecified** thoracic, thoracolumbar and lumbosacral intervertebral disc disorder
- M53 Other and unspecified dorsopathies, not elsewhere classified
  - M53.0 Cervicocranial syndrome
    Posterior cervical sympathetic syndrome
  - M53.1 Cervicobrachial syndrome
    Excludes2 cervical disc disorder (M50.-)
    thoracic outlet syndrome (G54.0)
  - M53.2 Spinal **instabilities**
    - M53.2X Spinal **instabilities**
      - M53.2X1 Spinal instabilities, **occipito-atlanto-axial region**
      - M53.2X2 Spinal instabilities, **cervical region**
      - M53.2X3 Spinal instabilities, **cervicothoracic region**
      - M53.2X4 Spinal instabilities, **thoracic region**
      - M53.2X5 Spinal instabilities, **thoracolumbar region**
      - M53.2X6 Spinal instabilities, **lumbar region**
      - M53.2X7 Spinal instabilities, **lumbosacral region**
      - M53.2X8 Spinal instabilities, **sacral and sacrococcygeal region**
      - M53.2X9 Spinal instabilities, site **unspecified**
  - M53.3 Sacrococcygeal disorders, not elsewhere classified
    Coccygodynia

- M53.8 Other specified dorsopathies
  - M53.80 Other specified dorsopathies, site **unspecified**
  - M53.81 Other specified dorsopathies, **occipito-atlanto-axial region**
  - M53.82 Other specified dorsopathies, **cervical region**
  - M53.83 Other specified dorsopathies, **cervicothoracic region**
  - M53.84 Other specified dorsopathies, **thoracic region**
  - M53.85 Other specified dorsopathies, **thoracolumbar region**
  - M53.86 Other specified dorsopathies, **lumbar region**
  - M53.87 Other specified dorsopathies, **lumbosacral region**
  - M53.88 Other specified dorsopathies, **sacral and sacrococcygeal region**
  - M53.9 Dorsopathy, **unspecified**
- M54 Dorsalgia
  Excludes1 psychogenic dorsalgia (F45.41)
  - M54.0 Panniculitis affecting regions of neck and back
    Excludes1 lupus panniculitis (L93.2)
    panniculitis NOS (M79.3)
    relapsing [Weber-Christian] panniculitis (M35.6)
    - M54.00 Panniculitis affecting regions of neck and back, site **unspecified**
    - M54.01 Panniculitis affecting regions of neck and back, **occipito-atlanto-axial region**
    - M54.02 Panniculitis affecting regions of neck and back, **cervical region**
    - M54.03 Panniculitis affecting regions of neck and back, **cervicothoracic region**
    - M54.04 Panniculitis affecting regions of neck and back, **thoracic region**
    - M54.05 Panniculitis affecting regions of neck and back, **thoracolumbar region**
    - M54.06 Panniculitis affecting regions of neck and back, **lumbar region**
    - M54.07 Panniculitis affecting regions of neck and back, **lumbosacral region**
    - M54.08 Panniculitis affecting regions of neck and back, **sacral and sacrococcygeal region**
    - M54.09 Panniculitis affecting regions, neck and back, **multiple sites** in spine
  - M54.1 Radiculopathy
    Brachial neuritis or radiculitis NOS
    Lumbar neuritis or radiculitis NOS
    Lumbosacral neuritis or radiculitis NOS
    Thoracic neuritis or radiculitis NOS
    Radiculitis NOS
    Excludes1 neuralgia and neuritis NOS (M79.2)
    radiculopathy with cervical disc disorder (M50.1)
    radiculopathy with lumbar and other intervertebral disc disorder (M51.1-)
    radiculopathy with spondylosis (M47.2-)
    - M54.10 Radiculopathy, site **unspecified**
    - M54.11 Radiculopathy, **occipito-atlanto-axial region**
    - M54.12 Radiculopathy, **cervical region**
    - M54.13 Radiculopathy, **cervicothoracic region**
    - M54.14 Radiculopathy, **thoracic region**
    - M54.15 Radiculopathy, **thoracolumbar region**
    - M54.16 Radiculopathy, **lumbar region**
    - M54.17 Radiculopathy, **lumbosacral region**
    - M54.18 Radiculopathy, **sacral and sacrococcygeal region**

M54.2 Cervicalgia
> **Excludes1** cervicalgia due to intervertebral cervical disc disorder (M50.-)

M54.3 Sciatica
> **Excludes1** lesion of sciatic nerve (G57.0)
> sciatica due to intervertebral disc disorder (M51.1-)
> sciatica with lumbago (M54.4-)

  M54.30 Sciatica, unspecified side
  M54.31 Sciatica, right side
  M54.32 Sciatica, left side

M54.4 Lumbago with sciatica
> **Excludes1** lumbago with sciatica due to intervertebral disc disorder (M51.1-)

  M54.40 Lumbago with sciatica, unspecified side
  M54.41 Lumbago with sciatica, right side
  M54.42 Lumbago with sciatica, left side
    Coding Clinic: 2016, Q2, P7

M54.5 Low back pain
  Loin pain
  Lumbago NOS
> **Excludes1** low back strain (S39.012)
> lumbago due to intervertebral disc displacement (M51.2-)
> lumbago with sciatica (M54.4-)

M54.6 Pain in thoracic spine
> **Excludes1** pain in thoracic spine due to intervertebral disc disorder (M51.)

M54.8 Other dorsalgia
> **Excludes1** dorsalgia in thoracic region (M54.6)
> low back pain (M54.5)

  M54.81 Occipital neuralgia
  M54.89 Other dorsalgia

M54.9 Dorsalgia, unspecified
  Backache NOS
  Back pain NOS

SOFT TISSUE DISORDERS (M60-M79)

DISORDERS OF MUSCLES (M60-M63)

> **Excludes1** dermatopolymyositis (M33.-)
> muscular dystrophies and myopathies (G71-G72)
> myopathy in amyloidosis (E85.-)
> myopathy in polyarteritis nodosa (M30.0)
> myopathy in rheumatoid arthritis (M05.32)
> myopathy in scleroderma (M34.-)
> myopathy in Sjögren's syndrome (M35.03)
> myopathy in systemic lupus erythematosus (M32.-)

M60 Myositis
> **Excludes2** inclusion body myositis [IBM] (G72.41)

M60.0 Infective myositis
  Tropical pyomyositis
  Use additional code (B95-B97) to identify infectious agent

  M60.00 Infective myositis, unspecified site
    M60.000 Infective myositis, unspecified right arm
      Infective myositis, right upper limb NOS
    M60.001 Infective myositis, unspecified left arm
      Infective myositis, left upper limb NOS
    M60.002 Infective myositis, unspecified arm
      Infective myositis, upper limb NOS

    M60.003 Infective myositis, unspecified right leg
      Infective myositis, right lower limb NOS
    M60.004 Infective myositis, unspecified left leg
      Infective myositis, left lower limb NOS
    M60.005 Infective myositis, unspecified leg
      Infective myositis, lower limb NOS
    M60.009 Infective myositis, unspecified site

M60.01 Infective myositis, shoulder
  M60.011 Infective myositis, right shoulder
  M60.012 Infective myositis, left shoulder
  M60.019 Infective myositis, unspecified shoulder

M60.02 Infective myositis, upper arm
  M60.021 Infective myositis, right upper arm
  M60.022 Infective myositis, left upper arm
  M60.029 Infective myositis, unspecified upper arm

M60.03 Infective myositis, forearm
  M60.031 Infective myositis, right forearm
  M60.032 Infective myositis, left forearm
  M60.039 Infective myositis, unspecified forearm

M60.04 Infective myositis, hand and fingers
  M60.041 Infective myositis, right hand
  M60.042 Infective myositis, left hand
  M60.043 Infective myositis, unspecified hand
  M60.044 Infective myositis, right finger(s)
  M60.045 Infective myositis, left finger(s)
  M60.046 Infective myositis, unspecified finger(s)

M60.05 Infective myositis, thigh
  M60.051 Infective myositis, right thigh
  M60.052 Infective myositis, left thigh
  M60.059 Infective myositis, unspecified thigh

M60.06 Infective myositis, lower leg
  M60.061 Infective myositis, right lower leg
  M60.062 Infective myositis, left lower leg
  M60.069 Infective myositis, unspecified lower leg

M60.07 Infective myositis, ankle, foot and toes
  M60.070 Infective myositis, right ankle
  M60.071 Infective myositis, left ankle
  M60.072 Infective myositis, unspecified ankle
  M60.073 Infective myositis, right foot
  M60.074 Infective myositis, left foot
  M60.075 Infective myositis, unspecified foot
  M60.076 Infective myositis, right toe(s)
  M60.077 Infective myositis, left toe(s)
  M60.078 Infective myositis, unspecified toe(s)

  M60.08 Infective myositis, other site
  M60.09 Infective myositis, multiple sites

M60.1 Interstitial myositis
  M60.10 Interstitial myositis of unspecified site

M60.11 Interstitial myositis, shoulder
  M60.111 Interstitial myositis, right shoulder
  M60.112 Interstitial myositis, left shoulder
  M60.119 Interstitial myositis, unspecified shoulder

● M60.12 Interstitial myositis, upper arm
   M60.121 Interstitial myositis, right upper arm
   M60.122 Interstitial myositis, left upper arm
   M60.129 Interstitial myositis, unspecified upper arm

● M60.13 Interstitial myositis, forearm
   M60.131 Interstitial myositis, right forearm
   M60.132 Interstitial myositis, left forearm
   M60.139 Interstitial myositis, unspecified forearm

● M60.14 Interstitial myositis, hand
   M60.141 Interstitial myositis, right hand
   M60.142 Interstitial myositis, left hand
   M60.149 Interstitial myositis, unspecified hand

● M60.15 Interstitial myositis, thigh
   M60.151 Interstitial myositis, right thigh
   M60.152 Interstitial myositis, left thigh
   M60.159 Interstitial myositis, unspecified thigh

● M60.16 Interstitial myositis, lower leg
   M60.161 Interstitial myositis, right lower leg
   M60.162 Interstitial myositis, left lower leg
   M60.169 Interstitial myositis, unspecified lower leg

● M60.17 Interstitial myositis, ankle and foot
   M60.171 Interstitial myositis, right ankle and foot
   M60.172 Interstitial myositis, left ankle and foot
   M60.179 Interstitial myositis, unspecified ankle and foot

   M60.18 Interstitial myositis, other site
   M60.19 Interstitial myositis, multiple sites

● M60.2 Foreign body granuloma of soft tissue, not elsewhere classified
   Use additional code to identify the type of retained foreign body (Z18.-)
   Excludes1 foreign body granuloma of skin and subcutaneous tissue (L92.3)

   M60.20 Foreign body granuloma of soft tissue, not elsewhere classified, unspecified site

● M60.21 Foreign body granuloma of soft tissue, not elsewhere classified, shoulder
   M60.211 Foreign body granuloma of soft tissue, not elsewhere classified, right shoulder
   M60.212 Foreign body granuloma of soft tissue, not elsewhere classified, left shoulder
   M60.219 Foreign body granuloma of soft tissue, not elsewhere classified, unspecified shoulder

● M60.22 Foreign body granuloma of soft tissue, not elsewhere classified, upper arm
   M60.221 Foreign body granuloma of soft tissue, not elsewhere classified, right upper arm
   M60.222 Foreign body granuloma of soft tissue, not elsewhere classified, left upper arm
   M60.229 Foreign body granuloma of soft tissue, not elsewhere classified, unspecified upper arm

● M60.23 Foreign body granuloma of soft tissue, not elsewhere classified, forearm
   M60.231 Foreign body granuloma of soft tissue, not elsewhere classified, right forearm
   M60.232 Foreign body granuloma of soft tissue, not elsewhere classified, left forearm
   M60.239 Foreign body granuloma of soft tissue, not elsewhere classified, unspecified forearm

● M60.24 Foreign body granuloma of soft tissue, not elsewhere classified, hand
   M60.241 Foreign body granuloma of soft tissue, not elsewhere classified, right hand
   M60.242 Foreign body granuloma of soft tissue, not elsewhere classified, left hand
   M60.249 Foreign body granuloma of soft tissue, not elsewhere classified, unspecified hand

● M60.25 Foreign body granuloma of soft tissue, not elsewhere classified, thigh
   M60.251 Foreign body granuloma of soft tissue, not elsewhere classified, right thigh
   M60.252 Foreign body granuloma of soft tissue, not elsewhere classified, left thigh
   M60.259 Foreign body granuloma of soft tissue, not elsewhere classified, unspecified thigh

● M60.26 Foreign body granuloma of soft tissue, not elsewhere classified, lower leg
   M60.261 Foreign body granuloma of soft tissue, not elsewhere classified, right lower leg
   M60.262 Foreign body granuloma of soft tissue, not elsewhere classified, left lower leg
   M60.269 Foreign body granuloma of soft tissue, not elsewhere classified, unspecified lower leg

● M60.27 Foreign body granuloma of soft tissue, not elsewhere classified, ankle and foot
   M60.271 Foreign body granuloma of soft tissue, not elsewhere classified, right ankle and foot
   M60.272 Foreign body granuloma of soft tissue, not elsewhere classified, left ankle and foot
   M60.279 Foreign body granuloma of soft tissue, not elsewhere classified, unspecified ankle and foot

   M60.28 Foreign body granuloma of soft tissue, not elsewhere classified, other site

● M60.8 Other myositis
   M60.80 Other myositis, unspecified site
● M60.81 Other myositis shoulder
   M60.811 Other myositis, right shoulder
   M60.812 Other myositis, left shoulder
   M60.819 Other myositis, unspecified shoulder
● M60.82 Other myositis, upper arm
   M60.821 Other myositis, right upper arm
   M60.822 Other myositis, left upper arm
   M60.829 Other myositis, unspecified upper arm

● M60.83   Other myositis, forearm
     M60.831   Other myositis, right forearm
     M60.832   Other myositis, left forearm
     M60.839   Other myositis, unspecified forearm
● M60.84   Other myositis, hand
     M60.841   Other myositis, right hand
     M60.842   Other myositis, left hand
     M60.849   Other myositis, unspecified hand
● M60.85   Other myositis, thigh
     M60.851   Other myositis, right thigh
     M60.852   Other myositis, left thigh
     M60.859   Other myositis, unspecified thigh
● M60.86   Other myositis, lower leg
     M60.861   Other myositis, right lower leg
     M60.862   Other myositis, left lower leg
     M60.869   Other myositis, unspecified lower leg
● M60.87   Other myositis, ankle and foot
     M60.871   Other myositis, right ankle and foot
     M60.872   Other myositis, left ankle and foot
     M60.879   Other myositis, unspecified ankle and foot
   M60.88   Other myositis, other site
   M60.89   Other myositis, multiple sites
  M60.9   Myositis, unspecified

● M61   Calcification and ossification of muscle
  ● M61.0   Myositis ossificans traumatica
     M61.00   Myositis ossificans traumatica, unspecified site
   ● M61.01   Myositis ossificans traumatica, shoulder
     M61.011   Myositis ossificans traumatica, right shoulder
     M61.012   Myositis ossificans traumatica, left shoulder
     M61.019   Myositis ossificans traumatica, unspecified shoulder
   ● M61.02   Myositis ossificans traumatica, upper arm
     M61.021   Myositis ossificans traumatica, right upper arm
     M61.022   Myositis ossificans traumatica, left upper arm
     M61.029   Myositis ossificans traumatica, unspecified upper arm
   ● M61.03   Myositis ossificans traumatica, forearm
     M61.031   Myositis ossificans traumatica, right forearm
     M61.032   Myositis ossificans traumatica, left forearm
     M61.039   Myositis ossificans traumatica, unspecified forearm
   ● M61.04   Myositis ossificans traumatica, hand
     M61.041   Myositis ossificans traumatica, right hand
     M61.042   Myositis ossificans traumatica, left hand
     M61.049   Myositis ossificans traumatica, unspecified hand
   ● M61.05   Myositis ossificans traumatica, thigh
     M61.051   Myositis ossificans traumatica, right thigh
     M61.052   Myositis ossificans traumatica, left thigh
     M61.059   Myositis ossificans traumatica, unspecified thigh

● M61.06   Myositis ossificans traumatica, lower leg
     M61.061   Myositis ossificans traumatica, right lower leg
     M61.062   Myositis ossificans traumatica, left lower leg
     M61.069   Myositis ossificans traumatica, unspecified lower leg
● M61.07   Myositis ossificans traumatica, ankle and foot
     M61.071   Myositis ossificans traumatica, right ankle and foot
     M61.072   Myositis ossificans traumatica, left ankle and foot
     M61.079   Myositis ossificans traumatica, unspecified ankle and foot
   M61.08   Myositis ossificans traumatica, other site
   M61.09   Myositis ossificans traumatica, multiple sites
● M61.1   Myositis ossificans progressiva
    Fibrodysplasia ossificans progressiva
   M61.10   Myositis ossificans progressiva, unspecified site
   ● M61.11   Myositis ossificans progressiva, shoulder
     M61.111   Myositis ossificans progressiva, right shoulder
     M61.112   Myositis ossificans progressiva, left shoulder
     M61.119   Myositis ossificans progressiva, unspecified shoulder
   ● M61.12   Myositis ossificans progressiva, upper arm
     M61.121   Myositis ossificans progressiva, right upper arm
     M61.122   Myositis ossificans progressiva, left upper arm
     M61.129   Myositis ossificans progressiva, unspecified arm
   ● M61.13   Myositis ossificans progressiva, forearm
     M61.131   Myositis ossificans progressiva, right forearm
     M61.132   Myositis ossificans progressiva, left forearm
     M61.139   Myositis ossificans progressiva, unspecified forearm
   ● M61.14   Myositis ossificans progressiva, hand and finger(s)
     M61.141   Myositis ossificans progressiva, right hand
     M61.142   Myositis ossificans progressiva, left hand
     M61.143   Myositis ossificans progressiva, unspecified hand
     M61.144   Myositis ossificans progressiva, right finger(s)
     M61.145   Myositis ossificans progressiva, left finger(s)
     M61.146   Myositis ossificans progressiva, unspecified finger(s)
   ● M61.15   Myositis ossificans progressiva, thigh
     M61.151   Myositis ossificans progressiva, right thigh
     M61.152   Myositis ossificans progressiva, left thigh
     M61.159   Myositis ossificans progressiva, unspecified thigh
   ● M61.16   Myositis ossificans progressiva, lower leg
     M61.161   Myositis ossificans progressiva, right lower leg
     M61.162   Myositis ossificans progressiva, left lower leg
     M61.169   Myositis ossificans progressiva, unspecified lower leg

CHAPTER 13 (M00-M99)

● M61.17 Myositis ossificans progressiva, ankle, foot and toe(s)

    M61.171 Myositis ossificans progressiva, right ankle

    M61.172 Myositis ossificans progressiva, left ankle

    M61.173 Myositis ossificans progressiva, unspecified ankle

    M61.174 Myositis ossificans progressiva, right foot

    M61.175 Myositis ossificans progressiva, left foot

    M61.176 Myositis ossificans progressiva, unspecified foot

    M61.177 Myositis ossificans progressiva, right toe(s)

    M61.178 Myositis ossificans progressiva, left toe(s)

    M61.179 Myositis ossificans progressiva, unspecified toe(s)

M61.18 Myositis ossificans progressiva, other site

M61.19 Myositis ossificans progressiva, multiple sites

● M61.2 Paralytic calcification and ossification of muscle

    Myositis ossificans associated with quadriplegia or paraplegia

M61.20 Paralytic calcification and ossification of muscle, unspecified site

● M61.21 Paralytic calcification and ossification of muscle, shoulder

    M61.211 Paralytic calcification and ossification of muscle, right shoulder

    M61.212 Paralytic calcification and ossification of muscle, left shoulder

    M61.219 Paralytic calcification and ossification of muscle, unspecified shoulder

● M61.22 Paralytic calcification and ossification of muscle, upper arm

    M61.221 Paralytic calcification and ossification of muscle, right upper arm

    M61.222 Paralytic calcification and ossification of muscle, left upper arm

    M61.229 Paralytic calcification and ossification of muscle, unspecified upper arm

● M61.23 Paralytic calcification and ossification of muscle, forearm

    M61.231 Paralytic calcification and ossification of muscle, right forearm

    M61.232 Paralytic calcification and ossification of muscle, left forearm

    M61.239 Paralytic calcification and ossification of muscle, unspecified forearm

● M61.24 Paralytic calcification and ossification of muscle, hand

    M61.241 Paralytic calcification and ossification of muscle, right hand

    M61.242 Paralytic calcification and ossification of muscle, left hand

    M61.249 Paralytic calcification and ossification of muscle, unspecified hand

● M61.25 Paralytic calcification and ossification of muscle, thigh

    M61.251 Paralytic calcification and ossification of muscle, right thigh

    M61.252 Paralytic calcification and ossification of muscle, left thigh

    M61.259 Paralytic calcification and ossification of muscle, unspecified thigh

● M61.26 Paralytic calcification and ossification of muscle, lower leg

    M61.261 Paralytic calcification and ossification of muscle, right lower leg

    M61.262 Paralytic calcification and ossification of muscle, left lower leg

    M61.269 Paralytic calcification and ossification of muscle, unspecified lower leg

● M61.27 Paralytic calcification and ossification of muscle, ankle and foot

    M61.271 Paralytic calcification and ossification of muscle, right ankle and foot

    M61.272 Paralytic calcification and ossification of muscle, left ankle and foot

    M61.279 Paralytic calcification and ossification of muscle, unspecified ankle and foot

M61.28 Paralytic calcification and ossification of muscle, other site

M61.29 Paralytic calcification and ossification of muscle, multiple sites

● M61.3 Calcification and ossification of muscles associated with burns

    Myositis ossificans associated with burns

M61.30 Calcification and ossification of muscles associated with burns, unspecified site

● M61.31 Calcification and ossification of muscles associated with burns, shoulder

    M61.311 Calcification and ossification of muscles associated with burns, right shoulder

    M61.312 Calcification and ossification of muscles associated with burns, left shoulder

    M61.319 Calcification and ossification of muscles associated with burns, unspecified shoulder

● M61.32 Calcification and ossification of muscles associated with burns, upper arm

    M61.321 Calcification and ossification of muscles associated with burns, right upper arm

    M61.322 Calcification and ossification of muscles associated with burns, left upper arm

    M61.329 Calcification and ossification of muscles associated with burns, unspecified upper arm

● M61.33 Calcification and ossification of muscles associated with burns, forearm

    M61.331 Calcification and ossification of muscles associated with burns, right forearm

    M61.332 Calcification and ossification of muscles associated with burns, left forearm

    M61.339 Calcification and ossification of muscles associated with burns, unspecified forearm

● M61.34 Calcification and ossification of muscles associated with burns, hand

    M61.341 Calcification and ossification of muscles associated with burns, right hand

    M61.342 Calcification and ossification of muscles associated with burns, left hand

    M61.349 Calcification and ossification of muscles associated with burns, unspecified hand

CHAPTER 13 (M00-M99)

▶ New   ⇛ Revised   ~~deleted~~ Deleted   Excludes 1   Excludes 2   Includes   Use additional   Code first   Code also   Key words

OGCR Official Guidelines   X Assign placeholder X   ● Use Additional Character(s)   ▶ Manifestation Code   Coding Clinic

● M61.35   Calcification and ossification of muscles associated with burns, thigh

     M61.351   Calcification and ossification of muscles associated with burns, right thigh

     M61.352   Calcification and ossification of muscles associated with burns, left thigh

     M61.359   Calcification and ossification of muscles associated with burns, unspecified thigh

● M61.36   Calcification and ossification of muscles associated with burns, lower leg

     M61.361   Calcification and ossification of muscles associated with burns, right lower leg

     M61.362   Calcification and ossification of muscles associated with burns, left lower leg

     M61.369   Calcification and ossification of muscles associated with burns, unspecified lower leg

● M61.37   Calcification and ossification of muscles associated with burns, ankle and foot

     M61.371   Calcification and ossification of muscles associated with burns, right ankle and foot

     M61.372   Calcification and ossification of muscles associated with burns, left ankle and foot

     M61.379   Calcification and ossification of muscles associated with burns, unspecified ankle and foot

M61.38   Calcification and ossification of muscles associated with burns, other site

M61.39   Calcification and ossification of muscles associated with burns, multiple sites

● M61.4   Other calcification of muscle

     Excludes1   calcific tendinitis NOS (M65.2-)
                   calcific tendinitis of shoulder (M75.3)

M61.40   Other calcification of muscle, unspecified site

● M61.41   Other calcification of muscle, shoulder

     M61.411   Other calcification of muscle, right shoulder

     M61.412   Other calcification of muscle, left shoulder

     M61.419   Other calcification of muscle, unspecified shoulder

● M61.42   Other calcification of muscle, upper arm

     M61.421   Other calcification of muscle, right upper arm

     M61.422   Other calcification of muscle, left upper arm

     M61.429   Other calcification of muscle, unspecified upper arm

● M61.43   Other calcification of muscle, forearm

     M61.431   Other calcification of muscle, right forearm

     M61.432   Other calcification of muscle, left forearm

     M61.439   Other calcification of muscle, unspecified forearm

● M61.44   Other calcification of muscle, hand

     M61.441   Other calcification of muscle, right hand

     M61.442   Other calcification of muscle, left hand

     M61.449   Other calcification of muscle, unspecified hand

● M61.45   Other calcification of muscle, thigh

     M61.451   Other calcification of muscle, right thigh

     M61.452   Other calcification of muscle, left thigh

     M61.459   Other calcification of muscle, unspecified thigh

● M61.46   Other calcification of muscle, lower leg

     M61.461   Other calcification of muscle, right lower leg

     M61.462   Other calcification of muscle, left lower leg

     M61.469   Other calcification of muscle, unspecified lower leg

● M61.47   Other calcification of muscle, ankle and foot

     M61.471   Other calcification of muscle, right ankle and foot

     M61.472   Other calcification of muscle, left ankle and foot

     M61.479   Other calcification of muscle, unspecified ankle and foot

M61.48   Other calcification of muscle, other site

M61.49   Other calcification of muscle, multiple sites

● M61.5   Other ossification of muscle

M61.50   Other ossification of muscle, unspecified site

● M61.51   Other ossification of muscle, shoulder

     M61.511   Other ossification of muscle, right shoulder

     M61.512   Other ossification of muscle, left shoulder

     M61.519   Other ossification of muscle, unspecified shoulder

● M61.52   Other ossification of muscle, upper arm

     M61.521   Other ossification of muscle, right upper arm

     M61.522   Other ossification of muscle, left upper arm

     M61.529   Other ossification of muscle, unspecified upper arm

● M61.53   Other ossification of muscle, forearm

     M61.531   Other ossification of muscle, right forearm

     M61.532   Other ossification of muscle, left forearm

     M61.539   Other ossification of muscle, unspecified forearm

● M61.54   Other ossification of muscle, hand

     M61.541   Other ossification of muscle, right hand

     M61.542   Other ossification of muscle, left hand

     M61.549   Other ossification of muscle, unspecified hand

● M61.55   Other ossification of muscle, thigh

     M61.551   Other ossification of muscle, right thigh

     M61.552   Other ossification of muscle, left thigh

     M61.559   Other ossification of muscle, unspecified thigh

● M61.56   Other ossification of muscle, lower leg

     M61.561   Other ossification of muscle, right lower leg

     M61.562   Other ossification of muscle, left lower leg

     M61.569   Other ossification of muscle, unspecified lower leg

CHAPTER 13 (M00-M99)

● M61.57   Other ossification of muscle, ankle and foot
    M61.571   Other ossification of muscle, right ankle and foot
    M61.572   Other ossification of muscle, left ankle and foot
    M61.579   Other ossification of muscle, unspecified ankle and foot
  M61.58   Other ossification of muscle, other site
  M61.59   Other ossification of muscle, multiple sites
 M61.9   Calcification and ossification of muscle, unspecified

● M62   Other disorders of muscle

  Excludes1   alcoholic myopathy (G72.1)
       cramp and spasm (R25.2)
       drug-induced myopathy (G72.0)
      ➡ myalgia (M79.1-)
       stiff-man syndrome (G25.82)

  Excludes2   nontraumatic hematoma of muscle (M79.81)

● M62.0   Separation of muscle (nontraumatic)
   Diastasis of muscle

   Excludes1   diastasis recti complicating pregnancy, labor and delivery (O71.8)
        traumatic separation of muscle - see strain of muscle by body region

  M62.00   Separation of muscle (nontraumatic), unspecified site
● M62.01   Separation of muscle (nontraumatic), shoulder
    M62.011   Separation of muscle (nontraumatic), right shoulder
    M62.012   Separation of muscle (nontraumatic), left shoulder
    M62.019   Separation of muscle (nontraumatic), unspecified shoulder
● M62.02   Separation of muscle (nontraumatic), upper arm
    M62.021   Separation of muscle (nontraumatic), right upper arm
    M62.022   Separation of muscle (nontraumatic), left upper arm
    M62.029   Separation of muscle (nontraumatic), unspecified upper arm
● M62.03   Separation of muscle (nontraumatic), forearm
    M62.031   Separation of muscle (nontraumatic), right forearm
    M62.032   Separation of muscle (nontraumatic), left forearm
    M62.039   Separation of muscle (nontraumatic), unspecified forearm
● M62.04   Separation of muscle (nontraumatic), hand
    M62.041   Separation of muscle (nontraumatic), right hand
    M62.042   Separation of muscle (nontraumatic), left hand
    M62.049   Separation of muscle (nontraumatic), unspecified hand
● M62.05   Separation of muscle (nontraumatic), thigh
    M62.051   Separation of muscle (nontraumatic), right thigh
    M62.052   Separation of muscle (nontraumatic), left thigh
    M62.059   Separation of muscle (nontraumatic), unspecified thigh
● M62.06   Separation of muscle (nontraumatic), lower leg
    M62.061   Separation of muscle (nontraumatic), right lower leg
    M62.062   Separation of muscle (nontraumatic), left lower leg
    M62.069   Separation of muscle (nontraumatic), unspecified lower leg

● M62.07   Separation of muscle (nontraumatic), ankle and foot
    M62.071   Separation of muscle (nontraumatic), right ankle and foot
    M62.072   Separation of muscle (nontraumatic), left ankle and foot
    M62.079   Separation of muscle (nontraumatic), unspecified ankle and foot
  M62.08   Separation of muscle (nontraumatic), other site

● M62.1   Other rupture of muscle (nontraumatic)

   Excludes1   traumatic rupture of muscle - see strain of muscle by body region

   Excludes2   rupture of tendon (M66.-)

  M62.10   Other rupture of muscle (nontraumatic), unspecified site
● M62.11   Other rupture of muscle (nontraumatic), shoulder
    M62.111   Other rupture of muscle (nontraumatic), right shoulder
    M62.112   Other rupture of muscle (nontraumatic), left shoulder
    M62.119   Other rupture of muscle (nontraumatic), unspecified shoulder
● M62.12   Other rupture of muscle (nontraumatic), upper arm
    M62.121   Other rupture of muscle (nontraumatic), right upper arm
    M62.122   Other rupture of muscle (nontraumatic), left upper arm
    M62.129   Other rupture of muscle (nontraumatic), unspecified upper arm
● M62.13   Other rupture of muscle (nontraumatic), forearm
    M62.131   Other rupture of muscle (nontraumatic), right forearm
    M62.132   Other rupture of muscle (nontraumatic), left forearm
    M62.139   Other rupture of muscle (nontraumatic), unspecified forearm
● M62.14   Other rupture of muscle (nontraumatic), hand
    M62.141   Other rupture of muscle (nontraumatic), right hand
    M62.142   Other rupture of muscle (nontraumatic), left hand
    M62.149   Other rupture of muscle (nontraumatic), unspecified hand
● M62.15   Other rupture of muscle (nontraumatic), thigh
    M62.151   Other rupture of muscle (nontraumatic), right thigh
    M62.152   Other rupture of muscle (nontraumatic), left thigh
    M62.159   Other rupture of muscle (nontraumatic), unspecified thigh
● M62.16   Other rupture of muscle (nontraumatic), lower leg
    M62.161   Other rupture of muscle (nontraumatic), right lower leg
    M62.162   Other rupture of muscle (nontraumatic), left lower leg
    M62.169   Other rupture of muscle (nontraumatic), unspecified lower leg

▶ New   ⇒ Revised   ~~deleted~~ Deleted   Excludes 1   Excludes 2   Includes   Use additional   Code first   Code also   Key words
OGCR Official Guidelines   X Assign placeholder X   ● Use Additional Character(s)   ▷ Manifestation Code   Coding Clinic

● M62.17   Other rupture of muscle (nontraumatic), ankle and foot
    M62.171   Other rupture of muscle (nontraumatic), right ankle and foot
    M62.172   Other rupture of muscle (nontraumatic), left ankle and foot
    M62.179   Other rupture of muscle (nontraumatic), unspecified ankle and foot
   M62.18   Other rupture of muscle (nontraumatic), other site

● M62.2   Nontraumatic ischemic infarction of muscle
    Excludes1   compartment syndrome (traumatic) (T79.A-)
                   nontraumatic compartment syndrome (M79.A-)
                   traumatic ischemia of muscle (T79.6)
                   rhabdomyolysis (M62.82)
                   Volkmann's ischemic contracture (T79.6)
   M62.20   Nontraumatic ischemic infarction of muscle, unspecified site
● M62.21   Nontraumatic ischemic infarction of muscle, shoulder
    M62.211   Nontraumatic ischemic infarction of muscle, right shoulder
    M62.212   Nontraumatic ischemic infarction of muscle, left shoulder
    M62.219   Nontraumatic ischemic infarction of muscle, unspecified shoulder
● M62.22   Nontraumatic ischemic infarction of muscle, upper arm
    M62.221   Nontraumatic ischemic infarction of muscle, right upper arm
    M62.222   Nontraumatic ischemic infarction of muscle, left upper arm
    M62.229   Nontraumatic ischemic infarction of muscle, unspecified upper arm
● M62.23   Nontraumatic ischemic infarction of muscle, forearm
    M62.231   Nontraumatic ischemic infarction of muscle, right forearm
    M62.232   Nontraumatic ischemic infarction of muscle, left forearm
    M62.239   Nontraumatic ischemic infarction of muscle, unspecified forearm
● M62.24   Nontraumatic ischemic infarction of muscle, hand
    M62.241   Nontraumatic ischemic infarction of muscle, right hand
    M62.242   Nontraumatic ischemic infarction of muscle, left hand
    M62.249   Nontraumatic ischemic infarction of muscle, unspecified hand
● M62.25   Nontraumatic ischemic infarction of muscle, thigh
    M62.251   Nontraumatic ischemic infarction of muscle, right thigh
    M62.252   Nontraumatic ischemic infarction of muscle, left thigh
    M62.259   Nontraumatic ischemic infarction of muscle, unspecified thigh

● M62.26   Nontraumatic ischemic infarction of muscle, lower leg
    M62.261   Nontraumatic ischemic infarction of muscle, right lower leg
    M62.262   Nontraumatic ischemic infarction of muscle, left lower leg
    M62.269   Nontraumatic ischemic infarction of muscle, unspecified lower leg
● M62.27   Nontraumatic ischemic infarction of muscle, ankle and foot
    M62.271   Nontraumatic ischemic infarction of muscle, right ankle and foot
    M62.272   Nontraumatic ischemic infarction of muscle, left ankle and foot
    M62.279   Nontraumatic ischemic infarction of muscle, unspecified ankle and foot
   M62.28   Nontraumatic ischemic infarction of muscle, other site

M62.3   Immobility syndrome (paraplegic)
M62.4   Contracture of muscle
    Contracture of tendon (sheath)
    Excludes1   contracture of joint (M24.5-)
   M62.40   Contracture of muscle, unspecified site
● M62.41   Contracture of muscle, shoulder
    M62.411   Contracture of muscle, right shoulder
    M62.412   Contracture of muscle, left shoulder
    M62.419   Contracture of muscle, unspecified shoulder
● M62.42   Contracture of muscle, upper arm
    M62.421   Contracture of muscle, right upper arm
    M62.422   Contracture of muscle, left upper arm
    M62.429   Contracture of muscle, unspecified upper arm
● M62.43   Contracture of muscle, forearm
    M62.431   Contracture of muscle, right forearm
    M62.432   Contracture of muscle, left forearm
    M62.439   Contracture of muscle, unspecified forearm
● M62.44   Contracture of muscle, hand
    M62.441   Contracture of muscle, right hand
    M62.442   Contracture of muscle, left hand
    M62.449   Contracture of muscle, unspecified hand
● M62.45   Contracture of muscle, thigh
    M62.451   Contracture of muscle, right thigh
    M62.452   Contracture of muscle, left thigh
    M62.459   Contracture of muscle, unspecified thigh
● M62.46   Contracture of muscle, lower leg
    M62.461   Contracture of muscle, right lower leg
    M62.462   Contracture of muscle, left lower leg
    M62.469   Contracture of muscle, unspecified lower leg
● M62.47   Contracture of muscle, ankle and foot
    M62.471   Contracture of muscle, right ankle and foot
    M62.472   Contracture of muscle, left ankle and foot
    M62.479   Contracture of muscle, unspecified ankle and foot
   M62.48   Contracture of muscle, other site
   M62.49   Contracture of muscle, multiple sites

● **M62.5** **Muscle wasting and atrophy, not elsewhere classified**
Disuse atrophy NEC

> **Excludes1**　neuralgic amyotrophy (G54.5)
> progressive muscular atrophy (G12.21)
> sarcopenia (M62.84)

> **Excludes2**　pelvic muscle wasting (N81.84)

　M62.50 Muscle wasting and atrophy, not elsewhere classified, unspecified site

● **M62.51** Muscle wasting and atrophy, not elsewhere classified, shoulder

　　M62.511 Muscle wasting and atrophy, not elsewhere classified, right shoulder

　　M62.512 Muscle wasting and atrophy, not elsewhere classified, left shoulder

　　M62.519 Muscle wasting and atrophy, not elsewhere classified, unspecified shoulder

● **M62.52** Muscle wasting and atrophy, not elsewhere classified, upper arm

　　M62.521 Muscle wasting and atrophy, not elsewhere classified, right upper arm

　　M62.522 Muscle wasting and atrophy, not elsewhere classified, left upper arm

　　M62.529 Muscle wasting and atrophy, not elsewhere classified, unspecified upper arm

● **M62.53** Muscle wasting and atrophy, not elsewhere classified, forearm

　　M62.531 Muscle wasting and atrophy, not elsewhere classified, right forearm

　　M62.532 Muscle wasting and atrophy, not elsewhere classified, left forearm

　　M62.539 Muscle wasting and atrophy, not elsewhere classified, unspecified forearm

● **M62.54** Muscle wasting and atrophy, not elsewhere classified, hand

　　M62.541 Muscle wasting and atrophy, not elsewhere classified, right hand

　　M62.542 Muscle wasting and atrophy, not elsewhere classified, left hand

　　M62.549 Muscle wasting and atrophy, not elsewhere classified, unspecified hand

● **M62.55** Muscle wasting and atrophy, not elsewhere classified, thigh

　　M62.551 Muscle wasting and atrophy, not elsewhere classified, right thigh

　　M62.552 Muscle wasting and atrophy, not elsewhere classified, left thigh

　　M62.559 Muscle wasting and atrophy, not elsewhere classified, unspecified thigh

● **M62.56** Muscle wasting and atrophy, not elsewhere classified, lower leg

　　M62.561 Muscle wasting and atrophy, not elsewhere classified, right lower leg

　　M62.562 Muscle wasting and atrophy, not elsewhere classified, left lower leg

　　M62.569 Muscle wasting and atrophy, not elsewhere classified, unspecified lower leg

● **M62.57** Muscle wasting and atrophy, not elsewhere classified, ankle and foot

　　M62.571 Muscle wasting and atrophy, not elsewhere classified, right ankle and foot

　　M62.572 Muscle wasting and atrophy, not elsewhere classified, left ankle and foot

　　M62.579 Muscle wasting and atrophy, not elsewhere classified, unspecified ankle and foot

　M62.58 Muscle wasting and atrophy, not elsewhere classified, other site

　M62.59 Muscle wasting and atrophy, not elsewhere classified, multiple sites

● **M62.8** **Other specified disorders of muscle**

> **Excludes2**　nontraumatic hematoma of muscle (M79.81)

　M62.81 Muscle weakness (generalized)

> **Excludes1**　muscle weakness in sarcopenia (M62.84)

　M62.82 Rhabdomyolysis

> **Excludes1**　traumatic rhabdomyolysis (T79.6)

● **M62.83** Muscle spasm

　　M62.830 Muscle spasm of back

　　M62.831 Muscle spasm of calf
Charley-horse

　　M62.838 Other muscle spasm

　M62.84 Sarcopenia
Age-related sarcopenia

> *Code first* underlying disease, if applicable, such as:
> disorders of myoneural junction and muscle disease in diseases classified elsewhere (G73.-)
> other and unspecified myopathies (G72.-)
> primary disorders of muscles (G71.-)

Coding Clinic: 2016, Q4, P41

　M62.89 Other specified disorders of muscle
Muscle (sheath) hernia

　M62.9 Disorder of muscle, unspecified

● **M63** **Disorders of muscle in diseases classified elsewhere**

> *Code first* underlying disease, such as:
> leprosy (A30.-)
> neoplasm (C49.-, C79.89, D21.-, D48.1)
> schistosomiasis (B65.-)
> trichinellosis (B75)

> **Excludes1**　myopathy in cysticercosis (B69.81)
> myopathy in endocrine diseases (G73.7)
> myopathy in metabolic diseases (G73.7)
> myopathy in sarcoidosis (D86.87)
> myopathy in secondary syphilis (A51.49)
> myopathy in syphilis (late) (A52.78)
> myopathy in toxoplasmosis (B58.82)
> myopathy in tuberculosis (A18.09)

● **M63.8** **Disorders of muscle in diseases classified elsewhere**

▷ *M63.80* *Disorders of muscle in diseases classified elsewhere, unspecified site*

● *M63.81* *Disorders of muscle in diseases classified elsewhere, shoulder*

　▷ *M63.811* *Disorders of muscle in diseases classified elsewhere, right shoulder*

　▷ *M63.812* *Disorders of muscle in diseases classified elsewhere, left shoulder*

　▷ *M63.819* *Disorders of muscle in diseases classified elsewhere, unspecified shoulder*

● *M63.82* *Disorders of muscle in diseases classified elsewhere, upper arm*

　▷ *M63.821* *Disorders of muscle in diseases classified elsewhere, right upper arm*

　▷ *M63.822* *Disorders of muscle in diseases classified elsewhere, left upper arm*

　▷ *M63.829* *Disorders of muscle in diseases classified elsewhere, unspecified upper arm*

● **M63.83** Disorders of muscle in diseases classified elsewhere, forearm
- *M63.831 Disorders of muscle in diseases classified elsewhere, right forearm*
- *M63.832 Disorders of muscle in diseases classified elsewhere, left forearm*
- *M63.839 Disorders of muscle in diseases classified elsewhere, unspecified forearm*

● **M63.84** Disorders of muscle in diseases classified elsewhere, hand
- *M63.841 Disorders of muscle in diseases classified elsewhere, right hand*
- *M63.842 Disorders of muscle in diseases classified elsewhere, left hand*
- *M63.849 Disorders of muscle in diseases classified elsewhere, unspecified hand*

● **M63.85** Disorders of muscle in diseases classified elsewhere, thigh
- *M63.851 Disorders of muscle in diseases classified elsewhere, right thigh*
- *M63.852 Disorders of muscle in diseases classified elsewhere, left thigh*
- *M63.859 Disorders of muscle in diseases classified elsewhere, unspecified thigh*

● **M63.86** Disorders of muscle in diseases classified elsewhere, lower leg
- *M63.861 Disorders of muscle in diseases classified elsewhere, right lower leg*
- *M63.862 Disorders of muscle in diseases classified elsewhere, left lower leg*
- *M63.869 Disorders of muscle in diseases classified elsewhere, unspecified lower leg*

● **M63.87** Disorders of muscle in diseases classified elsewhere, ankle and foot
- *M63.871 Disorders of muscle in diseases classified elsewhere, right ankle and foot*
- *M63.872 Disorders of muscle in diseases classified elsewhere, left ankle and foot*
- *M63.879 Disorders of muscle in diseases classified elsewhere, unspecified ankle and foot*

- *M63.88 Disorders of muscle in diseases classified elsewhere, other site*
- *M63.89 Disorders of muscle in diseases classified elsewhere, multiple sites*

DISORDERS OF SYNOVIUM AND TENDON (M65-M67)

● **M65 Synovitis and tenosynovitis**
- **Excludes1** chronic crepitant synovitis of hand and wrist (M70.0-)
  current injury - see injury of ligament or tendon by body region
  soft tissue disorders related to use, overuse and pressure (M70.-)

● **M65.0 Abscess of tendon sheath**
  Use additional code (B95-B96) to identify bacterial agent
- **M65.00** Abscess of tendon sheath, unspecified site
- ● **M65.01** Abscess of tendon sheath, shoulder
  - M65.011 Abscess of tendon sheath, right shoulder
  - M65.012 Abscess of tendon sheath, left shoulder
  - M65.019 Abscess of tendon sheath, unspecified shoulder

Item 13-11 Synovitis is an inflammation of a synovial membrane resulting in pain on motion and is characterized by fluctuating swelling due to effusion in a synovial sac. **Tenosynovitis** is an inflammation of a tendon sheath and occurs most commonly in the wrists, hands, and feet. Bursitis is inflammation of a bursa (fluid-filled sac) caused by repetitive use, trauma, infection, or systemic inflammatory disease. Bursae act as protectors and facilitate movement between bones and overlapping muscles (deep bursae) or between bones and tendons/skin (superficial bursae).

● **M65.02** Abscess of tendon sheath, upper arm
  - M65.021 Abscess of tendon sheath, right upper arm
  - M65.022 Abscess of tendon sheath, left upper arm
  - M65.029 Abscess of tendon sheath, unspecified upper arm

● **M65.03** Abscess of tendon sheath, forearm
  - M65.031 Abscess of tendon sheath, right forearm
  - M65.032 Abscess of tendon sheath, left forearm
  - M65.039 Abscess of tendon sheath, unspecified forearm

● **M65.04** Abscess of tendon sheath, hand
  - M65.041 Abscess of tendon sheath, right hand
  - M65.042 Abscess of tendon sheath, left hand
  - M65.049 Abscess of tendon sheath, unspecified hand

● **M65.05** Abscess of tendon sheath, thigh
  - M65.051 Abscess of tendon sheath, right thigh
  - M65.052 Abscess of tendon sheath, left thigh
  - M65.059 Abscess of tendon sheath, unspecified thigh

● **M65.06** Abscess of tendon sheath, lower leg
  - M65.061 Abscess of tendon sheath, right lower leg
  - M65.062 Abscess of tendon sheath, left lower leg
  - M65.069 Abscess of tendon sheath, unspecified lower leg

● **M65.07** Abscess of tendon sheath, ankle and foot
  - M65.071 Abscess of tendon sheath, right ankle and foot
  - M65.072 Abscess of tendon sheath, left ankle and foot
  - M65.079 Abscess of tendon sheath, unspecified ankle and foot

- **M65.08** Abscess of tendon sheath, other site
● **M65.1** Other infective (teno)synovitis
  - **M65.10** Other infective (teno)synovitis, unspecified site
  - ● **M65.11** Other infective (teno)synovitis, shoulder
    - M65.111 Other infective (teno)synovitis, right shoulder
    - M65.112 Other infective (teno)synovitis, left shoulder
    - M65.119 Other infective (teno)synovitis, unspecified shoulder
  - ● **M65.12** Other infective (teno)synovitis, elbow
    - M65.121 Other infective (teno)synovitis, right elbow
    - M65.122 Other infective (teno)synovitis, left elbow
    - M65.129 Other infective (teno)synovitis, unspecified elbow

CHAPTER 13 (M00-M99)

CHAPTER 13 (MØØ-M99)

- ● M65.13   Other infective (teno)synovitis, wrist
    - M65.131   Other infective (teno)synovitis, right wrist
    - M65.132   Other infective (teno)synovitis, left wrist
    - M65.139   Other infective (teno)synovitis, unspecified wrist
- ● M65.14   Other infective (teno)synovitis, hand
    - M65.141   Other infective (teno)synovitis, right hand
    - M65.142   Other infective (teno)synovitis, left hand
    - M65.149   Other infective (teno)synovitis, unspecified hand
- ● M65.15   Other infective (teno)synovitis, hip
    - M65.151   Other infective (teno)synovitis, right hip
    - M65.152   Other infective (teno)synovitis, left hip
    - M65.159   Other infective (teno)synovitis, unspecified hip
- ● M65.16   Other infective (teno)synovitis, knee
    - M65.161   Other infective (teno)synovitis, right knee
    - M65.162   Other infective (teno)synovitis, left knee
    - M65.169   Other infective (teno)synovitis, unspecified knee
- ● M65.17   Other infective (teno)synovitis, ankle and foot
    - M65.171   Other infective (teno)synovitis, right ankle and foot
    - M65.172   Other infective (teno)synovitis, left ankle and foot
    - M65.179   Other infective (teno)synovitis, unspecified ankle and foot
- M65.18   Other infective (teno)synovitis, other site
- M65.19   Other infective (teno)synovitis, multiple sites
- ● M65.2   Calcific tendinitis
    - **Excludes1**   tendinitis as classified in M75-M77
    -                 calcified tendinitis of shoulder (M75.3)
    - M65.20   Calcific tendinitis, unspecified site
    - ● M65.22   Calcific tendinitis, upper arm
        - M65.221   Calcific tendinitis, right upper arm
        - M65.222   Calcific tendinitis, left upper arm
        - M65.229   Calcific tendinitis, unspecified upper arm
    - ● M65.23   Calcific tendinitis, forearm
        - M65.231   Calcific tendinitis, right forearm
        - M65.232   Calcific tendinitis, left forearm
        - M65.239   Calcific tendinitis, unspecified forearm
    - ● M65.24   Calcific tendinitis, hand
        - M65.241   Calcific tendinitis, right hand
        - M65.242   Calcific tendinitis, left hand
        - M65.249   Calcific tendinitis, unspecified hand
    - ● M65.25   Calcific tendinitis, thigh
        - M65.251   Calcific tendinitis, right thigh
        - M65.252   Calcific tendinitis, left thigh
        - M65.259   Calcific tendinitis, unspecified thigh
    - ● M65.26   Calcific tendinitis, lower leg
        - M65.261   Calcific tendinitis, right lower leg
        - M65.262   Calcific tendinitis, left lower leg
        - M65.269   Calcific tendinitis, unspecified lower leg

- ● M65.27   Calcific tendinitis, ankle and foot
    - M65.271   Calcific tendinitis, right ankle and foot
    - M65.272   Calcific tendinitis, left ankle and foot
    - M65.279   Calcific tendinitis, unspecified ankle and foot
- M65.28   Calcific tendinitis, other site
- M65.29   Calcific tendinitis, multiple sites
- ● M65.3   Trigger finger
    - Nodular tendinous disease
    - M65.30   Trigger finger, unspecified finger
    - ● M65.31   Trigger thumb
        - M65.311   Trigger thumb, right thumb
        - M65.312   Trigger thumb, left thumb
        - M65.319   Trigger thumb, unspecified thumb
    - ● M65.32   Trigger finger, index finger
        - M65.321   Trigger finger, right index finger
        - M65.322   Trigger finger, left index finger
        - M65.329   Trigger finger, unspecified index finger
    - ● M65.33   Trigger finger, middle finger
        - M65.331   Trigger finger, right middle finger
        - M65.332   Trigger finger, left middle finger
        - M65.339   Trigger finger, unspecified middle finger
    - ● M65.34   Trigger finger, ring finger
        - M65.341   Trigger finger, right ring finger
        - M65.342   Trigger finger, left ring finger
        - M65.349   Trigger finger, unspecified ring finger
    - ● M65.35   Trigger finger, little finger
        - M65.351   Trigger finger, right little finger
        - M65.352   Trigger finger, left little finger
        - M65.359   Trigger finger, unspecified little finger
- M65.4   Radial styloid tenosynovitis [de Quervain]
- ● M65.8   Other synovitis and tenosynovitis
    - M65.80   Other synovitis and tenosynovitis, unspecified site
    - ● M65.81   Other synovitis and tenosynovitis, shoulder
        - M65.811   Other synovitis and tenosynovitis, right shoulder
        - M65.812   Other synovitis and tenosynovitis, left shoulder
        - M65.819   Other synovitis and tenosynovitis, unspecified shoulder
    - ● M65.82   Other synovitis and tenosynovitis, upper arm
        - M65.821   Other synovitis and tenosynovitis, right upper arm
        - M65.822   Other synovitis and tenosynovitis, left upper arm
        - M65.829   Other synovitis and tenosynovitis, unspecified upper arm
    - ● M65.83   Other synovitis and tenosynovitis, forearm
        - M65.831   Other synovitis and tenosynovitis, right forearm
        - M65.832   Other synovitis and tenosynovitis, left forearm
        - M65.839   Other synovitis and tenosynovitis, unspecified forearm
    - ● M65.84   Other synovitis and tenosynovitis, hand
        - M65.841   Other synovitis and tenosynovitis, right hand
        - M65.842   Other synovitis and tenosynovitis, left hand
        - M65.849   Other synovitis and tenosynovitis, unspecified hand

▶ New   ⫸ Revised   ~~deleted~~ Deleted   Excludes 1   Excludes 2   Includes   Use additional   Code first   Code also   Key words
     OGCR Official Guidelines   X Assign placeholder X   ● Use Additional Character(s)   ▶ Manifestation Code   **Coding Clinic**

●M65.85   Other synovitis and tenosynovitis, thigh

    M65.851   Other synovitis and tenosynovitis, right thigh

    M65.852   Other synovitis and tenosynovitis, left thigh

    M65.859   Other synovitis and tenosynovitis, unspecified thigh

●M65.86   Other synovitis and tenosynovitis, lower leg

    M65.861   Other synovitis and tenosynovitis, right lower leg

    M65.862   Other synovitis and tenosynovitis, left lower leg

    M65.869   Other synovitis and tenosynovitis, unspecified lower leg

●M65.87   Other synovitis and tenosynovitis, ankle and foot

    M65.871   Other synovitis and tenosynovitis, right ankle and foot

    M65.872   Other synovitis and tenosynovitis, left ankle and foot

    M65.879   Other synovitis and tenosynovitis, unspecified ankle and foot

   M65.88   Other synovitis and tenosynovitis, other site

   M65.89   Other synovitis and tenosynovitis, multiple sites

M65.9   Synovitis and tenosynovitis, unspecified

●M66   Spontaneous rupture of synovium and tendon

    Includes   rupture that occurs when a normal force is applied to tissues that are inferred to have less than normal strength

    Excludes2   rotator cuff syndrome (M75.1-)

       rupture where an abnormal force is applied to normal tissue - see injury of tendon by body region

M66.0   Rupture of popliteal cyst

●M66.1   Rupture of synovium

    Rupture of synovial cyst

    Excludes2   rupture of popliteal cyst (M66.0)

   M66.10   Rupture of synovium, unspecified joint

●M66.11   Rupture of synovium, shoulder

    M66.111   Rupture of synovium, right shoulder

    M66.112   Rupture of synovium, left shoulder

    M66.119   Rupture of synovium, unspecified shoulder

●M66.12   Rupture of synovium, elbow

    M66.121   Rupture of synovium, right elbow

    M66.122   Rupture of synovium, left elbow

    M66.129   Rupture of synovium, unspecified elbow

●M66.13   Rupture of synovium, wrist

    M66.131   Rupture of synovium, right wrist

    M66.132   Rupture of synovium, left wrist

    M66.139   Rupture of synovium, unspecified wrist

●M66.14   Rupture of synovium, hand and fingers

    M66.141   Rupture of synovium, right hand

    M66.142   Rupture of synovium, left hand

    M66.143   Rupture of synovium, unspecified hand

    M66.144   Rupture of synovium, right finger(s)

    M66.145   Rupture of synovium, left finger(s)

    M66.146   Rupture of synovium, unspecified finger(s)

●M66.15   Rupture of synovium, hip

    M66.151   Rupture of synovium, right hip

    M66.152   Rupture of synovium, left hip

    M66.159   Rupture of synovium, unspecified hip

●M66.17   Rupture of synovium, ankle, foot and toes

    M66.171   Rupture of synovium, right ankle

    M66.172   Rupture of synovium, left ankle

    M66.173   Rupture of synovium, unspecified ankle

    M66.174   Rupture of synovium, right foot

    M66.175   Rupture of synovium, left foot

    M66.176   Rupture of synovium, unspecified foot

    M66.177   Rupture of synovium, right toe(s)

    M66.178   Rupture of synovium, left toe(s)

    M66.179   Rupture of synovium, unspecified toe(s)

   M66.18   Rupture of synovium, other site

●M66.2   Spontaneous rupture of extensor tendons

   M66.20   Spontaneous rupture of extensor tendons, unspecified site

●M66.21   Spontaneous rupture of extensor tendons, shoulder

    M66.211   Spontaneous rupture of extensor tendons, right shoulder

    M66.212   Spontaneous rupture of extensor tendons, left shoulder

    M66.219   Spontaneous rupture of extensor tendons, unspecified shoulder

●M66.22   Spontaneous rupture of extensor tendons, upper arm

    M66.221   Spontaneous rupture of extensor tendons, right upper arm

    M66.222   Spontaneous rupture of extensor tendons, left upper arm

    M66.229   Spontaneous rupture of extensor tendons, unspecified upper arm

●M66.23   Spontaneous rupture of extensor tendons, forearm

    M66.231   Spontaneous rupture of extensor tendons, right forearm

    M66.232   Spontaneous rupture of extensor tendons, left forearm

    M66.239   Spontaneous rupture of extensor tendons, unspecified forearm

●M66.24   Spontaneous rupture of extensor tendons, hand

    M66.241   Spontaneous rupture of extensor tendons, right hand

    M66.242   Spontaneous rupture of extensor tendons, left hand

    M66.249   Spontaneous rupture of extensor tendons, unspecified hand

●M66.25   Spontaneous rupture of extensor tendons, thigh

    M66.251   Spontaneous rupture of extensor tendons, right thigh

    M66.252   Spontaneous rupture of extensor tendons, left thigh

    M66.259   Spontaneous rupture of extensor tendons, unspecified thigh

●M66.26   Spontaneous rupture of extensor tendons, lower leg

    M66.261   Spontaneous rupture of extensor tendons, right lower leg

    M66.262   Spontaneous rupture of extensor tendons, left lower leg

    M66.269   Spontaneous rupture of extensor tendons, unspecified lower leg

CHAPTER 13 (M00-M99)

CHAPTER 13 (M00-M99)

● M66.27 Spontaneous rupture of extensor tendons, ankle and foot

    M66.271 Spontaneous rupture of extensor tendons, right ankle and foot

    M66.272 Spontaneous rupture of extensor tendons, left ankle and foot

    M66.279 Spontaneous rupture of extensor tendons, unspecified ankle and foot

  M66.28 Spontaneous rupture of extensor tendons, other site

  M66.29 Spontaneous rupture of extensor tendons, multiple sites

● M66.3 Spontaneous rupture of flexor tendons

  M66.30 Spontaneous rupture of flexor tendons, unspecified site

● M66.31 Spontaneous rupture of flexor tendons, shoulder

    M66.311 Spontaneous rupture of flexor tendons, right shoulder

    M66.312 Spontaneous rupture of flexor tendons, left shoulder

    M66.319 Spontaneous rupture of flexor tendons, unspecified shoulder

● M66.32 Spontaneous rupture of flexor tendons, upper arm

    M66.321 Spontaneous rupture of flexor tendons, right upper arm

    M66.322 Spontaneous rupture of flexor tendons, left upper arm

    M66.329 Spontaneous rupture of flexor tendons, unspecified upper arm

● M66.33 Spontaneous rupture of flexor tendons, forearm

    M66.331 Spontaneous rupture of flexor tendons, right forearm

    M66.332 Spontaneous rupture of flexor tendons, left forearm

    M66.339 Spontaneous rupture of flexor tendons, unspecified forearm

● M66.34 Spontaneous rupture of flexor tendons, hand

    M66.341 Spontaneous rupture of flexor tendons, right hand

    M66.342 Spontaneous rupture of flexor tendons, left hand

    M66.349 Spontaneous rupture of flexor tendons, unspecified hand

● M66.35 Spontaneous rupture of flexor tendons, thigh

    M66.351 Spontaneous rupture of flexor tendons, right thigh

    M66.352 Spontaneous rupture of flexor tendons, left thigh

    M66.359 Spontaneous rupture of flexor tendons, unspecified thigh

● M66.36 Spontaneous rupture of flexor tendons, lower leg

    M66.361 Spontaneous rupture of flexor tendons, right lower leg

    M66.362 Spontaneous rupture of flexor tendons, left lower leg

    M66.369 Spontaneous rupture of flexor tendons, unspecified lower leg

● M66.37 Spontaneous rupture of flexor tendons, ankle and foot

    M66.371 Spontaneous rupture of flexor tendons, right ankle and foot

    M66.372 Spontaneous rupture of flexor tendons, left ankle and foot

    M66.379 Spontaneous rupture of flexor tendons, unspecified ankle and foot

  M66.38 Spontaneous rupture of flexor tendons, other site

  M66.39 Spontaneous rupture of flexor tendons, multiple sites

● M66.8 Spontaneous rupture of other tendons

  M66.80 Spontaneous rupture of other tendons, unspecified site

● M66.81 Spontaneous rupture of other tendons, shoulder

    M66.811 Spontaneous rupture of other tendons, right shoulder

    M66.812 Spontaneous rupture of other tendons, left shoulder

    M66.819 Spontaneous rupture of other tendons, unspecified shoulder

● M66.82 Spontaneous rupture of other tendons, upper arm

    M66.821 Spontaneous rupture of other tendons, right upper arm

    M66.822 Spontaneous rupture of other tendons, left upper arm

    M66.829 Spontaneous rupture of other tendons, unspecified upper arm

● M66.83 Spontaneous rupture of other tendons, forearm

    M66.831 Spontaneous rupture of other tendons, right forearm

    M66.832 Spontaneous rupture of other tendons, left forearm

    M66.839 Spontaneous rupture of other tendons, unspecified forearm

● M66.84 Spontaneous rupture of other tendons, hand

    M66.841 Spontaneous rupture of other tendons, right hand

    M66.842 Spontaneous rupture of other tendons, left hand

    M66.849 Spontaneous rupture of other tendons, unspecified hand

● M66.85 Spontaneous rupture of other tendons, thigh

    M66.851 Spontaneous rupture of other tendons, right thigh

    M66.852 Spontaneous rupture of other tendons, left thigh

    M66.859 Spontaneous rupture of other tendons, unspecified thigh

● M66.86 Spontaneous rupture of other tendons, lower leg

    M66.861 Spontaneous rupture of other tendons, right lower leg

    M66.862 Spontaneous rupture of other tendons, left lower leg

    M66.869 Spontaneous rupture of other tendons, unspecified lower leg

● M66.87 Spontaneous rupture of other tendons, ankle and foot

    M66.871 Spontaneous rupture of other tendons, right ankle and foot

    M66.872 Spontaneous rupture of other tendons, left ankle and foot

    M66.879 Spontaneous rupture of other tendons, unspecified ankle and foot

  M66.88 Spontaneous rupture of other tendons, other

  M66.89 Spontaneous rupture of other tendons, multiple sites

M66.9 Spontaneous rupture of unspecified tendon

    Rupture at musculotendinous junction, nontraumatic

▶ New   ⇛ Revised   ~~deleted~~ Deleted   Excludes 1   Excludes 2   Includes   Use additional   Code first   Code also   Key words

OGCR Official Guidelines   X Assign placeholder X   ● Use Additional Character(s)   ▶ Manifestation Code   Coding Clinic

● **M67 Other disorders of synovium and tendon**
     Excludes1   palmar fascial fibromatosis [Dupuytren] (M72.0)
                    tendinitis NOS (M77.9-)
                    xanthomatosis localized to tendons (E78.2)

● **M67.0 Short Achilles tendon (acquired)**
     M67.00 Short Achilles tendon (acquired), **unspecified ankle**
     M67.01 Short Achilles tendon (acquired), **right ankle**
     M67.02 Short Achilles tendon (acquired), **left ankle**

● **M67.2 Synovial hypertrophy, not elsewhere classified**
     Excludes1   villonodular synovitis (pigmented) (M12.2-)
     M67.20 Synovial hypertrophy, not elsewhere classified, **unspecified site**
   ● **M67.21** Synovial hypertrophy, not elsewhere classified, **shoulder**
       M67.211 Synovial hypertrophy, not elsewhere classified, **right shoulder**
       M67.212 Synovial hypertrophy, not elsewhere classified, **left shoulder**
       M67.219 Synovial hypertrophy, not elsewhere classified, **unspecified shoulder**
   ● **M67.22** Synovial hypertrophy, not elsewhere classified, **upper arm**
       M67.221 Synovial hypertrophy, not elsewhere classified, **right upper arm**
       M67.222 Synovial hypertrophy, not elsewhere classified, **left upper arm**
       M67.229 Synovial hypertrophy, not elsewhere classified, **unspecified upper arm**
   ● **M67.23** Synovial hypertrophy, not elsewhere classified, **forearm**
       M67.231 Synovial hypertrophy, not elsewhere classified, **right forearm**
       M67.232 Synovial hypertrophy, not elsewhere classified, **left forearm**
       M67.239 Synovial hypertrophy, not elsewhere classified, **unspecified forearm**
   ● **M67.24** Synovial hypertrophy, not elsewhere classified, **hand**
       M67.241 Synovial hypertrophy, not elsewhere classified, **right hand**
       M67.242 Synovial hypertrophy, not elsewhere classified, **left hand**
       M67.249 Synovial hypertrophy, not elsewhere classified, **unspecified hand**
   ● **M67.25** Synovial hypertrophy, not elsewhere classified, **thigh**
       M67.251 Synovial hypertrophy, not elsewhere classified, **right thigh**
       M67.252 Synovial hypertrophy, not elsewhere classified, **left thigh**
       M67.259 Synovial hypertrophy, not elsewhere classified, **unspecified thigh**
   ● **M67.26** Synovial hypertrophy, not elsewhere classified, **lower leg**
       M67.261 Synovial hypertrophy, not elsewhere classified, **right lower leg**
       M67.262 Synovial hypertrophy, not elsewhere classified, **left lower leg**
       M67.269 Synovial hypertrophy, not elsewhere classified, **unspecified lower leg**
   ● **M67.27** Synovial hypertrophy, not elsewhere classified, **ankle and foot**
       M67.271 Synovial hypertrophy, not elsewhere classified, **right ankle and foot**
       M67.272 Synovial hypertrophy, not elsewhere classified, **left ankle and foot**
       M67.279 Synovial hypertrophy, not elsewhere classified, **unspecified ankle and foot**

     M67.28 Synovial hypertrophy, not elsewhere classified, **other site**
     M67.29 Synovial hypertrophy, not elsewhere classified, **multiple sites**

● **M67.3 Transient synovitis**
     Toxic synovitis
     Excludes1   palindromic rheumatism (M12.3-)
     M67.30 Transient synovitis, **unspecified site**
   ● **M67.31** Transient synovitis, **shoulder**
       M67.311 Transient synovitis, **right shoulder**
       M67.312 Transient synovitis, **left shoulder**
       M67.319 Transient synovitis, **unspecified shoulder**
   ● **M67.32** Transient synovitis, **elbow**
       M67.321 Transient synovitis, **right elbow**
       M67.322 Transient synovitis, **left elbow**
       M67.329 Transient synovitis, **unspecified elbow**
   ● **M67.33** Transient synovitis, **wrist**
       M67.331 Transient synovitis, **right wrist**
       M67.332 Transient synovitis, **left wrist**
       M67.339 Transient synovitis, **unspecified wrist**
   ● **M67.34** Transient synovitis, **hand**
       M67.341 Transient synovitis, **right hand**
       M67.342 Transient synovitis, **left hand**
       M67.349 Transient synovitis, **unspecified hand**
   ● **M67.35** Transient synovitis, **hip**
       M67.351 Transient synovitis, **right hip**
       M67.352 Transient synovitis, **left hip**
       M67.359 Transient synovitis, **unspecified hip**
   ● **M67.36** Transient synovitis, **knee**
       M67.361 Transient synovitis, **right knee**
       M67.362 Transient synovitis, **left knee**
       M67.369 Transient synovitis, **unspecified knee**
   ● **M67.37** Transient synovitis, **ankle and foot**
       M67.371 Transient synovitis, **right ankle and foot**
       M67.372 Transient synovitis, **left ankle and foot**
       M67.379 Transient synovitis, **unspecified ankle and foot**
     M67.38 Transient synovitis, **other site**
     M67.39 Transient synovitis, **multiple sites**

● **M67.4 Ganglion**
     Ganglion of joint or tendon (sheath)
     Excludes1   ganglion in yaws (A66.6)
     Excludes2   cyst of bursa (M71.2-M71.3)
                  cyst of synovium (M71.2-M71.3)
     M67.40 Ganglion, **unspecified site**
   ● **M67.41** Ganglion, **shoulder**
       M67.411 Ganglion, **right shoulder**
       M67.412 Ganglion, **left shoulder**
       M67.419 Ganglion, **unspecified shoulder**
   ● **M67.42** Ganglion, **elbow**
       M67.421 Ganglion, **right elbow**
       M67.422 Ganglion, **left elbow**
       M67.429 Ganglion, **unspecified elbow**
   ● **M67.43** Ganglion, **wrist**
       M67.431 Ganglion, **right wrist**
       M67.432 Ganglion, **left wrist**
       M67.439 Ganglion, **unspecified wrist**
   ● **M67.44** Ganglion, **hand**
       M67.441 Ganglion, **right hand**
       M67.442 Ganglion, **left hand**
       M67.449 Ganglion, **unspecified hand**

CHAPTER 13 (M00-M99)

● M67.45   Ganglion, hip
      M67.451   Ganglion, right hip
      M67.452   Ganglion, left hip
      M67.459   Ganglion, unspecified hip

● M67.46   Ganglion, knee
      M67.461   Ganglion, right knee
      M67.462   Ganglion, left knee
      M67.469   Ganglion, unspecified knee

● M67.47   Ganglion, ankle and foot
      M67.471   Ganglion, right ankle and foot
      M67.472   Ganglion, left ankle and foot
      M67.479   Ganglion, unspecified ankle and foot

   M67.48   Ganglion, other site
   M67.49   Ganglion, multiple sites

● M67.5   Plica syndrome
      Plica knee
   M67.50   Plica syndrome, unspecified knee
   M67.51   Plica syndrome, right knee
   M67.52   Plica syndrome, left knee

● M67.8   Other specified disorders of synovium and tendon
   M67.80   Other specified disorders of synovium and tendon, unspecified site

● M67.81   Other specified disorders of synovium and tendon, shoulder
      M67.811   Other specified disorders of synovium, right shoulder
      M67.812   Other specified disorders of synovium, left shoulder
      M67.813   Other specified disorders of tendon, right shoulder
      M67.814   Other specified disorders of tendon, left shoulder
      M67.819   Other specified disorders of synovium and tendon, unspecified shoulder

● M67.82   Other specified disorders of synovium and tendon, elbow
      M67.821   Other specified disorders of synovium, right elbow
      M67.822   Other specified disorders of synovium, left elbow
      M67.823   Other specified disorders of tendon, right elbow
      M67.824   Other specified disorders of tendon, left elbow
      M67.829   Other specified disorders of synovium and tendon, unspecified elbow

● M67.83   Other specified disorders of synovium and tendon, wrist
      M67.831   Other specified disorders of synovium, right wrist
      M67.832   Other specified disorders of synovium, left wrist
      M67.833   Other specified disorders of tendon, right wrist
      M67.834   Other specified disorders of tendon, left wrist
      M67.839   Other specified disorders of synovium and tendon, unspecified forearm

● M67.84   Other specified disorders of synovium and tendon, hand
      M67.841   Other specified disorders of synovium, right hand
      M67.842   Other specified disorders of synovium, left hand
      M67.843   Other specified disorders of tendon, right hand
      M67.844   Other specified disorders of tendon, left hand
      M67.849   Other specified disorders of synovium and tendon, unspecified hand

● M67.85   Other specified disorders of synovium and tendon, hip
      M67.851   Other specified disorders of synovium, right hip
      M67.852   Other specified disorders of synovium, left hip
      M67.853   Other specified disorders of tendon, right hip
      M67.854   Other specified disorders of tendon, left hip
      M67.859   Other specified disorders of synovium and tendon, unspecified hip

● M67.86   Other specified disorders of synovium and tendon, knee
      M67.861   Other specified disorders of synovium, right knee
      M67.862   Other specified disorders of synovium, left knee
      M67.863   Other specified disorders of tendon, right knee
      M67.864   Other specified disorders of tendon, left knee
      M67.869   Other specified disorders of synovium and tendon, unspecified knee

● M67.87   Other specified disorders of synovium and tendon, ankle and foot
      M67.871   Other specified disorders of synovium, right ankle and foot
      M67.872   Other specified disorders of synovium, left ankle and foot
      M67.873   Other specified disorders of tendon, right ankle and foot
      M67.874   Other specified disorders of tendon, left ankle and foot
      M67.879   Other specified disorders of synovium and tendon, unspecified ankle and foot

   M67.88   Other specified disorders of synovium and tendon, other site
   M67.89   Other specified disorders of synovium and tendon, multiple sites

● M67.9   Unspecified disorder of synovium and tendon
   M67.90   Unspecified disorder of synovium and tendon, unspecified site

● M67.91   Unspecified disorder of synovium and tendon, shoulder
      M67.911   Unspecified disorder of synovium and tendon, right shoulder
      M67.912   Unspecified disorder of synovium and tendon, left shoulder
      M67.919   Unspecified disorder of synovium and tendon, unspecified shoulder

● M67.92   Unspecified disorder of synovium and tendon, upper arm
      M67.921   Unspecified disorder of synovium and tendon, right upper arm
      M67.922   Unspecified disorder of synovium and tendon, left upper arm
      M67.929   Unspecified disorder of synovium and tendon, unspecified upper arm

▶ New   ⇢ Revised   ~~deleted~~ Deleted   Excludes 1   Excludes 2   Includes   Use additional   Code first   Code also   Key words

OGCR Official Guidelines   X Assign placeholder X   ● Use Additional Character(s)   ▶ Manifestation Code   Coding Clinic

● **M67.93** Unspecified disorder of synovium and tendon, forearm

     M67.931   Unspecified disorder of synovium and tendon, right forearm

     M67.932   Unspecified disorder of synovium and tendon, left forearm

     M67.939   Unspecified disorder of synovium and tendon, unspecified forearm

● **M67.94** Unspecified disorder of synovium and tendon, hand

     M67.941   Unspecified disorder of synovium and tendon, right hand

     M67.942   Unspecified disorder of synovium and tendon, left hand

     M67.949   Unspecified disorder of synovium and tendon, unspecified hand

● **M67.95** Unspecified disorder of synovium and tendon, thigh

     M67.951   Unspecified disorder of synovium and tendon, right thigh

     M67.952   Unspecified disorder of synovium and tendon, left thigh

     M67.959   Unspecified disorder of synovium and tendon, unspecified thigh

● **M67.96** Unspecified disorder of synovium and tendon, lower leg

     M67.961   Unspecified disorder of synovium and tendon, right lower leg

     M67.962   Unspecified disorder of synovium and tendon, left lower leg

     M67.969   Unspecified disorder of synovium and tendon, unspecified lower leg

● **M67.97** Unspecified disorder of synovium and tendon, ankle and foot

     M67.971   Unspecified disorder of synovium and tendon, right ankle and foot

     M67.972   Unspecified disorder of synovium and tendon, left ankle and foot

     M67.979   Unspecified disorder of synovium and tendon, unspecified ankle and foot

     M67.98   Unspecified disorder of synovium and tendon, other site

     M67.99   Unspecified disorder of synovium and tendon, multiple sites

OTHER SOFT TISSUE DISORDERS (M70-M79)

● **M70** Soft tissue disorders related to use, overuse and pressure

     Includes   soft tissue disorders of occupational origin

     Use additional external cause code to identify activity causing disorder (Y93.-)

     Excludes1   bursitis NOS (M71.9-)

     Excludes2   bursitis of shoulder (M75.5)
                enthesopathies (M76-M77)
                pressure ulcer (pressure area) (L89.-)

● **M70.0** Crepitant synovitis (acute) (chronic) of hand and wrist

     ● **M70.03** Crepitant synovitis (acute) (chronic), wrist

         M70.031   Crepitant synovitis (acute) (chronic), right wrist

         M70.032   Crepitant synovitis (acute) (chronic), left wrist

         M70.039   Crepitant synovitis (acute) (chronic), unspecified wrist

     ● **M70.04** Crepitant synovitis (acute) (chronic), hand

         M70.041   Crepitant synovitis (acute) (chronic), right hand

         M70.042   Crepitant synovitis (acute) (chronic), left hand

         M70.049   Crepitant synovitis (acute) (chronic), unspecified hand

● **M70.1** Bursitis of hand

     M70.10   Bursitis, unspecified hand

     M70.11   Bursitis, right hand

     M70.12   Bursitis, left hand

● **M70.2** Olecranon bursitis

     M70.20   Olecranon bursitis, unspecified elbow

     M70.21   Olecranon bursitis, right elbow

     M70.22   Olecranon bursitis, left elbow

● **M70.3** Other bursitis of elbow

     M70.30   Other bursitis of elbow, unspecified elbow

     M70.31   Other bursitis of elbow, right elbow

     M70.32   Other bursitis of elbow, left elbow

● **M70.4** Prepatellar bursitis

     M70.40   Prepatellar bursitis, unspecified knee

     M70.41   Prepatellar bursitis, right knee

     M70.42   Prepatellar bursitis, left knee

● **M70.5** Other bursitis of knee

     M70.50   Other bursitis of knee, unspecified knee

     M70.51   Other bursitis of knee, right knee

     M70.52   Other bursitis of knee, left knee

● **M70.6** Trochanteric bursitis

     Trochanteric tendinitis

     M70.60   Trochanteric bursitis, unspecified hip

     M70.61   Trochanteric bursitis, right hip

     M70.62   Trochanteric bursitis, left hip

● **M70.7** Other bursitis of hip

     Ischial bursitis

     M70.70   Other bursitis of hip, unspecified hip

     M70.71   Other bursitis of hip, right hip

     M70.72   Other bursitis of hip, left hip

● **M70.8** Other soft tissue disorders related to use, overuse and pressure

     M70.80   Other soft tissue disorders related to use, overuse and pressure of unspecified site

     ● **M70.81** Other soft tissue disorders related to use, overuse and pressure of shoulder

         M70.811   Other soft tissue disorders related to use, overuse and pressure, right shoulder

         M70.812   Other soft tissue disorders related to use, overuse and pressure, left shoulder

         M70.819   Other soft tissue disorders related to use, overuse and pressure, unspecified shoulder

     ● **M70.82** Other soft tissue disorders related to use, overuse and pressure of upper arm

         M70.821   Other soft tissue disorders related to use, overuse and pressure, right upper arm

         M70.822   Other soft tissue disorders related to use, overuse and pressure, left upper arm

         M70.829   Other soft tissue disorders related to use, overuse and pressure, unspecified upper arms

     ● **M70.83** Other soft tissue disorders related to use, overuse and pressure of forearm

         M70.831   Other soft tissue disorders related to use, overuse and pressure, right forearm

         M70.832   Other soft tissue disorders related to use, overuse and pressure, left forearm

         M70.839   Other soft tissue disorders related to use, overuse and pressure, unspecified forearm

● M70.84 Other soft tissue disorders related to use, overuse and pressure of hand
 M70.841 Other soft tissue disorders related to use, overuse and pressure, right hand
 M70.842 Other soft tissue disorders related to use, overuse and pressure, left hand
 M70.849 Other soft tissue disorders related to use, overuse and pressure, unspecified hand

● M70.85 Other soft tissue disorders related to use, overuse and pressure of thigh
 M70.851 Other soft tissue disorders related to use, overuse and pressure, right thigh
 M70.852 Other soft tissue disorders related to use, overuse and pressure, left thigh
 M70.859 Other soft tissue disorders related to use, overuse and pressure, unspecified thigh

● M70.86 Other soft tissue disorders related to use, overuse and pressure lower leg
 M70.861 Other soft tissue disorders related to use, overuse and pressure, right lower leg
 M70.862 Other soft tissue disorders related to use, overuse and pressure, left lower leg
 M70.869 Other soft tissue disorders related to use, overuse and pressure, unspecified leg

● M70.87 Other soft tissue disorders related to use, overuse and pressure of ankle and foot
 M70.871 Other soft tissue disorders related to use, overuse and pressure, right ankle and foot
 M70.872 Other soft tissue disorders related to use, overuse and pressure, left ankle and foot
 M70.879 Other soft tissue disorders related to use, overuse and pressure, unspecified ankle and foot

M70.88 Other soft tissue disorders related to use, overuse and pressure other site

M70.89 Other soft tissue disorders related to use, overuse and pressure multiple sites

● M70.9 Unspecified soft tissue disorder related to use, overuse and pressure
M70.90 Unspecified soft tissue disorder related to use, overuse and pressure of unspecified site

● M70.91 Unspecified soft tissue disorder related to use, overuse and pressure of shoulder
 M70.911 Unspecified soft tissue disorder related to use, overuse and pressure, right shoulder
 M70.912 Unspecified soft tissue disorder related to use, overuse and pressure, left shoulder
 M70.919 Unspecified soft tissue disorder related to use, overuse and pressure, unspecified shoulder

● M70.92 Unspecified soft tissue disorder related to use, overuse and pressure of upper arm
 M70.921 Unspecified soft tissue disorder related to use, overuse and pressure, right upper arm
 M70.922 Unspecified soft tissue disorder related to use, overuse and pressure, left upper arm
 M70.929 Unspecified soft tissue disorder related to use, overuse and pressure, unspecified upper arm

● M70.93 Unspecified soft tissue disorder related to use, overuse and pressure of forearm
 M70.931 Unspecified soft tissue disorder related to use, overuse and pressure, right forearm
 M70.932 Unspecified soft tissue disorder related to use, overuse and pressure, left forearm
 M70.939 Unspecified soft tissue disorder related to use, overuse and pressure, unspecified forearm

● M70.94 Unspecified soft tissue disorder related to use, overuse and pressure of hand
 M70.941 Unspecified soft tissue disorder related to use, overuse and pressure, right hand
 M70.942 Unspecified soft tissue disorder related to use, overuse and pressure, left hand
 M70.949 Unspecified soft tissue disorder related to use, overuse and pressure, unspecified hand

● M70.95 Unspecified soft tissue disorder related to use, overuse and pressure of thigh
 M70.951 Unspecified soft tissue disorder related to use, overuse and pressure, right thigh
 M70.952 Unspecified soft tissue disorder related to use, overuse and pressure, left thigh
 M70.959 Unspecified soft tissue disorder related to use, overuse and pressure, unspecified thigh

● M70.96 Unspecified soft tissue disorder related to use, overuse and pressure lower leg
 M70.961 Unspecified soft tissue disorder related to use, overuse and pressure, right lower leg
 M70.962 Unspecified soft tissue disorder related to use, overuse and pressure, left lower leg
 M70.969 Unspecified soft tissue disorder related to use, overuse and pressure, unspecified lower leg

● M70.97 Unspecified soft tissue disorder related to use, overuse and pressure of ankle and foot
 M70.971 Unspecified soft tissue disorder related to use, overuse and pressure, right ankle and foot
 M70.972 Unspecified soft tissue disorder related to use, overuse and pressure, left ankle and foot
 M70.979 Unspecified soft tissue disorder related to use, overuse and pressure, unspecified ankle and foot

M70.98 Unspecified soft tissue disorder related to use, overuse and pressure other

M70.99 Unspecified soft tissue disorder related to use, overuse and pressure multiple sites

● M71 Other bursopathies
 Excludes1 bunion (M20.1)
   bursitis related to use, overuse or pressure (M70.-)
   enthesopathies (M76-M77)

● M71.0 Abscess of bursa
 Use additional code (B95.-, B96.-) to identify causative organism
 M71.00 Abscess of bursa, unspecified site
 ● M71.01 Abscess of bursa, shoulder
  M71.011 Abscess of bursa, right shoulder
  M71.012 Abscess of bursa, left shoulder
  M71.019 Abscess of bursa, unspecified shoulder

▶ New ⇒ Revised ~~deleted~~ Deleted Excludes 1 Excludes 2 Includes Use additional Code first Code also Key words
OGCR Official Guidelines X Assign placeholder X ● Use Additional Character(s) ▷ Manifestation Code **Coding Clinic**

● M71.02   Abscess of bursa, elbow
     M71.021   Abscess of bursa, right elbow
     M71.022   Abscess of bursa, left elbow
     M71.029   Abscess of bursa, unspecified elbow
● M71.03   Abscess of bursa, wrist
     M71.031   Abscess of bursa, right wrist
     M71.032   Abscess of bursa, left wrist
     M71.039   Abscess of bursa, unspecified wrist
● M71.04   Abscess of bursa, hand
     M71.041   Abscess of bursa, right hand
     M71.042   Abscess of bursa, left hand
     M71.049   Abscess of bursa, unspecified hand
● M71.05   Abscess of bursa, hip
     M71.051   Abscess of bursa, right hip
     M71.052   Abscess of bursa, left hip
     M71.059   Abscess of bursa, unspecified hip
● M71.06   Abscess of bursa, knee
     M71.061   Abscess of bursa, right knee
     M71.062   Abscess of bursa, left knee
     M71.069   Abscess of bursa, unspecified knee
● M71.07   Abscess of bursa, ankle and foot
     M71.071   Abscess of bursa, right ankle and foot
     M71.072   Abscess of bursa, left ankle and foot
     M71.079   Abscess of bursa, unspecified ankle and foot
   M71.08   Abscess of bursa, other site
   M71.09   Abscess of bursa, multiple sites
● M71.1   Other infective bursitis
     Use additional code (B95.-, B96.-) to identify causative organism
   M71.10   Other infective bursitis, unspecified site
● M71.11   Other infective bursitis, shoulder
     M71.111   Other infective bursitis, right shoulder
     M71.112   Other infective bursitis, left shoulder
     M71.119   Other infective bursitis, unspecified shoulder
● M71.12   Other infective bursitis, elbow
     M71.121   Other infective bursitis, right elbow
     M71.122   Other infective bursitis, left elbow
     M71.129   Other infective bursitis, unspecified elbow
● M71.13   Other infective bursitis, wrist
     M71.131   Other infective bursitis, right wrist
     M71.132   Other infective bursitis, left wrist
     M71.139   Other infective bursitis, unspecified wrist
● M71.14   Other infective bursitis, hand
     M71.141   Other infective bursitis, right hand
     M71.142   Other infective bursitis, left hand
     M71.149   Other infective bursitis, unspecified hand
● M71.15   Other infective bursitis, hip
     M71.151   Other infective bursitis, right hip
     M71.152   Other infective bursitis, left hip
     M71.159   Other infective bursitis, unspecified hip
● M71.16   Other infective bursitis, knee
     M71.161   Other infective bursitis, right knee
     M71.162   Other infective bursitis, left knee
     M71.169   Other infective bursitis, unspecified knee

● M71.17   Other infective bursitis, ankle and foot
     M71.171   Other infective bursitis, right ankle and foot
     M71.172   Other infective bursitis, left ankle and foot
     M71.179   Other infective bursitis, unspecified ankle and foot
   M71.18   Other infective bursitis, other site
   M71.19   Other infective bursitis, multiple sites
● M71.2   Synovial cyst of popliteal space [Baker]
     Popliteal space = popliteal cavity, popliteal fossa. Depression in the posterior aspect of the knee (behind the knee).
     Excludes1   synovial cyst of popliteal space with rupture (M66.0)
   M71.20   Synovial cyst of popliteal space [Baker], unspecified knee
   M71.21   Synovial cyst of popliteal space [Baker], right knee
   M71.22   Synovial cyst of popliteal space [Baker], left knee
● M71.3   Other bursal cyst
     Synovial cyst NOS
     Excludes1   synovial cyst with rupture (M66.1-)
   M71.30   Other bursal cyst, unspecified site
● M71.31   Other bursal cyst, shoulder
     M71.311   Other bursal cyst, right shoulder
     M71.312   Other bursal cyst, left shoulder
     M71.319   Other bursal cyst, unspecified shoulder
● M71.32   Other bursal cyst, elbow
     M71.321   Other bursal cyst, right elbow
     M71.322   Other bursal cyst, left elbow
     M71.329   Other bursal cyst, unspecified elbow
● M71.33   Other bursal cyst, wrist
     M71.331   Other bursal cyst, right wrist
     M71.332   Other bursal cyst, left wrist
     M71.339   Other bursal cyst, unspecified wrist
● M71.34   Other bursal cyst, hand
     M71.341   Other bursal cyst, right hand
     M71.342   Other bursal cyst, left hand
     M71.349   Other bursal cyst, unspecified hand
● M71.35   Other bursal cyst, hip
     M71.351   Other bursal cyst, right hip
     M71.352   Other bursal cyst, left hip
     M71.359   Other bursal cyst, unspecified hip
● M71.37   Other bursal cyst, ankle and foot
     M71.371   Other bursal cyst, right ankle and foot
     M71.372   Other bursal cyst, left ankle and foot
     M71.379   Other bursal cyst, unspecified ankle and foot
   M71.38   Other bursal cyst, other site
   M71.39   Other bursal cyst, multiple sites
● M71.4   Calcium deposit in bursa
     Excludes2   calcium deposit in bursa of shoulder (M75.3)
   M71.40   Calcium deposit in bursa, unspecified site
● M71.42   Calcium deposit in bursa, elbow
     M71.421   Calcium deposit in bursa, right elbow
     M71.422   Calcium deposit in bursa, left elbow
     M71.429   Calcium deposit in bursa, unspecified elbow
● M71.43   Calcium deposit in bursa, wrist
     M71.431   Calcium deposit in bursa, right wrist
     M71.432   Calcium deposit in bursa, left wrist
     M71.439   Calcium deposit in bursa, unspecified wrist

CHAPTER 13 (M00-M99)

CHAPTER 13 (M00-M99)

● M71.44   Calcium deposit in bursa, hand
     M71.441   Calcium deposit in bursa, right hand
     M71.442   Calcium deposit in bursa, left hand
     M71.449   Calcium deposit in bursa, unspecified hand
● M71.45   Calcium deposit in bursa, hip
     M71.451   Calcium deposit in bursa, right hip
     M71.452   Calcium deposit in bursa, left hip
     M71.459   Calcium deposit in bursa, unspecified hip
● M71.46   Calcium deposit in bursa, knee
     M71.461   Calcium deposit in bursa, right knee
     M71.462   Calcium deposit in bursa, left knee
     M71.469   Calcium deposit in bursa, unspecified knee
● M71.47   Calcium deposit in bursa, ankle and foot
     M71.471   Calcium deposit in bursa, right ankle and foot
     M71.472   Calcium deposit in bursa, left ankle and foot
     M71.479   Calcium deposit in bursa, unspecified ankle and foot
   M71.48   Calcium deposit in bursa, other site
   M71.49   Calcium deposit in bursa, multiple sites
● M71.5   Other bursitis, not elsewhere classified

Excludes1	bursitis NOS (M71.9-)
Excludes2	bursitis of shoulder (M75.5)
	bursitis of tibial collateral [Pellegrini-Stieda] (M76.4-)

   M71.50   Other bursitis, not elsewhere classified, unspecified site
● M71.52   Other bursitis, not elsewhere classified, elbow
     M71.521   Other bursitis, not elsewhere classified, right elbow
     M71.522   Other bursitis, not elsewhere classified, left elbow
     M71.529   Other bursitis, not elsewhere classified, unspecified elbow
● M71.53   Other bursitis, not elsewhere classified, wrist
     M71.531   Other bursitis, not elsewhere classified, right wrist
     M71.532   Other bursitis, not elsewhere classified, left wrist
     M71.539   Other bursitis, not elsewhere classified, unspecified wrist
● M71.54   Other bursitis, not elsewhere classified, hand
     M71.541   Other bursitis, not elsewhere classified, right hand
     M71.542   Other bursitis, not elsewhere classified, left hand
     M71.549   Other bursitis, not elsewhere classified, unspecified hand
● M71.55   Other bursitis, not elsewhere classified, hip
     M71.551   Other bursitis, not elsewhere classified, right hip
     M71.552   Other bursitis, not elsewhere classified, left hip
     M71.559   Other bursitis, not elsewhere classified, unspecified hip
● M71.56   Other bursitis, not elsewhere classified, knee
     M71.561   Other bursitis, not elsewhere classified, right knee
     M71.562   Other bursitis, not elsewhere classified, left knee
     M71.569   Other bursitis, not elsewhere classified, unspecified knee

● M71.57   Other bursitis, not elsewhere classified, ankle and foot
     M71.571   Other bursitis, not elsewhere classified, right ankle and foot
     M71.572   Other bursitis, not elsewhere classified, left ankle and foot
     M71.579   Other bursitis, not elsewhere classified, unspecified ankle and foot
   M71.58   Other bursitis, not elsewhere classified, other site
● M71.8   Other specified bursopathies
   M71.80   Other specified bursopathies, unspecified site
● M71.81   Other specified bursopathies, shoulder
     M71.811   Other specified bursopathies, right shoulder
     M71.812   Other specified bursopathies, left shoulder
     M71.819   Other specified bursopathies, unspecified shoulder
● M71.82   Other specified bursopathies, elbow
     M71.821   Other specified bursopathies, right elbow
     M71.822   Other specified bursopathies, left elbow
     M71.829   Other specified bursopathies, unspecified elbow
● M71.83   Other specified bursopathies, wrist
     M71.831   Other specified bursopathies, right wrist
     M71.832   Other specified bursopathies, left wrist
     M71.839   Other specified bursopathies, unspecified wrist
● M71.84   Other specified bursopathies, hand
     M71.841   Other specified bursopathies, right hand
     M71.842   Other specified bursopathies, left hand
     M71.849   Other specified bursopathies, unspecified hand
● M71.85   Other specified bursopathies, hip
     M71.851   Other specified bursopathies, right hip
     M71.852   Other specified bursopathies, left hip
     M71.859   Other specified bursopathies, unspecified hip
● M71.86   Other specified bursopathies, knee
     M71.861   Other specified bursopathies, right knee
     M71.862   Other specified bursopathies, left knee
     M71.869   Other specified bursopathies, unspecified knee
● M71.87   Other specified bursopathies, ankle and foot
     M71.871   Other specified bursopathies, right ankle and foot
     M71.872   Other specified bursopathies, left ankle and foot
     M71.879   Other specified bursopathies, unspecified ankle and foot
   M71.88   Other specified bursopathies, other site
   M71.89   Other specified bursopathies, multiple sites
   M71.9   Bursopathy, unspecified
     Bursitis NOS

▶ New   ⇒ Revised   ~~deleted~~ Deleted   Excludes 1   Excludes 2   Includes   Use additional   Code first   Code also   Key words
OGCR Official Guidelines   X Assign placeholder X   ● Use Additional Character(s)   ▌ Manifestation Code   **Coding Clinic**

● **M72 Fibroblastic disorders**

    Excludes2   retroperitoneal fibromatosis (D48.3)

    M72.0 **Palmar fascial fibromatosis [Dupuytren]**   A

    M72.1 **Knuckle pads**

    M72.2 **Plantar fascial fibromatosis**
         Plantar fasciitis

    M72.4 **Pseudosarcomatous fibromatosis**
         Nodular fasciitis

    M72.6 **Necrotizing fasciitis**
         Use additional code (B95.-, B96.-) to identify causative
         organism

    M72.8 **Other fibroblastic disorders**
         Abscess of fascia
         Fasciitis NEC
         Other infective fasciitis
         Use additional code to (B95.-, B96.-) identify causative
         organism

         Excludes1   diffuse (eosinophilic) fasciitis (M35.4)
                    necrotizing fasciitis (M72.6)
                    nodular fasciitis (M72.4)
                    perirenal fasciitis NOS (N13.5)
                    perirenal fasciitis with infection (N13.6)
                    plantar fasciitis (M72.2)

    M72.9 **Fibroblastic disorder, unspecified**
         Fasciitis NOS
         Fibromatosis NOS

● **M75 Shoulder lesions**

    Excludes2   shoulder-hand syndrome (M89.0-)

   ● M75.0 **Adhesive capsulitis of shoulder**
         Frozen shoulder
         Periarthritis of shoulder

       M75.00 **Adhesive capsulitis of unspecified shoulder**

       M75.01 **Adhesive capsulitis of right shoulder**

       M75.02 **Adhesive capsulitis of left shoulder**
          Coding Clinic: 2015, Q2, P23

   ● M75.1 **Rotator cuff tear or rupture, not specified as traumatic**
         Rotator cuff syndrome
         Supraspinatus syndrome
         Supraspinatus tear or rupture, not specified as
           traumatic

         Excludes1   tear of rotator cuff, traumatic (S46.01-)

         Gradual onset due to repetitive stress to rotator cuff

    ● M75.10 **Unspecified rotator cuff tear or rupture, not specified as traumatic**

       M75.100 **Unspecified rotator cuff tear or rupture of unspecified shoulder, not specified as traumatic**

       M75.101 **Unspecified rotator cuff tear or rupture of right shoulder, not specified as traumatic**

       M75.102 **Unspecified rotator cuff tear or rupture of left shoulder, not specified as traumatic**

    ● M75.11 **Incomplete rotator cuff tear or rupture not specified as traumatic**

       M75.110 **Incomplete rotator cuff tear or rupture of unspecified shoulder, not specified as traumatic**

       M75.111 **Incomplete rotator cuff tear or rupture of right shoulder, not specified as traumatic**

       M75.112 **Incomplete rotator cuff tear or rupture of left shoulder, not specified as traumatic**

    ● M75.12 **Complete rotator cuff tear or rupture not specified as traumatic**

       M75.120 **Complete rotator cuff tear or rupture of unspecified shoulder, not specified as traumatic**

       M75.121 **Complete rotator cuff tear or rupture of right shoulder, not specified as traumatic**

       M75.122 **Complete rotator cuff tear or rupture of left shoulder, not specified as traumatic**

   ● M75.2 **Bicipital tendinitis**

       M75.20 **Bicipital tendinitis, unspecified shoulder**

       M75.21 **Bicipital tendinitis, right shoulder**

       M75.22 **Bicipital tendinitis, left shoulder**

   ● M75.3 **Calcific tendinitis of shoulder**
         Calcified bursa of shoulder

       M75.30 **Calcific tendinitis of unspecified shoulder**

       M75.31 **Calcific tendinitis of right shoulder**

       M75.32 **Calcific tendinitis of left shoulder**

   ● M75.4 **Impingement syndrome of shoulder**

       M75.40 **Impingement syndrome of unspecified shoulder**

       M75.41 **Impingement syndrome of right shoulder**

       M75.42 **Impingement syndrome of left shoulder**

   ● M75.5 **Bursitis of shoulder**

       M75.50 **Bursitis of unspecified shoulder**

       M75.51 **Bursitis of right shoulder**

       M75.52 **Bursitis of left shoulder**

   ● M75.8 **Other shoulder lesions**

       M75.80 **Other shoulder lesions, unspecified shoulder**

       M75.81 **Other shoulder lesions, right shoulder**

       M75.82 **Other shoulder lesions, left shoulder**

   ● M75.9 **Shoulder lesion, unspecified**

       M75.90 **Shoulder lesion, unspecified, unspecified shoulder**

       M75.91 **Shoulder lesion, unspecified, right shoulder**

       M75.92 **Shoulder lesion, unspecified, left shoulder**

● **M76 Enthesopathies, lower limb, excluding foot**

    Excludes2   bursitis due to use, overuse and pressure (M70.-)
                  enthesopathies of ankle and foot (M77.5-)

   ● M76.0 **Gluteal tendinitis**

       M76.00 **Gluteal tendinitis, unspecified hip**

       M76.01 **Gluteal tendinitis, right hip**

       M76.02 **Gluteal tendinitis, left hip**

   ● M76.1 **Psoas tendinitis**

       M76.10 **Psoas tendinitis, unspecified hip**

       M76.11 **Psoas tendinitis, right hip**

       M76.12 **Psoas tendinitis, left hip**

   ● M76.2 **Iliac crest spur**

       M76.20 **Iliac crest spur, unspecified hip**

       M76.21 **Iliac crest spur, right hip**

       M76.22 **Iliac crest spur, left hip**

   ● M76.3 **Iliotibial band syndrome**

       M76.30 **Iliotibial band syndrome, unspecified leg**

       M76.31 **Iliotibial band syndrome, right leg**

       M76.32 **Iliotibial band syndrome, left leg**

   ● M76.4 **Tibial collateral bursitis [Pellegrini-Stieda]**

       M76.40 **Tibial collateral bursitis [Pellegrini-Stieda], unspecified leg**

       M76.41 **Tibial collateral bursitis [Pellegrini-Stieda], right leg**

       M76.42 **Tibial collateral bursitis [Pellegrini-Stieda], left leg**

CHAPTER 13 (M00-M99)

● **M76.5 Patellar tendinitis**
     M76.50   Patellar tendinitis, unspecified knee
     M76.51   Patellar tendinitis, right knee
     M76.52   Patellar tendinitis, left knee

● **M76.6 Achilles tendinitis**
     Achilles bursitis
     M76.60   Achilles tendinitis, unspecified leg
     M76.61   Achilles tendinitis, right leg
     M76.62   Achilles tendinitis, left leg

● **M76.7 Peroneal tendinitis**
     M76.70   Peroneal tendinitis, unspecified leg
     M76.71   Peroneal tendinitis, right leg
     M76.72   Peroneal tendinitis, left leg

● **M76.8 Other specified enthesopathies of lower limb, excluding foot**
     ● M76.81   Anterior tibial syndrome
         M76.811   Anterior tibial syndrome, right leg
         M76.812   Anterior tibial syndrome, left leg
         M76.819   Anterior tibial syndrome, unspecified leg
     ● M76.82   Posterior tibial tendinitis
         M76.821   Posterior tibial tendinitis, right leg
         M76.822   Posterior tibial tendinitis, left leg
         M76.829   Posterior tibial tendinitis, unspecified leg
     ● M76.89   Other specified enthesopathies of lower limb, excluding foot
         M76.891   Other specified enthesopathies of right lower limb, excluding foot
         M76.892   Other specified enthesopathies of left lower limb, excluding foot
         M76.899   Other specified enthesopathies of unspecified lower limb, excluding foot

M76.9 Unspecified enthesopathy, lower limb, excluding foot

● **M77 Other enthesopathies**
     Excludes1   bursitis NOS (M71.9-)
     Excludes2   bursitis due to use, overuse and pressure (M70.-)
         osteophyte (M25.7)
         spinal enthesopathy (M46.0-)

● **M77.0 Medial epicondylitis**
     M77.00   Medial epicondylitis, unspecified elbow
     M77.01   Medial epicondylitis, right elbow
     M77.02   Medial epicondylitis, left elbow

● **M77.1 Lateral epicondylitis**
     Tennis elbow
     M77.10   Lateral epicondylitis, unspecified elbow
     M77.11   Lateral epicondylitis, right elbow
     M77.12   Lateral epicondylitis, left elbow

● **M77.2 Periarthritis of wrist**
     M77.20   Periarthritis, unspecified wrist
     M77.21   Periarthritis, right wrist
     M77.22   Periarthritis, left wrist

● **M77.3 Calcaneal spur**
     M77.30   Calcaneal spur, unspecified foot
     M77.31   Calcaneal spur, right foot
     M77.32   Calcaneal spur, left foot

● **M77.4 Metatarsalgia**
     Excludes1   Morton's metatarsalgia (G57.6)
     M77.40   Metatarsalgia, unspecified foot
     M77.41   Metatarsalgia, right foot
     M77.42   Metatarsalgia, left foot

● **M77.5 Other enthesopathy of foot**
     M77.50   Other enthesopathy of unspecified foot
     M77.51   Other enthesopathy of right foot
     M77.52   Other enthesopathy of left foot

M77.8 Other enthesopathies, not elsewhere classified

M77.9 Enthesopathy, unspecified
     Bone spur NOS
     Capsulitis NOS
     Periarthritis NOS
     Tendinitis NOS

● **M79 Other and unspecified soft tissue disorders, not elsewhere classified**
     Excludes1   psychogenic rheumatism (F45.8)
         soft tissue pain, psychogenic (F45.41)

M79.0 Rheumatism, unspecified
     Excludes1   fibromyalgia (M79.7)
         palindromic rheumatism (M12.3-)

● **M79.1 Myalgia**
     Myofascial pain syndrome
     ▶ M79.10   Myalgia, unspecified site
     ▶ M79.11   Myalgia of mastication muscle
     ▶ M79.12   Myalgia of auxiliary muscles, head and neck
     ▶ M79.18   Myalgia, other site
         Excludes1   fibromyalgia (M79.7)
             myositis (M60.-)

M79.2 Neuralgia and neuritis, unspecified
     Excludes1   brachial radiculitis NOS (M54.1)
         lumbosacral radiculitis NOS (M54.1)
         mononeuropathies (G56-G58)
         radiculitis NOS (M54.1)
         sciatica (M54.3-M54.4)

M79.3 Panniculitis, unspecified
     Excludes1   lupus panniculitis (L93.2)
         neck and back panniculitis (M54.0-)
         relapsing [Weber-Christian] panniculitis (M35.6)

M79.4 Hypertrophy of (infrapatellar) fat pad

M79.5 Residual foreign body in soft tissue
     Excludes1   foreign body granuloma of skin and subcutaneous tissue (L92.3)
         foreign body granuloma of soft tissue (M60.2-)

● **M79.6 Pain in limb, hand, foot, fingers and toes**
     Excludes2   pain in joint (M25.5-)
     ● M79.60   Pain in limb, unspecified
         M79.601   Pain in right arm
             Pain in right upper limb NOS
         M79.602   Pain in left arm
             Pain in left upper limb NOS
         M79.603   Pain in arm, unspecified
             Pain in upper limb NOS
         M79.604   Pain in right leg
             Pain in right lower limb NOS
         M79.605   Pain in left leg
             Pain in left lower limb NOS
         M79.606   Pain in leg, unspecified
             Pain in lower limb NOS
         M79.609   Pain in unspecified limb
             Pain in limb NOS
     ● M79.62   Pain in upper arm
         Pain in axillary region
         M79.621   Pain in right upper arm
         M79.622   Pain in left upper arm
         M79.629   Pain in unspecified upper arm
     ● M79.63   Pain in forearm
         M79.631   Pain in right forearm
         M79.632   Pain in left forearm
         M79.639   Pain in unspecified forearm

▶ New   ⇒ Revised   ~~deleted~~ Deleted   Excludes 1   Excludes 2   Includes   Use additional   Code first   Code also   Key words

OGCR Official Guidelines   X Assign placeholder X   ● Use Additional Character(s)   ▶ Manifestation Code   **Coding Clinic**

1046

● M79.64   Pain in hand and fingers
     M79.641   Pain in right hand
     M79.642   Pain in left hand
     M79.643   Pain in unspecified hand
     M79.644   Pain in right finger(s)
     M79.645   Pain in left finger(s)
     M79.646   Pain in unspecified finger(s)

● M79.65   Pain in thigh
     M79.651   Pain in right thigh
     M79.652   Pain in left thigh
     M79.659   Pain in unspecified thigh

● M79.66   Pain in lower leg
     M79.661   Pain in right lower leg
     M79.662   Pain in left lower leg
     M79.669   Pain in unspecified lower leg

● M79.67   Pain in foot and toes
     M79.671   Pain in right foot
     M79.672   Pain in left foot
     M79.673   Pain in unspecified foot
     M79.674   Pain in right toe(s)
     M79.675   Pain in left toe(s)
     M79.676   Pain in unspecified toe(s)

M79.7   Fibromyalgia
     Fibromyositis
     Fibrositis
     Myofibrositis

● M79.A   Nontraumatic compartment syndrome
     Code first, if applicable, associated postprocedural complication

     Excludes1   compartment syndrome NOS (T79.A-)
                 fibromyalgia (M79.7) nontraumatic ischemic infarction of muscle (M62.2-)
                 traumatic compartment syndrome (T79.A-)

● M79.A1   Nontraumatic compartment syndrome of upper extremity
     Nontraumatic compartment syndrome of shoulder, arm, forearm, wrist, hand, and fingers

     M79.A11   Nontraumatic compartment syndrome of right upper extremity
     M79.A12   Nontraumatic compartment syndrome of left upper extremity
     M79.A19   Nontraumatic compartment syndrome of unspecified upper extremity

● M79.A2   Nontraumatic compartment syndrome of lower extremity
     Nontraumatic compartment syndrome of hip, buttock, thigh, leg, foot, and toes

     M79.A21   Nontraumatic compartment syndrome of right lower extremity
     M79.A22   Nontraumatic compartment syndrome of left lower extremity
     M79.A29   Nontraumatic compartment syndrome of unspecified lower extremity

     M79.A3   Nontraumatic compartment syndrome of abdomen
     M79.A9   Nontraumatic compartment syndrome of other sites

● M79.8   Other specified soft tissue disorders
     M79.81   Nontraumatic hematoma of soft tissue
         Nontraumatic hematoma of muscle
         Nontraumatic seroma of muscle and soft tissue
     M79.89   Other specified soft tissue disorders
         Polyalgia

M79.9   Soft tissue disorder, unspecified

OGCR   **See Section I.C., Chapter 13.d.**

Osteoporosis

Osteoporosis is a systemic condition, meaning that all bones of the musculoskeletal system are affected. Therefore, site is not a component of the codes under category M81, Osteoporosis without current pathological fracture. The site codes under category M80, Osteoporosis with current pathological fracture, identify the site of the fracture, not the osteoporosis.

1) Osteoporosis without pathological fracture

Category M81, Osteoporosis without current pathological fracture, is for use for patients with osteoporosis who do not currently have a pathologic fracture due to the osteoporosis, even if they have had a fracture in the past. For patients with a history of osteoporosis fractures, status code Z87.310, Personal history of (healed) osteoporosis fracture, should follow the code from M81.

2) Osteoporosis with current pathological fracture

Category M80, Osteoporosis with current pathological fracture, is for patients who have a current pathologic fracture at the time of an encounter. The codes under M80 identify the site of the fracture. A code from category M80, not a traumatic fracture code, should be used for any patient with known osteoporosis who suffers a fracture, even if the patient had a minor fall or trauma, if that fall or trauma would not usually break a normal, healthy bone.

OSTEOPATHIES AND CHONDROPATHIES (M80-M94)

DISORDERS OF BONE DENSITY AND STRUCTURE (M80-M85)

M80   **Osteoporosis with current pathological fracture**
Excessive skeletal fragility (porous bone) resulting in bone fractures

     Includes   osteoporosis with current fragility fracture

Use additional code to identify major osseous defect, if applicable (M89.7-)

     Excludes1   collapsed vertebra NOS (M48.5)
                pathological fracture NOS (M84.4)
                wedging of vertebra NOS (M48.5)

     Excludes2   personal history of (healed) osteoporosis fracture (Z87.310)

Coding Clinic: 2018, Q2, P12

The appropriate 7th character is to be added to each code from category M80:

A	initial encounter for fracture *All encounters involving diagnosis and treatment*
D	subsequent encounter for fracture with routine healing
G	subsequent encounter for fracture with delayed healing *Encounters for attention to casting or fixation devices, medication, and follow-up visits during the healing phase*
K	subsequent encounter for fracture with nonunion *Total failure of fracture healing*
P	subsequent encounter for fracture with malunion *Fracture ends do not heal together correctly.*
S	sequela

● M80.0   **Age-related osteoporosis with current pathological fracture**
     Involutional osteoporosis with current pathological fracture
     Osteoporosis NOS with current pathological fracture
     Postmenopausal osteoporosis with current pathological fracture
     Senile osteoporosis with current pathological fracture

X ● M80.00   Age-related osteoporosis with current pathological fracture, unspecified site   A

● M80.01   Age-related osteoporosis with current pathological fracture, shoulder

     ● M80.011   Age-related osteoporosis with current pathological fracture, right shoulder   A
     ● M80.012   Age-related osteoporosis with current pathological fracture, left shoulder   A
     ● M80.019   Age-related osteoporosis with current pathological fracture, unspecified shoulder   A

CHAPTER 13 (M00-M99)

CHAPTER 13 (M00-M99)

● M80.02   Age-related osteoporosis with current pathological fracture, humerus
   ● M80.021   Age-related osteoporosis with current pathological fracture, right humerus   A
   ● M80.022   Age-related osteoporosis with current pathological fracture, left humerus   A
   ● M80.029   Age-related osteoporosis with current pathological fracture, unspecified humerus   A

● M80.03   Age-related osteoporosis with current pathological fracture, forearm
    Age-related osteoporosis with current pathological fracture of wrist
   ● M80.031   Age-related osteoporosis with current pathological fracture, right forearm   A
   ● M80.032   Age-related osteoporosis with current pathological fracture, left forearm   A
   ● M80.039   Age-related osteoporosis with current pathological fracture, unspecified forearm   A

● M80.04   Age-related osteoporosis with current pathological fracture, hand
   ● M80.041   Age-related osteoporosis with current pathological fracture, right hand   A
   ● M80.042   Age-related osteoporosis with current pathological fracture, left hand   A
   ● M80.049   Age-related osteoporosis with current pathological fracture, unspecified hand   A

● M80.05   Age-related osteoporosis with current pathological fracture, femur
    Age-related osteoporosis with current pathological fracture of hip
   ● M80.051   Age-related osteoporosis with current pathological fracture, right femur   A
   ● M80.052   Age-related osteoporosis with current pathological fracture, left femur
        Coding Clinic: 2018, Q2, P12   A
   ● M80.059   Age-related osteoporosis with current pathological fracture, unspecified femur   A

● M80.06   Age-related osteoporosis with current pathological fracture, lower leg
   ● M80.061   Age-related osteoporosis with current pathological fracture, right lower leg   A
   ● M80.062   Age-related osteoporosis with current pathological fracture, left lower leg   A
   ● M80.069   Age-related osteoporosis with current pathological fracture, unspecified lower leg   A

● M80.07   Age-related osteoporosis with current pathological fracture, ankle and foot
   ● M80.071   Age-related osteoporosis with current pathological fracture, right ankle and foot   A
   ● M80.072   Age-related osteoporosis with current pathological fracture, left ankle and foot   A
   ● M80.079   Age-related osteoporosis with current pathological fracture, unspecified ankle and foot   A

X ● M80.08   Age-related osteoporosis with current pathological fracture, vertebra(e)   A

● M80.8   Other osteoporosis with current pathological fracture
    Drug-induced osteoporosis with current pathological fracture
    Idiopathic osteoporosis with current pathological fracture
    Osteoporosis of disuse with current pathological fracture
    Postoophorectomy osteoporosis with current pathological fracture
    Postsurgical malabsorption osteoporosis with current pathological fracture
    Post-traumatic osteoporosis with current pathological fracture
    Use additional code for adverse effect, if applicable, to identify drug (T36-T50 with fifth or sixth character 5)

X ● M80.80   Other osteoporosis with current pathological fracture, unspecified site   A

● M80.81   Other osteoporosis with pathological fracture, shoulder
   ● M80.811   Other osteoporosis with current pathological fracture, right shoulder
   ● M80.812   Other osteoporosis with current pathological fracture, left shoulder
   ● M80.819   Other osteoporosis with current pathological fracture, unspecified shoulder

● M80.82   Other osteoporosis with current pathological fracture, humerus
   ● M80.821   Other osteoporosis with current pathological fracture, right humerus
   ● M80.822   Other osteoporosis with current pathological fracture, left humerus
   ● M80.829   Other osteoporosis with current pathological fracture, unspecified humerus

● M80.83   Other osteoporosis with current pathological fracture, forearm
    Other osteoporosis with current pathological fracture of wrist
   ● M80.831   Other osteoporosis with current pathological fracture, right forearm
   ● M80.832   Other osteoporosis with current pathological fracture, left forearm
   ● M80.839   Other osteoporosis with current pathological fracture, unspecified forearm

● M80.84   Other osteoporosis with current pathological fracture, hand
   ● M80.841   Other osteoporosis with current pathological fracture, right hand
   ● M80.842   Other osteoporosis with current pathological fracture, left hand
   ● M80.849   Other osteoporosis with current pathological fracture, unspecified hand

● M80.85   Other osteoporosis with current pathological fracture, femur
    Other osteoporosis with current pathological fracture of hip
   ● M80.851   Other osteoporosis with current pathological fracture, right femur
   ● M80.852   Other osteoporosis with current pathological fracture, left femur
   ● M80.859   Other osteoporosis with current pathological fracture, unspecified femur

▶ New   ⇒ Revised   ~~deleted~~ Deleted   Excludes 1   Excludes 2   Includes   Use additional   Code first   Code also   Key words
OGCR Official Guidelines   X Assign placeholder X   ● Use Additional Character(s)   ▷ Manifestation Code   **Coding Clinic**

● **M80.86** Other osteoporosis with current pathological fracture, lower leg

    ● **M80.861** Other osteoporosis with current pathological fracture, right lower leg

    ● **M80.862** Other osteoporosis with current pathological fracture, left lower leg

    ● **M80.869** Other osteoporosis with current pathological fracture, unspecified lower leg

● **M80.87** Other osteoporosis with current pathological fracture, ankle and foot

    ● **M80.871** Other osteoporosis with current pathological fracture, right ankle and foot

    ● **M80.872** Other osteoporosis with current pathological fracture, left ankle and foot

    ● **M80.879** Other osteoporosis with current pathological fracture, unspecified ankle and foot

X ● **M80.88** Other osteoporosis with current pathological fracture, vertebra(e)

● **M81** **Osteoporosis without current pathological fracture**

Use additional code to identify:
major osseous defect, if applicable (M89.7-)
personal history of (healed) osteoporosis fracture, if applicable (Z87.310)

    Excludes1   osteoporosis with current pathological fracture (M80.-)
                Sudeck's atrophy (M89.0)

M81.0 **Age-related osteoporosis without current pathological fracture**   A
Involutional osteoporosis without current pathological fracture
Osteoporosis NOS
Postmenopausal osteoporosis without current pathological fracture
Senile osteoporosis without current pathological fracture

M81.6 **Localized osteoporosis [Lequesne]**
    Excludes1   Sudeck's atrophy (M89.0)

M81.8 **Other osteoporosis without current pathological fracture**
Drug-induced osteoporosis without current pathological fracture
Idiopathic osteoporosis without current pathological fracture
Osteoporosis of disuse without current pathological fracture
Postoophorectomy osteoporosis without current pathological fracture
Postsurgical malabsorption osteoporosis without current pathological fracture
Post-traumatic osteoporosis without current pathological fracture
Use additional code for adverse effect, if applicable, to identify drug (T36-T50 with fifth or sixth character 5)

● **M83** **Adult osteomalacia**
    Excludes1   infantile and juvenile osteomalacia (E55.0)
                renal osteodystrophy (N25.0)
                rickets (active) (E55.0)
                rickets (active) sequelae (E64.3)
                vitamin D-resistant osteomalacia (E83.3)
                vitamin D-resistant rickets (active) (E83.3)

M83.0 **Puerperal osteomalacia** ♀   M

M83.1 **Senile osteomalacia**   A

M83.2 **Adult osteomalacia due to malabsorption**   A
Postsurgical malabsorption osteomalacia in adults

M83.3 **Adult osteomalacia due to malnutrition**   A

M83.4 **Aluminum bone disease**

M83.5 **Other drug-induced osteomalacia in adults**   A
Use additional code for adverse effect, if applicable, to identify drug (T36-T50 with fifth or sixth character 5)

M83.8 **Other adult osteomalacia**   A

M83.9 **Adult osteomalacia, unspecified**   A

● **M84** **Disorder of continuity of bone**
    Excludes2   traumatic fracture of bone-see fracture, by site

  ● **M84.3** **Stress fracture**
Fatigue fracture
March fracture
Stress fracture NOS
Stress reaction
Use additional external cause code(s) to identify the cause of the stress fracture

    Excludes1   pathological fracture NOS (M84.4.-)
                pathological fracture due to osteoporosis (M80.-)
                traumatic fracture (S12.-, S22.-, S32.-, S42.-, S52.-, S62.-, S72.-, S82.-, S92.-)

    Excludes2   personal history of (healed) stress (fatigue) fracture (Z87.312)
                stress fracture of vertebra (M48.4-)

The appropriate 7th character is to be added to each code from subcategory M84.3:

A	initial encounter for fracture
D	subsequent encounter for fracture with routine healing
G	subsequent encounter for fracture with delayed healing
K	subsequent encounter for fracture with nonunion
P	subsequent encounter for fracture with malunion
S	sequela

X ● **M84.30** Stress fracture, unspecified site

● **M84.31** Stress fracture, shoulder

    ● **M84.311** Stress fracture, right shoulder

    ● **M84.312** Stress fracture, left shoulder

    ● **M84.319** Stress fracture, unspecified shoulder

● **M84.32** Stress fracture, humerus

    ● **M84.321** Stress fracture, right humerus

    ● **M84.322** Stress fracture, left humerus

    ● **M84.329** Stress fracture, unspecified humerus

● **M84.33** Stress fracture, ulna and radius

    ● **M84.331** Stress fracture, right ulna

    ● **M84.332** Stress fracture, left ulna

    ● **M84.333** Stress fracture, right radius

    ● **M84.334** Stress fracture, left radius

    ● **M84.339** Stress fracture, unspecified ulna and radius

● **M84.34** Stress fracture, hand and fingers

    ● **M84.341** Stress fracture, right hand

    ● **M84.342** Stress fracture, left hand

    ● **M84.343** Stress fracture, unspecified hand

    ● **M84.344** Stress fracture, right finger(s)

    ● **M84.345** Stress fracture, left finger(s)

    ● **M84.346** Stress fracture, unspecified finger(s)

● **M84.35** Stress fracture, pelvis and femur
Stress fracture, hip

    ● **M84.350** Stress fracture, pelvis

    ● **M84.351** Stress fracture, right femur

    ● **M84.352** Stress fracture, left femur

    ● **M84.353** Stress fracture, unspecified femur

    ● **M84.359** Stress fracture, hip, unspecified

CHAPTER 13 (M00-M99)

● M84.36 Stress fracture, tibia and fibula
   ● M84.361 Stress fracture, right tibia
   ● M84.362 Stress fracture, left tibia
   ● M84.363 Stress fracture, right fibula
   ● M84.364 Stress fracture, left fibula
   ● M84.369 Stress fracture, unspecified tibia and fibula
● M84.37 Stress fracture, ankle, foot and toes
   ● M84.371 Stress fracture, right ankle
   ● M84.372 Stress fracture, left ankle
   ● M84.373 Stress fracture, unspecified ankle
   ● M84.374 Stress fracture, right foot
   ● M84.375 Stress fracture, left foot
   ● M84.376 Stress fracture, unspecified foot
   ● M84.377 Stress fracture, right toe(s)
   ● M84.378 Stress fracture, left toe(s)
   ● M84.379 Stress fracture, unspecified toe(s)
X ● M84.38 Stress fracture, other site
       Excludes2   stress fracture of vertebra (M48.4-)

● M84.4 Pathological fracture, not elsewhere classified
    Chronic fracture
    Pathological fracture NOS
    Excludes1   collapsed vertebra NEC (M48.5)
               pathological fracture in neoplastic disease (M84.5-)
               pathological fracture in osteoporosis (M80.-)
               pathological fracture in other disease (M84.6-)
               stress fracture (M84.3-)
               traumatic fracture (S12.-, S22.-, S32.-, S42.-, S52.-, S62.-, S72.-, S82.-, S92.-)
    Excludes2   personal history of (healed) pathological fracture (Z87.311)
    The appropriate 7th character is to be added to each code from subcategory M84.4:

> A   initial encounter for fracture
> D   subsequent encounter for fracture with routine healing
> G   subsequent encounter for fracture with delayed healing
> K   subsequent encounter for fracture with nonunion
> P   subsequent encounter for fracture with malunion
> S   sequela

X ● M84.40 Pathological fracture, unspecified site
● M84.41 Pathological fracture, shoulder
   ● M84.411 Pathological fracture, right shoulder
   ● M84.412 Pathological fracture, left shoulder
   ● M84.419 Pathological fracture, unspecified shoulder
● M84.42 Pathological fracture, humerus
   ● M84.421 Pathological fracture, right humerus
   ● M84.422 Pathological fracture, left humerus
   ● M84.429 Pathological fracture, unspecified humerus

● M84.43 Pathological fracture, ulna and radius
   ● M84.431 Pathological fracture, right ulna
   ● M84.432 Pathological fracture, left ulna
   ● M84.433 Pathological fracture, right radius
   ● M84.434 Pathological fracture, left radius
   ● M84.439 Pathological fracture, unspecified ulna and radius
● M84.44 Pathological fracture, hand and fingers
   ● M84.441 Pathological fracture, right hand
   ● M84.442 Pathological fracture, left hand
   ● M84.443 Pathological fracture, unspecified hand
   ● M84.444 Pathological fracture, right finger(s)
   ● M84.445 Pathological fracture, left finger(s)
   ● M84.446 Pathological fracture, unspecified finger(s)
● M84.45 Pathological fracture, femur and pelvis
   ● M84.451 Pathological fracture, right femur
   ● M84.452 Pathological fracture, left femur
   ● M84.453 Pathological fracture, unspecified femur
   ● M84.454 Pathological fracture, pelvis
           Coding Clinic: 2016, Q4, P43
   ● M84.459 Pathological fracture, hip, unspecified
● M84.46 Pathological fracture, tibia and fibula
   ● M84.461 Pathological fracture, right tibia
   ● M84.462 Pathological fracture, left tibia
   ● M84.463 Pathological fracture, right fibula
   ● M84.464 Pathological fracture, left fibula
   ● M84.469 Pathological fracture, unspecified tibia and fibula
● M84.47 Pathological fracture, ankle, foot and toes
   ● M84.471 Pathological fracture, right ankle
   ● M84.472 Pathological fracture, left ankle
   ● M84.473 Pathological fracture, unspecified ankle
   ● M84.474 Pathological fracture, right foot
   ● M84.475 Pathological fracture, left foot
   ● M84.476 Pathological fracture, unspecified foot
   ● M84.477 Pathological fracture, right toe(s)
   ● M84.478 Pathological fracture, left toe(s)
   ● M84.479 Pathological fracture, unspecified toe(s)
X ● M84.48 Pathological fracture, other site

OGCR Section I.C. 13.C.

Coding of Pathologic Fractures

7th character A is for use as long as the patient is receiving active treatment for the fracture. While the patient may be seen by a new or different provider over the course of treatment for a pathological fracture, assignment of the 7th character is based on whether the patient is undergoing active treatment and not whether the provider is seeing the patient for the first time.

7th character, D is to be used for encounters after the patient has completed active treatment for the fracture and is receiving routine care for the fracture during the healing or recovery phase. The other 7th characters, listed under each subcategory in the Tabular List, are to be used for subsequent encounters for treatment of problems associated with the healing, such as malunions, nonunions, and sequelae.

Care for complications of surgical treatment for fracture repairs during the healing or recovery phase should be coded with the appropriate complication codes.

See Section I.C.19. Coding of traumatic fractures.

▶ New   ⇒ Revised   ~~deleted~~ Deleted   Excludes 1   Excludes 2   Includes   Use additional   Code first   Code also   Key words
     OGCR Official Guidelines   X Assign placeholder X   ● Use Additional Character(s)   ▸ Manifestation Code   **Coding Clinic**

● **M84.5 Pathological fracture in neoplastic disease**

    Code also underlying neoplasm

    The appropriate 7th character is to be added to each
       code from subcategory M84.5:

A	initial encounter for fracture
D	subsequent encounter for fracture with routine healing
G	subsequent encounter for fracture with delayed healing
K	subsequent encounter for fracture with nonunion
P	subsequent encounter for fracture with malunion
S	sequela

X ● **M84.50 Pathological fracture in neoplastic disease, unspecified site**

● **M84.51 Pathological fracture in neoplastic disease, shoulder**

    ● **M84.511 Pathological fracture in neoplastic disease, right shoulder**

    ● **M84.512 Pathological fracture in neoplastic disease, left shoulder**

    ● **M84.519 Pathological fracture in neoplastic disease, unspecified shoulder**

● **M84.52 Pathological fracture in neoplastic disease, humerus**

    ● **M84.521 Pathological fracture in neoplastic disease, right humerus**

    ● **M84.522 Pathological fracture in neoplastic disease, left humerus**

    ● **M84.529 Pathological fracture in neoplastic disease, unspecified humerus**

● **M84.53 Pathological fracture in neoplastic disease, ulna and radius**

    ● **M84.531 Pathological fracture in neoplastic disease, right ulna**

    ● **M84.532 Pathological fracture in neoplastic disease, left ulna**

    ● **M84.533 Pathological fracture in neoplastic disease, right radius**

    ● **M84.534 Pathological fracture in neoplastic disease, left radius**

    ● **M84.539 Pathological fracture in neoplastic disease, unspecified ulna and radius**

● **M84.54 Pathological fracture in neoplastic disease, hand**

    ● **M84.541 Pathological fracture in neoplastic disease, right hand**

    ● **M84.542 Pathological fracture in neoplastic disease, left hand**

    ● **M84.549 Pathological fracture in neoplastic disease, unspecified hand**

● **M84.55 Pathological fracture in neoplastic disease, pelvis and femur**

    ● **M84.550 Pathological fracture in neoplastic disease, pelvis**

    ● **M84.551 Pathological fracture in neoplastic disease, right femur**

    ● **M84.552 Pathological fracture in neoplastic disease, left femur**

    ● **M84.553 Pathological fracture in neoplastic disease, unspecified femur**

    ● **M84.559 Pathological fracture in neoplastic disease, hip, unspecified**

● **M84.56 Pathological fracture in neoplastic disease, tibia and fibula**

    ● **M84.561 Pathological fracture in neoplastic disease, right tibia**

    ● **M84.562 Pathological fracture in neoplastic disease, left tibia**

    ● **M84.563 Pathological fracture in neoplastic disease, right fibula**

    ● **M84.564 Pathological fracture in neoplastic disease, left fibula**

    ● **M84.569 Pathological fracture in neoplastic disease, unspecified tibia and fibula**

● **M84.57 Pathological fracture in neoplastic disease, ankle and foot**

    ● **M84.571 Pathological fracture in neoplastic disease, right ankle**

    ● **M84.572 Pathological fracture in neoplastic disease, left ankle**

    ● **M84.573 Pathological fracture in neoplastic disease, unspecified ankle**

    ● **M84.574 Pathological fracture in neoplastic disease, right foot**

    ● **M84.575 Pathological fracture in neoplastic disease, left foot**

    ● **M84.576 Pathological fracture in neoplastic disease, unspecified foot**

X ● **M84.58 Pathological fracture in neoplastic disease, other specified site**

    Pathological fracture in neoplastic disease, vertebrae

● **M84.6 Pathological fracture in other disease**

    Code also underlying condition

    Excludes1   pathological fracture in osteoporosis (M80.-)

    The appropriate 7th character is to be added to each
       code from subcategory M84.6:

A	initial encounter for fracture
D	subsequent encounter for fracture with routine healing
G	subsequent encounter for fracture with delayed healing
K	subsequent encounter for fracture with nonunion
P	subsequent encounter for fracture with malunion
S	sequela

X ● **M84.60 Pathological fracture in other disease, unspecified site**

● **M84.61 Pathological fracture in other disease, shoulder**

    ● **M84.611 Pathological fracture in other disease, right shoulder**

    ● **M84.612 Pathological fracture in other disease, left shoulder**

    ● **M84.619 Pathological fracture in other disease, unspecified shoulder**

● **M84.62 Pathological fracture in other disease, humerus**

    ● **M84.621 Pathological fracture in other disease, right humerus**

    ● **M84.622 Pathological fracture in other disease, left humerus**

    ● **M84.629 Pathological fracture in other disease, unspecified humerus**

● **M84.63** Pathological fracture in other disease, ulna and radius
  - ● **M84.631** Pathological fracture in other disease, right ulna
  - ● **M84.632** Pathological fracture in other disease, left ulna
  - ● **M84.633** Pathological fracture in other disease, right radius
  - ● **M84.634** Pathological fracture in other disease, left radius
  - ● **M84.639** Pathological fracture in other disease, unspecified ulna and radius

● **M84.64** Pathological fracture in other disease, hand
  - ● **M84.641** Pathological fracture in other disease, right hand
  - ● **M84.642** Pathological fracture in other disease, left hand
  - ● **M84.649** Pathological fracture in other disease, unspecified hand

● **M84.65** Pathological fracture in other disease, pelvis and femur
  - ● **M84.650** Pathological fracture in other disease, pelvis
  - ● **M84.651** Pathological fracture in other disease, right femur
  - ● **M84.652** Pathological fracture in other disease, left femur
  - ● **M84.653** Pathological fracture in other disease, unspecified femur
  - ● **M84.659** Pathological fracture in other disease, hip, unspecified

● **M84.66** Pathological fracture in other disease, tibia and fibula
  - ● **M84.661** Pathological fracture in other disease, right tibia
  - ● **M84.662** Pathological fracture in other disease, left tibia
  - ● **M84.663** Pathological fracture in other disease, right fibula
  - ● **M84.664** Pathological fracture in other disease, left fibula
  - ● **M84.669** Pathological fracture in other disease, unspecified tibia and fibula

● **M84.67** Pathological fracture in other disease, ankle and foot
  - ● **M84.671** Pathological fracture in other disease, right ankle
  - ● **M84.672** Pathological fracture in other disease, left ankle
  - ● **M84.673** Pathological fracture in other disease, unspecified ankle
  - ● **M84.674** Pathological fracture in other disease, right foot
  - ● **M84.675** Pathological fracture in other disease, left foot
  - ● **M84.676** Pathological fracture in other disease, unspecified foot

X ● **M84.68** Pathological fracture in other disease, other site

● **M84.7** Nontraumatic fracture, not elsewhere classified
  - ● **M84.75** Atypical femoral fracture

    The appropriate 7th character is to be added to each code from M84.75:

A	initial encounter for fracture
D	subsequent encounter for fracture with routine healing
G	subsequent encounter for fracture with delayed healing
K	subsequent encounter for fracture with nonunion
P	subsequent encounter for fracture with malunion
S	sequela

    Coding Clinic: 2016, Q4, P41

    - ● **M84.750** Atypical femoral fracture, unspecified
    - ● **M84.751** Incomplete atypical femoral fracture, right leg
    - ● **M84.752** Incomplete atypical femoral fracture, left leg
    - ● **M84.753** Incomplete atypical femoral fracture, unspecified leg
    - ● **M84.754** Complete transverse atypical femoral fracture, right leg
    - ● **M84.755** Complete transverse atypical femoral fracture, left leg
    - ● **M84.756** Complete transverse atypical femoral fracture, unspecified leg
    - ● **M84.757** Complete oblique atypical femoral fracture, right leg
    - ● **M84.758** Complete oblique atypical femoral fracture, left leg
    - ● **M84.759** Complete oblique atypical femoral fracture, unspecified leg

● **M84.8** Other disorders of continuity of bone
  - **M84.80** Other disorders of continuity of bone, unspecified site
  - ● **M84.81** Other disorders of continuity of bone, shoulder
    - **M84.811** Other disorders of continuity of bone, right shoulder
    - **M84.812** Other disorders of continuity of bone, left shoulder
    - **M84.819** Other disorders of continuity of bone, unspecified shoulder
  - ● **M84.82** Other disorders of continuity of bone, humerus
    - **M84.821** Other disorders of continuity of bone, right humerus
    - **M84.822** Other disorders of continuity of bone, left humerus
    - **M84.829** Other disorders of continuity of bone, unspecified humerus
  - ● **M84.83** Other disorders of continuity of bone, ulna and radius
    - **M84.831** Other disorders of continuity of bone, right ulna
    - **M84.832** Other disorders of continuity of bone, left ulna
    - **M84.833** Other disorders of continuity of bone, right radius
    - **M84.834** Other disorders of continuity of bone, left radius
    - **M84.839** Other disorders of continuity of bone, unspecified ulna and radius

CHAPTER 13 (M00-M99)

● M84.84   Other disorders of continuity of bone, hand

    M84.841   Other disorders of continuity of bone, right hand

    M84.842   Other disorders of continuity of bone, left hand

    M84.849   Other disorders of continuity of bone, unspecified hand

● M84.85   Other disorders of continuity of bone, pelvic region and thigh

    M84.851   Other disorders of continuity of bone, right pelvic region and thigh

    M84.852   Other disorders of continuity of bone, left pelvic region and thigh

    M84.859   Other disorders of continuity of bone, unspecified pelvic region and thigh

● M84.86   Other disorders of continuity of bone, tibia and fibula

    M84.861   Other disorders of continuity of bone, right tibia

    M84.862   Other disorders of continuity of bone, left tibia

    M84.863   Other disorders of continuity of bone, right fibula

    M84.864   Other disorders of continuity of bone, left fibula

    M84.869   Other disorders of continuity of bone, unspecified tibia and fibula

● M84.87   Other disorders of continuity of bone, ankle and foot

    M84.871   Other disorders of continuity of bone, right ankle and foot

    M84.872   Other disorders of continuity of bone, left ankle and foot

    M84.879   Other disorders of continuity of bone, unspecified ankle and foot

    M84.88   Other disorders of continuity of bone, other site

M84.9   Disorder of continuity of bone, unspecified

● M85   Other disorders of bone density and structure

    Excludes1   osteogenesis imperfecta (Q78.0)
                 osteopetrosis (Q78.2)
                 osteopoikilosis (Q78.8)
                 polyostotic fibrous dysplasia (Q78.1)

● M85.0   Fibrous dysplasia (monostotic)

    Excludes2   fibrous dysplasia of jaw (M27.8)

    M85.00   Fibrous dysplasia (monostotic), unspecified site

● M85.01   Fibrous dysplasia (monostotic), shoulder

    M85.011   Fibrous dysplasia (monostotic), right shoulder

    M85.012   Fibrous dysplasia (monostotic), left shoulder

    M85.019   Fibrous dysplasia (monostotic), unspecified shoulder

● M85.02   Fibrous dysplasia (monostotic), upper arm

    M85.021   Fibrous dysplasia (monostotic), right upper arm

    M85.022   Fibrous dysplasia (monostotic), left upper arm

    M85.029   Fibrous dysplasia (monostotic), unspecified upper arm

● M85.03   Fibrous dysplasia (monostotic), forearm

    M85.031   Fibrous dysplasia (monostotic), right forearm

    M85.032   Fibrous dysplasia (monostotic), left forearm

    M85.039   Fibrous dysplasia (monostotic), unspecified forearm

● M85.04   Fibrous dysplasia (monostotic), hand

    M85.041   Fibrous dysplasia (monostotic), right hand

    M85.042   Fibrous dysplasia (monostotic), left hand

    M85.049   Fibrous dysplasia (monostotic), unspecified hand

● M85.05   Fibrous dysplasia (monostotic), thigh

    M85.051   Fibrous dysplasia (monostotic), right thigh

    M85.052   Fibrous dysplasia (monostotic), left thigh

    M85.059   Fibrous dysplasia (monostotic), unspecified thigh

● M85.06   Fibrous dysplasia (monostotic), lower leg

    M85.061   Fibrous dysplasia (monostotic), right lower leg

    M85.062   Fibrous dysplasia (monostotic), left lower leg

    M85.069   Fibrous dysplasia (monostotic), unspecified lower leg

● M85.07   Fibrous dysplasia (monostotic), ankle and foot

    M85.071   Fibrous dysplasia (monostotic), right ankle and foot

    M85.072   Fibrous dysplasia (monostotic), left ankle and foot

    M85.079   Fibrous dysplasia (monostotic), unspecified ankle and foot

    M85.08   Fibrous dysplasia (monostotic), other site

    M85.09   Fibrous dysplasia (monostotic), multiple sites

● M85.1   Skeletal fluorosis

    M85.10   Skeletal fluorosis, unspecified site

● M85.11   Skeletal fluorosis, shoulder

    M85.111   Skeletal fluorosis, right shoulder

    M85.112   Skeletal fluorosis, left shoulder

    M85.119   Skeletal fluorosis, unspecified shoulder

● M85.12   Skeletal fluorosis, upper arm

    M85.121   Skeletal fluorosis, right upper arm

    M85.122   Skeletal fluorosis, left upper arm

    M85.129   Skeletal fluorosis, unspecified upper arm

● M85.13   Skeletal fluorosis, forearm

    M85.131   Skeletal fluorosis, right forearm

    M85.132   Skeletal fluorosis, left forearm

    M85.139   Skeletal fluorosis, unspecified forearm

● M85.14   Skeletal fluorosis, hand

    M85.141   Skeletal fluorosis, right hand

    M85.142   Skeletal fluorosis, left hand

    M85.149   Skeletal fluorosis, unspecified hand

● M85.15   Skeletal fluorosis, thigh

    M85.151   Skeletal fluorosis, right thigh

    M85.152   Skeletal fluorosis, left thigh

    M85.159   Skeletal fluorosis, unspecified thigh

● M85.16   Skeletal fluorosis, lower leg

    M85.161   Skeletal fluorosis, right lower leg

    M85.162   Skeletal fluorosis, left lower leg

    M85.169   Skeletal fluorosis, unspecified lower leg

● M85.17   Skeletal fluorosis, ankle and foot

    M85.171   Skeletal fluorosis, right ankle and foot

    M85.172   Skeletal fluorosis, left ankle and foot

    M85.179   Skeletal fluorosis, unspecified ankle and foot

    M85.18   Skeletal fluorosis, other site

    M85.19   Skeletal fluorosis, multiple sites

M85.2 Hyperostosis of skull
● M85.3 Osteitis condensans
  M85.30 Osteitis condensans, unspecified site
  ● M85.31 Osteitis condensans, shoulder
    M85.311 Osteitis condensans, right shoulder
    M85.312 Osteitis condensans, left shoulder
    M85.319 Osteitis condensans, unspecified shoulder
  ● M85.32 Osteitis condensans, upper arm
    M85.321 Osteitis condensans, right upper arm
    M85.322 Osteitis condensans, left upper arm
    M85.329 Osteitis condensans, unspecified upper arm
  ● M85.33 Osteitis condensans, forearm
    M85.331 Osteitis condensans, right forearm
    M85.332 Osteitis condensans, left forearm
    M85.339 Osteitis condensans, unspecified forearm
  ● M85.34 Osteitis condensans, hand
    M85.341 Osteitis condensans, right hand
    M85.342 Osteitis condensans, left hand
    M85.349 Osteitis condensans, unspecified hand
  ● M85.35 Osteitis condensans, thigh
    M85.351 Osteitis condensans, right thigh
    M85.352 Osteitis condensans, left thigh
    M85.359 Osteitis condensans, unspecified thigh
  ● M85.36 Osteitis condensans, lower leg
    M85.361 Osteitis condensans, right lower leg
    M85.362 Osteitis condensans, left lower leg
    M85.369 Osteitis condensans, unspecified lower leg
  ● M85.37 Osteitis condensans, ankle and foot
    M85.371 Osteitis condensans, right ankle and foot
    M85.372 Osteitis condensans, left ankle and foot
    M85.379 Osteitis condensans, unspecified ankle and foot
  M85.38 Osteitis condensans, other site
  M85.39 Osteitis condensans, multiple sites
● M85.4 Solitary bone cyst
  Excludes2 solitary cyst of jaw (M27.4)
  M85.40 Solitary bone cyst, unspecified site
  ● M85.41 Solitary bone cyst, shoulder
    M85.411 Solitary bone cyst, right shoulder
    M85.412 Solitary bone cyst, left shoulder
    M85.419 Solitary bone cyst, unspecified shoulder
  ● M85.42 Solitary bone cyst, humerus
    M85.421 Solitary bone cyst, right humerus
    M85.422 Solitary bone cyst, left humerus
    M85.429 Solitary bone cyst, unspecified humerus
  ● M85.43 Solitary bone cyst, ulna and radius
    M85.431 Solitary bone cyst, right ulna and radius
    M85.432 Solitary bone cyst, left ulna and radius
    M85.439 Solitary bone cyst, unspecified ulna and radius

● M85.44 Solitary bone cyst, hand
    M85.441 Solitary bone cyst, right hand
    M85.442 Solitary bone cyst, left hand
    M85.449 Solitary bone cyst, unspecified hand
● M85.45 Solitary bone cyst, pelvis
    M85.451 Solitary bone cyst, right pelvis
    M85.452 Solitary bone cyst, left pelvis
    M85.459 Solitary bone cyst, unspecified pelvis
● M85.46 Solitary bone cyst, tibia and fibula
    M85.461 Solitary bone cyst, right tibia and fibula
    M85.462 Solitary bone cyst, left tibia and fibula
    M85.469 Solitary bone cyst, unspecified tibia and fibula
● M85.47 Solitary bone cyst, ankle and foot
    M85.471 Solitary bone cyst, right ankle and foot
    M85.472 Solitary bone cyst, left ankle and foot
    M85.479 Solitary bone cyst, unspecified ankle and foot
  M85.48 Solitary bone cyst, other site
● M85.5 Aneurysmal bone cyst
  Excludes2 aneurysmal cyst of jaw (M27.4)
  M85.50 Aneurysmal bone cyst, unspecified site
  ● M85.51 Aneurysmal bone cyst, shoulder
    M85.511 Aneurysmal bone cyst, right shoulder
    M85.512 Aneurysmal bone cyst, left shoulder
    M85.519 Aneurysmal bone cyst, unspecified shoulder
  ● M85.52 Aneurysmal bone cyst, upper arm
    M85.521 Aneurysmal bone cyst, right upper arm
    M85.522 Aneurysmal bone cyst, left upper arm
    M85.529 Aneurysmal bone cyst, unspecified upper arm
  ● M85.53 Aneurysmal bone cyst, forearm
    M85.531 Aneurysmal bone cyst, right forearm
    M85.532 Aneurysmal bone cyst, left forearm
    M85.539 Aneurysmal bone cyst, unspecified forearm
  ● M85.54 Aneurysmal bone cyst, hand
    M85.541 Aneurysmal bone cyst, right hand
    M85.542 Aneurysmal bone cyst, left hand
    M85.549 Aneurysmal bone cyst, unspecified hand
  ● M85.55 Aneurysmal bone cyst, thigh
    M85.551 Aneurysmal bone cyst, right thigh
    M85.552 Aneurysmal bone cyst, left thigh
    M85.559 Aneurysmal bone cyst, unspecified thigh
  ● M85.56 Aneurysmal bone cyst, lower leg
    M85.561 Aneurysmal bone cyst, right lower leg
    M85.562 Aneurysmal bone cyst, left lower leg
    M85.569 Aneurysmal bone cyst, unspecified lower leg
  ● M85.57 Aneurysmal bone cyst, ankle and foot
    M85.571 Aneurysmal bone cyst, right ankle and foot
    M85.572 Aneurysmal bone cyst, left ankle and foot
    M85.579 Aneurysmal bone cyst, unspecified ankle and foot
  M85.58 Aneurysmal bone cyst, other site
  M85.59 Aneurysmal bone cyst, multiple sites

● **M85.6**   **Other cyst of bone**
    Excludes1   cyst of jaw NEC (M27.4)
                  osteitis fibrosa cystica generalisata [von
                      Recklinghausen's disease of bone]
                      (E21.0)
    M85.60   Other cyst of bone, unspecified site
  ● M85.61   Other cyst of bone, shoulder
       M85.611   Other cyst of bone, right shoulder
       M85.612   Other cyst of bone, left shoulder
       M85.619   Other cyst of bone, unspecified
                 shoulder
  ● M85.62   Other cyst of bone, upper arm
       M85.621   Other cyst of bone, right upper arm
       M85.622   Other cyst of bone, left upper arm
       M85.629   Other cyst of bone, unspecified upper
                 arm
  ● M85.63   Other cyst of bone, forearm
       M85.631   Other cyst of bone, right forearm
       M85.632   Other cyst of bone, left forearm
       M85.639   Other cyst of bone, unspecified
                 forearm
  ● M85.64   Other cyst of bone, hand
       M85.641   Other cyst of bone, right hand
       M85.642   Other cyst of bone, left hand
       M85.649   Other cyst of bone, unspecified hand
  ● M85.65   Other cyst of bone, thigh
       M85.651   Other cyst of bone, right thigh
       M85.652   Other cyst of bone, left thigh
       M85.659   Other cyst of bone, unspecified thigh
  ● M85.66   Other cyst of bone, lower leg
       M85.661   Other cyst of bone, right lower leg
       M85.662   Other cyst of bone, left lower leg
       M85.669   Other cyst of bone, unspecified lower
                 leg
  ● M85.67   Other cyst of bone, ankle and foot
       M85.671   Other cyst of bone, right ankle and
                 foot
       M85.672   Other cyst of bone, left ankle and foot
       M85.679   Other cyst of bone, unspecified ankle
                 and foot
    M85.68   Other cyst of bone, other site
    M85.69   Other cyst of bone, multiple sites
● **M85.8**   **Other specified disorders of bone density and structure**
    Hyperostosis of bones, except skull
    Osteosclerosis, acquired
    Excludes1   diffuse idiopathic skeletal hyperostosis
                  [DISH] (M48.1)
                  osteosclerosis congenita (Q77.4)
                  osteosclerosis fragilitas (generalista)
                      (Q78.2)
                  osteosclerosis myelofibrosis (D75.81)
    M85.80   Other specified disorders of bone density and
                 structure, unspecified site
  ● M85.81   Other specified disorders of bone density and
                 structure, shoulder
       M85.811   Other specified disorders of bone
                 density and structure, right shoulder
       M85.812   Other specified disorders of bone
                 density and structure, left shoulder
       M85.819   Other specified disorders of bone
                 density and structure, unspecified
                 shoulder

  ● M85.82   Other specified disorders of bone density and
                 structure, upper arm
       M85.821   Other specified disorders of bone
                 density and structure, right upper arm
       M85.822   Other specified disorders of bone
                 density and structure, left upper arm
       M85.829   Other specified disorders of bone
                 density and structure, unspecified
                 upper arm
  ● M85.83   Other specified disorders of bone density and
                 structure, forearm
       M85.831   Other specified disorders of bone
                 density and structure, right forearm
       M85.832   Other specified disorders of bone
                 density and structure, left forearm
       M85.839   Other specified disorders of bone
                 density and structure, unspecified
                 forearm
  ● M85.84   Other specified disorders of bone density and
                 structure, hand
       M85.841   Other specified disorders of bone
                 density and structure, right hand
       M85.842   Other specified disorders of bone
                 density and structure, left hand
       M85.849   Other specified disorders of bone
                 density and structure, unspecified
                 hand
  ● M85.85   Other specified disorders of bone density and
                 structure, thigh
       M85.851   Other specified disorders of bone
                 density and structure, right thigh
       M85.852   Other specified disorders of bone
                 density and structure, left thigh
       M85.859   Other specified disorders of bone
                 density and structure, unspecified
                 thigh
  ● M85.86   Other specified disorders of bone density and
                 structure, lower leg
       M85.861   Other specified disorders of bone
                 density and structure, right lower leg
       M85.862   Other specified disorders of bone
                 density and structure, left lower leg
       M85.869   Other specified disorders of bone
                 density and structure, unspecified
                 lower leg
  ● M85.87   Other specified disorders of bone density and
                 structure, ankle and foot
       M85.871   Other specified disorders of bone
                 density and structure, right ankle and
                 foot
       M85.872   Other specified disorders of bone
                 density and structure, left ankle and
                 foot
       M85.879   Other specified disorders of bone
                 density and structure, unspecified
                 ankle and foot
    M85.88   Other specified disorders of bone density and
                 structure, other site
    M85.89   Other specified disorders of bone density and
                 structure, multiple sites
  M85.9   **Disorder of bone density and structure, unspecified**

Figure 13-6 Osteomyelitis of the spine. A lateral view of the lower thoracic spine demonstrates destruction of the disk space *(arrow)* as well as destruction of the adjoining vertebral bodies. (From Mettler: Essentials of Radiology, ed 2, Saunders, An Imprint of Elsevier, 2005)

Item 13–12　Osteomyelitis is an inflammation of the bone. **Acute osteomyelitis** is a rapidly destructive, pus-producing infection capable of causing severe bone destruction. **Chronic osteomyelitis** can remain long after the initial acute episode has passed and may lead to a recurrence of the acute phase. **Brodie's abscess** is an encapsulated focal abscess that must be surgically drained. **Periostitis** is an inflammation of the periosteum, a dense membrane composed of fibrous connective tissue that closely wraps all bone, except those with articulating surfaces in joints, which are covered by synovial membranes.

OTHER OSTEOPATHIES (M86-M90)

> **Excludes1** postprocedural osteopathies (M96.-)

● **M86　Osteomyelitis**

Use additional code (B95-B97) to identify infectious agent

Use additional code to identify major osseous defect, if applicable (M89.7-)

> **Excludes1** osteomyelitis due to:
> echinococcus (B67.2)
> gonococcus (A54.43)
> salmonella (A02.24)

> **Excludes2** ostemyelitis of:
> orbit (H05.0-)
> petrous bone (H70.2-)
> vertebra (M46.2-)

● **M86.0　Acute hematogenous** osteomyelitis

　M86.00 Acute hematogenous osteomyelitis, unspecified site

　● **M86.01** Acute hematogenous osteomyelitis, shoulder

　　M86.011 Acute hematogenous osteomyelitis, right shoulder

　　M86.012 Acute hematogenous osteomyelitis, left shoulder

　　M86.019 Acute hematogenous osteomyelitis, unspecified shoulder

　● **M86.02** Acute hematogenous osteomyelitis, humerus

　　M86.021 Acute hematogenous osteomyelitis, right humerus

　　M86.022 Acute hematogenous osteomyelitis, left humerus

　　M86.029 Acute hematogenous osteomyelitis, unspecified humerus

　● **M86.03** Acute hematogenous osteomyelitis, radius and ulna

　　M86.031 Acute hematogenous osteomyelitis, right radius and ulna

　　M86.032 Acute hematogenous osteomyelitis, left radius and ulna

　　M86.039 Acute hematogenous osteomyelitis, unspecified radius and ulna

　● **M86.04** Acute hematogenous osteomyelitis, hand

　　M86.041 Acute hematogenous osteomyelitis, right hand

　　M86.042 Acute hematogenous osteomyelitis, left hand

　　M86.049 Acute hematogenous osteomyelitis, unspecified hand

● **M86.05** Acute hematogenous osteomyelitis, femur

　M86.051 Acute hematogenous osteomyelitis, right femur

　M86.052 Acute hematogenous osteomyelitis, left femur

　M86.059 Acute hematogenous osteomyelitis, unspecified femur

● **M86.06** Acute hematogenous osteomyelitis, tibia and fibula

　M86.061 Acute hematogenous osteomyelitis, right tibia and fibula

　M86.062 Acute hematogenous osteomyelitis, left tibia and fibula

　M86.069 Acute hematogenous osteomyelitis, unspecified tibia and fibula

● **M86.07** Acute hematogenous osteomyelitis, ankle and foot

　M86.071 Acute hematogenous osteomyelitis, right ankle and foot

　M86.072 Acute hematogenous osteomyelitis, left ankle and foot

　M86.079 Acute hematogenous osteomyelitis, unspecified ankle and foot

　M86.08 Acute hematogenous osteomyelitis, other sites

　M86.09 Acute hematogenous osteomyelitis, multiple sites

● **M86.1　Other acute** osteomyelitis

　M86.10 Other acute osteomyelitis, unspecified site

　● **M86.11** Other acute osteomyelitis, shoulder

　　M86.111 Other acute osteomyelitis, right shoulder

　　M86.112 Other acute osteomyelitis, left shoulder

　　M86.119 Other acute osteomyelitis, unspecified shoulder

　● **M86.12** Other acute osteomyelitis, humerus

　　M86.121 Other acute osteomyelitis, right humerus

　　M86.122 Other acute osteomyelitis, left humerus

　　M86.129 Other acute osteomyelitis, unspecified humerus

　● **M86.13** Other acute osteomyelitis, radius and ulna

　　M86.131 Other acute osteomyelitis, right radius and ulna

　　M86.132 Other acute osteomyelitis, left radius and ulna

　　M86.139 Other acute osteomyelitis, unspecified radius and ulna

　● **M86.14** Other acute osteomyelitis, hand

　　M86.141 Other acute osteomyelitis, right hand

　　M86.142 Other acute osteomyelitis, left hand

　　M86.149 Other acute osteomyelitis, unspecified hand

　● **M86.15** Other acute osteomyelitis, femur

　　M86.151 Other acute osteomyelitis, right femur

　　M86.152 Other acute osteomyelitis, left femur

　　M86.159 Other acute osteomyelitis, unspecified femur

　● **M86.16** Other acute osteomyelitis, tibia and fibula

　　M86.161 Other acute osteomyelitis, right tibia and fibula

　　M86.162 Other acute osteomyelitis, left tibia and fibula

　　M86.169 Other acute osteomyelitis, unspecified tibia and fibula

▶ New　⇒ Revised　~~deleted~~ Deleted　Excludes 1　Excludes 2　Includes　Use additional　Code first　Code also　Key words

OGCR Official Guidelines　X Assign placeholder X　● Use Additional Character(s)　▌ Manifestation Code　**Coding Clinic**

● M86.17   Other acute osteomyelitis, ankle and foot

    M86.171   Other acute osteomyelitis, right ankle and foot

    M86.172   Other acute osteomyelitis, left ankle and foot

    M86.179   Other acute osteomyelitis, unspecified ankle and foot

   M86.18   Other acute osteomyelitis, other site

   M86.19   Other acute osteomyelitis, multiple sites

● M86.2   Subacute osteomyelitis

   M86.20   Subacute osteomyelitis, unspecified site

● M86.21   Subacute osteomyelitis, shoulder

    M86.211   Subacute osteomyelitis, right shoulder

    M86.212   Subacute osteomyelitis, left shoulder

    M86.219   Subacute osteomyelitis, unspecified shoulder

● M86.22   Subacute osteomyelitis, humerus

    M86.221   Subacute osteomyelitis, right humerus

    M86.222   Subacute osteomyelitis, left humerus

    M86.229   Subacute osteomyelitis, unspecified humerus

● M86.23   Subacute osteomyelitis, radius and ulna

    M86.231   Subacute osteomyelitis, right radius and ulna

    M86.232   Subacute osteomyelitis, left radius and ulna

    M86.239   Subacute osteomyelitis, unspecified radius and ulna

● M86.24   Subacute osteomyelitis, hand

    M86.241   Subacute osteomyelitis, right hand

    M86.242   Subacute osteomyelitis, left hand

    M86.249   Subacute osteomyelitis, unspecified hand

● M86.25   Subacute osteomyelitis, femur

    M86.251   Subacute osteomyelitis, right femur

    M86.252   Subacute osteomyelitis, left femur

    M86.259   Subacute osteomyelitis, unspecified femur

● M86.26   Subacute osteomyelitis, tibia and fibula

    M86.261   Subacute osteomyelitis, right tibia and fibula

    M86.262   Subacute osteomyelitis, left tibia and fibula

    M86.269   Subacute osteomyelitis, unspecified tibia and fibula

● M86.27   Subacute osteomyelitis, ankle and foot

    M86.271   Subacute osteomyelitis, right ankle and foot

    M86.272   Subacute osteomyelitis, left ankle and foot

    M86.279   Subacute osteomyelitis, unspecified ankle and foot

   M86.28   Subacute osteomyelitis, other site

   M86.29   Subacute osteomyelitis, multiple sites

● M86.3   Chronic multifocal osteomyelitis

   M86.30   Chronic multifocal osteomyelitis, unspecified site

● M86.31   Chronic multifocal osteomyelitis, shoulder

    M86.311   Chronic multifocal osteomyelitis, right shoulder

    M86.312   Chronic multifocal osteomyelitis, left shoulder

    M86.319   Chronic multifocal osteomyelitis, unspecified shoulder

● M86.32   Chronic multifocal osteomyelitis, humerus

    M86.321   Chronic multifocal osteomyelitis, right humerus

    M86.322   Chronic multifocal osteomyelitis, left humerus

    M86.329   Chronic multifocal osteomyelitis, unspecified humerus

● M86.33   Chronic multifocal osteomyelitis, radius and ulna

    M86.331   Chronic multifocal osteomyelitis, right radius and ulna

    M86.332   Chronic multifocal osteomyelitis, left radius and ulna

    M86.339   Chronic multifocal osteomyelitis, unspecified radius and ulna

● M86.34   Chronic multifocal osteomyelitis, hand

    M86.341   Chronic multifocal osteomyelitis, right hand

    M86.342   Chronic multifocal osteomyelitis, left hand

    M86.349   Chronic multifocal osteomyelitis, unspecified hand

● M86.35   Chronic multifocal osteomyelitis, femur

    M86.351   Chronic multifocal osteomyelitis, right femur

    M86.352   Chronic multifocal osteomyelitis, left femur

    M86.359   Chronic multifocal osteomyelitis, unspecified femur

● M86.36   Chronic multifocal osteomyelitis, tibia and fibula

    M86.361   Chronic multifocal osteomyelitis, right tibia and fibula

    M86.362   Chronic multifocal osteomyelitis, left tibia and fibula

    M86.369   Chronic multifocal osteomyelitis, unspecified tibia and fibula

● M86.37   Chronic multifocal osteomyelitis, ankle and foot

    M86.371   Chronic multifocal osteomyelitis, right ankle and foot

    M86.372   Chronic multifocal osteomyelitis, left ankle and foot

    M86.379   Chronic multifocal osteomyelitis, unspecified ankle and foot

   M86.38   Chronic multifocal osteomyelitis, other site

   M86.39   Chronic multifocal osteomyelitis, multiple sites

● M86.4   Chronic osteomyelitis with draining sinus

   M86.40   Chronic osteomyelitis with draining sinus, unspecified site

● M86.41   Chronic osteomyelitis with draining sinus, shoulder

    M86.411   Chronic osteomyelitis with draining sinus, right shoulder

    M86.412   Chronic osteomyelitis with draining sinus, left shoulder

    M86.419   Chronic osteomyelitis with draining sinus, unspecified shoulder

● M86.42   Chronic osteomyelitis with draining sinus, humerus

    M86.421   Chronic osteomyelitis with draining sinus, right humerus

    M86.422   Chronic osteomyelitis with draining sinus, left humerus

    M86.429   Chronic osteomyelitis with draining sinus, unspecified humerus

CHAPTER 13 (M00-M99)

CHAPTER 13 (M00–M99)

● M86.43 Chronic osteomyelitis with draining sinus, radius and ulna
    M86.431 Chronic osteomyelitis with draining sinus, right radius and ulna
    M86.432 Chronic osteomyelitis with draining sinus, left radius and ulna
    M86.439 Chronic osteomyelitis with draining sinus, unspecified radius and ulna
● M86.44 Chronic osteomyelitis with draining sinus, hand
    M86.441 Chronic osteomyelitis with draining sinus, right hand
    M86.442 Chronic osteomyelitis with draining sinus, left hand
    M86.449 Chronic osteomyelitis with draining sinus, unspecified hand
● M86.45 Chronic osteomyelitis with draining sinus, femur
    M86.451 Chronic osteomyelitis with draining sinus, right femur
    M86.452 Chronic osteomyelitis with draining sinus, left femur
    M86.459 Chronic osteomyelitis with draining sinus, unspecified femur
● M86.46 Chronic osteomyelitis with draining sinus, tibia and fibula
    M86.461 Chronic osteomyelitis with draining sinus, right tibia and fibula
    M86.462 Chronic osteomyelitis with draining sinus, left tibia and fibula
    M86.469 Chronic osteomyelitis with draining sinus, unspecified tibia and fibula
● M86.47 Chronic osteomyelitis with draining sinus, ankle and foot
    M86.471 Chronic osteomyelitis with draining sinus, right ankle and foot
    M86.472 Chronic osteomyelitis with draining sinus, left ankle and foot
    M86.479 Chronic osteomyelitis with draining sinus, unspecified ankle and foot
  M86.48 Chronic osteomyelitis with draining sinus, other site
  M86.49 Chronic osteomyelitis with draining sinus, multiple sites
● M86.5 Other chronic hematogenous osteomyelitis
  M86.50 Other chronic hematogenous osteomyelitis, unspecified site
● M86.51 Other chronic hematogenous osteomyelitis, shoulder
    M86.511 Other chronic hematogenous osteomyelitis, right shoulder
    M86.512 Other chronic hematogenous osteomyelitis, left shoulder
    M86.519 Other chronic hematogenous osteomyelitis, unspecified shoulder
● M86.52 Other chronic hematogenous osteomyelitis, humerus
    M86.521 Other chronic hematogenous osteomyelitis, right humerus
    M86.522 Other chronic hematogenous osteomyelitis, left humerus
    M86.529 Other chronic hematogenous osteomyelitis, unspecified humerus

● M86.53 Other chronic hematogenous osteomyelitis, radius and ulna
    M86.531 Other chronic hematogenous osteomyelitis, right radius and ulna
    M86.532 Other chronic hematogenous osteomyelitis, left radius and ulna
    M86.539 Other chronic hematogenous osteomyelitis, unspecified radius and ulna
● M86.54 Other chronic hematogenous osteomyelitis, hand
    M86.541 Other chronic hematogenous osteomyelitis, right hand
    M86.542 Other chronic hematogenous osteomyelitis, left hand
    M86.549 Other chronic hematogenous osteomyelitis, unspecified hand
● M86.55 Other chronic hematogenous osteomyelitis, femur
    M86.551 Other chronic hematogenous osteomyelitis, right femur
    M86.552 Other chronic hematogenous osteomyelitis, left femur
    M86.559 Other chronic hematogenous osteomyelitis, unspecified femur
● M86.56 Other chronic hematogenous osteomyelitis, tibia and fibula
    M86.561 Other chronic hematogenous osteomyelitis, right tibia and fibula
    M86.562 Other chronic hematogenous osteomyelitis, left tibia and fibula
    M86.569 Other chronic hematogenous osteomyelitis, unspecified tibia and fibula
● M86.57 Other chronic hematogenous osteomyelitis, ankle and foot
    M86.571 Other chronic hematogenous osteomyelitis, right ankle and foot
    M86.572 Other chronic hematogenous osteomyelitis, left ankle and foot
    M86.579 Other chronic hematogenous osteomyelitis, unspecified ankle and foot
  M86.58 Other chronic hematogenous osteomyelitis, other site
  M86.59 Other chronic hematogenous osteomyelitis, multiple sites
● M86.6 Other chronic osteomyelitis
  M86.60 Other chronic osteomyelitis, unspecified site
● M86.61 Other chronic osteomyelitis, shoulder
    M86.611 Other chronic osteomyelitis, right shoulder
    M86.612 Other chronic osteomyelitis, left shoulder
    M86.619 Other chronic osteomyelitis, unspecified shoulder
● M86.62 Other chronic osteomyelitis, humerus
    M86.621 Other chronic osteomyelitis, right humerus
    M86.622 Other chronic osteomyelitis, left humerus
    M86.629 Other chronic osteomyelitis, unspecified humerus
● M86.63 Other chronic osteomyelitis, radius and ulna
    M86.631 Other chronic osteomyelitis, right radius and ulna
    M86.632 Other chronic osteomyelitis, left radius and ulna
    M86.639 Other chronic osteomyelitis, unspecified radius and ulna

▶ New   ⇒ Revised   ~~deleted~~ Deleted   Excludes 1   Excludes 2   Includes   Use additional   Code first   Code also   Key words

OGCR Official Guidelines   X Assign placeholder X   ▷ Use Additional Character(s)   ▷ Manifestation Code   **Coding Clinic**

● **M86.64**   Other chronic osteomyelitis, hand
    M86.641   Other chronic osteomyelitis, right hand
    M86.642   Other chronic osteomyelitis, left hand
    M86.649   Other chronic osteomyelitis, unspecified hand

● **M86.65**   Other chronic osteomyelitis, thigh
    M86.651   Other chronic osteomyelitis, right thigh
    M86.652   Other chronic osteomyelitis, left thigh
    M86.659   Other chronic osteomyelitis, unspecified thigh

● **M86.66**   Other chronic osteomyelitis, tibia and fibula
    M86.661   Other chronic osteomyelitis, right tibia and fibula
    M86.662   Other chronic osteomyelitis, left tibia and fibula
    M86.669   Other chronic osteomyelitis, unspecified tibia and fibula

● **M86.67**   Other chronic osteomyelitis, ankle and foot
    M86.671   Other chronic osteomyelitis, right ankle and foot
       Coding Clinic: 2016, Q1, P13
    M86.672   Other chronic osteomyelitis, left ankle and foot
    M86.679   Other chronic osteomyelitis, unspecified ankle and foot

    M86.68   Other chronic osteomyelitis, other site
    M86.69   Other chronic osteomyelitis, multiple sites

● **M86.8**   Other osteomyelitis
    Brodie's abscess
  ● **M86.8X**   Other osteomyelitis
    M86.8X0   Other osteomyelitis, multiple sites
    M86.8X1   Other osteomyelitis, shoulder
    M86.8X2   Other osteomyelitis, upper arm
    M86.8X3   Other osteomyelitis, forearm
    M86.8X4   Other osteomyelitis, hand
    M86.8X5   Other osteomyelitis, thigh
    M86.8X6   Other osteomyelitis, lower leg
    M86.8X7   Other osteomyelitis, ankle and foot
    M86.8X8   Other osteomyelitis, other site
    M86.8X9   Other osteomyelitis, unspecified sites

  M86.9   Osteomyelitis, unspecified
    Infection of bone NOS
    Periostitis without osteomyelitis

● **M87**   **Osteonecrosis**
    Includes   avascular necrosis of bone
    Use additional code to identify major osseous defect, if applicable (M89.7-)
    Excludes1   juvenile osteonecrosis (M91-M92)
         osteochondropathies (M90-M93)

  ● **M87.0**   Idiopathic aseptic necrosis of bone
    M87.00   Idiopathic aseptic necrosis of unspecified bone
   ● M87.01   Idiopathic aseptic necrosis of shoulder
       Idiopathic aseptic necrosis of clavicle and scapula
    M87.011   Idiopathic aseptic necrosis of right shoulder
    M87.012   Idiopathic aseptic necrosis of left shoulder
    M87.019   Idiopathic aseptic necrosis of unspecified shoulder

● **M87.02**   Idiopathic aseptic necrosis of humerus
    M87.021   Idiopathic aseptic necrosis of right humerus
    M87.022   Idiopathic aseptic necrosis of left humerus
    M87.029   Idiopathic aseptic necrosis of unspecified humerus

● **M87.03**   Idiopathic aseptic necrosis of radius, ulna and carpus
    M87.031   Idiopathic aseptic necrosis of right radius
    M87.032   Idiopathic aseptic necrosis of left radius
    M87.033   Idiopathic aseptic necrosis of unspecified radius
    M87.034   Idiopathic aseptic necrosis of right ulna
    M87.035   Idiopathic aseptic necrosis of left ulna
    M87.036   Idiopathic aseptic necrosis of unspecified ulna
    M87.037   Idiopathic aseptic necrosis of right carpus
    M87.038   Idiopathic aseptic necrosis of left carpus
    M87.039   Idiopathic aseptic necrosis of unspecified carpus

● **M87.04**   Idiopathic aseptic necrosis of hand and fingers
    Idiopathic aseptic necrosis of metacarpals and phalanges of hands
    M87.041   Idiopathic aseptic necrosis of right hand
    M87.042   Idiopathic aseptic necrosis of left hand
    M87.043   Idiopathic aseptic necrosis of unspecified hand
    M87.044   Idiopathic aseptic necrosis of right finger(s)
    M87.045   Idiopathic aseptic necrosis of left finger(s)
    M87.046   Idiopathic aseptic necrosis of unspecified finger(s)

● **M87.05**   Idiopathic aseptic necrosis of pelvis and femur
    M87.050   Idiopathic aseptic necrosis of pelvis
    M87.051   Idiopathic aseptic necrosis of right femur
    M87.052   Idiopathic aseptic necrosis of left femur
    M87.059   Idiopathic aseptic necrosis of unspecified femur
       Idiopathic aseptic necrosis of hip NOS

● **M87.06**   Idiopathic aseptic necrosis of tibia and fibula
    M87.061   Idiopathic aseptic necrosis of right tibia
    M87.062   Idiopathic aseptic necrosis of left tibia
    M87.063   Idiopathic aseptic necrosis of unspecified tibia
    M87.064   Idiopathic aseptic necrosis of right fibula
    M87.065   Idiopathic aseptic necrosis of left fibula
    M87.066   Idiopathic aseptic necrosis of unspecified fibula

CHAPTER 13 (M00-M99)

● **M87.07** Idiopathic aseptic necrosis of ankle, foot and toes
  Idiopathic aseptic necrosis of metatarsus, tarsus, and phalanges of toes
  M87.071 Idiopathic aseptic necrosis of right ankle
  M87.072 Idiopathic aseptic necrosis of left ankle
  M87.073 Idiopathic aseptic necrosis of unspecified ankle
  M87.074 Idiopathic aseptic necrosis of right foot
  M87.075 Idiopathic aseptic necrosis of left foot
  M87.076 Idiopathic aseptic necrosis of unspecified foot
  M87.077 Idiopathic aseptic necrosis of right toe(s)
  M87.078 Idiopathic aseptic necrosis of left toe(s)
  M87.079 Idiopathic aseptic necrosis of unspecified toe(s)
  M87.08 Idiopathic aseptic necrosis of bone, other site
  M87.09 Idiopathic aseptic necrosis of bone, multiple sites

● **M87.1** Osteonecrosis due to drugs
  Use additional code for adverse effect, if applicable, to identify drug (T36-T50 with fifth or sixth character 5)
  M87.10 Osteonecrosis due to drugs, unspecified bone
● M87.11 Osteonecrosis due to drugs, shoulder
  M87.111 Osteonecrosis due to drugs, right shoulder
  M87.112 Osteonecrosis due to drugs, left shoulder
  M87.119 Osteonecrosis due to drugs, unspecified shoulder
● M87.12 Osteonecrosis due to drugs, humerus
  M87.121 Osteonecrosis due to drugs, right humerus
  M87.122 Osteonecrosis due to drugs, left humerus
  M87.129 Osteonecrosis due to drugs, unspecified humerus
● M87.13 Osteonecrosis due to drugs of radius, ulna and carpus
  M87.131 Osteonecrosis due to drugs of right radius
  M87.132 Osteonecrosis due to drugs of left radius
  M87.133 Osteonecrosis due to drugs of unspecified radius
  M87.134 Osteonecrosis due to drugs of right ulna
  M87.135 Osteonecrosis due to drugs of left ulna
  M87.136 Osteonecrosis due to drugs of unspecified ulna
  M87.137 Osteonecrosis due to drugs of right carpus
  M87.138 Osteonecrosis due to drugs of left carpus
  M87.139 Osteonecrosis due to drugs of unspecified carpus

● **M87.14** Osteonecrosis due to drugs, hand and fingers
  M87.141 Osteonecrosis due to drugs, right hand
  M87.142 Osteonecrosis due to drugs, left hand
  M87.143 Osteonecrosis due to drugs, unspecified hand
  M87.144 Osteonecrosis due to drugs, right finger(s)
  M87.145 Osteonecrosis due to drugs, left finger(s)
  M87.146 Osteonecrosis due to drugs, unspecified finger(s)
● M87.15 Osteonecrosis due to drugs, pelvis and femur
  M87.150 Osteonecrosis due to drugs, pelvis
  M87.151 Osteonecrosis due to drugs, right femur
  M87.152 Osteonecrosis due to drugs, left femur
  M87.159 Osteonecrosis due to drugs, unspecified femur
● M87.16 Osteonecrosis due to drugs, tibia and fibula
  M87.161 Osteonecrosis due to drugs, right tibia
  M87.162 Osteonecrosis due to drugs, left tibia
  M87.163 Osteonecrosis due to drugs, unspecified tibia
  M87.164 Osteonecrosis due to drugs, right fibula
  M87.165 Osteonecrosis due to drugs, left fibula
  M87.166 Osteonecrosis due to drugs, unspecified fibula
● M87.17 Osteonecrosis due to drugs, ankle, foot and toes
  M87.171 Osteonecrosis due to drugs, right ankle
  M87.172 Osteonecrosis due to drugs, left ankle
  M87.173 Osteonecrosis due to drugs, unspecified ankle
  M87.174 Osteonecrosis due to drugs, right foot
  M87.175 Osteonecrosis due to drugs, left foot
  M87.176 Osteonecrosis due to drugs, unspecified foot
  M87.177 Osteonecrosis due to drugs, right toe(s)
  M87.178 Osteonecrosis due to drugs, left toe(s)
  M87.179 Osteonecrosis due to drugs, unspecified toe(s)
● M87.18 Osteonecrosis due to drugs, other site
  M87.180 Osteonecrosis due to drugs, jaw
  M87.188 Osteonecrosis due to drugs, other site
  M87.19 Osteonecrosis due to drugs, multiple sites
● **M87.2** Osteonecrosis due to previous trauma
  M87.20 Osteonecrosis due to previous trauma, unspecified bone
● M87.21 Osteonecrosis due to previous trauma, shoulder
  M87.211 Osteonecrosis due to previous trauma, right shoulder
  M87.212 Osteonecrosis due to previous trauma, left shoulder
  M87.219 Osteonecrosis due to previous trauma, unspecified shoulder
● M87.22 Osteonecrosis due to previous trauma, humerus
  M87.221 Osteonecrosis due to previous trauma, right humerus
  M87.222 Osteonecrosis due to previous trauma, left humerus
  M87.229 Osteonecrosis due to previous trauma, unspecified humerus

▶ New   ⇒ Revised   deleted Deleted   Excludes 1   Excludes 2   Includes   Use additional   Code first   Code also   Key words
OGCR Official Guidelines   X Assign placeholder X   ● Use Additional Character(s)   ▶ Manifestation Code   **Coding Clinic**

● M87.23 Osteonecrosis due to previous trauma of radius, ulna and carpus

    M87.231 Osteonecrosis due to previous trauma of right radius

    M87.232 Osteonecrosis due to previous trauma of left radius

    M87.233 Osteonecrosis due to previous trauma of unspecified radius

    M87.234 Osteonecrosis due to previous trauma of right ulna

    M87.235 Osteonecrosis due to previous trauma of left ulna

    M87.236 Osteonecrosis due to previous trauma of unspecified ulna

    M87.237 Osteonecrosis due to previous trauma of right carpus

    M87.238 Osteonecrosis due to previous trauma of left carpus

    M87.239 Osteonecrosis due to previous trauma of unspecified carpus

● M87.24 Osteonecrosis due to previous trauma, hand and fingers

    M87.241 Osteonecrosis due to previous trauma, right hand

    M87.242 Osteonecrosis due to previous trauma, left hand

    M87.243 Osteonecrosis due to previous trauma, unspecified hand

    M87.244 Osteonecrosis due to previous trauma, right finger(s)

    M87.245 Osteonecrosis due to previous trauma, left finger(s)

    M87.246 Osteonecrosis due to previous trauma, unspecified finger(s)

● M87.25 Osteonecrosis due to previous trauma, pelvis and femur

    M87.250 Osteonecrosis due to previous trauma, pelvis

    M87.251 Osteonecrosis due to previous trauma, right femur

    M87.252 Osteonecrosis due to previous trauma, left femur

    M87.256 Osteonecrosis due to previous trauma, unspecified femur

● M87.26 Osteonecrosis due to previous trauma, tibia and fibula

    M87.261 Osteonecrosis due to previous trauma, right tibia

    M87.262 Osteonecrosis due to previous trauma, left tibia

    M87.263 Osteonecrosis due to previous trauma, unspecified tibia

    M87.264 Osteonecrosis due to previous trauma, right fibula

    M87.265 Osteonecrosis due to previous trauma, left fibula

    M87.266 Osteonecrosis due to previous trauma, unspecified fibula

● M87.27 Osteonecrosis due to previous trauma, ankle, foot and toes

    M87.271 Osteonecrosis due to previous trauma, right ankle

    M87.272 Osteonecrosis due to previous trauma, left ankle

    M87.273 Osteonecrosis due to previous trauma, unspecified ankle

    M87.274 Osteonecrosis due to previous trauma, right foot

    M87.275 Osteonecrosis due to previous trauma, left foot

    M87.276 Osteonecrosis due to previous trauma, unspecified foot

    M87.277 Osteonecrosis due to previous trauma, right toe(s)

    M87.278 Osteonecrosis due to previous trauma, left toe(s)

    M87.279 Osteonecrosis due to previous trauma, unspecified toe(s)

  M87.28 Osteonecrosis due to previous trauma, other site

  M87.29 Osteonecrosis due to previous trauma, multiple sites

● M87.3 Other secondary osteonecrosis

  M87.30 Other secondary osteonecrosis, unspecified bone

● M87.31 Other secondary osteonecrosis, shoulder

    M87.311 Other secondary osteonecrosis, right shoulder

    M87.312 Other secondary osteonecrosis, left shoulder

    M87.319 Other secondary osteonecrosis, unspecified shoulder

● M87.32 Other secondary osteonecrosis, humerus

    M87.321 Other secondary osteonecrosis, right humerus

    M87.322 Other secondary osteonecrosis, left humerus

    M87.329 Other secondary osteonecrosis, unspecified humerus

● M87.33 Other secondary osteonecrosis of radius, ulna and carpus

    M87.331 Other secondary osteonecrosis of right radius

    M87.332 Other secondary osteonecrosis of left radius

    M87.333 Other secondary osteonecrosis of unspecified radius

    M87.334 Other secondary osteonecrosis of right ulna

    M87.335 Other secondary osteonecrosis of left ulna

    M87.336 Other secondary osteonecrosis of unspecified ulna

    M87.337 Other secondary osteonecrosis of right carpus

    M87.338 Other secondary osteonecrosis of left carpus

    M87.339 Other secondary osteonecrosis of unspecified carpus

● M87.34 Other secondary osteonecrosis, hand and fingers

    M87.341 Other secondary osteonecrosis, right hand

    M87.342 Other secondary osteonecrosis, left hand

    M87.343 Other secondary osteonecrosis, unspecified hand

    M87.344 Other secondary osteonecrosis, right finger(s)

    M87.345 Other secondary osteonecrosis, left finger(s)

    M87.346 Other secondary osteonecrosis, unspecified finger(s)

CHAPTER 13 (MØØ-M99)

● M87.35 Other secondary osteonecrosis, pelvis and femur
  M87.350 Other secondary osteonecrosis, pelvis
  M87.351 Other secondary osteonecrosis, right femur
  M87.352 Other secondary osteonecrosis, left femur
  M87.353 Other secondary osteonecrosis, unspecified femur
● M87.36 Other secondary osteonecrosis, tibia and fibula
  M87.361 Other secondary osteonecrosis, right tibia
  M87.362 Other secondary osteonecrosis, left tibia
  M87.363 Other secondary osteonecrosis, unspecified tibia
  M87.364 Other secondary osteonecrosis, right fibula
  M87.365 Other secondary osteonecrosis, left fibula
  M87.366 Other secondary osteonecrosis, unspecified fibula
● M87.37 Other secondary osteonecrosis, ankle and foot
  M87.371 Other secondary osteonecrosis, right ankle
  M87.372 Other secondary osteonecrosis, left ankle
  M87.373 Other secondary osteonecrosis, unspecified ankle
  M87.374 Other secondary osteonecrosis, right foot
  M87.375 Other secondary osteonecrosis, left foot
  M87.376 Other secondary osteonecrosis, unspecified foot
  M87.377 Other secondary osteonecrosis, right toe(s)
  M87.378 Other secondary osteonecrosis, left toe(s)
  M87.379 Other secondary osteonecrosis, unspecified toe(s)
  M87.38 Other secondary osteonecrosis, other site
  M87.39 Other secondary osteonecrosis, multiple sites
● M87.8 Other osteonecrosis
  M87.80 Other osteonecrosis, unspecified bone
● M87.81 Other osteonecrosis, shoulder
  M87.811 Other osteonecrosis, right shoulder
  M87.812 Other osteonecrosis, left shoulder
  M87.819 Other osteonecrosis, unspecified shoulder
● M87.82 Other osteonecrosis, humerus
  M87.821 Other osteonecrosis, right humerus
  M87.822 Other osteonecrosis, left humerus
  M87.829 Other osteonecrosis, unspecified humerus
● M87.83 Other osteonecrosis of radius, ulna and carpus
  M87.831 Other osteonecrosis of right radius
  M87.832 Other osteonecrosis of left radius
  M87.833 Other osteonecrosis of unspecified radius
  M87.834 Other osteonecrosis of right ulna
  M87.835 Other osteonecrosis of left ulna
  M87.836 Other osteonecrosis of unspecified ulna
  M87.837 Other osteonecrosis of right carpus
  M87.838 Other osteonecrosis of left carpus
  M87.839 Other osteonecrosis of unspecified carpus

● M87.84 Other osteonecrosis, hand and fingers
  M87.841 Other osteonecrosis, right hand
  M87.842 Other osteonecrosis, left hand
  M87.843 Other osteonecrosis, unspecified hand
  M87.844 Other osteonecrosis, right finger(s)
  M87.845 Other osteonecrosis, left finger(s)
  M87.849 Other osteonecrosis, unspecified finger(s)
● M87.85 Other osteonecrosis, pelvis and femur
  M87.850 Other osteonecrosis, pelvis
  M87.851 Other osteonecrosis, right femur
  M87.852 Other osteonecrosis, left femur
  M87.859 Other osteonecrosis, unspecified femur
● M87.86 Other osteonecrosis, tibia and fibula
  M87.861 Other osteonecrosis, right tibia
  M87.862 Other osteonecrosis, left tibia
  M87.863 Other osteonecrosis, unspecified tibia
  M87.864 Other osteonecrosis, right fibula
  M87.865 Other osteonecrosis, left fibula
  M87.869 Other osteonecrosis, unspecified fibula
● M87.87 Other osteonecrosis, ankle, foot and toes
  M87.871 Other osteonecrosis, right ankle
  M87.872 Other osteonecrosis, left ankle
  M87.873 Other osteonecrosis, unspecified ankle
  M87.874 Other osteonecrosis, right foot
  M87.875 Other osteonecrosis, left foot
  M87.876 Other osteonecrosis, unspecified foot
  M87.877 Other osteonecrosis, right toe(s)
  M87.878 Other osteonecrosis, left toe(s)
  M87.879 Other osteonecrosis, unspecified toe(s)
  M87.88 Other osteonecrosis, other site
  M87.89 Other osteonecrosis, multiple sites
M87.9 Osteonecrosis, unspecified
  Necrosis of bone NOS

● M88 Osteitis deformans [Paget's disease of bone]
  Chronic disorder that results in enlarged and deformed bones. The excessive breakdown and formation of bone tissue causes bones to weaken and results in bone pain, arthritis, deformities, and fractures.
  Excludes1 osteitis deformans in neoplastic disease (M90.6)
M88.0 Osteitis deformans of skull
M88.1 Osteitis deformans of vertebrae
● M88.8 Osteitis deformans of other bones
  ● M88.81 Osteitis deformans of shoulder
    M88.811 Osteitis deformans of right shoulder
    M88.812 Osteitis deformans of left shoulder
    M88.819 Osteitis deformans of unspecified shoulder
  ● M88.82 Osteitis deformans of upper arm
    M88.821 Osteitis deformans of right upper arm
    M88.822 Osteitis deformans of left upper arm
    M88.829 Osteitis deformans of unspecified upper arm
  ● M88.83 Osteitis deformans of forearm
    M88.831 Osteitis deformans of right forearm
    M88.832 Osteitis deformans of left forearm
    M88.839 Osteitis deformans of unspecified forearm

▶ New   ⟹ Revised   ~~deleted~~ Deleted   Excludes 1   Excludes 2   Includes   Use additional   Code first   Code also   Key words

OGCR Official Guidelines   X Assign placeholder X   ● Use Additional Character(s)   ▶ Manifestation Code   **Coding Clinic**

- M88.84   Osteitis deformans of hand
  - M88.841   Osteitis deformans of right hand
  - M88.842   Osteitis deformans of left hand
  - M88.849   Osteitis deformans of unspecified hand
- M88.85   Osteitis deformans of thigh
  - M88.851   Osteitis deformans of right thigh
  - M88.852   Osteitis deformans of left thigh
  - M88.859   Osteitis deformans of unspecified thigh
- M88.86   Osteitis deformans of lower leg
  - M88.861   Osteitis deformans of right lower leg
  - M88.862   Osteitis deformans of left lower leg
  - M88.869   Osteitis deformans of unspecified lower leg
- M88.87   Osteitis deformans of ankle and foot
  - M88.871   Osteitis deformans of right ankle and foot
  - M88.872   Osteitis deformans of left ankle and foot
  - M88.879   Osteitis deformans of unspecified ankle and foot
- M88.88   Osteitis deformans of other bones
  - **Excludes2**   osteitis deformans of skull (M88.0)
    - osteitis deformans of vertebrae (M88.1)
- M88.89   Osteitis deformans of multiple sites
- M88.9   Osteitis deformans of unspecified bone

- M89   **Other disorders of bone**
  - M89.0   **Algoneurodystrophy**
    - Shoulder-hand syndrome
    - Sudeck's atrophy
    - **Excludes1**   causalgia, lower limb (G57.7-)
      - causalgia, upper limb (G56.4-)
      - complex regional pain syndrome II, lower limb (G57.7-)
      - complex regional pain syndrome II, upper limb (G56.4-)
      - reflex sympathetic dystrophy (G90.5-)
    - M89.00   Algoneurodystrophy, unspecified site
    - M89.01   Algoneurodystrophy, shoulder
      - M89.011   Algoneurodystrophy, right shoulder
      - M89.012   Algoneurodystrophy, left shoulder
      - M89.019   Algoneurodystrophy, unspecified shoulder
    - M89.02   Algoneurodystrophy, upper arm
      - M89.021   Algoneurodystrophy, right upper arm
      - M89.022   Algoneurodystrophy, left upper arm
      - M89.029   Algoneurodystrophy, unspecified upper arm
    - M89.03   Algoneurodystrophy, forearm
      - M89.031   Algoneurodystrophy, right forearm
      - M89.032   Algoneurodystrophy, left forearm
      - M89.039   Algoneurodystrophy, unspecified forearm
    - M89.04   Algoneurodystrophy, hand
      - M89.041   Algoneurodystrophy, right hand
      - M89.042   Algoneurodystrophy, left hand
      - M89.049   Algoneurodystrophy, unspecified hand
    - M89.05   Algoneurodystrophy, thigh
      - M89.051   Algoneurodystrophy, right thigh
      - M89.052   Algoneurodystrophy, left thigh
      - M89.059   Algoneurodystrophy, unspecified thigh

  - M89.06   Algoneurodystrophy, lower leg
    - M89.061   Algoneurodystrophy, right lower leg
    - M89.062   Algoneurodystrophy, left lower leg
    - M89.069   Algoneurodystrophy, unspecified lower leg
  - M89.07   Algoneurodystrophy, ankle and foot
    - M89.071   Algoneurodystrophy, right ankle and foot
    - M89.072   Algoneurodystrophy, left ankle and foot
    - M89.079   Algoneurodystrophy, unspecified ankle and foot
  - M89.08   Algoneurodystrophy, other site
  - M89.09   Algoneurodystrophy, multiple sites
  - M89.1   **Physeal arrest**
    - Arrest of growth plate
    - Epiphyseal arrest
    - Growth plate arrest
    - M89.12   Physeal arrest, humerus
      - M89.121   Complete physeal arrest, right proximal humerus
      - M89.122   Complete physeal arrest, left proximal humerus
      - M89.123   Partial physeal arrest, right proximal humerus
      - M89.124   Partial physeal arrest, left proximal humerus
      - M89.125   Complete physeal arrest, right distal humerus
      - M89.126   Complete physeal arrest, left distal humerus
      - M89.127   Partial physeal arrest, right distal humerus
      - M89.128   Partial physeal arrest, left distal humerus
      - M89.129   Physeal arrest, humerus, unspecified
    - M89.13   Physeal arrest, forearm
      - M89.131   Complete physeal arrest, right distal radius
      - M89.132   Complete physeal arrest, left distal radius
      - M89.133   Partial physeal arrest, right distal radius
      - M89.134   Partial physeal arrest, left distal radius
      - M89.138   Other physeal arrest of forearm
      - M89.139   Physeal arrest, forearm, unspecified
    - M89.15   Physeal arrest, femur
      - M89.151   Complete physeal arrest, right proximal femur
      - M89.152   Complete physeal arrest, left proximal femur
      - M89.153   Partial physeal arrest, right proximal femur
      - M89.154   Partial physeal arrest, left proximal femur
      - M89.155   Complete physeal arrest, right distal femur
      - M89.156   Complete physeal arrest, left distal femur
      - M89.157   Partial physeal arrest, right distal femur
      - M89.158   Partial physeal arrest, left distal femur
      - M89.159   Physeal arrest, femur, unspecified

CHAPTER 13 (M00–M99)

CHAPTER 13 (M00-M99)

● M89.16 Physeal arrest, lower leg
- M89.160 Complete physeal arrest, right proximal tibia
- M89.161 Complete physeal arrest, left proximal tibia
- M89.162 Partial physeal arrest, right proximal tibia
- M89.163 Partial physeal arrest, left proximal tibia
- M89.164 Complete physeal arrest, right distal tibia
- M89.165 Complete physeal arrest, left distal tibia
- M89.166 Partial physeal arrest, right distal tibia
- M89.167 Partial physeal arrest, left distal tibia
- M89.168 Other physeal arrest of lower leg
- M89.169 Physeal arrest, lower leg, unspecified

M89.18 Physeal arrest, other site

● M89.2 Other disorders of bone development and growth

M89.20 Other disorders of bone development and growth, unspecified site

● M89.21 Other disorders of bone development and growth, shoulder
- M89.211 Other disorders of bone development and growth, right shoulder
- M89.212 Other disorders of bone development and growth, left shoulder
- M89.219 Other disorders of bone development and growth, unspecified shoulder

● M89.22 Other disorders of bone development and growth, humerus
- M89.221 Other disorders of bone development and growth, right humerus
- M89.222 Other disorders of bone development and growth, left humerus
- M89.229 Other disorders of bone development and growth, unspecified humerus

● M89.23 Other disorders of bone development and growth, ulna and radius
- M89.231 Other disorders of bone development and growth, right ulna
- M89.232 Other disorders of bone development and growth, left ulna
- M89.233 Other disorders of bone development and growth, right radius
- M89.234 Other disorders of bone development and growth, left radius
- M89.239 Other disorders of bone development and growth, unspecified ulna and radius

● M89.24 Other disorders of bone development and growth, hand
- M89.241 Other disorders of bone development and growth, right hand
- M89.242 Other disorders of bone development and growth, left hand
- M89.249 Other disorders of bone development and growth, unspecified hand

● M89.25 Other disorders of bone development and growth, femur
- M89.251 Other disorders of bone development and growth, right femur
- M89.252 Other disorders of bone development and growth, left femur
- M89.259 Other disorders of bone development and growth, unspecified femur

● M89.26 Other disorders of bone development and growth, tibia and fibula
- M89.261 Other disorders of bone development and growth, right tibia
- M89.262 Other disorders of bone development and growth, left tibia
- M89.263 Other disorders of bone development and growth, right fibula
- M89.264 Other disorders of bone development and growth, left fibula
- M89.269 Other disorders of bone development and growth, unspecified lower leg

● M89.27 Other disorders of bone development and growth, ankle and foot
- M89.271 Other disorders of bone development and growth, right ankle and foot
- M89.272 Other disorders of bone development and growth, left ankle and foot
- M89.279 Other disorders of bone development and growth, unspecified ankle and foot

M89.28 Other disorders of bone development and growth, other site

M89.29 Other disorders of bone development and growth, multiple sites

● M89.3 Hypertrophy of bone

M89.30 Hypertrophy of bone, unspecified site

● M89.31 Hypertrophy of bone, shoulder
- M89.311 Hypertrophy of bone, right shoulder
- M89.312 Hypertrophy of bone, left shoulder
- M89.319 Hypertrophy of bone, unspecified shoulder

● M89.32 Hypertrophy of bone, humerus
- M89.321 Hypertrophy of bone, right humerus
- M89.322 Hypertrophy of bone, left humerus
- M89.329 Hypertrophy of bone, unspecified humerus

● M89.33 Hypertrophy of bone, ulna and radius
- M89.331 Hypertrophy of bone, right ulna
- M89.332 Hypertrophy of bone, left ulna
- M89.333 Hypertrophy of bone, right radius
- M89.334 Hypertrophy of bone, left radius
- M89.339 Hypertrophy of bone, unspecified ulna and radius

● M89.34 Hypertrophy of bone, hand
- M89.341 Hypertrophy of bone, right hand
- M89.342 Hypertrophy of bone, left hand
- M89.349 Hypertrophy of bone, unspecified hand

● M89.35 Hypertrophy of bone, femur
- M89.351 Hypertrophy of bone, right femur
- M89.352 Hypertrophy of bone, left femur
- M89.359 Hypertrophy of bone, unspecified femur

● M89.36 Hypertrophy of bone, tibia and fibula
- M89.361 Hypertrophy of bone, right tibia
- M89.362 Hypertrophy of bone, left tibia
- M89.363 Hypertrophy of bone, right fibula
- M89.364 Hypertrophy of bone, left fibula
- M89.369 Hypertrophy of bone, unspecified tibia and fibula

- M89.37   Hypertrophy of bone, ankle and foot
  - M89.371   Hypertrophy of bone, right ankle and foot
  - M89.372   Hypertrophy of bone, left ankle and foot
  - M89.379   Hypertrophy of bone, unspecified ankle and foot
  - M89.38   Hypertrophy of bone, other site
  - M89.39   Hypertrophy of bone, multiple sites
- M89.4   Other hypertrophic osteoarthropathy
  Marie-Bamberger disease
  Pachydermoperiostosis
  - M89.40   Other hypertrophic osteoarthropathy, unspecified site
- M89.41   Other hypertrophic osteoarthropathy, shoulder
  - M89.411   Other hypertrophic osteoarthropathy, right shoulder
  - M89.412   Other hypertrophic osteoarthropathy, left shoulder
  - M89.419   Other hypertrophic osteoarthropathy, unspecified shoulder
- M89.42   Other hypertrophic osteoarthropathy, upper arm
  - M89.421   Other hypertrophic osteoarthropathy, right upper arm
  - M89.422   Other hypertrophic osteoarthropathy, left upper arm
  - M89.429   Other hypertrophic osteoarthropathy, unspecified upper arm
- M89.43   Other hypertrophic osteoarthropathy, forearm
  - M89.431   Other hypertrophic osteoarthropathy, right forearm
  - M89.432   Other hypertrophic osteoarthropathy, left forearm
  - M89.439   Other hypertrophic osteoarthropathy, unspecified forearm
- M89.44   Other hypertrophic osteoarthropathy, hand
  - M89.441   Other hypertrophic osteoarthropathy, right hand
  - M89.442   Other hypertrophic osteoarthropathy, left hand
  - M89.449   Other hypertrophic osteoarthropathy, unspecified hand
- M89.45   Other hypertrophic osteoarthropathy, thigh
  - M89.451   Other hypertrophic osteoarthropathy, right thigh
  - M89.452   Other hypertrophic osteoarthropathy, left thigh
  - M89.459   Other hypertrophic osteoarthropathy, unspecified thigh
- M89.46   Other hypertrophic osteoarthropathy, lower leg
  - M89.461   Other hypertrophic osteoarthropathy, right lower leg
  - M89.462   Other hypertrophic osteoarthropathy, left lower leg
  - M89.469   Other hypertrophic osteoarthropathy, unspecified lower leg
- M89.47   Other hypertrophic osteoarthropathy, ankle and foot
  - M89.471   Other hypertrophic osteoarthropathy, right ankle and foot
  - M89.472   Other hypertrophic osteoarthropathy, left ankle and foot
  - M89.479   Other hypertrophic osteoarthropathy, unspecified ankle and foot
  - M89.48   Other hypertrophic osteoarthropathy, other site
  - M89.49   Other hypertrophic osteoarthropathy, multiple sites

- M89.5   Osteolysis
  Use additional code to identify major osseous defect, if applicable (M89.7-)
  Excludes2   periprosthetic osteolysis of internal prosthetic joint (T84.05-)
  - M89.50   Osteolysis, unspecified site
- M89.51   Osteolysis, shoulder
  - M89.511   Osteolysis, right shoulder
  - M89.512   Osteolysis, left shoulder
  - M89.519   Osteolysis, unspecified shoulder
- M89.52   Osteolysis, upper arm
  - M89.521   Osteolysis, right upper arm
  - M89.522   Osteolysis, left upper arm
  - M89.529   Osteolysis, unspecified upper arm
- M89.53   Osteolysis, forearm
  - M89.531   Osteolysis, right forearm
  - M89.532   Osteolysis, left forearm
  - M89.539   Osteolysis, unspecified forearm
- M89.54   Osteolysis, hand
  - M89.541   Osteolysis, right hand
  - M89.542   Osteolysis, left hand
  - M89.549   Osteolysis, unspecified hand
- M89.55   Osteolysis, thigh
  - M89.551   Osteolysis, right thigh
  - M89.552   Osteolysis, left thigh
  - M89.559   Osteolysis, unspecified thigh
- M89.56   Osteolysis, lower leg
  - M89.561   Osteolysis, right lower leg
  - M89.562   Osteolysis, left lower leg
  - M89.569   Osteolysis, unspecified lower leg
- M89.57   Osteolysis, ankle and foot
  - M89.571   Osteolysis, right ankle and foot
  - M89.572   Osteolysis, left ankle and foot
  - M89.579   Osteolysis, unspecified ankle and foot
  - M89.58   Osteolysis, other site
  - M89.59   Osteolysis, multiple sites
- M89.6   Osteopathy after poliomyelitis
  Use additional code (B91) to identify previous poliomyelitis
  Excludes1   postpolio syndrome (G14)
  - M89.60   Osteopathy after poliomyelitis, unspecified site
- M89.61   Osteopathy after poliomyelitis, shoulder
  - M89.611   Osteopathy after poliomyelitis, right shoulder
  - M89.612   Osteopathy after poliomyelitis, left shoulder
  - M89.619   Osteopathy after poliomyelitis, unspecified shoulder
- M89.62   Osteopathy after poliomyelitis, upper arm
  - M89.621   Osteopathy after poliomyelitis, right upper arm
  - M89.622   Osteopathy after poliomyelitis, left upper arm
  - M89.629   Osteopathy after poliomyelitis, unspecified upper arm
- M89.63   Osteopathy after poliomyelitis, forearm
  - M89.631   Osteopathy after poliomyelitis, right forearm
  - M89.632   Osteopathy after poliomyelitis, left forearm
  - M89.639   Osteopathy after poliomyelitis, unspecified forearm

CHAPTER 13 (M00-M99)

● **M89.64** Osteopathy after poliomyelitis, hand
    M89.641 Osteopathy after poliomyelitis, right hand
    M89.642 Osteopathy after poliomyelitis, left hand
    M89.649 Osteopathy after poliomyelitis, unspecified hand

● **M89.65** Osteopathy after poliomyelitis, thigh
    M89.651 Osteopathy after poliomyelitis, right thigh
    M89.652 Osteopathy after poliomyelitis, left thigh
    M89.659 Osteopathy after poliomyelitis, unspecified thigh

● **M89.66** Osteopathy after poliomyelitis, lower leg
    M89.661 Osteopathy after poliomyelitis, right lower leg
    M89.662 Osteopathy after poliomyelitis, left lower leg
    M89.669 Osteopathy after poliomyelitis, unspecified lower leg

● **M89.67** Osteopathy after poliomyelitis, ankle and foot
    M89.671 Osteopathy after poliomyelitis, right ankle and foot
    M89.672 Osteopathy after poliomyelitis, left ankle and foot
    M89.679 Osteopathy after poliomyelitis, unspecified ankle and foot

  M89.68 Osteopathy after poliomyelitis, other site
  M89.69 Osteopathy after poliomyelitis, multiple sites

● **M89.7** **Major osseous defect**
    Code first underlying disease, if known, such as:
      aseptic necrosis of bone (M87.-)
      malignant neoplasm of bone (C40.-)
      osteolysis (M89.5)
      osteomyelitis (M86.-)
      osteonecrosis (M87.-)
      osteoporosis (M80.-, M81.-)
      periprosthetic osteolysis (T84.05-)

  M89.70 Major osseous defect, unspecified site

● **M89.71** Major osseous defect, shoulder region
    Major osseous defect clavicle or scapula
    M89.711 Major osseous defect, right shoulder region
    M89.712 Major osseous defect, left shoulder region
    M89.719 Major osseous defect, unspecified shoulder region

● **M89.72** Major osseous defect, humerus
    M89.721 Major osseous defect, right humerus
    M89.722 Major osseous defect, left humerus
    M89.729 Major osseous defect, unspecified humerus

● **M89.73** Major osseous defect, forearm
    Major osseous defect of radius and ulna
    M89.731 Major osseous defect, right forearm
    M89.732 Major osseous defect, left forearm
    M89.739 Major osseous defect, unspecified forearm

● **M89.74** Major osseous defect, hand
    Major osseous defect of carpus, fingers, metacarpus
    M89.741 Major osseous defect, right hand
    M89.742 Major osseous defect, left hand
    M89.749 Major osseous defect, unspecified hand

● **M89.75** Major osseous defect, pelvic region and thigh
    Major osseous defect of femur and pelvis
    M89.751 Major osseous defect, right pelvic region and thigh
    M89.752 Major osseous defect, left pelvic region and thigh
    M89.759 Major osseous defect, unspecified pelvic region and thigh

● **M89.76** Major osseous defect, lower leg
    Major osseous defect of fibula and tibia
    M89.761 Major osseous defect, right lower leg
    M89.762 Major osseous defect, left lower leg
    M89.769 Major osseous defect, unspecified lower leg

● **M89.77** Major osseous defect, ankle and foot
    Major osseous defect of metatarsus, tarsus, toes
    M89.771 Major osseous defect, right ankle and foot
    M89.772 Major osseous defect, left ankle and foot
    M89.779 Major osseous defect, unspecified ankle and foot

  M89.78 Major osseous defect, other site
  M89.79 Major osseous defect, multiple sites

● **M89.8** **Other specified disorders** of bone
    Infantile cortical hyperostoses
    Post-traumatic subperiosteal ossification

● **M89.8X** Other specified disorders of bone
    M89.8X0 Other specified disorders of bone, multiple sites
    M89.8X1 Other specified disorders of bone, shoulder
    M89.8X2 Other specified disorders of bone, upper arm
    M89.8X3 Other specified disorders of bone, forearm
    M89.8X4 Other specified disorders of bone, hand
    M89.8X5 Other specified disorders of bone, thigh
    M89.8X6 Other specified disorders of bone, lower leg
    M89.8X7 Other specified disorders of bone, ankle and foot
    M89.8X8 Other specified disorders of bone, other site
    M89.8X9 Other specified disorders of bone, unspecified site

  M89.9 Disorder of bone, unspecified

▶ New   ⇒ Revised   ~~deleted~~ Deleted   Excludes 1   Excludes 2   Includes   Use additional   Code first   Code also   Key words
OGCR Official Guidelines   X Assign placeholder X   ● Use Additional Character(s)   ▌ Manifestation Code   **Coding Clinic**

●M90   Osteopathies in diseases classified elsewhere

     Excludes1   osteochondritis, osteomyelitis, and osteopathy (in):
         cryptococcosis (B45.3)
         diabetes mellitus (E08-E13 with .69-)
         gonococcal (A54.43)
         neurogenic syphilis (A52.11)
         renal osteodystrophy (N25.0)
         salmonellosis (A02.24)
         secondary syphilis (A51.46)
         syphilis (late) (A52.77)

●M90.5   Osteonecrosis in diseases classified elsewhere

     Code first underlying disease, such as:
         caisson disease (T70.3)
         hemoglobinopathy (D50-D64)

   ▌*M90.50*   *Osteonecrosis in diseases classified elsewhere, unspecified site*

   ●M90.51   Osteonecrosis in diseases classified elsewhere, shoulder

     ▌*M90.511*   *Osteonecrosis in diseases classified elsewhere, right shoulder*

     ▌*M90.512*   *Osteonecrosis in diseases classified elsewhere, left shoulder*

     ▌*M90.519*   *Osteonecrosis in diseases classified elsewhere, unspecified shoulder*

   ●M90.52   Osteonecrosis in diseases classified elsewhere, upper arm

     ▌*M90.521*   *Osteonecrosis in diseases classified elsewhere, right upper arm*

     ▌*M90.522*   *Osteonecrosis in diseases classified elsewhere, left upper arm*

     ▌*M90.529*   *Osteonecrosis in diseases classified elsewhere, unspecified upper arm*

   ●M90.53   Osteonecrosis in diseases classified elsewhere, forearm

     ▌*M90.531*   *Osteonecrosis in diseases classified elsewhere, right forearm*

     ▌*M90.532*   *Osteonecrosis in diseases classified elsewhere, left forearm*

     ▌*M90.539*   *Osteonecrosis in diseases classified elsewhere, unspecified forearm*

   ●M90.54   Osteonecrosis in diseases classified elsewhere, hand

     ▌*M90.541*   *Osteonecrosis in diseases classified elsewhere, right hand*

     ▌*M90.542*   *Osteonecrosis in diseases classified elsewhere, left hand*

     ▌*M90.549*   *Osteonecrosis in diseases classified elsewhere, unspecified hand*

   ●M90.55   Osteonecrosis in diseases classified elsewhere, thigh

     ▌*M90.551*   *Osteonecrosis in diseases classified elsewhere, right thigh*

     ▌*M90.552*   *Osteonecrosis in diseases classified elsewhere, left thigh*

     ▌*M90.559*   *Osteonecrosis in diseases classified elsewhere, unspecified thigh*

   ●M90.56   Osteonecrosis in diseases classified elsewhere, lower leg

     ▌*M90.561*   *Osteonecrosis in diseases classified elsewhere, right lower leg*

     ▌*M90.562*   *Osteonecrosis in diseases classified elsewhere, left lower leg*

     ▌*M90.569*   *Osteonecrosis in diseases classified elsewhere, unspecified lower leg*

   ●M90.57   Osteonecrosis in diseases classified elsewhere, ankle and foot

     ▌*M90.571*   *Osteonecrosis in diseases classified elsewhere, right ankle and foot*

     ▌*M90.572*   *Osteonecrosis in diseases classified elsewhere, left ankle and foot*

     ▌*M90.579*   *Osteonecrosis in diseases classified elsewhere, unspecified ankle and foot*

   ▌*M90.58*   *Osteonecrosis in diseases classified elsewhere, other site*

   ▌*M90.59*   *Osteonecrosis in diseases classified elsewhere, multiple sites*

●M90.6   Osteitis deformans in neoplastic diseases

     Osteitis deformans in malignant neoplasm of bone

     Code first the neoplasm (C40.-, C41.-)

     Excludes1   osteitis deformans [Paget's disease of bone] (M88.-)

   ▌*M90.60*   *Osteitis deformans in neoplastic diseases, unspecified site*

   ●M90.61   Osteitis deformans in neoplastic diseases, shoulder

     ▌*M90.611*   *Osteitis deformans in neoplastic diseases, right shoulder*

     ▌*M90.612*   *Osteitis deformans in neoplastic diseases, left shoulder*

     ▌*M90.619*   *Osteitis deformans in neoplastic diseases, unspecified shoulder*

   ●M90.62   Osteitis deformans in neoplastic diseases, upper arm

     ▌*M90.621*   *Osteitis deformans in neoplastic diseases, right upper arm*

     ▌*M90.622*   *Osteitis deformans in neoplastic diseases, left upper arm*

     ▌*M90.629*   *Osteitis deformans in neoplastic diseases, unspecified upper arm*

   ●M90.63   Osteitis deformans in neoplastic diseases, forearm

     ▌*M90.631*   *Osteitis deformans in neoplastic diseases, right forearm*

     ▌*M90.632*   *Osteitis deformans in neoplastic diseases, left forearm*

     ▌*M90.639*   *Osteitis deformans in neoplastic diseases, unspecified forearm*

   ●M90.64   Osteitis deformans in neoplastic diseases, hand

     ▌*M90.641*   *Osteitis deformans in neoplastic diseases, right hand*

     ▌*M90.642*   *Osteitis deformans in neoplastic diseases, left hand*

     ▌*M90.649*   *Osteitis deformans in neoplastic diseases, unspecified hand*

   ●M90.65   Osteitis deformans in neoplastic diseases, thigh

     ▌*M90.651*   *Osteitis deformans in neoplastic diseases, right thigh*

     ▌*M90.652*   *Osteitis deformans in neoplastic diseases, left thigh*

     ▌*M90.659*   *Osteitis deformans in neoplastic diseases, unspecified thigh*

   ●M90.66   Osteitis deformans in neoplastic diseases, lower leg

     ▌*M90.661*   *Osteitis deformans in neoplastic diseases, right lower leg*

     ▌*M90.662*   *Osteitis deformans in neoplastic diseases, left lower leg*

     ▌*M90.669*   *Osteitis deformans in neoplastic diseases, unspecified lower leg*

● M90.67 Osteitis deformans in neoplastic diseases, ankle and foot

▷ *M90.671 Osteitis deformans in neoplastic diseases, right ankle and foot*

▷ *M90.672 Osteitis deformans in neoplastic diseases, left ankle and foot*

▷ *M90.679 Osteitis deformans in neoplastic diseases, unspecified ankle and foot*

▷ *M90.68 Osteitis deformans in neoplastic diseases, other site*

▷ *M90.69 Osteitis deformans in neoplastic diseases, multiple sites*

● M90.8 Osteopathy in diseases classified elsewhere

Code first underlying disease, such as:
rickets (E55.0)
vitamin-D-resistant rickets (E83.3)

▷ *M90.80 Osteopathy in diseases classified elsewhere, unspecified site*

● M90.81 Osteopathy in diseases classified elsewhere, shoulder

▷ *M90.811 Osteopathy in diseases classified elsewhere, right shoulder*

▷ *M90.812 Osteopathy in diseases classified elsewhere, left shoulder*

▷ *M90.819 Osteopathy in diseases classified elsewhere, unspecified shoulder*

● M90.82 Osteopathy in diseases classified elsewhere, upper arm

▷ *M90.821 Osteopathy in diseases classified elsewhere, right upper arm*

▷ *M90.822 Osteopathy in diseases classified elsewhere, left upper arm*

▷ *M90.829 Osteopathy in diseases classified elsewhere, unspecified upper arm*

● M90.83 Osteopathy in diseases classified elsewhere, forearm

▷ *M90.831 Osteopathy in diseases classified elsewhere, right forearm*

▷ *M90.832 Osteopathy in diseases classified elsewhere, left forearm*

▷ *M90.839 Osteopathy in diseases classified elsewhere, unspecified forearm*

● M90.84 Osteopathy in diseases classified elsewhere, hand

▷ *M90.841 Osteopathy in diseases classified elsewhere, right hand*

▷ *M90.842 Osteopathy in diseases classified elsewhere, left hand*

▷ *M90.849 Osteopathy in diseases classified elsewhere, unspecified hand*

● M90.85 Osteopathy in diseases classified elsewhere, thigh

▷ *M90.851 Osteopathy in diseases classified elsewhere, right thigh*

▷ *M90.852 Osteopathy in diseases classified elsewhere, left thigh*

▷ *M90.859 Osteopathy in diseases classified elsewhere, unspecified thigh*

● M90.86 Osteopathy in diseases classified elsewhere, lower leg

▷ *M90.861 Osteopathy in diseases classified elsewhere, right lower leg*

▷ *M90.862 Osteopathy in diseases classified elsewhere, left lower leg*

▷ *M90.869 Osteopathy in diseases classified elsewhere, unspecified lower leg*

● M90.87 Osteopathy in diseases classified elsewhere, ankle and foot

▷ *M90.871 Osteopathy in diseases classified elsewhere, right ankle and foot*

▷ *M90.872 Osteopathy in diseases classified elsewhere, left ankle and foot*

▷ *M90.879 Osteopathy in diseases classified elsewhere, unspecified ankle and foot*

▷ *M90.88 Osteopathy in diseases classified elsewhere, other site*

▷ *M90.89 Osteopathy in diseases classified elsewhere, multiple sites*

CHONDROPATHIES (M91-M94)

Excludes1 postprocedural chondropathies (M96.-)

● M91 Juvenile osteochondrosis of hip and pelvis

Excludes1 slipped upper femoral epiphysis (nontraumatic) (M93.0)

M91.0 Juvenile osteochondrosis of pelvis
Osteochondrosis (juvenile) of acetabulum
Osteochondrosis (juvenile) of iliac crest [Buchanan]
Osteochondrosis (juvenile) of ischiopubic synchondrosis [van Neck]
Osteochondrosis (juvenile) of symphysis pubis [Pierson]

● M91.1 Juvenile osteochondrosis of head of femur [Legg-Calvé-Perthes]

M91.10 Juvenile osteochondrosis of head of femur [Legg-Calvé-Perthes], unspecified leg

M91.11 Juvenile osteochondrosis of head of femur [Legg-Calvé-Perthes], right leg

M91.12 Juvenile osteochondrosis of head of femur [Legg-Calvé-Perthes], left leg

● M91.2 Coxa plana
Hip deformity due to previous juvenile osteochondrosis

M91.20 Coxa plana, unspecified hip

M91.21 Coxa plana, right hip

M91.22 Coxa plana, left hip

● M91.3 Pseudocoxalgia

M91.30 Pseudocoxalgia, unspecified hip

M91.31 Pseudocoxalgia, right hip

M91.32 Pseudocoxalgia, left hip

● M91.4 Coxa magna

M91.40 Coxa magna, unspecified hip

M91.41 Coxa magna, right hip

M91.42 Coxa magna, left hip

● M91.8 Other juvenile osteochondrosis of hip and pelvis
Juvenile osteochondrosis after reduction of congenital dislocation of hip

M91.80 Other juvenile osteochondrosis of hip and pelvis, unspecified leg

M91.81 Other juvenile osteochondrosis of hip and pelvis, right leg

M91.82 Other juvenile osteochondrosis of hip and pelvis, left leg

● M91.9 Juvenile osteochondrosis of hip and pelvis, unspecified

M91.90 Juvenile osteochondrosis of hip and pelvis, unspecified, unspecified leg

M91.91 Juvenile osteochondrosis of hip and pelvis, unspecified, right leg

M91.92 Juvenile osteochondrosis of hip and pelvis, unspecified, left leg

▶ New ⇒ Revised ~~deleted~~ Deleted Excludes 1 Excludes 2 Includes Use additional Code first Code also Key words

OGCR Official Guidelines X Assign placeholder X ● Use Additional Character(s) ▷ Manifestation Code **Coding Clinic**

CHAPTER 13 (M00-M99)

● **M92   Other juvenile osteochondrosis**
  ● **M92.0   Juvenile osteochondrosis of humerus**
       Osteochondrosis (juvenile) of capitulum of humerus [Panner]
       Osteochondrosis (juvenile) of head of humerus [Haas]
     M92.00   Juvenile osteochondrosis of humerus, unspecified arm
     M92.01   Juvenile osteochondrosis of humerus, right arm
     M92.02   Juvenile osteochondrosis of humerus, left arm
  ● **M92.1   Juvenile osteochondrosis of radius and ulna**
       Osteochondrosis (juvenile) of lower ulna [Burns]
       Osteochondrosis (juvenile) of radial head [Brailsford]
     M92.10   Juvenile osteochondrosis of radius and ulna, unspecified arm
     M92.11   Juvenile osteochondrosis of radius and ulna, right arm
     M92.12   Juvenile osteochondrosis of radius and ulna, left arm
  ● **M92.2   Juvenile osteochondrosis, hand**
    ● **M92.20   Unspecified juvenile osteochondrosis, hand**
       M92.201   Unspecified juvenile osteochondrosis, right hand
       M92.202   Unspecified juvenile osteochondrosis, left hand
       M92.209   Unspecified juvenile osteochondrosis, unspecified hand
    ● **M92.21   Osteochondrosis (juvenile) of carpal lunate [Kienböck]**
       M92.211   Osteochondrosis (juvenile) of carpal lunate [Kienböck], right hand
       M92.212   Osteochondrosis (juvenile) of carpal lunate [Kienböck], left hand
       M92.219   Osteochondrosis (juvenile) of carpal lunate [Kienböck], unspecified hand
    ● **M92.22   Osteochondrosis (juvenile) of metacarpal heads [Mauclaire]**
       M92.221   Osteochondrosis (juvenile) of metacarpal heads [Mauclaire], right hand
       M92.222   Osteochondrosis (juvenile) of metacarpal heads [Mauclaire], left hand
       M92.229   Osteochondrosis (juvenile) of metacarpal heads [Mauclaire], unspecified hand
    ● **M92.29   Other juvenile osteochondrosis, hand**
       M92.291   Other juvenile osteochondrosis, right hand
       M92.292   Other juvenile osteochondrosis, left hand
       M92.299   Other juvenile osteochondrosis, unspecified hand
  ● **M92.3   Other juvenile osteochondrosis, upper limb**
     M92.30   Other juvenile osteochondrosis, unspecified upper limb
     M92.31   Other juvenile osteochondrosis, right upper limb
     M92.32   Other juvenile osteochondrosis, left upper limb
  ● **M92.4   Juvenile osteochondrosis of patella**
       Osteochondrosis (juvenile) of primary patellar center [Köhler]
       Osteochondrosis (juvenile) of secondary patellar center [Sinding Larsen]
     M92.40   Juvenile osteochondrosis of patella, unspecified knee
     M92.41   Juvenile osteochondrosis of patella, right knee
     M92.42   Juvenile osteochondrosis of patella, left knee

  ● **M92.5   Juvenile osteochondrosis of tibia and fibula**
       Osteochondrosis (juvenile) of proximal tibia [Blount]
       Osteochondrosis (juvenile) of tibial tubercle [Osgood-Schlatter]
       Tibia vara
     M92.50   Juvenile osteochondrosis of tibia and fibula, unspecified leg
     M92.51   Juvenile osteochondrosis of tibia and fibula, right leg
     M92.52   Juvenile osteochondrosis of tibia and fibula, left leg
  ● **M92.6   Juvenile osteochondrosis of tarsus**
       Osteochondrosis (juvenile) of calcaneum [Sever]
       Osteochondrosis (juvenile) of os tibiale externum [Haglund]
       Osteochondrosis (juvenile) of talus [Diaz]
       Osteochondrosis (juvenile) of tarsal navicular [Köhler]
     M92.60   Juvenile osteochondrosis of tarsus, unspecified ankle
     M92.61   Juvenile osteochondrosis of tarsus, right ankle
     M92.62   Juvenile osteochondrosis of tarsus, left ankle
  ● **M92.7   Juvenile osteochondrosis of metatarsus**
       Osteochondrosis (juvenile) of fifth metatarsus [Iselin]
       Osteochondrosis (juvenile) of second metatarsus [Freiberg]
     M92.70   Juvenile osteochondrosis of metatarsus, unspecified foot
     M92.71   Juvenile osteochondrosis of metatarsus, right foot
     M92.72   Juvenile osteochondrosis of metatarsus, left foot
     M92.8   Other specified juvenile osteochondrosis
       Calcaneal apophysitis
     M92.9   Juvenile osteochondrosis, unspecified
       Juvenile apophysitis NOS
       Juvenile epiphysitis NOS
       Juvenile osteochondritis NOS
       Juvenile osteochondrosis NOS

● **M93   Other osteochondropathies**
     Excludes2   osteochondrosis of spine (M42.-)
  ● **M93.0   Slipped upper femoral epiphysis (nontraumatic)**
       Use additional code for associated chondrolysis (M94.3)
    ● **M93.00   Unspecified slipped upper femoral epiphysis (nontraumatic)**
       M93.001   Unspecified slipped upper femoral epiphysis (nontraumatic), right hip
       M93.002   Unspecified slipped upper femoral epiphysis (nontraumatic), left hip
       M93.003   Unspecified slipped upper femoral epiphysis (nontraumatic), unspecified hip
    ● **M93.01   Acute slipped upper femoral epiphysis (nontraumatic)**
       M93.011   Acute slipped upper femoral epiphysis (nontraumatic), right hip
       M93.012   Acute slipped upper femoral epiphysis (nontraumatic), left hip
       M93.013   Acute slipped upper femoral epiphysis (nontraumatic), unspecified hip
    ● **M93.02   Chronic slipped upper femoral epiphysis (nontraumatic)**
       M93.021   Chronic slipped upper femoral epiphysis (nontraumatic), right hip
       M93.022   Chronic slipped upper femoral epiphysis (nontraumatic), left hip
       M93.023   Chronic slipped upper femoral epiphysis (nontraumatic), unspecified hip

CHAPTER 13 (M00-M99)

CHAPTER 13 (M00-M99)

● M93.03　Acute on chronic slipped upper femoral epiphysis (nontraumatic)
　　　M93.031　Acute on chronic slipped upper femoral epiphysis (nontraumatic), right hip
　　　M93.032　Acute on chronic slipped upper femoral epiphysis (nontraumatic), left hip
　　　M93.033　Acute on chronic slipped upper femoral epiphysis (nontraumatic), unspecified hip

M93.1　Kienböck's disease of adults　　　　　　　　　　A
　　　Adult osteochondrosis of carpal lunates

● M93.2　Osteochondritis dissecans
　　M93.20　Osteochondritis dissecans of unspecified site
　● M93.21　Osteochondritis dissecans of shoulder
　　　M93.211　Osteochondritis dissecans, right shoulder
　　　M93.212　Osteochondritis dissecans, left shoulder
　　　M93.219　Osteochondritis dissecans, unspecified shoulder
　● M93.22　Osteochondritis dissecans of elbow
　　　M93.221　Osteochondritis dissecans, right elbow
　　　M93.222　Osteochondritis dissecans, left elbow
　　　M93.229　Osteochondritis dissecans, unspecified elbow
　● M93.23　Osteochondritis dissecans of wrist
　　　M93.231　Osteochondritis dissecans, right wrist
　　　M93.232　Osteochondritis dissecans, left wrist
　　　M93.239　Osteochondritis dissecans, unspecified wrist
　● M93.24　Osteochondritis dissecans of joints of hand
　　　M93.241　Osteochondritis dissecans, joints of right hand
　　　M93.242　Osteochondritis dissecans, joints of left hand
　　　M93.249　Osteochondritis dissecans, joints of unspecified hand
　● M93.25　Osteochondritis dissecans of hip
　　　M93.251　Osteochondritis dissecans, right hip
　　　M93.252　Osteochondritis dissecans, left hip
　　　M93.259　Osteochondritis dissecans, unspecified hip
　● M93.26　Osteochondritis dissecans knee
　　　M93.261　Osteochondritis dissecans, right knee
　　　M93.262　Osteochondritis dissecans, left knee
　　　M93.269　Osteochondritis dissecans, unspecified knee
　● M93.27　Osteochondritis dissecans of ankle and joints of foot
　　　M93.271　Osteochondritis dissecans, right ankle and joints of right foot
　　　M93.272　Osteochondritis dissecans, left ankle and joints of left foot
　　　M93.279　Osteochondritis dissecans, unspecified ankle and joints of foot
　　M93.28　Osteochondritis dissecans other site
　　M93.29　Osteochondritis dissecans multiple sites

● M93.8　Other specified osteochondropathies
　　M93.80　Other specified osteochondropathies of unspecified site
　● M93.81　Other specified osteochondropathies of shoulder
　　　M93.811　Other specified osteochondropathies, right shoulder
　　　M93.812　Other specified osteochondropathies, left shoulder
　　　M93.819　Other specified osteochondropathies, unspecified shoulder
　● M93.82　Other specified osteochondropathies of upper arm
　　　M93.821　Other specified osteochondropathies, right upper arm
　　　M93.822　Other specified osteochondropathies, left upper arm
　　　M93.829　Other specified osteochondropathies, unspecified upper arm
　● M93.83　Other specified osteochondropathies of forearm
　　　M93.831　Other specified osteochondropathies, right forearm
　　　M93.832　Other specified osteochondropathies, left forearm
　　　M93.839　Other specified osteochondropathies, unspecified forearm
　● M93.84　Other specified osteochondropathies of hand
　　　M93.841　Other specified osteochondropathies, right hand
　　　M93.842　Other specified osteochondropathies, left hand
　　　M93.849　Other specified osteochondropathies, unspecified hand
　● M93.85　Other specified osteochondropathies of thigh
　　　M93.851　Other specified osteochondropathies, right thigh
　　　M93.852　Other specified osteochondropathies, left thigh
　　　M93.859　Other specified osteochondropathies, unspecified thigh
　● M93.86　Other specified osteochondropathies lower leg
　　　M93.861　Other specified osteochondropathies, right lower leg
　　　M93.862　Other specified osteochondropathies, left lower leg
　　　M93.869　Other specified osteochondropathies, unspecified lower leg
　● M93.87　Other specified osteochondropathies of ankle and foot
　　　M93.871　Other specified osteochondropathies, right ankle and foot
　　　M93.872　Other specified osteochondropathies, left ankle and foot
　　　M93.879　Other specified osteochondropathies, unspecified ankle and foot
　　M93.88　Other specified osteochondropathies other
　　M93.89　Other specified osteochondropathies multiple sites

▶ New　⇒ Revised　deleted Deleted　Excludes 1　Excludes 2　Includes　Use additional　Code first　Code also　Key words
OGCR Official Guidelines　X Assign placeholder X　● Use Additional Character(s)　▷ Manifestation Code　Coding Clinic

M93.9 Osteochondropathy, unspecified
     Apophysitis NOS
     Epiphysitis NOS
     Osteochondritis NOS
     Osteochondrosis NOS

    M93.90 Osteochondropathy, unspecified of unspecified site

  ● M93.91 Osteochondropathy, unspecified of shoulder
       M93.911 Osteochondropathy, unspecified, right shoulder
       M93.912 Osteochondropathy, unspecified, left shoulder
       M93.919 Osteochondropathy, unspecified, unspecified shoulder

  ● M93.92 Osteochondropathy, unspecified of upper arm
       M93.921 Osteochondropathy, unspecified, right upper arm
       M93.922 Osteochondropathy, unspecified, left upper arm
       M93.929 Osteochondropathy, unspecified, unspecified upper arm

  ● M93.93 Osteochondropathy, unspecified of forearm
       M93.931 Osteochondropathy, unspecified, right forearm
       M93.932 Osteochondropathy, unspecified, left forearm
       M93.939 Osteochondropathy, unspecified, unspecified forearm

  ● M93.94 Osteochondropathy, unspecified of hand
       M93.941 Osteochondropathy, unspecified, right hand
       M93.942 Osteochondropathy, unspecified, left hand
       M93.949 Osteochondropathy, unspecified, unspecified hand

  ● M93.95 Osteochondropathy, unspecified of thigh
       M93.951 Osteochondropathy, unspecified, right thigh
       M93.952 Osteochondropathy, unspecified, left thigh
       M93.959 Osteochondropathy, unspecified, unspecified thigh

  ● M93.96 Osteochondropathy, unspecified lower leg
       M93.961 Osteochondropathy, unspecified, right lower leg
       M93.962 Osteochondropathy, unspecified, left lower leg
       M93.969 Osteochondropathy, unspecified, unspecified lower leg

  ● M93.97 Osteochondropathy, unspecified of ankle and foot
       M93.971 Osteochondropathy, unspecified, right ankle and foot
       M93.972 Osteochondropathy, unspecified, left ankle and foot
       M93.979 Osteochondropathy, unspecified, unspecified ankle and foot

    M93.98 Osteochondropathy, unspecified other

    M93.99 Osteochondropathy, unspecified multiple sites

● M94 Other disorders of cartilage
  M94.0 Chondrocostal junction syndrome [Tietze]
     Costochondritis
  M94.1 Relapsing polychondritis
● M94.2 Chondromalacia
    Excludes1   chondromalacia patellae (M22.4)

    M94.20 Chondromalacia, unspecified site

  ● M94.21 Chondromalacia, shoulder
       M94.211 Chondromalacia, right shoulder
       M94.212 Chondromalacia, left shoulder
       M94.219 Chondromalacia, unspecified shoulder

  ● M94.22 Chondromalacia, elbow
       M94.221 Chondromalacia, right elbow
       M94.222 Chondromalacia, left elbow
       M94.229 Chondromalacia, unspecified elbow

  ● M94.23 Chondromalacia, wrist
       M94.231 Chondromalacia, right wrist
       M94.232 Chondromalacia, left wrist
       M94.239 Chondromalacia, unspecified wrist

  ● M94.24 Chondromalacia, joints of hand
       M94.241 Chondromalacia, joints of right hand
       M94.242 Chondromalacia, joints of left hand
       M94.249 Chondromalacia, joints of unspecified hand

  ● M94.25 Chondromalacia, hip
       M94.251 Chondromalacia, right hip
       M94.252 Chondromalacia, left hip
       M94.259 Chondromalacia, unspecified hip

  ● M94.26 Chondromalacia, knee
       M94.261 Chondromalacia, right knee
       M94.262 Chondromalacia, left knee
       M94.269 Chondromalacia, unspecified knee

  ● M94.27 Chondromalacia, ankle and joints of foot
       M94.271 Chondromalacia, right ankle and joints of right foot
       M94.272 Chondromalacia, left ankle and joints of left foot
       M94.279 Chondromalacia, unspecified ankle and joints of foot

    M94.28 Chondromalacia, other site

    M94.29 Chondromalacia, multiple sites

● M94.3 Chondrolysis
    Code first any associated slipped upper femoral epiphysis (nontraumatic) (M93.0-)

  ● M94.35 Chondrolysis, hip
       M94.351 Chondrolysis, right hip
       M94.352 Chondrolysis, left hip
       M94.359 Chondrolysis, unspecified hip

● M94.8 Other specified disorders of cartilage
  ● M94.8X Other specified disorders of cartilage
       M94.8X0 Other specified disorders of cartilage, multiple sites
       M94.8X1 Other specified disorders of cartilage, shoulder
       M94.8X2 Other specified disorders of cartilage, upper arm
       M94.8X3 Other specified disorders of cartilage, forearm

CHAPTER 13 (M00-M99)

M94.8X4   Other specified disorders of cartilage, hand

M94.8X5   Other specified disorders of cartilage, thigh

M94.8X6   Other specified disorders of cartilage, lower leg

M94.8X7   Other specified disorders of cartilage, ankle and foot

M94.8X8   Other specified disorders of cartilage, other site

M94.8X9   Other specified disorders of cartilage, unspecified sites

M94.9   Disorder of cartilage, unspecified

OTHER DISORDERS OF THE MUSCULOSKELETAL SYSTEM AND CONNECTIVE TISSUE (M95)

● M95   Other acquired deformities of musculoskeletal system and connective tissue

    Excludes2   acquired absence of limbs and organs (Z89-Z90)
       acquired deformities of limbs (M20-M21)
       congenital malformations and deformations of the musculoskeletal system (Q65-Q79)
       deforming dorsopathies (M40-M43)
       dentofacial anomalies [including malocclusion] (M26.-)
       postprocedural musculoskeletal disorders (M96.-)

M95.0   Acquired deformity of nose

    Excludes2   deviated nasal septum (J34.2)

● M95.1   Cauliflower ear

    Excludes2   other acquired deformities of ear (H61.1)

M95.10   Cauliflower ear, unspecified ear

M95.11   Cauliflower ear, right ear

M95.12   Cauliflower ear, left ear

M95.2   Other acquired deformity of head

M95.3   Acquired deformity of neck

M95.4   Acquired deformity of chest and rib

M95.5   Acquired deformity of pelvis

    Excludes1   maternal care for known or suspected disproportion (O33.-)

M95.8   Other specified acquired deformities of musculoskeletal system

M95.9   Acquired deformity of musculoskeletal system, unspecified

INTRAOPERATIVE AND POSTPROCEDURAL COMPLICATIONS AND DISORDERS OF MUSCULOSKELETAL SYSTEM, NOT ELSEWHERE CLASSIFIED (M96)

● M96   Intraoperative and postprocedural complications and disorders of musculoskeletal system, not elsewhere classified

    Excludes2   arthropathy following intestinal bypass (M02.0-)
       complications of internal orthopedic prosthetic devices, implants and grafts (T84.-)
       disorders associated with osteoporosis (M80)
       periprosthetic fracture around internal prosthetic joint (M97.-)
       presence of functional implants and other devices (Z96-Z97)

M96.0   Pseudarthrosis after fusion or arthrodesis

M96.1   Postlaminectomy syndrome, not elsewhere classified

M96.2   Postradiation kyphosis

M96.3   Postlaminectomy kyphosis

M96.4   Postsurgical lordosis

M96.5   Postradiation scoliosis

● M96.6   Fracture of bone following insertion of orthopedic implant, joint prosthesis, or bone plate
       Intraoperative fracture of bone during insertion of orthopedic implant, joint prosthesis, or bone plate

    Excludes2   complication of internal orthopedic devices, implants or grafts (T84.-)

● M96.62   Fracture of humerus following insertion of orthopedic implant, joint prosthesis, or bone plate

M96.621   Fracture of humerus following insertion of orthopedic implant, joint prosthesis, or bone plate, right arm

M96.622   Fracture of humerus following insertion of orthopedic implant, joint prosthesis, or bone plate, left arm

M96.629   Fracture of humerus following insertion of orthopedic implant, joint prosthesis, or bone plate, unspecified arm

● M96.63   Fracture of radius or ulna following insertion of orthopedic implant, joint prosthesis, or bone plate

M96.631   Fracture of radius or ulna following insertion of orthopedic implant, joint prosthesis, or bone plate, right arm

M96.632   Fracture of radius or ulna following insertion of orthopedic implant, joint prosthesis, or bone plate, left arm

M96.639   Fracture of radius or ulna following insertion of orthopedic implant, joint prosthesis, or bone plate, unspecified arm

M96.65   Fracture of pelvis following insertion of orthopedic implant, joint prosthesis, or bone plate

● M96.66   Fracture of femur following insertion of orthopedic implant, joint prosthesis, or bone plate

M96.661   Fracture of femur following insertion of orthopedic implant, joint prosthesis, or bone plate, right leg

M96.662   Fracture of femur following insertion of orthopedic implant, joint prosthesis, or bone plate, left leg

M96.669   Fracture of femur following insertion of orthopedic implant, joint prosthesis, or bone plate, unspecified leg

● M96.67   Fracture of tibia or fibula following insertion of orthopedic implant, joint prosthesis, or bone plate

M96.671   Fracture of tibia or fibula following insertion of orthopedic implant, joint prosthesis, or bone plate, right leg

M96.672   Fracture of tibia or fibula following insertion of orthopedic implant, joint prosthesis, or bone plate, left leg

M96.679   Fracture of tibia or fibula following insertion of orthopedic implant, joint prosthesis, or bone plate, unspecified leg

M96.69   Fracture of other bone following insertion of orthopedic implant, joint prosthesis, or bone plate

▶ New   ⇒ Revised   ~~deleted~~ Deleted   Excludes 1   Excludes 2   Includes   Use additional   Code first   Code also   Key words

OGCR Official Guidelines   X Assign placeholder X   ● Use Additional Character(s)   ▶ Manifestation Code   **Coding Clinic**

● **M96.8**   **Other intraoperative and postprocedural complications and disorders of musculoskeletal system, not elsewhere classified**
     Coding Clinic: 2016, Q4, P10

   ● **M96.81**   **Intraoperative hemorrhage and hematoma of a musculoskeletal structure complicating a procedure**

        Excludes1   intraoperative hemorrhage and hematoma of a musculoskeletal structure due to accidental puncture and laceration during a procedure (M96.82-)

       M96.810   Intraoperative hemorrhage and hematoma of a musculoskeletal structure complicating a musculoskeletal system procedure

       M96.811   Intraoperative hemorrhage and hematoma of a musculoskeletal structure complicating other procedure

   ● **M96.82**   **Accidental puncture and laceration of a musculoskeletal structure during a procedure**

       M96.820   Accidental puncture and laceration of a musculoskeletal structure during a musculoskeletal system procedure

       M96.821   Accidental puncture and laceration of a musculoskeletal structure during other procedure

   ● **M96.83**   **Postprocedural hemorrhage of a musculoskeletal structure following a procedure**

       M96.830   Postprocedural hemorrhage of a musculoskeletal structure following a musculoskeletal system procedure

       M96.831   Postprocedural hemorrhage of a musculoskeletal structure following other procedure

   ● **M96.84**   **Postprocedural hematoma and seroma of a musculoskeletal structure following a procedure**

       M96.840   Postprocedural hematoma of a musculoskeletal structure following a musculoskeletal system procedure

       M96.841   Postprocedural hematoma of a musculoskeletal structure following other procedure
         Coding Clinic: 2016, Q4, P10

       M96.842   Postprocedural seroma of a musculoskeletal structure following a musculoskeletal system procedure

       M96.843   Postprocedural seroma of a musculoskeletal structure following other procedure

   M96.89   **Other intraoperative and postprocedural complications and disorders of the musculoskeletal system**
       Instability of joint secondary to removal of joint prosthesis
       Use additional code, if applicable, to further specify disorder

PERIPROSTHETIC FRACTURE AROUND INTERNAL PROSTHETIC JOINT (M97)

● **M97**   **Periprosthetic fracture around internal prosthetic joint**

     Excludes2   fracture of bone following insertion of orthopedic implant, joint prosthesis or bone plate (M96.6-)
               breakage (fracture) of prosthetic joint (T84.01-)
     Coding Clinic: 2016, Q4, P42

     The appropriate 7th character is to be added to each code from category M97:

A	initial encounter
D	subsequent encounter
S	sequela

   ● **M97.0**   **Periprosthetic fracture around internal prosthetic hip joint**

    X ● **M97.01**   Periprosthetic fracture around internal prosthetic right hip joint
         Coding Clinic: 2016, Q4, P43

    X ● **M97.02**   Periprosthetic fracture around internal prosthetic left hip joint

   ● **M97.1**   **Periprosthetic fracture around internal prosthetic knee joint**

    X ● **M97.11**   Periprosthetic fracture around internal prosthetic right knee joint

    X ● **M97.12**   Periprosthetic fracture around internal prosthetic left knee joint

   ● **M97.2**   **Periprosthetic fracture around internal prosthetic ankle joint**

    X ● **M97.21**   Periprosthetic fracture around internal prosthetic right ankle joint

    X ● **M97.22**   Periprosthetic fracture around internal prosthetic left ankle joint

   ● **M97.3**   **Periprosthetic fracture around internal prosthetic shoulder joint**

    X ● **M97.31**   Periprosthetic fracture around internal prosthetic right shoulder joint

    X ● **M97.32**   Periprosthetic fracture around internal prosthetic left shoulder joint

   ● **M97.4**   **Periprosthetic fracture around internal prosthetic elbow joint**

    X ● **M97.41**   Periprosthetic fracture around internal prosthetic right elbow joint

    X ● **M97.42**   Periprosthetic fracture around internal prosthetic left elbow joint

   X ● **M97.8**   **Periprosthetic fracture around other internal prosthetic joint**
       Periprosthetic fracture around internal prosthetic finger joint
       Periprosthetic fracture around internal prosthetic spinal joint
       Periprosthetic fracture around internal prosthetic toe joint
       Periprosthetic fracture around internal prosthetic wrist joint
       Use additional code to identify the joint (Z96.6-)

   X ● **M97.9**   **Periprosthetic fracture around unspecified internal prosthetic joint**

CHAPTER 13 (M00-M99)

BIOMECHANICAL LESIONS, NOT ELSEWHERE CLASSIFIED (M99)

● **M99 Biomechanical lesions, not elsewhere classified**
   Note: This category should not be used if the condition can be classified elsewhere.
   ● **M99.0 Segmental and somatic dysfunction**
      M99.00 Segmental and somatic dysfunction of head region
      M99.01 Segmental and somatic dysfunction of cervical region
      M99.02 Segmental and somatic dysfunction of thoracic region
      M99.03 Segmental and somatic dysfunction of lumbar region
      M99.04 Segmental and somatic dysfunction of sacral region
      M99.05 Segmental and somatic dysfunction of pelvic region
      M99.06 Segmental and somatic dysfunction of lower extremity
      M99.07 Segmental and somatic dysfunction of upper extremity
      M99.08 Segmental and somatic dysfunction of rib cage
      M99.09 Segmental and somatic dysfunction of abdomen and other regions
   ● **M99.1 Subluxation complex (vertebral)**
      M99.10 Subluxation complex (vertebral) of head region
      M99.11 Subluxation complex (vertebral) of cervical region
      M99.12 Subluxation complex (vertebral) of thoracic region
      M99.13 Subluxation complex (vertebral) of lumbar region
      M99.14 Subluxation complex (vertebral) of sacral region
      M99.15 Subluxation complex (vertebral) of pelvic region
      M99.16 Subluxation complex (vertebral) of lower extremity
      M99.17 Subluxation complex (vertebral) of upper extremity
      M99.18 Subluxation complex (vertebral) of rib cage
      M99.19 Subluxation complex (vertebral) of abdomen and other regions
   ● **M99.2 Subluxation stenosis of neural canal**
      M99.20 Subluxation stenosis of neural canal of head region
      M99.21 Subluxation stenosis of neural canal of cervical region
      M99.22 Subluxation stenosis of neural canal of thoracic region
      M99.23 Subluxation stenosis of neural canal of lumbar region
      M99.24 Subluxation stenosis of neural canal of sacral region
      M99.25 Subluxation stenosis of neural canal of pelvic region
      M99.26 Subluxation stenosis of neural canal of lower extremity
      M99.27 Subluxation stenosis of neural canal of upper extremity
      M99.28 Subluxation stenosis of neural canal of rib cage
      M99.29 Subluxation stenosis of neural canal of abdomen and other regions

● **M99.3 Osseous stenosis of neural canal**
      M99.30 Osseous stenosis of neural canal of head region
      M99.31 Osseous stenosis of neural canal of cervical region
      M99.32 Osseous stenosis of neural canal of thoracic region
      M99.33 Osseous stenosis of neural canal of lumbar region
      M99.34 Osseous stenosis of neural canal of sacral region
      M99.35 Osseous stenosis of neural canal of pelvic region
      M99.36 Osseous stenosis of neural canal of lower extremity
      M99.37 Osseous stenosis of neural canal of upper extremity
      M99.38 Osseous stenosis of neural canal of rib cage
      M99.39 Osseous stenosis of neural canal of abdomen and other regions
   ● **M99.4 Connective tissue stenosis of neural canal**
      M99.40 Connective tissue stenosis of neural canal of head region
      M99.41 Connective tissue stenosis of neural canal of cervical region
      M99.42 Connective tissue stenosis of neural canal of thoracic region
      M99.43 Connective tissue stenosis of neural canal of lumbar region
      M99.44 Connective tissue stenosis of neural canal of sacral region
      M99.45 Connective tissue stenosis of neural canal of pelvic region
      M99.46 Connective tissue stenosis of neural canal of lower extremity
      M99.47 Connective tissue stenosis of neural canal of upper extremity
      M99.48 Connective tissue stenosis of neural canal of rib cage
      M99.49 Connective tissue stenosis of neural canal of abdomen and other regions
   ● **M99.5 Intervertebral disc stenosis of neural canal**
      M99.50 Intervertebral disc stenosis of neural canal of head region
      M99.51 Intervertebral disc stenosis of neural canal of cervical region
      M99.52 Intervertebral disc stenosis of neural canal of thoracic region
      M99.53 Intervertebral disc stenosis of neural canal of lumbar region
      M99.54 Intervertebral disc stenosis of neural canal of sacral region
      M99.55 Intervertebral disc stenosis of neural canal of pelvic region
      M99.56 Intervertebral disc stenosis of neural canal of lower extremity
      M99.57 Intervertebral disc stenosis of neural canal of upper extremity
      M99.58 Intervertebral disc stenosis of neural canal of rib cage
      M99.59 Intervertebral disc stenosis of neural canal of abdomen and other regions

▶ New   ⇒ Revised   deleted Deleted   Excludes 1   Excludes 2   Includes   Use additional   Code first   Code also   Key words
OGCR Official Guidelines   X Assign placeholder X   ● Use Additional Character(s)   ▶ Manifestation Code   **Coding Clinic**

● M99.6   Osseous and subluxation stenosis of intervertebral foramina

     M99.60   Osseous and subluxation stenosis of intervertebral foramina of head region

     M99.61   Osseous and subluxation stenosis of intervertebral foramina of cervical region

     M99.62   Osseous and subluxation stenosis of intervertebral foramina of thoracic region

     M99.63   Osseous and subluxation stenosis of intervertebral foramina of lumbar region

     M99.64   Osseous and subluxation stenosis of intervertebral foramina of sacral region

     M99.65   Osseous and subluxation stenosis of intervertebral foramina of pelvic region

     M99.66   Osseous and subluxation stenosis of intervertebral foramina of lower extremity

     M99.67   Osseous and subluxation stenosis of intervertebral foramina of upper extremity

     M99.68   Osseous and subluxation stenosis of intervertebral foramina of rib cage

     M99.69   Osseous and subluxation stenosis of intervertebral foramina of abdomen and other regions

● M99.7   Connective tissue and disc stenosis of intervertebral foramina

     M99.70   Connective tissue and disc stenosis of intervertebral foramina of head region

     M99.71   Connective tissue and disc stenosis of intervertebral foramina of cervical region

     M99.72   Connective tissue and disc stenosis of intervertebral foramina of thoracic region

     M99.73   Connective tissue and disc stenosis of intervertebral foramina of lumbar region

     M99.74   Connective tissue and disc stenosis of intervertebral foramina of sacral region

     M99.75   Connective tissue and disc stenosis of intervertebral foramina of pelvic region

     M99.76   Connective tissue and disc stenosis of intervertebral foramina of lower extremity

     M99.77   Connective tissue and disc stenosis of intervertebral foramina of upper extremity

     M99.78   Connective tissue and disc stenosis of intervertebral foramina of rib cage

     M99.79   Connective tissue and disc stenosis of intervertebral foramina of abdomen and other regions

● M99.8   Other biomechanical lesions

     M99.80   Other biomechanical lesions of head region

     M99.81   Other biomechanical lesions of cervical region

     M99.82   Other biomechanical lesions of thoracic region

     M99.83   Other biomechanical lesions of lumbar region

     M99.84   Other biomechanical lesions of sacral region

     M99.85   Other biomechanical lesions of pelvic region

     M99.86   Other biomechanical lesions of lower extremity

     M99.87   Other biomechanical lesions of upper extremity

     M99.88   Other biomechanical lesions of rib cage

     M99.89   Other biomechanical lesions of abdomen and other regions

     M99.9   Biomechanical lesion, unspecified

CHAPTER 13 (M00-M99)

CHAPTER 14

DISEASES OF THE GENITOURINARY SYSTEM (N00-N99)

OGCR Chapter-Specific Coding Guidelines

14. Chapter 14: Diseases of Genitourinary System (N00-N99)

 a. Chronic kidney disease

 1) Stages of chronic kidney disease (CKD)

The ICD-10-CM classifies CKD based on severity. The severity of CKD is designated by stages 1-5. Stage 2, code N18.2, equates to mild CKD; stage 3, code N18.3, equates to moderate CKD; and stage 4, code N18.4, equates to severe CKD. Code N18.6, End stage renal disease (ESRD), is assigned when the provider has documented end-stage-renal disease (ESRD).

 If both a stage of CKD and ESRD are documented, assign code N18.6 only.

 2) Chronic kidney disease and kidney transplant status

Patients who have undergone kidney transplant may still have some form of chronic kidney disease CKD because the kidney transplant may not fully restore kidney function. Therefore, the presence of CKD alone does not constitute a transplant complication. Assign the appropriate N18 code for the patient's stage of CKD and code Z94.0, Kidney transplant status. If a transplant complication such as failure or rejection or other transplant complication is documented, see Section I.C.19.g for information on coding complications of a kidney transplant. If the documentation is unclear as to whether the patient has a complication of the transplant, query the provider.

 3) Chronic kidney disease with other conditions

Patients with CKD may also suffer from other serious conditions, most commonly diabetes mellitus and hypertension. The sequencing of the CKD code in relationship to codes for other contributing conditions is based on the conventions in the Tabular List.

 See I.C.9. Hypertensive chronic kidney disease.
 See I.C.19. Chronic kidney disease and kidney transplant complications.

Item 14–1 Nephritis (inflammation) or **nephropathy** (disease) **with lesion of proliferative glomerulonephritis** results from a streptococcal infection.

Nephritis (inflammation) or **nephropathy** (disease) **with lesion of membranous glomerulonephritis** is characterized by deposits along the epithelial side of the basement membrane.

Nephritis (inflammation) or **nephropathy** (disease) **with lesion of membranoproliferative glomerulonephritis** is characterized by alterations in the basement membranes of the kidney and the glomerular cells.

Nephritis (inflammation) or **nephropathy** (disease) **with lesion of rapidly progressive glomerulonephritis** is characterized by rapid and progressive decline in renal function.

Nephritis (inflammation) or **nephropathy** (disease) **with lesion of renal cortical necrosis** is characterized by death of the cortical tissues.

Nephritis (inflammation) or **nephropathy** (disease) **with lesion of renal medullary necrosis** is characterized by death of the tissues that collect urine.

Item 14–2 Glomerulonephritis is nephritis accompanied by inflammation of the glomeruli of the kidney, resulting in the degeneration of the glomeruli and the nephrons.

Acute glomerulonephritis primarily affects children and young adults and is usually a result of a streptococcal infection.

Proliferative glomerulonephritis is the acute form of the disease resulting from a streptococcal infection.

Rapidly progressive glomerulonephritis, also known as **crescentic** or **malignant glomerulonephritis,** is the acute form of the disease, which leads quickly to rapid and progressive decline in renal function.

CHAPTER 14

DISEASES OF THE GENITOURINARY SYSTEM (N00-N99)

Excludes2 certain conditions originating in the perinatal period (P04-P96)

 certain infectious and parasitic diseases (A00-B99)

 complications of pregnancy, childbirth and the puerperium (O00-O9A)

 congenital malformations, deformations and chromosomal abnormalities (Q00-Q99)

 endocrine, nutritional and metabolic diseases (E00-E88)

 injury, poisoning and certain other consequences of external causes (S00-T88)

 neoplasms (C00-D49)

 symptoms, signs and abnormal clinical and laboratory findings, not elsewhere classified (R00-R94)

This chapter contains the following blocks:

N00-N08	Glomerular diseases
N10-N16	Renal tubulo-interstitial diseases
N17-N19	Acute kidney failure and chronic kidney disease
N20-N23	Urolithiasis
N25-N29	Other disorders of kidney and ureter
N30-N39	Other diseases of the urinary system
N40-N53	Diseases of male genital organs
N60-N65	Disorders of breast
N70-N77	Inflammatory diseases of female pelvic organs
N80-N98	Noninflammatory disorders of female genital tract
N99	Intraoperative and postprocedural complications and disorders of genitourinary system, not elsewhere classified

GLOMERULAR DISEASES (N00-N08)

Code also any associated kidney failure (N17-N19)

Excludes1 hypertensive chronic kidney disease (I12.-)

● **N00 Acute nephritic syndrome**

 Includes acute glomerular disease
 acute glomerulonephritis
 acute nephritis

 Excludes1 acute tubulo-interstitial nephritis (N10)
 nephritic syndrome NOS (N05.-)

 N00.0 Acute nephritic syndrome with minor glomerular abnormality
 Acute nephritic syndrome with minimal change lesion

 N00.1 Acute nephritic syndrome with focal and segmental glomerular lesions
 Acute nephritic syndrome with focal and segmental hyalinosis
 Acute nephritic syndrome with focal and segmental sclerosis
 Acute nephritic syndrome with focal glomerulonephritis

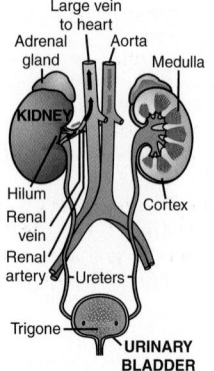

Figure 14-1 Kidneys within the urinary system.

▶ New   ⟾ Revised   ~~deleted~~ Deleted   Excludes 1   Excludes 2   Includes   Use additional   Code first   Code also   Key words

OGCR Official Guidelines   X Assign placeholder X   ● Use Additional Character(s)   ▷ Manifestation Code   **Coding Clinic**

N00.2   Acute nephritic syndrome with diffuse membranous glomerulonephritis

N00.3   Acute nephritic syndrome with diffuse mesangial proliferative glomerulonephritis

N00.4   Acute nephritic syndrome with diffuse endocapillary proliferative glomerulonephritis

N00.5   Acute nephritic syndrome with diffuse mesangiocapillary glomerulonephritis

Acute nephritic syndrome with membranoproliferative glomerulonephritis, types 1 and 3, or NOS

N00.6   Acute nephritic syndrome with dense deposit disease

Acute nephritic syndrome with membranoproliferative glomerulonephritis, type 2

N00.7   Acute nephritic syndrome with diffuse crescentic glomerulonephritis

Acute nephritic syndrome with extracapillary glomerulonephritis

N00.8   Acute nephritic syndrome with other morphologic changes

Acute nephritic syndrome with proliferative glomerulonephritis NOS

N00.9   Acute nephritic syndrome with unspecified morphologic changes

● **N01**   **Rapidly progressive nephritic syndrome**

Includes	rapidly progressive glomerular disease
	rapidly progressive glomerulonephritis
	rapidly progressive nephritis

Excludes1	nephritic syndrome NOS (N05.-)

N01.0   Rapidly progressive nephritic syndrome with minor glomerular abnormality

Rapidly progressive nephritic syndrome with minimal change lesion

N01.1   Rapidly progressive nephritic syndrome with focal and segmental glomerular lesions

Rapidly progressive nephritic syndrome with focal and segmental hyalinosis

Rapidly progressive nephritic syndrome with focal and segmental sclerosis

Rapidly progressive nephritic syndrome with focal glomerulonephritis

N01.2   Rapidly progressive nephritic syndrome with diffuse membranous glomerulonephritis

N01.3   Rapidly progressive nephritic syndrome with diffuse mesangial proliferative glomerulonephritis

N01.4   Rapidly progressive nephritic syndrome with diffuse endocapillary proliferative glomerulonephritis

N01.5   Rapidly progressive nephritic syndrome with diffuse mesangiocapillary glomerulonephritis

Rapidly progressive nephritic syndrome with membranoproliferative glomerulonephritis, types 1 and 3, or NOS

N01.6   Rapidly progressive nephritic syndrome with dense deposit disease

Rapidly progressive nephritic syndrome with membranoproliferative glomerulonephritis, type 2

N01.7   Rapidly progressive nephritic syndrome with diffuse crescentic glomerulonephritis

Rapidly progressive nephritic syndrome with extracapillary glomerulonephritis

N01.8   Rapidly progressive nephritic syndrome with other morphologic changes

Rapidly progressive nephritic syndrome with proliferative glomerulonephritis NOS

N01.9   Rapidly progressive nephritic syndrome with unspecified morphologic changes

● **N02**   **Recurrent and persistent hematuria**

Excludes1	acute cystitis with hematuria (N30.01)
	hematuria NOS (R31.9)
	hematuria not associated with specified morphologic lesions (R31.-)

N02.0   Recurrent and persistent hematuria with minor glomerular abnormality

Recurrent and persistent hematuria with minimal change lesion

N02.1   Recurrent and persistent hematuria with focal and segmental glomerular lesions

Recurrent and persistent hematuria with focal and segmental hyalinosis

Recurrent and persistent hematuria with focal and segmental sclerosis

Recurrent and persistent hematuria with focal glomerulonephritis

N02.2   Recurrent and persistent hematuria with diffuse membranous glomerulonephritis

N02.3   Recurrent and persistent hematuria with diffuse mesangial proliferative glomerulonephritis

N02.4   Recurrent and persistent hematuria with diffuse endocapillary proliferative glomerulonephritis

N02.5   Recurrent and persistent hematuria with diffuse mesangiocapillary glomerulonephritis

Recurrent and persistent hematuria with membranoproliferative glomerulonephritis, types 1 and 3, or NOS

N02.6   Recurrent and persistent hematuria with dense deposit disease

Recurrent and persistent hematuria with membranoproliferative glomerulonephritis, type 2

N02.7   Recurrent and persistent hematuria with diffuse crescentic glomerulonephritis

Recurrent and persistent hematuria with extracapillary glomerulonephritis

N02.8   Recurrent and persistent hematuria with other morphologic changes

Recurrent and persistent hematuria with proliferative glomerulonephritis NOS

N02.9   Recurrent and persistent hematuria with unspecified morphologic changes

Coding Clinic: 2017, Q2, P5

● **N03**   **Chronic nephritic syndrome**

Includes	chronic glomerular disease
	chronic glomerulonephritis
	chronic nephritis

Excludes1	chronic tubulo-interstitial nephritis (N11.-)
	diffuse sclerosing glomerulonephritis (N05.8-)
	nephritic syndrome NOS (N05.-)

N03.0   Chronic nephritic syndrome with minor glomerular abnormality

Chronic nephritic syndrome with minimal change lesion

N03.1   Chronic nephritic syndrome with focal and segmental glomerular lesions

Chronic nephritic syndrome with focal and segmental hyalinosis

Chronic nephritic syndrome with focal and segmental sclerosis

Chronic nephritic syndrome with focal glomerulonephritis

N03.2   Chronic nephritic syndrome with diffuse membranous glomerulonephritis

N03.3   Chronic nephritic syndrome with diffuse mesangial proliferative glomerulonephritis

N03.4   Chronic nephritic syndrome with diffuse endocapillary proliferative glomerulonephritis

Item 14–3 Chronic glomerulonephritis (GN) persists over a period of years, with remissions and exacerbation.

Chronic GN with lesion of proliferative glomerulonephritis results from a streptococcal infection.

Chronic GN with lesion of membranous glomerulonephritis, also known as membranous nephropathy, is characterized by deposits along the epithelial side of the basement membrane.

Chronic GN with lesion of membrano-proliferative glomerulonephritis (MPGN) is a group of disorders characterized by alterations in the basement membranes of the kidney and the glomerular cells.

Chronic GN with lesion of rapidly progressive glomerulonephritis is characterized by necrosis, endothelial proliferation, and mesangial proliferation. The condition is marked by rapid and progressive decline in renal function.

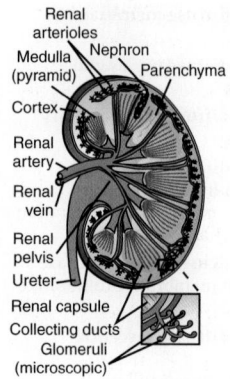

Figure 14-2   Kidney cross section.

Renal arterioles — Nephron — Medulla (pyramid) — Parenchyma — Cortex — Renal artery — Renal vein — Renal pelvis — Ureter — Renal capsule — Collecting ducts — Glomeruli (microscopic)

N03.5   **Chronic nephritic syndrome with diffuse mesangiocapillary glomerulonephritis**
      Chronic nephritic syndrome with membranoproliferative glomerulonephritis, types 1 and 3, or NOS

N03.6   **Chronic nephritic syndrome with dense deposit disease**
      Chronic nephritic syndrome with membranoproliferative glomerulonephritis, type 2

N03.7   **Chronic nephritic syndrome with diffuse crescentic glomerulonephritis**
      Chronic nephritic syndrome with extracapillary glomerulonephritis

N03.8   **Chronic nephritic syndrome with other morphologic changes**
      Chronic nephritic syndrome with proliferative glomerulonephritis NOS

N03.9   **Chronic nephritic syndrome with unspecified morphologic changes**

● N04   **Nephrotic syndrome**
      Includes   congenital nephrotic syndrome
                lipoid nephrosis

N04.0   **Nephrotic syndrome with minor glomerular abnormality**
      Nephrotic syndrome with minimal change lesion

N04.1   **Nephrotic syndrome with focal and segmental glomerular lesions**
      Nephrotic syndrome with focal and segmental hyalinosis
      Nephrotic syndrome with focal and segmental sclerosis
      Nephrotic syndrome with focal glomerulonephritis

N04.2   **Nephrotic syndrome with diffuse membranous glomerulonephritis**

N04.3   **Nephrotic syndrome with diffuse mesangial proliferative glomerulonephritis**

N04.4   **Nephrotic syndrome with diffuse endocapillary proliferative glomerulonephritis**

N04.5   **Nephrotic syndrome with diffuse mesangiocapillary glomerulonephritis**
      Nephrotic syndrome with membranoproliferative glomerulonephritis, types 1 and 3, or NOS

N04.6   **Nephrotic syndrome with dense deposit disease**
      Nephrotic syndrome with membranoproliferative glomerulonephritis, type 2

N04.7   **Nephrotic syndrome with diffuse crescentic glomerulonephritis**
      Nephrotic syndrome with extracapillary glomerulonephritis

N04.8   **Nephrotic syndrome with other morphologic changes**
      Nephrotic syndrome with proliferative glomerulonephritis NOS

N04.9   **Nephrotic syndrome with unspecified morphologic changes**

Item 14–4 Nephrotic syndrome (NS) is marked by massive proteinuria (protein in the urine) and water retention. Patients with NS are particularly vulnerable to staphylococcal and pneumococcal infections. NS with lesion of proliferative glomerulonephritis results from a streptococcal infection. NS with lesion of membranous glomerulonephritis results in thickening of the capillary walls. NS with lesion of minimal change glomerulonephritis is usually a benign disorder that occurs mostly in children and requires electron microscopy (biopsy) to verify changes in the glomeruli.

● N05   **Unspecified nephritic syndrome**
      Includes   glomerular disease NOS
                glomerulonephritis NOS
                nephritis NOS
                nephropathy NOS and renal disease NOS with morphological lesion specified in .0-.8
      Excludes1   nephropathy NOS with no stated morphological lesion (N28.9)
                renal disease NOS with no stated morphological lesion (N28.9)
                tubulo-interstitial nephritis NOS (N12)

N05.0   **Unspecified nephritic syndrome with minor glomerular abnormality**
      Unspecified nephritic syndrome with minimal change lesion

N05.1   **Unspecified nephritic syndrome with focal and segmental glomerular lesions**
      Unspecified nephritic syndrome with focal and segmental hyalinosis
      Unspecified nephritic syndrome with focal and segmental sclerosis
      Unspecified nephritic syndrome with focal glomerulonephritis

N05.2   **Unspecified nephritic syndrome with diffuse membranous glomerulonephritis**

N05.3   **Unspecified nephritic syndrome with diffuse mesangial proliferative glomerulonephritis**

N05.4   **Unspecified nephritic syndrome with diffuse endocapillary proliferative glomerulonephritis**

N05.5   **Unspecified nephritic syndrome with diffuse mesangiocapillary glomerulonephritis**
      Unspecified nephritic syndrome with membranoproliferative glomerulonephritis, types 1 and 3, or NOS

N05.6   **Unspecified nephritic syndrome with dense deposit disease**
      Unspecified nephritic syndrome with membranoproliferative glomerulonephritis, type 2

N05.7   **Unspecified nephritic syndrome with diffuse crescentic glomerulonephritis**
      Unspecified nephritic syndrome with extracapillary glomerulonephritis

N05.8   **Unspecified nephritic syndrome with other morphologic changes**
      Unspecified nephritic syndrome with proliferative glomerulonephritis NOS

N05.9   **Unspecified nephritic syndrome with unspecified morphologic changes**

● **N06**   **Isolated proteinuria with specified morphological lesion**

     Excludes1   proteinuria not associated with specific morphologic lesions (R80.0)

     N06.0   **Isolated proteinuria with minor glomerular abnormality**
         Isolated proteinuria with minimal change lesion

     N06.1   **Isolated proteinuria with focal and segmental glomerular lesions**
         Isolated proteinuria with focal and segmental hyalinosis
         Isolated proteinuria with focal and segmental sclerosis
         Isolated proteinuria with focal glomerulonephritis

     N06.2   **Isolated proteinuria with diffuse membranous glomerulonephritis**

     N06.3   **Isolated proteinuria with diffuse mesangial proliferative glomerulonephritis**

     N06.4   **Isolated proteinuria with diffuse endocapillary proliferative glomerulonephritis**

     N06.5   **Isolated proteinuria with diffuse mesangiocapillary glomerulonephritis**
         Isolated proteinuria with membranoproliferative glomerulonephritis, types 1 and 3, or NOS

     N06.6   **Isolated proteinuria with dense deposit disease**
         Isolated proteinuria with membranoproliferative glomerulonephritis, type 2

     N06.7   **Isolated proteinuria with diffuse crescentic glomerulonephritis**
         Isolated proteinuria with extracapillary glomerulonephritis

     N06.8   **Isolated proteinuria with other morphologic lesion**
         Isolated proteinuria with proliferative glomerulonephritis NOS

     N06.9   **Isolated proteinuria with unspecified morphologic lesion**

● **N07**   **Hereditary nephropathy, not elsewhere classified**

     Excludes2   Alport's syndrome (Q87.81-)
         hereditary amyloid nephropathy (E85.-)
         nail patella syndrome (Q87.2)
         non-neuropathic heredofamilial amyloidosis (E85.-)

     N07.0   **Hereditary nephropathy, not elsewhere classified with minor glomerular abnormality**
         Hereditary nephropathy, not elsewhere classified with minimal change lesion

     N07.1   **Hereditary nephropathy, not elsewhere classified with focal and segmental glomerular lesions**
         Hereditary nephropathy, not elsewhere classified with focal and segmental hyalinosis
         Hereditary nephropathy, not elsewhere classified with focal and segmental sclerosis
         Hereditary nephropathy, not elsewhere classified with focal glomerulonephritis

     N07.2   **Hereditary nephropathy, not elsewhere classified with diffuse membranous glomerulonephritis**

     N07.3   **Hereditary nephropathy, not elsewhere classified with diffuse mesangial proliferative glomerulonephritis**

     N07.4   **Hereditary nephropathy, not elsewhere classified with diffuse endocapillary proliferative glomerulonephritis**

     N07.5   **Hereditary nephropathy, not elsewhere classified with diffuse mesangiocapillary glomerulonephritis**
         Hereditary nephropathy, not elsewhere classified with membranoproliferative glomerulonephritis, types 1 and 3, or NOS

     N07.6   **Hereditary nephropathy, not elsewhere classified with dense deposit disease**
         Hereditary nephropathy, not elsewhere classified with membranoproliferative glomerulonephritis, type 2

     N07.7   **Hereditary nephropathy, not elsewhere classified with diffuse crescentic glomerulonephritis**
         Hereditary nephropathy, not elsewhere classified with extracapillary glomerulonephritis

     N07.8   **Hereditary nephropathy, not elsewhere classified with other morphologic lesions**
         Hereditary nephropathy, not elsewhere classified with proliferative glomerulonephritis NOS

     N07.9   **Hereditary nephropathy, not elsewhere classified with unspecified morphologic lesions**

▶ **N08**   *Glomerular disorders in diseases classified elsewhere*
     Glomerulonephritis
     Nephritis
     Nephropathy
     Code first underlying disease, such as:
         amyloidosis (E85.-)
         congenital syphilis (A50.5)
         cryoglobulinemia (D89.1)
         disseminated intravascular coagulation (D65)
         gout (M1A.-, M10.-)
         microscopic polyangiitis (M31.7)
         multiple myeloma (C90.0-)
         sepsis (A40.0-A41.9)
         sickle-cell disease (D57.0-D57.8)

     Excludes1   glomerulonephritis, nephritis and nephropathy (in):
         antiglomerular basement membrane disease (M31.0)
         diabetes (E08-E13 with .21)
         gonococcal (A54.21)
         Goodpasture's syndrome (M31.0)
         hemolytic-uremic syndrome (D59.3)
         lupus (M32.14)
         mumps (B26.83)
         syphilis (A52.75)
         systemic lupus erythematosus (M32.14)
         Wegener's granulomatosis (M31.31)
         pyelonephritis in diseases classified elsewhere (N16)
         renal tubulo-interstitial disorders classified elsewhere (N16)

RENAL TUBULO-INTERSTITIAL DISEASES (N10-N16)

     Includes   pyelonephritis
     Excludes1   pyeloureteritis cystica (N28.85)

N10   **Acute pyelonephritis**
     Acute infectious interstitial nephritis
     Acute pyelitis
     Acute tubulo-interstitial nephritis
     Hemoglobin nephrosis
     Myoglobin nephrosis
     Use additional code (B95-B97), to identify infectious agent

● **N11**   **Chronic tubulo-interstitial nephritis**

     Includes   chronic infectious interstitial nephritis
         chronic pyelitis
         chronic pyelonephritis

     Use additional code (B95-B97), to identify infectious agent

     N11.0   **Nonobstructive reflux-associated chronic pyelonephritis**
         Pyelonephritis (chronic) associated with (vesicoureteral) reflux

         Excludes1   vesicoureteral reflux NOS (N13.70)

     N11.1   **Chronic obstructive pyelonephritis**
         Pyelonephritis (chronic) associated with anomaly of pelviureteric junction
         Pyelonephritis (chronic) associated with anomaly of pyeloureteric junction
         Pyelonephritis (chronic) associated with crossing of vessel
         Pyelonephritis (chronic) associated with kinking of ureter
         Pyelonephritis (chronic) associated with obstruction of ureter
         Pyelonephritis (chronic) associated with stricture of pelviureteric junction
         Pyelonephritis (chronic) associated with stricture of ureter

         Excludes1   calculous pyelonephritis (N20.9)
                  obstructive uropathy (N13.-)

     N11.8   **Other chronic tubulo-interstitial nephritis**
         Nonobstructive chronic pyelonephritis NOS

     N11.9   **Chronic tubulo-interstitial nephritis, unspecified**
         Chronic interstitial nephritis NOS
         Chronic pyelitis NOS
         Chronic pyelonephritis NOS

CHAPTER 14 (N00-N99)

Figure 14-3   Acute pyelonephritis. Cortical surface exhibits grayish white areas of inflammation and abscess formation. (From Frazier MS, Drzymkowski JW: Essentials of Human Diseases and Conditions, St. Louis, Saunders/Elsevier, 2009)

Item 14–5 Pyelonephritis is an infection of the kidneys and ureters and may be chronic or acute in one or both kidneys.

N12   **Tubulo-interstitial nephritis, not specified as acute or chronic**
     Interstitial nephritis NOS
     Pyelitis NOS
     Pyelonephritis NOS
     Excludes1   calculous pyelonephritis (N20.9)

● **N13**   **Obstructive and reflux uropathy**
     Excludes2   calculus of kidney and ureter without hydronephrosis (N20.-)
                congenital obstructive defects of renal pelvis and ureter (Q62.0-Q62.3)
                hydronephrosis with ureteropelvic junction obstruction (Q62.11)
                obstructive pyelonephritis (N11.1)

     N13.0   **Hydronephrosis with ureteropelvic junction obstruction**
          Hydronephrosis due to acquired occlusion of ureteropelvic junction
          Excludes2   Hydronephrosis with ureteropelvic junction obstruction due to calculus (N13.2)
          Coding Clinic: 2016, Q4, P43

     N13.1   **Hydronephrosis with ureteral stricture, not elsewhere classified**
          Excludes1   hydronephrosis with ureteral stricture with infection (N13.6)

     N13.2   **Hydronephrosis with renal and ureteral calculous obstruction**
          Excludes1   hydronephrosis with renal and ureteral calculous obstruction with infection (N13.6)

●   **N13.3**   **Other and unspecified hydronephrosis**
          Excludes1   hydronephrosis with infection (N13.6)
         N13.30   **Unspecified hydronephrosis**
         N13.39   **Other hydronephrosis**

     N13.4   **Hydroureter**
          Excludes1   congenital hydroureter (Q62.3-)
                hydroureter with infection (N13.6)
                vesicoureteral-reflux with hydroureter (N13.73-)

     N13.5   **Crossing vessel and stricture of ureter without hydronephrosis**
          Kinking and stricture of ureter without hydronephrosis
          Excludes1   crossing vessel and stricture of ureter without hydronephrosis with infection (N13.6)
          Coding Clinic: 2016, Q4, P43

     N13.6   **Pyonephrosis**
          Conditions in N13.0-N13.5 with infection
          Obstructive uropathy with infection
          Use additional code (B95-B97), to identify infectious agent
          Coding Clinic: 2018, Q2, P21

●   **N13.7**   **Vesicoureteral-reflux**
          Excludes1   reflux-associated pyelonephritis (N11.0)
         N13.70   **Vesicoureteral-reflux, unspecified**
              Occurs when urine flows from bladder back into ureters
              Vesicoureteral-reflux NOS

         N13.71   **Vesicoureteral-reflux without reflux nephropathy**

●   **N13.72**   **Vesicoureteral-reflux with reflux nephropathy without hydroureter**
              N13.721   **Vesicoureteral-reflux with reflux nephropathy without hydroureter, unilateral**
              N13.722   **Vesicoureteral-reflux with reflux nephropathy without hydroureter, bilateral**
              N13.729   **Vesicoureteral-reflux with reflux nephropathy without hydroureter, unspecified**

●   **N13.73**   **Vesicoureteral-reflux with reflux nephropathy with hydroureter**
              N13.731   **Vesicoureteral-reflux with reflux nephropathy with hydroureter, unilateral**
              N13.732   **Vesicoureteral-reflux with reflux nephropathy with hydroureter, bilateral**
              N13.739   **Vesicoureteral-reflux with reflux nephropathy with hydroureter, unspecified**

     N13.8   **Other obstructive and reflux uropathy**
          Urinary tract obstruction due to specified cause
          Code first, if applicable, any causal condition first, such as: enlarged prostate (N40.1)

     N13.9   **Obstructive and reflux uropathy, unspecified**
          Urinary tract obstruction NOS

● **N14**   **Drug- and heavy-metal-induced tubulo-interstitial and tubular conditions**
     Code first poisoning due to drug or toxin, if applicable (T36-T65 with fifth or sixth character 1-4 or 6)
     Use additional code for adverse effect, if applicable, to identify drug (T36-T50 with fifth or sixth character 5)

     N14.0   **Analgesic nephropathy**
     N14.1   **Nephropathy induced by other drugs, medicaments and biological substances**
     N14.2   **Nephropathy induced by unspecified drug, medicament or biological substance**
     N14.3   **Nephropathy induced by heavy metals**
     N14.4   **Toxic nephropathy, not elsewhere classified**

● **N15**   **Other renal tubulo-interstitial diseases**
     N15.0   **Balkan nephropathy**
          Balkan endemic nephropathy
     N15.1   **Renal and perinephric abscess**
     N15.8   **Other specified renal tubulo-interstitial diseases**
     N15.9   **Renal tubulo-interstitial disease, unspecified**
          Infection of kidney NOS
          Excludes1   urinary tract infection NOS (N39.0)

Figure 14-4   Hydronephrosis of the kidney, with marked dilatation of pelvis and calyces and thinning of renal parenchyma. (From Kumar: Robbins and Cotran: Pathologic Basis of Disease, ed 8, Saunders, An Imprint of Elsevier, 2009)

▶ New   ⇒ Revised   ~~deleted~~ Deleted   Excludes 1   Excludes 2   Includes   Use additional   Code first   Code also   Key words
OGCR Official Guidelines   X Assign placeholder X   ● Use Additional Character(s)   ▷ Manifestation Code   **Coding Clinic**

▶ *N16*   *Renal tubulo-interstitial disorders in diseases classified elsewhere*
        Pyelonephritis
        Tubulo-interstitial nephritis

        Code first underlying disease, such as:
           brucellosis (A23.0-A23.9)
           cryoglobulinemia (D89.1)
           glycogen storage disease (E74.0)
           leukemia (C91-C95)
           lymphoma (C81.0-C85.9, C96.0-C96.9)
           multiple myeloma (C90.0-)
           sepsis (A40.0-A41.9)
           Wilson's disease (E83.0)

        Excludes1   diphtheritic pyelonephritis and tubulo-interstitial nephritis (A36.84)
                  pyelonephritis and tubulo-interstitial nephritis in candidiasis (B37.49)
                  pyelonephritis and tubulo-interstitial nephritis in cystinosis (E72.04)
                  pyelonephritis and tubulo-interstitial nephritis in salmonella infection (A02.25)
                  pyelonephritis and tubulo-interstitial nephritis in sarcoidosis (D86.84)
                  pyelonephritis and tubulo-interstitial nephritis in sicca syndrome [Sjogren's] (M35.04)
                  pyelonephritis and tubulo-interstitial nephritis in systemic lupus erythematosus (M32.15)
                  pyelonephritis and tubulo-interstitial nephritis in toxoplasmosis (B58.83)
                  renal tubular degeneration in diabetes (E08-E13 with .29)
                  syphilitic pyelonephritis and tubulo-interstitial nephritis (A52.75)

ACUTE KIDNEY FAILURE AND CHRONIC KIDNEY DISEASE (N17-N19)

        Excludes2   congenital renal failure (P96.0)
                  drug- and heavy-metal-induced tubulo-interstitial and tubular conditions (N14.-)
                  extrarenal uremia (R39.2)
                  hemolytic-uremic syndrome (D59.3)
                  hepatorenal syndrome (K76.7)
                  postpartum hepatorenal syndrome (O90.4)
                  posttraumatic renal failure (T79.5)
                  prerenal uremia (R39.2)
                  renal failure complicating abortion or ectopic or molar pregnancy (O00-O07, O08.4)
                  renal failure following labor and delivery (O90.4)
                  renal failure postprocedural (N99.0)

● **N17**   **Acute kidney failure**
        Code also associated underlying condition
        Excludes1   posttraumatic renal failure (T79.5)

     N17.0   **Acute kidney failure with tubular necrosis**
           Acute tubular necrosis
           Renal tubular necrosis
           Tubular necrosis NOS

     N17.1   **Acute kidney failure with acute cortical necrosis**
           Acute cortical necrosis
           Cortical necrosis NOS
           Renal cortical necrosis

     N17.2   **Acute kidney failure with medullary necrosis**
           Medullary [papillary] necrosis NOS
           Acute medullary [papillary] necrosis
           Renal medullary [papillary] necrosis

     N17.8   **Other acute kidney failure**

     N17.9   **Acute kidney failure, unspecified**
           Acute kidney injury (nontraumatic)
        Excludes2   traumatic kidney injury (S37.0-)

● **N18**   **Chronic kidney disease (CKD)**
        Code first any associated:
           diabetic chronic kidney disease (E08.22, E09.22, E10.22, E11.22, E13.22)
           hypertensive chronic kidney disease (I12.-, I13.-)
        Use additional code to identify kidney transplant status, if applicable, (Z94.0)
        Coding Clinic: 2016, Q4, P123

     N18.1   **Chronic kidney disease, stage 1**

     N18.2   **Chronic kidney disease, stage 2 (mild)**

     N18.3   **Chronic kidney disease, stage 3 (moderate)**

     N18.4   **Chronic kidney disease, stage 4 (severe)**
        Coding Clinic: 2013, Q1, P24

     N18.5   **Chronic kidney disease, stage 5**
        Excludes1   chronic kidney disease, stage 5 requiring chronic dialysis (N18.6)

     N18.6   **End stage renal disease**
           Chronic kidney disease requiring chronic dialysis
           Use additional code to identify dialysis status (Z99.2)
        Coding Clinic: 2016, Q3, P23, Q1, P13

     N18.9   **Chronic kidney disease, unspecified**
           Chronic renal disease
           Chronic renal failure NOS
           Chronic renal insufficiency
           Chronic uremia NOS
           Diffuse sclerosing glomerulonephritis NOS

  N19   **Unspecified kidney failure**
        Uremia NOS
        Excludes1   acute kidney failure (N17.-)
                  chronic kidney disease (N18.-)
                  chronic uremia (N18.9)
                  extrarenal uremia (R39.2)
                  prerenal uremia (R39.2)
                  renal insufficiency (acute) (N28.9)
                  uremia of newborn (P96.0)

UROLITHIASIS (N20-N23)

● **N20**   **Calculus of kidney and ureter**
        Calculous pyelonephritis
        Excludes1   nephrocalcinosis (E83.5)
                  that with hydronephrosis (N13.2)

     N20.0   **Calculus of kidney**
           Nephrolithiasis NOS   Staghorn calculus
           Renal calculus   Stone in kidney
           Renal stone
        Coding Clinic: 2017, Q1, P5

     N20.1   **Calculus of ureter**
           Ureteric stone
        Coding Clinic: 2016, Q3, P24

     N20.2   **Calculus of kidney with calculus of ureter**

     N20.9   **Urinary calculus, unspecified**

Figure 14-5   Multiple urinary calculi.

Multiple calculi

Item 14–6 Decreased blood flow is the usual cause of **acute renal failure** that offers a good prognosis for recovery.

    Chronic renal failure is usually the result of long-standing kidney disease and is a very serious condition that generally results in death.

CHAPTER 14 (N00-N99)

● **N21 Calculus of lower urinary tract**

    Includes calculus of lower urinary tract with cystitis and urethritis

    N21.0 Calculus in bladder
        Calculus in diverticulum of bladder
        Urinary bladder stone
        Excludes2 staghorn calculus (N20.0)
        Coding Clinic: 2015, Q2, P9

    N21.1 Calculus in urethra
        Excludes2 calculus of prostate (N42.0)

    N21.8 Other lower urinary tract calculus

    N21.9 Calculus of lower urinary tract, unspecified
        Excludes1 calculus of urinary tract NOS (N20.9)

▶ **N22 Calculus of urinary tract in diseases classified elsewhere**
    Code first underlying disease, such as:
      gout (M1A.-, M10.-)
      schistosomiasis (B65.0-B65.9)

N23 Unspecified renal colic

OTHER DISORDERS OF KIDNEY AND URETER (N25-N29)

    Excludes2 disorders of kidney and ureter with urolithiasis (N20-N23)

● **N25 Disorders resulting from impaired renal tubular function**

    N25.0 Renal osteodystrophy
        Azotemic osteodystrophy
        Phosphate-losing tubular disorders
        Renal rickets
        Renal short stature
        Excludes2 metabolic disorders classifiable to E70-E88

    N25.1 Nephrogenic diabetes insipidus
        Excludes1 diabetes insipidus NOS (E23.2)

  ● **N25.8 Other disorders resulting from impaired renal tubular function**
      N25.81 Secondary hyperparathyroidism of renal origin
          Excludes1 secondary hyperparathyroidism, non-renal (E21.1)
          Excludes2 metabolic disorders classifiable to E70-E88

      N25.89 Other disorders resulting from impaired renal tubular function
        Hypokalemic nephropathy
        Lightwood-Albright syndrome
        Renal tubular acidosis NOS

    N25.9 Disorder resulting from impaired renal tubular function, unspecified

● **N26 Unspecified contracted kidney**
    Excludes1 contracted kidney due to hypertension (I12.-)
        diffuse sclerosing glomerulonephritis (N05.8.-)
        hypertensive nephrosclerosis (arteriolar) (arteriosclerotic) (I12.-)
        small kidney of unknown cause (N27.-)

    N26.1 Atrophy of kidney (terminal)

    N26.2 Page kidney

    N26.9 Renal sclerosis, unspecified

● **N27 Small kidney of unknown cause**
    Includes oligonephronia
    N27.0 Small kidney, unilateral
    N27.1 Small kidney, bilateral
    N27.9 Small kidney, unspecified

● **N28 Other disorders of kidney and ureter, not elsewhere classified**

    N28.0 Ischemia and infarction of kidney
        Renal artery embolism
        Renal artery obstruction
        Renal artery occlusion
        Renal artery thrombosis
        Renal infarct
        Excludes1 atherosclerosis of renal artery (extrarenal part) (I70.1)
          congenital stenosis of renal artery (Q27.1)
          Goldblatt's kidney (I70.1)

    N28.1 Cyst of kidney, acquired
        Cyst (multiple) (solitary) of kidney, (acquired)
        Excludes1 cystic kidney disease (congenital) (Q61.-)

  ● **N28.8 Other specified disorders of kidney and ureter**
        Excludes1 hydroureter (N13.4)
          ureteric stricture with hydronephrosis (N13.1)
          ureteric stricture without hydronephrosis (N13.5)

      N28.81 Hypertrophy of kidney
      N28.82 Megaloureter
      N28.83 Nephroptosis
      N28.84 Pyelitis cystica
      N28.85 Pyeloureteritis cystica
      N28.86 Ureteritis cystica
      N28.89 Other specified disorders of kidney and ureter

    N28.9 Disorder of kidney and ureter, unspecified
        Nephropathy NOS
        Renal disease (acute) NOS
        Renal insufficiency (acute)
        Excludes1 chronic renal insufficiency (N18.9)
          unspecified nephritic syndrome (N05.-)
        Coding Clinic: 2016, Q1, P13

▶ **N29 Other disorders of kidney and ureter in diseases classified elsewhere**
    Code first underlying disease, such as:
      amyloidosis (E85.-)
      nephrocalcinosis (E83.5)
      schistosomiasis (B65.0-B65.9)
    Excludes1 disorders of kidney and ureter in:
        cystinosis (E72.0)
        gonorrhea (A54.21)
        syphilis (A52.75)
        tuberculosis (A18.11)

OTHER DISEASES OF THE URINARY SYSTEM (N30-N39)

    Excludes1 urinary infection (complicating):
        abortion or ectopic or molar pregnancy (O00-O07, O08.8)
        pregnancy, childbirth and the puerperium (O23.-, O75.3, O86.2-)

● **N30 Cystitis**
    Infection of bladder and irritation in lower urinary tract
    Use additional code to identify infectious agent (B95-B97)
    Excludes1 prostatocystitis (N41.3)

  ● **N30.0 Acute cystitis**
        Excludes1 irradiation cystitis (N30.4-)
          trigonitis (N30.3-)
      N30.00 Acute cystitis without hematuria
      N30.01 Acute cystitis with hematuria

  ● **N30.1 Interstitial cystitis (chronic)**
      Ongoing infection of kidney glomeruli and tubules
      N30.10 Interstitial cystitis (chronic) without hematuria
      N30.11 Interstitial cystitis (chronic) with hematuria

  ● **N30.2 Other chronic cystitis**
      N30.20 Other chronic cystitis without hematuria
      N30.21 Other chronic cystitis with hematuria

▶ New ⇒ Revised ~~deleted~~ Deleted Excludes 1 Excludes 2 Includes Use additional Code first Code also Key words
OGCR Official Guidelines X Assign placeholder X ● Use Additional Character(s) ▶ Manifestation Code **Coding Clinic**

● **N30.3**   **Trigonitis**
      Inflammation of triangular area of bladder (where the ureters
        and urethra come together)
      Urethrotrigonitis
      N30.30   **Trigonitis without hematuria**
      N30.31   **Trigonitis with hematuria**

● **N30.4**   **Irradiation cystitis**
      N30.40   **Irradiation cystitis without hematuria**
      N30.41   **Irradiation cystitis with hematuria**

● **N30.8**   **Other cystitis**
      Abscess of bladder
      N30.80   **Other cystitis without hematuria**
      N30.81   **Other cystitis with hematuria**

● **N30.9**   **Cystitis, unspecified**
      N30.90   **Cystitis, unspecified without hematuria**
      N30.91   **Cystitis, unspecified with hematuria**

● **N31**   **Neuromuscular dysfunction of bladder, not elsewhere classified**
      Use additional code to identify any associated urinary
        incontinence (N39.3-N39.4-)
      Excludes1   cord bladder NOS (G95.89)
          neurogenic bladder due to cauda equina
             syndrome (G83.4)
          neuromuscular dysfunction due to spinal cord
             lesion (G95.89)

      N31.0   **Uninhibited neuropathic bladder, not elsewhere classified**
      N31.1   **Reflex neuropathic bladder, not elsewhere classified**
      N31.2   **Flaccid neuropathic bladder, not elsewhere classified**
          Atonic (motor) (sensory) neuropathic bladder
          Diminished tone of bladder muscle
          Autonomous neuropathic bladder
          Nonreflex neuropathic bladder
      N31.8   **Other neuromuscular dysfunction of bladder**
      N31.9   **Neuromuscular dysfunction of bladder, unspecified**
          Neurogenic bladder dysfunction NOS

● **N32**   **Other disorders of bladder**
      Excludes2   calculus of bladder (N21.0)
          cystocele (N81.1-)
          hernia or prolapse of bladder, female (N81.1-)

      N32.0   **Bladder-neck obstruction**
          Bladder-neck stenosis (acquired)
          Excludes1   congenital bladder-neck obstruction
                 (Q64.3-)
      N32.1   **Vesicointestinal fistula**
          Vesicorectal fistula
      N32.2   **Vesical fistula, not elsewhere classified**
          Excludes1   fistula between bladder and female
                 genital tract (N82.0-N82.1)
      N32.3   **Diverticulum of bladder**
          Formation of sac from a herniation of wall of bladder
          Excludes1   congenital diverticulum of bladder (Q64.6)
                 diverticulitis of bladder (N30.8-)

● **N32.8**   **Other specified disorders of bladder**
      N32.81   **Overactive bladder**
          Detrusor muscle hyperactivity
          Excludes1   frequent urination due to
                 specified bladder condition-
                 code to condition
      N32.89   **Other specified disorders of bladder**
          Bladder hemorrhage
          Bladder hypertrophy
          Calcified bladder
          Contracted bladder
      N32.9   **Bladder disorder, unspecified**

▷ **N33**   *Bladder disorders in diseases classified elsewhere*
      Code first underlying disease, such as:
        schistosomiasis (B65.0-B65.9)
      Excludes1   bladder disorder in syphilis (A52.76)
          bladder disorder in tuberculosis (A18.12)
          candidal cystitis (B37.41)
          chlamydial cystitis (A56.01)
          cystitis in gonorrhea (A54.01)
          cystitis in neurogenic bladder (N31.-)
          diphtheritic cystitis (A36.85)
          syphilitic cystitis (A52.76)
          trichomonal cystitis (A59.03)

● **N34**   **Urethritis and urethral syndrome**
      Use additional code (B95-B97), to identify infectious agent
      Excludes2   Reiter's disease (M02.3-)
          urethritis in diseases with a predominantly sexual
             mode of transmission (A50-A64)
          urethrotrigonitis (N30.3-)

      N34.0   **Urethral abscess**
          Abscess (of) Cowper's gland
          Abscess (of) Littré's gland
          Abscess (of) urethral (gland)
          Periurethral abscess
          Excludes1   urethral caruncle (N36.2)
      N34.1   **Nonspecific urethritis**
          Nongonococcal urethritis
          Nonvenereal urethritis
      N34.2   **Other urethritis**
          Inflammation of urethra
          Meatitis, urethral
          Postmenopausal urethritis
          Ulcer of urethra (meatus)
          Urethritis NOS
      N34.3   **Urethral syndrome, unspecified**

● **N35**   **Urethral stricture**
      Narrowing of lumen of urethra caused by scarring due to infection or
        injury
      Excludes1   congenital urethral stricture (Q64.3-)
          postprocedural urethral stricture (N99.1-)

● **N35.0**   **Post-traumatic urethral stricture**
      Urethral stricture due to injury
      Excludes1   postprocedural urethral stricture (N99.1-)
      ● **N35.01**   **Post-traumatic urethral stricture, male**
          N35.010   **Post-traumatic urethral stricture,**
               male, meatal ♂
          N35.011   **Post-traumatic bulbous urethral**
               stricture ♂
          N35.012   **Post-traumatic membranous urethral**
               stricture ♂
          N35.013   **Post-traumatic anterior urethral**
               stricture ♂
          N35.014   **Post-traumatic urethral stricture,**
               male, unspecified ♂
       ▷ **N35.016**   **Post-traumatic urethral stricture,**
               male, overlapping sites
      ● **N35.02**   **Post-traumatic urethral stricture, female**
          N35.021   **Urethral stricture due to childbirth** ♀
          N35.028   **Other post-traumatic urethral**
               stricture, female ♀
● **N35.1**   **Postinfective urethral stricture, not elsewhere classified**
      Excludes1   urethral stricture associated with
             schistosomiasis (B65.-, N29)
          gonococcal urethral stricture (A54.01)
          syphilitic urethral stricture (A52.76)
      ● **N35.11**   **Postinfective urethral stricture, not elsewhere**
          classified, male
          N35.111   **Postinfective urethral stricture, not**
               elsewhere classified, male, meatal ♂
          N35.112   **Postinfective bulbous urethral stricture,**
               not elsewhere classified, male ♂

CHAPTER 14 (N00–N99)

CHAPTER 14 (N00-N99)

N35.113   Postinfective membranous urethral stricture, not elsewhere classified, male ♂

N35.114   Postinfective anterior urethral stricture, not elsewhere classified, male ♂

▶ N35.116   Postinfective urethral stricture, not elsewhere classified, male, overlapping sites ♂

N35.119   Postinfective urethral stricture, not elsewhere classified, male, unspecified ♂

N35.12   Postinfective urethral stricture, not elsewhere classified, female ♀

● N35.8   Other urethral stricture

     Excludes1   postprocedural urethral stricture (N99.1-)

▶ N35.81   Other urethral stricture, male

     ▶ N35.811   Other urethral stricture, male, meatal ♂

     ▶ N35.812   Other urethral bulbous stricture, male ♂

     ▶ N35.813   Other membranous urethral stricture, male ♂

     ▶ N35.814   Other anterior urethral stricture, male, anterior ♂

     ▶ N35.816   Other urethral stricture, male, overlapping sites ♂

     ▶ N35.819   Other urethral stricture, male, unspecified site ♂

▶ N35.82   Other urethral stricture, female ♀

N35.9   Urethral stricture, unspecified

▶ N35.91   Urethral stricture, unspecified, male

     ▶ N35.911   Unspecified urethral stricture, male, meatal

     ▶ N35.912   Unspecified bulbous urethral stricture, male

     ▶ N35.913   Unspecified membranous urethral stricture, male

     ▶ N35.914   Unspecified anterior urethral stricture, male

     ▶ N35.916   Unspecified urethral stricture, male, overlapping sites

     ▶ N35.919   Unspecified urethral stricture, male, unspecified site
         ▶ Pinhole meatus NOS
         ▶ Urethral stricture NOS

▶ N35.92   Unspecified urethral stricture, female

● **N36**   **Other disorders of urethra**

N36.0   Urethral fistula
     Urethroperineal fistula
     Urethrorectal fistula
     Urinary fistula NOS

     Excludes1   urethroscrotal fistula (N50.89)
         urethrovaginal fistula (N82.1)
         urethrovesicovaginal fistula (N82.1)

N36.1   Urethral diverticulum

N36.2   Urethral caruncle

● N36.4   Urethral functional and muscular disorders
     Use additional code to identify associated urinary stress incontinence (N39.3)

N36.41   **Hypermobility of urethra**

N36.42   **Intrinsic sphincter deficiency (ISD)**

N36.43   **Combined hypermobility of urethra and intrinsic sphincter deficiency**

N36.44   **Muscular disorders of urethra**
     Bladder sphincter dyssynergy

N36.5   Urethral false passage

N36.8   Other specified disorders of urethra

     Excludes1   congenital urethrocele (Q64.7)
         female urethrocele (N81.0)

N36.9   Urethral disorder, unspecified

▌ **N37**   *Urethral disorders in diseases classified elsewhere*
     Code first underlying disease

     Excludes1   urethritis (in):
         candidal infection (B37.41)
         chlamydial (A56.01)
         gonorrhea (A54.01)
         syphilis (A52.76)
         trichomonal infection (A59.03)
         tuberculosis (A18.13)

● **N39**   **Other disorders of urinary system**

     Excludes2   hematuria NOS (R31.-)
         recurrent or persistent hematuria (N02.-)
         recurrent or persistent hematuria with specified morphological lesion (N02.-)
         proteinuria NOS (R80.-)

N39.0   Urinary tract infection, site not specified
     Use additional code (B95-B97), to identify infectious agent

     Excludes1   candidiasis of urinary tract (B37.4-)
         neonatal urinary tract infection (P39.3)
         urinary tract infection of specified site, such as:
            cystitis (N30.-)
            urethritis (N34.-)

     Coding Clinic: 2018, Q2, P22; Q1, P16; 2012, Q4, P94

N39.3   Stress incontinence (female) (male)
     Code also any associated overactive bladder (N32.81)

     Excludes1   mixed incontinence (N39.46)

● N39.4   Other specified urinary incontinence
     Code also any associated overactive bladder (N32.81)

     Excludes1   enuresis NOS (R32)
         functional urinary incontinence (R39.81)
         urinary incontinence associated with cognitive impairment (R39.81)
         urinary incontinence NOS (R32)
         urinary incontinence of nonorganic origin (F98.0)

N39.41   Urge incontinence

     Excludes1   mixed incontinence (N39.46)

N39.42   **Incontinence without sensory awareness**
     Insensible (urinary) incontinence

N39.43   **Post-void dribbling**

N39.44   **Nocturnal enuresis**

N39.45   **Continuous leakage**

N39.46   **Mixed incontinence**
     Urge and stress incontinence

● N39.49   Other specified urinary incontinence

N39.490   Overflow incontinence

N39.491   Coital incontinence
     Coding Clinic: 2016, Q4, P44

N39.492   Postural (urinary) incontinence
     Coding Clinic: 2016, Q4, P44

N39.498   Other specified urinary incontinence
     Reflex incontinence
     Total incontinence

N39.8   Other specified disorders of urinary system

N39.9   Disorder of urinary system, unspecified

▶ New   ⇒ Revised   ~~deleted~~ Deleted   Excludes 1   Excludes 2   Includes   Use additional   Code first   Code also   Key words

OGCR Official Guidelines   X Assign placeholder X   ● Use Additional Character(s)   ▌ Manifestation Code   **Coding Clinic**

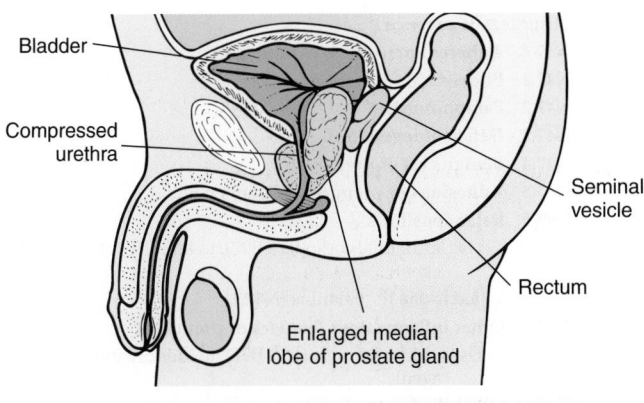

Figure 14-6 Benign prostatic hyperplasia. (From Shiland: Mastering Healthcare Terminology, ed 3, St. Louis, Mosby, 2010)

DISEASES OF MALE GENITAL ORGANS (N40-N53)

★ **(See Plate 387 on page 53.)**

● **N40 Benign prostatic hyperplasia**

> **Includes**   adenofibromatous hypertrophy of prostate
> benign hypertrophy of the prostate
> *Enlargement of prostate gland usually occurring
> with age and causing obstructed urine flow*
> benign prostatic hypertrophy
> BPH
> enlarged prostate
> nodular prostate
> polyp of prostate

> **Excludes1**   benign neoplasms of prostate (adenoma, benign)
> (fibroadenoma) (fibroma) (myoma) (D29.1)
> malignant neoplasm of prostate (C61)

N40.0   **Benign prostatic hyperplasia without lower urinary tract symptoms** ♂   A
> Enlarged prostate without LUTS
> Enlarged prostate NOS

N40.1   **Benign prostatic hyperplasia with lower urinary tract symptoms** ♂   A
> Enlarged prostate with LUTS
> Use additional code for associated symptoms, when specified:
> incomplete bladder emptying (R39.14)
> nocturia (R35.1)
> straining on urination (R39.16)
> urinary frequency (R35.0)
> urinary hesitancy (R39.11)
> urinary incontinence (N39.4-)
> urinary obstruction (N13.8)
> urinary retention (R33.8)
> urinary urgency (R39.15)
> weak urinary stream (R39.12)

N40.2   **Nodular prostate without lower urinary tract symptoms** ♂   A
> Nodular prostate without LUTS

N40.3   **Nodular prostate with lower urinary tract symptoms** ♂   A
> Use additional code for associated symptoms, when specified:
> incomplete bladder emptying (R39.14)
> nocturia (R35.1)
> straining on urination (R39.16)
> urinary frequency (R35.0)
> urinary hesitancy (R39.11)
> urinary incontinence (N39.4-)
> urinary obstruction (N13.8)
> urinary retention (R33.8)
> urinary urgency (R39.15)
> weak urinary stream (R39.12)

● **N41 Inflammatory diseases of prostate**
> Use additional code (B95-B97), to identify infectious agent

N41.0   Acute prostatitis ♂   A
N41.1   Chronic prostatitis ♂   A
N41.2   Abscess of prostate ♂   A
N41.3   Prostatocystitis ♂   A
N41.4   Granulomatous prostatitis ♂   A
N41.8   Other inflammatory diseases of prostate ♂   A
N41.9   Inflammatory disease of prostate, unspecified ♂   A
> Prostatitis NOS

● **N42 Other and unspecified disorders of prostate**

N42.0   **Calculus of prostate** ♂   A
> Prostatic stone

N42.1   **Congestion and hemorrhage of prostate** ♂   A
> **Excludes1**   enlarged prostate (N40.-)
> hematuria (R31.-)
> hyperplasia of prostate (N40.-)
> inflammatory diseases of prostate (N41.-)

● **N42.3   Dysplasia of prostate**
> Coding Clinic: 2016, Q4, P44

N42.30   Unspecified dysplasia of prostate ♂
N42.31   Prostatic intraepithelial neoplasia ♂
> PIN
> Prostatic intraepithelial neoplasia I (PIN I)
> Prostatic intraepithelial neoplasia II (PIN II)
> **Excludes1**   prostatic intraepithelial neoplasia
> III (PIN III) (D07.5)

N42.32   Atypical small acinar proliferation of prostate ♂
N42.39   Other dysplasia of prostate ♂

● **N42.8   Other specified disorders of prostate**
N42.81   Prostatodynia syndrome ♂   A
> Painful prostate syndrome
N42.82   Prostatosis syndrome ♂   A
N42.83   Cyst of prostate ♂   A
N42.89   Other specified disorders of prostate ♂   A
N42.9   Disorder of prostate, unspecified ♂   A

● **N43 Hydrocele and spermatocele**
> **Includes**   hydrocele of spermatic cord, testis or tunica
> vaginalis
> **Excludes1**   congenital hydrocele (P83.5)

N43.0   Encysted hydrocele ♂
N43.1   Infected hydrocele ♂
> Use additional code (B95-B97), to identify infectious agent
N43.2   Other hydrocele ♂
N43.3   Hydrocele, unspecified ♂
● **N43.4   Spermatocele of epididymis**
> Spermatic cyst
N43.40   Spermatocele of epididymis, unspecified ♂
N43.41   Spermatocele of epididymis, single ♂
N43.42   Spermatocele of epididymis, multiple ♂

Item 14–7   Hydrocele is a sac of fluid accumulating in the testes membrane.

Figure 14-7   A. Hydrocele. **B.** Newborn with large right hydrocele. (**B** from Nelson WE, Kliegman R: Nelson Textbook of Pediatrics, Philadelphia, Saunders Elsevier, 2011)

CHAPTER 14 (N00-N99)

● **N44 Noninflammatory disorders of testis**
    ● **N44.0 Torsion of testis**
        N44.00 Torsion of testis, unspecified ♂
        N44.01 Extravaginal torsion of spermatic cord ♂
        N44.02 Intravaginal torsion of spermatic cord ♂
            Torsion of spermatic cord NOS
        N44.03 Torsion of appendix testis ♂
        N44.04 Torsion of appendix epididymis ♂
    N44.1 Cyst of tunica albuginea testis ♂
    N44.2 Benign cyst of testis ♂
    N44.8 Other noninflammatory disorders of the testis ♂

● **N45 Orchitis and epididymitis**
    Orchitis is inflammation of one or both of the testes as a result of mumps or other infection, trauma, or metastasis. Epididymitis is inflammation of the tubular structure that connects the testicle with the vas deferens.
    Use additional code (B95-B97), to identify infectious agent
    N45.1 Epididymitis ♂
    N45.2 Orchitis ♂
    N45.3 Epididymo-orchitis ♂
    N45.4 Abscess of epididymis or testis ♂

● **N46 Male infertility**
    Excludes1   vasectomy status (Z98.52)
    ● **N46.0 Azoospermia**
        Absolute male infertility
        Male infertility due to germinal (cell) aplasia
        Male infertility due to spermatogenic arrest (complete)
        N46.01 Organic azoospermia   A
            Azoospermia NOS
      ● **N46.02 Azoospermia due to extratesticular causes**
            Code also associated cause
        N46.021 Azoospermia due to drug therapy ♂ A
        N46.022 Azoospermia due to infection ♂   A
        N46.023 Azoospermia due to obstruction of efferent ducts ♂   A
        N46.024 Azoospermia due to radiation ♂   A
        N46.025 Azoospermia due to systemic disease ♂   A
        N46.029 Azoospermia due to other extratesticular causes ♂   A
    ● **N46.1 Oligospermia**
        Male infertility due to germinal cell desquamation
        Male infertility due to hypospermatogenesis
        Male infertility due to incomplete spermatogenic arrest
        N46.11 Organic oligospermia ♂   A
            Oligospermia NOS
      ● **N46.12 Oligospermia due to extratesticular causes**
            Code also associated cause
        N46.121 Oligospermia due to drug therapy ♂ A
        N46.122 Oligospermia due to infection ♂   A
        N46.123 Oligospermia due to obstruction of efferent ducts ♂   A
        N46.124 Oligospermia due to radiation ♂   A
        N46.125 Oligospermia due to systemic disease ♂   A
        N46.129 Oligospermia due to other extratesticular causes ♂   A
    N46.8 Other male infertility ♂   A
    N46.9 Male infertility, unspecified ♂   A

● **N47 Disorders of prepuce**
    N47.0 Adherent prepuce, newborn ♂   N
    N47.1 Phimosis ♂
    N47.2 Paraphimosis ♂
    N47.3 Deficient foreskin ♂
    N47.4 Benign cyst of prepuce ♂
    N47.5 Adhesions of prepuce and glans penis ♂
    N47.6 Balanoposthitis ♂
        Use additional code (B95-B97), to identify infectious agent
        Excludes1   balanitis (N48.1)
    N47.7 Other inflammatory diseases of prepuce ♂
        Use additional code (B95-B97), to identify infectious agent
    N47.8 Other disorders of prepuce ♂

● **N48 Other disorders of penis**
    N48.0 Leukoplakia of penis ♂
        Balanitis xerotica obliterans
        Kraurosis of penis
        Lichen sclerosus of external male genital organs
        Excludes1   carcinoma in situ of penis (D07.4)
    N48.1 Balanitis ♂
        Use additional code (B95-B97), to identify infectious agent
        Excludes1   amebic balanitis (A06.8)
                 balanitis xerotica obliterans (N48.0)
                 candidal balanitis (B37.42)
                 gonococcal balanitis (A54.23)
                 herpesviral [herpes simplex] balanitis (A60.01)
    ● **N48.2 Other inflammatory disorders of penis**
        Use additional code (B95-B97), to identify infectious agent
        Excludes1   balanitis (N48.1)
                 balanitis xerotica obliterans (N48.0)
                 balanoposthitis (N47.6)
        N48.21 Abscess of corpus cavernosum and penis ♂
        N48.22 Cellulitis of corpus cavernosum and penis ♂
        N48.29 Other inflammatory disorders of penis ♂
    ● **N48.3 Priapism**
        Painful erection
        Code first underlying cause
        N48.30 Priapism, unspecified ♂
        N48.31 Priapism due to trauma ♂
      ▷ *N48.32 Priapism due to disease classified elsewhere* ♂
        N48.33 Priapism, drug-induced ♂
        N48.39 Other priapism ♂
    N48.5 Ulcer of penis ♂
    N48.6 Induration penis plastica ♂
        Peyronie's disease
        Plastic induration of penis
    ● **N48.8 Other specified disorders of penis**
        N48.81 Thrombosis of superficial vein of penis ♂
        N48.82 Acquired torsion of penis ♂
            Acquired torsion of penis NOS
            Excludes1   congenital torsion of penis (Q55.63)
        N48.83 Acquired buried penis ♂
            Excludes1   congenital hidden penis (Q55.64)
        N48.89 Other specified disorders of penis ♂
    N48.9 Disorder of penis, unspecified ♂

Item 14-8 Male infertility is the inability of the female sex partner to conceive after one year of unprotected intercourse.
    Azoospermia is no sperm ejaculated and **oligospermia** is few sperm ejaculated—both resulting in infertility. Extratesticular causes such as injury, infections, radiation, and chemotherapy may also cause male infertility.

▶ New   ⇒ Revised   ~~deleted~~ Deleted   Excludes 1   Excludes 2   Includes   Use additional   Code first   Code also   Key words
OGCR Official Guidelines   X Assign placeholder X   ● Use Additional Character(s)   ▷ Manifestation Code   **Coding Clinic**

● **N49 Inflammatory disorders of male genital organs, not elsewhere classified**

Use additional code (B95-B97), to identify infectious agent

Excludes1	inflammation of penis (N48.1, N48.2-)
	orchitis and epididymitis (N45.-)

N49.0 Inflammatory disorders of seminal vesicle ♂
Vesiculitis NOS

N49.1 Inflammatory disorders of spermatic cord, tunica vaginalis and vas deferens ♂
Vasitis

N49.2 Inflammatory disorders of scrotum ♂

N49.3 Fournier gangrene ♂

N49.8 Inflammatory disorders of other specified male genital organs ♂
Inflammation of multiple sites in male genital organs

N49.9 Inflammatory disorder of unspecified male genital organ ♂
Abscess of unspecified male genital organ
Boil of unspecified male genital organ
Carbuncle of unspecified male genital organ
Cellulitis of unspecified male genital organ

● **N50 Other and unspecified disorders of male genital organs**

Excludes2   torsion of testis (N44.0-)

N50.0 Atrophy of testis ♂

N50.1 Vascular disorders of male genital organs ♂
Hematocele, NOS, of male genital organs
Hemorrhage of male genital organs
Thrombosis of male genital organs

N50.3 Cyst of epididymis ♂

● **N50.8 Other specified disorders of male genital organs**
Coding Clinic: 2016, Q4, P45

    ● **N50.81 Testicular pain**

       N50.811 Right testicular pain ♂
       N50.812 Left testicular pain ♂
       N50.819 Testicular pain, unspecified ♂

    N50.82 Scrotal pain ♂

    N50.89 Other specified disorders of the male genital organs ♂
Atrophy of scrotum, seminal vesicle, spermatic cord, tunica vaginalis and vas deferens
Chylocele, tunica vaginalis (nonfilarial) NOS
Edema of scrotum, seminal vesicle, spermatic cord, tunica vaginalis and vas deferens
Hypertrophy of scrotum, seminal vesicle, spermatic cord, tunica vaginalis and vas deferens
Stricture of spermatic cord, tunica vaginalis, and vas deferens
Ulcer of scrotum, seminal vesicle, spermatic cord, testis, tunica vaginalis and vas deferens
Urethroscrotal fistula

N50.9 Disorder of male genital organs, unspecified ♂

▷ *N51 Disorders of male genital organs in diseases classified elsewhere* ♂

Code first underlying disease, such as:
filariasis (B74.0-B74.9)

Excludes1	amebic balanitis (A06.8)
	candidal balanitis (B37.42)
	gonococcal balanitis (A54.23)
	gonococcal prostatitis (A54.22)
	herpesviral [herpes simplex] balanitis (A60.01)
	trichomonal prostatitis (A59.02)
	tuberculous prostatitis (A18.14)

Item 14–9 Seminal vesiculitis is an inflammation of the seminal vesicle. **Spermatocele** is a benign cystic accumulation of sperm arising from the head of the epididymis. **Torsion of the testis** is a medical emergency occurring most commonly in boys 7 to 12 years of age and results from a congenital abnormality of the covering of the testis allowing the testis to twist within its sac and cutting off the blood supply to the testis.

Figure 14-8   A. Torsion of testis. **B.** Torsion of the testis. (**B** from Kliegman R, Nelson WE: Nelson Textbook of Pediatrics, Philadelphia, Saunders, 2007)

● **N52 Male erectile dysfunction**

Excludes1   psychogenic impotence (F52.21)

● **N52.0 Vasculogenic erectile dysfunction**

    N52.01 Erectile dysfunction due to arterial insufficiency ♂   A

    N52.02 Corporo-venous occlusive erectile dysfunction ♂   A

    N52.03 Combined arterial insufficiency and corporo-venous occlusive erectile dysfunction ♂   A

▷ *N52.1 Erectile dysfunction due to diseases classified elsewhere* ♂   A

     Code first underlying disease

N52.2 Drug-induced erectile dysfunction ♂   A

● **N52.3 Postprocedural erectile dysfunction**

    N52.31 Erectile dysfunction following radical prostatectomy ♂   A

    N52.32 Erectile dysfunction following radical cystectomy ♂   A

    N52.33 Erectile dysfunction following urethral surgery ♂   A

    N52.34 Erectile dysfunction following simple prostatectomy ♂   A

    N52.35 Erectile dysfunction following radiation therapy ♂   A
      Coding Clinic: 2016, Q4, P45

    N52.36 Erectile dysfunction following interstitial seed therapy ♂   A
      Coding Clinic: 2016, Q4, P45

    N52.37 Erectile dysfunction following prostate ablative therapy ♂   A
Erectile dysfunction following cryotherapy
Erectile dysfunction following other prostate ablative therapies
Erectile dysfunction following ultrasound ablative therapies
      Coding Clinic: 2016, Q4, P45

    N52.39 Other and unspecified postprocedural erectile dysfunction ♂   A

N52.8 Other male erectile dysfunction ♂   A

N52.9 Male erectile dysfunction, unspecified ♂   A
Impotence NOS

● N53   **Other male sexual dysfunction**
   Excludes1   psychogenic sexual dysfunction (F52.-)
   ● N53.1   **Ejaculatory dysfunction**
      Excludes1   premature ejaculation (F52.4)
      N53.11   **Retarded ejaculation** ♂
      N53.12   **Painful ejaculation** ♂
      N53.13   **Anejaculatory orgasm** ♂
      N53.14   **Retrograde ejaculation** ♂
      N53.19   **Other ejaculatory dysfunction** ♂
             Ejaculatory dysfunction NOS
   N53.8   **Other male sexual dysfunction** ♂
   N53.9   **Unspecified male sexual dysfunction** ♂

DISORDERS OF BREAST (N60-N65)

   Excludes1   disorders of breast associated with childbirth
              (O91-O92)

● N60   **Benign mammary dysplasia**
   Benign lumpiness of breast
   Includes   fibrocystic mastopathy
   ● N60.0   **Solitary cyst of breast**
          Cyst of breast
      N60.01   **Solitary cyst of right breast**
      N60.02   **Solitary cyst of left breast**
      N60.09   **Solitary cyst of unspecified breast**
   ● N60.1   **Diffuse cystic mastopathy**
          Cystic breast
          Fibrocystic disease of breast
      Excludes1   diffuse cystic mastopathy with epithelial
                 proliferation (N60.3-)
      N60.11   **Diffuse cystic mastopathy of right breast**   A
      N60.12   **Diffuse cystic mastopathy of left breast**   A
      N60.19   **Diffuse cystic mastopathy of unspecified
             breast**   A
   ● N60.2   **Fibroadenosis of breast**
          Adenofibrosis of breast
      Excludes2   fibroadenoma of breast (D24.-)
      N60.21   **Fibroadenosis of right breast**
      N60.22   **Fibroadenosis of left breast**
      N60.29   **Fibroadenosis of unspecified breast**
   ● N60.3   **Fibrosclerosis of breast**
          Cystic mastopathy with epithelial proliferation
      N60.31   **Fibrosclerosis of right breast**
      N60.32   **Fibrosclerosis of left breast**
      N60.39   **Fibrosclerosis of unspecified breast**
   ● N60.4   **Mammary duct ectasia**
      N60.41   **Mammary duct ectasia of right breast**
      N60.42   **Mammary duct ectasia of left breast**
      N60.49   **Mammary duct ectasia of unspecified breast**
   ● N60.8   **Other benign mammary dysplasias**
      N60.81   **Other benign mammary dysplasias of right
             breast**
      N60.82   **Other benign mammary dysplasias of left
             breast**
      N60.89   **Other benign mammary dysplasias of
             unspecified breast**
   ● N60.9   **Unspecified benign mammary dysplasia**
      N60.91   **Unspecified benign mammary dysplasia of
             right breast**
      N60.92   **Unspecified benign mammary dysplasia of left
             breast**
      N60.99   **Unspecified benign mammary dysplasia of
             unspecified breast**

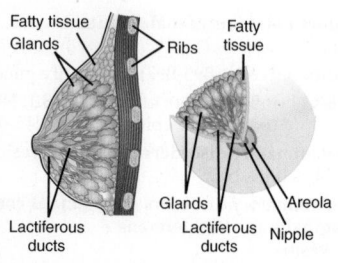

Figure 14-9   Breast.

● N61   **Inflammatory disorders of breast**
   Excludes1   inflammatory carcinoma of breast (C50.9)
              inflammatory disorder of breast associated with
                 childbirth (O91.-)
              neonatal infective mastitis (P39.0)
              thrombophlebitis of breast [Mondor's disease]
                 (I80.8)
   N61.0   **Mastitis without abscess**
          Infective mastitis (acute) (nonpuerperal) (subacute)
          Mastitis (acute) (nonpuerperal) (subacute) NOS
          Cellulitis (acute) (nonpuerperal) (subacute) of breast
             NOS
          Cellulitis (acute) (nonpuerperal) (subacute) of nipple
             NOS
   N61.1   **Abscess of the breast and nipple**
          Abscess (acute) (chronic) (nonpuerperal) of areola
          Abscess (acute) (chronic) (nonpuerperal) of breast
          Carbuncle of breast
          Mastitis with abscess

● N62   **Hypertrophy of breast**
       Gynecomastia
       Hypertrophy of breast NOS
       Massive pubertal hypertrophy of breast
   Excludes1   breast engorgement of newborn (P83.4)
              disproportion of reconstructed breast (N65.1)

● N63   **Unspecified lump in breast**
       Nodule(s) NOS in breast
   N63.0   **Unspecified lump in unspecified breast**
   ● N63.1   **Unspecified lump in the right breast**
      N63.10   **Unspecified lump in the right breast,
             unspecified quadrant**
      N63.11   **Unspecified lump in the right breast, upper
             outer quadrant**
             Coding Clinic: 2017, Q4, P19
      N63.12   **Unspecified lump in the right breast, upper
             inner quadrant**
      N63.13   **Unspecified lump in the right breast, lower
             outer quadrant**
      N63.14   **Unspecified lump in the right breast, lower
             inner quadrant**
   ● N63.2   **Unspecified lump in the left breast**
      N63.20   **Unspecified lump in the left breast, unspecified
             quadrant**
      N63.21   **Unspecified lump in the left breast, upper outer
             quadrant**
      N63.22   **Unspecified lump in the left breast, upper inner
             quadrant**
      N63.23   **Unspecified lump in the left breast, lower outer
             quadrant**
      N63.24   **Unspecified lump in the left breast, lower inner
             quadrant**

▶ New   ⇨ Revised   ~~deleted~~ Deleted   Excludes 1   Excludes 2   Includes   Use additional   Code first   Code also   Key words
OGCR Official Guidelines   X Assign placeholder X   ● Use Additional Character(s)   ▷ Manifestation Code   **Coding Clinic**

● **N63.3** Unspecified lump in axillary tail
    N63.31 Unspecified lump in axillary tail of the right breast
    N63.32 Unspecified lump in axillary tail of the left breast
● **N63.4** Unspecified lump in breast, subareolar
    N63.41 Unspecified lump in right breast, subareolar
    N63.42 Unspecified lump in left breast, subareolar

● **N64** Other disorders of breast
    Excludes2 mechanical complication of breast prosthesis and implant (T85.4-)
    N64.0 Fissure and fistula of nipple
    N64.1 Fat necrosis of breast
        Fat necrosis (segmental) of breast
        Code first breast necrosis due to breast graft (T85.898)
    N64.2 Atrophy of breast
    N64.3 Galactorrhea not associated with childbirth
        Excessive or spontaneous flow of milk
    N64.4 Mastodynia
●   **N64.5** Other signs and symptoms in breast
        Excludes2 abnormal findings on diagnostic imaging of breast (R92.-)
    N64.51 Induration of breast
    N64.52 Nipple discharge
        Excludes1 abnormal findings in nipple discharge (R89.-)
    N64.53 Retraction of nipple
    N64.59 Other signs and symptoms in breast
●   **N64.8** Other specified disorders of breast
    N64.81 Ptosis of breast   A
        Excludes1 ptosis of native breast in relation to reconstructed breast (N65.1)
    N64.82 Hypoplasia of breast   A
        Micromastia
        Excludes1 congenital absence of breast (Q83.0)
                hypoplasia of native breast in relation to reconstructed breast (N65.1)
    N64.89 Other specified disorders of breast
        Galactocele
        Subinvolution of breast (postlactational)
        Coding Clinic: 2018, Q1, P4
    N64.9 Disorder of breast, unspecified
        Coding Clinic: 2018, Q1, P4

● **N65** Deformity and disproportion of reconstructed breast
    N65.0 Deformity of reconstructed breast   A
        Contour irregularity in reconstructed breast
        Excess tissue in reconstructed breast
        Misshapen reconstructed breast
    N65.1 Disproportion of reconstructed breast   A
        Breast asymmetry between native breast and reconstructed breast
        Disproportion between native breast and reconstructed breast

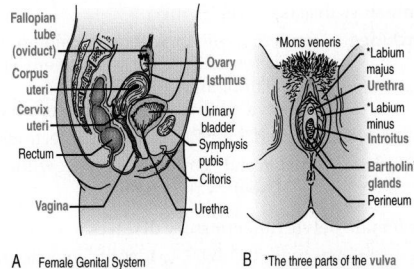

A   Female Genital System   B   *The three parts of the vulva

Figure 14-10 **A.** Female genital system. **B.** External female genital system. (From Buck CJ: Step-by-Step Medical Coding, ed 2016, St. Louis, Elsevier, 2016)

Item 14–10 Salpingitis is an infection of one or both fallopian tubes. **Oophoritis** is an infection of one or both ovaries.

INFLAMMATORY DISEASES OF FEMALE PELVIC ORGANS (N70-N77)

    Excludes1 inflammatory diseases of female pelvic organs complicating:
        abortion or ectopic or molar pregnancy (O00-O07, O08.0)
        pregnancy, childbirth and the puerperium (O23.-, O75.3, O85, O86.-)

★ **(See Plate 360 on page 80.)**

● **N70** Salpingitis and oophoritis
    Oophoritis = inflammation of ovary
    Salpingitis = inflammation of falloplan tube
    Includes   abscess (of) fallopian tube
                abscess (of) ovary
                pyosalpinx
                salpingo-oophoritis
                tubo-ovarian abscess
                tubo-ovarian inflammatory disease
    Use additional code (B95-B97), to identify infectious agent
    Excludes1 gonococcal infection (A54.24)
              tuberculous infection (A18.17)
  ● **N70.0** Acute salpingitis and oophoritis
    N70.01 Acute salpingitis ♀
    N70.02 Acute oophoritis ♀
    N70.03 Acute salpingitis and oophoritis ♀
  ● **N70.1** Chronic salpingitis and oophoritis
        Hydrosalpinx
    N70.11 Chronic salpingitis ♀
    N70.12 Chronic oophoritis ♀
    N70.13 Chronic salpingitis and oophoritis ♀
  ● **N70.9** Salpingitis and oophoritis, unspecified
    N70.91 Salpingitis, unspecified ♀
    N70.92 Oophoritis, unspecified ♀
    N70.93 Salpingitis and oophoritis, unspecified ♀

● **N71** Inflammatory disease of uterus, except cervix
    Includes   endo (myo) metritis
                metritis
                myometritis
                pyometra
                uterine abscess
    Use additional code (B95-B97), to identify infectious agent
    Excludes1 hyperplastic endometritis (N85.0-)
              infection of uterus following delivery (O85, O86.-)
    N71.0 Acute inflammatory disease of uterus ♀
    N71.1 Chronic inflammatory disease of uterus ♀
    N71.9 Inflammatory disease of uterus, unspecified ♀

CHAPTER 14 (N00–N99)

N72   Inflammatory disease of cervix uteri ♀

    Includes   cervicitis (with or without erosion or ectropion)
                     endocervicitis (with or without erosion or
                       ectropion)
                     exocervicitis (with or without erosion or ectropion)

    Use additional code (B95-B97), to identify infectious agent

    Excludes1   erosion and ectropion of cervix without cervicitis
                     (N86)

● **N73   Other female pelvic inflammatory diseases**

    Use additional code (B95-B97), to identify infectious agent

    N73.0   Acute parametritis and pelvic cellulitis ♀
        Abscess of broad ligament
        Abscess of parametrium
        Pelvic cellulitis, female

    N73.1   Chronic parametritis and pelvic cellulitis ♀
        Any condition in N73.0 specified as chronic

        Excludes1   tuberculous parametritis and pelvic
                      cellultis (A18.17)

    N73.2   Unspecified parametritis and pelvic cellulitis ♀
        Any condition in N73.0 unspecified whether acute or
           chronic

    N73.3   Female acute pelvic peritonitis ♀

    N73.4   Female chronic pelvic peritonitis ♀

        Excludes1   tuberculous pelvic (female) peritonitis
                      (A18.17)

    N73.5   Female pelvic peritonitis, unspecified ♀

    N73.6   Female pelvic peritoneal adhesions (postinfective) ♀

        Excludes2   postprocedural pelvic peritoneal
                      adhesions (N99.4)

    N73.8   Other specified female pelvic inflammatory diseases ♀

    N73.9   Female pelvic inflammatory disease, unspecified ♀
        Female pelvic infection or inflammation NOS

▷ *N74   Female pelvic inflammatory disorders in diseases classified
       elsewhere* ♀

    Code first underlying disease

    Excludes1   chlamydial cervicitis (A56.02)
                     chlamydial pelvic inflammatory disease (A56.11)
                     gonococcal cervicitis (A54.03)
                     gonococcal pelvic inflammatory disease (A54.24)
                     herpesviral [herpes simplex] cervicitis (A60.03)
                     herpesviral [herpes simplex] pelvic inflammatory
                      disease (A60.09)
                     syphilitic cervicitis (A52.76)
                     syphilitic pelvic inflammatory disease (A52.76)
                     trichomonal cervicitis (A59.09)
                     tuberculous cervicitis (A18.16)
                     tuberculous pelvic inflammatory disease (A18.17)

● **N75   Diseases of Bartholin's gland**

    N75.0   Cyst of Bartholin's gland ♀
        Cysts filled with liquid or semisolid material

    N75.1   Abscess of Bartholin's gland ♀
        Localized collection of pus

    N75.8   Other diseases of Bartholin's gland ♀
        Bartholinitis

    N75.9   Disease of Bartholin's gland, unspecified ♀

● **N76   Other inflammation of vagina and vulva**

    Use additional code (B95-B97), to identify infectious agent

    Excludes2   senile (atrophic) vaginitis (N95.2)
                     vulvar vestibulitis (N94.810)

    N76.0   Acute vaginitis ♀
        Acute vulvovaginitis
        Vaginitis NOS
        Vulvovaginitis NOS

    N76.1   Subacute and chronic vaginitis ♀
        Chronic vulvovaginitis
        Subacute vulvovaginitis

    N76.2   Acute vulvitis ♀
        Vulvitis NOS

    N76.3   Subacute and chronic vulvitis ♀

    N76.4   Abscess of vulva ♀
        Furuncle of vulva

    N76.5   Ulceration of vagina ♀

    N76.6   Ulceration of vulva ♀

    ● **N76.8   Other specified inflammation of vagina and vulva**

        N76.81   Mucositis (ulcerative) of vagina and vulva ♀

           Code also type of associated therapy, such as:
              antineoplastic and immunosuppressive
                  drugs (T45.1X-)
              radiological procedure and radiotherapy
                  (Y84.2)

           Excludes2   gastrointestinal mucositis
                           (ulcerative) (K92.81)
                         nasal mucositis (ulcerative)
                           (J34.81)
                         oral mucositis (ulcerative) (K12.3-)

        **N76.89   Other specified inflammation of vagina and
              vulva** ♀

● **N77   Vulvovaginal ulceration and inflammation in diseases classified
    elsewhere**

    ▷ *N77.0   Ulceration of vulva in diseases classified elsewhere* ♀

        Code first underlying disease, such as:
        Behçet's disease (M35.2)

        Excludes1   ulceration of vulva in gonococcal
                      infection (A54.02)
                      ulceration of vulva in herpesviral [herpes
                        simplex] infection (A60.04)
                      ulceration of vulva in syphilis (A51.0)
                      ulceration of vulva in tuberculosis (A18.18)

    ▷ *N77.1   Vaginitis, vulvitis and vulvovaginitis in diseases
        classified elsewhere* ♀

        Code first underlying disease, such as:
        pinworm (B80)

        Excludes1   candidial vulvovaginitis (B37.3)
                      chlamydial vulvovaginitis (A56.02)
                      gonococcal vulvovaginitis (A54.02)
                      herpesviral [herpes simplex]
                        vulvovaginitis (A60.04)
                      trichomonal vulvovaginitis (A59.01)
                      tuberculous vulvovaginitis (A18.18)
                      vulvovaginitis in early syphilis (A51.0)
                      vulvovaginitis in late syphilis (A52.76)

▶ New   ⇒ Revised   ~~deleted~~ Deleted   Excludes 1   Excludes 2   Includes   Use additional   Code first   Code also   Key words

OGCR Official Guidelines   X Assign placeholder X   ● Use Additional Character(s)   ▷ Manifestation Code   **Coding Clinic**

Item 14–11 Endometriosis is a condition for which no clear cause has been identified. Endometrial tissue is expelled from the uterus into the abdominal cavity and can implant onto a variety of organs. Classification is based on the site of implant of the endometrial tissue.

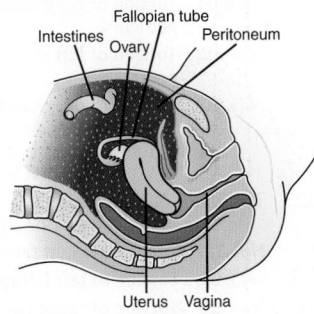

Fallopian tube
Intestines Ovary   Peritoneum

Uterus Vagina

Figure 14-11   Sites of potential endometrial implants.

NONINFLAMMATORY DISORDERS OF FEMALE GENITAL TRACT (N80–N98)

● N80   Endometriosis

  N80.0   **Endometriosis of uterus** ♀
     Adenomyosis
     Excludes1   stromal endometriosis (D39.0)

  N80.1   **Endometriosis of ovary** ♀
  N80.2   **Endometriosis of fallopian tube** ♀
  N80.3   **Endometriosis of pelvic peritoneum** ♀
  N80.4   **Endometriosis of rectovaginal septum and vagina** ♀
  N80.5   **Endometriosis of intestine** ♀
  N80.6   **Endometriosis in cutaneous scar** ♀
  N80.8   **Other endometriosis** ♀
     Endometriosis of thorax

  N80.9   **Endometriosis, unspecified** ♀

● N81   Female genital prolapse
     Excludes1   genital prolapse complicating pregnancy, labor or delivery (O34.5-)
        prolapse and hernia of ovary and fallopian tube (N83.4-)
        prolapse of vaginal vault after hysterectomy (N99.3)

  N81.0   **Urethrocele** ♀
     Excludes1   urethrocele with cystocele (N81.1-)
        urethrocele with prolapse of uterus (N81.2-N81.4)

● N81.1   **Cystocele**
     Cystocele with urethrocele
     Cystourethrocele
     Excludes1   cystocele with prolapse of uterus (N81.2-N81.4)

  N81.10   **Cystocele, unspecified** ♀
     Prolapse of (anterior) vaginal wall NOS
  N81.11   **Cystocele, midline** ♀
  N81.12   **Cystocele, lateral** ♀
     Paravaginal cystocele

A   B   C

Figure 14-12   Three stages of uterine prolapse. **A.** Uterus is prolapsed. **B.** Vagina and uterus are prolapsed (incomplete uterovaginal prolapse). **C.** Vagina and uterus are completely prolapsed and are exposed through the external genitalia (complete uterovaginal prolapse).

  N81.2   **Incomplete uterovaginal prolapse** ♀
     First degree uterine prolapse
     Prolapse of cervix NOS
     Second degree uterine prolapse
     Excludes1   cervical stump prolapse (N81.85)

  N81.3   **Complete uterovaginal prolapse** ♀
     Procidentia (uteri) NOS
     Third degree uterine prolapse

  N81.4   **Uterovaginal prolapse, unspecified** ♀
     Prolapse of uterus NOS

  N81.5   **Vaginal enterocele** ♀
     Excludes1   enterocele with prolapse of uterus (N81.2-N81.4)

  N81.6   **Rectocele** ♀
     Prolapse of posterior vaginal wall
     Use additional code for any associated fecal incontinence, if applicable (R15.-)
     Excludes2   perineocele (N81.81)
        rectal prolapse (K62.3)
        rectocele with prolapse of uterus (N81.2-N81.4)

● N81.8   **Other female genital prolapse**
  N81.81   **Perineocele** ♀
  N81.82   **Incompetence or weakening of pubocervical tissue** ♀
  N81.83   **Incompetence or weakening of rectovaginal tissue** ♀
  N81.84   **Pelvic muscle wasting** ♀
     Disuse atrophy of pelvic muscles and anal sphincter
  N81.85   **Cervical stump prolapse** ♀
  N81.89   **Other female genital prolapse** ♀
     Deficient perineum
     Old laceration of muscles of pelvic floor

  N81.9   **Female genital prolapse, unspecified** ♀

● N82   Fistulae involving female genital tract
     Excludes1   vesicointestinal fistulae (N32.1)

  N82.0   **Vesicovaginal fistula** ♀
  N82.1   **Other female urinary-genital tract fistulae** ♀
     Cervicovesical fistula
     Ureterovaginal fistula
     Urethrovaginal fistula
     Uteroureteric fistula
     Uterovesical fistula
     Coding Clinic: 2017, Q3, P4

  N82.2   **Fistula of vagina to small intestine** ♀
  N82.3   **Fistula of vagina to large intestine** ♀
     Rectovaginal fistula
  N82.4   **Other female intestinal-genital tract fistulae** ♀
     Intestinouterine fistula
  N82.5   **Female genital tract-skin fistulae** ♀
     Uterus to abdominal wall fistula
     Vaginoperineal fistula
  N82.8   **Other female genital tract fistulae** ♀
  N82.9   **Female genital tract fistula, unspecified** ♀

● N83   Noninflammatory disorders of ovary, fallopian tube and broad ligament
     Excludes2   hydrosalpinx (N70.1-)

● N83.0   **Follicular cyst of ovary**
     Cyst of graafian follicle
     Hemorrhagic follicular cyst (of ovary)
     Coding Clinic: 2016, Q4, P46
  N83.00   **Follicular cyst of ovary, unspecified side** ♀
  N83.01   **Follicular cyst of right ovary** ♀
  N83.02   **Follicular cyst of left ovary** ♀

CHAPTER 14 (N00-N99)

● **N83.1** **Corpus luteum cyst**
     Hemorrhagic corpus luteum cyst
     Coding Clinic: 2016, Q4, P46

     N83.10   Corpus luteum cyst of ovary, unspecified side ♀

     N83.11   Corpus luteum cyst of right ovary ♀

     N83.12   Corpus luteum cyst of left ovary ♀

● **N83.2** **Other and unspecified ovarian cysts**
     Excludes1   developmental ovarian cyst (Q50.1)
                      neoplastic ovarian cyst (D27.-)
                      polycystic ovarian syndrome (E28.2)
                      Stein-Leventhal syndrome (E28.2)
     Coding Clinic: 2016, Q4, P46

     ● **N83.20**   Unspecified ovarian cysts

         N83.201   Unspecified ovarian cyst, right side ♀

         N83.202   Unspecified ovarian cyst, left side ♀

         N83.209   Unspecified ovarian cyst, unspecified side ♀
                   Ovarian cyst, NOS

     ● **N83.29**   Other ovarian cysts
         Retention cyst of ovary
         Simple cyst of ovary

         N83.291   Other ovarian cyst, right side ♀

         N83.292   Other ovarian cyst, left side ♀

         N83.299   Other ovarian cyst, unspecified side ♀

● **N83.3** **Acquired atrophy of ovary and fallopian tube**
     Coding Clinic: 2016, Q4, P46

     ● **N83.31**   Acquired atrophy of ovary

         N83.311   Acquired atrophy of right ovary ♀

         N83.312   Acquired atrophy of left ovary ♀

         N83.319   Acquired atrophy of ovary, unspecified side ♀
                   Acquired atrophy of ovary, NOS

     ● **N83.32**   Acquired atrophy of fallopian tube

         N83.321   Acquired atrophy of right fallopian tube ♀

         N83.322   Acquired atrophy of left fallopian tube ♀

         N83.329   Acquired atrophy of fallopian tube, unspecified side ♀
                   Acquired atrophy of fallopian tube, NOS

     ● **N83.33**   Acquired atrophy of ovary and fallopian tube

         N83.331   Acquired atrophy of right ovary and fallopian tube ♀

         N83.332   Acquired atrophy of left ovary and fallopian tube ♀

         N83.339   Acquired atrophy of ovary and fallopian tube, unspecified side ♀
                   Acquired atrophy of ovary and fallopian tube, NOS

● **N83.4** **Prolapse and hernia of ovary and fallopian tube**
     Coding Clinic: 2016, Q4, P46

     N83.40   Prolapse and hernia of ovary and fallopian tube, unspecified side ♀
         Prolapse and hernia of ovary and fallopian tube, NOS

     N83.41   Prolapse and hernia of right ovary and fallopian tube ♀

     N83.42   Prolapse and hernia of left ovary and fallopian tube ♀

● **N83.5** **Torsion of ovary, ovarian pedicle and fallopian tube**
     Torsion of accessory tube
     Coding Clinic: 2016, Q4, P46

     ● **N83.51**   Torsion of ovary and ovarian pedicle

         N83.511   Torsion of right ovary and ovarian pedicle ♀

         N83.512   Torsion of left ovary and ovarian pedicle ♀

         N83.519   Torsion of ovary and ovarian pedicle, unspecified side ♀
                   Torsion of ovary and ovarian pedicle, NOS

     ● **N83.52**   Torsion of fallopian tube
         Torsion of hydatid of Morgagni

         N83.521   Torsion of right fallopian tube ♀

         N83.522   Torsion of left fallopian tube ♀

         N83.529   Torsion of fallopian tube, unspecified side ♀
                   Torsion of fallopian tube, NOS

     N83.53   Torsion of ovary, ovarian pedicle and fallopian tube ♀

N83.6 **Hematosalpinx** ♀
     Excludes1   hematosalpinx (with) (in):
                      hematocolpos (N89.7)
                      hematometra (N85.7)
                      tubal pregnancy (O00.1-)

N83.7 **Hematoma of broad ligament** ♀

N83.8 **Other noninflammatory disorders of ovary, fallopian tube and broad ligament** ♀
     Broad ligament laceration syndrome [Allen-Masters]

N83.9 **Noninflammatory disorder of ovary, fallopian tube and broad ligament, unspecified** ♀

● **N84** **Polyp of female genital tract**
     Excludes1   adenomatous polyp (D28.-)
                      placental polyp (O90.89)

N84.0 **Polyp of corpus uteri** ♀
     Polyp of endometrium
     Polyp of uterus NOS
     Excludes1   polypoid endometrial hyperplasia (N85.0-)

N84.1 **Polyp of cervix uteri** ♀
     Mucous polyp of cervix

N84.2 **Polyp of vagina** ♀

N84.3 **Polyp of vulva** ♀
     Polyp of labia

N84.8 **Polyp of other parts of female genital tract** ♀

N84.9 **Polyp of female genital tract, unspecified** ♀

● **N85** **Other noninflammatory disorders of uterus, except cervix**
     Excludes1   endometriosis (N80.-)
                      inflammatory diseases of uterus (N71.-)
                      noninflammatory disorders of cervix, except malposition (N86-N88)
                      polyp of corpus uteri (N84.0)
                      uterine prolapse (N81.-)

● **N85.0** **Endometrial hyperplasia**

     N85.00   Endometrial hyperplasia, unspecified ♀
         Hyperplasia (adenomatous) (cystic) (glandular) of endometrium
         Hyperplastic endometritis

     N85.01   Benign endometrial hyperplasia ♀
         Endometrial hyperplasia (complex) (simple) without atypia

     N85.02   Endometrial intraepithelial neoplasia [EIN] ♀
         Endometrial hyperplasia with atypia
         Excludes1   malignant neoplasm of endometrium (with endometrial intraepithelial neoplasia [EIN]) (C54.1)

▶ New   ➡ Revised   ~~deleted~~ Deleted   Excludes 1   Excludes 2   Includes   Use additional   Code first   Code also   Key words
OGCR Official Guidelines   X Assign placeholder X   ● Use Additional Character(s)   ▶ Manifestation Code   **Coding Clinic**

N85.2   Hypertrophy of uterus ♀
Bulky or enlarged uterus
> **Excludes1**   puerperal hypertrophy of uterus (O90.89)

N85.3   Subinvolution of uterus ♀
> **Excludes1**   puerperal subinvolution of uterus (O90.89)

N85.4   Malposition of uterus ♀
Anteversion of uterus
Retroflexion of uterus
Retroversion of uterus
> **Excludes1**   malposition of uterus complicating pregnancy, labor or delivery (O34.5-, O65.5)

N85.5   Inversion of uterus ♀
> **Excludes1**   current obstetric trauma (O71.2)
> postpartum inversion of uterus (O71.2)

N85.6   Intrauterine synechiae ♀

N85.7   Hematometra ♀
Hematosalpinx with hematometra
> **Excludes1**   hematometra with hematocolpos (N89.7)

N85.8   Other specified noninflammatory disorders of uterus ♀
Atrophy of uterus, acquired
Fibrosis of uterus NOS

N85.9   Noninflammatory disorder of uterus, unspecified ♀
Disorder of uterus NOS

N86   Erosion and ectropion of cervix uteri ♀
Decubitus (trophic) ulcer of cervix
Eversion of cervix
> **Excludes1**   erosion and ectropion of cervix with cervicitis (N72)

● **N87   Dysplasia of cervix uteri**
> **Excludes1**   abnormal results from cervical cytologic examination without histologic confirmation (R87.61-)
> carcinoma in situ of cervix uteri (D06.-)
> cervical intraepithelial neoplasia III [CIN III] (D06.-)
> HGSIL of cervix (R87.613)
> severe dysplasia of cervix uteri (D06.-)

N87.0   Mild cervical dysplasia ♀
Cervical intraepithelial neoplasia I [CIN I]

N87.1   Moderate cervical dysplasia ♀
Cervical intraepithelial neoplasia II [CIN II]

N87.9   Dysplasia of cervix uteri, unspecified ♀
Anaplasia of cervix
Cervical atypism
Cervical dysplasia NOS

● **N88   Other noninflammatory disorders of cervix uteri**
> **Excludes2**   inflammatory disease of cervix (N72)
> polyp of cervix (N84.1)

N88.0   Leukoplakia of cervix uteri ♀

N88.1   Old laceration of cervix uteri ♀
Adhesions of cervix
> **Excludes1**   current obstetric trauma (O71.3)

N88.2   Stricture and stenosis of cervix uteri ♀
> **Excludes1**   stricture and stenosis of cervix uteri complicating labor (O65.5)

N88.3   Incompetence of cervix uteri ♀
Investigation and management of (suspected) cervical incompetence in a nonpregnant woman
> **Excludes1**   cervical incompetence complicating pregnancy (O34.3-)

N88.4   Hypertrophic elongation of cervix uteri ♀

N88.8   Other specified noninflammatory disorders of cervix uteri ♀
> **Excludes1**   current obstetric trauma (O71.3)

N88.9   Noninflammatory disorder of cervix uteri, unspecified ♀

● **N89   Other noninflammatory disorders of vagina**
> **Excludes1**   abnormal results from vaginal cytologic examination without histologic confirmation (R87.62-)
> carcinoma in situ of vagina (D07.2)
> HGSIL of vagina (R87.623)
> inflammation of vagina (N76.-)
> senile (atrophic) vaginitis (N95.2)
> severe dysplasia of vagina (D07.2)
> trichomonal leukorrhea (A59.00)
> vaginal intraepithelial neoplasia [VAIN], grade III (D07.2)

N89.0   Mild vaginal dysplasia ♀
Vaginal intraepithelial neoplasia [VAIN], grade I

N89.1   Moderate vaginal dysplasia ♀
Vaginal intraepithelial neoplasia [VAIN], grade II

N89.3   Dysplasia of vagina, unspecified ♀

N89.4   Leukoplakia of vagina ♀

N89.5   Stricture and atresia of vagina ♀
Vaginal adhesions   Vaginal stenosis
> **Excludes1**   congenital atresia or stricture (Q52.4)
> postprocedural adhesions of vagina (N99.2)

N89.6   Tight hymenal ring ♀
Rigid hymen   Tight introitus
> **Excludes1**   imperforate hymen (Q52.3)

N89.7   Hematocolpos ♀
Hematocolpos with hematometra or hematosalpinx
Coding Clinic: 2016, Q4, P59

N89.8   Other specified noninflammatory disorders of vagina ♀
Leukorrhea NOS
Old vaginal laceration
Pessary ulcer of vagina
> **Excludes1**   current obstetric trauma (O70.-, O71.4, O71.7-O71.8)
> old laceration involving muscles of pelvic floor (N81.8)

N89.9   Noninflammatory disorder of vagina, unspecified ♀

● **N90   Other noninflammatory disorders of vulva and perineum**
> **Excludes1**   anogenital (venereal) warts (A63.0)
> carcinoma in situ of vulva (D07.1)
> condyloma acuminatum (A63.0)
> current obstetric trauma (O70.-, O71.7-O71.8)
> inflammation of vulva (N76.-)
> severe dysplasia of vulva (D07.1)
> vulvar intraepithelial neoplasm III [VIN III] (D07.1)

N90.0   Mild vulvar dysplasia ♀
Vulvar intraepithelial neoplasia [VIN], grade I

N90.1   Moderate vulvar dysplasia ♀
Vulvar intraepithelial neoplasia [VIN], grade II

N90.3   Dysplasia of vulva, unspecified ♀

N90.4   Leukoplakia of vulva ♀
Dystrophy of vulva
Kraurosis of vulva
Lichen sclerosus of external female genital organs

N90.5   Atrophy of vulva ♀
Stenosis of vulva

● **N90.6   Hypertrophy of vulva**
Coding Clinic: 2016, Q4, P46

    N90.60   Unspecified hypertrophy of vulva ♀
Unspecified hypertrophy of labia

    N90.61   Childhood asymmetric labium majus enlargement ♀
CALME

    N90.69   Other specified hypertrophy of vulva ♀
Other specified hypertrophy of labia

N90.7   Vulvar cyst ♀

● N90.8   Other specified noninflammatory disorders of vulva and perineum

   ● N90.81   Female genital mutilation status
      Female genital cutting status

      N90.810   Female genital mutilation status, unspecified ♀
         Female genital cutting status, unspecified
         Female genital mutilation status NOS

      N90.811   Female genital mutilation Type I status
         Clitorectomy status
         Female genital cutting Type I status

      N90.812   Female genital mutilation Type II status ♀
         Clitorectomy with excision of labia minora status
         Female genital cutting Type II status

      N90.813   Female genital mutilation Type III status ♀
         Female genital cutting Type III status
         Infibulation status

      N90.818   Other female genital mutilation status ♀
         Female genital cutting Type IV status
         Female genital mutilation Type IV status
         Other female genital cutting status

   N90.89   Other specified noninflammatory disorders of vulva and perineum ♀
      Adhesions of vulva
      Hypertrophy of clitoris

N90.9   Noninflammatory disorder of vulva and perineum, unspecified ♀

● N91   Absent, scanty and rare menstruation
   Excludes1   ovarian dysfunction (E28.-)

N91.0   Primary amenorrhea ♀
N91.1   Secondary amenorrhea ♀
N91.2   Amenorrhea, unspecified ♀
N91.3   Primary oligomenorrhea ♀
N91.4   Secondary oligomenorrhea ♀
N91.5   Oligomenorrhea, unspecified ♀
      Hypomenorrhea NOS

● N92   Excessive, frequent and irregular menstruation
   Excludes1   postmenopausal bleeding (N95.0)
           precocious puberty (menstruation) (E30.1)

N92.0   Excessive and frequent menstruation with regular cycle ♀
      Heavy periods NOS   Polymenorrhea
      Menorrhagia NOS

N92.1   Excessive and frequent menstruation with irregular cycle ♀
      Irregular intermenstrual bleeding
      Irregular, shortened intervals between menstrual bleeding
      Menometrorrhagia
      Metrorrhagia

N92.2   Excessive menstruation at puberty ♀   P
      Excessive bleeding associated with onset of menstrual periods
      Pubertal menorrhagia
      Puberty bleeding

N92.3   Ovulation bleeding ♀
      Regular intermenstrual bleeding

N92.4   Excessive bleeding in the premenopausal period ♀
      Climacteric menorrhagia or metrorrhagia
      Menopausal menorrhagia or metrorrhagia
      Preclimacteric menorrhagia or metrorrhagia
      Premenopausal menorrhagia or metrorrhagia

N92.5   Other specified irregular menstruation ♀
N92.6   Irregular menstruation, unspecified ♀
      Irregular bleeding NOS
      Irregular periods NOS
   Excludes1   irregular menstruation with:
         lengthened intervals or scanty bleeding (N91.3-N91.5)
         shortened intervals or excessive bleeding (N92.1)

● N93   Other abnormal uterine and vaginal bleeding
   Excludes1   neonatal vaginal hemorrhage (P54.6)
           precocious puberty (menstruation) (E30.1)
           pseudomenses (P54.6)

N93.0   Postcoital and contact bleeding ♀
N93.1   Pre-pubertal vaginal bleeding ♀
      Coding Clinic: 2016, Q4, P47
N93.8   Other specified abnormal uterine and vaginal bleeding ♀
      Dysfunctional or functional uterine or vaginal bleeding NOS
N93.9   Abnormal uterine and vaginal bleeding, unspecified ♀

● N94   Pain and other conditions associated with female genital organs and menstrual cycle

N94.0   Mittelschmerz ♀
      Ovulation pain

● N94.1   Dyspareunia
      Painful intercourse/coitus
   Excludes1   psychogenic dyspareunia (F52.6)
      Coding Clinic: 2016, Q4, P47
   N94.10   Unspecified dyspareunia ♀
   N94.11   Superficial (introital) dyspareunia ♀
   N94.12   Deep dyspareunia ♀
   N94.19   Other specified dyspareunia ♀

N94.2   Vaginismus ♀
      Vagina tightness
   Excludes1   psychogenic vaginismus (F52.5)

N94.3   Premenstrual tension syndrome ♀
      AKA: PMS
      Code also associated menstrual migraine (G43.82-, G43.83-)
   Excludes1   Premenstrual dysphoric disorder (F32.81)
      Coding Clinic: 2016, Q4, P14

N94.4   Primary dysmenorrhea ♀
      Lifelong painful menstruation
N94.5   Secondary dysmenorrhea ♀
      Later onset of painful menstruation
N94.6   Dysmenorrhea, unspecified ♀
   Excludes1   psychogenic dysmenorrhea (F45.8)

● N94.8   Other specified conditions associated with female genital organs and menstrual cycle

   ● N94.81   Vulvodynia
      N94.810   Vulvar vestibulitis ♀
      N94.818   Other vulvodynia ♀
      N94.819   Vulvodynia, unspecified ♀
         Vulvodynia NOS

   N94.89   Other specified conditions associated with female genital organs and menstrual cycle ♀

N94.9   Unspecified condition associated with female genital organs and menstrual cycle ♀

▶ New   ⇒ Revised   ~~deleted~~ Deleted   Excludes 1   Excludes 2   Includes   Use additional   Code first   Code also   Key words
OGCR Official Guidelines   X Assign placeholder X   ● Use Additional Character(s)   ▷ Manifestation Code   **Coding Clinic**

● N95   Menopausal and other perimenopausal disorders
        Menopausal and other perimenopausal disorders due to
            naturally occurring (age-related) menopause and
            perimenopause
        Excludes1   excessive bleeding in the premenopausal period
                    (N92.4)
                    menopausal and perimenopausal disorders due
                        to artificial or premature menopause (E89.4-,
                        E28.31-)
                    premature menopause (E28.31-)
        Excludes2   postmenopausal osteoporosis (M81.0-)
                    postmenopausal osteoporosis with current
                        pathological fracture (M80.0-)
                    postmenopausal urethritis (N34.2)
        N95.0   Postmenopausal bleeding ♀
        N95.1   Menopausal and female climacteric states ♀
                Symptoms such as flushing, sleeplessness, headache,
                    lack of concentration, associated with natural (age-
                    related) menopause
                Use additional code for associated symptoms
                Excludes1   asymptomatic menopausal state (Z78.0)
                            symptoms associated with artificial
                                menopause (E89.41)
                            symptoms associated with premature
                                menopause (E28.310)
        N95.2   Postmenopausal atrophic vaginitis ♀
                Senile (atrophic) vaginitis
        N95.8   Other specified menopausal and perimenopausal
                disorders ♀
        N95.9   Unspecified menopausal and perimenopausal disorder ♀
    N96   Recurrent pregnancy loss ♀
        Investigation or care in a nonpregnant woman with history of
            recurrent pregnancy loss
        Excludes1   recurrent pregnancy loss with current pregnancy
                    (O26.2-)

● N97   Female infertility
        Includes   inability to achieve a pregnancy
                    sterility, female NOS
        Excludes1   female infertility associated with:
                    hypopituitarism (E23.0)
                    Stein-Leventhal syndrome (E28.2)
        Excludes2   incompetence of cervix uteri (N88.3)
        N97.0   Female infertility associated with anovulation ♀
        N97.1   Female infertility of tubal origin ♀
                Female infertility associated with congenital anomaly
                    of tube
                Female infertility due to tubal block
                Female infertility due to tubal occlusion
                Female infertility due to tubal stenosis
        N97.2   Female infertility of uterine origin ♀
                Female infertility associated with congenital anomaly
                    of uterus
                Female infertility due to nonimplantation of ovum
        N97.8   Female infertility of other origin ♀
        N97.9   Female infertility, unspecified ♀
● N98   Complications associated with artificial fertilization
        N98.0   Infection associated with artificial insemination ♀
        N98.1   Hyperstimulation of ovaries ♀
                Hyperstimulation of ovaries NOS
                Hyperstimulation of ovaries associated with induced
                    ovulation
        N98.2   Complications of attempted introduction of fertilized
                ovum following in vitro fertilization ♀
        N98.3   Complications of attempted introduction of embryo in
                embryo transfer ♀
        N98.8   Other complications associated with artificial
                fertilization ♀
        N98.9   Complication associated with artificial fertilization,
                unspecified ♀

**INTRAOPERATIVE AND POSTPROCEDURAL COMPLICATIONS AND DISORDERS
OF GENITOURINARY SYSTEM, NOT ELSEWHERE CLASSIFIED (N99)**

● N99   Intraoperative and postprocedural complications and disorders
        of genitourinary system, not elsewhere classified
        Excludes2   irradiation cystitis (N30.4-)
                    postoophorectomy osteoporosis with current
                        pathological fracture (M80.8-)
                    postoophorectomy osteoporosis without current
                        pathological fracture (M81.8)
        N99.0   Postprocedural (acute) (chronic) kidney failure
                Use additional code to type of kidney disease
● N99.1   Postprocedural urethral stricture
        Postcatheterization urethral stricture
        ● N99.11   Postprocedural urethral stricture, male
                N99.110   Postprocedural urethral stricture,
                          male, meatal ♂
                N99.111   Postprocedural bulbous urethral
                          stricture, male ♂
                N99.112   Postprocedural membranous urethral
                          stricture, male ♂
                N99.113   Postprocedural anterior bulbous
                          urethral stricture, male ♂
                          Coding Clinic: 2016, Q4, P48
                N99.114   Postprocedural urethral stricture,
                          male, unspecified ♂
                N99.115   Postprocedural fossa navicularis
                          urethral stricture ♂
                          Coding Clinic: 2016, Q4, P47
            ▶ N99.116   Postprocedural urethral stricture,
                          male, overlapping sites ♂
        N99.12   Postprocedural urethral stricture, female ♀
    N99.2   Postprocedural adhesions of vagina ♀
    N99.3   Prolapse of vaginal vault after hysterectomy ♀
    N99.4   Postprocedural pelvic peritoneal adhesions
            Excludes2   pelvic peritoneal adhesions NOS (N73.6)
                        postinfective pelvic peritoneal adhesions
                            (N73.6)
● N99.5   Complications of stoma of urinary tract
        Excludes2   mechanical complication of urinary
                    catheter (T83.0-)
        ● N99.51   Complication of cystostomy
                N99.510   Cystostomy hemorrhage
                N99.511   Cystostomy infection
                N99.512   Cystostomy malfunction
                N99.518   Other cystostomy complication
        ● N99.52   Complication of incontinent external stoma of
                urinary tract
                N99.520   Hemorrhage of incontinent external
                          stoma of urinary tract
                N99.521   Infection of incontinent external
                          stoma of urinary tract
                          Coding Clinic: 2016, Q4, P48
                N99.522   Malfunction of incontinent external
                          stoma of urinary tract
                N99.523   Herniation of incontinent stoma of
                          urinary tract
                          Coding Clinic: 2016, Q4, P48
                N99.524   Stenosis of incontinent stoma of
                          urinary tract
                          Coding Clinic: 2016, Q4, P48
                N99.528   Other complication of incontinent
                          external stoma of urinary tract

CHAPTER 14 (N00–N99)

● **N99.53** Complication of continent stoma of urinary tract

     N99.530 Hemorrhage of continent stoma of urinary tract

     N99.531 Infection of continent stoma of urinary tract

     N99.532 Malfunction of continent stoma of urinary tract

     N99.533 Herniation of continent stoma of urinary tract
         Coding Clinic: 2016, Q4, P48

     N99.534 Stenosis of continent stoma of urinary tract
         Coding Clinic: 2016, Q4, P48

     N99.538 Other complication of continent stoma of urinary tract

● **N99.6** Intraoperative hemorrhage and hematoma of a genitourinary system organ or structure complicating a procedure

     Excludes1 intraoperative hemorrhage and hematoma of a genitourinary system organ or structure due to accidental puncture or laceration during a procedure (N99.7-)

     N99.61 Intraoperative hemorrhage and hematoma of a genitourinary system organ or structure complicating a genitourinary system procedure

     N99.62 Intraoperative hemorrhage and hematoma of a genitourinary system organ or structure complicating other procedure

● **N99.7** Accidental puncture and laceration of a genitourinary system organ or structure during a procedure

     N99.71 Accidental puncture and laceration of a genitourinary system organ or structure during a genitourinary system procedure

     N99.72 Accidental puncture and laceration of a genitourinary system organ or structure during other procedure

● **N99.8** Other intraoperative and postprocedural complications and disorders of genitourinary system
     Coding Clinic: 2016, Q4, P10

     N99.81 Other intraoperative complications of genitourinary system

●   **N99.82** Postprocedural hemorrhage of a genitourinary system organ or structure following a procedure

     N99.820 Postprocedural hemorrhage of a genitourinary system organ or structure following a genitourinary system procedure

     N99.821 Postprocedural hemorrhage of a genitourinary system organ or structure following other procedure

   N99.83 Residual ovary syndrome ♀

●   **N99.84** Postprocedural hematoma and seroma of a genitourinary system organ or structure following a procedure

     N99.840 Postprocedural hematoma of a genitourinary system organ or structure following a genitourinary system procedure

     N99.841 Postprocedural hematoma of a genitourinary system organ or structure following other procedure

     N99.842 Postprocedural seroma of a genitourinary system organ or structure following a genitourinary system procedure

     N99.843 Postprocedural seroma of a genitourinary system organ or structure following other procedure 🔗

   N99.89 Other postprocedural complications and disorders of genitourinary system

▶ New   ⇒ Revised   ~~deleted~~ Deleted   Excludes 1   Excludes 2   Includes   Use additional   Code first   Code also   Key words
OGCR Official Guidelines   X Assign placeholder X   ● Use Additional Character(s)   ▶ Manifestation Code   **Coding Clinic**

CHAPTER 15

PREGNANCY, CHILDBIRTH, AND THE PUERPERIUM (O00-O9A)

OGCR Chapter-Specific Coding Guidelines

15. **Chapter 15: Pregnancy, Childbirth, and the Puerperium (O00-O9A)**

a. **General Rules for Obstetric Cases**

1) **Codes from chapter 15 and sequencing priority**

Obstetric cases require codes from chapter 15, codes in the range O00-O9A, Pregnancy, Childbirth, and the Puerperium. Chapter 15 codes have sequencing priority over codes from other chapters. Additional codes from other chapters may be used in conjunction with chapter 15 codes to further specify conditions. Should the provider document that the pregnancy is incidental to the encounter, then code Z33.1, Pregnant state, incidental, should be used in place of any chapter 15 codes. It is the provider's responsibility to state that the condition being treated is not affecting the pregnancy.

2) **Chapter 15 codes used only on the maternal record**

Chapter 15 codes are to be used only on the maternal record, never on the record of the newborn.

3) **Final character for trimester**

The majority of codes in Chapter 15 have a final character indicating the trimester of pregnancy. The timeframes for the trimesters are indicated at the beginning of the chapter. If trimester is not a component of a code it is because the condition always occurs in a specific trimester, or the concept of trimester of pregnancy is not applicable. Certain codes have characters for only certain trimesters because the condition does not occur in all trimesters, but it may occur in more than just one.

Assignment of the final character for trimester should be based on the provider's documentation of the trimester (or number of weeks) for the current admission/encounter. This applies to the assignment of trimester for pre-existing conditions as well as those that develop during or are due to the pregnancy. The provider's documentation of the number of weeks may be used to assign the appropriate code identifying the trimester.

Whenever delivery occurs during the current admission, and there is an "in childbirth" option for the obstetric complication being coded, the "in childbirth" code should be assigned.

4) **Selection of trimester for inpatient admissions that encompass more than one trimester**

In instances when a patient is admitted to a hospital for complications of pregnancy during one trimester and remains in the hospital into a subsequent trimester, the trimester character for the antepartum complication code should be assigned on the basis of the trimester when the complication developed, not the trimester of the discharge. If the condition developed prior to the current admission/encounter or represents a pre-existing condition, the trimester character for the trimester at the time of the admission/encounter should be assigned.

5) **Unspecified trimester**

Each category that includes codes for trimester has a code for "unspecified trimester." The "unspecified trimester" code should rarely be used, such as when the documentation in the record is insufficient to determine the trimester and it is not possible to obtain clarification.

6) **7th character for Fetus Identification**

Where applicable, a.7th character is to be assigned for certain categories (O31, O32, O33.3 - O33.6, O35, O36, O40, O41, O60.1, O60.2, O64, and O69) to identify the fetus for which the complication code applies.

Assign 7th character "0":
- For single gestations
- When the documentation in the record is insufficient to determine the fetus affected and it is not possible to obtain clarification.
- When it is not possible to clinically determine which fetus is affected.

b. **Selection of OB Principal or First-listed Diagnosis**

1) **Routine outpatient prenatal visits**

For routine outpatient prenatal visits when no complications are present, a code from category Z34, Encounter for supervision of normal pregnancy, should be used as the first-listed diagnosis. These codes should not be used in conjunction with chapter 15 codes.

2) **Supervision of High-Risk Pregnancy**

Codes from category O09, Supervision of high-risk pregnancy, are intended for use only during the prenatal period. For complications during the labor or delivery episode as a result of a high-risk pregnancy, assign the applicable complication codes from Chapter 15. If there are no complications during the labor or delivery episode, assign code O80, Encounter for full-term uncomplicated delivery.

For routine prenatal outpatient visits for patients with high-risk pregnancies, a code from category O09, Supervision of high-risk pregnancy, should be used as the first-listed diagnosis. Secondary Chapter 15 codes may be used in conjunction with these codes if appropriate.

3) **Episodes when no delivery occurs**

In episodes when no delivery occurs, the principal diagnosis should correspond to the principal complication of the pregnancy which necessitated the encounter. Should more than one complication exist, all of which are treated or monitored, any of the complications codes may be sequenced first.

4) **When a delivery occurs**

When an obstetric patient is admitted and delivers during that admission, the condition that prompted the admission should be sequenced as the principal diagnosis. If multiple conditions prompted the admission, sequence the one most related to the delivery as the principal diagnosis. A code for any complication of the delivery should be assigned as an additional diagnosis. In cases of cesarean delivery, if the patient was admitted with a condition that resulted in the performance of a cesarean procedure, that condition should be selected as the principal diagnosis. If the reason for the admission was unrelated to the condition resulting in the cesarean delivery, the condition related to the reason for the admission should be selected as the principal diagnosis.

5) **Outcome of delivery**

A code from category Z37, Outcome of delivery, should be included on every maternal record when a delivery has occurred. These codes are not to be used on subsequent records or on the newborn record.

c. **Pre-existing conditions versus conditions due to the pregnancy**

Certain categories in Chapter 15 distinguish between conditions of the mother that existed prior to pregnancy (pre-existing) and those that are a direct result of pregnancy. When assigning codes from Chapter 15, it is important to assess if a condition was pre-existing prior to pregnancy or developed during or due to the pregnancy in order to assign the correct code.

Categories that do not distinguish between pre-existing and pregnancy-related conditions may be used for either. It is acceptable to use codes specifically for the puerperium with codes complicating pregnancy and childbirth if a condition arises postpartum during the delivery encounter.

d. **Pre-existing hypertension in pregnancy**

Category O10, Pre-existing hypertension complicating pregnancy, childbirth and the puerperium, includes codes for hypertensive heart and hypertensive chronic kidney disease. When assigning one of the O10 codes that includes hypertensive heart disease or hypertensive chronic kidney disease, it is necessary to add a secondary code from the appropriate hypertension category to specify the type of heart failure or chronic kidney disease.

See Section I.C.9. Hypertension.

e. **Fetal Conditions Affecting the Management of the Mother**

1) **Codes from categories O35 and O36**

Codes from categories O35, Maternal care for known or suspected fetal abnormality and damage, and O36, Maternal care for other fetal problems, are assigned only when the fetal condition is actually responsible for modifying the management of the mother, i.e., by requiring diagnostic studies, additional observation, special care, or termination of pregnancy. The fact that the fetal condition exists does not justify assigning a code from this series to the mother's record.

2) **In utero surgery**

In cases when surgery is performed on the fetus, a diagnosis code from category O35, Maternal care for known or suspected fetal abnormality and damage, should be assigned identifying the fetal condition. Assign the appropriate procedure code for the procedure performed.

No code from Chapter 16, the perinatal codes, should be used on the mother's record to identify fetal conditions. Surgery performed in utero on a fetus is still to be coded as an obstetric encounter.

f. **HIV Infection in Pregnancy, Childbirth, and the Puerperium**

During pregnancy, childbirth or the puerperium, a patient admitted because of an HIV-related illness should receive a principal diagnosis from subcategory O98.7-, Human immunodeficiency [HIV] disease complicating pregnancy, childbirth and the puerperium, followed by the code(s) for the HIV-related illness(es).

Patients with asymptomatic HIV infection status admitted during pregnancy, childbirth, or the puerperium should receive codes of O98.7- and Z21, Asymptomatic human immunodeficiency virus [HIV] infection status.

g. **Diabetes mellitus in pregnancy**

Diabetes mellitus is a significant complicating factor in pregnancy. Pregnant women who are diabetic should be assigned a code from category O24, Diabetes mellitus in pregnancy, childbirth, and the puerperium, first, followed by the appropriate diabetes code(s) (E08-E13) from Chapter 4.

h. Long term use of insulin and oral hypoglycemics
See section I.C.4.a.3 for information on the long term use of insulin and oral hypoglycemic.

i. Gestational (pregnancy induced) diabetes
Gestational (pregnancy induced) diabetes can occur during the second and third trimester of pregnancy in women who were not diabetic prior to pregnancy. Gestational diabetes can cause complications in the pregnancy similar to those of pre-existing diabetes mellitus. It also puts the woman at greater risk of developing diabetes after the pregnancy. Codes for gestational diabetes are in subcategory O24.4, Gestational diabetes mellitus. No other code from category O24, Diabetes mellitus in pregnancy, childbirth, and the puerperium, should be used with a code from O24.4.

The codes under subcategory O24.4 include diet controlled, insulin controlled, and controlled by oral hypoglycemic drugs. If a patient with gestational diabetes is treated with both diet and insulin, only the code for insulin-controlled is required. If a patient with gestational diabetes is treated with both diet and oral hypoglycemic medications, only the code for "controlled by oral hypoglycemic drugs" is required. Code Z79.4, Long-term (current) use of insulin or code Z79.84, Long-term (current) use of oral hypoglycemic drugs, should not be assigned with codes from subcategory O24.4.

An abnormal glucose tolerance in pregnancy is assigned a code from subcategory O99.81, Abnormal glucose complicating pregnancy, childbirth, and the puerperium.

j. Sepsis and septic shock complicating abortion, pregnancy, childbirth and the puerperium
When assigning a chapter 15 code for sepsis complicating abortion, pregnancy, childbirth, and the puerperium, a code for the specific type of infection should be assigned as an additional diagnosis. If severe sepsis is present, a code from subcategory R65.2, Severe sepsis, and code(s) for associated organ dysfunction(s) should also be assigned as additional diagnoses.

k. Puerperal sepsis
Code O85, Puerperal sepsis, should be assigned with a secondary code to identify the causal organism (e.g., for a bacterial infection, assign a code from category B95-B96, Bacterial infections in conditions classified elsewhere). A code from category A40, Streptococcal sepsis, or A41, Other sepsis, should not be used for puerperal sepsis. If applicable, use additional codes to identify severe sepsis (R65.2-) and any associated acute organ dysfunction.

l. Alcohol, tobacco *and drug* use during pregnancy, childbirth and the puerperium

1) Alcohol use during pregnancy, childbirth and the puerperium
Codes under subcategory O99.31, Alcohol use complicating pregnancy, childbirth, and the puerperium, should be assigned for any pregnancy case when a mother uses alcohol during the pregnancy or postpartum. A secondary code from category F10, Alcohol related disorders, should also be assigned to identify manifestations of the alcohol use.

2) Tobacco use during pregnancy, childbirth, and the puerperium
Codes under subcategory O99.33, Smoking (tobacco) complicating pregnancy, childbirth, and the puerperium, should be assigned for any pregnancy case when a mother uses any type of tobacco product during the pregnancy or postpartum. A secondary code from category F17, Nicotine dependence, should also be assigned to identify the type of nicotine dependence.

3) *Drug use during pregnancy, childbirth and the puerperium*
Codes under subcategory O99.32, Drug use complicating pregnancy, childbirth, and the puerperium, should be assigned for any pregnancy case when a mother uses drugs during the pregnancy or postpartum. This can involve illegal drugs, or inappropriate use or abuse of prescription drugs. Secondary code(s) from categories F11-F16 and F18F19 should also be assigned to identify manifestations of the drug use.

m. Poisoning, toxic effects, adverse effects and underdosing in a pregnant patient
A code from subcategory O9A.2, Injury, poisoning and certain other consequences of external causes complicating pregnancy, childbirth, and the puerperium, should be sequenced first, followed by the appropriate injury, poisoning, toxic effect, adverse effect or underdosing code, and then the additional code(s) that specifies the condition caused by the poisoning, toxic effect, adverse effect or underdosing.
See Section I.C.19. Adverse effects, poisoning, underdosing and toxic effects.

n. Normal Delivery, Code O80

1) Encounter for full term uncomplicated delivery
Code O80 should be assigned when a woman is admitted for a full-term normal delivery and delivers a single, healthy infant without any complications antepartum, during the delivery, or postpartum during the delivery episode. Code O80 is always a principal

diagnosis. It is not to be used if any other code from chapter 15 is needed to describe a current complication of the antenatal, delivery, or perinatal period. Additional codes from other chapters may be used with code O80 if they are not related to or are in any way complicating the pregnancy.

2) Uncomplicated delivery with resolved antepartum complication
Code O80 may be used if the patient had a complication at some point during the pregnancy, but the complication is not present at the time of the admission for delivery.

3) Outcome of delivery for O80
Z37.0, Single live birth, is the only outcome of delivery code appropriate for use with O80.

o. The Peripartum and Postpartum Periods

1) Peripartum and Postpartum periods
The postpartum period begins immediately after delivery and continues for six weeks following delivery. The peripartum period is defined as the last month of pregnancy to five months postpartum.

2) Peripartum and postpartum complication
A postpartum complication is any complication occurring within the six-week period.

3) Pregnancy-related complications after 6 week period
Chapter 15 codes may also be used to describe pregnancy-related complications after the peripartum or postpartum period if the provider documents that a condition is pregnancy related.

4) Admission for routine postpartum care following delivery outside hospital
When the mother delivers outside the hospital prior to admission and is admitted for routine postpartum care and no complications are noted, code Z39.0, Encounter for care and examination of mother immediately after delivery, should be assigned as the principal diagnosis.

5) Pregnancy associated cardiomyopathy
Pregnancy associated cardiomyopathy, code O90.3, is unique in that it may be diagnosed in the third trimester of pregnancy but may continue to progress months after delivery. For this reason, it is referred to as peripartum cardiomyopathy. Code O90.3 is only for use when the cardiomyopathy develops as a result of pregnancy in a woman who did not have pre-existing heart disease.

p. Code O94, Sequelae of complication of pregnancy, childbirth, and the puerperium

1) Code O94
Code O94, Sequelae of complication of pregnancy, childbirth, and the puerperium, is for use in those cases when an initial complication of a pregnancy develops a sequelae requiring care or treatment at a future date.

2) After the initial postpartum period
This code may be used at any time after the initial postpartum period.

3) Sequencing of Code O94
This code, like all sequela codes, is to be sequenced following the code describing the sequelae of the complication.

q. Termination of Pregnancy and Spontaneous abortions

1) Abortion with Liveborn Fetus
When an attempted termination of pregnancy results in a liveborn fetus assign code Z33.2, Encounter for elective termination of pregnancy and a code from category Z37, Outcome of Delivery.

2) Retained Products of Conception following an abortion
Subsequent encounters for retained products of conception following a spontaneous abortion or elective termination of pregnancy, without complications are assigned O03.4, Incomplete spontaneous, abortion without complication, or codes O07.4, Failed attempted termination of pregnancy without complication. This advice is appropriate even when the patient was discharged previously with a discharge diagnosis of complete abortion. If the patient has a specific complication associated with the spontaneous abortion or elective termination of pregnancy in addition to retained products of conception, assign the appropriate complication in category O03 or O07 instead of code O03.4 or O07.4

3) Complications leading to abortion
Codes from Chapter 15 may be used as additional codes to identify any documented complications of the pregnancy in conjunction with codes in categories in O04, O07 and O08.

r. Abuse in a pregnant patient
For suspected or confirmed cases of abuse of a pregnant patient, a code(s) from subcategories O9A.3, Physical abuse complicating pregnancy, childbirth, and the puerperium, O9A.4, Sexual abuse complicating pregnancy, childbirth, and the puerperium, and O9A.5, Psychological abuse complicating pregnancy, childbirth, and the puerperium, should be sequenced first, followed by the appropriate codes (if applicable) to identify any associated current injury due to physical abuse, sexual abuse, and the perpetrator of abuse.
See Section I.C.19. Adult and child abuse, neglect and other maltreatment.

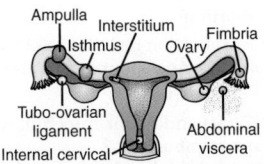

Figure 15-1   Implantation sites of ectopic pregnancy.

Item 15-1 Ectopic pregnancy most often occurs in the fallopian tube. Pregnancy outside the uterus may end in a lifethreatening rupture.

★**(See Plate 375 on page 52.)**

CHAPTER 15

PREGNANCY, CHILDBIRTH, AND THE PUERPERIUM (O00-O9A)

Note: CODES FROM THIS CHAPTER ARE FOR USE ONLY ON MATERNAL RECORDS, NEVER ON NEWBORN RECORDS

Codes from this chapter are for use for conditions related to or aggravated by the pregnancy, childbirth, or by the puerperium (maternal causes or obstetric causes)

Trimesters are counted from the first day of the last menstrual period. They are defined as follows:

1st trimester - less than 14 weeks 0 days

2nd trimester - 14 weeks 0 days to less than 28 weeks 0 days

3rd trimester - 28 weeks 0 days until delivery

Use additional code from category Z3A, Weeks of gestation, to identify the specific week of the pregnancy, if known.

Excludes1   supervision of normal pregnancy (Z34.-)

➡ **Excludes2**   mental and behavioral disorders associated with the puerperium (F53.-)
obstetrical tetanus (A34)
postpartum necrosis of pituitary gland (E23.0)
puerperal osteomalacia (M83.0)

This chapter contains the following blocks:

O00-O08	Pregnancy with abortive outcome
O09	Supervision of high risk pregnancy
O10-O16	Edema, proteinuria and hypertensive disorders in pregnancy, childbirth and the puerperium
O20-O29	Other maternal disorders predominantly related to pregnancy
O30-O48	Maternal care related to the fetus and amniotic cavity and possible delivery problems
O60-O77	Complications of labor and delivery
O80, O82	Encounter for delivery
O85-O92	Complications predominantly related to the puerperium
O94-O9A	Other obstetric conditions, not elsewhere classified

PREGNANCY WITH ABORTIVE OUTCOME (O00-O08)

Excludes1   continuing pregnancy in multiple gestation after abortion of one fetus or more (O31.1-, O31.3-)
Coding Clinic: 2016, Q4, P130

● **O00**   Ectopic pregnancy
    Includes   ruptured ectopic pregnancy
    Use additional code from category O08 to identify any associated complication

● **O00.0**   Abdominal pregnancy
    Excludes1   maternal care for viable fetus in abdominal pregnancy (O36.7-)
    Coding Clinic: 2016, Q4, P49

    O00.00   Abdominal pregnancy **without intrauterine pregnancy** ♀   M
           Abdominal pregnancy NOS

    O00.01   Abdominal pregnancy **with intrauterine pregnancy** ♀   M

● **O00.1**   Tubal pregnancy
    Fallopian pregnancy
    Rupture of (fallopian) tube due to pregnancy
    Tubal abortion
    Coding Clinic: 2016, Q4, P49

    ● O00.10   Tubal pregnancy **without intrauterine pregnancy**
           Tubal pregnancy NOS

       O00.101   **Right** tubal pregnancy without intrauterine pregnancy ♀   M

       O00.102   **Left** tubal pregnancy without intrauterine pregnancy ♀   M

       O00.109   **Unspecified** tubal pregnancy without intrauterine pregnancy ♀   M

    ● O00.11   Tubal pregnancy **with intrauterine pregnancy**

       O00.111   **Right** tubal pregnancy with intrauterine pregnancy ♀   M

       O00.112   **Left** tubal pregnancy with intrauterine pregnancy ♀   M

       O00.119   **Unspecified** tubal pregnancy with intrauterine pregnancy ♀   M

● **O00.2**   Ovarian pregnancy
    Coding Clinic: 2016, Q4, P49

    ● O00.20   Ovarian pregnancy **without intrauterine pregnancy**
           Ovarian pregnancy NOS

       O00.201   **Right** ovarian pregnancy without intrauterine pregnancy ♀   M

       O00.202   **Left** ovarian pregnancy without intrauterine pregnancy ♀   M

       O00.209   **Unspecified** ovarian pregnancy without intrauterine pregnancy ♀   M

    ● O00.21   Ovarian pregnancy **with intrauterine pregnancy**

       O00.211   **Right** ovarian pregnancy with intrauterine pregnancy ♀   M

       ➡ O00.212   **Left** ovarian pregnancy with intrauterine pregnancy ♀   M

       O00.219   **Unspecified** ovarian pregnancy with intrauterine pregnancy ♀   M

● **O00.8**   Other ectopic pregnancy
    Cervical pregnancy
    Cornual pregnancy
    Intraligamentous pregnancy
    Mural pregnancy
    Coding Clinic: 2016, Q4, P49

    O00.80   Other ectopic pregnancy **without intrauterine pregnancy** ♀   M
           Other ectopic pregnancy NOS

    O00.81   Other ectopic pregnancy **with intrauterine pregnancy** ♀   M

CHAPTER 15 (O00-O9A)

● **O00.9**   **Ectopic pregnancy, unspecified**
Coding Clinic: 2016, Q4, P49

     O00.90   **Unspecified ectopic pregnancy without intrauterine pregnancy** ♀   M
           Ectopic pregnancy NOS

     O00.91   **Unspecified ectopic pregnancy with intrauterine pregnancy** ♀   M

● **O01**   **Hydatidiform mole**
     Use additional code from category O08 to identify any associated complication

     Excludes1   chorioadenoma (destruens) (D39.2)
                  malignant hydatidiform mole (D39.2)

     O01.0   **Classical hydatidiform mole** ♀   M
         Complete hydatidiform mole

     O01.1   **Incomplete and partial hydatidiform mole** ♀   M

     O01.9   **Hydatidiform mole, unspecified** ♀   M
         Trophoblastic disease NOS
         Vesicular mole NOS

● **O02**   **Other abnormal products of conception**
     Use additional code from category O08 to identify any associated complication

     Excludes1   papyraceous fetus (O31.0-)

     O02.0   **Blighted ovum and nonhydatidiform mole** ♀   M
         Carneous mole   Molar pregnancy NEC
         Fleshy mole   Pathological ovum
         Intrauterine mole NOS

     O02.1   **Missed abortion** ♀   M
         Early fetal death, before completion of 20 weeks of gestation, with retention of dead fetus

         Excludes1   failed induced abortion (O07.-)
                    fetal death (intrauterine) (late) (O36.4)
                    missed abortion with blighted ovum (O02.0)
                    missed abortion with hydatidiform mole (O01.-)
                    missed abortion with nonhydatidiform (O02.0)
                    missed abortion with other abnormal products of conception (O02.8-)
                    missed delivery (O36.4)
                    stillbirth (P95)

● **O02.8**   **Other specified abnormal products of conception**
     Excludes1   abnormal products of conception with blighted ovum (O02.0)
                abnormal products of conception with hydatidiform mole (O01.-)
                abnormal products of conception with nonhydatidiform mole (O02.0)

     O02.81   **Inappropriate change in quantitative human chorionic gonadotropin (hCG) in early pregnancy** ♀   M
         Biochemical pregnancy
         Chemical pregnancy
         Inappropriate level of quantitative human chorionic gonadotropin (hCG) for gestational age in early pregnancy

     O02.89   **Other abnormal products of conception** ♀   M

     O02.9   **Abnormal product of conception, unspecified** ♀   M

● **O03**   **Spontaneous abortion**
     Note: Incomplete abortion includes retained products of conception following spontaneous abortion.
     Includes   miscarriage

     O03.0   **Genital tract and pelvic infection following incomplete spontaneous abortion** ♀   M
         Endometritis following incomplete spontaneous abortion
         Oophoritis following incomplete spontaneous abortion
         Parametritis following incomplete spontaneous abortion
         Pelvic peritonitis following incomplete spontaneous abortion
         Salpingitis following incomplete spontaneous abortion
         Salpingo-oophoritis following incomplete spontaneous abortion

         Excludes1   sepsis following incomplete spontaneous abortion (O03.37)
                    urinary tract infection following incomplete spontaneous abortion (O03.38)

     O03.1   **Delayed or excessive hemorrhage following incomplete spontaneous abortion** ♀   M
         Afibrinogenemia following incomplete spontaneous abortion
         Defibrination syndrome following incomplete spontaneous abortion
         Hemolysis following incomplete spontaneous abortion
         Intravascular coagulation following incomplete spontaneous abortion

     O03.2   **Embolism following incomplete spontaneous abortion** ♀   M
         Air embolism following incomplete spontaneous abortion
         Amniotic fluid embolism following incomplete spontaneous abortion
         Blood-clot embolism following incomplete spontaneous abortion
         Embolism NOS following incomplete spontaneous abortion
         Fat embolism following incomplete spontaneous abortion
         Pulmonary embolism following incomplete spontaneous abortion
         Pyemic embolism following incomplete spontaneous abortion
         Septic or septicopyemic embolism following incomplete spontaneous abortion
         Soap embolism following incomplete spontaneous abortion

● **O03.3**   **Other and unspecified complications following incomplete spontaneous abortion**
     O03.30   **Unspecified complication following incomplete spontaneous abortion** ♀   M

     O03.31   **Shock following incomplete spontaneous abortion** ♀   M
         Circulatory collapse following incomplete spontaneous abortion
         Shock (postprocedural) following incomplete spontaneous abortion

         Excludes1   shock due to infection following incomplete spontaneous abortion (O03.37)

     O03.32   **Renal failure following incomplete spontaneous abortion** ♀   M
         Kidney failure (acute) following incomplete spontaneous abortion
         Oliguria following incomplete spontaneous abortion
         Renal shutdown following incomplete spontaneous abortion
         Renal tubular necrosis following incomplete spontaneous abortion
         Uremia following incomplete spontaneous abortion

Item 15–2 A **hydatidiform** mole is an overproduction of placental tissue. The tumor secretes a hormone, chorionic gonadotropic hormone (CGH), that indicates a positive pregnancy test. There is no viable fetus. More than 80% of hydatidiform moles are noncancerous.

▶ New   ⇒ Revised   ~~deleted~~ Deleted   Excludes 1   Excludes 2   Includes   Use additional   Code first   Code also   Key words
OGCR Official Guidelines   X Assign placeholder X   ● Use Additional Character(s)   ▶ Manifestation Code   **Coding Clinic**

O03.33　**Metabolic disorder** following incomplete spontaneous abortion ♀　　M

O03.34　**Damage to pelvic organs** following incomplete spontaneous abortion ♀　　M
　　　　Laceration, perforation, tear or chemical damage of bladder following incomplete spontaneous abortion
　　　　Laceration, perforation, tear or chemical damage of bowel following incomplete spontaneous abortion
　　　　Laceration, perforation, tear or chemical damage of broad ligament following incomplete spontaneous abortion
　　　　Laceration, perforation, tear or chemical damage of cervix following incomplete spontaneous abortion
　　　　Laceration, perforation, tear or chemical damage of periurethral tissue following incomplete spontaneous abortion
　　　　Laceration, perforation, tear or chemical damage of uterus following incomplete spontaneous abortion
　　　　Laceration, perforation, tear or chemical damage of vagina following incomplete spontaneous abortion

O03.35　**Other venous complications** following incomplete spontaneous abortion ♀　　M

O03.36　**Cardiac arrest** following incomplete spontaneous abortion ♀　　M

O03.37　**Sepsis** following incomplete spontaneous abortion ♀　　M
　　　　Use additional code to identify infectious agent (B95-B97)
　　　　Use additional code to identify severe sepsis, if applicable (R65.2-)
　　　　Excludes1　septic or septicopyemic embolism following incomplete spontaneous abortion (O03.2)

O03.38　**Urinary tract infection** following incomplete spontaneous abortion ♀　　M
　　　　Cystitis following incomplete spontaneous abortion

O03.39　Incomplete spontaneous abortion **with other complications** ♀　　M

O03.4　Incomplete spontaneous abortion **without complication** ♀　　M

O03.5　**Genital tract and pelvic infection** following complete or unspecified spontaneous abortion ♀　　M
　　　　Endometritis following complete or unspecified spontaneous abortion
　　　　Oophoritis following complete or unspecified spontaneous abortion
　　　　Parametritis following complete or unspecified spontaneous abortion
　　　　Pelvic peritonitis following complete or unspecified spontaneous abortion
　　　　Salpingitis following complete or unspecified spontaneous abortion
　　　　Salpingo-oophoritis following complete or unspecified spontaneous abortion
　　　　Excludes1　sepsis following complete or unspecified spontaneous abortion (O03.87)
　　　　　　　　　urinary tract infection following complete or unspecified spontaneous abortion (O03.88)

O03.6　**Delayed or excessive hemorrhage** following complete or unspecified spontaneous abortion ♀　　M
　　　　Afibrinogenemia following complete or unspecified spontaneous abortion
　　　　Defibrination syndrome following complete or unspecified spontaneous abortion
　　　　Hemolysis following complete or unspecified spontaneous abortion
　　　　Intravascular coagulation following complete or unspecified spontaneous abortion

O03.7　**Embolism** following complete or unspecified spontaneous abortion ♀　　M
　　　　Air embolism following complete or unspecified spontaneous abortion
　　　　Amniotic fluid embolism following complete or unspecified spontaneous abortion
　　　　Blood-clot embolism following complete or unspecified spontaneous abortion
　　　　Embolism NOS following complete or unspecified spontaneous abortion
　　　　Fat embolism following complete or unspecified spontaneous abortion
　　　　Pulmonary embolism following complete or unspecified spontaneous abortion
　　　　Pyemic embolism following complete or unspecified spontaneous abortion
　　　　Septic or septicopyemic embolism following complete or unspecified spontaneous abortion
　　　　Soap embolism following complete or unspecified spontaneous abortion

● O03.8　**Other and unspecified complications** following complete or unspecified spontaneous abortion

　　O03.80　**Unspecified complication** following complete or unspecified spontaneous abortion ♀　　M

　　O03.81　**Shock** following complete or unspecified spontaneous abortion ♀　　M
　　　　　Circulatory collapse following complete or unspecified spontaneous abortion
　　　　　Shock (postprocedural) following complete or unspecified spontaneous abortion
　　　　　Excludes1　shock due to infection following complete or unspecified spontaneous abortion (O03.87)

　　O03.82　**Renal failure** following complete or unspecified spontaneous abortion ♀　　M
　　　　　Kidney failure (acute) following complete or unspecified spontaneous abortion
　　　　　Oliguria following complete or unspecified spontaneous abortion
　　　　　Renal shutdown following complete or unspecified spontaneous abortion
　　　　　Renal tubular necrosis following complete or unspecified spontaneous abortion
　　　　　Uremia following complete or unspecified spontaneous abortion

　　O03.83　**Metabolic disorder** following complete or unspecified spontaneous abortion ♀　　M

　　O03.84　**Damage to pelvic organs** following complete or unspecified spontaneous abortion ♀　　M
　　　　　Laceration, perforation, tear or chemical damage of bladder following complete or unspecified spontaneous abortion
　　　　　Laceration, perforation, tear or chemical damage of bowel following complete or unspecified spontaneous abortion
　　　　　Laceration, perforation, tear or chemical damage of broad ligament following complete or unspecified spontaneous abortion
　　　　　Laceration, perforation, tear or chemical damage of cervix following complete or unspecified spontaneous abortion
　　　　　Laceration, perforation, tear or chemical damage of periurethral tissue following complete or unspecified spontaneous abortion
　　　　　Laceration, perforation, tear or chemical damage of uterus following complete or unspecified spontaneous abortion
　　　　　Laceration, perforation, tear or chemical damage of vagina following complete or unspecified spontaneous abortion

O03.85 Other venous complications following complete or unspecified spontaneous abortion ♀ M

O03.86 Cardiac arrest following complete or unspecified spontaneous abortion ♀ M

O03.87 Sepsis following complete or unspecified spontaneous abortion ♀ M

Use additional code to identify infectious agent (B95-B97)

Use additional code to identify severe sepsis, if applicable (R65.2-)

Excludes1   septic or septicopyemic embolism following complete or unspecified spontaneous abortion (O03.7)

O03.88 Urinary tract infection following complete or unspecified spontaneous abortion ♀ M

Cystitis following complete or unspecified spontaneous abortion

O03.89 Complete or unspecified spontaneous abortion with other complications ♀ M

O03.9 Complete or unspecified spontaneous abortion without complication ♀ M

Miscarriage NOS

Spontaneous abortion NOS

● **O04** Complications following (induced) termination of pregnancy

Includes   complications following (induced) termination of pregnancy

Excludes1   encounter for elective termination of pregnancy, uncomplicated (Z33.2)

failed attempted termination of pregnancy (O07.-)

O04.5 Genital tract and pelvic infection following (induced) termination of pregnancy ♀ M

Endometritis following (induced) termination of pregnancy

Oophoritis following (induced) termination of pregnancy

Parametritis following (induced) termination of pregnancy

Pelvic peritonitis following (induced) termination of pregnancy

Salpingitis following (induced) termination of pregnancy

Salpingo-oophoritis following (induced) termination of pregnancy

Excludes1   sepsis following (induced) termination of pregnancy (O04.87)

urinary tract infection following (induced) termination of pregnancy (O04.88)

O04.6 Delayed or excessive hemorrhage following (induced) termination of pregnancy ♀ M

Afibrinogenemia following (induced) termination of pregnancy

Defibrination syndrome following (induced) termination of pregnancy

Hemolysis following (induced) termination of pregnancy

Intravascular coagulation following (induced) termination of pregnancy

O04.7 Embolism following (induced) termination of pregnancy ♀ M

Air embolism following (induced) termination of pregnancy

Amniotic fluid embolism following (induced) termination of pregnancy

Blood-clot embolism following (induced) termination of pregnancy

Embolism NOS following (induced) termination of pregnancy

Fat embolism following (induced) termination of pregnancy

Pulmonary embolism following (induced) termination of pregnancy

Pyemic embolism following (induced) termination of pregnancy

Septic or septicopyemic embolism following (induced) termination of pregnancy

Soap embolism following (induced) termination of pregnancy

● **O04.8** (Induced) termination of pregnancy with other and unspecified complications

O04.80 (Induced) termination of pregnancy with unspecified complications ♀ M

O04.81 Shock following (induced) termination of pregnancy ♀ M

Circulatory collapse following (induced) termination of pregnancy

Shock (postprocedural) following (induced) termination of pregnancy

Excludes1   shock due to infection following (induced) termination of pregnancy (O04.87)

O04.82 Renal failure following (induced) termination of pregnancy ♀ M

Kidney failure (acute) following (induced) termination of pregnancy

Oliguria following (induced) termination of pregnancy

Renal shutdown following (induced) termination of pregnancy

Renal tubular necrosis following (induced) termination of pregnancy

Uremia following (induced) termination of pregnancy

O04.83 Metabolic disorder following (induced) termination of pregnancy ♀ M

O04.84 Damage to pelvic organs following (induced) termination of pregnancy ♀ M

Laceration, perforation, tear or chemical damage of bladder following (induced) termination of pregnancy

Laceration, perforation, tear or chemical damage of bowel following (induced) termination of pregnancy

Laceration, perforation, tear or chemical damage of broad ligament following (induced) termination of pregnancy

Laceration, perforation, tear or chemical damage of cervix following (induced) termination of pregnancy

Laceration, perforation, tear or chemical damage of periurethral tissue following (induced) termination of pregnancy

Laceration, perforation, tear or chemical damage of uterus following (induced) termination of pregnancy

Laceration, perforation, tear or chemical damage of vagina following (induced) termination of pregnancy

▶ New   ⟹ Revised   ~~deleted~~ Deleted   Excludes 1   Excludes 2   Includes   Use additional   Code first   Code also   Key words

OGCR Official Guidelines   X Assign placeholder X   ● Use Additional Character(s)   ▷ Manifestation Code   Coding Clinic

O04.85 **Other venous complications following (induced) termination of pregnancy** ♀   M

O04.86 **Cardiac arrest following (induced) termination of pregnancy** ♀   M

O04.87 **Sepsis following (induced) termination of pregnancy** ♀   M

    Use additional code to identify infectious agent (B95-B97)

    Use additional code to identify severe sepsis, if applicable (R65.2-)

    Excludes1   septic or septicopyemic embolism following (induced) termination of pregnancy (O04.7)

O04.88 **Urinary tract infection following (induced) termination of pregnancy** ♀   M

    Cystitis following (induced) termination of pregnancy

O04.89 **(Induced) termination of pregnancy with other complications** ♀   M

● **O07** **Failed attempted termination of pregnancy**

    Includes   failure of attempted induction of termination of pregnancy

        incomplete elective abortion

    Excludes1   incomplete spontaneous abortion (O03.0-)

O07.0 **Genital tract and pelvic infection following failed attempted termination of pregnancy** ♀   M

    Endometritis following failed attempted termination of pregnancy

    Oophoritis following failed attempted termination of pregnancy

    Parametritis following failed attempted termination of pregnancy

    Pelvic peritonitis following failed termination of pregnancy

    Salpingitis following failed attempted termination of pregnancy

    Salpingo-oophoritis following failed attempted termination of pregnancy

    Excludes1   sepsis following failed attempted termination of pregnancy (O07.37)

        urinary tract infection following failed attempted termination of pregnancy (O07.38)

O07.1 **Delayed or excessive hemorrhage following failed attempted termination of pregnancy** ♀   M

    Afibrinogenemia following failed attempted termination of pregnancy

    Defibrination syndrome following failed attempted termination of pregnancy

    Hemolysis following failed attempted termination of pregnancy

    Intravascular coagulation following failed attempted termination of pregnancy

O07.2 **Embolism following failed attempted termination of pregnancy** ♀   M

    Air embolism following failed attempted termination of pregnancy

    Amniotic fluid embolism following failed attempted termination of pregnancy

    Blood-clot embolism following failed attempted termination of pregnancy

    Embolism NOS following failed attempted termination of pregnancy

    Fat embolism following failed attempted termination of pregnancy

    Pulmonary embolism following failed attempted termination of pregnancy

    Pyemic embolism following failed attempted termination of pregnancy

    Septic or septicopyemic embolism following failed attempted termination of pregnancy

    Soap embolism following failed attempted termination of pregnancy

● O07.3 **Failed attempted termination of pregnancy with other and unspecified complications**

O07.30 **Failed attempted termination of pregnancy with unspecified complications** ♀   M

O07.31 **Shock following failed attempted termination of pregnancy** ♀   M

    Circulatory collapse following failed attempted termination of pregnancy

    Shock (postprocedural) following failed attempted termination of pregnancy

    Excludes1   shock due to infection following failed attempted termination of pregnancy (O07.37)

O07.32 **Renal failure following failed attempted termination of pregnancy** ♀   M

    Kidney failure (acute) following failed attempted termination of pregnancy

    Oliguria following failed attempted termination of pregnancy

    Renal shutdown following failed attempted termination of pregnancy

    Renal tubular necrosis following failed attempted termination of pregnancy

    Uremia following failed attempted termination of pregnancy

O07.33 **Metabolic disorder following failed attempted termination of pregnancy** ♀   M

O07.34 **Damage to pelvic organs following failed attempted termination of pregnancy** ♀   M

    Laceration, perforation, tear or chemical damage of bladder following failed attempted termination of pregnancy

    Laceration, perforation, tear or chemical damage of bowel following failed attempted termination of pregnancy

    Laceration, perforation, tear or chemical damage of broad ligament following failed attempted termination of pregnancy

    Laceration, perforation, tear or chemical damage of cervix following failed attempted termination of pregnancy

    Laceration, perforation, tear or chemical damage of periurethral tissue following failed attempted termination of pregnancy

    Laceration, perforation, tear or chemical damage of uterus following failed attempted termination of pregnancy

    Laceration, perforation, tear or chemical damage of vagina following failed attempted termination of pregnancy

O07.35 **Other venous complications following failed attempted termination of pregnancy** ♀   M

O07.36 **Cardiac arrest following failed attempted termination of pregnancy** ♀   M

O07.37 **Sepsis following failed attempted termination of pregnancy** ♀   M

    Use additional code (B95-B97), to identify infectious agent

    Use additional code (R65.2-) to identify severe sepsis, if applicable

    Excludes1   septic or septicopyemic embolism following failed attempted termination of pregnancy (O07.2)

O07.38 **Urinary tract infection following failed attempted termination of pregnancy** ♀   M

    Cystitis following failed attempted termination of pregnancy

O07.39 **Failed attempted termination of pregnancy with other complications** ♀   M

O07.4 **Failed attempted termination of pregnancy without complication** ♀   M

● **O08**   **Complications following ectopic and molar pregnancy**
This category is for use with categories O00-O02 to identify any associated complications.

  O08.0   **Genital tract and pelvic infection** following ectopic and molar pregnancy ♀   M
    Endometritis following ectopic and molar pregnancy
    Oophoritis following ectopic and molar pregnancy
    Parametritis following ectopic and molar pregnancy
    Pelvic peritonitis following ectopic and molar pregnancy
    Salpingitis following ectopic and molar pregnancy
    Salpingo-oophoritis following ectopic and molar pregnancy
      Excludes1   sepsis following ectopic and molar pregnancy (O08.82)
                urinary tract infection (O08.83)

  O08.1   **Delayed or excessive hemorrhage** following ectopic and molar pregnancy ♀   M
    Afibrinogenemia following ectopic and molar pregnancy
    Defibrination syndrome following ectopic and molar pregnancy
    Hemolysis following ectopic and molar pregnancy
    Intravascular coagulation following ectopic and molar pregnancy
      Excludes1   delayed or excessive hemorrhage due to incomplete abortion (O03.1)

  O08.2   **Embolism following ectopic and molar pregnancy** ♀   M
    Air embolism following ectopic and molar pregnancy
    Amniotic fluid embolism following ectopic and molar pregnancy
    Blood-clot embolism following ectopic and molar pregnancy
    Embolism NOS following ectopic and molar pregnancy
    Fat embolism following ectopic and molar pregnancy
    Pulmonary embolism following ectopic and molar pregnancy
    Pyemic embolism following ectopic and molar pregnancy
    Septic or septicopyemic embolism following ectopic and molar pregnancy
    Soap embolism following ectopic and molar pregnancy

  O08.3   **Shock following ectopic and molar pregnancy** ♀   M
    Circulatory collapse following ectopic and molar pregnancy
    Shock (postprocedural) following ectopic and molar pregnancy
      Excludes1   shock due to infection following ectopic and molar pregnancy (O08.82)

  O08.4   **Renal failure following ectopic and molar pregnancy** ♀   M
    Kidney failure (acute) following ectopic and molar pregnancy
    Oliguria following ectopic and molar pregnancy
    Renal shutdown following ectopic and molar pregnancy
    Renal tubular necrosis following ectopic and molar pregnancy
    Uremia following ectopic and molar pregnancy

  O08.5   **Metabolic disorders following an ectopic and molar pregnancy** ♀   M

  O08.6   **Damage to pelvic organs and tissues following an ectopic and molar pregnancy** ♀   M
    Laceration, perforation, tear or chemical damage of bladder following an ectopic and molar pregnancy
    Laceration, perforation, tear or chemical damage of bowel following an ectopic and molar pregnancy
    Laceration, perforation, tear or chemical damage of broad ligament following an ectopic and molar pregnancy
    Laceration, perforation, tear or chemical damage of cervix following an ectopic and molar pregnancy
    Laceration, perforation, tear or chemical damage of periurethral tissue following an ectopic and molar pregnancy
    Laceration, perforation, tear or chemical damage of uterus following an ectopic and molar pregnancy
    Laceration, perforation, tear or chemical damage of vagina following an ectopic and molar pregnancy

  O08.7   **Other venous complications** following an ectopic and molar pregnancy ♀   M

● **O08.8**   **Other complications following an ectopic and molar pregnancy**
    O08.81   **Cardiac arrest** following an ectopic and molar pregnancy ♀   M
    O08.82   **Sepsis** following ectopic and molar pregnancy ♀   M
        Use additional code (B95-B97), to identify infectious agent
        Use additional code (R65.2-) to identify severe sepsis, if applicable
        Excludes1   septic or septicopyemic embolism following ectopic and molar pregnancy (O08.2)
    O08.83   **Urinary tract infection** following an ectopic and molar pregnancy ♀   M
        Cystitis following an ectopic and molar pregnancy
    O08.89   **Other complications** following an ectopic and molar pregnancy ♀   M

  O08.9   **Unspecified** complication following an ectopic and molar pregnancy ♀   M

SUPERVISION OF HIGH RISK PREGNANCY (O09)

● **O09**   **Supervision of high risk pregnancy**
Coding Clinic: 2016, Q4, P125, 150

  ● **O09.0**   **Supervision of pregnancy with history of infertility**
    O09.00   Supervision of pregnancy with history of infertility, **unspecified trimester** ♀   M
    O09.01   Supervision of pregnancy with history of infertility, **first trimester** ♀   M
    O09.02   Supervision of pregnancy with history of infertility, **second trimester** ♀   M
    O09.03   Supervision of pregnancy with history of infertility, **third trimester** ♀   M

  ● **O09.1**   **Supervision of pregnancy with history of ectopic pregnancy**
Coding Clinic: 2016, Q4, P49-50
    O09.10   Supervision of pregnancy with history of ectopic pregnancy, **unspecified trimester** ♀   M
    O09.11   Supervision of pregnancy with history of ectopic pregnancy, **first trimester** ♀   M
    O09.12   Supervision of pregnancy with history of ectopic pregnancy, **second trimester** ♀   M
    O09.13   Supervision of pregnancy with history of ectopic pregnancy, **third trimester** ♀   M

  ● **O09.A**   **Supervision of pregnancy with history of molar pregnancy**
Coding Clinic: 2016, Q4, P50
    O09.A0   Supervision of pregnancy with history of molar pregnancy, **unspecified trimester** ♀   M
    O09.A1   Supervision of pregnancy with history of molar pregnancy, **first trimester** ♀   M
    O09.A2   Supervision of pregnancy with history of molar pregnancy, **second trimester** ♀   M
    O09.A3   Supervision of pregnancy with history of molar pregnancy, **third trimester** ♀   M

▶ New   ➡ Revised   ~~deleted~~ Deleted   Excludes 1   Excludes 2   Includes   Use additional   Code first   Code also   Key words
OGCR Official Guidelines   X Assign placeholder X   ● Use Additional Character(s)   ▷ Manifestation Code   **Coding Clinic**

● **O09.2   Supervision of pregnancy with other poor reproductive or obstetric history**
    Excludes2   pregnancy care for patient with history of recurrent pregnancy loss (O26.2-)

● **O09.21   Supervision of pregnancy with history of pre-term labor**
    O09.211   Supervision of pregnancy with history of pre-term labor, first trimester ♀   M
    O09.212   Supervision of pregnancy with history of pre-term labor, second trimester ♀ M
    O09.213   Supervision of pregnancy with history of pre-term labor, third trimester ♀   M
    O09.219   Supervision of pregnancy with history of pre-term labor, unspecified trimester ♀   M

● **O09.29   Supervision of pregnancy with other poor reproductive or obstetric history**
    Supervision of pregnancy with history of neonatal death
    Supervision of pregnancy with history of stillbirth
    O09.291   Supervision of pregnancy with other poor reproductive or obstetric history, first trimester ♀   M
    O09.292   Supervision of pregnancy with other poor reproductive or obstetric history, second trimester ♀   M
    O09.293   Supervision of pregnancy with other poor reproductive or obstetric history, third trimester ♀   M
    O09.299   Supervision of pregnancy with other poor reproductive or obstetric history, unspecified trimester ♀   M

● **O09.3   Supervision of pregnancy with insufficient antenatal care**
    Supervision of concealed pregnancy
    Supervision of hidden pregnancy
    O09.30   Supervision of pregnancy with insufficient antenatal care, unspecified trimester ♀   M
    O09.31   Supervision of pregnancy with insufficient antenatal care, first trimester ♀   M
    O09.32   Supervision of pregnancy with insufficient antenatal care, second trimester ♀   M
    O09.33   Supervision of pregnancy with insufficient antenatal care, third trimester ♀   M

● **O09.4   Supervision of pregnancy with grand multiparity**
    O09.40   Supervision of pregnancy with grand multiparity, unspecified trimester ♀   M
    O09.41   Supervision of pregnancy with grand multiparity, first trimester ♀   M
    O09.42   Supervision of pregnancy with grand multiparity, second trimester ♀   M
    O09.43   Supervision of pregnancy with grand multiparity, third trimester ♀   M

● **O09.5   Supervision of elderly primigravida and multigravida**
    Pregnancy for a female 35 years and older at expected date of delivery

● **O09.51   Supervision of elderly primigravida**
    O09.511   Supervision of elderly primigravida, first trimester ♀   M
    O09.512   Supervision of elderly primigravida, second trimester ♀   M
    O09.513   Supervision of elderly primigravida, third trimester ♀   M
    O09.519   Supervision of elderly primigravida, unspecified trimester ♀   M

● **O09.52   Supervision of elderly multigravida**
    O09.521   Supervision of elderly multigravida, first trimester ♀   M
    O09.522   Supervision of elderly multigravida, second trimester ♀   M
    O09.523   Supervision of elderly multigravida, third trimester ♀   M
        Coding Clinic: 2016, Q4, P150
    O09.529   Supervision of elderly multigravida, unspecified trimester ♀   M

● **O09.6   Supervision of young primigravida and multigravida**
    Supervision of pregnancy for a female less than 16 years old at expected date of delivery

● **O09.61   Supervision of young primigravida**
    O09.611   Supervision of young primigravida, first trimester ♀   M
    O09.612   Supervision of young primigravida, second trimester ♀   M
    O09.613   Supervision of young primigravida, third trimester ♀   M
    O09.619   Supervision of young primigravida, unspecified trimester ♀   M

● **O09.62   Supervision of young multigravida**
    O09.621   Supervision of young multigravida, first trimester ♀   M
    O09.622   Supervision of young multigravida, second trimester ♀   M
    O09.623   Supervision of young multigravida, third trimester ♀   M
    O09.629   Supervision of young multigravida, unspecified trimester ♀   M

● **O09.7   Supervision of high risk pregnancy due to social problems**
    O09.70   Supervision of high risk pregnancy due to social problems, unspecified trimester ♀   M
    O09.71   Supervision of high risk pregnancy due to social problems, first trimester ♀   M
    O09.72   Supervision of high risk pregnancy due to social problems, second trimester ♀   M
    O09.73   Supervision of high risk pregnancy due to social problems, third trimester ♀   M

● **O09.8   Supervision of other high risk pregnancies**

● **O09.81   Supervision of pregnancy resulting from assisted reproductive technology**
    Supervision of pregnancy resulting from in-vitro fertilization
    Excludes2   gestational carrier status (Z33.3)
    O09.811   Supervision of pregnancy resulting from assisted reproductive technology, first trimester ♀   M
    O09.812   Supervision of pregnancy resulting from assisted reproductive technology, second trimester ♀   M
    O09.813   Supervision of pregnancy resulting from assisted reproductive technology, third trimester ♀   M
    O09.819   Supervision of pregnancy resulting from assisted reproductive technology, unspecified trimester ♀   M

CHAPTER 15 (O00-O9A)

● **O09.82** **Supervision of pregnancy with history of in utero procedure during previous pregnancy**

O09.821 Supervision of pregnancy with history of in utero procedure during previous pregnancy, first trimester ♀   M

O09.822 Supervision of pregnancy with history of in utero procedure during previous pregnancy, second trimester ♀   M

O09.823 Supervision of pregnancy with history of in utero procedure during previous pregnancy, third trimester ♀   M

O09.829 Supervision of pregnancy with history of in utero procedure during previous pregnancy, unspecified trimester ♀   M

Excludes1 supervision of pregnancy affected by in utero procedure during current pregnancy (O35.7)

● **O09.89** **Supervision of other high risk pregnancies**

O09.891 Supervision of other high risk pregnancies, first trimester ♀   M

O09.892 Supervision of other high risk pregnancies, second trimester ♀   M

O09.893 Supervision of other high risk pregnancies, third trimester ♀   M

O09.899 Supervision of other high risk pregnancies, unspecified trimester ♀   M

● **O09.9** **Supervision of high risk pregnancy, unspecified**

O09.90 Supervision of high risk pregnancy, unspecified, unspecified trimester ♀   M

O09.91 Supervision of high risk pregnancy, unspecified, first trimester ♀   M

O09.92 Supervision of high risk pregnancy, unspecified, second trimester ♀   M

O09.93 Supervision of high risk pregnancy, unspecified, third trimester ♀   M

EDEMA, PROTEINURIA AND HYPERTENSIVE DISORDERS IN PREGNANCY, CHILDBIRTH AND THE PUERPERIUM (O10-O16)

● **O10** **Pre-existing hypertension complicating pregnancy, childbirth and the puerperium**

Includes pre-existing hypertension with pre-existing proteinuria complicating pregnancy, childbirth and the puerperium

Excludes2 pre-existing hypertension with superimposed pre-eclampsia complicating pregnancy, childbirth and the puerperium (O11.-)

Coding Clinic: 2016, Q4, P50

● **O10.0** **Pre-existing essential hypertension complicating pregnancy, childbirth and the puerperium**

Any condition in I10 specified as a reason for obstetric care during pregnancy, childbirth or the puerperium

● **O10.01** **Pre-existing essential hypertension complicating pregnancy**

O10.011 Pre-existing essential hypertension complicating pregnancy, first trimester ♀   M

O10.012 Pre-existing essential hypertension complicating pregnancy, second trimester ♀   M

O10.013 Pre-existing essential hypertension complicating pregnancy, third trimester ♀   M

O10.019 Pre-existing essential hypertension complicating pregnancy, unspecified trimester ♀   M

O10.02 Pre-existing essential hypertension complicating childbirth ♀   M

O10.03 Pre-existing essential hypertension complicating the puerperium ♀   M

● **O10.1** **Pre-existing hypertensive heart disease complicating pregnancy, childbirth and the puerperium**

Any condition in I11 specified as a reason for obstetric care during pregnancy, childbirth or the puerperium

Use additional code from I11 to identify the type of hypertensive heart disease

● **O10.11** **Pre-existing hypertensive heart disease complicating pregnancy**

O10.111 Pre-existing hypertensive heart disease complicating pregnancy, first trimester ♀   M

O10.112 Pre-existing hypertensive heart disease complicating pregnancy, second trimester ♀   M

O10.113 Pre-existing hypertensive heart disease complicating pregnancy, third trimester ♀   M

O10.119 Pre-existing hypertensive heart disease complicating pregnancy, unspecified trimester ♀   M

O10.12 Pre-existing hypertensive heart disease complicating childbirth ♀   M

O10.13 Pre-existing hypertensive heart disease complicating the puerperium ♀   M

● **O10.2** **Pre-existing hypertensive chronic kidney disease complicating pregnancy, childbirth and the puerperium**

Any condition in I12 specified as a reason for obstetric care during pregnancy, childbirth or the puerperium

Use additional code from I12 to identify the type of hypertensive chronic kidney disease

● **O10.21** **Pre-existing hypertensive chronic kidney disease complicating pregnancy**

O10.211 Pre-existing hypertensive chronic kidney disease complicating pregnancy, first trimester ♀   M

O10.212 Pre-existing hypertensive chronic kidney disease complicating pregnancy, second trimester ♀   M

O10.213 Pre-existing hypertensive chronic kidney disease complicating pregnancy, third trimester ♀   M

O10.219 Pre-existing hypertensive chronic kidney disease complicating pregnancy, unspecified trimester ♀   M

O10.22 Pre-existing hypertensive chronic kidney disease complicating childbirth ♀   M

O10.23 Pre-existing hypertensive chronic kidney disease complicating the puerperium ♀   M

▶ New   ⇛ Revised   ~~deleted~~ Deleted   Excludes 1   Excludes 2   Includes   Use additional   Code first   Code also   Key words

OGCR Official Guidelines   X Assign placeholder X   ● Use Additional Character(s)   ▶ Manifestation Code   **Coding Clinic**

● **O10.3**   **Pre-existing hypertensive heart and chronic kidney disease complicating pregnancy, childbirth and the puerperium**

> Any condition in I13 specified as a reason for obstetric care during pregnancy, childbirth or the puerperium
>
> Use additional code from I13 to identify the type of hypertensive heart and chronic kidney disease

    ● **O10.31**   **Pre-existing hypertensive heart and chronic kidney disease complicating pregnancy**

       O10.311   Pre-existing hypertensive heart and chronic kidney disease complicating pregnancy, first trimester ♀   M

       O10.312   Pre-existing hypertensive heart and chronic kidney disease complicating pregnancy, second trimester ♀   M

       O10.313   Pre-existing hypertensive heart and chronic kidney disease complicating pregnancy, third trimester ♀   M

       O10.319   Pre-existing hypertensive heart and chronic kidney disease complicating pregnancy, unspecified trimester ♀   M

      O10.32   Pre-existing hypertensive heart and chronic kidney disease complicating childbirth ♀   M

      O10.33   Pre-existing hypertensive heart and chronic kidney disease complicating the puerperium ♀   M

● **O10.4**   **Pre-existing secondary hypertension complicating pregnancy, childbirth and the puerperium**

> Any condition in I15 specified as a reason for obstetric care during pregnancy, childbirth or the puerperium
>
> Use additional code from I15 to identify the type of secondary hypertension

    ● **O10.41**   **Pre-existing secondary hypertension complicating pregnancy**

       O10.411   Pre-existing secondary hypertension complicating pregnancy, first trimester ♀   M

       O10.412   Pre-existing secondary hypertension complicating pregnancy, second trimester ♀   M

       O10.413   Pre-existing secondary hypertension complicating pregnancy, third trimester ♀   M

       O10.419   Pre-existing secondary hypertension complicating pregnancy, unspecified trimester ♀   M

      O10.42   Pre-existing secondary hypertension complicating childbirth ♀   M

      O10.43   Pre-existing secondary hypertension complicating the puerperium ♀   M

● **O10.9**   **Unspecified pre-existing hypertension complicating pregnancy, childbirth and the puerperium**

    ● **O10.91**   **Unspecified pre-existing hypertension complicating pregnancy**

       O10.911   Unspecified pre-existing hypertension complicating pregnancy, first trimester ♀   M

       O10.912   Unspecified pre-existing hypertension complicating pregnancy, second trimester ♀   M

       O10.913   Unspecified pre-existing hypertension complicating pregnancy, third trimester ♀   M

       O10.919   Unspecified pre-existing hypertension complicating pregnancy, unspecified trimester ♀   M

      O10.92   Unspecified pre-existing hypertension complicating childbirth ♀   M

      O10.93   Unspecified pre-existing hypertension complicating the puerperium ♀   M

● **O11**   **Pre-existing hypertension with pre-eclampsia**

> **Includes**   conditions in O10 complicated by pre-eclampsia pre-eclampsia superimposed pre-existing hypertension
>
> Use additional code from O10 to identify the type of hypertension

    Coding Clinic: 2016, Q4, P50

    O11.1   Pre-existing hypertension with pre-eclampsia, first trimester ♀   M

    O11.2   Pre-existing hypertension with pre-eclampsia, second trimester ♀   M

    O11.3   Pre-existing hypertension with pre-eclampsia, third trimester ♀   M

    O11.4   Pre-existing hypertension with pre-eclampsia, complicating childbirth ♀   M

    O11.5   Pre-existing hypertension with pre-eclampsia, complicating the puerperium ♀   M

    O11.9   Pre-existing hypertension with pre-eclampsia, unspecified trimester ♀   M

● **O12**   **Gestational [pregnancy-induced] edema and proteinuria without hypertension**

    Coding Clinic: 2016, Q4, P50

    ● **O12.0**   **Gestational edema**

       O12.00   Gestational edema, unspecified trimester ♀   M

       O12.01   Gestational edema, first trimester ♀   M

       O12.02   Gestational edema, second trimester ♀   M

       O12.03   Gestational edema, third trimester ♀   M

       O12.04   Gestational edema, complicating childbirth ♀   M

       O12.05   Gestational edema, complicating the puerperium ♀   M

    ● **O12.1**   **Gestational proteinuria**

       O12.10   Gestational proteinuria, unspecified trimester ♀   M

       O12.11   Gestational proteinuria, first trimester ♀   M

       O12.12   Gestational proteinuria, second trimester ♀   M

       O12.13   Gestational proteinuria, third trimester ♀   M

       O12.14   Gestational proteinuria, complicating childbirth ♀   M

       O12.15   Gestational proteinuria, complicating the puerperium ♀   M

    ● **O12.2**   **Gestational edema with proteinuria**

       O12.20   Gestational edema with proteinuria, unspecified trimester ♀   M

       O12.21   Gestational edema with proteinuria, first trimester ♀   M

       O12.22   Gestational edema with proteinuria, second trimester ♀   M

       O12.23   Gestational edema with proteinuria, third trimester ♀   M

       O12.24   Gestational edema with proteinuria, complicating childbirth ♀   M

       O12.25   Gestational edema with proteinuria, complicating the puerperium ♀   M

CHAPTER 15 (O00–O9A)

● **O13   Gestational [pregnancy-induced] hypertension without significant proteinuria**

     Includes   gestational hypertension NOS
                 transient hypertension of pregnancy
     Coding Clinic: 2016, Q4, P50

   O13.1   Gestational [pregnancy-induced] hypertension without significant proteinuria, first trimester ♀   M

   O13.2   Gestational [pregnancy-induced] hypertension without significant proteinuria, second trimester ♀   M

   O13.3   Gestational [pregnancy-induced] hypertension without significant proteinuria, third trimester ♀   M

   O13.4   Gestational [pregnancy-induced] hypertension without significant proteinuria, complicating childbirth ♀   M

   O13.5   Gestational [pregnancy-induced] hypertension without significant proteinuria, complicating the puerperium ♀   M

   O13.9   Gestational [pregnancy-induced] hypertension without significant proteinuria, unspecified trimester ♀   M

● **O14   Pre-eclampsia**

     Excludes1   pre-existing hypertension with pre-eclampsia (O11)
     Coding Clinic: 2016, Q4, P50

  ● **O14.0**   Mild to moderate pre-eclampsia

     O14.00   Mild to moderate pre-eclampsia, unspecified trimester ♀   M

     O14.02   Mild to moderate pre-eclampsia, second trimester ♀   M

     O14.03   Mild to moderate pre-eclampsia, third trimester ♀   M

     O14.04   Mild to moderate pre-eclampsia, complicating childbirth ♀   M

     O14.05   Mild to moderate pre-eclampsia, complicating the puerperium ♀   M

  ● **O14.1**   Severe pre-eclampsia

     Excludes1   HELLP syndrome (O14.2-)

     H=hemolysis, EL=elevated liver enzymes, LP=low platelet count

     O14.10   Severe pre-eclampsia, unspecified trimester ♀   M

     O14.12   Severe pre-eclampsia, second trimester ♀   M

     O14.13   Severe pre-eclampsia, third trimester ♀   M

     O14.14   Severe pre-eclampsia complicating childbirth ♀   M

     O14.15   Severe pre-eclampsia, complicating the puerperium ♀   M

  ● **O14.2**   HELLP syndrome

     Severe pre-eclampsia with hemolysis, elevated liver enzymes and low platelet count (HELLP)

     O14.20   HELLP syndrome (HELLP), unspecified trimester ♀   M

     O14.22   HELLP syndrome (HELLP), second trimester ♀   M

     O14.23   HELLP syndrome (HELLP), third trimester ♀   M

     O14.24   HELLP syndrome, complicating childbirth ♀ M

     O14.25   HELLP syndrome, complicating the puerperium ♀   M

  ● **O14.9**   Unspecified pre-eclampsia

     O14.90   Unspecified pre-eclampsia, unspecified trimester ♀   M

     O14.92   Unspecified pre-eclampsia, second trimester ♀   M

     O14.93   Unspecified pre-eclampsia, third trimester ♀   M

     O14.94   Unspecified pre-eclampsia, complicating childbirth ♀   M

     O14.95   Unspecified pre-eclampsia, complicating the puerperium ♀   M

● **O15   Eclampsia**

     Includes   convulsions following conditions in O10-O14 and O16

  ● **O15.0**   Eclampsia complicating pregnancy
     Coding Clinic: 2016, Q4, P50

     O15.00   Eclampsia complicating pregnancy, unspecified trimester ♀   M

     O15.02   Eclampsia complicating pregnancy, second trimester ♀   M

     O15.03   Eclampsia complicating pregnancy, third trimester ♀   M

   O15.1   Eclampsia complicating labor ♀   M

   O15.2   Eclampsia complicating the puerperium ♀   M

   O15.9   Eclampsia, unspecified as to time period ♀   M
          Eclampsia NOS

● **O16   Unspecified maternal hypertension**
     Coding Clinic: 2016, Q4, P50

   O16.1   Unspecified maternal hypertension, first trimester ♀   M

   O16.2   Unspecified maternal hypertension, second trimester ♀   M

   O16.3   Unspecified maternal hypertension, third trimester ♀   M

   O16.4   Unspecified maternal hypertension, complicating childbirth ♀   M

   O16.5   Unspecified maternal hypertension, complicating the puerperium ♀   M

   O16.9   Unspecified maternal hypertension, unspecified trimester ♀   M

OTHER MATERNAL DISORDERS PREDOMINANTLY RELATED TO PREGNANCY (O20-O29)

     Excludes2   maternal care related to the fetus and amniotic cavity and possible delivery problems (O30-O48)
                 maternal diseases classifiable elsewhere but complicating pregnancy, labor and delivery, and the puerperium (O98-O99)

● **O20   Hemorrhage in early pregnancy**

     Includes   hemorrhage before completion of 20 weeks gestation

     Excludes1   pregnancy with abortive outcome (O00-O08)

   O20.0   Threatened abortion ♀   M
          Hemorrhage specified as due to threatened abortion

   O20.8   Other hemorrhage in early pregnancy ♀   M

   O20.9   Hemorrhage in early pregnancy, unspecified ♀   M

● **O21   Excessive vomiting in pregnancy**

   O21.0   Mild hyperemesis gravidarum ♀   M
          Hyperemesis gravidarum, mild or unspecified, starting before the end of the 20th week of gestation

   O21.1   Hyperemesis gravidarum with metabolic disturbance ♀   M
          Hyperemesis gravidarum, starting before the end of the 20th week of gestation, with metabolic disturbance such as carbohydrate depletion
          Hyperemesis gravidarum, starting before the end of the 20th week of gestation, with metabolic disturbance such as dehydration
          Hyperemesis gravidarum, starting before the end of the 20th week of gestation, with metabolic disturbance such as electrolyte imbalance

   O21.2   Late vomiting of pregnancy ♀   M
          Excessive vomiting starting after 20 completed weeks of gestation

   O21.8   Other vomiting complicating pregnancy ♀   M
          Vomiting due to diseases classified elsewhere, complicating pregnancy
          Use additional code, to identify cause

   O21.9   Vomiting of pregnancy, unspecified ♀   M

▶ New   ⇒ Revised   ~~deleted~~ Deleted   Excludes 1   Excludes 2   Includes   Use additional   Code first   Code also   Key words

OGCR Official Guidelines   X Assign placeholder X   ● Use Additional Character(s)   ▷ Manifestation Code   **Coding Clinic**

● **O22   Venous complications and hemorrhoids in pregnancy**

     Excludes1   venous complications of:
                    abortion NOS (O03.9)
                    ectopic or molar pregnancy (O08.7)
                    failed attempted abortion (O07.35)
                    induced abortion (O04.85)
                    spontaneous abortion (O03.89)

     Excludes2   obstetric pulmonary embolism (O88.-)
                    venous complications and hemorrhoids of childbirth and the puerperium (O87.-)

● **O22.0   Varicose veins of lower extremity in pregnancy**
       Varicose veins NOS in pregnancy

     O22.00   Varicose veins of lower extremity in pregnancy, unspecified trimester ♀   M

     O22.01   Varicose veins of lower extremity in pregnancy, first trimester ♀   M

     O22.02   Varicose veins of lower extremity in pregnancy, second trimester ♀   M

     O22.03   Varicose veins of lower extremity in pregnancy, third trimester ♀   M

● **O22.1   Genital varices in pregnancy**
       Perineal varices in pregnancy
       Vaginal varices in pregnancy
       Vulval varices in pregnancy

     O22.10   Genital varices in pregnancy, unspecified trimester ♀   M

     O22.11   Genital varices in pregnancy, first trimester ♀ M

     O22.12   Genital varices in pregnancy, second trimester ♀   M

     O22.13   Genital varices in pregnancy, third trimester ♀ M

● **O22.2   Superficial thrombophlebitis in pregnancy**
       Phlebitis in pregnancy NOS
       Thrombophlebitis of legs in pregnancy
       Thrombosis in pregnancy NOS

       Use additional code to identify the superficial thrombophlebitis (I80.0-)

     O22.20   Superficial thrombophlebitis in pregnancy, unspecified trimester ♀   M

     O22.21   Superficial thrombophlebitis in pregnancy, first trimester ♀   M

     O22.22   Superficial thrombophlebitis in pregnancy, second trimester ♀   M

     O22.23   Superficial thrombophlebitis in pregnancy, third trimester ♀   M

● **O22.3   Deep phlebothrombosis in pregnancy**
       Deep vein thrombosis, antepartum

       Use additional code to identify the deep vein thrombosis (I82.4-, I82.5-, I82.62-. I82.72-)

       Use additional code, if applicable, for associated long-term (current) use of anticoagulants (Z79.01)

     O22.30   Deep phlebothrombosis in pregnancy, unspecified trimester ♀   M

     O22.31   Deep phlebothrombosis in pregnancy, first trimester ♀   M

     O22.32   Deep phlebothrombosis in pregnancy, second trimester ♀   M

     O22.33   Deep phlebothrombosis in pregnancy, third trimester ♀   M

● **O22.4   Hemorrhoids in pregnancy**

     O22.40   Hemorrhoids in pregnancy, unspecified trimester ♀   M

     O22.41   Hemorrhoids in pregnancy, first trimester ♀ M

     O22.42   Hemorrhoids in pregnancy, second trimester ♀   M

     O22.43   Hemorrhoids in pregnancy, third trimester ♀ M

● **O22.5   Cerebral venous thrombosis in pregnancy**
       Cerebrovenous sinus thrombosis in pregnancy

     O22.50   Cerebral venous thrombosis in pregnancy, unspecified trimester ♀   M

     O22.51   Cerebral venous thrombosis in pregnancy, first trimester ♀   M

     O22.52   Cerebral venous thrombosis in pregnancy, second trimester ♀   M

     O22.53   Cerebral venous thrombosis in pregnancy, third trimester ♀   M

● **O22.8   Other venous complications in pregnancy**

  ● **O22.8X   Other venous complications in pregnancy**

     O22.8X1   Other venous complications in pregnancy, first trimester ♀   M

     O22.8X2   Other venous complications in pregnancy, second trimester ♀   M

     O22.8X3   Other venous complications in pregnancy, third trimester ♀   M

     O22.8X9   Other venous complications in pregnancy, unspecified trimester ♀ M

● **O22.9   Venous complication in pregnancy, unspecified**
       Gestational phlebitis NOS
       Gestational phlebopathy NOS
       Gestational thrombosis NOS

     O22.90   Venous complication in pregnancy, unspecified, unspecified trimester ♀   M

     O22.91   Venous complication in pregnancy, unspecified, first trimester ♀   M

     O22.92   Venous complication in pregnancy, unspecified, second trimester ♀   M

     O22.93   Venous complication in pregnancy, unspecified, third trimester ♀   M

● **O23   Infections of genitourinary tract in pregnancy**

       Use additional code to identify organism (B95.-, B96.-)

     Excludes2   gonococcal infections complicating pregnancy, childbirth and the puerperium (O98.2)
                    infections with a predominantly sexual mode of transmission NOS complicating pregnancy, childbirth and the puerperium (O98.3)
                    syphilis complicating pregnancy, childbirth and the puerperium (O98.1)
                    tuberculosis of genitourinary system complicating pregnancy, childbirth and the puerperium (O98.0)
                    venereal disease NOS complicating pregnancy, childbirth and the puerperium (O98.3)

● **O23.0   Infections of kidney in pregnancy**
       Pyelonephritis in pregnancy

     O23.00   Infections of kidney in pregnancy, unspecified trimester ♀   M

     O23.01   Infections of kidney in pregnancy, first trimester ♀   M

     O23.02   Infections of kidney in pregnancy, second trimester ♀   M

     O23.03   Infections of kidney in pregnancy, third trimester ♀   M

● **O23.1   Infections of bladder in pregnancy**

     O23.10   Infections of bladder in pregnancy, unspecified trimester ♀   M

     O23.11   Infections of bladder in pregnancy, first trimester ♀   M

     O23.12   Infections of bladder in pregnancy, second trimester ♀   M

     O23.13   Infections of bladder in pregnancy, third trimester ♀   M

CHAPTER 15 (O00-O9A)

CHAPTER 15 (O00-O9A)

● **O23.2** Infections of urethra in pregnancy
- **O23.20** Infections of urethra in pregnancy, unspecified trimester ♀   M
- **O23.21** Infections of urethra in pregnancy, first trimester ♀   M
- **O23.22** Infections of urethra in pregnancy, second trimester ♀   M
- **O23.23** Infections of urethra in pregnancy, third trimester ♀   M

● **O23.3** Infections of other parts of urinary tract in pregnancy
- **O23.30** Infections of other parts of urinary tract in pregnancy, unspecified trimester ♀   M
- **O23.31** Infections of other parts of urinary tract in pregnancy, first trimester ♀   M
- **O23.32** Infections of other parts of urinary tract in pregnancy, second trimester ♀   M
- **O23.33** Infections of other parts of urinary tract in pregnancy, third trimester ♀   M

● **O23.4** Unspecified infection of urinary tract in pregnancy
- **O23.40** Unspecified infection of urinary tract in pregnancy, unspecified trimester ♀   M
- **O23.41** Unspecified infection of urinary tract in pregnancy, first trimester ♀   M
- **O23.42** Unspecified infection of urinary tract in pregnancy, second trimester ♀   M
- **O23.43** Unspecified infection of urinary tract in pregnancy, third trimester ♀   M

● **O23.5** Infections of the genital tract in pregnancy
- ● **O23.51** Infection of cervix in pregnancy
  - **O23.511** Infections of cervix in pregnancy, first trimester ♀   M
  - **O23.512** Infections of cervix in pregnancy, second trimester ♀   M
  - **O23.513** Infections of cervix in pregnancy, third trimester ♀   M
  - **O23.519** Infections of cervix in pregnancy, unspecified trimester ♀   M
- ● **O23.52** Salpingo-oophoritis in pregnancy
  Oophoritis = inflammation of ovary
  Salpingitis = inflammation of fallopian tube
  Oophoritis in pregnancy
  Salpingitis in pregnancy
  - **O23.521** Salpingo-oophoritis in pregnancy, first trimester ♀   M
  - **O23.522** Salpingo-oophoritis in pregnancy, second trimester ♀   M
  - **O23.523** Salpingo-oophoritis in pregnancy, third trimester ♀   M
  - **O23.529** Salpingo-oophoritis in pregnancy, unspecified trimester ♀   M
- ● **O23.59** Infection of other part of genital tract in pregnancy
  - **O23.591** Infection of other part of genital tract in pregnancy, first trimester ♀   M
  - **O23.592** Infection of other part of genital tract in pregnancy, second trimester ♀   M
  - **O23.593** Infection of other part of genital tract in pregnancy, third trimester ♀   M
  - **O23.599** Infection of other part of genital tract in pregnancy, unspecified trimester ♀   M

● **O23.9** Unspecified genitourinary tract infection in pregnancy
Genitourinary tract infection in pregnancy NOS
- **O23.90** Unspecified genitourinary tract infection in pregnancy, unspecified trimester ♀   M
- **O23.91** Unspecified genitourinary tract infection in pregnancy, first trimester ♀   M
- **O23.92** Unspecified genitourinary tract infection in pregnancy, second trimester ♀   M
- **O23.93** Unspecified genitourinary tract infection in pregnancy, third trimester ♀   M

OGCR Section I.C.15.g.

Diabetes mellitus in pregnancy
Diabetes mellitus is a significant complicating factor in pregnancy. Pregnant women who are diabetic should be assigned a code from category O24, Diabetes mellitus in pregnancy, childbirth, and the puerperium, first, followed by the appropriate diabetes code(s) (E08-E13) from Chapter 4.

● **O24** Diabetes mellitus in pregnancy, childbirth, and the puerperium
- ● **O24.0** Pre-existing type 1 diabetes mellitus, in pregnancy, childbirth and the puerperium
  Juvenile onset diabetes mellitus, in pregnancy, childbirth and the puerperium
  Ketosis-prone diabetes mellitus in pregnancy, childbirth and the puerperium
  Use additional code from category E10 to further identify any manifestations
  - ● **O24.01** Pre-existing type 1 diabetes mellitus, in pregnancy
    - **O24.011** Pre-existing type 1 diabetes mellitus, in pregnancy, first trimester ♀   M
    - **O24.012** Pre-existing type 1 diabetes mellitus, in pregnancy, second trimester ♀   M
    - **O24.013** Pre-existing type 1 diabetes mellitus, in pregnancy, third trimester ♀   M
    - **O24.019** Pre-existing type 1 diabetes mellitus, in pregnancy, unspecified trimester ♀   M
  - **O24.02** Pre-existing type 1 diabetes mellitus, in childbirth ♀   M
  - **O24.03** Pre-existing type 1 diabetes mellitus, in the puerperium ♀   M
- ● **O24.1** Pre-existing type 2 diabetes mellitus, in pregnancy, childbirth and the puerperium
  Insulin-resistant diabetes mellitus in pregnancy, childbirth and the puerperium
  Use additional code (for):
  from category E11 to further identify any manifestations
  long-term (current) use of insulin (Z79.4)
  - ● **O24.11** Pre-existing type 2 diabetes mellitus, in pregnancy
    - **O24.111** Pre-existing type 2 diabetes mellitus, in pregnancy, first trimester ♀   M
    - **O24.112** Pre-existing type 2 diabetes mellitus, in pregnancy, second trimester ♀   M
    - **O24.113** Pre-existing type 2 diabetes mellitus, in pregnancy, third trimester ♀   M
    - **O24.119** Pre-existing type 2 diabetes mellitus, in pregnancy, unspecified trimester ♀   M
  - **O24.12** Pre-existing type 2 diabetes mellitus, in childbirth ♀   M
  - **O24.13** Pre-existing type 2 diabetes mellitus, in the puerperium ♀   M

▶ New   ⇒ Revised   ~~deleted~~ Deleted   Excludes 1   Excludes 2   Includes   Use additional   Code first   Code also   Key words
OGCR Official Guidelines   X Assign placeholder X   ● Use Additional Character(s)   ▶ Manifestation Code   **Coding Clinic**

● **O24.3**   **Unspecified pre-existing diabetes mellitus in pregnancy, childbirth and the puerperium**

Use additional code (for):
  from category E11 to further identify any manifestation
  long-term (current) use of insulin (Z79.4)

  ● **O24.31**   Unspecified pre-existing diabetes mellitus in pregnancy

     O24.311   Unspecified pre-existing diabetes mellitus in pregnancy, first trimester ♀   M

     O24.312   Unspecified pre-existing diabetes mellitus in pregnancy, second trimester ♀   M

     O24.313   Unspecified pre-existing diabetes mellitus in pregnancy, third trimester ♀   M

     O24.319   Unspecified pre-existing diabetes mellitus in pregnancy, unspecified trimester ♀   M

     O24.32   Unspecified pre-existing diabetes mellitus in childbirth ♀   M

     O24.33   Unspecified pre-existing diabetes mellitus in the puerperium ♀   M

OGCR Section I.C.15.i.

Gestational (pregnancy induced) diabetes

Gestational (pregnancy induced) diabetes can occur during the second and third trimester of pregnancy in women who were not diabetic prior to pregnancy. Gestational diabetes can cause complications in the pregnancy similar to those of pre-existing diabetes mellitus. It also puts the woman at greater risk of developing diabetes after the pregnancy. Codes for gestational diabetes are in subcategory O24.4, Gestational diabetes mellitus. No other code from category O24, Diabetes mellitus in pregnancy, childbirth, and the puerperium, should be used with a code from O24.4

The codes under subcategory O24.4 include diet controlled, insulin controlled, **and controlled by oral hypoglycemic drugs.** If a patient with gestational diabetes is treated with both diet and insulin, only the code for insulin-controlled is required. **If a patient with gestational diabetes is treated with both diet and oral hypoglycemic medications, only the code for "controlled by oral hypoglycemic drugs" is required.** Code Z79.4, Long-term (current) use of insulin **or code Z79.84, Long-term (current) use of oral hypoglycemic drugs,** should not be assigned with codes from subcategory O24.4.

An abnormal glucose tolerance in pregnancy is assigned a code from subcategory O99.81, Abnormal glucose complicating pregnancy, childbirth, and the puerperium.

● **O24.4**   **Gestational diabetes mellitus**
  Diabetes mellitus arising in pregnancy
  Gestational diabetes mellitus NOS
  Coding Clinic: 2016, Q4, P50, 126

  ● **O24.41**   Gestational diabetes mellitus in pregnancy

     O24.410   Gestational diabetes mellitus in pregnancy, diet controlled ♀   M

     O24.414   Gestational diabetes mellitus in pregnancy, insulin controlled ♀   M

     O24.415   Gestational diabetes mellitus in pregnancy, controlled by oral hypoglycemic drugs ♀   M
         Gestational diabetes mellitus in pregnancy, controlled by oral antidiabetic drugs
         Coding Clinic: 2016, Q4, P50

     O24.419   Gestational diabetes mellitus in pregnancy, unspecified control ♀   M
         Coding Clinic: 2015, Q4, P34

● **O24.42**   Gestational diabetes mellitus in childbirth

     O24.420   Gestational diabetes mellitus in childbirth, diet controlled ♀   M

     O24.424   Gestational diabetes mellitus in childbirth, insulin controlled ♀   M

     O24.425   Gestational diabetes mellitus in childbirth, controlled by oral hypoglycemic drugs ♀   M
         Gestational diabetes mellitus in childbirth, controlled by oral antidiabetic drugs
         Coding Clinic: 2016, Q4, P50

     O24.429   Gestational diabetes mellitus in childbirth, unspecified control ♀   M

● **O24.43**   Gestational diabetes mellitus in the puerperium

     O24.430   Gestational diabetes mellitus in the puerperium, diet controlled ♀   M

     O24.434   Gestational diabetes mellitus in the puerperium, insulin controlled ♀   M

     O24.435   Gestational diabetes mellitus in puerperium, controlled by oral hypoglycemic drugs ♀   M
         Gestational diabetes mellitus in puerperium, controlled by oral antidiabetic drugs
         Coding Clinic: 2016, Q4, P50

     O24.439   Gestational diabetes mellitus in the puerperium, unspecified control ♀   M

● **O24.8**   **Other pre-existing diabetes mellitus in pregnancy, childbirth, and the puerperium**

Use additional code (for):
  from categories E08, E09 and E13 to further identify any manifestation
  long-term (current) use of insulin (Z79.4)

  ● **O24.81**   Other pre-existing diabetes mellitus in pregnancy

     O24.811   Other pre-existing diabetes mellitus in pregnancy, first trimester ♀   M

     O24.812   Other pre-existing diabetes mellitus in pregnancy, second trimester ♀   M

     O24.813   Other pre-existing diabetes mellitus in pregnancy, third trimester ♀   M

     O24.819   Other pre-existing diabetes mellitus in pregnancy, unspecified trimester ♀   M

     O24.82   Other pre-existing diabetes mellitus in childbirth ♀   M

     O24.83   Other pre-existing diabetes mellitus in the puerperium ♀   M

● **O24.9**   **Unspecified diabetes mellitus in pregnancy, childbirth and the puerperium**

Use additional code for long-term (current) use of insulin (Z79.4)
Unknown whether patient was diabetic before pregnancy occurred

  ● **O24.91**   Unspecified diabetes mellitus in pregnancy

     O24.911   Unspecified diabetes mellitus in pregnancy, first trimester ♀   M

     O24.912   Unspecified diabetes mellitus in pregnancy, second trimester ♀   M

     O24.913   Unspecified diabetes mellitus in pregnancy, third trimester ♀   M

     O24.919   Unspecified diabetes mellitus in pregnancy, unspecified trimester ♀   M

     O24.92   Unspecified diabetes mellitus in childbirth ♀   M

     O24.93   Unspecified diabetes mellitus in the puerperium   M

CHAPTER 15 (O00-O9A)

● **O25**   **Malnutrition** in pregnancy, childbirth and the puerperium
  ● **O25.1**   Malnutrition in **pregnancy**
     O25.10   Malnutrition in pregnancy, **unspecified trimester** ♀   M
     O25.11   Malnutrition in pregnancy, **first trimester** ♀   M
     O25.12   Malnutrition in pregnancy, **second trimester** ♀ M
     O25.13   Malnutrition in pregnancy, **third trimester** ♀   M
   O25.2   Malnutrition in **childbirth** ♀   M
   O25.3   Malnutrition in the **puerperium** ♀   M

● **O26**   Maternal care for other conditions predominantly related to pregnancy
  ● **O26.0**   Excessive weight gain in pregnancy
     Excludes2   gestational edema (O12.0, O12.2)
     O26.00   Excessive weight gain in pregnancy, **unspecified trimester** ♀   M
     O26.01   Excessive weight gain in pregnancy, **first trimester** ♀   M
     O26.02   Excessive weight gain in pregnancy, **second trimester** ♀   M
     O26.03   Excessive weight gain in pregnancy, **third trimester** ♀   M
  ● **O26.1**   Low weight gain in pregnancy
     O26.10   Low weight gain in pregnancy, **unspecified trimester** ♀   M
     O26.11   Low weight gain in pregnancy, **first trimester** ♀   M
     O26.12   Low weight gain in pregnancy, **second trimester** ♀   M
     O26.13   Low weight gain in pregnancy, **third trimester** ♀   M
  ● **O26.2**   Pregnancy care for patient with **recurrent pregnancy loss**
     O26.20   Pregnancy care for patient with recurrent pregnancy loss, **unspecified trimester** ♀   M
     O26.21   Pregnancy care for patient with recurrent pregnancy loss, **first trimester** ♀   M
     O26.22   Pregnancy care for patient with recurrent pregnancy loss, **second trimester** ♀   M
     O26.23   Pregnancy care for patient with recurrent pregnancy loss, **third trimester** ♀   M
  ● **O26.3**   Retained intrauterine contraceptive device in pregnancy
     O26.30   Retained intrauterine contraceptive device in pregnancy, **unspecified trimester** ♀   M
     O26.31   Retained intrauterine contraceptive device in pregnancy, **first trimester** ♀   M
     O26.32   Retained intrauterine contraceptive device in pregnancy, **second trimester** ♀   M
     O26.33   Retained intrauterine contraceptive device in pregnancy, **third trimester** ♀   M
  ● **O26.4**   Herpes gestationis
     O26.40   Herpes gestationis, **unspecified trimester** ♀   M
     O26.41   Herpes gestationis, **first trimester** ♀   M
     O26.42   Herpes gestationis, **second trimester** ♀   M
     O26.43   Herpes gestationis, **third trimester** ♀   M
  ● **O26.5**   Maternal hypotension syndrome
     Supine hypotensive syndrome
     O26.50   Maternal hypotension syndrome, **unspecified trimester** ♀   M
     O26.51   Maternal hypotension syndrome, **first trimester** ♀   M
     O26.52   Maternal hypotension syndrome, **second trimester** ♀   M
     O26.53   Maternal hypotension syndrome, **third trimester** ♀   M

● **O26.6**   Liver and biliary tract disorders in pregnancy, childbirth and the puerperium
     Use additional code to identify the specific disorder
     Excludes2   hepatorenal syndrome following labor and delivery (O90.4)
  ● **O26.61**   Liver and biliary tract disorders in **pregnancy**
     O26.611   Liver and biliary tract disorders in pregnancy, **first trimester** ♀   M
     O26.612   Liver and biliary tract disorders in pregnancy, **second trimester** ♀   M
     O26.613   Liver and biliary tract disorders in pregnancy, **third trimester** ♀   M
     O26.619   Liver and biliary tract disorders in pregnancy, **unspecified trimester** ♀   M
   O26.62   Liver and biliary tract disorders in **childbirth** ♀   M
   O26.63   Liver and biliary tract disorders in the **puerperium** ♀   M
 ● **O26.7**   Subluxation of symphysis (pubis) in pregnancy, childbirth and the puerperium
     Excludes1   traumatic separation of symphysis (pubis) during childbirth (O71.6)
  ● **O26.71**   Subluxation of symphysis (pubis) in **pregnancy**
     O26.711   Subluxation of symphysis (pubis) in pregnancy, **first trimester** ♀   M
     O26.712   Subluxation of symphysis (pubis) in pregnancy, **second trimester** ♀   M
     O26.713   Subluxation of symphysis (pubis) in pregnancy, **third trimester** ♀   M
     O26.719   Subluxation of symphysis (pubis) in pregnancy, **unspecified trimester** ♀   M
   O26.72   Subluxation of symphysis (pubis) in **childbirth** ♀   M
   O26.73   Subluxation of symphysis (pubis) in the **puerperium** ♀   M
 ● **O26.8**   Other specified pregnancy related conditions
  ● **O26.81**   Pregnancy related **exhaustion and fatigue**
     O26.811   Pregnancy related exhaustion and fatigue, **first trimester** ♀   M
     O26.812   Pregnancy related exhaustion and fatigue, **second trimester** ♀   M
     O26.813   Pregnancy related exhaustion and fatigue, **third trimester** ♀   M
     O26.819   Pregnancy related exhaustion and fatigue, **unspecified trimester** ♀   M
  ● **O26.82**   Pregnancy related **peripheral neuritis**
     O26.821   Pregnancy related peripheral neuritis, **first trimester** ♀   M
     O26.822   Pregnancy related peripheral neuritis, **second trimester** ♀   M
     O26.823   Pregnancy related peripheral neuritis, **third trimester** ♀   M
     O26.829   Pregnancy related peripheral neuritis, **unspecified trimester** ♀   M
  ● **O26.83**   Pregnancy related **renal disease**
     Use additional code to identify the specific disorder
     O26.831   Pregnancy related renal disease, **first trimester** ♀   M
     O26.832   Pregnancy related renal disease, **second trimester** ♀   M
     O26.833   Pregnancy related renal disease, **third trimester** ♀   M
     O26.839   Pregnancy related renal disease, **unspecified trimester** ♀   M

▶ New   ⇒ Revised   ~~deleted~~ Deleted   Excludes 1   Excludes 2   Includes   Use additional   Code first   Code also   Key words
OGCR Official Guidelines   X Assign placeholder X   ● Use Additional Character(s)   ▌ Manifestation Code   **Coding Clinic**

● O26.84 **Uterine size-date discrepancy complicating pregnancy**

    Excludes1   encounter for suspected problem with fetal growth ruled out (ZØ3.74)

   O26.841 **Uterine size-date discrepancy, first trimester** ♀   M

   O26.842 **Uterine size-date discrepancy, second trimester** ♀   M

   O26.843 **Uterine size-date discrepancy, third trimester** ♀   M

   O26.849 **Uterine size-date discrepancy, unspecified trimester** ♀   M

● O26.85 **Spotting complicating pregnancy**

   O26.851 **Spotting complicating pregnancy, first trimester** ♀   M

   O26.852 **Spotting complicating pregnancy, second trimester** ♀   M

   O26.853 **Spotting complicating pregnancy, third trimester** ♀   M

   O26.859 **Spotting complicating pregnancy, unspecified trimester** ♀   M

  O26.86 **Pruritic urticarial papules and plaques of pregnancy (PUPPP)** ♀   M
      Polymorphic eruption of pregnancy

● O26.87 **Cervical shortening**

    Excludes1   encounter for suspected cervical shortening ruled out (ZØ3.75)

   O26.872 **Cervical shortening, second trimester** ♀   M

   O26.873 **Cervical shortening, third trimester** ♀   M

   O26.879 **Cervical shortening, unspecified trimester** ♀   M

● O26.89 **Other specified pregnancy related conditions**

   O26.891 **Other specified pregnancy related conditions, first trimester** ♀   M

   O26.892 **Other specified pregnancy related conditions, second trimester** ♀   M

   O26.893 **Other specified pregnancy related conditions, third trimester** ♀   M
       Coding Clinic: 2015, Q3, P40

   O26.899 **Other specified pregnancy related conditions, unspecified trimester** ♀ M

● O26.9 **Pregnancy related conditions, unspecified**

   O26.90 **Pregnancy related conditions, unspecified, unspecified trimester** ♀   M

   O26.91 **Pregnancy related conditions, unspecified, first trimester** ♀   M

   O26.92 **Pregnancy related conditions, unspecified, second trimester** ♀   M

   O26.93 **Pregnancy related conditions, unspecified, third trimester** ♀   M

● O28 **Abnormal findings on antenatal screening of mother**

    Excludes1   diagnostic findings classified elsewhere - see Alphabetical Index

  O28.0 **Abnormal hematological finding on antenatal screening of mother** ♀   M

  O28.1 **Abnormal biochemical finding on antenatal screening of mother** ♀   M

  O28.2 **Abnormal cytological finding on antenatal screening of mother** ♀   M

  O28.3 **Abnormal ultrasonic finding on antenatal screening of mother** ♀   M
      Coding Clinic: 2016, Q4, P5

  O28.4 **Abnormal radiological finding on antenatal screening of mother** ♀   M

  O28.5 **Abnormal chromosomal and genetic finding on antenatal screening of mother** ♀   M

  O28.8 **Other abnormal findings on antenatal screening of mother** ♀   M

  O28.9 **Unspecified abnormal findings on antenatal screening of mother** ♀   M

● O29 **Complications of anesthesia during pregnancy**

    Includes   maternal complications arising from the administration of a general, regional or local anesthetic, analgesic or other sedation during pregnancy

   Use additional code, if necessary, to identify the complication

    Excludes2   complications of anesthesia during labor and delivery (O74.-)
         complications of anesthesia during the puerperium (O89.-)

● O29.0 **Pulmonary complications of anesthesia during pregnancy**

  ● O29.01 **Aspiration pneumonitis due to anesthesia during pregnancy**
      Inhalation of stomach contents or secretions NOS due to anesthesia during pregnancy
      Mendelson's syndrome due to anesthesia during pregnancy

    O29.011 **Aspiration pneumonitis due to anesthesia during pregnancy, first trimester** ♀   M

    O29.012 **Aspiration pneumonitis due to anesthesia during pregnancy, second trimester** ♀   M

    O29.013 **Aspiration pneumonitis due to anesthesia during pregnancy, third trimester** ♀   M

    O29.019 **Aspiration pneumonitis due to anesthesia during pregnancy, unspecified trimester** ♀   M

  ● O29.02 **Pressure collapse of lung due to anesthesia during pregnancy**

    O29.021 **Pressure collapse of lung due to anesthesia during pregnancy, first trimester** ♀   M

    O29.022 **Pressure collapse of lung due to anesthesia during pregnancy, second trimester** ♀   M

    O29.023 **Pressure collapse of lung due to anesthesia during pregnancy, third trimester** ♀   M

    O29.029 **Pressure collapse of lung due to anesthesia during pregnancy, unspecified trimester** ♀   M

  ● O29.09 **Other pulmonary complications of anesthesia during pregnancy**

    O29.091 **Other pulmonary complications of anesthesia during pregnancy, first trimester** ♀   M

    O29.092 **Other pulmonary complications of anesthesia during pregnancy, second trimester** ♀   M

    O29.093 **Other pulmonary complications of anesthesia during pregnancy, third trimester** ♀   M

    O29.099 **Other pulmonary complications of anesthesia during pregnancy, unspecified trimester** ♀   M

CHAPTER 15 (OØØ-O9A)

CHAPTER 15 (O00-O9A)

● **O29.1** Cardiac complications of anesthesia during pregnancy
- ● **O29.11** Cardiac arrest due to anesthesia during pregnancy
  - O29.111 Cardiac arrest due to anesthesia during pregnancy, first trimester ♀ M
  - O29.112 Cardiac arrest due to anesthesia during pregnancy, second trimester ♀ M
  - O29.113 Cardiac arrest due to anesthesia during pregnancy, third trimester ♀ M
  - O29.119 Cardiac arrest due to anesthesia during pregnancy, unspecified trimester ♀ M
- ● **O29.12** Cardiac failure due to anesthesia during pregnancy
  - O29.121 Cardiac failure due to anesthesia during pregnancy, first trimester ♀ M
  - O29.122 Cardiac failure due to anesthesia during pregnancy, second trimester ♀ M
  - O29.123 Cardiac failure due to anesthesia during pregnancy, third trimester ♀ M
  - O29.129 Cardiac failure due to anesthesia during pregnancy, unspecified trimester ♀ M
- ● **O29.19** Other cardiac complications of anesthesia during pregnancy
  - O29.191 Other cardiac complications of anesthesia during pregnancy, first trimester ♀ M
  - O29.192 Other cardiac complications of anesthesia during pregnancy, second trimester ♀ M
  - O29.193 Other cardiac complications of anesthesia during pregnancy, third trimester ♀ M
  - O29.199 Other cardiac complications of anesthesia during pregnancy, unspecified trimester ♀ M

● **O29.2** Central nervous system complications of anesthesia during pregnancy
- ● **O29.21** Cerebral anoxia due to anesthesia during pregnancy
  - O29.211 Cerebral anoxia due to anesthesia during pregnancy, first trimester ♀ M
  - O29.212 Cerebral anoxia due to anesthesia during pregnancy, second trimester ♀ M
  - O29.213 Cerebral anoxia due to anesthesia during pregnancy, third trimester ♀ M
  - O29.219 Cerebral anoxia due to anesthesia during pregnancy, unspecified trimester ♀ M
- ● **O29.29** Other central nervous system complications of anesthesia during pregnancy
  - O29.291 Other central nervous system complications of anesthesia during pregnancy, first trimester ♀ M
  - O29.292 Other central nervous system complications of anesthesia during pregnancy, second trimester ♀ M
  - O29.293 Other central nervous system complications of anesthesia during pregnancy, third trimester ♀ M
  - O29.299 Other central nervous system complications of anesthesia during pregnancy, unspecified trimester ♀ M

● **O29.3** Toxic reaction to local anesthesia during pregnancy
- ● **O29.3X** Toxic reaction to local anesthesia during pregnancy
  - O29.3X1 Toxic reaction to local anesthesia during pregnancy, first trimester ♀ M
  - O29.3X2 Toxic reaction to local anesthesia during pregnancy, second trimester ♀ M
  - O29.3X3 Toxic reaction to local anesthesia during pregnancy, third trimester ♀ M
  - O29.3X9 Toxic reaction to local anesthesia during pregnancy, unspecified trimester ♀ M

● **O29.4** Spinal and epidural anesthesia induced headache during pregnancy
- O29.40 Spinal and epidural anesthesia induced headache during pregnancy, unspecified trimester ♀ M
- O29.41 Spinal and epidural anesthesia induced headache during pregnancy, first trimester ♀ M
- O29.42 Spinal and epidural anesthesia induced headache during pregnancy, second trimester ♀ M
- O29.43 Spinal and epidural anesthesia induced headache during pregnancy, third trimester ♀ M

● **O29.5** Other complications of spinal and epidural anesthesia during pregnancy
- ● **O29.5X** Other complications of spinal and epidural anesthesia during pregnancy
  - O29.5X1 Other complications of spinal and epidural anesthesia during pregnancy, first trimester ♀ M
  - O29.5X2 Other complications of spinal and epidural anesthesia during pregnancy, second trimester ♀ M
  - O29.5X3 Other complications of spinal and epidural anesthesia during pregnancy, third trimester ♀ M
  - O29.5X9 Other complications of spinal and epidural anesthesia during pregnancy, unspecified trimester ♀ M

● **O29.6** Failed or difficult intubation for anesthesia during pregnancy
- O29.60 Failed or difficult intubation for anesthesia during pregnancy, unspecified trimester ♀ M
- O29.61 Failed or difficult intubation for anesthesia during pregnancy, first trimester ♀ M
- O29.62 Failed or difficult intubation for anesthesia during pregnancy, second trimester ♀ M
- O29.63 Failed or difficult intubation for anesthesia during pregnancy, third trimester ♀ M

● **O29.8** Other complications of anesthesia during pregnancy
- ● **O29.8X** Other complications of anesthesia during pregnancy
  - O29.8X1 Other complications of anesthesia during pregnancy, first trimester ♀ M
  - O29.8X2 Other complications of anesthesia during pregnancy, second trimester ♀ M
  - O29.8X3 Other complications of anesthesia during pregnancy, third trimester ♀ M
  - O29.8X9 Other complications of anesthesia during pregnancy, unspecified trimester ♀ M

▶ New ⇒ Revised ~~deleted~~ Deleted Excludes 1 Excludes 2 Includes Use additional Code first Code also Key words

OGCR Official Guidelines X Assign placeholder X ● Use Additional Character(s) ▷ Manifestation Code **Coding Clinic**

● **O29.9**   Unspecified complication of anesthesia during pregnancy
-    **O29.90**   Unspecified complication of anesthesia during pregnancy, unspecified trimester ♀   M
-    **O29.91**   Unspecified complication of anesthesia during pregnancy, first trimester ♀   M
-    **O29.92**   Unspecified complication of anesthesia during pregnancy, second trimester ♀   M
-    **O29.93**   Unspecified complication of anesthesia during pregnancy, third trimester ♀   M

MATERNAL CARE RELATED TO THE FETUS AND AMNIOTIC CAVITY AND POSSIBLE DELIVERY PROBLEMS (O30–O48)

● **O30**   Multiple gestation
     Code also any complications specific to multiple gestation
     Coding Clinic: 2016, Q4, P51

● **O30.0**   Twin pregnancy

   ● **O30.00**   Twin pregnancy, unspecified number of placenta and unspecified number of amniotic sacs
-      **O30.001**   Twin pregnancy, unspecified number of placenta and unspecified number of amniotic sacs, first trimester ♀   M
-      **O30.002**   Twin pregnancy, unspecified number of placenta and unspecified number of amniotic sacs, second trimester ♀ M
-      **O30.003**   Twin pregnancy, unspecified number of placenta and unspecified number of amniotic sacs, third trimester ♀   M
-      **O30.009**   Twin pregnancy, unspecified number of placenta and unspecified number of amniotic sacs, unspecified trimester ♀   M

   ● **O30.01**   Twin pregnancy, monochorionic/monoamniotic
       Twin pregnancy, one placenta, one amniotic sac
       Excludes1   conjoined twins (O30.02-)
-      **O30.011**   Twin pregnancy, monochorionic/monoamniotic, first trimester ♀   M
-      **O30.012**   Twin pregnancy, monochorionic/monoamniotic, second trimester ♀   M
-      **O30.013**   Twin pregnancy, monochorionic/monoamniotic, third trimester ♀   M
-      **O30.019**   Twin pregnancy, monochorionic/monoamniotic, unspecified trimester ♀   M

   ● **O30.02**   Conjoined twin pregnancy
-      **O30.021**   Conjoined twin pregnancy, first trimester ♀   M
-      **O30.022**   Conjoined twin pregnancy, second trimester ♀   M
-      **O30.023**   Conjoined twin pregnancy, third trimester ♀   M
-      **O30.029**   Conjoined twin pregnancy, unspecified trimester ♀   M

   ● **O30.03**   Twin pregnancy, monochorionic/diamniotic
       Twin pregnancy, one placenta, two amniotic sacs
-      **O30.031**   Twin pregnancy, monochorionic/diamniotic, first trimester ♀   M
-      **O30.032**   Twin pregnancy, monochorionic/diamniotic, second trimester ♀   M
-      **O30.033**   Twin pregnancy, monochorionic/diamniotic, third trimester ♀   M
-      **O30.039**   Twin pregnancy, monochorionic/diamniotic, unspecified trimester ♀ M

● **O30.04**   Twin pregnancy, dichorionic/diamniotic
     Twin pregnancy, two placentae, two amniotic sacs
-      **O30.041**   Twin pregnancy, dichorionic/diamniotic, first trimester ♀   M
-      **O30.042**   Twin pregnancy, dichorionic/diamniotic, second trimester ♀   M
-      **O30.043**   Twin pregnancy, dichorionic/diamniotic, third trimester ♀   M
-      **O30.049**   Twin pregnancy, dichorionic/diamniotic, unspecified trimester ♀ M

● **O30.09**   Twin pregnancy, unable to determine number of placenta and number of amniotic sacs
-      **O30.091**   Twin pregnancy, unable to determine number of placenta and number of amniotic sacs, first trimester ♀   M
-      **O30.092**   Twin pregnancy, unable to determine number of placenta and number of amniotic sacs, second trimester ♀   M
-      **O30.093**   Twin pregnancy, unable to determine number of placenta and number of amniotic sacs, third trimester ♀   M
-      **O30.099**   Twin pregnancy, unable to determine number of placenta and number of amniotic sacs, unspecified trimester ♀   M

● **O30.1**   Triplet pregnancy

   ● **O30.10**   Triplet pregnancy, unspecified number of placenta and unspecified number of amniotic sacs
-      **O30.101**   Triplet pregnancy, unspecified number of placenta and unspecified number of amniotic sacs, first trimester ♀   M
-      **O30.102**   Triplet pregnancy, unspecified number of placenta and unspecified number of amniotic sacs, second trimester ♀   M
-      **O30.103**   Triplet pregnancy, unspecified number of placenta and unspecified number of amniotic sacs, third trimester ♀   M
       Coding Clinic: 2016, Q2, P8
-      **O30.109**   Triplet pregnancy, unspecified number of placenta and unspecified number of amniotic sacs, unspecified trimester ♀ M

   ● **O30.11**   Triplet pregnancy with two or more monochorionic fetuses
-      **O30.111**   Triplet pregnancy with two or more monochorionic fetuses, first trimester ♀   M
-      **O30.112**   Triplet pregnancy with two or more monochorionic fetuses, second trimester ♀   M
-      **O30.113**   Triplet pregnancy with two or more monochorionic fetuses, third trimester ♀   M
-      **O30.119**   Triplet pregnancy with two or more monochorionic fetuses, unspecified trimester ♀   M

   ● **O30.12**   Triplet pregnancy with two or more monoamniotic fetuses
-      **O30.121**   Triplet pregnancy with two or more monoamniotic fetuses, first trimester ♀   M
-      **O30.122**   Triplet pregnancy with two or more monoamniotic fetuses, second trimester ♀   M
-      **O30.123**   Triplet pregnancy with two or more monoamniotic fetuses, third trimester ♀   M
-      **O30.129**   Triplet pregnancy with two or more monoamniotic fetuses, unspecified trimester ♀   M

▶ **O30.13**   Triplet pregnancy, trichorionic/triamniotic

     ▶ **O30.131**   Triplet pregnancy, trichorionic/ triamniotic, first trimester

     ▶ **O30.132**   Triplet pregnancy, trichorionic/ triamniotic, second trimester

     ▶ **O30.133**   Triplet pregnancy, trichorionic/ triamniotic, third trimester

     ▶ **O30.139**   Triplet pregnancy, trichorionic/ triamniotic, unspecified trimester

● **O30.19**   Triplet pregnancy, unable to determine number of placenta and number of amniotic sacs

     O30.191   Triplet pregnancy, unable to determine number of placenta and number of amniotic sacs, first trimester ♀   M

     O30.192   Triplet pregnancy, unable to determine number of placenta and number of amniotic sacs, second trimester ♀   M

     O30.193   Triplet pregnancy, unable to determine number of placenta and number of amniotic sacs, third trimester ♀   M

     O30.199   Triplet pregnancy, unable to determine number of placenta and number of amniotic sacs, unspecified trimester ♀ M

● **O30.2**   Quadruplet pregnancy

   ● **O30.20**   Quadruplet pregnancy, unspecified number of placenta and unspecified number of amniotic sacs

     O30.201   Quadruplet pregnancy, unspecified number of placenta and unspecified number of amniotic sacs, first trimester ♀   M

     O30.202   Quadruplet pregnancy, unspecified number of placenta and unspecified number of amniotic sacs, second trimester ♀   M

     O30.203   Quadruplet pregnancy, unspecified number of placenta and unspecified number of amniotic sacs, third trimester ♀   M

     O30.209   Quadruplet pregnancy, unspecified number of placenta and unspecified number of amniotic sacs, unspecified trimester ♀   M

   ● **O30.21**   Quadruplet pregnancy with two or more monochorionic fetuses

     O30.211   Quadruplet pregnancy with two or more monochorionic fetuses, first trimester ♀   M

     O30.212   Quadruplet pregnancy with two or more monochorionic fetuses, second trimester ♀   M

     O30.213   Quadruplet pregnancy with two or more monochorionic fetuses, third trimester ♀   M

     O30.219   Quadruplet pregnancy with two or more monochorionic fetuses, unspecified trimester ♀

   ● **O30.22**   Quadruplet pregnancy with two or more monoamniotic fetuses

     O30.221   Quadruplet pregnancy with two or more monoamniotic fetuses, first trimester ♀   M

     O30.222   Quadruplet pregnancy with two or more monoamniotic fetuses, second trimester ♀   M

     O30.223   Quadruplet pregnancy with two or more monoamniotic fetuses, third trimester ♀   M

     O30.229   Quadruplet pregnancy with two or more monoamniotic fetuses, unspecified trimester ♀   M

▶ **O30.23**   Quadruplet pregnancy, quadrachorionic/ quadra-amniotic

     ▶ **O30.231**   Quadruplet pregnancy, quadrachorionic/quadra-amniotic, first trimester

     ▶ **O30.232**   Quadruplet pregnancy, quadrachorionic/quadra-amniotic, second trimester

     ▶ **O30.233**   Quadruplet pregnancy, quadrachorionic/quadra-amniotic, third trimester

     ▶ **O30.239**   Quadruplet pregnancy, quadrachorionic/quadra-amniotic, unspecifiedtrimester

● **O30.29**   Quadruplet pregnancy, unable to determine number of placenta and number of amniotic sacs

     O30.291   Quadruplet pregnancy, unable to determine number of placenta and number of amniotic sacs, first trimester ♀   M

     O30.292   Quadruplet pregnancy, unable to determine number of placenta and number of amniotic sacs, second trimester ♀   M

     O30.293   Quadruplet pregnancy, unable to determine number of placenta and number of amniotic sacs, third trimester ♀   M

     O30.299   Quadruplet pregnancy, unable to determine number of placenta and number of amniotic sacs, unspecified trimester ♀   M

● **O30.8**   Other specified multiple gestation

     Multiple gestation pregnancy greater then quadruplets

   ● **O30.80**   Other specified multiple gestation, unspecified number of placenta and unspecified number of amniotic sacs

     O30.801   Other specified multiple gestation, unspecified number of placenta and unspecified number of amniotic sacs, first trimester ♀   M

     O30.802   Other specified multiple gestation, unspecified number of placenta and unspecified number of amniotic sacs, second trimester ♀   M

     O30.803   Other specified multiple gestation, unspecified number of placenta and unspecified number of amniotic sacs, third trimester ♀   M

     O30.809   Other specified multiple gestation, unspecified number of placenta and unspecified number of amniotic sacs, unspecified trimester ♀   M

   ● **O30.81**   Other specified multiple gestation with two or more monochorionic fetuses

     O30.811   Other specified multiple gestation with two or more monochorionic fetuses, first trimester ♀   M

     O30.812   Other specified multiple gestation with two or more monochorionic fetuses, second trimester ♀   M

     O30.813   Other specified multiple gestation with two or more monochorionic fetuses, third trimester ♀   M

     O30.819   Other specified multiple gestation with two or more monochorionic fetuses, unspecified trimester ♀   M

● **O30.82** **Other specified multiple gestation with two or more monoamniotic fetuses**

     O30.821   Other specified multiple gestation with two or more monoamniotic fetuses, first trimester ♀   M

     O30.822   Other specified multiple gestation with two or more monoamniotic fetuses, second trimester ♀   M

     O30.823   Other specified multiple gestation with two or more monoamniotic fetuses, third trimester ♀   M

     O30.829   Other specified multiple gestation with two or more monoamniotic fetuses, unspecified trimester ♀   M

▶ **O30.83** **Other specified multiple gestation, number of chorions and amnions are both equal to the number of fetuses**

     ▶Pentachorionic, penta-amniotic pregnancy (quintuplets)

     ▶Hexachorionic, hexa-amniotic pregnancy (sextuplets)

     ▶Heptachorionic, hepta-amniotic pregnancy (septuplets)

   ▶ O30.831   Other specified multiple gestation, number of chorions and amnions are both equal to the number of fetuses, first trimester

   ▶ O30.832   Other specified multiple gestation, number of chorions and amnions are both equal to the number of fetuses, second trimester

   ▶ O30.833   Other specified multiple gestation, number of chorions and amnions are both equal to the number of fetuses, third trimester

   ▶ O30.839   Other specified multiple gestation, number of chorions and amnions are both equal to the number of fetuses, unspecified trimester

● **O30.89** **Other specified multiple gestation, unable to determine number of placenta and number of amniotic sacs**

     O30.891   Other specified multiple gestation, unable to determine number of placenta and number of amniotic sacs, first trimester ♀   M

     O30.892   Other specified multiple gestation, unable to determine number of placenta and number of amniotic sacs, second trimester ♀   M

     O30.893   Other specified multiple gestation, unable to determine number of placenta and number of amniotic sacs, third trimester ♀   M

     O30.899   Other specified multiple gestation, unable to determine number of placenta and number of amniotic sacs, unspecified trimester ♀   M

● **O30.9** **Multiple gestation, unspecified**
     Multiple pregnancy NOS

     O30.90   Multiple gestation, unspecified, unspecified trimester ♀   M

     O30.91   Multiple gestation, unspecified, first trimester ♀   M

     O30.92   Multiple gestation, unspecified, second trimester ♀   M

     O30.93   Multiple gestation, unspecified, third trimester ♀   M

● **O31** **Complications specific to multiple gestation**

     Excludes2   delayed delivery of second twin, triplet, etc. (O63.2)
                 malpresentation of one fetus or more (O32.9)
                 placental transfusion syndromes (O43.0-)

     Coding Clinic: 2012, Q4, P107

One of the following 7th characters is to be assigned to each code under category O31. 7th character 0 is for single gestations and multiple gestations where the fetus is unspecified. 7th characters 1 through 9 are for cases of multiple gestations to identify the fetus for which the code applies. The appropriate code from category O30, Multiple gestation, must also be assigned when assigning a code from category O31 that has a 7th character of 1 through 9.

0	not applicable or unspecified
1	fetus 1
2	fetus 2
3	fetus 3
4	fetus 4
5	fetus 5
9	other fetus

● **O31.0** **Papyraceous fetus**
     Fetus compressus

   X● O31.00   Papyraceous fetus, unspecified trimester ♀   M

   X● O31.01   Papyraceous fetus, first trimester ♀   M

   X● O31.02   Papyraceous fetus, second trimester ♀   M

   X● O31.03   Papyraceous fetus, third trimester ♀   M

● **O31.1** **Continuing pregnancy after spontaneous abortion of one fetus or more**

   X● O31.10   Continuing pregnancy after spontaneous abortion of one fetus or more, unspecified trimester ♀   M

   X● O31.11   Continuing pregnancy after spontaneous abortion of one fetus or more, first trimester ♀ M

   X● O31.12   Continuing pregnancy after spontaneous abortion of one fetus or more, second trimester ♀   M

   X● O31.13   Continuing pregnancy after spontaneous abortion of one fetus or more, third trimester ♀   M

● **O31.2** **Continuing pregnancy after intrauterine death of one fetus or more**

   X● O31.20   Continuing pregnancy after intrauterine death of one fetus or more, unspecified trimester ♀   M

   X● O31.21   Continuing pregnancy after intrauterine death of one fetus or more, first trimester ♀   M

   X● O31.22   Continuing pregnancy after intrauterine death of one fetus or more, second trimester ♀   M

   X● O31.23   Continuing pregnancy after intrauterine death of one fetus or more, third trimester ♀   M

● **O31.3** **Continuing pregnancy after elective fetal reduction of one fetus or more**
     Continuing pregnancy after selective termination of one fetus or more

   X● O31.30   Continuing pregnancy after elective fetal reduction of one fetus or more, unspecified trimester ♀   M

   X● O31.31   Continuing pregnancy after elective fetal reduction of one fetus or more, first trimester ♀   M

   X● O31.32   Continuing pregnancy after elective fetal reduction of one fetus or more, second trimester ♀   M

   X● O31.33   Continuing pregnancy after elective fetal reduction of one fetus or more, third trimester ♀   M

- ● **O31.8** Other complications specific to multiple gestation
  - ● **O31.8X** Other complications specific to multiple gestation
    - ● **O31.8X1** Other complications specific to multiple gestation, first trimester ♀ M
    - ● **O31.8X2** Other complications specific to multiple gestation, second trimester ♀ M
    - ● **O31.8X3** Other complications specific to multiple gestation, third trimester ♀ M
    - ● **O31.8X9** Other complications specific to multiple gestation, unspecified trimester ♀ M

- ● **O32** Maternal care for malpresentation of fetus

  Includes the listed conditions as a reason for observation, hospitalization or other obstetric care of the mother, or for cesarean delivery before onset of labor

  Excludes1 malpresentation of fetus with obstructed labor (O64.-)

  Coding Clinic: 2012, Q4, P107

  One of the following 7th characters is to be assigned to each code under category O32. 7th character 0 is for single gestations and multiple gestations where the fetus is unspecified. 7th characters 1 through 9 are for cases of multiple gestations to identify the fetus for which the code applies. The appropriate code from category O30, Multiple gestation, must also be assigned when assigning a code from category O32 that has a 7th character of 1 through 9.

0	not applicable or unspecified
1	fetus 1
2	fetus 2
3	fetus 3
4	fetus 4
5	fetus 5
9	other fetus

  - X ● **O32.0** Maternal care for unstable lie ♀ M
  - X ● **O32.1** Maternal care for breech presentation ♀ M
    Maternal care for buttocks presentation
    Maternal care for complete breech
    Maternal care for frank breech
    Excludes1 footling presentation (O32.8)
    incomplete breech (O32.8)
  - X ● **O32.2** Maternal care for transverse and oblique lie ♀ M
    Maternal care for oblique presentation
    Maternal care for transverse presentation
  - X ● **O32.3** Maternal care for face, brow and chin presentation ♀ M
  - X ● **O32.4** Maternal care for high head at term ♀ M
    Maternal care for failure of head to enter pelvic brim
  - X ● **O32.6** Maternal care for compound presentation ♀ M
  - X ● **O32.8** Maternal care for other malpresentation of fetus ♀ M
    Maternal care for footling presentation
    Maternal care for incomplete breech
  - X ● **O32.9** Maternal care for malpresentation of fetus, unspecified ♀ M

- ● **O33** Maternal care for disproportion

  Includes the listed conditions as a reason for observation, hospitalization or other obstetric care of the mother, or for cesarean delivery before onset of labor

  Excludes1 disproportion with obstructed labor (O65-O66)

  - **O33.0** Maternal care for disproportion due to deformity of maternal pelvic bones ♀ M
    Maternal care for disproportion due to pelvic deformity causing disproportion NOS
  - **O33.1** Maternal care for disproportion due to generally contracted pelvis ♀ M
    Maternal care for disproportion due to contracted pelvis NOS causing disproportion
  - **O33.2** Maternal care for disproportion due to inlet contraction of pelvis ♀ M
    Maternal care for disproportion due to inlet contraction (pelvis) causing disproportion

- X ● **O33.3** Maternal care for disproportion due to outlet contraction of pelvis ♀ M
  Maternal care for disproportion due to mid-cavity contraction (pelvis)
  Maternal care for disproportion due to outlet contraction (pelvis)

  One of the following 7th characters is to be assigned to code O33.3. 7th character 0 is for single gestations and multiple gestations where the fetus is unspecified. 7th characters 1 through 9 are for cases of multiple gestations to identify the fetus for which the code applies. The appropriate code from category O30, Multiple gestation, must also be assigned when assigning code O33.3 with a 7th character of 1 through 9.

0	not applicable or unspecified
1	fetus 1
2	fetus 2
3	fetus 3
4	fetus 4
5	fetus 5
9	other fetus

- X ● **O33.4** Maternal care for disproportion of mixed maternal and fetal origin ♀ M

  One of the following 7th characters is to be assigned to code O33.4. 7th character 0 is for single gestations and multiple gestations where the fetus is unspecified. 7th characters 1 through 9 are for cases of multiple gestations to identify the fetus for which the code applies. The appropriate code from category O30, Multiple gestation, must also be assigned when assigning code O33.4 with a 7th character of 1 through 9.

0	not applicable or unspecified
1	fetus 1
2	fetus 2
3	fetus 3
4	fetus 4
5	fetus 5
9	other fetus

- X ● **O33.5** Maternal care for disproportion due to unusually large fetus ♀ M
  Maternal care for disproportion due to disproportion of fetal origin with normally formed fetus
  Maternal care for disproportion due to fetal disproportion NOS

  One of the following 7th characters is to be assigned to code O33.5. 7th character 0 is for single gestations and multiple gestations where the fetus is unspecified. 7th characters 1 through 9 are for cases of multiple gestations to identify the fetus for which the code applies. The appropriate code from category O30, Multiple gestation, must also be assigned when assigning code O33.5 with a 7th character of 1 through 9.

0	not applicable or unspecified
1	fetus 1
2	fetus 2
3	fetus 3
4	fetus 4
5	fetus 5
9	other fetus

▶ New ⇒ Revised ~~deleted~~ Deleted | Excludes 1 | Excludes 2 | Includes | Use additional | Code first | Code also | Key words
OGCR Official Guidelines   X Assign placeholder X   ● Use Additional Character(s)   ▷ Manifestation Code   **Coding Clinic**

X ● **O33.6** **Maternal care for disproportion due to hydrocephalic fetus** ♀   M

One of the following 7th characters is to be assigned to code O33.6. 7th character Ø is for single gestations and multiple gestations where the fetus is unspecified. 7th characters 1 through 9 are for cases of multiple gestations to identify the fetus for which the code applies. The appropriate code from category O30, Multiple gestation, must also be assigned when assigning code O33.6 with a 7th character of 1 through 9.

Ø	not applicable or unspecified
1	fetus 1
2	fetus 2
3	fetus 3
4	fetus 4
5	fetus 5
9	other fetus

X ● **O33.7** **Maternal care for disproportion due to other fetal deformities** ♀   M

Maternal care for disproportion due to fetal ascites
Maternal care for disproportion due to fetal hydrops
Maternal care for disproportion due to fetal meningomyelocele
Maternal care for disproportion due to fetal sacral teratoma
Maternal care for disproportion due to fetal tumor

Excludes1   obstructed labor due to other fetal deformities (O66.3)

Coding Clinic: 2016, Q4, P51

One of the following 7th characters is to be assigned to code O33.7. 7th character Ø is for single gestations and multiple gestations where the fetus is unspecified. 7th characters 1 through 9 are for cases of multiple gestations to identify the fetus for which the code applies. The appropriate code from category O30, Multiple gestation, must also be assigned when assigning code O33.7 with a 7th character of 1 through 9.

Ø	not applicable or unspecified
1	fetus 1
2	fetus 2
3	fetus 3
4	fetus 4
5	fetus 5
9	other fetus

O33.8 **Maternal care for disproportion of other origin** ♀   M

O33.9 **Maternal care for disproportion, unspecified** ♀   M

Maternal care for disproportion due to cephalopelvic disproportion NOS
Maternal care for disproportion due to fetopelvic disproportion NOS

● **O34** **Maternal care for abnormality of pelvic organs**

Includes   the listed conditions as a reason for hospitalization or other obstetric care of the mother, or for cesarean delivery before onset of labor

Code first any associated obstructed labor (O65.5)

Use additional code for specific condition

● **O34.0** **Maternal care for congenital malformation of uterus**

Maternal care for double uterus
Maternal care for uterus bicornis

O34.00 **Maternal care for unspecified congenital malformation of uterus, unspecified trimester** ♀   M

O34.01 **Maternal care for unspecified congenital malformation of uterus, first trimester** ♀   M

O34.02 **Maternal care for unspecified congenital malformation of uterus, second trimester** ♀   M

O34.03 **Maternal care for unspecified congenital malformation of uterus, third trimester** ♀   M

● **O34.1** **Maternal care for benign tumor of corpus uteri**

Excludes2   maternal care for benign tumor of cervix (O34.4-)
maternal care for malignant neoplasm of uterus (O9A.1-)

O34.10 **Maternal care for benign tumor of corpus uteri, unspecified trimester** ♀   M

O34.11 **Maternal care for benign tumor of corpus uteri, first trimester** ♀   M

O34.12 **Maternal care for benign tumor of corpus uteri, second trimester** ♀   M

O34.13 **Maternal care for benign tumor of corpus uteri, third trimester** ♀   M

● **O34.2** **Maternal care due to uterine scar from previous surgery**
Coding Clinic: 2016, Q4, P76

● **O34.21** **Maternal care for scar from previous cesarean delivery**
Coding Clinic: 2016, Q4, P51

O34.211 **Maternal care for low transverse scar from previous cesarean delivery** ♀   M

O34.212 **Maternal care for vertical scar from previous cesarean delivery** ♀   M
Maternal care for classical scar from previous cesarean delivery

O34.219 **Maternal care for unspecified type scar from previous cesarean delivery** ♀   M

O34.29 **Maternal care due to uterine scar from other previous surgery** ♀   M
Maternal care due to uterine scar from other transmural uterine incision

● **O34.3** **Maternal care for cervical incompetence**
Maternal care for cerclage with or without cervical incompetence
Maternal care for Shirodkar suture with or without cervical incompetence

O34.30 **Maternal care for cervical incompetence, unspecified trimester** ♀   M

O34.31 **Maternal care for cervical incompetence, first trimester** ♀   M

O34.32 **Maternal care for cervical incompetence, second trimester** ♀   M

O34.33 **Maternal care for cervical incompetence, third trimester** ♀   M

● **O34.4** **Maternal care for other abnormalities of cervix**

O34.40 **Maternal care for other abnormalities of cervix, unspecified trimester** ♀   M

O34.41 **Maternal care for other abnormalities of cervix, first trimester** ♀   M

O34.42 **Maternal care for other abnormalities of cervix, second trimester** ♀   M

O34.43 **Maternal care for other abnormalities of cervix, third trimester** ♀   M

● **O34.5** **Maternal care for other abnormalities of gravid uterus**

● **O34.51** **Maternal care for incarceration of gravid uterus**

O34.511 **Maternal care for incarceration of gravid uterus, first trimester** ♀   M

O34.512 **Maternal care for incarceration of gravid uterus, second trimester** ♀   M

O34.513 **Maternal care for incarceration of gravid uterus, third trimester** ♀   M

O34.519 **Maternal care for incarceration of gravid uterus, unspecified trimester** ♀   M

CHAPTER 15 (O00–O9A)

● **O34.52** Maternal care for prolapse of gravid uterus

O34.521   Maternal care for prolapse of gravid uterus, first trimester ♀   M

O34.522   Maternal care for prolapse of gravid uterus, second trimester ♀   M

O34.523   Maternal care for prolapse of gravid uterus, third trimester ♀   M

O34.529   Maternal care for prolapse of gravid uterus, unspecified trimester ♀   M

● **O34.53** Maternal care for retroversion of gravid uterus

O34.531   Maternal care for retroversion of gravid uterus, first trimester ♀   M

O34.532   Maternal care for retroversion of gravid uterus, second trimester ♀   M

O34.533   Maternal care for retroversion of gravid uterus, third trimester ♀   M

O34.539   Maternal care for retroversion of gravid uterus, unspecified trimester ♀   M

● **O34.59** Maternal care for other abnormalities of gravid uterus

O34.591   Maternal care for other abnormalities of gravid uterus, first trimester ♀   M

O34.592   Maternal care for other abnormalities of gravid uterus, second trimester ♀ M

O34.593   Maternal care for other abnormalities of gravid uterus, third trimester ♀   M

O34.599   Maternal care for other abnormalities of gravid uterus, unspecified trimester ♀   M

● **O34.6** Maternal care for abnormality of vagina

    Excludes2   maternal care for vaginal varices in pregnancy (O22.1-)

O34.60   Maternal care for abnormality of vagina, unspecified trimester ♀   M

O34.61   Maternal care for abnormality of vagina, first trimester ♀   M

O34.62   Maternal care for abnormality of vagina, second trimester ♀   M

O34.63   Maternal care for abnormality of vagina, third trimester ♀   M

● **O34.7** Maternal care for abnormality of vulva and perineum

    Excludes2   maternal care for perineal and vulval varices in pregnancy (O22.1-)

O34.70   Maternal care for abnormality of vulva and perineum, unspecified trimester ♀   M

O34.71   Maternal care for abnormality of vulva and perineum, first trimester ♀   M

O34.72   Maternal care for abnormality of vulva and perineum, second trimester ♀   M

O34.73   Maternal care for abnormality of vulva and perineum, third trimester ♀   M

● **O34.8** Maternal care for other abnormalities of pelvic organs

O34.80   Maternal care for other abnormalities of pelvic organs, unspecified trimester ♀   M

O34.81   Maternal care for other abnormalities of pelvic organs, first trimester ♀   M

O34.82   Maternal care for other abnormalities of pelvic organs, second trimester ♀   M

O34.83   Maternal care for other abnormalities of pelvic organs, third trimester ♀   M

● **O34.9** Maternal care for abnormality of pelvic organ, unspecified

O34.90   Maternal care for abnormality of pelvic organ, unspecified, unspecified trimester ♀   M

O34.91   Maternal care for abnormality of pelvic organ, unspecified, first trimester ♀   M

O34.92   Maternal care for abnormality of pelvic organ, unspecified, second trimester ♀   M

O34.93   Maternal care for abnormality of pelvic organ, unspecified, third trimester ♀   M

● **O35** Maternal care for known or suspected fetal abnormality and damage

    Includes   the listed conditions in the fetus as a reason for hospitalization or other obstetric care to the mother, or for termination of pregnancy

Code also any associated maternal condition

    Excludes1   encounter for suspected maternal and fetal conditions ruled out (Z03.7-)

One of the following 7th characters is to be assigned to each code under category O35. 7th character Ø is for single gestations and multiple gestations where the fetus is unspecified. 7th characters 1 through 9 are for cases of multiple gestations to identify the fetus for which the code applies. The appropriate code from category O30, Multiple gestation, must also be assigned when assigning a code from category O35 that has a 7th character of 1 through 9.

Ø	not applicable or unspecified
1	fetus 1
2	fetus 2
3	fetus 3
4	fetus 4
5	fetus 5
9	other fetus

X ● **O35.Ø** Maternal care for (suspected) central nervous system malformation in fetus ♀   M

    Maternal care for fetal anencephaly

    Maternal care for fetal hydrocephalus

    Maternal care for fetal spina bifida

    Excludes2   chromosomal abnormality in fetus (O35.1)

X ● **O35.1** Maternal care for (suspected) chromosomal abnormality in fetus ♀   M

X ● **O35.2** Maternal care for (suspected) hereditary disease in fetus ♀   M

    Excludes2   chromosomal abnormality in fetus (O35.1)

X ● **O35.3** Maternal care for (suspected) damage to fetus from viral disease in mother ♀   M

    Maternal care for damage to fetus from maternal cytomegalovirus infection

    Maternal care for damage to fetus from maternal rubella

    Coding Clinic: 2016, Q4, P6

X ● **O35.4** Maternal care for (suspected) damage to fetus from alcohol ♀   M

X ● **O35.5** Maternal care for (suspected) damage to fetus by drugs ♀   M

    Maternal care for damage to fetus from drug addiction

X ● **O35.6** Maternal care for (suspected) damage to fetus by radiation ♀   M

X ● **O35.7** Maternal care for (suspected) damage to fetus by other medical procedures ♀   M

    Maternal care for damage to fetus by amniocentesis

    Maternal care for damage to fetus by biopsy procedures

    Maternal care for damage to fetus by hematological investigation

    Maternal care for damage to fetus by intrauterine contraceptive device

    Maternal care for damage to fetus by intrauterine surgery

X ● **O35.8** Maternal care for other (suspected) fetal abnormality and damage ♀   M

    Maternal care for damage to fetus from maternal listeriosis

    Maternal care for damage to fetus from maternal toxoplasmosis

X ● **O35.9** Maternal care for (suspected) fetal abnormality and damage, unspecified ♀   M

▶ New   ⇨ Revised   ~~deleted~~ Deleted   Excludes 1   Excludes 2   Includes   Use additional   Code first   Code also   Key words

OGCR Official Guidelines   X Assign placeholder X   ● Use Additional Character(s)   ▷ Manifestation Code   **Coding Clinic**

Fetal Conditions Affecting the Management of the Mother

1) Code from categories O35 and O36

Codes from categories O35, Maternal care for known or suspected fetal abnormality and damage, and O36, Maternal care for other fetal problems, are assigned only when the fetal condition is actually responsible for modifying the management of the mother, i.e., by requiring diagnostic studies, additional observation, special care, or termination of pregnancy. The fact that the fetal condition exists does not justify assigning a code from this series to the mother's record.

2) In utero surgery

In cases when surgery is performed on the fetus, a diagnosis code from category O35, Maternal care for known or suspected fetal abnormality and damage, should be assigned identifying the fetal condition. Assign the appropriate procedure code for the procedure performed.

No code from Chapter 16, the perinatal codes, should be used on the mother's record to identify fetal conditions. Surgery performed in utero on a fetus is still to be coded as an obstetric encounter.

● **O36**   **Maternal care for other fetal problems**

     Includes   the listed conditions in the fetus as a reason for hospitalization or other obstetric care of the mother, or for termination of pregnancy

     Excludes1   encounter for suspected maternal and fetal conditions ruled out (Z03.7-)
                    placental transfusion syndromes (O43.0-)

     Excludes2   labor and delivery complicated by fetal stress (O77.-)

One of the following 7th characters is to be assigned to each code under category O36. 7th character Ø is for single gestations and multiple gestations where the fetus is unspecified. 7th characters 1 through 9 are for cases of multiple gestations to identify the fetus for which the code applies. The appropriate code from category O30, Multiple gestation, must also be assigned when assigning a code from category O36 that has a 7th character of 1 through 9.

Ø	not applicable or unspecified
1	fetus 1
2	fetus 2
3	fetus 3
4	fetus 4
5	fetus 5
9	other fetus

Coding Clinic: 2015, Q3, P4Ø

● **O36.Ø**   **Maternal care for rhesus isoimmunization**
     Maternal care for Rh incompatibility (with hydrops fetalis)

   ● **O36.Ø1**   **Maternal care for anti-D [Rh] antibodies**

     ● **O36.Ø11**   **Maternal care for anti-D [Rh] antibodies, first trimester** ♀   M

     ● **O36.Ø12**   **Maternal care for anti-D [Rh] antibodies, second trimester** ♀   M

     ● **O36.Ø13**   **Maternal care for anti-D [Rh] antibodies, third trimester** ♀   M

     ● **O36.Ø19**   **Maternal care for anti-D [Rh] antibodies, unspecified trimester** ♀   M

   ● **O36.Ø9**   **Maternal care for other rhesus isoimmunization**

     ● **O36.Ø91**   **Maternal care for other rhesus isoimmunization, first trimester** ♀   M

     ● **O36.Ø92**   **Maternal care for other rhesus isoimmunization, second trimester** ♀   M

     ● **O36.Ø93**   **Maternal care for other rhesus isoimmunization, third trimester** ♀   M
           Coding Clinic: 2015, Q3, P4Ø

     ● **O36.Ø99**   **Maternal care for other rhesus isoimmunization, unspecified trimester** ♀   M

● **O36.1**   **Maternal care for other isoimmunization**
     Maternal care for ABO isoimmunization

   ● **O36.11**   **Maternal care for Anti-A sensitization**
     Maternal care for isoimmunization NOS (with hydrops fetalis)

     ● **O36.111**   **Maternal care for Anti-A sensitization, first trimester** ♀   M

     ● **O36.112**   **Maternal care for Anti-A sensitization, second trimester** ♀   M

     ● **O36.113**   **Maternal care for Anti-A sensitization, third trimester** ♀   M

     ● **O36.119**   **Maternal care for Anti-A sensitization, unspecified trimester** ♀   M

   ● **O36.19**   **Maternal care for other isoimmunization**
     Maternal care for Anti-B sensitization

     ● **O36.191**   **Maternal care for other isoimmunization, first trimester** ♀   M

     ● **O36.192**   **Maternal care for other isoimmunization, second trimester** ♀   M

     ● **O36.193**   **Maternal care for other isoimmunization, third trimester** ♀   M

     ● **O36.199**   **Maternal care for other isoimmunization, unspecified trimester** ♀   M

● **O36.2**   **Maternal care for hydrops fetalis**
     Maternal care for hydrops fetalis NOS
     Maternal care for hydrops fetalis not associated with isoimmunization

     Excludes1   hydrops fetalis associated with ABO isoimmunization (O36.1-)
                    hydrops fetalis associated with rhesus isoimmunization (O36.Ø-)

   ● **O36.20**   **Maternal care for hydrops fetalis, unspecified trimester** ♀   M

   ● **O36.21**   **Maternal care for hydrops fetalis, first trimester** ♀   M

   ● **O36.22**   **Maternal care for hydrops fetalis, second trimester** ♀   M

   ● **O36.23**   **Maternal care for hydrops fetalis, third trimester** ♀   M

● **O36.4**   **Maternal care for intrauterine death** ♀   M
     Maternal care for intrauterine fetal death NOS
     Maternal care for intrauterine fetal death after completion of 2Ø weeks of gestation
     Maternal care for late fetal death
     Maternal care for missed delivery

     Excludes1   missed abortion (O02.1)
                    stillbirth (P95)

● **O36.5**   **Maternal care for known or suspected poor fetal growth**

   ● **O36.51**   **Maternal care for known or suspected placental insufficiency**

     ● **O36.511**   **Maternal care for known or suspected placental insufficiency, first trimester** ♀   M

     ● **O36.512**   **Maternal care for known or suspected placental insufficiency, second trimester** ♀   M

     ● **O36.513**   **Maternal care for known or suspected placental insufficiency, third trimester** ♀   M

     ● **O36.519**   **Maternal care for known or suspected placental insufficiency, unspecified trimester** ♀   M

CHAPTER 15 (OØØ-O9A)

● **O36.59** **Maternal care for other known or suspected poor fetal growth**
Maternal care for known or suspected light-for-dates NOS
Maternal care for known or suspected small-for-dates NOS

    ● **O36.591** Maternal care for other known or suspected poor fetal growth, **first trimester** ♀   M

    ● **O36.592** Maternal care for other known or suspected poor fetal growth, **second trimester** ♀   M

    ● **O36.593** Maternal care for other known or suspected poor fetal growth, **third trimester** ♀   M

    ● **O36.599** Maternal care for other known or suspected poor fetal growth, **unspecified trimester** ♀   M

● **O36.6** **Maternal care for excessive fetal growth**
Maternal care for known or suspected large-for-dates

  X ● **O36.60** Maternal care for excessive fetal growth, **unspecified trimester** ♀   M

  X ● **O36.61** Maternal care for excessive fetal growth, **first trimester** ♀   M

  X ● **O36.62** Maternal care for excessive fetal growth, **second trimester** ♀   M

  X ● **O36.63** Maternal care for excessive fetal growth, **third trimester** ♀   M

● **O36.7** **Maternal care for viable fetus in abdominal pregnancy**

  X ● **O36.70** Maternal care for viable fetus in abdominal pregnancy, **unspecified trimester** ♀   M

  X ● **O36.71** Maternal care for viable fetus in abdominal pregnancy, **first trimester** ♀   M

  X ● **O36.72** Maternal care for viable fetus in abdominal pregnancy, **second trimester** ♀   M

  X ● **O36.73** Maternal care for viable fetus in abdominal pregnancy, **third trimester** ♀   M

● **O36.8** **Maternal care for other specified fetal problems**

  X ● **O36.80** Pregnancy with inconclusive fetal viability ♀   M
Encounter to determine fetal viability of pregnancy

  ● **O36.81** **Decreased fetal movements**

    ● **O36.812** Decreased fetal movements, **second trimester** ♀   M

    ● **O36.813** Decreased fetal movements, **third trimester** ♀   M

    ● **O36.819** Decreased fetal movements, **unspecified trimester** ♀   M

  ● **O36.82** **Fetal anemia and thrombocytopenia**

    ● **O36.821** Fetal anemia and thrombocytopenia, **first trimester** ♀   M

    ● **O36.822** Fetal anemia and thrombocytopenia, **second trimester** ♀   M

    ● **O36.823** Fetal anemia and thrombocytopenia, **third trimester** ♀   M

    ● **O36.829** Fetal anemia and thrombocytopenia, **unspecified trimester** ♀   M

  ● **O36.83** **Maternal care for abnormalities of the fetal heart rate or rhythm**

    ● **O36.831** Maternal care for abnormalities of the fetal heart rate or rhythm, **first trimester** ♀   M

    ● **O36.832** Maternal care for abnormalities of the fetal heart rate or rhythm, **second trimester** ♀   M

    ● **O36.833** Maternal care for abnormalities of the fetal heart rate or rhythm, **third trimester** ♀   M

    ● **O36.839** Maternal care for abnormalities of the fetal heart rate or rhythm, **unspecified trimester** ♀   M

● **O36.89** **Maternal care for** other **specified fetal problems**

  ● **O36.891** Maternal care for other specified fetal problems, **first trimester** ♀   M

  ● **O36.892** Maternal care for other specified fetal problems, **second trimester** ♀   M

  ● **O36.893** Maternal care for other specified fetal problems, **third trimester** ♀   M

  ● **O36.899** Maternal care for other specified fetal problems, **unspecified trimester** ♀   M

● **O36.9** **Maternal care for fetal problem, unspecified**

  X ● **O36.90** Maternal care for fetal problem, unspecified, **unspecified trimester** ♀   M

  X ● **O36.91** Maternal care for fetal problem, unspecified, **first trimester** ♀   M

  X ● **O36.92** Maternal care for fetal problem, unspecified, **second trimester** ♀   M

  X ● **O36.93** Maternal care for fetal problem, unspecified, **third trimester** ♀   M

● **O40** **Polyhydramnios**
Overabundance of amniotic fluid

  Includes   hydramnios

  Excludes1   encounter for suspected maternal and fetal conditions ruled out (Z03.7-)

One of the following 7th characters is to be assigned to each code under category O40. 7th character Ø is for single gestations and multiple gestations where the fetus is unspecified. 7th characters 1 through 9 are for cases of multiple gestations to identify the fetus for which the code applies. The appropriate code from category O3Ø, Multiple gestation, must also be assigned when assigning a code from category O40 that has a 7th character of 1 through 9.

Ø	not applicable or unspecified
1	fetus 1
2	fetus 2
3	fetus 3
4	fetus 4
5	fetus 5
9	other fetus

  X ● **O40.1** **Polyhydramnios, first trimester** ♀   M

  X ● **O40.2** **Polyhydramnios, second trimester** ♀   M

  X ● **O40.3** **Polyhydramnios, third trimester** ♀   M

  X ● **O40.9** **Polyhydramnios, unspecified trimester** ♀   M

● **O41** **Other disorders of amniotic fluid and membranes**

  Excludes1   encounter for suspected maternal and fetal conditions ruled out (Z03.7-)

One of the following 7th characters is to be assigned to each code under category O41. 7th character Ø is for single gestations and multiple gestations where the fetus is unspecified. 7th characters 1 through 9 are for cases of multiple gestations to identify the fetus for which the code applies. The appropriate code from category O3Ø, Multiple gestation, must also be assigned when assigning a code from category O41 that has a 7th character of 1 through 9.

Ø	not applicable or unspecified
1	fetus 1
2	fetus 2
3	fetus 3
4	fetus 4
5	fetus 5
9	other fetus

● **O41.Ø** **Oligohydramnios**
Scant volume of amniotic fluid
Oligohydramnios without rupture of membranes

  X ● **O41.00** Oligohydramnios, **unspecified trimester** ♀   M

  X ● **O41.01** Oligohydramnios, **first trimester** ♀   M

  X ● **O41.02** Oligohydramnios, **second trimester** ♀   M

  X ● **O41.03** Oligohydramnios, **third trimester** ♀   M

▶ New   ⇒ Revised   ~~deleted~~ Deleted   Excludes 1   Excludes 2   Includes   Use additional   Code first   Code also   Key words

OGCR Official Guidelines   X Assign placeholder X   ● Use Additional Character(s)   ▷ Manifestation Code   **Coding Clinic**

● **O41.1 Infection of amniotic sac and membranes**
  ● **O41.10 Infection of amniotic sac and membranes, unspecified**
    ● O41.101 Infection of amniotic sac and membranes, unspecified, first trimester ♀   M
    ● O41.102 Infection of amniotic sac and membranes, unspecified, second trimester ♀   M
    ● O41.103 Infection of amniotic sac and membranes, unspecified, third trimester ♀   M
    ● O41.109 Infection of amniotic sac and membranes, unspecified, unspecified trimester ♀   M
  ● **O41.12 Chorioamnionitis**
    ● O41.121 Chorioamnionitis, first trimester ♀ M
    ● O41.122 Chorioamnionitis, second trimester ♀   M
    ● O41.123 Chorioamnionitis, third trimester ♀ M
    ● O41.129 Chorioamnionitis, unspecified trimester ♀   M
  ● **O41.14 Placentitis**
    ● O41.141 Placentitis, first trimester ♀ M
    ● O41.142 Placentitis, second trimester ♀ M
    ● O41.143 Placentitis, third trimester ♀ M
    ● O41.149 Placentitis, unspecified trimester ♀ M
● **O41.8 Other specified disorders of amniotic fluid and membranes**
  ● **O41.8X Other specified disorders of amniotic fluid and membranes**
    ● O41.8X1 Other specified disorders of amniotic fluid and membranes, first trimester ♀   M
    ● O41.8X2 Other specified disorders of amniotic fluid and membranes, second trimester ♀   M
    ● O41.8X3 Other specified disorders of amniotic fluid and membranes, third trimester ♀   M
    ● O41.8X9 Other specified disorders of amniotic fluid and membranes, unspecified trimester ♀   M
● **O41.9 Disorder of amniotic fluid and membranes, unspecified**
  X ● **O41.90 Disorder of amniotic fluid and membranes, unspecified, unspecified trimester ♀   M**
  X ● **O41.91 Disorder of amniotic fluid and membranes, unspecified, first trimester ♀   M**
  X ● **O41.92 Disorder of amniotic fluid and membranes, unspecified, second trimester ♀   M**
  X ● **O41.93 Disorder of amniotic fluid and membranes, unspecified, third trimester ♀   M**

● **O42 Premature rupture of membranes**
  ● **O42.0 Premature rupture of membranes, onset of labor within 24 hours of rupture**
    O42.00 Premature rupture of membranes, onset of labor within 24 hours of rupture, unspecified weeks of gestation ♀   M
    ● **O42.01 Preterm premature rupture of membranes, onset of labor within 24 hours of rupture**
      Premature rupture of membranes before 37 completed weeks of gestation
      O42.011 Preterm premature rupture of membranes, onset of labor within 24 hours of rupture, first trimester ♀   M
      O42.012 Preterm premature rupture of membranes, onset of labor within 24 hours of rupture, second trimester ♀ M

      O42.013 Preterm premature rupture of membranes, onset of labor within 24 hours of rupture, third trimester ♀   M
      O42.019 Preterm premature rupture of membranes, onset of labor within 24 hours of rupture, unspecified trimester ♀   M
    O42.02 Full-term premature rupture of membranes, onset of labor within 24 hours of rupture ♀   M
      Premature rupture of membranes at or after 37 completed weeks of gestation, onset of labor within 24 hours of rupture
  ● **O42.1 Premature rupture of membranes, onset of labor more than 24 hours following rupture**
    O42.10 Premature rupture of membranes, onset of labor more than 24 hours following rupture, unspecified weeks of gestation ♀   M
    ● **O42.11 Preterm premature rupture of membranes, onset of labor more than 24 hours following rupture**
      Premature rupture of membranes before 37 completed weeks of gestation
      O42.111 Preterm premature rupture of membranes, onset of labor more than 24 hours following rupture, first trimester ♀   M
      O42.112 Preterm premature rupture of membranes, onset of labor more than 24 hours following rupture, second trimester ♀   M
      O42.113 Preterm premature rupture of membranes, onset of labor more than 24 hours following rupture, third trimester ♀   M
      O42.119 Preterm premature rupture of membranes, onset of labor more than 24 hours following rupture, unspecified trimester ♀   M
    O42.12 Full-term premature rupture of membranes, onset of labor more than 24 hours following rupture ♀   M
      Premature rupture of membranes at or after 37 completed weeks of gestation, onset of labor more than 24 hours following rupture
  ● **O42.9 Premature rupture of membranes, unspecified as to length of time between rupture and onset of labor**
    O42.90 Premature rupture of membranes, unspecified as to length of time between rupture and onset of labor, unspecified weeks of gestation ♀   M
    ● **O42.91 Preterm premature rupture of membranes, unspecified as to length of time between rupture and onset of labor**
      Premature rupture of membranes before 37 completed weeks of gestation
      O42.911 Preterm premature rupture of membranes, unspecified as to length of time between rupture and onset of labor, first trimester ♀   M
      O42.912 Preterm premature rupture of membranes, unspecified as to length of time between rupture and onset of labor, second trimester ♀   M
      O42.913 Preterm premature rupture of membranes, unspecified as to length of time between rupture and onset of labor, third trimester ♀   M
      O42.919 Preterm premature rupture of membranes, unspecified as to length of time between rupture and onset of labor, unspecified trimester ♀   M

O42.92   **Full-term premature rupture of membranes, unspecified as to length of time between rupture and onset of labor** ♀   M
      Premature rupture of membranes at or after 37 completed weeks of gestation, unspecified as to length of time between rupture and onset of labor

● **O43**   **Placental disorders**
    Excludes2   maternal care for poor fetal growth due to placental insufficiency (O36.5-)
       placenta previa (O44.-)
       placental polyp (O90.89)
       placentitis (O41.14-)
       premature separation of placenta [abruptio placentae] (O45.-)

● **O43.0**   **Placental transfusion syndromes**
 ● **O43.01**   **Fetomaternal placental transfusion syndrome**
     Maternofetal placental transfusion syndrome
    O43.011   **Fetomaternal placental transfusion syndrome, first trimester** ♀   M
    O43.012   **Fetomaternal placental transfusion syndrome, second trimester** ♀   M
    O43.013   **Fetomaternal placental transfusion syndrome, third trimester** ♀   M
    O43.019   **Fetomaternal placental transfusion syndrome, unspecified trimester** ♀   M

 ● **O43.02**   **Fetus-to-fetus placental transfusion syndrome**
    O43.021   **Fetus-to-fetus placental transfusion syndrome, first trimester** ♀   M
    O43.022   **Fetus-to-fetus placental transfusion syndrome, second trimester** ♀   M
    O43.023   **Fetus-to-fetus placental transfusion syndrome, third trimester** ♀   M
    O43.029   **Fetus-to-fetus placental transfusion syndrome, unspecified trimester** ♀   M

● **O43.1**   **Malformation of placenta**
 ● **O43.10**   **Malformation of placenta, unspecified**
     Abnormal placenta NOS
    O43.101   **Malformation of placenta, unspecified, first trimester** ♀   M
    O43.102   **Malformation of placenta, unspecified, second trimester** ♀   M
    O43.103   **Malformation of placenta, unspecified, third trimester** ♀   M
    O43.109   **Malformation of placenta, unspecified, unspecified trimester** ♀   M

 ● **O43.11**   **Circumvallate placenta**
    O43.111   **Circumvallate placenta, first trimester** ♀   M
    O43.112   **Circumvallate placenta, second trimester** ♀   M
    O43.113   **Circumvallate placenta, third trimester** ♀   M
    O43.119   **Circumvallate placenta, unspecified trimester** ♀   M

 ● **O43.12**   **Velamentous insertion of umbilical cord**
    O43.121   **Velamentous insertion of umbilical cord, first trimester** ♀   M
    O43.122   **Velamentous insertion of umbilical cord, second trimester** ♀   M
    O43.123   **Velamentous insertion of umbilical cord, third trimester** ♀   M
    O43.129   **Velamentous insertion of umbilical cord, unspecified trimester** ♀   M

 ● **O43.19**   **Other malformation of placenta**
    O43.191   **Other malformation of placenta, first trimester** ♀   M
    O43.192   **Other malformation of placenta, second trimester** ♀   M
    O43.193   **Other malformation of placenta, third trimester** ♀   M
    O43.199   **Other malformation of placenta, unspecified trimester** ♀   M

● **O43.2**   **Morbidly adherent placenta**
    Code also associated third stage postpartum hemorrhage, if applicable (O72.0)
    Excludes1   retained placenta (O73.-)
 ● **O43.21**   **Placenta accreta**
    O43.211   **Placenta accreta, first trimester** ♀   M
    O43.212   **Placenta accreta, second trimester** ♀   M
    O43.213   **Placenta accreta, third trimester** ♀   M
    O43.219   **Placenta accreta, unspecified trimester** ♀   M

 ● **O43.22**   **Placenta increta**
    O43.221   **Placenta increta, first trimester** ♀   M
    O43.222   **Placenta increta, second trimester** ♀   M
    O43.223   **Placenta increta, third trimester** ♀   M
    O43.229   **Placenta increta, unspecified trimester** ♀   M

 ● **O43.23**   **Placenta percreta**
    O43.231   **Placenta percreta, first trimester** ♀   M
    O43.232   **Placenta percreta, second trimester** ♀ M
    O43.233   **Placenta percreta, third trimester** ♀   M
    O43.239   **Placenta percreta, unspecified trimester** ♀   M

● **O43.8**   **Other placental disorders**
 ● **O43.81**   **Placental infarction**
    O43.811   **Placental infarction, first trimester** ♀ M
    O43.812   **Placental infarction, second trimester** ♀   M
    O43.813   **Placental infarction, third trimester** ♀   M
    O43.819   **Placental infarction, unspecified trimester** ♀   M

 ● **O43.89**   **Other placental disorders**
     Placental dysfunction
    O43.891   **Other placental disorders, first trimester** ♀   M
    O43.892   **Other placental disorders, second trimester** ♀   M
    O43.893   **Other placental disorders, third trimester** ♀   M
    O43.899   **Other placental disorders, unspecified trimester** ♀   M

● **O43.9**   **Unspecified placental disorder**
    O43.90   **Unspecified placental disorder, unspecified trimester** ♀   M
    O43.91   **Unspecified placental disorder, first trimester** ♀   M
    O43.92   **Unspecified placental disorder, second trimester** ♀   M
    O43.93   **Unspecified placental disorder, third trimester** ♀   M

▶ New   ⇒ Revised   ~~deleted~~ Deleted   Excludes 1   Excludes 2   Includes   Use additional   Code first   Code also   Key words
OGCR Official Guidelines   X Assign placeholder X   ● Use Additional Character(s)   ▶ Manifestation Code   **Coding Clinic**

Figure 15-2 **A.** Marginal placento previa. **B.** Partial placenta previa. **C.** Total placento previa.

Item 15-3 **Placenta previa** is a condition in which the opening of the cervix is obstructed by the displaced placenta. The three types, marginal, partial, and total, are varying degrees of placenta displacement. Placenta abruption is the premature breaking away of the placenta from the site of the uterine implant before the delivery of the fetus.

● **O44   Placenta previa**
     Coding Clinic: 2016, Q4, P52

   ● **O44.0   Complete placenta previa NOS or without hemorrhage**
       Placenta previa NOS

       O44.00   Complete placenta previa NOS or without hemorrhage, unspecified trimester ♀   M

       O44.01   Complete placenta previa NOS or without hemorrhage, first trimester ♀   M

       O44.02   Complete placenta previa NOS or without hemorrhage, second trimester ♀   M

       O44.03   Complete placenta previa NOS or without hemorrhage, third trimester ♀   M

   ● **O44.1   Complete placenta previa with hemorrhage**
       Excludes1   labor and delivery complicated by hemorrhage from vasa previa (O69.4)

       O44.10   Complete placenta previa with hemorrhage, unspecified trimester ♀   M

       O44.11   Complete placenta previa with hemorrhage, first trimester ♀   M

       O44.12   Complete placenta previa with hemorrhage, second trimester ♀   M

       O44.13   Complete placenta previa with hemorrhage, third trimester ♀   M

   ● **O44.2   Partial placenta previa without hemorrhage**
       Marginal placenta previa, NOS or without hemorrhage

       O44.20   Partial placenta previa NOS or without hemorrhage, unspecified trimester ♀   M

       O44.21   Partial placenta previa NOS or without hemorrhage, first trimester ♀   M

       O44.22   Partial placenta previa NOS or without hemorrhage, second trimester ♀   M

       O44.23   Partial placenta previa NOS or without hemorrhage, third trimester ♀   M

   ● **O44.3   Partial placenta previa with hemorrhage**
       Marginal placenta previa with hemorrhage

       O44.30   Partial placenta previa with hemorrhage, unspecified trimester ♀   M

       O44.31   Partial placenta previa with hemorrhage, first trimester ♀   M

       O44.32   Partial placenta previa with hemorrhage, second trimester ♀   M

       O44.33   Partial placenta previa with hemorrhage, third trimester ♀   M

   ● **O44.4   Low lying placenta NOS or without hemorrhage**
       Low implantation of placenta NOS or without hemorrhage

       O44.40   Low lying placenta NOS or without hemorrhage, unspecified trimester ♀   M

       O44.41   Low lying placenta NOS or without hemorrhage, first trimester ♀   M

       O44.42   Low lying placenta NOS or without hemorrhage, second trimester ♀   M

       O44.43   Low lying placenta NOS or without hemorrhage, third trimester ♀   M

   ● **O44.5   Low lying placenta with hemorrhage**
       Low implantation of placenta with hemorrhage

       O44.50   Low lying placenta with hemorrhage, unspecified trimester ♀   M

       O44.51   Low lying placenta with hemorrhage, first trimester ♀   M

       O44.52   Low lying placenta with hemorrhage, second trimester ♀   M

       O44.53   Low lying placenta with hemorrhage, third trimester ♀   M

● **O45   Premature separation of placenta [abruptio placentae]**

   ● **O45.0   Premature separation of placenta with coagulation defect**

     ● **O45.00   Premature separation of placenta with coagulation defect, unspecified**

       O45.001   Premature separation of placenta with coagulation defect, unspecified, first trimester ♀   M

       O45.002   Premature separation of placenta with coagulation defect, unspecified, second trimester ♀   M

       O45.003   Premature separation of placenta with coagulation defect, unspecified, third trimester ♀   M

       O45.009   Premature separation of placenta with coagulation defect, unspecified, unspecified trimester ♀   M

     ● **O45.01   Premature separation of placenta with afibrinogenemia**
       Premature separation of placenta with hypofibrinogenemia

       O45.011   Premature separation of placenta with afibrinogenemia, first trimester ♀   M

       O45.012   Premature separation of placenta with afibrinogenemia, second trimester ♀ M

       O45.013   Premature separation of placenta with afibrinogenemia, third trimester ♀   M

       O45.019   Premature separation of placenta with afibrinogenemia, unspecified trimester ♀   M

Figure 15-3 Abruptio placentae is classified according to the grade of separation of the placenta from the uterine wall. **A.** Mild separation in which hemorrhage is internal. **B.** Moderate separation in which there is external hemorrhage. **C.** Severe separation in which there is external hemorrhage and extreme separation.

CHAPTER 15 (O00-O9A)

CHAPTER 15 (O00-O9A)

● O45.02   Premature separation of placenta with disseminated intravascular coagulation

     O45.021   Premature separation of placenta with disseminated intravascular coagulation, first trimester ♀   M

     O45.022   Premature separation of placenta with disseminated intravascular coagulation, second trimester ♀   M

     O45.023   Premature separation of placenta with disseminated intravascular coagulation, third trimester ♀   M

     O45.029   Premature separation of placenta with disseminated intravascular coagulation, unspecified trimester ♀ M

● O45.09   Premature separation of placenta with other coagulation defect

     O45.091   Premature separation of placenta with other coagulation defect, first trimester ♀   M

     O45.092   Premature separation of placenta with other coagulation defect, second trimester ♀   M

     O45.093   Premature separation of placenta with other coagulation defect, third trimester ♀   M

     O45.099   Premature separation of placenta with other coagulation defect, unspecified trimester ♀   M

● O45.8   Other premature separation of placenta

 ● O45.8X   Other premature separation of placenta

     O45.8X1   Other premature separation of placenta, first trimester ♀   M

     O45.8X2   Other premature separation of placenta, second trimester ♀   M

     O45.8X3   Other premature separation of placenta, third trimester ♀   M

     O45.8X9   Other premature separation of placenta, unspecified trimester ♀   M

● O45.9   Premature separation of placenta, unspecified
     Abruptio placentae NOS

     O45.90   Premature separation of placenta, unspecified, unspecified trimester ♀   M

     O45.91   Premature separation of placenta, unspecified, first trimester ♀   M

     O45.92   Premature separation of placenta, unspecified, second trimester ♀   M

     O45.93   Premature separation of placenta, unspecified, third trimester ♀   M

● O46   Antepartum hemorrhage, not elsewhere classified

    Excludes1   hemorrhage in early pregnancy (O20.-)
                intrapartum hemorrhage NEC (O67.-)
                placenta previa (O44.-)
                premature separation of placenta [abruptio placentae] (O45.-)

● O46.0   Antepartum hemorrhage with coagulation defect

 ● O46.00   Antepartum hemorrhage with coagulation defect, unspecified

     O46.001   Antepartum hemorrhage with coagulation defect, unspecified, first trimester ♀   M

     O46.002   Antepartum hemorrhage with coagulation defect, unspecified, second trimester ♀   M

     O46.003   Antepartum hemorrhage with coagulation defect, unspecified, third trimester ♀   M

     O46.009   Antepartum hemorrhage with coagulation defect, unspecified, unspecified trimester ♀   M

● O46.01   Antepartum hemorrhage with afibrinogenemia
     Antepartum hemorrhage with hypofibrinogenemia

     O46.011   Antepartum hemorrhage with afibrinogenemia, first trimester ♀   M

     O46.012   Antepartum hemorrhage with afibrinogenemia, second trimester ♀ M

     O46.013   Antepartum hemorrhage with afibrinogenemia, third trimester ♀   M

     O46.019   Antepartum hemorrhage with afibrinogenemia, unspecified trimester ♀   M

● O46.02   Antepartum hemorrhage with disseminated intravascular coagulation

     O46.021   Antepartum hemorrhage with disseminated intravascular coagulation, first trimester ♀   M

     O46.022   Antepartum hemorrhage with disseminated intravascular coagulation, second trimester ♀   M

     O46.023   Antepartum hemorrhage with disseminated intravascular coagulation, third trimester ♀   M

     O46.029   Antepartum hemorrhage with disseminated intravascular coagulation, unspecified trimester ♀ M

● O46.09   Antepartum hemorrhage with other coagulation defect

     O46.091   Antepartum hemorrhage with other coagulation defect, first trimester ♀ M

     O46.092   Antepartum hemorrhage with other coagulation defect, second trimester ♀   M

     O46.093   Antepartum hemorrhage with other coagulation defect, third trimester ♀ M

     O46.099   Antepartum hemorrhage with other coagulation defect, unspecified trimester ♀   M

● O46.8   Other antepartum hemorrhage

 ● O46.8x   Other antepartum hemorrhage

     O46.8x1   Other antepartum hemorrhage, first trimester ♀   M

     O46.8x2   Other antepartum hemorrhage, second trimester ♀   M

     O46.8x3   Other antepartum hemorrhage, third trimester ♀   M

     O46.8x9   Other antepartum hemorrhage, unspecified trimester ♀   M

● O46.9   Antepartum hemorrhage, unspecified

     O46.90   Antepartum hemorrhage, unspecified, unspecified trimester ♀   M

     O46.91   Antepartum hemorrhage, unspecified, first trimester ♀   M

     O46.92   Antepartum hemorrhage, unspecified, second trimester ♀   M

     O46.93   Antepartum hemorrhage, unspecified, third trimester ♀   M

▶ New   ⟹ Revised   ~~deleted~~ Deleted   Excludes 1   Excludes 2   Includes   Use additional   Code first   Code also   Key words

OGCR Official Guidelines   X Assign placeholder X   ● Use Additional Character(s)   ▌ Manifestation Code   **Coding Clinic**

● **O47   False labor**

> **Includes**   Braxton Hicks contractions
>   threatened labor
>
> **Excludes1**   preterm labor (O60.-)

● **O47.0   False labor before 37 completed weeks of gestation**

> **O47.00   False labor before 37 completed gestation, unspecified trimester** ♀   M
>
> **O47.02   False labor before 37 completed gestation, second trimester** ♀   M
>
> **O47.03   False labor before 37 completed gestation, third trimester** ♀   M

O47.1   False labor at or after 37 completed weeks of gestation ♀   M

O47.9   False labor, unspecified ♀   M

● **O48   Late pregnancy**

O48.0   Post-term pregnancy ♀   M
> Pregnancy over 40 completed weeks to 42 completed weeks gestation

O48.1   Prolonged pregnancy ♀   M
> Pregnancy which has advanced beyond 42 completed weeks gestation

COMPLICATIONS OF LABOR AND DELIVERY (O60-O77)

● **O60   Preterm labor**

> **Includes**   onset (spontaneous) of labor before 37 completed weeks of gestation
>
> **Excludes1**   false labor (O47.0-)
>   threatened labor NOS (O47.0-)

● **O60.0   Preterm labor without delivery**

> **O60.00   Preterm labor without delivery, unspecified trimester** ♀   M
>
> **O60.02   Preterm labor without delivery, second trimester** ♀   M
>
> **O60.03   Preterm labor without delivery, third trimester** ♀   M

● **O60.1   Preterm labor with preterm delivery**

> One of the following 7th characters is to be assigned to each code under subcategory O60.1. 7th character 0 is for single gestations and multiple gestations where the fetus is unspecified. 7th characters 1 through 9 are for cases of multiple gestations to identify the fetus for which the code applies. The appropriate code from category O30, Multiple gestation, must also be assigned when assigning a code from subcategory O60.1 that has a 7th character of 1 through 9.

> | | |
> |---|---|
> | 0 | not applicable or unspecified |
> | 1 | fetus 1 |
> | 2 | fetus 2 |
> | 3 | fetus 3 |
> | 4 | fetus 4 |
> | 5 | fetus 5 |
> | 9 | other fetus |

> *Coding Clinic: 2016, Q2, P11*

X● **O60.10   Preterm labor with preterm delivery, unspecified trimester** ♀   M
> Preterm labor with delivery NOS

X● **O60.12   Preterm labor second trimester with preterm delivery second trimester** ♀   M

X● **O60.13   Preterm labor second trimester with preterm delivery third trimester** ♀   M

X● **O60.14   Preterm labor third trimester with preterm delivery third trimester** ♀   M
> *Coding Clinic: 2016, Q2, P10*

● **O60.2   Term delivery with preterm labor**

> One of the following 7th characters is to be assigned to each code under subcategory O60.2. 7th character 0 is for single gestations and multiple gestations where the fetus is unspecified. 7th characters 1 through 9 are for cases of multiple gestations to identify the fetus for which the code applies. The appropriate code from category O30, Multiple gestation, must also be assigned when assigning a code from subcategory O60.2 that has a 7th character of 1 through 9.

> | | |
> |---|---|
> | 0 | not applicable or unspecified |
> | 1 | fetus 1 |
> | 2 | fetus 2 |
> | 3 | fetus 3 |
> | 4 | fetus 4 |
> | 5 | fetus 5 |
> | 9 | other fetus |

X● **O60.20   Term delivery with preterm labor, unspecified trimester** ♀   M

X● **O60.22   Term delivery with preterm labor, second trimester** ♀   M

X● **O60.23   Term delivery with preterm labor, third trimester** ♀   M

● **O61   Failed induction of labor**

O61.0   Failed medical induction of labor ♀   M
> Failed induction (of labor) by oxytocin
> Failed induction (of labor) by prostaglandins

O61.1   Failed instrumental induction of labor ♀   M
> Failed mechanical induction (of labor)
> Failed surgical induction (of labor)

O61.8   Other failed induction of labor ♀   M

O61.9   Failed induction of labor, unspecified ♀   M

● **O62   Abnormalities of forces of labor**

O62.0   Primary inadequate contractions ♀   M
> Failure of cervical dilatation
> Primary hypotonic uterine dysfunction
> Uterine inertia during latent phase of labor

O62.1   Secondary uterine inertia ♀   M
> Arrested active phase of labor
> Secondary hypotonic uterine dysfunction

O62.2   Other uterine inertia ♀   M
> Atony of uterus without hemorrhage
> Atony of uterus NOS
> Desultory labor
> Hypotonic uterine dysfunction NOS
> Irregular labor
> Poor contractions
> Slow slope active phase of labor
> Uterine inertia NOS
>
> > **Excludes1**   atony of uterus with hemorrhage (postpartum) (O72.1)
> >   postpartum atony of uterus without hemorrhage (O75.89)

O62.3   Precipitate labor ♀   M

O62.4   Hypertonic, incoordinate, and prolonged uterine contractions ♀   M
> Cervical spasm
> Contraction ring dystocia
> Dyscoordinate labor
> Hour-glass contraction of uterus
> Hypertonic uterine dysfunction
> Incoordinate uterine action
> Tetanic contractions
> Uterine dystocia NOS
> Uterine spasm
>
> > **Excludes1**   dystocia (fetal) (maternal) NOS (O66.9)

O62.8   Other abnormalities of forces of labor ♀   M

O62.9   Abnormality of forces of labor, unspecified ♀   M

CHAPTER 15 (O00-O9A)

Figure 15-5 Hydrocephalic fetus causing disproportion.

X ● **O64.2** **Obstructed labor due to face presentation** ♀   M
    Obstructed labor due to chin presentation

X ● **O64.3** **Obstructed labor due to brow presentation** ♀   M

X ● **O64.4** **Obstructed labor due to shoulder presentation** ♀   M
    Prolapsed arm
    Excludes 1   impacted shoulders (O66.0)
               shoulder dystocia (O66.0)

X ● **O64.5** **Obstructed labor due to compound presentation** ♀   M

X ● **O64.8** **Obstructed labor due to other malposition and malpresentation** ♀   M
    Obstructed labor due to footling presentation
    Obstructed labor due to incomplete breech presentation

X ● **O64.9** **Obstructed labor due to malposition and malpresentation, unspecified** ♀   M

● **O65** **Obstructed labor due to maternal pelvic abnormality**

O65.0 **Obstructed labor due to deformed pelvis** ♀   M

O65.1 **Obstructed labor due to generally contracted pelvis** ♀   M

O65.2 **Obstructed labor due to pelvic inlet contraction** ♀   M

O65.3 **Obstructed labor due to pelvic outlet and mid-cavity contraction** ♀   M

O65.4 **Obstructed labor due to fetopelvic disproportion, unspecified** ♀   M
    Excludes 1   dystocia due to abnormality of fetus
               (O66.2-O66.3)

O65.5 **Obstructed labor due to abnormality of maternal pelvic organs** ♀
    Obstructed labor due to conditions listed in O34.-
    Use additional code to identify abnormality of pelvic organs O34.-

O65.8 **Obstructed labor due to other maternal pelvic abnormalities** ♀   M

O65.9 **Obstructed labor due to maternal pelvic abnormality, unspecified** ♀   M

● **O66** **Other obstructed labor**

O66.0 **Obstructed labor due to shoulder dystocia** ♀   M
    Impacted shoulders

O66.1 **Obstructed labor due to locked twins** ♀   M

O66.2 **Obstructed labor due to unusually large fetus** ♀   M

O66.3 **Obstructed labor due to other abnormalities of fetus** ♀   M
    Dystocia due to fetal ascites
    Dystocia due to fetal hydrops
    Dystocia due to fetal meningomyelocele
    Dystocia due to fetal sacral teratoma
    Dystocia due to fetal tumor
    Dystocia due to hydrocephalic fetus
    Use additional code to identify cause of obstruction

● **O66.4** **Failed trial of labor**

O66.40 **Failed trial of labor, unspecified** ♀   M

O66.41 **Failed attempted vaginal birth after previous cesarean delivery** ♀   M
    *Code first rupture of uterus, if applicable
    (O71.0-, O71.1)*

O66.5 **Attempted application of vacuum extractor and forceps** ♀   M
    Attempted application of vacuum or forceps, with subsequent delivery by forceps or cesarean delivery

Figure 15-4 Five types of malposition and malpresentation of the fetus: **A.** Breech. **B.** Vertex. **C.** Face. **D.** Brow. **E.** Shoulder.

● **O63** **Long labor**

O63.0 **Prolonged first stage (of labor)** ♀   M

O63.1 **Prolonged second stage (of labor)** ♀   M

O63.2 **Delayed delivery of second twin, triplet, etc.** ♀   M

O63.9 **Long labor, unspecified** ♀   M
    Prolonged labor NOS

● **O64** **Obstructed labor due to malposition and malpresentation of fetus**

One of the following 7th characters is to be assigned to each code under category O64. 7th character Ø is for single gestations and multiple gestations where the fetus is unspecified. 7th characters 1 through 9 are for cases of multiple gestations to identify the fetus for which the code applies. The appropriate code from category O3Ø, Multiple gestation, must also be assigned when assigning a code from category O64 that has a 7th character of 1 through 9.

Ø	not applicable or unspecified
1	fetus 1
2	fetus 2
3	fetus 3
4	fetus 4
5	fetus 5
9	other fetus

X ● **O64.0** **Obstructed labor due to incomplete rotation of fetal head** ♀   M
    Deep transverse arrest
    Obstructed labor due to persistent occipitoiliac (position)
    Obstructed labor due to persistent occipitoposterior (position)
    Obstructed labor due to persistent occipitosacral (position)
    Obstructed labor due to persistent occipitotransverse (position)

X ● **O64.1** **Obstructed labor due to breech presentation** ♀   M
    Obstructed labor due to buttocks presentation
    Obstructed labor due to complete breech presentation
    Obstructed labor due to frank breech presentation

▶ New   ⏵ Revised   d̶e̶l̶e̶t̶e̶d̶ Deleted   Excludes 1   Excludes 2   Includes   Use additional   Code first   Code also   Key words

OGCR Official Guidelines   X Assign placeholder X   ● Use Additional Character(s)   ▶ Manifestation Code   **Coding Clinic**

O66.6   **Obstructed labor due to** other multiple fetuses ♀   M

O66.8   **Other specified obstructed labor** ♀   M
     Use additional code to identify cause of obstruction

O66.9   **Obstructed labor, unspecified** ♀   M
     Dystocia NOS
     Fetal dystocia NOS
     Maternal dystocia NOS

● **O67**   **Labor and delivery complicated by intrapartum hemorrhage, not elsewhere classified**
     Excludes1   antepartum hemorrhage NEC (O46.-)
              placenta previa (O44.-)
              premature separation of placenta [abruptio placentae] (O45.-)
     Excludes2   postpartum hemorrhage (O72.-)

O67.0   **Intrapartum hemorrhage with** coagulation defect ♀   M
     Intrapartum hemorrhage (excessive) associated with afibrinogenemia
     Intrapartum hemorrhage (excessive) associated with disseminated intravascular coagulation
     Intrapartum hemorrhage (excessive) associated with hyperfibrinolysis
     Intrapartum hemorrhage (excessive) associated with hypofibrinogenemia

O67.8   **Other intrapartum hemorrhage** ♀   M
     Excessive intrapartum hemorrhage

O67.9   **Intrapartum hemorrhage, unspecified** ♀   M

O68   **Labor and delivery complicated by abnormality of fetal acid-base balance** ♀   M
     Fetal acidemia complicating labor and delivery
     Fetal acidosis complicating labor and delivery
     Fetal alkalosis complicating labor and delivery
     Fetal metabolic acidemia complicating labor and delivery
     Excludes1   fetal stress NOS (O77.9)
              labor and delivery complicated by electrocardiographic evidence of fetal stress (O77.8)
              labor and delivery complicated by ultrasonic evidence of fetal stress (O77.8)
     Excludes2   abnormality in fetal heart rate or rhythm (O76)
              labor and delivery complicated by meconium in amniotic fluid (O77.0)

● **O69**   **Labor and delivery complicated by** umbilical cord complications
     One of the following 7th characters is to be assigned to each code under category O69. 7th character 0 is for single gestations and multiple gestations where the fetus is unspecified. 7th characters 1 through 9 are for cases of multiple gestations to identify the fetus for which the code applies. The appropriate code from category O30, Multiple gestation, must also be assigned when assigning a code from category O69 that has a 7th character of 1 through 9.

> 0   not applicable or unspecified
> 1   fetus 1
> 2   fetus 2
> 3   fetus 3
> 4   fetus 4
> 5   fetus 5
> 9   other fetus

X ● O69.0   **Labor and delivery complicated by** prolapse of cord ♀   M

X ● O69.1   **Labor and delivery complicated by** cord around neck, with compression ♀   M
     Excludes1   labor and delivery complicated by cord around neck, without compression (O69.81)

X ● O69.2   **Labor and delivery complicated by other cord entanglement, with compression** ♀   M
     Labor and delivery complicated by compression of cord NOS
     Labor and delivery complicated by entanglement of cords of twins in monoamniotic sac
     Labor and delivery complicated by knot in cord
     Excludes1   labor and delivery complicated by other cord entanglement, without compression (O69.82)

X ● O69.3   **Labor and delivery complicated by** short cord ♀   M

X ● O69.4   **Labor and delivery complicated by** vasa previa ♀   M
     Labor and delivery complicated by hemorrhage from vasa previa

X ● O69.5   **Labor and delivery complicated by** vascular lesion of cord ♀   M
     Labor and delivery complicated by cord bruising
     Labor and delivery complicated by cord hematoma
     Labor and delivery complicated by thrombosis of umbilical vessels

● O69.8   **Labor and delivery complicated by other cord complications**
   X ● O69.81   **Labor and delivery complicated by** cord around neck, without compression ♀   M
   X ● O69.82   **Labor and delivery complicated by other cord entanglement, without compression** ♀   M
   X ● O69.89   **Labor and delivery complicated by** other cord complications ♀   M

X ● O69.9   **Labor and delivery complicated by cord complication, unspecified** ♀   M

● **O70**   **Perineal laceration during delivery**
     Includes   episiotomy extended by laceration
     Excludes1   obstetric high vaginal laceration alone (O71.4)

O70.0   **First degree perineal laceration during delivery** ♀   M
     Perineal laceration, rupture or tear involving fourchette during delivery
     Perineal laceration, rupture or tear involving labia during delivery
     Perineal laceration, rupture or tear involving skin during delivery
     Perineal laceration, rupture or tear involving vagina during delivery
     Perineal laceration, rupture or tear involving vulva during delivery
     Slight perineal laceration, rupture or tear during delivery

O70.1   **Second degree perineal laceration during delivery** ♀   M
     Perineal laceration, rupture or tear during delivery as in O70.0, also involving pelvic floor
     Perineal laceration, rupture or tear during delivery as in O70.0, also involving perineal muscles
     Perineal laceration, rupture or tear during delivery as in O70.0, also involving vaginal muscles
     Excludes1   perineal laceration involving anal sphincter (O70.2)
     Coding Clinic: 2016, CODING CIQ4, P53, Q2, P34

Figure 15-6 Perineal lacerations: **A.** First-degree is laceration of superficial tissues. **B.** Second-degree is limited to the pelvic floor and may involve the perineal or vaginal muscles. **C.** Third-degree involves the anal sphincter. **D.** Fourth-degree involves anal or rectal mucosa.

● **O70.2 Third degree perineal laceration during delivery**
    Perineal laceration, rupture or tear during delivery as in O70.1, also involving anal sphincter
    Perineal laceration, rupture or tear during delivery as in O70.1, also involving rectovaginal septum
    Perineal laceration, rupture or tear during delivery as in O70.1, also involving sphincter NOS

    Excludes1   anal sphincter tear during delivery without third degree perineal laceration (O70.4)
                    perineal laceration involving anal or rectal mucosa (O70.3)

    O70.20 Third degree perineal laceration during delivery, unspecified ♀   M

    O70.21 Third degree perineal laceration during delivery, IIIa ♀   M
        Third degree perineal laceration during delivery with less than 50% of external anal sphincter (EAS) thickness torn

    O70.22 Third degree perineal laceration during delivery, IIIb ♀   M
        Third degree perineal laceration during delivery with more than 50% external anal sphincter (EAS) thickness torn

    O70.23 Third degree perineal laceration during delivery, IIIc ♀   M
        Third degree perineal laceration during delivery with both external anal sphincter (EAS) and internal anal sphincter (IAS) torn

O70.3 Fourth degree perineal laceration during delivery ♀   M
    Perineal laceration, rupture or tear during delivery as in O70.2, also involving anal mucosa
    Perineal laceration, rupture or tear during delivery as in O70.2, also involving rectal mucosa

O70.4 Anal sphincter tear complicating delivery, not associated with third degree laceration ♀   M
    Excludes1   anal sphincter tear with third degree perineal laceration (O70.2)

O70.9 Perineal laceration during delivery, unspecified ♀   M

● **O71 Other obstetric trauma**
    Includes   obstetric damage from instruments

  ● **O71.0 Rupture of uterus (spontaneous) before onset of labor**
    Excludes1   disruption of (current) cesarean delivery wound (O90.0)
                laceration of uterus, NEC (O71.81)

    O71.00 Rupture of uterus before onset of labor, unspecified trimester ♀   M

    O71.02 Rupture of uterus before onset of labor, second trimester ♀   M

    O71.03 Rupture of uterus before onset of labor, third trimester ♀   M

O71.1 Rupture of uterus during labor ♀   M
    Rupture of uterus not stated as occurring before onset of labor
    Excludes1   disruption of cesarean delivery wound (O90.0)
                laceration of uterus, NEC (O71.81)

O71.2 Postpartum inversion of uterus ♀   M

O71.3 Obstetric laceration of cervix ♀   M
    Annular detachment of cervix

O71.4 Obstetric high vaginal laceration alone ♀   M
    Laceration of vaginal wall without perineal laceration
    Excludes1   obstetric high vaginal laceration with perineal laceration (O70.-)

O71.5 Other obstetric injury to pelvic organs ♀   M
    Obstetric injury to bladder
    Obstetric injury to urethra
    Excludes2   obstetric periurethral trauma (O71.82)

O71.6 Obstetric damage to pelvic joints and ligaments ♀   M
    Obstetric avulsion of inner symphyseal cartilage
    Obstetric damage to coccyx
    Obstetric traumatic separation of symphysis (pubis)

O71.7 Obstetric hematoma of pelvis ♀   M
    Obstetric hematoma of perineum
    Obstetric hematoma of vagina
    Obstetric hematoma of vulva

● **O71.8 Other specified obstetric trauma**

    O71.81 Laceration of uterus, not elsewhere classified ♀   M

    O71.82 Other specified trauma to perineum and vulva ♀   M
        Obstetric periurethral trauma

    O71.89 Other specified obstetric trauma ♀   M

O71.9 Obstetric trauma, unspecified ♀   M

● **O72 Postpartum hemorrhage**
    Includes   hemorrhage after delivery of fetus or infant

O72.0 Third-stage hemorrhage ♀   M
    Hemorrhage associated with retained, trapped or adherent placenta
    Retained placenta NOS
    Code also type of adherent placenta (O43.2-)

O72.1 Other immediate postpartum hemorrhage ♀   M
    Hemorrhage following delivery of placenta
    Postpartum hemorrhage (atonic) NOS
    Uterine atony with hemorrhage
    Excludes1   uterine atony NOS (O62.2)
                uterine atony without hemorrhage (O62.2)
                postpartum atony of uterus without hemorrhage (O75.89)

O72.2 Delayed and secondary postpartum hemorrhage ♀   M
    Hemorrhage associated with retained portions of placenta or membranes after the first 24 hours following delivery of placenta
    Retained products of conception NOS, following delivery

O72.3 Postpartum coagulation defects ♀   M
    Postpartum afibrinogenemia
    Postpartum fibrinolysis

▶ New   ⟫ Revised   ~~deleted~~ Deleted   Excludes 1   Excludes 2   Includes   Use additional   Code first   Code also   Key words

OGCR Official Guidelines   X Assign placeholder X   ● Use Additional Character(s)   ▌ Manifestation Code   Coding Clinic

● **O73** **Retained placenta and membranes, without hemorrhage**

    Excludes1 placenta accreta (O43.21-)
                   placenta increta (O43.22-)
                   placenta percreta (O43.23-)

    O73.0 **Retained placenta without hemorrhage** ♀   **M**
           Adherent placenta, without hemorrhage
           Trapped placenta without hemorrhage

    O73.1 **Retained portions of placenta and membranes, without hemorrhage** ♀   **M**
           Retained products of conception following delivery, without hemorrhage

● **O74** **Complications of anesthesia during labor and delivery**

    Includes   maternal complications arising from the administration of a general, regional or local anesthetic, analgesic or other sedation during labor and delivery

    Use additional code, if applicable, to identify specific complication

    O74.0 **Aspiration pneumonitis due to anesthesia during labor and delivery** ♀   **M**
           Inhalation of stomach contents or secretions NOS due to anesthesia during labor and delivery
           Mendelson's syndrome due to anesthesia during labor and delivery

    O74.1 **Other pulmonary complications of anesthesia during labor and delivery** ♀   **M**

    O74.2 **Cardiac complications of anesthesia during labor and delivery** ♀   **M**

    O74.3 **Central nervous system complications of anesthesia during labor and delivery** ♀   **M**

    O74.4 **Toxic reaction to local anesthesia during labor and delivery** ♀   **M**

    O74.5 **Spinal and epidural anesthesia-induced headache during labor and delivery** ♀   **M**

    O74.6 **Other complications of spinal and epidural anesthesia during labor and delivery** ♀   **M**

    O74.7 **Failed or difficult intubation for anesthesia during labor and delivery** ♀   **M**

    O74.8 **Other complications of anesthesia during labor and delivery** ♀   **M**

    O74.9 **Complication of anesthesia during labor and delivery, unspecified** ♀   **M**

● **O75** **Other complications of labor and delivery, not elsewhere classified**

    Excludes2 puerperal (postpartum) infection (O86.-)
                   puerperal (postpartum) sepsis (O85)

    O75.0 **Maternal distress during labor and delivery** ♀   **M**

    O75.1 **Shock during or following labor and delivery** ♀   **M**
           Obstetric shock following labor and delivery

    O75.2 **Pyrexia during labor, not elsewhere classified** ♀   **M**

    O75.3 **Other infection during labor** ♀   **M**
           Sepsis during labor
           Use additional code (B95-B97), to identify infectious agent

    O75.4 **Other complications of obstetric surgery and procedures** ♀   **M**
           Cardiac arrest following obstetric surgery or procedures
           Cardiac failure following obstetric surgery or procedures
           Cerebral anoxia following obstetric surgery or procedures
           Pulmonary edema following obstetric surgery or procedures
           Use additional code to identify specific complication
           Excludes2 complications of anesthesia during labor and delivery (O74.-)
                       disruption of obstetrical (surgical) wound (O90.0-O90.1)
                       hematoma of obstetrical (surgical) wound (O90.2)
                       ➠ infection of obstetrical (surgical) wound (O86.0-)

    O75.5 **Delayed delivery after artificial rupture of membranes** ♀   **M**

● **O75.8** **Other specified complications of labor and delivery**

    O75.81 **Maternal exhaustion complicating labor and delivery** ♀   **M**

    O75.82 **Onset (spontaneous) of labor after 37 completed weeks of gestation but before 39 completed weeks gestation, with delivery by (planned) cesarean section** ♀   **M**
           Delivery by (planned) cesarean section occurring after 37 completed weeks of gestation but before 39 completed weeks gestation due to (spontaneous) onset of labor
           Code first to specify reason for planned cesarean section such as:
               cephalopelvic disproportion (normally formed fetus) (O33.9)
               previous cesarean delivery (O34.21)

    O75.89 **Other specified complications of labor and delivery** ♀   **M**

    O75.9 **Complication of labor and delivery, unspecified** ♀   **M**

  O76 **Abnormality in fetal heart rate and rhythm complicating labor and delivery** ♀   **M**
        Depressed fetal heart rate tones complicating labor and delivery
        Fetal bradycardia complicating labor and delivery
        Fetal heart rate decelerations complicating labor and delivery
        Fetal heart rate irregularity complicating labor and delivery
        Fetal heart rate abnormal variability complicating labor and delivery
        Fetal tachycardia complicating labor and delivery
        Non-reassuring fetal heart rate or rhythm complicating labor and delivery
        Excludes1 fetal stress NOS (O77.9)
                 labor and delivery complicated by electrocardiographic evidence of fetal stress (O77.8)
                 labor and delivery complicated by ultrasonic evidence of fetal stress (O77.8)
        Excludes2 fetal metabolic acidemia (O68)
                 other fetal stress (O77.0-O77.1)

● **O77** **Other fetal stress complicating labor and delivery**

    O77.0 **Labor and delivery complicated by meconium in amniotic fluid** ♀   **M**

    O77.1 **Fetal stress in labor or delivery due to drug administration** ♀   **M**

    O77.8 **Labor and delivery complicated by other evidence of fetal stress** ♀   **M**
           Labor and delivery complicated by electrocardiographic evidence of fetal stress
           Labor and delivery complicated by ultrasonic evidence of fetal stress
        Excludes1 abnormality of fetal acid-base balance (O68)
                 abnormality in fetal heart rate or rhythm (O76)
                 fetal metabolic acidemia (O68)

    O77.9 **Labor and delivery complicated by fetal stress, unspecified** ♀   **M**
        Excludes1 abnormality of fetal acid-base balance (O68)
                 abnormality in fetal heart rate or rhythm (O76)
                 fetal metabolic acidemia (O68)

CHAPTER 15 (O00-O9A)

Figure 15-7 The four stages of normal delivery: **I.** Lightening, which occurs 2 to 4 weeks before birth, at which time the fetus turns with head toward the vagina. **II.** Regular contractions begin, the amniotic sac ruptures, and dilation is complete. **III.** Delivery of the head and rotation. **IV.** Expulsion of placenta.

OGCR Section I.C., Chapter 15.n.

Normal Delivery, Code O80

1) Encounter for full term uncomplicated delivery

Code O80 should be assigned when a woman is admitted for a full-term normal delivery and delivers a single, healthy infant without any complications antepartum, during the delivery, or postpartum during the delivery episode. Code O80 is always a principal diagnosis. It is not to be used if any other code from Chapter 15 is needed to describe a current complication of the antenatal, delivery, or perinatal period. Additional codes from other chapters may be used with code O80 if they are not related to or are in any way complicating the pregnancy.

2) Uncomplicated delivery with resolved antepartum complication

Code O80 may be used if the patient had a complication at some point during the pregnancy, but the complication is not present at the time of the admission for delivery.

3) Outcome of delivery for O80

Z37.0, Single live brith, is the only outcome of delivery code appropriate for use with O80.

ENCOUNTER FOR DELIVERY (O80-O82)

O80   Encounter for full-term uncomplicated delivery ♀   M
　　　Delivery requiring minimal or no assistance, with or without episiotomy, without fetal manipulation [e.g., rotation version] or instrumentation [forceps] of a spontaneous, cephalic, vaginal, full-term, single, live-born infant. This code is for use as a single diagnosis code and is not to be used with any other code from chapter 15.

　　　Use additional code to indicate outcome of delivery (Z37.0)
　　　Coding Clinic: 2016, Q4, P124, 150

O82   Encounter for cesarean delivery without indication ♀   M
　　　Use additional code to indicate outcome of delivery (Z37.0)

COMPLICATIONS PREDOMINANTLY RELATED TO THE PUERPERIUM (O85-O92)

　　⟹ **Excludes2** mental and behavioral disorders associated with the puerperium (F53.-)
　　　　　　　obstetrical tetanus (A34)
　　　　　　　puerperal osteomalacia (M83.0)

O85   Puerperal sepsis ♀   M
　　　Postpartum sepsis
　　　Puerperal peritonitis
　　　Puerperal pyemia
　　　Use additional code (B95-B97), to identify infectious agent
　　　Use additional code (R65.2-) to identify severe sepsis, if applicable
　　　Excludes1 fever of unknown origin following delivery (O86.4)
　　　　　　　genital tract infection following delivery (O86.1-)
　　　　　　　obstetric pyemic and septic embolism (O88.3-)
　　　　　　　puerperal septic thrombophlebitis (O86.81)
　　　　　　　urinary tract infection following delivery (O86.2-)
　　　Excludes2 sepsis during labor (O75.3)

● **O86   Other puerperal infections**
　　　Use additional code (B95-B97), to identify infectious agent
　　　Excludes2 infection during labor (O75.3)
　　　　　　　obstetrical tetanus (A34)

O86.0   Infection of obstetric surgical wound ♀   M
　　　Infected cesarean delivery wound following delivery
　　　Infected perineal repair following delivery
　　▶ **Excludes1** complications of procedures, not elsewhere classified (T81.44)
　　　　▶postprocedural fever NOS (R50.82)
　　　　▶postprocedural retroperitoneal abscess (K68.11)

　▶ **O86.00   Infection of obstetric surgical wound, unspecified**
　▶ **O86.01   Infection of obstetric surgical wound, superficial incisional site**
　　　▶Subcutaneous abscess following an obstetrical procedure
　　　▶Stitch abscess following an obstetrical procedure
　▶ **O86.02   Infection of obstetric surgical wound, deep incisional site**
　　　▶Intramuscular abscess following an obstetrical procedure
　　　▶Sub-fascial abscess following a procedure
　▶ **O86.03   Infection of obstetric surgical wound, organ and space site**
　　　▶Intraabdominal abscess following an obstetrical procedure
　　　▶Subphrenic abscess following an obstetrical procedure
　▶ **O86.04   Sepsis following an obstetrical procedure**
　　　▶ Use additional code to identify the sepsis
　▶ **O86.08   Infection of obstetric surgical wound, other surgical site**

● **O86.1   Other infection of genital tract following delivery**
　　　O86.11   Cervicitis following delivery ♀   M
　　　O86.12   Endometritis following delivery ♀   M
　　　O86.13   Vaginitis following delivery ♀   M
　　　O86.19   Other infection of genital tract following delivery ♀   M

● **O86.2** **Urinary tract infection following delivery**

     O86.20 **Urinary tract infection following delivery, unspecified** ♀   M

         Puerperal urinary tract infection NOS

     O86.21 **Infection of kidney following delivery** ♀   M

     O86.22 **Infection of bladder following delivery** ♀   M

         Infection of urethra following delivery

     O86.29 **Other urinary tract infection following delivery** ♀   M

● **O86.4** **Pyrexia of unknown origin following delivery** ♀   M

     Puerperal infection NOS following delivery

     Puerperal pyrexia NOS following delivery

     Excludes2   pyrexia during labor (O75.2)

● **O86.8** **Other specified puerperal infections**

     O86.81 **Puerperal septic thrombophlebitis** ♀   M

     O86.89 **Other specified puerperal infections** ♀   M

● **O87** **Venous complications and hemorrhoids in the puerperium**

     Includes   venous complications in labor, delivery and the puerperium

     Excludes2   obstetric embolism (O88.-)

         puerperal septic thrombophlebitis (O86.81)

         venous complications in pregnancy (O22.-)

O87.0 **Superficial thrombophlebitis in the puerperium** ♀   M

     Puerperal phlebitis NOS

     Puerperal thrombosis NOS

O87.1 **Deep phlebothrombosis in the puerperium** ♀   M

     Deep vein thrombosis, postpartum

     Pelvic thrombophlebitis, postpartum

     Use additional code to identify the deep vein thrombosis (I82.4-, I82.5-, I82.62-. I82.72-)

     Use additional code, if applicable, for associated long-term (current) use of anticoagulants (Z79.01)

O87.2 **Hemorrhoids in the puerperium** ♀   M

O87.3 **Cerebral venous thrombosis in the puerperium** ♀   M

     Cerebrovenous sinus thrombosis in the puerperium

O87.4 **Varicose veins of lower extremity in the puerperium** ♀   M

O87.8 **Other venous complications in the puerperium** ♀   M

     Genital varices in the puerperium

O87.9 **Venous complication in the puerperium, unspecified** ♀ M

     Puerperal phlebopathy NOS

O88 **Obstetric embolism**

     Excludes1   embolism complicating abortion NOS (O03.2)

         embolism complicating ectopic or molar pregnancy (O08.2)

         embolism complicating failed attempted abortion (O07.2)

         embolism complicating induced abortion (O04.7)

         embolism complicating spontaneous abortion (O03.2, O03.7)

● **O88.0** **Obstetric air embolism**

     ● **O88.01** **Obstetric air embolism in pregnancy**

         O88.011 **Air embolism in pregnancy, first trimester** ♀   M

         O88.012 **Air embolism in pregnancy, second trimester** ♀   M

         O88.013 **Air embolism in pregnancy, third trimester** ♀   M

         O88.019 **Air embolism in pregnancy, unspecified trimester** ♀   M

     O88.02 **Air embolism in childbirth** ♀   M

     O88.03 **Air embolism in the puerperium** ♀   M

● **O88.1** **Amniotic fluid embolism**

     Anaphylactoid syndrome in pregnancy

     ● **O88.11** **Amniotic fluid embolism in pregnancy**

         O88.111 **Amniotic fluid embolism in pregnancy, first trimester** ♀   M

         O88.112 **Amniotic fluid embolism in pregnancy, second trimester** ♀   M

         O88.113 **Amniotic fluid embolism in pregnancy, third trimester** ♀   M

         O88.119 **Amniotic fluid embolism in pregnancy, unspecified trimester** ♀   M

     O88.12 **Amniotic fluid embolism in childbirth** ♀   M

     O88.13 **Amniotic fluid embolism in the puerperium** ♀   M

● **O88.2** **Obstetric thromboembolism**

     ● **O88.21** **Thromboembolism in pregnancy**

         Obstetric (pulmonary) embolism NOS

         O88.211 **Thromboembolism in pregnancy, first trimester** ♀   M

         O88.212 **Thromboembolism in pregnancy, second trimester** ♀   M

         O88.213 **Thromboembolism in pregnancy, third trimester** ♀   M

         O88.219 **Thromboembolism in pregnancy, unspecified trimester** ♀   M

     O88.22 **Thromboembolism in childbirth** ♀   M

     O88.23 **Thromboembolism in the puerperium** ♀   M

         Puerperal (pulmonary) embolism NOS

● **O88.3** **Obstetric pyemic and septic embolism**

     ● **O88.31** **Pyemic and septic embolism in pregnancy**

         O88.311 **Pyemic and septic embolism in pregnancy, first trimester** ♀   M

         O88.312 **Pyemic and septic embolism in pregnancy, second trimester** ♀   M

         O88.313 **Pyemic and septic embolism in pregnancy, third trimester** ♀   M

         O88.319 **Pyemic and septic embolism in pregnancy, unspecified trimester** ♀   M

     O88.32 **Pyemic and septic embolism in childbirth** ♀   M

     O88.33 **Pyemic and septic embolism in the puerperium** ♀   M

● **O88.8** **Other obstetric embolism**

     Obstetric fat embolism

     ● **O88.81** **Other embolism in pregnancy**

         O88.811 **Other embolism in pregnancy, first trimester** ♀   M

         O88.812 **Other embolism in pregnancy, second trimester** ♀   M

         O88.813 **Other embolism in pregnancy, third trimester** ♀   M

         O88.819 **Other embolism in pregnancy, unspecified trimester** ♀   M

     O88.82 **Other embolism in childbirth** ♀   M

     O88.83 **Other embolism in the puerperium** ♀   M

CHAPTER 15 (O00-O9A)

● **O89 Complications of anesthesia during the puerperium**

    Includes   maternal complications arising from the administration of a general, regional or local anesthetic, analgesic or other sedation during the puerperium

    Use additional code, if applicable, to identify specific complication

● **O89.0 Pulmonary complications of anesthesia during the puerperium**

    O89.01 Aspiration pneumonitis due to anesthesia during the puerperium ♀   M

        Inhalation of stomach contents or secretions NOS due to anesthesia during the puerperium

        Mendelson's syndrome due to anesthesia during the puerperium

    O89.09 Other pulmonary complications of anesthesia during the puerperium ♀   M

  O89.1 Cardiac complications of anesthesia during the puerperium ♀   M

  O89.2 Central nervous system complications of anesthesia during the puerperium ♀   M

  O89.3 Toxic reaction to local anesthesia during the puerperium ♀   M

  O89.4 Spinal and epidural anesthesia-induced headache during the puerperium ♀   M

  O89.5 Other complications of spinal and epidural anesthesia during the puerperium ♀   M

  O89.6 Failed or difficult intubation for anesthesia during the puerperium ♀   M

  O89.8 Other complications of anesthesia during the puerperium ♀   M

  O89.9 Complication of anesthesia during the puerperium, unspecified ♀   M

● **O90 Complications of the puerperium, not elsewhere classified**

  O90.0 Disruption of cesarean delivery wound ♀   M

    Dehiscence of cesarean delivery wound

    Excludes1   rupture of uterus (spontaneous) before onset of labor (O71.0-)

                rupture of uterus during labor (O71.1)

  O90.1 Disruption of perineal obstetric wound ♀   M

    Disruption of wound of episiotomy

    Disruption of wound of perineal laceration

    Secondary perineal tear

  O90.2 Hematoma of obstetric wound ♀   M

  O90.3 Peripartum cardiomyopathy ♀   M

    Conditions in I42.- arising during pregnancy and the puerperium

    Excludes1   pre-existing heart disease complicating pregnancy and the puerperium (O99.4-)

  O90.4 Postpartum acute kidney failure ♀   M

    Hepatorenal syndrome following labor and delivery

  O90.5 Postpartum thyroiditis ♀   M

  O90.6 Postpartum mood disturbance ♀   M

    Postpartum blues   Postpartum sadness

    Postpartum dysphoria

    ➡ **Excludes1**   postpartum depression (F53.0)

             ➡ puerperal psychosis (F53.1)

● **O90.8 Other complications of the puerperium, not elsewhere classified**

    O90.81 Anemia of the puerperium ♀   M

        Postpartum anemia NOS

        Excludes1   pre-existing anemia complicating the puerperium (O99.03)

    O90.89 Other complications of the puerperium, not elsewhere classified ♀   M

        Placental polyp

  O90.9 Complication of the puerperium, unspecified ♀   M

● **O91 Infections of breast associated with pregnancy, the puerperium and lactation**

    Use additional code to identify infection

● **O91.0 Infection of nipple associated with pregnancy, the puerperium and lactation**

  ● **O91.01 Infection of nipple associated with pregnancy**

    Gestational abscess of nipple

    O91.011 Infection of nipple associated with pregnancy, first trimester ♀   M

    O91.012 Infection of nipple associated with pregnancy, second trimester ♀   M

    O91.013 Infection of nipple associated with pregnancy, third trimester ♀   M

    O91.019 Infection of nipple associated with pregnancy, unspecified trimester ♀   M

  O91.02 Infection of nipple associated with the puerperium ♀   M

    Puerperal abscess of nipple

  O91.03 Infection of nipple associated with lactation ♀ M

    Abscess of nipple associated with lactation

● **O91.1 Abscess of breast associated with pregnancy, the puerperium and lactation**

  ● **O91.11 Abscess of breast associated with pregnancy**

    Gestational mammary abscess

    Gestational purulent mastitis

    Gestational subareolar abscess

    O91.111 Abscess of breast associated with pregnancy, first trimester ♀   M

    O91.112 Abscess of breast associated with pregnancy, second trimester ♀   M

    O91.113 Abscess of breast associated with pregnancy, third trimester ♀   M

    O91.119 Abscess of breast associated with pregnancy, unspecified trimester ♀   M

  O91.12 Abscess of breast associated with the puerperium ♀   M

    Puerperal mammary abscess

    Puerperal purulent mastitis

    Puerperal subareolar abscess

  O91.13 Abscess of breast associated with lactation ♀   M

    Mammary abscess associated with lactation

    Purulent mastitis associated with lactation

    Subareolar abscess associated with lactation

● **O91.2 Nonpurulent mastitis associated with pregnancy, the puerperium and lactation**

  ● **O91.21 Nonpurulent mastitis associated with pregnancy**

    Gestational interstitial mastitis

    Gestational lymphangitis of breast

    Gestational mastitis NOS

    Gestational parenchymatous mastitis

    O91.211 Nonpurulent mastitis associated with pregnancy, first trimester ♀   M

    O91.212 Nonpurulent mastitis associated with pregnancy, second trimester ♀   M

    O91.213 Nonpurulent mastitis associated with pregnancy, third trimester ♀   M

    O91.219 Nonpurulent mastitis associated with pregnancy, unspecified trimester ♀ M

  O91.22 Nonpurulent mastitis associated with the puerperium ♀   M

    Puerperal interstitial mastitis

    Puerperal lymphangitis of breast

    Puerperal mastitis NOS

    Puerperal parenchymatous mastitis

  O91.23 Nonpurulent mastitis associated with lactation ♀   M

    Interstitial mastitis associated with lactation

    Lymphangitis of breast associated with lactation

    Mastitis NOS associated with lactation

    Parenchymatous mastitis associated with lactation

▶ New   ➡ Revised   ~~deleted~~ Deleted   Excludes 1   Excludes 2   Includes   Use additional   Code first   Code also   Key words

OGCR Official Guidelines   X Assign placeholder X   ● Use Additional Character(s)   ▌ Manifestation Code   **Coding Clinic**

● **O92**   **Other disorders of breast and disorders of lactation associated with pregnancy and the puerperium**
  ● **O92.0**   **Retracted nipple associated with pregnancy, the puerperium, and lactation**
    ● **O92.01**   **Retracted nipple associated with pregnancy**
       O92.011   Retracted nipple associated with pregnancy, first trimester ♀   M
       O92.012   Retracted nipple associated with pregnancy, second trimester ♀   M
       O92.013   Retracted nipple associated with pregnancy, third trimester ♀   M
       O92.019   Retracted nipple associated with pregnancy, unspecified trimester ♀   M
     O92.02   Retracted nipple associated with the puerperium ♀   M
     O92.03   Retracted nipple associated with lactation ♀   M
  ● **O92.1**   **Cracked nipple associated with pregnancy, the puerperium, and lactation**
     Fissure of nipple, gestational or puerperal
    ● **O92.11**   **Cracked nipple associated with pregnancy**
       O92.111   Cracked nipple associated with pregnancy, first trimester ♀   M
       O92.112   Cracked nipple associated with pregnancy, second trimester ♀   M
       O92.113   Cracked nipple associated with pregnancy, third trimester ♀   M
       O92.119   Cracked nipple associated with pregnancy, unspecified trimester ♀   M
     O92.12   Cracked nipple associated with the puerperium ♀   M
     O92.13   Cracked nipple associated with lactation ♀   M
  ● **O92.2**   **Other and unspecified disorders of breast associated with pregnancy and the puerperium**
     O92.20   Unspecified disorder of breast associated with pregnancy and the puerperium ♀   M
     O92.29   Other disorders of breast associated with pregnancy and the puerperium ♀   M
   O92.3   **Agalactia** ♀   M
     Primary agalactia
     Excludes1   elective agalactia (O92.5)
              secondary agalactia (O92.5)
              therapeutic agalactia (O92.5)
   O92.4   **Hypogalactia** ♀   M
   O92.5   **Suppressed lactation** ♀   M
     Elective agalactia   Therapeutic agalactia
     Secondary agalactia
     Excludes1   primary agalactia (O92.3)
   O92.6   **Galactorrhea** ♀   M
  ● **O92.7**   **Other and unspecified disorders of lactation**
     O92.70   Unspecified disorders of lactation ♀   M
     O92.79   Other disorders of lactation ♀   M
       Puerperal galactocele

OTHER OBSTETRIC CONDITIONS, NOT ELSEWHERE CLASSIFIED (O94-O9A)

  O94   **Sequelae of complication of pregnancy, childbirth, and the puerperium** ♀   M
     Note: This category is to be used to indicate conditions in O00-O77.-, O85-O94 and O98-O9A.- as the cause of late effects. The "sequelae" include conditions specified as such, or as late effects, which may occur at any time after the puerperium.
     Code first condition resulting from (sequela) of complication of pregnancy, childbirth, and the puerperium

  O98   **Maternal infectious and parasitic diseases classifiable elsewhere but complicating pregnancy, childbirth and the puerperium**
     Includes   the listed conditions when complicating the pregnant state, when aggravated by the pregnancy, or as a reason for obstetric care
     Use additional code (Chapter 1), to identify specific infectious or parasitic disease
     Excludes2   herpes gestationis (O26.4-)
              infectious carrier state (O99.82-, O99.83-)
              obstetrical tetanus (A34)
              puerperal infection (O86.-)
              puerperal sepsis (O85)
              when the reason for maternal care is that the disease is known or suspected to have affected the fetus (O35-O36)
  ● **O98.0**   **Tuberculosis complicating pregnancy, childbirth and the puerperium**
     Conditions in A15-A19
    ● **O98.01**   **Tuberculosis complicating pregnancy**
       O98.011   Tuberculosis complicating pregnancy, first trimester ♀   M
       O98.012   Tuberculosis complicating pregnancy, second trimester ♀   M
       O98.013   Tuberculosis complicating pregnancy, third trimester ♀   M
       O98.019   Tuberculosis complicating pregnancy, unspecified trimester ♀   M
     O98.02   Tuberculosis complicating childbirth ♀   M
     O98.03   Tuberculosis complicating the puerperium ♀   M
  ● **O98.1**   **Syphilis complicating pregnancy, childbirth and the puerperium**
     Conditions in A50-A53
    ● **O98.11**   **Syphilis complicating pregnancy**
       O98.111   Syphilis complicating pregnancy, first trimester ♀   M
       O98.112   Syphilis complicating pregnancy, second trimester ♀   M
       O98.113   Syphilis complicating pregnancy, third trimester ♀   M
       O98.119   Syphilis complicating pregnancy, unspecified trimester ♀   M
     O98.12   Syphilis complicating childbirth ♀   M
     O98.13   Syphilis complicating the puerperium ♀   M
  ● **O98.2**   **Gonorrhea complicating pregnancy, childbirth and the puerperium**
     Conditions in A54.-
    ● **O98.21**   **Gonorrhea complicating pregnancy**
       O98.211   Gonorrhea complicating pregnancy, first trimester ♀   M
       O98.212   Gonorrhea complicating pregnancy, second trimester ♀   M
       O98.213   Gonorrhea complicating pregnancy, third trimester ♀   M
       O98.219   Gonorrhea complicating pregnancy, unspecified trimester ♀   M
     O98.22   Gonorrhea complicating childbirth ♀   M
     O98.23   Gonorrhea complicating the puerperium ♀   M

CHAPTER 15 (O00-O9A)

● **O98.3 Other infections with a predominantly sexual mode of transmission complicating pregnancy, childbirth and the puerperium**
Conditions in A55-A64

   ● **O98.31 Other infections with a predominantly sexual mode of transmission complicating pregnancy**

      O98.311 Other infections with a predominantly sexual mode of transmission complicating pregnancy, **first trimester** ♀   M

      O98.312 Other infections with a predominantly sexual mode of transmission complicating pregnancy, **second trimester** ♀   M

      O98.313 Other infections with a predominantly sexual mode of transmission complicating pregnancy, **third trimester** ♀   M

      O98.319 Other infections with a predominantly sexual mode of transmission complicating pregnancy, **unspecified trimester** ♀   M

      O98.32 Other infections with a predominantly sexual mode of transmission complicating **childbirth** ♀   M

      O98.33 Other infections with a predominantly sexual mode of transmission complicating the **puerperium** ♀   M

● **O98.4 Viral hepatitis complicating pregnancy, childbirth and the puerperium**
Conditions in B15-B19

   ● **O98.41 Viral hepatitis complicating pregnancy**

      O98.411 Viral hepatitis complicating pregnancy, **first trimester** ♀   M

      O98.412 Viral hepatitis complicating pregnancy, **second trimester** ♀   M

      O98.413 Viral hepatitis complicating pregnancy, **third trimester** ♀   M

      O98.419 Viral hepatitis complicating pregnancy, **unspecified trimester** ♀   M

      O98.42 Viral hepatitis complicating **childbirth** ♀   M

      O98.43 Viral hepatitis complicating the **puerperium** ♀   M

● **O98.5 Other viral diseases complicating pregnancy, childbirth and the puerperium**
Conditions in A80-B09, B25-B34, R87.81-, R87.82-

   Excludes:1 human immunodeficiency virus [HIV] disease complicating pregnancy, childbirth and the puerperium (O98.7-)

   ● **O98.51 Other viral diseases complicating pregnancy**

      O98.511 Other viral diseases complicating pregnancy, **first trimester** ♀   M

      O98.512 Other viral diseases complicating pregnancy, **second trimester** ♀   M
          Coding Clinic: 2016, Q4, P5-6

      O98.513 Other viral diseases complicating pregnancy, **third trimester** ♀   M
          Coding Clinic: 2016, Q4, P6

      O98.519 Other viral diseases complicating pregnancy, **unspecified trimester** ♀   M

      O98.52 Other viral diseases complicating **childbirth** ♀   M

      O98.53 Other viral diseases complicating the **puerperium** ♀   M

● **O98.6 Protozoal diseases complicating pregnancy, childbirth and the puerperium**
Conditions in B50-B64

   ● **O98.61 Protozoal diseases complicating pregnancy**

      O98.611 Protozoal diseases complicating pregnancy, **first trimester** ♀   M

      O98.612 Protozoal diseases complicating pregnancy, **second trimester** ♀   M

      O98.613 Protozoal diseases complicating pregnancy, **third trimester** ♀   M

      O98.619 Protozoal diseases complicating pregnancy, **unspecified trimester** ♀   M

      O98.62 Protozoal diseases complicating **childbirth** ♀   M

      O98.63 Protozoal diseases complicating the **puerperium** ♀   M

● **O98.7 Human immunodeficiency virus [HIV] disease complicating pregnancy, childbirth and the puerperium**

   Use additional code to identify the type of HIV disease:
      Acquired immune deficiency syndrome (AIDS) (B20)
      Asymptomatic HIV status (Z21)
      HIV positive NOS (Z21)
      Symptomatic HIV disease (B20)

   OGCR Section I.C.15.f.

   HIV Infection in Pregnancy, Childbirth and the Puerperium

   During pregnancy, childbirth or the puerperium, a patient admitted because of an HIV-related illness should receive a principal diagnosis from subcategory O98.7-. Human immunodeficiency [HIV] disease complicating pregnancy, childbirth and the puerperium, followed by the code(s) for the HIV-related illness(es).

   Patients with asymptomatic HIV infection status admitted during pregnancy, childbirth, or the puerperium should receive codes of O98.7- and Z21, Asymptomatic human immunodeficiency virus [HIV] infection status.

   ● **O98.71 Human immunodeficiency virus [HIV] disease complicating pregnancy**

      O98.711 Human immunodeficiency virus [HIV] disease complicating pregnancy, **first trimester** ♀   M

      O98.712 Human immunodeficiency virus [HIV] disease complicating pregnancy, **second trimester** ♀   M

      O98.713 Human immunodeficiency virus [HIV] disease complicating pregnancy, **third trimester** ♀   M

      O98.719 Human immunodeficiency virus [HIV] disease complicating pregnancy, **unspecified trimester** ♀   M

      O98.72 Human immunodeficiency virus [HIV] disease complicating **childbirth** ♀   M

      O98.73 Human immunodeficiency virus [HIV] disease complicating the **puerperium** ♀   M

● **O98.8 Other maternal infectious and parasitic diseases complicating pregnancy, childbirth and the puerperium**

   ● **O98.81 Other maternal infectious and parasitic diseases complicating pregnancy**

      O98.811 Other maternal infectious and parasitic diseases complicating pregnancy, **first trimester** ♀   M

      O98.812 Other maternal infectious and parasitic diseases complicating pregnancy, **second trimester** ♀   M

O98.813   Other maternal infectious and parasitic diseases complicating pregnancy, **third trimester** ♀   M

O98.819   Other maternal infectious and parasitic diseases complicating pregnancy, **unspecified trimester** ♀   M

O98.82   Other maternal infectious and parasitic diseases complicating **childbirth** ♀   M

O98.83   Other maternal infectious and parasitic diseases complicating the **puerperium** ♀   M

● **O98.9**   Unspecified maternal infectious and parasitic disease complicating pregnancy, childbirth and the puerperium

   ● **O98.91**   Unspecified maternal infectious and parasitic disease complicating **pregnancy**

O98.911   Unspecified maternal infectious and parasitic disease complicating pregnancy, **first trimester** ♀   M

O98.912   Unspecified maternal infectious and parasitic disease complicating pregnancy, **second trimester** ♀   M

O98.913   Unspecified maternal infectious and parasitic disease complicating pregnancy, **third trimester** ♀   M

O98.919   Unspecified maternal infectious and parasitic disease complicating pregnancy, **unspecified trimester** ♀   M

   O98.92   Unspecified maternal infectious and parasitic disease complicating **childbirth** ♀   M

   O98.93   Unspecified maternal infectious and parasitic disease complicating the **puerperium** ♀   M

● **O99**   Other maternal diseases classifiable elsewhere but complicating pregnancy, childbirth and the puerperium

Includes: conditions which complicate the pregnant state, are aggravated by the pregnancy or are a main reason for obstetric care

Use additional code to identify specific condition

Excludes2   when the reason for maternal care is that the condition is known or suspected to have affected the fetus (O35-O36)

● **O99.0**   Anemia complicating pregnancy, childbirth and the puerperium
Conditions in D50-D64

Excludes1   anemia arising in the puerperium (O90.81)
postpartum anemia NOS (O90.81)

   ● **O99.01**   Anemia complicating **pregnancy**

O99.011   Anemia complicating pregnancy, **first trimester** ♀   M

O99.012   Anemia complicating pregnancy, **second trimester** ♀   M

O99.013   Anemia complicating pregnancy, **third trimester** ♀   M

O99.019   Anemia complicating pregnancy, **unspecified trimester** ♀   M

   O99.02   Anemia complicating **childbirth** ♀   M

   O99.03   Anemia complicating the **puerperium** ♀   M

Excludes1   postpartum anemia not pre-existing prior to delivery (O90.81)

● **O99.1**   Other diseases of the blood and blood-forming organs and certain disorders involving the immune mechanism complicating pregnancy, childbirth and the puerperium
Conditions in D65-D89

Excludes1   hemorrhage with coagulation defects (O45.-, O46.0-, O67.0, O72.3)

   ● **O99.11**   Other diseases of the blood and blood-forming organs and certain disorders involving the immune mechanism complicating **pregnancy**

O99.111   Other diseases of the blood and blood-forming organs and certain disorders involving the immune mechanism complicating pregnancy, **first trimester** ♀   M

O99.112   Other diseases of the blood and blood-forming organs and certain disorders involving the immune mechanism complicating pregnancy, **second trimester** ♀   M

O99.113   Other diseases of the blood and blood-forming organs and certain disorders involving the immune mechanism complicating pregnancy, **third trimester** ♀   M

O99.119   Other diseases of the blood and blood-forming organs and certain disorders involving the immune mechanism complicating pregnancy, **unspecified trimester** ♀   M

   O99.12   Other diseases of the blood and blood-forming organs and certain disorders involving the immune mechanism complicating **childbirth** ♀   M

   O99.13   Other diseases of the blood and blood-forming organs and certain disorders involving the immune mechanism complicating the **puerperium** ♀   M

● **O99.2**   Endocrine, nutritional and metabolic diseases complicating pregnancy, childbirth and the puerperium
Conditions in E00-E88

Excludes2   diabetes mellitus (O24.-)
malnutrition (O25.-)
postpartum thyroiditis (O90.5)

   ● **O99.21**   Obesity complicating pregnancy, childbirth, and the puerperium

Use additional code to identify the type of obesity (E66.-)

O99.210   Obesity complicating pregnancy, **unspecified trimester** ♀   M

O99.211   Obesity complicating pregnancy, **first trimester** ♀   M

O99.212   Obesity complicating pregnancy, **second trimester** ♀   M

O99.213   Obesity complicating pregnancy, **third trimester** ♀   M

O99.214   Obesity complicating **childbirth** ♀   M

O99.215   Obesity complicating the **puerperium** ♀   M

CHAPTER 15 (O00-O9A)

● **O99.28** Other endocrine, nutritional and metabolic diseases complicating pregnancy, childbirth and the puerperium

　　　O99.280 Endocrine, nutritional and metabolic diseases complicating pregnancy, unspecified trimester ♀　　M

　　　O99.281 Endocrine, nutritional and metabolic diseases complicating pregnancy, first trimester ♀　　M

　　　O99.282 Endocrine, nutritional and metabolic diseases complicating pregnancy, second trimester ♀　　M

　　　O99.283 Endocrine, nutritional and metabolic diseases complicating pregnancy, third trimester ♀　　M

　　　O99.284 Endocrine, nutritional and metabolic diseases complicating childbirth ♀　　M

　　　O99.285 Endocrine, nutritional and metabolic diseases complicating the puerperium ♀　　M

● **O99.3** Mental disorders and diseases of the nervous system complicating pregnancy, childbirth and the puerperium

● **O99.31** Alcohol use complicating pregnancy, childbirth, and the puerperium

　　Use additional code(s) from F10 to identify manifestations of the alcohol use

　　　O99.310 Alcohol use complicating pregnancy, unspecified trimester ♀　　M

　　　O99.311 Alcohol use complicating pregnancy, first trimester ♀　　M

　　　O99.312 Alcohol use complicating pregnancy, second trimester ♀　　M

　　　O99.313 Alcohol use complicating pregnancy, third trimester ♀　　M

　　　O99.314 Alcohol use complicating childbirth ♀　　M

　　　O99.315 Alcohol use complicating the puerperium ♀　　M

● **O99.32** Drug use complicating pregnancy, childbirth, and the puerperium

　　Use additional code(s) from F11-F16 and F18-F19 to identify manifestations of the drug use

　　　O99.320 Drug use complicating pregnancy, unspecified trimester ♀　　M

　　　O99.321 Drug use complicating pregnancy, first trimester ♀　　M

　　　O99.322 Drug use complicating pregnancy, second trimester ♀　　M

　　　O99.323 Drug use complicating pregnancy, third trimester ♀　　M

　　　O99.324 Drug use complicating childbirth ♀　　M

　　　O99.325 Drug use complicating the puerperium ♀　　M

● **O99.33** Tobacco use disorder complicating pregnancy, childbirth, and the puerperium

　　Smoking complicating pregnancy, childbirth, and the puerperium

　　Use additional code from category F17 to identify type of tobacco nicotine dependence

　　　O99.330 Smoking (tobacco) complicating pregnancy, unspecified trimester ♀　　M

　　　O99.331 Smoking (tobacco) complicating pregnancy, first trimester ♀　　M

　　　O99.332 Smoking (tobacco) complicating pregnancy, second trimester ♀　　M

　　　O99.333 Smoking (tobacco) complicating pregnancy, third trimester ♀　　M

　　　O99.334 Smoking (tobacco) complicating childbirth ♀　　M

　　　O99.335 Smoking (tobacco) complicating the puerperium ♀　　M

● **O99.34** Other mental disorders complicating pregnancy, childbirth, and the puerperium

　　Conditions in F01-F09 and F20-F99

　　Excludes2 postpartum mood disturbance (O90.6)
　　　　　　➡ postnatal psychosis (F53.1)
　　　　　　➡ puerperal psychosis (F53.1)

　　　O99.340 Other mental disorders complicating pregnancy, unspecified trimester ♀　　M

　　　O99.341 Other mental disorders complicating pregnancy, first trimester ♀　　M

　　　O99.342 Other mental disorders complicating pregnancy, second trimester ♀　　M

　　　O99.343 Other mental disorders complicating pregnancy, third trimester ♀　　M

　　　O99.344 Other mental disorders complicating childbirth ♀　　M

　　　O99.345 Other mental disorders complicating the puerperium ♀　　M

● **O99.35** Diseases of the nervous system complicating pregnancy, childbirth, and the puerperium

　　Conditions in G00-G99

　　Excludes2 pregnancy related peripheral neuritis (O26.8-)

　　　O99.350 Diseases of the nervous system complicating pregnancy, unspecified trimester ♀　　M

　　　O99.351 Diseases of the nervous system complicating pregnancy, first trimester ♀　　M

　　　O99.352 Diseases of the nervous system complicating pregnancy, second trimester ♀　　M

　　　O99.353 Diseases of the nervous system complicating pregnancy, third trimester ♀　　M

　　　O99.354 Diseases of the nervous system complicating childbirth ♀　　M

　　　O99.355 Diseases of the nervous system complicating the puerperium ♀　　M

● **O99.4** Diseases of the circulatory system complicating pregnancy, childbirth and the puerperium

　　Conditions in I00-I99

　　Excludes1 peripartum cardiomyopathy (O90.3)
　　Excludes2 hypertensive disorders (O10-O16)
　　　　　　obstetric embolism (O88.-)
　　　　　　venous complications and cerebrovenous sinus thrombosis in labor, childbirth and the puerperium (O87.-)
　　　　　　venous complications and cerebrovenous sinus thrombosis in pregnancy (O22.-)

● **O99.41** Diseases of the circulatory system complicating pregnancy
　　Coding Clinic: 2016, Q2, P8

　　　O99.411 Diseases of the circulatory system complicating pregnancy, first trimester ♀　　M

　　　O99.412 Diseases of the circulatory system complicating pregnancy, second trimester ♀　　M

　　　O99.413 Diseases of the circulatory system complicating pregnancy, third trimester ♀　　M

　　　O99.419 Diseases of the circulatory system complicating pregnancy, unspecified trimester ♀　　M

　　O99.42 Diseases of the circulatory system complicating childbirth ♀　　M

　　O99.43 Diseases of the circulatory system complicating the puerperium ♀　　M

▶ New　　⇒ Revised　　~~deleted~~ Deleted　　Excludes 1　　Excludes 2　　Includes　　Use additional　　Code first　　Code also　　Key words

OGCR Official Guidelines　　X Assign placeholder X　　● Use Additional Character(s)　　▷ Manifestation Code　　Coding Clinic

● **O99.5** **Diseases of the respiratory system** complicating pregnancy, childbirth and the puerperium
Conditions in J00-J99

  ● **O99.51** Diseases of the respiratory system complicating **pregnancy**

     O99.511 Diseases of the respiratory system complicating pregnancy, **first trimester** ♀   M

     O99.512 Diseases of the respiratory system complicating pregnancy, **second trimester** ♀   M

     O99.513 Diseases of the respiratory system complicating pregnancy, **third trimester** ♀   M

     O99.519 Diseases of the respiratory system complicating pregnancy, **unspecified trimester** ♀   M

     O99.52 Diseases of the respiratory system complicating **childbirth** ♀   M

     O99.53 Diseases of the respiratory system complicating the **puerperium** ♀   M

● **O99.6** **Diseases of the digestive system** complicating pregnancy, childbirth and the puerperium
Conditions in K00-K93

   Excludes2   hemorrhoids in pregnancy (O22.4-)
       liver and biliary tract disorders in pregnancy, childbirth and the puerperium (O26.6-)

  ● **O99.61** Diseases of the digestive system complicating **pregnancy**

     O99.611 Diseases of the digestive system complicating pregnancy, **first trimester** ♀   M

     O99.612 Diseases of the digestive system complicating pregnancy, **second trimester** ♀   M

     O99.613 Diseases of the digestive system complicating pregnancy, **third trimester** ♀   M

     O99.619 Diseases of the digestive system complicating pregnancy, **unspecified trimester** ♀   M

     O99.62 Diseases of the digestive system complicating **childbirth** ♀   M

     O99.63 Diseases of the digestive system complicating the **puerperium** ♀   M

● **O99.7** **Diseases of the skin and subcutaneous tissue** complicating pregnancy, childbirth and the puerperium
Conditions in L00-L99

   Excludes2   herpes gestationis (O26.4)
       pruritic urticarial papules and plaques of pregnancy (PUPPP) (O26.86)

  ● **O99.71** Diseases of the skin and subcutaneous tissue complicating **pregnancy**

     O99.711 Diseases of the skin and subcutaneous tissue complicating pregnancy, **first trimester** ♀   M

     O99.712 Diseases of the skin and subcutaneous tissue complicating pregnancy, **second trimester** ♀   M

     O99.713 Diseases of the skin and subcutaneous tissue complicating pregnancy, **third trimester** ♀   M

     O99.719 Diseases of the skin and subcutaneous tissue complicating pregnancy, **unspecified trimester** ♀   M

     O99.72 Diseases of the skin and subcutaneous tissue complicating **childbirth** ♀   M

     O99.73 Diseases of the skin and subcutaneous tissue complicating the **puerperium** ♀   M

● **O99.8** **Other specified diseases and conditions** complicating pregnancy, childbirth and the puerperium
Conditions in D00-D48, H00-H95, M00-N99, and Q00-Q99

   Use additional code to identify condition

   Excludes2   genitourinary infections in pregnancy (O23.-)
       infection of genitourinary tract following delivery (O86.1-O86.3)
       malignant neoplasm complicating pregnancy, childbirth and the puerperium (O9A.1-)
       maternal care for known or suspected abnormality of maternal pelvic organs (O34.-)
       postpartum acute kidney failure (O90.4)
       traumatic injuries in pregnancy (O9A.2-)

  ● **O99.81** **Abnormal glucose** complicating pregnancy, childbirth and the puerperium

     Excludes1   gestational diabetes (O24.4-)

     O99.810 Abnormal glucose complicating **pregnancy** ♀   M

     O99.814 Abnormal glucose complicating **childbirth** ♀   M

     O99.815 Abnormal glucose complicating the **puerperium** ♀   M

  ● **O99.82** **Streptococcus B carrier state** complicating pregnancy, childbirth and the puerperium

     Excludes1   Carrier of streptococcus group B (GBS) in a nonpregnant woman (Z22.330)

     O99.820 Streptococcus B carrier state complicating **pregnancy** ♀   M

     O99.824 Streptococcus B carrier state complicating **childbirth** ♀   M

     O99.825 Streptococcus B carrier state complicating the **puerperium** ♀   M

  ● **O99.83** **Other infection carrier state** complicating pregnancy, childbirth and the puerperium

     Use additional code to identify the carrier state (Z22.-)

     O99.830 Other infection carrier state complicating **pregnancy** ♀   M

     O99.834 Other infection carrier state complicating **childbirth** ♀   M

     O99.835 Other infection carrier state complicating the **puerperium** ♀   M

  ● **O99.84** **Bariatric surgery status** complicating pregnancy, childbirth and the puerperium
     Gastric banding status complicating pregnancy, childbirth and the puerperium
     Gastric bypass status for obesity complicating pregnancy, childbirth and the puerperium
     Obesity surgery status complicating pregnancy, childbirth and the puerperium

     O99.840 Bariatric surgery status complicating pregnancy, **unspecified trimester** ♀ M

     O99.841 Bariatric surgery status complicating pregnancy, **first trimester** ♀   M

     O99.842 Bariatric surgery status complicating pregnancy, **second trimester** ♀   M

     O99.843 Bariatric surgery status complicating pregnancy, **third trimester** ♀   M

     O99.844 Bariatric surgery status complicating **childbirth** ♀   M

     O99.845 Bariatric surgery status complicating the **puerperium** ♀   M

     O99.89 **Other specified diseases and conditions** complicating pregnancy, childbirth and the puerperium ♀   M

OGCR Section I.C.2.l.3.

> Malignant neoplasm in a pregnant patient
>
> When a pregnant woman has a malignant neoplasm, a code from subcategory O9A.1-, Malignant neoplasm complicating pregnancy, childbirth, and the puerperium, should be sequenced first, followed by the appropriate code from Chapter 2 to indicate the type of neoplasm.

● **O9A**   **Maternal malignant neoplasms, traumatic injuries and abuse classifiable elsewhere but complicating pregnancy, childbirth and the puerperium**

   ● **O9A.1**   **Malignant neoplasm complicating pregnancy, childbirth and the puerperium**

        Conditions in C00-C96

        Use additional code to identify neoplasm

        Excludes2   maternal care for benign tumor of corpus uteri (O34.1-)

                maternal care for benign tumor of cervix (O34.4-)

      ● **O9A.11**   Malignant neoplasm complicating pregnancy

          O9A.111   Malignant neoplasm complicating pregnancy, first trimester ♀   M

          O9A.112   Malignant neoplasm complicating pregnancy, second trimester ♀   M

          O9A.113   Malignant neoplasm complicating pregnancy, third trimester ♀   M

          O9A.119   Malignant neoplasm complicating pregnancy, unspecified trimester ♀   M

      O9A.12   Malignant neoplasm complicating childbirth ♀   M

      O9A.13   Malignant neoplasm complicating the puerperium ♀   M

          Coding Clinic: 2015, Q3, P19

   ● **O9A.2**   **Injury, poisoning and certain other consequences of external causes complicating pregnancy, childbirth and the puerperium**

        Conditions in S00-T88, except T74 and T76

        Use additional code(s) to identify the injury or poisoning

        Excludes2   physical, sexual and psychological abuse complicating pregnancy, childbirth and the puerperium (O9A.3-, O9A.4-, O9A.5-)

      ● **O9A.21**   Injury, poisoning and certain other consequences of external causes complicating pregnancy

          O9A.211   Injury, poisoning and certain other consequences of external causes complicating pregnancy, first trimester ♀   M

          O9A.212   Injury, poisoning and certain other consequences of external causes complicating pregnancy, second trimester ♀   M

          O9A.213   Injury, poisoning and certain other consequences of external causes complicating pregnancy, third trimester ♀   M

          O9A.219   Injury, poisoning and certain other consequences of external causes complicating pregnancy, unspecified trimester ♀   M

      O9A.22   Injury, poisoning and certain other consequences of external causes complicating childbirth ♀   M

      O9A.23   Injury, poisoning and certain other consequences of external causes complicating the puerperium ♀   M

● **O9A.3**   **Physical abuse complicating pregnancy, childbirth and the puerperium**

        Conditions in T74.11 or T76.11

        Use additional code (if applicable):

          to identify any associated current injury due to physical abuse

          to identify the perpetrator of abuse (Y07.-)

        Excludes2   sexual abuse complicating pregnancy, childbirth and the puerperium (O9A.4)

   ● **O9A.31**   Physical abuse complicating pregnancy

          O9A.311   Physical abuse complicating pregnancy, first trimester ♀   M

          O9A.312   Physical abuse complicating pregnancy, second trimester ♀   M

          O9A.313   Physical abuse complicating pregnancy, third trimester ♀   M

          O9A.319   Physical abuse complicating pregnancy, unspecified trimester ♀   M

      O9A.32   Physical abuse complicating childbirth ♀   M

      O9A.33   Physical abuse complicating the puerperium ♀   M

● **O9A.4**   **Sexual abuse complicating pregnancy, childbirth and the puerperium**

        Conditions in T74.21 or T76.21

        Use additional code (if applicable):

          to identify any associated current injury due to sexual abuse

          to identify the perpetrator of abuse (Y07.-)

   ● **O9A.41**   Sexual abuse complicating pregnancy

          O9A.411   Sexual abuse complicating pregnancy, first trimester ♀   M

          O9A.412   Sexual abuse complicating pregnancy, second trimester ♀   M

          O9A.413   Sexual abuse complicating pregnancy, third trimester ♀   M

          O9A.419   Sexual abuse complicating pregnancy, unspecified trimester ♀   M

      O9A.42   Sexual abuse complicating childbirth ♀   M

      O9A.43   Sexual abuse complicating the puerperium ♀   M

● **O9A.5**   **Psychological abuse complicating pregnancy, childbirth and the puerperium**

        Conditions in T74.31 or T76.31

        Use additional code to identify the perpetrator of abuse (Y07.-)

   ● **O9A.51**   Psychological abuse complicating pregnancy

          O9A.511   Psychological abuse complicating pregnancy, first trimester ♀   M

          O9A.512   Psychological abuse complicating pregnancy, second trimester ♀   M

          O9A.513   Psychological abuse complicating pregnancy, third trimester ♀   M

          O9A.519   Psychological abuse complicating pregnancy, unspecified trimester ♀   M

      O9A.52   Psychological abuse complicating childbirth ♀ M

      O9A.53   Psychological abuse complicating the puerperium ♀   M

▶ New   ⇥ Revised   ~~deleted~~ Deleted   Excludes 1   Excludes 2   Includes   Use additional   Code first   Code also   Key words

OGCR Official Guidelines   X Assign placeholder X   ● Use Additional Character(s)   ▶ Manifestation Code   **Coding Clinic**

CHAPTER 16

CERTAIN CONDITIONS ORIGINATING IN THE PERINATAL PERIOD (P00-P96)

OGCR Chapter-Specific Coding Guidelines

16. **Chapter 16: Certain Conditions Originating in the Perinatal Period (P00-P96)**

For coding and reporting purposes the perinatal period is defined as before birth through the 28th day following birth. The following guidelines are provided for reporting purposes

a. **General Perinatal Rules**

1) **Use of Chapter 16 Codes**

Codes in this chapter are never for use on the maternal record. Codes from Chapter 15, the obstetric chapter, are never permitted on the newborn record. Chapter 16 codes may be used throughout the life of the patient if the condition is still present.

2) **Principal Diagnosis for Birth Record**

When coding the birth episode in a newborn record, assign a code from category Z38, Liveborn infants according to place of birth and type of delivery, as the principal diagnosis. A code from category Z38 is assigned only once, to a newborn at the time of birth. If a newborn is transferred to another institution, a code from category Z38 should not be used at the receiving hospital.

A code from category Z38 is used only on the newborn record, not on the mother's record.

3) **Use of Codes from other Chapters with Codes from Chapter 16**

Codes from other chapters may be used with codes from chapter 16 if the codes from the other chapters provide more specific detail. Codes for signs and symptoms may be assigned when a definitive diagnosis has not been established. If the reason for the encounter is a perinatal condition, the code from chapter 16 should be sequenced first.

4) **Use of Chapter 16 Codes after the Perinatal Period**

Should a condition originate in the perinatal period, and continue throughout the life of the patient, the perinatal code should continue to be used regardless of the patient's age.

5) **Birth process or community acquired conditions**

If a newborn has a condition that may be either due to the birth process or community acquired and the documentation does not indicate which it is, the default is due to the birth process and the code from Chapter 16 should be used. If the condition is community-acquired, a code from Chapter 16 should not be assigned.

6) **Code all clinically significant conditions**

All clinically significant conditions noted on routine newborn examination should be coded. A condition is clinically significant if it requires:
- clinical evaluation; or
- therapeutic treatment; or
- diagnostic procedures; or
- extended length of hospital stay; or
- increased nursing care and/or monitoring; or
- has implications for future health care needs

Note: The perinatal guidelines listed above are the same as the general coding guidelines for "additional diagnoses", except for the final point regarding implications for future health care needs. Codes should be assigned for conditions that have been specified by the provider as having implications for future health care needs.

b. **Observation and Evaluation of Newborns for Suspected Conditions Not Found**

1) **Use of Z05 codes**

Assign a code from category Z05, Observation and evaluation of newborns and infants for suspected conditions ruled out, to identify those instances when a healthy newborn is evaluated for a suspected condition that is determined after study not to be present. Do not use a code from category Z05 when the patient has identified signs or symptoms of a suspected problem; in such cases code the sign or symptom.

2) **Z05 on Other than the Birth Record**

A code from category Z05 may also be assigned as a principal or first-listed code for readmissions or encounters when the code from category Z38 code no longer applies. Codes from category Z05 are for use only for healthy newborns and infants for which no condition after study is found to be present.

3) **Z05 on a birth record**

A code from category Z05 is to be used as a secondary code after the code from category Z38, Liveborn infants according to place of birth and type of delivery.

c. **Coding Additional Perinatal Diagnoses**

1) **Assigning codes for conditions that require treatment**

Assign codes for conditions that require treatment or further investigation, prolong the length of stay, or require resource utilization.

2) **Codes for conditions specified as having implications for future health care needs**

Assign codes for conditions that have been specified by the provider as having implications for future health care needs.

Note: This guideline should not be used for adult patients.

d. **Prematurity and Fetal Growth Retardation**

Providers utilize different criteria in determining prematurity. A code for prematurity should not be assigned unless it is documented. Assignment of codes in categories P05, Disorders of newborn related to slow fetal growth and fetal malnutrition, and P07, Disorders of newborn related to short gestation and low birth weight, not elsewhere classified, should be based on the recorded birth weight and estimated gestational age.

When both birth weight and gestational age are available, two codes from category P07 should be assigned, with the code for birth weight sequenced before the code for gestational age.

e. **Low birth weight and immaturity status**

Codes from category P07, Disorders of newborn related to short gestation and low birth weight, not elsewhere classified, are for use for a child or adult who was premature or had a low birth weight as a newborn and this is affecting the patient's current health status.

See Section I.C.21. Factors influencing health status and contact with health services, Status.

f. **Bacterial Sepsis of Newborn**

Category P36, Bacterial sepsis of newborn, includes congenital sepsis. If a perinate is documented as having sepsis without documentation of congenital or community acquired, the default is congenital and a code from category P36 should be assigned. If the P36 code includes the causal organism, an additional code from category B95, Streptococcus, Staphylococcus, and Enterococcus as the cause of diseases classified elsewhere, or B96, Other bacterial agents as the cause of diseases classified elsewhere, should not be assigned. If the P36 code does not include the causal organism, assign an additional code from category B96. If applicable, use additional codes to identify severe sepsis (R65.2-) and any associated acute organ dysfunction.

g. **Stillbirth**

Code P95, Stillbirth, is only for use in institutions that maintain separate records for stillbirths. No other code should be used with P95. Code P95 should not be used on the mother's record.

CHAPTER 16

CERTAIN CONDITIONS ORIGINATING IN THE PERINATAL PERIOD (P00-P96)

Note: Codes from this chapter are for use on newborn records only, never on maternal records.

Includes conditions that have their origin in the fetal or perinatal period (before birth through the first 28 days after birth) even if morbidity occurs later

Excludes2 congenital malformations, deformations and chromosomal abnormalities (Q00-Q99)
endocrine, nutritional and metabolic diseases (E00-E88)
injury, poisoning and certain other consequences of external causes (S00-T88)
neoplasms (C00-D49)
tetanus neonatorum (A33)

This chapter contains the following blocks:

P00-P04	Newborn affected by maternal factors and by complications of pregnancy, labor, and delivery
P05-P08	Disorders of newborns related to length of gestation and fetal growth
P09	Abnormal findings on neonatal screening
P10-P15	Birth trauma
P19-P29	Respiratory and cardiovascular disorders specific to the perinatal period
P35-P39	Infections specific to the perinatal period
P50-P61	Hemorrhagic and hematological disorders of newborn
P70-P74	Transitory endocrine and metabolic disorders specific to newborn
P76-P78	Digestive system disorders of newborn
P80-P83	Conditions involving the integument and temperature regulation of newborn
P84	Other problems with newborn
P90-P96	Other disorders originating in the perinatal period

NEWBORN AFFECTED BY MATERNAL FACTORS AND BY COMPLICATIONS OF PREGNANCY, LABOR, AND DELIVERY (P00–P04)

Note: These codes are for use when the listed maternal conditions are specified as the cause of confirmed morbidity or potential morbidity which have their origin in the perinatal period (before birth through the first 28 days after birth).

● **P00** **Newborn affected by maternal conditions that may be unrelated to present pregnancy**
Code first any current condition in newborn
Excludes2 encounter for observation of newborn for suspected diseases and conditions ruled out (Z05.-)
newborn affected by maternal complications of pregnancy (P01.-)
newborn affected by maternal endocrine and metabolic disorders (P70–P74)
newborn affected by noxious substances transmitted via placenta or breast milk (P04.-)
Coding Clinic: 2016, Q4, P54

P00.0 **Newborn affected by maternal hypertensive disorders**
Newborn affected by maternal conditions classifiable to O10-O11, O13-O16

P00.1 **Newborn affected by maternal renal and urinary tract diseases**
Newborn affected by maternal conditions classifiable to N00-N39

P00.2 **Newborn affected by maternal infectious and parasitic diseases**
Newborn affected by maternal infectious disease classifiable to A00-B99, J09 and J10
Excludes1 maternal genital tract or other localized infections (P00.8)
Excludes2 infections specific to the perinatal period (P35-P39)
Coding Clinic: 2015, Q3, P21

P00.3 **Newborn affected by other maternal circulatory and respiratory diseases**
Newborn affected by maternal conditions classifiable to I00-I99, J00-J99, Q20-Q34 and not included in P00.0, P00.2

P00.4 **Newborn affected by maternal nutritional disorders**
Newborn affected by maternal disorders classifiable to E40-E64
Maternal malnutrition NOS

P00.5 **Newborn affected by maternal injury**
Newborn affected by maternal conditions classifiable to O9A.2-

P00.6 **Newborn affected by surgical procedure on mother**
Newborn affected by amniocentesis
Excludes1 Cesarean delivery for present delivery (P03.4)
damage to placenta from amniocentesis, cesarean delivery or surgical induction (P02.1)
previous surgery to uterus or pelvic organs (P03.89)
Excludes2 newborn affected by complication of (fetal) intrauterine procedure (P96.5)

P00.7 **Newborn affected by other medical procedures on mother, not elsewhere classified**
Newborn affected by radiation to mother
Excludes1 damage to placenta from amniocentesis, cesarean delivery or surgical induction (P02.1)
newborn affected by other complications of labor and delivery (P03.-)

● **P00.8** **Newborn affected by other maternal conditions**

P00.81 **Newborn affected by periodontal disease in mother**

P00.89 **Newborn affected by other maternal conditions**
Newborn affected by conditions classifiable to T80-T88
Newborn affected by maternal genital tract or other localized infections
Newborn affected by maternal systemic lupus erythematosus

P00.9 **Newborn affected by unspecified maternal condition**

● **P01** **Newborn affected by maternal complications of pregnancy**
Code first any current condition in newborn
Excludes2 encounter for observation of newborn for suspected diseases and conditions ruled out (Z05.-)
Coding Clinic: 2016, Q4, P54

P01.0 **Newborn affected by incompetent cervix**

P01.1 **Newborn affected by premature rupture of membranes**

P01.2 **Newborn affected by oligohydramnios**
Excludes1 oligohydramnios due to premature rupture of membranes (P01.1)

P01.3 **Newborn affected by polyhydramnios**
Excess of amniotic fluid, usually > 2000 mL
Newborn affected by hydramnios

P01.4   **Newborn affected by** ectopic pregnancy
         Newborn affected by abdominal pregnancy

P01.5   **Newborn affected by** multiple pregnancy
         Newborn affected by triplet (pregnancy)
         Newborn affected by twin (pregnancy)

P01.6   **Newborn affected by** maternal death

P01.7   **Newborn affected by** malpresentation before labor
         Newborn affected by breech presentation before labor
         Newborn affected by external version before labor
         Newborn affected by face presentation before labor
         Newborn affected by transverse lie before labor
         Newborn affected by unstable lie before labor

P01.8   **Newborn affected by** other maternal complications of pregnancy

P01.9   **Newborn affected by** maternal complication of pregnancy, unspecified

● **P02   Newborn affected by complications of placenta, cord and membranes**

         Code first any current condition in newborn

         Excludes2   encounter for observation of newborn for suspected diseases and conditions ruled out (Z05.-)

         Coding Clinic: 2016, Q4, P54

P02.0   **Newborn affected by** placenta previa

P02.1   **Newborn affected by other forms of** placental separation and hemorrhage
         Newborn affected by abruptio placenta
         Newborn affected by accidental hemorrhage
         Newborn affected by antepartum hemorrhage
         Newborn affected by damage to placenta from amniocentesis, cesarean delivery or surgical induction
         Newborn affected by maternal blood loss
         Newborn affected by premature separation of placenta

● P02.2   **Newborn affected by other and unspecified morphological and functional abnormalities of placenta**

         P02.20   **Newborn affected by** unspecified **morphological and functional abnormalities of placenta**

         P02.29   **Newborn affected by** other **morphological and functional abnormalities of placenta**
                  Newborn affected by placental dysfunction
                  Newborn affected by placental infarction
                  Newborn affected by placental insufficiency

P02.3   **Newborn affected by** placental transfusion syndromes
         Newborn affected by placental and cord abnormalities resulting in twin-to-twin or other transplacental transfusion

P02.4   **Newborn affected by** prolapsed cord

P02.5   **Newborn affected by** other compression of umbilical cord
         Newborn affected by umbilical cord (tightly) around neck
         Newborn affected by entanglement of umbilical cord
         Newborn affected by knot in umbilical cord

● P02.6   **Newborn affected by other and unspecified** conditions of umbilical cord

         P02.60   **Newborn affected by** unspecified conditions of umbilical cord

         P02.69   **Newborn affected by** other conditions of umbilical cord
                  Newborn affected by short umbilical cord
                  Newborn affected by vasa previa

                  Excludes1   newborn affected by single umbilical artery (Q27.0)

● P02.7   **Newborn affected by** chorioamnionitis
         Inflammation of chorion and amnion
         ~~Newborn affected by amnionitis~~
         ~~Newborn affected by membranitis~~
         ~~Newborn affected by placentitis~~

   ▶ P02.70   **Newborn affected by fetal inflammatory response syndrome**
              ▶ Newborn affected by FIRS

   ▶ P02.78   **Newborn affected by other conditions from chorioamnionitis**
              ▶ Newborn affected by amnionitis
              ▶ Newborn affected by membranitis
              ▶ Newborn affected by placentitis

P02.8   **Newborn affected by** other abnormalities of membranes

P02.9   **Newborn affected by** abnormality of membranes, unspecified

● **P03   Newborn affected by** other complications of labor and delivery**

         Code first any current condition in newborn

         Excludes2   encounter for observation of newborn for suspected diseases and conditions ruled out (Z05.-)

         Coding Clinic: 2016, Q4, P54

P03.0   **Newborn affected by** breech delivery and extraction

P03.1   **Newborn affected by other** malpresentation, malposition and disproportion **during labor and delivery**
         Newborn affected by contracted pelvis
         Newborn affected by conditions classifiable to O64-O66
         Newborn affected by persistent occipitoposterior
         Newborn affected by transverse lie

P03.2   **Newborn affected by** forceps delivery

P03.3   **Newborn affected by delivery by** vacuum extractor **[ventouse]**

P03.4   **Newborn affected by** Cesarean delivery

P03.5   **Newborn affected by** precipitate delivery
         Newborn affected by rapid second stage

P03.6   **Newborn affected by** abnormal uterine contractions
         Newborn affected by conditions classifiable to O62.-, except O62.3
         Newborn affected by hypertonic labor
         Newborn affected by uterine inertia

● P03.8   **Newborn affected by other specified complications of labor and delivery**

   ● P03.81   **Newborn affected by** abnormality in fetal (intrauterine) heart rate or rhythm

              Excludes1   neonatal cardiac dysrhythmia (P29.1-)

              P03.810   **Newborn affected by abnormality in fetal (intrauterine) heart rate or rhythm** before the onset of labor

              P03.811   **Newborn affected by abnormality in fetal (intrauterine) heart rate or rhythm** during labor

              P03.819   **Newborn affected by abnormality in fetal (intrauterine) heart rate or rhythm,** unspecified **as to time of onset**

      P03.82   **Meconium passage during delivery**

              Excludes1   meconium aspiration (P24.00, P24.01)
                              meconium staining (P96.83)

      P03.89   **Newborn affected by** other specified **complications of labor and delivery**
               Newborn affected by abnormality of maternal soft tissues
               Newborn affected by conditions classifiable to O60-O75 and by procedures used in labor and delivery not included in P02.- and P03.0-P03.6
               Newborn affected by induction of labor

P03.9   **Newborn affected by complication of labor and delivery, unspecified**

● **P04** **Newborn affected by noxious substances transmitted via placenta or breast milk**

Includes   nonteratogenic effects of substances transmitted via placenta

Excludes2   congenital malformations (Q00-Q99)

encounter for observation of newborn for suspected diseases and conditions ruled out (Z05.-)

neonatal jaundice from excessive hemolysis due to drugs or toxins transmitted from mother (P58.4)

newborn in contact with and (suspected) exposures hazardous to health not transmitted via placenta or breast milk (Z77.-)

Coding Clinic: 2016, Q4, P54

P04.0 **Newborn affected by maternal anesthesia and analgesia in pregnancy, labor and delivery**

⇒Newborn affected by reactions and intoxications from maternal opiates and tranquilizers administered for procedures during pregnancy or labor and delivery

▶ **Excludes2**   newborn affected by other maternal medication (P04.1-)

● **P04.1** **Newborn affected by other maternal medication**

~~Newborn affected by cancer chemotherapy~~
~~Newborn affected by cytotoxic drugs~~

▶ *Code first withdrawal symptoms from maternal use of drugs of addiction, if applicable (P96.1)*

Excludes1   dysmorphism due to warfarin (Q86.2)

fetal hydantoin syndrome (Q86.1)

~~maternal use of drugs of addiction (P04.4-)~~

▶ **Excludes2**   maternal anesthesia and analgesia in pregnancy, labor and delivery (P04.0)

maternal use of drugs of addiction (P04.4-)

▶ **P04.11** **Newborn affected by maternal antineoplastic chemotherapy**

▶ **P04.12** **Newborn affected by maternal cytotoxic drugs**

▶ **P04.13** **Newborn affected by maternal use of anticonvulsants**

▶ **P04.14** **Newborn affected by maternal use of opiates**

▶ **P04.15** **Newborn affected by maternal use of antidepressants**

▶ **P04.16** **Newborn affected by maternal use of amphetamines**

▶ **P04.17** **Newborn affected by maternal use of sedative-hypnotics**

▶ **P04.1A** **Newborn affected by maternal use of anxiolytics**

▶ **P04.18** **Newborn affected by other maternal medication**

▶ **P04.19** **Newborn affected by maternal use of unspecified medication**

Coding Clinic: 2016, Q4, P55

P04.2 **Newborn affected by maternal use of tobacco**

Newborn affected by exposure in utero to tobacco smoke

Excludes2   newborn exposure to environmental tobacco smoke (P96.81)

P04.3 **Newborn affected by maternal use of alcohol**

Excludes1   fetal alcohol syndrome (Q86.0)

● **P04.4** **Newborn affected by maternal use of drugs of addiction**

▶ **P04.40** **Newborn affected by maternal use of unspecified drugs of addiction**

P04.41 **Newborn affected by maternal use of cocaine**
"Crack baby"

▶ **P04.42** **Newborn affected by maternal use of hallucinogens**

▶ **Excludes2**   newborn affected by other maternal medication (P04.1-)

P04.49 **Newborn affected by maternal use of other drugs of addiction**

Excludes2   newborn affected by maternal anesthesia and analgesia (P04.0)

withdrawal symptoms from maternal use of drugs of addiction (P96.1)

P04.5 **Newborn affected by maternal use of nutritional chemical substances**

P04.6 **Newborn affected by maternal exposure to environmental chemical substances**

● **P04.8** **Newborn affected by other maternal noxious substances**

▶ **P04.81** **Newborn affected by maternal use of cannabis**

▶ **P04.89** **Newborn affected by other maternal noxious substances**

P04.9 **Newborn affected by maternal noxious substance, unspecified**

OGCR Section I.C.16.d.

Prematurity and Fetal Growth Retardation

Providers utilize different criteria in determining prematurity. A code for prematurity should not be assigned unless it is documented. Assignment of codes in categories P05, Disorders of newborn related to slow fetal growth and fetal malnutrition, and P07, Disorders of newborn related to short gestation and low birth weight, not elsewhere classified, should be based on the recorded birth weight and estimated gestational age.

When both birth weight and gestational age are available, two codes from category P07 should be assigned, with the code for birth weight sequenced before the code for gestational age.

DISORDERS OF NEWBORN RELATED TO LENGTH OF GESTATION AND FETAL GROWTH (P05-P08)

● **P05** **Disorders of newborn related to slow fetal growth and fetal malnutrition**

Coding Clinic: 2016, Q4, P56

● **P05.0** **Newborn light for gestational age**

Newborn light-for-dates

Weight below but length above 10th percentile for gestational age

P05.00 **Newborn light for gestational age, unspecified weight**

P05.01 **Newborn light for gestational age, less than 500 grams**

P05.02 **Newborn light for gestational age, 500-749 grams**

P05.03 **Newborn light for gestational age, 750-999 grams**

P05.04 **Newborn light for gestational age, 1000-1249 grams**

P05.05 **Newborn light for gestational age, 1250-1499 grams**

P05.06 **Newborn light for gestational age, 1500-1749 grams**

P05.07 **Newborn light for gestational age, 1750-1999 grams**

P05.08 **Newborn light for gestational age, 2000-2499 grams**

P05.09 **Newborn light for gestational age, 2500 grams and over**

Newborn light for gestational age, other

Coding Clinic: 2016, Q4, P55

▶ New   ⇒ Revised   ~~deleted~~ Deleted   Excludes 1   Excludes 2   Includes   Use additional   Code first   Code also   Key words

OGCR Official Guidelines   X Assign placeholder X   ● Use Additional Character(s)   ▶ Manifestation Code   **Coding Clinic**

● **P05.1**   **Newborn small for gestational age**
       Newborn small-and-light-for-dates
       Newborn small-for-dates
       Weight and length below 10th percentile for gestational age

     P05.10   **Newborn small for gestational age, unspecified weight**

     P05.11   **Newborn small for gestational age, less than 500 grams**

     P05.12   **Newborn small for gestational age, 500-749 grams**

     P05.13   **Newborn small for gestational age, 750-999 grams**

     P05.14   **Newborn small for gestational age, 1000-1249 grams**

     P05.15   **Newborn small for gestational age, 1250-1499 grams**

     P05.16   **Newborn small for gestational age, 1500-1749 grams**

     P05.17   **Newborn small for gestational age, 1750-1999 grams**

     P05.18   **Newborn small for gestational age, 2000-2499 grams**

     P05.19   **Newborn small for gestational age, other**
         Newborn small for gestational age, 2500 grams and over
         Coding Clinic: 2016, Q4, P55

● **P05.2**   **Newborn affected by fetal (intrauterine) malnutrition not light or small for gestational age**
       Infant, not light or small for gestational age, showing signs of fetal malnutrition, such as dry, peeling skin and loss of subcutaneous tissue

     Excludes1   newborn affected by fetal malnutrition with light for gestational age (P05.0-)
            newborn affected by fetal malnutrition with small for gestational age (P05.1-)

P05.9   **Newborn affected by slow intrauterine growth, unspecified**
       Newborn affected by fetal growth retardation NOS

● **P07**   **Disorders of newborn related to short gestation and low birth weight, not elsewhere classified**
     Note: When both birth weight and gestational age of the newborn are available, both should be coded with birth weight sequenced before gestational age.

     Includes   the listed conditions, without further specification, as the cause of morbidity or additional care, in newborn

● **P07.0**   **Extremely low birth weight newborn**
       Newborn birth weight 999 g. or less

     Excludes1   low birth weight due to slow fetal growth and fetal malnutrition (P05.-)

     P07.00   **Extremely low birth weight newborn, unspecified weight**

     P07.01   **Extremely low birth weight newborn, less than 500 grams**

     P07.02   **Extremely low birth weight newborn, 500-749 grams**

     P07.03   **Extremely low birth weight newborn, 750-999 grams**

● **P07.1**   **Other low birth weight newborn**
       Newborn birth weight 1000-2499 g.

     Excludes1   low birth weight due to slow fetal growth and fetal malnutrition (P05.-)

     P07.10   **Other low birth weight newborn, unspecified weight**

     P07.14   **Other low birth weight newborn, 1000-1249 grams**

     P07.15   **Other low birth weight newborn, 1250-1499 grams**

     P07.16   **Other low birth weight newborn, 1500-1749 grams**

     P07.17   **Other low birth weight newborn, 1750-1999 grams**

     P07.18   **Other low birth weight newborn, 2000-2499 grams**

● **P07.2**   **Extreme immaturity of newborn**
       Less than 28 completed weeks (less than 196 completed days) of gestation

     P07.20   **Extreme immaturity of newborn, unspecified weeks of gestation**
         Gestational age less than 28 completed weeks NOS

     P07.21   **Extreme immaturity of newborn, gestational age less than 23 completed weeks**
         Extreme immaturity of newborn, gestational age less than 23 weeks, 0 days

     P07.22   **Extreme immaturity of newborn, gestational age 23 completed weeks**
         Extreme immaturity of newborn, gestational age 23 weeks, 0 days through 23 weeks, 6 days

     P07.23   **Extreme immaturity of newborn, gestational age 24 completed weeks**
         Extreme immaturity of newborn, gestational age 24 weeks, 0 days through 24 weeks, 6 days

     P07.24   **Extreme immaturity of newborn, gestational age 25 completed weeks**
         Extreme immaturity of newborn, gestational age 25 weeks, 0 days through 25 weeks, 6 days

     P07.25   **Extreme immaturity of newborn, gestational age 26 completed weeks**
         Extreme immaturity of newborn, gestational age 26 weeks, 0 days through 26 weeks, 6 days

     P07.26   **Extreme immaturity of newborn, gestational age 27 completed weeks**
         Extreme immaturity of newborn, gestational age 27 weeks, 0 days through 27 weeks, 6 days

● **P07.3**   **Preterm [premature] newborn [other]**
       28 completed weeks or more but less than 37 completed weeks (196 completed days but less than 259 completed days) of gestation
       Prematurity NOS

     P07.30   **Preterm newborn, unspecified weeks of gestation**

     P07.31   **Preterm newborn, gestational age 28 completed weeks**
         Preterm newborn, gestational age 28 weeks, 0 days through 28 weeks, 6 days

     P07.32   **Preterm newborn, gestational age 29 completed weeks**
         Preterm newborn, gestational age 29 weeks, 0 days through 29 weeks, 6 days

CHAPTER 16 (P00-P96)

P07.33   Preterm newborn, gestational age 30 completed weeks
     Preterm newborn, gestational age 30 weeks, 0 days through 30 weeks, 6 days

P07.34   Preterm newborn, gestational age 31 completed weeks
     Preterm newborn, gestational age 31 weeks, 0 days through 31 weeks, 6 days

P07.35   Preterm newborn, gestational age 32 completed weeks
     Preterm newborn, gestational age 32 weeks, 0 days through 32 weeks, 6 days

P07.36   Preterm newborn, gestational age 33 completed weeks
     Preterm newborn, gestational age 33 weeks, 0 days through 33 weeks, 6 days

P07.37   Preterm newborn, gestational age 34 completed weeks
     Preterm newborn, gestational age 34 weeks, 0 days through 34 weeks, 6 days
     Coding Clinic: 2017, Q2, P7

P07.38   Preterm newborn, gestational age 35 completed weeks
     Preterm newborn, gestational age 35 weeks, 0 days through 35 weeks, 6 days

P07.39   Preterm newborn, gestational age 36 completed weeks
     Preterm newborn, gestational age 36 weeks, 0 days through 36 weeks, 6 days
     Coding Clinic: 2017, Q3, P26

● **P08   Disorders of newborn related to long gestation and high birth weight**
     Note: When both birth weight and gestational age of the newborn are available, priority of assignment should be given to birth weight.
     Includes   the listed conditions, without further specification, as causes of morbidity or additional care, in newborn

P08.0   Exceptionally large newborn baby
     Usually implies a birth weight of 4500 g. or more
     Excludes1   syndrome of infant of diabetic mother (P70.1)
         syndrome of infant of mother with gestational diabetes (P70.0)

P08.1   Other heavy for gestational age newborn
     Other newborn heavy- or large-for-dates regardless of period of gestation
     Usually implies a birth weight of 4000 g. to 4499 g.
     Excludes1   newborn with a birth weight of 4500 or more (P08.0)
         syndrome of infant of diabetic mother (P70.1)
         syndrome of infant of mother with gestational diabetes (P70.0)

● **P08.2   Late newborn, not heavy for gestational age**

P08.21   Post-term newborn
     Newborn with gestation period over 40 completed weeks to 42 completed weeks

P08.22   Prolonged gestation of newborn
     Newborn with gestation period over 42 completed weeks (294 days or more), not heavy- or large-for-dates
     Postmaturity NOS

ABNORMAL FINDINGS ON NEONATAL SCREENING (P09)

P09   Abnormal findings on neonatal screening
     Use additional code to identify signs, symptoms and conditions associated with the screening
     Excludes2   nonspecific serologic evidence of human immunodeficiency virus [HIV] (R75)

BIRTH TRAUMA (P10-P15)

● **P10   Intracranial laceration and hemorrhage due to birth injury**
     Excludes1   intracranial hemorrhage of newborn NOS (P52.9)
         intracranial hemorrhage of newborn due to anoxia or hypoxia (P52.-)
         nontraumatic intracranial hemorrhage of newborn (P52.-)

P10.0   Subdural hemorrhage due to birth injury
     Subdural hematoma (localized) due to birth injury
     Excludes1   subdural hemorrhage accompanying tentorial tear (P10.4)

P10.1   Cerebral hemorrhage due to birth injury

P10.2   Intraventricular hemorrhage due to birth injury

P10.3   Subarachnoid hemorrhage due to birth injury

P10.4   Tentorial tear due to birth injury
     Pertaining to tentorium of cerebellum (extension of dura mater that separates cerebellum from inferior portion of occipital lobes)

P10.8   Other intracranial lacerations and hemorrhages due to birth injury

P10.9   Unspecified intracranial laceration and hemorrhage due to birth injury

● **P11   Other birth injuries to central nervous system**

P11.0   Cerebral edema due to birth injury

P11.1   Other specified brain damage due to birth injury

P11.2   Unspecified brain damage due to birth injury

P11.3   Birth injury to facial nerve
     Facial palsy due to birth injury

P11.4   Birth injury to other cranial nerves

P11.5   Birth injury to spine and spinal cord
     Fracture of spine due to birth injury

P11.9   Birth injury to central nervous system, unspecified

● **P12   Birth injury to scalp**

P12.0   Cephalhematoma due to birth injury

P12.1   Chignon (from vacuum extraction) due to birth injury

P12.2   Epicranial subaponeurotic hemorrhage due to birth injury
     Subgaleal hemorrhage

P12.3   Bruising of scalp due to birth injury

P12.4   Injury of scalp of newborn due to monitoring equipment
     Sampling incision of scalp of newborn
     Scalp clip (electrode) injury of newborn

● **P12.8   Other birth injuries to scalp**

P12.81   Caput succedaneum

P12.89   Other birth injuries to scalp

P12.9   Birth injury to scalp, unspecified

● **P13   Birth injury to skeleton**
     Excludes2   birth injury to spine (P11.5)

P13.0   Fracture of skull due to birth injury

P13.1   Other birth injuries to skull
     Excludes1   cephalhematoma (P12.0)

P13.2   Birth injury to femur

P13.3   Birth injury to other long bones

P13.4   Fracture of clavicle due to birth injury

P13.8   Birth injuries to other parts of skeleton

P13.9   Birth injury to skeleton, unspecified

Item 16-1　The **peripheral nervous system** consists of 31 pairs of spinal nerves, 12 pairs of cranial nerves, and the autonomic nerves, which are divided into the parasympathetic and sympathetic nerves. The cranial nerves are: olfactory (I), optic (II), oculomotor (III), trochlear (IV), trigeminal (V), abducens (VI), facial (VII), vestibulocochlear (VIII), glossopharyngeal (IX), vagus (X), accessory (XI), and hypoglossal (XII).

Central
Nervous System

• Brain
• Spinal cord

Peripheral
Nervous System

• Cranial nerves (12)
• Spinal nerves
　cervical (8)
　thoracic (12)
　lumbar (5)
　sacral (5)
　coccyx (1)

Figure 16-1　The central nervous system consists of the brain and spinal cord. The peripheral nervous system consists of nerves that lie outside the skull and spinal cord. (From Stoy: Mosby's EMT-Basic Textbook, ed 2, St. Louis, Mosby, 2007)

● **P14**　Birth injury to peripheral nervous system
　　P14.0　Erb's paralysis due to birth injury
　　P14.1　Klumpke's paralysis due to birth injury
　　P14.2　Phrenic nerve paralysis due to birth injury
　　P14.3　Other brachial plexus birth injuries
　　P14.8　Birth injuries to other parts of peripheral nervous system
　　P14.9　Birth injury to peripheral nervous system, unspecified

● **P15**　Other birth injuries
　　P15.0　Birth injury to liver
　　　　Rupture of liver due to birth injury
　　P15.1　Birth injury to spleen
　　　　Rupture of spleen due to birth injury
　　P15.2　Sternomastoid injury due to birth injury
　　P15.3　Birth injury to eye
　　　　Subconjunctival hemorrhage due to birth injury
　　　　Traumatic glaucoma due to birth injury
　　P15.4　Birth injury to face
　　　　Facial congestion due to birth injury
　　P15.5　Birth injury to external genitalia
　　P15.6　Subcutaneous fat necrosis due to birth injury
　　P15.8　Other specified birth injuries
　　P15.9　Birth injury, unspecified

RESPIRATORY AND CARDIOVASCULAR DISORDERS SPECIFIC TO THE PERINATAL PERIOD (P19-P29)

● **P19**　Metabolic acidemia in newborn
　　Includes　　metabolic acidemia in newborn
　　P19.0　Metabolic acidemia in newborn first noted before onset of labor
　　P19.1　Metabolic acidemia in newborn first noted during labor
　　P19.2　Metabolic acidemia noted at birth
　　P19.9　Metabolic acidemia, unspecified

● **P22**　Respiratory distress of newborn
　　Excludes1　　respiratory arrest of newborn (P28.81)
　　　　　　respiratory failure of newborn NOS (P28.5)
　　P22.0　Respiratory distress syndrome of newborn
　　　　Cardiorespiratory distress syndrome of newborn
　　　　Hyaline membrane disease
　　　　Idiopathic respiratory distress syndrome [IRDS or RDS] of newborn
　　　　Pulmonary hypoperfusion syndrome
　　　　Respiratory distress syndrome, type I
　　P22.1　Transient tachypnea of newborn
　　　　Idiopathic tachypnea of newborn
　　　　Respiratory distress syndrome, type II
　　　　Wet lung syndrome
　　P22.8　Other respiratory distress of newborn
　　P22.9　Respiratory distress of newborn, unspecified

● **P23**　Congenital pneumonia
　　Includes　　infective pneumonia acquired in utero or during birth
　　Excludes1　　neonatal pneumonia resulting from aspiration (P24.-)
　　P23.0　Congenital pneumonia due to viral agent
　　　　Use additional code (B97) to identify organism
　　　　Excludes1　　congenital rubella pneumonitis (P35.0)
　　P23.1　Congenital pneumonia due to Chlamydia
　　P23.2　Congenital pneumonia due to staphylococcus
　　P23.3　Congenital pneumonia due to streptococcus, group B
　　P23.4　Congenital pneumonia due to Escherichia coli
　　P23.5　Congenital pneumonia due to Pseudomonas
　　P23.6　Congenital pneumonia due to other bacterial agents
　　　　Congenital pneumonia due to Hemophilus influenzae
　　　　Congenital pneumonia due to Klebsiella pneumoniae
　　　　Congenital pneumonia due to Mycoplasma
　　　　Congenital pneumonia due to Streptococcus, except group B
　　　　Use additional code (B95-B96) to identify organism
　　P23.8　Congenital pneumonia due to other organisms
　　P23.9　Congenital pneumonia, unspecified

● **P24**　Neonatal aspiration
　　Includes　　aspiration in utero and during delivery
● 　**P24.0**　Meconium aspiration
　　　　Excludes1　　meconium passage (without aspiration) during delivery (P03.82)
　　　　　　meconium staining (P96.83)
　　　　P24.00　Meconium aspiration without respiratory symptoms
　　　　　　Meconium aspiration NOS
　　　　P24.01　Meconium aspiration with respiratory symptoms
　　　　　　Meconium aspiration pneumonia
　　　　　　Meconium aspiration pneumonitis
　　　　　　Meconium aspiration syndrome NOS
　　　　　　Use additional code to identify any secondary pulmonary hypertension, if applicable (I27.2-)

CHAPTER 16 (P00-P96)

CHAPTER 16 (P00–P96)

● **P24.1 Neonatal aspiration of (clear) amniotic fluid and mucus**
Neonatal aspiration of liquor (amnii)

    P24.10 Neonatal aspiration of (clear) amniotic fluid and mucus without respiratory symptoms
        Neonatal aspiration of amniotic fluid and mucus NOS

    P24.11 Neonatal aspiration of (clear) amniotic fluid and mucus with respiratory symptoms
        Neonatal aspiration of amniotic fluid and mucus with pneumonia
        Neonatal aspiration of amniotic fluid and mucus with pneumonitis
        Use additional code to identify any secondary pulmonary hypertension, if applicable (I27.2-)

● **P24.2 Neonatal aspiration of blood**

    P24.20 Neonatal aspiration of blood without respiratory symptoms
        Neonatal aspiration of blood NOS

    P24.21 Neonatal aspiration of blood with respiratory symptoms
        Neonatal aspiration of blood with pneumonia
        Neonatal aspiration of blood with pneumonitis
        Use additional code to identify any secondary pulmonary hypertension, if applicable (I27.2-)

● **P24.3 Neonatal aspiration of milk and regurgitated food**
Neonatal aspiration of stomach contents

    P24.30 Neonatal aspiration of milk and regurgitated food without respiratory symptoms
        Neonatal aspiration of milk and regurgitated food NOS

    P24.31 Neonatal aspiration of milk and regurgitated food with respiratory symptoms
        Neonatal aspiration of milk and regurgitated food with pneumonia
        Neonatal aspiration of milk and regurgitated food with pneumonitis
        Use additional code to identify any secondary pulmonary hypertension, if applicable (I27.2-)

● **P24.8 Other neonatal aspiration**

    P24.80 Other neonatal aspiration without respiratory symptoms
        Neonatal aspiration NEC

    P24.81 Other neonatal aspiration with respiratory symptoms
        Neonatal aspiration pneumonia NEC
        Neonatal aspiration with pneumonitis NEC
        Neonatal aspiration with pneumonia NOS
        Neonatal aspiration with pneumonitis NOS
        Use additional code to identify any secondary pulmonary hypertension, if applicable (I27.2-)

    P24.9 Neonatal aspiration, unspecified

● **P25 Interstitial emphysema and related conditions originating in the perinatal period**

    P25.0 Interstitial emphysema originating in the perinatal period

    P25.1 Pneumothorax originating in the perinatal period

    P25.2 Pneumomediastinum originating in the perinatal period

    P25.3 Pneumopericardium originating in the perinatal period

    P25.8 Other conditions related to interstitial emphysema originating in the perinatal period

● **P26 Pulmonary hemorrhage originating in the perinatal period**
    Excludes1   acute idiopathic hemorrhage in infants over 28 days old (R04.81)

    P26.0 Tracheobronchial hemorrhage originating in the perinatal period

    P26.1 Massive pulmonary hemorrhage originating in the perinatal period

    P26.8 Other pulmonary hemorrhages originating in the perinatal period

    P26.9 Unspecified pulmonary hemorrhage originating in the perinatal period

● **P27 Chronic respiratory disease originating in the perinatal period**
    Excludes2   respiratory distress of newborn (P22.0-P22.9)

    P27.0 Wilson-Mikity syndrome
        Pulmonary dysmaturity

    P27.1 Bronchopulmonary dysplasia originating in the perinatal period

    P27.8 Other chronic respiratory diseases originating in the perinatal period
        Congenital pulmonary fibrosis
        Ventilator lung in newborn

    P27.9 Unspecified chronic respiratory disease originating in the perinatal period

● **P28 Other respiratory conditions originating in the perinatal period**
    Excludes1   congenital malformations of the respiratory system (Q30-Q34)

    P28.0 Primary atelectasis of newborn
        Failure of lungs to expand properly at birth
        Primary failure to expand terminal respiratory units
        Pulmonary hypoplasia associated with short gestation
        Pulmonary immaturity NOS

● **P28.1 Other and unspecified atelectasis of newborn**

    P28.10 Unspecified atelectasis of newborn
        Atelectasis of newborn NOS

    P28.11 Resorption atelectasis without respiratory distress syndrome
        Excludes1   resorption atelectasis with respiratory distress syndrome (P22.0)

    P28.19 Other atelectasis of newborn
        Partial atelectasis of newborn
        Secondary atelectasis of newborn

    P28.2 Cyanotic attacks of newborn
        Excludes1   apnea of newborn (P28.3-P28.4)

    P28.3 Primary sleep apnea of newborn
        Central sleep apnea of newborn
        Obstructive sleep apnea of newborn
        Sleep apnea of newborn NOS

    P28.4 Other apnea of newborn
        Apnea of prematurity
        Obstructive apnea of newborn
        Excludes1   obstructive sleep apnea of newborn (P28.3)

    P28.5 Respiratory failure of newborn
        Excludes1   respiratory arrest of newborn (P28.81)
                     respiratory distress of newborn (P22.0-)

● **P28.8 Other specified respiratory conditions of newborn**

    P28.81 Respiratory arrest of newborn
        Coding Clinic: 2017, Q2, P6

    P28.89 Other specified respiratory conditions of newborn
        Congenital laryngeal stridor
        Sniffles in newborn
        Snuffles in newborn
        Excludes1   early congenital syphilitic rhinitis (A50.05)

    P28.9 Respiratory condition of newborn, unspecified
        Respiratory depression in newborn

▶ New   ⇒ Revised   ~~deleted~~ Deleted   Excludes 1   Excludes 2   Includes   Use additional   Code first   Code also   Key words
OGCR Official Guidelines   X Assign placeholder X   ● Use Additional Character(s)   ▌ Manifestation Code   **Coding Clinic**

● **P29**   **Cardiovascular disorders originating in the perinatal period**
> **Excludes1**   congenital malformations of the circulatory system (Q20-Q28)

   P29.0   **Neonatal cardiac failure**

● **P29.1**   **Neonatal cardiac dysrhythmia**
     P29.11   Neonatal tachycardia
     P29.12   Neonatal bradycardia

   P29.2   **Neonatal hypertension**

● **P29.3**   **Persistent fetal circulation**
     P29.30   Pulmonary hypertension of newborn
           Persistent pulmonary hypertension of newborn
     P29.38   Other persistent fetal circulation
           Delayed closure of ductus arteriosus

   P29.4   **Transient myocardial ischemia in newborn**

● **P29.8**   **Other cardiovascular disorders originating in the perinatal period**
     P29.81   Cardiac arrest of newborn
     P29.89   Other cardiovascular disorders originating in the perinatal period

   P29.9   **Cardiovascular disorder originating in the perinatal period, unspecified**

INFECTIONS SPECIFIC TO THE PERINATAL PERIOD (P35-P39)

Infections acquired in utero, during birth via the umbilicus, or during the first 28 days after birth

> **Excludes2**   asymptomatic human immunodeficiency virus [HIV] infection status (Z21)
> congenital gonococcal infection (A54.-)
> congenital pneumonia (P23.-)
> congenital syphilis (A50.-)
> human immunodeficiency virus [HIV] disease (B20)
> infant botulism (A48.51)
> infectious diseases not specific to the perinatal period (A00-B99, J09, J10.-)
> intestinal infectious disease (A00-A09)
> laboratory evidence of human immunodeficiency virus [HIV] (R75)
> tetanus neonatorum (A33)

● **P35**   **Congenital viral diseases**
> **Includes**   infections acquired in utero or during birth

   P35.0   **Congenital rubella syndrome**
      Congenital rubella pneumonitis

   P35.1   **Congenital cytomegalovirus infection**
      Viruses transmitted by multiple routes that cause mild/subclinical infection

   P35.2   **Congenital herpesviral [herpes simplex] infection**

   P35.3   **Congenital viral hepatitis**

▶ **P35.4**   **Congenital Zika virus disease**
     ▶ Use additional code to identify manifestations of congenital Zika virus disease

   P35.8   **Other congenital viral diseases**
      Congenital varicella [chickenpox]
      Coding Clinic: 2016, Q4, P7

   P35.9   **Congenital viral disease, unspecified**

● **P36**   **Bacterial sepsis of newborn**
> **Includes**   congenital sepsis
> Use additional code(s), if applicable, to identify severe sepsis (R65.2-) and associated acute organ dysfunction(s)

   P36.0   **Sepsis of newborn due to streptococcus, group B**

● **P36.1**   **Sepsis of newborn due to other and unspecified streptococci**
     P36.10   Sepsis of newborn due to unspecified streptococci
     P36.19   Sepsis of newborn due to other streptococci

   P36.2   **Sepsis of newborn due to Staphylococcus aureus**

● **P36.3**   **Sepsis of newborn due to other and unspecified staphylococci**
     P36.30   Sepsis of newborn due to unspecified staphylococci
     P36.39   Sepsis of newborn due to other staphylococci

   P36.4   **Sepsis of newborn due to Escherichia coli**

   P36.5   **Sepsis of newborn due to anaerobes**

   P36.8   **Other bacterial sepsis of newborn**
      Use additional code from category B96 to identify organism

   P36.9   **Bacterial sepsis of newborn, unspecified**

● **P37**   **Other congenital infectious and parasitic diseases**
> **Excludes2**   congenital syphilis (A50.-)
> infectious neonatal diarrhea (A00-A09)
> necrotizing enterocolitis in newborn (P77.-)
> noninfectious neonatal diarrhea (P78.3)
> ophthalmia neonatorum due to gonococcus (A54.31)
> tetanus neonatorum (A33)

   P37.0   **Congenital tuberculosis**

   P37.1   **Congenital toxoplasmosis**
      Parasitic infection, often causing mild flu-like illness
      Hydrocephalus due to congenital toxoplasmosis

   P37.2   **Neonatal (disseminated) listeriosis**
      Acquired transplacentally or during/after parturition in which symptoms are those of sepsis

   P37.3   **Congenital falciparum malaria**

   P37.4   **Other congenital malaria**

   P37.5   **Neonatal candidiasis**

   P37.8   **Other specified congenital infectious and parasitic diseases**

   P37.9   **Congenital infectious or parasitic disease, unspecified**

● **P38**   **Omphalitis of newborn**
     Inflammation of umbilicus
> **Excludes1**   omphalitis not of newborn (L08.82)
> tetanus omphalitis (A33)
> umbilical hemorrhage of newborn (P51.-)

   P38.1   **Omphalitis with mild hemorrhage**

   P38.9   **Omphalitis without hemorrhage**
      Omphalitis of newborn NOS

● **P39**   **Other infections specific to the perinatal period**
     Use additional code to identify organism or specific infection

   P39.0   **Neonatal infective mastitis**
> **Excludes1**   breast engorgement of newborn (P83.4)
> noninfective mastitis of newborn (P83.4)

   P39.1   **Neonatal conjunctivitis and dacryocystitis**
      Neonatal chlamydial conjunctivitis
      Ophthalmia neonatorum NOS
      Neonate = newborn
> **Excludes1**   gonococcal conjunctivitis (A54.31)

   P39.2   **Intra-amniotic infection affecting newborn, not elsewhere classified**

   P39.3   **Neonatal urinary tract infection**

   P39.4   **Neonatal skin infection**
      Neonatal pyoderma
> **Excludes1**   pemphigus neonatorum (L00)
> staphylococcal scalded skin syndrome (L00)

   P39.8   **Other specified infections specific to the perinatal period**

   P39.9   **Infection specific to the perinatal period, unspecified**

HEMORRHAGIC AND HEMATOLOGICAL DISORDERS OF NEWBORN (P50-P61)

Excludes1 congenital stenosis and stricture of bile ducts (Q44.3)
Crigler-Najjar syndrome (E80.5)
Dubin-Johnson syndrome (E80.6)
Gilbert syndrome (E80.4)
hereditary hemolytic anemias (D55-D58)

● **P50** **Newborn affected by intrauterine (fetal) blood loss**
Excludes1 congenital anemia from intrauterine (fetal) blood loss (P61.3)

P50.0 **Newborn affected by intrauterine (fetal) blood loss from vasa previa**

P50.1 **Newborn affected by intrauterine (fetal) blood loss from ruptured cord**

P50.2 **Newborn affected by intrauterine (fetal) blood loss from placenta**

P50.3 **Newborn affected by hemorrhage into co-twin**

P50.4 **Newborn affected by hemorrhage into maternal circulation**

P50.5 **Newborn affected by intrauterine (fetal) blood loss from cut end of co-twin's cord**

P50.8 **Newborn affected by other intrauterine (fetal) blood loss**

P50.9 **Newborn affected by intrauterine (fetal) blood loss, unspecified**
Newborn affected by fetal hemorrhage NOS

● **P51** **Umbilical hemorrhage of newborn**
Excludes1 omphalitis with mild hemorrhage (P38.1)
umbilical hemorrhage from cut end of co-twins cord (P50.5)

P51.0 **Massive umbilical hemorrhage of newborn**

P51.8 **Other umbilical hemorrhages of newborn**
Slipped umbilical ligature NOS

P51.9 **Umbilical hemorrhage of newborn, unspecified**

● **P52** **Intracranial nontraumatic hemorrhage of newborn**
Includes intracranial hemorrhage due to anoxia or hypoxia
Excludes1 intracranial hemorrhage due to birth injury (P10.-)
intracranial hemorrhage due to other injury (S06.-)

P52.0 **Intraventricular (nontraumatic) hemorrhage, grade 1, of newborn**
Subependymal hemorrhage (without intraventricular extension)
Bleeding into germinal matrix

P52.1 **Intraventricular (nontraumatic) hemorrhage, grade 2, of newborn**
Subependymal hemorrhage with intraventricular extension
Bleeding into ventricle

● **P52.2** **Intraventricular (nontraumatic) hemorrhage, grade 3 and grade 4, of newborn**

P52.21 **Intraventricular (nontraumatic) hemorrhage, grade 3, of newborn**
Subependymal hemorrhage with intraventricular extension with enlargement of ventricle

P52.22 **Intraventricular (nontraumatic) hemorrhage, grade 4, of newborn**
Bleeding into cerebral cortex
Subependymal hemorrhage with intracerebral extension

P52.3 **Unspecified intraventricular (nontraumatic) hemorrhage of newborn**

P52.4 **Intracerebral (nontraumatic) hemorrhage of newborn**

P52.5 **Subarachnoid (nontraumatic) hemorrhage of newborn**

P52.6 **Cerebellar (nontraumatic) and posterior fossa hemorrhage of newborn**

P52.8 **Other intracranial (nontraumatic) hemorrhages of newborn**

P52.9 **Intracranial (nontraumatic) hemorrhage of newborn, unspecified**

P53 **Hemorrhagic disease of newborn**
Vitamin K deficiency of newborn

● **P54** **Other neonatal hemorrhages**
Excludes1 newborn affected by (intrauterine) blood loss (P50.-)
pulmonary hemorrhage originating in the perinatal period (P26.-)

P54.0 **Neonatal hematemesis**
Vomiting of blood
Excludes1 neonatal hematemesis due to swallowed maternal blood (P78.2)

P54.1 **Neonatal melena**
Dark-colored feces stained with blood pigments
Excludes1 neonatal melena due to swallowed maternal blood (P78.2)

P54.2 **Neonatal rectal hemorrhage**

P54.3 **Other neonatal gastrointestinal hemorrhage**

P54.4 **Neonatal adrenal hemorrhage**

P54.5 **Neonatal cutaneous hemorrhage**
Neonatal bruising
Neonatal ecchymoses
Neonatal petechiae
Neonatal superficial hematomata
Excludes2 bruising of scalp due to birth injury (P12.3)
cephalhematoma due to birth injury (P12.0)

P54.6 **Neonatal vaginal hemorrhage** ♀
Neonatal pseudomenses

P54.8 **Other specified neonatal hemorrhages**

P54.9 **Neonatal hemorrhage, unspecified**

● **P55** **Hemolytic disease of newborn**
AKA erythroblastosis fetalis and is due to Rh isoimmunization, result of Rh blood factor incompatibilities between mother (Rh negative) and fetus (Rh positive)

P55.0 **Rh isoimmunization of newborn**

P55.1 **ABO isoimmunization of newborn**
Coding Clinic: 2015, Q3, P20

P55.8 **Other hemolytic diseases of newborn**

P55.9 **Hemolytic disease of newborn, unspecified**

● **P56** **Hydrops fetalis due to hemolytic disease**
Caused by maternal sensitization to fetal blood group antigen
Excludes1 hydrops fetalis NOS (P83.2)

P56.0 **Hydrops fetalis due to isoimmunization**

● **P56.9** **Hydrops fetalis due to other and unspecified hemolytic disease**

P56.90 **Hydrops fetalis due to unspecified hemolytic disease**

P56.99 **Hydrops fetalis due to other hemolytic disease**

● **P57** **Kernicterus**
High levels of bilirubin in blood, with severe neural symptoms

P57.0 **Kernicterus due to isoimmunization**

P57.8 **Other specified kernicterus**
Excludes1 Crigler-Najjar syndrome (E80.5)

P57.9 **Kernicterus, unspecified**

● **P58** **Neonatal jaundice due to other excessive hemolysis**

    Excludes1   jaundice due to isoimmunization (P55-P57)

    P58.0 **Neonatal jaundice due to bruising**

    P58.1 **Neonatal jaundice due to bleeding**

    P58.2 **Neonatal jaundice due to infection**

    P58.3 **Neonatal jaundice due to polycythemia**

●   **P58.4** **Neonatal jaundice due to drugs or toxins transmitted from mother or given to newborn**

        Code first poisoning due to drug or toxin, if applicable (T36-T65 with fifth or sixth character 1-4 or 6)

        Use additional code for adverse effect, if applicable, to identify drug (T36-T50 with fifth or sixth character 5)

        P58.41 **Neonatal jaundice due to drugs or toxins transmitted from mother**

        P58.42 **Neonatal jaundice due to drugs or toxins given to newborn**

    P58.5 **Neonatal jaundice due to swallowed maternal blood**

    P58.8 **Neonatal jaundice due to other specified excessive hemolysis**

    P58.9 **Neonatal jaundice due to excessive hemolysis, unspecified**

● **P59** **Neonatal jaundice from other and unspecified causes**

    Excludes1   jaundice due to inborn errors of metabolism (E70-E88)

                kernicterus (P57.-)

    P59.0 **Neonatal jaundice associated with preterm delivery**

        Hyperbilirubinemia of prematurity

        Jaundice due to delayed conjugation associated with preterm delivery

    P59.1 **Inspissated bile syndrome**

●   **P59.2** **Neonatal jaundice from other and unspecified hepatocellular damage**

        Excludes1   congenital viral hepatitis (P35.3)

        P59.20 **Neonatal jaundice from unspecified hepatocellular damage**

        P59.29 **Neonatal jaundice from other hepatocellular damage**

            Neonatal giant cell hepatitis

            Neonatal (idiopathic) hepatitis

    P59.3 **Neonatal jaundice from breast milk inhibitor**

    P59.8 **Neonatal jaundice from other specified causes**

    P59.9 **Neonatal jaundice, unspecified**

        Neonatal physiological jaundice (intense)(prolonged) NOS

        Coding Clinic: 2015, Q3, P20

  P60 **Disseminated intravascular coagulation of newborn**

    Defibrination syndrome of newborn

● **P61** **Other perinatal hematological disorders**

    Excludes1   transient hypogammaglobulinemia of infancy (D80.7)

    P61.0 **Transient neonatal thrombocytopenia**

        Lack of sufficient numbers of circulating thrombocytes (platelets)

        Neonatal thrombocytopenia due to exchange transfusion

        Neonatal thrombocytopenia due to idiopathic maternal thrombocytopenia

        Neonatal thrombocytopenia due to isoimmunization

    P61.1 **Polycythemia neonatorum**

        Neonate = newborn

    P61.2 **Anemia of prematurity**

    P61.3 **Congenital anemia from fetal blood loss**

    P61.4 **Other congenital anemias, not elsewhere classified**

        Congenital anemia NOS

    P61.5 **Transient neonatal neutropenia**

        Low levels of granulocytic neutrophilic white blood cells

        Excludes1   congenital neutropenia (nontransient) (D70.0)

    P61.6 **Other transient neonatal disorders of coagulation**

    P61.8 **Other specified perinatal hematological disorders**

    P61.9 **Perinatal hematological disorder, unspecified**

TRANSITORY ENDOCRINE AND METABOLIC DISORDERS SPECIFIC TO NEWBORN (P70-P74)

    Includes   transitory endocrine and metabolic disturbances caused by the infant's response to maternal endocrine and metabolic factors, or its adjustment to extrauterine environment

● **P70** **Transitory disorders of carbohydrate metabolism specific to newborn**

    P70.0 **Syndrome of infant of mother with gestational diabetes**

        Newborn (with hypoglycemia) affected by maternal gestational diabetes

        Excludes1   newborn (with hypoglycemia) affected by maternal (pre-existing) diabetes mellitus (P70.1)

                syndrome of infant of a diabetic mother (P70.1)

    P70.1 **Syndrome of infant of a diabetic mother**

        Newborn (with hypoglycemia) affected by maternal (pre-existing) diabetes mellitus

        Excludes1   newborn (with hypoglycemia) affected by maternal gestational diabetes (P70.0)

                syndrome of infant of mother with gestational diabetes (P70.0)

    P70.2 **Neonatal diabetes mellitus**

    P70.3 **Iatrogenic neonatal hypoglycemia**

    P70.4 **Other neonatal hypoglycemia**

        Transitory neonatal hypoglycemia

    P70.8 **Other transitory disorders of carbohydrate metabolism of newborn**

    P70.9 **Transitory disorder of carbohydrate metabolism of newborn, unspecified**

● **P71** **Transitory neonatal disorders of calcium and magnesium metabolism**

    P71.0 **Cow's milk hypocalcemia in newborn**

    P71.1 **Other neonatal hypocalcemia**

        Excludes1   neonatal hypoparathyroidism (P71.4)

    P71.2 **Neonatal hypomagnesemia**

    P71.3 **Neonatal tetany without calcium or magnesium deficiency**

        Neonatal tetany NOS

    P71.4 **Transitory neonatal hypoparathyroidism**

    P71.8 **Other transitory neonatal disorders of calcium and magnesium metabolism**

        Coding Clinic: 2016, Q4, P55

    P71.9 **Transitory neonatal disorder of calcium and magnesium metabolism, unspecified**

● **P72** **Other transitory neonatal endocrine disorders**

    Excludes1   congenital hypothyroidism with or without goiter (E03.0-E03.1)

                dyshormogenetic goiter (E07.1)

                Pendred's syndrome (E07.1)

    P72.0 **Neonatal goiter, not elsewhere classified**

        Transitory congenital goiter with normal functioning

    P72.1 **Transitory neonatal hyperthyroidism**

        Neonatal thyrotoxicosis

    P72.2 **Other transitory neonatal disorders of thyroid function, not elsewhere classified**

        Transitory neonatal hypothyroidism

    P72.8 **Other specified transitory neonatal endocrine disorders**

    P72.9 **Transitory neonatal endocrine disorder, unspecified**

CHAPTER 16 (P00-P96)

CHAPTER 16 (P00-P96)

● **P74**   **Other transitory neonatal electrolyte and metabolic disturbances**

     P74.0   **Late metabolic acidosis of newborn**

         Excludes1   (fetal) metabolic acidosis of newborn (P19)

     P74.1   **Dehydration of newborn**

●   **P74.2**   **Disturbances of sodium balance of newborn**
         Coding Clinic: 2018, Q2, P6

     ▶ **P74.21**   **Hypernatremia of newborn**

     ▶ **P74.22**   **Hyponatremia of newborn**

●   **P74.3**   **Disturbances of potassium balance of newborn**

     ▶ **P74.31**   **Hyperkalemia of newborn**

     ▶ **P74.32**   **Hypokalemia of newborn**

●   **P74.4**   **Other transitory electrolyte disturbances of newborn**

     ▶ **P74.41**   **Alkalosis of newborn**
            Hyperbicarbonatemia

    ▶● **P74.42**   **Disturbances of chlorine balance of newborn**

       ▶ **P74.421**   **Hyperchloremia of newborn**
               Hyperchloremic metabolic acidosis

          ▶ **Excludes2**   late metabolic acidosis of the newborn (P77.0)

       ▶ **P74.422**   **Hypochloremia of newborn**

     ▶ **P74.49**   **Other transitory electrolyte disturbance of newborn**

     P74.5   **Transitory tyrosinemia of newborn**

     P74.6   **Transitory hyperammonemia of newborn**

     P74.8   **Other transitory metabolic disturbances of newborn**
          Amino-acid metabolic disorders described as transitory

     P74.9   **Transitory metabolic disturbance of newborn, unspecified**

DIGESTIVE SYSTEM DISORDERS OF NEWBORN (P76-P78)

● **P76**   **Other intestinal obstruction of newborn**

     P76.0   **Meconium plug syndrome**
          Fetal stool obstruction in large intestine, present at birth; may be symptom of organic disease.
          Meconium ileus NOS

         Excludes1   meconium ileus in cystic fibrosis (E84.11)

     P76.1   **Transitory ileus of newborn**
          Temporary obstruction of ileus (small intestine)

         Excludes1   Hirschsprung's disease (Q43.1)

     P76.2   **Intestinal obstruction due to inspissated milk**
          Being thickened, dried, or made less fluid

     P76.8   **Other specified intestinal obstruction of newborn**

         Excludes1   intestinal obstruction classifiable to K56.-

     P76.9   **Intestinal obstruction of newborn, unspecified**

● **P77**   **Necrotizing enterocolitis of newborn**

     P77.1   **Stage 1 necrotizing enterocolitis in newborn**
          Necrotizing enterocolitis without pneumatosis, without perforation

     P77.2   **Stage 2 necrotizing enterocolitis in newborn**
          Necrotizing enterocolitis with pneumatosis, without perforation

     P77.3   **Stage 3 necrotizing enterocolitis in newborn**
          Necrotizing enterocolitis with perforation
          Necrotizing enterocolitis with pneumatosis and perforation

     P77.9   **Necrotizing enterocolitis in newborn, unspecified**
          Necrotizing enterocolitis in newborn, NOS

● **P78**   **Other perinatal digestive system disorders**

         Excludes1   cystic fibrosis (E84.0-E84.9)
               neonatal gastrointestinal hemorrhages (P54.0-P54.3)

     P78.0   **Perinatal intestinal perforation**
          Meconium peritonitis

     P78.1   **Other neonatal peritonitis**
          Neonatal peritonitis NOS

     P78.2   **Neonatal hematemesis and melena due to swallowed maternal blood**

     P78.3   **Noninfective neonatal diarrhea**
          Neonatal diarrhea NOS

●   **P78.8**   **Other specified perinatal digestive system disorders**

       P78.81   **Congenital cirrhosis (of liver)**

       P78.82   **Peptic ulcer of newborn**

       P78.83   **Newborn esophageal reflux**
           Neonatal esophageal reflux

       P78.84   **Gestational alloimmune liver disease**
           GALD
           Neonatal hemochromatosis

         Excludes1   hemochromatosis (E83.11-)

       P78.89   **Other specified perinatal digestive system disorders**

     P78.9   **Perinatal digestive system disorder, unspecified**

CONDITIONS INVOLVING THE INTEGUMENT AND TEMPERATURE REGULATION OF NEWBORN (P80-P83)

● **P80**   **Hypothermia of newborn**

     P80.0   **Cold injury syndrome**
          Severe and usually chronic hypothermia associated with a pink flushed appearance, edema and neurological and biochemical abnormalities.

         Excludes1   mild hypothermia of newborn (P80.8)

     P80.8   **Other hypothermia of newborn**
          Mild hypothermia of newborn

     P80.9   **Hypothermia of newborn, unspecified**

● **P81**   **Other disturbances of temperature regulation of newborn**

     P81.0   **Environmental hyperthermia of newborn**

     P81.8   **Other specified disturbances of temperature regulation of newborn**

     P81.9   **Disturbance of temperature regulation of newborn, unspecified**
          Fever of newborn NOS

● **P83**   **Other conditions of integument specific to newborn**

         Excludes1   congenital malformations of skin and integument (Q80-Q84)
               hydrops fetalis due to hemolytic disease (P56.-)
               neonatal skin infection (P39.4)
               staphylococcal scalded skin syndrome (L00)

         Excludes2   cradle cap (L21.0)
               diaper [napkin] dermatitis (L22)

     P83.0   **Sclerema neonatorum**
          Neonate = newborn

     P83.1   **Neonatal erythema toxicum**
          Benign, generalized, transient pustules that become firm vesicles

     P83.2   **Hydrops fetalis not due to hemolytic disease**
          Severe, life-threatening problem of severe edema (swelling) as result of too much fluid leaving blood and entering tissue
          Hydrops fetalis NOS

● P83.3 **Other and unspecified edema specific to newborn**

    P83.30 Unspecified edema specific to newborn

    P83.39 Other edema specific to newborn

    P83.4 **Breast engorgement of newborn**
        Noninfective mastitis of newborn

    P83.5 **Congenital hydrocele** ♂

    P83.6 **Umbilical polyp of newborn**

● P83.8 **Other specified conditions of integument specific to newborn**

    P83.81 **Umbilical granuloma**

        Excludes2 Granulomatous disorder of the skin and subcutaneous tissue, unspecified (L92.9)

    P83.88 **Other specified conditions of integument specific to newborn**
        Bronze baby syndrome
        Neonatal scleroderma
        Urticaria neonatorum

    P83.9 **Condition of the integument specific to newborn, unspecified**

OTHER PROBLEMS WITH NEWBORN (P84)

P84 **Other problems with newborn**
    Acidemia of newborn
    Acidosis of newborn
    Anoxia of newborn NOS
    Asphyxia of newborn NOS
    Hypercapnia of newborn
    Hypoxemia of newborn
    Hypoxia of newborn NOS
    Mixed metabolic and respiratory acidosis of newborn

    Excludes1 intracranial hemorrhage due to anoxia or hypoxia (P52.-)
        hypoxic ischemic encephalopathy [HIE] (P91.6-)
        late metabolic acidosis of newborn (P74.0)

OTHER DISORDERS ORIGINATING IN THE PERINATAL PERIOD (P90-P96)

P90 **Convulsions of newborn**

    Excludes1 benign myoclonic epilepsy in infancy (G40.3-)
        benign neonatal convulsions (familial) (G40.3-)

● P91 **Other disturbances of cerebral status of newborn**

    P91.0 **Neonatal cerebral ischemia**

    P91.1 **Acquired periventricular cysts of newborn**

    P91.2 **Neonatal cerebral leukomalacia**
        Degeneration of white matter adjacent to cerebral ventricles following cerebral hypoxia or brain ischemia in neonates
        Periventricular leukomalacia

    P91.3 **Neonatal cerebral irritability**

    P91.4 **Neonatal cerebral depression**

    P91.5 **Neonatal coma**

● P91.6 **Hypoxic ischemic encephalopathy [HIE]**

    Excludes1 Neonatal cerebral depression (P91.4)
        Neonatal cerebral irritability (P91.3)
        Neonatal coma (P91.5)

    P91.60 **Hypoxic ischemic encephalopathy [HIE], unspecified**

    P91.61 **Mild hypoxic ischemic encephalopathy [HIE]**

    P91.62 **Moderate hypoxic ischemic encephalopathy [HIE]**

    P91.63 **Severe hypoxic ischemic encephalopathy [HIE]**

● P91.8 **Other specified disturbances of cerebral status of newborn**

    ● P91.81 **Neonatal encephalopathy**

        ▷ *P91.811 Neonatal encephalopathy in diseases classified elsewhere*

        Code first underlying condition, if known, such as:
        ➡congenital cirrhosis (of liver) (P78.81)
        intracranial nontraumatic hemorrhage of newborn (P52.-)
        kernicterus (P57.-)

        P91.819 **Neonatal encephalopathy, unspecified**

    P91.88 **Other specified disturbances of cerebral status of newborn**

    P91.9 **Disturbance of cerebral status of newborn, unspecified**

● P92 **Feeding problems of newborn**

    Excludes1 eating disorders (F50.-)
        feeding problems in child over 28 days old (R63.3)
    Coding Clinic: 2017, Q1, P28; 2016, Q3, P19

● P92.0 **Vomiting of newborn**

    Excludes1 vomiting of child over 28 days old (R11.-)

    P92.01 **Bilious vomiting of newborn**

        Excludes1 bilious vomiting in child over 28 days old (R11.14)

    P92.09 **Other vomiting of newborn**

        Excludes1 regurgitation of food in newborn (P92.1)

    P92.1 **Regurgitation and rumination of newborn**

    P92.2 **Slow feeding of newborn**

    P92.3 **Underfeeding of newborn**

    P92.4 **Overfeeding of newborn**

    P92.5 **Neonatal difficulty in feeding at breast**
        Coding Clinic: 2017, Q1, P28; 2016, Q3, P19

    P92.6 **Failure to thrive in newborn**

        Excludes1 failure to thrive in child over 28 days old (R62.51)

    P92.8 **Other feeding problems of newborn**

    P92.9 **Feeding problem of newborn, unspecified**

● P93 **Reactions and intoxications due to drugs administered to newborn**

    Includes reactions and intoxications due to drugs administered to fetus affecting newborn

    Excludes1 jaundice due to drugs or toxins transmitted from mother or given to newborn (P58.4-)
        ➡reactions and intoxications from maternal opiates, tranquilizers and other medication (P04.0-P04.1, P04.4-)
        withdrawal symptoms from maternal use of drugs of addiction (P96.1)
        withdrawal symptoms from therapeutic use of drugs in newborn (P96.2)

    P93.0 **Grey baby syndrome**
        Grey syndrome from chloramphenicol administration in newborn

    P93.8 **Other reactions and intoxications due to drugs administered to newborn**

        Use additional code for adverse effect, if applicable, to identify drug (T36-T50 with fifth or sixth character 5)

CHAPTER 16 (P00-P96)

● **P94   Disorders of muscle tone of newborn**

P94.0   Transient neonatal myasthenia gravis

> **Excludes1**   myasthenia gravis (G70.0)

P94.1   Congenital hypertonia

P94.2   Congenital hypotonia

> Floppy baby syndrome, unspecified

P94.8   Other disorders of muscle tone of newborn

P94.9   Disorder of muscle tone of newborn, unspecified

OGCR Section I.C.16.g.

> Stillbirth
>
> Code P95, Stillbirth, is only for use for institutions that maintain separate records for stillbirths. No other code should be used with P95. Code P95 should not be used on the mother's record.

P95   Stillbirth

> Deadborn fetus NOS
> Fetal death of unspecified cause
> Stillbirth NOS
>
> **Excludes1**   maternal care for intrauterine death (O36.4)
>   missed abortion (O02.1)
>   outcome of delivery, stillbirth (Z37.1, Z37.3, Z37.4, Z37.7)

● **P96   Other conditions originating in the perinatal period**

P96.0   Congenital renal failure

> Uremia of newborn

P96.1   Neonatal withdrawal symptoms from maternal use of drugs of addiction

> Drug withdrawal syndrome in infant of dependent mother
> Neonatal abstinence syndrome
>
> **Excludes1**   reactions and intoxications from maternal opiates and tranquilizers administered during labor and delivery (P04.0)

P96.2   Withdrawal symptoms from therapeutic use of drugs in newborn

P96.3   Wide cranial sutures of newborn

> Neonatal craniotabes

P96.5   Complication to newborn due to (fetal) intrauterine procedure

> **Excludes2**   newborn affected by amniocentesis (P00.6)

● **P96.8   Other specified conditions originating in the perinatal period**

P96.81   Exposure to (parental) (environmental) tobacco smoke in the perinatal period

> **Excludes2**   newborn affected by in utero exposure to tobacco (P04.2)
>   exposure to environmental tobacco smoke after the perinatal period (Z77.22)

P96.82   Delayed separation of umbilical cord

P96.83   Meconium staining

> **Excludes1**   meconium aspiration (P24.00, P24.01)
>   meconium passage during delivery (P03.82)

P96.89   Other specified conditions originating in the perinatal period

> Use additional code to specify condition

P96.9   Condition originating in the perinatal period, unspecified

> Congenital debility NOS

▶ New   ⟹ Revised   ~~deleted~~ Deleted   Excludes 1   Excludes 2   Includes   Use additional   Code first   Code also   Key words

OGCR Official Guidelines   X Assign placeholder X   ● Use Additional Character(s)   ▶ Manifestation Code   **Coding Clinic**

CHAPTER 17

CONGENITAL MALFORMATIONS, DEFORMATIONS, AND CHROMOSOMAL ABNORMALITIES (Q00–Q99)

OGCR Chapter-Specific Coding Guidelines

17. **Chapter 17: Congenital malformations, deformations, and chromosomal abnormalities (Q00-Q99)**
Assign an appropriate code(s) from categories Q00-Q99, Congenital malformations, deformations, and chromosomal abnormalities when a malformation/deformation or chromosomal abnormality is documented. A malformation/deformation/ or chromosomal abnormality may be the principal/first-listed diagnosis on a record or a secondary diagnosis.

When a malformation/deformation/or chromosomal abnormality does not have a unique code assignment, assign additional code(s) for any manifestations that may be present.

When the code assignment specifically identifies the malformation/deformation/or chromosomal abnormality, manifestations that are an inherent component of the anomaly should not be coded separately. Additional codes should be assigned for manifestations that are not an inherent component.

Codes from Chapter 17 may be used throughout the life of the patient. If a congenital malformation or deformity has been corrected, a personal history code should be used to identify the history of the malformation or deformity. Although present at birth, malformation/deformation/or chromosomal abnormality may not be identified until later in life. Whenever the condition is diagnosed by the physician, it is appropriate to assign a code from codes Q00-Q99.

For the birth admission, the appropriate code from category Z38, Liveborn infants, according to place of birth and type of delivery, should be sequenced as the principal diagnosis, followed by any congenital anomaly codes, Q00-Q99.

CHAPTER 17

CONGENITAL MALFORMATIONS, DEFORMATIONS, AND CHROMOSOMAL ABNORMALITIES (Q00–Q99)

➡ **Note:** Codes from this chapter are not for use on maternal records

Excludes2 inborn errors of metabolism (E70-E88)

This chapter contains the following blocks:

Q00-Q07	Congenital malformations of the nervous system
Q10-Q18	Congenital malformations of eye, ear, face and neck
Q20-Q28	Congenital malformations of the circulatory system
Q30-Q34	Congenital malformations of the respiratory system
Q35-Q37	Cleft lip and cleft palate
Q38-Q45	Other congenital malformations of the digestive system
Q50-Q56	Congenital malformations of genital organs
Q60-Q64	Congenital malformations of the urinary system
Q65-Q79	Congenital malformations and deformations of the musculoskeletal system
Q80-Q89	Other congenital malformations
Q90-Q99	Chromosomal abnormalities, not elsewhere classified

Figure 17-1 An infant with a large occipital encephalocele. The large skin-covered encephalocele is visible. (From Swaiman KF, Ashwal S, Ferriero DM: Pediatric Neurology: Principles and Practice, Philadelphia, Saunders, 2012)

CONGENITAL MALFORMATIONS OF THE NERVOUS SYSTEM (Q00–Q07)

● **Q00   Anencephaly and similar malformations**

Q00.0   Anencephaly
Absence of skull with cerebral hemispheres missing or reduced to small masses attached to base of cranium
Acephaly
Acrania
Amyelencephaly
Hemianencephaly
Hemicephaly

Q00.1   Craniorachischisis
Developmental anomaly consisting of fissure of cranium and vertebral column

Q00.2   Iniencephaly
Developmental anomaly characterized by enlargement of foramen magnum and absence of laminae and spinous processes of cervical, dorsal

● **Q01   Encephalocele**
Sac-like protrusions of brain and membranes visible through an opening in skull

Includes   Arnold-Chiari syndrome, type III
encephalocystocele
encephalomyelocele
hydroencephalocele
hydromeningocele, cranial
meningocele, cerebral
meningoencephalocele

Excludes1   Meckel-Gruber syndrome (Q61.9)

Q01.0   Frontal encephalocele
Q01.1   Nasofrontal encephalocele
Q01.2   Occipital encephalocele
Q01.8   Encephalocele of other sites
Q01.9   Encephalocele, unspecified

Q02   Microcephaly
Head size measures significantly below normal based on standardized charts

Includes   hydromicrocephaly
micrencephalon

▶ Use additional code, if applicable, to identify congenital Zika virus disease

Excludes1   Meckel-Gruber syndrome (Q61.9)

Coding Clinic: 2016, Q4, P7

● **Q03   Congenital hydrocephalus**
Accumulation of cerebrospinal fluid in ventricles resulting in swelling and enlargement

Includes   hydrocephalus in newborn
Excludes1   Arnold-Chiari syndrome, type II (Q07.0-)
acquired hydrocephalus (G91.-)
hydrocephalus due to congenital toxoplasmosis (P37.1)
hydrocephalus with spina bifida (Q05.0-Q05.4)

Q03.0   Malformations of aqueduct of Sylvius
Anomaly of aqueduct of Sylvius
Obstruction of aqueduct of Sylvius, congenital
Stenosis of aqueduct of Sylvius

Q03.1   Atresia of foramina of Magendie and Luschka
Dandy-Walker syndrome

Q03.8   Other congenital hydrocephalus

Q03.9   Congenital hydrocephalus, unspecified

● **Q04   Other congenital malformations of brain**

> **Excludes1**   cyclopia (Q87.0)
> macrocephaly (Q75.3)

Q04.0   Congenital malformations of corpus callosum
Agenesis of corpus callosum

Q04.1   Arhinencephaly
Congenital absence of olfactory bulbs, tract, or nerves

Q04.2   Holoprosencephaly
Failure of cleavage of forebrain (prosencephalon) resulting in incomplete or absent cortical separation and deficits in midline facial development

Q04.3   Other reduction deformities of brain
Absence of part of brain
Agenesis of part of brain
> *Cerebral cortex are not fully formed, brain surface is smooth*

Agyria
Aplasia of part of brain
Hydranencephaly
Hypoplasia of part of brain
Lissencephaly
> *Congenital malformation or absence of convolutions of cerebral cortex*

Microgyria
> *Malformation of brain characterized by excessive number of small convolutions (gyri) on surface*

Pachygyria
> *Reduction in number of sulci of cerebrum*

> **Excludes1**   congenital malformations of corpus callosum (Q04.0)

Q04.4   Septo-optic dysplasia of brain

Q04.5   Megalencephaly
Abnormally large brain

Q04.6   Congenital cerebral cysts
Porencephaly   Schizencephaly
> **Excludes1**   acquired porencephalic cyst (G93.0)

Q04.8   Other specified congenital malformations of brain
Arnold-Chiari syndrome, type IV
Macrogyria

Q04.9   Congenital malformation of brain, unspecified
Congenital anomaly NOS of brain
Congenital deformity NOS of brain
Congenital disease or lesion NOS of brain
Multiple anomalies NOS of brain, congenital

● **Q05   Spina bifida**

> *Developmental anomaly characterized by defective closure of vertebral arch, through which spinal cord and meninges may protrude*

> **Includes**   hydromeningocele (spinal)
> meningocele (spinal)
> meningomyelocele
> myelocele
> myelomeningocele
> rachischisis
> spina bifida (aperta)(cystica)
> syringomyelocele

Use additional code for any associated paraplegia (paraparesis) (G82.2-)

> **Excludes1**   Arnold-Chiari syndrome, type II (Q07.0-)
> spina bifida occulta (Q76.0)

Q05.0   Cervical spina bifida with hydrocephalus

Q05.1   Thoracic spina bifida with hydrocephalus
Dorsal spina bifida with hydrocephalus
Thoracolumbar spina bifida with hydrocephalus

Q05.2   Lumbar spina bifida with hydrocephalus
Lumbosacral spina bifida with hydrocephalus

Q05.3   Sacral spina bifida with hydrocephalus

Q05.4   Unspecified spina bifida with hydrocephalus

Q05.5   Cervical spina bifida without hydrocephalus

Q05.6   Thoracic spina bifida without hydrocephalus
Dorsal spina bifida NOS
Thoracolumbar spina bifida NOS

Q05.7   Lumbar spina bifida without hydrocephalus
Lumbosacral spina bifida NOS

Q05.8   Sacral spina bifida without hydrocephalus

Q05.9   Spina bifida, unspecified

● **Q06   Other congenital malformations of spinal cord**

Q06.0   Amyelia
Congenital absence of spinal cord

Q06.1   Hypoplasia and dysplasia of spinal cord
Underdevelopment of spinal cord
Atelomyelia
> *Congenitally incomplete development of spinal cord*

Myelatelia
Myelodysplasia of spinal cord
> *Defective development of spinal cord, especially lower segments*

Q06.2   Diastematomyelia
Congenital anomaly, associated with spina bifida, in which spinal cord is split into halves and surrounded by dural sac

Q06.3   Other congenital cauda equina malformations

Q06.4   Hydromyelia
Dilation of central canal of spinal cord with increased fluid accumulation
Hydrorachis

Q06.8   Other specified congenital malformations of spinal cord

Q06.9   Congenital malformation of spinal cord, unspecified
Congenital anomaly NOS of spinal cord
Congenital deformity NOS of spinal cord
Congenital disease or lesion NOS of spinal cord

● **Q07   Other congenital malformations of nervous system**

> **Excludes2**   congenital central alveolar hypoventilation syndrome (G47.35)
> familial dysautonomia [Riley-Day] (G90.1)
> neurofibromatosis (nonmalignant) (Q85.0-)

● **Q07.0   Arnold-Chiari syndrome**
Herniation of cerebellar tonsils and vermis through foramen magnum into spinal canal
Arnold-Chiari syndrome, type II

> **Excludes1**   Arnold-Chiari syndrome, type III (Q01.-)
> Arnold-Chiari syndrome, type IV (Q04.8)

Q07.00   Arnold-Chiari syndrome without spina bifida or hydrocephalus

Q07.01   Arnold-Chiari syndrome with spina bifida

Q07.02   Arnold-Chiari syndrome with hydrocephalus

Q07.03   Arnold-Chiari syndrome with spina bifida and hydrocephalus

Q07.8   Other specified congenital malformations of nervous system
Agenesis of nerve
Displacement of brachial plexus
Jaw-winking syndrome
Marcus Gunn's syndrome

Q07.9   Congenital malformation of nervous system, unspecified
Congenital anomaly NOS of nervous system
Congenital deformity NOS of nervous system
Congenital disease or lesion NOS of nervous system

▶ New   ⟹ Revised   ~~deleted~~ Deleted   Excludes 1   Excludes 2   Includes   Use additional   Code first   Code also   Key words

OGCR Official Guidelines   X Assign placeholder X   ● Use Additional Character(s)   ▌ Manifestation Code   **Coding Clinic**

CONGENITAL MALFORMATIONS OF EYE, EAR, FACE AND NECK (Q10-Q18)

Excludes2   cleft lip and cleft palate (Q35-Q37)
congenital malformation of cervical spine (Q05.0, Q05.5, Q67.5, Q76.0-Q76.4)
congenital malformation of larynx (Q31.-)
congenital malformation of lip NEC (Q38.0)
congenital malformation of nose (Q30.-)
congenital malformation of parathyroid gland (Q89.2)
congenital malformation of thyroid gland (Q89.2)

● **Q10** Congenital malformations of eyelid, lacrimal apparatus and orbit

Excludes1   cryptophthalmos NOS (Q11.2)
cryptophthalmos syndrome (Q87.0)

Q10.0 Congenital ptosis
Prolapse or drooping of upper eyelid from paralysis of third nerve or from sympathetic innervations

Q10.1 Congenital ectropion
Outward turning of eyelid

Q10.2 Congenital entropion
Inward turning of eyelid

Q10.3 Other congenital malformations of eyelid
Ablepharon
Blepharophimosis, congenital
Coloboma of eyelid
Congenital absence or agenesis of cilia
Congenital absence or agenesis of eyelid
Congenital accessory eyelid
Congenital accessory eye muscle
Congenital malformation of eyelid NOS

Q10.4 Absence and agenesis of lacrimal apparatus
Congenital absence of punctum lacrimale

Q10.5 Congenital stenosis and stricture of lacrimal duct

Q10.6 Other congenital malformations of lacrimal apparatus
Congenital malformation of lacrimal apparatus NOS

Q10.7 Congenital malformation of orbit

● **Q11** Anophthalmos, microphthalmos and macrophthalmos
Absence of eye and optic pit

Q11.0 Cystic eyeball

Q11.1 Other anophthalmos
Anophthalmos NOS
Agenesis of eye
Absence of eye
Aplasia of eye

Q11.2 Microphthalmos
Partial absence of eye and optic pit
Cryptophthalmos NOS
Dysplasia of eye
Hypoplasia of eye
Rudimentary eye

Excludes1   cryptophthalmos syndrome (Q87.0)

Q11.3 Macrophthalmos
Congenital enlargement of eyes

Excludes1   macrophthalmos in congenital glaucoma (Q15.0)

● **Q12** Congenital lens malformations

Q12.0 Congenital cataract

Q12.1 Congenital displaced lens

Q12.2 Coloboma of lens

Q12.3 Congenital aphakia

Q12.4 Spherophakia
Smaller, more spherical optic lens than normal

Q12.8 Other congenital lens malformations
Microphakia

Q12.9 Congenital lens malformation, unspecified

● **Q13** Congenital malformations of anterior segment of eye

Q13.0 Coloboma of iris
Coloboma NOS

Q13.1 Absence of iris
Aniridia
Use additional code for associated glaucoma (H42)

Q13.2 Other congenital malformations of iris
Anisocoria, congenital
Atresia of pupil
Congenital malformation of iris NOS
Corectopia

Q13.3 Congenital corneal opacity

Q13.4 Other congenital corneal malformations
Congenital malformation of cornea NOS
Microcornea
Peter's anomaly

Q13.5 Blue sclera
Condition of unusual blueness of sclera; not harmful

● **Q13.8** Other congenital malformations of anterior segment of eye

Q13.81 Rieger's anomaly
Use additional code for associated glaucoma (H42)

Q13.89 Other congenital malformations of anterior segment of eye

Q13.9 Congenital malformation of anterior segment of eye, unspecified

● **Q14** Congenital malformations of posterior segment of eye

Excludes2   optic nerve hypoplasia (H47.03-)

Q14.0 Congenital malformation of vitreous humor
Congenital vitreous opacity

Q14.1 Congenital malformation of retina
Congenital retinal aneurysm

Q14.2 Congenital malformation of optic disc
Coloboma of optic disc

Q14.3 Congenital malformation of choroid

Q14.8 Other congenital malformations of posterior segment of eye
Coloboma of the fundus

Q14.9 Congenital malformation of posterior segment of eye, unspecified

CHAPTER 17 (Q00-Q99)

Figure 17-2 Bilateral congenital **hydrophthalmia,** in which the eyes are very large in comparison to the other facial features due to glaucoma.

CHAPTER 17 (Q00-Q99)

● **Q15 Other congenital malformations of eye**
> **Excludes1**   congenital nystagmus (H55.01)
> ocular albinism (E70.31-)
> optic nerve hypoplasia (H47.03-)
> retinitis pigmentosa (H35.52)

   Q15.0 Congenital glaucoma
       Axenfeld's anomaly
       Buphthalmos
> *Congenital syndrome characterized by enlargement of the eye with sympotoms of glaucoma.*

       Glaucoma of childhood
       Glaucoma of newborn
       Hydrophthalmos
       Keratoglobus, congenital, with glaucoma
       Macrocornea with glaucoma
       Macrophthalmos in congenital glaucoma
       Megalocornea with glaucoma

   Q15.8 Other specified congenital malformations of eye

   Q15.9 Congenital malformation of eye, unspecified
       Congenital anomaly of eye
       Congenital deformity of eye

● **Q16 Congenital malformations of ear causing impairment of hearing**
> **Excludes1**   congenital deafness (H90.-)

   Q16.0 Congenital absence of (ear) auricle

   Q16.1 Congenital absence, atresia and stricture of auditory canal (external)
       Congenital atresia or stricture of osseous meatus

   Q16.2 Absence of eustachian tube

   Q16.3 Congenital malformation of ear ossicles
       Congenital fusion of ear ossicles

   Q16.4 Other congenital malformations of middle ear
       Congenital malformation of middle ear NOS

   Q16.5 Congenital malformation of inner ear
       Congenital anomaly of membranous labyrinth
       Congenital anomaly of organ of Corti

   Q16.9 Congenital malformation of ear causing impairment of hearing, unspecified
       Congenital absence of ear NOS

● **Q17 Other congenital malformations of ear**
> **Excludes1**   congenital malformations of ear with impairment of hearing (Q16.0-Q16.9)
> preauricular sinus (Q18.1)

   Q17.0 Accessory auricle
       Accessory tragus
       Polyotia
       Preauricular appendage or tag
       Supernumerary ear
       Supernumerary lobule

   Q17.1 Macrotia
       Enlarged ears

   Q17.2 Microtia
       An abnormally small or underdeveloped external ear

   Q17.3 Other misshapen ear
       Pointed ear

   Q17.4 Misplaced ear
       Low-set ears
> **Excludes1**   cervical auricle (Q18.2)

   Q17.5 Prominent ear
       Bat ear

   Q17.8 Other specified congenital malformations of ear
       Congenital absence of lobe of ear

   Q17.9 Congenital malformation of ear, unspecified
       Congenital anomaly of ear NOS

● **Q18 Other congenital malformations of face and neck**
> **Excludes1**   cleft lip and cleft palate (Q35-Q37)
> conditions classified to Q67.0-Q67.4
> congenital malformations of skull and face bones (Q75.-)
> cyclopia (Q87.0)
> dentofacial anomalies [including malocclusion] (M26.-)
> malformation syndromes affecting facial appearance (Q87.0)
> persistent thyroglossal duct (Q89.2)

   Q18.0 Sinus, fistula and cyst of branchial cleft
       Branchial vestige
> *Brachial remnants (cysts, fistula, skin tags) that are developmental anomalies*

   Q18.1 Preauricular sinus and cyst
       Fistula of auricle, congenital
       Cervicoaural fistula
> *Abnormal passage in neck originating from first branchial cleft*

   Q18.2 Other branchial cleft malformations
       Branchial cleft malformation NOS
       Cervical auricle
       Otocephaly

   Q18.3 Webbing of neck
       Pterygium colli
> *Thick fold of skin on side of neck*

   Q18.4 Macrostomia
> *Results from failure of union of maxillary and mandibular processes, results in abnormally large mouth*

   Q18.5 Microstomia

   Q18.6 Macrocheilia
> *Excessive size of lips*
       Hypertrophy of lip, congenital

   Q18.7 Microcheilia
> *Abnormal smallness of lips*

   Q18.8 Other specified congenital malformations of face and neck
       Medial cyst of face and neck
       Medial fistula of face and neck
       Medial sinus of face and neck

   Q18.9 Congenital malformation of face and neck, unspecified
       Congenital anomaly NOS of face and neck

CONGENITAL MALFORMATIONS OF VTHE CIRCULATORY SYSTEM (Q20-Q28)

● **Q20 Congenital malformations of cardiac chambers and connections**
> **Excludes1**   dextrocardia with situs inversus (Q89.3)
> mirror-image atrial arrangement with situs inversus (Q89.3)

   Q20.0 Common arterial trunk
       Persistent truncus arteriosus
> **Excludes1**   aortic septal defect (Q21.4)

   Q20.1 Double outlet right ventricle
       Taussig-Bing syndrome

   Q20.2 Double outlet left ventricle

   Q20.3 Discordant ventriculoarterial connection
       Dextrotransposition of aorta
       Transposition of great vessels (complete)

   Q20.4 Double inlet ventricle
       Common ventricle
       Cor triloculare biatriatum
       Single ventricle

   Q20.5 Discordant atrioventricular connection
       Corrected transposition
       Levotransposition
       Ventricular inversion

   Q20.6 Isomerism of atrial appendages
       Isomerism of atrial appendages with asplenia or polysplenia

   Q20.8 Other congenital malformations of cardiac chambers and connections
       Cor binoculare

   Q20.9 Congenital malformation of cardiac chambers and connections, unspecified

▶ New   ⇒ Revised   ~~deleted~~ Deleted   Excludes 1   Excludes 2   Includes   Use additional   Code first   Code also   Key words

OGCR Official Guidelines   X Assign placeholder X   ● Use Additional Character(s)   ▌ Manifestation Code   **Coding Clinic**

● **Q21   Congenital malformations of cardiac septa**

     Excludes1   acquired cardiac septal defect (I51.0)

   Q21.0   Ventricular septal defect
       Roger's disease

   Q21.1   Atrial septal defect
       Coronary sinus defect
       Patent or persistent foramen ovale
       Patent or persistent ostium secundum defect (type II)
       Patent or persistent sinus venosus defect

   Q21.2   Atrioventricular septal defect
       Common atrioventricular canal
       Endocardial cushion defect
       Ostium primum atrial septal defect (type I)

   Q21.3   Tetralogy of Fallot
       Ventricular septal defect with pulmonary stenosis or atresia, dextroposition of aorta and hypertrophy of right ventricle.

   Q21.4   Aortopulmonary septal defect
       Aortic septal defect
       Aortopulmonary window

   Q21.8   Other congenital malformations of cardiac septa
       Eisenmenger's defect
       Pentalogy of Fallot

       Code also if applicable:
         Eisenmenger's complex (I27.83)
         Eisenmenger's syndrome (I27.83)

   Q21.9   Congenital malformation of cardiac septum, unspecified
       Septal (heart) defect NOS

● **Q22   Congenital malformations of pulmonary and tricuspid valves**

   Q22.0   Pulmonary valve atresia

   Q22.1   Congenital pulmonary valve stenosis

   Q22.2   Congenital pulmonary valve insufficiency
       Congenital pulmonary valve regurgitation

   Q22.3   Other congenital malformations of pulmonary valve
       Congenital malformation of pulmonary valve NOS
       Supernumerary cusps of pulmonary valve

   Q22.4   Congenital tricuspid stenosis
       Congenital tricuspid atresia

   Q22.5   Ebstein's anomaly
       Malformation of tricuspid valve

   Q22.6   Hypoplastic right heart syndrome

   Q22.8   Other congenital malformations of tricuspid valve

   Q22.9   Congenital malformation of tricuspid valve, unspecified

● **Q23   Congenital malformations of aortic and mitral valves**

   Q23.0   Congenital stenosis of aortic valve
       Congenital aortic atresia
       Congenital aortic stenosis NOS

     Excludes1   congenital stenosis of aortic valve in hypoplastic left heart syndrome (Q23.4)
         congenital subaortic stenosis (Q24.4)
         supravalvular aortic stenosis (congenital) (Q25.3)

   Q23.1   Congenital insufficiency of aortic valve
       Bicuspid aortic valve
       Congenital aortic insufficiency

   Q23.2   Congenital mitral stenosis
       Congenital mitral atresia

   Q23.3   Congenital mitral insufficiency

   Q23.4   Hypoplastic left heart syndrome

   Q23.8   Other congenital malformations of aortic and mitral valves

   Q23.9   Congenital malformation of aortic and mitral valves, unspecified

● **Q24   Other congenital malformations of heart**

     Excludes1   endocardial fibroelastosis (I42.4)

   Q24.0   Dextrocardia
       Heart is located in right hemithorax

     Excludes1   dextrocardia with situs inversus (Q89.3)
         isomerism of atrial appendages (with asplenia or polysplenia) (Q20.6)
         mirror-image atrial arrangement with situs inversus (Q89.3)

   Q24.1   Levocardia
       Normal position of heart but related structures on wrong side

   Q24.2   Cor triatriatum
       Congenital heart defect; left atrium is subdivided

   Q24.3   Pulmonary infundibular stenosis
       Subvalvular pulmonic stenosis

   Q24.4   Congenital subaortic stenosis

   Q24.5   Malformation of coronary vessels
       Congenital coronary (artery) aneurysm

   Q24.6   Congenital heart block

   Q24.8   Other specified congenital malformations of heart
       Congenital diverticulum of left ventricle
       Congenital malformation of myocardium
       Congenital malformation of pericardium
       Malposition of heart
       Uhl's disease

   Q24.9   Congenital malformation of heart, unspecified
       Congenital anomaly of heart
       Congenital disease of heart

● **Q25   Congenital malformations of great arteries**

   Q25.0   Patent ductus arteriosus
       Fetal blood vessel connecting left pulmonary artery directly to descending aorta
       Patent ductus Botallo
       Persistent ductus arteriosus

   Q25.1   Coarctation of aorta
       Coarctation of aorta (preductal) (postductal)
       Stenosis of aorta
       Coding Clinic: 2016, Q4, P56-57

●   **Q25.2   Atresia of aorta**
       Coding Clinic: 2016, Q4, P56

     Q25.21   Interruption of aortic arch
         Atresia of aortic arch

     Q25.29   Other atresia of aorta
         Atresia of aorta

   Q25.3   Supravalvular aortic stenosis
     Excludes1   congenital aortic stenosis NOS (Q23.0)
         congenital stenosis of aortic valve (Q23.0)

●   **Q25.4   Other congenital malformations of aorta**
     Excludes1   hypoplasia of aorta in hypoplastic left heart syndrome (Q23.4)
       Coding Clinic: 2016, Q4, P57

     Q25.40   Congenital malformation of aorta unspecified

     Q25.41   Absence and aplasia of aorta

     Q25.42   Hypoplasia of aorta

     Q25.43   Congenital aneurysm of aorta
         Congenital aneurysm of aortic root
         Congenital aneurysm of aortic sinus

     Q25.44   Congenital dilation of aorta

     Q25.45   Double aortic arch
         Vascular ring of aorta

     Q25.46   Tortuous aortic arch
         Persistent convolutions of aortic arch

     Q25.47   Right aortic arch
         Persistent right aortic arch

     Q25.48   Anomalous origin of subclavian artery

     Q25.49   Other congenital malformations of aorta
         Aortic arch
         Bovine arch

Q25.5   **Atresia of pulmonary artery**

Q25.6   **Stenosis of pulmonary artery**
        Supravalvular pulmonary stenosis

● Q25.7   **Other congenital malformations of pulmonary artery**

     Q25.71   Coarctation of pulmonary artery

     Q25.72   **Congenital pulmonary arteriovenous malformation**
            Congenital pulmonary arteriovenous aneurysm

     Q25.79   **Other congenital malformations of pulmonary artery**
            Aberrant pulmonary artery
            Agenesis of pulmonary artery
            Congenital aneurysm of pulmonary artery
            Congenital anomaly of pulmonary artery
            Hypoplasia of pulmonary artery

Q25.8   **Other congenital malformations of other great arteries**

Q25.9   **Congenital malformation of great arteries, unspecified**

● Q26   **Congenital malformations of great veins**

   Q26.0   **Congenital stenosis of vena cava**
        Congenital stenosis of vena cava (inferior)(superior)

   Q26.1   **Persistent left superior vena cava**

   Q26.2   **Total anomalous pulmonary venous connection**
        Total anomalous pulmonary venous return [TAPVR], subdiaphragmatic
        Total anomalous pulmonary venous return [TAPVR], supradiaphragmatic

   Q26.3   **Partial anomalous pulmonary venous connection**
        Partial anomalous pulmonary venous return

   Q26.4   **Anomalous pulmonary venous connection, unspecified**

   Q26.5   **Anomalous portal venous connection**

   Q26.6   **Portal vein-hepatic artery fistula**

   Q26.8   **Other congenital malformations of great veins**
        Absence of vena cava (inferior) (superior)
        Azygos continuation of inferior vena cava
        Persistent left posterior cardinal vein
        Scimitar syndrome

   Q26.9   **Congenital malformation of great vein, unspecified**
        Congenital anomaly of vena cava (inferior) (superior) NOS

● Q27   **Other congenital malformations of peripheral vascular system**

     Excludes2   anomalies of cerebral and precerebral vessels (Q28.0-Q28.3)
            anomalies of coronary vessels (Q24.5)
            anomalies of pulmonary artery (Q25.5-Q25.7)
            congenital retinal aneurysm (Q14.1)
            hemangioma and lymphangioma (D18.-)

   Q27.0   **Congenital absence and hypoplasia of umbilical artery**
        Single umbilical artery

   Q27.1   **Congenital renal artery stenosis**

   Q27.2   **Other congenital malformations of renal artery**
        Congenital malformation of renal artery NOS
        Multiple renal arteries

● Q27.3   **Arteriovenous malformation (peripheral)**
        Arteriovenous aneurysm

     Excludes1   acquired arteriovenous aneurysm (I77.0)

     Excludes2   arteriovenous malformation of cerebral vessels (Q28.2)
            arteriovenous malformation of precerebral vessels (Q28.0)

     Q27.30   **Arteriovenous malformation, site unspecified**

     Q27.31   **Arteriovenous malformation of vessel of upper limb**

     Q27.32   **Arteriovenous malformation of vessel of lower limb**

     Q27.33   **Arteriovenous malformation of digestive system vessel**

     Q27.34   **Arteriovenous malformation of renal vessel**

     Q27.39   **Arteriovenous malformation, other site**

   Q27.4   **Congenital phlebectasia**

   Q27.8   **Other specified congenital malformations of peripheral vascular system**
        Absence of peripheral vascular system
        Atresia of peripheral vascular system
        Congenital aneurysm (peripheral)
        Congenital stricture, artery
        Congenital varix

     Excludes1   arteriovenous malformation (Q27.3-)

   Q27.9   **Congenital malformation of peripheral vascular system, unspecified**
        Anomaly of artery or vein NOS

● Q28   **Other congenital malformations of circulatory system**

     Excludes1   congenital aneurysm NOS (Q27.8)
            congenital coronary aneurysm (Q24.5)
            ruptured cerebral arteriovenous malformation (I60.8)
            ruptured malformation of precerebral vessels (I72.0)

     Excludes2   congenital peripheral aneurysm (Q27.8)
            congenital pulmonary aneurysm (Q25.79)
            congenital retinal aneurysm (Q14.1)

   Q28.0   **Arteriovenous malformation of precerebral vessels**
        Congenital arteriovenous precerebral aneurysm (nonruptured)

   Q28.1   **Other malformations of precerebral vessels**
        Congenital malformation of precerebral vessels NOS
        Congenital precerebral aneurysm (nonruptured)

   Q28.2   **Arteriovenous malformation of cerebral vessels**
        Arteriovenous malformation of brain NOS
        Congenital arteriovenous cerebral aneurysm (nonruptured)

   Q28.3   **Other malformations of cerebral vessels**
        Congenital cerebral aneurysm (nonruptured)
        Congenital malformation of cerebral vessels NOS
        Developmental venous anomaly

   Q28.8   **Other specified congenital malformations of circulatory system**
        Congenital aneurysm, specified site NEC
        Spinal vessel anomaly

   Q28.9   **Congenital malformation of circulatory system, unspecified**

CONGENITAL MALFORMATIONS OF THE RESPIRATORY SYSTEM (Q30-Q34)

● Q30   **Congenital malformations of nose**

     Excludes1   congenital deviation of nasal septum (Q67.4)

   Q30.0   **Choanal atresia**
        Atresia of nares (anterior) (posterior)
        Congenital stenosis of nares (anterior) (posterior)

   Q30.1   **Agenesis and underdevelopment of nose**
        Congenital absent of nose

   Q30.2   **Fissured, notched and cleft nose**

   Q30.3   **Congenital perforated nasal septum**

   Q30.8   **Other congenital malformations of nose**
        Accessory nose
        Congenital anomaly of nasal sinus wall

   Q30.9   **Congenital malformation of nose, unspecified**

▶ New   ⇒ Revised   ~~deleted~~ Deleted   Excludes 1   Excludes 2   Includes   Use additional   Code first   Code also   Key words

OGCR Official Guidelines   X Assign placeholder X   ● Use Additional Character(s)   ▶ Manifestation Code   **Coding Clinic**

● **Q31 Congenital malformations of larynx**
    Excludes1 congenital laryngeal stridor NOS (P28.89)

  Q31.0 Web of larynx
    Glottic web of larynx
    Subglottic web of larynx
    Web of larynx NOS

  Q31.1 Congenital subglottic stenosis

  Q31.2 Laryngeal hypoplasia

  Q31.3 Laryngocele

  Q31.5 Congenital laryngomalacia

  Q31.8 Other congenital malformations of larynx
    Absence of larynx
    Agenesis of larynx
    Atresia of larynx
    Congenital cleft thyroid cartilage
    Congenital fissure of epiglottis
    Congenital stenosis of larynx NEC
    Posterior cleft of cricoid cartilage

  Q31.9 Congenital malformation of larynx, unspecified

● **Q32 Congenital malformations of trachea and bronchus**
    Excludes1 congenital bronchiectasis (Q33.4)

  Q32.0 Congenital tracheomalacia

  Q32.1 Other congenital malformations of trachea
    Atresia of trachea
    Congenital anomaly of tracheal cartilage
    Congenital dilatation of trachea
    Congenital malformation of trachea
    Congenital stenosis of trachea
    Congenital tracheocele

  Q32.2 Congenital bronchomalacia

  Q32.3 Congenital stenosis of bronchus

  Q32.4 Other congenital malformations of bronchus
    Absence of bronchus
    Agenesis of bronchus
    Atresia of bronchus
    Congenital diverticulum of bronchus
    Congenital malformation of bronchus NOS

● **Q33 Congenital malformations of lung**

  Q33.0 Congenital cystic lung
    Congenital cystic lung disease
    Congenital honeycomb lung
    Congenital polycystic lung disease
    Excludes1 cystic fibrosis (E84.0)
             cystic lung disease, acquired or
               unspecified (J98.4)

  Q33.1 Accessory lobe of lung
    Azygos lobe (fissured), lung

  Q33.2 Sequestration of lung

  Q33.3 Agenesis of lung
    Congenital absence of lung (lobe)

  Q33.4 Congenital bronchiectasis

  Q33.5 Ectopic tissue in lung

  Q33.6 Congenital hypoplasia and dysplasia of lung
    Excludes1 pulmonary hypoplasia associated with
             short gestation (P28.0)

  Q33.8 Other congenital malformations of lung

  Q33.9 Congenital malformation of lung, unspecified

● **Q34 Other congenital malformations of respiratory system**
    Excludes2 congenital central alveolar hypoventilation
             syndrome (G47.35)

  Q34.0 Anomaly of pleura

  Q34.1 Congenital cyst of mediastinum

  Q34.8 Other specified congenital malformations of respiratory system
    Atresia of nasopharynx

  Q34.9 Congenital malformation of respiratory system, unspecified
    Congenital absence of respiratory system
    Congenital anomaly of respiratory system NOS

Figure 17-3 Cleft palate.

CLEFT LIP AND CLEFT PALATE (Q35-Q37)

Use additional code to identify associated malformation of the nose (Q30.2)
    Excludes1 Robin's syndrome (Q87.0)

● **Q35 Cleft palate**
    Includes fissure of palate
             palatoschisis
    Excludes1 cleft palate with cleft lip (Q37.-)

  Q35.1 Cleft hard palate

  Q35.3 Cleft soft palate

  Q35.5 Cleft hard palate with cleft soft palate

  Q35.7 Cleft uvula

  Q35.9 Cleft palate, unspecified
    Cleft palate NOS

● **Q36 Cleft lip**
    Includes cheiloschisis
             congenital fissure of lip
             harelip
             labium leporinum
    Excludes1 cleft lip with cleft palate (Q37.-)

  Q36.0 Cleft lip, bilateral

  Q36.1 Cleft lip, median

  Q36.9 Cleft lip, unilateral
    Cleft lip NOS

● **Q37 Cleft palate with cleft lip**
    Includes cheilopalatoschisis

  Q37.0 Cleft hard palate with bilateral cleft lip

  Q37.1 Cleft hard palate with unilateral cleft lip
    Cleft hard palate with cleft lip NOS

  Q37.2 Cleft soft palate with bilateral cleft lip

  Q37.3 Cleft soft palate with unilateral cleft lip
    Cleft soft palate with cleft lip NOS

  Q37.4 Cleft hard and soft palate with bilateral cleft lip

  Q37.5 Cleft hard and soft palate with unilateral cleft lip
    Cleft hard and soft palate with cleft lip NOS

  Q37.8 Unspecified cleft palate with bilateral cleft lip

  Q37.9 Unspecified cleft palate with unilateral cleft lip
    Cleft palate with cleft lip NOS

CHAPTER 17 (Q00-Q99)

OTHER CONGENITAL MALFORMATIONS OF THE DIGESTIVE SYSTEM (Q38-Q45)

● Q38 **Other congenital malformations of tongue, mouth and pharynx**

Excludes1 dentofacial anomalies (M26.-)
macrostomia (Q18.4)
microstomia (Q18.5)

Q38.0 **Congenital malformations of lips, not elsewhere classified**
Congenital fistula of lip
Congenital malformation of lip NOS
Van der Woude's syndrome
Excludes1 cleft lip (Q36.-)
cleft lip with cleft palate (Q37.-)
macrocheilia (Q18.6)
microcheilia (Q18.7)

Q38.1 **Ankyloglossia**
Restricted movement of tongue resulting in speech difficulty
Tongue tie

Q38.2 **Macroglossia**
Excessive size of tongue
Congenital hypertrophy of tongue

Q38.3 **Other congenital malformations of tongue**
Aglossia
Bifid tongue
Congenital adhesion of tongue
Congenital fissure of tongue
Congenital malformation of tongue NOS
Double tongue
Hypoglossia
Hypoplasia of tongue
Microglossia

Q38.4 **Congenital malformations of salivary glands and ducts**
Atresia of salivary glands and ducts
Congenital absence of salivary glands and ducts
Congenital accessory salivary glands and ducts
Congenital fistula of salivary gland

Q38.5 **Congenital malformations of palate, not elsewhere classified**
Congenital absence of uvula
Congenital malformation of palate NOS
Congenital high arched palate
Excludes1 cleft palate (Q35.-)
cleft palate with cleft lip (Q37.-)

Q38.6 **Other congenital malformations of mouth**
Congenital malformation of mouth NOS

Q38.7 **Congenital pharyngeal pouch**
Congenital diverticulum of pharynx
Excludes1 pharyngeal pouch syndrome (D82.1)

Q38.8 **Other congenital malformations of pharynx**
Congenital malformation of pharynx NOS
Imperforate pharynx

● Q39 **Congenital malformations of esophagus**

Q39.0 **Atresia of esophagus without fistula**
Atresia of esophagus NOS

Q39.1 **Atresia of esophagus with tracheo-esophageal fistula**
Atresia of esophagus with broncho-esophageal fistula

Q39.2 **Congenital tracheo-esophageal fistula without atresia**
Congenital tracheo-esophageal fistula NOS

Q39.3 **Congenital stenosis and stricture of esophagus**

Q39.4 **Esophageal web**

Q39.5 **Congenital dilatation of esophagus**
Congenital cardiospasm

Q39.6 **Congenital diverticulum of esophagus**
Congenital esophageal pouch

Q39.8 **Other congenital malformations of esophagus**
Congenital absence of esophagus
Congenital displacement of esophagus
Congenital duplication of esophagus

Q39.9 **Congenital malformation of esophagus, unspecified**

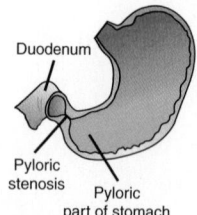

Figure 17-4 Pyloric stenosis.

Duodenum

Pyloric stenosis

Pyloric part of stomach

● Q40 **Other congenital malformations of upper alimentary tract**

Q40.0 **Congenital hypertrophic pyloric stenosis**
Congenital or infantile constriction
Congenital or infantile hypertrophy
Congenital or infantile spasm
Congenital or infantile stenosis
Congenital or infantile stricture

Q40.1 **Congenital hiatus hernia**
Congenital displacement of cardia through esophageal hiatus
Excludes1 congenital diaphragmatic hernia (Q79.0)

Q40.2 **Other specified congenital malformations of stomach**
Congenital displacement of stomach
Congenital diverticulum of stomach
Congenital hourglass stomach
Congenital duplication of stomach
Megalogastria
Microgastria

Q40.3 **Congenital malformation of stomach, unspecified**

Q40.8 **Other specified congenital malformations of upper alimentary tract**

Q40.9 **Congenital malformation of upper alimentary tract, unspecified**
Congenital anomaly of upper alimentary tract
Congenital deformity of upper alimentary tract

● Q41 **Congenital absence, atresia and stenosis of small intestine**

Includes congenital obstruction, occlusion or stricture of small intestine or intestine NOS

Excludes1 cystic fibrosis with intestinal manifestation (E84.11)
meconium ileus NOS (without cystic fibrosis) (P76.0)

Q41.0 **Congenital absence, atresia and stenosis of duodenum**

Q41.1 **Congenital absence, atresia and stenosis of jejunum**
Apple peel syndrome
Imperforate jejunum

Q41.2 **Congenital absence, atresia and stenosis of ileum**

Q41.8 **Congenital absence, atresia and stenosis of other specified parts of small intestine**

Q41.9 **Congenital absence, atresia and stenosis of small intestine, part unspecified**
Congenital absence, atresia and stenosis of intestine NOS

● Q42 **Congenital absence, atresia and stenosis of large intestine**

Includes congenital obstruction, occlusion and stricture of large intestine

Q42.0 **Congenital absence, atresia and stenosis of rectum with fistula**

Q42.1 **Congenital absence, atresia and stenosis of rectum without fistula**
Imperforate rectum

Q42.2 **Congenital absence, atresia and stenosis of anus with fistula**

Q42.3 **Congenital absence, atresia and stenosis of anus without fistula**
Imperforate anus

Q42.8 **Congenital absence, atresia and stenosis of other parts of large intestine**

Q42.9 **Congenital absence, atresia and stenosis of large intestine, part unspecified**

▶ New   ⇒ Revised   ~~deleted~~ Deleted   Excludes 1   Excludes 2   Includes   Use additional   Code first   Code also   Key words
OGCR Official Guidelines   X Assign placeholder X   ● Use Additional Character(s)   ▶ Manifestation Code   **Coding Clinic**

- **Q43   Other congenital malformations of intestine**
  - **Q43.0   Meckel's diverticulum (displaced) (hypertrophic)**
    Congenital abnormality in which a pouch remains on the lower end of the small intestine
    Persistent omphalomesenteric duct
    Persistent vitelline duct
  - **Q43.1   Hirschsprung's disease**
    Developmental disorder of enteric nervous system characterized by absence of ganglion cells in distal colon resulting in functional obstruction
    Aganglionosis
    Congenital (aganglionic) megacolon
  - **Q43.2   Other congenital functional disorders of colon**
    Congenital dilatation of colon
  - **Q43.3   Congenital malformations of intestinal fixation**
    Congenital omental, anomalous adhesions [bands]
    Congenital peritoneal adhesions [bands]
    Incomplete rotation of cecum and colon
    Insufficient rotation of cecum and colon
    Jackson's membrane
    Malrotation of colon
    Rotation failure of cecum and colon
    Universal mesentery
  - **Q43.4   Duplication of intestine**
  - **Q43.5   Ectopic anus**
    Anal opening in abnormal location
  - **Q43.6   Congenital fistula of rectum and anus**
    - **Excludes1**   congenital fistula of anus with absence, atresia and stenosis (Q42.2)
      congenital fistula of rectum with absence, atresia and stenosis (Q42.0)
      congenital rectovaginal fistula (Q52.2)
      congenital urethrorectal fistula (Q64.73)
      pilonidal fistula or sinus (L05.-)
  - **Q43.7   Persistent cloaca**
    Malformation in which rectum, vagina, and urinary tract form one channel AKA congenital cloaca
    Cloaca NOS
  - **Q43.8   Other specified congenital malformations of intestine**
    Congenital blind loop syndrome
    Congenital diverticulitis, colon
    Congenital diverticulum, intestine
    Dolichocolon
    Megaloappendix
    Megaloduodenum
    Microcolon
    Transposition of appendix
    Transposition of colon
    Transposition of intestine
  - **Q43.9   Congenital malformation of intestine, unspecified**

- **Q44   Congenital malformations of gallbladder, bile ducts and liver**
  - **Q44.0   Agenesis, aplasia and hypoplasia of gallbladder**
    Congenital absence of gallbladder
  - **Q44.1   Other congenital malformations of gallbladder**
    Congenital malformation of gallbladder NOS
    Intrahepatic gallbladder
  - **Q44.2   Atresia of bile ducts**
  - **Q44.3   Congenital stenosis and stricture of bile ducts**
  - **Q44.4   Choledochal cyst**
  - **Q44.5   Other congenital malformations of bile ducts**
    Accessory hepatic duct
    Biliary duct duplication
    Congenital malformation of bile duct NOS
    Cystic duct duplication
  - **Q44.6   Cystic disease of liver**
    Fibrocystic disease of liver
  - **Q44.7   Other congenital malformations of liver**
    Accessory liver
    Alagille's syndrome
    Congenital absence of liver
    Congenital hepatomegaly
    Congenital malformation of liver NOS

- **Q45   Other congenital malformations of digestive system**
  - **Excludes2**   congenital diaphragmatic hernia (Q79.0)
    congenital hiatus hernia (Q40.1)
  - **Q45.0   Agenesis, aplasia and hypoplasia of pancreas**
    Congenital absence of pancreas
  - **Q45.1   Annular pancreas**
  - **Q45.2   Congenital pancreatic cyst**
  - **Q45.3   Other congenital malformations of pancreas and pancreatic duct**
    Accessory pancreas
    Congenital malformation of pancreas or pancreatic duct NOS
    - **Excludes1**   congenital diabetes mellitus (E10.-)
      cystic fibrosis (E84.0-E84.9)
      fibrocystic disease of pancreas (E84.-)
      neonatal diabetes mellitus (P70.2)
  - **Q45.8   Other specified congenital malformations of digestive system**
    Absence (complete) (partial) of alimentary tract NOS
    Duplication of digestive system
    Malposition, congenital of digestive system
  - **Q45.9   Congenital malformation of digestive system, unspecified**
    Congenital anomaly of digestive system
    Congenital deformity of digestive system

CONGENITAL MALFORMATIONS OF GENITAL ORGANS (Q50-Q56)

- **Excludes1**   androgen insensitivity syndrome (E34.5-)
  syndromes associated with anomalies in the number and form of chromosomes (Q90-Q99)

- **Q50   Congenital malformations of ovaries, fallopian tubes and broad ligaments**
  - **Q50.0   Congenital absence of ovary**
    - **Excludes1**   Turner's syndrome (Q96.-)
    - **Q50.01   Congenital absence of ovary, unilateral** ♀
    - **Q50.02   Congenital absence of ovary, bilateral** ♀
  - **Q50.1   Developmental ovarian cyst** ♀
  - **Q50.2   Congenital torsion of ovary** ♀
  - **Q50.3   Other congenital malformations of ovary**
    - **Q50.31   Accessory ovary** ♀
    - **Q50.32   Ovarian streak** ♀
      Inadequate ovaries with absent follicular and hormonal function
      46, XX with streak gonads
    - **Q50.39   Other congenital malformation of ovary** ♀
      Congenital malformation of ovary NOS
  - **Q50.4   Embryonic cyst of fallopian tube** ♀
    Fimbrial cyst
  - **Q50.5   Embryonic cyst of broad ligament** ♀
    Epoophoron cyst
    Parovarian cyst
  - **Q50.6   Other congenital malformations of fallopian tube and broad ligament** ♀
    Absence of fallopian tube and broad ligament
    Accessory fallopian tube and broad ligament
    Atresia of fallopian tube and broad ligament
    Congenital malformation of fallopian tube or broad ligament NOS

- **Q51   Congenital malformations of uterus and cervix**
  - **Q51.0   Agenesis and aplasia of uterus** ♀
    Congenital absence of uterus
  - **Q51.1   Doubling of uterus with doubling of cervix and vagina**
    - **Q51.10   Doubling of uterus with doubling of cervix and vagina without obstruction** ♀
      Doubling of uterus with doubling of cervix and vagina NOS
    - **Q51.11   Doubling of uterus with doubling of cervix and vagina with obstruction** ♀

CHAPTER 17 (Q00-Q99)

● **Q51.2** **Other doubling of uterus** ♀
    Doubling of uterus NOS
    ⇒Septate uterus

▶ **Q51.20** **Other doubling of uterus, unspecified**
        ▶Septate uterus, unspecified

▶ **Q51.21** **Other complete doubling of uterus**
        ▶Complete septate uterus

▶ **Q51.22** **Other partial doubling of uterus**
        ▶Partial septate uterus

▶ **Q51.28** **Other doubling of uterus, other specified**
        ▶Septate uterus, other specified

Q51.3 **Bicornate uterus** ♀
    Bicornate uterus, complete or partial
    Birth defect in which uterus has two separate 'horns' that form top of uterus

Q51.4 **Unicornate uterus** ♀
    Unicornate uterus with or without a separate uterine horn
    Uterus with only one functioning horn
    Uterus with half being undeveloped

Q51.5 **Agenesis and aplasia of cervix** ♀
    Congenital absence of cervix

Q51.6 **Embryonic cyst of cervix** ♀

Q51.7 **Congenital fistulae between uterus and digestive and urinary tracts** ♀

● **Q51.8** **Other congenital malformations of uterus and cervix**

● **Q51.81** **Other congenital malformations of uterus**

Q51.810 **Arcuate uterus** ♀
    Arcuatus uterus

Q51.811 **Hypoplasia of uterus** ♀

Q51.818 **Other congenital malformations of uterus** ♀
    Müllerian anomaly of uterus NEC

● **Q51.82** **Other congenital malformations of cervix**

Q51.820 **Cervical duplication** ♀

Q51.821 **Hypoplasia of cervix** ♀

Q51.828 **Other congenital malformations of cervix** ♀

Q51.9 **Congenital malformation of uterus and cervix, unspecified** ♀

● **Q52** **Other congenital malformations of female genitalia**

Q52.0 **Congenital absence of vagina** ♀
    Vaginal agenesis, total or partial

● **Q52.1** **Doubling of vagina**
    Excludes1   doubling of vagina with doubling of uterus and cervix (Q51.1-)

Q52.10 **Doubling of vagina, unspecified** ♀
    Septate vagina NOS

Q52.11 **Transverse vaginal septum** ♀

● **Q52.12** **Longitudinal vaginal septum**
    Coding Clinic: 2016, Q4, P58

Q52.120 **Longitudinal vaginal septum, nonobstructing** ♀

Q52.121 **Longitudinal vaginal septum, obstructing, right side** ♀

Q52.122 **Longitudinal vaginal septum, obstructing, left side** ♀

Q52.123 **Longitudinal vaginal septum, microperforate, right side** ♀

Q52.124 **Longitudinal vaginal septum, microperforate, left side** ♀
    Coding Clinic: 2016, Q4, P59

Q52.129 **Other and unspecified longitudinal vaginal septum** ♀

Q52.2 **Congenital rectovaginal fistula** ♀
    Excludes1   cloaca (Q43.7)

Q52.3 **Imperforate hymen** ♀
    Membrane (hymen) completely closes vaginal orifice

Q52.4 **Other congenital malformations of vagina** ♀
    Canal of Nuck cyst, congenital
    Congenital malformation of vagina NOS
    Embryonic vaginal cyst
    Gartner's duct cyst

Q52.5 **Fusion of labia** ♀

Q52.6 **Congenital malformation of clitoris** ♀

● **Q52.7** **Other and unspecified congenital malformations of vulva**

Q52.70 **Unspecified congenital malformations of vulva** ♀
    Congenital malformation of vulva NOS

Q52.71 **Congenital absence of vulva** ♀

Q52.79 **Other congenital malformations of vulva** ♀
    Congenital cyst of vulva

Q52.8 **Other specified congenital malformations of female genitalia** ♀

Q52.9 **Congenital malformation of female genitalia, unspecified** ♀

● **Q53** **Undescended and ectopic testicle**

● **Q53.0** **Ectopic testis**

Q53.00 Ectopic testis, unspecified ♂

Q53.01 Ectopic testis, unilateral ♂

Q53.02 Ectopic testes, bilateral ♂

● **Q53.1** **Undescended testicle, unilateral**

Q53.10 **Unspecified undescended testicle, unilateral** ♂

● **Q53.11** **Abdominal testis, unilateral**

Q53.111 Unilateral intraabdominal testis ♂

Q53.112 Unilateral inguinal testis ♂

Q53.12 Ectopic perineal testis, unilateral ♂

Q53.13 Unilateral high scrotal testis ♂

● **Q53.2** **Undescended testicle, bilateral**

Q53.20 Undescended testicle, unspecified, bilateral ♂

● **Q53.21** **Abdominal testis, bilateral**

Q53.211 Bilateral intraabdominal testes ♂

Q53.212 Bilateral inguinal testes ♂

Q53.22 Ectopic perineal testis, bilateral ♂

Q53.23 Bilateral high scrotal testes ♂

Q53.9 Undescended testicle, unspecified ♂
    Cryptorchism NOS

Item 17–1 Testes form in the abdomen of the male and only descend into the scrotum during normal embryonic development. "Ectopic" testes are out of their normal place or "retained" (left behind) in the abdomen. Crypto (hidden) orchism (testicle) is a major risk factor for testicular cancer.

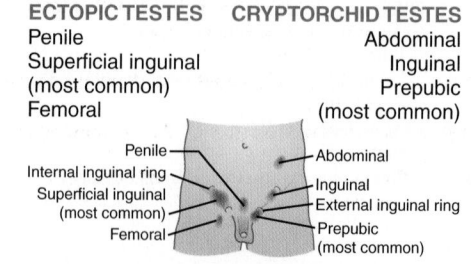

ECTOPIC TESTES	CRYPTORCHID TESTES
Penile	Abdominal
Superficial inguinal (most common)	Inguinal
	Prepubic
Femoral	(most common)

Figure 17-5 Undescended testes and the positions of the testes in various types of cryptorchidism or abnormal paths of descent.

▶ New   ⇒ Revised   ~~deleted~~ Deleted   Excludes 1   Excludes 2   Includes   Use additional   Code first   Code also   Key words

1164   OGCR Official Guidelines   X Assign placeholder X   ● Use Additional Character(s)   ▶ Manifestation Code   **Coding Clinic**

● **Q54   Hypospadias**
Birth defect of male; urethra opens in abnormal location on shaft
> **Excludes1**   epispadias (Q64.0)

   Q54.0   Hypospadias, balanic ♂
     Hypospadias, coronal
     Hypospadias, glandular

   Q54.1   Hypospadias, penile ♂

   Q54.2   Hypospadias, penoscrotal ♂

   Q54.3   Hypospadias, perineal ♂

   Q54.4   Congenital chordee ♂
     Chordee without hypospadias

   Q54.8   Other hypospadias ♂
     Hypospadias with intersex state

   Q54.9   Hypospadias, unspecified ♂

● **Q55   Other congenital malformations of male genital organs**
> **Excludes1**   congenital hydrocele (P83.5)
>   hypospadias (Q54.-)

   Q55.0   Absence and aplasia of testis ♂
     Monorchism

   Q55.1   Hypoplasia of testis and scrotum ♂
     Fusion of testes

●   **Q55.2   Other and unspecified congenital malformations of testis and scrotum**

     Q55.20   Unspecified congenital malformations of testis and scrotum ♂
         Congenital malformation of testis or scrotum NOS

     Q55.21   Polyorchism ♂
         Developmental anomaly characterized by presence of more than two testes

     Q55.22   Retractile testis ♂

     Q55.23   Scrotal transposition ♂

     Q55.29   Other congenital malformations of testis and scrotum ♂

   Q55.3   Atresia of vas deferens ♂
     Code first any associated cystic fibrosis (E84.-)

   Q55.4   Other congenital malformations of vas deferens, epididymis, seminal vesicles and prostate ♂
     Absence or aplasia of prostate
     Absence or aplasia of spermatic cord
     Congenital malformation of vas deferens, epididymis, seminal vesicles or prostate NOS

   Q55.5   Congenital absence and aplasia of penis ♂

●   **Q55.6   Other congenital malformations of penis**

     Q55.61   Curvature of penis (lateral) ♂

     Q55.62   Hypoplasia of penis ♂
         Underdevelopment penis
         Micropenis

     Q55.63   Congenital torsion of penis ♂
>   **Excludes1**   acquired torsion of penis (N48.82)

     Q55.64   Hidden penis ♂
         Buried penis
         Concealed penis
>   **Excludes1**   acquired buried penis (N48.83)

     Q55.69   Other congenital malformation of penis ♂
         Congenital malformation of penis NOS

   Q55.7   Congenital vasocutaneous fistula ♂
     Abnormal opening between vas deferens and skin

   Q55.8   Other specified congenital malformations of male genital organs ♂

   Q55.9   Congenital malformation of male genital organ, unspecified ♂
     Congenital anomaly of male genital organ
     Congenital deformity of male genital organ

● **Q56   Indeterminate sex and pseudohermaphroditism**
Internal reproductive organs are opposite external physical characteristics.
> **Excludes1**   46,XX true hermaphrodite (Q99.1)
>   androgen insensitivity syndrome (E34.5-)
>   chimera 46,XX/46,XY true hermaphrodite (Q99.0)
>   female pseudohermaphroditism with adrenocortical disorder (E25.-)
>   pseudohermaphroditism with specified chromosomal anomaly (Q96-Q99)
>   pure gonadal dysgenesis (Q99.1)

   Q56.0   Hermaphroditism, not elsewhere classified
     Ovotestis

   Q56.1   Male pseudohermaphroditism, not elsewhere classified ♂
     46, XY with streak gonads
     Male pseudohermaphroditism NOS

   Q56.2   Female pseudohermaphroditism, not elsewhere classified ♀
     Female pseudohermaphroditism NOS

   Q56.3   Pseudohermaphroditism, unspecified

   Q56.4   Indeterminate sex, unspecified
     Ambiguous genitalia

CONGENITAL MALFORMATIONS OF THE URINARY SYSTEM (Q60-Q64)

● **Q60   Renal agenesis and other reduction defects of kidney**
> **Includes**   congenital absence of kidney
>   congenital atrophy of kidney
>   infantile atrophy of kidney

   Q60.0   Renal agenesis, unilateral

   Q60.1   Renal agenesis, bilateral

   Q60.2   Renal agenesis, unspecified

   Q60.3   Renal hypoplasia, unilateral

   Q60.4   Renal hypoplasia, bilateral

   Q60.5   Renal hypoplasia, unspecified

   Q60.6   Potter's syndrome

● **Q61   Cystic kidney disease**
Cysts that develop in failing kidney due to end-stage renal disease
> **Excludes1**   acquired cyst of kidney (N28.1)
>   Potter's syndrome (Q60.6)

●   **Q61.0   Congenital renal cyst**

     Q61.00   Congenital renal cyst, unspecified
         Cyst of kidney NOS (congenital)

     Q61.01   Congenital single renal cyst

     Q61.02   Congenital multiple renal cysts

●   **Q61.1   Polycystic kidney, infantile type**
     Polycystic kidney, autosomal recessive

     Q61.11   Cystic dilatation of collecting ducts

     Q61.19   Other polycystic kidney, infantile type

   Q61.2   Polycystic kidney, adult type
     Polycystic kidney, autosomal dominant

   Q61.3   Polycystic kidney, unspecified
     Coding Clinic: 2016, Q3, P23

   Q61.4   Renal dysplasia
     Multicystic dysplastic kidney
     Multicystic kidney (development)
     Multicystic kidney disease
     Multicystic renal dysplasia
>   **Excludes1**   polycystic kidney disease (Q61.11-Q61.3)

   Q61.5   Medullary cystic kidney
     Nephronopthisis
     Sponge kidney NOS

   Q61.8   Other cystic kidney diseases
     Fibrocystic kidney
     Fibrocystic renal degeneration or disease

   Q61.9   Cystic kidney disease, unspecified
     Meckel-Gruber syndrome

CHAPTER 17 (Q00-Q99)

● **Q62   Congenital obstructive defects of renal pelvis and congenital malformations of ureter**

    Q62.0   Congenital hydronephrosis

●   **Q62.1   Congenital occlusion of ureter**
        Atresia and stenosis of ureter

        Q62.10   Congenital occlusion of ureter, unspecified

        Q62.11   Congenital occlusion of ureteropelvic junction

        Q62.12   Congenital occlusion of ureterovesical orifice

    Q62.2   Congenital megaureter
        Congenital dilatation of ureter

●   **Q62.3   Other obstructive defects of renal pelvis and ureter**

        Q62.31   Congenital ureterocele, orthotopic

        Q62.32   Cecoureterocele
            Ectopic ureterocele

        Q62.39   Other obstructive defects of renal pelvis and ureter
            Ureteropelvic junction obstruction NOS

    Q62.4   Agenesis of ureter
        Congenital absence ureter

    Q62.5   Duplication of ureter
        Accessory ureter
        Double ureter

●   **Q62.6   Malposition of ureter**

        Q62.60   Malposition of ureter, unspecified

        Q62.61   Deviation of ureter

        Q62.62   Displacement of ureter

        Q62.63   Anomalous implantation of ureter
            Ectopia of ureter
            Ectopic ureter

        Q62.69   Other malposition of ureter

    Q62.7   Congenital vesico-uretero-renal reflux

    Q62.8   Other congenital malformations of ureter
        Anomaly of ureter NOS

● **Q63   Other congenital malformations of kidney**

    Excludes1   congenital nephrotic syndrome (N04.-)

    Q63.0   Accessory kidney

    Q63.1   Lobulated, fused and horseshoe kidney

    Q63.2   Ectopic kidney
        Congenital displaced kidney
        Malrotation of kidney

    Q63.3   Hyperplastic and giant kidney
        Compensatory hypertrophy of kidney

    Q63.8   Other specified congenital malformations of kidney
        Congenital renal calculi

    Q63.9   Congenital malformation of kidney, unspecified

● **Q64   Other congenital malformations of urinary system**

    Q64.0   Epispadias
        Urethral opening somewhere on dorsum of penis

        Excludes1   hypospadias (Q54.-)

●   **Q64.1   Exstrophy of urinary bladder**
        Bladder is exposed, inside out, and protrudes through abdominal wall

        Q64.10   Exstrophy of urinary bladder, unspecified
            Ectopia vesicae

        Q64.11   Supravesical fissure of urinary bladder

        Q64.12   Cloacal exstrophy of urinary bladder

        Q64.19   Other exstrophy of urinary bladder
            Extroversion of bladder

    Q64.2   Congenital posterior urethral valves

    Q64.3   Other atresia and stenosis of urethra and bladder neck

        Q64.31   Congenital bladder neck obstruction
            Congenital obstruction of vesicourethral orifice

        Q64.32   Congenital stricture of urethra

        Q64.33   Congenital stricture of urinary meatus

        Q64.39   Other atresia and stenosis of urethra and bladder neck
            Atresia and stenosis of urethra and bladder neck NOS

    Q64.4   Malformation of urachus
        Cyst of urachus
        Patent urachus
        Prolapse of urachus

    Q64.5   Congenital absence of bladder and urethra

    Q64.6   Congenital diverticulum of bladder

●   **Q64.7   Other and unspecified congenital malformations of bladder and urethra**

        Excludes1   congenital prolapse of bladder (mucosa) (Q79.4)

        Q64.70   Unspecified congenital malformation of bladder and urethra
            Malformation of bladder or urethra NOS

        Q64.71   Congenital prolapse of urethra

        Q64.72   Congenital prolapse of urinary meatus

        Q64.73   Congenital urethrorectal fistula

        Q64.74   Double urethra

        Q64.75   Double urinary meatus

        Q64.79   Other congenital malformations of bladder and urethra

    Q64.8   Other specified congenital malformations of urinary system

    Q64.9   Congenital malformation of urinary system, unspecified
        Congenital anomaly NOS of urinary system
        Congenital deformity NOS of urinary system

CONGENITAL MALFORMATIONS AND DEFORMATIONS OF THE MUSCULOSKELETAL SYSTEM (Q65-Q79)

● **Q65   Congenital deformities of hip**

    Excludes1   clicking hip (R29.4)

●   **Q65.0   Congenital dislocation of hip, unilateral**

        Q65.00   Congenital dislocation of unspecified hip, unilateral

        Q65.01   Congenital dislocation of right hip, unilateral

        Q65.02   Congenital dislocation of left hip, unilateral

    Q65.1   Congenital dislocation of hip, bilateral

    Q65.2   Congenital dislocation of hip, unspecified

●   **Q65.3   Congenital partial dislocation of hip, unilateral**

        Q65.30   Congenital partial dislocation of unspecified hip, unilateral

        Q65.31   Congenital partial dislocation of right hip, unilateral

        Q65.32   Congenital partial dislocation of left hip, unilateral

    Q65.4   Congenital partial dislocation of hip, bilateral

    Q65.5   Congenital partial dislocation of hip, unspecified

    Q65.6   Congenital unstable hip
        Congenital dislocatable hip

●   **Q65.8   Other congenital deformities of hip**

        Q65.81   Congenital coxa valga

        Q65.82   Congenital coxa vara

        Q65.89   Other specified congenital deformities of hip
            Anteversion of femoral neck
            Congenital acetabular dysplasia

    Q65.9   Congenital deformity of hip, unspecified

▶ New   ⇒ Revised   ~~deleted~~ Deleted   Excludes 1   Excludes 2   Includes   Use additional   Code first   Code also   Key words

OGCR Official Guidelines   X Assign placeholder X   ● Use Additional Character(s)   ▶ Manifestation Code   **Coding Clinic**

Item 17–2   **Equinus foot** is a term referring to the hoof of a horse. The deformity is usually congenital or spastic. **Talipes equinovarus** is referred to as clubfoot. The foot tends to be smaller than normal, with the heel pointing downward and the forefoot turning inward. The heel cord (Achilles tendon) is tight, causing the heel to be drawn up toward the leg.

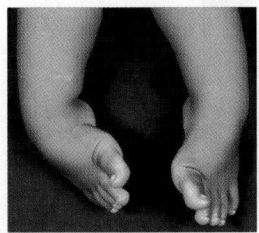

Figure 17-6   Supination and cavus deformity of forefoot. (From Kliegman R, Nelson WE: Nelson Textbook of Pediatrics, Philadelphia, Saunders, 2007)

Figure 17-7   Talipes. (From Dorland: Dorland's Illustrated Medical Dictionary, ed 31, Saunders, 2007, p 1893)

● **Q66**   **Congenital deformities of feet**

     Excludes1   reduction defects of feet (Q72.-)
                   valgus deformities (acquired) (M21.0-)
                   varus deformities (acquired) (M21.1-)

   Q66.0   **Congenital talipes equinovarus**
         Heel is turned inward from midline and foot is plantar flexed; AKA clubfoot

   Q66.1   **Congenital talipes calcaneovarus**
         Deformity of foot in which heel is turned toward midline of body and anterior of foot is elevated

● **Q66.2**   **Congenital metatarsus (primus) varus**
         Angulation of first metatarsal bone toward midline of body
         Coding Clinic: 2016, Q4, P59

       Q66.21   **Congenital metatarsus primus varus**

       Q66.22   **Congenital metatarsus adductus**
               Congenital metatarsus varus

   Q66.3   **Other congenital varus deformities of feet**
         Hallux varus, congenital

   Q66.4   **Congenital talipes calcaneovalgus**

● **Q66.5**   **Congenital pes planus**
         Congenital flat foot
         Congenital rigid flat foot
         Congenital spastic (everted) flat foot
         Excludes1   pes planus, acquired (M21.4)

       Q66.50   **Congenital pes planus, unspecified foot**

       Q66.51   **Congenital pes planus, right foot**

       Q66.52   **Congenital pes planus, left foot**

   Q66.6   **Other congenital valgus deformities of feet**
         Inward angulation
         Congenital metatarsus valgus

   Q66.7   **Congenital pes cavus**

● **Q66.8**   **Other congenital deformities of feet**

       Q66.80   **Congenital vertical talus deformity, unspecified foot**

       Q66.81   **Congenital vertical talus deformity, right foot**

       Q66.82   **Congenital vertical talus deformity, left foot**

       Q66.89   **Other specified congenital deformities of feet**
               Congenital asymmetric talipes
               Congenital clubfoot NOS
               Congenital talipes NOS
               Congenital tarsal coalition
               Hammer toe, congenital

   Q66.9   **Congenital deformity of feet, unspecified**

● **Q67**   **Congenital musculoskeletal deformities of head, face, spine and chest**

     Excludes1   congenital malformation syndromes classified to Q87.-
                   Potter's syndrome (Q60.6)

   Q67.0   **Congenital facial asymmetry**

   Q67.1   **Congenital compression facies**

   Q67.2   **Dolichocephaly**
         Long head dimension

   Q67.3   **Plagiocephaly**
         Asymmetric shape of head resulting from irregular closure of cranial sutures

   Q67.4   **Other congenital deformities of skull, face and jaw**
         Congenital depressions in skull
         Congenital hemifacial atrophy or hypertrophy
         Deviation of nasal septum, congenital
         Squashed or bent nose, congenital
         Excludes1   dentofacial anomalies [including malocclusion] (M26.-)
                          syphilitic saddle nose (A50.5)

   Q67.5   **Congenital deformity of spine**
         Congenital postural scoliosis
         Congenital scoliosis NOS
         Excludes1   infantile idiopathic scoliosis (M41.0)
                          scoliosis due to congenital bony malformation (Q76.3)

   Q67.6   **Pectus excavatum**
         Congenital funnel chest
         Funnel-shaped chest depression

   Q67.7   **Pectus carinatum**
         Congenital pigeon chest

   Q67.8   **Other congenital deformities of chest**
         Congenital deformity of chest wall NOS

CHAPTER 17 (Q00-Q99)

CHAPTER 17 (Q00-Q99)

Figure 17-8 Mild to moderate inbowing of the lower leg. (From Lissauer T, Clayden G: Illustrated Textbook of Paediatrics, Edinburgh, Mosby, 2011)

Figure 17-9 Thumb and index finger. (From Chung K: Hand and Upper Extremity Reconstruction, 1e, Saunders, 2008)

● **Q68 Other congenital musculoskeletal deformities**
  Excludes1 reduction defects of limb(s) (Q71-Q73)
  Excludes2 congenital myotonic chondrodystrophy (G71.13)
  Q68.0 Congenital deformity of sternocleidomastoid muscle
    Congenital contracture of sternocleidomastoid (muscle)
    Congenital (sternomastoid) torticollis
    Sternomastoid tumor (congenital)
  Q68.1 Congenital deformity of finger(s) and hand
    Congenital clubfinger
    Spade-like hand (congenital)
  Q68.2 Congenital deformity of knee
    Congenital dislocation of knee
    Congenital genu recurvatum
      Hyperextension of knee resulting from hypermobility
  Q68.3 Congenital bowing of femur
    Excludes1 anteversion of femur (neck) (Q65.89)
  Q68.4 Congenital bowing of tibia and fibula
  Q68.5 Congenital bowing of long bones of leg, unspecified
  Q68.6 Discoid meniscus
  Q68.8 Other specified congenital musculoskeletal deformities
    Congenital deformity of clavicle
    Congenital deformity of elbow
    Congenital deformity of forearm
    Congenital deformity of scapula
    Congenital deformity of wrist
    Congenital dislocation of elbow
    Congenital dislocation of shoulder
    Congenital dislocation of wrist

● **Q69 Polydactyly**
  AKA hyperdactyly, consists of supernumerary fingers or toes
  Q69.0 Accessory finger(s)
  Q69.1 Accessory thumb(s)
  Q69.2 Accessory toe(s)
    Accessory hallux
  Q69.9 Polydactyly, unspecified
    Supernumerary digit(s) NOS

● **Q70 Syndactyly**
  Webbing between distal phalanges of adjacent digits
  ● **Q70.0 Fused fingers**
    Complex syndactyly of fingers with synostosis
    Q70.00 Fused fingers, unspecified hand
    Q70.01 Fused fingers, right hand
    Q70.02 Fused fingers, left hand
    Q70.03 Fused fingers, bilateral
  ● **Q70.1 Webbed fingers**
    Simple syndactyly of fingers without synostosis
    Q70.10 Webbed fingers, unspecified hand
    Q70.11 Webbed fingers, right hand
    Q70.12 Webbed fingers, left hand
    Q70.13 Webbed fingers, bilateral

● **Q70.2 Fused toes**
    Complex syndactyly of toes with synostosis
    Q70.20 Fused toes, unspecified foot
    Q70.21 Fused toes, right foot
    Q70.22 Fused toes, left foot
    Q70.23 Fused toes, bilateral
● **Q70.3 Webbed toes**
    Simple syndactyly of toes without synostosis
    Q70.30 Webbed toes, unspecified foot
    Q70.31 Webbed toes, right foot
    Q70.32 Webbed toes, left foot
    Q70.33 Webbed toes, bilateral
  Q70.4 Polysyndactyly, unspecified
    Excludes1 specified syndactyly of hand and feet - code to specified conditions (Q70.0- -Q70.3-)
    Extra and webbed digits
  Q70.9 Syndactyly, unspecified
    Symphalangy NOS

● **Q71 Reduction defects of upper limb**
  ● **Q71.0 Congenital complete absence of upper limb**
    Q71.00 Congenital complete absence of unspecified upper limb
    Q71.01 Congenital complete absence of right upper limb
    Q71.02 Congenital complete absence of left upper limb
    Q71.03 Congenital complete absence of upper limb, bilateral
  ● **Q71.1 Congenital absence of upper arm and forearm with hand present**
    Q71.10 Congenital absence of unspecified upper arm and forearm with hand present
    Q71.11 Congenital absence of right upper arm and forearm with hand present
    Q71.12 Congenital absence of left upper arm and forearm with hand present
    Q71.13 Congenital absence of upper arm and forearm with hand present, bilateral
  ● **Q71.2 Congenital absence of both forearm and hand**
    Q71.20 Congenital absence of both forearm and hand, unspecified upper limb
    Q71.21 Congenital absence of both forearm and hand, right upper limb
    Q71.22 Congenital absence of both forearm and hand, left upper limb
    Q71.23 Congenital absence of both forearm and hand, bilateral
  ● **Q71.3 Congenital absence of hand and finger**
    Q71.30 Congenital absence of unspecified hand and finger
    Q71.31 Congenital absence of right hand and finger
    Q71.32 Congenital absence of left hand and finger
    Q71.33 Congenital absence of hand and finger, bilateral

▶ New   ⇒ Revised   ~~deleted~~ Deleted   Excludes 1   Excludes 2   Includes   Use additional   Code first   Code also   Key words
OGCR Official Guidelines   X Assign placeholder X   ● Use Additional Character(s)   ▷ Manifestation Code   **Coding Clinic**

● Q71.4 **Longitudinal reduction defect of radius**
Clubhand (congenital)
Radial clubhand

  Q71.40 Longitudinal reduction defect of unspecified radius

  Q71.41 Longitudinal reduction defect of right radius

  Q71.42 Longitudinal reduction defect of left radius

  Q71.43 Longitudinal reduction defect of radius, bilateral

● Q71.5 **Longitudinal reduction defect of ulna**

  Q71.50 Longitudinal reduction defect of unspecified ulna

  Q71.51 Longitudinal reduction defect of right ulna

  Q71.52 Longitudinal reduction defect of left ulna

  Q71.53 Longitudinal reduction defect of ulna, bilateral

● Q71.6 **Lobster-claw hand**

  Q71.60 Lobster-claw hand, unspecified hand

  Q71.61 Lobster-claw right hand

  Q71.62 Lobster-claw left hand

  Q71.63 Lobster-claw hand, bilateral

● Q71.8 **Other reduction defects of upper limb**

  ● Q71.81 **Congenital shortening of upper limb**

    Q71.811 Congenital shortening of right upper limb

    Q71.812 Congenital shortening of left upper limb

    Q71.813 Congenital shortening of upper limb, bilateral

    Q71.819 Congenital shortening of unspecified upper limb

  ● Q71.89 **Other reduction defects of upper limb**

    Q71.891 Other reduction defects of right upper limb

    Q71.892 Other reduction defects of left upper limb

    Q71.893 Other reduction defects of upper limb, bilateral

    Q71.899 Other reduction defects of unspecified upper limb

● Q71.9 **Unspecified reduction defect of upper limb**

  Q71.90 Unspecified reduction defect of unspecified upper limb

  Q71.91 Unspecified reduction defect of right upper limb

  Q71.92 Unspecified reduction defect of left upper limb

  Q71.93 Unspecified reduction defect of upper limb, bilateral

● Q72 **Reduction defects of lower limb**

  ● Q72.0 **Congenital complete absence of lower limb**

    Q72.00 Congenital complete absence of unspecified lower limb

    Q72.01 Congenital complete absence of right lower limb

    Q72.02 Congenital complete absence of left lower limb

    Q72.03 Congenital complete absence of lower limb, bilateral

  ● Q72.1 **Congenital absence of thigh and lower leg with foot present**

    Q72.10 Congenital absence of unspecified thigh and lower leg with foot present

    Q72.11 Congenital absence of right thigh and lower leg with foot present

    Q72.12 Congenital absence of left thigh and lower leg with foot present

    Q72.13 Congenital absence of thigh and lower leg with foot present, bilateral

● Q72.2 **Congenital absence of both lower leg and foot**

  Q72.20 Congenital absence of both lower leg and foot, unspecified lower limb

  Q72.21 Congenital absence of both lower leg and foot, right lower limb

  Q72.22 Congenital absence of both left lower leg and foot, left lower limb

  Q72.23 Congenital absence of both lower leg and foot, bilateral

● Q72.3 **Congenital absence of foot and toe(s)**

  Q72.30 Congenital absence of unspecified foot and toe(s)

  Q72.31 Congenital absence of right foot and toe(s)

  Q72.32 Congenital absence of left foot and toe(s)

  Q72.33 Congenital absence of foot and toe(s), bilateral

● Q72.4 **Longitudinal reduction defect of femur**
Proximal femoral focal deficiency

  Q72.40 Longitudinal reduction defect of unspecified femur

  Q72.41 Longitudinal reduction defect of right femur

  Q72.42 Longitudinal reduction defect of left femur

  Q72.43 Longitudinal reduction defect of femur, bilateral

● Q72.5 **Longitudinal reduction defect of tibia**

  Q72.50 Longitudinal reduction defect of unspecified tibia

  Q72.51 Longitudinal reduction defect of right tibia

  Q72.52 Longitudinal reduction defect of left tibia

  Q72.53 Longitudinal reduction defect of tibia, bilateral

● Q72.6 **Longitudinal reduction defect of fibula**

  Q72.60 Longitudinal reduction defect of unspecified fibula

  Q72.61 Longitudinal reduction defect of right fibula

  Q72.62 Longitudinal reduction defect of left fibula

  Q72.63 Longitudinal reduction defect of fibula, bilateral

● Q72.7 **Split foot**

  Q72.70 Split foot, unspecified lower limb

  Q72.71 Split foot, right lower limb

  Q72.72 Split foot, left lower limb

  Q72.73 Split foot, bilateral

● Q72.8 **Other reduction defects of lower limb**

  ● Q72.81 **Congenital shortening of lower limb**

    Q72.811 Congenital shortening of right lower limb

    Q72.812 Congenital shortening of left lower limb

    Q72.813 Congenital shortening of lower limb, bilateral

    Q72.819 Congenital shortening of unspecified lower limb

  ● Q72.89 **Other reduction defects of lower limb**

    Q72.891 Other reduction defects of right lower limb

    Q72.892 Other reduction defects of left lower limb

    Q72.893 Other reduction defects of lower limb, bilateral

    Q72.899 Other reduction defects of unspecified lower limb

● Q72.9 **Unspecified reduction defect of lower limb**

  Q72.90 Unspecified reduction defect of unspecified lower limb

  Q72.91 Unspecified reduction defect of right lower limb

  Q72.92 Unspecified reduction defect of left lower limb

  Q72.93 Unspecified reduction defect of lower limb, bilateral

CHAPTER 17 (Q00-Q99)

CHAPTER 17 (Q00-Q99)

● **Q73 Reduction defects of unspecified limb**

    Q73.0 Congenital absence of unspecified limb(s)
        Amelia NOS

    Q73.1 Phocomelia, unspecified limb(s)
        Phocomelia NOS
          Absence/shortening of long bones primarily as a result of thalidomide

    Q73.8 Other reduction defects of unspecified limb(s)
        Longitudinal reduction deformity of unspecified limb(s)
        Ectromelia of limb NOS
          Gross hypoplasia or aplasia of one or more long bones of limb(s)
        Hemimelia of limb NOS
          Absence of one-half of long bone
        Reduction defect of limb NOS

● **Q74 Other congenital malformations of limb(s)**
    Excludes1 polydactyly (Q69.-)
               reduction defect of limb (Q71-Q73)
               syndactyly (Q70.-)

    Q74.0 Other congenital malformations of upper limb(s), including shoulder girdle
        Accessory carpal bones
        Cleidocranial dysostosis
        Congenital pseudarthrosis of clavicle
        Macrodactylia (fingers)
        Madelung's deformity
        Radioulnar synostosis
        Sprengel's deformity
        Triphalangeal thumb

    Q74.1 Congenital malformation of knee
        Congenital absence of patella
        Congenital dislocation of patella
        Congenital genu valgum
        Congenital genu varum
        Rudimentary patella
        Excludes1 congenital dislocation of knee (Q68.2)
                   congenital genu recurvatum (Q68.2)
                   nail patella syndrome (Q87.2)

    Q74.2 Other congenital malformations of lower limb(s), including pelvic girdle
        Congenital fusion of sacroiliac joint
        Congenital malformation of ankle joint
        Congenital malformation of sacroiliac joint
        Excludes1 anteversion of femur (neck) (Q65.89)

    Q74.3 Arthrogryposis multiplex congenita
    Q74.8 Other specified congenital malformations of limb(s)
    Q74.9 Unspecified congenital malformation of limb(s)
        Congenital anomaly of limb(s) NOS

● **Q75 Other congenital malformations of skull and face bones**
    Excludes1 congenital malformation of face NOS (Q18.-)
               congenital malformation syndromes classified to Q87.-
               dentofacial anomalies [including malocclusion] (M26.-)
               musculoskeletal deformities of head and face (Q67.0-Q67.4)
               skull defects associated with congenital anomalies of brain such as:
                 anencephaly (Q00.0)
                 encephalocele (Q01.-)
                 hydrocephalus (Q03.-)
                 microcephaly (Q02)

    Q75.0 Craniosynostosis
        Premature closure of sutures of skull
        Acrocephaly
        Imperfect fusion of skull
        Oxycephaly
        Trigonocephaly

    Q75.1 Craniofacial dysostosis
        Congenital deformity of head
        Crouzon's disease

Item 17–3 Anencephalus is a congenital deformity of the cranial vault. **Craniosynostosis,** also known as craniostenosis and stenocephaly, signifies any form of congenital deformity of the skull that results from the premature closing of the sutures of the skull. **Iniencephaly** is a deformity in which the head and neck are flexed backward to a great extent and the head is very large in comparison to the shortened body.

Figure 17-10 Generalized craniosynostosis without symptoms or signs of increased intracranial pressure. (From Goetz C: Textbook of Clinical Neurology, St. Louis, MO, Elsevier, 2007)

    Q75.2 Hypertelorism
    Q75.3 Macrocephaly
        Unusually large size of head; AKA megalocephaly
    Q75.4 Mandibulofacial dysostosis
        Franceschetti syndrome
        Treacher Collins syndrome
    Q75.5 Oculomandibular dysostosis
        Ossification of occular and mandibular bones
    Q75.8 Other specified congenital malformations of skull and face bones
        Absence of skull bone, congenital
        Congenital deformity of forehead
        Platybasia
    Q75.9 Congenital malformation of skull and face bones, unspecified
        Congenital anomaly of face bones NOS
        Congenital anomaly of skull NOS

● **Q76 Congenital malformations of spine and bony thorax**
    Excludes1 congenital musculoskeletal deformities of spine and chest (Q67.5-Q67.8)
    Q76.0 Spina bifida occulta
        Excludes1 meningocele (spinal) (Q05.-)
                   spina bifida (aperta) (cystica) (Q05.-)
    Q76.1 Klippel-Feil syndrome
        Cervical fusion syndrome
    Q76.2 Congenital spondylolisthesis
        Congenital spondylolysis
        Excludes1 spondylolisthesis (acquired) (M43.1-)
                   spondylolysis (acquired) (M43.0-)
    Q76.3 Congenital scoliosis due to congenital bony malformation
        Hemivertebra fusion or failure of segmentation with scoliosis
●   **Q76.4 Other congenital malformations of spine, not associated with scoliosis**
●   **Q76.41 Congenital kyphosis**
             Abnormal increase in convexity curvature of thoracic spinal column; AKA humpback
             Q76.411 Congenital kyphosis, occipito-atlanto-axial region
             Q76.412 Congenital kyphosis, cervical region
             Q76.413 Congenital kyphosis, cervicothoracic region
             Q76.414 Congenital kyphosis, thoracic region
             Q76.415 Congenital kyphosis, thoracolumbar region
             Q76.419 Congenital kyphosis, unspecified region

▶ New   ➡ Revised   ~~deleted~~ Deleted   Excludes 1   Excludes 2   Includes   Use additional   Code first   Code also   Key words
OGCR Official Guidelines   X Assign placeholder X   ● Use Additional Character(s)   ▶ Manifestation Code   **Coding Clinic**

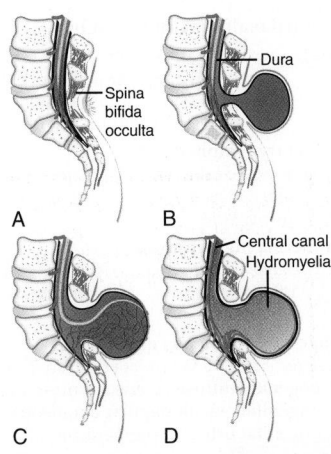

Figure 17-11   A. Spina bifida occulta. **B.** Meningocele.
C. Myelomeningocele. **D.** Myelocystocele (syringomyelocele)
or hydromyelia.

Item 17–4   Spina bifida is a midline spinal defect in which one or more vertebrae fail to fuse, leaving an opening in the vertebral canal. When the defect is not visible, it is called spina bifida occulta, and when it is visible, it is called spina bifida cystica.

● **Q76.42   Congenital lordosis**
    An abnormal increase in curvature of lumbar spine (sway back)
    Q76.425   Congenital lordosis, thoracolumbar region
    Q76.426   Congenital lordosis, lumbar region
    Q76.427   Congenital lordosis, lumbosacral region
    Q76.428   Congenital lordosis, sacral and sacrococcygeal region
    Q76.429   Congenital lordosis, unspecified region
    Q76.49   Other congenital malformations of spine, not associated with scoliosis
        Congenital absence of vertebra NOS
        Congenital fusion of spine NOS
        Congenital malformation of lumbosacral (joint) (region) NOS
        Congenital malformation of spine NOS
        Hemivertebra NOS
        Malformation of spine NOS
        Platyspondylisis NOS
        Supernumerary vertebra NOS
    Q76.5   Cervical rib
        Supernumerary rib in cervical region
    Q76.6   Other congenital malformations of ribs
        Accessory rib
        Congenital absence of rib
        Congenital fusion of ribs
        Congenital malformation of ribs NOS
        Excludes1   short rib syndrome (Q77.2)
    Q76.7   Congenital malformation of sternum
        Congenital absence of sternum
        Sternum bifidum
    Q76.8   Other congenital malformations of bony thorax
    Q76.9   Congenital malformation of bony thorax, unspecified

● **Q77   Osteochondrodysplasia with defects of growth of tubular bones and spine**
    Excludes1   mucopolysaccharidosis (E76.0-E76.3)
    Excludes2   congenital myotonic chondrodystrophy (G71.13)
    Q77.0   Achondrogenesis
        Hypochondrogenesis
    Q77.1   Thanatophoric short stature
    Q77.2   Short rib syndrome
        Asphyxiating thoracic dysplasia [Jeune]
    Q77.3   Chondrodysplasia punctata
        Benign cartilaginous neoplasms
        Excludes1   rhizomelic chondrodysplasia punctata (E71.43)
    Q77.4   Achondroplasia
        Disturbance of epiphyseal chondroblastic growth and maturation, results in dwarfism
        Hypochondroplasia
        Osteosclerosis congenita
    Q77.5   Diastrophic dysplasia
    Q77.6   Chondroectodermal dysplasia
        Defective development of skin, hair, teeth, with polydactyly and defect of cardiac septum
        Ellis-van Creveld syndrome
    Q77.7   Spondyloepiphyseal dysplasia
    Q77.8   Other osteochondrodysplasia with defects of growth of tubular bones and spine
    Q77.9   Osteochondrodysplasia with defects of growth of tubular bones and spine, unspecified

● **Q78   Other osteochondrodysplasias**
    Disorder of development of bone and cartilage; common cause of dwarfism
    Excludes2   congenital myotonic chondrodystrophy (G71.13)
    Q78.0   Osteogenesis imperfecta
        Fragilitas ossium
        Osteopsathyrosis
    Q78.1   Polyostotic fibrous dysplasia
        Albright(-McCune)(-Sternberg) syndrome
    Q78.2   Osteopetrosis
        Abnormally dense bone; AKA marble bones disease, ivory bones
        Albers-Schönberg syndrome
        Osteosclerosis NOS
    Q78.3   Progressive diaphyseal dysplasia
        Camurati-Engelmann syndrome
    Q78.4   Enchondromatosis
        Thinning of overlying cortex of bone and distorted length
        Maffucci's syndrome
        Ollier's disease
    Q78.5   Metaphyseal dysplasia
        Disturbance in enchondral bone growth, causing ends of shafts to remain larger than normal in circumference
        Pyle's syndrome
    Q78.6   Multiple congenital exostoses
        Diaphyseal aclasis
    Q78.8   Other specified osteochondrodysplasias
        Osteopoikilosis
    Q78.9   Osteochondrodysplasia, unspecified
        Chondrodystrophy NOS
        AKA skeletal dysplasia (dwarfism) caused by genetic mutations affecting hyaline cartilage capping long bones and vertebrae
        Osteodystrophy NOS

CHAPTER 17 (Q00-Q99)

● **Q79** **Congenital malformations of musculoskeletal system, not elsewhere classified**

    Excludes2   congenital (sternomastoid) torticollis (Q68.0)

Q79.0 **Congenital diaphragmatic hernia**

    Excludes1   congenital hiatus hernia (Q40.1)

Q79.1 **Other congenital malformations of diaphragm**
    Absence of diaphragm
    Congenital malformation of diaphragm NOS
    Eventration of diaphragm

Q79.2 **Exomphalos**
    Abdominal hernia in which part of intestine protrudes at umbilicus; AKA exomphalos and exumbilication
    Omphalocele

      Excludes1   umbilical hernia (K42.-)

Q79.3 **Gastroschisis**
    Congenital fissure of anterior abdominal wall often with protrusion of small/large intestine

Q79.4 **Prune belly syndrome**
    Congenital prolapse of bladder mucosa
    Eagle-Barrett syndrome

● **Q79.5** **Other congenital malformations of abdominal wall**

    Excludes1   umbilical hernia (K42.-)

    Q79.51   **Congenital hernia of bladder**

    Q79.59   **Other congenital malformations of abdominal wall**

Q79.6 **Ehlers-Danlos syndrome**
    Group of inherited disorders of connective tissue; AKA cutis hyperelastica

Q79.8 **Other congenital malformations of musculoskeletal system**
    Absence of muscle
    Absence of tendon
    Accessory muscle
    Amyotrophia congenita
    Congenital constricting bands
    Congenital shortening of tendon
    Poland syndrome

Q79.9 **Congenital malformation of musculoskeletal system, unspecified**
    Congenital anomaly of musculoskeletal system NOS
    Congenital deformity of musculoskeletal system NOS

OTHER CONGENITAL MALFORMATIONS (Q80-Q89)

● **Q80** **Congenital ichthyosis**
    Characterized by increased keratinization, resulting in noninflammatory scaling of skin

    Excludes1   Refsum's disease (G60.1)

Q80.0 **Ichthyosis vulgaris**

Q80.1 **X-linked ichthyosis**

Q80.2 **Lamellar ichthyosis**
    Collodion baby

Q80.3 **Congenital bullous ichthyosiform erythroderma**

Q80.4 **Harlequin fetus**

Q80.8 **Other congenital ichthyosis**

Q80.9 **Congenital ichthyosis, unspecified**

● **Q81** **Epidermolysis bullosa**
    Loosening of epidermis

Q81.0 **Epidermolysis bullosa simplex**

    Excludes1   Cockayne's syndrome (Q87.1)

Q81.1 **Epidermolysis bullosa letalis**
    Herlitz' syndrome

Q81.2 **Epidermolysis bullosa dystrophica**

Q81.8 **Other epidermolysis bullosa**

Q81.9 **Epidermolysis bullosa, unspecified**

● **Q82** **Other congenital malformations of skin**

    Excludes1   acrodermatitis enteropathica (E83.2)
              congenital erythropoietic porphyria (E80.0)
              pilonidal cyst or sinus (L05.-)
              Sturge-Weber (-Dimitri) syndrome (Q85.8)

Q82.0 **Hereditary lymphedema**
    Characterized by swelling of subcutaneous tissue caused by obstruction of lymphatic vessels and resulting edema of lymph fluid

Q82.1 **Xeroderma pigmentosum**
    Extreme sensitivity to ultraviolet rays that most commonly affects the eyes and skin, but may also involve the nervous system

Q82.2 **Congenital cutaneous mastocytosis**
    Characterized by infiltrates of mast cells in tissues/organs
    Congenital diffuse cutaneous mastocytosis
    Congenital maculopapular cutaneous mastocytosis
    Congenital urticaria pigmentosa

    Excludes1   cutaneous mastocytosis NOS (D47.01)
            diffuse cutaneous mastocytosis (with onset after newborn period) (D47.01)
            malignant mastocytosis (C96.2-)
            systemic mastocytosis (D47.02)
            urticaria pigmentosa (non-congenital) (with onset after newborn period) (D47.01)

Q82.3 **Incontinentia pigmenti**
    Characterized by hypopigmented cutaneous in adults and early childhood

Q82.4 **Ectodermal dysplasia (anhidrotic)**
    Absence/deficiency of tissues/structures, including teeth, hair, nails, and certain glands

    Excludes1   Ellis-van Creveld syndrome (Q77.6)

Q82.5 **Congenital non-neoplastic nevus**
    Birthmark NOS
    Flammeus Nevus
    Portwine Nevus
    Sanguineous Nevus
    Strawberry Nevus
    Vascular Nevus NOS
    Verrucous Nevus

    Excludes2   Café au lait spots (L81.3)
            lentigo (L81.4)
            nevus NOS (D22.-)
            araneus nevus (I78.1)
            melanocytic nevus (D22.-)
            pigmented nevus (D22.-)
            spider nevus (I78.1)
            stellar nevus (I78.1)

Q82.6 **Congenital sacral dimple**
    Parasacral dimple

    Excludes2   pilonidal cyst with abscess (L05.01)
            pilonidal cyst without abscess (L05.91)
    Coding Clinic: 2016, Q4, P60

Q82.8 **Other specified congenital malformations of skin**
    Abnormal palmar creases
    Accessory skin tags
    Benign familial pemphigus [Hailey-Hailey]
    Congenital poikiloderma
    Cutis laxa (hyperelastica)
    Dermatoglyphic anomalies
    Inherited keratosis palmaris et plantaris
    Keratosis follicularis [Darier-White]

    Excludes1   Ehlers-Danlos syndrome (Q79.6)
    Coding Clinic: 2016, Q1, P17

Q82.9 **Congenital malformation of skin, unspecified**

▶ New   ⇒ Revised   ~~deleted~~ Deleted   Excludes 1   Excludes 2   Includes   Use additional   Code first   Code also   Key words
    OGCR Official Guidelines   X Assign placeholder X   ● Use Additional Character(s)   � Manifestation Code   **Coding Clinic**

● **Q83**   **Congenital malformations of breast**

     Excludes2   absence of pectoral muscle (Q79.8)
                          hypoplasia of breast (N64.82)
                          micromastia (N64.82)

   Q83.0   **Congenital absence of breast with absent nipple**

   Q83.1   **Accessory breast**
          Supernumerary breast

   Q83.2   **Absent nipple**

   Q83.3   **Accessory nipple**
          Supernumerary nipple

   Q83.8   **Other congenital malformations of breast**

   Q83.9   **Congenital malformation of breast, unspecified**

● **Q84**   **Other congenital malformations of integument**

   Q84.0   **Congenital alopecia**
          Congenital atrichosis

   Q84.1   **Congenital morphological disturbances of hair, not elsewhere classified**
          Beaded hair
          Monilethrix
          Pili annulati

       Excludes1   Menkes' kinky hair syndrome (E83.0)

   Q84.2   **Other congenital malformations of hair**
          Congenital hypertrichosis
          Congenital malformation of hair NOS
          Persistent lanugo

   Q84.3   **Anonychia**
          Absence of nail

       Excludes1   nail patella syndrome (Q87.2)

   Q84.4   **Congenital leukonychia**
          Opaque, whitish discoloration of nails; AKA leukopathia unguium

   Q84.5   **Enlarged and hypertrophic nails**
          Congenital onychauxis
          Pachyonychia

   Q84.6   **Other congenital malformations of nails**
          Congenital clubnail
          Congenital koilonychia
          Congenital malformation of nail NOS

   Q84.8   **Other specified congenital malformations of integument**
          Aplasia cutis congenita

   Q84.9   **Congenital malformation of integument, unspecified**
          Congenital anomaly of integument NOS
          Congenital deformity of integument NOS

● **Q85**   **Phakomatoses, not elsewhere classified**

       Excludes1   ataxia telangiectasia [Louis-Bar] (G11.3)
                          familial dysautonomia [Riley-Day] (G90.1)

   ● **Q85.0**   **Neurofibromatosis (nonmalignant)**
          Developmental changes in nervous system and other structures, with formation of neurofibromas

     Q85.00   **Neurofibromatosis, unspecified**

     Q85.01   **Neurofibromatosis, type 1**
            Von Recklinghausen disease

     Q85.02   **Neurofibromatosis, type 2**
            Acoustic neurofibromatosis

     Q85.03   **Schwannomatosis**

     Q85.09   **Other neurofibromatosis**

   Q85.1   **Tuberous sclerosis**
          Bourneville's disease
          Epiloia

   Q85.8   **Other phakomatoses, not elsewhere classified**
          Peutz-Jeghers Syndrome
          Sturge-Weber(-Dimitri) syndrome
          von Hippel-Lindau syndrome

       Excludes1   Meckel-Gruber syndrome (Q61.9)

   Q85.9   **Phakomatosis, unspecified**
          Hamartosis NOS

● **Q86**   **Congenital malformation syndromes due to known exogenous causes, not elsewhere classified**

       Excludes2   iodine-deficiency-related hypothyroidism (E00-E02)
                          nonteratogenic effects of substances transmitted via placenta or breast milk (P04.-)

   Q86.0   **Fetal alcohol syndrome (dysmorphic)**

   Q86.1   **Fetal hydantoin syndrome**
          Meadow's syndrome

   Q86.2   **Dysmorphism due to warfarin**

   Q86.8   **Other congenital malformation syndromes due to known exogenous causes**

● **Q87**   **Other specified congenital malformation syndromes affecting multiple systems**
       Use additional code(s) to identify all associated manifestations

   Q87.0   **Congenital malformation syndromes predominantly affecting facial appearance**
          Acrocephalopolysyndactyly
          Acrocephalosyndactyly [Apert]
          Cryptophthalmos syndrome
          Cyclopia
          Goldenhar syndrome
          Moebius syndrome
          Oro-facial-digital syndrome
          Robin syndrome
          Whistling face

   Q87.1   **Congenital malformation syndromes predominantly associated with short stature**
          Aarskog syndrome
          Cockayne syndrome
          De Lange syndrome
          Dubowitz syndrome
          Noonan syndrome
          Prader-Willi syndrome
          Robinow-Silverman-Smith syndrome
          Russell-Silver syndrome
          Seckel syndrome

       Excludes1   Ellis-van Creveld syndrome (Q77.6)
                          Smith-Lemli-Opitz syndrome (E78.72)

   Q87.2   **Congenital malformation syndromes predominantly involving limbs**
          Holt-Oram syndrome
          Klippel-Trenaunay-Weber syndrome
          Nail patella syndrome
          Rubinstein-Taybi syndrome
          Sirenomelia syndrome
          Thrombocytopenia with absent radius [TAR] syndrome
          VATER syndrome

   Q87.3   **Congenital malformation syndromes involving early overgrowth**
          Beckwith-Wiedemann syndrome
          Sotos' syndrome
          Weaver syndrome

   ● **Q87.4**   **Marfan's syndrome**

     Q87.40   **Marfan's syndrome, unspecified**

     ● **Q87.41**   **Marfan's syndrome with cardiovascular manifestations**

       Q87.410   **Marfan's syndrome with aortic dilation**

       Q87.418   **Marfan's syndrome with other cardiovascular manifestations**

     Q87.42   **Marfan's syndrome with ocular manifestations**

     Q87.43   **Marfan's syndrome with skeletal manifestation**

   Q87.5   **Other congenital malformation syndromes with other skeletal changes**

CHAPTER 17 (Q00-Q99)

CHAPTER 17 (Q00-Q99)

● **Q87.8** **Other specified congenital malformation syndromes, not elsewhere classified**

     Excludes1   Zellweger syndrome (E71.510)

     Q87.81 **Alport syndrome**
         Progressive sensorineural hearing loss, progressive pyelonephritis or glomerulonephritis, and ocular defects
         Use additional code to identify stage of chronic kidney disease (N18.1-N18.6)

     Q87.82 **Arterial tortuosity syndrome**
         Coding Clinic: 2016, Q4, P60-61

     Q87.89 **Other specified congenital malformation syndromes, not elsewhere classified**
         Laurence-Moon (-Bardet)-Biedl syndrome

● **Q89** **Other congenital malformations, not elsewhere classified**

   ● **Q89.0** **Congenital absence and malformations of spleen**
       Excludes1   isomerism of atrial appendages (with asplenia or polysplenia) (Q20.6)

     Q89.01 **Asplenia (congenital)**
     Q89.09 **Congenital malformations of spleen**
         Congenital splenomegaly

   Q89.1 **Congenital malformations of adrenal gland**
       Excludes1   adrenogenital disorders (E25.-)
                    congenital adrenal hyperplasia (E25.0)

   Q89.2 **Congenital malformations of other endocrine glands**
     Congenital malformation of parathyroid or thyroid gland
     Persistent thyroglossal duct
     Thyroglossal cyst
       Excludes1   congenital goiter (E03.0)
                    congenital hypothyroidism (E03.1)

   Q89.3 **Situs inversus**
     Lateral transposition of viscera of thorax and abdomen
     Dextrocardia with situs inversus
     Mirror-image atrial arrangement with situs inversus
     Situs inversus or transversus abdominalis
     Situs inversus or transversus thoracis
     Transposition of abdominal viscera
     Transposition of thoracic viscera
       Excludes1   dextrocardia NOS (Q24.0)

   Q89.4 **Conjoined twins**
     Craniopagus
     Dicephaly
     Pygopagus
     Thoracopagus

   Q89.7 **Multiple congenital malformations, not elsewhere classified**
     Multiple congenital anomalies NOS
     Multiple congenital deformities NOS
       Excludes1   congenital malformation syndromes affecting multiple systems (Q87.-)

   Q89.8 **Other specified congenital malformations**
     Use additional code(s) to identify all associated manifestations

   Q89.9 **Congenital malformation, unspecified**
     Congenital anomaly NOS
     Congenital deformity NOS

CHROMOSOMAL ABNORMALITIES, NOT ELSEWHERE CLASSIFIED (Q90-Q99)

     Excludes2   mitochondrial metabolic disorders (E88.4-)

● **Q90** **Down syndrome**
     Use additional code(s) to identify any associated physical conditions and degree of intellectual disabilities (F70-F79)

   Q90.0 **Trisomy 21, nonmosaicism (meiotic nondisjunction)**
     Trisomy 21, nondisjunction, accounts for 95% of Downs syndrome cases

   Q90.1 **Trisomy 21, mosaicism (mitotic nondisjunction)**
   Q90.2 **Trisomy 21, translocation**
   Q90.9 **Down syndrome, unspecified**
     Trisomy 21 NOS

● **Q91** **Trisomy 18 and Trisomy 13**

   Q91.0 **Trisomy 18, nonmosaicism (meiotic nondisjunction)**
   Q91.1 **Trisomy 18, mosaicism (mitotic nondisjunction)**
   Q91.2 **Trisomy 18, translocation**
   Q91.3 **Trisomy 18, unspecified**
   Q91.4 **Trisomy 13, nonmosaicism (meiotic nondisjunction)**
   Q91.5 **Trisomy 13, mosaicism (mitotic nondisjunction)**
   Q91.6 **Trisomy 13, translocation**
   Q91.7 **Trisomy 13, unspecified**

● **Q92** **Other trisomies and partial trisomies of the autosomes, not elsewhere classified**

     Includes   unbalanced translocations and insertions
     Excludes1   trisomies of chromosomes 13, 18, 21 (Q90-Q91)

   Q92.0 **Whole chromosome trisomy, nonmosaicism (meiotic nondisjunction)**
   Q92.1 **Whole chromosome trisomy, mosaicism (mitotic nondisjunction)**
   Q92.2 **Partial trisomy**
     Less than whole arm duplicated
     Whole arm or more duplicated
       Excludes1   partial trisomy due to unbalanced translocation (Q92.5)

   Q92.5 **Duplications with other complex rearrangements**
     Partial trisomy due to unbalanced translocations
     Code also any associated deletions due to unbalanced translocations, inversions and insertions (Q93.7)

   ● **Q92.6** **Marker chromosomes**
     Trisomies due to dicentrics
     Trisomies due to extra rings
     Trisomies due to isochromosomes
     Individual with marker heterochromatin

     Q92.61 **Marker chromosomes in normal individual**
     Q92.62 **Marker chromosomes in abnormal individual**

   Q92.7 **Triploidy and polyploidy**
   Q92.8 **Other specified trisomies and partial trisomies of autosomes**
     Duplications identified by fluorescence in situ hybridization (FISH)
     Duplications identified by in situ hybridization (ISH)
     Duplications seen only at prometaphase

   Q92.9 **Trisomy and partial trisomy of autosomes, unspecified**

● **Q93** **Monosomies and deletions from the autosomes, not elsewhere classified**

   Q93.0 **Whole chromosome monosomy, nonmosaicism (meiotic nondisjunction)**
   Q93.1 **Whole chromosome monosomy, mosaicism (mitotic nondisjunction)**
   Q93.2 **Chromosome replaced with ring, dicentric or isochromosome**
   Q93.3 **Deletion of short arm of chromosome 4**
     Wolff-Hirschorn syndrome
   Q93.4 **Deletion of short arm of chromosome 5**
     Cri-du-chat syndrome
   ● **Q93.5** **Other deletions of part of a chromosome**
     ~~Angelman syndrome~~
     ▶ **Q93.51** **Angelman syndrome**
     ▶ **Q93.59** **Other deletions of part of a chromosome**
   Q93.7 **Deletions with other complex rearrangements**
     Deletions due to unbalanced translocations, inversions and insertions
     Code also any associated duplications due to unbalanced translocations, inversions and insertions (Q92.5)

▶ New   ⇒ Revised   ~~deleted~~ Deleted   Excludes 1   Excludes 2   Includes   Use additional   Code first   Code also   Key words

OGCR Official Guidelines   X Assign placeholder X   ● Use Additional Character(s)   ▷ Manifestation Code   **Coding Clinic**

● **Q93.8 Other deletions from the autosomes**

    Q93.81 Velo-cardio-facial syndrome
        Deletion 22q11.2

▶   **Q93.82 Williams syndrome**

    Q93.88 Other microdeletions Miller-Dieker syndrome
        Smith-Magenis syndrome

    Q93.89 Other deletions from the autosomes
        Deletions identified by fluorescence in situ
          hybridization (FISH)
        Deletions identified by in situ hybridization
          (ISH)
        Deletions seen only at prometaphase

  Q93.9 Deletion from autosomes, unspecified

● **Q95 Balanced rearrangements and structural markers, not elsewhere classified**

    Includes   Robertsonian and balanced reciprocal
             translocations and insertions

  Q95.0 Balanced translocation and insertion in normal individual

  Q95.1 Chromosome inversion in normal individual

  Q95.2 Balanced autosomal rearrangement in abnormal individual

  Q95.3 Balanced sex/autosomal rearrangement in abnormal individual

  Q95.5 Individual with autosomal fragile site

  Q95.8 Other balanced rearrangements and structural markers

  Q95.9 Balanced rearrangement and structural marker, unspecified

● **Q96 Turner's syndrome**

    Caused by missing or incomplete X chromosome affecting growth and sexual development

    Excludes1   Noonan syndrome (Q87.1)

  Q96.0 Karyotype 45, X ♀

  Q96.1 Karyotype 46, X iso (Xq) ♀
        Karyotype 46, isochromosome Xq

  Q96.2 Karyotype 46, X with abnormal sex chromosome, except iso (Xq) ♀
        Karyotype 46, X with abnormal sex chromosome, except
          isochromosome Xq

  Q96.3 Mosaicism, 45, X/46, XX or XY ♀

  Q96.4 Mosaicism, 45, X/other cell line(s) with abnormal sex chromosome ♀

  Q96.8 Other variants of Turner's syndrome ♀

  Q96.9 Turner's syndrome, unspecified ♀

● **Q97 Other sex chromosome abnormalities, female phenotype, not elsewhere classified**

    Excludes1   Turner's syndrome (Q96.-)

  Q97.0 Karyotype 47, XXX ♀

  Q97.1 Female with more than three X chromosomes ♀

  Q97.2 Mosaicism, lines with various numbers of X chromosomes ♀

  Q97.3 Female with 46, XY karyotype ♀

  Q97.8 Other specified sex chromosome abnormalities, female phenotype ♀

  Q97.9 Sex chromosome abnormality, female phenotype, unspecified ♀

● **Q98 Other sex chromosome abnormalities, male phenotype, not elsewhere classified**

  Q98.0 Klinefelter syndrome karyotype 47, XXY ♂

  Q98.1 Klinefelter syndrome, male with more than two X chromosomes ♂

  Q98.3 Other male with 46, XX karyotype ♂

  Q98.4 Klinefelter syndrome, unspecified ♂

  Q98.5 Karyotype 47, XYY

  Q98.6 Male with structurally abnormal sex chromosome ♂

  Q98.7 Male with sex chromosome mosaicism ♂

  Q98.8 Other specified sex chromosome abnormalities, male phenotype ♂

  Q98.9 Sex chromosome abnormality, male phenotype, unspecified ♂

● **Q99 Other chromosome abnormalities, not elsewhere classified**

  Q99.0 Chimera 46, XX/46, XY
        Chimera 46, XX/46, XY true hermaphrodite

  Q99.1 46, XX true hermaphrodite
        46, XX with streak gonads
        46, XY with streak gonads
        Pure gonadal dysgenesis

  Q99.2 Fragile X chromosome
        Fragile X syndrome

  Q99.8 Other specified chromosome abnormalities

  Q99.9 Chromosomal abnormality, unspecified

CHAPTER 17 (Q00-Q99)

CHAPTER 18

SYMPTOMS, SIGNS, AND ABNORMAL CLINICAL AND LABORATORY FINDINGS, NOT ELSEWHERE CLASSIFIED (R00-R99)

OGCR Chapter-Specific Coding Guidelines

18. **Chapter 18: Symptoms, signs, and abnormal clinical and laboratory findings, not elsewhere classified (R00-R99)**
Chapter 18 includes symptoms, signs, abnormal results of clinical or other investigative procedures, and ill-defined conditions regarding which no diagnosis classifiable elsewhere is recorded. Signs and symptoms that point to a specific diagnosis have been assigned to a category in other chapters of the classification.

a. **Use of symptom codes**
Codes that describe symptoms and signs are acceptable for reporting purposes when a related definitive diagnosis has not been established (confirmed) by the provider.

b. **Use of a symptom code with a definitive diagnosis code**
Codes for signs and symptoms may be reported in addition to a related definitive diagnosis when the sign or symptom is not routinely associated with that diagnosis, such as the various signs and symptoms associated with complex syndromes. The definitive diagnosis code should be sequenced before the symptom code.

Signs or symptoms that are associated routinely with a disease process should not be assigned as additional codes, unless otherwise instructed by the classification.

c. **Combination codes that include symptoms**
ICD-10-CM contains a number of combination codes that identify both the definitive diagnosis and common symptoms of that diagnosis. When using one of these combination codes, an additional code should not be assigned for the symptom.

d. **Repeated falls**
Code R29.6, Repeated falls, is for use for encounters when a patient has recently fallen and the reason for the fall is being investigated.

Code Z91.81, History of falling, is for use when a patient has fallen in the past and is at risk for future falls. When appropriate, both codes R29.6 and Z91.81 may be assigned together.

e. **Coma scale**
The coma scale codes (R40.2-) can be used in conjunction with traumatic brain injury codes, acute cerebrovascular disease or sequelae of cerebrovascular disease codes. These codes are primarily for use by trauma registries, but they may be used in any setting where this information is collected. The coma scale may also be used to assess the status of the central nervous system for other non-trauma conditions, such as monitoring patients in the intensive care unit regardless of medical condition. The coma scale codes should be sequenced after the diagnosis code(s).

These codes, one from each subcategory, are needed to complete the scale. The 7th character indicates when the scale was recorded. The 7th character should match for all three codes.

At a minimum, report the initial score documented on presentation at your facility. This may be a score from the emergency medicine technician (EMT) or in the emergency department. If desired, a facility may choose to capture multiple coma scale scores.

Assign code R40.24, Glasgow coma scale, total score, when only the total score is documented in the medical record and not the individual score(s).

Do not report codes for individual or total Glasgow coma scale scores for a patient with a medically induced coma or a sedated patient.

See Section I.B.14 for coma scale documentation by clinicians other than patient's provider

f. **Functional quadriplegia**
GUIDELINE HAS BEEN DELETED EFFECTIVE OCTOBER 1, 2017

g. **SIRS due to Non-Infectious Process**
The systemic inflammatory response syndrome (SIRS) can develop as a result of certain non-infectious disease processes, such as trauma, malignant neoplasm, or pancreatitis. When SIRS is documented with a noninfectious condition, and no subsequent infection is documented, the code for the underlying condition, such as an injury, should be assigned, followed by code R65.10, Systemic inflammatory response syndrome (SIRS) of non-infectious origin without acute organ dysfunction, or code R65.11, Systemic inflammatory response syndrome (SIRS) of non-infectious origin with acute organ dysfunction. If an associated acute organ dysfunction is documented, the appropriate code(s) for the specific type of organ dysfunction(s) should be assigned in addition to code R65.11. If acute organ dysfunction is documented, but it cannot be determined if the acute organ dysfunction is associated with SIRS or due to another condition (e.g., directly due to the trauma), the provider should be queried.

h. **Death NOS**
Code R99, Ill-defined and unknown cause of mortality, is only for use in the very limited circumstance when a patient who has already died is brought into an emergency department or other healthcare facility and is pronounced dead upon arrival. It does not represent the discharge disposition of death.

i. **NIHSS Stroke Scale**
The NIH stroke scale (NIHSS) codes (R29.7- -) can be used in conjunction with acute stroke codes (I63) to identify the patient's neurological status and the severity of the stroke. The stroke scale codes should be sequenced after the acute stroke diagnosis code(s).

At a minimum, report the initial score documented. If desired, a facility may choose to capture multiple stroke scale scores.

See Section I.B.14 for NIHSS stroke scale documentation by clinicians other than patient's provider

CHAPTER 18

SYMPTOMS, SIGNS, AND ABNORMAL CLINICAL AND LABORATORY FINDINGS, NOT ELSEWHERE CLASSIFIED (R00-R99)

Note: This chapter includes symptoms, signs, abnormal results of clinical or other investigative procedures, and ill-defined conditions regarding which no diagnosis classifiable elsewhere is recorded.

Signs and symptoms that point rather definitely to a given diagnosis have been assigned to a category in other chapters of the classification. In general, categories in this chapter include the less well-defined conditions and symptoms that, without the necessary study of the case to establish a final diagnosis, point perhaps equally to two or more diseases or to two or more systems of the body. Practically all categories in the chapter could be designated "not otherwise specified", "unknown etiology" or "transient". The Alphabetical Index should be consulted to determine which symptoms and signs are to be allocated here and which to other chapters. The residual subcategories, numbered .8, are generally provided for other relevant symptoms that cannot be allocated elsewhere in the classification.

The conditions and signs or symptoms included in categories R00-R94 consist of:
(a) cases for which no more specific diagnosis can be made even after all the facts bearing on the case have been investigated;
(b) signs or symptoms existing at the time of initial encounter that proved to be transient and whose causes could not be determined;
(c) provisional diagnosis in a patient who failed to return for further investigation or care;
(d) cases referred elsewhere for investigation or treatment before the diagnosis was made;
(e) cases in which a more precise diagnosis was not available for any other reason;
(f) certain symptoms, for which supplementary information is provided, that represent important problems in medical care in their own right.

Excludes2   abnormal findings on antenatal screening of mother (O28.-)
certain conditions originating in the perinatal period (P04-P96)
signs and symptoms classified in the body system chapters
signs and symptoms of breast (N63, N64.5)

This chapter contains the following blocks:

R00-R09	Symptoms and signs involving the circulatory and respiratory systems
R10-R19	Symptoms and signs involving the digestive system and abdomen
R20-R23	Symptoms and signs involving the skin and subcutaneous tissue
R25-R29	Symptoms and signs involving the nervous and musculoskeletal systems
R30-R39	Symptoms and signs involving the genitourinary system
R40-R46	Symptoms and signs involving cognition, perception, emotional state and behavior
R47-R49	Symptoms and signs involving speech and voice
R50-R69	General symptoms and signs
R70-R79	Abnormal findings on examination of blood, without diagnosis
R80-R82	Abnormal findings on examination of urine, without diagnosis
R83-R89	Abnormal findings on examination of other body fluids, substances and tissues, without diagnosis
R90-R94	Abnormal findings on diagnostic imaging and in function studies, without diagnosis
R97	Abnormal tumor markers
R99	Ill-defined and unknown cause of mortality

SYMPTOMS AND SIGNS INVOLVING THE CIRCULATORY AND RESPIRATORY SYSTEMS (R00-R09)

● **R00**   **Abnormalities of heart beat**

    Excludes1   abnormalities originating in the perinatal period (P29.1-)

    Excludes2   specified arrhythmias (I47-I49)

  R00.0   **Tachycardia, unspecified**
    Rapid heart rate >100 beats
    Rapid heart beat
    Sinoauricular tachycardia NOS
    Sinus [sinusal] tachycardia NOS
      Excludes1   neonatal tachycardia (P29.11)
                  paroxysmal tachycardia (I47.-)

  R00.1   **Bradycardia, unspecified**
    Slow heart rate, <60
    Sinoatrial bradycardia
    Sinus bradycardia
    Slow heart beat
    Vagal bradycardia
    Use additional code for adverse effect, if applicable, to identify drug (T36-T50 with fifth or sixth character 5)
      Excludes1   neonatal bradycardia (P29.12)

  R00.2   **Palpitations**
    Awareness of heart beat

  R00.8   **Other abnormalities of heart beat**

  R00.9   **Unspecified abnormalities of heart beat**

● **R01**   **Cardiac murmurs and other cardiac sounds**

> **Excludes1**   cardiac murmurs and sounds originating in the perinatal period (P29.8)

  R01.0   **Benign and innocent cardiac murmurs**
> Functional cardiac murmur

  R01.1   **Cardiac murmur, unspecified**
> Cardiac bruit NOS
> Heart murmur NOS
> Systolic murmur NOS

  R01.2   **Other cardiac sounds**
> Cardiac dullness, increased or decreased
> Precordial friction

  OGCR Section I.C.9.a.7.

> Hypertension, Transient
>
> Assign code R03.0, Elevated blood pressure reading without diagnosis of hypertension, unless patient has an established diagnosis of hypertension. Assign code O13.-, Gestational [pregnancy-induced] hypertension with significant proteinuria, or O14.-, Pre-eclampsia, for transient hypertension of pregnancy.

● **R03**   **Abnormal blood-pressure reading, without diagnosis**

  R03.0   **Elevated blood-pressure reading, without diagnosis of hypertension**
> **Note:** This category is to be used to record an episode of elevated blood pressure in a patient in whom no formal diagnosis of hypertension has been made, or as an isolated incidental finding.

  R03.1   **Nonspecific low blood-pressure reading**
> **Excludes1**   hypotension (I95.-)
> maternal hypotension syndrome (O26.5-)
> neurogenic orthostatic hypotension (G90.3)

● **R04**   **Hemorrhage from respiratory passages**

  R04.0   **Epistaxis**
> Hemorrhage from nose
> Nosebleed

  R04.1   **Hemorrhage from throat**
> **Excludes2**   hemoptysis (R04.2)

  R04.2   **Hemoptysis**
> Blood-stained sputum
> Cough with hemorrhage

● **R04.8**   **Hemorrhage from other sites in respiratory passages**

    R04.81   **Acute idiopathic pulmonary hemorrhage in infants**   P
> AIPHI
> Acute idiopathic hemorrhage in infants over 28 days old
> **Excludes1**   perinatal pulmonary hemorrhage (P26.-)
> von Willebrand's disease (D68.0)

    R04.89   **Hemorrhage from other sites in respiratory passages**
> Pulmonary hemorrhage NOS

  R04.9   **Hemorrhage from respiratory passages, unspecified**

R05   **Cough**
> **Excludes1**   cough with hemorrhage (R04.2)
> smoker's cough (J41.0)

● **R06**   **Abnormalities of breathing**

> **Excludes1**   acute respiratory distress syndrome (J80)
> respiratory arrest (R09.2)
> respiratory arrest of newborn (P28.81)
> respiratory distress syndrome of newborn (P22.-)
> respiratory failure (J96.-)
> respiratory failure of newborn (P28.5)

● **R06.0**   **Dyspnea**

> **Excludes1**   tachypnea NOS (R06.82)
> transient tachypnea of newborn (P22.1)

  R06.00   **Dyspnea, unspecified**
> **Coding Clinic: 2017, Q1, P26-27**

  R06.01   **Orthopnea**

  R06.02   **Shortness of breath**

  R06.03   **Acute respiratory distress**

  R06.09   **Other forms of dyspnea**

  R06.1   **Stridor**
> *Harsh, high-pitched breath sound*
> **Excludes1**   congenital laryngeal stridor (P28.89)
> laryngismus (stridulus) (J38.5)

  R06.2   **Wheezing**
> **Excludes1**   Asthma (J45.-)
> **Coding Clinic: 2016, Q2, P34**

  R06.3   **Periodic breathing**
> Cheyne-Stokes breathing
> *An abnormal pattern of breathing with gradually increasing and decreasing tidal volume with some periods of apnea*

  R06.4   **Hyperventilation**
> **Excludes1**   psychogenic hyperventilation (F45.8)

  R06.5   **Mouth breathing**
> **Excludes2**   dry mouth NOS (R68.2)

  R06.6   **Hiccough**
> **Excludes1**   psychogenic hiccough (F45.8)

  R06.7   **Sneezing**

● **R06.8**   **Other abnormalities of breathing**

    R06.81   **Apnea, not elsewhere classified**
> Apnea NOS
> **Excludes1**   apnea (of) newborn (P28.4)
> sleep apnea (G47.3-)
> sleep apnea of newborn (primary) (P28.3)

    R06.82   **Tachypnea, not elsewhere classified**
> Tachypnea NOS
> **Excludes1**   transitory tachypnea of newborn (P22.1)

    R06.83   **Snoring**

    R06.89   **Other abnormalities of breathing**
> Breath-holding (spells)
> Sighing

  R06.9   **Unspecified abnormalities of breathing**

● **R07**   **Pain in throat and chest**

> **Excludes1**   epidemic myalgia (B33.0)
> **Excludes2**   jaw pain R68.84
> pain in breast (N64.4)

  R07.0   **Pain in throat**
> **Excludes1**   chronic sore throat (J31.2)
> sore throat (acute) NOS (J02.9)
> **Excludes2**   dysphagia (R13.1-)
> pain in neck (M54.2)

  R07.1   **Chest pain on breathing**
> Painful respiration

  R07.2   **Precordial pain**

● R07.8　**Other chest pain**
　　R07.81　**Pleurodynia**
　　　　　　Pleurodynia NOS
　　　　　　　Excludes1　epidemic pleurodynia (B33.0)
　　R07.82　**Intercostal pain**
　　R07.89　**Other chest pain**
　　　　　　Anterior chest-wall pain NOS
　　R07.9　**Chest pain, unspecified**

● R09　**Other symptoms and signs involving the circulatory and respiratory system**
　　　Excludes1　acute respiratory distress syndrome (J80)
　　　　　　respiratory arrest of newborn (P28.81)
　　　　　　respiratory distress syndrome of newborn (P22.0)
　　　　　　respiratory failure (J96.-)
　　　　　　respiratory failure of newborn (P28.5)

● R09.0　**Asphyxia and hypoxemia**
　　　Excludes1　asphyxia due to carbon monoxide (T58.-)
　　　　　　asphyxia due to foreign body in respiratory tract (T17.-)
　　　　　　birth (intrauterine) asphyxia (P84)
　　　　　　hyperventilation (R06.4)
　　　　　　traumatic asphyxia (T71.-)
　　　Excludes2　hypercapnia (R06.89)
　　R09.01　**Asphyxia**
　　R09.02　**Hypoxemia**
　　R09.1　**Pleurisy**
　　　　　Occurs when double membrane (pleura) lining chest cavity and lung surface becomes inflamed causing sharp pain on inspiration/expiration
　　　Excludes1　pleurisy with effusion (J90)
　　R09.2　**Respiratory arrest**
　　　　　Cardiorespiratory failure
　　　Excludes1　cardiac arrest (I46.-)
　　　　　　respiratory arrest of newborn (P28.81)
　　　　　　respiratory distress of newborn (P22.0)
　　　　　　respiratory failure (J96.-)
　　　　　　respiratory failure of newborn (P28.5)
　　　　　　respiratory insufficiency (R06.89)
　　　　　　respiratory insufficiency of newborn (P28.5)
　　R09.3　**Abnormal sputum**
　　　　　Abnormal amount of sputum
　　　　　Abnormal color of sputum
　　　　　Abnormal odor of sputum
　　　　　Excessive sputum
　　　Excludes1　blood-stained sputum (R04.2)

● R09.8　**Other specified symptoms and signs involving the circulatory and respiratory systems**
　　R09.81　**Nasal congestion**
　　R09.82　**Postnasal drip**
　　R09.89　**Other specified symptoms and signs involving the circulatory and respiratory systems**
　　　　　Bruit (arterial)
　　　　　Abnormal chest percussion
　　　　　Feeling of foreign body in throat
　　　　　Friction sounds in chest
　　　　　Chest tympany
　　　　　Choking sensation
　　　　　Rales
　　　　　　Wet rattling, clicking, crackling sounds on auscultation
　　　　　Weak pulse
　　　Excludes2　foreign body in throat (T17.2-)
　　　　　　wheezing (R06.2)

SYMPTOMS AND SIGNS INVOLVING THE DIGESTIVE SYSTEM AND ABDOMEN (R10-R19)

　Excludes2　congenital or infantile pylorospasm (Q40.0)
　　　　gastrointestinal hemorrhage (K92.0-K92.2)
　　　　intestinal obstruction (K56.-)
　　　　newborn gastrointestinal hemorrhage (P54.0-P54.3)
　　　　newborn intestinal obstruction (P76.-)
　　　　pylorospasm (K31.3)
　　　　signs and symptoms involving the urinary system (R30-R39)
　　　　symptoms referable to female genital organs (N94.-)
　　　　symptoms referable to male genital organs (N48-N50)

● R10　**Abdominal and pelvic pain**
　　　Excludes1　renal colic (N23)
　　　Excludes2　dorsalgia (M54.-)
　　　　　flatulence and related conditions (R14.-)
　　R10.0　**Acute abdomen**
　　　　　Severe abdominal pain (generalized) (with abdominal rigidity)
　　　Excludes1　abdominal rigidity NOS (R19.3)
　　　　　generalized abdominal pain NOS (R10.84)
　　　　　localized abdominal pain (R10.1-R10.3-)

● R10.1　**Pain localized to upper abdomen**
　　R10.10　**Upper abdominal pain, unspecified**
　　R10.11　**Right upper quadrant pain**
　　R10.12　**Left upper quadrant pain**
　　R10.13　**Epigastric pain**
　　　　　Dyspepsia
　　　Excludes1　functional dyspepsia (K30)
　　R10.2　**Pelvic and perineal pain**
　　　Excludes1　vulvodynia (N94.81)

● R10.3　**Pain localized to other parts of lower abdomen**
　　R10.30　**Lower abdominal pain, unspecified**
　　R10.31　**Right lower quadrant pain**
　　R10.32　**Left lower quadrant pain**
　　R10.33　**Periumbilical pain**

● R10.8　**Other abdominal pain**
　● R10.81　**Abdominal tenderness**
　　　　　Abdominal tenderness NOS
　　　　R10.811　**Right upper quadrant abdominal tenderness**
　　　　R10.812　**Left upper quadrant abdominal tenderness**
　　　　R10.813　**Right lower quadrant abdominal tenderness**
　　　　R10.814　**Left lower quadrant abdominal tenderness**
　　　　R10.815　**Periumbilic abdominal tenderness**
　　　　R10.816　**Epigastric abdominal tenderness**
　　　　R10.817　**Generalized abdominal tenderness**
　　　　R10.819　**Abdominal tenderness, unspecified site**

● **R10.82**   **Rebound** abdominal tenderness

R10.821   **Right upper** quadrant rebound abdominal tenderness

R10.822   **Left upper** quadrant rebound abdominal tenderness

R10.823   **Right lower** quadrant rebound abdominal tenderness

R10.824   **Left lower** quadrant rebound abdominal tenderness

R10.825   **Periumbilic** rebound abdominal tenderness

R10.826   **Epigastric** rebound abdominal tenderness

R10.827   **Generalized** rebound abdominal tenderness

R10.829   Rebound abdominal tenderness, unspecified site

R10.83   **Colic**   P
Colic NOS
Infantile colic
Excludes1   colic in adult and child over 12 months old (R10.84)

R10.84   **Generalized** abdominal pain
Excludes1   generalized abdominal pain associated with acute abdomen (R10.0)

R10.9   **Unspecified** abdominal pain

● **R11**   **Nausea and vomiting**
Excludes1   cyclical vomiting associated with migraine (G43.A-)
excessive vomiting in pregnancy (O21.-)
hematemesis (K92.0)
neonatal hematemesis (P54.0)
newborn vomiting (P92.0-)
psychogenic vomiting (F50.89)
vomiting associated with bulimia nervosa (F50.2)
vomiting following gastrointestinal surgery (K91.0)
Coding Clinic: 2017, Q1, P27

● **R11.0**   **Nausea**
Nausea NOS
Nausea without vomiting

● **R11.1**   **Vomiting**
R11.10   **Vomiting, unspecified**
Vomiting NOS
R11.11   **Vomiting without nausea**
R11.12   **Projectile vomiting**
R11.13   **Vomiting of fecal matter**
R11.14   **Bilious vomiting**
Bilious emesis

R11.2   **Nausea with vomiting, unspecified**
Persistent nausea with vomiting NOS

R12   **Heartburn**
Excludes1   dyspepsia NOS (R10.13)
functional dyspepsia (K30)

● **R13**   **Aphagia and dysphagia**
R13.0   **Aphagia**
Inability to swallow
Excludes1   psychogenic aphagia (F50.9)

● **R13.1**   **Dysphagia**
Difficulty swallowing
Code first, if applicable, dysphagia following cerebrovascular disease (I69. with final characters -91)
Excludes1   psychogenic dysphagia (F45.8)
R13.10   **Dysphagia, unspecified**
Difficulty in swallowing NOS
R13.11   **Dysphagia, oral phase**
R13.12   **Dysphagia, oropharyngeal phase**
R13.13   **Dysphagia, pharyngeal phase**
R13.14   **Dysphagia, pharyngoesophageal phase**
R13.19   **Other dysphagia**
Cervical dysphagia
Neurogenic dysphagia

● **R14**   **Flatulence and related conditions**
Excludes1   psychogenic aerophagy (F45.8)
R14.0   **Abdominal distension (gaseous)**
Bloating
Tympanites (abdominal) (intestinal)
R14.1   **Gas pain**
R14.2   **Eructation**
Belching air from stomach through mouth
R14.3   **Flatulence**

● **R15**   **Fecal incontinence**
Includes   encopresis NOS
Excludes1   fecal incontinence of nonorganic origin (F98.1)
R15.0   **Incomplete defecation**
Excludes1   constipation (K59.0-)
fecal impaction (K56.41)
R15.1   **Fecal smearing**
Fecal soiling
R15.2   **Fecal urgency**
R15.9   **Full incontinence of feces**
Fecal incontinence NOS

● **R16**   **Hepatomegaly and splenomegaly, not elsewhere classified**
Enlargement of liver or spleen
R16.0   **Hepatomegaly, not elsewhere classified**
Hepatomegaly NOS
R16.1   **Splenomegaly, not elsewhere classified**
Splenomegaly NOS
R16.2   **Hepatomegaly with splenomegaly, not elsewhere classified**
Hepatosplenomegaly NOS

R17   **Unspecified jaundice**
Excludes1   neonatal jaundice (P55, P57-P59)

● **R18**   **Ascites**
Includes   fluid in peritoneal cavity
Excludes1   ascites in alcoholic cirrhosis (K70.31)
ascites in alcoholic hepatitis (K70.11)
ascites in toxic liver disease with chronic active hepatitis (K71.51)
R18.0   **Malignant ascites**
Code first malignancy, such as:
malignant neoplasm of ovary (C56.-)
secondary malignant neoplasm of retroperitoneum and peritoneum (C78.6)
R18.8   **Other ascites**
Ascites NOS
Peritoneal effusion (chronic)
Coding Clinic: 2018, Q1, P4

▶ New   ⇒ Revised   ~~deleted~~ Deleted   Excludes 1   Excludes 2   Includes   Use additional   Code first   Code also   Key words
OGCR Official Guidelines   X Assign placeholder X   ● Use Additional Character(s)   ▌ Manifestation Code   Coding Clinic

● **R19** **Other symptoms and signs involving the digestive system and abdomen**
　　Excludes1　acute abdomen (R10.0)
● **R19.0** **Intra-abdominal and pelvic swelling, mass and lump**
　　　Excludes1　abdominal distension (gaseous) (R14.-)
　　　　　　　　　　ascites (R18.-)
　　R19.00　**Intra-abdominal and pelvic swelling, mass and lump, unspecified site**
　　R19.01　**Right upper quadrant abdominal swelling, mass and lump**
　　R19.02　**Left upper quadrant abdominal swelling, mass and lump**
　　R19.03　**Right lower quadrant abdominal swelling, mass and lump**
　　R19.04　**Left lower quadrant abdominal swelling, mass and lump**
　　R19.05　**Periumbilic swelling, mass or lump**
　　　　　　　Diffuse or generalized umbilical swelling or mass
　　R19.06　**Epigastric swelling, mass or lump**
　　R19.07　**Generalized intra-abdominal and pelvic swelling, mass and lump**
　　　　　　　Diffuse or generalized intra-abdominal swelling or mass NOS
　　　　　　　Diffuse or generalized pelvic swelling or mass NOS
　　R19.09　**Other intra-abdominal and pelvic swelling, mass and lump**
● **R19.1** **Abnormal bowel sounds**
　　R19.11　**Absent bowel sounds**
　　R19.12　**Hyperactive bowel sounds**
　　R19.15　**Other abnormal bowel sounds**
　　　　　　　Abnormal bowel sounds NOS
　R19.2 **Visible peristalsis**
　　　　　Hyperperistalsis
● **R19.3** **Abdominal rigidity**
　　　Excludes1　abdominal rigidity with severe abdominal pain (R10.0)
　　R19.30　**Abdominal rigidity, unspecified site**
　　R19.31　**Right upper quadrant abdominal rigidity**
　　R19.32　**Left upper quadrant abdominal rigidity**
　　R19.33　**Right lower quadrant abdominal rigidity**
　　R19.34　**Left lower quadrant abdominal rigidity**
　　R19.35　**Periumbilic abdominal rigidity**
　　R19.36　**Epigastric abdominal rigidity**
　　R19.37　**Generalized abdominal rigidity**
　R19.4 **Change in bowel habit**
　　　Excludes1　constipation (K59.0-)
　　　　　　　　　functional diarrhea (K59.1)
　R19.5 **Other fecal abnormalities**
　　　　　Abnormal stool color
　　　　　Bulky stools
　　　　　Mucus in stools
　　　　　Occult blood in feces
　　　　　Occult blood in stools
　　　Excludes1　melena (K92.1)
　　　　　　　　　neonatal melena (P54.1)
　R19.6 **Halitosis**
　R19.7 **Diarrhea, unspecified**
　　　　　Diarrhea NOS
　　　Excludes1　functional diarrhea (K59.1)
　　　　　　　　　neonatal diarrhea (P78.3)
　　　　　　　　　psychogenic diarrhea (F45.8)
　R19.8 **Other specified symptoms and signs involving the digestive system and abdomen**

SYMPTOMS AND SIGNS INVOLVING THE SKIN AND SUBCUTANEOUS TISSUE (R20-R23)
　　Excludes2　symptoms relating to breast (N64.4-N64.5)
● **R20** **Disturbances of skin sensation**
　　　Excludes1　dissociative anesthesia and sensory loss (F44.6)
　　　　　　　　　psychogenic disturbances (F45.8)
　R20.0 **Anesthesia of skin**
　　　　　Loss of sensation
　R20.1 **Hypoesthesia of skin**
　　　　　Unpleasant abnormal sensation
　R20.2 **Paresthesia of skin**
　　　　　Abnormal touch sensation, including burning, prickling, often in absence of external stimulus
　　　　　Formication　　　　　　　Tingling skin
　　　　　Pins and needles
　　　Excludes1　acroparesthesia (I73.8)
　R20.3 **Hyperesthesia**
　R20.8 **Other disturbances of skin sensation**
　R20.9 **Unspecified disturbances of skin sensation**
　R21 **Rash and other nonspecific skin eruption**
　　　Includes　rash NOS
　　　Excludes1　specified type of rash- code to condition
　　　　　　　　　vesicular eruption (R23.8)
● **R22** **Localized swelling, mass and lump of skin and subcutaneous tissue**
　　　Includes　subcutaneous nodules (localized) (superficial)
　　　Excludes1　abnormal findings on diagnostic imaging (R90-R93)
　　　　　　　　　edema (R60.-)
　　　　　　　　　enlarged lymph nodes (R59.-)
　　　　　　　　　localized adiposity (E65)
　　　　　　　　　swelling of joint (M25.4-)
　R22.0 **Localized swelling, mass and lump, head**
　R22.1 **Localized swelling, mass and lump, neck**
　R22.2 **Localized swelling, mass and lump, trunk**
　　　Excludes1　intra-abdominal or pelvic mass and lump (R19.0-)
　　　　　　　　　intra-abdominal or pelvic swelling (R19.0-)
　　　Excludes2　breast mass and lump (N63)
● **R22.3** **Localized swelling, mass and lump, upper limb**
　　R22.30　**Localized swelling, mass and lump, unspecified upper limb**
　　R22.31　**Localized swelling, mass and lump, right upper limb**
　　R22.32　**Localized swelling, mass and lump, left upper limb**
　　R22.33　**Localized swelling, mass and lump, upper limb, bilateral**
● **R22.4** **Localized swelling, mass and lump, lower limb**
　　R22.40　**Localized swelling, mass and lump, unspecified lower limb**
　　R22.41　**Localized swelling, mass and lump, right lower limb**
　　R22.42　**Localized swelling, mass and lump, left lower limb**
　　R22.43　**Localized swelling, mass and lump, lower limb, bilateral**
　R22.9 **Localized swelling, mass and lump, unspecified**

CHAPTER 18 (R00-R99)

CHAPTER 18 (R00-R99)

● **R23** **Other skin changes**

R23.0 **Cyanosis**
> **Excludes1** acrocyanosis (I73.8)
> cyanotic attacks of newborn (P28.2)

R23.1 **Pallor**
Clammy skin

R23.2 **Flushing**
Excessive blushing
Code first, if applicable, menopausal and female climacteric states (N95.1)

R23.3 **Spontaneous ecchymoses**
Small hemorrhagic spot of skin; AKA black and blue spot
Petechiae
> **Excludes1** ecchymoses of newborn (P54.5)
> purpura (D69.-)

R23.4 **Changes in skin texture**
Desquamation of skin   Scaling of skin
Induration of skin
> **Excludes1** epidermal thickening NOS (L85.9)

R23.8 **Other skin changes**

R23.9 **Unspecified skin changes**

SYMPTOMS AND SIGNS INVOLVING THE NERVOUS AND MUSCULOSKELETAL SYSTEMS (R25-R29)

● **R25** **Abnormal involuntary movements**
> **Excludes1** specific movement disorders (G20-G26)
> stereotyped movement disorders (F98.4)
> tic disorders (F95.-)

R25.0 **Abnormal head movements**

R25.1 **Tremor, unspecified**
> **Excludes1** chorea NOS (G25.5)
> essential tremor (G25.0)
> hysterical tremor (F44.4)
> intention tremor (G25.2)

R25.2 **Cramp and spasm**
> **Excludes2** carpopedal spasm (R29.0)
> charley-horse (M62.831)
> infantile spasms (G40.4-)
> muscle spasm of back (M62.830)
> muscle spasm of calf (M62.831)

R25.3 **Fasciculation**
Twitching NOS

R25.8 **Other abnormal involuntary movements**

R25.9 **Unspecified abnormal involuntary movements**

● **R26** **Abnormalities of gait and mobility**
> **Excludes1** ataxia NOS (R27.0)
> hereditary ataxia (G11.-)
> locomotor (syphilitic) ataxia (A52.11)
> immobility syndrome (paraplegic) (M62.3)

R26.0 **Ataxic gait**
Staggering gait

R26.1 **Paralytic gait**
Spastic gait

R26.2 **Difficulty in walking, not elsewhere classified**
> **Excludes1** falling (R29.6)
> unsteadiness on feet (R26.81)
> Coding Clinic: 2016, Q2, P7

● **R26.8** **Other abnormalities of gait and mobility**
R26.81 **Unsteadiness on feet**
R26.89 **Other abnormalities of gait and mobility**

R26.9 **Unspecified abnormalities of gait and mobility**

● **R27** **Other lack of coordination**
> **Excludes1** ataxic gait (R26.0)
> hereditary ataxia (G11.-)
> vertigo NOS (R42)

R27.0 **Ataxia, unspecified**
> **Excludes1** ataxia following cerebrovascular disease
> (I69. with final characters -93)

R27.8 **Other lack of coordination**

R27.9 **Unspecified lack of coordination**

● **R29** **Other symptoms and signs involving the nervous and musculoskeletal systems**

R29.0 **Tetany**
Hyperexcitability of nerves and muscles characterized by spasm, twitching, and cramps
Carpopedal spasm
> **Excludes1** hysterical tetany (F44.5)
> neonatal tetany (P71.3)
> parathyroid tetany (E20.9)
> post-thyroidectomy tetany (E89.2)

R29.1 **Meningismus**

R29.2 **Abnormal reflex**
> **Excludes2** abnormal pupillary reflex (H57.0)
> hyperactive gag reflex (J39.2)
> vasovagal reaction or syncope (R55)

R29.3 **Abnormal posture**

R29.4 **Clicking hip**
> **Excludes1** congenital deformities of hip (Q65.-)

R29.5 **Transient paralysis**
Code first any associated spinal cord injury (S14.0, S14.1-, S24.0, S24.1-, S34.0-, S34.1-)
> **Excludes1** transient ischemic attack (G45.9)

R29.6 **Repeated falls**
Falling
Tendency to fall
> **Excludes2** at risk for falling (Z91.81)
> history of falling (Z91.81)

OGCR Section I.C.18.d.
> Repeated falls
> Code R29.6, Repeated falls, is for use for encounters when a patient has recently fallen and the reason for the fall is being investigated.
> Code Z91.81, History of falling, is for use when a patient has fallen in the past and is at risk for future falls. When appropriate, both codes R29.6 and Z91.81 may be assigned together.

Coding Clinic: 2016, Q2, P7

● **R29.7** **National Institutes of Health Stroke Scale (NIHSS) score**
Code first the type of cerebral infarction (I63-)
Coding Clinic: 2016, Q4, P61, 127

● **R29.70** **NIHSS score 0-9**
R29.700 **NIHSS score 0**
R29.701 **NIHSS score 1**
R29.702 **NIHSS score 2**
R29.703 **NIHSS score 3**
R29.704 **NIHSS score 4**
R29.705 **NIHSS score 5**
R29.706 **NIHSS score 6**
R29.707 **NIHSS score 7**
R29.708 **NIHSS score 8**
R29.709 **NIHSS score 9**

● **R29.71** **NIHSS score 10-19**
R29.710 **NIHSS score 10**
R29.711 **NIHSS score 11**
R29.712 **NIHSS score 12**
R29.713 **NIHSS score 13**
R29.714 **NIHSS score 14**
R29.715 **NIHSS score 15**
R29.716 **NIHSS score 16**
R29.717 **NIHSS score 17**
R29.718 **NIHSS score 18**
R29.719 **NIHSS score 19**

▶ New   ⇒ Revised   ~~deleted~~ Deleted   Excludes 1   Excludes 2   Includes   Use additional   Code first   Code also   Key words

OGCR Official Guidelines   X Assign placeholder X   ● Use Additional Character(s)   �Ⅰ Manifestation Code   **Coding Clinic**

● R29.72 NIHSS score 20-29

  R29.720 NIHSS score 20
  R29.721 NIHSS score 21
  R29.722 NIHSS score 22
  R29.723 NIHSS score 23
  R29.724 NIHSS score 24
  R29.725 NIHSS score 25
  R29.726 NIHSS score 26
  R29.727 NIHSS score 27
  R29.728 NIHSS score 28
  R29.729 NIHSS score 29

OGCR Section I.C.18.i.

NIHSS Stroke Scale

The NIH stroke scale (NIHSS) codes (R29.7- -) can be used in conjunction with acute stroke codes (I63) to identify the patient's neurological status and the severity of the stroke. The stroke scale codes should be sequenced after the acute stroke diagnosis code(s). At a minimum, report the initial score documented. If desired, a facility may choose to capture multiple stroke scale scores.

● R29.73 NIHSS score 30-39

  R29.730 NIHSS score 30
           Coding Clinic: 2016, Q4, P62
  R29.731 NIHSS score 31
  R29.732 NIHSS score 32
  R29.733 NIHSS score 33
  R29.734 NIHSS score 34
  R29.735 NIHSS score 35
  R29.736 NIHSS score 36
  R29.737 NIHSS score 37
  R29.738 NIHSS score 38
  R29.739 NIHSS score 39

● R29.74 NIHSS score 40-42

  R29.740 NIHSS score 40
  R29.741 NIHSS score 41
  R29.742 NIHSS score 42

● R29.8 Other symptoms and signs involving the nervous and musculoskeletal systems

  ● R29.81 Other symptoms and signs involving the nervous system

    R29.810 **Facial weakness**
             Facial droop
             Excludes1 Bell's palsy (G51.0)
                            facial weakness
                            following cerebro-
                            vascular disease
                            (I69. with final
                            characters -92)

    R29.818 **Other symptoms and signs involving the nervous system**

  ● R29.89 Other symptoms and signs involving the musculoskeletal system
            Excludes2 pain in limb (M79.6-)

    R29.890 **Loss of height**
             Excludes1 osteoporosis
                            (M80-M81)

    R29.891 **Ocular torticollis**
             Excludes1 congenital (sterno-
                            mastoid)
                            torticollis Q68.0
                            psychogenic torticollis
                            (F45.8)
                            spasmodic torticollis
                            (G24.3)
                            torticollis due to birth
                            injury (P15.8)
                            torticollis NOS M43.6

    R29.898 **Other symptoms and signs involving the musculoskeletal system**

● R29.9 Unspecified symptoms and signs involving the nervous and musculoskeletal systems

  R29.90 **Unspecified symptoms and signs involving the nervous system**

  R29.91 **Unspecified symptoms and signs involving the musculoskeletal system**

SYMPTOMS AND SIGNS INVOLVING THE GENITOURINARY SYSTEM (R30-R39)

● R30 Pain associated with micturition
       Excludes1 psychogenic pain associated with micturition (F45.8)

  R30.0 **Dysuria**
         Painful urination
         Strangury

  R30.1 **Vesical tenesmus**
         Straining to urinate, with sensation of a full bladder even when empty

  R30.9 **Painful micturition, unspecified**
         Painful urination NOS

● R31 Hematuria
       Excludes1 hematuria included with underlying conditions, such as:
                      acute cystitis with hematuria (N30.01)
                      recurrent and persistent hematuria in glomerular diseases (N02.-)

  R31.0 **Gross hematuria**
         Coding Clinic: 2017, Q1, P17

  R31.1 **Benign essential microscopic hematuria**

  ● R31.2 Other microscopic hematuria
           Coding Clinic: 2016, Q4, P62

    R31.21 **Asymptomatic microscopic hematuria**
            AMH

    R31.29 **Other microscopic hematuria**

  R31.9 **Hematuria, unspecified**
         Coding Clinic: 2017, Q1, P6

R32 **Unspecified urinary incontinence**
     Enuresis NOS
     Excludes1 functional urinary incontinence (R39.81)
                    nonorganic enuresis (F98.0)
                    stress incontinence and other specified urinary incontinence (N39.3-N39.4-)
                    urinary incontinence associated with cognitive impairment (R39.81)

● R33 Retention of urine
       Excludes1 psychogenic retention of urine (F45.8)

  R33.0 **Drug induced retention of urine**
         Use additional code for adverse effect, if applicable, to identify drug (T36-T50 with fifth or sixth character 5)

  R33.8 **Other retention of urine**
         Code first, if applicable, any causal condition, such as:
         enlarged prostate (N40.1)

  R33.9 **Retention of urine, unspecified**

R34 Anuria and oliguria
     Excludes1 anuria and oliguria complicating abortion or ectopic or molar pregnancy (O00-O07, O08.4)
                    anuria and oliguria complicating pregnancy (O26.83-)
                    anuria and oliguria complicating the puerperium (O90.4)

● **R35**   **Polyuria**
Passage of excessive volume of urine
Code first, if applicable, any causal condition, such as:
    enlarged prostate (N4Ø.1)
    Excludes1   psychogenic polyuria (F45.8)

    R35.Ø   **Frequency of micturition**
        Discharge or passage of urine; AKA uresis

    R35.1   **Nocturia**
        Urinary frequency at night

    R35.8   **Other polyuria**
        Polyuria NOS

● **R36**   **Urethral discharge**
    R36.Ø   **Urethral discharge without blood**
    R36.1   **Hematospermia** ♂
        Presence of blood in semen

    R36.9   **Urethral discharge, unspecified**
        Penile discharge NOS
        Urethrorrhea

  R37   **Sexual dysfunction, unspecified**

● **R39**   **Other and unspecified symptoms and signs involving the genitourinary system**
    R39.Ø   **Extravasation of urine**
        Leakage, discharge

  ● **R39.1**   **Other difficulties with micturition**
        Code first, if applicable, any causal condition, such as:
            enlarged prostate (N4Ø.1)
        R39.11   **Hesitancy of micturition**
        R39.12   **Poor urinary stream**
            Weak urinary steam
        R39.13   **Splitting of urinary stream**
        R39.14   **Feeling of incomplete bladder emptying**
        R39.15   **Urgency of urination**
            Excludes1   urge incontinence (N39.41, N39.46)
        R39.16   **Straining to void**
      ● **R39.19**   **Other difficulties with micturition**
            Coding Clinic: 2Ø16, Q4, P63
            R39.191   **Need to immediately re-void**
            R39.192   **Position dependent micturition**
            R39.198   **Other difficulties with micturition**

    R39.2   **Extrarenal uremia**
        Prerenal uremia
        Excludes1   uremia NOS (N19)

  ● **R39.8**   **Other symptoms and signs involving the genitourinary system**
        R39.81   **Functional urinary incontinence**
            Urinary incontinence due to cognitive impairment, or severe physical disability or immobility
            Excludes1   stress incontinence and other specified urinary incontinence (N39.3-N39.4-)
                urinary incontinence NOS (R32)
        R39.82   **Chronic bladder pain**
            Coding Clinic: 2Ø16, Q4, P64
        R39.83   **Unilateral non-palpable testicle** ♂
        R39.84   **Bilateral non-palpable testicles** ♂
        R39.89   **Other symptoms and signs involving the genitourinary system**
            Coding Clinic: 2Ø16, Q4, P64

    R39.9   **Unspecified symptoms and signs involving the genitourinary system**

SYMPTOMS AND SIGNS INVOLVING COGNITION, PERCEPTION, EMOTIONAL STATE AND BEHAVIOR (R4Ø-R46)

  Excludes2   symptoms and signs constituting part of a pattern of mental disorder (FØ1-F99)
        Coding Clinic: 2Ø15, Q4, P4Ø

● **R4Ø**   **Somnolence, stupor and coma**
    Excludes1   neonatal coma (P91.5)
        somnolence, stupor and coma in diabetes (EØ8-E13)
        somnolence, stupor and coma in hepatic failure (K72.-)
        somnolence, stupor and coma in hypoglycemia (nondiabetic) (E15)

    R4Ø.Ø   **Somnolence**
        Drowsiness
        Excludes1   coma (R4Ø.2-)

    R4Ø.1   **Stupor**
        Lowered level of consciousness
        Catatonic stupor
        Semicoma
        Excludes1   catatonic schizophrenia (F2Ø.2)
            coma (R4Ø.2-)
            depressive stupor (F31-F33)
            dissociative stupor (F44.2)
            manic stupor (F3Ø.2)

OGCR   Section I.C.18.e.

Coma scale

The coma scale codes (R4Ø.2-) can be used in conjunction with traumatic brain injury codes, acute cerebrovascular disease or sequelae of cerebrovascular disease codes. These codes are primarily for use by trauma registries, but they may be used in any setting where this information is collected. The coma scale may also be used to assess the status of the central nervous system for other non-trauma conditions, such as monitoring patients in the intensive care unit regardless of medical condition. The coma scale codes should be sequenced after the diagnosis code(s).

These codes, one from each subcategory, are needed to complete the scale. The 7th character indicates when the scale was recorded. The 7th character should match for all three codes.

At a minimum, report the initial score documented on presentation at your facility. This may be a score from the emergency medicine technician (EMT) or in the emergency department. If desired, a facility may choose to capture multiple coma scale scores.

Assign code R4Ø.24, Glasgow coma scale, total score, when only the total score is documented in the medical record and not the individual score(s).

● **R4Ø.2**   **Coma**
    Code first any associated:
        fracture of skull (SØ2.-)
        intracranial injury (SØ6.-)
    Note: One code from each subcategory R4Ø.21-R4Ø-23 is required to complete the coma scale
        Coding Clinic: 2Ø16, Q4, P127

    R4Ø.2Ø   **Unspecified coma**
        Coma NOS
        Unconsciousness NOS

  ● **R4Ø.21**   **Coma scale, eyes open**
        The following appropriate 7th character is to be added to subcategory R4Ø.21-:

Ø	unspecified time
1	in the field [EMT or ambulance]
2	at arrival to emergency department
3	at hospital admission
4	24 hours or more after hospital admission

        Coding Clinic: 2Ø17, Q4, P25; 2Ø15, Q2, P18

    ● **R4Ø.211**   **Coma scale, eyes open, never**
        ▶Coma scale eye opening score of 1

▶ New   ⇒ Revised   ~~deleted~~ Deleted   Excludes 1   Excludes 2   Includes   Use additional   Code first   Code also   Key words

1184   **OGCR** Official Guidelines   X Assign placeholder X   ● Use Additional Character(s)   ▌ Manifestation Code   **Coding Clinic**

- ● R40.212   **Coma scale, eyes open, to pain**
  - ▶Coma scale eye opening score of 2
- ● R40.213   **Coma scale, eyes open, to sound**
  - ▶Coma scale eye opening score of 3
- ● R40.214   **Coma scale, eyes open, spontaneous**
  - ▶Coma scale eye opening score of 4
- ● R40.22   **Coma scale, best verbal response**

The following appropriate 7th character is to be added to subcategory R40.22-:

Ø	unspecified time
1	in the field [EMT or ambulance]
2	at arrival to emergency department
3	at hospital admission
4	24 hours or more after hospital admission

Coding Clinic: 2017, Q4, P25; 2015, Q2, P18

- ● R40.221   **Coma scale, best verbal response, none**
  - ▶Coma scale verbal score of 1
- ● R40.222   **Coma scale, best verbal response, incomprehensible words**
  - ▶Coma scale verbal score of 2
    Incomprehensible sounds (2-5 years of age)
    Moans/grunts to pain; restless (<2 years old)
- ● R40.223   **Coma scale, best verbal response, inappropriate words**
  - ▶Coma scale verbal score of 3
    Inappropriate crying or screaming (< 2 years of age)
    Screaming (2-5 years of age)
- ● R40.224   **Coma scale, best verbal response, confused conversation**
  - ▶Coma scale verbal score of 4
    Inappropriate words (2-5 years of age)
    Irritable cries (< 2 years of age)
- ● R40.225   **Coma scale, best verbal response, oriented**
  - ▶Coma scale verbal score of 5
    Cooing or babbling or crying appropriately (< 2 years of age)
    Uses appropriate words (2- 5 years of age)
- ● R40.23   **Coma scale, best motor response**

The following appropriate 7th character is to be added to subcategory R40.23-:

Ø	unspecified time
1	in the field [EMT or ambulance]
2	at arrival to emergency department
3	at hospital admission
4	24 hours or more after hospital admission

Coding Clinic: 2017, Q4, P25; 2015, Q2, P18

- ● R40.231   **Coma scale, best motor response, none**
  - ▶Coma scale motor score of 1
- ● R40.232   **Coma scale, best motor response, extension**
    Abnormal extensor posturing to pain or noxious stimuli (< 2 years of age)
  - ▶Coma scale motor score of 2
    Extensor posturing to pain or noxious stimuli (2-5 years of age)

Glasgow Coma Scale

Eye Opening Response	
• Spontaneous--open with blinking at baseline	4 points
• To verbal stimuli, command, speech	3 points
• To pain only (not applied to face)	2 points
• No response	1 point
Verbal Response	
• Oriented	5 points
• Confused conversation, but able to answer questions	4 points
• Inappropriate words	3 points
• Incomprehensible speech	2 points
• No response	1 point
Motor Response	
• Obeys commands for movement	6 points
• Purposeful movement to painful stimulus	5 points
• Withdraws in response to pain	4 points
• Flexion in response to pain (decorticate posturing)	3 points
• Extension response in response to pain (decerebrate posturing)	2 points
• No response	1 point

Categorization:
Coma: No eye opening, no ability to follow commands, no word verbalizations (3-8)

Head Injury Classification:
Severe Head Injury--GCS score of 8 or less
Moderate Head Injury--GCS score of 9 to 12
Mild head injury--GCS score of 13 to 15

(Adapted from: Advanced Trauma Life Support: Course for Physicians, American College of Surgeons, 1993). http://www.bt.cdc.gov/masscasulatires/gscale.asp

Figure 18-1

- ● R40.233   **Coma scale, best motor response, abnormal flexion**
  - ▶Coma scale motor score of 3
  - ➡Abnormal flexure posturing to pain or noxious stimuli (2-5 years of age)
    Flexion/decorticate posturing (< 2 years of age)
- ● R40.234   **Coma scale, best motor response, flexion withdrawal**
  - ▶Coma scale motor score of 4
  - ➡Withdraws from pain or noxious stimuli (2-5 years of age)
- ● R40.235   **Coma scale, best motor response, localizes pain**
  - ▶Coma scale motor score of 5
    Localizes pain (2-5 years of age)
    Withdraws to touch (< 2 years of age)
- ● R40.236   **Coma scale, best motor response, obeys commands**
  - ▶Coma scale motor score of 6
    Normal or spontaneous movement (< 2 years of age)
    Obeys commands (2-5 years of age)

CHAPTER 18 (R00-R99)

● **R40.24**   **Glasgow coma scale, total score**
Note: Assign a code from subcategory R40.24, when only the total coma score is documented
The following appropriate 7th character is to be added to subcategory R40.24-:

0	unspecified time
1	in the field [EMT or ambulance]
2	at arrival to emergency department
3	at hospital admission
4	24 hours or more after hospital admission

Coding Clinic: 2016, Q4, P64; 2015, Q2, P18

● **R40.241**   Glasgow coma scale score **13-15**
● **R40.242**   Glasgow coma scale score **9-12**
● **R40.243**   Glasgow coma scale score **3-8**
● **R40.244**   **Other coma, without documented Glasgow coma scale score, or with partial score reported**

R40.3   **Persistent vegetative state**
R40.4   **Transient alteration of awareness**

● **R41**   **Other symptoms and signs involving cognitive functions and awareness**
   Excludes1   dissociative [conversion] disorders (F44.-)
                mild cognitive impairment, so stated (G31.84)

R41.0   **Disorientation, unspecified**
   Confusion NOS   Delirium NOS
   Coding Clinic: 2016, Q4, P71

R41.1   **Anterograde amnesia**
R41.2   **Retrograde amnesia**
R41.3   **Other amnesia**
   Amnesia NOS
   Memory loss NOS
   Excludes1   amnestic disorder due to known physiologic condition (F04)
             amnestic syndrome due to psychoactive substance use (F10-F19 with 5th character .6)
             mild memory disturbance due to known physiological condition (F06.8)
             transient global amnesia (G45.4)

R41.4   **Neurologic neglect syndrome**
   Asomatognosia   Left-sided neglect
   Hemi-akinesia   Sensory neglect
   Hemi-inattention   Visuospatial neglect
   Hemispatial neglect
   Excludes1   visuospatial deficit (R41.842)

● **R41.8**   **Other symptoms and signs involving cognitive functions and awareness**
R41.81   **Age-related cognitive decline**   A
   Senility NOS
R41.82   **Altered mental status, unspecified**
   Change in mental status NOS
   Excludes1   altered level of consciousness (R40.-)
             altered mental status due to known condition - code to condition
             delirium NOS (R41.0)
   Coding Clinic: 2012, Q4, P98
R41.83   **Borderline intellectual functioning**
   IQ level 71 to 84
   Excludes1   intellectual disabilities (F70-F79)

● **R41.84**   **Other specified cognitive deficit**
   Excludes1   cognitive deficits as sequelae of cerebrovascular disease (I69.01-, I69.11-, I69.21-, I69.31-, I69.81-, I69.91-)
R41.840   **Attention and concentration deficit**
   Excludes1   attention-deficit hyperactivity disorders (F90.-)
R41.841   **Cognitive communication deficit**
R41.842   **Visuospatial deficit**
R41.843   **Psychomotor deficit**
R41.844   **Frontal lobe and executive function deficit**
R41.89   **Other symptoms and signs involving cognitive functions and awareness**
   Anosognosia

R41.9   **Unspecified symptoms and signs involving cognitive functions and awareness**
   Unspecified neurocognitive disorder

R42   **Dizziness and giddiness**
   Light-headedness
   Vertigo NOS
   Excludes1   vertiginous syndromes (H81.-)
             vertigo from infrasound (T75.23)
   Coding Clinic: 2015, Q4, P40

● **R43**   **Disturbances of smell and taste**
R43.0   **Anosmia**
   Absence of sense of smell; AKA anosphresia and olfactory anesthesia
R43.1   **Parosmia**
R43.2   **Parageusia**
   Perversion of sense of taste or bad taste in mouth; AKA dysgeusia
R43.8   **Other disturbances of smell and taste**
   Mixed disturbance of smell and taste
R43.9   **Unspecified disturbances of smell and taste**

● **R44**   **Other symptoms and signs involving general sensations and perceptions**
   Excludes1   alcoholic hallucinations (F1.5)
             hallucinations in drug psychosis (F11-F19 with .5)
             hallucinations in mood disorders with psychotic symptoms (F30.2, F31.5, F32.3, F33.3)
             hallucinations in schizophrenia, schizotypal and delusional disorders (F20-F29)
   Excludes2   disturbances of skin sensation (R20.-)
R44.0   **Auditory hallucinations**
R44.1   **Visual hallucinations**
R44.2   **Other hallucinations**
R44.3   **Hallucinations, unspecified**
R44.8   **Other symptoms and signs involving general sensations and perceptions**
R44.9   **Unspecified symptoms and signs involving general sensations and perceptions**

● **R45**   **Symptoms and signs involving emotional state**
R45.0   **Nervousness**
   Nervous tension
R45.1   **Restlessness and agitation**
R45.2   **Unhappiness**
R45.3   **Demoralization and apathy**
   Excludes1   anhedonia (R45.84)

R45.4   Irritability and anger
R45.5   Hostility
R45.6   Violent behavior
R45.7   State of emotional shock and stress, unspecified
● R45.8   Other symptoms and signs involving emotional state
  R45.81   Low self-esteem
  R45.82   Worries
  R45.83   Excessive crying of child, adolescent or adult
    Excludes1   excessive crying of infant (baby) R68.11
  R45.84   Anhedonia
    Total loss of feeling of pleasure in pleasurable acts
● R45.85   Homicidal and suicidal ideations
    Excludes1   suicide attempt (T14.91)
    R45.850   Homicidal ideations
    R45.851   Suicidal ideations
  R45.86   Emotional lability
  R45.87   Impulsiveness
  R45.89   Other symptoms and signs involving emotional state

● R46   Symptoms and signs involving appearance and behavior
  Excludes1   appearance and behavior in schizophrenia, schizotypal and delusional disorders (F20-F29)
    mental and behavioral disorders (F01-F99)
  R46.0   Very low level of personal hygiene
  R46.1   Bizarre personal appearance
  R46.2   Strange and inexplicable behavior
  R46.3   Overactivity
  R46.4   Slowness and poor responsiveness
    Excludes1   stupor (R40.1)
  R46.5   Suspiciousness and marked evasiveness
  R46.6   Undue concern and preoccupation with stressful events
  R46.7   Verbosity and circumstantial detail obscuring reason for contact
● R46.8   Other symptoms and signs involving appearance and behavior
  R46.81   Obsessive-compulsive behavior
    Excludes1   obsessive-compulsive disorder (F42-)
  R46.89   Other symptoms and signs involving appearance and behavior

SYMPTOMS AND SIGNS INVOLVING SPEECH AND VOICE (R47-R49)

● R47   Speech disturbances, not elsewhere classified
  Excludes1   autism (F84.0)
    cluttering (F80.81)
    specific developmental disorders of speech and language (F80.-)
    stuttering (F80.81)
● R47.0   Dysphasia and aphasia
  R47.01   Aphasia
    Excludes1   aphasia following cerebrovascular disease (I69. with final characters -20)
      progressive isolated aphasia (G31.01)
  R47.02   Dysphasia
    Impairment in comprehension of speech, caused by left-sided brain damage
    Excludes1   dysphasia following cerebrovascular disease (I69. with final characters -21)

R47.1   Dysarthria and anarthria
  Motor speech disorder
    Excludes1   dysarthria following cerebrovascular disease (I69. with final characters -22)
● R47.8   Other speech disturbances
    Excludes1   dysarthria following cerebrovascular disease (I69. with final characters -28)
  R47.81   Slurred speech
  ▷ R47.82   *Fluency disorder in conditions classified elsewhere*
    Stuttering in conditions classified elsewhere
    Code first underlying disease or condition, such as: Parkinson's disease (G20)
    Excludes1   adult onset fluency disorder (F98.5)
      childhood onset fluency disorder (F80.81)
      fluency disorder (stuttering) following cerebrovascular disease (I69. with final characters -23)
  R47.89   Other speech disturbances
R47.9   Unspecified speech disturbances

● R48   Dyslexia and other symbolic dysfunctions, not elsewhere classified
  Excludes1   specific developmental disorders of scholastic skills (F81.-)
  R48.0   Dyslexia and alexia
  R48.1   Agnosia
    Loss of ability to recognize objects, persons, sounds, shapes, or smells
    Astereognosia (astereognosis)
    Autotopagnosia
    Excludes1   visual object agnosia (R48.3)
  R48.2   Apraxia
    Loss of ability to execute or carry out learned purposeful movements
    Excludes1   apraxia following cerebrovascular disease (I69. with final characters -90)
  R48.3   Visual agnosia
    Prosopagnosia
    Simultanagnosia (asimultagnosia)
  R48.8   Other symbolic dysfunctions
    Acalculia
      Difficulty performing simple mathematical tasks resulting from neurological injury
    Agraphia
    Coding Clinic: 2017, Q1, P27
  R48.9   Unspecified symbolic dysfunctions

● R49   Voice and resonance disorders
  Excludes1   psychogenic voice and resonance disorders (F44.4)
  R49.0   Dysphonia
    Hoarseness
  R49.1   Aphonia
    Loss of voice
● R49.2   Hypernasality and hyponasality
  R49.21   Hypernasality
  R49.22   Hyponasality
  R49.8   Other voice and resonance disorders
  R49.9   Unspecified voice and resonance disorder
    Change in voice NOS
    Resonance disorder NOS

CHAPTER 18 (R00-R99)

CHAPTER 18 (R00-R99)

GENERAL SYMPTOMS AND SIGNS (R50-R69)

● **R50   Fever of other and unknown origin**

     Excludes1   chills without fever (R68.83)
                         febrile convulsions (R56.0-)
                         fever of unknown origin during labor (O75.2)
                         fever of unknown origin in newborn (P81.9)
                         hypothermia due to illness (R68.0)
                         malignant hyperthermia due to anesthesia (T88.3)
                         puerperal pyrexia NOS (O86.4)

     R50.2   Drug induced fever
         Use additional code for adverse effect, if applicable, to identify drug (T36-T50 with fifth or sixth character 5)

         Excludes1   postvaccination (postimmunization) fever (R50.83)

●   **R50.8   Other specified fever**

  ▶   *R50.81   Fever presenting with conditions classified elsewhere*

         Code first underlying condition when associated fever is present, such as with:
                leukemia (C91-C95)
                neutropenia (D70.-)
                sickle-cell disease (D57.-)

     R50.82   Postprocedural fever

         Excludes1   postprocedural infection (T81.44)
                     posttransfusion fever (R50.84)
                     postvaccination (postimmunization) fever (R50.83)

     R50.83   Postvaccination fever
         Postimmunization fever

     R50.84   Febrile nonhemolytic transfusion reaction
         FNHTR
         Posttransfusion fever

     R50.9   Fever, unspecified
         Fever NOS
         Fever of unknown origin [FUO]
         Fever with chills
         Fever with rigors
         Hyperpyrexia NOS
         Persistent fever
         Pyrexia NOS

R51   Headache
     Facial pain NOS

     Excludes1   atypical face pain (G50.1)
                     migraine and other headache syndromes (G43-G44)
                     trigeminal neuralgia (G50.0)

R52   Pain, unspecified
     Acute pain NOS   Pain NOS
     Generalized pain NOS

     Excludes1   acute and chronic pain, not elsewhere classified (G89.-)
                     localized pain, unspecified type - code to pain by site, such as:
                         abdomen pain (R10.-)
                         back pain (M54.9)
                         breast pain (N64.4)
                         chest pain (R07.1-R07.9)
                         ear pain (H92.0-)
                         eye pain (H57.1)
                         headache (R51)
                         joint pain (M25.5-)
                         limb pain (M79.6-)
                         lumbar region pain (M54.5)
                         pelvic and perineal pain (R10.2)
                         shoulder pain (M25.51-)
                         spine pain (M54.-)
                         throat pain (R07.0)
                         tongue pain (K14.6)
                         tooth pain (K08.8)
                         renal colic (N23)
                     pain disorders exclusively related to psychological factors (F45.41)

● **R53   Malaise and fatigue**

     R53.0   Neoplastic (malignant) related fatigue
         Code first associated neoplasm

     R53.1   Weakness
         Asthenia NOS

         Excludes1   age-related weakness (R54)
                     muscle weakness (M62.8-)
                     sarcopenia (M62.84)
                     senile asthenia (R54)

         Coding Clinic: 2017, Q1, P7

     R53.2   Functional quadriplegia
         Complete immobility due to severe physical disability or frailty

         Excludes1   frailty NOS (R54)
                     hysterical paralysis (F44.4)
                     immobility syndrome (M62.3)
                     neurologic quadriplegia (G82.5-)
                     quadriplegia (G82.50)

         Coding Clinic: 2016, Q2, P6

●   **R53.8   Other malaise and fatigue**

         Excludes1   combat exhaustion and fatigue (F43.0)
                     congenital debility (P96.9)
                     exhaustion and fatigue due to excessive exertion (T73.3)
                     exhaustion and fatigue due to exposure (T73.2)
                     exhaustion and fatigue due to heat (T67.-)
                     exhaustion and fatigue due to pregnancy (O26.8-)
                     exhaustion and fatigue due to recurrent depressive episode (F33)
                     exhaustion and fatigue due to senile debility (R54)

     R53.81   Other malaise
         Chronic debility
         Debility NOS
         General physical deterioration
         Malaise NOS
         Nervous debility

         Excludes1   age-related physical debility (R54)

     R53.82   Chronic fatigue, unspecified
         Chronic fatigue syndrome NOS

         Excludes1   postviral fatigue syndrome (G93.3)

     R53.83   Other fatigue
         Fatigue NOS
         Lack of energy
         Lethargy
         Tiredness

         Excludes2   exhaustion and fatigue due to depressive episode (F32.-)

         Coding Clinic: 2017, Q1, P7

R54   Age-related physical debility   A
     Frailty
     Old age
     Senescence
     Senile asthenia
     Senile debility

     Excludes1   age-related cognitive decline (R41.81)
                     sarcopenia (M62.84)
                     senile psychosis (F03)
                     senility NOS (R41.81)

▶ New   ⇒ Revised   ~~deleted~~ Deleted   Excludes 1   Excludes 2   Includes   Use additional   Code first   Code also   Key words
OGCR Official Guidelines   X Assign placeholder X   ● Use Additional Character(s)   ▌ Manifestation Code   Coding Clinic

● R55   **Syncope and collapse**
         Blackout
         Fainting
         Vasovagal attack
         Excludes1   cardiogenic shock (R57.Ø)
                          carotid sinus syncope (G9Ø.Ø1)
                          heat syncope (T67.1)
                          neurocirculatory asthenia (F45.8)
                          neurogenic orthostatic hypotension (G9Ø.3)
                          orthostatic hypotension (I95.1)
                          postprocedural shock (T81.1-)
                          psychogenic syncope (F48.8)
                          shock NOS (R57.9)
                          shock complicating or following abortion or
                              ectopic or molar pregnancy (OØØ-OØ7, OØ8.3)
                          shock complicating or following labor and
                              delivery (O75.1)
                          Stokes-Adams attack (I45.9)
                          unconsciousness NOS (R4Ø.2-)

● R56   **Convulsions, not elsewhere classified**
         Excludes1   dissociative convulsions and seizures (F44.5)
                          epileptic convulsions and seizures (G4Ø.-)
                          newborn convulsions and seizures (P9Ø)

  ● R56.Ø   **Febrile convulsions**
         R56.ØØ   **Simple febrile convulsions**
                      Febrile convulsion NOS
                      Febrile seizure NOS

         R56.Ø1   **Complex febrile convulsions**
                      Atypical febrile seizure
                      Complex febrile seizure
                      Complicated febrile seizure
                      Excludes1   status epilepticus (G4Ø.9Ø1)

    R56.1   **Post traumatic seizures**
             Excludes1   post traumatic epilepsy (G4Ø.-)

    R56.9   **Unspecified convulsions**
             Convulsion disorder   Recurrent convulsions
             Fit NOS   Seizure(s) (convulsive) NOS

● R57   **Shock, not elsewhere classified**
         Excludes1   anaphylactic shock NOS (T78.2)
                          anaphylactic reaction or shock due to adverse
                              food reaction (T78.Ø-)
                          anaphylactic shock due to adverse effect of
                              correct drug or medicament properly
                              administered (T88.6)
                          anaphylactic shock due to serum (T8Ø.5-)
                          anesthetic shock (T88.3)
                          electric shock (T75.4)
                          obstetric shock (O75.1)
                          postprocedural shock (T81.1-)
                          psychic shock (F43.Ø)
                          shock complicating or following ectopic or molar
                              pregnancy (OØØ-OØ7, OØ8.3)
                          shock due to lightning (T75.Ø1)
                          traumatic shock (T79.4)
                          toxic shock syndrome (A48.3)

    R57.Ø   **Cardiogenic shock**
             Excludes2   septic shock (R65.21)

    R57.1   **Hypovolemic shock**
             Decreased blood volume (loss)

    R57.8   **Other shock**

    R57.9   **Shock, unspecified**
             Failure of peripheral circulation NOS
             Resulting in significant blood pressure drop

● R58   **Hemorrhage, not elsewhere classified**
         Hemorrhage NOS
         Excludes1   hemorrhage included with underlying
                              conditions, such as:
                          acute duodenal ulcer with hemorrhage (K26.Ø)
                          acute gastritis with bleeding (K29.Ø1)
                          ulcerative enterocolitis with rectal bleeding
                              (K51.Ø1)

● R59   **Enlarged lymph nodes**
         Includes   swollen glands
         Excludes1   lymphadenitis NOS (I88.9)
                          acute lymphadenitis (LØ4.-)
                          chronic lymphadenitis (I88.1)
                          mesenteric (acute) (chronic) lymphadenitis (I88.Ø)

    R59.Ø   **Localized enlarged lymph nodes**
    R59.1   **Generalized enlarged lymph nodes**
             Lymphadenopathy NOS
    R59.9   **Enlarged lymph nodes, unspecified**

● R60   **Edema, not elsewhere classified**
         Excludes1   angioneurotic edema (T78.3)
                          ascites (R18.-)
                          cerebral edema (G93.6)
                          cerebral edema due to birth injury (P11.Ø)
                          edema of larynx (J38.4)
                          edema of nasopharynx (J39.2)
                          edema of pharynx (J39.2)
                          gestational edema (O12.Ø-)
                          hereditary edema (Q82.Ø)
                          hydrops fetalis NOS (P83.2)
                          hydrothorax (J94.8)
                          hydrops fetalis NOS (P83.2)
                          newborn edema (P83.3)
                          pulmonary edema (J81.-)

    R60.Ø   **Localized edema**
    R60.1   **Generalized edema**
             Excludes2   nutritional edema (E4Ø-E46)
    R60.9   **Edema, unspecified**
             Fluid retention NOS

  R61   **Generalized hyperhidrosis**
         Excessive sweating
         Night sweats
         Secondary hyperhidrosis
         *Code first, if applicable, menopausal and female climacteric states
         (N95.1)*
         Excludes1   focal (primary) (secondary) hyperhidrosis (L74.5-)
                          Frey's syndrome (L74.52)
                          localized (primary) (secondary) hyperhidrosis
                              (L74.5-)

● R62   **Lack of expected normal physiological development in
         childhood and adults**
         Excludes1   delayed puberty (E3Ø.Ø)
                          gonadal dysgenesis (Q99.1)
                          hypopituitarism (E23.Ø)

    R62.Ø   **Delayed milestone in childhood**   P
             Delayed attainment of expected physiological
                 developmental stage
             Late talker
             Late walker

  ● R62.5   **Other and unspecified lack of expected normal
             physiological development in childhood**
             Excludes1   HIV disease resulting in failure to thrive
                                  (B2Ø)
                              physical retardation due to malnutrition
                                  (E45)

         R62.5Ø   **Unspecified lack of expected normal
                      physiological development in childhood**
                      Infantilism NOS

         R62.51   **Failure to thrive (child)**   P
                      Failure to gain weight
                      Excludes1   failure to thrive in child under 28
                                       days old (P92.6)

         R62.52   **Short stature (child)**
                      Lack of growth   Short stature NOS
                      Physical retardation
                      Excludes1   short stature due to endocrine
                                       disorder (E34.3)

         R62.59   **Other lack of expected normal physiological
                      development in childhood**

    R62.7   **Adult failure to thrive**   A

● **R63   Symptoms and signs concerning food and fluid intake**

    Excludes1   bulimia NOS (F50.2)
                 eating disorders of nonorganic origin (F50.-)
                 malnutrition (E40-E46)

    R63.0   Anorexia
        Loss of appetite
        Excludes1   anorexia nervosa (F50.0-)
                 loss of appetite of nonorganic origin
                    (F50.89)

    R63.1   Polydipsia
        Excessive thirst

    R63.2   Polyphagia
        Excessive eating   Hyperalimentation NOS

    R63.3   Feeding difficulties
        Feeding problem (elderly) (infant) NOS
        Picky eater
        Excludes1   eating disorders (F50.-)
                 feeding problems of newborn (P92.-)
                 infant feeding disorder of nonorganic
                    origin (F98.2-)
        Coding Clinic: 2017, Q1, P27; 2016, Q3, P19

    R63.4   Abnormal weight loss

    R63.5   Abnormal weight gain
        Excludes1   excessive weight gain in pregnancy
                    (O26.0-)
                 obesity (E66.-)

    R63.6   Underweight
        Use additional code to identify body mass index (BMI),
           if known (Z68.-)
        Excludes1   abnormal weight loss (R63.4)
                 anorexia nervosa (F50.0-)
                 malnutrition (E40-E46)

    **R63.8   Other symptoms and signs concerning food and fluid
            intake**

  R64   Cachexia
        Wasting syndrome
        Code first underlying condition, if known
        Excludes1   abnormal weight loss (R63.4)
                 nutritional marasmus (E41)
        Coding Clinic: 2017, Q3, P25

● **R65   Symptoms and signs specifically associated with systemic
      inflammation and infection**

  ● **R65.1   Systemic inflammatory response syndrome (SIRS) of
          non-infectious origin**
        Code first underlying condition, such as:
           heatstroke (T67.0)
           injury and trauma (S00-T88)
        Excludes1   sepsis - code to infection
                 severe sepsis (R65.2)

        **R65.10   Systemic inflammatory response syndrome
                 (SIRS) of non-infectious origin without acute
                 organ dysfunction**
                 Systemic inflammatory response syndrome
                    (SIRS) NOS

        **R65.11   Systemic inflammatory response syndrome
                 (SIRS) of non-infectious origin with acute
                 organ dysfunction**
                 Use additional code to identify specific acute
                    organ dysfunction, such as:
                    acute kidney failure (N17.-)
                    acute respiratory failure (J96.0-)
                    critical illness myopathy (G72.81)
                    critical illness polyneuropathy (G62.81)
                    disseminated intravascular coagulopathy
                      [DIC] (D65)
                    encephalopathy (metabolic) (septic) (G93.41)
                    hepatic failure (K72.0-)

OGCR Section I.C.18.g.

SIRS due to Non-Infectious Process

The systemic inflammatory response syndrome (SIRS) can develop as a result of certain non-infectious disease processes, such as trauma, malignant neoplasm, or pancreatitis. When SIRS is documented with a noninfectious condition, and no subsequent infection is documented, the code for the underlying condition, such as an injury, should be assigned, followed by code R65.10. Systemic inflammatory response syndrome (SIRS) of non-infectious origin without acute organ dysfunction, or code R65.11, Systemic inflammatory response syndrome (SIRS) of non-infectious origin with acute organ dysfunction. If an associated acute organ dysfunction is documented, the appropriate code(s) for the specific type of organ dysfunction(s) should be assigned in addition to code R65.11. If acute organ dysfunction is documented, but it cannot be determined if the acute organ dysfunction is associated with SIRS or due to another condition (e.g., directly due to the trauma), the provider should be queried.

  ● **R65.2   Severe sepsis**
        Infection with associated acute organ dysfunction
        Sepsis with acute organ dysfunction
        Sepsis with multiple organ dysfunction
        Systemic inflammatory response syndrome due to
           infectious process with acute organ dysfunction
        Code first underlying infection, such as:
           infection following a procedure (T81.44)
           infections following infusion, transfusion and
               therapeutic injection (T80.2-)
           puerperal sepsis (O85)
           sepsis following complete or unspecified
               spontaneous abortion (O03.87)
           sepsis following ectopic and molar pregnancy (O08.82)
           sepsis following incomplete spontaneous abortion
               (O03.37)
           sepsis following (induced) termination of pregnancy
               (O04.87)
           sepsis NOS (A41.9)
        Use additional code to identify specific acute organ
           dysfunction, such as:
           acute kidney failure (N17.-)
           acute respiratory failure (J96.0-)
           critical illness myopathy (G72.81)
           critical illness polyneuropathy (G62.81)
           disseminated intravascular coagulopathy [DIC] (D65)
           encephalopathy (metabolic) (septic) (G93.41)
           hepatic failure (K72.0-)
        Coding Clinic: 2017, Q4, P99; 2016, Q3, P8

        R65.20   Severe sepsis without septic shock
                 Severe sepsis NOS
                 Coding Clinic: 2016, Q3, P14

        R65.21   Severe sepsis with septic shock

● **R68   Other general symptoms and signs**

    **R68.0   Hypothermia, not associated with low environmental
            temperature**
        Excludes1   hypothermia NOS (accidental) (T68)
                 hypothermia due to anesthesia (T88.51)
                 hypothermia due to low environmental
                    temperature (T68)
                 newborn hypothermia (P80.-)

  ● **R68.1   Nonspecific symptoms peculiar to infancy**
        Excludes1   colic, infantile (R10.83)
                 neonatal cerebral irritability (P91.3)
                 teething syndrome (K00.7)

        R68.11   Excessive crying of infant (baby)   P
                 Excludes1   excessive crying of child,
                        adolescent, or adult (R45.83)

        R68.12   Fussy infant (baby)   P
                 Irritable infant

▶ New   ⟹ Revised   ~~deleted~~ Deleted   Excludes 1   Excludes 2   Includes   Use additional   Code first   Code also   Key words
OGCR Official Guidelines   X Assign placeholder X   ● Use Additional Character(s)   ▌ Manifestation Code   **Coding Clinic**

R68.13   **Apparent life threatening event in infant (ALTE)**   P

     Apparent life threatening event in newborn
     Brief resolved unexplained event (BRUE)

     Code first confirmed diagnosis, if known

     Use additional code(s) for associated signs and symptoms if no confirmed diagnosis established, or if signs and symptoms are not associated routinely with confirmed diagnosis, or provide additional information for cause of ALTE

R68.19   **Other nonspecific symptoms peculiar to infancy**   P

R68.2   **Dry mouth, unspecified**

     Excludes1   dry mouth due to dehydration (E86.0)
                 dry mouth due to sicca syndrome [Sjögren] (M35.0-)
                 salivary gland hyposecretion (K11.7)

R68.3   **Clubbing of fingers**

     Clubbing of nails

     Excludes1   congenital clubfinger (Q68.1)

● **R68.8**   **Other general symptoms and signs**

    R68.81   **Early satiety**

    R68.82   **Decreased libido**   A

         Decreased sexual desire

    R68.83   **Chills (without fever)**

         Chills NOS

         Excludes1   chills with fever (R50.9)

    R68.84   **Jaw pain**

         Mandibular pain
         Maxilla pain

         Excludes1   temporomandibular joint arthralgia (M26.62-)

    R68.89   **Other general symptoms and signs**

R69   **Illness, unspecified**

     Unknown and unspecified cases of morbidity

ABNORMAL FINDINGS ON EXAMINATION OF BLOOD, WITHOUT DIAGNOSIS (R70-R79)

     Excludes2   abnormal findings on antenatal screening of mother (O28.-)
                 abnormalities of lipids (E78.-)
                 abnormalities of platelets and thrombocytes (D69.-)
                 abnormalities of white blood cells classified elsewhere (D70-D72)
                 coagulation hemorrhagic disorders (D65-D68)
                 diagnostic abnormal findings classified elsewhere —*see* Alphabetical Index
                 hemorrhagic and hematological disorders of newborn (P50-P61)

● **R70**   **Elevated erythrocyte sedimentation rate and abnormality of plasma viscosity**

    R70.0   **Elevated erythrocyte sedimentation rate**

    R70.1   **Abnormal plasma viscosity**

● **R71**   **Abnormality of red blood cells**

     Excludes1   anemias (D50-D64)
                 anemia of premature infant (P61.2)
                 benign (familial) polycythemia (D75.0)
                 congenital anemias (P61.2-P61.4)
                 newborn anemia due to isoimmunization (P55.-)
                 polycythemia neonatorum (P61.1)
                 polycythemia NOS (D75.1)
                 polycythemia vera (D45)
                 secondary polycythemia (D75.1)

    R71.0   **Precipitous drop in hematocrit**

         Drop (precipitous) in hemoglobin
         Drop in hematocrit
         Blood volume that has decreased red blood cells

    R71.8   **Other abnormality of red blood cells**

         Abnormal red-cell morphology NOS
         Abnormal red-cell volume NOS
         Anisocytosis
         Red blood cells of unequal size
         Poikilocytosis
         Red blood cells of abnormal shape

● **R73**   **Elevated blood glucose level**

     Excludes1   diabetes mellitus (E08-E13)
                 diabetes mellitus in pregnancy, childbirth and the puerperium (O24.-)
                 neonatal disorders (P70.0-P70.2)
                 postsurgical hypoinsulinemia (E89.1)

    ● **R73.0**   **Abnormal glucose**

         Excludes1   abnormal glucose in pregnancy (O99.81-)
                       diabetes mellitus (E08-E13)
                       dysmetabolic syndrome X (E88.81)
                       gestational diabetes (O24.4-)
                       glycosuria (R81)
                       hypoglycemia (E16.2)

      R73.01   **Impaired fasting glucose**

           Elevated fasting glucose

      R73.02   **Impaired glucose tolerance (oral)**

           Elevated glucose tolerance

      R73.03   **Prediabetes**

           Latent diabetes
           Coding Clinic: 2016, Q4, P65

      R73.09   **Other abnormal glucose**

           Abnormal glucose NOS
           Abnormal non-fasting glucose tolerance
           Coding Clinic: 2016, Q4, P65

    R73.9   **Hyperglycemia, unspecified**

● **R74**   **Abnormal serum enzyme levels**

    R74.0   **Nonspecific elevation of levels of transaminase and lactic acid dehydrogenase [LDH]**

    R74.8   **Abnormal levels of other serum enzymes**

         Abnormal level of acid phosphatase
         Abnormal level of alkaline phosphatase
         Abnormal level of amylase
         Abnormal level of lipase [triacylglycerol lipase]

    R74.9   **Abnormal serum enzyme level, unspecified**

OGCR   Section I.C.1.e and f.

Patients with inconclusive HIV serology

e. Patients with inconclusive HIV serology, but no definitive diagnosis or manifestations of the illness, may be assigned code R75, Inconclusive laboratory evidence of human immunodeficiency virus [HIV].

f. Previously diagnosed HIV-related illness

Patients with any known prior diagnosis of an HIV-related illness should be coded to B20. Once a patient has developed an HIV-related illness, the patient should always be assigned code B20 on every subsequent admission/encounter. Patients previously diagnosed with any HIV illness (B20) should never be assigned to R75 or Z21, Asymptomatic human immunodeficiency virus [HIV] infection status.

R75   **Inconclusive laboratory evidence of human immunodeficiency virus [HIV]**

     Nonconclusive HIV-test finding in infants

     Excludes1   asymptomatic human immunodeficiency virus [HIV] infection status (Z21)
                 human immunodeficiency virus [HIV] disease (B20)

● R76 Other abnormal immunological findings in serum

R76.0 Raised antibody titer

Excludes1 isoimmunization in pregnancy (O36.0-O36.1)
isoimmunization affecting newborn (P55.-)

● R76.1 Nonspecific reaction to test for tuberculosis

R76.11 **Nonspecific reaction to tuberculin skin test without active tuberculosis**
Abnormal result of Mantoux test
PPD positive
Tuberculin (skin test) positive
Tuberculin (skin test) reactor

Excludes1 nonspecific reaction to cell mediated immunity measurement of gamma interferon antigen response without active tuberculosis (R76.12)

R76.12 **Nonspecific reaction to cell mediated immunity measurement of gamma interferon antigen response without active tuberculosis**
Nonspecific reaction to QuantiFERON-TB test (QFT) without active tuberculosis

Excludes1 nonspecific reaction to tuberculin skin test without active tuberculosis (R76.11)
positive tuberculin skin test (R76.11)

R76.8 **Other specified abnormal immunological findings in serum**
Raised level of immunoglobulins NOS

R76.9 **Abnormal immunological finding in serum, unspecified**

● R77 Other abnormalities of plasma proteins

⮕ **Excludes1** disorders of plasma-protein metabolism (E88.0-)

R77.0 **Abnormality of albumin**

R77.1 **Abnormality of globulin**
Hyperglobulinemia NOS

R77.2 **Abnormality of alphafetoprotein**

R77.8 **Other specified abnormalities of plasma proteins**

R77.9 **Abnormality of plasma protein, unspecified**

● R78 Findings of drugs and other substances, not normally found in blood

Use additional code to identify any retained foreign body, if applicable (Z18.-)

Excludes1 mental or behavioral disorders due to psychoactive substance use (F10-F19)

R78.0 **Finding of alcohol in blood**
Use additional external cause code (Y90.-), for detail regarding alcohol level.

R78.1 **Finding of opiate drug in blood**

R78.2 **Finding of cocaine in blood**

R78.3 **Finding of hallucinogen in blood**

R78.4 **Finding of other drugs of addictive potential in blood**

R78.5 **Finding of other psychotropic drug in blood**

R78.6 **Finding of steroid agent in blood**

● R78.7 **Finding of abnormal level of heavy metals in blood**

R78.71 **Abnormal lead level in blood**

Excludes1 lead poisoning (T56.0-)

R78.79 **Finding of abnormal level of heavy metals in blood**

● R78.8 **Finding of other specified substances, not normally found in blood**

R78.81 **Bacteremia**
Blood poisoning/bacteremia

Excludes1 sepsis-code to specified infection

R78.89 **Finding of other specified substances, not normally found in blood**
Finding of abnormal level of lithium in blood

R78.9 **Finding of unspecified substance, not normally found in blood**

● R79 Other abnormal findings of blood chemistry

Use additional code to identify any retained foreign body, if applicable (Z18.-)

Excludes1 asymptomatic hyperuricemia (E79.0)
hyperglycemia NOS (R73.9)
hypoglycemia NOS (E16.2)
neonatal hypoglycemia (P70.3-P70.4)
specific findings indicating disorder of amino-acid metabolism (E70-E72)
specific findings indicating disorder of carbohydrate metabolism (E73-E74)
specific findings indicating disorder of lipid metabolism (E75.-)

R79.0 **Abnormal level of blood mineral**
Abnormal blood level of cobalt
Abnormal blood level of copper
Abnormal blood level of iron
Abnormal blood level of magnesium
Abnormal blood level of mineral NEC
Abnormal blood level of zinc

Excludes1 abnormal level of lithium (R78.89)
disorders of mineral metabolism (E83.-)
neonatal hypomagnesemia (P71.2)
nutritional mineral deficiency (E58-E61)

R79.1 **Abnormal coagulation profile**
Abnormal or prolonged bleeding time
Abnormal or prolonged coagulation time
Abnormal or prolonged partial thromboplastin time [PTT]
Abnormal or prolonged prothrombin time [PT]

Excludes1 coagulation defects (D68.-)

Excludes2 abnormality of fluid, electrolyte or acid-base balance (E86-E87)

● R79.8 **Other specified abnormal findings of blood chemistry**

R79.81 **Abnormal blood-gas level**

R79.82 **Elevated C-reactive protein (CRP)**

R79.89 **Other specified abnormal findings of blood chemistry**

R79.9 **Abnormal finding of blood chemistry, unspecified**

ABNORMAL FINDINGS ON EXAMINATION OF URINE, WITHOUT DIAGNOSIS (R80-R82)

Excludes1 abnormal findings on antenatal screening of mother (O28.-)
diagnostic abnormal findings classified elsewhere - see Alphabetical Index
specific findings indicating disorder of amino-acid metabolism (E70-E72)
specific findings indicating disorder of carbohydrate metabolism (E73-E74)

● R80 Proteinuria

Excludes1 gestational proteinuria (O12.1-)

R80.0 **Isolated proteinuria**
Idiopathic proteinuria

Excludes1 isolated proteinuria with specific morphological lesion (N06.-)

R80.1 **Persistent proteinuria, unspecified**

R80.2 **Orthostatic proteinuria, unspecified**
Postural proteinuria

R80.3 **Bence Jones proteinuria**

R80.8 **Other proteinuria**

R80.9 **Proteinuria, unspecified**
Albuminuria NOS

R81 Glycosuria

Excludes1 renal glycosuria (E74.8)

▶ New   ⮕ Revised   ~~deleted~~ Deleted   Excludes 1   Excludes 2   Includes   Use additional   Code first   Code also   Key words

OGCR Official Guidelines   X Assign placeholder X   ● Use Additional Character(s)   ▶ Manifestation Code   **Coding Clinic**

● **R82**   **Other and unspecified abnormal findings in urine**

> **Includes**   chromoabnormalities in urine

> Use additional code to identify any retained foreign body, if applicable (Z18.-)

> **Excludes2**   hematuria (R31.-)

R82.0   **Chyluria**
> *White milky urine*
>> **Excludes1**   filarial chyluria (B74.-)

R82.1   **Myoglobinuria**
> *Presence of myoglobin (iron containing protein) in urine*

R82.2   **Biliuria**
> *Presence of bile pigments/salts in urine*

R82.3   **Hemoglobinuria**
> *Presence of hemoglobin in urine*
>> **Excludes1**   hemoglobinuria due to hemolysis from external causes NEC (D59.6)
>> hemoglobinuria due to paroxysmal nocturnal [Marchiafava-Micheli] (D59.5)

R82.4   **Acetonuria**
> Ketonuria

R82.5   **Elevated urine levels of drugs, medicaments and biological substances**
> Elevated urine levels of catecholamines
> Elevated urine levels of indoleacetic acid
> Elevated urine levels of 17-ketosteroids
> Elevated urine levels of steroids

R82.6   **Abnormal urine levels of substances chiefly nonmedicinal as to source**
> Abnormal urine level of heavy metals

● **R82.7**   **Abnormal findings on microbiological examination of urine**
> **Excludes1**   colonization status (Z22.-)
> **Coding Clinic: 2016, Q4, P65**

> **R82.71**   **Bacteriuria**

> **R82.79**   **Other abnormal findings on microbiological examination of urine**
>> Positive culture findings of urine

R82.8   **Abnormal findings on cytological and histological examination of urine**

● **R82.9**   **Other and unspecified abnormal findings in urine**

> **R82.90**   Unspecified abnormal findings in urine

> **R82.91**   Other chromoabnormalities of urine
>> Chromoconversion (dipstick)
>> Idiopathic dipstick converts positive for blood with no cellular forms in sediment
>>> **Excludes1**   hemoglobinuria (R82.3)
>>> myoglobinuria (R82.1)

> ● **R82.99**   **Other abnormal findings in urine**
>> ~~Cells and casts in urine~~
>> ~~Crystalluria~~
>> ~~Melanuria~~
>>> ▶ **R82.991**   **Hypocitraturia**
>>> ▶ **R82.992**   **Hyperoxaluria**
>>>> ▶ **Excludes1**   Primary hyperoxaluria (E72.53)
>>> ▶ **R82.993**   **Hyperuricoscuria**
>>> ▶ **R82.994**   **Hypercalciuria**
>>>> ▶Idiopathic hypercalciuria
>>> ▶ **R82.998**   **Other abnormal findings in urine**
>>>> ▶Cells and casts in urine
>>>> ▶Crystalluria
>>>> ▶Melanuria

ABNORMAL FINDINGS ON EXAMINATION OF OTHER BODY FLUIDS, SUBSTANCES AND TISSUES, WITHOUT DIAGNOSIS (R83-R89)

> **Excludes1**   abnormal findings on antenatal screening of mother (O28.-)
> diagnostic abnormal findings classified elsewhere - see Alphabetical Index

> **Excludes2**   abnormal findings on examination of blood, without diagnosis (R70-R79)
> abnormal findings on examination of urine, without diagnosis (R80-R82)
> abnormal tumor markers (R97.-)

● **R83**   **Abnormal findings in cerebrospinal fluid**

R83.0   **Abnormal level of enzymes in cerebrospinal fluid**

R83.1   **Abnormal level of hormones in cerebrospinal fluid**

R83.2   **Abnormal level of other drugs, medicaments and biological substances in cerebrospinal fluid**

R83.3   **Abnormal level of substances chiefly nonmedicinal as to source in cerebrospinal fluid**

R83.4   **Abnormal immunological findings in cerebrospinal fluid**

R83.5   **Abnormal microbiological findings in cerebrospinal fluid**
> Positive culture findings in cerebrospinal fluid
>> **Excludes1**   colonization status (Z22.-)

R83.6   **Abnormal cytological findings in cerebrospinal fluid**

R83.8   **Other abnormal findings in cerebrospinal fluid**
> Abnormal chromosomal findings in cerebrospinal fluid

R83.9   **Unspecified abnormal finding in cerebrospinal fluid**

● **R84**   **Abnormal findings in specimens from respiratory organs and thorax**

> **Includes**   abnormal findings in bronchial washings
> abnormal findings in nasal secretions
> abnormal findings in pleural fluid
> abnormal findings in sputum
> abnormal findings in throat scrapings

> **Excludes1**   blood-stained sputum (R04.2)

R84.0   **Abnormal level of enzymes in specimens from respiratory organs and thorax**

R84.1   **Abnormal level of hormones in specimens from respiratory organs and thorax**

R84.2   **Abnormal level of other drugs, medicaments and biological substances in specimens from respiratory organs and thorax**

R84.3   **Abnormal level of substances chiefly nonmedicinal as to source in specimens from respiratory organs and thorax**

R84.4   **Abnormal immunological findings in specimens from respiratory organs and thorax**

R84.5   **Abnormal microbiological findings in specimens from respiratory organs and thorax**
> Positive culture findings in specimens from respiratory organs and thorax
>> **Excludes1**   colonization status (Z22.-)

R84.6   **Abnormal cytological findings in specimens from respiratory organs and thorax**

R84.7   **Abnormal histological findings in specimens from respiratory organs and thorax**

R84.8   **Other abnormal findings in specimens from respiratory organs and thorax**
> Abnormal chromosomal findings in specimens from respiratory organs and thorax

R84.9   **Unspecified abnormal finding in specimens from respiratory organs and thorax**

CHAPTER 18 (R00-R99)

● R85   Abnormal findings in specimens from digestive organs and abdominal cavity

   Includes   abnormal findings in peritoneal fluid
                   abnormal findings in saliva

   Excludes1   cloudy peritoneal dialysis effluent (R88.0)
                   fecal abnormalities (R19.5)

   R85.0   Abnormal level of enzymes in specimens from digestive organs and abdominal cavity

   R85.1   Abnormal level of hormones in specimens from digestive organs and abdominal cavity

   R85.2   Abnormal level of other drugs, medicaments and biological substances in specimens from digestive organs and abdominal cavity

   R85.3   Abnormal level of substances chiefly nonmedicinal as to source in specimens from digestive organs and abdominal cavity

   R85.4   Abnormal immunological findings in specimens from digestive organs and abdominal cavity

   R85.5   Abnormal microbiological findings in specimens from digestive organs and abdominal cavity
            Positive culture findings in specimens from digestive organs and abdominal cavity
            Excludes1   colonization status (Z22.-)

● R85.6   Abnormal cytological findings in specimens from digestive organs and abdominal cavity

    ● R85.61   Abnormal cytologic smear of anus
              Excludes1   abnormal cytological findings in specimens from other digestive organs and abdominal cavity (R85.69)
                               carcinoma in situ of anus (histologically confirmed) (D01.3)
                               anal intraepithelial neoplasia I [AIN I] (K62.82)
                               anal intraepithelial neoplasia II [AIN II] (K62.82)
                               anal intraepithelial neoplasia III [AIN III] (D01.3)
                               dysplasia (mild) (moderate) of anus (histologically confirmed) (K62.82)
                               severe dysplasia of anus (histologically confirmed) (D01.3)
              Excludes2   anal high risk human papillomavirus (HPV) DNA test positive (R85.81)
                               anal low risk human papillomavirus (HPV) DNA test positive (R85.82)

        R85.610   Atypical squamous cells of undetermined significance on cytologic smear of anus (ASC-US)

        R85.611   Atypical squamous cells cannot exclude high grade squamous intraepithelial lesion on cytologic smear of anus (ASC-H)

        R85.612   Low grade squamous intraepithelial lesion on cytologic smear of anus (LGSIL)

        R85.613   High grade squamous intraepithelial lesion on cytologic smear of anus (HGSIL)

        R85.614   Cytologic evidence of malignancy on smear of anus

        R85.615   Unsatisfactory cytologic smear of anus
                   Inadequate sample of cytologic smear of anus

        R85.616   Satisfactory anal smear but lacking transformation zone

        R85.618   Other abnormal cytological findings on specimens from anus

        R85.619   Unspecified abnormal cytological findings in specimens from anus
                   Abnormal anal cytology NOS
                   Atypical glandular cells of anus NOS

    R85.69   Abnormal cytological findings in specimens from other digestive organs and abdominal cavity

   R85.7   Abnormal histological findings in specimens from digestive organs and abdominal cavity

● R85.8   Other abnormal findings in specimens from digestive organs and abdominal cavity

    R85.81   Anal high risk human papillomavirus (HPV) DNA test positive
              Excludes1   anogenital warts due to human papillomavirus (HPV) (A63.0)
                               condyloma acuminatum (A63.0)

    R85.82   Anal low risk human papillomavirus (HPV) DNA test positive
              Use additional code for associated human papillomavirus (B97.7)

    R85.89   Other abnormal findings in specimens from digestive organs and abdominal cavity
              Abnormal chromosomal findings in specimens from digestive organs and abdominal cavity

   R85.9   Unspecified abnormal finding in specimens from digestive organs and abdominal cavity

● R86   Abnormal findings in specimens from male genital organs

   Includes   abnormal findings in prostatic secretions
                   abnormal findings in semen, seminal fluid
                   abnormal spermatozoa

   Excludes1   azoospermia (N46.0-)
                   oligospermia (N46.1-)

   R86.0   Abnormal level of enzymes in specimens from male genital organs ♂

   R86.1   Abnormal level of hormones in specimens from male genital organs ♂

   R86.2   Abnormal level of other drugs, medicaments and biological substances in specimens from male genital organs ♂

   R86.3   Abnormal level of substances chiefly nonmedicinal as to source in specimens from male genital organs ♂

   R86.4   Abnormal immunological findings in specimens from male genital organs ♂

   R86.5   Abnormal microbiological findings in specimens from male genital organs ♂
            Positive culture findings in specimens from male genital organs
            Excludes1   colonization status (Z22.-)

   R86.6   Abnormal cytological findings in specimens from male genital organs ♂

   R86.7   Abnormal histological findings in specimens from male genital organs ♂

   R86.8   Other abnormal findings in specimens from male genital organs ♂
            Abnormal chromosomal findings in specimens from male genital organs

   R86.9   Unspecified abnormal finding in specimens from male genital organs ♂

▶ New   ⇒ Revised   ~~deleted~~ Deleted   Excludes 1   Excludes 2   Includes   Use additional   Code first   Code also   Key words
OGCR Official Guidelines   X Assign placeholder X   ● Use Additional Character(s)   ▶ Manifestation Code   **Coding Clinic**

● **R87**   **Abnormal findings in specimens from female genital organs**

     Includes   abnormal findings in secretion and smears from cervix uteri

                 abnormal findings in secretion and smears from vagina

                 abnormal findings in secretion and smears from vulva

R87.0   **Abnormal level of enzymes in specimens from female genital organs** ♀

R87.1   **Abnormal level of hormones in specimens from female genital organs** ♀

R87.2   **Abnormal level of other drugs, medicaments and biological substances in specimens from female genital organs** ♀

R87.3   **Abnormal level of substances chiefly nonmedicinal as to source in specimens from female genital organs** ♀

R87.4   **Abnormal immunological findings in specimens from female genital organs** ♀

R87.5   **Abnormal microbiological findings in specimens from female genital organs** ♀

     Positive culture findings in specimens from female genital organs

     Excludes1   colonization status (Z22.-)

● **R87.6**   **Abnormal cytological findings in specimens from female genital organs**

   ● **R87.61**   **Abnormal cytological findings in specimens from cervix uteri**

       Excludes1   abnormal cytological findings in specimens from other female genital organs (R87.69)

                   abnormal cytological findings in specimens from vagina (R87.62-)

                   carcinoma in situ of cervix uteri (histologically confirmed) (D06.-)

                   cervical intraepithelial neoplasia I [CIN I] (N87.0)

                   cervical intraepithelial neoplasia II [CIN II] (N87.1)

                   cervical intraepithelial neoplasia III [CIN III] (D06.-)

                   dysplasia (mild) (moderate) of cervix uteri (histologically confirmed) (N87.-)

                   severe dysplasia of cervix uteri (histologically confirmed) (D06.-)

       Excludes2   cervical high risk human papillomavirus (HPV) DNA test positive (R87.810)

                   cervical low risk human papillomavirus (HPV) DNA test positive (R87.820)

     R87.610   **Atypical squamous cells of undetermined significance on cytologic smear of cervix (ASC-US)** ♀

     R87.611   **Atypical squamous cells cannot exclude high grade squamous intraepithelial lesion on cytologic smear of cervix (ASC-H)** ♀

     R87.612   **Low grade squamous intraepithelial lesion on cytologic smear of cervix (LGSIL)** ♀

     R87.613   **High grade squamous intraepithelial lesion on cytologic smear of cervix (HGSIL)** ♀

     R87.614   **Cytologic evidence of malignancy on smear of cervix** ♀

     R87.615   **Unsatisfactory cytologic smear of cervix** ♀

       Inadequate sample of cytologic smear of cervix

R87.616   **Satisfactory cervical smear but lacking transformation zone** ♀

R87.618   **Other abnormal cytological findings on specimens from cervix uteri** ♀

R87.619   **Unspecified abnormal cytological findings in specimens from cervix uteri** ♀

     Abnormal cervical cytology NOS

     Abnormal Papanicolaou smear of cervix NOS

     Abnormal thin preparation smear of cervix NOS

     Atypical endocervical cells of cervix NOS

     Atypical endometrial cells of cervix NOS

     Atypical glandular cells of cervix NOS

● **R87.62**   **Abnormal cytological findings in specimens from vagina**

     Use additional code to identify acquired absence of uterus and cervix, if applicable (Z90.71-)

     Excludes1   abnormal cytological findings in specimens from cervix uteri (R87.61-)

                   abnormal cytological findings in specimens from other female genital organs (R87.69)

                   carcinoma in situ of vagina (histologically confirmed) (D07.2)

                   vaginal intraepithelial neoplasia I [VAIN I] (N89.0)

                   vaginal intraepithelial neoplasia II [VAIN II] (N89.1)

                   vaginal intraepithelial neoplasia III [VAIN III] (D07.2)

                   dysplasia (mild) (moderate) of vagina (histologically confirmed) (N89.-)

                   severe dysplasia of vagina (histologically confirmed) (D07.2)

     Excludes2   vaginal high risk human papillomavirus (HPV) DNA test positive (R87.811)

                   vaginal low risk human papillomavirus (HPV) DNA test positive (R87.821)

     R87.620   **Atypical squamous cells of undetermined significance on cytologic smear of vagina (ASC-US)** ♀

     R87.621   **Atypical squamous cells cannot exclude high grade squamous intraepithelial lesion on cytologic smear of vagina (ASC-H)** ♀

     R87.622   **Low grade squamous intraepithelial lesion on cytologic smear of vagina (LGSIL)** ♀

     R87.623   **High grade squamous intraepithelial lesion on cytologic smear of vagina (HGSIL)** ♀

     R87.624   **Cytologic evidence of malignancy on smear of vagina** ♀

     R87.625   **Unsatisfactory cytologic smear of vagina** ♀

       Inadequate sample of cytologic smear of vagina

     R87.628   **Other abnormal cytological findings on specimens from vagina** ♀

R87.629   **Unspecified** abnormal cytological findings in specimens from vagina ♀
Abnormal Papanicolaou smear of vagina NOS
Abnormal thin preparation smear of vagina NOS
Abnormal vaginal cytology NOS
Atypical endocervical cells of vagina NOS
Atypical endometrial cells of vagina NOS
Atypical glandular cells of vagina NOS

R87.69   Abnormal cytological findings in specimens from other female genital organs ♀
Abnormal cytological findings in specimens from female genital organs NOS
Excludes1   dysplasia of vulva (histologically confirmed) (N90.Ø-N90.3)

R87.7   Abnormal **histological** findings in specimens from female genital organs ♀
Excludes1   carcinoma in situ (histologically confirmed) of female genital organs (DØ6-DØ7.3)
cervical intraepithelial neoplasia I [CIN I] (N87.Ø)
cervical intraepithelial neoplasia II [CIN II] (N87.1)
cervical intraepithelial neoplasia III [CIN III] (DØ6.-)
dysplasia (mild) (moderate) of cervix uteri (histologically confirmed) (N87.-)
dysplasia (mild) (moderate) of vagina (histologically confirmed) (N89.-)
vaginal intraepithelial neoplasia I [VAIN I] (N89.Ø)
vaginal intraepithelial neoplasia II [VAIN II] (N89.1)
vaginal intraepithelial neoplasia III [VAIN III] (DØ7.2)
severe dysplasia of cervix uteri (histologically confirmed) (DØ6.-)
severe dysplasia of vagina (histologically confirmed) (DØ7.2)

● R87.8   **Other** abnormal findings in specimens from female genital organs
● R87.81   High risk human papillomavirus (HPV) DNA test positive from female genital organs
Excludes1   anogenital warts due to human papillomavirus (HPV) (A63.Ø)
condyloma acuminatum (A63.Ø)
R87.81Ø   Cervical high risk human papillomavirus (HPV) DNA test positive ♀
R87.811   **Vaginal** high risk human papillomavirus (HPV) DNA test positive ♀

● R87.82   Low risk human papillomavirus (HPV) DNA test positive from female genital organs
Use additional code for associated human papillomavirus (B97.7)
R87.82Ø   Cervical low risk human papillomavirus (HPV) DNA test positive ♀
R87.821   Vaginal low risk human papillomavirus (HPV) DNA test positive ♀

R87.89   Other abnormal findings in specimens from female genital organs ♀
Abnormal chromosomal findings in specimens from female genital organs

R87.9   **Unspecified** abnormal finding in specimens from female genital organs ♀

● R88   **Abnormal findings in other body fluids and substances**
R88.Ø   Cloudy (hemodialysis) (peritoneal) dialysis effluent
R88.8   Abnormal findings in other body fluids and substances

● R89   Abnormal findings in specimens from **other organs, systems and tissues**
Includes   abnormal findings in nipple discharge
abnormal findings in synovial fluid
abnormal findings in wound secretions

R89.Ø   Abnormal level of **enzymes** in specimens from other organs, systems and tissues

R89.1   Abnormal level of **hormones** in specimens from other organs, systems and tissues

R89.2   Abnormal level of **other drugs, medicaments and biological substances** in specimens from other organs, systems and tissues

R89.3   Abnormal level of **substances chiefly nonmedicinal** as to source in specimens from other organs, systems and tissues

R89.4   Abnormal **immunological** findings in specimens from other organs, systems and tissues

R89.5   Abnormal **microbiological** findings in specimens from other organs, systems and tissues
Positive culture findings in specimens from other organs, systems and tissues
Excludes1   colonization status (Z22.-)

R89.6   Abnormal **cytological** findings in specimens from other organs, systems and tissues

R89.7   Abnormal **histological** findings in specimens from other organs, systems and tissues

R89.8   **Other** abnormal findings in specimens from other organs, systems and tissues
Abnormal chromosomal findings in specimens from other organs, systems and tissues

R89.9   **Unspecified** abnormal finding in specimens from other organs, systems and tissues

---

ABNORMAL FINDINGS ON DIAGNOSTIC IMAGING AND IN FUNCTION STUDIES, WITHOUT DIAGNOSIS (R9Ø-R94)

Includes   nonspecific abnormal findings on diagnostic imaging by computerized axial tomography [CAT scan]
nonspecific abnormal findings on diagnostic imaging by magnetic resonance imaging [MRI][NMR]
nonspecific abnormal findings on diagnostic imaging by positron emission tomography [PET scan]
nonspecific abnormal findings on diagnostic imaging by thermography
nonspecific abnormal findings on diagnostic imaging by ultrasound [echogram]
nonspecific abnormal findings on diagnostic imaging by X-ray examination

Excludes1   abnormal findings on antenatal screening of mother (O28.-)
diagnostic abnormal findings classified elsewhere - see Alphabetical Index

● R9Ø   Abnormal findings on **diagnostic imaging of central nervous system**
R9Ø.Ø   **Intracranial space-occupying lesion** found on diagnostic imaging of central nervous system
● R9Ø.8   Other abnormal findings on diagnostic imaging of central nervous system
R9Ø.81   Abnormal echoencephalogram
R9Ø.82   White matter disease, **unspecified**
R9Ø.89   Other abnormal findings on diagnostic imaging of central nervous system
Other cerebrovascular abnormality found on diagnostic imaging of central nervous system

---

▶ New   ⇒ Revised   ~~deleted~~ Deleted   Excludes 1   Excludes 2   Includes   Use additional   Code first   Code also   Key words
OGCR Official Guidelines   X Assign placeholder X   ● Use Additional Character(s)   ▷ Manifestation Code   **Coding Clinic**
1196

● **R91**   **Abnormal findings on diagnostic imaging of lung**

     R91.1   **Solitary pulmonary nodule**
         Coin lesion lung
         Solitary pulmonary nodule, subsegmental branch of the bronchial tree

     R91.8   **Other nonspecific abnormal finding of lung field**
         Lung mass NOS found on diagnostic imaging of lung
         Pulmonary infiltrate NOS
         Shadow, lung

● **R92**   **Abnormal and inconclusive findings on diagnostic imaging of breast**

     R92.0   **Mammographic microcalcification found on diagnostic imaging of breast**
         Excludes2   mammographic calcification (calculus) found on diagnostic imaging of breast (R92.1)

     R92.1   **Mammographic calcification found on diagnostic imaging of breast**
         Mammographic calculus found on diagnostic imaging of breast

     R92.2   **Inconclusive mammogram**
         Dense breasts NOS
         Inconclusive mammogram NEC
         Inconclusive mammography due to dense breasts
         Inconclusive mammography NEC
         Coding Clinic: 2015, Q1, P24

     R92.8   **Other abnormal and inconclusive findings on diagnostic imaging of breast**

● **R93**   **Abnormal findings on diagnostic imaging of other body structures**

     R93.0   **Abnormal findings on diagnostic imaging of skull and head, not elsewhere classified**
         Excludes1   intracranial space-occupying lesion found on diagnostic imaging (R90.0)

     R93.1   **Abnormal findings on diagnostic imaging of heart and coronary circulation**
         Abnormal echocardiogram NOS
         Abnormal heart shadow

     R93.2   **Abnormal findings on diagnostic imaging of liver and biliary tract**
         Nonvisualization of gallbladder

     R93.3   **Abnormal findings on diagnostic imaging of other parts of digestive tract**

●   **R93.4**   **Abnormal findings on diagnostic imaging of urinary organs**
         Excludes2   hypertrophy of kidney (N28.81)
         Coding Clinic: 2016, Q4, P66

         R93.41   **Abnormal radiologic findings on diagnostic imaging of renal pelvis, ureter, or bladder**
            Filling defect of bladder found on diagnostic imaging
            Filling defect of renal pelvis found on diagnostic imaging
            Filling defect of ureter found on diagnostic imaging

●   **R93.42**   **Abnormal radiologic findings on diagnostic imaging of kidney**
            R93.421   **Abnormal radiologic findings on diagnostic imaging of right kidney**
            R93.422   **Abnormal radiologic findings on diagnostic imaging of left kidney**
            R93.429   **Abnormal radiologic findings on diagnostic imaging of unspecified kidney**

         R93.49   **Abnormal radiologic findings on diagnostic imaging of other urinary organs**

     R93.5   **Abnormal findings on diagnostic imaging of other abdominal regions, including retroperitoneum**

     R93.6   **Abnormal findings on diagnostic imaging of limbs**
         ⇒ **Excludes2**   abnormal finding in skin and subcutaneous tissue (R93.8-)

     R93.7   **Abnormal findings on diagnostic imaging of other parts of musculoskeletal system**
         Excludes2   abnormal findings on diagnostic imaging of skull (R93.0)

●   **R93.8**   **Abnormal findings on diagnostic imaging of other specified body structures**
         ~~Abnormal finding by radioisotope localization of placenta~~
         ~~Abnormal radiological finding in skin and subcutaneous tissue~~
         ~~Mediastinal shift~~

▶   **R93.81**   **Abnormal radiologic findings on diagnostic imaging of testis**
         ▶ **R93.811**   **Abnormal radiologic findings on diagnostic imaging of right testicle**
         ▶ **R93.812**   **Abnormal radiologic findings on diagnostic imaging of left testicle**
         ▶ **R93.813**   **Abnormal radiologic findings on diagnostic imaging of testicles, bilateral**
         ▶ **R93.819**   **Abnormal radiologic findings on diagnostic imaging of unspecified testicle**

▶   **R93.89**   **Abnormal findings on diagnostic imaging of other specified body structures**
         ▶ Abnormal finding by radioisotope localization of placenta
         ▶ Abnormal radiological finding in skin and subcutaneous tissue
         ▶ Mediastinal shift

     R93.9   **Diagnostic imaging inconclusive due to excess body fat of patient**

● **R94**   **Abnormal results of function studies**
     Includes   abnormal results of radionuclide [radioisotope] uptake studies
               abnormal results of scintigraphy

●   **R94.0**   **Abnormal results of function studies of central nervous system**
         R94.01   **Abnormal electroencephalogram [EEG]**
         R94.02   **Abnormal brain scan**
         R94.09   **Abnormal results of other function studies of central nervous system**

●   **R94.1**   **Abnormal results of function studies of peripheral nervous system and special senses**

●   **R94.11**   **Abnormal results of function studies of eye**
            R94.110   **Abnormal electro-oculogram [EOG]**
            R94.111   **Abnormal electroretinogram [ERG]**
               Abnormal retinal function study
            R94.112   **Abnormal visually evoked potential [VEP]**
            R94.113   **Abnormal oculomotor study**
            R94.118   **Abnormal results of other function studies of eye**

●   **R94.12**   **Abnormal results of function studies of ear and other special senses**
            R94.120   **Abnormal auditory function study**
               Coding Clinic: 2016, Q3, P17
            R94.121   **Abnormal vestibular function study**
            R94.128   **Abnormal results of other function studies of ear and other special senses**

CHAPTER 18 (R00-R99)

CHAPTER 18 (R00–R99)

Trochlear nerve (IV)
Optic nerve (II)
Olfactory nerve (I)
Abducens nerve (VI)
Oculomotor nerve (III)
Facial nerve (VII)
Trigeminal nerve (V)
Vestibulocochlear nerve (VIII)
Glossopharyngeal nerve (IX)
Vagus nerve (X)
Accessory nerve (XI)
Hypoglossal nerve (XII)

Figure 18-2   Cranial nerves. (From Patton and Thibodeau: Anatomy and physiology, ed 7, St. Louis, Mosby, 2009)

Item 18–1 The **peripheral nervous system** consists of 31 pairs of spinal nerves, 12 pairs of cranial nerves, and the autonomic nerves, which are divided into the parasympathetic and sympathetic nerves. The cranial nerves are: olfactory (I), optic (II), oculomotor (III), trochlear (IV), trigeminal (V), abducens (VI), facial (VII), vestibulocochlear (VIII), glossopharyngeal (IX), vagus (X), accessory (XI), and hypoglossal (XII).

● **R94.13**   **Abnormal results of function studies of peripheral nervous system**

     R94.130   **Abnormal response to nerve stimulation, unspecified**

     R94.131   **Abnormal electromyogram [EMG]**
         Excludes1   electromyogram of eye (R94.113)

     R94.138   **Abnormal results of other function studies of peripheral nervous system**

R94.2   **Abnormal results of pulmonary function studies**
     Reduced ventilatory capacity
     Reduced vital capacity

● **R94.3**   **Abnormal results of cardiovascular function studies**

     R94.30   **Abnormal result of cardiovascular function study, unspecified**

     R94.31   **Abnormal electrocardiogram [ECG] [EKG]**
         Excludes1   long QT syndrome (I45.81)

     R94.39   **Abnormal result of other cardiovascular function study**
         Abnormal electrophysiological intracardiac studies
         Abnormal phonocardiogram
         Abnormal vectorcardiogram

R94.4   **Abnormal results of kidney function studies**
     Abnormal renal function test

R94.5   **Abnormal results of liver function studies**

R94.6   **Abnormal results of thyroid function studies**

R94.7   **Abnormal results of other endocrine function studies**
     Excludes2   abnormal glucose (R73.0-)

R94.8   **Abnormal results of function studies of other organs and systems**
     Abnormal basal metabolic rate [BMR]
     Abnormal bladder function test
     Abnormal splenic function test

ABNORMAL TUMOR MARKERS (R97)

● **R97**   **Abnormal tumor markers**
     Elevated tumor associated antigens [TAA]
     Elevated tumor specific antigens [TSA]

R97.0   **Elevated carcinoembryonic antigen [CEA]**

R97.1   **Elevated cancer antigen 125 [CA 125]**

● **R97.2**   **Elevated prostate specific antigen [PSA]**
     Coding Clinic: 2016, Q4, P66

     R97.20   **Elevated prostate specific antigen [PSA]** ♂   A

     R97.21   **Rising PSA following treatment for malignant neoplasm of prostate** ♂   A

R97.8   **Other abnormal tumor markers**

ILL-DEFINED AND UNKNOWN CAUSE OF MORTALITY (R99)

R99   **Ill-defined and unknown cause of mortality**
     Death (unexplained) NOS
     Unspecified cause of mortality

     OGCR   Section I.C.18.h.

     Death NOS

     Code R99, Ill-defined and unknown cause of mortality, is only for use in the very limited circumstance when a patient who has already died is brought into the emergency department or other healthcare facility and is pronounced dead upon arrival. It does not represent the discharge disposition of death.

▶ New   ⇒ Revised   ~~deleted~~ Deleted   Excludes 1   Excludes 2   Includes   Use additional   Code first   Code also   Key words

OGCR Official Guidelines   X Assign placeholder X   ● Use Additional Character(s)   ▶ Manifestation Code   **Coding Clinic**

CHAPTER 19

INJURY, POISONING AND CERTAIN OTHER CONSEQUENCES OF EXTERNAL CAUSES (S00-T88)

OGCR Chapter-Specific Coding Guidelines

19. **Chapter 19: Injury, poisoning, and certain other consequences of external causes (S00-T88)**

a. **Application of 7th Characters in Chapter 19**
Most categories in Chapter 19 have a 7th character requirement for each applicable code. Most categories in this chapter have three 7th character values (with the exception of fractures): A, initial encounter, D, subsequent encounter and S, sequela. Categories for traumatic fractures have additional 7th character values. While the patient may be seen by a new or different provider over the course of treatment for an injury, assignment of the 7th character is based on whether the patient is undergoing active treatment and not whether the provider is seeing the patient for the first time.

For complication codes, active treatment refers to treatment for the condition described by the code, even though it may be related to an earlier precipitating problem. For example, code T84.50XA, Infection and inflammatory reaction due to unspecified internal joint prosthesis, initial encounter, is used when active treatment is provided for the infection, even though the condition relates to the prosthetic device, implant or graft that was placed at a previous encounter.

7th character "A", initial encounter is used for each encounter where the patient is receiving active treatment for the condition.

7th character "D" subsequent encounter is used for encounters after the patient has completed active treatment of the condition and is receiving routine care for the condition during the healing or recovery phase.

The aftercare Z codes should not be used for aftercare for conditions such as injuries or poisonings, where 7th characters are provided to identify subsequent care. For example, for aftercare of an injury, assign the acute injury code with the 7th character "D" (subsequent encounter).

7th character "S", sequela, is for use for complications or conditions that arise as a direct result of a condition, such as scar formation after a burn. The scars are sequelae of the burn. When using 7th character "S", it is necessary to use both the injury code that precipitated the sequela and the code for the sequela itself. The "S" is added only to the injury code, not the sequela code. The 7th character "S" identifies the injury responsible for the sequela. The specific type of sequela (e.g. scar) is sequenced first, followed by the injury code.

See Section I.B.10. Sequelae, (Late Effects)

b. **Coding of Injuries**
When coding injuries, assign separate codes for each injury unless a combination code is provided, in which case the combination code is assigned. Codes from category T07, Unspecified multiple injuries should not be assigned in the inpatient setting unless information for a more specific code is not available. Traumatic injury codes (S00-T14.9) are not to be used for normal, healing surgical wounds or to identify complications of surgical wounds.

The code for the most serious injury, as determined by the provider and the focus of treatment, is sequenced first.

1) **Superficial injuries**
Superficial injuries such as abrasions or contusions are not coded when associated with more severe injuries of the same site.

2) **Primary injury with damage to nerves/blood vessels**
When a primary injury results in minor damage to peripheral nerves or blood vessels, the primary injury is sequenced first with additional code(s) for injuries to nerves and spinal cord (such as category S04), and/or injury to blood vessels (such as category S15). When the primary injury is to the blood vessels or nerves, that injury should be sequenced first.

c. **Coding of Traumatic Fractures**
The principles of multiple coding of injuries should be followed in coding fractures. Fractures of specified sites are coded individually by site in accordance with both the provisions within

categories S02, S12, S22, S32, S42, S49, S52, S59, S62, S72, S79, S82, S89, S92 and the level of detail furnished by medical record content.

A fracture not indicated as open or closed should be coded to closed. A fracture not indicated whether displaced or not displaced should be coded to displaced.

More specific guidelines are as follows:

1) **Initial vs. Subsequent Encounter for Fractures**
Traumatic fractures are coded using the appropriate 7th character for initial encounter (A, B, C) for each encounter where the patient is receiving active treatment for the fracture. The appropriate 7th character for initial encounter should also be assigned for a patient who delayed seeking treatment for the fracture or nonunion.

Fractures are coded using the appropriate 7th character for subsequent care for encounters after the patient has completed active treatment of the fracture and is receiving routine care for the fracture during the healing or recovery phase.

Care for complications of surgical treatment for fracture repairs during the healing or recovery phase should be coded with the appropriate complication codes.

Care of complications of fractures, such as malunion and nonunion, should be reported with the appropriate 7th character for subsequent care with nonunion (K, M, N,) or subsequent care with malunion (P, Q, R).

Malunion/nonunion: The appropriate 7th character for initial encounter should also be assigned for a patient who delayed seeking treatment for the fracture or nonunion.

The open fracture designations in the assignment of the 7th character for fractures of the forearm, femur and lower leg, including ankle are based on the Gustilo open fracture classification. When the Gustilo classification type is not specified for an open fracture, the 7th character for open fracture type I or II should be assigned (B, E, H, M, Q).

A code from category M80, not a traumatic fracture code, should be used for any patient with known osteoporosis who suffers a fracture, even if the patient had a minor fall or trauma, if that fall or trauma would not usually break a normal, healthy bone.

See Section I.C.13. Osteoporosis.

The aftercare Z codes should not be used for aftercare for traumatic fractures. For aftercare of a traumatic fracture, assign the acute fracture code with the appropriate 7th character.

2) **Multiple fractures sequencing**
Multiple fractures are sequenced in accordance with the severity of the fracture.

d. **Coding of Burns and Corrosions**
The ICD-10-CM makes a distinction between burns and corrosions. The burn codes are for thermal burns, except sunburns, that come from a heat source, such as a fire or hot appliance. The burn codes are also for burns resulting from electricity and radiation. Corrosions are burns due to chemicals. The guidelines are the same for burns and corrosions.

Current burns (T20-T25) are classified by depth, extent and by agent (X code). Burns are classified by depth as first degree (erythema), second degree (blistering), and third degree (full-thickness involvement). Burns of the eye and internal organs (T26-T28) are classified by site, but not by degree.

1) **Sequencing of burn and related condition codes**
Sequence first the code that reflects the highest degree of burn when more than one burn is present.

a. When the reason for the admission or encounter is for treatment of external multiple burns, sequence first the code that reflects the burn of the highest degree.

b. When a patient has both internal and external burns, the circumstances of admission govern the selection of the principal diagnosis or first-listed diagnosis.

c. When a patient is admitted for burn injuries and other related conditions such as smoke inhalation and/or respiratory failure, the circumstances of admission govern the selection of the principal or first-listed diagnosis.

2) Burns of the same *anatomic* site

Classify burns of the same **anatomic** site **and on the same side** but of different degrees to the subcategory identifying the highest degree recorded in the diagnosis **(e.g., for second and third degree burns of right thigh, assign only code T24.311-).**

3) Non-healing burns

Non-healing burns are coded as acute burns.

Necrosis of burned skin should be coded as a non-healed burn.

4) Infected Burn

For any documented infected burn site, use an additional code for the infection.

5) Assign separate codes for each burn site

When coding burns, assign separate codes for each burn site. Category T30, Burn and corrosion, body region unspecified is extremely vague and should rarely be used.

Codes for burns of "multiple sites" should only be assigned when the medical record documentation does not specify the individual sites.

6) Burns and Corrosions Classified According to Extent of Body Surface Involved

Assign codes from category T31, Burns classified according to extent of body surface involved, or T32, Corrosions classified according to extent of body surface involved, when the site of the burn is not specified or when there is a need for additional data. It is advisable to use category T31 as additional coding when needed to provide data for evaluating burn mortality, such as that needed by burn units. It is also advisable to use category T31 as an additional code for reporting purposes when there is mention of a third-degree burn involving 20 percent or more of the body surface.

Categories T31 and T32 are based on the classic "rule of nines" in estimating body surface involved: head and neck are assigned nine percent, each arm nine percent, each leg 18 percent, the anterior trunk 18 percent, posterior trunk 18 percent, and genitalia one percent. Providers may change these percentage assignments where necessary to accommodate infants and children who have proportionately larger heads than adults, and patients who have large buttocks, thighs, or abdomen that involve burns.

7) Encounters for treatment of sequela of burns

Encounters for the treatment of the late effects of burns or corrosions (i.e., scars or joint contractures) should be coded with a burn or corrosion code with the 7th character "S" for sequela.

8) Sequelae with a late effect code and current burn

When appropriate, both a code for a current burn or corrosion with 7th character "A" or "D" and a burn or corrosion code with 7th character "S" may be assigned on the same record (when both a current burn and sequelae of an old burn exist). Burns and corrosions do not heal at the same rate and a current healing wound may still exist with sequela of a healed burn or corrosion.

See Section I.B.10. Sequela, (Late Effects)

9) Use of an external cause code with burns and corrosions

An external cause code should be used with burns and corrosions to identify the source and intent of the burn, as well as the place where it occurred.

e. Adverse Effects, Poisoning , Underdosing and Toxic Effects

Codes in categories T36-T65 are combination codes that include the substance that was taken as well as the intent. No additional external cause code is required for poisonings, toxic effects, adverse effects and underdosing codes.

1) Do not code directly from the Table of Drugs

Do not code directly from the Table of Drugs and Chemicals. Always refer back to the Tabular List.

2) Use as many codes as necessary to describe

Use as many codes as necessary to describe completely all drugs, medicinal or biological substances.

3) If the same code would describe the causative agent

If the same code would describe the causative agent for more than one adverse reaction, poisoning, toxic effect or underdosing, assign the code only once.

4) If two or more drugs, medicinal or biological substances

If two or more drugs, medicinal or biological substances are reported, code each individually unless a combination code is listed in the Table of Drugs and Chemicals.

5) The occurrence of drug toxicity is classified in ICD-10-CM as follows:

(a) Adverse Effect

When coding an adverse effect of a drug that has been correctly prescribed and properly administered, assign the appropriate code for the nature of the adverse effect followed by the appropriate code for the adverse effect of the drug (T36-T50). The code for the drug should have a 5th or 6th character "5" (for example T36.0X5-) Examples of the nature of an adverse effect are tachycardia, delirium, gastrointestinal hemorrhaging, vomiting, hypokalemia, hepatitis, renal failure, or respiratory failure.

(b) Poisoning

When coding a poisoning or reaction to the improper use of a medication (e.g., overdose, wrong substance given or taken in error, wrong route of administration), first assign the appropriate code from categories T36-T50. The poisoning codes have an associated intent as their 5th or 6th character (accidental, intentional self-harm, assault and undetermined). If the intent of the poisoning is unknown or unspecified, code the intent as accidental intent. The undetermined intent is only for use if the documentation in the record specifies that the intent cannot be determined. Use additional code(s) for all manifestations of poisonings.

If there is also a diagnosis of abuse or dependence of the substance, the abuse or dependence is assigned as an additional code.

Examples of poisoning include:

(i) Error was made in drug prescription
Errors made in drug prescription or in the administration of the drug by provider, nurse, patient, or other person.

(ii) Overdose of a drug intentionally taken If an overdose of a drug was intentionally taken or administered and resulted in drug toxicity, it would be coded as a poisoning.

(iii) Nonprescribed drug taken with correctly prescribed and properly administered drug. If a nonprescribed drug or medicinal agent was taken in combination with a correctly prescribed and properly administered drug, any drug toxicity or other reaction resulting from the interaction of the two drugs would be classified as a poisoning.

(iv) Interaction of drug(s) and alcohol.
When a reaction results from the interaction of a drug(s) and alcohol, this would be classified as poisoning.

See Section I.C.4. if poisoning is the result of insulin pump malfunctions.

(c) Underdosing

Underdosing refers to taking less of a medication than is prescribed by a provider or a manufacturer's instruction. **Discontinuing the use of a prescribed medication on the patient's own initiative (not directed by the patient's provider) is also classified as an underdosing.** For underdosing, assign the code from categories T36-T50 (fifth or sixth character "6").

Codes for underdosing should never be assigned as principal or first-listed codes. If a patient has a relapse or exacerbation of the medical condition for which the drug is prescribed because of the reduction in dose, then the medical condition itself should be coded.

Noncompliance (Z91.12-, Z91.13- **and Z91.14-**) or complication of care (Y63.6-Y63.9) codes are to be used with an underdosing code to indicate intent, if known.

(d) Toxic Effects

When a harmful substance is ingested or comes in contact with a person, this is classified as a toxic effect. The toxic effect codes are in categories T51-T65.

Toxic effect codes have an associated intent: accidental, intentional self-harm, assault and undetermined.

f. Adult and child abuse, neglect and other maltreatment

Sequence first the appropriate code from categories T74 (Adult and child abuse, neglect and other maltreatment, confirmed) or T76 (Adult and child abuse, neglect and other maltreatment, suspected) for abuse, neglect and other maltreatment, followed by any accompanying mental health or injury code(s).

If the documentation in the medical record states abuse or neglect it is coded as confirmed (T74.-). It is coded as suspected if it is documented as suspected (T76.-).

For cases of confirmed abuse or neglect an external cause code from the assault section (X92-Y09) should be added to identify the cause of any physical injuries. A perpetrator code (Y07) should be added when the perpetrator of the abuse is known. For suspected cases of abuse or neglect, do not report external cause or perpetrator code.

If a suspected case of abuse, neglect or mistreatment is ruled out during an encounter code Z04.71, Encounter for examination and observation following alleged physical adult abuse, ruled out, or code Z04.72, Encounter for examination and observation following alleged child physical abuse, ruled out, should be used, not a code from T76.

If a suspected case of alleged rape or sexual abuse is ruled out during an encounter code Z04.41, Encounter for examination and observation following alleged adult rape or code Z04.42, Encounter for examination and observation following alleged child rape, should be used, not a code from T76.

If a suspected case of forced sexual exploitation or forced labor exploitation is ruled out during an encounter, code Z04.81, Encounter for examination and observation of victim following forced sexual exploitation, or code Z04.82, Encounter for examination and observation of victim following forced labor exploitation, should be used, not a code from T76.

See Section I.C.15. Abuse in a pregnant patient.

g. Complications of care

1) General guidelines for complications of care

(a) Documentation of complications of care

See Section I.B.16. for information on documentation of complications of care.

2) Pain due to medical devices

Pain associated with devices, implants or grafts left in a surgical site (for example painful hip prosthesis) is assigned to the appropriate code(s) found in Chapter 19, Injury, poisoning, and certain other consequences of external causes. Specific codes for pain due to medical devices are found in the T code section of the ICD-10-CM. Use additional code(s) from category G89 to identify acute or chronic pain due to presence of the device, implant or graft (G89.18 or G89.28).

3) Transplant complications

(a) Transplant complications other than kidney

Codes under category T86, Complications of transplanted organs and tissues, are for use for both complications and rejection of transplanted organs. A transplant complication code is only assigned if the complication affects the function of the transplanted organ. Two codes are required to fully describe a transplant complication: the appropriate code from category T86 and a secondary code that identifies the complication.

Pre-existing conditions or conditions that develop after the transplant are not coded as complications unless they affect the function of the transplanted organs.

See I.C.21. for transplant organ removal status
See I.C.2. for malignant neoplasm associated with transplanted organ.

(b) Kidney transplant complications

Patients who have undergone kidney transplant may still have some form of chronic kidney disease (CKD) because the kidney transplant may not fully restore kidney function. Code T86.1- should be assigned for documented complications of a kidney transplant, such as transplant failure or rejection or other transplant complication. Code T86.1- should not be assigned for post kidney transplant patients who have chronic kidney (CKD) unless a transplant complication such as transplant failure or rejection is documented. If the documentation is unclear as to whether the patient has a complication of the transplant, query the provider.

Conditions that affect the function of the transplanted kidney, other than CKD, should be assigned a code from subcategory T86.1, Complications of transplanted organ, Kidney, and a secondary code that identifies the complication.

For patients with CKD following a kidney transplant, but who do not have a complication such as failure or rejection, *see Section I.C.14. Chronic kidney disease and kidney transplant status.*

4) Complication codes that include the external cause

As with certain other T codes, some of the complications of care codes have the external cause included in the code. The code includes the nature of the complication as well as the type of procedure that caused the complication. No external cause code indicating the type of procedure is necessary for these codes.

5) Complications of care codes within the body system chapters

Intraoperative and postprocedural complication codes are found within the body system chapters with codes specific to the organs and structures of that body system. These codes should be sequenced first, followed by a code(s) for the specific complication, if applicable.

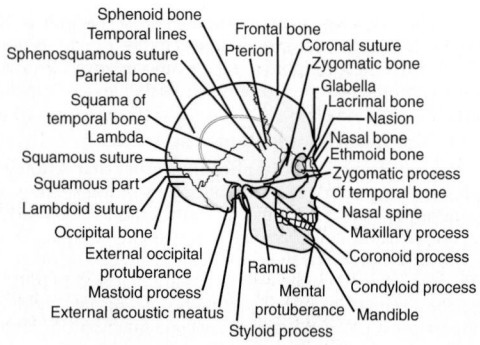

Figure 19-1 Lateral view of skull.

Figure 19-2 Frontal view of skull.

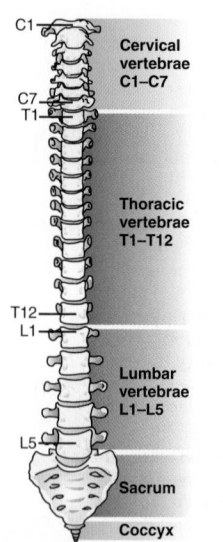

Figure 19-3 Anterior view of vertebral column.

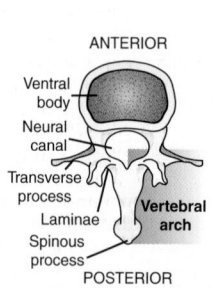

Figure 19-4 Vertebra viewed from above.

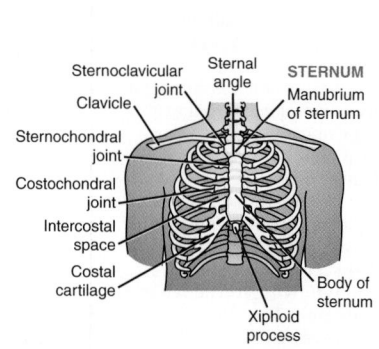

Figure 19-5 Anterior view of rib cage.

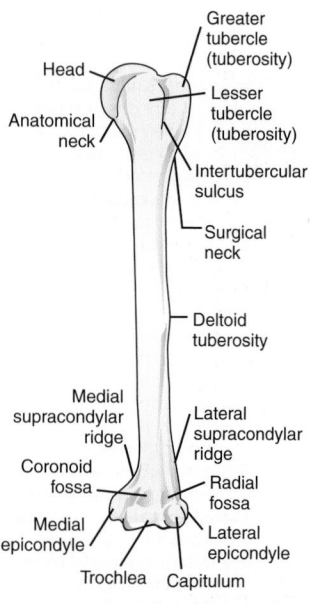

Figure 19-6 Anterior aspect of left humerus.

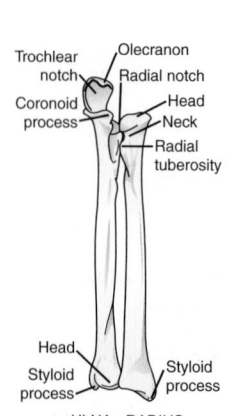

Figure 19-7 Anterior aspect of left radius and ulna.

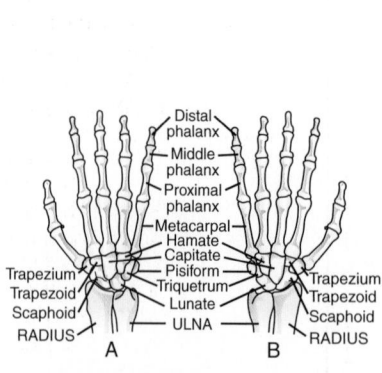

Figure 19-8 Right hand and wrist: **A.** Dorsal surface. **B.** Palmar surface.

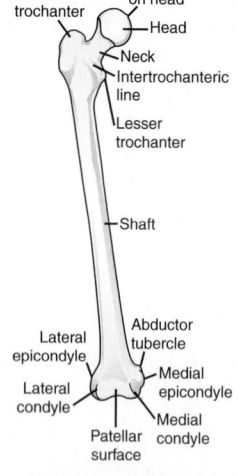

Figure 19-9 Anterior aspect of right femur.

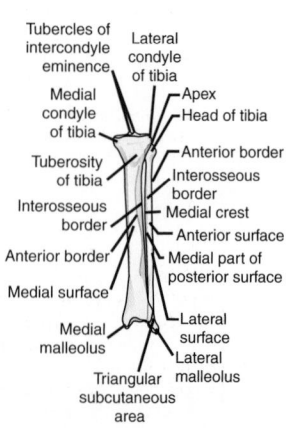

Figure 19-10 Anterior aspect of left tibia and fibula.

▶ New   ⇒ Revised   ~~deleted~~ Deleted   Excludes 1   Excludes 2   Includes   Use additional   Code first   Code also   Key words

OGCR Official Guidelines   X Assign placeholder X   ● Use Additional Character(s)   ▷ Manifestation Code   **Coding Clinic**

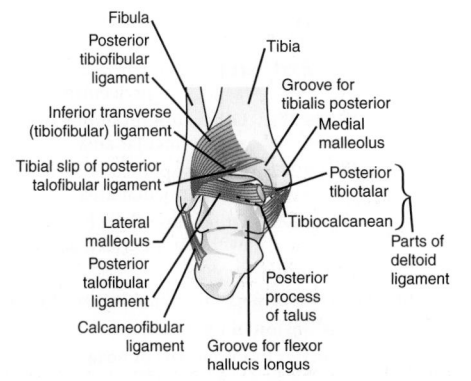

Figure 19-11   Posterior aspect of the left ankle joint.

Figure 19-12   Right foot viewed from above.

CHAPTER 19

INJURY, POISONING AND CERTAIN OTHER CONSEQUENCES OF EXTERNAL CAUSES (S00-T88)

Note: Use secondary code(s) from Chapter 20, External causes of morbidity, to indicate cause of injury. Codes within the T section that include the external cause do not require an additional external cause code.

> Use additional code to identify any retained foreign body, if applicable (Z18.-)
>
> **Excludes1**   birth trauma (P10-P15)
> obstetric trauma (O70-O71)

Note: The chapter uses the S-section for coding different types of injuries related to single body regions and the T-section to cover injuries to unspecified body regions as well as poisoning and certain other consequences of external causes.

This chapter contains the following blocks:

S00-S09	Injuries to the head
S10-S19	Injuries to the neck
S20-S29	Injuries to the thorax
S30-S39	Injuries to the abdomen, lower back, lumbar spine, pelvis and external genitals
S40-S49	Injuries to the shoulder and upper arm
S50-S59	Injuries to the elbow and forearm
S60-S69	Injuries to the wrist, hand, and fingers
S70-S79	Injuries to the hip and thigh
S80-S89	Injuries to the knee and lower leg
S90-S99	Injuries to the ankle and foot

T07	Injuries involving multiple body regions
T14	Injury of unspecified body region
T15-T19	Effects of foreign body entering through natural orifice
T20-T25	Burns and corrosions of external body surface, specified by site
T26-T28	Burns and corrosions confined to eye and internal organs
T30-T32	Burns and corrosions of multiple and unspecified body regions
T33-T34	Frostbite
T36-T50	Poisoning by, adverse effect of and underdosing of drugs, medicaments and biological substances
T51-T65	Toxic effects of substances chiefly nonmedicinal as to source
T66-T78	Other and unspecified effects of external causes
T79	Certain early complications of trauma
T80-T88	Complications of surgical and medical care, not elsewhere classified

INJURIES TO THE HEAD (S00-S09)

Includes   injuries of ear
injuries of eye
injuries of face [any part]
injuries of gum
injuries of jaw
injuries of oral cavity
injuries of palate
injuries of periocular area
injuries of scalp
injuries of temporomandibular joint area
injuries of tongue
injuries of tooth

Code also for any associated infection

Excludes2   burns and corrosions (T20-T32)
effects of foreign body in ear (T16)
effects of foreign body in larynx (T17.3)
effects of foreign body in mouth NOS (T18.0)
effects of foreign body in nose (T17.0-T17.1)
effects of foreign body in pharynx (T17.2)
effects of foreign body on external eye (T15.-)
frostbite (T33-T34)
insect bite or sting, venomous (T63.4)

● **S00**   **Superficial injury of head**

> **Excludes1**   diffuse cerebral contusion (S06.2-)
> focal cerebral contusion (S06.3-)
> injury of eye and orbit (S05.-)
> open wound of head (S01.-)

The appropriate 7th character is to be added to each code from category S00

A	initial encounter
	All encounters involving diagnosis and treatment
D	subsequent encounter
	Encounters during the healing phase
S	sequela

● **S00.0**   **Superficial injury of scalp**
   X ● **S00.00**   **Unspecified superficial injury of scalp**
   X ● **S00.01**   **Abrasion of scalp**
   X ● **S00.02**   **Blister** (nonthermal) **of scalp**
   X ● **S00.03**   **Contusion of scalp**
      Bruise of scalp
      Hematoma of scalp
   X ● **S00.04**   **External constriction of part of scalp**
   X ● **S00.05**   **Superficial foreign body of scalp**
      Splinter in the scalp
   X ● **S00.06**   **Insect bite** (nonvenomous) **of scalp**
   X ● **S00.07**   **Other superficial bite of scalp**
      Excludes1   open bite of scalp (S01.05)

● **S00.1** Contusion of eyelid and periocular area
Black eye
Excludes2 contusion of eyeball and orbital tissues
(S05.1)
X● **S00.10** Contusion of unspecified eyelid and periocular
area
X● **S00.11** Contusion of right eyelid and periocular area
X● **S00.12** Contusion of left eyelid and periocular area
● **S00.2** Other and unspecified superficial injuries of eyelid and
periocular area
Excludes2 superficial injury of conjunctiva and
cornea (S05.0-)
● **S00.20** Unspecified superficial injury of eyelid and
periocular area
● **S00.201** Unspecified superficial injury of right
eyelid and periocular area
● **S00.202** Unspecified superficial injury of left
eyelid and periocular area
● **S00.209** Unspecified superficial injury of
unspecified eyelid and periocular area
● **S00.21** Abrasion of eyelid and periocular area
● **S00.211** Abrasion of right eyelid and
periocular area
● **S00.212** Abrasion of left eyelid and periocular
area
● **S00.219** Abrasion of unspecified eyelid and
periocular area
● **S00.22** Blister (nonthermal) of eyelid and periocular
area
● **S00.221** Blister (nonthermal) of right eyelid
and periocular area
● **S00.222** Blister (nonthermal) of left eyelid and
periocular area
● **S00.229** Blister (nonthermal) of unspecified
eyelid and periocular area
● **S00.24** External constriction of eyelid and periocular
area
● **S00.241** External constriction of right eyelid
and periocular area
● **S00.242** External constriction of left eyelid
and periocular area
● **S00.249** External constriction of unspecified
eyelid and periocular area
● **S00.25** Superficial foreign body of eyelid and
periocular area
Splinter of eyelid and periocular area
Excludes2 retained foreign body in eyelid
(H02.81-)
● **S00.251** Superficial foreign body of right
eyelid and periocular area
● **S00.252** Superficial foreign body of left eyelid
and periocular area
● **S00.259** Superficial foreign body of
unspecified eyelid and periocular area
● **S00.26** Insect bite (nonvenomous) of eyelid and
periocular area
● **S00.261** Insect bite (nonvenomous) of right
eyelid and periocular area
● **S00.262** Insect bite (nonvenomous) of left
eyelid and periocular area
● **S00.269** Insect bite (nonvenomous) of
unspecified eyelid and periocular area

● **S00.27** Other superficial bite of eyelid and periocular
area
Excludes1 open bite of eyelid and
periocular area (S01.15)
● **S00.271** Other superficial bite of right eyelid
and periocular area
● **S00.272** Other superficial bite of left eyelid
and periocular area
● **S00.279** Other superficial bite of unspecified
eyelid and periocular area
● **S00.3** Superficial injury of nose
X● **S00.30** Unspecified superficial injury of nose
X● **S00.31** Abrasion of nose
X● **S00.32** Blister (nonthermal) of nose
X● **S00.33** Contusion of nose
Bruise of nose
Hematoma of nose
X● **S00.34** External constriction of nose
X● **S00.35** Superficial foreign body of nose
Splinter in the nose
X● **S00.36** Insect bite (nonvenomous) of nose
X● **S00.37** Other superficial bite of nose
Excludes1 open bite of nose (S01.25)
● **S00.4** Superficial injury of ear
● **S00.40** Unspecified superficial injury of ear
● **S00.401** Unspecified superficial injury of right
ear
● **S00.402** Unspecified superficial injury of left
ear
● **S00.409** Unspecified superficial injury of
unspecified ear
● **S00.41** Abrasion of ear
● **S00.411** Abrasion of right ear
● **S00.412** Abrasion of left ear
● **S00.419** Abrasion of unspecified ear
● **S00.42** Blister (nonthermal) of ear
● **S00.421** Blister (nonthermal) of right ear
● **S00.422** Blister (nonthermal) of left ear
● **S00.429** Blister (nonthermal) of unspecified
ear
● **S00.43** Contusion of ear
Bruise of ear
Hematoma of ear
● **S00.431** Contusion of right ear
● **S00.432** Contusion of left ear
● **S00.439** Contusion of unspecified ear
● **S00.44** External constriction of ear
● **S00.441** External constriction of right ear
● **S00.442** External constriction of left ear
● **S00.449** External constriction of unspecified
ear
● **S00.45** Superficial foreign body of ear
Splinter in the ear
● **S00.451** Superficial foreign body of right ear
● **S00.452** Superficial foreign body of left ear
● **S00.459** Superficial foreign body of
unspecified ear
● **S00.46** Insect bite (nonvenomous) of ear
● **S00.461** Insect bite (nonvenomous) of right
ear
● **S00.462** Insect bite (nonvenomous) of left ear
● **S00.469** Insect bite (nonvenomous) of
unspecified ear

● S00.47   **Other superficial bite of ear**
     Excludes1   open bite of ear (S01.35)
     ● S00.471   Other superficial bite of **right** ear
     ● S00.472   Other superficial bite of **left** ear
     ● S00.479   Other superficial bite of **unspecified** ear

● S00.5   **Superficial injury of lip and oral cavity**
   ● S00.50   **Unspecified superficial injury of lip and oral cavity**
     ● S00.501   Unspecified superficial injury of **lip**
     ● S00.502   Unspecified superficial injury of **oral cavity**
   ● S00.51   **Abrasion of lip and oral cavity**
     ● S00.511   Abrasion of **lip**
     ● S00.512   Abrasion of **oral cavity**
   ● S00.52   **Blister (nonthermal) of lip and oral cavity**
     ● S00.521   Blister (nonthermal) of **lip**
     ● S00.522   Blister (nonthermal) of **oral cavity**
   ● S00.53   **Contusion of lip and oral cavity**
     ● S00.531   Contusion of **lip**
       Bruise of lip
       Hematoma of lip
     ● S00.532   Contusion of **oral cavity**
       Bruise of oral cavity
       Hematoma of oral cavity
   ● S00.54   **External constriction of lip and oral cavity**
     ● S00.541   External constriction of **lip**
     ● S00.542   External constriction of **oral cavity**
   ● S00.55   **Superficial foreign body of lip and oral cavity**
     ● S00.551   Superficial foreign body of **lip**
       Splinter of lip and oral cavity
     ● S00.552   Superficial foreign body of **oral cavity**
       Splinter of lip and oral cavity
   ● S00.56   **Insect bite (nonvenomous) of lip and oral cavity**
     ● S00.561   Insect bite (nonvenomous) of **lip**
     ● S00.562   Insect bite (nonvenomous) of **oral cavity**
   ● S00.57   **Other superficial bite of lip and oral cavity**
     ● S00.571   Other superficial bite of **lip**
       Excludes1   open bite of lip (S01.551)
     ● S00.572   Other superficial bite of **oral cavity**
       Excludes1   open bite of oral cavity (S01.552)

● S00.8   **Superficial injury of other parts of head**
   Superficial injuries of face [any part]
X ● S00.80   **Unspecified superficial injury of other part of head**
X ● S00.81   **Abrasion of other part of head**
X ● S00.82   **Blister (nonthermal) of other part of head**
X ● S00.83   **Contusion of other part of head**
     Bruise of other part of head
     Hematoma of other part of head
X ● S00.84   **External constriction of other part of head**
X ● S00.85   **Superficial foreign body of other part of head**
     Splinter in other part of head
X ● S00.86   **Insect bite (nonvenomous) of other part of head**
X ● S00.87   **Other superficial bite of other part of head**
     Excludes1   open bite of other part of head (S01.85)

● S00.9   **Superficial injury of unspecified part of head**
X ● S00.90   **Unspecified superficial injury of unspecified part of head**
X ● S00.91   **Abrasion of unspecified part of head**
X ● S00.92   **Blister (nonthermal) of unspecified part of head**

X ● S00.93   **Contusion of unspecified part of head**
     Bruise of head
     Hematoma of head
X ● S00.94   **External constriction of unspecified part of head**
X ● S00.95   **Superficial foreign body of unspecified part of head**
     Splinter of head
X ● S00.96   **Insect bite (nonvenomous) of unspecified part of head**
X ● S00.97   **Other superficial bite of unspecified part of head**
     Excludes1   open bite of head (S01.95)

● S01   **Open wound of head**
   Code also any associated:
     injury of cranial nerve (S04.-)
     injury of muscle and tendon of head (S09.1-)
     intracranial injury (S06.-)
     wound infection
   Excludes1   open skull fracture (S02.- with 7th character B)
   Excludes2   injury of eye and orbit (S05.-)
       traumatic amputation of part of head (S08.-)
   The appropriate 7th character is to be added to each code from category S01

A	initial encounter
D	subsequent encounter
S	sequela

● S01.0   **Open wound of scalp**
   Excludes1   avulsion of scalp (S08.0)
X ● S01.00   **Unspecified open wound of scalp**
X ● S01.01   **Laceration without foreign body of scalp**
X ● S01.02   **Laceration with foreign body of scalp**
     Coding Clinic: 2015, Q1, P5-7
X ● S01.03   **Puncture wound without foreign body of scalp**
X ● S01.04   **Puncture wound with foreign body of scalp**
X ● S01.05   **Open bite of scalp**
     Bite of scalp NOS
     Excludes1   superficial bite of scalp (S00.06, S00.07-)

● S01.1   **Open wound of eyelid and periocular area**
   Open wound of eyelid and periocular area with or without involvement of lacrimal passages
   ● S01.10   **Unspecified open wound of eyelid and periocular area**
     ● S01.101   Unspecified open wound of **right** eyelid and periocular area
     ● S01.102   Unspecified open wound of **left** eyelid and periocular area
     ● S01.109   Unspecified open wound of **unspecified** eyelid and periocular area
   ● S01.11   **Laceration without foreign body of eyelid and periocular area**
     ● S01.111   Laceration without foreign body of **right** eyelid and periocular area
     ● S01.112   Laceration without foreign body of **left** eyelid and periocular area
     ● S01.119   Laceration without foreign body of **unspecified** eyelid and periocular area
   ● S01.12   **Laceration with foreign body of eyelid and periocular area**
     ● S01.121   Laceration with foreign body of **right** eyelid and periocular area
     ● S01.122   Laceration with foreign body of **left** eyelid and periocular area
     ● S01.129   Laceration with foreign body of **unspecified** eyelid and periocular area

CHAPTER 19 (S00-T88)

● **S01.13**   Puncture wound without foreign body of eyelid and periocular area

     ● **S01.131**   Puncture wound without foreign body of right eyelid and periocular area

     ● **S01.132**   Puncture wound without foreign body of left eyelid and periocular area

     ● **S01.139**   Puncture wound without foreign body of unspecified eyelid and periocular area

● **S01.14**   Puncture wound with foreign body of eyelid and periocular area

     ● **S01.141**   Puncture wound with foreign body of right eyelid and periocular area

     ● **S01.142**   Puncture wound with foreign body of left eyelid and periocular area

     ● **S01.149**   Puncture wound with foreign body of unspecified eyelid and periocular area

● **S01.15**   Open bite of eyelid and periocular area
       Bite of eyelid and periocular area NOS

       Excludes1   superficial bite of eyelid and periocular area (S00.26, S00.27)

     ● **S01.151**   Open bite of right eyelid and periocular area

     ● **S01.152**   Open bite of left eyelid and periocular area

     ● **S01.159**   Open bite of unspecified eyelid and periocular area

● **S01.2**   Open wound of nose

   X ● **S01.20**   Unspecified open wound of nose

   X ● **S01.21**   Laceration without foreign body of nose
       Coding Clinic: 2015, Q1, P5-6

   X ● **S01.22**   Laceration with foreign body of nose

   X ● **S01.23**   Puncture wound without foreign body of nose

   X ● **S01.24**   Puncture wound with foreign body of nose

   X ● **S01.25**   Open bite of nose
       Bite of nose NOS

       Excludes1   superficial bite of nose (S00.36, S00.37)

● **S01.3**   Open wound of ear

     ● **S01.30**   Unspecified open wound of ear

       ● **S01.301**   Unspecified open wound of right ear

       ● **S01.302**   Unspecified open wound of left ear

       ● **S01.309**   Unspecified open wound of unspecified ear

     ● **S01.31**   Laceration without foreign body of ear

       ● **S01.311**   Laceration without foreign body of right ear

       ● **S01.312**   Laceration without foreign body of left ear

       ● **S01.319**   Laceration without foreign body of unspecified ear

     ● **S01.32**   Laceration with foreign body of ear

       ● **S01.321**   Laceration with foreign body of right ear

       ● **S01.322**   Laceration with foreign body of left ear

       ● **S01.329**   Laceration with foreign body of unspecified ear

● **S01.33**   Puncture wound without foreign body of ear

     ● **S01.331**   Puncture wound without foreign body of right ear

     ● **S01.332**   Puncture wound without foreign body of left ear

     ● **S01.339**   Puncture wound without foreign body of unspecified ear

● **S01.34**   Puncture wound with foreign body of ear

     ● **S01.341**   Puncture wound with foreign body of right ear

     ● **S01.342**   Puncture wound with foreign body of left ear

     ● **S01.349**   Puncture wound with foreign body of unspecified ear

● **S01.35**   Open bite of ear
       Bite of ear NOS

       Excludes1   superficial bite of ear (S00.46, S00.47)

     ● **S01.351**   Open bite of right ear

     ● **S01.352**   Open bite of left ear

     ● **S01.359**   Open bite of unspecified ear

● **S01.4**   Open wound of cheek and temporomandibular area

     ● **S01.40**   Unspecified open wound of cheek and temporomandibular area

       ● **S01.401**   Unspecified open wound of right cheek and temporomandibular area

       ● **S01.402**   Unspecified open wound of left cheek and temporomandibular area

       ● **S01.409**   Unspecified open wound of unspecified cheek and temporomandibular area

     ● **S01.41**   Laceration without foreign body of cheek and temporomandibular area

       ● **S01.411**   Laceration without foreign body of right cheek and temporomandibular area
         Coding Clinic: 2015, Q1, P5-7

       ● **S01.412**   Laceration without foreign body of left cheek and temporomandibular area

       ● **S01.419**   Laceration without foreign body of unspecified cheek and temporomandibular area

     ● **S01.42**   Laceration with foreign body of cheek and temporomandibular area

       ● **S01.421**   Laceration with foreign body of right cheek and temporomandibular area

       ● **S01.422**   Laceration with foreign body of left cheek and temporomandibular area

       ● **S01.429**   Laceration with foreign body of unspecified cheek and temporomandibular area

     ● **S01.43**   Puncture wound without foreign body of cheek and temporomandibular area

       ● **S01.431**   Puncture wound without foreign body of right cheek and temporomandibular area

       ● **S01.432**   Puncture wound without foreign body of left cheek and temporomandibular area

       ● **S01.439**   Puncture wound without foreign body of unspecified cheek and temporomandibular area

● S01.44   Puncture wound with foreign body of cheek and temporomandibular area
   ● S01.441   Puncture wound with foreign body of right cheek and temporomandibular area
   ● S01.442   Puncture wound with foreign body of left cheek and temporomandibular area
   ● S01.449   Puncture wound with foreign body of unspecified cheek and temporomandibular area
● S01.45   Open bite of cheek and temporomandibular area
     Bite of cheek and temporomandibular area NOS
     Excludes2   superficial bite of cheek and temporomandibular area (S00.86, S00.87)
   ● S01.451   Open bite of right cheek and temporomandibular area
   ● S01.452   Open bite of left cheek and temporomandibular area
   ● S01.459   Open bite of unspecified cheek and temporomandibular area
● S01.5   Open wound of lip and oral cavity
     Excludes2   tooth dislocation (S03.2)
                  tooth fracture (S02.5)
   ● S01.50   Unspecified open wound of lip and oral cavity
     ● S01.501   Unspecified open wound of lip
     ● S01.502   Unspecified open wound of oral cavity
   ● S01.51   Laceration of lip and oral cavity without foreign body
     ● S01.511   Laceration without foreign body of lip
     ● S01.512   Laceration without foreign body of oral cavity
   ● S01.52   Laceration of lip and oral cavity with foreign body
     ● S01.521   Laceration with foreign body of lip
     ● S01.522   Laceration with foreign body of oral cavity
   ● S01.53   Puncture wound of lip and oral cavity without foreign body
     ● S01.531   Puncture wound without foreign body of lip
     ● S01.532   Puncture wound without foreign body of oral cavity
   ● S01.54   Puncture wound of lip and oral cavity with foreign body
     ● S01.541   Puncture wound with foreign body of lip
     ● S01.542   Puncture wound with foreign body of oral cavity
   ● S01.55   Open bite of lip and oral cavity
     ● S01.551   Open bite of lip
         Bite of lip NOS
         Excludes1   superficial bite of lip (S00.571)
     ● S01.552   Open bite of oral cavity
         Bite of oral cavity NOS
         Excludes1   superficial bite of oral cavity (S00.572)

● S01.8   Open wound of other parts of head
   X● S01.80   Unspecified open wound of other part of head
   X● S01.81   Laceration without foreign body of other part of head
   X● S01.82   Laceration with foreign body of other part of head
   X● S01.83   Puncture wound without foreign body of other part of head
   X● S01.84   Puncture wound with foreign body of other part of head
   X● S01.85   Open bite of other part of head
     Bite of other part of head NOS
     Excludes1   superficial bite of other part of head (S00.87)
● S01.9   Open wound of unspecified part of head
   X● S01.90   Unspecified open wound of unspecified part of head
   X● S01.91   Laceration without foreign body of unspecified part of head
   X● S01.92   Laceration with foreign body of unspecified part of head
   X● S01.93   Puncture wound without foreign body of unspecified part of head
   X● S01.94   Puncture wound with foreign body of unspecified part of head
   X● S01.95   Open bite of unspecified part of head
     Bite of head NOS
     Excludes1   superficial bite of head NOS (S00.97)

● S02   Fracture of skull and facial bones
     Note: A fracture not indicated as open or closed should be coded to closed
     The appropriate 7th character is to be added to each code from category S02

A	initial encounter for closed fracture
B	initial encounter for open fracture
D	subsequent encounter for fracture with routine healing
G	subsequent encounter for fracture with delayed healing
K	subsequent encounter for fracture with nonunion
S	sequela

     Code also any associated intracranial injury (S06.-)
   X● S02.0   Fracture of vault of skull
     Fracture of frontal bone
     Fracture of parietal bone
   ● S02.1   Fracture of base of skull
     Excludes1   orbit NOS (S02.8)
     Excludes2   orbital floor (S02.3-)
     Coding Clinic: 2016, Q4, P66
     ● S02.10   Unspecified fracture of base of skull
       ● S02.101   Fracture of base of skull, right side
       ● S02.102   Fracture of base of skull, left side
       ● S02.109   Fracture of base of skull, unspecified side
     ● S02.11   Fracture of occiput
       ● S02.110   Type I occipital condyle fracture, unspecified side
       ● S02.111   Type II occipital condyle fracture, unspecified side
       ● S02.112   Type III occipital condyle fracture, unspecified side

● S02.113   Unspecified occipital condyle fracture

● S02.118   Other fracture of occiput, unspecified side

● S02.119   Unspecified fracture of occiput

● S02.11A   Type I occipital condyle fracture, right side

● S02.11B   Type I occipital condyle fracture, left side

● S02.11C   Type II occipital condyle fracture, right side

● S02.11D   Type II occipital condyle fracture, left side

● S02.11E   Type III occipital condyle fracture, right side

● S02.11F   Type III occipital condyle fracture, left side

● S02.11G   Other fracture of occiput, right side

● S02.11H   Other fracture of occiput, left side

X ● **S02.19**   Other fracture of base of skull
     Fracture of anterior fossa of base of skull
     Fracture of ethmoid sinus
     Fracture of frontal sinus
     Fracture of middle fossa of base of skull
     Fracture of orbital roof
     Fracture of posterior fossa of base of skull
     Fracture of sphenoid
     Fracture of temporal bone

X ● **S02.2**   Fracture of nasal bones

● **S02.3**   Fracture of orbital floor
     Excludes1   orbit NOS (S02.8)
     Excludes2   orbital roof (S02.1-)
     Coding Clinic: 2016, Q4, P66

X ● **S02.30**   Fracture of orbital floor, unspecified side

X ● **S02.31**   Fracture of orbital floor, right side

X ● **S02.32**   Fracture of orbital floor, left side

● **S02.4**   Fracture of malar, maxillary and zygoma bones
     Fracture of superior maxilla
     Fracture of upper jaw (bone)
     Fracture of zygomatic process of temporal bone
     Coding Clinic: 2016, Q4, P66

● **S02.40**   Fracture of malar, maxillary and zygoma bones, unspecified

   ● S02.400   Malar fracture unspecified side

   ● S02.401   Maxillary fracture, unspecified side

   ● S02.402   Zygomatic fracture, unspecified side

   ● S02.40A   Malar fracture, right side

   ● S02.40B   Malar fracture, left side

   ● S02.40C   Maxillary fracture, right side

   ● S02.40D   Maxillary fracture, left side

   ● S02.40E   Zygomatic fracture, right side

   ● S02.40F   Zygomatic fracture, left side

● **S02.41**   LeFort fracture

   ● S02.411   LeFort I fracture

   ● S02.412   LeFort II fracture

   ● S02.413   LeFort III fracture

X ● **S02.42**   Fracture of alveolus of maxilla

X ● **S02.5**   Fracture of tooth (traumatic) Broken tooth
     Excludes1   cracked tooth (nontraumatic) (K03.81)

● **S02.6**   Fracture of mandible
     Fracture of lower jaw (bone)
     Coding Clinic: 2016, Q4, P66

● **S02.60**   Fracture of mandible of unspecified site

   ● S02.600   Fracture of unspecified part of body of mandible, unspecified side

   ● S02.601   Fracture of unspecified part of body of right mandible

   ● S02.602   Fracture of unspecified part of body of left mandible

   ● S02.609   Fracture of mandible, unspecified

● **S02.61**   Fracture of condylar process of mandible

   ● S02.610   Fracture of condylar process of mandible, unspecified side

   ● S02.611   Fracture of condylar process of right mandible

   ● S02.612   Fracture of condylar process of left mandible

● **S02.62**   Fracture of subcondylar process of mandible

   ● S02.620   Fracture of subcondylar process of mandible, unspecified side

   ● S02.621   Fracture of subcondylar process of right mandible

   ● S02.622   Fracture of subcondylar process of left mandible

● **S02.63**   Fracture of coronoid process of mandible

   ● S02.630   Fracture of coronoid process of mandible, unspecified side

   ● S02.631   Fracture of coronoid process of right mandible

   ● S02.632   Fracture of coronoid process of left mandible

● **S02.64**   Fracture of ramus of mandible

   ● S02.640   Fracture of ramus of mandible, unspecified side

   ● S02.641   Fracture of ramus of right mandible

   ● S02.642   Fracture of ramus of left mandible

● **S02.65**   Fracture of angle of mandible

   ● S02.650   Fracture of angle of mandible, unspecified side

   ● S02.651   Fracture of angle of right mandible

   ● S02.652   Fracture of angle of left mandible

X ● **S02.66**   Fracture of symphysis of mandible

● **S02.67**   Fracture of alveolus of mandible

   ● S02.670   Fracture of alveolus of mandible, unspecified side

   ● S02.671   Fracture of alveolus of right mandible

   ● S02.672   Fracture of alveolus of left mandible

X ● **S02.69**   Fracture of mandible of other specified site

● **S02.8**   Fractures of other specified skull and facial bones
     Fracture of orbit NOS
     Fracture of palate
     Excludes1   fracture of orbital floor (S02.3-)
                fracture of orbital roof (S02.1-)
     Coding Clinic: 2016, Q4, P66

X ● **S02.80**   Fracture of other specified skull and facial bones, unspecified side

X ● **S02.81**   Fracture of other specified skull and facial bones, right side

X ● **S02.82**   Fracture of other specified skull and facial bones, left side

● **S02.9**   Fracture of unspecified skull and facial bones

X ● **S02.91**   Unspecified fracture of skull

X ● **S02.92**   Unspecified fracture of facial bones

▶ New   ⇒ Revised   ~~deleted~~ Deleted   Excludes 1   Excludes 2   Includes   Use additional   Code first   Code also   Key words

OGCR Official Guidelines   X Assign placeholder X   ● Use Additional Character(s)   ▷ Manifestation Code   **Coding Clinic**

● **S03**   **Dislocation and sprain of joints and ligaments of head**

     Includes   avulsion of joint (capsule) or ligament of head
                 laceration of cartilage, joint (capsule) or ligament of head
                 sprain of cartilage, joint (capsule) or ligament of head
                 traumatic hemarthrosis of joint or ligament of head
                 traumatic rupture of joint or ligament of head
                 traumatic subluxation of joint or ligament of head
                 traumatic tear of joint or ligament of head

     Code also any associated open wound

     Excludes2   Strain of muscle or tendon of head (S09.1)

     The appropriate 7th character is to be added to each code from category S03

> A   initial encounter
> D   subsequent encounter
> S   sequela

● **S03.0**   **Dislocation of jaw**
       Dislocation of jaw (cartilage) (meniscus)
       Dislocation of mandible
       Dislocation of temporomandibular (joint)
       Coding Clinic: 2016, Q4, P67

    X● **S03.00**   Dislocation of jaw, **unspecified** side
    X● **S03.01**   Dislocation of jaw, **right** side
    X● **S03.02**   Dislocation of jaw, **left** side
    X● **S03.03**   Dislocation of jaw, **bilateral** side

X● **S03.1**   **Dislocation of septal cartilage of nose**

X● **S03.2**   **Dislocation of tooth**

● **S03.4**   **Sprain of jaw**
       Sprain of temporomandibular (joint) (ligament)
       Coding Clinic: 2016, Q4, P67

    X● **S03.40**   Sprain of jaw, **unspecified** side
    X● **S03.41**   Sprain of jaw, **right** side
    X● **S03.42**   Sprain of jaw, **left** side
    X● **S03.43**   Sprain of jaw, **bilateral** side

X● **S03.8**   **Sprain of joints and ligaments of other parts of head**
X● **S03.9**   **Sprain of joints and ligaments of unspecified parts of head**

● **S04**   **Injury of cranial nerve**
       The selection of side should be based on the side of the body being affected
       Code first any associated intracranial injury (S06.-)
       Code also any associated:
         open wound of head (S01.-)
         skull fracture (S02.-)
       The appropriate 7th character is to be added to each code from category S04

> A   initial encounter
> D   subsequent encounter
> S   sequela

● **S04.0**   **Injury of optic nerve and pathways**
       Use additional code to identify any visual field defect or blindness (H53.4-, H54.-)

   ● **S04.01**   **Injury of optic nerve**
          Injury of 2nd cranial nerve

     ● **S04.011**   Injury of optic nerve, **right** eye
     ● **S04.012**   Injury of optic nerve, **left** eye
     ● **S04.019**   Injury of optic nerve, **unspecified** eye
              Injury of optic nerve NOS

   X● **S04.02**   **Injury of optic chiasm**

   ● **S04.03**   **Injury of optic tract and pathways**
          Injury of optic radiation

     ● **S04.031**   Injury of optic tract and pathways, **right** side
     ● **S04.032**   Injury of optic tract and pathways, **left** side
     ● **S04.039**   Injury of optic tract and pathways, **unspecified** side
              Injury of optic tract and pathways NOS

Figure 19-13   Cranial nerves. (From Patton and Thibodeau: Anatomy and physiology, ed 7, St. Louis, Mosby, 2009)

CHAPTER 19 (S00–T88)

- S04.04   Injury of visual cortex
  - S04.041   Injury of visual cortex, right side
  - S04.042   Injury of visual cortex, left side
  - S04.049   Injury of visual cortex, unspecified side
    - Injury of visual cortex NOS
- S04.1   Injury of oculomotor nerve
  - Injury of 3rd cranial nerve
  - X S04.10   Injury of oculomotor nerve, unspecified side
  - X S04.11   Injury of oculomotor nerve, right side
  - X S04.12   Injury of oculomotor nerve, left side
- S04.2   Injury of trochlear nerve
  - Injury of 4th cranial nerve
  - X S04.20   Injury of trochlear nerve, unspecified side
  - X S04.21   Injury of trochlear nerve, right side
  - X S04.22   Injury of trochlear nerve, left side
- S04.3   Injury of trigeminal nerve
  - Injury of 5th cranial nerve
  - X S04.30   Injury of trigeminal nerve, unspecified side
  - X S04.31   Injury of trigeminal nerve, right side
  - X S04.32   Injury of trigeminal nerve, left side
- S04.4   Injury of abducent nerve
  - Injury of 6th cranial nerve
  - X S04.40   Injury of abducent nerve, unspecified side
  - X S04.41   Injury of abducent nerve, right side
  - X S04.42   Injury of abducent nerve, left side
- S04.5   Injury of facial nerve
  - Injury of 7th cranial nerve
  - X S04.50   Injury of facial nerve, unspecified side
  - X S04.51   Injury of facial nerve, right side
  - X S04.52   Injury of facial nerve, left side
- S04.6   Injury of acoustic nerve
  - Injury of auditory nerve
  - Injury of 8th cranial nerve
  - X S04.60   Injury of acoustic nerve, unspecified side
  - X S04.61   Injury of acoustic nerve, right side
  - X S04.62   Injury of acoustic nerve, left side
- S04.7   Injury of accessory nerve
  - Injury of 11th cranial nerve
  - X S04.70   Injury of accessory nerve, unspecified side
  - X S04.71   Injury of accessory nerve, right side
  - X S04.72   Injury of accessory nerve, left side
- S04.8   Injury of other cranial nerves
  - S04.81   Injury of olfactory [1st] nerve
    - S04.811   Injury of olfactory [1st] nerve, right side
    - S04.812   Injury of olfactory [1st] nerve, left side
    - S04.819   Injury of olfactory [1st] nerve, unspecified side
  - S04.89   Injury of other cranial nerves
    - Injury of vagus [10th] nerve
    - S04.891   Injury of other cranial nerves, right side
    - S04.892   Injury of other cranial nerves, left side
    - S04.899   Injury of other cranial nerves, unspecified side
- X S04.9   Injury of unspecified cranial nerve

- S05   Injury of eye and orbit
  - **Includes**   open wound of eye and orbit
  - **Excludes2**   2nd cranial [optic] nerve injury (S04.0-)
    3rd cranial [oculomotor] nerve injury (S04.1-)
    open wound of eyelid and periocular area (S01.1-)
    orbital bone fracture (S02.1-, S02.3-, S02.8-)
    superficial injury of eyelid (S00.1-S00.2)

  The appropriate 7th character is to be added to each code from category S05

A	initial encounter
D	subsequent encounter
S	sequela

  - S05.0   Injury of conjunctiva and corneal abrasion without foreign body
    - **Excludes1**   foreign body in conjunctival sac (T15.1)
      foreign body in cornea (T15.0)
    - X S05.00   Injury of conjunctiva and corneal abrasion without foreign body, unspecified eye
    - X S05.01   Injury of conjunctiva and corneal abrasion without foreign body, right eye
    - X S05.02   Injury of conjunctiva and corneal abrasion without foreign body, left eye
  - S05.1   Contusion of eyeball and orbital tissues
    - Traumatic hyphema
    - **Excludes2**   black eye NOS (S00.1)
      contusion of eyelid and periocular area (S00.1)
    - X S05.10   Contusion of eyeball and orbital tissues, unspecified eye
    - X S05.11   Contusion of eyeball and orbital tissues, right eye
    - X S05.12   Contusion of eyeball and orbital tissues, left eye
  - S05.2   Ocular laceration and rupture with prolapse or loss of intraocular tissue
    - X S05.20   Ocular laceration and rupture with prolapse or loss of intraocular tissue, unspecified eye
    - X S05.21   Ocular laceration and rupture with prolapse or loss of intraocular tissue, right eye
    - X S05.22   Ocular laceration and rupture with prolapse or loss of intraocular tissue, left eye
  - S05.3   Ocular laceration without prolapse or loss of intraocular tissue
    - Laceration of eye NOS
    - X S05.30   Ocular laceration without prolapse or loss of intraocular tissue, unspecified eye
    - X S05.31   Ocular laceration without prolapse or loss of intraocular tissue, right eye
    - X S05.32   Ocular laceration without prolapse or loss of intraocular tissue, left eye
  - S05.4   Penetrating wound of orbit with or without foreign body
    - **Excludes2**   retained (old) foreign body following penetrating wound in orbit (H05.5-)
    - X S05.40   Penetrating wound of orbit with or without foreign body, unspecified eye
    - X S05.41   Penetrating wound of orbit with or without foreign body, right eye
    - X S05.42   Penetrating wound of orbit with or without foreign body, left eye
  - S05.5   Penetrating wound with foreign body of eyeball
    - **Excludes2**   retained (old) intraocular foreign body (H44.6-, H44.7)
    - X S05.50   Penetrating wound with foreign body of unspecified eyeball
    - X S05.51   Penetrating wound with foreign body of right eyeball
    - X S05.52   Penetrating wound with foreign body of left eyeball

▶ New   ⇒ Revised   deleted Deleted   Excludes 1   Excludes 2   Includes   Use additional   Code first   Code also   Key words
OGCR Official Guidelines   X Assign placeholder X   ● Use Additional Character(s)   ▷ Manifestation Code   Coding Clinic

● **S05.6** **Penetrating wound without foreign body of eyeball**
Ocular penetration NOS

   X ● **S05.60** **Penetrating wound without foreign body of unspecified eyeball**

   X ● **S05.61** **Penetrating wound without foreign body of right eyeball**

   X ● **S05.62** **Penetrating wound without foreign body of left eyeball**

● **S05.7** **Avulsion of eye**
Traumatic enucleation

   X ● **S05.70** Avulsion of unspecified eye

   X ● **S05.71** Avulsion of right eye

   X ● **S05.72** Avulsion of left eye

● **S05.8** **Other injuries of eye and orbit**
Lacrimal duct injury

   ● **S05.8X** Other injuries of eye and orbit

     ● **S05.8X1** Other injuries of right eye and orbit

     ● **S05.8X2** Other injuries of left eye and orbit

     ● **S05.8X9** Other injuries of unspecified eye and orbit

● **S05.9** **Unspecified injury of eye and orbit**
Injury of eye NOS

   X ● **S05.90** Unspecified injury of unspecified eye and orbit

   X ● **S05.91** Unspecified injury of right eye and orbit

   X ● **S05.92** Unspecified injury of left eye and orbit

● **S06** **Intracranial injury**

   Includes   traumatic brain injury

   Code also any associated:
     open wound of head (S01.-)
     skull fracture (S02.-)

   Excludes1   head injury NOS (S09.90)

   The appropriate 7th character is to be added to each code from category S06

A	initial encounter
D	subsequent encounter
S	sequela

   Note: 7th characters D and S do not apply to codes in category S06 with 6th character 7 - death due to brain injury prior to regaining consciousness, or 8 - death due to other cause prior to regaining consciousness.
   Coding Clinic: 2015, Q4, P40

● **S06.0** **Concussion**
Commotio cerebri

   Excludes1   concussion with other intracranial injuries classified in subcategories S06.1- to S06.6- , S06.81- and S06.82- code to specified intracranial injury
   Coding Clinic: 2016, Q4, P67

   ● **S06.0X** Concussion

     ● **S06.0X0** Concussion without loss of consciousness

     ● **S06.0X1** Concussion with loss of consciousness of 30 minutes or less

     ● **S06.0X9** Concussion with loss of consciousness of unspecified duration
Concussion NOS
Coding Clinic: 2016, Q4, P68

● **S06.1** **Traumatic cerebral edema**
Diffuse traumatic cerebral edema
Focal traumatic cerebral edema
Coding Clinic: 2016, Q4, P67

   ● **S06.1X** Traumatic cerebral edema

     ● **S06.1X0** Traumatic cerebral edema without loss of consciousness
Coding Clinic: 2015, Q1, P12

     ● **S06.1X1** Traumatic cerebral edema with loss of consciousness of 30 minutes or less

     ● **S06.1X2** Traumatic cerebral edema with loss of consciousness of 31 minutes to 59 minutes

     ● **S06.1X3** Traumatic cerebral edema with loss of consciousness of 1 hour to 5 hours 59 minutes

     ● **S06.1X4** Traumatic cerebral edema with loss of consciousness of 6 hours to 24 hours

     ● **S06.1X5** Traumatic cerebral edema with loss of consciousness greater than 24 hours with return to pre-existing conscious level

     ● **S06.1X6** Traumatic cerebral edema with loss of consciousness greater than 24 hours without return to pre-existing conscious level with patient surviving

     ● **S06.1X7** Traumatic cerebral edema with loss of consciousness of any duration with death due to brain injury prior to regaining consciousness

     ● **S06.1X8** Traumatic cerebral edema with loss of consciousness of any duration with death due to other cause prior to regaining consciousness

     ● **S06.1X9** Traumatic cerebral edema with loss of consciousness of unspecified duration
Traumatic cerebral edema NOS

● **S06.2** **Diffuse traumatic brain injury**
Diffuse axonal brain injury

   Excludes1   traumatic diffuse cerebral edema (S06.1X-)

   ● **S06.2X** Diffuse traumatic brain injury

     ● **S06.2X0** Diffuse traumatic brain injury without loss of consciousness

     ● **S06.2X1** Diffuse traumatic brain injury with loss of consciousness of 30 minutes or less

     ● **S06.2X2** Diffuse traumatic brain injury with loss of consciousness of 31 minutes to 59 minutes

     ● **S06.2X3** Diffuse traumatic brain injury with loss of consciousness of 1 hour to 5 hours 59 minutes

     ● **S06.2X4** Diffuse traumatic brain injury with loss of consciousness of 6 hours to 24 hours

     ● **S06.2X5** Diffuse traumatic brain injury with loss of consciousness greater than 24 hours with return to pre-existing conscious levels

     ● **S06.2X6** Diffuse traumatic brain injury with loss of consciousness greater than 24 hours without return to pre-existing conscious level with patient surviving

● S06.2X7 Diffuse traumatic brain injury with loss of consciousness of any duration with death due to brain injury prior to regaining consciousness

● S06.2X8 Diffuse traumatic brain injury with loss of consciousness of any duration with death due to other cause prior to regaining consciousness

● S06.2X9 Diffuse traumatic brain injury with loss of consciousness of unspecified duration
Diffuse traumatic brain injury NOS

● S06.3 Focal traumatic brain injury
Excludes1 any condition classifiable to S06.4-S06.6
focal cerebral edema (S06.1)

● S06.30 Unspecified focal traumatic brain injury

● S06.300 Unspecified focal traumatic brain injury without loss of consciousness

● S06.301 Unspecified focal traumatic brain injury with loss of consciousness of 30 minutes or less

● S06.302 Unspecified focal traumatic brain injury with loss of consciousness of 31 minutes to 59 minutes

● S06.303 Unspecified focal traumatic brain injury with loss of consciousness of 1 hour to 5 hours 59 minutes

● S06.304 Unspecified focal traumatic brain injury with loss of consciousness of 6 hours to 24 hours

● S06.305 Unspecified focal traumatic brain injury with loss of consciousness greater than 24 hours with return to pre-existing conscious level

● S06.306 Unspecified focal traumatic brain injury with loss of consciousness greater than 24 hours without return to pre-existing conscious level with patient surviving

● S06.307 Unspecified focal traumatic brain injury with loss of consciousness of any duration with death due to brain injury prior to regaining consciousness

● S06.308 Unspecified focal traumatic brain injury with loss of consciousness of any duration with death due to other cause prior to regaining consciousness

● S06.309 Unspecified focal traumatic brain injury with loss of consciousness of unspecified duration
Unspecified focal traumatic brain injury NOS

● S06.31 Contusion and laceration of right cerebrum

● S06.310 Contusion and laceration of right cerebrum without loss of consciousness

● S06.311 Contusion and laceration of right cerebrum with loss of consciousness of 30 minutes or less

● S06.312 Contusion and laceration of right cerebrum with loss of consciousness of 31 minutes to 59 minutes

● S06.313 Contusion and laceration of right cerebrum with loss of consciousness of 1 hour to 5 hours 59 minutes

● S06.314 Contusion and laceration of right cerebrum with loss of consciousness of 6 hours to 24 hours

● S06.315 Contusion and laceration of right cerebrum with loss of consciousness greater than 24 hours with return to pre-existing conscious level

● S06.316 Contusion and laceration of right cerebrum with loss of consciousness greater than 24 hours without return to pre-existing conscious level with patient surviving

● S06.317 Contusion and laceration of right cerebrum with loss of consciousness of any duration with death due to brain injury prior to regaining consciousness

● S06.318 Contusion and laceration of right cerebrum with loss of consciousness of any duration with death due to other cause prior to regaining consciousness

● S06.319 Contusion and laceration of right cerebrum with loss of consciousness of unspecified duration
Contusion and laceration of right cerebrum NOS

● S06.32 Contusion and laceration of left cerebrum

● S06.320 Contusion and laceration of left cerebrum without loss of consciousness

● S06.321 Contusion and laceration of left cerebrum with loss of consciousness of 30 minutes or less

● S06.322 Contusion and laceration of left cerebrum with loss of consciousness of 31 minutes to 59 minutes

● S06.323 Contusion and laceration of left cerebrum with loss of consciousness of 1 hour to 5 hours 59 minutes

● S06.324 Contusion and laceration of left cerebrum with loss of consciousness of 6 hours to 24 hours

● S06.325 Contusion and laceration of left cerebrum with loss of consciousness greater than 24 hours with return to pre-existing conscious level

● S06.326 Contusion and laceration of left cerebrum with loss of consciousness greater than 24 hours without return to pre-existing conscious level with patient surviving

● S06.327 Contusion and laceration of left cerebrum with loss of consciousness of any duration with death due to brain injury prior to regaining consciousness

● S06.328 Contusion and laceration of left cerebrum with loss of consciousness of any duration with death due to other cause prior to regaining consciousness

● S06.329 Contusion and laceration of left cerebrum with loss of consciousness of unspecified duration
Contusion and laceration of left cerebrum NOS

▶ New   ⇒ Revised   deleted Deleted   Excludes 1   Excludes 2   Includes   Use additional   Code first   Code also   Key words
OGCR Official Guidelines   X Assign placeholder X   ● Use Additional Character(s)   ▷ Manifestation Code   Coding Clinic

● **S06.33**   Contusion and laceration of cerebrum, unspecified

    ● **S06.330**   Contusion and laceration of cerebrum, unspecified, without loss of consciousness

    ● **S06.331**   Contusion and laceration of cerebrum, unspecified, with loss of consciousness of 30 minutes or less

    ● **S06.332**   Contusion and laceration of cerebrum, unspecified, with loss of consciousness of 31 minutes to 59 minutes

    ● **S06.333**   Contusion and laceration of cerebrum, unspecified, with loss of consciousness of 1 hour to 5 hours 59 minutes

    ● **S06.334**   Contusion and laceration of cerebrum, unspecified, with loss of consciousness of 6 hours to 24 hours

    ● **S06.335**   Contusion and laceration of cerebrum, unspecified, with loss of consciousness greater than 24 hours with return to pre-existing conscious level

    ● **S06.336**   Contusion and laceration of cerebrum, unspecified, with loss of consciousness greater than 24 hours without return to pre-existing conscious level with patient surviving

    ● **S06.337**   Contusion and laceration of cerebrum, unspecified, with loss of consciousness of any duration with death due to brain injury prior to regaining consciousness

    ● **S06.338**   Contusion and laceration of cerebrum, unspecified, with loss of consciousness of any duration with death due to other cause prior to regaining consciousness

    ● **S06.339**   Contusion and laceration of cerebrum, unspecified, with loss of consciousness of unspecified duration
       Contusion and laceration of cerebrum NOS

● **S06.34**   Traumatic hemorrhage of right cerebrum
     Traumatic intracerebral hemorrhage and hematoma of right cerebrum

    ● **S06.340**   Traumatic hemorrhage of right cerebrum without loss of consciousness
       Coding Clinic: 2015, Q1, P12

    ● **S06.341**   Traumatic hemorrhage of right cerebrum with loss of consciousness of 30 minutes or less

    ● **S06.342**   Traumatic hemorrhage of right cerebrum with loss of consciousness of 31 minutes to 59 minutes

    ● **S06.343**   Traumatic hemorrhage of right cerebrum with loss of consciousness of 1 hours to 5 hours 59 minutes

    ● **S06.344**   Traumatic hemorrhage of right cerebrum with loss of consciousness of 6 hours to 24 hours

    ● **S06.345**   Traumatic hemorrhage of right cerebrum with loss of consciousness greater than 24 hours with return to pre-existing conscious level

    ● **S06.346**   Traumatic hemorrhage of right cerebrum with loss of consciousness greater than 24 hours without return to pre-existing conscious level with patient surviving

    ● **S06.347**   Traumatic hemorrhage of right cerebrum with loss of consciousness of any duration with death due to brain injury prior to regaining consciousness

    ● **S06.348**   Traumatic hemorrhage of right cerebrum with loss of consciousness of any duration with death due to other cause prior to regaining consciousness

    ● **S06.349**   Traumatic hemorrhage of right cerebrum with loss of consciousness of unspecified duration
       Traumatic hemorrhage of right cerebrum NOS

● **S06.35**   Traumatic hemorrhage of left cerebrum
     Traumatic intracerebral hemorrhage and hematoma of left cerebrum

    ● **S06.350**   Traumatic hemorrhage of left cerebrum without loss of consciousness

    ● **S06.351**   Traumatic hemorrhage of left cerebrum with loss of consciousness of 30 minutes or less

    ● **S06.352**   Traumatic hemorrhage of left cerebrum with loss of consciousness of 31 minutes to 59 minutes

    ● **S06.353**   Traumatic hemorrhage of left cerebrum with loss of consciousness of 1 hours to 5 hours 59 minutes

    ● **S06.354**   Traumatic hemorrhage of left cerebrum with loss of consciousness of 6 hours to 24 hours

    ● **S06.355**   Traumatic hemorrhage of left cerebrum with loss of consciousness greater than 24 hours with return to pre-existing conscious level

    ● **S06.356**   Traumatic hemorrhage of left cerebrum with loss of consciousness greater than 24 hours without return to pre-existing conscious level with patient surviving

    ● **S06.357**   Traumatic hemorrhage of left cerebrum with loss of consciousness of any duration with death due to brain injury prior to regaining consciousness

    ● **S06.358**   Traumatic hemorrhage of left cerebrum with loss of consciousness of any duration with death due to other cause prior to regaining consciousness

    ● **S06.359**   Traumatic hemorrhage of left cerebrum with loss of consciousness of unspecified duration
       Traumatic hemorrhage of left cerebrum NOS

CHAPTER 19 (S00-T88)

CHAPTER 19 (S00-T88)

● S06.36   **Traumatic hemorrhage of cerebrum, unspecified**
Traumatic intracerebral hemorrhage and hematoma, unspecified

    ● S06.360   Traumatic hemorrhage of cerebrum, unspecified, without loss of consciousness

    ● S06.361   Traumatic hemorrhage of cerebrum, unspecified, with loss of consciousness of 30 minutes or less

    ● S06.362   Traumatic hemorrhage of cerebrum, unspecified, with loss of consciousness of 31 minutes to 59 minutes

    ● S06.363   Traumatic hemorrhage of cerebrum, unspecified, with loss of consciousness of 1 hours to 5 hours 59 minutes

    ● S06.364   Traumatic hemorrhage of cerebrum, unspecified, with loss of consciousness of 6 hours to 24 hours

    ● S06.365   Traumatic hemorrhage of cerebrum, unspecified, with loss of consciousness greater than 24 hours with return to pre-existing conscious level

    ● S06.366   Traumatic hemorrhage of cerebrum, unspecified, with loss of consciousness greater than 24 hours without return to pre-existing conscious level with patient surviving

    ● S06.367   Traumatic hemorrhage of cerebrum, unspecified, with loss of consciousness of any duration with death due to brain injury prior to regaining consciousness

    ● S06.368   Traumatic hemorrhage of cerebrum, unspecified, with loss of consciousness of any duration with death due to other cause prior to regaining consciousness

    ● S06.369   Traumatic hemorrhage of cerebrum, unspecified, with loss of consciousness of unspecified duration
       Traumatic hemorrhage of cerebrum NOS

● S06.37   Contusion, laceration, and hemorrhage of cerebellum

    ● S06.370   Contusion, laceration, and hemorrhage of cerebellum without loss of consciousness

    ● S06.371   Contusion, laceration, and hemorrhage of cerebellum with loss of consciousness of 30 minutes or less

    ● S06.372   Contusion, laceration, and hemorrhage of cerebellum with loss of consciousness of 31 minutes to 59 minutes

    ● S06.373   Contusion, laceration, and hemorrhage of cerebellum with loss of consciousness of 1 hour to 5 hours 59 minutes

    ● S06.374   Contusion, laceration, and hemorrhage of cerebellum with loss of consciousness of 6 hours to 24 hours

    ● S06.375   Contusion, laceration, and hemorrhage of cerebellum with loss of consciousness greater than 24 hours with return to pre-existing conscious level

    ● S06.376   Contusion, laceration, and hemorrhage of cerebellum with loss of consciousness greater than 24 hours without return to pre-existing conscious level with patient surviving

    ● S06.377   Contusion, laceration, and hemorrhage of cerebellum with loss of consciousness of any duration with death due to brain injury prior to regaining consciousness

    ● S06.378   Contusion, laceration, and hemorrhage of cerebellum with loss of consciousness of any duration with death due to other cause prior to regaining consciousness

    ● S06.379   Contusion, laceration, and hemorrhage of cerebellum with loss of consciousness of unspecified duration
       Contusion, laceration, and hemorrhage of cerebellum NOS

● S06.38   Contusion, laceration, and hemorrhage of brainstem

    ● S06.380   Contusion, laceration, and hemorrhage of brainstem without loss of consciousness

    ● S06.381   Contusion, laceration, and hemorrhage of brainstem with loss of consciousness of 30 minutes or less

    ● S06.382   Contusion, laceration, and hemorrhage of brainstem with loss of consciousness of 31 minutes to 59 minutes

    ● S06.383   Contusion, laceration, and hemorrhage of brainstem with loss of consciousness of 1 hour to 5 hours 59 minutes

    ● S06.384   Contusion, laceration, and hemorrhage of brainstem with loss of consciousness of 6 hours to 24 hours

    ● S06.385   Contusion, laceration, and hemorrhage of brainstem with loss of consciousness greater than 24 hours with return to pre-existing conscious level

    ● S06.386   Contusion, laceration, and hemorrhage of brainstem with loss of consciousness greater than 24 hours without return to pre-existing conscious level with patient surviving

    ● S06.387   Contusion, laceration, and hemorrhage of brainstem with loss of consciousness of any duration with death due to brain injury prior to regaining consciousness

    ● S06.388   Contusion, laceration, and hemorrhage of brainstem with loss of consciousness of any duration with death due to other cause prior to regaining consciousness

    ● S06.389   Contusion, laceration, and hemorrhage of brainstem with loss of consciousness of unspecified duration
       Contusion, laceration, and hemorrhage of brainstem NOS

▶ New   ⇒ Revised   ~~deleted~~ Deleted   Excludes 1   Excludes 2   Includes   Use additional   Code first   Code also   Key words

OGCR Official Guidelines   X Assign placeholder X   ● Use Additional Character(s)   ▷ Manifestation Code   **Coding Clinic**

- **S06.4　Epidural hemorrhage**
  Situated outside dura mater
  Extradural hemorrhage NOS
  Intracranial hemorrhage due to trauma
  Extradural hemorrhage (traumatic)
  - **S06.4X　Epidural hemorrhage**
    - **S06.4X0　Epidural hemorrhage without loss of consciousness**
    - **S06.4X1　Epidural hemorrhage with loss of consciousness of 30 minutes or less**
    - **S06.4X2　Epidural hemorrhage with loss of consciousness of 31 minutes to 59 minutes**
    - **S06.4X3　Epidural hemorrhage with loss of consciousness of 1 hour to 5 hours 59 minutes**
    - **S06.4X4　Epidural hemorrhage with loss of consciousness of 6 hours to 24 hours**
    - **S06.4X5　Epidural hemorrhage with loss of consciousness greater than 24 hours with return to pre-existing conscious level**
    - **S06.4X6　Epidural hemorrhage with loss of consciousness greater than 24 hours without return to pre-existing conscious level with patient surviving**
    - **S06.4X7　Epidural hemorrhage with loss of consciousness of any duration with death due to brain injury prior to regaining consciousness**
    - **S06.4X8　Epidural hemorrhage with loss of consciousness of any duration with death due to other causes prior to regaining consciousness**
    - **S06.4X9　Epidural hemorrhage with loss of consciousness of unspecified duration**
      Epidural hemorrhage NOS
- **S06.5　Traumatic subdural hemorrhage**
  - **S06.5X　Traumatic subdural hemorrhage**
    - **S06.5X0　Traumatic subdural hemorrhage without loss of consciousness**
      Coding Clinic: 2018, Q2, P13; 2015, Q3, P37
    - **S06.5X1　Traumatic subdural hemorrhage with loss of consciousness of 30 minutes or less**
    - **S06.5X2　Traumatic subdural hemorrhage with loss of consciousness of 31 minutes to 59 minutes**
    - **S06.5X3　Traumatic subdural hemorrhage with loss of consciousness of 1 hour to 5 hours 59 minutes**
    - **S06.5X4　Traumatic subdural hemorrhage with loss of consciousness of 6 hours to 24 hours**
    - **S06.5X5　Traumatic subdural hemorrhage with loss of consciousness greater than 24 hours with return to pre-existing conscious level**
    - **S06.5X6　Traumatic subdural hemorrhage with loss of consciousness greater than 24 hours without return to pre-existing conscious level with patient surviving**
    - **S06.5X7　Traumatic subdural hemorrhage with loss of consciousness of any duration with death due to brain injury before regaining consciousness**

- **S06.5X8　Traumatic subdural hemorrhage with loss of consciousness of any duration with death due to other cause before regaining consciousness**
- **S06.5X9　Traumatic subdural hemorrhage with loss of consciousness of unspecified duration**
  Traumatic subdural hemorrhage NOS
- **S06.6　Traumatic subarachnoid hemorrhage**
  Between arachnoid and pia mater
  Coding Clinic: 2016, Q4, P67
  - **S06.6X　Traumatic subarachnoid hemorrhage**
    - **S06.6X0　Traumatic subarachnoid hemorrhage without loss of consciousness**
      Coding Clinic: 2015, Q3, P37
    - **S06.6X1　Traumatic subarachnoid hemorrhage with loss of consciousness of 30 minutes or less**
    - **S06.6X2　Traumatic subarachnoid hemorrhage with loss of consciousness of 31 minutes to 59 minutes**
    - **S06.6X3　Traumatic subarachnoid hemorrhage with loss of consciousness of 1 hour to 5 hours 59 minutes**
    - **S06.6X4　Traumatic subarachnoid hemorrhage with loss of consciousness of 6 hours to 24 hours**
    - **S06.6X5　Traumatic subarachnoid hemorrhage with loss of consciousness greater than 24 hours with return to pre-existing conscious level**
    - **S06.6X6　Traumatic subarachnoid hemorrhage with loss of consciousness greater than 24 hours without return to pre-existing conscious level with patient surviving**
    - **S06.6X7　Traumatic subarachnoid hemorrhage with loss of consciousness of any duration with death due to brain injury prior to regaining consciousness**
    - **S06.6X8　Traumatic subarachnoid hemorrhage with loss of consciousness of any duration with death due to other cause prior to regaining consciousness**
    - **S06.6X9　Traumatic subarachnoid hemorrhage with loss of consciousness of unspecified duration**
      Traumatic subarachnoid hemorrhage NOS
- **S06.8　Other specified intracranial injuries**
  - **S06.81　Injury of right internal carotid artery, intracranial portion, not elsewhere classified**
    Coding Clinic: 2016, Q4, P67
    - **S06.810　Injury of right internal carotid artery, intracranial portion, not elsewhere classified without loss of consciousness**
    - **S06.811　Injury of right internal carotid artery, intracranial portion, not elsewhere classified with loss of consciousness of 30 minutes or less**
    - **S06.812　Injury of right internal carotid artery, intracranial portion, not elsewhere classified with loss of consciousness of 31 minutes to 59 minutes**

CHAPTER 19 (S00-T88)

● **S06.813** Injury of right internal carotid artery, intracranial portion, not elsewhere classified with loss of consciousness of 1 hour to 5 hours 59 minutes

● **S06.814** Injury of right internal carotid artery, intracranial portion, not elsewhere classified with loss of consciousness of 6 hours to 24 hours

● **S06.815** Injury of right internal carotid artery, intracranial portion, not elsewhere classified with loss of consciousness greater than 24 hours with return to pre-existing conscious level

● **S06.816** Injury of right internal carotid artery, intracranial portion, not elsewhere classified with loss of consciousness greater than 24 hours without return to pre-existing conscious level with patient surviving

● **S06.817** Injury of right internal carotid artery, intracranial portion, not elsewhere classified with loss of consciousness of any duration with death due to brain injury prior to regaining consciousness

● **S06.818** Injury of right internal carotid artery, intracranial portion, not elsewhere classified with loss of consciousness of any duration with death due to other cause prior to regaining consciousness

● **S06.819** Injury of right internal carotid artery, intracranial portion, not elsewhere classified with loss of consciousness of unspecified duration
Injury of right internal carotid artery, intracranial portion, not elsewhere classified NOS

● **S06.82** Injury of left internal carotid artery, intracranial portion, not elsewhere classified
Coding Clinic: 2016, Q4, P67

● **S06.820** Injury of left internal carotid artery, intracranial portion, not elsewhere classified without loss of consciousness

● **S06.821** Injury of left internal carotid artery, intracranial portion, not elsewhere classified with loss of consciousness of 30 minutes or less

● **S06.822** Injury of left internal carotid artery, intracranial portion, not elsewhere classified with loss of consciousness of 31 minutes to 59 minutes

● **S06.823** Injury of left internal carotid artery, intracranial portion, not elsewhere classified with loss of consciousness of 1 hour to 5 hours 59 minutes

● **S06.824** Injury of left internal carotid artery, intracranial portion, not elsewhere classified with loss of consciousness of 6 hours to 24 hours

● **S06.825** Injury of left internal carotid artery, intracranial portion, not elsewhere classified with loss of consciousness greater than 24 hours with return to pre-existing conscious level

● **S06.826** Injury of left internal carotid artery, intracranial portion, not elsewhere classified with loss of consciousness greater than 24 hours without return to pre-existing conscious level with patient surviving

● **S06.827** Injury of left internal carotid artery, intracranial portion, not elsewhere classified with loss of consciousness of any duration with death due to brain injury prior to regaining consciousness

● **S06.828** Injury of left internal carotid artery, intracranial portion, not elsewhere classified with loss of consciousness of any duration with death due to other cause prior to regaining consciousness

● **S06.829** Injury of left internal carotid artery, intracranial portion, not elsewhere classified with loss of consciousness of unspecified duration
Injury of left internal carotid artery, intracranial portion, not elsewhere classified NOS

● **S06.89** Other specified intracranial injury
Excludes1 concussion (S06.0X-)

● **S06.890** Other specified intracranial injury without loss of consciousness

● **S06.891** Other specified intracranial injury with loss of consciousness of 30 minutes or less

● **S06.892** Other specified intracranial injury with loss of consciousness of 31 minutes to 59 minutes

● **S06.893** Other specified intracranial injury with loss of consciousness of 1 hour to 5 hours 59 minutes

● **S06.894** Other specified intracranial injury with loss of consciousness of 6 hours to 24 hours

● **S06.895** Other specified intracranial injury with loss of consciousness greater than 24 hours with return to pre-existing conscious level

● **S06.896** Other specified intracranial injury with loss of consciousness greater than 24 hours without return to pre-existing conscious level with patient surviving

● **S06.897** Other specified intracranial injury with loss of consciousness of any duration with death due to brain injury prior to regaining consciousness

● **S06.898** Other specified intracranial injury with loss of consciousness of any duration with death due to other cause prior to regaining consciousness

● **S06.899** Other specified intracranial injury with loss of consciousness of unspecified duration

● **S06.9**   **Unspecified intracranial injury**
    Brain injury NOS
    Head injury NOS with loss of consciousness
    Traumatic brain injury NOS
    Excludes1   conditions classifiable to S06.0- to
                    S06.8-code to specified intracranial
                    injury
                head injury NOS (S09.90)

   ● **S06.9X**   **Unspecified intracranial injury**

     ● **S06.9X0**   Unspecified intracranial injury
                 without loss of consciousness

     ● **S06.9X1**   Unspecified intracranial injury with
                 loss of consciousness of 30 minutes or
                 less

     ● **S06.9X2**   Unspecified intracranial injury with
                 loss of consciousness of 31 minutes to
                 59 minutes

     ● **S06.9X3**   Unspecified intracranial injury with
                 loss of consciousness of 1 hour to
                 5 hours 59 minutes

     ● **S06.9X4**   Unspecified intracranial injury with
                 loss of consciousness of 6 hours to
                 24 hours

     ● **S06.9X5**   Unspecified intracranial injury with
                 loss of consciousness greater than
                 24 hours with return to pre-existing
                 conscious level

     ● **S06.9X6**   Unspecified intracranial injury with
                 loss of consciousness greater than
                 24 hours without return to pre-
                 existing conscious level with patient
                 surviving

     ● **S06.9X7**   Unspecified intracranial injury with
                 loss of consciousness of any duration
                 with death due to brain injury prior
                 to regaining consciousness

     ● **S06.9X8**   Unspecified intracranial injury with
                 loss of consciousness of any duration
                 with death due to other cause prior to
                 regaining consciousness

     ● **S06.9X9**   Unspecified intracranial injury with
                 loss of consciousness of unspecified
                 duration

● **S07**   **Crushing injury of head**
    Use additional code for all associated injuries, such as:
       intracranial injuries (S06.-)
       skull fractures (S02.-)
    The appropriate 7th character is to be added to each code from
      category S07

> A   initial encounter
> D   subsequent encounter
> S   sequela

  X ● **S07.0**   Crushing injury of face
  X ● **S07.1**   Crushing injury of skull
  X ● **S07.8**   Crushing injury of other parts of head
  X ● **S07.9**   Crushing injury of head, part unspecified

● **S08**   **Avulsion and traumatic amputation of part of head**
    An amputation not identified as partial or complete should be
      coded to complete
    The appropriate 7th character is to be added to each code from
      category S08

> A   initial encounter
> D   subsequent encounter
> S   sequela

  X ● **S08.0**   **Avulsion of scalp**
   ● **S08.1**   **Traumatic amputation of ear**

     ● **S08.11**   **Complete traumatic amputation of ear**

       ● **S08.111**   Complete traumatic amputation of
                   right ear

       ● **S08.112**   Complete traumatic amputation of
                   left ear

       ● **S08.119**   Complete traumatic amputation of
                   unspecified ear

     ● **S08.12**   **Partial traumatic amputation of ear**

       ● **S08.121**   Partial traumatic amputation of right
                   ear

       ● **S08.122**   Partial traumatic amputation of left
                   ear

       ● **S08.129**   Partial traumatic amputation of
                   unspecified ear

   ● **S08.8**   **Traumatic amputation of other parts of head**

     ● **S08.81**   **Traumatic amputation of nose**

       ● **S08.811**   Complete traumatic amputation of
                   nose

       ● **S08.812**   Partial traumatic amputation of nose

     X ● **S08.89**   Traumatic amputation of other parts of head

● **S09**   **Other and unspecified injuries of head**
    The appropriate 7th character is to be added to each code from
      category S09

> A   initial encounter
> D   subsequent encounter
> S   sequela

  X ● **S09.0**   **Injury of blood vessels of head, not elsewhere classified**
      Excludes1   injury of cerebral blood vessels (S06.-)
                   injury of precerebral blood vessels (S15.-)

   ● **S09.1**   **Injury of muscle and tendon of head**
      Code also any associated open wound (S01.-)
      Excludes2   sprain to joints and ligament of head
                   (S03.9)

    X ● **S09.10**   Unspecified injury of muscle and tendon of
                 head
                   Injury of muscle and tendon of head NOS

    X ● **S09.11**   Strain of muscle and tendon of head
    X ● **S09.12**   Laceration of muscle and tendon of head
    X ● **S09.19**   Other specified injury of muscle and tendon of
                 head

   ● **S09.2**   **Traumatic rupture of ear drum**
      Excludes1   traumatic rupture of ear drum due to
                   blast injury (S09.31-)

    X ● **S09.20**   Traumatic rupture of unspecified ear drum
    X ● **S09.21**   Traumatic rupture of right ear drum
    X ● **S09.22**   Traumatic rupture of left ear drum

● **S09.3** Other specified and unspecified injury of middle and inner ear

　　Excludes1 injury to ear NOS (S09.91-)

　　Excludes2 injury to external ear (S00.4-, S01.3-, S08.1-)

　● **S09.30** Unspecified injury of middle and inner ear

　　● **S09.301** Unspecified injury of right middle and inner ear

　　● **S09.302** Unspecified injury of left middle and inner ear

　　● **S09.309** Unspecified injury of unspecified middle and inner ear

　● **S09.31** Primary blast injury of ear
　　　Blast injury of ear NOS

　　● **S09.311** Primary blast injury of right ear

　　● **S09.312** Primary blast injury of left ear

　　● **S09.313** Primary blast injury of ear, bilateral

　　● **S09.319** Primary blast injury of unspecified ear

　● **S09.39** Other specified injury of middle and inner ear
　　　Secondary blast injury to ear

　　● **S09.391** Other specified injury of right middle and inner ear

　　● **S09.392** Other specified injury of left middle and inner ear

　　● **S09.399** Other specified injury of unspecified middle and inner ear

X ● **S09.8** Other specified injuries of head

● **S09.9** Unspecified injury of face and head

　X ● **S09.90** Unspecified injury of head
　　　Head injury NOS

　　Excludes1 brain injury NOS (S06.9-)
　　　　　head injury NOS with loss of consciousness (S06.9-)
　　　　　intracranial injury NOS (S06.9-)

　X ● **S09.91** Unspecified injury of ear
　　　Injury of ear NOS

　X ● **S09.92** Unspecified injury of nose
　　　Injury of nose NOS

　X ● **S09.93** Unspecified injury of face
　　　Injury of face NOS

INJURIES TO THE NECK (S10-S19)

Includes injuries of nape
　　　injuries of supraclavicular region
　　　injuries of throat

Excludes2 burns and corrosions (T20-T32)
　　　effects of foreign body in esophagus (T18.1)
　　　effects of foreign body in larynx (T17.3)
　　　effects of foreign body in pharynx (T17.2)
　　　effects of foreign body in trachea (T17.4)
　　　frostbite (T33-T34)
　　　insect bite or sting, venomous (T63.4)

● **S10** Superficial injury of neck

The appropriate 7th character is to be added to each code from category S10

A	initial encounter
D	subsequent encounter
S	sequela

X ● **S10.0** Contusion of throat
　　　Contusion of cervical esophagus
　　　Contusion of larynx
　　　Contusion of pharynx
　　　Contusion of trachea

● **S10.1** Other and unspecified superficial injuries of throat

　X ● **S10.10** Unspecified superficial injuries of throat

　X ● **S10.11** Abrasion of throat

　X ● **S10.12** Blister (nonthermal) of throat

　X ● **S10.14** External constriction of part of throat

　X ● **S10.15** Superficial foreign body of throat
　　　Splinter in the throat

　X ● **S10.16** Insect bite (nonvenomous) of throat

　X ● **S10.17** Other superficial bite of throat

　　Excludes1 open bite of throat (S11.85)

● **S10.8** Superficial injury of other specified parts of neck

　X ● **S10.80** Unspecified superficial injury of other specified part of neck

　X ● **S10.81** Abrasion of other specified part of neck

　X ● **S10.82** Blister (nonthermal) of other specified part of neck

　X ● **S10.83** Contusion of other specified part of neck

　X ● **S10.84** External constriction of other specified part of neck

　X ● **S10.85** Superficial foreign body of other specified part of neck
　　　Splinter in other part of neck

　X ● **S10.86** Insect bite of other specified part of neck

　X ● **S10.87** Other superficial bite of other specified part of neck

　　Excludes1 open bite of other specified parts of neck (S11.85)

● **S10.9** Superficial injury of unspecified part of neck

　X ● **S10.90** Unspecified superficial injury of unspecified part of neck

　X ● **S10.91** Abrasion of unspecified part of neck

　X ● **S10.92** Blister (nonthermal) of unspecified part of neck

　X ● **S10.93** Contusion of unspecified part of neck

　X ● **S10.94** External constriction of unspecified part of neck

　X ● **S10.95** Superficial foreign body of unspecified part of neck

　X ● **S10.96** Insect bite of unspecified part of neck

　X ● **S10.97** Other superficial bite of unspecified part of neck

● **S11** Open wound of neck

Code also any associated:
　　spinal cord injury (S14.0, S14.1-)
　　wound infection

Excludes2 open fracture of vertebra (S12.- with 7th character B)

The appropriate 7th character is to be added to each code from category S11

A	initial encounter
D	subsequent encounter
S	sequela

● **S11.0** Open wound of larynx and trachea

　● **S11.01** Open wound of larynx

　　Excludes2 open wound of vocal cord (S11.03)

　　● **S11.011** Laceration without foreign body of larynx

　　● **S11.012** Laceration with foreign body of larynx

　　● **S11.013** Puncture wound without foreign body of larynx

　　● **S11.014** Puncture wound with foreign body of larynx

　　● **S11.015** Open bite of larynx
　　　　Bite of larynx NOS

　　● **S11.019** Unspecified open wound of larynx

● S11.02   Open wound of trachea
             Open wound of cervical trachea
             Open wound of trachea NOS
             Excludes2   open wound of thoracic trachea
                             (S27.5-)
     ● S11.021   Laceration without foreign body of
                 trachea
     ● S11.022   Laceration with foreign body of
                 trachea
     ● S11.023   Puncture wound without foreign
                 body of trachea
     ● S11.024   Puncture wound with foreign body of
                 trachea
     ● S11.025   Open bite of trachea
                 Bite of trachea NOS
     ● S11.029   Unspecified open wound of trachea
  ● S11.03   Open wound of vocal cord
     ● S11.031   Laceration without foreign body of
                 vocal cord
     ● S11.032   Laceration with foreign body of vocal
                 cord
     ● S11.033   Puncture wound without foreign
                 body of vocal cord
     ● S11.034   Puncture wound with foreign body of
                 vocal cord
     ● S11.035   Open bite of vocal cord
                 Bite of vocal cord NOS
     ● S11.039   Unspecified open wound of vocal
                 cord
● S11.1   Open wound of thyroid gland
  X ● S11.10   Unspecified open wound of thyroid gland
  X ● S11.11   Laceration without foreign body of thyroid
              gland
  X ● S11.12   Laceration with foreign body of thyroid gland
  X ● S11.13   Puncture wound without foreign body of
              thyroid gland
  X ● S11.14   Puncture wound with foreign body of thyroid
              gland
  X ● S11.15   Open bite of thyroid gland
              Bite of thyroid gland NOS
● S11.2   Open wound of pharynx and cervical esophagus
          Excludes1   open wound of esophagus NOS (S27.8-)
  X ● S11.20   Unspecified open wound of pharynx and
              cervical esophagus
  X ● S11.21   Laceration without foreign body of pharynx
              and cervical esophagus
  X ● S11.22   Laceration with foreign body of pharynx and
              cervical esophagus
  X ● S11.23   Puncture wound without foreign body of
              pharynx and cervical esophagus
  X ● S11.24   Puncture wound with foreign body of pharynx
              and cervical esophagus
  X ● S11.25   Open bite of pharynx and cervical esophagus
              Bite of pharynx and cervical esophagus NOS
● S11.8   Open wound of other specified parts of neck
  X ● S11.80   Unspecified open specified wound of other part
              of neck
  X ● S11.81   Laceration without foreign body of other
              specified part of neck
  X ● S11.82   Laceration with foreign body of other specified
              part of neck
  X ● S11.83   Puncture wound without foreign body of other
              specified part of neck
  X ● S11.84   Puncture wound with foreign body of other
              specified part of neck
  X ● S11.85   Open bite of other specified part of neck
              Bite of other part of neck NOS
              Excludes1   superficial bite of other specified
                             part of neck (S10.87)
  X ● S11.89   Other open wound of other part of neck

● S11.9   Open wound of unspecified part of neck
  X ● S11.90   Unspecified open wound of unspecified part of
              neck
  X ● S11.91   Laceration without foreign body of unspecified
              part of neck
  X ● S11.92   Laceration with foreign body of unspecified
              part of neck
  X ● S11.93   Puncture wound without foreign body of
              unspecified part of neck
  X ● S11.94   Puncture wound with foreign body of
              unspecified part of neck
  X ● S11.95   Open bite of unspecified part of neck
              Bite of neck NOS
              Excludes1   superficial bite of neck (S10.97)
● S12   Fracture of cervical vertebra and other parts of neck
        Note: A fracture not indicated as displaced or nondisplaced
                  should be coded to displaced
                  A fracture not indicated as open or closed should be coded to
                  closed
        Includes   fracture of cervical neural arch
                     fracture of cervical spine
                     fracture of cervical spinous process
                     fracture of cervical transverse process
                     fracture of cervical vertebral arch
                     fracture of neck
        Code first any associated cervical spinal cord injury (S14.0, S14.1-)
        The appropriate 7th character is to be added to all codes from
        subcategories S12.0-S12.6

A	initial encounter for closed fracture
B	initial encounter for open fracture
D	subsequent encounter for fracture with routine healing
G	subsequent encounter for fracture with delayed healing
K	subsequent encounter for fracture with nonunion
S	sequela

● S12.0   Fracture of first cervical vertebra
          Atlas
  ● S12.00   Unspecified fracture of first cervical vertebra
     ● S12.000   Unspecified displaced fracture of first
                 cervical vertebra
     ● S12.001   Unspecified nondisplaced fracture of
                 first cervical vertebra
  X ● S12.01   Stable burst fracture of first cervical vertebra
  X ● S12.02   Unstable burst fracture of first cervical vertebra
  ● S12.03   Posterior arch fracture of first cervical vertebra
     ● S12.030   Displaced posterior arch fracture of
                 first cervical vertebra
     ● S12.031   Nondisplaced posterior arch fracture
                 of first cervical vertebra
  ● S12.04   Lateral mass fracture of first cervical vertebra
     ● S12.040   Displaced lateral mass fracture of first
                 cervical vertebra
     ● S12.041   Nondisplaced lateral mass fracture of
                 first cervical vertebra
  ● S12.09   Other fracture of first cervical vertebra
     ● S12.090   Other displaced fracture of first
                 cervical vertebra
     ● S12.091   Other nondisplaced fracture of first
                 cervical vertebra
● S12.1   Fracture of second cervical vertebra
          Axis
  ● S12.10   Unspecified fracture of second cervical vertebra
     ● S12.100   Unspecified displaced fracture of
                 second cervical vertebra
     ● S12.101   Unspecified nondisplaced fracture of
                 second cervical vertebra

CHAPTER 19 (S00-T88)

- S12.11   Type II dens fracture
  - S12.110   Anterior displaced Type II dens fracture
  - S12.111   Posterior displaced Type II dens fracture
  - S12.112   Nondisplaced Type II dens fracture
- S12.12   Other dens fracture
  - S12.120   Other displaced dens fracture
  - S12.121   Other nondisplaced dens fracture
- S12.13   Unspecified traumatic spondylolisthesis of second cervical vertebra
  - S12.130   Unspecified traumatic displaced spondylolisthesis of second cervical vertebra
  - S12.131   Unspecified traumatic nondisplaced spondylolisthesis of second cervical vertebra
- X S12.14   Type III traumatic spondylolisthesis of second cervical vertebra
- S12.15   Other traumatic spondylolisthesis of second cervical vertebra
  - S12.150   Other traumatic displaced spondylolisthesis of second cervical vertebra
  - S12.151   Other traumatic nondisplaced spondylolisthesis of second cervical vertebra
- S12.19   Other fracture of second cervical vertebra
  - S12.190   Other displaced fracture of second cervical vertebra
  - S12.191   Other nondisplaced fracture of second cervical vertebra
- S12.2   Fracture of third cervical vertebra
  - S12.20   Unspecified fracture of third cervical vertebra
    - S12.200   Unspecified displaced fracture of third cervical vertebra
    - S12.201   Unspecified nondisplaced fracture of third cervical vertebra
  - S12.23   Unspecified traumatic spondylolisthesis of third cervical vertebra
    - S12.230   Unspecified traumatic displaced spondylolisthesis of third cervical vertebra
    - S12.231   Unspecified traumatic nondisplaced spondylolisthesis of third cervical vertebra
  - X S12.24   Type III traumatic spondylolisthesis of third cervical vertebra
  - S12.25   Other traumatic spondylolisthesis of third cervical vertebra
    - S12.250   Other traumatic displaced spondylolisthesis of third cervical vertebra
    - S12.251   Other traumatic nondisplaced spondylolisthesis of third cervical vertebra
  - S12.29   Other fracture of third cervical vertebra
    - S12.290   Other displaced fracture of third cervical vertebra
    - S12.291   Other nondisplaced fracture of third cervical vertebra
- S12.3   Fracture of fourth cervical vertebra
  - S12.30   Unspecified fracture of fourth cervical vertebra
    - S12.300   Unspecified displaced fracture of fourth cervical vertebra
    - S12.301   Unspecified nondisplaced fracture of fourth cervical vertebra

- S12.33   Unspecified traumatic spondylolisthesis of fourth cervical vertebra
  - S12.330   Unspecified traumatic displaced spondylolisthesis of fourth cervical vertebra
  - S12.331   Unspecified traumatic nondisplaced spondylolisthesis of fourth cervical vertebra
- X S12.34   Type III traumatic spondylolisthesis of fourth cervical vertebra
- S12.35   Other traumatic spondylolisthesis of fourth cervical vertebra
  - S12.350   Other traumatic displaced spondylolisthesis of fourth cervical vertebra
  - S12.351   Other traumatic nondisplaced spondylolisthesis of fourth cervical vertebra
- S12.39   Other fracture of fourth cervical vertebra
  - S12.390   Other displaced fracture of fourth cervical vertebra
  - S12.391   Other nondisplaced fracture of fourth cervical vertebra
- S12.4   Fracture of fifth cervical vertebra
  - S12.40   Unspecified fracture of fifth cervical vertebra
    - S12.400   Unspecified displaced fracture of fifth cervical vertebra
    - S12.401   Unspecified nondisplaced fracture of fifth cervical vertebra
  - S12.43   Unspecified traumatic spondylolisthesis of fifth cervical vertebra
    - S12.430   Unspecified traumatic displaced spondylolisthesis of fifth cervical vertebra
    - S12.431   Unspecified traumatic nondisplaced spondylolisthesis of fifth cervical vertebra
  - X S12.44   Type III traumatic spondylolisthesis of fifth cervical vertebra
  - S12.45   Other traumatic spondylolisthesis of fifth cervical vertebra
    - S12.450   Other traumatic displaced spondylolisthesis of fifth cervical vertebra
    - S12.451   Other traumatic nondisplaced spondylolisthesis of fifth cervical vertebra
  - S12.49   Other fracture of fifth cervical vertebra
    - S12.490   Other displaced fracture of fifth cervical vertebra
    - S12.491   Other nondisplaced fracture of fifth cervical vertebra
- S12.5   Fracture of sixth cervical vertebra
  - S12.50   Unspecified fracture of sixth cervical vertebra
    - S12.500   Unspecified displaced fracture of sixth cervical vertebra
    - S12.501   Unspecified nondisplaced fracture of sixth cervical vertebra
  - S12.53   Unspecified traumatic spondylolisthesis of sixth cervical vertebra
    - S12.530   Unspecified traumatic displaced spondylolisthesis of sixth cervical vertebra
    - S12.531   Unspecified traumatic nondisplaced spondylolisthesis of sixth cervical vertebra

▶ New   ⇒ Revised   ~~deleted~~ Deleted   Excludes 1   Excludes 2   Includes   Use additional   Code first   Code also   Key words

OGCR Official Guidelines   X Assign placeholder X   ● Use Additional Character(s)   ▶ Manifestation Code   **Coding Clinic**

X ● **S12.54**   **Type III** traumatic spondylolisthesis of sixth cervical vertebra

● **S12.55**   **Other** traumatic spondylolisthesis of sixth cervical vertebra

   ● **S12.550**   Other traumatic **displaced** spondylolisthesis of sixth cervical vertebra

   ● **S12.551**   Other traumatic **nondisplaced** spondylolisthesis of sixth cervical vertebra

● **S12.59**   Other fracture of sixth cervical vertebra

   ● **S12.590**   Other **displaced** fracture of sixth cervical vertebra

   ● **S12.591**   Other **nondisplaced** fracture of sixth cervical vertebra

● **S12.6**   Fracture of **seventh** cervical vertebra

   S12.60   **Unspecified** fracture of seventh cervical vertebra

     ● **S12.600**   Unspecified **displaced** fracture of seventh cervical vertebra

     ● **S12.601**   Unspecified **nondisplaced** fracture of seventh cervical vertebra

   ● **S12.63**   **Unspecified** traumatic spondylolisthesis of seventh cervical vertebra

     ● **S12.630**   Unspecified traumatic **displaced** spondylolisthesis of seventh cervical vertebra

     ● **S12.631**   Unspecified traumatic **nondisplaced** spondylolisthesis of seventh cervical vertebra

X ● **S12.64**   **Type III** traumatic spondylolisthesis of seventh cervical vertebra

● **S12.65**   **Other** traumatic spondylolisthesis of seventh cervical vertebra

   ● **S12.650**   Other traumatic **displaced** spondylolisthesis of seventh cervical vertebra

   ● **S12.651**   Other traumatic **nondisplaced** spondylolisthesis of seventh cervical vertebra

● **S12.69**   Other fracture of seventh cervical vertebra

   ● **S12.690**   Other **displaced** fracture of seventh cervical vertebra

   ● **S12.691**   Other **nondisplaced** fracture of seventh cervical vertebra

X ● **S12.8**   Fracture of **other parts** of neck

   Hyoid bone   Thyroid cartilage
   Larynx   Trachea

   The appropriate 7th character is to be added to code S12.8

A	initial encounter
D	subsequent encounter
S	sequela

X ● **S12.9**   Fracture of neck, **unspecified**

   Fracture of neck NOS
   Fracture of cervical spine NOS
   Fracture of cervical vertebra NOS

   The appropriate 7th character is to be added to code S12.9

A	initial encounter
D	subsequent encounter
S	sequela

● **S13**   Dislocation and sprain of joints and ligaments at neck level

   Includes   avulsion of joint or ligament at neck level
     laceration of cartilage, joint or ligament at neck level
     sprain of cartilage, joint or ligament at neck level
     traumatic hemarthrosis of joint or ligament at neck level
     traumatic rupture of joint or ligament at neck level
     traumatic subluxation of joint or ligament at neck level
     traumatic tear of joint or ligament at neck level

   Code also any associated open wound

   Excludes2   strain of muscle or tendon at neck level (S16.1)

   The appropriate 7th character is to be added to each code from category S13

A	initial encounter
D	subsequent encounter
S	sequela

X ● **S13.0**   **Traumatic rupture** of cervical intervertebral disc

   Excludes1   rupture or displacement (nontraumatic) of cervical intervertebral disc NOS (M50.-)

● **S13.1**   Subluxation and dislocation of **cervical vertebrae**

   Code also any associated:
     open wound of neck (S11.-)
     spinal cord injury (S14.1-)

   Excludes2   fracture of cervical vertebrae (S12.0-S12.3-)

   ● **S13.10**   Subluxation and dislocation of **unspecified** cervical vertebrae

     ● **S13.100**   **Subluxation** of unspecified cervical vertebrae

     ● **S13.101**   **Dislocation** of unspecified cervical vertebrae

   ● **S13.11**   Subluxation and dislocation of **C0/C1** cervical vertebrae

     Subluxation and dislocation of atlantooccipital joint
     Subluxation and dislocation of atloidooccipital joint
     Subluxation and dislocation of occipitoatloid joint

     ● **S13.110**   **Subluxation** of C0/C1 cervical vertebrae

     ● **S13.111**   **Dislocation** of C0/C1 cervical vertebrae

   ● **S13.12**   Subluxation and dislocation of **C1/C2** cervical vertebrae

     Subluxation and dislocation of atlantoaxial joint

     ● **S13.120**   **Subluxation** of C1/C2 cervical vertebrae

     ● **S13.121**   **Dislocation** of C1/C2 cervical vertebrae

   ● **S13.13**   Subluxation and dislocation of **C2/C3** cervical vertebrae

     ● **S13.130**   **Subluxation** of C2/C3 cervical vertebrae

     ● **S13.131**   **Dislocation** of C2/C3 cervical vertebrae

   ● **S13.14**   Subluxation and dislocation of **C3/C4** cervical vertebrae

     ● **S13.140**   **Subluxation** of C3/C4 cervical vertebrae

     ● **S13.141**   **Dislocation** of C3/C4 cervical vertebrae

● **S13.15** Subluxation and dislocation of C4/C5 cervical vertebrae
- ● **S13.150** Subluxation of C4/C5 cervical vertebrae
- ● **S13.151** Dislocation of C4/C5 cervical vertebrae

● **S13.16** Subluxation and dislocation of C5/C6 cervical vertebrae
- ● **S13.160** Subluxation of C5/C6 cervical vertebrae
- ● **S13.161** Dislocation of C5/C6 cervical vertebrae

● **S13.17** Subluxation and dislocation of C6/C7 cervical vertebrae
- ● **S13.170** Subluxation of C6/C7 cervical vertebrae
- ● **S13.171** Dislocation of C6/C7 cervical vertebrae

● **S13.18** Subluxation and dislocation of C7/T1 cervical vertebrae
- ● **S13.180** Subluxation of C7/T1 cervical vertebrae
- ● **S13.181** Dislocation of C7/T1 cervical vertebrae

● **S13.2** Dislocation of other and unspecified parts of neck
- X ● **S13.20** Dislocation of unspecified parts of neck
- X ● **S13.29** Dislocation of other parts of neck

X ● **S13.4** Sprain of ligaments of cervical spine
Sprain of anterior longitudinal (ligament), cervical
Sprain of atlanto-axial (joints)
Sprain of atlanto-occipital (joints)
Whiplash injury of cervical spine

X ● **S13.5** Sprain of thyroid region
Sprain of cricoarytenoid (joint) (ligament)
Sprain of cricothyroid (joint) (ligament)
Sprain of thyroid cartilage

X ● **S13.8** Sprain of joints and ligaments of other parts of neck

X ● **S13.9** Sprain of joints and ligaments of unspecified parts of neck

● **S14** Injury of nerves and spinal cord at neck level
Note: Code to highest level of cervical cord injury
Code also any associated:
fracture of cervical vertebra (S12.0--S12.6.-)
open wound of neck (S11.-)
transient paralysis (R29.5)

The appropriate 7th character is to be added to each code from category S14

A	initial encounter
D	subsequent encounter
S	sequela

X ● **S14.0** Concussion and edema of cervical spinal cord

● **S14.1** Other and unspecified injuries of cervical spinal cord
- ● **S14.10** Unspecified injury of cervical spinal cord
  - ● **S14.101** Unspecified injury at C1 level of cervical spinal cord
  - ● **S14.102** Unspecified injury at C2 level of cervical spinal cord
  - ● **S14.103** Unspecified injury at C3 level of cervical spinal cord
  - ● **S14.104** Unspecified injury at C4 level of cervical spinal cord
  - ● **S14.105** Unspecified injury at C5 level of cervical spinal cord
  - ● **S14.106** Unspecified injury at C6 level of cervical spinal cord
  - ● **S14.107** Unspecified injury at C7 level of cervical spinal cord
  - ● **S14.108** Unspecified injury at C8 level of cervical spinal cord
  - ● **S14.109** Unspecified injury at unspecified level of cervical spinal cord
    Injury of cervical spinal cord NOS

● **S14.11** Complete lesion of cervical spinal cord
- ● **S14.111** Complete lesion at C1 level of cervical spinal cord
- ● **S14.112** Complete lesion at C2 level of cervical spinal cord
- ● **S14.113** Complete lesion at C3 level of cervical spinal cord
- ● **S14.114** Complete lesion at C4 level of cervical spinal cord
- ● **S14.115** Complete lesion at C5 level of cervical spinal cord
- ● **S14.116** Complete lesion at C6 level of cervical spinal cord
- ● **S14.117** Complete lesion at C7 level of cervical spinal cord
- ● **S14.118** Complete lesion at C8 level of cervical spinal cord
- ● **S14.119** Complete lesion at unspecified level of cervical spinal cord

● **S14.12** Central cord syndrome of cervical spinal cord
- ● **S14.121** Central cord syndrome at C1 level of cervical spinal cord
- ● **S14.122** Central cord syndrome at C2 level of cervical spinal cord
- ● **S14.123** Central cord syndrome at C3 level of cervical spinal cord
- ● **S14.124** Central cord syndrome at C4 level of cervical spinal cord
- ● **S14.125** Central cord syndrome at C5 level of cervical spinal cord
- ● **S14.126** Central cord syndrome at C6 level of cervical spinal cord
- ● **S14.127** Central cord syndrome at C7 level of cervical spinal cord
- ● **S14.128** Central cord syndrome at C8 level of cervical spinal cord
- ● **S14.129** Central cord syndrome at unspecified level of cervical spinal cord

● **S14.13** Anterior cord syndrome of cervical spinal cord
- ● **S14.131** Anterior cord syndrome at C1 level of cervical spinal cord
- ● **S14.132** Anterior cord syndrome at C2 level of cervical spinal cord
- ● **S14.133** Anterior cord syndrome at C3 level of cervical spinal cord
- ● **S14.134** Anterior cord syndrome at C4 level of cervical spinal cord
- ● **S14.135** Anterior cord syndrome at C5 level of cervical spinal cord
- ● **S14.136** Anterior cord syndrome at C6 level of cervical spinal cord
- ● **S14.137** Anterior cord syndrome at C7 level of cervical spinal cord
- ● **S14.138** Anterior cord syndrome at C8 level of cervical spinal cord
- ● **S14.139** Anterior cord syndrome at unspecified level of cervical spinal cord

▶ New ⇒ Revised ~~deleted~~ Deleted Excludes 1 Excludes 2 Includes Use additional Code first Code also Key words
OGCR Official Guidelines X Assign placeholder X ● Use Additional Character(s) ▶ Manifestation Code **Coding Clinic**

● S14.14   **Brown-Séquard syndrome** of cervical spinal cord
  ● S14.141   Brown-Séquard syndrome at **C1 level** of cervical spinal cord
  ● S14.142   Brown-Séquard syndrome at **C2 level** of cervical spinal cord
  ● S14.143   Brown-Séquard syndrome at **C3 level** of cervical spinal cord
  ● S14.144   Brown-Séquard syndrome at **C4 level** of cervical spinal cord
  ● S14.145   Brown-Séquard syndrome at **C5 level** of cervical spinal cord
  ● S14.146   Brown-Séquard syndrome at **C6 level** of cervical spinal cord
  ● S14.147   Brown-Séquard syndrome at **C7 level** of cervical spinal cord
  ● S14.148   Brown-Séquard syndrome at **C8 level** of cervical spinal cord
  ● S14.149   Brown-Séquard syndrome at **unspecified level** of cervical spinal cord

● S14.15   **Other incomplete lesions** of cervical spinal cord
  Incomplete lesion of cervical spinal cord NOS
  Posterior cord syndrome of cervical spinal cord
  ● S14.151   Other incomplete lesion at **C1 level** of cervical spinal cord
  ● S14.152   Other incomplete lesion at **C2 level** of cervical spinal cord
  ● S14.153   Other incomplete lesion at **C3 level** of cervical spinal cord
  ● S14.154   Other incomplete lesion at **C4 level** of cervical spinal cord
  ● S14.155   Other incomplete lesion at **C5 level** of cervical spinal cord
  ● S14.156   Other incomplete lesion at **C6 level** of cervical spinal cord
  ● S14.157   Other incomplete lesion at **C7 level** of cervical spinal cord
  ● S14.158   Other incomplete lesion at **C8 level** of cervical spinal cord
  ● S14.159   Other incomplete lesion at **unspecified level** of cervical spinal cord

X ● S14.2   Injury of **nerve root of cervical spine**
X ● S14.3   Injury of **brachial plexus**
X ● S14.4   Injury of **peripheral nerves of neck**
X ● S14.5   Injury of **cervical sympathetic nerves**
X ● S14.8   Injury of **other** specified nerves of neck
X ● S14.9   Injury of **unspecified** nerves of neck

● S15   **Injury of blood vessels at neck level**
  Code also any associated open wound (S11.-)
  The appropriate 7th character is to be added to each code from category S15

> | A | initial encounter |
> |---|---|
> | D | subsequent encounter |
> | S | sequela |

● S15.0   **Injury of carotid artery** of neck
  Injury of carotid artery (common) (external) (internal, extracranial portion)
  Injury of carotid artery NOS
    Excludes1   injury of internal carotid artery, intracranial portion (S06.8)
  ● S15.00   **Unspecified injury** of carotid artery
    ● S15.001   Unspecified injury of **right carotid** artery
    ● S15.002   Unspecified injury of **left carotid** artery
    ● S15.009   Unspecified injury of **unspecified** carotid artery

● S15.01   **Minor laceration** of carotid artery
  Incomplete transection of carotid artery
  Laceration of carotid artery NOS
  Superficial laceration of carotid artery
  ● S15.011   Minor laceration of **right carotid** artery
  ● S15.012   Minor laceration of **left carotid** artery
  ● S15.019   Minor laceration of **unspecified** carotid artery

● S15.02   **Major laceration** of carotid artery
  Complete transection of carotid artery
  Traumatic rupture of carotid artery
  ● S15.021   Major laceration of **right carotid** artery
  ● S15.022   Major laceration of **left carotid** artery
  ● S15.029   Major laceration of **unspecified** carotid artery

● S15.09   **Other** specified injury of carotid artery
  ● S15.091   Other specified injury of **right carotid** artery
  ● S15.092   Other specified injury of **left carotid** artery
  ● S15.099   Other specified injury of **unspecified** carotid artery

● S15.1   Injury of **vertebral artery**
  ● S15.10   **Unspecified** injury of vertebral artery
    ● S15.101   Unspecified injury of **right** vertebral artery
    ● S15.102   Unspecified injury of **left** vertebral artery
    ● S15.109   Unspecified injury of **unspecified** vertebral artery

  ● S15.11   **Minor laceration** of vertebral artery
    Incomplete transection of vertebral artery
    Laceration of vertebral artery NOS
    Superficial laceration of vertebral artery
    ● S15.111   Minor laceration of **right** vertebral artery
    ● S15.112   Minor laceration of **left** vertebral artery
    ● S15.119   Minor laceration of **unspecified** vertebral artery

  ● S15.12   **Major laceration** of vertebral artery
    Complete transection of vertebral artery
    Traumatic rupture of vertebral artery
    ● S15.121   Major laceration of **right** vertebral artery
    ● S15.122   Major laceration of **left** vertebral artery
    ● S15.129   Major laceration of **unspecified** vertebral artery

  ● S15.19   **Other** specified injury of vertebral artery
    ● S15.191   Other specified injury of **right** vertebral artery
    ● S15.192   Other specified injury of **left** vertebral artery
    ● S15.199   Other specified injury of **unspecified** vertebral artery

● S15.2   Injury of **external jugular vein**
  ● S15.20   **Unspecified** injury of external jugular vein
    ● S15.201   Unspecified injury of **right** external jugular vein
    ● S15.202   Unspecified injury of **left** external jugular vein
    ● S15.209   Unspecified injury of **unspecified** external jugular vein

CHAPTER 19 (S00-T88)

CHAPTER 19 (S00-T88)

● S15.21   **Minor laceration** of external jugular vein
    Incomplete transection of external jugular vein
    Laceration of external jugular vein NOS
    Superficial laceration of external jugular vein
  ● S15.211   **Minor laceration** of **right** external jugular vein
  ● S15.212   **Minor laceration** of **left** external jugular vein
  ● S15.219   **Minor laceration** of **unspecified** external jugular vein
● S15.22   **Major laceration** of external jugular vein
    Complete transection of external jugular vein
    Traumatic rupture of external jugular vein
  ● S15.221   **Major laceration** of **right** external jugular vein
  ● S15.222   **Major laceration** of **left** external jugular vein
  ● S15.229   **Major laceration** of **unspecified** external jugular vein
● S15.29   **Other** specified injury of external jugular vein
  ● S15.291   **Other** specified injury of **right** external jugular vein
  ● S15.292   **Other** specified injury of **left** external jugular vein
  ● S15.299   **Other** specified injury of **unspecified** external jugular vein
● S15.3   Injury of **internal jugular vein**
  ● S15.30   **Unspecified** injury of internal jugular vein
    ● S15.301   **Unspecified** injury of **right** internal jugular vein
    ● S15.302   **Unspecified** injury of **left** internal jugular vein
    ● S15.309   **Unspecified** injury of **unspecified** internal jugular vein
  ● S15.31   **Minor laceration** of internal jugular vein
    Incomplete transection of internal jugular vein
    Laceration of internal jugular vein NOS
    Superficial laceration of internal jugular vein
    ● S15.311   **Minor laceration** of **right** internal jugular vein
    ● S15.312   **Minor laceration** of **left** internal jugular vein
    ● S15.319   **Minor laceration** of **unspecified** internal jugular vein
  ● S15.32   **Major laceration** of internal jugular vein
    Complete transection of internal jugular vein
    Traumatic rupture of internal jugular vein
    ● S15.321   **Major laceration** of **right** internal jugular vein
    ● S15.322   **Major laceration** of **left** internal jugular vein
    ● S15.329   **Major laceration** of **unspecified** internal jugular vein
  ● S15.39   **Other** specified injury of internal jugular vein
    ● S15.391   **Other** specified injury of **right** internal jugular vein
    ● S15.392   **Other** specified injury of **left** internal jugular vein
    ● S15.399   **Other** specified injury of **unspecified** internal jugular vein
X ● S15.8   Injury of **other** specified blood vessels at neck level
X ● S15.9   Injury of **unspecified** blood vessel at neck level

● S16   Injury of muscle, fascia and tendon at neck level
    Code also any associated open wound (S11.-)
    Excludes2   sprain of joint or ligament at neck level (S13.9)
    The appropriate 7th character is to be added to each code from category S16

A	initial encounter
D	subsequent encounter
S	sequela

X ● S16.1   **Strain** of muscle, fascia and tendon at neck level
X ● S16.2   **Laceration** of muscle, fascia and tendon at neck level
X ● S16.8   **Other** specified injury of muscle, fascia and tendon at neck level
X ● S16.9   **Unspecified** injury of muscle, fascia and tendon at neck level

● S17   Crushing injury of neck
    Use additional code for all associated injuries, such as:
      injury of blood vessels (S15.-)
      open wound of neck (S11.-)
      spinal cord injury (S14.0, S14.1-)
      vertebral fracture (S12.0--S12.3-)
    The appropriate 7th character is to be added to each code from category S17

A	initial encounter
D	subsequent encounter
S	sequela

X ● S17.0   Crushing injury of **larynx and trachea**
X ● S17.8   Crushing injury of **other** specified parts of neck
X ● S17.9   Crushing injury of neck, part **unspecified**

● S19   Other and unspecified injuries of neck
    The appropriate 7th character is to be added to each code from category S19

A	initial encounter
D	subsequent encounter
S	sequela

  ● S19.8   **Other** specified injuries of neck
    X ● S19.80   Other specified injuries of **unspecified** part of neck
    X ● S19.81   Other specified injuries of **larynx**
    X ● S19.82   Other specified injuries of **cervical trachea**
      Excludes2   other specified injury of thoracic trachea (S27.5-)
    X ● S19.83   Other specified injuries of **vocal cord**
    X ● S19.84   Other specified injuries of **thyroid gland**
    X ● S19.85   Other specified injuries of **pharynx and cervical esophagus**
    X ● S19.89   **Other** specified injuries of other specified part of neck
X ● S19.9   **Unspecified** injury of neck

▶ New   ⇛ Revised   ~~deleted~~ Deleted   Excludes 1   Excludes 2   Includes   Use additional   Code first   Code also   Key words
OGCR Official Guidelines   X Assign placeholder X   ● Use Additional Character(s)   ▶ Manifestation Code   **Coding Clinic**

INJURIES TO THE THORAX (S20-S29)

Includes   injuries of breast
injuries of chest (wall)
injuries of interscapular area

Excludes2   burns and corrosions (T20-T32)
effects of foreign body in bronchus (T17.5)
effects of foreign body in esophagus (T18.1)
effects of foreign body in lung (T17.8)
effects of foreign body in trachea (T17.4)
frostbite (T33-T34)
injuries of axilla
injuries of clavicle
injuries of scapular region
injuries of shoulder
insect bite or sting, venomous (T63.4)

● **S20**   **Superficial injury of thorax**

The appropriate 7th character is to be added to each code from category S20

A	initial encounter
D	subsequent encounter
S	sequela

● **S20.0**   **Contusion of breast**

X ● **S20.00**   Contusion of breast, unspecified breast

X ● **S20.01**   Contusion of right breast

X ● **S20.02**   Contusion of left breast

● **S20.1**   **Other and unspecified superficial injuries of breast**

● **S20.10**   Unspecified superficial injuries of breast

     ● **S20.101**   Unspecified superficial injuries of breast, right breast

     ● **S20.102**   Unspecified superficial injuries of breast, left breast

     ● **S20.109**   Unspecified superficial injuries of breast, unspecified breast

● **S20.11**   Abrasion of breast

     ● **S20.111**   Abrasion of breast, right breast

     ● **S20.112**   Abrasion of breast, left breast

     ● **S20.119**   Abrasion of breast, unspecified breast

● **S20.12**   Blister (nonthermal) of breast

     ● **S20.121**   Blister (nonthermal) of breast, right breast

     ● **S20.122**   Blister (nonthermal) of breast, left breast

     ● **S20.129**   Blister (nonthermal) of breast, unspecified breast

● **S20.14**   External constriction of part of breast

     ● **S20.141**   External constriction of part of breast, right breast

     ● **S20.142**   External constriction of part of breast, left breast

     ● **S20.149**   External constriction of part of breast, unspecified breast

● **S20.15**   Superficial foreign body of breast
Splinter in the breast

     ● **S20.151**   Superficial foreign body of breast, right breast

     ● **S20.152**   Superficial foreign body of breast, left breast

     ● **S20.159**   Superficial foreign body of breast, unspecified breast

● **S20.16**   Insect bite (nonvenomous) of breast

     ● **S20.161**   Insect bite (nonvenomous) of breast, right breast

     ● **S20.162**   Insect bite (nonvenomous) of breast, left breast

     ● **S20.169**   Insect bite (nonvenomous) of breast, unspecified breast

● **S20.17**   Other superficial bite of breast

Excludes1   open bite of breast (S21.05-)

     ● **S20.171**   Other superficial bite of breast, right breast

     ● **S20.172**   Other superficial bite of breast, left breast

     ● **S20.179**   Other superficial bite of breast, unspecified breast

● **S20.2**   **Contusion of thorax**

X ● **S20.20**   Contusion of thorax, unspecified

● **S20.21**   Contusion of front wall of thorax

     ● **S20.211**   Contusion of right front wall of thorax

     ● **S20.212**   Contusion of left front wall of thorax

     ● **S20.219**   Contusion of unspecified front wall of thorax

● **S20.22**   Contusion of back wall of thorax

     ● **S20.221**   Contusion of right back wall of thorax

     ● **S20.222**   Contusion of left back wall of thorax

     ● **S20.229**   Contusion of unspecified back wall of thorax

● **S20.3**   **Other and unspecified superficial injuries of front wall of thorax**

● **S20.30**   Unspecified superficial injuries of front wall of thorax

     ● **S20.301**   Unspecified superficial injuries of right front wall of thorax

     ● **S20.302**   Unspecified superficial injuries of left front wall of thorax

     ● **S20.309**   Unspecified superficial injuries of unspecified front wall of thorax

● **S20.31**   Abrasion of front wall of thorax

     ● **S20.311**   Abrasion of right front wall of thorax

     ● **S20.312**   Abrasion of left front wall of thorax

     ● **S20.319**   Abrasion of unspecified front wall of thorax

● **S20.32**   Blister (nonthermal) of front wall of thorax

     ● **S20.321**   Blister (nonthermal) of right front wall of thorax

     ● **S20.322**   Blister (nonthermal) of left front wall of thorax

     ● **S20.329**   Blister (nonthermal) of unspecified front wall of thorax

● **S20.34**   External constriction of front wall of thorax

     ● **S20.341**   External constriction of right front wall of thorax

     ● **S20.342**   External constriction of left front wall of thorax

     ● **S20.349**   External constriction of unspecified front wall of thorax

● **S20.35**   Superficial foreign body of front wall of thorax
Splinter in front wall of thorax

     ● **S20.351**   Superficial foreign body of right front wall of thorax

     ● **S20.352**   Superficial foreign body of left front wall of thorax

     ● **S20.359**   Superficial foreign body of unspecified front wall of thorax

● **S20.36**   Insect bite (nonvenomous) of front wall of thorax

     ● **S20.361**   Insect bite (nonvenomous) of right front wall of thorax

     ● **S20.362**   Insect bite (nonvenomous) of left front wall of thorax

     ● **S20.369**   Insect bite (nonvenomous) of unspecified front wall of thorax

CHAPTER 19 (S00-T88)

● S20.37   Other superficial bite of front wall of thorax
            Excludes1   open bite of front wall of thorax
                             (S21.14)
     ● S20.371   Other superficial bite of **right** front
                  wall of thorax
     ● S20.372   Other superficial bite of **left** front
                  wall of thorax
     ● S20.379   Other superficial bite of **unspecified**
                  front wall of thorax
● S20.4   Other and unspecified superficial injuries of **back wall**
           of thorax
  ● S20.40   **Unspecified** superficial injuries of back wall of
              thorax
     ● S20.401   Unspecified superficial injuries of
                  right back wall of thorax
     ● S20.402   Unspecified superficial injuries of **left**
                  back wall of thorax
     ● S20.409   Unspecified superficial injuries of
                  unspecified back wall of thorax
  ● S20.41   **Abrasion** of back wall of thorax
     ● S20.411   Abrasion of **right** back wall of thorax
     ● S20.412   Abrasion of **left** back wall of thorax
     ● S20.419   Abrasion of **unspecified** back wall of
                  thorax
  ● S20.42   **Blister (nonthermal)** of back wall of thorax
     ● S20.421   Blister (nonthermal) of **right** back
                  wall of thorax
     ● S20.422   Blister (nonthermal) of **left** back wall
                  of thorax
     ● S20.429   Blister (nonthermal) of **unspecified**
                  back wall of thorax
  ● S20.44   **External constriction** of back wall of thorax
     ● S20.441   External constriction of **right** back
                  wall of thorax
     ● S20.442   External constriction of **left** back wall
                  of thorax
     ● S20.449   External constriction of **unspecified**
                  back wall of thorax
  ● S20.45   **Superficial foreign body** of back wall of thorax
              Splinter of back wall of thorax
     ● S20.451   Superficial foreign body of **right** back
                  wall of thorax
     ● S20.452   Superficial foreign body of **left** back
                  wall of thorax
     ● S20.459   Superficial foreign body of
                  unspecified back wall of thorax
  ● S20.46   **Insect bite (nonvenomous)** of back wall of
              thorax
     ● S20.461   Insect bite (nonvenomous) of **right**
                  back wall of thorax
     ● S20.462   Insect bite (nonvenomous) of **left**
                  back wall of thorax
     ● S20.469   Insect bite (nonvenomous) of
                  unspecified back wall of thorax
  ● S20.47   **Other superficial bite** of back wall of thorax
              Excludes1   open bite of back wall of thorax
                               (S21.24)
     ● S20.471   Other superficial bite of **right** back
                  wall of thorax
     ● S20.472   Other superficial bite of **left** back wall
                  of thorax
     ● S20.479   Other superficial bite of **unspecified**
                  back wall of thorax

● S20.9   Superficial injury of unspecified parts of thorax
           Excludes1   contusion of thorax NOS (S20.20)
  X ● S20.90   **Unspecified** superficial injury of unspecified
                parts of thorax
                Superficial injury of thoracic wall NOS
  X ● S20.91   **Abrasion** of unspecified parts of thorax
  X ● S20.92   **Blister (nonthermal)** of unspecified parts of
                thorax
  X ● S20.94   **External constriction** of unspecified parts of
                thorax
  X ● S20.95   **Superficial foreign body** of unspecified parts of
                thorax
                Splinter in thorax NOS
  X ● S20.96   **Insect bite (nonvenomous)** of unspecified parts
                of thorax
  X ● S20.97   Other superficial bite of unspecified parts of
                thorax
                Excludes1   open bite of thorax NOS (S21.95)
● S21   Open wound of thorax
         Code also any associated injury such as:
            injury of heart (S26.-)
            injury of intrathoracic organs (S27.-)
            rib fracture (S22.3-, S22.4-)
            spinal cord injury (S24.0-, S24.1-)
            traumatic hemothorax (S27.1)
            traumatic hemopneumothorax (S27.3)
            traumatic pneumothorax (S27.0)
            wound infection
         Excludes1   traumatic amputation (partial) of thorax (S28.1)
         The appropriate 7th character is to be added to each code from
            category S21

         | A | initial encounter |
         | D | subsequent encounter |
         | S | sequela |

  ● S21.0   Open wound of breast
     ● S21.00   **Unspecified** open wound of breast
        ● S21.001   Unspecified open wound of **right**
                     breast
        ● S21.002   Unspecified open wound of **left**
                     breast
        ● S21.009   Unspecified open wound of
                     unspecified breast
     ● S21.01   Laceration **without foreign body** of breast
        ● S21.011   Laceration without foreign body of
                     right breast
        ● S21.012   Laceration without foreign body of
                     left breast
        ● S21.019   Laceration without foreign body of
                     unspecified breast
     ● S21.02   Laceration **with foreign body** of breast
        ● S21.021   Laceration with foreign body of **right**
                     breast
        ● S21.022   Laceration with foreign body of **left**
                     breast
        ● S21.029   Laceration with foreign body of
                     unspecified breast

Item 19–1   Pneumothorax is a collection of gas (positive air pressure) in
the pleural space resulting in the lung collapsing. A **tension pneumothorax**
is life-threatening and is a result of air in the pleural space causing a displacement
in the mediastinal structures and cardiopulmonary function compromise. A
traumatic pneumothorax results from blunt or penetrating injury that
disrupts the parietal/visceral pleura. **Hemothorax** is blood or bloody fluid in
the pleural cavity as a result of traumatic blood vessel rupture or inflammation of
the lungs from pneumonia.

▶ New   ⇒ Revised   ~~deleted~~ Deleted   Excludes 1   Excludes 2   Includes   Use additional   Code first   Code also   Key words

OGCR Official Guidelines   X Assign placeholder X   ● Use Additional Character(s)   ▷ Manifestation Code   **Coding Clinic**

- ⬤ S21.03 Puncture wound without foreign body of breast
  - ⬤ S21.031 Puncture wound without foreign body of right breast
  - ⬤ S21.032 Puncture wound without foreign body of left breast
  - ⬤ S21.039 Puncture wound without foreign body of unspecified breast
- ⬤ S21.04 Puncture wound with foreign body of breast
  - ⬤ S21.041 Puncture wound with foreign body of right breast
  - ⬤ S21.042 Puncture wound with foreign body of left breast
  - ⬤ S21.049 Puncture wound with foreign body of unspecified breast
- ⬤ S21.05 Open bite of breast
  Bite of breast NOS
  > **Excludes1** superficial bite of breast (S20.17)
  - ⬤ S21.051 Open bite of right breast
  - ⬤ S21.052 Open bite of left breast
  - ⬤ S21.059 Open bite of unspecified breast
- ⬤ S21.1 Open wound of front wall of thorax without penetration into thoracic cavity
  Open wound of chest without penetration into thoracic cavity
  - ⬤ S21.10 Unspecified open wound of front wall of thorax without penetration into thoracic cavity
    - ⬤ S21.101 Unspecified open wound of right front wall of thorax without penetration into thoracic cavity
    - ⬤ S21.102 Unspecified open wound of left front wall of thorax without penetration into thoracic cavity
    - ⬤ S21.109 Unspecified open wound of unspecified front wall of thorax without penetration into thoracic cavity
  - ⬤ S21.11 Laceration without foreign body of front wall of thorax without penetration into thoracic cavity
    - ⬤ S21.111 Laceration without foreign body of right front wall of thorax without penetration into thoracic cavity
    - ⬤ S21.112 Laceration without foreign body of left front wall of thorax without penetration into thoracic cavity
    - ⬤ S21.119 Laceration without foreign body of unspecified front wall of thorax without penetration into thoracic cavity
  - ⬤ S21.12 Laceration with foreign body of front wall of thorax without penetration into thoracic cavity
    - ⬤ S21.121 Laceration with foreign body of right front wall of thorax without penetration into thoracic cavity
    - ⬤ S21.122 Laceration with foreign body of left front wall of thorax without penetration into thoracic cavity
    - ⬤ S21.129 Laceration with foreign body of unspecified front wall of thorax without penetration into thoracic cavity

- ⬤ S21.13 Puncture wound without foreign body of front wall of thorax without penetration into thoracic cavity
  - ⬤ S21.131 Puncture wound without foreign body of right front wall of thorax without penetration into thoracic cavity
  - ⬤ S21.132 Puncture wound without foreign body of left front wall of thorax without penetration into thoracic cavity
  - ⬤ S21.139 Puncture wound without foreign body of unspecified front wall of thorax without penetration into thoracic cavity
- ⬤ S21.14 Puncture wound with foreign body of front wall of thorax without penetration into thoracic cavity
  - ⬤ S21.141 Puncture wound with foreign body of right front wall of thorax without penetration into thoracic cavity
  - ⬤ S21.142 Puncture wound with foreign body of left front wall of thorax without penetration into thoracic cavity
  - ⬤ S21.149 Puncture wound with foreign body of unspecified front wall of thorax without penetration into thoracic cavity
- ⬤ S21.15 Open bite of front wall of thorax without penetration into thoracic cavity
  Bite of front wall of thorax NOS
  > **Excludes1** superficial bite of front wall of thorax (S20.37)
  - ⬤ S21.151 Open bite of right front wall of thorax without penetration into thoracic cavity
  - ⬤ S21.152 Open bite of left front wall of thorax without penetration into thoracic cavity
  - ⬤ S21.159 Open bite of unspecified front wall of thorax without penetration into thoracic cavity
- ⬤ S21.2 Open wound of back wall of thorax without penetration into thoracic cavity
  - ⬤ S21.20 Unspecified open wound of back wall of thorax without penetration into thoracic cavity
    - ⬤ S21.201 Unspecified open wound of right back wall of thorax without penetration into thoracic cavity
    - ⬤ S21.202 Unspecified open wound of left back wall of thorax without penetration into thoracic cavity
    - ⬤ S21.209 Unspecified open wound of unspecified back wall of thorax without penetration into thoracic cavity
  - ⬤ S21.21 Laceration without foreign body of back wall of thorax without penetration into thoracic cavity
    - ⬤ S21.211 Laceration without foreign body of right back wall of thorax without penetration into thoracic cavity
    - ⬤ S21.212 Laceration without foreign body of left back wall of thorax without penetration into thoracic cavity
    - ⬤ S21.219 Laceration without foreign body of unspecified back wall of thorax without penetration into thoracic cavity

CHAPTER 19 (S00-T88)

CHAPTER 19 (S00-T88)

● S21.22   **Laceration with foreign body** of back wall of thorax without penetration into thoracic cavity

  ● S21.221   Laceration with foreign body of **right** back wall of thorax without penetration into thoracic cavity

  ● S21.222   Laceration with foreign body of **left** back wall of thorax without penetration into thoracic cavity

  ● S21.229   Laceration with foreign body of **unspecified** back wall of thorax without penetration into thoracic cavity

● S21.23   **Puncture wound without foreign body** of back wall of thorax without penetration into thoracic cavity

  ● S21.231   Puncture wound without foreign body of **right** back wall of thorax without penetration into thoracic cavity

  ● S21.232   Puncture wound without foreign body of **left** back wall of thorax without penetration into thoracic cavity

  ● S21.239   Puncture wound without foreign body of **unspecified** back wall of thorax without penetration into thoracic cavity

● S21.24   **Puncture wound with foreign body** of back wall of thorax without penetration into thoracic cavity

  ● S21.241   Puncture wound with foreign body of **right** back wall of thorax without penetration into thoracic cavity

  ● S21.242   Puncture wound with foreign body of **left** back wall of thorax without penetration into thoracic cavity

  ● S21.249   Puncture wound with foreign body of **unspecified** back wall of thorax without penetration into thoracic cavity

● S21.25   Open bite of back wall of thorax without penetration into thoracic cavity
       Bite of back wall of thorax NOS

     Excludes1   superficial bite of back wall of thorax (S20.47)

  ● S21.251   Open bite of **right** back wall of thorax without penetration into thoracic cavity

  ● S21.252   Open bite of **left** back wall of thorax without penetration into thoracic cavity

  ● S21.259   Open bite of **unspecified** back wall of thorax without penetration into thoracic cavity

● S21.3   Open wound of **front wall** of thorax **with penetration into thoracic cavity**
       Open wound of chest with penetration into thoracic cavity

  ● S21.30   **Unspecified** open wound of front wall of thorax with penetration into thoracic cavity

    ● S21.301   Unspecified open wound of **right** front wall of thorax with penetration into thoracic cavity

    ● S21.302   Unspecified open wound of **left** front wall of thorax with penetration into thoracic cavity

    ● S21.309   Unspecified open wound of **unspecified** front wall of thorax with penetration into thoracic cavity

● S21.31   **Laceration without foreign body** of front wall of thorax with penetration into thoracic cavity

  ● S21.311   Laceration without foreign body of **right** front wall of thorax with penetration into thoracic cavity

  ● S21.312   Laceration without foreign body of **left** front wall of thorax with penetration into thoracic cavity

  ● S21.319   Laceration without foreign body of **unspecified** front wall of thorax with penetration into thoracic cavity

● S21.32   **Laceration with foreign body** of front wall of thorax with penetration into thoracic cavity

  ● S21.321   Laceration with foreign body of **right** front wall of thorax with penetration into thoracic cavity

  ● S21.322   Laceration with foreign body of **left** front wall of thorax with penetration into thoracic cavity

  ● S21.329   Laceration with foreign body of **unspecified** front wall of thorax with penetration into thoracic cavity

● S21.33   **Puncture wound without foreign body** of front wall of thorax with penetration into thoracic cavity

  ● S21.331   Puncture wound without foreign body of **right** front wall of thorax with penetration into thoracic cavity

  ● S21.332   Puncture wound without foreign body of **left** front wall of thorax with penetration into thoracic cavity

  ● S21.339   Puncture wound without foreign body of **unspecified** front wall of thorax with penetration into thoracic cavity

● S21.34   **Puncture wound with foreign body** of front wall of thorax with penetration into thoracic cavity

  ● S21.341   Puncture wound with foreign body of **right** front wall of thorax with penetration into thoracic cavity

  ● S21.342   Puncture wound with foreign body of **left** front wall of thorax with penetration into thoracic cavity

  ● S21.349   Puncture wound with foreign body of **unspecified** front wall of thorax with penetration into thoracic cavity

● S21.35   Open bite of front wall of thorax with penetration into thoracic cavity

     Excludes1   superficial bite of front wall of thorax (S20.37)

  ● S21.351   Open bite of **right** front wall of thorax with penetration into thoracic cavity

  ● S21.352   Open bite of **left** front wall of thorax with penetration into thoracic cavity

  ● S21.359   Open bite of **unspecified** front wall of thorax with penetration into thoracic cavity

● S21.4   Open wound of back wall of thorax with **penetration into thoracic cavity**

  ● S21.40   **Unspecified** open wound of back wall of thorax with penetration into thoracic cavity

    ● S21.401   Unspecified open wound of **right** back wall of thorax with penetration into thoracic cavity

    ● S21.402   Unspecified open wound of **left** back wall of thorax with penetration into thoracic cavity

    ● S21.409   Unspecified open wound of **unspecified** back wall of thorax with penetration into thoracic cavity

● S21.41   Laceration without foreign body of back wall of thorax with penetration into thoracic cavity

  ● S21.411   Laceration without foreign body of **right** back wall of thorax with penetration into thoracic cavity

  ● S21.412   Laceration without foreign body of **left** back wall of thorax with penetration into thoracic cavity

  ● S21.419   Laceration without foreign body of **unspecified** back wall of thorax with penetration into thoracic cavity

● S21.42   Laceration with foreign body of back wall of thorax with penetration into thoracic cavity

  ● S21.421   Laceration with foreign body of **right** back wall of thorax with penetration into thoracic cavity

  ● S21.422   Laceration with foreign body of **left** back wall of thorax with penetration into thoracic cavity

  ● S21.429   Laceration with foreign body of **unspecified** back wall of thorax with penetration into thoracic cavity

● S21.43   Puncture wound without foreign body of back wall of thorax with penetration into thoracic cavity

  ● S21.431   Puncture wound without foreign body of **right** back wall of thorax with penetration into thoracic cavity

  ● S21.432   Puncture wound without foreign body of **left** back wall of thorax with penetration into thoracic cavity

  ● S21.439   Puncture wound without foreign body of **unspecified** back wall of thorax with penetration into thoracic cavity

● S21.44   Puncture wound with foreign body of back wall of thorax with penetration into thoracic cavity

  ● S21.441   Puncture wound with foreign body of **right** back wall of thorax with penetration into thoracic cavity

  ● S21.442   Puncture wound with foreign body of **left** back wall of thorax with penetration into thoracic cavity

  ● S21.449   Puncture wound with foreign body of **unspecified** back wall of thorax with penetration into thoracic cavity

● S21.45   Open bite of back wall of thorax with penetration into thoracic cavity
Bite of back wall of thorax NOS

> **Excludes1**   superficial bite of back wall of thorax (S20.47)

  ● S21.451   Open bite of **right** back wall of thorax with penetration into thoracic cavity

  ● S21.452   Open bite of **left** back wall of thorax with penetration into thoracic cavity

  ● S21.459   Open bite of **unspecified** back wall of thorax with penetration into thoracic cavity

● S21.9   Open wound of **unspecified** part of thorax
Open wound of thoracic wall NOS

X ● S21.90   **Unspecified** open wound of unspecified part of thorax

X ● S21.91   Laceration without foreign body of unspecified part of thorax

X ● S21.92   Laceration with foreign body of unspecified part of thorax

X ● S21.93   Puncture wound without foreign body of unspecified part of thorax

X ● S21.94   Puncture wound with foreign body of unspecified part of thorax

X ● S21.95   Open bite of unspecified part of thorax

> **Excludes1**   superficial bite of thorax (S20.97)

● S22   Fracture of rib(s), sternum and thoracic spine

Note: A fracture not indicated as displaced or nondisplaced should be coded to displaced

A fracture not indicated as open or closed should be coded to closed

Includes   fracture of thoracic neural arch
fracture of thoracic spinous process
fracture of thoracic transverse process
fracture of thoracic vertebra
fracture of thoracic vertebral arch

Code first any associated:
injury of intrathoracic organ (S27.-)
spinal cord injury (S24.0-, S24.1-)

Excludes1   transection of thorax (S28.1)

Excludes2   fracture of clavicle (S42.0-)
fracture of scapula (S42.1-)

The appropriate 7th character is to be added to each code from category S22

> A   initial encounter for closed fracture
> B   initial encounter for open fracture
> D   subsequent encounter for fracture with routine healing
> G   subsequent encounter for fracture with delayed healing
> K   subsequent encounter for fracture with nonunion
> S   sequela

● S22.0   Fracture of thoracic vertebra

  ● S22.00   Fracture of **unspecified** thoracic vertebra

    ● S22.000   **Wedge compression** fracture of unspecified thoracic vertebra

    ● S22.001   **Stable burst** fracture of unspecified thoracic vertebra

    ● S22.002   **Unstable burst** fracture of unspecified thoracic vertebra

    ● S22.008   **Other** fracture of unspecified thoracic vertebra

    ● S22.009   **Unspecified** fracture of unspecified thoracic vertebra

  ● S22.01   Fracture of **first** thoracic vertebra

    ● S22.010   **Wedge compression** fracture of first thoracic vertebra

    ● S22.011   **Stable burst** fracture of first thoracic vertebra

    ● S22.012   **Unstable burst** fracture of first thoracic vertebra

    ● S22.018   **Other** fracture of first thoracic vertebra

    ● S22.019   **Unspecified** fracture of first thoracic vertebra

  ● S22.02   Fracture of **second** thoracic vertebra

    ● S22.020   **Wedge compression** fracture of second thoracic vertebra

    ● S22.021   **Stable burst** fracture of second thoracic vertebra

    ● S22.022   **Unstable burst** fracture of second thoracic vertebra

    ● S22.028   **Other** fracture of second thoracic vertebra

    ● S22.029   **Unspecified** fracture of second thoracic vertebra

  ● S22.03   Fracture of **third** thoracic vertebra

    ● S22.030   **Wedge compression** fracture of third thoracic vertebra

    ● S22.031   **Stable burst** fracture of third thoracic vertebra

    ● S22.032   **Unstable burst** fracture of third thoracic vertebra

    ● S22.038   **Other** fracture of third thoracic vertebra

    ● S22.039   **Unspecified** fracture of third thoracic vertebra

● S22.04   Fracture of fourth thoracic vertebra
   ● S22.040   Wedge compression fracture of fourth thoracic vertebra
   ● S22.041   Stable burst fracture of fourth thoracic vertebra
   ● S22.042   Unstable burst fracture of fourth thoracic vertebra
   ● S22.048   Other fracture of fourth thoracic vertebra
   ● S22.049   Unspecified fracture of fourth thoracic vertebra

● S22.05   Fracture of T5-T6 vertebra
   ● S22.050   Wedge compression fracture of T5-T6 vertebra
   ● S22.051   Stable burst fracture of T5-T6 vertebra
   ● S22.052   Unstable burst fracture of T5-T6 vertebra
   ● S22.058   Other fracture of T5-T6 vertebra
   ● S22.059   Unspecified fracture of T5-T6 vertebra

● S22.06   Fracture of T7-T8 vertebra
   ● S22.060   Wedge compression fracture of T7-T8 vertebra
   ● S22.061   Stable burst fracture of T7-T8 vertebra
   ● S22.062   Unstable burst fracture of T7-T8 vertebra
   ● S22.068   Other fracture of T7-T8 thoracic vertebra
   ● S22.069   Unspecified fracture of T7-T8 vertebra

● S22.07   Fracture of T9-T10 vertebra
   ● S22.070   Wedge compression fracture of T9-T10 vertebra
   ● S22.071   Stable burst fracture of T9-T10 vertebra
   ● S22.072   Unstable burst fracture of T9-T10 vertebra
   ● S22.078   Other fracture of T9-T10 vertebra
   ● S22.079   Unspecified fracture of T9-T10 vertebra

● S22.08   Fracture of T11-T12 vertebra
   ● S22.080   Wedge compression fracture of T11-T12 vertebra
   ● S22.081   Stable burst fracture of T11-T12 vertebra
   ● S22.082   Unstable burst fracture of T11-T12 vertebra
   ● S22.088   Other fracture of T11-T12 vertebra
   ● S22.089   Unspecified fracture of T11-T12 vertebra

● S22.2   Fracture of sternum
  X ● S22.20   Unspecified fracture of sternum
  X ● S22.21   Fracture of manubrium
  X ● S22.22   Fracture of body of sternum
  X ● S22.23   Sternal manubrial dissociation
  X ● S22.24   Fracture of xiphoid process

● S22.3 Fracture of one rib
  X ● S22.31   Fracture of one rib, right side
  X ● S22.32   Fracture of one rib, left side
  X ● S22.39   Fracture of one rib, unspecified side

● S22.4   Multiple fractures of ribs
   Fractures of two or more ribs
   Excludes1   flail chest (S22.5-)
  X ● S22.41   Multiple fractures of ribs, right side
  X ● S22.42   Multiple fractures of ribs, left side
  X ● S22.43   Multiple fractures of ribs, bilateral
  X ● S22.49   Multiple fractures of ribs, unspecified side

X ● S22.5   Flail chest
   Unstable chest due to sternum and/or rib fracture

X ● S22.9   Fracture of bony thorax, part unspecified

● S23   Dislocation and sprain of joints and ligaments of thorax
  Includes   avulsion of joint or ligament of thorax
   laceration of cartilage, joint or ligament of thorax
   sprain of cartilage, joint or ligament of thorax
   traumatic hemarthrosis of joint or ligament of thorax
   traumatic rupture of joint or ligament of thorax
   traumatic subluxation of joint or ligament of thorax
   traumatic tear of joint or ligament of thorax
  Code also any associated open wound
  Excludes2   dislocation, sprain of sternoclavicular joint (S43.2, S43.6)
   strain of muscle or tendon of thorax (S29.01-)
  The appropriate 7th character is to be added to each code from category S23

   A   initial encounter
   D   subsequent encounter
   S   sequela

X ● S23.0   Traumatic rupture of thoracic intervertebral disc
  Excludes1   rupture or displacement (nontraumatic) of thoracic intervertebral disc NOS (M51.- with fifth character 4)

● S23.1   Subluxation and dislocation of thoracic vertebra
  Code also any associated
   open wound of thorax (S21.-)
   spinal cord injury (S24.0-, S24.1-)
  Excludes2   fracture of thoracic vertebrae (S22.0-)
  ● S23.10   Subluxation and dislocation of unspecified thoracic vertebra
   ● S23.100   Subluxation of unspecified thoracic vertebra
   ● S23.101   Dislocation of unspecified thoracic vertebra
  ● S23.11   Subluxation and dislocation of T1/T2 thoracic vertebra
   ● S23.110   Subluxation of T1/T2 thoracic vertebra
   ● S23.111   Dislocation of T1/T2 thoracic vertebra
  ● S23.12   Subluxation and dislocation of T2/T3-T3/T4 thoracic vertebra
   ● S23.120   Subluxation of T2/T3 thoracic vertebra
   ● S23.121   Dislocation of T2/T3 thoracic vertebra
   ● S23.122   Subluxation of T3/T4 thoracic vertebra
   ● S23.123   Dislocation of T3/T4 thoracic vertebra
  ● S23.13   Subluxation and dislocation of T4/T5-T5/T6 thoracic vertebra
   ● S23.130   Subluxation of T4/T5 thoracic vertebra
   ● S23.131   Dislocation of T4/T5 thoracic vertebra
   ● S23.132   Subluxation of T5/T6 thoracic vertebra
   ● S23.133   Dislocation of T5/T6 thoracic vertebra
  ● S23.14   Subluxation and dislocation of T6/T7-T7/T8 thoracic vertebra
   ● S23.140   Subluxation of T6/T7 thoracic vertebra
   ● S23.141   Dislocation of T6/T7 thoracic vertebra
   ● S23.142   Subluxation of T7/T8 thoracic vertebra
   ● S23.143   Dislocation of T7/T8 thoracic vertebra

▶ New   ⇛ Revised   ~~deleted~~ Deleted   Excludes 1   Excludes 2   Includes   Use additional   Code first   Code also   Key words
OGCR Official Guidelines   X Assign placeholder X   ● Use Additional Character(s)   ▎ Manifestation Code   **Coding Clinic**

● S23.15   Subluxation and dislocation of T8/T9-T9/T10
           thoracic vertebra
   ● S23.150   Subluxation of T8/T9 thoracic
              vertebra
   ● S23.151   Dislocation of T8/T9 thoracic vertebra
   ● S23.152   Subluxation of T9/T10 thoracic
              vertebra
   ● S23.153   Dislocation of T9/T10 thoracic
              vertebra
● S23.16   Subluxation and dislocation of T10/T11-T11/T12
           thoracic vertebra
   ● S23.160   Subluxation of T10/T11 thoracic
              vertebra
   ● S23.161   Dislocation of T10/T11 thoracic
              vertebra
   ● S23.162   Subluxation of T11/T12 thoracic
              vertebra
   ● S23.163   Dislocation of T11/T12 thoracic
              vertebra
● S23.17   Subluxation and dislocation of T12/L1 thoracic
           vertebra
   ● S23.170   Subluxation of T12/L1 thoracic
              vertebra
   ● S23.171   Dislocation of T12/L1 thoracic
              vertebra
● S23.2   Dislocation of other and unspecified parts of thorax
   X ● S23.20   Dislocation of unspecified part of thorax
   X ● S23.29   Dislocation of other parts of thorax
X ● S23.3   Sprain of ligaments of thoracic spine
● S23.4   Sprain of ribs and sternum
   X ● S23.41   Sprain of ribs
   ● S23.42   Sprain of sternum
      ● S23.420   Sprain of sternoclavicular (joint)
                 (ligament)
      ● S23.421   Sprain of chondrosternal joint
      ● S23.428   Other sprain of sternum
      ● S23.429   Unspecified sprain of sternum
X ● S23.8   Sprain of other specified parts of thorax
X ● S23.9   Sprain of unspecified parts of thorax

● S24   Injury of nerves and spinal cord at thorax level
        Note: Code to highest level of thoracic spinal cord injury.
        Injuries to the spinal cord (S24.0 and S24.1) refer to the cord
        level and not bone level injury, and can affect nerve roots at
        and below the level given.
        Code also any associated:
           fracture of thoracic vertebra (S22.0-)
           open wound of thorax (S21.-)
           transient paralysis (R29.5)
        Excludes2   injury of brachial plexus (S14.3)
        The appropriate 7th character is to be added to each code from
           category S24

        ┌─────────────────────────────┐
        │ A   initial encounter   │
        │ D   subsequent encounter   │
        │ S   sequela   │
        └─────────────────────────────┘

X ● S24.0   Concussion and edema of thoracic spinal cord
● S24.1   Other and unspecified injuries of thoracic spinal cord
   ● S24.10   Unspecified injury of thoracic spinal cord
      ● S24.101   Unspecified injury at T1 level of
                 thoracic spinal cord
      ● S24.102   Unspecified injury at T2-T6 level of
                 thoracic spinal cord
      ● S24.103   Unspecified injury at T7-T10 level of
                 thoracic spinal cord
      ● S24.104   Unspecified injury at T11-T12 level of
                 thoracic spinal cord
      ● S24.109   Unspecified injury at unspecified level
                 of thoracic spinal cord
                 Injury of thoracic spinal cord NOS

● S24.11   Complete lesion of thoracic spinal cord
   ● S24.111   Complete lesion at T1 level of
              thoracic spinal cord
   ● S24.112   Complete lesion at T2-T6 level of
              thoracic spinal cord
   ● S24.113   Complete lesion at T7-T10 level of
              thoracic spinal cord
   ● S24.114   Complete lesion at T11-T12 level of
              thoracic spinal cord
   ● S24.119   Complete lesion at unspecified level
              of thoracic spinal cord
● S24.13   Anterior cord syndrome of thoracic spinal cord
   ● S24.131   Anterior cord syndrome at T1 level of
              thoracic spinal cord
   ● S24.132   Anterior cord syndrome at T2-T6 level
              of thoracic spinal cord
   ● S24.133   Anterior cord syndrome at T7-T10
              level of thoracic spinal cord
   ● S24.134   Anterior cord syndrome at T11-T12
              level of thoracic spinal cord
   ● S24.139   Anterior cord syndrome at
              unspecified level of thoracic spinal
              cord
● S24.14   Brown-Séquard syndrome of thoracic spinal
           cord
   ● S24.141   Brown-Séquard syndrome at T1 level
              of thoracic spinal cord
   ● S24.142   Brown-Séquard syndrome at T2-T6
              level of thoracic spinal cord
   ● S24.143   Brown-Séquard syndrome at T7-T10
              level of thoracic spinal cord
   ● S24.144   Brown-Séquard syndrome at T11-T12
              level of thoracic spinal cord
   ● S24.149   Brown-Séquard syndrome at
              unspecified level of thoracic spinal
              cord
● S24.15   Other incomplete lesions of thoracic spinal cord
           Incomplete lesion of thoracic spinal cord NOS
           Posterior cord syndrome of thoracic spinal
              cord
   ● S24.151   Other incomplete lesion at T1 level of
              thoracic spinal cord
   ● S24.152   Other incomplete lesion at T2-T6
              level of thoracic spinal cord
   ● S24.153   Other incomplete lesion at T7-T10
              level of thoracic spinal cord
   ● S24.154   Other incomplete lesion at T11-T12
              level of thoracic spinal cord
   ● S24.159   Other incomplete lesion at
              unspecified level of thoracic spinal
              cord
X ● S24.2   Injury of nerve root of thoracic spine
X ● S24.3   Injury of peripheral nerves of thorax
X ● S24.4   Injury of thoracic sympathetic nervous system
           Injury of cardiac plexus
           Injury of esophageal plexus
           Injury of pulmonary plexus
           Injury of stellate ganglion
           Injury of thoracic sympathetic ganglion
X ● S24.8   Injury of other specified nerves of thorax
X ● S24.9   Injury of unspecified nerve of thorax

● **S25**   **Injury of blood vessels of thorax**

The appropriate 7th character is to be added to each code from category S25

A	initial encounter
D	subsequent encounter
S	sequela

Code also any associated open wound (S21.-)

● **S25.0**   **Injury of thoracic aorta**
     Injury of aorta NOS

   X ● **S25.00**   **Unspecified injury of thoracic aorta**

   X ● **S25.01**   **Minor laceration of thoracic aorta**
       Incomplete transection of thoracic aorta
       Laceration of thoracic aorta NOS
       Superficial laceration of thoracic aorta

   X ● **S25.02**   **Major laceration of thoracic aorta**
       Complete transection of thoracic aorta
       Traumatic rupture of thoracic aorta

   X ● **S25.09**   **Other specified injury of thoracic aorta**

● **S25.1**   **Injury of innominate or subclavian artery**

   ● **S25.10**   **Unspecified injury of innominate or subclavian artery**

     ● **S25.101**   **Unspecified injury of right innominate or subclavian artery**

     ● **S25.102**   **Unspecified injury of left innominate or subclavian artery**

     ● **S25.109**   **Unspecified injury of unspecified innominate or subclavian artery**

   ● **S25.11**   **Minor laceration of innominate or subclavian artery**
       Incomplete transection of innominate or subclavian artery
       Laceration of innominate or subclavian artery NOS
       Superficial laceration of innominate or subclavian artery

     ● **S25.111**   **Minor laceration of right innominate or subclavian artery**

     ● **S25.112**   **Minor laceration of left innominate or subclavian artery**

     ● **S25.119**   **Minor laceration of unspecified innominate or subclavian artery**

   ● **S25.12**   **Major laceration of innominate or subclavian artery**
       Complete transection of innominate or subclavian artery
       Traumatic rupture of innominate or subclavian artery

     ● **S25.121**   **Major laceration of right innominate or subclavian artery**

     ● **S25.122**   **Major laceration of left innominate or subclavian artery**

     ● **S25.129**   **Major laceration of unspecified innominate or subclavian artery**

   ● **S25.19**   **Other specified injury of innominate or subclavian artery**

     ● **S25.191**   **Other specified injury of right innominate or subclavian artery**

     ● **S25.192**   **Other specified injury of left innominate or subclavian artery**

     ● **S25.199**   **Other specified injury of unspecified innominate or subclavian artery**

● **S25.2**   **Injury of superior vena cava**
     Injury of vena cava NOS

   X ● **S25.20**   **Unspecified injury of superior vena cava**

   X ● **S25.21**   **Minor laceration of superior vena cava**
       Incomplete transection of superior vena cava
       Laceration of superior vena cava NOS
       Superficial laceration of superior vena cava

   X ● **S25.22**   **Major laceration of superior vena cava**
       Complete transection of superior vena cava
       Traumatic rupture of superior vena cava

   X ● **S25.29**   **Other specified injury of superior vena cava**

● **S25.3**   **Injury of innominate or subclavian vein**

   ● **S25.30**   **Unspecified injury of innominate or subclavian vein**

     ● **S25.301**   **Unspecified injury of right innominate or subclavian vein**

     ● **S25.302**   **Unspecified injury of left innominate or subclavian vein**

     ● **S25.309**   **Unspecified injury of unspecified innominate or subclavian vein**

   ● **S25.31**   **Minor laceration of innominate or subclavian vein**
       Incomplete transection of innominate or subclavian vein
       Laceration of innominate or subclavian vein NOS
       Superficial laceration of innominate or subclavian vein

     ● **S25.311**   **Minor laceration of right innominate or subclavian vein**

     ● **S25.312**   **Minor laceration of left innominate or subclavian vein**

     ● **S25.319**   **Minor laceration of unspecified innominate or subclavian vein**

   ● **S25.32**   **Major laceration of innominate or subclavian vein**
       Complete transection of innominate or subclavian vein
       Traumatic rupture of innominate or subclavian vein

     ● **S25.321**   **Major laceration of right innominate or subclavian vein**

     ● **S25.322**   **Major laceration of left innominate or subclavian vein**

     ● **S25.329**   **Major laceration of unspecified innominate or subclavian vein**

   ● **S25.39**   **Other specified injury of innominate or subclavian vein**

     ● **S25.391**   **Other specified injury of right innominate or subclavian vein**

     ● **S25.392**   **Other specified injury of left innominate or subclavian vein**

     ● **S25.399**   **Other specified injury of unspecified innominate or subclavian vein**

● **S25.4**   **Injury of pulmonary blood vessels**

   ● **S25.40**   **Unspecified injury of pulmonary blood vessels**

     ● **S25.401**   **Unspecified injury of right pulmonary blood vessels**

     ● **S25.402**   **Unspecified injury of left pulmonary blood vessels**

     ● **S25.409**   **Unspecified injury of unspecified pulmonary blood vessels**

▶ New   ⇒ Revised   ~~deleted~~ Deleted   Excludes 1   Excludes 2   Includes   Use additional   Code first   Code also   Key words
OGCR Official Guidelines   X Assign placeholder X   ● Use Additional Character(s)   ▶ Manifestation Code   **Coding Clinic**

- **S25.41   Minor laceration of pulmonary blood vessels**
  - Incomplete transection of pulmonary blood vessels
  - Laceration of pulmonary blood vessels NOS
  - Superficial laceration of pulmonary blood vessels
  - **S25.411   Minor laceration of right pulmonary blood vessels**
  - **S25.412   Minor laceration of left pulmonary blood vessels**
  - **S25.419   Minor laceration of unspecified pulmonary blood vessels**
- **S25.42   Major laceration of pulmonary blood vessels**
  - Complete transection of pulmonary blood vessels
  - Traumatic rupture of pulmonary blood vessels
  - **S25.421   Major laceration of right pulmonary blood vessels**
  - **S25.422   Major laceration of left pulmonary blood vessels**
  - **S25.429   Major laceration of unspecified pulmonary blood vessels**
- **S25.49   Other specified injury of pulmonary blood vessels**
  - **S25.491   Other specified injury of right pulmonary blood vessels**
  - **S25.492   Other specified injury of left pulmonary blood vessels**
  - **S25.499   Other specified injury of unspecified pulmonary blood vessels**
- **S25.5   Injury of intercostal blood vessels**
  - **S25.50   Unspecified injury of intercostal blood vessels**
    - **S25.501   Unspecified injury of intercostal blood vessels, right side**
    - **S25.502   Unspecified injury of intercostal blood vessels, left side**
    - **S25.509   Unspecified injury of intercostal blood vessels, unspecified side**
  - **S25.51   Laceration of intercostal blood vessels**
    - **S25.511   Laceration of intercostal blood vessels, right side**
    - **S25.512   Laceration of intercostal blood vessels, left side**
    - **S25.519   Laceration of intercostal blood vessels, unspecified side**
  - **S25.59   Other specified injury of intercostal blood vessels**
    - **S25.591   Other specified injury of intercostal blood vessels, right side**
    - **S25.592   Other specified injury of intercostal blood vessels, left side**
    - **S25.599   Other specified injury of intercostal blood vessels, unspecified side**
- **S25.8   Injury of other blood vessels of thorax**
  - Injury of azygos vein
  - Injury of mammary artery or vein
  - **S25.80   Unspecified injury of other blood vessels of thorax**
    - **S25.801   Unspecified injury of other blood vessels of thorax, right side**
    - **S25.802   Unspecified injury of other blood vessels of thorax, left side**
    - **S25.809   Unspecified injury of other blood vessels of thorax, unspecified side**

- **S25.81   Laceration of other blood vessels of thorax**
  - **S25.811   Laceration of other blood vessels of thorax, right side**
  - **S25.812   Laceration of other blood vessels of thorax, left side**
  - **S25.819   Laceration of other blood vessels of thorax, unspecified side**
- **S25.89   Other specified injury of other blood vessels of thorax**
  - **S25.891   Other specified injury of other blood vessels of thorax, right side**
  - **S25.892   Other specified injury of other blood vessels of thorax, left side**
  - **S25.899   Other specified injury of other blood vessels of thorax, unspecified side**
- **S25.9   Injury of unspecified blood vessel of thorax**
  - X **S25.90   Unspecified injury of unspecified blood vessel of thorax**
  - X **S25.91   Laceration of unspecified blood vessel of thorax**
  - X **S25.99   Other specified injury of unspecified blood vessel of thorax**

- **S26   Injury of heart**

  The appropriate 7th character is to be added to each code from category S26

A	initial encounter
D	subsequent encounter
S	sequela

  Code also any associated:
  - open wound of thorax (S21.-)
  - traumatic hemopneumothorax (S27.2)
  - traumatic hemothorax (S27.1)
  - traumatic pneumothorax (S27.0)
  - **S26.0   Injury of heart with hemopericardium**
    - *Hemopericardium: effusion of blood within pericardium*
    - X **S26.00   Unspecified injury of heart with hemopericardium**
    - X **S26.01   Contusion of heart with hemopericardium**
    - **S26.02   Laceration of heart with hemopericardium**
      - **S26.020   Mild laceration of heart with hemopericardium**
        - Laceration of heart without penetration of heart chamber
      - **S26.021   Moderate laceration of heart with hemopericardium**
        - Laceration of heart with penetration of heart chamber
      - **S26.022   Major laceration of heart with hemopericardium**
        - Laceration of heart with penetration of multiple heart chambers
    - X **S26.09   Other injury of heart with hemopericardium**
  - **S26.1   Injury of heart without hemopericardium**
    - *Hemopericardium: effusion of blood within pericardium*
    - X **S26.10   Unspecified injury of heart without hemopericardium**
    - X **S26.11   Contusion of heart without hemopericardium**
    - X **S26.12   Laceration of heart without hemopericardium**
    - X **S26.19   Other injury of heart without hemopericardium**

Item 19–2   Pneumothorax is a collection of gas (positive air pressure) in the pleural space resulting in the lung collapsing. A **tension pneumothorax** is life-threatening and is a result of air in the pleural space causing a displacement in the mediastinal structures and cardiopulmonary function compromise. A **traumatic pneumothorax** results from blunt or penetrating injury that disrupts the parietal/visceral pleura. **Hemothorax** is blood or bloody fluid in the pleural cavity as a result of traumatic blood vessel rupture or inflammation of the lungs from pneumonia.

CHAPTER 19 (S00–T88)

● **S26.9**   **Injury of heart, unspecified with or without hemopericardium**
　　　　　Hemopericardium: effusion of blood within pericardium

X● **S26.90**   Unspecified injury of heart, unspecified with or without hemopericardium

X● **S26.91**   Contusion of heart, unspecified with or without hemopericardium

X● **S26.92**   Laceration of heart, unspecified with or without hemopericardium
　　　　　　　Laceration of heart NOS

X● **S26.99**   Other injury of heart, unspecified with or without hemopericardium

● **S27**   **Injury of other and unspecified intrathoracic organs**
　　　Code also any associated open wound of thorax (S21.-)
　　　Excludes2　injury of cervical esophagus (S10-S19)
　　　　　　　　injury of trachea (cervical) (S10-S19)

　　　The appropriate 7th character is to be added to each code from category S27

┌─────────────────────────────┐
│ A   initial encounter   │
│ D   subsequent encounter │
│ S   sequela   │
└─────────────────────────────┘

X● **S27.0**   **Traumatic pneumothorax**
　　　Excludes1　spontaneous pneumothorax (J93.-)

X● **S27.1**   **Traumatic hemothorax**

X● **S27.2**   **Traumatic hemopneumothorax**

● **S27.3**   **Other and unspecified injuries of lung**

　● **S27.30**   Unspecified injury of lung
　　　● **S27.301**   Unspecified injury of lung, unilateral
　　　● **S27.302**   Unspecified injury of lung, bilateral
　　　● **S27.309**   Unspecified injury of lung, unspecified

　● **S27.31**   Primary blast injury of lung
　　　　　Blast injury of lung NOS
　　　● **S27.311**   Primary blast injury of lung, unilateral
　　　● **S27.312**   Primary blast injury of lung, bilateral
　　　● **S27.319**   Primary blast injury of lung, unspecified

　● **S27.32**   Contusion of lung
　　　● **S27.321**   Contusion of lung, unilateral
　　　● **S27.322**   Contusion of lung, bilateral
　　　● **S27.329**   Contusion of lung, unspecified

　● **S27.33**   Laceration of lung
　　　● **S27.331**   Laceration of lung, unilateral
　　　● **S27.332**   Laceration of lung, bilateral
　　　● **S27.339**   Laceration of lung, unspecified

　● **S27.39**   Other injuries of lung
　　　　　Secondary blast injury of lung
　　　● **S27.391**   Other injuries of lung, unilateral
　　　● **S27.392**   Other injuries of lung, bilateral
　　　● **S27.399**   Other injuries of lung, unspecified

● **S27.4**   **Injury of bronchus**
　● **S27.40**   Unspecified injury of bronchus
　　　● **S27.401**   Unspecified injury of bronchus, unilateral
　　　● **S27.402**   Unspecified injury of bronchus, bilateral
　　　● **S27.409**   Unspecified injury of bronchus, unspecified

● **S27.41**   Primary blast injury of bronchus
　　　　Blast injury of bronchus NOS
　● **S27.411**   Primary blast injury of bronchus, unilateral
　● **S27.412**   Primary blast injury of bronchus, bilateral
　● **S27.419**   Primary blast injury of bronchus, unspecified

● **S27.42**   Contusion of bronchus
　● **S27.421**   Contusion of bronchus, unilateral
　● **S27.422**   Contusion of bronchus, bilateral
　● **S27.429**   Contusion of bronchus, unspecified

● **S27.43**   Laceration of bronchus
　● **S27.431**   Laceration of bronchus, unilateral
　● **S27.432**   Laceration of bronchus, bilateral
　● **S27.439**   Laceration of bronchus, unspecified

● **S27.49**   Other injury of bronchus
　　　Secondary blast injury of bronchus
　● **S27.491**   Other injury of bronchus, unilateral
　● **S27.492**   Other injury of bronchus, bilateral
　● **S27.499**   Other injury of bronchus, unspecified

● **S27.5**   **Injury of thoracic trachea**
　X● **S27.50**   Unspecified injury of thoracic trachea
　X● **S27.51**   Primary blast injury of thoracic trachea
　　　　　Blast injury of thoracic trachea NOS
　X● **S27.52**   Contusion of thoracic trachea
　X● **S27.53**   Laceration of thoracic trachea
　X● **S27.59**   Other injury of thoracic trachea
　　　　　Secondary blast injury of thoracic trachea

● **S27.6**   **Injury of pleura**
　X● **S27.60**   Unspecified injury of pleura
　X● **S27.63**   Laceration of pleura
　X● **S27.69**   Other injury of pleura

● **S27.8**   **Injury of other specified intrathoracic organs**
　● **S27.80**   Injury of diaphragm
　　　● **S27.802**   Contusion of diaphragm
　　　● **S27.803**   Laceration of diaphragm
　　　● **S27.808**   Other injury of diaphragm
　　　● **S27.809**   Unspecified injury of diaphragm

　● **S27.81**   Injury of esophagus (thoracic part)
　　　● **S27.812**   Contusion of esophagus (thoracic part)
　　　● **S27.813**   Laceration of esophagus (thoracic part)
　　　● **S27.818**   Other injury of esophagus (thoracic part)
　　　● **S27.819**   Unspecified injury of esophagus (thoracic part)

　● **S27.89**   Injury of other specified intrathoracic organs
　　　　Injury of lymphatic thoracic duct
　　　　Injury of thymus gland
　　　● **S27.892**   Contusion of other specified intrathoracic organs
　　　● **S27.893**   Laceration of other specified intrathoracic organs
　　　● **S27.898**   Other injury of other specified intrathoracic organs
　　　● **S27.899**   Unspecified injury of other specified intrathoracic organs

X● **S27.9**   **Injury of unspecified intrathoracic organ**

▶ New　➡ Revised　~~deleted~~ Deleted　Excludes 1　Excludes 2　Includes　Use additional　Code first　Code also　Key words
OGCR Official Guidelines　X Assign placeholder X　● Use Additional Character(s)　▶ Manifestation Code　**Coding Clinic**

● **S28** **Crushing injury of thorax, and traumatic amputation of part of thorax**

> The appropriate 7th character is to be added to each code from category S28

> A   initial encounter
> D   subsequent encounter
> S   sequela

X ● **S28.0** **Crushed chest**
> Use additional code for all associated injuries
> **Excludes1**   flail chest (S22.5)

X ● **S28.1** **Traumatic amputation (partial) of part of thorax, except breast**

● **S28.2** **Traumatic amputation of breast**

> ● **S28.21** **Complete traumatic amputation of breast**
> Traumatic amputation of breast NOS

>> ● **S28.211** **Complete traumatic amputation of right breast**

>> ● **S28.212** **Complete traumatic amputation of left breast**

>> ● **S28.219** **Complete traumatic amputation of unspecified breast**

> ● **S28.22** **Partial traumatic amputation of breast**

>> ● **S28.221** **Partial traumatic amputation of right breast**

>> ● **S28.222** **Partial traumatic amputation of left breast**

>> ● **S28.229** **Partial traumatic amputation of unspecified breast**

● **S29** **Other and unspecified injuries of thorax**

> Code also any associated open wound (S21.-)

> The appropriate 7th character is to be added to each code from category S29

> A   initial encounter
> D   subsequent encounter
> S   sequela

● **S29.0** **Injury of muscle and tendon at thorax level**

> ● **S29.00** **Unspecified injury of muscle and tendon of thorax**

>> ● **S29.001** **Unspecified injury of muscle and tendon of front wall of thorax**

>> ● **S29.002** **Unspecified injury of muscle and tendon of back wall of thorax**

>> ● **S29.009** **Unspecified injury of muscle and tendon of unspecified wall of thorax**

> ● **S29.01** **Strain of muscle and tendon of thorax**

>> ● **S29.011** **Strain of muscle and tendon of front wall of thorax**

>> ● **S29.012** **Strain of muscle and tendon of back wall of thorax**

>> ● **S29.019** **Strain of muscle and tendon of unspecified wall of thorax**

> ● **S29.02** **Laceration of muscle and tendon of thorax**

>> ● **S29.021** **Laceration of muscle and tendon of front wall of thorax**

>> ● **S29.022** **Laceration of muscle and tendon of back wall of thorax**

>> ● **S29.029** **Laceration of muscle and tendon of unspecified wall of thorax**

> ● **S29.09** **Other injury of muscle and tendon of thorax**

>> ● **S29.091** **Other injury of muscle and tendon of front wall of thorax**

>> ● **S29.092** **Other injury of muscle and tendon of back wall of thorax**

>> ● **S29.099** **Other injury of muscle and tendon of unspecified wall of thorax**

X ● **S29.8** **Other specified injuries of thorax**

X ● **S29.9** **Unspecified injury of thorax**

INJURIES TO THE ABDOMEN, LOWER BACK, LUMBAR SPINE PELVIS AND EXTERNAL GENITALS (S30-S39)

> **Includes**   injuries to the abdominal wall
> injuries to the anus
> injuries to the buttock
> injuries to the external genitalia
> injuries to the flank
> injuries to the groin

> **Excludes2**   burns and corrosions (T20-T32)
> effects of foreign body in anus and rectum (T18.5)
> effects of foreign body in genitourinary tract (T19.-)
> effects of foreign body in stomach, small intestine and colon (T18.2-T18.4)
> frostbite (T33-T34)
> insect bite or sting, venomous (T63.4)

● **S30** **Superficial injury of abdomen, lower back, pelvis and external genitals**

> **Excludes2**   superficial injury of hip (S70.-)

> The appropriate 7th character is to be added to each code from category S30

> A   initial encounter
> D   subsequent encounter
> S   sequela

X ● **S30.0** **Contusion of lower back and pelvis**
> Contusion of buttock

X ● **S30.1** **Contusion of abdominal wall**
> Contusion of flank
> Contusion of groin

● **S30.2** **Contusion of external genital organs**

> ● **S30.20** **Contusion of unspecified external genital organ**

>> ● **S30.201** **Contusion of unspecified external genital organ, male ♂**

>> ● **S30.202** **Contusion of unspecified external genital organ, female ♀**

> X ● **S30.21** **Contusion of penis ♂**

> X ● **S30.22** **Contusion of scrotum and testes ♂**

> X ● **S30.23** **Contusion of vagina and vulva ♀**

X ● **S30.3** **Contusion of anus**

● **S30.8** **Other superficial injuries of abdomen, lower back, pelvis and external genitals**

> ● **S30.81** **Abrasion of abdomen, lower back, pelvis and external genitals**

>> ● **S30.810** **Abrasion of lower back and pelvis**

>> ● **S30.811** **Abrasion of abdominal wall**

>> ● **S30.812** **Abrasion of penis ♂**

>> ● **S30.813** **Abrasion of scrotum and testes ♂**

>> ● **S30.814** **Abrasion of vagina and vulva ♀**

>> ● **S30.815** **Abrasion of unspecified external genital organs, male ♂**

>> ● **S30.816** **Abrasion of unspecified external genital organs, female ♀**

>> ● **S30.817** **Abrasion of anus**

> ● **S30.82** **Blister (nonthermal) of abdomen, lower back, pelvis and external genitals**

>> ● **S30.820** **Blister (nonthermal) of lower back and pelvis**

>> ● **S30.821** **Blister (nonthermal) of abdominal wall**

>> ● **S30.822** **Blister (nonthermal) of penis ♂**

>> ● **S30.823** **Blister (nonthermal) of scrotum and testes ♂**

>> ● **S30.824** **Blister (nonthermal) of vagina and vulva ♀**

>> ● **S30.825** **Blister (nonthermal) of unspecified external genital organs, male ♂**

>> ● **S30.826** **Blister (nonthermal) of unspecified external genital organs, female ♀**

>> ● **S30.827** **Blister (nonthermal) of anus**

CHAPTER 19 (S00-T88)

● S30.84   **External constriction of abdomen, lower back, pelvis and external genitals**

    ● S30.840   **External constriction of lower back and pelvis**

    ● S30.841   **External constriction of abdominal wall**

    ● S30.842   **External constriction of penis ♂**
         Hair tourniquet syndrome of penis
         Use additional cause code to identify the constricting item (W49.0-)

    ● S30.843   **External constriction of scrotum and testes ♂**

    ● S30.844   **External constriction of vagina and vulva ♀**

    ● S30.845   **External constriction of unspecified external genital organs, male ♂**

    ● S30.846   **External constriction of unspecified external genital organs, female ♀**

● S30.85   **Superficial foreign body of abdomen, lower back, pelvis and external genitals**
      Splinter in the abdomen, lower back, pelvis and external genitals

    ● S30.850   **Superficial foreign body of lower back and pelvis**

    ● S30.851   **Superficial foreign body of abdominal wall**

    ● S30.852   **Superficial foreign body of penis ♂**

    ● S30.853   **Superficial foreign body of scrotum and testes ♂**

    ● S30.854   **Superficial foreign body of vagina and vulva ♀**

    ● S30.855   **Superficial foreign body of unspecified external genital organs, male ♂**

    ● S30.856   **Superficial foreign body of unspecified external genital organs, female ♀**

    ● S30.857   **Superficial foreign body of anus**

● S30.86   **Insect bite (nonvenomous) of abdomen, lower back, pelvis and external genitals**

    ● S30.860   **Insect bite (nonvenomous) of lower back and pelvis**

    ● S30.861   **Insect bite (nonvenomous) of abdominal wall**

    ● S30.862   **Insect bite (nonvenomous) of penis ♂**

    ● S30.863   **Insect bite (nonvenomous) of scrotum and testes ♂**

    ● S30.864   **Insect bite (nonvenomous) of vagina and vulva ♀**

    ● S30.865   **Insect bite (nonvenomous) of unspecified external genital organs, male ♂**

    ● S30.866   **Insect bite (nonvenomous) of unspecified external genital organs, female ♀**

    ● S30.867   **Insect bite (nonvenomous) of anus**

● S30.87   **Other superficial bite of abdomen, lower back, pelvis and external genitals**

    Excludes1   open bite of abdomen, lower back, pelvis and external genitals (S31.05, S31.15, S31.25, S31.35, S31.45, S31.55)

    ● S30.870   **Other superficial bite of lower back and pelvis**

    ● S30.871   **Other superficial bite of abdominal wall**

● S30.872   **Other superficial bite of penis ♂**

● S30.873   **Other superficial bite of scrotum and testes ♂**

● S30.874   **Other superficial bite of vagina and vulva ♀**

● S30.875   **Other superficial bite of unspecified external genital organs, male ♂**

● S30.876   **Other superficial bite of unspecified external genital organs, female ♀**

● S30.877   **Other superficial bite of anus**

● S30.9   **Unspecified superficial injury of abdomen, lower back, pelvis and external genitals**

  X ● S30.91   **Unspecified superficial injury of lower back and pelvis**

  X ● S30.92   **Unspecified superficial injury of abdominal wall**

  X ● S30.93   **Unspecified superficial injury of penis ♂**

  X ● S30.94   **Unspecified superficial injury of scrotum and testes ♂**

  X ● S30.95   **Unspecified superficial injury of vagina and vulva ♀**

  X ● S30.96   **Unspecified superficial injury of unspecified external genital organs, male ♂**

  X ● S30.97   **Unspecified superficial injury of unspecified external genital organs, female ♀**

  X ● S30.98   **Unspecified superficial injury of anus**

● S31   **Open wound of abdomen, lower back, pelvis and external genitals**

    Code also any associated:
      spinal cord injury (S24.0, S24.1-, S34.0-, S34.1-)
      wound infection

    Excludes1   traumatic amputation of part of abdomen, lower back and pelvis (S38.2-, S38.3)

    Excludes2   open wound of hip (S71.00-S71.02)
           open fracture of pelvis (S32.1--S32.9 with 7th character B)

    The appropriate 7th character is to be added to each code from category S31

A	initial encounter
D	subsequent encounter
S	sequela

● S31.0   **Open wound of lower back and pelvis**

    ● S31.00   **Unspecified open wound of lower back and pelvis**

      ● S31.000   **Unspecified open wound of lower back and pelvis without penetration into retroperitoneum**
         Unspecified open wound of lower back and pelvis NOS

      ● S31.001   **Unspecified open wound of lower back and pelvis with penetration into retroperitoneum**

    ● S31.01   **Laceration without foreign body of lower back and pelvis**

      ● S31.010   **Laceration without foreign body of lower back and pelvis without penetration into retroperitoneum**
         Laceration without foreign body of lower back and pelvis NOS

      ● S31.011   **Laceration without foreign body of lower back and pelvis with penetration into retroperitoneum**

▶ New   ⇒ Revised   ~~deleted~~ Deleted   Excludes 1   Excludes 2   Includes   Use additional   Code first   Code also   Key words

OGCR Official Guidelines   X Assign placeholder X   ● Use Additional Character(s)   ▶ Manifestation Code   **Coding Clinic**

- S31.02 Laceration with foreign body of lower back and pelvis
    - S31.020 Laceration with foreign body of lower back and pelvis without penetration into retroperitoneum
        Laceration with foreign body of lower back and pelvis NOS
    - S31.021 Laceration with foreign body of lower back and pelvis with penetration into retroperitoneum
- S31.03 Puncture wound without foreign body of lower back and pelvis
    - S31.030 Puncture wound without foreign body of lower back and pelvis without penetration into retroperitoneum
        Puncture wound without foreign body of lower back and pelvis NOS
    - S31.031 Puncture wound without foreign body of lower back and pelvis with penetration into retroperitoneum
- S31.04 Puncture wound with foreign body of lower back and pelvis
    - S31.040 Puncture wound with foreign body of lower back and pelvis without penetration into retroperitoneum
        Puncture wound with foreign body of lower back and pelvis NOS
    - S31.041 Puncture wound with foreign body of lower back and pelvis with penetration into retroperitoneum
- S31.05 Open bite of lower back and pelvis
    Bite of lower back and pelvis NOS
    Excludes1 superficial bite of lower back and pelvis (S30.860, S30.870)
    - S31.050 Open bite of lower back and pelvis without penetration into retroperitoneum
        Open bite of lower back and pelvis NOS
    - S31.051 Open bite of lower back and pelvis with penetration into retroperitoneum
- S31.1 Open wound of abdominal wall without penetration into peritoneal cavity
    Open wound of abdominal wall NOS
    Excludes2 open wound of abdominal wall with penetration into peritoneal cavity (S31.6-)
    - S31.10 Unspecified open wound of abdominal wall without penetration into peritoneal cavity
        - S31.100 Unspecified open wound of abdominal wall, right upper quadrant without penetration into peritoneal cavity
        - S31.101 Unspecified open wound of abdominal wall, left upper quadrant without penetration into peritoneal cavity
        - S31.102 Unspecified open wound of abdominal wall, epigastric region without penetration into peritoneal cavity
        - S31.103 Unspecified open wound of abdominal wall, right lower quadrant without penetration into peritoneal cavity
        - S31.104 Unspecified open wound of abdominal wall, left lower quadrant without penetration into peritoneal cavity
        - S31.105 Unspecified open wound of abdominal wall, periumbilic region without penetration into peritoneal cavity
        - S31.109 Unspecified open wound of abdominal wall, unspecified quadrant without penetration into peritoneal cavity
            Unspecified open wound of abdominal wall NOS
    - S31.11 Laceration without foreign body of abdominal wall without penetration into peritoneal cavity
        - S31.110 Laceration without foreign body of abdominal wall, right upper quadrant without penetration into peritoneal cavity
        - S31.111 Laceration without foreign body of abdominal wall, left upper quadrant without penetration into peritoneal cavity
        - S31.112 Laceration without foreign body of abdominal wall, epigastric region without penetration into peritoneal cavity
        - S31.113 Laceration without foreign body of abdominal wall, right lower quadrant without penetration into peritoneal cavity
        - S31.114 Laceration without foreign body of abdominal wall, left lower quadrant without penetration into peritoneal cavity
        - S31.115 Laceration without foreign body of abdominal wall, periumbilic region without penetration into peritoneal cavity
        - S31.119 Laceration without foreign body of abdominal wall, unspecified quadrant without penetration into peritoneal cavity
    - S31.12 Laceration with foreign body of abdominal wall without penetration into peritoneal cavity
        - S31.120 Laceration of abdominal wall with foreign body, right upper quadrant without penetration into peritoneal cavity
        - S31.121 Laceration of abdominal wall with foreign body, left upper quadrant without penetration into peritoneal cavity
        - S31.122 Laceration of abdominal wall with foreign body, epigastric region without penetration into peritoneal cavity
        - S31.123 Laceration of abdominal wall with foreign body, right lower quadrant without penetration into peritoneal cavity
        - S31.124 Laceration of abdominal wall with foreign body, left lower quadrant without penetration into peritoneal cavity
        - S31.125 Laceration of abdominal wall with foreign body, periumbilic region without penetration into peritoneal cavity
        - S31.129 Laceration of abdominal wall with foreign body, unspecified quadrant without penetration into peritoneal cavity

CHAPTER 19 (S00–T88)

● S31.13 Puncture wound of abdominal wall without foreign body without penetration into peritoneal cavity

  ● S31.130 Puncture wound of abdominal wall without foreign body, right upper quadrant without penetration into peritoneal cavity

  ● S31.131 Puncture wound of abdominal wall without foreign body, left upper quadrant without penetration into peritoneal cavity

  ● S31.132 Puncture wound of abdominal wall without foreign body, epigastric region without penetration into peritoneal cavity

  ● S31.133 Puncture wound of abdominal wall without foreign body, right lower quadrant without penetration into peritoneal cavity

  ● S31.134 Puncture wound of abdominal wall without foreign body, left lower quadrant without penetration into peritoneal cavity

  ● S31.135 Puncture wound of abdominal wall without foreign body, periumbilic region without penetration into peritoneal cavity

  ● S31.139 Puncture wound of abdominal wall without foreign body, unspecified quadrant without penetration into peritoneal cavity

● S31.14 Puncture wound of abdominal wall with foreign body without penetration into peritoneal cavity

  ● S31.140 Puncture wound of abdominal wall with foreign body, right upper quadrant without penetration into peritoneal cavity

  ● S31.141 Puncture wound of abdominal wall with foreign body, left upper quadrant without penetration into peritoneal cavity

  ● S31.142 Puncture wound of abdominal wall with foreign body, epigastric region without penetration into peritoneal cavity

  ● S31.143 Puncture wound of abdominal wall with foreign body, right lower quadrant without penetration into peritoneal cavity

  ● S31.144 Puncture wound of abdominal wall with foreign body, left lower quadrant without penetration into peritoneal cavity

  ● S31.145 Puncture wound of abdominal wall with foreign body, periumbilic region without penetration into peritoneal cavity

  ● S31.149 Puncture wound of abdominal wall with foreign body, unspecified quadrant without penetration into peritoneal cavity

● S31.15 Open bite of abdominal wall without penetration into peritoneal cavity
           Bite of abdominal wall NOS

    Excludes1 superficial bite of abdominal wall (S30.871)

  ● S31.150 Open bite of abdominal wall, right upper quadrant without penetration into peritoneal cavity

  ● S31.151 Open bite of abdominal wall, left upper quadrant without penetration into peritoneal cavity

  ● S31.152 Open bite of abdominal wall, epigastric region without penetration into peritoneal cavity

  ● S31.153 Open bite of abdominal wall, right lower quadrant without penetration into peritoneal cavity

  ● S31.154 Open bite of abdominal wall, left lower quadrant without penetration into peritoneal cavity

  ● S31.155 Open bite of abdominal wall, periumbilic region without penetration into peritoneal cavity

  ● S31.159 Open bite of abdominal wall, unspecified quadrant without penetration into peritoneal cavity

● S31.2 Open wound of penis

  X ● S31.20 Unspecified open wound of penis ♂
  X ● S31.21 Laceration without foreign body of penis ♂
  X ● S31.22 Laceration with foreign body of penis ♂
  X ● S31.23 Puncture wound without foreign body of penis ♂
  X ● S31.24 Puncture wound with foreign body of penis ♂
  X ● S31.25 Open bite of penis ♂
             Bite of penis NOS

    Excludes1 superficial bite of penis (S30.862, S30.872)

● S31.3 Open wound of scrotum and testes

  X ● S31.30 Unspecified open wound of scrotum and testes ♂
  X ● S31.31 Laceration without foreign body of scrotum and testes ♂
  X ● S31.32 Laceration with foreign body of scrotum and testes ♂
  X ● S31.33 Puncture wound without foreign body of scrotum and testes ♂
  X ● S31.34 Puncture wound with foreign body of scrotum and testes ♂
  X ● S31.35 Open bite of scrotum and testes ♂
             Bite of scrotum and testes NOS

    Excludes1 superficial bite of scrotum and testes (S30.863, S30.873)

● S31.4 Open wound of vagina and vulva

    Excludes1 injury to vagina and vulva during delivery (O70.-, O71.4)

  X ● S31.40 Unspecified open wound of vagina and vulva ♀
  X ● S31.41 Laceration without foreign body of vagina and vulva ♀
  X ● S31.42 Laceration with foreign body of vagina and vulva ♀
  X ● S31.43 Puncture wound without foreign body of vagina and vulva ♀
  X ● S31.44 Puncture wound with foreign body of vagina and vulva ♀
  X ● S31.45 Open bite of vagina and vulva ♀
             Bite of vagina and vulva NOS

    Excludes1 superficial bite of vagina and vulva (S30.864, S30.874)

● S31.5 Open wound of unspecified external genital organs

    Excludes1 traumatic amputation of external genital organs (S38.21, S38.22)

  ● S31.50 Unspecified open wound of unspecified external genital organs

    ● S31.501 Unspecified open wound of unspecified external genital organs, male ♂

    ● S31.502 Unspecified open wound of unspecified external genital organs, female ♀

● **S31.51**   Laceration without foreign body of unspecified external genital organs

    ● S31.511   Laceration without foreign body of unspecified external genital organs, male ♂

    ● S31.512   Laceration without foreign body of unspecified external genital organs, female ♀

● **S31.52**   Laceration with foreign body of unspecified external genital organs

    ● S31.521   Laceration with foreign body of unspecified external genital organs, male ♂

    ● S31.522   Laceration with foreign body of unspecified external genital organs, female ♀

● **S31.53**   Puncture wound without foreign body of unspecified external genital organs

    ● S31.531   Puncture wound without foreign body of unspecified external genital organs, male ♂

    ● S31.532   Puncture wound without foreign body of unspecified external genital organs, female ♀

● **S31.54**   Puncture wound with foreign body of unspecified external genital organs

    ● S31.541   Puncture wound with foreign body of unspecified external genital organs, male ♂

    ● S31.542   Puncture wound with foreign body of unspecified external genital organs, female ♀

● **S31.55**   Open bite of unspecified external genital organs

    Bite of unspecified external genital organs NOS

    Excludes1   superficial bite of unspecified external genital organs (S30.865, S30.866, S30.875, S30.876)

    ● S31.551   Open bite of unspecified external genital organs, male ♂

    ● S31.552   Open bite of unspecified external genital organs, female ♀

● **S31.6**   Open wound of abdominal wall with penetration into peritoneal cavity

  ● **S31.60**   Unspecified open wound of abdominal wall with penetration into peritoneal cavity

    ● S31.600   Unspecified open wound of abdominal wall, right upper quadrant with penetration into peritoneal cavity

    ● S31.601   Unspecified open wound of abdominal wall, left upper quadrant with penetration into peritoneal cavity

    ● S31.602   Unspecified open wound of abdominal wall, epigastric region with penetration into peritoneal cavity

    ● S31.603   Unspecified open wound of abdominal wall, right lower quadrant with penetration into peritoneal cavity

    ● S31.604   Unspecified open wound of abdominal wall, left lower quadrant with penetration into peritoneal cavity

    ● S31.605   Unspecified open wound of abdominal wall, periumbilic region with penetration into peritoneal cavity

    ● S31.609   Unspecified open wound of abdominal wall, unspecified quadrant with penetration into peritoneal cavity

  ● **S31.61**   Laceration without foreign body of abdominal wall with penetration into peritoneal cavity

    ● S31.610   Laceration without foreign body of abdominal wall, right upper quadrant with penetration into peritoneal cavity

    ● S31.611   Laceration without foreign body of abdominal wall, left upper quadrant with penetration into peritoneal cavity

    ● S31.612   Laceration without foreign body of abdominal wall, epigastric region with penetration into peritoneal cavity

    ● S31.613   Laceration without foreign body of abdominal wall, right lower quadrant with penetration into peritoneal cavity

        Coding Clinic: 2015, Q4, P37

    ● S31.614   Laceration without foreign body of abdominal wall, left lower quadrant with penetration into peritoneal cavity

    ● S31.615   Laceration without foreign body of abdominal wall, periumbilic region with penetration into peritoneal cavity

    ● S31.619   Laceration without foreign body of abdominal wall, unspecified quadrant with penetration into peritoneal cavity

  ● **S31.62**   Laceration with foreign body of abdominal wall with penetration into peritoneal cavity

    ● S31.620   Laceration with foreign body of abdominal wall, right upper quadrant with penetration into peritoneal cavity

    ● S31.621   Laceration with foreign body of abdominal wall, left upper quadrant with penetration into peritoneal cavity

    ● S31.622   Laceration with foreign body of abdominal wall, epigastric region with penetration into peritoneal cavity

    ● S31.623   Laceration with foreign body of abdominal wall, right lower quadrant with penetration into peritoneal cavity

    ● S31.624   Laceration with foreign body of abdominal wall, left lower quadrant with penetration into peritoneal cavity

    ● S31.625   Laceration with foreign body of abdominal wall, periumbilic region with penetration into peritoneal cavity

    ● S31.629   Laceration with foreign body of abdominal wall, unspecified quadrant with penetration into peritoneal cavity

CHAPTER 19 (S00-T88)

● S31.63   **Puncture wound without foreign body**
of abdominal wall with penetration into
peritoneal cavity

   ● S31.630   Puncture wound without foreign
body of abdominal wall, right upper
quadrant with penetration into
peritoneal cavity

   ● S31.631   Puncture wound without foreign
body of abdominal wall, left upper
quadrant with penetration into
peritoneal cavity

   ● S31.632   Puncture wound without foreign
body of abdominal wall, epigastric
region with penetration into
peritoneal cavity

   ● S31.633   Puncture wound without foreign
body of abdominal wall, right lower
quadrant with penetration into
peritoneal cavity

   ● S31.634   Puncture wound without foreign
body of abdominal wall, left lower
quadrant with penetration into
peritoneal cavity

   ● S31.635   Puncture wound without foreign
body of abdominal wall, periumbilic
region with penetration into
peritoneal cavity

   ● S31.639   Puncture wound without foreign
body of abdominal wall, unspecified
quadrant with penetration into
peritoneal cavity

● S31.64   **Puncture wound with foreign body of**
abdominal wall with penetration into
peritoneal cavity

   ● S31.640   Puncture wound with foreign body of
abdominal wall, right upper quadrant
with penetration into peritoneal
cavity

   ● S31.641   Puncture wound with foreign body of
abdominal wall, left upper quadrant
with penetration into peritoneal
cavity

   ● S31.642   Puncture wound with foreign body
of abdominal wall, epigastric region
with penetration into peritoneal
cavity

   ● S31.643   Puncture wound with foreign body of
abdominal wall, right lower quadrant
with penetration into peritoneal
cavity

   ● S31.644   Puncture wound with foreign body of
abdominal wall, left lower quadrant
with penetration into peritoneal
cavity

   ● S31.645   Puncture wound with foreign body of
abdominal wall, periumbilic region
with penetration into peritoneal
cavity

   ● S31.649   Puncture wound with foreign body of
abdominal wall, unspecified quadrant
with penetration into peritoneal
cavity

● S31.65   Open bite of abdominal wall with penetration
into peritoneal cavity

     Excludes1   superficial bite of abdominal
wall (S30.861, S30.871)

   ● S31.650   Open bite of abdominal wall, right
upper quadrant with penetration into
peritoneal cavity

   ● S31.651   Open bite of abdominal wall, left
upper quadrant with penetration into
peritoneal cavity

● S31.652   Open bite of abdominal wall,
epigastric region with penetration
into peritoneal cavity

● S31.653   Open bite of abdominal wall, right
lower quadrant with penetration into
peritoneal cavity

● S31.654   Open bite of abdominal wall, left
lower quadrant with penetration into
peritoneal cavity

● S31.655   Open bite of abdominal wall,
periumbilic region with penetration
into peritoneal cavity

● S31.659   Open bite of abdominal wall,
unspecified quadrant with penetration
into peritoneal cavity

● S31.8   Open wound of other parts of abdomen, lower back and
pelvis

  ● S31.80   Open wound of unspecified buttock

   ● S31.801   Laceration without foreign body of
unspecified buttock

   ● S31.802   Laceration with foreign body of
unspecified buttock

   ● S31.803   Puncture wound without foreign
body of unspecified buttock

   ● S31.804   Puncture wound with foreign body of
unspecified buttock

   ● S31.805   Open bite of unspecified buttock
Bite of buttock NOS

      Excludes1   superficial bite of
buttock (S30.870)

   ● S31.809   Unspecified open wound of
unspecified buttock

  ● S31.81   Open wound of right buttock

   ● S31.811   Laceration without foreign body of
right buttock

   ● S31.812   Laceration with foreign body of right
buttock

   ● S31.813   Puncture wound without foreign
body of right buttock

   ● S31.814   Puncture wound with foreign body of
right buttock

   ● S31.815   Open bite of right buttock
Bite of right buttock NOS

      Excludes1   superficial bite of
buttock (S30.870)

   ● S31.819   Unspecified open wound of right
buttock

  ● S31.82   Open wound of left buttock

   ● S31.821   Laceration without foreign body of
left buttock

   ● S31.822   Laceration with foreign body of left
buttock

   ● S31.823   Puncture wound without foreign
body of left buttock

   ● S31.824   Puncture wound with foreign body of
left buttock

   ● S31.825   Open bite of left buttock
Bite of left buttock NOS

      Excludes1   superficial bite of
buttock (S30.870)

   ● S31.829   Unspecified open wound of left
buttock

  ● S31.83   Open wound of anus

   ● S31.831   Laceration without foreign body of
anus

   ● S31.832   Laceration with foreign body of anus

   ● S31.833   Puncture wound without foreign
body of anus

▶ New   ⇒ Revised   ~~deleted~~ Deleted   Excludes 1   Excludes 2   Includes   Use additional   Code first   Code also   Key words

OGCR Official Guidelines   X Assign placeholder X   ● Use Additional Character(s)   ▷ Manifestation Code   **Coding Clinic**

● S31.834   **Puncture wound with foreign body of anus**

● S31.835   **Open bite of anus**
Bite of anus NOS
Excludes1   superficial bite of anus (S30.877)

● S31.839   **Unspecified open wound of anus**

● S32   **Fracture of lumbar spine and pelvis**
Note: A fracture not indicated as displaced or nondisplaced should be coded to displaced
A fracture not indicated as opened or closed should be coded to closed
Includes   fracture of lumbosacral neural arch
fracture of lumbosacral spinous process
fracture of lumbosacral transverse process
fracture of lumbosacral vertebra
fracture of lumbosacral vertebral arch
Code first any associated spinal cord and spinal nerve injury (S34.-)
Excludes1   transection of abdomen (S38.3)
Excludes2   fracture of hip NOS (S72.0-)
The appropriate 7th character is to be added to each code from category S32

A	initial encounter for closed fracture
B	initial encounter for open fracture
D	subsequent encounter for fracture with routine healing
G	subsequent encounter for fracture with delayed healing
K	subsequent encounter for fracture with nonunion
S	sequela

● S32.0   **Fracture of lumbar vertebra**
Fracture of lumbar spine NOS

  ● S32.00   **Fracture of unspecified lumbar vertebra**
    ● S32.000   **Wedge compression** fracture of unspecified lumbar vertebra
    ● S32.001   **Stable burst** fracture of unspecified lumbar vertebra
    ● S32.002   **Unstable burst** fracture of unspecified lumbar vertebra
    ● S32.008   **Other** fracture of unspecified lumbar vertebra
    ● S32.009   **Unspecified** fracture of unspecified lumbar vertebra

  ● S32.01   **Fracture of first lumbar vertebra**
    ● S32.010   **Wedge compression** fracture of first lumbar vertebra
    ● S32.011   **Stable burst** fracture of first lumbar vertebra
    ● S32.012   **Unstable burst** fracture of first lumbar vertebra
    ● S32.018   **Other** fracture of first lumbar vertebra
    ● S32.019   **Unspecified** fracture of first lumbar vertebra

  ● S32.02   **Fracture of second lumbar vertebra**
    ● S32.020   **Wedge compression** fracture of second lumbar vertebra
    ● S32.021   **Stable burst** fracture of second lumbar vertebra
    ● S32.022   **Unstable burst** fracture of second lumbar vertebra
    ● S32.028   **Other** fracture of second lumbar vertebra
    ● S32.029   **Unspecified** fracture of second lumbar vertebra

● S32.03   **Fracture of third lumbar vertebra**
    ● S32.030   **Wedge compression** fracture of third lumbar vertebra
    ● S32.031   **Stable burst** fracture of third lumbar vertebra
    ● S32.032   **Unstable burst** fracture of third lumbar vertebra
    ● S32.038   **Other** fracture of third lumbar vertebra
    ● S32.039   **Unspecified** fracture of third lumbar vertebra

● S32.04   **Fracture of fourth lumbar vertebra**
    ● S32.040   **Wedge compression** fracture of fourth lumbar vertebra
    ● S32.041   **Stable burst** fracture of fourth lumbar vertebra
    ● S32.042   **Unstable burst** fracture of fourth lumbar vertebra
    ● S32.048   **Other** fracture of fourth lumbar vertebra
    ● S32.049   **Unspecified** fracture of fourth lumbar vertebra

● S32.05   **Fracture of fifth lumbar vertebra**
    ● S32.050   **Wedge compression** fracture of fifth lumbar vertebra
    ● S32.051   **Stable burst** fracture of fifth lumbar vertebra
    ● S32.052   **Unstable burst** fracture of fifth lumbar vertebra
    ● S32.058   **Other** fracture of fifth lumbar vertebra
    ● S32.059   **Unspecified** fracture of fifth lumbar vertebra

● S32.1   **Fracture of sacrum**
For vertical fractures, code to most medial fracture extension
Use two codes if both a vertical and transverse fracture are present
Code also any associated fracture of pelvic ring (S32.8-)

  X ● S32.10   **Unspecified** fracture of sacrum
  ● S32.11   **Zone I** fracture of sacrum
Vertical sacral ala fracture of sacrum
    ● S32.110   **Nondisplaced** Zone I fracture of sacrum
    ● S32.111   **Minimally displaced** Zone I fracture of sacrum
    ● S32.112   **Severely displaced** Zone I fracture of sacrum
    ● S32.119   **Unspecified** Zone I fracture of sacrum

  ● S32.12   **Zone II** fracture of sacrum
Vertical foraminal region fracture of sacrum
    ● S32.120   **Nondisplaced** Zone II fracture of sacrum
    ● S32.121   **Minimally displaced** Zone II fracture of sacrum
    ● S32.122   **Severely displaced** Zone II fracture of sacrum
    ● S32.129   **Unspecified** Zone II fracture of sacrum

  ● S32.13   **Zone III** fracture of sacrum
Vertical fracture into spinal canal region of sacrum
    ● S32.130   **Nondisplaced** Zone III fracture of sacrum
    ● S32.131   **Minimally displaced** Zone III fracture of sacrum
    ● S32.132   **Severely displaced** Zone III fracture of sacrum
    ● S32.139   **Unspecified** Zone III fracture of sacrum

CHAPTER 19 (S00-T88)

CHAPTER 19 (S00-T88)

X ● **S32.14**   **Type 1** fracture of sacrum
       Transverse flexion fracture of sacrum without displacement

X ● **S32.15**   **Type 2** fracture of sacrum
       Transverse flexion fracture of sacrum with posterior displacement

X ● **S32.16**   **Type 3** fracture of sacrum
       Transverse extension fracture of sacrum with anterior displacement

X ● **S32.17**   **Type 4** fracture of sacrum
       Transverse segmental comminution of upper sacrum

X ● **S32.19**   **Other** fracture of sacrum

X ● **S32.2**   Fracture of **coccyx**

● **S32.3**   Fracture of **ilium**
     Excludes1   fracture of ilium with associated disruption of pelvic ring (S32.8-)

  ● **S32.30**   **Unspecified** fracture of ilium
     ● **S32.301**   Unspecified fracture of **right** ilium
     ● **S32.302**   Unspecified fracture of **left** ilium
     ● **S32.309**   Unspecified fracture of **unspecified** ilium

  ● **S32.31**   **Avulsion** fracture of ilium
     ● **S32.311**   Displaced avulsion fracture of **right** ilium
     ● **S32.312**   Displaced avulsion fracture of **left** ilium
     ● **S32.313**   Displaced avulsion fracture of **unspecified** ilium
     ● **S32.314**   Nondisplaced avulsion fracture of **right** ilium
     ● **S32.315**   Nondisplaced avulsion fracture of **left** ilium
     ● **S32.316**   Nondisplaced avulsion fracture of **unspecified** ilium

  ● **S32.39**   **Other** fracture of ilium
     ● **S32.391**   Other fracture of **right** ilium
     ● **S32.392**   Other fracture of **left** ilium
     ● **S32.399**   Other fracture of **unspecified** ilium

● **S32.4**   Fracture of **acetabulum**
     Code also any associated fracture of pelvic ring (S32.8-)

  ● **S32.40**   **Unspecified** fracture of acetabulum
     ● **S32.401**   Unspecified fracture of **right** acetabulum
     ● **S32.402**   Unspecified fracture of **left** acetabulum
     ● **S32.409**   Unspecified fracture of **unspecified** acetabulum

  ● **S32.41**   Fracture of **anterior wall** of acetabulum
     ● **S32.411**   Displaced fracture of anterior wall of **right** acetabulum
     ● **S32.412**   Displaced fracture of anterior wall of **left** acetabulum
     ● **S32.413**   Displaced fracture of anterior wall of **unspecified** acetabulum
     ● **S32.414**   Nondisplaced fracture of anterior wall of **right** acetabulum
     ● **S32.415**   Nondisplaced fracture of anterior wall of **left** acetabulum
     ● **S32.416**   Nondisplaced fracture of anterior wall of **unspecified** acetabulum

  ● **S32.42**   Fracture of **posterior wall** of acetabulum
     ● **S32.421**   Displaced fracture of posterior wall of **right** acetabulum
     ● **S32.422**   Displaced fracture of posterior wall of **left** acetabulum
     ● **S32.423**   Displaced fracture of posterior wall of **unspecified** acetabulum

     ● **S32.424**   Nondisplaced fracture of posterior wall of **right** acetabulum
     ● **S32.425**   Nondisplaced fracture of posterior wall of **left** acetabulum
     ● **S32.426**   Nondisplaced fracture of posterior wall of **unspecified** acetabulum

  ● **S32.43**   Fracture of **anterior column [iliopubic]** of acetabulum
     ● **S32.431**   Displaced fracture of anterior column [iliopubic] of **right** acetabulum
     ● **S32.432**   Displaced fracture of anterior column [iliopubic] of **left** acetabulum
     ● **S32.433**   Displaced fracture of anterior column [iliopubic] of **unspecified** acetabulum
     ● **S32.434**   Nondisplaced fracture of anterior column [iliopubic] of **right** acetabulum
     ● **S32.435**   Nondisplaced fracture of anterior column [iliopubic] of **left** acetabulum
     ● **S32.436**   Nondisplaced fracture of anterior column [iliopubic] of **unspecified** acetabulum

  ● **S32.44**   Fracture of **posterior column [ilioischial]** of acetabulum
     ● **S32.441**   Displaced fracture of posterior column [ilioischial] of **right** acetabulum
     ● **S32.442**   Displaced fracture of posterior column [ilioischial] of **left** acetabulum
     ● **S32.443**   Displaced fracture of posterior column [ilioischial] of **unspecified** acetabulum
     ● **S32.444**   Nondisplaced fracture of posterior column [ilioischial] of **right** acetabulum
     ● **S32.445**   Nondisplaced fracture of posterior column [ilioischial] of **left** acetabulum
     ● **S32.446**   Nondisplaced fracture of posterior column [ilioischial] of **unspecified** acetabulum

  ● **S32.45**   **Transverse** fracture of acetabulum
     ● **S32.451**   Displaced transverse fracture of **right** acetabulum
     ● **S32.452**   Displaced transverse fracture of **left** acetabulum
     ● **S32.453**   Displaced transverse fracture of **unspecified** acetabulum
     ● **S32.454**   Nondisplaced transverse fracture of **right** acetabulum
     ● **S32.455**   Nondisplaced transverse fracture of **left** acetabulum
     ● **S32.456**   Nondisplaced transverse fracture of **unspecified** acetabulum

  ● **S32.46**   **Associated transverse-posterior** fracture of acetabulum
     ● **S32.461**   Displaced associated transverse-posterior fracture of **right** acetabulum
     ● **S32.462**   Displaced associated transverse-posterior fracture of **left** acetabulum
     ● **S32.463**   Displaced associated transverse-posterior fracture of **unspecified** acetabulum
     ● **S32.464**   Nondisplaced associated transverse-posterior fracture of **right** acetabulum
     ● **S32.465**   Nondisplaced associated transverse-posterior fracture of **left** acetabulum
     ● **S32.466**   Nondisplaced associated transverse-posterior fracture of **unspecified** acetabulum

► New   ⇒ Revised   ~~deleted~~ Deleted   Excludes 1   Excludes 2   Includes   Use additional   Code first   Code also   Key words

OGCR Official Guidelines   X Assign placeholder X   ● Use Additional Character(s)   ▌ Manifestation Code   **Coding Clinic**

- **S32.47** Fracture of medial wall of acetabulum
    - **S32.471** Displaced fracture of medial wall of right acetabulum
    - **S32.472** Displaced fracture of medial wall of left acetabulum
    - **S32.473** Displaced fracture of medial wall of unspecified acetabulum
    - **S32.474** Nondisplaced fracture of medial wall of right acetabulum
    - **S32.475** Nondisplaced fracture of medial wall of left acetabulum
    - **S32.476** Nondisplaced fracture of medial wall of unspecified acetabulum
- **S32.48** Dome fracture of acetabulum
    - **S32.481** Displaced dome fracture of right acetabulum
    - **S32.482** Displaced dome fracture of left acetabulum
    - **S32.483** Displaced dome fracture of unspecified acetabulum
    - **S32.484** Nondisplaced dome fracture of right acetabulum
    - **S32.485** Nondisplaced dome fracture of left acetabulum
    - **S32.486** Nondisplaced dome fracture of unspecified acetabulum
- **S32.49** Other fracture of acetabulum
    - **S32.491** Other fracture of right acetabulum
    - **S32.492** Other fracture of left acetabulum
    - **S32.499** Other fracture of unspecified acetabulum
- **S32.5** Fracture of pubis
    - **Excludes1**   fracture of pubis with associated disruption of pelvic ring (S32.8-)
    - **S32.50** Unspecified fracture of pubis
        - **S32.501** Unspecified fracture of right pubis
        - **S32.502** Unspecified fracture of left pubis
        - **S32.509** Unspecified fracture of unspecified pubis
    - **S32.51** Fracture of superior rim of pubis
        - **S32.511** Fracture of superior rim of right pubis
        - **S32.512** Fracture of superior rim of left pubis
        - **S32.519** Fracture of superior rim of unspecified pubis
    - **S32.59** Other specified fracture of pubis
        - **S32.591** Other specified fracture of right pubis
        - **S32.592** Other specified fracture of left pubis
        - **S32.599** Other specified fracture of unspecified pubis
- **S32.6** Fracture of ischium
    - **Excludes1**   fracture of ischium with associated disruption of pelvic ring (S32.8-)
    - **S32.60** Unspecified fracture of ischium
        - **S32.601** Unspecified fracture of right ischium
        - **S32.602** Unspecified fracture of left ischium
        - **S32.609** Unspecified fracture of unspecified ischium
    - **S32.61** Avulsion fracture of ischium
        - **S32.611** Displaced avulsion fracture of right ischium
        - **S32.612** Displaced avulsion fracture of left ischium
        - **S32.613** Displaced avulsion fracture of unspecified ischium
        - **S32.614** Nondisplaced avulsion fracture of right ischium

- **S32.615** Nondisplaced avulsion fracture of left ischium
- **S32.616** Nondisplaced avulsion fracture of unspecified ischium
- **S32.69** Other specified fracture of ischium
    - **S32.691** Other specified fracture of right ischium
    - **S32.692** Other specified fracture of left ischium
    - **S32.699** Other specified fracture of unspecified ischium
- **S32.8** Fracture of other parts of pelvis

    Code also any associated:
    fracture of acetabulum (S32.4-)
    sacral fracture (S32.1-)
    - **S32.81** Multiple fractures of pelvis with disruption of pelvic ring

        Multiple pelvic fractures with disruption of pelvic circle
        - **S32.810** Multiple fractures of pelvis with stable disruption of pelvic ring
        - **S32.811** Multiple fractures of pelvis with unstable disruption of pelvic ring
    - X ● **S32.82** Multiple fractures of pelvis without disruption of pelvic ring

        Multiple pelvic fractures without disruption of pelvic circle
    - X ● **S32.89** Fracture of other parts of pelvis
- X ● **S32.9** Fracture of unspecified parts of lumbosacral spine and pelvis

    Fracture of lumbosacral spine NOS
    Fracture of pelvis NOS
    Coding Clinic: 2012, Q4, P93

- **S33** Dislocation and sprain of joints and ligaments of lumbar spine and pelvis
    - **Includes**   avulsion of joint or ligament of lumbar spine and pelvis
      laceration of cartilage, joint or ligament of lumbar spine and pelvis
      sprain of cartilage, joint or ligament of lumbar spine and pelvis
      traumatic hemarthrosis of joint or ligament of lumbar spine and pelvis
      traumatic rupture of joint or ligament of lumbar spine and pelvis
      traumatic subluxation of joint or ligament of lumbar spine and pelvis
      traumatic tear of joint or ligament of lumbar spine and pelvis

    Code also any associated open wound
    - **Excludes1**   nontraumatic rupture or displacement of lumbar intervertebral disc NOS (M51.-)
      obstetric damage to pelvic joints and ligaments (O71.6)
    - **Excludes2**   dislocation and sprain of joints and ligaments of hip (S73.-)
      strain of muscle of lower back and pelvis (S39.01-)

    The appropriate 7th character is to be added to each code from category S33

A	initial encounter
D	subsequent encounter
S	sequela

- X ● **S33.0** Traumatic rupture of lumbar intervertebral disc
    - **Excludes1**   rupture or displacement (nontraumatic) of lumbar intervertebral disc NOS (M51.- with fifth character 6)

CHAPTER 19 (S00-T88)

● **S33.1**   **Subluxation and dislocation of lumbar vertebra**
     Code also any associated:
         open wound of abdomen, lower back and pelvis (S31)
         spinal cord injury (S24.0, S24.1-, S34.0-, S34.1-)
     Excludes2   fracture of lumbar vertebrae (S32.0-)

   ● **S33.10**   **Subluxation and dislocation of unspecified lumbar vertebra**
     ● **S33.100**   **Subluxation of unspecified lumbar vertebra**
     ● **S33.101**   **Dislocation of unspecified lumbar vertebra**

   ● **S33.11**   **Subluxation and dislocation of L1/L2 lumbar vertebra**
     ● **S33.110**   **Subluxation of L1/L2 lumbar vertebra**
     ● **S33.111**   **Dislocation of L1/L2 lumbar vertebra**

   ● **S33.12**   **Subluxation and dislocation of L2/L3 lumbar vertebra**
     ● **S33.120**   **Subluxation of L2/L3 lumbar vertebra**
     ● **S33.121**   **Dislocation of L2/L3 lumbar vertebra**

   ● **S33.13**   **Subluxation and dislocation of L3/L4 lumbar vertebra**
     ● **S33.130**   **Subluxation of L3/L4 lumbar vertebra**
     ● **S33.131**   **Dislocation of L3/L4 lumbar vertebra**

   ● **S33.14**   **Subluxation and dislocation of L4/L5 lumbar vertebra**
     ● **S33.140**   **Subluxation of L4/L5 lumbar vertebra**
     ● **S33.141**   **Dislocation of L4/L5 lumbar vertebra**

X ● **S33.2**   **Dislocation of sacroiliac and sacrococcygeal joint**

● **S33.3**   **Dislocation of other and unspecified parts of lumbar spine and pelvis**
   X ● **S33.30**   **Dislocation of unspecified parts of lumbar spine and pelvis**
   X ● **S33.39**   **Dislocation of other parts of lumbar spine and pelvis**

X ● **S33.4**   **Traumatic rupture of symphysis pubis**
X ● **S33.5**   **Sprain of ligaments of lumbar spine**
X ● **S33.6**   **Sprain of sacroiliac joint**
X ● **S33.8**   **Sprain of other parts of lumbar spine and pelvis**
X ● **S33.9**   **Sprain of unspecified parts of lumbar spine and pelvis**

● **S34**   **Injury of lumbar and sacral spinal cord and nerves at abdomen, lower back and pelvis level**
   Note: Code to highest level of lumbar cord injury
     Injuries to the spinal cord (S34.0 and S34.1) refer to the cord level and not bone level injury, and can affect nerve roots at and below the level given.
   The appropriate 7th character is to be added to each code from category S34

     | | |
     A   initial encounter
     D   subsequent encounter
     S   sequela

   Code also any associated:
     fracture of vertebra (S22.0-, S32.0-)
     open wound of abdomen, lower back and pelvis (S31.-)
     transient paralysis (R29.5)

   ● **S34.0**   **Concussion and edema of lumbar and sacral spinal cord**
     X ● **S34.01**   **Concussion and edema of lumbar spinal cord**
     X ● **S34.02**   **Concussion and edema of sacral spinal cord**
       Concussion and edema of conus medullaris

● **S34.1**   **Other and unspecified injury of lumbar and sacral spinal cord**

   ● **S34.10**   **Unspecified injury to lumbar spinal cord**
     ● **S34.101**   **Unspecified injury to L$_1$ level of lumbar spinal cord**
       Unspecified injury to lumbar spinal cord level 1
     ● **S34.102**   **Unspecified injury to L$_2$ level of lumbar spinal cord**
       Unspecified injury to lumbar spinal cord level 2
     ● **S34.103**   **Unspecified injury to L$_3$ level of lumbar spinal cord**
       Unspecified injury to lumbar spinal cord level 3
     ● **S34.104**   **Unspecified injury to L$_4$ level of lumbar spinal cord**
       Unspecified injury to lumbar spinal cord level 4
     ● **S34.105**   **Unspecified injury to L$_5$ level of lumbar spinal cord**
       Unspecified injury to lumbar spinal cord level 5
     ● **S34.109**   **Unspecified injury to unspecified level of lumbar spinal cord**

   ● **S34.11**   **Complete lesion of lumbar spinal cord**
     ● **S34.111**   **Complete lesion of L$_1$ level of lumbar spinal cord**
       Complete lesion of lumbar spinal cord level 1
     ● **S34.112**   **Complete lesion of L$_2$ level of lumbar spinal cord**
       Complete lesion of lumbar spinal cord level 2
     ● **S34.113**   **Complete lesion of L$_3$ level of lumbar spinal cord**
       Complete lesion of lumbar spinal cord level 3
     ● **S34.114**   **Complete lesion of L$_4$ level of lumbar spinal cord**
       Complete lesion of lumbar spinal cord level 4
     ● **S34.115**   **Complete lesion of L$_5$ level of lumbar spinal cord**
       Complete lesion of lumbar spinal cord level 5
     ● **S34.119**   **Complete lesion of unspecified level of lumbar spinal cord**

   ● **S34.12**   **Incomplete lesion of lumbar spinal cord**
     ● **S34.121**   **Incomplete lesion of L$_1$ level of lumbar spinal cord**
       Incomplete lesion of lumbar spinal cord level 1
     ● **S34.122**   **Incomplete lesion of L$_2$ level of lumbar spinal cord**
       Incomplete lesion of lumbar spinal cord level 2
     ● **S34.123**   **Incomplete lesion of L$_3$ level of lumbar spinal cord**
       Incomplete lesion of lumbar spinal cord level 3
     ● **S34.124**   **Incomplete lesion of L$_4$ level of lumbar spinal cord**
       Incomplete lesion of lumbar spinal cord level 4
     ● **S34.125**   **Incomplete lesion of L$_5$ level of lumbar spinal cord**
       Incomplete lesion of lumbar spinal cord level 5
     ● **S34.129**   **Incomplete lesion of unspecified level of lumbar spinal cord**

▶ New   ⇒ Revised   ~~deleted~~ Deleted   Excludes 1   Excludes 2   Includes   Use additional   Code first   Code also   Key words
OGCR Official Guidelines   X Assign placeholder X   ● Use Additional Character(s)   ▌ Manifestation Code   **Coding Clinic**

● S34.13   **Other and unspecified injury to** sacral spinal
cord
Other injury to conus medullaris

● S34.131   **Complete lesion of** sacral spinal cord
Complete lesion of conus medullaris

● S34.132   **Incomplete lesion of** sacral spinal
cord
Incomplete lesion of conus
medullaris

● S34.139   **Unspecified injury to** sacral spinal
cord
Unspecified injury of conus
medullaris

● S34.2   **Injury of** nerve root of lumbar and sacral spine

X● S34.21   **Injury of nerve root of** lumbar **spine**

X● S34.22   **Injury of nerve root of** sacral **spine**

X● S34.3   **Injury of cauda equina**

X● S34.4   **Injury of lumbosacral plexus**

X● S34.5   **Injury of lumbar, sacral and pelvic sympathetic nerves**
Injury of celiac ganglion or plexus
Injury of hypogastric plexus
Injury of mesenteric plexus (inferior) (superior)
Injury of splanchnic nerve

X● S34.6   **Injury of peripheral nerve(s) at abdomen, lower back and pelvis level**

X● S34.8   **Injury of other nerves at abdomen, lower back and pelvis level**

X● S34.9   **Injury of** unspecified **nerves at abdomen, lower back and pelvis level**

● S35   **Injury of blood vessels at abdomen, lower back and pelvis level**
The appropriate 7th character is to be added to each code from
category S35

A	initial encounter
D	subsequent encounter
S	sequela

Code also any associated open wound (S31.-)

● S35.0   **Injury of abdominal aorta**

> **Excludes1**   injury of aorta NOS (S25.0)

X● S35.00   **Unspecified injury of abdominal aorta**

X● S35.01   **Minor laceration of abdominal aorta**
Incomplete transection of abdominal aorta
Laceration of abdominal aorta NOS
Superficial laceration of abdominal aorta

X● S35.02   **Major laceration of abdominal aorta**
Complete transection of abdominal aorta
Traumatic rupture of abdominal aorta

X● S35.09   **Other injury of abdominal aorta**

● S35.1   **Injury of** inferior vena cava
Injury of hepatic vein

> **Excludes1**   injury of vena cava NOS (S25.2)

X● S35.10   **Unspecified injury of inferior vena cava**

X● S35.11   **Minor laceration of inferior vena cava**
Incomplete transection of inferior vena cava
Laceration of inferior vena cava NOS
Superficial laceration of inferior vena cava

X● S35.12   **Major laceration of inferior vena cava**
Complete transection of inferior vena cava
Traumatic rupture of inferior vena cava

X● S35.19   **Other injury of inferior vena cava**

● S35.2   **Injury of celiac or mesenteric artery and branches**

● S35.21   **Injury of** celiac artery

● S35.211   **Minor laceration of celiac artery**
Incomplete transection of celiac
artery
Laceration of celiac artery NOS
Superficial laceration of celiac artery

● S35.212   **Major laceration of celiac artery**
Complete transection of celiac artery
Traumatic rupture of celiac artery

● S35.218   **Other injury of celiac artery**

● S35.219   **Unspecified injury of celiac artery**

● S35.22   **Injury of** superior mesenteric artery

● S35.221   **Minor laceration of superior
mesenteric artery**
Incomplete transection of superior
mesenteric artery
Laceration of superior mesenteric
artery NOS
Superficial laceration of superior
mesenteric artery

● S35.222   **Major laceration of superior
mesenteric artery**
Complete transection of superior
mesenteric artery
Traumatic rupture of superior
mesenteric artery

● S35.228   **Other injury of superior mesenteric
artery**

● S35.229   **Unspecified injury of superior
mesenteric artery**

● S35.23   **Injury of** inferior mesenteric artery

● S35.231   **Minor laceration of inferior
mesenteric artery**
Incomplete transection of inferior
mesenteric artery
Laceration of inferior mesenteric
artery NOS
Superficial laceration of inferior
mesenteric artery

● S35.232   **Major laceration of inferior
mesenteric artery**
Complete transection of inferior
mesenteric artery
Traumatic rupture of inferior
mesenteric artery

● S35.238   **Other injury of inferior mesenteric
artery**

● S35.239   **Unspecified injury of inferior
mesenteric artery**

● S35.29   **Injury of branches of celiac and mesenteric
artery**
Injury of gastric artery
Injury of gastroduodenal artery
Injury of hepatic artery
Injury of splenic artery

● S35.291   **Minor laceration of branches of celiac
and mesenteric artery**
Incomplete transection of branches
of celiac and mesenteric artery
Laceration of branches of celiac and
mesenteric artery NOS
Superficial laceration of branches of
celiac and mesenteric artery

● S35.292   **Major laceration of branches of celiac
and mesenteric artery**
Complete transection of branches of
celiac and mesenteric artery
Traumatic rupture of branches of
celiac and mesenteric artery

● S35.298   **Other injury of branches of celiac and
mesenteric artery**

● S35.299   **Unspecified injury of branches of
celiac and mesenteric artery**

CHAPTER 19 (S00-T88)

- S35.3   Injury of portal or splenic vein and branches
  - S35.31   Injury of portal vein
    - S35.311   Laceration of portal vein
    - S35.318   Other specified injury of portal vein
    - S35.319   Unspecified injury of portal vein
  - S35.32   Injury of splenic vein
    - S35.321   Laceration of splenic vein
    - S35.328   Other specified injury of splenic vein
    - S35.329   Unspecified injury of splenic vein
  - S35.33   Injury of superior mesenteric vein
    - S35.331   Laceration of superior mesenteric vein
    - S35.338   Other specified injury of superior mesenteric vein
    - S35.339   Unspecified injury of superior mesenteric vein
  - S35.34   Injury of inferior mesenteric vein
    - S35.341   Laceration of inferior mesenteric vein
    - S35.348   Other specified injury of inferior mesenteric vein
    - S35.349   Unspecified injury of inferior mesenteric vein
- S35.4   Injury of renal blood vessels
  - S35.40   Unspecified injury of renal blood vessel
    - S35.401   Unspecified injury of right renal artery
    - S35.402   Unspecified injury of left renal artery
    - S35.403   Unspecified injury of unspecified renal artery
    - S35.404   Unspecified injury of right renal vein
    - S35.405   Unspecified injury of left renal vein
    - S35.406   Unspecified injury of unspecified renal vein
  - S35.41   Laceration of renal blood vessel
    - S35.411   Laceration of right renal artery
    - S35.412   Laceration of left renal artery
    - S35.413   Laceration of unspecified renal artery
    - S35.414   Laceration of right renal vein
    - S35.415   Laceration of left renal vein
    - S35.416   Laceration of unspecified renal vein
  - S35.49   Other specified injury of renal blood vessel
    - S35.491   Other specified injury of right renal artery
    - S35.492   Other specified injury of left renal artery
    - S35.493   Other specified injury of unspecified renal artery
    - S35.494   Other specified injury of right renal vein
    - S35.495   Other specified injury of left renal vein
    - S35.496   Other specified injury of unspecified renal vein
- S35.5   Injury of iliac blood vessels
  - X S35.50   Injury of unspecified iliac blood vessel(s)
  - S35.51   Injury of iliac artery or vein
    Injury of hypogastric artery or vein
    - S35.511   Injury of right iliac artery
    - S35.512   Injury of left iliac artery
    - S35.513   Injury of unspecified iliac artery
    - S35.514   Injury of right iliac vein
    - S35.515   Injury of left iliac vein
    - S35.516   Injury of unspecified iliac vein

- S35.53   Injury of uterine artery or vein
  - S35.531   Injury of right uterine artery ♀
  - S35.532   Injury of left uterine artery ♀
  - S35.533   Injury of unspecified uterine artery ♀
  - S35.534   Injury of right uterine vein ♀
  - S35.535   Injury of left uterine vein ♀
  - S35.536   Injury of unspecified uterine vein ♀
  - X S35.59   Injury of other iliac blood vessels
- S35.8   Injury of other blood vessels at abdomen, lower back and pelvis level
    Injury of ovarian artery or vein
  - S35.8X   Injury of other blood vessels at abdomen, lower back and pelvis level
    - S35.8X1   Laceration of other blood vessels at abdomen, lower back and pelvis level
    - S35.8X8   Other specified injury of other blood vessels at abdomen, lower back and pelvis level
    - S35.8X9   Unspecified injury of other blood vessels at abdomen, lower back and pelvis level
- S35.9   Injury of unspecified blood vessel at abdomen, lower back and pelvis level
  - X S35.90   Unspecified injury of unspecified blood vessel at abdomen, lower back and pelvis level
  - X S35.91   Laceration of unspecified blood vessel at abdomen, lower back and pelvis level
  - X S35.99   Other specified injury of unspecified blood vessel at abdomen, lower back and pelvis level
- S36   Injury of intra-abdominal organs
    The appropriate 7th character is to be added to each code from category S36

A	initial encounter
D	subsequent encounter
S	sequela

    Code also any associated open wound (S31.-)
  - S36.0   Injury of spleen
    - X S36.00   Unspecified injury of spleen
    - S36.02   Contusion of spleen
      - S36.020   Minor contusion of spleen
        Contusion of spleen less than 2 cm
      - S36.021   Major contusion of spleen
        Contusion of spleen greater than 2 cm
      - S36.029   Unspecified contusion of spleen
        Coding Clinic: 2015, Q2, P36, Q1, P11
    - S36.03   Laceration of spleen
      - S36.030   Superficial (capsular) laceration of spleen
        Laceration of spleen less than 1 cm
        Minor laceration of spleen
      - S36.031   Moderate laceration of spleen
        Laceration of spleen 1 to 3 cm
        Coding Clinic: 2015, Q2, P36, Q1, P11
      - S36.032   Major laceration of spleen
        Avulsion of spleen
        Laceration of spleen greater than 3 cm
        Massive laceration of spleen
        Multiple moderate lacerations of spleen
        Stellate laceration of spleen
      - S36.039   Unspecified laceration of spleen
    - X S36.09   Other injury of spleen

▶ New   ⇒ Revised   ~~deleted~~ Deleted   Excludes 1   Excludes 2   Includes   Use additional   Code first   Code also   Key words
OGCR Official Guidelines   X Assign placeholder X   ● Use Additional Character(s)   ▸ Manifestation Code   Coding Clinic

● S36.1   Injury of liver and gallbladder and bile duct
   ● S36.11   **Injury of liver**
     ● S36.112   Contusion of liver
     ● S36.113   Laceration of liver, unspecified degree
     ● S36.114   Minor laceration of liver
          Laceration involving capsule only, or, without significant involvement of hepatic parenchyma [i.e., less than 1 cm deep]
     ● S36.115   Moderate laceration of liver
          Laceration involving parenchyma but without major disruption of parenchyma [i.e., less than 10 cm long and less than 3 cm deep]
     ● S36.116   Major laceration of liver
          Laceration with significant disruption of hepatic parenchyma [i.e., greater than 10 cm long and 3 cm deep]
          Multiple moderate lacerations, with or without hematoma
          Stellate laceration of liver
     ● S36.118   Other injury of liver
     ● S36.119   Unspecified injury of liver
          Coding Clinic: 2015, Q2, P17
   ● S36.12   Injury of gallbladder
     ● S36.122   Contusion of gallbladder
     ● S36.123   Laceration of gallbladder
     ● S36.128   Other injury of gallbladder
     ● S36.129   Unspecified injury of gallbladder
   X ● S36.13   Injury of bile duct
● S36.2   Injury of pancreas
   ● S36.20   Unspecified injury of pancreas
     ● S36.200   Unspecified injury of head of pancreas
     ● S36.201   Unspecified injury of body of pancreas
     ● S36.202   Unspecified injury of tail of pancreas
     ● S36.209   Unspecified injury of unspecified part of pancreas
   ● S36.22   Contusion of pancreas
     ● S36.220   Contusion of head of pancreas
     ● S36.221   Contusion of body of pancreas
     ● S36.222   Contusion of tail of pancreas
     ● S36.229   Contusion of unspecified part of pancreas
   ● S36.23   Laceration of pancreas, unspecified degree
     ● S36.230   Laceration of head of pancreas, unspecified degree
     ● S36.231   Laceration of body of pancreas, unspecified degree
     ● S36.232   Laceration of tail of pancreas, unspecified degree
     ● S36.239   Laceration of unspecified part of pancreas, unspecified degree
   ● S36.24   Minor laceration of pancreas
     ● S36.240   Minor laceration of head of pancreas
     ● S36.241   Minor laceration of body of pancreas
     ● S36.242   Minor laceration of tail of pancreas
     ● S36.249   Minor laceration of unspecified part of pancreas

● S36.25   Moderate laceration of pancreas
     ● S36.250   Moderate laceration of head of pancreas
     ● S36.251   Moderate laceration of body of pancreas
     ● S36.252   Moderate laceration of tail of pancreas
     ● S36.259   Moderate laceration of unspecified part of pancreas
● S36.26   Major laceration of pancreas
     ● S36.260   Major laceration of head of pancreas
     ● S36.261   Major laceration of body of pancreas
     ● S36.262   Major laceration of tail of pancreas
     ● S36.269   Major laceration of unspecified part of pancreas
● S36.29   Other injury of pancreas
     ● S36.290   Other injury of head of pancreas
     ● S36.291   Other injury of body of pancreas
     ● S36.292   Other injury of tail of pancreas
     ● S36.299   Other injury of unspecified part of pancreas
● S36.3   Injury of stomach
   X ● S36.30   Unspecified injury of stomach
   X ● S36.32   Contusion of stomach
   X ● S36.33   Laceration of stomach
   X ● S36.39   Other injury of stomach
● S36.4   Injury of small intestine
   ● S36.40   Unspecified injury of small intestine
     ● S36.400   Unspecified injury of duodenum
     ● S36.408   Unspecified injury of other part of small intestine
     ● S36.409   Unspecified injury of unspecified part of small intestine
   ● S36.41   Primary blast injury of small intestine
          Blast injury of small intestine NOS
     ● S36.410   Primary blast injury of duodenum
     ● S36.418   Primary blast injury of other part of small intestine
     ● S36.419   Primary blast injury of unspecified part of small intestine
   ● S36.42   Contusion of small intestine
     ● S36.420   Contusion of duodenum
     ● S36.428   Contusion of other part of small intestine
     ● S36.429   Contusion of unspecified part of small intestine
   ● S36.43   Laceration of small intestine
     ● S36.430   Laceration of duodenum
     ● S36.438   Laceration of other part of small intestine
     ● S36.439   Laceration of unspecified part of small intestine
   ● S36.49   Other injury of small intestine
     ● S36.490   Other injury of duodenum
     ● S36.498   Other injury of other part of small intestine
     ● S36.499   Other injury of unspecified part of small intestine

CHAPTER 19 (S00-T88)

S36.5 **Injury of colon**
>**Excludes2**   injury of rectum (S36.6-)

    S36.50   Unspecified injury of colon

        S36.500   Unspecified injury of ascending [right] colon

        S36.501   Unspecified injury of transverse colon

        S36.502   Unspecified injury of descending [left] colon

        S36.503   Unspecified injury of sigmoid colon

        S36.508   Unspecified injury of other part of colon

        S36.509   Unspecified injury of unspecified part of colon

    S36.51   Primary blast injury of colon
>Blast injury of colon NOS

        S36.510   Primary blast injury of ascending [right] colon

        S36.511   Primary blast injury of transverse colon

        S36.512   Primary blast injury of descending [left] colon

        S36.513   Primary blast injury of sigmoid colon

        S36.518   Primary blast injury of other part of colon

        S36.519   Primary blast injury of unspecified part of colon

    S36.52   Contusion of colon

        S36.520   Contusion of ascending [right] colon

        S36.521   Contusion of transverse colon

        S36.522   Contusion of descending [left] colon

        S36.523   Contusion of sigmoid colon

        S36.528   Contusion of other part of colon

        S36.529   Contusion of unspecified part of colon

    S36.53   Laceration of colon

        S36.530   Laceration of ascending [right] colon

        S36.531   Laceration of transverse colon

        S36.532   Laceration of descending [left] colon

        S36.533   Laceration of sigmoid colon

        S36.538   Laceration of other part of colon

        S36.539   Laceration of unspecified part of colon

    S36.59   Other injury of colon
>Secondary blast injury of colon

        S36.590   Other injury of ascending [right] colon

        S36.591   Other injury of transverse colon

        S36.592   Other injury of descending [left] colon

        S36.593   Other injury of sigmoid colon

        S36.598   Other injury of other part of colon

        S36.599   Other injury of unspecified part of colon

S36.6 **Injury of rectum**

  X **S36.60**   Unspecified injury of rectum

  X **S36.61**   Primary blast injury of rectum
>Blast injury of rectum NOS

  X **S36.62**   Contusion of rectum

  X **S36.63**   Laceration of rectum

  X **S36.69**   Other injury of rectum
>Secondary blast injury of rectum

S36.8 **Injury of other intra-abdominal organs**

  X **S36.81**   Injury of peritoneum

    S36.89   Injury of other intra-abdominal organs
>Injury of retroperitoneum

        S36.892   Contusion of other intra-abdominal organs

        S36.893   Laceration of other intra-abdominal organs

        S36.898   Other injury of other intra-abdominal organs

        S36.899   Unspecified injury of other intra-abdominal organs

S36.9 **Injury of unspecified intra-abdominal organ**

  X **S36.90**   Unspecified injury of unspecified intra-abdominal organ

  X **S36.92**   Contusion of unspecified intra-abdominal organ

  X **S36.93**   Laceration of unspecified intra-abdominal organ

  X **S36.99**   Other injury of unspecified intra-abdominal organ

S37   **Injury of urinary and pelvic organs**
>Code also any associated open wound (S31.-)
>
>**Excludes1**   obstetric trauma to pelvic organs (O71.-)
>
>**Excludes2**   injury of peritoneum (S36.81)
>injury of retroperitoneum (S36.89-)

The appropriate 7th character is to be added to each code from category S37

A	initial encounter
D	subsequent encounter
S	sequela

S37.0   **Injury of kidney**
>**Excludes2**   acute kidney injury (nontraumatic) (N17.9)

    S37.00   Unspecified injury of kidney

        S37.001   Unspecified injury of right kidney

        S37.002   Unspecified injury of left kidney

        S37.009   Unspecified injury of unspecified kidney

    S37.01   Minor contusion of kidney
>Contusion of kidney less than 2 cm
>Contusion of kidney NOS

        S37.011   Minor contusion of right kidney

        S37.012   Minor contusion of left kidney

        S37.019   Minor contusion of unspecified kidney

    S37.02   Major contusion of kidney
>Contusion of kidney greater than 2 cm

        S37.021   Major contusion of right kidney

        S37.022   Major contusion of left kidney

        S37.029   Major contusion of unspecified kidney

    S37.03   Laceration of kidney, unspecified degree

        S37.031   Laceration of right kidney, unspecified degree

        S37.032   Laceration of left kidney, unspecified degree

        S37.039   Laceration of unspecified kidney, unspecified degree

    S37.04   Minor laceration of kidney
>Laceration of kidney less than 1 cm

        S37.041   Minor laceration of right kidney

        S37.042   Minor laceration of left kidney

        S37.049   Minor laceration of unspecified kidney

- S37.05   **Moderate laceration of kidney**
  - Laceration of kidney 1 to 3 cm
  - S37.051   Moderate laceration of right kidney
  - S37.052   Moderate laceration of left kidney
  - S37.059   Moderate laceration of unspecified kidney
- S37.06   **Major laceration of kidney**
  - Avulsion of kidney
  - Laceration of kidney greater than 3 cm
  - Massive laceration of kidney
  - Multiple moderate lacerations of kidney
  - Stellate laceration of kidney
  - S37.061   Major laceration of right kidney
  - S37.062   Major laceration of left kidney
  - S37.069   Major laceration of unspecified kidney
- S37.09   **Other injury of kidney**
  - S37.091   Other injury of right kidney
  - S37.092   Other injury of left kidney
  - S37.099   Other injury of unspecified kidney
- S37.1   **Injury of ureter**
  - X S37.10   **Unspecified injury of ureter**
  - X S37.12   **Contusion of ureter**
  - X S37.13   **Laceration of ureter**
  - X S37.19   **Other injury of ureter**
- S37.2   **Injury of bladder**
  - X S37.20   **Unspecified injury of bladder**
  - X S37.22   **Contusion of bladder**
  - X S37.23   **Laceration of bladder**
  - X S37.29   **Other injury of bladder**
- S37.3   **Injury of urethra**
  - X S37.30   **Unspecified injury of urethra**
  - X S37.32   **Contusion of urethra**
  - X S37.33   **Laceration of urethra**
  - X S37.39   **Other injury of urethra**
- S37.4   **Injury of ovary**
  - S37.40   **Unspecified injury of ovary**
    - S37.401   Unspecified injury of ovary, unilateral ♀
    - S37.402   Unspecified injury of ovary, bilateral ♀
    - S37.409   Unspecified injury of ovary, unspecified ♀
  - S37.42   **Contusion of ovary**
    - S37.421   Contusion of ovary, unilateral ♀
    - S37.422   Contusion of ovary, bilateral ♀
    - S37.429   Contusion of ovary, unspecified ♀
  - S37.43   **Laceration of ovary**
    - S37.431   Laceration of ovary, unilateral ♀
    - S37.432   Laceration of ovary, bilateral ♀
    - S37.439   Laceration of ovary, unspecified ♀
  - S37.49   **Other injury of ovary**
    - S37.491   Other injury of ovary, unilateral ♀
    - S37.492   Other injury of ovary, bilateral ♀
    - S37.499   Other injury of ovary, unspecified ♀
- S37.5   **Injury of fallopian tube**
  - S37.50   **Unspecified injury of fallopian tube**
    - S37.501   Unspecified injury of fallopian tube, unilateral ♀
    - S37.502   Unspecified injury of fallopian tube, bilateral ♀
    - S37.509   Unspecified injury of fallopian tube, unspecified ♀

- S37.51   **Primary blast injury of fallopian tube**
  - Blast injury of fallopian tube NOS
  - S37.511   Primary blast injury of fallopian tube, unilateral ♀
  - S37.512   Primary blast injury of fallopian tube, bilateral ♀
  - S37.519   Primary blast injury of fallopian tube, unspecified ♀
- S37.52   **Contusion of fallopian tube**
  - S37.521   Contusion of fallopian tube, unilateral ♀
  - S37.522   Contusion of fallopian tube, bilateral ♀
  - S37.529   Contusion of fallopian tube, unspecified ♀
- S37.53   **Laceration of fallopian tube**
  - S37.531   Laceration of fallopian tube, unilateral ♀
  - S37.532   Laceration of fallopian tube, bilateral ♀
  - S37.539   Laceration of fallopian tube, unspecified ♀
- S37.59   **Other injury of fallopian tube**
  - Secondary blast injury of fallopian tube
  - S37.591   Other injury of fallopian tube, unilateral ♀
  - S37.592   Other injury of fallopian tube, bilateral ♀
  - S37.599   Other injury of fallopian tube, unspecified ♀
- S37.6   **Injury of uterus**
  - **Excludes1**   injury to gravid uterus (O9A.2-)
  - injury to uterus during delivery (O71.-)
  - X S37.60   **Unspecified injury of uterus** ♀
  - X S37.62   **Contusion of uterus** ♀
  - X S37.63   **Laceration of uterus** ♀
  - X S37.69   **Other injury of uterus** ♀
- S37.8   **Injury of other urinary and pelvic organs**
  - S37.81   **Injury of adrenal gland**
    - S37.812   Contusion of adrenal gland
    - S37.813   Laceration of adrenal gland
    - S37.818   Other injury of adrenal gland
    - S37.819   Unspecified injury of adrenal gland
  - S37.82   **Injury of prostate**
    - S37.822   Contusion of prostate ♂
    - S37.823   Laceration of prostate ♂
    - S37.828   Other injury of prostate ♂
    - S37.829   Unspecified injury of prostate ♂
  - S37.89   **Injury of other urinary and pelvic organ**
    - S37.892   Contusion of other urinary and pelvic organ
    - S37.893   Laceration of other urinary and pelvic organ
    - S37.898   Other injury of other urinary and pelvic organ
    - S37.899   Unspecified injury of other urinary and pelvic organ
- S37.9   **Injury of unspecified urinary and pelvic organ**
  - X S37.90   **Unspecified injury of unspecified urinary and pelvic organ**
  - X S37.92   **Contusion of unspecified urinary and pelvic organ**
  - X S37.93   **Laceration of unspecified urinary and pelvic organ**
  - X S37.99   **Other injury of unspecified urinary and pelvic organ**

CHAPTER 19 (SØØ-T88)

● **S38　Crushing injury and traumatic amputation of abdomen, lower back, pelvis and external genitals**

An amputation not identified as partial or complete should be coded to complete

The appropriate 7th character is to be added to each code from category S38

A	initial encounter
D	subsequent encounter
S	sequela

● **S38.0　Crushing injury of external genital organs**

Use additional code for any associated injuries

● **S38.00　Crushing injury of unspecified external genital organs**

● **S38.001　Crushing injury of unspecified external genital organs, male ♂**

● **S38.002　Crushing injury of unspecified external genital organs, female ♀**

X● **S38.01　Crushing injury of penis ♂**

X● **S38.02　Crushing injury of scrotum and testis ♂**

X● **S38.03　Crushing injury of vulva ♀**

X● **S38.1　Crushing injury of abdomen, lower back, and pelvis**

Use additional code for all associated injuries, such as:
fracture of thoracic or lumbar spine and pelvis (S22.0-, S32.-)
injury to intra-abdominal organs (S36.-)
injury to urinary and pelvic organs (S37.-)
open wound of abdominal wall (S31.-)
spinal cord injury (S34.0, S34.1-)

Excludes2　crushing injury of external genital organs (S38.0-)

● **S38.2　Traumatic amputation of external genital organs**

● **S38.21　Traumatic amputation of female external genital organs**

Traumatic amputation of clitoris
Traumatic amputation of labium (majus) (minus)
Traumatic amputation of vulva

● **S38.211　Complete traumatic amputation of female external genital organs ♀**

● **S38.212　Partial traumatic amputation of female external genital organs ♀**

● **S38.22　Traumatic amputation of penis**

● **S38.221　Complete traumatic amputation of penis ♂**

● **S38.222　Partial traumatic amputation of penis ♂**

● **S38.23　Traumatic amputation of scrotum and testis**

● **S38.231　Complete traumatic amputation of scrotum and testis ♂**

● **S38.232　Partial traumatic amputation of scrotum and testis ♂**

X● **S38.3　Transection (partial) of abdomen**

● **S39　Other and unspecified injuries of abdomen, lower back, pelvis and external genitals**

Code also any associated open wound (S31.-)

Excludes2　sprain of joints and ligaments of lumbar spine and pelvis (S33.-)

The appropriate 7th character is to be added to each code from category S39

A	initial encounter
D	subsequent encounter
S	sequela

● **S39.0　Injury of muscle, fascia and tendon of abdomen, lower back and pelvis**

● **S39.00　Unspecified injury of muscle, fascia and tendon of abdomen, lower back and pelvis**

● **S39.001　Unspecified injury of muscle, fascia and tendon of abdomen**

● **S39.002　Unspecified injury of muscle, fascia and tendon of lower back**

● **S39.003　Unspecified injury of muscle, fascia and tendon of pelvis**

● **S39.01　Strain of muscle, fascia and tendon of abdomen, lower back and pelvis**

● **S39.011　Strain of muscle, fascia and tendon of abdomen**

● **S39.012　Strain of muscle, fascia and tendon of lower back**

Coding Clinic: 2016, Q4, P74

● **S39.013　Strain of muscle, fascia and tendon of pelvis**

● **S39.02　Laceration of muscle, fascia and tendon of abdomen, lower back and pelvis**

● **S39.021　Laceration of muscle, fascia and tendon of abdomen**

● **S39.022　Laceration of muscle, fascia and tendon of lower back**

● **S39.023　Laceration of muscle, fascia and tendon of pelvis**

● **S39.09　Other injury of muscle, fascia and tendon of abdomen, lower back and pelvis**

● **S39.091　Other injury of muscle, fascia and tendon of abdomen**

● **S39.092　Other injury of muscle, fascia and tendon of lower back**

● **S39.093　Other injury of muscle, fascia and tendon of pelvis**

● **S39.8　Other specified injuries of abdomen, lower back, pelvis and external genitals**

X● **S39.81　Other specified injuries of abdomen**

X● **S39.82　Other specified injuries of lower back**

X● **S39.83　Other specified injuries of pelvis**

● **S39.84　Other specified injuries of external genitals**

● **S39.840　Fracture of corpus cavernosum penis ♂**

● **S39.848　Other specified injuries of external genitals**

● **S39.9　Unspecified injury of abdomen, lower back, pelvis and external genitals**

X● **S39.91　Unspecified injury of abdomen**

X● **S39.92　Unspecified injury of lower back**

X● **S39.93　Unspecified injury of pelvis**

X● **S39.94　Unspecified injury of external genitals**

INJURIES TO THE SHOULDER AND UPPER ARM (S40-S49)

Includes　injuries of axilla injuries of scapular region

Excludes2　burns and corrosions (T20-T32)
frostbite (T33-T34)
injuries of elbow (S50-S59)
insect bite or sting, venomous (T63.4)

● **S40　Superficial injury of shoulder and upper arm**

The appropriate 7th character is to be added to each code from category S40

A	initial encounter
D	subsequent encounter
S	sequela

● **S40.0　Contusion of shoulder and upper arm**

● **S40.01　Contusion of shoulder**

● **S40.011　Contusion of right shoulder**

● **S40.012　Contusion of left shoulder**

● **S40.019　Contusion of unspecified shoulder**

● **S40.02　Contusion of upper arm**

● **S40.021　Contusion of right upper arm**

● **S40.022　Contusion of left upper arm**

● **S40.029　Contusion of unspecified upper arm**

▶ New　⇒ Revised　~~deleted~~ Deleted　Excludes 1　Excludes 2　Includes　Use additional　Code first　Code also　Key words
OGCR Official Guidelines　X Assign placeholder X　● Use Additional Character(s)　▷ Manifestation Code　Coding Clinic

- S40.2   Other superficial injuries of shoulder
  - S40.21   Abrasion of shoulder
    - S40.211   Abrasion of right shoulder
    - S40.212   Abrasion of left shoulder
    - S40.219   Abrasion of unspecified shoulder
  - S40.22   Blister (nonthermal) of shoulder
    - S40.221   Blister (nonthermal) of right shoulder
    - S40.222   Blister (nonthermal) of left shoulder
    - S40.229   Blister (nonthermal) of unspecified shoulder
  - S40.24   External constriction of shoulder
    - S40.241   External constriction of right shoulder
    - S40.242   External constriction of left shoulder
    - S40.249   External constriction of unspecified shoulder
  - S40.25   Superficial foreign body of shoulder
    Splinter in the shoulder
    - S40.251   Superficial foreign body of right shoulder
    - S40.252   Superficial foreign body of left shoulder
    - S40.259   Superficial foreign body of unspecified shoulder
  - S40.26   Insect bite (nonvenomous) of shoulder
    - S40.261   Insect bite (nonvenomous) of right shoulder
    - S40.262   Insect bite (nonvenomous) of left shoulder
    - S40.269   Insect bite (nonvenomous) of unspecified shoulder
  - S40.27   Other superficial bite of shoulder
    - **Excludes1**   open bite of shoulder (S41.05)
    - S40.271   Other superficial bite of right shoulder
    - S40.272   Other superficial bite of left shoulder
    - S40.279   Other superficial bite of unspecified shoulder
- S40.8   Other superficial injuries of upper arm
  - S40.81   Abrasion of upper arm
    - S40.811   Abrasion of right upper arm
    - S40.812   Abrasion of left upper arm
    - S40.819   Abrasion of unspecified upper arm
  - S40.82   Blister (nonthermal) of upper arm
    - S40.821   Blister (nonthermal) of right upper arm
    - S40.822   Blister (nonthermal) of left upper arm
    - S40.829   Blister (nonthermal) of unspecified upper arm
  - S40.84   External constriction of upper arm
    - S40.841   External constriction of right upper arm
    - S40.842   External constriction of left upper arm
    - S40.849   External constriction of unspecified upper arm
  - S40.85   Superficial foreign body of upper arm
    Splinter in the upper arm
    - S40.851   Superficial foreign body of right upper arm
    - S40.852   Superficial foreign body of left upper arm
    - S40.859   Superficial foreign body of unspecified upper arm
  - S40.86   Insect bite (nonvenomous) of upper arm
    - S40.861   Insect bite (nonvenomous) of right upper arm
    - S40.862   Insect bite (nonvenomous) of left upper arm
    - S40.869   Insect bite (nonvenomous) of unspecified upper arm
  - S40.87   Other superficial bite of upper arm
    - **Excludes1**   open bite of upper arm (S41.14)
    - **Excludes2**   other superficial bite of shoulder (S40.27-)
    - S40.871   Other superficial bite of right upper arm
    - S40.872   Other superficial bite of left upper arm
    - S40.879   Other superficial bite of unspecified upper arm
- S40.9   Unspecified superficial injury of shoulder and upper arm
  - S40.91   Unspecified superficial injury of shoulder
    - S40.911   Unspecified superficial injury of right shoulder
    - S40.912   Unspecified superficial injury of left shoulder
    - S40.919   Unspecified superficial injury of unspecified shoulder
  - S40.92   Unspecified superficial injury of upper arm
    - S40.921   Unspecified superficial injury of right upper arm
    - S40.922   Unspecified superficial injury of left upper arm
    - S40.929   Unspecified superficial injury of unspecified upper arm
- S41   Open wound of shoulder and upper arm
  Code also any associated wound infection
  - **Excludes1**   traumatic amputation of shoulder and upper arm (S48.-)
  - **Excludes2**   open fracture of shoulder and upper arm (S42.- with 7th character B or C)

  The appropriate 7th character is to be added to each code from category S41

A	initial encounter
D	subsequent encounter
S	sequela

  - S41.0   Open wound of shoulder
    - S41.00   Unspecified open wound of shoulder
      - S41.001   Unspecified open wound of right shoulder
      - S41.002   Unspecified open wound of left shoulder
      - S41.009   Unspecified open wound of unspecified shoulder
    - S41.01   Laceration without foreign body of shoulder
      - S41.011   Laceration without foreign body of right shoulder
      - S41.012   Laceration without foreign body of left shoulder
      - S41.019   Laceration without foreign body of unspecified shoulder
    - S41.02   Laceration with foreign body of shoulder
      - S41.021   Laceration with foreign body of right shoulder
      - S41.022   Laceration with foreign body of left shoulder
      - S41.029   Laceration with foreign body of unspecified shoulder

● **S41.03 Puncture wound without foreign body of shoulder**
  ● S41.031   Puncture wound without foreign body of **right shoulder**
  ● S41.032   Puncture wound without foreign body of **left shoulder**
  ● S41.039   Puncture wound without foreign body of **unspecified shoulder**

● **S41.04 Puncture wound with foreign body of shoulder**
  ● S41.041   Puncture wound with foreign body of **right shoulder**
  ● S41.042   Puncture wound with foreign body of **left shoulder**
  ● S41.049   Puncture wound with foreign body of **unspecified shoulder**

● **S41.05 Open bite of shoulder**
    Bite of shoulder NOS
    Excludes1 superficial bite of shoulder (S40.27)
  ● S41.051   Open bite of **right shoulder**
  ● S41.052   Open bite of **left shoulder**
  ● S41.059   Open bite of **unspecified shoulder**

● **S41.1 Open wound of upper arm**
  ● **S41.10 Unspecified open wound of upper arm**
    ● S41.101   Unspecified open wound of **right upper arm**
    ● S41.102   Unspecified open wound of **left upper arm**
    ● S41.109   Unspecified open wound of **unspecified upper arm**

  ● **S41.11 Laceration without foreign body of upper arm**
    ● S41.111   Laceration without foreign body of **right upper arm**
    ● S41.112   Laceration without foreign body of **left upper arm**
    ● S41.119   Laceration without foreign body of **unspecified upper arm**

  ● **S41.12 Laceration with foreign body of upper arm**
    ● S41.121   Laceration with foreign body of **right upper arm**
    ● S41.122   Laceration with foreign body of **left upper arm**
    ● S41.129   Laceration with foreign body of **unspecified upper arm**

  ● **S41.13 Puncture wound without foreign body of upper arm**
    ● S41.131   Puncture wound without foreign body of **right upper arm**
    ● S41.132   Puncture wound without foreign body of **left upper arm**
    ● S41.139   Puncture wound without foreign body of **unspecified upper arm**

  ● **S41.14 Puncture wound with foreign body of upper arm**
    ● S41.141   Puncture wound with foreign body of **right upper arm**
    ● S41.142   Puncture wound with foreign body of **left upper arm**
    ● S41.149   Puncture wound with foreign body of **unspecified upper arm**

  ● **S41.15 Open bite of upper arm**
      Bite of upper arm NOS
      Excludes1 superficial bite of upper arm (S40.87)
    ● S41.151   Open bite of **right upper arm**
    ● S41.152   Open bite of **left upper arm**
    ● S41.159   Open bite of **unspecified upper arm**

● **S42 Fracture of shoulder and upper arm**
  Note: A fracture not indicated as displaced or nondisplaced should be coded to displaced
    A fracture not indicated as open or closed should be coded to closed
  Excludes1 traumatic amputation of shoulder and upper arm (S48.-)
  The appropriate 7th character is to be added to all codes from category S42

A	initial encounter for closed fracture
B	initial encounter for open fracture
D	subsequent encounter for fracture with routine healing
G	subsequent encounter for fracture with delayed healing
K	subsequent encounter for fracture with nonunion
P	subsequent encounter for fracture with malunion
S	sequela

● **S42.0 Fracture of clavicle**
  ● **S42.00 Fracture of unspecified part of clavicle**
    ● S42.001   Fracture of unspecified part of **right clavicle**
    ● S42.002   Fracture of unspecified part of **left clavicle**
    ● S42.009   Fracture of unspecified part of **unspecified clavicle**
        Coding Clinic: 2012, Q4, P3

  ● **S42.01 Fracture of sternal end of clavicle**
    ● S42.011   **Anterior displaced** fracture of sternal end of **right clavicle**
    ● S42.012   **Anterior displaced** fracture of sternal end of **left clavicle**
    ● S42.013   **Anterior displaced** fracture of sternal end of **unspecified clavicle**
        Displaced fracture of sternal end of clavicle NOS
    ● S42.014   **Posterior displaced** fracture of sternal end of **right clavicle**
    ● S42.015   **Posterior displaced** fracture of sternal end of **left clavicle**
    ● S42.016   **Posterior displaced** fracture of sternal end of **unspecified clavicle**
    ● S42.017   **Nondisplaced** fracture of sternal end of **right clavicle**
    ● S42.018   **Nondisplaced** fracture of sternal end of **left clavicle**
    ● S42.019   **Nondisplaced** fracture of sternal end of **unspecified clavicle**

  ● **S42.02 Fracture of shaft of clavicle**
    ● S42.021   **Displaced** fracture of shaft of **right clavicle**
    ● S42.022   **Displaced** fracture of shaft of **left clavicle**
    ● S42.023   **Displaced** fracture of shaft of **unspecified clavicle**
    ● S42.024   **Nondisplaced** fracture of shaft of **right clavicle**
    ● S42.025   **Nondisplaced** fracture of shaft of **left clavicle**
    ● S42.026   **Nondisplaced** fracture of shaft of **unspecified clavicle**

  ● **S42.03 Fracture of lateral end of clavicle**
      Fracture of acromial end of clavicle
    ● S42.031   **Displaced** fracture of lateral end of **right clavicle**
    ● S42.032   **Displaced** fracture of lateral end of **left clavicle**

▶ New   ⇒ Revised   ~~deleted~~ Deleted   Excludes 1   Excludes 2   Includes   Use additional   Code first   Code also   Key words
OGCR Official Guidelines   X Assign placeholder X   ● Use Additional Character(s)   ▶ Manifestation Code   Coding Clinic

- S42.033   Displaced fracture of lateral end of unspecified clavicle
- S42.034   Nondisplaced fracture of lateral end of right clavicle
- S42.035   Nondisplaced fracture of lateral end of left clavicle
- S42.036   Nondisplaced fracture of lateral end of unspecified clavicle

- S42.1   **Fracture of scapula**
  - S42.10   Fracture of unspecified part of scapula
    - S42.101   Fracture of unspecified part of scapula, right shoulder
    - S42.102   Fracture of unspecified part of scapula, left shoulder
    - S42.109   Fracture of unspecified part of scapula, unspecified shoulder
  - S42.11   Fracture of body of scapula
    - S42.111   Displaced fracture of body of scapula, right shoulder
    - S42.112   Displaced fracture of body of scapula, left shoulder
    - S42.113   Displaced fracture of body of scapula, unspecified shoulder
    - S42.114   Nondisplaced fracture of body of scapula, right shoulder
    - S42.115   Nondisplaced fracture of body of scapula, left shoulder
    - S42.116   Nondisplaced fracture of body of scapula, unspecified shoulder
  - S42.12   Fracture of acromial process
    - S42.121   Displaced fracture of acromial process, right shoulder
    - S42.122   Displaced fracture of acromial process, left shoulder
    - S42.123   Displaced fracture of acromial process, unspecified shoulder
    - S42.124   Nondisplaced fracture of acromial process, right shoulder
    - S42.125   Nondisplaced fracture of acromial process, left shoulder
    - S42.126   Nondisplaced fracture, of acromial process, unspecified shoulder
  - S42.13   Fracture of coracoid process
    - S42.131   Displaced fracture of coracoid process, right shoulder
    - S42.132   Displaced fracture of coracoid process, left shoulder
    - S42.133   Displaced fracture of coracoid process, unspecified shoulder
    - S42.134   Nondisplaced fracture of coracoid process, right shoulder
    - S42.135   Nondisplaced fracture of coracoid process, left shoulder
    - S42.136   Nondisplaced fracture of coracoid process, unspecified shoulder
  - S42.14   Fracture of glenoid cavity of scapula
    - S42.141   Displaced fracture of glenoid cavity of scapula, right shoulder
    - S42.142   Displaced fracture of glenoid cavity of scapula, left shoulder
    - S42.143   Displaced fracture of glenoid cavity of scapula, unspecified shoulder
    - S42.144   Nondisplaced fracture of glenoid cavity of scapula, right shoulder

- S42.145   Nondisplaced fracture of glenoid cavity of scapula, left shoulder
- S42.146   Nondisplaced fracture of glenoid cavity of scapula, unspecified shoulder
- S42.15   Fracture of neck of scapula
  - S42.151   Displaced fracture of neck of scapula, right shoulder
  - S42.152   Displaced fracture of neck of scapula, left shoulder
  - S42.153   Displaced fracture of neck of scapula, unspecified shoulder
  - S42.154   Nondisplaced fracture of neck of scapula, right shoulder
  - S42.155   Nondisplaced fracture of neck of scapula, left shoulder
  - S42.156   Nondisplaced fracture of neck of scapula, unspecified shoulder
- S42.19   Fracture of other part of scapula
  - S42.191   Fracture of other part of scapula, right shoulder
  - S42.192   Fracture of other part of scapula, left shoulder
  - S42.199   Fracture of other part of scapula, unspecified shoulder

- S42.2   **Fracture of upper end of humerus**
  Fracture of proximal end of humerus

  Excludes2   fracture of shaft of humerus (S42.3-)
  physeal fracture of upper end of humerus (S49.0-)

  - S42.20   Unspecified fracture of upper end of humerus
    - S42.201   Unspecified fracture of upper end of right humerus
    - S42.202   Unspecified fracture of upper end of left humerus
    - S42.209   Unspecified fracture of upper end of unspecified humerus
  - S42.21   Unspecified fracture of surgical neck of humerus
    Fracture of neck of humerus NOS
    - S42.211   Unspecified displaced fracture of surgical neck of right humerus
    - S42.212   Unspecified displaced fracture of surgical neck of left humerus
    - S42.213   Unspecified displaced fracture of surgical neck of unspecified humerus
    - S42.214   Unspecified nondisplaced fracture of surgical neck of right humerus
    - S42.215   Unspecified nondisplaced fracture of surgical neck of left humerus
    - S42.216   Unspecified nondisplaced fracture of surgical neck of unspecified humerus
  - S42.22   2-part fracture of surgical neck of humerus
    - S42.221   2-part displaced fracture of surgical neck of right humerus
    - S42.222   2-part displaced fracture of surgical neck of left humerus
    - S42.223   2-part displaced fracture of surgical neck of unspecified humerus
    - S42.224   2-part nondisplaced fracture of surgical neck of right humerus
    - S42.225   2-part nondisplaced fracture of surgical neck of left humerus
    - S42.226   2-part nondisplaced fracture of surgical neck of unspecified humerus

S42.23 3-part fracture of surgical neck of humerus

- **S42.231** 3-part fracture of surgical neck of right humerus
- **S42.232** 3-part fracture of surgical neck of left humerus
- **S42.239** 3-part fracture of surgical neck of unspecified humerus

S42.24 4-part fracture of surgical neck of humerus

- **S42.241** 4-part fracture of surgical neck of right humerus
- **S42.242** 4-part fracture of surgical neck of left humerus
- **S42.249** 4-part fracture of surgical neck of unspecified humerus

S42.25 Fracture of greater tuberosity of humerus

- **S42.251** Displaced fracture of greater tuberosity of right humerus
- **S42.252** Displaced fracture of greater tuberosity of left humerus
- **S42.253** Displaced fracture of greater tuberosity of unspecified humerus
- **S42.254** Nondisplaced fracture of greater tuberosity of right humerus
- **S42.255** Nondisplaced fracture of greater tuberosity of left humerus
- **S42.256** Nondisplaced fracture of greater tuberosity of unspecified humerus

S42.26 Fracture of lesser tuberosity of humerus

- **S42.261** Displaced fracture of lesser tuberosity of right humerus
- **S42.262** Displaced fracture of lesser tuberosity of left humerus
- **S42.263** Displaced fracture of lesser tuberosity of unspecified humerus
- **S42.264** Nondisplaced fracture of lesser tuberosity of right humerus
- **S42.265** Nondisplaced fracture of lesser tuberosity of left humerus
- **S42.266** Nondisplaced fracture of lesser tuberosity of unspecified humerus

S42.27 Torus fracture of upper end of humerus

The appropriate 7th character is to be added to all codes in subcategory S42.27

A	initial encounter for closed fracture
D	subsequent encounter for fracture with routine healing
G	subsequent encounter for fracture with delayed healing
K	subsequent encounter for fracture with nonunion
P	subsequent encounter for fracture with malunion
S	sequela

- **S42.271** Torus fracture of upper end of right humerus
- **S42.272** Torus fracture of upper end of left humerus
- **S42.279** Torus fracture of upper end of unspecified humerus

S42.29 Other fracture of upper end of humerus

Fracture of anatomical neck of humerus
Fracture of articular head of humerus

- **S42.291** Other displaced fracture of upper end of right humerus
- **S42.292** Other displaced fracture of upper end of left humerus
- **S42.293** Other displaced fracture of upper end of unspecified humerus

- **S42.294** Other nondisplaced fracture of upper end of right humerus
- **S42.295** Other nondisplaced fracture of upper end of left humerus
- **S42.296** Other nondisplaced fracture of upper end of unspecified humerus

S42.3 Fracture of shaft of humerus

Fracture of humerus NOS
Fracture of upper arm NOS

Excludes2 physeal fractures of upper end of humerus (S49.0-)
physeal fractures of lower end of humerus (S49.1-)

S42.30 Unspecified fracture of shaft of humerus

- **S42.301** Unspecified fracture of shaft of humerus, right arm
- **S42.302** Unspecified fracture of shaft of humerus, left arm
- **S42.309** Unspecified fracture of shaft of humerus, unspecified arm

S42.31 Greenstick fracture of shaft of humerus

The appropriate 7th character is to be added to all codes in subcategory S42.31

A	initial encounter for closed fracture
D	subsequent encounter for fracture with routine healing
G	subsequent encounter for fracture with delayed healing
K	subsequent encounter for fracture with nonunion
P	subsequent encounter for fracture with malunion
S	sequela

- **S42.311** Greenstick fracture of shaft of humerus, right arm
- **S42.312** Greenstick fracture of shaft of humerus, left arm
- **S42.319** Greenstick fracture of shaft of humerus, unspecified arm

S42.32 Transverse fracture of shaft of humerus

- **S42.321** Displaced transverse fracture of shaft of humerus, right arm
- **S42.322** Displaced transverse fracture of shaft of humerus, left arm
- **S42.323** Displaced transverse fracture of shaft of humerus, unspecified arm
- **S42.324** Nondisplaced transverse fracture of shaft of humerus, right arm
- **S42.325** Nondisplaced transverse fracture of shaft of humerus, left arm
- **S42.326** Nondisplaced transverse fracture of shaft of humerus, unspecified arm

S42.33 Oblique fracture of shaft of humerus

- **S42.331** Displaced oblique fracture of shaft of humerus, right arm
- **S42.332** Displaced oblique fracture of shaft of humerus, left arm
- **S42.333** Displaced oblique fracture of shaft of humerus, unspecified arm
- **S42.334** Nondisplaced oblique fracture of shaft of humerus, right arm
- **S42.335** Nondisplaced oblique fracture of shaft of humerus, left arm
- **S42.336** Nondisplaced oblique fracture of shaft of humerus, unspecified arm

▶ New   ⇒ Revised   ~~deleted~~ Deleted   Excludes 1   Excludes 2   Includes   Use additional   Code first   Code also   Key words

OGCR Official Guidelines   X Assign placeholder X   ● Use Additional Character(s)   ▶ Manifestation Code   **Coding Clinic**

● **S42.34**   Spiral fracture of shaft of humerus
- ● **S42.341**   Displaced spiral fracture of shaft of humerus, right arm
- ● **S42.342**   Displaced spiral fracture of shaft of humerus, left arm
- ● **S42.343**   Displaced spiral fracture of shaft of humerus, unspecified arm
- ● **S42.344**   Nondisplaced spiral fracture of shaft of humerus, right arm
- ● **S42.345**   Nondisplaced spiral fracture of shaft of humerus, left arm
- ● **S42.346**   Nondisplaced spiral fracture of shaft of humerus, unspecified arm

● **S42.35**   Comminuted fracture of shaft of humerus
- ● **S42.351**   Displaced comminuted fracture of shaft of humerus, right arm
- ● **S42.352**   Displaced comminuted fracture of shaft of humerus, left arm
- ● **S42.353**   Displaced comminuted fracture of shaft of humerus, unspecified arm
- ● **S42.354**   Nondisplaced comminuted fracture of shaft of humerus, right arm
- ● **S42.355**   Nondisplaced comminuted fracture of shaft of humerus, left arm
- ● **S42.356**   Nondisplaced comminuted fracture of shaft of humerus, unspecified arm

● **S42.36**   Segmental fracture of shaft of humerus
- ● **S42.361**   Displaced segmental fracture of shaft of humerus, right arm
- ● **S42.362**   Displaced segmental fracture of shaft of humerus, left arm
- ● **S42.363**   Displaced segmental fracture of shaft of humerus, unspecified arm
- ● **S42.364**   Nondisplaced segmental fracture of shaft of humerus, right arm
- ● **S42.365**   Nondisplaced segmental fracture of shaft of humerus, left arm
- ● **S42.366**   Nondisplaced segmental fracture of shaft of humerus, unspecified arm

● **S42.39**   Other fracture of shaft of humerus
- ● **S42.391**   Other fracture of shaft of right humerus
- ● **S42.392**   Other fracture of shaft of left humerus
- ● **S42.399**   Other fracture of shaft of unspecified humerus

● **S42.4**   Fracture of lower end of humerus
Fracture of distal end of humerus

> **Excludes2**   fracture of shaft of humerus (S42.3-)
> physeal fracture of lower end of humerus (S49.1-)

● **S42.40**   Unspecified fracture of lower end of humerus
Fracture of elbow NOS
- ● **S42.401**   Unspecified fracture of lower end of right humerus
- ● **S42.402**   Unspecified fracture of lower end of left humerus
- ● **S42.409**   Unspecified fracture of lower end of unspecified humerus

● **S42.41**   Simple supracondylar fracture without intercondylar fracture of humerus
- ● **S42.411**   Displaced simple supracondylar fracture without intercondylar fracture of right humerus
- ● **S42.412**   Displaced simple supracondylar fracture without intercondylar fracture of left humerus
- ● **S42.413**   Displaced simple supracondylar fracture without intercondylar fracture of unspecified humerus
- ● **S42.414**   Nondisplaced simple supracondylar fracture without intercondylar fracture of right humerus
- ● **S42.415**   Nondisplaced simple supracondylar fracture without intercondylar fracture of left humerus
- ● **S42.416**   Nondisplaced simple supracondylar fracture without intercondylar fracture of unspecified humerus

● **S42.42**   Comminuted supracondylar fracture without intercondylar fracture of humerus
- ● **S42.421**   Displaced comminuted supracondylar fracture without intercondylar fracture of right humerus
- ● **S42.422**   Displaced comminuted supracondylar fracture without intercondylar fracture of left humerus
- ● **S42.423**   Displaced comminuted supracondylar fracture without intercondylar fracture of unspecified humerus
- ● **S42.424**   Nondisplaced comminuted supracondylar fracture without intercondylar fracture of right humerus
- ● **S42.425**   Nondisplaced comminuted supracondylar fracture without intercondylar fracture of left humerus
- ● **S42.426**   Nondisplaced comminuted supracondylar fracture without intercondylar fracture of unspecified humerus

● **S42.43**   Fracture (avulsion) of lateral epicondyle of humerus
- ● **S42.431**   Displaced fracture (avulsion) of lateral epicondyle of right humerus
- ● **S42.432**   Displaced fracture (avulsion) of lateral epicondyle of left humerus
- ● **S42.433**   Displaced fracture (avulsion) of lateral epicondyle of unspecified humerus
- ● **S42.434**   Nondisplaced fracture (avulsion) of lateral epicondyle of right humerus
- ● **S42.435**   Nondisplaced fracture (avulsion) of lateral epicondyle of left humerus
- ● **S42.436**   Nondisplaced fracture (avulsion) of lateral epicondyle of unspecified humerus

● **S42.44**   Fracture (avulsion) of medial epicondyle of humerus
- ● **S42.441**   Displaced fracture (avulsion) of medial epicondyle of right humerus
- ● **S42.442**   Displaced fracture (avulsion) of medial epicondyle of left humerus
- ● **S42.443**   Displaced fracture (avulsion) of medial epicondyle of unspecified humerus
- ● **S42.444**   Nondisplaced fracture (avulsion) of medial epicondyle of right humerus
- ● **S42.445**   Nondisplaced fracture (avulsion) of medial epicondyle of left humerus
- ● **S42.446**   Nondisplaced fracture (avulsion) of medial epicondyle of unspecified humerus
- ● **S42.447**   Incarcerated fracture (avulsion) of medial epicondyle of right humerus
- ● **S42.448**   Incarcerated fracture (avulsion) of medial epicondyle of left humerus
- ● **S42.449**   Incarcerated fracture (avulsion) of medial epicondyle of unspecified humerus

CHAPTER 19 (SØØ-T88)

● **S42.45**   **Fracture of lateral condyle of humerus**
Fracture of capitellum of humerus

    ● **S42.451**   **Displaced fracture of lateral condyle of right humerus**

    ● **S42.452**   **Displaced fracture of lateral condyle of left humerus**

    ● **S42.453**   **Displaced fracture of lateral condyle of unspecified humerus**

    ● **S42.454**   **Nondisplaced fracture of lateral condyle of right humerus**

    ● **S42.455**   **Nondisplaced fracture of lateral condyle of left humerus**

    ● **S42.456**   **Nondisplaced fracture of lateral condyle of unspecified humerus**

● **S42.46**   **Fracture of medial condyle of humerus**
Trochlea fracture of humerus

    ● **S42.461**   **Displaced fracture of medial condyle of right humerus**

    ● **S42.462**   **Displaced fracture of medial condyle of left humerus**

    ● **S42.463**   **Displaced fracture of medial condyle of unspecified humerus**

    ● **S42.464**   **Nondisplaced fracture of medial condyle of right humerus**

    ● **S42.465**   **Nondisplaced fracture of medial condyle of left humerus**

    ● **S42.466**   **Nondisplaced fracture of medial condyle of unspecified humerus**

● **S42.47**   **Transcondylar fracture of humerus**

    ● **S42.471**   **Displaced transcondylar fracture of right humerus**

    ● **S42.472**   **Displaced transcondylar fracture of left humerus**

    ● **S42.473**   **Displaced transcondylar fracture of unspecified humerus**

    ● **S42.474**   **Nondisplaced transcondylar fracture of right humerus**

    ● **S42.475**   **Nondisplaced transcondylar fracture of left humerus**

    ● **S42.476**   **Nondisplaced transcondylar fracture of unspecified humerus**

● **S42.48**   **Torus fracture of lower end of humerus**

The appropriate 7th character is to be added to all codes in subcategory S42.48

A	initial encounter for closed fracture
D	subsequent encounter for fracture with routine healing
G	subsequent encounter for fracture with delayed healing
K	subsequent encounter for fracture with nonunion
P	subsequent encounter for fracture with malunion
S	sequela

    ● **S42.481**   **Torus fracture of lower end of right humerus**

    ● **S42.482**   **Torus fracture of lower end of left humerus**

    ● **S42.489**   **Torus fracture of lower end of unspecified humerus**

● **S42.49**   **Other fracture of lower end of humerus**

    ● **S42.491**   **Other displaced fracture of lower end of right humerus**

    ● **S42.492**   **Other displaced fracture of lower end of left humerus**

    ● **S42.493**   **Other displaced fracture of lower end of unspecified humerus**

    ● **S42.494**   **Other nondisplaced fracture of lower end of right humerus**

    ● **S42.495**   **Other nondisplaced fracture of lower end of left humerus**

    ● **S42.496**   **Other nondisplaced fracture of lower end of unspecified humerus**

● **S42.9**   **Fracture of shoulder girdle, part unspecified**
Fracture of shoulder NOS

   X ● **S42.90**   **Fracture of unspecified shoulder girdle, part unspecified**

   X ● **S42.91**   **Fracture of right shoulder girdle, part unspecified**

   X ● **S42.92**   **Fracture of left shoulder girdle, part unspecified**

● **S43**   **Dislocation and sprain of joints and ligaments of shoulder girdle**

   Includes   avulsion of joint or ligament of shoulder girdle
laceration of cartilage, joint or ligament of shoulder girdle
sprain of cartilage, joint or ligament of shoulder girdle
traumatic hemarthrosis of joint or ligament of shoulder girdle
traumatic rupture of joint or ligament of shoulder girdle
traumatic subluxation of joint or ligament of shoulder girdle
traumatic tear of joint or ligament of shoulder girdle

Code also any associated open wound

   Excludes2   strain of muscle, fascia and tendon of shoulder and upper arm (S46.-)

The appropriate 7th character is to be added to each code from category S43

A	initial encounter
D	subsequent encounter
S	sequela

● **S43.0**   **Subluxation and dislocation of shoulder joint**
Dislocation of glenohumeral joint
Subluxation of glenohumeral joint

    ● **S43.00**   **Unspecified subluxation and dislocation of shoulder joint**
Dislocation of humerus NOS
Subluxation of humerus NOS

      ● **S43.001**   **Unspecified subluxation of right shoulder joint**

      ● **S43.002**   **Unspecified subluxation of left shoulder joint**

      ● **S43.003**   **Unspecified subluxation of unspecified shoulder joint**

      ● **S43.004**   **Unspecified dislocation of right shoulder joint**

      ● **S43.005**   **Unspecified dislocation of left shoulder joint**

      ● **S43.006**   **Unspecified dislocation of unspecified shoulder joint**

    ● **S43.01**   **Anterior subluxation and dislocation of humerus**

      ● **S43.011**   **Anterior subluxation of right humerus**

      ● **S43.012**   **Anterior subluxation of left humerus**

      ● **S43.013**   **Anterior subluxation of unspecified humerus**

      ● **S43.014**   **Anterior dislocation of right humerus**

      ● **S43.015**   **Anterior dislocation of left humerus**

      ● **S43.016**   **Anterior dislocation of unspecified humerus**

● S43.02   Posterior subluxation and dislocation of humerus
  ● S43.021   Posterior subluxation of right humerus
  ● S43.022   Posterior subluxation of left humerus
  ● S43.023   Posterior subluxation of unspecified humerus
  ● S43.024   Posterior dislocation of right humerus
  ● S43.025   Posterior dislocation of left humerus
  ● S43.026   Posterior dislocation of unspecified humerus
● S43.03   Inferior subluxation and dislocation of humerus
  ● S43.031   Inferior subluxation of right humerus
  ● S43.032   Inferior subluxation of left humerus
  ● S43.033   Inferior subluxation of unspecified humerus
  ● S43.034   Inferior dislocation of right humerus
  ● S43.035   Inferior dislocation of left humerus
  ● S43.036   Inferior dislocation of unspecified humerus
● S43.08   Other subluxation and dislocation of shoulder joint
  ● S43.081   Other subluxation of right shoulder joint
  ● S43.082   Other subluxation of left shoulder joint
  ● S43.083   Other subluxation of unspecified shoulder joint
  ● S43.084   Other dislocation of right shoulder joint
  ● S43.085   Other dislocation of left shoulder joint
  ● S43.086   Other dislocation of unspecified shoulder joint
● S43.1   Subluxation and dislocation of acromioclavicular joint
  ● S43.10   Unspecified dislocation of acromioclavicular joint
    ● S43.101   Unspecified dislocation of right acromioclavicular joint
    ● S43.102   Unspecified dislocation of left acromioclavicular joint
    ● S43.109   Unspecified dislocation of unspecified acromioclavicular joint
  ● S43.11   Subluxation of acromioclavicular joint
    ● S43.111   Subluxation of right acromioclavicular joint
    ● S43.112   Subluxation of left acromioclavicular joint
    ● S43.119   Subluxation of unspecified acromioclavicular joint
  ● S43.12   Dislocation of acromioclavicular joint, 100%-200% displacement
    ● S43.121   Dislocation of right acromioclavicular joint, 100%-200% displacement
    ● S43.122   Dislocation of left acromioclavicular joint, 100%-200% displacement
    ● S43.129   Dislocation of unspecified acromioclavicular joint, 100%-200% displacement

● S43.13   Dislocation of acromioclavicular joint, greater than 200% displacement
  ● S43.131   Dislocation of right acromioclavicular joint, greater than 200% displacement
  ● S43.132   Dislocation of left acromioclavicular joint, greater than 200% displacement
  ● S43.139   Dislocation of unspecified acromioclavicular joint, greater than 200% displacement
● S43.14   Inferior dislocation of acromioclavicular joint
  ● S43.141   Inferior dislocation of right acromioclavicular joint
  ● S43.142   Inferior dislocation of left acromioclavicular joint
  ● S43.149   Inferior dislocation of unspecified acromioclavicular joint
● S43.15   Posterior dislocation of acromioclavicular joint
  ● S43.151   Posterior dislocation of right acromioclavicular joint
  ● S43.152   Posterior dislocation of left acromioclavicular joint
  ● S43.159   Posterior dislocation of unspecified acromioclavicular joint
● S43.2   Subluxation and dislocation of sternoclavicular joint
  ● S43.20   Unspecified subluxation and dislocation of sternoclavicular joint
    ● S43.201   Unspecified subluxation of right sternoclavicular joint
    ● S43.202   Unspecified subluxation of left sternoclavicular joint
    ● S43.203   Unspecified subluxation of unspecified sternoclavicular joint
    ● S43.204   Unspecified dislocation of right sternoclavicular joint
    ● S43.205   Unspecified dislocation of left sternoclavicular joint
    ● S43.206   Unspecified dislocation of unspecified sternoclavicular joint
  ● S43.21   Anterior subluxation and dislocation of sternoclavicular joint
    ● S43.211   Anterior subluxation of right sternoclavicular joint
    ● S43.212   Anterior subluxation of left sternoclavicular joint
    ● S43.213   Anterior subluxation of unspecified sternoclavicular joint
    ● S43.214   Anterior dislocation of right sternoclavicular joint
    ● S43.215   Anterior dislocation of left sternoclavicular joint
    ● S43.216   Anterior dislocation of unspecified sternoclavicular joint
  ● S43.22   Posterior subluxation and dislocation of sternoclavicular joint
    ● S43.221   Posterior subluxation of right sternoclavicular joint
    ● S43.222   Posterior subluxation of left sternoclavicular joint
    ● S43.223   Posterior subluxation of unspecified sternoclavicular joint
    ● S43.224   Posterior dislocation of right sternoclavicular joint
    ● S43.225   Posterior dislocation of left sternoclavicular joint
    ● S43.226   Posterior dislocation of unspecified sternoclavicular joint

CHAPTER 19 (S00-T88)

● **S43.3** **Subluxation and dislocation of other and unspecified parts of shoulder girdle**

  ● **S43.30** **Subluxation and dislocation of unspecified parts of shoulder girdle**
Dislocation of shoulder girdle NOS
Subluxation of shoulder girdle NOS

    ● **S43.301** **Subluxation of unspecified parts of right shoulder girdle**

    ● **S43.302** **Subluxation of unspecified parts of left shoulder girdle**

    ● **S43.303** **Subluxation of unspecified parts of unspecified shoulder girdle**

    ● **S43.304** **Dislocation of unspecified parts of right shoulder girdle**

    ● **S43.305** **Dislocation of unspecified parts of left shoulder girdle**

    ● **S43.306** **Dislocation of unspecified parts of unspecified shoulder girdle**

  ● **S43.31** **Subluxation and dislocation of scapula**

    ● **S43.311** **Subluxation of right scapula**

    ● **S43.312** **Subluxation of left scapula**

    ● **S43.313** **Subluxation of unspecified scapula**

    ● **S43.314** **Dislocation of right scapula**

    ● **S43.315** **Dislocation of left scapula**

    ● **S43.316** **Dislocation of unspecified scapula**

  ● **S43.39** **Subluxation and dislocation of other parts of shoulder girdle**

    ● **S43.391** **Subluxation of other parts of right shoulder girdle**

    ● **S43.392** **Subluxation of other parts of left shoulder girdle**

    ● **S43.393** **Subluxation of other parts of unspecified shoulder girdle**

    ● **S43.394** **Dislocation of other parts of right shoulder girdle**

    ● **S43.395** **Dislocation of other parts of left shoulder girdle**

    ● **S43.396** **Dislocation of other parts of unspecified shoulder girdle**

● **S43.4** **Sprain of shoulder joint**

  ● **S43.40** **Unspecified sprain of shoulder joint**

    ● **S43.401** **Unspecified sprain of right shoulder joint**

    ● **S43.402** **Unspecified sprain of left shoulder joint**

    ● **S43.409** **Unspecified sprain of unspecified shoulder joint**

  ● **S43.41** **Sprain of coracohumeral (ligament)**

    ● **S43.411** **Sprain of right coracohumeral (ligament)**

    ● **S43.412** **Sprain of left coracohumeral (ligament)**

    ● **S43.419** **Sprain of unspecified coracohumeral (ligament)**

  ● **S43.42** **Sprain of rotator cuff capsule**
Encounters during the healing phase

    Excludes1   rotator cuff syndrome (complete) (incomplete), not specified as traumatic (M75.1-)

    Excludes2   injury of tendon of rotator cuff (S46.0-)

    ● **S43.421** **Sprain of right rotator cuff capsule**

    ● **S43.422** **Sprain of left rotator cuff capsule**

    ● **S43.429** **Sprain of unspecified rotator cuff capsule**

● **S43.43** **Superior glenoid labrum lesion**
SLAP lesion

  ● **S43.431** **Superior glenoid labrum lesion of right shoulder**

  ● **S43.432** **Superior glenoid labrum lesion of left shoulder**

  ● **S43.439** **Superior glenoid labrum lesion of unspecified shoulder**

  ● **S43.49** **Other sprain of shoulder joint**

    ● **S43.491** **Other sprain of right shoulder joint**

    ● **S43.492** **Other sprain of left shoulder joint**

    ● **S43.499** **Other sprain of unspecified shoulder joint**

● **S43.5** **Sprain of acromioclavicular joint**
Sprain of acromioclavicular ligament

  X ● **S43.50** **Sprain of unspecified acromioclavicular joint**

  X ● **S43.51** **Sprain of right acromioclavicular joint**

  X ● **S43.52** **Sprain of left acromioclavicular joint**

● **S43.6** **Sprain of sternoclavicular joint**

  X ● **S43.60** **Sprain of unspecified sternoclavicular joint**

  X ● **S43.61** **Sprain of right sternoclavicular joint**

  X ● **S43.62** **Sprain of left sternoclavicular joint**

● **S43.8** **Sprain of other specified parts of shoulder girdle**

  X ● **S43.80** **Sprain of other specified parts of unspecified shoulder girdle**

  X ● **S43.81** **Sprain of other specified parts of right shoulder girdle**

  X ● **S43.82** **Sprain of other specified parts of left shoulder girdle**

● **S43.9** **Sprain of unspecified parts of shoulder girdle**

  X ● **S43.90** **Sprain of unspecified parts of unspecified shoulder girdle**
Sprain of shoulder girdle NOS

  X ● **S43.91** **Sprain of unspecified parts of right shoulder girdle**

  X ● **S43.92** **Sprain of unspecified parts of left shoulder girdle**

● **S44** **Injury of nerves at shoulder and upper arm level**
Code also any associated open wound (S41.-)

  Excludes2   injury of brachial plexus (S14.3-)

The appropriate 7th character is to be added to each code from category S44

A	initial encounter
D	subsequent encounter
S	sequela

● **S44.0** **Injury of ulnar nerve at upper arm level**

    Excludes1   ulnar nerve NOS (S54.0)

  X ● **S44.00** **Injury of ulnar nerve at upper arm level, unspecified arm**

  X ● **S44.01** **Injury of ulnar nerve at upper arm level, right arm**

  X ● **S44.02** **Injury of ulnar nerve at upper arm level, left arm**

● **S44.1** **Injury of median nerve at upper arm level**

    Excludes1   median nerve NOS (S54.1)

  X ● **S44.10** **Injury of median nerve at upper arm level, unspecified arm**

  X ● **S44.11** **Injury of median nerve at upper arm level, right arm**

  X ● **S44.12** **Injury of median nerve at upper arm level, left arm**

● **S44.2**   Injury of radial nerve at upper arm level
     Excludes1   radial nerve NOS (S54.2)
X ● **S44.20**   Injury of radial nerve at upper arm level, unspecified arm
X ● **S44.21**   Injury of radial nerve at upper arm level, right arm
X ● **S44.22**   Injury of radial nerve at upper arm level, left arm

● **S44.3**   Injury of axillary nerve
X ● **S44.30**   Injury of axillary nerve, unspecified arm
X ● **S44.31**   Injury of axillary nerve, right arm
X ● **S44.32**   Injury of axillary nerve, left arm

● **S44.4**   Injury of musculocutaneous nerve
X ● **S44.40**   Injury of musculocutaneous nerve, unspecified arm
X ● **S44.41**   Injury of musculocutaneous nerve, right arm
X ● **S44.42**   Injury of musculocutaneous nerve, left arm

● **S44.5**   Injury of cutaneous sensory nerve at shoulder and upper arm level
X ● **S44.50**   Injury of cutaneous sensory nerve at shoulder and upper arm level, unspecified arm
X ● **S44.51**   Injury of cutaneous sensory nerve at shoulder and upper arm level, right arm
X ● **S44.52**   Injury of cutaneous sensory nerve at shoulder and upper arm level, left arm

● **S44.8**   Injury of other nerves at shoulder and upper arm level
● **S44.8X**   Injury of other nerves at shoulder and upper arm level
● **S44.8X1**   Injury of other nerves at shoulder and upper arm level, right arm
● **S44.8X2**   Injury of other nerves at shoulder and upper arm level, left arm
● **S44.8X9**   Injury of other nerves at shoulder and upper arm level, unspecified arm

● **S44.9**   Injury of unspecified nerve at shoulder and upper arm level
X ● **S44.90**   Injury of unspecified nerve at shoulder and upper arm level, unspecified arm
X ● **S44.91**   Injury of unspecified nerve at shoulder and upper arm level, right arm
X ● **S44.92**   Injury of unspecified nerve at shoulder and upper arm level, left arm

● **S45**   Injury of blood vessels at shoulder and upper arm level
     Code also any associated open wound (S41.-)
     Excludes2   injury of subclavian artery (S25.1)
         injury of subclavian vein (S25.3)
     The appropriate 7th character is to be added to each code from category S45

A	initial encounter
D	subsequent encounter
S	sequela

● **S45.0**   Injury of axillary artery
● **S45.00**   Unspecified injury of axillary artery
● **S45.001**   Unspecified injury of axillary artery, right side
● **S45.002**   Unspecified injury of axillary artery, left side
● **S45.009**   Unspecified injury of axillary artery, unspecified side
● **S45.01**   Laceration of axillary artery
● **S45.011**   Laceration of axillary artery, right side
● **S45.012**   Laceration of axillary artery, left side
● **S45.019**   Laceration of axillary artery, unspecified side

● **S45.09**   Other specified injury of axillary artery
● **S45.091**   Other specified injury of axillary artery, right side
● **S45.092**   Other specified injury of axillary artery, left side
● **S45.099**   Other specified injury of axillary artery, unspecified side

● **S45.1**   Injury of brachial artery
● **S45.10**   Unspecified injury of brachial artery
● **S45.101**   Unspecified injury of brachial artery, right side
● **S45.102**   Unspecified injury of brachial artery, left side
● **S45.109**   Unspecified injury of brachial artery, unspecified side
● **S45.11**   Laceration of brachial artery
● **S45.111**   Laceration of brachial artery, right side
● **S45.112**   Laceration of brachial artery, left side
● **S45.119**   Laceration of brachial artery, unspecified side
● **S45.19**   Other specified injury of brachial artery
● **S45.191**   Other specified injury of brachial artery, right side
● **S45.192**   Other specified injury of brachial artery, left side
● **S45.199**   Other specified injury of brachial artery, unspecified side

● **S45.2**   Injury of axillary or brachial vein
● **S45.20**   Unspecified injury of axillary or brachial vein
● **S45.201**   Unspecified injury of axillary or brachial vein, right side
● **S45.202**   Unspecified injury of axillary or brachial vein, left side
● **S45.209**   Unspecified injury of axillary or brachial vein, unspecified side
● **S45.21**   Laceration of axillary or brachial vein
● **S45.211**   Laceration of axillary or brachial vein, right side
● **S45.212**   Laceration of axillary or brachial vein, left side
● **S45.219**   Laceration of axillary or brachial vein, unspecified side
● **S45.29**   Other specified injury of axillary or brachial vein
● **S45.291**   Other specified injury of axillary or brachial vein, right side
● **S45.292**   Other specified injury of axillary or brachial vein, left side
● **S45.299**   Other specified injury of axillary or brachial vein, unspecified side

● **S45.3**   Injury of superficial vein at shoulder and upper arm level
● **S45.30**   Unspecified injury of superficial vein at shoulder and upper arm level
● **S45.301**   Unspecified injury of superficial vein at shoulder and upper arm level, right arm
● **S45.302**   Unspecified injury of superficial vein at shoulder and upper arm level, left arm
● **S45.309**   Unspecified injury of superficial vein at shoulder and upper arm level, unspecified arm

CHAPTER 19 (S00-T88)

● **S45.31** **Laceration** of superficial vein at shoulder and upper arm level

  ● **S45.311** Laceration of superficial vein at shoulder and upper arm level, **right arm**

  ● **S45.312** Laceration of superficial vein at shoulder and upper arm level, **left arm**

  ● **S45.319** Laceration of superficial vein at shoulder and upper arm level, **unspecified arm**

● **S45.39** **Other** specified injury of superficial vein at shoulder and upper arm level

  ● **S45.391** Other specified injury of superficial vein at shoulder and upper arm level, **right arm**

  ● **S45.392** Other specified injury of superficial vein at shoulder and upper arm level, **left arm**

  ● **S45.399** Other specified injury of superficial vein at shoulder and upper arm level, **unspecified arm**

● **S45.8** Injury of other specified blood vessels at shoulder and upper arm level

  ● **S45.80** **Unspecified** injury of other specified blood vessels at shoulder and upper arm level

    ● **S45.801** Unspecified injury of other specified blood vessels at shoulder and upper arm level, **right arm**

    ● **S45.802** Unspecified injury of other specified blood vessels at shoulder and upper arm level, **left arm**

    ● **S45.809** Unspecified injury of other specified blood vessels at shoulder and upper arm level, **unspecified arm**

  ● **S45.81** **Laceration** of other specified blood vessels at shoulder and upper arm level

    ● **S45.811** Laceration of other specified blood vessels at shoulder and upper arm level, **right arm**

    ● **S45.812** Laceration of other specified blood vessels at shoulder and upper arm level, **left arm**

    ● **S45.819** Laceration of other specified blood vessels at shoulder and upper arm level, **unspecified arm**

  ● **S45.89** **Other** specified injury of other specified blood vessels at shoulder and upper arm level

    ● **S45.891** Other specified injury of other specified blood vessels at shoulder and upper arm level, **right arm**

    ● **S45.892** Other specified injury of other specified blood vessels at shoulder and upper arm level, **left arm**

    ● **S45.899** Other specified injury of other specified blood vessels at shoulder and upper arm level, **unspecified arm**

● **S45.9** Injury of unspecified blood vessel at shoulder and upper arm level

  ● **S45.90** **Unspecified** injury of unspecified blood vessel at shoulder and upper arm level

    ● **S45.901** Unspecified injury of unspecified blood vessel at shoulder and upper arm level, **right arm**

    ● **S45.902** Unspecified injury of unspecified blood vessel at shoulder and upper arm level, **left arm**

    ● **S45.909** Unspecified injury of unspecified blood vessel at shoulder and upper arm level, **unspecified arm**

● **S45.91** **Laceration** of unspecified blood vessel at shoulder and upper arm level

  ● **S45.911** Laceration of unspecified blood vessel at shoulder and upper arm level, **right arm**

  ● **S45.912** Laceration of unspecified blood vessel at shoulder and upper arm level, **left arm**

  ● **S45.919** Laceration of unspecified blood vessel at shoulder and upper arm level, **unspecified arm**

● **S45.99** **Other** specified injury of unspecified blood vessel at shoulder and upper arm level

  ● **S45.991** Other specified injury of unspecified blood vessel at shoulder and upper arm level, **right arm**

  ● **S45.992** Other specified injury of unspecified blood vessel at shoulder and upper arm level, **left arm**

  ● **S45.999** Other specified injury of unspecified blood vessel at shoulder and upper arm level, **unspecified arm**

● **S46** Injury of muscle, fascia and tendon at shoulder and upper arm level

  Code also any associated open wound (S41.-)

  Excludes2 injury of muscle, fascia and tendon at elbow (S56.-)

           sprain of joints and ligaments of shoulder girdle (S43.9)

  The appropriate 7th character is to be added to each code from category S46

A	initial encounter
D	subsequent encounter
S	sequela

● **S46.0** Injury of muscle(s) and tendon(s) of the rotator cuff of shoulder

  ● **S46.00** **Unspecified** injury of muscle(s) and tendon(s) of the rotator cuff of shoulder

    ● **S46.001** Unspecified injury of muscle(s) and tendon(s) of the rotator cuff of **right** shoulder

    ● **S46.002** Unspecified injury of muscle(s) and tendon(s) of the rotator cuff of **left** shoulder

    ● **S46.009** Unspecified injury of muscle(s) and tendon(s) of the rotator cuff of **unspecified** shoulder

  ● **S46.01** **Strain** of muscle(s) and tendon(s) of the rotator cuff of shoulder

    Acute onset due to trauma to rotator cuff muscle/tendon

    ● **S46.011** Strain of muscle(s) and tendon(s) of the rotator cuff of **right** shoulder

    ● **S46.012** Strain of muscle(s) and tendon(s) of the rotator cuff of **left** shoulder

    ● **S46.019** Strain of muscle(s) and tendon(s) of the rotator cuff of **unspecified** shoulder

  ● **S46.02** **Laceration** of muscle(s) and tendon(s) of the rotator cuff of shoulder

    ● **S46.021** Laceration of muscle(s) and tendon(s) of the rotator cuff of **right** shoulder

    ● **S46.022** Laceration of muscle(s) and tendon(s) of the rotator cuff of **left** shoulder

    ● **S46.029** Laceration of muscle(s) and tendon(s) of the rotator cuff of **unspecified** shoulder

▶ New   ⇒ Revised   ~~deleted~~ Deleted   Excludes 1   Excludes 2   Includes   Use additional   Code first   Code also   Key words

OGCR Official Guidelines   X Assign placeholder X   ● Use Additional Character(s)   ▶ Manifestation Code   **Coding Clinic**

- S46.09   Other injury of muscle(s) and tendon(s) of the rotator cuff of shoulder
  - S46.091   Other injury of muscle(s) and tendon(s) of the rotator cuff of right shoulder
  - S46.092   Other injury of muscle(s) and tendon(s) of the rotator cuff of left shoulder
  - S46.099   Other injury of muscle(s) and tendon(s) of the rotator cuff of unspecified shoulder
- S46.1   Injury of muscle, fascia and tendon of long head of biceps
  - S46.10   Unspecified injury of muscle, fascia and tendon of long head of biceps
    - S46.101   Unspecified injury of muscle, fascia and tendon of long head of biceps, right arm
    - S46.102   Unspecified injury of muscle, fascia and tendon of long head of biceps, left arm
    - S46.109   Unspecified injury of muscle, fascia and tendon of long head of biceps, unspecified arm
  - S46.11   Strain of muscle, fascia and tendon of long head of biceps
    - S46.111   Strain of muscle, fascia and tendon of long head of biceps, right arm
    - S46.112   Strain of muscle, fascia and tendon of long head of biceps, left arm
    - S46.119   Strain of muscle, fascia and tendon of long head of biceps, unspecified arm
  - S46.12   Laceration of muscle, fascia and tendon of long head of biceps
    - S46.121   Laceration of muscle, fascia and tendon of long head of biceps, right arm
    - S46.122   Laceration of muscle, fascia and tendon of long head of biceps, left arm
    - S46.129   Laceration of muscle, fascia and tendon of long head of biceps, unspecified arm
  - S46.19   Other injury of muscle, fascia and tendon of long head of biceps
    - S46.191   Other injury of muscle, fascia and tendon of long head of biceps, right arm
    - S46.192   Other injury of muscle, fascia and tendon of long head of biceps, left arm
    - S46.199   Other injury of muscle, fascia and tendon of long head of biceps, unspecified arm
- S46.2   Injury of muscle, fascia and tendon of other parts of biceps
  - S46.20   Unspecified injury of muscle, fascia and tendon of other parts of biceps
    - S46.201   Unspecified injury of muscle, fascia and tendon of other parts of biceps, right arm
    - S46.202   Unspecified injury of muscle, fascia and tendon of other parts of biceps, left arm
    - S46.209   Unspecified injury of muscle, fascia and tendon of other parts of biceps, unspecified arm
  - S46.21   Strain of muscle, fascia and tendon of other parts of biceps
    - S46.211   Strain of muscle, fascia and tendon of other parts of biceps, right arm
    - S46.212   Strain of muscle, fascia and tendon of other parts of biceps, left arm
    - S46.219   Strain of muscle, fascia and tendon of other parts of biceps, unspecified arm
  - S46.22   Laceration of muscle, fascia and tendon of other parts of biceps
    - S46.221   Laceration of muscle, fascia and tendon of other parts of biceps, right arm
    - S46.222   Laceration of muscle, fascia and tendon of other parts of biceps, left arm
    - S46.229   Laceration of muscle, fascia and tendon of other parts of biceps, unspecified arm
  - S46.29   Other injury of muscle, fascia and tendon of other parts of biceps
    - S46.291   Other injury of muscle, fascia and tendon of other parts of biceps, right arm
    - S46.292   Other injury of muscle, fascia and tendon of other parts of biceps, left arm
    - S46.299   Other injury of muscle, fascia and tendon of other parts of biceps, unspecified arm
- S46.3   Injury of muscle, fascia and tendon of triceps
  - S46.30   Unspecified injury of muscle, fascia and tendon of triceps
    - S46.301   Unspecified injury of muscle, fascia and tendon of triceps, right arm
    - S46.302   Unspecified injury of muscle, fascia and tendon of triceps, left arm
    - S46.309   Unspecified injury of muscle, fascia and tendon of triceps, unspecified arm
  - S46.31   Strain of muscle, fascia and tendon of triceps
    - S46.311   Strain of muscle, fascia and tendon of triceps, right arm
    - S46.312   Strain of muscle, fascia and tendon of triceps, left arm
    - S46.319   Strain of muscle, fascia and tendon of triceps, unspecified arm
  - S46.32   Laceration of muscle, fascia and tendon of triceps
    - S46.321   Laceration of muscle, fascia and tendon of triceps, right arm
    - S46.322   Laceration of muscle, fascia and tendon of triceps, left arm
    - S46.329   Laceration of muscle, fascia and tendon of triceps, unspecified arm
  - S46.39   Other injury of muscle, fascia and tendon of triceps
    - S46.391   Other injury of muscle, fascia and tendon of triceps, right arm
    - S46.392   Other injury of muscle, fascia and tendon of triceps, left arm
    - S46.399   Other injury of muscle, fascia and tendon of triceps, unspecified arm

CHAPTER 19 (S00-T88)

CHAPTER 19 (S00-T88)

● **S46.8**   Injury of other muscles, fascia and tendons at shoulder and upper arm level

   ● **S46.80**   Unspecified injury of other muscles, fascia and tendons at shoulder and upper arm level

     ● **S46.801**   Unspecified injury of other muscles, fascia and tendons at shoulder and upper arm level, right arm

     ● **S46.802**   Unspecified injury of other muscles, fascia and tendons at shoulder and upper arm level, left arm

     ● **S46.809**   Unspecified injury of other muscles, fascia and tendons at shoulder and upper arm level, unspecified arm

   ● **S46.81**   Strain of other muscles, fascia and tendons at shoulder and upper arm level

     ● **S46.811**   Strain of other muscles, fascia and tendons at shoulder and upper arm level, right arm

     ● **S46.812**   Strain of other muscles, fascia and tendons at shoulder and upper arm level, left arm

     ● **S46.819**   Strain of other muscles, fascia and tendons at shoulder and upper arm level, unspecified arm

   ● **S46.82**   Laceration of other muscles, fascia and tendons at shoulder and upper arm level

     ● **S46.821**   Laceration of other muscles, fascia and tendons at shoulder and upper arm level, right arm

     ● **S46.822**   Laceration of other muscles, fascia and tendons at shoulder and upper arm level, left arm

     ● **S46.829**   Laceration of other muscles, fascia and tendons at shoulder and upper arm level, unspecified arm

   ● **S46.89**   Other injury of other muscles, fascia and tendons at shoulder and upper arm level

     ● **S46.891**   Other injury of other muscles, fascia and tendons at shoulder and upper arm level, right arm

     ● **S46.892**   Other injury of other muscles, fascia and tendons at shoulder and upper arm level, left arm

     ● **S46.899**   Other injury of other muscles, fascia and tendons at shoulder and upper arm level, unspecified arm

● **S46.9**   Injury of unspecified muscle, fascia and tendon at shoulder and upper arm level

   ● **S46.90**   Unspecified injury of unspecified muscle, fascia and tendon at shoulder and upper arm level

     ● **S46.901**   Unspecified injury of unspecified muscle, fascia and tendon at shoulder and upper arm level, right arm

     ● **S46.902**   Unspecified injury of unspecified muscle, fascia and tendon at shoulder and upper arm level, left arm

     ● **S46.909**   Unspecified injury of unspecified muscle, fascia and tendon at shoulder and upper arm level, unspecified arm

   ● **S46.91**   Strain of unspecified muscle, fascia and tendon at shoulder and upper arm level

     ● **S46.911**   Strain of unspecified muscle, fascia and tendon at shoulder and upper arm level, right arm

     ● **S46.912**   Strain of unspecified muscle, fascia and tendon at shoulder and upper arm level, left arm

     ● **S46.919**   Strain of unspecified muscle, fascia and tendon at shoulder and upper arm level, unspecified arm

   ● **S46.92**   Laceration of unspecified muscle, fascia and tendon at shoulder and upper arm level

     ● **S46.921**   Laceration of unspecified muscle, fascia and tendon at shoulder and upper arm level, right arm

     ● **S46.922**   Laceration of unspecified muscle, fascia and tendon at shoulder and upper arm level, left arm

     ● **S46.929**   Laceration of unspecified muscle, fascia and tendon at shoulder and upper arm level, unspecified arm

   ● **S46.99**   Other injury of unspecified muscle, fascia and tendon at shoulder and upper arm level

     ● **S46.991**   Other injury of unspecified muscle, fascia and tendon at shoulder and upper arm level, right arm

     ● **S46.992**   Other injury of unspecified muscle, fascia and tendon at shoulder and upper arm level, left arm

     ● **S46.999**   Other injury of unspecified muscle, fascia and tendon at shoulder and upper arm level, unspecified arm

● **S47**   **Crushing injury of shoulder and upper arm**

   Use additional code for all associated injuries

   Excludes2   crushing injury of elbow (S57.0-)

   The appropriate 7th character is to be added to each code from category S47

A	initial encounter
D	subsequent encounter
S	sequela

X ● **S47.1**   Crushing injury of right shoulder and upper arm

X ● **S47.2**   Crushing injury of left shoulder and upper arm

X ● **S47.9**   Crushing injury of shoulder and upper arm, unspecified arm

● **S48**   **Traumatic amputation of shoulder and upper arm**

   An amputation not identified as partial or complete should be coded to complete

   Excludes1   traumatic amputation at elbow level (S58.0)

   The appropriate 7th character is to be added to each code from category S48

A	initial encounter
D	subsequent encounter
S	sequela

● **S48.0**   Traumatic amputation at shoulder joint

   ● **S48.01**   Complete traumatic amputation at shoulder joint

     ● **S48.011**   Complete traumatic amputation at right shoulder joint

     ● **S48.012**   Complete traumatic amputation at left shoulder joint

     ● **S48.019**   Complete traumatic amputation at unspecified shoulder joint

   ● **S48.02**   Partial traumatic amputation at shoulder joint

     ● **S48.021**   Partial traumatic amputation at right shoulder joint

     ● **S48.022**   Partial traumatic amputation at left shoulder joint

     ● **S48.029**   Partial traumatic amputation at unspecified shoulder joint

- ● **S48.1**   Traumatic amputation at level between shoulder and elbow
  - ● **S48.11**   Complete traumatic amputation at level between shoulder and elbow
    - ● S48.111   Complete traumatic amputation at level between right shoulder and elbow
    - ● S48.112   Complete traumatic amputation at level between left shoulder and elbow
    - ● S48.119   Complete traumatic amputation at level between unspecified shoulder and elbow
  - ● **S48.12**   Partial traumatic amputation at level between shoulder and elbow
    - ● S48.121   Partial traumatic amputation at level between right shoulder and elbow
    - ● S48.122   Partial traumatic amputation at level between left shoulder and elbow
    - ● S48.129   Partial traumatic amputation at level between unspecified shoulder and elbow
- ● **S48.9**   Traumatic amputation of shoulder and upper arm, level unspecified
  - ● **S48.91**   Complete traumatic amputation of shoulder and upper arm, level unspecified
    - ● S48.911   Complete traumatic amputation of right shoulder and upper arm, level unspecified
    - ● S48.912   Complete traumatic amputation of left shoulder and upper arm, level unspecified
    - ● S48.919   Complete traumatic amputation of unspecified shoulder and upper arm, level unspecified
  - ● **S48.92**   Partial traumatic amputation of shoulder and upper arm, level unspecified
    - ● S48.921   Partial traumatic amputation of right shoulder and upper arm, level unspecified
    - ● S48.922   Partial traumatic amputation of left shoulder and upper arm, level unspecified
    - ● S48.929   Partial traumatic amputation of unspecified shoulder and upper arm, level unspecified

- ● **S49**   Other and unspecified injuries of shoulder and upper arm

  The appropriate 7th character is to be added to each code from subcategories S49.0 and S49.1

A	initial encounter for closed fracture
D	subsequent encounter for fracture with routine healing
G	subsequent encounter for fracture with delayed healing
K	subsequent encounter for fracture with nonunion
P	subsequent encounter for fracture with malunion
S	sequela

  - ● **S49.0**   Physeal fracture of upper end of humerus
    - ● **S49.00**   Unspecified physeal fracture of upper end of humerus
      - ● S49.001   Unspecified physeal fracture of upper end of humerus, right arm
      - ● S49.002   Unspecified physeal fracture of upper end of humerus, left arm
      - ● S49.009   Unspecified physeal fracture of upper end of humerus, unspecified arm

Item 19–3 SALTER-HARRIS TYPE 1: epiphysis is completely separated from end of bone, or metaphysic growth plate remains attached to epiphysis
SALTER-HARRIS TYPE 2: epiphysis and growth plate are partially separated from metaphysis, which is cracked—most common type
SALTER-HARRIS TYPE 3: fracture occurring through epiphysis and separates part of epiphysis and growth plate from metaphysis fracture, usually at distal end of tibia
SALTER-HARRIS TYPE 4: fracture runs through epiphysis, across growth plate, into metaphysic, surgery is required to restore joint surface to normal and align growth plate

  - ● **S49.01**   Salter-Harris Type I physeal fracture of upper end of humerus
    - ● S49.011   Salter-Harris Type I physeal fracture of upper end of humerus, right arm
    - ● S49.012   Salter-Harris Type I physeal fracture of upper end of humerus, left arm
    - ● S49.019   Salter-Harris Type I physeal fracture of upper end of humerus, unspecified arm
  - ● **S49.02**   Salter-Harris Type II physeal fracture of upper end of humerus
    - ● S49.021   Salter-Harris Type II physeal fracture of upper end of humerus, right arm
    - ● S49.022   Salter-Harris Type II physeal fracture of upper end of humerus, left arm
    - ● S49.029   Salter-Harris Type II physeal fracture of upper end of humerus, unspecified arm
  - ● **S49.03**   Salter-Harris Type III physeal fracture of upper end of humerus
    - ● S49.031   Salter-Harris Type III physeal fracture of upper end of humerus, right arm
    - ● S49.032   Salter-Harris Type III physeal fracture of upper end of humerus, left arm
    - ● S49.039   Salter-Harris Type III physeal fracture of upper end of humerus, unspecified arm
  - ● **S49.04**   Salter-Harris Type IV physeal fracture of upper end of humerus
    - ● S49.041   Salter-Harris Type IV physeal fracture of upper end of humerus, right arm
    - ● S49.042   Salter-Harris Type IV physeal fracture of upper end of humerus, left arm
    - ● S49.049   Salter-Harris Type IV physeal fracture of upper end of humerus, unspecified arm
  - ● **S49.09**   Other physeal fracture of upper end of humerus
    - ● S49.091   Other physeal fracture of upper end of humerus, right arm
    - ● S49.092   Other physeal fracture of upper end of humerus, left arm
    - ● S49.099   Other physeal fracture of upper end of humerus, unspecified arm
  - ● **S49.1**   Physeal fracture of lower end of humerus
    - ● **S49.10**   Unspecified physeal fracture of lower end of humerus
      - ● S49.101   Unspecified physeal fracture of lower end of humerus, right arm
      - ● S49.102   Unspecified physeal fracture of lower end of humerus, left arm
      - ● S49.109   Unspecified physeal fracture of lower end of humerus, unspecified arm

CHAPTER 19 (S00-T88)

CHAPTER 19 (S00-T88)

● S49.11   **Salter-Harris Type I** physeal fracture of lower end of humerus
    ● S49.111   Salter-Harris Type I physeal fracture of lower end of humerus, **right arm**
    ● S49.112   Salter-Harris Type I physeal fracture of lower end of humerus, **left arm**
    ● S49.119   Salter-Harris Type I physeal fracture of lower end of humerus, **unspecified arm**

● S49.12   **Salter-Harris Type II** physeal fracture of lower end of humerus
    ● S49.121   Salter-Harris Type II physeal fracture of lower end of humerus, **right arm**
    ● S49.122   Salter-Harris Type II physeal fracture of lower end of humerus, **left arm**
    ● S49.129   Salter-Harris Type II physeal fracture of lower end of humerus, **unspecified arm**

● S49.13   **Salter-Harris Type III** physeal fracture of lower end of humerus
    ● S49.131   Salter-Harris Type III physeal fracture of lower end of humerus, **right arm**
    ● S49.132   Salter-Harris Type III physeal fracture of lower end of humerus, **left arm**
    ● S49.139   Salter-Harris Type III physeal fracture of lower end of humerus, **unspecified arm**

● S49.14   **Salter-Harris Type IV** physeal fracture of lower end of humerus
    ● S49.141   Salter-Harris Type IV physeal fracture of lower end of humerus, **right arm**
    ● S49.142   Salter-Harris Type IV physeal fracture of lower end of humerus, **left arm**
    ● S49.149   Salter-Harris Type IV physeal fracture of lower end of humerus, **unspecified arm**

● S49.19   **Other** physeal fracture of lower end of humerus
    ● S49.191   Other physeal fracture of lower end of humerus, **right arm**
    ● S49.192   Other physeal fracture of lower end of humerus, **left arm**
    ● S49.199   Other physeal fracture of lower end of humerus, **unspecified arm**

● S49.8   **Other** specified injuries of shoulder and upper arm

The appropriate 7th character is to be added to each code in subcategory S49.8

A	initial encounter
D	subsequent encounter
S	sequela

X ● S49.80   Other specified injuries of shoulder and upper arm, **unspecified arm**
X ● S49.81   Other specified injuries of **right** shoulder and upper arm
X ● S49.82   Other specified injuries of **left** shoulder and upper arm

● S49.9   **Unspecified** injury of shoulder and upper arm

The appropriate 7th character is to be added to each code in subcategory S49.9

A	initial encounter
D	subsequent encounter
S	sequela

X ● S49.90   Unspecified injury of shoulder and upper arm, **unspecified** arm
X ● S49.91   Unspecified injury of **right** shoulder and upper arm
X ● S49.92   Unspecified injury of **left** shoulder and upper arm

---

INJURIES TO THE ELBOW AND FOREARM (S50-S59)

Excludes2   burns and corrosions (T20-T32)
         frostbite (T33-T34)
         injuries of wrist and hand (S60-S69)
         insect bite or sting, venomous (T63.4)

● S50   Superficial injury of elbow and forearm
   Excludes2   superficial injury of wrist and hand (S60.-)

The appropriate 7th character is to be added to each code from category S50

A	initial encounter
D	subsequent encounter
S	sequela

● S50.0   Contusion of **elbow**
  X ● S50.00   Contusion of **unspecified** elbow
  X ● S50.01   Contusion of **right** elbow
  X ● S50.02   Contusion of **left** elbow

● S50.1   Contusion of **forearm**
  X ● S50.10   Contusion of **unspecified** forearm
  X ● S50.11   Contusion of **right** forearm
  X ● S50.12   Contusion of **left** forearm

● S50.3   Other superficial injuries of **elbow**
  ● S50.31   **Abrasion** of elbow
    ● S50.311   Abrasion of **right** elbow
    ● S50.312   Abrasion of **left** elbow
    ● S50.319   Abrasion of **unspecified** elbow
  ● S50.32   **Blister** (nonthermal) of elbow
    ● S50.321   Blister (nonthermal) of **right** elbow
    ● S50.322   Blister (nonthermal) of **left** elbow
    ● S50.329   Blister (nonthermal) of **unspecified** elbow
  ● S50.34   **External constriction** of elbow
    ● S50.341   External constriction of **right** elbow
    ● S50.342   External constriction of **left** elbow
    ● S50.349   External constriction of **unspecified** elbow
  ● S50.35   **Superficial foreign body** of elbow
     Splinter in the elbow
    ● S50.351   Superficial foreign body of **right** elbow
    ● S50.352   Superficial foreign body of **left** elbow
    ● S50.359   Superficial foreign body of **unspecified** elbow
  ● S50.36   **Insect bite** (nonvenomous) of elbow
    ● S50.361   Insect bite (nonvenomous) of **right** elbow
    ● S50.362   Insect bite (nonvenomous) of **left** elbow
    ● S50.369   Insect bite (nonvenomous) of **unspecified** elbow
  ● S50.37   **Other** superficial bite of elbow
     Excludes1   open bite of elbow (S51.04)
    ● S50.371   Other superficial bite of **right** elbow
    ● S50.372   Other superficial bite of **left** elbow
    ● S50.379   Other superficial bite of **unspecified** elbow

● S50.8   Other superficial injuries of **forearm**
  ● S50.81   **Abrasion** of forearm
    ● S50.811   Abrasion of **right** forearm
    ● S50.812   Abrasion of **left** forearm
    ● S50.819   Abrasion of **unspecified** forearm
  ● S50.82   **Blister** (nonthermal) of forearm
    ● S50.821   Blister (nonthermal) of **right** forearm
    ● S50.822   Blister (nonthermal) of **left** forearm
    ● S50.829   Blister (nonthermal) of **unspecified** forearm

▶ New   ⇒ Revised   ~~deleted~~ Deleted   Excludes 1   Excludes 2   Includes   Use additional   Code first   Code also   Key words

OGCR Official Guidelines   X Assign placeholder X   ● Use Additional Character(s)   ▶ Manifestation Code   **Coding Clinic**

● S50.84   External constriction of forearm
   ● S50.841   External constriction of right forearm
   ● S50.842   External constriction of left forearm
   ● S50.849   External constriction of unspecified forearm
● S50.85   Superficial foreign body of forearm
            Splinter in the forearm
   ● S50.851   Superficial foreign body of right forearm
   ● S50.852   Superficial foreign body of left forearm
   ● S50.859   Superficial foreign body of unspecified forearm
● S50.86   Insect bite (nonvenomous) of forearm
   ● S50.861   Insect bite (nonvenomous) of right forearm
   ● S50.862   Insect bite (nonvenomous) of left forearm
   ● S50.869   Insect bite (nonvenomous) of unspecified forearm
● S50.87   Other superficial bite of forearm
            Excludes1   open bite of forearm (S51.84)
   ● S50.871   Other superficial bite of right forearm
   ● S50.872   Other superficial bite of left forearm
   ● S50.879   Other superficial bite of unspecified forearm
● S50.9   Unspecified superficial injury of elbow and forearm
   ● S50.90   Unspecified superficial injury of elbow
      ● S50.901   Unspecified superficial injury of right elbow
      ● S50.902   Unspecified superficial injury of left elbow
      ● S50.909   Unspecified superficial injury of unspecified elbow
   ● S50.91   Unspecified superficial injury of forearm
      ● S50.911   Unspecified superficial injury of right forearm
      ● S50.912   Unspecified superficial injury of left forearm
      ● S50.919   Unspecified superficial injury of unspecified forearm

● S51   Open wound of elbow and forearm
         Code also any associated wound infection
         Excludes1   open fracture of elbow and forearm (S52.- with open fracture 7th character)
                          traumatic amputation of elbow and forearm (S58.-)
         Excludes2   open wound of wrist and hand (S61.-)
         The appropriate 7th character is to be added to each code from category S51

         ┌─────────────────────────────────┐
         │ A   initial encounter   │
         │ D   subsequent encounter   │
         │ S   sequela   │
         └─────────────────────────────────┘

● S51.0   Open wound of elbow
   ● S51.00   Unspecified open wound of elbow
      ● S51.001   Unspecified open wound of right elbow
                  Coding Clinic: 2012, Q4, P108
      ● S51.002   Unspecified open wound of left elbow
      ● S51.009   Unspecified open wound of unspecified elbow
                  Open wound of elbow NOS

● S51.01   Laceration without foreign body of elbow
   ● S51.011   Laceration without foreign body of right elbow
   ● S51.012   Laceration without foreign body of left elbow
   ● S51.019   Laceration without foreign body of unspecified elbow
● S51.02   Laceration with foreign body of elbow
   ● S51.021   Laceration with foreign body of right elbow
   ● S51.022   Laceration with foreign body of left elbow
   ● S51.029   Laceration with foreign body of unspecified elbow
● S51.03   Puncture wound without foreign body of elbow
   ● S51.031   Puncture wound without foreign body of right elbow
   ● S51.032   Puncture wound without foreign body of left elbow
   ● S51.039   Puncture wound without foreign body of unspecified elbow
● S51.04   Puncture wound with foreign body of elbow
   ● S51.041   Puncture wound with foreign body of right elbow
   ● S51.042   Puncture wound with foreign body of left elbow
   ● S51.049   Puncture wound with foreign body of unspecified elbow
● S51.05   Open bite of elbow
            Bite of elbow NOS
            Excludes1   superficial bite of elbow (S50.36, S50.37)
   ● S51.051   Open bite, right elbow
   ● S51.052   Open bite, left elbow
   ● S51.059   Open bite, unspecified elbow
● S51.8   Open wound of forearm
          Excludes2   open wound of elbow (S51.0-)
   ● S51.80   Unspecified open wound of forearm
      ● S51.801   Unspecified open wound of right forearm
      ● S51.802   Unspecified open wound of left forearm
      ● S51.809   Unspecified open wound of unspecified forearm
                  Open wound of forearm NOS
   ● S51.81   Laceration without foreign body of forearm
      ● S51.811   Laceration without foreign body of right forearm
      ● S51.812   Laceration without foreign body of left forearm
      ● S51.819   Laceration without foreign body of unspecified forearm
   ● S51.82   Laceration with foreign body of forearm
      ● S51.821   Laceration with foreign body of right forearm
      ● S51.822   Laceration with foreign body of left forearm
      ● S51.829   Laceration with foreign body of unspecified forearm
   ● S51.83   Puncture wound without foreign body of forearm
      ● S51.831   Puncture wound without foreign body of right forearm
      ● S51.832   Puncture wound without foreign body of left forearm
      ● S51.839   Puncture wound without foreign body of unspecified forearm

CHAPTER 19 (S00-T88)

CHAPTER 19 (S00-T88)

● S51.84   **Puncture wound with foreign body of forearm**
- ● S51.841   **Puncture wound with foreign body of right forearm**
- ● S51.842   **Puncture wound with foreign body of left forearm**
- ● S51.849   **Puncture wound with foreign body of unspecified forearm**

● S51.85   **Open bite of forearm**
Bite of forearm NOS

Excludes1   superficial bite of forearm (S50.86, S50.87)

- ● S51.851   **Open bite of right forearm**
- ● S51.852   **Open bite of left forearm**
- ● S51.859   **Open bite of unspecified forearm**

● S52   **Fracture of forearm**

Note: A fracture not identified as displaced or nondisplaced should be coded to displaced

A fracture not designated as open or closed should be coded to closed

The open fracture designations are based on the Gustilo open fracture classification

Excludes1   traumatic amputation of forearm (S58.-)

Excludes2   fracture at wrist and hand level (S62.-)

The appropriate 7th character is to be added to all codes from category S52

A	initial encounter for closed fracture
B	initial encounter for open fracture type I or II
	initial encounter for open fracture NOS
C	initial encounter for open fracture type IIIA, IIIB, or IIIC
D	subsequent encounter for closed fracture with routine healing
E	subsequent encounter for open fracture type I or II with routine healing
F	subsequent encounter for open fracture type IIIA, IIIB, or IIIC with routine healing
G	subsequent encounter for closed fracture with delayed healing
H	subsequent encounter for open fracture type I or II with delayed healing
J	subsequent encounter for open fracture type IIIA, IIIB, or IIIC with delayed healing
K	subsequent encounter for closed fracture with nonunion
M	subsequent encounter for open fracture type I or II with nonunion
N	subsequent encounter for open fracture type IIIA, IIIB, or IIIC with nonunion
P	subsequent encounter for closed fracture with malunion
Q	subsequent encounter for open fracture type I or II with malunion
R	subsequent encounter for open fracture type IIIA, IIIB, or IIIC with malunion
S	sequela

Coding Clinic: 2016, Q1, P33

● S52.0   **Fracture of upper end of ulna**
Fracture of proximal end of ulna

Excludes2   fracture of elbow NOS (S42.40-)
fractures of shaft of ulna (S52.2-)

● S52.00   **Unspecified fracture of upper end of ulna**
- ● S52.001   **Unspecified fracture of upper end of right ulna**
- ● S52.002   **Unspecified fracture of upper end of left ulna**
- ● S52.009   **Unspecified fracture of upper end of unspecified ulna**

● S52.01   **Torus fracture of upper end of ulna**

The appropriate 7th character is to be added to all codes in subcategory S52.01

A	initial encounter for closed fracture
D	subsequent encounter for fracture with routine healing
G	subsequent encounter for fracture with delayed healing
K	subsequent encounter for fracture with nonunion
P	subsequent encounter for fracture with malunion
S	sequela

- ● S52.011   **Torus fracture of upper end of right ulna**
- ● S52.012   **Torus fracture of upper end of left ulna**
- ● S52.019   **Torus fracture of upper end of unspecified ulna**

● S52.02   **Fracture of olecranon process without intraarticular extension of ulna**
- ● S52.021   **Displaced fracture of olecranon process without intraarticular extension of right ulna**
- ● S52.022   **Displaced fracture of olecranon process without intraarticular extension of left ulna**
- ● S52.023   **Displaced fracture of olecranon process without intraarticular extension of unspecified ulna**
- ● S52.024   **Nondisplaced fracture of olecranon process without intraarticular extension of right ulna**
- ● S52.025   **Nondisplaced fracture of olecranon process without intraarticular extension of left ulna**
- ● S52.026   **Nondisplaced fracture of olecranon process without intraarticular extension of unspecified ulna**

● S52.03   **Fracture of olecranon process with intraarticular extension of ulna**
- ● S52.031   **Displaced fracture of olecranon process with intraarticular extension of right ulna**
- ● S52.032   **Displaced fracture of olecranon process with intraarticular extension of left ulna**
- ● S52.033   **Displaced fracture of olecranon process with intraarticular extension of unspecified ulna**
- ● S52.034   **Nondisplaced fracture of olecranon process with intraarticular extension of right ulna**
- ● S52.035   **Nondisplaced fracture of olecranon process with intraarticular extension of left ulna**
- ● S52.036   **Nondisplaced fracture of olecranon process with intraarticular extension of unspecified ulna**

● S52.04   **Fracture of coronoid process of ulna**
- ● S52.041   **Displaced fracture of coronoid process of right ulna**
- ● S52.042   **Displaced fracture of coronoid process of left ulna**
- ● S52.043   **Displaced fracture of coronoid process of unspecified ulna**
- ● S52.044   **Nondisplaced fracture of coronoid process of right ulna**

▶ New   ⇒ Revised   ~~deleted~~ Deleted   Excludes 1   Excludes 2   Includes   Use additional   Code first   Code also   Key words

OGCR Official Guidelines   X Assign placeholder X   ● Use Additional Character(s)   ▷ Manifestation Code   **Coding Clinic**

● S52.045　Nondisplaced fracture of coronoid process of left ulna

● S52.046　Nondisplaced fracture of coronoid process of unspecified ulna

● S52.09　Other fracture of upper end of ulna

　● S52.091　Other fracture of upper end of right ulna

　● S52.092　Other fracture of upper end of left ulna

　● S52.099　Other fracture of upper end of unspecified ulna

● S52.1　Fracture of upper end of radius
　　Fracture of proximal end of radius

　　Excludes2　physeal fractures of upper end of radius (S59.2-)
　　　　　　　　fracture of shaft of radius (S52.3-)

● S52.10　Unspecified fracture of upper end of radius

　● S52.101　Unspecified fracture of upper end of right radius

　● S52.102　Unspecified fracture of upper end of left radius

　● S52.109　Unspecified fracture of upper end of unspecified radius

● S52.11　Torus fracture of upper end of radius

　　The appropriate 7th character is to be added to all codes in subcategory S52.11

A	initial encounter for closed fracture
D	subsequent encounter for fracture with routine healing
G	subsequent encounter for fracture with delayed healing
K	subsequent encounter for fracture with nonunion
P	subsequent encounter for fracture with malunion
S	sequela

　● S52.111　Torus fracture of upper end of right radius

　● S52.112　Torus fracture of upper end of left radius

　● S52.119　Torus fracture of upper end of unspecified radius

● S52.12　Fracture of head of radius

　● S52.121　Displaced fracture of head of right radius

　● S52.122　Displaced fracture of head of left radius

　● S52.123　Displaced fracture of head of unspecified radius

　● S52.124　Nondisplaced fracture of head of right radius

　● S52.125　Nondisplaced fracture of head of left radius

　● S52.126　Nondisplaced fracture of head of unspecified radius

● S52.13　Fracture of neck of radius

　● S52.131　Displaced fracture of neck of right radius

　● S52.132　Displaced fracture of neck of left radius

　● S52.133　Displaced fracture of neck of unspecified radius

　● S52.134　Nondisplaced fracture of neck of right radius

　● S52.135　Nondisplaced fracture of neck of left radius

　● S52.136　Nondisplaced fracture of neck of unspecified radius

● S52.18　Other fracture of upper end of radius

　● S52.181　Other fracture of upper end of right radius

　● S52.182　Other fracture of upper end of left radius

　● S52.189　Other fracture of upper end of unspecified radius

● S52.2　Fracture of shaft of ulna

● S52.20　Unspecified fracture of shaft of ulna
　　Fracture of ulna NOS

　● S52.201　Unspecified fracture of shaft of right ulna

　● S52.202　Unspecified fracture of shaft of left ulna

　● S52.209　Unspecified fracture of shaft of unspecified ulna

● S52.21　Greenstick fracture of shaft of ulna

　　The appropriate 7th character is to be added to all codes in subcategory S52.21

A	initial encounter for closed fracture
D	subsequent encounter for fracture with routine healing
G	subsequent encounter for fracture with delayed healing
K	subsequent encounter for fracture with nonunion
P	subsequent encounter for fracture with malunion
S	sequela

　● S52.211　Greenstick fracture of shaft of right ulna

　● S52.212　Greenstick fracture of shaft of left ulna

　● S52.219　Greenstick fracture of shaft of unspecified ulna

● S52.22　Transverse fracture of shaft of ulna

　● S52.221　Displaced transverse fracture of shaft of right ulna

　● S52.222　Displaced transverse fracture of shaft of left ulna

　● S52.223　Displaced transverse fracture of shaft of unspecified ulna

　● S52.224　Nondisplaced transverse fracture of shaft of right ulna

　● S52.225　Nondisplaced transverse fracture of shaft of left ulna

　● S52.226　Nondisplaced transverse fracture of shaft of unspecified ulna

● S52.23　Oblique fracture of shaft of ulna

　● S52.231　Displaced oblique fracture of shaft of right ulna

　● S52.232　Displaced oblique fracture of shaft of left ulna

　● S52.233　Displaced oblique fracture of shaft of unspecified ulna

　● S52.234　Nondisplaced oblique fracture of shaft of right ulna

　● S52.235　Nondisplaced oblique fracture of shaft of left ulna

　● S52.236　Nondisplaced oblique fracture of shaft of unspecified ulna

CHAPTER 19 (S00-T88)

● **S52.24**   **Spiral** fracture of shaft of ulna

   ● **S52.241**   Displaced spiral fracture of shaft of ulna, **right arm**

   ● **S52.242**   Displaced spiral fracture of shaft of ulna, **left arm**

   ● **S52.243**   Displaced spiral fracture of shaft of ulna, **unspecified arm**

   ● **S52.244**   Nondisplaced spiral fracture of shaft of ulna, **right arm**

   ● **S52.245**   Nondisplaced spiral fracture of shaft of ulna, **left arm**

   ● **S52.246**   Nondisplaced spiral fracture of shaft of ulna, **unspecified arm**

● **S52.25**   **Comminuted** fracture of shaft of ulna

   ● **S52.251**   Displaced comminuted fracture of shaft of ulna, **right arm**

   ● **S52.252**   Displaced comminuted fracture of shaft of ulna, **left arm**

   ● **S52.253**   Displaced comminuted fracture of shaft of ulna, **unspecified arm**

   ● **S52.254**   Nondisplaced comminuted fracture of shaft of ulna, **right arm**

   ● **S52.255**   Nondisplaced comminuted fracture of shaft of ulna, **left arm**

   ● **S52.256**   Nondisplaced comminuted fracture of shaft of ulna, **unspecified arm**

● **S52.26**   **Segmental** fracture of shaft of ulna

   ● **S52.261**   Displaced segmental fracture of shaft of ulna, **right arm**

   ● **S52.262**   Displaced segmental fracture of shaft of ulna, **left arm**

   ● **S52.263**   Displaced segmental fracture of shaft of ulna, **unspecified arm**

   ● **S52.264**   Nondisplaced segmental fracture of shaft of ulna, **right arm**

   ● **S52.265**   Nondisplaced segmental fracture of shaft of ulna, **left arm**

   ● **S52.266**   Nondisplaced segmental fracture of shaft of ulna, **unspecified arm**

● **S52.27**   **Monteggia's** fracture of ulna

      Fracture of upper shaft of ulna with dislocation of radial head

   ● **S52.271**   Monteggia's fracture of **right** ulna

   ● **S52.272**   Monteggia's fracture of **left** ulna

   ● **S52.279**   Monteggia's fracture of **unspecified** ulna

● **S52.28**   **Bent bone** of ulna

   ● **S52.281**   Bent bone of **right** ulna

   ● **S52.282**   Bent bone of **left** ulna

   ● **S52.283**   Bent bone of **unspecified** ulna

● **S52.29**   **Other** fracture of shaft of ulna

   ● **S52.291**   Other fracture of shaft of **right** ulna

   ● **S52.292**   Other fracture of shaft of **left** ulna

   ● **S52.299**   Other fracture of shaft of **unspecified** ulna

● **S52.3**   Fracture of **shaft** of radius

 ● **S52.30**   **Unspecified** fracture of shaft of radius

   ● **S52.301**   Unspecified fracture of shaft of **right** radius

   ● **S52.302**   Unspecified fracture of shaft of **left** radius

   ● **S52.309**   Unspecified fracture of shaft of **unspecified** radius

● **S52.31**   **Greenstick** fracture of shaft of radius

      The appropriate 7th character is to be added to all codes in subcategory S52.31

> | | |
> |---|---|
> | A | initial encounter for closed fracture |
> | D | subsequent encounter for fracture with routine healing |
> | G | subsequent encounter for fracture with delayed healing |
> | K | subsequent encounter for fracture with nonunion |
> | P | subsequent encounter for fracture with malunion |
> | S | sequela |

   ● **S52.311**   Greenstick fracture of shaft of radius, **right arm**

   ● **S52.312**   Greenstick fracture of shaft of radius, **left arm**

   ● **S52.319**   Greenstick fracture of shaft of radius, **unspecified arm**

● **S52.32**   **Transverse** fracture of shaft of radius

   ● **S52.321**   Displaced transverse fracture of shaft of **right radius**

   ● **S52.322**   Displaced transverse fracture of shaft of **left radius**

   ● **S52.323**   Displaced transverse fracture of shaft of **unspecified radius**

   ● **S52.324**   Nondisplaced transverse fracture of shaft of **right radius**

   ● **S52.325**   Nondisplaced transverse fracture of shaft of **left radius**

   ● **S52.326**   Nondisplaced transverse fracture of shaft of **unspecified radius**

● **S52.33**   **Oblique** fracture of shaft of radius

   ● **S52.331**   Displaced oblique fracture of shaft of **right radius**

   ● **S52.332**   Displaced oblique fracture of shaft of **left radius**

   ● **S52.333**   Displaced oblique fracture of shaft of **unspecified radius**

   ● **S52.334**   Nondisplaced oblique fracture of shaft of **right radius**

   ● **S52.335**   Nondisplaced oblique fracture of shaft of **left radius**

   ● **S52.336**   Nondisplaced oblique fracture of shaft of **unspecified radius**

● **S52.34**   **Spiral** fracture of shaft of radius

   ● **S52.341**   Displaced spiral fracture of shaft of radius, **right arm**

   ● **S52.342**   Displaced spiral fracture of shaft of radius, **left arm**

   ● **S52.343**   Displaced spiral fracture of shaft of radius, **unspecified arm**

   ● **S52.344**   Nondisplaced spiral fracture of shaft of radius, **right arm**

   ● **S52.345**   Nondisplaced spiral fracture of shaft of radius, **left arm**

   ● **S52.346**   Nondisplaced spiral fracture of shaft of radius, **unspecified arm**

● **S52.35**   **Comminuted** fracture of shaft of radius

   ● **S52.351**   Displaced comminuted fracture of shaft of radius, **right arm**

   ● **S52.352**   Displaced comminuted fracture of shaft of radius, **left arm**

▶ New   ⇒ Revised   ~~deleted~~ Deleted   Excludes 1   Excludes 2   Includes   Use additional   Code first   Code also   Key words

OGCR Official Guidelines   X Assign placeholder X   ● Use Additional Character(s)   ▶ Manifestation Code   **Coding Clinic**

● **S52.353 Displaced** comminuted fracture of shaft of radius, **unspecified arm**

● **S52.354 Nondisplaced** comminuted fracture of shaft of radius, **right arm**

● **S52.355 Nondisplaced** comminuted fracture of shaft of radius, **left arm**

● **S52.356 Nondisplaced** comminuted fracture of shaft of radius, **unspecified arm**

● **S52.36 Segmental** fracture of shaft of radius

  ● **S52.361 Displaced segmental** fracture of shaft of radius, **right arm**

  ● **S52.362 Displaced segmental** fracture of shaft of radius, **left arm**

  ● **S52.363 Displaced segmental** fracture of shaft of radius, **unspecified arm**

  ● **S52.364 Nondisplaced segmental** fracture of shaft of radius, **right arm**

  ● **S52.365 Nondisplaced segmental** fracture of shaft of radius, **left arm**

  ● **S52.366 Nondisplaced segmental** fracture of shaft of radius, **unspecified arm**

● **S52.37 Galeazzi's** fracture
    Fracture of lower shaft of radius with radioulnar joint dislocation

  ● **S52.371 Galeazzi's** fracture of **right radius**

  ● **S52.372 Galeazzi's** fracture of **left radius**

  ● **S52.379 Galeazzi's** fracture of **unspecified radius**

● **S52.38 Bent bone** of radius

  ● **S52.381 Bent bone of right** radius

  ● **S52.382 Bent bone of left** radius

  ● **S52.389 Bent bone of unspecified** radius

● **S52.39 Other** fracture of shaft of radius

  ● **S52.391 Other** fracture of shaft of radius, **right arm**

  ● **S52.392 Other** fracture of shaft of radius, **left arm**

  ● **S52.399 Other** fracture of shaft of radius, **unspecified arm**

● **S52.5 Fracture of lower end of radius**
    Fracture of distal end of radius

    Excludes2   physeal fractures of lower end of radius (S59.2-)

● **S52.50 Unspecified** fracture of the lower end of radius

  ● **S52.501 Unspecified** fracture of the lower end of **right radius**

  ● **S52.502 Unspecified** fracture of the lower end of **left radius**

  ● **S52.509 Unspecified** fracture of the lower end of **unspecified radius**

● **S52.51 Fracture of radial styloid process**

  ● **S52.511 Displaced** fracture of **right** radial styloid process

  ● **S52.512 Displaced** fracture of **left** radial styloid process

  ● **S52.513 Displaced** fracture of **unspecified** radial styloid process

  ● **S52.514 Nondisplaced** fracture of **right** radial styloid process

  ● **S52.515 Nondisplaced** fracture of **left** radial styloid process

  ● **S52.516 Nondisplaced** fracture of **unspecified** radial styloid process

● **S52.52 Torus** fracture of lower end of radius

  The appropriate 7th character is to be added to all codes in subcategory S52.52

A	initial encounter for closed fracture
D	subsequent encounter for fracture with routine healing
G	subsequent encounter for fracture with delayed healing
K	subsequent encounter for fracture with nonunion
P	subsequent encounter for fracture with malunion
S	sequela

  ● **S52.521 Torus** fracture of lower end of **right** radius

  ● **S52.522 Torus** fracture of lower end of **left** radius

  ● **S52.529 Torus** fracture of lower end of **unspecified** radius

● **S52.53 Colles'** fracture

  ● **S52.531 Colles'** fracture of **right** radius

  ● **S52.532 Colles'** fracture of **left** radius
      Coding Clinic: 2016, Q2, P5

  ● **S52.539 Colles'** fracture of **unspecified** radius

● **S52.54 Smith's** fracture

  ● **S52.541 Smith's** fracture of **right** radius

  ● **S52.542 Smith's** fracture of **left** radius

  ● **S52.549 Smith's** fracture of **unspecified** radius

● **S52.55 Other extraarticular** fracture of lower end of radius

  ● **S52.551 Other extraarticular** fracture of lower end of **right** radius

  ● **S52.552 Other extraarticular** fracture of lower end of **left** radius

  ● **S52.559 Other extraarticular** fracture of lower end of **unspecified** radius

● **S52.56 Barton's** fracture

  ● **S52.561 Barton's** fracture of **right** radius

  ● **S52.562 Barton's** fracture of **left** radius

  ● **S52.569 Barton's** fracture of **unspecified** radius

● **S52.57 Other intraarticular** fracture of lower end of radius

  ● **S52.571 Other intraarticular** fracture of lower end of **right** radius

  ● **S52.572 Other intraarticular** fracture of lower end of **left** radius

  ● **S52.579 Other intraarticular** fracture of lower end of **unspecified** radius

● **S52.59 Other fractures** of lower end of radius

  ● **S52.591 Other fractures** of lower end of **right** radius

  ● **S52.592 Other fractures** of lower end of **left** radius

  ● **S52.599 Other fractures** of lower end of **unspecified** radius

● **S52.6 Fracture of lower end of ulna**

  ● **S52.60 Unspecified** fracture of lower end of ulna ‑

    ● **S52.601 Unspecified** fracture of lower end of **right** ulna

    ● **S52.602 Unspecified** fracture of lower end of **left** ulna

    ● **S52.609 Unspecified** fracture of lower end of **unspecified** ulna

CHAPTER 19 (S00–T88)

● **S52.61** Fracture of ulna styloid process
   ● **S52.611** **Displaced fracture of right ulna styloid process**
   ● **S52.612** **Displaced fracture of left ulna styloid process**
   ● **S52.613** **Displaced fracture of unspecified ulna styloid process**
   ● **S52.614** **Nondisplaced fracture of right ulna styloid process**
   ● **S52.615** **Nondisplaced fracture of left ulna styloid process**
   ● **S52.616** **Nondisplaced fracture of unspecified ulna styloid process**
● **S52.62** Torus fracture of lower end of ulna

The appropriate 7th character is to be added to all codes in subcategory S52.62

A	initial encounter for closed fracture
D	subsequent encounter for fracture with routine healing
G	subsequent encounter for fracture with delayed healing
K	subsequent encounter for fracture with nonunion
P	subsequent encounter for fracture with malunion
S	sequela

   ● **S52.621** **Torus fracture of lower end of right ulna**
   ● **S52.622** **Torus fracture of lower end of left ulna**
   ● **S52.629** **Torus fracture of lower end of unspecified ulna**
● **S52.69** Other fracture of lower end of ulna
   ● **S52.691** **Other fracture of lower end of right ulna**
   ● **S52.692** **Other fracture of lower end of left ulna**
   ● **S52.699** **Other fracture of lower end of unspecified ulna**
● **S52.9** Unspecified fracture of forearm
  X● **S52.90** **Unspecified fracture of unspecified forearm**
  X● **S52.91** **Unspecified fracture of right forearm**
  X● **S52.92** **Unspecified fracture of left forearm**

● **S53** **Dislocation and sprain of joints and ligaments of elbow**

Includes   avulsion of joint or ligament of elbow
laceration of cartilage, joint or ligament of elbow
sprain of cartilage, joint or ligament of elbow
traumatic hemarthrosis of joint or ligament of elbow
traumatic rupture of joint or ligament of elbow
traumatic subluxation of joint or ligament of elbow
traumatic tear of joint or ligament of elbow

Code also any associated open wound
Excludes2   strain of muscle, fascia and tendon at forearm level (S56.-)

The appropriate 7th character is to be added to each code from category S53

A	initial encounter
D	subsequent encounter
S	sequela

● **S53.0** **Subluxation and dislocation of radial head**
Dislocation of radiohumeral joint
Subluxation of radiohumeral joint
  Excludes1   Monteggia's fracture-dislocation (S52.27-)
  ● **S53.00** **Unspecified subluxation and dislocation of radial head**
    ● **S53.001** **Unspecified subluxation of right radial head**
    ● **S53.002** **Unspecified subluxation of left radial head**
    ● **S53.003** **Unspecified subluxation of unspecified radial head**
    ● **S53.004** **Unspecified dislocation of right radial head**
    ● **S53.005** **Unspecified dislocation of left radial head**
    ● **S53.006** **Unspecified dislocation of unspecified radial head**
  ● **S53.01** **Anterior subluxation and dislocation of radial head**
Anteriomedial subluxation and dislocation of radial head
    ● **S53.011** **Anterior subluxation of right radial head**
    ● **S53.012** **Anterior subluxation of left radial head**
    ● **S53.013** **Anterior subluxation of unspecified radial head**
    ● **S53.014** **Anterior dislocation of right radial head**
    ● **S53.015** **Anterior dislocation of left radial head**
    ● **S53.016** **Anterior dislocation of unspecified radial head**
  ● **S53.02** **Posterior subluxation and dislocation of radial head**
Posteriolateral subluxation and dislocation of radial head
    ● **S53.021** **Posterior subluxation of right radial head**
    ● **S53.022** **Posterior subluxation of left radial head**
    ● **S53.023** **Posterior subluxation of unspecified radial head**
    ● **S53.024** **Posterior dislocation of right radial head**
    ● **S53.025** **Posterior dislocation of left radial head**
    ● **S53.026** **Posterior dislocation of unspecified radial head**
  ● **S53.03** **Nursemaid's elbow**
    ● **S53.031** **Nursemaid's elbow, right elbow**
        Coding Clinic: 2015, Q1, P7-8
    ● **S53.032** **Nursemaid's elbow, left elbow**
    ● **S53.033** **Nursemaid's elbow, unspecified elbow**
  ● **S53.09** **Other subluxation and dislocation of radial head**
    ● **S53.091** **Other subluxation of right radial head**
    ● **S53.092** **Other subluxation of left radial head**
    ● **S53.093** **Other subluxation of unspecified radial head**
    ● **S53.094** **Other dislocation of right radial head**
    ● **S53.095** **Other dislocation of left radial head**
    ● **S53.096** **Other dislocation of unspecified radial head**
● **S53.1** **Subluxation and dislocation of ulnohumeral joint**
Subluxation and dislocation of elbow NOS
  Excludes1   dislocation of radial head alone (S53.0-)
  ● **S53.10** **Unspecified subluxation and dislocation of ulnohumeral joint**
    ● **S53.101** **Unspecified subluxation of right ulnohumeral joint**
    ● **S53.102** **Unspecified subluxation of left ulnohumeral joint**
    ● **S53.103** **Unspecified subluxation of unspecified ulnohumeral joint**
    ● **S53.104** **Unspecified dislocation of right ulnohumeral joint**

▶ New   ⇒ Revised   ~~deleted~~ Deleted   Excludes 1   Excludes 2   Includes   Use additional   Code first   Code also   Key words
OGCR Official Guidelines   X Assign placeholder X   ● Use Additional Character(s)   ▌ Manifestation Code   **Coding Clinic**

● S53.105   Unspecified dislocation of left ulnohumeral joint

● S53.106   Unspecified dislocation of unspecified ulnohumeral joint

● S53.11   Anterior subluxation and dislocation of ulnohumeral joint

  ● S53.111   Anterior subluxation of right ulnohumeral joint

  ● S53.112   Anterior subluxation of left ulnohumeral joint

  ● S53.113   Anterior subluxation of unspecified ulnohumeral joint

  ● S53.114   Anterior dislocation of right ulnohumeral joint
        Coding Clinic: 2012, Q4, P108

  ● S53.115   Anterior dislocation of left ulnohumeral joint

  ● S53.116   Anterior dislocation of unspecified ulnohumeral joint

● S53.12   Posterior subluxation and dislocation of ulnohumeral joint

  ● S53.121   Posterior subluxation of right ulnohumeral joint

  ● S53.122   Posterior subluxation of left ulnohumeral joint

  ● S53.123   Posterior subluxation of unspecified ulnohumeral joint

  ● S53.124   Posterior dislocation of right ulnohumeral joint

  ● S53.125   Posterior dislocation of left ulnohumeral joint

  ● S53.126   Posterior dislocation of unspecified ulnohumeral joint

● S53.13   Medial subluxation and dislocation of ulnohumeral joint

  ● S53.131   Medial subluxation of right ulnohumeral joint

  ● S53.132   Medial subluxation of left ulnohumeral joint

  ● S53.133   Medial subluxation of unspecified ulnohumeral joint

  ● S53.134   Medial dislocation of right ulnohumeral joint

  ● S53.135   Medial dislocation of left ulnohumeral joint

  ● S53.136   Medial dislocation of unspecified ulnohumeral joint

● S53.14   Lateral subluxation and dislocation of ulnohumeral joint

  ● S53.141   Lateral subluxation of right ulnohumeral joint

  ● S53.142   Lateral subluxation of left ulnohumeral joint

  ● S53.143   Lateral subluxation of unspecified ulnohumeral joint

  ● S53.144   Lateral dislocation of right ulnohumeral joint

  ● S53.145   Lateral dislocation of left ulnohumeral joint

  ● S53.146   Lateral dislocation of unspecified ulnohumeral joint

● S53.19   Other subluxation and dislocation of ulnohumeral joint

  ● S53.191   Other subluxation of right ulnohumeral joint

  ● S53.192   Other subluxation of left ulnohumeral joint

  ● S53.193   Other subluxation of unspecified ulnohumeral joint

● S53.194   Other dislocation of right ulnohumeral joint

● S53.195   Other dislocation of left ulnohumeral joint

● S53.196   Other dislocation of unspecified ulnohumeral joint

● S53.2   Traumatic rupture of radial collateral ligament
    Excludes1   sprain of radial collateral ligament NOS (S53.43-)

X ● S53.20   Traumatic rupture of unspecified radial collateral ligament

X ● S53.21   Traumatic rupture of right radial collateral ligament

X ● S53.22   Traumatic rupture of left radial collateral ligament

● S53.3   Traumatic rupture of ulnar collateral ligament
    Excludes1   sprain of ulnar collateral ligament (S53.44-)

X ● S53.30   Traumatic rupture of unspecified ulnar collateral ligament

X ● S53.31   Traumatic rupture of right ulnar collateral ligament

X ● S53.32   Traumatic rupture of left ulnar collateral ligament

● S53.4   Sprain of elbow
    Excludes2   traumatic rupture of radial collateral ligament (S53.2-)
                traumatic rupture of ulnar collateral ligament (S53.3-)

● S53.40   Unspecified sprain of elbow

  ● S53.401   Unspecified sprain of right elbow

  ● S53.402   Unspecified sprain of left elbow

  ● S53.409   Unspecified sprain of unspecified elbow
       Sprain of elbow NOS

● S53.41   Radiohumeral (joint) sprain

  ● S53.411   Radiohumeral (joint) sprain of right elbow

  ● S53.412   Radiohumeral (joint) sprain of left elbow

  ● S53.419   Radiohumeral (joint) sprain of unspecified elbow

● S53.42   Ulnohumeral (joint) sprain

  ● S53.421   Ulnohumeral (joint) sprain of right elbow

  ● S53.422   Ulnohumeral (joint) sprain of left elbow

  ● S53.429   Ulnohumeral (joint) sprain of unspecified elbow

● S53.43   Radial collateral ligament sprain

  ● S53.431   Radial collateral ligament sprain of right elbow

  ● S53.432   Radial collateral ligament sprain of left elbow

  ● S53.439   Radial collateral ligament sprain of unspecified elbow

● S53.44   Ulnar collateral ligament sprain

  ● S53.441   Ulnar collateral ligament sprain of right elbow

  ● S53.442   Ulnar collateral ligament sprain of left elbow

  ● S53.449   Ulnar collateral ligament sprain of unspecified elbow

● S53.49   Other sprain of elbow

  ● S53.491   Other sprain of right elbow

  ● S53.492   Other sprain of left elbow

  ● S53.499   Other sprain of unspecified elbow

CHAPTER 19 (S00–T88)

CHAPTER 19 (S00-T88)

● **S54**   **Injury of nerves at forearm level**

     Code also any associated open wound (S51.-)

     Excludes2   injury of nerves at wrist and hand level (S64.-)

     The appropriate 7th character is to be added to each code from category S54

A	initial encounter
D	subsequent encounter
S	sequela

● **S54.0**   **Injury of ulnar nerve at forearm level**

       Injury of ulnar nerve NOS

   X ● **S54.00**   Injury of ulnar nerve at forearm level, unspecified arm

   X ● **S54.01**   Injury of ulnar nerve at forearm level, right arm

   X ● **S54.02**   Injury of ulnar nerve at forearm level, left arm

● **S54.1**   **Injury of median nerve at forearm level**

       Injury of median nerve NOS

   X ● **S54.10**   Injury of median nerve at forearm level, unspecified arm

   X ● **S54.11**   Injury of median nerve at forearm level, right arm

   X ● **S54.12**   Injury of median nerve at forearm level, left arm

● **S54.2**   **Injury of radial nerve at forearm level**

       Injury of radial nerve NOS

   X ● **S54.20**   Injury of radial nerve at forearm level, unspecified arm

   X ● **S54.21**   Injury of radial nerve at forearm level, right arm

   X ● **S54.22**   Injury of radial nerve at forearm level, left arm

● **S54.3**   **Injury of cutaneous sensory nerve at forearm level**

   X ● **S54.30**   Injury of cutaneous sensory nerve at forearm level, unspecified arm

   X ● **S54.31**   Injury of cutaneous sensory nerve at forearm level, right arm

   X ● **S54.32**   Injury of cutaneous sensory nerve at forearm level, left arm

● **S54.8**   **Injury of other nerves at forearm level**

   ● **S54.8X**   Injury of other nerves at forearm level

     ● **S54.8X1**   Injury of other nerves at forearm level, right arm

     ● **S54.8X2**   Injury of other nerves at forearm level, left arm

     ● **S54.8X9**   Injury of other nerves at forearm level, unspecified arm

● **S54.9**   **Injury of unspecified nerve at forearm level**

   X ● **S54.90**   Injury of unspecified nerve at forearm level, unspecified arm

   X ● **S54.91**   Injury of unspecified nerve at forearm level, right arm

   X ● **S54.92**   Injury of unspecified nerve at forearm level, left arm

● **S55**   **Injury of blood vessels at forearm level**

     Code also any associated open wound (S51.-)

     Excludes2   injury of blood vessels at wrist and hand level (S65.-)

              injury of brachial vessels (S45.1-S45.2)

     The appropriate 7th character is to be added to each code from category S55

A	initial encounter
D	subsequent encounter
S	sequela

● **S55.0**   **Injury of ulnar artery at forearm level**

   ● **S55.00**   Unspecified injury of ulnar artery at forearm level

     ● **S55.001**   Unspecified injury of ulnar artery at forearm level, right arm

     ● **S55.002**   Unspecified injury of ulnar artery at forearm level, left arm

     ● **S55.009**   Unspecified injury of ulnar artery at forearm level, unspecified arm

   ● **S55.01**   Laceration of ulnar artery at forearm level

     ● **S55.011**   Laceration of ulnar artery at forearm level, right arm

     ● **S55.012**   Laceration of ulnar artery at forearm level, left arm

     ● **S55.019**   Laceration of ulnar artery at forearm level, unspecified arm

   ● **S55.09**   Other specified injury of ulnar artery at forearm level

     ● **S55.091**   Other specified injury of ulnar artery at forearm level, right arm

     ● **S55.092**   Other specified injury of ulnar artery at forearm level, left arm

     ● **S55.099**   Other specified injury of ulnar artery at forearm level, unspecified arm

● **S55.1**   **Injury of radial artery at forearm level**

   ● **S55.10**   Unspecified injury of radial artery at forearm level

     ● **S55.101**   Unspecified injury of radial artery at forearm level, right arm

     ● **S55.102**   Unspecified injury of radial artery at forearm level, left arm

     ● **S55.109**   Unspecified injury of radial artery at forearm level, unspecified arm

   ● **S55.11**   Laceration of radial artery at forearm level

     ● **S55.111**   Laceration of radial artery at forearm level, right arm

     ● **S55.112**   Laceration of radial artery at forearm level, left arm

     ● **S55.119**   Laceration of radial artery at forearm level, unspecified arm

   ● **S55.19**   Other specified injury of radial artery at forearm level

     ● **S55.191**   Other specified injury of radial artery at forearm level, right arm

     ● **S55.192**   Other specified injury of radial artery at forearm level, left arm

     ● **S55.199**   Other specified injury of radial artery at forearm level, unspecified arm

▶ New   ⇒ Revised   ~~deleted~~ Deleted   Excludes 1   Excludes 2   Includes   Use additional   Code first   Code also   Key words

OGCR Official Guidelines   X Assign placeholder X   ● Use Additional Character(s)   ▷ Manifestation Code   **Coding Clinic**

● S55.2   Injury of vein at forearm level
   ● S55.20   Unspecified injury of vein at forearm level
      ● S55.201   Unspecified injury of vein at forearm level, right arm
      ● S55.202   Unspecified injury of vein at forearm level, left arm
      ● S55.209   Unspecified injury of vein at forearm level, unspecified arm
   ● S55.21   Laceration of vein at forearm level
      ● S55.211   Laceration of vein at forearm level, right arm
      ● S55.212   Laceration of vein at forearm level, left arm
      ● S55.219   Laceration of vein at forearm level, unspecified arm
   ● S55.29   Other specified injury of vein at forearm level
      ● S55.291   Other specified injury of vein at forearm level, right arm
      ● S55.292   Other specified injury of vein at forearm level, left arm
      ● S55.299   Other specified injury of vein at forearm level, unspecified arm

● S55.8   Injury of other blood vessels at forearm level
   ● S55.80   Unspecified injury of other blood vessels at forearm level
      ● S55.801   Unspecified injury of other blood vessels at forearm level, right arm
      ● S55.802   Unspecified injury of other blood vessels at forearm level, left arm
      ● S55.809   Unspecified injury of other blood vessels at forearm level, unspecified arm
   ● S55.81   Laceration of other blood vessels at forearm level
      ● S55.811   Laceration of other blood vessels at forearm level, right arm
      ● S55.812   Laceration of other blood vessels at forearm level, left arm
      ● S55.819   Laceration of other blood vessels at forearm level, unspecified arm
   ● S55.89   Other specified injury of other blood vessels at forearm level
      ● S55.891   Other specified injury of other blood vessels at forearm level, right arm
      ● S55.892   Other specified injury of other blood vessels at forearm level, left arm
      ● S55.899   Other specified injury of other blood vessels at forearm level, unspecified arm

● S55.9   Injury of unspecified blood vessel at forearm level
   ● S55.90   Unspecified injury of unspecified blood vessel at forearm level
      ● S55.901   Unspecified injury of unspecified blood vessel at forearm level, right arm
      ● S55.902   Unspecified injury of unspecified blood vessel at forearm level, left arm
      ● S55.909   Unspecified injury of unspecified blood vessel at forearm level, unspecified arm
   ● S55.91   Laceration of unspecified blood vessel at forearm level
      ● S55.911   Laceration of unspecified blood vessel at forearm level, right arm
      ● S55.912   Laceration of unspecified blood vessel at forearm level, left arm
      ● S55.919   Laceration of unspecified blood vessel at forearm level, unspecified arm

● S55.99   Other specified injury of unspecified blood vessel at forearm level
   ● S55.991   Other specified injury of unspecified blood vessel at forearm level, right arm
   ● S55.992   Other specified injury of unspecified blood vessel at forearm level, left arm
   ● S55.999   Other specified injury of unspecified blood vessel at forearm level, unspecified arm

● S56   Injury of muscle, fascia and tendon at forearm level
   Code also any associated open wound (S51.-)
   Excludes2   injury of muscle, fascia and tendon at or below wrist (S66.-)
                sprain of joints and ligaments of elbow (S53.4-)
   The appropriate 7th character is to be added to each code from category S56

A	initial encounter
D	subsequent encounter
S	sequela

● S56.0   Injury of flexor muscle, fascia and tendon of thumb at forearm level
   ● S56.00   Unspecified injury of flexor muscle, fascia and tendon of thumb at forearm level
      ● S56.001   Unspecified injury of flexor muscle, fascia and tendon of right thumb at forearm level
      ● S56.002   Unspecified injury of flexor muscle, fascia and tendon of left thumb at forearm level
      ● S56.009   Unspecified injury of flexor muscle, fascia and tendon of unspecified thumb at forearm level
   ● S56.01   Strain of flexor muscle, fascia and tendon of thumb at forearm level
      ● S56.011   Strain of flexor muscle, fascia and tendon of right thumb at forearm level
      ● S56.012   Strain of flexor muscle, fascia and tendon of left thumb at forearm level
      ● S56.019   Strain of flexor muscle, fascia and tendon of unspecified thumb at forearm level
   ● S56.02   Laceration of flexor muscle, fascia and tendon of thumb at forearm level
      ● S56.021   Laceration of flexor muscle, fascia and tendon of right thumb at forearm level
      ● S56.022   Laceration of flexor muscle, fascia and tendon of left thumb at forearm level
      ● S56.029   Laceration of flexor muscle, fascia and tendon of unspecified thumb at forearm level
   ● S56.09   Other injury of flexor muscle, fascia and tendon of thumb at forearm level
      ● S56.091   Other injury of flexor muscle, fascia and tendon of right thumb at forearm level
      ● S56.092   Other injury of flexor muscle, fascia and tendon of left thumb at forearm level
      ● S56.099   Other injury of flexor muscle, fascia and tendon of unspecified thumb at forearm level

- ● S56.1 Injury of flexor muscle, fascia and tendon of other and unspecified finger at forearm level
  - ● S56.10 Unspecified injury of flexor muscle, fascia and tendon of other and unspecified finger at forearm level
    - ● S56.101 Unspecified injury of flexor muscle, fascia and tendon of right index finger at forearm level
    - ● S56.102 Unspecified injury of flexor muscle, fascia and tendon of left index finger at forearm level
    - ● S56.103 Unspecified injury of flexor muscle, fascia and tendon of right middle finger at forearm level
    - ● S56.104 Unspecified injury of flexor muscle, fascia and tendon of left middle finger at forearm level
    - ● S56.105 Unspecified injury of flexor muscle, fascia and tendon of right ring finger at forearm level
    - ● S56.106 Unspecified injury of flexor muscle, fascia and tendon of left ring finger at forearm level
    - ● S56.107 Unspecified injury of flexor muscle, fascia and tendon of right little finger at forearm level
    - ● S56.108 Unspecified injury of flexor muscle, fascia and tendon of left little finger at forearm level
    - ● S56.109 Unspecified injury of flexor muscle, fascia and tendon of unspecified finger at forearm level
  - ● S56.11 Strain of flexor muscle, fascia and tendon of other and unspecified finger at forearm level
    - ● S56.111 Strain of flexor muscle, fascia and tendon of right index finger at forearm level
    - ● S56.112 Strain of flexor muscle, fascia and tendon of left index finger at forearm level
    - ● S56.113 Strain of flexor muscle, fascia and tendon of right middle finger at forearm level
    - ● S56.114 Strain of flexor muscle, fascia and tendon of left middle finger at forearm level
    - ● S56.115 Strain of flexor muscle, fascia and tendon of right ring finger at forearm level
    - ● S56.116 Strain of flexor muscle, fascia and tendon of left ring finger at forearm level
    - ● S56.117 Strain of flexor muscle, fascia and tendon of right little finger at forearm level
    - ● S56.118 Strain of flexor muscle, fascia and tendon of left little finger at forearm level
    - ● S56.119 Strain of flexor muscle, fascia and tendon of finger of unspecified finger at forearm level
  - ● S56.12 Laceration of flexor muscle, fascia and tendon of other and unspecified finger at forearm level
    - ● S56.121 Laceration of flexor muscle, fascia and tendon of right index finger at forearm level
    - ● S56.122 Laceration of flexor muscle, fascia and tendon of left index finger at forearm level
    - ● S56.123 Laceration of flexor muscle, fascia and tendon of right middle finger at forearm level
    - ● S56.124 Laceration of flexor muscle, fascia and tendon of left middle finger at forearm level
    - ● S56.125 Laceration of flexor muscle, fascia and tendon of right ring finger at forearm level
    - ● S56.126 Laceration of flexor muscle, fascia and tendon of left ring finger at forearm level
    - ● S56.127 Laceration of flexor muscle, fascia and tendon of right little finger at forearm level
    - ● S56.128 Laceration of flexor muscle, fascia and tendon of left little finger at forearm level
    - ● S56.129 Laceration of flexor muscle, fascia and tendon of unspecified finger at forearm level
  - ● S56.19 Other injury of flexor muscle, fascia and tendon of other and unspecified finger at forearm level
    - ● S56.191 Other injury of flexor muscle, fascia and tendon of right index finger at forearm level
    - ● S56.192 Other injury of flexor muscle, fascia and tendon of left index finger at forearm level
    - ● S56.193 Other injury of flexor muscle, fascia and tendon of right middle finger at forearm level
    - ● S56.194 Other injury of flexor muscle, fascia and tendon of left middle finger at forearm level
    - ● S56.195 Other injury of flexor muscle, fascia and tendon of right ring finger at forearm level
    - ● S56.196 Other injury of flexor muscle, fascia and tendon of left ring finger at forearm level
    - ● S56.197 Other injury of flexor muscle, fascia and tendon of right little finger at forearm level
    - ● S56.198 Other injury of flexor muscle, fascia and tendon of left little finger at forearm level
    - ● S56.199 Other injury of flexor muscle, fascia and tendon of unspecified finger at forearm level
- ● S56.2 Injury of other flexor muscle, fascia and tendon at forearm level
  - ● S56.20 Unspecified injury of other flexor muscle, fascia and tendon at forearm level
    - ● S56.201 Unspecified injury of other flexor muscle, fascia and tendon at forearm level, right arm
    - ● S56.202 Unspecified injury of other flexor muscle, fascia and tendon at forearm level, left arm
    - ● S56.209 Unspecified injury of other flexor muscle, fascia and tendon at forearm level, unspecified arm
  - ● S56.21 Strain of other flexor muscle, fascia and tendon at forearm level
    - ● S56.211 Strain of other flexor muscle, fascia and tendon at forearm level, right arm
    - ● S56.212 Strain of other flexor muscle, fascia and tendon at forearm level, left arm
    - ● S56.219 Strain of other flexor muscle, fascia and tendon at forearm level, unspecified arm

▶ New ⇒ Revised deleted Deleted Excludes 1 Excludes 2 Includes Use additional Code first Code also Key words

OGCR Official Guidelines X Assign placeholder X ● Use Additional Character(s) ▶ Manifestation Code **Coding Clinic**

● S56.22   Laceration of other flexor muscle, fascia and tendon at forearm level

    ● S56.221   Laceration of other flexor muscle, fascia and tendon at forearm level, right arm

    ● S56.222   Laceration of other flexor muscle, fascia and tendon at forearm level, left arm

    ● S56.229   Laceration of other flexor muscle, fascia and tendon at forearm level, unspecified arm

● S56.29   Other injury of other flexor muscle, fascia and tendon at forearm level

    ● S56.291   Other injury of other flexor muscle, fascia and tendon at forearm level, right arm

    ● S56.292   Other injury of other flexor muscle, fascia and tendon at forearm level, left arm

    ● S56.299   Other injury of other flexor muscle, fascia and tendon at forearm level, unspecified arm

● S56.3   Injury of extensor or abductor muscles, fascia and tendons of thumb at forearm level

    ● S56.30   Unspecified injury of extensor or abductor muscles, fascia and tendons of thumb at forearm level

      ● S56.301   Unspecified injury of extensor or abductor muscles, fascia and tendons of right thumb at forearm level

      ● S56.302   Unspecified injury of extensor or abductor muscles, fascia and tendons of left thumb at forearm level

      ● S56.309   Unspecified injury of extensor or abductor muscles, fascia and tendons of unspecified thumb at forearm level

    ● S56.31   Strain of extensor or abductor muscles, fascia and tendons of thumb at forearm level

      ● S56.311   Strain of extensor or abductor muscles, fascia and tendons of right thumb at forearm level

      ● S56.312   Strain of extensor or abductor muscles, fascia and tendons of left thumb at forearm level

      ● S56.319   Strain of extensor or abductor muscles, fascia and tendons of unspecified thumb at forearm level

    ● S56.32   Laceration of extensor or abductor muscles, fascia and tendons of thumb at forearm level

      ● S56.321   Laceration of extensor or abductor muscles, fascia and tendons of right thumb at forearm level

      ● S56.322   Laceration of extensor or abductor muscles, fascia and tendons of left thumb at forearm level

      ● S56.329   Laceration of extensor or abductor muscles, fascia and tendons of unspecified thumb at forearm level

    ● S56.39   Other injury of extensor or abductor muscles, fascia and tendons of thumb at forearm level

      ● S56.391   Other injury of extensor or abductor muscles, fascia and tendons of right thumb at forearm level

      ● S56.392   Other injury of extensor or abductor muscles, fascia and tendons of left thumb at forearm level

      ● S56.399   Other injury of extensor or abductor muscles, fascia and tendons of unspecified thumb at forearm level

● S56.4   Injury of extensor muscle, fascia and tendon of other and unspecified finger at forearm level

    ● S56.40   Unspecified injury of extensor muscle, fascia and tendon of other and unspecified finger at forearm level

      ● S56.401   Unspecified injury of extensor muscle, fascia and tendon of right index finger at forearm level

      ● S56.402   Unspecified injury of extensor muscle, fascia and tendon of left index finger at forearm level

      ● S56.403   Unspecified injury of extensor muscle, fascia and tendon of right middle finger at forearm level

      ● S56.404   Unspecified injury of extensor muscle, fascia and tendon of left middle finger at forearm level

      ● S56.405   Unspecified injury of extensor muscle, fascia and tendon of right ring finger at forearm level

      ● S56.406   Unspecified injury of extensor muscle, fascia and tendon of left ring finger at forearm level

      ● S56.407   Unspecified injury of extensor muscle, fascia and tendon of right little finger at forearm level

      ● S56.408   Unspecified injury of extensor muscle, fascia and tendon of left little finger at forearm level

      ● S56.409   Unspecified injury of extensor muscle, fascia and tendon of unspecified finger at forearm level

    ● S56.41   Strain of extensor muscle, fascia and tendon of other and unspecified finger at forearm level

      ● S56.411   Strain of extensor muscle, fascia and tendon of right index finger at forearm level

      ● S56.412   Strain of extensor muscle, fascia and tendon of left index finger at forearm level

      ● S56.413   Strain of extensor muscle, fascia and tendon of right middle finger at forearm level

      ● S56.414   Strain of extensor muscle, fascia and tendon of left middle finger at forearm level

      ● S56.415   Strain of extensor muscle, fascia and tendon of right ring finger at forearm level

      ● S56.416   Strain of extensor muscle, fascia and tendon of left ring finger at forearm level

      ● S56.417   Strain of extensor muscle, fascia and tendon of right little finger at forearm level

      ● S56.418   Strain of extensor muscle, fascia and tendon of left little finger at forearm level

      ● S56.419   Strain of extensor muscle, fascia and tendon of finger, unspecified finger at forearm level

    ● S56.42   Laceration of extensor muscle, fascia and tendon of other and unspecified finger at forearm level

      ● S56.421   Laceration of extensor muscle, fascia and tendon of right index finger at forearm level

      ● S56.422   Laceration of extensor muscle, fascia and tendon of left index finger at forearm level

● S56.423   Laceration of extensor muscle, fascia and tendon of right middle finger at forearm level

● S56.424   Laceration of extensor muscle, fascia and tendon of left middle finger at forearm level

● S56.425   Laceration of extensor muscle, fascia and tendon of right ring finger at forearm level

● S56.426   Laceration of extensor muscle, fascia and tendon of left ring finger at forearm level

● S56.427   Laceration of extensor muscle, fascia and tendon of right little finger at forearm level

● S56.428   Laceration of extensor muscle, fascia and tendon of left little finger at forearm level

● S56.429   Laceration of extensor muscle, fascia and tendon of unspecified finger at forearm level

● S56.49   Other injury of extensor muscle, fascia and tendon of other and unspecified finger at forearm level

    ● S56.491   Other injury of extensor muscle, fascia and tendon of right index finger at forearm level

    ● S56.492   Other injury of extensor muscle, fascia and tendon of left index finger at forearm level

    ● S56.493   Other injury of extensor muscle, fascia and tendon of right middle finger at forearm level

    ● S56.494   Other injury of extensor muscle, fascia and tendon of left middle finger at forearm level

    ● S56.495   Other injury of extensor muscle, fascia and tendon of right ring finger at forearm level

    ● S56.496   Other injury of extensor muscle, fascia and tendon of left ring finger at forearm level

    ● S56.497   Other injury of extensor muscle, fascia and tendon of right little finger at forearm level

    ● S56.498   Other injury of extensor muscle, fascia and tendon of left little finger at forearm level

    ● S56.499   Other injury of extensor muscle, fascia and tendon of unspecified finger at forearm level

● S56.5   Injury of other extensor muscle, fascia and tendon at forearm level

   ● S56.50   Unspecified injury of other extensor muscle, fascia and tendon at forearm level

    ● S56.501   Unspecified injury of other extensor muscle, fascia and tendon at forearm level, right arm

    ● S56.502   Unspecified injury of other extensor muscle, fascia and tendon at forearm level, left arm

    ● S56.509   Unspecified injury of other extensor muscle, fascia and tendon at forearm level, unspecified arm

   ● S56.51   Strain of other extensor muscle, fascia and tendon at forearm level

    ● S56.511   Strain of other extensor muscle, fascia and tendon at forearm level, right arm

    ● S56.512   Strain of other extensor muscle, fascia and tendon at forearm level, left arm

    ● S56.519   Strain of other extensor muscle, fascia and tendon at forearm level, unspecified arm

● S56.52   Laceration of other extensor muscle, fascia and tendon at forearm level

    ● S56.521   Laceration of other extensor muscle, fascia and tendon at forearm level, right arm

    ● S56.522   Laceration of other extensor muscle, fascia and tendon at forearm level, left arm

    ● S56.529   Laceration of other extensor muscle, fascia and tendon at forearm level, unspecified arm

   ● S56.59   Other injury of other extensor muscle, fascia and tendon at forearm level

    ● S56.591   Other injury of other extensor muscle, fascia and tendon at forearm level, right arm

    ● S56.592   Other injury of other extensor muscle, fascia and tendon at forearm level, left arm

    ● S56.599   Other injury of other extensor muscle, fascia and tendon at forearm level, unspecified arm

● S56.8   Injury of other muscles, fascia and tendons at forearm level

   ● S56.80   Unspecified injury of other muscles, fascia and tendons at forearm level

    ● S56.801   Unspecified injury of other muscles, fascia and tendons at forearm level, right arm

    ● S56.802   Unspecified injury of other muscles, fascia and tendons at forearm level, left arm

    ● S56.809   Unspecified injury of other muscles, fascia and tendons at forearm level, unspecified arm

   ● S56.81   Strain of other muscles, fascia and tendons at forearm level

    ● S56.811   Strain of other muscles, fascia and tendons at forearm level, right arm

    ● S56.812   Strain of other muscles, fascia and tendons at forearm level, left arm

    ● S56.819   Strain of other muscles, fascia and tendons at forearm level, unspecified arm

   ● S56.82   Laceration of other muscles, fascia and tendons at forearm level

    ● S56.821   Laceration of other muscles, fascia and tendons at forearm level, right arm

    ● S56.822   Laceration of other muscles, fascia and tendons at forearm level, left arm

    ● S56.829   Laceration of other muscles, fascia and tendons at forearm level, unspecified arm

   ● S56.89   Other injury of other muscles, fascia and tendons at forearm level

    ● S56.891   Other injury of other muscles, fascia and tendons at forearm level, right arm

    ● S56.892   Other injury of other muscles, fascia and tendons at forearm level, left arm

    ● S56.899   Other injury of other muscles, fascia and tendons at forearm level, unspecified arm

▶ New   ⇒ Revised   ~~deleted~~ Deleted   Excludes 1   Excludes 2   Includes   Use additional   Code first   Code also   Key words

OGCR Official Guidelines   X Assign placeholder X   ● Use Additional Character(s)   ▶ Manifestation Code   **Coding Clinic**

● S56.9   Injury of unspecified muscles, fascia and tendons at forearm level

  ● S56.90   Unspecified injury of unspecified muscles, fascia and tendons at forearm level

    ● S56.901   Unspecified injury of unspecified muscles, fascia and tendons at forearm level, right arm

    ● S56.902   Unspecified injury of unspecified muscles, fascia and tendons at forearm level, left arm

    ● S56.909   Unspecified injury of unspecified muscles, fascia and tendons at forearm level, unspecified arm

  ● S56.91   Strain of unspecified muscles, fascia and tendons at forearm level

    ● S56.911   Strain of unspecified muscles, fascia and tendons at forearm level, right arm

    ● S56.912   Strain of unspecified muscles, fascia and tendons at forearm level, left arm

    ● S56.919   Strain of unspecified muscles, fascia and tendons at forearm level, unspecified arm

  ● S56.92   Laceration of unspecified muscles, fascia and tendons at forearm level

    ● S56.921   Laceration of unspecified muscles, fascia and tendons at forearm level, right arm

    ● S56.922   Laceration of unspecified muscles, fascia and tendons at forearm level, left arm

    ● S56.929   Laceration of unspecified muscles, fascia and tendons at forearm level, unspecified arm

  ● S56.99   Other injury of unspecified muscles, fascia and tendons at forearm level

    ● S56.991   Other injury of unspecified muscles, fascia and tendons at forearm level, right arm

    ● S56.992   Other injury of unspecified muscles, fascia and tendons at forearm level, left arm

    ● S56.999   Other injury of unspecified muscles, fascia and tendons at forearm level, unspecified arm

● S57   Crushing injury of elbow and forearm

  Use additional code(s) for all associated injuries

  Excludes2   crushing injury of wrist and hand (S67.-)

  The appropriate 7th character is to be added to each code from category S57

A	initial encounter
D	subsequent encounter
S	sequela

  ● S57.0   Crushing injury of elbow

    X ● S57.00   Crushing injury of unspecified elbow

    X ● S57.01   Crushing injury of right elbow

    X ● S57.02   Crushing injury of left elbow

  ● S57.8   Crushing injury of forearm

    X ● S57.80   Crushing injury of unspecified forearm

    X ● S57.81   Crushing injury of right forearm

    X ● S57.82   Crushing injury of left forearm

● S58   Traumatic amputation of elbow and forearm

  An amputation not identified as partial or complete should be coded to complete

  Excludes1   traumatic amputation of wrist and hand (S68.-)

  The appropriate 7th character is to be added to each code from category S58

A	initial encounter
D	subsequent encounter
S	sequela

  ● S58.0   Traumatic amputation at elbow level

    ● S58.01   Complete traumatic amputation at elbow level

      ● S58.011   Complete traumatic amputation at elbow level, right arm

      ● S58.012   Complete traumatic amputation at elbow level, left arm

      ● S58.019   Complete traumatic amputation at elbow level, unspecified arm

    ● S58.02   Partial traumatic amputation at elbow level

      ● S58.021   Partial traumatic amputation at elbow level, right arm

      ● S58.022   Partial traumatic amputation at elbow level, left arm

      ● S58.029   Partial traumatic amputation at elbow level, unspecified arm

  ● S58.1   Traumatic amputation at level between elbow and wrist

    ● S58.11   Complete traumatic amputation at level between elbow and wrist

      ● S58.111   Complete traumatic amputation at level between elbow and wrist, right arm

      ● S58.112   Complete traumatic amputation at level between elbow and wrist, left arm

      ● S58.119   Complete traumatic amputation at level between elbow and wrist, unspecified arm

    ● S58.12   Partial traumatic amputation at level between elbow and wrist

      ● S58.121   Partial traumatic amputation at level between elbow and wrist, right arm

      ● S58.122   Partial traumatic amputation at level between elbow and wrist, left arm

      ● S58.129   Partial traumatic amputation at level between elbow and wrist, unspecified arm

  ● S58.9   Traumatic amputation of forearm, level unspecified

    Excludes1   traumatic amputation of wrist (S68.-)

    ● S58.91   Complete traumatic amputation of forearm, level unspecified

      ● S58.911   Complete traumatic amputation of right forearm, level unspecified

      ● S58.912   Complete traumatic amputation of left forearm, level unspecified

      ● S58.919   Complete traumatic amputation of unspecified forearm, level unspecified

    ● S58.92   Partial traumatic amputation of forearm, level unspecified

      ● S58.921   Partial traumatic amputation of right forearm, level unspecified

      ● S58.922   Partial traumatic amputation of left forearm, level unspecified

      ● S58.929   Partial traumatic amputation of unspecified forearm, level unspecified

CHAPTER 19 (S00-T88)

● **S59   Other and unspecified injuries of elbow and forearm**

    Excludes2   other and unspecified injuries of wrist and hand (S69.-)

    The appropriate 7th character is to be added to each code from subcategories S59.0, S59.1, and S59.2

A	initial encounter for closed fracture
D	subsequent encounter for fracture with routine healing
G	subsequent encounter for fracture with delayed healing
K	subsequent encounter for fracture with nonunion
P	subsequent encounter for fracture with malunion
S	sequela

● **S59.0   Physeal fracture of lower end of ulna**

  ● **S59.00   Unspecified physeal fracture of lower end of ulna**

    ● S59.001   Unspecified physeal fracture of lower end of ulna, **right arm**

    ● S59.002   Unspecified physeal fracture of lower end of ulna, **left arm**

    ● S59.009   Unspecified physeal fracture of lower end of ulna, **unspecified arm**

  ● **S59.01   Salter-Harris Type I physeal fracture of lower end of ulna**

    ● S59.011   Salter-Harris Type I physeal fracture of lower end of ulna, **right arm**

    ● S59.012   Salter-Harris Type I physeal fracture of lower end of ulna, **left arm**

    ● S59.019   Salter-Harris Type I physeal fracture of lower end of ulna, **unspecified arm**

  ● **S59.02   Salter-Harris Type II physeal fracture of lower end of ulna**

    ● S59.021   Salter-Harris Type II physeal fracture of lower end of ulna, **right arm**

    ● S59.022   Salter-Harris Type II physeal fracture of lower end of ulna, **left arm**

    ● S59.029   Salter-Harris Type II physeal fracture of lower end of ulna, **unspecified arm**

  ● **S59.03   Salter-Harris Type III physeal fracture of lower end of ulna**

    ● S59.031   Salter-Harris Type III physeal fracture of lower end of ulna, **right arm**

    ● S59.032   Salter-Harris Type III physeal fracture of lower end of ulna, **left arm**

    ● S59.039   Salter-Harris Type III physeal fracture of lower end of ulna, **unspecified arm**

  ● **S59.04   Salter-Harris Type IV physeal fracture of lower end of ulna**

    ● S59.041   Salter-Harris Type IV physeal fracture of lower end of ulna, **right arm**

    ● S59.042   Salter-Harris Type IV physeal fracture of lower end of ulna, **left arm**

    ● S59.049   Salter-Harris Type IV physeal fracture of lower end of ulna, **unspecified arm**

  ● **S59.09   Other physeal fracture of lower end of ulna**

    ● S59.091   Other physeal fracture of lower end of ulna, **right arm**

    ● S59.092   Other physeal fracture of lower end of ulna, **left arm**

    ● S59.099   Other physeal fracture of lower end of ulna, **unspecified arm**

Item 19–4   SALTER-HARRIS TYPE 1: epiphysis is completely separated from end of bone, or metaphysic growth plate remains attached to epiphysis

  SALTER-HARRIS TYPE 2: epiphysis and growth plate are partially separated from metaphysis, which is cracked—most common type

  SALTER-HARRIS TYPE 3: fracture occurring through epiphysis and separates part of epiphysis and growth plate from metaphysis fracture, usually at distal end of tibia

  SALTER-HARRIS TYPE 4: fracture runs through epiphysis, across growth plate, into metaphysic, surgery is required to restore joint surface to normal and align growth plate

● **S59.1   Physeal fracture of upper end of radius**

  ● **S59.10   Unspecified physeal fracture of upper end of radius**

    ● S59.101   Unspecified physeal fracture of upper end of radius, **right arm**

    ● S59.102   Unspecified physeal fracture of upper end of radius, **left arm**

    ● S59.109   Unspecified physeal fracture of upper end of radius, **unspecified arm**

  ● **S59.11   Salter-Harris Type I physeal fracture of upper end of radius**

    ● S59.111   Salter-Harris Type I physeal fracture of upper end of radius, **right arm**

    ● S59.112   Salter-Harris Type I physeal fracture of upper end of radius, **left arm**

    ● S59.119   Salter-Harris Type I physeal fracture of upper end of radius, **unspecified arm**

  ● **S59.12   Salter-Harris Type II physeal fracture of upper end of radius**

    ● S59.121   Salter-Harris Type II physeal fracture of upper end of radius, **right arm**

    ● S59.122   Salter-Harris Type II physeal fracture of upper end of radius, **left arm**

    ● S59.129   Salter-Harris Type II physeal fracture of upper end of radius, **unspecified arm**

  ● **S59.13   Salter-Harris Type III physeal fracture of upper end of radius**

    ● S59.131   Salter-Harris Type III physeal fracture of upper end of radius, **right arm**

    ● S59.132   Salter-Harris Type III physeal fracture of upper end of radius, **left arm**

    ● S59.139   Salter-Harris Type III physeal fracture of upper end of radius, **unspecified arm**

  ● **S59.14   Salter-Harris Type IV physeal fracture of upper end of radius**

    ● S59.141   Salter-Harris Type IV physeal fracture of upper end of radius, **right arm**

    ● S59.142   Salter-Harris Type IV physeal fracture of upper end of radius, **left arm**

    ● S59.149   Salter-Harris Type IV physeal fracture of upper end of radius, **unspecified arm**

  ● **S59.19   Other physeal fracture of upper end of radius**

    ● S59.191   Other physeal fracture of upper end of radius, **right arm**

    ● S59.192   Other physeal fracture of upper end of radius, **left arm**

    ● S59.199   Other physeal fracture of upper end of radius, **unspecified arm**

● **S59.2   Physeal fracture of lower end of radius**

  ● **S59.20   Unspecified physeal fracture of lower end of radius**

    ● S59.201   Unspecified physeal fracture of lower end of radius, **right arm**

    ● S59.202   Unspecified physeal fracture of lower end of radius, **left arm**

    ● S59.209   Unspecified physeal fracture of lower end of radius, **unspecified arm**

  ● **S59.21   Salter-Harris Type I physeal fracture of lower end of radius**

    ● S59.211   Salter-Harris Type I physeal fracture of lower end of radius, **right arm**

    ● S59.212   Salter-Harris Type I physeal fracture of lower end of radius, **left arm**

    ● S59.219   Salter-Harris Type I physeal fracture of lower end of radius, **unspecified arm**

▶ New　⟹ Revised　~~deleted~~ Deleted　Excludes 1　Excludes 2　Includes　Use additional　Code first　Code also　Key words

OGCR Official Guidelines　X Assign placeholder X　● Use Additional Character(s)　▷ Manifestation Code　**Coding Clinic**

● S59.22   **Salter-Harris Type II** physeal fracture of lower end of radius

    ● S59.221   Salter-Harris Type II physeal fracture of lower end of radius, **right arm**

    ● S59.222   Salter-Harris Type II physeal fracture of lower end of radius, **left arm**

    ● S59.229   Salter-Harris Type II physeal fracture of lower end of radius, **unspecified arm**

● S59.23   **Salter-Harris Type III** physeal fracture of lower end of radius

    ● S59.231   Salter-Harris Type III physeal fracture of lower end of radius, **right arm**

    ● S59.232   Salter-Harris Type III physeal fracture of lower end of radius, **left arm**

    ● S59.239   Salter-Harris Type III physeal fracture of lower end of radius, **unspecified arm**

● S59.24   **Salter-Harris Type IV** physeal fracture of lower end of radius

    ● S59.241   Salter-Harris Type IV physeal fracture of lower end of radius, **right arm**

    ● S59.242   Salter-Harris Type IV physeal fracture of lower end of radius, **left arm**

    ● S59.249   Salter-Harris Type IV physeal fracture of lower end of radius, **unspecified arm**

● S59.29   **Other** physeal fracture of lower end of radius

    ● S59.291   Other physeal fracture of lower end of radius, **right arm**

    ● S59.292   Other physeal fracture of lower end of radius, **left arm**

    ● S59.299   Other physeal fracture of lower end of radius, **unspecified arm**

● S59.8   **Other** specified injuries of elbow and forearm

The appropriate 7th character is to be added to each code in subcategory S59.8

> A   initial encounter
> D   subsequent encounter
> S   sequela

   ● S59.80   Other specified injuries of **elbow**

     ● S59.801   Other specified injuries of **right elbow**

     ● S59.802   Other specified injuries of **left elbow**

     ● S59.809   Other specified injuries of **unspecified elbow**

   ● S59.81   Other specified injuries of **forearm**

     ● S59.811   Other specified injuries **right forearm**

     ● S59.812   Other specified injuries **left forearm**

     ● S59.819   Other specified injuries **unspecified forearm**

● S59.9   **Unspecified** injury of elbow and forearm

The appropriate 7th character is to be added to each code in subcategory S59.9

> A   initial encounter
> D   subsequent encounter
> S   sequela

   ● S59.90   Unspecified injury of **elbow**

     ● S59.901   Unspecified injury of **right elbow**

     ● S59.902   Unspecified injury of **left elbow**

     ● S59.909   Unspecified injury of **unspecified elbow**

   ● S59.91   Unspecified injury of **forearm**

     ● S59.911   Unspecified injury of **right forearm**

     ● S59.912   Unspecified injury of **left forearm**

     ● S59.919   Unspecified injury of **unspecified forearm**

INJURIES TO THE WRIST, HAND AND FINGERS (S60-S69)

Excludes2   burns and corrosions (T20-T32)
           frostbite (T33-T34)
           insect bite or sting, venomous (T63.4)

● S60   **Superficial injury of wrist, hand and fingers**

The appropriate 7th character is to be added to each code from category S60

> A   initial encounter
> D   subsequent encounter
> S   sequela

   ● S60.0   Contusion of **finger** without damage to nail

     Excludes1   contusion involving nail (matrix) (S60.1)

   X ● S60.00   Contusion of **unspecified** finger without damage to nail
            Contusion of finger(s) NOS

   ● S60.01   Contusion of **thumb** without damage to nail

     ● S60.011   Contusion of **right thumb** without damage to nail

     ● S60.012   Contusion of **left thumb** without damage to nail

     ● S60.019   Contusion of **unspecified thumb** without damage to nail

   ● S60.02   Contusion of **index** finger without damage to nail

     ● S60.021   Contusion of **right** index finger without damage to nail

     ● S60.022   Contusion of **left** index finger without damage to nail

     ● S60.029   Contusion of **unspecified** index finger without damage to nail

   ● S60.03   Contusion of **middle** finger without damage to nail

     ● S60.031   Contusion of **right** middle finger without damage to nail

     ● S60.032   Contusion of **left** middle finger without damage to nail

     ● S60.039   Contusion of **unspecified** middle finger without damage to nail

   ● S60.04   Contusion of **ring** finger without damage to nail

     ● S60.041   Contusion of **right** ring finger without damage to nail

     ● S60.042   Contusion of **left** ring finger without damage to nail

     ● S60.049   Contusion of **unspecified** ring finger without damage to nail

   ● S60.05   Contusion of **little** finger without damage to nail

     ● S60.051   Contusion of **right** little finger without damage to nail

     ● S60.052   Contusion of **left** little finger without damage to nail

     ● S60.059   Contusion of **unspecified** little finger without damage to nail

   ● S60.1   Contusion of **finger** with damage to nail

   X ● S60.10   Contusion of **unspecified** finger with damage to nail

   ● S60.11   Contusion of **thumb** with damage to nail

     ● S60.111   Contusion of **right thumb** with damage to nail

     ● S60.112   Contusion of **left thumb** with damage to nail

     ● S60.119   Contusion of **unspecified thumb** with damage to nail

● **S60.12** Contusion of index finger with damage to nail
  - ● **S60.121** Contusion of right index finger with damage to nail
  - ● **S60.122** Contusion of left index finger with damage to nail
  - ● **S60.129** Contusion of unspecified index finger with damage to nail
● **S60.13** Contusion of middle finger with damage to nail
  - ● **S60.131** Contusion of right middle finger with damage to nail
  - ● **S60.132** Contusion of left middle finger with damage to nail
  - ● **S60.139** Contusion of unspecified middle finger with damage to nail
● **S60.14** Contusion of ring finger with damage to nail
  - ● **S60.141** Contusion of right ring finger with damage to nail
  - ● **S60.142** Contusion of left ring finger with damage to nail
  - ● **S60.149** Contusion of unspecified ring finger with damage to nail
● **S60.15** Contusion of little finger with damage to nail
  - ● **S60.151** Contusion of right little finger with damage to nail
  - ● **S60.152** Contusion of left little finger with damage to nail
  - ● **S60.159** Contusion of unspecified little finger with damage to nail
● **S60.2** Contusion of wrist and hand
  Excludes2 contusion of fingers (S60.0-, S60.1-)
  - ● **S60.21** Contusion of wrist
    - ● **S60.211** Contusion of right wrist
    - ● **S60.212** Contusion of left wrist
    - ● **S60.219** Contusion of unspecified wrist
  - ● **S60.22** Contusion of hand
    - ● **S60.221** Contusion of right hand
    - ● **S60.222** Contusion of left hand
    - ● **S60.229** Contusion of unspecified hand
● **S60.3** Other superficial injuries of thumb
  - ● **S60.31** Abrasion of thumb
    - ● **S60.311** Abrasion of right thumb
    - ● **S60.312** Abrasion of left thumb
    - ● **S60.319** Abrasion of unspecified thumb
  - ● **S60.32** Blister (nonthermal) of thumb
    - ● **S60.321** Blister (nonthermal) of right thumb
    - ● **S60.322** Blister (nonthermal) of left thumb
    - ● **S60.329** Blister (nonthermal) of unspecified thumb
  - ● **S60.34** External constriction of thumb
    Hair tourniquet syndrome of thumb
    Use additional cause code to identify the constricting item (W49.0-)
    - ● **S60.341** External constriction of right thumb
    - ● **S60.342** External constriction of left thumb
    - ● **S60.349** External constriction of unspecified thumb
  - ● **S60.35** Superficial foreign body of thumb
    Splinter in the thumb
    - ● **S60.351** Superficial foreign body of right thumb
    - ● **S60.352** Superficial foreign body of left thumb
    - ● **S60.359** Superficial foreign body of unspecified thumb

● **S60.36** Insect bite (nonvenomous) of thumb
  - ● **S60.361** Insect bite (nonvenomous) of right thumb
  - ● **S60.362** Insect bite (nonvenomous) of left thumb
  - ● **S60.369** Insect bite (nonvenomous) of unspecified thumb
● **S60.37** Other superficial bite of thumb
  Excludes1 open bite of thumb (S61.05-, S61.15-)
  - ● **S60.371** Other superficial bite of right thumb
  - ● **S60.372** Other superficial bite of left thumb
  - ● **S60.379** Other superficial bite of unspecified thumb
● **S60.39** Other superficial injuries of thumb
  - ● **S60.391** Other superficial injuries of right thumb
  - ● **S60.392** Other superficial injuries of left thumb
  - ● **S60.399** Other superficial injuries of unspecified thumb
● **S60.4** Other superficial injuries of other fingers
  - ● **S60.41** Abrasion of fingers
    - ● **S60.410** Abrasion of right index finger
    - ● **S60.411** Abrasion of left index finger
    - ● **S60.412** Abrasion of right middle finger
    - ● **S60.413** Abrasion of left middle finger
    - ● **S60.414** Abrasion of right ring finger
    - ● **S60.415** Abrasion of left ring finger
    - ● **S60.416** Abrasion of right little finger
    - ● **S60.417** Abrasion of left little finger
    - ● **S60.418** Abrasion of other finger
      Abrasion of specified finger with unspecified laterality
    - ● **S60.419** Abrasion of unspecified finger
  - ● **S60.42** Blister (nonthermal) of fingers
    - ● **S60.420** Blister (nonthermal) of right index finger
    - ● **S60.421** Blister (nonthermal) of left index finger
    - ● **S60.422** Blister (nonthermal) of right middle finger
    - ● **S60.423** Blister (nonthermal) of left middle finger
    - ● **S60.424** Blister (nonthermal) of right ring finger
    - ● **S60.425** Blister (nonthermal) of left ring finger
    - ● **S60.426** Blister (nonthermal) of right little finger
    - ● **S60.427** Blister (nonthermal) of left little finger
    - ● **S60.428** Blister (nonthermal) of other finger
      Blister (nonthermal) of specified finger with unspecified laterality
    - ● **S60.429** Blister (nonthermal) of unspecified finger

● **S60.44**   **External constriction of fingers**
Hair tourniquet syndrome of finger
Use additional cause code to identify the constricting item (W49.0-)

    ● **S60.440**   External constriction of right index finger

    ● **S60.441**   External constriction of left index finger

    ● **S60.442**   External constriction of right middle finger

    ● **S60.443**   External constriction of left middle finger

    ● **S60.444**   External constriction of right ring finger

    ● **S60.445**   External constriction of left ring finger

    ● **S60.446**   External constriction of right little finger

    ● **S60.447**   External constriction of left little finger

    ● **S60.448**   External constriction of other finger
External constriction of specified finger with unspecified laterality

    ● **S60.449**   External constriction of unspecified finger

● **S60.45**   **Superficial foreign body of fingers**
Splinter in the finger(s)

    ● **S60.450**   Superficial foreign body of right index finger

    ● **S60.451**   Superficial foreign body of left index finger

    ● **S60.452**   Superficial foreign body of right middle finger

    ● **S60.453**   Superficial foreign body of left middle finger

    ● **S60.454**   Superficial foreign body of right ring finger

    ● **S60.455**   Superficial foreign body of left ring finger

    ● **S60.456**   Superficial foreign body of right little finger

    ● **S60.457**   Superficial foreign body of left little finger

    ● **S60.458**   Superficial foreign body of other finger
Superficial foreign body of specified finger with unspecified laterality

    ● **S60.459**   Superficial foreign body of unspecified finger

● **S60.46**   **Insect bite (nonvenomous) of fingers**

    ● **S60.460**   Insect bite (nonvenomous) of right index finger

    ● **S60.461**   Insect bite (nonvenomous) of left index finger

    ● **S60.462**   Insect bite (nonvenomous) of right middle finger

    ● **S60.463**   Insect bite (nonvenomous) of left middle finger

    ● **S60.464**   Insect bite (nonvenomous) of right ring finger

    ● **S60.465**   Insect bite (nonvenomous) of left ring finger

    ● **S60.466**   Insect bite (nonvenomous) of right little finger

    ● **S60.467**   Insect bite (nonvenomous) of left little finger

    ● **S60.468**   Insect bite (nonvenomous) of other finger
Insect bite (nonvenomous) of specified finger with unspecified laterality

    ● **S60.469**   Insect bite (nonvenomous) of unspecified finger

● **S60.47**   **Other superficial bite of fingers**
   Excludes1   open bite of fingers (S61.25-, S61.35-)

    ● **S60.470**   Other superficial bite of right index finger

    ● **S60.471**   Other superficial bite of left index finger

    ● **S60.472**   Other superficial bite of right middle finger

    ● **S60.473**   Other superficial bite of left middle finger

    ● **S60.474**   Other superficial bite of right ring finger

    ● **S60.475**   Other superficial bite of left ring finger

    ● **S60.476**   Other superficial bite of right little finger

    ● **S60.477**   Other superficial bite of left little finger

    ● **S60.478**   Other superficial bite of other finger
Other superficial bite of specified finger with unspecified laterality

    ● **S60.479**   Other superficial bite of unspecified finger

● **S60.5**   **Other superficial injuries of hand**
   Excludes2   superficial injuries of fingers (S60.3-, S60.4-)

    ● **S60.51**   **Abrasion of hand**

      ● **S60.511**   Abrasion of right hand

      ● **S60.512**   Abrasion of left hand

      ● **S60.519**   Abrasion of unspecified hand

    ● **S60.52**   **Blister (nonthermal) of hand**

      ● **S60.521**   Blister (nonthermal) of right hand

      ● **S60.522**   Blister (nonthermal) of left hand

      ● **S60.529**   Blister (nonthermal) of unspecified hand

    ● **S60.54**   **External constriction of hand**

      ● **S60.541**   External constriction of right hand

      ● **S60.542**   External constriction of left hand

      ● **S60.549**   External constriction of unspecified hand

    ● **S60.55**   **Superficial foreign body of hand**
Splinter in the hand

      ● **S60.551**   Superficial foreign body of right hand

      ● **S60.552**   Superficial foreign body of left hand

      ● **S60.559**   Superficial foreign body of unspecified hand

    ● **S60.56**   **Insect bite (nonvenomous) of hand**

      ● **S60.561**   Insect bite (nonvenomous) of right hand

      ● **S60.562**   Insect bite (nonvenomous) of left hand

      ● **S60.569**   Insect bite (nonvenomous) of unspecified hand

CHAPTER 19 (S00-T88)

● S60.57 **Other superficial bite of hand**
  Excludes1 open bite of hand (S61.45-)
  ● S60.571 Other superficial bite of hand of **right** hand
  ● S60.572 Other superficial bite of hand of **left** hand
  ● S60.579 Other superficial bite of hand of **unspecified** hand
● S60.8 **Other superficial injuries of wrist**
  ● S60.81 **Abrasion** of wrist
    ● S60.811 Abrasion of **right** wrist
    ● S60.812 Abrasion of **left** wrist
    ● S60.819 Abrasion of **unspecified** wrist
  ● S60.82 **Blister (nonthermal)** of wrist
    ● S60.821 Blister (nonthermal) of **right** wrist
    ● S60.822 Blister (nonthermal) of **left** wrist
    ● S60.829 Blister (nonthermal) of **unspecified** wrist
  ● S60.84 **External constriction** of wrist
    ● S60.841 External constriction of **right** wrist
    ● S60.842 External constriction of **left** wrist
    ● S60.849 External constriction of **unspecified** wrist
  ● S60.85 **Superficial foreign body** of wrist
    Splinter in the wrist
    ● S60.851 Superficial foreign body of **right wrist**
    ● S60.852 Superficial foreign body of **left wrist**
    ● S60.859 Superficial foreign body of **unspecified** wrist
  ● S60.86 **Insect bite (nonvenomous)** of wrist
    ● S60.861 Insect bite (nonvenomous) of **right** wrist
    ● S60.862 Insect bite (nonvenomous) of **left** wrist
    ● S60.869 Insect bite (nonvenomous) of **unspecified** wrist
  ● S60.87 **Other superficial bite of wrist**
    Excludes1 open bite of wrist (S61.55)
    ● S60.871 Other superficial bite of **right** wrist
    ● S60.872 Other superficial bite of **left** wrist
    ● S60.879 Other superficial bite of **unspecified** wrist
● S60.9 **Unspecified superficial injury of wrist, hand and fingers**
  ● S60.91 **Unspecified** superficial injury of **wrist**
    ● S60.911 Unspecified superficial injury of **right** wrist
    ● S60.912 Unspecified superficial injury of **left** wrist
    ● S60.919 Unspecified superficial injury of **unspecified** wrist
  ● S60.92 **Unspecified** superficial injury of **hand**
    ● S60.921 Unspecified superficial injury of **right** hand
    ● S60.922 Unspecified superficial injury of **left** hand
    ● S60.929 Unspecified superficial injury of **unspecified** hand
  ● S60.93 **Unspecified** superficial injury of **thumb**
    ● S60.931 Unspecified superficial injury of **right** thumb
    ● S60.932 Unspecified superficial injury of **left** thumb
    ● S60.939 Unspecified superficial injury of **unspecified** thumb

● S60.94 **Unspecified superficial injury of other fingers**
  ● S60.940 Unspecified superficial injury of **right index** finger
  ● S60.941 Unspecified superficial injury of **left index** finger
  ● S60.942 Unspecified superficial injury of **right middle** finger
  ● S60.943 Unspecified superficial injury of **left middle** finger
  ● S60.944 Unspecified superficial injury of **right ring** finger
  ● S60.945 Unspecified superficial injury of **left ring** finger
  ● S60.946 Unspecified superficial injury of **right little** finger
  ● S60.947 Unspecified superficial injury of **left little** finger
  ● S60.948 Unspecified superficial injury of **other** finger
    Unspecified superficial injury of specified finger with unspecified laterality
  ● S60.949 Unspecified superficial injury of **unspecified** finger
● S61 **Open wound of wrist, hand and fingers**
  Code also any associated wound infection
  Excludes1 open fracture of wrist, hand and finger (S62.- with 7th character B)
    traumatic amputation of wrist and hand (S68.-)
  The appropriate 7th character is to be added to each code from category S61

A	initial encounter
D	subsequent encounter
S	sequela

● S61.0 **Open wound of thumb without damage to nail**
  Excludes1 open wound of thumb with damage to nail (S61.1-)
  ● S61.00 **Unspecified open** wound of thumb without damage to nail
    ● S61.001 Unspecified open wound of **right** thumb without damage to nail
    ● S61.002 Unspecified open wound of **left** thumb without damage to nail
    ● S61.009 Unspecified open wound of **unspecified** thumb without damage to nail
  ● S61.01 **Laceration without foreign body** of thumb without damage to nail
    ● S61.011 Laceration without foreign body of **right** thumb without damage to nail
    ● S61.012 Laceration without foreign body of **left** thumb without damage to nail
    ● S61.019 Laceration without foreign body of **unspecified** thumb without damage to nail
  ● S61.02 **Laceration with foreign body** of thumb without damage to nail
    ● S61.021 Laceration with foreign body of **right** thumb without damage to nail
    ● S61.022 Laceration with foreign body of **left** thumb without damage to nail
    ● S61.029 Laceration with foreign body of **unspecified** thumb without damage to nail

▶ New ⇒ Revised ~~deleted~~ Deleted Excludes 1 Excludes 2 Includes Use additional Code first Code also Key words
OGCR Official Guidelines X Assign placeholder X ● Use Additional Character(s) ▌ Manifestation Code **Coding Clinic**

● **S61.03**   **Puncture wound without foreign body** of thumb without damage to nail

   ● S61.031   Puncture wound without foreign body of **right** thumb without damage to nail

   ● S61.032   Puncture wound without foreign body of **left** thumb without damage to nail

   ● S61.039   Puncture wound without foreign body of **unspecified** thumb without damage to nail

● **S61.04**   **Puncture wound with foreign body** of thumb without damage to nail

   ● S61.041   Puncture wound with foreign body of **right** thumb without damage to nail

   ● S61.042   Puncture wound with foreign body of **left** thumb without damage to nail

   ● S61.049   Puncture wound with foreign body of **unspecified** thumb without damage to nail

● **S61.05**   **Open bite of thumb without damage to nail**
Bite of thumb NOS

   Excludes1   superficial bite of thumb (S60.36-, S60.37-)

   ● S61.051   Open bite of **right** thumb without damage to nail

   ● S61.052   Open bite of **left** thumb without damage to nail

   ● S61.059   Open bite of **unspecified** thumb without damage to nail

● **S61.1**   Open wound of **thumb with damage to nail**

   ● **S61.10**   **Unspecified** open wound of thumb with damage to nail

     ● S61.101   Unspecified open wound of **right** thumb with damage to nail

     ● S61.102   Unspecified open wound of **left** thumb with damage to nail

     ● S61.109   Unspecified open wound of **unspecified** thumb with damage to nail

   ● **S61.11**   **Laceration without foreign body** of thumb with damage to nail

     ● S61.111   Laceration without foreign body of **right** thumb with damage to nail

     ● S61.112   Laceration without foreign body of **left** thumb with damage to nail

     ● S61.119   Laceration without foreign body of **unspecified** thumb with damage to nail

   ● **S61.12**   **Laceration with foreign body** of thumb with damage to nail

     ● S61.121   Laceration with foreign body of **right** thumb with damage to nail

     ● S61.122   Laceration with foreign body of **left** thumb with damage to nail

     ● S61.129   Laceration with foreign body of **unspecified** thumb with damage to nail

   ● **S61.13**   **Puncture wound without foreign body** of thumb with damage to nail

     ● S61.131   Puncture wound without foreign body of **right** thumb with damage to nail

     ● S61.132   Puncture wound without foreign body of **left** thumb with damage to nail

     ● S61.139   Puncture wound without foreign body of **unspecified** thumb with damage to nail

● **S61.14**   **Puncture wound with foreign body** of thumb with damage to nail

   ● S61.141   Puncture wound with foreign body of **right** thumb with damage to nail

   ● S61.142   Puncture wound with foreign body of **left** thumb with damage to nail

   ● S61.149   Puncture wound with foreign body of **unspecified** thumb with damage to nail

● **S61.15**   Open bite of **thumb with damage to nail**
Bite of thumb with damage to nail NOS

   Excludes1   superficial bite of thumb (S60.36-, S60.37-)

   ● S61.151   Open bite of **right** thumb with damage to nail

   ● S61.152   Open bite of **left** thumb with damage to nail

   ● S61.159   Open bite of **unspecified** thumb with damage to nail

● **S61.2**   Open wound of **other finger without damage to nail**

   Excludes1   open wound of finger involving nail (matrix) (S61.3-)

   Excludes2   open wound of thumb without damage to nail (S61.0-)

   ● **S61.20**   **Unspecified** open wound of other finger without damage to nail

     ● S61.200   Unspecified open wound of **right index** finger without damage to nail

     ● S61.201   Unspecified open wound of **left index** finger without damage to nail

     ● S61.202   Unspecified open wound of **right middle** finger without damage to nail

     ● S61.203   Unspecified open wound of **left middle** finger without damage to nail

     ● S61.204   Unspecified open wound of **right ring** finger without damage to nail

     ● S61.205   Unspecified open wound of **left ring** finger without damage to nail

     ● S61.206   Unspecified open wound of **right little** finger without damage to nail

     ● S61.207   Unspecified open wound of **left little** finger without damage to nail

     ● S61.208   Unspecified open wound of **other** finger without damage to nail
Unspecified open wound of specified finger with unspecified laterality without damage to nail

     ● S61.209   Unspecified open wound of **unspecified** finger without damage to nail

   ● **S61.21**   **Laceration without foreign body** of finger without damage to nail

     ● S61.210   Laceration without foreign body of **right index** finger without damage to nail

     ● S61.211   Laceration without foreign body of **left index** finger without damage to nail

     ● S61.212   Laceration without foreign body of **right middle** finger without damage to nail

     ● S61.213   Laceration without foreign body of **left middle** finger without damage to nail

     ● S61.214   Laceration without foreign body of **right ring** finger without damage to nail

     ● S61.215   Laceration without foreign body of **left ring** finger without damage to nail

     ● S61.216   Laceration without foreign body of **right little** finger without damage to nail

● S61.217   Laceration without foreign body of left little finger without damage to nail

● S61.218   Laceration without foreign body of other finger without damage to nail
Laceration without foreign body of specified finger with unspecified laterality without damage to nail

● S61.219   Laceration without foreign body of unspecified finger without damage to nail

● S61.22   Laceration with foreign body of finger without damage to nail

  ● S61.220   Laceration with foreign body of right index finger without damage to nail

  ● S61.221   Laceration with foreign body of left index finger without damage to nail

  ● S61.222   Laceration with foreign body of right middle finger without damage to nail

  ● S61.223   Laceration with foreign body of left middle finger without damage to nail

  ● S61.224   Laceration with foreign body of right ring finger without damage to nail

  ● S61.225   Laceration with foreign body of left ring finger without damage to nail

  ● S61.226   Laceration with foreign body of right little finger without damage to nail

  ● S61.227   Laceration with foreign body of left little finger without damage to nail

  ● S61.228   Laceration with foreign body of other finger without damage to nail
Laceration with foreign body of specified finger with unspecified laterality without damage to nail

  ● S61.229   Laceration with foreign body of unspecified finger without damage to nail

● S61.23   Puncture wound without foreign body of finger without damage to nail

  ● S61.230   Puncture wound without foreign body of right index finger without damage to nail

  ● S61.231   Puncture wound without foreign body of left index finger without damage to nail

  ● S61.232   Puncture wound without foreign body of right middle finger without damage to nail

  ● S61.233   Puncture wound without foreign body of left middle finger without damage to nail

  ● S61.234   Puncture wound without foreign body of right ring finger without damage to nail

  ● S61.235   Puncture wound without foreign body of left ring finger without damage to nail

  ● S61.236   Puncture wound without foreign body of right little finger without damage to nail

  ● S61.237   Puncture wound without foreign body of left little finger without damage to nail

  ● S61.238   Puncture wound without foreign body of other finger without damage to nail
Puncture wound without foreign body of specified finger with unspecified laterality without damage to nail

  ● S61.239   Puncture wound without foreign body of unspecified finger without damage to nail

● S61.24   Puncture wound with foreign body of finger without damage to nail

  ● S61.240   Puncture wound with foreign body of right index finger without damage to nail

  ● S61.241   Puncture wound with foreign body of left index finger without damage to nail

  ● S61.242   Puncture wound with foreign body of right middle finger without damage to nail

  ● S61.243   Puncture wound with foreign body of left middle finger without damage to nail

  ● S61.244   Puncture wound with foreign body of right ring finger without damage to nail

  ● S61.245   Puncture wound with foreign body of left ring finger without damage to nail

  ● S61.246   Puncture wound with foreign body of right little finger without damage to nail

  ● S61.247   Puncture wound with foreign body of left little finger without damage to nail

  ● S61.248   Puncture wound with foreign body of other finger without damage to nail
Puncture wound with foreign body of specified finger with unspecified laterality without damage to nail

  ● S61.249   Puncture wound with foreign body of unspecified finger without damage to nail

● S61.25   Open bite of finger without damage to nail
Bite of finger without damage to nail NOS

  Excludes 1   superficial bite of finger (S60.46-, S60.47-)

  ● S61.250   Open bite of right index finger without damage to nail

  ● S61.251   Open bite of left index finger without damage to nail

  ● S61.252   Open bite of right middle finger without damage to nail

  ● S61.253   Open bite of left middle finger without damage to nail

  ● S61.254   Open bite of right ring finger without damage to nail

  ● S61.255   Open bite of left ring finger without damage to nail

  ● S61.256   Open bite of right little finger without damage to nail

  ● S61.257   Open bite of left little finger without damage to nail

  ● S61.258   Open bite of other finger without damage to nail
Open bite of specified finger with unspecified laterality without damage to nail

  ● S61.259   Open bite of unspecified finger without damage to nail

● S61.3   Open wound of other finger with damage to nail

  ● S61.30   Unspecified open wound of finger with damage to nail

  ● S61.300   Unspecified open wound of right index finger with damage to nail

  ● S61.301   Unspecified open wound of left index finger with damage to nail

  ● S61.302   Unspecified open wound of right middle finger with damage to nail

  ● S61.303   Unspecified open wound of left middle finger with damage to nail

▶ New   ⟹ Revised   ~~deleted~~ Deleted   Excludes 1   Excludes 2   Includes   Use additional   Code first   Code also   Key words
OGCR Official Guidelines   X Assign placeholder X   ● Use Additional Character(s)   ▶ Manifestation Code   **Coding Clinic**

● S61.304   Unspecified open wound of right ring finger with damage to nail

● S61.305   Unspecified open wound of left ring finger with damage to nail

● S61.306   Unspecified open wound of right little finger with damage to nail

● S61.307   Unspecified open wound of left little finger with damage to nail

● S61.308   Unspecified open wound of other finger with damage to nail

> Unspecified open wound of specified finger with unspecified laterality with damage to nail

● S61.309   Unspecified open wound of unspecified finger with damage to nail

● S61.31   Laceration without foreign body of finger with damage to nail

● S61.310   Laceration without foreign body of right index finger with damage to nail

● S61.311   Laceration without foreign body of left index finger with damage to nail

● S61.312   Laceration without foreign body of right middle finger with damage to nail

● S61.313   Laceration without foreign body of left middle finger with damage to nail

● S61.314   Laceration without foreign body of right ring finger with damage to nail

● S61.315   Laceration without foreign body of left ring finger with damage to nail

● S61.316   Laceration without foreign body of right little finger with damage to nail

● S61.317   Laceration without foreign body of left little finger with damage to nail

● S61.318   Laceration without foreign body of other finger with damage to nail

> Laceration without foreign body of specified finger with unspecified laterality with damage to nail

● S61.319   Laceration without foreign body of unspecified finger with damage to nail

● S61.32   Laceration with foreign body of finger with damage to nail

● S61.320   Laceration with foreign body of right index finger with damage to nail

● S61.321   Laceration with foreign body of left index finger with damage to nail

● S61.322   Laceration with foreign body of right middle finger with damage to nail

● S61.323   Laceration with foreign body of left middle finger with damage to nail

● S61.324   Laceration with foreign body of right ring finger with damage to nail

● S61.325   Laceration with foreign body of left ring finger with damage to nail

● S61.326   Laceration with foreign body of right little finger with damage to nail

● S61.327   Laceration with foreign body of left little finger with damage to nail

● S61.328   Laceration with foreign body of other finger with damage to nail

> Laceration with foreign body of specified finger with unspecified laterality with damage to nail

● S61.329   Laceration with foreign body of unspecified finger with damage to nail

● S61.33   Puncture wound without foreign body of finger with damage to nail

● S61.330   Puncture wound without foreign body of right index finger with damage to nail

● S61.331   Puncture wound without foreign body of left index finger with damage to nail

● S61.332   Puncture wound without foreign body of right middle finger with damage to nail

● S61.333   Puncture wound without foreign body of left middle finger with damage to nail

● S61.334   Puncture wound without foreign body of right ring finger with damage to nail

● S61.335   Puncture wound without foreign body of left ring finger with damage to nail

● S61.336   Puncture wound without foreign body of right little finger with damage to nail

● S61.337   Puncture wound without foreign body of left little finger with damage to nail

● S61.338   Puncture wound without foreign body of other finger with damage to nail

> Puncture wound without foreign body of specified finger with unspecified laterality with damage to nail

● S61.339   Puncture wound without foreign body of unspecified finger with damage to nail

● S61.34   Puncture wound with foreign body of finger with damage to nail

● S61.340   Puncture wound with foreign body of right index finger with damage to nail

● S61.341   Puncture wound with foreign body of left index finger with damage to nail

● S61.342   Puncture wound with foreign body of right middle finger with damage to nail

● S61.343   Puncture wound with foreign body of left middle finger with damage to nail

● S61.344   Puncture wound with foreign body of right ring finger with damage to nail

● S61.345   Puncture wound with foreign body of left ring finger with damage to nail

● S61.346   Puncture wound with foreign body of right little finger with damage to nail

● S61.347   Puncture wound with foreign body of left little finger with damage to nail

● S61.348   Puncture wound with foreign body of other finger with damage to nail

> Puncture wound with foreign body of specified finger with unspecified laterality with damage to nail

● S61.349   Puncture wound with foreign body of unspecified finger with damage to nail

● **S61.35** **Open bite of finger with damage to nail**
Bite of finger with damage to nail NOS
> **Excludes1** superficial bite of finger (S60.46-, S60.47-)

● **S61.350** Open bite of **right index** finger with damage to nail

● **S61.351** Open bite of **left index** finger with damage to nail

● **S61.352** Open bite of **right middle** finger with damage to nail

● **S61.353** Open bite of **left middle** finger with damage to nail

● **S61.354** Open bite of **right ring** finger with damage to nail

● **S61.355** Open bite of **left ring** finger with damage to nail

● **S61.356** Open bite of **right little** finger with damage to nail

● **S61.357** Open bite of **left little** finger with damage to nail

● **S61.358** Open bite of **other** finger with damage to nail
Open bite of specified finger with unspecified laterality with damage to nail

● **S61.359** Open bite of **unspecified** finger with damage to nail

● **S61.4** **Open wound of hand**

● **S61.40** **Unspecified** open wound of hand

● **S61.401** Unspecified open wound of **right** hand

● **S61.402** Unspecified open wound of **left** hand

● **S61.409** Unspecified open wound of **unspecified** hand

● **S61.41** **Laceration without foreign body of hand**

● **S61.411** Laceration without foreign body of **right** hand

● **S61.412** Laceration without foreign body of **left** hand

● **S61.419** Laceration without foreign body of **unspecified** hand

● **S61.42** **Laceration with foreign body of hand**

● **S61.421** Laceration with foreign body of **right** hand

● **S61.422** Laceration with foreign body of **left** hand

● **S61.429** Laceration with foreign body of **unspecified** hand

● **S61.43** **Puncture wound without foreign body of hand**

● **S61.431** Puncture wound without foreign body of **right** hand

● **S61.432** Puncture wound without foreign body of **left** hand

● **S61.439** Puncture wound without foreign body of **unspecified** hand

● **S61.44** **Puncture wound with foreign body of hand**

● **S61.441** Puncture wound with foreign body of **right** hand

● **S61.442** Puncture wound with foreign body of **left** hand

● **S61.449** Puncture wound with foreign body of **unspecified** hand

● **S61.45** **Open bite of hand**
Bite of hand NOS
> **Excludes1** superficial bite of hand (S60.56-, S60.57-)

● **S61.451** Open bite of **right** hand

● **S61.452** Open bite of **left** hand

● **S61.459** Open bite of **unspecified** hand

● **S61.5** **Open wound of wrist**

● **S61.50** **Unspecified** open wound of wrist

● **S61.501** Unspecified open wound of **right** wrist

● **S61.502** Unspecified open wound of **left** wrist

● **S61.509** Unspecified open wound of **unspecified** wrist

● **S61.51** **Laceration without foreign body of wrist**

● **S61.511** Laceration without foreign body of **right** wrist

● **S61.512** Laceration without foreign body of **left** wrist

● **S61.519** Laceration without foreign body of **unspecified** wrist

● **S61.52** **Laceration with foreign body of wrist**

● **S61.521** Laceration with foreign body of **right** wrist

● **S61.522** Laceration with foreign body of **left** wrist

● **S61.529** Laceration with foreign body of **unspecified** wrist

● **S61.53** **Puncture wound without foreign body of wrist**

● **S61.531** Puncture wound without foreign body of **right** wrist

● **S61.532** Puncture wound without foreign body of **left** wrist

● **S61.539** Puncture wound without foreign body of **unspecified** wrist

● **S61.54** **Puncture wound with foreign body of wrist**

● **S61.541** Puncture wound with foreign body of **right** wrist

● **S61.542** Puncture wound with foreign body of **left** wrist

● **S61.549** Puncture wound with foreign body of **unspecified** wrist

● **S61.55** **Open bite of wrist**
Bite of wrist NOS
> **Excludes1** superficial bite of wrist (S60.86-, S60.87-)

● **S61.551** Open bite of **right** wrist

● **S61.552** Open bite of **left** wrist

● **S61.559** Open bite of **unspecified** wrist

● **S62** **Fracture at wrist and hand level**
Note: A fracture not indicated as displaced or nondisplaced should be coded to displaced
A fracture not indicated as open or closed should be coded to closed
> **Excludes1** traumatic amputation of wrist and hand (S68.-)
> **Excludes2** fracture of distal parts of ulna and radius (S52.-)

The appropriate 7th character is to be added to each code from category S62

A	initial encounter for closed fracture
B	initial encounter for open fracture
D	subsequent encounter for fracture with routine healing
G	subsequent encounter for fracture with delayed healing
K	subsequent encounter for fracture with nonunion
P	subsequent encounter for fracture with malunion
S	sequela

● **S62.0** **Fracture of navicular [scaphoid] bone of wrist**

● **S62.00** **Unspecified** fracture of navicular [scaphoid] bone of wrist

● **S62.001** Unspecified fracture of navicular [scaphoid] bone of **right** wrist

● **S62.002** Unspecified fracture of navicular [scaphoid] bone of **left** wrist
Coding Clinic: 2012, Q4, P106

● **S62.009** Unspecified fracture of navicular [scaphoid] bone of **unspecified** wrist

▶ New   ⇒ Revised   ~~deleted~~ Deleted   Excludes 1   Excludes 2   Includes   Use additional   Code first   Code also   Key words
OGCR Official Guidelines   X Assign placeholder X   ▌ Use Additional Character(s)   ▌ Manifestation Code   **Coding Clinic**

● **S62.01**   Fracture of distal pole of navicular [scaphoid] bone of wrist
     Fracture of volar tuberosity of navicular [scaphoid] bone of wrist

   ● **S62.011**   Displaced fracture of distal pole of navicular [scaphoid] bone of right wrist

   ● **S62.012**   Displaced fracture of distal pole of navicular [scaphoid] bone of left wrist

   ● **S62.013**   Displaced fracture of distal pole of navicular [scaphoid] bone of unspecified wrist

   ● **S62.014**   Nondisplaced fracture of distal pole of navicular [scaphoid] bone of right wrist

   ● **S62.015**   Nondisplaced fracture of distal pole of navicular [scaphoid] bone of left wrist

   ● **S62.016**   Nondisplaced fracture of distal pole of navicular [scaphoid] bone of unspecified wrist

● **S62.02**   Fracture of middle third of navicular [scaphoid] bone of wrist

   ● **S62.021**   Displaced fracture of middle third of navicular [scaphoid] bone of right wrist

   ● **S62.022**   Displaced fracture of middle third of navicular [scaphoid] bone of left wrist

   ● **S62.023**   Displaced fracture of middle third of navicular [scaphoid] bone of unspecified wrist

   ● **S62.024**   Nondisplaced fracture of middle third of navicular [scaphoid] bone of right wrist

   ● **S62.025**   Nondisplaced fracture of middle third of navicular [scaphoid] bone of left wrist

   ● **S62.026**   Nondisplaced fracture of middle third of navicular [scaphoid] bone of unspecified wrist

● **S62.03**   Fracture of proximal third of navicular [scaphoid] bone of wrist

   ● **S62.031**   Displaced fracture of proximal third of navicular [scaphoid] bone of right wrist

   ● **S62.032**   Displaced fracture of proximal third of navicular [scaphoid] bone of left wrist

   ● **S62.033**   Displaced fracture of proximal third of navicular [scaphoid] bone of unspecified wrist

   ● **S62.034**   Nondisplaced fracture of proximal third of navicular [scaphoid] bone of right wrist

   ● **S62.035**   Nondisplaced fracture of proximal third of navicular [scaphoid] bone of left wrist

   ● **S62.036**   Nondisplaced fracture of proximal third of navicular [scaphoid] bone of unspecified wrist

● **S62.1**   Fracture of other and unspecified carpal bone(s)
     Excludes2   fracture of scaphoid of wrist (S62.0-)

● **S62.10**   Fracture of unspecified carpal bone
     Fracture of wrist NOS

   ● **S62.101**   Fracture of unspecified carpal bone, right wrist

   ● **S62.102**   Fracture of unspecified carpal bone, left wrist
       Coding Clinic: 2012, Q4, P95

   ● **S62.109**   Fracture of unspecified carpal bone, unspecified wrist

● **S62.11**   Fracture of triquetrum [cuneiform] bone of wrist

   ● **S62.111**   Displaced fracture of triquetrum [cuneiform] bone, right wrist

   ● **S62.112**   Displaced fracture of triquetrum [cuneiform] bone, left wrist

   ● **S62.113**   Displaced fracture of triquetrum [cuneiform] bone, unspecified wrist

   ● **S62.114**   Nondisplaced fracture of triquetrum [cuneiform] bone, right wrist

   ● **S62.115**   Nondisplaced fracture of triquetrum [cuneiform] bone, left wrist

   ● **S62.116**   Nondisplaced fracture of triquetrum [cuneiform] bone, unspecified wrist

● **S62.12**   Fracture of lunate [semilunar]

   ● **S62.121**   Displaced fracture of lunate [semilunar], right wrist

   ● **S62.122**   Displaced fracture of lunate [semilunar], left wrist

   ● **S62.123**   Displaced fracture of lunate [semilunar], unspecified wrist

   ● **S62.124**   Nondisplaced fracture of lunate [semilunar], right wrist

   ● **S62.125**   Nondisplaced fracture of lunate [semilunar], left wrist

   ● **S62.126**   Nondisplaced fracture of lunate [semilunar], unspecified wrist

● **S62.13**   Fracture of capitate [os magnum] bone

   ● **S62.131**   Displaced fracture of capitate [os magnum] bone, right wrist

   ● **S62.132**   Displaced fracture of capitate [os magnum] bone, left wrist

   ● **S62.133**   Displaced fracture of capitate [os magnum] bone, unspecified wrist

   ● **S62.134**   Nondisplaced fracture of capitate [os magnum] bone, right wrist

   ● **S62.135**   Nondisplaced fracture of capitate [os magnum] bone, left wrist

   ● **S62.136**   Nondisplaced fracture of capitate [os magnum] bone, unspecified wrist

● **S62.14**   Fracture of body of hamate [unciform] bone
     Fracture of hamate [unciform] bone NOS

   ● **S62.141**   Displaced fracture of body of hamate [unciform] bone, right wrist

   ● **S62.142**   Displaced fracture of body of hamate [unciform] bone, left wrist

   ● **S62.143**   Displaced fracture of body of hamate [unciform] bone, unspecified wrist

   ● **S62.144**   Nondisplaced fracture of body of hamate [unciform] bone, right wrist

   ● **S62.145**   Nondisplaced fracture of body of hamate [unciform] bone, left wrist

   ● **S62.146**   Nondisplaced fracture of body of hamate [unciform] bone, unspecified wrist

● **S62.15**   Fracture of hook process of hamate [unciform] bone
     Fracture of unciform process of hamate [unciform] bone

   ● **S62.151**   Displaced fracture of hook process of hamate [unciform] bone, right wrist

   ● **S62.152**   Displaced fracture of hook process of hamate [unciform] bone, left wrist

   ● **S62.153**   Displaced fracture of hook process of hamate [unciform] bone, unspecified wrist

   ● **S62.154**   Nondisplaced fracture of hook process of hamate [unciform] bone, right wrist

   ● **S62.155**   Nondisplaced fracture of hook process of hamate [unciform] bone, left wrist

   ● **S62.156**   Nondisplaced fracture of hook process of hamate [unciform] bone, unspecified wrist

CHAPTER 19 (S00-T88)

● **S62.16**   Fracture of pisiform
  ● S62.161   Displaced fracture of pisiform, right wrist
  ● S62.162   Displaced fracture of pisiform, left wrist
  ● S62.163   Displaced fracture of pisiform, unspecified wrist
  ● S62.164   Nondisplaced fracture of pisiform, right wrist
  ● S62.165   Nondisplaced fracture of pisiform, left wrist
  ● S62.166   Nondisplaced fracture of pisiform, unspecified wrist

● **S62.17**   Fracture of trapezium [larger multangular]
  ● S62.171   Displaced fracture of trapezium [larger multangular], right wrist
  ● S62.172   Displaced fracture of trapezium [larger multangular], left wrist
  ● S62.173   Displaced fracture of trapezium [larger multangular], unspecified wrist
  ● S62.174   Nondisplaced fracture of trapezium [larger multangular], right wrist
  ● S62.175   Nondisplaced fracture of trapezium [larger multangular], left wrist
  ● S62.176   Nondisplaced fracture of trapezium [larger multangular], unspecified wrist

● **S62.18**   Fracture of trapezoid [smaller multangular]
  ● S62.181   Displaced fracture of trapezoid [smaller multangular], right wrist
  ● S62.182   Displaced fracture of trapezoid [smaller multangular], left wrist
  ● S62.183   Displaced fracture of trapezoid [smaller multangular], unspecified wrist
  ● S62.184   Nondisplaced fracture of trapezoid [smaller multangular], right wrist
  ● S62.185   Nondisplaced fracture of trapezoid [smaller multangular], left wrist
  ● S62.186   Nondisplaced fracture of trapezoid [smaller multangular], unspecified wrist

● **S62.2**   Fracture of first metacarpal bone
  ● **S62.20**   Unspecified fracture of first metacarpal bone
    ● S62.201   Unspecified fracture of first metacarpal bone, right hand
    ● S62.202   Unspecified fracture of first metacarpal bone, left hand
    ● S62.209   Unspecified fracture of first metacarpal bone, unspecified hand
  ● **S62.21**   Bennett's fracture
    ● S62.211   Bennett's fracture, right hand
    ● S62.212   Bennett's fracture, left hand
    ● S62.213   Bennett's fracture, unspecified hand
  ● **S62.22**   Rolando's fracture
    ● S62.221   Displaced Rolando's fracture, right hand
    ● S62.222   Displaced Rolando's fracture, left hand
    ● S62.223   Displaced Rolando's fracture, unspecified hand
    ● S62.224   Nondisplaced Rolando's fracture, right hand
    ● S62.225   Nondisplaced Rolando's fracture, left hand
    ● S62.226   Nondisplaced Rolando's fracture, unspecified hand

● **S62.23**   Other fracture of base of first metacarpal bone
  ● S62.231   Other displaced fracture of base of first metacarpal bone, right hand
  ● S62.232   Other displaced fracture of base of first metacarpal bone, left hand
  ● S62.233   Other displaced fracture of base of first metacarpal bone, unspecified hand
  ● S62.234   Other nondisplaced fracture of base of first metacarpal bone, right hand
  ● S62.235   Other nondisplaced fracture of base of first metacarpal bone, left hand
  ● S62.236   Other nondisplaced fracture of base of first metacarpal bone, unspecified hand

● **S62.24**   Fracture of shaft of first metacarpal bone
  ● S62.241   Displaced fracture of shaft of first metacarpal bone, right hand
  ● S62.242   Displaced fracture of shaft of first metacarpal bone, left hand
  ● S62.243   Displaced fracture of shaft of first metacarpal bone, unspecified hand
  ● S62.244   Nondisplaced fracture of shaft of first metacarpal bone, right hand
  ● S62.245   Nondisplaced fracture of shaft of first metacarpal bone, left hand
  ● S62.246   Nondisplaced fracture of shaft of first metacarpal bone, unspecified hand

● **S62.25**   Fracture of neck of first metacarpal bone
  ● S62.251   Displaced fracture of neck of first metacarpal bone, right hand
  ● S62.252   Displaced fracture of neck of first metacarpal bone, left hand
  ● S62.253   Displaced fracture of neck of first metacarpal bone, unspecified hand
  ● S62.254   Nondisplaced fracture of neck of first metacarpal bone, right hand
  ● S62.255   Nondisplaced fracture of neck of first metacarpal bone, left hand
  ● S62.256   Nondisplaced fracture of neck of first metacarpal bone, unspecified hand

● **S62.29**   Other fracture of first metacarpal bone
  ● S62.291   Other fracture of first metacarpal bone, right hand
  ● S62.292   Other fracture of first metacarpal bone, left hand
  ● S62.299   Other fracture of first metacarpal bone, unspecified hand

● **S62.3**   Fracture of other and unspecified metacarpal bone
  Excludes2   fracture of first metacarpal bone (S62.2-)
  ● **S62.30**   Unspecified fracture of other metacarpal bone
    ● S62.300   Unspecified fracture of second metacarpal bone, right hand
    ● S62.301   Unspecified fracture of second metacarpal bone, left hand
    ● S62.302   Unspecified fracture of third metacarpal bone, right hand
    ● S62.303   Unspecified fracture of third metacarpal bone, left hand
    ● S62.304   Unspecified fracture of fourth metacarpal bone, right hand
    ● S62.305   Unspecified fracture of fourth metacarpal bone, left hand
    ● S62.306   Unspecified fracture of fifth metacarpal bone, right hand
    ● S62.307   Unspecified fracture of fifth metacarpal bone, left hand

▶ New   ⇒ Revised   ~~deleted~~ Deleted   Excludes 1   Excludes 2   Includes   Use additional   Code first   Code also   Key words

OGCR Official Guidelines   X Assign placeholder X   ● Use Additional Character(s)   ⟩ Manifestation Code   **Coding Clinic**

● **S62.308**   Unspecified fracture of other metacarpal bone
  Unspecified fracture of specified metacarpal bone with unspecified laterality

● **S62.309**   Unspecified fracture of unspecified metacarpal bone

● **S62.31**   Displaced fracture of base of other metacarpal bone

● **S62.310**   Displaced fracture of base of second metacarpal bone, right hand

● **S62.311**   Displaced fracture of base of second metacarpal bone, left hand

● **S62.312**   Displaced fracture of base of third metacarpal bone, right hand

● **S62.313**   Displaced fracture of base of third metacarpal bone, left hand

● **S62.314**   Displaced fracture of base of fourth metacarpal bone, right hand

● **S62.315**   Displaced fracture of base of fourth metacarpal bone, left hand

● **S62.316**   Displaced fracture of base of fifth metacarpal bone, right hand

● **S62.317**   Displaced fracture of base of fifth metacarpal bone, left hand

● **S62.318**   Displaced fracture of base of other metacarpal bone
  Displaced fracture of base of specified metacarpal bone with unspecified laterality

● **S62.319**   Displaced fracture of base of unspecified metacarpal bone

● **S62.32**   Displaced fracture of shaft of other metacarpal bone

● **S62.320**   Displaced fracture of shaft of second metacarpal bone, right hand

● **S62.321**   Displaced fracture of shaft of second metacarpal bone, left hand

● **S62.322**   Displaced fracture of shaft of third metacarpal bone, right hand

● **S62.323**   Displaced fracture of shaft of third metacarpal bone, left hand

● **S62.324**   Displaced fracture of shaft of fourth metacarpal bone, right hand

● **S62.325**   Displaced fracture of shaft of fourth metacarpal bone, left hand

● **S62.326**   Displaced fracture of shaft of fifth metacarpal bone, right hand

● **S62.327**   Displaced fracture of shaft of fifth metacarpal bone, left hand

● **S62.328**   Displaced fracture of shaft of other metacarpal bone
  Displaced fracture of shaft of specified metacarpal bone with unspecified laterality

● **S62.329**   Displaced fracture of shaft of unspecified metacarpal bone

● **S62.33**   Displaced fracture of neck of other metacarpal bone

● **S62.330**   Displaced fracture of neck of second metacarpal bone, right hand

● **S62.331**   Displaced fracture of neck of second metacarpal bone, left hand

● **S62.332**   Displaced fracture of neck of third metacarpal bone, right hand

● **S62.333**   Displaced fracture of neck of third metacarpal bone, left hand

● **S62.334**   Displaced fracture of neck of fourth metacarpal bone, right hand

● **S62.335**   Displaced fracture of neck of fourth metacarpal bone, left hand

● **S62.336**   Displaced fracture of neck of fifth metacarpal bone, right hand

● **S62.337**   Displaced fracture of neck of fifth metacarpal bone, left hand

● **S62.338**   Displaced fracture of neck of other metacarpal bone
  Displaced fracture of neck of specified metacarpal bone with unspecified laterality

● **S62.339**   Displaced fracture of neck of unspecified metacarpal bone

● **S62.34**   Nondisplaced fracture of base of other metacarpal bone

● **S62.340**   Nondisplaced fracture of base of second metacarpal bone, right hand

● **S62.341**   Nondisplaced fracture of base of second metacarpal bone, left hand

● **S62.342**   Nondisplaced fracture of base of third metacarpal bone, right hand

● **S62.343**   Nondisplaced fracture of base of third metacarpal bone, left hand

● **S62.344**   Nondisplaced fracture of base of fourth metacarpal bone, right hand

● **S62.345**   Nondisplaced fracture of base of fourth metacarpal bone, left hand

● **S62.346**   Nondisplaced fracture of base of fifth metacarpal bone, right hand

● **S62.347**   Nondisplaced fracture of base of fifth metacarpal bone, left hand

● **S62.348**   Nondisplaced fracture of base of other metacarpal bone
  Nondisplaced fracture of base of specified metacarpal bone with unspecified laterality

● **S62.349**   Nondisplaced fracture of base of unspecified metacarpal bone

● **S62.35**   Nondisplaced fracture of shaft of other metacarpal bone

● **S62.350**   Nondisplaced fracture of shaft of second metacarpal bone, right hand

● **S62.351**   Nondisplaced fracture of shaft of second metacarpal bone, left hand

● **S62.352**   Nondisplaced fracture of shaft of third metacarpal bone, right hand

● **S62.353**   Nondisplaced fracture of shaft of third metacarpal bone, left hand

● **S62.354**   Nondisplaced fracture of shaft of fourth metacarpal bone, right hand

● **S62.355**   Nondisplaced fracture of shaft of fourth metacarpal bone, left hand

● **S62.356**   Nondisplaced fracture of shaft of fifth metacarpal bone, right hand

● **S62.357**   Nondisplaced fracture of shaft of fifth metacarpal bone, left hand

● **S62.358**   Nondisplaced fracture of shaft of other metacarpal bone
  Nondisplaced fracture of shaft of specified metacarpal bone with unspecified laterality

● **S62.359**   Nondisplaced fracture of shaft of unspecified metacarpal bone

CHAPTER 19 (S00–T88)

● **S62.36** Nondisplaced fracture of neck of other metacarpal bone

  ● **S62.360** Nondisplaced fracture of neck of second metacarpal bone, right hand

  ● **S62.361** Nondisplaced fracture of neck of second metacarpal bone, left hand

  ● **S62.362** Nondisplaced fracture of neck of third metacarpal bone, right hand

  ● **S62.363** Nondisplaced fracture of neck of third metacarpal bone, left hand

  ● **S62.364** Nondisplaced fracture of neck of fourth metacarpal bone, right hand

  ● **S62.365** Nondisplaced fracture of neck of fourth metacarpal bone, left hand

  ● **S62.366** Nondisplaced fracture of neck of fifth metacarpal bone, right hand

  ● **S62.367** Nondisplaced fracture of neck of fifth metacarpal bone, left hand

  ● **S62.368** Nondisplaced fracture of neck of other metacarpal bone

      Nondisplaced fracture of neck of specified metacarpal bone with unspecified laterality

  ● **S62.369** Nondisplaced fracture of neck of unspecified metacarpal bone

● **S62.39** Other fracture of other metacarpal bone

  ● **S62.390** Other fracture of second metacarpal bone, right hand

  ● **S62.391** Other fracture of second metacarpal bone, left hand

  ● **S62.392** Other fracture of third metacarpal bone, right hand

  ● **S62.393** Other fracture of third metacarpal bone, left hand

  ● **S62.394** Other fracture of fourth metacarpal bone, right hand

  ● **S62.395** Other fracture of fourth metacarpal bone, left hand

  ● **S62.396** Other fracture of fifth metacarpal bone, right hand

  ● **S62.397** Other fracture of fifth metacarpal bone, left hand

  ● **S62.398** Other fracture of other metacarpal bone

      Other fracture of specified metacarpal bone with unspecified laterality

  ● **S62.399** Other fracture of unspecified metacarpal bone

● **S62.5** Fracture of thumb

  ● **S62.50** Fracture of unspecified phalanx of thumb

  ● **S62.501** Fracture of unspecified phalanx of right thumb

  ● **S62.502** Fracture of unspecified phalanx of left thumb

  ● **S62.509** Fracture of unspecified phalanx of unspecified thumb

  ● **S62.51** Fracture of proximal phalanx of thumb

  ● **S62.511** Displaced fracture of proximal phalanx of right thumb

  ● **S62.512** Displaced fracture of proximal phalanx of left thumb

  ● **S62.513** Displaced fracture of proximal phalanx of unspecified thumb

  ● **S62.514** Nondisplaced fracture of proximal phalanx of right thumb

  ● **S62.515** Nondisplaced fracture of proximal phalanx of left thumb

  ● **S62.516** Nondisplaced fracture of proximal phalanx of unspecified thumb

● **S62.52** Fracture of distal phalanx of thumb

  ● **S62.521** Displaced fracture of distal phalanx of right thumb

  ● **S62.522** Displaced fracture of distal phalanx of left thumb

  ● **S62.523** Displaced fracture of distal phalanx of unspecified thumb

  ● **S62.524** Nondisplaced fracture of distal phalanx of right thumb

  ● **S62.525** Nondisplaced fracture of distal phalanx of left thumb

  ● **S62.526** Nondisplaced fracture of distal phalanx of unspecified thumb

● **S62.6** Fracture of other and unspecified finger(s)

  Excludes2   fracture of thumb (S62.5-)

  ● **S62.60** Fracture of unspecified phalanx of finger

  ● **S62.600** Fracture of unspecified phalanx of right index finger

  ● **S62.601** Fracture of unspecified phalanx of left index finger

  ● **S62.602** Fracture of unspecified phalanx of right middle finger

  ● **S62.603** Fracture of unspecified phalanx of left middle finger

  ● **S62.604** Fracture of unspecified phalanx of right ring finger

  ● **S62.605** Fracture of unspecified phalanx of left ring finger

  ● **S62.606** Fracture of unspecified phalanx of right little finger

  ● **S62.607** Fracture of unspecified phalanx of left little finger

  ● **S62.608** Fracture of unspecified phalanx of other finger

      Fracture of unspecified phalanx of specified finger with unspecified laterality

  ● **S62.609** Fracture of unspecified phalanx of unspecified finger

  ● **S62.61** Displaced fracture of proximal phalanx of finger

  ● **S62.610** Displaced fracture of proximal phalanx of right index finger

  ● **S62.611** Displaced fracture of proximal phalanx of left index finger

  ● **S62.612** Displaced fracture of proximal phalanx of right middle finger

  ● **S62.613** Displaced fracture of proximal phalanx of left middle finger

  ● **S62.614** Displaced fracture of proximal phalanx of right ring finger

  ● **S62.615** Displaced fracture of proximal phalanx of left ring finger

  ● **S62.616** Displaced fracture of proximal phalanx of right little finger

  ● **S62.617** Displaced fracture of proximal phalanx of left little finger

  ● **S62.618** Displaced fracture of proximal phalanx of other finger

      Displaced fracture of proximal phalanx of specified finger with unspecified laterality

  ● **S62.619** Displaced fracture of proximal phalanx of unspecified finger

  ● **S62.62** Displaced fracture of middle phalanx of finger

  ● **S62.620** Displaced fracture of middle phalanx of right index finger

  ● **S62.621** Displaced fracture of middle phalanx of left index finger

▶ New   ⇒ Revised   ~~deleted~~ Deleted   Excludes 1   Excludes 2   Includes   Use additional   Code first   Code also   Key words

OGCR Official Guidelines   X Assign placeholder X   ● Use Additional Character(s)   ▷ Manifestation Code   **Coding Clinic**

● S62.622 Displaced fracture of middle phalanx
              of right middle finger

● S62.623 Displaced fracture of middle phalanx
              of left middle finger

● S62.624 Displaced fracture of middle phalanx
              of right ring finger

● S62.625 Displaced fracture of middle phalanx
              of left ring finger

➡● S62.626 Displaced fracture of middle phalanx
              of right little finger

➡● S62.627 Displaced fracture of middle phalanx
              of left little finger

➡● S62.628 Displaced fracture of middle phalanx
              of other finger
                ➡Displaced fracture of middle
                    phalanx of specified finger with
                    unspecified laterality

➡● S62.629 Displaced fracture of middle phalanx
              of unspecified finger

● S62.63 Displaced fracture of distal phalanx of finger

● S62.630 Displaced fracture of distal phalanx
              of right index finger

● S62.631 Displaced fracture of distal phalanx
              of left index finger

● S62.632 Displaced fracture of distal phalanx
              of right middle finger

● S62.633 Displaced fracture of distal phalanx
              of left middle finger

● S62.634 Displaced fracture of distal phalanx
              of right ring finger

● S62.635 Displaced fracture of distal phalanx
              of left ring finger

● S62.636 Displaced fracture of distal phalanx
              of right little finger

● S62.637 Displaced fracture of distal phalanx
              of left little finger

● S62.638 Displaced fracture of distal phalanx
              of other finger
                Displaced fracture of distal phalanx
                    of specified finger with
                    unspecified laterality

● S62.639 Displaced fracture of distal phalanx
              of unspecified finger

● S62.64 Nondisplaced fracture of proximal phalanx of
            finger

● S62.640 Nondisplaced fracture of proximal
              phalanx of right index finger

● S62.641 Nondisplaced fracture of proximal
              phalanx of left index finger

● S62.642 Nondisplaced fracture of proximal
              phalanx of right middle finger

● S62.643 Nondisplaced fracture of proximal
              phalanx of left middle finger

● S62.644 Nondisplaced fracture of proximal
              phalanx of right ring finger

● S62.645 Nondisplaced fracture of proximal
              phalanx of left ring finger

● S62.646 Nondisplaced fracture of proximal
              phalanx of right little finger

● S62.647 Nondisplaced fracture of proximal
              phalanx of left little finger

● S62.648 Nondisplaced fracture of proximal
              phalanx of other finger
                Nondisplaced fracture of proximal
                    phalanx of specified finger with
                    unspecified laterality

● S62.649 Nondisplaced fracture of proximal
              phalanx of unspecified finger

Figure 19-14 Dorsal dislocation of the distal phalanx of the index
finger. (From Hardy M, Snaith B: Musculoskeletal Trauma: A Guide to
Assessment and Diagnosis, 1e, Elsevier, 2011)

● S62.65 Nondisplaced fracture of middle phalanx of
            finger

● S62.650 Nondisplaced fracture of middle
              phalanx of right index finger

● S62.651 Nondisplaced fracture of middle
              phalanx of left index finger

● S62.652 Nondisplaced fracture of middle
              phalanx of right middle finger

● S62.653 Nondisplaced fracture of middle
              phalanx of left middle finger

➡● S62.654 Nondisplaced fracture of middle
              phalanx of right ring finger

➡● S62.655 Nondisplaced fracture of middle
              phalanx of left ring finger

➡● S62.656 Nondisplaced fracture of middle
              phalanx of right little finger

➡● S62.657 Nondisplaced fracture of middle
              phalanx of left little finger

➡● S62.658 Nondisplaced fracture of middle
              phalanx of other finger
                ➡Nondisplaced fracture of middle
                    phalanx of specified finger with
                    unspecified laterality

➡● S62.659 Nondisplaced fracture of middle
              phalanx of unspecified finger

● S62.66 Nondisplaced fracture of distal phalanx of finger

● S62.660 Nondisplaced fracture of distal
              phalanx of right index finger

● S62.661 Nondisplaced fracture of distal
              phalanx of left index finger

● S62.662 Nondisplaced fracture of distal
              phalanx of right middle finger

● S62.663 Nondisplaced fracture of distal
              phalanx of left middle finger

● S62.664 Nondisplaced fracture of distal
              phalanx of right ring finger

● S62.665 Nondisplaced fracture of distal
              phalanx of left ring finger

● S62.666 Nondisplaced fracture of distal
              phalanx of right little finger

● S62.667 Nondisplaced fracture of distal
              phalanx of left little finger

● S62.668   **Nondisplaced** fracture of distal phalanx of **other** finger
    Nondisplaced fracture of distal phalanx of specified finger with unspecified laterality

● S62.669   **Nondisplaced** fracture of distal phalanx of **unspecified** finger

● S62.9   **Unspecified** fracture of wrist and hand

X● S62.90   Unspecified fracture of **unspecified** wrist and hand

X● S62.91   Unspecified fracture of **right** wrist and hand

X● S62.92   Unspecified fracture of **left** wrist and hand

● S63   **Dislocation and sprain of joints and ligaments at wrist and hand level**

    Includes   avulsion of joint or ligament at wrist and hand level
        laceration of cartilage, joint or ligament at wrist and hand level
        sprain of cartilage, joint or ligament at wrist and hand level
        traumatic hemarthrosis of joint or ligament at wrist and hand level
        traumatic rupture of joint or ligament at wrist and hand level
        traumatic subluxation of joint or ligament at wrist and hand level
        traumatic tear of joint or ligament at wrist and hand level

    Code also any associated open wound

    Excludes2   strain of muscle, fascia and tendon of wrist and hand (S66.-)

    The appropriate 7th character is to be added to each code from category S63

A	initial encounter
D	subsequent encounter
S	sequela

● S63.0   **Subluxation and dislocation of wrist and hand joints**

● S63.00   **Unspecified** subluxation and dislocation of wrist and hand
    Dislocation of carpal bone NOS
    Dislocation of distal end of radius NOS
    Subluxation of carpal bone NOS
    Subluxation of distal end of radius NOS

● S63.001   Unspecified **subluxation** of **right** wrist and hand

● S63.002   Unspecified **subluxation** of **left** wrist and hand

● S63.003   Unspecified **subluxation** of **unspecified** wrist and hand

● S63.004   Unspecified **dislocation** of **right** wrist and hand

● S63.005   Unspecified **dislocation** of **left** wrist and hand

● S63.006   Unspecified **dislocation** of **unspecified** wrist and hand

● S63.01   Subluxation and dislocation of **distal radioulnar** joint

● S63.011   **Subluxation** of distal radioulnar joint of **right** wrist

● S63.012   **Subluxation** of distal radioulnar joint of **left** wrist

● S63.013   **Subluxation** of distal radioulnar joint of **unspecified** wrist

● S63.014   **Dislocation** of distal radioulnar joint of **right** wrist

● S63.015   **Dislocation** of distal radioulnar joint of **left** wrist

● S63.016   **Dislocation** of distal radioulnar joint of **unspecified** wrist

● S63.02   Subluxation and dislocation of **radiocarpal** joint

● S63.021   **Subluxation** of radiocarpal joint of **right** wrist

● S63.022   **Subluxation** of radiocarpal joint of **left** wrist

● S63.023   **Subluxation** of radiocarpal joint of **unspecified** wrist

● S63.024   **Dislocation** of radiocarpal joint of **right** wrist

● S63.025   **Dislocation** of radiocarpal joint of **left** wrist

● S63.026   **Dislocation** of radiocarpal joint of **unspecified** wrist

● S63.03   Subluxation and dislocation of **midcarpal** joint

● S63.031   **Subluxation** of midcarpal joint of **right** wrist

● S63.032   **Subluxation** of midcarpal joint of **left** wrist

● S63.033   **Subluxation** of midcarpal joint of **unspecified** wrist

● S63.034   **Dislocation** of midcarpal joint of **right** wrist

● S63.035   **Dislocation** of midcarpal joint of **left** wrist

● S63.036   **Dislocation** of midcarpal joint of **unspecified** wrist

● S63.04   Subluxation and dislocation of **carpometacarpal** joint of thumb

    Excludes2   interphalangeal subluxation and dislocation of thumb (S63.1-)

● S63.041   **Subluxation** of carpometacarpal joint of **right** thumb

● S63.042   **Subluxation** of carpometacarpal joint of **left** thumb

● S63.043   **Subluxation** of carpometacarpal joint of **unspecified** thumb

● S63.044   **Dislocation** of carpometacarpal joint of **right** thumb

● S63.045   **Dislocation** of carpometacarpal joint of **left** thumb

● S63.046   **Dislocation** of carpometacarpal joint of **unspecified** thumb

● S63.05   Subluxation and dislocation of **other** carpometacarpal joint

    Excludes2   subluxation and dislocation of carpometacarpal joint of thumb (S63.04-)

● S63.051   **Subluxation** of other carpometacarpal joint of **right** hand

● S63.052   **Subluxation** of other carpometacarpal joint of **left** hand

● S63.053   **Subluxation** of other carpometacarpal joint of **unspecified** hand

● S63.054   **Dislocation** of other carpometacarpal joint of **right** hand

● S63.055   **Dislocation** of other carpometacarpal joint of **left** hand

● S63.056   **Dislocation** of other carpometacarpal joint of **unspecified** hand

● S63.06   Subluxation and dislocation of **metacarpal** (bone), proximal end

● S63.061   **Subluxation** of metacarpal (bone), proximal end of **right** hand

● S63.062   **Subluxation** of metacarpal (bone), proximal end of **left** hand

● S63.063   **Subluxation** of metacarpal (bone), proximal end of **unspecified** hand

● S63.064   **Dislocation** of metacarpal (bone), proximal end of **right** hand

● S63.065   Dislocation of metacarpal (bone), proximal end of left hand

● S63.066   Dislocation of metacarpal (bone), proximal end of unspecified hand

● S63.07   Subluxation and dislocation of distal end of ulna

   ● S63.071   Subluxation of distal end of right ulna

   ● S63.072   Subluxation of distal end of left ulna

   ● S63.073   Subluxation of distal end of unspecified ulna

   ● S63.074   Dislocation of distal end of right ulna

   ● S63.075   Dislocation of distal end of left ulna

   ● S63.076   Dislocation of distal end of unspecified ulna

● S63.09   Other subluxation and dislocation of wrist and hand

   ● S63.091   Other subluxation of right wrist and hand

   ● S63.092   Other subluxation of left wrist and hand

   ● S63.093   Other subluxation of unspecified wrist and hand

   ● S63.094   Other dislocation of right wrist and hand

   ● S63.095   Other dislocation of left wrist and hand

   ● S63.096   Other dislocation of unspecified wrist and hand

● S63.1   Subluxation and dislocation of thumb

   ● S63.10   Unspecified subluxation and dislocation of thumb

      ● S63.101   Unspecified subluxation of right thumb

      ● S63.102   Unspecified subluxation of left thumb

      ● S63.103   Unspecified subluxation of unspecified thumb

      ● S63.104   Unspecified dislocation of right thumb

      ● S63.105   Unspecified dislocation of left thumb

      ● S63.106   Unspecified dislocation of unspecified thumb

   ● S63.11   Subluxation and dislocation of metacarpophalangeal joint of thumb

      ● S63.111   Subluxation of metacarpophalangeal joint of right thumb

      ● S63.112   Subluxation of metacarpophalangeal joint of left thumb

      ● S63.113   Subluxation of metacarpophalangeal joint of unspecified thumb

      ● S63.114   Dislocation of metacarpophalangeal joint of right thumb

      ● S63.115   Dislocation of metacarpophalangeal joint of left thumb

      ● S63.116   Dislocation of metacarpophalangeal joint of unspecified thumb

   ● S63.12   Subluxation and dislocation of interphalangeal joint of thumb

      ● S63.121   Subluxation of interphalangeal joint of right thumb

      ● S63.122   Subluxation of interphalangeal joint of left thumb

      ● S63.123   Subluxation of interphalangeal joint of unspecified thumb

      ● S63.124   Dislocation of interphalangeal joint of right thumb

      ● S63.125   Dislocation of interphalangeal joint of left thumb

      ● S63.126   Dislocation of interphalangeal joint of unspecified thumb

● S63.2   Subluxation and dislocation of other finger(s)

   Excludes2   subluxation and dislocation of thumb (S63.1-)

   ● S63.20   Unspecified subluxation of other finger

      ● S63.200   Unspecified subluxation of right index finger

      ● S63.201   Unspecified subluxation of left index finger

      ● S63.202   Unspecified subluxation of right middle finger

      ● S63.203   Unspecified subluxation of left middle finger

      ● S63.204   Unspecified subluxation of right ring finger

      ● S63.205   Unspecified subluxation of left ring finger

      ● S63.206   Unspecified subluxation of right little finger

      ● S63.207   Unspecified subluxation of left little finger

      ● S63.208   Unspecified subluxation of other finger
                   Unspecified subluxation of specified finger with unspecified laterality

      ● S63.209   Unspecified subluxation of unspecified finger

   ● S63.21   Subluxation of metacarpophalangeal joint of finger

      ● S63.210   Subluxation of metacarpophalangeal joint of right index finger

      ● S63.211   Subluxation of metacarpophalangeal joint of left index finger

      ● S63.212   Subluxation of metacarpophalangeal joint of right middle finger

      ● S63.213   Subluxation of metacarpophalangeal joint of left middle finger

      ● S63.214   Subluxation of metacarpophalangeal joint of right ring finger

      ● S63.215   Subluxation of metacarpophalangeal joint of left ring finger

      ● S63.216   Subluxation of metacarpophalangeal joint of right little finger

      ● S63.217   Subluxation of metacarpophalangeal joint of left little finger

      ● S63.218   Subluxation of metacarpophalangeal joint of other finger
                   Subluxation of metacarpophalangeal joint of specified finger with unspecified laterality

      ● S63.219   Subluxation of metacarpophalangeal joint of unspecified finger

   ● S63.22   Subluxation of unspecified interphalangeal joint of finger

      ● S63.220   Subluxation of unspecified interphalangeal joint of right index finger

      ● S63.221   Subluxation of unspecified interphalangeal joint of left index finger

      ● S63.222   Subluxation of unspecified interphalangeal joint of right middle finger

      ● S63.223   Subluxation of unspecified interphalangeal joint of left middle finger

      ● S63.224   Subluxation of unspecified interphalangeal joint of right ring finger

      ● S63.225   Subluxation of unspecified interphalangeal joint of left ring finger

● S63.226 Subluxation of unspecified interphalangeal joint of right little finger

● S63.227 Subluxation of unspecified interphalangeal joint of left little finger

● S63.228 Subluxation of unspecified interphalangeal joint of other finger
  Subluxation of unspecified interphalangeal joint of specified finger with unspecified laterality

● S63.229 Subluxation of unspecified interphalangeal joint of unspecified finger

● S63.23 Subluxation of proximal interphalangeal joint of finger

  ● S63.230 Subluxation of proximal interphalangeal joint of right index finger

  ● S63.231 Subluxation of proximal interphalangeal joint of left index finger

  ● S63.232 Subluxation of proximal interphalangeal joint of right middle finger

  ● S63.233 Subluxation of proximal interphalangeal joint of left middle finger

  ● S63.234 Subluxation of proximal interphalangeal joint of right ring finger

  ● S63.235 Subluxation of proximal interphalangeal joint of left ring finger

  ● S63.236 Subluxation of proximal interphalangeal joint of right little finger

  ● S63.237 Subluxation of proximal interphalangeal joint of left little finger

  ● S63.238 Subluxation of proximal interphalangeal joint of other finger
    Subluxation of proximal interphalangeal joint of specified finger with unspecified laterality

  ● S63.239 Subluxation of proximal interphalangeal joint of unspecified finger

● S63.24 Subluxation of distal interphalangeal joint of finger

  ● S63.240 Subluxation of distal interphalangeal joint of right index finger

  ● S63.241 Subluxation of distal interphalangeal joint of left index finger

  ● S63.242 Subluxation of distal interphalangeal joint of right middle finger

  ● S63.243 Subluxation of distal interphalangeal joint of left middle finger

  ● S63.244 Subluxation of distal interphalangeal joint of right ring finger

  ● S63.245 Subluxation of distal interphalangeal joint of left ring finger

  ● S63.246 Subluxation of distal interphalangeal joint of right little finger

  ● S63.247 Subluxation of distal interphalangeal joint of left little finger

● S63.248 Subluxation of distal interphalangeal joint of other finger
  Subluxation of distal interphalangeal joint of specified finger with unspecified laterality

● S63.249 Subluxation of distal interphalangeal joint of unspecified finger

● S63.25 Unspecified dislocation of other finger

  ● S63.250 Unspecified dislocation of right index finger

  ● S63.251 Unspecified dislocation of left index finger

  ● S63.252 Unspecified dislocation of right middle finger

  ● S63.253 Unspecified dislocation of left middle finger

  ● S63.254 Unspecified dislocation of right ring finger

  ● S63.255 Unspecified dislocation of left ring finger

  ● S63.256 Unspecified dislocation of right little finger

  ● S63.257 Unspecified dislocation of left little finger

  ● S63.258 Unspecified dislocation of other finger
    Unspecified dislocation of specified finger with unspecified laterality

  ● S63.259 Unspecified dislocation of unspecified finger
    Unspecified dislocation of unspecified finger with unspecified laterality

● S63.26 Dislocation of metacarpophalangeal joint of finger

  ● S63.260 Dislocation of metacarpophalangeal joint of right index finger

  ● S63.261 Dislocation of metacarpophalangeal joint of left index finger

  ● S63.262 Dislocation of metacarpophalangeal joint of right middle finger

  ● S63.263 Dislocation of metacarpophalangeal joint of left middle finger

  ● S63.264 Dislocation of metacarpophalangeal joint of right ring finger

  ● S63.265 Dislocation of metacarpophalangeal joint of left ring finger

  ● S63.266 Dislocation of metacarpophalangeal joint of right little finger

  ● S63.267 Dislocation of metacarpophalangeal joint of left little finger

  ● S63.268 Dislocation of metacarpophalangeal joint of other finger
    Dislocation of metacarpophalangeal joint of specified finger with unspecified laterality

  ● S63.269 Dislocation of metacarpophalangeal joint of unspecified finger

● S63.27 Dislocation of unspecified interphalangeal joint of finger

  ● S63.270 Dislocation of unspecified interphalangeal joint of right index finger

  ● S63.271 Dislocation of unspecified interphalangeal joint of left index finger

▶ New ⇶ Revised ~~deleted~~ Deleted Excludes 1 Excludes 2 Includes Use additional Code first Code also Key words
OGCR Official Guidelines X Assign placeholder X ● Use Additional Character(s) ▷ Manifestation Code Coding Clinic

● S63.272   Dislocation of unspecified interphalangeal joint of right middle finger

● S63.273   Dislocation of unspecified interphalangeal joint of left middle finger

● S63.274   Dislocation of unspecified interphalangeal joint of right ring finger

● S63.275   Dislocation of unspecified interphalangeal joint of left ring finger

● S63.276   Dislocation of unspecified interphalangeal joint of right little finger

● S63.277   Dislocation of unspecified interphalangeal joint of left little finger

● S63.278   Dislocation of unspecified interphalangeal joint of other finger
     Dislocation of unspecified interphalangeal joint of specified finger with unspecified laterality

● S63.279   Dislocation of unspecified interphalangeal joint of unspecified finger
     Dislocation of unspecified interphalangeal joint of unspecified finger without specified laterality

● S63.28   Dislocation of proximal interphalangeal joint of finger

● S63.280   Dislocation of proximal interphalangeal joint of right index finger

● S63.281   Dislocation of proximal interphalangeal joint of left index finger

● S63.282   Dislocation of proximal interphalangeal joint of right middle finger

● S63.283   Dislocation of proximal interphalangeal joint of left middle finger

● S63.284   Dislocation of proximal interphalangeal joint of right ring finger

● S63.285   Dislocation of proximal interphalangeal joint of left ring finger

● S63.286   Dislocation of proximal interphalangeal joint of right little finger

● S63.287   Dislocation of proximal interphalangeal joint of left little finger

● S63.288   Dislocation of proximal interphalangeal joint of other finger
     Dislocation of proximal interphalangeal joint of specified finger with unspecified laterality

● S63.289   Dislocation of proximal interphalangeal joint of unspecified finger

● S63.29   Dislocation of distal interphalangeal joint of finger

● S63.290   Dislocation of distal interphalangeal joint of right index finger

● S63.291   Dislocation of distal interphalangeal joint of left index finger

● S63.292   Dislocation of distal interphalangeal joint of right middle finger

● S63.293   Dislocation of distal interphalangeal joint of left middle finger

● S63.294   Dislocation of distal interphalangeal joint of right ring finger

● S63.295   Dislocation of distal interphalangeal joint of left ring finger

● S63.296   Dislocation of distal interphalangeal joint of right little finger

● S63.297   Dislocation of distal interphalangeal joint of left little finger

● S63.298   Dislocation of distal interphalangeal joint of other finger
     Dislocation of distal interphalangeal joint of specified finger with unspecified laterality

● S63.299   Dislocation of distal interphalangeal joint of unspecified finger

● S63.3   Traumatic rupture of ligament of wrist

● S63.30   Traumatic rupture of unspecified ligament of wrist

● S63.301   Traumatic rupture of unspecified ligament of right wrist

● S63.302   Traumatic rupture of unspecified ligament of left wrist

● S63.309   Traumatic rupture of unspecified ligament of unspecified wrist

● S63.31   Traumatic rupture of collateral ligament of wrist

● S63.311   Traumatic rupture of collateral ligament of right wrist

● S63.312   Traumatic rupture of collateral ligament of left wrist

● S63.319   Traumatic rupture of collateral ligament of unspecified wrist

● S63.32   Traumatic rupture of radiocarpal ligament

● S63.321   Traumatic rupture of right radiocarpal ligament

● S63.322   Traumatic rupture of left radiocarpal ligament

● S63.329   Traumatic rupture of unspecified radiocarpal ligament

● S63.33   Traumatic rupture of ulnocarpal (palmar) ligament

● S63.331   Traumatic rupture of right ulnocarpal (palmar) ligament

● S63.332   Traumatic rupture of left ulnocarpal (palmar) ligament

● S63.339   Traumatic rupture of unspecified ulnocarpal (palmar) ligament

● S63.39   Traumatic rupture of other ligament of wrist

● S63.391   Traumatic rupture of other ligament of right wrist

● S63.392   Traumatic rupture of other ligament of left wrist

● S63.399   Traumatic rupture of other ligament of unspecified wrist

CHAPTER 19 (S00-T88)

CHAPTER 19 (S00-T88)

● S63.4   Traumatic rupture of ligament of finger at metacarpophalangeal and interphalangeal joint(s)

● S63.40   Traumatic rupture of unspecified ligament of finger at metacarpophalangeal and interphalangeal joint

● S63.400   Traumatic rupture of unspecified ligament of right index finger at metacarpophalangeal and interphalangeal joint

● S63.401   Traumatic rupture of unspecified ligament of left index finger at metacarpophalangeal and interphalangeal joint

● S63.402   Traumatic rupture of unspecified ligament of right middle finger at metacarpophalangeal and interphalangeal joint

● S63.403   Traumatic rupture of unspecified ligament of left middle finger at metacarpophalangeal and interphalangeal joint

● S63.404   Traumatic rupture of unspecified ligament of right ring finger at metacarpophalangeal and interphalangeal joint

● S63.405   Traumatic rupture of unspecified ligament of left ring finger at metacarpophalangeal and interphalangeal joint

● S63.406   Traumatic rupture of unspecified ligament of right little finger at metacarpophalangeal and interphalangeal joint

● S63.407   Traumatic rupture of unspecified ligament of left little finger at metacarpophalangeal and interphalangeal joint

● S63.408   Traumatic rupture of unspecified ligament of other finger at metacarpophalangeal and interphalangeal joint

Traumatic rupture of unspecified ligament of specified finger with unspecified laterality at metacarpophalangeal and interphalangeal joint

● S63.409   Traumatic rupture of unspecified ligament of unspecified finger at metacarpophalangeal and interphalangeal joint

● S63.41   Traumatic rupture of collateral ligament of finger at metacarpophalangeal and interphalangeal joint

● S63.410   Traumatic rupture of collateral ligament of right index finger at metacarpophalangeal and interphalangeal joint

● S63.411   Traumatic rupture of collateral ligament of left index finger at metacarpophalangeal and interphalangeal joint

● S63.412   Traumatic rupture of collateral ligament of right middle finger at metacarpophalangeal and interphalangeal joint

● S63.413   Traumatic rupture of collateral ligament of left middle finger at metacarpophalangeal and interphalangeal joint

● S63.414   Traumatic rupture of collateral ligament of right ring finger at metacarpophalangeal and interphalangeal joint

● S63.415   Traumatic rupture of collateral ligament of left ring finger at metacarpophalangeal and interphalangeal joint

● S63.416   Traumatic rupture of collateral ligament of right little finger at metacarpophalangeal and interphalangeal joint

● S63.417   Traumatic rupture of collateral ligament of left little finger at metacarpophalangeal and interphalangeal joint

● S63.418   Traumatic rupture of collateral ligament of other finger at metacarpophalangeal and interphalangeal joint

Traumatic rupture of collateral ligament of specified finger with unspecified laterality at metacarpophalangeal and interphalangeal joint

● S63.419   Traumatic rupture of collateral ligament of unspecified finger at metacarpophalangeal and interphalangeal joint

● S63.42   Traumatic rupture of palmar ligament of finger at metacarpophalangeal and interphalangeal joint

● S63.420   Traumatic rupture of palmar ligament of right index finger at metacarpophalangeal and interphalangeal joint

● S63.421   Traumatic rupture of palmar ligament of left index finger at metacarpophalangeal and interphalangeal joint

● S63.422   Traumatic rupture of palmar ligament of right middle finger at metacarpophalangeal and interphalangeal joint

● S63.423   Traumatic rupture of palmar ligament of left middle finger at metacarpophalangeal and interphalangeal joint

● S63.424   Traumatic rupture of palmar ligament of right ring finger at metacarpophalangeal and interphalangeal joint

● S63.425   Traumatic rupture of palmar ligament of left ring finger at metacarpophalangeal and interphalangeal joint

● S63.426   Traumatic rupture of palmar ligament of right little finger at metacarpophalangeal and interphalangeal joint

● S63.427   Traumatic rupture of palmar ligament of left little finger at metacarpophalangeal and interphalangeal joint

● S63.428   Traumatic rupture of palmar ligament of other finger at metacarpophalangeal and interphalangeal joint

Traumatic rupture of palmar ligament of specified finger with unspecified laterality at metacarpophalangeal and interphalangeal joint

● S63.429   Traumatic rupture of palmar ligament of unspecified finger at metacarpophalangeal and interphalangeal joint

▶ New   ⇒ Revised   ~~deleted~~ Deleted   Excludes 1   Excludes 2   Includes   Use additional   Code first   Code also   Key words

OGCR Official Guidelines   X Assign placeholder X   ● Use Additional Character(s)   ▌ Manifestation Code   **Coding Clinic**

● S63.43   Traumatic rupture of volar plate of finger at metacarpophalangeal and interphalangeal joint

  ● S63.430   Traumatic rupture of volar plate of right index finger at metacarpophalangeal and interphalangeal joint

  ● S63.431   Traumatic rupture of volar plate of left index finger at metacarpophalangeal and interphalangeal joint

  ● S63.432   Traumatic rupture of volar plate of right middle finger at metacarpophalangeal and interphalangeal joint

  ● S63.433   Traumatic rupture of volar plate of left middle finger at metacarpophalangeal and interphalangeal joint

  ● S63.434   Traumatic rupture of volar plate of right ring finger at metacarpophalangeal and interphalangeal joint

  ● S63.435   Traumatic rupture of volar plate of left ring finger at metacarpophalangeal and interphalangeal joint

  ● S63.436   Traumatic rupture of volar plate of right little finger at metacarpophalangeal and interphalangeal joint

  ● S63.437   Traumatic rupture of volar plate of left little finger at metacarpophalangeal and interphalangeal joint

  ● S63.438   Traumatic rupture of volar plate of other finger at metacarpophalangeal and interphalangeal joint
     Traumatic rupture of volar plate of specified finger with unspecified laterality at metacarpophalangeal and interphalangeal joint

  ● S63.439   Traumatic rupture of volar plate of unspecified finger at metacarpophalangeal and interphalangeal joint

● S63.49   Traumatic rupture of other ligament of finger at metacarpophalangeal and interphalangeal joint

  ● S63.490   Traumatic rupture of other ligament of right index finger at metacarpophalangeal and interphalangeal joint

  ● S63.491   Traumatic rupture of other ligament of left index finger at metacarpophalangeal and interphalangeal joint

  ● S63.492   Traumatic rupture of other ligament of right middle finger at metacarpophalangeal and interphalangeal joint

  ● S63.493   Traumatic rupture of other ligament of left middle finger at metacarpophalangeal and interphalangeal joint

  ● S63.494   Traumatic rupture of other ligament of right ring finger at metacarpophalangeal and interphalangeal joint

  ● S63.495   Traumatic rupture of other ligament of left ring finger at metacarpophalangeal and interphalangeal joint

  ● S63.496   Traumatic rupture of other ligament of right little finger at metacarpophalangeal and interphalangeal joint

  ● S63.497   Traumatic rupture of other ligament of left little finger at metacarpophalangeal and interphalangeal joint

  ● S63.498   Traumatic rupture of other ligament of other finger at metacarpophalangeal and interphalangeal joint
     Traumatic rupture of ligament of specified finger with unspecified laterality at metacarpophalangeal and interphalangeal joint

  ● S63.499   Traumatic rupture of other ligament of unspecified finger at metacarpophalangeal and interphalangeal joint

● S63.5   Other and unspecified sprain of wrist

  ● S63.50   Unspecified sprain of wrist

    ● S63.501   Unspecified sprain of right wrist

    ● S63.502   Unspecified sprain of left wrist

    ● S63.509   Unspecified sprain of unspecified wrist

  ● S63.51   Sprain of carpal (joint)

    ● S63.511   Sprain of carpal joint of right wrist

    ● S63.512   Sprain of carpal joint of left wrist

    ● S63.519   Sprain of carpal joint of unspecified wrist

  ● S63.52   Sprain of radiocarpal joint
     Excludes1   traumatic rupture of radiocarpal ligament (S63.32-)

    ● S63.521   Sprain of radiocarpal joint of right wrist

    ● S63.522   Sprain of radiocarpal joint of left wrist

    ● S63.529   Sprain of radiocarpal joint of unspecified wrist

  ● S63.59   Other specified sprain of wrist

    ● S63.591   Other specified sprain of right wrist

    ● S63.592   Other specified sprain of left wrist

    ● S63.599   Other specified sprain of unspecified wrist

● S63.6   Other and unspecified sprain of finger(s)
   Excludes1   traumatic rupture of ligament of finger at metacarpophalangeal and interphalangeal joint(s) (S63.4-)

  ● S63.60   Unspecified sprain of thumb

    ● S63.601   Unspecified sprain of right thumb

    ● S63.602   Unspecified sprain of left thumb

    ● S63.609   Unspecified sprain of unspecified thumb

  ● S63.61   Unspecified sprain of other and unspecified finger(s)

    ● S63.610   Unspecified sprain of right index finger

    ● S63.611   Unspecified sprain of left index finger

    ● S63.612   Unspecified sprain of right middle finger

    ● S63.613   Unspecified sprain of left middle finger

    ● S63.614   Unspecified sprain of right ring finger

    ● S63.615   Unspecified sprain of left ring finger

    ● S63.616   Unspecified sprain of right little finger

CHAPTER 19 (S00-T88)

- S63.617   Unspecified sprain of left little finger
- S63.618   Unspecified sprain of other finger
  - Unspecified sprain of specified finger with unspecified laterality
- S63.619   Unspecified sprain of unspecified finger
- S63.62   Sprain of interphalangeal joint of thumb
  - S63.621   Sprain of interphalangeal joint of right thumb
  - S63.622   Sprain of interphalangeal joint of left thumb
  - S63.629   Sprain of interphalangeal joint of unspecified thumb
- S63.63   Sprain of interphalangeal joint of other and unspecified finger(s)
  - S63.630   Sprain of interphalangeal joint of right index finger
  - S63.631   Sprain of interphalangeal joint of left index finger
  - S63.632   Sprain of interphalangeal joint of right middle finger
  - S63.633   Sprain of interphalangeal joint of left middle finger
  - S63.634   Sprain of interphalangeal joint of right ring finger
  - S63.635   Sprain of interphalangeal joint of left ring finger
  - S63.636   Sprain of interphalangeal joint of right little finger
  - S63.637   Sprain of interphalangeal joint of left little finger
  - S63.638   Sprain of interphalangeal joint of other finger
  - S63.639   Sprain of interphalangeal joint of unspecified finger
- S63.64   Sprain of metacarpophalangeal joint of thumb
  - S63.641   Sprain of metacarpophalangeal joint of right thumb
  - S63.642   Sprain of metacarpophalangeal joint of left thumb
  - S63.649   Sprain of metacarpophalangeal joint of unspecified thumb
- S63.65   Sprain of metacarpophalangeal joint of other and unspecified finger(s)
  - S63.650   Sprain of metacarpophalangeal joint of right index finger
  - S63.651   Sprain of metacarpophalangeal joint of left index finger
  - S63.652   Sprain of metacarpophalangeal joint of right middle finger
  - S63.653   Sprain of metacarpophalangeal joint of left middle finger
  - S63.654   Sprain of metacarpophalangeal joint of right ring finger
  - S63.655   Sprain of metacarpophalangeal joint of left ring finger
  - S63.656   Sprain of metacarpophalangeal joint of right little finger
  - S63.657   Sprain of metacarpophalangeal joint of left little finger
  - S63.658   Sprain of metacarpophalangeal joint of other finger
    - Sprain of metacarpophalangeal joint of specified finger with unspecified laterality
  - S63.659   Sprain of metacarpophalangeal joint of unspecified finger

- S63.68   Other sprain of thumb
  - S63.681   Other sprain of right thumb
  - S63.682   Other sprain of left thumb
  - S63.689   Other sprain of unspecified thumb
- S63.69   Other sprain of other and unspecified finger(s)
  - S63.690   Other sprain of right index finger
  - S63.691   Other sprain of left index finger
  - S63.692   Other sprain of right middle finger
  - S63.693   Other sprain of left middle finger
  - S63.694   Other sprain of right ring finger
  - S63.695   Other sprain of left ring finger
  - S63.696   Other sprain of right little finger
  - S63.697   Other sprain of left little finger
  - S63.698   Other sprain of other finger
    - Other sprain of specified finger with unspecified laterality
  - S63.699   Other sprain of unspecified finger
- S63.8   Sprain of other part of wrist and hand
  - S63.8X   Sprain of other part of wrist and hand
    - S63.8X1   Sprain of other part of right wrist and hand
    - S63.8X2   Sprain of other part of left wrist and hand
    - S63.8X9   Sprain of other part of unspecified wrist and hand
- S63.9   Sprain of unspecified part of wrist and hand
  - X S63.90   Sprain of unspecified part of unspecified wrist and hand
  - X S63.91   Sprain of unspecified part of right wrist and hand
  - X S63.92   Sprain of unspecified part of left wrist and hand

- S64   Injury of nerves at wrist and hand level

  The appropriate 7th character is to be added to each code from category S64

A	initial encounter
D	subsequent encounter
S	sequela

  Code also any associated open wound (S61.-)

  - S64.0   Injury of ulnar nerve at wrist and hand level
    - X S64.00   Injury of ulnar nerve at wrist and hand level of unspecified arm
    - X S64.01   Injury of ulnar nerve at wrist and hand level of right arm
    - X S64.02   Injury of ulnar nerve at wrist and hand level of left arm
  - S64.1   Injury of median nerve at wrist and hand level
    - X S64.10   Injury of median nerve at wrist and hand level of unspecified arm
    - X S64.11   Injury of median nerve at wrist and hand level of right arm
    - X S64.12   Injury of median nerve at wrist and hand level of left arm
  - S64.2   Injury of radial nerve at wrist and hand level
    - X S64.20   Injury of radial nerve at wrist and hand level of unspecified arm
    - X S64.21   Injury of radial nerve at wrist and hand level of right arm
    - X S64.22   Injury of radial nerve at wrist and hand level of left arm
  - S64.3   Injury of digital nerve of thumb
    - X S64.30   Injury of digital nerve of unspecified thumb
    - X S64.31   Injury of digital nerve of right thumb
    - X S64.32   Injury of digital nerve of left thumb

● **S64.4**   Injury of digital nerve of other and unspecified finger
   X ● **S64.40**   Injury of digital nerve of unspecified finger
     ● **S64.49**   Injury of digital nerve of other finger
       ● **S64.490**   Injury of digital nerve of right index finger
       ● **S64.491**   Injury of digital nerve of left index finger
       ● **S64.492**   Injury of digital nerve of right middle finger
       ● **S64.493**   Injury of digital nerve of left middle finger
       ● **S64.494**   Injury of digital nerve of right ring finger
       ● **S64.495**   Injury of digital nerve of left ring finger
       ● **S64.496**   Injury of digital nerve of right little finger
       ● **S64.497**   Injury of digital nerve of left little finger
       ● **S64.498**   Injury of digital nerve of other finger
           Injury of digital nerve of specified finger with unspecified laterality

● **S64.8**   Injury of other nerves at wrist and hand level
     ● **S64.8X**   Injury of other nerves at wrist and hand level
       ● **S64.8X1**   Injury of other nerves at wrist and hand level of right arm
       ● **S64.8X2**   Injury of other nerves at wrist and hand level of left arm
       ● **S64.8X9**   Injury of other nerves at wrist and hand level of unspecified arm

● **S64.9**   Injury of unspecified nerve at wrist and hand level
   X ● **S64.90**   Injury of unspecified nerve at wrist and hand level of unspecified arm
   X ● **S64.91**   Injury of unspecified nerve at wrist and hand level of right arm
   X ● **S64.92**   Injury of unspecified nerve at wrist and hand level of left arm

● **S65**   **Injury of blood vessels at wrist and hand level**
     The appropriate 7th character is to be added to each code from category S65

A	initial encounter
D	subsequent encounter
S	sequela

     Code also any associated open wound (S61.-)

● **S65.0**   Injury of ulnar artery at wrist and hand level
     ● **S65.00**   Unspecified injury of ulnar artery at wrist and hand level
       ● **S65.001**   Unspecified injury of ulnar artery at wrist and hand level of right arm
       ● **S65.002**   Unspecified injury of ulnar artery at wrist and hand level of left arm
       ● **S65.009**   Unspecified injury of ulnar artery at wrist and hand level of unspecified arm
     ● **S65.01**   Laceration of ulnar artery at wrist and hand level
       ● **S65.011**   Laceration of ulnar artery at wrist and hand level of right arm
       ● **S65.012**   Laceration of ulnar artery at wrist and hand level of left arm
       ● **S65.019**   Laceration of ulnar artery at wrist and hand level of unspecified arm

● **S65.09**   Other specified injury of ulnar artery at wrist and hand level
       ● **S65.091**   Other specified injury of ulnar artery at wrist and hand level of right arm
       ● **S65.092**   Other specified injury of ulnar artery at wrist and hand level of left arm
       ● **S65.099**   Other specified injury of ulnar artery at wrist and hand level of unspecified arm

● **S65.1**   Injury of radial artery at wrist and hand level
     ● **S65.10**   Unspecified injury of radial artery at wrist and hand level
       ● **S65.101**   Unspecified injury of radial artery at wrist and hand level of right arm
       ● **S65.102**   Unspecified injury of radial artery at wrist and hand level of left arm
       ● **S65.109**   Unspecified injury of radial artery at wrist and hand level of unspecified arm
     ● **S65.11**   Laceration of radial artery at wrist and hand level
       ● **S65.111**   Laceration of radial artery at wrist and hand level of right arm
       ● **S65.112**   Laceration of radial artery at wrist and hand level of left arm
       ● **S65.119**   Laceration of radial artery at wrist and hand level of unspecified arm
     ● **S65.19**   Other specified injury of radial artery at wrist and hand level
       ● **S65.191**   Other specified injury of radial artery at wrist and hand level of right arm
       ● **S65.192**   Other specified injury of radial artery at wrist and hand level of left arm
       ● **S65.199**   Other specified injury of radial artery at wrist and hand level of unspecified arm

● **S65.2**   Injury of superficial palmar arch
     ● **S65.20**   Unspecified injury of superficial palmar arch
       ● **S65.201**   Unspecified injury of superficial palmar arch of right hand
       ● **S65.202**   Unspecified injury of superficial palmar arch of left hand
       ● **S65.209**   Unspecified injury of superficial palmar arch of unspecified hand
     ● **S65.21**   Laceration of superficial palmar arch
       ● **S65.211**   Laceration of superficial palmar arch of right hand
       ● **S65.212**   Laceration of superficial palmar arch of left hand
       ● **S65.219**   Laceration of superficial palmar arch of unspecified hand
     ● **S65.29**   Other specified injury of superficial palmar arch
       ● **S65.291**   Other specified injury of superficial palmar arch of right hand
       ● **S65.292**   Other specified injury of superficial palmar arch of left hand
       ● **S65.299**   Other specified injury of superficial palmar arch of unspecified hand

● **S65.3**   Injury of deep palmar arch
     ● **S65.30**   Unspecified injury of deep palmar arch
       ● **S65.301**   Unspecified injury of deep palmar arch of right hand
       ● **S65.302**   Unspecified injury of deep palmar arch of left hand
       ● **S65.309**   Unspecified injury of deep palmar arch of unspecified hand

CHAPTER 19 (S00-T88)

● S65.31　Laceration of deep palmar arch
　● S65.311　Laceration of deep palmar arch of right hand
　● S65.312　Laceration of deep palmar arch of left hand
　● S65.319　Laceration of deep palmar arch of unspecified hand
● S65.39　Other specified injury of deep palmar arch
　● S65.391　Other specified injury of deep palmar arch of right hand
　● S65.392　Other specified injury of deep palmar arch of left hand
　● S65.399　Other specified injury of deep palmar arch of unspecified hand
● S65.4　Injury of blood vessel of thumb
　● S65.40　Unspecified injury of blood vessel of thumb
　　● S65.401　Unspecified injury of blood vessel of right thumb
　　● S65.402　Unspecified injury of blood vessel of left thumb
　　● S65.409　Unspecified injury of blood vessel of unspecified thumb
　● S65.41　Laceration of blood vessel of thumb
　　● S65.411　Laceration of blood vessel of right thumb
　　● S65.412　Laceration of blood vessel of left thumb
　　● S65.419　Laceration of blood vessel of unspecified thumb
　● S65.49　Other specified injury of blood vessel of thumb
　　● S65.491　Other specified injury of blood vessel of right thumb
　　● S65.492　Other specified injury of blood vessel of left thumb
　　● S65.499　Other specified injury of blood vessel of unspecified thumb
● S65.5　Injury of blood vessel of other and unspecified finger
　● S65.50　Unspecified injury of blood vessel of other and unspecified finger
　　● S65.500　Unspecified injury of blood vessel of right index finger
　　● S65.501　Unspecified injury of blood vessel of left index finger
　　● S65.502　Unspecified injury of blood vessel of right middle finger
　　● S65.503　Unspecified injury of blood vessel of left middle finger
　　● S65.504　Unspecified injury of blood vessel of right ring finger
　　● S65.505　Unspecified injury of blood vessel of left ring finger
　　● S65.506　Unspecified injury of blood vessel of right little finger
　　● S65.507　Unspecified injury of blood vessel of left little finger
　　● S65.508　Unspecified injury of blood vessel of other finger
　　　　　　Unspecified injury of blood vessel of specified finger with unspecified laterality
　　● S65.509　Unspecified injury of blood vessel of unspecified finger

● S65.51　Laceration of blood vessel of other and unspecified finger
　● S65.510　Laceration of blood vessel of right index finger
　● S65.511　Laceration of blood vessel of left index finger
　● S65.512　Laceration of blood vessel of right middle finger
　● S65.513　Laceration of blood vessel of left middle finger
　● S65.514　Laceration of blood vessel of right ring finger
　● S65.515　Laceration of blood vessel of left ring finger
　● S65.516　Laceration of blood vessel of right little finger
　● S65.517　Laceration of blood vessel of left little finger
　● S65.518　Laceration of blood vessel of other finger
　　　　　Laceration of blood vessel of specified finger with unspecified laterality
　● S65.519　Laceration of blood vessel of unspecified finger
● S65.59　Other specified injury of blood vessel of other and unspecified finger
　● S65.590　Other specified injury of blood vessel of right index finger
　● S65.591　Other specified injury of blood vessel of left index finger
　● S65.592　Other specified injury of blood vessel of right middle finger
　● S65.593　Other specified injury of blood vessel of left middle finger
　● S65.594　Other specified injury of blood vessel of right ring finger
　● S65.595　Other specified injury of blood vessel of left ring finger
　● S65.596　Other specified injury of blood vessel of right little finger
　● S65.597　Other specified injury of blood vessel of left little finger
　● S65.598　Other specified injury of blood vessel of other finger
　　　　　Other specified injury of blood vessel of specified finger with unspecified laterality
　● S65.599　Other specified injury of blood vessel of unspecified finger
● S65.8　Injury of other blood vessels at wrist and hand level
　● S65.80　Unspecified injury of other blood vessels at wrist and hand level
　　● S65.801　Unspecified injury of other blood vessels at wrist and hand level of right arm
　　● S65.802　Unspecified injury of other blood vessels at wrist and hand level of left arm
　　● S65.809　Unspecified injury of other blood vessels at wrist and hand level of unspecified arm
　● S65.81　Laceration of other blood vessels at wrist and hand level
　　● S65.811　Laceration of other blood vessels at wrist and hand level of right arm
　　● S65.812　Laceration of other blood vessels at wrist and hand level of left arm
　　● S65.819　Laceration of other blood vessels at wrist and hand level of unspecified arm

▶ New　⇒ Revised　deleted Deleted　Excludes 1　Excludes 2　Includes　Use additional　Code first　Code also　Key words
OGCR Official Guidelines　X Assign placeholder X　▶ Use Additional Character(s)　▶ Manifestation Code　Coding Clinic

● **S65.89**   Other specified injury of other blood vessels at wrist and hand level

    ● **S65.891**   Other specified injury of other blood vessels at wrist and hand level of right arm

    ● **S65.892**   Other specified injury of other blood vessels at wrist and hand level of left arm

    ● **S65.899**   Other specified injury of other blood vessels at wrist and hand level of unspecified arm

● **S65.9**   Injury of unspecified blood vessel at wrist and hand level

   ● **S65.90**   Unspecified injury of unspecified blood vessel at wrist and hand level

    ● **S65.901**   Unspecified injury of unspecified blood vessel at wrist and hand level of right arm

    ● **S65.902**   Unspecified injury of unspecified blood vessel at wrist and hand level of left arm

    ● **S65.909**   Unspecified injury of unspecified blood vessel at wrist and hand level of unspecified arm

   ● **S65.91**   Laceration of unspecified blood vessel at wrist and hand level

    ● **S65.911**   Laceration of unspecified blood vessel at wrist and hand level of right arm

    ● **S65.912**   Laceration of unspecified blood vessel at wrist and hand level of left arm

    ● **S65.919**   Laceration of unspecified blood vessel at wrist and hand level of unspecified arm

   ● **S65.99**   Other specified injury of unspecified blood vessel at wrist and hand level

    ● **S65.991**   Other specified injury of unspecified blood vessel at wrist and hand of right arm

    ● **S65.992**   Other specified injury of unspecified blood vessel at wrist and hand of left arm

    ● **S65.999**   Other specified injury of unspecified blood vessel at wrist and hand of unspecified arm

● **S66**   **Injury of muscle, fascia and tendon at wrist and hand level**

   Code also any associated open wound (S61.-)

   Excludes2   sprain of joints and ligaments of wrist and hand (S63.-)

   The appropriate 7th character is to be added to each code from category S66

A	initial encounter
D	subsequent encounter
S	sequela

  ● **S66.0**   Injury of long flexor muscle, fascia and tendon of thumb at wrist and hand level

   ● **S66.00**   Unspecified injury of long flexor muscle, fascia and tendon of thumb at wrist and hand level

    ● **S66.001**   Unspecified injury of long flexor muscle, fascia and tendon of right thumb at wrist and hand level

    ● **S66.002**   Unspecified injury of long flexor muscle, fascia and tendon of left thumb at wrist and hand level

    ● **S66.009**   Unspecified injury of long flexor muscle, fascia and tendon of unspecified thumb at wrist and hand level

● **S66.01**   Strain of long flexor muscle, fascia and tendon of thumb at wrist and hand level

   ● **S66.011**   Strain of long flexor muscle, fascia and tendon of right thumb at wrist and hand level

   ● **S66.012**   Strain of long flexor muscle, fascia and tendon of left thumb at wrist and hand level

   ● **S66.019**   Strain of long flexor muscle, fascia and tendon of unspecified thumb at wrist and hand level

● **S66.02**   Laceration of long flexor muscle, fascia and tendon of thumb at wrist and hand level

   ● **S66.021**   Laceration of long flexor muscle, fascia and tendon of right thumb at wrist and hand level

   ● **S66.022**   Laceration of long flexor muscle, fascia and tendon of left thumb at wrist and hand level

   ● **S66.029**   Laceration of long flexor muscle, fascia and tendon of unspecified thumb at wrist and hand level

● **S66.09**   Other specified injury of long flexor muscle, fascia and tendon of thumb at wrist and hand level

   ● **S66.091**   Other specified injury of long flexor muscle, fascia and tendon of right thumb at wrist and hand level

   ● **S66.092**   Other specified injury of long flexor muscle, fascia and tendon of left thumb at wrist and hand level

   ● **S66.099**   Other specified injury of long flexor muscle, fascia and tendon of unspecified thumb at wrist and hand level

● **S66.1**   Injury of flexor muscle, fascia and tendon of other and unspecified finger at wrist and hand level

   Excludes2   injury of long flexor muscle, fascia and tendon of thumb at wrist and hand level (S66.0-)

  ● **S66.10**   Unspecified injury of flexor muscle, fascia and tendon of other and unspecified finger at wrist and hand level

   ● **S66.100**   Unspecified injury of flexor muscle, fascia and tendon of right index finger at wrist and hand level

   ● **S66.101**   Unspecified injury of flexor muscle, fascia and tendon of left index finger at wrist and hand level

   ● **S66.102**   Unspecified injury of flexor muscle, fascia and tendon of right middle finger at wrist and hand level

   ● **S66.103**   Unspecified injury of flexor muscle, fascia and tendon of left middle finger at wrist and hand level

   ● **S66.104**   Unspecified injury of flexor muscle, fascia and tendon of right ring finger at wrist and hand level

   ● **S66.105**   Unspecified injury of flexor muscle, fascia and tendon of left ring finger at wrist and hand level

   ● **S66.106**   Unspecified injury of flexor muscle, fascia and tendon of right little finger at wrist and hand level

   ● **S66.107**   Unspecified injury of flexor muscle, fascia and tendon of left little finger at wrist and hand level

● S66.108 Unspecified injury of flexor muscle, fascia and tendon of other finger at wrist and hand level
         Unspecified injury of flexor muscle, fascia and tendon of specified finger with unspecified laterality at wrist and hand level

● S66.109 Unspecified injury of flexor muscle, fascia and tendon of unspecified finger at wrist and hand level

● S66.11 Strain of flexor muscle, fascia and tendon of other and unspecified finger at wrist and hand level

● S66.110 Strain of flexor muscle, fascia and tendon of right index finger at wrist and hand level

● S66.111 Strain of flexor muscle, fascia and tendon of left index finger at wrist and hand level

● S66.112 Strain of flexor muscle, fascia and tendon of right middle finger at wrist and hand level

● S66.113 Strain of flexor muscle, fascia and tendon of left middle finger at wrist and hand level

● S66.114 Strain of flexor muscle, fascia and tendon of right ring finger at wrist and hand level

● S66.115 Strain of flexor muscle, fascia and tendon of left ring finger at wrist and hand level

● S66.116 Strain of flexor muscle, fascia and tendon of right little finger at wrist and hand level

● S66.117 Strain of flexor muscle, fascia and tendon of left little finger at wrist and hand level

● S66.118 Strain of flexor muscle, fascia and tendon of other finger at wrist and hand level
         Strain of flexor muscle, fascia and tendon of specified finger with unspecified laterality at wrist and hand level

● S66.119 Strain of flexor muscle, fascia and tendon of unspecified finger at wrist and hand level

● S66.12 Laceration of flexor muscle, fascia and tendon of other and unspecified finger at wrist and hand level

● S66.120 Laceration of flexor muscle, fascia and tendon of right index finger at wrist and hand level

● S66.121 Laceration of flexor muscle, fascia and tendon of left index finger at wrist and hand level

● S66.122 Laceration of flexor muscle, fascia and tendon of right middle finger at wrist and hand level

● S66.123 Laceration of flexor muscle, fascia and tendon of left middle finger at wrist and hand level

● S66.124 Laceration of flexor muscle, fascia and tendon of right ring finger at wrist and hand level

● S66.125 Laceration of flexor muscle, fascia and tendon of left ring finger at wrist and hand level

● S66.126 Laceration of flexor muscle, fascia and tendon of right little finger at wrist and hand level

● S66.127 Laceration of flexor muscle, fascia and tendon of left little finger at wrist and hand level

● S66.128 Laceration of flexor muscle, fascia and tendon of other finger at wrist and hand level
         Laceration of flexor muscle, fascia and tendon of specified finger with unspecified laterality at wrist and hand level

● S66.129 Laceration of flexor muscle, fascia and tendon of unspecified finger at wrist and hand level

● S66.19 Other injury of flexor muscle, fascia and tendon of other and unspecified finger at wrist and hand level

● S66.190 Other injury of flexor muscle, fascia and tendon of right index finger at wrist and hand level

● S66.191 Other injury of flexor muscle, fascia and tendon of left index finger at wrist and hand level

● S66.192 Other injury of flexor muscle, fascia and tendon of right middle finger at wrist and hand level

● S66.193 Other injury of flexor muscle, fascia and tendon of left middle finger at wrist and hand level

● S66.194 Other injury of flexor muscle, fascia and tendon of right ring finger at wrist and hand level

● S66.195 Other injury of flexor muscle, fascia and tendon of left ring finger at wrist and hand level

● S66.196 Other injury of flexor muscle, fascia and tendon of right little finger at wrist and hand level

● S66.197 Other injury of flexor muscle, fascia and tendon of left little finger at wrist and hand level

● S66.198 Other injury of flexor muscle, fascia and tendon of other finger at wrist and hand level
         Other injury of flexor muscle, fascia and tendon of specified finger with unspecified laterality at wrist and hand level

● S66.199 Other injury of flexor muscle, fascia and tendon of unspecified finger at wrist and hand level

● S66.2 Injury of extensor muscle, fascia and tendon of thumb at wrist and hand level

● S66.20 Unspecified injury of extensor muscle, fascia and tendon of thumb at wrist and hand level

● S66.201 Unspecified injury of extensor muscle, fascia and tendon of right thumb at wrist and hand level

● S66.202 Unspecified injury of extensor muscle, fascia and tendon of left thumb at wrist and hand level

● S66.209 Unspecified injury of extensor muscle, fascia and tendon of unspecified thumb at wrist and hand level

▶ New   ⇒ Revised   ~~deleted~~ Deleted   Excludes 1   Excludes 2   Includes   Use additional   Code first   Code also   Key words
OGCR Official Guidelines   X Assign placeholder X   ● Use Additional Character(s)   ▶ Manifestation Code   Coding Clinic

CHAPTER 19 (S00-T88)

● **S66.21**   Strain of extensor muscle, fascia and tendon of thumb at wrist and hand level

    ● **S66.211**   Strain of extensor muscle, fascia and tendon of right thumb at wrist and hand level

    ● **S66.212**   Strain of extensor muscle, fascia and tendon of left thumb at wrist and hand level

    ● **S66.219**   Strain of extensor muscle, fascia and tendon of unspecified thumb at wrist and hand level

● **S66.22**   Laceration of extensor muscle, fascia and tendon of thumb at wrist and hand level

    ● **S66.221**   Laceration of extensor muscle, fascia and tendon of right thumb at wrist and hand level

    ● **S66.222**   Laceration of extensor muscle, fascia and tendon of left thumb at wrist and hand level

    ● **S66.229**   Laceration of extensor muscle, fascia and tendon of unspecified thumb at wrist and hand level

● **S66.29**   Other specified injury of extensor muscle, fascia and tendon of thumb at wrist and hand level

    ● **S66.291**   Other specified injury of extensor muscle, fascia and tendon of right thumb at wrist and hand level

    ● **S66.292**   Other specified injury of extensor muscle, fascia and tendon of left thumb at wrist and hand level

    ● **S66.299**   Other specified injury of extensor muscle, fascia and tendon of unspecified thumb at wrist and hand level

● **S66.3**   Injury of extensor muscle, fascia and tendon of other and unspecified finger at wrist and hand level

    Excludes2   injury of extensor muscle, fascia and tendon of thumb at wrist and hand level (S66.2-)

  ● **S66.30**   Unspecified injury of extensor muscle, fascia and tendon of other and unspecified finger at wrist and hand level

    ● **S66.300**   Unspecified injury of extensor muscle, fascia and tendon of right index finger at wrist and hand level

    ● **S66.301**   Unspecified injury of extensor muscle, fascia and tendon of left index finger at wrist and hand level

    ● **S66.302**   Unspecified injury of extensor muscle, fascia and tendon of right middle finger at wrist and hand level

    ● **S66.303**   Unspecified injury of extensor muscle, fascia and tendon of left middle finger at wrist and hand level

    ● **S66.304**   Unspecified injury of extensor muscle, fascia and tendon of right ring finger at wrist and hand level

    ● **S66.305**   Unspecified injury of extensor muscle, fascia and tendon of left ring finger at wrist and hand level

    ● **S66.306**   Unspecified injury of extensor muscle, fascia and tendon of right little finger at wrist and hand level

    ● **S66.307**   Unspecified injury of extensor muscle, fascia and tendon of left little finger at wrist and hand level

● **S66.308**   Unspecified injury of extensor muscle, fascia and tendon of other finger at wrist and hand level

    Unspecified injury of extensor muscle, fascia and tendon of specified finger with unspecified laterality at wrist and hand level

● **S66.309**   Unspecified injury of extensor muscle, fascia and tendon of unspecified finger at wrist and hand level

● **S66.31**   Strain of extensor muscle, fascia and tendon of other and unspecified finger at wrist and hand level

    ● **S66.310**   Strain of extensor muscle, fascia and tendon of right index finger at wrist and hand level

    ● **S66.311**   Strain of extensor muscle, fascia and tendon of left index finger at wrist and hand level

    ● **S66.312**   Strain of extensor muscle, fascia and tendon of right middle finger at wrist and hand level

    ● **S66.313**   Strain of extensor muscle, fascia and tendon of left middle finger at wrist and hand level

    ● **S66.314**   Strain of extensor muscle, fascia and tendon of right ring finger at wrist and hand level

    ● **S66.315**   Strain of extensor muscle, fascia and tendon of left ring finger at wrist and hand level

    ● **S66.316**   Strain of extensor muscle, fascia and tendon of right little finger at wrist and hand level

    ● **S66.317**   Strain of extensor muscle, fascia and tendon of left little finger at wrist and hand level

    ● **S66.318**   Strain of extensor muscle, fascia and tendon of other finger at wrist and hand level

    Strain of extensor muscle, fascia and tendon of specified finger with unspecified laterality at wrist and hand level

    ● **S66.319**   Strain of extensor muscle, fascia and tendon of unspecified finger at wrist and hand level

● **S66.32**   Laceration of extensor muscle, fascia and tendon of other and unspecified finger at wrist and hand level

    ● **S66.320**   Laceration of extensor muscle, fascia and tendon of right index finger at wrist and hand level

    ● **S66.321**   Laceration of extensor muscle, fascia and tendon of left index finger at wrist and hand level

    ● **S66.322**   Laceration of extensor muscle, fascia and tendon of right middle finger at wrist and hand level

    ● **S66.323**   Laceration of extensor muscle, fascia and tendon of left middle finger at wrist and hand level

    ● **S66.324**   Laceration of extensor muscle, fascia and tendon of right ring finger at wrist and hand level

CHAPTER 19 (S00-T88)

S66.325   Laceration of extensor muscle, fascia and tendon of left ring finger at wrist and hand level

S66.326   Laceration of extensor muscle, fascia and tendon of right little finger at wrist and hand level

S66.327   Laceration of extensor muscle, fascia and tendon of left little finger at wrist and hand level

S66.328   Laceration of extensor muscle, fascia and tendon of other finger at wrist and hand level

     Laceration of extensor muscle, fascia and tendon of specified finger with unspecified laterality at wrist and hand level

S66.329   Laceration of extensor muscle, fascia and tendon of unspecified finger at wrist and hand level

● S66.39   Other injury of extensor muscle, fascia and tendon of other and unspecified finger at wrist and hand level

    S66.390   Other injury of extensor muscle, fascia and tendon of right index finger at wrist and hand level

    S66.391   Other injury of extensor muscle, fascia and tendon of left index finger at wrist and hand level

    S66.392   Other injury of extensor muscle, fascia and tendon of right middle finger at wrist and hand level

    S66.393   Other injury of extensor muscle, fascia and tendon of left middle finger at wrist and hand level

    S66.394   Other injury of extensor muscle, fascia and tendon of right ring finger at wrist and hand level

    S66.395   Other injury of extensor muscle, fascia and tendon of left ring finger at wrist and hand level

    S66.396   Other injury of extensor muscle, fascia and tendon of right little finger at wrist and hand level

    S66.397   Other injury of extensor muscle, fascia and tendon of left little finger at wrist and hand level

    S66.398   Other injury of extensor muscle, fascia and tendon of other finger at wrist and hand level

      Other injury of extensor muscle, fascia and tendon of specified finger with unspecified laterality at wrist and hand level

    S66.399   Other injury of extensor muscle, fascia and tendon of unspecified finger at wrist and hand level

● S66.4   Injury of intrinsic muscle, fascia and tendon of thumb at wrist and hand level

● S66.40   Unspecified injury of intrinsic muscle, fascia and tendon of thumb at wrist and hand level

    ● S66.401   Unspecified injury of intrinsic muscle, fascia and tendon of right thumb at wrist and hand level

    S66.402   Unspecified injury of intrinsic muscle, fascia and tendon of left thumb at wrist and hand level

    S66.409   Unspecified injury of intrinsic muscle, fascia and tendon of unspecified thumb at wrist and hand level

● S66.41   Strain of intrinsic muscle, fascia and tendon of thumb at wrist and hand level

    ● S66.411   Strain of intrinsic muscle, fascia and tendon of right thumb at wrist and hand level

    ● S66.412   Strain of intrinsic muscle, fascia and tendon of left thumb at wrist and hand level

    ● S66.419   Strain of intrinsic muscle, fascia and tendon of unspecified thumb at wrist and hand level

● S66.42   Laceration of intrinsic muscle, fascia and tendon of thumb at wrist and hand level

    ● S66.421   Laceration of intrinsic muscle, fascia and tendon of right thumb at wrist and hand level

    ● S66.422   Laceration of intrinsic muscle, fascia and tendon of left thumb at wrist and hand level

    S66.429   Laceration of intrinsic muscle, fascia and tendon of unspecified thumb at wrist and hand level

● S66.49   Other specified injury of intrinsic muscle, fascia and tendon of thumb at wrist and hand level

    ● S66.491   Other specified injury of intrinsic muscle, fascia and tendon of right thumb at wrist and hand level

    ● S66.492   Other specified injury of intrinsic muscle, fascia and tendon of left thumb at wrist and hand level

    ● S66.499   Other specified injury of intrinsic muscle, fascia and tendon of unspecified thumb at wrist and hand level

● S66.5   Injury of intrinsic muscle, fascia and tendon of other and unspecified finger at wrist and hand level

    Excludes2   injury of intrinsic muscle, fascia and tendon of thumb at wrist and hand level (S66.4-)

● S66.50   Unspecified injury of intrinsic muscle, fascia and tendon of other and unspecified finger at wrist and hand level

    ● S66.500   Unspecified injury of intrinsic muscle, fascia and tendon of right index finger at wrist and hand level

    ● S66.501   Unspecified injury of intrinsic muscle, fascia and tendon of left index finger at wrist and hand level

    ● S66.502   Unspecified injury of intrinsic muscle, fascia and tendon of right middle finger at wrist and hand level

    ● S66.503   Unspecified injury of intrinsic muscle, fascia and tendon of left middle finger at wrist and hand level

    ● S66.504   Unspecified injury of intrinsic muscle, fascia and tendon of right ring finger at wrist and hand level

    ● S66.505   Unspecified injury of intrinsic muscle, fascia and tendon of left ring finger at wrist and hand level

    ● S66.506   Unspecified injury of intrinsic muscle, fascia and tendon of right little finger at wrist and hand level

    ● S66.507   Unspecified injury of intrinsic muscle, fascia and tendon of left little finger at wrist and hand level

▶ New   ⇒ Revised   ~~deleted~~ Deleted   Excludes 1   Excludes 2   Includes   Use additional   Code first   Code also   Key words

OGCR Official Guidelines   X Assign placeholder X   ● Use Additional Character(s)   ▶ Manifestation Code   **Coding Clinic**

● S66.508   Unspecified injury of intrinsic muscle, fascia and tendon of other finger at wrist and hand level
     Unspecified injury of intrinsic muscle, fascia and tendon of specified finger with unspecified laterality at wrist and hand level

● S66.509   Unspecified injury of intrinsic muscle, fascia and tendon of unspecified finger at wrist and hand level

● S66.51   Strain of intrinsic muscle, fascia and tendon of other and unspecified finger at wrist and hand level

● S66.510   Strain of intrinsic muscle, fascia and tendon of right index finger at wrist and hand level

● S66.511   Strain of intrinsic muscle, fascia and tendon of left index finger at wrist and hand level

● S66.512   Strain of intrinsic muscle, fascia and tendon of right middle finger at wrist and hand level

● S66.513   Strain of intrinsic muscle, fascia and tendon of left middle finger at wrist and hand level

● S66.514   Strain of intrinsic muscle, fascia and tendon of right ring finger at wrist and hand level

● S66.515   Strain of intrinsic muscle, fascia and tendon of left ring finger at wrist and hand level

● S66.516   Strain of intrinsic muscle, fascia and tendon of right little finger at wrist and hand level

● S66.517   Strain of intrinsic muscle, fascia and tendon of left little finger at wrist and hand level

● S66.518   Strain of intrinsic muscle, fascia and tendon of other finger at wrist and hand level
     Strain of intrinsic muscle, fascia and tendon of specified finger with unspecified laterality at wrist and hand level

● S66.519   Strain of intrinsic muscle, fascia and tendon of unspecified finger at wrist and hand level

● S66.52   Laceration of intrinsic muscle, fascia and tendon of other and unspecified finger at wrist and hand level

● S66.520   Laceration of intrinsic muscle, fascia and tendon of right index finger at wrist and hand level

● S66.521   Laceration of intrinsic muscle, fascia and tendon of left index finger at wrist and hand level

● S66.522   Laceration of intrinsic muscle, fascia and tendon of right middle finger at wrist and hand level

● S66.523   Laceration of intrinsic muscle, fascia and tendon of left middle finger at wrist and hand level

● S66.524   Laceration of intrinsic muscle, fascia and tendon of right ring finger at wrist and hand level

● S66.525   Laceration of intrinsic muscle, fascia and tendon of left ring finger at wrist and hand level

● S66.526   Laceration of intrinsic muscle, fascia and tendon of right little finger at wrist and hand level

● S66.527   Laceration of intrinsic muscle, fascia and tendon of left little finger at wrist and hand level

● S66.528   Laceration of intrinsic muscle, fascia and tendon of other finger at wrist and hand level
     Laceration of intrinsic muscle, fascia and tendon of specified finger with unspecified laterality at wrist and hand level

● S66.529   Laceration of intrinsic muscle, fascia and tendon of unspecified finger at wrist and hand level

● S66.59   Other injury of intrinsic muscle, fascia and tendon of other and unspecified finger at wrist and hand level

● S66.590   Other injury of intrinsic muscle, fascia and tendon of right index finger at wrist and hand level

● S66.591   Other injury of intrinsic muscle, fascia and tendon of left index finger at wrist and hand level

● S66.592   Other injury of intrinsic muscle, fascia and tendon of right middle finger at wrist and hand level

● S66.593   Other injury of intrinsic muscle, fascia and tendon of left middle finger at wrist and hand level

● S66.594   Other injury of intrinsic muscle, fascia and tendon of right ring finger at wrist and hand level

● S66.595   Other injury of intrinsic muscle, fascia and tendon of left ring finger at wrist and hand level

● S66.596   Other injury of intrinsic muscle, fascia and tendon of right little finger at wrist and hand level

● S66.597   Other injury of intrinsic muscle, fascia and tendon of left little finger at wrist and hand level

● S66.598   Other injury of intrinsic muscle, fascia and tendon of other finger at wrist and hand level
     Other injury of intrinsic muscle, fascia and tendon of specified finger with unspecified laterality at wrist and hand level

● S66.599   Other injury of intrinsic muscle, fascia and tendon of unspecified finger at wrist and hand level

● S66.8   Injury of other specified muscles, fascia and tendons at wrist and hand level

● S66.80   Unspecified injury of other specified muscles, fascia and tendons at wrist and hand level

● S66.801   Unspecified injury of other specified muscles, fascia and tendons at wrist and hand level, right hand

● S66.802   Unspecified injury of other specified muscles, fascia and tendons at wrist and hand level, left hand

● S66.809   Unspecified injury of other specified muscles, fascia and tendons at wrist and hand level, unspecified hand

● **S66.81** Strain of other specified muscles, fascia and tendons at wrist and hand level
- ● **S66.811** Strain of other specified muscles, fascia and tendons at wrist and hand level, right hand
- ● **S66.812** Strain of other specified muscles, fascia and tendons at wrist and hand level, left hand
- ● **S66.819** Strain of other specified muscles, fascia and tendons at wrist and hand level, unspecified hand

● **S66.82** Laceration of other specified muscles, fascia and tendons at wrist and hand level
- ● **S66.821** Laceration of other specified muscles, fascia and tendons at wrist and hand level, right hand
- ● **S66.822** Laceration of other specified muscles, fascia and tendons at wrist and hand level, left hand
- ● **S66.829** Laceration of other specified muscles, fascia and tendons at wrist and hand level, unspecified hand

● **S66.89** Other injury of other specified muscles, fascia and tendons at wrist and hand level
- ● **S66.891** Other injury of other specified muscles, fascia and tendons at wrist and hand level, right hand
- ● **S66.892** Other injury of other specified muscles, fascia and tendons at wrist and hand level, left hand
- ● **S66.899** Other injury of other specified muscles, fascia and tendons at wrist and hand level, unspecified hand

● **S66.9** Injury of unspecified muscle, fascia and tendon at wrist and hand level
- ● **S66.90** Unspecified injury of unspecified muscle, fascia and tendon at wrist and hand level
  - ● **S66.901** Unspecified injury of unspecified muscle, fascia and tendon at wrist and hand level, right hand
  - ● **S66.902** Unspecified injury of unspecified muscle, fascia and tendon at wrist and hand level, left hand
  - ● **S66.909** Unspecified injury of unspecified muscle, fascia and tendon at wrist and hand level, unspecified hand
- ● **S66.91** Strain of unspecified muscle, fascia and tendon at wrist and hand level
  - ● **S66.911** Strain of unspecified muscle, fascia and tendon at wrist and hand level, right hand
  - ● **S66.912** Strain of unspecified muscle, fascia and tendon at wrist and hand level, left hand
  - ● **S66.919** Strain of unspecified muscle, fascia and tendon at wrist and hand level, unspecified hand
- ● **S66.92** Laceration of unspecified muscle, fascia and tendon at wrist and hand level
  - ● **S66.921** Laceration of unspecified muscle, fascia and tendon at wrist and hand level, right hand
  - ● **S66.922** Laceration of unspecified muscle, fascia and tendon at wrist and hand level, left hand
  - ● **S66.929** Laceration of unspecified muscle, fascia and tendon at wrist and hand level, unspecified hand

● **S66.99** Other injury of unspecified muscle, fascia and tendon at wrist and hand level
- ● **S66.991** Other injury of unspecified muscle, fascia and tendon at wrist and hand level, right hand
- ● **S66.992** Other injury of unspecified muscle, fascia and tendon at wrist and hand level, left hand
- ● **S66.999** Other injury of unspecified muscle, fascia and tendon at wrist and hand level, unspecified hand

● **S67** Crushing injury of wrist, hand and fingers

Use additional code for all associated injuries, such as:
fracture of wrist and hand (S62.-)
open wound of wrist and hand (S61.-)

The appropriate 7th character is to be added to each code from category S67

A	initial encounter
D	subsequent encounter
S	sequela

● **S67.0** Crushing injury of thumb
- X ● **S67.00** Crushing injury of unspecified thumb
- X ● **S67.01** Crushing injury of right thumb
- X ● **S67.02** Crushing injury of left thumb

● **S67.1** Crushing injury of other and unspecified finger(s)
> **Excludes2**   crushing injury of thumb (S67.0-)
- X ● **S67.10** Crushing injury of unspecified finger(s)
- ● **S67.19** Crushing injury of other finger(s)
  - ● **S67.190** Crushing injury of right index finger
  - ● **S67.191** Crushing injury of left index finger
  - ● **S67.192** Crushing injury of right middle finger
  - ● **S67.193** Crushing injury of left middle finger
  - ● **S67.194** Crushing injury of right ring finger
  - ● **S67.195** Crushing injury of left ring finger
  - ● **S67.196** Crushing injury of right little finger
  - ● **S67.197** Crushing injury of left little finger
  - ● **S67.198** Crushing injury of other finger
    Crushing injury of specified finger with unspecified laterality

● **S67.2** Crushing injury of hand
> **Excludes2**   crushing injury of fingers (S67.1-)
>   crushing injury of thumb (S67.0-)
- X ● **S67.20** Crushing injury of unspecified hand
- X ● **S67.21** Crushing injury of right hand
- X ● **S67.22** Crushing injury of left hand

● **S67.3** Crushing injury of wrist
- X ● **S67.30** Crushing injury of unspecified wrist
- X ● **S67.31** Crushing injury of right wrist
- X ● **S67.32** Crushing injury of left wrist

● **S67.4** Crushing injury of wrist and hand
> **Excludes1**   crushing injury of hand alone (S67.2-)
>   crushing injury of wrist alone (S67.3-)
>
> **Excludes2**   crushing injury of fingers (S67.1-)
>   crushing injury of thumb (S67.0-)
- X ● **S67.40** Crushing injury of unspecified wrist and hand
- X ● **S67.41** Crushing injury of right wrist and hand
- X ● **S67.42** Crushing injury of left wrist and hand

● **S67.9** Crushing injury of unspecified part(s) of wrist, hand and fingers
- X ● **S67.90** Crushing injury of unspecified part(s) of unspecified wrist, hand and fingers
- X ● **S67.91** Crushing injury of unspecified part(s) of right wrist, hand and fingers
- X ● **S67.92** Crushing injury of unspecified part(s) of left wrist, hand and fingers

▶ New   ⟹ Revised   ~~deleted~~ Deleted   Excludes 1   Excludes 2   Includes   Use additional   Code first   Code also   Key words

OGCR Official Guidelines   X Assign placeholder X   ● Use Additional Character(s)   ▶ Manifestation Code   **Coding Clinic**

● **S68**   Traumatic amputation of wrist, hand and fingers

    An amputation not identified as partial or complete should be coded to complete

    The appropriate 7th character is to be added to each code from category S68

A	initial encounter
D	subsequent encounter
S	sequela

  ● **S68.0**   Traumatic metacarpophalangeal amputation of thumb

      Traumatic amputation of thumb NOS

    ● **S68.01**   Complete traumatic metacarpophalangeal amputation of thumb

      ● **S68.011**   Complete traumatic metacarpophalangeal amputation of right thumb

      ● **S68.012**   Complete traumatic metacarpophalangeal amputation of left thumb

      ● **S68.019**   Complete traumatic metacarpophalangeal amputation of unspecified thumb

    ● **S68.02**   Partial traumatic metacarpophalangeal amputation of thumb

      ● **S68.021**   Partial traumatic metacarpophalangeal amputation of right thumb

      ● **S68.022**   Partial traumatic metacarpophalangeal amputation of left thumb

      ● **S68.029**   Partial traumatic metacarpophalangeal amputation of unspecified thumb

  ● **S68.1**   Traumatic metacarpophalangeal amputation of other and unspecified finger

      Traumatic amputation of finger NOS

      Excludes2   traumatic metacarpophalangeal amputation of thumb (S68.0-)

    ● **S68.11**   Complete traumatic metacarpophalangeal amputation of other and unspecified finger

      ● **S68.110**   Complete traumatic metacarpophalangeal amputation of right index finger

      ● **S68.111**   Complete traumatic metacarpophalangeal amputation of left index finger

      ● **S68.112**   Complete traumatic metacarpophalangeal amputation of right middle finger

      ● **S68.113**   Complete traumatic metacarpophalangeal amputation of left middle finger

      ● **S68.114**   Complete traumatic metacarpophalangeal amputation of right ring finger

      ● **S68.115**   Complete traumatic metacarpophalangeal amputation of left ring finger

      ● **S68.116**   Complete traumatic metacarpophalangeal amputation of right little finger

      ● **S68.117**   Complete traumatic metacarpophalangeal amputation of left little finger

      ● **S68.118**   Complete traumatic metacarpophalangeal amputation of other finger

        Complete traumatic metacarpophalangeal amputation of specified finger with unspecified laterality

      ● **S68.119**   Complete traumatic metacarpophalangeal amputation of unspecified finger

  ● **S68.12**   Partial traumatic metacarpophalangeal amputation of other and unspecified finger

    ● **S68.120**   Partial traumatic metacarpophalangeal amputation of right index finger

    ● **S68.121**   Partial traumatic metacarpophalangeal amputation of left index finger

    ● **S68.122**   Partial traumatic metacarpophalangeal amputation of right middle finger

    ● **S68.123**   Partial traumatic metacarpophalangeal amputation of left middle finger

    ● **S68.124**   Partial traumatic metacarpophalangeal amputation of right ring finger

    ● **S68.125**   Partial traumatic metacarpophalangeal amputation of left ring finger

    ● **S68.126**   Partial traumatic metacarpophalangeal amputation of right little finger

    ● **S68.127**   Partial traumatic metacarpophalangeal amputation of left little finger

    ● **S68.128**   Partial traumatic metacarpophalangeal amputation of other finger

      Partial traumatic metacarpophalangeal amputation of specified finger with unspecified laterality

    ● **S68.129**   Partial traumatic metacarpophalangeal amputation of unspecified finger

  ● **S68.4**   Traumatic amputation of hand at wrist level

    Traumatic amputation of hand NOS

    Traumatic amputation of wrist

    ● **S68.41**   Complete traumatic amputation of hand at wrist level

      ● **S68.411**   Complete traumatic amputation of right hand at wrist level

      ● **S68.412**   Complete traumatic amputation of left hand at wrist level

      ● **S68.419**   Complete traumatic amputation of unspecified hand at wrist level

    ● **S68.42**   Partial traumatic amputation of hand at wrist level

      ● **S68.421**   Partial traumatic amputation of right hand at wrist level

      ● **S68.422**   Partial traumatic amputation of left hand at wrist level

      ● **S68.429**   Partial traumatic amputation of unspecified hand at wrist level

  ● **S68.5**   Traumatic transphalangeal amputation of thumb

    Traumatic interphalangeal joint amputation of thumb

    ● **S68.51**   Complete traumatic transphalangeal amputation of thumb

      ● **S68.511**   Complete traumatic transphalangeal amputation of right thumb

      ● **S68.512**   Complete traumatic transphalangeal amputation of left thumb

      ● **S68.519**   Complete traumatic transphalangeal amputation of unspecified thumb

CHAPTER 19 (S00-T88)

CHAPTER 19 (S00-T88)

● **S68.52** **Partial** traumatic transphalangeal amputation of thumb
    ● S68.521   Partial traumatic transphalangeal amputation of **right** thumb
    ● S68.522   Partial traumatic transphalangeal amputation of **left** thumb
    ● S68.529   Partial traumatic transphalangeal amputation of **unspecified** thumb

● **S68.6**   Traumatic **transphalangeal** amputation of other and unspecified **finger**
  ● **S68.61**   **Complete** traumatic transphalangeal amputation of other and unspecified **finger(s)**
    ● S68.610   Complete traumatic transphalangeal amputation of **right index** finger
    ● S68.611   Complete traumatic transphalangeal amputation of **left index** finger
    ● S68.612   Complete traumatic transphalangeal amputation of **right middle** finger
    ● S68.613   Complete traumatic transphalangeal amputation of **left middle** finger
    ● S68.614   Complete traumatic transphalangeal amputation of **right ring** finger
    ● S68.615   Complete traumatic transphalangeal amputation of **left ring** finger
    ● S68.616   Complete traumatic transphalangeal amputation of **right little** finger
    ● S68.617   Complete traumatic transphalangeal amputation of **left little** finger
    ● S68.618   Complete traumatic transphalangeal amputation of **other** finger
          Complete traumatic transphalangeal amputation of specified finger with unspecified laterality
    ● S68.619   Complete traumatic transphalangeal amputation of **unspecified** finger
  ● **S68.62**   **Partial** traumatic transphalangeal amputation of other and unspecified finger
    ● S68.620   Partial traumatic transphalangeal amputation of **right index** finger
    ● S68.621   Partial traumatic transphalangeal amputation of **left index** finger
    ● S68.622   Partial traumatic transphalangeal amputation of **right middle** finger
    ● S68.623   Partial traumatic transphalangeal amputation of **left middle** finger
    ● S68.624   Partial traumatic transphalangeal amputation of **right ring** finger
    ● S68.625   Partial traumatic transphalangeal amputation of **left ring** finger
    ● S68.626   Partial traumatic transphalangeal amputation of **right little** finger
    ● S68.627   Partial traumatic transphalangeal amputation of **left little** finger
    ● S68.628   Partial traumatic transphalangeal amputation of **other** finger
          Partial traumatic transphalangeal amputation of specified finger with unspecified laterality
    ● S68.629   Partial traumatic transphalangeal amputation of **unspecified** finger

● **S68.7**   Traumatic **transmetacarpal** amputation of hand
  ● **S68.71**   **Complete** traumatic transmetacarpal amputation of hand
    ● S68.711   Complete traumatic transmetacarpal amputation of **right** hand
    ● S68.712   Complete traumatic transmetacarpal amputation of **left** hand
    ● S68.719   Complete traumatic transmetacarpal amputation of **unspecified** hand

● **S68.72**   **Partial** traumatic transmetacarpal amputation of hand
    ● S68.721   Partial traumatic transmetacarpal amputation of **right** hand
    ● S68.722   Partial traumatic transmetacarpal amputation of **left** hand
    ● S68.729   Partial traumatic transmetacarpal amputation of **unspecified** hand

● **S69**   Other and unspecified injuries of wrist, hand and finger(s)
     The appropriate 7th character is to be added to each code from category S69

> A   initial encounter
> D   subsequent encounter
> S   sequela

  ● **S69.8**   Other specified injuries of wrist, hand and finger(s)
    X ● S69.80   Other specified injuries of **unspecified** wrist, hand and finger(s)
    X ● S69.81   Other specified injuries of **right** wrist, hand and finger(s)
    X ● S69.82   Other specified injuries of **left** wrist, hand and finger(s)
  ● **S69.9**   **Unspecified** injury of wrist, hand and finger(s)
    X ● S69.90   Unspecified injury of **unspecified** wrist, hand and finger(s)
    X ● S69.91   Unspecified injury of **right** wrist, hand and finger(s)
    X ● S69.92   Unspecified injury of **left** wrist, hand and finger(s)

INJURIES TO THE HIP AND THIGH (S70-S79)

Excludes2   burns and corrosions (T20-T32)
               frostbite (T33-T34)
               snake bite (T63.0-)
               venomous insect bite or sting (T63.4-)

● **S70**   Superficial injury of hip and thigh
     The appropriate 7th character is to be added to each code from category S70

> A   initial encounter
> D   subsequent encounter
> S   sequela

  ● **S70.0**   Contusion of hip
    X ● S70.00   Contusion of **unspecified** hip
    X ● S70.01   Contusion of **right** hip
    X ● S70.02   Contusion of **left** hip
  ● **S70.1**   Contusion of thigh
    X ● S70.10   Contusion of **unspecified** thigh
    X ● S70.11   Contusion of **right** thigh
    X ● S70.12   Contusion of **left** thigh
  ● **S70.2**   Other superficial injuries of **hip**
    ● **S70.21**   **Abrasion** of hip
      ● S70.211   Abrasion, **right** hip
      ● S70.212   Abrasion, **left** hip
      ● S70.219   Abrasion, **unspecified** hip
    ● **S70.22**   **Blister** (nonthermal) of hip
      ● S70.221   Blister (nonthermal), **right** hip
      ● S70.222   Blister (nonthermal), **left** hip
      ● S70.229   Blister (nonthermal), **unspecified** hip
    ● **S70.24**   **External constriction** of hip
      ● S70.241   External constriction, **right** hip
      ● S70.242   External constriction, **left** hip
      ● S70.249   External constriction, **unspecified** hip

▶ New   ⮕ Revised   ~~deleted~~ Deleted   Excludes 1   Excludes 2   Includes   Use additional   Code first   Code also   Key words
OGCR Official Guidelines   X Assign placeholder X   ● Use Additional Character(s)   ▮ Manifestation Code   **Coding Clinic**

- S70.25 **Superficial foreign body of hip**
  Splinter in the hip
  - S70.251 **Superficial foreign body, right hip**
  - S70.252 **Superficial foreign body, left hip**
  - S70.259 **Superficial foreign body, unspecified hip**
- S70.26 **Insect bite (nonvenomous) of hip**
  - S70.261 **Insect bite (nonvenomous), right hip**
  - S70.262 **Insect bite (nonvenomous), left hip**
  - S70.269 **Insect bite (nonvenomous), unspecified hip**
- S70.27 **Other superficial bite of hip**
    Excludes1 open bite of hip (S71.05-)
  - S70.271 **Other superficial bite of hip, right hip**
  - S70.272 **Other superficial bite of hip, left hip**
  - S70.279 **Other superficial bite of hip, unspecified hip**
- S70.3 **Other superficial injuries of thigh**
  - S70.31 **Abrasion of thigh**
    - S70.311 **Abrasion, right thigh**
    - S70.312 **Abrasion, left thigh**
    - S70.319 **Abrasion, unspecified thigh**
  - S70.32 **Blister (nonthermal) of thigh**
    - S70.321 **Blister (nonthermal), right thigh**
    - S70.322 **Blister (nonthermal), left thigh**
    - S70.329 **Blister (nonthermal), unspecified thigh**
  - S70.34 **External constriction of thigh**
    - S70.341 **External constriction, right thigh**
    - S70.342 **External constriction, left thigh**
    - S70.349 **External constriction, unspecified thigh**
  - S70.35 **Superficial foreign body of thigh**
    Splinter in the thigh
    - S70.351 **Superficial foreign body, right thigh**
    - S70.352 **Superficial foreign body, left thigh**
    - S70.359 **Superficial foreign body, unspecified thigh**
  - S70.36 **Insect bite (nonvenomous) of thigh**
    - S70.361 **Insect bite (nonvenomous), right thigh**
    - S70.362 **Insect bite (nonvenomous), left thigh**
    - S70.369 **Insect bite (nonvenomous), unspecified thigh**
  - S70.37 **Other superficial bite of thigh**
      Excludes1 open bite of thigh (S71.15)
    - S70.371 **Other superficial bite of right thigh**
    - S70.372 **Other superficial bite of left thigh**
    - S70.379 **Other superficial bite of unspecified thigh**
- S70.9 **Unspecified superficial injury of hip and thigh**
  - S70.91 **Unspecified superficial injury of hip**
    - S70.911 **Unspecified superficial injury of right hip**
    - S70.912 **Unspecified superficial injury of left hip**
    - S70.919 **Unspecified superficial injury of unspecified hip**
  - S70.92 **Unspecified superficial injury of thigh**
    - S70.921 **Unspecified superficial injury of right thigh**
    - S70.922 **Unspecified superficial injury of left thigh**
    - S70.929 **Unspecified superficial injury of unspecified thigh**

- S71 **Open wound of hip and thigh**
  Code also any associated wound infection
    Excludes1 open fracture of hip and thigh (S72.-)
         traumatic amputation of hip and thigh (S78.-)
    Excludes2 bite of venomous animal (T63.-)
         open wound of ankle, foot and toes (S91.-)
         open wound of knee and lower leg (S81.-)

  The appropriate 7th character is to be added to each code from category S71

A	initial encounter
D	subsequent encounter
S	sequela

  - S71.0 **Open wound of hip**
    - S71.00 **Unspecified open wound of hip**
      - S71.001 **Unspecified open wound, right hip**
      - S71.002 **Unspecified open wound, left hip**
      - S71.009 **Unspecified open wound, unspecified hip**
    - S71.01 **Laceration without foreign body of hip**
      - S71.011 **Laceration without foreign body, right hip**
      - S71.012 **Laceration without foreign body, left hip**
      - S71.019 **Laceration without foreign body, unspecified hip**
    - S71.02 **Laceration with foreign body of hip**
      - S71.021 **Laceration with foreign body, right hip**
      - S71.022 **Laceration with foreign body, left hip**
      - S71.029 **Laceration with foreign body, unspecified hip**
    - S71.03 **Puncture wound without foreign body of hip**
      - S71.031 **Puncture wound without foreign body, right hip**
      - S71.032 **Puncture wound without foreign body, left hip**
      - S71.039 **Puncture wound without foreign body, unspecified hip**
    - S71.04 **Puncture wound with foreign body of hip**
      - S71.041 **Puncture wound with foreign body, right hip**
      - S71.042 **Puncture wound with foreign body, left hip**
      - S71.049 **Puncture wound with foreign body, unspecified hip**
    - S71.05 **Open bite of hip**
      Bite of hip NOS
        Excludes1 superficial bite of hip (S70.26, S70.27)
      - S71.051 **Open bite, right hip**
      - S71.052 **Open bite, left hip**
      - S71.059 **Open bite, unspecified hip**
  - S71.1 **Open wound of thigh**
    - S71.10 **Unspecified open wound of thigh**
      - S71.101 **Unspecified open wound, right thigh**
      - S71.102 **Unspecified open wound, left thigh**
      - S71.109 **Unspecified open wound, unspecified thigh**
    - S71.11 **Laceration without foreign body of thigh**
      - S71.111 **Laceration without foreign body, right thigh**
      - S71.112 **Laceration without foreign body, left thigh**
      - S71.119 **Laceration without foreign body, unspecified thigh**

CHAPTER 19 (S00-T88)

● **S71.12**   **Laceration with foreign body of thigh**
- ● **S71.121**   Laceration with foreign body, right thigh
- ● **S71.122**   Laceration with foreign body, left thigh
- ● **S71.129**   Laceration with foreign body, unspecified thigh

● **S71.13**   **Puncture wound without foreign body of thigh**
- ● **S71.131**   Puncture wound without foreign body, right thigh
- ● **S71.132**   Puncture wound without foreign body, left thigh
- ● **S71.139**   Puncture wound without foreign body, unspecified thigh

● **S71.14**   **Puncture wound with foreign body of thigh**
- ● **S71.141**   Puncture wound with foreign body, right thigh
- ● **S71.142**   Puncture wound with foreign body, left thigh
- ● **S71.149**   Puncture wound with foreign body, unspecified thigh

● **S71.15**   **Open bite of thigh**
Bite of thigh NOS
> **Excludes1**   superficial bite of thigh (S70.37-)
- ● **S71.151**   Open bite, right thigh
- ● **S71.152**   Open bite, left thigh
- ● **S71.159**   Open bite, unspecified thigh

● **S72**   **Fracture of femur**

Note: A fracture not indicated as displaced or nondisplaced should be coded to displaced

A fracture not indicated as open or closed should be coded to closed

The open fracture designations are based on the Gustilo open fracture classification

> **Excludes1**   traumatic amputation of hip and thigh (S78.-)
> **Excludes2**   fracture of lower leg and ankle (S82.-)
> fracture of foot (S92.-)
> periprosthetic fracture of prosthetic implant of hip (M97.0-)

The appropriate 7th character is to be added to all codes from category S72

A	initial encounter for closed fracture
B	initial encounter for open fracture type I or II
	initial encounter for open fracture NOS
C	initial encounter for open fracture type IIIA, IIIB, or IIIC
D	subsequent encounter for closed fracture with routine healing
E	subsequent encounter for open fracture type I or II with routine healing
F	subsequent encounter for open fracture type IIIA, IIIB, or IIIC with routine healing
G	subsequent encounter for closed fracture with delayed healing
H	subsequent encounter for open fracture type I or II with delayed healing
J	subsequent encounter for open fracture type IIIA, IIIB, or IIIC with delayed healing
K	subsequent encounter for closed fracture with nonunion
M	subsequent encounter for open fracture type I or II with nonunion
N	subsequent encounter for open fracture type IIIA, IIIB, or IIIC with nonunion
P	subsequent encounter for closed fracture with malunion
Q	subsequent encounter for open fracture type I or II with malunion
R	subsequent encounter for open fracture type IIIA, IIIB, or IIIC with malunion
S	sequela

● **S72.0**   **Fracture of head and neck of femur**
> **Excludes2**   physeal fracture of upper end of femur (S79.0-)

● **S72.00**   **Fracture of unspecified part of neck of femur**
Fracture of hip NOS
Fracture of neck of femur NOS
- ● **S72.001**   Fracture of unspecified part of neck of right femur
- ● **S72.002**   Fracture of unspecified part of neck of left femur
  > **Coding Clinic: 2015, Q4, P37, Q1, P17**
- ● **S72.009**   Fracture of unspecified part of neck of unspecified femur

● **S72.01**   **Unspecified intracapsular fracture of femur**
Subcapital fracture of femur
- ● **S72.011**   Unspecified intracapsular fracture of right femur
- ● **S72.012**   Unspecified intracapsular fracture of left femur
- ● **S72.019**   Unspecified intracapsular fracture of unspecified femur

● **S72.02**   **Fracture of epiphysis (separation) (upper) of femur**
Transepiphyseal fracture of femur
Fracture and separation across growth plate
> **Excludes1**   capital femoral epiphyseal fracture (pediatric) of femur (S79.01-)
> Salter-Harris Type I physeal fracture of upper end of femur (S79.01-)
- ● **S72.021**   Displaced fracture of epiphysis (separation) (upper) of right femur
- ● **S72.022**   Displaced fracture of epiphysis (separation) (upper) of left femur
- ● **S72.023**   Displaced fracture of epiphysis (separation) (upper) of unspecified femur
- ● **S72.024**   Nondisplaced fracture of epiphysis (separation) (upper) of right femur
- ● **S72.025**   Nondisplaced fracture of epiphysis (separation) (upper) of left femur
- ● **S72.026**   Nondisplaced fracture of epiphysis (separation) (upper) of unspecified femur

● **S72.03**   **Midcervical fracture of femur**
Transcervical fracture of femur NOS
- ● **S72.031**   Displaced midcervical fracture of right femur
- ● **S72.032**   Displaced midcervical fracture of left femur
- ● **S72.033**   Displaced midcervical fracture of unspecified femur
- ● **S72.034**   Nondisplaced midcervical fracture of right femur
- ● **S72.035**   Nondisplaced midcervical fracture of left femur
- ● **S72.036**   Nondisplaced midcervical fracture of unspecified femur

● **S72.04**   **Fracture of base of neck of femur**
Cervicotrochanteric fracture of femur
- ● **S72.041**   Displaced fracture of base of neck of right femur
- ● **S72.042**   Displaced fracture of base of neck of left femur
- ● **S72.043**   Displaced fracture of base of neck of unspecified femur
- ● **S72.044**   Nondisplaced fracture of base of neck of right femur
- ● **S72.045**   Nondisplaced fracture of base of neck of left femur
- ● **S72.046**   Nondisplaced fracture of base of neck of unspecified femur

▶ New   ⇒ Revised   ~~deleted~~ Deleted   Excludes 1   Excludes 2   Includes   Use additional   Code first   Code also   Key words
OGCR Official Guidelines   X Assign placeholder X   ● Use Additional Character(s)   ⫠ Manifestation Code   **Coding Clinic**

- S72.05   Unspecified fracture of head of femur
             Fracture of head of femur NOS
  - S72.051   Unspecified fracture of head of right femur
  - S72.052   Unspecified fracture of head of left femur
  - S72.059   Unspecified fracture of head of unspecified femur
- S72.06   Articular fracture of head of femur
  - S72.061   Displaced articular fracture of head of right femur
  - S72.062   Displaced articular fracture of head of left femur
  - S72.063   Displaced articular fracture of head of unspecified femur
  - S72.064   Nondisplaced articular fracture of head of right femur
  - S72.065   Nondisplaced articular fracture of head of left femur
  - S72.066   Nondisplaced articular fracture of head of unspecified femur
- S72.09   Other fracture of head and neck of femur
  - S72.091   Other fracture of head and neck of right femur
  - S72.092   Other fracture of head and neck of left femur
  - S72.099   Other fracture of head and neck of unspecified femur
- S72.1   Pertrochanteric fracture
          Fracture extending close to, but not into, joint
  - S72.10   Unspecified trochanteric fracture of femur
               Fracture of trochanter NOS
    - S72.101   Unspecified trochanteric fracture of right femur
    - S72.102   Unspecified trochanteric fracture of left femur
    - S72.109   Unspecified trochanteric fracture of unspecified femur
  - S72.11   Fracture of greater trochanter of femur
    - S72.111   Displaced fracture of greater trochanter of right femur
    - S72.112   Displaced fracture of greater trochanter of left femur
    - S72.113   Displaced fracture of greater trochanter of unspecified femur
    - S72.114   Nondisplaced fracture of greater trochanter of right femur
    - S72.115   Nondisplaced fracture of greater trochanter of left femur
    - S72.116   Nondisplaced fracture of greater trochanter of unspecified femur
  - S72.12   Fracture of lesser trochanter of femur
    - S72.121   Displaced fracture of lesser trochanter of right femur
    - S72.122   Displaced fracture of lesser trochanter of left femur
    - S72.123   Displaced fracture of lesser trochanter of unspecified femur
    - S72.124   Nondisplaced fracture of lesser trochanter of right femur
    - S72.125   Nondisplaced fracture of lesser trochanter of left femur
    - S72.126   Nondisplaced fracture of lesser trochanter of unspecified femur

- S72.13   Apophyseal fracture of femur
             Pertaining to articulations between articular facets of adjacent vertebrae
             Excludes1   chronic (nontraumatic) slipped upper femoral epiphysis (M93.0-)
  - S72.131   Displaced apophyseal fracture of right femur
  - S72.132   Displaced apophyseal fracture of left femur
  - S72.133   Displaced apophyseal fracture of unspecified femur
  - S72.134   Nondisplaced apophyseal fracture of right femur
  - S72.135   Nondisplaced apophyseal fracture of left femur
  - S72.136   Nondisplaced apophyseal fracture of unspecified femur
- S72.14   Intertrochanteric fracture of femur
  - S72.141   Displaced intertrochanteric fracture of right femur
                Coding Clinic: 2016, Q3, P17
  - S72.142   Displaced intertrochanteric fracture of left femur
  - S72.143   Displaced intertrochanteric fracture of unspecified femur
  - S72.144   Nondisplaced intertrochanteric fracture of right femur
  - S72.145   Nondisplaced intertrochanteric fracture of left femur
  - S72.146   Nondisplaced intertrochanteric fracture of unspecified femur
- S72.2   Subtrochanteric fracture of femur
          Subtrochanteric: inferior to trochanter
  - X ● S72.21   Displaced subtrochanteric fracture of right femur
  - X ● S72.22   Displaced subtrochanteric fracture of left femur
  - X ● S72.23   Displaced subtrochanteric fracture of unspecified femur
  - X ● S72.24   Nondisplaced subtrochanteric fracture of right femur
  - X ● S72.25   Nondisplaced subtrochanteric fracture of left femur
  - X ● S72.26   Nondisplaced subtrochanteric fracture of unspecified femur
- S72.3   Fracture of shaft of femur
  - S72.30   Unspecified fracture of shaft of femur
    - S72.301   Unspecified fracture of shaft of right femur
                  Coding Clinic: 2018, Q2, P12
    - S72.302   Unspecified fracture of shaft of left femur
    - S72.309   Unspecified fracture of shaft of unspecified femur
  - S72.32   Transverse fracture of shaft of femur
    - S72.321   Displaced transverse fracture of shaft of right femur
    - S72.322   Displaced transverse fracture of shaft of left femur
    - S72.323   Displaced transverse fracture of shaft of unspecified femur
    - S72.324   Nondisplaced transverse fracture of shaft of right femur
    - S72.325   Nondisplaced transverse fracture of shaft of left femur
    - S72.326   Nondisplaced transverse fracture of shaft of unspecified femur

CHAPTER 19 (S00-T88)

● **S72.33**   Oblique fracture of shaft of femur
- ● S72.331   Displaced oblique fracture of shaft of right femur
- ● S72.332   Displaced oblique fracture of shaft of left femur
- ● S72.333   Displaced oblique fracture of shaft of unspecified femur
- ● S72.334   Nondisplaced oblique fracture of shaft of right femur
- ● S72.335   Nondisplaced oblique fracture of shaft of left femur
- ● S72.336   Nondisplaced oblique fracture of shaft of unspecified femur

● **S72.34**   Spiral fracture of shaft of femur
- ● S72.341   Displaced spiral fracture of shaft of right femur
- ● S72.342   Displaced spiral fracture of shaft of left femur
- ● S72.343   Displaced spiral fracture of shaft of unspecified femur
- ● S72.344   Nondisplaced spiral fracture of shaft of right femur
- ● S72.345   Nondisplaced spiral fracture of shaft of left femur
- ● S72.346   Nondisplaced spiral fracture of shaft of unspecified femur

● **S72.35**   Comminuted fracture of shaft of femur
- ● S72.351   Displaced comminuted fracture of shaft of right femur
- ● S72.352   Displaced comminuted fracture of shaft of left femur
- ● S72.353   Displaced comminuted fracture of shaft of unspecified femur
- ● S72.354   Nondisplaced comminuted fracture of shaft of right femur
- ● S72.355   Nondisplaced comminuted fracture of shaft of left femur
- ● S72.356   Nondisplaced comminuted fracture of shaft of unspecified femur

● **S72.36**   Segmental fracture of shaft of femur
- ● S72.361   Displaced segmental fracture of shaft of right femur
- ● S72.362   Displaced segmental fracture of shaft of left femur
- ● S72.363   Displaced segmental fracture of shaft of unspecified femur
- ● S72.364   Nondisplaced segmental fracture of shaft of right femur
- ● S72.365   Nondisplaced segmental fracture of shaft of left femur
- ● S72.366   Nondisplaced segmental fracture of shaft of unspecified femur

● **S72.39**   Other fracture of shaft of femur
- ● S72.391   Other fracture of shaft of right femur
- ● S72.392   Other fracture of shaft of left femur
- ● S72.399   Other fracture of shaft of unspecified femur

● **S72.4**   Fracture of lower end of femur
     Fracture of distal end of femur
     Excludes2   fracture of shaft of femur (S72.3-)
                 physeal fracture of lower end of femur (S79.1-)

● **S72.40**   Unspecified fracture of lower end of femur
- ● S72.401   Unspecified fracture of lower end of right femur
  - **Coding Clinic: 2016, Q4, P43**
- ● S72.402   Unspecified fracture of lower end of left femur
- ● S72.409   Unspecified fracture of lower end of unspecified femur

● **S72.41**   Unspecified condyle fracture of lower end of femur
     Condyle fracture of femur NOS
- ● S72.411   Displaced unspecified condyle fracture of lower end of right femur
- ● S72.412   Displaced unspecified condyle fracture of lower end of left femur
- ● S72.413   Displaced unspecified condyle fracture of lower end of unspecified femur
- ● S72.414   Nondisplaced unspecified condyle fracture of lower end of right femur
- ● S72.415   Nondisplaced unspecified condyle fracture of lower end of left femur
- ● S72.416   Nondisplaced unspecified condyle fracture of lower end of unspecified femur

● **S72.42**   Fracture of lateral condyle of femur
- ● S72.421   Displaced fracture of lateral condyle of right femur
- ● S72.422   Displaced fracture of lateral condyle of left femur
- ● S72.423   Displaced fracture of lateral condyle of unspecified femur
- ● S72.424   Nondisplaced fracture of lateral condyle of right femur
- ● S72.425   Nondisplaced fracture of lateral condyle of left femur
- ● S72.426   Nondisplaced fracture of lateral condyle of unspecified femur

● **S72.43**   Fracture of medial condyle of femur
- ● S72.431   Displaced fracture of medial condyle of right femur
- ● S72.432   Displaced fracture of medial condyle of left femur
- ● S72.433   Displaced fracture of medial condyle of unspecified femur
- ● S72.434   Nondisplaced fracture of medial condyle of right femur
- ● S72.435   Nondisplaced fracture of medial condyle of left femur
- ● S72.436   Nondisplaced fracture of medial condyle of unspecified femur

● **S72.44**   Fracture of lower epiphysis (separation) of femur
     Excludes1   Salter-Harris Type I physeal fracture of lower end of femur (S79.11-)
- ● S72.441   Displaced fracture of lower epiphysis (separation) of right femur
- ● S72.442   Displaced fracture of lower epiphysis (separation) of left femur
- ● S72.443   Displaced fracture of lower epiphysis (separation) of unspecified femur
- ● S72.444   Nondisplaced fracture of lower epiphysis (separation) of right femur
- ● S72.445   Nondisplaced fracture of lower epiphysis (separation) of left femur
- ● S72.446   Nondisplaced fracture of lower epiphysis (separation) of unspecified femur

▶ New   ⇒ Revised   ~~deleted~~ Deleted   Excludes 1   Excludes 2   Includes   Use additional   Code first   Code also   Key words

OGCR Official Guidelines   X Assign placeholder X   ● Use Additional Character(s)   ▮ Manifestation Code   **Coding Clinic**

- S72.45 **Supracondylar fracture without intracondylar extension of lower end of femur**
  Supracondylar fracture of lower end of femur NOS
  - **Excludes1** supracondylar fracture with intracondylar extension of lower end of femur (S72.46-)
  - S72.451 Displaced supracondylar fracture without intracondylar extension of lower end of right femur
  - S72.452 Displaced supracondylar fracture without intracondylar extension of lower end of left femur
  - S72.453 Displaced supracondylar fracture without intracondylar extension of lower end of unspecified femur
  - S72.454 Nondisplaced supracondylar fracture without intracondylar extension of lower end of right femur
  - S72.455 Nondisplaced supracondylar fracture without intracondylar extension of lower end of left femur
  - S72.456 Nondisplaced supracondylar fracture without intracondylar extension of lower end of unspecified femur
- S72.46 **Supracondylar fracture with intracondylar extension of lower end of femur**
  - **Excludes1** supracondylar fracture without intracondylar extension of lower end of femur (S72.45-)
  - S72.461 Displaced supracondylar fracture with intracondylar extension of lower end of right femur
  - S72.462 Displaced supracondylar fracture with intracondylar extension of lower end of left femur
  - S72.463 Displaced supracondylar fracture with intracondylar extension of lower end of unspecified femur
  - S72.464 Nondisplaced supracondylar fracture with intracondylar extension of lower end of right femur
  - S72.465 Nondisplaced supracondylar fracture with intracondylar extension of lower end of left femur
  - S72.466 Nondisplaced supracondylar fracture with intracondylar extension of lower end of unspecified femur
- S72.47 **Torus fracture of lower end of femur**
  The appropriate 7th character is to be added to all codes in subcategory S72.47

A	initial encounter for closed fracture
D	subsequent encounter for fracture with routine healing
G	subsequent encounter for fracture with delayed healing
K	subsequent encounter for fracture with nonunion
P	subsequent encounter for fracture with malunion
S	sequela

  - S72.471 Torus fracture of lower end of right femur
  - S72.472 Torus fracture of lower end of left femur
  - S72.479 Torus fracture of lower end of unspecified femur

- S72.49 **Other fracture of lower end of femur**
  - S72.491 Other fracture of lower end of right femur
  - S72.492 Other fracture of lower end of left femur
  - S72.499 Other fracture of lower end of unspecified femur
- S72.8 **Other fracture of femur**
  - S72.8X Other fracture of femur
    - S72.8X1 Other fracture of right femur
    - S72.8X2 Other fracture of left femur
    - S72.8X9 Other fracture of unspecified femur
- S72.9 **Unspecified fracture of femur**
  Fracture of thigh NOS
  Fracture of upper leg NOS
  - **Excludes1** fracture of hip NOS (S72.00-, S72.01-)
  - X S72.90 Unspecified fracture of unspecified femur
    Coding Clinic: 2012, Q4, P94
  - X S72.91 Unspecified fracture of right femur
  - X S72.92 Unspecified fracture of left femur
- S73 **Dislocation and sprain of joint and ligaments of hip**
  - **Includes** avulsion of joint or ligament of hip
    laceration of cartilage, joint or ligament of hip
    sprain of cartilage, joint or ligament of hip
    traumatic hemarthrosis of joint or ligament of hip
    traumatic rupture of joint or ligament of hip
    traumatic subluxation of joint or ligament of hip
    traumatic tear of joint or ligament of hip

  Code also any associated open wound
  - **Excludes2** strain of muscle, fascia and tendon of hip and thigh (S76.-)

  The appropriate 7th character is to be added to each code from category S73

A	initial encounter
D	subsequent encounter
S	sequela

  - S73.0 **Subluxation and dislocation of hip**
    Out of position
    - **Excludes2** dislocation and subluxation of hip prosthesis (T84.020, T84.021)
    - S73.00 Unspecified subluxation and dislocation of hip
      Dislocation of hip NOS
      Subluxation of hip NOS
      - S73.001 Unspecified subluxation of right hip
      - S73.002 Unspecified subluxation of left hip
      - S73.003 Unspecified subluxation of unspecified hip
      - S73.004 Unspecified dislocation of right hip
      - S73.005 Unspecified dislocation of left hip
      - S73.006 Unspecified dislocation of unspecified hip
    - S73.01 Posterior subluxation and dislocation of hip
      - S73.011 Posterior subluxation of right hip
      - S73.012 Posterior subluxation of left hip
      - S73.013 Posterior subluxation of unspecified hip
      - S73.014 Posterior dislocation of right hip
      - S73.015 Posterior dislocation of left hip
      - S73.016 Posterior dislocation of unspecified hip

● S73.02   Obturator subluxation and dislocation of hip
- ● S73.021   Obturator subluxation of right hip
- ● S73.022   Obturator subluxation of left hip
- ● S73.023   Obturator subluxation of unspecified hip
- ● S73.024   Obturator dislocation of right hip
- ● S73.025   Obturator dislocation of left hip
- ● S73.026   Obturator dislocation of unspecified hip

● S73.03   Other anterior subluxation and dislocation of hip
- ● S73.031   Other anterior subluxation of right hip
- ● S73.032   Other anterior subluxation of left hip
- ● S73.033   Other anterior subluxation of unspecified hip
- ● S73.034   Other anterior dislocation of right hip
- ● S73.035   Other anterior dislocation of left hip
- ● S73.036   Other anterior dislocation of unspecified hip

● S73.04   Central subluxation and dislocation of hip
- ● S73.041   Central subluxation of right hip
- ● S73.042   Central subluxation of left hip
- ● S73.043   Central subluxation of unspecified hip
- ● S73.044   Central dislocation of right hip
- ● S73.045   Central dislocation of left hip
- ● S73.046   Central dislocation of unspecified hip

● S73.1   Sprain of hip
- ● S73.10   Unspecified sprain of hip
  - ● S73.101   Unspecified sprain of right hip
  - ● S73.102   Unspecified sprain of left hip
  - ● S73.109   Unspecified sprain of unspecified hip
- ● S73.11   Iliofemoral ligament sprain of hip
  - ● S73.111   Iliofemoral ligament sprain of right hip
  - ● S73.112   Iliofemoral ligament sprain of left hip
  - ● S73.119   Iliofemoral ligament sprain of unspecified hip
- ● S73.12   Ischiocapsular (ligament) sprain of hip
  - ● S73.121   Ischiocapsular ligament sprain of right hip
  - ● S73.122   Ischiocapsular ligament sprain of left hip
  - ● S73.129   Ischiocapsular ligament sprain of unspecified hip
- ● S73.19   Other sprain of hip
  - ● S73.191   Other sprain of right hip
  - ● S73.192   Other sprain of left hip
  - ● S73.199   Other sprain of unspecified hip

● S74   Injury of nerves at hip and thigh level

Code also any associated open wound (S71.-)

Excludes2   injury of nerves at ankle and foot level (S94.-)
injury of nerves at lower leg level (S84.-)

The appropriate 7th character is to be added to each code from category S74

A	initial encounter
D	subsequent encounter
S	sequela

● S74.0   Injury of sciatic nerve at hip and thigh level
- X ● S74.00   Injury of sciatic nerve at hip and thigh level, unspecified leg
- X ● S74.01   Injury of sciatic nerve at hip and thigh level, right leg
- X ● S74.02   Injury of sciatic nerve at hip and thigh level, left leg

● S74.1   Injury of femoral nerve at hip and thigh level
- X ● S74.10   Injury of femoral nerve at hip and thigh level, unspecified leg
- X ● S74.11   Injury of femoral nerve at hip and thigh level, right leg
- X ● S74.12   Injury of femoral nerve at hip and thigh level, left leg

● S74.2   Injury of cutaneous sensory nerve at hip and thigh level
- X ● S74.20   Injury of cutaneous sensory nerve at hip and thigh level, unspecified leg
- X ● S74.21   Injury of cutaneous sensory nerve at hip and high level, right leg
- X ● S74.22   Injury of cutaneous sensory nerve at hip and thigh level, left leg

● S74.8   Injury of other nerves at hip and thigh level
- ● S74.8X   Injury of other nerves at hip and thigh level
  - ● S74.8X1   Injury of other nerves at hip and thigh level, right leg
  - ● S74.8X2   Injury of other nerves at hip and thigh level, left leg
  - ● S74.8X9   Injury of other nerves at hip and thigh level, unspecified leg

● S74.9   Injury of unspecified nerve at hip and thigh level
- X ● S74.90   Injury of unspecified nerve at hip and thigh level, unspecified leg
- X ● S74.91   Injury of unspecified nerve at hip and thigh level, right leg
- X ● S74.92   Injury of unspecified nerve at hip and thigh level, left leg

● S75   Injury of blood vessels at hip and thigh level

Code also any associated open wound (S71.-)

Excludes2   injury of blood vessels at lower leg level (S85.-)
injury of popliteal artery (S85.0)

The appropriate 7th character is to be added to each code from category S75

A	initial encounter
D	subsequent encounter
S	sequela

● S75.0   Injury of femoral artery
- ● S75.00   Unspecified injury of femoral artery
  - ● S75.001   Unspecified injury of femoral artery, right leg
  - ● S75.002   Unspecified injury of femoral artery, left leg
  - ● S75.009   Unspecified injury of femoral artery, unspecified leg
- ● S75.01   Minor laceration of femoral artery
  Incomplete transection of femoral artery
  Laceration of femoral artery NOS
  Superficial laceration of femoral artery
  - ● S75.011   Minor laceration of femoral artery, right leg
  - ● S75.012   Minor laceration of femoral artery, left leg
  - ● S75.019   Minor laceration of femoral artery, unspecified leg
- ● S75.02   Major laceration of femoral artery
  Complete transection of femoral artery
  Traumatic rupture of femoral artery
  - ● S75.021   Major laceration of femoral artery, right leg
  - ● S75.022   Major laceration of femoral artery, left leg
  - ● S75.029   Major laceration of femoral artery, unspecified leg

▶ New   ⏩ Revised   ~~deleted~~ Deleted   Excludes 1   Excludes 2   Includes   Use additional   Code first   Code also   Key words

OGCR Official Guidelines   X Assign placeholder X   ● Use Additional Character(s)   ▶ Manifestation Code   **Coding Clinic**

● **S75.09 Other** specified injury of femoral artery

   ● **S75.091 Other** specified injury of femoral artery, **right** leg

   ● **S75.092 Other** specified injury of femoral artery, **left** leg

   ● **S75.099 Other** specified injury of femoral artery, **unspecified** leg

● **S75.1 Injury of femoral vein at hip and thigh level**

   ● **S75.10 Unspecified** injury of femoral vein at hip and thigh level

      ● **S75.101 Unspecified** injury of femoral vein at hip and thigh level, **right** leg

      ● **S75.102 Unspecified** injury of femoral vein at hip and thigh level, **left** leg

      ● **S75.109 Unspecified** injury of femoral vein at hip and thigh level, **unspecified** leg

   ● **S75.11 Minor laceration** of femoral vein at hip and thigh level

      Incomplete transection of femoral vein at hip and thigh level

      Laceration of femoral vein at hip and thigh level NOS

      Superficial laceration of femoral vein at hip and thigh level

      ● **S75.111 Minor laceration** of femoral vein at hip and thigh level, **right** leg

      ● **S75.112 Minor laceration** of femoral vein at hip and thigh level, **left** leg

      ● **S75.119 Minor laceration** of femoral vein at hip and thigh level, **unspecified** leg

   ● **S75.12 Major laceration** of femoral vein at hip and thigh level

      Complete transection of femoral vein at hip and thigh level

      Traumatic rupture of femoral vein at hip and thigh level

      ● **S75.121 Major laceration** of femoral vein at hip and thigh level, **right** leg

      ● **S75.122 Major laceration** of femoral vein at hip and thigh level, **left** leg

      ● **S75.129 Major laceration** of femoral vein at hip and thigh level, **unspecified** leg

   ● **S75.19 Other** specified injury of femoral vein at hip and thigh level

      ● **S75.191 Other** specified injury of femoral vein at hip and thigh level, **right** leg

      ● **S75.192 Other** specified injury of femoral vein at hip and thigh level, **left** leg

      ● **S75.199 Other** specified injury of femoral vein at hip and thigh level, **unspecified** leg

● **S75.2 Injury of greater saphenous vein at hip and thigh level**

   Excludes1   greater saphenous vein NOS (S85.3)

   ● **S75.20 Unspecified** injury of greater saphenous vein at hip and thigh level

      ● **S75.201 Unspecified** injury of greater saphenous vein at hip and thigh level, **right** leg

      ● **S75.202 Unspecified** injury of greater saphenous vein at hip and thigh level, **left** leg

      ● **S75.209 Unspecified** injury of greater saphenous vein at hip and thigh level, **unspecified** leg

● **S75.21 Minor laceration** of greater saphenous vein at hip and thigh level

   Incomplete transection of greater saphenous vein at hip and thigh level

   Laceration of greater saphenous vein at hip and thigh level NOS

   Superficial laceration of greater saphenous vein at hip and thigh level

   ● **S75.211 Minor laceration** of greater saphenous vein at hip and thigh level, **right** leg

   ● **S75.212 Minor laceration** of greater saphenous vein at hip and thigh level, **left** leg

   ● **S75.219 Minor laceration** of greater saphenous vein at hip and thigh level, **unspecified** leg

● **S75.22 Major laceration** of greater saphenous vein at hip and thigh level

   Complete transection of greater saphenous vein at hip and thigh level

   Traumatic rupture of greater saphenous vein at hip and thigh level

   ● **S75.221 Major laceration** of greater saphenous vein at hip and thigh level, **right** leg

   ● **S75.222 Major laceration** of greater saphenous vein at hip and thigh level, **left** leg

   ● **S75.229 Major laceration** of greater saphenous vein at hip and thigh level, **unspecified** leg

● **S75.29 Other** specified injury of greater saphenous vein at hip and thigh level

   ● **S75.291 Other** specified injury of greater saphenous vein at hip and thigh level, **right** leg

   ● **S75.292 Other** specified injury of greater saphenous vein at hip and thigh level, **left** leg

   ● **S75.299 Other** specified injury of greater saphenous vein at hip and thigh level, **unspecified** leg

● **S75.8 Injury of other blood vessels at hip and thigh level**

   ● **S75.80 Unspecified** injury of other blood vessels at hip and thigh level

      ● **S75.801 Unspecified** injury of other blood vessels at hip and thigh level, **right** leg

      ● **S75.802 Unspecified** injury of other blood vessels at hip and thigh level, **left** leg

      ● **S75.809 Unspecified** injury of other blood vessels at hip and thigh level, **unspecified** leg

   ● **S75.81 Laceration** of other blood vessels at hip and thigh level

      ● **S75.811 Laceration** of other blood vessels at hip and thigh level, **right** leg

      ● **S75.812 Laceration** of other blood vessels at hip and thigh level, **left** leg

      ● **S75.819 Laceration** of other blood vessels at hip and thigh level, **unspecified** leg

   ● **S75.89 Other** specified injury of other blood vessels at hip and thigh level

      ● **S75.891 Other** specified injury of other blood vessels at hip and thigh level, **right** leg

      ● **S75.892 Other** specified injury of other blood vessels at hip and thigh level, **left** leg

      ● **S75.899 Other** specified injury of other blood vessels at hip and thigh level, **unspecified** leg

● S75.9   Injury of unspecified blood vessel at hip and thigh level
  ● S75.90   Unspecified injury of unspecified blood vessel at hip and thigh level
    ● S75.901   Unspecified injury of unspecified blood vessel at hip and thigh level, right leg
    ● S75.902   Unspecified injury of unspecified blood vessel at hip and thigh level, left leg
    ● S75.909   Unspecified injury of unspecified blood vessel at hip and thigh level, unspecified leg
  ● S75.91   Laceration of unspecified blood vessel at hip and thigh level
    ● S75.911   Laceration of unspecified blood vessel at hip and thigh level, right leg
    ● S75.912   Laceration of unspecified blood vessel at hip and thigh level, left leg
    ● S75.919   Laceration of unspecified blood vessel at hip and thigh level, unspecified leg
  ● S75.99   Other specified injury of unspecified blood vessel at hip and thigh level
    ● S75.991   Other specified injury of unspecified blood vessel at hip and thigh level, right leg
    ● S75.992   Other specified injury of unspecified blood vessel at hip and thigh level, left leg
    ● S75.999   Other specified injury of unspecified blood vessel at hip and thigh level, unspecified leg

● S76   Injury of muscle, fascia and tendon at hip and thigh level
  Code also any associated open wound (S71.-)
  Excludes2   injury of muscle, fascia and tendon at lower leg level (S86)
    sprain of joint and ligament of hip (S73.1)
  The appropriate 7th character is to be added to each code from category S76

A	initial encounter
D	subsequent encounter
S	sequela

  ● S76.0   Injury of muscle, fascia and tendon of hip
    ● S76.00   Unspecified injury of muscle, fascia and tendon of hip
      ● S76.001   Unspecified injury of muscle, fascia and tendon of right hip
      ● S76.002   Unspecified injury of muscle, fascia and tendon of left hip
      ● S76.009   Unspecified injury of muscle, fascia and tendon of unspecified hip
    ● S76.01   Strain of muscle, fascia and tendon of hip
      ● S76.011   Strain of muscle, fascia and tendon of right hip
      ● S76.012   Strain of muscle, fascia and tendon of left hip
      ● S76.019   Strain of muscle, fascia and tendon of unspecified hip
    ● S76.02   Laceration of muscle, fascia and tendon of hip
      ● S76.021   Laceration of muscle, fascia and tendon of right hip
      ● S76.022   Laceration of muscle, fascia and tendon of left hip
      ● S76.029   Laceration of muscle, fascia and tendon of unspecified hip

● S76.09   Other specified injury of muscle, fascia and tendon of hip
  ● S76.091   Other specified injury of muscle, fascia and tendon of right hip
  ● S76.092   Other specified injury of muscle, fascia and tendon of left hip
  ● S76.099   Other specified injury of muscle, fascia and tendon of unspecified hip
● S76.1   Injury of quadriceps muscle, fascia and tendon
  Injury of patellar ligament (tendon)
  ● S76.10   Unspecified injury of quadriceps muscle, fascia and tendon
    ● S76.101   Unspecified injury of right quadriceps muscle, fascia and tendon
    ● S76.102   Unspecified injury of left quadriceps muscle, fascia and tendon
    ● S76.109   Unspecified injury of unspecified quadriceps muscle, fascia and tendon
  ● S76.11   Strain of quadriceps muscle, fascia and tendon
    ● S76.111   Strain of right quadriceps muscle, fascia and tendon
    ● S76.112   Strain of left quadriceps muscle, fascia and tendon
    ● S76.119   Strain of unspecified quadriceps muscle, fascia and tendon
  ● S76.12   Laceration of quadriceps muscle, fascia and tendon
    ● S76.121   Laceration of right quadriceps muscle, fascia and tendon
    ● S76.122   Laceration of left quadriceps muscle, fascia and tendon
    ● S76.129   Laceration of unspecified quadriceps muscle, fascia and tendon
  ● S76.19   Other specified injury of quadriceps muscle, fascia and tendon
    ● S76.191   Other specified injury of right quadriceps muscle, fascia and tendon
    ● S76.192   Other specified injury of left quadriceps muscle, fascia and tendon
    ● S76.199   Other specified injury of unspecified quadriceps muscle, fascia and tendon
● S76.2   Injury of adductor muscle, fascia and tendon of thigh
  ● S76.20   Unspecified injury of adductor muscle, fascia and tendon of thigh
    ● S76.201   Unspecified injury of adductor muscle, fascia and tendon of right thigh
    ● S76.202   Unspecified injury of adductor muscle, fascia and tendon of left thigh
    ● S76.209   Unspecified injury of adductor muscle, fascia and tendon of unspecified thigh
  ● S76.21   Strain of adductor muscle, fascia and tendon of thigh
    ● S76.211   Strain of adductor muscle, fascia and tendon of right thigh
    ● S76.212   Strain of adductor muscle, fascia and tendon of left thigh
    ● S76.219   Strain of adductor muscle, fascia and tendon of unspecified thigh
  ● S76.22   Laceration of adductor muscle, fascia and tendon of thigh
    ● S76.221   Laceration of adductor muscle, fascia and tendon of right thigh
    ● S76.222   Laceration of adductor muscle, fascia and tendon of left thigh
    ● S76.229   Laceration of adductor muscle, fascia and tendon of unspecified thigh

▶ New   ⇒ Revised   ~~deleted~~ Deleted   Excludes 1   Excludes 2   Includes   Use additional   Code first   Code also   Key words
OGCR Official Guidelines   X Assign placeholder X   ▶ Use Additional Character(s)   ▶ Manifestation Code   Coding Clinic

- ● S76.29   **Other** injury of adductor muscle, fascia and tendon of thigh
  - ● S76.291   Other injury of adductor muscle, fascia and tendon of **right** thigh
  - ● S76.292   Other injury of adductor muscle, fascia and tendon of **left** thigh
  - ● S76.299   Other injury of adductor muscle, fascia and tendon of **unspecified** thigh
- ● S76.3   Injury of muscle, fascia and tendon of the **posterior muscle group** at thigh level
  - ● S76.30   **Unspecified** injury of muscle, fascia and tendon of the posterior muscle group at thigh level
    - ● S76.301   Unspecified injury of muscle, fascia and tendon of the posterior muscle group at thigh level, **right** thigh
    - ● S76.302   Unspecified injury of muscle, fascia and tendon of the posterior muscle group at thigh level, **left** thigh
    - ● S76.309   Unspecified injury of muscle, fascia and tendon of the posterior muscle group at thigh level, **unspecified** thigh
  - ● S76.31   **Strain** of muscle, fascia and tendon of the posterior muscle group at thigh level
    - ● S76.311   Strain of muscle, fascia and tendon of the posterior muscle group at thigh level, **right** thigh
    - ● S76.312   Strain of muscle, fascia and tendon of the posterior muscle group at thigh level, **left** thigh
    - ● S76.319   Strain of muscle, fascia and tendon of the posterior muscle group at thigh level, **unspecified** thigh
  - ● S76.32   **Laceration** of muscle, fascia and tendon of the posterior muscle group at thigh level
    - ● S76.321   Laceration of muscle, fascia and tendon of the posterior muscle group at thigh level, **right** thigh
    - ● S76.322   Laceration of muscle, fascia and tendon of the posterior muscle group at thigh level, **left** thigh
    - ● S76.329   Laceration of muscle, fascia and tendon of the posterior muscle group at thigh level, **unspecified** thigh
  - ● S76.39   **Other** specified injury of muscle, fascia and tendon of the posterior muscle group at thigh level
    - ● S76.391   Other specified injury of muscle, fascia and tendon of the posterior muscle group at thigh level, **right** thigh
    - ● S76.392   Other specified injury of muscle, fascia and tendon of the posterior muscle group at thigh level, **left** thigh
    - ● S76.399   Other specified injury of muscle, fascia and tendon of the posterior muscle group at thigh level, **unspecified** thigh
- ● S76.8   Injury of **other specified muscles**, fascia and tendons at thigh level
  - ● S76.80   **Unspecified** injury of other specified muscles, fascia and tendons at thigh level
    - ● S76.801   Unspecified injury of other specified muscles, fascia and tendons at thigh level, **right** thigh
    - ● S76.802   Unspecified injury of other specified muscles, fascia and tendons at thigh level, **left** thigh
    - ● S76.809   Unspecified injury of other specified muscles, fascia and tendons at thigh level, **unspecified** thigh

- ● S76.81   **Strain** of other specified specified muscles, fascia and tendons at thigh level
  - ● S76.811   Strain of other specified muscles, fascia and tendons at thigh level, **right** thigh
  - ● S76.812   Strain of other specified muscles, fascia and tendons at thigh level, **left** thigh
  - ● S76.819   Strain of other specified muscles, fascia and tendons at thigh level, **unspecified** thigh
- ● S76.82   **Laceration** of other specified muscles, fascia and tendons at thigh level
  - ● S76.821   Laceration of other specified muscles, fascia and tendons at thigh level, **right** thigh
  - ● S76.822   Laceration of other specified muscles, fascia and tendons at thigh level, **left** thigh
  - ● S76.829   Laceration of other specified muscles, fascia and tendons at thigh level, **unspecified** thigh
- ● S76.89   **Other** injury of other specified muscles, fascia and tendons at thigh level
  - ● S76.891   Other injury of other specified muscles, fascia and tendons at thigh level, **right** thigh
  - ● S76.892   Other injury of other specified muscles, fascia and tendons at thigh level, **left** thigh
  - ● S76.899   Other injury of other specified muscles, fascia and tendons at thigh level, **unspecified** thigh
- ● S76.9   Injury of **unspecified muscles**, fascia and tendons at thigh level
  - ● S76.90   **Unspecified** injury of unspecified muscles, fascia and tendons at thigh level
    - ● S76.901   Unspecified injury of unspecified muscles, fascia and tendons at thigh level, **right** thigh
    - ● S76.902   Unspecified injury of unspecified muscles, fascia and tendons at thigh level, **left** thigh
    - ● S76.909   Unspecified injury of unspecified muscles, fascia and tendons at thigh level, **unspecified** thigh
  - ● S76.91   **Strain** of unspecified muscles, fascia and tendons at thigh level
    - ● S76.911   Strain of unspecified muscles, fascia and tendons at thigh level, **right** thigh
    - ● S76.912   Strain of unspecified muscles, fascia and tendons at thigh level, **left** thigh
    - ● S76.919   Strain of unspecified muscles fascia and tendons at thigh level, **unspecified** thigh
  - ● S76.92   **Laceration** of unspecified muscles, fascia and tendons at thigh level
    - ● S76.921   Laceration of unspecified muscles, fascia and tendons at thigh level, **right** thigh
    - ● S76.922   Laceration of unspecified muscles, fascia and tendons at thigh level, **left** thigh
    - ● S76.929   Laceration of unspecified muscles, fascia and tendons at thigh level, **unspecified** thigh

CHAPTER 19 (S00-T88)

● **S76.99** **Other** specified injury of unspecified muscles, fascia and tendons at thigh level

  ● **S76.991** Other specified injury of unspecified muscles, fascia and tendons at thigh level, **right** thigh

  ● **S76.992** Other specified injury of unspecified muscles, fascia and tendons at thigh level, **left** thigh

  ● **S76.999** Other specified injury of unspecified muscles, fascia and tendons at thigh level, **unspecified** thigh

● **S77** **Crushing injury of hip and thigh**

Use additional code(s) for all associated injuries

Excludes2 crushing injury of ankle and foot (S97.-)
crushing injury of lower leg (S87.-)

The appropriate 7th character is to be added to each code from category S77

A	initial encounter
D	subsequent encounter
S	sequela

 ● **S77.0** Crushing injury of **hip**

  X● **S77.00** Crushing injury of **unspecified** hip

  X● **S77.01** Crushing injury of **right** hip

  X● **S77.02** Crushing injury of **left** hip

 ● **S77.1** Crushing injury of **thigh**

  X● **S77.10** Crushing injury of **unspecified** thigh

  X● **S77.11** Crushing injury of **right** thigh

  X● **S77.12** Crushing injury of **left** thigh

 ● **S77.2** Crushing injury of **hip with thigh**

  X● **S77.20** Crushing injury of **unspecified** hip with thigh

  X● **S77.21** Crushing injury of **right** hip with thigh

  X● **S77.22** Crushing injury of **left** hip with thigh

● **S78** **Traumatic amputation of hip and thigh**

An amputation not identified as partial or complete should be coded to complete

Excludes1 traumatic amputation of knee (S88.0-)

The appropriate 7th character is to be added to each code from category S78

A	initial encounter
D	subsequent encounter
S	sequela

 ● **S78.0** Traumatic amputation **at hip joint**

  ● **S78.01** **Complete** traumatic amputation at hip joint

   ● **S78.011** Complete traumatic amputation at **right** hip joint

   ● **S78.012** Complete traumatic amputation at **left** hip joint

   ● **S78.019** Complete traumatic amputation at **unspecified** hip joint

  ● **S78.02** **Partial** traumatic amputation at hip joint

   ● **S78.021** Partial traumatic amputation at **right** hip joint

   ● **S78.022** Partial traumatic amputation at **left** hip joint

   ● **S78.029** Partial traumatic amputation at **unspecified** hip joint

● **S78.1** Traumatic amputation at level **between hip and knee**

Excludes1 traumatic amputation of knee (S88.0-)

 ● **S78.11** **Complete** traumatic amputation at level between hip and knee

  ● **S78.111** Complete traumatic amputation at level between **right** hip and knee

  ● **S78.112** Complete traumatic amputation at level between **left** hip and knee

  ● **S78.119** Complete traumatic amputation at level between **unspecified** hip and knee

 ● **S78.12** **Partial** traumatic amputation at level between hip and knee

  ● **S78.121** Partial traumatic amputation at level between **right** hip and knee

  ● **S78.122** Partial traumatic amputation at level between **left** hip and knee

  ● **S78.129** Partial traumatic amputation at level between **unspecified** hip and knee

● **S78.9** Traumatic amputation of hip and thigh, **level unspecified**

 ● **S78.91** **Complete** traumatic amputation of hip and thigh, level unspecified

  ● **S78.911** Complete traumatic amputation of **right** hip and thigh, level unspecified

  ● **S78.912** Complete traumatic amputation of **left** hip and thigh, level unspecified

  ● **S78.919** Complete traumatic amputation of **unspecified** hip and thigh, level unspecified

 ● **S78.92** **Partial** traumatic amputation of hip and thigh, level unspecified

  ● **S78.921** Partial traumatic amputation of **right** hip and thigh, level unspecified

  ● **S78.922** Partial traumatic amputation of **left** hip and thigh, level unspecified

  ● **S78.929** Partial traumatic amputation of **unspecified** hip and thigh, level unspecified

● **S79** **Other and unspecified injuries of hip and thigh**

Note: A fracture not indicated as open or closed should be coded to closed

The appropriate 7th character is to be added to each code from subcategories S79.0 and S79.1

A	initial encounter for closed fracture
D	subsequent encounter for fracture with routine healing
G	subsequent encounter for fracture with delayed healing
K	subsequent encounter for fracture with nonunion
P	subsequent encounter for fracture with malunion
S	sequela

 ● **S79.0** **Physeal fracture of upper end of femur**

Excludes1 apophyseal fracture of upper end of femur (S72.13-)
nontraumatic slipped upper femoral epiphysis (M93.0-)

  ● **S79.00** Unspecified physeal fracture of upper end of femur

   ● **S79.001** Unspecified physeal fracture of upper end of **right** femur

   ● **S79.002** Unspecified physeal fracture of upper end of **left** femur

   ● **S79.009** Unspecified physeal fracture of upper end of **unspecified** femur

Item 19–5   SALTER-HARRIS TYPE 1: epiphysis is completely separated from end of bone, or metaphysic growth plate remains attached to epiphysis

    SALTER-HARRIS TYPE 2: epiphysis and growth plate are partially separated from metaphysis, which is cracked—most common type

    SALTER-HARRIS TYPE 3: fracture occurring through epiphysis and separates part of epiphysis and growth plate from metaphysis fracture, usually at distal end of tibia

    SALTER-HARRIS TYPE 4: fracture runs through epiphysis, across growth plate, into metaphysic, surgery is required to restore joint surface to normal and align growth plate

- **S79.01**   **Salter-Harris Type I physeal fracture of upper end of femur**
  - Acute on chronic slipped capital femoral epiphysis (traumatic)
  - Acute slipped capital femoral epiphysis (traumatic)
  - Capital femoral epiphyseal fracture
  - **Excludes1**   chronic slipped upper femoral epiphysis (nontraumatic) (M93.02-)
  - **S79.011**   Salter-Harris Type I physeal fracture of upper end of right femur
  - **S79.012**   Salter-Harris Type I physeal fracture of upper end of left femur
  - **S79.019**   Salter-Harris Type I physeal fracture of upper end of unspecified femur
- **S79.09**   Other physeal fracture of upper end of femur
  - **S79.091**   Other physeal fracture of upper end of right femur
  - **S79.092**   Other physeal fracture of upper end of left femur
  - **S79.099**   Other physeal fracture of upper end of unspecified femur
- **S79.1**   **Physeal fracture of lower end of femur**
  - **S79.10**   **Unspecified physeal fracture of lower end of femur**
    - **S79.101**   Unspecified physeal fracture of lower end of right femur
    - **S79.102**   Unspecified physeal fracture of lower end of left femur
    - **S79.109**   Unspecified physeal fracture of lower end of unspecified femur
  - **S79.11**   **Salter-Harris Type I physeal fracture of lower end of femur**
    - **S79.111**   Salter-Harris Type I physeal fracture of lower end of right femur
    - **S79.112**   Salter-Harris Type I physeal fracture of lower end of left femur
    - **S79.119**   Salter-Harris Type I physeal fracture of lower end of unspecified femur
  - **S79.12**   **Salter-Harris Type II physeal fracture of lower end of femur**
    - **S79.121**   Salter-Harris Type II physeal fracture of lower end of right femur
    - **S79.122**   Salter-Harris Type II physeal fracture of lower end of left femur
    - **S79.129**   Salter-Harris Type II physeal fracture of lower end of unspecified femur

- **S79.13**   **Salter-Harris Type III physeal fracture of lower end of femur**
  - **S79.131**   Salter-Harris Type III physeal fracture of lower end of right femur
  - **S79.132**   Salter-Harris Type III physeal fracture of lower end of left femur
  - **S79.139**   Salter-Harris Type III physeal fracture of lower end of unspecified femur
- **S79.14**   **Salter-Harris Type IV physeal fracture of lower end of femur**
  - **S79.141**   Salter-Harris Type IV physeal fracture of lower end of right femur
  - **S79.142**   Salter-Harris Type IV physeal fracture of lower end of left femur
  - **S79.149**   Salter-Harris Type IV physeal fracture of lower end of unspecified femur
- **S79.19**   **Other physeal fracture of lower end of femur**
  - **S79.191**   Other physeal fracture of lower end of right femur
  - **S79.192**   Other physeal fracture of lower end of left femur
  - **S79.199**   Other physeal fracture of lower end of unspecified femur
- **S79.8 Other specified injuries of hip and thigh**
  - The appropriate 7th character is to be added to each code in subcategory S79.8

A	initial encounter
D	subsequent encounter
S	sequela

  - **S79.81**   **Other specified injuries of hip**
    - **S79.811**   Other specified injuries of right hip
    - **S79.812**   Other specified injuries of left hip
    - **S79.819**   Other specified injuries of unspecified hip
  - **S79.82**   **Other specified injuries of thigh**
    - **S79.821**   Other specified injuries of right thigh
    - **S79.822**   Other specified injuries of left thigh
    - **S79.829**   Other specified injuries of unspecified thigh
- **S79.9**   **Unspecified injury of hip and thigh**
  - The appropriate 7th character is to be added to each code in subcategory S79.9

A	initial encounter
D	subsequent encounter
S	sequela

  - **S79.91**   **Unspecified injury of hip**
    - **S79.911**   Unspecified injury of right hip
    - **S79.912**   Unspecified injury of left hip
    - **S79.919**   Unspecified injury of unspecified hip
  - **S79.92**   **Unspecified injury of thigh**
    - **S79.921**   Unspecified injury of right thigh
    - **S79.922**   Unspecified injury of left thigh
    - **S79.929**   Unspecified injury of unspecified thigh

CHAPTER 19 (S00-T88)

INJURIES TO THE KNEE AND LOWER LEG (S80-S89)

Excludes2   burns and corrosions (T20-T32)
frostbite (T33-T34)
injuries of ankle and foot, except fracture of ankle and malleolus (S90-S99)
insect bite or sting, venomous (T63.4)

● **S80   Superficial injury of knee and lower leg**

Excludes2   superficial injury of ankle and foot (S90.-)

The appropriate 7th character is to be added to each code from category S80

> A   initial encounter
> D   subsequent encounter
> S   sequela

● **S80.0   Contusion of knee**
    X ● S80.00   Contusion of unspecified knee
    X ● S80.01   Contusion of right knee
    X ● S80.02   Contusion of left knee
● **S80.1   Contusion of lower leg**
    X ● S80.10   Contusion of unspecified lower leg
    X ● S80.11   Contusion of right lower leg
    X ● S80.12   Contusion of left lower leg
● **S80.2   Other superficial injuries of knee**
    ● S80.21   Abrasion of knee
       ● S80.211   Abrasion, right knee
       ● S80.212   Abrasion, left knee
       ● S80.219   Abrasion, unspecified knee
    ● S80.22   Blister (nonthermal) of knee
       ● S80.221   Blister (nonthermal), right knee
       ● S80.222   Blister (nonthermal), left knee
       ● S80.229   Blister (nonthermal), unspecified knee
    ● S80.24   External constriction of knee
       ● S80.241   External constriction, right knee
       ● S80.242   External constriction, left knee
       ● S80.249   External constriction, unspecified knee
    ● S80.25   Superficial foreign body of knee
       Splinter in the knee
       ● S80.251   Superficial foreign body, right knee
       ● S80.252   Superficial foreign body, left knee
       ● S80.259   Superficial foreign body, unspecified knee
    ● S80.26   Insect bite (nonvenomous) of knee
       ● S80.261   Insect bite (nonvenomous), right knee
       ● S80.262   Insect bite (nonvenomous), left knee
       ● S80.269   Insect bite (nonvenomous), unspecified knee
    ● S80.27   Other superficial bite of knee
       Excludes1   open bite of knee (S81.05-)
       ● S80.271   Other superficial bite of right knee
       ● S80.272   Other superficial bite of left knee
       ● S80.279   Other superficial bite of unspecified knee
● **S80.8   Other superficial injuries of lower leg**
    ● S80.81   Abrasion of lower leg
       ● S80.811   Abrasion, right lower leg
       ● S80.812   Abrasion, left lower leg
       ● S80.819   Abrasion, unspecified lower leg
    ● S80.82   Blister (nonthermal) of lower leg
       ● S80.821   Blister (nonthermal), right lower leg
       ● S80.822   Blister (nonthermal), left lower leg
       ● S80.829   Blister (nonthermal), unspecified lower leg

● S80.84   **External constriction of lower leg**
    ● S80.841   External constriction, right lower leg
    ● S80.842   External constriction, left lower leg
    ● S80.849   External constriction, unspecified lower leg
● S80.85   **Superficial foreign body of lower leg**
    Splinter in the lower leg
    ● S80.851   Superficial foreign body, right lower leg
    ● S80.852   Superficial foreign body, left lower leg
    ● S80.859   Superficial foreign body, unspecified lower leg
● S80.86   **Insect bite (nonvenomous) of lower leg**
    ● S80.861   Insect bite (nonvenomous), right lower leg
    ● S80.862   Insect bite (nonvenomous), left lower leg
    ● S80.869   Insect bite (nonvenomous), unspecified lower leg
● S80.87   **Other superficial bite of lower leg**
    Excludes1   open bite of lower leg (S81.85-)
    ● S80.871   Other superficial bite, right lower leg
    ● S80.872   Other superficial bite, left lower leg
    ● S80.879   Other superficial bite, unspecified lower leg
● S80.9   **Unspecified superficial injury of knee and lower leg**
    ● S80.91   Unspecified superficial injury of knee
       ● S80.911   Unspecified superficial injury of right knee
       ● S80.912   Unspecified superficial injury of left knee
       ● S80.919   Unspecified superficial injury of unspecified knee
    ● S80.92   Unspecified superficial injury of lower leg
       ● S80.921   Unspecified superficial injury of right lower leg
       ● S80.922   Unspecified superficial injury of left lower leg
       ● S80.929   Unspecified superficial injury of unspecified lower leg

● **S81   Open wound of knee and lower leg**
    Code also any associated wound infection
    Excludes1   open fracture of knee and lower leg (S82.-)
              traumatic amputation of lower leg (S88.-)
    Excludes2   open wound of ankle and foot (S91.-)
    The appropriate 7th character is to be added to each code from category S81

> A   initial encounter
> D   subsequent encounter
> S   sequela

● S81.0   **Open wound of knee**
    ● S81.00   Unspecified open wound of knee
       ● S81.001   Unspecified open wound, right knee
       ● S81.002   Unspecified open wound, left knee
       ● S81.009   Unspecified open wound, unspecified knee
    ● S81.01   Laceration without foreign body of knee
       ● S81.011   Laceration without foreign body, right knee
       ● S81.012   Laceration without foreign body, left knee
       ● S81.019   Laceration without foreign body, unspecified knee

● **S81.02**   **Laceration with foreign body of knee**
   ● **S81.021**   Laceration with foreign body, **right** knee
   ● **S81.022**   Laceration with foreign body, **left** knee
   ● **S81.029**   Laceration with foreign body, **unspecified** knee
● **S81.03**   **Puncture wound without foreign body of knee**
   ● **S81.031**   Puncture wound without foreign body, **right** knee
   ● **S81.032**   Puncture wound without foreign body, **left** knee
   ● **S81.039**   Puncture wound without foreign body, **unspecified** knee
● **S81.04**   **Puncture wound with foreign body of knee**
   ● **S81.041**   Puncture wound with foreign body, **right** knee
   ● **S81.042**   Puncture wound with foreign body, **left** knee
   ● **S81.049**   Puncture wound with foreign body, **unspecified** knee
● **S81.05**   **Open bite of knee**
     Bite of knee NOS
     Excludes1   superficial bite of knee (S80.27-)
   ● **S81.051**   Open bite, **right** knee
   ● **S81.052**   Open bite, **left** knee
   ● **S81.059**   Open bite, **unspecified** knee
● **S81.8**   **Open wound of lower leg**
   ● **S81.80**   **Unspecified open wound of lower leg**
     ● **S81.801**   Unspecified open wound, **right** lower leg
     ● **S81.802**   Unspecified open wound, **left** lower leg
     ● **S81.809**   Unspecified open wound, **unspecified** lower leg
   ● **S81.81**   **Laceration without foreign body of lower leg**
     ● **S81.811**   Laceration without foreign body, **right** lower leg
     ● **S81.812**   Laceration without foreign body, **left** lower leg
     ● **S81.819**   Laceration without foreign body, **unspecified** lower leg
   ● **S81.82**   **Laceration with foreign body of lower leg**
     ● **S81.821**   Laceration with foreign body, **right** lower leg
     ● **S81.822**   Laceration with foreign body, **left** lower leg
     ● **S81.829**   Laceration with foreign body, **unspecified** lower leg
   ● **S81.83**   **Puncture wound without foreign body of lower leg**
     ● **S81.831**   Puncture wound without foreign body, **right** lower leg
     ● **S81.832**   Puncture wound without foreign body, **left** lower leg
     ● **S81.839**   Puncture wound without foreign body, **unspecified** lower leg
   ● **S81.84**   **Puncture wound with foreign body of lower leg**
     ● **S81.841**   Puncture wound with foreign body, **right** lower leg
        Coding Clinic: 2016, Q3, P46
     ● **S81.842**   Puncture wound with foreign body, **left** lower leg
     ● **S81.849**   Puncture wound with foreign body, **unspecified** lower leg

● **S81.85**   **Open bite of lower leg**
     Bite of lower leg NOS
     Excludes1   superficial bite of lower leg (S80.86-, S80.87-)
   ● **S81.851**   Open bite, **right** lower leg
   ● **S81.852**   Open bite, **left** lower leg
   ● **S81.859**   Open bite, **unspecified** lower leg

● **S82**   **Fracture of lower leg, including ankle**
   Note: A fracture not indicated as displaced or nondisplaced should be coded to displaced
   A fracture not indicated as open or closed should be coded to closed
   The open fracture designations are based on the Gustilo open fracture classification
   Includes   fracture of malleolus
   Excludes1   traumatic amputation of lower leg (S88.-)
   Excludes2   fracture of foot, except ankle (S92.-)
     periprosthetic fracture of prosthetic implant of knee (M97.0-)
   The appropriate 7th character is to be added to all codes from category S82

A	initial encounter for closed fracture
B	initial encounter for open fracture type I or II initial encounter for open fracture NOS
C	initial encounter for open fracture type IIIA, IIIB, or IIIC
D	subsequent encounter for closed fracture with routine healing
E	subsequent encounter for open fracture type I or II with routine healing
F	subsequent encounter for open fracture type IIIA, IIIB, or IIIC with routine healing
G	subsequent encounter for closed fracture with delayed healing
H	subsequent encounter for open fracture type I or II with delayed healing
J	subsequent encounter for open fracture type IIIA, IIIB, or IIIC with delayed healing
K	subsequent encounter for closed fracture with nonunion
M	subsequent encounter for open fracture type I or II with nonunion
N	subsequent encounter for open fracture type IIIA, IIIB, or IIIC with nonunion
P	subsequent encounter for closed fracture with malunion
Q	subsequent encounter for open fracture type I or II with malunion
R	subsequent encounter for open fracture type IIIA, IIIB, or IIIC with malunion
S	sequela

   ● **S82.0**   **Fracture of patella**
     Knee cap
     ● **S82.00**   **Unspecified fracture of patella**
       ● **S82.001**   Unspecified fracture of **right** patella
       ● **S82.002**   Unspecified fracture of **left** patella
       ● **S82.009**   Unspecified fracture of **unspecified** patella
     ● **S82.01**   **Osteochondral fracture of patella**
       ● **S82.011**   **Displaced** osteochondral fracture of **right** patella
       ● **S82.012**   **Displaced** osteochondral fracture of **left** patella
       ● **S82.013**   **Displaced** osteochondral fracture of **unspecified** patella
       ● **S82.014**   **Nondisplaced** osteochondral fracture of **right** patella
       ● **S82.015**   **Nondisplaced** osteochondral fracture of **left** patella
       ● **S82.016**   **Nondisplaced** osteochondral fracture of **unspecified** patella

CHAPTER 19 (S00-T88)

- **S82.02**   **Longitudinal fracture of patella**
  - **S82.021**   Displaced longitudinal fracture of right patella
  - **S82.022**   Displaced longitudinal fracture of left patella
  - **S82.023**   Displaced longitudinal fracture of unspecified patella
  - **S82.024**   Nondisplaced longitudinal fracture of right patella
  - **S82.025**   Nondisplaced longitudinal fracture of left patella
  - **S82.026**   Nondisplaced longitudinal fracture of unspecified patella
- **S82.03**   **Transverse fracture of patella**
  - **S82.031**   Displaced transverse fracture of right patella
  - **S82.032**   Displaced transverse fracture of left patella
  - **S82.033**   Displaced transverse fracture of unspecified patella
  - **S82.034**   Nondisplaced transverse fracture of right patella
  - **S82.035**   Nondisplaced transverse fracture of left patella
  - **S82.036**   Nondisplaced transverse fracture of unspecified patella
- **S82.04**   **Comminuted fracture of patella**
  - **S82.041**   Displaced comminuted fracture of right patella
  - **S82.042**   Displaced comminuted fracture of left patella
  - **S82.043**   Displaced comminuted fracture of unspecified patella
  - **S82.044**   Nondisplaced comminuted fracture of right patella
  - **S82.045**   Nondisplaced comminuted fracture of left patella
  - **S82.046**   Nondisplaced comminuted fracture of unspecified patella
- **S82.09**   **Other fracture of patella**
  - **S82.091**   Other fracture of right patella
  - **S82.092**   Other fracture of left patella
  - **S82.099**   Other fracture of unspecified patella
- **S82.1**   **Fracture of upper end of tibia**
  Fracture of proximal end of tibia
  > **Excludes2**   fracture of shaft of tibia (S82.2-)
  > physeal fracture of upper end of tibia (S89.0-)
  - **S82.10**   **Unspecified fracture of upper end of tibia**
    - **S82.101**   Unspecified fracture of upper end of right tibia
    - **S82.102**   Unspecified fracture of upper end of left tibia
    - **S82.109**   Unspecified fracture of upper end of unspecified tibia
  - **S82.11**   **Fracture of tibial spine**
    - **S82.111**   Displaced fracture of right tibial spine
    - **S82.112**   Displaced fracture of left tibial spine
    - **S82.113**   Displaced fracture of unspecified tibial spine
    - **S82.114**   Nondisplaced fracture of right tibial spine
    - **S82.115**   Nondisplaced fracture of left tibial spine
    - **S82.116**   Nondisplaced fracture of unspecified tibial spine

- **S82.12**   **Fracture of lateral condyle of tibia**
  - **S82.121**   Displaced fracture of lateral condyle of right tibia
  - **S82.122**   Displaced fracture of lateral condyle of left tibia
  - **S82.123**   Displaced fracture of lateral condyle of unspecified tibia
  - **S82.124**   Nondisplaced fracture of lateral condyle of right tibia
  - **S82.125**   Nondisplaced fracture of lateral condyle of left tibia
  - **S82.126**   Nondisplaced fracture of lateral condyle of unspecified tibia
- **S82.13**   **Fracture of medial condyle of tibia**
  - **S82.131**   Displaced fracture of medial condyle of right tibia
  - **S82.132**   Displaced fracture of medial condyle of left tibia
  - **S82.133**   Displaced fracture of medial condyle of unspecified tibia
  - **S82.134**   Nondisplaced fracture of medial condyle of right tibia
  - **S82.135**   Nondisplaced fracture of medial condyle of left tibia
  - **S82.136**   Nondisplaced fracture of medial condyle of unspecified tibia
- **S82.14**   **Bicondylar fracture of tibia**
  Fracture of tibial plateau NOS
  - **S82.141**   Displaced bicondylar fracture of right tibia
  - **S82.142**   Displaced bicondylar fracture of left tibia
  - **S82.143**   Displaced bicondylar fracture of unspecified tibia
  - **S82.144**   Nondisplaced bicondylar fracture of right tibia
  - **S82.145**   Nondisplaced bicondylar fracture of left tibia
  - **S82.146**   Nondisplaced bicondylar fracture of unspecified tibia
- **S82.15**   **Fracture of tibial tuberosity**
  - **S82.151**   Displaced fracture of right tibial tuberosity
  - **S82.152**   Displaced fracture of left tibial tuberosity
  - **S82.153**   Displaced fracture of unspecified tibial tuberosity
  - **S82.154**   Nondisplaced fracture of right tibial tuberosity
  - **S82.155**   Nondisplaced fracture of left tibial tuberosity
  - **S82.156**   Nondisplaced fracture of unspecified tibial tuberosity
- **S82.16**   **Torus fracture of upper end of tibia**
  The appropriate 7th character is to be added to all codes in subcategory S82.16

  > | | |
  > |---|---|
  > | A | initial encounter for closed fracture |
  > | D | subsequent encounter for fracture with routine healing |
  > | G | subsequent encounter for fracture with delayed healing |
  > | K | subsequent encounter for fracture with nonunion |
  > | P | subsequent encounter for fracture with malunion |
  > | S | sequela |

  - **S82.161**   Torus fracture of upper end of right tibia
  - **S82.162**   Torus fracture of upper end of left tibia
  - **S82.169**   Torus fracture of upper end of unspecified tibia

● S82.19   Other fracture of upper end of tibia
   ● S82.191   Other fracture of upper end of **right** tibia
   ● S82.192   Other fracture of upper end of **left** tibia
   ● S82.199   Other fracture of upper end of **unspecified** tibia

● S82.2   Fracture of **shaft** of tibia
   ● S82.20   **Unspecified** fracture of shaft of tibia
      Fracture of tibia NOS
     ● S82.201   Unspecified fracture of shaft of **right** tibia
     ● S82.202   Unspecified fracture of shaft of **left** tibia
     ● S82.209   Unspecified fracture of shaft of **unspecified** tibia
   ● S82.22   **Transverse** fracture of shaft of tibia
     ● S82.221   Displaced transverse fracture of shaft of **right** tibia
     ● S82.222   Displaced transverse fracture of shaft of **left** tibia
     ● S82.223   Displaced transverse fracture of shaft of **unspecified** tibia
     ● S82.224   Nondisplaced transverse fracture of shaft of **right** tibia
     ● S82.225   Nondisplaced transverse fracture of shaft of **left** tibia
     ● S82.226   Nondisplaced transverse fracture of shaft of **unspecified** tibia
   ● S82.23   **Oblique** fracture of shaft of tibia
     ● S82.231   Displaced oblique fracture of shaft of **right** tibia
     ● S82.232   Displaced oblique fracture of shaft of **left** tibia
     ● S82.233   Displaced oblique fracture of shaft of **unspecified** tibia
     ● S82.234   Nondisplaced oblique fracture of shaft of **right** tibia
        Coding Clinic: 2015, Q1, P9-10
     ● S82.235   Nondisplaced oblique fracture of shaft of **left** tibia
     ● S82.236   Nondisplaced oblique fracture of shaft of **unspecified** tibia
   ● S82.24   **Spiral** fracture of shaft of tibia
      Toddler fracture
     ● S82.241   Displaced spiral fracture of shaft of **right** tibia
     ● S82.242   Displaced spiral fracture of shaft of **left** tibia
     ● S82.243   Displaced spiral fracture of shaft of **unspecified** tibia
     ● S82.244   Nondisplaced spiral fracture of shaft of **right** tibia
     ● S82.245   Nondisplaced spiral fracture of shaft of **left** tibia
     ● S82.246   Nondisplaced spiral fracture of shaft of **unspecified** tibia
   ● S82.25   **Comminuted** fracture of shaft of tibia
     ● S82.251   Displaced comminuted fracture of shaft of **right** tibia
        Coding Clinic: 2015, Q2, P6
     ● S82.252   Displaced comminuted fracture of shaft of **left** tibia
     ● S82.253   Displaced comminuted fracture of shaft of **unspecified** tibia

     ● S82.254   Nondisplaced comminuted fracture of shaft of **right** tibia
     ● S82.255   Nondisplaced comminuted fracture of shaft of **left** tibia
     ● S82.256   Nondisplaced comminuted fracture of shaft of **unspecified** tibia
   ● S82.26   **Segmental** fracture of shaft of tibia
     ● S82.261   Displaced segmental fracture of shaft of **right** tibia
     ● S82.262   Displaced segmental fracture of shaft of **left** tibia
     ● S82.263   Displaced segmental fracture of shaft of **unspecified** tibia
     ● S82.264   Nondisplaced segmental fracture of shaft of **right** tibia
     ● S82.265   Nondisplaced segmental fracture of shaft of **left** tibia
     ● S82.266   Nondisplaced segmental fracture of shaft of **unspecified** tibia
   ● S82.29   **Other** fracture of shaft of tibia
     ● S82.291   Other fracture of shaft of **right** tibia
     ● S82.292   Other fracture of shaft of **left** tibia
     ● S82.299   Other fracture of shaft of **unspecified** tibia

● S82.3   Fracture of **lower end** of tibia
    Excludes1   bimalleolar fracture of lower leg (S82.84-)
             fracture of medial malleolus alone (S82.5-)
             Maisonneuve's fracture (S82.86-)
             pilon fracture of distal tibia (S82.87-)
             trimalleolar fractures of lower leg (S82.85-)
   ● S82.30   **Unspecified** fracture of lower end of tibia
     ● S82.301   Unspecified fracture of lower end of **right** tibia
     ● S82.302   Unspecified fracture of lower end of **left** tibia
     ● S82.309   Unspecified fracture of lower end of **unspecified** tibia
   ● S82.31   **Torus** fracture of lower end of tibia
      The appropriate 7th character is to be added to all codes in subcategory S82.31

> A   initial encounter for closed fracture
> D   subsequent encounter for fracture with routine healing
> G   subsequent encounter for fracture with delayed healing
> K   subsequent encounter for fracture with nonunion
> P   subsequent encounter for fracture with malunion
> S   sequela

     ● S82.311   Torus fracture of lower end of **right** tibia
     ● S82.312   Torus fracture of lower end of **left** tibia
     ● S82.319   Torus fracture of lower end of **unspecified** tibia
   ● S82.39   **Other** fracture of lower end of tibia
     ● S82.391   Other fracture of lower end of **right** tibia
     ● S82.392   Other fracture of lower end of **left** tibia
        Coding Clinic: 2015, Q1, P25
     ● S82.399   Other fracture of lower end of **unspecified** tibia

CHAPTER 19 (S00-T88)

● S82.4   Fracture of shaft of fibula
     Excludes2   fracture of lateral malleolus alone (S82.6-)
   ● S82.40   Unspecified fracture of shaft of fibula
     ● S82.401   Unspecified fracture of shaft of right fibula
     ● S82.402   Unspecified fracture of shaft of left fibula
     ● S82.409   Unspecified fracture of shaft of unspecified fibula
   ● S82.42   Transverse fracture of shaft of fibula
     ● S82.421   Displaced transverse fracture of shaft of right fibula
     ● S82.422   Displaced transverse fracture of shaft of left fibula
     ● S82.423   Displaced transverse fracture of shaft of unspecified fibula
     ● S82.424   Nondisplaced transverse fracture of shaft of right fibula
     ● S82.425   Nondisplaced transverse fracture of shaft of left fibula
     ● S82.426   Nondisplaced transverse fracture of shaft of unspecified fibula
   ● S82.43   Oblique fracture of shaft of fibula
     ● S82.431   Displaced oblique fracture of shaft of right fibula
     ● S82.432   Displaced oblique fracture of shaft of left fibula
     ● S82.433   Displaced oblique fracture of shaft of unspecified fibula
     ● S82.434   Nondisplaced oblique fracture of shaft of right fibula
     ● S82.435   Nondisplaced oblique fracture of shaft of left fibula
     ● S82.436   Nondisplaced oblique fracture of shaft of unspecified fibula
   ● S82.44   Spiral fracture of shaft of fibula
     ● S82.441   Displaced spiral fracture of shaft of right fibula
     ● S82.442   Displaced spiral fracture of shaft of left fibula
     ● S82.443   Displaced spiral fracture of shaft of unspecified fibula
     ● S82.444   Nondisplaced spiral fracture of shaft of right fibula
     ● S82.445   Nondisplaced spiral fracture of shaft of left fibula
     ● S82.446   Nondisplaced spiral fracture of shaft of unspecified fibula
   ● S82.45   Comminuted fracture of shaft of fibula
     ● S82.451   Displaced comminuted fracture of shaft of right fibula
     ● S82.452   Displaced comminuted fracture of shaft of left fibula
     ● S82.453   Displaced comminuted fracture of shaft of unspecified fibula
     ● S82.454   Nondisplaced comminuted fracture of shaft of right fibula
     ● S82.455   Nondisplaced comminuted fracture of shaft of left fibula
     ● S82.456   Nondisplaced comminuted fracture of shaft of unspecified fibula
   ● S82.46   Segmental fracture of shaft of fibula
     ● S82.461   Displaced segmental fracture of shaft of right fibula
     ● S82.462   Displaced segmental fracture of shaft of left fibula

     ● S82.463   Displaced segmental fracture of shaft of unspecified fibula
     ● S82.464   Nondisplaced segmental fracture of shaft of right fibula
     ● S82.465   Nondisplaced segmental fracture of shaft of left fibula
     ● S82.466   Nondisplaced segmental fracture of shaft of unspecified fibula
   ● S82.49   Other fracture of shaft of fibula
     ● S82.491   Other fracture of shaft of right fibula
     ● S82.492   Other fracture of shaft of left fibula
     ● S82.499   Other fracture of shaft of unspecified fibula
● S82.5   Fracture of medial malleolus
     Excludes1   pilon fracture of distal tibia (S82.87-)
                  Salter-Harris type III of lower end of tibia (S89.13-)
                  Salter-Harris type IV of lower end of tibia (S89.14-)
   X ● S82.51   Displaced fracture of medial malleolus of right tibia
   X ● S82.52   Displaced fracture of medial malleolus of left tibia
   X ● S82.53   Displaced fracture of medial malleolus of unspecified tibia
   X ● S82.54   Nondisplaced fracture of medial malleolus of right tibia
   X ● S82.55   Nondisplaced fracture of medial malleolus of left tibia
   X ● S82.56   Nondisplaced fracture of medial malleolus of unspecified tibia
● S82.6   Fracture of lateral malleolus
     Excludes1   pilon fracture of distal tibia (S82.87-)
   X ● S82.61   Displaced fracture of lateral malleolus of right fibula
   X ● S82.62   Displaced fracture of lateral malleolus of left fibula
   X ● S82.63   Displaced fracture of lateral malleolus of unspecified fibula
   X ● S82.64   Nondisplaced fracture of lateral malleolus of right fibula
   X ● S82.65   Nondisplaced fracture of lateral malleolus of left fibula
   X ● S82.66   Nondisplaced fracture of lateral malleolus of unspecified fibula
● S82.8   Other fractures of lower leg
   ● S82.81   Torus fracture of upper end of fibula
     The appropriate 7th character is to be added to all codes in subcategory S82.81

A	initial encounter for closed fracture
D	subsequent encounter for fracture with routine healing
G	subsequent encounter for fracture with delayed healing
K	subsequent encounter for fracture with nonunion
P	subsequent encounter for fracture with malunion
S	sequela

     ● S82.811   Torus fracture of upper end of right fibula
     ● S82.812   Torus fracture of upper end of left fibula
     ● S82.819   Torus fracture of upper end of unspecified fibula

▶ New   ⇒ Revised   ~~deleted~~ Deleted   Excludes 1   Excludes 2   Includes   Use additional   Code first   Code also   Key words
OGCR Official Guidelines   X Assign placeholder X   ● Use Additional Character(s)   ▷ Manifestation Code   Coding Clinic

● **S82.82**   **Torus fracture of lower end of fibula**

> The appropriate 7th character is to be added to all codes in subcategory S82.82

> | | |
> |---|---|
> | A | initial encounter for closed fracture |
> | D | subsequent encounter for fracture with routine healing |
> | G | subsequent encounter for fracture with delayed healing |
> | K | subsequent encounter for fracture with nonunion |
> | P | subsequent encounter for fracture with malunion |
> | S | sequela |

   ● **S82.821**   Torus fracture of lower end of **right** fibula

   ● **S82.822**   Torus fracture of lower end of **left** fibula

   ● **S82.829**   Torus fracture of lower end of **unspecified** fibula

● **S82.83**   **Other** fracture of upper and lower end of fibula

   ● **S82.831**   Other fracture of upper and lower end of **right** fibula

   ● **S82.832**   Other fracture of upper and lower end of **left** fibula
      Coding Clinic: 2015, Q1, P9-10

   ● **S82.839**   Other fracture of upper and lower end of **unspecified** fibula

● **S82.84**   **Bimalleolar** fracture of lower leg

   ● **S82.841**   Displaced bimalleolar fracture of **right** lower leg

   ● **S82.842**   Displaced bimalleolar fracture of **left** lower leg

   ● **S82.843**   Displaced bimalleolar fracture of **unspecified** lower leg

   ● **S82.844**   Nondisplaced bimalleolar fracture of **right** lower leg

   ● **S82.845**   Nondisplaced bimalleolar fracture of **left** lower leg

   ● **S82.846**   Nondisplaced bimalleolar fracture of **unspecified** lower leg

● **S82.85**   **Trimalleolar** fracture of lower leg

   ● **S82.851**   Displaced trimalleolar fracture of **right** lower leg

   ● **S82.852**   Displaced trimalleolar fracture of **left** lower leg

   ● **S82.853**   Displaced trimalleolar fracture of **unspecified** lower leg

   ● **S82.854**   Nondisplaced trimalleolar fracture of **right** lower leg

   ● **S82.855**   Nondisplaced trimalleolar fracture of **left** lower leg

   ● **S82.856**   Nondisplaced trimalleolar fracture of **unspecified** lower leg

● **S82.86**   **Maisonneuve's fracture**

   ● **S82.861**   Displaced Maisonneuve's fracture of **right** leg

   ● **S82.862**   Displaced Maisonneuve's fracture of **left** leg

   ● **S82.863**   Displaced Maisonneuve's fracture of **unspecified** leg

   ● **S82.864**   Nondisplaced Maisonneuve's fracture of **right** leg

   ● **S82.865**   Nondisplaced Maisonneuve's fracture of **left** leg

   ● **S82.866**   Nondisplaced Maisonneuve's fracture of **unspecified** leg

● **S82.87**   **Pilon** fracture of tibia

   ● **S82.871**   Displaced pilon fracture of **right tibia**

   ● **S82.872**   Displaced pilon fracture of **left tibia**

   ● **S82.873**   Displaced pilon fracture of **unspecified** tibia

   ● **S82.874**   Nondisplaced pilon fracture of **right** tibia

   ● **S82.875**   Nondisplaced pilon fracture of **left** tibia

   ● **S82.876**   Nondisplaced pilon fracture of **unspecified** tibia

● **S82.89**   **Other** fractures of lower leg
> Fracture of ankle NOS

   ● **S82.891**   Other fracture of **right** lower leg

   ● **S82.892**   Other fracture of **left** lower leg

   ● **S82.899**   Other fracture of **unspecified** lower leg

● **S82.9**   **Unspecified** fracture of lower leg

   X ● **S82.90**   Unspecified fracture of **unspecified** lower leg

   X ● **S82.91**   Unspecified fracture of **right** lower leg

   X ● **S82.92**   Unspecified fracture of **left** lower leg

● **S83**   **Dislocation and sprain of joints and ligaments of knee**

> | **Includes** | avulsion of joint or ligament of knee |
> |---|---|
> | | laceration of cartilage, joint or ligament of knee |
> | | sprain of cartilage, joint or ligament of knee |
> | | traumatic hemarthrosis of joint or ligament of knee |
> | | traumatic rupture of joint or ligament of knee |
> | | traumatic subluxation of joint or ligament of knee |
> | | traumatic tear of joint or ligament of knee |

> **Code also** any associated open wound

> | **Excludes1** | derangement of patella (M22.0-M22.3) |
> |---|---|
> | | injury of patellar ligament (tendon) (S76.1-) |
> | | internal derangement of knee (M23.-) |
> | | old dislocation of knee (M24.36) |
> | | pathological dislocation of knee (M24.36) |
> | | recurrent dislocation of knee (M22.0) |

> | **Excludes2** | strain of muscle, fascia and tendon of lower leg (S86.-) |
> |---|---|

> The appropriate 7th character is to be added to each code from category S83

> | | |
> |---|---|
> | A | initial encounter |
> | D | subsequent encounter |
> | S | sequela |

● **S83.0**   **Subluxation and dislocation of patella**

   ● **S83.00**   **Unspecified** subluxation and dislocation of patella

     ● **S83.001**   Unspecified subluxation of **right** patella

     ● **S83.002**   Unspecified subluxation of **left** patella

     ● **S83.003**   Unspecified subluxation of **unspecified** patella

     ● **S83.004**   Unspecified dislocation of **right** patella

     ● **S83.005**   Unspecified dislocation of **left** patella

     ● **S83.006**   Unspecified dislocation of **unspecified** patella

   ● **S83.01**   **Lateral** subluxation and dislocation of patella

     ● **S83.011**   Lateral subluxation of **right** patella

     ● **S83.012**   Lateral subluxation of **left** patella

     ● **S83.013**   Lateral subluxation of **unspecified** patella

     ● **S83.014**   Lateral dislocation of **right** patella

     ● **S83.015**   Lateral dislocation of **left** patella

     ● **S83.016**   Lateral dislocation of **unspecified** patella

CHAPTER 19 (S00-T88)

- S83.09   Other subluxation and dislocation of patella
  - S83.091   Other subluxation of right patella
  - S83.092   Other subluxation of left patella
  - S83.093   Other subluxation of unspecified patella
  - S83.094   Other dislocation of right patella
  - S83.095   Other dislocation of left patella
  - S83.096   Other dislocation of unspecified patella
- S83.1   Subluxation and dislocation of knee
  - **Excludes2**   instability of knee prosthesis (T84.022, T84.023)
  - S83.10   Unspecified subluxation and dislocation of knee
    - S83.101   Unspecified subluxation of right knee
    - S83.102   Unspecified subluxation of left knee
    - S83.103   Unspecified subluxation of unspecified knee
    - S83.104   Unspecified dislocation of right knee
    - S83.105   Unspecified dislocation of left knee
    - S83.106   Unspecified dislocation of unspecified knee
  - S83.11   Anterior subluxation and dislocation of proximal end of tibia
    - Posterior subluxation and dislocation of distal end of femur
    - S83.111   Anterior subluxation of proximal end of tibia, right knee
    - S83.112   Anterior subluxation of proximal end of tibia, left knee
    - S83.113   Anterior subluxation of proximal end of tibia, unspecified knee
    - S83.114   Anterior dislocation of proximal end of tibia, right knee
    - S83.115   Anterior dislocation of proximal end of tibia, left knee
    - S83.116   Anterior dislocation of proximal end of tibia, unspecified knee
  - S83.12   Posterior subluxation and dislocation of proximal end of tibia
    - Anterior dislocation of distal end of femur
    - S83.121   Posterior subluxation of proximal end of tibia, right knee
    - S83.122   Posterior subluxation of proximal end of tibia, left knee
    - S83.123   Posterior subluxation of proximal end of tibia, unspecified knee
    - S83.124   Posterior dislocation of proximal end of tibia, right knee
    - S83.125   Posterior dislocation of proximal end of tibia, left knee
    - S83.126   Posterior dislocation of proximal end of tibia, unspecified knee
  - S83.13   Medial subluxation and dislocation of proximal end of tibia
    - S83.131   Medial subluxation of proximal end of tibia, right knee
    - S83.132   Medial subluxation of proximal end of tibia, left knee
    - S83.133   Medial subluxation of proximal end of tibia, unspecified knee
    - S83.134   Medial dislocation of proximal end of tibia, right knee
    - S83.135   Medial dislocation of proximal end of tibia, left knee
    - S83.136   Medial dislocation of proximal end of tibia, unspecified knee
- S83.14   Lateral subluxation and dislocation of proximal end of tibia
  - S83.141   Lateral subluxation of proximal end of tibia, right knee
  - S83.142   Lateral subluxation of proximal end of tibia, left knee
  - S83.143   Lateral subluxation of proximal end of tibia, unspecified knee
  - S83.144   Lateral dislocation of proximal end of tibia, right knee
  - S83.145   Lateral dislocation of proximal end of tibia, left knee
  - S83.146   Lateral dislocation of proximal end of tibia, unspecified knee
- S83.19   Other subluxation and dislocation of knee
  - S83.191   Other subluxation of right knee
  - S83.192   Other subluxation of left knee
  - S83.193   Other subluxation of unspecified knee
  - S83.194   Other dislocation of right knee
  - S83.195   Other dislocation of left knee
  - S83.196   Other dislocation of unspecified knee
- S83.2   Tear of meniscus, current injury
  - **Excludes1**   old bucket-handle tear (M23.2)
  - S83.20   Tear of unspecified meniscus, current injury
    - Tear of meniscus of knee NOS
    - S83.200   Bucket-handle tear of unspecified meniscus, current injury, right knee
    - S83.201   Bucket-handle tear of unspecified meniscus, current injury, left knee
    - S83.202   Bucket-handle tear of unspecified meniscus, current injury, unspecified knee
    - S83.203   Other tear of unspecified meniscus, current injury, right knee
    - S83.204   Other tear of unspecified meniscus, current injury, left knee
    - S83.205   Other tear of unspecified meniscus, current injury, unspecified knee
    - S83.206   Unspecified tear of unspecified meniscus, current injury, right knee
    - S83.207   Unspecified tear of unspecified meniscus, current injury, left knee
    - S83.209   Unspecified tear of unspecified meniscus, current injury, unspecified knee
  - S83.21   Bucket-handle tear of medial meniscus, current injury
    - S83.211   Bucket-handle tear of medial meniscus, current injury, right knee
    - S83.212   Bucket-handle tear of medial meniscus, current injury, left knee
    - S83.219   Bucket-handle tear of medial meniscus, current injury, unspecified knee
  - S83.22   Peripheral tear of medial meniscus, current injury
    - S83.221   Peripheral tear of medial meniscus, current injury, right knee
    - S83.222   Peripheral tear of medial meniscus, current injury, left knee
    - S83.229   Peripheral tear of medial meniscus, current injury, unspecified knee

● S83.23 Complex tear of medial meniscus, current injury
   ● S83.231 Complex tear of medial meniscus, current injury, right knee
   ● S83.232 Complex tear of medial meniscus, current injury, left knee
   ● S83.239 Complex tear of medial meniscus, current injury, unspecified knee
● S83.24 Other tear of medial meniscus, current injury
   ● S83.241 Other tear of medial meniscus, current injury, right knee
   ● S83.242 Other tear of medial meniscus, current injury, left knee
   ● S83.249 Other tear of medial meniscus, current injury, unspecified knee
● S83.25 Bucket-handle tear of lateral meniscus, current injury
   ● S83.251 Bucket-handle tear of lateral meniscus, current injury, right knee
   ● S83.252 Bucket-handle tear of lateral meniscus, current injury, left knee
   ● S83.259 Bucket-handle tear of lateral meniscus, current injury, unspecified knee
● S83.26 Peripheral tear of lateral meniscus, current injury
   ● S83.261 Peripheral tear of lateral meniscus, current injury, right knee
   ● S83.262 Peripheral tear of lateral meniscus, current injury, left knee
   ● S83.269 Peripheral tear of lateral meniscus, current injury, unspecified knee
● S83.27 Complex tear of lateral meniscus, current injury
   ● S83.271 Complex tear of lateral meniscus, current injury, right knee
   ● S83.272 Complex tear of lateral meniscus, current injury, left knee
   ● S83.279 Complex tear of lateral meniscus, current injury, unspecified knee
● S83.28 Other tear of lateral meniscus, current injury
   ● S83.281 Other tear of lateral meniscus, current injury, right knee
   ● S83.282 Other tear of lateral meniscus, current injury, left knee
   ● S83.289 Other tear of lateral meniscus, current injury, unspecified knee
● S83.3 Tear of articular cartilage of knee, current
  X ● S83.30 Tear of articular cartilage of unspecified knee, current
  X ● S83.31 Tear of articular cartilage of right knee, current
  X ● S83.32 Tear of articular cartilage of left knee, current
● S83.4 Sprain of collateral ligament of knee
   ● S83.40 Sprain of unspecified collateral ligament of knee
     ● S83.401 Sprain of unspecified collateral ligament of right knee
     ● S83.402 Sprain of unspecified collateral ligament of left knee
     ● S83.409 Sprain of unspecified collateral ligament of unspecified knee
   ● S83.41 Sprain of medial collateral ligament of knee
     Sprain of tibial collateral ligament
     ● S83.411 Sprain of medial collateral ligament of right knee
     ● S83.412 Sprain of medial collateral ligament of left knee
     ● S83.419 Sprain of medial collateral ligament of unspecified knee

● S83.42 Sprain of lateral collateral ligament of knee
   Sprain of fibular collateral ligament
   ● S83.421 Sprain of lateral collateral ligament of right knee
   ● S83.422 Sprain of lateral collateral ligament of left knee
   ● S83.429 Sprain of lateral collateral ligament of unspecified knee
● S83.5 Sprain of cruciate ligament of knee
   ● S83.50 Sprain of unspecified cruciate ligament of knee
     ● S83.501 Sprain of unspecified cruciate ligament of right knee
     ● S83.502 Sprain of unspecified cruciate ligament of left knee
     ● S83.509 Sprain of unspecified cruciate ligament of unspecified knee
   ● S83.51 Sprain of anterior cruciate ligament of knee
     ● S83.511 Sprain of anterior cruciate ligament of right knee
       Coding Clinic: 2016, Q2, P4
     ● S83.512 Sprain of anterior cruciate ligament of left knee
     ● S83.519 Sprain of anterior cruciate ligament of unspecified knee
   ● S83.52 Sprain of posterior cruciate ligament of knee
     ● S83.521 Sprain of posterior cruciate ligament of right knee
     ● S83.522 Sprain of posterior cruciate ligament of left knee
     ● S83.529 Sprain of posterior cruciate ligament of unspecified knee
● S83.6 Sprain of the superior tibiofibular joint and ligament
  X ● S83.60 Sprain of the superior tibiofibular joint and ligament, unspecified knee
  X ● S83.61 Sprain of the superior tibiofibular joint and ligament, right knee
  X ● S83.62 Sprain of the superior tibiofibular joint and ligament, left knee
● S83.8 Sprain of other specified parts of knee
   ● S83.8X Sprain of other specified parts of knee
     ● S83.8X1 Sprain of other specified parts of right knee
     ● S83.8X2 Sprain of other specified parts of left knee
     ● S83.8X9 Sprain of other specified parts of unspecified knee
● S83.9 Sprain of unspecified site of knee
  X ● S83.90 Sprain of unspecified site of unspecified knee
  X ● S83.91 Sprain of unspecified site of right knee
  X ● S83.92 Sprain of unspecified site of left knee
● S84 Injury of nerves at lower leg level
   Code also any associated open wound (S81.-)
   Excludes2 injury of nerves at ankle and foot level (S94.-)
   The appropriate 7th character is to be added to each code from category S84

A	initial encounter
D	subsequent encounter
S	sequela

● S84.0 Injury of tibial nerve at lower leg level
  X ● S84.00 Injury of tibial nerve at lower leg level, unspecified leg
  X ● S84.01 Injury of tibial nerve at lower leg level, right leg
  X ● S84.02 Injury of tibial nerve at lower leg level, left leg

CHAPTER 19 (S00-T88)

● **S84.1　Injury of peroneal nerve at lower leg level**
　X ● S84.10　Injury of peroneal nerve at lower leg level, unspecified leg
　X ● S84.11　Injury of peroneal nerve at lower leg level, right leg
　X ● S84.12　Injury of peroneal nerve at lower leg level, left leg
● **S84.2　Injury of cutaneous sensory nerve at lower leg level**
　X ● S84.20　Injury of cutaneous sensory nerve at lower leg level, unspecified leg
　X ● S84.21　Injury of cutaneous sensory nerve at lower leg level, right leg
　X ● S84.22　Injury of cutaneous sensory nerve at lower leg level, left leg
● **S84.8　Injury of other nerves at lower leg level**
　● S84.80　Injury of other nerves at lower leg level
　　● S84.801　Injury of other nerves at lower leg level, right leg
　　● S84.802　Injury of other nerves at lower leg level, left leg
　　● S84.809　Injury of other nerves at lower leg level, unspecified leg
● **S84.9　Injury of unspecified nerve at lower leg level**
　X ● S84.90　Injury of unspecified nerve at lower leg level, unspecified leg
　X ● S84.91　Injury of unspecified nerve at lower leg level, right leg
　X ● S84.92　Injury of unspecified nerve at lower leg level, left leg

● **S85　Injury of blood vessels at lower leg level**
　　Code also any associated open wound (S81.-)
　　Excludes2　injury of blood vessels at ankle and foot level (S95.-)

　　The appropriate 7th character is to be added to each code from category S85

A	initial encounter
D	subsequent encounter
S	sequela

● **S85.0　Injury of popliteal artery**
　● S85.00　Unspecified injury of popliteal artery
　　● S85.001　Unspecified injury of popliteal artery, right leg
　　● S85.002　Unspecified injury of popliteal artery, left leg
　　● S85.009　Unspecified injury of popliteal artery, unspecified leg
　● S85.01　Laceration of popliteal artery
　　● S85.011　Laceration of popliteal artery, right leg
　　● S85.012　Laceration of popliteal artery, left leg
　　● S85.019　Laceration of popliteal artery, unspecified leg
　● S85.09　Other specified injury of popliteal artery
　　● S85.091　Other specified injury of popliteal artery, right leg
　　● S85.092　Other specified injury of popliteal artery, left leg
　　● S85.099　Other specified injury of popliteal artery, unspecified leg
● **S85.1　Injury of tibial artery**
　● S85.10　Unspecified injury of unspecified tibial artery
　　　Injury of tibial artery NOS
　　● S85.101　Unspecified injury of unspecified tibial artery, right leg
　　● S85.102　Unspecified injury of unspecified tibial artery, left leg
　　● S85.109　Unspecified injury of unspecified tibial artery, unspecified leg

● S85.11　Laceration of unspecified tibial artery
　● S85.111　Laceration of unspecified tibial artery, right leg
　● S85.112　Laceration of unspecified tibial artery, left leg
　● S85.119　Laceration of unspecified tibial artery, unspecified leg
● S85.12　Other specified injury of unspecified tibial artery
　● S85.121　Other specified injury of unspecified tibial artery, right leg
　● S85.122　Other specified injury of unspecified tibial artery, left leg
　● S85.129　Other specified injury of unspecified tibial artery, unspecified leg
● S85.13　Unspecified injury of anterior tibial artery
　● S85.131　Unspecified injury of anterior tibial artery, right leg
　● S85.132　Unspecified injury of anterior tibial artery, left leg
　● S85.139　Unspecified injury of anterior tibial artery, unspecified leg
● S85.14　Laceration of anterior tibial artery
　● S85.141　Laceration of anterior tibial artery, right leg
　● S85.142　Laceration of anterior tibial artery, left leg
　● S85.149　Laceration of anterior tibial artery, unspecified leg
● S85.15　Other specified injury of anterior tibial artery
　● S85.151　Other specified injury of anterior tibial artery, right leg
　● S85.152　Other specified injury of anterior tibial artery, left leg
　● S85.159　Other specified injury of anterior tibial artery, unspecified leg
● S85.16　Unspecified injury of posterior tibial artery
　● S85.161　Unspecified injury of posterior tibial artery, right leg
　● S85.162　Unspecified injury of posterior tibial artery, left leg
　● S85.169　Unspecified injury of posterior tibial artery, unspecified leg
● S85.17　Laceration of posterior tibial artery
　● S85.171　Laceration of posterior tibial artery, right leg
　● S85.172　Laceration of posterior tibial artery, left leg
　● S85.179　Laceration of posterior tibial artery, unspecified leg
● S85.18　Other specified injury of posterior tibial artery
　● S85.181　Other specified injury of posterior tibial artery, right leg
　● S85.182　Other specified injury of posterior tibial artery, left leg
　● S85.189　Other specified injury of posterior tibial artery, unspecified leg
● **S85.2　Injury of peroneal artery**
　● S85.20　Unspecified injury of peroneal artery
　　● S85.201　Unspecified injury of peroneal artery, right leg
　　● S85.202　Unspecified injury of peroneal artery, left leg
　　● S85.209　Unspecified injury of peroneal artery, unspecified leg

● S85.21　Laceration of peroneal artery
　　● S85.211　Laceration of peroneal artery, right leg
　　● S85.212　Laceration of peroneal artery, left leg
　　● S85.219　Laceration of peroneal artery, unspecified leg
● S85.29　Other specified injury of peroneal artery
　　● S85.291　Other specified injury of peroneal artery, right leg
　　● S85.292　Other specified injury of peroneal artery, left leg
　　● S85.299　Other specified injury of peroneal artery, unspecified leg
● S85.3　Injury of greater saphenous vein at lower leg level
　　Injury of greater saphenous vein NOS
　　Injury of saphenous vein NOS
　　● S85.30　Unspecified injury of greater saphenous vein at lower leg level
　　　　● S85.301　Unspecified injury of greater saphenous vein at lower leg level, right leg
　　　　● S85.302　Unspecified injury of greater saphenous vein at lower leg level, left leg
　　　　● S85.309　Unspecified injury of greater saphenous vein at lower leg level, unspecified leg
　　● S85.31　Laceration of greater saphenous vein at lower leg level
　　　　● S85.311　Laceration of greater saphenous vein at lower leg level, right leg
　　　　● S85.312　Laceration of greater saphenous vein at lower leg level, left leg
　　　　● S85.319　Laceration of greater saphenous vein at lower leg level, unspecified leg
　　● S85.39　Other specified injury of greater saphenous vein at lower leg level
　　　　● S85.391　Other specified injury of greater saphenous vein at lower leg level, right leg
　　　　● S85.392　Other specified injury of greater saphenous vein at lower leg level, left leg
　　　　● S85.399　Other specified injury of greater saphenous vein at lower leg level, unspecified leg
● S85.4　Injury of lesser saphenous vein at lower leg level
　　● S85.40　Unspecified injury of lesser saphenous vein at lower leg level
　　　　● S85.401　Unspecified injury of lesser saphenous vein at lower leg level, right leg
　　　　● S85.402　Unspecified injury of lesser saphenous vein at lower leg level, left leg
　　　　● S85.409　Unspecified injury of lesser saphenous vein at lower leg level, unspecified leg
　　● S85.41　Laceration of lesser saphenous vein at lower leg level
　　　　● S85.411　Laceration of lesser saphenous vein at lower leg level, right leg
　　　　● S85.412　Laceration of lesser saphenous vein at lower leg level, left leg
　　　　● S85.419　Laceration of lesser saphenous vein at lower leg level, unspecified leg

● S85.49　Other specified injury of lesser saphenous vein at lower leg level
　　● S85.491　Other specified injury of lesser saphenous vein at lower leg level, right leg
　　● S85.492　Other specified injury of lesser saphenous vein at lower leg level, left leg
　　● S85.499　Other specified injury of lesser saphenous vein at lower leg level, unspecified leg
● S85.5　Injury of popliteal vein
　　● S85.50　Unspecified injury of popliteal vein
　　　　● S85.501　Unspecified injury of popliteal vein, right leg
　　　　● S85.502　Unspecified injury of popliteal vein, left leg
　　　　● S85.509　Unspecified injury of popliteal vein, unspecified leg
　　● S85.51　Laceration of popliteal vein
　　　　● S85.511　Laceration of popliteal vein, right leg
　　　　● S85.512　Laceration of popliteal vein, left leg
　　　　● S85.519　Laceration of popliteal vein, unspecified leg
　　● S85.59　Other specified injury of popliteal vein
　　　　● S85.591　Other specified injury of popliteal vein, right leg
　　　　● S85.592　Other specified injury of popliteal vein, left leg
　　　　● S85.599　Other specified injury of popliteal vein, unspecified leg
● S85.8　Injury of other blood vessels at lower leg level
　　● S85.80　Unspecified injury of other blood vessels at lower leg level
　　　　● S85.801　Unspecified injury of other blood vessels at lower leg level, right leg
　　　　● S85.802　Unspecified injury of other blood vessels at lower leg level, left leg
　　　　● S85.809　Unspecified injury of other blood vessels at lower leg level, unspecified leg
　　● S85.81　Laceration of other blood vessels at lower leg level
　　　　● S85.811　Laceration of other blood vessels at lower leg level, right leg
　　　　● S85.812　Laceration of other blood vessels at lower leg level, left leg
　　　　● S85.819　Laceration of other blood vessels at lower leg level, unspecified leg
　　● S85.89　Other specified injury of other blood vessels at lower leg level
　　　　● S85.891　Other specified injury of other blood vessels at lower leg level, right leg
　　　　● S85.892　Other specified injury of other blood vessels at lower leg level, left leg
　　　　● S85.899　Other specified injury of other blood vessels at lower leg level, unspecified leg
● S85.9　Injury of unspecified blood vessel at lower leg level
　　● S85.90　Unspecified injury of unspecified blood vessel at lower leg level
　　　　● S85.901　Unspecified injury of unspecified blood vessel at lower leg level, right leg
　　　　● S85.902　Unspecified injury of unspecified blood vessel at lower leg level, left leg
　　　　● S85.909　Unspecified injury of unspecified blood vessel at lower leg level, unspecified leg

CHAPTER 19 (S00-T88)

- S85.91 **Laceration** of unspecified blood vessel at lower leg level
  - S85.911 Laceration of unspecified blood vessel at lower leg level, **right** leg
  - S85.912 Laceration of unspecified blood vessel at lower leg level, **left** leg
  - S85.919 Laceration of unspecified blood vessel at lower leg level, **unspecified** leg
  - S85.99 **Other** specified injury of unspecified blood vessel at lower leg level
    - S85.991 Other specified injury of unspecified blood vessel at lower leg level, **right** leg
    - S85.992 Other specified injury of unspecified blood vessel at lower leg level, **left** leg
    - S85.999 Other specified injury of unspecified blood vessel at lower leg level, **unspecified** leg

- S86 Injury of muscle, fascia and tendon at lower leg level

  Code also any associated open wound (S81.-)

  Excludes2 injury of muscle, fascia and tendon at ankle (S96.-)
  injury of patellar ligament (tendon) (S76.1-)
  sprain of joints and ligaments of knee (S83.-)

  The appropriate 7th character is to be added to each code from category S86

A	initial encounter
D	subsequent encounter
S	sequela

  - S86.0 Injury of **Achilles tendon**
    - S86.00 **Unspecified** injury of Achilles tendon
      - S86.001 Unspecified injury of **right** Achilles tendon
      - S86.002 Unspecified injury of **left** Achilles tendon
      - S86.009 Unspecified injury of **unspecified** Achilles tendon
    - S86.01 **Strain** of Achilles tendon
      - S86.011 Strain of **right** Achilles tendon
      - S86.012 Strain of **left** Achilles tendon
      - S86.019 Strain of **unspecified** Achilles tendon
    - S86.02 **Laceration** of Achilles tendon
      - S86.021 Laceration of **right** Achilles tendon
      - S86.022 Laceration of **left** Achilles tendon
      - S86.029 Laceration of **unspecified** Achilles tendon
    - S86.09 **Other** specified injury of Achilles tendon
      - S86.091 Other specified injury of **right** Achilles tendon
      - S86.092 Other specified injury of **left** Achilles tendon
      - S86.099 Other specified injury of **unspecified** Achilles tendon
  - S86.1 Injury of other muscle(s) and tendon(s) of **posterior** muscle group at lower leg level
    - S86.10 **Unspecified** injury of other muscle(s) and tendon(s) of posterior muscle group at lower leg level
      - S86.101 Unspecified injury of other muscle(s) and tendon(s) of posterior muscle group at lower leg level, **right** leg
      - S86.102 Unspecified injury of other muscle(s) and tendon(s) of posterior muscle group at lower leg level, **left** leg
      - S86.109 Unspecified injury of other muscle(s) and tendon(s) of posterior muscle group at lower leg level, **unspecified** leg

  - S86.11 **Strain** of other muscle(s) and tendon(s) of posterior muscle group at lower leg level
    - S86.111 Strain of other muscle(s) and tendon(s) of posterior muscle group at lower leg level, **right** leg
    - S86.112 Strain of other muscle(s) and tendon(s) of posterior muscle group at lower leg level, **left** leg
    - S86.119 Strain of other muscle(s) and tendon(s) of posterior muscle group at lower leg level, **unspecified** leg
  - S86.12 **Laceration** of other muscle(s) and tendon(s) of posterior muscle group at lower leg level
    - S86.121 Laceration of other muscle(s) and tendon(s) of posterior muscle group at lower leg level, **right** leg
    - S86.122 Laceration of other muscle(s) and tendon(s) of posterior muscle group at lower leg level, **left** leg
    - S86.129 Laceration of other muscle(s) and tendon(s) of posterior muscle group at lower leg level, **unspecified** leg
  - S86.19 **Other** injury of other muscle(s) and tendon(s) of posterior muscle group at lower leg level
    - S86.191 Other injury of other muscle(s) and tendon(s) of posterior muscle group at lower leg level, **right** leg
    - S86.192 Other injury of other muscle(s) and tendon(s) of posterior muscle group at lower leg level, **left** leg
    - S86.199 Other injury of other muscle(s) and tendon(s) of posterior muscle group at lower leg level, **unspecified** leg
- S86.2 Injury of muscle(s) and tendon(s) of **anterior muscle group** at lower leg level
  - S86.20 **Unspecified** injury of muscle(s) and tendon(s) of anterior muscle group at lower leg level
    - S86.201 Unspecified injury of muscle(s) and tendon(s) of anterior muscle group at lower leg level, **right** leg
    - S86.202 Unspecified injury of muscle(s) and tendon(s) of anterior muscle group at lower leg level, **left** leg
    - S86.209 Unspecified injury of muscle(s) and tendon(s) of anterior muscle group at lower leg level, **unspecified** leg
  - S86.21 **Strain** of muscle(s) and tendon(s) of anterior muscle group at lower leg level
    - S86.211 Strain of muscle(s) and tendon(s) of anterior muscle group at lower leg level, **right** leg
    - S86.212 Strain of muscle(s) and tendon(s) of anterior muscle group at lower leg level, **left** leg
    - S86.219 Strain of muscle(s) and tendon(s) of anterior muscle group at lower leg level, **unspecified** leg
  - S86.22 **Laceration** of muscle(s) and tendon(s) of anterior muscle group at lower leg level
    - S86.221 Laceration of muscle(s) and tendon(s) of anterior muscle group at lower leg level, **right** leg
    - S86.222 Laceration of muscle(s) and tendon(s) of anterior muscle group at lower leg level, **left** leg
    - S86.229 Laceration of muscle(s) and tendon(s) of anterior muscle group at lower leg level, **unspecified** leg

- S86.29   Other injury of muscle(s) and tendon(s) of anterior muscle group at lower leg level
  - S86.291   Other injury of muscle(s) and tendon(s) of anterior muscle group at lower leg level, right leg
  - S86.292   Other injury of muscle(s) and tendon(s) of anterior muscle group at lower leg level, left leg
  - S86.299   Other injury of muscle(s) and tendon(s) of anterior muscle group at lower leg level, unspecified leg
- S86.3   Injury of muscle(s) and tendon(s) of peroneal muscle group at lower leg level
  - S86.30   Unspecified injury of muscle(s) and tendon(s) of peroneal muscle group at lower leg level
    - S86.301   Unspecified injury of muscle(s) and tendon(s) of peroneal muscle group at lower leg level, right leg
    - S86.302   Unspecified injury of muscle(s) and tendon(s) of peroneal muscle group at lower leg level, left leg
    - S86.309   Unspecified injury of muscle(s) and tendon(s) of peroneal muscle group at lower leg level, unspecified leg
  - S86.31   Strain of muscle(s) and tendon(s) of peroneal muscle group at lower leg level
    - S86.311   Strain of muscle(s) and tendon(s) of peroneal muscle group at lower leg level, right leg
    - S86.312   Strain of muscle(s) and tendon(s) of peroneal muscle group at lower leg level, left leg
    - S86.319   Strain of muscle(s) and tendon(s) of peroneal muscle group at lower leg level, unspecified leg
  - S86.32   Laceration of muscle(s) and tendon(s) of peroneal muscle group at lower leg level
    - S86.321   Laceration of muscle(s) and tendon(s) of peroneal muscle group at lower leg level, right leg
    - S86.322   Laceration of muscle(s) and tendon(s) of peroneal muscle group at lower leg level, left leg
    - S86.329   Laceration of muscle(s) and tendon(s) of peroneal muscle group at lower leg level, unspecified leg
  - S86.39   Other injury of muscle(s) and tendon(s) of peroneal muscle group at lower leg level
    - S86.391   Other injury of muscle(s) and tendon(s) of peroneal muscle group at lower leg level, right leg
    - S86.392   Other injury of muscle(s) and tendon(s) of peroneal muscle group at lower leg level, left leg
    - S86.399   Other injury of muscle(s) and tendon(s) of peroneal muscle group at lower leg level, unspecified leg
- S86.8   Injury of other muscles and tendons at lower leg level
  - S86.80   Unspecified injury of other muscles and tendons at lower leg level
    - S86.801   Unspecified injury of other muscle(s) and tendon(s) at lower leg level, right leg
    - S86.802   Unspecified injury of other muscle(s) and tendon(s) at lower leg level, left leg
    - S86.809   Unspecified injury of other muscle(s) and tendon(s) at lower leg level, unspecified leg

- S86.81   Strain of other muscles and tendons at lower leg level
  - S86.811   Strain of other muscle(s) and tendon(s) at lower leg level, right leg
  - S86.812   Strain of other muscle(s) and tendon(s) at lower leg level, left leg
  - S86.819   Strain of other muscle(s) and tendon(s) at lower leg level, unspecified leg
- S86.82   Laceration of other muscles and tendons at lower leg level
  - S86.821   Laceration of other muscle(s) and tendon(s) at lower leg level, right leg
  - S86.822   Laceration of other muscle(s) and tendon(s) at lower leg level, left leg
  - S86.829   Laceration of other muscle(s) and tendon(s) at lower leg level, unspecified leg
- S86.89   Other injury of other muscles and tendons at lower leg level
  - S86.891   Other injury of other muscle(s) and tendon(s) at lower leg level, right leg
  - S86.892   Other injury of other muscle(s) and tendon(s) at lower leg level, left leg
  - S86.899   Other injury of other muscle(s) and tendon(s) at lower leg level, unspecified leg
- S86.9   Injury of unspecified muscle and tendon at lower leg level
  - S86.90   Unspecified injury of unspecified muscle and tendon at lower leg level
    - S86.901   Unspecified injury of unspecified muscle(s) and tendon(s) at lower leg level, right leg
    - S86.902   Unspecified injury of unspecified muscle(s) and tendon(s) at lower leg level, left leg
    - S86.909   Unspecified injury of unspecified muscle(s) and tendon(s) at lower leg level, unspecified leg
  - S86.91   Strain of unspecified muscle and tendon at lower leg level
    - S86.911   Strain of unspecified muscle(s) and tendon(s) at lower leg level, right leg
    - S86.912   Strain of unspecified muscle(s) and tendon(s) at lower leg level, left leg
    - S86.919   Strain of unspecified muscle(s) and tendon(s) at lower leg level, unspecified leg
  - S86.92   Laceration of unspecified muscle and tendon at lower leg level
    - S86.921   Laceration of unspecified muscle(s) and tendon(s) at lower leg level, right leg
    - S86.922   Laceration of unspecified muscle(s) and tendon(s) at lower leg level, left leg
    - S86.929   Laceration of unspecified muscle(s) and tendon(s) at lower leg level, unspecified leg
  - S86.99   Other injury of unspecified muscle and tendon at lower leg level
    - S86.991   Other injury of unspecified muscle(s) and tendon(s) at lower leg level, right leg
    - S86.992   Other injury of unspecified muscle(s) and tendon(s) at lower leg level, left leg
    - S86.999   Other injury of unspecified muscle(s) and tendon(s) at lower leg level, unspecified leg

● **S87**   **Crushing injury of lower leg**

     Use additional code(s) for all associated injuries

     Excludes2   crushing injury of ankle and foot (S97.-)

     The appropriate 7th character is to be added to each code from category S87

> A   initial encounter
> D   subsequent encounter
> S   sequela

   ● **S87.0**   **Crushing injury of knee**

     X● **S87.00**   Crushing injury of unspecified knee

     X● **S87.01**   Crushing injury of right knee

     X● **S87.02**   Crushing injury of left knee

   ● **S87.8**   **Crushing injury of lower leg**

     X● **S87.80**   Crushing injury of unspecified lower leg

     X● **S87.81**   Crushing injury of right lower leg

     X● **S87.82**   Crushing injury of left lower leg

● **S88**   **Traumatic amputation of lower leg**

     An amputation not identified as partial or complete should be coded to complete

     Excludes1   traumatic amputation of ankle and foot (S98.-)

     The appropriate 7th character is to be added to each code from category S88

> A   initial encounter
> D   subsequent encounter
> S   sequela

   ● **S88.0**   **Traumatic amputation at knee level**

     ● **S88.01**   **Complete traumatic amputation at knee level**

       ● **S88.011**   Complete traumatic amputation at knee level, right lower leg

       ● **S88.012**   Complete traumatic amputation at knee level, left lower leg

       ● **S88.019**   Complete traumatic amputation at knee level, unspecified lower leg

     ● **S88.02**   **Partial traumatic amputation at knee level**

       ● **S88.021**   Partial traumatic amputation at knee level, right lower leg

       ● **S88.022**   Partial traumatic amputation at knee level, left lower leg

       ● **S88.029**   Partial traumatic amputation at knee level, unspecified lower leg

   ● **S88.1**   **Traumatic amputation at level between knee and ankle**

     ● **S88.11**   **Complete traumatic amputation at level between knee and ankle**

       ● **S88.111**   Complete traumatic amputation at level between knee and ankle, right lower leg

       ● **S88.112**   Complete traumatic amputation at level between knee and ankle, left lower leg

       ● **S88.119**   Complete traumatic amputation at level between knee and ankle, unspecified lower leg

     ● **S88.12**   **Partial traumatic amputation at level between knee and ankle**

       ● **S88.121**   Partial traumatic amputation at level between knee and ankle, right lower leg

       ● **S88.122**   Partial traumatic amputation at level between knee and ankle, left lower leg

       ● **S88.129**   Partial traumatic amputation at level between knee and ankle, unspecified lower leg

   ● **S88.9**   **Traumatic amputation of lower leg, level unspecified**

     ● **S88.91**   **Complete traumatic amputation of lower leg, level unspecified**

       ● **S88.911**   Complete traumatic amputation of right lower leg, level unspecified

       ● **S88.912**   Complete traumatic amputation of left lower leg, level unspecified

       ● **S88.919**   Complete traumatic amputation of unspecified lower leg, level unspecified

     ● **S88.92**   **Partial traumatic amputation of lower leg, level unspecified**

       ● **S88.921**   Partial traumatic amputation of right lower leg, level unspecified

       ● **S88.922**   Partial traumatic amputation of left lower leg, level unspecified

       ● **S88.929**   Partial traumatic amputation of unspecified lower leg, level unspecified

● **S89**   **Other and unspecified injuries of lower leg**

     Note: A fracture not indicated as open or closed should be coded to closed

     Excludes2   other and unspecified injuries of ankle and foot (S99.-)

     The appropriate 7th character is to be added to each code from subcategories S89.0, S89.1, S89.2, and S89.3

> A   initial encounter for closed fracture
> D   subsequent encounter for fracture with routine healing
> G   subsequent encounter for fracture with delayed healing
> K   subsequent encounter for fracture with nonunion
> P   subsequent encounter for fracture with malunion
> S   sequela

   ● **S89.0**   **Physeal fracture of upper end of tibia**

     ● **S89.00**   **Unspecified physeal fracture of upper end of tibia**

       ● **S89.001**   Unspecified physeal fracture of upper end of right tibia

       ● **S89.002**   Unspecified physeal fracture of upper end of left tibia

       ● **S89.009**   Unspecified physeal fracture of upper end of unspecified tibia

     ● **S89.01**   **Salter-Harris Type I physeal fracture of upper end of tibia**

       ● **S89.011**   Salter-Harris Type I physeal fracture of upper end of right tibia

       ● **S89.012**   Salter-Harris Type I physeal fracture of upper end of left tibia

       ● **S89.019**   Salter-Harris Type I physeal fracture of upper end of unspecified tibia

     ● **S89.02**   **Salter-Harris Type II physeal fracture of upper end of tibia**

       ● **S89.021**   Salter-Harris Type II physeal fracture of upper end of right tibia

       ● **S89.022**   Salter-Harris Type II physeal fracture of upper end of left tibia

       ● **S89.029**   Salter-Harris Type II physeal fracture of upper end of unspecified tibia

     ● **S89.03**   **Salter-Harris Type III physeal fracture of upper end of tibia**

       ● **S89.031**   Salter-Harris Type III physeal fracture of upper end of right tibia

       ● **S89.032**   Salter-Harris Type III physeal fracture of upper end of left tibia

       ● **S89.039**   Salter-Harris Type III physeal fracture of upper end of unspecified tibia

- ● S89.04   Salter-Harris Type IV physeal fracture of upper end of tibia
  - ● S89.041   Salter-Harris Type IV physeal fracture of upper end of right tibia
  - ● S89.042   Salter-Harris Type IV physeal fracture of upper end of left tibia
  - ● S89.049   Salter-Harris Type IV physeal fracture of upper end of unspecified tibia
- ● S89.09   Other physeal fracture of upper end of tibia
  - ● S89.091   Other physeal fracture of upper end of right tibia
  - ● S89.092   Other physeal fracture of upper end of left tibia
  - ● S89.099   Other physeal fracture of upper end of unspecified tibia
- ● S89.1   Physeal fracture of lower end of tibia
  - ● S89.10   Unspecified physeal fracture of lower end of tibia
    - ● S89.101   Unspecified physeal fracture of lower end of right tibia
    - ● S89.102   Unspecified physeal fracture of lower end of left tibia
    - ● S89.109   Unspecified physeal fracture of lower end of unspecified tibia
  - ● S89.11   Salter-Harris Type I physeal fracture of lower end of tibia
    - ● S89.111   Salter-Harris Type I physeal fracture of lower end of right tibia
    - ● S89.112   Salter-Harris Type I physeal fracture of lower end of left tibia
    - ● S89.119   Salter-Harris Type I physeal fracture of lower end of unspecified tibia
  - ● S89.12   Salter-Harris Type II physeal fracture of lower end of tibia
    - ● S89.121   Salter-Harris Type II physeal fracture of lower end of right tibia
    - ● S89.122   Salter-Harris Type II physeal fracture of lower end of left tibia
    - ● S89.129   Salter-Harris Type II physeal fracture of lower end of unspecified tibia
  - ● S89.13   Salter-Harris Type III physeal fracture of lower end of tibia
    - **Excludes1**   fracture of medial malleolus (adult) (S82.5-)
    - ● S89.131   Salter-Harris Type III physeal fracture of lower end of right tibia
    - ● S89.132   Salter-Harris Type III physeal fracture of lower end of left tibia
    - ● S89.139   Salter-Harris Type III physeal fracture of lower end of unspecified tibia
  - ● S89.14   Salter-Harris Type IV physeal fracture of lower end of tibia
    - **Excludes1**   fracture of medial malleolus (adult) (S82.5-)
    - ● S89.141   Salter-Harris Type IV physeal fracture of lower end of right tibia
    - ● S89.142   Salter-Harris Type IV physeal fracture of lower end of left tibia
    - ● S89.149   Salter-Harris Type IV physeal fracture of lower end of unspecified tibia
  - ● S89.19   Other physeal fracture of lower end of tibia
    - ● S89.191   Other physeal fracture of lower end of right tibia
    - ● S89.192   Other physeal fracture of lower end of left tibia
    - ● S89.199   Other physeal fracture of lower end of unspecified tibia
- ● S89.2   Physeal fracture of upper end of fibula
  - ● S89.20   Unspecified physeal fracture of upper end of fibula
    - ● S89.201   Unspecified physeal fracture of upper end of right fibula
    - ● S89.202   Unspecified physeal fracture of upper end of left fibula
    - ● S89.209   Unspecified physeal fracture of upper end of unspecified fibula
  - ● S89.21   Salter-Harris Type I physeal fracture of upper end of fibula
    - ● S89.211   Salter-Harris Type I physeal fracture of upper end of right fibula
    - ● S89.212   Salter-Harris Type I physeal fracture of upper end of left fibula
    - ● S89.219   Salter-Harris Type I physeal fracture of upper end of unspecified fibula
  - ● S89.22   Salter-Harris Type II physeal fracture of upper end of fibula
    - ● S89.221   Salter-Harris Type II physeal fracture of upper end of right fibula
    - ● S89.222   Salter-Harris Type II physeal fracture of upper end of left fibula
    - ● S89.229   Salter-Harris Type II physeal fracture of upper end of unspecified fibula
  - ● S89.29   Other physeal fracture of upper end of fibula
    - ● S89.291   Other physeal fracture of upper end of right fibula
    - ● S89.292   Other physeal fracture of upper end of left fibula
    - ● S89.299   Other physeal fracture of upper end of unspecified fibula
- ● S89.3   Physeal fracture of lower end of fibula
  - ● S89.30   Unspecified physeal fracture of lower end of fibula
    - ● S89.301   Unspecified physeal fracture of lower end of right fibula
    - ● S89.302   Unspecified physeal fracture of lower end of left fibula
    - ● S89.309   Unspecified physeal fracture of lower end of unspecified fibula
  - ● S89.31   Salter-Harris Type I physeal fracture of lower end of fibula
    - ● S89.311   Salter-Harris Type I physeal fracture of lower end of right fibula
    - ● S89.312   Salter-Harris Type I physeal fracture of lower end of left fibula
    - ● S89.319   Salter-Harris Type I physeal fracture of lower end of unspecified fibula
  - ● S89.32   Salter-Harris Type II physeal fracture of lower end of fibula
    - ● S89.321   Salter-Harris Type II physeal fracture of lower end of right fibula
    - ● S89.322   Salter-Harris Type II physeal fracture of lower end of left fibula
    - ● S89.329   Salter-Harris Type II physeal fracture of lower end of unspecified fibula
  - ● S89.39   Other physeal fracture of lower end of fibula
    - ● S89.391   Other physeal fracture of lower end of right fibula
    - ● S89.392   Other physeal fracture of lower end of left fibula
    - ● S89.399   Other physeal fracture of lower end of unspecified fibula

CHAPTER 19 (S00-T88)

● **S89.8**   **Other specified injuries of lower leg**

The appropriate 7th character is to be added to each code in subcategory S89.8

> A   initial encounter
> D   subsequent encounter
> S   sequela

    X● **S89.80**   **Other specified injuries of unspecified lower leg**
    X● **S89.81**   **Other specified injuries of right lower leg**
    X● **S89.82**   **Other specified injuries of left lower leg**

● **S89.9**   **Unspecified injury of lower leg**

The appropriate 7th character is to be added to each code in subcategory S89.9

> A   initial encounter
> D   subsequent encounter
> S   sequela

    X● **S89.90**   **Unspecified injury of unspecified lower leg**
    X● **S89.91**   **Unspecified injury of right lower leg**
    X● **S89.92**   **Unspecified injury of left lower leg**

INJURIES TO THE ANKLE AND FOOT (S90-S99)

Excludes2   burns and corrosions (T20-T32)
fracture of ankle and malleolus (S82.-)
frostbite (T33-T34)
insect bite or sting, venomous (T63.4)

● **S90**   **Superficial injury of ankle, foot and toes**

The appropriate 7th character is to be added to each code from category S90

> A   initial encounter
> D   subsequent encounter
> S   sequela

● **S90.0**   **Contusion of ankle**
    X● **S90.00**   **Contusion of unspecified ankle**
    X● **S90.01**   **Contusion of right ankle**
    X● **S90.02**   **Contusion of left ankle**

● **S90.1**   **Contusion of toe without damage to nail**
   ● **S90.11**   **Contusion of great toe without damage to nail**
     ● **S90.111**   **Contusion of right great toe without damage to nail**
     ● **S90.112**   **Contusion of left great toe without damage to nail**
     ● **S90.119**   **Contusion of unspecified great toe without damage to nail**
   ● **S90.12**   **Contusion of lesser toe without damage to nail**
     ● **S90.121**   **Contusion of right lesser toe(s) without damage to nail**
     ● **S90.122**   **Contusion of left lesser toe(s) without damage to nail**
     ● **S90.129**   **Contusion of unspecified lesser toe(s) without damage to nail**
Contusion of toe NOS

● **S90.2**   **Contusion of toe with damage to nail**
   ● **S90.21**   **Contusion of great toe with damage to nail**
     ● **S90.211**   **Contusion of right great toe with damage to nail**
     ● **S90.212**   **Contusion of left great toe with damage to nail**
     ● **S90.219**   **Contusion of unspecified great toe with damage to nail**
   ● **S90.22**   **Contusion of lesser toe with damage to nail**
     ● **S90.221**   **Contusion of right lesser toe(s) with damage to nail**
     ● **S90.222**   **Contusion of left lesser toe(s) with damage to nail**
     ● **S90.229**   **Contusion of unspecified lesser toe(s) with damage to nail**

● **S90.3**   **Contusion of foot**
   Excludes2   contusion of toes (S90.1-, S90.2-)
   X● **S90.30**   **Contusion of unspecified foot**
Contusion of foot NOS
   X● **S90.31**   **Contusion of right foot**
   X● **S90.32**   **Contusion of left foot**

● **S90.4**   **Other superficial injuries of toe**
   ● **S90.41**   **Abrasion of toe**
     ● **S90.411**   **Abrasion, right great toe**
     ● **S90.412**   **Abrasion, left great toe**
     ● **S90.413**   **Abrasion, unspecified great toe**
     ● **S90.414**   **Abrasion, right lesser toe(s)**
     ● **S90.415**   **Abrasion, left lesser toe(s)**
     ● **S90.416**   **Abrasion, unspecified lesser toe(s)**
   ● **S90.42**   **Blister (nonthermal) of toe**
     ● **S90.421**   **Blister (nonthermal), right great toe**
     ● **S90.422**   **Blister (nonthermal), left great toe**
     ● **S90.423**   **Blister (nonthermal), unspecified great toe**
     ● **S90.424**   **Blister (nonthermal), right lesser toe(s)**
     ● **S90.425**   **Blister (nonthermal), left lesser toe(s)**
     ● **S90.426**   **Blister (nonthermal), unspecified lesser toe(s)**
   ● **S90.44**   **External constriction of toe**
Hair tourniquet syndrome of toe
     ● **S90.441**   **External constriction, right great toe**
     ● **S90.442**   **External constriction, left great toe**
     ● **S90.443**   **External constriction, unspecified great toe**
     ● **S90.444**   **External constriction, right lesser toe(s)**
     ● **S90.445**   **External constriction, left lesser toe(s)**
     ● **S90.446**   **External constriction, unspecified lesser toe(s)**
   ● **S90.45**   **Superficial foreign body of toe**
Splinter in the toe
     ● **S90.451**   **Superficial foreign body, right great toe**
     ● **S90.452**   **Superficial foreign body, left great toe**
     ● **S90.453**   **Superficial foreign body, unspecified great toe**
     ● **S90.454**   **Superficial foreign body, right lesser toe(s)**
     ● **S90.455**   **Superficial foreign body, left lesser toe(s)**
     ● **S90.456**   **Superficial foreign body, unspecified lesser toe(s)**
   ● **S90.46**   **Insect bite (nonvenomous) of toe**
     ● **S90.461**   **Insect bite (nonvenomous), right great toe**
     ● **S90.462**   **Insect bite (nonvenomous), left great toe**
     ● **S90.463**   **Insect bite (nonvenomous), unspecified great toe**
     ● **S90.464**   **Insect bite (nonvenomous), right lesser toe(s)**
     ● **S90.465**   **Insect bite (nonvenomous), left lesser toe(s)**
     ● **S90.466**   **Insect bite (nonvenomous), unspecified lesser toe(s)**
   ● **S90.47**   **Other superficial bite of toe**
     Excludes1   open bite of toe (S91.15-, S91.25-)
     ● **S90.471**   **Other superficial bite of right great toe**
     ● **S90.472**   **Other superficial bite of left great toe**

▶ New   ⇒ Revised   ~~deleted~~ Deleted   Excludes 1   Excludes 2   Includes   Use additional   Code first   Code also   Key words

1334   OGCR Official Guidelines   X Assign placeholder X   ● Use Additional Character(s)   ▷ Manifestation Code   **Coding Clinic**

● S90.473 Other superficial bite of unspecified great toe
● S90.474 Other superficial bite of right lesser toe(s)
● S90.475 Other superficial bite of left lesser toe(s)
● S90.476 Other superficial bite of unspecified lesser toe(s)

● S90.5 Other superficial injuries of ankle
  ● S90.51 Abrasion of ankle
    ● S90.511 Abrasion, right ankle
    ● S90.512 Abrasion, left ankle
    ● S90.519 Abrasion, unspecified ankle
  ● S90.52 Blister (nonthermal) of ankle
    ● S90.521 Blister (nonthermal), right ankle
    ● S90.522 Blister (nonthermal), left ankle
    ● S90.529 Blister (nonthermal), unspecified ankle
  ● S90.54 External constriction of ankle
    ● S90.541 External constriction, right ankle
    ● S90.542 External constriction, left ankle
    ● S90.549 External constriction, unspecified ankle
  ● S90.55 Superficial foreign body of ankle
            Splinter in the ankle
    ● S90.551 Superficial foreign body, right ankle
    ● S90.552 Superficial foreign body, left ankle
    ● S90.559 Superficial foreign body, unspecified ankle
  ● S90.56 Insect bite (nonvenomous) of ankle
    ● S90.561 Insect bite (nonvenomous), right ankle
    ● S90.562 Insect bite (nonvenomous), left ankle
    ● S90.569 Insect bite (nonvenomous), unspecified ankle
  ● S90.57 Other superficial bite of ankle
            Excludes1 open bite of ankle (S91.05-)
    ● S90.571 Other superficial bite of ankle, right ankle
    ● S90.572 Other superficial bite of ankle, left ankle
    ● S90.579 Other superficial bite of ankle, unspecified ankle

● S90.8 Other superficial injuries of foot
  ● S90.81 Abrasion of foot
    ● S90.811 Abrasion, right foot
    ● S90.812 Abrasion, left foot
    ● S90.819 Abrasion, unspecified foot
  ● S90.82 Blister (nonthermal) of foot
    ● S90.821 Blister (nonthermal), right foot
    ● S90.822 Blister (nonthermal), left foot
    ● S90.829 Blister (nonthermal), unspecified foot
  ● S90.84 External constriction of foot
    ● S90.841 External constriction, right foot
    ● S90.842 External constriction, left foot
    ● S90.849 External constriction, unspecified foot
  ● S90.85 Superficial foreign body of foot
            Splinter in the foot
    ● S90.851 Superficial foreign body, right foot
    ● S90.852 Superficial foreign body, left foot
    ● S90.859 Superficial foreign body, unspecified foot

● S90.86 Insect bite (nonvenomous) of foot
    ● S90.861 Insect bite (nonvenomous), right foot
    ● S90.862 Insect bite (nonvenomous), left foot
    ● S90.869 Insect bite (nonvenomous), unspecified foot
● S90.87 Other superficial bite of foot
          Excludes1 open bite of foot (S91.35-)
    ● S90.871 Other superficial bite of right foot
    ● S90.872 Other superficial bite of left foot
    ● S90.879 Other superficial bite of unspecified foot

● S90.9 Unspecified superficial injury of ankle, foot and toe
  ● S90.91 Unspecified superficial injury of ankle
    ● S90.911 Unspecified superficial injury of right ankle
    ● S90.912 Unspecified superficial injury of left ankle
    ● S90.919 Unspecified superficial injury of unspecified ankle
  ● S90.92 Unspecified superficial injury of foot
    ● S90.921 Unspecified superficial injury of right foot
    ● S90.922 Unspecified superficial injury of left foot
    ● S90.929 Unspecified superficial injury of unspecified foot
  S90.93 Unspecified superficial injury of toes
    ● S90.931 Unspecified superficial injury of right great toe
    ● S90.932 Unspecified superficial injury of left great toe
    ● S90.933 Unspecified superficial injury of unspecified great toe
    ● S90.934 Unspecified superficial injury of right lesser toe(s)
    ● S90.935 Unspecified superficial injury of left lesser toe(s)
    ● S90.936 Unspecified superficial injury of unspecified lesser toe(s)

● S91 Open wound of ankle, foot and toes
       Code also any associated wound infection
       Excludes1 open fracture of ankle, foot and toes (S92.-with 7th character B)
                 traumatic amputation of ankle and foot (S98.-)
       The appropriate 7th character is to be added to each code from category S91

A	initial encounter
D	subsequent encounter
S	sequela

  ● S91.0 Open wound of ankle
    ● S91.00 Unspecified open wound of ankle
      ● S91.001 Unspecified open wound, right ankle
      ● S91.002 Unspecified open wound, left ankle
      ● S91.009 Unspecified open wound, unspecified ankle
    ● S91.01 Laceration without foreign body of ankle
      ● S91.011 Laceration without foreign body, right ankle
      ● S91.012 Laceration without foreign body, left ankle
      ● S91.019 Laceration without foreign body, unspecified ankle

CHAPTER 19 (S00-T88)

- S91.02 **Laceration with foreign body** of ankle
  - S91.021 Laceration with foreign body, **right** ankle
  - S91.022 Laceration with foreign body, **left** ankle
  - S91.029 Laceration with foreign body, **unspecified** ankle
- S91.03 **Puncture wound without foreign body** of ankle
  - S91.031 Puncture wound without foreign body, **right** ankle
  - S91.032 Puncture wound without foreign body, **left** ankle
  - S91.039 Puncture wound without foreign body, **unspecified** ankle
- S91.04 **Puncture wound with foreign body** of ankle
  - S91.041 Puncture wound with foreign body, **right** ankle
  - S91.042 Puncture wound with foreign body, **left** ankle
  - S91.049 Puncture wound with foreign body, **unspecified** ankle
- S91.05 **Open bite of ankle**
  - **Excludes1** superficial bite of ankle (S90.56-, S90.57-)
  - S91.051 Open bite, **right** ankle
  - S91.052 Open bite, **left** ankle
  - S91.059 Open bite, **unspecified** ankle
- S91.1 **Open wound of toe without damage to nail**
  - S91.10 **Unspecified** open wound of toe without damage to nail
    - S91.101 Unspecified open wound of **right great** toe without damage to nail
    - S91.102 Unspecified open wound of **left great** toe without damage to nail
    - S91.103 Unspecified open wound of **unspecified great** toe without damage to nail
    - S91.104 Unspecified open wound of **right lesser** toe(s) without damage to nail
    - S91.105 Unspecified open wound of **left lesser** toe(s) without damage to nail
    - S91.106 Unspecified open wound of **unspecified lesser** toe(s) without damage to nail
    - S91.109 Unspecified open wound of **unspecified toe**(s) without damage to nail
  - S91.11 **Laceration without foreign body** of toe without damage to nail
    - S91.111 Laceration without foreign body of **right great** toe without damage to nail
    - S91.112 Laceration without foreign body of **left great** toe without damage to nail
    - S91.113 Laceration without foreign body of **unspecified great** toe without damage to nail
    - S91.114 Laceration without foreign body of **right lesser** toe(s) without damage to nail
    - S91.115 Laceration without foreign body of **left lesser** toe(s) without damage to nail
    - S91.116 Laceration without foreign body of **unspecified lesser** toe(s) without damage to nail
    - S91.119 Laceration without foreign body of **unspecified toe** without damage to nail

- S91.12 **Laceration with foreign body** of toe without damage to nail
  - S91.121 Laceration with foreign body of **right great** toe without damage to nail
  - S91.122 Laceration with foreign body of **left great** toe without damage to nail
  - S91.123 Laceration with foreign body of **unspecified great** toe without damage to nail
  - S91.124 Laceration with foreign body of **right lesser** toe(s) without damage to nail
  - S91.125 Laceration with foreign body of **left lesser** toe(s) without damage to nail
  - S91.126 Laceration with foreign body of **unspecified lesser** toe(s) without damage to nail
  - S91.129 Laceration with foreign body of **unspecified toe**(s) without damage to nail
- S91.13 **Puncture wound without foreign body** of toe without damage to nail
  - S91.131 Puncture wound without foreign body of **right great** toe without damage to nail
  - S91.132 Puncture wound without foreign body of **left great** toe without damage to nail
  - S91.133 Puncture wound without foreign body of **unspecified great** toe without damage to nail
  - S91.134 Puncture wound without foreign body of **right lesser** toe(s) without damage to nail
  - S91.135 Puncture wound without foreign body of **left lesser** toe(s) without damage to nail
  - S91.136 Puncture wound without foreign body of **unspecified lesser** toe(s) without damage to nail
  - S91.139 Puncture wound without foreign body of **unspecified toe**(s) without damage to nail
- S91.14 **Puncture wound with foreign body** of toe without damage to nail
  - S91.141 Puncture wound with foreign body of **right great** toe without damage to nail
  - S91.142 Puncture wound with foreign body of **left great** toe without damage to nail
  - S91.143 Puncture wound with foreign body of **unspecified great** toe without damage to nail
  - S91.144 Puncture wound with foreign body of **right lesser** toe(s) without damage to nail
  - S91.145 Puncture wound with foreign body of **left lesser** toe(s) without damage to nail
  - S91.146 Puncture wound with foreign body of **unspecified lesser** toe(s) without damage to nail
  - S91.149 Puncture wound with foreign body of **unspecified toe**(s) without damage to nail
- S91.15 **Open bite of toe** without damage to nail
  - Bite of toe NOS
  - **Excludes1** superficial bite of toe (S90.46-, S90.47-)
  - S91.151 Open bite of **right great** toe without damage to nail
  - S91.152 Open bite of **left great** toe without damage to nail

---

▶ New   ⇒ Revised   ~~deleted~~ Deleted   Excludes 1   Excludes 2   Includes   Use additional   Code first   Code also   Key words

OGCR Official Guidelines   X Assign placeholder X   ● Use Additional Character(s)   ▷ Manifestation Code   **Coding Clinic**

CHAPTER 19 (S00-T88)

- S91.153   Open bite of unspecified great toe without damage to nail
- S91.154   Open bite of right lesser toe(s) without damage to nail
- S91.155   Open bite of left lesser toe(s) without damage to nail
- S91.156   Open bite of unspecified lesser toe(s) without damage to nail
- S91.159   Open bite of unspecified toe(s) without damage to nail

- S91.2   Open wound of toe with damage to nail
  - S91.20   Unspecified open wound of toe with damage to nail
    - S91.201   Unspecified open wound of right great toe with damage to nail
    - S91.202   Unspecified open wound of left great toe with damage to nail
    - S91.203   Unspecified open wound of unspecified great toe with damage to nail
    - S91.204   Unspecified open wound of right lesser toe(s) with damage to nail
    - S91.205   Unspecified open wound of left lesser toe(s) with damage to nail
    - S91.206   Unspecified open wound of unspecified lesser toe(s) with damage to nail
    - S91.209   Unspecified open wound of unspecified toe(s) with damage to nail
  - S91.21   Laceration without foreign body of toe with damage to nail
    - S91.211   Laceration without foreign body of right great toe with damage to nail
    - S91.212   Laceration without foreign body of left great toe with damage to nail
    - S91.213   Laceration without foreign body of unspecified great toe with damage to nail
    - S91.214   Laceration without foreign body of right lesser toe(s) with damage to nail
    - S91.215   Laceration without foreign body of left lesser toe(s) with damage to nail
    - S91.216   Laceration without foreign body of unspecified lesser toe(s) with damage to nail
    - S91.219   Laceration without foreign body of unspecified toe(s) with damage to nail
  - S91.22   Laceration with foreign body of toe with damage to nail
    - S91.221   Laceration with foreign body of right great toe with damage to nail
    - S91.222   Laceration with foreign body of left great toe with damage to nail
    - S91.223   Laceration with foreign body of unspecified great toe with damage to nail
    - S91.224   Laceration with foreign body of right lesser toe(s) with damage to nail
    - S91.225   Laceration with foreign body of left lesser toe(s) with damage to nail
    - S91.226   Laceration with foreign body of unspecified lesser toe(s) with damage to nail
    - S91.229   Laceration with foreign body of unspecified toe(s) with damage to nail

- S91.23   Puncture wound without foreign body of toe with damage to nail
  - S91.231   Puncture wound without foreign body of right great toe with damage to nail
  - S91.232   Puncture wound without foreign body of left great toe with damage to nail
  - S91.233   Puncture wound without foreign body of unspecified great toe with damage to nail
  - S91.234   Puncture wound without foreign body of right lesser toe(s) with damage to nail
  - S91.235   Puncture wound without foreign body of left lesser toe(s) with damage to nail
  - S91.236   Puncture wound without foreign body of unspecified lesser toe(s) with damage to nail
  - S91.239   Puncture wound without foreign body of unspecified toe(s) with damage to nail
- S91.24   Puncture wound with foreign body of toe with damage to nail
  - S91.241   Puncture wound with foreign body of right great toe with damage to nail
  - S91.242   Puncture wound with foreign body of left great toe with damage to nail
  - S91.243   Puncture wound with foreign body of unspecified great toe with damage to nail
  - S91.244   Puncture wound with foreign body of right lesser toe(s) with damage to nail
  - S91.245   Puncture wound with foreign body of left lesser toe(s) with damage to nail
  - S91.246   Puncture wound with foreign body of unspecified lesser toe(s) with damage to nail
  - S91.249   Puncture wound with foreign body of unspecified toe(s) with damage to nail
- S91.25   Open bite of toe with damage to nail
  Bite of toe with damage to nail NOS
  > **Excludes1**   superficial bite of toe (S90.46-, S90.47-)
  - S91.251   Open bite of right great toe with damage to nail
  - S91.252   Open bite of left great toe with damage to nail
  - S91.253   Open bite of unspecified great toe with damage to nail
  - S91.254   Open bite of right lesser toe(s) with damage to nail
  - S91.255   Open bite of left lesser toe(s) with damage to nail
  - S91.256   Open bite of unspecified lesser toe(s) with damage to nail
  - S91.259   Open bite of unspecified toe(s) with damage to nail

- S91.3   Open wound of foot
  - S91.30   Unspecified open wound of foot
    - S91.301   Unspecified open wound, right foot
    - S91.302   Unspecified open wound, left foot
    - S91.309   Unspecified open wound, unspecified foot

● **S91.31**   Laceration without foreign body of foot
    ● **S91.311**   Laceration without foreign body, **right** foot
    ● **S91.312**   Laceration without foreign body, **left** foot
    ● **S91.319**   Laceration without foreign body, **unspecified** foot
● **S91.32**   Laceration with foreign body of foot
    ● **S91.321**   Laceration with foreign body, **right** foot
    ● **S91.322**   Laceration with foreign body, **left foot**
    ● **S91.329**   Laceration with foreign body, **unspecified** foot
● **S91.33**   Puncture wound without foreign body of foot
    ● **S91.331**   Puncture wound without foreign body, **right** foot
    ● **S91.332**   Puncture wound without foreign body, **left** foot
    ● **S91.339**   Puncture wound without foreign body, **unspecified** foot
● **S91.34**   Puncture wound with foreign body of foot
    ● **S91.341**   Puncture wound with foreign body, **right foot**
    ● **S91.342**   Puncture wound with foreign body, **left foot**
    ● **S91.349**   Puncture wound with foreign body, **unspecified** foot
● **S91.35**   Open bite of foot
    Excludes1   superficial bite of foot (S90.86-, S90.87-)
    ● **S91.351**   Open bite, **right** foot
    ● **S91.352**   Open bite, **left** foot
    ● **S91.359**   Open bite, **unspecified** foot

● **S92**   Fracture of foot and toe, except ankle

Note: A fracture not indicated as displaced or nondisplaced should be coded to displaced

    A fracture not indicated as open or closed should be coded to closed

Excludes1   traumatic amputation of ankle and foot (S98.-)
Excludes2   fracture of ankle (S82.-)
                fracture of malleolus (S82.-)

The appropriate 7th character is to be added to each code from category S92

A	initial encounter for closed fracture
B	initial encounter for open fracture
D	subsequent encounter for fracture with routine healing
G	subsequent encounter for fracture with delayed healing
K	subsequent encounter for fracture with nonunion
P	subsequent encounter for fracture with malunion
S	sequela

● **S92.0**   Fracture of calcaneus
    Heel bone   Os calcis
    Excludes2   Physeal fracture of calcaneus (S99.0-)

    ● **S92.00**   Unspecified fracture of calcaneus
       ● **S92.001**   Unspecified fracture of **right** calcaneus
       ● **S92.002**   Unspecified fracture of **left** calcaneus
       ● **S92.009**   Unspecified fracture of **unspecified** calcaneus
    ● **S92.01**   Fracture of body of calcaneus
       ● **S92.011**   Displaced fracture of body of **right** calcaneus
       ● **S92.012**   Displaced fracture of body of **left** calcaneus
       ● **S92.013**   Displaced fracture of body of **unspecified** calcaneus
       ● **S92.014**   Nondisplaced fracture of body of **right** calcaneus

● **S92.015**   Nondisplaced fracture of body of **left** calcaneus
● **S92.016**   Nondisplaced fracture of body of **unspecified** calcaneus
● **S92.02**   Fracture of anterior process of calcaneus
    ● **S92.021**   Displaced fracture of anterior process of **right** calcaneus
    ● **S92.022**   Displaced fracture of anterior process of **left** calcaneus
    ● **S92.023**   Displaced fracture of anterior process of **unspecified** calcaneus
    ● **S92.024**   Nondisplaced fracture of anterior process of **right** calcaneus
    ● **S92.025**   Nondisplaced fracture of anterior process of **left** calcaneus
    ● **S92.026**   Nondisplaced fracture of anterior process of **unspecified** calcaneus
● **S92.03**   Avulsion fracture of tuberosity of calcaneus
    ● **S92.031**   Displaced avulsion fracture of tuberosity of **right** calcaneus
    ● **S92.032**   Displaced avulsion fracture of tuberosity of **left** calcaneus
    ● **S92.033**   Displaced avulsion fracture of tuberosity of **unspecified** calcaneus
    ● **S92.034**   Nondisplaced avulsion fracture of tuberosity of **right** calcaneus
    ● **S92.035**   Nondisplaced avulsion fracture of tuberosity of **left** calcaneus
    ● **S92.036**   Nondisplaced avulsion fracture of tuberosity of **unspecified** calcaneus
● **S92.04**   Other fracture of tuberosity of calcaneus
    ● **S92.041**   Displaced other fracture of tuberosity of **right** calcaneus
    ● **S92.042**   Displaced other fracture of tuberosity of **left** calcaneus
    ● **S92.043**   Displaced other fracture of tuberosity of **unspecified** calcaneus
    ● **S92.044**   Nondisplaced other fracture of tuberosity of **right** calcaneus
    ● **S92.045**   Nondisplaced other fracture of tuberosity of **left** calcaneus
    ● **S92.046**   Nondisplaced other fracture of tuberosity of **unspecified** calcaneus
● **S92.05**   Other extraarticular fracture of calcaneus
    ● **S92.051**   Displaced other extraarticular fracture of **right** calcaneus
    ● **S92.052**   Displaced other extraarticular fracture of **left** calcaneus
    ● **S92.053**   Displaced other extraarticular fracture of **unspecified** calcaneus
    ● **S92.054**   Nondisplaced other extraarticular fracture of **right** calcaneus
    ● **S92.055**   Nondisplaced other extraarticular fracture of **left** calcaneus
    ● **S92.056**   Nondisplaced other extraarticular fracture of **unspecified** calcaneus
● **S92.06**   Intraarticular fracture of calcaneus
    ● **S92.061**   Displaced intraarticular fracture of **right** calcaneus
    ● **S92.062**   Displaced intraarticular fracture of **left** calcaneus
    ● **S92.063**   Displaced intraarticular fracture of **unspecified** calcaneus
    ● **S92.064**   Nondisplaced intraarticular fracture of **right** calcaneus
    ● **S92.065**   Nondisplaced intraarticular fracture of **left** calcaneus
    ● **S92.066**   Nondisplaced intraarticular fracture of **unspecified** calcaneus

▶ New   ⇒ Revised   ~~deleted~~ Deleted   Excludes 1   Excludes 2   Includes   Use additional   Code first   Code also   Key words
    OGCR Official Guidelines   X Assign placeholder X   ● Use Additional Character(s)   ▷ Manifestation Code   **Coding Clinic**

- ● S92.1　Fracture of talus
  Astragalus
  - ● S92.10　Unspecified fracture of talus
    - ● S92.101　Unspecified fracture of right talus
    - ● S92.102　Unspecified fracture of left talus
    - ● S92.109　Unspecified fracture of unspecified talus
  - ● S92.11　Fracture of neck of talus
    - ● S92.111　Displaced fracture of neck of right talus
    - ● S92.112　Displaced fracture of neck of left talus
    - ● S92.113　Displaced fracture of neck of unspecified talus
    - ● S92.114　Nondisplaced fracture of neck of right talus
    - ● S92.115　Nondisplaced fracture of neck of left talus
    - ● S92.116　Nondisplaced fracture of neck of unspecified talus
  - ● S92.12　Fracture of body of talus
    - ● S92.121　Displaced fracture of body of right talus
    - ● S92.122　Displaced fracture of body of left talus
    - ● S92.123　Displaced fracture of body of unspecified talus
    - ● S92.124　Nondisplaced fracture of body of right talus
    - ● S92.125　Nondisplaced fracture of body of left talus
    - ● S92.126　Nondisplaced fracture of body of unspecified talus
  - ● S92.13　Fracture of posterior process of talus
    - ● S92.131　Displaced fracture of posterior process of right talus
    - ● S92.132　Displaced fracture of posterior process of left talus
    - ● S92.133　Displaced fracture of posterior process of unspecified talus
    - ● S92.134　Nondisplaced fracture of posterior process of right talus
    - ● S92.135　Nondisplaced fracture of posterior process of left talus
    - ● S92.136　Nondisplaced fracture of posterior process of unspecified talus
  - ● S92.14　Dome fracture of talus
    - **Excludes1**　osteochondritis dissecans (M93.2)
    - ● S92.141　Displaced dome fracture of right talus
    - ● S92.142　Displaced dome fracture of left talus
    - ● S92.143　Displaced dome fracture of unspecified talus
    - ● S92.144　Nondisplaced dome fracture of right talus
    - ● S92.145　Nondisplaced dome fracture of left talus
    - ● S92.146　Nondisplaced dome fracture of unspecified talus
  - ● S92.15　Avulsion fracture (chip fracture) of talus
    - ● S92.151　Displaced avulsion fracture (chip fracture) of right talus
    - ● S92.152　Displaced avulsion fracture (chip fracture) of left talus
    - ● S92.153　Displaced avulsion fracture (chip fracture) of unspecified talus
    - ● S92.154　Nondisplaced avulsion fracture (chip fracture) of right talus

- ● S92.155　Nondisplaced avulsion fracture (chip fracture) of left talus
- ● S92.156　Nondisplaced avulsion fracture (chip fracture) of unspecified talus
  - ● S92.19　Other fracture of talus
    - ● S92.191　Other fracture of right talus
    - ● S92.192　Other fracture of left talus
    - ● S92.199　Other fracture of unspecified talus
- ● S92.2　Fracture of other and unspecified tarsal bone(s)
  - ● S92.20　Fracture of unspecified tarsal bone(s)
    - ● S92.201　Fracture of unspecified tarsal bone(s) of right foot
    - ● S92.202　Fracture of unspecified tarsal bone(s) of left foot
    - ● S92.209　Fracture of unspecified tarsal bone(s) of unspecified foot
  - ● S92.21　Fracture of cuboid bone
    - ● S92.211　Displaced fracture of cuboid bone of right foot
    - ● S92.212　Displaced fracture of cuboid bone of left foot
    - ● S92.213　Displaced fracture of cuboid bone of unspecified foot
    - ● S92.214　Nondisplaced fracture of cuboid bone of right foot
    - ● S92.215　Nondisplaced fracture of cuboid bone of left foot
    - ● S92.216　Nondisplaced fracture of cuboid bone of unspecified foot
  - ● S92.22　Fracture of lateral cuneiform
    - ● S92.221　Displaced fracture of lateral cuneiform of right foot
    - ● S92.222　Displaced fracture of lateral cuneiform of left foot
    - ● S92.223　Displaced fracture of lateral cuneiform of unspecified foot
    - ● S92.224　Nondisplaced fracture of lateral cuneiform of right foot
    - ● S92.225　Nondisplaced fracture of lateral cuneiform of left foot
    - ● S92.226　Nondisplaced fracture of lateral cuneiform of unspecified foot
  - ● S92.23　Fracture of intermediate cuneiform
    - ● S92.231　Displaced fracture of intermediate cuneiform of right foot
    - ● S92.232　Displaced fracture of intermediate cuneiform of left foot
    - ● S92.233　Displaced fracture of intermediate cuneiform of unspecified foot
    - ● S92.234　Nondisplaced fracture of intermediate cuneiform of right foot
    - ● S92.235　Nondisplaced fracture of intermediate cuneiform of left foot
    - ● S92.236　Nondisplaced fracture of intermediate cuneiform of unspecified foot
  - ● S92.24　Fracture of medial cuneiform
    - ● S92.241　Displaced fracture of medial cuneiform of right foot
    - ● S92.242　Displaced fracture of medial cuneiform of left foot
    - ● S92.243　Displaced fracture of medial cuneiform of unspecified foot
    - ● S92.244　Nondisplaced fracture of medial cuneiform of right foot
    - ● S92.245　Nondisplaced fracture of medial cuneiform of left foot
    - ● S92.246　Nondisplaced fracture of medial cuneiform of unspecified foot

CHAPTER 19 (S00-T88)

CHAPTER 19 (S00-T88)

● **S92.25**   Fracture of navicular [scaphoid] of foot
- ● **S92.251**   Displaced fracture of navicular [scaphoid] of right foot
- ● **S92.252**   Displaced fracture of navicular [scaphoid] of left foot
- ● **S92.253**   Displaced fracture of navicular [scaphoid] of unspecified foot
- ● **S92.254**   Nondisplaced fracture of navicular [scaphoid] of right foot
- ● **S92.255**   Nondisplaced fracture of navicular [scaphoid] of left foot
- ● **S92.256**   Nondisplaced fracture of navicular [scaphoid] of unspecified foot

● **S92.3**   Fracture of metatarsal bone(s)

     Excludes2   Physeal fracture of metatarsal (S99.1-)

- ● **S92.30**   Fracture of unspecified metatarsal bone(s)
  - ● **S92.301**   Fracture of unspecified metatarsal bone(s), right foot
  - ● **S92.302**   Fracture of unspecified metatarsal bone(s), left foot
  - ● **S92.309**   Fracture of unspecified metatarsal bone(s), unspecified foot
- ● **S92.31**   Fracture of first metatarsal bone
  - ● **S92.311**   Displaced fracture of first metatarsal bone, right foot
  - ● **S92.312**   Displaced fracture of first metatarsal bone, left foot
  - ● **S92.313**   Displaced fracture of first metatarsal bone, unspecified foot
  - ● **S92.314**   Nondisplaced fracture of first metatarsal bone, right foot
  - ● **S92.315**   Nondisplaced fracture of first metatarsal bone, left foot
  - ● **S92.316**   Nondisplaced fracture of first metatarsal bone, unspecified foot
- ● **S92.32**   Fracture of second metatarsal bone
  - ● **S92.321**   Displaced fracture of second metatarsal bone, right foot
  - ● **S92.322**   Displaced fracture of second metatarsal bone, left foot
  - ● **S92.323**   Displaced fracture of second metatarsal bone, unspecified foot
  - ● **S92.324**   Nondisplaced fracture of second metatarsal bone, right foot
  - ● **S92.325**   Nondisplaced fracture of second metatarsal bone, left foot
  - ● **S92.326**   Nondisplaced fracture of second metatarsal bone, unspecified foot
- ● **S92.33**   Fracture of third metatarsal bone

    Coding Clinic: 2018, Q1, P3
  - ● **S92.331**   Displaced fracture of third metatarsal bone, right foot
  - ● **S92.332**   Displaced fracture of third metatarsal bone, left foot
  - ● **S92.333**   Displaced fracture of third metatarsal bone, unspecified foot
  - ● **S92.334**   Nondisplaced fracture of third metatarsal bone, right foot
  - ● **S92.335**   Nondisplaced fracture of third metatarsal bone, left foot
  - ● **S92.336**   Nondisplaced fracture of third metatarsal bone, unspecified foot

● **S92.34**   Fracture of fourth metatarsal bone
- ● **S92.341**   Displaced fracture of fourth metatarsal bone, right foot
- ● **S92.342**   Displaced fracture of fourth metatarsal bone, left foot
- ● **S92.343**   Displaced fracture of fourth metatarsal bone, unspecified foot
- ● **S92.344**   Nondisplaced fracture of fourth metatarsal bone, right foot
- ● **S92.345**   Nondisplaced fracture of fourth metatarsal bone, left foot
- ● **S92.346**   Nondisplaced fracture of fourth metatarsal bone, unspecified foot

● **S92.35**   Fracture of fifth metatarsal bone
- ● **S92.351**   Displaced fracture of fifth metatarsal bone, right foot
- ● **S92.352**   Displaced fracture of fifth metatarsal bone, left foot
- ● **S92.353**   Displaced fracture of fifth metatarsal bone, unspecified foot
- ● **S92.354**   Nondisplaced fracture of fifth metatarsal bone, right foot
- ● **S92.355**   Nondisplaced fracture of fifth metatarsal bone, left foot
- ● **S92.356**   Nondisplaced fracture of fifth metatarsal bone, unspecified foot

● **S92.4**   Fracture of great toe

     Excludes2   Physeal fracture of phalanx of toe (S99.2-)

- ● **S92.40**   Unspecified fracture of great toe
  - ● **S92.401**   Displaced unspecified fracture of right great toe
  - ● **S92.402**   Displaced unspecified fracture of left great toe
  - ● **S92.403**   Displaced unspecified fracture of unspecified great toe
  - ● **S92.404**   Nondisplaced unspecified fracture of right great toe
  - ● **S92.405**   Nondisplaced unspecified fracture of left great toe
  - ● **S92.406**   Nondisplaced unspecified fracture of unspecified great toe
- ● **S92.41**   Fracture of proximal phalanx of great toe
  - ● **S92.411**   Displaced fracture of proximal phalanx of right great toe
  - ● **S92.412**   Displaced fracture of proximal phalanx of left great toe
  - ● **S92.413**   Displaced fracture of proximal phalanx of unspecified great toe
  - ● **S92.414**   Nondisplaced fracture of proximal phalanx of right great toe
  - ● **S92.415**   Nondisplaced fracture of proximal phalanx of left great toe
  - ● **S92.416**   Nondisplaced fracture of proximal phalanx of unspecified great toe
- ● **S92.42**   Fracture of distal phalanx of great toe
  - ● **S92.421**   Displaced fracture of distal phalanx of right great toe
  - ● **S92.422**   Displaced fracture of distal phalanx of left great toe
  - ● **S92.423**   Displaced fracture of distal phalanx of unspecified great toe
  - ● **S92.424**   Nondisplaced fracture of distal phalanx of right great toe
  - ● **S92.425**   Nondisplaced fracture of distal phalanx of left great toe
  - ● **S92.426**   Nondisplaced fracture of distal phalanx of unspecified great toe

▶ New   ➡ Revised   ~~deleted~~ Deleted   Excludes 1   Excludes 2   Includes   Use additional   Code first   Code also   Key words

OGCR Official Guidelines   X Assign placeholder X   ● Use Additional Character(s)   ▶ Manifestation Code   **Coding Clinic**

- S92.49   Other fracture of great toe
  - S92.491   Other fracture of right great toe
  - S92.492   Other fracture of left great toe
  - S92.499   Other fracture of unspecified great toe
- S92.5   Fracture of lesser toe(s)

  Excludes2   Physeal fracture of phalanx of toe (S99.2-)

  - S92.50   Unspecified fracture of lesser toe(s)
    - S92.501   Displaced unspecified fracture of right lesser toe(s)
    - S92.502   Displaced unspecified fracture of left lesser toe(s)
    - S92.503   Displaced unspecified fracture of unspecified lesser toe(s)
    - S92.504   Nondisplaced unspecified fracture of right lesser toe(s)
    - S92.505   Nondisplaced unspecified fracture of left lesser toe(s)
    - S92.506   Nondisplaced unspecified fracture of unspecified lesser toe(s)
  - S92.51   Fracture of proximal phalanx of lesser toe(s)
    - S92.511   Displaced fracture of proximal phalanx of right lesser toe(s)
    - S92.512   Displaced fracture of proximal phalanx of left lesser toe(s)
    - S92.513   Displaced fracture of proximal phalanx of unspecified lesser toe(s)
    - S92.514   Nondisplaced fracture of proximal phalanx of right lesser toe(s)
    - S92.515   Nondisplaced fracture of proximal phalanx of left lesser toe(s)
    - S92.516   Nondisplaced fracture of proximal phalanx of unspecified lesser toe(s)
  - S92.52   Fracture of middle phalanx of lesser toe(s)
    - S92.521   Displaced fracture of middle phalanx of right lesser toe(s)
    - S92.522   Displaced fracture of middle phalanx of left lesser toe(s)
    - S92.523   Displaced fracture of middle phalanx of unspecified lesser toe(s)
    - S92.524   Nondisplaced fracture of middle phalanx of right lesser toe(s)
    - S92.525   Nondisplaced fracture of middle phalanx of left lesser toe(s)
    - S92.526   Nondisplaced fracture of middle phalanx of unspecified lesser toe(s)
  - S92.53   Fracture of distal phalanx of lesser toe(s)
    - S92.531   Displaced fracture of distal phalanx of right lesser toe(s)
    - S92.532   Displaced fracture of distal phalanx of left lesser toe(s)
    - S92.533   Displaced fracture of distal phalanx of unspecified lesser toe(s)
    - S92.534   Nondisplaced fracture of distal phalanx of right lesser toe(s)
    - S92.535   Nondisplaced fracture of distal phalanx of left lesser toe(s)
    - S92.536   Nondisplaced fracture of distal phalanx of unspecified lesser toe(s)
  - S92.59   Other fracture of lesser toe(s)
    - S92.591   Other fracture of right lesser toe(s)
    - S92.592   Other fracture of left lesser toe(s)
    - S92.599   Other fracture of unspecified lesser toe(s)
- S92.8   Other fracture of foot, except ankle
  - S92.81   Other fracture of foot

    Sesamoid fracture of foot

    Coding Clinic: 2016, Q4, P68

    - S92.811   Other fracture of right foot
    - S92.812   Other fracture of left foot
    - S92.819   Other fracture of unspecified foot
- S92.9   Unspecified fracture of foot and toe
  - S92.90   Unspecified fracture of foot
    - S92.901   Unspecified fracture of right foot
    - S92.902   Unspecified fracture of left foot
    - S92.909   Unspecified fracture of unspecified foot
  - S92.91   Unspecified fracture of toe
    - S92.911   Unspecified fracture of right toe(s)
    - S92.912   Unspecified fracture of left toe(s)
    - S92.919   Unspecified fracture of unspecified toe(s)
- S93   Dislocation and sprain of joints and ligaments at ankle, foot and toe level

  Includes   avulsion of joint or ligament of ankle, foot and toe

  laceration of cartilage, joint or ligament of ankle, foot and toe

  sprain of cartilage, joint or ligament of ankle, foot and toe

  traumatic hemarthrosis of joint or ligament of ankle, foot and toe

  traumatic rupture of joint or ligament of ankle, foot and toe

  traumatic subluxation of joint or ligament of ankle, foot and toe

  traumatic tear of joint or ligament of ankle, foot and toe

  Code also any associated open wound

  Excludes2   strain of muscle and tendon of ankle and foot (S96.-)

  The appropriate 7th character is to be added to each code from category S93

A	initial encounter
D	subsequent encounter
S	sequela

  - S93.0   Subluxation and dislocation of ankle joint

    Subluxation and dislocation of astragalus

    Subluxation and dislocation of fibula, lower end

    Subluxation and dislocation of talus

    Subluxation and dislocation of tibia, lower end

    - X ● S93.01   Subluxation of right ankle joint
    - X ● S93.02   Subluxation of left ankle joint
    - X ● S93.03   Subluxation of unspecified ankle joint
    - X ● S93.04   Dislocation of right ankle joint
    - X ● S93.05   Dislocation of left ankle joint
    - X ● S93.06   Dislocation of unspecified ankle joint
  - S93.1   Subluxation and dislocation of toe
    - S93.10   Unspecified subluxation and dislocation of toe

      Dislocation of toe NOS

      Subluxation of toe NOS

      - S93.101   Unspecified subluxation of right toe(s)
      - S93.102   Unspecified subluxation of left toe(s)
      - S93.103   Unspecified subluxation of unspecified toe(s)
      - S93.104   Unspecified dislocation of right toe(s)
      - S93.105   Unspecified dislocation of left toe(s)
      - S93.106   Unspecified dislocation of unspecified toe(s)

- S93.11 **Dislocation** of interphalangeal joint
  - S93.111 Dislocation of interphalangeal joint of **right great** toe
  - S93.112 Dislocation of interphalangeal joint of **left great** toe
  - S93.113 Dislocation of interphalangeal joint of **unspecified great** toe
  - S93.114 Dislocation of interphalangeal joint of **right lesser** toe(s)
  - S93.115 Dislocation of interphalangeal joint of **left lesser** toe(s)
  - S93.116 Dislocation of interphalangeal joint of **unspecified lesser** toe(s)
  - S93.119 Dislocation of interphalangeal joint of **unspecified** toe(s)
- S93.12 **Dislocation** of metatarsophalangeal joint
  - S93.121 Dislocation of metatarsophalangeal joint of **right great** toe
  - S93.122 Dislocation of metatarsophalangeal joint of **left great** toe
  - S93.123 Dislocation of metatarsophalangeal joint of **unspecified great** toe
  - S93.124 Dislocation of metatarsophalangeal joint of **right lesser** toe(s)
  - S93.125 Dislocation of metatarsophalangeal joint of **left lesser** toe(s)
  - S93.126 Dislocation of metatarsophalangeal joint of **unspecified lesser** toe(s)
  - S93.129 Dislocation of metatarsophalangeal joint of **unspecified** toe(s)
- S93.13 **Subluxation** of interphalangeal joint
  - S93.131 Subluxation of interphalangeal joint of **right great** toe
  - S93.132 Subluxation of interphalangeal joint of **left great** toe
  - S93.133 Subluxation of interphalangeal joint of **unspecified great** toe
  - S93.134 Subluxation of interphalangeal joint of **right lesser** toe(s)
  - S93.135 Subluxation of interphalangeal joint of **left lesser** toe(s)
  - S93.136 Subluxation of interphalangeal joint of **unspecified lesser** toe(s)
  - S93.139 Subluxation of interphalangeal joint of **unspecified** toe(s)
- S93.14 **Subluxation** of metatarsophalangeal joint
  - S93.141 Subluxation of metatarsophalangeal joint of **right great** toe
  - S93.142 Subluxation of metatarsophalangeal joint of **left great** toe
  - S93.143 Subluxation of metatarsophalangeal joint of **unspecified great** toe
  - S93.144 Subluxation of metatarsophalangeal joint of **right lesser** toe(s)
  - S93.145 Subluxation of metatarsophalangeal joint of **left lesser** toe(s)
  - S93.146 Subluxation of metatarsophalangeal joint of **unspecified lesser** toe(s)
  - S93.149 Subluxation of metatarsophalangeal joint of **unspecified** toe(s)
- S93.3 Subluxation and dislocation of **foot**
  - **Excludes2** dislocation of toe (S93.1-)
  - S93.30 **Unspecified** subluxation and dislocation of foot
    Dislocation of foot NOS
    Subluxation of foot NOS
    - S93.301 Unspecified **subluxation** of **right** foot
    - S93.302 Unspecified **subluxation** of **left** foot
    - S93.303 Unspecified **subluxation** of **unspecified** foot

- S93.304 Unspecified **dislocation of right** foot
- S93.305 Unspecified **dislocation of left** foot
- S93.306 Unspecified **dislocation of unspecified** foot
- S93.31 Subluxation and dislocation of **tarsal** joint
  - S93.311 **Subluxation** of tarsal joint of **right** foot
  - S93.312 **Subluxation** of tarsal joint of **left** foot
  - S93.313 **Subluxation** of tarsal joint of **unspecified** foot
  - S93.314 **Dislocation** of tarsal joint of **right** foot
  - S93.315 **Dislocation** of tarsal joint of **left** foot
  - S93.316 **Dislocation** of tarsal joint of **unspecified** foot
- S93.32 Subluxation and dislocation of **tarsometatarsal** joint
  - S93.321 **Subluxation** of tarsometatarsal joint of **right** foot
  - S93.322 **Subluxation** of tarsometatarsal joint of **left** foot
  - S93.323 **Subluxation** of tarsometatarsal joint of **unspecified** foot
  - S93.324 **Dislocation** of tarsometatarsal joint of **right** foot
  - S93.325 **Dislocation** of tarsometatarsal joint of **left** foot
  - S93.326 **Dislocation** of tarsometatarsal joint of **unspecified** foot
- S93.33 Other subluxation and dislocation of foot
  - S93.331 Other **subluxation** of **right** foot
  - S93.332 Other **subluxation** of **left** foot
  - S93.333 Other **subluxation** of **unspecified** foot
  - S93.334 Other **dislocation** of **right** foot
  - S93.335 Other **dislocation** of **left** foot
  - S93.336 Other **dislocation** of **unspecified** foot
- S93.4 Sprain of **ankle**
  Injury to ligaments when one or more is stretched/torn
  Excludes2 injury of Achilles tendon (S86.0-)
  - S93.40 Sprain of **unspecified** ligament of ankle
    Sprain of ankle NOS
    Sprained ankle NOS
    - S93.401 Sprain of unspecified ligament of **right** ankle
    - S93.402 Sprain of unspecified ligament of **left** ankle
    - S93.409 Sprain of unspecified ligament of **unspecified** ankle
  - S93.41 Sprain of **calcaneofibular** ligament
    - S93.411 Sprain of calcaneofibular ligament of **right** ankle
    - S93.412 Sprain of calcaneofibular ligament of **left** ankle
    - S93.419 Sprain of calcaneofibular ligament of **unspecified** ankle
  - S93.42 Sprain of **deltoid** ligament
    - S93.421 Sprain of deltoid ligament of **right** ankle
    - S93.422 Sprain of deltoid ligament of **left** ankle
    - S93.429 Sprain of deltoid ligament of **unspecified** ankle
  - S93.43 Sprain of **tibiofibular** ligament
    - S93.431 Sprain of tibiofibular ligament of **right** ankle
    - S93.432 Sprain of tibiofibular ligament of **left** ankle
    - S93.439 Sprain of tibiofibular ligament of **unspecified** ankle

● **S93.49**   Sprain of other ligament of ankle
      Sprain of internal collateral ligament
      Sprain of talofibular ligament
   ● **S93.491**   Sprain of other ligament of right ankle
   ● **S93.492**   Sprain of other ligament of left ankle
   ● **S93.499**   Sprain of other ligament of unspecified ankle

● **S93.5**   Sprain of toe
   ● **S93.50**   Unspecified sprain of toe
     ● **S93.501**   Unspecified sprain of right great toe
     ● **S93.502**   Unspecified sprain of left great toe
     ● **S93.503**   Unspecified sprain of unspecified great toe
     ● **S93.504**   Unspecified sprain of right lesser toe(s)
     ● **S93.505**   Unspecified sprain of left lesser toe(s)
     ● **S93.506**   Unspecified sprain of unspecified lesser toe(s)
     ● **S93.509**   Unspecified sprain of unspecified toe(s)
   ● **S93.51**   Sprain of interphalangeal joint of toe
     ● **S93.511**   Sprain of interphalangeal joint of right great toe
     ● **S93.512**   Sprain of interphalangeal joint of left great toe
     ● **S93.513**   Sprain of interphalangeal joint of unspecified great toe
     ● **S93.514**   Sprain of interphalangeal joint of right lesser toe(s)
     ● **S93.515**   Sprain of interphalangeal joint of left lesser toe(s)
     ● **S93.516**   Sprain of interphalangeal joint of unspecified lesser toe(s)
     ● **S93.519**   Sprain of interphalangeal joint of unspecified toe(s)
   ● **S93.52**   Sprain of metatarsophalangeal joint of toe
     ● **S93.521**   Sprain of metatarsophalangeal joint of right great toe
     ● **S93.522**   Sprain of metatarsophalangeal joint of left great toe
     ● **S93.523**   Sprain of metatarsophalangeal joint of unspecified great toe
     ● **S93.524**   Sprain of metatarsophalangeal joint of right lesser toe(s)
     ● **S93.525**   Sprain of metatarsophalangeal joint of left lesser toe(s)
     ● **S93.526**   Sprain of metatarsophalangeal joint of unspecified lesser toe(s)
     ● **S93.529**   Sprain of metatarsophalangeal joint of unspecified toe(s)

● **S93.6**   Sprain of foot
     Excludes2   sprain of metatarsophalangeal joint of toe (S93.52-)
                 sprain of toe (S93.5-)
   ● **S93.60**   Unspecified sprain of foot
     ● **S93.601**   Unspecified sprain of right foot
     ● **S93.602**   Unspecified sprain of left foot
     ● **S93.609**   Unspecified sprain of unspecified foot
   ● **S93.61**   Sprain of tarsal ligament of foot
     ● **S93.611**   Sprain of tarsal ligament of right foot
     ● **S93.612**   Sprain of tarsal ligament of left foot
     ● **S93.619**   Sprain of tarsal ligament of unspecified foot

   ● **S93.62**   Sprain of tarsometatarsal ligament of foot
     ● **S93.621**   Sprain of tarsometatarsal ligament of right foot
     ● **S93.622**   Sprain of tarsometatarsal ligament of left foot
     ● **S93.629**   Sprain of tarsometatarsal ligament of unspecified foot
   ● **S93.69**   Other sprain of foot
     ● **S93.691**   Other sprain of right foot
     ● **S93.692**   Other sprain of left foot
     ● **S93.699**   Other sprain of unspecified foot

● **S94**   Injury of nerves at ankle and foot level
     The appropriate 7th character is to be added to each code from category S94

A	initial encounter
D	subsequent encounter
S	sequela

     Code also any associated open wound (S91.-)
● **S94.0**   Injury of lateral plantar nerve
   X ● **S94.00**   Injury of lateral plantar nerve, unspecified leg
   X ● **S94.01**   Injury of lateral plantar nerve, right leg
   X ● **S94.02**   Injury of lateral plantar nerve, left leg
● **S94.1**   Injury of medial plantar nerve
   X ● **S94.10**   Injury of medial plantar nerve, unspecified leg
   X ● **S94.11**   Injury of medial plantar nerve, right leg
   X ● **S94.12**   Injury of medial plantar nerve, left leg
● **S94.2**   Injury of deep peroneal nerve at ankle and foot level
     Injury of terminal, lateral branch of deep peroneal nerve
   X ● **S94.20**   Injury of deep peroneal nerve at ankle and foot level, unspecified leg
   X ● **S94.21**   Injury of deep peroneal nerve at ankle and foot level, right leg
   X ● **S94.22**   Injury of deep peroneal nerve at ankle and foot level, left leg
● **S94.3**   Injury of cutaneous sensory nerve at ankle and foot level
   X ● **S94.30**   Injury of cutaneous sensory nerve at ankle and foot level, unspecified leg
   X ● **S94.31**   Injury of cutaneous sensory nerve at ankle and foot level, right leg
   X ● **S94.32**   Injury of cutaneous sensory nerve at ankle and foot level, left leg
● **S94.8**   Injury of other nerves at ankle and foot level
   ● **S94.8X**   Injury of other nerves at ankle and foot level
     ● **S94.8X1**   Injury of other nerves at ankle and foot level, right leg
     ● **S94.8X2**   Injury of other nerves at ankle and foot level, left leg
     ● **S94.8X9**   Injury of other nerves at ankle and foot level, unspecified leg
● **S94.9**   Injury of unspecified nerve at ankle and foot level
   X ● **S94.90**   Injury of unspecified nerve at ankle and foot level, unspecified leg
   X ● **S94.91**   Injury of unspecified nerve at ankle and foot level, right leg
   X ● **S94.92**   Injury of unspecified nerve at ankle and foot level, left leg

CHAPTER 19 (S00-T88)

● **S95**   **Injury of blood vessels at ankle and foot level**

> Code also any associated open wound (S91.-)
>
> **Excludes2**   injury of posterior tibial artery and vein (S85.1-, S85.8-)
>
> The appropriate 7th character is to be added to each code from category S95

> | | |
> |---|---|
> | A | initial encounter |
> | D | subsequent encounter |
> | S | sequela |

● **S95.0**   **Injury of dorsal artery of foot**

     ● **S95.00**   **Unspecified** injury of dorsal artery of foot

         ● **S95.001**   Unspecified injury of dorsal artery of **right** foot

         ● **S95.002**   Unspecified injury of dorsal artery of **left** foot

         ● **S95.009**   Unspecified injury of dorsal artery of **unspecified** foot

     ● **S95.01**   **Laceration** of dorsal artery of foot

         ● **S95.011**   Laceration of dorsal artery of **right** foot

         ● **S95.012**   Laceration of dorsal artery of **left** foot

         ● **S95.019**   Laceration of dorsal artery of **unspecified** foot

     ● **S95.09**   **Other** specified injury of dorsal artery of foot

         ● **S95.091**   Other specified injury of dorsal artery of **right** foot

         ● **S95.092**   Other specified injury of dorsal artery of **left** foot

         ● **S95.099**   Other specified injury of dorsal artery of **unspecified** foot

● **S95.1**   **Injury of plantar artery of foot**

     ● **S95.10**   **Unspecified** injury of plantar artery of foot

         ● **S95.101**   Unspecified injury of plantar artery of **right** foot

         ● **S95.102**   Unspecified injury of plantar artery of **left** foot

         ● **S95.109**   Unspecified injury of plantar artery of **unspecified** foot

     ● **S95.11**   **Laceration** of plantar artery of foot

         ● **S95.111**   Laceration of plantar artery of **right** foot

         ● **S95.112**   Laceration of plantar artery of **left** foot

         ● **S95.119**   Laceration of plantar artery of **unspecified** foot

     ● **S95.19**   **Other** specified injury of plantar artery of foot

         ● **S95.191**   Other specified injury of plantar artery of **right** foot

         ● **S95.192**   Other specified injury of plantar artery of **left** foot

         ● **S95.199**   Other specified injury of plantar artery of **unspecified** foot

● **S95.2**   **Injury of dorsal vein of foot**

     ● **S95.20**   Unspecified injury of dorsal vein of foot

         ● **S95.201**   Unspecified injury of dorsal vein of **right** foot

         ● **S95.202**   Unspecified injury of dorsal vein of **left** foot

         ● **S95.209**   Unspecified injury of dorsal vein of **unspecified** foot

     ● **S95.21**   **Laceration** of dorsal vein of foot

         ● **S95.211**   Laceration of dorsal vein of **right** foot

         ● **S95.212**   Laceration of dorsal vein of **left** foot

         ● **S95.219**   Laceration of dorsal vein of **unspecified** foot

● **S95.29**   **Other** specified injury of dorsal vein of foot

     ● **S95.291**   Other specified injury of dorsal vein of **right** foot

     ● **S95.292**   Other specified injury of dorsal vein of **left** foot

     ● **S95.299**   Other specified injury of dorsal vein of **unspecified** foot

● **S95.8**   **Injury of other blood vessels at ankle and foot level**

     ● **S95.80**   **Unspecified** injury of other blood vessels at ankle and foot level

         ● **S95.801**   Unspecified injury of other blood vessels at ankle and foot level, **right leg**

         ● **S95.802**   Unspecified injury of other blood vessels at ankle and foot level, **left leg**

         ● **S95.809**   Unspecified injury of other blood vessels at ankle and foot level, **unspecified leg**

     ● **S95.81**   **Laceration** of other blood vessels at ankle and foot level

         ● **S95.811**   Laceration of other blood vessels at ankle and foot level, **right leg**

         ● **S95.812**   Laceration of other blood vessels at ankle and foot level, **left leg**

         ● **S95.819**   Laceration of other blood vessels at ankle and foot level, **unspecified** leg

     ● **S95.89**   **Other** specified injury of other blood vessels at ankle and foot level

         ● **S95.891**   Other specified injury of other blood vessels at ankle and foot level, **right leg**

         ● **S95.892**   Other specified injury of other blood vessels at ankle and foot level, **left leg**

         ● **S95.899**   Other specified injury of other blood vessels at ankle and foot level, **unspecified** leg

● **S95.9**   **Injury of unspecified blood vessel at ankle and foot level**

     ● **S95.90**   **Unspecified** injury of unspecified blood vessel at ankle and foot level

         ● **S95.901**   Unspecified injury of unspecified blood vessel at ankle and foot level, **right leg**

         ● **S95.902**   Unspecified injury of unspecified blood vessel at ankle and foot level, **left leg**

         ● **S95.909**   Unspecified injury of unspecified blood vessel at ankle and foot level, **unspecified** leg

     ● **S95.91**   **Laceration** of unspecified blood vessel at ankle and foot level

         ● **S95.911**   Laceration of unspecified blood vessel at ankle and foot level, **right leg**

         ● **S95.912**   Laceration of unspecified blood vessel at ankle and foot level, **left leg**

         ● **S95.919**   Laceration of unspecified blood vessel at ankle and foot level, **unspecified** leg

     ● **S95.99**   **Other** specified injury of unspecified blood vessel at ankle and foot level

         ● **S95.991**   Other specified injury of unspecified blood vessel at ankle and foot level, **right leg**

         ● **S95.992**   Other specified injury of unspecified blood vessel at ankle and foot level, **left leg**

         ● **S95.999**   Other specified injury of unspecified blood vessel at ankle and foot level, **unspecified** leg

● S96   **Injury of muscle and tendon at ankle and foot level**
       Code also any associated open wound (S91.-)
       Excludes2   injury of Achilles tendon (S86.0-)
                    sprain of joints and ligaments of ankle and foot
                    (S93.-)

       The appropriate 7th character is to be added to each code from
       category S96

> A   initial encounter
> D   subsequent encounter
> S   sequela

● S96.0   **Injury of muscle and tendon of long flexor muscle of toe at ankle and foot level**

    ● S96.00   **Unspecified** injury of muscle and tendon of long flexor muscle of toe at ankle and foot level

       ● S96.001   Unspecified injury of muscle and tendon of long flexor muscle of toe at ankle and foot level, **right** foot

       ● S96.002   Unspecified injury of muscle and tendon of long flexor muscle of toe at ankle and foot level, **left** foot

       ● S96.009   Unspecified injury of muscle and tendon of long flexor muscle of toe at ankle and foot level, **unspecified** foot

    ● S96.01   **Strain** of muscle and tendon of long flexor muscle of toe at ankle and foot level

       ● S96.011   Strain of muscle and tendon of long flexor muscle of toe at ankle and foot level, **right** foot

       ● S96.012   Strain of muscle and tendon of long flexor muscle of toe at ankle and foot level, **left** foot

       ● S96.019   Strain of muscle and tendon of long flexor muscle of toe at ankle and foot level, **unspecified** foot

    ● S96.02   **Laceration** of muscle and tendon of long flexor muscle of toe at ankle and foot level

       ● S96.021   Laceration of muscle and tendon of long flexor muscle of toe at ankle and foot level, **right** foot

       ● S96.022   Laceration of muscle and tendon of long flexor muscle of toe at ankle and foot level, **left** foot

       ● S96.029   Laceration of muscle and tendon of long flexor muscle of toe at ankle and foot level, **unspecified** foot

    ● S96.09   **Other** injury of muscle and tendon of long flexor muscle of toe at ankle and foot level

       ● S96.091   Other injury of muscle and tendon of long flexor muscle of toe at ankle and foot level, **right** foot

       ● S96.092   Other injury of muscle and tendon of long flexor muscle of toe at ankle and foot level, **left** foot

       ● S96.099   Other injury of muscle and tendon of long flexor muscle of toe at ankle and foot level, **unspecified** foot

● S96.1   **Injury of muscle and tendon of long extensor muscle of toe at ankle and foot level**

    ● S96.10   **Unspecified** injury of muscle and tendon of long extensor muscle of toe at ankle and foot level

       ● S96.101   Unspecified injury of muscle and tendon of long extensor muscle of toe at ankle and foot level, **right** foot

       ● S96.102   Unspecified injury of muscle and tendon of long extensor muscle of toe at ankle and foot level, **left** foot

       ● S96.109   Unspecified injury of muscle and tendon of long extensor muscle of toe at ankle and foot level, **unspecified** foot

● S96.11   **Strain of muscle and tendon of long extensor muscle of toe at ankle and foot level**

       ● S96.111   Strain of muscle and tendon of long extensor muscle of toe at ankle and foot level, **right** foot

       ● S96.112   Strain of muscle and tendon of long extensor muscle of toe at ankle and foot level, **left** foot

       ● S96.119   Strain of muscle and tendon of long extensor muscle of toe at ankle and foot level, **unspecified** foot

● S96.12   **Laceration** of muscle and tendon of long extensor muscle of toe at ankle and foot level

       ● S96.121   Laceration of muscle and tendon of long extensor muscle of toe at ankle and foot level, **right** foot

       ● S96.122   Laceration of muscle and tendon of long extensor muscle of toe at ankle and foot level, **left** foot

       ● S96.129   Laceration of muscle and tendon of long extensor muscle of toe at ankle and foot level, **unspecified** foot

● S96.19   **Other** specified injury of muscle and tendon of long extensor muscle of toe at ankle and foot level

       ● S96.191   Other specified injury of muscle and tendon of long extensor muscle of toe at ankle and foot level, **right** foot

       ● S96.192   Other specified injury of muscle and tendon of long extensor muscle of toe at ankle and foot level, **left** foot

       ● S96.199   Other specified injury of muscle and tendon of long extensor muscle of toe at ankle and foot level, **unspecified** foot

● S96.2   **Injury of intrinsic muscle and tendon at ankle and foot level**

    ● S96.20   **Unspecified** injury of intrinsic muscle and tendon at ankle and foot level

       ● S96.201   Unspecified injury of intrinsic muscle and tendon at ankle and foot level, **right** foot

       ● S96.202   Unspecified injury of intrinsic muscle and tendon at ankle and foot level, **left** foot

       ● S96.209   Unspecified injury of intrinsic muscle and tendon at ankle and foot level, **unspecified** foot

    ● S96.21   **Strain** of intrinsic muscle and tendon at ankle and foot level

       ● S96.211   Strain of intrinsic muscle and tendon at ankle and foot level, **right** foot

       ● S96.212   Strain of intrinsic muscle and tendon at ankle and foot level, **left** foot

       ● S96.219   Strain of intrinsic muscle and tendon at ankle and foot level, **unspecified** foot

    ● S96.22   **Laceration** of intrinsic muscle and tendon at ankle and foot level

       ● S96.221   Laceration of intrinsic muscle and tendon at ankle and foot level, **right** foot

       ● S96.222   Laceration of intrinsic muscle and tendon at left ankle and foot level, **left** foot

       ● S96.229   Laceration of intrinsic muscle and tendon at ankle and foot level, **unspecified** foot

- S96.29 Other specified injury of intrinsic muscle and tendon at ankle and foot level
  - S96.291 Other specified injury of intrinsic muscle and tendon at ankle and foot level, right foot
  - S96.292 Other specified injury of intrinsic muscle and tendon at ankle and foot level, left foot
  - S96.299 Other specified injury of intrinsic muscle and tendon at ankle and foot level, unspecified foot
- S96.8 Injury of other specified muscles and tendons at ankle and foot level
  - S96.80 Unspecified injury of other specified muscles and tendons at ankle and foot level
    - S96.801 Unspecified injury of other specified muscles and tendons at ankle and foot level, right foot
    - S96.802 Unspecified injury of other specified muscles and tendons at ankle and foot level, left foot
    - S96.809 Unspecified injury of other specified muscles and tendons at ankle and foot level, unspecified foot
  - S96.81 Strain of other specified muscles and tendons at ankle and foot level
    - S96.811 Strain of other specified muscles and tendons at ankle and foot level, right foot
    - S96.812 Strain of other specified muscles and tendons at ankle and foot level, left foot
    - S96.819 Strain of other specified muscles and tendons at ankle and foot level, unspecified foot
  - S96.82 Laceration of other specified muscles and tendons at ankle and foot level
    - S96.821 Laceration of other specified muscles and tendons at ankle and foot level, right foot
    - S96.822 Laceration of other specified muscles and tendons at ankle and foot level, left foot
    - S96.829 Laceration of other specified muscles and tendons at ankle and foot level, unspecified foot
  - S96.89 Other specified injury of other specified muscles and tendons at ankle and foot level
    - S96.891 Other specified injury of other specified muscles and tendons at ankle and foot level, right foot
    - S96.892 Other specified injury of other specified muscles and tendons at ankle and foot level, left foot
    - S96.899 Other specified injury of other specified muscles and tendons at ankle and foot level, unspecified foot
- S96.9 Injury of unspecified muscle and tendon at ankle and foot level
  - S96.90 Unspecified injury of unspecified muscle and tendon at ankle and foot level
    - S96.901 Unspecified injury of unspecified muscle and tendon at ankle and foot level, right foot
    - S96.902 Unspecified injury of unspecified muscle and tendon at ankle and foot level, left foot
    - S96.909 Unspecified injury of unspecified muscle and tendon at ankle and foot level, unspecified foot

- S96.91 Strain of unspecified muscle and tendon at ankle and foot level
  - S96.911 Strain of unspecified muscle and tendon at ankle and foot level, right foot
  - S96.912 Strain of unspecified muscle and tendon at ankle and foot level, left foot
  - S96.919 Strain of unspecified muscle and tendon at ankle and foot level, unspecified foot
- S96.92 Laceration of unspecified muscle and tendon at ankle and foot level
  - S96.921 Laceration of unspecified muscle and tendon at ankle and foot level, right foot
  - S96.922 Laceration of unspecified muscle and tendon at ankle and foot level, left foot
  - S96.929 Laceration of unspecified muscle and tendon at ankle and foot level, unspecified foot
- S96.99 Other specified injury of unspecified muscle and tendon at ankle and foot level
  - S96.991 Other specified injury of unspecified muscle and tendon at ankle and foot level, right foot
  - S96.992 Other specified injury of unspecified muscle and tendon at ankle and foot level, left foot
  - S96.999 Other specified injury of unspecified muscle and tendon at ankle and foot level, unspecified foot

- S97 Crushing injury of ankle and foot

  Use additional code(s) for all associated injuries

  The appropriate 7th character is to be added to each code from category S97

A	initial encounter
D	subsequent encounter
S	sequela

  - S97.0 Crushing injury of ankle
    - X ● S97.00 Crushing injury of unspecified ankle
    - X ● S97.01 Crushing injury of right ankle
    - X ● S97.02 Crushing injury of left ankle
  - S97.1 Crushing injury of toe
    - S97.10 Crushing injury of unspecified toe(s)
      - S97.101 Crushing injury of unspecified right toe(s)
      - S97.102 Crushing injury of unspecified left toe(s)
      - S97.109 Crushing injury of unspecified toe(s)
        Crushing injury of toe NOS
    - S97.11 Crushing injury of great toe
      - S97.111 Crushing injury of right great toe
      - S97.112 Crushing injury of left great toe
      - S97.119 Crushing injury of unspecified great toe
    - S97.12 Crushing injury of lesser toe(s)
      - S97.121 Crushing injury of right lesser toe(s)
      - S97.122 Crushing injury of left lesser toe(s)
      - S97.129 Crushing injury of lesser toe(s), unspecified toe(s)
  - S97.8 Crushing injury of foot
    - X ● S97.80 Crushing injury of foot, unspecified side
      Crushing injury of foot NOS
    - X ● S97.81 Crushing injury of right foot
    - X ● S97.82 Crushing injury of left foot

▶ New   ⇒ Revised   ~~deleted~~ Deleted   Excludes 1   Excludes 2   Includes   Use additional   Code first   Code also   Key words

OGCR Official Guidelines   X Assign placeholder X   ● Use Additional Character(s)   ▷ Manifestation Code   **Coding Clinic**

● S98   Traumatic amputation of ankle and foot

An amputation not identified as partial or complete should be coded to complete

The appropriate 7th character is to be added to each code from category S98

A	initial encounter
D	subsequent encounter
S	sequela

● S98.0   Traumatic amputation of foot at ankle level

   ● S98.01   Complete traumatic amputation of foot at ankle level

     ● S98.011   Complete traumatic amputation of right foot at ankle level

     ● S98.012   Complete traumatic amputation of left foot at ankle level

     ● S98.019   Complete traumatic amputation of unspecified foot at ankle level

   ● S98.02   Partial traumatic amputation of foot at ankle level

     ● S98.021   Partial traumatic amputation of right foot at ankle level

     ● S98.022   Partial traumatic amputation of left foot at ankle level

     ● S98.029   Partial traumatic amputation of unspecified foot at ankle level

● S98.1   Traumatic amputation of one toe

   ● S98.11   Complete traumatic amputation of great toe

     ● S98.111   Complete traumatic amputation of right great toe

     ● S98.112   Complete traumatic amputation of left great toe

     ● S98.119   Complete traumatic amputation of unspecified great toe

   ● S98.12   Partial traumatic amputation of great toe

     ● S98.121   Partial traumatic amputation of right great toe

     ● S98.122   Partial traumatic amputation of left great toe

     ● S98.129   Partial traumatic amputation of unspecified great toe

   ● S98.13   Complete traumatic amputation of one lesser toe

       Traumatic amputation of toe NOS

     ● S98.131   Complete traumatic amputation of one right lesser toe

     ● S98.132   Complete traumatic amputation of one left lesser toe

     ● S98.139   Complete traumatic amputation of one unspecified lesser toe

   ● S98.14   Partial traumatic amputation of one lesser toe

     ● S98.141   Partial traumatic amputation of one right lesser toe

     ● S98.142   Partial traumatic amputation of one left lesser toe

     ● S98.149   Partial traumatic amputation of one unspecified lesser toe

● S98.2   Traumatic amputation of two or more lesser toes

   ● S98.21   Complete traumatic amputation of two or more lesser toes

     ● S98.211   Complete traumatic amputation of two or more right lesser toes

     ● S98.212   Complete traumatic amputation of two or more left lesser toes

     ● S98.219   Complete traumatic amputation of two or more unspecified lesser toes

   ● S98.22   Partial traumatic amputation of two or more lesser toes

     ● S98.221   Partial traumatic amputation of two or more right lesser toes

     ● S98.222   Partial traumatic amputation of two or more left lesser toes

     ● S98.229   Partial traumatic amputation of two or more unspecified lesser toes

● S98.3   Traumatic amputation of midfoot

   ● S98.31   Complete traumatic amputation of midfoot

     ● S98.311   Complete traumatic amputation of right midfoot

     ● S98.312   Complete traumatic amputation of left midfoot

     ● S98.319   Complete traumatic amputation of unspecified midfoot

   ● S98.32   Partial traumatic amputation of midfoot

     ● S98.321   Partial traumatic amputation of right midfoot

     ● S98.322   Partial traumatic amputation of left midfoot

     ● S98.329   Partial traumatic amputation of unspecified midfoot

● S98.9   Traumatic amputation of foot, level unspecified

   ● S98.91   Complete traumatic amputation of foot, level unspecified

     ● S98.911   Complete traumatic amputation of right foot, level unspecified

     ● S98.912   Complete traumatic amputation of left foot, level unspecified

     ● S98.919   Complete traumatic amputation of unspecified foot, level unspecified

   ● S98.92   Partial traumatic amputation of foot, level unspecified

     ● S98.921   Partial traumatic amputation of right foot, level unspecified

     ● S98.922   Partial traumatic amputation of left foot, level unspecified

     ● S98.929   Partial traumatic amputation of unspecified foot, level unspecified

● S99   Other and unspecified injuries of ankle and foot

     Coding Clinic: 2016, Q4, P68

● S99.0   Physeal fracture of calcaneus

The appropriate 7th character is to be added to each code from subcategories S99.0

A	initial encounter for closed fracture
B	initial encounter for open fracture
D	subsequent encounter for fracture with routine healing
G	subsequent encounter for fracture with delayed healing
K	subsequent encounter for fracture with nonunion
P	subsequent encounter for fracture with malunion
S	sequela

   ● S99.00   Unspecified physeal fracture of calcaneus

     ● S99.001   Unspecified physeal fracture of right calcaneus

     ● S99.002   Unspecified physeal fracture of left calcaneus

     ● S99.009   Unspecified physeal fracture of unspecified calcaneus

CHAPTER 19 (S00-T88)

● S99.01   **Salter-Harris Type I** physeal fracture of calcaneus
     Coding Clinic: 2016, Q4, P69

    ● S99.011   Salter-Harris Type I physeal fracture of right calcaneus

    ● S99.012   Salter-Harris Type I physeal fracture of left calcaneus

    ● S99.019   Salter-Harris Type I physeal fracture of unspecified calcaneus

● S99.02   **Salter-Harris Type II** physeal fracture of calcaneus
     Coding Clinic: 2016, Q4, P69

    ● S99.021   Salter-Harris Type II physeal fracture of right calcaneus

    ● S99.022   Salter-Harris Type II physeal fracture of left calcaneus

    ● S99.029   Salter-Harris Type II physeal fracture of unspecified calcaneus

● S99.03   **Salter-Harris Type III** physeal fracture of calcaneus
     Coding Clinic: 2016, Q4, P69

    ● S99.031   Salter-Harris Type III physeal fracture of right calcaneus

    ● S99.032   Salter-Harris Type III physeal fracture of left calcaneus

    ● S99.039   Salter-Harris Type III physeal fracture of unspecified calcaneus

● S99.04   **Salter-Harris Type IV** physeal fracture of calcaneus
     Coding Clinic: 2016, Q4, P69

    ● S99.041   Salter-Harris Type IV physeal fracture of right calcaneus

    ● S99.042   Salter-Harris Type IV physeal fracture of left calcaneus

    ● S99.049   Salter-Harris Type IV physeal fracture of unspecified calcaneus

● S99.09   Other physeal fracture of calcaneus
     Coding Clinic: 2016, Q4, P69

    ● S99.091   Other physeal fracture of right calcaneus

    ● S99.092   Other physeal fracture of left calcaneus

    ● S99.099   Other physeal fracture of unspecified calcaneus

● S99.1   Physeal fracture of metatarsal

     The appropriate 7th character is to be added to each code from subcategories S99.1

A	initial encounter for closed fracture
B	initial encounter for open fracture
D	subsequent encounter for fracture with routine healing
G	subsequent encounter for fracture with delayed healing
K	subsequent encounter for fracture with nonunion
P	subsequent encounter for fracture with malunion
S	sequela

● S99.10   Unspecified physeal fracture of metatarsal

    ● S99.101   Unspecified physeal fracture of right metatarsal

    ● S99.102   Unspecified physeal fracture of left metatarsal

    ● S99.109   Unspecified physeal fracture of unspecified metatarsal

● S99.11   **Salter-Harris Type I** physeal fracture of metatarsal
     Coding Clinic: 2016, Q4, P69

    ● S99.111   Salter-Harris Type I physeal fracture of right metatarsal

    ● S99.112   Salter-Harris Type I physeal fracture of left metatarsal
         Coding Clinic: 2018, Q1, P3

    ● S99.119   Salter-Harris Type I physeal fracture of unspecified metatarsal

● S99.12   **Salter-Harris Type II** physeal fracture of metatarsal
     Coding Clinic: 2016, Q4, P69

    ● S99.121   Salter-Harris Type II physeal fracture of right metatarsal

    ● S99.122   Salter-Harris Type II physeal fracture of left metatarsal

    ● S99.129   Salter-Harris Type II physeal fracture of unspecified metatarsal

● S99.13   **Salter-Harris Type III** physeal fracture of metatarsal
     Coding Clinic: 2016, Q4, P69

    ● S99.131   Salter-Harris Type III physeal fracture of right metatarsal

    ● S99.132   Salter-Harris Type III physeal fracture of left metatarsal

    ● S99.139   Salter-Harris Type III physeal fracture of unspecified metatarsal

● S99.14   **Salter-Harris Type IV** physeal fracture of metatarsal
     Coding Clinic: 2016, Q4, P69

    ● S99.141   Salter-Harris Type IV physeal fracture of right metatarsal

    ● S99.142   Salter-Harris Type IV physeal fracture of left metatarsal

    ● S99.149   Salter-Harris Type IV physeal fracture of unspecified metatarsal

● S99.19   Other physeal fracture of metatarsal
     Coding Clinic: 2016, Q4, P69

    ● S99.191   Other physeal fracture of right metatarsal

    ● S99.192   Other physeal fracture of left metatarsal

    ● S99.199   Other physeal fracture of unspecified metatarsal

● S99.2   Physeal fracture of phalanx of toe

     The appropriate 7th character is to be added to each code from subcategories S99.2

A	initial encounter for closed fracture
B	initial encounter for open fracture
D	subsequent encounter for fracture with routine healing
G	subsequent encounter for fracture with delayed healing
K	subsequent encounter for fracture with nonunion
P	subsequent encounter for fracture with malunion
S	sequela

● S99.20   Unspecified physeal fracture of phalanx of toe

    ● S99.201   Unspecified physeal fracture of phalanx of right toe

    ● S99.202   Unspecified physeal fracture of phalanx of right toe

    ● S99.209   Unspecified physeal fracture of phalanx of unspecified toe

▶ New   ⇒ Revised   ~~deleted~~ Deleted   Excludes 1   Excludes 2   Includes   Use additional   Code first   Code also   Key words

OGCR Official Guidelines   X Assign placeholder X   ● Use Additional Character(s)   ▸ Manifestation Code   **Coding Clinic**

● S99.21   **Salter-Harris Type I physeal fracture of phalanx of toe**
Coding Clinic: 2016, Q4, P69
  ● S99.211   Salter-Harris Type I physeal fracture of phalanx of right toe
  ● S99.212   Salter-Harris Type I physeal fracture of phalanx of left toe
  ● S99.219   Salter-Harris Type I physeal fracture of phalanx of unspecified toe

● S99.22   **Salter-Harris Type II physeal fracture of phalanx of toe**
Coding Clinic: 2016, Q4, P69
  ● S99.221   Salter-Harris Type II physeal fracture of phalanx of right toe
  ● S99.222   Salter-Harris Type II physeal fracture of phalanx of left toe
  ● S99.229   Salter-Harris Type II physeal fracture of phalanx of unspecified toe

● S99.23   **Salter-Harris Type III physeal fracture of phalanx of toe**
Coding Clinic: 2016, Q4, P69
  ● S99.231   Salter-Harris Type III physeal fracture of phalanx of right toe
  ● S99.232   Salter-Harris Type III physeal fracture of phalanx of left toe
  ● S99.239   Salter-Harris Type III physeal fracture of phalanx of unspecified toe

● S99.24   **Salter-Harris Type IV physeal fracture of phalanx of toe**
Coding Clinic: 2016, Q4, P69
  ● S99.241   Salter-Harris Type IV physeal fracture of phalanx of right toe
  ● S99.242   Salter-Harris Type IV physeal fracture of phalanx of left toe
  ● S99.249   Salter-Harris Type IV physeal fracture of phalanx of unspecified toe

● S99.29   **Other physeal fracture of phalanx of toe**
Coding Clinic: 2016, Q4, P69
  ● S99.291   Other physeal fracture of phalanx of right toe
  ● S99.292   Other physeal fracture of phalanx of left toe
  ● S99.299   Other physeal fracture of phalanx of unspecified toe

● S99.8   **Other specified injuries of ankle and foot**
The appropriate 7th character is to be added to each code from subcategory S99.8

A	initial encounter
D	subsequent encounter
S	sequela

  ● S99.81   **Other specified injuries of ankle**
    ● S99.811   Other specified injuries of right ankle
    ● S99.812   Other specified injuries of left ankle
    ● S99.819   Other specified injuries of unspecified ankle

● S99.82   **Other specified injuries of foot**
  ● S99.821   Other specified injuries of right foot
  ● S99.822   Other specified injuries of left foot
  ● S99.829   Other specified injuries of unspecified foot

● S99.9   **Unspecified injury of ankle and foot**
The appropriate 7th character is to be added to each code from subcategory S99.9

A	initial encounter
D	subsequent encounter
S	sequela

● S99.91   **Unspecified injury of ankle**
  ● S99.911   Unspecified injury of right ankle
  ● S99.912   Unspecified injury of left ankle
  ● S99.919   Unspecified injury of unspecified ankle
● S99.92   **Unspecified injury of foot**
  ● S99.921   Unspecified injury of right foot
  ● S99.922   Unspecified injury of left foot
  ● S99.929   Unspecified injury of unspecified foot

INJURY, POISONING AND CERTAIN OTHER CONSEQUENCES OF EXTERNAL CAUSES (T07-T88)

INJURIES INVOLVING MULTIPLE BODY REGIONS (T07)

Excludes1   burns and corrosions (T20-T32)
           frostbite (T33-T34)
           insect bite or sting, venomous (T63.4)
           sunburn (L55.-)

X ● T07   **Unspecified multiple injuries**
The appropriate 7th character is to be added to code T07

A	initial encounter
D	subsequent encounter
S	sequela

Excludes1   injury NOS (T14.90)

INJURY OF UNSPECIFIED BODY REGION (T14)

● T14   **Injury of unspecified body region**
The appropriate 7th character is to be added to each code from category T14

A	initial encounter
D	subsequent encounter
S	sequela

Excludes1   multiple unspecified injuries (T07)
X ● T14.8   **Other injury of unspecified body region**
  Abrasion NOS   Skin injury NOS
  Contusion NOS   Vascular injury NOS
  Crush injury NOS   Wound NOS
  Fracture NOS
● T14.9   **Unspecified injury**
  X ● T14.90   **Injury, unspecified**
    Injury NOS
  X ● T14.91   **Suicide attempt**
    Attempted suicide NOS

EFFECTS OF FOREIGN BODY ENTERING THROUGH NATURAL ORIFICE (T15-T19)

Excludes2   foreign body accidentally left in operation wound (T81.5-)
foreign body in penetrating wound - see open wound by body region
residual foreign body in soft tissue (M79.5)
splinter, without open wound - see superficial injury by body region

● **T15**   **Foreign body on external eye**

Excludes2   foreign body in penetrating wound of orbit and eye ball (S05.4-, S05.5-)
open wound of eyelid and periocular area (S01.1-)
retained foreign body in eyelid (H02.8-)
retained (old) foreign body in penetrating wound of orbit and eye ball (H05.5-, H44.6-, H44.7-)
superficial foreign body of eyelid and periocular area (S00.25-)

The appropriate 7th character is to be added to each code from category T15

A	initial encounter
D	subsequent encounter
S	sequela

● **T15.0**   **Foreign body in cornea**
   X ● **T15.00**   Foreign body in cornea, unspecified eye
   X ● **T15.01**   Foreign body in cornea, right eye
   X ● **T15.02**   Foreign body in cornea, left eye

● **T15.1**   **Foreign body in conjunctival sac**
   X ● **T15.10**   Foreign body in conjunctival sac, unspecified eye
   X ● **T15.11**   Foreign body in conjunctival sac, right eye
   X ● **T15.12**   Foreign body in conjunctival sac, left eye

● **T15.8**   **Foreign body in other and multiple parts of external eye**
Foreign body in lacrimal punctum
   X ● **T15.80**   Foreign body in other and multiple parts of external eye, unspecified eye
   X ● **T15.81**   Foreign body in other and multiple parts of external eye, right eye
   X ● **T15.82**   Foreign body in other and multiple parts of external eye, left eye

● **T15.9**   **Foreign body on external eye, part unspecified**
   X ● **T15.90**   Foreign body on external eye, part unspecified, unspecified eye
   X ● **T15.91**   Foreign body on external eye, part unspecified, right eye
   X ● **T15.92**   Foreign body on external eye, part unspecified, left eye

● **T16**   **Foreign body in ear**

Includes   foreign body in auditory canal

The appropriate 7th character is to be added to each code from category T16

A	initial encounter
D	subsequent encounter
S	sequela

   X ● **T16.1**   Foreign body in right ear
   X ● **T16.2**   Foreign body in left ear
   X ● **T16.9**   Foreign body in ear, unspecified ear

● **T17**   **Foreign body in respiratory tract**

The appropriate 7th character is to be added to each code from category T17

A	initial encounter
D	subsequent encounter
S	sequela

X ● **T17.0**   **Foreign body in nasal sinus**
X ● **T17.1**   **Foreign body in nostril**
    Foreign body in nose NOS

● **T17.2**   **Foreign body in pharynx**
   Foreign body in nasopharynx
   Foreign body in throat NOS
   ● **T17.20**   Unspecified foreign body in pharynx
     ● **T17.200**   Unspecified foreign body in pharynx causing asphyxiation
     ● **T17.208**   Unspecified foreign body in pharynx causing other injury
   ● **T17.21**   Gastric contents in pharynx
     Aspiration of gastric contents into pharynx
     Vomitus in pharynx
     ● **T17.210**   Gastric contents in pharynx causing asphyxiation
     ● **T17.218**   Gastric contents in pharynx causing other injury
   ● **T17.22**   Food in pharynx
     Bones in pharynx
     Seeds in pharynx
     ● **T17.220**   Food in pharynx causing asphyxiation
     ● **T17.228**   Food in pharynx causing other injury
   ● **T17.29**   Other foreign object in pharynx
     ● **T17.290**   Other foreign object in pharynx causing asphyxiation
     ● **T17.298**   Other foreign object in pharynx causing other injury

● **T17.3**   **Foreign body in larynx**
   ● **T17.30**   Unspecified foreign body in larynx
     ● **T17.300**   Unspecified foreign body in larynx causing asphyxiation
     ● **T17.308**   Unspecified foreign body in larynx causing other injury
   ● **T17.31**   Gastric contents in larynx
     Aspiration of gastric contents into larynx
     Vomitus in larynx
     ● **T17.310**   Gastric contents in larynx causing asphyxiation
     ● **T17.318**   Gastric contents in larynx causing other injury
   ● **T17.32**   Food in larynx
     Bones in larynx
     Seeds in larynx
     ● **T17.320**   Food in larynx causing asphyxiation
     ● **T17.328**   Food in larynx causing other injury
   ● **T17.39**   Other foreign object in larynx
     ● **T17.390**   Other foreign object in larynx causing asphyxiation
     ● **T17.398**   Other foreign object in larynx causing other injury

● **T17.4**   **Foreign body in trachea**
   ● **T17.40**   Unspecified foreign body in trachea
     ● **T17.400**   Unspecified foreign body in trachea causing asphyxiation
     ● **T17.408**   Unspecified foreign body in trachea causing other injury

▶ New   ⇒ Revised   ~~deleted~~ Deleted   Excludes 1   Excludes 2   Includes   Use additional   Code first   Code also   Key words

OGCR Official Guidelines   X Assign placeholder X   ● Use Additional Character(s)   ▶ Manifestation Code   **Coding Clinic**

● **T17.41**   **Gastric contents in trachea**
     Aspiration of gastric contents into trachea
     Vomitus in trachea

   ● **T17.410**   **Gastric contents in trachea causing asphyxiation**

   ● **T17.418**   **Gastric contents in trachea causing other injury**

● **T17.42**   **Food in trachea**
     Bones in trachea
     Seeds in trachea

   ● **T17.420**   **Food in trachea causing asphyxiation**

   ● **T17.428**   **Food in trachea causing other injury**

● **T17.49**   **Other foreign object in trachea**

   ● **T17.490**   **Other foreign object in trachea causing asphyxiation**

   ● **T17.498**   **Other foreign object in trachea causing other injury**

● **T17.5**   **Foreign body in bronchus**

  ● **T17.50**   **Unspecified foreign body in bronchus**

   ● **T17.500**   **Unspecified foreign body in bronchus causing asphyxiation**

   ● **T17.508**   **Unspecified foreign body in bronchus causing other injury**

  ● **T17.51**   **Gastric contents in bronchus**
     Aspiration of gastric contents into bronchus
     Vomitus in bronchus

   ● **T17.510**   **Gastric contents in bronchus causing asphyxiation**

   ● **T17.518**   **Gastric contents in bronchus causing other injury**

  ● **T17.52**   **Food in bronchus**
     Bones in bronchus
     Seeds in bronchus

   ● **T17.520**   **Food in bronchus causing asphyxiation**

   ● **T17.528**   **Food in bronchus causing other injury**

  ● **T17.59**   **Other foreign object in bronchus**

   ● **T17.590**   **Other foreign object in bronchus causing asphyxiation**

   ● **T17.598**   **Other foreign object in bronchus causing other injury**

● **T17.8**   **Foreign body in other parts of respiratory tract**
     Foreign body in bronchioles
     Foreign body in lung

  ● **T17.80**   **Unspecified foreign body in other parts of respiratory tract**

   ● **T17.800**   **Unspecified foreign body in other parts of respiratory tract causing asphyxiation**

   ● **T17.808**   **Unspecified foreign body in other parts of respiratory tract causing other injury**

  ● **T17.81**   **Gastric contents in other parts of respiratory tract**
     Aspiration of gastric contents into other parts of respiratory tract
     Vomitus in other parts of respiratory tract

   ● **T17.810**   **Gastric contents in other parts of respiratory tract causing asphyxiation**

   ● **T17.818**   **Gastric contents in other parts of respiratory tract causing other injury**

  ● **T17.82**   **Food in other parts of respiratory tract**
     Bones in other parts of respiratory tract
     Seeds in other parts of respiratory tract

   ● **T17.820**   **Food in other parts of respiratory tract causing asphyxiation**

   ● **T17.828**   **Food in other parts of respiratory tract causing other injury**

● **T17.89**   **Other foreign object in other parts of respiratory tract**

   ● **T17.890**   **Other foreign object in other parts of respiratory tract causing asphyxiation**

   ● **T17.898**   **Other foreign object in other parts of respiratory tract causing other injury**

● **T17.9**   **Foreign body in respiratory tract, part unspecified**

  ● **T17.90**   **Unspecified foreign body in respiratory tract, part unspecified**

   ● **T17.900**   **Unspecified foreign body in respiratory tract, part unspecified causing asphyxiation**

   ● **T17.908**   **Unspecified foreign body in respiratory tract, part unspecified causing other injury**

  ● **T17.91**   **Gastric contents in respiratory tract, part unspecified**
     Aspiration of gastric contents into respiratory tract, part unspecified
     Vomitus in trachea respiratory tract, part unspecified

   ● **T17.910**   **Gastric contents in respiratory tract, part unspecified causing asphyxiation**

   ● **T17.918**   **Gastric contents in respiratory tract, part unspecified causing other injury**

  ● **T17.92**   **Food in respiratory tract, part unspecified**
     Bones in respiratory tract, part unspecified
     Seeds in respiratory tract, part unspecified

   ● **T17.920**   **Food in respiratory tract, part unspecified causing asphyxiation**

   ● **T17.928**   **Food in respiratory tract, part unspecified causing other injury**

  ● **T17.99**   **Other foreign object in respiratory tract, part unspecified**

   ● **T17.990**   **Other foreign object in respiratory tract, part unspecified in causing asphyxiation**

   ● **T17.998**   **Other foreign object in respiratory tract, part unspecified causing other injury**

● **T18**   **Foreign body in alimentary tract**

    Excludes2   foreign body in pharynx (T17.2-)

    The appropriate 7th character is to be added to each code from category T18

A	initial encounter
D	subsequent encounter
S	sequela

X ● **T18.0**   **Foreign body in mouth**

X ● **T18.1**   **Foreign body in esophagus**

    Excludes2   foreign body in respiratory tract (T17.-)

  ● **T18.10**   **Unspecified foreign body in esophagus**

   ● **T18.100**   **Unspecified foreign body in esophagus causing compression of trachea**
      Unspecified foreign body in esophagus causing obstruction of respiration

   ● **T18.108**   **Unspecified foreign body in esophagus causing other injury**

  ● **T18.11**   **Gastric contents in esophagus**
     Vomitus in esophagus

   ● **T18.110**   **Gastric contents in esophagus causing compression of trachea**
      Gastric contents in esophagus causing obstruction of respiration

   ● **T18.118**   **Gastric contents in esophagus causing other injury**

CHAPTER 19 (SØØ-T88)

● **T18.12**   **Food in esophagus**
     Bones in esophagus
     Seeds in esophagus

    ● **T18.120**   **Food in esophagus causing compression of trachea**
        Food in esophagus causing obstruction of respiration

    ● **T18.128**   **Food in esophagus causing other injury**

   ● **T18.19**   **Other foreign object in esophagus**

    ● **T18.190**   **Other foreign object in esophagus causing compression of trachea**
        Other foreign body in esophagus causing obstruction of respiration
        Coding Clinic: 2015, Q1, P24

    ● **T18.198**   **Other foreign object in esophagus causing other injury**
        Coding Clinic: 2015, Q1, P24

X ● **T18.2**   **Foreign body in stomach**

X ● **T18.3**   **Foreign body in small intestine**

X ● **T18.4**   **Foreign body in colon**

X ● **T18.5**   **Foreign body in anus and rectum**
     Foreign body in rectosigmoid (junction)

X ● **T18.8**   **Foreign body in other parts of alimentary tract**

X ● **T18.9**   **Foreign body in alimentary tract, part unspecified**
     Foreign body in digestive system NOS
     Swallowed foreign body NOS

● **T19**   **Foreign body in genitourinary tract**

    Excludes2   complications due to implanted mesh (T83.7-)
       mechanical complications of contraceptive device (intrauterine) (vaginal) (T83.3-)
       presence of contraceptive device (intrauterine) (vaginal) (Z97.5)

    The appropriate 7th character is to be added to each code from category T19

A	initial encounter
D	subsequent encounter
S	sequela

X ● **T19.0**   **Foreign body in urethra**

X ● **T19.1**   **Foreign body in bladder**

X ● **T19.2**   **Foreign body in vulva and vagina ♀**

X ● **T19.3**   **Foreign body in uterus ♀**

X ● **T19.4**   **Foreign body in penis ♂**

X ● **T19.8**   **Foreign body in other parts of genitourinary tract**

X ● **T19.9**   **Foreign body in genitourinary tract, part unspecified**

BURNS AND CORROSIONS (T20-T32)

    Includes   burns (thermal) from electrical heating appliances
       burns (thermal) from electricity
       burns (thermal) from flame
       burns (thermal) from friction
       burns (thermal) from hot air and hot gases
       burns (thermal) from hot objects
       burns (thermal) from lightning
       burns (thermal) from radiation chemical
       burn [corrosion] (external) (internal) scalds

    Excludes2   erythema [dermatitis] ab igne (L59.0)
       radiation-related disorders of the skin and subcutaneous tissue (L55-L59)
       sunburn (L55.-)

OGCR Section I.C.19.d.

Burns and Corrosions

The ICD-10-CM makes a distinction between burn and corrosions. The burn codes are for thermal burns, except sunburns, that come from a heat source, such as a fire or hot appliance. The burn codes are also for burns resulting from electricity and radiation. Corrosions are burns due to chemicals. The guidelines for burns and corrosions are the same.

Current burns (T20-T25) are classified by depth, extent and by agent (X code). Burns are classified by depth as first degree (erythema), second degree (blistering), and third degree (full-thickness involvement). Burns of the eye and internal organs (T26-T28) are classified by site, but not by degree.

1) Sequencing of burn and related condition codes

Sequence first the code that reflects the highest degree of burn when more than one burn is present.

a. When the reason for the admission or encounter is for treatment of external multiple burns, sequence first the code that reflects the burn of the highest degree.

b. When a patient has both internal and external burns, the circumstances of admission govern the selection of the principal diagnosis or first-listed diagnosis.

c. When a patient is admitted for burn injuries and other related conditions such as smoke inhalation and/or respiratory failure, the circumstances of admission govern the selection of the principal or first-listed diagnosis.

2) Burns of the same local site

Classify burns of the same local site (three-character category level, T20-T28) but of different degrees to the subcategory identifying the highest degree recorded in the diagnosis.

BURNS AND CORROSIONS OF EXTERNAL BODY SURFACE, SPECIFIED BY SITE (T20-T25)

    Includes   burns and corrosions of first degree [erythema]
       burns and corrosions of second degree [blisters] [epidermal loss]
       burns and corrosions of third degree [deep necrosis of underlying tissue] [full-thickness skin loss]

    Use additional code from category T31 or T32 to identify extent of body surface involved

● **T20**   **Burn and corrosion of head, face, and neck**

    Excludes2   burn and corrosion of ear drum (T28.41, T28.91)
       burn and corrosion of eye and adnexa (T26.-)
       burn and corrosion of mouth and pharynx (T28.0)

    The appropriate 7th character is to be added to each code from category T20

A	initial encounter
D	subsequent encounter
S	sequela

   ● **T20.0**   **Burn of unspecified degree of head, face, and neck**
     Use additional external cause code to identify the source, place and intent of the burn (X00-X19, X75-X77, X96-X98, Y92)

    X ● **T20.00**   **Burn of unspecified degree of head, face, and neck, unspecified site**

    ● **T20.01**   **Burn of unspecified degree of ear [any part, except ear drum]**
       Excludes2   burn of ear drum (T28.41-)

     ● **T20.011**   **Burn of unspecified degree of right ear [any part, except ear drum]**

     ● **T20.012**   **Burn of unspecified degree of left ear [any part, except ear drum]**

     ● **T20.019**   **Burn of unspecified degree of unspecified ear [any part, except ear drum]**

▶ New   ⇒ Revised   ~~deleted~~ Deleted   Excludes 1   Excludes 2   Includes   Use additional   Code first   Code also   Key words
OGCR Official Guidelines   X Assign placeholder X   ● Use Additional Character(s)   ▶ Manifestation Code   **Coding Clinic**

Figure 19-15 A. Second-degree burn. **B.** Third-degree burn. (A. From Black J, Hawks J: Medical-Surgical Nursing: Clinical Management for Positive Outcomes, 8e, Saunders, 2008. B. From Marx J, Hockberger R, Walls R: Rosen's Emergency Medicine - Concepts and Clinical Practice, 7e, Mosby, 2009)

X● T20.02   Burn of unspecified degree of lip(s)

X● T20.03   Burn of unspecified degree of chin

X● T20.04   Burn of unspecified degree of nose (septum)

X● T20.05   Burn of unspecified degree of scalp [any part]

X● T20.06   Burn of unspecified degree of forehead and cheek

X● T20.07   Burn of unspecified degree of neck

X● T20.09   Burn of unspecified degree of multiple sites of head, face, and neck

● T20.1   Burn of first degree of head, face, and neck

     Use additional external cause code to identify the source, place and intent of the burn (X00-X19, X75-X77, X96-X98, Y92)

X● T20.10   Burn of first degree of head, face, and neck, unspecified site

● T20.11   Burn of first degree of ear [any part, except ear drum]

     Excludes2   burn of ear drum (T28.41-)

● T20.111   Burn of first degree of right ear [any part, except ear drum]

● T20.112   Burn of first degree of left ear [any part, except ear drum]

● T20.119   Burn of first degree of unspecified ear [any part, except ear drum]

X● T20.12   Burn of first degree of lip(s)

X● T20.13   Burn of first degree of chin

X● T20.14   Burn of first degree of nose (septum)

X● T20.15   Burn of first degree of scalp [any part]

X● T20.16   Burn of first degree of forehead and cheek

X● T20.17   Burn of first degree of neck

X● T20.19   Burn of first degree of multiple sites of head, face, and neck

● T20.2   Burn of second degree of head, face, and neck

     Use additional external cause code to identify the source, place and intent of the burn (X00-X19, X75-X77, X96-X98, Y92)

X● T20.20   Burn of second degree of head, face, and neck, unspecified site

● T20.21   Burn of second degree of ear [any part, except ear drum]

     Excludes2   burn of ear drum (T28.41-)

● T20.211   Burn of second degree of right ear [any part, except ear drum]

● T20.212   Burn of second degree of left ear [any part, except ear drum]

● T20.219   Burn of second degree of unspecified ear [any part, except ear drum]

X● T20.22   Burn of second degree of lip(s)

X● T20.23   Burn of second degree of chin

X● T20.24   Burn of second degree of nose (septum)

X● T20.25   Burn of second degree of scalp [any part]
     Coding Clinic: 2015, Q1, P19

X● T20.26   Burn of second degree of forehead and cheek

X● T20.27   Burn of second degree of neck

X● T20.29   Burn of second degree of multiple sites of head, face, and neck

● T20.3   Burn of third degree of head, face, and neck

     Use additional external cause code to identify the source, place and intent of the burn (X00-X19, X75-X77, X96-X98, Y92)

X● T20.30   Burn of third degree of head, face, and neck, unspecified site

● T20.31   Burn of third degree of ear [any part, except ear drum]

     Excludes2   burn of ear drum (T28.41-)

● T20.311   Burn of third degree of right ear [any part, except ear drum]

● T20.312   Burn of third degree of left ear [any part, except ear drum]
     Coding Clinic: 2015, Q1, P18

● T20.319   Burn of third degree of unspecified ear [any part, except ear drum]

X● T20.32   Burn of third degree of lip(s)

X● T20.33   Burn of third degree of chin

X● T20.34   Burn of third degree of nose (septum)

X● T20.35   Burn of third degree of scalp [any part]

X● T20.36   Burn of third degree of forehead and cheek

X● T20.37   Burn of third degree of neck

X● T20.39   Burn of third degree of multiple sites of head, face, and neck

● T20.4   Corrosion of unspecified degree of head, face, and neck

     Code first (T51-T65) to identify chemical and intent

     Use additional external cause code to identify place (Y92)

X● T20.40   Corrosion of unspecified degree of head, face, and neck, unspecified site

● T20.41   Corrosion of unspecified degree of ear [any part, except ear drum]

     Excludes2   corrosion of ear drum (T28.91-)

● T20.411   Corrosion of unspecified degree of right ear [any part, except ear drum]

● T20.412   Corrosion of unspecified degree of left ear [any part, except ear drum]

● T20.419   Corrosion of unspecified degree of unspecified ear [any part, except ear drum]

X● T20.42   Corrosion of unspecified degree of lip(s)

X● T20.43   Corrosion of unspecified degree of chin

X● T20.44   Corrosion of unspecified degree of nose (septum)

X● T20.45   Corrosion of unspecified degree of scalp [any part]

X● T20.46   Corrosion of unspecified degree of forehead and cheek

X● T20.47   Corrosion of unspecified degree of neck

X● T20.49   Corrosion of unspecified degree of multiple sites of head, face, and neck

● T20.5   Corrosion of first degree of head, face, and neck

     Code first (T51-T65) to identify chemical and intent

     Use additional external cause code to identify place (Y92)

X● T20.50   Corrosion of first degree of head, face, and neck, unspecified site

● T20.51   Corrosion of first degree of ear [any part, except ear drum]

     Excludes2   corrosion of ear drum (T28.91-)

● T20.511   Corrosion of first degree of right ear [any part, except ear drum]

● T20.512   Corrosion of first degree of left ear [any part, except ear drum]

● T20.519   Corrosion of first degree of unspecified ear [any part, except ear drum]

CHAPTER 19 (S00-T88)

X● **T20.52** Corrosion of first degree of lip(s)

X● **T20.53** Corrosion of first degree of chin

X● **T20.54** Corrosion of first degree of nose (septum)

X● **T20.55** Corrosion of first degree of scalp [any part]

X● **T20.56** Corrosion of first degree of forehead and cheek

X● **T20.57** Corrosion of first degree of neck

X● **T20.59** Corrosion of first degree of multiple sites of head, face, and neck

●**T20.6** Corrosion of second degree of head, face, and neck

Code first (T51-T65) to identify chemical and intent

Use additional external cause code to identify place (Y92)

X● **T20.60** Corrosion of second degree of head, face, and neck, unspecified site

●**T20.61** Corrosion of second degree of ear [any part, except ear drum]

Excludes2 corrosion of ear drum (T28.91-)

●**T20.611** Corrosion of second degree of right ear [any part, except ear drum]

●**T20.612** Corrosion of second degree of left ear [any part, except ear drum]

●**T20.619** Corrosion of second degree of unspecified ear [any part, except ear drum]

X● **T20.62** Corrosion of second degree of lip(s)

X● **T20.63** Corrosion of second degree of chin

X● **T20.64** Corrosion of second degree of nose (septum)

X● **T20.65** Corrosion of second degree of scalp [any part]

X● **T20.66** Corrosion of second degree of forehead and cheek

X● **T20.67** Corrosion of second degree of neck

X● **T20.69** Corrosion of second degree of multiple sites of head, face, and neck

●**T20.7** Corrosion of third degree of head, face, and neck

Code first (T51-T65) to identify chemical and intent

Use additional external cause code to identify place (Y92)

X● **T20.70** Corrosion of third degree of head, face, and neck, unspecified site

●**T20.71** Corrosion of third degree of ear [any part, except ear drum]

Excludes2 corrosion of ear drum (T28.91-)

●**T20.711** Corrosion of third degree of right ear [any part, except ear drum]

●**T20.712** Corrosion of third degree of left ear [any part, except ear drum]

●**T20.719** Corrosion of third degree of unspecified ear [any part, except ear drum]

X● **T20.72** Corrosion of third degree of lip(s)

X● **T20.73** Corrosion of third degree of chin

X● **T20.74** Corrosion of third degree of nose (septum)

X● **T20.75** Corrosion of third degree of scalp [any part]

X● **T20.76** Corrosion of third degree of forehead and cheek

X● **T20.77** Corrosion of third degree of neck

X● **T20.79** Corrosion of third degree of multiple sites of head, face, and neck

●**T21** Burn and corrosion of trunk

Includes burns and corrosion of hip region

Excludes2 burns and corrosion of axilla (T22.- with fifth character 4)

burns and corrosion of scapular region (T22.- with fifth character 6)

burns and corrosion of shoulder (T22.- with fifth character 5)

The appropriate 7th character is to be added to each code from category T21

A	initial encounter
D	subsequent encounter
S	sequela

●**T21.0** Burn of unspecified degree of trunk

Use additional external cause code to identify the source, place and intent of the burn (X00-X19, X75-X77, X96-X98, Y92)

X● **T21.00** Burn of unspecified degree of trunk, unspecified site

X● **T21.01** Burn of unspecified degree of chest wall

⮕Burn of unspecified degree of breast

X● **T21.02** Burn of unspecified degree of abdominal wall

Burn of unspecified degree of flank

Burn of unspecified degree of groin

X● **T21.03** Burn of unspecified degree of upper back

Burn of unspecified degree of interscapular region

X● **T21.04** Burn of unspecified degree of lower back

X● **T21.05** Burn of unspecified degree of buttock

Burn of unspecified degree of anus

X● **T21.06** Burn of unspecified degree of male genital region ♂

Burn of unspecified degree of penis

Burn of unspecified degree of scrotum

Burn of unspecified degree of testis

X● **T21.07** Burn of unspecified degree of female genital region ♀

Burn of unspecified degree of labium (majus) (minus)

Burn of unspecified degree of perineum

Burn of unspecified degree of vulva

Excludes2 burn of vagina (T28.3)

X● **T21.09** Burn of unspecified degree of other site of trunk

●**T21.1** Burn of first degree of trunk

Use additional external cause code to identify the source, place and intent of the burn (X00-X19, X75-X77, X96-X98, Y92)

X● **T21.10** Burn of first degree of trunk, unspecified site

X● **T21.11** Burn of first degree of chest wall

Burn of first degree of breast

X● **T21.12** Burn of first degree of abdominal wall

Burn of first degree of flank

Burn of first degree of groin

X● **T21.13** Burn of first degree of upper back

Burn of first degree of interscapular region

X● **T21.14** Burn of first degree of lower back

X● **T21.15** Burn of first degree of buttock

Burn of first degree of anus

X● **T21.16** Burn of first degree of male genital region ♂

Burn of first degree of penis

Burn of first degree of scrotum

Burn of first degree of testis

X● **T21.17** Burn of first degree of female genital region ♀

Burn of first degree of labium (majus) (minus)

Burn of first degree of perineum

Burn of first degree of vulva

Excludes2 burn of vagina (T28.3)

X● **T21.19** Burn of first degree of other site of trunk

▶ New　⮕ Revised　~~deleted~~ Deleted　Excludes 1　Excludes 2　Includes　Use additional　Code first　Code also　Key words

OGCR Official Guidelines　X Assign placeholder X　● Use Additional Character(s)　▷ Manifestation Code　**Coding Clinic**

● **T21.2   Burn of second degree of trunk**

> Use additional external cause code to identify the source, place and intent of the burn (X00-X19, X75-X77, X96-X98, Y92)

X ● **T21.20   Burn of second degree of trunk, unspecified site**

X ● **T21.21   Burn of second degree of chest wall**
   Burn of second degree of breast

X ● **T21.22   Burn of second degree of abdominal wall**
   Burn of second degree of flank
   Burn of second degree of groin

X ● **T21.23   Burn of second degree of upper back**
   Burn of second degree of interscapular region

X ● **T21.24   Burn of second degree of lower back**

X ● **T21.25   Burn of second degree of buttock**
   Burn of second degree of anus

X ● **T21.26   Burn of second degree of male genital region** ♂
   Burn of second degree of penis
   Burn of second degree of scrotum
   Burn of second degree of testis

X ● **T21.27   Burn of second degree of female genital region** ♀
   Burn of second degree of labium (majus) (minus)
   Burn of second degree of perineum
   Burn of second degree of vulva

> **Excludes2**   burn of vagina (T28.3)

X ● **T21.29   Burn of second degree of other site of trunk**

● **T21.3   Burn of third degree of trunk**

> Use additional external cause code to identify the source, place and intent of the burn (X00-X19, X75-X77, X96-X98, Y92)

X ● **T21.30   Burn of third degree of trunk, unspecified site**

X ● **T21.31   Burn of third degree of chest wall**
   Burn of third degree of breast
   Coding Clinic: 2016, Q2, P6

X ● **T21.32   Burn of third degree of abdominal wall**
   Burn of third degree of flank
   Burn of third degree of groin

X ● **T21.33   Burn of third degree of upper back**
   Burn of third degree of interscapular region

X ● **T21.34   Burn of third degree of lower back**

X ● **T21.35   Burn of third degree of buttock**
   Burn of third degree of anus

X ● **T21.36   Burn of third degree of male genital region** ♂
   Burn of third degree of penis
   Burn of third degree of scrotum
   Burn of third degree of testis

X ● **T21.37   Burn of third degree of female genital region** ♀
   Burn of third degree of labium (majus) (minus)
   Burn of third degree of perineum
   Burn of third degree of vulva

> **Excludes2**   burn of vagina (T28.3)

X ● **T21.39   Burn of third degree of other site of trunk**

● **T21.4   Corrosion of unspecified degree of trunk**

> *Code first* (T51-T65) *to identify chemical and intent*
> Use additional external cause code to identify place (Y92)

X ● **T21.40   Corrosion of unspecified degree of trunk, unspecified site**

X ● **T21.41   Corrosion of unspecified degree of chest wall**
   Corrosion of unspecified degree of breast

X ● **T21.42   Corrosion of unspecified degree of abdominal wall**
   Corrosion of unspecified degree of flank
   Corrosion of unspecified degree of groin

X ● **T21.43   Corrosion of unspecified degree of upper back**
   Corrosion of unspecified degree of interscapular region

X ● **T21.44   Corrosion of unspecified degree of lower back**

X ● **T21.45   Corrosion of unspecified degree of buttock**
   Corrosion of unspecified degree of anus

X ● **T21.46   Corrosion of unspecified degree of male genital region** ♂
   Corrosion of unspecified degree of penis
   Corrosion of unspecified degree of scrotum
   Corrosion of unspecified degree of testis

X ● **T21.47   Corrosion of unspecified degree of female genital region** ♀
   Corrosion of unspecified degree of labium (majus) (minus)
   Corrosion of unspecified degree of perineum
   Corrosion of unspecified degree of vulva

> **Excludes2**   corrosion of vagina (T28.8)

X ● **T21.49   Corrosion of unspecified degree of other site of trunk**

● **T21.5   Corrosion of first degree of trunk**

> *Code first* (T51-T65) *to identify chemical and intent*
> Use additional external cause code to identify place (Y92)

X ● **T21.50   Corrosion of first degree of trunk, unspecified site**

X ● **T21.51   Corrosion of first degree of chest wall**
   Corrosion of first degree of breast

X ● **T21.52   Corrosion of first degree of abdominal wall**
   Corrosion of first degree of flank
   Corrosion of first degree of groin

X ● **T21.53   Corrosion of first degree of upper back**
   Corrosion of first degree of interscapular region

X ● **T21.54   Corrosion of first degree of lower back**

X ● **T21.55   Corrosion of first degree of buttock**
   Corrosion of first degree of anus

X ● **T21.56   Corrosion of first degree of male genital region** ♂
   Corrosion of first degree of penis
   Corrosion of first degree of scrotum
   Corrosion of first degree of testis

X ● **T21.57   Corrosion of first degree of female genital region** ♀
   Corrosion of first degree of labium (majus) (minus)
   Corrosion of first degree of perineum
   Corrosion of first degree of vulva

> **Excludes2**   corrosion of vagina (T28.8)

X ● **T21.59   Corrosion of first degree of other site of trunk**

● **T21.6   Corrosion of second degree of trunk**

> *Code first* (T51-T65) *to identify chemical and intent*
> Use additional external cause code to identify place (Y92)

X ● **T21.60   Corrosion of second degree of trunk, unspecified site**

X ● **T21.61   Corrosion of second degree of chest wall**
   Corrosion of second degree of breast

X ● **T21.62   Corrosion of second degree of abdominal wall**
   Corrosion of second degree of flank
   Corrosion of second degree of groin

X ● **T21.63   Corrosion of second degree of upper back**
   Corrosion of second degree of interscapular region

X ● **T21.64   Corrosion of second degree of lower back**

X ● **T21.65   Corrosion of second degree of buttock**
   Corrosion of second degree of anus

X ● **T21.66   Corrosion of second degree of male genital region** ♂
   Corrosion of second degree of penis
   Corrosion of second degree of scrotum
   Corrosion of second degree of testis

X ● **T21.67   Corrosion of second degree of female genital region** ♀
   Corrosion of second degree of labium (majus) (minus)
   Corrosion of second degree of perineum
   Corrosion of second degree of vulva

> **Excludes2**   corrosion of vagina (T28.8)

X ● **T21.69   Corrosion of second degree of other site of trunk**

CHAPTER 19 (S00-T88)

CHAPTER 19 (S00-T88)

● **T21.7**   **Corrosion of third degree of trunk**
     Code first (T51-T65) to identify chemical and intent
     Use additional external cause code to identify place (Y92)

X ● **T21.70**   **Corrosion of third degree of trunk, unspecified site**

X ● **T21.71**   **Corrosion of third degree of chest wall**
     Corrosion of third degree of breast

X ● **T21.72**   **Corrosion of third degree of abdominal wall**
     Corrosion of third degree of flank
     Corrosion of third degree of groin

X ● **T21.73**   **Corrosion of third degree of upper back**
     Corrosion of third degree of interscapular region

X ● **T21.74**   **Corrosion of third degree of lower back**

X ● **T21.75**   **Corrosion of third degree of buttock**
     Corrosion of third degree of anus

X ● **T21.76**   **Corrosion of third degree of male genital region** ♂
     Corrosion of third degree of penis
     Corrosion of third degree of scrotum
     Corrosion of third degree of testis

X ● **T21.77**   **Corrosion of third degree of female genital region** ♀
     Corrosion of third degree of labium (majus) (minus)
     Corrosion of third degree of perineum
     Corrosion of third degree of vulva
     Excludes2   corrosion of vagina (T28.8)

X ● **T21.79**   **Corrosion of third degree of other site of trunk**

● **T22**   **Burn and corrosion of shoulder and upper limb, except wrist and hand**
     Excludes2   burn and corrosion of interscapular region (T21.-)
                 burn and corrosion of wrist and hand (T23.-)
     The appropriate 7th character is to be added to each code from category T22

> A   initial encounter
> D   subsequent encounter
> S   sequela

● **T22.0**   **Burn of unspecified degree of shoulder and upper limb, except wrist and hand**
     Use additional external cause code to identify the source, place and intent of the burn (X00-X19, X75-X77, X96-X98, Y92)

X ● **T22.00**   **Burn of unspecified degree of shoulder and upper limb, except wrist and hand, unspecified site**

● **T22.01**   **Burn of unspecified degree of forearm**

   ● **T22.011**   **Burn of unspecified degree of right forearm**

   ● **T22.012**   **Burn of unspecified degree of left forearm**

   ● **T22.019**   **Burn of unspecified degree of unspecified forearm**

● **T22.02**   **Burn of unspecified degree of elbow**

   ● **T22.021**   **Burn of unspecified degree of right elbow**

   ● **T22.022**   **Burn of unspecified degree of left elbow**

   ● **T22.029**   **Burn of unspecified degree of unspecified elbow**

● **T22.03**   **Burn of unspecified degree of upper arm**

   ● **T22.031**   **Burn of unspecified degree of right upper arm**

   ● **T22.032**   **Burn of unspecified degree of left upper arm**

   ● **T22.039**   **Burn of unspecified degree of unspecified upper arm**

● **T22.04**   **Burn of unspecified degree of axilla**

   ● **T22.041**   **Burn of unspecified degree of right axilla**

   ● **T22.042**   **Burn of unspecified degree of left axilla**

   ● **T22.049**   **Burn of unspecified degree of unspecified axilla**

● **T22.05**   **Burn of unspecified degree of shoulder**

   ● **T22.051**   **Burn of unspecified degree of right shoulder**

   ● **T22.052**   **Burn of unspecified degree of left shoulder**

   ● **T22.059**   **Burn of unspecified degree of unspecified shoulder**

● **T22.06**   **Burn of unspecified degree of scapular region**

   ● **T22.061**   **Burn of unspecified degree of right scapular region**

   ● **T22.062**   **Burn of unspecified degree of left scapular region**

   ● **T22.069**   **Burn of unspecified degree of unspecified scapular region**

● **T22.09**   **Burn of unspecified degree of multiple sites of shoulder and upper limb, except wrist and hand**

   ● **T22.091**   **Burn of unspecified degree of multiple sites of right shoulder and upper limb, except wrist and hand**

   ● **T22.092**   **Burn of unspecified degree of multiple sites of left shoulder and upper limb, except wrist and hand**

   ● **T22.099**   **Burn of unspecified degree of multiple sites of unspecified shoulder and upper limb, except wrist and hand**

● **T22.1**   **Burn of first degree of shoulder and upper limb, except wrist and hand**
     Use additional external cause code to identify the source, place and intent of the burn (X00-X19, X75-X77, X96-X98, Y92)

X ● **T22.10**   **Burn of first degree of shoulder and upper limb, except wrist and hand, unspecified site**

● **T22.11**   **Burn of first degree of forearm**

   ● **T22.111**   **Burn of first degree of right forearm**

   ● **T22.112**   **Burn of first degree of left forearm**

   ● **T22.119**   **Burn of first degree of unspecified forearm**

● **T22.12**   **Burn of first degree of elbow**

   ● **T22.121**   **Burn of first degree of right elbow**

   ● **T22.122**   **Burn of first degree of left elbow**

   ● **T22.129**   **Burn of first degree of unspecified elbow**

● **T22.13**   **Burn of first degree of upper arm**

   ● **T22.131**   **Burn of first degree of right upper arm**

   ● **T22.132**   **Burn of first degree of left upper arm**

   ● **T22.139**   **Burn of first degree of unspecified upper arm**

● **T22.14**   **Burn of first degree of axilla**

   ● **T22.141**   **Burn of first degree of right axilla**

   ● **T22.142**   **Burn of first degree of left axilla**

   ● **T22.149**   **Burn of first degree of unspecified axilla**

● **T22.15**   **Burn of first degree of shoulder**

   ● **T22.151**   **Burn of first degree of right shoulder**

   ● **T22.152**   **Burn of first degree of left shoulder**

   ● **T22.159**   **Burn of first degree of unspecified shoulder**

● T22.16   Burn of first degree of scapular region
  - ● T22.161   Burn of first degree of right scapular region
  - ● T22.162   Burn of first degree of left scapular region
  - ● T22.169   Burn of first degree of unspecified scapular region
- ● T22.19   Burn of first degree of multiple sites of shoulder and upper limb, except wrist and hand
  - ● T22.191   Burn of first degree of multiple sites of right shoulder and upper limb, except wrist and hand
  - ● T22.192   Burn of first degree of multiple sites of left shoulder and upper limb, except wrist and hand
  - ● T22.199   Burn of first degree of multiple sites of unspecified shoulder and upper limb, except wrist and hand
- ● T22.2   Burn of second degree of shoulder and upper limb, except wrist and hand

  Use additional external cause code to identify the source, place and intent of the burn (X00-X19, X75-X77, X96-X98, Y92)

  - X ● T22.20   Burn of second degree of shoulder and upper limb, except wrist and hand, unspecified site
  - ● T22.21   Burn of second degree of forearm
    - ● T22.211   Burn of second degree of right forearm
    - ● T22.212   Burn of second degree of left forearm
    - ● T22.219   Burn of second degree of unspecified forearm
  - ● T22.22   Burn of second degree of elbow
    - ● T22.221   Burn of second degree of right elbow
    - ● T22.222   Burn of second degree of left elbow
    - ● T22.229   Burn of second degree of unspecified elbow
  - ● T22.23   Burn of second degree of upper arm
    - ● T22.231   Burn of second degree of right upper arm
    - ● T22.232   Burn of second degree of left upper arm
    - ● T22.239   Burn of second degree of unspecified upper arm
  - ● T22.24   Burn of second degree of axilla
    - ● T22.241   Burn of second degree of right axilla
    - ● T22.242   Burn of second degree of left axilla
    - ● T22.249   Burn of second degree of unspecified axilla
  - ● T22.25   Burn of second degree of shoulder
    - ● T22.251   Burn of second degree of right shoulder
    - ● T22.252   Burn of second degree of left shoulder
    - ● T22.259   Burn of second degree of unspecified shoulder
  - ● T22.26   Burn of second degree of scapular region
    - ● T22.261   Burn of second degree of right scapular region
    - ● T22.262   Burn of second degree of left scapular region
    - ● T22.269   Burn of second degree of unspecified scapular region

- ● T22.29   Burn of second degree of multiple sites of shoulder and upper limb, except wrist and hand
  - ● T22.291   Burn of second degree of multiple sites of right shoulder and upper limb, except wrist and hand
  - ● T22.292   Burn of second degree of multiple sites of left shoulder and upper limb, except wrist and hand
  - ● T22.299   Burn of second degree of multiple sites of unspecified shoulder and upper limb, except wrist and hand
- ● T22.3   Burn of third degree of shoulder and upper limb, except wrist and hand

  Use additional external cause code to identify the source, place and intent of the burn (X00-X19, X75-X77, X96-X98, Y92)

  - X ● T22.30   Burn of third degree of shoulder and upper limb, except wrist and hand, unspecified site
  - ● T22.31   Burn of third degree of forearm
    - ● T22.311   Burn of third degree of right forearm
    - ● T22.312   Burn of third degree of left forearm
    - ● T22.319   Burn of third degree of unspecified forearm
  - ● T22.32   Burn of third degree of elbow
    - ● T22.321   Burn of third degree of right elbow
    - ● T22.322   Burn of third degree of left elbow
    - ● T22.329   Burn of third degree of unspecified elbow
  - ● T22.33   Burn of third degree of upper arm
    - ● T22.331   Burn of third degree of right upper arm
    - ● T22.332   Burn of third degree of left upper arm
    - ● T22.339   Burn of third degree of unspecified upper arm
  - ● T22.34   Burn of third degree of axilla
    - ● T22.341   Burn of third degree of right axilla
    - ● T22.342   Burn of third degree of left axilla
    - ● T22.349   Burn of third degree of unspecified axilla
  - ● T22.35   Burn of third degree of shoulder
    - ● T22.351   Burn of third degree of right shoulder
    - ● T22.352   Burn of third degree of left shoulder
    - ● T22.359   Burn of third degree of unspecified shoulder
  - ● T22.36   Burn of third degree of scapular region
    - ● T22.361   Burn of third degree of right scapular region
    - ● T22.362   Burn of third degree of left scapular region
    - ● T22.369   Burn of third degree of unspecified scapular region
  - ● T22.39   Burn of third degree of multiple sites of shoulder and upper limb, except wrist and hand
    - ● T22.391   Burn of third degree of multiple sites of right shoulder and upper limb, except wrist and hand
    - ● T22.392   Burn of third degree of multiple sites of left shoulder and upper limb, except wrist and hand
    - ● T22.399   Burn of third degree of multiple sites of unspecified shoulder and upper limb, except wrist and hand

CHAPTER 19 (S00-T88)

● **T22.4**   **Corrosion of unspecified degree of shoulder and upper limb, except wrist and hand**

Code first (T51-T65) to identify chemical and intent

Use additional external cause code to identify place (Y92)

X ● **T22.40**   Corrosion of unspecified degree of shoulder and upper limb, except wrist and hand, unspecified site

● **T22.41**   Corrosion of unspecified degree of forearm

    ● **T22.411**   Corrosion of unspecified degree of right forearm

    ● **T22.412**   Corrosion of unspecified degree of left forearm

    ● **T22.419**   Corrosion of unspecified degree of unspecified forearm

● **T22.42**   Corrosion of unspecified degree of elbow

    ● **T22.421**   Corrosion of unspecified degree of right elbow

    ● **T22.422**   Corrosion of unspecified degree of left elbow

    ● **T22.429**   Corrosion of unspecified degree of unspecified elbow

● **T22.43**   Corrosion of unspecified degree of upper arm

    ● **T22.431**   Corrosion of unspecified degree of right upper arm

    ● **T22.432**   Corrosion of unspecified degree of left upper arm

    ● **T22.439**   Corrosion of unspecified degree of unspecified upper arm

● **T22.44**   Corrosion of unspecified degree of axilla

    ● **T22.441**   Corrosion of unspecified degree of right axilla

    ● **T22.442**   Corrosion of unspecified degree of left axilla

    ● **T22.449**   Corrosion of unspecified degree of unspecified axilla

● **T22.45**   Corrosion of unspecified degree of shoulder

    ● **T22.451**   Corrosion of unspecified degree of right shoulder

    ● **T22.452**   Corrosion of unspecified degree of left shoulder

    ● **T22.459**   Corrosion of unspecified degree of unspecified shoulder

● **T22.46**   Corrosion of unspecified degree of scapular region

    ● **T22.461**   Corrosion of unspecified degree of right scapular region

    ● **T22.462**   Corrosion of unspecified degree of left scapular region

    ● **T22.469**   Corrosion of unspecified degree of unspecified scapular region

● **T22.49**   Corrosion of unspecified degree of multiple sites of shoulder and upper limb, except wrist and hand

    ● **T22.491**   Corrosion of unspecified degree of multiple sites of right shoulder and upper limb, except wrist and hand

    ● **T22.492**   Corrosion of unspecified degree of multiple sites of left shoulder and upper limb, except wrist and hand

    ● **T22.499**   Corrosion of unspecified degree of multiple sites of unspecified shoulder and upper limb, except wrist and hand

● **T22.5**   **Corrosion of first degree of shoulder and upper limb, except wrist and hand**

Code first (T51-T65) to identify chemical and intent

Use additional external cause code to identify place (Y92)

X ● **T22.50**   Corrosion of first degree of shoulder and upper limb, except wrist and hand unspecified site

● **T22.51**   Corrosion of first degree of forearm

    ● **T22.511**   Corrosion of first degree of right forearm

    ● **T22.512**   Corrosion of first degree of left forearm

    ● **T22.519**   Corrosion of first degree of unspecified forearm

● **T22.52**   Corrosion of first degree of elbow

    ● **T22.521**   Corrosion of first degree of right elbow

    ● **T22.522**   Corrosion of first degree of left elbow

    ● **T22.529**   Corrosion of first degree of unspecified elbow

● **T22.53**   Corrosion of first degree of upper arm

    ● **T22.531**   Corrosion of first degree of right upper arm

    ● **T22.532**   Corrosion of first degree of left upper arm

    ● **T22.539**   Corrosion of first degree of unspecified upper arm

● **T22.54**   Corrosion of first degree of axilla

    ● **T22.541**   Corrosion of first degree of right axilla

    ● **T22.542**   Corrosion of first degree of left axilla

    ● **T22.549**   Corrosion of first degree of unspecified axilla

● **T22.55**   Corrosion of first degree of shoulder

    ● **T22.551**   Corrosion of first degree of right shoulder

    ● **T22.552**   Corrosion of first degree of left shoulder

    ● **T22.559**   Corrosion of first degree of unspecified shoulder

● **T22.56**   Corrosion of first degree of scapular region

    ● **T22.561**   Corrosion of first degree of right scapular region

    ● **T22.562**   Corrosion of first degree of left scapular region

    ● **T22.569**   Corrosion of first degree of unspecified scapular region

● **T22.59**   Corrosion of first degree of multiple sites of shoulder and upper limb, except wrist and hand

    ● **T22.591**   Corrosion of first degree of multiple sites of right shoulder and upper limb, except wrist and hand

    ● **T22.592**   Corrosion of first degree of multiple sites of left shoulder and upper limb, except wrist and hand

    ● **T22.599**   Corrosion of first degree of multiple sites of unspecified shoulder and upper limb, except wrist and hand

▶ New   ⇒ Revised   ~~deleted~~ Deleted   Excludes 1   Excludes 2   Includes   Use additional   Code first   Code also   Key words

OGCR Official Guidelines   X Assign placeholder X   ● Use Additional Character(s)   ▸ Manifestation Code   **Coding Clinic**

● **T22.6** Corrosion of second degree of shoulder and upper limb, except wrist and hand

    Code first (T51-T65) to identify chemical and intent

    Use additional external cause code to identify place (Y92)

X ● **T22.60** Corrosion of second degree of shoulder and upper limb, except wrist and hand, unspecified site

● **T22.61** Corrosion of second degree of forearm

    ● **T22.611** Corrosion of second degree of right forearm

    ● **T22.612** Corrosion of second degree of left forearm

    ● **T22.619** Corrosion of second degree of unspecified forearm

● **T22.62** Corrosion of second degree of elbow

    ● **T22.621** Corrosion of second degree of right elbow

    ● **T22.622** Corrosion of second degree of left elbow

    ● **T22.629** Corrosion of second degree of unspecified elbow

● **T22.63** Corrosion of second degree of upper arm

    ● **T22.631** Corrosion of second degree of right upper arm

    ● **T22.632** Corrosion of second degree of left upper arm

    ● **T22.639** Corrosion of second degree of unspecified upper arm

● **T22.64** Corrosion of second degree of axilla

    ● **T22.641** Corrosion of second degree of right axilla

    ● **T22.642** Corrosion of second degree of left axilla

    ● **T22.649** Corrosion of second degree of unspecified axilla

● **T22.65** Corrosion of second degree of shoulder

    ● **T22.651** Corrosion of second degree of right shoulder

    ● **T22.652** Corrosion of second degree of left shoulder

    ● **T22.659** Corrosion of second degree of unspecified shoulder

● **T22.66** Corrosion of second degree of scapular region

    ● **T22.661** Corrosion of second degree of right scapular region

    ● **T22.662** Corrosion of second degree of left scapular region

    ● **T22.669** Corrosion of second degree of unspecified scapular region

● **T22.69** Corrosion of second degree of multiple sites of shoulder and upper limb, except wrist and hand

    ● **T22.691** Corrosion of second degree of multiple sites of right shoulder and upper limb, except wrist and hand

    ● **T22.692** Corrosion of second degree of multiple sites of left shoulder and upper limb, except wrist and hand

    ● **T22.699** Corrosion of second degree of multiple sites of unspecified shoulder and upper limb, except wrist and hand

● **T22.7** Corrosion of third degree of shoulder and upper limb, except wrist and hand

    Code first (T51-T65) to identify chemical and intent

    Use additional external cause code to identify place (Y92)

X ● **T22.70** Corrosion of third degree of shoulder and upper limb, except wrist and hand, unspecified site

● **T22.71** Corrosion of third degree of forearm

    ● **T22.711** Corrosion of third degree of right forearm

    ● **T22.712** Corrosion of third degree of left forearm

    ● **T22.719** Corrosion of third degree of unspecified forearm

● **T22.72** Corrosion of third degree of elbow

    ● **T22.721** Corrosion of third degree of right elbow

    ● **T22.722** Corrosion of third degree of left elbow

    ● **T22.729** Corrosion of third degree of unspecified elbow

● **T22.73** Corrosion of third degree of upper arm

    ● **T22.731** Corrosion of third degree of right upper arm

    ● **T22.732** Corrosion of third degree of left upper arm

    ● **T22.739** Corrosion of third degree of unspecified upper arm

● **T22.74** Corrosion of third degree of axilla

    ● **T22.741** Corrosion of third degree of right axilla

    ● **T22.742** Corrosion of third degree of left axilla

    ● **T22.749** Corrosion of third degree of unspecified axilla

● **T22.75** Corrosion of third degree of shoulder

    ● **T22.751** Corrosion of third degree of right shoulder

    ● **T22.752** Corrosion of third degree of left shoulder

    ● **T22.759** Corrosion of third degree of unspecified shoulder

● **T22.76** Corrosion of third degree of scapular region

    ● **T22.761** Corrosion of third degree of right scapular region

    ● **T22.762** Corrosion of third degree of left scapular region

    ● **T22.769** Corrosion of third degree of unspecified scapular region

● **T22.79** Corrosion of third degree of multiple sites of shoulder and upper limb, except wrist and hand

    ● **T22.791** Corrosion of third degree of multiple sites of right shoulder and upper limb, except wrist and hand

    ● **T22.792** Corrosion of third degree of multiple sites of left shoulder and upper limb, except wrist and hand

    ● **T22.799** Corrosion of third degree of multiple sites of unspecified shoulder and upper limb, except wrist and hand

CHAPTER 19 (S00-T88)

● **T23 Burn and corrosion of wrist and hand**

The appropriate 7th character is to be added to each code from category T23

A	initial encounter
D	subsequent encounter
S	sequela

● **T23.0 Burn of unspecified degree of wrist and hand**

Use additional external cause code to identify the source, place and intent of the burn (X00-X19, X75-X77, X96-X98, Y92)

● **T23.00 Burn of unspecified degree of hand, unspecified site**

    ● T23.001 Burn of unspecified degree of right hand, unspecified site

    ● T23.002 Burn of unspecified degree of left hand, unspecified site

    ● T23.009 Burn of unspecified degree of unspecified hand, unspecified site

● **T23.01 Burn of unspecified degree of thumb (nail)**

    ● T23.011 Burn of unspecified degree of right thumb (nail)

    ● T23.012 Burn of unspecified degree of left thumb (nail)

    ● T23.019 Burn of unspecified degree of unspecified thumb (nail)

● **T23.02 Burn of unspecified degree of single finger (nail) except thumb**

    ● T23.021 Burn of unspecified degree of single right finger (nail) except thumb

    ● T23.022 Burn of unspecified degree of single left finger (nail) except thumb

    ● T23.029 Burn of unspecified degree of unspecified single finger (nail) except thumb

● **T23.03 Burn of unspecified degree of multiple fingers (nail), not including thumb**

    ● T23.031 Burn of unspecified degree of multiple right fingers (nail), not including thumb

    ● T23.032 Burn of unspecified degree of multiple left fingers (nail), not including thumb

    ● T23.039 Burn of unspecified degree of unspecified multiple fingers (nail), not including thumb

● **T23.04 Burn of unspecified degree of multiple fingers (nail), including thumb**

    ● T23.041 Burn of unspecified degree of multiple right fingers (nail), including thumb

    ● T23.042 Burn of unspecified degree of multiple left fingers (nail), including thumb

    ● T23.049 Burn of unspecified degree of unspecified multiple fingers (nail), including thumb

● **T23.05 Burn of unspecified degree of palm**

    ● T23.051 Burn of unspecified degree of right palm

    ● T23.052 Burn of unspecified degree of left palm

    ● T23.059 Burn of unspecified degree of unspecified palm

● **T23.06 Burn of unspecified degree of back of hand**

    ● T23.061 Burn of unspecified degree of back of right hand

    ● T23.062 Burn of unspecified degree of back of left hand

    ● T23.069 Burn of unspecified degree of back of unspecified hand

● **T23.07 Burn of unspecified degree of wrist**

    ● T23.071 Burn of unspecified degree of right wrist

    ● T23.072 Burn of unspecified degree of left wrist

    ● T23.079 Burn of unspecified degree of unspecified wrist

● **T23.09 Burn of unspecified degree of multiple sites of wrist and hand**

    ● T23.091 Burn of unspecified degree of multiple sites of right wrist and hand

    ● T23.092 Burn of unspecified degree of multiple sites of left wrist and hand

    ● T23.099 Burn of unspecified degree of multiple sites of unspecified wrist and hand

● **T23.1 Burn of first degree of wrist and hand**

Use additional external cause code to identify the source, place and intent of the burn (X00-X19, X75-X77, X96-X98, Y92)

● **T23.10 Burn of first degree of hand, unspecified site**

    ● T23.101 Burn of first degree of right hand, unspecified site

    ● T23.102 Burn of first degree of left hand, unspecified site

    ● T23.109 Burn of first degree of unspecified hand, unspecified site

● **T23.11 Burn of first degree of thumb (nail)**

    ● T23.111 Burn of first degree of right thumb (nail)

    ● T23.112 Burn of first degree of left thumb (nail)

    ● T23.119 Burn of first degree of unspecified thumb (nail)

● **T23.12 Burn of first degree of single finger (nail) except thumb**

    ● T23.121 Burn of first degree of single right finger (nail) except thumb

    ● T23.122 Burn of first degree of single left finger (nail) except thumb

    ● T23.129 Burn of first degree of unspecified single finger (nail) except thumb

● **T23.13 Burn of first degree of multiple fingers (nail), not including thumb**

    ● T23.131 Burn of first degree of multiple right fingers (nail), not including thumb

    ● T23.132 Burn of first degree of multiple left fingers (nail), not including thumb

    ● T23.139 Burn of first degree of unspecified multiple fingers (nail), not including thumb

● **T23.14 Burn of first degree of multiple fingers (nail), including thumb**

    ● T23.141 Burn of first degree of multiple right fingers (nail), including thumb

    ● T23.142 Burn of first degree of multiple left fingers (nail), including thumb

    ● T23.149 Burn of first degree of unspecified multiple fingers (nail), including thumb

▶ New	⇒ Revised	~~deleted~~ Deleted	Excludes 1	Excludes 2	Includes	Use additional	Code first	Code also	Key words

OGCR Official Guidelines   X Assign placeholder X   ● Use Additional Character(s)   ▷ Manifestation Code   **Coding Clinic**

- T23.15   Burn of first degree of palm
  - T23.151   Burn of first degree of right palm
  - T23.152   Burn of first degree of left palm
  - T23.159   Burn of first degree of unspecified palm
- T23.16   Burn of first degree of back of hand
  - T23.161   Burn of first degree of back of right hand
  - T23.162   Burn of first degree of back of left hand
  - T23.169   Burn of first degree of back of unspecified hand
- T23.17   Burn of first degree of wrist
  - T23.171   Burn of first degree of right wrist
  - T23.172   Burn of first degree of left wrist
  - T23.179   Burn of first degree of unspecified wrist
- T23.19   Burn of first degree of multiple sites of wrist and hand
  - T23.191   Burn of first degree of multiple sites of right wrist and hand
  - T23.192   Burn of first degree of multiple sites of left wrist and hand
  - T23.199   Burn of first degree of multiple sites of unspecified wrist and hand
- T23.2   Burn of second degree of wrist and hand
  Use additional external cause code to identify the source, place and intent of the burn (X00-X19, X75-X77, X96-X98, Y92)
  - T23.20   Burn of second degree of hand, unspecified site
    - T23.201   Burn of second degree of right hand, unspecified site
    - T23.202   Burn of second degree of left hand, unspecified site
    - T23.209   Burn of second degree of unspecified hand, unspecified site
  - T23.21   Burn of second degree of thumb (nail)
    - T23.211   Burn of second degree of right thumb (nail)
    - T23.212   Burn of second degree of left thumb (nail)
    - T23.219   Burn of second degree of unspecified thumb (nail)
  - T23.22   Burn of second degree of single finger (nail) except thumb
    - T23.221   Burn of second degree of single right finger (nail) except thumb
    - T23.222   Burn of second degree of single left finger (nail) except thumb
    - T23.229   Burn of second degree of unspecified single finger (nail) except thumb
  - T23.23   Burn of second degree of multiple fingers (nail), not including thumb
    - T23.231   Burn of second degree of multiple right fingers (nail), not including thumb
    - T23.232   Burn of second degree of multiple left fingers (nail), not including thumb
    - T23.239   Burn of second degree of unspecified multiple fingers (nail), not including thumb
  - T23.24   Burn of second degree of multiple fingers (nail), including thumb
    - T23.241   Burn of second degree of multiple right fingers (nail), including thumb
    - T23.242   Burn of second degree of multiple left fingers (nail), including thumb
    - T23.249   Burn of second degree of unspecified multiple fingers (nail), including thumb

- T23.25   Burn of second degree of palm
  - T23.251   Burn of second degree of right palm
  - T23.252   Burn of second degree of left palm
  - T23.259   Burn of second degree of unspecified palm
- T23.26   Burn of second degree of back of hand
  - T23.261   Burn of second degree of back of right hand
  - T23.262   Burn of second degree of back of left hand
  - T23.269   Burn of second degree of back of unspecified hand
- T23.27   Burn of second degree of wrist
  - T23.271   Burn of second degree of right wrist
  - T23.272   Burn of second degree of left wrist
  - T23.279   Burn of second degree of unspecified wrist
- T23.29   Burn of second degree of multiple sites of wrist and hand
  - T23.291   Burn of second degree of multiple sites of right wrist and hand
  - T23.292   Burn of second degree of multiple sites of left wrist and hand
  - T23.299   Burn of second degree of multiple sites of unspecified wrist and hand
- T23.3   Burn of third degree of wrist and hand
  Use additional external cause code to identify the source, place and intent of the burn (X00-X19, X75-X77, X96-X98, Y92)
  - T23.30   Burn of third degree of hand, unspecified site
    - T23.301   Burn of third degree of right hand, unspecified site
      Coding Clinic: 2015, Q1, P19
    - T23.302   Burn of third degree of left hand, unspecified site
      Coding Clinic: 2016, Q2, P5
    - T23.309   Burn of third degree of unspecified hand, unspecified site
  - T23.31   Burn of third degree of thumb (nail)
    - T23.311   Burn of third degree of right thumb (nail)
    - T23.312   Burn of third degree of left thumb (nail)
    - T23.319   Burn of third degree of unspecified thumb (nail)
  - T23.32   Burn of third degree of single finger (nail) except thumb
    - T23.321   Burn of third degree of single right finger (nail) except thumb
    - T23.322   Burn of third degree of single left finger (nail) except thumb
    - T23.329   Burn of third degree of unspecified single finger (nail) except thumb
  - T23.33   Burn of third degree of multiple fingers (nail), not including thumb
    - T23.331   Burn of third degree of multiple right fingers (nail), not including thumb
    - T23.332   Burn of third degree of multiple left fingers (nail), not including thumb
    - T23.339   Burn of third degree of unspecified multiple fingers (nail), not including thumb
  - T23.34   Burn of third degree of multiple fingers (nail), including thumb
    - T23.341   Burn of third degree of multiple right fingers (nail), including thumb
    - T23.342   Burn of third degree of multiple left fingers (nail), including thumb
    - T23.349   Burn of third degree of unspecified multiple fingers (nail), including thumb

CHAPTER 19 (S00-T88)

CHAPTER 19 (S00-T88)

● **T23.35**   Burn of third degree of palm
    ● **T23.351**   Burn of third degree of right palm
    ● **T23.352**   Burn of third degree of left palm
    ● **T23.359**   Burn of third degree of unspecified palm
● **T23.36**   Burn of third degree of back of hand
    ● **T23.361**   Burn of third degree of back of right hand
    ● **T23.362**   Burn of third degree of back of left hand
    ● **T23.369**   Burn of third degree of back of unspecified hand
● **T23.37**   Burn of third degree of wrist
    ● **T23.371**   Burn of third degree of right wrist
    ● **T23.372**   Burn of third degree of left wrist
    ● **T23.379**   Burn of third degree of unspecified wrist
● **T23.39**   Burn of third degree of multiple sites of wrist and hand
    ● **T23.391**   Burn of third degree of multiple sites of right wrist and hand
    ● **T23.392**   Burn of third degree of multiple sites of left wrist and hand
    ● **T23.399**   Burn of third degree of multiple sites of unspecified wrist and hand

● **T23.4**   Corrosion of unspecified degree of wrist and hand
Code first (T51-T65) to identify chemical and intent
Use additional external cause code to identify place (Y92)
● **T23.40**   Corrosion of unspecified degree of hand, unspecified site
    ● **T23.401**   Corrosion of unspecified degree of right hand, unspecified site
    ● **T23.402**   Corrosion of unspecified degree of left hand, unspecified site
    ● **T23.409**   Corrosion of unspecified degree of unspecified hand, unspecified site
● **T23.41**   Corrosion of unspecified degree of thumb (nail)
    ● **T23.411**   Corrosion of unspecified degree of right thumb (nail)
    ● **T23.412**   Corrosion of unspecified degree of left thumb (nail)
    ● **T23.419**   Corrosion of unspecified degree of unspecified thumb (nail)
● **T23.42**   Corrosion of unspecified degree of single finger (nail) except thumb
    ● **T23.421**   Corrosion of unspecified degree of single right finger (nail) except thumb
    ● **T23.422**   Corrosion of unspecified degree of single left finger (nail) except thumb
    ● **T23.429**   Corrosion of unspecified degree of unspecified single finger (nail) except thumb
● **T23.43**   Corrosion of unspecified degree of multiple fingers (nail), not including thumb
    ● **T23.431**   Corrosion of unspecified degree of multiple right fingers (nail), not including thumb
    ● **T23.432**   Corrosion of unspecified degree of multiple left fingers (nail), not including thumb
    ● **T23.439**   Corrosion of unspecified degree of unspecified multiple fingers (nail), not including thumb

● **T23.44**   Corrosion of unspecified degree of multiple fingers (nail), including thumb
    ● **T23.441**   Corrosion of unspecified degree of multiple right fingers (nail), including thumb
    ● **T23.442**   Corrosion of unspecified degree of multiple left fingers (nail), including thumb
    ● **T23.449**   Corrosion of unspecified degree of unspecified multiple fingers (nail), including thumb
● **T23.45**   Corrosion of unspecified degree of palm
    ● **T23.451**   Corrosion of unspecified degree of right palm
    ● **T23.452**   Corrosion of unspecified degree of left palm
    ● **T23.459**   Corrosion of unspecified degree of unspecified palm
● **T23.46**   Corrosion of unspecified degree of back of hand
    ● **T23.461**   Corrosion of unspecified degree of back of right hand
    ● **T23.462**   Corrosion of unspecified degree of back of left hand
    ● **T23.469**   Corrosion of unspecified degree of back of unspecified hand
● **T23.47**   Corrosion of unspecified degree of wrist
    ● **T23.471**   Corrosion of unspecified degree of right wrist
    ● **T23.472**   Corrosion of unspecified degree of left wrist
    ● **T23.479**   Corrosion of unspecified degree of unspecified wrist
● **T23.49**   Corrosion of unspecified degree of multiple sites of wrist and hand
    ● **T23.491**   Corrosion of unspecified degree of multiple sites of right wrist and hand
    ● **T23.492**   Corrosion of unspecified degree of multiple sites of left wrist and hand
    ● **T23.499**   Corrosion of unspecified degree of multiple sites of unspecified wrist and hand

● **T23.5**   Corrosion of first degree of wrist and hand
Code first (T51-T65) to identify chemical and intent
Use additional external cause code to identify place (Y92)
● **T23.50**   Corrosion of first degree of hand, unspecified site
    ● **T23.501**   Corrosion of first degree of right hand, unspecified site
    ● **T23.502**   Corrosion of first degree of left hand, unspecified site
    ● **T23.509**   Corrosion of first degree of unspecified hand, unspecified site
● **T23.51**   Corrosion of first degree of thumb (nail)
    ● **T23.511**   Corrosion of first degree of right thumb (nail)
    ● **T23.512**   Corrosion of first degree of left thumb (nail)
    ● **T23.519**   Corrosion of first degree of unspecified thumb (nail)
● **T23.52**   Corrosion of first degree of single finger (nail) except thumb
    ● **T23.521**   Corrosion of first degree of single right finger (nail) except thumb
    ● **T23.522**   Corrosion of first degree of single left finger (nail) except thumb
    ● **T23.529**   Corrosion of first degree of unspecified single finger (nail) except thumb

▶ New   ⇒ Revised   ~~deleted~~ Deleted   Excludes 1   Excludes 2   Includes   Use additional   Code first   Code also   Key words
OGCR Official Guidelines   X Assign placeholder X   ● Use Additional Character(s)   ▶ Manifestation Code   **Coding Clinic**

● **T23.53** Corrosion of first degree of multiple fingers (nail), not including thumb

  ● **T23.531** Corrosion of first degree of multiple right fingers (nail), not including thumb

  ● **T23.532** Corrosion of first degree of multiple left fingers (nail), not including thumb

  ● **T23.539** Corrosion of first degree of unspecified multiple fingers (nail), not including thumb

● **T23.54** Corrosion of first degree of multiple fingers (nail), including thumb

  ● **T23.541** Corrosion of first degree of multiple right fingers (nail), including thumb

  ● **T23.542** Corrosion of first degree of multiple left fingers (nail), including thumb

  ● **T23.549** Corrosion of first degree of unspecified multiple fingers (nail), including thumb

● **T23.55** Corrosion of first degree of palm

  ● **T23.551** Corrosion of first degree of right palm

  ● **T23.552** Corrosion of first degree of left palm

  ● **T23.559** Corrosion of first degree of unspecified palm

● **T23.56** Corrosion of first degree of back of hand

  ● **T23.561** Corrosion of first degree of back of right hand

  ● **T23.562** Corrosion of first degree of back of left hand

  ● **T23.569** Corrosion of first degree of back of unspecified hand

● **T23.57** Corrosion of first degree of wrist

  ● **T23.571** Corrosion of first degree of right wrist

  ● **T23.572** Corrosion of first degree of left wrist

  ● **T23.579** Corrosion of first degree of unspecified wrist

● **T23.59** Corrosion of first degree of multiple sites of wrist and hand

  ● **T23.591** Corrosion of first degree of multiple sites of right wrist and hand

  ● **T23.592** Corrosion of first degree of multiple sites of left wrist and hand

  ● **T23.599** Corrosion of first degree of multiple sites of unspecified wrist and hand

● **T23.6** Corrosion of second degree of wrist and hand

  Code first (T51-T65) to identify chemical and intent

  Use additional external cause code to identify place (Y92)

● **T23.60** Corrosion of second degree of hand, unspecified site

  ● **T23.601** Corrosion of second degree of right hand, unspecified site

  ● **T23.602** Corrosion of second degree of left hand, unspecified site

  ● **T23.609** Corrosion of second degree of unspecified hand, unspecified site

● **T23.61** Corrosion of second degree of thumb (nail)

  ● **T23.611** Corrosion of second degree of right thumb (nail)

  ● **T23.612** Corrosion of second degree of left thumb (nail)

  ● **T23.619** Corrosion of second degree of unspecified thumb (nail)

● **T23.62** Corrosion of second degree of single finger (nail) except thumb

  ● **T23.621** Corrosion of second degree of single right finger (nail) except thumb

  ● **T23.622** Corrosion of second degree of single left finger (nail) except thumb

  ● **T23.629** Corrosion of second degree of unspecified single finger (nail) except thumb

● **T23.63** Corrosion of second degree of multiple fingers (nail), not including thumb

  ● **T23.631** Corrosion of second degree of multiple right fingers (nail), not including thumb

  ● **T23.632** Corrosion of second degree of multiple left fingers (nail), not including thumb

  ● **T23.639** Corrosion of second degree of unspecified multiple fingers (nail), not including thumb

● **T23.64** Corrosion of second degree of multiple fingers (nail), including thumb

  ● **T23.641** Corrosion of second degree of multiple right fingers (nail), including thumb

  ● **T23.642** Corrosion of second degree of multiple left fingers (nail), including thumb

  ● **T23.649** Corrosion of second degree of unspecified multiple fingers (nail), including thumb

● **T23.65** Corrosion of second degree of palm

  ● **T23.651** Corrosion of second degree of right palm

  ● **T23.652** Corrosion of second degree of left palm

  ● **T23.659** Corrosion of second degree of unspecified palm

● **T23.66** Corrosion of second degree of back of hand

  ● **T23.661** Corrosion of second degree back of right hand

  ● **T23.662** Corrosion of second degree back of left hand

  ● **T23.669** Corrosion of second degree back of unspecified hand

● **T23.67** Corrosion of second degree of wrist

  ● **T23.671** Corrosion of second degree of right wrist

  ● **T23.672** Corrosion of second degree of left wrist

  ● **T23.679** Corrosion of second degree of unspecified wrist

● **T23.69** Corrosion of second degree of multiple sites of wrist and hand

  ● **T23.691** Corrosion of second degree of multiple sites of right wrist and hand

  ● **T23.692** Corrosion of second degree of multiple sites of left wrist and hand

  ● **T23.699** Corrosion of second degree of multiple sites of unspecified wrist and hand

● **T23.7 Corrosion of third degree of wrist and hand**

Code first (T51-T65) to identify chemical and intent

Use additional external cause code to identify place (Y92)

● **T23.70 Corrosion of third degree of hand, unspecified site**

● T23.701 Corrosion of third degree of right hand, unspecified site

● T23.702 Corrosion of third degree of left hand, unspecified site

● T23.709 Corrosion of third degree of unspecified hand, unspecified site

● **T23.71 Corrosion of third degree of thumb (nail)**

● T23.711 Corrosion of third degree of right thumb (nail)

● T23.712 Corrosion of third degree of left thumb (nail)

● T23.719 Corrosion of third degree of unspecified thumb (nail)

● **T23.72 Corrosion of third degree of single finger (nail) except thumb**

● T23.721 Corrosion of third degree of single right finger (nail) except thumb

● T23.722 Corrosion of third degree of single left finger (nail) except thumb

● T23.729 Corrosion of third degree of unspecified single finger (nail) except thumb

● **T23.73 Corrosion of third degree of multiple fingers (nail), not including thumb**

● T23.731 Corrosion of third degree of multiple right fingers (nail), not including thumb

● T23.732 Corrosion of third degree of multiple left fingers (nail), not including thumb

● T23.739 Corrosion of third degree of unspecified multiple fingers (nail), not including thumb

● **T23.74 Corrosion of third degree of multiple fingers (nail), including thumb**

● T23.741 Corrosion of third degree of multiple right fingers (nail), including thumb

● T23.742 Corrosion of third degree of multiple left fingers (nail), including thumb

● T23.749 Corrosion of third degree of unspecified multiple fingers (nail), including thumb

● **T23.75 Corrosion of third degree of palm**

● T23.751 Corrosion of third degree of right palm

● T23.752 Corrosion of third degree of left palm

● T23.759 Corrosion of third degree of unspecified palm

● **T23.76 Corrosion of third degree of back of hand**

● T23.761 Corrosion of third degree of back of right hand

● T23.762 Corrosion of third degree of back of left hand

● T23.769 Corrosion of third degree of back of unspecified hand

● **T23.77 Corrosion of third degree of wrist**

● T23.771 Corrosion of third degree of right wrist

● T23.772 Corrosion of third degree of left wrist

● T23.779 Corrosion of third degree of unspecified wrist

● **T23.79 Corrosion of third degree of multiple sites of wrist and hand**

● T23.791 Corrosion of third degree of multiple sites of right wrist and hand

● T23.792 Corrosion of third degree of multiple sites of left wrist and hand

● T23.799 Corrosion of third degree of multiple sites of unspecified wrist and hand

● **T24 Burn and corrosion of lower limb, except ankle and foot**

Excludes2   burn and corrosion of ankle and foot (T25.-)

burn and corrosion of hip region (T21.-)

The appropriate 7th character is to be added to each code from category T24

A	initial encounter
D	subsequent encounter
S	sequela

● **T24.0 Burn of unspecified degree of lower limb, except ankle and foot**

Use additional external cause code to identify the source, place and intent of the burn (X00-X19, X75-X77, X96-X98, Y92)

● **T24.00 Burn of unspecified degree of unspecified site of lower limb, except ankle and foot**

● T24.001 Burn of unspecified degree of unspecified site of right lower limb, except ankle and foot

● T24.002 Burn of unspecified degree of unspecified site of left lower limb, except ankle and foot

● T24.009 Burn of unspecified degree of unspecified site of unspecified lower limb, except ankle and foot

● **T24.01 Burn of unspecified degree of thigh**

● T24.011 Burn of unspecified degree of right thigh

● T24.012 Burn of unspecified degree of left thigh

● T24.019 Burn of unspecified degree of unspecified thigh

● **T24.02 Burn of unspecified degree of knee**

● T24.021 Burn of unspecified degree of right knee

● T24.022 Burn of unspecified degree of left knee

● T24.029 Burn of unspecified degree of unspecified knee

● **T24.03 Burn of unspecified degree of lower leg**

● T24.031 Burn of unspecified degree of right lower leg

● T24.032 Burn of unspecified degree of left lower leg

● T24.039 Burn of unspecified degree of unspecified lower leg

● **T24.09 Burn of unspecified degree of multiple sites of lower limb, except ankle and foot**

● T24.091 Burn of unspecified degree of multiple sites of right lower limb, except ankle and foot

● T24.092 Burn of unspecified degree of multiple sites of left lower limb, except ankle and foot

● T24.099 Burn of unspecified degree of multiple sites of unspecified lower limb, except ankle and foot

▶ New   ⇒ Revised   ~~deleted~~ Deleted   Excludes 1   Excludes 2   Includes   Use additional   Code first   Code also   Key words

OGCR Official Guidelines   X Assign placeholder X   ● Use Additional Character(s)   ▶ Manifestation Code   **Coding Clinic**

● **T24.1**   Burn of first degree of lower limb, except ankle and foot

> Use additional external cause code to identify the source, place and intent of the burn (X00-X19, X75-X77, X96-X98, Y92)

  ● **T24.10**   Burn of first degree of unspecified site of lower limb, except ankle and foot

    ● T24.101   Burn of first degree of unspecified site of right lower limb, except ankle and foot

    ● T24.102   Burn of first degree of unspecified site of left lower limb, except ankle and foot

    ● T24.109   Burn of first degree of unspecified site of unspecified lower limb, except ankle and foot

  ● **T24.11**   Burn of first degree of thigh

    ● T24.111   Burn of first degree of right thigh

    ● T24.112   Burn of first degree of left thigh

    ● T24.119   Burn of first degree of unspecified thigh

  ● **T24.12**   Burn of first degree of knee

    ● T24.121   Burn of first degree of right knee

    ● T24.122   Burn of first degree of left knee

    ● T24.129   Burn of first degree of unspecified knee

  ● **T24.13**   Burn of first degree of lower leg

    ● T24.131   Burn of first degree of right lower leg

    ● T24.132   Burn of first degree of left lower leg

    ● T24.139   Burn of first degree of unspecified lower leg

  ● **T24.19**   Burn of first degree of multiple sites of lower limb, except ankle and foot

    ● T24.191   Burn of first degree of multiple sites of right lower limb, except ankle and foot

    ● T24.192   Burn of first degree of multiple sites of left lower limb, except ankle and foot

    ● T24.199   Burn of first degree of multiple sites of unspecified lower limb, except ankle and foot

● **T24.2**   Burn of second degree of lower limb, except ankle and foot

> Use additional external cause code to identify the source, place and intent of the burn (X00-X19, X75-X77, X96-X98, Y92)

  ● **T24.20**   Burn of second degree of unspecified site of lower limb, except ankle and foot

    ● T24.201   Burn of second degree of unspecified site of right lower limb, except ankle and foot

    ● T24.202   Burn of second degree of unspecified site of left lower limb, except ankle and foot

    ● T24.209   Burn of second degree of unspecified site of unspecified lower limb, except ankle and foot

  ● **T24.21**   Burn of second degree of thigh

    ● T24.211   Burn of second degree of right thigh

    ● T24.212   Burn of second degree of left thigh

    ● T24.219   Burn of second degree of unspecified thigh

  ● **T24.22**   Burn of second degree of knee

    ● T24.221   Burn of second degree of right knee

    ● T24.222   Burn of second degree of left knee

    ● T24.229   Burn of second degree of unspecified knee

● **T24.23**   Burn of second degree of lower leg

    ● T24.231   Burn of second degree of right lower leg

    ● T24.232   Burn of second degree of left lower leg

    ● T24.239   Burn of second degree of unspecified lower leg

● **T24.29**   Burn of second degree of multiple sites of lower limb, except ankle and foot

    ● T24.291   Burn of second degree of multiple sites of right lower limb, except ankle and foot

    ● T24.292   Burn of second degree of multiple sites of left lower limb, except ankle and foot

    ● T24.299   Burn of second degree of multiple sites of unspecified lower limb, except ankle and foot

● **T24.3**   Burn of third degree of lower limb, except ankle and foot

> Use additional external cause code to identify the source, place and intent of the burn (X00-X19, X75-X77, X96-X98, Y92)

  ● **T24.30**   Burn of third degree of unspecified site of lower limb, except ankle and foot

    ● T24.301   Burn of third degree of unspecified site of right lower limb, except ankle and foot

    ● T24.302   Burn of third degree of unspecified site of left lower limb, except ankle and foot

    ● T24.309   Burn of third degree of unspecified site of unspecified lower limb, except ankle and foot

  ● **T24.31**   Burn of third degree of thigh

    ● T24.311   Burn of third degree of right thigh

    ● T24.312   Burn of third degree of left thigh

    ● T24.319   Burn of third degree of unspecified thigh

  ● **T24.32**   Burn of third degree of knee

    ● T24.321   Burn of third degree of right knee

    ● T24.322   Burn of third degree of left knee

    ● T24.329   Burn of third degree of unspecified knee

  ● **T24.33**   Burn of third degree of lower leg

    ● T24.331   Burn of third degree of right lower leg

    ● T24.332   Burn of third degree of left lower leg

    ● T24.339   Burn of third degree of unspecified lower leg

  ● **T24.39**   Burn of third degree of multiple sites of lower limb, except ankle and foot

    ● T24.391   Burn of third degree of multiple sites of right lower limb, except ankle and foot

      Coding Clinic: 2016, Q2, P5

    ● T24.392   Burn of third degree of multiple sites of left lower limb, except ankle and foot

    ● T24.399   Burn of third degree of multiple sites of unspecified lower limb, except ankle and foot

- T24.4 Corrosion of unspecified degree of lower limb, except ankle and foot

    Code first (T51-T65) to identify chemical and intent

    Use additional external cause code to identify place (Y92)

    - T24.40 Corrosion of unspecified degree of unspecified site of lower limb, except ankle and foot
        - T24.401 Corrosion of unspecified degree of unspecified site of right lower limb, except ankle and foot
        - T24.402 Corrosion of unspecified degree of unspecified site of left lower limb, except ankle and foot
        - T24.409 Corrosion of unspecified degree of unspecified site of unspecified lower limb, except ankle and foot
    - T24.41 Corrosion of unspecified degree of thigh
        - T24.411 Corrosion of unspecified degree of right thigh
        - T24.412 Corrosion of unspecified degree of left thigh
        - T24.419 Corrosion of unspecified degree of unspecified thigh
    - T24.42 Corrosion of unspecified degree of knee
        - T24.421 Corrosion of unspecified degree of right knee
        - T24.422 Corrosion of unspecified degree of left knee
        - T24.429 Corrosion of unspecified degree of unspecified knee
    - T24.43 Corrosion of unspecified degree of lower leg
        - T24.431 Corrosion of unspecified degree of right lower leg
        - T24.432 Corrosion of unspecified degree of left lower leg
        - T24.439 Corrosion of unspecified degree of unspecified lower leg
    - T24.49 Corrosion of unspecified degree of multiple sites of lower limb, except ankle and foot
        - T24.491 Corrosion of unspecified degree of multiple sites of right lower limb, except ankle and foot
        - T24.492 Corrosion of unspecified degree of multiple sites of left lower limb, except ankle and foot
        - T24.499 Corrosion of unspecified degree of multiple sites of unspecified lower limb, except ankle and foot

- T24.5 Corrosion of first degree of lower limb, except ankle and foot

    Code first (T51-T65) to identify chemical and intent

    Use additional external cause code to identify place (Y92)

    - T24.50 Corrosion of first degree of unspecified site of lower limb, except ankle and foot
        - T24.501 Corrosion of first degree of unspecified site of right lower limb, except ankle and foot
        - T24.502 Corrosion of first degree of unspecified site of left lower limb, except ankle and foot
        - T24.509 Corrosion of first degree of unspecified site of unspecified lower limb, except ankle and foot

- T24.51 Corrosion of first degree of thigh
    - T24.511 Corrosion of first degree of right thigh
    - T24.512 Corrosion of first degree of left thigh
    - T24.519 Corrosion of first degree of unspecified thigh
- T24.52 Corrosion of first degree of knee
    - T24.521 Corrosion of first degree of right knee
    - T24.522 Corrosion of first degree of left knee
    - T24.529 Corrosion of first degree of unspecified knee
- T24.53 Corrosion of first degree of lower leg
    - T24.531 Corrosion of first degree of right lower leg
    - T24.532 Corrosion of first degree of left lower leg
    - T24.539 Corrosion of first degree of unspecified lower leg
- T24.59 Corrosion of first degree of multiple sites of lower limb, except ankle and foot
    - T24.591 Corrosion of first degree of multiple sites of right lower limb, except ankle and foot
    - T24.592 Corrosion of first degree of multiple sites of left lower limb, except ankle and foot
    - T24.599 Corrosion of first degree of multiple sites of unspecified lower limb, except ankle and foot

- T24.6 Corrosion of second degree of lower limb, except ankle and foot

    Code first (T51-T65) to identify chemical and intent

    Use additional external cause code to identify place (Y92)

    - T24.60 Corrosion of second degree of unspecified site of lower limb, except ankle and foot
        - T24.601 Corrosion of second degree of unspecified site of right lower limb, except ankle and foot
        - T24.602 Corrosion of second degree of unspecified site of left lower limb, except ankle and foot
        - T24.609 Corrosion of second degree of unspecified site of unspecified lower limb, except ankle and foot
    - T24.61 Corrosion of second degree of thigh
        - T24.611 Corrosion of second degree of right thigh
        - T24.612 Corrosion of second degree of left thigh
        - T24.619 Corrosion of second degree of unspecified thigh
    - T24.62 Corrosion of second degree of knee
        - T24.621 Corrosion of second degree of right knee
        - T24.622 Corrosion of second degree of left knee
        - T24.629 Corrosion of second degree of unspecified knee

● **T24.63**   Corrosion of second degree of lower leg
    ● **T24.631**   Corrosion of second degree of right lower leg
    ● **T24.632**   Corrosion of second degree of left lower leg
    ● **T24.639**   Corrosion of second degree of unspecified lower leg
● **T24.69**   Corrosion of second degree of multiple sites of lower limb, except ankle and foot
    ● **T24.691**   Corrosion of second degree of multiple sites of right lower limb, except ankle and foot
    ● **T24.692**   Corrosion of second degree of multiple sites of left lower limb, except ankle and foot
    ● **T24.699**   Corrosion of second degree of multiple sites of unspecified lower limb, except ankle and foot

● **T24.7**   Corrosion of third degree of lower limb, except ankle and foot

Code first (T51-T65) *to identify chemical and intent*

Use additional external cause code to identify place (Y92)

    ● **T24.70**   Corrosion of third degree of unspecified site of lower limb, except ankle and foot
      ● **T24.701**   Corrosion of third degree of unspecified site of right lower limb, except ankle and foot
      ● **T24.702**   Corrosion of third degree of unspecified site of left lower limb, except ankle and foot
      ● **T24.709**   Corrosion of third degree of unspecified site of unspecified lower limb, except ankle and foot
    ● **T24.71**   Corrosion of third degree of thigh
      ● **T24.711**   Corrosion of third degree of right thigh
      ● **T24.712**   Corrosion of third degree of left thigh
      ● **T24.719**   Corrosion of third degree of unspecified thigh
    ● **T24.72**   Corrosion of third degree of knee
      ● **T24.721**   Corrosion of third degree of right knee
      ● **T24.722**   Corrosion of third degree of left knee
      ● **T24.729**   Corrosion of third degree of unspecified knee
    ● **T24.73**   Corrosion of third degree of lower leg
      ● **T24.731**   Corrosion of third degree of right lower leg
      ● **T24.732**   Corrosion of third degree of left lower leg
      ● **T24.739**   Corrosion of third degree of unspecified lower leg
    ● **T24.79**   Corrosion of third degree of multiple sites of lower limb, except ankle and foot
      ● **T24.791**   Corrosion of third degree of multiple sites of right lower limb, except ankle and foot
      ● **T24.792**   Corrosion of third degree of multiple sites of left lower limb, except ankle and foot
      ● **T24.799**   Corrosion of third degree of multiple sites of unspecified lower limb, except ankle and foot

● **T25**   Burn and corrosion of ankle and foot

The appropriate 7th character is to be added to each code from category T25

A	initial encounter
D	subsequent encounter
S	sequela

● **T25.0**   Burn of unspecified degree of ankle and foot

Use additional external cause code to identify the source, place and intent of the burn (X00-X19, X75-X77, X96-X98, Y92)

    ● **T25.01**   Burn of unspecified degree of ankle
      ● **T25.011**   Burn of unspecified degree of right ankle
      ● **T25.012**   Burn of unspecified degree of left ankle
      ● **T25.019**   Burn of unspecified degree of unspecified ankle
    ● **T25.02**   Burn of unspecified degree of foot

      Excludes2   burn of unspecified degree of toe(s) (nail) (T25.03-)

      ● **T25.021**   Burn of unspecified degree of right foot
      ● **T25.022**   Burn of unspecified degree of left foot
      ● **T25.029**   Burn of unspecified degree of unspecified foot
    ● **T25.03**   Burn of unspecified degree of toe(s) (nail)
      ● **T25.031**   Burn of unspecified degree of right toe(s) (nail)
      ● **T25.032**   Burn of unspecified degree of left toe(s) (nail)
      ● **T25.039**   Burn of unspecified degree of unspecified toe(s) (nail)
    ● **T25.09**   Burn of unspecified degree of multiple sites of ankle and foot
      ● **T25.091**   Burn of unspecified degree of multiple sites of right ankle and foot
      ● **T25.092**   Burn of unspecified degree of multiple sites of left ankle and foot
      ● **T25.099**   Burn of unspecified degree of multiple sites of unspecified ankle and foot

● **T25.1**   Burn of first degree of ankle and foot

Use additional external cause code to identify the source, place and intent of the burn (X00-X19, X75-X77, X96-X98, Y92)

    ● **T25.11**   Burn of first degree of ankle
      ● **T25.111**   Burn of first degree of right ankle
      ● **T25.112**   Burn of first degree of left ankle
      ● **T25.119**   Burn of first degree of unspecified ankle
    ● **T25.12**   Burn of first degree of foot

      Excludes2   burn of first degree of toe(s) (nail) (T25.13-)

      ● **T25.121**   Burn of first degree of right foot
      ● **T25.122**   Burn of first degree of left foot
      ● **T25.129**   Burn of first degree of unspecified foot
    ● **T25.13**   Burn of first degree of toe(s) (nail)
      ● **T25.131**   Burn of first degree of right toe(s) (nail)
      ● **T25.132**   Burn of first degree of left toe(s) (nail)
      ● **T25.139**   Burn of first degree of unspecified toe(s) (nail)

CHAPTER 19 (S00-T88)

● **T25.19** Burn of first degree of multiple sites of ankle and foot
   ● **T25.191** Burn of first degree of multiple sites of right ankle and foot
   ● **T25.192** Burn of first degree of multiple sites of left ankle and foot
   ● **T25.199** Burn of first degree of multiple sites of unspecified ankle and foot

● **T25.2** Burn of second degree of ankle and foot
   Use additional external cause code to identify the source, place and intent of the burn (X00-X19, X75-X77, X96-X98, Y92)
   ● **T25.21** Burn of second degree of ankle
      ● **T25.211** Burn of second degree of right ankle
      ● **T25.212** Burn of second degree of left ankle
      ● **T25.219** Burn of second degree of unspecified ankle
   ● **T25.22** Burn of second degree of foot
      Excludes2 burn of second degree of toe(s) (nail) (T25.23-)
      ● **T25.221** Burn of second degree of right foot
      ● **T25.222** Burn of second degree of left foot
      ● **T25.229** Burn of second degree of unspecified foot
   ● **T25.23** Burn of second degree of toe(s) (nail)
      ● **T25.231** Burn of second degree of right toe(s) (nail)
      ● **T25.232** Burn of second degree of left toe(s) (nail)
      ● **T25.239** Burn of second degree of unspecified toe(s) (nail)
   ● **T25.29** Burn of second degree of multiple sites of ankle and foot
      ● **T25.291** Burn of second degree of multiple sites of right ankle and foot
      ● **T25.292** Burn of second degree of multiple sites of left ankle and foot
      ● **T25.299** Burn of second degree of multiple sites of unspecified ankle and foot

● **T25.3** Burn of third degree of ankle and foot
   Use additional external cause code to identify the source, place and intent of the burn (X00-X19, X75-X77, X96-X98, Y92)
   ● **T25.31** Burn of third degree of ankle
      ● **T25.311** Burn of third degree of right ankle
      ● **T25.312** Burn of third degree of left ankle
      ● **T25.319** Burn of third degree of unspecified ankle
   ● **T25.32** Burn of third degree of foot
      Excludes2 burn of third degree of toe(s) (nail) (T25.33-)
      ● **T25.321** Burn of third degree of right foot
      ● **T25.322** Burn of third degree of left foot
      ● **T25.329** Burn of third degree of unspecified foot
   ● **T25.33** Burn of third degree of toe(s) (nail)
      ● **T25.331** Burn of third degree of right toe(s) (nail)
      ● **T25.332** Burn of third degree of left toe(s) (nail)
      ● **T25.339** Burn of third degree of unspecified toe(s) (nail)

● **T25.39** Burn of third degree of multiple sites of ankle and foot
   ● **T25.391** Burn of third degree of multiple sites of right ankle and foot
   ● **T25.392** Burn of third degree of multiple sites of left ankle and foot
   ● **T25.399** Burn of third degree of multiple sites of unspecified ankle and foot

● **T25.4** Corrosion of unspecified degree of ankle and foot
   Code first (T51-T65) to identify chemical and intent
   Use additional external cause code to identify place (Y92)
   ● **T25.41** Corrosion of unspecified degree of ankle
      ● **T25.411** Corrosion of unspecified degree of right ankle
      ● **T25.412** Corrosion of unspecified degree of left ankle
      ● **T25.419** Corrosion of unspecified degree of unspecified ankle
   ● **T25.42** Corrosion of unspecified degree of foot
      Excludes2 corrosion of unspecified degree of toe(s) (nail) (T25.43-)
      ● **T25.421** Corrosion of unspecified degree of right foot
      ● **T25.422** Corrosion of unspecified degree of left foot
      ● **T25.429** Corrosion of unspecified degree of unspecified foot
   ● **T25.43** Corrosion of unspecified degree of toe(s) (nail)
      ● **T25.431** Corrosion of unspecified degree of right toe(s) (nail)
      ● **T25.432** Corrosion of unspecified degree of left toe(s) (nail)
      ● **T25.439** Corrosion of unspecified degree of unspecified toe(s) (nail)
   ● **T25.49** Corrosion of unspecified degree of multiple sites of ankle and foot
      ● **T25.491** Corrosion of unspecified degree of multiple sites of right ankle and foot
      ● **T25.492** Corrosion of unspecified degree of multiple sites of left ankle and foot
      ● **T25.499** Corrosion of unspecified degree of multiple sites of unspecified ankle and foot

● **T25.5** Corrosion of first degree of ankle and foot
   Code first (T51-T65) to identify chemical and intent
   Use additional external cause code to identify place (Y92)
   ● **T25.51** Corrosion of first degree of ankle
      ● **T25.511** Corrosion of first degree of right ankle
      ● **T25.512** Corrosion of first degree of left ankle
      ● **T25.519** Corrosion of first degree of unspecified ankle
   ● **T25.52** Corrosion of first degree of foot
      Excludes2 corrosion of first degree of toe(s) (nail) (T25.53-)
      ● **T25.521** Corrosion of first degree of right foot
      ● **T25.522** Corrosion of first degree of left foot
      ● **T25.529** Corrosion of first degree of unspecified foot

● **T25.53**   Corrosion of first degree of toe(s) (nail)

  ● **T25.531**   Corrosion of first degree of right toe(s) (nail)

  ● **T25.532**   Corrosion of first degree of left toe(s) (nail)

  ● **T25.539**   Corrosion of first degree of unspecified toe(s) (nail)

● **T25.59**   Corrosion of first degree of multiple sites of ankle and foot

  ● **T25.591**   Corrosion of first degree of multiple sites of right ankle and foot

  ● **T25.592**   Corrosion of first degree of multiple sites of left ankle and foot

  ● **T25.599**   Corrosion of first degree of multiple sites of unspecified ankle and foot

● **T25.6**   Corrosion of second degree of ankle and foot

  Code first (T51-T65) *to identify chemical and intent*

  Use additional external cause code to identify place (Y92)

  ● **T25.61**   Corrosion of second degree of ankle

    ● **T25.611**   Corrosion of second degree of right ankle

    ● **T25.612**   Corrosion of second degree of left ankle

    ● **T25.619**   Corrosion of second degree of unspecified ankle

  ● **T25.62**   Corrosion of second degree of foot

    Excludes2   corrosion of second degree of toe(s) (nail) (T25.63-)

    ● **T25.621**   Corrosion of second degree of right foot

    ● **T25.622**   Corrosion of second degree of left foot

    ● **T25.629**   Corrosion of second degree of unspecified foot

  ● **T25.63**   Corrosion of second degree of toe(s) (nail)

    ● **T25.631**   Corrosion of second degree of right toe(s) (nail)

    ● **T25.632**   Corrosion of second degree of left toe(s) (nail)

    ● **T25.639**   Corrosion of second degree of unspecified toe(s) (nail)

  ● **T25.69**   Corrosion of second degree of multiple sites of ankle and foot

    ● **T25.691**   Corrosion of second degree of right ankle and foot

    ● **T25.692**   Corrosion of second degree of left ankle and foot

    ● **T25.699**   Corrosion of second degree of unspecified ankle and foot

● **T25.7**   Corrosion of third degree of ankle and foot

  Code first (T51-T65) *to identify chemical and intent*

  Use additional external cause code to identify place (Y92)

  ● **T25.71**   Corrosion of third degree of ankle

    ● **T25.711**   Corrosion of third degree of right ankle

    ● **T25.712**   Corrosion of third degree of left ankle

    ● **T25.719**   Corrosion of third degree of unspecified ankle

● **T25.72**   Corrosion of third degree of foot

  Excludes2   corrosion of third degree of toe(s) (nail) (T25.73-)

  ● **T25.721**   Corrosion of third degree of right foot

  ● **T25.722**   Corrosion of third degree of left foot

  ● **T25.729**   Corrosion of third degree of unspecified foot

● **T25.73**   Corrosion of third degree of toe(s) (nail)

  ● **T25.731**   Corrosion of third degree of right toe(s) (nail)

  ● **T25.732**   Corrosion of third degree of left toe(s) (nail)

  ● **T25.739**   Corrosion of third degree of unspecified toe(s) (nail)

● **T25.79**   Corrosion of third degree of multiple sites of ankle and foot

  ● **T25.791**   Corrosion of third degree of multiple sites of right ankle and foot

  ● **T25.792**   Corrosion of third degree of multiple sites of left ankle and foot

  ● **T25.799**   Corrosion of third degree of multiple sites of unspecified ankle and foot

---

BURNS AND CORROSIONS CONFINED TO EYE AND INTERNAL ORGANS (T26-T28)

● **T26**   Burn and corrosion confined to eye and adnexa

  The appropriate 7th character is to be added to each code from category T26

A	initial encounter
D	subsequent encounter
S	sequela

  ● **T26.0**   Burn of eyelid and periocular area

    Use additional external cause code to identify the source, place and intent of the burn (X00-X19, X75-X77, X96-X98, Y92)

    X ● **T26.00**   Burn of unspecified eyelid and periocular area

    X ● **T26.01**   Burn of right eyelid and periocular area

    X ● **T26.02**   Burn of left eyelid and periocular area

  ● **T26.1**   Burn of cornea and conjunctival sac

    Use additional external cause code to identify the source, place and intent of the burn (X00-X19, X75-X77, X96-X98, Y92)

    X ● **T26.10**   Burn of cornea and conjunctival sac, unspecified eye

    X ● **T26.11**   Burn of cornea and conjunctival sac, right eye

    X ● **T26.12**   Burn of cornea and conjunctival sac, left eye

  ● **T26.2**   Burn with resulting rupture and destruction of eyeball

    Use additional external cause code to identify the source, place and intent of the burn (X00-X19, X75-X77, X96-X98, Y92)

    X ● **T26.20**   Burn with resulting rupture and destruction of unspecified eyeball

    X ● **T26.21**   Burn with resulting rupture and destruction of right eyeball

    X ● **T26.22**   Burn with resulting rupture and destruction of left eyeball

CHAPTER 19 (S00-T88)

CHAPTER 19 (S00-T88)

● **T26.3** **Burns of other specified parts** of eye and adnexa

Use additional external cause code to identify the source, place and intent of the burn (X00-X19, X75-X77, X96-X98, Y92)

X ● **T26.30** Burns of other specified parts of **unspecified eye** and adnexa

X ● **T26.31** Burns of other specified parts of **right eye** and adnexa

X ● **T26.32** Burns of other specified parts of **left eye** and adnexa

● **T26.4** **Burn of eye and adnexa, part unspecified**

Use additional external cause code to identify the source, place and intent of the burn (X00-X19, X75-X77, X96-X98, Y92)

X ● **T26.40** Burn of **unspecified eye** and adnexa, part unspecified

X ● **T26.41** Burn of **right eye** and adnexa, part unspecified

X ● **T26.42** Burn of **left eye** and adnexa, part unspecified

● **T26.5** **Corrosion of eyelid and periocular area**

Code first (T51-T65) to identify chemical and intent

Use additional external cause code to identify place (Y92)

X ● **T26.50** Corrosion of **unspecified** eyelid and periocular area

X ● **T26.51** Corrosion of **right** eyelid and periocular area

X ● **T26.52** Corrosion of **left** eyelid and periocular area

● **T26.6** **Corrosion of cornea and conjunctival sac**

Code first (T51-T65) to identify chemical and intent

Use additional external cause code to identify place (Y92)

X ● **T26.60** Corrosion of cornea and conjunctival sac, **unspecified eye**

X ● **T26.61** Corrosion of cornea and conjunctival sac, **right eye**

X ● **T26.62** Corrosion of cornea and conjunctival sac, **left eye**

● **T26.7** **Corrosion with resulting rupture and destruction of eyeball**

Code first (T51-T65) to identify chemical and intent

Use additional external cause code to identify place (Y92)

X ● **T26.70** Corrosion with resulting rupture and destruction of **unspecified** eyeball

X ● **T26.71** Corrosion with resulting rupture and destruction of **right** eyeball

X ● **T26.72** Corrosion with resulting rupture and destruction of **left** eyeball

● **T26.8** **Corrosions of other specified parts** of eye and adnexa

Code first (T51-T65) to identify chemical and intent

Use additional external cause code to identify place (Y92)

X ● **T26.80** Corrosions of other specified parts of **unspecified eye** and adnexa

X ● **T26.81** Corrosions of other specified parts of **right eye** and adnexa

X ● **T26.82** Corrosions of other specified parts of **left eye** and adnexa

● **T26.9** **Corrosion of eye and adnexa, part unspecified**

Code first (T51-T65) to identify chemical and intent

Use additional external cause code to identify place (Y92)

X ● **T26.90** Corrosion of **unspecified eye** and adnexa, part unspecified

X ● **T26.91** Corrosion of **right** eye and adnexa, part unspecified

X ● **T26.92** Corrosion of **left** eye and adnexa, part unspecified

● **T27** Burn and corrosion of **respiratory tract**

Use additional external cause code to identify the source and intent of the burn (X00-X19, X75-X77, X96-X98)

Use additional external cause code to identify place (Y92)

The appropriate 7th character is to be added to each code from category T27

A	initial encounter
D	subsequent encounter
S	sequela

X ● **T27.0** **Burn of larynx and trachea**

X ● **T27.1** **Burn involving larynx and trachea with lung**

X ● **T27.2** **Burn of other parts of respiratory tract**
Burn of thoracic cavity

X ● **T27.3** **Burn of respiratory tract, part unspecified**

X ● **T27.4** **Corrosion of larynx and trachea**
Code first (T51-T65) to identify chemical and intent

X ● **T27.5** **Corrosion involving larynx and trachea with lung**

X ● **T27.6** **Corrosion of other parts of respiratory tract**
Code first (T51-T65) to identify chemical and intent

X ● **T27.7** **Corrosion of respiratory tract, part unspecified**
Code first (T51-T65) to identify chemical and intent

● **T28** Burn and corrosion of **other internal organs**

Use additional external cause code to identify the source and intent of the burn (X00-X19, X75-X77, X96-X98)

Use additional external cause code to identify place (Y92)

The appropriate 7th character is to be added to each code from category T28

A	initial encounter
D	subsequent encounter
S	sequela

X ● **T28.0** **Burn of mouth and pharynx**

X ● **T28.1** **Burn of esophagus**

X ● **T28.2** **Burn of other parts of alimentary tract**

X ● **T28.3** **Burn of internal genitourinary organs**

X ● **T28.4** **Burns of other and unspecified internal organs**
Code first (T51-T65) to identify chemical and intent

  X ● **T28.40** Burn of **unspecified** internal organ

  ● **T28.41** Burn of **ear drum**

    ● **T28.411** Burn of **right ear drum**

    ● **T28.412** Burn of **left ear drum**

    ● **T28.419** Burn of **unspecified ear drum**

  X ● **T28.49** Burn of **other internal organ**

X ● **T28.5** **Corrosion of mouth and pharynx**
Code first (T51-T65) to identify chemical and intent

X ● **T28.6** **Corrosion of esophagus**
Code first (T51-T65) to identify chemical and intent

X ● **T28.7** **Corrosion of other parts of alimentary tract**
Code first (T51-T65) to identify chemical and intent

X ● **T28.8** **Corrosion of internal genitourinary organs**
Code first (T51-T65) to identify chemical and intent

● **T28.9** **Corrosions of other and unspecified internal organs**
Code first (T51-T65) to identify chemical and intent

  X ● **T28.90** Corrosions of **unspecified** internal organs

  ● **T28.91** Corrosions of **ear drum**

    ● **T28.911** Corrosions of **right ear drum**

    ● **T28.912** Corrosions of **left ear drum**

    ● **T28.919** Corrosions of **unspecified ear drum**

  X ● **T28.99** Corrosions of **other internal organs**

▶ New   ⇛ Revised   ~~deleted~~ Deleted   Excludes 1   Excludes 2   Includes   Use additional   Code first   Code also   Key words

OGCR Official Guidelines   X Assign placeholder X   ● Use Additional Character(s)   ▶ Manifestation Code   **Coding Clinic**

OGCR Section I.C.19.d.5.

Assign separate code for each burn site
When coding burns, assign separate codes for each burn site. Category T30, Burn and corrosion, body region unspecified is extremely vague and should rarely be used.

BURNS AND CORROSIONS OF MULTIPLE AND UNSPECIFIED BODY REGIONS (T30-T32)

- **T30**   **Burn and corrosion, body region unspecified**
    - **T30.0**   **Burn of unspecified body region, unspecified degree**
        This code is not for inpatient use. Code to specified site and degree of burns
        Burn NOS
        Multiple burns NOS
    - **T30.4**   **Corrosion of unspecified body region, unspecified degree**
        This code is not for inpatient use. Code to specified site and degree of corrosion
        Corrosion NOS
        Multiple corrosion NOS

- **T31**   **Burns classified according to extent of body surface involved**
    Note: This category is to be used as the primary code only when the site of the burn is unspecified. It should be used as a supplementary code with categories T20-T25 when the site is specified.
    - **T31.0**   **Burns involving less than 10% of body surface**
    - **T31.1**   **Burns involving 10-19% of body surface**
        - **T31.10**   **Burns involving 10-19% of body surface with 0% to 9% third degree burns**
            Burns involving 10-19% of body surface NOS
        - **T31.11**   **Burns involving 10-19% of body surface with 10-19% third degree burns**
    - **T31.2**   **Burns involving 20-29% of body surface**
        - **T31.20**   **Burns involving 20-29% of body surface with 0% to 9% third degree burns**
            Burns involving 20-29% of body surface NOS
        - **T31.21**   **Burns involving 20-29% of body surface with 10-19% third degree burns**
        - **T31.22**   **Burns involving 20-29% of body surface with 20-29% third degree burns**
    - **T31.3**   **Burns involving 30-39% of body surface**
        - **T31.30**   **Burns involving 30-39% of body surface with 0% to 9% third degree burns**
            Burns involving 30-39% of body surface NOS
        - **T31.31**   **Burns involving 30-39% of body surface with 10-19% third degree burns**
        - **T31.32**   **Burns involving 30-39% of body surface with 20-29% third degree burns**
        - **T31.33**   **Burns involving 30-39% of body surface with 30-39% third degree burns**
    - **T31.4**   **Burns involving 40-49% of body surface**
        - **T31.40**   **Burns involving 40-49% of body surface with 0% to 9% third degree burns**
            Burns involving 40-49% of body surface NOS
        - **T31.41**   **Burns involving 40-49% of body surface with 10-19% third degree burns**
        - **T31.42**   **Burns involving 40-49% of body surface with 20-29% third degree burns**
        - **T31.43**   **Burns involving 40-49% of body surface with 30-39% third degree burns**
        - **T31.44**   **Burns involving 40-49% of body surface with 40-49% third degree burns**
    - **T31.5**   **Burns involving 50-59% of body surface**
        - **T31.50**   **Burns involving 50-59% of body surface with 0% to 9% third degree burns**
            Burns involving 50-59% of body surface NOS
        - **T31.51**   **Burns involving 50-59% of body surface with 10-19% third degree burns**

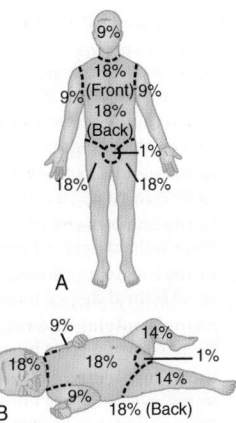

Figure 19-16   Rule of nines: percentages of total body area. (From Marx: Rosen's Emergency Medicine: Concepts and Clinical Practice, ed 6, Mosby, 2006)

- **T31.52**   **Burns involving 50-59% of body surface with 20-29% third degree burns**
- **T31.53**   **Burns involving 50-59% of body surface with 30-39% third degree burns**
- **T31.54**   **Burns involving 50-59% of body surface with 40-49% third degree burns**
- **T31.55**   **Burns involving 50-59% of body surface with 50-59% third degree burns**
- **T31.6**   **Burns involving 60-69% of body surface**
    - **T31.60**   **Burns involving 60-69% of body surface with 0% to 9% third degree burns**
        Burns involving 60-69% of body surface NOS
    - **T31.61**   **Burns involving 60-69% of body surface with 10-19% third degree burns**
    - **T31.62**   **Burns involving 60-69% of body surface with 20-29% third degree burns**
    - **T31.63**   **Burns involving 60-69% of body surface with 30-39% third degree burns**
    - **T31.64**   **Burns involving 60-69% of body surface with 40-49% third degree burns**
    - **T31.65**   **Burns involving 60-69% of body surface with 50-59% third degree burns**
    - **T31.66**   **Burns involving 60-69% of body surface with 60-69% third degree burns**
- **T31.7**   **Burns involving 70-79% of body surface**
    - **T31.70**   **Burns involving 70-79% of body surface with 0% to 9% third degree burns**
        Burns involving 70-79% of body surface NOS
    - **T31.71**   **Burns involving 70-79% of body surface with 10-19% third degree burns**
    - **T31.72**   **Burns involving 70-79% of body surface with 20-29% third degree burns**
    - **T31.73**   **Burns involving 70-79% of body surface with 30-39% third degree burns**
    - **T31.74**   **Burns involving 70-79% of body surface with 40-49% third degree burns**
    - **T31.75**   **Burns involving 70-79% of body surface with 50-59% third degree burns**
    - **T31.76**   **Burns involving 70-79% of body surface with 60-69% third degree burns**
    - **T31.77**   **Burns involving 70-79% of body surface with 70-79% third degree burns**

CHAPTER 19 (S00-T88)

● **T31.8**   **Burns involving 80-89% of body surface**

    T31.80   **Burns involving 80-89% of body surface with 0% to 9% third degree burns**
        Burns involving 80-89% of body surface NOS

    T31.81   **Burns involving 80-89% of body surface with 10-19% third degree burns**

    T31.82   **Burns involving 80-89% of body surface with 20-29% third degree burns**

    T31.83   **Burns involving 80-89% of body surface with 30-39% third degree burns**

    T31.84   **Burns involving 80-89% of body surface with 40-49% third degree burns**

    T31.85   **Burns involving 80-89% of body surface with 50-59% third degree burns**

    T31.86   **Burns involving 80-89% of body surface with 60-69% third degree burns**

    T31.87   **Burns involving 80-89% of body surface with 70-79% third degree burns**

    T31.88   **Burns involving 80-89% of body surface with 80-89% third degree burns**

● **T31.9**   **Burns involving 90% or more of body surface**

    T31.90   **Burns involving 90% or more of body surface with 0% to 9% third degree burns**
        Burns involving 90% or more of body surface NOS

    T31.91   **Burns involving 90% or more of body surface with 10-19% third degree burns**

    T31.92   **Burns involving 90% or more of body surface with 20-29% third degree burns**

    T31.93   **Burns involving 90% or more of body surface with 30-39% third degree burns**

    T31.94   **Burns involving 90% or more of body surface with 40-49% third degree burns**

    T31.95   **Burns involving 90% or more of body surface with 50-59% third degree burns**

    T31.96   **Burns involving 90% or more of body surface with 60-69% third degree burns**

    T31.97   **Burns involving 90% or more of body surface with 70-79% third degree burns**

    T31.98   **Burns involving 90% or more of body surface with 80-89% third degree burns**

    T31.99   **Burns involving 90% or more of body surface with 90% or more third degree burns**

● **T32**   **Corrosions classified according to extent of body surface involved**

    Note: This category is to be used as the primary code only when the site of the corrosion is unspecified. It may be used as a supplementary code with categories T20-T25 when the site is specified.

    T32.0   **Corrosions involving less than 10% of body surface**

● **T32.1**   **Corrosions involving 10-19% of body surface**

    T32.10   **Corrosions involving 10-19% of body surface with 0% to 9% third degree corrosion**
        Corrosions involving 10-19% of body surface NOS

    T32.11   **Corrosions involving 10-19% of body surface with 10-19% third degree corrosion**

● **T32.2**   **Corrosions involving 20-29% of body surface**

    T32.20   **Corrosions involving 20-29% of body surface with 0% to 9% third degree corrosion**

    T32.21   **Corrosions involving 20-29% of body surface with 10-19% third degree corrosion**

    T32.22   **Corrosions involving 20-29% of body surface with 20-29% third degree corrosion**

● **T32.3**   **Corrosions involving 30-39% of body surface**

    T32.30   **Corrosions involving 30-39% of body surface with 0% to 9% third degree corrosion**

    T32.31   **Corrosions involving 30-39% of body surface with 10-19% third degree corrosion**

    T32.32   **Corrosions involving 30-39% of body surface with 20-29% third degree corrosion**

    T32.33   **Corrosions involving 30-39% of body surface with 30-39% third degree corrosion**

● **T32.4**   **Corrosions involving 40-49% of body surface**

    T32.40   **Corrosions involving 40-49% of body surface with 0% to 9% third degree corrosion**

    T32.41   **Corrosions involving 40-49% of body surface with 10-19% third degree corrosion**

    T32.42   **Corrosions involving 40-49% of body surface with 20-29% third degree corrosion**

    T32.43   **Corrosions involving 40-49% of body surface with 30-39% third degree corrosion**

    T32.44   **Corrosions involving 40-49% of body surface with 40-49% third degree corrosion**

● **T32.5**   **Corrosions involving 50-59% of body surface**

    T32.50   **Corrosions involving 50-59% of body surface with 0% to 9% third degree corrosion**

    T32.51   **Corrosions involving 50-59% of body surface with 10-19% third degree corrosion**

    T32.52   **Corrosions involving 50-59% of body surface with 20-29% third degree corrosion**

    T32.53   **Corrosions involving 50-59% of body surface with 30-39% third degree corrosion**

    T32.54   **Corrosions involving 50-59% of body surface with 40-49% third degree corrosion**

    T32.55   **Corrosions involving 50-59% of body surface with 50-59% third degree corrosion**

● **T32.6**   **Corrosions involving 60-69% of body surface**

    T32.60   **Corrosions involving 60-69% of body surface with 0% to 9% third degree corrosion**

    T32.61   **Corrosions involving 60-69% of body surface with 10-19% third degree corrosion**

    T32.62   **Corrosions involving 60-69% of body surface with 20-29% third degree corrosion**

    T32.63   **Corrosions involving 60-69% of body surface with 30-39% third degree corrosion**

    T32.64   **Corrosions involving 60-69% of body surface with 40-49% third degree corrosion**

    T32.65   **Corrosions involving 60-69% of body surface with 50-59% third degree corrosion**

    T32.66   **Corrosions involving 60-69% of body surface with 60-69% third degree corrosion**

● **T32.7**   **Corrosions involving 70-79% of body surface**

    T32.70   **Corrosions involving 70-79% of body surface with 0% to 9% third degree corrosion**

    T32.71   **Corrosions involving 70-79% of body surface with 10-19% third degree corrosion**

    T32.72   **Corrosions involving 70-79% of body surface with 20-29% third degree corrosion**

    T32.73   **Corrosions involving 70-79% of body surface with 30-39% third degree corrosion**

    T32.74   **Corrosions involving 70-79% of body surface with 40-49% third degree corrosion**

    T32.75   **Corrosions involving 70-79% of body surface with 50-59% third degree corrosion**

    T32.76   **Corrosions involving 70-79% of body surface with 60-69% third degree corrosion**

    T32.77   **Corrosions involving 70-79% of body surface with 70-79% third degree corrosion**

▶ New   ⇒ Revised   ~~deleted~~ Deleted   Excludes 1   Excludes 2   Includes   Use additional   Code first   Code also   Key words

OGCR Official Guidelines   X Assign placeholder X   ● Use Additional Character(s)   ▶ Manifestation Code   **Coding Clinic**

● **T32.8**   Corrosions involving 80-89% of body surface

     T32.80   Corrosions involving 80-89% of body surface with 0% to 9% third degree corrosion

     T32.81   Corrosions involving 80-89% of body surface with 10-19% third degree corrosion

     T32.82   Corrosions involving 80-89% of body surface with 20-29% third degree corrosion

     T32.83   Corrosions involving 80-89% of body surface with 30-39% third degree corrosion

     T32.84   Corrosions involving 80-89% of body surface with 40-49% third degree corrosion

     T32.85   Corrosions involving 80-89% of body surface with 50-59% third degree corrosion

     T32.86   Corrosions involving 80-89% of body surface with 60-69% third degree corrosion

     T32.87   Corrosions involving 80-89% of body surface with 70-79% third degree corrosion

     T32.88   Corrosions involving 80-89% of body surface with 80-89% third degree corrosion

● **T32.9**   Corrosions involving 90% or more of body surface

     T32.90   Corrosions involving 90% or more of body surface with 0% to 9% third degree corrosion

     T32.91   Corrosions involving 90% or more of body surface with 10-19% third degree corrosion

     T32.92   Corrosions involving 90% or more of body surface with 20-29% third degree corrosion

     T32.93   Corrosions involving 90% or more of body surface with 30-39% third degree corrosion

     T32.94   Corrosions involving 90% or more of body surface with 40-49% third degree corrosion

     T32.95   Corrosions involving 90% or more of body surface with 50-59% third degree corrosion

     T32.96   Corrosions involving 90% or more of body surface with 60-69% third degree corrosion

     T32.97   Corrosions involving 90% or more of body surface with 70-79% third degree corrosion

     T32.98   Corrosions involving 90% or more of body surface with 80-89% third degree corrosion

     T32.99   Corrosions involving 90% or more of body surface with 90% or more third degree corrosion

FROSTBITE (T33-T34)

Excludes2   hypothermia and other effects of reduced temperature (T68, T69.-)

● **T33**   **Superficial frostbite**

   Includes   frostbite with partial thickness skin loss

   The appropriate 7th character is to be added to each code from category T33

     A   initial encounter
     D   subsequent encounter
     S   sequela

● **T33.0**   Superficial frostbite of head

    ● T33.01   Superficial frostbite of ear

      ● T33.011   Superficial frostbite of right ear

      ● T33.012   Superficial frostbite of left ear

      ● T33.019   Superficial frostbite of unspecified ear

   X ● T33.02   Superficial frostbite of nose

   X ● T33.09   Superficial frostbite of other part of head

X ● **T33.1**   Superficial frostbite of neck

X ● **T33.2**   Superficial frostbite of thorax

X ● **T33.3**   Superficial frostbite of abdominal wall, lower back and pelvis

● **T33.4**   Superficial frostbite of arm

   Excludes2   superficial frostbite of wrist and hand (T33.5-)

   X ● T33.40   Superficial frostbite of unspecified arm

   X ● T33.41   Superficial frostbite of right arm

   X ● T33.42   Superficial frostbite of left arm

● **T33.5**   Superficial frostbite of wrist, hand, and fingers

    ● T33.51   Superficial frostbite of wrist

      ● T33.511   Superficial frostbite of right wrist

      ● T33.512   Superficial frostbite of left wrist

      ● T33.519   Superficial frostbite of unspecified wrist

    ● T33.52   Superficial frostbite of hand

      Excludes2   superficial frostbite of fingers (T33.53-)

      ● T33.521   Superficial frostbite of right hand

      ● T33.522   Superficial frostbite of left hand

      ● T33.529   Superficial frostbite of unspecified hand

    ● T33.53   Superficial frostbite of finger(s)

      ● T33.531   Superficial frostbite of right finger(s)

      ● T33.532   Superficial frostbite of left finger(s)

      ● T33.539   Superficial frostbite of unspecified finger(s)

● **T33.6**   Superficial frostbite of hip and thigh

   X ● T33.60   Superficial frostbite of unspecified hip and thigh

   X ● T33.61   Superficial frostbite of right hip and thigh

   X ● T33.62   Superficial frostbite of left hip and thigh

● **T33.7**   Superficial frostbite of knee and lower leg

   Excludes2   superficial frostbite of ankle and foot (T33.8-)

   X ● T33.70   Superficial frostbite of unspecified knee and lower leg

   X ● T33.71   Superficial frostbite of right knee and lower leg

   X ● T33.72   Superficial frostbite of left knee and lower leg

● **T33.8**   Superficial frostbite of ankle, foot, and toe(s)

    ● T33.81   Superficial frostbite of ankle

      ● T33.811   Superficial frostbite of right ankle

      ● T33.812   Superficial frostbite of left ankle

      ● T33.819   Superficial frostbite of unspecified ankle

    ● T33.82   Superficial frostbite of foot

      ● T33.821   Superficial frostbite of right foot

      ● T33.822   Superficial frostbite of left foot

      ● T33.829   Superficial frostbite of unspecified foot

    ● T33.83   Superficial frostbite of toe(s)

      ● T33.831   Superficial frostbite of right toe(s)

      ● T33.832   Superficial frostbite of left toe(s)

      ● T33.839   Superficial frostbite of unspecified toe(s)

● **T33.9**   Superficial frostbite of other and unspecified sites

   X ● T33.90   Superficial frostbite of unspecified sites
      Superficial frostbite NOS

   X ● T33.99   Superficial frostbite of other sites
      Superficial frostbite of leg NOS
      Superficial frostbite of trunk NOS

CHAPTER 19 (S00-T88)

● **T34   Frostbite with tissue necrosis**

The appropriate 7th character is to be added to each code from category T34

A	initial encounter
D	subsequent encounter
S	sequela

● **T34.0   Frostbite with tissue necrosis of head**

● **T34.01   Frostbite with tissue necrosis of ear**

● **T34.011   Frostbite with tissue necrosis of right ear**

● **T34.012   Frostbite with tissue necrosis of left ear**

● **T34.019   Frostbite with tissue necrosis of unspecified ear**

X ● **T34.02   Frostbite with tissue necrosis of nose**

X ● **T34.09   Frostbite with tissue necrosis of other part of head**

X ● **T34.1   Frostbite with tissue necrosis of neck**

X ● **T34.2   Frostbite with tissue necrosis of thorax**

X ● **T34.3   Frostbite with tissue necrosis of abdominal wall, lower back and pelvis**

● **T34.4   Frostbite with tissue necrosis of arm**

Excludes2   frostbite with tissue necrosis of wrist and hand (T34.5-)

X ● **T34.40   Frostbite with tissue necrosis of unspecified arm**

X ● **T34.41   Frostbite with tissue necrosis of right arm**

X ● **T34.42   Frostbite with tissue necrosis of left arm**

● **T34.5   Frostbite with tissue necrosis of wrist, hand, and finger(s)**

● **T34.51   Frostbite with tissue necrosis of wrist**

● **T34.511   Frostbite with tissue necrosis of right wrist**

● **T34.512   Frostbite with tissue necrosis of left wrist**

● **T34.519   Frostbite with tissue necrosis of unspecified wrist**

● **T34.52   Frostbite with tissue necrosis of hand**

Excludes2   frostbite with tissue necrosis of finger(s) (T34.53-)

● **T34.521   Frostbite with tissue necrosis of right hand**

● **T34.522   Frostbite with tissue necrosis of left hand**

● **T34.529   Frostbite with tissue necrosis of unspecified hand**

● **T34.53   Frostbite with tissue necrosis of finger(s)**

● **T34.531   Frostbite with tissue necrosis of right finger(s)**

● **T34.532   Frostbite with tissue necrosis of left finger(s)**

● **T34.539   Frostbite with tissue necrosis of unspecified finger(s)**

● **T34.6   Frostbite with tissue necrosis of hip and thigh**

X ● **T34.60   Frostbite with tissue necrosis of unspecified hip and thigh**

X ● **T34.61   Frostbite with tissue necrosis of right hip and thigh**

X ● **T34.62   Frostbite with tissue necrosis of left hip and thigh**

● **T34.7   Frostbite with tissue necrosis of knee and lower leg**

Excludes2   frostbite with tissue necrosis of ankle and foot (T34.8-)

X ● **T34.70   Frostbite with tissue necrosis of unspecified knee and lower leg**

X ● **T34.71   Frostbite with tissue necrosis of right knee and lower leg**

X ● **T34.72   Frostbite with tissue necrosis of left knee and lower leg**

● **T34.8   Frostbite with tissue necrosis of ankle, foot, and toe(s)**

● **T34.81   Frostbite with tissue necrosis of ankle**

● **T34.811   Frostbite with tissue necrosis of right ankle**

● **T34.812   Frostbite with tissue necrosis of left ankle**

● **T34.819   Frostbite with tissue necrosis of unspecified ankle**

● **T34.82   Frostbite with tissue necrosis of foot**

● **T34.821   Frostbite with tissue necrosis of right foot**

● **T34.822   Frostbite with tissue necrosis of left foot**

● **T34.829   Frostbite with tissue necrosis of unspecified foot**

● **T34.83   Frostbite with tissue necrosis of toe(s)**

● **T34.831   Frostbite with tissue necrosis of right toe(s)**

● **T34.832   Frostbite with tissue necrosis of left toe(s)**

● **T34.839   Frostbite with tissue necrosis of unspecified toe(s)**

● **T34.9   Frostbite with tissue necrosis of other and unspecified sites**

X ● **T34.90   Frostbite with tissue necrosis of unspecified sites**

Frostbite with tissue necrosis NOS

X ● **T34.99   Frostbite with tissue necrosis of other sites**

Frostbite with tissue necrosis of leg NOS
Frostbite with tissue necrosis of trunk NOS

OGCR See Section I.C.19.e.

Adverse Effects, Poisoning , Underdosing and Toxic Effects
Codes in categories T36-T65 are combination codes that include the substance that was taken as well as the intent. No additional external cause code is required for poisonings, toxic effects, adverse effects and underdosing codes.

POISONING BY, ADVERSE EFFECTS OF AND UNDERDOSING OF DRUGS MEDICAMENTS AND BIOLOGICAL SUBSTANCES (T36-T50)

Includes   adverse effect of correct substance properly administered
poisoning by overdose of substance
poisoning by wrong substance given or taken in error
underdosing by (inadvertently) (deliberately) taking less substance than prescribed or instructed

Code first, for adverse effects, the nature of the adverse effect, such as:
adverse effect NOS (T88.7)
aspirin gastritis (K29.-)
blood disorders (D56-D76)
contact dermatitis (L23-L25)
dermatitis due to substances taken internally (L27.-)
nephropathy (N14.0-N14.2)

Note: The drug giving rise to the adverse effect should be identified by use of codes from categories T36-T50 with fifth or sixth character 5.

Use additional code(s) to specify:
manifestations of poisoning
underdosing or failure in dosage during medical and surgical care (Y63.6, Y63.8-Y63.9)
underdosing of medication regimen (Z91.12-, Z91.13-)

Excludes1   toxic reaction to local anesthesia in pregnancy (O29.3-)

Excludes2   abuse and dependence of psychoactive substances (F10-F19)
abuse of non-dependence-producing substances (F55.-)
drug reaction and poisoning affecting newborn (P00-P96)
pathological drug intoxication (inebriation) (F10-F19)

▶ New   ⟾ Revised   ~~deleted~~ Deleted   Excludes 1   Excludes 2   Includes   Use additional   Code first   Code also   Key words

OGCR Official Guidelines   X Assign placeholder X   ● Use Additional Character(s)   ▷ Manifestation Code   **Coding Clinic**

● **T36   Poisoning by, adverse effect of and underdosing of systemic antibiotics**

> **Excludes1**   antineoplastic antibiotics (T45.1-)
> locally applied antibiotic NEC (T49.0)
> topically used antibiotic for ear, nose and throat (T49.6)
> topically used antibiotic for eye (T49.5)

> The appropriate 7th character is to be added to each code from category T36

> | | |
> |---|---|
> | A | initial encounter |
> | D | subsequent encounter |
> | S | sequela |

● **T36.0   Poisoning by, adverse effect of and underdosing of penicillins**

  ● **T36.0X   Poisoning by, adverse effect of and underdosing of penicillins**

    ● **T36.0X1   Poisoning by penicillins, accidental (unintentional)**
    Poisoning by penicillins NOS

    ● **T36.0X2   Poisoning by penicillins, intentional self-harm**

    ● **T36.0X3   Poisoning by penicillins, assault**

    ● **T36.0X4   Poisoning by penicillins, undetermined**

    ● **T36.0X5   Adverse effect of penicillins**

    ● **T36.0X6   Underdosing of penicillins**

● **T36.1   Poisoning by, adverse effect of and underdosing of cephalosporins and other betalactam antibiotics**

  ● **T36.1X   Poisoning by, adverse effect of and underdosing of cephalosporins and other beta-lactam antibiotics**

    ● **T36.1X1   Poisoning by cephalosporins and other beta-lactam antibiotics, accidental (unintentional)**
    Poisoning by cephalosporins and other beta-lactam antibiotics NOS

    ● **T36.1X2   Poisoning by cephalosporins and other beta-lactam antibiotics, intentional self-harm**

    ● **T36.1X3   Poisoning by cephalosporins and other beta-lactam antibiotics, assault**

    ● **T36.1X4   Poisoning by cephalosporins and other beta-lactam antibiotics, undetermined**

    ● **T36.1X5   Adverse effect of cephalosporins and other beta-lactam antibiotics**

    ● **T36.1X6   Underdosing of cephalosporins and other beta-lactam antibiotics**

● **T36.2   Poisoning by, adverse effect of and underdosing of chloramphenicol group**

  ● **T36.2X   Poisoning by, adverse effect of and underdosing of chloramphenicol group**

    ● **T36.2X1   Poisoning by chloramphenicol group, accidental (unintentional)**
    Poisoning by chloramphenicol group NOS

    ● **T36.2X2   Poisoning by chloramphenicol group, intentional self-harm**

    ● **T36.2X3   Poisoning by chloramphenicol group, assault**

    ● **T36.2X4   Poisoning by chloramphenicol group, undetermined**

    ● **T36.2X5   Adverse effect of chloramphenicol group**

    ● **T36.2X6   Underdosing of chloramphenicol group**

● **T36.3   Poisoning by, adverse effect of and underdosing of macrolides**

  ● **T36.3X   Poisoning by, adverse effect of and underdosing of macrolides**

    ● **T36.3X1   Poisoning by macrolides, accidental (unintentional)**
    Poisoning by macrolides NOS

    ● **T36.3X2   Poisoning by macrolides, intentional self-harm**

    ● **T36.3X3   Poisoning by macrolides, assault**

    ● **T36.3X4   Poisoning by macrolides, undetermined**

    ● **T36.3X5   Adverse effect of macrolides**

    ● **T36.3X6   Underdosing of macrolides**

● **T36.4   Poisoning by, adverse effect of and underdosing of tetracyclines**

  ● **T36.4X   Poisoning by, adverse effect of and underdosing of tetracyclines**

    ● **T36.4X1   Poisoning by tetracyclines, accidental (unintentional)**
    Poisoning by tetracyclines NOS

    ● **T36.4X2   Poisoning by tetracyclines, intentional self-harm**

    ● **T36.4X3   Poisoning by tetracyclines, assault**

    ● **T36.4X4   Poisoning by tetracyclines, undetermined**

    ● **T36.4X5   Adverse effect of tetracyclines**

    ● **T36.4X6   Underdosing of tetracyclines**

● **T36.5   Poisoning by, adverse effect of and underdosing of aminoglycosides**
Poisoning by, adverse effect of and underdosing of streptomycin

  ● **T36.5X   Poisoning by, adverse effect of and underdosing of aminoglycosides**

    ● **T36.5X1   Poisoning by aminoglycosides, accidental (unintentional)**
    Poisoning by aminoglycosides NOS

    ● **T36.5X2   Poisoning by aminoglycosides, intentional self-harm**

    ● **T36.5X3   Poisoning by aminoglycosides, assault**

    ● **T36.5X4   Poisoning by aminoglycosides, undetermined**

    ● **T36.5X5   Adverse effect of aminoglycosides**

    ● **T36.5X6   Underdosing of aminoglycosides**

● **T36.6   Poisoning by, adverse effect of and underdosing of rifampicins**

  ● **T36.6X   Poisoning by, adverse effect of and underdosing of rifampicins**

    ● **T36.6X1   Poisoning by rifampicins, accidental (unintentional)**
    Poisoning by rifampicins NOS

    ● **T36.6X2   Poisoning by rifampicins, intentional self-harm**

    ● **T36.6X3   Poisoning by rifampicins, assault**

    ● **T36.6X4   Poisoning by rifampicins, undetermined**

    ● **T36.6X5   Adverse effect of rifampicins**

    ● **T36.6X6   Underdosing of rifampicins**

CHAPTER 19 (S00-T88)

CHAPTER 19 (S00-T88)

● T36.7   Poisoning by, adverse effect of and underdosing of antifungal antibiotics, systemically used

  ● T36.7X   Poisoning by, adverse effect of and underdosing of antifungal antibiotics, systemically used

    ● T36.7X1   Poisoning by antifungal antibiotics, systemically used, accidental (unintentional)
      Poisoning by antifungal antibiotics, systemically used NOS

    ● T36.7X2   Poisoning by antifungal antibiotics, systemically used, intentional self-harm

    ● T36.7X3   Poisoning by antifungal antibiotics, systemically used, assault

    ● T36.7X4   Poisoning by antifungal antibiotics, systemically used, undetermined

    ● T36.7X5   Adverse effect of antifungal antibiotics, systemically used

    ● T36.7X6   Underdosing of antifungal antibiotics, systemically used

● T36.8   Poisoning by, adverse effect of and underdosing of other systemic antibiotics

  ● T36.8X   Poisoning by, adverse effect of and underdosing of other systemic antibiotics

    ● T36.8X1   Poisoning by other systemic antibiotics, accidental (unintentional)
      Poisoning by other systemic antibiotics NOS

    ● T36.8X2   Poisoning by other systemic antibiotics, intentional self-harm

    ● T36.8X3   Poisoning by other systemic antibiotics, assault

    ● T36.8X4   Poisoning by other systemic antibiotics, undetermined

    ● T36.8X5   Adverse effect of other systemic antibiotics
      Coding Clinic: 2017, Q1, P39

    ● T36.8X6   Underdosing of other systemic antibiotics

● T36.9   Poisoning by, adverse effect of and underdosing of unspecified systemic antibiotic

  X ● T36.91   Poisoning by unspecified systemic antibiotic, accidental (unintentional)
      Poisoning by systemic antibiotic NOS

  X ● T36.92   Poisoning by unspecified systemic antibiotic, intentional self-harm

  X ● T36.93   Poisoning by unspecified systemic antibiotic, assault

  X ● T36.94   Poisoning by unspecified systemic antibiotic, undetermined

  X ● T36.95   Adverse effect of unspecified systemic antibiotic

  X ● T36.96   Underdosing of unspecified systemic antibiotic

● T37   Poisoning by, adverse effect of and underdosing of other systemic anti-infectives and antiparasitics

  Excludes1   anti-infectives topically used for ear, nose and throat (T49.6-)
    anti-infectives topically used for eye (T49.5-)
    locally applied anti-infectives NEC (T49.0-)

  The appropriate 7th character is to be added to each code from category T37

A	initial encounter
D	subsequent encounter
S	sequela

● T37.0   Poisoning by, adverse effect of and underdosing of sulfonamides

  ● T37.0X   Poisoning by, adverse effect of and underdosing of sulfonamides

    ● T37.0X1   Poisoning by sulfonamides, accidental (unintentional)
      Poisoning by sulfonamides NOS

    ● T37.0X2   Poisoning by sulfonamides, intentional self-harm

    ● T37.0X3   Poisoning by sulfonamides, assault

    ● T37.0X4   Poisoning by sulfonamides, undetermined

    ● T37.0X5   Adverse effect of sulfonamides

    ● T37.0X6   Underdosing of sulfonamides

● T37.1   Poisoning by, adverse effect of and underdosing of antimycobacterial drugs

  Excludes1   rifampicins (T36.6-) streptomycin (T36.5-)

  ● T37.1X   Poisoning by, adverse effect of and underdosing of antimycobacterial drugs

    ● T37.1X1   Poisoning by antimycobacterial drugs, accidental (unintentional)
      Poisoning by antimycobacterial drugs NOS

    ● T37.1X2   Poisoning by antimycobacterial drugs, intentional self-harm

    ● T37.1X3   Poisoning by antimycobacterial drugs, assault

    ● T37.1X4   Poisoning by antimycobacterial drugs, undetermined

    ● T37.1X5   Adverse effect of antimycobacterial drugs

    ● T37.1X6   Underdosing of antimycobacterial drugs

● T37.2   Poisoning by, adverse effect of and underdosing of antimalarials and drugs acting on other blood protozoa

  Excludes1   hydroxyquinoline derivatives (T37.8-)

  ● T37.2X   Poisoning by, adverse effect of and underdosing of antimalarials and drugs acting on other blood protozoa

    ● T37.2X1   Poisoning by antimalarials and drugs acting on other blood protozoa, accidental (unintentional)
      Poisoning by antimalarials and drugs acting on other blood protozoa NOS

    ● T37.2X2   Poisoning by antimalarials and drugs acting on other blood protozoa, intentional self-harm

    ● T37.2X3   Poisoning by antimalarials and drugs acting on other blood protozoa, assault

    ● T37.2X4   Poisoning by antimalarials and drugs acting on other blood protozoa, undetermined

    ● T37.2X5   Adverse effect of antimalarials and drugs acting on other blood protozoa

    ● T37.2X6   Underdosing of antimalarials and drugs acting on other blood protozoa

● T37.3   Poisoning by, adverse effect of and underdosing of other antiprotozoal drugs

  ● T37.3X   Poisoning by, adverse effect of and underdosing of other antiprotozoal drugs

    ● T37.3X1   Poisoning by other antiprotozoal drugs, accidental (unintentional)
      Poisoning by other antiprotozoal drugs NOS

    ● T37.3X2   Poisoning by other antiprotozoal drugs, intentional self-harm

    ● T37.3X3   Poisoning by other antiprotozoal drugs, assault

    ● T37.3X4   Poisoning by other antiprotozoal drugs, undetermined

    ● T37.3X5   Adverse effect of other antiprotozoal drugs

    ● T37.3X6   Underdosing of other antiprotozoal drugs

▶ New   ⇒ Revised   d̶e̶l̶e̶t̶e̶d̶ Deleted   Excludes 1   Excludes 2   Includes   Use additional   Code first   Code also   Key words
OGCR Official Guidelines   X Assign placeholder X   ● Use Additional Character(s)   ▷ Manifestation Code   **Coding Clinic**

● **T37.4** Poisoning by, adverse effect of and underdosing of anthelminthics
  ● **T37.4X** Poisoning by, adverse effect of and underdosing of anthelminthics
    ● **T37.4X1** Poisoning by anthelminthics, accidental (unintentional)
        Poisoning by anthelminthics NOS
    ● **T37.4X2** Poisoning by anthelminthics, intentional self-harm
    ● **T37.4X3** Poisoning by anthelminthics, assault
    ● **T37.4X4** Poisoning by anthelminthics, undetermined
    ● **T37.4X5** Adverse effect of anthelminthics
    ● **T37.4X6** Underdosing of anthelminthics
● **T37.5** Poisoning by, adverse effect of and underdosing of antiviral drugs
    Excludes1 amantadine (T42.8-)
                   cytarabine (T45.1-)
  ● **T37.5X** Poisoning by, adverse effect of and underdosing of antiviral drugs
    ● **T37.5X1** Poisoning by antiviral drugs, accidental (unintentional)
        Poisoning by antiviral drugs NOS
    ● **T37.5X2** Poisoning by antiviral drugs, intentional self-harm
    ● **T37.5X3** Poisoning by antiviral drugs, assault
    ● **T37.5X4** Poisoning by antiviral drugs, undetermined
    ● **T37.5X5** Adverse effect of antiviral drugs
    ● **T37.5X6** Underdosing of antiviral drugs
● **T37.8** Poisoning by, adverse effect of and underdosing of other specified systemic anti-infectives and antiparasitics
        Poisoning by, adverse effect of and underdosing of hydroxyquinoline derivatives
    Excludes1 antimalarial drugs (T37.2-)
  ● **T37.8X** Poisoning by, adverse effect of and underdosing of other specified systemic anti-infectives and antiparasitics
    ● **T37.8X1** Poisoning by other specified systemic anti-infectives and antiparasitics, accidental (unintentional)
        Poisoning by other specified systemic anti-infectives and antiparasitics NOS
    ● **T37.8X2** Poisoning by other specified systemic anti-infectives and antiparasitics, intentional self-harm
    ● **T37.8X3** Poisoning by other specified systemic anti-infectives and antiparasitics, assault
    ● **T37.8X4** Poisoning by other specified systemic anti-infectives and antiparasitics, undetermined
    ● **T37.8X5** Adverse effect of other specified systemic anti-infectives and antiparasitics
    ● **T37.8X6** Underdosing of other specified systemic anti-infectives and antiparasitics
● **T37.9** Poisoning by, adverse effect of and underdosing of unspecified systemic anti-infective and antiparasitics
  X● **T37.91** Poisoning by unspecified systemic anti-infective and antiparasitics, accidental (unintentional)
        Poisoning by, adverse effect of and underdosing of systemic anti-infective and antiparasitics NOS
  X● **T37.92** Poisoning by unspecified systemic anti-infective and antiparasitics, intentional self-harm

  X● **T37.93** Poisoning by unspecified systemic anti-infective and antiparasitics, assault
  X● **T37.94** Poisoning by unspecified systemic anti-infective and antiparasitics, undetermined
  X● **T37.95** Adverse effect of unspecified systemic anti-infective and antiparasitic
  X● **T37.96** Underdosing of unspecified systemic anti-infectives and antiparasitics
● **T38** Poisoning by, adverse effect of and underdosing of hormones and their synthetic substitutes and antagonists, not elsewhere classified
    Excludes1 mineralocorticoids and their antagonists (T50.0-)
                   oxytocic hormones (T48.0-)
                   parathyroid hormones and derivatives (T50.9-)
    The appropriate 7th character is to be added to each code from category T38

A	initial encounter
D	subsequent encounter
S	sequela

● **T38.0** Poisoning by, adverse effect of and underdosing of glucocorticoids and synthetic analogues
    Excludes1 glucocorticoids, topically used (T49.-)
  ● **T38.0X** Poisoning by, adverse effect of and underdosing of glucocorticoids and synthetic analogues
    ● **T38.0X1** Poisoning by glucocorticoids and synthetic analogues, accidental (unintentional)
        Poisoning by glucocorticoids and synthetic analogues NOS
    ● **T38.0X2** Poisoning by glucocorticoids and synthetic analogues, intentional self-harm
    ● **T38.0X3** Poisoning by glucocorticoids and synthetic analogues, assault
    ● **T38.0X4** Poisoning by glucocorticoids and synthetic analogues, undetermined
    ● **T38.0X5** Adverse effect of glucocorticoids and synthetic analogues
    ● **T38.0X6** Underdosing of glucocorticoids and synthetic analogues
● **T38.1** Poisoning by, adverse effect of and underdosing of thyroid hormones and substitutes
  ● **T38.1X** Poisoning by, adverse effect of and underdosing of thyroid hormones and substitutes
    ● **T38.1X1** Poisoning by thyroid hormones and substitutes, accidental (unintentional)
        Poisoning by thyroid hormones and substitutes NOS
    ● **T38.1X2** Poisoning by thyroid hormones and substitutes, intentional self-harm
    ● **T38.1X3** Poisoning by thyroid hormones and substitutes, assault
    ● **T38.1X4** Poisoning by thyroid hormones and substitutes, undetermined
    ● **T38.1X5** Adverse effect of thyroid hormones and substitutes
    ● **T38.1X6** Underdosing of thyroid hormones and substitutes
● **T38.2** Poisoning by, adverse effect of and underdosing of antithyroid drugs
  ● **T38.2X** Poisoning by, adverse effect of and underdosing of antithyroid drugs
    ● **T38.2X1** Poisoning by antithyroid drugs, accidental (unintentional)
        Poisoning by antithyroid drugs NOS
    ● **T38.2X2** Poisoning by antithyroid drugs, intentional self-harm
    ● **T38.2X3** Poisoning by antithyroid drugs, assault

CHAPTER 19 (S00-T88)

- **T38.2X4** Poisoning by antithyroid drugs, undetermined
- **T38.2X5** Adverse effect of antithyroid drugs
- **T38.2X6** Underdosing of antithyroid drugs
- **T38.3** Poisoning by, adverse effect of and underdosing of insulin and oral hypoglycemic [antidiabetic] drugs
  - **T38.3X** Poisoning by, adverse effect of and underdosing of insulin and oral hypoglycemic [antidiabetic] drugs
    - **T38.3X1** Poisoning by insulin and oral hypoglycemic [antidiabetic] drugs, accidental (unintentional)
      Poisoning by insulin and oral hypoglycemic [antidiabetic] drugs NOS
    - **T38.3X2** Poisoning by insulin and oral hypoglycemic [antidiabetic] drugs, intentional self-harm
    - **T38.3X3** Poisoning by insulin and oral hypoglycemic [antidiabetic] drugs, assault
    - **T38.3X4** Poisoning by insulin and oral hypoglycemic [antidiabetic] drugs, undetermined
    - **T38.3X5** Adverse effect of insulin and oral hypoglycemic [antidiabetic] drugs
    - **T38.3X6** Underdosing of insulin and oral hypoglycemic [antidiabetic] drugs
- **T38.4** Poisoning by, adverse effect of and underdosing of oral contraceptives
  Poisoning by, adverse effect of and underdosing of multiple- and single-ingredient oral contraceptive preparations
  - **T38.4X** Poisoning by, adverse effect of and underdosing of oral contraceptives
    - **T38.4X1** Poisoning by oral contraceptives, accidental (unintentional)
      Poisoning by oral contraceptives NOS
    - **T38.4X2** Poisoning by oral contraceptives, intentional self-harm
    - **T38.4X3** Poisoning by oral contraceptives, assault
    - **T38.4X4** Poisoning by oral contraceptives, undetermined
    - **T38.4X5** Adverse effect of oral contraceptives
    - **T38.4X6** Underdosing of oral contraceptives
- **T38.5** Poisoning by, adverse effect of and underdosing of other estrogens and progestogens
  Poisoning by, adverse effect of and underdosing of estrogens and progestogens mixtures and substitutes
  - **T38.5X** Poisoning by, adverse effect of and underdosing of other estrogens and progestogens
    - **T38.5X1** Poisoning by other estrogens and progestogens, accidental (unintentional)
      Poisoning by other estrogens and progestogens NOS
    - **T38.5X2** Poisoning by other estrogens and progestogens, intentional self-harm
    - **T38.5X3** Poisoning by other estrogens and progestogens, assault
    - **T38.5X4** Poisoning by other estrogens and progestogens, undetermined
    - **T38.5X5** Adverse effect of other estrogens and progestogens
    - **T38.5X6** Underdosing of other estrogens and progestogens

- **T38.6** Poisoning by, adverse effect of and underdosing of antigonadotrophins, antiestrogens, antiandrogens, not elsewhere classified
  Poisoning by, adverse effect of and underdosing of tamoxifen
  - **T38.6X** Poisoning by, adverse effect of and underdosing of antigonadotrophins, antiestrogens, antiandrogens, not elsewhere classified
    - **T38.6X1** Poisoning by antigonadotrophins, antiestrogens, antiandrogens, not elsewhere classified, accidental (unintentional)
      Poisoning by antigonadotrophins, antiestrogens, antiandrogens, not elsewhere classified NOS
    - **T38.6X2** Poisoning by antigonadotrophins, antiestrogens, antiandrogens, not elsewhere classified, intentional self-harm
    - **T38.6X3** Poisoning by antigonadotrophins, antiestrogens, antiandrogens, not elsewhere classified, assault
    - **T38.6X4** Poisoning by antigonadotrophins, antiestrogens, antiandrogens, not elsewhere classified, undetermined
    - **T38.6X5** Adverse effect of antigonadotrophins, antiestrogens, antiandrogens, not elsewhere classified
    - **T38.6X6** Underdosing of antigonadotrophins, antiestrogens, antiandrogens, not elsewhere classified
- **T38.7** Poisoning by, adverse effect of and underdosing of androgens and anabolic congeners
  - **T38.7X** Poisoning by, adverse effect of and underdosing of androgens and anabolic congeners
    - **T38.7X1** Poisoning by androgens and anabolic congeners, accidental (unintentional)
      Poisoning by androgens and anabolic congeners NOS
    - **T38.7X2** Poisoning by androgens and anabolic congeners, intentional self-harm
    - **T38.7X3** Poisoning by androgens and anabolic congeners, assault
    - **T38.7X4** Poisoning by androgens and anabolic congeners, undetermined
    - **T38.7X5** Adverse effect of androgens and anabolic congeners
    - **T38.7X6** Underdosing of androgens and anabolic congeners
- **T38.8** Poisoning by, adverse effect of and underdosing of other and unspecified hormones and synthetic substitutes
  - **T38.80** Poisoning by, adverse effect of and underdosing of unspecified hormones and synthetic substitutes
    - **T38.801** Poisoning by unspecified hormones and synthetic substitutes, accidental (unintentional)
      Poisoning by unspecified hormones and synthetic substitutes NOS
    - **T38.802** Poisoning by unspecified hormones and synthetic substitutes, intentional self-harm
    - **T38.803** Poisoning by unspecified hormones and synthetic substitutes, assault
    - **T38.804** Poisoning by unspecified hormones and synthetic substitutes, undetermined
    - **T38.805** Adverse effect of unspecified hormones and synthetic substitutes
    - **T38.806** Underdosing of unspecified hormones and synthetic substitutes

▶ New   ⇒ Revised   ~~deleted~~ Deleted   Excludes 1   Excludes 2   Includes   Use additional   Code first   Code also   Key words

OGCR Official Guidelines   X Assign placeholder X   ● Use Additional Character(s)   ▶ Manifestation Code   **Coding Clinic**

● T38.81   Poisoning by, adverse effect of and underdosing of anterior pituitary [adenohypophyseal] hormones

     ● T38.811   Poisoning by anterior pituitary [adenohypophyseal] hormones, accidental (unintentional)
         Poisoning by anterior pituitary [adenohypophyseal] hormones NOS

     ● T38.812   Poisoning by anterior pituitary [adenohypophyseal] hormones, intentional self-harm

     ● T38.813   Poisoning by anterior pituitary [adenohypophyseal] hormones, assault

     ● T38.814   Poisoning by anterior pituitary [adenohypophyseal] hormones, undetermined

     ● T38.815   Adverse effect of anterior pituitary [adenohypophyseal] hormones

     ● T38.816   Underdosing of anterior pituitary [adenohypophyseal] hormones

● T38.89   Poisoning by, adverse effect of and underdosing of other hormones and synthetic substitutes

     ● T38.891   Poisoning by other hormones and synthetic substitutes, accidental (unintentional)
         Poisoning by other hormones and synthetic substitutes NOS

     ● T38.892   Poisoning by other hormones and synthetic substitutes, intentional self-harm

     ● T38.893   Poisoning by other hormones and synthetic substitutes, assault

     ● T38.894   Poisoning by other hormones and synthetic substitutes, undetermined

     ● T38.895   Adverse effect of other hormones and synthetic substitutes

     ● T38.896   Underdosing of other hormones and synthetic substitutes

● T38.9   Poisoning by, adverse effect of and underdosing of other and unspecified hormone antagonists

     ● T38.90   Poisoning by, adverse effect of and underdosing of unspecified hormone antagonists

         ● T38.901   Poisoning by unspecified hormone antagonists, accidental (unintentional)
             Poisoning by unspecified hormone antagonists NOS

         ● T38.902   Poisoning by unspecified hormone antagonists, intentional self-harm

         ● T38.903   Poisoning by unspecified hormone antagonists, assault

         ● T38.904   Poisoning by unspecified hormone antagonists, undetermined

         ● T38.905   Adverse effect of unspecified hormone antagonists

         ● T38.906   Underdosing of unspecified hormone antagonists

     ● T38.99   Poisoning by, adverse effect of and underdosing of other hormone antagonists

         ● T38.991   Poisoning by other hormone antagonists, accidental (unintentional)
             Poisoning by other hormone antagonists NOS

         ● T38.992   Poisoning by other hormone antagonists, intentional self-harm

         ● T38.993   Poisoning by other hormone antagonists, assault

         ● T38.994   Poisoning by other hormone antagonists, undetermined

         ● T38.995   Adverse effect of other hormone antagonists

         ● T38.996   Underdosing of other hormone antagonists

● T39   Poisoning by, adverse effect of and underdosing of nonopioid analgesics, antipyretics and antirheumatics

     The appropriate 7th character is to be added to each code from category T39

A	initial encounter
D	subsequent encounter
S	sequela

     ● T39.0   Poisoning by, adverse effect of and underdosing of salicylates

         ● T39.01   Poisoning by, adverse effect of and underdosing of aspirin
             Poisoning by, adverse effect of and underdosing of acetylsalicylic acid

             ● T39.011   Poisoning by aspirin, accidental (unintentional)

             ● T39.012   Poisoning by aspirin, intentional self-harm

             ● T39.013   Poisoning by aspirin, assault

             ● T39.014   Poisoning by aspirin, undetermined

             ● T39.015   Adverse effect of aspirin
                 Coding Clinic: 2016, Q1, P15

             ● T39.016   Underdosing of aspirin

         ● T39.09   Poisoning by, adverse effect of and underdosing of other salicylates

             ● T39.091   Poisoning by salicylates, accidental (unintentional)
                 Poisoning by salicylates NOS

             ● T39.092   Poisoning by salicylates, intentional self-harm

             ● T39.093   Poisoning by salicylates, assault

             ● T39.094   Poisoning by salicylates, undetermined

             ● T39.095   Adverse effect of salicylates

             ● T39.096   Underdosing of salicylates

     ● T39.1   Poisoning by, adverse effect of and underdosing of 4-Aminophenol derivatives

         ● T39.1X   Poisoning by, adverse effect of and underdosing of 4-Aminophenol derivatives

             ● T39.1X1   Poisoning by 4-Aminophenol derivatives, accidental (unintentional)
                 Poisoning by 4-Aminophenol derivatives NOS

             ● T39.1X2   Poisoning by 4-Aminophenol derivatives, intentional self-harm

             ● T39.1X3   Poisoning by 4-Aminophenol derivatives, assault

             ● T39.1X4   Poisoning by 4-Aminophenol derivatives, undetermined

             ● T39.1X5   Adverse effect of 4-Aminophenol derivatives

             ● T39.1X6   Underdosing of 4-Aminophenol derivatives

● **T39.2　Poisoning by, adverse effect of and underdosing of pyrazolone derivatives**

　● **T39.2X　Poisoning by, adverse effect of and underdosing of pyrazolone derivatives**

　　● **T39.2X1　Poisoning by pyrazolone derivatives, accidental (unintentional)**
　　　　　Poisoning by pyrazolone derivatives NOS

　　● **T39.2X2　Poisoning by pyrazolone derivatives, intentional self-harm**

　　● **T39.2X3　Poisoning by pyrazolone derivatives, assault**

　　● **T39.2X4　Poisoning by pyrazolone derivatives, undetermined**

　　● **T39.2X5　Adverse effect of pyrazolone derivatives**

　　● **T39.2X6　Underdosing of pyrazolone derivatives**

● **T39.3　Poisoning by, adverse effect of and underdosing of other nonsteroidal anti-inflammatory drugs [NSAID]**

　● **T39.31　Poisoning by, adverse effect of and underdosing of propionic acid derivatives**
　　　Poisoning by, adverse effect of and underdosing of fenoprofen
　　　Poisoning by, adverse effect of and underdosing of flurbiprofen
　　　Poisoning by, adverse effect of and underdosing of ibuprofen
　　　Poisoning by, adverse effect of and underdosing of ketoprofen
　　　Poisoning by, adverse effect of and underdosing of naproxen
　　　Poisoning by, adverse effect of and underdosing of oxaprozin

　　● **T39.311　Poisoning by propionic acid derivatives, accidental (unintentional)**

　　● **T39.312　Poisoning by propionic acid derivatives, intentional self-harm**

　　● **T39.313　Poisoning by propionic acid derivatives, assault**

　　● **T39.314　Poisoning by propionic acid derivatives, undetermined**

　　● **T39.315　Adverse effect of propionic acid derivatives**

　　● **T39.316　Underdosing of propionic acid derivatives**

　● **T39.39　Poisoning by, adverse effect of and underdosing of other nonsteroidal anti-inflammatory drugs [NSAID]**

　　● **T39.391　Poisoning by other nonsteroidal anti-inflammatory drugs [NSAID], accidental (unintentional)**
　　　　　Poisoning by other nonsteroidal anti-inflammatory drugs NOS

　　● **T39.392　Poisoning by other nonsteroidal anti-inflammatory drugs [NSAID], intentional self-harm**

　　● **T39.393　Poisoning by other nonsteroidal anti-inflammatory drugs [NSAID], assault**

　　● **T39.394　Poisoning by other nonsteroidal anti-inflammatory drugs [NSAID], undetermined**

　　● **T39.395　Adverse effect of other nonsteroidal anti-inflammatory drugs [NSAID]**

　　● **T39.396　Underdosing of other nonsteroidal anti-inflammatory drugs [NSAID]**

● **T39.4　Poisoning by, adverse effect of and underdosing of antirheumatics, not elsewhere classified**

　Excludes1　poisoning by, adverse effect of and underdosing of glucocorticoids (T38.0-)
　　　poisoning by, adverse effect of and underdosing of salicylates (T39.0-)

　● **T39.4X　Poisoning by, adverse effect of and underdosing of antirheumatics, not elsewhere classified**

　　● **T39.4X1　Poisoning by antirheumatics, not elsewhere classified, accidental (unintentional)**
　　　　　Poisoning by antirheumatics, not elsewhere classified NOS

　　● **T39.4X2　Poisoning by antirheumatics, not elsewhere classified, intentional self-harm**

　　● **T39.4X3　Poisoning by antirheumatics, not elsewhere classified, assault**

　　● **T39.4X4　Poisoning by antirheumatics, not elsewhere classified, undetermined**

　　● **T39.4X5　Adverse effect of antirheumatics, not elsewhere classified**

　　● **T39.4X6　Underdosing of antirheumatics, not elsewhere classified**

● **T39.8　Poisoning by, adverse effect of and underdosing of other nonopioid analgesics and antipyretics, not elsewhere classified**

　● **T39.8X　Poisoning by, adverse effect of and underdosing of other nonopioid analgesics and antipyretics, not elsewhere classified**

　　● **T39.8X1　Poisoning by other nonopioid analgesics and antipyretics, not elsewhere classified, accidental (unintentional)**
　　　　　Poisoning by other nonopioid analgesics and antipyretics, not elsewhere classified NOS

　　● **T39.8X2　Poisoning by other nonopioid analgesics and antipyretics, not elsewhere classified, intentional self-harm**

　　● **T39.8X3　Poisoning by other nonopioid analgesics and antipyretics, not elsewhere classified, assault**

　　● **T39.8X4　Poisoning by other nonopioid analgesics and antipyretics, not elsewhere classified, undetermined**

　　● **T39.8X5　Adverse effect of other nonopioid analgesics and antipyretics, not elsewhere classified**

　　● **T39.8X6　Underdosing of other nonopioid analgesics and antipyretics, not elsewhere classified**

● **T39.9　Poisoning by, adverse effect of and underdosing of unspecified nonopioid analgesic, antipyretic and antirheumatic**

　X ● **T39.91　Poisoning by unspecified nonopioid analgesic, antipyretic and antirheumatic, accidental (unintentional)**
　　　　Poisoning by nonopioid analgesic, antipyretic and antirheumatic NOS

　X ● **T39.92　Poisoning by unspecified nonopioid analgesic, antipyretic and antirheumatic, intentional self-harm**

　X ● **T39.93　Poisoning by unspecified nonopioid analgesic, antipyretic and antirheumatic, assault**

▶ New　⇒ Revised　~~deleted~~ Deleted　Excludes 1　Excludes 2　Includes　Use additional　Code first　Code also　Key words
OGCR Official Guidelines　X Assign placeholder X　● Use Additional Character(s)　▶ Manifestation Code　Coding Clinic
1380

X● **T39.94** Poisoning by unspecified nonopioid analgesic, antipyretic and antirheumatic, undetermined

X● **T39.95** Adverse effect of unspecified nonopioid analgesic, antipyretic and antirheumatic

X● **T39.96** Underdosing of unspecified nonopioid analgesic, antipyretic and antirheumatic

● **T40** Poisoning by, adverse effect of and underdosing of narcotics and psychodysleptics [hallucinogens]

    Excludes2 drug dependence and related mental and behavioral disorders due to psychoactive substance use (F10.-F19.-)

    The appropriate 7th character is to be added to each code from category T40

> A   initial encounter
> D   subsequent encounter
> S   sequela

● **T40.0** Poisoning by, adverse effect of and underdosing of opium

  ● **T40.0X** Poisoning by, adverse effect of and underdosing of opium

    ● **T40.0X1** Poisoning by opium, accidental (unintentional)
        Poisoning by opium NOS

    ● **T40.0X2** Poisoning by opium, intentional self-harm

    ● **T40.0X3** Poisoning by opium, assault

    ● **T40.0X4** Poisoning by opium, undetermined

    ● **T40.0X5** Adverse effect of opium

    ● **T40.0X6** Underdosing of opium

● **T40.1** Poisoning by and adverse effect of heroin

  ● **T40.1X** Poisoning by and adverse effect of heroin

    ● **T40.1X1** Poisoning by heroin, accidental (unintentional)
        Poisoning by heroin NOS

    ● **T40.1X2** Poisoning by heroin, intentional self-harm

    ● **T40.1X3** Poisoning by heroin, assault

    ● **T40.1X4** Poisoning by heroin, undetermined

● **T40.2** Poisoning by, adverse effect of and underdosing of other opioids

  ● **T40.2X** Poisoning by, adverse effect of and underdosing of other opioids

    ● **T40.2X1** Poisoning by other opioids, accidental (unintentional)
        Poisoning by other opioids NOS

    ● **T40.2X2** Poisoning by other opioids, intentional self-harm

    ● **T40.2X3** Poisoning by other opioids, assault

    ● **T40.2X4** Poisoning by other opioids, undetermined

    ● **T40.2X5** Adverse effect of other opioids

    ● **T40.2X6** Underdosing of other opioids

● **T40.3** Poisoning by, adverse effect of and underdosing of methadone

  ● **T40.3X** Poisoning by, adverse effect of and underdosing of methadone

    ● **T40.3X1** Poisoning by methadone, accidental (unintentional)
        Poisoning by methadone NOS

    ● **T40.3X2** Poisoning by methadone, intentional self-harm

    ● **T40.3X3** Poisoning by methadone, assault

    ● **T40.3X4** Poisoning by methadone, undetermined

    ● **T40.3X5** Adverse effect of methadone

    ● **T40.3X6** Underdosing of methadone

● **T40.4** Poisoning by, adverse effect of and underdosing of other synthetic narcotics

  ● **T40.4X** Poisoning by, adverse effect of and underdosing of other synthetic narcotics

    ● **T40.4X1** Poisoning by other synthetic narcotics, accidental (unintentional)
        Poisoning by other synthetic narcotics NOS

    ● **T40.4X2** Poisoning by other synthetic narcotics, intentional self-harm

    ● **T40.4X3** Poisoning by other synthetic narcotics, assault

    ● **T40.4X4** Poisoning by other synthetic narcotics, undetermined

    ● **T40.4X5** Adverse effect of other synthetic narcotics

    ● **T40.4X6** Underdosing of other synthetic narcotics

● **T40.5** Poisoning by, adverse effect of and underdosing of cocaine

  ● **T40.5X** Poisoning by, adverse effect of and underdosing of cocaine

    ● **T40.5X1** Poisoning by cocaine, accidental (unintentional)
        Poisoning by cocaine NOS
        Coding Clinic: 2016, Q2, P9

    ● **T40.5X2** Poisoning by cocaine, intentional self-harm

    ● **T40.5X3** Poisoning by cocaine, assault

    ● **T40.5X4** Poisoning by cocaine, undetermined

    ● **T40.5X5** Adverse effect of cocaine

    ● **T40.5X6** Underdosing of cocaine

● **T40.6** Poisoning by, adverse effect of and underdosing of other and unspecified narcotics

  ● **T40.60** Poisoning by, adverse effect of and underdosing of unspecified narcotics

    ● **T40.601** Poisoning by unspecified narcotics, accidental (unintentional)
        Poisoning by narcotics NOS

    ● **T40.602** Poisoning by unspecified narcotics, intentional self-harm

    ● **T40.603** Poisoning by unspecified narcotics, assault

    ● **T40.604** Poisoning by unspecified narcotics, undetermined

    ● **T40.605** Adverse effect of unspecified narcotics

    ● **T40.606** Underdosing of unspecified narcotics

  ● **T40.69** Poisoning by, adverse effect of and underdosing of other narcotics

    ● **T40.691** Poisoning by other narcotics, accidental (unintentional)
        Poisoning by other narcotics NOS

    ● **T40.692** Poisoning by other narcotics, intentional self-harm

    ● **T40.693** Poisoning by other narcotics, assault

    ● **T40.694** Poisoning by other narcotics, undetermined

    ● **T40.695** Adverse effect of other narcotics

    ● **T40.696** Underdosing of other narcotics

CHAPTER 19 (S00-T88)

CHAPTER 19 (S00-T88)

●T40.7   Poisoning by, adverse effect of and underdosing of cannabis (derivatives)

   ●T40.7X   Poisoning by, adverse effect of and underdosing of cannabis (derivatives)

      ●T40.7X1   Poisoning by cannabis (derivatives), accidental (unintentional)
         Poisoning by cannabis NOS

      ●T40.7X2   Poisoning by cannabis (derivatives), intentional self-harm

      ●T40.7X3   Poisoning by cannabis (derivatives), assault

      ●T40.7X4   Poisoning by cannabis (derivatives), undetermined

      ●T40.7X5   Adverse effect of cannabis (derivatives)

      ●T40.7X6   Underdosing of cannabis (derivatives)

●T40.8   Poisoning by and adverse effect of lysergide [LSD]

   ●T40.8X   Poisoning by and adverse effect of lysergide [LSD]

      ●T40.8X1   Poisoning by lysergide [LSD], accidental (unintentional)
         Poisoning by lysergide [LSD] NOS

      ●T40.8X2   Poisoning by lysergide [LSD], intentional self-harm

      ●T40.8X3   Poisoning by lysergide [LSD], assault

      ●T40.8X4   Poisoning by lysergide [LSD], undetermined

●T40.9   Poisoning by, adverse effect of and underdosing of other and unspecified psychodysleptics [hallucinogens]

   ●T40.90   Poisoning by, adverse effect of and underdosing of unspecified psychodysleptics [hallucinogens]

      ●T40.901   Poisoning by unspecified psychodysleptics [hallucinogens], accidental (unintentional)

      ●T40.902   Poisoning by unspecified psychodysleptics [hallucinogens], intentional self-harm

      ●T40.903   Poisoning by unspecified psychodysleptics [hallucinogens], assault

      ●T40.904   Poisoning by unspecified psychodysleptics [hallucinogens], undetermined

      ●T40.905   Adverse effect of unspecified psychodysleptics [hallucinogens]

      ●T40.906   Underdosing of unspecified psychodysleptics

   ●T40.99   Poisoning by, adverse effect of and underdosing of other psychodysleptics [hallucinogens]

      ●T40.991   Poisoning by other psychodysleptics [hallucinogens], accidental (unintentional)
         Poisoning by other psychodysleptics [hallucinogens] NOS

      ●T40.992   Poisoning by other psychodysleptics [hallucinogens], intentional self-harm

      ●T40.993   Poisoning by other psychodysleptics [hallucinogens], assault

      ●T40.994   Poisoning by other psychodysleptics [hallucinogens], undetermined

      ●T40.995   Adverse effect of other psychodysleptics [hallucinogens]

      ●T40.996   Underdosing of other psychodysleptics

●T41   Poisoning by, adverse effect of and underdosing of anesthetics and therapeutic gases

   Excludes1   benzodiazepines (T42.4-)
      cocaine (T40.5-)
      complications of anesthesia during pregnancy (O29.-)
      complications of anesthesia during labor and delivery (O74.-)
      complications of anesthesia during the puerperium (O89.-) opioids (T40.0-T40.2-)

   The appropriate 7th character is to be added to each code from category T41

      A   initial encounter
      D   subsequent encounter
      S   sequela

●T41.0   Poisoning by, adverse effect of and underdosing of inhaled anesthetics

   Excludes1   oxygen (T41.5-)

   ●T41.0X   Poisoning by, adverse effect of and underdosing of inhaled anesthetics

      ●T41.0X1   Poisoning by inhaled anesthetics, accidental (unintentional)
         Poisoning by inhaled anesthetics NOS

      ●T41.0X2   Poisoning by inhaled anesthetics, intentional self-harm

      ●T41.0X3   Poisoning by inhaled anesthetics, assault

      ●T41.0X4   Poisoning by inhaled anesthetics, undetermined

      ●T41.0X5   Adverse effect of inhaled anesthetics

      ●T41.0X6   Underdosing of inhaled anesthetics

●T41.1   Poisoning by, adverse effect of and underdosing of intravenous anesthetics
   Poisoning by, adverse effect of and underdosing of thiobarbiturates

   ●T41.1X   Poisoning by, adverse effect of and underdosing of intravenous anesthetics

      ●T41.1X1   Poisoning by intravenous anesthetics, accidental (unintentional)
         Poisoning by intravenous anesthetics NOS

      ●T41.1X2   Poisoning by intravenous anesthetics, intentional self-harm

      ●T41.1X3   Poisoning by intravenous anesthetics, assault

      ●T41.1X4   Poisoning by intravenous anesthetics, undetermined

      ●T41.1X5   Adverse effect of intravenous anesthetics

      ●T41.1X6   Underdosing of intravenous anesthetics

●T41.2   Poisoning by, adverse effect of and underdosing of other and unspecified general anesthetics

   ●T41.20   Poisoning by, adverse effect of and underdosing of unspecified general anesthetics

      ●T41.201   Poisoning by unspecified general anesthetics, accidental (unintentional)
         Poisoning by general anesthetics NOS

      ●T41.202   Poisoning by unspecified general anesthetics, intentional self-harm

      ●T41.203   Poisoning by unspecified general anesthetics, assault

      ●T41.204   Poisoning by unspecified general anesthetics, undetermined

      ●T41.205   Adverse effect of unspecified general anesthetics
         Coding Clinic: 2016, Q4, P73

      ●T41.206   Underdosing of unspecified general anesthetics

▶ New   ⇒ Revised   ~~deleted~~ Deleted   Excludes 1   Excludes 2   Includes   Use additional   Code first   Code also   Key words

OGCR Official Guidelines   X Assign placeholder X   ● Use Additional Character(s)   ❱ Manifestation Code   Coding Clinic

● **T41.29**   Poisoning by, adverse effect of and underdosing of other general anesthetics

    ● **T41.291**   Poisoning by other general anesthetics, accidental (unintentional)
        Poisoning by other general anesthetics NOS

    ● **T41.292**   Poisoning by other general anesthetics, intentional self-harm

    ● **T41.293**   Poisoning by other general anesthetics, assault

    ● **T41.294**   Poisoning by other general anesthetics, undetermined

    ● **T41.295**   Adverse effect of other general anesthetics

    ● **T41.296**   Underdosing of other general anesthetics

● **T41.3**   Poisoning by, adverse effect of and underdosing of local anesthetics

    Cocaine (topical)

    Excludes2   poisoning by cocaine used as a central nervous system stimulant (T40.5X1-T40.5X4)

    ● **T41.3X**   Poisoning by, adverse effect of and underdosing of local anesthetics

       ● **T41.3X1**   Poisoning by local anesthetics, accidental (unintentional)
          Poisoning by local anesthetics NOS

       ● **T41.3X2**   Poisoning by local anesthetics, intentional self-harm

       ● **T41.3X3**   Poisoning by local anesthetics, assault

       ● **T41.3X4**   Poisoning by local anesthetics, undetermined

       ● **T41.3X5**   Adverse effect of local anesthetics

       ● **T41.3X6**   Underdosing of local anesthetics

● **T41.4**   Poisoning by, adverse effect of and underdosing of unspecified anesthetic

    X ● **T41.41**   Poisoning by unspecified anesthetic, accidental (unintentional)
        Poisoning by anesthetic NOS

    X ● **T41.42**   Poisoning by unspecified anesthetic, intentional self-harm

    X ● **T41.43**   Poisoning by unspecified anesthetic, assault

    X ● **T41.44**   Poisoning by unspecified anesthetic, undetermined

    X ● **T41.45**   Adverse effect of unspecified anesthetic

    X ● **T41.46**   Underdosing of unspecified anesthetics

● **T41.5**   Poisoning by, adverse effect of and underdosing of therapeutic gases

    ● **T41.5X**   Poisoning by, adverse effect of and underdosing of therapeutic gases

       ● **T41.5X1**   Poisoning by therapeutic gases, accidental (unintentional)
          Poisoning by therapeutic gases NOS

       ● **T41.5X2**   Poisoning by therapeutic gases, intentional self-harm

       ● **T41.5X3**   Poisoning by therapeutic gases, assault

       ● **T41.5X4**   Poisoning by therapeutic gases, undetermined

       ● **T41.5X5**   Adverse effect of therapeutic gases

       ● **T41.5X6**   Underdosing of therapeutic gases

● **T42**   Poisoning by, adverse effect of and underdosing of antiepileptic, sedative-hypnotic and antiparkinsonism drugs

    Excludes2   drug dependence and related mental and behavioral disorders due to psychoactive substance use (F10.--F19.-)

    The appropriate 7th character is to be added to each code from category T42

    | | |
    A   initial encounter
    D   subsequent encounter
    S   sequela

● **T42.0**   Poisoning by, adverse effect of and underdosing of hydantoin derivatives

    ● **T42.0X**   Poisoning by, adverse effect of and underdosing of hydantoin derivatives

       ● **T42.0X1**   Poisoning by hydantoin derivatives, accidental (unintentional)
          Poisoning by hydantoin derivatives NOS

       ● **T42.0X2**   Poisoning by hydantoin derivatives, intentional self-harm

       ● **T42.0X3**   Poisoning by hydantoin derivatives, assault

       ● **T42.0X4**   Poisoning by hydantoin derivatives, undetermined

       ● **T42.0X5**   Adverse effect of hydantoin derivatives

       ● **T42.0X6**   Underdosing of hydantoin derivatives

● **T42.1**   Poisoning by, adverse effect of and underdosing of iminostilbenes

    Poisoning by, adverse effect of and underdosing of carbamazepine

    ● **T42.1X**   Poisoning by, adverse effect of and underdosing of iminostilbenes

       ● **T42.1X1**   Poisoning by iminostilbenes, accidental (unintentional)
          Poisoning by iminostilbenes NOS

       ● **T42.1X2**   Poisoning by iminostilbenes, intentional self-harm

       ● **T42.1X3**   Poisoning by iminostilbenes, assault

       ● **T42.1X4**   Poisoning by iminostilbenes, undetermined

       ● **T42.1X5**   Adverse effect of iminostilbenes

       ● **T42.1X6**   Underdosing of iminostilbenes

● **T42.2**   Poisoning by, adverse effect of and underdosing of succinimides and oxazolidinediones

    ● **T42.2X**   Poisoning by, adverse effect of and underdosing of succinimides and oxazolidinediones

       ● **T42.2X1**   Poisoning by succinimides and oxazolidinediones, accidental (unintentional)
          Poisoning by succinimides and oxazolidinediones NOS

       ● **T42.2X2**   Poisoning by succinimides and oxazolidinediones, intentional self-harm

       ● **T42.2X3**   Poisoning by succinimides and oxazolidinediones, assault

       ● **T42.2X4**   Poisoning by succinimides and oxazolidinediones, undetermined

       ● **T42.2X5**   Adverse effect of succinimides and oxazolidinediones

       ● **T42.2X6**   Underdosing of succinimides and oxazolidinediones

CHAPTER 19 (S00-T88)

● **T42.3** Poisoning by, adverse effect of and underdosing of barbiturates

    Excludes1   poisoning by, adverse effect of and underdosing of thiobarbiturates (T41.1-)

  ● **T42.3X** Poisoning by, adverse effect of and underdosing of barbiturates

    ● **T42.3X1** Poisoning by barbiturates, accidental (unintentional)
        Poisoning by barbiturates NOS

    ● **T42.3X2** Poisoning by barbiturates, intentional self-harm

    ● **T42.3X3** Poisoning by barbiturates, assault

    ● **T42.3X4** Poisoning by barbiturates, undetermined

    ● **T42.3X5** Adverse effect of barbiturates

    ● **T42.3X6** Underdosing of barbiturates

● **T42.4** Poisoning by, adverse effect of and underdosing of benzodiazepines

  ● **T42.4X** Poisoning by, adverse effect of and underdosing of benzodiazepines

    ● **T42.4X1** Poisoning by benzodiazepines, accidental (unintentional)
        Poisoning by benzodiazepines NOS

    ● **T42.4X2** Poisoning by benzodiazepines, intentional self-harm

    ● **T42.4X3** Poisoning by benzodiazepines, assault

    ● **T42.4X4** Poisoning by benzodiazepines, undetermined

    ● **T42.4X5** Adverse effect of benzodiazepines

    ● **T42.4X6** Underdosing of benzodiazepines

● **T42.5** Poisoning by, adverse effect of and underdosing of mixed antiepileptics

  ● **T42.5X** Poisoning by, adverse effect of and underdosing of antiepileptics

    ● **T42.5X1** Poisoning by mixed antiepileptics, accidental (unintentional)
        Poisoning by mixed antiepileptics NOS

    ● **T42.5X2** Poisoning by mixed antiepileptics, intentional self-harm

    ● **T42.5X3** Poisoning by mixed antiepileptics, assault

    ● **T42.5X4** Poisoning by mixed antiepileptics, undetermined

    ● **T42.5X5** Adverse effect of mixed antiepileptics

    ● **T42.5X6** Underdosing of mixed antiepileptics

● **T42.6** Poisoning by, adverse effect of and underdosing of other antiepileptic and sedative-hypnotic drugs

    Poisoning by, adverse effect of and underdosing of methaqualone
    Poisoning by, adverse effect of and underdosing of valproic acid

    Excludes1   poisoning by, adverse effect of and underdosing of carbamazepine (T42.1-)

  ● **T42.6X** Poisoning by, adverse effect of and underdosing of other antiepileptic and sedative-hypnotic drugs

    ● **T42.6X1** Poisoning by other antiepileptic and sedative-hypnotic drugs, accidental (unintentional)
        Poisoning by other antiepileptic and sedative-hypnotic drugs NOS

    ● **T42.6X2** Poisoning by other antiepileptic and sedative-hypnotic drugs, intentional self-harm

    ● **T42.6X3** Poisoning by other antiepileptic and sedative-hypnotic drugs, assault

    ● **T42.6X4** Poisoning by other antiepileptic and sedative-hypnotic drugs, undetermined

    ● **T42.6X5** Adverse effect of other antiepileptic and sedative-hypnotic drugs

    ● **T42.6X6** Underdosing of other antiepileptic and sedative-hypnotic drugs

● **T42.7** Poisoning by, adverse effect of and underdosing of unspecified antiepileptic and sedative-hypnotic drugs

  X ● **T42.71** Poisoning by unspecified antiepileptic and sedative-hypnotic drugs, accidental (unintentional)
        Poisoning by antiepileptic and sedative-hypnotic drugs NOS

  X ● **T42.72** Poisoning by unspecified antiepileptic and sedative-hypnotic drugs, intentional self-harm

  X ● **T42.73** Poisoning by unspecified antiepileptic and sedative-hypnotic drugs, assault

  X ● **T42.74** Poisoning by unspecified antiepileptic and sedative-hypnotic drugs, undetermined

  X ● **T42.75** Adverse effect of unspecified antiepileptic and sedative-hypnotic drugs

  X ● **T42.76** Underdosing of unspecified antiepileptic and sedative-hypnotic drugs

● **T42.8** Poisoning by, adverse effect of and underdosing of antiparkinsonism drugs and other central muscle-tone depressants

    Poisoning by, adverse effect of and underdosing of amantadine

  ● **T42.8X** Poisoning by, adverse effect of and underdosing of antiparkinsonism drugs and other central muscle-tone depressants

    ● **T42.8X1** Poisoning by antiparkinsonism drugs and other central muscle-tone depressants, accidental (unintentional)
        Poisoning by antiparkinsonism drugs and other central muscle-tone depressants NOS

    ● **T42.8X2** Poisoning by antiparkinsonism drugs and other central muscle-tone depressants, intentional self-harm

    ● **T42.8X3** Poisoning by antiparkinsonism drugs and other central muscle-tone depressants, assault

    ● **T42.8X4** Poisoning by antiparkinsonism drugs and other central muscle-tone depressants, undetermined

    ● **T42.8X5** Adverse effect of antiparkinsonism drugs and other central muscle-tone depressants

    ● **T42.8X6** Underdosing of antiparkinsonism drugs and other central muscle-tone depressants

▶ New   ⇒ Revised   ~~deleted~~ Deleted   Excludes 1   Excludes 2   Includes   Use additional   Code first   Code also   Key words
OGCR Official Guidelines   X Assign placeholder X   ● Use Additional Character(s)   ▮ Manifestation Code   **Coding Clinic**

● **T43**   **Poisoning by, adverse effect of and underdosing of psychotropic drugs, not elsewhere classified**

     Excludes1   appetite depressants (T50.5-)
                     barbiturates (T42.3-)
                     benzodiazepines (T42.4-)
                     methaqualone (T42.6-)
                     psychodysleptics [hallucinogens] (T40.7-T40.9-)

     Excludes2   drug dependence and related mental and behavioral disorders due to psychoactive substance use (F10.--F19.-)

The appropriate 7th character is to be added to each code from category T43

A	initial encounter
D	subsequent encounter
S	sequela

● **T43.0**   **Poisoning by, adverse effect of and underdosing of tricyclic and tetracyclic antidepressants**

   ● **T43.01**   Poisoning by, adverse effect of and underdosing of tricyclic antidepressants

     ● **T43.011**   Poisoning by tricyclic antidepressants, accidental (unintentional)
                 Poisoning by tricyclic antidepressants NOS

     ● **T43.012**   Poisoning by tricyclic antidepressants, intentional self-harm

     ● **T43.013**   Poisoning by tricyclic antidepressants, assault

     ● **T43.014**   Poisoning by tricyclic antidepressants, undetermined

     ● **T43.015**   Adverse effect of tricyclic antidepressants

     ● **T43.016**   Underdosing of tricyclic antidepressants

   ● **T43.02**   Poisoning by, adverse effect of and underdosing of tetracyclic antidepressants

     ● **T43.021**   Poisoning by tetracyclic antidepressants, accidental (unintentional)
                 Poisoning by tetracyclic antidepressants NOS

     ● **T43.022**   Poisoning by tetracyclic antidepressants, intentional self-harm

     ● **T43.023**   Poisoning by tetracyclic antidepressants, assault

     ● **T43.024**   Poisoning by tetracyclic antidepressants, undetermined

     ● **T43.025**   Adverse effect of tetracyclic antidepressants

     ● **T43.026**   Underdosing of tetracyclic antidepressants

● **T43.1**   **Poisoning by, adverse effect of and underdosing of monoamine-oxidase-inhibitor antidepressants**

   ● **T43.1X**   Poisoning by, adverse effect of and underdosing of monoamine-oxidase-inhibitor antidepressants

     ● **T43.1X1**   Poisoning by monoamine-oxidase-inhibitor antidepressants, accidental (unintentional)
                 Poisoning by monoamine-oxidase-inhibitor antidepressants NOS

     ● **T43.1X2**   Poisoning by monoamine-oxidase-inhibitor antidepressants, intentional self-harm

     ● **T43.1X3**   Poisoning by monoamine-oxidase-inhibitor antidepressants, assault

     ● **T43.1X4**   Poisoning by monoamine-oxidase-inhibitor antidepressants, undetermined

     ● **T43.1X5**   Adverse effect of monoamine-oxidase-inhibitor antidepressants

     ● **T43.1X6**   Underdosing of monoamine-oxidase-inhibitor antidepressants

● **T43.2**   **Poisoning by, adverse effect of and underdosing of other and unspecified antidepressants**

   ● **T43.20**   Poisoning by, adverse effect of and underdosing of unspecified antidepressants

     ● **T43.201**   Poisoning by unspecified antidepressants, accidental (unintentional)
                 Poisoning by antidepressants NOS

     ● **T43.202**   Poisoning by unspecified antidepressants, intentional self-harm

     ● **T43.203**   Poisoning by unspecified antidepressants, assault

     ● **T43.204**   Poisoning by unspecified antidepressants, undetermined

     ● **T43.205**   Adverse effect of unspecified antidepressants
                 Antidepressant discontinuation syndrome

     ● **T43.206**   Underdosing of unspecified antidepressants

   ● **T43.21**   Poisoning by, adverse effect of and underdosing of selective serotonin and norepinephrine reuptake inhibitors
         Poisoning by, adverse effect of and underdosing of SSNRI antidepressants

     ● **T43.211**   Poisoning by selective serotonin and norepinephrine reuptake inhibitors, accidental (unintentional)

     ● **T43.212**   Poisoning by selective serotonin and norepinephrine reuptake inhibitors, intentional self-harm

     ● **T43.213**   Poisoning by selective serotonin and norepinephrine reuptake inhibitors, assault

     ● **T43.214**   Poisoning by selective serotonin and norepinephrine reuptake inhibitors, undetermined

     ● **T43.215**   Adverse effect of selective serotonin and norepinephrine reuptake inhibitors

     ● **T43.216**   Underdosing of selective serotonin and norepinephrine reuptake inhibitors

   ● **T43.22**   Poisoning by, adverse effect of and underdosing of selective serotonin reuptake inhibitors
         Poisoning by, adverse effect of and underdosing of SSRI antidepressants

     ● **T43.221**   Poisoning by selective serotonin reuptake inhibitors, accidental (unintentional)

     ● **T43.222**   Poisoning by selective serotonin reuptake inhibitors, intentional self-harm

     ● **T43.223**   Poisoning by selective serotonin reuptake inhibitors, assault

     ● **T43.224**   Poisoning by selective serotonin reuptake inhibitors, undetermined

     ● **T43.225**   Adverse effect of selective serotonin reuptake inhibitors

     ● **T43.226**   Underdosing of selective serotonin reuptake inhibitors

CHAPTER 19 (S00-T88)

● **T43.29** Poisoning by, adverse effect of and underdosing of other antidepressants

  ● **T43.291** Poisoning by other antidepressants, accidental (unintentional)

    Poisoning by other antidepressants NOS

  ● **T43.292** Poisoning by other antidepressants, intentional self-harm

  ● **T43.293** Poisoning by other antidepressants, assault

  ● **T43.294** Poisoning by other antidepressants, undetermined

  ● **T43.295** Adverse effect of other antidepressants

  ● **T43.296** Underdosing of other antidepressants

● **T43.3** Poisoning by, adverse effect of and underdosing of phenothiazine antipsychotics and neuroleptics

 ● **T43.3X** Poisoning by, adverse effect of and underdosing of phenothiazine antipsychotics and neuroleptics

  ● **T43.3X1** Poisoning by phenothiazine antipsychotics and neuroleptics, accidental (unintentional)

    Poisoning by phenothiazine antipsychotics and neuroleptics NOS

  ● **T43.3X2** Poisoning by phenothiazine antipsychotics and neuroleptics, intentional self-harm

  ● **T43.3X3** Poisoning by phenothiazine antipsychotics and neuroleptics, assault

  ● **T43.3X4** Poisoning by phenothiazine antipsychotics and neuroleptics, undetermined

  ● **T43.3X5** Adverse effect of phenothiazine antipsychotics and neuroleptics

  ● **T43.3X6** Underdosing of phenothiazine antipsychotics and neuroleptics

● **T43.4** Poisoning by, adverse effect of and underdosing of butyrophenone and thiothixene neuroleptics

 ● **T43.4X** Poisoning by, adverse effect of and underdosing of butyrophenone and thiothixene neuroleptics

  ● **T43.4X1** Poisoning by butyrophenone and thiothixene neuroleptics, accidental (unintentional)

    Poisoning by butyrophenone and thiothixene neuroleptics NOS

  ● **T43.4X2** Poisoning by butyrophenone and thiothixene neuroleptics, intentional self-harm

  ● **T43.4X3** Poisoning by butyrophenone and thiothixene neuroleptics, assault

  ● **T43.4X4** Poisoning by butyrophenone and thiothixene neuroleptics, undetermined

  ● **T43.4X5** Adverse effect of butyrophenone and thiothixene neuroleptics

  ● **T43.4X6** Underdosing of butyrophenone and thiothixene neuroleptics

● **T43.5** Poisoning by, adverse effect of and underdosing of other and unspecified antipsychotics and neuroleptics

  Excludes1   poisoning by, adverse effect of and underdosing of rauwolfia (T46.5-)

 ● **T43.50** Poisoning by, adverse effect of and underdosing of unspecified antipsychotics and neuroleptics

  ● **T43.501** Poisoning by unspecified antipsychotics and neuroleptics, accidental (unintentional)

    Poisoning by antipsychotics and neuroleptics NOS

  ● **T43.502** Poisoning by unspecified antipsychotics and neuroleptics, intentional self-harm

  ● **T43.503** Poisoning by unspecified antipsychotics and neuroleptics, assault

  ● **T43.504** Poisoning by unspecified antipsychotics and neuroleptics, undetermined

  ● **T43.505** Adverse effect of unspecified antipsychotics and neuroleptics

  ● **T43.506** Underdosing of unspecified antipsychotics and neuroleptics

 ● **T43.59** Poisoning by, adverse effect of and underdosing of other antipsychotics and neuroleptics

  ● **T43.591** Poisoning by other antipsychotics and neuroleptics, accidental (unintentional)

    Poisoning by other antipsychotics and neuroleptics NOS

  ● **T43.592** Poisoning by other antipsychotics and neuroleptics, intentional self-harm

    Coding Clinic: 2017, Q1, P40

  ● **T43.593** Poisoning by other antipsychotics and neuroleptics, assault

  ● **T43.594** Poisoning by other antipsychotics and neuroleptics, undetermined

  ● **T43.595** Adverse effect of other antipsychotics and neuroleptics

  ● **T43.596** Underdosing of other antipsychotics and neuroleptics

● **T43.6** Poisoning by, adverse effect of and underdosing of psychostimulants

  Excludes1   poisoning by, adverse effect of and underdosing of cocaine (T40.5-)

 ● **T43.60** Poisoning by, adverse effect of and underdosing of unspecified psychostimulant

  ● **T43.601** Poisoning by unspecified psychostimulants, accidental (unintentional)

    Poisoning by psychostimulants NOS

  ● **T43.602** Poisoning by unspecified psychostimulants, intentional self-harm

  ● **T43.603** Poisoning by unspecified psychostimulants, assault

  ● **T43.604** Poisoning by unspecified psychostimulants, undetermined

  ● **T43.605** Adverse effect of unspecified psychostimulants

  ● **T43.606** Underdosing of unspecified psychostimulants

▶ New   ⇒ Revised   ~~deleted~~ Deleted   Excludes 1   Excludes 2   Includes   Use additional   Code first   Code also   Key words

OGCR Official Guidelines   X Assign placeholder X   ● Use Additional Character(s)   ▶ Manifestation Code   **Coding Clinic**

● **T43.61** Poisoning by, adverse effect of and underdosing of caffeine
- ● **T43.611** Poisoning by caffeine, accidental (unintentional)
  Poisoning by caffeine NOS
- ● **T43.612** Poisoning by caffeine, intentional self-harm
- ● **T43.613** Poisoning by caffeine, assault
- ● **T43.614** Poisoning by caffeine, undetermined
- ● **T43.615** Adverse effect of caffeine
- ● **T43.616** Underdosing of caffeine

● **T43.62** Poisoning by, adverse effect of and underdosing of amphetamines
  Poisoning by, adverse effect of and underdosing of methamphetamines
- ● **T43.621** Poisoning by amphetamines, accidental (unintentional)
  Poisoning by amphetamines NOS
- ● **T43.622** Poisoning by amphetamines, intentional self-harm
- ● **T43.623** Poisoning by amphetamines, assault
- ● **T43.624** Poisoning by amphetamines, undetermined
- ● **T43.625** Adverse effect of amphetamines
- ● **T43.626** Underdosing of amphetamines

● **T43.63** Poisoning by, adverse effect of and underdosing of methylphenidate
- ● **T43.631** Poisoning by methylphenidate, accidental (unintentional)
  Poisoning by methylphenidate NOS
- ● **T43.632** Poisoning by methylphenidate, intentional self-harm
- ● **T43.633** Poisoning by methylphenidate, assault
- ● **T43.634** Poisoning by methylphenidate, undetermined
- ● **T43.635** Adverse effect of methylphenidate
- ● **T43.636** Underdosing of methylphenidate

▶ ● **T43.64** Poisoning by ecstasy
  ▶ Poisoning by MDMA
  ▶ Poisoning by 3,4-methylenedioxymethamphetamine
- ▶ ● **T43.641** Poisoning by ecstasy, accidental (unintentional)
  ▶ Poisoning by ecstasy NOS
- ▶ ● **T43.642** Poisoning by ecstasy, intentional self-harm
- ▶ ● **T43.643** Poisoning by ecstasy, assault
- ▶ ● **T43.644** Poisoning by ecstasy, undetermined

● **T43.69** Poisoning by, adverse effect of and underdosing of other psychostimulants
- ● **T43.691** Poisoning by other psychostimulants, accidental (unintentional)
  Poisoning by other psychostimulants NOS
- ● **T43.692** Poisoning by other psychostimulants, intentional self-harm
- ● **T43.693** Poisoning by other psychostimulants, assault
- ● **T43.694** Poisoning by other psychostimulants, undetermined
- ● **T43.695** Adverse effect of other psychostimulants
- ● **T43.696** Underdosing of other psychostimulants

● **T43.8** Poisoning by, adverse effect of and underdosing of other psychotropic drugs
- ● **T43.8X** Poisoning by, adverse effect of and underdosing of other psychotropic drugs
  - ● **T43.8X1** Poisoning by other psychotropic drugs, accidental (unintentional)
    Poisoning by other psychotropic drugs NOS
  - ● **T43.8X2** Poisoning by other psychotropic drugs, intentional self-harm
  - ● **T43.8X3** Poisoning by other psychotropic drugs, assault
  - ● **T43.8X4** Poisoning by other psychotropic drugs, undetermined
  - ● **T43.8X5** Adverse effect of other psychotropic drugs
  - ● **T43.8X6** Underdosing of other psychotropic drugs

● **T43.9** Poisoning by, adverse effect of and underdosing of unspecified psychotropic drug
- X ● **T43.91** Poisoning by unspecified psychotropic drug, accidental (unintentional)
  Poisoning by psychotropic drug NOS
- X ● **T43.92** Poisoning by unspecified psychotropic drug, intentional self-harm
- X ● **T43.93** Poisoning by unspecified psychotropic drug, assault
- X ● **T43.94** Poisoning by unspecified psychotropic drug, undetermined
- X ● **T43.95** Adverse effect of unspecified psychotropic drug
- X ● **T43.96** Underdosing of unspecified psychotropic drug

● **T44** Poisoning by, adverse effect of and underdosing of drugs primarily affecting the autonomic nervous system
  The appropriate 7th character is to be added to each code from category T44

A	initial encounter
D	subsequent encounter
S	sequela

● **T44.0** Poisoning by, adverse effect of and underdosing of anticholinesterase agents
- ● **T44.0X** Poisoning by, adverse effect of and underdosing of anticholinesterase agents
  - ● **T44.0X1** Poisoning by anticholinesterase agents, accidental (unintentional)
    Poisoning by anticholinesterase agents NOS
  - ● **T44.0X2** Poisoning by anticholinesterase agents, intentional self-harm
  - ● **T44.0X3** Poisoning by anticholinesterase agents, assault
  - ● **T44.0X4** Poisoning by anticholinesterase agents, undetermined
  - ● **T44.0X5** Adverse effect of anticholinesterase agents
  - ● **T44.0X6** Underdosing of anticholinesterase agents

CHAPTER 19 (S00-T88)

●**T44.1** **Poisoning by, adverse effect of and underdosing of other parasympathomimetics [cholinergics]**

  ●**T44.1X** Poisoning by, adverse effect of and underdosing of other parasympathomimetics [cholinergics]

    ●**T44.1X1** Poisoning by other parasympathomimetics [cholinergics], accidental (unintentional)
        Poisoning by other parasympathomimetics [cholinergics] NOS

    ●**T44.1X2** Poisoning by other parasympathomimetics [cholinergics], intentional self-harm

    ●**T44.1X3** Poisoning by other parasympathomimetics [cholinergics], assault

    ●**T44.1X4** Poisoning by other parasympathomimetics [cholinergics], undetermined

    ●**T44.1X5** Adverse effect of other parasympathomimetics [cholinergics]

    ●**T44.1X6** Underdosing of other parasympathomimetics

●**T44.2** **Poisoning by, adverse effect of and underdosing of ganglionic blocking drugs**

  ●**T44.2X** Poisoning by, adverse effect of and underdosing of ganglionic blocking drugs

    ●**T44.2X1** Poisoning by ganglionic blocking drugs, accidental (unintentional)
        Poisoning by ganglionic blocking drugs NOS

    ●**T44.2X2** Poisoning by ganglionic blocking drugs, intentional self-harm

    ●**T44.2X3** Poisoning by ganglionic blocking drugs, assault

    ●**T44.2X4** Poisoning by ganglionic blocking drugs, undetermined

    ●**T44.2X5** Adverse effect of ganglionic blocking drugs

    ●**T44.2X6** Underdosing of ganglionic blocking drugs

●**T44.3** **Poisoning by, adverse effect of and underdosing of other parasympatholytics [anticholinergics and antimuscarinics] and spasmolytics**
    Poisoning by, adverse effect of and underdosing of papaverine

  ●**T44.3X** Poisoning by, adverse effect of and underdosing of other parasympatholytics [anticholinergics and antimuscarinics] and spasmolytics

    ●**T44.3X1** Poisoning by other parasympatholytics [anticholinergics and antimuscarinics] and spasmolytics, accidental (unintentional)
        Poisoning by other parasympatholytics [anticholinergics and antimuscarinics] and spasmolytics NOS

    ●**T44.3X2** Poisoning by other parasympatholytics [anticholinergics and antimuscarinics] and spasmolytics, intentional self-harm

●**T44.3X3** Poisoning by other parasympatholytics [anticholinergics and antimuscarinics] and spasmolytics, assault

●**T44.3X4** Poisoning by other parasympatholytics [anticholinergics and antimuscarinics] and spasmolytics, undetermined

●**T44.3X5** Adverse effect of other parasympatholytics [anticholinergics and antimuscarinics] and spasmolytics

●**T44.3X6** Underdosing of other parasympatholytics [anticholinergics and antimuscarinics] and spasmolytics

●**T44.4** **Poisoning by, adverse effect of and underdosing of predominantly alpha-adrenoreceptor agonists**
    Poisoning by, adverse effect of and underdosing of metaraminol

  ●**T44.4X** Poisoning by, adverse effect of and underdosing of predominantly alpha-adrenoreceptor agonists

    ●**T44.4X1** Poisoning by predominantly alpha-adrenoreceptor agonists, accidental (unintentional)
        Poisoning by predominantly alpha-adrenoreceptor agonists NOS

    ●**T44.4X2** Poisoning by predominantly alpha-adrenoreceptor agonists, intentional self-harm

    ●**T44.4X3** Poisoning by predominantly alpha-adrenoreceptor agonists, assault

    ●**T44.4X4** Poisoning by predominantly alpha-adrenoreceptor agonists, undetermined

    ●**T44.4X5** Adverse effect of predominantly alpha-adrenoreceptor agonists

    ●**T44.4X6** Underdosing of predominantly alpha-adrenoreceptor agonists

●**T44.5** **Poisoning by, adverse effect of and underdosing of predominantly beta-adrenoreceptor agonists**

  Excludes1 poisoning by, adverse effect of and underdosing of beta-adrenoreceptor agonists used in asthma therapy (T48.6-)

  ●**T44.5X** Poisoning by, adverse effect of and underdosing of predominantly beta-adrenoreceptor agonists

    ●**T44.5X1** Poisoning by predominantly beta-adrenoreceptor agonists, accidental (unintentional)
        Poisoning by predominantly beta-adrenoreceptor agonists NOS

    ●**T44.5X2** Poisoning by predominantly beta-adrenoreceptor agonists, intentional self-harm

    ●**T44.5X3** Poisoning by predominantly beta-adrenoreceptor agonists, assault

    ●**T44.5X4** Poisoning by predominantly beta-adrenoreceptor agonists, undetermined

    ●**T44.5X5** Adverse effect of predominantly beta-adrenoreceptor agonists

    ●**T44.5X6** Underdosing of predominantly beta-adrenoreceptor agonists

● **T44.6**   **Poisoning by, adverse effect of and underdosing of alpha-adrenoreceptor antagonists**

> **Excludes1**   poisoning by, adverse effect of and underdosing of ergot alkaloids (T48.0)

  ● **T44.6X**   **Poisoning by, adverse effect of and underdosing of alpha-adrenoreceptor antagonists**

    ● **T44.6X1**   **Poisoning by alpha-adrenoreceptor antagonists, accidental (unintentional)**
> Poisoning by alpha-adrenoreceptor antagonists NOS

    ● **T44.6X2**   **Poisoning by alpha-adrenoreceptor antagonists, intentional self-harm**

    ● **T44.6X3**   **Poisoning by alpha-adrenoreceptor antagonists, assault**

    ● **T44.6X4**   **Poisoning by alpha-adrenoreceptor antagonists, undetermined**

    ● **T44.6X5**   **Adverse effect of alpha-adrenoreceptor antagonists**

    ● **T44.6X6**   **Underdosing of alpha-adrenoreceptor antagonists**

● **T44.7**   **Poisoning by, adverse effect of and underdosing of beta-adrenoreceptor antagonists**

  ● **T44.7X**   **Poisoning by, adverse effect of and underdosing of beta-adrenoreceptor antagonists**

    ● **T44.7X1**   **Poisoning by beta-adrenoreceptor antagonists, accidental (unintentional)**
> Poisoning by beta-adrenoreceptor antagonists NOS

    ● **T44.7X2**   **Poisoning by beta-adrenoreceptor antagonists, intentional self-harm**

    ● **T44.7X3**   **Poisoning by beta-adrenoreceptor antagonists, assault**

    ● **T44.7X4**   **Poisoning by beta-adrenoreceptor antagonists, undetermined**

    ● **T44.7X5**   **Adverse effect of beta-adrenoreceptor antagonists**

    ● **T44.7X6**   **Underdosing of beta-adrenoreceptor antagonists**

● **T44.8**   **Poisoning by, adverse effect of and underdosing of centrally-acting and adrenergic-neuron-blocking agents**

> **Excludes1**   poisoning by, adverse effect of and underdosing of clonidine (T46.5)
> poisoning by, adverse effect of and underdosing of guanethidine (T46.5)

  ● **T44.8X**   **Poisoning by, adverse effect of and underdosing of centrally-acting and adrenergic-neuron-blocking agents**

    ● **T44.8X1**   **Poisoning by centrally-acting and adrenergic-neuron-blocking agents, accidental (unintentional)**
> Poisoning by centrally-acting and adrenergic-neuron-blocking agents NOS

    ● **T44.8X2**   **Poisoning by centrally-acting and adrenergic-neuron-blocking agents, intentional self-harm**

    ● **T44.8X3**   **Poisoning by centrally-acting and adrenergic-neuron-blocking agents, assault**

    ● **T44.8X4**   **Poisoning by centrally-acting and adrenergic-neuron-blocking agents, undetermined**

    ● **T44.8X5**   **Adverse effect of centrally-acting and adrenergic-neuron-blocking agents**

    ● **T44.8X6**   **Underdosing of centrally-acting and adrenergic-neuron-blocking agents**

● **T44.9**   **Poisoning by, adverse effect of and underdosing of other and unspecified drugs primarily affecting the autonomic nervous system**
> Poisoning by, adverse effect of and underdosing of drug stimulating both alpha and beta-adrenoreceptors

  ● **T44.90**   **Poisoning by, adverse effect of and underdosing of unspecified drugs primarily affecting the autonomic nervous system**

    ● **T44.901**   **Poisoning by unspecified drugs primarily affecting the autonomic nervous system, accidental (unintentional)**
> Poisoning by unspecified drugs primarily affecting the autonomic nervous system NOS

    ● **T44.902**   **Poisoning by unspecified drugs primarily affecting the autonomic nervous system, intentional self-harm**

    ● **T44.903**   **Poisoning by unspecified drugs primarily affecting the autonomic nervous system, assault**

    ● **T44.904**   **Poisoning by unspecified drugs primarily affecting the autonomic nervous system, undetermined**

    ● **T44.905**   **Adverse effect of unspecified drugs primarily affecting the autonomic nervous system**

    ● **T44.906**   **Underdosing of unspecified drugs primarily affecting the autonomic nervous system**

  ● **T44.99**   **Poisoning by, adverse effect of and underdosing of other drugs primarily affecting the autonomic nervous system**

    ● **T44.991**   **Poisoning by other drug primarily affecting the autonomic nervous system, accidental (unintentional)**
> Poisoning by other drugs primarily affecting the autonomic nervous system NOS

    ● **T44.992**   **Poisoning by other drug primarily affecting the autonomic nervous system, intentional self-harm**

    ● **T44.993**   **Poisoning by other drug primarily affecting the autonomic nervous system, assault**

    ● **T44.994**   **Poisoning by other drug primarily affecting the autonomic nervous system, undetermined**

    ● **T44.995**   **Adverse effect of other drug primarily affecting the autonomic nervous system**

    ● **T44.996**   **Underdosing of other drug primarily affecting the autonomic nervous system**

CHAPTER 19 (S00-T88)

CHAPTER 19 (S00-T88)

● T45   Poisoning by, adverse effect of and underdosing of primarily systemic and hematological agents, not elsewhere classified

The appropriate 7th character is to be added to each code from category T45

A	initial encounter
D	subsequent encounter
S	sequela

● T45.0   Poisoning by, adverse effect of and underdosing of antiallergic and antiemetic drugs

Excludes1   poisoning by, adverse effect of and underdosing of phenothiazine-based neuroleptics (T43.3)

● T45.0X   Poisoning by, adverse effect of and underdosing of antiallergic and antiemetic drugs

● T45.0X1   Poisoning by antiallergic and antiemetic drugs, accidental (unintentional)
Poisoning by antiallergic and antiemetic drugs NOS

● T45.0X2   Poisoning by antiallergic and antiemetic drugs, intentional self-harm

● T45.0X3   Poisoning by antiallergic and antiemetic drugs, assault

● T45.0X4   Poisoning by antiallergic and antiemetic drugs, undetermined

● T45.0X5   Adverse effect of antiallergic and antiemetic drugs

● T45.0X6   Underdosing of antiallergic and antiemetic drugs

● T45.1   Poisoning by, adverse effect of and underdosing of antineoplastic and immunosuppressive drugs

Excludes1   poisoning by, adverse effect of and underdosing of tamoxifen (T38.6)

● T45.1X   Poisoning by, adverse effect of and underdosing of antineoplastic and immunosuppressive drugs

● T45.1X1   Poisoning by antineoplastic and immunosuppressive drugs, accidental (unintentional)
Poisoning by antineoplastic and immunosuppressive drugs NOS

● T45.1X2   Poisoning by antineoplastic and immunosuppressive drugs, intentional self-harm

● T45.1X3   Poisoning by antineoplastic and immunosuppressive drugs, assault

● T45.1X4   Poisoning by antineoplastic and immunosuppressive drugs, undetermined

● T45.1X5   Adverse effect of antineoplastic and immunosuppressive drugs

● T45.1X6   Underdosing of antineoplastic and immunosuppressive drugs

● T45.2   Poisoning by, adverse effect of and underdosing of vitamins

Excludes2   poisoning by, adverse effect of and underdosing of nicotinic acid (derivatives) (T46.7)
poisoning by, adverse effect of and underdosing of iron (T45.4)
poisoning by, adverse effect of and underdosing of vitamin K (T45.7)

● T45.2X   Poisoning by, adverse effect of and underdosing of vitamins

● T45.2X1   Poisoning by vitamins, accidental (unintentional)
Poisoning by vitamins NOS

● T45.2X2   Poisoning by vitamins, intentional self-harm

● T45.2X3   Poisoning by vitamins, assault

● T45.2X4   Poisoning by vitamins, undetermined

● T45.2X5   Adverse effect of vitamins

● T45.2X6   Underdosing of vitamins
Excludes1   vitamin deficiencies (E50-E56)

● T45.3   Poisoning by, adverse effect of and underdosing of enzymes

● T45.3X   Poisoning by, adverse effect of and underdosing of enzymes

● T45.3X1   Poisoning by enzymes, accidental (unintentional)
Poisoning by enzymes NOS

● T45.3X2   Poisoning by enzymes, intentional self-harm

● T45.3X3   Poisoning by enzymes, assault

● T45.3X4   Poisoning by enzymes, undetermined

● T45.3X5   Adverse effect of enzymes

● T45.3X6   Underdosing of enzymes

● T45.4   Poisoning by, adverse effect of and underdosing of iron and its compounds

● T45.4X   Poisoning by, adverse effect of and underdosing of iron and its compounds

● T45.4X1   Poisoning by iron and its compounds, accidental (unintentional)
Poisoning by iron and its compounds NOS

● T45.4X2   Poisoning by iron and its compounds, intentional self-harm

● T45.4X3   Poisoning by iron and its compounds, assault

● T45.4X4   Poisoning by iron and its compounds, undetermined

● T45.4X5   Adverse effect of iron and its compounds

● T45.4X6   Underdosing of iron and its compounds
Excludes1   iron deficiency (E61.1)

● T45.5   Poisoning by, adverse effect of and underdosing of anticoagulants and antithrombotic drugs

● T45.51   Poisoning by, adverse effect of and underdosing of anticoagulants

● T45.511   Poisoning by anticoagulants, accidental (unintentional)
Poisoning by anticoagulants NOS

● T45.512   Poisoning by anticoagulants, intentional self-harm

● T45.513   Poisoning by anticoagulants, assault

● T45.514   Poisoning by anticoagulants, undetermined

● T45.515   Adverse effect of anticoagulants
Coding Clinic: 2016, Q1, P14; 2013, Q2, P35

● T45.516   Underdosing of anticoagulants

▶ New   ⇒ Revised   deleted Deleted   Excludes 1   Excludes 2   Includes   Use additional   Code first   Code also   Key words

OGCR Official Guidelines   X Assign placeholder X   ● Use Additional Character(s)   ▷ Manifestation Code   Coding Clinic

● **T45.52**   Poisoning by, adverse effect of and underdosing of antithrombotic drugs
    Poisoning by, adverse effect of and underdosing of antiplatelet drugs

    Excludes2   poisoning by, adverse effect of and underdosing of aspirin (T39.01-)
        poisoning by, adverse effect of and underdosing of acetylsalicylic acid (T39.01-)

    ● **T45.521**   Poisoning by antithrombotic drugs, accidental (unintentional)
        Poisoning by antithrombotic drug NOS

    ● **T45.522**   Poisoning by antithrombotic drugs, intentional self-harm

    ● **T45.523**   Poisoning by antithrombotic drugs, assault

    ● **T45.524**   Poisoning by antithrombotic drugs, undetermined

    ● **T45.525**   Adverse effect of antithrombotic drugs
        Coding Clinic: 2016, Q1, P15

    ● **T45.526**   Underdosing of antithrombotic drugs

● **T45.6**   Poisoning by, adverse effect of and underdosing of fibrinolysis-affecting drugs

   ● **T45.60**   Poisoning by, adverse effect of and underdosing of unspecified fibrinolysis-affecting drugs

    ● **T45.601**   Poisoning by unspecified fibrinolysis-affecting drugs, accidental (unintentional)
        Poisoning by fibrinolysis-affecting drug NOS

    ● **T45.602**   Poisoning by unspecified fibrinolysis-affecting drugs, intentional self-harm

    ● **T45.603**   Poisoning by unspecified fibrinolysis-affecting drugs, assault

    ● **T45.604**   Poisoning by unspecified fibrinolysis-affecting drugs, undetermined

    ● **T45.605**   Adverse effect of unspecified fibrinolysis-affecting drugs

    ● **T45.606**   Underdosing of unspecified fibrinolysis-affecting drugs

   ● **T45.61**   Poisoning by, adverse effect of and underdosing of thrombolytic drugs

    ● **T45.611**   Poisoning by thrombolytic drug, accidental (unintentional)
        Poisoning by thrombolytic drug NOS

    ● **T45.612**   Poisoning by thrombolytic drug, intentional self-harm

    ● **T45.613**   Poisoning by thrombolytic drug, assault

    ● **T45.614**   Poisoning by thrombolytic drug, undetermined

    ● **T45.615**   Adverse effect of thrombolytic drugs
        Coding Clinic: 2017, Q2, P10

    ● **T45.616**   Underdosing of thrombolytic drugs

   ● **T45.62**   Poisoning by, adverse effect of and underdosing of hemostatic drugs

    ● **T45.621**   Poisoning by hemostatic drug, accidental (unintentional)
        Poisoning by hemostatic drug NOS

    ● **T45.622**   Poisoning by hemostatic drug, intentional self-harm

    ● **T45.623**   Poisoning by hemostatic drug, assault

    ● **T45.624**   Poisoning by hemostatic drug, undetermined

    ● **T45.625**   Adverse effect of hemostatic drug

    ● **T45.626**   Underdosing of hemostatic drugs

● **T45.69**   Poisoning by, adverse effect of and underdosing of other fibrinolysis-affecting drugs

    ● **T45.691**   Poisoning by other fibrinolysis-affecting drugs, accidental (unintentional)
        Poisoning by other fibrinolysis-affecting drug NOS

    ● **T45.692**   Poisoning by other fibrinolysis-affecting drugs, intentional self-harm

    ● **T45.693**   Poisoning by other fibrinolysis-affecting drugs, assault

    ● **T45.694**   Poisoning by other fibrinolysis-affecting drugs, undetermined

    ● **T45.695**   Adverse effect of other fibrinolysis-affecting drugs

    ● **T45.696**   Underdosing of other fibrinolysis-affecting drugs

● **T45.7**   Poisoning by, adverse effect of and underdosing of anticoagulant antagonists, vitamin K and other coagulants

   ● **T45.7X**   Poisoning by, adverse effect of and underdosing of anticoagulant antagonists, vitamin K and other coagulants

    ● **T45.7X1**   Poisoning by anticoagulant antagonists, vitamin K and other coagulants, accidental (unintentional)
        Poisoning by anticoagulant antagonists, vitamin K and other coagulants NOS

    ● **T45.7X2**   Poisoning by anticoagulant antagonists, vitamin K and other coagulants, intentional self-harm

    ● **T45.7X3**   Poisoning by anticoagulant antagonists, vitamin K and other coagulants, assault

    ● **T45.7X4**   Poisoning by anticoagulant antagonists, vitamin K and other coagulants, undetermined

    ● **T45.7X5**   Adverse effect of anticoagulant antagonists, vitamin K and other coagulants

    ● **T45.7X6**   Underdosing of anticoagulant antagonist, vitamin K and other coagulants

       Excludes1   vitamin K deficiency (E56.1)

● **T45.8**   Poisoning by, adverse effect of and underdosing of other primarily systemic and hematological agents
    Poisoning by, adverse effect of and underdosing of liver preparations and other antianemic agents
    Poisoning by, adverse effect of and underdosing of natural blood and blood products
    Poisoning by, adverse effect of and underdosing of plasma substitute

    Excludes2   poisoning by, adverse effect of and underdosing of immunoglobulin (T50.Z1)
        poisoning by, adverse effect of and underdosing of iron (T45.4)
        transfusion reactions (T80.-)

   ● **T45.8X**   Poisoning by, adverse effect of and underdosing of other primarily systemic and hematological agents

    ● **T45.8X1**   Poisoning by other primarily systemic and hematological agents, accidental (unintentional)
        Poisoning by other primarily systemic and hematological agents NOS

    ● **T45.8X2**   Poisoning by other primarily systemic and hematological agents, intentional self-harm

CHAPTER 19 (S00-T88)

- T45.8X3 Poisoning by other primarily systemic and hematological agents, assault
- T45.8X4 Poisoning by other primarily systemic and hematological agents, undetermined
- T45.8X5 Adverse effect of other primarily systemic and hematological agents
  Coding Clinic: 2016, Q4, P42
- T45.8X6 Underdosing of other primarily systemic and hematological agents
- T45.9 Poisoning by, adverse effect of and underdosing of unspecified primarily systemic and hematological agent
  - X T45.91 Poisoning by unspecified primarily systemic and hematological agent, accidental (unintentional)
    Poisoning by primarily systemic and hematological agent NOS
  - X T45.92 Poisoning by unspecified primarily systemic and hematological agent, intentional self-harm
  - X T45.93 Poisoning by unspecified primarily systemic and hematological agent, assault
  - X T45.94 Poisoning by unspecified primarily systemic and hematological agent, undetermined
  - X T45.95 Adverse effect of unspecified primarily systemic and hematological agent
  - X T45.96 Underdosing of unspecified primarily systemic and hematological agent
- T46 Poisoning by, adverse effect of and underdosing of agents primarily affecting the cardiovascular system
  Excludes1 poisoning by, adverse effect of and underdosing of metaraminol (T44.4)
  The appropriate 7th character is to be added to each code from category T46

A	initial encounter
D	subsequent encounter
S	sequela

- T46.0 Poisoning by, adverse effect of and underdosing of cardiac-stimulant glycosides and drugs of similar action
  - T46.0X Poisoning by, adverse effect of and underdosing of cardiac-stimulant glycosides and drugs of similar action
    - T46.0X1 Poisoning by cardiac-stimulant glycosides and drugs of similar action, accidental (unintentional)
      Poisoning by cardiac-stimulant glycosides and drugs of similar action NOS
    - T46.0X2 Poisoning by cardiac-stimulant glycosides and drugs of similar action, intentional self-harm
    - T46.0X3 Poisoning by cardiac-stimulant glycosides and drugs of similar action, assault
    - T46.0X4 Poisoning by cardiac-stimulant glycosides and drugs of similar action, undetermined
    - T46.0X5 Adverse effect of cardiac-stimulant glycosides and drugs of similar action
    - T46.0X6 Underdosing of cardiac-stimulant glycosides and drugs of similar action
- T46.1 Poisoning by, adverse effect of and underdosing of calcium-channel blockers
  - T46.1X Poisoning by, adverse effect of and underdosing of calcium-channel blockers
    - T46.1X1 Poisoning by calcium-channel blockers, accidental (unintentional)
      Poisoning by calcium-channel blockers NOS
    - T46.1X2 Poisoning by calcium-channel blockers, intentional self-harm

- T46.1X3 Poisoning by calcium-channel blockers, assault
- T46.1X4 Poisoning by calcium-channel blockers, undetermined
- T46.1X5 Adverse effect of calcium-channel blockers
- T46.1X6 Underdosing of calcium-channel blockers
- T46.2 Poisoning by, adverse effect of and underdosing of other antidysrhythmic drugs, not elsewhere classified
  Excludes1 poisoning by, adverse effect of and underdosing of beta-adrenoreceptor antagonists (T44.7-)
  - T46.2X Poisoning by, adverse effect of and underdosing of other antidysrhythmic drugs
    - T46.2X1 Poisoning by other antidysrhythmic drugs, accidental (unintentional)
      Poisoning by other antidysrhythmic drugs NOS
    - T46.2X2 Poisoning by other antidysrhythmic drugs, intentional self-harm
    - T46.2X3 Poisoning by other antidysrhythmic drugs, assault
    - T46.2X4 Poisoning by other antidysrhythmic drugs, undetermined
    - T46.2X5 Adverse effect of other antidysrhythmic drugs
    - T46.2X6 Underdosing of other antidysrhythmic drugs
- T46.3 Poisoning by, adverse effect of and underdosing of coronary vasodilators
  Poisoning by, adverse effect of and underdosing of dipyridamole
  Excludes1 poisoning by, adverse effect of and underdosing of calcium-channel blockers (T46.1)
  - T46.3X Poisoning by, adverse effect of and underdosing of coronary vasodilators
    - T46.3X1 Poisoning by coronary vasodilators, accidental (unintentional)
      Poisoning by coronary vasodilators NOS
    - T46.3X2 Poisoning by coronary vasodilators, intentional self-harm
    - T46.3X3 Poisoning by coronary vasodilators, assault
    - T46.3X4 Poisoning by coronary vasodilators, undetermined
    - T46.3X5 Adverse effect of coronary vasodilators
    - T46.3X6 Underdosing of coronary vasodilators
- T46.4 Poisoning by, adverse effect of and underdosing of angiotensin-converting-enzyme inhibitors
  - T46.4X Poisoning by, adverse effect of and underdosing of angiotensin-converting-enzyme inhibitors
    - T46.4X1 Poisoning by angiotensin-converting-enzyme inhibitors, accidental (unintentional)
      Poisoning by angiotensin-converting-enzyme inhibitors NOS
    - T46.4X2 Poisoning by angiotensin-converting-enzyme inhibitors, intentional self-harm
    - T46.4X3 Poisoning by angiotensin-converting-enzyme inhibitors, assault
    - T46.4X4 Poisoning by angiotensin-converting-enzyme inhibitors, undetermined
    - T46.4X5 Adverse effect of angiotensin-converting-enzyme inhibitors
    - T46.4X6 Underdosing of angiotensin-converting-enzyme inhibitors

● T46.5   **Poisoning by, adverse effect of and underdosing of other antihypertensive drugs**

     Excludes2   poisoning by, adverse effect of and underdosing of beta-adrenoreceptor antagonists (T44.7)

                 poisoning by, adverse effect of and underdosing of calcium-channel blockers (T46.1)

                 poisoning by, adverse effect of and underdosing of diuretics (T50.0-T50.2)

  ● T46.5X   **Poisoning by, adverse effect of and underdosing of other antihypertensive drugs**

    ● T46.5X1   **Poisoning by other antihypertensive drugs, accidental (unintentional)**

          Poisoning by other antihypertensive drugs NOS

    ● T46.5X2   **Poisoning by other antihypertensive drugs, intentional self-harm**

    ● T46.5X3   **Poisoning by other antihypertensive drugs, assault**

    ● T46.5X4   **Poisoning by other antihypertensive drugs, undetermined**

    ● T46.5X5   **Adverse effect of other antihypertensive drugs**

    ● T46.5X6   **Underdosing of other antihypertensive drugs**

● T46.6   **Poisoning by, adverse effect of and underdosing of antihyperlipidemic and antiarteriosclerotic drugs**

  ● T46.6X   **Poisoning by, adverse effect of and underdosing of antihyperlipidemic and antiarteriosclerotic drugs**

    ● T46.6X1   **Poisoning by antihyperlipidemic and antiarteriosclerotic drugs, accidental (unintentional)**

          Poisoning by antihyperlipidemic and antiarteriosclerotic drugs NOS

    ● T46.6X2   **Poisoning by antihyperlipidemic and antiarteriosclerotic drugs, intentional self-harm**

    ● T46.6X3   **Poisoning by antihyperlipidemic and antiarteriosclerotic drugs, assault**

    ● T46.6X4   **Poisoning by antihyperlipidemic and antiarteriosclerotic drugs, undetermined**

    ● T46.6X5   **Adverse effect of antihyperlipidemic and antiarteriosclerotic drugs**

    ● T46.6X6   **Underdosing of antihyperlipidemic and antiarteriosclerotic drugs**

● T46.7   **Poisoning by, adverse effect of and underdosing of peripheral vasodilators**

     Poisoning by, adverse effect of and underdosing of nicotinic acid (derivatives)

     Excludes1   poisoning by, adverse effect of and underdosing of papaverine (T44.3)

  ● T46.7X   **Poisoning by, adverse effect of and underdosing of peripheral vasodilators**

    ● T46.7X1   **Poisoning by peripheral vasodilators, accidental (unintentional)**

          Poisoning by peripheral vasodilators NOS

    ● T46.7X2   **Poisoning by peripheral vasodilators, intentional self-harm**

    ● T46.7X3   **Poisoning by peripheral vasodilators, assault**

    ● T46.7X4   **Poisoning by peripheral vasodilators, undetermined**

    ● T46.7X5   **Adverse effect of peripheral vasodilators**

    ● T46.7X6   **Underdosing of peripheral vasodilators**

● T46.8   **Poisoning by, adverse effect of and underdosing of antivaricose drugs, including sclerosing agents**

  ● T46.8X   **Poisoning by, adverse effect of and underdosing of antivaricose drugs, including sclerosing agents**

    ● T46.8X1   **Poisoning by antivaricose drugs, including sclerosing agents, accidental (unintentional)**

          Poisoning by antivaricose drugs, including sclerosing agents NOS

    ● T46.8X2   **Poisoning by antivaricose drugs, including sclerosing agents, intentional self-harm**

    ● T46.8X3   **Poisoning by antivaricose drugs, including sclerosing agents, assault**

    ● T46.8X4   **Poisoning by antivaricose drugs, including sclerosing agents, undetermined**

    ● T46.8X5   **Adverse effect of antivaricose drugs, including sclerosing agents**

    ● T46.8X6   **Underdosing of antivaricose drugs, including sclerosing agents**

● T46.9   **Poisoning by, adverse effect of and underdosing of other and unspecified agents primarily affecting the cardiovascular system**

  ● T46.90   **Poisoning by, adverse effect of and underdosing of unspecified agents primarily affecting the cardiovascular system**

    ● T46.901   **Poisoning by unspecified agents primarily affecting the cardiovascular system, accidental (unintentional)**

    ● T46.902   **Poisoning by unspecified agents primarily affecting the cardiovascular system, intentional self-harm**

    ● T46.903   **Poisoning by unspecified agents primarily affecting the cardiovascular system, assault**

    ● T46.904   **Poisoning by unspecified agents primarily affecting the cardiovascular system, undetermined**

    ● T46.905   **Adverse effect of unspecified agents primarily affecting the cardiovascular system**

    ● T46.906   **Underdosing of unspecified agents primarily affecting the cardiovascular system**

  ● T46.99   **Poisoning by, adverse effect of and underdosing of other agents primarily affecting the cardiovascular system**

    ● T46.991   **Poisoning by other agents primarily affecting the cardiovascular system, accidental (unintentional)**

    ● T46.992   **Poisoning by other agents primarily affecting the cardiovascular system, intentional self-harm**

    ● T46.993   **Poisoning by other agents primarily affecting the cardiovascular system, assault**

    ● T46.994   **Poisoning by other agents primarily affecting the cardiovascular system, undetermined**

    ● T46.995   **Adverse effect of other agents primarily affecting the cardiovascular system**

    ● T46.996   **Underdosing of other agents primarily affecting the cardiovascular system**

CHAPTER 19 (S00-T88)

T47   Poisoning by, adverse effect of and underdosing of agents primarily affecting the gastrointestinal system

The appropriate 7th character is to be added to each code from category T47

A	initial encounter
D	subsequent encounter
S	sequela

T47.0   Poisoning by, adverse effect of and underdosing of histamine H2-receptor blockers

   T47.0X   Poisoning by, adverse effect of and underdosing of histamine H2-receptor blockers

     T47.0X1   Poisoning by histamine H2-receptor blockers, accidental (unintentional)
       Poisoning by histamine H2-receptor blockers NOS

     T47.0X2   Poisoning by histamine H2-receptor blockers, intentional self-harm

     T47.0X3   Poisoning by histamine H2-receptor blockers, assault

     T47.0X4   Poisoning by histamine H2-receptor blockers, undetermined

     T47.0X5   Adverse effect of histamine H2-receptor blockers

     T47.0X6   Underdosing of histamine H2-receptor blockers

T47.1   Poisoning by, adverse effect of and underdosing of other antacids and anti-gastric-secretion drugs

   T47.1X   Poisoning by, adverse effect of and underdosing of other antacids and anti-gastric-secretion drugs

     T47.1X1   Poisoning by other antacids and anti-gastric-secretion drugs, accidental (unintentional)
       Poisoning by other antacids and anti-gastric-secretion drugs NOS

     T47.1X2   Poisoning by other antacids and anti-gastric-secretion drugs, intentional self-harm

     T47.1X3   Poisoning by other antacids and anti-gastric-secretion drugs, assault

     T47.1X4   Poisoning by other antacids and anti-gastric-secretion drugs, undetermined

     T47.1X5   Adverse effect of other antacids and anti-gastric-secretion drugs

     T47.1X6   Underdosing of other antacids and anti-gastric-secretion drugs

T47.2   Poisoning by, adverse effect of and underdosing of stimulant laxatives

   T47.2X   Poisoning by, adverse effect of and underdosing of stimulant laxatives

     T47.2X1   Poisoning by stimulant laxatives, accidental (unintentional)
       Poisoning by stimulant laxatives NOS

     T47.2X2   Poisoning by stimulant laxatives, intentional self-harm

     T47.2X3   Poisoning by stimulant laxatives, assault

     T47.2X4   Poisoning by stimulant laxatives, undetermined

     T47.2X5   Adverse effect of stimulant laxatives

     T47.2X6   Underdosing of stimulant laxatives

T47.3   Poisoning by, adverse effect of and underdosing of saline and osmotic laxatives

   T47.3X   Poisoning by and adverse effect of saline and osmotic laxatives

     T47.3X1   Poisoning by saline and osmotic laxatives, accidental (unintentional)
       Poisoning by saline and osmotic laxatives NOS

     T47.3X2   Poisoning by saline and osmotic laxatives, intentional self-harm

     T47.3X3   Poisoning by saline and osmotic laxatives, assault

     T47.3X4   Poisoning by saline and osmotic laxatives, undetermined

     T47.3X5   Adverse effect of saline and osmotic laxatives

     T47.3X6   Underdosing of saline and osmotic laxatives

T47.4   Poisoning by, adverse effect of and underdosing of other laxatives

   T47.4X   Poisoning by, adverse effect of and underdosing of other laxatives

     T47.4X1   Poisoning by other laxatives, accidental (unintentional)
       Poisoning by other laxatives NOS

     T47.4X2   Poisoning by other laxatives, intentional self-harm

     T47.4X3   Poisoning by other laxatives, assault

     T47.4X4   Poisoning by other laxatives, undetermined

     T47.4X5   Adverse effect of other laxatives

     T47.4X6   Underdosing of other laxatives

T47.5   Poisoning by, adverse effect of and underdosing of digestants

   T47.5X   Poisoning by, adverse effect of and underdosing of digestants

     T47.5X1   Poisoning by digestants, accidental (unintentional)
       Poisoning by digestants NOS

     T47.5X2   Poisoning by digestants, intentional self-harm

     T47.5X3   Poisoning by digestants, assault

     T47.5X4   Poisoning by digestants, undetermined

     T47.5X5   Adverse effect of digestants

     T47.5X6   Underdosing of digestants

T47.6   Poisoning by, adverse effect of and underdosing of antidiarrheal drugs

   Excludes2   poisoning by, adverse effect of and underdosing of systemic antibiotics and other anti-infectives (T36-T37)

   T47.6X   Poisoning by, adverse effect of and underdosing of antidiarrheal drugs

     T47.6X1   Poisoning by antidiarrheal drugs, accidental (unintentional)
       Poisoning by antidiarrheal drugs NOS

     T47.6X2   Poisoning by antidiarrheal drugs, intentional self-harm

     T47.6X3   Poisoning by antidiarrheal drugs, assault

     T47.6X4   Poisoning by antidiarrheal drugs, undetermined

     T47.6X5   Adverse effect of antidiarrheal drugs

     T47.6X6   Underdosing of antidiarrheal drugs

► New   ⮕ Revised   ~~deleted~~ Deleted   Excludes 1   Excludes 2   Includes   Use additional   Code first   Code also   Key words

OGCR Official Guidelines   X Assign placeholder X   ● Use Additional Character(s)   ▷ Manifestation Code   **Coding Clinic**

- **T47.7** Poisoning by, adverse effect of and underdosing of emetics
  - **T47.7X** Poisoning by, adverse effect of and underdosing of emetics
    - **T47.7X1** Poisoning by emetics, accidental (unintentional)
      Poisoning by emetics NOS
    - **T47.7X2** Poisoning by emetics, intentional self-harm
    - **T47.7X3** Poisoning by emetics, assault
    - **T47.7X4** Poisoning by emetics, undetermined
    - **T47.7X5** Adverse effect of emetics
    - **T47.7X6** Underdosing of emetics
- **T47.8** Poisoning by, adverse effect of and underdosing of other agents primarily affecting gastrointestinal system
  - **T47.8X** Poisoning by, adverse effect of and underdosing of other agents primarily affecting gastrointestinal system
    - **T47.8X1** Poisoning by other agents primarily affecting gastrointestinal system, accidental (unintentional)
      Poisoning by other agents primarily affecting gastrointestinal system NOS
    - **T47.8X2** Poisoning by other agents primarily affecting gastrointestinal system, intentional self-harm
    - **T47.8X3** Poisoning by other agents primarily affecting gastrointestinal system, assault
    - **T47.8X4** Poisoning by other agents primarily affecting gastrointestinal system, undetermined
    - **T47.8X5** Adverse effect of other agents primarily affecting gastrointestinal system
    - **T47.8X6** Underdosing of other agents primarily affecting gastrointestinal system
- **T47.9** Poisoning by, adverse effect of and underdosing of unspecified agents primarily affecting the gastrointestinal system
  - X **T47.91** Poisoning by unspecified agents primarily affecting the gastrointestinal system, accidental (unintentional)
    Poisoning by agents primarily affecting the gastrointestinal system NOS
  - X **T47.92** Poisoning by unspecified agents primarily affecting the gastrointestinal system, intentional self-harm
  - X **T47.93** Poisoning by unspecified agents primarily affecting the gastrointestinal system, assault
  - X **T47.94** Poisoning by unspecified agents primarily affecting the gastrointestinal system, undetermined
  - X **T47.95** Adverse effect of unspecified agents primarily affecting the gastrointestinal system
  - X **T47.96** Underdosing of unspecified agents primarily affecting the gastrointestinal system

- **T48** Poisoning by, adverse effect of and underdosing of agents primarily acting on smooth and skeletal muscles and the respiratory system

  The appropriate 7th character is to be added to each code from category T48

A	initial encounter
D	subsequent encounter
S	sequela

  - **T48.0** Poisoning by, adverse effect of and underdosing of oxytocic drugs

    Excludes1   poisoning by, adverse effect of and underdosing of estrogens, progestogens and antagonists (T38.4-T38.6)

    - **T48.0X** Poisoning by, adverse effect of and underdosing of oxytocic drugs
      - **T48.0X1** Poisoning by oxytocic drugs, accidental (unintentional)
        Poisoning by oxytocic drugs NOS
      - **T48.0X2** Poisoning by oxytocic drugs, intentional self-harm
      - **T48.0X3** Poisoning by oxytocic drugs, assault
      - **T48.0X4** Poisoning by oxytocic drugs, undetermined
      - **T48.0X5** Adverse effect of oxytocic drugs
      - **T48.0X6** Underdosing of oxytocic drugs
  - **T48.1** Poisoning by, adverse effect of and underdosing of skeletal muscle relaxants [neuromuscular blocking agents]
    - **T48.1X** Poisoning by, adverse effect of and underdosing of skeletal muscle relaxants [neuromuscular blocking agents]
      - **T48.1X1** Poisoning by skeletal muscle relaxants [neuromuscular blocking agents], accidental (unintentional)
        Poisoning by skeletal muscle relaxants [neuromuscular blocking agents] NOS
      - **T48.1X2** Poisoning by skeletal muscle relaxants [neuromuscular blocking agents], intentional self-harm
      - **T48.1X3** Poisoning by skeletal muscle relaxants [neuromuscular blocking agents], assault
      - **T48.1X4** Poisoning by skeletal muscle relaxants [neuromuscular blocking agents], undetermined
      - **T48.1X5** Adverse effect of skeletal muscle relaxants [neuromuscular blocking agents]
      - **T48.1X6** Underdosing of skeletal muscle relaxants [neuromuscular blocking agents]
  - **T48.2** Poisoning by, adverse effect of and underdosing of other and unspecified drugs acting on muscles
    - **T48.20** Poisoning by, adverse effect of and underdosing of unspecified drugs acting on muscles
      - **T48.201** Poisoning by unspecified drugs acting on muscles, accidental (unintentional)
        Poisoning by unspecified drugs acting on muscles NOS
      - **T48.202** Poisoning by unspecified drugs acting on muscles, intentional self-harm
      - **T48.203** Poisoning by unspecified drugs acting on muscles, assault
      - **T48.204** Poisoning by unspecified drugs acting on muscles, undetermined
      - **T48.205** Adverse effect of unspecified drugs acting on muscles
      - **T48.206** Underdosing of unspecified drugs acting on muscles

CHAPTER 19 (S00-T88)

● **T48.29** Poisoning by, adverse effect of and underdosing of other drugs acting on muscles

  ● **T48.291** Poisoning by other drugs acting on muscles, accidental (unintentional)
       Poisoning by other drugs acting on muscles NOS

  ● **T48.292** Poisoning by other drugs acting on muscles, intentional self-harm

  ● **T48.293** Poisoning by other drugs acting on muscles, assault

  ● **T48.294** Poisoning by other drugs acting on muscles, undetermined

  ● **T48.295** Adverse effect of other drugs acting on muscles

  ● **T48.296** Underdosing of other drugs acting on muscles

● **T48.3** Poisoning by, adverse effect of and underdosing of antitussives

  ● **T48.3X** Poisoning by, adverse effect of and underdosing of antitussives

    ● **T48.3X1** Poisoning by antitussives, accidental (unintentional)
        Poisoning by antitussives NOS

    ● **T48.3X2** Poisoning by antitussives, intentional self-harm

    ● **T48.3X3** Poisoning by antitussives, assault

    ● **T48.3X4** Poisoning by antitussives, undetermined

    ● **T48.3X5** Adverse effect of antitussives

    ● **T48.3X6** Underdosing of antitussives

● **T48.4** Poisoning by, adverse effect of and underdosing of expectorants

  ● **T48.4X** Poisoning by, adverse effect of and underdosing of expectorants

    ● **T48.4X1** Poisoning by expectorants, accidental (unintentional)
        Poisoning by expectorants NOS

    ● **T48.4X2** Poisoning by expectorants, intentional self-harm

    ● **T48.4X3** Poisoning by expectorants, assault

    ● **T48.4X4** Poisoning by expectorants, undetermined

    ● **T48.4X5** Adverse effect of expectorants

    ● **T48.4X6** Underdosing of expectorants

● **T48.5** Poisoning by, adverse effect of and underdosing of other anti-common-cold drugs
     Poisoning by, adverse effect of and underdosing of decongestants

     Excludes2 poisoning by, adverse effect of and underdosing of antipyretics, NEC (T39.9-)
          poisoning by, adverse effect of and underdosing of non-steroidal antiinflammatory drugs (T39.3-)
          poisoning by, adverse effect of and underdosing of salicylates (T39.0-)

  ● **T48.5X** Poisoning by, adverse effect of and underdosing of other anti-common-cold drugs

    ● **T48.5X1** Poisoning by other anti-common-cold drugs, accidental (unintentional)
        Poisoning by other anti-common-cold drugs NOS

    ● **T48.5X2** Poisoning by other anti-common-cold drugs, intentional self-harm

    ● **T48.5X3** Poisoning by other anti-common-cold drugs, assault

    ● **T48.5X4** Poisoning by other anti-common-cold drugs, undetermined

    ● **T48.5X5** Adverse effect of other anti-common-cold drugs

    ● **T48.5X6** Underdosing of other anti-common-cold drugs

● **T48.6** Poisoning by, adverse effect of and underdosing of antiasthmatics, not elsewhere classified
     Poisoning by, adverse effect of and underdosing of beta-adrenoreceptor agonists used in asthma therapy

     Excludes1 poisoning by, adverse effect of and underdosing of beta-adrenoreceptor agonists not used in asthma therapy (T44.5)
          poisoning by, adverse effect of and underdosing of anterior pituitary [adenohypophyseal] hormones (T38.8)

  ● **T48.6X** Poisoning by, adverse effect of and underdosing of antiasthmatics

    ● **T48.6X1** Poisoning by antiasthmatics, accidental (unintentional)
        Poisoning by antiasthmatics NOS

    ● **T48.6X2** Poisoning by antiasthmatics, intentional self-harm

    ● **T48.6X3** Poisoning by antiasthmatics, assault

    ● **T48.6X4** Poisoning by antiasthmatics, undetermined

    ● **T48.6X5** Adverse effect of antiasthmatics

    ● **T48.6X6** Underdosing of antiasthmatics

● **T48.9** Poisoning by, adverse effect of and underdosing of other and unspecified agents primarily acting on the respiratory system

  ● **T48.90** Poisoning by, adverse effect of and underdosing of unspecified agents primarily acting on the respiratory system

    ● **T48.901** Poisoning by unspecified agents primarily acting on the respiratory system, accidental (unintentional)

    ● **T48.902** Poisoning by unspecified agents primarily acting on the respiratory system, intentional self-harm

    ● **T48.903** Poisoning by unspecified agents primarily acting on the respiratory system, assault

    ● **T48.904** Poisoning by unspecified agents primarily acting on the respiratory system, undetermined

    ● **T48.905** Adverse effect of unspecified agents primarily acting on the respiratory system

    ● **T48.906** Underdosing of unspecified agents primarily acting on the respiratory system

  ● **T48.99** Poisoning by, adverse effect of and underdosing of other agents primarily acting on the respiratory system

    ● **T48.991** Poisoning by other agents primarily acting on the respiratory system, accidental (unintentional)

    ● **T48.992** Poisoning by other agents primarily acting on the respiratory system, intentional self-harm

    ● **T48.993** Poisoning by other agents primarily acting on the respiratory system, assault

    ● **T48.994** Poisoning by other agents primarily acting on the respiratory system, undetermined

    ● **T48.995** Adverse effect of other agents primarily acting on the respiratory system

    ● **T48.996** Underdosing of other agents primarily acting on the respiratory system

▶ New   ⇒ Revised   ~~deleted~~ Deleted   Excludes 1   Excludes 2   Includes   Use additional   Code first   Code also   Key words

OGCR Official Guidelines   X Assign placeholder X   ▶ Use Additional Character(s)   ▶ Manifestation Code   **Coding Clinic**

1396

- **T49**   **Poisoning by, adverse effect of and underdosing of topical agents primarily affecting skin and mucous membrane and by ophthalmological, otorhinolaryngological and dental drugs**

  > **Includes**   poisoning by, adverse effect of and underdosing of glucocorticoids, topically used

  The appropriate 7th character is to be added to each code from category T49

A	initial encounter
D	subsequent encounter
S	sequela

  - **T49.0**   **Poisoning by, adverse effect of and underdosing of local antifungal, anti-infective and anti-inflammatory drugs**
    - **T49.0X**   **Poisoning by, adverse effect of and underdosing of local antifungal, anti-infective and anti-inflammatory drugs**
      - **T49.0X1**   Poisoning by local antifungal, anti-infective and anti-inflammatory drugs, accidental (unintentional)
        > Poisoning by local antifungal, anti-infective and anti-inflammatory drugs NOS
      - **T49.0X2**   Poisoning by local antifungal, anti-infective and anti-inflammatory drugs, intentional self-harm
      - **T49.0X3**   Poisoning by local antifungal, anti-infective and anti-inflammatory drugs, assault
      - **T49.0X4**   Poisoning by local antifungal, anti-infective and anti-inflammatory drugs, undetermined
      - **T49.0X5**   Adverse effect of local antifungal, anti-infective and anti-inflammatory drugs
      - **T49.0X6**   Underdosing of local antifungal, anti-infective and anti-inflammatory drugs
  - **T49.1**   **Poisoning by, adverse effect of and underdosing of antipruritics**
    - **T49.1X**   **Poisoning by, adverse effect of and underdosing of antipruritics**
      - **T49.1X1**   Poisoning by antipruritics, accidental (unintentional)
        > Poisoning by antipruritics NOS
      - **T49.1X2**   Poisoning by antipruritics, intentional self-harm
      - **T49.1X3**   Poisoning by antipruritics, assault
      - **T49.1X4**   Poisoning by antipruritics, undetermined
      - **T49.1X5**   Adverse effect of antipruritics
      - **T49.1X6**   Underdosing of antipruritics
  - **T49.2**   **Poisoning by, adverse effect of and underdosing of local astringents and local detergents**
    - **T49.2X**   **Poisoning by, adverse effect of and underdosing of local astringents and local detergents**
      - **T49.2X1**   Poisoning by local astringents and local detergents, accidental (unintentional)
        > Poisoning by local astringents and local detergents NOS
      - **T49.2X2**   Poisoning by local astringents and local detergents, intentional self-harm
      - **T49.2X3**   Poisoning by local astringents and local detergents, assault
      - **T49.2X4**   Poisoning by local astringents and local detergents, undetermined
      - **T49.2X5**   Adverse effect of local astringents and local detergents
      - **T49.2X6**   Underdosing of local astringents and local detergents

- **T49.3**   **Poisoning by, adverse effect of and underdosing of emollients, demulcents and protectants**
  - **T49.3X**   **Poisoning by, adverse effect of and underdosing of emollients, demulcents and protectants**
    - **T49.3X1**   Poisoning by emollients, demulcents and protectants, accidental (unintentional)
      > Poisoning by emollients, demulcents and protectants NOS
    - **T49.3X2**   Poisoning by emollients, demulcents and protectants, intentional self-harm
    - **T49.3X3**   Poisoning by emollients, demulcents and protectants, assault
    - **T49.3X4**   Poisoning by emollients, demulcents and protectants, undetermined
    - **T49.3X5**   Adverse effect of emollients, demulcents and protectants
    - **T49.3X6**   Underdosing of emollients, demulcents and protectants
- **T49.4**   **Poisoning by, adverse effect of and underdosing of keratolytics, keratoplastics, and other hair treatment drugs and preparations**
  - **T49.4X**   **Poisoning by, adverse effect of and underdosing of keratolytics, keratoplastics, and other hair treatment drugs and preparations**
    - **T49.4X1**   Poisoning by keratolytics, keratoplastics, and other hair treatment drugs and preparations, accidental (unintentional)
      > Poisoning by keratolytics, keratoplastics, and other hair treatment drugs and preparations NOS
    - **T49.4X2**   Poisoning by keratolytics, keratoplastics, and other hair treatment drugs and preparations, intentional self-harm
    - **T49.4X3**   Poisoning by keratolytics, keratoplastics, and other hair treatment drugs and preparations, assault
    - **T49.4X4**   Poisoning by keratolytics, keratoplastics, and other hair treatment drugs and preparations, undetermined
    - **T49.4X5**   Adverse effect of keratolytics, keratoplastics, and other hair treatment drugs and preparations
    - **T49.4X6**   Underdosing of keratolytics, keratoplastics, and other hair treatment drugs and preparations
- **T49.5**   **Poisoning by, adverse effect of and underdosing of ophthalmological drugs and preparations**
  - **T49.5X**   **Poisoning by, adverse effect of and underdosing of ophthalmological drugs and preparations**
    - **T49.5X1**   Poisoning by ophthalmological drugs and preparations, accidental (unintentional)
      > Poisoning by ophthalmological drugs and preparations NOS
    - **T49.5X2**   Poisoning by ophthalmological drugs and preparations, intentional self-harm
    - **T49.5X3**   Poisoning by ophthalmological drugs and preparations, assault
    - **T49.5X4**   Poisoning by ophthalmological drugs and preparations, undetermined
    - **T49.5X5**   Adverse effect of ophthalmological drugs and preparations
    - **T49.5X6**   Underdosing of ophthalmological drugs and preparations

CHAPTER 19 (S00–T88)

● **T49.6** Poisoning by, adverse effect of and underdosing of otorhinolaryngological drugs and preparations

  ● **T49.6X** Poisoning by, adverse effect of and underdosing of otorhinolaryngological drugs and preparations

    ● **T49.6X1** Poisoning by otorhinolaryngological drugs and preparations, accidental (unintentional)
         Poisoning by otorhinolaryngological drugs and preparations NOS

    ● **T49.6X2** Poisoning by otorhinolaryngological drugs and preparations, intentional self-harm

    ● **T49.6X3** Poisoning by otorhinolaryngological drugs and preparations, assault

    ● **T49.6X4** Poisoning by otorhinolaryngological drugs and preparations, undetermined

    ● **T49.6X5** Adverse effect of otorhinolaryngological drugs and preparations

    ● **T49.6X6** Underdosing of otorhinolaryngological drugs and preparations

● **T49.7** Poisoning by, adverse effect of and underdosing of dental drugs, topically applied

  ● **T49.7X** Poisoning by, adverse effect of and underdosing of dental drugs, topically applied

    ● **T49.7X1** Poisoning by dental drugs, topically applied, accidental (unintentional)
         Poisoning by dental drugs, topically applied NOS

    ● **T49.7X2** Poisoning by dental drugs, topically applied, intentional self-harm

    ● **T49.7X3** Poisoning by dental drugs, topically applied, assault

    ● **T49.7X4** Poisoning by dental drugs, topically applied, undetermined

    ● **T49.7X5** Adverse effect of dental drugs, topically applied

    ● **T49.7X6** Underdosing of dental drugs, topically applied

● **T49.8** Poisoning by, adverse effect of and underdosing of other topical agents
     Poisoning by, adverse effect of and underdosing of spermicides

  ● **T49.8X** Poisoning by, adverse effect of and underdosing of other topical agents

    ● **T49.8X1** Poisoning by other topical agents, accidental (unintentional)
         Poisoning by other topical agents NOS

    ● **T49.8X2** Poisoning by other topical agents, intentional self-harm

    ● **T49.8X3** Poisoning by other topical agents, assault

    ● **T49.8X4** Poisoning by other topical agents, undetermined

    ● **T49.8X5** Adverse effect of other topical agents

    ● **T49.8X6** Underdosing of other topical agents

● **T49.9** Poisoning by, adverse effect of and underdosing of unspecified topical agent

  X● **T49.91** Poisoning by unspecified topical agent, accidental (unintentional)

  X● **T49.92** Poisoning by unspecified topical agent, intentional self-harm

  X● **T49.93** Poisoning by unspecified topical agent, assault

  X● **T49.94** Poisoning by unspecified topical agent, undetermined

  X● **T49.95** Adverse effect of unspecified topical agent

  X● **T49.96** Underdosing of unspecified topical agent

● **T50** Poisoning by, adverse effect of and underdosing of diuretics and other and unspecified drugs, medicaments and biological substances

     The appropriate 7th character is to be added to each code from category T50

     | | |
     | A | initial encounter |
     | D | subsequent encounter |
     | S | sequela |

● **T50.0** Poisoning by, adverse effect of and underdosing of mineralocorticoids and their antagonists

  ● **T50.0X** Poisoning by, adverse effect of and underdosing of mineralocorticoids and their antagonists

    ● **T50.0X1** Poisoning by mineralocorticoids and their antagonists, accidental (unintentional)
         Poisoning by mineralocorticoids and their antagonists NOS

    ● **T50.0X2** Poisoning by mineralocorticoids and their antagonists, intentional self-harm

    ● **T50.0X3** Poisoning by mineralocorticoids and their antagonists, assault

    ● **T50.0X4** Poisoning by mineralocorticoids and their antagonists, undetermined

    ● **T50.0X5** Adverse effect of mineralocorticoids and their antagonists

    ● **T50.0X6** Underdosing of mineralocorticoids and their antagonists

● **T50.1** Poisoning by, adverse effect of and underdosing of loop [high-ceiling] diuretics

  ● **T50.1X** Poisoning by, adverse effect of and underdosing of loop [high-ceiling] diuretics

    ● **T50.1X1** Poisoning by loop [high-ceiling] diuretics, accidental (unintentional)
         Poisoning by loop [high-ceiling] diuretics NOS

    ● **T50.1X2** Poisoning by loop [high-ceiling] diuretics, intentional self-harm

    ● **T50.1X3** Poisoning by loop [high-ceiling] diuretics, assault

    ● **T50.1X4** Poisoning by loop [high-ceiling] diuretics, undetermined

    ● **T50.1X5** Adverse effect of loop [high-ceiling] diuretics

    ● **T50.1X6** Underdosing of loop [high-ceiling] diuretics

● **T50.2** Poisoning by, adverse effect of and underdosing of carbonic-anhydrase inhibitors, benzothiadiazides and other diuretics
     Poisoning by, adverse effect of and underdosing of acetazolamide

  ● **T50.2X** Poisoning by, adverse effect of and underdosing of carbonic-anhydrase inhibitors, benzothiadiazides and other diuretics

    ● **T50.2X1** Poisoning by carbonic-anhydrase inhibitors, benzothiadiazides and other diuretics, accidental (unintentional)
         Poisoning by carbonic-anhydrase inhibitors, benzothiadiazides and other diuretics NOS

    ● **T50.2X2** Poisoning by carbonic-anhydrase inhibitors, benzothiadiazides and other diuretics, intentional self-harm

    ● **T50.2X3** Poisoning by carbonic-anhydrase inhibitors, benzothiadiazides and other diuretics, assault

    ● **T50.2X4** Poisoning by carbonic-anhydrase inhibitors, benzothiadiazides and other diuretics, undetermined

CHAPTER 19 (S00-T88)

▶ New   ⇒ Revised   ~~deleted~~ Deleted   Excludes 1   Excludes 2   Includes   Use additional   Code first   Code also   Key words
OGCR Official Guidelines   X Assign placeholder X   ● Use Additional Character(s)   ▷ Manifestation Code   **Coding Clinic**

● **T50.2X5** Adverse effect of carbonic-anhydrase inhibitors, benzothiadiazides and other diuretics

● **T50.2X6** Underdosing of carbonic-anhydrase inhibitors, benzothiadiazides and other diuretics

● **T50.3** Poisoning by, adverse effect of and underdosing of electrolytic, caloric and water-balance agents
Poisoning by, adverse effect of and underdosing of oral rehydration salts

● **T50.3X** Poisoning by, adverse effect of and underdosing of electrolytic, caloric and water-balance agents

● **T50.3X1** Poisoning by electrolytic, caloric and water-balance agents, accidental (unintentional)
Poisoning by electrolytic, caloric and water-balance agents NOS

● **T50.3X2** Poisoning by electrolytic, caloric and water-balance agents, intentional self-harm

● **T50.3X3** Poisoning by electrolytic, caloric and water-balance agents, assault

● **T50.3X4** Poisoning by electrolytic, caloric and water-balance agents, undetermined

● **T50.3X5** Adverse effect of electrolytic, caloric and water-balance agents

● **T50.3X6** Underdosing of electrolytic, caloric and water-balance agents

● **T50.4** Poisoning by, adverse effect of and underdosing of drugs affecting uric acid metabolism

● **T50.4X** Poisoning by, adverse effect of and underdosing of drugs affecting uric acid metabolism

● **T50.4X1** Poisoning by drugs affecting uric acid metabolism, accidental (unintentional)
Poisoning by drugs affecting uric acid metabolism NOS

● **T50.4X2** Poisoning by drugs affecting uric acid metabolism, intentional self-harm

● **T50.4X3** Poisoning by drugs affecting uric acid metabolism, assault

● **T50.4X4** Poisoning by drugs affecting uric acid metabolism, undetermined

● **T50.4X5** Adverse effect of drugs affecting uric acid metabolism

● **T50.4X6** Underdosing of drugs affecting uric acid metabolism

● **T50.5** Poisoning by, adverse effect of and underdosing of appetite depressants

● **T50.5X** Poisoning by, adverse effect of and underdosing of appetite depressants

● **T50.5X1** Poisoning by appetite depressants, accidental (unintentional)
Poisoning by appetite depressants NOS

● **T50.5X2** Poisoning by appetite depressants, intentional self-harm

● **T50.5X3** Poisoning by appetite depressants, assault

● **T50.5X4** Poisoning by appetite depressants, undetermined

● **T50.5X5** Adverse effect of appetite depressants

● **T50.5X6** Underdosing of appetite depressants

● **T50.6** Poisoning by, adverse effect of and underdosing of antidotes and chelating agents
Poisoning by, adverse effect of and underdosing of alcohol deterrents

● **T50.6X** Poisoning by, adverse effect of and underdosing of antidotes and chelating agents

● **T50.6X1** Poisoning by antidotes and chelating agents, accidental (unintentional)
Poisoning by antidotes and chelating agents NOS

● **T50.6X2** Poisoning by antidotes and chelating agents, intentional self-harm

● **T50.6X3** Poisoning by antidotes and chelating agents, assault

● **T50.6X4** Poisoning by antidotes and chelating agents, undetermined

● **T50.6X5** Adverse effect of antidotes and chelating agents

● **T50.6X6** Underdosing of antidotes and chelating agents

● **T50.7** Poisoning by, adverse effect of and underdosing of analeptics and opioid receptor antagonists

● **T50.7X** Poisoning by, adverse effect of and underdosing of analeptics and opioid receptor antagonists

● **T50.7X1** Poisoning by analeptics and opioid receptor antagonists, accidental (unintentional)
Poisoning by analeptics and opioid receptor antagonists NOS

● **T50.7X2** Poisoning by analeptics and opioid receptor antagonists, intentional self-harm

● **T50.7X3** Poisoning by analeptics and opioid receptor antagonists, assault

● **T50.7X4** Poisoning by analeptics and opioid receptor antagonists, undetermined

● **T50.7X5** Adverse effect of analeptics and opioid receptor antagonists

● **T50.7X6** Underdosing of analeptics and opioid receptor antagonists

● **T50.8** Poisoning by, adverse effect of and underdosing of diagnostic agents

● **T50.8X** Poisoning by, adverse effect of and underdosing of diagnostic agents

● **T50.8X1** Poisoning by diagnostic agents, accidental (unintentional)
Poisoning by diagnostic agents NOS

● **T50.8X2** Poisoning by diagnostic agents, intentional self-harm

● **T50.8X3** Poisoning by diagnostic agents, assault

● **T50.8X4** Poisoning by diagnostic agents, undetermined

● **T50.8X5** Adverse effect of diagnostic agents

● **T50.8X6** Underdosing of diagnostic agents

● **T50.A** Poisoning by, adverse effect of and underdosing of bacterial vaccines

● **T50.A1** Poisoning by, adverse effect of and underdosing of pertussis vaccine, including combinations with a pertussis component

● **T50.A11** Poisoning by pertussis vaccine, including combinations with a pertussis component, accidental (unintentional)

● **T50.A12** Poisoning by pertussis vaccine, including combinations with a pertussis component, intentional self-harm

N Newborn Age: 0 **P** Pediatric Age: 0–17 **M** Maternity DX: 12–55 **A** Adult Age: 15–124 ♀ Females Only ♂ Males Only **1399**

CHAPTER 19 (S00-T88)

● T50.A13   Poisoning by pertussis vaccine, including combinations with a pertussis component, assault

● T50.A14   Poisoning by pertussis vaccine, including combinations with a pertussis component, undetermined

● T50.A15   Adverse effect of pertussis vaccine, including combinations with a pertussis component

● T50.A16   Underdosing of pertussis vaccine, including combinations with a pertussis component

● T50.A2   Poisoning by, adverse effect of and underdosing of mixed bacterial vaccines without a pertussis component

● T50.A21   Poisoning by mixed bacterial vaccines without a pertussis component, accidental (unintentional)

● T50.A22   Poisoning by mixed bacterial vaccines without a pertussis component, intentional self-harm

● T50.A23   Poisoning by mixed bacterial vaccines without a pertussis component, assault

● T50.A24   Poisoning by mixed bacterial vaccines without a pertussis component, undetermined

● T50.A25   Adverse effect of mixed bacterial vaccines without a pertussis component

● T50.A26   Underdosing of mixed bacterial vaccines without a pertussis component

● T50.A9   Poisoning by, adverse effect of and underdosing of other bacterial vaccines

● T50.A91   Poisoning by other bacterial vaccines, accidental (unintentional)

● T50.A92   Poisoning by other bacterial vaccines, intentional self-harm

● T50.A93   Poisoning by other bacterial vaccines, assault

● T50.A94   Poisoning by other bacterial vaccines, undetermined

● T50.A95   Adverse effect of other bacterial vaccines

● T50.A96   Underdosing of other bacterial vaccines

● T50.B   Poisoning by, adverse effect of and underdosing of viral vaccines

● T50.B1   Poisoning by, adverse effect of and underdosing of smallpox vaccines

● T50.B11   Poisoning by smallpox vaccines, accidental (unintentional)

● T50.B12   Poisoning by smallpox vaccines, intentional self-harm

● T50.B13   Poisoning by smallpox vaccines, assault

● T50.B14   Poisoning by smallpox vaccines, undetermined

● T50.B15   Adverse effect of smallpox vaccines

● T50.B16   Underdosing of smallpox vaccines

● T50.B9   Poisoning by, adverse effect of and underdosing of other viral vaccines

● T50.B91   Poisoning by other viral vaccines, accidental (unintentional)

● T50.B92   Poisoning by other viral vaccines, intentional self-harm

● T50.B93   Poisoning by other viral vaccines, assault

● T50.B94   Poisoning by other viral vaccines, undetermined

● T50.B95   Adverse effect of other viral vaccines

● T50.B96   Underdosing of other viral vaccines

● T50.Z   Poisoning by, adverse effect of and underdosing of other vaccines and biological substances

● T50.Z1   Poisoning by, adverse effect of and underdosing of immunoglobulin

● T50.Z11   Poisoning by immunoglobulin, accidental (unintentional)

● T50.Z12   Poisoning by immunoglobulin, intentional self-harm

● T50.Z13   Poisoning by immunoglobulin, assault

● T50.Z14   Poisoning by immunoglobulin, undetermined

● T50.Z15   Adverse effect of immunoglobulin

● T50.Z16   Underdosing of immunoglobulin

● T50.Z9   Poisoning by, adverse effect of and underdosing of other vaccines and biological substances

● T50.Z91   Poisoning by other vaccines and biological substances, accidental (unintentional)

● T50.Z92   Poisoning by other vaccines and biological substances, intentional self-harm

● T50.Z93   Poisoning by other vaccines and biological substances, assault

● T50.Z94   Poisoning by other vaccines and biological substances, undetermined

● T50.Z95   Adverse effect of other vaccines and biological substances

● T50.Z96   Underdosing of other vaccines and biological substances

● T50.9   Poisoning by, adverse effect of and underdosing of other and unspecified drugs, medicaments and biological substances

● T50.90   Poisoning by, adverse effect of and underdosing of unspecified drugs, medicaments and biological substances

● T50.901   Poisoning by unspecified drugs, medicaments and biological substances, accidental (unintentional)
    Coding Clinic: 2015, Q1, P21

● T50.902   Poisoning by unspecified drugs, medicaments and biological substances, intentional self-harm

● T50.903   Poisoning by unspecified drugs, medicaments and biological substances, assault

● T50.904   Poisoning by unspecified drugs, medicaments and biological substances, undetermined

● T50.905   Adverse effect of unspecified drugs, medicaments and biological substances

● T50.906   Underdosing of unspecified drugs, medicaments and biological substances

● T50.99   Poisoning by, adverse effect of and underdosing of other drugs, medicaments and biological substances

● T50.991   Poisoning by other drugs, medicaments and biological substances, accidental (unintentional)

● T50.992   Poisoning by other drugs, medicaments and biological substances, intentional self-harm

● T50.993   Poisoning by other drugs, medicaments and biological substances, assault

● **T50.994** Poisoning by other drugs, medicaments and biological substances, undetermined

● **T50.995** Adverse effect of other drugs, medicaments and biological substances

● **T50.996** Underdosing of other drugs, medicaments and biological substances

TOXIC EFFECTS OF SUBSTANCES CHIEFLY NONMEDICINAL AS TO SOURCE (T51-T65)

Note: When no intent is indicated code to accidental. Undetermined intent is only for use when there is specific documentation in the record that the intent of the toxic effect cannot be determined.

Use additional code(s): for all associated manifestations of toxic effect, such as:
respiratory conditions due to external agents (J60-J70)
personal history of foreign body fully removed (Z87.821)
to identify any retained foreign body, if applicable (Z18.-)

Excludes1 contact with and (suspected) exposure to toxic substances (Z77.-)

● **T51** Toxic effect of alcohol

The appropriate 7th character is to be added to each code from category T51

A	initial encounter
D	subsequent encounter
S	sequela

● **T51.0** Toxic effect of ethanol
Toxic effect of ethyl alcohol

Excludes2 acute alcohol intoxication or 'hangover' effects (F10.129, F10.229, F10.929)
drunkenness (F10.129, F10.229, F10.929)
pathological alcohol intoxication (F10.129, F10.229, F10.929)

● **T51.0X** Toxic effect of ethanol

● **T51.0X1** Toxic effect of ethanol, accidental (unintentional)
Toxic effect of ethanol NOS

● **T51.0X2** Toxic effect of ethanol, intentional self-harm

● **T51.0X3** Toxic effect of ethanol, assault

● **T51.0X4** Toxic effect of ethanol, undetermined

● **T51.1** Toxic effect of methanol
Toxic effect of methyl alcohol

● **T51.1X** Toxic effect of methanol

● **T51.1X1** Toxic effect of methanol, accidental (unintentional)
Toxic effect of methanol NOS

● **T51.1X2** Toxic effect of methanol, intentional self-harm

● **T51.1X3** Toxic effect of methanol, assault

● **T51.1X4** Toxic effect of methanol, undetermined

● **T51.2** Toxic effect of 2-Propanol
Toxic effect of isopropyl alcohol

● **T51.2X** Toxic effect of 2-Propanol

● **T51.2X1** Toxic effect of 2-Propanol, accidental (unintentional)
Toxic effect of 2-Propanol NOS

● **T51.2X2** Toxic effect of 2-Propanol, intentional self-harm

● **T51.2X3** Toxic effect of 2-Propanol, assault

● **T51.2X4** Toxic effect of 2-Propanol, undetermined

● **T51.3** Toxic effect of fusel oil
Toxic effect of amyl alcohol
Toxic effect of butyl [1-butanol] alcohol
Toxic effect of propyl [1-propanol] alcohol

● **T51.3X** Toxic effect of fusel oil

● **T51.3X1** Toxic effect of fusel oil, accidental (unintentional)
Toxic effect of fusel oil NOS

● **T51.3X2** Toxic effect of fusel oil, intentional self-harm

● **T51.3X3** Toxic effect of fusel oil, assault

● **T51.3X4** Toxic effect of fusel oil, undetermined

● **T51.8** Toxic effect of other alcohols

● **T51.8X** Toxic effect of other alcohols

● **T51.8X1** Toxic effect of other alcohols, accidental (unintentional)
Toxic effect of other alcohols NOS

● **T51.8X2** Toxic effect of other alcohols, intentional self-harm

● **T51.8X3** Toxic effect of other alcohols, assault

● **T51.8X4** Toxic effect of other alcohols, undetermined

● **T51.9** Toxic effect of unspecified alcohol

X ● **T51.91** Toxic effect of unspecified alcohol, accidental (unintentional)

X ● **T51.92** Toxic effect of unspecified alcohol, intentional self-harm

X ● **T51.93** Toxic effect of unspecified alcohol, assault

X ● **T51.94** Toxic effect of unspecified alcohol, undetermined

● **T52** Toxic effect of organic solvents

Excludes1 halogen derivatives of aliphatic and aromatic hydrocarbons (T53.-)

The appropriate 7th character is to be added to each code from category T52

A	initial encounter
D	subsequent encounter
S	sequela

● **T52.0** Toxic effects of petroleum products
Toxic effects of gasoline [petrol]
Toxic effects of kerosene [paraffin oil]
Toxic effects of paraffin wax
Toxic effects of ether petroleum
Toxic effects of naphtha petroleum
Toxic effects of spirit petroleum

● **T52.0X** Toxic effects of petroleum products

● **T52.0X1** Toxic effect of petroleum products, accidental (unintentional)
Toxic effects of petroleum products NOS

● **T52.0X2** Toxic effect of petroleum products, intentional self-harm

● **T52.0X3** Toxic effect of petroleum products, assault

● **T52.0X4** Toxic effect of petroleum products, undetermined

● **T52.1** Toxic effects of benzene

Excludes1 homologues of benzene (T52.2)
nitroderivatives and aminoderivatives of benzene and its homologues (T65.3)

● **T52.1X** Toxic effects of benzene

● **T52.1X1** Toxic effect of benzene, accidental (unintentional)
Toxic effects of benzene NOS

● **T52.1X2** Toxic effect of benzene, intentional self-harm

● **T52.1X3** Toxic effect of benzene, assault

● **T52.1X4** Toxic effect of benzene, undetermined

CHAPTER 19 (S00-T88)

CHAPTER 19 (S00-T88)

● **T52.2 Toxic effects of homologues of benzene**
Toxic effects of toluene [methylbenzene]
Toxic effects of xylene [dimethylbenzene]
  ● **T52.2X Toxic effects of homologues of benzene**
    ● **T52.2X1 Toxic effect of homologues of benzene, accidental (unintentional)**
      Toxic effects of homologues of benzene NOS
    ● **T52.2X2 Toxic effect of homologues of benzene, intentional self-harm**
    ● **T52.2X3 Toxic effect of homologues of benzene, assault**
    ● **T52.2X4 Toxic effect of homologues of benzene, undetermined**

● **T52.3 Toxic effects of glycols**
  ● **T52.3X Toxic effects of glycols**
    ● **T52.3X1 Toxic effect of glycols, accidental (unintentional)**
      Toxic effects of glycols NOS
    ● **T52.3X2 Toxic effect of glycols, intentional self-harm**
    ● **T52.3X3 Toxic effect of glycols, assault**
    ● **T52.3X4 Toxic effect of glycols, undetermined**

● **T52.4 Toxic effects of ketones**
  ● **T52.4X Toxic effects of ketones**
    ● **T52.4X1 Toxic effect of ketones, accidental (unintentional)**
      Toxic effects of ketones NOS
    ● **T52.4X2 Toxic effect of ketones, intentional self-harm**
    ● **T52.4X3 Toxic effect of ketones, assault**
    ● **T52.4X4 Toxic effect of ketones, undetermined**

● **T52.8 Toxic effects of other organic solvents**
  ● **T52.8X Toxic effects of other organic solvents**
    ● **T52.8X1 Toxic effect of other organic solvents, accidental (unintentional)**
      Toxic effects of other organic solvents NOS
    ● **T52.8X2 Toxic effect of other organic solvents, intentional self-harm**
    ● **T52.8X3 Toxic effect of other organic solvents, assault**
    ● **T52.8X4 Toxic effect of other organic solvents, undetermined**

● **T52.9 Toxic effects of unspecified organic solvent**
  X ● **T52.91 Toxic effect of unspecified organic solvent, accidental (unintentional)**
  X ● **T52.92 Toxic effect of unspecified organic solvent, intentional self-harm**
  X ● **T52.93 Toxic effect of unspecified organic solvent, assault**
  X ● **T52.94 Toxic effect of unspecified organic solvent, undetermined**

● **T53 Toxic effect of halogen derivatives of aliphatic and aromatic hydrocarbons**
The appropriate 7th character is to be added to each code from category T53

A	initial encounter
D	subsequent encounter
S	sequela

● **T53.0 Toxic effects of carbon tetrachloride**
Toxic effects of tetrachloromethane
  ● **T53.0X Toxic effects of carbon tetrachloride**
    ● **T53.0X1 Toxic effect of carbon tetrachloride, accidental (unintentional)**
      Toxic effects of carbon tetrachloride NOS
    ● **T53.0X2 Toxic effect of carbon tetrachloride, intentional self-harm**

    ● **T53.0X3 Toxic effect of carbon tetrachloride, assault**
    ● **T53.0X4 Toxic effect of carbon tetrachloride, undetermined**

● **T53.1 Toxic effects of chloroform**
Toxic effects of trichloromethane
  ● **T53.1X Toxic effects of chloroform**
    ● **T53.1X1 Toxic effect of chloroform, accidental (unintentional)**
      Toxic effects of chloroform NOS
    ● **T53.1X2 Toxic effect of chloroform, intentional self-harm**
    ● **T53.1X3 Toxic effect of chloroform, assault**
    ● **T53.1X4 Toxic effect of chloroform, undetermined**

● **T53.2 Toxic effects of trichloroethylene**
Toxic effects of trichloroethene
  ● **T53.2X Toxic effects of trichloroethylene**
    ● **T53.2X1 Toxic effect of trichloroethylene, accidental (unintentional)**
      Toxic effects of trichloroethylene NOS
    ● **T53.2X2 Toxic effect of trichloroethylene, intentional self-harm**
    ● **T53.2X3 Toxic effect of trichloroethylene, assault**
    ● **T53.2X4 Toxic effect of trichloroethylene, undetermined**

● **T53.3 Toxic effects of tetrachloroethylene**
Toxic effects of perchloroethylene
Toxic effect of tetrachloroethene
  ● **T53.3X Toxic effects of tetrachloroethylene**
    ● **T53.3X1 Toxic effect of tetrachloroethylene, accidental (unintentional)**
      Toxic effects of tetrachloroethylene NOS
    ● **T53.3X2 Toxic effect of tetrachloroethylene, intentional self-harm**
    ● **T53.3X3 Toxic effect of tetrachloroethylene, assault**
    ● **T53.3X4 Toxic effect of tetrachloroethylene, undetermined**

● **T53.4 Toxic effects of dichloromethane**
Toxic effects of methylene chloride
  ● **T53.4X Toxic effects of dichloromethane**
    ● **T53.4X1 Toxic effect of dichloromethane, accidental (unintentional)**
      Toxic effects of dichloromethane NOS
    ● **T53.4X2 Toxic effect of dichloromethane, intentional self-harm**
    ● **T53.4X3 Toxic effect of dichloromethane, assault**
    ● **T53.4X4 Toxic effect of dichloromethane, undetermined**

● **T53.5 Toxic effects of chlorofluorocarbons**
  ● **T53.5X Toxic effects of chlorofluorocarbons**
    ● **T53.5X1 Toxic effect of chlorofluorocarbons, accidental (unintentional)**
      Toxic effects of chlorofluorocarbons NOS
    ● **T53.5X2 Toxic effect of chlorofluorocarbons, intentional self-harm**
    ● **T53.5X3 Toxic effect of chlorofluorocarbons, assault**
    ● **T53.5X4 Toxic effect of chlorofluorocarbons, undetermined**

▶ New   ⇒ Revised   ~~deleted~~ Deleted   Excludes 1   Excludes 2   Includes   Use additional   Code first   Code also   Key words
OGCR Official Guidelines   X Assign placeholder X   ● Use Additional Character(s)   ▷ Manifestation Code   **Coding Clinic**

● **T53.6** Toxic effects of other halogen derivatives of aliphatic hydrocarbons
  ● **T53.6X** Toxic effects of other halogen derivatives of aliphatic hydrocarbons
    ● **T53.6X1** Toxic effect of other halogen derivatives of aliphatic hydrocarbons, accidental (unintentional)
      Toxic effects of other halogen derivatives of aliphatic hydrocarbons NOS
    ● **T53.6X2** Toxic effect of other halogen derivatives of aliphatic hydrocarbons, intentional self-harm
    ● **T53.6X3** Toxic effect of other halogen derivatives of aliphatic hydrocarbons, assault
    ● **T53.6X4** Toxic effect of other halogen derivatives of aliphatic hydrocarbons, undetermined

● **T53.7** Toxic effects of other halogen derivatives of aromatic hydrocarbons
  ● **T53.7X** Toxic effects of other halogen derivatives of aromatic hydrocarbons
    ● **T53.7X1** Toxic effect of other halogen derivatives of aromatic hydrocarbons, accidental (unintentional)
      Toxic effects of other halogen derivatives of aromatic hydrocarbons NOS
    ● **T53.7X2** Toxic effect of other halogen derivatives of aromatic hydrocarbons, intentional self-harm
    ● **T53.7X3** Toxic effect of other halogen derivatives of aromatic hydrocarbons, assault
    ● **T53.7X4** Toxic effect of other halogen derivatives of aromatic hydrocarbons, undetermined

● **T53.9** Toxic effects of unspecified halogen derivatives of aliphatic and aromatic hydrocarbons
  X● **T53.91** Toxic effect of unspecified halogen derivatives of aliphatic and aromatic hydrocarbons, accidental (unintentional)
  X● **T53.92** Toxic effect of unspecified halogen derivatives of aliphatic and aromatic hydrocarbons, intentional self-harm
  X● **T53.93** Toxic effect of unspecified halogen derivatives of aliphatic and aromatic hydrocarbons, assault
  X● **T53.94** Toxic effect of unspecified halogen derivatives of aliphatic and aromatic hydrocarbons, undetermined

● **T54** Toxic effect of corrosive substances
  The appropriate 7th character is to be added to each code from category T54

> A   initial encounter
> D   subsequent encounter
> S   sequela

● **T54.0** Toxic effects of phenol and phenol homologues
  ● **T54.0X** Toxic effects of phenol and phenol homologues
    ● **T54.0X1** Toxic effect of phenol and phenol homologues, accidental (unintentional)
      Toxic effects of phenol and phenol homologues NOS
    ● **T54.0X2** Toxic effect of phenol and phenol homologues, intentional self-harm

    ● **T54.0X3** Toxic effect of phenol and phenol homologues, assault
    ● **T54.0X4** Toxic effect of phenol and phenol homologues, undetermined

● **T54.1** Toxic effects of other corrosive organic compounds
  ● **T54.1X** Toxic effects of other corrosive organic compounds
    ● **T54.1X1** Toxic effect of other corrosive organic compounds, accidental (unintentional)
      Toxic effects of other corrosive organic compounds NOS
    ● **T54.1X2** Toxic effect of other corrosive organic compounds, intentional self-harm
    ● **T54.1X3** Toxic effect of other corrosive organic compounds, assault
    ● **T54.1X4** Toxic effect of other corrosive organic compounds, undetermined

● **T54.2** Toxic effects of corrosive acids and acid-like substances
  Toxic effects of hydrochloric acid
  Toxic effects of sulfuric acid
  ● **T54.2X** Toxic effects of corrosive acids and acid-like substances
    ● **T54.2X1** Toxic effect of corrosive acids and acid-like substances, accidental (unintentional)
      Toxic effects of corrosive acids and acid-like substances NOS
    ● **T54.2X2** Toxic effect of corrosive acids and acid-like substances, intentional self-harm
    ● **T54.2X3** Toxic effect of corrosive acids and acid-like substances, assault
    ● **T54.2X4** Toxic effect of corrosive acids and acid-like substances, undetermined

● **T54.3** Toxic effects of corrosive alkalis and alkali-like substances
  Toxic effects of potassium hydroxide
  Toxic effects of sodium hydroxide
  ● **T54.3X** Toxic effects of corrosive alkalis and alkali-like substances
    ● **T54.3X1** Toxic effect of corrosive alkalis and alkali-like substances, accidental (unintentional)
      Toxic effects of corrosive alkalis and alkali-like substances NOS
    ● **T54.3X2** Toxic effect of corrosive alkalis and alkali-like substances, intentional self-harm
    ● **T54.3X3** Toxic effect of corrosive alkalis and alkali-like substances, assault
    ● **T54.3X4** Toxic effect of corrosive alkalis and alkali-like substances, undetermined

● **T54.9** Toxic effects of unspecified corrosive substance
  X● **T54.91** Toxic effect of unspecified corrosive substance, accidental (unintentional)
  X● **T54.92** Toxic effect of unspecified corrosive substance, intentional self-harm
  X● **T54.93** Toxic effect of unspecified corrosive substance, assault
  X● **T54.94** Toxic effect of unspecified corrosive substance, undetermined

CHAPTER 19 (S00-T88)

CHAPTER 19 (S00-T88)

● **T55   Toxic effect of soaps and detergents**

    The appropriate 7th character is to be added to each code from category T55

A	initial encounter
D	subsequent encounter
S	sequela

  ● **T55.0   Toxic effect of soaps**

    ● **T55.0X   Toxic effect of soaps**

      ● **T55.0X1   Toxic effect of soaps, accidental (unintentional)**
          Toxic effect of soaps NOS

      ● **T55.0X2   Toxic effect of soaps, intentional self-harm**

      ● **T55.0X3   Toxic effect of soaps, assault**

      ● **T55.0X4   Toxic effect of soaps, undetermined**

  ● **T55.1   Toxic effect of detergents**

    ● **T55.1X   Toxic effect of detergents**

      ● **T55.1X1   Toxic effect of detergents, accidental (unintentional)**
          Toxic effect of detergents NOS

      ● **T55.1X2   Toxic effect of detergents, intentional self-harm**

      ● **T55.1X3   Toxic effect of detergents, assault**

      ● **T55.1X4   Toxic effect of detergents, undetermined**

● **T56   Toxic effect of metals**

    Includes   toxic effects of fumes and vapors of metals
               toxic effects of metals from all sources, except medicinal substances

    Use additional code to identify any retained metal foreign body, if applicable (Z18.0-, T18.1-)

    Excludes1   arsenic and its compounds (T57.0)
                manganese and its compounds (T57.2)

    The appropriate 7th character is to be added to each code from category T56

A	initial encounter
D	subsequent encounter
S	sequela

  ● **T56.0   Toxic effects of lead and its compounds**

    ● **T56.0X   Toxic effects of lead and its compounds**

      ● **T56.0X1   Toxic effect of lead and its compounds, accidental (unintentional)**
          Toxic effects of lead and its compounds NOS

      ● **T56.0X2   Toxic effect of lead and its compounds, intentional self-harm**

      ● **T56.0X3   Toxic effect of lead and its compounds, assault**

      ● **T56.0X4   Toxic effect of lead and its compounds, undetermined**

  ● **T56.1   Toxic effects of mercury and its compounds**

    ● **T56.1X   Toxic effects of mercury and its compounds**

      ● **T56.1X1   Toxic effect of mercury and its compounds, accidental (unintentional)**
          Toxic effects of mercury and its compounds NOS

      ● **T56.1X2   Toxic effect of mercury and its compounds, intentional self-harm**

      ● **T56.1X3   Toxic effect of mercury and its compounds, assault**

      ● **T56.1X4   Toxic effect of mercury and its compounds, undetermined**

  ● **T56.2   Toxic effects of chromium and its compounds**

    ● **T56.2X   Toxic effects of chromium and its compounds**

      ● **T56.2X1   Toxic effect of chromium and its compounds, accidental (unintentional)**
          Toxic effects of chromium and its compounds NOS

      ● **T56.2X2   Toxic effect of chromium and its compounds, intentional self-harm**

      ● **T56.2X3   Toxic effect of chromium and its compounds, assault**

      ● **T56.2X4   Toxic effect of chromium and its compounds, undetermined**

  ● **T56.3   Toxic effects of cadmium and its compounds**

    ● **T56.3X   Toxic effects of cadmium and its compounds**

      ● **T56.3X1   Toxic effect of cadmium and its compounds, accidental (unintentional)**
          Toxic effects of cadmium and its compounds NOS

      ● **T56.3X2   Toxic effect of cadmium and its compounds, intentional self-harm**

      ● **T56.3X3   Toxic effect of cadmium and its compounds, assault**

      ● **T56.3X4   Toxic effect of cadmium and its compounds, undetermined**

  ● **T56.4   Toxic effects of copper and its compounds**

    ● **T56.4X   Toxic effects of copper and its compounds**

      ● **T56.4X1   Toxic effect of copper and its compounds, accidental (unintentional)**
          Toxic effects of copper and its compounds NOS

      ● **T56.4X2   Toxic effect of copper and its compounds, intentional self-harm**

      ● **T56.4X3   Toxic effect of copper and its compounds, assault**

      ● **T56.4X4   Toxic effect of copper and its compounds, undetermined**

  ● **T56.5   Toxic effects of zinc and its compounds**

    ● **T56.5X   Toxic effects of zinc and its compounds**

      ● **T56.5X1   Toxic effect of zinc and its compounds, accidental (unintentional)**
          Toxic effects of zinc and its compounds NOS

      ● **T56.5X2   Toxic effect of zinc and its compounds, intentional self-harm**

      ● **T56.5X3   Toxic effect of zinc and its compounds, assault**

      ● **T56.5X4   Toxic effect of zinc and its compounds, undetermined**

  ● **T56.6   Toxic effects of tin and its compounds**

    ● **T56.6X   Toxic effects of tin and its compounds**

      ● **T56.6X1   Toxic effect of tin and its compounds, accidental (unintentional)**
          Toxic effects of tin and its compounds NOS

      ● **T56.6X2   Toxic effect of tin and its compounds, intentional self-harm**

      ● **T56.6X3   Toxic effect of tin and its compounds, assault**

      ● **T56.6X4   Toxic effect of tin and its compounds, undetermined**

● **T56.7**   Toxic effects of beryllium and its compounds
   ● **T56.7X**   Toxic effects of beryllium and its compounds
     ● **T56.7X1**   Toxic effects of beryllium and its compounds, accidental (unintentional)
         Toxic effects of beryllium and its compounds NOS
     ● **T56.7X2**   Toxic effect of beryllium and its compounds, intentional self-harm
     ● **T56.7X3**   Toxic effect of beryllium and its compounds, assault
     ● **T56.7X4**   Toxic effect of beryllium and its compounds, undetermined

● **T56.8**   Toxic effects of other metals
   ● **T56.81**   Toxic effect of thallium
     ● **T56.811**   Toxic effect of thallium, accidental (unintentional)
         Toxic effect of thallium NOS
     ● **T56.812**   Toxic effect of thallium, intentional self-harm
     ● **T56.813**   Toxic effect of thallium, assault
     ● **T56.814**   Toxic effect of thallium, undetermined
   ● **T56.89**   Toxic effects of other metals
     ● **T56.891**   Toxic effect of other metals, accidental (unintentional)
         Toxic effects of other metals NOS
     ● **T56.892**   Toxic effect of other metals, intentional self-harm
     ● **T56.893**   Toxic effect of other metals, assault
     ● **T56.894**   Toxic effect of other metals, undetermined

● **T56.9**   Toxic effects of unspecified metal
   X ● **T56.91**   Toxic effect of unspecified metal, accidental (unintentional)
   X ● **T56.92**   Toxic effect of unspecified metal, intentional self-harm
   X ● **T56.93**   Toxic effect of unspecified metal, assault
   X ● **T56.94**   Toxic effect of unspecified metal, undetermined

● **T57**   Toxic effect of other inorganic substances
   The appropriate 7th character is to be added to each code from category T57

A	initial encounter
D	subsequent encounter
S	sequela

● **T57.0**   Toxic effect of arsenic and its compounds
   ● **T57.0X**   Toxic effect of arsenic and its compounds
     ● **T57.0X1**   Toxic effect of arsenic and its compounds, accidental (unintentional)
         Toxic effect of arsenic and its compounds NOS
     ● **T57.0X2**   Toxic effect of arsenic and its compounds, intentional self-harm
     ● **T57.0X3**   Toxic effect of arsenic and its compounds, assault
     ● **T57.0X4**   Toxic effect of arsenic and its compounds, undetermined

● **T57.1**   Toxic effect of phosphorus and its compounds
     Excludes1   organophosphate insecticides (T60.0)
   ● **T57.1X**   Toxic effect of phosphorus and its compounds
     ● **T57.1X1**   Toxic effect of phosphorus and its compounds, accidental (unintentional)
         Toxic effect of phosphorus and its compounds NOS
     ● **T57.1X2**   Toxic effect of phosphorus and its compounds, intentional self-harm
     ● **T57.1X3**   Toxic effect of phosphorus and its compounds, assault
     ● **T57.1X4**   Toxic effect of phosphorus and its compounds, undetermined

● **T57.2**   Toxic effect of manganese and its compounds
   ● **T57.2X**   Toxic effect of manganese and its compounds
     ● **T57.2X1**   Toxic effect of manganese and its compounds, accidental (unintentional)
         Toxic effect of manganese and its compounds NOS
     ● **T57.2X2**   Toxic effect of manganese and its compounds, intentional self-harm
     ● **T57.2X3**   Toxic effect of manganese and its compounds, assault
     ● **T57.2X4**   Toxic effect of manganese and its compounds, undetermined

● **T57.3**   Toxic effect of hydrogen cyanide
   ● **T57.3X**   Toxic effect of hydrogen cyanide
     ● **T57.3X1**   Toxic effect of hydrogen cyanide, accidental (unintentional)
         Toxic effect of hydrogen cyanide NOS
     ● **T57.3X2**   Toxic effect of hydrogen cyanide, intentional self-harm
     ● **T57.3X3**   Toxic effect of hydrogen cyanide, assault
     ● **T57.3X4**   Toxic effect of hydrogen cyanide, undetermined

● **T57.8**   Toxic effect of other specified inorganic substances
   ● **T57.8X**   Toxic effect of other specified inorganic substances
     ● **T57.8X1**   Toxic effect of other specified inorganic substances, accidental (unintentional)
         Toxic effect of other specified inorganic substances NOS
     ● **T57.8X2**   Toxic effect of other specified inorganic substances, intentional self-harm
     ● **T57.8X3**   Toxic effect of other specified inorganic substances, assault
     ● **T57.8X4**   Toxic effect of other specified inorganic substances, undetermined

● **T57.9**   Toxic effect of unspecified inorganic substance
   X ● **T57.91**   Toxic effect of unspecified inorganic substance, accidental (unintentional)
   X ● **T57.92**   Toxic effect of unspecified inorganic substance, intentional self-harm
   X ● **T57.93**   Toxic effect of unspecified inorganic substance, assault
   X ● **T57.94**   Toxic effect of unspecified inorganic substance, undetermined

CHAPTER 19 (S00-T88)

● **T58**   **Toxic effect of carbon monoxide**

> **Includes**   asphyxiation from carbon monoxide
> toxic effect of carbon monoxide from all sources

The appropriate 7th character is to be added to each code from category T58

> A   initial encounter
> D   subsequent encounter
> S   sequela

● **T58.0**   **Toxic effect of carbon monoxide from motor vehicle exhaust**
> Toxic effect of exhaust gas from gas engine
> Toxic effect of exhaust gas from motor pump

   X● **T58.01**   Toxic effect of carbon monoxide from motor vehicle exhaust, accidental (unintentional)

   X● **T58.02**   Toxic effect of carbon monoxide from motor vehicle exhaust, intentional self-harm

   X● **T58.03**   Toxic effect of carbon monoxide from motor vehicle exhaust, assault

   X● **T58.04**   Toxic effect of carbon monoxide from motor vehicle exhaust, undetermined

● **T58.1**   **Toxic effect of carbon monoxide from utility gas**
> Toxic effect of acetylene
> Toxic effect of gas NOS used for lighting, heating, cooking
> Toxic effect of water gas

   X● **T58.11**   Toxic effect of carbon monoxide from utility gas, accidental (unintentional)

   X● **T58.12**   Toxic effect of carbon monoxide from utility gas, intentional self-harm

   X● **T58.13**   Toxic effect of carbon monoxide from utility gas, assault

   X● **T58.14**   Toxic effect of carbon monoxide from utility gas, undetermined

● **T58.2**   **Toxic effect of carbon monoxide from incomplete combustion of other domestic fuels**
> Toxic effect of carbon monoxide from incomplete combustion of coal, coke, kerosene, wood

   ● **T58.2X**   **Toxic effect of carbon monoxide from incomplete combustion of other domestic fuels**

     ● **T58.2X1**   Toxic effect of carbon monoxide from incomplete combustion of other domestic fuels, accidental (unintentional)

     ● **T58.2X2**   Toxic effect of carbon monoxide from incomplete combustion of other domestic fuels, intentional self-harm

     ● **T58.2X3**   Toxic effect of carbon monoxide from incomplete combustion of other domestic fuels, assault

     ● **T58.2X4**   Toxic effect of carbon monoxide from incomplete combustion of other domestic fuels, undetermined

● **T58.8**   **Toxic effect of carbon monoxide from other source**
> Toxic effect of carbon monoxide from blast furnace gas
> Toxic effect of carbon monoxide from fuels in industrial use
> Toxic effect of carbon monoxide from kiln vapor

   ● **T58.8X**   **Toxic effect of carbon monoxide from other source**

     ● **T58.8X1**   Toxic effect of carbon monoxide from other source, accidental (unintentional)

     ● **T58.8X2**   Toxic effect of carbon monoxide from other source, intentional self-harm

     ● **T58.8X3**   Toxic effect of carbon monoxide from other source, assault

     ● **T58.8X4**   Toxic effect of carbon monoxide from other source, undetermined

● **T58.9**   **Toxic effect of carbon monoxide from unspecified source**

   X● **T58.91**   Toxic effect of carbon monoxide from unspecified source, accidental (unintentional)

   X● **T58.92**   Toxic effect of carbon monoxide from unspecified source, intentional self-harm

   X● **T58.93**   Toxic effect of carbon monoxide from unspecified source, assault

   X● **T58.94**   Toxic effect of carbon monoxide from unspecified source, undetermined

● **T59**   **Toxic effect of other gases, fumes and vapors**

> **Includes**   aerosol propellants
> **Excludes1**   chlorofluorocarbons (T53.5)

The appropriate 7th character is to be added to each code from category T59

> A   initial encounter
> D   subsequent encounter
> S   sequela

● **T59.0**   **Toxic effect of nitrogen oxides**

   ● **T59.0X**   **Toxic effect of nitrogen oxides**

     ● **T59.0X1**   Toxic effect of nitrogen oxides, accidental (unintentional)
> Toxic effect of nitrogen oxides NOS

     ● **T59.0X2**   Toxic effect of nitrogen oxides, intentional self-harm

     ● **T59.0X3**   Toxic effect of nitrogen oxides, assault

     ● **T59.0X4**   Toxic effect of nitrogen oxides, undetermined

● **T59.1**   **Toxic effect of sulfur dioxide**

   ● **T59.1X**   **Toxic effect of sulfur dioxide**

     ● **T59.1X1**   Toxic effect of sulfur dioxide, accidental (unintentional)
> Toxic effect of sulfur dioxide NOS

     ● **T59.1X2**   Toxic effect of sulfur dioxide, intentional self-harm

     ● **T59.1X3**   Toxic effect of sulfur dioxide, assault

     ● **T59.1X4**   Toxic effect of sulfur dioxide, undetermined

● **T59.2**   **Toxic effect of formaldehyde**

   ● **T59.2X**   **Toxic effect of formaldehyde**

     ● **T59.2X1**   Toxic effect of formaldehyde, accidental (unintentional)
> Toxic effect of formaldehyde NOS

     ● **T59.2X2**   Toxic effect of formaldehyde, intentional self-harm

     ● **T59.2X3**   Toxic effect of formaldehyde, assault

     ● **T59.2X4**   Toxic effect of formaldehyde, undetermined

● **T59.3**   **Toxic effect of lacrimogenic gas**
> Toxic effect of tear gas

   ● **T59.3X**   **Toxic effect of lacrimogenic gas**

     ● **T59.3X1**   Toxic effect of lacrimogenic gas, accidental (unintentional)
> Toxic effect of lacrimogenic gas NOS

     ● **T59.3X2**   Toxic effect of lacrimogenic gas, intentional self-harm

     ● **T59.3X3**   Toxic effect of lacrimogenic gas, assault

     ● **T59.3X4**   Toxic effect of lacrimogenic gas, undetermined

● **T59.4**   **Toxic effect of chlorine gas**

   ● **T59.4X**   **Toxic effect of chlorine gas**

     ● **T59.4X1**   Toxic effect of chlorine gas, accidental (unintentional)
> Toxic effect of chlorine gas NOS

     ● **T59.4X2**   Toxic effect of chlorine gas, intentional self-harm

     ● **T59.4X3**   Toxic effect of chlorine gas, assault

     ● **T59.4X4**   Toxic effect of chlorine gas, undetermined

▶ New   ⇒ Revised   ~~deleted~~ Deleted   Excludes 1   Excludes 2   Includes   Use additional   Code first   Code also   Key words

1406   OGCR Official Guidelines   X Assign placeholder X   ● Use Additional Character(s)   ▷ Manifestation Code   **Coding Clinic**

● **T59.5**   Toxic effect of fluorine gas and hydrogen fluoride
  ● **T59.5X**   Toxic effect of fluorine gas and hydrogen fluoride
    ● **T59.5X1**   Toxic effect of fluorine gas and hydrogen fluoride, accidental (unintentional)
         Toxic effect of fluorine gas and hydrogen fluoride NOS
    ● **T59.5X2**   Toxic effect of fluorine gas and hydrogen fluoride, intentional self-harm
    ● **T59.5X3**   Toxic effect of fluorine gas and hydrogen fluoride, assault
    ● **T59.5X4**   Toxic effect of fluorine gas and hydrogen fluoride, undetermined

● **T59.6**   Toxic effect of hydrogen sulfide
  ● **T59.6X**   Toxic effect of hydrogen sulfide
    ● **T59.6X1**   Toxic effect of hydrogen sulfide, accidental (unintentional)
         Toxic effect of hydrogen sulfide NOS
    ● **T59.6X2**   Toxic effect of hydrogen sulfide, intentional self-harm
    ● **T59.6X3**   Toxic effect of hydrogen sulfide, assault
    ● **T59.6X4**   Toxic effect of hydrogen sulfide, undetermined

● **T59.7**   Toxic effect of carbon dioxide
  ● **T59.7X**   Toxic effect of carbon dioxide
    ● **T59.7X1**   Toxic effect of carbon dioxide, accidental (unintentional)
         Toxic effect of carbon dioxide NOS
    ● **T59.7X2**   Toxic effect of carbon dioxide, intentional self-harm
    ● **T59.7X3**   Toxic effect of carbon dioxide, assault
    ● **T59.7X4**   Toxic effect of carbon dioxide, undetermined

● **T59.8**   Toxic effect of other specified gases, fumes and vapors
  ● **T59.81**   Toxic effect of smoke
     Smoke inhalation
     Excludes2   toxic effect of cigarette (tobacco) smoke (T65.22-)
    ● **T59.811**   Toxic effect of smoke, accidental (unintentional)
         Toxic effect of smoke NOS
    ● **T59.812**   Toxic effect of smoke, intentional self-harm
    ● **T59.813**   Toxic effect of smoke, assault
    ● **T59.814**   Toxic effect of smoke, undetermined
  ● **T59.89**   Toxic effect of other specified gases, fumes and vapors
    ● **T59.891**   Toxic effect of other specified gases, fumes and vapors, accidental (unintentional)
    ● **T59.892**   Toxic effect of other specified gases, fumes and vapors, intentional self-harm
    ● **T59.893**   Toxic effect of other specified gases, fumes and vapors, assault
    ● **T59.894**   Toxic effect of other specified gases, fumes and vapors, undetermined

● **T59.9**   Toxic effect of unspecified gases, fumes and vapors
  X ● **T59.91**   Toxic effect of unspecified gases, fumes and vapors, accidental (unintentional)
  X ● **T59.92**   Toxic effect of unspecified gases, fumes and vapors, intentional self-harm
  X ● **T59.93**   Toxic effect of unspecified gases, fumes and vapors, assault
  X ● **T59.94**   Toxic effect of unspecified gases, fumes and vapors, undetermined

● **T60**   Toxic effect of pesticides
   Includes   toxic effect of wood preservatives
   The appropriate 7th character is to be added to each code from category T60

A	initial encounter
D	subsequent encounter
S	sequela

● **T60.0**   Toxic effect of organophosphate and carbamate insecticides
  ● **T60.0X**   Toxic effect of organophosphate and carbamate insecticides
    ● **T60.0X1**   Toxic effect of organophosphate and carbamate insecticides, accidental (unintentional)
         Toxic effect of organophosphate and carbamate insecticides NOS
    ● **T60.0X2**   Toxic effect of organophosphate and carbamate insecticides, intentional self-harm
    ● **T60.0X3**   Toxic effect of organophosphate and carbamate insecticides, assault
    ● **T60.0X4**   Toxic effect of organophosphate and carbamate insecticides, undetermined

● **T60.1**   Toxic effect of halogenated insecticides
   Excludes1   chlorinated hydrocarbon (T53.-)
  ● **T60.1X**   Toxic effect of halogenated insecticides
    ● **T60.1X1**   Toxic effect of halogenated insecticides, accidental (unintentional)
         Toxic effect of halogenated insecticides NOS
    ● **T60.1X2**   Toxic effect of halogenated insecticides, intentional self-harm
    ● **T60.1X3**   Toxic effect of halogenated insecticides, assault
    ● **T60.1X4**   Toxic effect of halogenated insecticides, undetermined

● **T60.2**   Toxic effect of other insecticides
  ● **T60.2X**   Toxic effect of other insecticides
    ● **T60.2X1**   Toxic effect of other insecticides, accidental (unintentional)
         Toxic effect of other insecticides NOS
    ● **T60.2X2**   Toxic effect of other insecticides, intentional self-harm
    ● **T60.2X3**   Toxic effect of other insecticides, assault
    ● **T60.2X4**   Toxic effect of other insecticides, undetermined

● **T60.3**   Toxic effect of herbicides and fungicides
  ● **T60.3X**   Toxic effect of herbicides and fungicides
    ● **T60.3X1**   Toxic effect of herbicides and fungicides, accidental (unintentional)
         Toxic effect of herbicides and fungicides NOS
    ● **T60.3X2**   Toxic effect of herbicides and fungicides, intentional self-harm
    ● **T60.3X3**   Toxic effect of herbicides and fungicides, assault
    ● **T60.3X4**   Toxic effect of herbicides and fungicides, undetermined

CHAPTER 19 (S00-T88)

● **T60.4 Toxic effect of rodenticides**
     Excludes1   strychnine and its salts (T65.1)
                     thallium (T56.81-)
   ● **T60.4X Toxic effect of rodenticides**
      ● **T60.4X1 Toxic effect of rodenticides, accidental (unintentional)**
           Toxic effect of rodenticides NOS
      ● **T60.4X2 Toxic effect of rodenticides, intentional self-harm**
      ● **T60.4X3 Toxic effect of rodenticides, assault**
      ● **T60.4X4 Toxic effect of rodenticides, undetermined**
● **T60.8 Toxic effect of other pesticides**
   ● **T60.8X Toxic effect of other pesticides**
      ● **T60.8X1 Toxic effect of other pesticides, accidental (unintentional)**
           Toxic effect of other pesticides NOS
      ● **T60.8X2 Toxic effect of other pesticides, intentional self-harm**
      ● **T60.8X3 Toxic effect of other pesticides, assault**
      ● **T60.8X4 Toxic effect of other pesticides, undetermined**
● **T60.9 Toxic effect of unspecified pesticide**
   X ● **T60.91 Toxic effect of unspecified pesticide, accidental (unintentional)**
   X ● **T60.92 Toxic effect of unspecified pesticide, intentional self-harm**
   X ● **T60.93 Toxic effect of unspecified pesticide, assault**
   X ● **T60.94 Toxic effect of unspecified pesticide, undetermined**

● **T61 Toxic effect of noxious substances eaten as seafood**
     Excludes1   allergic reaction to food, such as:
                  anaphylactic reaction or shock due to adverse food reaction (T78.0-)
                  bacterial foodborne intoxications (A05.-)
                  dermatitis (L23.6, L25.4, L27.2)
                  food protein-induced enterocolitis syndrome (K52.21)
                  food protein-induced enteropathy (K52.22)
                  gastroenteritis (noninfective) (K52.29)
                  toxic effect of aflatoxin and other mycotoxins (T64)
                  toxic effect of cyanides (T65.0-)
                  toxic effect of harmful algae bloom (T65.82-)
                  toxic effect of hydrogen cyanide (T57.3-)
                  toxic effect of mercury (T56.1-)
                  toxic effect of red tide (T65.82-)

The appropriate 7th character is to be added to each code from category T61

A	initial encounter
D	subsequent encounter
S	sequela

● **T61.0 Ciguatera fish poisoning**
   X ● **T61.01 Ciguatera fish poisoning, accidental (unintentional)**
   X ● **T61.02 Ciguatera fish poisoning, intentional self-harm**
   X ● **T61.03 Ciguatera fish poisoning, assault**
   X ● **T61.04 Ciguatera fish poisoning, undetermined**
● **T61.1 Scombroid fish poisoning**
     Histamine-like syndrome
   X ● **T61.11 Scombroid fish poisoning, accidental (unintentional)**
   X ● **T61.12 Scombroid fish poisoning, intentional self-harm**
   X ● **T61.13 Scombroid fish poisoning, assault**
   X ● **T61.14 Scombroid fish poisoning, undetermined**

● **T61.7 Other fish and shellfish poisoning**
   ● **T61.77 Other fish poisoning**
      ● **T61.771 Other fish poisoning, accidental (unintentional)**
      ● **T61.772 Other fish poisoning, intentional self-harm**
      ● **T61.773 Other fish poisoning, assault**
      ● **T61.774 Other fish poisoning, undetermined**
   ● **T61.78 Other shellfish poisoning**
      ● **T61.781 Other shellfish poisoning, accidental (unintentional)**
      ● **T61.782 Other shellfish poisoning, intentional self-harm**
      ● **T61.783 Other shellfish poisoning, assault**
      ● **T61.784 Other shellfish poisoning, undetermined**
● **T61.8 Toxic effect of other seafood**
   ● **T61.8X Toxic effect of other seafood**
      ● **T61.8X1 Toxic effect of other seafood, accidental (unintentional)**
      ● **T61.8X2 Toxic effect of other seafood, intentional self-harm**
      ● **T61.8X3 Toxic effect of other seafood, assault**
      ● **T61.8X4 Toxic effect of other seafood, undetermined**
● **T61.9 Toxic effect of unspecified seafood**
   X ● **T61.91 Toxic effect of unspecified seafood, accidental (unintentional)**
   X ● **T61.92 Toxic effect of unspecified seafood, intentional self-harm**
   X ● **T61.93 Toxic effect of unspecified seafood, assault**
   X ● **T61.94 Toxic effect of unspecified seafood, undetermined**

● **T62 Toxic effect of other noxious substances eaten as food**
     Excludes1   allergic reaction to food, such as:
                  anaphylactic shock (reaction) due to adverse food reaction (T78.0-)
                  dermatitis (L23.6, L25.4, L27.2)
                  food protein-induced enterocolitis syndrome (K52.21)
                  food protein-induced enteropathy (K52.22)
                  gastroenteritis (noninfective) (K52.29)
                  bacterial food borne intoxications (A05.-)
                  toxic effect of aflatoxin and other mycotoxins (T64)
                  toxic effect of cyanides (T65.0-)
                  toxic effect of hydrogen cyanide (T57.3-)
                  toxic effect of mercury (T56.1-)

The appropriate 7th character is to be added to each code from category T62

A	initial encounter
D	subsequent encounter
S	sequela

● **T62.0 Toxic effect of ingested mushrooms**
   ● **T62.0X Toxic effect of ingested mushrooms**
      ● **T62.0X1 Toxic effect of ingested mushrooms, accidental (unintentional)**
           Toxic effect of ingested mushrooms NOS
      ● **T62.0X2 Toxic effect of ingested mushrooms, intentional self-harm**
      ● **T62.0X3 Toxic effect of ingested mushrooms, assault**
      ● **T62.0X4 Toxic effect of ingested mushrooms, undetermined**

● **T62.1**   Toxic effect of ingested berries
    ● **T62.1X**   Toxic effect of ingested berries
       ● **T62.1X1**   Toxic effect of ingested berries, accidental (unintentional)
           Toxic effect of ingested berries NOS
       ● **T62.1X2**   Toxic effect of ingested berries, intentional self-harm
       ● **T62.1X3**   Toxic effect of ingested berries, assault
       ● **T62.1X4**   Toxic effect of ingested berries, undetermined

● **T62.2**   Toxic effect of other ingested (parts of) plant(s)
    ● **T62.2X**   Toxic effect of other ingested (parts of) plant(s)
       ● **T62.2X1**   Toxic effect of other ingested (parts of) plant(s), accidental (unintentional)
           Toxic effect of other ingested (parts of) plant(s) NOS
       ● **T62.2X2**   Toxic effect of other ingested (parts of) plant(s), intentional self-harm
       ● **T62.2X3**   Toxic effect of other ingested (parts of) plant(s), assault
       ● **T62.2X4**   Toxic effect of other ingested (parts of) plant(s), undetermined

● **T62.8**   Toxic effect of other specified noxious substances eaten as food
    ● **T62.8X**   Toxic effect of other specified noxious substances eaten as food
       ● **T62.8X1**   Toxic effect of other specified noxious substances eaten as food, accidental (unintentional)
           Toxic effect of other specified noxious substances eaten as food NOS
       ● **T62.8X2**   Toxic effect of other specified noxious substances eaten as food, intentional self-harm
       ● **T62.8X3**   Toxic effect of other specified noxious substances eaten as food, assault
       ● **T62.8X4**   Toxic effect of other specified noxious substances eaten as food, undetermined

● **T62.9**   Toxic effect of unspecified noxious substance eaten as food
    X ● **T62.91**   Toxic effect of unspecified noxious substance eaten as food, accidental (unintentional)
       Toxic effect of unspecified noxious substance eaten as food NOS
    X ● **T62.92**   Toxic effect of unspecified noxious substance eaten as food, intentional self-harm
    X ● **T62.93**   Toxic effect of unspecified noxious substance eaten as food, assault
    X ● **T62.94**   Toxic effect of unspecified noxious substance eaten as food, undetermined

● **T63**   Toxic effect of contact with venomous animals and plants

    | **Includes** | bite or touch of venomous animal |
    | | pricked or stuck by thorn or leaf |

    | **Excludes2** | ingestion of toxic animal or plant (T61.-, T62.-) |

    The appropriate 7th character is to be added to each code from category T63

    | A | initial encounter |
    | D | subsequent encounter |
    | S | sequela |

    ● **T63.0**   Toxic effect of snake venom
       ● **T63.00**   Toxic effect of unspecified snake venom
          ● **T63.001**   Toxic effect of unspecified snake venom, accidental (unintentional)
            Toxic effect of unspecified snake venom NOS
          ● **T63.002**   Toxic effect of unspecified snake venom, intentional self-harm

● **T63.003**   Toxic effect of unspecified snake venom, assault
● **T63.004**   Toxic effect of unspecified snake venom, undetermined

● **T63.01**   Toxic effect of rattlesnake venom
    ● **T63.011**   Toxic effect of rattlesnake venom, accidental (unintentional)
       Toxic effect of rattlesnake venom NOS
    ● **T63.012**   Toxic effect of rattlesnake venom, intentional self-harm
    ● **T63.013**   Toxic effect of rattlesnake venom, assault
    ● **T63.014**   Toxic effect of rattlesnake venom, undetermined

● **T63.02**   Toxic effect of coral snake venom
    ● **T63.021**   Toxic effect of coral snake venom, accidental (unintentional)
       Toxic effect of coral snake venom NOS
    ● **T63.022**   Toxic effect of coral snake venom, intentional self-harm
    ● **T63.023**   Toxic effect of coral snake venom, assault
    ● **T63.024**   Toxic effect of coral snake venom, undetermined

● **T63.03**   Toxic effect of taipan venom
    ● **T63.031**   Toxic effect of taipan venom, accidental (unintentional)
       Toxic effect of taipan venom NOS
    ● **T63.032**   Toxic effect of taipan venom, intentional self-harm
    ● **T63.033**   Toxic effect of taipan venom, assault
    ● **T63.034**   Toxic effect of taipan venom, undetermined

● **T63.04**   Toxic effect of cobra venom
    ● **T63.041**   Toxic effect of cobra venom, accidental (unintentional)
       Toxic effect of cobra venom NOS
    ● **T63.042**   Toxic effect of cobra venom, intentional self-harm
    ● **T63.043**   Toxic effect of cobra venom, assault
    ● **T63.044**   Toxic effect of cobra venom, undetermined

● **T63.06**   Toxic effect of venom of other North and South American snake
    ● **T63.061**   Toxic effect of venom of other North and South American snake, accidental (unintentional)
       Toxic effect of venom of other North and South American snake NOS
    ● **T63.062**   Toxic effect of venom of other North and South American snake, intentional self-harm
    ● **T63.063**   Toxic effect of venom of other North and South American snake, assault
    ● **T63.064**   Toxic effect of venom of other North and South American snake, undetermined

● **T63.07**   Toxic effect of venom of other Australian snake
    ● **T63.071**   Toxic effect of venom of other Australian snake, accidental (unintentional)
       Toxic effect of venom of other Australian snake NOS
    ● **T63.072**   Toxic effect of venom of other Australian snake, intentional self-harm
    ● **T63.073**   Toxic effect of venom of other Australian snake, assault
    ● **T63.074**   Toxic effect of venom of other Australian snake, undetermined

CHAPTER 19 (S00-T88)

● **T63.08** Toxic effect of venom of other African and Asian snake

  ● **T63.081** Toxic effect of venom of other African and Asian snake, accidental (unintentional)
    Toxic effect of venom of other African and Asian snake NOS

  ● **T63.082** Toxic effect of venom of other African and Asian snake, intentional self-harm

  ● **T63.083** Toxic effect of venom of other African and Asian snake, assault

  ● **T63.084** Toxic effect of venom of other African and Asian snake, undetermined

● **T63.09** Toxic effect of venom of other snake

  ● **T63.091** Toxic effect of venom of other snake, accidental (unintentional)
    Toxic effect of venom of other snake NOS

  ● **T63.092** Toxic effect of venom of other snake, intentional self-harm

  ● **T63.093** Toxic effect of venom of other snake, assault

  ● **T63.094** Toxic effect of venom of other snake, undetermined

● **T63.1** Toxic effect of venom of other reptiles

  ● **T63.11** Toxic effect of venom of gila monster

    ● **T63.111** Toxic effect of venom of gila monster, accidental (unintentional)
      Toxic effect of venom of gila monster NOS

    ● **T63.112** Toxic effect of venom of gila monster, intentional self-harm

    ● **T63.113** Toxic effect of venom of gila monster, assault

    ● **T63.114** Toxic effect of venom of gila monster, undetermined

  ● **T63.12** Toxic effect of venom of other venomous lizard

    ● **T63.121** Toxic effect of venom of other venomous lizard, accidental (unintentional)
      Toxic effect of venom of other venomous lizard NOS

    ● **T63.122** Toxic effect of venom of other venomous lizard, intentional self-harm

    ● **T63.123** Toxic effect of venom of other venomous lizard, assault

    ● **T63.124** Toxic effect of venom of other venomous lizard, undetermined

  ● **T63.19** Toxic effect of venom of other reptiles

    ● **T63.191** Toxic effect of venom of other reptiles, accidental (unintentional)
      Toxic effect of venom of other reptiles NOS

    ● **T63.192** Toxic effect of venom of other reptiles, intentional self-harm

    ● **T63.193** Toxic effect of venom of other reptiles, assault

    ● **T63.194** Toxic effect of venom of other reptiles, undetermined

● **T63.2** Toxic effect of venom of scorpion

  ● **T63.2X** Toxic effect of venom of scorpion

    ● **T63.2X1** Toxic effect of venom of scorpion, accidental (unintentional)
      Toxic effect of venom of scorpion NOS

    ● **T63.2X2** Toxic effect of venom of scorpion, intentional self-harm

    ● **T63.2X3** Toxic effect of venom of scorpion, assault

    ● **T63.2X4** Toxic effect of venom of scorpion, undetermined

● **T63.3** Toxic effect of venom of spider

  ● **T63.30** Toxic effect of unspecified spider venom

    ● **T63.301** Toxic effect of unspecified spider venom, accidental (unintentional)

    ● **T63.302** Toxic effect of unspecified spider venom, intentional self-harm

    ● **T63.303** Toxic effect of unspecified spider venom, assault

    ● **T63.304** Toxic effect of unspecified spider venom, undetermined

  ● **T63.31** Toxic effect of venom of black widow spider

    ● **T63.311** Toxic effect of venom of black widow spider, accidental (unintentional)

    ● **T63.312** Toxic effect of venom of black widow spider, intentional self-harm

    ● **T63.313** Toxic effect of venom of black widow spider, assault

    ● **T63.314** Toxic effect of venom of black widow spider, undetermined

  ● **T63.32** Toxic effect of venom of tarantula

    ● **T63.321** Toxic effect of venom of tarantula, accidental (unintentional)

    ● **T63.322** Toxic effect of venom of tarantula, intentional self-harm

    ● **T63.323** Toxic effect of venom of tarantula, assault

    ● **T63.324** Toxic effect of venom of tarantula, undetermined

  ● **T63.33** Toxic effect of venom of brown recluse spider

    ● **T63.331** Toxic effect of venom of brown recluse spider, accidental (unintentional)

    ● **T63.332** Toxic effect of venom of brown recluse spider, intentional self-harm

    ● **T63.333** Toxic effect of venom of brown recluse spider, assault

    ● **T63.334** Toxic effect of venom of brown recluse spider, undetermined

  ● **T63.39** Toxic effect of venom of other spider

    ● **T63.391** Toxic effect of venom of other spider, accidental (unintentional)

    ● **T63.392** Toxic effect of venom of other spider, intentional self-harm

    ● **T63.393** Toxic effect of venom of other spider, assault

    ● **T63.394** Toxic effect of venom of other spider, undetermined

● **T63.4** Toxic effect of venom of other arthropods

  ● **T63.41** Toxic effect of venom of centipedes and venomous millipedes

    ● **T63.411** Toxic effect of venom of centipedes and venomous millipedes, accidental (unintentional)

    ● **T63.412** Toxic effect of venom of centipedes and venomous millipedes, intentional self-harm

    ● **T63.413** Toxic effect of venom of centipedes and venomous millipedes, assault

    ● **T63.414** Toxic effect of venom of centipedes and venomous millipedes, undetermined

▶ New   ⇒ Revised   ~~deleted~~ Deleted   Excludes 1   Excludes 2   Includes   Use additional   Code first   Code also   Key words

OGCR Official Guidelines   X Assign placeholder X   ● Use Additional Character(s)   ▶ Manifestation Code   **Coding Clinic**

● T63.42   Toxic effect of venom of ants
   ● T63.421   Toxic effect of venom of ants, accidental (unintentional)
   ● T63.422   Toxic effect of venom of ants, intentional self-harm
   ● T63.423   Toxic effect of venom of ants, assault
   ● T63.424   Toxic effect of venom of ants, undetermined
● T63.43   Toxic effect of venom of caterpillars
   ● T63.431   Toxic effect of venom of caterpillars, accidental (unintentional)
   ● T63.432   Toxic effect of venom of caterpillars, intentional self-harm
   ● T63.433   Toxic effect of venom of caterpillars, assault
   ● T63.434   Toxic effect of venom of caterpillars, undetermined
● T63.44   Toxic effect of venom of bees
   ● T63.441   Toxic effect of venom of bees, accidental (unintentional)
   ● T63.442   Toxic effect of venom of bees, intentional self-harm
   ● T63.443   Toxic effect of venom of bees, assault
   ● T63.444   Toxic effect of venom of bees, undetermined
● T63.45   Toxic effect of venom of hornets
   ● T63.451   Toxic effect of venom of hornets, accidental (unintentional)
   ● T63.452   Toxic effect of venom of hornets, intentional self-harm
   ● T63.453   Toxic effect of venom of hornets, assault
   ● T63.454   Toxic effect of venom of hornets, undetermined
● T63.46   Toxic effect of venom of wasps
         Toxic effect of yellow jacket
   ● T63.461   Toxic effect of venom of wasps, accidental (unintentional)
   ● T63.462   Toxic effect of venom of wasps, intentional self-harm
   ● T63.463   Toxic effect of venom of wasps, assault
   ● T63.464   Toxic effect of venom of wasps, undetermined
● T63.48   Toxic effect of venom of other arthropod
   ● T63.481   Toxic effect of venom of other arthropod, accidental (unintentional)
   ● T63.482   Toxic effect of venom of other arthropod, intentional self-harm
   ● T63.483   Toxic effect of venom of other arthropod, assault
   ● T63.484   Toxic effect of venom of other arthropod, undetermined
● T63.5   Toxic effect of contact with venomous fish
      Excludes2   poisoning by ingestion of fish (T61.-)
   ● T63.51   Toxic effect of contact with stingray
      ● T63.511   Toxic effect of contact with stingray, accidental (unintentional)
      ● T63.512   Toxic effect of contact with stingray, intentional self-harm
      ● T63.513   Toxic effect of contact with stingray, assault
      ● T63.514   Toxic effect of contact with stingray, undetermined

● T63.59   Toxic effect of contact with other venomous fish
   ● T63.591   Toxic effect of contact with other venomous fish, accidental (unintentional)
   ● T63.592   Toxic effect of contact with other venomous fish, intentional self-harm
   ● T63.593   Toxic effect of contact with other venomous fish, assault
   ● T63.594   Toxic effect of contact with other venomous fish, undetermined
● T63.6   Toxic effect of contact with other venomous marine animals
      Excludes1   sea-snake venom (T63.09)
      Excludes2   poisoning by ingestion of shellfish (T61.78-)
   ● T63.61   Toxic effect of contact with Portugese Man-o-war
         Toxic effect of contact with bluebottle
      ● T63.611   Toxic effect of contact with Portugese Man-o-war, accidental (unintentional)
      ● T63.612   Toxic effect of contact with Portugese Man-o-war, intentional self-harm
      ● T63.613   Toxic effect of contact with Portugese Man-o-war, assault
      ● T63.614   Toxic effect of contact with Portugese Man-o-war, undetermined
   ● T63.62   Toxic effect of contact with other jellyfish
      ● T63.621   Toxic effect of contact with other jellyfish, accidental (unintentional)
      ● T63.622   Toxic effect of contact with other jellyfish, intentional self-harm
      ● T63.623   Toxic effect of contact with other jellyfish, assault
      ● T63.624   Toxic effect of contact with other jellyfish, undetermined
   ● T63.63   Toxic effect of contact with sea anemone
      ● T63.631   Toxic effect of contact with sea anemone, accidental (unintentional)
      ● T63.632   Toxic effect of contact with sea anemone, intentional self-harm
      ● T63.633   Toxic effect of contact with sea anemone, assault
      ● T63.634   Toxic effect of contact with sea anemone, undetermined
   ● T63.69   Toxic effect of contact with other venomous marine animals
      ● T63.691   Toxic effect of contact with other venomous marine animals, accidental (unintentional)
      ● T63.692   Toxic effect of contact with other venomous marine animals, intentional self-harm
      ● T63.693   Toxic effect of contact with other venomous marine animals, assault
      ● T63.694   Toxic effect of contact with other venomous marine animals, undetermined
● T63.7   Toxic effect of contact with venomous plant
   ● T63.71   Toxic effect of contact with venomous marine plant
      ● T63.711   Toxic effect of contact with venomous marine plant, accidental (unintentional)
      ● T63.712   Toxic effect of contact with venomous marine plant, intentional self-harm
      ● T63.713   Toxic effect of contact with venomous marine plant, assault
      ● T63.714   Toxic effect of contact with venomous marine plant, undetermined

- T63.79　Toxic effect of contact with other venomous plant
  - T63.791　Toxic effect of contact with other venomous plant, accidental (unintentional)
  - T63.792　Toxic effect of contact with other venomous plant, intentional self-harm
  - T63.793　Toxic effect of contact with other venomous plant, assault
  - T63.794　Toxic effect of contact with other venomous plant, undetermined
- T63.8　Toxic effect of contact with other venomous animals
  - T63.81　Toxic effect of contact with venomous frog
    - **Excludes1**　contact with nonvenomous frog (W62.0)
    - T63.811　Toxic effect of contact with venomous frog, accidental (unintentional)
    - T63.812　Toxic effect of contact with venomous frog, intentional self-harm
    - T63.813　Toxic effect of contact with venomous frog, assault
    - T63.814　Toxic effect of contact with venomous frog, undetermined
  - T63.82　Toxic effect of contact with venomous toad
    - **Excludes1**　contact with nonvenomous toad (W62.1)
    - T63.821　Toxic effect of contact with venomous toad, accidental (unintentional)
    - T63.822　Toxic effect of contact with venomous toad, intentional self-harm
    - T63.823　Toxic effect of contact with venomous toad, assault
    - T63.824　Toxic effect of contact with venomous toad, undetermined
  - T63.83　Toxic effect of contact with other venomous amphibian
    - **Excludes1**　contact with nonvenomous amphibian (W62.9)
    - T63.831　Toxic effect of contact with other venomous amphibian, accidental (unintentional)
    - T63.832　Toxic effect of contact with other venomous amphibian, intentional self-harm
    - T63.833　Toxic effect of contact with other venomous amphibian, assault
    - T63.834　Toxic effect of contact with other venomous amphibian, undetermined
  - T63.89　Toxic effect of contact with other venomous animals
    - T63.891　Toxic effect of contact with other venomous animals, accidental (unintentional)
    - T63.892　Toxic effect of contact with other venomous animals, intentional self-harm
    - T63.893　Toxic effect of contact with other venomous animals, assault
    - T63.894　Toxic effect of contact with other venomous animals, undetermined
- T63.9　Toxic effect of contact with unspecified venomous animal
  - X● T63.91　Toxic effect of contact with unspecified venomous animal, accidental (unintentional)
  - X● T63.92　Toxic effect of contact with unspecified venomous animal, intentional self-harm
  - X● T63.93　Toxic effect of contact with unspecified venomous animal, assault
  - X● T63.94　Toxic effect of contact with unspecified venomous animal, undetermined

- T64　Toxic effect of aflatoxin and other mycotoxin food contaminants

  The appropriate 7th character is to be added to each code from category T64

A	initial encounter
D	subsequent encounter
S	sequela

  - T64.0　Toxic effect of aflatoxin
    - X● T64.01　Toxic effect of aflatoxin, accidental (unintentional)
    - X● T64.02　Toxic effect of aflatoxin, intentional self-harm
    - X● T64.03　Toxic effect of aflatoxin, assault
    - X● T64.04　Toxic effect of aflatoxin, undetermined
  - T64.8　Toxic effect of other mycotoxin food contaminants
    - X● T64.81　Toxic effect of other mycotoxin food contaminants, accidental (unintentional)
    - X● T64.82　Toxic effect of other mycotoxin food contaminants, intentional self-harm
    - X● T64.83　Toxic effect of other mycotoxin food contaminants, assault
    - X● T64.84　Toxic effect of other mycotoxin food contaminants, undetermined

- T65　Toxic effect of other and unspecified substances

  The appropriate 7th character is to be added to each code from category T65

A	initial encounter
D	subsequent encounter
S	sequela

  - T65.0　Toxic effect of cyanides
    - **Excludes1**　hydrogen cyanide (T57.3-)
    - T65.0X　Toxic effect of cyanides
      - T65.0X1　Toxic effect of cyanides, accidental (unintentional)
        Toxic effect of cyanides NOS
      - T65.0X2　Toxic effect of cyanides, intentional self-harm
      - T65.0X3　Toxic effect of cyanides, assault
      - T65.0X4　Toxic effect of cyanides, undetermined
  - T65.1　Toxic effect of strychnine and its salts
    - T65.1X　Toxic effect of strychnine and its salts
      - T65.1X1　Toxic effect of strychnine and its salts, accidental (unintentional)
        Toxic effect of strychnine and its salts NOS
      - T65.1X2　Toxic effect of strychnine and its salts, intentional self-harm
      - T65.1X3　Toxic effect of strychnine and its salts, assault
      - T65.1X4　Toxic effect of strychnine and its salts, undetermined
  - T65.2　Toxic effect of tobacco and nicotine
    - **Excludes2**　nicotine dependence (F17.-)
    - T65.21　Toxic effect of chewing tobacco
      - T65.211　Toxic effect of chewing tobacco, accidental (unintentional)
        Toxic effect of chewing tobacco NOS
      - T65.212　Toxic effect of chewing tobacco, intentional self-harm
      - T65.213　Toxic effect of chewing tobacco, assault
      - T65.214　Toxic effect of chewing tobacco, undetermined

● **T65.22** Toxic effect of tobacco cigarettes
Toxic effect of tobacco smoke

Use additional code for exposure to second
hand tobacco smoke (Z57.31, Z77.22)

● **T65.221** Toxic effect of tobacco cigarettes,
accidental (unintentional)
Toxic effect of tobacco cigarettes
NOS

● **T65.222** Toxic effect of tobacco cigarettes,
intentional self-harm

● **T65.223** Toxic effect of tobacco cigarettes,
assault

● **T65.224** Toxic effect of tobacco cigarettes,
undetermined

● **T65.29** Toxic effect of other tobacco and nicotine

● **T65.291** Toxic effect of other tobacco and
nicotine, accidental (unintentional)
Toxic effect of other tobacco and
nicotine NOS

● **T65.292** Toxic effect of other tobacco and
nicotine, intentional self-harm

● **T65.293** Toxic effect of other tobacco and
nicotine, assault

● **T65.294** Toxic effect of other tobacco and
nicotine, undetermined

● **T65.3** Toxic effect of nitroderivatives and aminoderivatives of
benzene and its homologues
Toxic effect of anilin [benzenamine]
Toxic effect of nitrobenzene
Toxic effect of trinitrotoluene

● **T65.3X** Toxic effect of nitroderivatives and
aminoderivatives of benzene and its
homologues

● **T65.3X1** Toxic effect of nitroderivatives
and aminoderivatives of benzene
and its homologues, accidental
(unintentional)
Toxic effect of nitroderivatives and
aminoderivatives of benzene
and its homologues NOS

● **T65.3X2** Toxic effect of nitroderivatives and
aminoderivatives of benzene and its
homologues, intentional self-harm

● **T65.3X3** Toxic effect of nitroderivatives and
aminoderivatives of benzene and its
homologues, assault

● **T65.3X4** Toxic effect of nitroderivatives and
aminoderivatives of benzene and its
homologues, undetermined

● **T65.4** Toxic effect of carbon disulfide

● **T65.4X** Toxic effect of carbon disulfide

● **T65.4X1** Toxic effect of carbon disulfide,
accidental (unintentional)
Toxic effect of carbon disulfide NOS

● **T65.4X2** Toxic effect of carbon disulfide,
intentional self-harm

● **T65.4X3** Toxic effect of carbon disulfide,
assault

● **T65.4X4** Toxic effect of carbon disulfide,
undetermined

● **T65.5** Toxic effect of nitroglycerin and other nitric acids and
esters
Toxic effect of 1,2,3-Propanetriol trinitrate

● **T65.5X** Toxic effect of nitroglycerin and other nitric
acids and esters

● **T65.5X1** Toxic effect of nitroglycerin and other
nitric acids and esters, accidental
(unintentional)
Toxic effect of nitroglycerin and other
nitric acids and esters NOS

● **T65.5X2** Toxic effect of nitroglycerin and other
nitric acids and esters, intentional
self-harm

● **T65.5X3** Toxic effect of nitroglycerin and other
nitric acids and esters, assault

● **T65.5X4** Toxic effect of nitroglycerin and other
nitric acids and esters, undetermined

● **T65.6** Toxic effect of paints and dyes, not elsewhere classified

● **T65.6X** Toxic effect of paints and dyes, not elsewhere
classified

● **T65.6X1** Toxic effect of paints and dyes, not
elsewhere classified, accidental
(unintentional)
Toxic effect of paints and dyes NOS

● **T65.6X2** Toxic effect of paints and dyes, not
elsewhere classified, intentional
self-harm

● **T65.6X3** Toxic effect of paints and dyes, not
elsewhere classified, assault

● **T65.6X4** Toxic effect of paints and dyes, not
elsewhere classified, undetermined

● **T65.8** Toxic effect of other specified substances

● **T65.81** Toxic effect of latex

● **T65.811** Toxic effect of latex, accidental
(unintentional)
Toxic effect of latex NOS

● **T65.812** Toxic effect of latex, intentional
self-harm

● **T65.813** Toxic effect of latex, assault

● **T65.814** Toxic effect of latex, undetermined

● **T65.82** Toxic effect of harmful algae and algae toxins
Toxic effect of (harmful) algae bloom NOS
Toxic effect of blue-green algae bloom
Toxic effect of brown tide
Toxic effect of cyanobacteria bloom
Toxic effect of Florida red tide
Toxic effect of pfiesteria piscicida
Toxic effect of red tide

● **T65.821** Toxic effect of harmful algae
and algae toxins, accidental
(unintentional)
Toxic effect of harmful algae and
algae toxins NOS

● **T65.822** Toxic effect of harmful algae and
algae toxins, intentional self-harm

● **T65.823** Toxic effect of harmful algae and
algae toxins, assault

● **T65.824** Toxic effect of harmful algae and
algae toxins, undetermined

● **T65.83** Toxic effect of fiberglass

● **T65.831** Toxic effect of fiberglass, accidental
(unintentional)
Toxic effect of fiberglass NOS

● **T65.832** Toxic effect of fiberglass, intentional
self-harm

● **T65.833** Toxic effect of fiberglass, assault

● **T65.834** Toxic effect of fiberglass,
undetermined

● **T65.89** Toxic effect of other specified substances

● **T65.891** Toxic effect of other specified
substances, accidental (unintentional)
Toxic effect of other specified
substances NOS
Coding Clinic: 2018, Q1, P5

● **T65.892** Toxic effect of other specified
substances, intentional self-harm

● **T65.893** Toxic effect of other specified
substances, assault

● **T65.894** Toxic effect of other specified
substances, undetermined

CHAPTER 19 (S00-T88)

● **T65.9 Toxic effect of unspecified substance**
  X● **T65.91 Toxic effect of unspecified substance, accidental (unintentional)**
         Poisoning NOS
  X● **T65.92 Toxic effect of unspecified substance, intentional self-harm**
  X● **T65.93 Toxic effect of unspecified substance, assault**
  X● **T65.94 Toxic effect of unspecified substance, undetermined**

OTHER AND UNSPECIFIED EFFECTS OF EXTERNAL CAUSES (T66-T78)

● **T66 Radiation sickness, unspecified**
  Excludes1 specified adverse effects of radiation, such as:
             burns (T20-T31)
             leukemia (C91-C95)
             radiation gastroenteritis and colitis (K52.0)
             radiation pneumonitis (J70.0)
             radiation related disorders of the skin and subcutaneous tissue (L55-L59)
             sunburn (L55.-)

  The appropriate 7th character is to be added to code T66

A	initial encounter
D	subsequent encounter
S	sequela

● **T67 Effects of heat and light**
  Excludes1 erythema [dermatitis] ab igne (L59.0)
             malignant hyperpyrexia due to anesthesia (T88.3)
             radiation-related disorders of the skin and subcutaneous tissue (L55-L59)
  Excludes2 burns (T20-T31)
             sunburn (L55.-)
             sweat disorder due to heat (L74-L75)

  The appropriate 7th character is to be added to each code from category T67

A	initial encounter
D	subsequent encounter
S	sequela

  X● **T67.0 Heatstroke and sunstroke**
         Heat apoplexy
         Heat pyrexia
         Siriasis
         Thermoplegia
         Use additional code(s) to identify any associated complications of heatstroke, such as:
             coma and stupor (R40.-)
             systemic inflammatory response syndrome (R65.1-)
  X● **T67.1 Heat syncope**
         Heat collapse
  X● **T67.2 Heat cramp**
  X● **T67.3 Heat exhaustion, anhydrotic**
         Heat prostration due to water depletion
         Excludes1 heat exhaustion due to salt depletion (T67.4)
  X● **T67.4 Heat exhaustion due to salt depletion**
         Heat prostration due to salt (and water) depletion
  X● **T67.5 Heat exhaustion, unspecified**
         Heat prostration NOS
  X● **T67.6 Heat fatigue, transient**
  X● **T67.7 Heat edema**
  X● **T67.8 Other effects of heat and light**
  X● **T67.9 Effect of heat and light, unspecified**

X● **T68 Hypothermia**
       Accidental hypothermia
       Hypothermia NOS
       Use additional code to identify source of exposure:
           Exposure to excessive cold of man-made origin (W93)
           Exposure to excessive cold of natural origin (X31)
       Excludes1 hypothermia following anesthesia (T88.51)
                  hypothermia not associated with low environmental temperature (R68.0)
                  hypothermia of newborn (P80.-)
       Excludes2 frostbite (T33-T34)
       The appropriate 7th character is to be added to code T68

A	initial encounter
D	subsequent encounter
S	sequela

● **T69 Other effects of reduced temperature**
       Use additional code to identify source of exposure:
           Exposure to excessive cold of man-made origin (W93)
           Exposure to excessive cold of natural origin (X31)
       Excludes2 frostbite (T33-T34)
       The appropriate 7th character is to be added to each code from category T69

A	initial encounter
D	subsequent encounter
S	sequela

  ● **T69.0 Immersion hand and foot**
    ● **T69.01 Immersion hand**
        ● **T69.011 Immersion hand, right hand**
        ● **T69.012 Immersion hand, left hand**
        ● **T69.019 Immersion hand, unspecified hand**
    ● **T69.02 Immersion foot**
        Trench foot
        ● **T69.021 Immersion foot, right foot**
        ● **T69.022 Immersion foot, left foot**
        ● **T69.029 Immersion foot, unspecified foot**
  X● **T69.1 Chilblains**
  X● **T69.8 Other specified effects of reduced temperature**
  X● **T69.9 Effect of reduced temperature, unspecified**

● **T70 Effects of air pressure and water pressure**
       The appropriate 7th character is to be added to each code from category T70

A	initial encounter
D	subsequent encounter
S	sequela

  X● **T70.0 Otitic barotrauma**
         Aero-otitis media
         Effects of change in ambient atmospheric pressure or water pressure on ears
  X● **T70.1 Sinus barotrauma**
         Aerosinusitis
         Effects of change in ambient atmospheric pressure on sinuses
  ● **T70.2 Other and unspecified effects of high altitude**
         Excludes2 polycythemia due to high altitude (D75.1)
    X● **T70.20 Unspecified effects of high altitude**
    X● **T70.29 Other effects of high altitude**
           Alpine sickness
           Anoxia due to high altitude
           Barotrauma NOS
           Hypobaropathy
           Mountain sickness

▶ New   ⟹ Revised   ~~deleted~~ Deleted   Excludes 1   Excludes 2   Includes   Use additional   Code first   Code also   Key words
OGCR Official Guidelines   X Assign placeholder X   ● Use Additional Character(s)   ▷ Manifestation Code   **Coding Clinic**

X● **T70.3**   **Caisson disease [decompression sickness]**
     Compressed-air disease
     Diver's palsy or paralysis

X● **T70.4**   **Effects of high-pressure fluids**
     Hydraulic jet injection (industrial)
     Pneumatic jet injection (industrial)
     Traumatic jet injection (industrial)

X● **T70.8**   **Other effects of air pressure and water pressure**

X● **T70.9**   **Effect of air pressure and water pressure, unspecified**

● **T71**   **Asphyxiation**
     Mechanical suffocation
     Traumatic suffocation

     Excludes1   acute respiratory distress (syndrome) (J80)
                anoxia due to high altitude (T70.2)
                asphyxia NOS (R09.01)
                asphyxia from carbon monoxide (T58.-)
                asphyxia from inhalation of food or foreign body
                   (T17.-)
                asphyxia from other gases, fumes and vapors
                   (T59.-)
                respiratory distress (syndrome) in newborn
                   (P22.-)

     The appropriate 7th character is to be added to each code from
        category T71

> | | |
> |---|---|
> | A | initial encounter |
> | D | subsequent encounter |
> | S | sequela |

● **T71.1**   **Asphyxiation due to mechanical threat to breathing**
     Suffocation due to mechanical threat to breathing

   ● **T71.11**   **Asphyxiation due to smothering under pillow**

     ● **T71.111**   **Asphyxiation due to smothering under pillow, accidental**
            Asphyxiation due to smothering under pillow NOS

     ● **T71.112**   **Asphyxiation due to smothering under pillow, intentional self-harm**

     ● **T71.113**   **Asphyxiation due to smothering under pillow, assault**

     ● **T71.114**   **Asphyxiation due to smothering under pillow, undetermined**

   ● **T71.12**   **Asphyxiation due to plastic bag**

     ● **T71.121**   **Asphyxiation due to plastic bag, accidental**
            Asphyxiation due to plastic bag NOS

     ● **T71.122**   **Asphyxiation due to plastic bag, intentional self-harm**

     ● **T71.123**   **Asphyxiation due to plastic bag, assault**

     ● **T71.124**   **Asphyxiation due to plastic bag, undetermined**

   ● **T71.13**   **Asphyxiation due to being trapped in bed linens**

     ● **T71.131**   **Asphyxiation due to being trapped in bed linens, accidental**
            Asphyxiation due to being trapped in bed linens NOS

     ● **T71.132**   **Asphyxiation due to being trapped in bed linens, intentional self-harm**

     ● **T71.133**   **Asphyxiation due to being trapped in bed linens, assault**

     ● **T71.134**   **Asphyxiation due to being trapped in bed linens, undetermined**

● **T71.14**   **Asphyxiation due to smothering under another person's body (in bed)**

   ● **T71.141**   **Asphyxiation due to smothering under another person's body (in bed), accidental**
            Asphyxiation due to smothering under another person's body (in bed) NOS

   ● **T71.143**   **Asphyxiation due to smothering under another person's body (in bed), assault**

   ● **T71.144**   **Asphyxiation due to smothering under another person's body (in bed), undetermined**

● **T71.15**   **Asphyxiation due to smothering in furniture**

   ● **T71.151**   **Asphyxiation due to smothering in furniture, accidental**
            Asphyxiation due to smothering in furniture NOS

   ● **T71.152**   **Asphyxiation due to smothering in furniture, intentional self-harm**

   ● **T71.153**   **Asphyxiation due to smothering in furniture, assault**

   ● **T71.154**   **Asphyxiation due to smothering in furniture, undetermined**

● **T71.16**   **Asphyxiation due to hanging**
     Hanging by window shade cord

     Use additional code for any associated injuries, such as:
         crushing injury of neck (S17.-)
         fracture of cervical vertebrae (S12.0-S12.2-)
         open wound of neck (S11.-)

   ● **T71.161**   **Asphyxiation due to hanging, accidental**
            Asphyxiation due to hanging NOS
            Hanging NOS

   ● **T71.162**   **Asphyxiation due to hanging, intentional self-harm**

   ● **T71.163**   **Asphyxiation due to hanging, assault**

   ● **T71.164**   **Asphyxiation due to hanging, undetermined**

● **T71.19**   **Asphyxiation due to mechanical**
     Threat to breathing due to other causes

   ● **T71.191**   **Asphyxiation due to mechanical threat to breathing due to other causes, accidental**
            Asphyxiation due to other causes NOS
            Coding Clinic: 2016, Q4, P76

   ● **T71.192**   **Asphyxiation due to mechanical threat to breathing due to other causes, intentional self-harm**

   ● **T71.193**   **Asphyxiation due to mechanical threat to breathing due to other causes, assault**

   ● **T71.194**   **Asphyxiation due to mechanical threat to breathing due to other causes, undetermined**

● **T71.2**   **Asphyxiation due to systemic oxygen deficiency due to low oxygen content in ambient air**
     Suffocation due to systemic oxygen deficiency due to low oxygen content in ambient air

X● **T71.20**   **Asphyxiation due to systemic oxygen deficiency due to low oxygen content in ambient air due to unspecified cause**

X● **T71.21**   **Asphyxiation due to cave-in or falling earth**
     Use additional code for any associated cataclysm (X34-X38)

CHAPTER 19 (S00-T88)

●T71.22 Asphyxiation due to being trapped in a car trunk
    ●T71.221 Asphyxiation due to being trapped in a car trunk, accidental
    ●T71.222 Asphyxiation due to being trapped in a car trunk, intentional self-harm
    ●T71.223 Asphyxiation due to being trapped in a car trunk, assault
    ●T71.224 Asphyxiation due to being trapped in a car trunk, undetermined
●T71.23 Asphyxiation due to being trapped in a (discarded) refrigerator
    ●T71.231 Asphyxiation due to being trapped in a (discarded) refrigerator, accidental
    ●T71.232 Asphyxiation due to being trapped in a (discarded) refrigerator, intentional self-harm
    ●T71.233 Asphyxiation due to being trapped in a (discarded) refrigerator, assault
    ●T71.234 Asphyxiation due to being trapped in a (discarded) refrigerator, undetermined
X●T71.29 Asphyxiation due to being trapped in other low oxygen environment
X●T71.9 Asphyxiation due to unspecified cause
    Suffocation (by strangulation) due to unspecified cause
    Suffocation NOS
    Systemic oxygen deficiency due to low oxygen content in ambient air due to unspecified cause
    Systemic oxygen deficiency due to mechanical threat to breathing due to unspecified cause
    Traumatic asphyxia NOS

●T73 Effects of other deprivation
    The appropriate 7th character is to be added to each code from category T73

A	initial encounter
D	subsequent encounter
S	sequela

X●T73.0 Starvation
    Deprivation of food
X●T73.1 Deprivation of water
X●T73.2 Exhaustion due to exposure
X●T73.3 Exhaustion due to excessive exertion
    Exhaustion due to overexertion
X●T73.8 Other effects of deprivation
X●T73.9 Effect of deprivation, unspecified

●T74 Adult and child abuse, neglect and other maltreatment, confirmed
    Use additional code, if applicable, to identify any associated current injury
    Use additional external cause code to identify perpetrator, if known (Y07.-)
    Excludes1 abuse and maltreatment in pregnancy (O9A.3-, O9A.4-, O9A.5-)
        adult and child maltreatment, suspected (T76.-)
    The appropriate 7th character is to be added to each code from category T74

A	initial encounter
D	subsequent encounter
S	sequela

●T74.0 Neglect or abandonment, confirmed
    X●T74.01 Adult neglect or abandonment, confirmed   A
    X●T74.02 Child neglect or abandonment, confirmed   P

●T74.1 Physical abuse, confirmed
    Excludes2 sexual abuse (T74.2-)
    X●T74.11 Adult physical abuse, confirmed   A
    X●T74.12 Child physical abuse, confirmed   P
        Excludes2 shaken infant syndrome (T74.4)
●T74.2 Sexual abuse, confirmed
    Rape, confirmed
    Sexual assault, confirmed
    X●T74.21 Adult sexual abuse, confirmed   A
    X●T74.22 Child sexual abuse, confirmed   P
●T74.3 Psychological abuse, confirmed
    ▶Bullying and intimidation, confirmed
    ▶Intimidation through social media, confirmed
    X●T74.31 Adult psychological abuse, confirmed   A
    X●T74.32 Child psychological abuse, confirmed   P
X●T74.4 Shaken infant syndrome   P
▶●T74.5 Forced sexual exploitation, confirmed
    ▶X●T74.51 Adult forced sexual exploitation, confirmed
    ▶X●T74.52 Child sexual exploitation, confirmed
▶●T74.6 Forced labor exploitation, confirmed
    ▶X●T74.61 Adult forced labor exploitation, confirmed
    ▶X●T74.62 Child forced labor exploitation, confirmed
●T74.9 Unspecified maltreatment, confirmed
    X●T74.91 Unspecified adult maltreatment, confirmed   A
    X●T74.92 Unspecified child maltreatment, confirmed   P

●T75 Other and unspecified effects of other external causes
    Excludes1 adverse effects NEC (T78.-)
    Excludes2 burns (electric) (T20-T31)
    The appropriate 7th character is to be added to each code from category T75

A	initial encounter
D	subsequent encounter
S	sequela

●T75.0 Effects of lightning
    Struck by lightning
    X●T75.00 Unspecified effects of lightning
        Struck by lightning NOS
    X●T75.01 Shock due to being struck by lightning
    X●T75.09 Other effects of lightning
        Use additional code for other effects of lightning
X●T75.1 Unspecified effects of drowning and nonfatal submersion
    Immersion
    Excludes1 specified effects of drowning code to effects
●T75.2 Effects of vibration
    X●T75.20 Unspecified effects of vibration
    X●T75.21 Pneumatic hammer syndrome
    X●T75.22 Traumatic vasospastic syndrome
    X●T75.23 Vertigo from infrasound
        Excludes1 vertigo NOS (R42)
    X●T75.29 Other effects of vibration
X●T75.3 Motion sickness
    Airsickness   Travel sickness
    Seasickness
    Use additional external cause code to identify vehicle or type of motion (Y92.81-, Y93.5-)
X●T75.4 Electrocution
    Shock from electric current
    Shock from electroshock gun (taser)
●T75.8 Other specified effects of external causes
    X●T75.81 Effects of abnormal gravitation [G] forces
    X●T75.82 Effects of weightlessness
    X●T75.89 Other specified effects of external causes

▶ New   ⇒ Revised   ~~deleted~~ Deleted   Excludes 1   Excludes 2   Includes   Use additional   Code first   Code also   Key words
OGCR Official Guidelines   X Assign placeholder X   ● Use Additional Character(s)   ▷ Manifestation Code   **Coding Clinic**

● **T76** **Adult and child abuse, neglect and other maltreatment, suspected**

     Use additional code, if applicable, to identify any associated current injury

     Excludes1   adult and child maltreatment, confirmed (T74.-)
                   suspected abuse and maltreatment in pregnancy (O9A.3-, O9A.4-, O9A.5-)
                   suspected adult physical abuse, ruled out (Z04.71)
                   suspected adult sexual abuse, ruled out (Z04.41)
                   suspected child physical abuse, ruled out (Z04.72)
                   suspected child sexual abuse, ruled out (Z04.42)

     The appropriate 7th character is to be added to each code from category T76

> | | |
> |---|---|
> | A | initial encounter |
> | D | subsequent encounter |
> | S | sequela |

     Coding Clinic: 2016, Q4, P129

● **T76.0**   **Neglect or abandonment, suspected**
     X● **T76.01**   **Adult** neglect or abandonment, suspected   A
     X● **T76.02**   **Child** neglect or abandonment, suspected   P

● **T76.1**   **Physical abuse, suspected**
     X● **T76.11**   **Adult** physical abuse, suspected   A
     X● **T76.12**   **Child** physical abuse, suspected   P

● **T76.2**   **Sexual abuse, suspected**
     Rape, suspected
       Excludes1   alleged abuse, ruled out (Z04.7)
     X● **T76.21**   **Adult** sexual abuse, suspected   A
     X● **T76.22**   **Child** sexual abuse, suspected   P

● **T76.3**   **Psychological abuse, suspected**
     ▶Bullying and intimidation, suspected
     ▶Intimidation through social media, suspected
     X● **T76.31**   **Adult** psychological abuse, suspected   A
     X● **T76.32**   **Child** psychological abuse, suspected   P

▶● **T76.5**   **Forced sexual exploitation, suspected**
     ▶X● **T76.51**   **Adult** forced sexual exploitation, suspected
     ▶X● **T76.52**   **Child** sexual exploitation, suspected

▶● **T76.6**   **Forced labor exploitation, suspected**
     ▶X● **T76.61**   **Adult** forced labor exploitation, suspected
     ▶X● **T76.62**   **Child** forced labor exploitation, suspected

● **T76.9**   **Unspecified maltreatment, suspected**
     X● **T76.91**   Unspecified **adult** maltreatment, suspected   A
     X● **T76.92**   Unspecified **child** maltreatment, suspected   P

● **T78**   **Adverse effects, not elsewhere classified**
     Excludes2   complications of surgical and medical care NEC (T80-T88)

     The appropriate 7th character is to be added to each code from category T78

> | | |
> |---|---|
> | A | initial encounter |
> | D | subsequent encounter |
> | S | sequela |

● **T78.0**   **Anaphylactic reaction due to food**
     Anaphylactic reaction due to adverse food reaction
     Anaphylactic shock or reaction due to nonpoisonous foods
     Anaphylactoid reaction due to food
     X● **T78.00**   Anaphylactic reaction due to unspecified food
     X● **T78.01**   Anaphylactic reaction due to peanuts
     X● **T78.02**   Anaphylactic reaction due to shellfish (crustaceans)
     X● **T78.03**   Anaphylactic reaction due to other fish
     X● **T78.04**   Anaphylactic reaction due to fruits and vegetables

     X● **T78.05**   Anaphylactic reaction due to tree nuts and seeds
         Excludes2   anaphylactic reaction due to peanuts (T78.01)
     X● **T78.06**   Anaphylactic reaction due to food additives
     X● **T78.07**   Anaphylactic reaction due to milk and dairy products
     X● **T78.08**   Anaphylactic reaction due to eggs
     X● **T78.09**   Anaphylactic reaction due to other food products

X● **T78.1**   **Other adverse food reactions, not elsewhere classified**
     Use additional code to identify the type of reaction, if applicable
     Excludes1   anaphylactic reaction or shock due to adverse food reaction (T78.0-)
                   anaphylactic reaction due to food (T78.0-)
                   bacterial food borne intoxications (A05.-)
     Excludes2   allergic and dietetic gastroenteritis and colitis (K52.29)
                   allergic rhinitis due to food (J30.5)
                   dermatitis due to food in contact with skin (L23.6, L24.6, L25.4)
                   dermatitis due to ingested food (L27.2)
                   food protein-induced enterocolitis syndrome (K52.21)
                   food protein-induced enteropathy (K52.22)

X● **T78.2**   **Anaphylactic shock, unspecified**
     Occurs when allergic response triggers large quantities of histamines, prostaglandins, leukotrienes resulting in systemic vasodilation
     Allergic shock
     Anaphylactic reaction
     Anaphylaxis
     Excludes1   anaphylactic reaction or shock due to adverse effect of correct medicinal substance properly administered (T88.6)
                   anaphylactic reaction or shock due to adverse food reaction (T78.0-)
                   anaphylactic reaction or shock due to serum (T80.5-)

X● **T78.3**   **Angioneurotic edema**
     Allergic angioedema
     Giant urticaria
     Vascular disorder resulting from abnormalities of autonomic nervous system fibers supplying blood vessels
     Quincke's edema
     Excludes1   serum urticaria (T80.6-)
                   urticaria (L50.-)

● **T78.4**   **Other and unspecified allergy**
     Excludes1   specified types of allergic reaction such as:
                   allergic diarrhea (K52.29)
                   allergic gastroenteritis and colitis (K52.29)
                   dermatitis (L23-L25, L27.-)
                   food protein-induced enterocolitis syndrome (K52.21)
                   food protein-induced enteropathy (K52.22)
                   hay fever (J30.1)
     X● **T78.40**   **Allergy, unspecified**
           Allergic reaction NOS
           Hypersensitivity NOS
     X● **T78.41**   **Arthus phenomenon**
           Arthus reaction
     X● **T78.49**   **Other allergy**

X● **T78.8**   **Other adverse effects, not elsewhere classified**

CHAPTER 19 (S00-T88)

CERTAIN EARLY COMPLICATIONS OF TRAUMA (T79)

● **T79   Certain early complications of trauma, not elsewhere classified**

Excludes2   acute respiratory distress syndrome (J80)
complications occurring during or following
  medical procedures (T80-T88)
complications of surgical and medical care NEC
  (T80-T88)
newborn respiratory distress syndrome (P22.0)

The appropriate 7th character is to be added to each code from
category T79

> A   initial encounter
> D   subsequent encounter
> S   sequela

X ● **T79.0   Air embolism (traumatic)**

Excludes1   air embolism complicating abortion
  or ectopic or molar pregnancy
  (O00-O07, O08.2)
air embolism complicating pregnancy,
  childbirth and the puerperium (O88.0)
air embolism following infusion,
  transfusion, and therapeutic injection
  (T80.0)
air embolism following procedure NEC
  (T81.7-)

X ● **T79.1   Fat embolism (traumatic)**

Excludes1   fat embolism complicating:
  abortion or ectopic or molar pregnancy
    (O00-O07, O08.2)
  pregnancy, childbirth and the
    puerperium (O88.8)

X ● **T79.2   Traumatic secondary and recurrent hemorrhage and
seroma**

X ● **T79.4   Traumatic shock**
Shock (immediate) (delayed) following injury

Excludes1   anaphylactic shock due to adverse food
  reaction (T78.0-)
anaphylactic shock due to correct
  medicinal substance properly
  administered (T88.6)
anaphylactic shock due to serum (T80.5-)
anaphylactic shock NOS (T78.2)
anesthetic shock (T88.2)
electric shock (T75.4)
nontraumatic shock NEC (R57.-)
obstetric shock (O75.1)
postprocedural shock (T81.1-)
septic shock (R65.21)
shock complicating abortion or ectopic or
  molar pregnancy (O00-O07, O08.3)
shock due to lightning (T75.01)
shock NOS (R57.9)

X ● **T79.5   Traumatic anuria**
Crush syndrome
Renal failure following crushing

X ● **T79.6   Traumatic ischemia of muscle**
Traumatic rhabdomyolysis
Volkmann's ischemic contracture

Excludes2   anterior tibial syndrome (M76.8)
compartment syndrome (traumatic)
  (T79.A-)
nontraumatic ischemia of muscle (M62.2-)

X ● **T79.7   Traumatic subcutaneous emphysema**

Excludes1   emphysema NOS (J43)
emphysema (subcutaneous) resulting
  from a procedure (T81.82)

● **T79.A   Traumatic compartment syndrome**

Excludes1   fibromyalgia (M79.7)
nontraumatic compartment syndrome
  (M79.A-)
traumatic ischemic infarction of muscle
  (T79.6)

X ● **T79.A0   Compartment syndrome, unspecified**
Compartment syndrome NOS

● **T79.A1   Traumatic compartment syndrome of upper
extremity**
Traumatic compartment syndrome of shoulder,
  arm, forearm, wrist, hand, and fingers

● **T79.A11   Traumatic compartment syndrome of
right upper extremity**

● **T79.A12   Traumatic compartment syndrome of
left upper extremity**

● **T79.A19   Traumatic compartment syndrome of
unspecified upper extremity**

● **T79.A2   Traumatic compartment syndrome of lower
extremity**
Traumatic compartment syndrome of hip,
  buttock, thigh, leg, foot, and toes

● **T79.A21   Traumatic compartment syndrome of
right lower extremity**

● **T79.A22   Traumatic compartment syndrome of
left lower extremity**

● **T79.A29   Traumatic compartment syndrome of
unspecified lower extremity**

X ● **T79.A3   Traumatic compartment syndrome of abdomen**

X ● **T79.A9   Traumatic compartment syndrome of other sites**

X ● **T79.8   Other early complications of trauma**

X ● **T79.9   Unspecified early complication of trauma**

COMPLICATIONS OF SURGICAL AND MEDICAL CARE
NOT ELSEWHERE CLASSIFIED (T80-T88)

Use additional code for adverse effect, if applicable, to identify
  drug (T36-T50 with fifth or sixth character 5)

Use additional code(s) to identify the specified condition
  resulting from the complication.

Use additional code to identify devices involved and details of
  circumstances (Y62-Y82)

Excludes2   any encounters with medical care for
  postprocedural conditions in which no
  complications are present, such as:
    artificial opening status (Z93.-)
    closure of external stoma (Z43.-)
    fitting and adjustment of external prosthetic
      device (Z44.-)
burns and corrosions from local applications and
  irradiation (T20-T32)
complications of surgical procedures during
  pregnancy, childbirth and the puerperium
  (O00-O9A)
mechanical complication of respirator [ventilator]
  (J95.850)
poisoning and toxic effects of drugs and
  chemicals (T36-T65 with fifth or sixth
  character 1-4 or 6)
postprocedural fever (R50.82)
specified complications classified elsewhere,
  such as:
    cerebrospinal fluid leak from spinal puncture
      (G97.0)
    colostomy malfunction (K94.0-)
    disorders of fluid and electrolyte imbalance
      (E86-E87)
    functional disturbances following cardiac
      surgery (I97.0-I97.1)
    intraoperative and postprocedural
      complications of specified body systems
      (D78.-, E36.-, E89.-, G97.3-, G97.4, H59.3-,
      H59.-, H95.2-, H95.3, I97.4-, I97.5, J95.6-,
      J95.7, K91.6-, L76.-, M96.-, N99.-)
    ostomy complications (J95.0-, K94.-, N99.5-)
    postgastric surgery syndromes (K91.1)
    postlaminectomy syndrome NEC (M96.1)
    postmastectomy lymphedema syndrome
      (I97.2)
    postsurgical blind-loop syndrome (K91.2)
    ventilator associated pneumonia (J95.851)

▶ New   ⇒ Revised   ~~deleted~~ Deleted   Excludes 1   Excludes 2   Includes   Use additional   Code first   Code also   Key words
OGCR Official Guidelines   X Assign placeholder X   ● Use Additional Character(s)   ⟩ Manifestation Code   **Coding Clinic**

● **T80** **Complications following infusion, transfusion and therapeutic injection**

> **Includes**   complications following perfusion
> **Excludes2**   bone marrow transplant rejection (T86.01)
> febrile nonhemolytic transfusion reaction (R50.84)
> fluid overload due to transfusion (E87.71)
> posttransfusion purpura (D69.51)
> transfusion associated circulatory overload (TACO) (E87.71)
> transfusion (red blood cell) associated hemochromatosis (E83.111)
> transfusion related acute lung injury (TRALI) (J95.84)

The appropriate 7th character is to be added to each code from category T80

> | | |
> |---|---|
> | A | initial encounter |
> | D | subsequent encounter |
> | S | sequela |

X● **T80.0** **Air embolism** following infusion, transfusion and therapeutic injection

X● **T80.1** **Vascular complications** following infusion, transfusion and therapeutic injection

> Use additional code to identify the vascular complication
> **Excludes2**   extravasation of vesicant agent (T80.81-)
> infiltration of vesicant agent (T80.81-)
> vascular complications specified as due to prosthetic devices, implants and grafts (T82.8- T83.8-, T84.8-, T85.8-)
> postprocedural vascular complications (T81.7-)

● **T80.2** **Infections** following infusion, transfusion and therapeutic injection

> Use additional code to identify the specific infection, such as:
> sepsis (A41.9)
> Use additional code (R65.2-) to identify severe sepsis, if applicable
> **Excludes2**   infections specified as due to prosthetic devices, implants and grafts (T82.6-T82.7, T83.5-T83.6, T84.5-T84.7, T85.7)
> postprocedural infections (T81.44)

> ● **T80.21** **Infection due to central venous catheter**
> Infection due to pulmonary artery catheter (Swan-Ganz catheter)

> > ● **T80.211** **Bloodstream** infection due to central venous catheter
> > Catheter-related bloodstream infection (CRBSI) NOS
> > Central line-associated bloodstream infection (CLABSI)
> > Bloodstream infection due to Hickman catheter
> > Bloodstream infection due to peripherally inserted central catheter (PICC)
> > Bloodstream infection due to portacath (port-a-cath)
> > Bloodstream infection due to pulmonary artery catheter
> > Bloodstream infection due to triple lumen catheter
> > Bloodstream infection due to umbilical venous catheter

> > ● **T80.212** **Local** infection due to central venous catheter
> > Exit or insertion site infection
> > Local infection due to Hickman catheter
> > Local infection due to peripherally inserted central catheter (PICC)
> > Local infection due to portacath (port-a-cath)
> > Local infection due to pulmonary artery catheter
> > Local infection due to triple lumen catheter
> > Local infection due to umbilical venous catheter
> > Port or reservoir infection
> > Tunnel infection

> > ● **T80.218** **Other** infection due to central venous catheter
> > Other central line-associated infection
> > Other infection due to Hickman catheter
> > Other infection due to peripherally inserted central catheter (PICC)
> > Other infection due to portacath (port-a-cath)
> > Other infection due to pulmonary artery catheter
> > Other infection due to triple lumen catheter
> > Other infection due to umbilical venous catheter

> > ● **T80.219** **Unspecified** infection due to central venous catheter
> > Central line-associated infection NOS
> > Unspecified infection due to Hickman catheter
> > Unspecified infection due to peripherally inserted central catheter (PICC)
> > Unspecified infection due to portacath (port-a-cath)
> > Unspecified infection due to pulmonary artery catheter
> > Unspecified infection due to triple lumen catheter
> > Unspecified infection due to umbilical venous catheter

> X● **T80.22** **Acute infection following transfusion, infusion, or injection of blood and blood products**

> X● **T80.29** **Infection following other infusion, transfusion and therapeutic injection**

● **T80.3** **ABO incompatibility** reaction due to transfusion of blood or blood products

> ⟹ **Excludes1**   minor blood group antigens reactions (Duffy) (E) (K) (Kell) (Kidd) (Lewis) (M) (N) (P) (S) (T80.A-)

> X● **T80.30** **ABO incompatibility reaction due to transfusion of blood or blood products, unspecified**
> ABO incompatibility blood transfusion NOS
> Reaction to ABO incompatibility from transfusion NOS

CHAPTER 19 (S00-T88)

CHAPTER 19 (S00-T88)

● T80.31   **ABO incompatibility with** hemolytic transfusion reaction
  - ● T80.310   **ABO incompatibility with** acute **hemolytic transfusion reaction**
      ABO incompatibility with hemolytic transfusion reaction less than 24 hours after transfusion
      Acute hemolytic transfusion reaction (AHTR) due to ABO incompatibility
  - ● T80.311   **ABO incompatibility with** delayed **hemolytic transfusion reaction**
      ABO incompatibility with hemolytic transfusion reaction 24 hours or more after transfusion
      Delayed hemolytic transfusion reaction (DHTR) due to ABO incompatibility
  - ● T80.319   **ABO incompatibility with hemolytic transfusion reaction,** unspecified
      ABO incompatibility with hemolytic transfusion reaction at unspecified time after transfusion
      Hemolytic transfusion reaction (HTR) due to ABO incompatibility NOS

X ● T80.39   **Other ABO incompatibility reaction due to transfusion of blood or blood products**
    Delayed serologic transfusion reaction (DSTR) from ABO incompatibility
    Other ABO incompatible blood transfusion
    Other reaction to ABO incompatible blood transfusion

● T80.4   **Rh incompatibility reaction due to transfusion of blood or blood products**
    Reaction due to incompatibility of Rh antigens (C) (c) (D) (E) (e)

X ● T80.40   **Rh incompatibility reaction due to transfusion of blood or blood products,** unspecified
    Reaction due to Rh factor in transfusion NOS
    Rh incompatible blood transfusion NOS

● T80.41   **Rh incompatibility with** hemolytic transfusion reaction
  - ● T80.410   **Rh incompatibility with** acute **hemolytic transfusion reaction**
      Acute hemolytic transfusion reaction (AHTR) due to Rh incompatibility
      Rh incompatibility with hemolytic transfusion reaction less than 24 hours after transfusion
  - ● T80.411   **Rh incompatibility with** delayed **hemolytic transfusion reaction**
      Delayed hemolytic transfusion reaction (DHTR) due to Rh incompatibility
      Rh incompatibility with hemolytic transfusion reaction 24 hours or more after transfusion
  - ● T80.419   **Rh incompatibility with hemolytic transfusion reaction,** unspecified
      Rh incompatibility with hemolytic transfusion reaction at unspecified time after transfusion
      Hemolytic transfusion reaction (HTR) due to Rh incompatibility NOS

X ● T80.49   **Other Rh incompatibility reaction due to transfusion of blood or blood products**
    Delayed serologic transfusion reaction (DSTR) from Rh incompatibility
    Other reaction to Rh incompatible blood transfusion

● T80.A   **Non-ABO incompatibility reaction due to transfusion of blood or blood products**
    Reaction due to incompatibility of minor antigens (Duffy) (Kell) (Kidd) (Lewis) (M) (N) (P) (S)

X ● T80.A0   **Non-ABO incompatibility reaction due to transfusion of blood or blood products,** unspecified
    Non-ABO antigen incompatibility reaction from transfusion NOS

● T80.A1   **Non-ABO incompatibility with** hemolytic transfusion reaction
  - ● T80.A10   **Non-ABO incompatibility with** acute **hemolytic transfusion reaction**
      Acute hemolytic transfusion reaction (AHTR) due to non-ABO incompatibility
      Non-ABO incompatibility with hemolytic transfusion reaction less than 24 hours after transfusion
  - ● T80.A11   **Non-ABO incompatibility with** delayed **hemolytic transfusion reaction**
      Delayed hemolytic transfusion reaction (DHTR) due to non-ABO incompatibility
      Non-ABO incompatibility with hemolytic transfusion reaction 24 or more hours after transfusion
  - ● T80.A19   **Non-ABO incompatibility with hemolytic transfusion reaction,** unspecified
      Hemolytic transfusion reaction (HTR) due to non-ABO incompatibility NOS
      Non-ABO incompatibility with hemolytic transfusion reaction at unspecified time after transfusion

X ● T80.A9   **Other non-ABO incompatibility reaction due to transfusion of blood or blood products**
    Delayed serologic transfusion reaction (DSTR) from non-ABO incompatibility
    Other reaction to non-ABO incompatible blood transfusion

● T80.5   **Anaphylactic reaction due to serum**
    Allergic reaction due to serum
    Anaphylactic shock due to serum
    Anaphylactoid reaction due to serum
    Anaphylaxis due to serum

    Excludes1   ABO incompatibility reaction due to transfusion of blood or blood products (T80.3-)
    allergic reaction or shock NOS (T78.2)
    anaphylactic reaction or shock NOS (T78.2)
    anaphylactic reaction or shock due to adverse effect of correct medicinal substance properly administered (T88.6)
    other serum reaction (T80.6-)

X ● T80.51   **Anaphylactic reaction due to** administration of blood and blood products

X ● T80.52   **Anaphylactic reaction due to** vaccination

X ● T80.59   **Anaphylactic reaction due to** other serum

▶ New   ⇒ Revised   ~~deleted~~ Deleted   Excludes 1   Excludes 2   Includes   Use additional   Code first   Code also   Key words
OGCR Official Guidelines   X Assign placeholder X   ● Use Additional Character(s)   ▷ Manifestation Code   **Coding Clinic**

● **T80.6**   **Other serum reactions**
     Intoxication by serum
     Protein sickness
     Serum rash
     Serum sickness
     Serum urticaria
     Excludes2   serum hepatitis (B16-B19)

X● **T80.61**   **Other serum reaction due to administration of blood and blood products**

X● **T80.62**   **Other serum reaction due to vaccination**

X● **T80.69**   **Other serum reaction due to other serum**
     Code also, if applicable, arthropathy in hypersensitivity reactions classified elsewhere (M36.4)

● **T80.8**   **Other complications following infusion, transfusion and therapeutic injection**

   ● **T80.81**   **Extravasation of vesicant agent**
     Infiltration of vesicant agent

     ● **T80.810**   **Extravasation of vesicant antineoplastic chemotherapy**
       Infiltration of vesicant antineoplastic chemotherapy

     ● **T80.818**   **Extravasation of other vesicant agent**
       Infiltration of other vesicant agent

X● **T80.89**   **Other complications following infusion, transfusion and therapeutic injection**
     Delayed serologic transfusion reaction (DSTR), unspecified incompatibility
     Use additional code to identify graft-versus-host reaction, if applicable, (D89.81-)

● **T80.9**   **Unspecified complication following infusion, transfusion and therapeutic injection**

X● **T80.90**   **Unspecified complication following infusion and therapeutic injection**

   ● **T80.91**   **Hemolytic transfusion reaction, unspecified incompatibility**
     Excludes1   ABO incompatibility with hemolytic transfusion reaction (T80.31-)
       Non-ABO incompatibility with hemolytic transfusion reaction (T80.A1-)
       Rh incompatibility with hemolytic transfusion reaction (T80.41-)

     ● **T80.910**   **Acute hemolytic transfusion reaction, unspecified incompatibility**

     ● **T80.911**   **Delayed hemolytic transfusion reaction, unspecified incompatibility**

     ● **T80.919**   **Hemolytic transfusion reaction, unspecified incompatibility, unspecified as acute or delayed**
       Hemolytic transfusion reaction NOS

X● **T80.92**   **Unspecified transfusion reaction**
     Transfusion reaction NOS

● **T81**   **Complications of procedures, not elsewhere classified**
     Use additional code for adverse effect, if applicable, to identify drug (T36-T50 with fifth or sixth character 5)
     Excludes2   complications following immunization (T88.0-T88.1)
       complications following infusion, transfusion and therapeutic injection (T80.-)
       complications of transplanted organs and tissue (T86.-)
       poisoning and toxic effects of drugs and chemicals (T36-T65 with fifth or sixth character 1-4 or 6)
       specified complications classified elsewhere, such as:
         complication of prosthetic devices, implants and grafts (T82-T85)
         dermatitis due to drugs and medicaments (L23.3, L24.4, L25.1, L27.0-L27.1)
         endosseous dental implant failure (M27.6-)
         floppy iris syndrome (IFIS) (intraoperative) H21.81
         intraoperative and postprocedural complications of specific body system (D78.-, E36.-, E89.-, G97.3-, G97.4, H59.3-, H59.-, H95.2-, H95.3, I97.4-, I97.5, J95, K91.-, L76.-, M96.-, N99.-)
         ostomy complications (J95.0-, K94.-, N99.5-)
         plateau iris syndrome (post-iridectomy) (postprocedural) H21.82

Coding Clinic: 2016, Q4, P29

The appropriate 7th character is to be added to each code from category T81

A	initial encounter
D	subsequent encounter
S	sequela

● **T81.1**   **Postprocedural shock**
     Shock during or resulting from a procedure, not elsewhere classified
     Excludes1   anaphylactic shock NOS (T78.2)
       anaphylactic shock due to correct substance properly administered (T88.6)
       anaphylactic shock due to serum (T80.5-)
       anesthetic shock (T88.2)
       electric shock (T75.4)
       obstetric shock (O75.1)
       septic shock (R65.21)
       shock following abortion or ectopic or molar pregnancy (O00-O07, O08.3)
       traumatic shock (T79.4)

X● **T81.10**   **Postprocedural shock unspecified**
     Collapse NOS during or resulting from a procedure, not elsewhere classified
     Postprocedural failure of peripheral circulation
     Postprocedural shock NOS

X● **T81.11**   **Postprocedural cardiogenic shock**

X● **T81.12**   **Postprocedural septic shock**
     Postprocedural endotoxic shock resulting from a procedure, not elsewhere classified
     Postprocedural gram-negative shock resulting from a procedure, not elsewhere classified
     Code first underlying infection
     Use additional code, to identify any associated acute organ dysfunction, if applicable

X● **T81.19**   **Other postprocedural shock**
     Postprocedural hypovolemic shock

CHAPTER 19 (S00-T88)

- ● **T81.3** **Disruption of wound, not elsewhere classified**
  Disruption of any suture materials or other closure methods
  - **Excludes1**   breakdown (mechanical) of permanent sutures (T85.612)
    displacement of permanent sutures (T85.622)
    disruption of cesarean delivery wound (O90.0)
    disruption of perineal obstetric wound (O90.1)
    mechanical complication of permanent sutures NEC (T85.692)
  - X● **T81.30** **Disruption of wound, unspecified**
    Disruption of wound NOS
  - X● **T81.31** **Disruption of external operation (surgical) wound, not elsewhere classified**
    - **Excludes1**   dehiscence of amputation stump (T87.81)
    Dehiscence of operation wound NOS
    Disruption of operation wound NOS
    Disruption or dehiscence of closure of cornea
    Disruption or dehiscence of closure of mucosa
    Disruption or dehiscence of closure of skin and subcutaneous tissue
    Full-thickness skin disruption or dehiscence
    Superficial disruption or dehiscence of operation wound
    Coding Clinic: 2015, Q1, P20
  - X● **T81.32** **Disruption of internal operation (surgical) wound, not elsewhere classified**
    Deep disruption or dehiscence of operation wound NOS
    Disruption or dehiscence of closure of internal organ or other internal tissue
    Disruption or dehiscence of closure of muscle or muscle flap
    Disruption or dehiscence of closure of ribs or rib cage
    Disruption or dehiscence of closure of skull or craniotomy
    Disruption or dehiscence of closure of sternum or sternotomy
    Disruption or dehiscence of closure of tendon or ligament
    Disruption or dehiscence of closure of superficial or muscular fascia
    Coding Clinic: 2017, Q3, P4
  - X● **T81.33** **Disruption of traumatic injury wound repair**
    Disruption or dehiscence of closure of traumatic laceration (external) (internal)
- ● **T81.4** **Infection following a procedure**
  ~~Intra-abdominal abscess following a procedure~~
  ~~Postprocedural infection, not elsewhere classified~~
  ~~Sepsis following a procedure~~
  ~~Stitch abscess following a procedure~~
  ~~Subphrenic abscess following a procedure~~
  ~~Wound abscess following a procedure~~
  Use additional code to identify infection
  Use additional code (R65.2-) to identify severe sepsis, if applicable
  - ~~Excludes1~~ ~~obstetric surgical wound infection (O86.0)~~
    ~~postprocedural fever NOS (R50.82)~~
    ~~postprocedural retroperitoneal abscess (K68.11)~~
  - **Excludes2**   bleb associated endophthalmitis (H59.4-)
    infection due to infusion, transfusion and therapeutic injection (T80.2-)
    infection due to prosthetic devices, implants and grafts (T82.6-T82.7, T83.5-T83.6, T84.5-T84.7, T85.7)
    ▶obstetric surgical wound infection (O86.0-)
    ▶postprocedural fever NOS (R50.82)
    ▶postprocedural retroperitoneal abscess (K68.11)

- ▶X● **T81.40** Infection following a procedure, unspecified
- ▶X● **T81.41** Infection following a procedure, superficial incisional surgical site
  ▶Subcutaneous abscess following a procedure
  ▶Stitch abscess following a procedure
- ▶X● **T81.42** Infection following a procedure, deep incisional surgical site
  ▶Intra-muscular abscess following a procedure
- ▶X● **T81.43** Infection following a procedure, organ and space surgical site
  ▶Intra-abdominal abscess following a procedure
  ▶Subphrenic abscess following a procedure
- ▶X● **T81.44** Sepsis following a procedure
  ▶Use additional code to identify the sepsis
- ▶X● **T81.49** Infection following a procedure, other surgical site
  Coding Clinic: 2015, Q4, P37
- ● **T81.5** **Complications of foreign body accidentally left in body following procedure**
  - ● **T81.50** Unspecified complication of foreign body accidentally left in body following procedure
    - ● **T81.500** Unspecified complication of foreign body accidentally left in body following surgical operation
    - ● **T81.501** Unspecified complication of foreign body accidentally left in body following infusion or transfusion
    - ● **T81.502** Unspecified complication of foreign body accidentally left in body following kidney dialysis
    - ● **T81.503** Unspecified complication of foreign body accidentally left in body following injection or immunization
    - ● **T81.504** Unspecified complication of foreign body accidentally left in body following endoscopic examination
    - ● **T81.505** Unspecified complication of foreign body accidentally left in body following heart catheterization
    - ● **T81.506** Unspecified complication of foreign body accidentally left in body following aspiration, puncture or other catheterization
    - ● **T81.507** Unspecified complication of foreign body accidentally left in body following removal of catheter or packing
    - ● **T81.508** Unspecified complication of foreign body accidentally left in body following other procedure
    - ● **T81.509** Unspecified complication of foreign body accidentally left in body following unspecified procedure
  - ● **T81.51** Adhesions due to foreign body accidentally left in body following procedure
    - ● **T81.510** Adhesions due to foreign body accidentally left in body following surgical operation
    - ● **T81.511** Adhesions due to foreign body accidentally left in body following infusion or transfusion
    - ● **T81.512** Adhesions due to foreign body accidentally left in body following kidney dialysis
    - ● **T81.513** Adhesions due to foreign body accidentally left in body following injection or immunization
    - ● **T81.514** Adhesions due to foreign body accidentally left in body following endoscopic examination

▶ New   ⇒ Revised   ~~deleted~~ Deleted   Excludes 1   Excludes 2   Includes   Use additional   Code first   Code also   Key words
OGCR Official Guidelines   X Assign placeholder X   ● Use Additional Character(s)   ▶ Manifestation Code   **Coding Clinic**

● T81.515   Adhesions due to foreign body accidentally left in body following heart catheterization

● T81.516   Adhesions due to foreign body accidentally left in body following aspiration, puncture or other catheterization

● T81.517   Adhesions due to foreign body accidentally left in body following removal of catheter or packing

● T81.518   Adhesions due to foreign body accidentally left in body following other procedure

● T81.519   Adhesions due to foreign body accidentally left in body following unspecified procedure

● T81.52   Obstruction due to foreign body accidentally left in body following procedure

● T81.520   Obstruction due to foreign body accidentally left in body following surgical operation

● T81.521   Obstruction due to foreign body accidentally left in body following infusion or transfusion

● T81.522   Obstruction due to foreign body accidentally left in body following kidney dialysis

● T81.523   Obstruction due to foreign body accidentally left in body following injection or immunization

● T81.524   Obstruction due to foreign body accidentally left in body following endoscopic examination

● T81.525   Obstruction due to foreign body accidentally left in body following heart catheterization

● T81.526   Obstruction due to foreign body accidentally left in body following aspiration, puncture or other catheterization

● T81.527   Obstruction due to foreign body accidentally left in body following removal of catheter or packing

● T81.528   Obstruction due to foreign body accidentally left in body following other procedure

● T81.529   Obstruction due to foreign body accidentally left in body following unspecified procedure

● T81.53   Perforation due to foreign body accidentally left in body following procedure

● T81.530   Perforation due to foreign body accidentally left in body following surgical operation

● T81.531   Perforation due to foreign body accidentally left in body following infusion or transfusion

● T81.532   Perforation due to foreign body accidentally left in body following kidney dialysis

● T81.533   Perforation due to foreign body accidentally left in body following injection or immunization

● T81.534   Perforation due to foreign body accidentally left in body following endoscopic examination

● T81.535   Perforation due to foreign body accidentally left in body following heart catheterization

● T81.536   Perforation due to foreign body accidentally left in body following aspiration, puncture or other catheterization

● T81.537   Perforation due to foreign body accidentally left in body following removal of catheter or packing

● T81.538   Perforation due to foreign body accidentally left in body following other procedure

● T81.539   Perforation due to foreign body accidentally left in body following unspecified procedure

● T81.59   Other complications of foreign body accidentally left in body following procedure

     Excludes2   obstruction or perforation due to prosthetic devices and implants intentionally left in body (T82.0-T82.5, T83.0-T83.4, T83.7, T84.0-T84.4, T85.0-T85.6)

● T81.590   Other complications of foreign body accidentally left in body following surgical operation

● T81.591   Other complications of foreign body accidentally left in body following infusion or transfusion

● T81.592   Other complications of foreign body accidentally left in body following kidney dialysis

● T81.593   Other complications of foreign body accidentally left in body following injection or immunization

● T81.594   Other complications of foreign body accidentally left in body following endoscopic examination

● T81.595   Other complications of foreign body accidentally left in body following heart catheterization

● T81.596   Other complications of foreign body accidentally left in body following aspiration, puncture or other catheterization

● T81.597   Other complications of foreign body accidentally left in body following removal of catheter or packing

● T81.598   Other complications of foreign body accidentally left in body following other procedure

● T81.599   Other complications of foreign body accidentally left in body following unspecified procedure

● T81.6   Acute reaction to foreign substance accidentally left during a procedure

     Excludes2   complications of foreign body accidentally left in body cavity or operation wound following procedure (T81.5-)

X ● T81.60   Unspecified acute reaction to foreign substance accidentally left during a procedure

X ● T81.61   Aseptic peritonitis due to foreign substance accidentally left during a procedure
         Chemical peritonitis

X ● T81.69   Other acute reaction to foreign substance accidentally left during a procedure

- **T81.7** **Vascular complications following a procedure, not elsewhere classified**
  Air embolism following procedure NEC
  Phlebitis or thrombophlebitis resulting from a procedure
  - **Excludes1** embolism complicating abortion or ectopic or molar pregnancy (O00-O07, O08.2)
    embolism complicating pregnancy, childbirth and the puerperium (O88.-)
    traumatic embolism (T79.0)
  - **Excludes2** embolism due to prosthetic devices, implants and grafts (T82.8, T83.81, T84.8-, T85.1-)
    embolism following infusion, transfusion and therapeutic injection (T80.0)
  - **T81.71** **Complication of artery following a procedure, not elsewhere classified**
    - **T81.710** Complication of mesenteric artery following a procedure, not elsewhere classified
    - **T81.711** Complication of renal artery following a procedure, not elsewhere classified
    - **T81.718** Complication of other artery following a procedure, not elsewhere classified
    - **T81.719** Complication of unspecified artery following a procedure, not elsewhere classified
  - X **T81.72** **Complication of vein following a procedure, not elsewhere classified**
- **T81.8** **Other complications of procedures, not elsewhere classified**
  - **Excludes2** hypothermia following anesthesia (T88.51)
    malignant hyperpyrexia due to anesthesia (T88.3)
  - X **T81.81** **Complication of inhalation therapy**
  - X **T81.82** **Emphysema (subcutaneous) resulting from a procedure**
  - X **T81.83** **Persistent postprocedural fistula**
    Coding Clinic: 2017, Q3, P3-5
  - X **T81.89** **Other complications of procedures, not elsewhere classified**
    Use additional code to specify complication, such as:
    postprocedural delirium (F05)
- X **T81.9** **Unspecified complication of procedure**
- **T82** **Complications of cardiac and vascular prosthetic devices, implants and grafts**
  - **Excludes2** failure and rejection of transplanted organs and tissue (T86.-)

  The appropriate 7th character is to be added to each code from category T82

A	initial encounter
D	subsequent encounter
S	sequela

  - **T82.0** **Mechanical complication of heart valve prosthesis**
    Mechanical complication of artificial heart valve
    - **Excludes1** mechanical complication of biological heart valve graft (T82.22-)
    - X **T82.01** **Breakdown (mechanical) of heart valve prosthesis**
    - X **T82.02** **Displacement of heart valve prosthesis**
      Malposition of heart valve prosthesis
    - X **T82.03** **Leakage of heart valve prosthesis**
    - X **T82.09** **Other mechanical complication of heart valve prosthesis**
      Obstruction (mechanical) of heart valve prosthesis
      Perforation of heart valve prosthesis
      Protrusion of heart valve prosthesis

- **T82.1** **Mechanical complication of cardiac electronic device**
  - **T82.11** **Breakdown (mechanical) of cardiac electronic device**
    - **T82.110** Breakdown (mechanical) of cardiac electrode
    - **T82.111** Breakdown (mechanical) of cardiac pulse generator (battery)
    - **T82.118** Breakdown (mechanical) of other cardiac electronic device
    - **T82.119** Breakdown (mechanical) of unspecified cardiac electronic device
  - **T82.12** **Displacement of cardiac electronic device**
    Malposition of cardiac electronic device
    - **T82.120** Displacement of cardiac electrode
    - **T82.121** Displacement of cardiac pulse generator (battery)
    - **T82.128** Displacement of other cardiac electronic device
    - **T82.129** Displacement of unspecified cardiac electronic device
  - **T82.19** **Other mechanical complication of cardiac electronic device**
    Leakage of cardiac electronic device
    Obstruction of cardiac electronic device
    Perforation of cardiac electronic device
    Protrusion of cardiac electronic device
    - **T82.190** Other mechanical complication of cardiac electrode
    - **T82.191** Other mechanical complication of cardiac pulse generator (battery)
    - **T82.198** Other mechanical complication of other cardiac electronic device
    - **T82.199** Other mechanical complication of unspecified cardiac device
- **T82.2** **Mechanical complication of coronary artery bypass graft and biological heart valve graft**
  - **Excludes1** mechanical complication of artificial heart valve prosthesis (T82.0-)
  - **T82.21** **Mechanical complication of coronary artery bypass graft**
    - **T82.211** Breakdown (mechanical) of coronary artery bypass graft
    - **T82.212** Displacement of coronary artery bypass graft
      Malposition of coronary artery bypass graft
    - **T82.213** Leakage of coronary artery bypass graft
    - **T82.218** Other mechanical complication of coronary artery bypass graft
      Obstruction, mechanical of coronary artery bypass graft
      Perforation of coronary artery bypass graft
      Protrusion of coronary artery bypass graft
  - **T82.22** **Mechanical complication of biological heart valve graft**
    - **T82.221** Breakdown (mechanical) of biological heart valve graft
    - **T82.222** Displacement of biological heart valve graft
      Malposition of biological heart valve graft
    - **T82.223** Leakage of biological heart valve graft
    - **T82.228** Other mechanical complication of biological heart valve graft
      Obstruction of biological heart valve graft
      Perforation of biological heart valve graft
      Protrusion of biological heart valve graft

► New ⟹ Revised ~~deleted~~ Deleted Excludes 1 Excludes 2 Includes Use additional Code first Code also Key words
OGCR Official Guidelines X Assign placeholder X ● Use Additional Character(s) ▌ Manifestation Code Coding Clinic

● **T82.3 Mechanical complication of other vascular grafts**
- ● **T82.31 Breakdown (mechanical) of other vascular grafts**
  - ● T82.310 Breakdown (mechanical) of aortic (bifurcation) graft (replacement)
  - ● T82.311 Breakdown (mechanical) of carotid arterial graft (bypass)
  - ● T82.312 Breakdown (mechanical) of femoral arterial graft (bypass)
  - ● T82.318 Breakdown (mechanical) of other vascular grafts
  - ● T82.319 Breakdown (mechanical) of unspecified vascular grafts
- ● **T82.32 Displacement of other vascular grafts**
  Malposition of other vascular grafts
  - ● T82.320 Displacement of aortic (bifurcation) graft (replacement)
  - ● T82.321 Displacement of carotid arterial graft (bypass)
  - ● T82.322 Displacement of femoral arterial graft (bypass)
  - ● T82.328 Displacement of other vascular grafts
  - ● T82.329 Displacement of unspecified vascular grafts
- ● **T82.33 Leakage of other vascular grafts**
  - ● T82.330 Leakage of aortic (bifurcation) graft (replacement)
  - ● T82.331 Leakage of carotid arterial graft (bypass)
  - ● T82.332 Leakage of femoral arterial graft (bypass)
  - ● T82.338 Leakage of other vascular grafts
  - ● T82.339 Leakage of unspecified vascular graft
- ● **T82.39 Other mechanical complication of other vascular grafts**
  Obstruction (mechanical) of other vascular grafts
  Perforation of other vascular grafts
  Protrusion of other vascular grafts
  - ● T82.390 Other mechanical complication of aortic (bifurcation) graft (replacement)
  - ● T82.391 Other mechanical complication of carotid arterial graft (bypass)
  - ● T82.392 Other mechanical complication of femoral arterial graft (bypass)
  - ● T82.398 Other mechanical complication of other vascular grafts
  - ● T82.399 Other mechanical complication of unspecified vascular grafts
● **T82.4 Mechanical complication of vascular dialysis catheter**
  Mechanical complication of hemodialysis catheter
  Excludes1 mechanical complication of intraperitoneal dialysis catheter (T85.62)
- X ● **T82.41 Breakdown (mechanical) of vascular dialysis catheter**
- X ● **T82.42 Displacement of vascular dialysis catheter**
  Malposition of vascular dialysis catheter
- X ● **T82.43 Leakage of vascular dialysis catheter**
- X ● **T82.49 Other complication of vascular dialysis catheter**
  Obstruction (mechanical) of vascular dialysis catheter
  Perforation of vascular dialysis catheter
  Protrusion of vascular dialysis catheter

● **T82.5 Mechanical complication of other cardiac and vascular devices and implants**
  Excludes2 mechanical complication of epidural and subdural infusion catheter (T85.61)
- ● **T82.51 Breakdown (mechanical) of other cardiac and vascular devices and implants**
  - ● T82.510 Breakdown (mechanical) of surgically created arteriovenous fistula
  - ● T82.511 Breakdown (mechanical) of surgically created arteriovenous shunt
  - ● T82.512 Breakdown (mechanical) of artificial heart
  - ● T82.513 Breakdown (mechanical) of balloon (counterpulsation) device
  - ● T82.514 Breakdown (mechanical) of infusion catheter
  - ● T82.515 Breakdown (mechanical) of umbrella device
  - ● T82.518 Breakdown (mechanical) of other cardiac and vascular devices and implants
  - ● T82.519 Breakdown (mechanical) of unspecified cardiac and vascular devices and implants
- ● **T82.52 Displacement of other cardiac and vascular devices and implants**
  Malposition of other cardiac and vascular devices and implants
  - ● T82.520 Displacement of surgically created arteriovenous fistula
  - ● T82.521 Displacement of surgically created arteriovenous shunt
  - ● T82.522 Displacement of artificial heart
  - ● T82.523 Displacement of balloon (counterpulsation) device
  - ● T82.524 Displacement of infusion catheter
  - ● T82.525 Displacement of umbrella device
  - ● T82.528 Displacement of other cardiac and vascular devices and implants
  - ● T82.529 Displacement of unspecified cardiac and vascular devices and implants
- ● **T82.53 Leakage of other cardiac and vascular devices and implants**
  - ● T82.530 Leakage of surgically created arteriovenous fistula
  - ● T82.531 Leakage of surgically created arteriovenous shunt
  - ● T82.532 Leakage of artificial heart
  - ● T82.533 Leakage of balloon (counterpulsation) device
  - ● T82.534 Leakage of infusion catheter
  - ● T82.535 Leakage of umbrella device
  - ● T82.538 Leakage of other cardiac and vascular devices and implants
  - ● T82.539 Leakage of unspecified cardiac and vascular devices and implants
- ● **T82.59 Other mechanical complication of other cardiac and vascular devices and implants**
  Obstruction (mechanical) of other cardiac and vascular devices and implants
  Perforation of other cardiac and vascular devices and implants
  Protrusion of other cardiac and vascular devices and implants
  - ● T82.590 Other mechanical complication of surgically created arteriovenous fistula
  - ● T82.591 Other mechanical complication of surgically created arteriovenous shunt

● T82.592   Other mechanical complication of artificial heart

● T82.593   Other mechanical complication of balloon (counterpulsation) device

● T82.594   Other mechanical complication of infusion catheter

● T82.595   Other mechanical complication of umbrella device

● T82.598   Other mechanical complication of other cardiac and vascular devices and implants

● T82.599   Other mechanical complication of unspecified cardiac and vascular devices and implants

X ● T82.6   Infection and inflammatory reaction due to cardiac valve prosthesis

> Use additional code to identify infection

X ● T82.7   Infection and inflammatory reaction due to other cardiac and vascular devices, implants and grafts

> Use additional code to identify infection

● T82.8   Other specified complications of cardiac and vascular prosthetic devices, implants and grafts

● T82.81   Embolism due to cardiac and vascular prosthetic devices, implants and grafts
> Coding Clinic: 2016, Q4, P70

● T82.817   Embolism due to cardiac prosthetic devices, implants and grafts
> Coding Clinic: 2016, Q4, P70; 2015, Q1, P20

● T82.818   Embolism due to vascular prosthetic devices, implants and grafts

● T82.82   Fibrosis due to cardiac and vascular prosthetic devices, implants and grafts
> Coding Clinic: 2016, Q4, P70

● T82.827   Fibrosis due to cardiac prosthetic devices, implants and grafts

● T82.828   Fibrosis due to vascular prosthetic devices, implants and grafts

● T82.83   Hemorrhage due to cardiac and vascular prosthetic devices, implants and grafts
> Coding Clinic: 2016, Q4, P70

● T82.837   Hemorrhage due to cardiac prosthetic devices, implants and grafts

● T82.838   Hemorrhage due to vascular prosthetic devices, implants and grafts

● T82.84   Pain due to cardiac and vascular prosthetic devices, implants and grafts
> Coding Clinic: 2016, Q4, P70

● T82.847   Pain due to cardiac prosthetic devices, implants and grafts

● T82.848   Pain due to vascular prosthetic devices, implants and grafts

● T82.85   Stenosis due to cardiac and vascular prosthetic devices, implants and grafts

● T82.855   Stenosis of coronary artery stent
> In-stent stenosis (restenosis) of coronary artery stent
> Restenosis of coronary artery stent
> Coding Clinic: 2016, Q4, P70

● T82.856   Stenosis of peripheral vascular stent
> In-stent stenosis (restenosis) of peripheral vascular stent
> Restenosis of peripheral vascular stent
> Coding Clinic: 2016, Q4, P70

● T82.857   Stenosis of other cardiac prosthetic devices, implants and grafts
> Coding Clinic: 2016, Q4, P70

● T82.858   Stenosis of other vascular prosthetic devices, implants and grafts

> Coding Clinic: 2016, Q4, P70

● T82.86   Thrombosis of cardiac and vascular prosthetic devices, implants and grafts

● T82.867   Thrombosis due to cardiac prosthetic devices, implants and grafts

● T82.868   Thrombosis due to vascular prosthetic devices, implants and grafts

● T82.89   Other specified complication of cardiac and vascular prosthetic devices, implants and grafts

● T82.897   Other specified complication of cardiac prosthetic devices, implants and grafts

● T82.898   Other specified complication of vascular prosthetic devices, implants and grafts

X ● T82.9   Unspecified complication of cardiac and vascular prosthetic device, implant and graft

● T83   Complications of genitourinary prosthetic devices, implants and grafts

> **Excludes2**   failure and rejection of transplanted organs and tissue (T86.-)

> The appropriate 7th character is to be added to each code from category T83

> | A | initial encounter |
> |---|---|
> | D | subsequent encounter |
> | S | sequela |

> Coding Clinic: 2016, Q4, P70-71

● T83.0   Mechanical complication of urinary catheter

> **Excludes2**   complications of stoma of urinary tract (N99.5-)

> Coding Clinic: 2016, Q4, P70

● T83.01   Breakdown (mechanical) of urinary catheter

● T83.010   Breakdown (mechanical) of cystostomy catheter

● T83.011   Breakdown (mechanical) of indwelling urethral catheter

● T83.012   Breakdown (mechanical) of nephrostomy catheter

● T83.018   Breakdown (mechanical) of other urinary catheter
> Breakdown (mechanical) of Hopkins catheter
> Breakdown (mechanical) of ileostomy catheter
> Breakdown (mechanical) urostomy catheter

● T83.02   Displacement of urinary catheter
> Malposition of urinary catheter

● T83.020   Displacement of cystostomy catheter

● T83.021   Displacement of indwelling urethral catheter

● T83.022   Displacement of nephrostomy catheter

● T83.028   Displacement of other urinary catheter
> Displacement of Hopkins catheter
> Displacement of ileostomy catheter
> Displacement of urostomy catheter

● T83.03   Leakage of urinary catheter

● T83.030   Leakage of cystostomy catheter

● T83.031   Leakage of indwelling urethral catheter

● T83.032   Leakage of nephrostomy catheter

● T83.038   Leakage of other urinary catheter
> Leakage of Hopkins catheter
> Leakage of ileostomy catheter
> Leakage of urostomy catheter

▶ New   ⇒ Revised   ~~deleted~~ Deleted   Excludes 1   Excludes 2   Includes   Use additional   Code first   Code also   Key words

OGCR Official Guidelines   X Assign placeholder X   ● Use Additional Character(s)   ▷ Manifestation Code   **Coding Clinic**

● **T83.09** **Other mechanical complication of urinary catheter**
     Obstruction (mechanical) of urinary catheter
     Perforation of urinary catheter
     Protrusion of urinary catheter

     ● **T83.090** **Other mechanical complication of cystostomy catheter**

     ● **T83.091** **Other mechanical complication of indwelling urethral catheter**

     ● **T83.092** **Other mechanical complication of nephrostomy catheter**

     ● **T83.098** **Other mechanical complication of other urinary catheter**
         Other mechanical complication of Hopkins catheter
         Other mechanical complication of ileostomy catheter
         Other mechanical complication of urostomy catheter

● **T83.1** **Mechanical complication of other urinary devices and implants**
     Coding Clinic: 2016, Q4, P70

     ● **T83.11** **Breakdown (mechanical) of other urinary devices and implants**

         ● **T83.110** **Breakdown (mechanical) of urinary electronic stimulator device**
             Excludes2 Breakdown (mechanical) of electrode (lead) for sacral nerve neurostimulator (T85.111)
                 Breakdown (mechanical) of implanted electronic sacral neurostimulator, pulse generator or receiver (T85.113)

         ● **T83.111** **Breakdown (mechanical) of implanted urinary sphincter**

         ● **T83.112** **Breakdown (mechanical) of indwelling ureteral stent**

         ● **T83.113** **Breakdown (mechanical) of other urinary stents**
             Breakdown (mechanical) of ileal conduit stent
             Breakdown (mechanical) of nephroureteral stent

         ● **T83.118** **Breakdown (mechanical) of other urinary devices and implants**

     ● **T83.12** **Displacement of other urinary devices and implants**
         Malposition of other urinary devices and implants

         ● **T83.120** **Displacement of urinary electronic stimulator device**
             Excludes2 Displacement of electrode (lead) for sacral nerve neurostimulator (T85.121)
                 Displacement of implanted electronic sacral neurostimulator, pulse generator or receiver (T85.123)

         ● **T83.121** **Displacement of implanted urinary sphincter**

         ● **T83.122** **Displacement of indwelling ureteral stent**

         ● **T83.123** **Displacement of other urinary stents**
             Displacement of ileal conduit stent
             Displacement of nephroureteral stent

         ● **T83.128** **Displacement of other urinary devices and implants**

     ● **T83.19** **Other mechanical complication of other urinary devices and implants**
         Leakage of other urinary devices and implants
         Obstruction (mechanical) of other urinary devices and implants
         Perforation of other urinary devices and implants
         Protrusion of other urinary devices and implants

         ● **T83.190** **Other mechanical complication of urinary electronic stimulator device**
             Excludes2 Other mechanical complication of electrode (lead) for sacral nerve neurostimulator (T85.191)
                 Other mechanical complication of implanted electronic sacral neurostimulator, pulse generator or receiver (T85.193)

         ● **T83.191** **Other mechanical complication of implanted urinary sphincter**

         ● **T83.192** **Other mechanical complication of indwelling ureteral stent**

         ● **T83.193** **Other mechanical complication of other urinary stent**
             Other mechanical complication of ileal conduit stent
             Other mechanical complication of nephroureteral stent

         ● **T83.198** **Other mechanical complication of other urinary devices and implants**

● **T83.2** **Mechanical complication of graft of urinary organ**
     Coding Clinic: 2016, Q4, P70

     X ● **T83.21** **Breakdown (mechanical) of graft of urinary organ**

     X ● **T83.22** **Displacement of graft of urinary organ**
         Malposition of graft of urinary organ

     X ● **T83.23** **Leakage of graft of urinary organ**

     X ● **T83.24** **Erosion of graft of urinary organ**
         Coding Clinic: 2016, Q4, P70

     X ● **T83.25** **Exposure of graft of urinary organ**
         Coding Clinic: 2016, Q4, P70

     X ● **T83.29** **Other mechanical complication of graft of urinary organ**
         Obstruction (mechanical) of graft of urinary organ
         Perforation of graft of urinary organ
         Protrusion of graft of urinary organ

● **T83.3** **Mechanical complication of intrauterine contraceptive device**

     X ● **T83.31** **Breakdown (mechanical) of intrauterine contraceptive device** ♀

     X ● **T83.32** **Displacement of intrauterine contraceptive device** ♀
         Malposition of intrauterine contraceptive device
         Missing string of intrauterine contraceptive device

     X ● **T83.39** **Other mechanical complication of intrauterine contraceptive device** ♀
         Leakage of intrauterine contraceptive device
         Obstruction (mechanical) of intrauterine contraceptive device
         Perforation of intrauterine contraceptive device
         Protrusion of intrauterine contraceptive device

● **T83.4**   **Mechanical complication of other prosthetic devices, implants and grafts of genital tract**
Coding Clinic: 2016, Q4, P71

   ● **T83.41**   **Breakdown (mechanical) of other prosthetic devices, implants and grafts of genital tract**

     ● **T83.410**   **Breakdown (mechanical) of implanted penile prosthesis** ♂
Breakdown (mechanical) of penile prosthesis cylinder
Breakdown (mechanical) of penile prosthesis pump
Breakdown (mechanical) of penile prosthesis reservoir

     ● **T83.411**   **Breakdown (mechanical) of implanted testicular prosthesis**

     ● **T83.418**   **Breakdown (mechanical) of other prosthetic devices, implants and grafts of genital tract**

   ● **T83.42**   **Displacement of other prosthetic devices, implants and grafts of genital tract**
Malposition of other prosthetic devices, implants and grafts of genital tract

     ● **T83.420**   **Displacement of implanted penile prosthesis** ♂
Displacement of penile prosthesis cylinder
Displacement of penile prosthesis pump
Displacement of penile prosthesis reservoir

     ● **T83.421**   **Displacement of implanted testicular prosthesis**

     ● **T83.428**   **Displacement of other prosthetic devices, implants and grafts of genital tract**
Coding Clinic: 2018, Q1, P6

   ● **T83.49**   **Other mechanical complication of other prosthetic devices, implants and grafts of genital tract**
Leakage of other prosthetic devices, implants and grafts of genital tract
Obstruction, mechanical of other prosthetic devices, implants and grafts of genital tract
Perforation of other prosthetic devices, implants and grafts of genital tract
Protrusion of other prosthetic devices, implants and grafts of genital tract

     ● **T83.490**   **Other mechanical complication of implanted penile prosthesis** ♂
Other mechanical complication of penile prosthesis cylinder
Other mechanical complication of penile prosthesis pump
Other mechanical complication of penile prosthesis reservoir

     ● **T83.491**   **Other mechanical complication of implanted testicular prosthesis**

     ● **T83.498**   **Other mechanical complication of other prosthetic devices, implants and grafts of genital tract**

● **T83.5**   **Infection and inflammatory reaction due to prosthetic device, implant and graft in urinary system**
Use additional code to identify infection
Coding Clinic: 2016, Q4, P71

   ● **T83.51**   **Infection and inflammatory reaction due to urinary catheter**
Excludes2   complications of stoma of urinary tract (N99.5-)

     ● **T83.510**   **Infection and inflammatory reaction due to cystostomy catheter**

     ● **T83.511**   **Infection and inflammatory reaction due to indwelling urethral catheter**

     ● **T83.512**   **Infection and inflammatory reaction due to nephrostomy catheter**

     ● **T83.518**   **Infection and inflammatory reaction due to other urinary catheter**
Infection and inflammatory reaction due to Hopkins catheter
Infection and inflammatory reaction due to ileostomy catheter
Infection and inflammatory reaction due to urostomy catheter

   ● **T83.59**   **Infection and inflammatory reaction due to prosthetic device, implant and graft in urinary system**

     ● **T83.590**   **Infection and inflammatory reaction due to implanted urinary neurostimulation device**
Excludes2   Infection and inflammatory reaction due to electrode lead of sacral nerve neurostimulator (T85.732)
Infection and inflammatory reaction due to pulse generator or receiver of sacral nerve neurostimulator (T85.734)

     ● **T83.591**   **Infection and inflammatory reaction due to implanted urinary sphincter**

     ● **T83.592**   **Infection and inflammatory reaction due to indwelling ureteral stent**

     ● **T83.593**   **Infection and inflammatory reaction due to other urinary stents**
Infection and inflammatory reaction due to ileal conduit stents
Infection and inflammatory reaction due to nephroureteral stent

     ● **T83.598**   **Infection and inflammatory reaction due to other prosthetic device, implant and graft in urinary system**

● **T83.6**   **Infection and inflammatory reaction due to prosthetic device, implant and graft in genital tract**
Use additional code to identify infection
Coding Clinic: 2016, Q4, P71

   ● **T83.61**   **Infection and inflammatory reaction due to implanted penile prosthesis**
Infection and inflammatory reaction due to penile prosthesis cylinder
Infection and inflammatory reaction due to penile prosthesis pump
Infection and inflammatory reaction due to penile prosthesis reservoir

   ● **T83.62**   **Infection and inflammatory reaction due to implanted testicular prosthesis**

   ● **T83.69**   **Infection and inflammatory reaction due to other prosthetic device, implant and graft in genital tract**

► New   ⇒ Revised   ~~deleted~~ Deleted   Excludes 1   Excludes 2   Includes   Use additional   Code first   Code also   Key words
OGCR Official Guidelines   X Assign placeholder X   Use Additional Character(s)   ▌ Manifestation Code   **Coding Clinic**

● **T83.7** **Complications due to** implanted mesh **and other** prosthetic materials
   Coding Clinic: 2016, Q4, P71

   ● **T83.71** **Erosion** of implanted mesh and other prosthetic materials to surrounding organ or tissue
      Coding Clinic: 2016, Q4, P71

      ● **T83.711** Erosion of implanted vaginal mesh to surrounding organ or tissue ♀
         Erosion of implanted vaginal mesh into pelvic floor muscles
         Coding Clinic: 2016, Q4, P71

      ● **T83.712** Erosion of implanted urethral mesh to surrounding organ or tissue
         Erosion of implanted female urethral sling
         Erosion of implanted male urethral sling
         Erosion of implanted urethral mesh into pelvic floor muscles

      ● **T83.713** Erosion of implanted urethral bulking agent to surrounding organ or tissue

      ● **T83.714** Erosion of implanted ureteral bulking agent to surrounding organ or tissue

      ● **T83.718** Erosion of other implanted mesh to organ or tissue
         Coding Clinic: 2016, Q4, P71

      ● **T83.719** Erosion of other prosthetic materials to surrounding organ or tissue
         Coding Clinic: 2016, Q4, P71

   ● **T83.72** **Exposure** of implanted mesh and other prosthetic materials into surrounding organ or tissue
      Extrusion of implanted mesh
      Coding Clinic: 2016, Q4, P71

      ● **T83.721** Exposure of implanted vaginal mesh into vagina ♀
         Exposure of implanted vaginal mesh through vaginal wall

      ● **T83.722** Exposure of implanted urethral mesh into urethra
         Exposure of implanted female urethral sling
         Exposure of implanted male urethral sling
         Exposure of implanted urethral mesh through urethral wall

      ● **T83.723** Exposure of implanted urethral bulking agent into urethra

      ● **T83.724** Exposure of implanted ureteral bulking agent into ureter

      ● **T83.728** Exposure of other implanted mesh into organ or tissue
         Coding Clinic: 2016, Q4, P71

      ● **T83.729** Exposure of other prosthetic materials into organ or tissue
         Coding Clinic: 2016, Q4, P71

   X ● **T83.79** Other specified complications due to other genitourinary prosthetic materials

● **T83.8** **Other specified complications** of genitourinary prosthetic devices, implants and grafts

   X ● **T83.81** Embolism due to genitourinary prosthetic devices, implants and grafts

   X ● **T83.82** Fibrosis due to genitourinary prosthetic devices, implants and grafts

   X ● **T83.83** Hemorrhage due to genitourinary prosthetic devices, implants and grafts

   X ● **T83.84** Pain due to genitourinary prosthetic devices, implants and grafts

   X ● **T83.85** Stenosis due to genitourinary prosthetic devices, implants and grafts

   X ● **T83.86** Thrombosis due to genitourinary prosthetic devices, implants and grafts

   X ● **T83.89** Other specified complication of genitourinary prosthetic devices, implants and grafts

X ● **T83.9** Unspecified complication of genitourinary prosthetic device, implant and graft

● **T84** **Complications of** internal orthopedic prosthetic devices, implants and grafts

   Excludes2 failure and rejection of transplanted organs and tissues (T86.-)
   fracture of bone following insertion of orthopedic implant, joint prosthesis or bone plate (M96.6)

   The appropriate 7th character is to be added to each code from category T84

A	initial encounter
D	subsequent encounter
S	sequela

   ● **T84.Ø** **Mechanical complication of** internal joint prosthesis

      ● **T84.Ø1** **Broken** internal joint prosthesis
         Breakage (fracture) of prosthetic joint
         Broken prosthetic joint implant
         Excludes1 periprosthetic joint implant fracture (M97-)
         Coding Clinic: 2016, Q4, P42

         ● **T84.Ø1Ø** Broken internal right hip prosthesis
         ● **T84.Ø11** Broken internal left hip prosthesis
         ● **T84.Ø12** Broken internal right knee prosthesis
         ● **T84.Ø13** Broken internal left knee prosthesis
         ● **T84.Ø18** Broken internal joint prosthesis, other site
            Use additional code to identify the joint (Z96.6-)
         ● **T84.Ø19** Broken internal joint prosthesis, unspecified site

      ● **T84.Ø2** **Dislocation of** internal joint prosthesis
         Instability of internal joint prosthesis
         Subluxation of internal joint prosthesis

         ● **T84.Ø2Ø** Dislocation of internal right hip prosthesis
         ● **T84.Ø21** Dislocation of internal left hip prosthesis
         ● **T84.Ø22** Instability of internal right knee prosthesis
         ● **T84.Ø23** Instability of internal left knee prosthesis
         ● **T84.Ø28** Dislocation of other internal joint prosthesis
            Use additional code to identify the joint (Z96.6-)
         ● **T84.Ø29** Dislocation of unspecified internal joint prosthesis

      ● **T84.Ø3** **Mechanical** loosening of internal prosthetic joint
         Aseptic loosening of prosthetic joint

         ● **T84.Ø3Ø** Mechanical loosening of internal right hip prosthetic joint
         ● **T84.Ø31** Mechanical loosening of internal left hip prosthetic joint
         ● **T84.Ø32** Mechanical loosening of internal right knee prosthetic joint
         ● **T84.Ø33** Mechanical loosening of internal left knee prosthetic joint
         ● **T84.Ø38** Mechanical loosening of other internal prosthetic joint
            Use additional code to identify the joint (Z96.6-)
         ● **T84.Ø39** Mechanical loosening of unspecified internal prosthetic joint

CHAPTER 19 (SØØ-T88)

- **T84.05** **Periprosthetic osteolysis** of internal prosthetic joint
  Use additional code to identify major osseous defect, if applicable (M89.7-)
  - T84.050 Periprosthetic osteolysis of internal prosthetic **right hip** joint
  - T84.051 Periprosthetic osteolysis of internal prosthetic **left hip** joint
  - T84.052 Periprosthetic osteolysis of internal prosthetic **right knee** joint
  - T84.053 Periprosthetic osteolysis of internal prosthetic **left knee** joint
  - T84.058 Periprosthetic osteolysis of **other** internal prosthetic joint
    Use additional code to identify the joint (Z96.6-)
  - T84.059 Periprosthetic osteolysis of **unspecified** internal prosthetic joint
- **T84.06** **Wear of articular bearing surface** of internal prosthetic joint
  - T84.060 Wear of articular bearing surface of internal prosthetic **right hip** joint
  - T84.061 Wear of articular bearing surface of internal prosthetic **left hip** joint
  - T84.062 Wear of articular bearing surface of internal prosthetic **right knee** joint
  - T84.063 Wear of articular bearing surface of internal prosthetic **left knee** joint
  - T84.068 Wear of articular bearing surface of **other** internal prosthetic joint
    Use additional code to identify the joint (Z96.6-)
  - T84.069 Wear of articular bearing surface of **unspecified** internal prosthetic joint
- **T84.09** **Other mechanical complication** of internal joint prosthesis
  Prosthetic joint implant failure NOS
  - T84.090 Other mechanical complication of internal **right hip** prosthesis
  - T84.091 Other mechanical complication of internal **left hip** prosthesis
  - T84.092 Other mechanical complication of internal **right knee** prosthesis
  - T84.093 Other mechanical complication of internal **left knee** prosthesis
  - T84.098 Other mechanical complication of **other** internal joint prosthesis
    Use additional code to identify the joint (Z96.6-)
  - T84.099 Other mechanical complication of **unspecified** internal joint prosthesis
- **T84.1** Mechanical complication of **internal fixation device** of **bones of limb**
  Excludes2 mechanical complication of internal fixation device of bones of feet (T84.2-)
    mechanical complication of internal fixation device of bones of fingers (T84.2-)
    mechanical complication of internal fixation device of bones of hands (T84.2-)
    mechanical complication of internal fixation device of bones of toes (T84.2-)
- **T84.11** **Breakdown (mechanical)** of internal fixation device of bones of limb
  - T84.110 Breakdown (mechanical) of internal fixation device of **right humerus**
  - T84.111 Breakdown (mechanical) of internal fixation device of **left humerus**
  - T84.112 Breakdown (mechanical) of internal fixation device of bone of **right forearm**
  - T84.113 Breakdown (mechanical) of internal fixation device of bone of **left forearm**
  - T84.114 Breakdown (mechanical) of internal fixation device of **right femur**
  - T84.115 Breakdown (mechanical) of internal fixation device of **left femur**
  - T84.116 Breakdown (mechanical) of internal fixation device of bone of **right lower leg**
  - T84.117 Breakdown (mechanical) of internal fixation device of bone of **left lower leg**
  - T84.119 Breakdown (mechanical) of internal fixation device of **unspecified** bone of limb
- **T84.12** Displacement of internal fixation device of bones of limb
  Malposition of internal fixation device of bones of limb
  - T84.120 Displacement of internal fixation device of **right humerus**
  - T84.121 Displacement of internal fixation device of **left humerus**
  - T84.122 Displacement of internal fixation device of bone of **right forearm**
  - T84.123 Displacement of internal fixation device of bone of **left forearm**
  - T84.124 Displacement of internal fixation device of **right femur**
  - T84.125 Displacement of internal fixation device of **left femur**
  - T84.126 Displacement of internal fixation device of bone of **right lower leg**
  - T84.127 Displacement of internal fixation device of bone of **left lower leg**
  - T84.129 Displacement of internal fixation device of **unspecified** bone of limb
- **T84.19** **Other mechanical complication** of internal fixation device of bones of limb
  Obstruction (mechanical) of internal fixation device of bones of limb
  Perforation of internal fixation device of bones of limb
  Protrusion of internal fixation device of bones of limb
  - T84.190 Other mechanical complication of internal fixation device of **right humerus**
  - T84.191 Other mechanical complication of internal fixation device of **left humerus**
  - T84.192 Other mechanical complication of internal fixation device of bone of **right forearm**
  - T84.193 Other mechanical complication of internal fixation device of bone of **left forearm**
  - T84.194 Other mechanical complication of internal fixation device of **right femur**
  - T84.195 Other mechanical complication of internal fixation device of **left femur**
  - T84.196 Other mechanical complication of internal fixation device of bone of **right lower leg**
  - T84.197 Other mechanical complication of internal fixation device of bone of **left lower leg**
  - T84.199 Other mechanical complication of internal fixation device of **unspecified** bone of limb

● **T84.2**   Mechanical complication of internal fixation device of other bones

   ● **T84.21**   Breakdown (mechanical) of internal fixation device of other bones

     ● **T84.210**   Breakdown (mechanical) of internal fixation device of bones of hand and fingers

     ● **T84.213**   Breakdown (mechanical) of internal fixation device of bones of foot and toes

     ● **T84.216**   Breakdown (mechanical) of internal fixation device of vertebrae

     ● **T84.218**   Breakdown (mechanical) of internal fixation device of other bones

   ● **T84.22**   Displacement of internal fixation device of other bones

     Malposition of internal fixation device of other bones

     ● **T84.220**   Displacement of internal fixation device of bones of hand and fingers

     ● **T84.223**   Displacement of internal fixation device of bones of foot and toes

     ● **T84.226**   Displacement of internal fixation device of vertebrae

     ● **T84.228**   Displacement of internal fixation device of other bones

   ● **T84.29**   Other mechanical complication of internal fixation device of other bones

     Obstruction (mechanical) of internal fixation device of other bones
     Perforation of internal fixation device of other bones
     Protrusion of internal fixation device of other bones

     ● **T84.290**   Other mechanical complication of internal fixation device of bones of hand and fingers

     ● **T84.293**   Other mechanical complication of internal fixation device of bones of foot and toes

     ● **T84.296**   Other mechanical complication of internal fixation device of vertebrae

     ● **T84.298**   Other mechanical complication of internal fixation device of other bones

● **T84.3**   Mechanical complication of other bone devices, implants and grafts

     Excludes2   other complications of bone graft (T86.83-)

   ● **T84.31**   Breakdown (mechanical) of other bone devices, implants and grafts

     ● **T84.310**   Breakdown (mechanical) of electronic bone stimulator

     ● **T84.318**   Breakdown (mechanical) of other bone devices, implants and grafts

   ● **T84.32**   Displacement of other bone devices, implants and grafts

     Malposition of other bone devices, implants and grafts

     ● **T84.320**   Displacement of electronic bone stimulator

     ● **T84.328**   Displacement of other bone devices, implants and grafts

● **T84.39**   Other mechanical complication of other bone devices, implants and grafts

     Obstruction (mechanical) of other bone devices, implants and grafts
     Perforation of other bone devices, implants and grafts
     Protrusion of other bone devices, implants and grafts

     ● **T84.390**   Other mechanical complication of electronic bone stimulator

     ● **T84.398**   Other mechanical complication of other bone devices, implants and grafts

● **T84.4**   Mechanical complication of other internal orthopedic devices, implants and grafts

   ● **T84.41**   Breakdown (mechanical) of other internal orthopedic devices, implants and grafts

     ● **T84.410**   Breakdown (mechanical) of muscle and tendon graft

     ● **T84.418**   Breakdown (mechanical) of other internal orthopedic devices, implants and grafts

   ● **T84.42**   Displacement of other internal orthopedic devices, implants and grafts

     Malposition of other internal orthopedic devices, implants and grafts

     ● **T84.420**   Displacement of muscle and tendon graft

     ● **T84.428**   Displacement of other internal orthopedic devices, implants and grafts

   ● **T84.49**   Other mechanical complication of other internal orthopedic devices, implants and grafts

     Mechanical complication of other internal orthopedic devices, implants and grafts NOS
     Obstruction (mechanical) of other internal orthopedic devices, implants and grafts
     Perforation of other internal orthopedic devices, implants and grafts
     Protrusion of other internal orthopedic devices, implants and grafts

     ● **T84.490**   Other mechanical complication of muscle and tendon graft

     ● **T84.498**   Other mechanical complication of other internal orthopedic devices, implants and grafts

● **T84.5**   Infection and inflammatory reaction due to internal joint prosthesis

     Use additional code to identify infection
     Coding Clinic: 2015, Q1, P16

   X ● **T84.50**   Infection and inflammatory reaction due to unspecified internal joint prosthesis
     Coding Clinic: 2015, Q1, P3

   X ● **T84.51**   Infection and inflammatory reaction due to internal right hip prosthesis
     Coding Clinic: 2015, Q4, P36

   X ● **T84.52**   Infection and inflammatory reaction due to internal left hip prosthesis
     Coding Clinic: 2015, Q1, P16-17

   X ● **T84.53**   Infection and inflammatory reaction due to internal right knee prosthesis

   X ● **T84.54**   Infection and inflammatory reaction due to internal left knee prosthesis

   X ● **T84.59**   Infection and inflammatory reaction due to other internal joint prosthesis

CHAPTER 19 (S00-T88)

CHAPTER 19 (S00-T88)

● **T84.6**   **Infection and inflammatory reaction due to internal fixation device**

     Use additional code to identify infection

X● **T84.60**   Infection and inflammatory reaction due to internal fixation device of unspecified site

● **T84.61**   Infection and inflammatory reaction due to internal fixation device of arm

    ● **T84.610**   Infection and inflammatory reaction due to internal fixation device of right humerus

    ● **T84.611**   Infection and inflammatory reaction due to internal fixation device of left humerus

    ● **T84.612**   Infection and inflammatory reaction due to internal fixation device of right radius

    ● **T84.613**   Infection and inflammatory reaction due to internal fixation device of left radius

    ● **T84.614**   Infection and inflammatory reaction due to internal fixation device of right ulna

    ● **T84.615**   Infection and inflammatory reaction due to internal fixation device of left ulna

    ● **T84.619**   Infection and inflammatory reaction due to internal fixation device of unspecified bone of arm

● **T84.62**   Infection and inflammatory reaction due to internal fixation device of leg

    ● **T84.620**   Infection and inflammatory reaction due to internal fixation device of right femur

    ● **T84.621**   Infection and inflammatory reaction due to internal fixation device of left femur

    ● **T84.622**   Infection and inflammatory reaction due to internal fixation device of right tibia

    ● **T84.623**   Infection and inflammatory reaction due to internal fixation device of left tibia

    ● **T84.624**   Infection and inflammatory reaction due to internal fixation device of right fibula

    ● **T84.625**   Infection and inflammatory reaction due to internal fixation device of left fibula

    ● **T84.629**   Infection and inflammatory reaction due to internal fixation device of unspecified bone of leg

X● **T84.63**   Infection and inflammatory reaction due to internal fixation device of spine

X● **T84.69**   Infection and inflammatory reaction due to internal fixation device of other site

● **T84.7**   **Infection and inflammatory reaction due to other internal orthopedic prosthetic devices, implants and grafts**

     Use additional code to identify infection

● **T84.8**   **Other specified complications of internal orthopedic prosthetic devices, implants and grafts**

X● **T84.81**   Embolism due to internal orthopedic prosthetic devices, implants and grafts

X● **T84.82**   Fibrosis due to internal orthopedic prosthetic devices, implants and grafts

X● **T84.83**   Hemorrhage due to internal orthopedic prosthetic devices, implants and grafts

X● **T84.84**   Pain due to internal orthopedic prosthetic devices, implants and grafts

X● **T84.85**   Stenosis due to internal orthopedic prosthetic devices, implants and grafts

X● **T84.86**   Thrombosis due to internal orthopedic prosthetic devices, implants and grafts

X● **T84.89**   Other specified complication of internal orthopedic prosthetic devices, implants and grafts

X● **T84.9**   **Unspecified complication of internal orthopedic prosthetic device, implant and graft**

● **T85**   **Complications of other internal prosthetic devices, implants and grafts**

    Excludes2   failure and rejection of transplanted organs and tissue (T86.-)

    The appropriate 7th character is to be added to each code from category T85

> | | |
> |---|---|
> | A | initial encounter |
> | D | subsequent encounter |
> | S | sequela |

Coding Clinic: 2016, Q4, P71

● **T85.0**   **Mechanical complication of ventricular intracranial (communicating) shunt**

X● **T85.01**   Breakdown (mechanical) of ventricular intracranial (communicating) shunt

X● **T85.02**   Displacement of ventricular intracranial (communicating) shunt

     Malposition of ventricular intracranial (communicating) shunt

X● **T85.03**   Leakage of ventricular intracranial (communicating) shunt

X● **T85.09**   Other mechanical complication of ventricular intracranial (communicating) shunt

     Obstruction (mechanical) of ventricular intracranial (communicating) shunt

     Perforation of ventricular intracranial (communicating) shunt

     Protrusion of ventricular intracranial (communicating) shunt

● **T85.1**   **Mechanical complication of implanted electronic stimulator of nervous system**

    Coding Clinic: 2016, Q4, P71

● **T85.11**   Breakdown (mechanical) of implanted electronic stimulator of nervous system

    ● **T85.110**   Breakdown (mechanical) of implanted electronic neurostimulator of brain electrode (lead)

    ● **T85.111**   Breakdown (mechanical) of implanted electronic neurostimulator of peripheral nerve electrode (lead)

      Breakdown of electrode (lead) for cranial nerve neurostimulators

      Breakdown of electrode (lead) for gastric neurostimulator

      Breakdown of electrode (lead) for sacral nerve neurostimulator

      Breakdown of electrode (lead) for vagal nerve neurostimulators

    ● **T85.112**   Breakdown (mechanical) of implanted electronic neurostimulator of spinal cord electrode (lead)

    ● **T85.113**   Breakdown (mechanical) of implanted electronic neurostimulator, generator

      ⮕ Breakdown (mechanical) of implanted electronic neurostimulator generator, brain, peripheral, gastric, spinal

      Breakdown (mechanical) of implanted electronic sacral neurostimulator, pulse generator or receiver

    ● **T85.118**   Breakdown (mechanical) of other implanted electronic stimulator of nervous system

▶ New   ⮕ Revised   ~~deleted~~ Deleted   Excludes 1   Excludes 2   Includes   Use additional   Code first   Code also   Key words

OGCR Official Guidelines   X Assign placeholder X   ● Use Additional Character(s)   ▷ Manifestation Code   **Coding Clinic**

● T85.12   **Displacement of implanted electronic stimulator of nervous system**
> Malposition of implanted electronic stimulator of nervous system

  ● T85.120   **Displacement of implanted electronic neurostimulator of brain electrode (lead)**

  ● T85.121   **Displacement of implanted electronic neurostimulator of peripheral nerve electrode (lead)**
> Displacement of electrode (lead) for cranial nerve neurostimulators
> Displacement of electrode (lead) for gastric neurostimulator
> Displacement of electrode (lead) for sacral nerve neurostimulator
> Displacement of electrode (lead) for vagal nerve neurostimulators

  ● T85.122   **Displacement of implanted electronic neurostimulator of spinal cord electrode (lead)**

  ● T85.123   **Displacement of implanted electronic neurostimulator, generator**
> Displacement of implanted electronic neurostimulator generator, brain, peripheral, gastric, spinal
> Displacement of implanted electronic sacral neurostimulator, pulse generator or receiver

  ● T85.128   **Displacement of other implanted electronic stimulator of nervous system**

● T85.19   **Other mechanical complication of implanted electronic stimulator of nervous system**
> Leakage of implanted electronic stimulator of nervous system
> Obstruction (mechanical) of implanted electronic stimulator of nervous system
> Perforation of implanted electronic stimulator of nervous system
> Protrusion of implanted electronic stimulator of nervous system

  ● T85.190   **Other mechanical complication of implanted electronic neurostimulator of brain electrode (lead)**

  ● T85.191   **Other mechanical complication of implanted electronic neurostimulator of peripheral nerve electrode (lead)**
> Other mechanical complication of electrode (lead) for cranial nerve neurostimulators
> Other mechanical complication of electrode (lead) for gastric neurostimulator
> Other mechanical complication of electrode (lead) for sacral nerve neurostimulator
> Other mechanical complication of electrode (lead) for vagal nerve neurostimulators

  ● T85.192   **Other mechanical complication of implanted electronic neurostimulator of spinal cord electrode (lead)**

  ● T85.193   **Other mechanical complication of implanted electronic neurostimulator, generator**
> Other mechanical complication of implanted electronic neurostimulator generator, brain, peripheral, gastric, spinal
> Other mechanical complication of implanted electronic sacral neurostimulator, pulse generator or receiver

  ● T85.199   **Other mechanical complication of other implanted electronic stimulator of nervous system**

● T85.2   **Mechanical complication of intraocular lens**

  X ● T85.21   **Breakdown (mechanical) of intraocular lens**

  X ● T85.22   **Displacement of intraocular lens**
> Malposition of intraocular lens

  X ● T85.29   **Other mechanical complication of intraocular lens**
> Obstruction (mechanical) of intraocular lens
> Perforation of intraocular lens
> Protrusion of intraocular lens

● T85.3   **Mechanical complication of other ocular prosthetic devices, implants and grafts**

    Excludes2   other complications of corneal graft (T86.84-)

  ● T85.31   **Breakdown (mechanical) of other ocular prosthetic devices, implants and grafts**

    ● T85.310   **Breakdown (mechanical) of prosthetic orbit of right eye**

    ● T85.311   **Breakdown (mechanical) of prosthetic orbit of left eye**

    ● T85.318   **Breakdown (mechanical) of other ocular prosthetic devices, implants and grafts**

  ● T85.32   **Displacement of other ocular prosthetic devices, implants and grafts**
> Malposition of other ocular prosthetic devices, implants and grafts

    ● T85.320   **Displacement of prosthetic orbit of right eye**

    ● T85.321   **Displacement of prosthetic orbit of left eye**

    ● T85.328   **Displacement of other ocular prosthetic devices, implants and grafts**

  ● T85.39   **Other mechanical complication of other ocular prosthetic devices, implants and grafts**
> Obstruction (mechanical) of other ocular prosthetic devices, implants and grafts
> Perforation of other ocular prosthetic devices, implants and grafts
> Protrusion of other ocular prosthetic devices, implants and grafts

    ● T85.390   **Other mechanical complication of prosthetic orbit of right eye**

    ● T85.391   **Other mechanical complication of prosthetic orbit of left eye**

    ● T85.398   **Other mechanical complication of other ocular prosthetic devices, implants and grafts**

CHAPTER 19 (S00-T88)

● **T85.4**   **Mechanical complication of breast prosthesis and implant**

     X ● **T85.41**   **Breakdown (mechanical) of breast prosthesis and implant**

     X ● **T85.42**   **Displacement of breast prosthesis and implant**
           Malposition of breast prosthesis and implant

     X ● **T85.43**   **Leakage of breast prosthesis and implant**

     X ● **T85.44**   **Capsular contracture of breast implant**

     X ● **T85.49**   **Other mechanical complication of breast prosthesis and implant**
           Obstruction (mechanical) of breast prosthesis and implant
           Perforation of breast prosthesis and implant
           Protrusion of breast prosthesis and implant

● **T85.5**   **Mechanical complication of gastrointestinal prosthetic devices, implants and grafts**

     ● **T85.51**   **Breakdown (mechanical) of gastrointestinal prosthetic devices, implants and grafts**

         ● **T85.510**   **Breakdown (mechanical) of bile duct prosthesis**

         ● **T85.511**   **Breakdown (mechanical) of esophageal anti-reflux device**

         ● **T85.518**   **Breakdown (mechanical) of other gastrointestinal prosthetic devices, implants and grafts**

     ● **T85.52**   **Displacement of gastrointestinal prosthetic devices, implants and grafts**
           Malposition of gastrointestinal prosthetic devices, implants and grafts

         ● **T85.520**   **Displacement of bile duct prosthesis**

         ● **T85.521**   **Displacement of esophageal anti-reflux device**

         ● **T85.528**   **Displacement of other gastrointestinal prosthetic devices, implants and grafts**

     ● **T85.59**   **Other mechanical complication of gastrointestinal prosthetic devices, implants and**
           Obstruction, mechanical of gastrointestinal prosthetic devices, implants and grafts
           Perforation of gastrointestinal prosthetic devices, implants and grafts
           Protrusion of gastrointestinal prosthetic devices, implants and grafts

         ● **T85.590**   **Other mechanical complication of bile duct prosthesis**

         ● **T85.591**   **Other mechanical complication of esophageal anti-reflux device**

         ● **T85.598**   **Other mechanical complication of other gastrointestinal prosthetic devices, implants and grafts**

● **T85.6**   **Mechanical complication of other specified internal and external prosthetic devices, implants and grafts**
     Coding Clinic: 2016, Q4, P71

     ● **T85.61**   **Breakdown (mechanical) of other specified internal prosthetic devices, implants and grafts**

         ● **T85.610**   **Breakdown (mechanical) of cranial or spinal infusion catheter**
             Breakdown (mechanical) of epidural infusion catheter
             Breakdown (mechanical) of intrathecal infusion catheter
             Breakdown (mechanical) of subarachnoid infusion catheter
             Breakdown (mechanical) of subdural infusion catheter

         ● **T85.611**   **Breakdown (mechanical) of intraperitoneal dialysis catheter**

            Excludes 1   mechanical complication of vascular dialysis catheter (T82.4-)

         ● **T85.612**   **Breakdown (mechanical) of permanent sutures**

            Excludes 1   mechanical complication of permanent (wire) suture used in bone repair (T84.1-T84.2)

         ● **T85.613**   **Breakdown (mechanical) of artificial skin graft and decellularized allodermis**
             Failure of artificial skin graft and decellularized allodermis
             Non-adherence of artificial skin graft and decellularized allodermis
             Poor incorporation of artificial skin graft and decellularized allodermis
             Shearing of artificial skin graft and decellularized allodermis

         ● **T85.614**   **Breakdown (mechanical) of insulin pump**

         ● **T85.615**   **Breakdown (mechanical) of other nervous system device, implant or graft**
             Breakdown (mechanical) of intrathecal infusion pump

         ● **T85.618**   **Breakdown (mechanical) of other specified internal prosthetic devices, implants and grafts**

     ● **T85.62**   **Displacement of other specified internal prosthetic devices, implants and grafts**
           Malposition of other specified internal prosthetic devices, implants and grafts

         ● **T85.620**   **Displacement of cranial or spinal infusion catheter**
             Displacement of epidural infusion catheter
             Displacement of intrathecal infusion catheter
             Displacement of subarachnoid infusion catheter
             Displacement of subdural infusion catheter

         ● **T85.621**   **Displacement of intraperitoneal dialysis catheter**

            Excludes 1   mechanical complication of vascular dialysis catheter (T82.4-)

         ● **T85.622**   **Displacement of permanent sutures**

            Excludes 1   mechanical complication of permanent (wire) suture used in bone repair (T84.1-T84.2)

         ● **T85.623**   **Displacement of artificial skin graft and decellularized allodermis**
             Dislodgement of artificial skin graft and decellularized allodermis

         ● **T85.624**   **Displacement of insulin pump**

         ● **T85.625**   **Displacement of other nervous system device, implant or graft**
             Displacement of intrathecal infusion pump

         ● **T85.628**   **Displacement of other specified internal prosthetic devices, implants and grafts**
             Coding Clinic: 2015, Q1, P15

▶ New   ⇒ Revised   ~~deleted~~ Deleted   Excludes 1   Excludes 2   Includes   Use additional   Code first   Code also   Key words

OGCR Official Guidelines   X Assign placeholder X   ● Use Additional Character(s)   ▶ Manifestation Code   **Coding Clinic**

● **T85.63 Leakage of other specified internal prosthetic devices, implants and grafts**

  ● **T85.630 Leakage of cranial or spinal infusion catheter**

      Leakage of epidural infusion catheter

      Leakage of intrathecal infusion catheter

      Leakage of subdural infusion catheter

      Leakage of subarachnoid infusion catheter

  ● **T85.631 Leakage of intraperitoneal dialysis catheter**

      Excludes1   mechanical complication of vascular dialysis catheter (T82.4)

  ● **T85.633 Leakage of insulin pump**

  ● **T85.635 Leakage of other nervous system device, implant or graft**

      Leakage of intrathecal infusion pump

  ● **T85.638 Leakage of other specified internal prosthetic devices, implants and grafts**

● **T85.69 Other mechanical complication of other specified internal prosthetic devices, implants and grafts**

    Obstruction, mechanical of other specified internal prosthetic devices, implants and grafts

    Perforation of other specified internal prosthetic devices, implants and grafts

    Protrusion of other specified internal prosthetic devices, implants and grafts

  ● **T85.690 Other mechanical complication of cranial or spinal infusion catheter**

      Other mechanical complication of epidural infusion catheter

      Other mechanical complication of intrathecal infusion catheter

      Other mechanical complication of subarachnoid infusion catheter

      Other mechanical complication of subdural infusion catheter

  ● **T85.691 Other mechanical complication of intraperitoneal dialysis catheter**

      Excludes1   mechanical complication of vascular dialysis catheter (T82.4)

  ● **T85.692 Other mechanical complication of permanent sutures**

      Excludes1   mechanical complication of permanent (wire) suture used in bone repair (T84.1-T84.2)

  ● **T85.693 Other mechanical complication of artificial skin graft and decellularized allodermis**

  ● **T85.694 Other mechanical complication of insulin pump**

● **T85.695 Other mechanical complication of other nervous system device, implant or graft**

    Other mechanical complication of intrathecal infusion pump

● **T85.698 Other mechanical complication of other specified internal prosthetic devices, implants and grafts**

    Mechanical complication of nonabsorbable surgical material NOS

● **T85.7 Infection and inflammatory reaction due to other internal prosthetic devices, implants and grafts**

    Use additional code to identify infection

    Coding Clinic: 2016, Q4, P72

X ● **T85.71 Infection and inflammatory reaction due to peritoneal dialysis catheter**

X ● **T85.72 Infection and inflammatory reaction due to insulin pump**

  ● **T85.73 Infection and inflammatory reaction due to nervous system devices, implants and graft**

    ● **T85.730 Infection and inflammatory reaction due to ventricular intracranial (communicating) shunt**

    ● **T85.731 Infection and inflammatory reaction due to implanted electronic neurostimulator of brain, electrode (lead)**

    ● **T85.732 Infection and inflammatory reaction due to implanted electronic neurostimulator of peripheral nerve, electrode (lead)**

      Infection and inflammatory reaction due to electrode (lead) for cranial nerve neurostimulators

      Infection and inflammatory reaction due to electrode (lead) for gastric neurostimulator

      Infection and inflammatory reaction due to electrode (lead) for sacral nerve neurostimulator

      Infection and inflammatory reaction due to electrode (lead) for vagal nerve neurostimulators

    ● **T85.733 Infection and inflammatory reaction due to implanted electronic neurostimulator of spinal cord, electrode (lead)**

    ● **T85.734 Infection and inflammatory reaction due to implanted electronic neurostimulator, generator**

      Generator pocket infection

    ● **T85.735 Infection and inflammatory reaction due to cranial or spinal infusion catheter**

      Infection and inflammatory reaction due to epidural catheter

      Infection and inflammatory reaction due to intrathecal infusion catheter

      Infection and inflammatory reaction due to subarachnoid catheter

      Infection and inflammatory reaction due to subdural catheter

    ● **T85.738 Infection and inflammatory reaction due to other nervous system device, implant or graft**

      Infection and inflammatory reaction due to intrathecal infusion pump

X ● **T85.79 Infection and inflammatory reaction due to other internal prosthetic devices, implants and grafts**

    Coding Clinic: 2016, Q4, P72

CHAPTER 19 (S00-T88)

● T85.8   Other specified complications of internal prosthetic devices, implants and grafts, not elsewhere classified
Coding Clinic: 2016, Q4, P72

    ● T85.81   Embolism due to internal prosthetic devices, implants and grafts, not elsewhere classified

       ● T85.810   Embolism due to nervous system prosthetic devices, implants and grafts

       ● T85.818   Embolism due to other internal prosthetic devices, implants and grafts

    ● T85.82   Fibrosis due to internal prosthetic devices, implants and grafts, not elsewhere classified

       ● T85.820   Fibrosis due to nervous system prosthetic devices, implants and grafts

       ● T85.828   Fibrosis due to other internal prosthetic devices, implants and grafts

    ● T85.83   Hemorrhage due to internal prosthetic devices, implants and grafts, not elsewhere classified

       ● T85.830   Hemorrhage due to nervous system prosthetic devices, implants and grafts

       ● T85.838   Hemorrhage due to other internal prosthetic devices, implants and grafts

    ● T85.84   Pain due to internal prosthetic devices, implants and grafts, not elsewhere classified

       ● T85.840   Pain due to nervous system prosthetic devices, implants and grafts

       ● T85.848   Pain due to other internal prosthetic devices, implants and grafts

    ● T85.85   Stenosis due to internal prosthetic devices, implants and grafts, not elsewhere classified

       ● T85.850   Stenosis due to nervous system prosthetic devices, implants and grafts

       ● T85.858   Stenosis due to other internal prosthetic devices, implants and grafts

    ● T85.86   Thrombosis due to internal prosthetic devices, implants and grafts, not elsewhere classified

       ● T85.860   Thrombosis due to nervous system prosthetic devices, implants and grafts

       ● T85.868   Thrombosis due to other internal prosthetic devices, implants and grafts

    ● T85.89   Other specified complication of internal prosthetic devices, implants and grafts, not elsewhere classified
Coding Clinic: 2016, Q4, P72

       ● T85.890   Other specified complication of nervous system prosthetic devices, implants and grafts

       ● T85.898   Other specified complication of other internal prosthetic devices, implants and grafts

X ● T85.9   Unspecified complication of internal prosthetic device, implant and graft

    Complication of internal prosthetic device, implant and graft NOS

OGCR Section I.C.19.g.3.

Organ Transplant Complications

Transplant Complications

(a) Transplant complications other than kidney

Codes under category T86, Complications of transplanted organs and tissues, are for use for both complications and rejection of transplanted organs. A transplant complication code is only assigned if the complication affects the function of the transplanted organ. Two codes are required to fully describe a transplant complication: the appropriate code from category T86 and a secondary code that identifies the complication.

Pre-existing conditions or conditions that develop after the transplant are not coded as complications unless they affect the function of the transplanted organs.

See I.C.21 for transplant organ removal status

See I.C.2 for malignant neoplasm associated with transplanted organ.

● T86   Complications of transplanted organs and tissue

    Use additional code to identify other transplant complications, such as:
    graft-versus-host disease (D89.81-)
    malignancy associated with organ transplant (C80.2)
    post-transplant lymphoproliferative disorders (PTLD) (D47.Z1)

    ● T86.0   Complications of bone marrow transplant

       T86.00   Unspecified complication of bone marrow transplant

       T86.01   Bone marrow transplant rejection

       T86.02   Bone marrow transplant failure

       T86.03   Bone marrow transplant infection

       T86.09   Other complications of bone marrow transplant

    ● T86.1   Complications of kidney transplant

       T86.10   Unspecified complication of kidney transplant

       T86.11   Kidney transplant rejection

       T86.12   Kidney transplant failure
Coding Clinic: 2013, Q1, P24

       T86.13   Kidney transplant infection
           Use additional code to specify infection

       T86.19   Other complication of kidney transplant

    ● T86.2   Complications of heart transplant

       Excludes1   complication of:
           artificial heart device (T82.5)
           heart-lung transplant (T86.3)

       T86.20   Unspecified complication of heart transplant

       T86.21   Heart transplant rejection

       T86.22   Heart transplant failure

       T86.23   Heart transplant infection
           Use additional code to specify infection

       ● T86.29   Other complications of heart transplant

          T86.290   Cardiac allograft vasculopathy

              Excludes1   atherosclerosis of coronary arteries (I25.75-, I25.76-, I25.81-)

          T86.298   Other complications of heart transplant

    ● T86.3   Complications of heart-lung transplant

       T86.30   Unspecified complication of heart-lung transplant

       T86.31   Heart-lung transplant rejection

       T86.32   Heart-lung transplant failure

       T86.33   Heart-lung transplant infection
           Use additional code to specify infection

       T86.39   Other complications of heart-lung transplant

▶ New   ⇒ Revised   ~~deleted~~ Deleted   Excludes 1   Excludes 2   Includes   Use additional   Code first   Code also   Key words

OGCR Official Guidelines   X Assign placeholder X   ● Use Additional Character(s)   ▮ Manifestation Code   **Coding Clinic**

● **T86.4**   **Complications of liver transplant**
     T86.40   Unspecified complication of liver transplant
     T86.41   Liver transplant rejection
     T86.42   Liver transplant failure
     T86.43   Liver transplant infection
           Use additional code to identify infection, such as:
              Cytomegalovirus (CMV) infection (B25.-)
     T86.49   Other complications of liver transplant
● **T86.5**   **Complications of stem cell transplant**
       Complications from stem cells from peripheral blood
       Complications from stem cells from umbilical cord
● **T86.8**   **Complications of other transplanted organs and tissues**
   ● **T86.81**   **Complications of lung transplant**
        Excludes1   complication of heart-lung transplant (T86.3-)
      T86.810   Lung transplant rejection
      T86.811   Lung transplant failure
      T86.812   Lung transplant infection
            Use additional code to specify infection
      T86.818   Other complications of lung transplant
      T86.819   Unspecified complication of lung transplant
   ● **T86.82**   **Complications of skin graft (allograft) (autograft)**
        Excludes2   complication of artificial skin graft (T85.693)
      T86.820   Skin graft (allograft) rejection
      T86.821   Skin graft (allograft) (autograft) failure
      T86.822   Skin graft (allograft) (autograft) infection
            Use additional code to specify infection
      T86.828   Other complications of skin graft (allograft) (autograft)
      T86.829   Unspecified complication of skin graft (allograft) (autograft)
   ● **T86.83**   **Complications of bone graft**
        Excludes2   mechanical complications of bone graft (T84.3-)
      T86.830   Bone graft rejection
      T86.831   Bone graft failure
      T86.832   Bone graft infection
            Use additional code to specify infection
      T86.838   Other complications of bone graft
      T86.839   Unspecified complication of bone graft
   ● **T86.84**   **Complications of corneal transplant**
        Excludes2   mechanical complications of corneal graft (T85.3-)
      T86.840   Corneal transplant rejection
      T86.841   Corneal transplant failure
      T86.842   Corneal transplant infection
            Use additional code to specify infection
      T86.848   Other complications of corneal transplant
      T86.849   Unspecified complication of corneal transplant

   ● **T86.85**   **Complication of intestine transplant**
      T86.850   Intestine transplant rejection
      T86.851   Intestine transplant failure
      T86.852   Intestine transplant infection
            Use additional code to specify infection
      T86.858   Other complications of intestine transplant
      T86.859   Unspecified complication of intestine transplant
   ● **T86.89**   **Complications of other transplanted tissue**
       Transplant failure or rejection of pancreas
      T86.890   Other transplanted tissue rejection
      T86.891   Other transplanted tissue failure
      T86.892   Other transplanted tissue infection
            Use additional code to specify infection
      T86.898   Other complications of other transplanted tissue
      T86.899   Unspecified complication of other transplanted tissue
   ● **T86.9**   **Complication of unspecified transplanted organ and tissue**
      T86.90   Unspecified complication of unspecified transplanted organ and tissue
      T86.91   Unspecified transplanted organ and tissue rejection
      T86.92   Unspecified transplanted organ and tissue failure
      T86.93   Unspecified transplanted organ and tissue infection
            Use additional code to specify infection
      T86.99   Other complications of unspecified transplanted organ and tissue
● **T87**   **Complications peculiar to reattachment and amputation**
   ● **T87.0**   **Complications of reattached (part of) upper extremity**
     ● **T87.0X**   **Complications of reattached (part of) upper extremity**
       T87.0X1   Complications of reattached (part of) right upper extremity
       T87.0X2   Complications of reattached (part of) left upper extremity
       T87.0X9   Complications of reattached (part of) unspecified upper extremity
   ● **T87.1**   **Complications of reattached (part of) lower extremity**
     ● **T87.1X**   **Complications of reattached (part of) lower extremity**
       T87.1X1   Complications of reattached (part of) right lower extremity
       T87.1X2   Complications of reattached (part of) left lower extremity
       T87.1X9   Complications of reattached (part of) unspecified lower extremity
     T87.2   **Complications of other reattached body part**
   ● **T87.3**   **Neuroma of amputation stump**
      T87.30   Neuroma of amputation stump, unspecified extremity
      T87.31   Neuroma of amputation stump, right upper extremity
      T87.32   Neuroma of amputation stump, left upper extremity
      T87.33   Neuroma of amputation stump, right lower extremity
      T87.34   Neuroma of amputation stump, left lower extremity

CHAPTER 19 (S00-T88)

● **T87.4**   **Infection of amputation stump**

     T87.40   **Infection of amputation stump, unspecified extremity**

     T87.41   **Infection of amputation stump, right upper extremity**

     T87.42   **Infection of amputation stump, left upper extremity**

     T87.43   **Infection of amputation stump, right lower extremity**

     T87.44   **Infection of amputation stump, left lower extremity**

● **T87.5**   **Necrosis of amputation stump**

     T87.50   **Necrosis of amputation stump, unspecified extremity**

     T87.51   **Necrosis of amputation stump, right upper extremity**

     T87.52   **Necrosis of amputation stump, left upper extremity**

     T87.53   **Necrosis of amputation stump, right lower extremity**

     T87.54   **Necrosis of amputation stump, left lower extremity**

● **T87.8**   **Other complications of amputation stump**

     T87.81   **Dehiscence of amputation stump**

     T87.89   **Other complications of amputation stump**
            Amputation stump contracture
            Amputation stump contracture of next proximal joint
            Amputation stump flexion
            Amputation stump edema
            Amputation stump hematoma

         Excludes2   phantom limb syndrome (G54.6-G54.7)

     T87.9   **Unspecified complications of amputation stump**

● **T88**   **Other complications of surgical and medical care, not elsewhere classified**

     Excludes2   complication following infusion, transfusion and therapeutic injection (T80.-)
           complication following procedure NEC (T81.-)
           complications of anesthesia in labor and delivery (O74.-)
           complications of anesthesia in pregnancy (O29.-)
           complications of anesthesia in puerperium (O89.-)
           complications of devices, implants and grafts (T82-T85)
           complications of obstetric surgery and procedure (O75.4)
           dermatitis due to drugs and medicaments (L23.3, L24.4, L25.1, L27.0-L27.1)
           poisoning and toxic effects of drugs and chemicals (T36-T65 with fifth or sixth character 1-4 or 6)
           specified complications classified elsewhere

     The appropriate 7th character is to be added to each code from category T88

> | A | initial encounter |
> |---|---|
> | D | subsequent encounter |
> | S | sequela |

X ● **T88.0**   **Infection following immunization**
         Sepsis following immunization

X ● **T88.1**   **Other complications following immunization, not elsewhere classified**
         Generalized vaccinia
         Rash following immunization

         Excludes1   vaccinia not from vaccine (B08.011)

         Excludes2   anaphylactic shock due to serum (T80.5-)
             other serum reactions (T80.6-)
             postimmunization arthropathy (M02.2)
             postimmunization encephalitis (G04.02)
             postimmunization fever (R50.83)

X ● **T88.2**   **Shock due to anesthesia**
         Use additional code for adverse effect, if applicable, to identify drug (T41.- with fifth or sixth character 5)

         Excludes1   complications of anesthesia (in):
             labor and delivery (O74.-)
             pregnancy (O29.-)
             puerperium (O89.-)
             postprocedural shock NOS (T81.1-)

X ● **T88.3**   **Malignant hyperthermia due to anesthesia**
         Use additional code for adverse effect, if applicable, to identify drug (T41.- with fifth or sixth character 5)

X ● **T88.4**   **Failed or difficult intubation**

● **T88.5**   **Other complications of anesthesia**
         Use additional code for adverse effect, if applicable, to identify drug (T41.- with fifth or sixth character 5)
         Coding Clinic: 2016, Q4, P72

     X ● **T88.51**   **Hypothermia following anesthesia**

     X ● **T88.52**   **Failed moderate sedation during procedure**
           Failed conscious sedation during procedure

           Excludes2   personal history of failed moderate sedation (Z92.83)

     X ● **T88.53**   **Unintended awareness under general anesthesia during procedure**

           Excludes2   personal history of unintended awareness under general anesthesia (Z92.84)
         Coding Clinic: 2016, Q4, P72-73

     X ● **T88.59**   **Other complications of anesthesia**

X ● **T88.6**   **Anaphylactic reaction due to adverse effect of correct drug or medicament properly administered**
         Anaphylactic shock due to adverse effect of correct drug or medicament properly administered
         Anaphylactoid reaction NOS

         Use additional code for adverse effect, if applicable, to identify drug (T36-T50 with fifth or sixth character 5)

         Excludes1   anaphylactic reaction due to serum (T80.5-)
             anaphylactic shock or reaction due to adverse food reaction (T78.0-)

X ● **T88.7**   **Unspecified adverse effect of drug or medicament**
         Drug hypersensitivity NOS
         Drug reaction NOS

         Use additional code for adverse effect, if applicable, to identify drug (T36-T50 with fifth or sixth character 5)

         Excludes1   specified adverse effects of drugs and medicaments (A00-R94 and T80-T88.6, T88.8)

X ● **T88.8**   **Other specified complications of surgical and medical care, not elsewhere classified**
         Use additional code to identify the complication

X ● **T88.9**   **Complication of surgical and medical care, unspecified**

CHAPTER 20

EXTERNAL CAUSES OF MORBIDITY
(V00-Y99)

OGCR Chapter-Specific Coding Guidelines

20. Chapter 20: External Causes of Morbidity (V00-Y99)

The external causes of morbidity codes should never be sequenced as the first-listed or principal diagnosis.

External cause codes are intended to provide data for injury research and evaluation of injury prevention strategies. These codes capture how the injury or health condition happened (cause), the intent (unintentional or accidental; or intentional, such as suicide or assault), the place where the event occurred the activity of the patient at the time of the event, and the person's status (e.g., civilian, military).

There is no national requirement for mandatory ICD-10-CM external cause code reporting. Unless a provider is subject to a state-based external cause code reporting mandate or these codes are required by a particular payer, reporting of ICD-10-CM codes in Chapter 20, External Causes of Morbidity, is not required. In the absence of a mandatory reporting requirement, providers are encouraged to voluntarily report external cause codes, as they provide valuable data for injury research and evaluation of injury prevention strategies.

a. General External Cause Coding Guidelines

1) Used with any code in the range of A00.0-T88.9, Z00-Z99

An external cause code may be used with any code in the range of A00.0-T88.9, Z00-Z99, classification that **represents** a health condition due to an external cause. Though they are most applicable to injuries, they are also valid for use with such things as infections or diseases due to an external source, and other health conditions, such as a heart attack that occurs during strenuous physical activity.

2) External cause code used for length of treatment

Assign the external cause code, with the appropriate 7th character (initial encounter, subsequent encounter or sequela) for each encounter for which the injury or condition is being treated.

Most categories in chapter 20 have a 7th character requirement for each applicable code. Most categories in this chapter have three 7th character values: A, initial encounter, D, subsequent encounter and S, sequela. While the patient may be seen by a new or different provider over the course of treatment for an injury or condition, assignment of the 7th character for external cause should match the 7th character of the code assigned for the associated injury or condition for the encounter.

3) Use the full range of external cause codes

Use the full range of external cause codes to completely describe the cause, the intent, the place of occurrence and if applicable, the activity of the patient at the time of the event, and the patient's status, for all injuries, and other health conditions due to an external cause.

4) Assign as many external cause codes as necessary

Assign as many external cause codes as necessary to fully explain each cause. If only one external code can be recorded, assign the code most related to the principal diagnosis.

5) The selection of the appropriate external cause code

The selection of the appropriate external cause code is guided by the Alphabetic Index of External Causes and by Inclusion and Exclusion notes in the Tabular List.

6) External cause code can never be a principal diagnosis

An external cause code can never be a principal (first-listed) diagnosis.

7) Combination external cause codes

Certain of the external cause codes are combination codes that identify sequential events that result in an injury, such as a fall which results in striking against an object. The injury may be due to either event or both. The combination external cause code used should correspond to the sequence of events regardless of which caused the most serious injury.

8) No external cause code needed in certain circumstances

No external cause code from Chapter 20 is needed if the external cause and intent are included in a code from another chapter (e.g., T36.0X1- Poisoning by penicillins, accidental (unintentional)).

b. Place of Occurrence Guideline

Codes from category Y92, Place of occurrence of the external cause, are secondary codes for use after other external cause codes to identify the location of the patient at the time of injury or other condition.

Generally, a place of occurrence code is assigned only once, at the initial encounter for treatment. However, in the rare instance that a new injury occurs during hospitalization, an additional place of occurrence code may be assigned. No 7th characters are used for Y92. Only one code from Y92 should be recorded on a medical record.

Do not use place of occurrence code Y92.9 if the place is not stated or is not applicable.

c. Activity Code

Assign a code from category Y93, Activity code, to describe the activity of the patient at the time the injury or other health condition occurred.

An activity code is used only once, at the initial encounter for treatment. Only one code from Y93 should be recorded on a medical record.

The activity codes are not applicable to poisonings, adverse effects, misadventures or sequela.

Do not assign Y93.9, Unspecified activity, if the activity is not stated.

A code from category Y93 is appropriate for use with external cause and intent codes if identifying the activity provides additional information about the event.

d. Place of Occurrence, Activity, and Status Codes Used with other External Cause Code

When applicable, place of occurrence, activity, and external cause status codes are sequenced after the main external cause code(s). Regardless of the number of external cause codes assigned, there should be only one place of occurrence code, one activity code, and one external cause status code assigned to an encounter.

e. If the Reporting Format Limits the Number of External Cause Codes

If the reporting format limits the number of external cause codes that can be used in reporting clinical data, report the code for the cause/intent most related to the principal diagnosis. If the format permits capture of additional external cause codes, the cause/intent, including medical misadventures, of the additional events should be reported rather than the codes for place, activity, or external status.

f. Multiple External Cause Coding Guidelines

More than one external cause code is required to fully describe the external cause of an illness or injury. The assignment of external cause codes should be sequenced in the following priority:

If two or more events cause separate injuries, an external cause code should be assigned for each cause. The first-listed external cause code will be selected in the following order:

External codes for child and adult abuse take priority over all other external cause codes.

See Section I.C.19., Child and Adult abuse guidelines.

External codes for terrorism events take priority over all other external cause codes except child and adult abuse.

External cause codes for cataclysmic events take priority over all other external cause codes except child and adult abuse and terrorism.

External cause codes for transport accidents take priority over all other external cause codes except cataclysmic events, child and adult abuse and terrorism.

Activity and external cause status codes are assigned following all causal (intent) external cause codes.

The first-listed external cause code should correspond to the cause of the most serious diagnosis due to an assault, accident, or self-harm, following the order of hierarchy listed above.

g. Child and Adult Abuse Guideline

Adult and child abuse, neglect and maltreatment are classified as assault. Any of the assault codes may be used to indicate the external cause of any injury resulting from the confirmed abuse.

For confirmed cases of abuse, neglect and maltreatment, when the perpetrator is known, a code from Y07, Perpetrator of maltreatment and neglect, should accompany any other assault codes.

See Section I.C.19. Adult and child abuse, neglect and other maltreatment

h. Unknown or Undetermined Intent Guideline

If the intent (accident, self-harm, assault) of the cause of an injury or other condition is unknown or unspecified, code the intent as accidental intent. All transport accident categories assume accidental intent.

1) Use of undetermined intent

External cause codes for events of undetermined intent are only for use if the documentation in the record specifies that the intent cannot be determined.

i. Sequelae (Late Effects) of External Cause Guidelines

1) Sequelae external cause codes

Sequela are reported using the external cause code with the 7th character "S" for sequela. These codes should be used with any report of a late effect or sequela resulting from a previous injury.

See Section I.B.10. Sequela, (Late Effects)

2) Sequela external cause code with a related current injury

A sequela external cause code should never be used with a related current nature of injury code.

3) Use of sequela external cause codes for subsequent visits

Use a late effect external cause code for subsequent visits when a late effect of the initial injury is being treated. Do not use a late effect external cause code for subsequent visits for follow-up care (e.g., to assess healing, to receive rehabilitative therapy) of the injury when no late effect of the injury has been documented.

j. Terrorism Guidelines

1) Cause of injury identified by the Federal Government (FBI) as terrorism

When the cause of an injury is identified by the Federal Government (FBI) as terrorism, the first-listed external cause code should be a code from category Y38, Terrorism. The definition of terrorism employed by the FBI is found at the inclusion note at the beginning of category Y38. Use additional code for place of occurrence (Y92.-). More than one Y38 code may be assigned if the injury is the result of more than one mechanism of terrorism.

2) Cause of an injury is suspected to be the result of terrorism

When the cause of an injury is suspected to be the result of terrorism a code from category Y38 should not be assigned. Suspected cases should be classified as assault.

3) Code Y38.9, Terrorism, secondary effects

Assign code Y38.9, Terrorism, secondary effects, for conditions occurring subsequent to the terrorist event. This code should not be assigned for conditions that are due to the initial terrorist act.

It is acceptable to assign code Y38.9 with another code from Y38 if there is an injury due to the initial terrorist event and an injury that is a subsequent result of the terrorist event.

k. External cause status

A code from category Y99, External cause status, should be assigned whenever any other external cause code is assigned for an encounter, including an Activity code, except for the events noted below. Assign a code from category Y99, External cause status, to indicate the work status of the person at the time the event occurred. The status code indicates whether the event occurred during military activity, whether a non-military person was at work, whether an individual including a student or volunteer was involved in a non-work activity at the time of the causal event.

A code from Y99, External cause status, should be assigned, when applicable, with other external cause codes, such as transport accidents and falls. The external cause status codes are not applicable to poisonings, adverse effects, misadventures or late effects.

Do not assign a code from category Y99 if no other external cause codes (cause, activity) are applicable for the encounter.

An external cause status code is used only once, at the initial encounter for treatment. Only one code from Y99 should be recorded on a medical record.

Do not assign code Y99.9, Unspecified external cause status, if the status is not stated.

CHAPTER 20

EXTERNAL CAUSES OF MORBIDITY (V00-Y99)

Note: This chapter permits the classification of environmental events and circumstances as the cause of injury, and other adverse effects. Where a code from this section is applicable, it is intended that it shall be used secondary to a code from another chapter of the Classification indicating the nature of the condition. Most often, the condition will be classifiable to Chapter 19, Injury, poisoning and certain other consequences of external causes (S00-T88). Other conditions that may be stated to be due to external causes are classified in Chapters 1 to 18. For these conditions, codes from Chapter 20 should be used to provide additional information as to the cause of the condition.

This chapter contains the following blocks:

V00-X58	Accidents
V00-V99	Transport accidents
V00-V09	Pedestrian injured in transport accident
V10-V19	Pedal cycle rider injured in transport accident
V20-V29	Motorcycle rider injured in transport accident
V30-V39	Occupant of three-wheeled motor vehicle injured in transport accident
V40-V49	Car occupant injured in transport accident
V50-V59	Occupant of pick-up truck or van injured in transport accident
V60-V69	Occupant of heavy transport vehicle injured in transport accident
V70-V79	Bus occupant injured in transport accident
V80-V89	Other land transport accidents
V90-V94	Water transport accidents
V95-V97	Air and space transport accidents
V98-V99	Other and unspecified transport accidents
W00-X58	Other external causes of accidental injury
W00-W19	Slipping, tripping, stumbling and falls
W20-W49	Exposure to inanimate mechanical forces
W50-W64	Exposure to animate mechanical forces
W65-W74	Accidental non-transport drowning and submersion
W85-W99	Exposure to electric current, radiation and extreme ambient air temperature and pressure
X00-X08	Exposure to smoke, fire and flames
X10-X19	Contact with heat and hot substances
X30-X39	Exposure to forces of nature
X50	Overexertion and strenuous or repetitive movements
X52, X58	Accidental exposure to other specified factors
X71-X83	Intentional self-harm
X92-Y09	Assault
Y21-Y33	Event of undetermined intent
Y35-Y38	Legal intervention, operations of war, military operations, and terrorism
Y62-Y84	Complications of medical and surgical care
Y62-Y69	Misadventures to patients during surgical and medical care
Y70-Y82	Medical devices associated with adverse incidents in diagnostic and therapeutic use
Y83-Y84	Surgical and other medical procedures as the cause of abnormal reaction of the patient, or of later complication, without mention of misadventure at the time of the procedure
Y90-Y99	Supplementary factors related to causes of morbidity classified elsewhere

ACCIDENTS (V00-X58)

TRANSPORT ACCIDENTS (V00-V99)

Note: This section is structured in 12 groups. Those relating to land transport accidents (V00-V89) reflect the victim's mode of transport and are subdivided to identify the victim's 'counterpart' or the type of event. The vehicle of which the injured person is an occupant is identified in the first two characters since it is seen as the most important factor to identify for prevention purposes. A transport accident is one in which the vehicle involved must be moving or running or in use for transport purposes at the time of the accident.

Use additional code to identify:
Airbag injury (W22.1)
Type of street or road (Y92.4-)
Use of cellular telephone and other electronic equipment at the time of the transport accident (Y93.C-)

Excludes1 agricultural vehicles in stationary use or maintenance (W31.-)
assault by crashing of motor vehicle (Y03.-)
automobile or motor cycle in stationary use or maintenance - code to type of accident
crashing of motor vehicle, undetermined intent (Y32)
intentional self-harm by crashing of motor vehicle (X82)

Excludes2 transport accidents due to cataclysm (X34-X38)

Note: Definitions related to transport accidents:

(a) A transport accident (V00-V99) is any accident involving a device designed primarily for, or used at the time primarily for, conveying persons or good from one place to another.

(b) A public highway [trafficway] or street is the entire width between property lines (or other boundary lines) of land open to the public as a matter of right or custom for purposes of moving persons or property from one place to another. A roadway is that part of the public highway designed, improved and customarily used for vehicular traffic.

(c) A traffic accident is any vehicle accident occurring on the public highway [i.e., originating on, terminating on, or involving a vehicle partially on the highway]. A vehicle accident is assumed to have occurred on the public highway unless another place is specified, except in the case of accidents involving only off-road motor vehicles, which are classified as nontraffic accidents unless the contrary is stated.

(d) A nontraffic accident is any vehicle accident that occurs entirely in any place other than a public highway.

(e) A pedestrian is any person involved in an accident who was not at the time of the accident riding in or on a motor vehicle, railway train, streetcar or animal-drawn or other vehicle, or on a pedal cycle or animal. This includes, a person changing a tire, working on a parked car, or a person on foot. It also includes the user of a pedestrian conveyance such as a baby stroller, ice-skates, skis, sled, roller skates, a skateboard, nonmotorized or motorized wheelchair, motorized mobility scooter, or nonmotorized scooter.

(f) A driver is an occupant of a transport vehicle who is operating or intending to operate it.

(g) A passenger is any occupant of a transport vehicle other than the driver, except a person traveling on the outside of the vehicle.

(h) A person on the outside of a vehicle is any person being transported by a vehicle but not occupying the space normally reserved for the driver or passengers, or the space intended for the transport of property. This includes a person travelling on the bodywork, bumper, fender, roof, running board or step of a vehicle, as well as, hanging on the outside of the vehicle.

(i) A pedal cycle is any land transport vehicle operated solely by nonmotorized pedals including a bicycle or tricycle.

(j) A pedal cyclist is any person riding a pedal cycle or in a sidecar or trailer attached to a pedal cycle.

(k) A motorcycle is a two-wheeled motor vehicle with one or two riding saddles and sometimes with a third wheel for the support of a sidecar. The sidecar is considered part of the motorcycle. This includes a moped, motor scooter, or motorized bicycle.

(l) A motorcycle rider is any person riding a motorcycle or in a sidecar or trailer attached to the motorcycle.

(m) A three-wheeled motor vehicle is a motorized tricycle designed primarily for on-road use. This includes a motor-driven tricycle, a motorized rickshaw, or a three-wheeled motor car.

(n) A car [automobile] is a four-wheeled motor vehicle designed primarily for carrying up to 7 persons. A trailer being towed by the car is considered part of the car. It does not include a van or minivan—see definition (o)

(o) A pick-up truck or van is a four or six-wheeled motor vehicle designed for carrying passengers as well as property or cargo weighing less than the local limit for classification as a heavy goods vehicle, and not requiring a special driver's license. This includes a minivan and a sport-utility vehicle (SUV).

(p) A heavy transport vehicle is a motor vehicle designed primarily for carrying property, meeting local criteria for classification as a heavy goods vehicle in terms of weight and requiring a special driver's license.

(q) A bus (coach) is a motor vehicle designed or adapted primarily for carrying more than 10 passengers, and requiring a special driver's license.

(r) A railway train or railway vehicle is any device, with or without freight or passenger cars coupled to it, designed for traffic on a railway track. This includes subterranean (subways) or elevated trains.

(s) A streetcar is a device designed and used primarily for transporting passengers within a municipality, running on rails, usually subject to normal traffic control signals, and operated principally on a right-of-way that forms part of the roadway. This includes a tram or trolley that runs on rails. A trailer being towed by a streetcar is considered part of the streetcar.

(t) A special vehicle mainly used on industrial premises is a motor vehicle designed primarily for use within the buildings and premises of industrial or commercial establishments. This includes battery-powered airport passenger vehicles or baggage/mail trucks, forklifts, coal-cars in a coal mine, logging cars and trucks used in mines or quarries.

(u) A special vehicle mainly used in agriculture is a motor vehicle designed specifically for use in farming and agriculture (horticulture), to work the land, tend and harvest crops and transport materials on the farm. This includes harvesters, farm machinery and tractor and trailers.

(v) A special construction vehicle is a motor vehicle designed specifically for use on construction and demolition sites. This includes bulldozers, diggers, earth levellers, dump trucks, backhoes, front-end loaders, pavers, and mechanical shovels.

(w) A special all-terrain vehicle is a motor vehicle of special design to enable it to negotiate over rough or soft terrain, snow or sand. Examples of special design are high construction, special wheels and tires, tracks, and support on a cushion of air. This includes snow mobiles, all-terrain vehicles (ATV), and dune buggies. It does not include passenger vehicle designated as sport utility vehicles (SUV).

(x) A watercraft is any device designed for transporting passengers or goods on water. This includes motor or sail boats, ships, and hovercraft.

(y) An aircraft is any device for transporting passengers or goods in the air. This includes hot-air balloons, gliders, helicopters and airplanes.

(z) A military vehicle is any motorized vehicle operating on a public roadway owned by the military and being operated by a member of the military.

PEDESTRIAN INJURED IN TRANSPORT ACCIDENT (V00-V09)

Includes   person changing tire on transport vehicle
person examining engine of vehicle broken down in (on side of) road

Excludes1   fall due to non-transport collision with other person (W03)
pedestrian on foot falling (slipping) on ice and snow (W00.-)
struck or bumped by another person (W51)

● V00   **Pedestrian conveyance accident**

Use additional place of occurrence and activity external cause codes, if known (Y92.-, Y93.-)

Excludes1   collision with another person without fall (W51)
fall due to person on foot colliding with another person on foot (W03)
fall from non-moving wheelchair, nonmotorized scooter and motorized mobility scooter without collision (W05.-)
pedestrian (conveyance) collision with other land transport vehicle (V01-V09)
pedestrian on foot falling (slipping) on ice and snow (W00.-)

The appropriate 7th character is to be added to each code from category V00

A	initial encounter
D	subsequent encounter
S	sequela

● **V00.0**   **Pedestrian on foot injured in collision with pedestrian conveyance**

X ● **V00.01**   **Pedestrian on foot injured in collision with roller-skater**

X ● **V00.02**   **Pedestrian on foot injured in collision with skateboarder**

X ● **V00.09**   **Pedestrian on foot injured in collision with other pedestrian conveyance**

● **V00.1**   **Rolling-type pedestrian conveyance accident**

➡ **Excludes1**   accident with baby stroller (V00.82-)
accident with wheelchair (powered) (V00.81-)
accident with motorized mobility scooter (V00.83-)

● **V00.11**   **In-line roller-skate accident**

● **V00.111**   **Fall from in-line roller-skates**

● **V00.112**   **In-line roller-skater colliding with stationary object**

● **V00.118**   **Other in-line roller-skate accident**

Excludes1   roller-skater collision with other land transport vehicle (V01-V09 with 5th character 1)

● **V00.12**   **Non-in-line roller-skate accident**

● **V00.121**   **Fall from non-in-line roller-skates**

● **V00.122**   **Non-in-line roller-skater colliding with stationary object**

● **V00.128**   **Other non-in-line roller-skating accident**

Excludes1   roller-skater collision with other land transport vehicle (V01-V09 with 5th character 1)

- V00.13   **Skateboard accident**
  - V00.131   **Fall from skateboard**
  - V00.132   **Skateboarder colliding with stationary object**
  - V00.138   **Other skateboard accident**
    - **Excludes1**   skateboarder collision with other land transport vehicle (V01-V09 with 5th character 2)
- V00.14   **Scooter (nonmotorized) accident**
  - **Excludes1**   motor scooter accident (V20-V29)
  - V00.141   **Fall from scooter (nonmotorized)**
  - V00.142   **Scooter (nonmotorized) colliding with stationary object**
  - V00.148   **Other scooter (nonmotorized) accident**
    - **Excludes1**   scooter (non-motorized) collision with other land transport vehicle (V01-V09 with fifth character 9)
- V00.15   **Heelies accident**
  - Rolling shoe
  - Wheeled shoe
  - Wheelies accident
  - V00.151   **Fall from heelies**
  - V00.152   **Heelies colliding with stationary object**
  - V00.158   **Other heelies accident**
- V00.18   **Accident on other rolling-type pedestrian conveyance**
  - V00.181   **Fall from other rolling-type pedestrian conveyance**
  - V00.182   **Pedestrian on other rolling-type pedestrian conveyance colliding with stationary object**
  - V00.188   **Other accident on other rolling-type pedestrian conveyance**
- V00.2   **Gliding-type pedestrian conveyance accident**
  - V00.21   **Ice-skates accident**
    - V00.211   **Fall from ice-skates**
    - V00.212   **Ice-skater colliding with stationary object**
    - V00.218   **Other ice-skates accident**
      - **Excludes1**   ice-skater collision with other land transport vehicle (V01-V09 with 5th character 9)
  - V00.22   **Sled accident**
    - V00.221   **Fall from sled**
    - V00.222   **Sledder colliding with stationary object**
    - V00.228   **Other sled accident**
      - **Excludes1**   sled collision with other land transport vehicle (V01-V09 with 5th character 9)

- V00.28   **Other gliding-type pedestrian conveyance accident**
  - V00.281   **Fall from other gliding-type pedestrian conveyance**
  - V00.282   **Pedestrian on other gliding-type pedestrian conveyance colliding with stationary object**
  - V00.288   **Other accident on other gliding-type pedestrian conveyance**
    - **Excludes1**   gliding-type pedestrian conveyance collision with other land transport vehicle (V01-V09 with 5th character 9)
- V00.3   **Flat-bottomed pedestrian conveyance accident**
  - V00.31   **Snowboard accident**
    - V00.311   **Fall from snowboard**
    - V00.312   **Snowboarder colliding with stationary object**
    - V00.318   **Other snowboard accident**
      - **Excludes1**   snowboarder collision with other land transport vehicle (V01-V09 with 5th character 9)
  - V00.32   **Snow-ski accident**
    - V00.321   **Fall from snow-skis**
      - Coding Clinic: 2015, Q1, P12
    - V00.322   **Snow-skier colliding with stationary object**
    - V00.328   **Other snow-ski accident**
      - **Excludes1**   snow-skier collision with other land transport vehicle (V01-V09 with 5th character 9)
  - V00.38   **Other flat-bottomed pedestrian conveyance accident**
    - V00.381   **Fall from other flat-bottomed pedestrian conveyance**
    - V00.382   **Pedestrian on other flat-bottomed pedestrian conveyance colliding with stationary object**
    - V00.388   **Other accident on other flat-bottomed pedestrian conveyance**
- V00.8   **Accident on other pedestrian conveyance**
  - V00.81   **Accident with wheelchair (powered)**
    - V00.811   **Fall from moving wheelchair (powered)**
      - **Excludes1**   fall from non-moving wheelchair (W05.0)
    - V00.812   **Wheelchair (powered) colliding with stationary object**
    - V00.818   **Other accident with wheelchair (powered)**
  - V00.82   **Accident with baby stroller**
    - V00.821   **Fall from baby stroller**
    - V00.822   **Baby stroller colliding with stationary object**
    - V00.828   **Other accident with baby stroller**

● **V00.83**   **Accident with** motorized mobility scooter

  ● **V00.831**   **Fall from motorized mobility scooter**

    Excludes1   fall from non-moving motorized mobility scooter (W05.2)

  ● **V00.832**   **Motorized mobility scooter** colliding **with stationary object**

  ● **V00.838**   **Other accident with motorized mobility scooter**

● **V00.89**   **Accident on** other **pedestrian conveyance**

  ● **V00.891**   **Fall from other pedestrian conveyance**

  ● **V00.892**   **Pedestrian on other pedestrian conveyance** colliding **with stationary object**

  ● **V00.898**   **Other accident on other pedestrian conveyance**

    ⇒ **Excludes1**   other pedestrian (conveyance) collision with other land transport vehicle (V01-V09 with 5th character 9)

● **V01**   **Pedestrian injured in collision with pedal cycle**

The appropriate 7th character is to be added to each code from category V01

> A   initial encounter
> D   subsequent encounter
> S   sequela

  ● **V01.0**   **Pedestrian injured in collision with pedal cycle in** nontraffic **accident**

    X ● **V01.00**   **Pedestrian on** foot **injured in collision with pedal cycle in nontraffic accident**

      Pedestrian NOS injured in collision with pedal cycle in nontraffic accident

    X ● **V01.01**   **Pedestrian on** roller-skates **injured in collision with pedal cycle in nontraffic accident**

    X ● **V01.02**   **Pedestrian on** skateboard **injured in collision with pedal cycle in nontraffic accident**

    X ● **V01.09**   **Pedestrian with** other **conveyance injured in collision with pedal cycle in nontraffic accident**

      ⇒ Pedestrian with baby stroller injured in collision with pedal cycle in nontraffic accident

      Pedestrian in wheelchair (powered) injured in collision with pedal cycle in nontraffic accident

      Pedestrian in motorized mobility scooter injured in collision with pedal cycle in nontraffic accident

      Pedestrian on ice-skates injured in collision with pedal cycle in nontraffic accident

      Pedestrian on nonmotorized scooter injured in collision with pedal cycle in nontraffic accident

      Pedestrian on sled injured in collision with pedal cycle in nontraffic accident

      Pedestrian on snowboard injured in collision with pedal cycle in nontraffic accident

      Pedestrian on snow-skis injured in collision with pedal cycle in nontraffic accident

  ● **V01.1**   **Pedestrian injured in collision with pedal cycle in** traffic **accident**

    X ● **V01.10**   **Pedestrian on** foot **injured in collision with pedal cycle in traffic accident**

      Pedestrian NOS injured in collision with pedal cycle in traffic accident

    X ● **V01.11**   **Pedestrian on** roller-skates **injured in collision with pedal cycle in traffic accident**

    X ● **V01.12**   **Pedestrian on** skateboard **injured in collision with pedal cycle in traffic accident**

    X ● **V01.19**   **Pedestrian with** other **conveyance injured in collision with pedal cycle in traffic accident**

      ⇒ Pedestrian with baby stroller injured in collision with pedal cycle in traffic accident

      Pedestrian in wheelchair (powered) injured in collision with pedal cycle in traffic accident

      Pedestrian in motorized mobility scooter injured in collision with pedal cycle in traffic accident

      Pedestrian on ice-skates injured in collision with pedal cycle in traffic accident

      Pedestrian on nonmotorized scooter injured in collision with pedal cycle in traffic accident

      Pedestrian on sled injured in collision with pedal cycle in traffic accident

      Pedestrian on snowboard injured in collision with pedal cycle in traffic accident

      Pedestrian on snow-skis injured in collision with pedal cycle in traffic accident

  ● **V01.9**   **Pedestrian injured in collision with pedal cycle, unspecified whether traffic or nontraffic accident**

    X ● **V01.90**   **Pedestrian on** foot **injured in collision with pedal cycle, unspecified whether traffic or nontraffic accident**

      Pedestrian NOS injured in collision with pedal cycle, unspecified whether traffic or nontraffic accident

    X ● **V01.91**   **Pedestrian on** roller-skates **injured in collision with pedal cycle, unspecified whether traffic or nontraffic accident**

    X ● **V01.92**   **Pedestrian on** skateboard **injured in collision with pedal cycle, unspecified whether traffic or nontraffic accident**

    X ● **V01.99**   **Pedestrian with** other **conveyance injured in collision with pedal cycle, unspecified whether traffic or nontraffic accident**

      ⇒ Pedestrian with baby stroller injured in collision with pedal cycle, unspecified whether traffic or nontraffic accident

      Pedestrian in wheelchair (powered) injured in collision with pedal cycle, unspecified whether traffic or nontraffic accident

      Pedestrian in motorized mobility scooter injured in collision with pedal cycle, unspecified whether traffic or nontraffic accident

      Pedestrian on ice-skates injured in collision with pedal cycle unspecified, whether traffic or nontraffic accident

      Pedestrian on nonmotorized scooter injured in collision with pedal cycle, unspecified whether traffic or nontraffic accident

      Pedestrian on sled injured in collision with pedal cycle unspecified, whether traffic or nontraffic accident

      Pedestrian on snowboard injured in collision with pedal cycle, unspecified whether traffic or nontraffic accident

      Pedestrian on snow-skis injured in collision with pedal cycle, unspecified whether traffic or nontraffic accident

▶ New   ⇒ Revised   ~~deleted~~ Deleted   Excludes 1   Excludes 2   Includes   Use additional   Code first   Code also   Key words

OGCR Official Guidelines   X Assign placeholder X   ● Use Additional Character(s)   ▷ Manifestation Code   **Coding Clinic**

● **V02 Pedestrian injured in collision with two- or three-wheeled motor vehicle**

The appropriate 7th character is to be added to each code from category V02

> A   initial encounter
> D   subsequent encounter
> S   sequela

● **V02.0 Pedestrian injured in collision with two- or three-wheeled motor vehicle in nontraffic accident**

X ● **V02.00 Pedestrian on foot injured in collision with two- or three-wheeled motor vehicle in nontraffic accident**

Pedestrian NOS injured in collision with two- or three-wheeled motor vehicle in nontraffic accident

X ● **V02.01 Pedestrian on roller-skates injured in collision with two- or three-wheeled motor vehicle in nontraffic accident**

X ● **V02.02 Pedestrian on skateboard injured in collision with two- or three-wheeled motor vehicle in nontraffic accident**

X ● **V02.09 Pedestrian with other conveyance injured in collision with two- or three-wheeled motor vehicle in nontraffic accident**

➠Pedestrian with baby stroller injured in collision with two- or three-wheeled motor vehicle in nontraffic accident

Pedestrian on ice-skates injured in collision with two- or three-wheeled motor vehicle in nontraffic accident

Pedestrian in wheelchair (powered) injured in collision with two- or three-wheeled motor vehicle in nontraffic accident

Pedestrian in motorized mobility scooter injured in collision with two- or three-wheeled motor vehicle in nontraffic accident

Pedestrian on nonmotorized scooter injured in collision with two- or three-wheeled motor vehicle in nontraffic accident

Pedestrian on sled injured in collision with two- or three-wheeled motor vehicle in nontraffic accident

Pedestrian on snowboard injured in collision with two- or three-wheeled motor vehicle in nontraffic accident

Pedestrian on snow-skis injured in collision with two- or three-wheeled motor vehicle in nontraffic accident

● **V02.1 Pedestrian injured in collision with two- or three-wheeled motor vehicle in traffic accident**

X ● **V02.10 Pedestrian on foot injured in collision with two- or three-wheeled motor vehicle in traffic accident**

Pedestrian NOS injured in collision with two- or three-wheeled motor vehicle in traffic accident

X ● **V02.11 Pedestrian on roller-skates injured in collision with two- or three-wheeled motor vehicle in traffic accident**

X ● **V02.12 Pedestrian on skateboard injured in collision with two- or three-wheeled motor vehicle in traffic accident**

X ● **V02.19 Pedestrian with other conveyance injured in collision with two- or three-wheeled motor vehicle in traffic accident**

➠Pedestrian with baby stroller injured in collision with two- or three-wheeled motor vehicle in traffic accident

Pedestrian in wheelchair (powered) injured in collision with two- or three-wheeled motor vehicle in traffic accident

Pedestrian in motorized mobility scooter injured in collision with two- or three-wheeled motor vehicle in traffic accident

Pedestrian on ice-skates injured in collision with two- or three-wheeled motor vehicle in traffic accident

Pedestrian on nonmotorized scooter injured in collision with two- or three-wheeled motor vehicle in traffic accident

Pedestrian on sled injured in collision with two- or three-wheeled motor vehicle in traffic accident

Pedestrian on snowboard injured in collision with two- or three-wheeled motor vehicle in traffic accident

Pedestrian on snow-skis injured in collision with two- or three-wheeled motor vehicle in traffic accident

● **V02.9 Pedestrian injured in collision with two- or three-wheeled motor vehicle, unspecified whether traffic or nontraffic accident**

X ● **V02.90 Pedestrian on foot injured in collision with two- or three-wheeled motor vehicle, unspecified whether traffic or nontraffic accident**

Pedestrian NOS injured in collision with two- or three-wheeled motor vehicle, unspecified whether traffic or nontraffic accident

X ● **V02.91 Pedestrian on roller-skates injured in collision with two- or three-wheeled motor vehicle, unspecified whether traffic or nontraffic accident**

X ● **V02.92 Pedestrian on skateboard injured in collision with two- or three-wheeled motor vehicle, unspecified whether traffic or nontraffic accident**

X ● **V02.99 Pedestrian with other conveyance injured in collision with two- or three-wheeled motor vehicle, unspecified whether traffic or nontraffic accident**
➧ Pedestrian with baby stroller injured in collision with two- or three-wheeled motor vehicle, unspecified whether traffic or nontraffic accident
Pedestrian in wheelchair (powered) injured in collision with two- or three-wheeled motor vehicle, unspecified whether traffic or nontraffic accident
Pedestrian in motorized mobility scooter injured in collision with two- or three-wheeled motor vehicle, unspecified whether traffic or nontraffic accident
Pedestrian on ice-skates injured in collision with two- or three-wheeled motor vehicle, unspecified whether traffic or nontraffic accident
Pedestrian on nonmotorized scooter injured in collision with two- or three-wheeled motor vehicle, unspecified whether traffic or nontraffic accident
Pedestrian on sled injured in collision with two- or three-wheeled motor vehicle, unspecified whether traffic or nontraffic accident
Pedestrian on snowboard injured in collision with two- or three-wheeled motor vehicle, unspecified whether traffic or nontraffic accident
Pedestrian on snow-skis injured in collision with two- or three-wheeled motor vehicle, unspecified whether traffic or nontraffic accident

● **V03 Pedestrian injured in collision with car, pick-up truck or van**
The appropriate 7th character is to be added to each code from category V03

A	initial encounter
D	subsequent encounter
S	sequela

● **V03.0 Pedestrian injured in collision with car, pick-up truck or van in nontraffic accident**

X ● **V03.00 Pedestrian on foot injured in collision with car, pick-up truck or van in nontraffic accident**
Pedestrian NOS injured in collision with car, pick-up truck or van in nontraffic accident

X ● **V03.01 Pedestrian on roller-skates injured in collision with car, pick-up truck or van in nontraffic accident**

X ● **V03.02 Pedestrian on skateboard injured in collision with car, pick-up truck or van in nontraffic accident**

X ● **V03.09 Pedestrian with other conveyance injured in collision with car, pick-up truck or van in nontraffic accident**
➧ Pedestrian with baby stroller injured in collision with car, pick-up truck or van in nontraffic accident
Pedestrian in wheelchair (powered) injured in collision with car, pick-up truck or van in nontraffic accident
Pedestrian in motorized mobility scooter injured in collision with car, pick-up truck or van in nontraffic accident
Pedestrian on ice-skates injured in collision with car, pick-up truck or van in nontraffic accident
Pedestrian on nonmotorized scooter injured in collision with car, pick-up truck or van in nontraffic accident
Pedestrian on sled injured in collision with car, pick-up truck or van in nontraffic accident
Pedestrian on snowboard injured in collision with car, pick-up truck or van in nontraffic accident
Pedestrian on snow-skis injured in collision with car, pick-up truck or van in nontraffic accident

● **V03.1 Pedestrian injured in collision with car, pick-up truck or van in traffic accident**

X ● **V03.10 Pedestrian on foot injured in collision with car, pick-up truck or van in traffic accident**
Pedestrian NOS injured in collision with car, pick-up truck or van in traffic accident

X ● **V03.11 Pedestrian on roller-skates injured in collision with car, pick-up truck or van in traffic accident**

X ● **V03.12 Pedestrian on skateboard injured in collision with car, pick-up truck or van in traffic accident**

X ● **V03.19 Pedestrian with other conveyance injured in collision with car, pick-up truck or van in traffic accident**
➧ Pedestrian with baby stroller injured in collision with car, pick-up truck or van in traffic accident
Pedestrian in wheelchair (powered) injured in collision with car, pick-up truck or van in traffic accident
Pedestrian in motorized mobility scooter injured in collision with car, pick-up truck or van in traffic accident
Pedestrian on ice-skates injured in collision with car, pick-up truck or van in traffic accident
Pedestrian on nonmotorized scooter injured in collision with car, pick-up truck or van in traffic accident
Pedestrian on sled injured in collision with car, pick-up truck or van in traffic accident
Pedestrian on snowboard injured in collision with car, pick-up truck or van in traffic accident
Pedestrian on snow-skis injured in collision with car, pick-up truck or van in traffic accident

▶ New ➧ Revised ~~deleted~~ Deleted Excludes 1 Excludes 2 Includes Use additional Code first Code also Key words
OGCR Official Guidelines X Assign placeholder X ● Use Additional Character(s) ▸ Manifestation Code Coding Clinic

● V03.9 **Pedestrian injured in collision with car, pick-up truck or van, unspecified whether traffic or nontraffic accident**

  X ● V03.90 **Pedestrian on foot injured in collision with car, pick-up truck or van, unspecified whether traffic or nontraffic accident**

      Pedestrian NOS injured in collision with car, pick-up truck or van, unspecified whether traffic or nontraffic accident

  X ● V03.91 **Pedestrian on roller-skates injured in collision with car, pick-up truck or van, unspecified whether traffic or nontraffic accident**

  X ● V03.92 **Pedestrian on skateboard injured in collision with car, pick-up truck or van, unspecified whether traffic or nontraffic accident**

  X ● V03.99 **Pedestrian with other conveyance injured in collision with car, pick-up truck or van, unspecified whether traffic or nontraffic accident**

    ➠ Pedestrian with baby stroller injured in collision with car, pick-up truck or van, unspecified whether traffic or nontraffic accident

      Pedestrian in wheelchair (powered) injured in collision with car, pick-up truck or van, unspecified whether traffic or nontraffic accident

      Pedestrian in motorized mobility scooter injured in collision with car, pick-up truck or van, unspecified whether traffic or nontraffic accident

      Pedestrian on ice-skates injured in collision with car, pick-up truck or van, unspecified whether traffic or nontraffic accident

      Pedestrian on nonmotorized scooter injured in collision with car, pick-up truck or van, unspecified whether traffic or nontraffic accident

      Pedestrian on sled injured in collision with car, pick-up truck or van in nontraffic accident

      Pedestrian on snowboard injured in collision with car, pick-up truck or van, unspecified whether traffic or nontraffic accident

      Pedestrian on snow-skis injured in collision with car, pick-up truck or van, unspecified whether traffic or nontraffic accident

● V04 **Pedestrian injured in collision with heavy transport vehicle or bus**

   Excludes1   pedestrian injured in collision with military vehicle (V09.01, V09.21)

  The appropriate 7th character is to be added to each code from category V04

A	initial encounter
D	subsequent encounter
S	sequela

● V04.0 **Pedestrian injured in collision with heavy transport vehicle or bus in nontraffic accident**

  X ● V04.00 **Pedestrian on foot injured in collision with heavy transport vehicle or bus in nontraffic accident**

      Pedestrian NOS injured in collision with heavy transport vehicle or bus in nontraffic accident

  X ● V04.01 **Pedestrian on roller-skates injured in collision with heavy transport vehicle or bus in nontraffic accident**

  X ● V04.02 **Pedestrian on skateboard injured in collision with heavy transport vehicle or bus in nontraffic accident**

  X ● V04.09 **Pedestrian with other conveyance injured in collision with heavy transport vehicle or bus in nontraffic accident**

    ➠ Pedestrian with baby stroller injured in collision with heavy transport vehicle or bus in nontraffic accident

      Pedestrian in wheelchair (powered) injured in collision with heavy transport vehicle or bus in nontraffic accident

      Pedestrian in motorized mobility scooter injured in collision with heavy transport vehicle or bus in nontraffic accident

      Pedestrian on ice-skates injured in collision with heavy transport vehicle or bus in nontraffic accident

      Pedestrian on nonmotorized scooter injured in collision with heavy transport vehicle or bus in nontraffic accident

      Pedestrian on sled injured in collision with heavy transport vehicle or bus in nontraffic accident

      Pedestrian on snowboard injured in collision with heavy transport vehicle or bus in nontraffic accident

      Pedestrian on snow-skis injured in collision with heavy transport vehicle or bus in nontraffic accident

● V04.1 **Pedestrian injured in collision with heavy transport vehicle or bus in traffic accident**

  X ● V04.10 **Pedestrian on foot injured in collision with heavy transport vehicle or bus in traffic accident**

      Pedestrian NOS injured in collision with heavy transport vehicle or bus in traffic accident

  X ● V04.11 **Pedestrian on roller-skates injured in collision with heavy transport vehicle or bus in traffic accident**

  X ● V04.12 **Pedestrian on skateboard injured in collision with heavy transport vehicle or bus in traffic accident**

  X ● V04.19 **Pedestrian with other conveyance injured in collision with heavy transport vehicle or bus in traffic accident**

    ➠ Pedestrian with baby stroller injured in collision with heavy transport vehicle or bus in traffic accident

      Pedestrian in wheelchair (powered) injured in collision with heavy transport vehicle or bus in traffic accident

      Pedestrian in motorized mobility scooter injured in collision with heavy transport vehicle or bus in traffic accident

      Pedestrian on ice-skates injured in collision with heavy transport vehicle or bus in traffic accident

      Pedestrian on nonmotorized scooter injured in collision with heavy transport vehicle or bus in traffic accident

      Pedestrian on sled injured in collision with heavy transport vehicle or bus in traffic accident

      Pedestrian on snowboard injured in collision with heavy transport vehicle or bus in traffic accident

      Pedestrian on snow-skis injured in collision with heavy transport vehicle or bus in traffic accident

CHAPTER 20 (V01-Y99)

● **V04.9** **Pedestrian injured in collision with heavy transport vehicle or bus, unspecified whether traffic or nontraffic accident**

  X ● **V04.90** **Pedestrian on foot injured in collision with heavy transport vehicle or bus, unspecified whether traffic or nontraffic accident**

        Pedestrian NOS injured in collision with heavy transport vehicle or bus, unspecified whether traffic or nontraffic accident

  X ● **V04.91** **Pedestrian on roller-skates injured in collision with heavy transport vehicle or bus, unspecified whether traffic or nontraffic accident**

  X ● **V04.92** **Pedestrian on skateboard injured in collision with heavy transport vehicle or bus, unspecified whether traffic or nontraffic accident**

  X ● **V04.99** **Pedestrian with other conveyance injured in collision with heavy transport vehicle or bus, unspecified whether traffic or nontraffic accident**

    ➠Pedestrian with baby stroller injured in collision with heavy transport vehicle or bus, unspecified whether traffic or nontraffic accident

    Pedestrian in wheelchair (powered) injured in collision with heavy transport vehicle or bus, unspecified whether traffic or nontraffic accident

    Pedestrian in motorized mobility scooter injured in collision with heavy transport vehicle or bus, unspecified whether traffic or nontraffic accident

    Pedestrian on ice-skates injured in collision with heavy transport vehicle or bus, unspecified whether traffic or nontraffic accident

    Pedestrian on nonmotorized scooter injured in collision with heavy transport vehicle or bus, unspecified whether traffic or nontraffic accident

    Pedestrian on sled injured in collision with heavy transport vehicle or bus, unspecified whether traffic or nontraffic accident

    Pedestrian on snowboard injured in collision with heavy transport vehicle or bus, unspecified whether traffic or nontraffic accident

    Pedestrian on snow-skis injured in collision with heavy transport vehicle or bus, unspecified whether traffic or nontraffic accident

● **V05** **Pedestrian injured in collision with railway train or railway vehicle**

  The appropriate 7th character is to be added to each code from category V05

A	initial encounter
D	subsequent encounter
S	sequela

● **V05.0** **Pedestrian injured in collision with railway train or railway vehicle in nontraffic accident**

  X ● **V05.00** **Pedestrian on foot injured in collision with railway train or railway vehicle in nontraffic accident**

        Pedestrian NOS injured in collision with railway train or railway vehicle in nontraffic accident

  X ● **V05.01** **Pedestrian on roller-skates injured in collision with railway train or railway vehicle in nontraffic accident**

  X ● **V05.02** **Pedestrian on skateboard injured in collision with railway train or railway vehicle in nontraffic accident**

  X ● **V05.09** **Pedestrian with other conveyance injured in collision with railway train or railway vehicle in nontraffic accident**

    ➠Pedestrian with baby stroller injured in collision with railway train or railway vehicle in nontraffic accident

    Pedestrian in wheelchair (powered) injured in collision with railway train or railway vehicle in nontraffic accident

    Pedestrian in motorized mobility scooter injured in collision with railway train or railway vehicle in nontraffic accident

    Pedestrian on ice-skates injured in collision with railway train or railway vehicle in nontraffic accident

    Pedestrian on nonmotorized scooter injured in collision with railway train or railway vehicle in nontraffic accident

    Pedestrian on sled injured in collision with railway train or railway vehicle in nontraffic accident

    Pedestrian on snowboard injured in collision with railway train or railway vehicle in nontraffic accident

    Pedestrian on snow-skis injured in collision with railway train or railway vehicle in nontraffic accident

● **V05.1** **Pedestrian injured in collision with railway train or railway vehicle in traffic accident**

  X ● **V05.10** **Pedestrian on foot injured in collision with railway train or railway vehicle in traffic accident**

        Pedestrian NOS injured in collision with railway train or railway vehicle in traffic accident

  X ● **V05.11** **Pedestrian on roller-skates injured in collision with railway train or railway vehicle in traffic accident**

  X ● **V05.12** **Pedestrian on skateboard injured in collision with railway train or railway vehicle in traffic accident**

  X ● **V05.19** **Pedestrian with other conveyance injured in collision with railway train or railway vehicle in traffic accident**

    ➠Pedestrian with baby stroller injured in collision with railway train or railway vehicle in traffic accident

    Pedestrian in wheelchair (powered) injured in collision with railway train or railway vehicle in traffic accident

    Pedestrian in motorized mobility scooter injured in collision with railway train or railway vehicle in traffic accident

    Pedestrian on ice-skates injured in collision with railway train or railway vehicle in traffic accident

    Pedestrian on nonmotorized scooter injured in collision with railway train or railway vehicle in traffic accident

    Pedestrian on sled injured in collision with railway train or railway vehicle in traffic accident

    Pedestrian on snowboard injured in collision with railway train or railway vehicle in traffic accident

    Pedestrian on snow-skis injured in collision with railway train or railway vehicle in traffic accident

● **V05.9**   **Pedestrian injured in collision with railway train or railway vehicle, unspecified whether traffic or nontraffic accident**

    X ● **V05.90**   **Pedestrian on foot injured in collision with railway train or railway vehicle, unspecified whether traffic or nontraffic accident**
       Pedestrian NOS injured in collision with railway train or railway vehicle, unspecified whether traffic or nontraffic accident

    X ● **V05.91**   **Pedestrian on roller-skates injured in collision with railway train or railway vehicle, unspecified whether traffic or nontraffic accident**

    X ● **V05.92**   **Pedestrian on skateboard injured in collision with railway train or railway vehicle, unspecified whether traffic or nontraffic accident**

    X ● **V05.99**   **Pedestrian with other conveyance injured in collision with railway train or railway vehicle, unspecified whether traffic or nontraffic accident**
       ➡ Pedestrian with baby stroller injured in collision with railway train or railway vehicle, unspecified whether traffic or nontraffic
       Pedestrian in wheelchair (powered) injured in collision with railway train or railway vehicle, unspecified whether traffic or nontraffic
       Pedestrian in motorized mobility scooter injured in collision with railway train or railway vehicle, unspecified whether traffic or nontraffic
       Pedestrian on ice-skates injured in collision with railway train or railway vehicle, unspecified whether traffic or nontraffic
       Pedestrian on nonmotorized scooter injured in collision with railway train or railway vehicle, unspecified whether traffic or nontraffic
       Pedestrian on sled injured in collision with railway train or railway vehicle, unspecified whether traffic or nontraffic
       Pedestrian on snowboard injured in collision with railway train or railway vehicle, unspecified whether traffic or nontraffic
       Pedestrian on snow-skis injured in collision with railway train or railway vehicle, unspecified whether traffic or nontraffic

● **V06**   **Pedestrian injured in collision with other nonmotor vehicle**

    | **Includes** | collision with animal-drawn vehicle, animal being ridden, nonpowered streetcar |

    | **Excludes1** | pedestrian injured in collision with pedestrian conveyance (V00.0-) |

    The appropriate 7th character is to be added to each code from category V06

    | A | initial encounter |
    | D | subsequent encounter |
    | S | sequela |

● **V06.0**   **Pedestrian injured in collision with other nonmotor vehicle in nontraffic accident**

    X ● **V06.00**   **Pedestrian on foot injured in collision with other nonmotor vehicle in nontraffic accident**
       Pedestrian NOS injured in collision with other nonmotor vehicle in nontraffic accident

    X ● **V06.01**   **Pedestrian on roller-skates injured in collision with other nonmotor vehicle in nontraffic accident**

    X ● **V06.02**   **Pedestrian on skateboard injured in collision with other nonmotor vehicle in nontraffic accident**

    X ● **V06.09**   **Pedestrian with other conveyance injured in collision with other nonmotor vehicle in nontraffic accident**
       ➡ Pedestrian with baby stroller injured in collision with other nonmotor vehicle in nontraffic accident
       Pedestrian in wheelchair (powered) injured in collision with other nonmotor vehicle in nontraffic accident
       Pedestrian in motorized mobility scooter injured in collision with other nonmotor vehicle in nontraffic accident
       Pedestrian on ice-skates injured in collision with other nonmotor vehicle in nontraffic accident
       Pedestrian on nonmotorized scooter injured in collision with other nonmotor vehicle in nontraffic accident
       Pedestrian on sled injured in collision with other nonmotor vehicle in nontraffic accident
       Pedestrian on snowboard injured in collision with other nonmotor vehicle in nontraffic accident
       Pedestrian on snow-skis injured in collision with other nonmotor vehicle in nontraffic accident

● **V06.1**   **Pedestrian injured in collision with other nonmotor vehicle in traffic accident**

    X ● **V06.10**   **Pedestrian on foot injured in collision with other nonmotor vehicle in traffic accident**
       Pedestrian NOS injured in collision with other nonmotor vehicle in traffic accident

    X ● **V06.11**   **Pedestrian on roller-skates injured in collision with other nonmotor vehicle in traffic accident**

    X ● **V06.12**   **Pedestrian on skateboard injured in collision with other nonmotor vehicle in traffic accident**

    X ● **V06.19**   **Pedestrian with other conveyance injured in collision with other nonmotor vehicle in traffic accident**
       ➡ Pedestrian with baby stroller injured in collision with other nonmotor vehicle in nontraffic accident
       Pedestrian in wheelchair (powered) injured in collision with other nonmotor vehicle in traffic accident
       Pedestrian in motorized mobility scooter injured in collision with other nonmotor vehicle in traffic accident
       Pedestrian on ice-skates injured in collision with other nonmotor vehicle in traffic accident
       Pedestrian on nonmotorized scooter injured in collision with other nonmotor vehicle in traffic accident
       Pedestrian on sled injured in collision with other nonmotor vehicle in traffic accident
       Pedestrian on snowboard injured in collision with other nonmotor vehicle in traffic accident
       Pedestrian on snow-skis injured in collision with other nonmotor vehicle in traffic accident

● **V06.9**   **Pedestrian injured in collision with other nonmotor vehicle, unspecified whether traffic or nontraffic accident**

    X ● **V06.90**   **Pedestrian on foot injured in collision with other nonmotor vehicle, unspecified whether traffic or nontraffic accident**
       Pedestrian NOS injured in collision with other nonmotor vehicle, unspecified whether traffic or nontraffic accident

    X ● **V06.91**   **Pedestrian on roller-skates injured in collision with other nonmotor vehicle, unspecified whether traffic or nontraffic accident**

CHAPTER 20 (V01-Y99)

X● **V06.92** **Pedestrian on** skateboard **injured in collision with other nonmotor vehicle, unspecified whether traffic or nontraffic accident**

X● **V06.99** **Pedestrian with** other conveyance **injured in collision with other nonmotor vehicle, unspecified whether traffic or nontraffic accident**

➡ Pedestrian with baby stroller injured in collision with other nonmotor vehicle, unspecified whether traffic or nontraffic accident

Pedestrian in wheelchair (powered) injured in collision with other nonmotor vehicle, unspecified whether traffic or nontraffic accident

Pedestrian in motorized mobility scooter injured in collision with other nonmotor vehicle, unspecified whether traffic or nontraffic accident

Pedestrian on ice-skates injured in collision with other nonmotor vehicle, unspecified whether traffic or nontraffic accident

Pedestrian on nonmotorized scooter injured in collision with other nonmotor vehicle, unspecified whether traffic or nontraffic accident

Pedestrian on sled injured in collision with other nonmotor vehicle, unspecified whether traffic or nontraffic accident

Pedestrian on snowboard injured in collision with other nonmotor vehicle, unspecified whether traffic or nontraffic accident

Pedestrian on snow-skis injured in collision with other nonmotor vehicle, unspecified whether traffic or nontraffic accident

● **V09** **Pedestrian injured in other and unspecified transport accidents**

The appropriate 7th character is to be added to each code from category V09

A	initial encounter
D	subsequent encounter
S	sequela

● **V09.0** **Pedestrian injured in** nontraffic accident **involving other and unspecified motor vehicles**

X● **V09.00** **Pedestrian injured in nontraffic accident involving** unspecified **motor vehicles**

X● **V09.01** **Pedestrian injured in nontraffic accident involving** military **vehicle**

X● **V09.09** **Pedestrian injured in nontraffic accident involving** other **motor vehicles**

Pedestrian injured in nontraffic accident by special vehicle

X● **V09.1** **Pedestrian injured in** unspecified nontraffic accident

● **V09.2** **Pedestrian injured in** traffic accident **involving other and unspecified motor vehicles**

X● **V09.20** **Pedestrian injured in traffic accident involving** unspecified **motor vehicles**

X● **V09.21** **Pedestrian injured in traffic accident involving** military **vehicle**

X● **V09.29** **Pedestrian injured in traffic accident involving** other **motor vehicles**

X● **V09.3** **Pedestrian injured in** unspecified traffic accident

X● **V09.9** **Pedestrian injured in** unspecified transport accident

PEDAL CYCLE RIDER INJURED IN TRANSPORT ACCIDENT (V10-V19)

Includes	any non-motorized vehicle, excluding an animal-drawn vehicle, or a sidecar or trailer attached to the pedal cycle
Excludes2	rupture of pedal cycle tire (W37.0)

● **V10** **Pedal cycle rider injured in collision with pedestrian or animal**

Excludes1	pedal cycle rider collision with animal-drawn vehicle or animal being ridden (V16.-)

The appropriate 7th character is to be added to each code from category V10

A	initial encounter
D	subsequent encounter
S	sequela

X● **V10.0** **Pedal cycle** driver **injured in collision with pedestrian or animal in** nontraffic accident

X● **V10.1** **Pedal cycle** passenger **injured in collision with pedestrian or animal in** nontraffic accident

X● **V10.2** Unspecified **pedal cyclist injured in collision with pedestrian or animal in** nontraffic accident

X● **V10.3** **Person** boarding or alighting **a pedal cycle injured in collision with pedestrian or animal**

X● **V10.4** **Pedal cycle** driver **injured in collision with pedestrian or animal in** traffic accident

X● **V10.5** **Pedal cycle** passenger **injured in collision with pedestrian or animal in** traffic accident

X● **V10.9** Unspecified **pedal cyclist injured in collision with pedestrian or animal in** traffic accident

● **V11** **Pedal cycle rider injured in collision with other pedal cycle**

The appropriate 7th character is to be added to each code from category V11

A	initial encounter
D	subsequent encounter
S	sequela

X● **V11.0** **Pedal cycle** driver **injured in collision with other pedal cycle in** nontraffic accident

X● **V11.1** **Pedal cycle** passenger **injured in collision with other pedal cycle in** nontraffic accident

X● **V11.2** Unspecified **pedal cyclist injured in collision with other pedal cycle in** nontraffic accident

X● **V11.3** **Person** boarding or alighting **a pedal cycle injured in collision with other pedal cycle**

X● **V11.4** **Pedal cycle** driver **injured in collision with other pedal cycle in** traffic accident

X● **V11.5** **Pedal cycle** passenger **injured in collision with other pedal cycle in** traffic accident

X● **V11.9** Unspecified **pedal cyclist injured in collision with other pedal cycle in** traffic accident

▶ New   ➡ Revised   ~~deleted~~ Deleted   Excludes 1   Excludes 2   Includes   Use additional   Code first   Code also   Key words

OGCR Official Guidelines   X Assign placeholder X   ● Use Additional Character(s)   ▶ Manifestation Code   **Coding Clinic**

● **V12   Pedal cycle rider injured in collision with two- or three-wheeled motor vehicle**

> The appropriate 7th character is to be added to each code from category V12

> | A | initial encounter |
> |---|---|
> | D | subsequent encounter |
> | S | sequela |

X ● **V12.0**   Pedal cycle **driver** injured in collision with two- or three-wheeled motor vehicle in **nontraffic accident**

X ● **V12.1**   Pedal cycle **passenger** injured in collision with two- or three-wheeled motor vehicle in **nontraffic accident**

X ● **V12.2**   **Unspecified** pedal cyclist injured in collision with two- or three-wheeled motor vehicle in **nontraffic accident**

X ● **V12.3**   Person **boarding or alighting** a pedal cycle injured in collision with two- or three-wheeled motor vehicle

X ● **V12.4**   Pedal cycle **driver** injured in collision with two- or three-wheeled motor vehicle in **traffic accident**

X ● **V12.5**   Pedal cycle **passenger** injured in collision with two- or three-wheeled motor vehicle in **traffic accident**

X ● **V12.9**   **Unspecified** pedal cyclist injured in collision with two- or three-wheeled motor vehicle in **traffic accident**

● **V13   Pedal cycle rider injured in collision with car, pick-up truck or van**

> The appropriate 7th character is to be added to each code from category V13

> | A | initial encounter |
> |---|---|
> | D | subsequent encounter |
> | S | sequela |

X ● **V13.0**   Pedal cycle **driver** injured in collision with car, pick-up truck or van in **nontraffic accident**

X ● **V13.1**   Pedal cycle **passenger** injured in collision with car, pick-up truck or van in **nontraffic accident**

X ● **V13.2**   **Unspecified** pedal cyclist injured in collision with car, pick-up truck or van in **nontraffic accident**

X ● **V13.3**   Person **boarding or alighting** a pedal cycle injured in collision with car, pick-up truck or van

X ● **V13.4**   Pedal cycle **driver** injured in collision with car, pick-up truck or van in **traffic accident**

X ● **V13.5**   Pedal cycle **passenger** injured in collision with car, pick-up truck or van in **traffic accident**

X ● **V13.9**   **Unspecified** pedal cyclist injured in collision with car, pick-up truck or van in **traffic accident**

● **V14   Pedal cycle rider injured in collision with heavy transport vehicle or bus**

> **Excludes1**   pedal cycle rider injured in collision with military vehicle (V19.81)

> The appropriate 7th character is to be added to each code from category V14

> | A | initial encounter |
> |---|---|
> | D | subsequent encounter |
> | S | sequela |

X ● **V14.0**   Pedal cycle **driver** injured in collision with heavy transport vehicle or bus in **nontraffic accident**

X ● **V14.1**   Pedal cycle **passenger** injured in collision with heavy transport vehicle or bus in **nontraffic accident**

X ● **V14.2**   **Unspecified** pedal cyclist injured in collision with heavy transport vehicle or bus in **nontraffic accident**

X ● **V14.3**   Person **boarding or alighting** a pedal cycle injured in collision with heavy transport vehicle or bus

X ● **V14.4**   Pedal cycle **driver** injured in collision with heavy transport vehicle or bus in **traffic accident**

X ● **V14.5**   Pedal cycle **passenger** injured in collision with heavy transport vehicle or bus in **traffic accident**

X ● **V14.9**   **Unspecified** pedal cyclist injured in collision with heavy transport vehicle or bus in **traffic accident**

● **V15   Pedal cycle rider injured in collision with railway train or railway vehicle**

> The appropriate 7th character is to be added to each code from category V15

> | A | initial encounter |
> |---|---|
> | D | subsequent encounter |
> | S | sequela |

X ● **V15.0**   Pedal cycle **driver** injured in collision with railway train or railway vehicle in **nontraffic accident**

X ● **V15.1**   Pedal cycle **passenger** injured in collision with railway train or railway vehicle in **nontraffic accident**

X ● **V15.2**   **Unspecified** pedal cyclist injured in collision with railway train or railway vehicle in **nontraffic accident**

X ● **V15.3**   Person **boarding or alighting** a pedal cycle injured in collision with railway train or railway vehicle

X ● **V15.4**   Pedal cycle **driver** injured in collision with railway train or railway vehicle in **traffic accident**

X ● **V15.5**   Pedal cycle **passenger** injured in collision with railway train or railway vehicle in **traffic accident**

X ● **V15.9**   **Unspecified** pedal cyclist injured in collision with railway train or railway vehicle in **traffic accident**

● **V16   Pedal cycle rider injured in collision with other nonmotor vehicle**

> **Includes**   collision with animal-drawn vehicle, animal being ridden, streetcar

> The appropriate 7th character is to be added to each code from category V16

> | A | initial encounter |
> |---|---|
> | D | subsequent encounter |
> | S | sequela |

X ● **V16.0**   Pedal cycle **driver** injured in collision with other nonmotor vehicle in **nontraffic accident**

X ● **V16.1**   Pedal cycle **passenger** injured in collision with other nonmotor vehicle in **nontraffic accident**

X ● **V16.2**   **Unspecified** pedal cyclist injured in collision with other nonmotor vehicle in **nontraffic accident**

X ● **V16.3**   Person **boarding or alighting** a pedal cycle injured in collision with other nonmotor vehicle in nontraffic accident

X ● **V16.4**   Pedal cycle **driver** injured in collision with other nonmotor vehicle in **traffic accident**

X ● **V16.5**   Pedal cycle **passenger** injured in collision with other nonmotor vehicle in **traffic accident**

X ● **V16.9**   **Unspecified** pedal cyclist injured in collision with other nonmotor vehicle in **traffic accident**

● **V17   Pedal cycle rider injured in collision with fixed or stationary object**

> The appropriate 7th character is to be added to each code from category V17

> | A | initial encounter |
> |---|---|
> | D | subsequent encounter |
> | S | sequela |

X ● **V17.0**   Pedal cycle **driver** injured in collision with fixed or stationary object in **nontraffic accident**

X ● **V17.1**   Pedal cycle **passenger** injured in collision with fixed or stationary object in **nontraffic accident**

X ● **V17.2**   **Unspecified** pedal cyclist injured in collision with fixed or stationary object in **nontraffic accident**

X ● **V17.3**   Person **boarding or alighting** a pedal cycle injured in collision with fixed or stationary object

X ● **V17.4**   Pedal cycle **driver** injured in collision with fixed or stationary object in **traffic accident**

X ● **V17.5**   Pedal cycle **passenger** injured in collision with fixed or stationary object in **traffic accident**

X ● **V17.9**   **Unspecified** pedal cyclist injured in collision with fixed or stationary object in **traffic accident**

CHAPTER 20 (V01–Y99)

● **V18**   **Pedal cycle rider injured in noncollision transport accident**

> **Includes**   fall or thrown from pedal cycle (without antecedent collision)
> overturning pedal cycle NOS
> overturning pedal cycle without collision

> The appropriate 7th character is to be added to each code from category V18

> | | |
> |---|---|
> | A | initial encounter |
> | D | subsequent encounter |
> | S | sequela |

X ● **V18.0**   Pedal cycle driver injured in noncollision transport accident in nontraffic accident

X ● **V18.1**   Pedal cycle passenger injured in noncollision transport accident in nontraffic accident

X ● **V18.2**   Unspecified pedal cyclist injured in noncollision transport accident in nontraffic accident

X ● **V18.3**   Person boarding or alighting a pedal cycle injured in noncollision transport accident

X ● **V18.4**   Pedal cycle driver injured in noncollision transport accident in traffic accident

X ● **V18.5**   Pedal cycle passenger injured in noncollision transport accident in traffic accident

X ● **V18.9**   Unspecified pedal cyclist injured in noncollision transport accident in traffic accident

● **V19**   **Pedal cycle rider injured in other and unspecified transport accidents**

> The appropriate 7th character is to be added to each code from category V19

> | | |
> |---|---|
> | A | initial encounter |
> | D | subsequent encounter |
> | S | sequela |

● **V19.0**   Pedal cycle driver injured in collision with other and unspecified motor vehicles in nontraffic accident

   X ● **V19.00**   Pedal cycle driver injured in collision with unspecified motor vehicles in nontraffic accident

   X ● **V19.09**   Pedal cycle driver injured in collision with other motor vehicles in nontraffic accident

● **V19.1**   Pedal cycle passenger injured in collision with other and unspecified motor vehicles in nontraffic accident

   X ● **V19.10**   Pedal cycle passenger injured in collision with unspecified motor vehicles in nontraffic accident

   X ● **V19.19**   Pedal cycle passenger injured in collision with other motor vehicles in nontraffic accident

● **V19.2**   Unspecified pedal cyclist injured in collision with other and unspecified motor vehicles in nontraffic accident

   X ● **V19.20**   Unspecified pedal cyclist injured in collision with unspecified motor vehicles in nontraffic accident
> Pedal cycle collision NOS, nontraffic

   X ● **V19.29**   Unspecified pedal cyclist injured in collision with other motor vehicles in nontraffic accident

X ● **V19.3**   Pedal cyclist (driver) (passenger) injured in unspecified nontraffic accident
> Pedal cycle accident NOS, nontraffic
> Pedal cyclist injured in nontraffic accident NOS

● **V19.4**   Pedal cycle driver injured in collision with other and unspecified motor vehicles in traffic accident

   X ● **V19.40**   Pedal cycle driver injured in collision with unspecified motor vehicles in traffic accident

   X ● **V19.49**   Pedal cycle driver injured in collision with other motor vehicles in traffic accident

● **V19.5**   Pedal cycle passenger injured in collision with other and unspecified motor vehicles in traffic accident

   X ● **V19.50**   Pedal cycle passenger injured in collision with unspecified motor vehicles in traffic accident

   X ● **V19.59**   Pedal cycle passenger injured in collision with other motor vehicles in traffic accident

● **V19.6**   Unspecified pedal cyclist injured in collision with other and unspecified motor vehicles in traffic accident

   X ● **V19.60**   Unspecified pedal cyclist injured in collision with unspecified motor vehicles in traffic accident
> Pedal cycle collision NOS (traffic)

   X ● **V19.69**   Unspecified pedal cyclist injured in collision with other motor vehicles in traffic accident

● **V19.8**   Pedal cyclist (driver) (passenger) injured in other specified transport accidents

   X ● **V19.81**   Pedal cyclist (driver) (passenger) injured in transport accident with military vehicle

   X ● **V19.88**   Pedal cyclist (driver) (passenger) injured in other specified transport accidents

X ● **V19.9**   Pedal cyclist (driver) (passenger) injured in unspecified traffic accident
> Pedal cycle accident NOS

MOTORCYCLE RIDER INJURED IN TRANSPORT ACCIDENT (V20-V29)

> **Includes**   moped motorcycle with sidecar motorized bicycle motor scooter

> **Excludes1**   three-wheeled motor vehicle (V30-V39)

● **V20**   **Motorcycle rider injured in collision with pedestrian or animal**

> **Excludes1**   motorcycle rider collision with animal-drawn vehicle or animal being ridden (V26.-)

> The appropriate 7th character is to be added to each code from category V20

> | | |
> |---|---|
> | A | initial encounter |
> | D | subsequent encounter |
> | S | sequela |

X ● **V20.0**   Motorcycle driver injured in collision with pedestrian or animal in nontraffic accident

X ● **V20.1**   Motorcycle passenger injured in collision with pedestrian or animal in nontraffic accident

X ● **V20.2**   Unspecified motorcycle rider injured in collision with pedestrian or animal in nontraffic accident

X ● **V20.3**   Person boarding or alighting a motorcycle injured in collision with pedestrian or animal

X ● **V20.4**   Motorcycle driver injured in collision with pedestrian or animal in traffic accident

X ● **V20.5**   Motorcycle passenger injured in collision with pedestrian or animal in traffic accident

X ● **V20.9**   Unspecified motorcycle rider injured in collision with pedestrian or animal in traffic accident

● **V21**   **Motorcycle rider injured in collision with pedal cycle**

> The appropriate 7th character is to be added to each code from category V21

> | | |
> |---|---|
> | A | initial encounter |
> | D | subsequent encounter |
> | S | sequela |

X ● **V21.0**   Motorcycle driver injured in collision with pedal cycle in nontraffic accident

X ● **V21.1**   Motorcycle passenger injured in collision with pedal cycle in nontraffic accident

X ● **V21.2**   Unspecified motorcycle rider injured in collision with pedal cycle in nontraffic accident

X ● **V21.3**   Person boarding or alighting a motorcycle injured in collision with pedal cycle

X ● **V21.4**   Motorcycle driver injured in collision with pedal cycle in traffic accident

X ● **V21.5**   Motorcycle passenger injured in collision with pedal cycle in traffic accident

X ● **V21.9**   Unspecified motorcycle rider injured in collision with pedal cycle in traffic accident

> ▶ New   ⇒ Revised   ~~deleted~~ Deleted   Excludes 1   Excludes 2   Includes   Use additional   Code first   Code also   Key words
>
> **OGCR** Official Guidelines   X Assign placeholder X   ▶ Use Additional Character(s)   ▶ Manifestation Code   **Coding Clinic**

● **V22** **Motorcycle rider injured in collision with two- or three-wheeled motor vehicle**

> The appropriate 7th character is to be added to each code from category V22

> | | |
> |---|---|
> | A | initial encounter |
> | D | subsequent encounter |
> | S | sequela |

X ● **V22.0** Motorcycle driver injured in collision with two- or three-wheeled motor vehicle in nontraffic accident

X ● **V22.1** Motorcycle passenger injured in collision with two- or three-wheeled motor vehicle in nontraffic accident

X ● **V22.2** Unspecified motorcycle rider injured in collision with two- or three-wheeled motor vehicle in nontraffic accident

X ● **V22.3** Person boarding or alighting a motorcycle injured in collision with two- or three-wheeled motor vehicle

X ● **V22.4** Motorcycle driver injured in collision with two- or three-wheeled motor vehicle in traffic accident

X ● **V22.5** Motorcycle passenger injured in collision with two- or three-wheeled motor vehicle in traffic accident

X ● **V22.9** Unspecified motorcycle rider injured in collision with two- or three-wheeled motor vehicle in traffic accident

● **V23** **Motorcycle rider injured in collision with car, pick-up truck or van**

> The appropriate 7th character is to be added to each code from category V23

> | | |
> |---|---|
> | A | initial encounter |
> | D | subsequent encounter |
> | S | sequela |

X ● **V23.0** Motorcycle driver injured in collision with car, pick-up truck or van in nontraffic accident

X ● **V23.1** Motorcycle passenger injured in collision with car, pick-up truck or van in nontraffic accident

X ● **V23.2** Unspecified motorcycle rider injured in collision with car, pick-up truck or van in nontraffic accident

X ● **V23.3** Person boarding or alighting a motorcycle injured in collision with car, pick-up truck or van

X ● **V23.4** Motorcycle driver injured in collision with car, pick-up truck or van in traffic accident

X ● **V23.5** Motorcycle passenger injured in collision with car, pick-up truck or van in traffic accident

X ● **V23.9** Unspecified motorcycle rider injured in collision with car, pick-up truck or van in traffic accident

● **V24** **Motorcycle rider injured in collision with heavy transport vehicle or bus**

> **Excludes1**   motorcycle rider injured in collision with military vehicle (V29.81)

> The appropriate 7th character is to be added to each code from category V24

> | | |
> |---|---|
> | A | initial encounter |
> | D | subsequent encounter |
> | S | sequela |

X ● **V24.0** Motorcycle driver injured in collision with heavy transport vehicle or bus in nontraffic accident

X ● **V24.1** Motorcycle passenger injured in collision with heavy transport vehicle or bus in nontraffic accident

X ● **V24.2** Unspecified motorcycle rider injured in collision with heavy transport vehicle or bus in nontraffic accident

X ● **V24.3** Person boarding or alighting a motorcycle injured in collision with heavy transport vehicle or bus

X ● **V24.4** Motorcycle driver injured in collision with heavy transport vehicle or bus in traffic accident

X ● **V24.5** Motorcycle passenger injured in collision with heavy transport vehicle or bus in traffic accident

X ● **V24.9** Unspecified motorcycle rider injured in collision with heavy transport vehicle or bus in traffic accident

● **V25** **Motorcycle rider injured in collision with railway train or railway vehicle**

> The appropriate 7th character is to be added to each code from category V25

> | | |
> |---|---|
> | A | initial encounter |
> | D | subsequent encounter |
> | S | sequela |

X ● **V25.0** Motorcycle driver injured in collision with railway train or railway vehicle in nontraffic accident

X ● **V25.1** Motorcycle passenger injured in collision with railway train or railway vehicle in nontraffic accident

X ● **V25.2** Unspecified motorcycle rider injured in collision with railway train or railway vehicle in nontraffic accident

X ● **V25.3** Person boarding or alighting a motorcycle injured in collision with railway train or railway vehicle

X ● **V25.4** Motorcycle driver injured in collision with railway train or railway vehicle in traffic accident

X ● **V25.5** Motorcycle passenger injured in collision with railway train or railway vehicle in traffic accident

X ● **V25.9** Unspecified motorcycle rider injured in collision with railway train or railway vehicle in traffic accident

● **V26** **Motorcycle rider injured in collision with other nonmotor vehicle**

> **Includes**   collision with animal-drawn vehicle, animal being ridden, streetcar

> The appropriate 7th character is to be added to each code from category V26

> | | |
> |---|---|
> | A | initial encounter |
> | D | subsequent encounter |
> | S | sequela |

X ● **V26.0** Motorcycle driver injured in collision with other nonmotor vehicle in nontraffic accident

X ● **V26.1** Motorcycle passenger injured in collision with other nonmotor vehicle in nontraffic accident

X ● **V26.2** Unspecified motorcycle rider injured in collision with other nonmotor vehicle in nontraffic accident

X ● **V26.3** Person boarding or alighting a motorcycle injured in collision with other nonmotor vehicle

X ● **V26.4** Motorcycle driver injured in collision with other nonmotor vehicle in traffic accident

X ● **V26.5** Motorcycle passenger injured in collision with other nonmotor vehicle in traffic accident

X ● **V26.9** Unspecified motorcycle rider injured in collision with other nonmotor vehicle in traffic accident

● **V27** **Motorcycle rider injured in collision with fixed or stationary object**

> The appropriate 7th character is to be added to each code from category V27

> | | |
> |---|---|
> | A | initial encounter |
> | D | subsequent encounter |
> | S | sequela |

X ● **V27.0** Motorcycle driver injured in collision with fixed or stationary object in nontraffic accident

X ● **V27.1** Motorcycle passenger injured in collision with fixed or stationary object in nontraffic accident

X ● **V27.2** Unspecified motorcycle rider injured in collision with fixed or stationary object in nontraffic accident

X ● **V27.3** Person boarding or alighting a motorcycle injured in collision with fixed or stationary object

X ● **V27.4** Motorcycle driver injured in collision with fixed or stationary object in traffic accident

X ● **V27.5** Motorcycle passenger injured in collision with fixed or stationary object in traffic accident

X ● **V27.9** Unspecified motorcycle rider injured in collision with fixed or stationary object in traffic accident

CHAPTER 20 (V01-Y99)

● **V28 Motorcycle rider injured in noncollision transport accident**

     Includes   fall or thrown from motorcycle (without antecedent collision)
                       overturning motorcycle NOS
                       overturning motorcycle without collision

     The appropriate 7th character is to be added to each code from category V28

     A   initial encounter
     D   subsequent encounter
     S   sequela

X ● **V28.0 Motorcycle driver injured in noncollision transport accident in nontraffic accident**

X ● **V28.1 Motorcycle passenger injured in noncollision transport accident in nontraffic accident**

X ● **V28.2 Unspecified motorcycle rider injured in noncollision transport accident in nontraffic accident**

X ● **V28.3 Person boarding or alighting a motorcycle injured in noncollision transport accident**

X ● **V28.4 Motorcycle driver injured in noncollision transport accident in traffic accident**

X ● **V28.5 Motorcycle passenger injured in noncollision transport accident in traffic accident**

X ● **V28.9 Unspecified motorcycle rider injured in noncollision transport accident in traffic accident**

● **V29 Motorcycle rider injured in other and unspecified transport accidents**

     The appropriate 7th character is to be added to each code from category V29

     A   initial encounter
     D   subsequent encounter
     S   sequela

     Coding Clinic: 2015, Q3, P20

● **V29.0 Motorcycle driver injured in collision with other and unspecified motor vehicles in nontraffic accident**

   X ● **V29.00 Motorcycle driver injured in collision with unspecified motor vehicles in nontraffic accident**

   X ● **V29.09 Motorcycle driver injured in collision with other motor vehicles in nontraffic accident**

● **V29.1 Motorcycle passenger injured in collision with other and unspecified motor vehicles in nontraffic accident**

   X ● **V29.10 Motorcycle passenger injured in collision with unspecified motor vehicles in nontraffic accident**

   X ● **V29.19 Motorcycle passenger injured in collision with other motor vehicles in nontraffic accident**

● **V29.2 Unspecified motorcycle rider injured in collision with other and unspecified motor vehicles in nontraffic accident**

   X ● **V29.20 Unspecified motorcycle rider injured in collision with unspecified motor vehicles in nontraffic accident**
             Motorcycle collision NOS, nontraffic

   X ● **V29.29 Unspecified motorcycle rider injured in collision with other motor vehicles in nontraffic accident**

X ● **V29.3 Motorcycle rider (driver) (passenger) injured in unspecified nontraffic accident**
         Motorcycle accident NOS, nontraffic
         Motorcycle rider injured in nontraffic accident NOS

● **V29.4 Motorcycle driver injured in collision with other and unspecified motor vehicles in traffic accident**

   X ● **V29.40 Motorcycle driver injured in collision with unspecified motor vehicles in traffic accident**

   X ● **V29.49 Motorcycle driver injured in collision with other motor vehicles in traffic accident**

● **V29.5 Motorcycle passenger injured in collision with other and unspecified motor vehicles in traffic accident**

   X ● **V29.50 Motorcycle passenger injured in collision with unspecified motor vehicles in traffic accident**

   X ● **V29.59 Motorcycle passenger injured in collision with other motor vehicles in traffic accident**

● **V29.6 Unspecified motorcycle rider injured in collision with other and unspecified motor vehicles in traffic accident**

   X ● **V29.60 Unspecified motorcycle rider injured in collision with unspecified motor vehicles in traffic accident**
             Motorcycle collision NOS (traffic)

   X ● **V29.69 Unspecified motorcycle rider injured in collision with other motor vehicles in traffic accident**

● **V29.8 Motorcycle rider (driver) (passenger) injured in other specified transport accidents**

   X ● **V29.81 Motorcycle rider (driver) (passenger) injured in transport accident with military vehicle**

   X ● **V29.88 Motorcycle rider (driver) (passenger) injured in other specified transport accidents**

X ● **V29.9 Motorcycle rider (driver) (passenger) injured in unspecified traffic accident**
         Motorcycle accident NOS

OCCUPANT OF THREE-WHEELED MOTOR VEHICLE INJURED IN TRANSPORT ACCIDENT (V30-V39)

     Includes   motorized tricycle
                       motorized rickshaw
                       three-wheeled motor car

     Excludes1   all-terrain vehicles (V86.-)
                       motorcycle with sidecar (V20-V29)
                       vehicle designed primarily for off-road use (V86.-)

● **V30 Occupant of three-wheeled motor vehicle injured in collision with pedestrian or animal**

     Excludes1   three-wheeled motor vehicle collision with animal-drawn vehicle or animal being ridden (V36.-)

     The appropriate 7th character is to be added to each code from category V30

     A   initial encounter
     D   subsequent encounter
     S   sequela

X ● **V30.0 Driver of three-wheeled motor vehicle injured in collision with pedestrian or animal in nontraffic accident**

X ● **V30.1 Passenger in three-wheeled motor vehicle injured in collision with pedestrian or animal in nontraffic accident**

X ● **V30.2 Person on outside of three-wheeled motor vehicle injured in collision with pedestrian or animal in nontraffic accident**

X ● **V30.3 Unspecified occupant of three-wheeled motor vehicle injured in collision with pedestrian or animal in nontraffic accident**

X ● **V30.4 Person boarding or alighting a three-wheeled motor vehicle injured in collision with pedestrian or animal**

X ● **V30.5 Driver of three-wheeled motor vehicle injured in collision with pedestrian or animal in traffic accident**

X ● **V30.6 Passenger in three-wheeled motor vehicle injured in collision with pedestrian or animal in traffic accident**

X ● **V30.7 Person on outside of three-wheeled motor vehicle injured in collision with pedestrian or animal in traffic accident**

X ● **V30.9 Unspecified occupant of three-wheeled motor vehicle injured in collision with pedestrian or animal in traffic accident**

▶ New   ⇒ Revised   ~~deleted~~ Deleted   Excludes 1   Excludes 2   Includes   Use additional   Code first   Code also   Key words
OGCR Official Guidelines   X Assign placeholder X   ● Use Additional Character(s)   ▶ Manifestation Code   **Coding Clinic**

● **V31** **Occupant of three-wheeled motor vehicle injured in collision with pedal cycle**

     The appropriate 7th character is to be added to each code from category V31

A	initial encounter
D	subsequent encounter
S	sequela

X● **V31.0** Driver of three-wheeled motor vehicle injured in collision with pedal cycle in nontraffic accident

X● **V31.1** Passenger in three-wheeled motor vehicle injured in collision with pedal cycle in nontraffic accident

X● **V31.2** Person on outside of three-wheeled motor vehicle injured in collision with pedal cycle in nontraffic accident

X● **V31.3** Unspecified occupant of three-wheeled motor vehicle injured in collision with pedal cycle in nontraffic accident

X● **V31.4** Person boarding or alighting a three-wheeled motor vehicle injured in collision with pedal cycle

X● **V31.5** Driver of three-wheeled motor vehicle injured in collision with pedal cycle in traffic accident

X● **V31.6** Passenger in three-wheeled motor vehicle injured in collision with pedal cycle in traffic accident

X● **V31.7** Person on outside of three-wheeled motor vehicle injured in collision with pedal cycle in traffic accident

X● **V31.9** Unspecified occupant of three-wheeled motor vehicle injured in collision with pedal cycle in traffic accident

● **V32** **Occupant of three-wheeled motor vehicle injured in collision with two- or three-wheeled motor vehicle**

     The appropriate 7th character is to be added to each code from category V32

A	initial encounter
D	subsequent encounter
S	sequela

X● **V32.0** Driver of three-wheeled motor vehicle injured in collision with two- or three-wheeled motor vehicle in nontraffic accident

X● **V32.1** Passenger in three-wheeled motor vehicle injured in collision with two- or three-wheeled motor vehicle in nontraffic accident

X● **V32.2** Person on outside of three-wheeled motor vehicle injured in collision with two- or three-wheeled motor vehicle in nontraffic accident

X● **V32.3** Unspecified occupant of three-wheeled motor vehicle injured in collision with two- or three-wheeled motor vehicle in nontraffic accident

X● **V32.4** Person boarding or alighting a three-wheeled motor vehicle injured in collision with two- or three-wheeled motor vehicle

X● **V32.5** Driver of three-wheeled motor vehicle injured in collision with two- or three-wheeled motor vehicle in traffic accident

X● **V32.6** Passenger in three-wheeled motor vehicle injured in collision with two- or three-wheeled motor vehicle in traffic accident

X● **V32.7** Person on outside of three-wheeled motor vehicle injured in collision with two- or three-wheeled motor vehicle in traffic accident

X● **V32.9** Unspecified occupant of three-wheeled motor vehicle injured in collision with two- or three-wheeled motor vehicle in traffic accident

● **V33** **Occupant of three-wheeled motor vehicle injured in collision with car, pick-up truck or van**

     The appropriate 7th character is to be added to each code from category V33

A	initial encounter
D	subsequent encounter
S	sequela

X● **V33.0** Driver of three-wheeled motor vehicle injured in collision with car, pick-up truck or van in nontraffic accident

X● **V33.1** Passenger in three-wheeled motor vehicle injured in collision with car, pick-up truck or van in nontraffic accident

X● **V33.2** Person on outside of three-wheeled motor vehicle injured in collision with car, pick-up truck or van in nontraffic accident

X● **V33.3** Unspecified occupant of three-wheeled motor vehicle injured in collision with car, pick-up truck or van in nontraffic accident

X● **V33.4** Person boarding or alighting a three-wheeled motor vehicle injured in collision with car, pick-up truck or van

X● **V33.5** Driver of three-wheeled motor vehicle injured in collision with car, pick-up truck or van in traffic accident

X● **V33.6** Passenger in three-wheeled motor vehicle injured in collision with car, pick-up truck or van in traffic accident

X● **V33.7** Person on outside of three-wheeled motor vehicle injured in collision with car, pick-up truck or van in traffic accident

X● **V33.9** Unspecified occupant of three-wheeled motor vehicle injured in collision with car, pick-up truck or van in traffic accident

● **V34** **Occupant of three-wheeled motor vehicle injured in collision with heavy transport vehicle or bus**

     Excludes1   occupant of three-wheeled motor vehicle injured in collision with military vehicle (V39.81)

     The appropriate 7th character is to be added to each code from category V34

A	initial encounter
D	subsequent encounter
S	sequela

X● **V34.0** Driver of three-wheeled motor vehicle injured in collision with heavy transport vehicle or bus in nontraffic accident

X● **V34.1** Passenger in three-wheeled motor vehicle injured in collision with heavy transport vehicle or bus in nontraffic accident

X● **V34.2** Person on outside of three-wheeled motor vehicle injured in collision with heavy transport vehicle or bus in nontraffic accident

X● **V34.3** Unspecified occupant of three-wheeled motor vehicle injured in collision with heavy transport vehicle or bus in nontraffic accident

X● **V34.4** Person boarding or alighting a three-wheeled motor vehicle injured in collision with heavy transport vehicle or bus

X● **V34.5** Driver of three-wheeled motor vehicle injured in collision with heavy transport vehicle or bus in traffic accident

X● **V34.6** Passenger in three-wheeled motor vehicle injured in collision with heavy transport vehicle or bus in traffic accident

X● **V34.7** Person on outside of three-wheeled motor vehicle injured in collision with heavy transport vehicle or bus in traffic accident

X● **V34.9** Unspecified occupant of three-wheeled motor vehicle injured in collision with heavy transport vehicle or bus in traffic accident

● **V35 Occupant of three-wheeled motor vehicle injured in collision with railway train or railway vehicle**

The appropriate 7th character is to be added to each code from category V35

A	initial encounter
D	subsequent encounter
S	sequela

X● **V35.0 Driver of three-wheeled motor vehicle injured in collision with railway train or railway vehicle in nontraffic accident**

X● **V35.1 Passenger in three-wheeled motor vehicle injured in collision with railway train or railway vehicle in nontraffic accident**

X● **V35.2 Person on outside of three-wheeled motor vehicle injured in collision with railway train or railway vehicle in nontraffic accident**

X● **V35.3 Unspecified occupant of three-wheeled motor vehicle injured in collision with railway train or railway vehicle in nontraffic accident**

X● **V35.4 Person boarding or alighting a three-wheeled motor vehicle injured in collision with railway train or railway vehicle**

X● **V35.5 Driver of three-wheeled motor vehicle injured in collision with railway train or railway vehicle in traffic accident**

X● **V35.6 Passenger in three-wheeled motor vehicle injured in collision with railway train or railway vehicle in traffic accident**

X● **V35.7 Person on outside of three-wheeled motor vehicle injured in collision with railway train or railway vehicle in traffic accident**

X● **V35.9 Unspecified occupant of three-wheeled motor vehicle injured in collision with railway train or railway vehicle in traffic accident**

● **V36 Occupant of three-wheeled motor vehicle injured in collision with other nonmotor vehicle**

Includes   collision with animal-drawn vehicle, animal being ridden, streetcar

The appropriate 7th character is to be added to each code from category V36

A	initial encounter
D	subsequent encounter
S	sequela

X● **V36.0 Driver of three-wheeled motor vehicle injured in collision with other nonmotor vehicle in nontraffic accident**

X● **V36.1 Passenger in three-wheeled motor vehicle injured in collision with other nonmotor vehicle in nontraffic accident**

X● **V36.2 Person on outside of three-wheeled motor vehicle injured in collision with other nonmotor vehicle in nontraffic accident**

X● **V36.3 Unspecified occupant of three-wheeled motor vehicle injured in collision with other nonmotor vehicle in nontraffic accident**

X● **V36.4 Person boarding or alighting a three-wheeled motor vehicle injured in collision with other nonmotor vehicle**

X● **V36.5 Driver of three-wheeled motor vehicle injured in collision with other nonmotor vehicle in traffic accident**

X● **V36.6 Passenger in three-wheeled motor vehicle injured in collision with other nonmotor vehicle in traffic accident**

X● **V36.7 Person on outside of three-wheeled motor vehicle injured in collision with other nonmotor vehicle in traffic accident**

X● **V36.9 Unspecified occupant of three-wheeled motor vehicle injured in collision with other nonmotor vehicle in traffic accident**

● **V37 Occupant of three-wheeled motor vehicle injured in collision with fixed or stationary object**

The appropriate 7th character is to be added to each code from category V37

A	initial encounter
D	subsequent encounter
S	sequela

X● **V37.0 Driver of three-wheeled motor vehicle injured in collision with fixed or stationary object in nontraffic accident**

X● **V37.1 Passenger in three-wheeled motor vehicle injured in collision with fixed or stationary object in nontraffic accident**

X● **V37.2 Person on outside of three-wheeled motor vehicle injured in collision with fixed or stationary object in nontraffic accident**

X● **V37.3 Unspecified occupant of three-wheeled motor vehicle injured in collision with fixed or stationary object in nontraffic accident**

X● **V37.4 Person boarding or alighting a three-wheeled motor vehicle injured in collision with fixed or stationary object**

X● **V37.5 Driver of three-wheeled motor vehicle injured in collision with fixed or stationary object in traffic accident**

X● **V37.6 Passenger in three-wheeled motor vehicle injured in collision with fixed or stationary object in traffic accident**

X● **V37.7 Person on outside of three-wheeled motor vehicle injured in collision with fixed or stationary object in traffic accident**

X● **V37.9 Unspecified occupant of three-wheeled motor vehicle injured in collision with fixed or stationary object in traffic accident**

● **V38 Occupant of three-wheeled motor vehicle injured in noncollision transport accident**

Includes   fall or thrown from three-wheeled motor vehicle overturning of three-wheeled motor vehicle NOS overturning of three-wheeled motor vehicle without collision

The appropriate 7th character is to be added to each code from category V38

A	initial encounter
D	subsequent encounter
S	sequela

X● **V38.0 Driver of three-wheeled motor vehicle injured in noncollision transport accident in nontraffic accident**

X● **V38.1 Passenger in three-wheeled motor vehicle injured in noncollision transport accident in nontraffic accident**

X● **V38.2 Person on outside of three-wheeled motor vehicle injured in noncollision transport accident in nontraffic accident**

X● **V38.3 Unspecified occupant of three-wheeled motor vehicle injured in noncollision transport accident in nontraffic accident**

X● **V38.4 Person boarding or alighting a three-wheeled motor vehicle injured in noncollision transport accident**

X● **V38.5 Driver of three-wheeled motor vehicle injured in noncollision transport accident in traffic accident**

X● **V38.6 Passenger in three-wheeled motor vehicle injured in noncollision transport accident in traffic accident**

X● **V38.7 Person on outside of three-wheeled motor vehicle injured in noncollision transport accident in traffic accident**

X● **V38.9 Unspecified occupant of three-wheeled motor vehicle injured in noncollision transport accident in traffic accident**

▶ New   ⇒ Revised   ~~deleted~~ Deleted   Excludes 1   Excludes 2   Includes   Use additional   Code first   Code also   Key words

OGCR Official Guidelines   X Assign placeholder X   ● Use Additional Character(s)   ▶ Manifestation Code   **Coding Clinic**

● **V39**   Occupant of three-wheeled motor vehicle injured in other and unspecified transport accidents

> The appropriate 7th character is to be added to each code from category V39

> | | |
> |---|---|
> | A | initial encounter |
> | D | subsequent encounter |
> | S | sequela |

● **V39.0**   Driver of three-wheeled motor vehicle injured in collision with other and unspecified motor vehicles in nontraffic accident

   X● **V39.00**   Driver of three-wheeled motor vehicle injured in collision with unspecified motor vehicles in nontraffic accident

   X● **V39.09**   Driver of three-wheeled motor vehicle injured in collision with other motor vehicles in nontraffic accident

● **V39.1**   Passenger in three-wheeled motor vehicle injured in collision with other and unspecified motor vehicles in nontraffic accident

   X● **V39.10**   Passenger in three-wheeled motor vehicle injured in collision with unspecified motor vehicles in nontraffic accident

   X● **V39.19**   Passenger in three-wheeled motor vehicle injured in collision with other motor vehicles in nontraffic accident

● **V39.2**   Unspecified occupant of three-wheeled motor vehicle injured in collision with other and unspecified motor vehicles in nontraffic accident

   X● **V39.20**   Unspecified occupant of three-wheeled motor vehicle injured in collision with unspecified motor vehicles in nontraffic accident

> Collision NOS involving three-wheeled motor vehicle, nontraffic

   X● **V39.29**   Unspecified occupant of three-wheeled motor vehicle injured in collision with other motor vehicles in nontraffic accident

X● **V39.3**   Occupant (driver) (passenger) of three-wheeled motor vehicle injured in unspecified nontraffic accident

> Accident NOS involving three-wheeled motor vehicle, nontraffic
> Occupant of three-wheeled motor vehicle injured in nontraffic accident NOS

● **V39.4**   Driver of three-wheeled motor vehicle injured in collision with other and unspecified motor vehicles in traffic accident

   X● **V39.40**   Driver of three-wheeled motor vehicle injured in collision with unspecified motor vehicles in traffic accident

   X● **V39.49**   Driver of three-wheeled motor vehicle injured in collision with other motor vehicles in traffic accident

● **V39.5**   Passenger in three-wheeled motor vehicle injured in collision with other and unspecified motor vehicles in traffic accident

   X● **V39.50**   Passenger in three-wheeled motor vehicle injured in collision with unspecified motor vehicles in traffic accident

   X● **V39.59**   Passenger in three-wheeled motor vehicle injured in collision with other motor vehicles in traffic accident

● **V39.6**   Unspecified occupant of three-wheeled motor vehicle injured in collision with other and unspecified motor vehicles in traffic accident

   X● **V39.60**   Unspecified occupant of three-wheeled motor vehicle injured in collision with unspecified motor vehicles in traffic accident

> Collision NOS involving three-wheeled motor vehicle (traffic)

   X● **V39.69**   Unspecified occupant of three-wheeled motor vehicle injured in collision with other motor vehicles in traffic accident

● **V39.8**   Occupant (driver) (passenger) of three-wheeled motor vehicle injured in other specified transport accidents

   X● **V39.81**   Occupant (driver) (passenger) of three-wheeled motor vehicle injured in transport accident with military vehicle

   X● **V39.89**   Occupant (driver) (passenger) of three-wheeled motor vehicle injured in other specified transport accidents

X● **V39.9**   Occupant (driver) (passenger) of three-wheeled motor vehicle injured in unspecified traffic accident

> Accident NOS involving three-wheeled motor vehicle

CAR OCCUPANT INJURED IN TRANSPORT ACCIDENT (V40-V49)

> **Includes**   a four-wheeled motor vehicle designed primarily for carrying passengers
> automobile (pulling a trailer or camper)

> **Excludes1**   bus (V50-V59)
> minibus (V50-V59)
> minivan (V50-V59)
> motorcoach (V70-V79)
> pick-up truck (V50-V59)
> sport utility vehicle (SUV) (V50-V59)

● **V40**   Car occupant injured in collision with pedestrian or animal

> **Excludes1**   car collision with animal-drawn vehicle or animal being ridden (V46.-)

> The appropriate 7th character is to be added to each code from category V40

> | | |
> |---|---|
> | A | initial encounter |
> | D | subsequent encounter |
> | S | sequela |

   X● **V40.0**   Car driver injured in collision with pedestrian or animal in nontraffic accident

   X● **V40.1**   Car passenger injured in collision with pedestrian or animal in nontraffic accident

   X● **V40.2**   Person on outside of car injured in collision with pedestrian or animal in nontraffic accident

   X● **V40.3**   Unspecified car occupant injured in collision with pedestrian or animal in nontraffic accident

   X● **V40.4**   Person boarding or alighting a car injured in collision with pedestrian or animal

   X● **V40.5**   Car driver injured in collision with pedestrian or animal in traffic accident

   X● **V40.6**   Car passenger injured in collision with pedestrian or animal in traffic accident

   X● **V40.7**   Person on outside of car injured in collision with pedestrian or animal in traffic accident

   X● **V40.9**   Unspecified car occupant injured in collision with pedestrian or animal in traffic accident

● **V41**   Car occupant injured in collision with pedal cycle

> The appropriate 7th character is to be added to each code from category V41

> | | |
> |---|---|
> | A | initial encounter |
> | D | subsequent encounter |
> | S | sequela |

   X● **V41.0**   Car driver injured in collision with pedal cycle in nontraffic accident

   X● **V41.1**   Car passenger injured in collision with pedal cycle in nontraffic accident

   X● **V41.2**   Person on outside of car injured in collision with pedal cycle in nontraffic accident

   X● **V41.3**   Unspecified car occupant injured in collision with pedal cycle in nontraffic accident

   X● **V41.4**   Person boarding or alighting a car injured in collision with pedal cycle

   X● **V41.5**   Car driver injured in collision with pedal cycle in traffic accident

   X● **V41.6**   Car passenger injured in collision with pedal cycle in traffic accident

CHAPTER 20 (V01-Y99)

X● **V41.7** Person on outside of car injured in collision with pedal cycle in traffic accident

X● **V41.9** Unspecified car occupant injured in collision with pedal cycle in traffic accident

●**V42** Car occupant injured in collision with two- or three-wheeled motor vehicle

The appropriate 7th character is to be added to each code from category V42

A	initial encounter
D	subsequent encounter
S	sequela

X● **V42.0** Car driver injured in collision with two- or three-wheeled motor vehicle in nontraffic accident

X● **V42.1** Car passenger injured in collision with two- or three-wheeled motor vehicle in nontraffic accident

X● **V42.2** Person on outside of car injured in collision with two- or three-wheeled motor vehicle in nontraffic accident

X● **V42.3** Unspecified car occupant injured in collision with two- or three-wheeled motor vehicle in nontraffic accident

X● **V42.4** Person boarding or alighting a car injured in collision with two- or three-wheeled motor vehicle

X● **V42.5** Car driver injured in collision with two- or three-wheeled motor vehicle in traffic accident

X● **V42.6** Car passenger injured in collision with two- or three-wheeled motor vehicle in traffic accident

X● **V42.7** Person on outside of car injured in collision with two- or three-wheeled motor vehicle in traffic accident

X● **V42.9** Unspecified car occupant injured in collision with two- or three-wheeled motor vehicle in traffic accident

●**V43** Car occupant injured in collision with car, pick-up truck or van

The appropriate 7th character is to be added to each code from category V43

A	initial encounter
D	subsequent encounter
S	sequela

●**V43.0** Car driver injured in collision with car, pick-up truck or van in nontraffic accident

X● **V43.01** Car driver injured in collision with sport utility vehicle in nontraffic accident

X● **V43.02** Car driver injured in collision with other type car in nontraffic accident

X● **V43.03** Car driver injured in collision with pick-up truck in nontraffic accident

X● **V43.04** Car driver injured in collision with van in nontraffic accident

●**V43.1** Car passenger injured in collision with car, pick-up truck or van in nontraffic accident

X● **V43.11** Car passenger injured in collision with sport utility vehicle in nontraffic accident

X● **V43.12** Car passenger injured in collision with other type car in nontraffic accident

X● **V43.13** Car passenger injured in collision with pick-up in nontraffic accident

X● **V43.14** Car passenger injured in collision with van in nontraffic accident

●**V43.2** Person on outside of car injured in collision with car, pick-up truck or van in nontraffic accident

X● **V43.21** Person on outside of car injured in collision with sport utility vehicle in nontraffic accident

X● **V43.22** Person on outside of car injured in collision with other type car in nontraffic accident

X● **V43.23** Person on outside of car injured in collision with pick-up truck in nontraffic accident

X● **V43.24** Person on outside of car injured in collision with van in nontraffic accident

●**V43.3** Unspecified car occupant injured in collision with car, pick-up truck or van in nontraffic accident

X● **V43.31** Unspecified car occupant injured in collision with sport utility vehicle in nontraffic accident

X● **V43.32** Unspecified car occupant injured in collision with other type car in nontraffic accident

X● **V43.33** Unspecified car occupant injured in collision with pick-up truck in nontraffic accident

X● **V43.34** Unspecified car occupant injured in collision with van in nontraffic accident

●**V43.4** Person boarding or alighting a car injured in collision with car, pick-up truck or van

X● **V43.41** Person boarding or alighting a car injured in collision with sport utility vehicle

X● **V43.42** Person boarding or alighting a car injured in collision with other type car

X● **V43.43** Person boarding or alighting a car injured in collision with pick-up truck

X● **V43.44** Person boarding or alighting a car injured in collision with van

●**V43.5** Car driver injured in collision with car, pick-up truck or van in traffic accident

X● **V43.51** Car driver injured in collision with sport utility vehicle in traffic accident

X● **V43.52** Car driver injured in collision with other type car in traffic accident

X● **V43.53** Car driver injured in collision with pick-up truck in traffic accident

X● **V43.54** Car driver injured in collision with van in traffic accident

●**V43.6** Car passenger injured in collision with car, pick-up truck or van in traffic accident

X● **V43.61** Car passenger injured in collision with sport utility vehicle in traffic accident
Coding Clinic: 2015, Q1, P5-7

X● **V43.62** Car passenger injured in collision with other type car in traffic accident

X● **V43.63** Car passenger injured in collision with pick-up truck in traffic accident

X● **V43.64** Car passenger injured in collision with van in traffic accident

●**V43.7** Person on outside of car injured in collision with car, pick-up truck or van in traffic accident

X● **V43.71** Person on outside of car injured in collision with sport utility vehicle in traffic accident

X● **V43.72** Person on outside of car injured in collision with other type car in traffic accident

X● **V43.73** Person on outside of car injured in collision with pick-up truck in traffic accident

X● **V43.74** Person on outside of car injured in collision with van in traffic accident

●**V43.9** Unspecified car occupant injured in collision with car, pick-up truck or van in traffic accident

X● **V43.91** Unspecified car occupant injured in collision with sport utility vehicle in traffic accident

X● **V43.92** Unspecified car occupant injured in collision with other type car in traffic accident

X● **V43.93** Unspecified car occupant injured in collision with pick-up truck in traffic accident

X● **V43.94** Unspecified car occupant injured in collision with van in traffic accident

▶ New   ⇒ Revised   ~~deleted~~ Deleted   Excludes 1   Excludes 2   Includes   Use additional   Code first   Code also   Key words

OGCR Official Guidelines   X Assign placeholder X   ▶ Use Additional Character(s)   ▶ Manifestation Code   **Coding Clinic**

● **V44** **Car occupant injured in collision with heavy transport vehicle or bus**

> **Excludes1** car occupant injured in collision with military vehicle (V49.81)

The appropriate 7th character is to be added to each code from category V44

> A initial encounter
> D subsequent encounter
> S sequela

X● **V44.0** Car **driver** injured in collision with heavy transport vehicle or bus in **nontraffic accident**

X● **V44.1** Car **passenger** injured in collision with heavy transport vehicle or bus in **nontraffic accident**

X● **V44.2** **Person on outside** of car injured in collision with heavy transport vehicle or bus in **nontraffic accident**

X● **V44.3** **Unspecified** car occupant injured in collision with heavy transport vehicle or bus in **nontraffic accident**

X● **V44.4** **Person boarding or alighting** a car injured in collision with heavy transport vehicle or bus

X● **V44.5** Car **driver** injured in collision with heavy transport vehicle or bus in **traffic accident**

X● **V44.6** Car **passenger** injured in collision with heavy transport vehicle or bus in **traffic accident**

X● **V44.7** **Person on outside** of car injured in collision with heavy transport vehicle or bus in **traffic accident**

X● **V44.9** **Unspecified** car occupant injured in collision with heavy transport vehicle or bus in **traffic accident**

● **V45** **Car occupant injured in collision with railway train or railway vehicle**

The appropriate 7th character is to be added to each code from category V45

> A initial encounter
> D subsequent encounter
> S sequela

X● **V45.0** Car **driver** injured in collision with railway train or railway vehicle in **nontraffic accident**

X● **V45.1** Car **passenger** injured in collision with railway train or railway vehicle in **nontraffic accident**

X● **V45.2** **Person on outside** of car injured in collision with railway train or railway vehicle in **nontraffic accident**

X● **V45.3** **Unspecified** car occupant injured in collision with railway train or railway vehicle in **nontraffic accident**

X● **V45.4** **Person boarding or alighting** a car injured in collision with railway train or railway vehicle

X● **V45.5** Car **driver** injured in collision with railway train or railway vehicle in **traffic accident**

X● **V45.6** Car **passenger** injured in collision with railway train or railway vehicle in **traffic accident**

X● **V45.7** **Person on outside** of car injured in collision with railway train or railway vehicle in **traffic accident**

X● **V45.9** **Unspecified** car occupant injured in collision with railway train or railway vehicle in **traffic accident**

● **V46** **Car occupant injured in collision with other nonmotor vehicle**

> **Includes** collision with animal-drawn vehicle, animal being ridden, streetcar

The appropriate 7th character is to be added to each code from category V46

> A initial encounter
> D subsequent encounter
> S sequela

X● **V46.0** Car **driver** injured in collision with other nonmotor vehicle in **nontraffic accident**

X● **V46.1** Car **passenger** injured in collision with other nonmotor vehicle in **nontraffic accident**

X● **V46.2** **Person on outside** of car injured in collision with other nonmotor vehicle in **nontraffic accident**

X● **V46.3** **Unspecified** car occupant injured in collision with other nonmotor vehicle in **nontraffic accident**

X● **V46.4** **Person boarding or alighting** a car injured in collision with other nonmotor vehicle

X● **V46.5** Car **driver** injured in collision with other nonmotor vehicle in **traffic accident**

X● **V46.6** Car **passenger** injured in collision with other nonmotor vehicle in **traffic accident**

X● **V46.7** **Person on outside** of car injured in collision with other nonmotor vehicle in **traffic accident**

X● **V46.9** **Unspecified** car occupant injured in collision with other nonmotor vehicle in **traffic accident**

● **V47** **Car occupant injured in collision with fixed or stationary object**

The appropriate 7th character is to be added to each code from category V47

> A initial encounter
> D subsequent encounter
> S sequela

Coding Clinic: 2016, Q4, P73

X● **V47.0** Car **driver** injured in collision with fixed or stationary object in **nontraffic accident**

X● **V47.1** Car **passenger** injured in collision with fixed or stationary object in **nontraffic accident**

X● **V47.2** **Person on outside** of car injured in collision with fixed or stationary object in **nontraffic accident**

X● **V47.3** **Unspecified** car occupant injured in collision with fixed or stationary object in **nontraffic accident**

X● **V47.4** **Person boarding or alighting** a car injured in collision with fixed or stationary object

X● **V47.5** Car **driver** injured in collision with fixed or stationary object in **traffic accident**

X● **V47.6** Car **passenger** injured in collision with fixed or stationary object in **traffic accident**

X● **V47.7** **Person on outside** of car injured in collision with fixed or stationary object in **traffic accident**

X● **V47.9** **Unspecified** car occupant injured in collision with fixed or stationary object in **traffic accident**

● **V48** **Car occupant injured in noncollision transport accident**

> **Includes** overturning car NOS
> overturning car without collision

The appropriate 7th character is to be added to each code from category V48

> A initial encounter
> D subsequent encounter
> S sequela

X● **V48.0** Car **driver** injured in noncollision transport accident in **nontraffic accident**

X● **V48.1** Car **passenger** injured in noncollision transport accident in **nontraffic accident**

X● **V48.2** **Person on outside** of car injured in noncollision transport accident in **nontraffic accident**

X● **V48.3** **Unspecified** car occupant injured in noncollision transport accident in **nontraffic accident**

X● **V48.4** **Person boarding or alighting** a car injured in noncollision transport accident

X● **V48.5** Car **driver** injured in noncollision transport accident in **traffic accident**

X● **V48.6** Car **passenger** injured in noncollision transport accident in **traffic accident**

X● **V48.7** **Person on outside** of car injured in noncollision transport accident in **traffic accident**

X● **V48.9** **Unspecified** car occupant injured in noncollision transport accident in **traffic accident**

CHAPTER 20 (V01-Y99)

● **V49**   **Car occupant injured in other and unspecified transport accidents**

The appropriate 7th character is to be added to each code from category V49

A	initial encounter
D	subsequent encounter
S	sequela

  ● **V49.Ø**   **Driver** injured in collision with other and unspecified motor vehicles in nontraffic accident

    X● **V49.ØØ**   Driver injured in collision with unspecified motor vehicles in nontraffic accident

    X● **V49.Ø9**   Driver injured in collision with other motor vehicles in nontraffic accident

  ● **V49.1**   **Passenger** injured in collision with other and unspecified motor vehicles in nontraffic accident

    X● **V49.1Ø**   Passenger injured in collision with unspecified motor vehicles in nontraffic accident

    X● **V49.19**   Passenger injured in collision with other motor vehicles in nontraffic accident

  ● **V49.2**   **Unspecified** car occupant injured in collision with other and unspecified motor vehicles in nontraffic accident

    X● **V49.2Ø**   Unspecified car occupant injured in collision with unspecified motor vehicles in nontraffic accident
         Car collision NOS, nontraffic

    X● **V49.29**   Unspecified car occupant injured in collision with other motor vehicles in nontraffic accident

  X● **V49.3**   Car occupant (driver) (passenger) injured in unspecified nontraffic accident
       Car accident NOS, nontraffic
       Car occupant injured in nontraffic accident NOS

  ● **V49.4**   **Driver** injured in collision with other and unspecified motor vehicles in traffic accident

    X● **V49.4Ø**   Driver injured in collision with unspecified motor vehicles in traffic accident

    X● **V49.49**   Driver injured in collision with other motor vehicles in traffic accident

  ● **V49.5**   **Passenger** injured in collision with other and unspecified motor vehicles in traffic accident

    X● **V49.5Ø**   Passenger injured in collision with unspecified motor vehicles in traffic accident

    X● **V49.59**   Passenger injured in collision with other motor vehicles in traffic accident

  ● **V49.6**   **Unspecified** car occupant injured in collision with other and unspecified motor vehicles in traffic accident

    X● **V49.6Ø**   Unspecified car occupant injured in collision with unspecified motor vehicles in traffic accident
         Car collision NOS (traffic)

    X● **V49.69**   Unspecified car occupant injured in collision with other motor vehicles in traffic accident

  ● **V49.8**   Car occupant (driver) (passenger) injured in other specified transport accidents

    X● **V49.81**   Car occupant (driver) (passenger) injured in transport accident with military vehicle

    X● **V49.88**   Car occupant (driver) (passenger) injured in other specified transport accidents

  X● **V49.9**   Car occupant (driver) (passenger) injured in unspecified traffic accident
       Car accident NOS
       Coding Clinic: 2Ø15, Q1, P11

OCCUPANT OF PICK-UP TRUCK OR VAN INJURED IN TRANSPORT ACCIDENT (V5Ø-V59)

Includes	a four- or six-wheel motor vehicle designed primarily for carrying passengers and property but weighing less than the local limit for classification as a heavy goods vehicle
	minibus
	minivan
	sport utility vehicle (SUV)
	truck
	van
Excludes1	heavy transport vehicle (V6Ø-V69)

● **V5Ø**   **Occupant of pick-up truck or van injured in collision with pedestrian or animal**

Excludes1	pick-up truck or van collision with animal-drawn vehicle or animal being ridden (V56.-)

The appropriate 7th character is to be added to each code from category V5Ø

A	initial encounter
D	subsequent encounter
S	sequela

  X● **V5Ø.Ø**   **Driver** of pick-up truck or van injured in collision with pedestrian or animal in nontraffic accident

  X● **V5Ø.1**   **Passenger** in pick-up truck or van injured in collision with pedestrian or animal in nontraffic accident

  X● **V5Ø.2**   **Person** on outside of pick-up truck or van injured in collision with pedestrian or animal in nontraffic accident

  X● **V5Ø.3**   **Unspecified** occupant of pick-up truck or van injured in collision with pedestrian or animal in nontraffic accident

  X● **V5Ø.4**   **Person** boarding or alighting a pick-up truck or van injured in collision with pedestrian or animal

  X● **V5Ø.5**   **Driver** of pick-up truck or van injured in collision with pedestrian or animal in traffic accident

  X● **V5Ø.6**   **Passenger** in pick-up truck or van injured in collision with pedestrian or animal in traffic accident

  X● **V5Ø.7**   **Person** on outside of pick-up truck or van injured in collision with pedestrian or animal in traffic accident

  X● **V5Ø.9**   **Unspecified** occupant of pick-up truck or van injured in collision with pedestrian or animal in traffic accident

● **V51**   **Occupant of pick-up truck or van injured in collision with pedal cycle**

The appropriate 7th character is to be added to each code from category V51

A	initial encounter
D	subsequent encounter
S	sequela

  X● **V51.Ø**   **Driver** of pick-up truck or van injured in collision with pedal cycle in nontraffic accident

  X● **V51.1**   **Passenger** in pick-up truck or van injured in collision with pedal cycle in nontraffic accident

  X● **V51.2**   **Person** on outside of pick-up truck or van injured in collision with pedal cycle in nontraffic accident

  X● **V51.3**   **Unspecified** occupant of pick-up truck or van injured in collision with pedal cycle in nontraffic accident

  X● **V51.4**   **Person** boarding or alighting a pick-up truck or van injured in collision with pedal cycle

  X● **V51.5**   **Driver** of pick-up truck or van injured in collision with pedal cycle in traffic accident

  X● **V51.6**   **Passenger** in pick-up truck or van injured in collision with pedal cycle in traffic accident

  X● **V51.7**   **Person** on outside of pick-up truck or van injured in collision with pedal cycle in traffic accident

  X● **V51.9**   **Unspecified** occupant of pick-up truck or van injured in collision with pedal cycle in traffic accident

---

▶ New   ⇒ Revised   ~~deleted~~ Deleted   Excludes 1   Excludes 2   Includes   Use additional   Code first   Code also   Key words

OGCR Official Guidelines   X Assign placeholder X   ● Use Additional Character(s)   ▶ Manifestation Code   **Coding Clinic**

● **V52** **Occupant of pick-up truck or van injured in collision with two- or three-wheeled motor vehicle**

> The appropriate 7th character is to be added to each code from category V52

> | A | initial encounter |
> |---|---|
> | D | subsequent encounter |
> | S | sequela |

X ● **V52.0** **Driver of pick-up truck or van injured in collision with two- or three-wheeled motor vehicle in nontraffic accident**

X ● **V52.1** **Passenger in pick-up truck or van injured in collision with two- or three-wheeled motor vehicle in nontraffic accident**

X ● **V52.2** **Person on outside of pick-up truck or van injured in collision with two- or three-wheeled motor vehicle in nontraffic accident**

X ● **V52.3** **Unspecified occupant of pick-up truck or van injured in collision with two- or three-wheeled motor vehicle in nontraffic accident**

X ● **V52.4** **Person boarding or alighting a pick-up truck or van injured in collision with two- or three-wheeled motor vehicle**

X ● **V52.5** **Driver of pick-up truck or van injured in collision with two- or three-wheeled motor vehicle in traffic accident**

X ● **V52.6** **Passenger in pick-up truck or van injured in collision with two- or three-wheeled motor vehicle in traffic accident**

X ● **V52.7** **Person on outside of pick-up truck or van injured in collision with two- or three-wheeled motor vehicle in traffic accident**

X ● **V52.9** **Unspecified occupant of pick-up truck or van injured in collision with two- or three-wheeled motor vehicle in traffic accident**

● **V53** **Occupant of pick-up truck or van injured in collision with car, pick-up truck or van**

> The appropriate 7th character is to be added to each code from category V53

> | A | initial encounter |
> |---|---|
> | D | subsequent encounter |
> | S | sequela |

X ● **V53.0** **Driver of pick-up truck or van injured in collision with car, pick-up truck or van in nontraffic accident**

X ● **V53.1** **Passenger in pick-up truck or van injured in collision with car, pick-up truck or van in nontraffic accident**

X ● **V53.2** **Person on outside of pick-up truck or van injured in collision with car, pick-up truck or van in nontraffic accident**

X ● **V53.3** **Unspecified occupant of pick-up truck or van injured in collision with car, pick-up truck or van in nontraffic accident**

X ● **V53.4** **Person boarding or alighting a pick-up truck or van injured in collision with car, pick-up truck or van**

X ● **V53.5** **Driver of pick-up truck or van injured in collision with car, pick-up truck or van in traffic accident**

X ● **V53.6** **Passenger in pick-up truck or van injured in collision with car, pick-up truck or van in traffic accident**

X ● **V53.7** **Person on outside of pick-up truck or van injured in collision with car, pick-up truck or van in traffic accident**

X ● **V53.9** **Unspecified occupant of pick-up truck or van injured in collision with car, pick-up truck or van in traffic accident**

● **V54** **Occupant of pick-up truck or van injured in collision with heavy transport vehicle or bus**

> **Excludes1**   occupant of pick-up truck or van injured in collision with military vehicle (V59.81)

> The appropriate 7th character is to be added to each code from category V54

> | A | initial encounter |
> |---|---|
> | D | subsequent encounter |
> | S | sequela |

X ● **V54.0** **Driver of pick-up truck or van injured in collision with heavy transport vehicle or bus in nontraffic accident**

X ● **V54.1** **Passenger in pick-up truck or van injured in collision with heavy transport vehicle or bus in nontraffic accident**

X ● **V54.2** **Person on outside of pick-up truck or van injured in collision with heavy transport vehicle or bus in nontraffic accident**

X ● **V54.3** **Unspecified occupant of pick-up truck or van injured in collision with heavy transport vehicle or bus in nontraffic accident**

X ● **V54.4** **Person boarding or alighting a pick-up truck or van injured in collision with heavy transport vehicle or bus**

X ● **V54.5** **Driver of pick-up truck or van injured in collision with heavy transport vehicle or bus in traffic accident**

X ● **V54.6** **Passenger in pick-up truck or van injured in collision with heavy transport vehicle or bus in traffic accident**

X ● **V54.7** **Person on outside of pick-up truck or van injured in collision with heavy transport vehicle or bus in traffic accident**

X ● **V54.9** **Unspecified occupant of pick-up truck or van injured in collision with heavy transport vehicle or bus in traffic accident**

● **V55** **Occupant of pick-up truck or van injured in collision with railway train or railway vehicle**

> The appropriate 7th character is to be added to each code from category V55

> | A | initial encounter |
> |---|---|
> | D | subsequent encounter |
> | S | sequela |

X ● **V55.0** **Driver of pick-up truck or van injured in collision with railway train or railway vehicle in nontraffic accident**

X ● **V55.1** **Passenger in pick-up truck or van injured in collision with railway train or railway vehicle in nontraffic accident**

X ● **V55.2** **Person on outside of pick-up truck or van injured in collision with railway train or railway vehicle in nontraffic accident**

X ● **V55.3** **Unspecified occupant of pick-up truck or van injured in collision with railway train or railway vehicle in nontraffic accident**

X ● **V55.4** **Person boarding or alighting a pick-up truck or van injured in collision with railway train or railway vehicle**

X ● **V55.5** **Driver of pick-up truck or van injured in collision with railway train or railway vehicle in traffic accident**

X ● **V55.6** **Passenger in pick-up truck or van injured in collision with railway train or railway vehicle in traffic accident**

X ● **V55.7** **Person on outside of pick-up truck or van injured in collision with railway train or railway vehicle in traffic accident**

X ● **V55.9** **Unspecified occupant of pick-up truck or van injured in collision with railway train or railway vehicle in traffic accident**

● **V56**   **Occupant of pick-up truck or van injured in collision with other nonmotor vehicle**

     Includes   collision with animal-drawn vehicle, animal being ridden, streetcar

     The appropriate 7th character is to be added to each code from category V56

       A   initial encounter
       D   subsequent encounter
       S   sequela

X● **V56.0**   Driver of pick-up truck or van injured in collision with other nonmotor vehicle in nontraffic accident

X● **V56.1**   Passenger in pick-up truck or van injured in collision with other nonmotor vehicle in nontraffic accident

X● **V56.2**   Person on outside of pick-up truck or van injured in collision with other nonmotor vehicle in nontraffic accident

X● **V56.3**   Unspecified occupant of pick-up truck or van injured in collision with other nonmotor vehicle in nontraffic accident

X● **V56.4**   Person boarding or alighting a pick-up truck or van injured in collision with other nonmotor vehicle

X● **V56.5**   Driver of pick-up truck or van injured in collision with other nonmotor vehicle in traffic accident

X● **V56.6**   Passenger in pick-up truck or van injured in collision with other nonmotor vehicle in traffic accident

X● **V56.7**   Person on outside of pick-up truck or van injured in collision with other nonmotor vehicle in traffic accident

X● **V56.9**   Unspecified occupant of pick-up truck or van injured in collision with other nonmotor vehicle in traffic accident

● **V57**   **Occupant of pick-up truck or van injured in collision with fixed or stationary object**

     The appropriate 7th character is to be added to each code from category V57

       A   initial encounter
       D   subsequent encounter
       S   sequela

X● **V57.0**   Driver of pick-up truck or van injured in collision with fixed or stationary object in nontraffic accident

X● **V57.1**   Passenger in pick-up truck or van injured in collision with fixed or stationary object in nontraffic accident

X● **V57.2**   Person on outside of pick-up truck or van injured in collision with fixed or stationary object in nontraffic accident

X● **V57.3**   Unspecified occupant of pick-up truck or van injured in collision with fixed or stationary object in nontraffic accident

X● **V57.4**   Person boarding or alighting a pick-up truck or van injured in collision with fixed or stationary object

X● **V57.5**   Driver of pick-up truck or van injured in collision with fixed or stationary object in traffic accident

X● **V57.6**   Passenger in pick-up truck or van injured in collision with fixed or stationary object in traffic accident

X● **V57.7**   Person on outside of pick-up truck or van injured in collision with fixed or stationary object in traffic accident

X● **V57.9**   Unspecified occupant of pick-up truck or van injured in collision with fixed or stationary object in traffic accident

● **V58**   **Occupant of pick-up truck or van injured in noncollision transport accident**

     Includes   overturning pick-up truck or van NOS
                overturning pick-up truck or van without collision

     The appropriate 7th character is to be added to each code from category V58

       A   initial encounter
       D   subsequent encounter
       S   sequela

X● **V58.0**   Driver of pick-up truck or van injured in noncollision transport accident in nontraffic accident

X● **V58.1**   Passenger in pick-up truck or van injured in noncollision transport accident in nontraffic accident

X● **V58.2**   Person on outside of pick-up truck or van injured in noncollision transport accident in nontraffic accident

X● **V58.3**   Unspecified occupant of pick-up truck or van injured in noncollision transport accident in nontraffic accident

X● **V58.4**   Person boarding or alighting a pick-up truck or van injured in noncollision transport accident

X● **V58.5**   Driver of pick-up truck or van injured in noncollision transport accident in traffic accident

X● **V58.6**   Passenger in pick-up truck or van injured in noncollision transport accident in traffic accident

X● **V58.7**   Person on outside of pick-up truck or van injured in noncollision transport accident in traffic accident

X● **V58.9**   Unspecified occupant of pick-up truck or van injured in noncollision transport accident in traffic accident

● **V59**   **Occupant of pick-up truck or van injured in other and unspecified transport accidents**

     The appropriate 7th character is to be added to each code from category V59

       A   initial encounter
       D   subsequent encounter
       S   sequela

● **V59.0**   Driver of pick-up truck or van injured in collision with other and unspecified motor vehicles in nontraffic accident

   X● **V59.00**   Driver of pick-up truck or van injured in collision with unspecified motor vehicles in nontraffic accident

   X● **V59.09**   Driver of pick-up truck or van injured in collision with other motor vehicles in nontraffic accident

● **V59.1**   Passenger in pick-up truck or van injured in collision with other and unspecified motor vehicles in nontraffic accident

   X● **V59.10**   Passenger in pick-up truck or van injured in collision with unspecified motor vehicles in nontraffic accident

   X● **V59.19**   Passenger in pick-up truck or van injured in collision with other motor vehicles in nontraffic accident

● **V59.2**   Unspecified occupant of pick-up truck or van injured in collision with other and unspecified motor vehicles in nontraffic accident

   X● **V59.20**   Unspecified occupant of pick-up truck or van injured in collision with unspecified motor vehicles in nontraffic accident
          Collision NOS involving pick-up truck or van, nontraffic

   X● **V59.29**   Unspecified occupant of pick-up truck or van injured in collision with other motor vehicles in nontraffic accident

X● **V59.3** Occupant (driver) (passenger) of pick-up truck or van injured in **unspecified nontraffic accident**
Accident NOS involving pick-up truck or van, nontraffic
Occupant of pick-up truck or van injured in nontraffic accident NOS

● **V59.4** Driver of pick-up truck or van injured in collision with other and unspecified motor vehicles in **traffic accident**

X● **V59.40** Driver of pick-up truck or van injured in collision with **unspecified** motor vehicles in traffic accident

X● **V59.49** Driver of pick-up truck or van injured in collision with **other** motor vehicles in traffic accident

● **V59.5** Passenger in pick-up truck or van injured in collision with other and unspecified motor vehicles in **traffic accident**

X● **V59.50** Passenger in pick-up truck or van injured in collision with **unspecified** motor vehicles in traffic accident

X● **V59.59** Passenger in pick-up truck or van injured in collision with **other** motor vehicles in traffic accident

● **V59.6** **Unspecified** occupant of pick-up truck or van injured in collision with other and unspecified motor vehicles in **traffic accident**

X● **V59.60** Unspecified occupant of pick-up truck or van injured in collision with **unspecified** motor vehicles in traffic accident
Collision NOS involving pick-up truck or van (traffic)

X● **V59.69** Unspecified occupant of pick-up truck or van injured in collision with **other** motor vehicles in traffic accident

● **V59.8** Occupant (driver) (passenger) of pick-up truck or van injured in other specified transport accidents

X● **V59.81** Occupant (driver) (passenger) of pick-up truck or van injured in transport accident with **military** vehicle

X● **V59.88** Occupant (driver) (passenger) of pick-up truck or van injured in **other** specified transport accidents

X● **V59.9** Occupant (driver) (passenger) of pick-up truck or van injured in **unspecified traffic accident**
Accident NOS involving pick-up truck or van

OCCUPANT OF HEAVY TRANSPORT VEHICLE INJURED IN TRANSPORT ACCIDENT (V60-V69)

Includes	18 wheeler
	armored car
	panel truck
Excludes1	bus
	motorcoach

● **V60** Occupant of heavy transport vehicle injured in collision with pedestrian or animal

Excludes1 heavy transport vehicle collision with animal-drawn vehicle or animal being ridden (V66.-)

The appropriate 7th character is to be added to each code from category V60

A	initial encounter
D	subsequent encounter
S	sequela

X● **V60.0** Driver of heavy transport vehicle injured in collision with pedestrian or animal in **nontraffic accident**

X● **V60.1** Passenger in heavy transport vehicle injured in collision with pedestrian or animal in **nontraffic accident**

X● **V60.2** Person on outside of heavy transport vehicle injured in collision with pedestrian or animal in **nontraffic accident**

X● **V60.3** **Unspecified** occupant of heavy transport vehicle injured in collision with pedestrian or animal in **nontraffic accident**

X● **V60.4** Person **boarding or alighting** a heavy transport vehicle injured in collision with pedestrian or animal

X● **V60.5** **Driver** of heavy transport vehicle injured in collision with pedestrian or animal in **traffic accident**

X● **V60.6** **Passenger** in heavy transport vehicle injured in collision with pedestrian or animal in **traffic accident**

X● **V60.7** **Person on outside** of heavy transport vehicle injured in collision with pedestrian or animal in **traffic accident**

X● **V60.9** **Unspecified** occupant of heavy transport vehicle injured in collision with pedestrian or animal in **traffic accident**

● **V61** Occupant of heavy transport vehicle injured in collision with pedal cycle

The appropriate 7th character is to be added to each code from category V61

A	initial encounter
D	subsequent encounter
S	sequela

X● **V61.0** Driver of heavy transport vehicle injured in collision with pedal cycle in **nontraffic accident**

X● **V61.1** Passenger in heavy transport vehicle injured in collision with pedal cycle in **nontraffic accident**

X● **V61.2** Person on outside of heavy transport vehicle injured in collision with pedal cycle in **nontraffic accident**

X● **V61.3** Unspecified occupant of heavy transport vehicle injured in collision with pedal cycle in **nontraffic accident**

X● **V61.4** Person **boarding or alighting** a heavy transport vehicle injured in collision with pedal cycle while boarding or alighting

X● **V61.5** Driver of heavy transport vehicle injured in collision with pedal cycle in **traffic accident**

X● **V61.6** Passenger in heavy transport vehicle injured in collision with pedal cycle in **traffic accident**

X● **V61.7** Person on outside of heavy transport vehicle injured in collision with pedal cycle in **traffic accident**

X● **V61.9** Unspecified occupant of heavy transport vehicle injured in collision with pedal cycle in **traffic accident**

● **V62** Occupant of heavy transport vehicle injured in collision with two- or three-wheeled motor vehicle

The appropriate 7th character is to be added to each code from category V62

A	initial encounter
D	subsequent encounter
S	sequela

X● **V62.0** Driver of heavy transport vehicle injured in collision with two- or three-wheeled motor vehicle in **nontraffic accident**

X● **V62.1** Passenger in heavy transport vehicle injured in collision with two- or three-wheeled motor vehicle in **nontraffic accident**

X● **V62.2** Person on outside of heavy transport vehicle injured in collision with two- or three-wheeled motor vehicle in **nontraffic accident**

X● **V62.3** Unspecified occupant of heavy transport vehicle injured in collision with two- or three-wheeled motor vehicle in **nontraffic accident**

X● **V62.4** Person **boarding or alighting** a heavy transport vehicle injured in collision with two- or three-wheeled motor vehicle

X● **V62.5** Driver of heavy transport vehicle injured in collision with two- or three-wheeled motor vehicle in **traffic accident**

X● **V62.6** Passenger in heavy transport vehicle injured in collision with two- or three-wheeled motor vehicle in **traffic accident**

CHAPTER 20 (V01-Y99)

CHAPTER 20 (V01-Y99)

X ● **V62.7** **Person on outside** of heavy transport vehicle injured in collision with two- or three-wheeled motor vehicle in traffic accident

X ● **V62.9** **Unspecified** occupant of heavy transport vehicle injured in collision with two- or three-wheeled motor vehicle in traffic accident

● **V63** Occupant of heavy transport vehicle injured in collision with car, pick-up truck or van

> The appropriate 7th character is to be added to each code from category V63

> | A | initial encounter |
> |---|---|
> | D | subsequent encounter |
> | S | sequela |

X ● **V63.0** **Driver** of heavy transport vehicle injured in collision with car, pick-up truck or van in nontraffic accident

X ● **V63.1** **Passenger** in heavy transport vehicle injured in collision with car, pick-up truck or van in nontraffic accident

X ● **V63.2** **Person on outside** of heavy transport vehicle injured in collision with car, pick-up truck or van in nontraffic accident

X ● **V63.3** **Unspecified** occupant of heavy transport vehicle injured in collision with car, pick-up truck or van in nontraffic accident

X ● **V63.4** **Person boarding or alighting** a heavy transport vehicle injured in collision with car, pick-up truck or van

X ● **V63.5** **Driver** of heavy transport vehicle injured in collision with car, pick-up truck or van in traffic accident

X ● **V63.6** **Passenger** in heavy transport vehicle injured in collision with car, pick-up truck or van in traffic accident

X ● **V63.7** **Person on outside** of heavy transport vehicle injured in collision with car, pick-up truck or van in traffic accident

X ● **V63.9** **Unspecified** occupant of heavy transport vehicle injured in collision with car, pick-up truck or van in traffic accident

● **V64** Occupant of heavy transport vehicle injured in collision with heavy transport vehicle or bus

> **Excludes1**   occupant of heavy transport vehicle injured in collision with military vehicle (V69.81)

> The appropriate 7th character is to be added to each code from category V64

> | A | initial encounter |
> |---|---|
> | D | subsequent encounter |
> | S | sequela |

X ● **V64.0** **Driver** of heavy transport vehicle injured in collision with heavy transport vehicle or bus in nontraffic accident

X ● **V64.1** **Passenger** in heavy transport vehicle injured in collision with heavy transport vehicle or bus in nontraffic accident

X ● **V64.2** **Person on outside** of heavy transport vehicle injured in collision with heavy transport vehicle or bus in nontraffic accident

X ● **V64.3** **Unspecified** occupant of heavy transport vehicle injured in collision with heavy transport vehicle or bus in nontraffic accident

X ● **V64.4** **Person boarding or alighting** a heavy transport vehicle injured in collision with heavy transport vehicle or bus while boarding or alighting

X ● **V64.5** **Driver** of heavy transport vehicle injured in collision with heavy transport vehicle or bus in traffic accident

X ● **V64.6** **Passenger** in heavy transport vehicle injured in collision with heavy transport vehicle or bus in traffic accident

X ● **V64.7** **Person on outside** of heavy transport vehicle injured in collision with heavy transport vehicle or bus in traffic accident

X ● **V64.9** **Unspecified** occupant of heavy transport vehicle injured in collision with heavy transport vehicle or bus in traffic accident

● **V65** Occupant of heavy transport vehicle injured in collision with railway train or railway vehicle

> The appropriate 7th character is to be added to each code from category V65

> | A | initial encounter |
> |---|---|
> | D | subsequent encounter |
> | S | sequela |

X ● **V65.0** **Driver** of heavy transport vehicle injured in collision with railway train or railway vehicle in nontraffic accident

X ● **V65.1** **Passenger** in heavy transport vehicle injured in collision with railway train or railway vehicle in nontraffic accident

X ● **V65.2** **Person on outside** of heavy transport vehicle injured in collision with railway train or railway vehicle in nontraffic accident

X ● **V65.3** **Unspecified** occupant of heavy transport vehicle injured in collision with railway train or railway vehicle in nontraffic accident

X ● **V65.4** **Person boarding or alighting** a heavy transport vehicle injured in collision with railway train or railway vehicle

X ● **V65.5** **Driver** of heavy transport vehicle injured in collision with railway train or railway vehicle in traffic accident

X ● **V65.6** **Passenger** in heavy transport vehicle injured in collision with railway train or railway vehicle in traffic accident

X ● **V65.7** **Person on outside** of heavy transport vehicle injured in collision with railway train or railway vehicle in traffic accident

X ● **V65.9** **Unspecified** occupant of heavy transport vehicle injured in collision with railway train or railway vehicle in traffic accident

● **V66** Occupant of heavy transport vehicle injured in collision with other nonmotor vehicle

> **Includes**   collision with animal-drawn vehicle, animal being ridden, streetcar

> The appropriate 7th character is to be added to each code from category V66

> | A | initial encounter |
> |---|---|
> | D | subsequent encounter |
> | S | sequela |

X ● **V66.0** **Driver** of heavy transport vehicle injured in collision with other nonmotor vehicle in nontraffic accident

X ● **V66.1** **Passenger** in heavy transport vehicle injured in collision with other nonmotor vehicle in nontraffic accident

X ● **V66.2** **Person on outside** of heavy transport vehicle injured in collision with other nonmotor vehicle in nontraffic accident

X ● **V66.3** **Unspecified** occupant of heavy transport vehicle injured in collision with other nonmotor vehicle in nontraffic accident

X ● **V66.4** **Person boarding or alighting** a heavy transport vehicle injured in collision with other nonmotor vehicle

X ● **V66.5** **Driver** of heavy transport vehicle injured in collision with other nonmotor vehicle in traffic accident

X ● **V66.6** **Passenger** in heavy transport vehicle injured in collision with other nonmotor vehicle in traffic accident

X ● **V66.7** **Person on outside** of heavy transport vehicle injured in collision with other nonmotor vehicle in traffic accident

X ● **V66.9** **Unspecified** occupant of heavy transport vehicle injured in collision with other nonmotor vehicle in traffic accident

▶ New   ⇒ Revised   ~~deleted~~ Deleted   Excludes 1   Excludes 2   Includes   Use additional   Code first   Code also   Key words

OGCR Official Guidelines   X Assign placeholder X   ● Use Additional Character(s)   ▷ Manifestation Code   **Coding Clinic**

● **V67**   **Occupant of heavy transport vehicle injured in collision with fixed or stationary object**

The appropriate 7th character is to be added to each code from category V67

A	initial encounter
D	subsequent encounter
S	sequela

X● **V67.0**   Driver of heavy transport vehicle injured in collision with fixed or stationary object in nontraffic accident

X● **V67.1**   Passenger in heavy transport vehicle injured in collision with fixed or stationary object in nontraffic accident

X● **V67.2**   Person on outside of heavy transport vehicle injured in collision with fixed or stationary object in nontraffic accident

X● **V67.3**   Unspecified occupant of heavy transport vehicle injured in collision with fixed or stationary object in nontraffic accident

X● **V67.4**   Person boarding or alighting a heavy transport vehicle injured in collision with fixed or stationary object

X● **V67.5**   Driver of heavy transport vehicle injured in collision with fixed or stationary object in traffic accident

X● **V67.6**   Passenger in heavy transport vehicle injured in collision with fixed or stationary object in traffic accident

X● **V67.7**   Person on outside of heavy transport vehicle injured in collision with fixed or stationary object in traffic accident

X● **V67.9**   Unspecified occupant of heavy transport vehicle injured in collision with fixed or stationary object in traffic accident

● **V68**   **Occupant of heavy transport vehicle injured in noncollision transport accident**

Includes   overturning heavy transport vehicle NOS
overturning heavy transport vehicle without collision

The appropriate 7th character is to be added to each code from category V68

A	initial encounter
D	subsequent encounter
S	sequela

X● **V68.0**   Driver of heavy transport vehicle injured in noncollision transport accident in nontraffic accident

X● **V68.1**   Passenger in heavy transport vehicle injured in noncollision transport accident in nontraffic accident

X● **V68.2**   Person on outside of heavy transport vehicle injured in noncollision transport accident in nontraffic accident

X● **V68.3**   Unspecified occupant of heavy transport vehicle injured in noncollision transport accident in nontraffic accident

X● **V68.4**   Person boarding or alighting a heavy transport vehicle injured in noncollision transport accident

X● **V68.5**   Driver of heavy transport vehicle injured in noncollision transport accident in traffic accident

X● **V68.6**   Passenger in heavy transport vehicle injured in noncollision transport accident in traffic accident

X● **V68.7**   Person on outside of heavy transport vehicle injured in noncollision transport accident in traffic accident

X● **V68.9**   Unspecified occupant of heavy transport vehicle injured in noncollision transport accident in traffic accident

● **V69**   **Occupant of heavy transport vehicle injured in other and unspecified transport accidents**

The appropriate 7th character is to be added to each code from category V69

A	initial encounter
D	subsequent encounter
S	sequela

● **V69.0**   Driver of heavy transport vehicle injured in collision with other and unspecified motor vehicles in nontraffic accident

X● **V69.00**   Driver of heavy transport vehicle injured in collision with unspecified motor vehicles in nontraffic accident

X● **V69.09**   Driver of heavy transport vehicle injured in collision with other motor vehicles in nontraffic accident

● **V69.1**   Passenger in heavy transport vehicle injured in collision with other and unspecified motor vehicles in nontraffic accident

X● **V69.10**   Passenger in heavy transport vehicle injured in collision with unspecified motor vehicles in nontraffic accident

X● **V69.19**   Passenger in heavy transport vehicle injured in collision with other motor vehicles in nontraffic accident

● **V69.2**   Unspecified occupant of heavy transport vehicle injured in collision with other and unspecified motor vehicles in nontraffic accident

X● **V69.20**   Unspecified occupant of heavy transport vehicle injured in collision with unspecified motor vehicles in nontraffic accident
Collision NOS involving heavy transport vehicle, nontraffic

X● **V69.29**   Unspecified occupant of heavy transport vehicle injured in collision with other motor vehicles in nontraffic accident

X● **V69.3**   Occupant (driver) (passenger) of heavy transport vehicle injured in unspecified nontraffic accident
Accident NOS involving heavy transport vehicle, nontraffic
Occupant of heavy transport vehicle injured in nontraffic accident NOS

● **V69.4**   Driver of heavy transport vehicle injured in collision with other and unspecified motor vehicles in traffic accident

X● **V69.40**   Driver of heavy transport vehicle injured in collision with unspecified motor vehicles in traffic accident

X● **V69.49**   Driver of heavy transport vehicle injured in collision with other motor vehicles in traffic accident

● **V69.5**   Passenger in heavy transport vehicle injured in collision with other and unspecified motor vehicles in traffic accident

X● **V69.50**   Passenger in heavy transport vehicle injured in collision with unspecified motor vehicles in traffic accident

X● **V69.59**   Passenger in heavy transport vehicle injured in collision with other motor vehicles in traffic accident

● **V69.6** Unspecified occupant of heavy transport vehicle injured in collision with other and unspecified motor vehicles in traffic accident

　　X● **V69.60** Unspecified occupant of heavy transport vehicle injured in collision with unspecified motor vehicles in traffic accident
　　　　　Collision NOS involving heavy transport vehicle (traffic)

　　X● **V69.69** Unspecified occupant of heavy transport vehicle injured in collision with other motor vehicles in traffic accident

● **V69.8** Occupant (driver) (passenger) of heavy transport vehicle injured in other specified transport accidents

　　X● **V69.81** Occupant (driver) (passenger) of heavy transport vehicle injured in transport accidents with military vehicle

　　X● **V69.88** Occupant (driver) (passenger) of heavy transport vehicle injured in other specified transport accidents

X● **V69.9** Occupant (driver) (passenger) of heavy transport vehicle injured in unspecified traffic accident
　　　Accident NOS involving heavy transport vehicle

BUS OCCUPANT INJURED IN TRANSPORT ACCIDENT (V70-V79)

Includes	motorcoach
Excludes1	minibus (V50-V59)

● **V70** Bus occupant injured in collision with pedestrian or animal

　　Excludes1 bus collision with animal-drawn vehicle or animal being ridden (V76.-)

The appropriate 7th character is to be added to each code from category V70

A	initial encounter
D	subsequent encounter
S	sequela

X● **V70.0** Driver of bus injured in collision with pedestrian or animal in nontraffic accident

X● **V70.1** Passenger on bus injured in collision with pedestrian or animal in nontraffic accident

X● **V70.2** Person on outside of bus injured in collision with pedestrian or animal in nontraffic accident

X● **V70.3** Unspecified occupant of bus injured in collision with pedestrian or animal in nontraffic accident

X● **V70.4** Person boarding or alighting from bus injured in collision with pedestrian or animal

X● **V70.5** Driver of bus injured in collision with pedestrian or animal in traffic accident

X● **V70.6** Passenger on bus injured in collision with pedestrian or animal in traffic accident

X● **V70.7** Person on outside of bus injured in collision with pedestrian or animal in traffic accident

X● **V70.9** Unspecified occupant of bus injured in collision with pedestrian or animal in traffic accident

● **V71** Bus occupant injured in collision with pedal cycle

The appropriate 7th character is to be added to each code from category V71

A	initial encounter
D	subsequent encounter
S	sequela

X● **V71.0** Driver of bus injured in collision with pedal cycle in nontraffic accident

X● **V71.1** Passenger on bus injured in collision with pedal cycle in nontraffic accident

X● **V71.2** Person on outside of bus injured in collision with pedal cycle in nontraffic accident

X● **V71.3** Unspecified occupant of bus injured in collision with pedal cycle in nontraffic accident

X● **V71.4** Person boarding or alighting from bus injured in collision with pedal cycle

X● **V71.5** Driver of bus injured in collision with pedal cycle in traffic accident

X● **V71.6** Passenger on bus injured in collision with pedal cycle in traffic accident

X● **V71.7** Person on outside of bus injured in collision with pedal cycle in traffic accident

X● **V71.9** Unspecified occupant of bus injured in collision with pedal cycle in traffic accident

● **V72** Bus occupant injured in collision with two- or three-wheeled motor vehicle

The appropriate 7th character is to be added to each code from category V72

A	initial encounter
D	subsequent encounter
S	sequela

X● **V72.0** Driver of bus injured in collision with two- or three-wheeled motor vehicle in nontraffic accident

X● **V72.1** Passenger on bus injured in collision with two- or three-wheeled motor vehicle in nontraffic accident

X● **V72.2** Person on outside of bus injured in collision with two- or three-wheeled motor vehicle in nontraffic accident

X● **V72.3** Unspecified occupant of bus injured in collision with two- or three-wheeled motor vehicle in nontraffic accident

X● **V72.4** Person boarding or alighting from bus injured in collision with two- or three-wheeled motor vehicle

X● **V72.5** Driver of bus injured in collision with two- or three-wheeled motor vehicle in traffic accident

X● **V72.6** Passenger on bus injured in collision with two- or three-wheeled motor vehicle in traffic accident

X● **V72.7** Person on outside of bus injured in collision with two- or three-wheeled motor vehicle in traffic accident

X● **V72.9** Unspecified occupant of bus injured in collision with two- or three-wheeled motor vehicle in traffic accident

● **V73** Bus occupant injured in collision with car, pick-up truck or van

The appropriate 7th character is to be added to each code from category V73

A	initial encounter
D	subsequent encounter
S	sequela

X● **V73.0** Driver of bus injured in collision with car, pick-up truck or van in nontraffic accident

X● **V73.1** Passenger on bus injured in collision with car, pick-up truck or van in nontraffic accident

X● **V73.2** Person on outside of bus injured in collision with car, pick-up truck or van in nontraffic accident

X● **V73.3** Unspecified occupant of bus injured in collision with car, pick-up truck or van in nontraffic accident

X● **V73.4** Person boarding or alighting from bus injured in collision with car, pick-up truck or van

X● **V73.5** Driver of bus injured in collision with car, pick-up truck or van in traffic accident

X● **V73.6** Passenger on bus injured in collision with car, pick-up truck or van in traffic accident

X● **V73.7** Person on outside of bus injured in collision with car, pick-up truck or van in traffic accident

X● **V73.9** Unspecified occupant of bus injured in collision with car, pick-up truck or van in traffic accident

● **V74** **Bus occupant injured in collision with heavy transport vehicle or bus**

> **Excludes1** bus occupant injured in collision with military vehicle (V79.81)

> The appropriate 7th character is to be added to each code from category V74

> | A | initial encounter |
> |---|---|
> | D | subsequent encounter |
> | S | sequela |

X● **V74.0** Driver of bus injured in collision with heavy transport vehicle or bus in nontraffic accident

X● **V74.1** Passenger on bus injured in collision with heavy transport vehicle or bus in nontraffic accident

X● **V74.2** Person on outside of bus injured in collision with heavy transport vehicle or bus in nontraffic accident

X● **V74.3** Unspecified occupant of bus injured in collision with heavy transport vehicle or bus in nontraffic accident

X● **V74.4** Person boarding or alighting from bus injured in collision with heavy transport vehicle or bus

X● **V74.5** Driver of bus injured in collision with heavy transport vehicle or bus in traffic accident

X● **V74.6** Passenger on bus injured in collision with heavy transport vehicle or bus in traffic accident

X● **V74.7** Person on outside of bus injured in collision with heavy transport vehicle or bus in traffic accident

X● **V74.9** Unspecified occupant of bus injured in collision with heavy transport vehicle or bus in traffic accident

● **V75** **Bus occupant injured in collision with railway train or railway vehicle**

> The appropriate 7th character is to be added to each code from category V75

> | A | initial encounter |
> |---|---|
> | D | subsequent encounter |
> | S | sequela |

X● **V75.0** Driver of bus injured in collision with railway train or railway vehicle in nontraffic accident

X● **V75.1** Passenger on bus injured in collision with railway train or railway vehicle in nontraffic accident

X● **V75.2** Person on outside of bus injured in collision with railway train or railway vehicle in nontraffic accident

X● **V75.3** Unspecified occupant of bus injured in collision with railway train or railway vehicle in nontraffic accident

X● **V75.4** Person boarding or alighting from bus injured in collision with railway train or railway vehicle

X● **V75.5** Driver of bus injured in collision with railway train or railway vehicle in traffic accident

X● **V75.6** Passenger on bus injured in collision with railway train or railway vehicle in traffic accident

X● **V75.7** Person on outside of bus injured in collision with railway train or railway vehicle in traffic accident

X● **V75.9** Unspecified occupant of bus injured in collision with railway train or railway vehicle in traffic accident

● **V76** **Bus occupant injured in collision with other nonmotor vehicle**

> **Includes** collision with animal-drawn vehicle, animal being ridden, streetcar

> The appropriate 7th character is to be added to each code from category V76

> | A | initial encounter |
> |---|---|
> | D | subsequent encounter |
> | S | sequela |

X● **V76.0** Driver of bus injured in collision with other nonmotor vehicle in nontraffic accident

X● **V76.1** Passenger on bus injured in collision with other nonmotor vehicle in nontraffic accident

X● **V76.2** Person on outside of bus injured in collision with other nonmotor vehicle in nontraffic accident

X● **V76.3** Unspecified occupant of bus injured in collision with other nonmotor vehicle in nontraffic accident

X● **V76.4** Person boarding or alighting from bus injured in collision with other nonmotor vehicle

X● **V76.5** Driver of bus injured in collision with other nonmotor vehicle in traffic accident

X● **V76.6** Passenger on bus injured in collision with other nonmotor vehicle in traffic accident

X● **V76.7** Person on outside of bus injured in collision with other nonmotor vehicle in traffic accident

X● **V76.9** Unspecified occupant of bus injured in collision with other nonmotor vehicle in traffic accident

● **V77** **Bus occupant injured in collision with fixed or stationary object**

> The appropriate 7th character is to be added to each code from category V77

> | A | initial encounter |
> |---|---|
> | D | subsequent encounter |
> | S | sequela |

X● **V77.0** Driver of bus injured in collision with fixed or stationary object in nontraffic accident

X● **V77.1** Passenger on bus injured in collision with fixed or stationary object in nontraffic accident

X● **V77.2** Person on outside of bus injured in collision with fixed or stationary object in nontraffic accident

X● **V77.3** Unspecified occupant of bus injured in collision with fixed or stationary object in nontraffic accident

X● **V77.4** Person boarding or alighting from bus injured in collision with fixed or stationary object

X● **V77.5** Driver of bus injured in collision with fixed or stationary object in traffic accident

X● **V77.6** Passenger on bus injured in collision with fixed or stationary object in traffic accident

X● **V77.7** Person on outside of bus injured in collision with fixed or stationary object in traffic accident

X● **V77.9** Unspecified occupant of bus injured in collision with fixed or stationary object in traffic accident

● **V78** **Bus occupant injured in noncollision transport accident**

> **Includes** overturning bus NOS
> overturning bus without collision

> The appropriate 7th character is to be added to each code from category V78

> | A | initial encounter |
> |---|---|
> | D | subsequent encounter |
> | S | sequela |

X● **V78.0** Driver of bus injured in noncollision transport accident in nontraffic accident

X● **V78.1** Passenger on bus injured in noncollision transport accident in nontraffic accident

X● **V78.2** Person on outside of bus injured in noncollision transport accident in nontraffic accident

X● **V78.3** Unspecified occupant of bus injured in noncollision transport accident in nontraffic accident

X● **V78.4** Person boarding or alighting from bus injured in noncollision transport accident

X● **V78.5** Driver of bus injured in noncollision transport accident in traffic accident

X● **V78.6** Passenger on bus injured in noncollision transport accident in traffic accident

X● **V78.7** Person on outside of bus injured in noncollision transport accident in traffic accident

X● **V78.9** Unspecified occupant of bus injured in noncollision transport accident in traffic accident

CHAPTER 20 (V01-Y99)

● V79   **Bus occupant injured in other and unspecified transport accidents**

The appropriate 7th character is to be added to each code from category V79

> A   initial encounter
> D   subsequent encounter
> S   sequela

● **V79.0**   Driver of bus injured in collision with other and unspecified motor vehicles in nontraffic accident

   X ● **V79.00**   Driver of bus injured in collision with unspecified motor vehicles in nontraffic accident

   X ● **V79.09**   Driver of bus injured in collision with other motor vehicles in nontraffic accident

● **V79.1**   Passenger on bus injured in collision with other and unspecified motor vehicles in nontraffic accident

   X ● **V79.10**   Passenger on bus injured in collision with unspecified motor vehicles in nontraffic accident

   X ● **V79.19**   Passenger on bus injured in collision with other motor vehicles in nontraffic accident

● **V79.2**   Unspecified bus occupant injured in collision with other and unspecified motor vehicles in nontraffic accident

   X ● **V79.20**   Unspecified bus occupant injured in collision with unspecified motor vehicles in nontraffic accident
> Bus collision NOS, nontraffic

   X ● **V79.29**   Unspecified bus occupant injured in collision with other motor vehicles in nontraffic accident

X ● **V79.3**   Bus occupant (driver) (passenger) injured in unspecified nontraffic accident
> Bus accident NOS, nontraffic
> Bus occupant injured in nontraffic accident NOS

● **V79.4**   Driver of bus injured in collision with other and unspecified motor vehicles in traffic accident

   X ● **V79.40**   Driver of bus injured in collision with unspecified motor vehicles in traffic accident

   X ● **V79.49**   Driver of bus injured in collision with other motor vehicles in traffic accident

● **V79.5**   Passenger on bus injured in collision with other and unspecified motor vehicles in traffic accident

   X ● **V79.50**   Passenger on bus injured in collision with unspecified motor vehicles in traffic accident

   X ● **V79.59**   Passenger on bus injured in collision with other motor vehicles in traffic accident

● **V79.6**   Unspecified bus occupant injured in collision with other and unspecified motor vehicles in traffic accident

   X ● **V79.60**   Unspecified bus occupant injured in collision with unspecified motor vehicles in traffic accident
> Bus collision NOS (traffic)

   X ● **V79.69**   Unspecified bus occupant injured in collision with other motor vehicles in traffic accident

● **V79.8**   Bus occupant (driver) (passenger) injured in other specified transport accidents

   X ● **V79.81**   Bus occupant (driver) (passenger) injured in transport accidents with military vehicle

   X ● **V79.88**   Bus occupant (driver) (passenger) injured in other specified transport accidents

X ● **V79.9**   Bus occupant (driver) (passenger) injured in unspecified traffic accident
> Bus accident NOS

OTHER LAND TRANSPORT ACCIDENTS (V80-V89)

● V80   **Animal-rider or occupant of animal-drawn vehicle injured in transport accident**

The appropriate 7th character is to be added to each code from category V80

> A   initial encounter
> D   subsequent encounter
> S   sequela

● **V80.0**   Animal-rider or occupant of animal drawn vehicle injured by fall from or being thrown from animal or animal-drawn vehicle in noncollision accident

   ● **V80.01**   Animal-rider injured by fall from or being thrown from animal in noncollision accident

     ● **V80.010**   Animal-rider injured by fall from or being thrown from horse in noncollision accident

     ● **V80.018**   Animal-rider injured by fall from or being thrown from other animal in noncollision accident

   X ● **V80.02**   Occupant of animal-drawn vehicle injured by fall from or being thrown from animal-drawn vehicle in noncollision accident
> Overturning animal-drawn vehicle NOS
> Overturning animal-drawn vehicle without collision

● **V80.1**   Animal-rider or occupant of animal-drawn vehicle injured in collision with pedestrian or animal

> **Excludes1**   animal-rider or animal-drawn vehicle collision with animal-drawn vehicle or animal being ridden (V80.7)

   X ● **V80.11**   Animal-rider injured in collision with pedestrian or animal

   X ● **V80.12**   Occupant of animal-drawn vehicle injured in collision with pedestrian or animal

● **V80.2**   Animal-rider or occupant of animal-drawn vehicle injured in collision with pedal cycle

   X ● **V80.21**   Animal-rider injured in collision with pedal cycle

   X ● **V80.22**   Occupant of animal-drawn vehicle injured in collision with pedal cycle

● **V80.3**   Animal-rider or occupant of animal-drawn vehicle injured in collision with two- or three-wheeled motor vehicle

   X ● **V80.31**   Animal-rider injured in collision with two- or three-wheeled motor vehicle

   X ● **V80.32**   Occupant of animal-drawn vehicle injured in collision with two- or three-wheeled motor vehicle

● **V80.4**   Animal-rider or occupant of animal-drawn vehicle injured in collision with car, pick-up truck, van, heavy transport vehicle or bus

> **Excludes1**   animal-rider injured in collision with military vehicle (V80.910)
> occupant of animal-drawn vehicle injured in collision with military vehicle (V80.920)

   X ● **V80.41**   Animal-rider injured in collision with car, pick-up truck, van, heavy transport vehicle or bus

   X ● **V80.42**   Occupant of animal-drawn vehicle injured in collision with car, pick-up truck, van, heavy transport vehicle or bus

▶ New   ⇒ Revised   ~~deleted~~ Deleted   Excludes 1   Excludes 2   Includes   Use additional   Code first   Code also   Key words

OGCR Official Guidelines   X Assign placeholder X   ● Use Additional Character(s)   ▶ Manifestation Code   **Coding Clinic**

● **V80.5** Animal-rider or occupant of animal-drawn vehicle injured in collision with other specified motor vehicle

  X● **V80.51** Animal-rider injured in collision with other specified motor vehicle

  X● **V80.52** Occupant of animal-drawn vehicle injured in collision with other specified motor vehicle

● **V80.6** Animal-rider or occupant of animal-drawn vehicle injured in collision with railway train or railway vehicle

  X● **V80.61** Animal-rider injured in collision with railway train or railway vehicle

  X● **V80.62** Occupant of animal-drawn vehicle injured in collision with railway train or railway vehicle

● **V80.7** Animal-rider or occupant of animal-drawn vehicle injured in collision with other nonmotor vehicles

  ● **V80.71** Animal-rider or occupant of animal-drawn vehicle injured in collision with animal being ridden

    ● **V80.710** Animal-rider injured in collision with other animal being ridden

    ● **V80.711** Occupant of animal-drawn vehicle injured in collision with animal being ridden

  ● **V80.72** Animal-rider or occupant of animal-drawn vehicle injured in collision with other animal-drawn vehicle

    ● **V80.720** Animal-rider injured in collision with animal-drawn vehicle

    ● **V80.721** Occupant of animal-drawn vehicle injured in collision with other animal-drawn vehicle

  ● **V80.73** Animal-rider or occupant of animal-drawn vehicle injured in collision with streetcar

    ● **V80.730** Animal-rider injured in collision with streetcar

    ● **V80.731** Occupant of animal-drawn vehicle injured in collision with streetcar

  ● **V80.79** Animal-rider or occupant of animal-drawn vehicle injured in collision with other nonmotor vehicles

    ● **V80.790** Animal-rider injured in collision with other nonmotor vehicles

    ● **V80.791** Occupant of animal-drawn vehicle injured in collision with other nonmotor vehicles

● **V80.8** Animal-rider or occupant of animal-drawn vehicle injured in collision with fixed or stationary object

  X● **V80.81** Animal-rider injured in collision with fixed or stationary object

  X● **V80.82** Occupant of animal-drawn vehicle injured in collision with fixed or stationary object

● **V80.9** Animal-rider or occupant of animal-drawn vehicle injured in other and unspecified transport accidents

  ● **V80.91** Animal-rider injured in other and unspecified transport accidents

    ● **V80.910** Animal-rider injured in transport accident with military vehicle

    ● **V80.918** Animal-rider injured in other transport accident

    ● **V80.919** Animal-rider injured in unspecified transport accident

      Animal rider accident NOS

● **V80.92** Occupant of animal-drawn vehicle injured in other and unspecified transport accidents

  ● **V80.920** Occupant of animal-drawn vehicle injured in transport accident with military vehicle

  ● **V80.928** Occupant of animal-drawn vehicle injured in other transport accident

  ● **V80.929** Occupant of animal-drawn vehicle injured in unspecified transport accident

      Animal-drawn vehicle accident NOS

● **V81** Occupant of railway train or railway vehicle injured in transport accident

  Includes   derailment of railway train or railway vehicle

         person on outside of train

  Excludes1   streetcar (V82.-)

  The appropriate 7th character is to be added to each code from category V81

A	initial encounter
D	subsequent encounter
S	sequela

  X● **V81.0** Occupant of railway train or railway vehicle injured in collision with motor vehicle in nontraffic accident

    Excludes1   occupant of railway train or railway vehicle injured due to collision with military vehicle (V81.83)

  X● **V81.1** Occupant of railway train or railway vehicle injured in collision with motor vehicle in traffic accident

    Excludes1   occupant of railway train or railway vehicle injured due to collision with military vehicle (V81.83)

  X● **V81.2** Occupant of railway train or railway vehicle injured in collision with or hit by rolling stock

  X● **V81.3** Occupant of railway train or railway vehicle injured in collision with other object

      Railway collision NOS

  X● **V81.4** Person injured while boarding or alighting from railway train or railway vehicle

  X● **V81.5** Occupant of railway train or railway vehicle injured by fall in railway train or railway vehicle

  X● **V81.6** Occupant of railway train or railway vehicle injured by fall from railway train or railway vehicle

  X● **V81.7** Occupant of railway train or railway vehicle injured in derailment without antecedent collision

  ● **V81.8** Occupant of railway train or railway vehicle injured in other specified railway accidents

    X● **V81.81** Occupant of railway train or railway vehicle injured due to explosion or fire on train

    X● **V81.82** Occupant of railway train or railway vehicle injured due to object falling onto train

        Occupant of railway train or railway vehicle injured due to falling earth onto train

        Occupant of railway train or railway vehicle injured due to falling rocks onto train

        Occupant of railway train or railway vehicle injured due to falling snow onto train

        Occupant of railway train or railway vehicle injured due to falling trees onto train

    X● **V81.83** Occupant of railway train or railway vehicle injured due to collision with military vehicle

    X● **V81.89** Occupant of railway train or railway vehicle injured due to other specified railway accident

  X● **V81.9** Occupant of railway train or railway vehicle injured in unspecified railway accident

      Railway accident NOS

CHAPTER 20 (V01-Y99)

● **V82** **Occupant of powered streetcar injured in transport accident**

> **Includes**   interurban electric car
> person on outside of streetcar
> tram (car)
> trolley (car)

> **Excludes1**   bus (V70-V79)
> motorcoach (V70-V79)
> nonpowered streetcar (V76.-)
> train (V81.-)

The appropriate 7th character is to be added to each code from category V82

> A   initial encounter
> D   subsequent encounter
> S   sequela

X ● **V82.0**   **Occupant of streetcar injured in collision with motor vehicle in nontraffic accident**

X ● **V82.1**   **Occupant of streetcar injured in collision with motor vehicle in traffic accident**

X ● **V82.2**   **Occupant of streetcar injured in collision with or hit by rolling stock**

X ● **V82.3**   **Occupant of streetcar injured in collision with other object**

> **Excludes1**   collision with animal-drawn vehicle or animal being ridden (V82.8)

X ● **V82.4**   **Person injured while boarding or alighting from streetcar**

X ● **V82.5**   **Occupant of streetcar injured by fall in streetcar**

> **Excludes1**   fall in streetcar:
>   while boarding or alighting (V82.4)
>   with antecedent collision (V82.0-V82.3)

X ● **V82.6**   **Occupant of streetcar injured by fall from streetcar**

> **Excludes1**   fall from streetcar:
>   while boarding or alighting (V82.4)
>   with antecedent collision (V82.0-V82.3)

X ● **V82.7**   **Occupant of streetcar injured in derailment without antecedent collision**

> **Excludes1**   occupant of streetcar injured in derailment with antecedent collision (V82.0-V82.3)

X ● **V82.8**   **Occupant of streetcar injured in other specified transport accidents**
> Streetcar collision with military vehicle
> Streetcar collision with train or nonmotor vehicles

X ● **V82.9**   **Occupant of streetcar injured in unspecified traffic accident**
> Streetcar accident NOS

● **V83** **Occupant of special vehicle mainly used on industrial premises injured in transport accident**

> **Includes**   battery-powered airport passenger vehicle
> battery-powered truck (baggage) (mail)
> coal-car in mine
> forklift (truck)
> logging car
> self-propelled industrial truck
> station baggage truck (powered)
> tram, truck, or tub (powered) in mine or quarry

> **Excludes1**   special construction vehicles (V85.-)
> special industrial vehicle in stationary use or maintenance (W31.-)

The appropriate 7th character is to be added to each code from category V83

> A   initial encounter
> D   subsequent encounter
> S   sequela

X ● **V83.0**   **Driver of special industrial vehicle injured in traffic accident**

X ● **V83.1**   **Passenger of special industrial vehicle injured in traffic accident**

X ● **V83.2**   **Person on outside of special industrial vehicle injured in traffic accident**

X ● **V83.3**   **Unspecified occupant of special industrial vehicle injured in traffic accident**

X ● **V83.4**   **Person injured while boarding or alighting from special industrial vehicle**

X ● **V83.5**   **Driver of special industrial vehicle injured in nontraffic accident**

X ● **V83.6**   **Passenger of special industrial vehicle injured in nontraffic accident**

X ● **V83.7**   **Person on outside of special industrial vehicle injured in nontraffic accident**

X ● **V83.9**   **Unspecified occupant of special industrial vehicle injured in nontraffic accident**
> Special-industrial-vehicle accident NOS

● **V84** **Occupant of special vehicle mainly used in agriculture injured in transport accident**

> **Includes**   self-propelled farm machinery
> tractor (and trailer)

> **Excludes1**   animal-powered farm machinery accident (W30.8-)
> contact with combine harvester (W30.0)
> special agricultural vehicle in stationary use or maintenance (W30.-)

The appropriate 7th character is to be added to each code from category V84

> A   initial encounter
> D   subsequent encounter
> S   sequela

X ● **V84.0**   **Driver of special agricultural vehicle injured in traffic accident**

X ● **V84.1**   **Passenger of special agricultural vehicle injured in traffic accident**

X ● **V84.2**   **Person on outside of special agricultural vehicle injured in traffic accident**

X ● **V84.3**   **Unspecified occupant of special agricultural vehicle injured in traffic accident**

X ● **V84.4**   **Person injured while boarding or alighting from special agricultural vehicle**

X ● **V84.5**   **Driver of special agricultural vehicle injured in nontraffic accident**

X ● **V84.6**   **Passenger of special agricultural vehicle injured in nontraffic accident**

X ● **V84.7**   **Person on outside of special agricultural vehicle injured in nontraffic accident**

X ● **V84.9**   **Unspecified occupant of special agricultural vehicle injured in nontraffic accident**
> Special-agricultural vehicle accident NOS

● **V85** **Occupant of special construction vehicle injured in transport accident**

> **Includes**   bulldozer
> digger
> dump truck
> earth-leveller
> mechanical shovel
> road-roller

> **Excludes1**   special industrial vehicle (V83.-)
> special construction vehicle in stationary use or maintenance (W31.-)

The appropriate 7th character is to be added to each code from category V85

> A   initial encounter
> D   subsequent encounter
> S   sequela

X ● **V85.0**   **Driver of special construction vehicle injured in traffic accident**

X ● **V85.1**   **Passenger of special construction vehicle injured in traffic accident**

▶ New   ⇒ Revised   ~~deleted~~ Deleted   Excludes 1   Excludes 2   Includes   Use additional   Code first   Code also   Key words

OGCR Official Guidelines   X Assign placeholder X   ● Use Additional Character(s)   ▷ Manifestation Code   **Coding Clinic**

X ● **V85.2** **Person on outside of special construction vehicle injured in** traffic accident

X ● **V85.3** **Unspecified occupant of special construction vehicle injured in** traffic accident

X ● **V85.4** **Person injured while** boarding or alighting **from special construction vehicle**

X ● **V85.5** **Driver of special construction vehicle injured in** nontraffic accident

X ● **V85.6** **Passenger of special construction vehicle injured in** nontraffic accident

X ● **V85.7** **Person on outside of special construction vehicle injured in** nontraffic accident

X ● **V85.9** **Unspecified occupant of special construction vehicle injured in** nontraffic accident
      Special-construction-vehicle accident NOS

● **V86** **Occupant of special all-terrain or other off-road motor vehicle, injured in transport accident**

    Excludes1 special all-terrain vehicle in stationary use or maintenance (W31.-)
                sport-utility vehicle (V50-V59)
                three-wheeled motor vehicle designed for on-road use (V30-V39)

The appropriate 7th character is to be added to each code from category V86

A	initial encounter
D	subsequent encounter
S	sequela

● **V86.0** **Driver of special all-terrain or other off-road motor vehicle injured in** traffic accident

X ● **V86.01** **Driver of** ambulance or fire engine **injured in traffic accident**

X ● **V86.02** **Driver of** snowmobile **injured in traffic accident**

X ● **V86.03** **Driver of** dune buggy **injured in traffic accident**

X ● **V86.04** **Driver of** military **vehicle injured in traffic accident**

X ● **V86.05** **Driver of** 3- or 4-wheeled all-terrain vehicle (ATV) **injured in traffic accident**

X ● **V86.06** **Driver of** dirt bike or motor/cross bike **injured in traffic accident**

X ● **V86.09** **Driver of** other off-road special all-terrain or other off-road vehicle **injured in traffic accident**
    Driver of dirt bike injured in traffic accident
    Driver of go cart injured in traffic accident
    Driver of golf cart injured in traffic accident

● **V86.1** **Passenger of special all-terrain or other off-road motor vehicle injured in** traffic accident

X ● **V86.11** **Passenger of** ambulance or fire engine **injured in traffic accident**

X ● **V86.12** **Passenger of** snowmobile **injured in traffic accident**

X ● **V86.13** **Passenger of** dune buggy **injured in traffic accident**

X ● **V86.14** **Passenger of** military **vehicle injured in traffic accident**

X ● **V86.15** **Passenger of** 3- or 4-wheeled all-terrain vehicle (ATV) **injured in traffic accident**

X ● **V86.16** **Passenger of** dirt bike or motor/cross bike **injured in traffic accident**

X ● **V86.19** **Passenger of** other off-road special all-terrain or other off-road off-road motor vehicle injured in **traffic accident**
    Passenger of dirt bike injured in traffic accident
    Passenger of go cart injured in traffic accident
    Passenger of golf cart injured in traffic accident

● **V86.2** **Person on outside of special all-terrain or other off-road motor vehicle injured in** traffic accident

X ● **V86.21** **Person on outside of** ambulance or fire engine **injured in traffic accident**

X ● **V86.22** **Person on outside of** snowmobile **injured in traffic accident**

X ● **V86.23** **Person on outside of** dune buggy **injured in traffic accident**

X ● **V86.24** **Person on outside of** military **vehicle injured in traffic accident**

X ● **V86.25** **Person on outside of** 3- or 4-wheeled all-terrain vehicle (ATV) **injured in traffic accident**

X ● **V86.26** **Person on outside of** dirt bike or motor/cross bike **injured in traffic accident**

X ● **V86.29** **Person on outside of** other special all-terrain or other off-road motor vehicle **injured in traffic accident**
    Person on outside of dirt bike injured in traffic accident
    Person on outside of go cart in traffic accident
    Person on outside of golf cart injured in traffic accident

● **V86.3** **Unspecified occupant of special all-terrain or other off-road motor vehicle injured in** traffic accident

X ● **V86.31** **Unspecified occupant of** ambulance or fire engine **injured in traffic accident**

X ● **V86.32** **Unspecified occupant of** snowmobile **injured in traffic accident**

X ● **V86.33** **Unspecified occupant of** dune buggy **injured in traffic accident**

X ● **V86.34** **Unspecified occupant of** military **vehicle injured in traffic accident**

X ● **V86.35** **Unspecified occupant of** 3- or 4-wheeled all-terrain vehicle (ATV) **injured in traffic accident**

X ● **V86.36** **Unspecified occupant of** dirt bike or motor/cross bike **injured in traffic accident**

X ● **V86.39** **Unspecified occupant of** other special all-terrain or other off-road motor vehicle **injured in traffic accident**
    Unspecified occupant of dirt bike injured in traffic accident
    Unspecified occupant of go cart injured in traffic accident
    Unspecified occupant of golf cart injured in traffic accident

● **V86.4** **Person injured while** boarding or alighting **from special all-terrain or other off-road motor vehicle**

X ● **V86.41** **Person injured while boarding or alighting from** ambulance or fire engine

X ● **V86.42** **Person injured while boarding or alighting from** snowmobile

X ● **V86.43** **Person injured while boarding or alighting from** dune buggy

X ● **V86.44** **Person injured while boarding or alighting from** military vehicle

X ● **V86.45** **Person injured while boarding or alighting from a** 3- or 4-wheeled all-terrain vehicle (ATV)

X ● **V86.46** **Person injured while boarding or alighting from a** dirt bike or motor/cross bike

X ● **V86.49** **Person injured while boarding or alighting from** other special all-terrain or other off-road motor vehicle
    Person injured while boarding or alighting from dirt bike
    Person injured while boarding or alighting from go cart
    Person injured while boarding or alighting from golf cart

● **V86.5**   **Driver of special all-terrain or other off-road motor vehicle injured in nontraffic accident**

   X● **V86.51**   Driver of ambulance or fire engine injured in nontraffic accident

   X● **V86.52**   Driver of snowmobile injured in nontraffic accident

   X● **V86.53**   Driver of dune buggy injured in nontraffic accident

   X● **V86.54**   Driver of military vehicle injured in nontraffic accident

   X● **V86.55**   Driver of 3- or 4-wheeled all-terrain vehicle (ATV) injured in nontraffic accident

   X● **V86.56**   Driver of dirt bike or motor/cross bike injured in nontraffic accident

   X● **V86.59**   Driver of other off-road special all-terrain or other off-road motor vehicle injured in nontraffic accident

      Driver of dirt bike injured in nontraffic accident

      Driver of go cart injured in nontraffic accident

      Driver of golf cart injured in nontraffic accident

● **V86.6**   **Passenger of special all-terrain or other off-road motor vehicle injured in nontraffic accident**

   X● **V86.61**   Passenger of ambulance or fire engine injured in nontraffic accident

   X● **V86.62**   Passenger of snowmobile injured in nontraffic accident

   X● **V86.63**   Passenger of dune buggy injured in nontraffic accident

   X● **V86.64**   Passenger of military vehicle injured in nontraffic accident

   X● **V86.65**   Passenger of 3- or 4-wheeled all-terrain vehicle (ATV) injured in nontraffic accident

   X● **V86.66**   Passenger of dirt bike or motor/cross bike injured in nontraffic accident

   X● **V86.69**   Passenger of other special all-terrain or other off-road vehicle injured in nontraffic accident

      Passenger of dirt bike injured in nontraffic accident

      Passenger of go cart injured in nontraffic accident

      Passenger of golf cart injured in nontraffic accident

● **V86.7**   **Person on outside of special all-terrain or other off-road motor vehicle injured in nontraffic accident**

   X● **V86.71**   Person on outside of ambulance or fire engine injured in nontraffic accident

   X● **V86.72**   Person on outside of snowmobile injured in nontraffic accident

   X● **V86.73**   Person on outside of dune buggy injured in nontraffic accident

   X● **V86.74**   Person on outside of military vehicle injured in nontraffic accident

   X● **V86.75**   Person on outside of 3- or 4-wheeled all-terrain vehicle (ATV) injured in nontraffic accident

   X● **V86.76**   Person on outside of dirt bike or motor/cross bike injured in nontraffic accident

   X● **V86.79**   Person on outside of other special all-terrain or other off-road motor vehicles injured in nontraffic accident

      Person on outside of dirt bike injured in nontraffic accident

      Person on outside of go cart injured in nontraffic accident

      Person on outside of golf cart injured in nontraffic accident

● **V86.9**   **Unspecified occupant of special all-terrain or other off-road motor vehicle injured in nontraffic accident**

   X● **V86.91**   Unspecified occupant of ambulance or fire engine injured in nontraffic accident

   X● **V86.92**   Unspecified occupant of snowmobile injured in nontraffic accident

   X● **V86.93**   Unspecified occupant of dune buggy injured in nontraffic accident

   X● **V86.94**   Unspecified occupant of military vehicle injured in nontraffic accident

   X● **V86.95**   Unspecified occupant of 3- or 4-wheeled all-terrain vehicle (ATV) injured in nontraffic accident

   X● **V86.96**   Unspecified occupant of dirt bike or motor/cross bike injured in nontraffic accident

   X● **V86.99**   Unspecified occupant of other special all-terrain or other off-road motor vehicle injured in nontraffic accident

      Off-road motor-vehicle accident NOS

      Other motor-vehicle accident NOS

      Unspecified occupant of go cart injured in nontraffic accident

      Unspecified occupant of golf cart injured in nontraffic accident

      Unspecified occupant of race car injured in nontraffic accident

● **V87**   **Traffic accident of specified type but victim's mode of transport unknown**

   Excludes1   collision involving:
      pedal cycle (V10-V19)
      pedestrian (V01-V09)

   The appropriate 7th character is to be added to each code from category V87

     | | |
     A   initial encounter
     D   subsequent encounter
     S   sequela

   X● **V87.0**   Person injured in collision between car and two- or three-wheeled powered vehicle (traffic)

   X● **V87.1**   Person injured in collision between other motor vehicle and two- or three-wheeled motor vehicle (traffic)

   X● **V87.2**   Person injured in collision between car and pick-up truck or van (traffic)

   X● **V87.3**   Person injured in collision between car and bus (traffic)

   X● **V87.4**   Person injured in collision between car and heavy transport vehicle (traffic)

   X● **V87.5**   Person injured in collision between heavy transport vehicle and bus (traffic)

   X● **V87.6**   Person injured in collision between railway train or railway vehicle and car (traffic)

   X● **V87.7**   Person injured in collision between other specified motor vehicles (traffic)

   X● **V87.8**   Person injured in other specified noncollision transport accidents involving motor vehicle (traffic)

   X● **V87.9**   Person injured in other specified (collision) (noncollision) transport accidents involving nonmotor vehicle (traffic)

● **V88**   **Nontraffic accident of specified type but victim's mode of transport unknown**

   Excludes1   collision involving:
      pedal cycle (V10-V19)
      pedestrian (V01-V09)

   The appropriate 7th character is to be added to each code from category V88

     | | |
     A   initial encounter
     D   subsequent encounter
     S   sequela

   X● **V88.0**   Person injured in collision between car and two- or three-wheeled motor vehicle, nontraffic

   X● **V88.1**   Person injured in collision between other motor vehicle and two- or three-wheeled motor vehicle, nontraffic

   X● **V88.2**   Person injured in collision between car and pick-up truck or van, nontraffic

---

▶ New   ⟹ Revised   ~~deleted~~ Deleted   Excludes 1   Excludes 2   Includes   Use additional   Code first   Code also   Key words

OGCR Official Guidelines   X Assign placeholder X   ● Use Additional Character(s)   ▶ Manifestation Code   **Coding Clinic**

X ● **V88.3** Person injured in collision between car and bus, nontraffic

X ● **V88.4** Person injured in collision between car and heavy transport vehicle, nontraffic

X ● **V88.5** Person injured in collision between heavy transport vehicle and bus, nontraffic

X ● **V88.6** Person injured in collision between railway train or railway vehicle and car, nontraffic

X ● **V88.7** Person injured in collision between other specified motor vehicle, nontraffic

X ● **V88.8** Person injured in other specified noncollision transport accidents involving motor vehicle, nontraffic

X ● **V88.9** Person injured in other specified (collision) (noncollision) transport accidents involving nonmotor vehicle, nontraffic

● **V89   Motor- or nonmotor-vehicle accident, type of vehicle unspecified**

The appropriate 7th character is to be added to each code from category V89

> A   initial encounter
> D   subsequent encounter
> S   sequela

X ● **V89.0** Person injured in unspecified motor-vehicle accident, nontraffic
> Motor-vehicle accident NOS, nontraffic

X ● **V89.1** Person injured in unspecified nonmotor-vehicle accident, nontraffic
> Nonmotor-vehicle accident NOS (nontraffic)

X ● **V89.2** Person injured in unspecified motor-vehicle accident, traffic
> Motor-vehicle accident [MVA] NOS
> Road (traffic) accident [RTA] NOS

X ● **V89.3** Person injured in unspecified nonmotor-vehicle accident, traffic
> Nonmotor-vehicle traffic accident NOS

X ● **V89.9** Person injured in unspecified vehicle accident
> Collision NOS

WATER TRANSPORT ACCIDENTS (V90-V94)

● **V90   Drowning and submersion due to accident to watercraft**

Excludes1   civilian water transport accident involving military watercraft (V94.81-)
fall into water not from watercraft (W16.-)
military watercraft accident in military or war operations (Y36.0-, Y37.0-)
water-transport–related drowning or submersion without accident to watercraft (V92.-)

The appropriate 7th character is to be added to each code from category V90

> A   initial encounter
> D   subsequent encounter
> S   sequela

● **V90.0   Drowning and submersion due to watercraft overturning**

X ● **V90.00** Drowning and submersion due to merchant ship overturning

X ● **V90.01** Drowning and submersion due to passenger ship overturning
> Drowning and submersion due to ferry-boat overturning
> Drowning and submersion due to liner overturning

X ● **V90.02** Drowning and submersion due to fishing boat overturning

X ● **V90.03** Drowning and submersion due to other powered watercraft overturning
> Drowning and submersion due to hovercraft (on open water) overturning
> Drowning and submersion due to jet ski overturning

X ● **V90.04** Drowning and submersion due to sailboat overturning

X ● **V90.05** Drowning and submersion due to canoe or kayak overturning

X ● **V90.06** Drowning and submersion due to (nonpowered) inflatable craft overturning

X ● **V90.08** Drowning and submersion due to other unpowered watercraft overturning
> Drowning and submersion due to windsurfer overturning

X ● **V90.09** Drowning and submersion due to unspecified watercraft overturning
> Drowning and submersion due to boat NOS overturning
> Drowning and submersion due to ship NOS overturning
> Drowning and submersion due to watercraft NOS overturning

● **V90.1   Drowning and submersion due to watercraft sinking**

X ● **V90.10** Drowning and submersion due to merchant ship sinking

X ● **V90.11** Drowning and submersion due to passenger ship sinking
> Drowning and submersion due to ferry-boat sinking
> Drowning and submersion due to liner sinking

X ● **V90.12** Drowning and submersion due to fishing boat sinking

X ● **V90.13** Drowning and submersion due to other powered watercraft sinking
> Drowning and submersion due to hovercraft (on open water) sinking
> Drowning and submersion due to jet ski sinking

X ● **V90.14** Drowning and submersion due to sailboat sinking

X ● **V90.15** Drowning and submersion due to canoe or kayak sinking

X ● **V90.16** Drowning and submersion due to (nonpowered) inflatable craft sinking

X ● **V90.18** Drowning and submersion due to other unpowered watercraft sinking

X ● **V90.19** Drowning and submersion due to unspecified watercraft sinking
> Drowning and submersion due to boat NOS sinking
> Drowning and submersion due to ship NOS sinking
> Drowning and submersion due to watercraft NOS sinking

● **V90.2   Drowning and submersion due to falling or jumping from burning watercraft**

X ● **V90.20** Drowning and submersion due to falling or jumping from burning merchant ship

X ● **V90.21** Drowning and submersion due to falling or jumping from burning passenger ship
> Drowning and submersion due to falling or jumping from burning ferry-boat
> Drowning and submersion due to falling or jumping from burning liner

X ● **V90.22** Drowning and submersion due to falling or jumping from burning fishing boat

X ● **V90.23** Drowning and submersion due to falling or jumping from other burning powered watercraft
> Drowning and submersion due to falling and jumping from burning hovercraft (on open water)
> Drowning and submersion due to falling and jumping from burning jet ski

X ● **V90.24** Drowning and submersion due to falling or jumping from burning sailboat

X ● **V90.25** **Drowning and submersion due to falling or jumping from burning** canoe or kayak

X ● **V90.26** **Drowning and submersion due to falling or jumping from burning (nonpowered)** inflatable craft

X ● **V90.27** **Drowning and submersion due to falling or jumping from burning** water-skis

X ● **V90.28** **Drowning and submersion due to falling or jumping from** other burning unpowered watercraft
　　Drowning and submersion due to falling and jumping from burning surf-board
　　Drowning and submersion due to falling and jumping from burning windsurfer

X ● **V90.29** **Drowning and submersion due to falling or jumping from** unspecified burning watercraft
　　Drowning and submersion due to falling or jumping from burning boat NOS
　　Drowning and submersion due to falling or jumping from burning ship NOS
　　Drowning and submersion due to falling or jumping from burning watercraft NOS

● **V90.3** **Drowning and submersion due to** falling or jumping from crushed watercraft

X ● **V90.30** **Drowning and submersion due to falling or jumping from crushed** merchant ship

X ● **V90.31** **Drowning and submersion due to falling or jumping from crushed** passenger ship
　　Drowning and submersion due to falling and jumping from crushed ferry-boat
　　Drowning and submersion due to falling and jumping from crushed liner

X ● **V90.32** **Drowning and submersion due to falling or jumping from crushed** fishing boat

X ● **V90.33** **Drowning and submersion due to falling or jumping from** other crushed powered watercraft
　　Drowning and submersion due to falling and jumping from crushed hovercraft
　　Drowning and submersion due to falling and jumping from crushed jet ski

X ● **V90.34** **Drowning and submersion due to falling or jumping from crushed** sailboat

X ● **V90.35** **Drowning and submersion due to falling or jumping from crushed** canoe or kayak

X ● **V90.36** **Drowning and submersion due to falling or jumping from crushed (nonpowered)** inflatable craft

X ● **V90.37** **Drowning and submersion due to falling or jumping from crushed** water-skis

X ● **V90.38** **Drowning and submersion due to falling or jumping from** other crushed unpowered watercraft
　　Drowning and submersion due to falling and jumping from crushed surf-board
　　Drowning and submersion due to falling and jumping from crushed windsurfer

X ● **V90.39** **Drowning and submersion due to falling or jumping from crushed** unspecified watercraft
　　Drowning and submersion due to falling and jumping from crushed boat NOS
　　Drowning and submersion due to falling and jumping from crushed ship NOS
　　Drowning and submersion due to falling and jumping from crushed watercraft NOS

● **V90.8** **Drowning and submersion due to** other accident to watercraft

X ● **V90.80** **Drowning and submersion due to other accident to** merchant ship

X ● **V90.81** **Drowning and submersion due to other accident to** passenger ship
　　Drowning and submersion due to other accident to ferry-boat
　　Drowning and submersion due to other accident to liner

X ● **V90.82** **Drowning and submersion due to other accident to** fishing boat

X ● **V90.83** **Drowning and submersion due to other accident to** other powered watercraft
　　Drowning and submersion due to other accident to hovercraft (on open water)
　　Drowning and submersion due to other accident to jet ski

X ● **V90.84** **Drowning and submersion due to other accident to** sailboat

X ● **V90.85** **Drowning and submersion due to other accident to** canoe or kayak

X ● **V90.86** **Drowning and submersion due to other accident to (nonpowered)** inflatable craft

X ● **V90.87** **Drowning and submersion due to other accident to** water-skis

X ● **V90.88** **Drowning and submersion due to other accident to** other unpowered watercraft
　　Drowning and submersion due to other accident to surf-board
　　Drowning and submersion due to other accident to windsurfer

X ● **V90.89** **Drowning and submersion due to other accident to** unspecified watercraft
　　Drowning and submersion due to other accident to boat NOS
　　Drowning and submersion due to other accident to ship NOS
　　Drowning and submersion due to other accident to watercraft NOS

● **V91** **Other injury due to accident to watercraft**

　Includes   any injury except drowning and submersion as a result of an accident to watercraft

　Excludes1   civilian water transport accident involving military watercraft (V94.81-)
　　　military watercraft accident in military or war operations (Y36, Y37.-)

　Excludes2   drowning and submersion due to accident to watercraft (V90.-)

The appropriate 7th character is to be added to each code from category V91

A	initial encounter
D	subsequent encounter
S	sequela

● **V91.0** **Burn due to watercraft on fire**

　Excludes1   burn from localized fire or explosion on board ship without accident to watercraft (V93.-)

X ● **V91.00** **Burn due to** merchant ship **on fire**

X ● **V91.01** **Burn due to** passenger ship **on fire**
　　Burn due to ferry-boat on fire
　　Burn due to liner on fire

X ● **V91.02** **Burn due to** fishing boat **on fire**

X ● **V91.03** **Burn due to** other powered watercraft **on fire**
　　Burn due to hovercraft (on open water) on fire
　　Burn due to jet ski on fire

X ● **V91.04** **Burn due to** sailboat **on fire**

X ● **V91.05** **Burn due to** canoe or kayak **on fire**

X ● **V91.06** **Burn due to (nonpowered)** inflatable craft **on fire**

X ● **V91.07** **Burn due to** water-skis **on fire**

X ● **V91.08** **Burn due to** other unpowered watercraft **on fire**

X ● **V91.09** **Burn due to** unspecified **watercraft on fire**
　　Burn due to boat NOS on fire
　　Burn due to ship NOS on fire
　　Burn due to watercraft NOS on fire

▶ New   ⇛ Revised   ~~deleted~~ Deleted   Excludes 1   Excludes 2   Includes   Use additional   Code first   Code also   Key words

OGCR Official Guidelines   X Assign placeholder X   ● Use Additional Character(s)   ▶ Manifestation Code   **Coding Clinic**

● **V91.1 Crushed between watercraft and other watercraft or other object due to collision**
> Crushed by lifeboat after abandoning ship in a collision
>
> **Note:** Select the specified type of watercraft that the victim was on at the time of the collision.

X● **V91.10 Crushed between merchant ship and other watercraft or other object due to collision**

X● **V91.11 Crushed between passenger ship and other watercraft or other object due to collision**
> Crushed between ferry-boat and other watercraft or other object due to collision
> Crushed between liner and other watercraft or other object due to collision

X● **V91.12 Crushed between fishing boat and other watercraft or other object due to collision**

X● **V91.13 Crushed between other powered watercraft and other watercraft or other object due to collision**
> Crushed between hovercraft (on open water) and other watercraft or other object due to collision
> Crushed between jet ski and other watercraft or other object due to collision

X● **V91.14 Crushed between sailboat and other watercraft or other object due to collision**

X● **V91.15 Crushed between canoe or kayak and other watercraft or other object due to collision**

X● **V91.16 Crushed between (nonpowered) inflatable craft and other watercraft or other object due to collision**

X● **V91.18 Crushed between other unpowered watercraft and other watercraft or other object due to collision**
> Crushed between surfboard and other watercraft or other object due to collision
> Crushed between windsurfer and other watercraft or other object due to collision

X● **V91.19 Crushed between unspecified watercraft and other watercraft or other object due to collision**
> Crushed between boat NOS and other watercraft or other object due to collision
> Crushed between ship NOS and other watercraft or other object due to collision
> Crushed between watercraft NOS and other watercraft or other object due to collision

● **V91.2 Fall due to collision between watercraft and other watercraft or other object**
> Fall while remaining on watercraft after collision
>
> **Note:** Select the specified type of watercraft that the victim was on at the time of the collision.
>
> **Excludes1**   crushed between watercraft and other watercraft and other object due to collision (V91.1-)
> drowning and submersion due to falling from crushed watercraft (V90.3-)

X● **V91.20 Fall due to collision between merchant ship and other watercraft or other object**

X● **V91.21 Fall due to collision between passenger ship and other watercraft or other object**
> Fall due to collision between ferry-boat and other watercraft or other object
> Fall due to collision between liner and other watercraft or other object

X● **V91.22 Fall due to collision between fishing boat and other watercraft or other object**

X● **V91.23 Fall due to collision between other powered watercraft and other watercraft or other object**
> Fall due to collision between hovercraft (on open water) and other watercraft or other object
> Fall due to collision between jet ski and other watercraft or other object

X● **V91.24 Fall due to collision between sailboat and other watercraft or other object**

X● **V91.25 Fall due to collision between canoe or kayak and other watercraft or other object**

X● **V91.26 Fall due to collision between (nonpowered) inflatable craft and other watercraft or other object**

X● **V91.29 Fall due to collision between unspecified watercraft and other watercraft or other object**
> Fall due to collision between boat NOS and other watercraft or other object
> Fall due to collision between ship NOS and other watercraft or other object
> Fall due to collision between watercraft NOS and other watercraft or other object

● **V91.3 Hit or struck by falling object due to accident to watercraft**
> Hit or struck by falling object (part of damaged watercraft or other object) after falling or jumping from damaged watercraft
>
> **Excludes2**   drowning or submersion due to fall or jumping from damaged watercraft (V90.2-, V90.3-)

X● **V91.30 Hit or struck by falling object due to accident to merchant ship**

X● **V91.31 Hit or struck by falling object due to accident to passenger ship**
> Hit or struck by falling object due to accident to ferry-boat
> Hit or struck by falling object due to accident to liner

X● **V91.32 Hit or struck by falling object due to accident to fishing boat**

X● **V91.33 Hit or struck by falling object due to accident to other powered watercraft**
> Hit or struck by falling object due to accident to hovercraft (on open water)
> Hit or struck by falling object due to accident to jet ski

X● **V91.34 Hit or struck by falling object due to accident to sailboat**

X● **V91.35 Hit or struck by falling object due to accident to canoe or kayak**

X● **V91.36 Hit or struck by falling object due to accident to (nonpowered) inflatable craft**

X● **V91.37 Hit or struck by falling object due to accident to water-skis**
> Hit by water-skis after jumping off of waterskis

X● **V91.38 Hit or struck by falling object due to accident to other unpowered watercraft**
> Hit or struck by surf-board after falling off damaged surf-board
> Hit or struck by object after falling off damaged windsurfer

X● **V91.39 Hit or struck by falling object due to accident to unspecified watercraft**
> Hit or struck by falling object due to accident to boat NOS
> Hit or struck by falling object due to accident to ship NOS
> Hit or struck by falling object due to accident to watercraft NOS

● **V91.8**   Other injury due to other accident to watercraft

X ● **V91.80**   Other injury due to other accident to merchant ship

X ● **V91.81**   Other injury due to other accident to passenger ship

> Other injury due to other accident to ferry-boat
> Other injury due to other accident to liner

X ● **V91.82**   Other injury due to other accident to fishing boat

X ● **V91.83**   Other injury due to other accident to other powered watercraft

> Other injury due to other accident to hovercraft (on open water)
> Other injury due to other accident to jet ski

X ● **V91.84**   Other injury due to other accident to sailboat

X ● **V91.85**   Other injury due to other accident to canoe or kayak

X ● **V91.86**   Other injury due to other accident to (nonpowered) inflatable craft

X ● **V91.87**   Other injury due to other accident to water-skis

X ● **V91.88**   Other injury due to other accident to other unpowered watercraft

> Other injury due to other accident to surf-board
> Other injury due to other accident to windsurfer

X ● **V91.89**   Other injury due to other accident to unspecified watercraft

> Other injury due to other accident to boat NOS
> Other injury due to other accident to ship NOS
> Other injury due to other accident to watercraft NOS

● **V92**   Drowning and submersion due to accident on board watercraft, without accident to watercraft

> **Excludes1**   civilian water transport accident involving military watercraft (V94.81-)
> drowning or submersion due to accident to watercraft (V90-V91)
> drowning or submersion of diver who voluntarily jumps from boat not involved in an accident (W16.711, W16.721)
> fall into water without watercraft (W16.-)
> military watercraft accident in military or war operations (Y36, Y37)

The appropriate 7th character is to be added to each code from category V92

> A   initial encounter
> D   subsequent encounter
> S   sequela

● **V92.0**   Drowning and submersion due to fall off watercraft

> Drowning and submersion due to fall from gangplank of watercraft
> Drowning and submersion due to fall overboard watercraft

> **Excludes2**   hitting head on object or bottom of body of water due to fall from watercraft (V94.0-)

X ● **V92.00**   Drowning and submersion due to fall off merchant ship

X ● **V92.01**   Drowning and submersion due to fall off passenger ship

> Drowning and submersion due to fall off ferry-boat
> Drowning and submersion due to fall off liner

X ● **V92.02**   Drowning and submersion due to fall off fishing boat

X ● **V92.03**   Drowning and submersion due to fall off other powered watercraft

> Drowning and submersion due to fall off hovercraft (on open water)
> Drowning and submersion due to fall off jet ski

X ● **V92.04**   Drowning and submersion due to fall off sailboat

X ● **V92.05**   Drowning and submersion due to fall off canoe or kayak

X ● **V92.06**   Drowning and submersion due to fall off (nonpowered) inflatable craft

X ● **V92.07**   Drowning and submersion due to fall off water-skis

> **Excludes1**   drowning and submersion due to falling off burning water-skis (V90.27)
> drowning and submersion due to falling off crushed water-skis (V90.37)
> hit by boat while water-skiing NOS (V94.X)

X ● **V92.08**   Drowning and submersion due to fall off other unpowered watercraft

> Drowning and submersion due to fall off surf-board
> Drowning and submersion due to fall off windsurfer

> **Excludes1**   drowning and submersion due to fall off burning unpowered watercraft (V90.28)
> drowning and submersion due to fall off crushed unpowered watercraft (V90.38)
> drowning and submersion due to fall off damaged unpowered watercraft (V90.88)
> drowning and submersion due to rider of nonpowered watercraft being hit by other watercraft (V94.-)
> other injury due to rider of nonpowered watercraft being hit by other watercraft (V94.-)

X ● **V92.09**   Drowning and submersion due to fall off unspecified watercraft

> Drowning and submersion due to fall off boat NOS
> Drowning and submersion due to fall off ship NOS
> Drowning and submersion due to fall off watercraft NOS

● **V92.1**   Drowning and submersion due to being thrown overboard by motion of watercraft

> **Excludes1**   drowning and submersion due to fall off surf-board (V92.08)
> drowning and submersion due to fall off water-skis (V92.07)
> drowning and submersion due to fall off windsurfer (V92.08)

X ● **V92.10**   Drowning and submersion due to being thrown overboard by motion of merchant ship

X ● **V92.11**   Drowning and submersion due to being thrown overboard by motion of passenger ship

> Drowning and submersion due to being thrown overboard by motion of ferry-boat
> Drowning and submersion due to being thrown overboard by motion of liner

X ● **V92.12** **Drowning and submersion due to being thrown overboard by motion of fishing boat**

X ● **V92.13** **Drowning and submersion due to being thrown overboard by motion of other powered watercraft**
Drowning and submersion due to being thrown overboard by motion of hovercraft

X ● **V92.14** **Drowning and submersion due to being thrown overboard by motion of sailboat**

X ● **V92.15** **Drowning and submersion due to being thrown overboard by motion of canoe or kayak**

X ● **V92.16** **Drowning and submersion due to being thrown overboard by motion of (nonpowered) inflatable craft**

X ● **V92.19** **Drowning and submersion due to being thrown overboard by motion of unspecified watercraft**
Drowning and submersion due to being thrown overboard by motion of boat NOS
Drowning and submersion due to being thrown overboard by motion of ship NOS
Drowning and submersion due to being thrown overboard by motion of watercraft NOS

● **V92.2** **Drowning and submersion due to being washed overboard from watercraft**
Code first any associated cataclysm (X37.0-)

X ● **V92.20** **Drowning and submersion due to being washed overboard from merchant ship**

X ● **V92.21** **Drowning and submersion due to being washed overboard from passenger ship**
Drowning and submersion due to being washed overboard from ferry-boat
Drowning and submersion due to being washed overboard from liner

X ● **V92.22** **Drowning and submersion due to being washed overboard from fishing boat**

X ● **V92.23** **Drowning and submersion due to being washed overboard from other powered watercraft**
Drowning and submersion due to being washed overboard from hovercraft (on open water)
Drowning and submersion due to being washed overboard from jet ski

X ● **V92.24** **Drowning and submersion due to being washed overboard from sailboat**

X ● **V92.25** **Drowning and submersion due to being washed overboard from canoe or kayak**

X ● **V92.26** **Drowning and submersion due to being washed overboard from (nonpowered) inflatable craft**

X ● **V92.27** **Drowning and submersion due to being washed overboard from water-skis**

Excludes1   drowning and submersion due to fall off water-skis (V92.07)

X ● **V92.28** **Drowning and submersion due to being washed overboard from other unpowered watercraft**
Drowning and submersion due to being washed overboard from surf-board
Drowning and submersion due to being washed overboard from windsurfer

X ● **V92.29** **Drowning and submersion due to being washed overboard from unspecified watercraft**
Drowning and submersion due to being washed overboard from boat NOS
Drowning and submersion due to being washed overboard from ship NOS
Drowning and submersion due to being washed overboard from watercraft NOS

● **V93** **Other injury due to accident on board watercraft, without accident to watercraft**

Excludes1   civilian water transport accident involving military watercraft (V94.81-)
other injury due to accident to watercraft (V91.-)
military watercraft accident in military or war operations (Y36, Y37.-)

Excludes2   drowning and submersion due to accident on board watercraft, without accident to watercraft (V92.-)

The appropriate 7th character is to be added to each code from category V93

A	initial encounter
D	subsequent encounter
S	sequela

● **V93.0** **Burn due to localized fire on board watercraft**

Excludes1   burn due to watercraft on fire (V91.0-)

X ● **V93.00** **Burn due to localized fire on board merchant vessel**

X ● **V93.01** **Burn due to localized fire on board passenger vessel**
Burn due to localized fire on board ferry-boat
Burn due to localized fire on board liner

X ● **V93.02** **Burn due to localized fire on board fishing boat**

X ● **V93.03** **Burn due to localized fire on board other powered watercraft**
Burn due to localized fire on board hovercraft
Burn due to localized fire on board jet ski

X ● **V93.04** **Burn due to localized fire on board sailboat**

X ● **V93.09** **Burn due to localized fire on board unspecified watercraft**
Burn due to localized fire on board boat NOS
Burn due to localized fire on board ship NOS
Burn due to localized fire on board watercraft NOS

● **V93.1** **Other burn on board watercraft**
Burn due to source other than fire on board watercraft

Excludes1   burn due to watercraft on fire (V91.0-)

X ● **V93.10** **Other burn on board merchant vessel**

X ● **V93.11** **Other burn on board passenger vessel**
Other burn on board ferry-boat
Other burn on board liner

X ● **V93.12** **Other burn on board fishing boat**

X ● **V93.13** **Other burn on board other powered watercraft**
Other burn on board hovercraft
Other burn on board jet ski

X ● **V93.14** **Other burn on board sailboat**

X ● **V93.19** **Other burn on board unspecified watercraft**
Other burn on board boat NOS
Other burn on board ship NOS
Other burn on board watercraft NOS

● **V93.2** **Heat exposure on board watercraft**

Excludes1   exposure to man-made heat not aboard watercraft (W92)
exposure to natural heat while on board watercraft (X30)
exposure to sunlight while on board watercraft (X32)

Excludes2   burn due to fire on board watercraft (V93.0-)

X ● **V93.20** **Heat exposure on board merchant ship**

X ● **V93.21** **Heat exposure on board passenger ship**
Heat exposure on board ferry-boat
Heat exposure on board liner

X ● **V93.22** **Heat exposure on board fishing boat**

X ● **V93.23** **Heat exposure on board other powered watercraft**
Heat exposure on board hovercraft

X ● **V93.24** **Heat exposure on board sailboat**

X ● **V93.29** **Heat exposure on board unspecified watercraft**
Heat exposure on board boat NOS
Heat exposure on board ship NOS
Heat exposure on board watercraft NOS

CHAPTER 20 (V01-Y99)

- **V93.3   Fall on board watercraft**
  - **Excludes1**   fall due to collision of watercraft (V91.2-)
  - X **V93.30   Fall on board merchant ship**
  - X **V93.31   Fall on board passenger ship**
    - Fall on board ferry-boat
    - Fall on board liner
  - X **V93.32   Fall on board fishing boat**
  - X **V93.33   Fall on board other powered watercraft**
    - Fall on board hovercraft (on open water)
    - Fall on board jet ski
  - X **V93.34   Fall on board sailboat**
  - X **V93.35   Fall on board canoe or kayak**
  - X **V93.36   Fall on board (nonpowered) inflatable craft**
  - X **V93.38   Fall on board other unpowered watercraft**
  - X **V93.39   Fall on board unspecified watercraft**
    - Fall on board boat NOS
    - Fall on board ship NOS
    - Fall on board watercraft NOS

- **V93.4   Struck by falling object on board watercraft**
  - Hit by falling object on board watercraft
  - **Excludes1**   struck by falling object due to accident to watercraft (V91.3)
  - X **V93.40   Struck by falling object on merchant ship**
  - X **V93.41   Struck by falling object on passenger ship**
    - Struck by falling object on ferry-boat
    - Struck by falling object on liner
  - X **V93.42   Struck by falling object on fishing boat**
  - X **V93.43   Struck by falling object on other powered watercraft**
    - Struck by falling object on hovercraft
  - X **V93.44   Struck by falling object on sailboat**
  - X **V93.48   Struck by falling object on other unpowered watercraft**
  - X **V93.49   Struck by falling object on unspecified watercraft**

- **V93.5   Explosion on board watercraft**
  - Boiler explosion on steamship
  - **Excludes2**   fire on board watercraft (V93.0-)
  - X **V93.50   Explosion on board merchant ship**
  - X **V93.51   Explosion on board passenger ship**
    - Explosion on board ferry-boat
    - Explosion on board liner
  - X **V93.52   Explosion on board fishing boat**
  - X **V93.53   Explosion on board other powered watercraft**
    - Explosion on board hovercraft
    - Explosion on board jet ski
  - X **V93.54   Explosion on board sailboat**
  - X **V93.59   Explosion on board unspecified watercraft**
    - Explosion on board boat NOS
    - Explosion on board ship NOS
    - Explosion on board watercraft NOS

- **V93.6   Machinery accident on board watercraft**
  - **Excludes1**   machinery explosion on board watercraft (V93.4-)
    - machinery fire on board watercraft (V93.0-)
  - X **V93.60   Machinery accident on board merchant ship**
  - X **V93.61   Machinery accident on board passenger ship**
    - Machinery accident on board ferry-boat
    - Machinery accident on board liner
  - X **V93.62   Machinery accident on board fishing boat**
  - X **V93.63   Machinery accident on board other powered watercraft**
    - Machinery accident on board hovercraft
  - X **V93.64   Machinery accident on board sailboat**
  - X **V93.69   Machinery accident on board unspecified watercraft**
    - Machinery accident on board boat NOS
    - Machinery accident on board ship NOS
    - Machinery accident on board watercraft NOS

- **V93.8   Other injury due to other accident on board watercraft**
  - Accidental poisoning by gases or fumes on watercraft
  - X **V93.80   Other injury due to other accident on board merchant ship**
  - X **V93.81   Other injury due to other accident on board passenger ship**
    - Other injury due to other accident on board ferry-boat
    - Other injury due to other accident on board liner
  - X **V93.82   Other injury due to other accident on board fishing boat**
  - X **V93.83   Other injury due to other accident on board other powered watercraft**
    - Other injury due to other accident on board hovercraft
    - Other injury due to other accident on board jet ski
  - X **V93.84   Other injury due to other accident on board sailboat**
  - X **V93.85   Other injury due to other accident on board canoe or kayak**
  - X **V93.86   Other injury due to other accident on board (nonpowered) inflatable craft**
  - X **V93.87   Other injury due to other accident on board water-skis**
    - Hit or struck by object while waterskiing
  - X **V93.88   Other injury due to other accident on board other unpowered watercraft**
    - Hit or struck by object while surfing
    - Hit or struck by object while on board windsurfer
  - X **V93.89   Other injury due to other accident on board unspecified watercraft**
    - Other injury due to other accident on board boat NOS
    - Other injury due to other accident on board ship NOS
    - Other injury due to other accident on board watercraft NOS

- **V94   Other and unspecified water transport accidents**
  - **Excludes1**   military watercraft accidents in military or war operations (Y36, Y37)
  - The appropriate 7th character is to be added to each code from category V94

A	initial encounter
D	subsequent encounter
S	sequela

  - X **V94.0   Hitting object or bottom of body of water due to fall from watercraft**
    - **Excludes2**   drowning and submersion due to fall from watercraft (V92.0-)
  - **V94.1   Bather struck by watercraft**
    - Swimmer hit by watercraft
    - X **V94.11   Bather struck by powered watercraft**
    - X **V94.12   Bather struck by nonpowered watercraft**
  - **V94.2   Rider of nonpowered watercraft struck by other watercraft**
    - X **V94.21   Rider of nonpowered watercraft struck by other nonpowered watercraft**
      - Canoer hit by other nonpowered watercraft
      - Surfer hit by other nonpowered watercraft
      - Windsurfer hit by other nonpowered watercraft
    - X **V94.22   Rider of nonpowered watercraft struck by powered watercraft**
      - Canoer hit by motorboat
      - Surfer hit by motorboat
      - Windsurfer hit by motorboat

▶ New   ⇒ Revised   ~~deleted~~ Deleted   Excludes 1   Excludes 2   Includes   Use additional   Code first   Code also   Key words

OGCR Official Guidelines   X Assign placeholder X   ● Use Additional Character(s)   ▶ Manifestation Code   **Coding Clinic**

● **V94.3**   **Injury to rider of (inflatable) watercraft being pulled behind other watercraft**

   X ● **V94.31**   **Injury to rider of (inflatable) recreational watercraft being pulled behind other watercraft**
     Injury to rider of inner-tube pulled behind motor boat

   X ● **V94.32**   **Injury to rider of non-recreational watercraft being pulled behind other watercraft**
     Injury to occupant of dingy being pulled behind boat or ship
     Injury to occupant of life-raft being pulled behind boat or ship

  X ● **V94.4**   **Injury to barefoot water-skier**
     Injury to person being pulled behind boat or ship

● **V94.8**   **Other water transport accident**

   ● **V94.81**   **Water transport accident involving military watercraft**

     ● **V94.810**   **Civilian watercraft involved in water transport accident with military watercraft**
       Passenger on civilian watercraft injured due to accident with military watercraft

     ● **V94.811**   **Civilian in water injured by military watercraft**

     ● **V94.818**   **Other water transport accident involving military watercraft**

   X ● **V94.89**   **Other water transport accident**

  X ● **V94.9**   **Unspecified water transport accident**
     Water transport accident NOS

AIR AND SPACE TRANSPORT ACCIDENTS (V95-V97)

Excludes1	military aircraft accidents in military or war operations (Y36, Y37)

● **V95**   **Accident to powered aircraft causing injury to occupant**
     The appropriate 7th character is to be added to each code from category V95

A	initial encounter
D	subsequent encounter
S	sequela

● **V95.0**   **Helicopter accident injuring occupant**

   X ● **V95.00**   **Unspecified helicopter accident injuring occupant**

   X ● **V95.01**   **Helicopter crash injuring occupant**

   X ● **V95.02**   **Forced landing of helicopter injuring occupant**

   X ● **V95.03**   **Helicopter collision injuring occupant**
     Helicopter collision with any object, fixed, movable or moving

   X ● **V95.04**   **Helicopter fire injuring occupant**

   X ● **V95.05**   **Helicopter explosion injuring occupant**

   X ● **V95.09**   **Other helicopter accident injuring occupant**

● **V95.1**   **Ultralight, microlight or powered-glider accident injuring occupant**

   X ● **V95.10**   **Unspecified ultralight, microlight or powered-glider accident injuring occupant**

   X ● **V95.11**   **Ultralight, microlight or powered-glider crash injuring occupant**

   X ● **V95.12**   **Forced landing of ultralight, microlight or powered-glider injuring occupant**

   X ● **V95.13**   **Ultralight, microlight or powered-glider collision injuring occupant**
     Ultralight, microlight or powered-glider collision with any object, fixed, movable or moving

   X ● **V95.14**   **Ultralight, microlight or powered-glider fire injuring occupant**

   X ● **V95.15**   **Ultralight, microlight or powered-glider explosion injuring occupant**

   X ● **V95.19**   **Other ultralight, microlight or powered-glider accident injuring occupant**

● **V95.2**   **Other private fixed-wing aircraft accident injuring occupant**

   X ● **V95.20**   **Unspecified accident to other private fixed-wing aircraft, injuring occupant**

   X ● **V95.21**   **Other private fixed-wing aircraft crash injuring occupant**

   X ● **V95.22**   **Forced landing of other private fixed-wing aircraft injuring occupant**

   X ● **V95.23**   **Other private fixed-wing aircraft collision injuring occupant**
     Other private fixed-wing aircraft collision with any object, fixed, movable or moving

   X ● **V95.24**   **Other private fixed-wing aircraft fire injuring occupant**

   X ● **V95.25**   **Other private fixed-wing aircraft explosion injuring occupant**

   X ● **V95.29**   **Other accident to other private fixed-wing aircraft injuring occupant**

● **V95.3**   **Commercial fixed-wing aircraft accident injuring occupant**

   X ● **V95.30**   **Unspecified accident to commercial fixed-wing aircraft injuring occupant**

   X ● **V95.31**   **Commercial fixed-wing aircraft crash injuring occupant**

   X ● **V95.32**   **Forced landing of commercial fixed-wing aircraft injuring occupant**

   X ● **V95.33**   **Commercial fixed-wing aircraft collision injuring occupant**
     Commercial fixed-wing aircraft collision with any object, fixed, movable or moving

   X ● **V95.34**   **Commercial fixed-wing aircraft fire injuring occupant**

   X ● **V95.35**   **Commercial fixed-wing aircraft explosion injuring occupant**

   X ● **V95.39**   **Other accident to commercial fixed-wing aircraft injuring occupant**

● **V95.4**   **Spacecraft accident injuring occupant**

   X ● **V95.40**   **Unspecified spacecraft accident injuring occupant**

   X ● **V95.41**   **Spacecraft crash injuring occupant**

   X ● **V95.42**   **Forced landing of spacecraft injuring occupant**

   X ● **V95.43**   **Spacecraft collision injuring occupant**
     Spacecraft collision with any object, fixed, moveable or moving

   X ● **V95.44**   **Spacecraft fire injuring occupant**

   X ● **V95.45**   **Spacecraft explosion injuring occupant**

   X ● **V95.49**   **Other spacecraft accident injuring occupant**

  X ● **V95.8**   **Other powered aircraft accidents injuring occupant**

  X ● **V95.9**   **Unspecified aircraft accident injuring occupant**
     Aircraft accident NOS
     Air transport accident NOS

CHAPTER 20 (V01-Y99)

● **V96　Accident to nonpowered aircraft causing injury to occupant**

The appropriate 7th character is to be added to each code from category V96

A	initial encounter
D	subsequent encounter
S	sequela

● **V96.0　Balloon accident injuring occupant**
X● **V96.00** Unspecified balloon accident injuring occupant
X● **V96.01** Balloon crash injuring occupant
X● **V96.02** Forced landing of balloon injuring occupant
X● **V96.03** Balloon collision injuring occupant
　　　　Balloon collision with any object, fixed, moveable or moving
X● **V96.04** Balloon fire injuring occupant
X● **V96.05** Balloon explosion injuring occupant
X● **V96.09** Other balloon accident injuring occupant

● **V96.1　Hang-glider accident injuring occupant**
X● **V96.10** Unspecified hang-glider accident injuring occupant
X● **V96.11** Hang-glider crash injuring occupant
X● **V96.12** Forced landing of hang-glider injuring occupant
X● **V96.13** Hang-glider collision injuring occupant
　　　　Hang-glider collision with any object, fixed, moveable or moving
X● **V96.14** Hang-glider fire injuring occupant
X● **V96.15** Hang-glider explosion injuring occupant
X● **V96.19** Other hang-glider accident injuring occupant

● **V96.2　Glider (nonpowered) accident injuring occupant**
X● **V96.20** Unspecified glider (nonpowered) accident injuring occupant
X● **V96.21** Glider (nonpowered) crash injuring occupant
X● **V96.22** Forced landing of glider (nonpowered) injuring occupant
X● **V96.23** Glider (nonpowered) collision injuring occupant
　　　　Glider (nonpowered) collision with any object, fixed, moveable or moving
X● **V96.24** Glider (nonpowered) fire injuring occupant
X● **V96.25** Glider (nonpowered) explosion injuring occupant
X● **V96.29** Other glider (nonpowered) accident injuring occupant

X● **V96.8** Other nonpowered-aircraft accidents injuring occupant
　　　　Kite carrying a person accident injuring occupant
X● **V96.9** Unspecified nonpowered-aircraft accident injuring occupant
　　　　Nonpowered-aircraft accident NOS

● **V97　Other specified air transport accidents**

The appropriate 7th character is to be added to each code from category V97

A	initial encounter
D	subsequent encounter
S	sequela

X● **V97.0** Occupant of aircraft injured in other specified air transport accidents
　　　　Fall in, on or from aircraft in air transport accident
　　　　Excludes1　accident while boarding or alighting aircraft (V97.1)
X● **V97.1** Person injured while boarding or alighting from aircraft

● **V97.2　Parachutist accident**
X● **V97.21** Parachutist entangled in object
　　　　Parachutist landing in tree
X● **V97.22** Parachutist injured on landing
X● **V97.29** Other parachutist accident

● **V97.3　Person on ground injured in air transport accident**
X● **V97.31** Hit by object falling from aircraft
　　　　Hit by crashing aircraft
　　　　Injured by aircraft hitting house
　　　　Injured by aircraft hitting car
X● **V97.32** Injured by rotating propeller
X● **V97.33** Sucked into jet engine
X● **V97.39** Other injury to person on ground due to air transport accident

● **V97.8　Other air transport accidents, not elsewhere classified**
　　　　Excludes1　aircraft accident NOS (V95.9)
　　　　　　　　exposure to changes in air pressure during ascent or descent (W94.-)

● **V97.81** Air transport accident involving military aircraft
● **V97.810** Civilian aircraft involved in air transport accident with military aircraft
　　　　Passenger in civilian aircraft injured due to accident with military aircraft
● **V97.811** Civilian injured by military aircraft
● **V97.818** Other air transport accident involving military aircraft

X● **V97.89** Other air transport accidents, not elsewhere classified
　　　　Injury from machinery on aircraft

OTHER AND UNSPECIFIED TRANSPORT ACCIDENTS (V98-V99)

Excludes1　vehicle accident, type of vehicle unspecified (V89.-)

● **V98　Other specified transport accidents**

The appropriate 7th character is to be added to each code from category V98

A	initial encounter
D	subsequent encounter
S	sequela

X● **V98.0** Accident to, on or involving cable-car, not on rails
　　　　Caught or dragged by cable-car, not on rails
　　　　Fall or jump from cable-car, not on rails
　　　　Object thrown from or in cable-car, not on rails
X● **V98.1** Accident to, on or involving land-yacht
X● **V98.2** Accident to, on or involving ice yacht
X● **V98.3** Accident to, on or involving ski lift
　　　　Accident to, on or involving ski chair-lift
　　　　Accident to, on or involving ski-lift with gondola
X● **V98.8** Other specified transport accidents

X● **V99　Unspecified transport accident**

The appropriate 7th character is to be added to code V99

A	initial encounter
D	subsequent encounter
S	sequela

▶ New　⇒ Revised　~~deleted~~ Deleted　Excludes 1　Excludes 2　Includes　Use additional　Code first　Code also　Key words
OGCR Official Guidelines　X Assign placeholder X　● Use Additional Character(s)　▶ Manifestation Code　Coding Clinic

OTHER EXTERNAL CAUSES OF ACCIDENTAL INJURY (W00-X58)

SLIPPING, TRIPPING, STUMBLING AND FALLS (W00-W19)

Excludes1   assault involving a fall (Y01-Y02)
fall from animal (V80.-)
fall (in) (from) machinery (in operation)
(W28-W31)
fall (in) (from) transport vehicle (V01-V99)
intentional self-harm involving a fall (X80-X81)

Excludes2   at risk for fall (history of fall) Z91.81
fall (in) (from) burning building (X00.-)
fall into fire (X00-X04, X08)

● **W00   Fall due to ice and snow**

     Includes   pedestrian on foot falling (slipping) on ice and
snow

     Excludes1   fall on (from) ice and snow involving pedestrian
conveyance (V00.-)
fall from stairs and steps not due to ice and snow
(W10.-)

The appropriate 7th character is to be added to each code from
category W00

A	initial encounter
D	subsequent encounter
S	sequela

X ● **W00.0   Fall on same level due to ice and snow**
      Coding Clinic: 2016, Q2, P5

X ● **W00.1   Fall from stairs and steps due to ice and snow**

X ● **W00.2   Other fall from one level to another due to ice and snow**

X ● **W00.9   Unspecified fall due to ice and snow**

● **W01   Fall on same level from slipping, tripping and stumbling**

     Includes   fall on moving sidewalk

     Excludes1   fall due to bumping (striking) against object
(W18.0-)
fall in shower or bathtub (W18.2-)
fall on same level NOS (W18.30)
fall on same level from slipping, tripping and
stumbling due to ice or snow (W00.0)
fall off or from toilet (W18.1-)
slipping, tripping and stumbling NOS (W18.40)
slipping, tripping and stumbling without falling
(W18.4-)

The appropriate 7th character is to be added to each code from
category W01

A	initial encounter
D	subsequent encounter
S	sequela

X ● **W01.0   Fall on same level from slipping, tripping and
stumbling without subsequent striking against object**
      Falling over animal

● **W01.1   Fall on same level from slipping, tripping and
stumbling with subsequent striking against object**

   X ● **W01.10   Fall on same level from slipping, tripping and
stumbling with subsequent striking against
unspecified object**

   ● **W01.11   Fall on same level from slipping, tripping and
stumbling with subsequent striking against
sharp object**

     ● **W01.110   Fall on same level from slipping,
tripping and stumbling with
subsequent striking against sharp
glass**

     ● **W01.111   Fall on same level from slipping,
tripping and stumbling with
subsequent striking against power
tool or machine**

     ● **W01.118   Fall on same level from slipping,
tripping and stumbling with
subsequent striking against other
sharp object**

     ● **W01.119   Fall on same level from slipping,
tripping and stumbling with
subsequent striking against
unspecified sharp object**

   ● **W01.19   Fall on same level from slipping, tripping and
stumbling with subsequent striking against
other object**

     ● **W01.190   Fall on same level from slipping,
tripping and stumbling with
subsequent striking against furniture**

     ● **W01.198   Fall on same level from slipping,
tripping and stumbling with
subsequent striking against other
object**

X ● **W03   Other fall on same level due to collision with another person**
     Fall due to non-transport collision with other person

     Excludes1   collision with another person without fall (W51)
crushed or pushed by a crowd or human
stampede (W52)
fall involving pedestrian conveyance (V00-V09)
fall due to ice or snow (W00)
fall on same level NOS (W18.30)

The appropriate 7th character is to be added to code W03

A	initial encounter
D	subsequent encounter
S	sequela

     Coding Clinic: 2015, Q1, P9-10; 2012, Q4, P108

X ● **W04   Fall while being carried or supported by other persons**
     Accidentally dropped while being carried

The appropriate 7th character is to be added to code W04

A	initial encounter
D	subsequent encounter
S	sequel

● **W05   Fall from non-moving wheelchair, nonmotorized scooter and
motorized mobility scooter**

     Excludes1   fall from moving wheelchair (powered) (V00.811)
fall from motorized mobility scooter
(V00.831)
fall from nonmotorized scooter (V00.141)

The appropriate 7th character is to be added to each code from
category W05

A	initial encounter
D	subsequent encounter
S	sequela

X ● **W05.0   Fall from non-moving wheelchair**

X ● **W05.1   Fall from non-moving nonmotorized scooter**

X ● **W05.2   Fall from non-moving motorized mobility scooter**

X ● **W06   Fall from bed**

The appropriate 7th character is to be added to code W06

A	initial encounter
D	subsequent encounter
S	sequela

X ● **W07   Fall from chair**

The appropriate 7th character is to be added to code W07

A	initial encounter
D	subsequent encounter
S	sequela

CHAPTER 20 (V01-Y99)

X ● **W08**   **Fall from other furniture**

> The appropriate 7th character is to be added to code W08

> | A | initial encounter |
> |---|---|
> | D | subsequent encounter |
> | S | sequela |

● **W09**   **Fall on and from playground equipment**

> **Excludes1**   fall involving recreational machinery (W31)

> The appropriate 7th character is to be added to each code from category W09

> | A | initial encounter |
> |---|---|
> | D | subsequent encounter |
> | S | sequela |

X ● **W09.0**   **Fall on or from playground slide**

X ● **W09.1**   **Fall from playground swing**

X ● **W09.2**   **Fall on or from jungle gym**

X ● **W09.8**   **Fall on or from other playground equipment**

● **W10**   **Fall on and from stairs and steps**

> **Excludes1**   fall from stairs and steps due to ice and snow (W00.1)

> The appropriate 7th character is to be added to each code from category W10

> | A | initial encounter |
> |---|---|
> | D | subsequent encounter |
> | S | sequela |

X ● **W10.0**   **Fall (on) (from) escalator**

X ● **W10.1**   **Fall (on) (from) sidewalk curb**

X ● **W10.2**   **Fall (on) (from) incline**
> Fall (on) (from) ramp

X ● **W10.8**   **Fall (on) (from) other stairs and steps**

X ● **W10.9**   **Fall (on) (from) unspecified stairs and steps**

X ● **W11**   **Fall on and from ladder**

> The appropriate 7th character is to be added to code W11

> | A | initial encounter |
> |---|---|
> | D | subsequent encounter |
> | S | sequela |

X ● **W12**   **Fall on and from scaffolding**

> The appropriate 7th character is to be added to code W12

> | A | initial encounter |
> |---|---|
> | D | subsequent encounter |
> | S | sequela |

● **W13**   **Fall from, out of or through building or structure**

> The appropriate 7th character is to be added to each code from category W13

> | A | initial encounter |
> |---|---|
> | D | subsequent encounter |
> | S | sequela |

X ● **W13.0**   **Fall from, out of or through balcony**
> Fall from, out of or through railing

X ● **W13.1**   **Fall from, out of or through bridge**

X ● **W13.2**   **Fall from, out of or through roof**

X ● **W13.3**   **Fall through floor**

X ● **W13.4**   **Fall from, out of or through window**
> **Excludes2**   fall with subsequent striking against sharp glass (W01.110)

X ● **W13.8**   **Fall from, out of or through other building or structure**
> Fall from, out of or through viaduct
> Fall from, out of or through wall
> Fall from, out of or through flag-pole

X ● **W13.9**   **Fall from, out of or through building, not otherwise specified**
> **Excludes1**   collapse of a building or structure (W20.-)
> fall or jump from burning building or structure (X00.-)

X ● **W14**   **Fall from tree**

> The appropriate 7th character is to be added to code W14

> | A | initial encounter |
> |---|---|
> | D | subsequent encounter |
> | S | sequela |

X ● **W15**   **Fall from cliff**

> The appropriate 7th character is to be added to code W15

> | A | initial encounter |
> |---|---|
> | D | subsequent encounter |
> | S | sequela |

● **W16**   **Fall, jump or diving into water**

> **Excludes1**   accidental non-watercraft drowning and submersion not involving fall (W65-W74)
> effects of air pressure from diving (W94.-)
> fall into water from watercraft (V90-V94)
> hitting an object or against bottom when falling from watercraft (V94.0)

> **Excludes2**   striking or hitting diving board (W21.4)

> The appropriate 7th character is to be added to each code from category W16

> | A | initial encounter |
> |---|---|
> | D | subsequent encounter |
> | S | sequela |

● **W16.0**   **Fall into swimming pool**
> Fall into swimming pool NOS
> **Excludes1**   fall into empty swimming pool (W17.3)

> ● **W16.01**   **Fall into swimming pool striking water surface**

>> ● **W16.011**   **Fall into swimming pool striking water surface causing drowning and submersion**
>>> **Excludes1**   drowning and submersion while in swimming pool without fall (W67)

>> ● **W16.012**   **Fall into swimming pool striking water surface causing other injury**

● W16.02 Fall into swimming pool striking bottom
  ● W16.021 Fall into swimming pool striking bottom causing drowning and submersion

    Excludes1   drowning and submersion while in swimming pool without fall (W67)

  ● W16.022 Fall into swimming pool striking bottom causing other injury
● W16.03 Fall into swimming pool striking wall
  ● W16.031 Fall into swimming pool striking wall causing drowning and submersion

    Excludes1   drowning and submersion while in swimming pool without fall (W67)

  ● W16.032 Fall into swimming pool striking wall causing other injury
● W16.1 Fall into natural body of water
      Fall into lake
      Fall into open sea
      Fall into river
      Fall into stream
  ● W16.11 Fall into natural body of water striking water surface
    ● W16.111 Fall into natural body of water striking water surface causing drowning and submersion

      Excludes1   drowning and submersion while in natural body of water without fall (W69)

    ● W16.112 Fall into natural body of water striking water surface causing other injury
  ● W16.12 Fall into natural body of water striking bottom
    ● W16.121 Fall into natural body of water striking bottom causing drowning and submersion

      Excludes1   drowning and submersion while in natural body of water without fall (W69)

    ● W16.122 Fall into natural body of water striking bottom causing other injury
  ● W16.13 Fall into natural body of water striking side
    ● W16.131 Fall into natural body of water striking side causing drowning and submersion

      Excludes1   drowning and submersion while in natural body of water without fall (W69)

    ● W16.132 Fall into natural body of water striking side causing other injury
● W16.2 Fall in (into) filled bathtub or bucket of water
  ● W16.21 Fall in (into) filled bathtub

    Excludes1   fall into empty bathtub (W18.2)

    ● W16.211 Fall in (into) filled bathtub causing drowning and submersion

      Excludes1   drowning and submersion while in filled bathtub without fall (W65)

    ● W16.212 Fall in (into) filled bathtub causing other injury

● W16.22 Fall in (into) bucket of water
  ● W16.221 Fall in (into) bucket of water causing drowning and submersion
  ● W16.222 Fall in (into) bucket of water causing other injury
● W16.3 Fall into other water
      Fall into fountain
      Fall into reservoir
  ● W16.31 Fall into other water striking water surface
    ● W16.311 Fall into other water striking water surface causing drowning and submersion

      Excludes1   drowning and submersion while in other water without fall (W73)

    ● W16.312 Fall into other water striking water surface causing other injury
  ● W16.32 Fall into other water striking bottom
    ● W16.321 Fall into other water striking bottom causing drowning and submersion

      Excludes1   drowning and submersion while in other water without fall (W73)

    ● W16.322 Fall into other water striking bottom causing other injury
  ● W16.33 Fall into other water striking wall
    ● W16.331 Fall into other water striking wall causing drowning and submersion

      Excludes1   drowning and submersion while in other water without fall (W73)

    ● W16.332 Fall into other water striking wall causing other injury
● W16.4 Fall into unspecified water
  X ● W16.41 Fall into unspecified water causing drowning and submersion
  X ● W16.42 Fall into unspecified water causing other injury
● W16.5 Jumping or diving into swimming pool
  ● W16.51 Jumping or diving into swimming pool striking water surface
    ● W16.511 Jumping or diving into swimming pool striking water surface causing drowning and submersion

      Excludes1   drowning and submersion while in swimming pool without jumping or diving (W67)

    ● W16.512 Jumping or diving into swimming pool striking water surface causing other injury
  ● W16.52 Jumping or diving into swimming pool striking bottom
    ● W16.521 Jumping or diving into swimming pool striking bottom causing drowning and submersion

      Excludes1   drowning and submersion while in swimming pool without jumping or diving (W67)

    ● W16.522 Jumping or diving into swimming pool striking bottom causing other injury

CHAPTER 20 (V01-Y99)

- **W16.53** Jumping or diving into swimming pool striking wall
  - **W16.531** Jumping or diving into swimming pool striking wall causing drowning and submersion
    - **Excludes1** drowning and submersion while in swimming pool without jumping or diving (W67)
  - **W16.532** Jumping or diving into swimming pool striking wall causing other injury
- **W16.6** Jumping or diving into natural body of water
  - Jumping or diving into lake
  - Jumping or diving into open sea
  - Jumping or diving into river
  - Jumping or diving into stream
  - **W16.61** Jumping or diving into natural body of water striking water surface
    - **W16.611** Jumping or diving into natural body of water striking water surface causing drowning and submersion
      - **Excludes1** drowning and submersion while in natural body of water without jumping or diving (W69)
    - **W16.612** Jumping or diving into natural body of water striking water surface causing other injury
  - **W16.62** Jumping or diving into natural body of water striking bottom
    - **W16.621** Jumping or diving into natural body of water striking bottom causing drowning and submersion
      - **Excludes1** drowning and submersion while in natural body of water without jumping or diving (W69)
    - **W16.622** Jumping or diving into natural body of water striking bottom causing other injury
- **W16.7** Jumping or diving from boat
  - **Excludes1** fall from boat into water - see watercraft accident (V9Ø-V94)
  - **W16.71** Jumping or diving from boat striking water surface
    - **W16.711** Jumping or diving from boat striking water surface causing drowning and submersion
    - **W16.712** Jumping or diving from boat striking water surface causing other injury
  - **W16.72** Jumping or diving from boat striking bottom
    - **W16.721** Jumping or diving from boat striking bottom causing drowning and submersion
    - **W16.722** Jumping or diving from boat striking bottom causing other injury

- **W16.8** Jumping or diving into other water
  - Jumping or diving into fountain
  - Jumping or diving into reservoir
  - **W16.81** Jumping or diving into other water striking water surface
    - **W16.811** Jumping or diving into other water striking water surface causing drowning and submersion
      - **Excludes1** drowning and submersion while in other water without jumping or diving (W73)
    - **W16.812** Jumping or diving into other water striking water surface causing other injury
  - **W16.82** Jumping or diving into other water striking bottom
    - **W16.821** Jumping or diving into other water striking bottom causing drowning and submersion
      - **Excludes1** drowning and submersion while in other water without jumping or diving (W73)
    - **W16.822** Jumping or diving into other water striking bottom causing other injury
  - **W16.83** Jumping or diving into other water striking wall
    - **W16.831** Jumping or diving into other water striking wall causing drowning and submersion
      - **Excludes1** drowning and submersion while in other water without jumping or diving (W73)
    - **W16.832** Jumping or diving into other water striking wall causing other injury
- **W16.9** Jumping or diving into unspecified water
  - X **W16.91** Jumping or diving into unspecified water causing drowning and submersion
  - X **W16.92** Jumping or diving into unspecified water causing other injury
- **W17** Other fall from one level to another

  The appropriate 7th character is to be added to each code from category W17

A	initial encounter
D	subsequent encounter
S	sequela

  - X **W17.Ø** Fall into well
  - X **W17.1** Fall into storm drain or manhole
  - X **W17.2** Fall into hole
    - Fall into pit
  - X **W17.3** Fall into empty swimming pool
    - **Excludes1** fall into filled swimming pool (W16.Ø-)
  - X **W17.4** Fall from dock
  - **W17.8** Other fall from one level to another
    - X **W17.81** Fall down embankment (hill)
    - X **W17.82** Fall from (out of) grocery cart
      - Fall due to grocery cart tipping over
    - X **W17.89** Other fall from one level to another
      - Fall from cherry picker
      - Fall from lifting device
      - Fall from mobile elevated work platform [MEWP]
      - Fall from sky lift
      - **Coding Clinic: 2Ø15, Q2, P6**

▶ New   ➠ Revised   ~~deleted~~ Deleted   Excludes 1   Excludes 2   Includes   Use additional   Code first   Code also   Key words

OGCR Official Guidelines   X Assign placeholder X   ● Use Additional Character(s)   ▶ Manifestation Code   **Coding Clinic**

● **W18 Other slipping, tripping and stumbling and falls**

The appropriate 7th character is to be added to each code from category W18

A	initial encounter
D	subsequent encounter
S	sequela

● **W18.0 Fall due to bumping against object**
Striking against object with subsequent fall

    Excludes1   fall on same level due to slipping, tripping, or stumbling with subsequent striking against object (W01.1-)

X● **W18.00 Striking against unspecified object with subsequent fall**

X● **W18.01 Striking against sports equipment with subsequent fall**

X● **W18.02 Striking against glass with subsequent fall**

X● **W18.09 Striking against other object with subsequent fall**

● **W18.1 Fall from or off toilet**

X● **W18.11 Fall from or off toilet without subsequent striking against object**
Fall from (off) toilet NOS

X● **W18.12 Fall from or off toilet with subsequent striking against object**

X● **W18.2 Fall in (into) shower or empty bathtub**

    Excludes1   fall in full bathtub causing drowning or submersion (W16.21-)

● **W18.3 Other and unspecified fall on same level**

X● **W18.30 Fall on same level, unspecified**

X● **W18.31 Fall on same level due to stepping on an object**
Fall on same level due to stepping on an animal

    Excludes1   slipping, tripping and stumbling without fall due to stepping on animal (W18.41)

X● **W18.39 Other fall on same level**

● **W18.4 Slipping, tripping and stumbling without falling**

    Excludes1   collision with another person without fall (W51)

X● **W18.40 Slipping, tripping and stumbling without falling, unspecified**

X● **W18.41 Slipping, tripping and stumbling without falling due to stepping on object**
Slipping, tripping and stumbling without falling due to stepping on animal

        Excludes1   slipping, tripping and stumbling with fall due to stepping on animal (W18.31)

X● **W18.42 Slipping, tripping and stumbling without falling due to stepping into hole or opening**

X● **W18.43 Slipping, tripping and stumbling without falling due to stepping from one level to another**

X● **W18.49 Other slipping, tripping and stumbling without falling**

X● **W19 Unspecified fall**
Accidental fall NOS

The appropriate 7th character is to be added to code W19

A	initial encounter
D	subsequent encounter
S	sequela

Coding Clinic: 2012, Q4, P95

EXPOSURE TO INANIMATE MECHANICAL FORCES (W20-W49)

    Excludes1   assault (X92-Y09)
            contact or collision with animals or persons (W50-W64)
            exposure to inanimate mechanical forces involving military or war operations (Y36.-, Y37.-)
            intentional self-harm (X71-X83)

Coding Clinic: 2016, Q4, P129

● **W20 Struck by thrown, projected or falling object**

Code first any associated:
cataclysm (X34-X39)
lightning strike (T75.00)

    Excludes1   falling object in machinery accident (W24, W28-W31)
            falling object in transport accident (V01-V99)
            object set in motion by explosion (W35-W40)
            object set in motion by firearm (W32-W34)
            struck by thrown sports equipment (W21.-)

The appropriate 7th character is to be added to each code from category W20

A	initial encounter
D	subsequent encounter
S	sequela

X● **W20.0 Struck by falling object in cave-in**

    Excludes2   asphyxiation due to cave-in (T71.21)

X● **W20.1 Struck by object due to collapse of building**

    Excludes1   struck by object due to collapse of burning building (X00.2, X02.2)

X● **W20.8 Other cause of strike by thrown, projected or falling object**

    Excludes1   struck by thrown sports equipment (W21.-)

● **W21 Striking against or struck by sports equipment**

    Excludes1   assault with sports equipment (Y08.0-)
            striking against or struck by sports equipment with subsequent fall (W18.01)

The appropriate 7th character is to be added to each code from category W21

A	initial encounter
D	subsequent encounter
S	sequela

● **W21.0 Struck by hit or thrown ball**

X● **W21.00 Struck by hit or thrown ball, unspecified type**

X● **W21.01 Struck by football**

X● **W21.02 Struck by soccer ball**

X● **W21.03 Struck by baseball**

X● **W21.04 Struck by golf ball**

X● **W21.05 Struck by basketball**

X● **W21.06 Struck by volleyball**

X● **W21.07 Struck by softball**

X● **W21.09 Struck by other hit or thrown ball**

● **W21.1 Struck by bat, racquet or club**

X● **W21.11 Struck by baseball bat**

X● **W21.12 Struck by tennis racquet**

X● **W21.13 Struck by golf club**

X● **W21.19 Struck by other bat, racquet or club**

● **W21.2 Struck by hockey stick or puck**

● **W21.21 Struck by hockey stick**

● **W21.210 Struck by ice hockey stick**

● **W21.211 Struck by field hockey stick**

● **W21.22 Struck by hockey puck**

● **W21.220 Struck by ice hockey puck**

● **W21.221 Struck by field hockey puck**

● **W21.3 Struck by sports foot wear**
  X● **W21.31 Struck by shoe cleats**
        Stepped on by shoe cleats
  X● **W21.32 Struck by skate blades**
        Skated over by skate blades
  X● **W21.39 Struck by other sports foot wear**
X● **W21.4 Striking against diving board**
      Use additional code for subsequent falling into water, if applicable (W16.-)
● **W21.8 Striking against or struck by other sports equipment**
  X● **W21.81 Striking against or struck by football helmet**
  X● **W21.89 Striking against or struck by other sports equipment**
X● **W21.9 Striking against or struck by unspecified sports equipment**

● **W22 Striking against or struck by other objects**
    Excludes1 striking against or struck by object with subsequent fall (W18.Ø9)
    The appropriate 7th character is to be added to each code from category W22

A	initial encounter
D	subsequent encounter
S	sequela

  ● **W22.Ø Striking against stationary object**
      Excludes1 striking against stationary sports equipment (W21.8)
    X● **W22.Ø1 Walked into wall**
    X● **W22.Ø2 Walked into lamppost**
    X● **W22.Ø3 Walked into furniture**
    ● **W22.Ø4 Striking against wall of swimming pool**
      ● **W22.Ø41 Striking against wall of swimming pool causing drowning and submersion**
            Excludes1 drowning and submersion while swimming without striking against wall (W67)
      ● **W22.Ø42 Striking against wall of swimming pool causing other injury**
    X● **W22.Ø9 Striking against other stationary object**
  ● **W22.1 Striking against or struck by automobile airbag**
    X● **W22.1Ø Striking against or struck by unspecified automobile airbag**
    X● **W22.11 Striking against or struck by driver side automobile airbag**
    X● **W22.12 Striking against or struck by front passenger side automobile airbag**
    X● **W22.19 Striking against or struck by other automobile airbag**
X● **W22.8 Striking against or struck by other objects**
      Striking against or struck by object NOS
      Excludes1 struck by thrown, projected or falling object (W20.-)

● **W23 Caught, crushed, jammed or pinched in or between objects**
    Excludes1 injury caused by cutting or piercing instruments (W25-W27)
          injury caused by firearms malfunction (W32.1, W33.1-, W34.1-)
          injury caused by lifting and transmission devices (W24.-)
          injury caused by machinery (W28-W31)
          injury caused by nonpowered hand tools (W27.-)
          injury caused by transport vehicle being used as a means of transportation (VØ1-V99)
          injury caused by struck by thrown, projected or falling object (W20.-)
    The appropriate 7th character is to be added to each code from category W23

A	initial encounter
D	subsequent encounter
S	sequela

  X● **W23.Ø Caught, crushed, jammed, or pinched between moving objects**
  X● **W23.1 Caught, crushed, jammed, or pinched between stationary objects**

● **W24 Contact with lifting and transmission devices, not elsewhere classified**
    Excludes1 transport accidents (VØ1-V99)
    The appropriate 7th character is to be added to each code from category W24

A	initial encounter
D	subsequent encounter
S	sequela

  X● **W24.Ø Contact with lifting devices, not elsewhere classified**
        Contact with chain hoist
        Contact with drive belt
        Contact with pulley (block)
  X● **W24.1 Contact with transmission devices, not elsewhere classified**
        Contact with transmission belt or cable

X● **W25 Contact with sharp glass**
      Code first any associated:
        injury due to flying glass from explosion or firearm discharge (W32-W4Ø)
        transport accident (VØØ-V99)
    Excludes1 fall on same level due to slipping, tripping and stumbling with subsequent striking against sharp glass (WØ1.1Ø)
          striking against sharp glass with subsequent fall (W18.Ø2)
    Excludes2 glass embedded in skin (W45)
    The appropriate 7th character is to be added to code W25

A	initial encounter
D	subsequent encounter
S	sequela

▶ New ⇒ Revised ~~deleted~~ Deleted Excludes 1 Excludes 2 Includes Use additional Code first Code also Key words
OGCR Official Guidelines X Assign placeholder X ● Use Additional Character(s) ▷ Manifestation Code **Coding Clinic**

● **W26 Contact with other sharp objects**

> **Excludes2**   sharp object(s) embedded in skin (W45)

> The appropriate 7th character is to be added to each code from category W26

> | | |
> |---|---|
> | A | initial encounter |
> | D | subsequent encounter |
> | S | sequela |

> Coding Clinic: 2016, Q4, P73

X ● **W26.0 Contact with knife**

> **Excludes1**   contact with electric knife (W29.1)

X ● **W26.1 Contact with sword or dagger**

X ● **W26.2 Contact with edge of stiff paper**
> Paper cut
> Coding Clinic: 2016, Q4, P73

X ● **W26.8 Contact with other sharp object(s), not elsewhere classified**
> Contact with tin can lid
> Coding Clinic: 2016, Q4, P73

X ● **W26.9 Contact with unspecified sharp object(s)**
> Coding Clinic: 2016, Q4, P73

● **W27 Contact with nonpowered hand tool**

> The appropriate 7th character is to be added to each code from category W27

> | | |
> |---|---|
> | A | initial encounter |
> | D | subsequent encounter |
> | S | sequela |

X ● **W27.0 Contact with workbench tool**
> Contact with auger
> Contact with axe
> Contact with chisel
> Contact with handsaw
> Contact with screwdriver

X ● **W27.1 Contact with garden tool**
> Contact with hoe
> Contact with nonpowered lawn mower
> Contact with pitchfork
> Contact with rake

X ● **W27.2 Contact with scissors**

X ● **W27.3 Contact with needle (sewing)**

> **Excludes1**   contact with hypodermic needle (W46.-)

X ● **W27.4 Contact with kitchen utensil**
> Contact with fork
> Contact with ice-pick
> Contact with can-opener NOS

X ● **W27.5 Contact with paper-cutter**

X ● **W27.8 Contact with other nonpowered hand tool**
> Contact with nonpowered sewing machine
> Contact with shovel

X ● **W28 Contact with powered lawn mower**
> Powered lawn mower (commercial) (residential)

> **Excludes1**   contact with nonpowered lawn mower (W27.1)

> **Excludes2**   exposure to electric current (W86.-)

> The appropriate 7th character is to be added to code W28

> | | |
> |---|---|
> | A | initial encounter |
> | D | subsequent encounter |
> | S | sequela |

● **W29 Contact with other powered hand tools and household machinery**

> **Excludes1**   contact with commercial machinery (W31.82)
> contact with hot household appliance (X15)
> contact with nonpowered hand tool (W27.-)
> exposure to electric current (W86.)

> The appropriate 7th character is to be added to each code from category W29

> | | |
> |---|---|
> | A | initial encounter |
> | D | subsequent encounter |
> | S | sequela |

X ● **W29.0 Contact with powered kitchen appliance**
> Contact with blender
> Contact with can-opener
> Contact with garbage disposal
> Contact with mixer

X ● **W29.1 Contact with electric knife**

X ● **W29.2 Contact with other powered household machinery**
> Contact with electric fan
> Contact with powered dryer (clothes) (powered) (spin)
> Contact with washing-machine
> Contact with sewing machine

X ● **W29.3 Contact with powered garden and outdoor hand tools and machinery**
> Contact with chainsaw
> Contact with edger
> Contact with garden cultivator (tiller)
> Contact with hedge trimmer
> Contact with other powered garden tool

> **Excludes1**   contact with powered lawn mower (W28)

X ● **W29.4 Contact with nail gun**

X ● **W29.8 Contact with other powered hand tools and household machinery**
> Contact with do-it-yourself tool NOS

● **W30 Contact with agricultural machinery**

> **Includes**   animal-powered farm machine

> **Excludes1**   agricultural transport vehicle accident (V01-V99)
> explosion of grain store (W40.8)
> exposure to electric current (W86.-)

> The appropriate 7th character is to be added to each code from category W30

> | | |
> |---|---|
> | A | initial encounter |
> | D | subsequent encounter |
> | S | sequela |

X ● **W30.0 Contact with combine harvester**
> Contact with reaper
> Contact with thresher

X ● **W30.1 Contact with power take-off devices (PTO)**

X ● **W30.2 Contact with hay derrick**

X ● **W30.3 Contact with grain storage elevator**

> **Excludes1**   explosion of grain store (W40.8)

● **W30.8 Contact with other specified agricultural machinery**

> X ● **W30.81 Contact with agricultural transport vehicle in stationary use**
> > Contact with agricultural transport vehicle under repair, not on public roadway

> > **Excludes1**   agricultural transport vehicle accident (V01-V99)

> X ● **W30.89 Contact with other specified agricultural machinery**

X ● **W30.9 Contact with unspecified agricultural machinery**
> Contact with farm machinery NOS

CHAPTER 20 (V01-Y99)

● **W31**   **Contact with other and unspecified machinery**

    Excludes1   contact with agricultural machinery (W30.-)
          contact with machinery in transport under
             own power or being towed by a vehicle
             (V01-V99)
          exposure to electric current (W86)

    The appropriate 7th character is to be added to each code from
    category W31

      A   initial encounter
      D   subsequent encounter
      S   sequela

X● **W31.0**   **Contact with mining and earth-drilling machinery**
        Contact with bore or drill (land) (seabed)
        Contact with shaft hoist
        Contact with shaft lift
        Contact with undercutter

X● **W31.1**   **Contact with metalworking machines**
        Contact with abrasive wheel
        Contact with forging machine
        Contact with lathe
        Contact with mechanical shears
        Contact with metal drilling machine
        Contact with milling machine
        Contact with power press
        Contact with rolling-mill
        Contact with metal sawing machine

X● **W31.2**   **Contact with powered woodworking and forming machines**
        Contact with band saw
        Contact with bench saw
        Contact with circular saw
        Contact with molding machine
        Contact with overhead plane
        Contact with powered saw
        Contact with radial saw
        Contact with sander
        Excludes1   nonpowered woodworking tools (W27.0)

X● **W31.3**   **Contact with prime movers**
        Contact with gas turbine
        Contact with internal combustion engine
        Contact with steam engine
        Contact with water driven turbine

● **W31.8**   **Contact with other specified machinery**

   X● **W31.81**   **Contact with recreational machinery**
          Contact with roller-coaster

   X● **W31.82**   **Contact with other commercial machinery**
          Contact with commercial electric fan
          Contact with commercial kitchen appliances
          Contact with commercial powered dryer
             (clothes) (powered) (spin)
          Contact with commercial washing-machine
          Contact with commercial sewing machine
          Excludes1   contact with household
                   machinery (W29.-)
                   contact with powered lawn
                   mower (W28)

   X● **W31.83**   **Contact with special construction vehicle in stationary use**
          Contact with special construction vehicle
             under repair, not on public roadway
          Excludes1   special construction vehicle
                   accident (V01-V99)

   X● **W31.89**   **Contact with other specified machinery**

X● **W31.9**   **Contact with unspecified machinery**
        Contact with machinery NOS

● **W32**   **Accidental handgun discharge and malfunction**

    Includes   accidental discharge and malfunction of gun for
           single hand use
          accidental discharge and malfunction of pistol
          accidental discharge and malfunction of revolver
          handgun discharge and malfunction NOS

    Excludes1   accidental airgun discharge and malfunction
             (W34.010, W34.110)
          accidental BB gun discharge and malfunction
             (W34.010, W34.110)
          accidental pellet gun discharge and malfunction
             (W34.010, W34.110)
          accidental shotgun discharge and malfunction
             (W33.01, W33.11)
          assault by handgun discharge (X93)
          handgun discharge involving legal intervention
             (Y35.0-)
          handgun discharge involving military or war
             operations (Y36.4-)
          intentional self-harm by handgun discharge (X72)
          Very pistol discharge and malfunction (W34.09,
             W34.19)

    The appropriate 7th character is to be added to each code from
    category W32

      A   initial encounter
      D   subsequent encounter
      S   sequela

X● **W32.0**   **Accidental handgun discharge**

X● **W32.1**   **Accidental handgun malfunction**
        Injury due to explosion of handgun (parts)
        Injury due to malfunction of mechanism or component
          of handgun
        Injury due to recoil of handgun
        Powder burn from handgun

● **W33**   **Accidental rifle, shotgun and larger firearm discharge and malfunction**

    Includes   rifle, shotgun and larger firearm discharge and
           malfunction NOS

    Excludes1   accidental airgun discharge and malfunction
             (W34.010, W34.110)
          accidental BB gun discharge and malfunction
             (W34.010, W34.110)
          accidental handgun discharge and malfunction
             (W32.-)
          accidental pellet gun discharge and malfunction
             (W34.010, W34.110)
          assault by rifle, shotgun and larger firearm
             discharge (X94)
          firearm discharge involving legal intervention
             (Y35.0-)
          firearm discharge involving military or war
             operations (Y36.4-)
          intentional self-harm by rifle, shotgun and larger
             firearm discharge (X73)

    The appropriate 7th character is to be added to each code from
    category W33

      A   initial encounter
      D   subsequent encounter
      S   sequela

● **W33.0**   **Accidental rifle, shotgun and larger firearm discharge**

   X● **W33.00**   **Accidental discharge of unspecified larger firearm**
          Discharge of unspecified larger firearm NOS

   X● **W33.01**   **Accidental discharge of shotgun**
          Discharge of shotgun NOS

   X● **W33.02**   **Accidental discharge of hunting rifle**
          Discharge of hunting rifle NOS

   X● **W33.03**   **Accidental discharge of machine gun**
          Discharge of machine gun NOS

   X● **W33.09**   **Accidental discharge of other larger firearm**
          Discharge of other larger firearm NOS

● **W33.1**   **Accidental rifle, shotgun and larger firearm malfunction**
     Injury due to explosion of rifle, shotgun and larger firearm (parts)
     Injury due to malfunction of mechanism or component of rifle, shotgun and larger firearm
     Injury due to piercing, cutting, crushing or pinching due to (by) slide trigger mechanism, scope or other gun part
     Injury due to recoil of rifle, shotgun and larger firearm
     Powder burn from rifle, shotgun and larger firearm

   X ● **W33.10**   **Accidental malfunction of unspecified larger firearm**
       Malfunction of unspecified larger firearm NOS

   X ● **W33.11**   **Accidental malfunction of shotgun**
       Malfunction of shotgun NOS

   X ● **W33.12**   **Accidental malfunction of hunting rifle**
       Malfunction of hunting rifle NOS

   X ● **W33.13**   **Accidental malfunction of machine gun**
       Malfunction of machine gun NOS

   X ● **W33.19**   **Accidental malfunction of other larger firearm**
       Malfunction of other larger firearm NOS

● **W34**   **Accidental discharge and malfunction from other and unspecified firearms and guns**

   The appropriate 7th character is to be added to each code from category W34

A	initial encounter
D	subsequent encounter
S	sequela

● **W34.0**   **Accidental discharge from other and unspecified firearms and guns**

   X ● **W34.00**   **Accidental discharge from unspecified firearms or gun**
       Discharge from firearm NOS
       Gunshot wound NOS
       Shot NOS
       Coding Clinic: 2015, Q1, P17

   ● **W34.01**   **Accidental discharge of gas, air or spring-operated guns**

     ● **W34.010**   **Accidental discharge of airgun**
         Accidental discharge of BB gun
         Accidental discharge of pellet gun

     ● **W34.011**   **Accidental discharge of paintball gun**
         Accidental injury due to paintball discharge

     ● **W34.018**   **Accidental discharge of other gas, air or spring-operated gun**

   X ● **W34.09**   **Accidental discharge from other specified firearms**
       Accidental discharge from Very pistol [flare]

● **W34.1**   **Accidental malfunction from other and unspecified firearms and guns**

   X ● **W34.10**   **Accidental malfunction from unspecified firearms or gun**
       Firearm malfunction NOS

   ● **W34.11**   **Accidental malfunction of gas, air or spring-operated guns**

     ● **W34.110**   **Accidental malfunction of airgun**
         Accidental malfunction of BB gun
         Accidental malfunction of pellet gun

     ● **W34.111**   **Accidental malfunction of paintball gun**
         Accidental injury due to paintball gun malfunction

     ● **W34.118**   **Accidental malfunction of other gas, air or spring-operated gun**

   X ● **W34.19**   **Accidental malfunction from other specified firearms**
       Accidental malfunction from Very pistol [flare]

X ● **W35**   **Explosion and rupture of boiler**

   Excludes1   explosion and rupture of boiler on watercraft (V93.4)

   The appropriate 7th character is to be added to code W35

A	initial encounter
D	subsequent encounter
S	sequela

● **W36**   **Explosion and rupture of gas cylinder**

   The appropriate 7th character is to be added to each code from category W36

A	initial encounter
D	subsequent encounter
S	sequela

   X ● **W36.1**   **Explosion and rupture of aerosol can**
   X ● **W36.2**   **Explosion and rupture of air tank**
   X ● **W36.3**   **Explosion and rupture of pressurized-gas tank**
   X ● **W36.8**   **Explosion and rupture of other gas cylinder**
   X ● **W36.9**   **Explosion and rupture of unspecified gas cylinder**

● **W37**   **Explosion and rupture of pressurized tire, pipe or hose**

   The appropriate 7th character is to be added to each code from category W37

A	initial encounter
D	subsequent encounter
S	sequela

   X ● **W37.0**   **Explosion of bicycle tire**
   X ● **W37.8**   **Explosion and rupture of other pressurized tire, pipe or hose**

X ● **W38**   **Explosion and rupture of other specified pressurized devices**

   The appropriate 7th character is to be added to code W38

A	initial encounter
D	subsequent encounter
S	sequela

X ● **W39**   **Discharge of firework**

   The appropriate 7th character is to be added to code W39

A	initial encounter
D	subsequent encounter
S	sequela

● **W40**   **Explosion of other materials**

   Excludes1   assault by explosive material (X96)
       explosion involving legal intervention (Y35.1-)
       explosion involving military or war operations (Y36.0-, Y36.2-)
       intentional self-harm by explosive material (X75)

   The appropriate 7th character is to be added to each code from category W40

A	initial encounter
D	subsequent encounter
S	sequela

   X ● **W40.0**   **Explosion of blasting material**
       Explosion of blasting cap
       Explosion of detonator
       Explosion of dynamite
       Explosion of explosive (any) used in blasting operations

   X ● **W40.1**   **Explosion of explosive gases**
       Explosion of acetylene
       Explosion of butane
       Explosion of coal gas
       Explosion in mine NOS
       Explosion of explosive gas
       Explosion of fire damp
       Explosion of gasoline fumes
       Explosion of methane
       Explosion of propane

CHAPTER 20 (V01-Y99)

X ● **W40.8 Explosion of other specified explosive materials**
Explosion in dump NOS
Explosion in factory NOS
Explosion in grain store
Explosion in munitions
Excludes1 explosion involving legal intervention
(Y35.1-)
explosion involving military or war
operations (Y36.0-, Y36.2-)

X ● **W40.9 Explosion of unspecified explosive materials**
Explosion NOS

● **W42 Exposure to noise**
The appropriate 7th character is to be added to each code from
category W42

A	initial encounter
D	subsequent encounter
S	sequela

X ● **W42.0 Exposure to supersonic waves**
X ● **W42.9 Exposure to other noise**
Exposure to sound waves NOS

● **W45 Foreign body or object entering through skin**
Includes foreign body or object embedded in skin
nail embedded in skin
Excludes2 contact with hand tools (nonpowered) (powered)
(W27-W29)
contact with other sharp object(s) (W26.-)
contact with sharp glass (W25.-)
struck by objects (W20-W22)
The appropriate 7th character is to be added to each code from
category W45

A	initial encounter
D	subsequent encounter
S	sequela

X ● **W45.0 Nail entering through skin**
X ● **W45.8 Other foreign body or object entering through skin**
Splinter in skin NOS

● **W46 Contact with hypodermic needle**
The appropriate 7th character is to be added to each code from
category W46

A	initial encounter
D	subsequent encounter
S	sequela

X ● **W46.0 Contact with hypodermic needle**
Hypodermic needle stick NOS
X ● **W46.1 Contact with contaminated hypodermic needle**

● **W49 Exposure to other inanimate mechanical forces**
Includes exposure to abnormal gravitational [G] forces
exposure to inanimate mechanical forces NEC
Excludes1 exposure to inanimate mechanical forces
involving military or war operations (Y36.-,
Y37.-)
The appropriate 7th character is to be added to each code from
category W49

A	initial encounter
D	subsequent encounter
S	sequela

● **W49.0 Item causing external constriction**
X ● **W49.01 Hair causing external constriction**
X ● **W49.02 String or thread causing external constriction**
X ● **W49.03 Rubber band causing external constriction**
X ● **W49.04 Ring or other jewelry causing external
constriction**
X ● **W49.09 Other item causing external constriction**
X ● **W49.9 Exposure to other inanimate mechanical forces**

EXPOSURE TO ANIMATE MECHANICAL FORCES (W50-W64)

Excludes1 toxic effect of contact with venomous animals
and plants (T63.-)

● **W50 Accidental hit, strike, kick, twist, bite or scratch by another person**
Includes hit, strike, kick, twist, bite, or scratch by another
person NOS
Excludes1 assault by bodily force (Y04)
struck by objects (W20-W22)
The appropriate 7th character is to be added to each code from
category W50

A	initial encounter
D	subsequent encounter
S	sequela

X ● **W50.0 Accidental hit or strike by another person**
Hit or strike by another person NOS
X ● **W50.1 Accidental kick by another person**
Kick by another person NOS
X ● **W50.2 Accidental twist by another person**
Twist by another person NOS
Coding Clinic: 2015, Q1, P8
X ● **W50.3 Accidental bite by another person**
Human bite
Bite by another person NOS
X ● **W50.4 Accidental scratch by another person**
Scratch by another person NOS

X ● **W51 Accidental striking against or bumped into by another person**
Excludes1 assault by striking against or bumping into by
another person (Y04.2)
fall due to collision with another person (W03)
The appropriate 7th character is to be added to code W51

A	initial encounter
D	subsequent encounter
S	sequela

X ● **W52 Crushed, pushed or stepped on by crowd or human stampede**
Crushed, pushed or stepped on by crowd or human stampede
with or without fall
The appropriate 7th character is to be added to code W52

A	initial encounter
D	subsequent encounter
S	sequela

● **W53 Contact with rodent**
Includes contact with saliva, feces or urine of rodent
The appropriate 7th character is to be added to each code from
category W53

A	initial encounter
D	subsequent encounter
S	sequela

● **W53.0 Contact with mouse**
X ● **W53.01 Bitten by mouse**
X ● **W53.09 Other contact with mouse**
● **W53.1 Contact with rat**
X ● **W53.11 Bitten by rat**
X ● **W53.19 Other contact with rat**
● **W53.2 Contact with squirrel**
X ● **W53.21 Bitten by squirrel**
X ● **W53.29 Other contact with squirrel**
● **W53.8 Contact with other rodent**
X ● **W53.81 Bitten by other rodent**
X ● **W53.89 Other contact with other rodent**

▶ New   ⇒ Revised   ~~deleted~~ Deleted   Excludes 1   Excludes 2   Includes   Use additional   Code first   Code also   Key words
OGCR Official Guidelines   X Assign placeholder X   ▷ Use Additional Character(s)   ▷ Manifestation Code   **Coding Clinic**

● **W54   Contact with dog**

     Includes   contact with saliva, feces or urine of dog

     The appropriate 7th character is to be added to each code from category W54

> A   initial encounter
> D   subsequent encounter
> S   sequela

X ● **W54.0   Bitten by dog**

X ● **W54.1   Struck by dog**
       Knocked over by dog

X ● **W54.8   Other contact with dog**

● **W55   Contact with other mammals**

     Includes   contact with saliva, feces or urine of mammal

     Excludes1   animal being ridden - see transport accidents
                bitten or struck by dog (W54)
                bitten or struck by rodent (W53.-)
                contact with marine mammals (W56.X-)

     The appropriate 7th character is to be added to each code from category W55

> A   initial encounter
> D   subsequent encounter
> S   sequela

● **W55.0   Contact with cat**

X ● **W55.01   Bitten by cat**

X ● **W55.03   Scratched by cat**

X ● **W55.09   Other contact with cat**

● **W55.1   Contact with horse**

X ● **W55.11   Bitten by horse**

X ● **W55.12   Struck by horse**

X ● **W55.19   Other contact with horse**

● **W55.2   Contact with cow**
       Contact with bull

X ● **W55.21   Bitten by cow**

X ● **W55.22   Struck by cow**
         Gored by bull

X ● **W55.29   Other contact with cow**

● **W55.3   Contact with other hoof stock**
       Contact with goats
       Contact with sheep

X ● **W55.31   Bitten by other hoof stock**

X ● **W55.32   Struck by other hoof stock**
         Gored by goat
         Gored by ram

X ● **W55.39   Other contact with other hoof stock**

● **W55.4   Contact with pig**

X ● **W55.41   Bitten by pig**

X ● **W55.42   Struck by pig**

X ● **W55.49   Other contact with pig**

● **W55.5   Contact with raccoon**

X ● **W55.51   Bitten by raccoon**

X ● **W55.52   Struck by raccoon**

X ● **W55.59   Other contact with raccoon**

● **W55.8   Contact with other mammals**

X ● **W55.81   Bitten by other mammals**

X ● **W55.82   Struck by other mammals**

X ● **W55.89   Other contact with other mammals**

● **W56   Contact with nonvenomous marine animal**

     Excludes1   contact with venomous marine animal (T63.-)

     The appropriate 7th character is to be added to each code from category W56

> A   initial encounter
> D   subsequent encounter
> S   sequela

● **W56.0   Contact with dolphin**

X ● **W56.01   Bitten by dolphin**

X ● **W56.02   Struck by dolphin**

X ● **W56.09   Other contact with dolphin**

● **W56.1   Contact with sea lion**

X ● **W56.11   Bitten by sea lion**

X ● **W56.12   Struck by sea lion**

X ● **W56.19   Other contact with sea lion**

● **W56.2   Contact with orca**
       Contact with killer whale

X ● **W56.21   Bitten by orca**

X ● **W56.22   Struck by orca**

X ● **W56.29   Other contact with orca**

● **W56.3   Contact with other marine mammals**

X ● **W56.31   Bitten by other marine mammals**

X ● **W56.32   Struck by other marine mammals**

X ● **W56.39   Other contact with other marine mammals**

● **W56.4   Contact with shark**

X ● **W56.41   Bitten by shark**

X ● **W56.42   Struck by shark**

X ● **W56.49   Other contact with shark**

● **W56.5   Contact with other fish**

X ● **W56.51   Bitten by other fish**

X ● **W56.52   Struck by other fish**

X ● **W56.59   Other contact with other fish**

● **W56.8   Contact with other nonvenomous marine animals**

X ● **W56.81   Bitten by other nonvenomous marine animals**

X ● **W56.82   Struck by other nonvenomous marine animals**

X ● **W56.89   Other contact with other nonvenomous marine animals**

X ● **W57   Bitten or stung by nonvenomous insect and other nonvenomous arthropods**

     Excludes1   contact with venomous insects and arthropods (T63.2-, T63.3-, T63.4-)

     The appropriate 7th character is to be added to code W57

> A   initial encounter
> D   subsequent encounter
> S   sequela

● **W58   Contact with crocodile or alligator**

     The appropriate 7th character is to be added to each code from category W58

> A   initial encounter
> D   subsequent encounter
> S   sequela

● **W58.0   Contact with alligator**

X ● **W58.01   Bitten by alligator**

X ● **W58.02   Struck by alligator**

X ● **W58.03   Crushed by alligator**

X ● **W58.09   Other contact with alligator**

● **W58.1   Contact with crocodile**

X ● **W58.11   Bitten by crocodile**

X ● **W58.12   Struck by crocodile**

X ● **W58.13   Crushed by crocodile**

X ● **W58.19   Other contact with crocodile**

CHAPTER 20 (V01-Y99)

CHAPTER 20 (V01-Y99)

● W59   Contact with other nonvenomous reptiles

> **Excludes1**   contact with venomous reptile (T63.0-, T63.1-)
>
> The appropriate 7th character is to be added to each code from category W59

A	initial encounter
D	subsequent encounter
S	sequela

  ● W59.0   Contact with nonvenomous lizards

     X ● W59.01   **Bitten by nonvenomous lizards**

     X ● W59.02   **Struck by nonvenomous lizards**

     X ● W59.09   **Other contact with nonvenomous lizards**
                Exposure to nonvenomous lizards

  ● W59.1   Contact with nonvenomous snakes

     X ● W59.11   **Bitten by nonvenomous snake**

     X ● W59.12   **Struck by nonvenomous snake**

     X ● W59.13   **Crushed by nonvenomous snake**

     X ● W59.19   **Other contact with nonvenomous snake**

  ● W59.2   Contact with turtles

> **Excludes1**   contact with tortoises (W59.8-)

     X ● W59.21   **Bitten by turtle**

     X ● W59.22   **Struck by turtle**

     X ● W59.29   **Other contact with turtle**
                Exposure to turtles

  ● W59.8   Contact with other nonvenomous reptiles

     X ● W59.81   **Bitten by other nonvenomous reptiles**

     X ● W59.82   **Struck by other nonvenomous reptiles**

     X ● W59.83   **Crushed by other nonvenomous reptiles**

     X ● W59.89   **Other contact with other nonvenomous reptiles**

X ● W60   Contact with nonvenomous plant thorns and spines and sharp leaves

> **Excludes1**   contact with venomous plants (T63.X7-)
>
> The appropriate 7th character is to be added to code W60

A	initial encounter
D	subsequent encounter
S	sequela

● W61   Contact with birds (domestic) (wild)

> **Includes**   contact with excreta of birds
>
> The appropriate 7th character is to be added to each code from category W61

A	initial encounter
D	subsequent encounter
S	sequela

  ● W61.0   Contact with parrot

     X ● W61.01   **Bitten by parrot**

     X ● W61.02   **Struck by parrot**

     X ● W61.09   **Other contact with parrot**
                Exposure to parrots

  ● W61.1   Contact with macaw

     X ● W61.11   **Bitten by macaw**

     X ● W61.12   **Struck by macaw**

     X ● W61.19   **Other contact with macaw**
                Exposure to macaws

  ● W61.2   Contact with other psittacines

     X ● W61.21   **Bitten by other psittacines**

     X ● W61.22   **Struck by other psittacines**

     X ● W61.29   **Other contact with other psittacines**
                Exposure to other psittacines

  ● W61.3   Contact with chicken

     X ● W61.32   **Struck by chicken**

     X ● W61.33   **Pecked by chicken**

     X ● W61.39   **Other contact with chicken**
                Exposure to chickens

  ● W61.4   Contact with turkey

     X ● W61.42   **Struck by turkey**

     X ● W61.43   **Pecked by turkey**

     X ● W61.49   **Other contact with turkey**

  ● W61.5   Contact with goose

     X ● W61.51   **Bitten by goose**

     X ● W61.52   **Struck by goose**

     X ● W61.59   **Other contact with goose**

  ● W61.6   Contact with duck

     X ● W61.61   **Bitten by duck**

     X ● W61.62   **Struck by duck**

     X ● W61.69   **Other contact with duck**

  ● W61.9   Contact with other birds

     X ● W61.91   **Bitten by other birds**

     X ● W61.92   **Struck by other birds**

     X ● W61.99   **Other contact with other birds**
                Contact with bird NOS

● W62   Contact with nonvenomous amphibians

> **Excludes1**   contact with venomous amphibians (T63.81-R63.83)
>
> The appropriate 7th character is to be added to each code from category W62

A	initial encounter
D	subsequent encounter
S	sequela

   X ● W62.0   Contact with nonvenomous frogs

   X ● W62.1   Contact with nonvenomous toads

   X ● W62.9   Contact with other nonvenomous amphibians

X ● W64   Exposure to other animate mechanical forces

> **Includes**   exposure to nonvenomous animal NOS
>
> **Excludes1**   contact with venomous animal (T63.-)
>
> The appropriate 7th character is to be added to code W64

A	initial encounter
D	subsequent encounter
S	sequela

ACCIDENTAL NON-TRANSPORT DROWNING AND SUBMERSION (W65-W74)

> **Excludes1**   accidental drowning and submersion due to fall into water (W16.-)
>
>   accidental drowning and submersion due to water transport accident (V90.-, V92.-)
>
> **Excludes2**   accidental drowning and submersion due to cataclysm (X34-X39)

X ● W65   Accidental drowning and submersion while in bathtub

> **Excludes1**   accidental drowning and submersion due to fall in (into) bathtub (W16.211)
>
> The appropriate 7th character is to be added to code W65

A	initial encounter
D	subsequent encounter
S	sequela

X ● W67   Accidental drowning and submersion while in swimming pool

> **Excludes1**   accidental drowning and submersion due to fall into swimming pool (W16.011, W16.021, W16.031)
>
>   accidental drowning and submersion due to striking into wall of swimming pool (W22.041)
>
> The appropriate 7th character is to be added to code W67

A	initial encounter
D	subsequent encounter
S	sequela

▶ New   ⇒ Revised   ~~deleted~~ Deleted   Excludes 1   Excludes 2   Includes   Use additional   Code first   Code also   Key words

OGCR Official Guidelines   X Assign placeholder X   ● Use Additional Character(s)   ▶ Manifestation Code   **Coding Clinic**

X ● **W69 Accidental drowning and submersion while in natural water**
Accidental drowning and submersion while in lake
Accidental drowning and submersion while in open sea
Accidental drowning and submersion while in river
Accidental drowning and submersion while in stream

> **Excludes1** accidental drowning and submersion due to fall into natural body of water (W16.111, W16.121, W16.131)

The appropriate 7th character is to be added to code W69

A	initial encounter
D	subsequent encounter
S	sequela

X ● **W73 Other specified cause of accidental non-transport drowning and submersion**
Accidental drowning and submersion while in quenching tank
Accidental drowning and submersion while in reservoir

> **Excludes1** accidental drowning and submersion due to fall into other water (W16.311, W16.321, W16.331)

The appropriate 7th character is to be added to code W73

A	initial encounter
D	subsequent encounter
S	sequela

X ● **W74 Unspecified cause of accidental drowning and submersion**
Drowning NOS

The appropriate 7th character is to be added to code W74

A	initial encounter
D	subsequent encounter
S	sequela

EXPOSURE TO ELECTRIC CURRENT, RADIATION AND EXTREME AMBIENT AIR TEMPERATURE AND PRESSURE (W85-W99)

> **Excludes1** exposure to:
> failure in dosage of radiation or temperature during surgical and medical care (Y63.2-Y63.5)
> lightning (T75.Ø-)
> natural cold (X31)
> natural heat (X3Ø)
> natural radiation NOS (X39)
> radiological procedure and radiotherapy (Y84.2)
> sunlight (X32)

X ● **W85 Exposure to electric transmission lines**
Broken power line

The appropriate 7th character is to be added to code W85

A	initial encounter
D	subsequent encounter
S	sequela

● **W86 Exposure to other specified electric current**

The appropriate 7th character is to be added to each code from category W86

A	initial encounter
D	subsequent encounter
S	sequela

X ● **W86.Ø Exposure to domestic wiring and appliances**
X ● **W86.1 Exposure to industrial wiring, appliances and electrical machinery**
Exposure to conductors
Exposure to control apparatus
Exposure to electrical equipment and machinery
Exposure to transformers

X ● **W86.8 Exposure to other electric current**
Exposure to wiring and appliances in or on farm (not farmhouse)
Exposure to wiring and appliances outdoors
Exposure to wiring and appliances in or on public building
Exposure to wiring and appliances in or on residential institutions
Exposure to wiring and appliances in or on schools

● **W88 Exposure to ionizing radiation**

> **Excludes1** exposure to sunlight (X32)

The appropriate 7th character is to be added to each code from category W88

A	initial encounter
D	subsequent encounter
S	sequela

X ● **W88.Ø Exposure to X-rays**
X ● **W88.1 Exposure to radioactive isotopes**
X ● **W88.8 Exposure to other ionizing radiation**

● **W89 Exposure to man-made visible and ultraviolet light**

> **Includes** exposure to welding light (arc)
> **Excludes1** exposure to sunlight (X32)

The appropriate 7th character is to be added to each code from category W89

A	initial encounter
D	subsequent encounter
S	sequela

X ● **W89.Ø Exposure to welding light (arc)**
X ● **W89.1 Exposure to tanning bed**
X ● **W89.8 Exposure to other man-made visible and ultraviolet light**
X ● **W89.9 Exposure to unspecified man-made visible and ultraviolet light**

● **W90 Exposure to other nonionizing radiation**

> **Excludes1** exposure to sunlight (X32)

The appropriate 7th character is to be added to each code from category W90

A	initial encounter
D	subsequent encounter
S	sequela

X ● **W90.Ø Exposure to radiofrequency**
X ● **W90.1 Exposure to infrared radiation**
X ● **W90.2 Exposure to laser radiation**
X ● **W90.8 Exposure to other nonionizing radiation**

X ● **W92 Exposure to excessive heat of man-made origin**

The appropriate 7th character is to be added to code W92

A	initial encounter
D	subsequent encounter
S	sequela

● **W93 Exposure to excessive cold of man-made origin**

The appropriate 7th character is to be added to each code from category W93

A	initial encounter
D	subsequent encounter
S	sequela

● **W93.Ø Contact with or inhalation of dry ice**
X ● **W93.Ø1 Contact with dry ice**
X ● **W93.Ø2 Inhalation of dry ice**

CHAPTER 2Ø (VØ1-Y99)

- ● W93.1 **Contact with or inhalation of liquid air**
  - X● W93.11 **Contact with liquid air**
    - Contact with liquid hydrogen
    - Contact with liquid nitrogen
  - X● W93.12 **Inhalation of liquid air**
    - Inhalation of liquid hydrogen
    - Inhalation of liquid nitrogen
- X● W93.2 **Prolonged exposure in deep freeze unit or refrigerator**
- X● W93.8 **Exposure to other excessive cold of man-made origin**

● W94 **Exposure to high and low air pressure and changes in air pressure**

The appropriate 7th character is to be added to each code from category W94

A	initial encounter
D	subsequent encounter
S	sequela

- X● W94.0 **Exposure to prolonged high air pressure**
- ● W94.1 **Exposure to prolonged low air pressure**
  - X● W94.11 **Exposure to residence or prolonged visit at high altitude**
  - X● W94.12 **Exposure to other prolonged low air pressure**
- ● W94.2 **Exposure to rapid changes in air pressure during ascent**
  - X● W94.21 **Exposure to reduction in atmospheric pressure while surfacing from deep-water diving**
  - X● W94.22 **Exposure to reduction in atmospheric pressure while surfacing from underground**
  - X● W94.23 **Exposure to sudden change in air pressure in aircraft during ascent**
  - X● W94.29 **Exposure to other rapid changes in air pressure during ascent**
- ● W94.3 **Exposure to rapid changes in air pressure during descent**
  - X● W94.31 **Exposure to sudden change in air pressure in aircraft during descent**
  - X● W94.32 **Exposure to high air pressure from rapid descent in water**
  - X● W94.39 **Exposure to other rapid changes in air pressure during descent**

X● W99 **Exposure to other man-made environmental factors**

The appropriate 7th character is to be added to code W99

A	initial encounter
D	subsequent encounter
S	sequela

EXPOSURE TO SMOKE, FIRE AND FLAMES (X00-X08)

Excludes1 arson (X97)
Excludes2 explosions (W35-W40)
lightning (T75.0-)
transport accident (V01-V99)

● X00 **Exposure to uncontrolled fire in building or structure**
Includes conflagration in building or structure
Code first any associated cataclysm
Excludes2 exposure to ignition or melting of nightwear (X05)
exposure to ignition or melting of other clothing and apparel (X06.-)
exposure to other specified smoke, fire and flames (X08.-)

The appropriate 7th character is to be added to each code from category X00

A	initial encounter
D	subsequent encounter
S	sequela

- X● X00.0 **Exposure to flames in uncontrolled fire in building or structure**
  Coding Clinic: 2016, Q2, P5-6; 2015, Q1, P19
- X● X00.1 **Exposure to smoke in uncontrolled fire in building or structure**
- X● X00.2 **Injury due to collapse of burning building or structure in uncontrolled fire**
  Excludes1 injury due to collapse of building not on fire (W20.1)
- X● X00.3 **Fall from burning building or structure in uncontrolled fire**
- X● X00.4 **Hit by object from burning building or structure in uncontrolled fire**
- X● X00.5 **Jump from burning building or structure in uncontrolled fire**
- X● X00.8 **Other exposure to uncontrolled fire in building or structure**

● X01 **Exposure to uncontrolled fire, not in building or structure**
Includes exposure to forest fire

The appropriate 7th character is to be added to each code from category X01

A	initial encounter
D	subsequent encounter
S	sequela

- X● X01.0 **Exposure to flames in uncontrolled fire, not in building or structure**
- X● X01.1 **Exposure to smoke in uncontrolled fire, not in building or structure**
- X● X01.3 **Fall due to uncontrolled fire, not in building or structure**
- X● X01.4 **Hit by object due to uncontrolled fire, not in building or structure**
- X● X01.8 **Other exposure to uncontrolled fire, not in building or structure**

● X02 **Exposure to controlled fire in building or structure**
Includes exposure to fire in fireplace exposure to fire in stove

The appropriate 7th character is to be added to each code from category X02

A	initial encounter
D	subsequent encounter
S	sequela

- X● X02.0 **Exposure to flames in controlled fire in building or structure**
- X● X02.1 **Exposure to smoke in controlled fire in building or structure**
- X● X02.2 **Injury due to collapse of burning building or structure in controlled fire**
  Excludes1 injury due to collapse of building not on fire (W20.1)
- X● X02.3 **Fall from burning building or structure in controlled fire**
- X● X02.4 **Hit by object from burning building or structure in controlled fire**
- X● X02.5 **Jump from burning building or structure in controlled fire**
- X● X02.8 **Other exposure to controlled fire in building or structure**

● X03 **Exposure to controlled fire, not in building or structure**
Includes exposure to bon fire exposure to camp fire exposure to trash fire

The appropriate 7th character is to be added to each code from category X03

A	initial encounter
D	subsequent encounter
S	sequela

- X● X03.0 **Exposure to flames in controlled fire, not in building or structure**
  Coding Clinic: 2015, Q1, P19
- X● X03.1 **Exposure to smoke in controlled fire, not in building or structure**
- X● X03.3 **Fall due to controlled fire, not in building or structure**
- X● X03.4 **Hit by object due to controlled fire, not in building or structure**
- X● X03.8 **Other exposure to controlled fire, not in building or structure**

▶ New   ⇒ Revised   ~~deleted~~ Deleted   Excludes 1   Excludes 2   Includes   Use additional   Code first   Code also   Key words
OGCR Official Guidelines   X Assign placeholder X   ● Use Additional Character(s)   ▌ Manifestation Code   **Coding Clinic**

X⬤**X04** **Exposure to ignition of highly flammable material**
      Exposure to ignition of gasoline
      Exposure to ignition of kerosene
      Exposure to ignition of petrol
      Excludes2   exposure to ignition or melting of nightwear
                        (X05)
                   exposure to ignition or melting of other clothing
                        and apparel (X06)

      The appropriate 7th character is to be added to code X04

A	initial encounter
D	subsequent encounter
S	sequela

      Coding Clinic: 2016, Q2, P4

X⬤**X05** **Exposure to ignition or melting of nightwear**
      Excludes2   exposure to uncontrolled fire in building or
                        structure (X00.-)
                   exposure to uncontrolled fire, not in building or
                        structure (X01.-)
                   exposure to controlled fire in building or
                        structure (X02.-)
                   exposure to controlled fire, not in building or
                        structure (X03.-)
                   exposure to ignition of highly flammable
                        materials (X04.-)

      The appropriate 7th character is to be added to code X05

A	initial encounter
D	subsequent encounter
S	sequela

⬤**X06** **Exposure to ignition or melting of other clothing and apparel**
      Excludes2   exposure to uncontrolled fire in building or
                        structure (X00.-)
                   exposure to uncontrolled fire, not in building or
                        structure (X01.-)
                   exposure to controlled fire in building or
                        structure (X02.-)
                   exposure to controlled fire, not in building or
                        structure (X03.-)
                   exposure to ignition of highly flammable
                        materials (X04.-)

      The appropriate 7th character is to be added to each code from
          category X06

A	initial encounter
D	subsequent encounter
S	sequela

  X⬤**X06.0** **Exposure to ignition of plastic jewelry**
  X⬤**X06.1** **Exposure to melting of plastic jewelry**
  X⬤**X06.2** **Exposure to ignition of other clothing and apparel**
  X⬤**X06.3** **Exposure to melting of other clothing and apparel**

⬤**X08** **Exposure to other specified smoke, fire and flames**
      The appropriate 7th character is to be added to each code from
          category X08

A	initial encounter
D	subsequent encounter
S	sequela

  ⬤**X08.0** **Exposure to bed fire**
        Exposure to mattress fire
    X⬤**X08.00** **Exposure to bed fire due to unspecified burning material**
    X⬤**X08.01** **Exposure to bed fire due to burning cigarette**
          Coding Clinic: 2015, Q1, P19
    X⬤**X08.09** **Exposure to bed fire due to other burning material**

  ⬤**X08.1** **Exposure to sofa fire**
    X⬤**X08.10** **Exposure to sofa fire due to unspecified burning material**
    X⬤**X08.11** **Exposure to sofa fire due to burning cigarette**
    X⬤**X08.19** **Exposure to sofa fire due to other burning material**

  ⬤**X08.2** **Exposure to other furniture fire**
    X⬤**X08.20** **Exposure to other furniture fire due to unspecified burning material**
    X⬤**X08.21** **Exposure to other furniture fire due to burning cigarette**
    X⬤**X08.29** **Exposure to other furniture fire due to other burning material**

  X⬤**X08.8** **Exposure to other specified smoke, fire and flames**

CONTACT WITH HEAT AND HOT SUBSTANCES (X10-X19)

      Excludes1   exposure to excessive natural heat (X30)
                   exposure to fire and flames (X00-X08)

⬤**X10** **Contact with hot drinks, food, fats and cooking oils**
      The appropriate 7th character is to be added to each code from
          category X10

A	initial encounter
D	subsequent encounter
S	sequela

  X⬤**X10.0** **Contact with hot drinks**
  X⬤**X10.1** **Contact with hot food**
  X⬤**X10.2** **Contact with fats and cooking oils**

⬤**X11** **Contact with hot tap-water**
      Includes   contact with boiling tap-water
                 contact with boiling water NOS
      Excludes1   contact with water heated on stove (X12)
      The appropriate 7th character is to be added to each code from
          category X11

A	initial encounter
D	subsequent encounter
S	sequela

  X⬤**X11.0** **Contact with hot water in bath or tub**
        Excludes1   contact with running hot water in bath or
                   tub (X11.1)
  X⬤**X11.1** **Contact with running hot water**
        Contact with hot water running out of hose
        Contact with hot water running out of tap
  X⬤**X11.8** **Contact with other hot tap-water**
        Contact with hot water in bucket
        Contact with hot tap-water NOS

X⬤**X12** **Contact with other hot fluids**
      Contact with water heated on stove
      Excludes1   hot (liquid) metals (X18)
      The appropriate 7th character is to be added to code X12

A	initial encounter
D	subsequent encounter
S	sequela

⬤**X13** **Contact with steam and other hot vapors**
      The appropriate 7th character is to be added to each code from
          category X13

A	initial encounter
D	subsequent encounter
S	sequela

  X⬤**X13.0** **Inhalation of steam and other hot vapors**
  X⬤**X13.1** **Other contact with steam and other hot vapors**

CHAPTER 20 (V01-Y99)

● **X14** **Contact with hot air and other hot gases**

The appropriate 7th character is to be added to each code from category X14

A	initial encounter
D	subsequent encounter
S	sequela

X ● **X14.0** **Inhalation of hot air and gases**

X ● **X14.1** **Other contact with hot air and other hot gases**

● **X15** **Contact with hot household appliances**

Excludes1   contact with heating appliances (X16)
contact with powered household appliances (W29.-)
exposure to controlled fire in building or structure due to household appliance (X02.8)
exposure to household appliances electrical current (W86.0)

The appropriate 7th character is to be added to each code from category X15

A	initial encounter
D	subsequent encounter
S	sequela

X ● **X15.0** **Contact with hot stove (kitchen)**

X ● **X15.1** **Contact with hot toaster**

X ● **X15.2** **Contact with hotplate**

X ● **X15.3** **Contact with hot saucepan or skillet**

X ● **X15.8** **Contact with other hot household appliances**
Contact with cooker
Contact with kettle
Contact with light bulbs

X ● **X16** **Contact with hot heating appliances, radiators and pipes**

Excludes1   contact with powered appliances (W29.-)
exposure to controlled fire in building or structure due to appliance (X02.8)
exposure to industrial appliances electrical current (W86.1)

The appropriate 7th character is to be added to code X16

A	initial encounter
D	subsequent encounter
S	sequela

X ● **X17** **Contact with hot engines, machinery and tools**

Excludes1   contact with hot heating appliances, radiators and pipes (X16)
contact with hot household appliances (X15)

The appropriate 7th character is to be added to code X17

A	initial encounter
D	subsequent encounter
S	sequela

X ● **X18** **Contact with other hot metals**
Contact with liquid metal

The appropriate 7th character is to be added to code X18

A	initial encounter
D	subsequent encounter
S	sequela

X ● **X19** **Contact with other heat and hot substances**

Excludes1   objects that are not normally hot, e.g., an object made hot by a house fire (X00-X08)

The appropriate 7th character is to be added to code X19

A	initial encounter
D	subsequent encounter
S	sequela

EXPOSURE TO FORCES OF NATURE (X30-X39)

X ● **X30** **Exposure to excessive natural heat**
Exposure to excessive heat as the cause of sunstroke
Exposure to heat NOS

Excludes1   excessive heat of man-made origin (W92)
exposure to man-made radiation (W89)
exposure to sunlight (X32)
exposure to tanning bed (W89)

The appropriate 7th character is to be added to code X30

A	initial encounter
D	subsequent encounter
S	sequela

X ● **X31** **Exposure to excessive natural cold**
Excessive cold as the cause of chilblains NOS
Excessive cold as the cause of immersion foot or hand
Exposure to cold NOS
Exposure to weather conditions

Excludes1   cold of man-made origin (W93.-)
contact with or inhalation of dry ice (W93.-)
contact with or inhalation of liquefied gas (W93.-)

The appropriate 7th character is to be added to code X31

A	initial encounter
D	subsequent encounter
S	sequela

X ● **X32** **Exposure to sunlight**

Excludes1   man-made radiation (tanning bed) (W89)

Excludes2   radiation-related disorders of the skin and subcutaneous tissue (L55-L59)

The appropriate 7th character is to be added to code X32

A	initial encounter
D	subsequent encounter
S	sequela

X ● **X34** **Earthquake**

Excludes2   tidal wave (tsunami) due to earthquake (X37.41)

The appropriate 7th character is to be added to code X34

A	initial encounter
D	subsequent encounter
S	sequela

X ● **X35** **Volcanic eruption**

Excludes2   tidal wave (tsunami) due to volcanic eruption (X37.41)

The appropriate 7th character is to be added to code X35

A	initial encounter
D	subsequent encounter
S	sequela

● **X36** **Avalanche, landslide and other earth movements**

Includes   victim of mudslide of cataclysmic nature

Excludes1   earthquake (X34)

Excludes2   transport accident involving collision with avalanche or landslide not in motion (V01-V99)

The appropriate 7th character is to be added to each code from category X36

A	initial encounter
D	subsequent encounter
S	sequela

X ● **X36.0** **Collapse of dam or man-made structure causing earth movement**

X ● **X36.1** **Avalanche, landslide, or mudslide**

▶ New   ⇒ Revised   ~~deleted~~ Deleted   Excludes 1   Excludes 2   Includes   Use additional   Code first   Code also   Key words

OGCR Official Guidelines   X Assign placeholder X   ● Use Additional Character(s)   ▶ Manifestation Code   **Coding Clinic**

● **X37   Cataclysmic storm**

The appropriate 7th character is to be added to each code from category X37

A	initial encounter
D	subsequent encounter
S	sequela

X ● **X37.0   Hurricane**
     Storm surge   Typhoon

X ● **X37.1   Tornado**
     Cyclone   Twister

X ● **X37.2   Blizzard (snow) (ice)**

X ● **X37.3   Dust storm**

● **X37.4   Tidalwave**

    X ● **X37.41   Tidal wave due to earthquake or volcanic eruption**
         Tidal wave NOS
         Tsunami

    X ● **X37.42   Tidal wave due to storm**

    X ● **X37.43   Tidal wave due to landslide**

X ● **X37.8   Other cataclysmic storms**
     Cloudburst
     Torrential rain

     Excludes2   flood (X38)

X ● **X37.9   Unspecified cataclysmic storm**
     Storm NOS

     ➡ **Excludes1**   collapse of dam or man-made structure causing earth movement (X36.0)

X ● **X38   Flood**

Flood arising from remote storm
Flood of cataclysmic nature arising from melting snow
Flood resulting directly from storm

➡ **Excludes1**   collapse of dam or man-made structure causing earth movement (X36.0)
           tidal wave NOS (X37.41)
           ➡tidal wave caused by storm (X37.42)

The appropriate 7th character is to be added to code X38

A	initial encounter
D	subsequent encounter
S	sequela

● **X39   Exposure to other forces of nature**

The appropriate 7th character is to be added to each code from category X39

A	initial encounter
D	subsequent encounter
S	sequela

● **X39.0   Exposure to natural radiation**

     ➡ **Excludes1**   contact with and (suspected) exposure to radon and other naturally occurring radiation (Z77.123)
           exposure to man-made radiation (W88-W90)
           exposure to sunlight (X32)

    X ● **X39.01   Exposure to radon**

    X ● **X39.08   Exposure to other natural radiation**

X ● **X39.8   Other exposure to forces of nature**

OVEREXERTION AND STRENUOUS OR REPETITIVE MOVEMENTS (X50)

● **X50   Overexertion and strenuous or repetitive movements**

The appropriate 7th character is to be added to each code from category X50

A	initial encounter
D	subsequent encounter
S	sequela

Coding Clinic: 2016, Q4, P73-74

X ● **X50.0   Overexertion from strenuous movement or load**
     Lifting heavy objects
     Lifting weights
     Coding Clinic: 2016, Q4, P74

X ● **X50.1   Overexertion from prolonged static or awkward postures**
     Prolonged bending
     Prolonged kneeling
     Prolonged reaching
     Prolonged sitting
     Prolonged standing
     Prolonged twisting
     Static bending
     Static kneeling
     Static reaching
     Static sitting
     Static standing
     Static twisting

X ● **X50.3   Overexertion from repetitive movements**
     Use of hand as hammer

     Excludes2   Overuse from prolonged static or awkward postures (X50.1)
     Coding Clinic: 2016, Q4, P74

X ● **X50.9   Other and unspecified overexertion or strenuous movements or postures**
     Contact pressure
     Contact stress

ACCIDENTAL EXPOSURE TO OTHER SPECIFIED FACTORS (X52, X58)

X ● **X52   Prolonged stay in weightless environment**
     Weightlessness in spacecraft (simulator)

The appropriate 7th character is to be added to code X52

A	initial encounter
D	subsequent encounter
S	sequela

X ● **X58   Exposure to other specified factors**
     Accident NOS
     Exposure NOS

The appropriate 7th character is to be added to code X58

A	initial encounter
D	subsequent encounter
S	sequela

INTENTIONAL SELF-HARM (X71-X83)

Purposely self-inflicted injury
Suicide (attempted)

● **X71   Intentional self-harm by drowning and submersion**

The appropriate 7th character is to be added to each code from category X71

A	initial encounter
D	subsequent encounter
S	sequela

X ● **X71.0   Intentional self-harm by drowning and submersion while in bathtub**

X ● **X71.1   Intentional self-harm by drowning and submersion while in swimming pool**

X ● **X71.2   Intentional self-harm by drowning and submersion after jump into swimming pool**

CHAPTER 20 (V01-Y99)

X⬤ **X71.3** **Intentional self-harm by drowning and submersion in natural water**

X⬤ **X71.8** **Other intentional self-harm by drowning and submersion**

X⬤ **X71.9** **Intentional self-harm by drowning and submersion, unspecified**

X⬤**X72**   **Intentional self-harm by handgun discharge**
Intentional self-harm by gun for single hand use
Intentional self-harm by pistol
Intentional self-harm by revolver

> **Excludes1**   Very pistol (X74.8)

The appropriate 7th character is to be added to code X72

A	initial encounter
D	subsequent encounter
S	sequela

⬤**X73**   **Intentional self-harm by rifle, shotgun and larger firearm discharge**

> **Excludes1**   airgun (X74.Ø1)

The appropriate 7th character is to be added to each code from category X73

A	initial encounter
D	subsequent encounter
S	sequela

X⬤ **X73.Ø** **Intentional self-harm by shotgun discharge**

X⬤ **X73.1** **Intentional self-harm by hunting rifle discharge**

X⬤ **X73.2** **Intentional self-harm by machine gun discharge**

X⬤ **X73.8** **Intentional self-harm by other larger firearm discharge**

X⬤ **X73.9** **Intentional self-harm by unspecified larger firearm discharge**

⬤**X74**   **Intentional self-harm by other and unspecified firearm and gun discharge**

The appropriate 7th character is to be added to each code from category X74

A	initial encounter
D	subsequent encounter
S	sequela

⬤**X74.Ø**   **Intentional self-harm by gas, air or spring-operated guns**

X⬤ **X74.Ø1**   **Intentional self-harm by airgun**
Intentional self-harm by BB gun discharge
Intentional self-harm by pellet gun discharge

X⬤ **X74.Ø2**   **Intentional self-harm by paintball gun**

X⬤ **X74.Ø9**   **Intentional self-harm by other gas, air or spring-operated gun**

X⬤ **X74.8** **Intentional self-harm by other firearm discharge**
Intentional self-harm by Very pistol [flare] discharge

X⬤ **X74.9** **Intentional self-harm by unspecified firearm discharge**

X⬤**X75**   **Intentional self-harm by explosive material**
The appropriate 7th character is to be added to code X75

A	initial encounter
D	subsequent encounter
S	sequela

X⬤**X76**   **Intentional self-harm by smoke, fire and flames**
The appropriate 7th character is to be added to code X76

A	initial encounter
D	subsequent encounter
S	sequela

⬤**X77**   **Intentional self-harm by steam, hot vapors and hot objects**
The appropriate 7th character is to be added to each code from category X77

A	initial encounter
D	subsequent encounter
S	sequela

X⬤ **X77.Ø** **Intentional self-harm by steam or hot vapors**

X⬤ **X77.1** **Intentional self-harm by hot tap water**

X⬤ **X77.2** **Intentional self-harm by other hot fluids**

X⬤ **X77.3** **Intentional self-harm by hot household appliances**

X⬤ **X77.8** **Intentional self-harm by other hot objects**

X⬤ **X77.9** **Intentional self-harm by unspecified hot objects**

⬤**X78**   **Intentional self-harm by sharp object**
The appropriate 7th character is to be added to each code from category X78

A	initial encounter
D	subsequent encounter
S	sequela

X⬤ **X78.Ø** **Intentional self-harm by sharp glass**

X⬤ **X78.1** **Intentional self-harm by knife**

X⬤ **X78.2** **Intentional self-harm by sword or dagger**

X⬤ **X78.8** **Intentional self-harm by other sharp object**

X⬤ **X78.9** **Intentional self-harm by unspecified sharp object**

X⬤**X79**   **Intentional self-harm by blunt object**
The appropriate 7th character is to be added to code X79

A	initial encounter
D	subsequent encounter
S	sequela

X⬤**X80**   **Intentional self-harm by jumping from a high place**
Intentional fall from one level to another
The appropriate 7th character is to be added to code X8Ø

A	initial encounter
D	subsequent encounter
S	sequela

⬤**X81**   **Intentional self-harm by jumping or lying in front of moving object**
The appropriate 7th character is to be added to each code from category X81

A	initial encounter
D	subsequent encounter
S	sequela

X⬤ **X81.Ø** **Intentional self-harm by jumping or lying in front of motor vehicle**

X⬤ **X81.1** **Intentional self-harm by jumping or lying in front of (subway) train**

X⬤ **X81.8** **Intentional self-harm by jumping or lying in front of other moving object**

⬤**X82**   **Intentional self-harm by crashing of motor vehicle**
The appropriate 7th character is to be added to each code from category X82

A	initial encounter
D	subsequent encounter
S	sequela

X⬤ **X82.Ø** **Intentional collision of motor vehicle with other motor vehicle**

X⬤ **X82.1** **Intentional collision of motor vehicle with train**

X⬤ **X82.2** **Intentional collision of motor vehicle with tree**

X⬤ **X82.8** **Other intentional self-harm by crashing of motor vehicle**

▶ New   ⟾ Revised   ~~deleted~~ Deleted   Excludes 1   Excludes 2   Includes   Use additional   Code first   Code also   Key words

OGCR Official Guidelines   X Assign placeholder X   ⬤ Use Additional Character(s)   ▶ Manifestation Code   **Coding Clinic**

● X83   **Intentional self-harm by other specified means**

    Excludes1   intentional self-harm by poisoning or contact
                 with toxic substance - see Table of Drugs and
                 Chemicals

    The appropriate 7th character is to be added to each code from
    category X83

A	initial encounter
D	subsequent encounter
S	sequela

X ● **X83.0**   Intentional self-harm by crashing of aircraft
X ● **X83.1**   Intentional self-harm by electrocution
X ● **X83.2**   Intentional self-harm by exposure to extremes of cold
X ● **X83.8**   Intentional self-harm by other specified means

ASSAULT (X92-Y09)

    Includes   homicide injuries inflicted by another person
                with intent to injure or kill, by any means

    Excludes1   injuries due to legal intervention (Y35.-)
                injuries due to operations of war (Y36.-)
                injuries due to terrorism (Y38.-)

● X92   **Assault by drowning and submersion**

    The appropriate 7th character is to be added to each code from
    category X92

A	initial encounter
D	subsequent encounter
S	sequela

X ● **X92.0**   Assault by drowning and submersion while in bathtub
X ● **X92.1**   Assault by drowning and submersion while in
           swimming pool
X ● **X92.2**   Assault by drowning and submersion after push into
           swimming pool
X ● **X92.3**   Assault by drowning and submersion in natural water
X ● **X92.8**   Other assault by drowning and submersion
X ● **X92.9**   Assault by drowning and submersion, unspecified

X ● X93   **Assault by handgun discharge**
    Assault by discharge of gun for single hand use
    Assault by discharge of pistol
    Assault by discharge of revolver

    Excludes1   Very pistol (X95.8)

    The appropriate 7th character is to be added to code X93

A	initial encounter
D	subsequent encounter
S	sequela

● X94   **Assault by rifle, shotgun and larger firearm discharge**

    Excludes1   airgun (X95.01)

    The appropriate 7th character is to be added to each code from
    category X94

A	initial encounter
D	subsequent encounter
S	sequela

X ● **X94.0**   Assault by shotgun
X ● **X94.1**   Assault by hunting rifle
X ● **X94.2**   Assault by machine gun
X ● **X94.8**   Assault by other larger firearm discharge
X ● **X94.9**   Assault by unspecified larger firearm discharge

● X95   **Assault by other and unspecified firearm and gun discharge**

    The appropriate 7th character is to be added to each code from
    category X95

A	initial encounter
D	subsequent encounter
S	sequela

  ● X95.0   **Assault by gas, air or spring-operated guns**
    X ● **X95.01**   Assault by airgun discharge
                Assault by BB gun discharge
                Assault by pellet gun discharge
    X ● **X95.02**   Assault by paintball gun discharge
    X ● **X95.09**   Assault by other gas, air or spring-operated gun
X ● **X95.8**   Assault by other firearm discharge
           Assault by very pistol [flare] discharge
X ● **X95.9**   Assault by unspecified firearm discharge
           Coding Clinic: 2016, Q3, P24

● X96   **Assault by explosive material**

    Excludes1   incendiary device (X97)
                terrorism involving explosive material (Y38.2-)

    The appropriate 7th character is to be added to each code from
    category X96

A	initial encounter
D	subsequent encounter
S	sequela

X ● **X96.0**   Assault by antipersonnel bomb
      Excludes1   antipersonnel bomb use in military or
                   war (Y36.2-)
X ● **X96.1**   Assault by gasoline bomb
X ● **X96.2**   Assault by letter bomb
X ● **X96.3**   Assault by fertilizer bomb
X ● **X96.4**   Assault by pipe bomb
X ● **X96.8**   Assault by other specified explosive
X ● **X96.9**   Assault by unspecified explosive

X ● X97   **Assault by smoke, fire and flames**
    Assault by arson
    Assault by cigarettes
    Assault by incendiary device

    The appropriate 7th character is to be added to code X97

A	initial encounter
D	subsequent encounter
S	sequela

● X98   **Assault by steam, hot vapors and hot objects**

    The appropriate 7th character is to be added to each code from
    category X98

A	initial encounter
D	subsequent encounter
S	sequela

X ● **X98.0**   Assault by steam or hot vapors
X ● **X98.1**   Assault by hot tap water
X ● **X98.2**   Assault by hot fluids
X ● **X98.3**   Assault by hot household appliances
X ● **X98.8**   Assault by other hot objects
X ● **X98.9**   Assault by unspecified hot objects

● **X99 Assault by sharp object**

> **Excludes1** assault by strike by sports equipment (Y08.0-)

> The appropriate 7th character is to be added to each code from category X99

> | A | initial encounter |
> |---|---|
> | D | subsequent encounter |
> | S | sequela |

X ● **X99.Ø Assault by sharp glass**

X ● **X99.1 Assault by knife**

X ● **X99.2 Assault by sword or dagger**

X ● **X99.8 Assault by other sharp object**

X ● **X99.9 Assault by unspecified sharp object**
> Assault by stabbing NOS

X ● **YØØ Assault by blunt object**

> **Excludes1** assault by strike by sports equipment (Y08.0)

> The appropriate 7th character is to be added to code YØØ

> | A | initial encounter |
> |---|---|
> | D | subsequent encounter |
> | S | sequela |

X ● **YØ1 Assault by pushing from high place**

> The appropriate 7th character is to be added to code YØ1

> | A | initial encounter |
> |---|---|
> | D | subsequent encounter |
> | S | sequela |

● **YØ2 Assault by pushing or placing victim in front of moving object**

> The appropriate 7th character is to be added to each code from category YØ2

> | A | initial encounter |
> |---|---|
> | D | subsequent encounter |
> | S | sequela |

X ● **YØ2.Ø Assault by pushing or placing victim in front of motor vehicle**

X ● **YØ2.1 Assault by pushing or placing victim in front of (subway) train**

X ● **YØ2.8 Assault by pushing or placing victim in front of other moving object**

● **YØ3 Assault by crashing of motor vehicle**

> The appropriate 7th character is to be added to each code from category YØ3

> | A | initial encounter |
> |---|---|
> | D | subsequent encounter |
> | S | sequela |

X ● **YØ3.Ø Assault by being hit or run over by motor vehicle**

X ● **YØ3.8 Other assault by crashing of motor vehicle**

● **YØ4 Assault by bodily force**

> **Excludes1** assault by:
> submersion (X92.-)
> use of weapon (X93-X95, X99, YØØ)

> The appropriate 7th character is to be added to each code from category YØ4

> | A | initial encounter |
> |---|---|
> | D | subsequent encounter |
> | S | sequela |

X ● **YØ4.Ø Assault by unarmed brawl or fight**

X ● **YØ4.1 Assault by human bite**

X ● **YØ4.2 Assault by strike against or bumped into by another person**

X ● **YØ4.8 Assault by other bodily force**
> Assault by bodily force NOS

OGCR Section I.C.19.f.

Adult and child abuse, neglect and other maltreatment

Sequence first the appropriate code from categories T74 or T76 for abuse, neglect and other maltreatment, followed by any accompanying mental health or injury code(s).

If the documentation in the medical record states abuse or neglect it is coded as confirmed (T74.-). It is coded as suspected if it is documented as suspected (T76.-).

For cases of confirmed abuse or neglect an external cause code from the assault section (X92-Y09) should be added to identify the cause of any physical injuries. A perpetrator code (Y07) should be added when the perpetrator of the abuse is known. For suspected cases of abuse or neglect, do not report external cause or perpetrator code.

If a suspected case of abuse, neglect or mistreatment is ruled out during an encounter code Z04.71, Encounter for examination and observation following alleged physical adult abuse, ruled out, or code Z04.72, Encounter for examination and observation following alleged adult rape, should be used, not a code from T76.

If a suspected case of alleged rape or sexual abuse is ruled out during an encounter code Z04.41, Encounter for examination and observation following alleged adult rape or code Z04.42, Encounter for examination and observation following alleged child rape should be used, not a code from T76.

● **Y07 Perpetrator of assault, maltreatment and neglect**

> **Note:** Codes from this category are for use only in cases of confirmed abuse (T74.-)

> Selection of the correct perpetrator code is based on the relationship between the perpetrator and the victim

> **Includes** perpetrator of abandonment
> perpetrator of emotional neglect
> perpetrator of mental cruelty
> perpetrator of physical abuse
> perpetrator of physical neglect
> perpetrator of sexual abuse
> perpetrator of torture

> **Coding Clinic: 2016, Q4, P129**

● **Y07.Ø Spouse or partner, perpetrator of maltreatment and neglect**
> Spouse or partner, perpetrator of maltreatment and neglect against spouse or partner

> **Y07.Ø1 Husband, perpetrator of maltreatment and neglect**

> **Y07.Ø2 Wife, perpetrator of maltreatment and neglect**

> **Y07.Ø3 Male partner, perpetrator of maltreatment and neglect**

> **Y07.Ø4 Female partner, perpetrator of maltreatment and neglect**

● **Y07.1 Parent (adoptive) (biological), perpetrator of maltreatment and neglect**

> **Y07.11 Biological father, perpetrator of maltreatment and neglect**

> **Y07.12 Biological mother, perpetrator of maltreatment and neglect**

> **Y07.13 Adoptive father, perpetrator of maltreatment and neglect**

> **Y07.14 Adoptive mother, perpetrator of maltreatment and neglect**

● **Y07.4 Other family member, perpetrator of maltreatment and neglect**

> ● **Y07.41 Sibling, perpetrator of maltreatment and neglect**

> > **Excludes1** stepsibling, perpetrator of maltreatment and neglect (Y07.435, Y07.436)

> > **Y07.410 Brother, perpetrator of maltreatment and neglect**

> > **Y07.411 Sister, perpetrator of maltreatment and neglect**

▶ New ⇒ Revised ~~deleted~~ Deleted Excludes 1 Excludes 2 Includes Use additional Code first Code also Key words
OGCR Official Guidelines X Assign placeholder X ● Use Additional Character(s) ▶ Manifestation Code **Coding Clinic**

● **Y07.42**   **Foster parent, perpetrator of maltreatment and neglect**
     Y07.420   **Foster father, perpetrator of maltreatment and neglect**
     Y07.421   **Foster mother, perpetrator of maltreatment and neglect**

● **Y07.43**   **Stepparent or stepsibling, perpetrator of maltreatment and neglect**
     Y07.430   **Stepfather, perpetrator of maltreatment and neglect**
     Y07.432   **Male friend of parent (co-residing in household), perpetrator of maltreatment and neglect**
     Y07.433   **Stepmother, perpetrator of maltreatment and neglect**
     Y07.434   **Female friend of parent (co-residing in household), perpetrator of maltreatment and neglect**
     Y07.435   **Stepbrother, perpetrator or maltreatment and neglect**
     Y07.436   **Stepsister, perpetrator of maltreatment and neglect**

● **Y07.49**   **Other family member, perpetrator of maltreatment and neglect**
     Y07.490   **Male cousin, perpetrator of maltreatment and neglect**
     Y07.491   **Female cousin, perpetrator of maltreatment and neglect**
     Y07.499   **Other family member, perpetrator of maltreatment and neglect**

● **Y07.5**   **Non-family member, perpetrator of maltreatment and neglect**
     Y07.50   **Unspecified non-family member, perpetrator of maltreatment and neglect**

● **Y07.51**   **Daycare provider, perpetrator of maltreatment and neglect**
     Y07.510   **At-home childcare provider, perpetrator of maltreatment and neglect**
     Y07.511   **Daycare center childcare provider, perpetrator of maltreatment and neglect**
     Y07.512   **At-home adultcare provider, perpetrator of maltreatment and neglect**
     Y07.513   **Adultcare center provider, perpetrator of maltreatment and neglect**
     Y07.519   **Unspecified daycare provider, perpetrator of maltreatment and neglect**

● **Y07.52**   **Healthcare provider, perpetrator of maltreatment and neglect**
     Y07.521   **Mental health provider, perpetrator of maltreatment and neglect**
     Y07.528   **Other therapist or healthcare provider, perpetrator of maltreatment and neglect**
         Nurse perpetrator of maltreatment and neglect
         Occupational therapist perpetrator of maltreatment and neglect
         Physical therapist perpetrator of maltreatment and neglect
         Speech therapist perpetrator of maltreatment and neglect
     Y07.529   **Unspecified healthcare provider, perpetrator of maltreatment and neglect**

     Y07.53   **Teacher or instructor, perpetrator of maltreatment and neglect**
         Coach, perpetrator of maltreatment and neglect
     Y07.59   **Other non-family member, perpetrator of maltreatment and neglect**

▶ **Y07.6**   **Multiple perpetrators of maltreatment and neglect**

   Y07.9   **Unspecified perpetrator of maltreatment and neglect**

● **Y08**   **Assault by other specified means**
     The appropriate 7th character is to be added to each code from category Y08

A	initial encounter
D	subsequent encounter
S	sequela

● **Y08.0**   **Assault by strike by sport equipment**
   X ● **Y08.01**   **Assault by strike by hockey stick**
   X ● **Y08.02**   **Assault by strike by baseball bat**
   X ● **Y08.09**   **Assault by strike by other specified type of sport equipment**

● **Y08.8**   **Assault by other specified means**
   X ● **Y08.81**   **Assault by crashing of aircraft**
   X ● **Y08.89**   **Assault by other specified means**

● **Y09**   **Assault by unspecified means**
     Assassination (attempted) NOS
     Homicide (attempted) NOS
     Manslaughter (attempted) NOS
     Murder (attempted) NOS

EVENT OF UNDETERMINED INTENT (Y21-Y33)

Undetermined intent is only for use when there is specific documentation in the record that the intent of the injury cannot be determined. If no such documentation is present, code to accidental (unintentional)

● **Y21**   **Drowning and submersion, undetermined intent**
     The appropriate 7th character is to be added to each code from category Y21

A	initial encounter
D	subsequent encounter
S	sequela

X ● **Y21.0**   **Drowning and submersion while in bathtub, undetermined intent**

X ● **Y21.1**   **Drowning and submersion after fall into bathtub, undetermined intent**

X ● **Y21.2**   **Drowning and submersion while in swimming pool, undetermined intent**

X ● **Y21.3**   **Drowning and submersion after fall into swimming pool, undetermined intent**

X ● **Y21.4**   **Drowning and submersion in natural water, undetermined intent**

X ● **Y21.8**   **Other drowning and submersion, undetermined intent**

X ● **Y21.9**   **Unspecified drowning and submersion, undetermined intent**

X ● **Y22**   **Handgun discharge, undetermined intent**
     Discharge of gun for single hand use, undetermined intent
     Discharge of pistol, undetermined intent
     Discharge of revolver, undetermined intent
     Excludes2   very pistol (Y24.8)
     The appropriate 7th character is to be added to code Y22

A	initial encounter
D	subsequent encounter
S	sequela

● **Y23**   **Rifle, shotgun and larger firearm** discharge, undetermined intent

> **Excludes2**   airgun (Y24.0)

> The appropriate 7th character is to be added to each code from category Y23

> | A | initial encounter |
> | D | subsequent encounter |
> | S | sequela |

X ● **Y23.0**   **Shotgun** discharge, undetermined intent
X ● **Y23.1**   **Hunting rifle** discharge, undetermined intent
X ● **Y23.2**   **Military firearm** discharge, undetermined intent
X ● **Y23.3**   **Machine gun** discharge, undetermined intent
X ● **Y23.8**   **Other** larger firearm discharge, undetermined intent
X ● **Y23.9**   **Unspecified** larger firearm discharge, undetermined intent

● **Y24**   **Other and unspecified firearm** discharge, undetermined intent

> The appropriate 7th character is to be added to each code from category Y24

> | A | initial encounter |
> | D | subsequent encounter |
> | S | sequela |

X ● **Y24.0**   **Airgun** discharge, undetermined intent
> BB gun discharge, undetermined intent
> Pellet gun discharge, undetermined intent
X ● **Y24.8**   **Other firearm** discharge, undetermined intent
> Paintball gun discharge, undetermined intent
> Very pistol [flare] discharge, undetermined intent
X ● **Y24.9**   **Unspecified firearm** discharge, undetermined intent

X ● **Y25**   **Contact with explosive material**, undetermined intent

> The appropriate 7th character is to be added to code Y25

> | A | initial encounter |
> | D | subsequent encounter |
> | S | sequela |

X ● **Y26**   **Exposure to smoke, fire and flames**, undetermined intent

> The appropriate 7th character is to be added to code Y26

> | A | initial encounter |
> | D | subsequent encounter |
> | S | sequela |

● **Y27**   **Contact with steam, hot vapors and hot objects**, undetermined intent

> The appropriate 7th character is to be added to each code from category Y27

> | A | initial encounter |
> | D | subsequent encounter |
> | S | sequela |

X ● **Y27.0**   Contact with **steam and hot vapors**, undetermined intent
X ● **Y27.1**   Contact with **hot tap water**, undetermined intent
X ● **Y27.2**   Contact with **hot fluids**, undetermined intent
X ● **Y27.3**   Contact with **hot household appliance**, undetermined intent
X ● **Y27.8**   Contact with **other hot objects**, undetermined intent
X ● **Y27.9**   Contact with **unspecified** hot objects, undetermined intent

● **Y28**   **Contact with sharp object**, undetermined intent

> The appropriate 7th character is to be added to each code from category Y28

> | A | initial encounter |
> | D | subsequent encounter |
> | S | sequela |

X ● **Y28.0**   Contact with **sharp glass**, undetermined intent
X ● **Y28.1**   Contact with **knife**, undetermined intent
X ● **Y28.2**   Contact with **sword or dagger**, undetermined intent
X ● **Y28.8**   Contact with **other** sharp object, undetermined intent
X ● **Y28.9**   Contact with **unspecified** sharp object, undetermined intent

X ● **Y29**   **Contact with blunt object**, undetermined intent

> The appropriate 7th character is to be added to code Y29

> | A | initial encounter |
> | D | subsequent encounter |
> | S | sequela |

X ● **Y30**   **Falling, jumping or pushed from a high place**, undetermined intent

> Victim falling from one level to another, undetermined intent

> The appropriate 7th character is to be added to code Y30

> | A | initial encounter |
> | D | subsequent encounter |
> | S | sequela |

X ● **Y31**   **Falling, lying or running before or into moving object**, undetermined intent

> The appropriate 7th character is to be added to code Y31

> | A | initial encounter |
> | D | subsequent encounter |
> | S | sequela |

X ● **Y32**   **Crashing of motor vehicle**, undetermined intent

> The appropriate 7th character is to be added to code Y32

> | A | initial encounter |
> | D | subsequent encounter |
> | S | sequela |

X ● **Y33**   **Other specified events**, undetermined intent

> The appropriate 7th character is to be added to code Y33

> | A | initial encounter |
> | D | subsequent encounter |
> | S | sequela |

▶ New   ⇒ Revised   ~~deleted~~ Deleted   Excludes 1   Excludes 2   Includes   Use additional   Code first   Code also   Key words

OGCR Official Guidelines   X Assign placeholder X   ● Use Additional Character(s)   ▶ Manifestation Code   **Coding Clinic**

LEGAL INTERVENTION, OPERATIONS OF WAR, MILITARY OPERATIONS, AND TERRORISM (Y35-Y38)

● **Y35**   **Legal intervention**

Includes   any injury sustained as a result of an encounter with any law enforcement official, serving in any capacity at the time of the encounter, whether on-duty or off-duty. Includes: injury to law enforcement official, suspect and bystander

The appropriate 7th character is to be added to each code from category Y35

A	initial encounter
D	subsequent encounter
S	sequela

● **Y35.0**   **Legal intervention involving firearm discharge**

● **Y35.00**   Legal intervention involving unspecified firearm discharge
Legal intervention involving gunshot wound
Legal intervention involving shot NOS

● **Y35.001**   Legal intervention involving unspecified firearm discharge, law enforcement official injured

● **Y35.002**   Legal intervention involving unspecified firearm discharge, bystander injured

● **Y35.003**   Legal intervention involving unspecified firearm discharge, suspect injured

● **Y35.01**   Legal intervention involving injury by machine gun

● **Y35.011**   Legal intervention involving injury by machine gun, law enforcement official injured

● **Y35.012**   Legal intervention involving injury by machine gun, bystander injured

● **Y35.013**   Legal intervention involving injury by machine gun, suspect injured

● **Y35.02**   Legal intervention involving injury by handgun

● **Y35.021**   Legal intervention involving injury by handgun, law enforcement official injured

● **Y35.022**   Legal intervention involving injury by handgun, bystander injured

● **Y35.023**   Legal intervention involving injury by handgun, suspect injured

● **Y35.03**   Legal intervention involving injury by rifle pellet

● **Y35.031**   Legal intervention involving injury by rifle pellet, law enforcement official injured

● **Y35.032**   Legal intervention involving injury by rifle pellet, bystander injured

● **Y35.033**   Legal intervention involving injury by rifle pellet, suspect injured

● **Y35.04**   Legal intervention involving injury by rubber bullet

● **Y35.041**   Legal intervention involving injury by rubber bullet, law enforcement official injured

● **Y35.042**   Legal intervention involving injury by rubber bullet, bystander injured

● **Y35.043**   Legal intervention involving injury by rubber bullet, suspect injured

● **Y35.09**   Legal intervention involving other firearm discharge

● **Y35.091**   Legal intervention involving other firearm discharge, law enforcement official injured

● **Y35.092**   Legal intervention involving other firearm discharge, bystander injured

● **Y35.093**   Legal intervention involving other firearm discharge, suspect injured

● **Y35.1**   **Legal intervention involving explosives**

● **Y35.10**   Legal intervention involving unspecified explosives

● **Y35.101**   Legal intervention involving unspecified explosives, law enforcement official injured

● **Y35.102**   Legal intervention involving unspecified explosives, bystander injured

● **Y35.103**   Legal intervention involving unspecified explosives, suspect injured

● **Y35.11**   Legal intervention involving injury by dynamite

● **Y35.111**   Legal intervention involving injury by dynamite, law enforcement official injured

● **Y35.112**   Legal intervention involving injury by dynamite, bystander injured

● **Y35.113**   Legal intervention involving injury by dynamite, suspect injured

● **Y35.12**   Legal intervention involving injury by explosive shell

● **Y35.121**   Legal intervention involving injury by explosive shell, law enforcement official injured

● **Y35.122**   Legal intervention involving injury by explosive shell, bystander injured

● **Y35.123**   Legal intervention involving injury by explosive shell, suspect injured

● **Y35.19**   Legal intervention involving other explosives
Legal intervention involving injury by grenade
Legal intervention involving injury by mortar bomb

● **Y35.191**   Legal intervention involving other explosives, law enforcement official injured

● **Y35.192**   Legal intervention involving other explosives, bystander injured

● **Y35.193**   Legal intervention involving other explosives, suspect injured

● **Y35.2**   **Legal intervention involving gas**
Legal intervention involving asphyxiation by gas
Legal intervention involving poisoning by gas

● **Y35.20**   Legal intervention involving unspecified gas

● **Y35.201**   Legal intervention involving unspecified gas, law enforcement official injured

● **Y35.202**   Legal intervention involving unspecified gas, bystander injured

● **Y35.203**   Legal intervention involving unspecified gas, suspect injured

CHAPTER 20 (V01-Y99)

● Y35.21   Legal intervention involving injury by tear gas
     ● Y35.211   Legal intervention involving injury by tear gas, law enforcement official injured
     ● Y35.212   Legal intervention involving injury by tear gas, bystander injured
     ● Y35.213   Legal intervention involving injury by tear gas, suspect injured
● Y35.29   Legal intervention involving other gas
     ● Y35.291   Legal intervention involving other gas, law enforcement official injured
     ● Y35.292   Legal intervention involving other gas, bystander injured
     ● Y35.293   Legal intervention involving other gas, suspect injured

● Y35.3   Legal intervention involving blunt objects
     Legal intervention involving being hit or struck by blunt object
   ● Y35.30   Legal intervention involving unspecified blunt objects
     ● Y35.301   Legal intervention involving unspecified blunt objects, law enforcement official injured
     ● Y35.302   Legal intervention involving unspecified blunt objects, bystander injured
     ● Y35.303   Legal intervention involving unspecified blunt objects, suspect injured
   ● Y35.31   Legal intervention involving baton
     ● Y35.311   Legal intervention involving baton, law enforcement official injured
     ● Y35.312   Legal intervention involving baton, bystander injured
     ● Y35.313   Legal intervention involving baton, suspect injured
   ● Y35.39   Legal intervention involving other blunt objects
     ● Y35.391   Legal intervention involving other blunt objects, law enforcement official injured
     ● Y35.392   Legal intervention involving other blunt objects, bystander injured
     ● Y35.393   Legal intervention involving other blunt objects, suspect injured

● Y35.4   Legal intervention involving sharp objects
     Legal intervention involving being cut by sharp objects
     Legal intervention involving being stabbed by sharp objects
   ● Y35.40   Legal intervention involving unspecified sharp objects
     ● Y35.401   Legal intervention involving unspecified sharp objects, law enforcement official injured
     ● Y35.402   Legal intervention involving unspecified sharp objects, bystander injured
     ● Y35.403   Legal intervention involving unspecified sharp objects, suspect injured
   ● Y35.41   Legal intervention involving bayonet
     ● Y35.411   Legal intervention involving bayonet, law enforcement official injured
     ● Y35.412   Legal intervention involving bayonet, bystander injured
     ● Y35.413   Legal intervention involving bayonet, suspect injured

● Y35.49   Legal intervention involving other sharp objects
     ● Y35.491   Legal intervention involving other sharp objects, law enforcement official injured
     ● Y35.492   Legal intervention involving other sharp objects, bystander injured
     ● Y35.493   Legal intervention involving other sharp objects, suspect injured
● Y35.8   Legal intervention involving other specified means
   ● Y35.81   Legal intervention involving manhandling
     ● Y35.811   Legal intervention involving manhandling, law enforcement official injured
     ● Y35.812   Legal intervention involving manhandling, bystander injured
     ● Y35.813   Legal intervention involving manhandling, suspect injured
   ● Y35.89   Legal intervention involving other specified means
     ● Y35.891   Legal intervention involving other specified means, law enforcement official injured
     ● Y35.892   Legal intervention involving other specified means, bystander injured
     ● Y35.893   Legal intervention involving other specified means, suspect injured
       Coding Clinic: 2018, Q1, P5
● Y35.9   Legal intervention, means unspecified
   X ● Y35.91   Legal intervention, means unspecified, law enforcement official injured
   X ● Y35.92   Legal intervention, means unspecified, bystander injured
   X ● Y35.93   Legal intervention, means unspecified, suspect injured

● Y36   Operations of war

   Includes   injuries to military personnel and civilians caused by war, civil insurrection, and peacekeeping missions

   Excludes1   injury to military personnel occurring during peacetime military operations (Y37.-)
       military vehicles involved in transport accidents with non-military vehicle during peacetime (V09.01, V09.21, V19.81, V29.81, V39.81, V49.81, V59.81, V69.81, V79.81)

The appropriate 7th character is to be added to each code from category Y36

> A   initial encounter
> D   subsequent encounter
> S   sequela

● Y36.0   War operations involving explosion of marine weapons
     Weapons and military watercraft
   ● Y36.00   War operations involving explosion of unspecified marine weapon
     War operations involving underwater blast NOS
     ● Y36.000   War operations involving explosion of unspecified marine weapon, military personnel
     ● Y36.001   War operations involving explosion of unspecified marine weapon, civilian
   ● Y36.01   War operations involving explosion of depth-charge
     ● Y36.010   War operations involving explosion of depth-charge, military personnel
     ● Y36.011   War operations involving explosion of depth-charge, civilian

▶ New   ⇒ Revised   ~~deleted~~ Deleted   Excludes 1   Excludes 2   Includes   Use additional   Code first   Code also   Key words
OGCR Official Guidelines   X Assign placeholder X   ● Use Additional Character(s)   ▷ Manifestation Code   Coding Clinic

● **Y36.02**　**War operations involving explosion of marine mine**

War operations involving explosion of marine mine, at sea or in harbor

● **Y36.020**　**War operations involving explosion of marine mine, military personnel**

● **Y36.021**　**War operations involving explosion of marine mine, civilian**

● **Y36.03**　**War operations involving explosion of sea-based artillery shell**

● **Y36.030**　**War operations involving explosion of sea-based artillery shell, military personnel**

● **Y36.031**　**War operations involving explosion of sea-based artillery shell, civilian**

● **Y36.04**　**War operations involving explosion of torpedo**

● **Y36.040**　**War operations involving explosion of torpedo, military personnel**

● **Y36.041**　**War operations involving explosion of torpedo, civilian**

● **Y36.05**　**War operations involving accidental detonation of onboard marine weapons**

● **Y36.050**　**War operations involving accidental detonation of onboard marine weapons, military personnel**

● **Y36.051**　**War operations involving accidental detonation of onboard marine weapons, civilian**

● **Y36.09**　**War operations involving explosion of other marine weapons**

● **Y36.090**　**War operations involving explosion of other marine weapons, military personnel**

● **Y36.091**　**War operations involving explosion of other marine weapons, civilian**

● **Y36.1**　**War operations involving destruction of aircraft**

● **Y36.10**　**War operations involving unspecified destruction of aircraft**

● **Y36.100**　**War operations involving unspecified destruction of aircraft, military personnel**

● **Y36.101**　**War operations involving unspecified destruction of aircraft, civilian**

● **Y36.11**　**War operations involving destruction of aircraft due to enemy fire or explosives**

War operations involving destruction of aircraft due to air to air missile

War operations involving destruction of aircraft due to explosive placed on aircraft

War operations involving destruction of aircraft due to rocket propelled grenade [RPG]

War operations involving destruction of aircraft due to small arms fire

War operations involving destruction of aircraft due to surface to air missile

● **Y36.110**　**War operations involving destruction of aircraft due to enemy fire or explosives, military personnel**

● **Y36.111**　**War operations involving destruction of aircraft due to enemy fire or explosives, civilian**

● **Y36.12**　**War operations involving destruction of aircraft due to collision with other aircraft**

● **Y36.120**　**War operations involving destruction of aircraft due to collision with other aircraft, military personnel**

● **Y36.121**　**War operations involving destruction of aircraft due to collision with other aircraft, civilian**

● **Y36.13**　**War operations involving destruction of aircraft due to onboard fire**

● **Y36.130**　**War operations involving destruction of aircraft due to onboard fire, military personnel**

● **Y36.131**　**War operations involving destruction of aircraft due to onboard fire, civilian**

● **Y36.14**　**War operations involving destruction of aircraft due to accidental detonation of onboard munitions and explosives**

● **Y36.140**　**War operations involving destruction of aircraft due to accidental detonation of onboard munitions and explosives, military personnel**

● **Y36.141**　**War operations involving destruction of aircraft due to accidental detonation of onboard munitions and explosives, civilian**

● **Y36.19**　**War operations involving other destruction of aircraft**

● **Y36.190**　**War operations involving other destruction of aircraft, military personnel**

● **Y36.191**　**War operations involving other destruction of aircraft, civilian**

● **Y36.2**　**War operations involving other explosions and fragments**

Excludes1　war operations involving explosion of aircraft (Y36.1-)

war operations involving explosion of marine weapons (Y36.0-)

war operations involving explosion of nuclear weapons (Y36.5-)

war operations involving explosion occurring after cessation of hostilities (Y36.8-)

● **Y36.20**　**War operations involving unspecified explosion and fragments**

War operations involving air blast NOS

War operations involving blast NOS

War operations involving blast fragments NOS

War operations involving blast wave NOS

War operations involving blast wind NOS

War operations involving explosion NOS

War operations involving explosion of bomb NOS

● **Y36.200**　**War operations involving unspecified explosion and fragments, military personnel**

● **Y36.201**　**War operations involving unspecified explosion and fragments, civilian**

● **Y36.21**　**War operations involving explosion of aerial bomb**

● **Y36.210**　**War operations involving explosion of aerial bomb, military personnel**

● **Y36.211**　**War operations involving explosion of aerial bomb, civilian**

● **Y36.22**　**War operations involving explosion of guided missile**

● **Y36.220**　**War operations involving explosion of guided missile, military personnel**

● **Y36.221**　**War operations involving explosion of guided missile, civilian**

CHAPTER 20 (V01-Y99)

CHAPTER 20 (V01-Y99)

● **Y36.23** **War operations involving explosion of improvised explosive device [IED]**
War operations involving explosion of person-borne improvised explosive device [IED]
War operations involving explosion of vehicle-borne improvised explosive device [IED]
War operations involving explosion of roadside improvised explosive device [IED]

  ● **Y36.230** **War operations involving explosion of improvised explosive device [IED], military personnel**

  ● **Y36.231** **War operations involving explosion of improvised explosive device [IED], civilian**

● **Y36.24** **War operations involving explosion due to accidental detonation and discharge of own munitions or munitions launch device**

  ● **Y36.240** **War operations involving explosion due to accidental detonation and discharge of own munitions or munitions launch device, military personnel**

  ● **Y36.241** **War operations involving explosion due to accidental detonation and discharge of own munitions or munitions launch device, civilian**

● **Y36.25** **War operations involving fragments from munitions**

  ● **Y36.250** **War operations involving fragments from munitions, military personnel**

  ● **Y36.251** **War operations involving fragments from munitions, civilian**

● **Y36.26** **War operations involving fragments of improvised explosive device [IED]**
War operations involving fragments of person-borne improvised explosive device [IED]
War operations involving fragments of vehicle-borne improvised explosive device [IED]
War operations involving fragments of roadside improvised explosive device [IED]

  ● **Y36.260** **War operations involving fragments of improvised explosive device [IED], military personnel**

  ● **Y36.261** **War operations involving fragments of improvised explosive device [IED], civilian**

● **Y36.27** **War operations involving fragments from weapons**

  ● **Y36.270** **War operations involving fragments from weapons, military personnel**

  ● **Y36.271** **War operations involving fragments from weapons, civilian**

● **Y36.29** **War operations involving other explosions and fragments**
War operations involving explosion of grenade
War operations involving explosions of land mine
War operations involving shrapnel NOS

  ● **Y36.290** **War operations involving other explosions and fragments, military personnel**

  ● **Y36.291** **War operations involving other explosions and fragments, civilian**

● **Y36.3** **War operations involving fires, conflagrations and hot substances**
War operations involving smoke, fumes, and heat from fires, conflagrations and hot substances

  Excludes1   war operations involving fires and conflagrations aboard military aircraft (Y36.1-)
war operations involving fires and conflagrations aboard military watercraft (Y36.0-)
war operations involving fires and conflagrations caused indirectly by conventional weapons (Y36.2-)
war operations involving fires and thermal effects of nuclear weapons (Y36.53-)

● **Y36.30** **War operations involving unspecified fire, conflagration and hot substance**

  ● **Y36.300** **War operations involving unspecified fire, conflagration and hot substance, military personnel**

  ● **Y36.301** **War operations involving unspecified fire, conflagration and hot substance, civilian**

● **Y36.31** **War operations involving gasoline bomb**
War operations involving incendiary bomb
War operations involving petrol bomb

  ● **Y36.310** **War operations involving gasoline bomb, military personnel**

  ● **Y36.311** **War operations involving gasoline bomb, civilian**

● **Y36.32** **War operations involving incendiary bullet**

  ● **Y36.320** **War operations involving incendiary bullet, military personnel**

  ● **Y36.321** **War operations involving incendiary bullet, civilian**

● **Y36.33** **War operations involving flamethrower**

  ● **Y36.330** **War operations involving flamethrower, military personnel**

  ● **Y36.331** **War operations involving flamethrower, civilian**

● **Y36.39** **War operations involving other fires, conflagrations and hot substances**

  ● **Y36.390** **War operations involving other fires, conflagrations and hot substances, military personnel**

  ● **Y36.391** **War operations involving other fires, conflagrations and hot substances, civilian**

● **Y36.4** **War operations involving firearm discharge and other forms of conventional warfare**

  ● **Y36.41** **War operations involving rubber bullets**

    ● **Y36.410** **War operations involving rubber bullets, military personnel**

    ● **Y36.411** **War operations involving rubber bullets, civilian**

  ● **Y36.42** **War operations involving firearms pellets**

    ● **Y36.420** **War operations involving firearms pellets, military personnel**

    ● **Y36.421** **War operations involving firearms pellets, civilian**

▶ New   ⟾ Revised   ~~deleted~~ Deleted   Excludes 1   Excludes 2   Includes   Use additional   Code first   Code also   Key words
OGCR Official Guidelines   X Assign placeholder X   ● Use Additional Character(s)   ▸ Manifestation Code   Coding Clinic

● **Y36.43** **War operations involving other firearms discharge**
War operations involving bullets NOS

> **Excludes1**   war operations involving munitions fragments (Y36.25-)
> war operations involving incendiary bullets (Y36.32-)

   ● **Y36.430** **War operations involving other firearms discharge, military personnel**

   ● **Y36.431** **War operations involving other firearms discharge, civilian**

● **Y36.44** **War operations involving unarmed hand to hand combat**

> **Excludes1**   war operations involving combat using blunt or piercing object (Y36.45-)
> war operations involving intentional restriction of air and airway (Y36.46-)
> war operations involving unintentional restriction of air and airway (Y36.47-)

   ● **Y36.440** **War operations involving unarmed hand to hand combat, military personnel**

   ● **Y36.441** **War operations involving unarmed hand to hand combat, civilian**

● **Y36.45** **War operations involving combat using blunt or piercing object**

   ● **Y36.450** **War operations involving combat using blunt or piercing object, military personnel**

   ● **Y36.451** **War operations involving combat using blunt or piercing object, civilian**

● **Y36.46** **War operations involving intentional restriction of air and airway**

   ● **Y36.460** **War operations involving intentional restriction of air and airway, military personnel**

   ● **Y36.461** **War operations involving intentional restriction of air and airway, civilian**

● **Y36.47** **War operations involving unintentional restriction of air and airway**

   ● **Y36.470** **War operations involving unintentional restriction of air and airway, military personnel**

   ● **Y36.471** **War operations involving unintentional restriction of air and airway, civilian**

● **Y36.49** **War operations involving other forms of conventional warfare**

   ● **Y36.490** **War operations involving other forms of conventional warfare, military personnel**

   ● **Y36.491** **War operations involving other forms of conventional warfare, civilian**

● **Y36.5** **War operations involving nuclear weapons**
War operations involving dirty bomb NOS

   ● **Y36.50** **War operations involving unspecified effect of nuclear weapon**

     ● **Y36.500** **War operations involving unspecified effect of nuclear weapon, military personnel**

     ● **Y36.501** **War operations involving unspecified effect of nuclear weapon, civilian**

● **Y36.51** **War operations involving direct blast effect of nuclear weapon**
War operations involving blast pressure of nuclear weapon

   ● **Y36.510** **War operations involving direct blast effect of nuclear weapon, military personnel**

   ● **Y36.511** **War operations involving direct blast effect of nuclear weapon, civilian**

● **Y36.52** **War operations involving indirect blast effect of nuclear weapon**
War operations involving being thrown by blast of nuclear weapon
War operations involving being struck or crushed by blast debris of nuclear weapon

   ● **Y36.520** **War operations involving indirect blast effect of nuclear weapon, military personnel**

   ● **Y36.521** **War operations involving indirect blast effect of nuclear weapon, civilian**

● **Y36.53** **War operations involving thermal radiation effect of nuclear weapon**
War operations involving direct heat from nuclear weapon
War operation involving fireball effects from nuclear weapon

   ● **Y36.530** **War operations involving thermal radiation effect of nuclear weapon, military personnel**

   ● **Y36.531** **War operations involving thermal radiation effect of nuclear weapon, civilian**

● **Y36.54** **War operation involving nuclear radiation effects of nuclear weapon**
War operation involving acute radiation exposure from nuclear weapon
War operation involving exposure to immediate ionizing radiation from nuclear weapon
War operation involving fallout exposure from nuclear weapon
War operation involving secondary effects of nuclear weapons

   ● **Y36.540** **War operation involving nuclear radiation effects of nuclear weapon, military personnel**

   ● **Y36.541** **War operation involving nuclear radiation effects of nuclear weapon, civilian**

● **Y36.59** **War operation involving other effects of nuclear weapons**

   ● **Y36.590** **War operation involving other effects of nuclear weapons, military personnel**

   ● **Y36.591** **War operation involving other effects of nuclear weapons, civilian**

● **Y36.6** **War operations involving biological weapons**

   ● **Y36.6X** **War operations involving biological weapons**

     ● **Y36.6X0** **War operations involving biological weapons, military personnel**

     ● **Y36.6X1** **War operations involving biological weapons, civilian**

CHAPTER 20 (V01-Y99)

CHAPTER 2Ø (VØ1-Y99)

● **Y36.7** **War operations involving chemical weapons and other forms of unconventional warfare**
     Excludes1   war operations involving incendiary devices (Y36.3-, Y36.5-)
    ● **Y36.7X** **War operations involving chemical weapons and other forms of unconventional warfare**
       ● **Y36.7XØ** **War operations involving chemical weapons and other forms of unconventional warfare, military personnel**
       ● **Y36.7X1** **War operations involving chemical weapons and other forms of unconventional warfare, civilian**
● **Y36.8** **War operations occurring after cessation of hostilities**
     War operations classifiable to categories Y36.Ø-Y36.8 but occurring after cessation of hostilities
    ● **Y36.81** **Explosion of mine placed during war operations but exploding after cessation of hostilities**
       ● **Y36.81Ø** **Explosion of mine placed during war operations but exploding after cessation of hostilities, military personnel**
       ● **Y36.811** **Explosion of mine placed during war operations but exploding after cessation of hostilities, civilian**
    ● **Y36.82** **Explosion of bomb placed during war operations but exploding after cessation of hostilities**
       ● **Y36.82Ø** **Explosion of bomb placed during war operations but exploding after cessation of hostilities, military personnel**
       ● **Y36.821** **Explosion of bomb placed during war operations but exploding after cessation of hostilities, civilian**
    ● **Y36.88** **Other war operations occurring after cessation of hostilities**
       ● **Y36.88Ø** **Other war operations occurring after cessation of hostilities, military personnel**
       ● **Y36.881** **Other war operations occurring after cessation of hostilities, civilian**
    ● **Y36.89** **Unspecified war operations occurring after cessation of hostilities**
       ● **Y36.89Ø** **Unspecified war operations occurring after cessation of hostilities, military personnel**
       ● **Y36.891** **Unspecified war operations occurring after cessation of hostilities, civilian**
● **Y36.9** **Other and unspecified war operations**
    X ● **Y36.9Ø** **War operations, unspecified**
    X ● **Y36.91** **War operations involving unspecified weapon of mass destruction [WMD]**
    X ● **Y36.92** **War operations involving friendly fire**

● **Y37** **Military operations**
    Includes   Injuries to military personnel and civilians occurring during peacetime on military property and during routine military exercises and operations
    Excludes1   military aircraft involved in aircraft accident with civilian aircraft (V97.81-)
       military vehicles involved in transport accident with civilian vehicle (VØ9.Ø1, VØ9.21, V19.81, V29.81, V39.81, V49.81, V59.81, V69.81, V79.81)
       military watercraft involved in water transport accident with civilian watercraft (V94.81-)
       war operations (Y36.-)
    The appropriate 7th character is to be added to each code from category Y37

A	initial encounter
D	subsequent encounter
S	sequela

● **Y37.Ø** **Military operations involving explosion of marine weapons**
    ● **Y37.ØØ** **Military operations involving explosion of unspecified marine weapon**
       Military operations involving underwater blast NOS
       ● **Y37.ØØØ** **Military operations involving explosion of unspecified marine weapon, military personnel**
       ● **Y37.ØØ1** **Military operations involving explosion of unspecified marine weapon, civilian**
    ● **Y37.Ø1** **Military operations involving explosion of depth-charge**
       ● **Y37.Ø1Ø** **Military operations involving explosion of depth-charge, military personnel**
       ● **Y37.Ø11** **Military operations involving explosion of depth-charge, civilian**
    ● **Y37.Ø2** **Military operations involving explosion of marine mine**
       Military operations involving explosion of marine mine, at sea or in harbor
       ● **Y37.Ø2Ø** **Military operations involving explosion of marine mine, military personnel**
       ● **Y37.Ø21** **Military operations involving explosion of marine mine, civilian**
    ● **Y37.Ø3** **Military operations involving explosion of sea-based artillery shell**
       ● **Y37.Ø3Ø** **Military operations involving explosion of sea-based artillery shell, military personnel**
       ● **Y37.Ø31** **Military operations involving explosion of sea-based artillery shell, civilian**
    ● **Y37.Ø4** **Military operations involving explosion of torpedo**
       ● **Y37.Ø4Ø** **Military operations involving explosion of torpedo, military personnel**
       ● **Y37.Ø41** **Military operations involving explosion of torpedo, civilian**
    ● **Y37.Ø5** **Military operations involving accidental detonation of onboard marine weapons**
       ● **Y37.Ø5Ø** **Military operations involving accidental detonation of onboard marine weapons, military personnel**
       ● **Y37.Ø51** **Military operations involving accidental detonation of onboard marine weapons, civilian**

▶ New   ⇒ Revised   ~~deleted~~ Deleted   Excludes 1   Excludes 2   Includes   Use additional   Code first   Code also   Key words
OGCR Official Guidelines   X Assign placeholder X   ● Use Additional Character(s)   ▶ Manifestation Code   **Coding Clinic**

- **Y37.09**   Military operations involving explosion of other marine weapons
  - **Y37.090**   Military operations involving explosion of other marine weapons, military personnel
  - **Y37.091**   Military operations involving explosion of other marine weapons, civilian
- **Y37.1**   Military operations involving destruction of aircraft
  - **Y37.10**   Military operations involving unspecified destruction of aircraft
    - **Y37.100**   Military operations involving unspecified destruction of aircraft, military personnel
    - **Y37.101**   Military operations involving unspecified destruction of aircraft, civilian
  - **Y37.11**   Military operations involving destruction of aircraft due to enemy fire or explosives
    Military operations involving destruction of aircraft due to air to air missile
    Military operations involving destruction of aircraft due to explosive placed on aircraft
    Military operations involving destruction of aircraft due to rocket propelled grenade [RPG]
    Military operations involving destruction of aircraft due to small arms fire
    Military operations involving destruction of aircraft due to surface to air missile
    - **Y37.110**   Military operations involving destruction of aircraft due to enemy fire or explosives, military personnel
    - **Y37.111**   Military operations involving destruction of aircraft due to enemy fire or explosives, civilian
  - **Y37.12**   Military operations involving destruction of aircraft due to collision with other aircraft
    - **Y37.120**   Military operations involving destruction of aircraft due to collision with other aircraft, military personnel
    - **Y37.121**   Military operations involving destruction of aircraft due to collision with other aircraft, civilian
  - **Y37.13**   Military operations involving destruction of aircraft due to onboard fire
    - **Y37.130**   Military operations involving destruction of aircraft due to onboard fire, military personnel
    - **Y37.131**   Military operations involving destruction of aircraft due to onboard fire, civilian
  - **Y37.14**   Military operations involving destruction of aircraft due to accidental detonation of onboard munitions and explosives
    - **Y37.140**   Military operations involving destruction of aircraft due to accidental detonation of onboard munitions and explosives, military personnel
    - **Y37.141**   Military operations involving destruction of aircraft due to accidental detonation of onboard munitions and explosives, civilian
  - **Y37.19**   Military operations involving other destruction of aircraft
    - **Y37.190**   Military operations involving other destruction of aircraft, military personnel
    - **Y37.191**   Military operations involving other destruction of aircraft, civilian

- **Y37.2**   Military operations involving other explosions and fragments
  - **Excludes1**   military operations involving explosion of aircraft (Y37.1-)
    military operations involving explosion of marine weapons (Y37.0-)
    military operations involving explosion of nuclear weapons (Y37.5-)
  - **Y37.20**   Military operations involving unspecified explosion and fragments
    Military operations involving air blast NOS
    Military operations involving blast NOS
    Military operations involving blast fragments NOS
    Military operations involving blast wave NOS
    Military operations involving blast wind NOS
    Military operations involving explosion NOS
    Military operations involving explosion of bomb NOS
    - **Y37.200**   Military operations involving unspecified explosion and fragments, military personnel
    - **Y37.201**   Military operations involving unspecified explosion and fragments, civilian
  - **Y37.21**   Military operations involving explosion of aerial bomb
    - **Y37.210**   Military operations involving explosion of aerial bomb, military personnel
    - **Y37.211**   Military operations involving explosion of aerial bomb, civilian
  - **Y37.22**   Military operations involving explosion of guided missile
    - **Y37.220**   Military operations involving explosion of guided missile, military personnel
    - **Y37.221**   Military operations involving explosion of guided missile, civilian
  - **Y37.23**   Military operations involving explosion of improvised explosive device [IED]
    Military operations involving explosion of person-borne improvised explosive device [IED]
    Military operations involving explosion of vehicle-borne improvised explosive device [IED]
    Military operations involving explosion of roadside improvised explosive device [IED]
    - **Y37.230**   Military operations involving explosion of improvised explosive device [IED], military personnel
    - **Y37.231**   Military operations involving explosion of improvised explosive device [IED], civilian
  - **Y37.24**   Military operations involving explosion due to accidental detonation and discharge of own munitions or munitions launch device
    - **Y37.240**   Military operations involving explosion due to accidental detonation and discharge of own munitions or munitions launch device, military personnel
    - **Y37.241**   Military operations involving explosion due to accidental detonation and discharge of own munitions or munitions launch device, civilian

● **Y37.25** Military operations involving fragments from munitions
   ● **Y37.250** Military operations involving fragments from munitions, military personnel
   ● **Y37.251** Military operations involving fragments from munitions, civilian
● **Y37.26** Military operations involving fragments of improvised explosive device [IED]
     Military operations involving fragments of person-borne improvised explosive device [IED]
     Military operations involving fragments of vehicle-borne improvised explosive device [IED]
     Military operations involving fragments of roadside improvised explosive device [IED]
   ● **Y37.260** Military operations involving fragments of improvised explosive device [IED], military personnel
   ● **Y37.261** Military operations involving fragments of improvised explosive device [IED], civilian
● **Y37.27** Military operations involving fragments from weapons
   ● **Y37.270** Military operations involving fragments from weapons, military personnel
   ● **Y37.271** Military operations involving fragments from weapons, civilian
● **Y37.29** Military operations involving other explosions and fragments
     Military operations involving explosion of grenade
     Military operations involving explosions of land mine
     Military operations involving shrapnel NOS
   ● **Y37.290** Military operations involving other explosions and fragments, military personnel
   ● **Y37.291** Military operations involving other explosions and fragments, civilian
● **Y37.3** Military operations involving fires, conflagrations and hot substances
     Military operations involving smoke, fumes, and heat from fires, conflagrations and hot substances
   Excludes1 military operations involving fires and conflagrations aboard military aircraft (Y37.1-)
         military operations involving fires and conflagrations aboard military watercraft (Y37.0-)
         military operations involving fires and conflagrations caused indirectly by conventional weapons (Y37.2-)
         military operations involving fires and thermal effects of nuclear weapons (Y36.53-)
  ● **Y37.30** Military operations involving unspecified fire, conflagration and hot substance
   ● **Y37.300** Military operations involving unspecified fire, conflagration and hot substance, military personnel
   ● **Y37.301** Military operations involving unspecified fire, conflagration and hot substance, civilian
  ● **Y37.31** Military operations involving gasoline bomb
     Military operations involving incendiary bomb
     Military operations involving petrol bomb
   ● **Y37.310** Military operations involving gasoline bomb, military personnel
   ● **Y37.311** Military operations involving gasoline bomb, civilian

● **Y37.32** Military operations involving incendiary bullet
   ● **Y37.320** Military operations involving incendiary bullet, military personnel
   ● **Y37.321** Military operations involving incendiary bullet, civilian
● **Y37.33** Military operations involving flamethrower
   ● **Y37.330** Military operations involving flamethrower, military personnel
   ● **Y37.331** Military operations involving flamethrower, civilian
● **Y37.39** Military operations involving other fires, conflagrations and hot substances
   ● **Y37.390** Military operations involving other fires, conflagrations and hot substances, military personnel
   ● **Y37.391** Military operations involving other fires, conflagrations and hot substances, civilian
● **Y37.4** Military operations involving firearm discharge and other forms of conventional warfare
  ● **Y37.41** Military operations involving rubber bullets
   ● **Y37.410** Military operations involving rubber bullets, military personnel
   ● **Y37.411** Military operations involving rubber bullets, civilian
  ● **Y37.42** Military operations involving firearms pellets
   ● **Y37.420** Military operations involving firearms pellets, military personnel
   ● **Y37.421** Military operations involving firearms pellets, civilian
  ● **Y37.43** Military operations involving other firearms discharge
     Military operations involving bullets NOS
   Excludes1 military operations involving munitions fragments (Y37.25-)
         military operations involving incendiary bullets (Y37.32-)
   ● **Y37.430** Military operations involving other firearms discharge, military personnel
   ● **Y37.431** Military operations involving other firearms discharge, civilian
  ● **Y37.44** Military operations involving unarmed hand to hand combat
   Excludes1 military operations involving combat using blunt or piercing object (Y37.45-)
         military operations involving intentional restriction of air and airway (Y37.46-)
         military operations involving unintentional restriction of air and airway (Y37.47-)
   ● **Y37.440** Military operations involving unarmed hand to hand combat, military personnel
   ● **Y37.441** Military operations involving unarmed hand to hand combat, civilian
  ● **Y37.45** Military operations involving combat using blunt or piercing object
   ● **Y37.450** Military operations involving combat using blunt or piercing object, military personnel
   ● **Y37.451** Military operations involving combat using blunt or piercing object, civilian

▶ New   ⏩ Revised   ~~deleted~~ Deleted   Excludes 1   Excludes 2   Includes   Use additional   Code first   Code also   Key words
OGCR Official Guidelines   X Assign placeholder X   ● Use Additional Character(s)   ▶ Manifestation Code   **Coding Clinic**

●Y37.46　Military operations involving intentional restriction of air and airway

　　●Y37.460　Military operations involving intentional restriction of air and airway, military personnel

　　●Y37.461　Military operations involving intentional restriction of air and airway, civilian

●Y37.47　Military operations involving unintentional restriction of air and airway

　　●Y37.470　Military operations involving unintentional restriction of air and airway, military personnel

　　●Y37.471　Military operations involving unintentional restriction of air and airway, civilian

●Y37.49　Military operations involving other forms of conventional warfare

　　●Y37.490　Military operations involving other forms of conventional warfare, military personnel

　　●Y37.491　Military operations involving other forms of conventional warfare, civilian

●Y37.5　Military operations involving nuclear weapons
　　　　Military operation involving dirty bomb NOS

●Y37.50　Military operations involving unspecified effect of nuclear weapon

　　●Y37.500　Military operations involving unspecified effect of nuclear weapon, military personnel

　　●Y37.501　Military operations involving unspecified effect of nuclear weapon, civilian

●Y37.51　Military operations involving direct blast effect of nuclear weapon
　　　　Military operations involving blast pressure of nuclear weapon

　　●Y37.510　Military operations involving direct blast effect of nuclear weapon, military personnel

　　●Y37.511　Military operations involving direct blast effect of nuclear weapon, civilian

●Y37.52　Military operations involving indirect blast effect of nuclear weapon
　　　　Military operations involving being thrown by blast of nuclear weapon
　　　　Military operations involving being struck or crushed by blast debris of nuclear weapon

　　●Y37.520　Military operations involving indirect blast effect of nuclear weapon, military personnel

　　●Y37.521　Military operations involving indirect blast effect of nuclear weapon, civilian

●Y37.53　Military operations involving thermal radiation effect of nuclear weapon
　　　　Military operations involving direct heat from nuclear weapon
　　　　Military operation involving fireball effects from nuclear weapon

　　●Y37.530　Military operations involving thermal radiation effect of nuclear weapon, military personnel

　　●Y37.531　Military operations involving thermal radiation effect of nuclear weapon, civilian

●Y37.54　Military operation involving nuclear radiation effects of nuclear weapon
　　　　Military operation involving acute radiation exposure from nuclear weapon
　　　　Military operation involving exposure to immediate ionizing radiation from nuclear weapon
　　　　Military operation involving fallout exposure from nuclear weapon
　　　　Military operation involving secondary effects of nuclear weapons

　　●Y37.540　Military operation involving nuclear radiation effects of nuclear weapon, military personnel

　　●Y37.541　Military operation involving nuclear radiation effects of nuclear weapon, civilian

●Y37.59　Military operation involving other effects of nuclear weapons

　　●Y37.590　Military operation involving other effects of nuclear weapons, military personnel

　　●Y37.591　Military operation involving other effects of nuclear weapons, civilian

●Y37.6　Military operations involving biological weapons

　　●Y37.6X　Military operations involving biological weapons

　　　　●Y37.6X0　Military operations involving biological weapons, military personnel

　　　　●Y37.6X1　Military operations involving biological weapons, civilian

●Y37.7　Military operations involving chemical weapons and other forms of unconventional warfare

　　Excludes1　military operations involving incendiary devices (Y36.3-, Y36.5-)

　　●Y37.7X　Military operations involving chemical weapons and other forms of unconventional warfare

　　　　●Y37.7X0　Military operations involving chemical weapons and other forms of unconventional warfare, military personnel

　　　　●Y37.7X1　Military operations involving chemical weapons and other forms of unconventional warfare, civilian

●Y37.9　Other and unspecified military operations

　　X●Y37.90　Military operations, unspecified

　　X●Y37.91　Military operations involving unspecified weapon of mass destruction [WMD]

　　X●Y37.92　Military operations involving friendly fire

CHAPTER 20 (V01-Y99)

● **Y38   Terrorism**
These codes are for use to identify injuries resulting from the unlawful use of force or violence against persons or property to intimidate or coerce a government, the civilian population, or any segment thereof, in furtherance of political or social objective

Use additional code for place of occurrence (Y92.-)

The appropriate 7th character is to be added to each code from category Y38

> A   initial encounter
> D   subsequent encounter
> S   sequela

● **Y38.0   Terrorism involving explosion of marine weapons**
Terrorism involving depth-charge
Terrorism involving marine mine
Terrorism involving mine NOS, at sea or in harbor
Terrorism involving sea-based artillery shell
Terrorism involving torpedo
Terrorism involving underwater blast

● **Y38.0X   Terrorism involving explosion of marine weapons**

● **Y38.0X1   Terrorism involving explosion of marine weapons, public safety official injured**

● **Y38.0X2   Terrorism involving explosion of marine weapons, civilian injured**

● **Y38.0X3   Terrorism involving explosion of marine weapons, terrorist injured**

● **Y38.1   Terrorism involving destruction of aircraft**
Terrorism involving aircraft burned
Terrorism involving aircraft exploded
Terrorism involving aircraft being shot down
Terrorism involving aircraft used as a weapon

● **Y38.1X   Terrorism involving destruction of aircraft**

● **Y38.1X1   Terrorism involving destruction of aircraft, public safety official injured**

● **Y38.1X2   Terrorism involving destruction of aircraft, civilian injured**

● **Y38.1X3   Terrorism involving destruction of aircraft, terrorist injured**

● **Y38.2   Terrorism involving other explosions and fragments**
Terrorism involving antipersonnel (fragments) bomb
Terrorism involving blast NOS
Terrorism involving explosion NOS
Terrorism involving explosion of breech block
Terrorism involving explosion of cannon block
Terrorism involving explosion (fragments) of artillery shell
Terrorism involving explosion (fragments) of bomb
Terrorism involving explosion (fragments) of grenade
Terrorism involving explosion (fragments) of guided missile
Terrorism involving explosion (fragments) of land mine
Terrorism involving explosion of mortar bomb
Terrorism involving explosion of munitions
Terrorism involving explosion (fragments) of rocket
Terrorism involving explosion (fragments) of shell
Terrorism involving shrapnel
Terrorism involving mine NOS, on land

> **Excludes1**   terrorism involving explosion of nuclear weapon (Y38.5)
> terrorism involving suicide bomber (Y38.81)

● **Y38.2X   Terrorism involving other explosions and fragments**

● **Y38.2X1   Terrorism involving other explosions and fragments, public safety official injured**

● **Y38.2X2   Terrorism involving other explosions and fragments, civilian injured**

● **Y38.2X3   Terrorism involving other explosions and fragments, terrorist injured**

● **Y38.3   Terrorism involving fires, conflagration and hot substances**
Terrorism involving conflagration NOS
Terrorism involving fire NOS
Terrorism involving petrol bomb

> **Excludes1**   terrorism involving fire or heat of nuclear weapon (Y38.5)

● **Y38.3X   Terrorism involving fires, conflagration and hot substances**

● **Y38.3X1   Terrorism involving fires, conflagration and hot substances, public safety official injured**

● **Y38.3X2   Terrorism involving fires, conflagration and hot substances, civilian injured**

● **Y38.3X3   Terrorism involving fires, conflagration and hot substances, terrorist injured**

● **Y38.4   Terrorism involving firearms**
Terrorism involving carbine bullet
Terrorism involving machine gun bullet
Terrorism involving pellets (shotgun)
Terrorism involving pistol bullet
Terrorism involving rifle bullet
Terrorism involving rubber (rifle) bullet

● **Y38.4X   Terrorism involving firearms**

● **Y38.4X1   Terrorism involving firearms, public safety official injured**

● **Y38.4X2   Terrorism involving firearms, civilian injured**

● **Y38.4X3   Terrorism involving firearms, terrorist injured**

● **Y38.5   Terrorism involving nuclear weapons**
Terrorism involving blast effects of nuclear weapon
Terrorism involving exposure to ionizing radiation from nuclear weapon
Terrorism involving fireball effect of nuclear weapon
Terrorism involving heat from nuclear weapon

● **Y38.5X   Terrorism involving nuclear weapons**

● **Y38.5X1   Terrorism involving nuclear weapons, public safety official injured**

● **Y38.5X2   Terrorism involving nuclear weapons, civilian injured**

● **Y38.5X3   Terrorism involving nuclear weapons, terrorist injured**

● **Y38.6   Terrorism involving biological weapons**
Terrorism involving anthrax
Terrorism involving cholera
A serious, often deadly, infectious disease of small intestine
Terrorism involving smallpox

● **Y38.6X   Terrorism involving biological weapons**

● **Y38.6X1   Terrorism involving biological weapons, public safety official injured**

● **Y38.6X2   Terrorism involving biological weapons, civilian injured**

● **Y38.6X3   Terrorism involving biological weapons, terrorist injured**

● **Y38.7   Terrorism involving chemical weapons**
Terrorism involving gases, fumes, chemicals
Terrorism involving hydrogen cyanide
Terrorism involving phosgene
Terrorism involving sarin

● **Y38.7X   Terrorism involving chemical weapons**

● **Y38.7X1   Terrorism involving chemical weapons, public safety official injured**

● **Y38.7X2   Terrorism involving chemical weapons, civilian injured**

● **Y38.7X3   Terrorism involving chemical weapons, terrorist injured**

▶ New   ⇢ Revised   ~~deleted~~ Deleted   Excludes 1   Excludes 2   Includes   Use additional   Code first   Code also   Key words
OGCR Official Guidelines   X Assign placeholder X   ▶ Use Additional Character(s)   ▶ Manifestation Code   **Coding Clinic**

● **Y38.8** **Terrorism involving other and unspecified means**
　● **Y38.80** **Terrorism involving unspecified means**
　　　Terrorism NOS
　● **Y38.81** **Terrorism involving suicide bomber**
　　● **Y38.811** **Terrorism involving suicide bomber, public safety official injured**
　　● **Y38.812** **Terrorism involving suicide bomber, civilian injured**
　● **Y38.89** **Terrorism involving other means**
　　　Terrorism involving drowning and submersion
　　　Terrorism involving lasers
　　　Terrorism involving piercing or stabbing instruments
　　● **Y38.891** **Terrorism involving other means, public safety official injured**
　　● **Y38.892** **Terrorism involving other means, civilian injured**
　　● **Y38.893** **Terrorism involving other means, terrorist injured**
● **Y38.9** **Terrorism, secondary effects**
　　Note: This code is for use to identify conditions occurring subsequent to a terrorist attack not those that are due to the initial terrorist attack.
　● **Y38.9X** **Terrorism, secondary effects**
　　● **Y38.9X1** **Terrorism, secondary effects, public safety official injured**
　　● **Y38.9X2** **Terrorism, secondary effects, civilian injured categories**

COMPLICATIONS OF MEDICAL AND SURGICAL CARE (Y62-Y84)

| **Includes** | complications of medical devices surgical and medical procedures as the cause of abnormal reaction of the patient, or of later complication, without mention of misadventure at the time of the procedure |

MISADVENTURES TO PATIENTS DURING SURGICAL AND MEDICAL CARE (Y62-Y69)

| **Excludes1** | surgical and medical procedures as the cause of abnormal reaction of the patient, without mention of misadventure at the time of the procedure (Y83-Y84) |
| | ~~breakdown or malfunctioning of medical device (during procedure) (after implantation) (ongoing use) (Y70-Y82)~~ |

● **Y62** **Failure of sterile precautions during surgical and medical care**
　Y62.0 **Failure of sterile precautions during surgical operation**
　Y62.1 **Failure of sterile precautions during infusion or transfusion**
　Y62.2 **Failure of sterile precautions during kidney dialysis and other perfusion**
　Y62.3 **Failure of sterile precautions during injection or immunization**
　Y62.4 **Failure of sterile precautions during endoscopic examination**
　Y62.5 **Failure of sterile precautions during heart catheterization**
　Y62.6 **Failure of sterile precautions during aspiration, puncture and other catheterization**
　Y62.8 **Failure of sterile precautions during other surgical and medical care**
　Y62.9 **Failure of sterile precautions during unspecified surgical and medical care**

● **Y63** **Failure in dosage during surgical and medical care**
　| **Excludes2** | accidental overdose of drug or wrong drug given in error (T36-T50) |
　Y63.0 **Excessive amount of blood or other fluid given during transfusion or infusion**
　Y63.1 **Incorrect dilution of fluid used during infusion**
　Y63.2 **Overdose of radiation given during therapy**
　Y63.3 **Inadvertent exposure of patient to radiation during medical care**
　Y63.4 **Failure in dosage in electroshock or insulin-shock therapy**
　Y63.5 **Inappropriate temperature in local application and packing**
　Y63.6 **Underdosing and nonadministration of necessary drug, medicament or biological substance**
　Y63.8 **Failure in dosage during other surgical and medical care**
　Y63.9 **Failure in dosage during unspecified surgical and medical care**

● **Y64** **Contaminated medical or biological substances**
　Y64.0 **Contaminated medical or biological substance, transfused or infused**
　Y64.1 **Contaminated medical or biological substance, injected or used for immunization**
　Y64.8 **Contaminated medical or biological substance administered by other means**
　Y64.9 **Contaminated medical or biological substance administered by unspecified means**
　　　Administered contaminated medical or biological substance NOS

● **Y65** **Other misadventures during surgical and medical care**
　Y65.0 **Mismatched blood in transfusion**
　Y65.1 **Wrong fluid used in infusion**
　Y65.2 **Failure in suture or ligature during surgical operation**
　Y65.3 **Endotracheal tube wrongly placed during anesthetic procedure**
　Y65.4 **Failure to introduce or to remove other tube or instrument**
　● **Y65.5** **Performance of wrong procedure (operation)**
　　● **Y65.51** **Performance of wrong procedure (operation) on correct patient**
　　　　Wrong device implanted into correct surgical site
　　　| **Excludes1** | performance of correct procedure (operation) on wrong side or body part (Y65.53) |
　　● **Y65.52** **Performance of procedure (operation) on patient not scheduled for surgery**
　　　　Performance of procedure (operation) intended for another patient
　　　　Performance of procedure (operation) on wrong patient
　　● **Y65.53** **Performance of correct procedure (operation) on wrong side or body part**
　　　　Performance of correct procedure (operation) on wrong side
　　　　Performance of correct procedure (operation) on wrong site
　Y65.8 **Other specified misadventures during surgical and medical care**

Y66 **Nonadministration of surgical and medical care**
　　Premature cessation of surgical and medical care
　　| **Excludes1** | DNR status (Z66) |
　　| | palliative care (Z51.5) |

Y69 **Unspecified misadventure during surgical and medical care**

MEDICAL DEVICES ASSOCIATED WITH ADVERSE INCIDENTS IN DIAGNOSTIC AND THERAPEUTIC USE (Y70-Y82)

Includes   breakdown or malfunction of medical devices (during use) (after implantation) (ongoing use)

Excludes2   ~~breakdown or malfunctioning of medical device (after implantation) (during procedure) (ongoing use) (Y70-Y82)~~

later complications following use of medical devices without breakdown or malfunctioning of device (Y83-Y84)

misadventure to patients during surgical and medical care, classifiable to (Y62-Y69)

surgical and other medical procedures as the cause of abnormal reaction of the patient, or of later complication, without mention of misadventure at the time of the procedure (Y83-Y84)

● **Y70**   **Anesthesiology** devices associated with adverse incidents

    Y70.0   Diagnostic and monitoring anesthesiology devices associated with adverse incidents

    Y70.1   Therapeutic (nonsurgical) and rehabilitative anesthesiology devices associated with adverse incidents

    Y70.2   Prosthetic and other implants, materials and accessory anesthesiology devices associated with adverse incidents

    Y70.3   Surgical instruments, materials and anesthesiology devices (including sutures) associated with adverse incidents

    Y70.8   Miscellaneous anesthesiology devices associated with adverse incidents, not elsewhere classified

● **Y71**   **Cardiovascular** devices associated with adverse incidents

    Y71.0   Diagnostic and monitoring cardiovascular devices associated with adverse incidents

    Y71.1   Therapeutic (nonsurgical) and rehabilitative cardiovascular devices associated with adverse incidents

    Y71.2   Prosthetic and other implants, materials and accessory cardiovascular devices associated with adverse incidents

    Y71.3   Surgical instruments, materials and cardiovascular devices (including sutures) associated with adverse incidents

    Y71.8   Miscellaneous cardiovascular devices associated with adverse incidents, not elsewhere classified

● **Y72**   **Otorhinolaryngological** devices associated with adverse incidents

    Y72.0   Diagnostic and monitoring otorhinolaryngological devices associated with adverse incidents

    Y72.1   Therapeutic (nonsurgical) and rehabilitative otorhinolaryngological devices associated with adverse incidents

    Y72.2   Prosthetic and other implants, materials and accessory otorhinolaryngological devices associated with adverse incidents

    Y72.3   Surgical instruments, materials and otorhinolaryngological devices (including sutures) associated with adverse incidents

    Y72.8   Miscellaneous otorhinolaryngological devices associated with adverse incidents, not elsewhere classified

● **Y73**   **Gastroenterology and urology** devices associated with adverse incidents

    Y73.0   Diagnostic and monitoring gastroenterology and urology devices associated with adverse incidents

    Y73.1   Therapeutic (nonsurgical) and rehabilitative gastroenterology and urology devices associated with adverse incidents

    Y73.2   Prosthetic and other implants, materials and accessory gastroenterology and urology devices associated with adverse incidents

    Y73.3   Surgical instruments, materials and gastroenterology and urology devices (including sutures) associated with adverse incidents

    Y73.8   Miscellaneous gastroenterology and urology devices associated with adverse incidents, not elsewhere classified

● **Y74**   **General hospital and personal-use** devices associated with adverse incidents

    Y74.0   Diagnostic and monitoring general hospital and personal-use devices associated with adverse incidents

    Y74.1   Therapeutic (nonsurgical) and rehabilitative general hospital and personal-use devices associated with adverse incidents

    Y74.2   Prosthetic and other implants, materials and accessory general hospital and personal-use devices associated with adverse incidents

    Y74.3   Surgical instruments, materials and general hospital and personal-use devices (including sutures) associated with adverse incidents

    Y74.8   Miscellaneous general hospital and personal-use devices associated with adverse incidents, not elsewhere classified

● **Y75**   **Neurological** devices associated with adverse incidents

    Y75.0   Diagnostic and monitoring neurological devices associated with adverse incidents

    Y75.1   Therapeutic (nonsurgical) and rehabilitative neurological devices associated with adverse incidents

    Y75.2   Prosthetic and other implants, materials and neurological devices associated with adverse incidents

    Y75.3   Surgical instruments, materials and neurological devices (including sutures) associated with adverse incidents

    Y75.8   Miscellaneous neurological devices associated with adverse incidents, not elsewhere classified

● **Y76**   **Obstetric and gynecological** devices associated with adverse incidents

    Y76.0   Diagnostic and monitoring obstetric and gynecological devices associated with adverse incidents ♀

    Y76.1   Therapeutic (nonsurgical) and rehabilitative obstetric and gynecological devices associated with adverse incidents ♀

    Y76.2   Prosthetic and other implants, materials and accessory obstetric and gynecological devices associated with adverse incidents ♀

    Y76.3   Surgical instruments, materials and obstetric and gynecological devices (including sutures) associated with adverse incidents ♀

    Y76.8   Miscellaneous obstetric and gynecological devices associated with adverse incidents, not elsewhere classified ♀

▶ New   ⇨ Revised   ~~deleted~~ Deleted   Excludes 1   Excludes 2   Includes   Use additional   Code first   Code also   Key words

OGCR Official Guidelines   X Assign placeholder X   ● Use Additional Character(s)   ▶ Manifestation Code   **Coding Clinic**

● Y77   Ophthalmic devices associated with adverse incidents

    Y77.0   Diagnostic and monitoring ophthalmic devices associated with adverse incidents

    Y77.1   Therapeutic (nonsurgical) and rehabilitative ophthalmic devices associated with adverse incidents

    Y77.2   Prosthetic and other implants, materials and accessory ophthalmic devices associated with adverse incidents

    Y77.3   Surgical instruments, materials and ophthalmic devices (including sutures) associated with adverse incidents

    Y77.8   Miscellaneous ophthalmic devices associated with adverse incidents, not elsewhere classified

● Y78   Radiological devices associated with adverse incidents

    Y78.0   Diagnostic and monitoring radiological devices associated with adverse incidents

    Y78.1   Therapeutic (nonsurgical) and rehabilitative radiological devices associated with adverse incidents

    Y78.2   Prosthetic and other implants, materials and accessory radiological devices associated with adverse incidents

    Y78.3   Surgical instruments, materials and radiological devices (including sutures) associated with adverse incidents

    Y78.8   Miscellaneous radiological devices associated with adverse incidents, not elsewhere classified

● Y79   Orthopedic devices associated with adverse incidents

    Y79.0   Diagnostic and monitoring orthopedic devices associated with adverse incidents

    Y79.1   Therapeutic (nonsurgical) and rehabilitative orthopedic devices associated with adverse incidents

    Y79.2   Prosthetic and other implants, materials and accessory orthopedic devices associated with adverse incidents

    Y79.3   Surgical instruments, materials and orthopedic devices (including sutures) associated with adverse incidents

    Y79.8   Miscellaneous orthopedic devices associated with adverse incidents, not elsewhere classified

● Y80   Physical medicine devices associated with adverse incidents

    Y80.0   Diagnostic and monitoring physical medicine devices associated with adverse incidents

    Y80.1   Therapeutic (nonsurgical) and rehabilitative physical medicine devices associated with adverse incidents

    Y80.2   Prosthetic and other implants, materials and accessory physical medicine devices associated with adverse incidents

    Y80.3   Surgical instruments, materials and physical medicine devices (including sutures) associated with adverse incidents

    Y80.8   Miscellaneous physical medicine devices associated with adverse incidents, not elsewhere classified

● Y81   General- and plastic-surgery devices associated with adverse incidents

    Y81.0   Diagnostic and monitoring general- and plastic-surgery devices associated with adverse incidents

    Y81.1   Therapeutic (nonsurgical) and rehabilitative general- and plastic-surgery devices associated with adverse incidents

    Y81.2   Prosthetic and other implants, materials and accessory general- and plastic-surgery devices associated with adverse incidents

    Y81.3   Surgical instruments, materials and general- and plastic-surgery devices (including sutures) associated with adverse incidents

    Y81.8   Miscellaneous general- and plastic-surgery devices associated with adverse incidents, not elsewhere classified

● Y82   Other and unspecified medical devices associated with adverse incidents

    Y82.8   Other medical devices associated with adverse incidents

    Y82.9   Unspecified medical devices associated with adverse incidents

---

SURGICAL AND OTHER MEDICAL PROCEDURES AS THE CAUSE OF ABNORMAL REACTION OF THE PATIENT, OR OF LATER COMPLICATION, WITHOUT MENTION OF MISADVENTURE AT THE TIME OF THE PROCEDURE (Y83-Y84)

Excludes1   misadventures to patients during surgical and medical care, classifiable to (Y62-Y69)

Excludes2   breakdown or malfunctioning of medical device (after implantation) (during procedure) (ongoing use) (Y70-Y82)

● Y83   Surgical operation and other surgical procedures as the cause of abnormal reaction of the patient, or of later complication, without mention of misadventure at the time of the procedure

    Y83.0   Surgical operation with transplant of whole organ as the cause of abnormal reaction of the patient, or of later complication, without mention of misadventure at the time of the procedure

    Y83.1   Surgical operation with implant of artificial internal device as the cause of abnormal reaction of the patient, or of later complication, without mention of misadventure at the time of the procedure

    Y83.2   Surgical operation with anastomosis, bypass or graft as the cause of abnormal reaction of the patient, or of later complication, without mention of misadventure at the time of the procedure

    Y83.3   Surgical operation with formation of external stoma as the cause of abnormal reaction of the patient, or of later complication, without mention of misadventure at the time of the procedure

    Y83.4   Other reconstructive surgery as the cause of abnormal reaction of the patient, or of later complication, without mention of misadventure at the time of the procedure

    Y83.5   Amputation of limb(s) as the cause of abnormal reaction of the patient, or of later complication, without mention of misadventure at the time of the procedure

    Y83.6   Removal of other organ (partial) (total) as the cause of abnormal reaction of the patient, or of later complication, without mention of misadventure at the time of the procedure

    Y83.8   Other surgical procedures as the cause of abnormal reaction of the patient, or of later complication, without mention of misadventure at the time of the procedure

    Y83.9   Surgical procedure, unspecified as the cause of abnormal reaction of the patient, or of later complication, without mention of misadventure at the time of the procedure

● Y84   Other medical procedures as the cause of abnormal reaction of the patient, or of later complication, without mention of misadventure at the time of the procedure

    Y84.0   Cardiac catheterization as the cause of abnormal reaction of the patient, or of later complication, without mention of misadventure at the time of the procedure

    Y84.1   Kidney dialysis as the cause of abnormal reaction of the patient, or of later complication, without mention of misadventure at the time of the procedure

    Y84.2   Radiological procedure and radiotherapy as the cause of abnormal reaction of the patient, or of later complication, without mention of misadventure at the time of the procedure
       Coding Clinic: 2017, Q1, P34

    Y84.3   Shock therapy as the cause of abnormal reaction of the patient, or of later complication, without mention of misadventure at the time of the procedure

    Y84.4   Aspiration of fluid as the cause of abnormal reaction of the patient, or of later complication, without mention of misadventure at the time of the procedure

    Y84.5   Insertion of gastric or duodenal sound as the cause of abnormal reaction of the patient, or of later complication, without mention of misadventure at the time of the procedure

    Y84.6   Urinary catheterization as the cause of abnormal reaction of the patient, or of later complication, without mention of misadventure at the time of the procedure

CHAPTER 20 (V01-Y99)

Y84.7   **Blood-sampling** as the cause of abnormal reaction of the patient, or of later complication, without mention of misadventure at the time of the procedure

Y84.8   **Other medical procedures** as the cause of abnormal reaction of the patient, or of later complication, without mention of misadventure at the time of the procedure

Y84.9   Medical procedure, **unspecified** as the cause of abnormal reaction of the patient, or of later complication, without mention of misadventure at the time of the procedure

---

SUPPLEMENTARY FACTORS RELATED TO CAUSES OF MORBIDITY CLASSIFIED ELSEWHERE (Y90-Y99)

Note: These categories may be used to provide supplementary information concerning causes of morbidity. They are not to be used for single-condition coding.

● **Y90   Evidence of alcohol involvement determined by blood alcohol level**
         Code first any associated alcohol related disorders (F10)
Y90.0   Blood alcohol level of **less than 20 mg/100 ml**
Y90.1   Blood alcohol level of **20-39 mg/100 ml**
Y90.2   Blood alcohol level of **40-59 mg/100 ml**
Y90.3   Blood alcohol level of **60-79 mg/100 ml**
Y90.4   Blood alcohol level of **80-99 mg/100 ml**
Y90.5   Blood alcohol level of **100-119 mg/100 ml**
Y90.6   Blood alcohol level of **120-199 mg/100 ml**
Y90.7   Blood alcohol level of **200-239 mg/100 ml**
Y90.8   Blood alcohol level of **240 mg/100 ml or more**
Y90.9   **Presence** of alcohol in blood, **level not specified**

OGCR Section I.C.20.b.

Place of Occurrence Guideline

Codes from category Y92, Place of occurrence of the external cause, are secondary codes for use after other external cause codes to identify the location of the patient at the time of injury or other condition.

Generally, a place of occurrence code is assigned only once, at the initial encounter for treatment. However, in the rare instance that a new injury occurs during hospitalization, an additional place of occurrence code may be assigned. No 7th characters are used for Y92. Only one code from Y92 should be recorded on a medical record.

Do not use place of occurrence code Y92.9 if the place is not stated or is not applicable.

● **Y92   Place of occurrence of the external cause**
         The following category is for use, when relevant, to identify the place of occurrence of the external cause. Use in conjunction with an activity code.
         Place of occurrence should be recorded only at the initial encounter for treatment

● **Y92.0   Non-institutional (private) residence** as the place of occurrence of the external cause
         Excludes1   abandoned or derelict house (Y92.89)
                         home under construction but not yet occupied (Y92.6-)
                         institutional place of residence (Y92.1-)

● Y92.00   **Unspecified** non-institutional (private) residence as the place of occurrence of the external cause
         Y92.000   **Kitchen** of unspecified non-institutional (private) residence as the place of occurrence of the external cause
         Y92.001   **Dining room** of unspecified non-institutional (private) residence as the place of occurrence of the external cause

Y92.002   **Bathroom** of unspecified non-institutional (private) residence single-family (private) house as the place of occurrence of the external cause

Y92.003   **Bedroom** of unspecified non-institutional (private) residence as the place of occurrence of the external cause

Y92.007   **Garden or yard** of unspecified non-institutional (private) residence as the place of occurrence of the external cause

Y92.008   **Other place** in unspecified non-institutional (private) residence as the place of occurrence of the external cause

Y92.009   **Unspecified place** in unspecified non-institutional (private) residence as the place of occurrence of the external cause
         Home (NOS) as the place of occurrence of the external cause

● **Y92.01   Single-family non-institutional (private) house as the place of occurrence of the external cause**
         Farmhouse as the place of occurrence of the external cause
         Excludes1   barn (Y92.71)
                         chicken coop or hen house (Y92.72)
                         farm field (Y92.73)
                         orchard (Y92.74)
                         single family mobile home or trailer (Y92.02-)
                         slaughter house (Y92.86)

Y92.010   **Kitchen** of single-family (private) house as the place of occurrence of the external cause

Y92.011   **Dining room** of single-family (private) house as the place of occurrence of the external cause

Y92.012   **Bathroom** of single-family (private) house as the place of occurrence of the external cause

Y92.013   **Bedroom** of single-family (private) house as the place of occurrence of the external cause

Y92.014   **Private driveway** to single-family (private) house as the place of occurrence of the external cause

Y92.015   **Private garage** of single-family (private) house as the place of occurrence of the external cause

Y92.016   **Swimming pool** in single-family (private) house or garden as the place of occurrence of the external cause

Y92.017   **Garden or yard** in single-family (private) house as the place of occurrence of the external cause

Y92.018   **Other place** in single-family (private) house as the place of occurrence of the external cause

Y92.019   **Unspecified** place in single-family (private) house as the place of occurrence of the external cause

● **Y92.02**   **Mobile home** as the place of occurrence of the external cause

Y92.020   **Kitchen** in mobile home as the place of occurrence of the external cause

Y92.021   **Dining room** in mobile home as the place of occurrence of the external cause

Y92.022   **Bathroom** in mobile home as the place of occurrence of the external cause

Y92.023   **Bedroom** in mobile home as the place of occurrence of the external cause

Y92.024   **Driveway** of mobile home as the place of occurrence of the external cause

Y92.025   **Garage** of mobile home as the place of occurrence of the external cause

Y92.026   **Swimming pool** of mobile home as the place of occurrence of the external cause

Y92.027   **Garden or yard** of mobile home as the place of occurrence of the external cause

Y92.028   **Other place** in mobile home as the place of occurrence of the external cause

Y92.029   **Unspecified** place in mobile home as the place of occurrence of the external cause

● **Y92.03**   **Apartment** as the place of occurrence of the external cause

Condominium as the place of occurrence of the external cause

Co-op apartment as the place of occurrence of the external cause

Y92.030   **Kitchen** in apartment as the place of occurrence of the external cause

Y92.031   **Bathroom** in apartment as the place of occurrence of the external cause

Y92.032   **Bedroom** in apartment as the place of occurrence of the external cause

Y92.038   **Other place** in apartment as the place of occurrence of the external cause

Y92.039   **Unspecified** place in apartment as the place of occurrence of the external cause

● **Y92.04**   **Boarding-house** as the place of occurrence of the external cause

Y92.040   **Kitchen** in boarding-house as the place of occurrence of the external cause

Y92.041   **Bathroom** in boarding-house as the place of occurrence of the external cause

Y92.042   **Bedroom** in boarding-house as the place of occurrence of the external cause

Y92.043   **Driveway** of boarding-house as the place of occurrence of the external cause

Y92.044   **Garage** of boarding-house as the place of occurrence of the external cause

Y92.045   **Swimming pool** of boarding-house as the place of occurrence of the external cause

Y92.046   **Garden or yard** of boarding-house as the place of occurrence of the external cause

Y92.048   **Other place** in boarding-house as the place of occurrence of the external cause

Y92.049   **Unspecified** place in boarding-house as the place of occurrence of the external cause

● **Y92.09**   **Other non-institutional residence** as the place of occurrence of the external cause

Y92.090   **Kitchen** in other non-institutional residence as the place of occurrence of the external cause

Y92.091   **Bathroom** in other non-institutional residence as the place of occurrence of the external cause

Y92.092   **Bedroom** in other non-institutional residence as the place of occurrence of the external cause

Y92.093   **Driveway** of other non-institutional residence as the place of occurrence of the external cause

Y92.094   **Garage** of other non-institutional residence as the place of occurrence of the external cause

Y92.095   **Swimming pool** of other non-institutional residence as the place of occurrence of the external cause

Y92.096   **Garden or yard** of other non-institutional residence as the place of occurrence of the external cause

Y92.098   **Other place** in other non-institutional residence as the place of occurrence of the external cause

Y92.099   **Unspecified** place in other non-institutional residence as the place of occurrence of the external cause

Coding Clinic: 2017, Q2, P10

● **Y92.1**   **Institutional (nonprivate) residence** as the place of occurrence of the external cause

Y92.10   **Unspecified** residential institution as the place of occurrence of the external cause

● **Y92.11**   **Children's home and orphanage** as the place of occurrence of the external cause

Y92.110   **Kitchen** in children's home and orphanage as the place of occurrence of the external cause

Y92.111   **Bathroom** in children's home and orphanage as the place of occurrence of the external cause

Y92.112   **Bedroom** in children's home and orphanage as the place of occurrence of the external cause

Y92.113   **Driveway** of children's home and orphanage as the place of occurrence of the external cause

Y92.114   **Garage** of children's home and orphanage as the place of occurrence of the external cause

Y92.115   **Swimming pool** of children's home and orphanage as the place of occurrence of the external cause

Y92.116   **Garden or yard** of children's home and orphanage as the place of occurrence of the external cause

Y92.118   **Other place** in children's home and orphanage as the place of occurrence of the external cause

Y92.119   **Unspecified** place in children's home and orphanage as the place of occurrence of the external cause

Y92.12 Nursing home as the place of occurrence of the external cause
Home for the sick as the place of occurrence of the external cause
Hospice as the place of occurrence of the external cause

Y92.120 **Kitchen** in nursing home as the place of occurrence of the external cause

Y92.121 **Bathroom** in nursing home as the place of occurrence of the external cause

Y92.122 **Bedroom** in nursing home as the place of occurrence of the external cause

Y92.123 **Driveway** of nursing home as the place of occurrence of the external cause

Y92.124 **Garage** of nursing home as the place of occurrence of the external cause

Y92.125 **Swimming pool** of nursing home as the place of occurrence of the external cause

Y92.126 **Garden or yard** of nursing home as the place of occurrence of the external cause

Y92.128 **Other place** in nursing home as the place of occurrence of the external cause

Y92.129 **Unspecified** place in nursing home as the place of occurrence of the external cause
Coding Clinic: 2017, Q2, P10

Y92.13 Military base as the place of occurrence of the external cause

Excludes1   military training grounds (Y92.83)

Y92.130 **Kitchen** on military base as the place of occurrence of the external cause

Y92.131 **Mess hall** on military base as the place of occurrence of the external cause

Y92.133 **Barracks** on military base as the place of occurrence of the external cause

Y92.135 **Garage** on military base as the place of occurrence of the external cause

Y92.136 **Swimming pool** on military base as the place of occurrence of the external cause

Y92.137 **Garden or yard** on military base as the place of occurrence of the external cause

Y92.138 **Other place** on military base as the place of occurrence of the external cause

Y92.139 **Unspecified** place military base as the place of occurrence of the external cause

Y92.14 Prison as the place of occurrence of the external cause

Y92.140 **Kitchen** in prison as the place of occurrence of the external cause

Y92.141 **Dining room** in prison as the place of occurrence of the external cause

Y92.142 **Bathroom** in prison as the place of occurrence of the external cause

Y92.143 **Cell** of prison as the place of occurrence of the external cause

Y92.146 **Swimming pool** of prison as the place of occurrence of the external cause

Y92.147 **Courtyard** of prison as the place of occurrence of the external cause

Y92.148 **Other place** in prison as the place of occurrence of the external cause

Y92.149 **Unspecified** place in prison as the place of occurrence of the external cause

Y92.15 Reform school as the place of occurrence of the external cause

Y92.150 **Kitchen** in reform school as the place of occurrence of the external cause

Y92.151 **Dining room** in reform school as the place of occurrence of the external cause

Y92.152 **Bathroom** in reform school as the place of occurrence of the external cause

Y92.153 **Bedroom** in reform school as the place of occurrence of the external cause

Y92.154 **Driveway** of reform school as the place of occurrence of the external cause

Y92.155 **Garage** of reform school as the place of occurrence of the external cause

Y92.156 **Swimming pool** of reform school as the place of occurrence of the external cause

Y92.157 **Garden or yard** of reform school as the place of occurrence of the external cause

Y92.158 **Other place** in reform school as the place of occurrence of the external cause

Y92.159 **Unspecified** place in reform school as the place of occurrence of the external cause

Y92.16 School dormitory as the place of occurrence of the external cause

Excludes1   reform school as the place of occurrence of the external cause (Y92.15-)
school buildings and grounds as the place of occurrence of the external cause (Y92.2-)
school sports and athletic areas as the place of occurrence of the external cause (Y92.3-)

Y92.160 **Kitchen** in school dormitory as the place of occurrence of the external cause

Y92.161 **Dining room** in school dormitory as the place of occurrence of the external cause

Y92.162 **Bathroom** in school dormitory as the place of occurrence of the external cause

Y92.163 **Bedroom** in school dormitory as the place of occurrence of the external cause

Y92.168 **Other place** in school dormitory as the place of occurrence of the external cause

Y92.169 **Unspecified** place in school dormitory as the place of occurrence of the external cause

▶ New   ⇒ Revised   ~~deleted~~ Deleted   Excludes 1   Excludes 2   Includes   Use additional   Code first   Code also   Key words
OGCR Official Guidelines   X Assign placeholder X   ▸ Use Additional Character(s)   ▸ Manifestation Code   Coding Clinic

● **Y92.19** **Other specified residential institution** as the place of occurrence of the external cause

　　Y92.190 **Kitchen** in other specified residential institution as the place of occurrence of the external cause

　　Y92.191 **Dining room** in other specified residential institution as the place of occurrence of the external cause

　　Y92.192 **Bathroom** in other specified residential institution as the place of occurrence of the external cause

　　Y92.193 **Bedroom** in other specified residential institution as the place of occurrence of the external cause

　　Y92.194 **Driveway** of other specified residential institution as the place of occurrence of the external cause

　　Y92.195 **Garage** of other specified residential institution as the place of occurrence of the external cause

　　Y92.196 **Pool** of other specified residential institution as the place of occurrence of the external cause

　　Y92.197 **Garden or yard** of other specified residential institution as the place of occurrence of the external cause

　　Y92.198 **Other place** in other specified residential institution as the place of occurrence of the external cause
　　　　　　Coding Clinic: 2017, Q2, P11

　　Y92.199 **Unspecified** place in other specified residential institution as the place of occurrence of the external cause
　　　　　　Coding Clinic: 2017, Q2, P10

● **Y92.2** **School, other institution and public administrative area** as the place of occurrence of the external cause

　　Building and adjacent grounds used by the general public or by a particular group of the public

　　Excludes1　building under construction as the place of occurrence of the external cause (Y92.6)

　　　　　　residential institution as the place of occurrence of the external cause (Y92.1)

　　　　　　school dormitory as the place of occurrence of the external cause (Y92.16-)

　　　　　　sports and athletics area of schools as the place of occurrence of the external cause (Y92.3-)

● **Y92.21** **School (private) (public) (state)** as the place of occurrence of the external cause

　　Y92.210 **Daycare center** as the place of occurrence of the external cause

　　Y92.211 **Elementary school** as the place of occurrence of the external cause
　　　　　　Kindergarten as the place of occurrence of the external cause

　　Y92.212 **Middle school** as the place of occurrence of the external cause

　　Y92.213 **High school** as the place of occurrence of the external cause
　　　　　　Coding Clinic: 2012, Q4, P108

　　Y92.214 **College** as the place of occurrence of the external cause
　　　　　　University as the place of occurrence of the external cause

　　Y92.215 **Trade school** as the place of occurrence of the external cause

　　Y92.218 **Other school** as the place of occurrence of the external cause

　　Y92.219 **Unspecified school** as the place of occurrence of the external cause

Y92.22 **Religious institution** as the place of occurrence of the external cause

　　Church as the place of occurrence of the external cause

　　Mosque as the place of occurrence of the external cause

　　Synagogue as the place of occurrence of the external cause

● **Y92.23** **Hospital** as the place of occurrence of the external cause

　　Excludes1　ambulatory (outpatient) health services establishments (Y92.53-)

　　　　　　home for the sick as the place of occurrence of the external cause (Y92.12-)

　　　　　　hospice as the place of occurrence of the external cause (Y92.12-)

　　　　　　nursing home as the place of occurrence of the external cause (Y92.12-)

　　Y92.230 **Patient room** in hospital as the place of occurrence of the external cause

　　Y92.231 **Patient bathroom** in hospital as the place of occurrence of the external cause

　　Y92.232 **Corridor** of hospital as the place of occurrence of the external cause

　　Y92.233 **Cafeteria** of hospital as the place of occurrence of the external cause

　　Y92.234 **Operating room** of hospital as the place of occurrence of the external cause

　　Y92.238 **Other place** in hospital as the place of occurrence of the external cause

　　Y92.239 **Unspecified** place in hospital as the place of occurrence of the external cause

● **Y92.24** **Public administrative building** as the place of occurrence of the external cause

　　Y92.240 **Courthouse** as the place of occurrence of the external cause

　　Y92.241 **Library** as the place of occurrence of the external cause

　　Y92.242 **Post office** as the place of occurrence of the external cause

　　Y92.243 **City hall** as the place of occurrence of the external cause

　　Y92.248 **Other** public administrative building as the place of occurrence of the external cause

● **Y92.25** **Cultural building** as the place of occurrence of the external cause

　　Y92.250 **Art gallery** as the place of occurrence of the external cause

　　Y92.251 **Museum** as the place of occurrence of the external cause

　　Y92.252 **Music hall** as the place of occurrence of the external cause

　　Y92.253 **Opera house** as the place of occurrence of the external cause

　　Y92.254 **Theater (live)** as the place of occurrence of the external cause

　　Y92.258 **Other** cultural public building as the place of occurrence of the external cause

Y92.26 **Movie house or cinema** as the place of occurrence of the external cause

Y92.29 **Other specified public building** as the place of occurrence of the external cause

　　Assembly hall as the place of occurrence of the external cause

　　Clubhouse as the place of occurrence of the external cause

● **Y92.3**　**Sports and athletics area** as the place of occurrence of the external cause

　● **Y92.31**　**Athletic court** as the place of occurrence of the external cause

　　　Excludes1　tennis court in private home or garden (Y92.09)

　　　Y92.310　**Basketball court** as the place of occurrence of the external cause

　　　Y92.311　**Squash court** as the place of occurrence of the external cause

　　　Y92.312　**Tennis court** as the place of occurrence of the external cause

　　　Y92.318　**Other athletic court** as the place of occurrence of the external cause

　● **Y92.32**　**Athletic field** as the place of occurrence of the external cause

　　　Y92.320　**Baseball field** as the place of occurrence of the external cause

　　　Y92.321　**Football field** as the place of occurrence of the external cause

　　　Y92.322　**Soccer field** as the place of occurrence of the external cause

　　　Y92.328　**Other athletic field** as the place of occurrence of the external cause
　　　　　　Cricket field as the place of occurrence of the external cause
　　　　　　Hockey field as the place of occurrence of the external cause

　● **Y92.33**　**Skating rink** as the place of occurrence of the external cause

　　　Y92.330　**Ice skating rink (indoor) (outdoor)** as the place of occurrence of the external cause

　　　Y92.331　**Roller skating rink** as the place of occurrence of the external cause

　　Y92.34　**Swimming pool (public)** as the place of occurrence of the external cause

　　　Excludes1　swimming pool in private home or garden (Y92.016)

　　Y92.39　**Other specified sports and athletic area** as the place of occurrence of the external cause
　　　　Golf-course as the place of occurrence of the external cause
　　　　Gymnasium as the place of occurrence of the external cause
　　　　Riding-school as the place of occurrence of the external cause
　　　　Stadium as the place of occurrence of the external cause

● **Y92.4**　**Street, highway and other paved roadways** as the place of occurrence of the external cause

　　Excludes1　private driveway of residence (Y92.014, Y92.024, Y92.043, Y92.093, Y92.113, Y92.123, Y92.154, Y92.194)

　● **Y92.41**　**Street and highway** as the place of occurrence of the external cause

　　　Y92.410　**Unspecified** street and highway as the place of occurrence of the external cause
　　　　　Road NOS as the place of occurrence of the external cause

　　　Y92.411　**Interstate highway** as the place of occurrence of the external cause
　　　　　Freeway as the place of occurrence of the external cause
　　　　　Motorway as the place of occurrence of the external cause

　　　Y92.412　**Parkway** as the place of occurrence of the external cause

　　　Y92.413　**State road** as the place of occurrence of the external cause

　　　Y92.414　**Local residential or business street** as the place of occurrence of the external cause

　　　Y92.415　**Exit ramp or entrance ramp** of street or highway as the place of occurrence of the external cause

　● **Y92.48**　**Other paved roadways** as the place of occurrence of the external cause

　　　Y92.480　**Sidewalk** as the place of occurrence of the external cause

　　　Y92.481　**Parking lot** as the place of occurrence of the external cause

　　　Y92.482　**Bike path** as the place of occurrence of the external cause

　　　Y92.488　**Other** paved roadways as the place of occurrence of the external cause

● **Y92.5**　**Trade and service area** as the place of occurrence of the external cause

　　Excludes1　garage in private home (Y92.015)
　　　　schools and other public administration buildings (Y92.2-)

　● **Y92.51**　**Private commercial establishments** as the place of occurrence of the external cause

　　　Y92.510　**Bank** as the place of occurrence of the external cause

　　　Y92.511　**Restaurant or café** as the place of occurrence of the external cause

　　　Y92.512　**Supermarket, store or market** as the place of occurrence of the external cause

　　　Y92.513　**Shop (commercial)** as the place of occurrence of the external cause

　● **Y92.52**　**Service areas** as the place of occurrence of the external cause

　　　Y92.520　**Airport** as the place of occurrence of the external cause

　　　Y92.521　**Bus station** as the place of occurrence of the external cause

　　　Y92.522　**Railway station** as the place of occurrence of the external cause

　　　Y92.523　**Highway rest stop** as the place of occurrence of the external cause

　　　Y92.524　**Gas station** as the place of occurrence of the external cause
　　　　　Petroleum station as the place of occurrence of the external cause
　　　　　Service station as the place of occurrence of the external cause

　● **Y92.53**　**Ambulatory health services establishments** as the place of occurrence of the external cause

　　　Y92.530　**Ambulatory surgery center** as the place of occurrence of the external cause
　　　　　Outpatient surgery center, including that connected with a hospital as the place of occurrence of the external cause
　　　　　Same day surgery center, including that connected with a hospital as the place of occurrence of the external cause

　　　Y92.531　**Health care provider office** as the place of occurrence of the external cause
　　　　　Physician office as the place of occurrence of the external cause

　　　Y92.532　**Urgent care center** as the place of occurrence of the external cause

　　　Y92.538　**Other ambulatory health services establishments** as the place of occurrence of the external cause

▶ New　⇒ Revised　~~deleted~~ Deleted　Excludes 1　Excludes 2　Includes　Use additional　Code first　Code also　Key words
OGCR Official Guidelines　X Assign placeholder X　● Use Additional Character(s)　▶ Manifestation Code　Coding Clinic

Y92.59   Other trade areas as the place of occurrence of the external cause
  Office building as the place of occurrence of the external cause
  Casino as the place of occurrence of the external cause
  Garage (commercial) as the place of occurrence of the external cause
  Hotel as the place of occurrence of the external cause
  Radio or television station as the place of occurrence of the external cause
  Shopping mall as the place of occurrence of the external cause
  Warehouse as the place of occurrence of the external cause

● Y92.6   Industrial and construction area as the place of occurrence of the external cause

Y92.61   Building [any] under construction as the place of occurrence of the external cause

Y92.62   Dock or shipyard as the place of occurrence of the external cause
  Dockyard as the place of occurrence of the external cause
  Dry dock as the place of occurrence of the external cause
  Shipyard as the place of occurrence of the external cause

Y92.63   Factory as the place of occurrence of the external cause
  Factory building as the place of occurrence of the external cause
  Factory premises as the place of occurrence of the external cause
  Industrial yard as the place of occurrence of the external cause

Y92.64   Mine or pit as the place of occurrence of the external cause
  Mine as the place of occurrence of the external cause

Y92.65   Oil rig as the place of occurrence of the external cause
  Pit (coal) (gravel) (sand) as the place of occurrence of the external cause

Y92.69   Other specified industrial and construction area as the place of occurrence of the external cause
  Gasworks as the place of occurrence of the external cause
  Power-station (coal) (nuclear) (oil) as the place of occurrence of the external cause
  Tunnel under construction as the place of occurrence of the external cause
  Workshop as the place of occurrence of the external cause

● Y92.7   Farm as the place of occurrence of the external cause
  Ranch as the place of occurrence of the external cause

  Excludes1   farmhouse and home premises of farm (Y92.01-)

Y92.71   Barn as the place of occurrence of the external cause

Y92.72   Chicken coop as the place of occurrence of the external cause
  Hen house as the place of occurrence of the external cause

Y92.73   Farm field as the place of occurrence of the external cause

Y92.74   Orchard as the place of occurrence of the external cause

Y92.79   Other farm location as the place of occurrence of the external cause

● Y92.8   Other places as the place of occurrence of the external cause

● Y92.81   Transport vehicle as the place of occurrence of the external cause

  Excludes1   transport accidents (V00-V99)

Y92.810   Car as the place of occurrence of the external cause

Y92.811   Bus as the place of occurrence of the external cause

Y92.812   Truck as the place of occurrence of the external cause

Y92.813   Airplane as the place of occurrence of the external cause

Y92.814   Boat as the place of occurrence of the external cause

Y92.815   Train as the place of occurrence of the external cause

Y92.816   Subway car as the place of occurrence of the external cause

Y92.818   Other transport vehicle as the place of occurrence of the external cause

● Y92.82   Wilderness area

Y92.820   Desert as the place of occurrence of the external cause

Y92.821   Forest as the place of occurrence of the external cause

Y92.828   Other wilderness area as the place of occurrence of the external cause
  Swamp as the place of occurrence of the external cause
  Mountain as the place of occurrence of the external cause
  Marsh as the place of occurrence of the external cause
  Prairie as the place of occurrence of the external cause

● Y92.83   Recreation area as the place of occurrence of the external cause

Y92.830   Public park as the place of occurrence of the external cause

Y92.831   Amusement park as the place of occurrence of the external cause

Y92.832   Beach as the place of occurrence of the external cause
  Seashore as the place of occurrence of the external cause

Y92.833   Campsite as the place of occurrence of the external cause

Y92.834   Zoological garden (zoo) as the place of occurrence of the external cause

Y92.838   Other recreation area as the place of occurrence of the external cause

Y92.84   Military training ground as the place of occurrence of the external cause

Y92.85   Railroad track as the place of occurrence of the external cause

Y92.86   Slaughter house as the place of occurrence of the external cause

Y92.89   Other specified places as the place of occurrence of the external cause
  Derelict house as the place of occurrence of the external cause

OGCR   Section I.C.20.b.

Do not use place of occurrence code Y92.9 if the place is not stated or is not applicable.

Y92.9   Unspecified place or not applicable

CHAPTER 20 (V01-Y99)

OGCR See Section I.C.20.c.

Activity Code

Assign a code from category Y93, Activity code, to describe the activity of the patient at the time the injury or other health condition occurred.

An activity code is used only once, at the initial encounter for treatment. Only one code from Y93 should be recorded on a medical record.

The activity codes are not applicable to poisonings, adverse effects, misadventures or sequela.

Do not assign Y93.9, Unspecified activity, if the activity is not stated.

A code from category Y93 is appropriate for use with external cause and intent codes if identifying the activity provides additional information about the event.

● **Y93   Activity codes**

     Note: Category Y93 is provided for use to indicate the activity of the person seeking healthcare for an injury or health condition, such as a heart attack while shoveling snow, which resulted from, or was contributed to, by the activity. These codes are appropriate for use for both acute injuries, such as those from Chapter 19, and conditions that are due to the long-term, cumulative effects of an activity, such as those from Chapter 13. They are also appropriate for use with external cause codes for cause and intent if identifying the activity provides additional information on the event. These codes should be used in conjunction with codes for external cause status (Y99) and place of occurrence (Y92).

     This section contains the following broad activity categories:

         Y93.0   Activities involving walking and running
         Y93.1   Activities involving water and water craft
         Y93.2   Activities involving ice and snow
         Y93.3   Activities involving climbing, rappelling, and jumping off
         Y93.4   Activities involving dancing and other rhythmic movement
         Y93.5   Activities involving other sports and athletics played individually
         Y93.6   Activities involving other sports and athletics played as a team or group
         Y93.7   Activities involving other specified sports and athletics
         Y93.A   Activities involving other cardiorespiratory exercise
         Y93.B   Activities involving other muscle strengthening exercises
         Y93.C   Activities involving computer technology and electronic devices
         Y93.D   Activities involving arts and handcrafts
         Y93.E   Activities involving personal hygiene and interior property and clothing maintenance
         Y93.F   Activities involving caregiving
         Y93.G   Activities involving food preparation, cooking and grilling
         Y93.H   Activities involving exterior property and land maintenance, building and construction
         Y93.I   Activities involving roller coasters and other types of external motion
         Y93.J   Activities involving playing musical instrument
         Y93.K   Activities involving animal care
         Y93.8   Activities, other specified
         Y93.9   Activity, unspecified

● **Y93.0   Activities involving walking and running**

     Excludes1   Activity, walking an animal (Y93.K1)
                 Activity, walking or running on a treadmill (Y93.A1)

     Y93.01   Activity, walking, marching and hiking
         Activity, walking, marching and hiking on level or elevated terrain

         Excludes1   activity, mountain climbing (Y93.31)

     Y93.02   Activity, running

● **Y93.1   Activities involving water and water craft**

     Excludes1   activities involving ice (Y93.2-)

     Y93.11   Activity, swimming

     Y93.12   Activity, springboard and platform diving

     Y93.13   Activity, water polo

     Y93.14   Activity, water aerobics and water exercise

     Y93.15   Activity, underwater diving and snorkeling
         Activity, SCUBA diving

     Y93.16   Activity, rowing, canoeing, kayaking, rafting and tubing
         Activity, canoeing, kayaking, rafting and tubing in calm and turbulent water

     Y93.17   Activity, water skiing and wake boarding

     Y93.18   Activity, surfing, windsurfing and boogie boarding
         Activity, water sliding

     Y93.19   Activity, other involving water and watercraft
         Activity involving water NOS
         Activity, parasailing
         Activity, water survival training and testing

● **Y93.2   Activities involving ice and snow**

     Excludes1   activity, shoveling ice and snow (Y93.H1)

     Y93.21   Activity, ice skating
         Activity, figure skating (singles) (pairs)
         Activity, ice dancing

         Excludes1   activity, ice hockey (Y93.22)

     Y93.22   Activity, ice hockey

⇒ **Y93.23   Activity, snow (alpine) (downhill) skiing, snowboarding, sledding, tobogganing and snow tubing**

         Excludes1   activity, cross country skiing (Y93.24)

     Y93.24   Activity, cross country skiing
         Activity, nordic skiing

     Y93.29   Activity, other activity involving ice and snow
         Activity, activity involving ice and snow NOS

● **Y93.3   Activities involving climbing, rappelling and jumping off**

     Excludes1   activity, hiking on level or elevated terrain (Y93.01)
               activity, jumping rope (Y93.56)
               activity, trampoline jumping (Y93.44)

     Y93.31   Activity, mountain climbing, rock climbing and wall climbing

     Y93.32   Activity, rappelling

     Y93.33   Activity, BASE jumping
         Activity, building, Antenna, Span, Earth jumping

     Y93.34   Activity, bungee jumping

     Y93.35   Activity, hang gliding

     Y93.39   Activity, other activity involving climbing, rappelling and jumping off

● **Y93.4   Activities involving dancing and other rhythmic movement**

     Excludes1   activity, martial arts (Y93.75)

     Y93.41   Activity, dancing
         Coding Clinic: 2012, Q4, P108

     Y93.42   Activity, yoga

     Y93.43   Activity, gymnastics
         Activity, rhythmic gymnastics

         Excludes1   activity, trampolining (Y93.44)

     Y93.44   Activity, trampolining

     Y93.45   Activity, cheerleading

     Y93.49   Activity, other involving dancing and other rhythmic movements

▶ New   ⇒ Revised   ~~deleted~~ Deleted   Excludes 1   Excludes 2   Includes   Use additional   Code first   Code also   Key words

     OGCR Official Guidelines   X Assign placeholder X   ● Use Additional Character(s)   ▶ Manifestation Code   **Coding Clinic**

● **Y93.5**   **Activities involving other sports and athletics played individually**

     Excludes1   activity, dancing (Y93.41)
                            activity, gymnastic (Y93.43)
                            activity, trampolining (Y93.44)
                            activity, yoga (Y93.42)

     Y93.51   **Activity, roller skating (inline) and skateboarding**

     Y93.52   **Activity, horseback riding**

     Y93.53   **Activity, golf**

     Y93.54   **Activity, bowling**

     Y93.55   **Activity, bike riding**

     Y93.56   **Activity, jumping rope**

     Y93.57   **Activity, non-running track and field events**

         Excludes1   activity, running (any form) (Y93.02)

     Y93.59   **Activity, other involving other sports and athletics played individually**

         Excludes1   activities involving climbing, rappelling, and jumping (Y93.3-)
                            activities involving ice and snow (Y93.2-)
                            activities involving walking and running (Y93.0-)
                            activities involving water and watercraft (Y93.1-)

● **Y93.6**   **Activities involving other sports and athletics played as a team or group**

     Excludes1   activity, ice hockey (Y93.22)
                            activity, water polo (Y93.13)

     Y93.61   **Activity, American tackle football**
               Activity, football NOS

     Y93.62   **Activity, American flag or touch football**

     Y93.63   **Activity, rugby**

     Y93.64   **Activity, baseball**
               Activity, softball

     Y93.65   **Activity, lacrosse and field hockey**
               Coding Clinic: 2015, Q1, P9

     Y93.66   **Activity, soccer**

     Y93.67   **Activity, basketball**

     Y93.68   **Activity, volleyball (beach) (court)**

     Y93.6A   **Activity, physical games generally associated with school recess, summer camp and children**
               Activity, capture the flag
               Activity, dodge ball
               Activity, four square
               Activity, kickball

     Y93.69   **Activity, other involving other sports and athletics played as a team or group**
               Cricket

● **Y93.7**   **Activities involving other specified sports and athletics**

     Y93.71   **Activity, boxing**

     Y93.72   **Activity, wrestling**

     Y93.73   **Activity, racquet and hand sports**
               Activity, handball
               Activity, racquetball
               Activity, squash
               Activity, tennis

     Y93.74   **Activity, frisbee**
               Activity, ultimate frisbee

     Y93.75   **Activity, martial arts**
               Activity, combatives

     Y93.79   **Activity, other specified sports and athletics**

         Excludes1   sports and athletics activities specified in categories Y93.0-Y93.6

● **Y93.A**   **Activities involving other cardiorespiratory exercise**
         Activities involving physical training

     Y93.A1   **Activity, exercise machines primarily for cardiorespiratory conditioning**
               Activity, elliptical and stepper machines
               Activity, stationary bike
               Activity, treadmill

     Y93.A2   **Activity, calisthenics**
               Activity, jumping jacks
               Activity, warm up and cool down

     Y93.A3   **Activity, aerobic and step exercise**

     Y93.A4   **Activity, circuit training**

     Y93.A5   **Activity, obstacle course**
               Activity, challenge course
               Activity, confidence course

     Y93.A6   **Activity, grass drills**
               Activity, guerilla drills

     Y93.A9   **Activity, other involving other cardiorespiratory exercise**

         Excludes1   activities involving cardiorespiratory exercise specified in categories Y93.0-Y93.7

● **Y93.B**   **Activity involving other muscle strengthening exercises**

     Y93.B1   **Activity, exercise machines primarily for muscle strengthening**

     Y93.B2   **Activity, push-ups, pull-ups, sit-ups**

     Y93.B3   **Activity, free weights**
               Activity, barbells
               Activity, dumbbells

     Y93.B4   **Activity, pilates**

     Y93.B9   **Activity, other involving other muscle strengthening exercises**

         Excludes1   activities involving muscle strengthening specified in categories Y93.0-Y93.A

● **Y93.C**   **Activities involving computer technology and electronic devices**

     Excludes1   activity, electronic musical keyboard or instruments (Y93.J-)

     Y93.C1   **Activity, computer keyboarding**
               Activity, electronic game playing using keyboard or other stationary device

     Y93.C2   **Activity, hand held interactive electronic device**
               Activity, cellular telephone and communication device
               Activity, electronic game playing using interactive device

         Excludes1   activity, electronic game playing using keyboard or other stationary device (Y93.C1)

     Y93.C9   **Activity, other involving computer technology and electronic devices**

● **Y93.D**   **Activities involving arts and handcrafts**

     Excludes1   activities involving playing musical instrument (Y93.J-)

     Y93.D1   **Knitting and crocheting**

     Y93.D2   **Sewing**

     Y93.D3   **Furniture building and finishing**
               Furniture repair

     Y93.D9   **Activity, other involving arts and handcrafts**

CHAPTER 20 (V01-Y99)

● **Y93.E** **Activities involving personal hygiene and interior property and clothing maintenance**

> **Excludes1** activities involving cooking and grilling (Y93.G-)
> activities involving exterior property and land maintenance, building and construction (Y93.H-)
> activity involving caregiving (Y93.F-)
> activity, dishwashing (Y93.G1)
> activity, food preparation (Y93.G1)
> activity, gardening (Y93.H2)

> **Y93.E1** Activity, personal bathing and showering
> **Y93.E2** Activity, laundry
> **Y93.E3** Activity, vacuuming
> **Y93.E4** Activity, ironing
> **Y93.E5** Activity, floor mopping and cleaning
> **Y93.E6** Activity, residential relocation
>> Activity, packing up and unpacking involved in moving to a new residence
> **Y93.E8** Activity, other personal hygiene activity
> **Y93.E9** Activity, other household maintenance

● **Y93.F** **Activities involving person providing caregiving**
> Activity involving the provider of caregiving
> **Y93.F1** Activity, caregiving involving bathing
> **Y93.F2** Activity, caregiving involving lifting
>> **Coding Clinic: 2016, Q4, P74**
> **Y93.F9** Activity, other caregiving

● **Y93.G** **Activities involving food preparation, cooking and grilling**
> **Y93.G1** Activity, food preparation and clean up
>> Activity, dishwashing
> **Y93.G2** Activity, grilling and smoking food
> **Y93.G3** Activity, cooking and baking
>> Activity, use of stove, oven and microwave oven
> **Y93.G9** Activity, other activity involving cooking and grilling

● **Y93.H** **Activities involving property and land maintenance, building and construction**
> **Y93.H1** Activity, digging, shoveling and raking
>> Activity, dirt digging
>> Activity, raking leaves
>> Activity, snow shoveling
> **Y93.H2** Activity, gardening and landscaping
>> Activity, pruning, trimming shrubs, weeding
> **Y93.H3** Activity, building and construction
> **Y93.H9** Activity, other activity involving property and land maintenance, building and construction

● **Y93.I** **Activities involving roller coasters and other types of external motion**
> **Y93.I1** Activity, rollercoaster riding
> **Y93.I9** Activity, other involving external motion

● **Y93.J** **Activities involving playing musical instrument**
> Activity involving playing electric musical instrument
> **Y93.J1** Activity, piano playing
>> Activity, musical keyboard (electronic) playing
> **Y93.J2** Activity, drum and other percussion instrument playing
> **Y93.J3** Activity, string instrument playing
> **Y93.J4** Activity, winds and brass instrument playing

● **Y93.K** **Activities involving animal care**
> **Excludes1** activity, horseback riding (Y93.52)
> **Y93.K1** Activity, walking an animal
> **Y93.K2** Activity, milking an animal
> **Y93.K3** Activity, grooming and shearing an animal
> **Y93.K9** Activity, other activity involving animal care

● **Y93.8** **Other activity**
> **Coding Clinic: 2016, Q4, P74**
> **Y93.81** Activity, refereeing a sports activity
> **Y93.82** Activity, spectator at an event
> **Y93.83** Activity, rough housing and horseplay
>> **Coding Clinic: 2015, Q1, P8**
> **Y93.84** Activity, sleeping
> **Y93.85** Activity, choking game
>> Activity, blackout game
>> Activity, fainting game
>> Activity, pass out game
>> **Coding Clinic: 2016, Q4, P74-76**
> **Y93.89** Activity, other specified

OGCR See Section I.C.20.c.

> Do not assign Y93.9, Unspecified activity, if the activity is not stated.

● **Y93.9** **Activity, unspecified**

Y95 **Nosocomial condition**

● **Y99** **External cause status**
> **Note:** A single code from category Y99 should be used in conjunction with the external cause code(s) assigned to a record to indicate the status of the person at the time the event occurred.
> **Coding Clinic: 2016, Q4, P74**

> **Y99.0** **Civilian activity done for income or pay**
>> Civilian activity done for financial or other compensation
>> **Excludes1** military activity (Y99.1)
>> volunteer activity (Y99.2)

> **Y99.1** **Military activity**
>> **Excludes1** activity of off duty military personnel (Y99.8)

> **Y99.2** **Volunteer activity**
>> **Excludes1** activity of child or other family member assisting in compensated work of other family member (Y99.8)

> **Y99.8** **Other external cause status**
>> Activity NEC
>> Activity of child or other family member assisting in compensated work of other family member
>> Hobby not done for income
>> Leisure activity
>> Off-duty activity of military personnel
>> Recreation or sport not for income or while a student
>> Student activity
>> **Excludes1** civilian activity done for income or compensation (Y99.0)
>> military activity (Y99.1)
>> **Coding Clinic: 2012, Q4, P108**

> **Y99.9** **Unspecified external cause status**

▶ New   ⇒ Revised   ~~deleted~~ Deleted   Excludes 1   Excludes 2   Includes   Use additional   Code first   Code also   Key words

OGCR Official Guidelines   X Assign placeholder X   ▶ Use Additional Character(s)   ▷ Manifestation Code   **Coding Clinic**

CHAPTER 21

FACTORS INFLUENCING HEALTH STATUS AND CONTACT WITH HEALTH SERVICES (Z00-Z99)

OGCR Chapter-Specific Coding Guidelines

21. **Chapter 21: Factors influencing health status and contact with health services (Z00-Z99)**
Note: The chapter specific guidelines provide additional information about the use of Z codes for specified encounters.

a. **Use of Z codes in any healthcare setting**
Z codes are for use in any healthcare setting. Z codes may be used as either a first-listed (principal diagnosis code in the inpatient setting) or secondary code, depending on the circumstances of the encounter. Certain Z codes may only be used as first-listed or principal diagnosis.

b. **Z Codes indicate a reason for an encounter**
Z codes are not procedure codes. A corresponding procedure code must accompany a Z code to describe any procedure performed.

c. **Categories of Z Codes**
1) **Contact/Exposure**
Category Z20 indicates contact with, and suspected exposure to, communicable diseases. These codes are for patients who do not show any sign or symptom of a disease but are suspected to have been exposed to it by close personal contact with an infected individual or are in an area where a disease is epidemic.

Category Z77, Other contact with and (suspected) exposures hazardous to health, indicates contact with and suspected exposures hazardous to health.

Contact/exposure codes may be used as a first-listed code to explain an encounter for testing, or, more commonly, as a secondary code to identify a potential risk.

2) **Inoculations and vaccinations**
Code Z23 is for encounters for inoculations and vaccinations. It indicates that a patient is being seen to receive a prophylactic inoculation against a disease. Procedure codes are required to identify the actual administration of the injection and the type(s) of immunizations given. Code Z23 may be used as a secondary code if the inoculation is given as a routine part of preventive health care, such as a well-baby visit.

3) **Status**
Status codes indicate that a patient is either a carrier of a disease or has the sequelae or residual of a past disease or condition. This includes such things as the presence of prosthetic or mechanical devices resulting from past treatment. A status code is informative, because the status may affect the course of treatment and its outcome. A status code is distinct from a history code. The history code indicates that the patient no longer has the condition.

A status code should not be used with a diagnosis code from one of the body system chapters, if the diagnosis code includes the information provided by the status code. For example, code Z94.1, Heart transplant status, should not be used with a code from subcategory T86.2, Complications of heart transplant. The status code does not provide additional information. The complication code indicates that the patient is a heart transplant patient.

For encounters for weaning from a mechanical ventilator, assign a code from subcategory J96.1, Chronic respiratory failure, followed by code Z99.11, Dependence on respirator [ventilator] status.

The status Z codes/categories are:

Z14 Genetic carrier
Genetic carrier status indicates that a person carries a gene, associated with a particular disease, which may be passed to offspring who may develop that disease. The person does not have the disease and is not at risk of developing the disease.

Z15 Genetic susceptibility to disease Genetic susceptibility indicates that a person has a gene that increases the risk of that person developing the disease.
Codes from category Z15 should not be used as principal or first-listed codes. If the patient has the condition to which he/she is susceptible, and that condition is the reason for the encounter, the code for the current condition should be sequenced first. If the patient is being seen for follow-up after completed treatment for this condition, and the condition no longer exists, a follow-up

code should be sequenced first, followed by the appropriate personal history and genetic susceptibility codes. If the purpose of the encounter is genetic counseling associated with procreative management, code Z31.5, Encounter for genetic counseling, should be assigned as the first-listed code, followed by a code from category Z15. Additional codes should be assigned for any applicable family or personal history.

Z16 Resistance to antimicrobial drugs
This code indicates that a patient has a condition that is resistant to antimicrobial drug treatment. Sequence the infection code first.

Z17 Estrogen receptor status
Z18 Retained foreign body fragments
Z19 Hormone sensitivity malignancy status
Z21 Asymptomatic HIV infection status This code indicates that a patient has tested positive for HIV but has manifested no signs or symptoms of the disease.
Z22 Carrier of infectious disease Carrier status indicates that a person harbors the specific organisms of a disease without manifest symptoms and is capable of transmitting the infection.
Z28.3 Underimmunization status
Z33.1 Pregnant state, incidental This code is a secondary code only for use when the pregnancy is in no way complicating the reason for visit. Otherwise, a code from the obstetric chapter is required.
Z66 Do not resuscitate
This code may be used when it is documented by the provider that a patient is on do not resuscitate status at any time during the stay.

Z67 Blood type
Z68 Body mass index (BMI)
BMI codes should only be assigned when the associated diagnosis (such as overweight or obesity) meets the definition of a reportable diagnosis (see Section III, Reporting Additional Diagnoses). Do not assign BMI codes during pregnancy. See Section I.B.14 for BMI documentation by clinicians other than the patient's provider.
Z74.01 Bed confinement status
Z76.82 Awaiting organ transplant status
Z78 Other specified health status
Code Z78.1, Physical restraint status, may be used when it is documented by the provider that a patient has been put in restraints during the current encounter. Please note that this code should not be reported when it is documented by the provider that a patient is temporarily restrained during a procedure.

Z79 Long-term (current) drug therapy
Codes from this category indicate a patient's continuous use of a prescribed drug (including such things as aspirin therapy) for the long-term treatment of a condition or for prophylactic use. It is not for use for patients who have addictions to drugs. This subcategory is not for use of medications for detoxification or maintenance programs to prevent withdrawal symptoms in patients with drug dependence (e.g., methadone maintenance for opiate dependence). Assign the appropriate code for the drug dependence instead.

Assign a code from Z79 if the patient is receiving a medication for an extended period as a prophylactic measure (such as for the prevention of deep vein thrombosis) or as treatment of a chronic condition (such as arthritis) or a disease requiring a lengthy course of treatment (such as cancer). Do not assign a code from category Z79 for medication being administered for a brief period of time to treat an acute illness or injury (such as a course of antibiotics to treat acute bronchitis).

Z88 Allergy status to drugs, medicaments and biological substances Except: Z88.9, Allergy status to unspecified drugs, medicaments and biological substances status
Z89 Acquired absence of limb
Z90 Acquired absence of organs, not elsewhere classified
Z91.0- Allergy status, other than to drugs and biological substances
Z92.82 Status post administration of tPA (rtPA) in a different facility within the last 24 hours prior to admission to a current facility Assign code Z92.82, Status post administration of tPA (rtPA) in a different facility within the last 24 hours prior to admission to current

facility, as a secondary diagnosis when a patient is received by transfer into a facility and documentation indicates they were administered tissue plasminogen activator (tPA) within the last 24 hours prior to admission to the current facility. This guideline applies even if the patient is still receiving the tPA at the time they are received into the current facility. The appropriate code for the condition for which the tPA was administered (such as cerebrovascular disease or myocardial infarction) should be assigned first. Code Z92.82 is only applicable to the receiving facility record and not to the transferring facility record.

Z93	Artificial opening status
Z94	Transplanted organ and tissue status
Z95	Presence of cardiac and vascular implants and grafts
Z96	Presence of other functional implants
Z97	Presence of other devices
Z98	Other postprocedural states

Assign code Z98.85, Transplanted organ removal status, to indicate that a transplanted organ has been previously removed. This code should not be assigned for the encounter in which the transplanted organ is removed. The complication necessitating removal of the transplant organ should be assigned for that encounter.

See Section I.C.19. for information on the coding of organ transplant complications.

Z99	Dependence on enabling machines and devices, not elsewhere classified

Note: Categories Z89-Z90 and Z93-Z99 are for use only if there are no complications or malfunctions of the organ or tissue replaced, the amputation site or the equipment on which the patient is dependent.

4) History (of)

There are two types of history Z codes, personal and family. Personal history codes explain a patient's past medical condition that no longer exists and is not receiving any treatment, but that has the potential for recurrence, and therefore may require continued monitoring.

Family history codes are for use when a patient has a family member(s) who has had a particular disease that causes the patient to be at higher risk of also contracting the disease.

Personal history codes may be used in conjunction with follow-up codes and family history codes may be used in conjunction with screening codes to explain the need for a test or procedure. History codes are also acceptable on any medical record regardless of the reason for visit. A history of an illness, even if no longer present, is important information that may alter the type of treatment ordered.

The history Z code categories are:

Z80	Family history of primary malignant neoplasm
Z81	Family history of mental and behavioral disorders
Z82	Family history of certain disabilities and chronic diseases (leading to disablement)
Z83	Family history of other specific disorders
Z84	Family history of other conditions
Z85	Personal history of malignant neoplasm
Z86	Personal history of certain other diseases
Z87	Personal history of other diseases and conditions
Z91.4-	Personal history of psychological trauma, not elsewhere classified
Z91.5	Personal history of self-harm
Z91.81	History of falling
Z91.82	Personal history of military deployment
Z92	Personal history of medical treatment Except: Z92.0, Personal history of contraception Except: Z92.82, Status post administration of tPA (rtPA) in a different facility within the last 24 hours prior to admission to a current facility

5) Screening

Screening is the testing for disease or disease precursors in seemingly well individuals so that early detection and treatment can be provided for those who test positive for the disease (e.g., screening mammogram).

The testing of a person to rule out or confirm a suspected diagnosis because the patient has some sign or symptom is a diagnostic examination, not a screening. In these cases, the sign or symptom is used to explain the reason for the test.

A screening code may be a first-listed code if the reason for the visit is specifically the screening exam. It may also be used as an additional code if the screening is done during an office visit for other health problems. A screening code is not necessary if the screening is inherent to a routine examination, such as a pap smear done during a routine pelvic examination.

Should a condition be discovered during the screening then the code for the condition may be assigned as an additional diagnosis.

The Z code indicates that a screening exam is planned. A procedure code is required to confirm that the screening was performed.

The screening Z codes/categories:

Z11	Encounter for screening for infectious and parasitic diseases
Z12	Encounter for screening for malignant neoplasms
Z13	Encounter for screening for other diseases and disorders Except: Z13.9, Encounter for screening, unspecified
Z36	Encounter for antenatal screening for mother

6) Observation

There are three observation Z code categories. They are for use in very limited circumstances when a person is being observed for a suspected condition that is ruled out. The observation codes are not for use if an injury or illness or any signs or symptoms related to the suspected condition are present. In such cases the diagnosis/symptom code is used with the corresponding external cause code.

The observation codes are to be used as principal diagnosis only. The only exception to this is when the principal diagnosis is required to be a code from category Z38, Liveborn infants according to place of birth and type of delivery. Then a code from category Z05, Encounter for observation and evaluation of newborn for suspected diseases and conditions ruled out, is sequenced after the Z38 code. Additional codes may be used in addition to the observation code but only if they are unrelated to the suspected condition being observed.

Codes from subcategory Z03.7 Encounter for suspected maternal and fetal conditions ruled out, may either be used as a first-listed or as an additional code assignment depending on the case. They are for use in very limited circumstances on a maternal record when an encounter is for a suspected maternal or fetal condition that is ruled out during that encounter (for example, a maternal or fetal condition may be suspected due to an abnormal test result). These codes should not be used when the condition is confirmed. In those cases, the confirmed condition should be coded. In addition, these codes are not for use if an illness or any signs or symptoms related to the suspected condition or problem are present. In such cases the diagnosis/symptom code is used.

Additional codes may be used in addition to the code from subcategory Z03.7, but only if they are unrelated to the suspected condition being evaluated.

Codes from subcategory Z03.7 may not be used for encounters for antenatal screening of mother. *See Section I.C.21. Screening.*

For encounters for suspected fetal condition that are inconclusive following testing and evaluation, assign the appropriate code from category O35, O36, O40 or O41.

The observation Z code categories:

Z03	Encounter for medical observation for suspected diseases and conditions ruled out
Z04	Encounter for examination and observation for other reasons Except: Z04.9, Encounter for examination and observation for unspecified reason
Z05	Encounter for observation and evaluation of newborn for suspected diseases and conditions ruled out

7) Aftercare

Aftercare visit codes cover situations when the initial treatment of a disease has been performed and the patient requires continued care during the healing or recovery phase, or for the long-term consequences of the disease. The aftercare Z code should not be used if treatment is directed at a current, acute disease. The diagnosis code is to be used in these cases.

Exceptions to this rule are codes Z51.0, Encounter for antineoplastic radiation therapy, and codes from subcategory Z51.1, Encounter for antineoplastic chemotherapy and immunotherapy. These codes are to be first-listed, followed by the diagnosis code when a patient's encounter is solely to receive radiation therapy, chemotherapy, or immunotherapy for the treatment of a neoplasm. If the reason for the encounter is more than one type of antineoplastic therapy, code Z51.0 and a code from subcategory Z51.1 may be assigned together, in which case one of these codes would be reported as a secondary diagnosis.

The aftercare Z codes should also not be used for aftercare for injuries. For aftercare of an injury, assign the acute injury code with the appropriate 7th character (for subsequent encounter).

The aftercare codes are generally first-listed to explain the specific reason for the encounter. An aftercare code may be used as an additional code when some type of aftercare is provided in addition to the reason for admission and no diagnosis code is applicable. An example of this would be the closure of a colostomy during an encounter for treatment of another condition.

Aftercare codes should be used in conjunction with other aftercare codes or diagnosis codes to provide better detail on the specifics of an aftercare encounter visit, unless otherwise directed by the classification. Should a patient receive multiple types of antineoplastic therapy during the same encounter, code Z51.0, Encounter for antineoplastic radiation therapy, and codes from subcategory Z51.1, Encounter for antineoplastic chemotherapy and immunotherapy, may be used together on a record. The sequencing of multiple aftercare codes depends on the circumstances of the encounter.

Certain aftercare Z code categories need a secondary diagnosis code to describe the resolving condition or sequelae. For others, the condition is included in the code title.

Additional Z code aftercare category terms include fitting and adjustment, and attention to artificial openings.

Status Z codes may be used with aftercare Z codes to indicate the nature of the aftercare. For example code Z95.1, Presence of aortocoronary bypass graft, may be used with code Z48.812, Encounter for surgical aftercare following surgery on the circulatory system, to indicate the surgery for which the aftercare is being performed. A status code should not be used when the aftercare code indicates the type of status, such as using Z43.0, Encounter for attention to tracheostomy, with Z93.0, Tracheostomy status.

The aftercare Z category/codes:

Z42	Encounter for plastic and reconstructive surgery following medical procedure or healed injury
Z43	Encounter for attention to artificial openings
Z44	Encounter for fitting and adjustment of external prosthetic device
Z45	Encounter for adjustment and management of implanted device
Z46	Encounter for fitting and adjustment of other devices
Z47	Orthopedic aftercare
Z48	Encounter for other postprocedural aftercare
Z49	Encounter for care involving renal dialysis
Z51	Encounter for other aftercare and medical care

8) Follow-up

The follow-up codes are used to explain continuing surveillance following completed treatment of a disease, condition, or injury. They imply that the condition has been fully treated and no longer exists. They should not be confused with aftercare codes, or injury codes with a 7th character for subsequent encounter, that explain ongoing care of a healing condition or its sequelae. Follow-up codes may be used in conjunction with history codes to provide the full picture of the healed condition and its treatment. The follow-up code is sequenced first, followed by the history code.

A follow-up code may be used to explain multiple visits. Should a condition be found to have recurred on the follow-up visit, then the diagnosis code for the condition should be assigned in place of the follow-up code.

The follow-up Z code categories:

Z08	Encounter for follow-up examination after completed treatment for malignant neoplasm
Z09	Encounter for follow-up examination after completed treatment for conditions other than malignant neoplasm
Z39	Encounter for maternal postpartum care and examination

9) Donor

Codes in category Z52, Donors of organs and tissues, are used for living individuals who are donating blood or other body tissue.

These codes are only for individuals donating for others, not for self-donations. They are not used to identify cadaveric donations.

10) Counseling

Counseling Z codes are used when a patient or family member receives assistance in the aftermath of an illness or injury, or when support is required in coping with family or social problems.

The counseling Z codes/categories:

Z30.0-	Encounter for general counseling and advice on contraception
Z31.5	Encounter for procreative genetic counseling
Z31.6-	Encounter for general counseling and advice on procreation
Z32.2	Encounter for childbirth instruction
Z32.3	Encounter for childcare instruction
Z69	Encounter for mental health services for victim and perpetrator of abuse
Z70	Counseling related to sexual attitude, behavior and orientation
Z71	Persons encountering health services for other counseling and medical advice, not elsewhere classified
Z76.81	Expectant mother prebirth pediatrician visit

11) Encounters for Obstetrical and Reproductive Services

See Section I.C.15. Pregnancy, Childbirth, and the Puerperium, for further instruction on the use of these codes.

Z codes for pregnancy are for use in those circumstances when none of the problems or complications included in the codes from the Obstetrics chapter exist (a routine prenatal visit or postpartum care). Codes in category Z34, Encounter for supervision of normal pregnancy, are always first listed and are not to be used with any other code from the OB chapter.

Codes in category Z3A, Weeks of gestation, may be assigned to provide additional information about the pregnancy. Category Z3A codes should not be assigned for pregnancies with abortive outcomes (categories O00-O08), elective termination of pregnancy (code Z33.2), nor for postpartum conditions, as category Z3A is not applicable to these conditions. The date of the admission should be used to determine weeks of gestation for inpatient admissions that encompass more than one gestational week.

The outcome of delivery, category Z37, should be included on all maternal delivery records. It is always a secondary code. Codes in category Z37 should not be used on the newborn record.

Z codes for family planning (contraceptive) or procreative management and counseling should be included on an obstetric record either during the pregnancy or the postpartum stage, if applicable.

Z codes/categories for obstetrical and reproductive services:

Z30	Encounter for contraceptive management
Z31	Encounter for procreative management
Z32.2	Encounter for childbirth instruction
Z32.3	Encounter for childcare instruction
Z33	Pregnant state
Z34	Encounter for supervision of normal pregnancy
Z36	Encounter for antenatal screening of mother
Z3A	Weeks of gestation
Z37	Outcome of delivery
Z39	Encounter for maternal postpartum care and examination
Z76.81	Expectant mother prebirth pediatrician visit

12) Newborns and Infants

See Section I.C.16. Newborn (Perinatal) Guidelines, for further instruction on the use of these codes.

Newborn Z codes/categories:

Z76.1	Encounter for health supervision and care of foundling
Z00.1-	Encounter for routine child health examination
Z38	Liveborn infants according to place of birth and type of delivery

13) Routine and administrative examinations

The Z codes allow for the description of encounters for routine examinations, such as, a general check-up, or, examinations for administrative purposes, such as, a pre-employment physical. The codes are not to be used if the examination is for diagnosis of a suspected condition or for treatment purposes. In such cases the diagnosis code is used. During a routine exam, should a diagnosis or condition be discovered, it should be coded as an additional code. Pre-existing and chronic conditions and history codes may also be included as additional codes as long as the examination is for administrative purposes and not focused on any particular condition.

Some of the codes for routine health examinations distinguish between "with" and "without" abnormal findings. Code assignment depends on the information that is known at the time the encounter is being coded. For example, if no abnormal findings were found during the examination, but the encounter is being coded before test results are back, it is acceptable to assign the code for "without abnormal findings." When assigning a code for "with abnormal findings," additional code(s) should be assigned to identify the specific abnormal finding(s).

Pre-operative examination and pre-procedural laboratory examination Z codes are for use only in those situations when a patient is being cleared for a procedure or surgery and no treatment is given.

The Z codes/categories for routine and administrative examinations:

Z00	Encounter for general examination without complaint, suspected or reported diagnosis
Z01	Encounter for other special examination without complaint, suspected or reported diagnosis
Z02	Encounter for administrative examination Except: Z02.9, Encounter for administrative examinations, unspecified
Z32.0-	Encounter for pregnancy test

14) Miscellaneous Z codes

The miscellaneous Z codes capture a number of other health care encounters that do not fall into one of the other categories. Certain of these codes identify the reason for the encounter; others are for use as additional codes that provide useful information on circumstances that may affect a patient's care and treatment.

Prophylactic Organ Removal

For encounters specifically for prophylactic removal of an organ (such as prophylactic removal of breasts due to a genetic susceptibility to cancer or a family history of cancer), the principal or first-listed code should be a code from category Z40, Encounter for prophylactic surgery, followed by the appropriate codes to identify the associated risk factor (such as genetic susceptibility or family history).

If the patient has a malignancy of one site and is having prophylactic removal at another site to prevent either a new primary malignancy or metastatic disease, a code for the malignancy should also be assigned in addition to a code from subcategory Z40.0, Encounter for prophylactic surgery for risk factors related to malignant neoplasms. A Z40.0 code should not be assigned if the patient is having organ removal for treatment of a malignancy, such as the removal of the testes for the treatment of prostate cancer.

Miscellaneous Z codes/categories:

Z28	Immunization not carried out Except: Z28.3, Underimmunization status
Z29	Encounter for other prophylactic measures
Z40	Encounter for prophylactic surgery
Z41	Encounter for procedures for purposes other than remedying health state Except: Z41.9, Encounter for procedure for purposes other than remedying health state, unspecified
Z53	Persons encountering health services for specific procedures and treatment, not carried out
Z55	Problems related to education and literacy
Z56	Problems related to employment and unemployment
Z57	Occupational exposure to risk factors
Z58	Problems related to physical environment
Z59	Problems related to housing and economic circumstances
Z60	Problems related to social environment
Z62	Problems related to upbringing
Z63	Other problems related to primary support group, including family circumstances
Z64	Problems related to certain psychosocial circumstances
Z65	Problems related to other psychosocial circumstances
Z72	Problems related to lifestyle Note: These codes should be assigned only when the documentation specifies that the patient has an associated problem
Z73	Problems related to life management difficulty

Z74	Problems related to care provider dependency Except: Z74.01, Bed confinement status
Z75	Problems related to medical facilities and other health care
Z76.0	Encounter for issue of repeat prescription
Z76.3	Healthy person accompanying sick person
Z76.4	Other boarder to healthcare facility
Z76.5	Malingerer [conscious simulation]
Z91.1-	Patient's noncompliance with medical treatment and regimen
Z91.83	Wandering in diseases classified elsewhere
Z91.84-	Oral health risk factors
Z91.89	Other specified personal risk factors, not elsewhere classified

See Section I.B.14 for Z55-Z65 Persons with potential health hazards related to socioeconomic and psychosocial circumstances, documentation by clinicians other than the patient's provider

15) Nonspecific Z codes

Certain Z codes are so non-specific, or potentially redundant with other codes in the classification, that there can be little justification for their use in the inpatient setting. Their use in the outpatient setting should be limited to those instances when there is no further documentation to permit more precise coding. Otherwise, any sign or symptom or any other reason for visit that is captured in another code should be used.

Nonspecific Z codes/categories:

Z02.9	Encounter for administrative examinations, unspecified
Z04.9	Encounter for examination and observation for unspecified reason
Z13.9	Encounter for screening, unspecified
Z41.9	Encounter for procedure for purposes other than remedying health state, unspecified
Z52.9	Donor of unspecified organ or tissue
Z86.59	Personal history of other mental and behavioral disorders
Z88.9	Allergy status to unspecified drugs, medicaments and biological substances status
Z92.0	Personal history of contraception

16) Z Codes That May Only Be Principal/First-Listed Diagnosis

The following Z codes/categories may only be reported as the principal/first-listed diagnosis, except when there are multiple encounters on the same day and the medical records for the encounters are combined:

Z00	Encounter for general examination without complaint, suspected or reported diagnosis Except: Z00.6
Z01	Encounter for other special examination without complaint, suspected or reported diagnosis
Z02	Encounter for administrative examination
Z03	Encounter for medical observation for suspected diseases and conditions ruled out
Z04	Encounter for examination and observation for other reasons
Z33.2	Encounter for elective termination of pregnancy
Z31.81	Encounter for male factor infertility in female patient
Z31.83	Encounter for assisted reproductive fertility procedure cycle
Z31.84	Encounter for fertility preservation procedure
Z34	Encounter for supervision of normal pregnancy
Z39	Encounter for maternal postpartum care and examination
Z38	Liveborn infants according to place of birth and type of delivery
Z40	Encounter for prophylactic surgery
Z42	Encounter for plastic and reconstructive surgery following medical procedure or healed injury
Z51.0	Encounter for antineoplastic radiation therapy
Z51.1-	Encounter for antineoplastic chemotherapy and immunotherapy
Z52	Donors of organs and tissues Except: Z52.9, Donor of unspecified organ or tissue
Z76.1	Encounter for health supervision and care of foundling
Z76.2	Encounter for health supervision and care of other healthy infant and child
Z99.12	Encounter for respirator [ventilator] dependence during power failure

CHAPTER 21

FACTORS INFLUENCING HEALTH STATUS AND CONTACT WITH HEALTH SERVICES (Z00–Z99)

Note: Z codes represent reasons for encounters. A corresponding procedure code must accompany a Z code if a procedure is performed. Categories Z00–Z99 are provided for occasions when circumstances other than a disease, injury or external cause classifiable to categories A00–Y89 are recorded as "diagnoses" or "problems." This can arise in two main ways:

(a) When a person who may or may not be sick encounters the health services for some specific purpose, such as to receive limited care or service for a current condition, to donate an organ or tissue, to receive prophylactic vaccination (immunization), or to discuss a problem which is in itself not a disease or injury.

(b) When some circumstance or problem is present which influences the person's health status but is not in itself a current illness or injury.

This chapter contains the following blocks:

Z00–Z13	Persons encountering health services for examination
Z14–Z15	Genetic carrier and genetic susceptibility to disease
Z16	Resistance to antimicrobial drugs
Z17	Estrogen receptor status
Z18	Retained foreign body fragments
▶Z19	Hormone sensitivity malignancy status
Z20–Z29	Persons with potential health hazards related to communicable diseases
Z30–Z39	Persons encountering health services in circumstances related to reproduction
Z40–Z53	Encounters for other specific health care
Z55–Z65	Persons with potential health hazards related to socioeconomic and psychosocial circumstances
Z66	Do not resuscitate status
Z67	Blood type
Z68	Body mass index (BMI)
Z69–Z76	Persons encountering health services in other circumstances
Z77–Z99	Persons with potential health hazards related to family and personal history and certain conditions influencing health status

PERSONS ENCOUNTERING HEALTH SERVICES FOR EXAMINATIONS (Z00–Z13)

Note: Nonspecific abnormal findings disclosed at the time of these examinations are classified to categories R70–R94.

   Excludes1   examinations related to pregnancy and reproduction (Z30–Z36, Z39.-)

● **Z00**   **Encounter for general examination without complaint, suspected or reported diagnosis**

   Excludes1   encounter for examination for administrative purposes (Z02.-)

   Excludes2   encounter for pre-procedural examinations (Z01.81-)
            special screening examinations (Z11–Z13)

 ● **Z00.0**   **Encounter for general adult medical examination**
      Encounter for adult periodic examination (annual) (physical) and any associated laboratory and radiologic examinations

    Excludes1   encounter for examination of sign or symptom - code to sign or symptom general health check-up of infant or child (Z00.12.-)

     Coding Clinic: 2016, Q4, P131

     Z00.00   **Encounter for general adult medical examination without abnormal findings**   A
         Encounter for adult health check-up NOS
         Coding Clinic: 2017, Q4, P95; 2016, Q1, P37

     Z00.01   **Encounter for general adult medical examination with abnormal findings**   A
         Use additional code to identify abnormal findings
         Coding Clinic: 2016, Q1, P36

 ● **Z00.1**   **Encounter for newborn, infant and child health examinations**

  ● **Z00.11**   **Newborn health examination**
      Health check for child under 29 days old
      Use additional code to identify any abnormal findings

     Excludes1   health check for child over 28 days old (Z00.12-)

     Z00.110   **Health examination for newborn under 8 days old**   N
         Health check for newborn under 8 days old

     Z00.111   **Health examination for newborn 8 to 28 days old**   N
         Health check for newborn 8 to 28 days old
         Newborn weight check

  ● **Z00.12**   **Encounter for routine child health examination**
      ~~Encounter for development testing of infant or child~~
     ▶Immunizations appropriate for age
      Health check (routine) for child over 28 days old
     ▶Routine developmental screening of infant or child
     ▶Routine vision and hearing testing

     Excludes1   health check for child under 29 days old (Z00.11-)
           health supervision of foundling or other healthy infant or child (Z76.1-Z76.2)
           newborn health examination (Z00.11-)

     Z00.121   **Encounter for routine child health examination with abnormal findings**   P
         Use additional code to identify abnormal findings
         Coding Clinic: 2017, Q4, P95; 2016, Q1, P34-35

     Z00.129   **Encounter for routine child health examination without abnormal findings**   P
         Encounter for routine child health examination NOS
         Coding Clinic: 2016, Q1, P34

 Z00.2   **Encounter for examination for period of rapid growth in childhood**   P

 Z00.3   **Encounter for examination for adolescent development state**   P
      Encounter for puberty development state

 Z00.5   **Encounter for examination of potential donor of organ and tissue**

 Z00.6   **Encounter for examination for normal comparison and control in clinical research program**
      Examination of participant or control in clinical research program

 ● **Z00.7**   **Encounter for examination for period of delayed growth in childhood**

     Z00.70   **Encounter for examination for period of delayed growth in childhood without abnormal findings**   P

     Z00.71   **Encounter for examination for period of delayed growth in childhood with abnormal findings**   P
         Use additional code to identify abnormal findings

 Z00.8   **Encounter for other general examination**
      Encounter for health examination in population surveys

CHAPTER 21 (Z00-Z99)

● **Z01** **Encounter for other special examination without complaint, suspected or reported diagnosis**

> **Includes**   routine examination of specific system
>
> **Note:** Codes from category Z01 represent the reason for the encounter. A separate procedure code is required to identify any examinations or procedures performed.
>
> **Excludes1**   encounter for examination for administrative purposes (Z02.-)
> encounter for examination for suspected conditions, proven not to exist (Z03.-)
> encounter for laboratory and radiologic examinations as a component of general medical examinations (Z00.0-)
> encounter for laboratory, radiologic and imaging examinations for sign(s) and symptom(s) - code to the sign(s) or symptom(s)
>
> **Excludes2**   screening examinations (Z11-Z13)

● **Z01.0** **Encounter for examination of eyes and vision**

> **Excludes1**   examination for driving license (Z02.4)

> **Z01.00** **Encounter for examination of eyes and vision without abnormal findings**
> Encounter for examination of eyes and vision NOS

> **Z01.01** **Encounter for examination of eyes and vision with abnormal findings**
> Use additional code to identify abnormal findings
> Coding Clinic: 2016, Q4, P21

● **Z01.1** **Encounter for examination of ears and hearing**

> **Z01.10** **Encounter for examination of ears and hearing without abnormal findings**
> Encounter for examination of ears and hearing NOS
> Coding Clinic: 2016, Q4, P25

> ● **Z01.11** **Encounter for examination of ears and hearing with abnormal findings**
> Coding Clinic: 2016, Q3, P18
>
>> **Z01.110** **Encounter for hearing examination following failed hearing screening**
>> Coding Clinic: 2016, Q3, P18-19
>
>> **Z01.118** **Encounter for examination of ears and hearing with other abnormal findings**
>> Use additional code to identify abnormal findings
>> Coding Clinic: 2016, Q3, P17

> **Z01.12** **Encounter for hearing conservation and treatment**

● **Z01.2** **Encounter for dental examination and cleaning**

> **Z01.20** **Encounter for dental examination and cleaning without abnormal findings**
> Encounter for dental examination and cleaning NOS

> **Z01.21** **Encounter for dental examination and cleaning with abnormal findings**
> Use additional code to identify abnormal findings

● **Z01.3** **Encounter for examination of blood pressure**

> **Z01.30** **Encounter for examination of blood pressure without abnormal findings**
> Encounter for examination of blood pressure NOS

> **Z01.31** **Encounter for examination of blood pressure with abnormal findings**
> Use additional code to identify abnormal findings

● **Z01.4** **Encounter for gynecological examination**

> **Excludes2**   pregnancy examination or test (Z32.0-)
> routine examination for contraceptive maintenance (Z30.4-)

● **Z01.41** **Encounter for routine gynecological examination**
> Encounter for general gynecological examination with or without cervical smear
> Encounter for gynecological examination (general) (routine) NOS
> Encounter for pelvic examination (annual) (periodic)
> Use additional code:
> for screening for human papillomavirus, if applicable (Z11.51)
> for screening vaginal pap smear, if applicable (Z12.72)
> to identify acquired absence of uterus, if applicable (Z90.71-)
>
>> **Excludes1**   gynecologic examination status-post hysterectomy for malignant condition (Z08)
>> screening cervical pap smear not a part of a routine gynecological examination (Z12.4)

>> **Z01.411** **Encounter for gynecological examination (general) (routine) with abnormal findings** ♀
>> Use additional code to identify any abnormal findings

>> **Z01.419** **Encounter for gynecological examination (general) (routine) without abnormal findings** ♀

> **Z01.42** **Encounter for cervical smear to confirm findings of recent normal smear following initial abnormal smear** ♀

● **Z01.8** **Encounter for other specified special examinations**

● **Z01.81** **Encounter for preprocedural examinations**
> Encounter for preoperative examinations
> Encounter for radiological and imaging examinations as part of preprocedural examination

>> **Z01.810** **Encounter for preprocedural cardiovascular examination**

>> **Z01.811** **Encounter for preprocedural respiratory examination**

>> **Z01.812** **Encounter for preprocedural laboratory examination**
>> Blood and urine tests prior to treatment or procedure

>> **Z01.818** **Encounter for other preprocedural examination**
>> Encounter for preprocedural examination NOS
>> Encounter for examinations prior to antineoplastic chemotherapy

> **Z01.82** **Encounter for allergy testing**
>> **Excludes1**   encounter for antibody response examination (Z01.84)

> **Z01.83** **Encounter for blood typing**
> Encounter for Rh typing

> **Z01.84** **Encounter for antibody response examination**
> Encounter for immunity status testing
>> **Excludes1**   encounter for allergy testing (Z01.82)

> **Z01.89** **Encounter for other specified special examinations**

▶ New   ⇛ Revised   ~~deleted~~ Deleted   Excludes 1   Excludes 2   Includes   Use additional   Code first   Code also   Key words

OGCR Official Guidelines   X Assign placeholder X   ● Use Additional Character(s)   ▶ Manifestation Code   **Coding Clinic**

● **Z02   Encounter for administrative examination**

   Z02.0   Encounter for examination for admission to educational institution

      Encounter for examination for admission to preschool (education)

      Encounter for examination for re-admission to school following illness or medical treatment

   Z02.1   Encounter for pre-employment examination

   Z02.2   Encounter for examination for admission to residential institution

      Excludes1   examination for admission to prison (Z02.89)

   Z02.3   Encounter for examination for recruitment to armed forces

   Z02.4   Encounter for examination for driving license

   Z02.5   Encounter for examination for participation in sport

      Excludes1   blood-alcohol and blood-drug test (Z02.83)

   Z02.6   Encounter for examination for insurance purposes

●   **Z02.7   Encounter for issue of medical certificate**

      Excludes1   encounter for general medical examination (Z00-Z01, Z02.0-Z02.6, Z02.8-Z02.9)

      Z02.71   Encounter for disability determination

         Encounter for issue of medical certificate of incapacity

         Encounter for issue of medical certificate of invalidity

      Z02.79   Encounter for issue of other medical certificate

●   **Z02.8   Encounter for other administrative examinations**

      Z02.81   Encounter for paternity testing

      Z02.82   Encounter for adoption services

      Z02.83   Encounter for blood-alcohol and blood-drug test

         Use additional code for findings of alcohol or drugs in blood (R78.-)

      Z02.89   Encounter for other administrative examinations

         Encounter for examination for admission to prison

         Encounter for examination for admission to summer camp

         Encounter for immigration examination

         Encounter for naturalization examination

         Encounter for premarital examination

         Excludes1   health supervision of foundling or other healthy infant or child (Z76.1-Z76.2)

   Z02.9   Encounter for administrative examinations, unspecified

Revised

OGCR Section II.C.21.c.6.

Observation

There are three observation Z code categories. They are for use in very limited circumstances when a person is being observed for a suspected condition that is ruled out. The observation codes are not for use if an injury or illnesses or any signs or symptoms related to the suspected condition are present. In such cases the diagnosis/symptom code is used with the corresponding external cause code.

The observation codes are to be used as principal diagnosis only. The only exception to this is when the principal diagnosis is required to be a code from category Z38, Liveborn infants according to place of birth and type of delivery. Then a code from category Z05, Encounter for observation and evaluation of newborn for suspected diseases and conditions ruled out, is sequenced after the Z38 code. Additional codes may be used in addition to the observation code but only if they are unrelated to the suspected condition being observed.

Codes from subcategory Z03.7 Encounter for suspected maternal and fetal conditions ruled out, may either be used as a first listed or as an additional code assignment depending on the case. They are for use in very limited circumstances on a maternal record when an encounter is for a suspected maternal or fetal condition that is ruled out during that encounter (for example, a maternal or fetal condition may be suspected due to an abnormal test result). These codes should not be used when the condition is confirmed. In those cases, the confirmed condition should be coded. In addition, these codes are not for use if an illness or any signs or symptoms related to the suspected condition or problem are present. In such cases the diagnosis/symptom code is used.

Additional codes may be used in addition to the code from subcategory Z03.7, but only if they are unrelated to the suspected condition being evaluated.

Codes from subcategory Z03.7 may not be used for encounters for antenatal screening of mother. *See Section I.C.21. Screening.*

For encounters for suspected fetal condition that are inconclusive following testing and evaluation, assign the appropriate code from category O35, O36, O40 or O41.

The observation Z code categories:

Z03   Encounter for medical observation for suspected diseases and conditions ruled out

Z04   Encounter for examination and observation for other reasons Except: Z04.9, Encounter for examination and observation for unspecified reason

Z05   Encounter for observation and evaluation of newborn for suspected diseases and conditions ruled out

● **Z03   Encounter for medical observation for suspected diseases and conditions ruled out**

      This category is to be used when a person without a diagnosis is suspected of having an abnormal condition, without signs or symptoms, which requires study, but after examination and observation, is ruled out. This category is also for use for administrative and legal observation status.

      Excludes1   contact with and (suspected) exposures hazardous to health (Z77.-)

         encounter for observation and evaluation of newborn for suspected diseases and conditions ruled out (Z05.-)

         person with feared complaint in whom no diagnosis is made (Z71.1)

         signs or symptoms under study - code to signs or symptoms

   Z03.6   Encounter for observation for suspected toxic effect from ingested substance ruled out

      Encounter for observation for suspected adverse effect from drug

      Encounter for observation for suspected poisoning

● **Z03.7   Encounter for suspected maternal and fetal conditions ruled out**
Encounter for suspected maternal and fetal conditions not found

> **Excludes1**   known or suspected fetal anomalies affecting management of mother, not ruled out (O26.-, O35.-, O36.-, O40.-, O41.-)

Z03.71   Encounter for suspected problem with amniotic cavity and membrane ruled out ♀   M
Encounter for suspected oligohydramnios ruled out
Encounter for suspected polyhydramnios ruled out

Z03.72   Encounter for suspected placental problem ruled out ♀   M

Z03.73   Encounter for suspected fetal anomaly ruled out ♀   M
Coding Clinic: 2016, Q4, P6

Z03.74   Encounter for suspected problem with fetal growth ruled out ♀   M

Z03.75   Encounter for suspected cervical shortening ruled out ♀   M

Z03.79   Encounter for other suspected maternal and fetal conditions ruled out ♀   M
Coding Clinic: 2016, Q4, P7

● **Z03.8   Encounter for observation for other suspected diseases and conditions ruled out**

● **Z03.81   Encounter for observation for suspected exposure to biological agents ruled out**

Z03.810   Encounter for observation for suspected exposure to anthrax ruled out

Z03.818   Encounter for observation for suspected exposure to other biological agents ruled out

Z03.89   Encounter for observation for other suspected diseases and conditions ruled out

● **Z04   Encounter for examination and observation for other reasons**

> **Includes**   encounter for examination for medicolegal reasons
This category is to be used when a person without a diagnosis is suspected of having an abnormal condition, without signs or symptoms, which requires study, but after examination and observation, is ruled-out. This category is also for use for administrative and legal observation status.

Z04.1   Encounter for examination and observation following transport accident

> **Excludes1**   encounter for examination and observation following work accident (Z04.2)

Z04.2   Encounter for examination and observation following work accident

Z04.3   Encounter for examination and observation following other accident

● **Z04.4   Encounter for examination and observation following alleged rape**
Encounter for examination and observation of victim following alleged rape
Encounter for examination and observation of victim following alleged sexual abuse
Coding Clinic: 2016, Q4, P129

Z04.41   Encounter for examination and observation following alleged adult rape   A
Suspected adult rape, ruled out
Suspected adult sexual abuse, ruled out

Z04.42   Encounter for examination and observation following alleged child rape   P
Suspected child rape, ruled out
Suspected child sexual abuse, ruled out

Z04.6   Encounter for general psychiatric examination, requested by authority

● **Z04.7   Encounter for examination and observation following alleged physical abuse**

Z04.71   Encounter for examination and observation following alleged adult physical abuse   A
Suspected adult physical abuse, ruled out

> **Excludes1**   confirmed case of adult physical abuse (T74.-)
> encounter for examination and observation following alleged adult sexual abuse (Z04.41)
> suspected case of adult physical abuse, not ruled out (T76.-)

Z04.72   Encounter for examination and observation following alleged child physical abuse   P
Suspected child physical abuse, ruled out

> **Excludes1**   confirmed case of child physical abuse (T74.-)
> encounter for examination and observation following alleged child sexual abuse (Z04.42)
> suspected case of child physical abuse, not ruled out (T76.-)

● **Z04.8   Encounter for examination and observation for other specified reasons**
Encounter for examination and observation for request for expert evidence

▶ **Z04.81   Encounter for examination and observation of victim following forced sexual exploitation**

▶ **Z04.82   Encounter for examination and observation of victim following forced labor exploitation**

▶ **Z04.89   Encounter for examination and observation for other specified reasons**

Z04.9   Encounter for examination and observation for unspecified reason
Encounter for observation NOS

● **Z05   Encounter for observation and evaluation of newborn for suspected diseases and conditions ruled out**
This category is to be used for newborns, within the neonatal period (the first 28 days of life), who are suspected of having an abnormal condition, but without signs or symptoms, and which, after examination and observation, is ruled out.
Coding Clinic: 2016, Q4, P54, 77, 126-127, 130

Z05.0   Observation and evaluation of newborn for suspected cardiac condition ruled out

Z05.1   Observation and evaluation of newborn for suspected infectious condition ruled out

Z05.2   Observation and evaluation of newborn for suspected neurological condition ruled out

Z05.3   Observation and evaluation of newborn for suspected respiratory condition ruled out

● **Z05.4   Observation and evaluation of newborn for suspected genetic, metabolic or immunologic condition ruled out**

Z05.41   Observation and evaluation of newborn for suspected genetic condition ruled out
Coding Clinic: 2016, Q4, P55

Z05.42   Observation and evaluation of newborn for suspected metabolic condition ruled out

Z05.43   Observation and evaluation of newborn for suspected immunologic condition ruled out

Z05.5   Observation and evaluation of newborn for suspected gastrointestinal condition ruled out

Z05.6   Observation and evaluation of newborn for suspected genitourinary condition ruled out

▶ New   ⇒ Revised   ~~deleted~~ Deleted   Excludes 1   Excludes 2   Includes   Use additional   Code first   Code also   Key words
OGCR Official Guidelines   X Assign placeholder X   ● Use Additional Character(s)   ▶ Manifestation Code   **Coding Clinic**

● **Z05.7** **Observation and evaluation of newborn for suspected skin, subcutaneous, musculoskeletal and connective tissue condition ruled out**

    Z05.71 Observation and evaluation of newborn for suspected skin and subcutaneous tissue condition ruled out

    Z05.72 Observation and evaluation of newborn for suspected musculoskeletal condition ruled out

    Z05.73 Observation and evaluation of newborn for suspected connective tissue condition ruled out

Z05.8 **Observation and evaluation of newborn for other specified suspected condition ruled out**

Z05.9 **Observation and evaluation of newborn for unspecified suspected condition ruled out**

OGCR See Section II.C.21.c.8.

> The follow-up codes are used to explain continuing surveillance following completed treatment of a disease, condition, or injury. They imply that the condition has been fully treated and no longer exists. They should not be confused with aftercare codes, or injury codes with 7th character "D," that explain ongoing care of a healing condition or its sequelae. Follow-up codes may be used in conjunction with history codes to provide the full picture of the healed condition and its treatment. The follow-up code is sequenced first, followed by the history code.
>
> A follow-up code may be used to explain multiple visits. Should a condition be found to have recurred on the follow-up visit, then the diagnosis code for the condition should be assigned in place of the follow-up code.
>
> The follow-up Z code categories:
>
> Z08   Encounter for follow-up examination after completed treatment for malignant neoplasm
>
> Z09   Encounter for follow-up examination after completed treatment for conditions other than malignant neoplasm
>
> Z39   Encounter for maternal postpartum care and examination

Z08 **Encounter for follow-up examination after completed treatment for malignant neoplasm**

    Medical surveillance following completed treatment

    Use additional code to identify any acquired absence of organs (Z90.-)

    Use additional code to identify the personal history of malignant neoplasm (Z85.-)

    Excludes1 aftercare following medical care (Z43-Z49, Z51)

Z09 **Encounter for follow-up examination after completed treatment for conditions other than malignant neoplasm**

    Medical surveillance following completed treatment

    Use additional code to identify any applicable history of disease code (Z86.-. Z87.-)

    Excludes1 aftercare following medical care (Z43-Z49, Z51)
            surveillance of contraception (Z30.4-)
            surveillance of prosthetic and other medical devices (Z44-Z46)

    Coding Clinic: 2017, Q1, P9; 2015, Q1, P8

OGCR Section II.C.21.c.5.

> Screening
>
> Screening is the testing for disease or disease precursors in seemingly well individuals so that early detection and treatment can be provided for those who test positive for the disease (e.g., screening mammogram).
>
> The testing of a person to rule out or confirm a suspected diagnosis because the patient has some sign or symptom is a diagnostic examination, not a screening. In these cases, the sign or symptom is used to explain the reason for the test.
>
> A screening code may be a first listed code if the reason for the visit is specifically the screening exam. It may also be used as an additional code if the screening is done during an office visit for other health problems. A screening code is not necessary if the screening is inherent to a routine examination, such as a pap smear done during a routine pelvic examination.
>
> Should a condition be discovered during the screening then the code for the condition may be assigned as an additional diagnosis.
>
> The Z code indicates that a screening exam is planned. A procedure code is required to confirm that the screening was performed.
>
> The screening Z codes /categories:
>
> Z11   Encounter for screening for infectious and parasitic diseases
>
> Z12   Encounter for screening for malignant neoplasms
>
> Z13   Encounter for screening for other diseases and disorders
>   Except: Z13.9, Encounter for screening, unspecified
>
> Z36   Encounter for antenatal screening for mother

● **Z11** **Encounter for screening for infectious and parasitic diseases**

    Screening is the testing for disease or disease precursors in asymptomatic individuals so that early detection and treatment can be provided for those who test positive for the disease.

    Excludes1 encounter for diagnostic examination - code to sign or symptom

    Z11.0 **Encounter for screening for intestinal infectious diseases**

    Z11.1 **Encounter for screening for respiratory tuberculosis**

    Z11.2 **Encounter for screening for other bacterial diseases**

    Z11.3 **Encounter for screening for infections with a predominantly sexual mode of transmission**

        Excludes2 encounter for screening for human immunodeficiency virus [HIV] (Z11.4)
                encounter for screening for human papillomavirus (Z11.51)

    Z11.4 **Encounter for screening for human immunodeficiency virus [HIV]**

●   **Z11.5** **Encounter for screening for other viral diseases**

        Excludes2 encounter for screening for viral intestinal disease (Z11.0)

        Z11.51 **Encounter for screening for human papillomavirus (HPV)**

        Z11.59 **Encounter for screening for other viral diseases**

    Z11.6 **Encounter for screening for other protozoal diseases and helminthiases**

       Diseases or infestations caused by parasitic worms

        Excludes2 encounter for screening for protozoal intestinal disease (Z11.0)

    Z11.8 **Encounter for screening for other infectious and parasitic diseases**

       Encounter for screening for chlamydia
       Encounter for screening for rickettsial
       Encounter for screening for spirochetal
       Encounter for screening for mycoses

    Z11.9 **Encounter for screening for infectious and parasitic diseases, unspecified**

CHAPTER 21 (Z00-Z99)

● **Z12   Encounter for screening for malignant neoplasms**
>   Screening is the testing for disease or disease precursors in asymptomatic individuals so that early detection and treatment can be provided for those who test positive for the disease.
>
>   Use additional code to identify any family history of malignant neoplasm (Z80.-)
>
>   **Excludes1**   encounter for diagnostic examination - code to sign or symptom

Z12.0   Encounter for screening for malignant neoplasm of stomach

● **Z12.1   Encounter for screening for malignant neoplasm of intestinal tract**

>   **Z12.10   Encounter for screening for malignant neoplasm of intestinal tract, unspecified**
>
>   **Z12.11   Encounter for screening for malignant neoplasm of colon**
>   >   Encounter for screening colonoscopy NOS
>   >   Coding Clinic: 2018, Q1, P7; 2017, Q1, P8-9
>
>   **Z12.12   Encounter for screening for malignant neoplasm of rectum**
>
>   **Z12.13   Encounter for screening for malignant neoplasm of small intestine**

Z12.2   Encounter for screening for malignant neoplasm of respiratory organs

● **Z12.3   Encounter for screening for malignant neoplasm of breast**

>   **Z12.31   Encounter for screening mammogram for malignant neoplasm of breast**
>   >   **Excludes1**   inconclusive mammogram (R92.2)
>   >   Coding Clinic: 2015, Q1, P24
>
>   **Z12.39   Encounter for other screening for malignant neoplasm of breast**

Z12.4   Encounter for screening for malignant neoplasm of cervix ♀
>   Encounter for screening pap smear for malignant neoplasm of cervix
>
>   **Excludes1**   when screening is part of general gynecological examination (Z01.4-)
>
>   **Excludes2**   encounter for screening for human papillomavirus (Z11.51)

Z12.5   Encounter for screening for malignant neoplasm of prostate ♂

Z12.6   Encounter for screening for malignant neoplasm of bladder

● **Z12.7   Encounter for screening for malignant neoplasm of other genitourinary organs**

>   **Z12.71   Encounter for screening for malignant neoplasm of testis ♂**
>
>   **Z12.72   Encounter for screening for malignant neoplasm of vagina ♀**
>   >   Vaginal pap smear status - post hysterectomy for non-malignant condition
>   >   Use additional code to identify acquired absence of uterus (Z90.71-)
>   >   **Excludes1**   vaginal pap smear status - post hysterectomy for malignant conditions (Z08)
>
>   **Z12.73   Encounter for screening for malignant neoplasm of ovary ♀**
>
>   **Z12.79   Encounter for screening for malignant neoplasm of other genitourinary organs**

● **Z12.8   Encounter for screening for malignant neoplasm of other sites**

>   **Z12.81   Encounter for screening for malignant neoplasm of oral cavity**
>
>   **Z12.82   Encounter for screening for malignant neoplasm of nervous system**

>   **Z12.83   Encounter for screening for malignant neoplasm of skin**
>
>   **Z12.89   Encounter for screening for malignant neoplasm of other sites**

Z12.9   Encounter for screening for malignant neoplasm, site unspecified

● **Z13   Encounter for screening for other diseases and disorders**
>   Screening is the testing for disease or disease precursors in asymptomatic individuals so that early detection and treatment can be provided for those who test positive for the disease.
>
>   **Excludes1**   encounter for diagnostic examination - code to sign or symptom

Z13.0   Encounter for screening for diseases of the blood and blood-forming organs and certain disorders involving the immune mechanism

Z13.1   Encounter for screening for diabetes mellitus

● **Z13.2   Encounter for screening for nutritional, metabolic and other endocrine disorders**

>   **Z13.21   Encounter for screening for nutritional disorder**
>
> ● **Z13.22   Encounter for screening for metabolic disorder**
>   >   **Z13.220   Encounter for screening for lipoid disorders**
>   >   >   Encounter for screening for cholesterol level
>   >   >   Encounter for screening for hypercholesterolemia
>   >   >   Encounter for screening for hyperlipidemia
>   >
>   >   **Z13.228   Encounter for screening for other metabolic disorders**
>
>   **Z13.29   Encounter for screening for other suspected endocrine disorder**
>   >   **Excludes1**   encounter for screening for diabetes mellitus (Z13.1)

▶● **Z13.3   Encounter for screening examination for mental health and behavioral disorders**

▶   **Z13.30   Encounter for screening examination for mental health and behavioral disorders, unspecified**

▶   **Z13.31   Encounter for screening for depression**
>   ▶Encounter for screening for depression, adult
>   ▶Encounter for screening for depression for child or adolescent

▶   **Z13.32   Encounter for screening for maternal depression**
>   ▶Encounter for screening for perinatal depression

▶   **Z13.39   Encounter for screening examination for other mental health and behavioral disorders**
>   ▶Encounter for screening for alcoholism
>   ▶Encounter for screening for intellectual disabilities

Z13.4   Encounter for screening for certain developmental disorders in childhood   P
>   ▶Encounter for development testing of infant or child
>   Encounter for screening for developmental handicaps in early childhood
>   ~~Excludes1   routine development testing of infant or child (Z00.1-)~~
>   **Excludes2**   encounter for routine child health examination (Z00.12-)

▶   **Z13.40   Encounter for screening for unspecified developmental delays**

▶   **Z13.41   Encounter for autism screening**

▶   **Z13.42   Encounter for screening for global developmental delays (milestones)**
>   ▶Encounter for screening for developmental handicaps in early childhood

▶   **Z13.49   Encounter for screening for other developmental delays**

Z13.5 Encounter for screening for eye and ear disorders

> **Excludes2** encounter for general hearing examination (Z01.1-)
> encounter for general vision examination (Z01.0-)

> Coding Clinic: 2016, Q3, P17

Z13.6 Encounter for screening for cardiovascular disorders

● **Z13.7** Encounter for screening for genetic and chromosomal anomalies

> **Excludes1** genetic testing for procreative management (Z31.4-)

Z13.71 Encounter for nonprocreative screening for genetic disease carrier status

Z13.79 Encounter for other screening for genetic and chromosomal anomalies

● **Z13.8** Encounter for screening for other specified diseases and disorders

> **Excludes2** screening for malignant neoplasms (Z12.-)

● **Z13.81** Encounter for screening for digestive system disorders

Z13.810 Encounter for screening for upper gastrointestinal disorder

Z13.811 Encounter for screening for lower gastrointestinal disorder

> **Excludes1** encounter for screening for intestinal infectious disease (Z11.0)

Z13.818 Encounter for screening for other digestive system disorders

● **Z13.82** Encounter for screening for musculoskeletal disorder

Z13.820 Encounter for screening for osteoporosis

Z13.828 Encounter for screening for other musculoskeletal disorder

Z13.83 Encounter for screening for respiratory disorder NEC

> **Excludes1** encounter for screening for respiratory tuberculosis (Z11.1)

Z13.84 Encounter for screening for dental disorders

● **Z13.85** Encounter for screening for nervous system disorders

Z13.850 Encounter for screening for traumatic brain injury

Z13.858 Encounter for screening for other nervous system disorders

Z13.88 Encounter for screening for disorder due to exposure to contaminants

> **Excludes1** those exposed to contaminants without suspected disorders (Z57-Z77.-)

Z13.89 Encounter for screening for other disorder

> Encounter for screening for genitourinary disorders

Z13.9 Encounter for screening, unspecified

GENETIC CARRIER AND GENETIC SUSCEPTIBILITY TO DISEASE (Z14-Z15)

● **Z14** Genetic carrier

● **Z14.0** Hemophilia A carrier

Z14.01 Asymptomatic hemophilia A carrier

Z14.02 Symptomatic hemophilia A carrier

Z14.1 Cystic fibrosis carrier

Z14.8 Genetic carrier of other disease

● **Z15** Genetic susceptibility to disease

> **Excludes1** chromosomal anomalies (Q90-Q99)
> **Includes** confirmed abnormal gene

> Use additional code, if applicable, for any associated family history of the disease (Z80-Z84)

● **Z15.0** Genetic susceptibility to malignant neoplasm

> *Code first if applicable, any current malignant neoplasm (C00-C75, C81-C96)*

> Use additional code, if applicable, for any personal history of malignant neoplasm (Z85.-)

Z15.01 Genetic susceptibility to malignant neoplasm of breast

Z15.02 Genetic susceptibility to malignant neoplasm of ovary ♀

Z15.03 Genetic susceptibility to malignant neoplasm of prostate ♂

Z15.04 Genetic susceptibility to malignant neoplasm of endometrium ♀

Z15.09 Genetic susceptibility to other malignant neoplasm

● **Z15.8** Genetic susceptibility to other disease

Z15.81 Genetic susceptibility to multiple endocrine neoplasia [MEN]

> **Excludes1** multiple endocrine neoplasia [MEN] syndromes (E31.2-)

Z15.89 Genetic susceptibility to other disease

RESISTANCE TO ANTIMICROBIAL DRUGS (Z16)

● **Z16** Resistance to antimicrobial drugs

> **Note:** The codes in this category are provided for use as additional codes to identify the resistance and non-responsiveness of a condition to antimicrobial drugs.

> *Code first the infection*

> **Excludes1** Methicillin resistant Staphylococcus aureus infection (A49.02)
> Methicillin resistant Staphylococcus aureus pneumonia (J15.212)
> Sepsis due to Methicillin resistant Staphylococcus aureus (A41.02)

● **Z16.1** Resistance to beta lactam antibiotics

Z16.10 Resistance to unspecified beta lactam antibiotics

Z16.11 Resistance to penicillins
> Resistance to amoxicillin
> Resistance to ampicillin

Z16.12 Extended spectrum beta lactamase (ESBL) resistance

> **Excludes2** Methicillin resistant Staphylococcus aureus infection in diseases classified elsewhere (B95.62)

Z16.19 Resistance to other specified beta lactam antibiotics
> Resistance to cephalosporins

● **Z16.2** Resistance to other antibiotics

Z16.20 Resistance to unspecified antibiotic
> Resistance to antibiotics NOS

Z16.21 Resistance to vancomycin

Z16.22 Resistance to vancomycin related antibiotics

Z16.23 Resistance to quinolones and fluoroquinolones

Z16.24 Resistance to multiple antibiotics

Z16.29 Resistance to other single specified antibiotic
> Resistance to aminoglycosides
> Resistance to macrolides
> Resistance to sulfonamides
> Resistance to tetracyclines

● **Z16.3 Resistance to other antimicrobial drugs**

> **Excludes1** resistance to antibiotics (Z16.1-, Z16.2-)

Z16.30 Resistance to unspecified antimicrobial drugs
Drug resistance NOS

Z16.31 Resistance to antiparasitic drug(s)
Resistance to quinine and related compounds

Z16.32 Resistance to antifungal drug(s)

Z16.33 Resistance to antiviral drug(s)

● **Z16.34 Resistance to antimycobacterial drug(s)**
Resistance to tuberculostatics

Z16.341 Resistance to single antimycobacterial drug
Resistance to antimycobacterial drug NOS

Z16.342 Resistance to multiple antimycobacterial drugs

Z16.35 Resistance to multiple antimicrobial drugs

> **Excludes1** Resistance to multiple antibiotics only (Z16.24)

Z16.39 Resistance to other specified antimicrobial drug

ESTROGEN RECEPTOR STATUS (Z17)

● **Z17 Estrogen receptor status**
Code first malignant neoplasm of breast (C50.-)

Z17.0 Estrogen receptor positive status [ER+]

Z17.1 Estrogen receptor negative status [ER-]

RETAINED FOREIGN BODY FRAGMENTS (Z18)

● **Z18 Retained foreign body fragments**

> **Includes** embedded fragment (status)
> embedded splinter (status)
> retained foreign body status

> **Excludes1** artificial joint prosthesis status (Z96.6-)
> foreign body accidentally left during a procedure (T81.5-)
> foreign body entering through orifice (T15-T19)
> in situ cardiac device (Z95.-)
> organ or tissue replaced by means other than transplant (Z96.-, Z97.-)
> organ or tissue replaced by transplant (Z94.-)
> personal history of retained foreign body fully removed Z87.821
> superficial foreign body (non-embedded splinter) - code to superficial foreign body, by site

● **Z18.0 Retained radioactive fragments**

Z18.01 Retained depleted uranium fragments

Z18.09 Other retained radioactive fragments
Other retained depleted isotope fragments
Retained nontherapeutic radioactive fragments

● **Z18.1 Retained metal fragments**

> **Excludes1** retained radioactive metal fragments (Z18.01-Z18.09)

Z18.10 Retained metal fragments, unspecified
Retained metal fragment NOS

Z18.11 Retained magnetic metal fragments

Z18.12 Retained nonmagnetic metal fragments

Z18.2 Retained plastic fragments
Acrylics fragments
Diethylhexylphthalates fragments
Isocyanate fragments

● **Z18.3 Retained organic fragments**

Z18.31 Retained animal quills or spines

Z18.32 Retained tooth

Z18.33 Retained wood fragments

Z18.39 Other retained organic fragments

● **Z18.8 Other specified retained foreign body**

Z18.81 Retained glass fragments

Z18.83 Retained stone or crystalline fragments
Retained concrete or cement fragments

Z18.89 Other specified retained foreign body fragments
Coding Clinic: 2016, Q3, P24

Z18.9 Retained foreign body fragments, unspecified material

HORMONE SENSITIVITY MALIGNANCY STATUS (Z19)

● **Z19 Hormone sensitivity malignancy status**
Code first malignant neoplasm —*see* Table of Neoplasms, by site, malignant
Coding Clinic: 2016, Q4, P129

Z19.1 Hormone sensitive malignancy status
Coding Clinic: 2016, Q4, P76

Z19.2 Hormone resistant malignancy status
Castrate resistant prostate malignancy status
Coding Clinic: 2016, Q4, P76

PERSONS WITH POTENTIAL HEALTH HAZARDS RELATED TO COMMUNICABLE DISEASES (Z20-Z29)

● **Z20 Contact with and (suspected) exposure to communicable diseases**

> **Excludes1** carrier of infectious disease (Z22.-)
> diagnosed current infectious or parasitic disease - see Alphabetic Index

> **Excludes2** personal history of infectious and parasitic diseases (Z86.1-)

● **Z20.0 Contact with and (suspected) exposure to intestinal infectious diseases**

Z20.01 Contact with and (suspected) exposure to intestinal infectious diseases due to Escherichia coli (E. coli)

Z20.09 Contact with and (suspected) exposure to other intestinal infectious diseases

Z20.1 Contact with and (suspected) exposure to tuberculosis

Z20.2 Contact with and (suspected) exposure to infections with a predominantly sexual mode of transmission

Z20.3 Contact with and (suspected) exposure to rabies

Z20.4 Contact with and (suspected) exposure to rubella

Z20.5 Contact with and (suspected) exposure to viral hepatitis

Z20.6 Contact with and (suspected) exposure to human immunodeficiency virus [HIV]

> **Excludes1** asymptomatic human immunodeficiency virus [HIV]
> HIV infection status (Z21)

Z20.7 Contact with and (suspected) exposure to pediculosis, acariasis and other infestations

● **Z20.8 Contact with and (suspected) exposure to other communicable diseases**

● **Z20.81 Contact with and (suspected) exposure to other bacterial communicable diseases**

Z20.810 Contact with and (suspected) exposure to anthrax

Z20.811 Contact with and (suspected) exposure to meningococcus

Z20.818 Contact with and (suspected) exposure to other bacterial communicable diseases

- **Z20.82** **Contact with and (suspected) exposure to other viral communicable diseases**
  - Z20.820 Contact with and (suspected) exposure to varicella
  - ▶ Z20.821 Contact with and (suspected) exposure to Zika virus
  - Z20.828 Contact with and (suspected) exposure to other viral communicable diseases
    - Coding Clinic: 2016, Q4, P6-7, 121
  - **Z20.89** Contact with and (suspected) exposure to other communicable diseases
- **Z20.9** Contact with and (suspected) exposure to unspecified communicable disease

Z21   Asymptomatic human immunodeficiency virus [HIV] infection status
  HIV positive NOS
  Code first Human immunodeficiency virus [HIV] disease complicating pregnancy, childbirth and the puerperium, if applicable (O98.7-)
  Excludes1 acquired immunodeficiency syndrome (B20)
  contact with human immunodeficiency virus [HIV] (Z20.6)
  exposure to human immunodeficiency virus [HIV] (Z20.6)
  human immunodeficiency virus [HIV] disease (B20)
  inconclusive laboratory evidence of human immunodeficiency virus [HIV] (R75)

- **Z22   Carrier of infectious disease**
  Includes colonization status
  suspected carrier
  Excludes2 carrier of viral hepatitis (B18.-)
  - **Z22.0** Carrier of typhoid
  - **Z22.1** Carrier of other intestinal infectious diseases
  - **Z22.2** Carrier of diphtheria
  - **Z22.3** Carrier of other specified bacterial diseases
    - Z22.31 Carrier of bacterial disease due to meningococci
    - Z22.32 Carrier of bacterial disease due to staphylococci
      - Z22.321 Carrier or suspected carrier of Methicillin susceptible Staphylococcus aureus
        - MSSA colonization
      - Z22.322 Carrier or suspected carrier of Methicillin resistant Staphylococcus aureus
        - MRSA colonization
    - Z22.33 Carrier of bacterial disease due to streptococci
      - Z22.330 Carrier of Group B streptococcus
        - **Excludes1** Carrier of streptococcus group B (GBS) complicating pregnancy, childbirth and the puerperium (O99.82-)
      - Z22.338 Carrier of other streptococcus
    - Z22.39 Carrier of other specified bacterial diseases
  - **Z22.4** Carrier of infections with a predominantly sexual mode of transmission
  - **Z22.6** Carrier of human T-lymphotropic virus type-1 [HTLV-1] infection
  - **Z22.8** Carrier of other infectious diseases
  - **Z22.9** Carrier of infectious disease, unspecified

Z23   Encounter for immunization
  Code first any routine childhood examination
  Note: Procedure codes are required to identify the types of immunizations given.

- **Z28   Immunization not carried out and underimmunization status**
  Includes vaccination not carried out
  - **Z28.0** **Immunization not carried out because of contraindication**
    - Z28.01 Immunization not carried out because of acute illness of patient
    - Z28.02 Immunization not carried out because of chronic illness or condition of patient
    - Z28.03 Immunization not carried out because of immune compromised state of patient
    - Z28.04 Immunization not carried out because of patient allergy to vaccine or component
    - Z28.09 Immunization not carried out because of other contraindication
  - **Z28.1** Immunization not carried out because of patient decision for reasons of belief or group pressure
    Immunization not carried out because of religious belief
  - **Z28.2** **Immunization not carried out because of patient decision for other and unspecified reason**
    - Z28.20 Immunization not carried out because of patient decision for unspecified reason
    - Z28.21 Immunization not carried out because of patient refusal
    - Z28.29 Immunization not carried out because of patient decision for other reason
  - **Z28.3** Underimmunization status
    Delinquent immunization status
    Lapsed immunization schedule status
  - **Z28.8** **Immunization not carried out for other reason**
    - Z28.81 Immunization not carried out due to patient having had the disease
    - Z28.82 Immunization not carried out because of caregiver refusal
      Immunization not carried out because of guardian refusal
      Immunization not carried out because of parent refusal
      - **Excludes1** immunization not carried out because of caregiver refusal because of religious belief (Z28.1)
    - ▶ Z28.83 Immunization not carried out due to unavailability of vaccine
      - ▶ Delay in delivery of vaccine
      - ▶ Lack of availability of vaccine
      - ▶ Manufacturer delay of vaccine
    - Z28.89 Immunization not carried out for other reason
  - **Z28.9** Immunization not carried out for unspecified reason

- **Z29   Encounter for other prophylactic measures**
  Excludes1 desensitization to allergens (Z51.6)
  prophylactic surgery (Z40.-)
  Coding Clinic: 2016, Q4, P130
  - **Z29.1** **Encounter for prophylactic immunotherapy**
    Encounter for administration of immunoglobulin
    Coding Clinic: 2016, Q4, P78-79
    - Z29.11 Encounter for prophylactic immunotherapy for respiratory syncytial virus (RSV)
    - Z29.12 Encounter for prophylactic antivenin
    - Z29.13 Encounter for prophylactic Rho(D) immune globulin
    - Z29.14 Encounter for prophylactic rabies immune globin
  - **Z29.3** Encounter for prophylactic fluoride administration
    Coding Clinic: 2016, Q4, P79
  - **Z29.8** Encounter for other specified prophylactic measures
    Coding Clinic: 2016, Q4, P79
  - **Z29.9** Encounter for prophylactic measures, unspecified
    Coding Clinic: 2016, Q4, P79

CHAPTER 21 (Z00-Z99)

CHAPTER 21 (Z00-Z99)

PERSONS ENCOUNTERING HEALTH SERVICES IN CIRCUMSTANCES RELATED TO REPRODUCTION (Z30-Z39)

● **Z30 Encounter for contraceptive management**

  ● **Z30.0 Encounter for general counseling and advice on contraception**

    ● **Z30.01 Encounter for initial prescription of contraceptives**

      Excludes1 encounter for surveillance of contraceptives (Z30.4-)

      Z30.011 Encounter for initial prescription of contraceptive pills ♀

      Z30.012 Encounter for prescription of emergency contraception ♀
Encounter for postcoital contraception

      Z30.013 Encounter for initial prescription of injectable contraceptive ♀

      Z30.014 Encounter for initial prescription of intrauterine contraceptive device ♀

        Excludes1 encounter for insertion of intrauterine contraceptive device (Z30.430, Z30.432)

      Z30.015 Encounter for initial prescription of vaginal ring hormonal contraceptive ♀
Coding Clinic: 2016, Q4, P78

      Z30.016 Encounter for initial prescription of transdermal patch hormonal contraceptive device
Coding Clinic: 2016, Q4, P78

      Z30.017 Encounter for initial prescription of implantable subdermal contraceptive
Coding Clinic: 2016, Q4, P78

      Z30.018 Encounter for initial prescription of other contraceptives ♀
Encounter for initial prescription of barrier contraception
Encounter for initial prescription of diaphragm

      Z30.019 Encounter for initial prescription of contraceptives, unspecified ♀

    Z30.02 Counseling and instruction in natural family planning to avoid pregnancy

    Z30.09 Encounter for other general counseling and advice on contraception
Encounter for family planning advice NOS

  Z30.2 Encounter for sterilization

  ● **Z30.4 Encounter for surveillance of contraceptives**

    Z30.40 Encounter for surveillance of contraceptives, unspecified

    Z30.41 Encounter for surveillance of contraceptive pills ♀
Encounter for repeat prescription for contraceptive pill

    Z30.42 Encounter for surveillance of injectable contraceptive ♀

    ● **Z30.43 Encounter for surveillance of intrauterine contraceptive device**

      Z30.430 Encounter for insertion of intrauterine contraceptive device ♀

      Z30.431 Encounter for routine checking of intrauterine contraceptive device ♀

      Z30.432 Encounter for removal of intrauterine contraceptive device ♀

      Z30.433 Encounter for removal and reinsertion of intrauterine contraceptive device ♀
Encounter for replacement of intrauterine contraceptive device

    Z30.44 Encounter for surveillance of vaginal ring hormonal contraceptive device ♀
Coding Clinic: 2016, Q4, P78

    Z30.45 Encounter for surveillance of transdermal patch hormonal contraceptive device ♀
Coding Clinic: 2016, Q4, P78

    Z30.46 Encounter for surveillance of implantable subdermal contraceptive ♀
Encounter for checking, reinsertion or removal of implantable subdermal contraceptive
Coding Clinic: 2016, Q4, P78

    Z30.49 Encounter for surveillance of other contraceptives ♀
Encounter for surveillance of barrier contraception
Encounter for surveillance of diaphragm

  Z30.8 Encounter for other contraceptive management
Encounter for postvasectomy sperm count
Encounter for routine examination for contraceptive maintenance

    Excludes1 sperm count following sterilization reversal (Z31.42)
sperm count for fertility testing (Z31.41)

  Z30.9 Encounter for contraceptive management, unspecified

● **Z31 Encounter for procreative management**

  Excludes1 complications associated with artificial fertilization (N98.-)
female infertility (N97.-)
male infertility (N46.-)

  Z31.0 Encounter for reversal of previous sterilization

  ● **Z31.4 Encounter for procreative investigation and testing**

    Excludes1 postvasectomy sperm count (Z30.8)

    Z31.41 Encounter for fertility testing
Encounter for fallopian tube patency testing
Encounter for sperm count for fertility testing

    Z31.42 Aftercare following sterilization reversal
Sperm count following sterilization reversal

    ● **Z31.43 Encounter for genetic testing of female for procreative management**
Use additional code for recurrent pregnancy loss, if applicable (N96, O26.2-)

      Excludes1 nonprocreative genetic testing (Z13.7-)

      Z31.430 Encounter of female for testing for genetic disease carrier status for procreative management ♀

      Z31.438 Encounter for other genetic testing of female for procreative management ♀

    ● **Z31.44 Encounter for genetic testing of male for procreative management**

      Excludes1 nonprocreative genetic testing (Z13.7-)

      Z31.440 Encounter of male for testing for genetic disease carrier status for procreative management ♂

      Z31.441 Encounter for testing of male partner of patient with recurrent pregnancy loss ♂ A

      Z31.448 Encounter for other genetic testing of male for procreative management ♂ A

    Z31.49 Encounter for other procreative investigation and testing

  Z31.5 Encounter for procreative genetic counseling

- **Z31.6 Encounter for general counseling and advice on procreation**
  - **Z31.61 Procreative counseling and advice using natural family planning**
  - **Z31.62 Encounter for fertility preservation counseling**
    Encounter for fertility preservation counseling prior to cancer therapy
    Encounter for fertility preservation counseling prior to surgical removal of gonads
  - **Z31.69 Encounter for other general counseling and advice on procreation**
- **Z31.7 Encounter for procreative management and counseling for gestational carrier**
  - **Excludes1**   pregnant state, gestational carrier (Z33.3)
    Coding Clinic: 2016, Q4, P78
- **Z31.8 Encounter for other procreative management**
  - **Z31.81 Encounter for male factor infertility in female patient ♀**
  - **Z31.82 Encounter for Rh incompatibility status ♀**
    Coding Clinic: 2015, Q3, P40
  - **Z31.83 Encounter for assisted reproductive fertility procedure cycle ♀**
    Patient undergoing in vitro fertilization cycle
    Use additional code to identify the type of infertility
    - **Excludes1**   pre-cycle diagnosis and testing - code to reason for encounter
  - **Z31.84 Encounter for fertility preservation procedure**
    Encounter for fertility preservation procedure prior to cancer therapy
    Encounter for fertility preservation procedure prior to surgical removal of gonads
  - **Z31.89 Encounter for other procreative management**
- **Z31.9 Encounter for procreative management, unspecified**
- **Z32 Encounter for pregnancy test and childbirth and childcare instruction**
  - **Z32.0 Encounter for pregnancy test**
    - **Z32.00 Encounter for pregnancy test, result unknown ♀**
      Encounter for pregnancy test NOS
    - **Z32.01 Encounter for pregnancy test, result positive ♀**   M
    - **Z32.02 Encounter for pregnancy test, result negative ♀**   M
  - **Z32.2 Encounter for childbirth instruction**
  - **Z32.3 Encounter for childcare instruction**
    Encounter for prenatal or postpartum childcare instruction
- **Z33 Pregnant state**
  - **Z33.1 Pregnant state, incidental ♀**   M
    Pregnant state NOS
    - **Excludes1**   complications of pregnancy (O00-O9A)
      pregnant state, gestational carrier (Z33.3)
  - **Z33.2 Encounter for elective termination of pregnancy ♀**   M
    - **Excludes1**   early fetal death with retention of dead fetus (O02.1)
      late fetal death (O36.4)
      spontaneous abortion (O03)
    Coding Clinic: 2016, Q4, P130
  - **Z33.3 Pregnant state, gestational carrier ♀**
    - **Excludes1**   encounter for procreative management and counseling for gestational carrier (Z31.7)
    Coding Clinic: 2016, Q4, P78

Figure 21-1 Trimesters. (From Shiland, Betsy J. Medical Terminology & Anatomy for ICD-10 Coding, ed 2, Mosby, 2015)

- **Z34 Encounter for supervision of normal pregnancy**
  - **Excludes1**   any complication of pregnancy (O00-O9A)
    encounter for pregnancy test (Z32.0-)
    encounter for supervision of high risk pregnancy (O09.-)
    Coding Clinic: 2016, Q4, P6
  - **Z34.0 Encounter for supervision of normal first pregnancy**
    - **Z34.00 Encounter for supervision of normal first pregnancy, unspecified trimester ♀**   M
    - **Z34.01 Encounter for supervision of normal first pregnancy, first trimester ♀**   M
    - **Z34.02 Encounter for supervision of normal first pregnancy, second trimester ♀**   M
    - **Z34.03 Encounter for supervision of normal first pregnancy, third trimester ♀**   M
  - **Z34.8 Encounter for supervision of other normal pregnancy**
    - **Z34.80 Encounter for supervision of other normal pregnancy, unspecified trimester ♀**   M
    - **Z34.81 Encounter for supervision of other normal pregnancy, first trimester ♀**   M
    - **Z34.82 Encounter for supervision of other normal pregnancy, second trimester ♀**   M
    - **Z34.83 Encounter for supervision of other normal pregnancy, third trimester ♀**   M
  - **Z34.9 Encounter for supervision of normal pregnancy, unspecified**
    - **Z34.90 Encounter for supervision of normal pregnancy, unspecified, unspecified trimester ♀**   M
    - **Z34.91 Encounter for supervision of normal pregnancy, unspecified, first trimester ♀**   M
    - **Z34.92 Encounter for supervision of normal pregnancy, unspecified, second trimester ♀**   M
    - **Z34.93 Encounter for supervision of normal pregnancy, unspecified, third trimester ♀**   M
- **Z36 Encounter for antenatal screening of mother ♀**
  - **Includes**   Encounter for placental sample (taken vaginally)
    Screening is the testing for disease or disease precursors in asymptomatic individuals so that early detection and treatment can be provided for those who test positive for the disease.
  - **Excludes1**   diagnostic examination - code to sign or symptom
    encounter for suspected maternal and fetal conditions ruled out (Z03.7-)
    suspected fetal condition affecting management of pregnancy - code to condition in Chapter 15
  - **Excludes2**   abnormal findings on antenatal screening of mother (O28.-)
    genetic counseling and testing (Z31.43-, Z31.5)
    routine prenatal care (Z34)
  - **Z36.0 Encounter for antenatal screening for chromosomal anomalies ♀**   M

CHAPTER 21 (Z00-Z99)

CHAPTER 21 (Z00-Z99)

Z36.1   **Encounter for antenatal screening for raised alphafetoprotein level** ♀   M
     Encounter for antenatal screening for elevated maternal serum alphafetoprotein level

Z36.2   **Encounter for other antenatal screening follow-up** ♀   M
     Non-visualized anatomy on a previous scan

Z36.3   **Encounter for antenatal screening for malformations** ♀ M
     Screening for a suspected anomaly

Z36.4   **Encounter for antenatal screening for fetal growth retardation** ♀   M
     Intrauterine growth restriction (IUGR)/small-for-dates

Z36.5   **Encounter for antenatal screening for isoimmunization** ♀   M

● Z36.8   **Encounter for other antenatal screening**

    Z36.81   **Encounter for antenatal screening for hydrops fetalis** ♀   M

    Z36.82   **Encounter for antenatal screening for nuchal translucency** ♀   M

    Z36.83   **Encounter for fetal screening for congenital cardiac abnormalities** ♀   M

    Z36.84   **Encounter for antenatal screening for fetal lung maturity** ♀   M

    Z36.85   **Encounter for antenatal screening for Streptococcus B** ♀   M

    Z36.86   **Encounter for antenatal screening for cervical length** ♀   M
       Screening for risk of pre-term labor

    Z36.87   **Encounter for antenatal screening for uncertain dates** ♀   M

    Z36.88   **Encounter for antenatal screening for fetal macrosomia** ♀   M
       Screening for large-for-dates

    Z36.89   **Encounter for other specified antenatal screening** ♀   M

    Z36.8A   **Encounter for antenatal screening for other genetic defects** ♀   M

Z36.9   **Encounter for antenatal screening, unspecified** ♀   M

● **Z3A**   **Weeks of gestation**
   Note: Codes from category Z3A are for use, only on the maternal record, to indicate the weeks of gestation of the pregnancy, if known.
   Code first complications of pregnancy, childbirth and the puerperium (O09-O9A)
   Coding Clinic: 2016, Q4, P130; 2013, Q2, P33

● Z3A.0   **Weeks of gestation of pregnancy, unspecified or less than 10 weeks**

    Z3A.00   **Weeks of gestation of pregnancy not specified** ♀   M

    Z3A.01   **Less than 8 weeks gestation of pregnancy** ♀   M

    Z3A.08   **8 weeks gestation of pregnancy** ♀   M

    Z3A.09   **9 weeks gestation of pregnancy** ♀   M

● Z3A.1   **Weeks of gestation of pregnancy, weeks 10-19**

    Z3A.10   **10 weeks gestation of pregnancy** ♀   M
    Z3A.11   **11 weeks gestation of pregnancy** ♀   M
    Z3A.12   **12 weeks gestation of pregnancy** ♀   M
    Z3A.13   **13 weeks gestation of pregnancy** ♀   M
    Z3A.14   **14 weeks gestation of pregnancy** ♀   M
    Z3A.15   **15 weeks gestation of pregnancy** ♀   M
    Z3A.16   **16 weeks gestation of pregnancy** ♀   M
       Coding Clinic: 2016, Q4, P5
    Z3A.17   **17 weeks gestation of pregnancy** ♀   M
    Z3A.18   **18 weeks gestation of pregnancy** ♀   M
    Z3A.19   **19 weeks gestation of pregnancy** ♀   M

● Z3A.2   **Weeks of gestation of pregnancy, weeks 20-29**

    Z3A.20   **20 weeks gestation of pregnancy** ♀   M
       Coding Clinic: 2016, Q4, P6
    Z3A.21   **21 weeks gestation of pregnancy** ♀   M
    Z3A.22   **22 weeks gestation of pregnancy** ♀   M
       Coding Clinic: 2016, Q4, P6
    Z3A.23   **23 weeks gestation of pregnancy** ♀   M
    Z3A.24   **24 weeks gestation of pregnancy** ♀   M
    Z3A.25   **25 weeks gestation of pregnancy** ♀   M
    Z3A.26   **26 weeks gestation of pregnancy** ♀   M
    Z3A.27   **27 weeks gestation of pregnancy** ♀   M
    Z3A.28   **28 weeks gestation of pregnancy** ♀   M
    Z3A.29   **29 weeks gestation of pregnancy** ♀   M

● Z3A.3   **Weeks of gestation of pregnancy, weeks 30-39**

    Z3A.30   **30 weeks gestation of pregnancy** ♀   M
    Z3A.31   **31 weeks gestation of pregnancy** ♀   M
    Z3A.32   **32 weeks gestation of pregnancy** ♀   M
       Coding Clinic: 2016, Q4, P6
    Z3A.33   **33 weeks gestation of pregnancy** ♀   M
    Z3A.34   **34 weeks gestation of pregnancy** ♀   M
    Z3A.35   **35 weeks gestation of pregnancy** ♀   M
    Z3A.36   **36 weeks gestation of pregnancy** ♀   M
    Z3A.37   **37 weeks gestation of pregnancy** ♀   M
    Z3A.38   **38 weeks gestation of pregnancy** ♀   M
       Coding Clinic: 2016, Q2, P34
    Z3A.39   **39 weeks gestation of pregnancy** ♀   M

● Z3A.4   **Weeks of gestation of pregnancy, weeks 40 or greater**

    Z3A.40   **40 weeks gestation of pregnancy** ♀   M
    Z3A.41   **41 weeks gestation of pregnancy** ♀   M
    Z3A.42   **42 weeks gestation of pregnancy** ♀   M
    Z3A.49   **Greater than 42 weeks gestation of pregnancy** ♀   M

● **Z37**   **Outcome of delivery**
   This category is intended for use as an additional code to identify the outcome of delivery on the mother's record. It is not for use on the newborn record.
   Excludes1   stillbirth (P95)

Z37.0   **Single live birth** ♀   M
     Coding Clinic: 2016, Q2, P34

Z37.1   **Single stillbirth** ♀   M

Z37.2   **Twins, both liveborn** ♀   M

Z37.3   **Twins, one liveborn and one stillborn** ♀   M

Z37.4   **Twins, both stillborn** ♀   M

● Z37.5   **Other multiple births, all liveborn**

    Z37.50   **Multiple births, unspecified, all liveborn** ♀   M
    Z37.51   **Triplets, all liveborn** ♀   M
    Z37.52   **Quadruplets, all liveborn** ♀   M
    Z37.53   **Quintuplets, all liveborn** ♀   M
    Z37.54   **Sextuplets, all liveborn** ♀   M
    Z37.59   **Other multiple births, all liveborn** ♀   M

● Z37.6   **Other multiple births, some liveborn**

    Z37.60   **Multiple births, unspecified, some liveborn** ♀ M
    Z37.61   **Triplets, some liveborn** ♀   M
    Z37.62   **Quadruplets, some liveborn** ♀   M
    Z37.63   **Quintuplets, some liveborn** ♀   M
    Z37.64   **Sextuplets, some liveborn** ♀   M
    Z37.69   **Other multiple births, some liveborn** ♀   M

Z37.7   **Other multiple births, all stillborn** ♀   M

Z37.9   **Outcome of delivery, unspecified** ♀   M
     Multiple birth NOS
     Single birth NOS

▶ New   ⇒ Revised   ~~deleted~~ Deleted   Excludes 1   Excludes 2   Includes   Use additional   Code first   Code also   Key words
OGCR Official Guidelines   X Assign placeholder X   ● Use Additional Character(s)   ▶ Manifestation Code   **Coding Clinic**

● **Z38**   **Liveborn infants according to place of birth and type of delivery**
This category is for use as the principal code on the initial record of a newborn baby. It is to be used for the initial birth record only. It is not to be used on the mother's record.
Coding Clinic: 2017, Q2, P6-7; 2016, Q4, P126-127, 130; 2015, Q2, P15

   ● **Z38.0**   **Single liveborn infant, born in hospital**
Single liveborn infant, born in birthing center or other health care facility
Coding Clinic: 2017, Q2, P5-7

     Z38.00   **Single liveborn infant, delivered vaginally**   N
Coding Clinic: 2016, Q4, P7, 55

     Z38.01   **Single liveborn infant, delivered by cesarean**   N
Coding Clinic: 2017, Q2, P7; 2016, Q3, P18

   Z38.1   Single liveborn infant, **born outside hospital**   N

   Z38.2   Single liveborn infant, **unspecified as to place of birth**   N
Single liveborn infant NOS

   ● **Z38.3**   Twin liveborn infant, **born in hospital**

     Z38.30   Twin liveborn infant, **delivered vaginally**   N

     Z38.31   Twin liveborn infant, **delivered by cesarean**   N

   Z38.4   Twin liveborn infant, **born outside hospital**   N

   Z38.5   Twin liveborn infant, **unspecified as to place of birth**   N

   ● **Z38.6**   Other multiple liveborn infant, **born in hospital**

     Z38.61   Triplet liveborn infant, **delivered vaginally**   N

     Z38.62   Triplet liveborn infant, **delivered by cesarean**   N

     Z38.63   Quadruplet liveborn infant, **delivered vaginally**   N

     Z38.64   Quadruplet liveborn infant, **delivered by cesarean**   N

     Z38.65   Quintuplet liveborn infant, **delivered vaginally**   N

     Z38.66   Quintuplet liveborn infant, **delivered by cesarean**   N

     Z38.68   Other multiple liveborn infant, **delivered vaginally**   N

     Z38.69   Other multiple liveborn infant, **delivered by cesarean**   N

   Z38.7   Other multiple liveborn infant, **born outside hospital**   N

   Z38.8   Other multiple liveborn infant, **unspecified as to place of birth**   N

● **Z39**   **Encounter for maternal postpartum care and examination**

   Z39.0   **Encounter for care and examination of mother immediately after delivery** ♀   M
Care and observation in uncomplicated cases when the delivery occurs outside a healthcare facility

     Excludes1   care for postpartum complication - see Alphabetic index

   Z39.1   **Encounter for care and examination of lactating mother** ♀   M
Encounter for supervision of lactation

     Excludes1   disorders of lactation (O92.-)

   Z39.2   **Encounter for routine postpartum follow-up** ♀   M

ENCOUNTERS FOR OTHER SPECIFIC HEALTH CARE (Z40-Z53)

Categories Z40-Z53 are intended for use to indicate a reason for care. They may be used for patients who have already been treated for a disease or injury, but who are receiving aftercare or prophylactic care, or care to consolidate the treatment, or to deal with a residual state

   Excludes2   follow-up examination for medical surveillance after treatment (Z08-Z09)

● **Z40**   **Encounter for prophylactic surgery**

   Excludes1   organ donations (Z52.-)
therapeutic organ removal - code to condition
Coding Clinic: 2016, Q4, P79

   ● **Z40.0**   **Encounter for prophylactic surgery for risk factors related to malignant neoplasms**
Admission for prophylactic organ removal
Use additional code to identify risk factor

     Z40.00   **Encounter for prophylactic removal of unspecified organ**

     Z40.01   **Encounter for prophylactic removal of breast**

     Z40.02   **Encounter for prophylactic removal of ovary(s)** ♀
Encounter for prophylactic removal of ovary(s) and fallopian tube(s)

     Z40.03   **Encounter for prophylactic removal of fallopian tube(s)** ♀

     Z40.09   **Encounter for prophylactic removal of other organ**

   Z40.8   Encounter for **other prophylactic surgery**

   Z40.9   Encounter for prophylactic surgery, **unspecified**

● **Z41**   **Encounter for procedures for purposes other than remedying health state**

   Z41.1   Encounter for **cosmetic surgery**
Encounter for cosmetic breast implant
Encounter for cosmetic procedure

     Excludes1   encounter for plastic and reconstructive surgery following medical procedure or healed injury (Z42.-)
encounter for post-mastectomy breast implantation (Z42.1)

   Z41.2   Encounter for routine and ritual **male circumcision** ♂

   Z41.3   Encounter for **ear piercing**

   Z41.8   Encounter for **other procedures** for purposes other than remedying health state

   Z41.9   Encounter for procedure for purposes other than remedying health state, **unspecified**

● **Z42**   **Encounter for plastic and reconstructive surgery following medical procedure or healed injury**

   Excludes1   encounter for cosmetic plastic surgery (Z41.1)
encounter for plastic surgery for treatment of current injury - code to relevent injury

   Z42.1   Encounter for **breast reconstruction following mastectomy**   A

     Excludes1   deformity and disproportion of reconstructed breast (N65.1-)

   Z42.8   Encounter for **other plastic and reconstructive surgery following medical procedure or healed injury**
Coding Clinic: 2017, Q1, P42

CHAPTER 21 (Z00-Z99)

● **Z43**   **Encounter for attention to artificial openings**

    Includes   closure of artificial openings
                    passage of sounds or bougies through artificial openings
                    reforming artificial openings
                    removal of catheter from artificial openings
                    toilet or cleansing of artificial openings

    Excludes1   complications of external stoma (J95.0-, K94.-, N99.5-)

    Excludes2   fitting and adjustment of prosthetic and other devices (Z44-Z46)

  Z43.0   **Encounter for attention to tracheostomy**

  Z43.1   **Encounter for attention to gastrostomy**

      Excludes2   artificial opening status only, without need for care (Z93.-)

  Z43.2   **Encounter for attention to ileostomy**
        Coding Clinic: 2016, Q3, P5

  Z43.3   **Encounter for attention to colostomy**

  Z43.4   **Encounter for attention to other artificial openings of digestive tract**

  Z43.5   **Encounter for attention to cystostomy**

  Z43.6   **Encounter for attention to other artificial openings of urinary tract**
       Encounter for attention to nephrostomy
       Encounter for attention to ureterostomy
       Encounter for attention to urethrostomy

  Z43.7   **Encounter for attention to artificial vagina**

  Z43.8   **Encounter for attention to other artificial openings**

  Z43.9   **Encounter for attention to unspecified artificial opening**

● **Z44**   **Encounter for fitting and adjustment of external prosthetic device**

    Includes   removal or replacement of external prosthetic device

    Excludes1   malfunction or other complications of device - see Alphabetical Index presence of prosthetic device (Z97.-)

  ● **Z44.0**   **Encounter for fitting and adjustment of artificial arm**

    ● **Z44.00**   **Encounter for fitting and adjustment of unspecified artificial arm**

      Z44.001   **Encounter for fitting and adjustment of unspecified right artificial arm**

      Z44.002   **Encounter for fitting and adjustment of unspecified left artificial arm**

      Z44.009   **Encounter for fitting and adjustment of unspecified artificial arm, unspecified arm**

    ● **Z44.01**   **Encounter for fitting and adjustment of complete artificial arm**

      Z44.011   **Encounter for fitting and adjustment of complete right artificial arm**

      Z44.012   **Encounter for fitting and adjustment of complete left artificial arm**

      Z44.019   **Encounter for fitting and adjustment of complete artificial arm, unspecified arm**

    ● **Z44.02**   **Encounter for fitting and adjustment of partial artificial arm**

      Z44.021   **Encounter for fitting and adjustment of partial artificial right arm**

      Z44.022   **Encounter for fitting and adjustment of partial artificial left arm**

      Z44.029   **Encounter for fitting and adjustment of partial artificial arm, unspecified arm**

● **Z44.1**   **Encounter for fitting and adjustment of artificial leg**

  ● **Z44.10**   **Encounter for fitting and adjustment of unspecified artificial leg**

    Z44.101   **Encounter for fitting and adjustment of unspecified right artificial leg**

    Z44.102   **Encounter for fitting and adjustment of unspecified left artificial leg**

    Z44.109   **Encounter for fitting and adjustment of unspecified artificial leg, unspecified leg**

  ● **Z44.11**   **Encounter for fitting and adjustment of complete artificial leg**

    Z44.111   **Encounter for fitting and adjustment of complete right artificial leg**

    Z44.112   **Encounter for fitting and adjustment of complete left artificial leg**

    Z44.119   **Encounter for fitting and adjustment of complete artificial leg, unspecified leg**

  ● **Z44.12**   **Encounter for fitting and adjustment of partial artificial leg**

    Z44.121   **Encounter for fitting and adjustment of partial artificial right leg**

    Z44.122   **Encounter for fitting and adjustment of partial artificial left leg**

    Z44.129   **Encounter for fitting and adjustment of partial artificial leg, unspecified leg**

● **Z44.2**   **Encounter for fitting and adjustment of artificial eye**

    Excludes1   mechanical complication of ocular prosthesis (T85.3)

  Z44.20   **Encounter for fitting and adjustment of artificial eye, unspecified**

  Z44.21   **Encounter for fitting and adjustment of artificial right eye**

  Z44.22   **Encounter for fitting and adjustment of artificial left eye**

● **Z44.3**   **Encounter for fitting and adjustment of external breast prosthesis**

    Excludes1   complications of breast implant (T85.4-)
               encounter for adjustment or removal of breast implant (Z45.81-)
               encounter for initial breast implant insertion for cosmetic breast augmentation (Z41.1)
               encounter for breast reconstruction following mastectomy (Z42.1)

  Z44.30   **Encounter for fitting and adjustment of external breast prosthesis, unspecified breast**

  Z44.31   **Encounter for fitting and adjustment of external right breast prosthesis**

  Z44.32   **Encounter for fitting and adjustment of external left breast prosthesis**

  Z44.8   **Encounter for fitting and adjustment of other external prosthetic devices**

  Z44.9   **Encounter for fitting and adjustment of unspecified external prosthetic device**

▶ New   ⇒ Revised   ~~deleted~~ Deleted   Excludes 1   Excludes 2   Includes   Use additional   Code first   Code also   Key words
OGCR Official Guidelines   X Assign placeholder X   ● Use Additional Character(s)   ▸ Manifestation Code   **Coding Clinic**

● **Z45**   **Encounter for adjustment and management of implanted device**

Includes	removal or replacement of implanted device
Excludes1	malfunction or other complications of device - see Alphabetical Index
Excludes2	encounter for fitting and adjustment of non-implanted device (Z46.-)

● **Z45.0**   **Encounter for adjustment and management of cardiac device**

  ● **Z45.01**   **Encounter for adjustment and management of cardiac pacemaker**
      Encounter for adjustment and management of cardiac resynchronization therapy pacemaker (CRT-P)

      Excludes1   encounter for adjustment and management of automatic implantable cardiac defibrillator with synchronous cardiac pacemaker (Z45.02)

     Z45.010   **Encounter for checking and testing of cardiac pacemaker pulse generator [battery]**
       Encounter for replacing cardiac pacemaker pulse generator [battery]

     Z45.018   **Encounter for adjustment and management of other part of cardiac pacemaker**

       Excludes2   presence of prosthetic and other devices (Z95-Z97)

     Z45.02   **Encounter for adjustment and management of automatic implantable cardiac defibrillator**
       Encounter for adjustment and management of automatic implantable cardiac defibrillator with synchronous cardiac pacemaker
       Encounter for adjustment and management of cardiac resynchronization therapy defibrillator (CRT-D)

     Z45.09   **Encounter for adjustment and management of other cardiac device**

Z45.1   **Encounter for adjustment and management of infusion pump**

Z45.2   **Encounter for adjustment and management of vascular access device**
   Encounter for adjustment and management of vascular catheters

   Excludes1   encounter for adjustment and management of renal dialysis catheter (Z49.01)

● **Z45.3**   **Encounter for adjustment and management of implanted devices of the special senses**

   Z45.31   **Encounter for adjustment and management of implanted visual substitution device**

  ● **Z45.32**   **Encounter for adjustment and management of implanted hearing device**

     Excludes1   encounter for fitting and adjustment of hearing aide (Z46.1)

     Z45.320   **Encounter for adjustment and management of bone conduction device**

     Z45.321   **Encounter for adjustment and management of cochlear device**

     Z45.328   **Encounter for adjustment and management of other implanted hearing device**

● **Z45.4**   **Encounter for adjustment and management of implanted nervous system device**

   Z45.41   **Encounter for adjustment and management of cerebrospinal fluid drainage device**
     Encounter for adjustment and management of cerebral ventricular (communicating) shunt

   Z45.42   **Encounter for adjustment and management of neuropacemaker (brain) (peripheral nerve) (spinal cord)**

   Z45.49   **Encounter for adjustment and management of other implanted nervous system device**

● **Z45.8**   **Encounter for adjustment and management of other implanted devices**

  ● **Z45.81**   **Encounter for adjustment or removal of breast implant**
     Encounter for elective implant exchange (different material) (different size)
     Encounter removal of tissue expander without synchronous insertion of permanent implant

     Excludes1   complications of breast implant (T85.4-)
       encounter for initial breast implant insertion for cosmetic breast augmentation (Z41.1)
       encounter for breast reconstruction following mastectomy (Z42.1)

     Z45.811   **Encounter for adjustment or removal of right breast implant**

     Z45.812   **Encounter for adjustment or removal of left breast implant**

     Z45.819   **Encounter for adjustment or removal of unspecified breast implant**

   Z45.82   **Encounter for adjustment or removal of myringotomy device (stent) (tube)**

   Z45.89   **Encounter for adjustment and management of other implanted devices**

Z45.9   **Encounter for adjustment and management of unspecified implanted device**

● **Z46**   **Encounter for fitting and adjustment of other devices**

Includes	removal or replacement of other device
Excludes1	malfunction or other complications of device - see Alphabetical Index
Excludes2	encounter for fitting and management of implanted devices (Z45.-)

       issue of repeat prescription only (Z76.0)
       presence of prosthetic and other devices (Z95-Z97)

Z46.0   **Encounter for fitting and adjustment of spectacles and contact lenses**

Z46.1   **Encounter for fitting and adjustment of hearing aid**

   Excludes1   encounter for adjustment and management of implanted hearing device (Z45.32-)

Z46.2   **Encounter for fitting and adjustment of other devices related to nervous system and special senses**

   Excludes2   encounter for adjustment and management of implanted nervous system device (Z45.4-)
     encounter for adjustment and management of implanted visual substitution device (Z45.31)

Z46.3   **Encounter for fitting and adjustment of dental prosthetic device**
   Encounter for fitting and adjustment of dentures

Z46.4   **Encounter for fitting and adjustment of orthodontic device**

CHAPTER 21 (Z00-Z99)

● **Z46.5** **Encounter for fitting and adjustment of other gastrointestinal appliance and device**

> **Excludes1** encounter for attention to artificial openings of digestive tract (Z43.1-Z43.4)

> **Z46.51** **Encounter for fitting and adjustment of gastric lap band**

> **Z46.59** **Encounter for fitting and adjustment of other gastrointestinal appliance and device**

Z46.6 **Encounter for fitting and adjustment of urinary device**

> **Excludes2** attention to artificial openings of urinary tract (Z43.5, Z43.6)

● **Z46.8** **Encounter for fitting and adjustment of other specified devices**

> **Z46.81** **Encounter for fitting and adjustment of insulin pump**
> > Encounter for insulin pump instruction and training
> > Encounter for insulin pump titration

> **Z46.82** **Encounter for fitting and adjustment of non-vascular catheter**

> **Z46.89** **Encounter for fitting and adjustment of other specified devices**
> > Encounter for fitting and adjustment of wheelchair

Z46.9 **Encounter for fitting and adjustment of unspecified device**

● **Z47** **Orthopedic aftercare**

> **Excludes1** aftercare for healing fracture - code to fracture with 7th character D

Z47.1 **Aftercare following joint replacement surgery**
> Use additional code to identify the joint (Z96.6-)

Z47.2 **Encounter for removal of internal fixation device**

> **Excludes1** encounter for adjustment of internal fixation device for fracture treatment - code to fracture with appropriate 7th character
> > encounter for removal of external fixation device - code to fracture with 7th character D
> > infection or inflammatory reaction to internal fixation device (T84.6-)
> > mechanical complication of internal fixation device (T84.1-)

● **Z47.3** **Aftercare following explantation of joint prosthesis**
> Aftercare following explantation of joint prosthesis, staged procedure
> Encounter for joint prosthesis insertion following prior explantation of joint prosthesis
> **Coding Clinic: 2015, Q1, P17**

> **Z47.31** **Aftercare following explantation of shoulder joint prosthesis**
> > **Excludes1** acquired absence of shoulder joint following prior explantation of shoulder joint prosthesis (Z89.23-)
> > > shoulder joint prosthesis explantation status (Z89.23-)

> **Z47.32** **Aftercare following explantation of hip joint prosthesis**
> > **Excludes1** acquired absence of hip joint following prior explantation of hip joint prosthesis (Z89.62-)
> > > hip joint prosthesis explantation status (Z89.62-)
> > **Coding Clinic: 2015, Q1, P17**

> **Z47.33** **Aftercare following explantation of knee joint prosthesis**
> > **Excludes1** acquired absence of knee joint following prior explantation of knee prosthesis (Z89.52-)
> > > knee joint prosthesis explantation status (Z89.52-)

● **Z47.8** **Encounter for other orthopedic aftercare**

> **Z47.81** **Encounter for orthopedic aftercare following surgical amputation**
> > Use additional code to identify the limb amputated (Z89.-)

> **Z47.82** **Encounter for orthopedic aftercare following scoliosis surgery**

> **Z47.89** **Encounter for other orthopedic aftercare**
> > **Coding Clinic: 2015, Q1, P8**

● **Z48** **Encounter for other postprocedural aftercare**

> **Excludes1** encounter for aftercare following injury - code to Injury, by site, with appropriate 7th character for subsequent encounter
> > encounter for follow-up examination after completed treatment (Z08-Z09)

> **Excludes2** encounter for attention to artificial openings (Z43.-)
> > encounter for fitting and adjustment of prosthetic and other devices (Z44-Z46)

● **Z48.0** **Encounter for attention to dressings, sutures and drains**

> **Excludes1** encounter for planned postprocedural wound closure (Z48.1)

> **Z48.00** **Encounter for change or removal of nonsurgical wound dressing**
> > Encounter for change or removal of wound dressing NOS

> **Z48.01** **Encounter for change or removal of surgical wound dressing**
> > **Coding Clinic: 2015, Q4, P38**

> **Z48.02** **Encounter for removal of sutures**
> > Encounter for removal of staples
> > **Coding Clinic: 2015, Q1, P6**

> **Z48.03** **Encounter for change or removal of drains**

Z48.1 **Encounter for planned postprocedural wound closure**

> **Excludes1** encounter for attention to dressings and sutures (Z48.0-)

● **Z48.2** **Encounter for aftercare following organ transplant**

> **Z48.21** **Encounter for aftercare following heart transplant**

> **Z48.22** **Encounter for aftercare following kidney transplant**

> **Z48.23** **Encounter for aftercare following liver transplant**

> **Z48.24** **Encounter for aftercare following lung transplant**

> ● **Z48.28** **Encounter for aftercare following multiple organ transplant**
> > **Z48.280** **Encounter for aftercare following heart-lung transplant**
> > **Z48.288** **Encounter for aftercare following multiple organ transplant**

> ● **Z48.29** **Encounter for aftercare following other organ transplant**
> > **Z48.290** **Encounter for aftercare following bone marrow transplant**
> > **Z48.298** **Encounter for aftercare following other organ transplant**

Z48.3 **Aftercare following surgery for neoplasm**
> Use additional code to identify the neoplasm

▶ New   ➡ Revised   ~~deleted~~ Deleted   Excludes 1   Excludes 2   Includes   Use additional   Code first   Code also   Key words

OGCR Official Guidelines   X Assign placeholder X   ● Use Additional Character(s)   ▷ Manifestation Code   **Coding Clinic**

- **Z48.8**   **Encounter for other specified postprocedural aftercare**
  - **Z48.81**   **Encounter for surgical aftercare following surgery on specified body systems**
    These codes identify the body system requiring aftercare. They are for use in conjunction with other aftercare codes to fully explain the aftercare encounter. The condition treated should also be coded if still present.

    Excludes1   aftercare for injury - code the injury with 7th character D
    aftercare following surgery for neoplasm (Z48.3)

    Excludes2   aftercare following organ transplant (Z48.2-)
    orthopedic aftercare (Z47.-)

    - **Z48.810**   Encounter for surgical aftercare following surgery on the sense organs
    - **Z48.811**   Encounter for surgical aftercare following surgery on the nervous system

      Excludes2   encounter for surgical aftercare following surgery on the sense organs (Z48.810)

    - **Z48.812**   Encounter for surgical aftercare following surgery on the circulatory system
      Coding Clinic: 2012, Q4, P96
    - **Z48.813**   Encounter for surgical aftercare following surgery on the respiratory system
    - **Z48.814**   Encounter for surgical aftercare following surgery on the teeth or oral cavity
    - **Z48.815**   Encounter for surgical aftercare following surgery on the digestive system
      Coding Clinic: 2015, Q4, P38
    - **Z48.816**   Encounter for surgical aftercare following surgery on the genitourinary system

      Excludes1   encounter for aftercare following sterilization reversal (Z31.42)

    - **Z48.817**   Encounter for surgical aftercare following surgery on the skin and subcutaneous tissue
      Coding Clinic: 2015, Q1, P6
  - **Z48.89**   Encounter for other specified surgical aftercare
- **Z49**   **Encounter for care involving renal dialysis**
  Code also associated end stage renal disease (N18.6)
  - **Z49.0**   **Preparatory care for renal dialysis**
    Encounter for dialysis instruction and training
    - **Z49.01**   Encounter for fitting and adjustment of extracorporeal dialysis catheter
      Removal or replacement of renal dialysis catheter
      Toilet or cleansing of renal dialysis catheter
    - **Z49.02**   Encounter for fitting and adjustment of peritoneal dialysis catheter
  - **Z49.3**   **Encounter for adequacy testing for dialysis**
    - **Z49.31**   Encounter for adequacy testing for hemodialysis
    - **Z49.32**   Encounter for adequacy testing for peritoneal dialysis
      Encounter for peritoneal equilibration test

- **Z51**   **Encounter for other aftercare and medical care**
  Code also condition requiring care

  Excludes1   follow-up examination after treatment (Z08-Z09)
  Coding Clinic: 2017, Q1, P49; 2016, Q4, P130
  - **Z51.0**   **Encounter for antineoplastic radiation therapy**
    Coding Clinic: 2017, Q4, P103
  - **Z51.1**   **Encounter for antineoplastic chemotherapy and immunotherapy**

    Excludes2   encounter for chemotherapy and immunotherapy for nonneoplastic condition-code to condition

    - **Z51.11**   Encounter for antineoplastic chemotherapy
      Coding Clinic: 2015, Q3, P19
    - **Z51.12**   Encounter for antineoplastic immunotherapy
  - **Z51.5**   **Encounter for palliative care**
    Coding Clinic: 2017, Q1, P48-49
  - **Z51.6**   **Encounter for desensitization to allergens**
    Coding Clinic: 2016, Q4, P77-79
  - **Z51.8**   **Encounter for other specified aftercare**

    Excludes1   holiday relief care (Z75.5)
    - **Z51.81**   Encounter for therapeutic drug level monitoring
      Code also any long-term (current) drug therapy (Z79.-)

      Excludes1   encounter for blood-drug test for administrative or medicolegal reasons (Z02.83)

    - **Z51.89**   Encounter for other specified aftercare
      Coding Clinic: 2012, Q4, P96-97
- **Z52**   **Donors of organs and tissues**

  Includes   autologous and other living donors
  Excludes1   cadaveric donor - omit code
  examination of potential donor (Z00.5)
  Coding Clinic: 2012, Q4, P100
  - **Z52.0**   **Blood donor**
    - **Z52.00**   Unspecified blood donor
      - Z52.000   Unspecified donor, whole blood
      - Z52.001   Unspecified donor, stem cells
      - Z52.008   Unspecified donor, other blood
    - **Z52.01**   Autologous blood donor
      - Z52.010   Autologous donor, whole blood
      - Z52.011   Autologous donor, stem cells
      - Z52.018   Autologous donor, other blood
    - **Z52.09**   Other blood donor
      Volunteer donor
      - Z52.090   Other blood donor, whole blood
      - Z52.091   Other blood donor, stem cells
      - Z52.098   Other blood donor, other blood
  - **Z52.1**   **Skin donor**
    - Z52.10   Skin donor, unspecified
    - Z52.11   Skin donor, autologous
    - Z52.19   Skin donor, other
  - **Z52.2**   **Bone donor**
    - Z52.20   Bone donor, unspecified
    - Z52.21   Bone donor, autologous
    - Z52.29   Bone donor, other
  - **Z52.3**   **Bone marrow donor**
  - **Z52.4**   **Kidney donor**
  - **Z52.5**   **Cornea donor**
  - **Z52.6**   **Liver donor**
    Coding Clinic: 2012, Q4, P100

● **Z52.8** Donor of other specified organs or tissues

  ● **Z52.81** Egg (Oocyte) donor

    Z52.810 Egg (Oocyte) donor under age 35, anonymous recipient ♀
      Egg donor under age 35 NOS

    Z52.811 Egg (Oocyte) donor under age 35, designated recipient ♀

    Z52.812 Egg (Oocyte) donor age 35 and over, anonymous recipient ♀
      Egg donor age 35 and over NOS

    Z52.813 Egg (Oocyte) donor age 35 and over, designated recipient ♀

    Z52.819 Egg (Oocyte) donor, unspecified ♀

  Z52.89 Donor of other specified organs or tissues

Z52.9 Donor of unspecified organ or tissue
  Donor NOS

● **Z53** Persons encountering health services for specific procedures and treatment, not carried out

  ● **Z53.0** Procedure and treatment not carried out because of contraindication

    Z53.01 Procedure and treatment not carried out due to patient smoking

    Z53.09 Procedure and treatment not carried out because of other contraindication

  Z53.1 Procedure and treatment not carried out because of patient's decision for reasons of belief and group pressure

  ● **Z53.2** Procedure and treatment not carried out because of patient's decision for other and unspecified reasons

    Z53.20 Procedure and treatment not carried out because of patient's decision for unspecified reasons

    Z53.21 Procedure and treatment not carried out due to patient leaving prior to being seen by health care provider

    Z53.29 Procedure and treatment not carried out because of patient's decision for other reasons

  ● **Z53.3** Procedure converted to open procedure
    Coding Clinic: 2016, Q4, P79

    Z53.31 Laparoscopic surgical procedure converted to open procedure
      Coding Clinic: 2016, Q4, P100

    Z53.32 Thoracoscopic surgical procedure converted to open procedure

    Z53.33 Arthroscopic surgical procedure converted to open procedure

    Z53.39 Other specified procedure converted to open procedure

  Z53.8 Procedure and treatment not carried out for other reasons

  Z53.9 Procedure and treatment not carried out, unspecified reason

---

PERSONS WITH POTENTIAL HEALTH HAZARDS RELATED TO SOCIOECONOMIC AND PSYCHOSOCIAL CIRCUMSTANCES (Z55-Z65)

● **Z55** Problems related to education and literacy

  Excludes1 disorders of psychological development (F80-F89)

  Z55.0 Illiteracy and low-level literacy

  Z55.1 Schooling unavailable and unattainable

  Z55.2 Failed school examinations

  Z55.3 Underachievement in school

  Z55.4 Educational maladjustment and discord with teachers and classmates

  Z55.8 Other problems related to education and literacy
    Problems related to inadequate teaching

  Z55.9 Problems related to education and literacy, unspecified
    Academic problems NOS

● **Z56** Problems related to employment and unemployment

  Excludes2 occupational exposure to risk factors (Z57.-) problems related to housing and economic circumstances (Z59.-)

  Z56.0 Unemployment, unspecified

  Z56.1 Change of job

  Z56.2 Threat of job loss

  Z56.3 Stressful work schedule

  Z56.4 Discord with boss and workmates

  Z56.5 Uncongenial work environment
    Difficult conditions at work

  Z56.6 Other physical and mental strain related to work

  ● **Z56.8** Other problems related to employment

    Z56.81 Sexual harassment on the job

    Z56.82 Military deployment status
      Individual (civilian or military) currently deployed in theater or in support of military war, peacekeeping and humanitarian operations

    Z56.89 Other problems related to employment

  Z56.9 Unspecified problems related to employment
    Occupational problems NOS

● **Z57** Occupational exposure to risk factors

  Z57.0 Occupational exposure to noise

  Z57.1 Occupational exposure to radiation

  Z57.2 Occupational exposure to dust

  ● **Z57.3** Occupational exposure to other air contaminants

    Z57.31 Occupational exposure to environmental tobacco smoke

      Excludes2 exposure to environmental tobacco smoke (Z77.22)

    Z57.39 Occupational exposure to other air contaminants

  Z57.4 Occupational exposure to toxic agents in agriculture
    Occupational exposure to solids, liquids, gases or vapors in agriculture

  Z57.5 Occupational exposure to toxic agents in other industries
    Occupational exposure to solids, liquids, gases or vapors in other industries

  Z57.6 Occupational exposure to extreme temperature

  Z57.7 Occupational exposure to vibration

  Z57.8 Occupational exposure to other risk factors

  Z57.9 Occupational exposure to unspecified risk factor

● **Z59** Problems related to housing and economic circumstances

  Excludes2 problems related to upbringing (Z62.-)

  Z59.0 Homelessness

  Z59.1 Inadequate housing
    Lack of heating
    Restriction of space
    Technical defects in home preventing adequate care
    Unsatisfactory surroundings

    Excludes1 problems related to the natural and physical environment (Z77.1-)

  Z59.2 Discord with neighbors, lodgers and landlord

  Z59.3 Problems related to living in residential institution
    Boarding-school resident

    Excludes1 institutional upbringing (Z62.2)

  Z59.4 Lack of adequate food and safe drinking water
    Inadequate drinking water supply

    Excludes1 effects of hunger (T73.0)
      inappropriate diet or eating habits (Z72.4)
      malnutrition (E40-E46)

  Z59.5 Extreme poverty

  Z59.6 Low income

  Z59.7 Insufficient social insurance and welfare support

A

▶ New   ➠ Revised   ~~deleted~~ Deleted   Excludes 1   Excludes 2   Includes   Use additional   Code first   Code also   Key words

OGCR Official Guidelines   X Assign placeholder X   ● Use Additional Character(s)   ▶ Manifestation Code   **Coding Clinic**

Z59.8   **Other problems related to housing and economic circumstances**
       Foreclosure on loan
       Isolated dwelling
       Problems with creditors

Z59.9   **Problem related to housing and economic circumstances, unspecified**

● **Z60**   **Problems related to social environment**

Z60.0   **Problems of adjustment to life-cycle transitions**
       Empty nest syndrome
       Phase of life problem
       Problem with adjustment to retirement [pension]

Z60.2   **Problems related to living alone**

Z60.3   **Acculturation difficulty**
       Problem with migration
       Problem with social transplantation

Z60.4   **Social exclusion and rejection**
       Exclusion and rejection on the basis of personal characteristics, such as unusual physical appearance, illness or behavior.

       Excludes1   target of adverse discrimination such as for racial or religious reasons (Z60.5)

Z60.5   **Target of (perceived) adverse discrimination and persecution**

       Excludes1   social exclusion and rejection (Z60.4)

Z60.8   **Other problems related to social environment**

Z60.9   **Problem related to social environment, unspecified**

● **Z62**   **Problems related to upbringing**

       Includes   current and past negative life events in childhood
                        current and past problems of a child related to upbringing

       Excludes2   maltreatment syndrome (T74.-)
                        problems related to housing and economic circumstances (Z59.-)

Z62.0   **Inadequate parental supervision and control**

Z62.1   **Parental overprotection**

● **Z62.2**   **Upbringing away from parents**

       Excludes1   problems with boarding school (Z59.3)

     Z62.21   **Child in welfare custody**   **P**
            Child in care of non-parental family member
            Child in foster care

            Excludes2   problem for parent due to child in welfare custody (Z63.5)

     Z62.22   **Institutional upbringing**
            Child living in orphanage or group home

     Z62.29   **Other upbringing away from parents**

Z62.3   **Hostility towards and scapegoating of child**   **P**

Z62.6   **Inappropriate (excessive) parental pressure**

● **Z62.8**   **Other specified problems related to upbringing**

     ● **Z62.81**   **Personal history of abuse in childhood**

         Z62.810   **Personal history of physical and sexual abuse in childhood**

             Excludes1   current child physical abuse (T74.12, T76.12)
                         current child sexual abuse (T74.22, T76.22)

         Z62.811   **Personal history of psychological abuse in childhood**

             Excludes1   current child psychological abuse (T74.32, T76.32)

         Z62.812   **Personal history of neglect in childhood**

             Excludes1   current child neglect (T74.02, T76.02)

▶   **Z62.813**   **Personal history of forced labor or sexual exploitation in childhood**

         Z62.819   **Personal history of unspecified abuse in childhood**

             Excludes1   current child abuse NOS (T74.92, T76.92)

● **Z62.82**   **Parent-child conflict**

     Z62.820   **Parent-biological child conflict**
            Parent-child problem NOS

     Z62.821   **Parent-adopted child conflict**

     Z62.822   **Parent-foster child conflict**

● **Z62.89**   **Other specified problems related to upbringing**

     Z62.890   **Parent-child estrangement NEC**

     Z62.891   **Sibling rivalry**

     Z62.898   **Other specified problems related to upbringing**

Z62.9   **Problem related to upbringing, unspecified**

● **Z63**   **Other problems related to primary support group, including family circumstances**

       Excludes2   maltreatment syndrome (T74.-, T76)
                        parent-child problems (Z62.-)
                        problems related to negative life events in childhood (Z62.-)
                        problems related to upbringing (Z62.-)

Z63.0   **Problems in relationship with spouse or partner**
       Relationship distress with spouse or intimate partner

       Excludes1   counseling for spousal or partner abuse problems (Z69.1)
                        counseling related to sexual attitude, behavior, and orientation (Z70.-)

Z63.1   **Problems in relationship with in-laws**

● **Z63.3**   **Absence of family member**

       Excludes1   absence of family member due to disappearance and death (Z63.4)
                        absence of family member due to separation and divorce (Z63.5)

     Z63.31   **Absence of family member due to military deployment**
            Individual or family affected by other family member being on military deployment

            Excludes1   family disruption due to return of family member from military deployment (Z63.71)

     Z63.32   **Other absence of family member**

Z63.4   **Disappearance and death of family member**
       Assumed death of family member
       Bereavement

Z63.5   **Disruption of family by separation and divorce**
       Marital estrangement

Z63.6   **Dependent relative needing care at home**

● **Z63.7**   **Other stressful life events affecting family and household**

     Z63.71   **Stress on family due to return of family member from military deployment**
            Individual or family affected by family member having returned from military deployment (current or past conflict)

     Z63.72   **Alcoholism and drug addiction in family**

     Z63.79   **Other stressful life events affecting family and household**
            Anxiety (normal) about sick person in family
            Health problems within family
            Ill or disturbed family member
            Isolated family

CHAPTER 21 (Z00-Z99)

Z63.8   Other specified problems related to primary support group
- Family discord NOS
- Family estrangement NOS
- High expressed emotional level within family
- Inadequate family support NOS
- Inadequate or distorted communication within family

Z63.9   Problem related to primary support group, unspecified
- Relationship disorder NOS

● **Z64   Problems related to certain psychosocial circumstances**

Z64.0   Problems related to unwanted pregnancy ♀

Z64.1   Problems related to multiparity ♀

Z64.4   Discord with counselors
- Discord with probation officer
- Discord with social worker

● **Z65   Problems related to other psychosocial circumstances**

Z65.0   Conviction in civil and criminal proceedings without imprisonment

Z65.1   Imprisonment and other incarceration

Z65.2   Problems related to release from prison

Z65.3   Problems related to other legal circumstances
- Arrest
- Child custody or support proceedings
- Litigation
- Prosecution

Z65.4   Victim of crime and terrorism
- Victim of torture

Z65.5   Exposure to disaster, war and other hostilities
> **Excludes1**   target of perceived discrimination or persecution (Z60.5)

Z65.8   Other specified problems related to psychosocial circumstances
- Religious or spiritual problem

Z65.9   Problem related to unspecified psychosocial circumstances

DO NOT RESUSCITATE STATUS (Z66)

Z66   Do not resuscitate
- DNR status

BLOOD TYPE (Z67)

● **Z67   Blood type**
Coding Clinic: 2015, Q3, P40

  ● **Z67.1   Type A blood**
- **Z67.10   Type A blood, Rh positive**
- **Z67.11   Type A blood, Rh negative**

  ● **Z67.2   Type B blood**
- **Z67.20   Type B blood, Rh positive**
- **Z67.21   Type B blood, Rh negative**

  ● **Z67.3   Type AB blood**
- **Z67.30   Type AB blood, Rh positive**
- **Z67.31   Type AB blood, Rh negative**

  ● **Z67.4   Type O blood**
- **Z67.40   Type O blood, Rh positive**
- **Z67.41   Type O blood, Rh negative**

  ● **Z67.9   Unspecified blood type**
- **Z67.90   Unspecified blood type, Rh positive**
- **Z67.91   Unspecified blood type, Rh negative**
  Coding Clinic: 2015, Q3, P40

BODY MASS INDEX [BMI] (Z68)

OGCR Section I.B.14.

General Coding Guidelines

14. Documentation for BMI, Depth of Non-pressure ulcers, Pressure Ulcer Stages, Coma Scale, and NIH Stroke Scale

For the Body Mass Index (BMI), depth of non-pressure chronic ulcers, pressure ulcer stage, coma scale, and NIH stroke scale (NIHSS) codes, code assignment may be based on medical record documentation from clinicians who are not the patient's provider (i.e., physician or other qualified healthcare practitioner legally accountable for establishing the patient's diagnosis), since this information is typically documented by other clinicians involved in the care of the patient (e.g., a dietitian often documents the BMI, a nurse often documents the pressure ulcer stages, and an emergency medical technician often documents the coma scale). However, the associated diagnosis (such as overweight, obesity, acute stroke, or pressure ulcer) must be documented by the patient's provider. If there is conflicting medical record documentation, either from the same clinician or different clinicians, the patient's attending provider should be queried for clarification.

The BMI, coma scale, and NIHSS codes should only be reported as secondary diagnoses.

● **Z68   Body mass index [BMI]**
Kilograms per meters squared

> **Note:** BMI adult codes are for use for persons 21 years of age or older.
>
> BMI pediatric codes are for use for persons 2-20 years of age. These percentiles are based on the growth charts published by the Centers for Disease Control and Prevention (CDC)

Coding Clinic: 2016, Q4, P129

Z68.1   Body mass index (BMI) 19.9 or less, adult A
Coding Clinic: 2017, Q1, P39

  ● **Z68.2   Body mass index (BMI) 20-29, adult**
- **Z68.20   Body mass index (BMI) 20.0-20.9, adult** A
- **Z68.21   Body mass index (BMI) 21.0-21.9, adult** A
- **Z68.22   Body mass index (BMI) 22.0-22.9, adult** A
- **Z68.23   Body mass index (BMI) 23.0-23.9, adult** A
- **Z68.24   Body mass index (BMI) 24.0-24.9, adult** A
- **Z68.25   Body mass index (BMI) 25.0-25.9, adult** A
- **Z68.26   Body mass index (BMI) 26.0-26.9, adult** A
- **Z68.27   Body mass index (BMI) 27.0-27.9, adult** A
- **Z68.28   Body mass index (BMI) 28.0-28.9, adult** A
- **Z68.29   Body mass index (BMI) 29.0-29.9, adult** A

  ● **Z68.3   Body mass index (BMI) 30-39, adult**
- **Z68.30   Body mass index (BMI) 30.0-30.9, adult** A
- **Z68.31   Body mass index (BMI) 31.0-31.9, adult** A
- **Z68.32   Body mass index (BMI) 32.0-32.9, adult** A
- **Z68.33   Body mass index (BMI) 33.0-33.9, adult** A
- **Z68.34   Body mass index (BMI) 34.0-34.9, adult** A
- **Z68.35   Body mass index (BMI) 35.0-35.9, adult** A
- **Z68.36   Body mass index (BMI) 36.0-36.9, adult** A
- **Z68.37   Body mass index (BMI) 37.0-37.9, adult** A
- **Z68.38   Body mass index (BMI) 38.0-38.9, adult** A
- **Z68.39   Body mass index (BMI) 39.0-39.9, adult** A

  ● **Z68.4   Body mass index (BMI) 40 or greater, adult**
- **Z68.41   Body mass index (BMI) 40.0-44.9, adult** A
- **Z68.42   Body mass index (BMI) 45.0-49.9, adult** A
- **Z68.43   Body mass index (BMI) 50-59.9, adult** A
- **Z68.44   Body mass index (BMI) 60.0-69.9, adult** A
- **Z68.45   Body mass index (BMI) 70 or greater, adult** A

▶ New   ⇒ Revised   ~~deleted~~ Deleted   Excludes 1   Excludes 2   Includes   Use additional   Code first   Code also   Key words

OGCR Official Guidelines   X Assign placeholder X   ● Use Additional Character(s)   ▶ Manifestation Code   **Coding Clinic**

- **Z68.5**   Body mass index (BMI) pediatric
  - **Z68.51**   Body mass index (BMI) pediatric, less than 5th percentile for age
  - **Z68.52**   Body mass index (BMI) pediatric, 5th percentile to less than 85th percentile for age
  - **Z68.53**   Body mass index (BMI) pediatric, 85th percentile to less than 95th percentile for age
  - **Z68.54**   Body mass index (BMI) pediatric, greater than or equal to 95th percentile for age

PERSONS ENCOUNTERING HEALTH SERVICES IN OTHER CIRCUMSTANCES (Z69-Z76)

- **Z69**   Encounter for mental health services for victim and perpetrator of abuse
  - **Includes**   counseling for victims and perpetrators of abuse
- **Z69.0**   Encounter for mental health services for child abuse problems
  - **Z69.01**   Encounter for mental health services for parental child abuse
    - **Z69.010**   Encounter for mental health services for victim of parental child abuse   P
      - Encounter for mental health services for victim of child abuse by parent
      - Encounter for mental health services for victim of child neglect by parent
      - Encounter for mental health services for victim of child psychological abuse by parent
      - Encounter for mental health services for victim of child sexual abuse by parent
    - **Z69.011**   Encounter for mental health services for perpetrator of parental child abuse
      - Encounter for mental health services for perpetrator of parental child neglect
      - Encounter for mental health services for perpetrator of parental child psychological abuse
      - Encounter for mental health services for perpetrator of parental child sexual abuse
      - **Excludes1**   encounter for mental health services for non-parental child abuse (Z69.02-)
  - **Z69.02**   Encounter for mental health services for non-parental child abuse
    - **Z69.020**   Encounter for mental health services for victim of non-parental child abuse   P
      - Encounter for mental health services for victim of non-parental child neglect
      - Encounter for mental health services for victim of non-parental child psychological abuse
      - Encounter for mental health services for victim of non-parental child sexual abuse
    - **Z69.021**   Encounter for mental health services for perpetrator of non- parental child abuse
      - Encounter for mental health services for perpetrator of non-parental child neglect
      - Encounter for mental health services for perpetrator of non-parental child psychological abuse
      - Encounter for mental health services for perpetrator of non-parental child sexual abuse

- **Z69.1**   Encounter for mental health services for spousal or partner abuse problems
  - **Z69.11**   Encounter for mental health services for victim of spousal or partner abuse
    - Encounter for mental health services for victim of spouse or partner neglect
    - Encounter for mental health services for victim of spouse or partner psychological abuse
    - Encounter for mental health services for victim of spouse or partner violence, physical
  - **Z69.12**   Encounter for mental health services for perpetrator of spousal or partner abuse
    - Encounter for mental health services for perpetrator of spouse or partner neglect
    - Encounter for mental health services for perpetrator of spouse or partner psychological abuse
    - Encounter for mental health services for perpetrator of spouse or partner violence, physical
    - Encounter for mental health services for perpetrator of spouse or partner violence, sexual
- **Z69.8**   Encounter for mental health services for victim or perpetrator of other abuse
  - **Z69.81**   Encounter for mental health services for victim of other abuse
    - Encounter for mental health services for perpetrator of non-spousal adult abuse
    - Encounter for mental health services for victim of non-spousal adult abuse
    - Encounter for mental health services for victim of spouse or partner violence, sexual
    - Encounter for rape victim counseling
  - **Z69.82**   Encounter for mental health services for perpetrator of other abuse
- **Z70**   Counseling related to sexual attitude, behavior and orientation
  - **Includes**   encounter for mental health services for sexual attitude, behavior and orientation
  - **Excludes2**   contraceptive or procreative counseling (Z30-Z31)
  - **Z70.0**   Counseling related to sexual attitude
  - **Z70.1**   Counseling related to patient's sexual behavior and orientation
    - Patient concerned regarding impotence
    - Patient concerned regarding non-responsiveness
    - Patient concerned regarding promiscuity
    - Patient concerned regarding sexual orientation
  - **Z70.2**   Counseling related to sexual behavior and orientation of third party
    - Advice sought regarding sexual behavior and orientation of child
    - Advice sought regarding sexual behavior and orientation of partner
    - Advice sought regarding sexual behavior and orientation of spouse
  - **Z70.3**   Counseling related to combined concerns regarding sexual attitude, behavior and orientation
  - **Z70.8**   Other sex counseling
    - Encounter for sex education
  - **Z70.9**   Sex counseling, unspecified

CHAPTER 21 (Z00-Z99)

CHAPTER 21 (Z00–Z99)

● **Z71   Persons encountering health services for other counseling and medical advice, not elsewhere classified**

     Excludes2   contraceptive or procreation counseling (Z30–Z31)

                 sex counseling (Z70.-)

   Z71.0   Person encountering health services to consult on behalf of another person

     Person encountering health services to seek advice or treatment for non-attending third party

     Excludes2   anxiety (normal) about sick person in family (Z63.7)

                 expectant (adoptive) parent(s) pre-birth pediatrician visit (Z76.81)

   Z71.1   Person with feared health complaint in whom no diagnosis is made

     Person encountering health services with feared condition which was not demonstrated

     Person encountering health services in which problem was normal state

     "Worried well"

     Excludes1   medical observation for suspected diseases and conditions proven not to exist (Z03.-)

     Coding Clinic: 2016, Q4, P7

   Z71.2   Person consulting for explanation of examination or test findings

   Z71.3   Dietary counseling and surveillance

     Use additional code for any associated underlying medical condition

     Use additional code to identify body mass index (BMI), if known (Z68.-)

● **Z71.4   Alcohol abuse counseling and surveillance**

     Use additional code for alcohol abuse or dependence (F10.-)

   Z71.41   Alcohol abuse counseling and surveillance of alcoholic

   Z71.42   Counseling for family member of alcoholic

     Counseling for significant other, partner, or friend of alcoholic

● **Z71.5   Drug abuse counseling and surveillance**

     Use additional code for drug abuse or dependence (F11-F16, F18-F19)

   Z71.51   Drug abuse counseling and surveillance of drug abuser

   Z71.52   Counseling for family member of drug abuser

     Counseling for significant other, partner, or friend of drug abuser

   Z71.6   Tobacco abuse counseling

     Use additional code for nicotine dependence (F17.-)

   Z71.7   Human immunodeficiency virus [HIV] counseling

● **Z71.8   Other specified counseling**

     Excludes2   counseling for contraception (Z30.0-)

   Z71.81   Spiritual or religious counseling

   Z71.82   Exercise counseling

   Z71.83   Encounter for nonprocreative genetic counseling

     Excludes1   counseling for procreative genetics (Z31.5)

                 counseling for procreative management (Z31.6)

   Z71.89   Other specified counseling

   Z71.9   Counseling, unspecified

     Encounter for medical advice NOS

● **Z72   Problems related to lifestyle**

     Excludes2   problems related to life-management difficulty (Z73.-)

                 problems related to socioeconomic and psychosocial circumstances (Z55-Z65)

   Coding Clinic: 2016, Q4, P130

   Z72.0   Tobacco use

     Tobacco use NOS

     Excludes1   history of tobacco dependence (Z87.891)

                 nicotine dependence (F17.2-)

                 tobacco dependence (F17.2-)

                 tobacco use during pregnancy (O99.33-)

   Z72.3   Lack of physical exercise

   Z72.4   Inappropriate diet and eating habits

     Excludes1   behavioral eating disorders of infancy or childhood (F98.2-F98.3)

                 eating disorders (F50.-)

                 lack of adequate food (Z59.4)

                 malnutrition and other nutritional deficiencies (E40-E64)

● **Z72.5   High risk sexual behavior**

     Promiscuity

     Excludes1   paraphilias (F65)

   Z72.51   High risk heterosexual behavior

   Z72.52   High risk homosexual behavior

   Z72.53   High risk bisexual behavior

   Z72.6   Gambling and betting

     Excludes1   compulsive or pathological gambling (F63.0)

● **Z72.8   Other problems related to lifestyle**

● **Z72.81   Antisocial behavior**

     Excludes1   conduct disorders (F91.-)

   Z72.810   Child and adolescent antisocial behavior   P

     Antisocial behavior (child) (adolescent) without manifest psychiatric disorder

     Delinquency NOS

     Group delinquency

     Offenses in the context of gang membership

     Stealing in company with others

     Truancy from school

   Z72.811   Adult antisocial behavior   A

     Adult antisocial behavior without manifest psychiatric disorder

● **Z72.82   Problems related to sleep**

   Z72.820   Sleep deprivation

     Lack of adequate sleep

     Excludes1   insomnia (G47.0-)

   Z72.821   Inadequate sleep hygiene

     Bad sleep habits

     Irregular sleep habits

     Unhealthy sleep wake schedule

     Excludes1   insomnia (F51.0-, G47.0-)

   Z72.89   Other problems related to lifestyle

     Self-damaging behavior

   Z72.9   Problem related to lifestyle, unspecified

▶ New   ⟹ Revised   ~~deleted~~ Deleted   Excludes 1   Excludes 2   Includes   Use additional   Code first   Code also   Key words

OGCR Official Guidelines   X Assign placeholder X   ● Use Additional Character(s)   ▶ Manifestation Code   **Coding Clinic**

● **Z73   Problems related to life management difficulty**

> **Excludes2**   problems related to socioeconomic and
> psychosocial circumstances (Z55-Z65)

Z73.Ø   Burn-out

Z73.1   Type A behavior pattern

Z73.2   Lack of relaxation and leisure

Z73.3   Stress, not elsewhere classified
Physical and mental strain NOS

> **Excludes1**   stress related to employment or
> unemployment (Z56.-)

Z73.4   Inadequate social skills, not elsewhere classified

Z73.5   Social role conflict, not elsewhere classified

Z73.6   Limitation of activities due to disability

> **Excludes1**   care-provider dependency (Z74.-)

● **Z73.8   Other problems related to life management difficulty**

● **Z73.81   Behavioral insomnia of childhood**

Z73.81Ø   Behavioral insomnia of childhood, sleep-onset association type   P

Z73.811   Behavioral insomnia of childhood, limit setting type   P

Z73.812   Behavioral insomnia of childhood, combined type   P

Z73.819   Behavioral insomnia of childhood, unspecified type   P

Z73.82   Dual sensory impairment

Z73.89   Other problems related to life management difficulty

Z73.9   Problem related to life management difficulty, unspecified

● **Z74   Problems related to care provider dependency**

> **Excludes2**   dependence on enabling machines or devices
> NEC (Z99.-)

● **Z74.Ø   Reduced mobility**

Z74.Ø1   Bed confinement status
Bedridden

Z74.Ø9   Other reduced mobility
Chairridden
Reduced mobility NOS

> **Excludes2**   wheelchair dependence (Z99.3)

Z74.1   Need for assistance with personal care

Z74.2   Need for assistance at home and no other household member able to render care

Z74.3   Need for continuous supervision

Z74.8   Other problems related to care provider dependency

Z74.9   Problem related to care provider dependency, unspecified

● **Z75   Problems related to medical facilities and other health care**

Z75.Ø   Medical services not available in home

> **Excludes1**   no other household member able to
> render care (Z74.2)

Z75.1   Person awaiting admission to adequate facility elsewhere

Z75.2   Other waiting period for investigation and treatment

Z75.3   Unavailability and inaccessibility of health care facilities

> **Excludes1**   bed unavailable (Z75.1)

Z75.4   Unavailability and inaccessibility of other helping agencies

Z75.5   Holiday relief care

Z75.8   Other problems related to medical facilities and other health care

Z75.9   Unspecified problem related to medical facilities and other health care

● **Z76   Persons encountering health services in other circumstances**

Z76.Ø   Encounter for issue of repeat prescription
Encounter for issue of repeat prescription for appliance
Encounter for issue of repeat prescription for medicaments
Encounter for issue of repeat prescription for spectacles

> **Excludes2**   issue of medical certificate (ZØ2.7)
> repeat prescription for contraceptive
> (Z3Ø.4-)

Z76.1   Encounter for health supervision and care of foundling

Z76.2   Encounter for health supervision and care of other healthy infant and child   P
Encounter for medical or nursing care or supervision of healthy infant under circumstances such as adverse socioeconomic conditions at home
Encounter for medical or nursing care or supervision of healthy infant under circumstances such as awaiting foster or adoptive placement
Encounter for medical or nursing care or supervision of healthy infant under circumstances such as maternal illness
Encounter for medical or nursing care or supervision of healthy infant under circumstances such as number of children at home preventing or interfering with normal care

Z76.3   Healthy person accompanying sick person

Z76.4   Other boarder to healthcare facility

> **Excludes1**   homelessness (Z59.Ø)

Z76.5   Malingerer [conscious simulation]
Person feigning illness (with obvious motivation)

> ⇒ **Excludes1**   factitious disorder (F68.1-, F68.A)
> peregrinating patient (F68.1-)

● **Z76.8   Persons encountering health services in other specified circumstances**

Z76.81   Expectant parent(s) prebirth pediatrician visit
Pre-adoption pediatrician visit for adoptive parent(s)

Z76.82   Awaiting organ transplant status
Patient waiting for organ availability

Z76.89   Persons encountering health services in other specified circumstances
Persons encountering health services NOS

PERSONS WITH POTENTIAL HEALTH HAZARDS RELATED TO FAMILY AND PERSONAL HISTORY AND CERTAIN CONDITIONS INFLUENCING HEALTH STATUS (Z77-Z99)

> Code also any follow-up examination (ZØ8-ZØ9)

● **Z77   Other contact with and (suspected) exposures hazardous to health**

> **Includes**   contact with and (suspected) exposures to
> potential hazards to health

> **Excludes2**   contact with and (suspected) exposure to
> communicable diseases (Z2Ø.-)
> exposure to (parental) (environmental) tobacco
> smoke in the perinatal period (P96.81)
> newborn affected by noxious substances
> transmitted via placenta or breast milk
> (PØ4.-)
> occupational exposure to risk factors (Z57.-)
> retained foreign body (Z18.-)
> retained foreign body fully removed (Z87.821)
> toxic effects of substances chiefly nonmedicinal as
> to source (T51-T65)

● **Z77.Ø   Contact with and (suspected) exposure to hazardous, chiefly nonmedicinal, chemicals**

● **Z77.Ø1   Contact with and (suspected) exposure to hazardous metals**

Z77.Ø1Ø   Contact with and (suspected) exposure to arsenic

Z77.Ø11   Contact with and (suspected) exposure to lead

CHAPTER 21 (ZØØ-Z99)

Z77.012 **Contact with and (suspected) exposure to** uranium
     Excludes1   retained depleted uranium fragments (Z18.01)

Z77.018 **Contact with and (suspected) exposure to** other hazardous metals
     Contact with and (suspected) exposure to chromium compounds
     Contact with and (suspected) exposure to nickel dust

● Z77.02 **Contact with and (suspected) exposure to** hazardous aromatic compounds

Z77.020 **Contact with and (suspected) exposure to** aromatic amines

Z77.021 **Contact with and (suspected) exposure to** benzene

Z77.028 **Contact with and (suspected) exposure to** other hazardous aromatic compounds
     Aromatic dyes NOS
     Polycyclic aromatic hydrocarbons

● Z77.09 **Contact with and (suspected) exposure to** other hazardous, chiefly nonmedicinal, chemicals

Z77.090 **Contact with and (suspected) exposure to** asbestos

Z77.098 **Contact with and (suspected) exposure to** other hazardous, chiefly nonmedicinal, chemicals
     Dyes NOS

● Z77.1 **Contact with and (suspected) exposure to** environmental pollution and hazards in the physical environment

● Z77.11 **Contact with and (suspected) exposure to** environmental pollution

Z77.110 **Contact with and (suspected) exposure to** air pollution

Z77.111 **Contact with and (suspected) exposure to** water pollution

Z77.112 **Contact with and (suspected) exposure to** soil pollution

Z77.118 **Contact with and (suspected) exposure to** other environmental pollution

● Z77.12 **Contact with and (suspected) exposure to** hazards in the physical environment

Z77.120 **Contact with and (suspected) exposure to** mold (toxic)

Z77.121 **Contact with and (suspected) exposure to** harmful algae and algae toxins
     Contact with and (suspected) exposure to (harmful) algae bloom NOS
     Contact with and (suspected) exposure to blue-green algae bloom
     Contact with and (suspected) exposure to brown tide
     Contact with and (suspected) exposure to cyanobacteria bloom
     Contact with and (suspected) exposure to Florida red tide
     Contact with and (suspected) exposure to pfiesteria piscicida
     Contact with and (suspected) exposure to red tide

Z77.122 **Contact with and (suspected) exposure to** noise

➡ Z77.123 **Contact with and (suspected) exposure to** radon and other naturally occurring radiation
     Excludes2   radiation exposure as the cause of a confirmed condition (W88-W90, X39.0-)
     radiation sickness NOS (T66)

Z77.128 **Contact with and (suspected) exposure to** other hazards in the physical environment

● Z77.2 **Contact with and (suspected) exposure to** other hazardous substances

Z77.21 **Contact with and (suspected) exposure to** potentially hazardous body fluids

Z77.22 **Contact with and (suspected) exposure to** environmental tobacco smoke (acute) (chronic)
     Exposure to second hand tobacco smoke (acute) (chronic)
     Passive smoking (acute) (chronic)
     Excludes1   nicotine dependence (F17.-)
     tobacco use (Z72.0)
     Excludes2   occupational exposure to environmental tobacco smoke (Z57.31)

Z77.29 **Contact with and (suspected) exposure to** other hazardous substances
     Coding Clinic: 2016, Q2, P34

Z77.9 **Other contact with and (suspected) exposures hazardous to health**

● Z78 **Other specified health status**
     Excludes2   asymptomatic human immunodeficiency virus [HIV] infection status (Z21)
     postprocedural status (Z93-Z99)
     sex reassignment status (Z87.890)

Z78.0 **Asymptomatic menopausal state** ♀   A
     Menopausal state NOS
     Postmenopausal status NOS
     Excludes2   symptomatic menopausal state (N95.1)

Z78.1 **Physical restraint status**
     Excludes1   physical restraint due to a procedure - omit code

Z78.9 **Other specified health status**

● Z79 **Long term (current) drug therapy**
     Includes   long term (current) drug use for prophylactic purposes
     Code also any therapeutic drug level monitoring (Z51.81)
     Excludes2   drug abuse and dependence (F11-F19)
     drug use complicating pregnancy, childbirth, and the puerperium (O99.32-)
     long term (current) use of oral antidiabetic drugs (Z79.84)
     long term (current) use of oral hypoglycemic drugs (Z79.84)

● Z79.0 **Long term (current) use of anticoagulants and antithrombotics/antiplatelets**
     Excludes2   long term (current) use of aspirin (Z79.82)

Z79.01 **Long term (current) use of anticoagulants**

Z79.02 **Long term (current) use of antithrombotics/ antiplatelets**

Z79.1 **Long term (current) use of non-steroidal anti-inflammatories (NSAID)**
     Excludes2   long term (current) use of aspirin (Z79.82)

Z79.2 **Long term (current) use of antibiotics**

Z79.3 **Long term (current) use of hormonal contraceptives**
     Long term (current) use of birth control pill or patch

▶ New   ⇒ Revised   ~~deleted~~ Deleted   Excludes 1   Excludes 2   Includes   Use additional   Code first   Code also   Key words

OGCR Official Guidelines   X Assign placeholder X   ● Use Additional Character(s)   ▷ Manifestation Code   **Coding Clinic**

Z79.4   Long term (current) use of insulin
     Coding Clinic: 2016, Q4, P121-122, 126

● **Z79.5**   Long term (current) use of steroids

     Z79.51   Long term (current) use of inhaled steroids

     Z79.52   Long term (current) use of systemic steroids

● **Z79.8**   Other long term (current) drug therapy

  ● **Z79.81**   Long term (current) use of agents affecting estrogen receptors and estrogen levels

     Code first, if applicable:
     malignant neoplasm of breast (C50.-)
     malignant neoplasm of prostate (C61)

     Use additional code, if applicable, to identify:
     estrogen receptor positive status (Z17.0)
     family history of breast cancer (Z80.3)
     genetic susceptibility to malignant neoplasm (cancer) (Z15.0-)
     personal history of breast cancer (Z85.3)
     personal history of prostate cancer (Z85.46)
     postmenopausal status (Z78.0)

     Excludes1   hormone replacement therapy (Z79.890)

     Z79.810   Long term (current) use of selective estrogen receptor modulators (SERMs)
       Long term (current) use of raloxifene (Evista)
       Long term (current) use of tamoxifen (Nolvadex)
       Long term (current) use of toremifene (Fareston)

     Z79.811   Long term (current) use of aromatase inhibitors
       Long term (current) use of anastrozole (Arimidex)
       Long term (current) use of exemestane (Aromasin)
       Long term (current) use of letrozole (Femara)

     Z79.818   Long term (current) use of other agents affecting estrogen receptors and estrogen levels
       Long term (current) use of estrogen receptor downregulators
       Long term (current) use of fulvestrant (Faslodex)
       Long term (current) use of gonadotropin-releasing hormone (GnRH) agonist
       Long term (current) use of goserelin acetate (Zoladex)
       Long term (current) use of leuprolide acetate (leuprorelin) (Lupron)
       Long term (current) use of megestrol acetate (Megace)

     Z79.82   Long term (current) use of aspirin

     Z79.83   Long term (current) use of bisphosphonates
       Coding Clinic: 2016, Q4, P42

     Z79.84   Long term (current) use of oral hypoglycemic drugs
       Long term (current) use of oral antidiabetic drugs

       Excludes2   long term (current) use of insulin (Z79.4)
       Coding Clinic: 2016, Q4, P76, 121-122, 126

● **Z79.89**   Other long term (current) drug therapy

     Z79.890   Hormone replacement therapy

     Z79.891   Long term (current) use of opiate analgesic
       Long term (current) use of methadone for pain management

       Excludes1   methadone use NOS (F11.9-)
         use of methadone for treatment of heroin addiction (F11.2-)

     Z79.899   Other long term (current) drug therapy
       Coding Clinic: 2015, Q4, P34, Q3, P21

● **Z80**   Family history of primary malignant neoplasm

   Z80.0   Family history of malignant neoplasm of digestive organs
     Conditions classifiable to C15-C26
     Coding Clinic: 2018, Q1, P7

   Z80.1   Family history of malignant neoplasm of trachea, bronchus and lung
     Conditions classifiable to C33-C34

   Z80.2   Family history of malignant neoplasm of other respiratory and intrathoracic organs
     Conditions classifiable to C30-C32, C37-C39

   Z80.3   Family history of malignant neoplasm of breast
     Conditions classifiable to C50.-

  ● **Z80.4**   Family history of malignant neoplasm of genital organs
     Conditions classifiable to C51-C63

     Z80.41   Family history of malignant neoplasm of ovary

     Z80.42   Family history of malignant neoplasm of prostate

     Z80.43   Family history of malignant neoplasm of testis

     Z80.49   Family history of malignant neoplasm of other genital organs

  ● **Z80.5**   Family history of malignant neoplasm of urinary tract
     Conditions classifiable to C64-C68

     Z80.51   Family history of malignant neoplasm of kidney

     Z80.52   Family history of malignant neoplasm of bladder

     Z80.59   Family history of malignant neoplasm of other urinary tract organ

   Z80.6   Family history of leukemia
     Conditions classifiable to C91-C95

   Z80.7   Family history of other malignant neoplasms of lymphoid, hematopoietic and related tissues
     Conditions classifiable to C81-C90, C96.-

   Z80.8   Family history of malignant neoplasm of other organs or systems
     Conditions classifiable to C00-C14, C40-C49, C69-C79

   Z80.9   Family history of malignant neoplasm, unspecified
     Conditions classifiable to C80.1

● **Z81**   Family history of mental and behavioral disorders

   Z81.0   Family history of intellectual disabilities
     Conditions classifiable to F70-F79

   Z81.1   Family history of alcohol abuse and dependence
     Conditions classifiable to F10.-

   Z81.2   Family history of tobacco abuse and dependence
     Conditions classifiable to F17.-

   Z81.3   Family history of other psychoactive substance abuse and dependence
     Conditions classifiable to F11-F16, F18-F19

   Z81.4   Family history of other substance abuse and dependence
     Conditions classifiable to F55

   Z81.8   Family history of other mental and behavioral disorders
     Conditions classifiable elsewhere in F01-F99

CHAPTER 21 (Z00-Z99)

CHAPTER 21 (Z00-Z99)

● **Z82　Family history of certain disabilities and chronic diseases (leading to disablement)**

Z82.0　Family history of epilepsy and other diseases of the nervous system
Conditions classifiable to G00-G99

Z82.1　Family history of blindness and visual loss
Conditions classifiable to H54.-

Z82.2　Family history of deafness and hearing loss
Conditions classifiable to H90-H91

Z82.3　Family history of stroke
Conditions classifiable to I60-I64

● **Z82.4　Family history of ischemic heart disease and other diseases of the circulatory system**
Conditions classifiable to I00-I52, I65-I99

　Z82.41　Family history of sudden cardiac death

　Z82.49　Family history of ischemic heart disease and other diseases of the circulatory system

Z82.5　Family history of asthma and other chronic lower respiratory diseases
Conditions classifiable to J40-J47

　Excludes2　family history of other diseases of the respiratory system (Z83.6)

● **Z82.6　Family history of arthritis and other diseases of the musculoskeletal system and connective tissue**
Conditions classifiable to M00-M99

　Z82.61　Family history of arthritis

　Z82.62　Family history of osteoporosis

　Z82.69　Family history of other diseases of the musculoskeletal system and connective tissue

● **Z82.7　Family history of congenital malformations, deformations and chromosomal abnormalities**
Conditions classifiable to Q00-Q99

　Z82.71　Family history of polycystic kidney

　Z82.79　Family history of other congenital malformations, deformations and chromosomal abnormalities

Z82.8　Family history of other disabilities and chronic diseases leading to disablement, not elsewhere classified

● **Z83　Family history of other specific disorders**

　Excludes2　contact with and (suspected) exposure to communicable disease in the family (Z20.-)

Z83.0　Family history of human immunodeficiency virus [HIV] disease
Conditions classifiable to B20

Z83.1　Family history of other infectious and parasitic diseases
Conditions classifiable to A00-B19, B25-B94, B99

Z83.2　Family history of diseases of the blood and blood-forming organs and certain disorders involving the immune mechanism
Conditions classifiable to D50-D89

Z83.3　Family history of diabetes mellitus
Conditions classifiable to E08-E13

● **Z83.4　Family history of other endocrine, nutritional and metabolic diseases**
Conditions classifiable to E00-E07, E15-E88

　Z83.41　Family history of multiple endocrine neoplasia [MEN] syndrome

　Z83.42　Family history of familial hypercholesterolemia
　　Coding Clinic: 2016, Q4, P77

▶● **Z83.43　Family history of other disorder of lipoprotein metabolism and other lipidemias**

　▶ **Z83.430　Family history of elevated lipoprotein(a)**
　　▶Family history of elevated Lp(a)

　▶ **Z83.438　Family history of other disorder of lipoprotein metabolism and other lipidemia**
　　▶Family history of familial combined hyperlipidemia

　Z83.49　Family history of other endocrine, nutritional and metabolic diseases

● **Z83.5　Family history of eye and ear disorders**

　● **Z83.51　Family history of eye disorders**
　　Conditions classifiable to H00-H53, H55-H59

　　Excludes2　family history of blindness and visual loss (Z82.1)

　　　Z83.511　Family history of glaucoma

　　　Z83.518　Family history of other specified eye disorder

　Z83.52　Family history of ear disorders
　　Conditions classifiable to H60-H83, H92-H95

　　Excludes2　family history of deafness and hearing loss (Z82.2)

Z83.6　Family history of other diseases of the respiratory system
Conditions classifiable to J00-J39, J60-J99

　Excludes2　family history of asthma and other chronic lower respiratory diseases (Z82.5)

● **Z83.7　Family history of diseases of the digestive system**
Conditions classifiable to K00-K93

　Z83.71　Family history of colonic polyps

　　Excludes2　family history of malignant neoplasm of digestive organs (Z80.0)

　Z83.79　Family history of other diseases of the digestive system

● **Z84　Family history of other conditions**

Z84.0　Family history of diseases of the skin and subcutaneous tissue
Conditions classifiable to L00-L99

Z84.1　Family history of disorders of kidney and ureter
Conditions classifiable to N00-N29

Z84.2　Family history of other diseases of the genitourinary system
Conditions classifiable to N30-N99
Coding Clinic: 2016, Q4, P77

Z84.3　Family history of consanguinity

● **Z84.8　Family history of other specified conditions**

　Z84.81　Family history of carrier of genetic disease

　Z84.82　Family history of sudden infant death syndrome
　　Family history of SIDS

　Z84.89　Family history of other specified conditions

● **Z85　Personal history of malignant neoplasm**

Code first any follow-up examination after treatment of malignant neoplasm (Z08)

Use additional code to identify:
　alcohol use and dependence (F10.-)
　exposure to environmental tobacco smoke (Z77.22)
　history of tobacco dependence (Z87.891)
　occupational exposure to environmental tobacco smoke (Z57.31)
　tobacco dependence (F17.-)
　tobacco use (Z72.0)

Excludes2　personal history of benign neoplasm (Z86.01-)
　　personal history of carcinoma-in-situ (Z86.00-)

● **Z85.0　Personal history of malignant neoplasm of digestive organs**

　Z85.00　Personal history of malignant neoplasm of unspecified digestive organ

　Z85.01　Personal history of malignant neoplasm of esophagus
　　Conditions classifiable to C15

　● **Z85.02　Personal history of malignant neoplasm of stomach**

　　　Z85.020　Personal history of malignant carcinoid tumor of stomach
　　　　Conditions classifiable to C7A.092

　　　Z85.028　Personal history of other malignant neoplasm of stomach
　　　　Conditions classifiable to C16

▶ New　⇒ Revised　~~deleted~~ Deleted　| Excludes 1 |　| Excludes 2 |　| Includes |　| Use additional |　| Code first |　| Code also |　| Key words |
OGCR Official Guidelines　X Assign placeholder X　● Use Additional Character(s)　▶ Manifestation Code　**Coding Clinic**

● **Z85.03** **Personal history of malignant neoplasm of large intestine**

    Z85.030 **Personal history of malignant carcinoid tumor of large intestine**
        Conditions classifiable to C7A.022-C7A.025, C7A.029

    Z85.038 **Personal history of other malignant neoplasm of large intestine**
        Conditions classifiable to C18

● **Z85.04** **Personal history of malignant neoplasm of rectum, rectosigmoid junction, and anus**

    Z85.040 **Personal history of malignant carcinoid tumor of rectum**
        Conditions classifiable to C7A.026

    Z85.048 **Personal history of other malignant neoplasm of rectum, rectosigmoid junction, and anus**
        Conditions classifiable to C19-C21

Z85.05 **Personal history of malignant neoplasm of liver**
    Conditions classifiable to C22

● **Z85.06** **Personal history of malignant neoplasm of small intestine**

    Z85.060 **Personal history of malignant carcinoid tumor of small intestine**
        Conditions classifiable to C7A.01-

    Z85.068 **Personal history of other malignant neoplasm of small intestine**
        Conditions classifiable to C17

Z85.07 **Personal history of malignant neoplasm of pancreas**
    Conditions classifiable to C25

Z85.09 **Personal history of malignant neoplasm of other digestive organs**

● **Z85.1** **Personal history of malignant neoplasm of trachea, bronchus and lung**

  ● **Z85.11** **Personal history of malignant neoplasm of bronchus and lung**

    Z85.110 **Personal history of malignant carcinoid tumor of bronchus and lung**
        Conditions classifiable to C7A.090

    Z85.118 **Personal history of other malignant neoplasm of bronchus and lung**
        Conditions classifiable to C34

  Z85.12 **Personal history of malignant neoplasm of trachea**
    Conditions classifiable to C33

● **Z85.2** **Personal history of malignant neoplasm of other respiratory and intrathoracic organs**

  Z85.20 **Personal history of malignant neoplasm of unspecified respiratory organ**

  Z85.21 **Personal history of malignant neoplasm of larynx**
    Conditions classifiable to C32

  Z85.22 **Personal history of malignant neoplasm of nasal cavities, middle ear, and accessory sinuses**
    Conditions classifiable to C30-C31

  ● **Z85.23** **Personal history of malignant neoplasm of thymus**

    Z85.230 **Personal history of malignant carcinoid tumor of thymus**
        Conditions classifiable to C7A.091

    Z85.238 **Personal history of other malignant neoplasm of thymus**
        Conditions classifiable to C37

  Z85.29 **Personal history of malignant neoplasm of other respiratory and intrathoracic organs**

Z85.3 **Personal history of malignant neoplasm of breast**
    Conditions classifiable to C50.-

● **Z85.4** **Personal history of malignant neoplasm of genital organs**
    Conditions classifiable to C51-C63

  Z85.40 **Personal history of malignant neoplasm of unspecified female genital organ** ♀

  Z85.41 **Personal history of malignant neoplasm of cervix uteri** ♀

  Z85.42 **Personal history of malignant neoplasm of other parts of uterus** ♀

  Z85.43 **Personal history of malignant neoplasm of ovary** ♀

  Z85.44 **Personal history of malignant neoplasm of other female genital organs** ♀

  Z85.45 **Personal history of malignant neoplasm of unspecified male genital organ** ♂

  Z85.46 **Personal history of malignant neoplasm of prostate** ♂

  Z85.47 **Personal history of malignant neoplasm of testis** ♂

  Z85.48 **Personal history of malignant neoplasm of epididymis** ♂

  Z85.49 **Personal history of malignant neoplasm of other male genital organs** ♂

● **Z85.5** **Personal history of malignant neoplasm of urinary tract**
    Conditions classifiable to C64-C68

  Z85.50 **Personal history of malignant neoplasm of unspecified urinary tract organ**

  Z85.51 **Personal history of malignant neoplasm of bladder**

  ● **Z85.52** **Personal history of malignant neoplasm of kidney**

    Excludes1   personal history of malignant neoplasm of renal pelvis (Z85.53)

    Z85.520 **Personal history of malignant carcinoid tumor of kidney**
        Conditions classifiable to C7A.093

    Z85.528 **Personal history of other malignant neoplasm of kidney**
        Conditions classifiable to C64

  Z85.53 **Personal history of malignant neoplasm of renal pelvis**

  Z85.54 **Personal history of malignant neoplasm of ureter**

  Z85.59 **Personal history of malignant neoplasm of other urinary tract organ**

Z85.6 **Personal history of leukemia**
    Conditions classifiable to C91-C95

    Excludes1   leukemia in remission C91.0-C95.9 with 5th character 1

● **Z85.7** **Personal history of other malignant neoplasms of lymphoid, hematopoietic and related tissues**

  Z85.71 **Personal history of Hodgkin lymphoma**
    Conditions classifiable to C81

  Z85.72 **Personal history of non-Hodgkin lymphomas**
    Conditions classifiable to C82-C85

  Z85.79 **Personal history of other malignant neoplasms of lymphoid, hematopoietic and related tissues**
    Conditions classifiable to C88-C90, C96

    Excludes1   multiple myeloma in remission (C90.01)
        plasma cell leukemia in remission (C90.11)
        plasmacytoma in remission (C90.21)

CHAPTER 21 (Z00-Z99)

● **Z85.8**　**Personal history of malignant neoplasms of other organs and systems**
　　　Conditions classifiable to C00-C14, C40-C49, C69-C75, C7A.098, C76-C79

● **Z85.81**　**Personal history of malignant neoplasm of lip, oral cavity, and pharynx**

　Z85.810　**Personal history of malignant neoplasm of tongue**

　Z85.818　**Personal history of malignant neoplasm of other sites of lip, oral cavity, and pharynx**

　Z85.819　**Personal history of malignant neoplasm of unspecified site of lip, oral cavity, and pharynx**

● **Z85.82**　**Personal history of malignant neoplasm of skin**

　Z85.820　**Personal history of malignant melanoma of skin**
　　　Conditions classifiable to C43

　Z85.821　**Personal history of Merkel cell carcinoma**
　　　Conditions classifiable to C4A

　Z85.828　**Personal history of other malignant neoplasm of skin**
　　　Conditions classifiable to C44

● **Z85.83**　**Personal history of malignant neoplasm of bone and soft tissue**

　Z85.830　**Personal history of malignant neoplasm of bone**

　Z85.831　**Personal history of malignant neoplasm of soft tissue**
　　　Excludes2　personal history of malignant neoplasm of skin (Z85.82-)

● **Z85.84**　**Personal history of malignant neoplasm of eye and nervous tissue**

　Z85.840　**Personal history of malignant neoplasm of eye**

　Z85.841　**Personal history of malignant neoplasm of brain**

　Z85.848　**Personal history of malignant neoplasm of other parts of nervous tissue**

● **Z85.85**　**Personal history of malignant neoplasm of endocrine glands**

　Z85.850　**Personal history of malignant neoplasm of thyroid**

　Z85.858　**Personal history of malignant neoplasm of other endocrine glands**

　Z85.89　**Personal history of malignant neoplasm of other organs and systems**

Z85.9　**Personal history of malignant neoplasm, unspecified**
　　　Conditions classifiable to C7A.00, C80.1

● **Z86**　**Personal history of certain other diseases**
　　　Code first any follow-up examination after treatment (Z09)

● **Z86.0**　**Personal history of in-situ and benign neoplasms and neoplasms of uncertain behavior**
　　　Excludes2　personal history of malignant neoplasms (Z85.-)

● **Z86.00**　**Personal history of in-situ neoplasm**
　　　Conditions classifiable to D00-D09

　Z86.000　**Personal history of in-situ neoplasm of breast**

　Z86.001　**Personal history of in-situ neoplasm of cervix uteri** ♀
　　　Personal history of cervical intraepithelial neoplasia III [CIN III]

　Z86.008　**Personal history of in-situ neoplasm of other site**
　　　Personal history of vaginal intraepithelial neoplasia III [VAIN III]
　　　Personal history of vulvar intraepithelial neoplasia III [VIN III]

● **Z86.01**　**Personal history of benign neoplasm**
　　　Coding Clinic: 2017, Q1, P14

　Z86.010　**Personal history of colonic polyps**
　　　Coding Clinic: 2017, Q1, P9, P14

　Z86.011　**Personal history of benign neoplasm of the brain**

　Z86.012　**Personal history of benign carcinoid tumor**

　Z86.018　**Personal history of other benign neoplasm**
　　　Coding Clinic: 2017, Q1, P14

　Z86.03　**Personal history of neoplasm of uncertain behavior**

● **Z86.1**　**Personal history of infectious and parasitic diseases**
　　　Conditions classifiable to A00-B89, B99
　　　Excludes1　personal history of infectious diseases specific to a body system sequelae of infectious and parasitic diseases (B90-B94)
　　　Coding Clinic: 2016, Q4, P5

　Z86.11　**Personal history of tuberculosis**

　Z86.12　**Personal history of poliomyelitis**

　Z86.13　**Personal history of malaria**

　Z86.14　**Personal history of Methicillin resistant Staphylococcus aureus infection**
　　　Personal history of MRSA infection

　Z86.19　**Personal history of other infectious and parasitic diseases**

　Z86.2　**Personal history of diseases of the blood and blood-forming organs and certain disorders involving the immune mechanism**
　　　Conditions classifiable to D50-D89

▶ New　⇒ Revised　~~deleted~~ Deleted　Excludes 1　Excludes 2　Includes　Use additional　Code first　Code also　Key words
OGCR Official Guidelines　X Assign placeholder X　● Use Additional Character(s)　▶ Manifestation Code　**Coding Clinic**

● **Z86.3**   **Personal history of endocrine, nutritional and metabolic diseases**
Conditions classifiable to E00-E88

    Z86.31   **Personal history of diabetic foot ulcer**

       Excludes2   current diabetic foot ulcer (E08.621, E09.621, E10.621, E11.621, E13.621)

    Z86.32   **Personal history of gestational diabetes** ♀
Personal history of conditions classifiable to O24.4-

       Excludes1   gestational diabetes mellitus in current pregnancy (O24.4-)

    Z86.39   **Personal history of other endocrine, nutritional and metabolic disease**

● **Z86.5**   **Personal history of mental and behavioral disorders**
Conditions classifiable to F40-F59

    Z86.51   **Personal history of combat and operational stress reaction**   A

    Z86.59   **Personal history of other mental and behavioral disorders**

● **Z86.6**   **Personal history of diseases of the nervous system and sense organs**
Conditions classifiable to G00-G99, H00-H95

    Z86.61   **Personal history of infections of the central nervous system**
Personal history of encephalitis
Personal history of meningitis

    Z86.69   **Personal history of other diseases of the nervous system and sense organs**
Coding Clinic: 2016, Q4, P25

● **Z86.7**   **Personal history of diseases of the circulatory system**
Conditions classifiable to I00-I99

       Excludes2   old myocardial infarction (I25.2)
personal history of anaphylactic shock (Z87.892)
postmyocardial infarction syndrome (I24.1)

●   **Z86.71**   **Personal history of venous thrombosis and embolism**

      Z86.711   **Personal history of pulmonary embolism**

      Z86.718   **Personal history of other venous thrombosis and embolism**

    Z86.72   **Personal history of thrombophlebitis**

    Z86.73   **Personal history of transient ischemic attack (TIA), and cerebral infarction without residual deficits**
Personal history of prolonged reversible ischemic neurological deficit (PRIND)
Personal history of stroke NOS without residual deficits

       Excludes1   personal history of traumatic brain injury (Z87.820)
sequelae of cerebrovascular disease (I69.-)

      Coding Clinic: 2012, Q4, P3

    Z86.74   **Personal history of sudden cardiac arrest**
Personal history of sudden cardiac death successfully resuscitated

    Z86.79   **Personal history of other diseases of the circulatory system**

● **Z87**   **Personal history of other diseases and conditions**
Code first any follow-up examination after treatment (Z09)

● **Z87.0**   **Personal history of diseases of the respiratory system**
Conditions classifiable to J00-J99

    Z87.01   **Personal history of pneumonia (recurrent)**

    Z87.09   **Personal history of other diseases of the respiratory system**

● **Z87.1**   **Personal history of diseases of the digestive system**
Conditions classifiable to K00-K93

    Z87.11   **Personal history of peptic ulcer disease**

    Z87.19   **Personal history of other diseases of the digestive system**
Coding Clinic: 2017, Q1, P14

   Z87.2   **Personal history of diseases of the skin and subcutaneous tissue**
Conditions classifiable to L00-L99

       Excludes2   personal history of diabetic foot ulcer (Z86.31)

● **Z87.3**   **Personal history of diseases of the musculoskeletal system and connective tissue**
Conditions classifiable to M00-M99

       Excludes2   personal history of (healed) traumatic fracture (Z87.81)

●   **Z87.31**   **Personal history of (healed) nontraumatic fracture**

      Z87.310   **Personal history of (healed) osteoporosis fracture**
Personal history of (healed) fragility fracture
Personal history of (healed) collapsed vertebra due to osteoporosis

      Z87.311   **Personal history of (healed) other pathological fracture**
Personal history of (healed) collapsed vertebra NOS

         Excludes2   personal history of osteoporosis fracture (Z87.310)

      Z87.312   **Personal history of (healed) stress fracture**
Personal history of (healed) fatigue fracture

    Z87.39   **Personal history of other diseases of the musculoskeletal system and connective tissue**

● **Z87.4**   **Personal history of diseases of genitourinary system**
Conditions classifiable to N00-N99

●   **Z87.41**   **Personal history of dysplasia of the female genital tract**

       Excludes1   personal history of intraepithelial neoplasia III of female genital tract (Z86.001, Z86.008)
personal history of malignant neoplasm of female genital tract (Z85.40-Z85.44)

      Z87.410   **Personal history of cervical dysplasia** ♀

      Z87.411   **Personal history of vaginal dysplasia** ♀

      Z87.412   **Personal history of vulvar dysplasia** ♀

    Z87.42   **Personal history of other diseases of the female genital tract** ♀

● **Z87.43** **Personal history of diseases of male genital organs**

    Z87.430 **Personal history of prostatic dysplasia** ♂

        Excludes1 personal history of malignant neoplasm of prostate (Z85.46)

    Z87.438 **Personal history of other diseases of male genital organs** ♂

● **Z87.44** **Personal history of diseases of urinary system**

    Excludes1 personal history of malignant neoplasm of cervix uteri (Z85.41)

    Z87.440 **Personal history of urinary (tract) infections**

    Z87.441 **Personal history of nephrotic syndrome**

    Z87.442 **Personal history of urinary calculi**
        Personal history of kidney stones

    Z87.448 **Personal history of other diseases of urinary system**

● **Z87.5** **Personal history of complications of pregnancy, childbirth and the puerperium**
    Conditions classifiable to O00-O9A

    Excludes2 recurrent pregnancy loss (N96)

  Z87.51 **Personal history of pre-term labor** ♀

    Excludes1 current pregnancy with history of pre-term labor (O09.21-)

  Z87.59 **Personal history of other complications of pregnancy, childbirth and the puerperium** ♀
    Personal history of trophoblastic disease

● **Z87.7** **Personal history of (corrected) congenital malformations**
    Conditions classifiable to Q00-Q89 that have been repaired or corrected

    Excludes1 congenital malformations that have been partially corrected or repair but which still require medical treatment - code to condition

    Excludes2 other postprocedural states (Z98.-)
        personal history of medical treatment (Z92.-)
        presence of cardiac and vascular implants and grafts (Z95.-)
        presence of other devices (Z97.-)
        presence of other functional implants (Z96.-)
        transplanted organ and tissue status (Z94.-)

● **Z87.71** **Personal history of (corrected) congenital malformations of genitourinary system**

    Z87.710 **Personal history of (corrected) hypospadias** ♂

    Z87.718 **Personal history of other specified (corrected) congenital malformations of genitourinary system**

● **Z87.72** **Personal history of (corrected) congenital malformations of nervous system and sense organs**

    Z87.720 **Personal history of (corrected) congenital malformations of eye**

    Z87.721 **Personal history of (corrected) congenital malformations of ear**

    Z87.728 **Personal history of other specified (corrected) congenital malformations of nervous system and sense organs**

● **Z87.73** **Personal history of (corrected) congenital malformations of digestive system**

    Z87.730 **Personal history of (corrected) cleft lip and palate**

    Z87.738 **Personal history of other specified (corrected) congenital malformations of digestive system**

  Z87.74 **Personal history of (corrected) congenital malformations of heart and circulatory system**

  Z87.75 **Personal history of (corrected) congenital malformations of respiratory system**

  Z87.76 **Personal history of (corrected) congenital malformations of integument, limbs and musculoskeletal system**

● **Z87.79** **Personal history of other (corrected) congenital malformations**

    Z87.790 **Personal history of (corrected) congenital malformations of face and neck**

    Z87.798 **Personal history of other (corrected) congenital malformations**

● **Z87.8** **Personal history of other specified conditions**

    Excludes2 personal history of self harm (Z91.5)

  Z87.81 **Personal history of (healed) traumatic fracture**

    Excludes2 personal history of (healed) nontraumatic fracture (Z87.31-)

● **Z87.82** **Personal history of other (healed) physical injury and trauma**
    Conditions classifiable to S00-T88, except traumatic fractures

    Z87.820 **Personal history of traumatic brain injury**

        Excludes1 personal history of transient ischemic attack (TIA), and cerebral infarction without residual deficits (Z86.73)

    Z87.821 **Personal history of retained foreign body fully removed**

    Z87.828 **Personal history of other (healed) physical injury and trauma**

● **Z87.89** **Personal history of other specified conditions**

    Z87.890 **Personal history of sex reassignment**

    Z87.891 **Personal history of nicotine dependence**

        Excludes1 current nicotine dependence (F17.2-)

        Coding Clinic: 2017, Q2, P27

    Z87.892 **Personal history of anaphylaxis**
        Code also allergy status such as:
        allergy status to drugs, medicaments and biological substances (Z88.-)
        allergy status, other than to drugs and biological substances (Z91.0-)

    Z87.898 **Personal history of other specified conditions**
        Coding Clinic: 2013, Q1, P21

▶ New ⇒ Revised ~~deleted~~ Deleted Excludes 1 Excludes 2 Includes Use additional Code first Code also Key words
OGCR Official Guidelines X Assign placeholder X ● Use Additional Character(s) ▷ Manifestation Code Coding Clinic

● **Z88**   **Allergy status to drugs, medicaments and biological substances**

     Excludes2   allergy status, other than to drugs and biological substances (Z91.0-)

   Z88.0   Allergy status to penicillin

   Z88.1   Allergy status to other antibiotic agents status

   Z88.2   Allergy status to sulfonamides status
       Coding Clinic: 2015, Q3, P23

   Z88.3   Allergy status to other anti-infective agents status

   Z88.4   Allergy status to anesthetic agent status

   Z88.5   Allergy status to narcotic agent status

   Z88.6   Allergy status to analgesic agent status

   Z88.7   Allergy status to serum and vaccine status

   Z88.8   Allergy status to other drugs, medicaments and biological substances status

   Z88.9   Allergy status to unspecified drugs, medicaments and biological substances status

● **Z89**   **Acquired absence of limb**

     Includes   amputation status
                 postprocedural loss of limb
                 post-traumatic loss of limb

     Excludes1   acquired deformities of limbs (M20-M21)
                 congenital absence of limbs (Q71-Q73)

   ● **Z89.0**   Acquired absence of thumb and other finger(s)

     ● **Z89.01**   Acquired absence of thumb

       Z89.011   Acquired absence of right thumb

       Z89.012   Acquired absence of left thumb

       Z89.019   Acquired absence of unspecified thumb

     ● **Z89.02**   Acquired absence of other finger(s)

       Excludes2   acquired absence of thumb (Z89.01-)

       Z89.021   Acquired absence of right finger(s)

       Z89.022   Acquired absence of left finger(s)

       Z89.029   Acquired absence of unspecified finger(s)

   ● **Z89.1**   Acquired absence of hand and wrist

     ● **Z89.11**   Acquired absence of hand

       Z89.111   Acquired absence of right hand

       Z89.112   Acquired absence of left hand

       Z89.119   Acquired absence of unspecified hand

     ● **Z89.12**   Acquired absence of wrist
          Disarticulation at wrist

       Z89.121   Acquired absence of right wrist

       Z89.122   Acquired absence of left wrist

       Z89.129   Acquired absence of unspecified wrist

   ● **Z89.2**   Acquired absence of upper limb above wrist

     ● **Z89.20**   Acquired absence of upper limb, unspecified level

       Z89.201   Acquired absence of right upper limb, unspecified level

       Z89.202   Acquired absence of left upper limb, unspecified level

       Z89.209   Acquired absence of unspecified upper limb, unspecified level
           Acquired absence of arm NOS

     ● **Z89.21**   Acquired absence of upper limb below elbow

       Z89.211   Acquired absence of right upper limb below elbow

       Z89.212   Acquired absence of left upper limb below elbow

       Z89.219   Acquired absence of unspecified upper limb below elbow

   ● **Z89.22**   Acquired absence of upper limb above elbow
       Disarticulation at elbow

       Z89.221   Acquired absence of right upper limb above elbow

       Z89.222   Acquired absence of left upper limb above elbow

       Z89.229   Acquired absence of unspecified upper limb above elbow

   ● **Z89.23**   Acquired absence of shoulder
       Acquired absence of shoulder joint following explantation of shoulder joint prosthesis, with or without presence of antibiotic-impregnated cement spacer

       Z89.231   Acquired absence of right shoulder

       Z89.232   Acquired absence of left shoulder

       Z89.239   Acquired absence of unspecified shoulder

● **Z89.4**   Acquired absence of toe(s), foot, and ankle

   ● **Z89.41**   Acquired absence of great toe

       Z89.411   Acquired absence of right great toe

       Z89.412   Acquired absence of left great toe

       Z89.419   Acquired absence of unspecified great toe

   ● **Z89.42**   Acquired absence of other toe(s)

       Excludes2   acquired absence of great toe (Z89.41-)

       Z89.421   Acquired absence of other right toe(s)

       Z89.422   Acquired absence of other left toe(s)

       Z89.429   Acquired absence of other toe(s), unspecified side

   ● **Z89.43**   Acquired absence of foot

       Z89.431   Acquired absence of right foot

       Z89.432   Acquired absence of left foot

       Z89.439   Acquired absence of unspecified foot

   ● **Z89.44**   Acquired absence of ankle
       Disarticulation of ankle

       Z89.441   Acquired absence of right ankle

       Z89.442   Acquired absence of left ankle

       Z89.449   Acquired absence of unspecified ankle

● **Z89.5**   Acquired absence of leg below knee

   ● **Z89.51**   Acquired absence of leg below knee

       Z89.511   Acquired absence of right leg below knee

       Z89.512   Acquired absence of left leg below knee

       Z89.519   Acquired absence of unspecified leg below knee

   ● **Z89.52**   Acquired absence of knee
       Acquired absence of knee joint following explantation of knee joint prosthesis, with or without presence of antibiotic-impregnated cement spacer

       Z89.521   Acquired absence of right knee

       Z89.522   Acquired absence of left knee

       Z89.529   Acquired absence of unspecified knee

CHAPTER 21 (Z00-Z99)

● **Z89.6**   **Acquired absence of leg above knee**

   ● **Z89.61**   **Acquired absence of leg above knee**
         Acquired absence of leg NOS
         Disarticulation at knee

       Z89.611   **Acquired absence of right leg above knee**

       Z89.612   **Acquired absence of left leg above knee**

       Z89.619   **Acquired absence of unspecified leg above knee**

   ● **Z89.62**   **Acquired absence of hip**
         Acquired absence of hip joint following explantation of hip joint prosthesis, with or without presence of antibiotic-impregnated cement spacer
         Disarticulation at hip

       Z89.621   **Acquired absence of right hip joint**

       Z89.622   **Acquired absence of left hip joint**

       Z89.629   **Acquired absence of unspecified hip joint**

    Z89.9   **Acquired absence of limb, unspecified**

● **Z90**   **Acquired absence of organs, not elsewhere classified**

    Includes   postprocedural or post-traumatic loss of body part NEC

    Excludes1   congenital absence - see Alphabetical Index

    Excludes2   postprocedural absence of endocrine glands (E89.-)

  ● **Z90.0**   **Acquired absence of part of head and neck**

    Z90.01   **Acquired absence of eye**

    Z90.02   **Acquired absence of larynx**

    Z90.09   **Acquired absence of other part of head and neck**
         Acquired absence of nose

       Excludes2   teeth (K08.1)

  ● **Z90.1**   **Acquired absence of breast and nipple**

    Z90.10   **Acquired absence of unspecified breast and nipple**

    Z90.11   **Acquired absence of right breast and nipple**

    Z90.12   **Acquired absence of left breast and nipple**

    Z90.13   **Acquired absence of bilateral breasts and nipples**

    Z90.2   **Acquired absence of lung [part of]**

    Z90.3   **Acquired absence of stomach [part of]**

  ● **Z90.4**   **Acquired absence of other specified parts of digestive tract**

   ● **Z90.41**   **Acquired absence of pancreas**

         Code also exocrine pancreatic insufficiency (K86.81)

         Use additional code to identify any associated:
         insulin use (Z79.4)
         diabetes mellitus, postpancreatectomy (E13.-)

       Z90.410   **Acquired total absence of pancreas**
           Acquired absence of pancreas NOS

       Z90.411   **Acquired partial absence of pancreas**

    Z90.49   **Acquired absence of other specified parts of digestive tract**

    Z90.5   **Acquired absence of kidney**

    Z90.6   **Acquired absence of other parts of urinary tract**
         Acquired absence of bladder

● **Z90.7**   **Acquired absence of genital organ(s)**

    Excludes1   personal history of sex reassignment (Z87.890)

    Excludes2   female genital mutilation status (N90.81-)

  ● **Z90.71**   **Acquired absence of cervix and uterus**

       Z90.710   **Acquired absence of both cervix and uterus** ♀
           Acquired absence of uterus NOS
           Status post total hysterectomy

       Z90.711   **Acquired absence of uterus with remaining cervical stump** ♀
           Status post partial hysterectomy with remaining cervical stump

       Z90.712   **Acquired absence of cervix with remaining uterus** ♀

  ● **Z90.72**   **Acquired absence of ovaries**

       Z90.721   **Acquired absence of ovaries, unilateral** ♀

       Z90.722   **Acquired absence of ovaries, bilateral** ♀

    Z90.79   **Acquired absence of other genital organ(s)**

● **Z90.8**   **Acquired absence of other organs**

    Z90.81   **Acquired absence of spleen**

    Z90.89   **Acquired absence of other organs**

● **Z91**   **Personal risk factors, not elsewhere classified**

    Excludes2   contact with and (suspected) exposures hazardous to health (Z77.-)
         exposure to pollution and other problems related to physical environment (Z77.1-)
         female genital mutilation status (N90.81-)
         occupational exposure to risk factors (Z57.-)
         personal history of physical injury and trauma (Z87.81, Z87.82-)

● **Z91.0**   **Allergy status, other than to drugs and biological substances**

    Excludes2   allergy status to drugs, medicaments, and biological substances (Z88.-)

  ● **Z91.01**   **Food allergy status**

       Excludes2   food additives allergy status (Z91.02)

       Z91.010   **Allergy to peanuts**

       Z91.011   **Allergy to milk products**

          Excludes1   lactose intolerance (E73.-)

       Z91.012   **Allergy to eggs**

       Z91.013   **Allergy to seafood**
          Allergy to shellfish
          Allergy to octopus or squid ink

       Z91.018   **Allergy to other foods**
          Allergy to nuts other than peanuts

    Z91.02   **Food additives allergy status**

  ● **Z91.03**   **Insect allergy status**

       Z91.030   **Bee allergy status**

       Z91.038   **Other insect allergy status**

  ● **Z91.04**   **Nonmedicinal substance allergy status**

       Z91.040   **Latex allergy status**
          Latex sensitivity status

       Z91.041   **Radiographic dye allergy status**
          Allergy status to contrast media used for diagnostic X-ray procedure

       Z91.048   **Other nonmedicinal substance allergy status**

    Z91.09   **Other allergy status, other than to drugs and biological substances**

▶ New   ⇒ Revised   ~~deleted~~ Deleted   Excludes 1   Excludes 2   Includes   Use additional   Code first   Code also   Key words

OGCR Official Guidelines   X Assign placeholder X   ● Use Additional Character(s)   ▶ Manifestation Code   **Coding Clinic**

● **Z91.1** **Patient's noncompliance with medical treatment and regimen**

    Z91.11 Patient's noncompliance with dietary regimen

● **Z91.12** Patient's intentional underdosing of medication regimen

      Code first underdosing of medication (T36-T50) with fifth or sixth character 6

      Excludes1 adverse effect of prescribed drug taken as directed - code to adverse effect

          poisoning (overdose) - code to poisoning

      Z91.120 Patient's intentional underdosing of medication regimen due to financial hardship

      Z91.128 Patient's intentional underdosing of medication regimen for other reason

● **Z91.13** Patient's unintentional underdosing of medication regimen

      Code first underdosing of medication (T36-T50) with fifth or sixth character 6

      Excludes1 adverse effect of prescribed drug taken as directed - code to adverse effect

          poisoning (overdose) - code to poisoning

      Z91.130 Patient's unintentional underdosing of medication regimen due to age-related debility

      Z91.138 Patient's unintentional underdosing of medication regimen for other reason

    Z91.14 Patient's other noncompliance with medication regimen

      Patient's underdosing of medication NOS

    Z91.15 Patient's noncompliance with renal dialysis

    Z91.19 Patient's noncompliance with other medical treatment and regimen

      Nonadherence to medical treatment

● **Z91.4** **Personal history of psychological trauma, not elsewhere classified**

● **Z91.41** Personal history of adult abuse

      Excludes2 personal history of abuse in childhood (Z62.81-)

      Z91.410 Personal history of adult physical and sexual abuse   A

          Excludes1 current adult physical abuse (T74.11, T76.11)

               current adult sexual abuse (T74.21, T76.11)

      Z91.411 Personal history of adult psychological abuse   A

      Z91.412 Personal history of adult neglect   A

          Excludes1 current adult neglect (T74.01, T76.01)

      Z91.419 Personal history of unspecified adult abuse   A

▶ **Z91.42** Personal history of forced labor or sexual exploitation

    Z91.49 Other personal history of psychological trauma, not elsewhere classified

Z91.5 **Personal history of self-harm**

    Personal history of parasuicide

    Personal history of self-poisoning

    Personal history of suicide attempt

● **Z91.8** **Other specified personal risk factors, not elsewhere classified**

    Z91.81 History of falling

      At risk for falling

    Z91.82 Personal history of military deployment   A

      Individual (civilian or military) with past history of military war, peacekeeping and humanitarian deployment (current or past conflict)

      Returned from military deployment

▶ **Z91.83** *Wandering in diseases classified elsewhere*

      Code first underlying disorder such as:

      Alzheimer's disease (G30.-)

      autism or pervasive developmental disorder (F84.-)

      intellectual disabilities (F70-F79)

      unspecified dementia with behavioral disturbance (F03.9-)

● **Z91.84** Oral health risk factors

      Z91.841 Risk for dental caries, low

      Z91.842 Risk for dental caries, moderate

      Z91.843 Risk for dental caries, high

      Z91.849 Unspecified risk for dental caries

    Z91.89 Other specified personal risk factors, not elsewhere classified

      Coding Clinic: 2017, Q1, P46

● **Z92** **Personal history of medical treatment**

    Excludes2 postprocedural states (Z98.-)

    Z92.0 **Personal history of contraception**

      Excludes1 counseling or management of current contraceptive practices (Z30.-)

          long term (current) use of contraception (Z79.3)

          presence of (intrauterine) contraceptive device (Z97.5)

● **Z92.2** **Personal history of drug therapy**

      Excludes2 long term (current) drug therapy (Z79.-)

    Z92.21 Personal history of antineoplastic chemotherapy

    Z92.22 Personal history of monoclonal drug therapy

    Z92.23 Personal history of estrogen therapy

● **Z92.24** Personal history of steroid therapy

      Z92.240 Personal history of inhaled steroid therapy

      Z92.241 Personal history of systemic steroid therapy

          Personal history of steroid therapy NOS

    Z92.25 Personal history of immunosupression therapy

      Excludes2 personal history of steroid therapy (Z92.24)

    Z92.29 Personal history of other drug therapy

    Z92.3 **Personal history of irradiation**

      Personal history of exposure to therapeutic radiation

      Excludes1 exposure to radiation in the physical environment (Z77.12)

          occupational exposure to radiation (Z57.1)

CHAPTER 21 (Z00-Z99)

● **Z92.8**   **Personal history of other medical treatment**
      Coding Clinic: 2016, Q4, P72

    Z92.81   **Personal history of extracorporeal membrane oxygenation (ECMO)**

    Z92.82   **Status post administration of tPA (rtPA) in a different facility within the last 24 hours prior to admission to current facility**
       Code first condition requiring tPA administration, such as:
       acute cerebral infarction (I63.-)
       acute myocardial infarction (I21.-, I22.-)

    Z92.83   **Personal history of failed moderate sedation**
       Personal history of failed conscious sedation
       Excludes2   failed moderate sedation during procedure (T88.52)

    Z92.84   **Personal history of unintended awareness under general anesthesia**
       Excludes2   unintended awareness under general anesthesia during procedure (T88.53)
       Coding Clinic: 2016, Q4, P72, 77

    Z92.89   **Personal history of other medical treatment**

● **Z93**   **Artificial opening status**
    Excludes1   artificial openings requiring attention or management (Z43.-)
       complications of external stoma (J95.0-, K94.-, N99.5-)

    Z93.0   **Tracheostomy status**
    Z93.1   **Gastrostomy status**
    Z93.2   **Ileostomy status**
    Z93.3   **Colostomy status**
    Z93.4   **Other artificial openings of gastrointestinal tract status**
●   **Z93.5**   **Cystostomy status**
      Z93.50   **Unspecified cystostomy status**
      Z93.51   **Cutaneous-vesicostomy status**
      Z93.52   **Appendico-vesicostomy status**
      Z93.59   **Other cystostomy status**

    Z93.6   **Other artificial openings of urinary tract status**
       Nephrostomy status
       Ureterostomy status
       Urethrostomy status

    Z93.8   **Other artificial opening status**
    Z93.9   **Artificial opening status, unspecified**

● **Z94**   **Transplanted organ and tissue status**
    Includes   organ or tissue replaced by heterogenous or homogenous transplant
    Excludes1   complications of transplanted organ or tissue - see Alphabetical Index
    Excludes2   presence of vascular grafts (Z95.-)

    Z94.0   **Kidney transplant status**
    Z94.1   **Heart transplant status**
      Excludes1   artificial heart status (Z95.812)
       heart-valve replacement status (Z95.2-Z95.4)

    Z94.2   **Lung transplant status**
    Z94.3   **Heart and lungs transplant status**
    Z94.4   **Liver transplant status**
    Z94.5   **Skin transplant status**
       Autogenous skin transplant status
    Z94.6   **Bone transplant status**

    Z94.7   **Corneal transplant status**
●   **Z94.8**   **Other transplanted organ and tissue status**
      Z94.81   **Bone marrow transplant status**
      Z94.82   **Intestine transplant status**
      Z94.83   **Pancreas transplant status**
      Z94.84   **Stem cells transplant status**
      Z94.89   **Other transplanted organ and tissue status**
    Z94.9   **Transplanted organ and tissue status, unspecified**

● **Z95**   **Presence of cardiac and vascular implants and grafts**
    Excludes2   complications of cardiac and vascular devices, implants and grafts (T82.-)

    Z95.0   **Presence of cardiac pacemaker**
       Presence of cardiac resynchronization therapy (CRT-P) pacemaker
      Excludes1   adjustment or management of cardiac device (Z45.0-)
       adjustment or management of cardiac pacemaker (Z45.0)
       presence of automatic (implantable) cardiac defibrillator with synchronous cardiac pacemaker (Z95.810)

    Z95.1   **Presence of aortocoronary bypass graft**
       Presence of coronary artery bypass graft

    Z95.2   **Presence of prosthetic heart valve**
       Presence of heart valve NOS

    Z95.3   **Presence of xenogenic heart valve**
    Z95.4   **Presence of other heart-valve replacement**
    Z95.5   **Presence of coronary angioplasty implant and graft**
      Excludes1   coronary angioplasty status without implant and graft (Z98.61)

●   **Z95.8**   **Presence of other cardiac and vascular implants and grafts**
●   **Z95.81**   **Presence of other cardiac implants and grafts**
      Z95.810   **Presence of automatic (implantable) cardiac defibrillator**
     ➠ Presence of automatic (implantable) cardiac defibrillator with synchronous cardiac pacemaker
       Presence of cardiac resynchronization therapy defibrillator (CRT-D)
       Presence of cardioverter-defribillator (ICD)

      Z95.811   **Presence of heart assist device**
      Z95.812   **Presence of fully implantable artificial heart**
      Z95.818   **Presence of other cardiac implants and grafts**

●   **Z95.82**   **Presence of other vascular implants and grafts**
      Z95.820   **Peripheral vascular angioplasty status with implants and grafts**
       Excludes1   peripheral vascular angioplasty without implant and graft (Z98.62)

      Z95.828   **Presence of other vascular implants and grafts**
       Presence of intravascular prosthesis NEC

    Z95.9   **Presence of cardiac and vascular implant and graft, unspecified**

▶ New   ⇒ Revised   ~~deleted~~ Deleted   Excludes 1   Excludes 2   Includes   Use additional   Code first   Code also   Key words
OGCR Official Guidelines   X Assign placeholder X   ● Use Additional Character(s)   ▸ Manifestation Code   **Coding Clinic**

● **Z96   Presence of other functional implants**

    Excludes2   complications of internal prosthetic devices, implants and grafts (T82-T85)

                fitting and adjustment of prosthetic and other devices (Z44-Z46)

    Z96.0   Presence of urogenital implants

    Z96.1   Presence of intraocular lens

        Presence of pseudophakia

  ● **Z96.2   Presence of otological and audiological implants**

        Z96.20   Presence of otological and audiological implant, unspecified

        Z96.21   Cochlear implant status

        Z96.22   Myringotomy tube(s) status

        Z96.29   Presence of other otological and audiological implants

            Presence of bone-conduction hearing device

            Presence of eustachian tube stent

            Stapes replacement

    Z96.3   Presence of artificial larynx

  ● **Z96.4   Presence of endocrine implants**

        Z96.41   Presence of insulin pump (external) (internal)

        Z96.49   Presence of other endocrine implants

    Z96.5   Presence of tooth-root and mandibular implants

  ● **Z96.6   Presence of orthopedic joint implants**

        Z96.60   Presence of unspecified orthopedic joint implant

      ● **Z96.61   Presence of artificial shoulder joint**

          Z96.611   Presence of right artificial shoulder joint

          Z96.612   Presence of left artificial shoulder joint

          Z96.619   Presence of unspecified artificial shoulder joint

      ● **Z96.62   Presence of artificial elbow joint**

          Z96.621   Presence of right artificial elbow joint

          Z96.622   Presence of left artificial elbow joint

          Z96.629   Presence of unspecified artificial elbow joint

      ● **Z96.63   Presence of artificial wrist joint**

          Z96.631   Presence of right artificial wrist joint

          Z96.632   Presence of left artificial wrist joint

          Z96.639   Presence of unspecified artificial wrist joint

      ● **Z96.64   Presence of artificial hip joint**

          Hip-joint replacement (partial) (total)

          Z96.641   Presence of right artificial hip joint

             Coding Clinic: 2016, Q3, P17

          Z96.642   Presence of left artificial hip joint

             Coding Clinic: 2015, Q1, P16

          Z96.643   Presence of artificial hip joint, bilateral

          Z96.649   Presence of unspecified artificial hip joint

      ● **Z96.65   Presence of artificial knee joint**

          Z96.651   Presence of right artificial knee joint

          Z96.652   Presence of left artificial knee joint

          Z96.653   Presence of artificial knee joint, bilateral

          Z96.659   Presence of unspecified artificial knee joint

      ● **Z96.66   Presence of artificial ankle joint**

          Z96.661   Presence of right artificial ankle joint

          Z96.662   Presence of left artificial ankle joint

          Z96.669   Presence of unspecified artificial ankle joint

      ● **Z96.69   Presence of other orthopedic joint implants**

          Z96.691   Finger-joint replacement of right hand

          Z96.692   Finger-joint replacement of left hand

          Z96.693   Finger-joint replacement, bilateral

          Z96.698   Presence of other orthopedic joint implants

    Z96.7   Presence of other bone and tendon implants

        Presence of skull plate

  ● **Z96.8   Presence of other specified functional implants**

        Z96.81   Presence of artificial skin

        Z96.89   Presence of other specified functional implants

    Z96.9   Presence of functional implant, unspecified

● **Z97   Presence of other devices**

    Excludes1   complications of internal prosthetic devices, implants and grafts (T82-T85)

                fitting and adjustment of prosthetic and other devices (Z44-Z46)

    Excludes2   presence of cerebrospinal fluid drainage device (Z98.2)

    Z97.0   Presence of artificial eye

  ● **Z97.1   Presence of artificial limb (complete) (partial)**

        Z97.10   Presence of artificial limb (complete) (partial), unspecified

        Z97.11   Presence of artificial right arm (complete) (partial)

        Z97.12   Presence of artificial left arm (complete) (partial)

        Z97.13   Presence of artificial right leg (complete) (partial)

        Z97.14   Presence of artificial left leg (complete) (partial)

        Z97.15   Presence of artificial arms, bilateral (complete) (partial)

        Z97.16   Presence of artificial legs, bilateral (complete) (partial)

    Z97.2   Presence of dental prosthetic device (complete) (partial)

        Presence of dentures (complete) (partial)

    Z97.3   Presence of spectacles and contact lenses

    Z97.4   Presence of external hearing-aid

    Z97.5   Presence of (intrauterine) contraceptive device ♀

        Excludes1   checking, reinsertion or removal of implantable subdermal contraceptive (Z30.46)

                    checking, reinsertion or removal of intrauterine contraceptive device (Z30.43-)

    Z97.8   Presence of other specified devices

● **Z98   Other postprocedural states**

    Excludes2   aftercare (Z43-Z49, Z51)

                follow-up medical care (Z08-Z09)

                postprocedural complication - see Alphabetical Index

    Z98.0   Intestinal bypass and anastomosis status

        Excludes2   bariatric surgery status (Z98.84)

                  gastric bypass status (Z98.84)

                  obesity surgery status (Z98.84)

    Z98.1   Arthrodesis status

    Z98.2   Presence of cerebrospinal fluid drainage device

        Presence of CSF shunt

    Z98.3   Post therapeutic collapse of lung status

        Code first underlying disease

● **Z98.4 Cataract extraction status**
Use additional code to identify intraocular lens implant status (Z96.1)
Excludes1 aphakia (H27.0)

Z98.41 Cataract extraction status, right eye
Z98.42 Cataract extraction status, left eye
Z98.49 Cataract extraction status, unspecified eye

● **Z98.5 Sterilization status**
Excludes1 female infertility (N97.-)
male infertility (N46.-)

Z98.51 Tubal ligation status ♀
Z98.52 Vasectomy status ♂   A

● **Z98.6 Angioplasty status**
Z98.61 Coronary angioplasty status
Excludes1 coronary angioplasty status with implant and graft (Z95.5)

Z98.62 Peripheral vascular angioplasty status
Excludes1 peripheral vascular angioplasty status with implant and graft (Z95.820)

● **Z98.8 Other specified postprocedural states**
Coding Clinic: 2016, Q4, P76

● **Z98.81 Dental procedure status**
Z98.810 Dental sealant status
Z98.811 Dental restoration status
Dental crown status
Dental fillings status
Z98.818 Other dental procedure status

Z98.82 Breast implant status
Excludes1 breast implant removal status (Z98.86)

Z98.83 Filtering (vitreous) bleb after glaucoma surgery status
Excludes1 inflammation (infection) of postprocedural bleb (H59.4-)

Z98.84 Bariatric surgery status
Gastric banding status
Gastric bypass status for obesity
Obesity surgery status
Excludes1 bariatric surgery status complicating pregnancy, childbirth, or the puerperium (O99.84)
Excludes2 intestinal bypass and anastomosis status (Z98.0)

Z98.85 Transplanted organ removal status
Transplanted organ previously removed due to complication, failure, rejection or infection
Excludes1 encounter for removal of transplanted organ
-code to complication of transplanted organ (T86.-)

Z98.86 Personal history of breast implant removal

● **Z98.87 Personal history of in utero procedure**
Z98.870 Personal history of in utero procedure during pregnancy ♀
Excludes2 complications from in utero procedure for current pregnancy (O35.7)
supervision of current pregnancy with history of in utero procedure during previous pregnancy (O09.82-)

Z98.871 Personal history of in utero procedure while a fetus

● **Z98.89 Other specified postprocedural states**
Coding Clinic: 2016, Q4, P76
Z98.890 Other specified postprocedural states
Personal history of surgery, not elsewhere classified

Z98.891 History of uterine scar from previous surgery
Excludes1 Maternal care due to uterine scar from previous surgery (O34.2-)
Coding Clinic: 2016, Q4, P52, P76

● **Z99 Dependence on enabling machines and devices, not elsewhere classified**
Excludes1 cardiac pacemaker status (Z95.0)

Z99.0 Dependence on aspirator

● **Z99.1 Dependence on respirator**
Dependence on ventilator
Z99.11 Dependence on respirator [ventilator] status
Coding Clinic: 2018, Q1, P14; 2015, Q1, P21
Z99.12 Encounter for respirator [ventilator] dependence during power failure
Excludes1 mechanical complication of respirator [ventilator] (J95.850)

Z99.2 Dependence on renal dialysis
Hemodialysis status
Peritoneal dialysis status
Presence of arteriovenous shunt for dialysis
Renal dialysis status NOS
Excludes1 encounter for fitting and adjustment of dialysis catheter (Z49.0-)
Excludes2 noncompliance with renal dialysis (Z91.15)
Coding Clinic: 2016, Q1, P13

Z99.3 Dependence on wheelchair
Wheelchair confinement status
Code first cause of dependence, such as:
⇒ muscular dystrophy (G71.0-)
obesity (E66.-)

● **Z99.8 Dependence on other enabling machines and devices**
Z99.81 Dependence on supplemental oxygen
Dependence on long-term oxygen
Z99.89 Dependence on other enabling machines and devices
Dependence on machine or device NOS

▶ New   ⇒ Revised   ~~deleted~~ Deleted   Excludes 1   Excludes 2   Includes   Use additional   Code first   Code also   Key words
OGCR Official Guidelines   X Assign placeholder X   ● Use Additional Character(s)   ▷ Manifestation Code   **Coding Clinic**

TRUST ELSEVIER to provide *your* complete curriculum solution!

ELSEVIER

CONTENT

978-0-323-58219-3

978-0-323-58261-2

978-1-4557-5199-0

STUDY TOOLS

978-0-323-58251-3

978-0-323-58257-5

More study tools available

Create a customized portfolio to show employers

SIMULATIONS

COURSES

978-0-323-60873-2

978-0-323-64197-5

978-0-323-43011-1

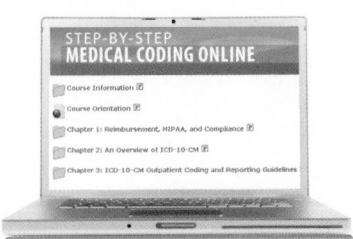
978-0-323-60874-9

1. Assess! Take the Pre-Exam

Use the Pre-Exam located on the companion Evolve site to gauge your strengths and weaknesses, develop a plan for focused study, and gain a better understanding of the testing process.

2. Study!

Use the quizzes in this book to sharpen your skills and build competency.

4. Test! Take the Final Exam

Gauge your readiness for the actual physician coding exam with the Final Exam. Boost your test-taking confidence and ensure certification success.

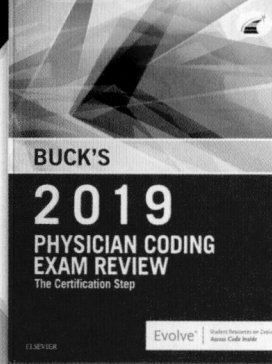

3. Apply! Take the Post-Exam

After studying, apply your knowledge to the Post-Exam located on the companion Evolve site. When finished, you'll receive scores for both the Pre- and Post-Exams and a breakdown of incorrect answers to help you identify areas where you need more detailed study and review.

ISBN: 978-0-323-58257-5

Perfect *your* understanding *and* prepare for certification
— START YOUR REVIEW NOW!

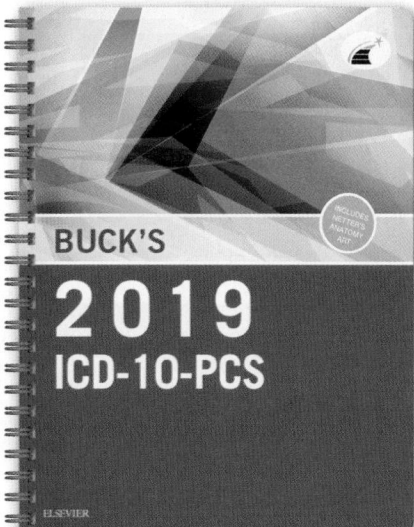

Trust Elsevier to take you through the levels *of* CODING SUCCESS

STEP**4:**
PROFESSIONAL

STEP**3:** CERTIFY

STEP**2:** PRACTICE

STEP**1:** LEARN

With the resources you need for every level of coding success, we are with you ever step of your coding career. From beginning to advanced, from the classroom to the workplace, from application to certification, the Step Series products are your guides to greater opportunities and successful career advancement.

Keep climbing with the most

Carol J. Buck, MS, CPC, CCS-P | Jackie Grass Koesterman, CP

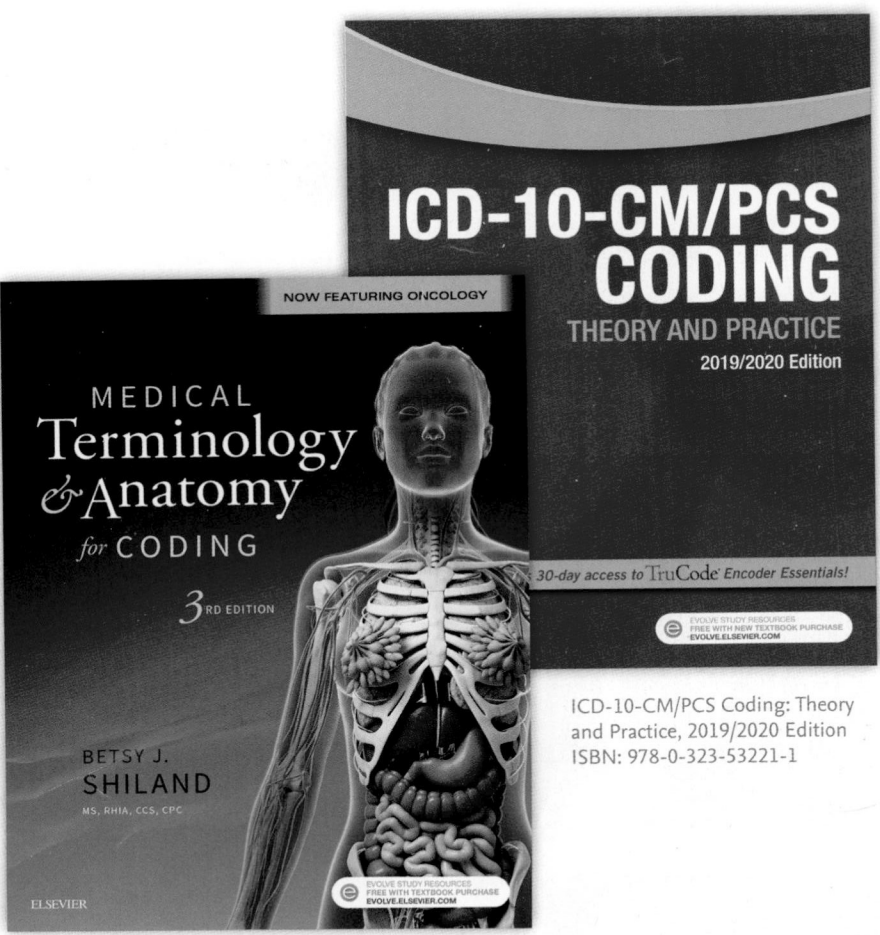